The
AMERICAN
RACING
MANUAL

●

2004 EDITION

Copyright © 2004 by Daily Racing Form LLC.
All rights reserved.
ISBN: 0-9726401-8-5
Library of Congress Control Number: 2003113622

All statistical information subsequent to July 22, 1998, provided by Equibase Company LLC. Pedigree and sales information provided by The Jockey Club Information Systems, Inc.

Published by
Daily Racing Form Press
100 Broadway, 7th Floor
New York, NY 10005

Acknowledgements

With a lengthy list of revived and added features, in combination with the already exhaustive material previously contained, the 2004 American Racing Manual continues to be the authoritative source of data and statistics on its subject. Only with essential contributions provided by both DRF employees and personnel from racing organizations throughout the world is such a book possible.

Special thanks goes to Managing Editor Duke Dosik; Graphics Editor William K. Scurry Jr., whose invaluable aid ranged far beyond the realm of graphics; programmer Duane Burke; Jeff Frank, for preparation of the chart pages; Ken Davis, an information source extraordinaire; Scott McKearney; and writers Jay Privman (U.S.); Bill Tallon (Canada); Alan Shuback (foreign); Glenye Cain (breeding and sales); Karen Johnson (steeplechase); Ira Kaplan and Noel Michaels. Finally, thanks in particular are due to Vice President Irwin Cohen, a tireless supporter of the American Racing Manual since its hardcover return in 2000.

No less important are the endless contributions from outside organizations, to whom the Daily Racing Form is indebted.

Sincerest thanks, once again, goes to Alan Marzelli, Chairman of Equibase Company LLC, and the President of The Jockey Club, who continues his strong personal support to the project; Christopher Scherf, Executive Vice President of Thoroughbred Racing Associations and Secretary of Equibase. Special mention also goes to Connie Brannen, Operations Manager at Equibase and liaison to this project, for her tireless contributions for the fourth straight year.

Thanks also to Breeders' Cup Limited and its Media Relations Director Jim Gluckson; the Thoroughbred Racing Associations' Karen Darling; the Breeders' Cup's McKay Smith; The Jockey Club's Janet Olson and John Cooney; and the National Thoroughbred Racing Association's Peggy Hendershot and Carol Paulick, all of whom provided timely material on behalf of their organizations. Thanks also to Andrew Beyer and photographer Frank Anderson of the Lexington Herald-Leader for their generous contributions. Particular thanks go to the many individuals at racing tracks across the United States and Canada who contributed updates on their facilities for the Track Directory section.

In the end, however, the greatest thanks go out to the racing industry professionals and racing fans who will make use of this book in their research endeavors.

Paula Welch Prather
Editor, American Racing Manual

Foreword

Now in its 109th year, the American Racing Manual continues to grow and enhance its status as the leading statistical resource for Thoroughbred racing. To that end, there will be more upgrades and additions to this year's ARM than perhaps any time in its history.

For the first time, *Daily Racing Form* National Handicapper Mike Watchmaker provides commentary on the top horses in every division. The feature is a year-end summary of the popular "Watchmaker Watch" feature which appears daily in DRF. There is a complete listing of graded stakes wins by Laffit Pincay, who ended his storied riding career in 2003.

Numerous lists make their ARM debut in 2004, including lifetime leaders among trainers and jockeys; fastest times at all common distances since 1991; best times at all distances at every track in 2003; progeny of leading broodmare sires; annual leading horses in races won; and the status of top yearlings, beginning with the yearling crop of 2001.

We have also revived a number of long-defunct ARM features including the year's necrology; a list of all-time leading horses in wins; the breeders and sires of millionaires; triple dead-heats for win; and in the foreign section, leading horses by money won in Europe, the Middle East, and the Far East.

Much of the credit for these improvements to the ARM goes to its new editor, Paula Welch Prather. Prather previously was Special Projects Editor for Daily Racing Form and developed the book "Champions" and the Graded Stakes Yearbook from 1995-98. She brings highly unique qualifications to the stewardship of the ARM, which will benefit greatly from her contributions.

Irwin Cohen
Vice President/Senior Editor
DRF

Index

GALLERY
OF
CHAMPIONS

MINESHAFT	HORSE OF THE YEAR
	OLDER MALE
ACTION THIS DAY	2-YEAR-OLD MALE
HALFBRIDLED	2-YEAR-OLD FILLY
FUNNY CIDE	3-YEAR-OLD MALE
BIRD TOWN	3-YEAR-OLD FILLY
AZERI	OLDER FEMALE
HIGH CHAPARRAL	GRASS HORSE, MALE
ISLINGTON	GRASS HORSE, FEMALE
ALDEBARAN	SPRINTER
MCDYNAMO	STEEPLECHASE

Older Male
Horse of the Year

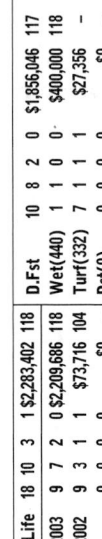

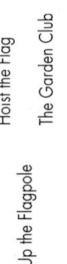

Robby Albarado

Neil Howard

MINESHAFT, 1999

Br: Farish & Elkins & Webber Jr (Ky.)

A.P. Indy 1989	Seattle Slew	Bold Reasoning
		My Charmer
	Weekend Surprise	Secretariat
		Lassie Dear
Prospectors Delite 1989	Mr. Prospector	Raise a Native
		Gold Digger
	Up the Flagpole	Hoist the Flag
		The Garden Club

Mineshaft
Own: Farish William S., Elkins Jr., James

Dk. b or b. h. 5 (May)
Sire: A.P. Indy (Seattle Slew) $300,000
Dam: Prospectors Delite (Mr. Prospector)
Br: W. S. Farish, James Elkins & W. T. Webber Jr. (Ky)
Tr: Howard Neil J(0 0 0 0 .00) 2003:(156 31 .20)

Life	18	10	3	1	$2,283,402	118		D.Fst	10	8	2	0	$1,856,046	117
2003	9	7	2	0	$2,209,686	118		Wet(440)	1	1	0	0	$400,000	118
2002	9	3	1	1	$73,716	104		Turf(332)	7	1	1	1	$27,356	–
	0	0	0	0	$0	–		Dst(0)	0	0	0	0	$0	–

27Sep03-10Bel	fst	1¼	:47^3 1:11 1:34^4 2:00^1	3↑ JkyClbGC-G1	**114**	3	3^2	2½	1½	1^5	14¼	Albarado R J	L126	*.40	93– 09	Mineshaft1264¼ Quest1262¾ Evening Attire1266½	When asked, ridden out	5
6Sep03- 9Bel	fst	1⅛	:47^2 1:11^1 1:34^2 1:46^1	3↑ Woodward-G1	**117**	2	43½	42½	3^2	12½	14¼	Albarado R J	L126	*.30	99– 13	*Mineshaft*1264¼ HoldThatTiger1224¾ Puzzlement12611¼	3 wide move, clear	5
5Jly03- 9Bel	fst	1¼	:48^3 1:12^3 1:37 2:01^2	3↑ SuburbnH-G1	**115**	1	21½	2½	1hd	1½	12¼	Albarado R J	L121	*.75	87– 13	*Mineshaft*1212¼ Volponi1214 Dollar Bill1152¼	Cruised when asked	8
14Jun03-10CD	fst	1⅛	:46^4 1:10^2 1:35 1:47^2	3↑ SFosterH-G1	**117**	10	52½	53½	11½	1^1	2hd	Albarado R J	L123	*.70	101– 04	*Perfect Drift*115hd *Mineshaft*1239½ *Aldebaran*120½	Bmp start,outgamed	10
16May03-11Pim	sly	1 3/16	:46^3 1:11 1:36^2 1:56	4↑ PimSpclH-G1	**118**	3	4^2	42¾	2^1	11½	13¾	Albarado R J	L121	*1.30	93– 23	Mineshaft1213¾ Western Pride116hd Judge's Case1131¾	Driving	9
25Apr03- 9Kee	fst	1⅛	:47^4 1:12 1:36^2 1:48^2	4↑ BenAli-G3	**116**	1	32½	3^3	2hd	12½	1^9	Albarado R J	L120	*.30	98– 02	*Mineshaft*1209 AmericanStyle1161¼ Mettron1161¾	Hand urging,much best	4
2Mar03- 9FG	fst	1⅛	:47^4 1:12^1 1:36^2 1:48^4	4↑ NwOrlnsH-G2	**116**	6	21½	22½	1hd	11½	13½	Albarado R J	L115	5.00	100– 17	*Mineshaft*1153½ Olmodavor1172½ Strive1141½	Took over, driving	11
9Feb03- 9FG	fst	1 1/16	:24 :47^4 1:12^4 1:43^3	4↑ WirlwayH-G3	**107**	7	57¼	45½	53½	42½	22½	Albarado R J	116	2.70	89– 20	Balto Star1182½ *Mineshaft*116¾ Bonapaw1153½	Up for second	8
19Jan03- 9FG	fst	1 1/16	:24^1 :47^2 1:11^3 1:43^4	4↑ DiplmtWayH75k	**103**	2	32½	31½	1hd	1^1	1no	Albarado R J	116	*1.00	91– 13	Mineshaft116no Learned1161¼ Discreet Hero1131	Shook free, all out	7

B. Wayne Hughes

David Flores

2-Year-Old Male

ACTION THIS DAY, 2001
Br: Jaime S. Carrion, trustee (Ky)

		Hail to Reason
	Roberto	Bramalea
Kris S. 1977		Princequillo
	Sharp Queen	Bridgework
		Sharpen Up
	Trempolino	Trephine
Najecam 1993		Forli
	Sue Warner	Bitty Girl

Life						$817,200	92	D.Fst	3	2	1	0	$817,200	92
	3	2	1	0				Wet(354)	0	0	0	0	$0	–
2003	3	2	1	0	$817,200	92		Turf(340)	0	0	0	0	$0	–
2002	0	M	0	0	$0	–		Dst(0)	0	0	0	0	$0	–

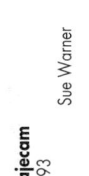

Action This Day
Own: Hughes B. W

B. c. 3 (Feb) KEEJUL02 $150,000
Sire: Kris S. (Roberto) $150,000
Dam: Najecam (Trempolino)
Br: Jaime S. Carrion, Trustee (Ky)
Tr: Mandella Richard E(0 0 0 0 .00) 2003:(253 51 .20)

25Oct03–7SA	fst	1 1/16	:221 :45 1:094 1:433	BesTBCJv-G1	92	2 12 13 1 213 106 1/4 31 1/2 12 3/4	Flores D R	LB122	26.80	86– 07	ActionThisDay122 3/4 MinisterEric122 5 ChpelRoyl122 no	4 wide, going away 12
28Sep03–1SA	fst	1 1/16	:232 :473 1:12 1:453	Md Sp Wt 45k	79	5 7 3/4 712 69 1/2 52 3/4	1 no Solis A	LB117	*1.00	76– 16	ActionThisDy117 no NtiveApprovl117 1/2 CourgeousAct117 4	Bid btwn,gamely 7
5Sep03–2Dmr	fst	1	:224 :463 1:104 1:37	Md Sp Wt 51k	74	5 66 66 3/4 57 1/2 46	27 Solis A	LB120	4.10	82– 10	Coldntight120 7 ActionThisDay120 nk ThtsnOutrge120 3	Bit tight 1/16,late 2d 6

2-Year-Old Female

HALFBRIDLED, 2001
Br: Wertheimer et Frere (Ky)

Unbridled 1987	Fappiano	Mr. Prospector
		Killaloe
	Gana Facil	Le Fabuleux
		Charedi
Half Queen 1996	Deputy Minister	Vice Regent
		Mint Copy
	At the Half	Seeking the Gold
		Knitted Gloves

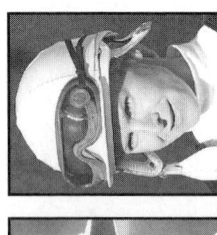

Richard Mandella

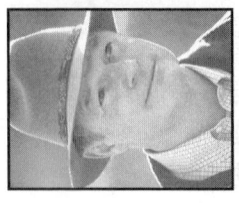

Julie Krone

Halfbridled
Own: Wertheimer Farm LLC

Dk. b or b. f. 3 (Feb)
Sire: Unbridled (Fappiano) $200,000
Dam: Half Queen (Deputy Minister)
Br: Wertheimer & Frere (Ky)
Tr: Mandella Richard E(0 0 0 0 .00) 2003:(253 51 20)

Life	4 4 0 0	$849,400	99	D.Fst 4 4 0 0	$849,400 99
2003	4 4 0 0	$849,400	99	Wet(413) 0 0 0 0	$0 −
2002	0 M 0 0	$0	−	Turf(282) 0 0 0 0	$0 −
				Dst(0) 0 0 0 0	$0 −

```
25Oct03-3SA fst 1¹⁄₁₆    :224 :464 1:104 1:423   99 14 74½ 51¾ 31  1½ 12½  Krone J A  ⒻBCJuvFil-G1  LB119 *2.30  91-07  Halfbridled1192½ Ashado119nk VictoryU.S.A.11993⁄4   Wide trip,drew off 14
28Sep03-9SA fst 1¹⁄₁₆    :24  :48  1:122 1:433   98  4 11½ 2½  11  12 14½  Krone J A  ⒻOakLeaf-G2   LB119  *.30  86-16  Halfbridled1194¼ Tarlow119¾ HollywoodStory1196½   Inside,clear,gamely  7
30Aug03-8Dmr fst 7f      :224 :451 1:093 1:221   99  1 4   42  2nd 11½ 15  Krone J A  ⒻDmrDeb-G1    LB116 1.60  91-13  Hlfbridled1165 HollywoodStory115no VictoryUSA1161½   Re-bid rail 1/4,clear  6
27Jly03-3Dmr fst 5½f     :22  :451 :574  1:04    87  1 4   65  64¼ 31 14½  Krone J A  ⒻMd Sp Wt 49k  B118 3.60  95-10  Halfbridled1184½ UppityKitty1182 HaleakalSunrise1182   4wd rally,drew off  6
```

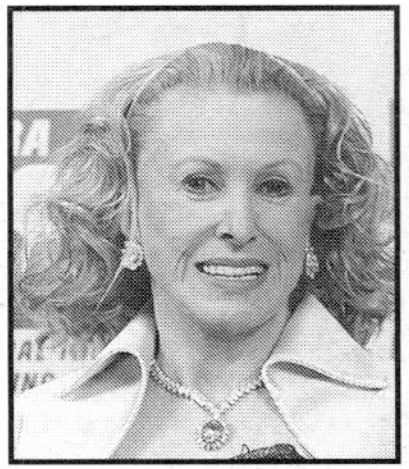

Marylou Whitney

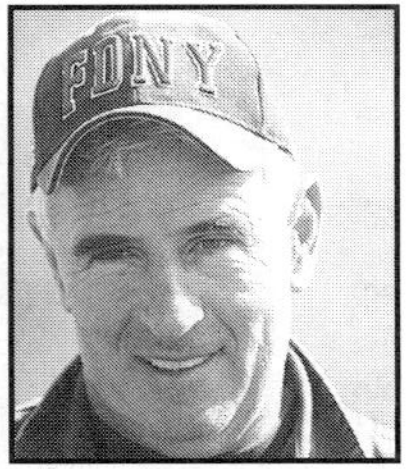

Nick Zito

3–Year–Old Female

BIRD TOWN, 2000

Br: Marylou Whitney Stables (Ky.)

		Mr. Prospector
	Seeking the Gold	
		Con Game
Cape Town 1995		
		Seattle Slew
	Seaside Attraction	
		Kamar
		Northern Dancer
	Storm Bird	
		South Ocean
Dear Birdie 1987		
		Silent Screen
	Hush Dear	
		You All

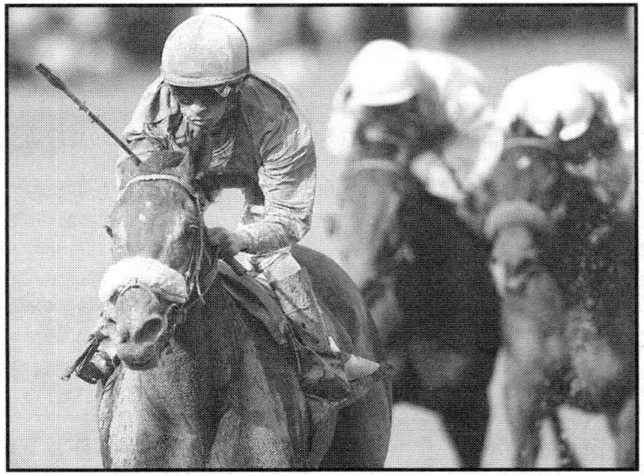

Bird Town
Own: Marylou Whitney Stables

B. f. 4 (Apr)
Sire: Cape Town (Seeking the Gold) $7,500
Dam: Dear Birdie (Storm Bird)
Br: Marylou Whitney Stables (Ky)
Tr: Zito Nicholas P(0 0 0 0 .00) 2003:(507 77 .15)

Life	**12**	**4**	**6**	**1**	**$871,251**	**101**	
2003	**8**	**3**	**4**	**0**	**$815,976**	**101**	
2002	**4**	**1**	**2**	**1**	**$55,275**	**80**	
	0	**0**	**0**	**0**	**$0**	**–**	

D.Fst	**10**	**3**	**5**	**1**	**$795,656**	**101**
Wet(372)	**2**	**1**	**1**	**0**	**$75,595**	**98**
Turf(302)	**0**	**0**	**0**	**0**	**$0**	**–**
Dst(0)	**0**	**0**	**0**	**0**	**$0**	**–**

4Oct03–9Bel	fst	1⅛	:474 1:122 1:363 1:491	3↑ ⒻBeldame-G1	**100**	5	1½	1½	1hd	22½	24½	Gryder A T	L120	11.20	79–26	Sightseek1234½ Bird Town1204¾ Buy the Sport120¾	Pace, second best	7
16Aug03–9Sar	fst	1¼	:482 1:124 1:374 2:05	ⒻAlabama-G1	**85**	5	33	32	22	57¾	511	Prado E S	L121	1.60	71–14	IslndFshion1216 AwesomeHumor1211 SpoknFur1211¼	Bumped after start	6
26Jly03–9Sar	fst	7f	:223 :451 1:081 1:204	ⒻTest-G1	**100**	7	1	31	3½	25½	24½	Prado E S	L122	*1.75	98–08	Lady Tak1224½ Bird Town1221½ *House Party*1221¾	3 wide, game finish	7
6Jun03–10Bel	fst	1	:232 :461 1:102 1:351	ⒻAcorn-G1	**96**	7	2hd	1hd	1½	11	1hd	Prado E S	L121	2.65	90–16	Bird Town121hd *Lady Tak*1211 Final Round1213¼	Game while drifting	7
2May03–10CD	fst	1⅛	:46 1:10 1:353 1:483	ⒻKyOaks-G1	**101**	5	87	86	74	4nk	13¼	Prado E S	L121	18.20	95–07	*Bird Town*1213¼ Santa Catarina121hd Yell121¾	Stumble start,6w,drv	12
10Apr03–8Kee	my	*7f	:214 :442 1:094 1:264	ⒻBeaumont-G2	**98**	7	1	2hd	11½	2hd	21¼	Coa E M	L118	3.30	91–15	My Boston Gal1201¼ *Bird Town*1184¾ Midnight Cry1184	Dueled, good try	9
23Feb03–5GP	fst	7f	:214 :444 1:101 1:224	ⒻCharon52k	**100**	5	3	25	22	17	112½	Coa E M	L120	3.40	94–13	Bird Town12012½ Crafty Brat1181¼ WesterlyBreeze1223¾	Kept to pressure	6
16Jan03–9GP	fst	170	:233 :482 1:132 1:421	ⒻAlw 34000N1x	**84**	6	11	11	1½	2hd	2nk	Day P	L119	2.80	90–18	*Yell*121nk *Bird Town*1195½ Marnesia Light1172¼	Inside, gamely	7

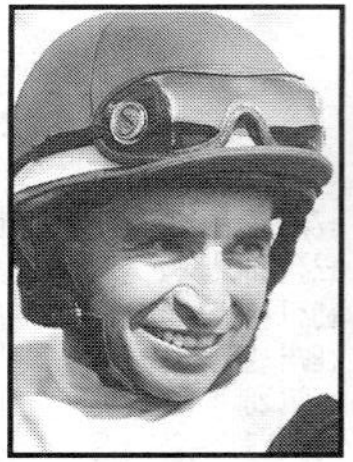
Jose Santos

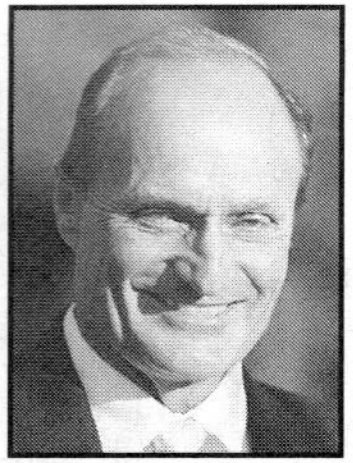
Barclay Tagg

3–Year–Old Male

FUNNY CIDE, 2000

Br: WinStar Farm LLC (NY)

Distorted Humor 1993	Forty Niner	Mr. Prospector
		File
	Danzig's Beauty	Danzig
		Sweetest Chant
Belle's Good Cide 1993	Slewacide	Seattle Slew
		Evasive
	Belle of Killarney	Little Current
		Cherished Moment

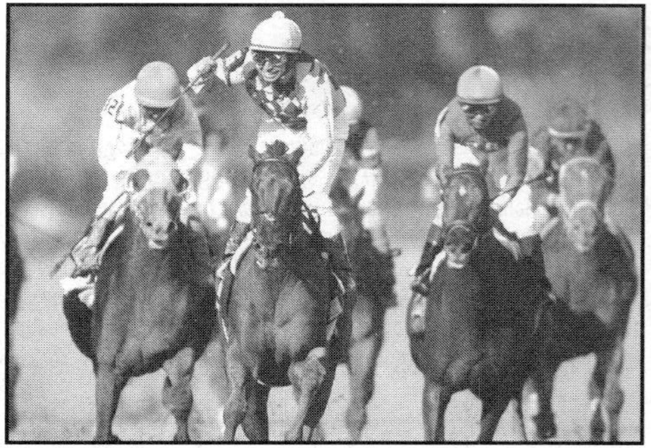

Funny Cide
Own: Sackatoga Stable

Ch. g. 4 (Apr) SARAUG01 $22,000
Sire: Distorted Humor (Forty Niner) $20,000
Dam: Belle's Good Cide (Slewacide)
Br: Win Star Farm, LLC (NY)
Tr: Tagg Barclay(0 0 0 0 .00) 2003:(166 16 .10)

Life	11	5	2	2	$2,099,385	114	D.Fst	8 4 1 1 $1,189,385 109
2003	8	2	2	2	$1,963,200	114	Wet(400)	3 1 1 1 $910,000 114
2002	3	3	0	0	$136,185	103	Turf(295)	0 0 0 0 $0 –
	0	0	0	0	$0	–	Dst(0)	0 0 0 0 $0 –

25Oct03–9SA	fst	1¼	:461 1:101 1:341 1:594	3↑ BCClasic-G1	97	4	52¼	65¼	78	1011	914¾	Krone J A	LB121	8.70	91– 07	PleasantlyPerfect1261½ MedglidOro126¾ Dynever121nk	Drifted wide, tired	10
3Aug03–11Mth	fst	1⅛	:47 1:104 1:36 1:491	HsklInvH-G1	94	5	52½	54½	55	47½	39	Santos J A	L123	*1.00	86– 08	Peace Rules1211¾ Sky Mesa1187¼ Funny Cide1231	Outside 1/4,mild bid	7
7Jun03–11Bel	sly	1½	:483 1:132 2:023 2:281	Belmont-G1	104	4	11	1hd	21	33	35	Santos J A	L126	*1.00	86– 14	EmpireMker126¾ TenMostWnted1264¼ FunnyCid1265¼	Set pace 3w, tired	6
17May03–12Pim	gd	1 3/16	:47 1:113 1:362 1:553	Preaknes-G1	114	9	32	21	2½	15	19¾	Santos J A	L126	*1.90	95– 12	FunnyCide1269¾ MidwayRod126¾ Scrimshw126no	Bmpd brk,ratd 3w,clear	10
3May03–10CD	fst	1¼	:461 1:102 1:353 2:01	KyDerby-G1	109	5	32	31½	2½	1hd	11¾	Santos J A	L126	12.80	94– 06	*Funny Cide*1261¾ *EmpireMaker*126hd PeaceRules126hd	Bmp start,stiff drive	16
12Apr03–8Aqu	my	1⅛	:471 1:11 1:354 1:483	WoodMem-G1	110	4	21½	21½	21	2hd	2½	Santos J A	L123	5.20	92– 12	Empire Maker123½ *Funny Cide*1237½ Kissin Saint1231	Bumped after start	8
9Mar03–9FG	fst	1 1/16	:232 :463 1:103 1:423	LaDerby-G2	99	2	11	11½	1½	43½	33¼	Santos J A	L122	6.10	94– 17	*Peace Rules*1222¼ [D]Kafwain1221 Funny Cide122½	Came again rail	10
Awarded second purse money																		
18Jan03–10GP	fst	1 1/16	:232 :471 1:112 1:43	HolyBull-G3	87	13	72¼	41½	44	44	56½	Santos J A	L122	5.30	87– 10	Offlee Wild116hd Powerful Touch1163 Bham1182½	Hit gate, wide, tired	13

3–Year–Old Female

BIRD TOWN, 2000

Br: Marylou Whitney Stables (Ky.)

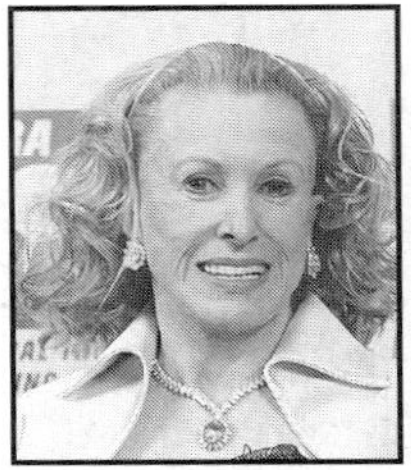

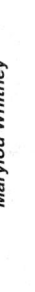

Marylou Whitney

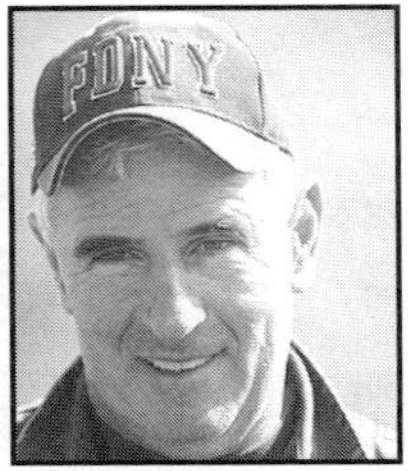

Nick Zito

		Mr. Prospector
	Seeking the Gold	
		Con Game
Cape Town 1995		
		Seattle Slew
	Seaside Attraction	
		Kamar
		Northern Dancer
	Storm Bird	
		South Ocean
Dear Birdie 1987		
		Silent Screen
	Hush Dear	
		You All

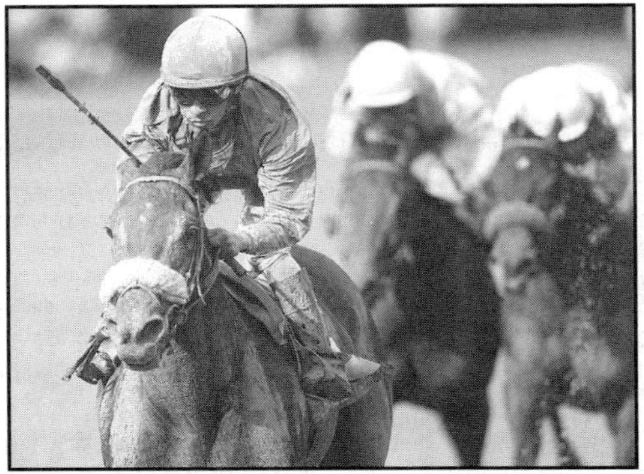

Bird Town
Own: Marylou Whitney Stables

B. f. 4 (Apr)
Sire: Cape Town (Seeking the Gold) $7,500
Dam: Dear Birdie (Storm Bird)
Br: Marylou Whitney Stables (Ky)
Tr: Zito Nicholas P(0 0 0 0 .00) 2003:(507 77 .15)

Life	12	4	6	1	$871,251	101
2003	8	3	4	0	$815,976	101
2002	4	1	2	1	$55,275	80
	0	0	0	0	$0	–

D.Fst	10	3	5	1	$795,656	101
Wet(372)	2	1	1	0	$75,595	98
Turf(302)	0	0	0	0	$0	–
Dst(0)	0	0	0	0	$0	–

4Oct03–9Bel	fst	1⅛	:474 1:122 1:363 1:491	3↑ⒻBeldame-G1	**100**	5	1½	1½	1hd	22½	24½	Gryder A T	L120	11.20	79– 26	Sightseek1234½ Bird Town1204¾ Buy the Sport120¾	Pace, second best	7
16Aug03–9Sar	fst	1¼	:482 1:124 1:374 2:05	ⒻAlabama-G1	**85**	5	33	32	22	57¾	511	Prado E S	L121	1.60	71– 14	IslndFshion1216 AwesomeHumor1211 SpoknFur1211¼	Bumped after start	6
26Jly03–9Sar	fst	7f	:223 :451 1:081 1:204	ⒻTest-G1	**100**	7	1	31	3½	25½	24½	Prado E S	L122	*1.75	98– 08	Lady Tak1224½ Bird Town1221½ *House Party*1221¾	3 wide, game finish	7
6Jun03–10Bel	fst	1	:232 :461 1:102 1:351	ⒻAcorn-G1	**96**	7	2hd	1hd	1½	11	1hd	Prado E S	L121	2.65	90– 16	Bird Town121hd *Lady Tak*1211 Final Round1213¼	Game while drifting	7
2May03–10CD	fst	1⅛	:46 1:10 1:353 1:483	ⒻKyOaks-G1	**101**	5	87	86	74	4nk	13¼	Prado E S	L121	18.20	95– 07	*Bird Town*1213¼ Santa Catarina121hd Yell121¾	Stumble start,6w,drv	12
10Apr03–8Kee	my	*7f	:214 :442 1:094 1:264	ⒻBeaumont-G2	**98**	7	1	2hd	11½	2hd	21¼	Coa E M	L118	3.30	91– 15	My Boston Gal1201¼ *Bird Town*1184¾ Midnight Cry1184	Dueled, good try	9
23Feb03–5GP	fst	7f	:214 :444 1:101 1:224	ⒻCharon52k	**100**	5	3	25	22	17	112½	Coa E M	L120	3.40	94– 13	Bird Town12012½ Crafty Brat1181¼ WesterlyBreeze1223¾	Kept to pressure	6
16Jan03–9GP	fst	170	:233 :482 1:132 1:421	ⒻAlw 34000N1x	**84**	6	11	11	1½	2hd	2nk	Day P	L119	2.80	90– 18	*Yell*121nk *Bird Town*1195½ Marnesia Light1172¼	Inside, gamely	7

3-Year-Old Male

FUNNY CIDE, 2000
Br: WinStar Farm LLC (NY)

Jose Santos

Barclay Tagg

Distorted Humor 1993	Forty Niner	Mr. Prospector
		File
	Danzig's Beauty	Danzig
		Sweetest Chant
Belle's Good Cide 1993	Slewacide	Seattle Slew
		Evasive
	Belle of Killarney	Little Current
		Cherished Moment

Funny Cide
Own: Sackatoga Stable

Ch. g. 4 (Apr) SARAUG01 $22,000
Sire: Distorted Humor (Forty Niner) $20,000
Dam: Belle's Good Cide (Slewacide)
Br: Win Star Farm, LLC (NY)
Tr: Tagg Barclay(0 0 0 0 .00) 2003:(166 16 .10)

Life	11	5	2	2	$2,099,385	114		
2003	8	2	2	2	$1,963,200	114		
2002	3	3	0	0	$136,185	103		
					$0	–		
D.Fst	8	4	1	1	$1,189,385	109		
Wet(400)	3	1	1	1	$910,000	114		
Turf(295)	0	0	0	0	$0	–		
Dst(0)	0	0	0	0	$0	–		

25Oct03-9SA fst 1¼ :46¹ 1:10¹ 1:34¹ 1:59⁴ 3↑BCClasic-G1 97 4 5²¼ 6⁵¼ 78 10¹¹ 9¹⁴¾ Krone J A LB121 8.70 91-07 PleasantlyPerfect126¹¼ MedglidOro126¾ Dynever121nk Drifted wide, tired 10

3Aug03-11Mth fst 1⅛ :47 1:10⁴ 1:36 1:49¹ HsklInvH-G1 94 5 5²½ 5⁴½ 55 47½ 39 Santos J A L123 *1.00 86-08 Peace Rules121¹¼ Sky Mesa118⁷¾ Funny Cide123¹ Outside 1/4,mild bid 7

7Jun03-11Bel sly 1½ :48³ 1:13² 2:02³ 2:28¹ Belmont-G1 104 4 11 1hd 21 33 35 Santos J A L126 *1.00 86-14 EmpireMker126¾ TenMostWnted126⁴¼ FunnyCid126⁵¼ Set pace 3w, tired 6

17May03-12Pim gd 1³⁄₁₆ :47 1:13 1:36² 1:55³ Preaknes-G1 114 9 32 21 2½ 15 19¾ Santos J A L126 *1.90 95-12 FunnyCide126⁹¾ MidwayRod126¾ Scrimshw126no Bmpd brk,ratd 3w,clear 10

3May03-10CD fst 1¼ :46¹ 1:10² 1:35² 2:01 KyDerby-G1 109 5 32 31½ 2½ 1hd 11¾ Santos J A L126 12.80 94-06 Funny Cide126¹¾ EmpireMaker126hd PeaceRules126hd Bmp start,stiff drive 16

12Apr03-8Aqu my 1⅛ :47¹ 1:11 1:35⁴ 1:48³ WoodMem-G1 110 4 2¹½ 2¹½ 21 2hd 2½ Santos J A L123 5.20 92-12 Empire Maker123¾ Funny Cide123⁷½ Kissin Saint123¹ Bumped after start 8

9Mar03-9FG fst 1⅛ :23² :46³ 1:10³ 1:42³ LaDerby-G2 99 2 11 11½ 1½ 43½ 33¼ Santos J A L122 6.10 94-17 Peace Rules122⁴¼ [D]Kafwain122¹ Funny Cide122½ Came again rail 10

Awarded second purse money

18Jan03-10GP fst 1¹⁄₁₆ :23² :47¹ 1:11² 1:43 HolyBull-G3 87 13 7²¼ 41½ 44 44 56½ Santos J A L122 5.30 87-10 Offlee Wild116hd Powerful Touch116³ Bham118²½ Hit gate, wide, tired 13

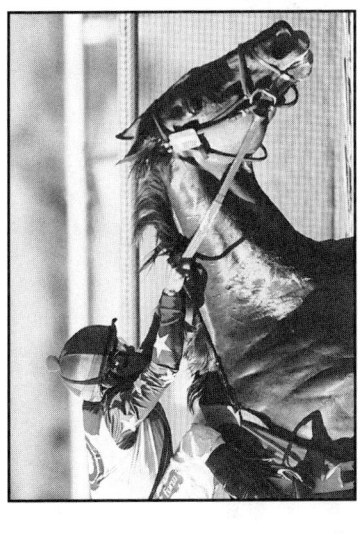

Older Female
AZERI, 1998
Br: Allen E. Paulson (Ky.)

Jade Hunter 1984	Mr. Prospector	Raise a Native
		Gold Digger
	Jadana	Pharly
		Janina
Zodiac Miss 1989	Ahonoora	Lorenzaccio
		Helen Nichols
	Capricornia	Try My Best
		Franconia

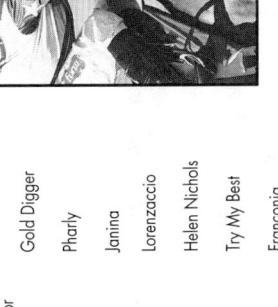

Mike Smith *Laura de Seroux*

	Life	16	14	2	0	$3,044,820	111		D.Fst	15	13	2	0	$2,004,820	110
	2003	5	4	1	0	$817,080	109		Wet(335)	1	1	0	0	$1,040,000	111
	2002	9	8	1	0	$2,181,540	111		Turf(265)	0	0	0	0	$0	–
		0	0	0	0	$0	–		Dst(0)	0	0	0	0	$0	–

Azeri
Own: Allen E. Paulson Living Trust

Ch. m. 6 (May) KEESEP99 $110,000
Sire: Jade Hunter (Mr. Prospector) $10,000
Dam: Zodiac Miss*Aus (Ahonoora*GB)
Br: Allen E. Paulson (Ky)
Tr: De Seroux Laura(0 0 0 0 .00) 2003:(111 14 .13)

28Sep03-6SA fst 1$\frac{1}{16}$:23² :47¹ 1:11¹ 1:42⁴ 3↑ⒻLdyScBCH-G2 101 5 54½ 53½ 53½ 32 32¼ Smith M E LB128 *.20 88- 16 Got Koko118¼ⒹElloluv116¹½ Azeri128¹ 3wd into lane,no bid 6
  Placed second through disqualification

10Aug03-8Dmr fst 1$\frac{1}{16}$:23¹ :47 1:11 1:42 3↑ⒻCLHrschH-G2 100 1 11 11½ 11½ 12½ 13¼ Smith M E LB127 *.30 95- 12 Azeri127³¼ *Got Koko*118ʰᵈ Tropical Blossom108⁴½ Bit off rail,handily 5

21Jun03-8Hol fst 1$\frac{1}{8}$:47¹ 1:10³ 1:35¹ 1:48² 3↑ⒻVanityH-G1 109 6 2½ 1ʰᵈ 2ⁿᵈ 11 12 Smith M E LB127 *.30 92- 14 Azeri127² Sister Girl Blues111½ *Bare Necessities*118⁴½ Dueled,inched clear 7

24May03-8Hol fst 1$\frac{1}{16}$:23 :46¹ 1:10 1:41⁴ 3↑ⒻMladyBCH-G1 109 4 2ʰᵈ 11 11½ 12½ 13 Smith M E LB125 *.20 95- 05 Azeri125³ Enjoy114³ Tropical Blossom111¹ Speed,met bids,clear 6

5Apr03-8OP fst 1$\frac{1}{16}$:24¹ :48³ 1:12¹ 1:43 4↑ⒻAplBlsmH-G1 105 6 3² 42 2½ 21½ 1ʰᵈ Smith M E L123 *.40 95- 11 Azeri123ʰᵈ Take ChargeLady118³½ *Mandy'sGold*116² Restrained,4-w, game 7

Turf Male

HIGH CHAPARRAL, 1999

Br: S. Coughlan (Ire)

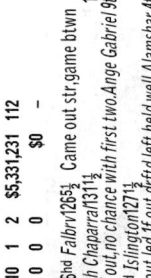

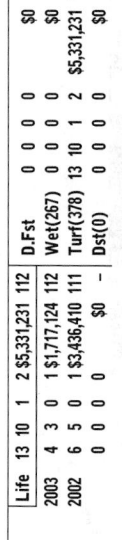

Sadler's Wells 1981	Northern Dancer	Nearctic	
		Natalma	
	Fairy Bridge	Bold Reason	
		Special	
Kasora 1993	Darshaan	Shirley Heights	
		Delsy	
	Kozana	Kris	
		Koblenza	

	Life	13	10	1	2	$5,331,231	112		D.Fst	0	0	0	0	$0	–
	2003	4	3	0	1	$1,717,124	112		Wet(267)	0	0	0	0	$0	–
	2002	6	5	0	1	$3,436,410	111		Turf(378)	13	10	1	2	$5,331,231	112
		0	0	0	0	$0	–		Dst(0)	0	0	0	0	$0	–

Aidan O'Brien   *Mick Kinane*

High Chaparral (Ire)

Own: Tabor Michael and Magnier, Mrs. John

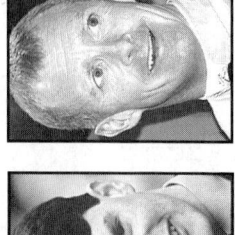
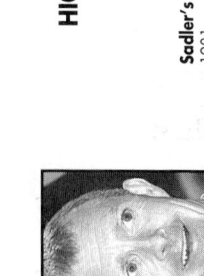

B. c. 5 (Mar)
Sire: Sadler's Wells (Northern Dancer)
Dam: Kasora (Darshaan*GB*)
Br: S. Coughlan (Ire)
Tr: O'Brien Aidan P(0 0 0 0 .00) 2003:(10 1 .10)

25Oct03–8SA   fm 1½ ⑪ :46³1:11² 2:00 2:24¹ 3♦BCTurf-G1   **112** 3 5² 3¹ 3² 3² 1ʰᵈ ♦Kinane M J   LB126 4.90 105– 04 ⒹⒽHighChaparral126 ⒹⒽJohar126ʰᵈ Falbrv126⁵¼ Came out str,game btwn 9
5Oct03♦Longchamp(Fr)   hy *1½ ⑪ RH 2:32¹ 3♦Prix de l'Arc de Triomphe-G1   35¾ Kinane M J   131 2.60 Dalakhani123¾ Mubtaker131⁵ High Chaparral131¹² 13
     Timeform rating: 124   Stk 18720000   4th on rail,3rd 2f out,no chance with first two.Ange Gabriel 9th
6Sep03♦Leopardstwn (Ire)   gd 1¼ ⑪ LH 2:03¹ 3♦Irish Champion Stakes-G1   1ⁿᵏ Kinane M J   130 4.00 High Chaparral130ⁿᵏ Falbrav130ʰᵈ Islington127¹¹ 7
     Timeform rating: 128   Stk 1110000   Trckd 4th,2nd 2f out,led 1f out,drft td left,held well.Alamshar 4th
10Aug03♦Curragh (Ire)   gd 1¼ ⑪ RH 2:04⁴ 3♦Royal Whip Stakes-G2   1⁴ Kinane M J   139 *.90 High Chaparral139⁴ Imperial Dancer132ⁿᵏ In Time's Eye132² 6
     Timeform rating: 128+   Stk 147000   Tracked in 3rd,2nd 1-1/2f out,led 1f out,driving

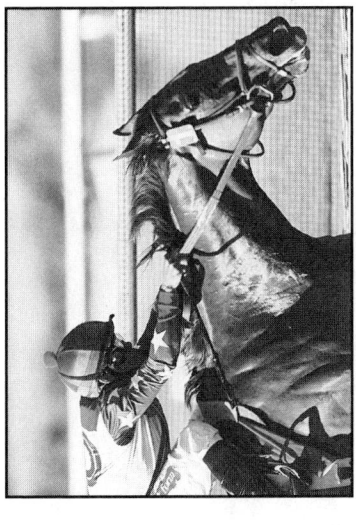

Older Female
AZERI, 1998
Br: Allen E. Paulson (Ky.)

Jade Hunter
1984
- Mr. Prospector
  - Raise a Native
  - Gold Digger
- Jadana
  - Pharly
  - Janina

Zodiac Miss
1989
- Ahonoora
  - Lorenzaccio
  - Helen Nichols
- Capricornia
  - Try My Best
  - Franconia

Mike Smith

Laura de Seroux

	Life	16	14	2	0	$3,044,820	111		D.Fst	15	13	2	0	$2,004,820	110
	2003	5	4	1	0	$817,080	109		Wet(335)	1	1	0	0	$1,040,000	111
	2002	9	8	1	0	$2,181,540	111		Turf(265)	0	0	0	0	$0	–
		0	0	0	0	$0	–		Dst(0)	0	0	0	0	$0	–

Azeri
Own: Allen E. Paulson Living Trust

Ch. m. 6 (May) KEESEP99 $110,000
Sire: Jade Hunter (Mr. Prospector) $10,000
Dam: Zodiac Miss*Aus (Ahonoora*GB)
Br: Allen E. Paulson (Ky)
Tr: De Seroux Laura(0 0 0 0 .00) 2003:(111 14 .13)

LB 128 88- 16 Got Koko118½ ⒹElloluv1161⅓ Azeri128¹ 3wd into lane,no bid 6

28Sep03-6SA fst 1¹⁄₁₆ :23² :47¹ 1:11¹1:42⁴ 3↑Ⓕ LdyScBCH-G2 101 5 54½ 53½ 53½ 32 32¾ Smith M E
  Placed second through disqualification

10Aug03-8Dmr fst 1¹⁄₁₆ :23¹ :47 1:11 1:42 3↑Ⓕ CLHrschH-G2 100 1 11 1½ 11½ 12½ 13¾ Smith M E LB127 95- 12 Azeri1273¼ Got Koko118hd Tropical Blossom1084¼ Bit off rail,handily 5

21Jun03-8Hol fst 1⅛ :47¹1:10³ 1:35¹1:48² 3↑Ⓕ VanityH-G1 109 6 2½ 1hd 2hd 11 12 Smith M E LB127 92- 14 Azeri1272 Sister Girl Blues111½ Bare Necessities1184½ Dueled,inched clear 7

24May03-8Hol fst 1⅛ :23 :46¹ 1:10 1:41⁴ 3↑Ⓕ MladyBCH-G1 109 4 2hd 11 12½ 12½ 13 Smith M E LB125 95- 05 Azeri125³ Enjoy1143 Tropical Blossom111¹ Speed,met bids,clear 6

5Apr03-8OP fst 1¹⁄₁₆ :24¹ :48³ 1:12¹1:43 4↑Ⓕ AplBlsmH-G1 105 6 32 42 2½ 21½ 1hd Smith M E L123 95- 11 Azeri123hd Take ChargeLady1183¾ Mandy'sGold116² Restrained, 4-w, game 7

Turf Male

HIGH CHAPARRAL, 1999

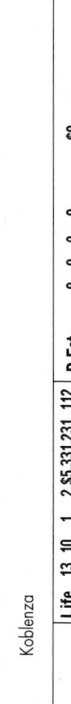

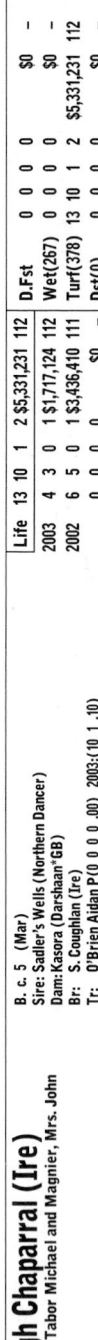

Aidan O'Brien   Mick Kinane

Br: S. Coughlan (Ire)

		Northern Dancer	Nearctic
			Natalma
Sadler's Wells		Fairy Bridge	Bold Reason
1981			Special
		Darshaan	Shirley Heights
			Delsy
Kasora		Kozana	Kris
1993			Koblenza

	Life	13	10	1	2	$5,331,231	112		D.Fst	0	0	0	0	$0	—
2003	4	3	0	1	$1,717,124	112		Wet(267)	0	0	0	0	$0	—
2002	6	5	0	0	$3,436,410	111		Turf(378)	13	10	1	2	$5,331,231	112
		0	0	0	0	$0	—		Dst(0)	0	0	0	0	$0	—

High Chaparral (Ire)

Own: Tabor Michael and Magnier, Mrs. John

B. c. 5 (Mar)
Sire: Sadler's Wells (Northern Dancer)
Dam: Kasora (Darshaan*GB)
Br: S. Coughlan (Ire)
Tr: O'Brien Aidan P(0 0 0 0 .00) 2003:(10 1 .10)

25Oct03-8SA fm 1½ ⑦ :48³1:11² 2:00 2:24¹ 3↑ BC Turf-G1   **112** 3 5² 3¹ 3² 3² 1hd ♦Kinane M J   LB126 *4.90 105– 04 [DH]HighChaparral126 [DH]Johar126hd Falbrv1265¼ Came out str,game btwn 9
5Oct03♦Longchamp(Fr) hy *1½ ⑦ RH 2:32¹ 3↑ Prix de l'Arc de Triomphe-G1   131   35¾ Kinane M J   2.60   Dalakhani123¾ Mubtaker131⁵ High Chaparral131½ 13
      Timeform rating: 124 Stk 18720000   4th on rail,3rd 2f out,no chance with first two,Ange Gabriel 9th
6Sep03♦Leopardstwn (Ire) gd 1¼ ⑦ LH 2:03¹ 3↑ Irish Champion Stakes-G1   130   1nk Kinane M J   4.00   High Chaparral130nk Falbrav130hd Islington1271½ 7
      Timeform rating: 128 Stk 1110000   Trckd 4th,2nd 2f out,led 1f out,drftd left,held well,Alamshar 4th
10Aug03♦Curragh (Ire) gd 1¼ ⑦ RH 2:04⁴ 3↑ Royal Whip Stakes-G2   139   1³ Kinane M J   *.90   High Chaparral139¾ Imperial Dancer132nk In Time's Eye1322 6
      Timeform rating: 128+ Stk 147000   Tracked in 3rd,2nd 1-1/2f out,led 1f out,driving

Turf Female

ISLINGTON, 1999

Br: Ballymacoll Stud Farm Ltd. (Ire)

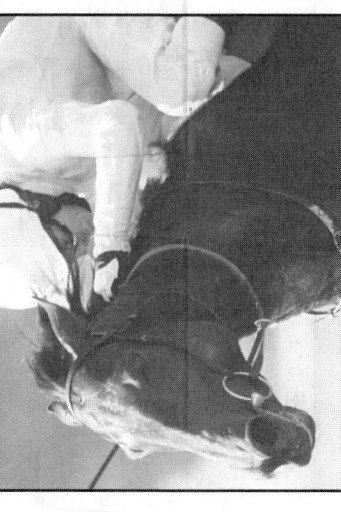

Sadler's Wells 1981	Northern Dancer	Nearctic
		Natalma
	Fairy Bridge	Bold Reason
		Special
Hellenic 1987	Darshaan	Shirley Heights
		Delsy
	Grecian Sea	Homeric
		Sea Venture

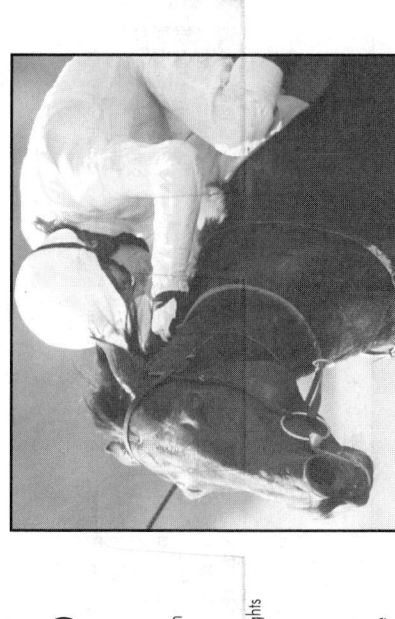

Kieran Fallon   Sir Michael Stoute

Islington (Ire)

Own: Executors Of The Late Lord Weinstock

B. f. 5   (Feb)
Sire: Sadler's Wells (Northern Dancer)
Dam: Hellenic (Darshaan*GB*)
Br: Ballymacoll Stud Farm Ltd (Ire)
Tr: Stoute Sir Michael R(0 0 0 0 .00)   2003:(2 1 .50)

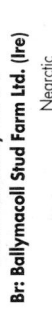

	Life	15	6	0	4	$1,553,043	109		D.Fst	0	0	0	0	$0	–
	2003	6	2	0	2	$955,142	109		Wet(267)	0	0	0	0	$0	–
	2002	7	4	0	1	$594,316	105	98–	Turf(378)	15	6	0	4	$1,553,043	109
		0	0	0	0	$0	–		Dst(0)	0	0	0	0	$0	–

30Nov03♦Tokyo (Jpn)   yl *1½① LH 2:28³ 3♣ Japan Cup-G1   9 13½ Fallon K   121   18.90   Tap Dance City129⁹ That's The Plenty121¾ *Symboli Kris* 5126ʰᵈ 18
  Timeform rating: 102   Stk 440000   Tracked in 4th,weakened over 1f out.Denon 8th,Johar 16th

25Oct03–6SA   fm   1¼ ①:46³ 1:10² 1:35¹1:59   3♣ⒷBCF&MTrf-G1   109   4   58   6¹¹   6¾   1ⁿᵏ Fallon K   LB123   *2.90   Islington123ⁿᵏ L'Ancresse118²¾ Yesterday118ⁿᵒ Pulled,bid,led,gamely 12
  Timeform rating: 124+   Stk 1110000   Rated at rear,pushed along after 4f,gaining late.Alamshar 4th

6Sep03♦Leopardstwn (Ire)   gd   1¼① LH 2:03¹   3♣ Irish Champion Stakes-G1   3ⁿᵏ Fallon K   127   16.00   High Chaparral130ⁿᵏ Falbrav130ʰᵈ Islington127¹¼ 7
  Timeform rating: Stk 1110000   Rated at rear,pushed along after 4f,gaining late.Alamshar 4th

20Aug03♦York (GB)   gf   1½① LH 2:27²   3♣Ⓕ Yorkshire Oaks-G1   11   Fallon K   130   *.70   Islington130¹ Ocean Silk120³ Summitville120¾ 8
  Timeform rating: 120   Stk 398000   3rd on rail,led over 2f out,held well.L'Ancresse5th,CasualLook7th

5Jly03♦Sandown Park (GB)   gd   1¼① RH 2:05²   3♣ Eclipse Stakes-G1   6 2¾ Fallon K   130   4.50   Falbrav133¾ Nayef133¹¼ Kaieteur133ⁿᵒ 15
  Timeform rating: 118   Stk 610000   Mid-pack on rail,3rd 1-1/2f out,faded late.Grandera 8th

18Jun03♦Ascot (GB)   gd   1¼① RH 2:05¹   4♣ Prince of Wales's Stakes-G1   3 3½ Fallon K   123   7.00   Nayef126²½ Ratt126¹ Islington123¹ 10
  Timeform rating: 118   Stk 587000   Trckd ldrs,angld out 1f out,drftd lft,held by first two.Falbrav5t

Robert Frankel

Jerry Bailey

Sprinter

ALDEBARAN, 1998
Br: Flaxman Holdings Ltd. (Ky)

Mr. Prospector 1970	Raise a Native → Native Dancer / Raise You
	Gold Digger → Nashua / Sequence
Chimes of Freedom 1987	Private Account → Damascus / Numbered Account
	Aviance → Northfields / Minnie Hauk

Aldebaran
Own: Flaxman Holdings Ltd

B. h. 6 (Feb)
Sire: Mr. Prospector (Raise a Native)
Dam: Chimes of Freedom (Private Account)
Br: Flaxman Holdings Ltd (Ky)
Tr: Frankel Robert J(0 0 0 0 .00) 2003:(411 114 .28)

Life	25	8	12	3	$1,739,186	122
2003	8	5	1	1	$1,110,606	122
2002	8	1	6	0	$428,800	113

D.Fst	12	5	5	1	$965,006	122
Wet(431)	3	1	2	0	$574,400	110
Turf(333)	10	2	5	2	$199,780	105
Dst(0)	0	0	0	0	$0	-

Steeplechase

McDynamo
Own: Moran Michael J

B. g. 7 (Apr)
Sire: Dynaformer (Roberto) $75,000
Dam: Rondonia (Monteverdi*Ire)
Br: Richard Fox, Nathan Fox & Richard Kaster (Ky)
Tr: Hendriks Sanna N(0 0 0 0 .00) 2003:(81 15 .19)

Life	19 10 3 0	$511,319	88			
Jumps	10 8 1 0	$466,429	–			
2003	3 3 0 0	$252,025	–	Wet	0 0 0 0	$0 –
2002	6 4 1 0	$199,404	–	Turf	9 2 2 0	$44,890 88

16Nov03–6Cam fm *2¾ Hurdles 5:05² 4♦ ColonlCp-G1 — 7 57½ 53¾ 12 12 14 Thornton C L156 – – McDynamo156⁴ Lord Zada156¹⁵¼ Pelagos156¹¼ Much the best 7

180ct03–4FH gd *2⅝ Hurdles 5:24 4♦⑧BrCupStp-G1 — 5 2² 11½ 12 14 115¼ Thornton C L156 – – McDynamo156¹⁵¼ Pelagos156² Mulahen156⁹¼ Easily 7

25Apr03–8Kee fm *2½ Hurdles 4:44¹ 4♦ RylChsHd-G1 — 1 76 76 66 11½ 17½ Thornton C L158 4.60 – – McDynmo158⁷½ ShmrockIsle158⁵ PrisethPrinc158ⁿᵏ Drew off,hand urging 8

Past Divisional Champions

Year	2-Year-Old Male	2-Year-Old Filly	3-Year-Old Male	3-Year-Old Filly	Handicap Horse	Handicap Mare	Grass Horse	Sprinter	Steeplechase	Horse of the Year
1936	Pompoon		Granville		Discovery			Myrtlewood	Bushranger	Granville
1937	Menow		War Admiral		Seabiscuit				Jungle King	War Admiral
1938	El Chico	Inscoelda	Stagehand		Seabiscuit	Marica				Seabiscuit
1939	Bimelech	Now What	Challedon	Unerring	Kayak II	Lady Maryland				Challedon
1940	Our Boots	Level Best	Bimelech		Challedon	War Plumage				Challedon
1941	Alsab	Petrify	Whirlaway	Painted Veil	Mioland	Fairy Chant			Speculate	Whirlaway
1942	Count Fleet	Ask Me Now	Alsab	Vagrancy	Whirlaway	Vagrancy			Elkridge	Whirlaway
1943	Platter	Duranza	Count Fleet	Stefanita	Market Wise	Mar-Kell			Brother Jones	Count Fleet
1944	Pavot	Busher	By Jimminy	Twilight Tear	Devil Diver	Twilight Tear			Rouge Dragon	Twilight Tear
1945	Star Pilot	Beaugay	Fighting Step	Busher	Stymie	Busher			Mercator	Busher
1946	Double Jay	First Flight	Assault	Bridal Flower	Armed	Gallorette		Polynesian	Elkridge	Assault
1947	Citation	Bewitch	Phalanx	But Why Not	Armed	But Why Not			War Battle	Armed
1948	Blue Peter	Myrtle Charm	Citation	Miss Request	Citation	Conniver		Coaltown	American Way	Citation
1949	Hill Prince	Bedo' Roses	Capot	Two Lea / Wistful	Coaltown	Bewitch		Delegate	Trough Hill	Capot
1950	Battlefield	Aunt Jinny	Hill Prince	Next Move	Noor	Two Lea		Royal Governor	Oedipus	Hill Prince
1951	Tom Fool	Rose Jet	Counterpoint	Kiss Me Kate	Hill Prince	Bed o' Roses		Sheilas Reward	Oedipus	Counterpoint
1952	Native Dancer	Sweet Patootie	One Count	Real Delight*	Crafty Admiral	Real Delight		Sheilas Reward	Jam*	One Count
1953	Porterhouse	Evening Out	Native Dancer	Grecian Queen	Tom Fool	Sickle's Image	Iceberg II	Tea-Maker	The Mast	Tom Fool
1954	Nashua	High Voltage	High Gun	Parlo*	Native Dancer	Parlo	Stan	Tom Fool	King Commander	Native Dancer
1955	Needles	Doubledogdare*	Nashua	Misty Morn	High Gun	Misty Morn*	St. Vincent	White Skies	Neji	Nashua
1956	Barbizon	Leallah*	Needles	Doubledogdare	Swaps	Blue Sparkler	Career Boy	Berseem	Shipboard	Swaps
1957	Nadir*	Idun	Bold Ruler	Bayou	Dedicate	Pucker Up	Round Table	Decathlon	Neji	Bold Ruler
1958	First Landing	Quill	Tim Tam	Idun	Round Table	Bornastar	Round Table	Decathlon	Neji	Round Table
1959	Warfare	My Dear Girl	Sword Dancer	Royal Native*	Sword Dancer*	Tempted	Round Table	Bold Ruler	Ancestor	Sword Dancer
1960	Hail to Reason	Bowl of Flowers	Kelso	Berlo	Bald Eagle	Royal Native		Intentionally	Benguala	Kelso
1961	Crimson Satan	Cicada	Carry Back	Bowl of Flowers	Kelso	Airmans Guide	T.V. Lark		Peal	Kelso
1962	Never Bend	Smart Deb	Jaipur	Cicada	Kelso	Primonetta			Barnabys Bluff	Kelso
1963	Hurry to Market	Tosmah*	Chateaugay	Lamb Chop	Kelso	Cicada	Mongo		Amber Diver	Kelso
1964	Bold Lad	Queen Empress	Northern Dancer	Tosmah*	Kelso	Tosmah			Bon Nouvel	Kelso
1965	Buckpasser	Moccasin	Tom Rolfe	What a Treat	Roman Brother	Old Hat	Parka	Affectionately	Bon Nouvel	Roman Brother*
1966	Successor	Regal Gleam	Buckpasser	Lady Pitt	Buckpasser*	Open Fire*	Assagai	Impressive	Mako*	Buckpasser
1967	Vitriolic	Queen of the Stage	Damascus	Full Sail	Damascus	Straight Deal	Fort Marcy	Dr. Fager	Quick Pitch	Damascus
1968	Top Knight	Gallant Bloom	Stage Door Johnny	Dark Mirage	Dr. Fager	Gamely	Dr. Fager	Dr. Fager	Bon Nouvel	Dr. Fager
1969	Silent Screen	Fast Attack*	Arts and Letters	Gallant Bloom	Arts and Letters*	Gallant Bloom*	Hawaii	Ta Wee	L'Escargot	Arts and Letters
1970	Hoist the Flag	Forward Gal	Personality	Office Queen*	Fort Marcy*	Shuvee	Fort Marcy	Ta Wee	Top Bid	Fort Marcy

Fillies voted Best 2-Year-Old: Beaugay (1945); First Flight (1946); Idun (1957)

Fillies voted Best 3-Year-Old: Twilight Tear (1944); Busher (1945); Dark Mirage (1968)

Eclipse Award Winners

Year	2-Year-Old Male	2-Year-Old Filly	3-Year-Old Male	3-Year-Old Filly	Handicap Horse	Handicap Mare	Grass Horse	Sprinter	Steeplechase	Horse of the Year
1971	Riva Ridge	Numbered Account	Canonero II	Turkish Trousers	Ack Ack	Shuvee	Run the Gauntlet	Ack Ack	Shadow Brook	Ack Ack
1972	Secretariat	La Prevoyante	Key to the Mint	Susan's Girl	Autobiography	Typecast	Cougar II	Chou Croute	Soothsayer	Secretariat
1973	Protagonist	Talking Picture	Secretariat	Desert Vixen	Riva Ridge	Susan's Girl	Secretariat	Shecky Greene	Athenian Idol	Secretariat
1974	Foolish Pleasure	Ruffian	Little Current	Chris Evert	Forego	Desert Vixen	Dahlia	Forego	Gran Kan	Forego
1975	Honest Pleasure	Dearly Precious	Wajima	Ruffian	Forego	Susan's Girl	Snow Knight	Gallant Bob	Life's Illusion	Forego
1976	Seattle Slew	Sensational	Bold Forbes	Revidere	Forego	Proud Delta	Youth	My Juliet	Straight and True	Forego
1977	Affirmed	Lakeville Miss	Seattle Slew	Our Mims	Forego	Cascapedia	Johnny D.	What a Summer	Cafe Prince	Seattle Slew
1978	Spectacular Bid	Candy Eclair / It's in the Air	Affirmed	Tempest Queen	Seattle Slew	Late Bloomer	Mac Diarmida	Dr. Patches / J.O. Tobin	Cafe Prince	Affirmed
1979	Rockhill Native	Smart Angle	Spectacular Bid	Davona Dale	Affirmed	Waya	Bowl Game (M) / Trillion (F)	Star de Naskra	Martie's Anger	Affirmed
1980	Lord Avie	Heavenly Cause	Temperence Hill	Genuine Risk	Spectacular Bid	Glorious Song	John Henry (M) / Just a Game II (F)	Plugged Nickle	Zaccio	Spectacular Bid
1981	Deputy Minister	Before Dawn	Pleasant Colony	Wayward Lass	John Henry	Relaxing	John Henry (M) / De La Rose (F)	Guilty Conscience	Zaccio	John Henry
1982	Roving Boy	Landaluce	Conquistador Cielo	Christmas Past	Lemhi Gold	Track Robbery	Perrault (M) / April Run (F)	Gold Beauty	Zaccio	Conq'st'dorCielo
1983	Devil's Bag	Althea	Slew o' Gold	Heartlight No. One	Bates Motel	Ambassador of Luck	John Henry (M) / All Along (F)	Chinook Pass	Flatterer	All Along
1984	Chief's Crown	Outstandingly	Swale	Life's Magic	Slew o' Gold	Princess Rooney	John Henry (M) / Royal Heroine (F)	Eillo	Flatterer	John Henry
1985	Tasso	Family Style	Spend a Buck	Mom's Command	Vanlandingham	Life's Magic	Cozzene (M) / Pebbles (F)	Precisionist	Flatterer	Spend a Buck
1986	Capote	Brave Raj	Snow Chief	Tiffany Lass	Turkoman	Lady's Secret	Manila (M) / Estrapade (F)	Smile	Flatterer	Lady's Secret
1987	Forty Niner	Epitome	Alysheba	Sacahuista	Ferdinand	North Sider	Theatrical (M) / Miesque (F)	Groovy	Inlander	Ferdinand
1988	Easy Goer	Open Mind	Risen Star	Winning Colors	Alysheba	Personal Ensign	Sunshine Forever (M) / Miesque (F)	Gulch	Jimmy Lorenzo	Alysheba
1989	Rhythm	Go for Wand	Sunday Silence	Open Mind	Blushing John	Bayakoa	Steinlen (M) / Brown Bess (F)	Safely Kept	Highland Bud	Sunday Silence
1990	Fly So Free	Meadow Star	Unbridled	Go for Wand	Criminal Type	Bayakoa	It'sallgreektome (M) / Laugh and Be Merry (F)	Housebuster	Morley Street	Criminal Type
1991	Arazi	Pleasant Stage	Hansel	Dance Smartly	Black Tie Affair	Queena	Tight Spot (M) / Miss Alleged (F)	Housebuster	Morley Street	Black Tie Affair

Year	2-Year-Old Male	2-Year-Old Filly	3-Year-Old Male	3-Year-Old Filly	Handicap Horse	Handicap Mare	Grass Horse	Sprinter	Steeplechase	Horse of the Year
1992	Gilded Time	Eliza	A.P. Indy	Saratoga Dew	Pleasant Tap	Paseana	Sky Classic (M) Flawlessly (F)	Rubiano	Lonesome Glory	A.P. Indy
1993	Dehere	Phone Chatter	Prairie Bayou	Hollywood Wildcat	Bertrando	Paseana	Kotashaan (M) Flawlessly (F)	Cardmania	Lonesome Glory	Kotashaan
1994	Timber Country	Flanders	Holy Bull	Heavenly Prize	The Wicked North	Sky Beauty	Paradise Creek (M) Hatoof (F)	Cherokee Run	Warm Spell	Holy Bull
1995	Maria's Mon	Golden Attraction	Thunder Gulch	Serena's Song	Cigar	Inside Information	Northern Spur (M) Possibly Perfect (F)	Not Surprising	Lonesome Glory	Cigar
1996	Boston Harbor	Storm Song	Skip Away	Yanks Music	Cigar	Jewel Princess	Singspiel (M) Wandesta (F)	Lit de Justice	Coreggio	Cigar
1997	Favorite Trick	Countess Diana	Silver Charm	Ajina	Skip Away	Hidden Lake	Chief Bearhart (M) Ryafan (F)	Smoke Glacken	Lonesome Glory	Favorite Trick
1998	Answer Lively	Silverbulletday	Real Quiet	Banshee Breeze	Skip Away	Escena	Buck's Boy (M) Fiji (F)	Reraise	Flat Top	Skip Away
1999	Anees	Chilukki	Charismatic	Silverbulletday	Victory Gallop	Beautiful Pleasure	Daylami (M) Soaring Softly (F)	Artax	Lonesome Glory	Charismatic
2000	Macho Uno	Caressing	Tiznow	Surfside	Lemon Drop Kid	Riboletta	Kalanisi (M) Perfect Sting (F)	Kona Gold	All Gong	Tiznow
2001	Johannesburg	Tempera	Point Given	Xtra Heat	Tiznow	Gourmet Girl	Fantastic Light (M) Banks Hill (F)	Squirtle Squirt	Pompeyo	Point Given
2002	Vindication	Storm Flag Flying	War Emblem	Farda Amiga	Left Bank	Azeri	High Chaparral (M) Golden Apples (F)	Orientate	Flat Top	Azeri
2003	Action This Day	Halfbridled	Funny Cide	Bird Town	Mineshaft	Azeri	High Chaparral (M) Islington (F)	Aldebaran	McDynamo	Mineshaft

*-Thoroughbred Racing Associations made alternate selection (listed below)

1952	Next Move–Handicap Mare	1966	Bold Bidder–Handicap Horse
1952	Oedipus–Steeplechase	1966	Summer Scandal–Handicap Mare
1954	Lavender Hill–Handicap Mare	1966	Tuscalee–Steeplechase
1955	Nasrina–2-Year-Old Filly	1967	Buckpasser–Handicap Horse
1955	Parlo–Handicap Mare	1967	Gamely–3-Year-Old Filly
1956	Romanita–2-Year-Old Filly	1968	Process Shot–2-Year-Old Filly
1957	Jewel's Reward–2-Year-Old Male	1968	Fort Marcy–Grass Horse
1959	Silver Spoon–3-Year-Old Filly	1969	Tudor Queen–2-Year-Old Filly
1959	Round Table–Handicap Horse	1969	Nodouble–Handicap Horse
1963	Castle Forbes–2-Year-Old Filly	1969	Gamely–Handicap Mare
1964	Old Hat–Handicap Mare	1970	Fanfreluche–3-Year-Old Filly
1965	Moccasin–Horse of the Year	1970	Nodouble–Handicap Horse

Previous Eclipse Award Winners

Year	Jockey
1971	Laffit Pincay Jr.
1972	Braulio Baeza
1973	Laffit Pincay Jr.
1974	Laffit Pincay Jr.
1975	Braulio Baeza
1976	Sandy Hawley
1977	Steve Cauthen
1978	Darrel McHargue
1979	Laffit Pincay Jr.
1980	Chris McCarron
1981	William Shoemaker
1982	Angel Cordero Jr.
1983	Angel Cordero Jr.
1984	Pat Day
1985	Laffit Pincay Jr.
1986	Pat Day
1987	Pat Day
1988	Jose Santos
1989	Kent Desormeaux
1990	Craig Perret
1991	Pat Day
1992	Kent Desormeaux
1993	Mike Smith
1994	Mike Smith
1995	Jerry Bailey
1996	Jerry Bailey
1997	Jerry Bailey
1998	Gary Stevens
1999	Jorge Chavez
2000	Jerry Bailey
2001	Jerry Bailey
2002	Jerry Bailey
2003	Jerry Bailey

Year	Trainer
1971	Charles Whittingham
1972	Lucien Laurin
1973	H. Allen Jerkens
1974	Sherill Ward
1975	Steve DiMauro
1976	Lazaro Barrera
1977	Lazaro Barrera
1978	Lazaro Barrera
1979	Lazaro Barrera
1980	Bud Delp
1981	Ron McAnally
1982	Charles Whittingham
1983	Woody Stephens
1984	Jack Van Berg
1985	D. Wayne Lukas
1986	D. Wayne Lukas
1987	D. Wayne Lukas
1988	Shug McGaughey
1989	Charles Whittingham
1990	Carl Nafzger
1991	Ron McAnally
1992	Ron McAnally
1993	Robert Frankel
1994	D. Wayne Lukas
1995	William I. Mott
1996	William I. Mott
1997	Bob Baffert
1998	Bob Baffert
1999	Bob Baffert
2000	Robert Frankel
2001	Robert Frankel
2002	Robert Frankel
2003	Robert Frankel

Year	Apprentice Jockey
1971	Gene St. Leon
1972	Thomas Wallis
1973	Steve Valdez
1974	Chris McCarron
1975	Jimmy Edwards
1976	George Martens
1977	Steve Cauthen
1978	Ron Franklin
1979	Cash Asmussen
1980	Frank Lovato Jr.
1981	Richard Migliore
1982	Alberto Delgado
1983	Declan Murphy
1984	Wesley Ward
1985	Art Madrid Jr.
1986	Allen Stacy
1987	Kent Desormeaux
1988	Steve Capanas
1989	Michael Luzzi
1990	Mark Johnston
1991	Mickey Walls
1992	Rosemary Homeister Jr.
1993	Juan Umana
1994	Dale Beckner
1995	Ramon Perez
1996	Neil Poznansky
1997	Roberto Rosado
	Philip Teator (tie)
1998	Shaun Bridgmohan
1999	Ariel Smith
2000	Tyler Baze
2001	Jeremy Rose
2002	Ryan Fogelsonger
2003	Eddie Castro

Owner-Breeder

1971	Paul Mellon
1972	Meadow Stable
1973	Meadow Stable

Owner

1971	Mr./Mrs. E.E. Fogelson
1974	Dan Lasater
1975	Dan Lasater
1976	Dan Lasater
1977	Maxwell Gluck
1978	Harbor View Farm
1979	Harbor View Farm
1980	Mr./Mrs. B. Firestone
1981	Dotsam Stable
1982	Viola Sommer
1983	John Franks
1984	John Franks
1985	Mr. and Mrs. Eugene Klein
1986	Mr. and Mrs. Eugene Klein
1987	Mr. and Mrs. Eugene Klein
1988	Ogden Phipps
1989	Ogden Phipps
1990	Frances Genter
1991	Sam-Son Farms
1992	Juddmonte Farms
1993	John Franks
1994	John Franks
1995	Allen Paulson
1996	Allen Paulson
1997	Carolyn Hine

1998	Frank Stronach
1999	Frank Stronach
2000	Frank Stronach
2001	Richard Englander
2002	Richard Englander
2003	Juddmonte Farms

Breeder

1974	John W. Galbreath
1975	Fred W. Hooper
1976	Nelson Bunker Hunt
1977	E.P. Taylor
1978	Harbor View Farm
1979	Claiborne Farm
1980	Mrs. Henry D. Paxson
1981	Golden Chance Farm
1982	Fred W. Hooper
1983	E.P. Taylor
1984	Claiborne Farm
1985	Nelson Bunker Hunt
1986	Paul Mellon
1987	Nelson Bunker Hunt
1988	Ogden Phipps
1989	North Ridge Farm
1990	Calumet Farm
1991	Mr./Mrs. John C. Mabee
1992	William S. Farish
1993	Allen Paulson
1994	William T. Young
1995	Juddmonte Farms
1996	Farnsworth Farms
1997	Mr./Mrs. John C. Mabee
1998	Mr./ Mrs. John C. Mabee
1999	William S. Farish
2000	Frank Stronach
2001	Juddmonte Farms
2002	Juddmonte Farms
2003	Juddmonte Farms

Award of Merit

1976	Jack Dreyfus
1977	Steve Cauthen
1978	Ogden Mills Phipps
1979	Frank E. Kilroe
1980	John D. Shapiro
1981	William Shoemaker
1984	John Gaines
1985	Keene Daingerfield
1986	Herman Cohen
1987	J.B. Faulconer
1988	John Forsythe
1989	Michael Sandler
1990	Warner L. Jones
1991	Fred W. Hooper
1992	Joe Hirsch
	Robert P. Strub
1993	Paul Mellon
1994	Alfred G. Vanderbilt
1995	James E. "Ted" Bassett III
1996	Allen Paulson
1997	Bob and Beverly Lewis
1998	D. G. Van Clief Jr.
2000	Jim McKay
2001	Pete Pedersen
	Harry Mangurian
2002	Ogden Phipps
	Howard Battle
2003	Richard Duchossois

Special Award
1971	Robert J. Kleberg
1974	Charles Hatton
1976	William Shoemaker
1980	John T. Landry
	Pierre E. Bellocq
1984	C.V. Whitney
1985	Arlington Park
1987	Anheuser-Busch
1988	Edward DeBartolo Sr.
1989	Richard L Duchossois
1994	Edward Arcaro
	John Longden
1995	Russell Baze
1998	Oak Tree Racing Association
1999	Laffit Pincay Jr.
2000	John Hettinger
2001	Sheikh Mohammed bin Rashid al Maktoum

Outstanding Achievement
1971	Charles Engelhard (posthumously)
1972	Arthur B. Hancock Jr. (posthumously)

Man of the Year
1972	John W. Galbreath
1973	Edward P. Taylor
1974	William L. McKnight
1975	John A. Morris

Outstanding Newspaper Writing
1971	Scott Young, Toronto Telegram
1972	Phil Ranallo, Buffalo Courier Express
1973	Red Smith, The New York Times
1974	William H. Rudy, New York Post
1975	Bob Harding, Newark Star-Ledger
1976	Edwin Pope, Miami Herald
1977	Skip Bayless, Los Angeles Times
1978	Joe Hirsch, Daily Racing Form
1979	Billy Reed, Louisville Courier-Journal
1980	Maryjean Wall, Lexington Herald
1981	Dave Kindred, Washington Post
1982	Edwin Pope, Miami Herald
1983	Dave Koerner, Louisville Times
1984	Bill Christine, Los Angeles Times
	Eddie Donnally, Dallas Morning News
1985	Paul Moran, Newsday
1986	Edwin Pope, Miami Herald
1987	Tim Layden, Capital Newspapers
1988	Billy Reed, Lexington Herald-Leader
1989	Ronnie Virgets, Gambit
1990	Paul Moran, Newsday
1992	James Wallace, Seattle Post Intelligencer
1993	Jennie Rees, Louisville Courier-Journal
1994	Mike Downey, Los Angeles Times
1995	Stephanie Diaz, Riverside Press-Enterprise
1996	Tom Keyser, The Baltimore Sun
1997	Maryjean Wall, Lexington Herald-Leader
1998	Tom Keyser, The Baltimore Sun
1999	Maryjean Wall, Lexington Herald-Leader

Outstanding Magazine Writing
1971	Bill Surface, Reader's Digest
1972	Edward L. Bowen, The Blood-Horse
1973	Pete Axthelm, Newsweek
1974	Chet Hagen, Spur
1975	Frank Deford, Sports Illustrated
1976	Whitney Tower, Classic
1977	Whitney Tower, Classic
1978	Bill Nack, Sports Illustrated
1979	William Leggett, Sports Illustrated
1980	Clive Gammon, Sports Illustrated
1981	Joseph P. Pons Jr., The Blood-Horse
1982	Jay Hovdey, Horsemen's Journal
1983	Arnold Kirkpatrick, Keeneland
1984	Frank Deford, Sports Illustrated
1985	Bill Mooney, Thoroughbred Record
1986	Bill Nack, Sports Illustrated
1987	Jack Mann, Spur
1988	Jennie Rees, Sunday Magazine, Louisville Courier-Journal
1989	Bill Nack, Sports Illustrated
1990	Bill Nack, Sports Illustrated
1992	Joseph P. Pons Jr., The Blood-Horse
1993	Stephanie Diaz, The Backstretch
1994	Jay Hovdey, The Blood-Horse
1995	Award vacated
1996	Don Clippinger, Mid-Atlantic Thoroughbred
1997	Bill Heller, The Backstretch
1998	Laura Hillenbrand, American Heritage
1999	Tom Keyser, Breeders' Cup Souvenir Magazine

Outstanding News Writing
1991	Bill Nack, Sports Illustrated

Outstanding Feature Writing
1991	Bill Nack, Sports Illustrated

Outstanding News/Commentary
2000	Jay Hovdey, Daily Racing Form
2001	Janet Patton, Lexington Herald-Leader
2002	Joe Drape, The New York Times
2003	Jay Hovdey, Daily Racing Form

Outstanding Feature/Enterprise
2000	Mary Simon, Thoroughbred Times
2001	Laura Hillenbrand, Equus
2002	John Jeremiah Sullivan, Harper's
2003	William Nack, GQ

Photography Achievement
1971	Art Rogers, Los Angeles Times
1972	Bob Coglianese, New York Racing Times
1973	Harry Leder, United Press International
1974	Michael Burns, Ontario Jockey Club
1975	John Pineda, Miami Herald
1976	John J. Vasile, Covina (Cal.) Sentinel
1977	John Walther, Miami Herald
1978	Douglas Lees, Fauquier Democrat
1979	Skip Ball, Maryland Horse
1980	Bob Coglianese, New York Racing Assn.
1981	Tony Baker, River Downs
1982	Kay Coyte, Horsemen's Journal
1983	Rayetta Burr, Paddock
1984	Bill Straus, Breeders' Cup Ltd.
1985	Kim Pratt, Garden State Park
1986	Janice Wilkman, Los Angeles Times
1987	Dan Farrell, New York Daily News
1988	Ben Van Hook, Louisville Courier-Journal
1989	Ron Cortes, Philadelphia Inquirer
1990	Michael Cartee, California Thoroughbred
1991	Rayetta Burr, Benoit and Associates

1992	Barbara Livingston, The Blood-Horse
1993	Michael Burns, Ontario Jockey Club
1994	Tony Leonard
1995	Michael J. Marten
1996	Skip Dickstein
1997	Jean Raftery Russell
1998	Ryan Haynes, Northlands Park
1999	Michael J. Marten
2000	Dave Landry
2001	Barbara Livingston
2002	Michael Clevenger, Louisville Courier-Journal
2003	Frank Anderson, Thoroughbred Times

Local Television Achievement

1975	Cawood Ledford, WHAS, Louisville
1976	NYRA-OTB Race of the Week
1977	Jane Chastain, KABC, Los Angeles
1978	Cawood Ledford, WHAS, Louisville
1979	Dave Johnson, ON-TV
1980	WCAU, Philadelphia
1981	WHAS, Louisville
1982	ON-TV, Los Angeles
1983	Cawood Ledford Productions
1984	NYRA/Cinema Mistral
1985	Oak Tree Racing Association
1986	Louisiana Downs
1987	Arlington Park
1988	Joseph Kwong. KCET-TV, Los Angeles
1989	Chris Thomas, WFLA-TV, Tampa
1990	Philip von Borries, WKPC-TV, Louisville
1991	WABC-TV, New York
1992	Rick Cushing, WKPC-TV, Louisville
1993	Stephen Sadis, KBTC, Tacoma
1994	Ronnie Virgets, WNXO, New Orleans
1995	JCM Productions, New York
1996	Kenny Rice, WTVQ-TV, Lexington
1997	Brian Blessing, Ontario Jockey Club
1998	Jeff Lifson, WHAS-TV, Louisville
1999	Fox Sports West 2 – The Best of Santa Anita
2000	Maryland Jockey Club, WMAR, Baltimore
2001	Steve Crump, WTVI-TV, Charlotte, NC
2002	Bryan Krantz, Fox SportsNet Southwest
2003	G.D. Hieronymus, WKYT-27, Lexington

National Television Achievement

1971	Burt Bacharach, CBS
1972	Chuck Milton, Tony Verna, CBS
1973	Chuck Milton, Tony Verna, CBS
1974	Pen Densham, John Watson, Insight Productions
1975	CBS
1976	CBS
1977	Jack Whitaker, CBS
1978	Roger Murphy, Public Broadcasting Service
1979	Don Ohlmeyer, NBC
1980	ABC
1981	Canadian Broadcasting Corporation
1982	ESPN
1983	CBS
1984	NBC
1985	CBS
1986	ABC
1987	ABC
1988	Thoroughbred Sports, Racing Across America
1989	ABC Sports

1990	ABC Sports
1991	CBS News, Sunday Morning with Charles Kuralt
1992	ABC Sports
1993	E.S. Lamoreaux III, CBS News, Sunday Morning with Charles Kuralt
1994	ABC's Wide World of Sports
1995	ABC's Wide World of Sports
1996	NBC Sports
1997	E.S. Lamoreaux III, CBS News, Sunday Morning with Charles Kuralt
1998	E.S. Lamoreaux III, CBS News, Sunday Morning with Charles Kuralt
1999	Live Racing – ABC Sports, Belmont coverage Feature – ESPN, Sports Century's 50 Greatest Athletes
2000	ABC Sports, Kentucky Derby coverage
2001	NBC, Breeders' Cup coverage

Live Racing

2002	David Michaels, NBC Sports, Preakness Stakes
2003	David Michaels, NBC Sports, Preakness Stakes

National Television Feature

2000	Paul Hutchinson, ABC Sports
2001	Mark Shapiro and Jim Cohen, ESPN, Sports Century Top 50 and Beyond
2002	Alexander Piper, NBC Sports
2003	Dora Militaru and Craig Deleval, MSNBC Joan Ciampi, ESPN2

Audio/Multi-Media Internet

2002	Shelby Whitfield, Premiere Radio Networks
2003	Hannan/Stauffer, KSPN ESPN Mark Miller, WBAL

Film Achievement

1972	Joseph Burnham

Radio Achievement

1971	Win Elliot
1976	Win Elliot
1978	Ted Patterson, WBAL, Baltimore
1979	Dick Woolley, WITH, Baltimore
1981	WBAL, Baltimore
1982	ABC Radio Network
1983	Tom Davis, WCBM, Baltimore
1984	WBAL, Baltimore
1985	Bob Lauder, WHAS, Louisville
1986	ABC Radio Network
1987	Bob Lauder, WHAS, Louisville
1988	John Asher, WAVG, Louisville
1989	John Asher, WAVG, Louisville
1990	John Asher, WHAS, Louisville
1991	Julia McEvoy, National Public Radio
1992	John Asher, WHAS, Louisville
1993	Tom Leach, WVLK, Lexington
1994	John Asher, WHAS, Louisville
1995	Vic Stauffer, KKAR, Omaha
1996	Robin Dawson, CJCL, Toronto
1997	John Patti, WBAL, Baltimore
1998	No award presented
1999	Tom Leach, WVLK, Lexington
2000	Premiere Radio
2001	Mark Miller, WBAL, Baltimore

2003 ECLIPSE AWARD

OUTSTANDING NEWS/COMMENTARY

BY JAY HOVDEY, DAILY RACING FORM

"Remembering laughter amid tears"
(Originally published in Daily Racing Form, Oct. 15, 2003)

ARCADIA, Calif. - Paddy Gallagher leaned on the wood railing at the mouth of his stable shed row and gazed up at a huge pepper tree swaying gently in the soft autumn breeze. In the distance, Trevor Denman's voice could be heard calling a race near the end of the Santa Anita program. It was almost four o'clock. Gallagher's horses were hungry, and they were letting him know.

"I remember the day I showed up to go to work for Bill at Hollywood Park," Gallagher said. "There was him and me, and just two horses. And a groom if I remember. I'm not sure what we were thinking, but before too long there were 35 horses in the barn. That was March of 1990."

It had been nine hours since Gallagher had learned that his best friend had died. Nine melancholy hours to deal with the fact that Bill Shoemaker would no longer be on the other end of the telephone for their daily calls, that Shoe would never again summon a tale from the good old days, nor laugh at one of Gallagher's famously off-color jokes.

"It was just like him, wasn't it?" Gallagher said. "Going quietly in his sleep. Never making a fuss."

When Bill Shoemaker closed his eyes and took his last, labored breath, some time between 4:30 and 6 a.m. Sunday in his San Marino home, a curtain softly descended upon the life of a man whose signature grace was the untroubled defiance of insurmountable odds.

He survived a premature birth weight of about two pounds. He defied the conventional prejudice against small jockeys. He survived the public pounding of a misjudged Kentucky Derby finish that dogged him for years. His answer, in the end, was 8,833 victories, four of them in the Derby, including his last at age 54.

In recent years, Shoemaker had all but disappeared from public view. The lonely free-

way accident that left him a quadriplegic occurred in April 1991, cutting short what was destined to be a successful second career as a Thoroughbred trainer.

Shoemaker continued to work alongside Gallagher, lending his name and considerable insight to the operation. But in the end, the hard work of mere survival became too great. Shoemaker officially retired in 1997.

"Here's the kind of horseman he was, the kind of trainer he would have been," Gallagher began.

"One morning that first season he went by the barn at Hollywood to get on a couple young fillies. On the way back to Santa Anita he calls me and says, 'You're gonna get mad at me when you see the work tab. They went kind of fast. But the one filly has more natural speed than maybe anything I've ever been on. And the other one is all class. She could be very special.'

"The one was Glen Kate," Gallagher said. "The other was Fire the Groom, and neither one had started."

Let the record show that Glen Kate went on to win the Laurel Dash and the Hong Kong International Bowl, and that Fire the Groom won the Beverly D.

Shoemaker, by then confined to a wheelchair, had to miss those races. He was busy learning how to deal with life without the ability to move his hands, arms, or legs.

"I could never imagine what he went through, just to get from one day to the next," Gallagher said. "He had to be handled for everything. Picked up to be showered, put in his chair, put in bed. They had to move his arms and legs to keep the circulation going, and breathing exercises to help him cough, to keep his lungs clear.

"But I never heard him complain," Gallagher said. "And he could still laugh. Laughed so hard sometimes that tears would come to his eyes. Only thing was, someone would have to reach over and wipe those tears away for him."

In what turned out to be his final visit,

Shoemaker dropped by Santa Anita earlier this month and spent the afternoon in the jockeys' room. That evening, he joined Gallagher for dinner in nearby Sierra Madre.

"He was talking about the new rider, Ryan Fogelsonger," Gallagher recalled. "Bill thought the kid looked pretty good on a horse. Thought he might make it out here. Then he said he was kind of mad at himself for not going over and introducing himself to the kid. Imagine that. Imagine being Bill Shoemaker, and being so humble."

In the coming days, Shoemaker tributes will pour forth. A memorial service is planned. Bill would be a little miffed at all the bother, but it's not for him - it is for his friends, his fans, his family, and especially for his daughter, Amanda. Not surprisingly, Shoemaker's preference was to keep things low key.

"We were talking about it one day," Gallagher said. "I don't remember what brought it up, but Bill said that for sure he wanted to be cremated. I told him not to worry, and for no extra charge I'd scatter his ashes on the finish line at Churchill Downs so he'd never forget where it was. That made him laugh."

He laughed so hard he cried.

"Lifetime's worth of great rides"
(Originally published in Daily Racing Form, Oct. 17, 2003)
ARCADIA, Calif. - It can be argued that Bill Shoemaker's greatest ride came on the summer day in 1991 when, in the first months of his quadriplegic existence following his one-car wreck, he successfully negotiated the hallway of a Colorado rehabilitation hospital using the sip-and-puff mechanism of his customized wheelchair. Later, he became so adept at its operation that he could run right over the tip of your shoe and make you think it was an accident.

Shoemaker spent more than 12 years in that wheelchair before his death last Sunday. He leaves behind a wealth of memories - Shoemaker stories have been flying this week - and there are some that even the humble Shoemaker enjoyed chewing on more than others.

First and foremost, there was the 1986 Kentucky Derby. Shoemaker was 54 at the time, making moves like a kid without a care.

"It was probably his greatest ride, but I wish he'd saved it for another day," said Chris McCarron, who finished second in that Derby aboard Bold Arrangement.

"Shoe made three perfect decisions that day," McCarron began. "First, he took his horse back to last from the inside post, otherwise he might have been put over the fence on the first turn. Then he made a move down the backstretch, cutting inside horses when he needed to. Finally, there was his move to the rail in the stretch. My colt was busy battling Broad Brush, and we had him beat. Then I look over and there's that little sonofagun going by us. I thought, 'Where'd he come from?' "

The companion piece to the 1986 Derby was the 1987 Breeders' Cup Classic at Hollywood Park, which hopefully will be highlighted during the NBC telecast of the Breeders' Cup on Oct. 25. Ferdinand and Shoemaker teamed to defeat Alysheba and McCarron in history's most exciting clash of Kentucky Derby winners.

"I could have gone to the lead at any time," Shoemaker said. "But I knew Ferdinand liked to pull himself up when he was in front. I knew Alysheba would be coming, but I had to wait as long as I could."

The sight of Shoemaker sitting chilly with barely a sixteenth of a mile to run in a $3 million race was unforgettable. When Shoemaker finally roused Ferdinand, the big red colt gave him just enough to win by a nose.

It was Shoemaker who rode Buckpasser to a nose victory over Abe's Hope in the 1966 Flamingo Stakes, dubbed the "Chicken Flamingo" because Hialeah management thought Buckpasser was such a lock that they made it a non-wagering event. Shoemaker was not fooled.

"The hardest race to win is the race you're supposed to win," he said.

John Henry was supposed to win the inaugural running of the Arlington Million in 1981, but all bets were scrambled when the course came up muddy and deep. John Henry hated the going, and Shoemaker knew it. But Shoe also knew his horse. Instead of pressing the issue, searching for good ground, or asking for too much, Shoemaker let John Henry get his sea legs. Ol' John found his rhythm just in time to catch The Bart on the line and win by a nose.

Shoemaker's work on Exceller in the 1979 Jockey Club Gold Cup ranks with his best. That day, in the wind and rain, Seattle Slew (under Angel Cordero) and Affirmed splashed through the Belmont mud in fast early fractions, while Shoemaker found himself more than 30 lengths off the pace halfway through the race. Then they began to move.

"I knew Cordero would be looking for me," Shoemaker said. "He'd try to shut me off or carry me wide like he always does. So I put my horse right behind him, in his blind spot. When he looked for me over his right shoulder, I took my horse to the inside and went to the lead. Still, Seattle Slew came back to make it close." The margin was a nose.

Shoemaker's all-time favorite ride came in the 1962 San Juan Capistrano Handicap, when he nursed the hard-core miler Olden Times to a narrow win at nearly 1 3/4 miles. It was a race later that year, however, that will always rank among the greatest in the Shoemaker canon, when Shoemaker rode Belmont winner Jaipur for Moody Jolley in the Travers against the brilliant Ridan.

"Maybe there was never a race like it," wrote veteran turf journalist Russ Harris. "It simply isn't possible for two horses to throw hooks into each other for a solid 1 1/4 miles, going as hard as they can every inch of the route, without giving way in the stretch. . . . It isn't possible, but Jaipur and Ridan did it. I never saw a horse race like it, and I couldn't find anyone at Saratoga who had."

Jaipur beat Ridan by a bob of the nose.

"Jolley proclaimed that Shoemaker was worth five pounds over any other rider, and Jaipur had finished well behind Ridan in earlier starts with other riders," Harris added. "If you switch the riders, would Ridan have won the Travers? I would have run on that ticket."

"Life and loss under red skies"
(Originally published in Daily Racing Form, Oct. 24, 2003)

ARCADIA, Calif. - Southern California is on fire again, so it must be time for a Breeders' Cup at Santa Anita Park.

When the international racing carnival last hit the Santa Anita side of town 10 years ago, the mountains rimming the L.A. basin were alive with the flames of a dozen distinct conflagrations. More fires burned to the south in Orange County, but the most dramatic - at least from the vantage point of Breeders' Cup participants - was the Sierra Madre fire that destroyed 151 homes in the foothills above the racetrack.

Hot and tinder-dry conditions were ripe for another outbreak this week, so it came as no real surprise Tuesday afternoon when the skies to the east, west, and south of Santa Anita filled with the sickly, reddish-gray smoke of brush in full burn. October in Southern California can be a very mean season.

The drama was not lost on the thousand or so faithful fans and friends of the family who gathered in the Santa Anita stands late Tuesday afternoon to spend a few precious moments in remembrance of Bill Shoemaker. Natural disasters mixed well with the emotions of personal loss.

The indomitable spirit of Bill Shoemaker permeates Santa Anita, from the histories of its greatest races, to the statuary in the paddock gardens, to the oldest corners of the jockeys' room, where Shoemaker reigned as a benign, accessible king and played his schoolboy pranks.

Shoemaker's death on the morning of Oct. 12, at age 72, trumped the sense of loss pervading the Southern California racing world since the summer of 2002, when a healthy Chris McCarron retired from riding. That was followed by career-ending injuries to Eddie Delahoussaye and Laffit Pincay, and the near-fatal experience of Gary Stevens in August at Arlington Park. Suddenly, everyone felt very mortal.

Shoemaker's death, however, rang a bell of finality. An era had ended, one populated by such formidable personalities as Charlie Whittingham, Eddie Arcaro, Johnny Longden, and Lazaro Barrera. The history of horse racing had come to a natural divide - those lucky enough to have lived in the time of Bill Shoemaker now had to deal with what comes next.

Tuesday's ceremony was anchored with dignity by Hollywood Park's Mike Willman. Amy Zimmerman's Santa Anita television team put together a full-blooded video montage of Shoemaker's life, highlighted by priceless archival film shot by the late Joe Burnham. An eloquent eulogy was delivered by John Gosden, the British trainer whose California career was graced by Shoemaker's friendship, as well as his active participation in a number of stakes wins.

The congregation was shaken briefly by the tearful appearance of Don Pierce, Shoemaker's closest running mate for 40 years and a ferociously competitive jockey in

his time. Pierce could barely deliver his tribute, leading once again to the nagging question: What happens when the tough guy
cries?

It was, however, that Mount Rushmore of
riders - Pincay, Delahoussaye, McCarron,
and Stevens - who stepped up to say what
needed to be said, leaving no doubt as to the
impact of their departed friend.

"Before Shoemaker, with very few excep-
tions, jockeys got little respect," McCarron
said. "Shoe forced people to respect jockeys.
They couldn't help respecting jockeys after
what he did on the track, and off the track."

True to form, Delahoussaye offered no
frills. "I love him, and I'll miss him," he said.
Then he read a poem titled "I'm Free,"
which contained the lines, "If parting has left
a void / then fill it with remembered joy."

"He was a great friend," Pincay said. "He's
probably laughing at all of us sitting in the
sun sweating, while he's having a drink with
Charlie."

Ten years ago, when the Breeders' Cup
was at Santa Anita Park, trainer Bill
Shoemaker sent out Diazo, who finished
sixth in the Breeders' Cup Classic. Shoe had
been in a wheelchair for two years, but that
did not stop him from being part of the
biggest day of the season.

Pincay, in addition to riding Diazo, won
the Juvenile Fillies that day aboard Phone
Chatter. Delahoussaye won the Distaff on
Hollywood Wildcat (after dropping his stick)
and the Sprint on Cardmania from out of the
clouds. McCarron endured tough losses in
both the Distaff, on Paseana, and the Turf,
aboard Bien Bien, while Stevens took the
Juvenile with Brocco and thought he was
home and dry in the Classic on Bertrando,
until the French longshot Arcangues ran
them down.

It was Stevens who sounded the sweetest
note as he concluded his remembrance of
his days as a young kid from Idaho learning
the ropes at Shoemaker's knee. Everyone
knew that Shoemaker lasted as long as he
did in a quadraplegic state because he did
not want to miss the formative years of his
daughter, now 23.

Looking down at Amanda Shoemaker, a
poised young woman who trains hunters and
jumpers at a San Francisco-area stable,
Stevens spoke for all of racing when he said,
"Thank you, Amanda, for giving us 12 more
years with your dad."

Eclipse Award-winning photograph
By Frank Anderson, Lexington Herald-Leader

Alphabetical Listing of North American Champions and Leading Sires and Broodmares

Horse	YOB	Title	Year
A.P. Indy	1989	Horse of the year	1992
A.P. Indy	1989	Champion 3-year-old colt	1992
A.P. Indy	1989	Leading sire	2003
A.P. Indy	1989	Among the leading sires	2000
A.P. Indy	1989	Among the leading sires	2001
Ace Card	1942	Broodmare of the year	1952
Ack Ack	1966	Horse of the year	1971
Ack Ack	1966	Champion sprinter	1971
Ack Ack	1966	Champion older horse	1971
Action This Day	2001	Champion 2-year-old colt	2003
Advising Anna	1930	Champion handicap mare	1934
Affectionately	1960	Champion 2-year-old filly	1962
Affectionately	1960	Champion sprinter	1965
Affectionately	1960	Champion older mare	1965
Affirmed	1975	Horse of the year	1978
Affirmed	1975	Horse of the year	1979
Affirmed	1975	Champion 2-year-old colt	1977
Affirmed	1975	Champion 3-year-old colt	1978
Affirmed	1975	Champion older horse	1979
Affirmed	1975	Among the leading bm sires	2003
Affirmed	1975	Triple Crown	1978
Afleet	1984	Among the leading sires	1996
Afleet	1984	Among the leading sires	1997
Ahoy	1960	Champion sprinter	1964
Airmans Guide	1957	Champion older mare	1961
Ajina	1994	Champion 3-year-old filly	1997
Alcibiades	1927	Champion 2-year-old filly	1929
Alcibiades	1927	Champion 3-year-old filly	1930
Aldebaran	1998	Champion sprinter	2003
All Along (FR)	1979	Horse of the year	1983
All Along (FR)	1979	Champion grass mare	1983
All Beautiful	1959	Broodmare of the year	1969
All Gong (GB)	1994	Champion steeplechaser	2000
Alleged	1974	Among the leading bm sires	2003
Alpenstock III	1936	Broodmare of the year	1951
Alsab	1939	Champion 2-year-old colt	1941
Alsab	1939	Champion 3-year-old colt	1942
Althea	1981	Champion 2-year-old filly	1983
Alydar	1975	Leading sire	1990
Alydar	1975	Among the leading sires	1986
Alydar	1975	Among the leading sires	1987
Alydar	1975	Among the leading sires	1988
Alydar	1975	Among the leading sires	1989
Alydar	1975	Among the leading sires	1992
Alydar	1975	Among the leading bm sires	1997
Alydar	1975	Among the leading bm sires	1999
Alydar	1975	Among the leading bm sires	2000
Alysheba	1984	Horse of the year	1988
Alysheba	1984	Champion 3-year-old colt	1987
Alysheba	1984	Champion older horse	1988
Ambassador of Luck	1979	Champion older mare	1983
Amber Diver	1954	Champion steeplechaser	1963
Ambiorix	1946	Leading sire	1961
American Flag	1922	Champion 3-year-old colt	1925
American Way	1942	Champion steeplechaser	1948
Ancestor	1949	Champion steeplechaser	1959
Anees	1997	Champion 2-year-old colt	1999
Anita Peabody	1925	Champion 2-year-old filly	1927
Anne Campbell	1973	Broodmare of the year	1999
Answer Lively	1996	Champion 2-year-old colt	1998
Apogee	1934	Champion 2-year-old filly	1936
April Run (IRE)	1978	Champion grass mare	1982
Arazi	1989	Champion 2-year-old colt	1991
Armed	1941	Horse of the year	1947
Armed	1941	Champion handicap horse	1946
Armed	1941	Champion handicap horse	1947
Artax	1995	Champion sprinter	1999
Arts and Letters	1966	Horse of the year	1969
Arts and Letters	1966	Champion 3-year-old colt	1969
Arts and Letters	1966	Champion older horse	1969
Askmenow	1940	Champion 2-year-old filly	1942
Assagai	1963	Champion grass horse	1966
Assault	1943	Horse of the year	1946
Assault	1943	Champion 3-year-old colt	1946
Assault	1943	Triple Crown	1946
Athenian Idol	1968	Champion steeplechaser	1973
Aunt Jinny	1948	Champion 2-year-old filly	1950
Autobiography	1968	Champion older horse	1972
Azeri	1998	Horse of the year	2002
Azeri	1998	Champion older mare	2002
Azeri	1998	Champion older mare	2003
Baba Kenny	1928	Champion 2-year-old filly	1930
Bald Eagle	1955	Champion older horse	1960
Balladier	1932	Champion 2-year-old colt	1934
Banja Luka	1968	Broodmare of the year	1987
Banks Hill (GB)	1998	Champion grass mare	2001
Banshee Breeze	1995	Champion 3-year-old filly	1998
Barbizon	1954	Champion 2-year-old colt	1956
Barn Swallow	1930	Champion 3-year-old filly	1933
Barnabys Bluff	1958	Champion steeplechaser	1962
Bateau	1925	Champion 3-year-old filly	1928
Bateau	1925	Champion handicap mare	1929
Bates Motel	1979	Champion older horse	1983
Battlefield	1948	Champion 2-year-old colt	1950
Bayakoa (ARG)	1984	Champion older mare	1989
Bayakoa (ARG)	1984	Champion older mare	1990
Bayou	1954	Champion 3-year-old filly	1957
Bazaar	1931	Champion 2-year-old filly	1933
Bazaar	1931	Champion 3-year-old filly	1934
Beaugay	1943	Champion 2-year-old filly	1945
Beautiful Pleasure	1995	Champion older mare	1999
Bed o' Roses	1947	Champion 2-year-old filly	1949
Bed o' Roses	1947	Champion older mare	1951
Before Dawn	1979	Champion 2-year-old filly	1981
Belle Jeep	1949	Broodmare of the year	1957
Benguala	1954	Champion steeplechaser	1960
Berlo	1957	Champion 3-year-old filly	1960
Berseem	1950	Champion sprinter	1955
Bertrando	1989	Champion older horse	1993
Best in Show	1965	Broodmare of the year	1982
Bewitch	1945	Champion 2-year-old filly	1947
Bewitch	1945	Champion older mare	1949
Big Pebble	1936	Champion handicap horse	1938
Bimelech	1937	Champion 2-year-old colt	1939
Bimelech	1937	Champion 3-year-old colt	1940
Bird Town	2000	Champion 3-year-old filly	2003
Black Helen	1932	Champion 3-year-old filly	1935
Black Maria	1923	Champion 3-year-old filly	1926
Black Maria	1923	Champion handicap mare	1927
Black Maria	1923	Champion handicap mare	1928
Black Tie Affair (Ire)	1986	Horse of the year	1991
Black Tie Affair (Ire)	1986	Champion older horse	1991
Blenheim II	1927	Leading sire	1941
Bloodroot	1932	Broodmare of the year	1946
Blue Larkspur	1926	Horse of the year	1929
Blue Larkspur	1926	Champion 3-year-old colt	1929

Horse	YOB	Title	Year
Blue Larkspur	1926	Champion handicap horse	1930
Blue Peter	1946	Champion 2-year-old colt	1948
Blue Sparkler	1952	Champion older mare	1956
Blushing Groom (Fr)	1974	Among the leading bm sires	1998
Blushing John	1985	Champion older horse	1989
Bold Bidder	1962	Champion older horse	1966
Bold Forbes	1973	Champion 3-year-old colt	1976
Bold Lad	1962	Champion 2-year-old	1964
Bold Liz	1970	2nd highweighted filly	1972
Bold Ruler	1954	Horse of the year	1957
Bold Ruler	1954	Champion 3-year-old colt	1957
Bold Ruler	1954	Champion sprinter	1958
Bold Ruler	1954	Leading sire	1963
Bold Ruler	1954	Leading sire	1964
Bold Ruler	1954	Leading sire	1965
Bold Ruler	1954	Leading sire	1966
Bold Ruler	1954	Leading sire	1967
Bold Ruler	1954	Leading sire	1968
Bold Ruler	1954	Leading sire	1969
Bold Ruler	1954	Leading sire	1973
Bold Venture	1933	Champion 3-year-old colt	1936
Bon Nouvel	1960	Champion steeplechaser	1964
Bon Nouvel	1960	Champion steeplechaser	1965
Bon Nouvel	1960	Champion steeplechaser	1968
Bornastar	1953	Champion older mare	1958
Boston Harbor	1994	Champion 2-year-old colt	1996
Bowl Game	1974	Champion grass horse	1979
Bowl of Flowers	1958	Champion 2-year-old filly	1960
Bowl of Flowers	1958	Champion 3-year-old filly	1961
Brave Raj	1984	Champion 2-year-old filly	1986
Bridal Flower	1943	Champion 3-year-old filly	1946
Broad Brush	1983	Leading sire	1994
Broad Brush	1983	Among the leading sires	1999
Broomstick	1901	Leading broodmare sire	1932
Broomstick	1901	Leading broodmare sire	1933
Brother Jones	1936	Champion steeplechaser	1943
Brown Bess	1982	Champion grass mare	1989
Buckaroo	1975	Leading sire	1985
Buckpasser	1963	Horse of the year	1966
Buckpasser	1963	Champion 2-year-old colt	1965
Buckpasser	1963	Champion 3-year-old colt	1966
Buckpasser	1963	Champion older horse	1966
Buckpasser	1963	Champion older horse	1967
Buckpasser	1963	Leading broodmare sire	1983
Buckpasser	1963	Leading broodmare sire	1984
Buckpasser	1963	Leading broodmare sire	1988
Buckpasser	1963	Leading broodmare sire	1989
Buck's Boy	1993	Champion grass horse	1998
Bull Dog	1927	Leading sire	1943
Bull Dog	1927	Leading broodmare sire	1953
Bull Dog	1927	Leading broodmare sire	1954
Bull Dog	1927	Leading broodmare sire	1956
Bull Lea	1935	Leading sire	1947
Bull Lea	1935	Leading sire	1948
Bull Lea	1935	Leading sire	1949
Bull Lea	1935	Leading sire	1952
Bull Lea	1935	Leading sire	1953
Bull Lea	1935	Leading broodmare sire	1958
Bull Lea	1935	Leading broodmare sire	1959
Bull Lea	1935	Leading broodmare sire	1960
Bull Lea	1935	Leading broodmare sire	1961
Burgoo King	1929	Champion 3-year-old colt	1932
Burning Blaze	1929	Champion 2-year-old colt	1931
Busher	1942	Horse of the year	1945
Busher	1942	Champion 2-year-old filly	1944
Busher	1942	Champion 3-year-old filly	1945
Busher	1942	Champion handicap mare	1945
Bushranger	1930	Champion steeplechaser	1936
But Why Not	1944	Champion 3-year-old filly	1947
But Why Not	1944	Champion handicap mare	1947
By Jimminy	1941	Champion 3-year-old colt	1944
Cafe Prince	1970	Champion steeplechaser	1977
Cafe Prince	1970	Champion steeplechaser	1978
Candy Eclair	1976	Champion 2-year-old filly	1978
Canonero II	1968	Champion 3-year-old colt	1971
Capot	1946	Horse of the year	1949
Capot	1946	Champion 3-year-old colt	1949
Capote	1984	Champion 2-year-old colt	1986
Capote	1984	Among the leading sires	1996
Cardmania	1986	Champion sprinter	1993
Career Boy	1953	Champion grass horse	1956
Careful	1918	Champion 2-year-old filly	1920
Careful	1918	Champion handicap mare	1922
Caressing	1998	Champion 2-year-old filly	2000
Carry Back	1958	Champion 3-year-old colt	1961
Cascapedia	1973	Champion older mare	1977
Castle Forbes	1961	Champion 2-year-old filly	1963
Cavalcade	1931	Horse of the year	1934
Cavalcade	1931	Champion 2-year-old colt	1933
Cavalcade	1931	Champion 3-year-old colt	1934
Celt	1905	Leading sire	1921
Celt	1905	Leading broodmare sire	1930
Chacolet	1918	Champion handicap mare	1923
Chacolet	1918	Champion handicap mare	1924
Challedon	1936	Horse of the year	1939
Challedon	1936	Horse of the year	1940
Challedon	1936	Champion 3-year-old	1939
Challedon	1936	Champion handicap horse	1940
Challenger II	1927	Leading sire	1939
Chance Play	1923	Horse of the year	1927
Chance Play	1923	Champion handicap horse	1927
Chance Play	1923	Leading sire	1935
Chance Play	1923	Leading sire	1944
Charismatic	1996	Horse of the year	1999
Charismatic	1996	Champion 3-year-old colt	1999
Chateaugay	1960	Champion 3-year-old colt	1963
Chatterton	1919	Leading sire	1932
Cherokee Run	1990	Champion sprinter	1994
Chicle	1913	Leading sire	1929
Chicle	1913	Leading broodmare sire	1942
Chief Bearhart	1993	Champion grass horse	1997
Chief's Crown	1982	Champion 2-year-old colt	1984
Chilukki	1997	Champion 2-year-old filly	1999
Chinook Pass	1979	Champion sprinter	1983
Chou Croute	1968	Champion sprinter	1972
Chris Evert	1971	Champion 3-year-old filly	1974
Chris Evert	1971	Filly Triple Crown	1974
Christmas Past	1979	Champion 3-year-old filly	1982
Cicada	1959	Champion 2-year-old filly	1961
Cicada	1959	Champion 3-year-old filly	1962
Cicada	1959	Champion older mare	1963
Cigar	1990	Horse of the year	1995
Cigar	1990	Horse of the year	1996
Cigar	1990	Champion older horse	1995
Cigar	1990	Champion older horse	1996
Citation	1945	Horse of the year	1948
Citation	1945	Champion 2-year-old colt	1947
Citation	1945	Champion 3-year-old colt	1948
Citation	1945	Champion older horse	1948
Citation	1945	Champion older horse	1951
Citation	1945	Triple Crown	1948
Cleopatra	1917	Champion 3-year-old filly	1920

Horse	YOB	Title	Year
Coaltown	1945	Horse of the year	1949
Coaltown	1945	Champion sprinter	1948
Coaltown	1945	Champion older horse	1949
Conniver	1944	Champion older mare	1948
Conquistador Cielo	1979	Horse of the year	1982
Conquistador Cielo	1979	Champion 3-year-old colt	1982
Constancy	1917	Champion 2-year-old filly	1919
Correggio (IRE)	1991	Champion steeplechaser	1996
Cosmah	1953	Broodmare of the year	1974
Cougar II	1966	Champion grass horse	1972
Count Fleet	1940	Horse of the year	1943
Count Fleet	1940	Champion 2-year-old colt	1942
Count Fleet	1940	Champion 3-year-old colt	1943
Count Fleet	1940	Leading sire	1951
Count Fleet	1940	Leading broodmare sire	1963
Count Fleet	1940	Triple Crown	1943
Counterpoint	1948	Horse of the year	1951
Counterpoint	1948	Champion 3-year-old colt	1951
Countess Diana	1995	Champion 2-year-old filly	1997
Courtly Dee	1968	Broodmare of the year	1983
Cox's Ridge	1974	Among the leading bm sires	2002
Cozzene	1980	Champion grass horse	1985
Cozzene	1980	Leading sire	1996
Crafty Admiral	1948	Champion older horse	1952
Crafty Admiral	1948	Leading broodmare sire	1978
Crafty Prospector	1979	Among the leading sires	1997
Criminal Type	1985	Horse of the year	1990
Criminal Type	1985	Champion older horse	1990
Crimson Satan	1959	Champion 2-year-old colt	1961
Crusader	1923	Horse of the year	1926
Crusader	1923	Champion 3-year-old colt	1926
Cudgel	1914	Champion handicap horse	1919
Current	1926	Champion 2-year-old filly	1928
Dahlia	1970	Champion grass horse	1974
Damascus	1964	Horse of the year	1967
Damascus	1964	Champion 3-year-old colt	1967
Damascus	1964	Champion handicap horse	1967
Dance Smartly	1988	Champion 3-year-old filly	1991
Danzig	1977	Leading sire	1991
Danzig	1977	Leading sire	1992
Danzig	1977	Leading sire	1993
Danzig	1977	Among the leading sires	1985
Danzig	1977	Among the leading sires	1986
Danzig	1977	Among the leading sires	1994
Danzig	1977	Among the leading bm sires	2000
Danzig	1977	Among the leading bm sires	2001
Dark Mirage	1965	Champion 3-year-old filly	1968
Dark Mirage	1965	Filly Triple Crown	1968
Dark Vintage	1956	2nd highweighted filly	1958
Darshaan (GB)	1981	Among the leading bm sires	2002
Davona Dale	1976	Champion 3-year-old filly	1979
Davona Dale	1976	Filly Triple Crown	1979
Dawn Play	1934	Champion 3-year-old filly	1937
Daylami (IRE)	1994	Champion grass horse	1999
De La Rose	1978	Champion grass mare	1981
Dearly Precious	1973	Champion 2-year-old filly	1975
Decathlon	1953	Champion sprinter	1956
Decathlon	1953	Champion sprinter	1957
Dedicate	1952	Champion older horse	1957
Dehere	1991	Champion 2-year-old colt	1993
Dehere	1991	Among the leading sires	2002
Delegate	1944	Champion sprinter	1949
Delta	1952	Broodmare of the year	1968
Deputy Minister	1979	Champion 2-year-old colt	1981
Deputy Minister	1979	Leading sire	1997
Deputy Minister	1979	Leading sire	1998
Deputy Minister	1979	Among the leading sires	1996
Deputy Minister	1979	Among the leading bm sires	2002
Deputy Minister	1979	Among the leading bm sires	2003
Desert Vixen	1970	Champion 3-year-old filly	1973
Desert Vixen	1970	Champion older mare	1974
Devil Diver	1939	Champion handicap horse	1943
Devil Diver	1939	Champion handicap horse	1944
Devil's Bag	1981	Champion 2-year-old colt	1983
Diavolo	1925	Champion handicap horse	1929
Dice	1925	Champion 2-year-old colt	1927
Discovery	1931	Horse of the year	1935
Discovery	1931	Champion handicap horse	1935
Discovery	1931	Champion handicap horse	1936
Dixieland Band	1980	Among the leading sires	1993
Dixieland Band	1980	Among the leading sires	1999
Dixieland Band	1980	Among the leading bm sires	2001
Double Jay	1944	Champion 2-year-old colt	1946
Double Jay	1944	Leading broodmare sire	1971
Double Jay	1944	Leading broodmare sire	1975
Double Jay	1944	Leading broodmare sire	1977
Double Jay	1944	Leading broodmare sire	1981
Doubledogdare	1953	Champion 2-year-old filly	1955
Doubledogdare	1953	Champion 3-year-old filly	1956
Dr. Fager	1964	Horse of the year	1968
Dr. Fager	1964	Champion sprinter	1967
Dr. Fager	1964	Champion sprinter	1968
Dr. Fager	1964	Champion grass horse	1968
Dr. Fager	1964	Champion older horse	1968
Dr. Fager	1964	Leading sire	1977
Dr. Patches	1974	Champion sprinter	1978
Dunce Cap II	1960	Broodmare of the year	1985
Durazna	1941	Champion 2-year-old filly	1943
Dynaformer	1985	Among the leading sires	2001
Dynaformer	1985	Among the leading sires	2002
Dynaformer	1985	Among the leading sires	2003
Easter Stockings	1925	Champion 3-year-old filly	1928
Easy Goer	1986	Champion 2-year-old colt	1988
Easy Lass	1940	Broodmare of the year	1949
Edith Cavell	1923	Champion 3-year-old filly	1926
Education	1944	Champion 2-year-old colt	1946
Eillo	1980	Champion sprinter	1984
El Chico	1936	Champion 2-year-old colt	1938
El Prado (IRE)	1989	Leading sire	2002
El Prado (IRE)	1989	Among the leading sires	2003
Eliza	1990	Champion 2-year-old filly	1992
Elkridge	1938	Champion steeplechaser	1942
Elkridge	1938	Champion steeplechaser	1946
Emotion	1919	Champion 3-year-old filly	1922
Epinard	1920	Champion handicap horse	1924
Epitome	1985	Champion 2-year-old filly	1987
Equipoise	1928	Horse of the year	1932
Equipoise	1928	Horse of the year	1933
Equipoise	1928	Champion 2-year-old colt	1930
Equipoise	1928	Champion handicap horse	1932
Equipoise	1928	Champion handicap horse	1933
Equipoise	1928	Champion handicap horse	1934
Equipoise	1928	Leading sire	1942
Escena	1993	Champion older mare	1998
Esposa	1932	Champion handicap mare	1937
Esposa	1932	Champion handicap mare	1938
Estrapade	1980	Champion grass mare	1986
Evening Out	1951	Champion 2-year-old filly	1953
Exclusive Native	1965	Leading sire	1978
Exclusive Native	1965	Leading sire	1979
Exterminator	1915	Horse of the year	1922
Exterminator	1915	Champion handicap horse	1920
Exterminator	1915	Champion handicap horse	1921
Exterminator	1915	Champion handicap horse	1922

Horse	YOB	Title	Year
Fair Play	1905	Leading sire	1920
Fair Play	1905	Leading sire	1924
Fair Play	1905	Leading sire	1927
Fair Play	1905	Leading broodmare sire	1931
Fair Play	1905	Leading broodmare sire	1934
Fair Play	1905	Leading broodmare sire	1938
Fair Star	1924	Champion 2-year-old filly	1926
Faireno	1929	Champion 3-year-old colt	1932
Fairy Chant	1937	Champion 3-year-old filly	1940
Fairy Chant	1937	Champion handicap mare	1941
Fall Aspen	1976	Broodmare of the year	1994
Family Style	1983	Champion 2-year-old filly	1985
Fanfreluche	1967	Champion 3-year-old filly	1970
Fantastic Light	1996	Champion grass horse	2001
Farda Amiga	1999	Champion 3-year-old filly	2002
Fast Attack	1967	Champion 2-year-old filly	1969
Favorite Trick	1995	Horse of the year	1997
Favorite Trick	1995	Champion 2-year-old colt	1997
Ferdinand	1983	Horse of the year	1987
Ferdinand	1983	Champion older horse	1987
Fighting Step	1942	Champion 3-year-old colt	1945
Fiji (GB)	1994	Champion grass mare	1998
First Flight	1944	Champion 2-year-old filly	1946
First Landing	1956	Champion 2-year-old colt	1958
Flanders	1992	Champion 2-year-old filly	1994
Flat Top	1993	Champion steeplechaser	1998
Flat Top	1993	Champion steeplechaser	2002
Flatterer	1979	Champion steeplechaser	1983
Flatterer	1979	Champion steeplechaser	1984
Flatterer	1979	Champion steeplechaser	1985
Flatterer	1979	Champion steeplechaser	1986
Flawlessly	1988	Champion grass mare	1992
Flawlessly	1988	Champion grass mare	1993
Florence Nightingale	1922	Champion 3-year-old filly	1925
Fluvanna	1921	Champion 2-year-old filly	1923
Fly So Free	1988	Champion 2-year-old colt	1990
Fly So Free	1988	Among the leading sires	2001
Foolish Pleasure	1972	Champion 2-year-old colt	1974
Forego	1970	Horse of the year	1974
Forego	1970	Horse of the year	1975
Forego	1970	Horse of the year	1976
Forego	1970	Champion sprinter	1974
Forego	1970	Champion older horse	1974
Forego	1970	Champion older horse	1975
Forego	1970	Champion older horse	1976
Forego	1970	Champion older horse	1977
Forever Yours	1933	Champion 2-year-old filly	1935
Fort Marcy	1964	Horse of the year	1970
Fort Marcy	1964	Champion grass horse	1967
Fort Marcy	1964	Champion grass horse	1970
Fort Marcy	1964	Champion older horse	1970
Forty Niner	1985	Champion 2-year-old colt	1987
Forty Niner	1985	Among the leading sires	1996
Forward Gal	1968	Champion 2-year-old filly	1970
Forward Pass	1965	Champion 3-year-old colt	1968
Friar's Carse	1923	Champion 2-year-old filly	1925
Funny Cide	2000	Champion 3-year-old colt	2003
Furl Sail	1964	Champion 3-year-old filly	1967
Gaga	1942	Broodmare of the year	1953
Gallant Bloom	1966	Champion 2-year-old filly	1968
Gallant Bloom	1966	Champion 3-year-old filly	1968
Gallant Bloom	1966	Champion handicap mare	1969
Gallant Bob	1972	Champion sprinter	1975
Gallant Fox	1927	Horse of the year	1930
Gallant Fox	1927	Champion 3-year-old colt	1930
Gallant Fox	1927	Triple Crown	1930
Gallorette	1942	Champion handicap mare	1946
Gamely	1964	Champion 3-year-old filly	1967
Gamely	1964	Champion older mare	1968
Gamely	1964	Champion older mare	1969
Gazala II	1964	Broodmare of the year	1976
Genuine Risk	1977	Champion 3-year-old filly	1980
Gilded Time	1990	Champion 2-year-old colt	1992
Glorious Song	1976	Champion older mare	1980
Glowing Tribute	1973	Broodmare of the year	1993
Go for Wand	1987	Champion 2-year-old filly	1989
Go for Wand	1987	Champion 3-year-old filly	1990
Gold Beauty	1979	Champion sprinter	1982
Golden Apples (IRE)	1998	Champion grass mare	2002
Golden Attraction	1993	Champion 2-year-old filly	1995
Gourmet Girl	1995	Champion older mare	2001
Gran Kan	1966	Champion steeplechaser	1974
Granville	1933	Horse of the year	1936
Granville	1933	Champion 3-year-old colt	1936
Graustark	1963	Among the leading bm sires	1993
Grecian Banner	1974	Broodmare of the year	1988
Grecian Queen	1950	Champion 3-year-old filly	1953
Grey Dawn II	1962	Leading broodmare sire	1990
Grey Lag	1918	Horse of the year	1921
Grey Lag	1918	Champion 3-year-old colt	1921
Grey Lag	1918	Champion handicap horse	1922
Grey Lag	1918	Champion handicap horse	1923
Groovy	1983	Champion sprinter	1987
Guilty Conscience	1976	Champion sprinter	1981
Gulch	1984	Champion sprinter	1988
Hail to Reason	1958	Champion 2-year-old colt	1960
Hail to Reason	1958	Leading sire	1970
Halfbridled	2001	Champion 2-year-old filly	2003
Halo	1969	Leading sire	1983
Halo	1969	Leading sire	1989
Halo	1969	Among the leading bm sires	2002
Handcuff	1935	Champion 3-year-old filly	1938
Hansel	1988	Champion 3-year-old colt	1991
Happy Gal	1930	Champion 2-year-old filly	1932
Hasty Queen II	1963	Broodmare of the year	1984
Hasty Road	1951	Champion 2-year-old colt	1953
Hatoof	1989	Champion grass mare	1994
Hawaii	1964	Champion grass horse	1969
Head Play	1930	Champion 3-year-old colt	1933
Heartlight No. One	1980	Champion 3-year-old filly	1983
Heavenly Cause	1978	Champion 2-year-old filly	1980
Heavenly Prize	1991	Champion 3-year-old filly	1994
Heliopolis	1936	Leading sire	1950
Heliopolis	1936	Leading sire	1954
Hidden Lake	1993	Champion older mare	1997
High Chaparral (Ire)	1999	Champion grass horse	2002
High Chaparral (Ire)	1999	Champion grass horse	2003
High Fleet	1933	Champion 3-year-old filly	1936
High Gun	1951	Champion 3-year-old colt	1954
High Gun	1951	Champion older horse	1955
High Strung	1926	Champion 2-year-old filly	1928
High Time	1916	Leading sire	1928
High Time	1916	Leading broodmare sire	1936
High Time	1916	Leading broodmare sire	1940
High Voltage	1952	Champion 2-year-old filly	1954
High Voltage	1952	Champion 3-year-old filly	1955
Highland Bud	1985	Champion steeplechaser	1989
Hildene	1938	Broodmare of the year	1950
Hill Prince	1947	Horse of the year	1950
Hill Prince	1947	Champion 2-year-old colt	1949
Hill Prince	1947	Champion 3-year-old colt	1950
Hill Prince	1947	Champion older horse	1951
His Majesty	1968	Leading sire	1982
Hoist the Flag	1968	Champion 2-year-old colt	1970

Horse	YOB	Title	Year	Horse	YOB	Title	Year
Hoist the Flag	1968	Leading broodmare sire	1987	La Prevoyante	1970	Champion 2-year-old filly	1972
Hollywood Wildcat	1990	Champion 3-year-old filly	1993	Lady Broadcast	1926	Champion handicap mare	1930
Holy Bull	1991	Horse of the year	1994	Lady Maryland	1934	Champion handicap mare	1939
Holy Bull	1991	Champion 3-year-old colt	1994	Lady Pitt	1963	Champion 3-year-old filly	1966
Honest Pleasure	1973	Champion 2-year-old colt	1975	Lady's Secret	1982	Horse of the year	1986
Housebuster	1987	Champion sprinter	1990	Lady's Secret	1982	Champion older mare	1986
Housebuster	1987	Champion sprinter	1991	Ladysman	1930	Champion 2-year-old colt	1932
Hurry to Market	1961	Champion 2-year-old colt	1963	Lakeville Miss	1975	Champion 3-year-old filly	1977
Iberia	1954	Broodmare of the year	1971	Lamb Chop	1960	Champion 3-year-old filly	1963
Iceberg II	1948	Champion grass horse	1953	Landaluce	1980	Champion 2-year-old filly	1982
Idun	1955	Champion 2-year-old filly	1957	Langfuhr	1992	Among the leading sires	2003
Idun	1955	Champion 3-year-old filly	1958	Late Bloomer	1974	Champion older mare	1978
Impressive	1963	Champion sprinter	1966	Late Date	1929	Champion handicap mare	1935
In Memoriam	1920	Champion 3-year-old colt	1923	Laugh and Be Merry	1985	Champion grass mare	1990
In Neon	1982	Broodmare of the year	1998	Lavender Hill	1949	Champion older mare	1954
Inlander (GB)	1981	Champion steeplechaser	1987	Leallah	1954	Champion 2-year-old filly	1956
Inscoelda	1936	Champion 2-year-old filly	1938	Left Bank	1997	Champion older horse	2002
Inside Information	1991	Champion older mare	1995	Lemhi Gold	1978	Champion older horse	1982
Intentionally	1956	Champion sprinter	1959	Lemon Drop Kid	1996	Champion older horse	2000
Iron Reward	1946	Broodmare of the year	1955	L'Escargot	1963	Champion steeplechaser	1969
Islington (IRE)	1999	Champion grass mare	2003	Levee	1953	Broodmare of the year	1970
It's in the Air	1976	Champion 3-year-old filly	1978	Level Best	1938	Champion 2-year-old filly	1940
Itsallgreektome	1987	Champion grass horse	1990	Life's Illusion	1971	Champion steeplechaser	1975
J. O. Tobin	1974	Champion sprinter	1978	Life's Magic	1981	Champion 3-year-old filly	1984
Jacola	1935	Champion 2-year-old filly	1937	Life's Magic	1981	Champion older mare	1985
Jaipur	1959	Champion 3-year-old colt	1962	Lit de Justice	1990	Champion sprinter	1996
Jam	1947	Champion steeplechaser	1952	Little Current	1971	Champion 3-year-old colt	1974
Jamestown	1928	Champion 2-year-old colt	1930	Lonesome Glory	1988	Champion steeplechaser	1992
Jewel Princess	1992	Champion older mare	1996	Lonesome Glory	1988	Champion steeplechaser	1993
Jewel's Reward	1955	Champion 2-year-old colt	1957	Lonesome Glory	1988	Champion steeplechaser	1995
Jimmy Lorenzo (GB)	1982	Champion steeplechaser	1988	Lonesome Glory	1988	Champion steeplechaser	1997
Johannesburg	1999	Champion 2-year-old colt	2001	Lonesome Glory	1988	Champion steeplechaser	1999
John Henry	1975	Horse of the year	1981	Lord Avie	1978	Champion 2-year-old colt	1980
John Henry	1975	Horse of the year	1984	Lyphard	1969	Leading sire	1986
John Henry	1975	Champion grass horse	1980	Mac Diarmida	1975	Champion grass horse	1978
John Henry	1975	Champion grass horse	1981	Macho Uno	1998	Champion 2-year-old colt	2000
John Henry	1975	Champion grass horse	1983	Mad Hatter	1916	Champion handicap horse	1921
John Henry	1975	Champion grass horse	1984	Mahmoud	1933	Leading sire	1946
John Henry	1975	Champion older horse	1981	Mahmoud	1933	Leading broodmare sire	1957
Johnny D.	1974	Champion grass horse	1977	Maid At Arms	1922	Champion 3-year-old filly	1925
Juliets Nurse	1948	Broodmare of the year	1966	Maid of Flight	1951	Broodmare of the year	1964
Jungle King	1930	Champion steeplechaser	1937	Mako	1960	Champion steeplechaser	1966
Just a Game (IRE)	1976	Champion grass mare	1980	Man o' War	1917	Horse of the year	1920
Kalanisi (IRE)	1996	Champion grass horse	2000	Man o' War	1917	Champion 2-year-old colt	1919
Kamar	1976	Broodmare of the year	1990	Man o' War	1917	Champion 3-year-old colt	1920
Kayak II	1935	Champion handicap horse	1939	Man o' War	1917	Leading sire	1926
Kelso	1957	Horse of the year	1960	Manila	1983	Champion grass horse	1986
Kelso	1957	Horse of the year	1961	Maria's Mon	1993	Champion 2-year-old colt	1995
Kelso	1957	Horse of the year	1962	Marica	1933	Champion handicap mare	1938
Kelso	1957	Horse of the year	1963	Mar-Kell	1939	Champion handicap mare	1943
Kelso	1957	Horse of the year	1964	Market Wise	1938	Champion handicap horse	1943
Kelso	1957	Champion 3-year-old colt	1960	Martie's Anger	1975	Champion steeplechaser	1979
Kelso	1957	Champion older horse	1961	Master Charlie	1922	Champion 2-year-old colt	1924
Kelso	1957	Champion older horse	1962	Mata Hari	1931	Champion 2-year-old filly	1933
Kelso	1957	Champion older horse	1963	Mata Hari	1931	Champion 3-year-old filly	1934
Kelso	1957	Champion older horse	1964	Maud Muller	1922	Champion 2-year-old filly	1924
Kerala	1958	Broodmare of the year	1967	McDynamo	1997	Champion steeplechaser	2003
Key Bridge	1959	Broodmare of the year	1980	McGee	1900	Leading sire	1922
Key to the Mint	1969	Champion 3-year-old colt	1972	Meadow Star	1988	Champion 2-year-old filly	1990
King Commander	1949	Champion steeplechaser	1954	Menow	1935	Champion 2-year-old colt	1937
Kiss Me Kate	1948	Champion 3-year-old filly	1951	Mercator	1939	Champion steeplechaser	1945
Knight's Daughter	1941	Broodmare of the year	1959	Miesque	1984	Champion grass mare	1987
Kona Gold	1994	Champion sprinter	2000	Miesque	1984	Champion grass mare	1988
Kotashaan (FR)	1988	Horse of the year	1993	Mike Hall	1924	Champion handicap horse	1928
Kotashaan (FR)	1988	Champion grass horse	1993	Milkmaid	1916	Champion 3-year-old filly	1919
Kris S.	1977	Among the leading sires	1993	Milkmaid	1916	Champion handicap mare	1920
Kris S.	1977	Among the leading sires	2003	Mineshaft	1999	Horse of the year	2003

Horse	YOB	Title	Year	Horse	YOB	Title	Year
Mineshaft	1999	Champion older horse	2003	Needles	1953	Champion 2-year-old colt	1955
Mioland	1937	Champion handicap horse	1941	Needles	1953	Champion 3-year-old colt	1956
Mira Femme	1964	Champion 2-year-old filly	1966	Neji	1950	Champion steeplechaser	1955
Miss Alleged	1987	Champion grass mare	1991	Neji	1950	Champion steeplechaser	1957
Miss Disco	1944	Broodmare of the year	1958	Neji	1950	Champion steeplechaser	1958
Miss Jemima	1917	Champion 2-year-old filly	1919	Nellie Flag	1932	Champion 2-year-old filly	1934
Miss Request	1945	Champion 3-year-old filly	1948	Nellie Morse	1921	Champion 3-year-old filly	1924
Misty Morn	1952	Champion 3-year-old filly	1955	Never Bend	1960	Champion 2-year-old colt	1962
Misty Morn	1952	Champion older mare	1955	Next Move	1947	Champion 3-year-old filly	1950
Misty Morn	1952	Broodmare of the year	1963	Next Move	1947	Champion older mare	1952
Miswaki	1978	Among the leading bm sires	1999	Nijinsky II	1967	Leading broodmare sire	1993
Moccasin	1963	Horse of the year	1965	Nijinsky II	1967	Leading broodmare sire	1994
Moccasin	1963	Champion 2-year-old filly	1965	Nijinsky II	1967	Among the leading bm sires	1996
Moment of Truth II	1959	Broodmare of the year	1972	Nijinsky II	1967	Among the leading bm sires	1998
Mom's Command	1982	Champion 3-year-old filly	1985	Nijinsky II	1967	Among the leading bm sires	1999
Mom's Command	1982	Filly Triple Crown	1985	Nijinsky II	1967	Among the leading bm sires	2000
Mongo	1959	Champion grass horse	1963	Nijinsky II	1967	Among the leading bm sires	2001
Morley Street	1984	Champion steeplechaser	1990	Nimba	1924	Champion 3-year-old filly	1927
Morley Street	1984	Champion steeplechaser	1991	Nodouble	1965	Champion older horse	1969
Morvich	1919	Champion 2-year-old colt	1921	Nodouble	1965	Champion older horse	1970
Mother Goose	1922	Champion 2-year-old filly	1924	Nodouble	1965	Leading sire	1981
Mr. Prospector	1970	Leading sire	1987	Noor	1945	Champion older horse	1950
Mr. Prospector	1970	Leading sire	1988	North Sider	1982	Champion older mare	1987
Mr. Prospector	1970	Leading broodmare sire	1997	Northern Dancer	1961	Champion 3-year-old colt	1964
Mr. Prospector	1970	Leading broodmare sire	1998	Northern Dancer	1961	Leading sire	1971
Mr. Prospector	1970	Leading broodmare sire	1999	Northern Dancer	1961	Leading broodmare sire	1991
Mr. Prospector	1970	Leading broodmare sire	2000	Northern Spur (Ire)	1991	Champion grass horse	1995
Mr. Prospector	1970	Leading broodmare sire	2001	Northern Sunset (Ire)	1977	Broodmare of the year	1995
Mr. Prospector	1970	Leading broodmare sire	2002	Not Surprising	1990	Champion sprinter	1995
Mr. Prospector	1970	Leading broodmare sire	2003	Now What	1937	Champion 2-year-old filly	1939
Mr. Prospector	1970	Among the leading sires	1980	Numbered Account	1969	Champion 2-year-old filly	1971
Mr. Prospector	1970	Among the leading sires	1981	Nureyev	1977	Among the leading bm sires	2003
Mr. Prospector	1970	Among the leading sires	1982	Occupy	1941	Champion 2-year-old colt	1943
Mr. Prospector	1970	Among the leading sires	1984	Oedipus	1946	Champion steeplechaser	1950
Mr. Prospector	1970	Among the leading sires	1989	Oedipus	1946	Champion steeplechaser	1951
Mr. Prospector	1970	Among the leading sires	1990	Oedipus	1946	Champion steeplechaser	1952
Mr. Prospector	1970	Among the leading sires	1991	Office Queen	1967	Champion 3-year-old filly	1970
Mr. Prospector	1970	Among the leading sires	1993	Oil Capitol	1947	Champion 2-year-old colt	1949
Mr. Prospector	1970	Among the leading sires	2000	Old Hat	1959	Champion older mare	1964
Mr. Prospector	1970	Among the leading bm sires	1990	Old Hat	1959	Champion older mare	1965
Mr. Prospector	1970	Among the leading bm sires	1993	Olympia	1946	Leading broodmare sire	1974
Mr. Prospector	1970	Among the leading bm sires	1994	Omaha	1932	Champion 3-year-old colt	1935
Mr. Prospector	1970	Among the leading bm sires	1995	Omaha	1932	Triple Crown	1935
Mr. Prospector	1970	Among the leading bm sires	1996	One Count	1949	Horse of the year	1952
My Dear	1917	Champion handicap mare	1921	One Count	1949	Champion 3-year-old colt	1952
My Dear Girl	1957	Champion 2-year-old filly	1959	Open Fire	1961	Champion older mare	1966
My Juliet	1972	Champion sprinter	1976	Open Mind	1986	Champion 2-year-old filly	1988
Myrtle Charm	1946	Champion 2-year-old filly	1948	Open Mind	1986	Champion 3-year-old filly	1989
Myrtlewood	1932	Champion sprinter	1936	Open Mind	1986	Filly Triple Crown	1989
Myrtlewood	1932	Champion handicap mare	1936	Orientate	1998	Champion sprinter	2002
Nadir	1955	Champion 2-year-old colt	1957	Our Boots	1938	Champion 2-year-old colt	1940
Nail	1953	Champion 2-year-old colt	1955	Our Mims	1974	Champion 3-year-old filly	1977
Nashua	1952	Horse of the year	1955	Our Page	1940	Broodmare of the year	1948
Nashua	1952	Champion 3-year-old colt	1954	Outstandingly	1982	Champion 2-year-old filly	1984
Nashua	1952	Champion 3-year-old colt	1955	Painted Veil	1938	Champion 3-year-old filly	1941
Nasrina	1953	Champion 2-year-old filly	1955	Palace Music	1981	Leading sire	1995
Nasrullah	1940	Leading sire	1955	Paradise Creek	1989	Champion grass horse	1994
Nasrullah	1940	Leading sire	1956	Parka	1958	Champion grass horse	1965
Nasrullah	1940	Leading sire	1959	Parlo	1951	Champion 3-year-old filly	1954
Nasrullah	1940	Leading sire	1960	Parlo	1951	Champion older mare	1954
Nasrullah	1940	Leading sire	1962	Parlo	1951	Champion older mare	1955
Natashka	1963	Broodmare of the year	1981	Paseana (ARG)	1987	Champion older mare	1992
Native Dancer	1950	Horse of the year	1952	Paseana (ARG)	1987	Champion older mare	1993
Native Dancer	1950	Horse of the year	1954	Pavot	1942	Champion 2-year-old colt	1944
Native Dancer	1950	Champion 2-year-old colt	1952	Peal	1956	Champion steeplechaser	1961
Native Dancer	1950	Champion 3-year-old colt	1953	Pebbles (GB)	1981	Champion grass mare	1985
Native Dancer	1950	Champion older horse	1954	Perfect Sting	1996	Champion grass mare	2000

Horse	YOB	Title	Year
Perrault (GB)	1977	Champion grass horse	1982
Personal Ensign	1984	Champion older mare	1988
Personal Ensign	1984	Broodmare of the year	1996
Personality	1967	Horse of the year	1970
Personality	1967	Champion 3-year-old colt	1970
Petrify	1939	Champion 2-year-old filly	1941
Phalanx	1944	Champion 3-year-old colt	1947
Phone Chatter	1991	Champion 2-year-old filly	1993
Platter	1941	Champion 2-year-old colt	1943
Pleasant Colony	1978	Champion 3-year-old colt	1981
Pleasant Stage	1989	Champion 2-year-old filly	1991
Pleasant Tap	1987	Champion older horse	1992
Plugged Nickle	1977	Champion sprinter	1980
Pocahontas	1955	Broodmare of the year	1965
Point Given	1998	Horse of the year	2001
Point Given	1998	Champion 3-year-old colt	2001
Polynesian	1942	Champion sprinter	1947
Pompey	1923	Champion 2-year-old colt	1925
Pompeyo (CHI)	1994	Champion steeplechaser	2001
Pompoon	1934	Champion 2-year-old colt	1936
Porterhouse	1951	Champion 2-year-old colt	1953
Possibly Perfect	1990	Champion grass mare	1995
Potheen	1928	Broodmare of the year	1947
Prairie Bayou	1990	Champion 3-year-old colt	1993
Precisionist	1981	Champion sprinter	1985
Primonetta	1958	Champion older mare	1962
Primonetta	1958	Broodmare of the year	1978
Prince John	1953	Leading broodmare sire	1979
Prince John	1953	Leading broodmare sire	1980
Prince John	1953	Leading broodmare sire	1982
Prince John	1953	Leading broodmare sire	1986
Princequillo	1940	Leading sire	1957
Princequillo	1940	Leading sire	1958
Princequillo	1940	Leading broodmare sire	1966
Princequillo	1940	Leading broodmare sire	1967
Princequillo	1940	Leading broodmare sire	1968
Princequillo	1940	Leading broodmare sire	1969
Princequillo	1940	Leading broodmare sire	1970
Princequillo	1940	Leading broodmare sire	1972
Princequillo	1940	Leading broodmare sire	1973
Princequillo	1940	Leading broodmare sire	1976
Princess Doreen	1921	Champion 3-year-old filly	1924
Princess Doreen	1921	Champion handicap mare	1925
Princess Doreen	1921	Champion handicap mare	1926
Princess Rooney	1980	Champion older mare	1984
Private Account	1976	Among the leading sires	1993
Process Shot	1966	Champion 2-year-old filly	1968
Protagonist	1971	Champion 2-year-old colt	1973
Proud Delta	1972	Champion older mare	1976
Prudery	1918	Champion 2-year-old filly	1920
Prudery	1918	Champion 3-year-old filly	1921
Pucker Up	1953	Champion older mare	1957
Queen Empress	1962	Champion 2-year-old filly	1964
Queen of the Stage	1965	Champion 2-year-old filly	1967
Queena	1986	Champion older mare	1991
Quick Pitch	1960	Champion steeplechaser	1967
Quill	1956	Champion 2-year-old filly	1958
Rahy	1985	Among the leading sires	2000
Rahy	1985	Among the leading sires	2001
Raise a Native	1961	Champion 2-year-old colt	1963
Raja Baba	1968	Leading sire	1980
Real Delight	1949	Champion 3-year-old filly	1952
Real Delight	1949	Champion older mare	1952
Real Quiet	1995	Champion 3-year-old colt	1998
Regal Gleam	1964	Champion 2-year-old filly	1966
Reigh Count	1925	Horse of the year	1928
Reigh Count	1925	Champion 2-year-old colt	1927
Reigh Count	1925	Champion 3-year-old colt	1928
Relaxing	1976	Champion older mare	1981
Relaxing	1976	Broodmare of the year	1989
Reraise	1995	Champion sprinter	1998
Revidere	1973	Champion 3-year-old filly	1976
Rhythm	1987	Champion 2-year-old colt	1989
Riboletta (BRZ)	1995	Champion older mare	2000
Ridan	1959	Champion 2-year-old colt	1961
Risen Star	1985	Champion 3-year-old colt	1988
Riva Ridge	1969	Champion 2-year-old colt	1971
Riva Ridge	1969	Champion older horse	1973
Riverman	1969	Among the leading bm sires	1997
Roberto	1969	Among the leading bm sires	1993
Rockhill Native	1977	Champion 2-year-old colt	1979
Roman	1937	Leading broodmare sire	1965
Roman Brother	1961	Horse of the year	1965
Roman Brother	1961	Champion older horse	1965
Romanita	1954	Champion 2-year-old filly	1956
Rose Jet	1949	Champion 2-year-old filly	1951
Rose of Sharon	1926	Champion 3-year-old filly	1929
Rouge Dragon	1938	Champion steeplechaser	1944
Round Table	1954	Horse of the year	1958
Round Table	1954	Champion grass horse	1957
Round Table	1954	Champion grass horse	1958
Round Table	1954	Champion grass horse	1959
Round Table	1954	Champion older horse	1958
Round Table	1954	Champion older horse	1959
Round Table	1954	Leading sire	1972
Roving Boy	1980	Champion 2-year-old colt	1982
Royal Governor	1944	Champion sprinter	1949
Royal Heroine (IRE)	1980	Champion grass mare	1984
Royal Native	1956	Champion 3-year-old filly	1959
Royal Native	1956	Champion older mare	1960
Rubiano	1987	Champion sprinter	1992
Ruffian	1972	Champion 2-year-old filly	1974
Ruffian	1972	Champion 3-year-old filly	1975
Ruffian	1972	Filly Triple Crown	1975
Run the Gantlet	1968	Champion grass horse	1971
Ryafan	1994	Champion grass mare	1997
Sacahuista	1984	Champion 3-year-old filly	1987
Safely Kept	1986	Champion sprinter	1989
Sally's Alley	1920	Champion 2-year-old filly	1922
Saratoga Dew	1989	Champion 3-year-old filly	1992
Sarazen	1921	Horse of the year	1924
Sarazen	1921	Horse of the year	1925
Sarazen	1921	Champion 3-year-old colt	1924
Sarazen	1921	Champion handicap horse	1925
Sarazen	1921	Champion handicap horse	1926
Scapa Flow	1924	Champion 2-year-old filly	1926
Seabiscuit	1933	Horse of the year	1938
Seabiscuit	1933	Champion handicap horse	1937
Seabiscuit	1933	Champion handicap horse	1938
Seattle Slew	1974	Horse of the year	1977
Seattle Slew	1974	Champion 2-year-old colt	1976
Seattle Slew	1974	Champion 3-year-old colt	1977
Seattle Slew	1974	Champion older horse	1978
Seattle Slew	1974	Leading sire	1984
Seattle Slew	1974	Leading broodmare sire	1995
Seattle Slew	1974	Leading broodmare sire	1996
Seattle Slew	1974	Among the leading sires	1986
Seattle Slew	1974	Among the leading sires	1989
Seattle Slew	1974	Among the leading sires	1992
Seattle Slew	1974	Among the leading bm sires	1998
Seattle Slew	1974	Triple Crown	1977
Secretariat	1970	Horse of the year	1972
Secretariat	1970	Horse of the year	1973
Secretariat	1970	Champion 2-year-old colt	1972

Horse	Year	Title	Year
Secretariat	1970	Champion 3-year-old colt	1973
Secretariat	1970	Champion grass horse	1973
Secretariat	1970	Leading broodmare sire	1992
Secretariat	1970	Among the leading bm sires	1996
Secretariat	1970	Among the leading bm sires	1997
Secretariat	1970	Triple Crown	1973
Seeking the Gold	1985	Among the leading sires	2000
Sensational	1974	Champion 2-year-old filly	1976
Serena's Song	1992	Champion 3-year-old filly	1995
Shadow Brook	1964	Champion steeplechaser	1971
Shannon II	1941	Champion handicap horse	1948
Shecky Greene	1970	Champion sprinter	1973
Sheilas Reward	1947	Champion sprinter	1950
Sheilas Reward	1947	Champion sprinter	1951
Shenanigans	1963	Broodmare of the year	1975
Shipboard	1950	Champion steeplechaser	1956
Shuvee	1966	Champion older mare	1970
Shuvee	1966	Champion older mare	1971
Shuvee	1966	Filly Triple Crown	1971
Siama	1947	Broodmare of the year	1960
Sickle	1924	Leading sire	1936
Sickle	1924	Leading sire	1938
Sickle's Image	1948	Champion older mare	1953
Silent Screen	1967	Champion 2-year-old colt	1969
Silver Buck	1978	Among the leading sires	1998
Silver Charm	1994	Champion 3-year-old colt	1997
Silver Deputy	1985	Among the leading sires	1998
Silver Deputy	1985	Among the leading sires	1999
Silver Spoon	1956	Champion 3-year-old filly	1959
Silverbulletday	1996	Champion 2-year-old filly	1998
Silverbulletday	1996	Champion 3-year-old filly	1999
Singspiel (IRE)	1992	Champion grass horse	1996
Sir Barton	1916	Horse of the year	1919
Sir Barton	1916	Champion 3-year-old colt	1919
Sir Barton	1916	Triple Crown	1919
Sir Gallahad III	1920	Leading sire	1930
Sir Gallahad III	1920	Leading sire	1933
Sir Gallahad III	1920	Leading sire	1934
Sir Gallahad III	1920	Leading sire	1940
Sir Gallahad III	1920	Leading broodmare sire	1939
Sir Gallahad III	1920	Leading broodmare sire	1943
Sir Gallahad III	1920	Leading broodmare sire	1944
Sir Gallahad III	1920	Leading broodmare sire	1945
Sir Gallahad III	1920	Leading broodmare sire	1946
Sir Gallahad III	1920	Leading broodmare sire	1947
Sir Gallahad III	1920	Leading broodmare sire	1948
Sir Gallahad III	1920	Leading broodmare sire	1949
Sir Gallahad III	1920	Leading broodmare sire	1950
Sir Gallahad III	1920	Leading broodmare sire	1951
Sir Gallahad III	1920	Leading broodmare sire	1952
Sir Gallahad III	1920	Leading broodmare sire	1955
Skip Away	1993	Horse of the year	1998
Skip Away	1993	Champion 3-year-old colt	1996
Skip Away	1993	Champion older horse	1997
Skip Away	1993	Champion older horse	1998
Skip Trial	1982	Among the leading sires	1997
Sky Beauty	1990	Champion older mare	1994
Sky Beauty	1990	Filly Triple Crown	1993
Sky Classic	1987	Champion grass horse	1992
Slew o' Gold	1980	Champion 3-year-old colt	1983
Slew o' Gold	1980	Champion older horse	1984
Slightly Dangerous	1979	Broodmare of the year	1997
Smart Angle	1977	Champion 2-year-old filly	1979
Smart Deb	1960	Champion 2-year-old filly	1962
Smartaire	1962	Broodmare of the year	1979
Smile	1982	Champion sprinter	1986
Smoke Glacken	1994	Champion sprinter	1997
Snow Chief	1983	Champion 3-year-old colt	1986
Snow Knight	1971	Champion grass horse	1975
Snowflake	1927	Champion 3-year-old filly	1930
Soaring Softly	1995	Champion grass mare	1999
Social Outcast	1950	Champion handicap horse	1955
Some Pomp	1931	Champion handicap mare	1935
Somethingroyal	1952	Broodmare of the year	1973
Soothsayer	1967	Champion steeplechaser	1972
Speak John	1958	Leading broodmare sire	1985
Spectacular Bid	1976	Horse of the year	1980
Spectacular Bid	1976	Champion 2-year-old colt	1978
Spectacular Bid	1976	Champion 3-year-old colt	1979
Spectacular Bid	1976	Champion older horse	1980
Speculate	1936	Champion steeplechaser	1941
Spend a Buck	1982	Horse of the year	1985
Spend a Buck	1982	Champion 3-year-old colt	1985
Squirtle Squirt	1998	Champion sprinter	2001
St. Germans	1921	Leading sire	1931
St. James	1921	Champion 2-year-old colt	1923
St. Vincent	1951	Champion grass horse	1955
Stage Door Johnny	1965	Champion 3-year-old colt	1968
Stagehand	1935	Champion 3-year-old colt	1938
Stan	1950	Champion grass horse	1954
Star de Naskra	1975	Champion sprinter	1979
Star Pilot	1943	Champion 2-year-old colt	1945
Star Shoot	1898	Leading sire	1919
Star Shoot	1898	Leading broodmare sire	1924
Star Shoot	1898	Leading broodmare sire	1925
Star Shoot	1898	Leading broodmare sire	1926
Star Shoot	1898	Leading broodmare sire	1928
Star Shoot	1898	Leading broodmare sire	1929
Startle	1919	Champion 2-year-old filly	1921
Stefanita	1940	Champion 3-year-old filly	1943
Steinlen (GB)	1983	Champion grass horse	1989
Storm Cat	1983	Leading sire	1999
Storm Cat	1983	Leading sire	2000
Storm Cat	1983	Among the leading sires	1997
Storm Cat	1983	Among the leading sires	2002
Storm Flag Flying	2000	Champion 2-year-old filly	2002
Storm Song	1994	Champion 2-year-old filly	1996
Straight and True	1970	Champion steeplechaser	1976
Straight Deal	1962	Champion older mare	1967
Strawberry Road (Aus)	1979	Among the leading sires	1998
Striking	1947	Broodmare of the year	1961
Stymie	1941	Champion handicap horse	1945
Successor	1964	Champion 2-year-old	1966
Summer Scandal	1962	Champion older mare	1966
Sun Beau	1925	Champion handicap horse	1929
Sun Beau	1925	Champion handicap horse	1930
Sun Beau	1925	Champion handicap horse	1931
Sun Briar	1915	Champion handicap horse	1919
Sunday Silence	1986	Horse of the year	1989
Sunday Silence	1986	Champion 3-year-old colt	1989
Sunshine Forever	1985	Champion grass horse	1988
Surfside	1997	Champion 2-year-old filly	2000
Susan's Girl	1969	Champion 3-year-old filly	1972
Susan's Girl	1969	Champion older mare	1973
Susan's Girl	1969	Champion older mare	1975
Swale	1981	Champion 3-year-old colt	1984
Swaps	1952	Horse of the year	1956
Swaps	1952	Champion older horse	1956
Sweep	1907	Leading sire	1925
Sweep	1907	Leading broodmare sire	1937
Sweep	1907	Leading broodmare sire	1941
Sweet Patootie	1950	Champion 2-year-old filly	1952
Sweet Tooth	1965	Broodmare of the year	1977
Swoon	1942	Broodmare of the year	1956

Sword Dancer	1956	Horse of the year	1959
Sword Dancer	1956	Champion 3-year-old colt	1959
Sword Dancer	1956	Champion older horse	1959
T. V. Lark	1957	Champion grass horse	1961
T. V. Lark	1957	Leading sire	1974
Ta Wee	1966	Champion sprinter	1969
Ta Wee	1966	Champion sprinter	1970
Talking Picture	1971	Champion 2-year-old filly	1973
Tambour	1928	Champion 3-year-old filly	1931
Tambour	1928	Champion handicap mare	1933
Tasso	1983	Champion 2-year-old colt	1985
Tea-Maker	1943	Champion sprinter	1952
Tempera	1999	Champion 2-year-old filly	2001
Temperence Hill	1977	Champion 3-year-old colt	1980
Tempest Queen	1975	Champion 3-year-old filly	1978
Tempted	1955	Champion older mare	1959
The Finn	1912	Leading sire	1923
The Mast	1947	Champion steeplechaser	1953
The Porter	1915	Leading sire	1937
The Wicked North	1989	Champion older horse	1994
Theatrical (IRE)	1982	Champion grass horse	1987
Thunder Gulch	1992	Champion 3-year-old colt	1995
Thunder Gulch	1992	Leading sire	2001
Tiffany Lass	1983	Champion 3-year-old filly	1986
Tight Spot	1987	Champion grass horse	1991
Tim Tam	1955	Champion 3-year-old colt	1958
Timber Country	1992	Champion 2-year-old colt	1994
Tintagel	1933	Champion 2-year-old colt	1935
Tiznow	1997	Horse of the year	2000
Tiznow	1997	Champion 3-year-old colt	2000
Tiznow	1997	Champion older horse	2001
Toll Booth	1971	Broodmare of the year	1991
Tom Fool	1949	Horse of the year	1953
Tom Fool	1949	Champion 2-year-old colt	1951
Tom Fool	1949	Champion sprinter	1953
Tom Fool	1949	Champion older horse	1953
Tom Rolfe	1962	Champion 3-year-old colt	1965
Too Bald	1964	Broodmare of the year	1986
Top Bid	1964	Champion steeplechaser	1970
Top Flight	1929	Champion 2-year-old filly	1931
Top Flight	1929	Champion 3-year-old filly	1932
Top Knight	1966	Champion 2-year-old colt	1968
Tosmah	1961	Champion 2-year-old filly	1963
Tosmah	1961	Champion 3-year-old filly	1964
Tosmah	1961	Champion older mare	1964
Track Medal	1950	Broodmare of the year	1962
Track Robbery	1976	Champion older mare	1982
Traffic Court	1938	Broodmare of the year	1954
Tred Avon	1928	Champion handicap mare	1932
Trillion	1974	Champion grass mare	1979
Trough Hill	1942	Champion steeplechaser	1949
Tryster	1918	Champion 2-year-old colt	1920
Tudor Queen	1967	Champion 2-year-old filly	1969
Turbo Jet II	1960	Champion grass horse	1964
Turkish Trousers	1968	Champion 3-year-old filly	1971
Turkoman	1982	Champion older horse	1986
Tuscalee	1960	Champion steeplechaser	1966
Twenty Grand	1928	Horse of the year	1931
Twenty Grand	1928	Champion 3-year-old colt	1931
Twilight Tear	1941	Horse of the year	1944
Twilight Tear	1941	Champion 2-year-old filly	1943
Twilight Tear	1941	Champion 3-year-old filly	1944
Twilight Tear	1941	Champion handicap mare	1944
Two Lea	1946	Champion 3-year-old filly	1949
Two Lea	1946	Champion older mare	1950
Typecast	1966	Champion older mare	1972
Unbridled	1987	Champion 3-year-old colt	1990
Unbridled	1987	Among the leading sires	1999
Unerring	1936	Champion 3-year-old filly	1939
Untidy	1920	Champion 3-year-old filly	1923
Vagrancy	1939	Champion 3-year-old filly	1942
Vagrancy	1939	Champion handicap mare	1942
Valenciennes	1927	Champion handicap mare	1931
Vanlandingham	1981	Champion older horse	1985
Vexatious	1916	Champion 3-year-old filly	1919
Vice Regent	1967	Among the leading bm sires	1993
Vice Regent	1967	Among the leading bm sires	1996
Vice Regent	1967	Among the leading bm sires	1998
Vice Regent	1967	Among the leading bm sires	1999
Vice Regent	1967	Among the leading bm sires	2000
Vice Regent	1967	Among the leading bm sires	2001
Victory Gallop	1995	Champion older horse	1999
Vindication	2000	Champion 2-year-old colt	2002
Vitriolic	1965	Champion 2-year-old colt	1967
Wajima	1972	Champion 3-year-old colt	1975
Wandesta (GB)	1991	Champion grass mare	1996
War Admiral	1934	Horse of the year	1937
War Admiral	1934	Champion 3-year-old colt	1937
War Admiral	1934	Leading sire	1945
War Admiral	1934	Leading broodmare sire	1962
War Admiral	1934	Leading broodmare sire	1964
War Admiral	1934	Triple Crown	1937
War Battle	1941	Champion steeplechaser	1947
War Emblem	1999	Champion 3-year-old colt	2002
War Plumage	1936	Champion 3-year-old filly	1939
War Plumage	1936	Champion handicap mare	1940
Warfare	1957	Champion 2-year-old colt	1959
Warm Spell	1988	Champion steeplechaser	1994
Waya (FR)	1974	Champion older mare	1979
Wayward Lass	1978	Champion 3-year-old filly	1981
Weekend Surprise	1980	Broodmare of the year	1992
What a Pleasure	1965	Leading sire	1975
What a Pleasure	1965	Leading sire	1976
What a Summer	1973	Champion sprinter	1977
What a Treat	1962	Champion 3-year-old filly	1965
Whichone	1927	Champion 2-year-old colt	1929
Whirlaway	1938	Horse of the year	1941
Whirlaway	1938	Horse of the year	1942
Whirlaway	1938	Champion 2-year-old colt	1940
Whirlaway	1938	Champion 3-year-old colt	1941
Whirlaway	1938	Champion handicap horse	1942
Whirlaway	1938	Triple Crown	1941
Whiskaway	1919	Champion 3-year-old colt	1922
Whiskery	1924	Champion 3-year-old colt	1927
White Skies	1949	Champion sprinter	1954
Wild Again	1980	Among the leading sires	1997
Wild Again	1980	Among the leading sires	2002
Winning Colors	1985	Champion 3-year-old filly	1988
Wise Counsellor	1921	Champion 2-year-old colt	1923
Wistful	1946	Champion 3-year-old filly	1949
Wrack	1909	Leading broodmare sire	1935
Xtra Heat	1998	Champion 3-year-old filly	2001
Yanks Music	1993	Champion 3-year-old filly	1996
Youth	1973	Champion grass horse	1976
Zaccio	1976	Champion steeplechaser	1980
Zaccio	1976	Champion steeplechaser	1981
Zaccio	1976	Champion steeplechaser	1982
Zev	1920	Horse of the year	1923
Zev	1920	Champion 2-year-old colt	1922
Zev	1920	Champion 3-year-old colt	1923

2003 SOVEREIGN RESULTS WITH POINT TOTALS

Horse of the Year
Wando 215
Perfect Soul. 61
Soaring Free 53

2-year-old filly
My Vintage Port 208
Silver Bird 107
America America 34

2-year-old colt/gelding
Judiths Wild Rush 183
Smoocher 97
A Bit O'Gold 77

3-year-old filly
Too Late Now 112
Winter Garden 111
Dancewithavixen 91

3-year-old colt/gelding
Wando 228
Mobil 107
Roscoe Pito 61

Older filly or mare
One for Rose 192
Brass in Pocket 125
Winning Chance 56

Older colt, horse or gelding
Phantom Light 104
Forever Grand 103
Wake At Noon 74

Turf filly or mare
Inish Glora 221
Chopinina 62
Strait From Texas 46

Turf colt, horse or gelding
Perfect Soul. 178
Soaring Free 128
Strut the Stage 57

Sprinter
Soaring Free 152
Forever Grand 123
Mulligan the Great 42

Jockey
Todd Kabel 224
Patrick Husbands 111
Emile Ramsammy 32

Apprentice jockey
Julia Brimo 179
Nicola Wright 132
Jillian Scharfstein 49

Trainer
Bob Tiller 193
Mike Keogh 95
Mark Frostad 54

Owner
Stronach Stable 139
Gustav Schickedanz 137
Sam-Son Farm 91

Breeder
Sam-Son Farm 155
Gustav Schickedanz 141
Adena Springs 81

Broodmare
Radiant Ring 122
Biddy Mulligan 64
Annasan 61

Canadian Horse of the Year

1951	Bull Page	1969	Jumpin Josephine	1987	Afleet
1952	Canadiana	1970	Fanfreluche	1988	Play the King
1953	King Maple	1971	Lauries Dancer	1989	With Approval
1954	Queen's Own	1972	La Prevoyante	1990	Izvestia
1955	Ace Marine	1973	Kennedy Road	1991	Dance Smartly
1956	Canadian Champ	1974	L' Enjoleur	1992	Benburb
1957	Hartney	1975	L' Enjoleur	1993	Peteski
1958	Nearctic	1976	Norcliffe	1994	Alywow
1959	Wonder Where	1977	L' Alezane	1995	Peaks and Valleys
1960	Victoria Park	1978	Overskate	1996	Mt. Sassafras
1961	Hidden Treasure	1979	Overskate	1997	Chief Bearhart
1962	Crafty Lace	1980	Glorious Song	1998	Chief Bearhart
1963	Canebora	1981	Deputy Minister	1999	Thornfield
1964	Northern Dancer	1982	Frost King	2000	Quiet Resolve
1965	George Royal	1983	Travelling Victor	2001	Win City
1966	Victorian Era	1984	Dauphin Fabuleux	2002	Wake at Noon
1967	He's A Smoothie	1985	Imperial Choice	2003	Wando
1968	Viceregal	1986	Ruling Angel		

2003 Sovereign Awards

By Bill Tallon

Wando, winner of the Canadian Triple Crown and $2,017,323 this season, received his just deserts when honored as Canada's Horse of the Year at the 2003 Sovereign Awards ceremony in Toronto on Dec. 6.

Winners of the Sovereign Awards, which honor the outstanding performers in Canadian Thoroughbred horseracing and breeding, were determined by 58 voters who listed their top three choices in each of 16 categories. Points were assigned on a 4-2-1 basis. To be eligible for Sovereign Awards, horses must have at least three starts in Canada in 2003 by Nov. 16.

Wando, owned and bred by Gustav Schickedanz and trained by Mike Keogh, was joined as a Horse of the Year finalist by Perfect Soul, winner of Keeneland's Grade 1 Shadwell Turf Mile and Canada's champion turf male, and Soaring Free, a multiple stakes winner on turf who was voted champion sprinter.

Soaring Free and Perfect Soul finished second and third, respectively, in Woodbine's Grade 1 Atto Mile, which was won by California invader Touch of the Blues.

Canada's other Grade 1 turf events, the Canadian International and E.P. Taylor Stakes, also were won by shippers who were ineligible for Sovereign Awards.

Phoenix Reach traveled over from England to win the Canadian International, while Volga was based in New York when she came in to take the E.P. Taylor.

But Wando kept the home fires burning.

In winning Woodbine's 1 1/4 mile Queen's Plate, Fort Erie's 1 3/16 mile Prince of Wales and Woodbine's Breeders' Stakes over 1 1/2 miles of turf, Wando became the seventh winner of the Candian Triple Crown and earned a bonus of $500,000.

In addition to his Canadian Horse of the Year title Wando also was the runaway winner of the Sovereign Award in the 3-year-old colt or gelding category where his stablemate, Mobil, was the runner-up.

But, surprisingly, Schickedanz himself was shut out in both the owner and breeder categories.

Stronach Stable, which was represented by champion older male Phantom Light, edged Schickedanz in the outstanding owner voting to take home its eighth award in the category.

Sam-Son Farm, whose homebred Soaring Free also was the runner-up in the turf male voting, collected its fourth consecutive award and sixth overall as outstanding breeder.

Wando's trainer, Mike Keogh, had been expected to be involved in a close vote in his category but was a distant second to Bob Tiller, who was Woodbine's leading trainer in races, money and stakes races won.

Tiller also was represented by four divisional finalists but was blanked on those fronts, suffering incredibly tough beats when Forever Grand was defeated by a single point in the older horse voting and Winter Garden lost by the same margin in the 3-year-old filly balloting.

Forever Grand also was runner-up in the sprinter vote and his stablemate Brass in Pocket was second in the older mare balloting.

Too Late Now, winner of the Grade 1 Selene and the Woodbine Oaks, was the 3-year-old filly champion while One for Rose, whose major success came in Woodbine's Grade 3 Maple Leaf, was champion older mare.

The votes in the other equine categories were decisive with My Vintage Port being honored as champion 2-year-old filly, Judiths Wild Rush as 2-year-old male, and Inish Glora as turf female.

Todd Kabel, Woodbine's leading rider in races, money and stakes races won, was a runaway winner of the outstanding jockey award, his third such success but his first since 1995.

The runner-up was Patrick Husbands, who was looking for his fifth consecutive award in the category.

Julia Brimo, Woodbine's leading apprentice rider, took home the Sovereign Award in her category. Nicola Wright, based at Hastings in Vancouver, was the runner-up for the second straight year.

Radiant Ring was honored as outstanding broodmare, which is a lifetime achievement award.

Sovereign Awards also were presented in four media categories, with the winners determined by the vote of a panel of judges.

Paul Wiecek, of the Winnipeg Free Press, was the winner of both the newspaper article and feature story awards. Michael Burns Jr. picked up his sixth award for outstanding photograph and Horse Racing Alberta & White Iron productions were honored in the film/video/broadcast category.

Alphabetical Listing of Canadian Champions and Leading Sires and Broodmares

Horse	YOB	Title	Year	Horse	YOB	Title	Year
A Fleets Dancer	1995	Champion older horse	2001	Cash Deposit	1994	Champion 2-year-old colt	1996
Ada Prospect	1981	Champion 2-year-old filly	1983	Catch the Ring	1997	Champion 3-year-old filly	2000
Added Edge	2000	Champion 2-year-old colt	2002	Cesca	1960	Champion 2-year-old filly	1962
Afleet	1984	Horse of the year	1987	Cesca	1960	Champion 3-year-old filly	1963
Afleet	1984	Champion 3-year-old colt	1987	Charlie Barley	1986	Champion grass horse	1989
Aim n Fire	1960	Champion 2-year-old	1962	Charming Sassafras	1985	Broodmare of the year	1997
Allan Blue	1977	Champion 2-year-old	1979	Chief Bearhart	1993	Horse of the year	1997
Almoner	1967	Champion 3-year-old colt	1970	Chief Bearhart	1993	Horse of the year	1998
Alydeed	1989	Leading sire	2001	Chief Bearhart	1993	Champion grass horse	1996
Alywow	1991	Horse of the year	1994	Chief Bearhart	1993	Champion grass horse	1997
Alywow	1991	Champion 3-year-old filly	1994	Chief Bearhart	1993	Champion grass horse	1998
Alywow	1991	Champion grass horse	1994	Chief Bearhart	1993	Champion older horse	1997
Amber Sherry	1966	Champion 2-year-old filly	1968	Choperion	1959	2nd highweighted	1962
Amelia Bearhart	1983	Broodmare of the year	1996	Chopinina	1998	Champion grass mare	2002
Apelia	1989	Champion sprinter	1993	Choral Group	1979	Champion 2-year-old filly	1981
Archers Bay	1995	Champion 3-year-old colt	1998	Christy's Mount	1973	Champion older mare	1978
Arctic Blizzard	1965	Champion 2-year-old	1967	Ciboulette	1961	2nd highweighted filly	1963
Arctic Vixen	1978	Broodmare of the year	1987	Claim	1985	Among the leading sires	1997
Ascot Knight	1984	Among the leading sires	1997	Classy 'n Smart	1981	Champion 3-year-old filly	1984
Ascot Knight	1984	Among the leading sires	1998	Classy 'n Smart	1981	Broodmare of the year	1991
Ascot Knight	1984	Among the leading sires	1999	Colorful Vices	1993	Champion grass mare	1998
Ascot Knight	1984	Among the leading sires	2001	Come in Dad	1970	Champion 3-year-old	1973
Ascot Knight	1984	Among the leading sires	2002	Comet Shine	1991	Champion 2-year-old colt	1993
Avant's Gold	1987	Champion older mare	1991	Connie Pat	1968	Champion handicap mare	1973
Avowal	1979	Champion 3-year-old filly	1982	Cool Reception	1964	Champion 2-year-old	1966
Avowal	1979	Champion sprinter	1982	Cotton Carnival	1994	Champion 3-year-old filly	1997
Balaklair	1960	2nd highweighted filly	1963	Coup d'Etat	1957	Champion older mare	1962
Ballade	1972	Broodmare of the year	1992	Court Royal	1959	Champion older mare	1963
Basqueian	1991	Champion older horse	1995	Cozzene's Prince	1987	Champion older horse	1993
Bayford	1978	Champion 2-year-old	1980	Crafty Lace	1959	Horse of the year	1962
Belle Geste	1968	Champion handicap mare	1972	Crafty Lace	1959	Champion 3-year-old	1962
Ben Fab	1977	Champion 3-year-old	1980	Cryptocloser	1994	Champion 3-year-old colt	1997
Ben Fab	1977	Champion grass horse	1981	Dance Act	1966	Champion handicap horse	1970
Benburb	1989	Horse of the year	1992	Dance Act	1966	Champion handicap horse	1971
Benburb	1989	Champion 3-year-old colt	1992	Dance for Donna	1989	Champion older mare	1993
Bessarabian	1982	Champion older mare	1986	Dance in Time	1974	Champion 3-year-old	1977
Blue Finn	1984	Champion 2-year-old colt	1986	Dance Smartly	1988	Horse of the year	1991
Blushing Katy	1986	Champion 3-year-old filly	1989	Dance Smartly	1988	Champion 2-year-old filly	1990
Bold Debra	1981	Broodmare of the year	1993	Dance Smartly	1988	Champion 3-year-old filly	1991
Bold Executive	1984	Leading sire	2003	Dance Smartly	1988	Broodmare of the year	2001
Bold Executive	1984	Among the leading sires	1998	Dance Smartly	1988	Triple Crown	1991
Bold Executive	1984	Among the leading sires	1999	Dance to Market	1967	Champion 2-year-old	1969
Bold Executive	1984	Among the leading sires	2001	Dancethruthedawn	1998	Champion 3-year-old filly	2001
Bold Executive	1984	Among the leading sires	2002	Dauphin Fabuleux	1982	Horse of the year	1984
Bold Ruckus	1976	Leading sire	1997	Dauphin Fabuleux	1982	Champion 2-year-old colt	1984
Bold Ruckus	1976	Leading sire	1998	Dawn Deluxe	1969	Champion 2-year-old filly	1971
Bold Ruckus	1976	Leading sire	1999	Dawson's Legacy	1995	Champion 2-year-old colt	1997
Bold Ruckus	1976	Among the leading sires	2001	Deceit Dancer	1982	Champion 2-year-old filly	1984
Bold Ruritana	1990	Champion grass mare	1995	Decidedly	1959	Champion older horse	1963
Bold Ruritana	1990	Champion older mare	1995	Deputy Inxs	1991	Champion sprinter	1998
Bolulight	1988	Champion 3-year-old	1991	Deputy Inxs	1991	Champion sprinter	1999
Bompago	1980	Champion 3-year-old colt	1983	Deputy Inxs	1991	Champion older horse	1999
Bounding Away	1981	Champion grass horse	1984	Deputy Jane West	1990	Champion 2-year-old filly	1992
Brave Front	1963	Champion 2-year-old filly	1965	Deputy Jane West	1990	Champion 3-year-old filly	1993
Bruce's Mill	1991	Champion 3-year-old	1994	Deputy Minister	1979	Horse of the year	1981
Brusque	2000	Champion 2-year-old filly	2002	Deputy Minister	1979	Champion 2-year-old colt	1981
Buckys Solution	1989	Champion 2-year-old filly	1991	Dianne's Lady	1974	Highweighted filly	1978
Bye and Near	1963	Champion handicap horse	1969	Diapason	1980	Champion sprinter	1984
Bye Bye Paris	1973	Champion 3-year-old filly	1976	Diva's Debut	1986	Champion older mare	1990
Canadian Factor	1980	Champion older horse	1984	Doris White	1966	Broodmare of the year	1977
Candle Bright	1980	Champion 2-year-old filly	1982	Double Ripple	1965	Highweighted filly	1969
Canebora	1960	Horse of the year	1963	Dr. Giddings	1960	2nd highweighted	1963
Canebora	1960	Champion 3-year-old	1963	Driving Home	1977	Champion older horse	1981
Canebora	1960	Triple Crown	1963	El Bandido	1957	Champion older horse	1962
Carotene	1983	Champion 3-year-old filly	1986	Eternal Search	1978	Champion sprinter	1981
Carotene	1983	Champion grass horse	1986	Eternal Search	1978	Champion older mare	1982
Carotene	1983	Champion grass horse	1987	Eternal Search	1978	Champion older mare	1983
Carotene	1983	Champion grass horse	1988	Etimota	1960	2nd highweighted filly	1962
Carotene	1983	Champion grass mare	1988	Exciting Story	1997	Champion 2-year-old colt	1999
Carotene	1983	Champion older mare	1987	Famous Road	1961	Champion 2-year-old filly	1963
Carotene	1983	Champion older mare	1988	Fanfreluche	1967	Horse of the year	1970

Horse	YOB	Title	Year	Horse	YOB	Title	Year
Fanfreluche	1967	Champion 3-year-old filly	1970	La Prevoyante	1970	Champion 2-year-old filly	1972
Fanfreluche	1967	Broodmare of the year	1978	La Prevoyante	1970	Champion older mare	1974
Fantasy Lake	1996	Champion 2-year-old filly	1998	La Voyageuse	1975	Champion 3-year-old filly	1978
First Class Gal	1988	Broodmare of the year	2002	La Voyageuse	1975	Champion sprinter	1980
Fitz's Fancy	1962	Broodmare of the year	1979	La Voyageuse	1975	Champion older mare	1979
Flaming Page	1959	Champion 3-year-old filly	1962	Lady Shari	1999	Champion 3-year-old filly	2002
Fleet Courage	1972	Broodmare of the year	1998	Lake Country	1981	Champion older mare	1985
Foxy Parent	1967	Champion 2-year-old filly	1969	L'Alezane	1975	Horse of the year	1977
Fraud Squad	1979	Champion sprinter	1983	L'Alezane	1975	Champion 2-year-old	1977
Free At Last	1989	Champion 2-year-old colt	1991	Langfuhr	1992	Champion sprinter	1996
Free Vacation	1996	Champion grass mare	1999	Larkwhistle	1994	Champion 2-year-old filly	1996
Friendly Ways	1968	Broodmare of the year	1984	Lauries Dancer	1968	Horse of the year	1971
Frost King	1978	Horse of the year	1982	Lauries Dancer	1968	Champion 3-year-old filly	1971
Frost King	1978	Champion 3-year-old colt	1981	Le Cinquieme Essai	1999	Champion 3-year-old colt	2002
Frost King	1978	Champion grass horse	1982	Legarto	1986	Champion 2-year-old filly	1988
Frost King	1978	Champion older horse	1982	L'Enjoleur	1972	Horse of the year	1974
Gandria	1996	Champion 3-year-old filly	1999	L'Enjoleur	1972	Horse of the year	1975
Gentleman Conn	1969	Champion 2-year-old colt	1971	L'Enjoleur	1972	Champion 2-year-old colt	1974
George Royal	1961	Horse of the year	1965	L'Enjoleur	1972	Champion 3-year-old colt	1975
Giboulee	1974	Champion older horse	1978	Let's Go Blue	1981	Champion older horse	1986
Ginger Gold	1999	Champion 2-year-old filly	2001	Liz's Pride	1976	Champion 2-year-old filly	1978
Glanmire	1990	Champion sprinter	1997	Lord Durham	1971	Champion 2-year-old	1973
Glorious Song	1976	Horse of the year	1980	Loudrangle	1974	Broodmare of the year	1986
Glorious Song	1976	Champion older mare	1980	Lubicon	1987	Champion 3-year-old filly	1990
Glorious Song	1976	Champion older mare	1981	Magic Code	1995	Champion older mare	1999
Glory Hill	1960	Champion 3-year-old filly	1963	Maudlin	1978	Among the leading sires	1999
Golden Choice	1983	Champion 3-year-old	1986	Medaille d'Or	1976	Champion 2-year-old	1978
Gomtuu	1993	Champion 2-year-old colt	1995	Mercedes Won	1986	Champion 2-year-old colt	1988
Good Old Mort	1962	Champion 2-year-old	1964	Minsky	1968	Champion 3-year-old	1971
Great Gladiator	1977	Among the leading sires	1998	Momigi	1972	Champion 3-year-old filly	1975
Great Gladiator	1977	Among the leading sires	1999	Momigi	1972	Champion grass horse	1977
Grey Classic	1983	Champion 2-year-old colt	1985	Momigi	1972	Champion handicap mare	1976
Hangin Round	1970	Broodmare of the year	1980	Mountain Angel	1997	Champion older mare	2001
Happy Victory	1969	Champion 3-year-old filly	1972	Mr. Epperson	1995	Champion sprinter	2001
Hasten To Add	1990	Champion grass horse	1995	Mr. Hot Shot	1985	Champion sprinter	1989
Heliotrope	1995	Champion grass mare	2000	Mt. Sassafras	1992	Horse of the year	1996
Hello Seattle	1997	Champion 2-year-old filly	1999	Mt. Sassafras	1992	Champion older horse	1996
Henry Tudor	1969	Champion older horse	1974	My Vintage Port	2001	Champion 2-year-old colt	2003
Hero's Love	1988	Champion grass horse	1993	Native Flower	1968	Broodmare of the year	1981
He's a Smoothie	1963	Horse of the year	1967	New Connection	1981	Champion sprinter	1986
He's a Smoothie	1963	Champion 3-year-old	1966	Nice Dancer	1969	Champion 3-year-old colt	1972
He's a Smoothie	1963	Champion handicap horse	1967	No Class	1974	Broodmare of the year	1985
He's a Smoothie	1963	Champion handicap horse	1968	Norcliffe	1973	Horse of the year	1976
Highland Legacy	1998	Champion 2-year-old colt	2000	Norcliffe	1973	Champion 3-year-old	1976
Hometown News	1965	Champion 3-year-old filly	1968	Norcliffe	1973	Champion handicap horse	1977
Honky Tonk Tune	1992	Champion 2-year-old filly	1994	Northern Blossom	1980	Champion 3-year-old filly	1983
Hope for a Breeze	1989	Champion 3-year-old filly	1992	Northern Dancer	1961	Horse of the year	1964
Ice Water	1963	Champion handicap mare	1968	Northern Dancer	1961	Champion 2-year-old colt	1963
Imperial Choice	1982	Horse of the year	1985	Northern Minx	1963	Broodmare of the year	1976
Imperial Choice	1982	Champion 3-year-old colt	1985	Northern Queen	1962	Champion 3-year-old filly	1965
Imperial Choice	1982	Champion grass horse	1985	Northernette	1974	Champion 2-year-old filly	1976
Inish Glora	1998	Champion grass mare	2003	Northernette	1974	Champion 3-year-old filly	1977
Izvestia	1987	Horse of the year	1990	Not Too Shy	1966	Champion 3-year-old filly	1969
Izvestia	1987	Champion 3-year-old colt	1990	Not Too Shy	1966	Champion handicap mare	1970
Izvestia	1987	Champion grass horse	1990	Not Too Shy	1966	Champion handicap mare	1971
Izvestia	1987	Triple Crown	1990	Numerous Times	1997	Champion grass horse	2001
Judiths Wild Rush	2001	Champion 2-year-old colt	2003	One for Rose	1999	Champion older mare	2003
Jumpin Joseph	1966	Horse of the year	1969	One From Heaven	1984	Champion 3-year-old filly	1987
Jumpin Joseph	1966	Champion 3-year-old colt	1969	One Way Love	1995	Champion sprinter	2000
Kamar	1976	Champion 3-year-old filly	1979	One Way Love	1995	Champion older horse	2000
Kennedy Road	1968	Horse of the year	1973	Overskate	1975	Horse of the year	1978
Kennedy Road	1968	Champion 2-year-old	1970	Overskate	1975	Horse of the year	1979
Kennedy Road	1968	Champion handicap horse	1972	Overskate	1975	Champion 2-year-old colt	1977
Kennedy Road	1968	Champion handicap horse	1973	Overskate	1975	Champion 3-year-old colt	1978
Kerensa	1963	Champion 3-year-old filly	1966	Overskate	1975	Champion grass horse	1978
Key to the Moon	1981	Champion 3-year-old colt	1984	Overskate	1975	Champion grass horse	1979
King Corrie	1988	Champion sprinter	1991	Overskate	1975	Champion grass horse	1980
King Corrie	1988	Champion sprinter	1992	Overskate	1975	Champion older horse	1979
King Ruckus	1990	Champion sprinter	1994	Overskate	1975	Champion older horse	1980
King Ruckus	1990	Champion older horse	1994	Par Excellance	1977	Champion 2-year-old filly	1979
Kingsbridge	1980	Champion grass horse	1983	Par Excellance	1977	Champion 3-year-old filly	1980
Kirby's Song	1995	Champion 3-year-old filly	1998	Passing Mood	1978	Broodmare of the year	1989
Kiss a Native	1997	Champion 3-year-old colt	2000	Peaks and Valleys	1992	Horse of the year	1995
La Lorgnette	1982	Champion 3-year-old filly	1985	Peaks and Valleys	1992	Champion 3-year-old colt	1995
La Prevoyante	1970	Horse of the year	1972	Pennyhill Park	1990	Champion older mare	1994

Horse	YOB	Title	Year
Perfect Soul (IRE)	1998	Champion grass horse	2003
Peteski	1990	Horse of the year	1993
Peteski	1990	Champion 3-year-old colt	1993
Peteski	1990	Triple Crown	1993
Phantom Light	1999	Champion older horse	2003
Phoenix Factor	1985	Champion 2-year-old filly	1987
Pine Point	1964	Champion 3-year-old	1967
Play the King	1983	Horse of the year	1988
Play the King	1983	Champion sprinter	1987
Play the King	1983	Champion sprinter	1988
Play the King	1983	Champion older horse	1987
Play the King	1983	Champion older horse	1988
Poetically	1998	Champion 2-year-old filly	2000
Polite Lady	1977	Broodmare of the year	1988
Portcullis	1999	Champion grass horse	2002
Primaly	1995	Champion 2-year-old filly	1997
Primarily	1988	Broodmare of the year	2000
Prince Avatar	1981	Champion 2-year-old	1983
Proper Evidence	1985	Champion older mare	1989
Proud Tobin	1973	Champion 2-year-old colt	1975
Queen Louie	1968	Champion 2-year-old filly	1970
Quiet Resolve	1995	Horse of the year	2000
Quiet Resolve	1995	Champion grass horse	2000
Radiant Ring	1988	Broodmare of the year	2003
Rainbow Connection	1978	Champion 2-year-old filly	1980
Rainbow Connection	1978	Champion 3-year-old filly	1981
Rainbow Connection	1978	Broodmare of the year	1994
Rainbows for Life	1988	Champion 2-year-old colt	1990
Rainbows for Life	1988	Champion grass horse	1992
Rainbows for Life	1988	Champion older horse	1992
Ramblin Road	1961	2nd highweighted	1963
Rare Friends	1999	Champion 2-year-old colt	2001
Rash Move	1971	Champion handicap horse	1975
Reasonable Wife	1968	Broodmare of the year	1975
Reasonable Win	1972	Champion handicap mare	1977
Regal Classic	1985	Champion 2-year-old colt	1987
Regal Classic	1985	Among the leading sires	1997
Regal Intention	1985	Champion 3-year-old colt	1988
Riddell's Creek	1996	Champion 2-year-old colt	1998
Rouletabille	1965	Champion 3-year-old	1968
Royal Tara	1961	Highweighted filly	1964
Royal Tara	1961	Highweighted older mare	1965
Ruling Angel	1984	Horse of the year	1986
Ruling Angel	1984	Champion 2-year-old filly	1986
Runaway Groom	1979	Champion 3-year-old colt	1982
Rushton's Corsair	1971	Champion 3-year-old	1974
Ruthie's Run	1972	Champion 2-year-old filly	1974
Santa Amelia	1993	Champion older mare	1998
Saoirse	1996	Champion older mare	2000
Scotzanna	1992	Champion 3-year-old filly	1995
Scotzanna	1992	Champion sprinter	1995
Sea Regent	1977	Broodmare of the year	1995
Seraphic	1973	Champion 2-year-old filly	1975
Sharpening Up	1983	Broodmare of the year	1999
Shy Spirit	1975	Broodmare of the year	1990
Silent Fleet	1993	Champion 3-year-old filly	1996
Silken Cat	1993	Champion 2-year-old filly	1995
Sintrillium	1978	Champion older mare	1984
Sky Classic	1987	Champion 2-year-old colt	1989
Sky Classic	1987	Champion grass horse	1991
Sky Classic	1987	Champion older horse	1991
Small Promises	1998	Champion older mare	2002
Soaring Free	1999	Champion sprinter	2003
Sonny Says Quick	1968	Highweighted filly	1970
Sound Reason	1974	Champion 2-year-old	1976
Sound Stage	1960	2nd highweighted	1962
Speedy Lament	1961	Champion older mare	1966
Square Angel	1970	Champion 3-year-old filly	1973
Stage Flite	1983	Champion 2-year-old filly	1985
Steady Growth	1976	Champion 3-year-old	1979
Steady Power	1984	Champion older horse	1989
Summer Mood	1981	Champion sprinter	1985
Sunny's Halo	1980	Champion 2-year-old	1982
Sweetest Thing	1998	Champion grass mare	2001
Talkin Man	1992	Champion 2-year-old	1994
Tejabo	1985	Among the leading sires	2002

Horse	YOB	Title	Year
Ten Gold Pots	1981	Champion older horse	1985
Term Limits	1991	Champion 2-year-old filly	1993
Terremoto	1991	Champion older horse	1998
Tethra	1992	Among the leading sires	2003
The Axe II	1958	Champion grass horse	1963
Thornfield	1994	Horse of the year	1999
Thornfield	1994	Champion grass horse	1999
Tilt My Halo	1985	Champion 3-year-old filly	1988
Titled Hero	1963	Champion 2-year-old	1965
Titled Hero	1963	Champion 3-year-old	1966
Too Late Now	2000	Champion 3-year-old filly	2003
Travelling Victor	1979	Horse of the year	1983
Travelling Victor	1979	Champion older horse	1983
Trudie Tudor	1971	Champion 2-year-old filly	1973
Trudie Tudor	1971	Champion 3-year-old filly	1974
Truth of It All	1990	Champion 2-year-old colt	1992
Twist the Snow	1986	Champion sprinter	1990
Twist the Snow	1986	Champion older horse	1990
Two Rings	1970	Broodmare of the year	1983
Vase	1959	2nd highweighted filly	1962
Vice Regent	1967	Among the leading sires	1997
Vice Regent	1967	Among the leading sires	1998
Viceregal	1966	Horse of the year	1968
Viceregal	1966	Champion 2-year-old colt	1968
Victor Cooley	1993	Champion 3-year-old colt	1996
Victorian Era	1962	Horse of the year	1966
Victorian Era	1962	Champion handicap horse	1966
Victorian Prince	1970	Champion grass horse	1976
Victorian Prince	1970	Champion older horse	1976
Victorian Queen	1971	Champion grass horse	1975
Victorian Queen	1971	Champion handicap mare	1975
Vying Victor	1989	Among the leading sires	2002
Vying Victor	1989	Among the leading sires	2003
Wake At Noon	1997	Horse of the year	2002
Wake At Noon	1997	Champion sprinter	2002
Wake At Noon	1997	Champion older horse	2002
Wando	2000	Horse of the year	2003
Wando	2000	Champion 3-year-old colt	2003
Wando	2000	Triple Crown	2003
War Deputy	1991	Leading sire	2002
War Deputy	1991	Among the leading sires	2001
War Deputy	1991	Among the leading sires	2003
Wavering Girl	1987	Champion 2-year-old filly	1989
Whiskey Wisdom	1993	Among the leading sires	2003
Wilderness Song	1988	Champion older mare	1992
Win City	1998	Horse of the year	2001
Win City	1998	Champion 3-year-old colt	2001
Windsharp	1991	Champion grass mare	1996
Windsharp	1991	Champion older mare	1996
With Approval	1986	Horse of the year	1989
With Approval	1986	Champion 3-year-old	1989
With Approval	1986	Triple Crown	1989
Woodcarver	1996	Champion 3-year-old colt	1999
Woolloomooloo	1992	Champion grass mare	1997
Woolloomooloo	1992	Champion older mare	1997
Yonnie Girl	1966	Broodmare of the year	1982
Zaca Spirit	1970	Champion 2-year-old	1972

PAST PERFORMANCES
OF
GREAT HORSES OF THE 20TH CENTURY

☆

AFFIRMED	LADY'S SECRET
BUCKPASSER	MAN O' WAR
CIGAR	NASHUA
CITATION	NATIVE DANCER
COLIN	PERSONAL ENSIGN
COUNT FLEET	RUFFIAN
DAMASCUS	SEABISCUIT
DR. FAGER	SEATTLE SLEW
EQUIPOISE	SECRETARIAT
EXTERMINATOR	SHUVEE
FOREGO	SKIP AWAY
HOLY BULL	SPECTACULAR BID
JOHN HENRY	SWAPS
KELSO	TOM FOOL
	TWILIGHT TEAR

Past Performances of Great Horses of the 20th Century

Affirmed — ch. c. 1975, by Exclusive Native (Raise a Native)–Won't Tell You, by Crafty Admiral — Lifetime record: 29 22 5 1 $2,393,818

Own.– Harbor View Farm
Br.– Harbor View Farm (Fla)
Tr.– Lazaro S. Barrera

6Oct79- 8Bel	fst	1½	:49 1:13^{1} 2:02^{2} 2:27^{2}	3↑ J C Gold Cup-G1	3	2	1½	1^{hd}	1½	1¾	Pincay L Jr	126	*.60	83-21	Affirmed126¾Spectacular Bid121^{3}Coastal121^{31}	Driving	4
22Sep79- 8Bel	sly	1¼	:47^{3} 1:11^{4} 1:36^{1} 2:01^{3}	3↑ Woodward-G1	2	2	2^{4}	1½	1^{3}	12½	Pincay L Jr	126	*.40	92-15	Affirmed1262½Coastal1203¾Czaravich1208½	Ridden out	5
29Aug79- 0Bel	sly	1	:22^{2} :45 1:09^{2} 1:34	3↑ Alw 30000	3	1	1½	1^{1}	1^{2}	1^{6}	Pincay L Jr	122	-	98-15	Affirmed122^{6}Island Sultan115^{14}Prefontaine117	Ridden out	3
	No wagering. Exhibition race run between 7th and 8th races																
24Jun79- 8Hol	fst	1¼	:45^{3} 1:09^{3} 1:34^{1} 1:58^{2}	3↑ Hol Gold Cup-G1	1	2	1^{hd}	1^{hd}	1^{hd}	1¾	Pincay L Jr	132	*.30	99-13	Affirmed132¾Sirlad120^{4}Text119^{5}	Driving	10
20May79- 8Hol	fst	1 1/16	:22^{2} :44^{4} 1:09^{1} 1:41^{1}	3↑ Californian-G1	2	1	1^{1}	1^{1}	1^{2}	1^{5}	Pincay L Jr	130	*.30	89-16	Affirmed130^{5}Syncopate114^{4}Harry's Love117¾	Driving	8
4Mar79- 8SA	fst	1¼	:46^{2} 1:10^{1} 1:34^{1} 1:58^{3}	4↑ S Anita H-G1	3	2	2^{1}	11½	1^{4}	14½	Pincay L Jr	128	*1.30	103-09	Affirmed1284½Tiller127^{3}[DH]PaintedWagon115	Speed to spare	8
4Feb79- 8SA	gd	1¼	:47 1:10^{4} 1:35^{3} 2:01	C H Strub-G1	8	2	3^{1}	1^{1}	1^{2}	1^{10}	Pincay L Jr	126	*.90	91-17	Affirmed126^{10}Johnny's Image115^{4}Quip115^{7}	Handily	9
20Jan79- 8SA	gd	1⅛	:45^{3} 1:09^{3} 1:35 1:48	San Fernando-G2	4	3	49½	57½	33½	22¾	Cauthen S	126	*.50	88-14	Radar Ahead1232¾Affirmed126^{nk}Little Reb120^{4}	Drifted out	8
7Jan79- 8SA	fst	7f	:22^{2} :45 1:08^{3} 1:21	Malibu-G2	2	1	3^{2}	32½	32½	32¼	Cauthen S	126	*.30	96-13	LittleReb1202¼RadarAhed123^{hd}Affrmd126^{3}	Hemmed in to str	5
14Oct78- 8Bel	sly	1½	:45^{1} 1:09^{2} 2:01^{4} 2:27^{1}	3↑ J C Gold Cup-G1	2	2	2^{hd}	3^{7}	4^{15}	518¾	Cauthen S	121	2.20e	65-13	Exceller126^{no}Seattle Slew126^{14}Great Contractor1264¾		6
	Saddle slipped																
16Sep78- 8Bel	fst	1⅛	:47 1:10^{1} 1:33^{3} 1:45^{4}	3↑ Marlboro Cup H-G1	1	2	22½	22½	2^{3}	2^{3}	Cauthen S	124	*.50	95-12	SeattleSlew128^{3}Affirmed124^{5}NastyandBold118^{4}	No excuse	6
19Aug78- 8Sar	fst	1¼	:48 1:11^{3} 1:36^{4} 2:02	Travers-G1	3	2	2^{hd}	11½	1^{2}	11¾	Pincay L Jr	126	*.70	91-14	[D]Affirmed1261¾Alydar1263¾NastyandBold126^{15}	Came over	4
	Disqualified and placed second																
8Aug78- 8Sar	gd	1⅛	:46^{3} 1:10^{1} 1:35 1:47^{4}	Jim Dandy-G3	4	2	2^{8}	2^{7}	2^{4}	1½	Cauthen S	128	*.05	96-04	Affirmed128½SensitivePrince119^{20}Addison1146½	Going away	5
10Jun78- 8Bel	fst	1½	:50 1:14 2:01^{3} 2:26^{4}	Belmont-G1	3	1	1^{1}	1^{hd}	1^{hd}	1^{hd}	Cauthen S	126	*.60	86-11	Affirmed126^{hd}Alydar126^{13}Darby Creek Road1267¾	Driving	5
20May78- 8Pim	fst	1 3/16	:47^{3} 1:11^{4} 1:36^{1} 1:54^{2}	Preakness-G1	6	2	1^{1}	1^{1}	1½	1^{nk}	Cauthen S	126	*.50	98-12	Affirmed126^{nk}Alydar1267½Believe It1262½	Brisk handling	7
6May78- 8CD	fst	1¼	:45^{3} 1:10^{4} 1:35^{4} 2:01^{1}	Ky Derby-G1	2	2	35½	2^{hd}	1^{2}	11½	Cauthen S	126	1.80	91-12	Affirmed1261½Alydar1261¼Believe It1264¼	Fully extended	11
16Apr78- 8Hol	fst	1⅛	:45 1:09^{2} 1:35 1:48^{1}	Hol Derby-G1	2	1	1^{hd}	1^{1}	12½	1^{2}	Cauthen S	122	*.30	91-17	Affirmed122^{2}Think Snow122^{3}Radar Ahead122^{2}	Driving	9
2Apr78- 8SA	fst	1⅛	:45^{4} 1:09^{4} 1:35^{3} 1:48	S Anita Derby-G1	7	2	1^{1}	11½	13½	1^{8}	Pincay L Jr	120	*.30	92-16	Affirmed120^{8}Balzac120^{1}Think Snow1202½	Handily	12
18Mar78- 8SA	fst	1 1/16	:24^{1} :48^{2} 1:12 1:42^{3}	San Felipe-G2	4	2	2^{1}	2^{hd}	1^{hd}	1^{2}	Cauthen S	126	*.30	89-17	Affirmed126^{2}Chance Dancer117^{6}Tampoy1181½	Driving	6
8Mar78- 6SA	fst	6½f	:21^{3} :44^{2} 1:09 1:15^{3}	Alw 30000	4	1	43½	11½	1^{4}	1^{5}	Cauthen S	124	*.20	92-16	Affirmed124^{5}Spotted Charger114½Don F.114^{hd}	Easily	5
29Oct77- 8Lrl	fst	1 1/16	:24 :48^{4} 1:13^{3} 1:44^{1}	Lrl Futurity-G1	3	2	2^{1}	2^{hd}	1^{hd}	1^{nk}	Cauthen S	122	1.40	92-27	Affirmed122^{nk}Alydar122^{10}StardeNskr122^{27}	Long,hard drive	4
15Oct77- 6Bel	my	1	:24^{2} :48^{1} 1:12^{2} 1:36^{3}	Champagne-G1	5	3	3^{2}	1^{hd}	1½	21¼	Cauthen S	122	*1.20	84-17	Alydar1221¼Affirmed1221¼Darby Creek Road1221½	2nd best	6
10Sep77- 8Bel	gd	7f	:23^{3} :46^{3} 1:09^{4} 1:21^{3}	Futurity-G1	2	2	2½	1^{hd}	2^{hd}	1no	Cauthen S	122	*1.20	94-10	Affirmed122^{no}Alydar122^{11}NastyandBold122^{hd}	Strong drive	5
27Aug77- 8Sar	fst	6½f	:22^{4} :45^{1} 1:09^{1} 1:15^{2}	Hopeful-G1	4	1	3^{2}	2^{hd}	1^{hd}	1½	Cauthen S	122	2.30	98-11	Affirmed122½Alydar1222½RegalandRoyal122^{hd}	Good handling	5
17Aug77- 8Sar	fst	6f	:21^{4} :44^{3} 1:09^{3}	Sanford-G2	3	2	35½	4^{3}	2½	12¾	Cauthen S	124	*1.30	92-15	Affirmed1242¾TltUp122^{hd}JtDplomcy124^{nk}	Driving,very wide	6
23Jly77- 5Hol	fst	6f	:21^{3} :44^{2} :56^{2} 1:09^{1}	Juv Champ (Div 1) 104k	6	3	1^{hd}	1½	1^{4}	1^{7}	Pincay L Jr	122	*.40	93-15	Affirmed122^{7}He's Dewan122^{6}Esops Foibles122¾	Easily	8
6Jly77- 8Bel	fst	5½f	:22^{2} :45^{4} :57^{2} 1:03^{3}	Great American 36k	1	1	1^{1}	2^{hd}	21½	23½	Cordero A Jr	122	4.60	93-16	Alydar1173½Affirmed122^{2}Going Investor122^{4}	No match	7
15Jun77- 8Bel	fst	5½f	:22^{2} :45^{3} :58^{2} 1:05	©Youthful 37k	1	1	2½	2½	1^{hd}	1^{nk}	Cordero A Jr	119	3.40	90-17	Affirmed119^{nk}Wood Native119½Sensitive Nose1192½	Driving	11
24May77- 4Bel	fst	5½f	:23 :47^{2} :59^{3} 1:06	Md Sp Wt	10	1	1½	11½	1^{2}	14½	Gonzalez B	117	14.30	85-21	Affirmed1174½Innocuous1223½Gymnast122^{2}	Ridden out	10

Past Performances of Great Horses of the 20th Century

Buckpasser

b. c. 1963, by Tom Fool (Menow)–Busanda, by War Admiral

Own.– O. Phipps
Br.– Ogden Phipps (Ky)
Tr.– E.A. Neloy

Lifetime record: 31 25 4 1 $1,462,014

30Sep67- 7Aqu	fst 1¼	:45^1 1:09^1 1:35^3 2:00^3 3↑	Woodward 107k	6	6	6^{14}	3^{3½}	3^8	2^{10}	Baeza B	126	b	*1.60e	85-15	Damascus120^{10}Buckpasser126^{½}Dr. Fager120^{13}	Good try	6
22Jly67- 7Aqu	fst 1¼	:46^2 1:09^4 1:34^2 2:00^1 3↑	Brooklyn H 106k	3	3	3^3	2^3	2^5	2^8	Baeza B	136	b	*.70	89-11	Handsome Boy116^{8}Bckpassr136^{4½}Mr. Right113^{3½}	No excuse	5
4Jly67- 7Aqu	fst 1¼	:47^4 1:11^4 1:36^3 2:02^1 3↑	Suburban H 109k	1	5	6^5	4^4	4^4	1^{½}	Baeza B	133	b	*.50	87-17	Buckpasser133^{½}RingTwice111^{2½}Yondr109^{1½}	Up final strides	7
17Jun67- 7Aqu	hd 1⅝Ⓣ	2:41^2 3↑	Bowling Green H 55k	3	4	4^{7½}	4^{6½}	3^5	3^{4½}	Baeza B	135	b	*.40e	82-13	Poker112^{1½}Assagai127^{3}Buckpasser135^{½}	Failed to respond	5
30May67- 7Aqu	fst 1	:23^2 :45^4 1:10 1:34^3 3↑	Metropolitan H 109k	5	3	3^2	3^{4½}	2^1	1^{1¼}	Baeza B	130	b	*.30	95-13	Buckpasser130^{1¼}Yonder108^{4½}Impressive113^1	Scored easily	6
14Jan67- 8SA	fst 1⅛	:46^2 1:10^3 1:35^4 1:48^1	San Fernando 56k	3	3	3^{7½}	4^{4½}	3^{2½}	1^{1½}	Baeza B	124	b	*.30	91-12	Buckpasser124^{1½}FleetHost121^{¾}Pretens118^{hd}	With authority	6
31Dec66- 6SA	fst 7f	:22^3 :45^1 1:09^3 1:22	Malibu 29k	2	9	7^{6½}	5^{4½}	2^1	1^{¾}	Baeza B	126	b	*.40	93-15	Buckpasser126^{¾}Drin120^{1}KingsFvor117^{1½}	Slow start,driving	9
29Oct66- 7Aqu	fst 2	:49^4 2:33^3 3:26^1 3↑	J C Gold Cup 110k	1	4	4^{4½}	1^{hd}	1^1	1^{1¾}	Baeza B	119	b	*.30e	65-21	Buckpasser119^{1¾}Niarkos124^{½}O'Hara124^8	Drew out handling	7
19Oct66- 7Aqu	sly 1⅝	:49^2 1:42^3 2:07^1 2:44^1	Lawrence Realizatn 54k	4	5	4^{4½}	3^{3½}	3^{2½}	1^{2½}	Baeza B	126	b	*.20e	84-19	Buckpasser126^{2½}Ring Twice116^{½}Poker116^{12}	Going away	5
1Oct66- 7Aqu	sly 1¼	:47 1:11^4 1:37^3 2:02^4 3↑	Woodward 112k	4	6	6^{4½}	3^{1½}	1^{hd}	1^{¾}	Baeza B	121	b	*.90e	84-24	Buckpasser121^{¾}Royal Gunner126^{¾}Buffle121^5	Ridden out	9
20Aug66- 6Sar	fst 1¼	:47^2 1:11^2 1:36^2 2:01^3	Travers 82k	6	5	5^{12}	4^{3½}	2^1	1^{¾}	Baeza B	126	b	*.30e	100-10	Buckpssr126^{¾}Ambrod123^{3½}Buffl120^{no}	Under strong handling	6
6Aug66- 8AP	fst 1⅛	:46^4 1:10^3 1:35^4 1:47	American Derby 129k	9	5	5^{9½}	6^8	4^2	1^{nk}	Baeza B	128	b	*.60e	101-09	Buckpasser128^{nk}Jolly Jet116^{1}Advocator116^3	Driving	9
23Jly66- 7Aqu	fst 1¼	:48^3 1:12^2 1:36^4 2:01^4 3↑	Brooklyn H 107k	2	2	2^{2½}	2^{1½}	1^{hd}	1^{hd}	Baeza B	120	b	*.60	89-16	Buckpasser120^{hd}Buffle113^{5}Pluck113^2	Faltered,came again	5
9Jly66- 8AP	fst 1⅛	:47^3 1:11^2 1:36^3 1:49^1	Chicagoan 103k	3	3	3^3	2^{½}	1^{hd}	1^{¾}	Baeza B	123	b	*.30	90-18	Buckpasser123^{¾}Whisper Jet114^{nk}Abe's Hope116^7	Mild drive	5
25Jun66- 8AP	fst 1	:22^1 :43^3 1:06^4 1:32^3	Arl Classic H 108k	4	6	7^9	5^9	3^4	1^{¾}	Baeza B	125	b	*.70e	103-04	Buckpasser125^{1¾}CremeDelaCreme123^{¾}HeJr.116^{nk}	Ridden out	8
18Jun66- 8Del	fst 1⅛	:46^3 1:10 1:36^4 1:49^2	Leonard Richards 41k	2	4	4^7	4^{8½}	2^{hd}	1^{¾}	Baeza B	126	b	*.30e	90-14	Buckpasser126^{¾}Buffle114^{¾}Deck Hand114^4	Under hand urging	6
4Jun66- 6Aqu	fst 6f	:22^2 :45^1 1:09^1 3↑	Alw 8500	5	3	2^2	1^{hd}	1^{hd}	1^2	Baeza B	115	b	*.40	97-14	Buckpasser115^{2}Tim'sStingry115^{2}Undrstudy121^{nk}	Mild drive	7
3Mar66- 0Hia	fst 1⅛	:46^2 1:10^4 1:36^3 1:50	Flamingo 136k	4	3	3^4	3^2	2^{½}	1no	Shoemaker W	122	b	-	85-18	Buckpasser122^{no}Abe'sHope122^{2¼}BlueSkyer122^{2½}	Came again	9
	Run between 7th and 8th races. No wagering																	
23Feb66- 8Hia	fst 1⅛	:45^2 1:09 1:34^3 1:47^4	Everglades 30k	6	2	2^3	2^1	2^{hd}	1^{hd}	Shoemaker W	122	b	*.20e	96-12	Buckpasser122^{hd}Stupendous115^{¾}Abe's Hope115^4	Swerved	8
14Feb66- 0Hia	fst 7f	:22^4 :45 1:08^4 1:21^4	Alw 5000	1	5	5^{14}	5^{12}	4^6	2^{4½}	Shoemaker W	124	b	-e	95-13	Impressive122^{4½}Buckpasser124^{1½}Stupendous113^{nk}	Rallied	5
	Exhibition race run between 7th and 8th races. No wagering;Previously trained by W.C. Winfrey																	
16Oct65- 7Aqu	fst 1	:22^3 :45^3 1:10^4 1:36^2	Champagne 223k	1	7	5^{4½}	5^{4½}	1^{½}	1^4	Baeza B	122	b	*.90e	86-20	Buckpasser122^{4}Our Michael122^{½}Advocator122^{1½}	Easily	9
25Sep65- 7Aqu	gd 6½f	:23 :46^2 1:10^4 1:17^1	Futurity 151k	7	6	4^{1¾}	2^1	2^1	2^{½}	Baeza B	122	b	*.70	93-20	PricelessGem119^{½}Buckpassr122^{10}ⒹAdvoctor122^3	No excuse	9
11Sep65- 8AP	fst 7f	:22^3 :45^2 1:10^2 1:23	Arl-Wash Futurity 335k	8	8	6^{6½}	5^{6¼}	1^4	1^{½}	Baeza B	122	b	*.80	92-15	Buckpasser122^{½}Fathers Image122^{2}Flame Tree122^{no}	Driving	10
28Aug65- 6Sar	fst 6½f	:22 :44^4 1:09^3 1:16	Hopeful 110k	7	7	4^{2½}	3^{1½}	3^{nk}	1^{2½}	Baeza B	122	b	*.30e	98-08	Buckpasser122^{2½}Impressive122^{¾}Indulto122^{2½}	Going away	7
7Aug65- 8Mth	fst 6f	:22 :45 1:10^3	Sapling 112k	1	7	6^{3¾}	3^{3½}	3^3	1^{½}	Baeza B	122	b	1.90	89-21	Buckpasser122^{½}Quinta122^{1½}OurMichael122^5	Left at post,up	7
30Jly65- 7Mth	fst 5½f	:22^1 :45^4 1:04	Alw 5000	3	5	4^2	3^3	1^1	1^7	Baeza B	122	b	*.90	97-19	Buckpasser122^{7}Model Fool116^{¾}Gary Dear119^3	Drew far out	6
7Jly65- 7Aqu	fst 5½f	:22^1 :45 :57^2 1:03^4	Tremont 34k	3	6	6^{6½}	4^{2½}	2^{½}	1^{nk}	Baeza B	118	b	*.70	94-13	Buckpasser118^{nk}SpringDouble118^{2½}Hospitalty118^{no}	Driving	6
28Jun65- 7Aqu	fst 5½f	:22^2 :45^2 :58 1:04^3	©National Stallion 32k	3	5	5^9	4^7	3^4	1$^{5•}$	Baeza B	122	b	*1.00	90-15	[DH]Hospitality117[DH]Buckpassr122^{5}KentuckyKn117^{no}	Just up	6
8Jun65- 6Aqu	fst 5½f	:22^3 :46^1 :58^3 1:05	Alw 5500	7	5	5^5	5^{2½}	2^{½}	1^{1½}	Baeza B	122		*1.90	88-21	Buckpassr122^{1½}KentuckyKin122^{2½}BanderaBeau119^4	Driving	9
29May65- 3Aqu	sly 5f	:23 :47^1 1:00	©Md Sp Wt	7	5	4^3	4^2	2^{½}	1^2	Baeza B	122		*1.25	85-20	Buckpasser122^{2}Exhibitionist122^{2½}Clique122^4	Easy score	8
13May65- 4Aqu	fst 5½f	:23^1 :48^2 1:00^3 1:07	©Md Sp Wt	8	10	6^6	5^7	5^5	4^{1¼}	Baeza B	122		5.30	77-26	LonelyGambler122^{½}HndsmeBy122^{no}MaskofPlay117^{¾}	Greenly	10

Past Performances of Great Horses of the 20th Century

Cigar   b. c. 1990, by Palace Music (The Minstrel)–Solar Slew, by Seattle Slew   Lifetime record: 33 19 4 5 $9,999,815

Own.– Allen E. Paulson
Br.– Allen E. Paulson (Md)
Tr.– William I. Mott

26Oct96–10WO fst 1¼	:46¹ 1:10⁴ 1:35² 2:01 3↑ B C Classic-G1		*.65	106-02	L 126	Bailey JD	7 7	85½	5¾	4¹	3ⁿᵏ		AlphabetSoup126ⁿᵒLouisQuatorze12¹ʰᵈCigar126½	5-wide bid 13
50ct96–10Bel fst 1¼	:47³ 1:11² 1:35⁴ 2:00⁴ 3↑ JC Gold Cup-G1		*.20	94-10	L 126	Bailey JD	6 3	34½	3½	3¹	2ⁿᵈ		SkipAway12¹ʰᵈCigar126²LousQutorz12¹¹	Drifted,outfinished 7
14Sep96–8Bel fst 1⅛	:46¹ 1:10² 1:34³ 1:47 3↑ Woodward-G1		*.35	95-10	L 126	Bailey JD	4 4	44½	3¹	1¹	1⁴		Cigar126⁴L`Carriere126½Golden Larch126¾	Ridden out 5
10Aug96–6Dmr fst 1¼	:45⁴ 1:09⁴ 1:33³ 1:59⁴ 3↑ Pacific Classic-G1		*.10	94-07	LB 124	Bailey JD	4 2	2¹	1ʰᵈ	2¼	23½		Dare and Go124³½Cigar124⁹Siphon124⁸	Led,outfinished 6
13Jly96–10AP fst 1⅛	:46⁴ 1:10¹ 1:35³ 1:48¹ 3↑ Citation Challnge 1075k		*.30	103-16	L 130	Bailey JD	10 7	6³	3¹¹	1½	1¾		Cigar130³¾Dramatic Gold118ⁿᵏEltish1182	Ridden out,wide 10
1Jun96–10Suf fst 1⅛	:45⁴ 1:10¹ 1:36¹ 1:49³ 3↑ Mass H 500k			95-08	LB 130	Bailey JD	3 4	3⁴	1²	1⁴	1½		Cigar130²PersonalMerit1110Prolanzr112ⁿᵏ	3 path,easily 6
27Mar96◆ NadAlSheba(Dub)fst*1¼LH	2:03⁴ 4↑ Dubai World Cup Stk4000000		–		124	Bailey JD					1½		Cigar124½Soul of the Matter1248¾L`Carriere1243½	11
												5th after 1f,bid 4f out,led 2f out,dueled 1¼f out,prevailed	
10Feb96–10GP fst 1⅛	:46¹ 1:10⁴ 1:35³ 1:49 3↑ Donn H-G1		*.20	92-12	L 128	Bailey JD	1 3	3²	13	1²	12		Cigar128⁴Wekiva Springs1174Heavenly Prize1153	8
	Six wide top str,easily best													
28Oct95–8Bel my 1¼	:48¹ 1:12¹ 1:35³ 1:59² 3↑ B C Classic-G1		*.70	97-08	L 126	Bailey JD	10 3	3¹	11½	12	1²½		Cgr1262½L`Crrr126¹UnccountdFor126¾	Four wide bid,driving 11
70ct95–10Bel wf 1¼	:48 1:12¹ 1:36 2:01¹ 3↑ JC Gold Cup-G1		*.35	88-14	LB 126	Bailey JD	6 3	3¹½	2½	12	11		Cigar126¹Unaccounted For1269½Star Standard121²	7
	Carried 7 wide,gamely													
16Sep95–9Bel fst 1⅛	:45⁴ 1:09³ 1:33⁴ 1:47 3↑ Woodward-G1		*.10	97-09	L 126	Bailey JD	5 3	3⁴	2½	13½	12¾		Cigar126²¾Star Standard12¹³Golden Larch126¾	Under wraps 6
2Jly95–6Hol fst 1¼	:45³ 1:09² 1:34 1:59² 3↑ Hol Gold Cup H-G1		*.90	103-04	LB 126	Bailey JD	1 4	4²	11	13	13½		Cigar126³Tinners Way118ⁿᵒTossofthecoin118½	8
	4 wide ¾,strong handling													
3Jun95–10Suf fst 1⅛	:47¹ 1:10² 1:35¹ 1:48 3↑ Mass H 750k		*.20	110-05	L 124	Bailey JD	6 4	3³	2½	13½	14		Cigar124⁴Poor but Honest1075½Double Calvados113ⁿᵏ	6
	Rated 3w,mild urging													
13May95–10Pim fst 1⅛	:48 1:11² 1:35¹ 1:53³ 4↑ Pim Special H-G1		*.40	106-02	L 122	Bailey JD	1 1	11½	11½	15	12½		Cigar122¹Devil His Due1212½Concern1214½	Ridden out 6
15Apr95–9OP fst 1⅛	:46² 1:10⁴ 1:35² 1:47⁴ 4↑ Oaklawn H-G1		*1.70	103-13	L 120	Bailey JD	4 4	45	4¹½	1ʰᵈ	12½		Cigar120²Silver Goblin1194Concern122¹	7
	Bumped,hit by opponent's whip,driving													
5Mar95–9GP fst 1¼	:47² 1:11⁴ 1:36⁴ 2:02⁴ 3↑ Gulf Park H-G1		*.50	88-19	L 118	Bailey JD	9 4	45	1ʰᵈ	15	17½		Cigar118⁷Pride of Burkaan1141Mahogany Hall1132	11
	Six wide bkstr,six wide top str,ridden out													
11Feb95–9GP fst 1⅛	:46² 1:10³ 1:36³ 1:49³ 3↑ Donn H-G1		4.00	89-13	L 115	Bailey JD	4 1	12	1ʰᵈ	1½	15½		Cigar115⁵Primitive Hall1121½Bonus Money1123½	9
22Jan95–10GP fst 1⅛	:46¹ :464 1:12¹ 1:431 4↑ Alw 33000		*.50	92-13	L 122	Bailey JD	5 1	1ʰᵈ	11	11½	12		Cigar122²Upping the Ante1198¾Chasin Gold122¹	8
	Crowded,bumped start,driving													
26Nov94–8Aqu fst 1	:23³ :454 1:11¹ 1:36 3↑ NYRA Mile-G1		8.90	88-28	111	Bailey JD	6 4	42	11½	17	17		Cigar1117DevilHisDue1242½PunchLine1121	Wide,ridden out 12
28Oct94–6Aqu fst 1	:22³ :443 1:09¹ 1:353 3↑ Alw 34000		3.50	90-23	117	Smith ME	6 2	12	13	16	18		Cigar1178Golden Plover1193½Gulliviegold1092	Handily 6
70ct94–8Bel fm 1⅛ Ⓣ	:23² :463 1:104 1:412 3↑ Alw 36000		3.40	80-15	117	Krone JA	2 4	35	25	34½	38½		UnaccountdFor1142½SameOldWish1196Cgr1172	Flattened out 6
16Sep94–7Bel fm 1⅛ Ⓣ	:23 :452 1:08³ 1:33 3↑ Alw 34000		*1.90	89-13	117	Bailey JD	10 8	87¼	45	66¾	78½		Jido1082½Brmuda Cedr1142Limtd Wr1132	Wide,flattened out 11
8Aug94–1Sar fm 1⅛ Ⓣ	:47² 1:12 1:36³ 1:483 3↑ Alw 34000		3.20	89-11	117	Smith ME	1 4	43½	42	3¹	33		MyMogul1191½NextEndvr1191½Cgr117ⁿᵏ	Lacked room stretch 8
8Jly94–7Bel fm 1⅛ Ⓣ	:24³ :482 1:12³ 1:43 3↑ Alw 34000		*1.70	72-16	117	Smith ME	5 2	1ʰᵈ	2ʰᵈ	43	49		DancingHuntr117½Compdr1173¹ʳmVryIrsh1115½	Dueled,tired 5
	Previously trained by Alex Hassinger Jr													
20Nov93–6Hol fm 1⅛ Ⓣ	:46¹ 1:10² 1:34¹ 1:464 Hol Derby-G1		24.80	76-08	LB 122	Valnzuela PA	9 4	55	4¹½	64½	1114½		ExplsiveRed1221¾JeuneHomm122ⁿᵏErlofBrkng122½	Wide trip 14
5Nov93–8SA fm 1⅛ Ⓣ	:48 1:12¹ 1:36 1:48 Volante H-G3		7.70	77-21	LB 118	Valnzuela PA	4 3	43	32½	2¹½	22		EasternMemories1132Cigar118ⁿᵏSnkEys120½	Bid,outfinished 9
25Sep93–5BM fm 1⅛ Ⓣ	:23 :453 1:10 1:413 Ascot H-G3		4.10	102-03	LB 117	Valnzuela PA	1 5	44	4¹½	12	3½		Siebe115ⁿᵏNonproductiveasset114ʰᵈCigar1172	Held well 11
3Sep93–8Dmr fm 1 Ⓣ	:224 :47 1:11 1:35 3↑ Alw 40000		3.30	95-04	LB 115	McCarron CJ	4 2	21	21	2ʰᵈ	2½		Kingdom of Spain119½Cigar115½Saturnino1173	Sharp effort 6
18Aug93–5Dmr fm 1 Ⓣ	:23¹ :472 1:11¹ 1:414 3↑ Alw 36000		*1.90	97-04	LB 115	McCarron CJ	5 4	53½	43½	3ⁿᵏ	12½		Cigar115²¾OurMotionGrantd122ʰᵈTheBerklyMn1142½	Driving 10

Past Performances of Great Horses of the 20th Century

12Jun93-10Hol	gd 1 1/16 (T)	:231 :48 1:113 1:412	Alw 39000	10 7 73 42 3½ 3¾	Valnzuela PA	LB 117	2.90	87-11	Nonprddctvast115½ Tossofthcn1191¼Cigar1172¾	4 wide stretch 10
23May93- 9Hol	fm 1 1/16 (T)	:232 :471 1:103 1:411	Alw 39000	11 3 31 2½ 1½ 4¾	Valnzuela PA	L 117	3.80	88-10	Pleasedontexplain117½Stately Warrior115½Fleet Wizard115¾	12
	Weakened a bit									
9May93- 3Hol	fst 6f	:22 :443 :564 1:092	Md Sp Wt	3 6 21 1½ 13 12¼	Valenzuela PA	117	5.20	93-11	Cigr1172¼GoldnSlwpy1165½FmousFn115hd	Off slowly,driving 6
21Feb93- 6SA	gd 6f	:214 :452 :58 1:104	Md Sp Wt	9 7 65½ 65¼ 68 713	Valenzuela PA	118	5.10	70-18	Demigod118nkCardiac1182[D]SirHutch1182½	Wide backstretch 9

Citation

b. c. 1945, by Bull Lea (Bull Dog)–Hydroplane II, by Hyperion — Lifetime record: 45 32 10 2 $1,085,760

Own.– Calumet Farm
Br.– Calumet Farm (Ky)
Tr.– H.A. Jones

14Jly51- 7Hol	fst 1¼	:464 1:103 2:01	3↑ Hol Gold Cup 137k	10 6 33 12 13 14	Brooks S	120 w	*.35e	94-10	Citation1204Bewitch108noBe Fleet1221	Ridden out 10
4Jly51- 7Hol	fst 1⅛	:464 1:11 1:36 1:482	3↑ American H 56k	5 5 52½ 4nk 2hd 1½	Brooks S	123 w	*.75e	98-07	Citation123½Bewitch1062¾Sturdy One112¾	Driving 8
14Jun51- 7Hol	fst 1	:232 :463 1:104 1:354	4↑ Handicap 15000	3 3 31 1hd 1½ 1½	Brooks S	120 w	*.95	98-10	Citation120½Be Fleet123¾Sturdy One110½	Driving 5
30May51- 7Hol	fst 1 1/16	:222 :45 1:101 1:42	3↑ Argonaut H 30k	6 5 59½ 44 24 23	Smith FA	121 w	*.45e	95-08	Be Fleet1183Citation121nkSturdy One111½	Closed well 10
11May51- 7Hol	fst 6f	:221 :452 :573 1:10	3↑ Premiere H 18k	3 8 86¼ 96¼ 84 52¾	Brooks S	120 w	*1.15	93-12	SpecilTouch122nkMnyunk1141¼BullrghJr.1101	Closed ground 10
26Apr51- 8BM	fst 6f	:223 :453 1:094	3↑ Alw 3000	2 5 55 43½ 33 32¼	Brooks S	120 w	*.60	97-10	Pancho Supreme1181¼A Lark1181Citation1203½	No excuse 5
18Apr51- 8BM	fst 6f	:223 :453 1:094	4↑ Alw 3250	4 3 46 43½ 32 31	Brooks S	120 w	*.55	98-13	A Lark109noPancho Supreme1201Citation1202¼	Good effort 6
24Jun50- 8GG	fst 1¼	:451 1:091 1:34 1:581	3↑ Golden Gate H 57k	3 2 313 37 34 23	Brooks S	126 w	1.20	105-12	Noor1273Citation1261On Trust1032½	No excuse 5
17Jun50- 8GG	fst 1⅛	:463 1:093 1:344 1:464	3↑ Forty-Niners H 10k	3 2 21½ 1hd 1hd 2nk	Brooks S	128 w	*.50	104-08	Noor123nkCitation1283Roman In1112	Outgamed 5
3Jun50- 8GG	fst 1	:221 :441 1:073 1:333	3↑ GG Mile H 23k	6 2 22 2½ 1hd 1¾	Brooks S	128 w	*.60	104-08	Citation128¾Bolero1235On Trust116nk	Driving 6
17May50- 7GG	fst 6f	:22 :442 1:082	4↑ Alw 4000	4 5 55 52¾ 21½ 2¾	Glisson G	120 w	*.25	99-10	Roman In120¾Citation1201¼Blue Border1173	Forced wide 6
4Mar50- 7SA	fst 1¾	:474 2:023 2:271 2:524	3↑ S Juan Capistrano H 64k	8 4 2hd 1hd 1hd 2no	Brooks S	130 w	*.60	127-06	Noor117noCitation13012½Mocopo107hd	Just failed 8
25Feb50- 7SA	fst 1¼	:462 1:11 1:351 2:00	3↑ S Anita H 135k	5 7 64 32½ 32 21¼	Arcaro E	132 w	*.35e	105-11	Noor1101¼Citation1321Two Lea113nk	Close quarters 11
11Feb50- 7SA	gd 1⅛	:471 1:113 1:372 1:501	3↑ San Antonio H 60k	7 4 35 22 2½ 21	Arcaro E	130 w	*.45e	91-17	Ponder1281Citation130½Noor114¾	Forced wide 9
26Jan50- 7SA	fst 6f	:223 :46 1:104	4↑ Handicap 6000	4 1 42¼ 31½ 2hd 2nk	Brooks S	130 w	*.25	93-15	Miche114nkCitation1303½Huon Kid107½	Close quarters 6
11Jan50- 4SA	sly 6f	:223 :461 1:112	4↑ Alw 5000	3 4 33 31½ 3nk 11½	Brooks S	124 w	*.15	90-19	Citation1241½Bold Gallant112nkRoman In1163½	Drew away 4
11Dec48- 7Tan	gd 1¼	:48 1:13 1:373 2:024	3↑ Tanforan H 54k	2 2 1½ 11½ 13½ 15	Arcaro E	123 w	*.05	103-12	Citation1235Stepfather1102½See-tee-see1172	Easily best 7
3Dec48- 7Tan	my 6f	:231 :463 1:12	Alw 5000	4 5 21½ 2hd 11½ 11½	Arcaro E	126 w	*.10	95-23	Citation1261½Bold Gallant1122Barsard1095	In hand 5
29Oct48- 6Pim	fst 1 3/16	:504 1:152 1:421 1:594	3↑ Pim Spl 10k	1 1 1 1 1 1	Arcaro E	120 w		83-11	Citation120	Breezing 1
	Walkover									
16Oct48- 7Bel	fst 1⅝	:48 1:381 2:034 2:424	3↑ Gold Cup 111k	8 3 33 12 14 12	Arcaro E	119 w	*.15	90-19	Citation1192Phalanx1265Carolyn A.1232½	In hand 9
	Geldings not eligible									
2Oct48- 6Bel	fst 2	:48 2:294 2:562 3:213	3↑ J C Gold Cup 108k	7 1 15 18 18 17	Arcaro E	117 w	*.30	96-09	Citation1177Phalanx12412Beauchef124hd	Easily 7
	Geldings not eligible									
29Sep48- 6Bel	fst 1	:224 :452 1:101 1:36	3↑ Sysonby Mile 29k	6 4 46 12 12 13	Arcaro E	119 w	*.10e	94-14	Citation1193First Flight123nkCoaltown1194	Eased up 6
28Aug48- 7Was	fst 1¼	:462 1:10 1:353 2:013	American Derby 88k	1 1 21½ 11½ 1hd 11	Arcaro E	126 w	*.10e	95-10	Citation1261Free America1181Volcanic1182	Driving 5
21Aug48- 4Was	fst 6f	:223 :45 1:104	Alw 4000	4 3 22 21 11 12½	Pierson NL	120 w	*.20	93-09	Citation1202½King Rhymer1141¼Speculation1176½	Easily 4
5Jly48- 7AP	fst 1⅛	:464 1:104 1:354 1:491	3↑ Stars & Stripes H 56k	6 5 53½ 3½ 11½ 12	Arcaro E	119 w	*.30e	100-07	Citation1192Eternal Reward116nkPellicle106hd	Driving 9
12Jun48- 6Bel	fst 1½	:482 1:123 2:023 2:281	Belmont 117k	1 1 1hd 14 15 18	Arcaro E	126 w	*.20	97-10	Citation1268Better Self126½Escadru1265	Much the best 8
	Geldings not eligible									
29May48- 6GS	fst 1¼	:47 1:113 1:36 2:03	Jersey 61k	4 4 1hd 13 18 111	Arcaro E	126 w	*.10	108-11	Citation12611Macbeth114¾[D]Bovard114¾	Eased up 5
15May48- 6Pim	hy 1 3/16	:502 1:16 1:43 2:022	Preakness 134k	4 1 11½ 12 12½ 15½	Arcaro E	126 w	*.10	70-43	Citation1265½Vulcan's Forge1263½Bovard126nk	Galloping 4

Past Performances of Great Horses of the 20th Century

	Previously trained by B.A. Jones																
1May48- 7CD	sly 1$\frac{1}{4}$	:46^3 1:11^2 1:38 2:05^2	Ky Derby 111k	1	2	2^6	2$\frac{1}{2}$	1^2	1$^{3\frac{1}{2}}$	Arcaro E	126	w	*.40e	80-22	Citation126$^{3\frac{1}{2}}$Coaltown126^{3}My Request126$^{1\frac{1}{2}}$	Drew away	6
27Apr48- 5CD	fst 1	:23 :46 1:10^3 1:37^2	Derby Trial 12k	2	2	2$\frac{1}{2}$	1^2	1$^{1\frac{1}{2}}$	1$^{1\frac{1}{4}}$	Arcaro E	118	w	*.10	92-23	Citation118$^{1\frac{1}{4}}$Escadru118$^{\frac{1}{2}}$Eagle Look110^{20}	Easily	4
	Previously trained by H.A. Jones																
17Apr48- 6HdG	gd 1$\frac{1}{16}$	:24 :48^3 1:13^2 1:45^4	Chesapeake 29k	4	3	3^1	1^1	1^3	1$^{4\frac{1}{2}}$	Arcaro E	122	w	*.20	84-16	Citation122$^{4\frac{1}{2}}$Bovard119^{5}Dr. Almac119^6	Easily	4
12Apr48- 6HdG	my 6f	:23^3 :47 1:12^2	Chesapeake Trial 12k	6	1	4$^{1\frac{3}{4}}$	4$^{1\frac{1}{2}}$	2^2	2^1	Arcaro E	126	w	*.30	88-27	Saggy122^{1}Citation126^{4}Dr. Almac122$^{1\frac{1}{2}}$	Carried wide	6
28Feb48- 6Hia	fst 1$\frac{1}{8}$	:46^2 1:10^3 1:35^4 1:48^4	Flamingo 62k	4	4	1^{hd}	1^{hd}	1^3	1^6	Snider A	126	w	*.20	97-09	Citation126^{6}Big Dial118^{4}Saggy122^1	Easily	7
18Feb48- 6Hia	fst 1$\frac{1}{8}$	:45^4 1:10 1:35^2 1:49	Everglades H 10k	1	2	2^3	1$\frac{1}{2}$	1^1	1^1	Snider A	126	w	*.15	96-11	Citation126^{1}Hypnos109^{4}Silverling112	Easily	3
11Feb48- 6Hia	fst 7f	:23^2 :46 1:10^1 1:23 3↑	Seminole H 12k	8	2	2^{hd}	2^{hd}	1^{hd}	1^1	Snider A	112	w	*.40e	97-16	Citation112^{1}Delegate123^{nk}Armed128^2	Drew out	9
2Feb48- 6Hia	fst 6f	:22^3 :45^4 1:10^2 3↑	Alw 5000	2	7	2^{hd}	2^{hd}	1^{hd}	1^1	Snider A	113	w	*.20e	96-10	Citation113^{1}Kitchen Police110$^{1\frac{3}{4}}$Say Blue107$^{1\frac{1}{2}}$	Handily	7
8Nov47- 5Pim	my 1$\frac{1}{16}$	:23^4 :48^3 1:14 1:48^4	Pim Futurity 48k	4	2	3$^{1\frac{1}{2}}$	2^{hd}	1$\frac{1}{2}$	1$^{1\frac{1}{2}}$	Dodson D	119	w	*.40	74-41	Citation119$^{1\frac{1}{2}}$Better Self119^{8}Ace Admiral122^2	Ridden out	5
4Oct47- 4Bel	fst 6$\frac{1}{2}$f-W	:22^1 :44^4 1:09^2 1:15^4	Futurity 106k	14	4		3$^{1\frac{1}{2}}$	1^3	1^3	Snider A	122	w	*.85e	93-10	Citation122^{3}Whirling Fox114^{nk}Bewitch123^1	Easily	14
	Geldings not eligible																
30Sep47- 4Bel	fst 6f-WC	:23^3 :45^3 1:11	Futurity Trial 10k	2	9		7^1	6$^{1\frac{1}{4}}$	1^1	Snider A	116	w	2.10	86-16	Citation116^{1}Gasparilla116^{nk}Up Beat116^{hd}	Drew away	14
16Aug47- 6Was	fst 6f	:22^3 :45 1:10^2	Was Futurity 78k	5	3	4^4	4^7	3^6	2^1	Brooks S	118	w	*.20e	97-07	Bewitch119^{1}Citation118^{hd}Free America118^2	Good effort	10
30Jly47- 7Was	fst 6f	:22^4 :45^3 1:10^3	Elementary 24k	10	5	2$^{1\frac{1}{2}}$	1$\frac{1}{2}$	1^1	1^2	Dodson D	122	w	*1.40	97-07	Citation122^{2}Salmagundi110^{no}Billings113^{nk}	Going away	10
24Jly47- 5AP	fst 5f	:22^3 :45^3 :58	Alw 4000	2	4	4^2	4$^{3\frac{1}{2}}$	3^2	1$\frac{1}{2}$	Dodson D	117	w	2.20	102-12	Citation117$^{\frac{1}{2}}$Kandy Comfort114$^{1\frac{1}{2}}$Queen Hairan114^2	Driving	8
21May47- 5HdG	gd 5f	:23 :46^4 :59^1	Alw 3500	1	4	2^2	2^3	2^2	1$^{1\frac{3}{4}}$	Snider A	119	w	*.40	99-18	Citation119$^{1\frac{3}{4}}$Little Tony113^{8}Grand Entry116^3	Going away	6
3May47- 4Pim	fst 5f	:23^1 :48^1 1:01^1	Alw 3500	1	1	1^1	1^{hd}	1$\frac{1}{2}$	1$^{3\frac{1}{2}}$	Snider A	119	w	*1.00	95-19	Citation119$^{3\frac{1}{2}}$Newsweekly119^{1}Still Champ119^{nk}	Going away	6
22Apr47- 3HdG	sl 4$\frac{1}{2}$f	:23 :48^2 :54^2	©Md Sp Wt	2	2		3^5	3^3	1$\frac{1}{2}$	Snider A	120	w	*1.60	93-07	Citation120$^{\frac{1}{2}}$Sunday Beau120^{nk}Brass Band120^{no}	Driving	11

Past Performances of Great Horses of the 20th Century

Colin

b. c. 1905, by Commando (Domino)–Pastorella, by Springfield **Lifetime record: 15 15 0 0 $180,912**

Own.– J.R. Keene
Br.– James R. Keene (Ky)
Tr.– J. Rowe

20Jun08- 4She	fst 1¼	:47 1:11^{3} 1:38 2:04	Tidal 20k	3	1	1^{2}	$1^{1½}$	1^{3}	1^{2}	Notter	126 w	*.20	103-06	Colin126^{2}Dorante126^{4}Stamin121^{8}	Bore out,tiring slightly	4
30May08- 3Bel	sly 1⅜		Belmont 25k	2	-			$1^{1½}$	1^{hd}	Notter	126 w	*.50	- -	Colin126^{hd}Fair Play126^{15}King James126^{10}	Eased up	4
	Driving rainstorm,no time taken															
23May08- 4Bel	hy 1	:24 :48 1:14 1:41	Withers 14k	2	1	1^{3}	1^{3}	1^{4}	1^{2}	Notter	126 w	*.40	82-19	Colin126^{2}Fair Play126^{¾}King James126^{8}	Eased up	6
16Oct07- 3Bel	fst 7f-Str	1:23	Champagne 7.2k	2	1	1^{3}	1^{4}	1^{5}	1^{6}	Miller W	122 w	*.14	103-06	Colin122^{6}Stamina119	Drawing away	2
7Oct07- 2Bel	fst 6f-Str	1:12	©Matron 10k	3	1	2^{4}	1^{5}	1^{4}	1^{3}	Miller W	129 w	*.14	90-11	Colin129^{3}Fair Play122^{4}Royal Tourist119^{½}	Easing up	4
30Sep07- 4Bri	my 6f	:24^{2} :47^{4} 1:12^{3}	©Produce (2nd half) 12k	1	1	$1^{1½}$	1^{4}	1^{4}	1^{5}	Miller W	125 w	*.25	96-13	Colin125^{5}Fair Play119^{hd}Royal Tourist119^{20}	Eased up	4
7Sep07- 3She	fst 7f-FC	1:24^{4}	Flatbush 10k	6	1	$1^{1½}$	$1^{1½}$	1^{3}	1^{3}	Miller W	120 w	*.35e	100-00	Colin120^{3}Celt105^{5}Bar None105^{1½}	Hard held	7
31Aug07- 4She	fst 6f-FC	1:11^{1}	Futurity 28k	5	1	2^{1}	2^{2}	$1^{½}$	$1^{1½}$	Miller W	125 w	*.33	97-03	Coln125^{1½}BrNon117^{1}Chpultpc117^{1½}	Blocked,as rider pleased	8
14Aug07- 3Sar	fst 6f	:24^{1} :48^{2} 1:13	Grand Union Hotel 10k	3	4	2^{hd}	2^{hd}	1^{hd}	1^{2}	Miller W	127 w	*.13e	95-05	Colin127^{2}Jim Gaffney112^{3}Ben Fleet117^{1}	Hard held	6
10Aug07- 3Sar	fst 6f	:23^{3} :47 :58^{2} 1:12	Sar Spl 9.5k	2	2	1^{hd}	1^{hd}	1^{1}	1^{1}	Miller W	122 w	*.40	100-04	Colin122^{1}Uncle122	Decisively	2
27Jly07- 4Bri	fst 6f	:23^{2} :47^{1} 1:12^{1}	Brighton Junior 15k	2	2	$1^{½}$	$1^{1½}$	$1^{1½}$	$1^{1½}$	Miller W	127 w	*.65	99-06	Coln127^{1½}Chpultpc125^{6}BrNon112^{½}	Repelled stretch challenge	8
29Jun07- 3She	sl 6f-FC	1:12^{2}	Great Trial 25k	7	2	2^{1}	1^{1}	1^{2}	1^{2}	Miller W	129 w	*2.60e	91-09	Colin129^{2}Meelick122^{1½}Monopolist122^{1½}	Mild restraint	14
5Jun07- 3Bel	my 5½f-Str	1:06^{3}	Eclipse 9.2k	6	2	1^{nk}	1^{hd}	1^{hd}	1^{hd}	Mountain	125 w	*.60	94-07	Colin125^{hd}Beaucoup117^{10}WvCrst117^{5}	Under pressure,gamely	6
1Jun07- 3Bel	fst 5f-Str	:58	National Stallion 10k	3	1	$1^{1½}$	$1^{1½}$	1^{2}	1^{3}	Miller W	122 w	*.75	102-00	Colin122^{3}Bar None117^{4}Ben Fleet122^{hd}	Never threatened	6
29May07- 2Bel	gd 5f-Str	1:01	Md Sp Wt	10	1	1^{2}	1^{3}	1^{2}	1^{2}	Miller W	110 w	*1.20	87-17	Colin110^{2}Bar None110^{8}Harcourt110^{1½}	Easily	23

Count Fleet

br. c. 1940, by Reigh Count (Sunreigh)–Quickly, by Haste **Lifetime record: 21 16 4 1 $250,300**

Own.– Mrs J. Hertz
Br.– Mrs John D. Hertz (Ky)
Tr.– G.D. Cameron

5Jun43- 6Bel	fst 1½	:48 1:12^{3} 2:03^{3} 2:28^{1}	Belmont 42k	2	1	1^{8}	1^{20}	1^{20}	1^{25}	Longden J	126wb	*.05	97-12	CountFleet126^{25}FairyManhurst126^{¾}Deseronto126	Galloping	3
	Geldings not eligible															
22May43- 6Bel	my 1	:23 :46^{2} 1:10^{3} 1:36	Withers 17k	2	1	$1^{1½}$	1^{3}	1^{2}	1^{5}	Longden J	126wb	*.05	94-21	Count Fleet126^{5}Slide Rule126^{12}Tip-Toe126	Wide,easily	3
	Geldings not eligible															
8May43- 6Pim	gd 1 3/16	:47^{2} 1:11^{4} 1:38^{1} 1:57^{2}	Preakness 60k	2	1	1^{4}	1^{4}	1^{5}	1^{8}	Longden J	126wb	*.15	95-15	Count Fleet126^{8}Blue Swords126^{5}Vincentive126^{20}	Easily	4
1May43- 7CD	fst 1¼	:46^{3} 1:12^{3} 1:37^{3} 2:04	Ky Derby 72k	5	1	1^{hd}	1^{2}	1^{2}	1^{3}	Longden J	126wb	*.40	87-12	Count Fleet126^{3}Blue Swords126^{6}Slide Rule126^{6}	Handily	10
17Apr43- 5Jam	fst 1 1/16	:23^{2} :46^{4} 1:11^{2} 1:43	Wood Mem 28k	4	1	1^{4}	1^{4}	1^{4}	$1^{3½}$	Longden J	126wb	*.25	98-06	Count Fleet126^{3½}Blue Swords126^{7}Twoses121^{2}	Much the best	8
13Apr43- 5Jam	sly 170	:23^{4} :47^{2} 1:12^{4} 1:42^{4}	Alw 3000	8	4	$3^{1½}$	2^{2}	2^{hd}	$1^{3½}$	Longden J	122wb	*.15	90-19	CountFlt122^{3½}Bossut113^{5}Towsr113^{hd}	Forced wide first turn	8
10Nov42- 6Pim	gd 1 1/16	:23^{1} :47^{3} 1:12 1:44^{4}	Walden 12k	3	1	1^{8}	1^{15}	1^{25}	1^{30}	Longden J	122 w	*.10	94-14	Count Fleet122^{30}Uncle Billies113^{15}Rough Doc113^{1}	Easily	4
31Oct42- 6Pim	fst 1 1/16	:23^{1} :46^{2} 1:11 1:43^{3}	Pim Futurity 34k	3	2	2^{hd}	$1^{½}$	1^{3}	1^{5}	Longden J	119wb	1.25	100-06	Count Fleet119^{5}Occupation122^{4}Vincentive122		3
	Geldings not eligible															
20Oct42- 5Jam	fst 170	:23^{4} :47^{3} 1:13 1:44	Alw 5000	5	5	1^{hd}	1^{4}	1^{5}	1^{6}	Longden J	122wb	*.25	84-16	Count Fleet122^{6}Towser116^{2½}Jack S.L.113^{3}	Easily	8
10Oct42- 5Bel	fst 1	:23^{1} :46 1:10 1:34^{4}	Champagne 12k	8	1	1^{2}	1^{3}	1^{3}	1^{6}	Longden J	116wb	*1.05	101-07	Count Fleet116^{6}Blue Swords119^{7}Attendant110^{1}	Easily	8
3Oct42- 4Bel	fst 6½f-W	:22^{2} :44^{3} 1:08^{3} 1:15^{1}	Futurity 69k	7	9	2^{2}	3^{4}	3^{4}	3^{5}	Longden J	119wb	*1.55	91-04	Occupation126^{5}Askmenow116^{hd}Count Fleet119^{1½}	Gamely	10
	Geldings not eligible															

Past Performances of Great Horses of the 20th Century

24Sep42- 6Bel	fst 6f-WC	:23 :461 1:103	Alw 2000	9	12	51¾	53	21	12½	Longden J	122wb	*1.40	94-06	CountFleet1222½BullsEye111nkJackS.L.111hd	Swerved start 13
15Sep42- 5Aqu	fst 6f	:224 :462 1:12	Alw 2500	2	1	21½	33	31	1nk	Longden J	118wb	*.70	92-12	CntFlt118nkVrySnooty1124NoondySun1121½	Bumped,driving 10
15Aug42- 6Was	fst 6f	:222 :454 1:12	Wash Park Futurity 68k	11	9	75	54¼	22	2nk	Longden J	117wb	4.80	91-12	Occupation122nkCntFleet1175BluSwords117hd	Wide,bumped 11
11Aug42- 6Was	gd 6f	:23 :463 1:13	Alw 1800	6	5	3½	2½	1½	1nk	Longden J	119wb	*.50	86-20	CountFleet119nkBlueSwords1084Hygrohour1223	Forced wide 9
22Jly42- 5Emp	fst 5¾f	:232 :463 1:074	Wakefield 6.8k	4	1	31¼	11	12	14	Longden J	116wb	*.65	98-10	CountFleet1164Rurales1132GoldShower1229	Speed to spare 4
15Jly42- 5Emp	fst 5¾f	:23 :454 1:08	©East View 7.1k	6	5	52	21½	22	21	Longden J	116wb	*.50	96-09	Gold Shower1161Count Fleet1167Rurales1122	Gamely 6
4Jly42- 4Emp	fst 5½f	:23 :462 :592 1:054	Alw 2000	5	5	53¾	42½	11	15	Longden J	111wb	*1.15	97-07	Count Fleet1115Samhar1143Bullpen114hd	Drew away easily 6
19Jun42- 3Aqu	fst 5½f	:23 :471 1:06	©Md Sp Wt	8	6	3¾	2½	3½	14	Longden J	116wb	*.75	97-08	CountFleet1164SewrdBound1161Crst116nk	Bore out str turn 10
15Jun42- 5Aqu	fst 5½f	:23 :473 1:061	Md Sp Wt	9	8	63	44½	22	21½	Longden J	116wb	*1.35	94-12	Supermont1161½Count Fleet1163Quiz116nk	Trouble early 14
1Jun42- 5Bel	fst 5f-WC	:572	©Md Sp Wt	13	5	3½	3½	32½	21½	Longden J	116wb	4.10	91-07	DoveShoot1161½CountFlet116noSuprmont116nk	Swerved start 16

Damascus

b. c. 1964, by Sword Dancer (Sunglow)–Kerala, by My Babu

Lifetime record: 32 21 7 3 $1,176,781

Own.– Mrs Edith W. Bancroft
Br.– Mrs Thomas Bancroft (Ky)
Tr.– F.Y. Whiteley Jr

26Oct68- 7Bel	gd 2	:502 2:313 3:224 3↑	J C Gold Cup 109k	1	3	48	612	624	637	Adams L	124	*1.30	48-16	QuickenTree1241¼FunnyFllow1193½Chmpon1193	Bowed tendon 6
28Sep68- 7Bel	fst 1¼	:472 1:113 1:37 2:03 3↑	Woodward 106k	3	2	1hd	1hd	1hd	2no	Baeza B	126	*.10	85-16	Mr. Right126noDamascus1267Grace Born12616	Just failed 4
14Sep68- 9Det	fst 1⅛	:471 1:111 1:361 1:49 3↑	Mich 1⅛ H 123k	1	9	1014	79½	66¾	22¾	Baeza B	133	*.30e	93-19	Nodouble1112¾Dmscs133hdMstyRun1092¼	Very wide stretch 12
2Sep68- 7Aqu	fst 1⅛	:47 1:11 1:354 1:482 3↑	Aqueduct 108k	4	3	35	33	2½	11½	Baeza B	134	*.40	94-13	Damascus1341½More Scents1148Fort Drum1143	Going away 6
10Aug68- 8Del	fst 1$\frac{1}{16}$	:24 :484 1:123 1:433 3↑	W Du Pont H 53k	4	5	31	2hd	1hd	12	Baeza B	134	*.20	91-20	Damascus1342BigRockCandy113¾CharlesElliott11010	Driving 5
20Jly68- 7Aqu	fst 1¼	:454 1:092 1:343 1:591 3↑	Brooklyn H 109k	2	5	511	2½	1½	12½	Ycaza M	130	1.40e	102-13	Damascus1302½Dr. Fager1353Mr. Right114hd	Won going away 7
13Jly68- 8Mth	fst 1¼	:48 1:121 1:371 2:03 3↑	AL Haskell H 111k	6	6	68	33	21	31½	Ycaza M	131	*.60	85-16	BoldHour1161¼Mr.Rght114nkDmscus1315	Stumbled after start 8
4Jly68- 7Aqu	fst 1¼	:482 1:11 1:343 1:593 3↑	Suburban H 107k	1	2	2½	2hd	22	35	Ycaza M	133	1.40	95-11	Dr. Fager1322Bold Hour1163Damascus1333½	Failed to rally 5
17Jun68- 5Del	fst 1 70	:234 :473 1:114 1:402 4↑	Alw 10000	3	3	24	2hd	11	13¾	Ycaza M	124	*.10	98-16	Damascus1243¾LighttheFuse1196ClassicWork120nk	Handily 5
10Feb68- 8SA	sl 1¼	:482 1:131 1:382 2:04	C H Strub 118k	1	5	57	1½	1hd	2hd	Turcotte R	126	*.20	78-22	Most Host114hdDamscs12610Ruken117½	Gave way gradually 6
20Jan68- 6SA	fst 1⅛	:49 1:13 1:371 1:484	San Fernando 56k	4	2	2½	1hd	11	12	Shoemaker W	126	*.10	88-12	Damascs1262Most Host113hdRuken1204½	Won drawing clear 6
6Jan68- 8SA	fst 7f	:223 :45 1:09 1:211	Malibu 45k	4	1	32½	3½	1½	12½	Shoemaker W	126	*.40	97-15	Damascus1262½Rising Market120nkRuken1231	Handily 8
11Nov67- 7Lrl	fm 1½Ⓣ	:491 1:14 2:03 2:27 3↑	D C Int'l 150k	2	4	43½	3½	2hd	2no	Shoemaker W	120	*.60	84-13	FortMarcy120noDmascus1202½TobinBronze1272½	Just failed 9
28Oct67- 7Aqu	fst 2	:494 2:302 2:554 3:201 3↑	J C Gold Cup 106k	1	2	22	2hd	14	14½	Shoemaker W	119	*.30	95-12	Dmascus1194½HandsomBoy1247½Successr1196½	Handy score 4
30Sep67- 7Aqu	fst 1¼	:451 1:091 1:353 2:003 3↑	Woodward 107k	5	5	512	1½	15	110	Shoemaker W	120	1.80e	95-15	Damascus12010Buckpasser126½Dr. Fager12013	Easy score 6
4Sep67- 7Aqu	fst 1⅛	:482 1:121 1:361 1:481 3↑	Aqueduct 106k	3	3	34	32	1hd	12	Shoemaker W	125	*.30	95-14	Damascus1252Ring Twice119½Straight Deal1166	Handily 5
19Aug67- 6Sar	sly 1¼	:454 1:11 1:364 2:013	Travers 80k	4	3	316	16	110	122	Shoemaker W	126	*.20	100-10	Damascus12622Reason to Hail1207Tumiga1175	Won eased up 4
5Aug67- 8AP	fst 1⅛	:46 1:101 1:343 1:464	American Derby 120k	2	6	612	66¼	14	17	Shoemaker W	126	*.80	101-16	Damascus1267InReality1203FavorableTurn1121½	Ridden out 7
15Jly67- 7Aqu	sly 1¼	:473 1:12 1:374 2:03	Dwyer H 83k	6	9	912	21	1hd	1¾	Shoemaker W	128	*.50	83-18	Damascus128¾FavorableTurn1122½BlastingChrg116hd	Driving 9
8Jly67- 8Del	fst 1$\frac{1}{16}$	:234 :471 1:104 1:421 3↑	W Du Pont Jr H 54k	4	5	58	43	21	2no	Shoemaker W	121	*.20	98-12	Exceedingly113noDamascus1214Flag Raiser1145	Hung 5
17Jun67- 8Del	fst 1⅛	:47 1:113 1:37 1:491	Leonard Richards 41k	4	4	32½	1½	1hd	13¼	Turcotte R	126	*.10	91-13	Damascus1263¼Misty Cloud1191½Favorable Turn1192½	Easily 6
3Jun67- 8Aqu	fst 1½	:47 1:122 2:023 2:284	Belmont 148k	1	6	59½	31	2hd	12½	Shoemaker W	126	*.80	87-15	Dmascus1262½CoolReception126½GentlmanJams1261	In hand 9
20May67- 8Pim	fst 1$\frac{3}{16}$	:462 1:104 1:364 1:551	Preakness 194k	2	9	811	86	13½	12¼	Shoemaker W	126	*1.80e	97-11	Damascus1262¼In Reality1264Proud Clarion126¾	Ridden out 10
6May67- 7CD	fst 1¼	:463 1:104 1:36 2:003	Ky Derby 162k	2	6	44	41½	32	34	Shoemaker W	126	*1.70	93-07	ProudClarion1261BarbsDelight1263Damascus1261¼	Bid,hung 14
22Apr67- 7Aqu	fst 1⅛	:462 1:104 1:363 1:493	Wood Memorial 112k	4	3	45	42	11	16	Shoemaker W	126	*.70	88-16	Damascus1266Gala Performance1263Dawn Glory1261½	Easily 9
15Apr67- 7Aqu	fst 1	:233 :461 1:102 1:351	Gotham 57k	9	2	23	2hd	1hd	2½	Shoemaker W	122	*1.30	91-14	Dr. Fager122½Damascus1225Reason to Hail1147	Game try 9

Past Performances of Great Horses of the 20th Century

25Mar67-7Aqu	my	7f	$:22^4\ :46^4\ 1{:}12^4\ 1{:}25^4$	Bay Shore 28k	1	4	4^6	$4^{5\frac{1}{2}}$	2^2	$1^{2\frac{1}{2}}$	Shoemaker W	115	2.40	77-35	Damascus115$^{2\frac{1}{2}}$Disciplinarian117$^{1\frac{1}{2}}$Nhoc'sBullt110^3	Driving	7
11Mar67-7Pim	fst	6f	$:23^3\ :47^2\ 1{:}12^1$	Alw 5000	8	3	$3^{1\frac{1}{2}}$	4^2	$5^{3\frac{1}{4}}$	1^{hd}	Shuk N	122	*.60	89-16	Dmascus122^{hd}Solar Bomb122$^{1\frac{1}{2}}$Last Cry119$^{\frac{1}{2}}$	Bumped late,up	8
30Nov66-7Aqu	gd	1	$:23^1\ :46\ 1{:}11^2\ 1{:}37$	Remsen 30k	2	3	2^{hd}	3^2	$4^{\frac{3}{4}}$	$1^{1\frac{1}{2}}$	Shoemaker W	117	*1.30	83-22	Damascus117$^{1\frac{1}{2}}$NativeGuile117$^{\frac{1}{2}}$ReflectedGlory119$^{\frac{3}{4}}$	Driving	14
29Oct66-3Lrl	fst	7f	$:22^4\ :46^2\ 1{:}12^1\ 1{:}25^1$	©Alw 4000	2	1	$1^{\frac{1}{2}}$	1^2	1^9	1^{12}	Shoemaker W	119	*.40	93-16	Damascus119^{12}Joxer115$^{3\frac{1}{2}}$Roman Away117$^{2\frac{1}{2}}$	Scored in hand	7
12Oct66-5Aqu	fst	7f	$:23\ :46^2\ 1{:}12\ 1{:}24^3$	©Md Sp Wt	8	1	1^1	1^1	1^4	1^8	Shoemaker W	122	*.90	83-18	Damascus122^{8}Winslow Homer122^{5}Gun Mount122^1	Easily	14
28Sep66-4Aqu	fst	7f	$:22^3\ :46\ 1{:}11^3\ 1{:}24^3$	©Md Sp Wt	11	9	7^6	$7^{7\frac{1}{2}}$	$3^{2\frac{1}{2}}$	$2^{2\frac{1}{2}}$	Shoemaker W	122	*2.60	80-19	Comprador122$^{2\frac{1}{2}}$Damascus122$^{\frac{3}{4}}$Air Rights122^1	Game try	14

Dr. Fager

b. c. 1964, by Rough'n Tumble (Free for All)–Aspidistra, by Better Self

Lifetime record: 22 18 2 1 $1,002,642

Own.– Tartan Stable
Br.– Tartan Farms (Fla)
Tr.– John A. Nerud

2Nov68-7Aqu	fst	7f	$:22^1\ :43^4\ 1{:}07^4\ 1{:}20^1$	3↑ Vosburgh H 57k	3	4	1^{hd}	1^{hd}	1^3	1^6	Baeza B	139	*.30	105-12	Dr.Fager139^{6}Kissin'George127^{6}JmJ.125^{hd}	Under mild drive	7
11Sep68-8Atl	fm	1$\frac{3}{16}$Ⓣ	$:48^4\ 1{:}12^3\ 1{:}36^4\ 1{:}55^1$	3↑ U Nations H 100k	6	1	1^{hd}	2^{hd}	1^{hd}	1^{nk}	Baeza B	134	*.80	94-10	Dr.Fgr134^{nk}Advoctor112$^{1\frac{1}{4}}$FortMrcy118$^{1\frac{1}{4}}$	Under stiff drive	9
24Aug68-8AP	fst	1	$:22^4\ :44\ 1{:}07^3\ 1{:}32^1$	3↑ Washington Park H 112k	9	6	2^{hd}	$1^{\frac{1}{2}}$	1^3	1^{10}	Baeza B	134	*.30	102-10	Dr. Fager134^{10}Racing Room116$^{1\frac{1}{2}}$Info112^1	Easily best	10
3Aug68-6Sar	fst	1⅛	$:47^1\ 1{:}11^3\ 1{:}36^3\ 1{:}48^4$	3↑ Whitney 53k	2	1	$1^{\frac{1}{2}}$	1^3	1^3	1^8	Baeza B	132	*.05	97-12	Dr. Fager132^{8}Spoon Bait114^{1}Fort Drum114^{15}	Much the best	4
20Jly68-7Aqu	fst	1¼	$:45^4\ 1{:}09^2\ 1{:}34^3\ 1{:}59^1$	3↑ Brooklyn H 109k	3	2	$2^{1\frac{1}{2}}$	$1^{\frac{1}{2}}$	$2^{\frac{1}{2}}$	$2^{2\frac{1}{2}}$	Baeza B	135	*.60	99-13	Damascus130$^{2\frac{1}{2}}$Dr.Fager135^{3}Mr.Right114^{hd}	Rank early going	7
4Jly68-7Aqu	fst	1¼	$:48^2\ 1{:}11\ 1{:}34^3\ 1{:}59^3$	3↑ Suburban H 107k	3	1	$1^{\frac{1}{2}}$	1^{hd}	1^2	1^2	Baeza B	132	*.80	100-11	Dr.Fager132^{2}BoldHour116^{3}Damascus133$^{3\frac{1}{2}}$	Under mild drive	5
18May68-8Hol	fst	1$\frac{1}{16}$	$:22^2\ :45\ 1{:}08^3\ 1{:}40^4$	3↑ Californian 119k	11	4	$2^{\frac{1}{2}}$	$1^{\frac{1}{2}}$	1^4	1^3	Baeza B	130	*1.20	91-13	Dr. Fager130^{3}Gamely116^{1}Rising Market121$^{1\frac{1}{2}}$	Much the best	14
4May68-7Aqu	fst	7f	$:22^2\ :45\ 1{:}08^4\ 1{:}21^2$	3↑ Roseben H 54k	5	1	$1^{\frac{1}{2}}$	1^1	1^3	1^3	Rotz JL	130	*.20	99-17	Dr. Fager130^{3}Tumiga121^{3}Diplomat Way121$^{\frac{3}{4}}$	Won eased up	5
7Nov67-7Aqu	fst	7f	$:22^2\ :45^1\ 1{:}09^3\ 1{:}21^3$	3↑ Vosburgh H 57k	6	8	$5^{2\frac{1}{2}}$	2^{hd}	1^{hd}	$1^{4\frac{1}{2}}$	Baeza B	128	*.20e	98-16	Dr. Fager128$^{4\frac{1}{2}}$Jim J.115$^{1\frac{1}{2}}$R. Thomas122^3	Wide,easily best	9
21Oct67-8Haw	fst	1¼	$:46^1\ 1{:}10^1\ 1{:}35^1\ 2{:}01^1$	3↑ Haw Gold Cup H 121k	1	1	$1^{\frac{1}{2}}$	1^{hd}	$1^{1\frac{1}{2}}$	$1^{2\frac{1}{2}}$	Baeza B	123	*.30	90-12	Dr.Fagr123$^{2\frac{1}{2}}$WhisprJt114$^{1\frac{1}{4}}$Pontmnow108$^{1\frac{1}{4}}$	Without urging	7
30Sep67-7Aqu	fst	1¼	$:45^1\ 1{:}09^1\ 1{:}35^3\ 2{:}00^3$	3↑ Woodward 107k	2	1	1^{hd}	$2^{\frac{1}{2}}$	2^5	$3^{10\frac{1}{2}}$	Boland W	120	1.80	84-15	Damascus120^{10}Buckpasser126$^{\frac{1}{2}}$Dr. Fager120^{13}	Faltered	6
2Sep67-8Rkm	fst	1¼	$:46^3\ 1{:}11\ 1{:}35^1\ 1{:}59^4$	NH Sweep Classic 265k	1	1	$1^{\frac{1}{2}}$	2^{hd}	2^{hd}	$1^{1\frac{1}{4}}$	Baeza B	120	*.20	115-17	Dr.Fager120$^{1\frac{1}{4}}$InReality126^{9}BarbsDelight115$^{2\frac{3}{4}}$	Mild drive	5
15Jly67-9Rkm	fst	1⅛	$:46^2\ 1{:}10^1\ 1{:}35^3\ 1{:}48^1$	Rkm Spl 85k	5	1	$1^{6\frac{1}{2}}$	$1^{3\frac{1}{2}}$	$1^{3\frac{1}{2}}$	$1^{4\frac{1}{4}}$	Baeza B	124	*.10	105-15	Dr.Fager124$^{4\frac{1}{4}}$ReasontoHail121$^{4\frac{3}{4}}$JackofAllTrds112$^{8\frac{1}{4}}$	Easily	7
24Jun67-8AP	sly	1	$:22^4\ :45\ 1{:}10^2\ 1{:}36$	AP Classic 106k	1	3	3^{nk}	1^3	1^6	1^{10}	Baeza B	120	*.40	83-25	Dr.Fagr120^{10}LightningOrphan116$^{1\frac{3}{4}}$DiplomatWay118^7	Easily	6
30May67-7GS	fst	1⅛	$:47\ 1{:}10^3\ 1{:}35^3\ 1{:}48$	Jersey Derby 119k	4	1	$1^{\frac{1}{2}}$	1^2	1^3	$1^{6\frac{1}{2}}$	Ycaza M	126	*.30	97-14	[D]Dr.Fager126$^{6\frac{1}{2}}$InReality126^{8}AirRghts126^{12}	Crowded field	4
	Disqualified and placed fourth																
13May67-7Aqu	fst	1	$:22^3\ :44^1\ 1{:}08\ 1{:}33^4$	Withers 58k	8	4	2^1	2^{hd}	$1^{1\frac{1}{2}}$	1^6	Baeza B	126	*.80	99-16	Dr. Fager126^{6}Tumiga126^{5}Reason to Hail126^5	Easy score	8
15Apr67-7Aqu	fst	1	$:23^3\ :46^1\ 1{:}10^2\ 1{:}35^1$	Gotham 57k	5	4	3^3	3^{nk}	2^{hd}	$1^{\frac{1}{2}}$	Ycaza M	122	*1.30e	92-14	Dr. Fager122$^{\frac{1}{2}}$Damascus122^{5}Reason to Hail114^7	Driving	9
15Oct66-7Aqu	fst	1	$:22^2\ :44^4\ 1{:}09^2\ 1{:}35$	Champagne 208k	7	4	$3^{\frac{1}{2}}$	1^{hd}	1^3	2^1	Shoemaker W	122	*1.00	92-14	Successor122^{1}Dr. Fager122^{4}Proviso122^4	Rank early,failed	10
5Oct66-7Aqu	gd	7f	$:22^4\ :46\ 1{:}11^3\ 1{:}24^4$	Cowdin 88k	1	10	3^1	3^2	$2^{1\frac{1}{2}}$	$1^{\frac{3}{4}}$	Shoemaker W	117	*.80	82-22	Dr.Fager117$^{\frac{3}{4}}$InRlty117$^{1\frac{1}{2}}$Succssor117$^{2\frac{1}{2}}$	Slow start,driving	10
10Sep66-8Atl	fst	7f	$:22^3\ :45^2\ 1{:}10^3\ 1{:}23^1$	World's Playground 28k	3	6	1^{hd}	$1^{\frac{1}{2}}$	1^4	1^{12}	Ycaza M	115	*.90	87-24	Dr. Fager115^{12}Glengary115$^{3\frac{1}{2}}$Pointsman115^{hd}	Much the best	11
13Aug66-4Sar	fst	6f	$:22^3\ :46^2\ 1{:}10^2$	Alw 5500	5	5	$2^{1\frac{1}{2}}$	2^2	1^2	1^8	Hidalgo D^5	117	*.90	96-09	Dr. Fager117^{8}Bandera Road117^{2}Quaker City115^2	Easily	8
15Jly66-3Aqu	fst	5½f	$:22^4\ :46^4\ :59\ 1{:}05$	©Md Sp Wt	8	8	8^3	2^1	$1^{1\frac{1}{2}}$	1^7	Hidalgo D^5	117	10.80	88-20	Dr. Fager117^{7}Lift Off122^{4}Rising Market122$^{\frac{1}{2}}$	Easily best	11

Past Performances of Great Horses of the 20th Century

Equipoise

ch. c. 1928, by Pennant (Peter Pan)–Swinging, by Broomstick
Own.– C.V. Whitney
Br.– H.P. Whitney (Ky)
Tr.– T.J. Healey

Lifetime record: 51 29 10 4 $338,610

Date/Race	Cond/Dist	Fractions	Race	PP St	Calls	Fin	Jockey	Wt	Odds	Speed	Top finishers	Comment	Field
23Feb35- 6SA	fst 1¼	:45 1:10 1:36 2:02^{1} 3↑	S Anita H 125k	19 12	12^{13} 12^{13} 74¼	77½	Workman R	130wb	*1.70e	--	Azucar117^{2}Ladysman117^{1}Time Supply118^{2}		20
	Off slowly,close quarters												
18Feb35- 5SA	fst 1 1/16	:24 :47^{3} 1:12 1:43^{2} 3↑	Handicap 1200	4 3	31½ 31 1^{hd}	11	Workman R	125wb	*.60	--	[D]Equipos125^{1}TwntyGrnd116^{3}Srd105^{1½}	Bumped rival,bore in	5
	Disqualified												
13Feb35- 5SA	fst 1	:23 :46^{3} 1:10^{2} 1:36^{3} 3↑	Handicap 1000	5 5	45 33 3½	21	Workman R	128wb	*.30	--	Sweping Light109^{1}Equipoise128^{nk}Ted Clark111^{1½}	Impeded	8
6Nov34- 3Bel	sly 1¼	:49^{3} 1:14^{3} 1:40^{4} 2:06^{3} 3↑	Whitney Trophy H 5.5k	5 1	51 21½ 2^{hd}	11½	Workman R	128wb	*.55	67-23	Equipoise128^{1½}Faireno122^{2}Mr. Khayyam120^{4}	Ridden out	6
31Oct34- 6Nar	fst 6f	:23 :45^{3} 1:10^{4} 3↑	Invitation 5.1k	5 2	45½ 44½ 43¾	3½	Workman R	130wb	*.45	100-07	Okapi130½All Forlorn127^{no}Equipoise130^{hd}	Closed fast	5
30May34- 5Bel	fst 1¼	:47^{1} 1:12 1:37^{1} 2:02^{3} 3↑	Suburban H 7.4k	1 4	53¼ 31¼ 2½	2no	Robertson A	134wb	*.50	87-16	Ladysman114^{no}Equipoise134^{10}War Glory115^{1½}	Just missed	8
19May34- 4Bel	fst 1	:23^{3} :47 1:11^{2} 1:37 3↑	Metropolitan H 4.3k	6 8	82¾ 4½ 1^{hd}	12	Workman R	132wb	*.70	90-15	[D]Equipoise132^{2}Mr.Khyym119^{1}SunArchr106^{5}	Swerved stretch	9
	Disqualified												
5May34- 5Pim	fst 1 3/16	:48^{3} 1:14 1:40 2:01^{4} 3↑	Dixie H 5.9k	4 1	2^{nk} 2½ 14	11½	Workman R	130wb	*.10	81-19	Equipoise130^{1½}Chatmoss110^{3}Flaming Mamie102^{7}	Easily	4
21Apr34- 5HdG	fst 1 1/16	:23^{2} :47^{2} 1:12^{2} 1:44^{2} 3↑	Philadelphia H 8.4k	4 4	32½ 21 11½	11	Workman R	130wb	*.50	98-08	Equipoise130^{1}Springsteel117^{4}Larranaga113^{6}	In hand	5
30Sep33- 5HdG	fst 1⅛	:48 1:11^{4} 1:37^{1} 1:49^{4} 3↑	Havre de Grace H 11k	1 4	42 31½ 21	21	Workman R	132wb	*1.60	100-09	Osculator104^{1}Equipoise132^{1½}Mate110^{1½}	Closed well	9
16Sep33- 5Bel	my 2	:50 2:34^{1} 3:25^{1} 3↑	J C Gold Cup 8.1k	1 2	21½ 21 31¼	312	Workman R	125wb	*.45	71-16	Dark Secret125^{4}Gusto125^{8}Equipoise125^{7}	No excuses	4
2Sep33- 5Sar	fst 1¾	:52 2:09^{2} 2:34^{4} 3:00 3↑	Sar Cup 6.9k	3 2	21½ 21 11	11½	Workman R	126 w	*.12	75-14	Equipoise126^{1½}Gusto126^{8}Keep Out118	Going away	3
24Aug33- 6Haw	fst 1¼	:48^{3} 1:13^{2} 1:38^{3} 2:02^{4} 3↑	Haw Gold Cup 27k	3 1	33 2½ 1^{hd}	12	Workman R	126wb	*.18	94-14	Equipoise126^{2}GallantSir126^{1½}Mr.Khayyam117^{1½}	Going away	5
3Aug33- 5Sar	fst 1	:24^{2} :48 1:13^{3} 1:39 3↑	Wilson 3.3k	3 3	31¾ 3^{nk} 1^{hd}	13	Workman R	126wb	*.20	86-15	Equipoise126^{3}Tambour106^{2}Mate111^{3}	Eased up	5
22Jly33- 6AP	fst 1¼	:47^{1} 1:11^{4} 1:37 2:02^{3} 3↑	Arlington H 12k	4 5	42 31½ 2^{nk}	11½	Workman R	135wb	*.75	96-13	Equipoise135^{1½}Watch Him106^{5}Gallant Sir125^{no}	Going away	7
7Jun33- 4Bel	fst 1¼	:47 1:11^{1} 1:36 2:02 3↑	Suburban H 8.9k	7 2	43½ 21½ 2^{hd}	12	Workman R	132wb	*.40	90-18	Equipoise132^{2}Osculator107^{6}Apprentice112^{nk}	Eased up	7
3Jun33- 5Bel	fst 1	:23^{2} :46^{4} 1:11^{4} 1:37^{2} 3↑	Metropolitan H 5.8k	7 5	32 2½ 11	14	Workman R	128wb	*.90	88-15	Equipoise128^{4}Okapi102^{1}Scotch Gold106^{1}	Eased up	10
22Apr33- 5HdG	fst 1 1/16	:23^{2} :47^{2} 1:12 1:44^{3} 3↑	Philadelphia H 8.9k	1 5	43 41¼ 12	11½	Workman R	128wb	*.90	99-05	Equipoise128^{1½}Tred Avon112^{2}Osculator105^{1}	Won easily	8
	Previously trained by F. Hopkins												
29Oct32- 5Lrl	gd 1¼	:48 1:13^{4} 1:39^{3} 2:05^{3} 3↑	Washington H 18k	6 4	86 21 2½	2^{hd}	Workman R	129wb	*1.10	82-25	Tred Avon112^{hd}Equipoise129^{no}Mate112^{6}	Finished fast	9
15Oct32- 5Lrl	fst 1	:23^{3} :47^{3} 1:13 1:37^{1} 2↑	Laurel 7.1k	1 7	54 41½ 3½	31½	Workman R	126wb	*.70	100-11	Jack High118^{no}Gallant Sir108^{1½}Equipoise126^{3}	No excuse	7
1Oct32- 5HdG	fst 1⅛	:46^{1} 1:11 1:36^{4} 1:50^{1} 3↑	H de Grace Cup H 26k	4 6	34½ 2½ 11½	11	Workman R	128wb	*1.05	99-06	Equipoise128^{1}Gallant Sir107^{3}Tred Avon110^{3}	Handily	13
24Sep32- 3HdG	gd 6f	:23 :46^{4} 1:12 3↑	Handicap 1500	3 5	54 53½ 58½	59	Workman R	129wb	*.65	86-08	Pairbypair107½Jack High123^{1½}Con Amore112^{5}	Dull effort	5
13Aug32- 5Sar	fst 1¼	:50 1:14^{2} 1:40 2:05^{3} 3↑	Whitney 6.9k	2 1	11½ 14 14	13	Workman R	126wb	*.14	81-16	Equipoise126^{3}Gusto117^{8}Rocky News116	Easily	3
6Aug32- 5Sar	fst 1	:23^{3} :46^{2} 1:11^{3} 1:38^{1} 3↑	Wilson 7.8k	2 3	32¼ 31 11	12	Workman R	126wb	*.13	90-11	Equipoise126^{2}Blind Bowboy121^{6}Pompeius113	Easily	3
23Jly32- 6AP	fst 1¼	:48 1:13 1:37^{2} 2:02^{1} 3↑	Arlington H 27k	3 4	32½ 2½ 2^{hd}	2^{nk}	Workman R	134wb	*.82	98-08	Plucky Play111^{nk}Equipoise134^{6}Pittsburgher105^{3}	Hard try	6
9Jly32- 6AP	fst 1¼	:48^{2} 1:13^{1} 1:37 2:02^{4} 3↑	Arl Gold Cup 24k	3 1	21½ 12½ 15	14	Workman R	126wb	*.24	95-04	Equipoise126^{4}Gusto114^{3½}Mate126	Easily	3
4Jly32- 5AP	hy 1⅛	:49^{2} 1:15 1:41^{2} 1:54^{4} 3↑	Stars & Stripes H 27k	1 2	1^{hd} 1^{hd} 13	1¾	Workman R	129wb	*.34	73-31	Equipoise129¾Tred Avon107^{5}Dr. Freeland110^{3}	Easily	6
30Jun32- 5AP	fst 1	:23^{1} :46 1:09^{1} 1:34^{2} 3↑	Handicap 1450	1 2	21½ 21½ 21	13	Workman R	128wb	*.90	106-02	Equipoise128^{3}Jamestown118^{3½}Spanish Play106	Easily	3
21May32- 4Bel	fst 1	:22^{4} :46^{2} 1:10^{2} 1:37 3↑	Metropolitan H 9k	6 5	33¼ 21½ 2^{hd}	12½	Workman R	127 w	*.60	90-15	Equipoise127^{2½}Sun Meadow118^{1½}Mate128^{4}	Easily	7
12May32- 4Bel	fst 6f-WC	1:09^{3} 3↑	Toboggan H 8.2k	10 6	21 1^{hd}	11	Workman R	129wb	*1.00	99-02	Equipoise129^{1}Ironclad108^{1½}Helianthus110^{4}	Handily	10
16Apr32- 5HdG	fst 6f	:23^{2} :47^{2} 1:12^{2} 3↑	Harford H 13k	9 5	72¼ 41½ 11½	13	Workman R	128wb	*.55	93-16	Equipoise128^{3}Happy Scot106.5^{hd}Evening105^{1}	Easily	12
13Apr32- 4Bow	fst 5f	:23^{1} :46 :59^{2} 3↑	Handicap 1400	7 2	51¾ 31½ 2^{nk}	1½	Workman R	126wb	*1.40	109-14	Equipoise126½Hygro112½Brandon Mint104^{6}	Drew out	7
9May31- 5Pim	fst 1 3/16	:48^{3} 1:13^{2} 1:38^{3} 1:59	Preakness 58k	2 7	63¼ 62¼ 41¾	42¾	Workman R	126wb	1.95	94-10	Mate126^{1½}Twenty Grand126^{nk}Ladder126^{1}	Impeded early	7
	Geldings not eligible												
25Apr31- 5HdG	fst 1 1/16	:24 :48^{3} 1:14^{3} 1:46^{4}	Cheseapeake 13k	6 6	64¼ 62¼ 611	613½	Robertson A	122wb	*.15	74-13	Anchors Aweigh114^{no}Soll Gills114^{3}Levante112^{1}	Distressed	6

Past Performances of Great Horses of the 20th Century

13Apr31- 4HdG fst 6f :231 :47 1:113 Alw 1400 4 1 21 2½ 1½ 1²½ Robertson A 123wb *.25 97-14 Equipoise1232½Panetian1084DarkHero1083 Outclassed field 5
5Nov30- 5Pim my 1 1/16 :234 :482 1:142 1:483 Pim Futurity 58k 2 8 87½ 54¾ 22 1½ Workman R 119wb *.95 79-26 Equipoise119½TwentyGrand119nkMat1194 Driving,great rush 8
Geldings not eligible;Previously owned by H.P. Whitney
16Oct30- 5CD fst 1 :231 :464 1:111 1:36 Ky Jockey Club 31k 4 2 2½ 12 2hd 2no Workman R 122wb *.76 101-13 Twenty Grand122noEquipoise12210Knight's Call1225 7
Going best at end
4Oct30- 3Aqu fst 1 :233 :473 1:13 1:38 Jr Champion 9.8k 4 5 53¼ 31¾ 21 21 Workman R 122wb *.20 89-15 Twenty Grand1111Equipoise1223Ormesby1168 Driving 7
27Sep30- 5HdG fst 6f :224 :463 1:122 Eastern Shore H 31k 2 8 52 2½ 11 15 Workman R 126wb *.60e 93-12 Equipoise1265Don Leon1192½Magnifico110hd Closed fast 15
13Sep30- 4Bel fst *7f-WC 1:203 Futurity 114k 7 6 2nk 32 2hd Workman R 130wb 3.60 92-11 Jamestown130hdEquipoise1303Mate1221 Driving,interfered 15
Geldings not eligible
6Sep30- 4Bel fst *7f-WC 1:214 Champagne 7.6k 9 6 2½ 1hd 2hd Workman R 132 w *1.20 86-15 Mate119hdEquipoise1323Sunny Lassie1135 Driving,faltered 10
9Aug30- 4Sar fst 6f :23 :46 1:112 Sar Spl 14k 1 4 21½ 21½ 21½ 22½ Workman R 122wb *.70 92-09 Jamestown1222½Eqpoise1228SunMedow1222 Not good enough 4
21Jun30- 3Aqu fst 5f 1:001 Great American 16k 3 1 11 12 12 Workman R 130wb *.45e 86-15 Equpos1302Polydorus1154HInthus1152½ Cleverly,mild drive 7
7Jun30- 3Bel fst 5f-WC :593 National Stallion 26k 7 4 21 13 16 Workman R 122wb *.40e 82-20 Equipoise1226Polydorus1222Baba Kenny119hd Easily 8
27May30- 4Bel gd 5f-WC :59 Juvenile 17k 1 4 34 31½ 1nk Workman R 125wb *.40e 85-24 Equipoise125nkHappy Scot122½Panasette1146 Driving 7
17May30- 3Bel sl 4½f-WC :523 Keene Mem 8.6k 2 2 3½ 2hd 12 Workman R 122wb *.60 92-13 Equipoise1222Happy Scot1228Avaricious1172 Easily 5
10May30- 3Jam fst 5f :231 :47 :591 Youthful 11k 1 2 4¾ 1nk 11 14 Workman R 117wb 3.50 97-14 [D]Equipoise1174Vander Pool1254Chouette1254 Drew away 8
Disqualified for impeding runner-up
2May30- 5Pim fst 4½f :223 :47 :534 Pim Nursery 7.6k 2 2 - - - - Workman R 122 w *1.65 -- Happy Scot1224Up1225St. Agnes1191 8
Stumbled after start,lost rider
23Apr30- 5HdG fst 4½f :23 :463 :53 Aberdeen 15k 7 9 55¼ 32¼ 34 Robertson A 122 w 4.25e 96-05 Vander Pool1221Up1173Equipoise1221½ Driving,closed well 10
15Apr30- 2HdG fst 4½f :233 :481 :542 Alw 1200 1 2 1½ 11½ 11½ Robertson A 118 w *.90 93-07 Equipoise1181½Schooner1123Uncle Sam1121 Driving 15
7Apr30- 3Bow hy 4f :232 :481 Alw 1200 8 4 1hd 1nk 14 Robertson A 111 w *2.15 92-08 Equipoise1114Glidelia1103Dry Dock112hd Won easily 11

Exterminator

ch. g. 1915, by McGee (White Knight)–Fair Empress, by Jim Gore **Lifetime record: 99 50 17 17 $252,996**

Own.– W.S. Kilmer
Br.– F.D. Knight (Ky)
Tr.– H. McDaniel

21Jun24- 5Dor gd 1 1/16 :232 :474 1:132 1:47 3↑ Queen's Hotel H 3k 4 3 31¼ 3¾ 42½ 35½ Wallace J 113 w *1.30 84-13 SpotCash1282½ForestLor1033Extrmntor113nk Pulled up lame 5
7Jun24- 6BB gd 1 :232 :473 1:132 1:394 3↑ Alw 1000 1 4 21½ 21 22 11 Wallace J 111 w 1.85 90-14 Exterminator1111Golden Rule1134Opperman1116 Handily 5
1May24- 6Pim fst 1 :242 :483 1:13 1:383 3↑ Handicap 2000 4 5 42½ 55¼ 46¼ 310½ Johnson A 126 w 4.80 84-11 Martingale120½SpicndSpn10610Extrmntor1261 Always outrun 6
19Apr24- 5HdG hy 1 1/16 :232 :482 1:153 1:492 3↑ Philadelphia H 5.1k 6 5 65½ 63 56¾ 58¼ Johnson A 125 w *1.20e 69-25 SpotCash111hdFlintStone118nkNewHampshire1124 No mishap 6
17Apr24- 5HdG fst 1 70 :244 :49 1:14 1:44 3↑ Alw 2000 2 2 21½ 1hd 1hd 1½ Walls P 107 w *.50 92-11 Exterminator107½GoldenSpher103½SttngSun10615 Ridden out 5
30Mar24- 6Tij fst 1¼ :474 1:124 1:39 2:052 3↑ Coffroth H 51k 11 7 65¾ 54¼ 53 41½ Johnson A 130 w *1.60e 97-14 Runstar123noOsprey123noCherryTree1171½ Challenged,tired 18
17Feb24- 4Tij fst 1 70 :241 :483 1:133 1:443 4↑ Alw 700 4 2 2¾ 21 11 11 Johnson A 113 w *.30 89-12 Extermintor1131Suprcrgo1161VnPtrck1011 Gentle hand ride 5
Previously trained by W. Shields
28Apr23- 5HdG my 1 70 :242 :493 1:143 1:452 3↑ Handicap 2500 3 4 31½ 21 2½ 2no Johnson A 132 w *1.10 85-21 Chickvl101noExtrmntor1321PulJons10810 Getting to winner 5
21Apr23- 5HdG fst 1 1/16 :24 :48 1:123 1:454 3↑ Philadelphia H 5.1k 2 4 53½ 42¼ 2¾ 1nk McAtee L 129 w *.80 95-10 Exterminator129nkPaul Jones1092Fair Phantom107nk Gamely 6
16Apr23- 4HdG my 6f :24 :49 1:15 3↑ Harford H 5.1k 4 5 64 62¾ 42½ 31¼ Sande E 132 w 3.70 80-32 Blazes106nkCareful116½Exterminator1326 Finished fast 8
Previously trained by E. Wayland
11Nov22- 4Pim fst 2¼ :50 2:34 3:04 3:532 3↑ Pim Cup H 10k 5 2 2hd 46 418 331½ Marineli B 126 w *.65 66-13 CaptanAlcock1061½PulJons9930Extrmntor126100 Forced pace 5
28Oct22- 5Lrl fst 1¼ :47 1:122 1:382 2:044 3↑ Washington H 28k 8 5 54 44½ 45 43½ Johnson A 132 w *.90 82-17 Oceanic104½Lucky Hour1202Paragon II1211 Finished fast 8

Past Performances of Great Horses of the 20th Century

21Oct22-5Lrl	fst 1	:24^4 :49 1:14 1:40	2↑ Laurel 13k	1	5	5^3	4^2	3^{1½}	1^{2½}	Johnson A	132 w	2.25	88-15	Extermintor132^{2½}[D]PrgonII125^{1½}Trystr123^{hd}	Won easing up	8
14Oct22-4Lrl	fst 6f	:23 :47 1:12^4	3↑ Handicap 2000	8	2	8^{6¾}	6^{4½}	6^5	4^{1½}	Johnson A	133 w	*2.25	92-16	CalamityJane113^{hd}OnWatch124^{1}TipptyWtcht112^{½}	Steady gain	8
30Sep22-5Haw	fst 1¼	:51^4 1:18^3 1:45^1 2:10	Special	-	1	1	1	1	1	Johnson A	126 w	-	73-19	Exterminator126	Good run	1
		Race against time														
20Sep22-5OW	fst 1¼	:46^3 1:11^3 1:38^2 2:05^1	3↑ Toronto Aut Cup H 16k	5	5	5^{3¼}	4^{2½}	3^{½}	1^{1½}	Johnson A	132 w	*.80	95-09	Exterminator132^{1½}Guy102^{hd}BitofWhit100^1	Rated,going away	8
31Aug22-4Sar	gd 1¾	:50 2:10 2:35 3:00^2	3↑ Sar Cup 8.3k	1	1	1^1	1^1	1^1	1^{nk}	Johnson A	126 w	1.40	80-18	Exterminatr126^{nk}MdHttr126^{12}BonHomm126	Outstayed rivals	3
1Aug22-4Sar	fst 1¼	:48^1 1:12^3 1:38 2:03^1	3↑ Saratoga H 9.2k	1	4	5^2	5^{3½}	5^7	5^{10¼}	Johnson A	137 w	5.00	83-09	Grey Lag130^{½}Bon Homme109^{1¼}Prudery114^6	Hard ridden	5
4Jly22-5Lat	gd 1½	:48^2 1:12^2 2:04^1 2:30^2	3↑ Independence H 18k	2	4	4^{4½}	5^{9½}	6^8	6^{12}	Johnson A	140 w	*.90	84-14	Firebrand116^{3}Devastation102^{6}Minto II116^1		8
		Appeared in distress after mile														
16Jun22-4Aqu	fst 1⅛	:47^3 1:12^3 1:37 1:50	3↑ Brooklyn H 9.8k	2	3	3^2	2^{½}	2^{hd}	1^{hd}	Johnson A	135 w	1.50	95-10	Exterminator135^{hd}GreyLag126^{4}PollyAnn103^{hd}	Strong finish	5
13Jun22-4Bel	fst 1 1/16	:23^4 :48 1:13^1 1:44	3↑ Handicap 1635	5	4	2^{1½}	2^2	1^1	1^{1½}	Johnson A	135 w	1.40	96-12	Exterminator135^{1½}Mad Hatter128^{6}Devastation102^{nk}	Rated	6
5Jun22-4Bel	gd 1⅛	:47 1:12^2 1:38^2 1:52^2	3↑ Handicap 1470	2	1	1no	1^{½}	1^{½}	1^{½}	Johnson A	133 w	*.07	83-11	Exterminator133^{½}Be Frank107	Won hard held	2
27May22-5CD	sl 1¼	:48 1:12^2 1:38^2 2:04^2	3↑ Kentucky H 12k	1	2	2^{hd}	1^1	1^{1½}	1^{1½}	Johnson A	138 w	*.45	94-15	Exterminator138^{1½}Firebrand119^{5}Blarney Stone95^8	Easily	4
20May22-5CD	fst 1⅛	:47^1 1:12 1:37 1:50	3↑ Clark H 13k	5	4	5^{1½}	2^{nk}	1^{½}	1^{1½}	Johnson A	133 w	*.60	99-10	Exterminator133^{1½}Lady Madcap111^{1}Rouleau107^4	Drew away	9
6May22-6Pim	sl 1 1/16	:24^3 :49^3 1:14 1:45^4	3↑ Pim Spring H 5.6k	3	2	2^1	1^{nk}	1^{hd}	1^{hd}	Johnson A	133 w	*.75	97-18	Exterminator133^{hd}Boniface125^{10}Registrar102^2	Hard drive	7
22Apr22-5HdG	fst 1 1/16	:24^4 :48^3 1:14^1 1:45	3↑ Philadelphia H 5.5k	2	2	3^{1¼}	3^{1½}	2^{hd}	2no	Johnson A	133 w	*.65	99-09	Boniface122^{no}Exterminator133^{6}BungaBuck110^{nk}	Cut off ⅜	6
15Apr22-4HdG	hy 6f	:23^4 :48^1 1:14^1	3↑ Harford H 5.2k	7	4	6^{4½}	4^3	4^2	1^1	Johnson A	132 wb	4.95	85-24	Exterminator132^{1}Billy Kelly132^{1}Dexterous102^1	Going away	12
		Previously trained by W. Knapp														
12Nov21-5Pim	hy 2¼	:55 2:46^2 3:12 4:08^1	3↑ Pim Cup H 9.8k	1	1	1^{½}	1^{½}	1^{hd}	1^{hd}	Johnson A	126 w	*.70	- -	Exterminator126^{hd}Boniface121^{20}Lady Emmeline96	Held on	3
29Oct21-5Lxt	fst 1½	:50^2 1:16^1 2:07 2:31^3	3↑ Lex Cup H 6.2k	5	3	3^3	2^3	3^{2½}	3^{6½}	Johnson A	135 w	*.80	84-10	Firbrnd118^{1½}UntdVrd105^{5}Extrmntor135^2	Tired under impost	5
22Oct21-4Lrl	fst 1¼	:47^1 1:12 1:38^2 2:04^2	3↑ Handicap 2038	6	3	3^7	3^4	2^{nk}	1^1	Johnson A	132 w	*1.65	88-14	Exterminator132^{1}My Dear115^{1½}Bygone Days96^{1½}	Driving	6
8Oct21-4Lrl	sly 1½	:48^3 1:14^1 2:06 2:35	3↑ Annapolis H 12k	6	4	1^{hd}	2^1	3^3	3^{8½}	Kelsay W	135 w	*2.15	64-23	ThePorter120^{2½}MyDer114^{6}Extrmntr135^{1½}	Eased when beaten	8
24Sep21-5OW	fst 1¼	:48 1:13^2 1:38^3 2:05^1	3↑ Toronto Aut Cup H 7.9k	6	4	4^{3½}	2^{½}	1^{½}	1^{nk}	Kelsay W	137 w	*1.40	95-12	Exterminator137^{nk}My Dear117^{2}Golden Sphere106^1	Gamely	9
16Sep21-4Bel	fst 2	:49^3 2:35^2 3:02 3:29^1	3↑ Autumn Gold Cup H 5.7k	2	2	1^{hd}	1^1	1^3	1^6	Kelsay W	130 w	*.33	63-19	Exterminator130^{6}Bellsolar104	In a canter	2
31Aug21-4Sar	sl 1¾	:55^4 2:13^2 2:39^3 3:04^3	3↑ Sar Cup 4.5k	-	1	1	1	1	1	Kelsay W	126 w	-	59-22	Exterminator126	Galloped	1
		Walkover														
27Aug21-4Sar	fst 1 3/16	:47^2 1:11^4 1:37^3 1:57^2	3↑ Merchants & Cits H 8.7k	6	5	5^{1¾}	2^1	1^{½}	1^1	Kelsay W	130 w	6.00	91-10	Exterminator130^{1}MadHattr132^{¾}Bllsolr104^{hd}	Outside,gamely	7
		Previously trained by F. Curtis														
12Jly21-4Wnr	fst 1⅛	:47^1 1:12 1:38^2 1:51^2	3↑ Frontier H 12k	7	4	5^{1¾}	3^{2½}	3^{1½}	3^2	Simpson R	132 w	4.20	97-07	BestPal119^{1½}IrishKiss108^{½}Extrmntor132^8	Closed with rush	8
9Jly21-5Lat	fst 1 3/16	:47^3 1:12^2 1:37^3 1:56^1	3↑ Daniel Boone H 14k	7	4	2^1	1^{½}	2^{1½}	3^2	Haynes E	135 w	2.20	100-08	Best Pal119^{1}La Rablee106^{1}Exterminator135^6		8
		Cut off by winner final ⅛														
4Jly21-5Lat	fst 1½	:49^3 1:14^1 2:05^2 2:30^1	3↑ Independence H 19k	5	3	3^2	2^1	1^{½}	1^1	Haynes E	130 w	*.55	97-07	Exterminator130^{1}Woodtrap111^{1½}La Rablee108^6	Handily	7
		Previously trained by W. McDaniel														
17Jun21-4Aqu	gd 1⅛	:46^2 1:11 1:36^2 1:49^4	3↑ Brooklyn H 9.8k	10	7	7^4	4^{2½}	4^{2½}	3^3	Ensor L	129 w	4.00	94-08	GreyLag112^{1½}JohnP.Grier124^{1½}Extrmntor129^1	Inside,gamely	11
4Jun21-4Bel	fst 1¼	:47^3 1:12 1:36^1 2:02^1	3↑ Suburban H 11k	8	5	5^{8½}	5^{9½}	5^{9½}	5^{8¾}	Johnson A	133 w	*1.20	80-09	Audacious120^{¾}MadHattr130^{6}SennngsPrk110^{no}	Always outrun	8
21May21-4Jam	fst 1⅛	:48 1:12^3 1:37^2 1:50	3↑ Long Beach H 5.8k	3	2	2^{1½}	1^{hd}	1^{½}	1^{¾}	Johnson A	130 w	*1.00	106-03	Exterminator130^{¾}Mad Hatter130^{5}Cirrus128^7	Drew clear	4
14May21-4Jam	my 1 1/16	:23^3 :48^1 1:14 1:47^1	3↑ Excelsior H 10k	1	5	5^3	4^{2½}	3^{1½}	2^1	Johnson A	129 w	3.60	89-15	Blazes118^{1}Exterminator129^{6}Naturalist126^{¾}	Slow late gain	7
7May21-4Jam	fst 1 1/16	:23^3 :47^2 1:12 1:45	3↑ Kings County H 6.1k	3	3	4^{4½}	3^5	2^5	2^3	Haynes E	129 w	2.20	98-08	MadHatter124^{3}Extrmintr129^{3}YllowHnd110^{1½}	Closed gamely	5
12Nov20-4Pim	fst 2¼	:47^2 2:32^1 2:58^3 3:53	3↑ Pim Cup H 10k	2	3	2^1	1^1	1^{½}	1no	Ensor L	126 w	*.75	20- -	Exterminator126^{no}Bonifc114^{10}PulJons110.5^6	Rated,all out	7
8Nov20-4Pim	fst 1½	:48^3 1:14^2 2:05^1 2:31^3	3↑ Bowie H 11k	3	7	7^{3½}	5^{3½}	6^{3¾}	5^{3½}	Fairbrother C	135 w	2.80	94-08	Mad Hatter120^{no}Boniface122^{1½}The Porter128^{no}	In a pocket	9
2Oct20-5OW	hy 2¼	:51^3 2:39^3 3:09^4 4:04^4	3↑ Ont Jockey Club Cup 7.7k	1	1	2^2	2^2	1^{nk}	1^{1¼}	Fairbrother C	134 w	*.15	49-26	Exterminator134^{1¼}Bondage110^{6}St. Germain90^{1½}	Easily	4
25Sep20-5OW	fst 1¼	:48^2 1:13^3 1:39^4 2:04^2	3↑ Toronto Aut Cup 7.8k	4	2	1^1	1^1	1^{½}	1^{hd}	Fairbrother C	132 w	*.25	99-10	Exterminator132^{hd}My Dear92^{12}Bondage108^1	Driving	5
		Previously trained by J.S. Healey														

Past Performances of Great Horses of the 20th Century

15Sep20-4Bel	fst	2	$:48^2$ $2:29^3$ $3:21^4$	3↑ Autumn Gold Cup 6.3k	2	3	$3^{2½}$	3^2	$2^{½}$	1^{hd}	Fairbrother C	128	w	*.70	--	Exterminator128^{hd}Damask$98^{2½}$Cleopatra105	Rated,driving	3
31Aug20-4Sar	sl	1¾	$:50^2$ $2:04^3$ $2:29^4$ $2:56^2$	3↑ Sar Cup 5.6k	2	1	1^1	$1^{1½}$	1^3	1^6	Fairbrother C	126	w	*.55	108-12	Exterminator126^6Cleopatra111	Easily	2
28Aug20-4Wnr	fst	1 1/16	:23 $:47^2$ 1:12 $1:44^4$	3↑ George Hendrie H 8.6k	4	3	$3^{1½}$	$3^{1¼}$	$2^{½}$	1^1	Fairbrother C	131	w	*1.15	98-09	Exterminator131^1Wildair114^3My Dear95^{hd}	Rated,going away	6
21Aug20-4Wnr	sl	1⅛	:48 $1:13^2$ $1:38^4$ $1:51^1$	3↑ Wnr Jockey Club H 11k	1	3	$2^{1½}$	$2^{1½}$	2^{nk}	$1^{1¼}$	Fairbrother C	125	w	2.50	100-17	Exterminator$125^{1¼}$Wildair110^{10}Boniface130^{nk}	Drew away	7
14Aug20-4Sar	gd	1⅛	$:48^4$ 1:14 $1:40^2$ $1:53^1$	3↑ Champlain H 4.1k	1	4	2^1	$3^{1½}$	$1^{½}$	$2^{1½}$	Schuttinger A	128	w	*2.20	82-19	Gnome$109^{1½}$Extrminatr128^1MadHatter117^5	Inside,no match	7
2Aug20-4Sar	fst	1¼	$:47^4$ 1:11 1:36 $2:01^4$	3↑ Saratoga H 6.7k	3	5	$5^{4¼}$	$2^{1½}$	$2^{2½}$	2^2	Schuttinger A	126	w	7.00	100-06	SirBarton129^2Exterminator126^3Wildair115^3	Gamely,no match	5
14Jly20-4Wnr	hy	1⅛	$:49^2$ $1:18^2$ 1:47 $2:01^1$	3↑ Frontier H 12k	5	3	4^4	2^2	$3^{2½}$	$3^{2½}$	Davies T	127	w	*1.25	47-48	Slippery Elm$109^{½}$The Porter129^2Exterminator127^5	Tired	8
3Jly20-4Aqu	my	1⅛	$:48^1$ $1:12^4$ $1:37^3$ $1:50^1$	3↑ Brookdale H 4.2k	2	3	$3^{½}$	2^1	$2^{½}$	$1^{1½}$	Schuttinger A	129	w	2.00	96-11	Exterminator$129^{1½}$Cirrus123^4Gladiator112^6	Hard ridden	4
29Jun20-4Aqu	fst	1 1/16	$:23^3$ $:46^2$ 1:11 1:44	3↑ Handicap 1290	3	3	3^4	3^3	3^1	$1^{¾}$	Schuttinger A	126	w	3.00	101-18	Exterminator$126^{¾}$Naturalist$120^{½}$Wildair114^{12}	Drew away	5
24Jun20-4Aqu	fst	1⅛	:47 1:11 $1:36^3$ 1:50	3↑ Brooklyn H 7.3k	7	7	7^5	7^6	4^6	$4^{8¼}$	Schuttinger A	124	w	6.00	89-09	Cirrus108^{hd}Boniface122^8Mad Hatter115^{hd}	Steadily	7
19Jun20-4Jam	gd	1⅛	$:47^4$ 1:13 $1:38^2$ $1:51^1$	3↑ Long Beach H 4k	2	3	$1^{½}$	1^1	1^1	1^1	Schuttinger A	119	w	2.20	102-06	Exterminator119^1Cirrus109^8Naturalist120^3	Handily	5
5Jun20-4Bel	my	1¼	:52 $1:16^3$ $1:43^2$ $2:09^3$	3↑ Suburban H 7.8k	5	5	$5^{8½}$	$4^{6½}$	4^7	3^6	Rice T	123	w	*2.20	46-30	Paul Jones106^{hd}Boniface115^6Exterminator$123^{½}$	Game try	5
29May20-5Bel	fst	1 1/16	$:24^2$:48 1:13 $1:44^3$	3↑ Handicap 1605	4	3	$2^{1½}$	3^1	$1^{½}$	2^{nk}	Davies T	128	w	*2.00	97-10	Alibi107^{nk}Exterminator128^2Sea Mint98^{no}	Led,tired	5
	Previously trained by H. McDaniel																	
13Nov19-4Pim	hy	2¼	$:52^3$ 2:50 $3:18^2$ 4:13	3↑ Pim Cup H 4.9k	1	1	2^2	1^4	1^2	1^4	Kummer C	121	w	*1.00	--	Extrminatr121^4RoycRools$105^{8½}$Woodtrp102^3	Won easing up	3
8Nov19-4Pim	fst	1½	$:49^3$ 1:15 $2:07^2$ $2:33^4$	3↑ Bowie H 10k	5	3	$5^{2¾}$	$5^{5½}$	5^{11}	$5^{13½}$	Kummer C	128	w	2.90	73-11	Royce Rools$107^{1½}$Cudgel131^4Mad Hatter113^2	Quit badly	5
18Oct19-5Lat	hy	2¼	:54 2:50 $3:18^4$ 4:17	3↑ Lat Cup 8.7k	4	3	1^1	2^{hd}	$2^{1½}$	2^2	Knapp W	134	w	*.45	--	Be Frank122^2Exterminator134^{20}Legal105^{20}	Tired	4
11Oct19-4Lrl	fst	1½	$:47^3$ 1:13 $2:03^3$ $2:29^3$	3↑ Annapolis H 8.3k	3	3	$3^{4½}$	2^1	$2^{1½}$	2^{hd}	Knapp W	128	w	2.05	107-06	Thunderclp108^{hd}Extrmntor128^3Cudgl132^1	Getting to winner	5
3Oct19-3Lrl	fst	1 1/16	$:24^2$:49 $1:15^3$ $1:46^1$	3↑ Alw 1200	2	1	1^1	1^{hd}	$1^{½}$	1^{nk}	Knapp W	120	w	*.05	86-15	Exterminator120^{nk}Orestes120^{10}Douglass S.113	Hard ridden	3
27Sep19-5HdG	fst	1⅛	$:47^1$ $1:12^2$ $1:37^3$ 1:50	3↑ Havre de Grace H 10k	5	6	$6^{4¾}$	$4^{¾}$	$4^{1¾}$	$2^{½}$	Knapp W	126	w	10.50	105-05	Cudgel$129^{½}$Extrmntr126^{no}SrBrton124^2	Impeded,game finish	8
22Sep19-5HdG	fst	1 1/16	:24 :48 1:13 1:45	3↑ Purse 2527	1	2	2^2	$2^{1½}$	2^1	$1^{¾}$	Schuttinger A	124	w	5.05	100-11	Exterminator$124^{¾}$Cudgel129^1Slippery Elm99^3	Gamely	5
11Sep19-4HdG	my	1 70	:25 :49 $1:14^3$ 1:45	3↑ Harford County H 5.4k	4	2	$3^{½}$	2^3	2^4	2^4	Schuttinger A	125	w	*.35	83-25	The Porter121^4Exterminator125^8Slippery Elm103^3	No match	5
30Aug19-4Sar	sl	1¾	:48 2:07 2:32 2:58	3↑ Sar Cup 6.3k	3	1	$1^{1½}$	1^2	$1^{½}$	$1^{1½}$	Schuttinger A	126	w	2.50	100-14	Extrmntr$126^{1½}$Purchs116^{50}ThTrump116	Challenged,drew away	3
23Aug19-4Sar	fst	1 3/16	$:48^4$ $1:13^3$ $1:37^2$ $1:57^2$	3↑ Merchants & Cits H 3.4k	1	1	1^1	$2^{½}$	$3^{2½}$	3^3	Loftus J	126	w	*1.10e	90-08	Cudgel132^1Star Master122^2Exterminator$126^{1½}$	No menace	5
9Aug19-4Sar	fst	1⅛	:48 $1:12^3$ $1:37^1$ 1:50	3↑ Champlain H 3.4k	6	4	$4^{2¾}$	3^1	2^1	2^1	Loftus J	120	w	*.90e	106-09	SunBriar128^1Extermintor$120^{½}$Hollstr$115^{1½}$	Not hard ridden	6
5Aug19-4Sar	fst	1	$:23^2$ $:46^2$ $1:11^2$ $1:36^1$	3↑ Delaware H 3.4k	6	5	$4^{4½}$	3^4	$3^{3½}$	3^1	Loftus J	121	w	*1.20e	99-08	FairyWand107^{hd}SunBriar128^1Exterminator$121^{½}$	Fast finish	8
14Jun19-4Jam	fst	1 1/16	$:24^4$ $:48^2$ 1:13 $1:45^2$	3↑ Excelsior H 4.8k	8	5	$4^{4½}$	$4^{5½}$	6^8	$5^{3¾}$	Loftus J	124	w	8.00	96-07	Naturalist122^1Star Master119^1Boniface108^{nk}	No threat	8
7Jun19-4Bel	fst	1¼	$:46^3$ $1:11^3$ 1:38 $2:02^1$	3↑ Suburban H 6.7k	1	4	$5^{7½}$	$7^{5¼}$	$7^{6¾}$	$5^{5¼}$	Rice T	128	w	5.00	84-16	Corn Tassel108^{nk}Sweep On$108^{1½}$Boniface107^3	Outrun	8
24May19-5CD	hy	1¼	$:48^2$ $1:14^3$ 1:42 $2:10^2$	3↑ Kentucky H 14k	1	4	$1^{½}$	1^{hd}	1^{hd}	3^1	Morys J	134	w	*2.15	64-31	Midway122^1Beaverkill108^{no}Exterminator134^2	Gamely	7
22May19-6CD	my	1	:25 :50 $1:15^3$ $1:42^3$	3↑ Handicap 1660	4	1	$1^{1½}$	1^2	$1^{1½}$	1^5	Morys J	134	w	*.60	74-39	Exterminator134^5Flyaway97^{nk}Drastic112^{10}	Ridden out	4
15May19-4CD	fst	1	:25 $:49^3$ $1:14^3$ $1:39^1$	3↑ Alw 1800	4	1	$1^{½}$	1^1	2^{hd}	2no	Morys J	115	w	*.20	91-11	Under Fire103^{no}Exterminator$115^{1½}$Bribed Voter108^8		4
	Tight restraint,tired																	
8May19-4Lxt	my	1¼	$:49^3$ $1:15^2$ 1:42 $2:07^3$	3↑ Camden H 2.5k	1	1	1^1	1^1	1^1	1^1	Morys J	132	w	*.35	81-28	Exterminator132^1Midway118	Drawing away	2
1May19-4Lxt	hy	1 1/16	$:24^3$ $:49^1$ 1:16 $1:50^2$	3↑ Ben Ali H 2.9k	4	3	$2^{1½}$	$2^{1½}$	$1^{1½}$	1^3	Morys J	124	w	*.60	70-33	Exterminator124^3AmericanAc99^6Mdwy120^{hd}	As rider pleased	5
31Mar19-4OP	fst	6f	$:23^3$:48	3↑ Handicap 800	3	1	$3^{1½}$	3^2	1^{hd}	$1^{1½}$	Haynes E	123	w	*1.00	96-09	Extrmntor$123^{1½}$UltmThul$114^{1½}$A.N.Akn107^2	As rider pleased	6
			$1:12^4$															
22Mar19-4OP	fst	1 70	$:24^2$:48 1:13 $1:43^2$	3↑ Handicap 800	2	2	$2^{½}$	$1^{1½}$	$1^{1½}$	1^3	Schuttinger A	126	w	*.80	109-09	Exterminator126^3Lucky B.$111^{1½}$Drastic111^3	Won eased up	4
28Nov18-5Lat	my	1 1/16	$:24^3$ $:49^3$ $1:15^3$ $1:50^3$	2↑ Handicap 2090	2	4	$3^{½}$	1^2	1^4	$1^{2½}$	Loftus J	126	w	*.85	64-37	Exterminator$126^{2½}$Drastic104^6WrMchn109^5	As rider pleased	8
23Nov18-5Lat	hy	2¼	:54 $2:43^3$ 3:11 $4:06^3$	3↑ Lat Cup H 8.9k	6	6	$1^{1½}$	1^1	1^{hd}	1no	Loftus J	121	w	*1.25	--	Exterminator121^{no}Beaverkill110^5Moscowa115^3	Gamely	6
12Nov18-4Pim	fst	1½	:49 $1:14^2$ $2:04^3$ $2:31^1$	3↑ Bowie H 12k	4	5	$1^{½}$	2^4	2^2	$3^{1¼}$	Loftus J	120	w	6.85	102-06	GeorgeSmith$130^{¾}$OmarKhayyam$115^{½}$Extrmntr120^6	Resolutely	15
6Nov18-4Pim	fst	1¼	$:49^2$ $1:14^1$ $1:39^3$ $2:05^3$	Pim Autumn H 5.4k	2	2	1^{hd}	2^{hd}	1^1	$1^{½}$	Ensor L	118	w	3.20	99-09	Extrmntor$118^{½}$Forground107^{nk}ThPortr127^6	Outstayed rivals	5
31Oct18-4Lrl	hy	1⅛	:50 1:16 $1:41^4$ $1:54^2$	3↑ National H 3k	1	1	1^{nk}	1^{nk}	1^{nk}	2^{hd}	Knapp W	117	w	1.75	76-25	Midway117^{hd}Exterminator117^{20}Tombolo98	Wide	3
26Oct18-6Lrl	fst	1⅛	:49 $1:14^1$ $1:39^3$ $1:52^1$	Ellicott City H 2.5k	5	1	1^{nk}	1^3	$1^{1½}$	$1^{2½}$	Knapp W	113	w	*.30	87-08	Extermintor$113^{2½}$Aurum$104.5^{1½}$RdSox105.5^{nk}	Never extended	5
12Oct18-5Lrl	gd	1⅛	:49 $1:14^3$ $1:40^2$ $1:51^2$	3↑ Washington H 2.5k	3	1	$1^{¾}$	2^2	3^2	$3^{3½}$	Knapp W	114	w	3.15	87-13	Midway111.5^2Cudgel$130^{1½}$Exterminator$113.5^{1½}$	Tired badly	4

Past Performances of Great Horses of the 20th Century

8Oct18-4Lrl	fst	1 1/16	:231 :464 1:124 1:441	Carrollton H 1.9k	4	1	1nk	1½	1½	1hd	Knapp W	118	w	12.70	96-11	Exterminator118hdThe Porter1265Sunny Slope1304	Gamely	4
4Oct18-4Lrl	fst	1 1/16	:24 :481 1:15 1:461	3↑ Alw 1408	4	1	12	11½	11	11	Kummer C	103	w	*.65	86-11	Exterminator1031Franklin1122John I. Day100no	Ridden out	4
30Aug18-4Sar	hy	1¼	:501 1:171 1:451 2:122	3↑ Handicap 1313	4	2	22	42½	47	39½	Knapp W	115	w	*2.20	48-34	Ticket1061½Bondage1068Extermntr1151½	Impeded by winner	5
17Aug18-4Sar	fst	1¼	:49 1:133 1:382 2:031	Travers 10k	2	2	44½	47	48	412	Schuttinger A	123	w	*1.10e	92-05	Sun Briar120hdJohren1266War Cloud1266	Outrun	4
3Aug18-4Sar	fst	1 3/16	:483 1:132 1:383 1:563	Kenner 4k	3	2	32½	33	31¾	22	Knapp W	129	w	5.00	105-02	Enfilade1142Exterminator129nkTippityWitcht1235	Game try	5
22Jun18-5Lat	fst	1½	:494 1:142 2:063 2:33	Lat Derby 12k	5	4	42½	35½	31½	22	Knapp W	124	w	8.75	85-11	Johren1272Exterminator124½Frecuttr1228	Hard ridden late	6
25May18-4BPT	fst	1		3↑ Turf and Field H .7k	-	-				21	Knapp W	122		*.45	- -	Kilts II1261Exterminator1221Square Dealer1262	Driving	6
	No time taken																	
11May18-5CD	my	1¼	:491 1:161 1:433 2:104	Ky Derby 18k	5	5	42½	1hd	2hd	11	Knapp W	114	w	29.60	63-25	Exterminator1141Escoba1178Viva America1134	Saved ground	8
	Previously owned and trained by J.C. Milam																	
26Jly17-2Knw	fst	5½f	:233 :473 1:004 1:071	Alw 800	3	7	64¾	45	66¾	4½	Morys J	112	w	*1.55	102-00	MissBryn112noOwnRoeO'Neil104½Salvstr112no	Finished fast	11
17Jly17-3Wnr	hy	5½f	:244 :51 1:052 1:13	Alw 800	2	6	43½	3nk	13	11	Kelsay W	105	w	7.85	63-41	Exterminator1051Fern Handley1031Lady Eileen1103	Handily	6
14Jly17-2Wnr	gd	5f	:23 :473 1:011	Alw 800	11	3	48	79¾	49	410	Morys J	105	w	14.35	84-18	Jack Hare Jr.1111High Cost1153Viva America1156	Bumped	11
30Jun17-1Lat	fst	6f	:233 :483 1:144	Md Sp Wt	2	2	12	12	11½	13	Morys J	109	w	5.20	81-12	Exterminator1093Mistress Polly1091Quito112½	Easily	12

Forego

b. g. 1970, by Forli (Aristophanes)–Lady Golconda, by Hasty Road

Lifetime record: 57 34 9 7 $1,938,957

Own.– Lazy F Ranch
Br.– Lazy F Ranch (Ky)
Tr.– Frank Y. Whiteley Jr

4Jly78-8Bel	sly	1¼	:483 1:123 1:37 2:014	3↑ Suburban H-G1	3	5	43½	68½	611	514	Shoemaker W	132		*.90	89-13	Upper Nile1131½Nearly on Time1092¼Great Contractor1143		6
	Tired after ¾																	
19Jun78-8Bel	fst	7f	:233 :462 1:094 1:213	3↑ Alw 25000	4	4	41½	31½	31½	1nk	Shoemaker W	122		*.30	94-12	Forego122nkDr. Patches1227Gabe Benzur1152	Ridden out	4
17Sep77-8Bel	sly	1⅛	:453 1:101 1:352 1:48	3↑ Woodward H-G1	3	8	79½	44	4¾	11½	Shoemaker W	133		*1.90	87-18	Forego1331½SilverSeries114nkGrtContrctor115nk	Ridden out	10
6Aug77-8Sar	sly	1⅛	:463 1:103 1:361 1:492	3↑ Whitney H-G2	7	6	712	716	716	718	Shoemaker W	136		*.80	70-16	Nearly on Time1034½American History1124¾Dancing Gun112¾		7
	Disliked going																	
23Jly77-8Bel	fst	1½	:49 1:124 2:023 2:261	3↑ Brooklyn H-G1	12	6	2hd	21½	25	211	Shoemaker W	137		*.70	78-17	GreatContractr11211Forego137nkAmrcnHstory112¾	Held 2nd	13
4Jly77-8Bel	fst	1¼	:472 1:113 1:373 2:03	3↑ Suburban H-G1	4	3	36½	45	42	2nk	Shoemaker W	138		*.30	84-16	QuietLittleTable114nkForego138nkNearlyonTm104¾	Bore out	6
13Jun77-8Bel	fst	1⅛	:471 1:111 1:354 1:481	3↑ Nassau County H-G3	3	5	54	51¼	4¾	1½	Shoemaker W	136		*.05	86-21	Forego136½Co Host110nkNorcliffe117½	Easily	7
30May77-8Bel	fst	1	:23 :451 1:101 1:344	3↑ Metropolitan H-G1	10	10	1014	86½	2hd	12	Shoemaker W	133		*.50	94-14	Forego1332Co Host1112Full Out1151½	Handily	12
23May77-6Bel	fst	7f	:242 :47 1:11 1:224	4↑ Alw 25000	2	3	31	32	2hd	1½	Shoemaker W	122		*.05	88-17	Forego122½Dance Spell1147Sawbones1092	Ridden out	5
2Oct76-8Bel	sly	1¼	:472 1:104 1:35 2:00	3↑ Marlboro Cup H-G1	10	4	86¼	67½	44	1hd	Shoemaker W	137		*1.10	99-11	Forego137hdHonestPleasure1191FthrHogn1102¾	Wide,just up	11
18Sep76-8Bel	fst	1⅛	:453 1:091 1:332 1:454	3↑ Woodward H-G1	2	7	76	76½	42½	11¼	Shoemaker W	135		*1.10	98-10	Forgo1351¼DanceSpell1152¾[DH]HonstPleasur121	Ridden out	10
21Aug76-8Mth	fst	1¼	:472 1:112 1:354 2:003	3↑ AL Haskell H-G1	7	5	33	22	21	31	Vasquez J	136		*.60	98-12	Hatchet Man1121Intrepid Hero119hdForego1366	Forced wide	8
24Jly76-8Aqu	fst	1¼	:464 1:111 1:362 2:011	3↑ Brooklyn H-G1	4	6	68½	21½	2hd	12	Gustines H	134		*.70	90-14	Forego1342LordRebeau1144½FoolishPleasur126no	Ridden out	8
5Jly76-8Aqu	fst	1 3/16	:474 1:112 1:361 1:552	3↑ Suburban H-G1	2	3	32½	21½	31½	2no	Gustines H	134		*.40	85-15	Foolish Pleasure125noForego134noLord Rebeau1164¼	Gamely	4
13Jun76-8Bel	fst	1⅛	:472 1:112 1:362 1:483	3↑ Nassau County H-G3	1	4	42½	32	1hd	12¾	Vasquez J	132		*.80	84-22	Forego1322¾El Pitirre1152¾Hatchet Man1142	Easily	5
31May76-8Bel	fst	1	:231 :453 1:092 1:344	3↑ Metropolitan H-G1	4	5	54½	44	41½	1hd	Gustines H	130		*1.10	94-16	Forego130hdMaster Derby1261¼Lord Rebeau1192¼		6
	Sluggish,just up																	
20May76-8Bel	fst	7f	:234 :464 1:10 1:22	4↑ Alw 25000	2	2	41½	3½	1hd	11¼	Gustines H	126		*.30	92-18	Forego1261¼Wishing Stone1196½Tiempazo III119½	Easily	4
	Previously trained by S.W. Ward																	

Past Performances of Great Horses of the 20th Century

27Sep75- 8Bel	fst 1½	:493 1:132 2:023 2:271 3↑	Woodward-G1	6	3	3½	1hd	1hd	1¾	Gustines H	126	*.90	84-19	Forego1261¾Wajima11911Group Plan126¾	Drew clear	6
13Sep75- 8Bel	fst 1¼	:472 1:104 1:352 2:00 3↑	Marlboro Cup Inv'l H-G1	3	7	76	32	1hd	2hd	Gustines H	129	*1.40	99-11	Wajima119hdForego1297½Ancient Title126¾	Bore out,missed	7
1Sep75- 8Bel	fst 1⅛	:452 1:09 1:341 1:471 3↑	Governor-G1	8	8	710	88¾	54½	42¾	Gustines H	134	*2.00	88-18	Wajima115hdFoolishPleasure1252AncntTtl130¾	Wide stretch	10
19Jly75- 8Bel	fst 1½	:484 1:132 2:024 2:274 3↑	Suburban H-G1	3	6	69½	42½	3½	1hd	Gustines H	134	*.60	81-18	Forego134hdArbees Boy1182¼Loud1147	Just up	7
4Jly75- 8Bel	fst 1¼	:463 1:101 1:344 1:594 3↑	Brooklyn H-G1	2	5	412	31½	1hd	1½	Gustines H	132	*.70	101-07	Frgo1321½MonetryPrncpl109noStopthMusc1215¾	Ridden out	8
26May75- 8Aqu	fst 1	:231 :453 1:084 1:333 3↑	Metropolitan H-G1	3	7	75¼	64¾	34	31	Gustines H	136	*.90	97-11	GoldandMyrrh121¾StoptheMusic124nkForego1363½	Rallied	7
17May75- 8Aqu	fst 7f	:223 :444 1:091 1:213 3↑	Carter H-G2	5	10	811	87¾	22	1hd	Gustines H	134	*.90	93-11	Forego134hdStop the Music1232½Orders1141¼	Brisk drive	10
15Feb75- 9Hia	fst 1¼	:463 1:102 1:35 2:014 3↑	Widener H-G1	5	9	813	45½	1hd	1¼	Gustines H	131	*.70	89-11	Forego1311¼Hat Full1111¼Gold and Myrrh115nk	Ridden out	9
1Feb75- 9Hia	fst 1⅛	:47 1:103 1:343 1:471 3↑	Seminole H-G2	5	8	85	32	2½	1¾	Gustines H	129	*.80	96-09	Forego129¾Mr. Door1151Lord Rebeau1152½	Ridden out	8
9Nov74- 8Aqu	fst 2	:493 2:304 2:56 3:211 3↑	J C Gold Cup-G1	2	8	42½	1hd	12½	12½	Gustines H	124	*.70	90-15	Forego1242½Copte124¾Group Plan1243¼	Ridden out	8
19Oct74- 8Aqu	fst 7f	:223 :452 1:094 1:213 3↑	Vosburgh H-G2	4	10	99½	77½	21	13½	Gustines H	131	*2.20	93-10	Forgo1313½StoptheMusic118noPrinceDantn1191¾	Ridden out	12
28Sep74- 8Bel	fst 1½	:49 1:132 2:022 2:272 3↑	Woodward-G1	5	10	1017	84¼	42	1nk	Gustines H	126	*2.30	83-13	Forego126nkArbees Boy1261¾Group Plan1262½	Driving	11
14Sep74- 8Bel	sly 1⅛	:46 1:102 1:343 1:463 3↑	Marlboro Cup H 250k	2	9	810	72¾	34½	34	Gustines H	126	2.70	90-12	Big Spruce1202¾Arbees Boy1191¼Forego126½	No final rally	10
2Sep74- 8Bel	fst 1⅛	:452 1:092 1:34 1:461 3↑	Governor-G1	10	8	812	65	57	45¼	Gustines H	128	*1.60	91-09	Big Spruce1182½Arbees Boy1211½Plunk1211¼	Wide	10
20Jly74- 8Aqu	fst 1¼	:472 1:111 1:361 2:012 3↑	Suburban H-G1	6	6	512	46½	44½	31½	Gustines H	131	*1.40	87-12	True Knight1271½Plunk114hdForego1312½	Rallied	10
4Jly74- 8Aqu	fst 1 3/16	:463 1:102 1:354 1:544 3↑	Brooklyn H-G1	6	6	615	48	2hd	1¾	Gustines H	129	*.40	88-14	Forego129¾BillyComeLately1142ArbeesBoy1166	Ridden out	7
26Jun74- 8Aqu	fst 7f	:223 :444 1:084 1:211 3↑	Nassau County H-G3	2	6	612	612	56½	2½	Gustines H	132	*.70	94-10	Timeless Moment112½Forego132½North Sea1142½	Fast finish	6
27May74- 8Bel	fst 1	:222 :443 1:09 1:342 3↑	Metropolitan H-G1	2	6	47½	2hd	11½	22	Gustines H	134	*1.30	94-11	Arbees Boy1122Forego134½Timeless Moment109hd	Gamely	8
18May74- 8Bel	fst 7f	:221 :45 1:092 1:221 3↑	Carter H-G2	7	8	89	63½	11½	12¼	Gustines H	129	*1.40	91-13	Forego1292¼Mr.Prospector1241TimelessMoment1132¾	Easily	8
23Mar74- 9Hia	fst 1¼	:471 1:11 1:354 2:011 3↑	Widener H-G1	5	5	58½	1½	11½	11	Gustines H	129	*.80	92-12	Forego1291True Knight1242Play the Field114no	Driving	7
23Feb74- 9GP	fst 1¼	:464 1:104 1:354 1:594 3↑	Gulf Park H-G2	2	4	413	22	1hd	1½	Gustines H	127	1.40	98-14	Forego127½True Knight1236Golden Don1183	Ridden out	6
9Feb74- 9GP	fst 1⅛	:471 1:112 1:362 1:483 3↑	Donn H-G3	2	4	35	32½	21	1no	Gustines H	125	*.70	91-19	Forego125noTrue Knight123½Proud and Bold122nk	Just up	5
8Dec73- 8Aqu	fst 1⅛	:454 1:10 1:35 1:471	Discovery H-G3	6	5	37	34	11½	1¾	Gustines H	127	*.60	100-13	Forego127¾MyGallant1225[D]KeytotheKingdom1131	Driving	7
24Nov73- 8Aqu	fst 1 3/16	:462 1:11 1:36 1:543	Roamer H-G2	9	4	514	32½	13	15	Gustines H	123	*2.10	89-13	Forego1235My Gallant1212½Twice a Prince1141	Handily	10
10Nov73- 6Aqu	fst 7f	:233 :463 1:102 1:223 3↑	Alw 12000	2	5	35½	36	34	34	Gustines H	122	*.90	84-22	North Sea1152¾Tap the Tree1141¼Forego1223½	Evenly	5
20Oct73- 8Aqu	fst 1	:233 :46 1:094 1:34	Jerome H-G2	7	6	63½	32½	2hd	2hd	Gustines H	124	2.20	97-14	Step Nicely118hdForego1243Linda's Chief1261¾	Gamely	10
8Oct73- 5Bel	fst 1	:234 :461 1:093 1:333 3↑	Alw 20000	3	3	31	1½	12½	15½	Gustines H	120	*1.60	100-07	Forego1205½Rule by Reason114noRoyal Owl12010	Ridden out	5
15Sep73- 8Bel	fst 1 1/16	:232 :462 1:102 1:402	Alw 20000	6	4	41½	1hd	13	12½	Gustines H	116	2.10	101-07	Forego1162½Arbees Boy1132Matinee Idol1133	Driving	8
1Sep73- 4Bel	fst 7f	:214 :442 1:091 1:221	Alw 20000	1	6	49½	25	13	1hd	Gustines H	113	*.60	91-10	Forego113hdCutlass113¾Jazziness116nk	Driving	6
24Aug73- 5Sar	fst 7f	:224 :451 1:083 1:21 3↑	Alw 12000	5	4	56½	56	47½	37¼	Anderson P	116	*.60	95-10	Prove Out1126½Cutlass109¾Forego1161¼	No excuse	6
9Jun73- 7Bel	fst 1 1/16	:232 :46 1:101 1:404	Alw 20000	4	5	53¼	12	17	19	Gustines H	111	*1.00	99-05	Forego1119AdaptiveAce114noIlIberightbck114no	Ridden out	10
30May73- 7Bel	fst 1	:231 :45 1:091 1:344	Withers-G2	3	5	56	45	43½	35	Anderson P	126	8.00	93-17	Lnda'sChief1263StoptheMusc1262Forgo126½	Between horses	6
5May73- 9CD	fst 1¼	:472 1:114 1:361 1:592	Ky Derby-G1	9	9	912	66	46½	411	Anderson P	126	28.60	92-10	Secretariat1262½Sham1268OurNative126½	Hit rail far turn	13
26Apr73- 6Kee	fst 1⅛	:463 1:11 1:37 1:493	Blue Grass-G1	5	6	611	52½	52¾	55	Anderson P	117	*2.60	84-18	My Gallant117hdOur Native1233½[DH]Warbucks117	No rally	9
31Mar73- 9GP	fst 1⅛	:471 1:102 1:342 1:472	Florida Derby-G1	6	4	56	33	23	23	Anderson P	118	*2.30	94-06	Royal and Regal1222Forego1181¼Restless Jet122hd	Gamely	8
24Mar73- 3GP	fst 7f	:221 :444 1:092 1:213	Alw 6500	1	8	65	53	11	12	Anderson P	119	*.30	96-12	Forego1192Cades Cove114noMalicious Music1143½	Driving	8
7Mar73- 9GP	fst 7f	:221 :443 1:082 1:204	Hutcheson-G3	1	7	56¾	37	24	23¼	Anderson P	116	2.40	97-10	Shecky Greene1223¼Forego1169Leo's Pisces1124½		7
	Away sluggishly															
10Feb73- 4Hia	fst 6f	:214 :452 1:094	Alw 6500	5	4	45½	32½	11	12½	Anderson P	122	*.60	95-18	Forego1222½Borage1152½Paternity1174	Easily	8
29Jan73- 1Hia	fst 6f	:222 :46 1:102	©Md Sp Wt	4	1	22	1hd	1½	18	Anderson P	122	*1.30	92-16	Forego1228Jonata1222Barclay Jet122½	Easily	11
17Jan73- 1Hia	fst 7f	:232 :461 1:11 1:233	©Md Sp Wt	9	11	97¼	89	79½	47	Anderson P	122	10.30	82-04	BuffaloLark1223¾TwoHarbrs1222CommandrLiz1221¼	Bumped	12

Past Performances of Great Horses of the 20th Century

Holy Bull

gr. c. 1991, by Great Above (Minnesota Mac)–Sharon Brown, by Al Hattab — Lifetime record: 16 13 0 0 $2,481,760

Own.– Warren A. Croll Jr
Br.– Pelican Stable (Fla)
Tr.– Warren A. Croll Jr

11Feb95- 9GP	fst 1⅛	:46^{2} 1:10^{3} 1:36^{3} 1:49^{3}	3↑ Donn H-G1	9 2 2^{2} — — —	Smith ME	127	*.30	--	Cigar115 5½ Primitive Hall112 1½ Bonus Money112 3½		9
	Pulled up 5½ furlong pole,lame left front										
22Jan95- 9GP	fst 7f	:22^{3} :45^{1} 1:09^{3} 1:22	3↑ Olympic H 100k	5 3 2^{1} 2^{hd} 1 1½ 1 2½	Smith ME	126	*.40	93-15	Holy Bull126 2½ Birdonthewire119 2¾ Patton115 ¾		6
	Raced well out in the track early,six wide top str,ridden out										
17Sep94- 8Bel	fst 1⅛	:46^{2} 1:10^{2} 1:34^{3} 1:46^{4}	3↑ Woodward-G1	5 2 2^{1} 1½ 1^{3} 1^{5}	Smith ME	121	*.90	97-10	Holy Bull121 5 Devil His Due126 1½ Colonial Affair126 3½		8
	Bump brk,ridden out										
20Aug94- 7Sar	wf 1¼	:46^{1} 1:10^{2} 1:35^{4} 2:02	Travers-G1	1 2 2^{hd} 1^{4} 1 1½ 1^{nk}	Smith ME	126	*.80	94-06	Holy Bull126 nk Concern126 17 Tabasco Cat126 1	Hard drive	5
31Jly94-10Mth	fst 1⅛	:47^{2} 1:11^{2} 1:35^{4} 1:48^{1}	Haskell Inv H-G1	3 1 1^{2} 1 2½ 1 1½ 1 1¾	Smith ME	126	*.20	93-07	Holy Bull126 1¾ Meadow Flight118 1¾ Concern118 1	Ridden out	6
3Jly94- 8Bel	fst 1 1/16	:22^{2} :45^{1} 1:09^{2} 1:41	Dwyer-G2	1 1 1^{1} 1 1½ 1^{3} 1 6¾	Smith ME	124	*.30	97-14	Holy Bull124 6¾ Twining122 5 Bay Street Star119 9	Handily	4
30May94- 8Bel	fst 1	:22^{4} :45 1:09^{2} 1:33^{4}	3↑ Metropolitan H-G1	6 1 1^{1} 1½ 1 2½ 1 5½	Smith ME	112	*1.00	94-09	HolyBull112 5½ CherokeeRun118 no DevilHisDue122 2	Driving	10
7May94- 8CD	sly 1¼	:47^{1} 1:11^{4} 1:37^{3} 2:03^{3}	Kentucky Derby-G1	4 6 5 3½ 9^{9} 12^{12} 12 18¼	Smith ME	126	*2.20	76-06	Go for Gin126 2 Strodes Creek126 2½ Blumin Affair126 ¾		14
	Off slow,in tight start,tired badly										
16Apr94- 9Kee	fst 1⅛	:47^{4} 1:12^{3} 1:37^{4} 1:50	Blue Grass-G2	1 1 1^{3} 1^{2} 1 1½ 1 3½	Smith ME	121	*.60	84-26	Holy Bull121 3½ Valiant Nature121 5 Mahogany Hall121 2¼		7
	Sharp,ridden out										
12Mar94-10GP	fst 1⅛	:46 1:10 1:34^{4} 1:47^{2}	Florida Derby-G1	6 1 1 2½ 1 2½ 1^{5} 1 5¾	Smith ME	122	2.70	100-06	HolyBull122 5¾ RidetheRails122 no Halo'sImag122 1	Ridden out	14
19Feb94- 9GP	gd 1 1/16	:22^{4} :45^{3} 1:10^{2} 1:44^{3}	Fountain of Youth-G2	4 1 1½ 2^{1} 6^{8} 6 24¼	Smith ME	119	*1.30	63-19	Dehere119 ¾ GoforGin119 1¼ RidetheRails117 3¾	Stopped badly	6
30Jan94- 9GP	fst 7f	:21^{3} :44 1:08^{1} 1:21^{1}	Hutcheson-G2	1 4 1 1½ 1 1½ 2 2½ 1¾	Smith ME	122	*.50	97-11	Holy Bull122 ¾ Patton113 3 You and I119 3		5
	Broke inward start,raced well off rail,ridden out										
23Oct93-11Crc	fst 1 1/16	:23 :46^{2} 1:11^{3} 1:46^{1}	Ⓡ In Reality 400k	9 1 1 1½ 1^{2} 1^{4} 1 7½	Smith ME	120	*.50	88-12	HolyBull120 7½ RusticLight120 1 ForwardtoLd120 1½	Ridden out	12
18Sep93- 6Bel	sly 7f	:22^{2} :45^{3} 1:10^{1} 1:23^{1}	Futurity-G1	2 1 1^{1} 1^{1} 1 2½ 1½	Smith ME	122	3.10	87-14	Holy Bull122 ½ Dehere122 5 Prenup122 8	All out	6
2Sep93- 7Bel	fst 6½f	:22 :44^{1} 1:09^{4} 1:17	Alw 28000	3 1 1½ 1^{hd} 1 2½ 1^{7}	Smith ME	119	*.90	88-15	Holy Bull119 7 Goodbye Doeny117 3 End Sweep119 ½	Ridden out	6
	Previously owned by Targan Stable										
14Aug93- 7Mth	fst 5½f	:21^{3} :44^{4} :57^{1} 1:03^{4}	Md Sp Wt	1 3 1^{1} 1 1½ 1 1½ 1 2½	Rivera L Jr	118	*1.10	95-17	Holy Bull118 2½ Palance118 7½ Hold My Tongue118 9	Driving	9

John Henry

b. g. 1975, by Ole Bob Bowers (Prince Blessed)–Once Double, by Double Jay — Lifetime record: 83 39 15 9 $6,597,947

Own.– Dotsam Stable
Br.– Golden Chance Farm Inc (Ky)
Tr.– Ronald McAnally

13Oct84- 8Med	fm 1⅜Ⓣ	:46^{4} 1:11 1:35^{1} 2:13	3↑ Ballantine H 900k	4 8 8^{9} 5 3½ 3 1½ 1 2¾	McCarron CJ	126	*.60	100-06	JohnHnry126 2¾ Who'sforDinner115 hd Win120 1	Came out,clear	12
22Sep84- 8Bel	fm 1½Ⓣ	:48^{4} 1:13 2:01^{3} 2:25^{1}	3↑ Turf Classic-G1	4 1 1 1½ 1½ 1½ 1^{nk}	McCarron CJ	126	*1.00	98-10	JohnHnry126 nk Win126 4 Majesty'sPrnc126 hd	Strong handling	6
26Aug84- 9AP	fm 1¼Ⓣ	:48^{2} 1:12^{2} 1:37^{2} 2:01^{2}	3↑ Bud Arl Million-G1	6 4 3 1½ 3^{2} 1^{hd} 1 1¾	McCarron CJ	126	*1.10	87-15	JohnHenry126 1¾ RoyalHeroine122 3 GatodelSol126 no	Drew out	12
23Jly84- 8Hol	fm 1½Ⓣ	:47^{1} 1:10^{3} 1:59^{4} 2:24^{4}	3↑ Sunset H-G1	7 5 4^{7} 3^{2} 2^{1} 1^{1}	McCarron CJ	126	*1.20	96-08	JhnHnry126 1 LoadtheCannons118 1½ PairofDeuces113 nk	Driving	9
24Jun84- 8Hol	fst 1¼	:47 1:10 1:35 2:00^{2}	3↑ Hol Gold Cup H-G1	4 4 4 3½ 3^{2} 3^{2} 2^{2}	McCarron CJ	125	2.60	87-20	DesertWine122 2 JohnHnry125 1½ Sari'sDreamer114 nk	Game try	8
28May84- 8Hol	fm 1½Ⓣ	:49 1:12^{3} 2:01^{1} 2:25	3↑ Hol Inv'l H-G1	1 2 3 1½ 3 1½ 3^{nk} 1½	McCarron CJ	126	*.80	95-08	JohnHnry126 ½ GalantVert116 2¾ LoadtheCannons120 1¼	Driving	9
6May84- 8GG	fm 1⅜Ⓣ	:47^{2} 1:12 1:35^{4} 2:13	3↑ Golden Gate H-G3	6 3 3 4½ 2^{2} 1½ 1^{2}	McCarron CJ	125	*.50	103-09	John Henry125 2 Silveyville117 6 Lucence116 6	Slow st.,clear	6

Past Performances of Great Horses of the 20th Century

1Apr84-8SA	fm 1½Ⓣ	:482 1:132 2:022 2:264	3↑ San Luis Rey-G1	4	2	21	1½	2½	3¾	McCarron CJ	126	1.60	80-17	Interco126nkGato del Sol126½John Henry1263½	Weakened	10
4Mar84-8SA	fst 1¼	:453 1:10 1:35 2:003	4↑ S Anita H-G1	10	7	76¼	45	56	58	McCarron CJ	127	*2.40	78-17	Interco1212¾Journey at Sea1171½Gato del Sol1171¾		12
	Stumble after start															
11Dec83-8Hol	gd 1⅜Ⓣ	:494 1:153 1:40 2:163	3↑ Hol Turf Cup-G1	4	2	22½	1½	2hd	1½	McCarron CJ	126	*1.50	72-27	John Henry126½Zalataia1231½Palikaraki1261¼	Came again	12
13Nov83-8SA	gd 1½Ⓣ	:472 1:131 2:034 2:291	3↑ Oak Tree Inv'l-G1	2	5	31	43½	31	2½	McCarron CJ	126	*.80	68-31	Zalataia123½JohnHnry1261½LoadthCnnons1223½	Held gamely	9
15Oct83-8Bel	fst 1½	:48 1:123 2:01 2:261	3↑ J C Gold Cup-G1	7	6	53	45	55	56¾	McCarron CJ	126	2.90	82-14	Slew o'Gold1213Highland Blade126nkBounding Basque1211½		11
	Weakened															
28Aug83-9AP	gd 1¼Ⓣ	:503 1:154 1:413 2:042	3↑ Arl Million-G1	13	3	21	2½	2½	2nk	McCarron CJ	126	*1.40	72-28	Tolomeo118nkJohnHenry126½Nijinsky'sSecret1262	Sharp try	14
4Jly83-8Hol	fm 1⅛Ⓣ	:49 1:13 1:363 1:482	3↑ American H-G2	1	3	33	21½	2½	11¼	McCarron CJ	127	2.10	88-12	JohnHenry1271¼PrinceFlorimund120½Tonzarun114no	Driving	8
28Nov82♦Tokyo(Jpn)	fm*1½ⓉLH	2:27	3↑ Japan Cup-G1 Stk801000						138	Shoemaker W	126	*.90		Half Iced121nkAll Along117nkApril Run1211	Prominent to stretch	15
13Nov82-6Med	gd 1¼	:473 1:121 1:37 2:012	3↑ Med Cup H-G2	2	5	37½	44¼	35½	35¾	Shoemaker W	129	*1.10	89-15	Mehmet1181¼ThirtyEghtPcs1134½JhnHnry1294½	Lacked a bid	9
31Oct82-8SA	fm 1½Ⓣ	:472 1:103 1:593 2:24	3↑ Oak Tree Inv'l-G1	6	4	44	21½	2½	12½	Shoemaker W	126	1.40	95-05	John Henry1262½Craelius1221½Regalberto1262	Drew clear	7
17Oct82-8SA	fm 1¼Ⓣ	:471 1:11 1:343 1:583	3↑ C F Burke H-G2	6	3	31½	42	42¾	41½	Shoemaker W	129	*.80	92-06	Mehmet117hdCraelius1141½It's the One124no	Evenly	7
28Mar82-8SA	fm 1½Ⓣ	:462 1:102 2:00 2:24	4↑ San Luis Rey-G1	3	3	33	33	43½	34¾	Shoemaker W	126	*.50	90-05	Perrault1263¼Exploded1261½John Henry126no	Evenly	5
7Mar82-8SA	fst 1¼	:45 1:09 1:342 1:59	4↑ S Anita H-G1	9	8	913	51¼	2½	2no	Shoemaker W	130	*1.30	94-07	ⒹPerrault126noJhnHenry1303¼It'stheOne123nk	Impeded end	11
	Placed first by disqualification															
6Dec81-8Hol	fm 1½Ⓣ	:49 1:13 2:03 2:264	3↑ Hol Turf Cup 550k	5	1	12	11	3½	42	Shoemaker W	126	*.40	84-11	Providential II126nkQueen to Conquer1231½Goldiko126nk		10
	Weakened;Previously trained by Victor J. Nickerson															
8Nov81-8SA	fm 1½Ⓣ	:472 1:102 1:593 2:232	3↑ Oak Tree Inv'l-G1	4	3	1½	1½	2hd	1nk	Shoemaker W	126	*.40	98-02	John Henry126nkSpence Bay1264½The Bart126no	Driving	7
10Oct81-8Bel	fst 1½	:48 1:123 2:021 2:282	3↑ J C Gold Cup-G1	8	5	42½	21	11½	1hd	Shoemaker W	126	*3.10	78-14	JohnHenry126hdPeatMoss126¾Relaxing123hd	Bore in,driving	11
	Previously trained by Ronald McAnally															
30Aug81-6AP	sf 1¼Ⓣ	:501 1:153 1:422 2:073	3↑ Arl Million 1000k	12	8	86½	56	31	1no	Shoemaker W	126	*1.10e	--	John Henry126noThe Bart1262¼Madam Gay117½	Just up	12
	Previously trained by Victor J. Nickerson															
11Jly81-8Bel	fm 1½Ⓣ	:494 1:142 2:03 2:264	3↑ Sword Dancer-G3	3	3	31½	11	11½	13½	Shoemaker W	126	*.30	90-13	JohnHnry1263½PassingZone1261¾PeatMoss1261¾	Ridden out	5
	Previously trained by Ronald McAnally															
14Jun81-8Hol	fst 1¼	:453 1:093 1:344 2:002	3↑ Hol Gold Cup H-G1	7	7	66¼	65¾	46½	42¾	Pincay L Jr	130	*1.20	86-16	ⒹCaterman120hdEleven Stitches1222½Super Moment117nk		10
	Wide late															
17May81-8Hol	fm 1½Ⓣ	:511 1:151 2:04 2:274	3↑ Hol Inv'l H-G1	5	2	2½	2½	1½	1¾	Pincay L Jr	130	*.40	81-12	John Henry130¾Caterman122hdGalaxy Libra118nk	Driving	7
29Mar81-8SA	fm 1½Ⓣ	:46 1:104 2:00 2:251	4↑ San Luis Rey-G1	1	2	21½	22	1hd	12¼	Pincay L Jr	126	*.20	89-11	John Henry1262¼Obraztsovy1261½Fiestero126hd	Easily	6
8Mar81-8SA	fst 1¼	:452 1:092 1:341 1:592	4↑ S Anita H-G1	3	7	65¼	22	1hd	11	Pincay L Jr	128	1.90	92-11	John Henry1281King Go Go1171¼Exploded115no	Driving	11
16Feb81-8SA	fm 1½Ⓣ	:474 1:113 1:59 2:24	4↑ San Luis Obispo H-G2	4	1	11	11	12½	11½	Pincay L Jr	127	*.50	95-05	John Henry1271½Galaxy Libra1195½Zor1151½	Ridden out	6
16Nov80-8SA	fm 1½Ⓣ	:454 1:101 1:582 2:232	3↑ Oak Tree Inv-G1	6	5	56½	66¾	37½	11½	Pincay L Jr	126	*1.50	98-02	John Henry1261½Balzac126½Bold Tropic126nk	Drew clear	10
	Previously trained by Victor J. Nickerson															
25Oct80-8Aqu	sf 1½Ⓣ	:514 1:192 2:13 2:393	3↑ Turf Classic-G1	4	1	12	23	25	38	Pincay L Jr	126	*2.00	35-57	Anifa1233Golden Act1265John Henry126nk	Weakened	8
4Oct80-8Bel	fst 1½	:494 1:15 2:051 2:301	3↑ J C Gold Cup-G1	3	2	21	2½	23	25½	Cordero A Jr	126	*.70	63-19	Temperence Hill1215½John Henry1262Ivory Hunter1263¼		7
	Best of others															
7Sep80-8Bel	fm 1¼Ⓣ	:483 1:122 1:362 1:592	3↑ Brighton Beach H-G3	5	1	1hd	11½	11½	1nk	Cordero A Jr	125	*.40	97-15	John Henry125nkPremier Ministre1174Match the Hatch1133		5
	Driving															
12Jly80-8Bel	fm 1½Ⓣ	:47 1:111 2:01 2:251	3↑ Sword Dancer 161k	2	2	21	1½	2hd	21¼	McHargue DG	126	*.80	97-15	Tiller1261¼John Henry1265Sten12612	Gamely	4
14Jun80-8Bel	fm 1⅜Ⓣ	:473 1:113 1:352 2:131	3↑ Bowling Green H-G2	3	1	1½	1hd	1½	2nk	McHargue DG	128	*1.80	96-15	Sten117nkJohn Henry1281Lyphard's Wish120nk	Brushed	9
	Previously trained by Ronald McAnally															
26May80-8Hol	fm 1½Ⓣ	:483 1:123 2:012 2:252	3↑ Hol Inv'l H-G1	4	1	14	12½	1½	1nk	McHargue DG	128	*.90	93-09	John Henry128nkBalzac1201½Go West Young Man1172½		10
	Fully extended															

Past Performances of Great Horses of the 20th Century

6Apr80- 8SA fm *1¾Ⓣ :46 1:594 2:464 4↑ S Juan Capistrano H-G1 3 1 12 11½ 12 11¼ McHargue DG 126 *2.20 93-08 John Henry1261¼Fiestero114nkThe Very One113hd Driving 11
16Mar80- 8SA fm 1½Ⓣ :464 1:104 1:592 2:23 4↑ San Luis Rey-G1 3 2 21 2½ 2½ 11½ McHargue DG 126 6.90 100-00 John Henry1261½Relaunch126noSilver Eagle126no Drew out 7
23Feb80-10Hia fm 1½Ⓣ 2:292 3↑ Hia Turf Cup H-G2 10 2 31½ 11 11½ 1½ McHargue DG 122 2.30 84-22 JohnHenry122½DancingMaster1135IvoryHunter111hd Driving 10
20Jan80- 8SA fst 1¼ :47 1:113 1:364 2:013 4↑ San Marcos H-G3 2 1 11½ 11 11 12½ McHargue DG 124 *.80 85-17 John Henry1242½El Fantastico1132¼Commemorativo110nk 5
Handily
1Jan80- 8SA gd 1⅛Ⓣ :48 1:121 1:371 1:494 4↑ San Gabriel H-G3 4 2 22 21½ 2½ 1hd McHargue DG 123 *1.70 78-22 John Henry123hdSmasher1115As de Copas1173 Driving 9
8Dec79- 8BM fm 1⅛Ⓣ :471 1:111 1:363 1:493 3↑ Bay Meadows H 114k 7 5 44½ 83¾ 1hd 21¼ McHargue DG 123 2.70 103-00 Leonotis1181¼John Henry1234Capt. Don117½ Held on 14
5Nov79- 8SA fm 1⅛Ⓣ :461 1:102 1:352 1:48 3↑ HP Russell H (Div 2) 45k 5 2 11 11 12 13¼ McHargue DG 122 *.70 87-15 JohnHenry1223¼Rusty Canyon114hdLeonotis1172 Ridden out 8
14Oct79- 8SA fm 1¼Ⓣ :454 1:10 1:343 1:591 3↑ C F Burke H-G2 5 3 21½ 1hd 1hd 21¼ McHargue DG 118 3.40 90-09 Silver Eagle1151¼John Henry118½Shagbark1181¼ Gamely 9
Previously trained by Victor J. Nickerson
10Sep79- 7Bel fm 1 1/16Ⓣ :24 :47 1:11 1:414 3↑ Alw 30000 2 1 13 11½ 12 12 Santiago A 117 1.90 87-17 John Henry1172Silent Cal117½Waya119no Ridden out 4
22Aug79- 7Sar fm 1⅛Ⓣ :462 1:111 1:343 1:462 3↑ Alw 27000 3 1 11½ 11½ 11½ 12½ Santiago A 115 *1.40 95-13 John Henry1152½Told114¾Poison Ivory1224 Driving 7
29Jly79- 7Pen sly 1 1/16 :232 :471 1:114 1:443 3↑ Capital City H 33k 7 5 41½ 31 41¼ 42 Santiago A 113 2.30 81-23 Horatius118nkTanthem1121½Shy Jester115nk Hung 7
14Jly79- 8Bel fm 1 1/16Ⓣ :233 :47 1:104 1:413 3↑ Sword Dancer 57k 2 1 2hd 21 22 22½ Santiago A 119 5.70 85-11 Darby Creek Road1192½John Henry1194Poison Ivory1191¾ 8
Best of others
6Jly79- 6Atl fm 1 1/16Ⓣ :23 :462 1:102 1:411 3↑ Sunrise H 35k 2 2 21½ 1½ 1hd 22¼ McCauley WH 111 *1.50 98-09 Chati1182¼John Henry111½Fed Funds1154 Tired 11
24Jun79-10Suf fst 1⅛ :453 1:10 1:36 1:483 3↑ Mass H-G3 9 4 68¾ 84¼ 96 108½ Borden DA 108 6.90 89-21 Island Sultan110¾Western Front113½Quiet Jay1161½ Tired 13
5Jun79- 8Mth fst 1 :232 :47 1:114 1:373 4↑ Alw 18000 1 3 2hd 13 18 114 McCauley WH 119 *.90 85-23 John Henry11914Thou Fool119noM.A.'s Date1131¾ Driving 7
26May79- 6Mth fst 6f :22 :443 1:104 4↑ Alw 16000 4 4 53½ 41¾ 21½ 2½ McCauley WH 117 6.90 85-19 ReallyandTruly117½JohnHnry1171¼Kintla'sFolly1153 Gamely 7
Previously trained by Robert A. Donato
29Oct78- 6Pen fm 1 1/16Ⓣ 1:412 Chcltetwn H (Div 2) 22k 5 2 21 1½ 12 11 Broussard R 124 *.70 -- John Henry1241Scythian Gold1166½Berlin's Burning1122 7
Ridden out
15Oct78- 5SA fm 1¼Ⓣ :453 1:094 1:342 1:59 3↑ C F Burke H (Div 1)-G2 2 1 1hd 1hd 44 65 Baltazar C 117 2.80 87-08 Star of Erin II113noImproviser1152¾Mr. Redoy1181¼ Tired 9
8Oct78- 8SA fm 1⅛Ⓣ :46 1:102 1:351 1:474 Volante H-G3 6 4 42 41 31½ 3½ Baltazar C 122 *2.30 87-12 WaysideStation117noAprilAxe120½JohnHenry1222 In close 11
16Sep78- 8AP gd 1 1/16Ⓣ :241 :484 1:131 1:454 Round Table H-G3 6 1 11 13 18 112 Amy J 121 *.50 80-30 JhnHnry12112GordieH.109noBringtheMoney111no Ridden out 9
9Sep78- 5Bel fm 7fⓉ :232 :46 1:093 1:22 3↑ Alw 21000 1 1 11½ 11½ 11 11½ Amy J 113 3.60 94-09 John Henry1131½Gab Bag1174Proud Arion1171¼ Hard ridden 8
18Aug78- 7Sar fm 1 1/16Ⓣ :251 :49 1:12 1:41 3↑ Alw 23000 7 2 2½ 2hd 44 47¼ Amy J 112 5.10 85-08 Blue Baron1172¼Quip1141Stir the Embers1194 Weakened 8
8Aug78- 7Sar gd 7f :223 :444 1:081 1:202 3↑ Alw 23000 2 2 31½ 24 38 514 Santiago A 113 2.90 89-04 DarbyCreekRoad11311Liberal117¾GoldenReserve117¾ Tired 6
29Jly78- 8Bel fm 1 1/16Ⓣ :233 :46 1:103 1:41 Lexington H-G2 5 1 12½ 12 11 2hd Santiago A 112 5.90 91-11 Mac Diarmida126hdJohn Henry1124¼Ashikaga110hd Gamely 9
19Jly78- 8Bel fm 1Ⓣ :24 :473 1:104 1:351 Hill Prince H 37k 5 1 2hd 2hd 2½ 21½ Santiago A 111 3.60 92-12 DarbyCreekRd1211½JhnHnry1112ScythianGold1116 Gamely 9
1Jly78- 8Mth fm 1 1/16Ⓣ :232 :47 1:11 1:432 Lamplighter H-G3 4 2 2hd 1hd 1½ 3½ Santiago A 112 *1.50 83-16 North Course112nkHoratius114nkJohnHenry112no Weakened 9
25Jun78- 6Bel hd 1 1/16Ⓣ :232 :47 1:102 1:411 3↑ Alw 18000 2 5 62½ 52 42 1nk Santiago A 112 3.40 90-07 John Henry112nkTurn of Coin1171¾Valinsky1171¾ Driving 9
1Jun78- 7Bel fm 1 1/16Ⓣ :231 :47 1:11 1:413 Clm 35000 1 2 21 1½ 17 114 Santiago A 117 3.30 88-12 JhnHnry11714ContinentalCousin117¾CptnPeter1132¼ Driving 10
21May78- 2Aqu fst 6f :224 :471 1:123 Clm 25000 4 4 32½ 1½ 11 12½ Santiago A 117 12.30 80-27 John Henry1172½Please See Me1171½Orfanik115nk Driving 9
Previously owned and trained by H. Snowden Jr
11Apr78- 7Kee fst 6f :22 :45 :59 1:093 Alw 8500 4 4 47½ 46 48½ 49½ McKnight J 113 6.40 84-15 Johnny Blade1074½Schottis112½Jester Beau1154½ No mishap 6
Previously owned by D. Lingo & C. Madere; previously trained by Phil Marino
22Mar78- 9FG fst 6f :23 :47 1:12 Clm 25000 7 6 78 89 64¾ 34 Copling D 114 25.10 81-16 Kim's Red1142Bunny Wag1122John Henry1141 Rallied 9
22Feb78- 9FG fst 6f :223 :463 1:113 Clm 20000 11 2 98¾ 98¾ 1015 1020 Elmer D 112 b 19.10 67-19 AdriaticEditions1144Bladesville113½Kim'sRed1141 Outrun 11
15Feb78- 6FG fst 6f :22 :462 1:113 Clm 25000 5 5 85¼ 61¼ 63¾ 66¼ Guajardo A 112 b 4.90 81-19 MercrCounty1121½Gen'sLTroy1121AdrtcEdtons1141 No mishap 8
4Feb78- 6FG fst 1 40 :252 :493 1:151 1:43 Alw 7500 2 9 84¾ 83½ 53¼ 55¾ Guajardo A 112 17.10 72-23 HogTown114¾TrafficWarning114hdSmokePole1092½ No mishap 10
23Jan78- 8FG gd 1 40 :241 :473 1:131 1:424 Alw 7500 7 4 42¾ 52¾ 86¾ 86½ Guajardo A 112 22.20 72-24 CabriniGreen117½DayTimeTudor1121As in Elbow112no Tired 9
31Dec77- 9FG fst 6f :22 :46 1:121 Sugar Bowl H 50k 4 12 127¾ 127½ 1210 1114 McKnight J 113 16.80 70-21 CabriniGreen122½CouponRate113¾SpecialHonr1101¼ Outrun 12

Past Performances of Great Horses of the 20th Century

17Dec77-6FG	gd 6f	:223 :472 1:122	©Alw 7000	1 6 64¼ 62¾ 53¾ 31¼	McKnight J	113	7.90	82-18	CabriniGreen1201¼CouponRate113hdJohnHenry113hd	Rallied	12
3Dec77-8FG	fst 6f	:222 :462 1:114	Alw 7000	1 7 75¾ 54 51¾ 43½	McKnight J	120	8.70	82-19	DragonTamer1171½TrafficWarnng1171¼HogTwn117¾	Rallied	11
19Nov77-9FG	fst 6f	:221 :464 1:124	©Sthern Hospitality 19k	8 12 105 63¼ 64¼ 59	Guajardo A	122	9.60	72-22	CbrniGreen1144MajesticSpiral1122½HogTown112hd	Late bid	12
5Sep77-11EvD	sly 6f	:232 :47 1:01 1:142	Lafayette Futurity 86k	1 6 45 32½ 1hd	Guajardo A	120	5.10	79-26	JohnHenry120hdLilLizaJayne1171SoundNote1203½	Driving	12
25Aug77-7EvD	gd 6f	:223 :462 1:002 1:13	Sp Wt 2700	8 5 33 32 2½	Guajardo A	120	4.10	85-21	Note to Mame117½John Henry1203Tudor Luck117hd		9
6Aug77-7EvD	sly 5f	:224 :483 1:001	Alw 2400	4 9 54½ 1hd 13	Guajardo A	120	3.00	82-19	John Henry1203Motor Dude1201½Bell's Chief1174	Driving	12
29Jly77-8JnD	fst *6f	:233 :473 1:02 1:152	Handicap 7500	9 9 - - - -	Munster L	102	3.90	- -	RunLikeHeck1191CapGardnr1072HarktheLedr1102	Lost rider	9
2Jly77-6JnD	sly 5f	:23 :481 1:011	Alw 4500	2 5 42 33 23	Spiehler G	116	*2.60	81-19	KindaNughty1133JhnHnry1161MossBluffKd1152	Bid,weakened	7
7Jun77-8JnD	fst 4f	:22 :471	Alw 3500	4 6 59 55½ 31	Spiehler G	120	14.60	89-11	DancngMeadw109¾DancingJudge120nkJhnHnry1201	Rallied	8
20May77-1JnD	fst 4f	:23 :481	Md Sp Wt	1 7 54½ 34 1no	Spiehler G	120	1.70	85-15	JhnHnry120noYouSexyThing1172Ricky'sChoice112¾	Driving	8

Kelso

dkbbr. g. 1957, by Your Host (Alibhai)–Maid of Flight, by Count Fleet
Lifetime record: 63 39 12 2 $1,977,896
Own.– Bohemia Stable
Br.– Mrs Richard C. duPont (Ky)
Tr.– C.H. Hanford

2Mar66-9Hia	fst 6f	:222 :444 1:10	4↑ Alw 10000	8 3 87¾ 89¾ 77¾ 44½	Boland W	113	3.30	89-13	DavusII119hdTimeTested1191CountryFrind1133½	Closed well	8
22Sep65-7Aqu	fst 1¼	:473 1:12 1:364 2:024	3↑ Stymie H 27k	6 4 45½ 1½ 16 18	Valenzuela I	128	*.30	84-17	Kelso1288[D]O'Har107¾Ky.Ponr110¾	With complete authority	6
6Sep65-7Aqu	fst 1⅛	:481 1:121 1:363 1:49	3↑ Aqueduct 108k	7 5 510 56 48 49	Valenzuela I	130	*1.00	82-14	Malicious1163Pluck116noRmnBrothr1216	Lacked any response	7
7Aug65-6Sar	fst 1⅛	:471 1:111 1:364 1:494	4↑ Whitney 54k	3 4 44 45 22½ 1no	Valenzuela I	130	*1.20	96-08	Kelso130noMalicious1146PiaStar127nk	Up in final strides	5
24Jly65-7Aqu	fst 1¼	:47 1:102 1:35 2:003	3↑ Brooklyn H 107k	1 5 56½ 43½ 33½ 34	Valenzuela I	132	*1.20	91-10	PiaStar1212RomnBrothr1212Kelso1321½	Hung under impost	5
10Jly65-8Del	fst 1 1/16	:241 :482 1:122 1:422	3↑ Diamond State H 21k	2 2 21½ 2½ 1½ 13¼	Valenzuela I	130	*.30	97-13	Kelso1303¼Kilmoray1093Big Brigade114no	Going away	4
29Jun65-8Mth	fst 6f	:222 :454 1:111	4↑ Alw 5000	8 3 56 86¾ 54¼ 3½	Boland W	122	*.50	85-23	Cachto117noCommunqu122½Klso122hd	Showed strong late bid	8
11Nov64-7Lrl	hd 1½Ⓣ	:464 1:102 2:00 2:234	3↑ D C Int'l 150k	5 2 24 1½ 13 14½	Valenzuela I	126	*1.20	112-00	Kelso1264½Gun Bow1269Aniline1223½	Drew out handily	8
31Oct64-7Aqu	fst 2	:484 2:533 3:191	3↑ J C Gold Cup 108k	2 5 43 11½ 14 15½	Valenzuela I	124	*.45	101-14	Kelso1245½Roman Brother1196Quadrangle11916	Easy score	6
3Oct64-7Aqu	gd 1¼	:481 1:121 1:371 2:022	3↑ Woodward 108k	3 2 21½ 2hd 1hd 2no	Valenzuela I	126	*.95	86-22	Gun Bow126noKelso1264Quadrangle12125	Bore in slightly	5
7Sep64-7Aqu	fst 1⅛	:463 1:104 1:353 1:483	3↑ Aqueduct 107k	3 2 25 21½ 1½ 1¾	Valenzuela I	128	2.20	98-16	Klso128¾GnBow1286Sadm1194½	Responded to strong urging	5
27Aug64-7Sar	hd 1⅛Ⓣ	1:463	3↑ Alw 9500	4 2 22½ 2hd 1½ 12½	Valenzuela I	118	*.30	102-00	Klso1182½Knghtsboro1161½RockyThumb1205	Scored in hand	8
25Jly64-7Aqu	fst 1¼	:461 1:101 1:35 1:593	3↑ Brooklyn H 110k	5 6 69 58½ 610 514	Valenzuela I	130	*.85	88-12	GnBow12212OldnTimes122noSunriseFlght113hd	Bumped gate	8
18Jly64-8Mth	fst 1¼	:451 1:101 1:353 2:014	3↑ Monmouth H 107k	1 5 56 43¼ 3½ 2nk	Valenzuela I	130	*.60	93-17	Mngo127nkKlso1304½GunBow12418	Hung through late stages	5
4Jly64-7Aqu	fst 1¼	:472 1:112 1:364 2:014	3↑ Suburban H 110k	6 4 34 32 31½ 2hd	Valenzuela I	131	*1.35	91-17	Iron Peg116hdKelso13140lden Times128¾	Getting to winner	8
25Jun64-7Aqu	fst 1⅛	:483 1:124 1:371 1:50	3↑ Handicap 15000	5 4 43½ 21½ 11½ 11¼	Valenzuela I	136	*.55	91-15	Kelso1361¼TropicalBreeze114½SunrisFlght12110	Mild drive	5
6Jun64-8Hol	fst 1 1/16	:224 :461 1:102 1:413	3↑ Californian 115k	3 5 65 75¼ 78¾ 68	Valenzuela I	127	*1.40	79-14	Mustard Plaster1111½Mr. Consistency1231½ColordoKing1232½		10
	Impeded										
23May64-8Hol	fst 7f	:214 :44 1:084 1:212	3↑ Los Angeles H 55k	9 1 713 98½ 913 89¼	Valenzuela I	130	*1.70	84-13	Cyrano124hdQuitaDude1142Admiral'sVoyag121no	Dull effort	9
11Nov63-7Lrl	fm 1½Ⓣ	:483 1:133 2:033 2:272	3↑ D C Int'l 150k	8 4 41½ 21 2½ 2½	Valenzuela I	126	*.50	93-14	Mongo126½Klso12612Nyrcos1223	Sluggish start,game effort	10
19Oct63-7Aqu	fst 2	:482 2:30 2:551 3:22	3↑ J C Gold Cup 108k	1 4 2hd 12 16 14	Valenzuela I	124	*.15	87-14	Kelso1244Guadalcanal1245Garwol1243½	Speed in reserve	7
28Sep63-7Aqu	fst 1¼	:473 1:114 1:362 2:004	3↑ Woodward 108k	2 3 34 2½ 1½ 13½	Valenzuela I	126	*.25	96-13	Kelso1263½NeverBend1201½CrimsonSatn1266	Speed to spare	5
2Sep63-7Aqu	fst 1⅛	:49 1:124 1:371 1:494	3↑ Aqueduct 110k	7 3 41½ 31 12 15½	Valenzuela I	134	*.70	92-17	Kelso1345½CrimsonSatan129hdGrwol116no	Under mild urging	8
3Aug63-6Sar	fst 1⅛	:48 1:12 1:372 1:502	4↑ Whitney 55k	2 4 42½ 42½ 11 12½	Valenzuela I	130	*.35	93-14	Kelso1302½Saidam1111Sunrise County117hd	Easily the best	7
4Jly63-7Aqu	fst 1¼	:484 1:131 1:381 2:014	3↑ Suburban H 108k	7 3 33 31½ 11½ 11¼	Valenzuela I	133	*.45	91-13	Kelso1331¼Saidam1111½Garwol1121	Retained a safe margin	7
19Jun63-7Aqu	fst 1⅛	:474 1:113 1:36 1:484	3↑ Nassau County 27k	3 3 31½ 31 12 11½	Valenzuela I	132	*.30	97-07	Kelso1321½Lnvn114noPolyld1143	Cleverly rated,easy score	5

Past Performances of Great Horses of the 20th Century

Date–Race	Cond	Time	Race/Purse	Jockey	Wt	Odds	Rating	Result / Comment
23Mar63-8Bow	fst 1 1/16	:242 :481 1:12 1:43	3↑ J B Campbell H 109k	Valenzuela I	131	*.80	99-15	Kelso131 1/2 Crimson Satan124 hd Gushing Wind116 6 — Hard drive 6
16Mar63-8GP	fst 1 1/8	:481 1:211 1:372 2:031	3↑ Gulf Park H 110k	Valenzuela I	130	*.20	83-20	Kelso130 3/4 Sensitivo1129 Jay Fox113 1/2 — Speed in reserve 6
23Feb63-7Hia	fst 1 1/8	:483 1:221 1:362 2:014	3↑ Widener H 128k	Valenzuela I	131	*.45	87-18	Beau Purple1252 1/4 Kelso1313 hd Heroshogala1104 — Best of others 9
9Feb63-7Hia	fst 1 1/8	:462 1:104 1:354 1:484	3↑ Seminole H 58k	Valenzuela I	128	2.35	91-19	Kelso1282 Ridan1129 1/2 Senstvo1153 1/2 — Rallied wide,drew away 6
30Jan63-8Hia	fst 7f	:23 :46 1:101 1:224	3↑ Palm Beach H 29k	Valenzuela I	128	2.45	89-16	Ridan1273 1/2 Jaipur1273 Merry Rulr1171 — Broke in stride,tired 5
1Dec62-8GS	fst 1 1/16	:491 1:15 2:051 2:301	3↑ Gov's Plate 54k	Valenzuela I	129	*.40	105-20	Kelso1295 Bass Clef1175 Polylad1178 — Drew away with ease 5
12Nov62-7Lrl	sf 1 1/16 T	:471 1:112 2:031 2:281	3↑ D C Int'l 125k	Valenzuela I	126	2.10	88-20	Matchl1128 1/2 Kelso1264 1/2 Carry Back126 5 — Easily best of rest 13
27Oct62-7Bel	sf 1 1/16 T	2:283	3↑ Man o' War 114k	Valenzuela I	126	*1.05	101-11	BeauPurple1262 Klso1265 1/2 ThAxII1261 1/2 — Finished very gamely 12
20Oct62-7Bel	fst 2	:493 2:282 2:533 3:194	3↑ J C Gold Cup 108k	Valenzuela I	124	*.25	103-08	Kelso1241 Guadalcanal1242 Nickel Boy1241 1/2 — Easily best 6
29Sep62-7Aqu	gd 1 1/4	:471 1:131 1:37 2:031	3↑ Woodward 115k	Valenzuela I	126	*.90	84-17	Kelso1264 1/2 Guadlcn1126 1/2 — Won as rider pleased 8
19Sep62-7Aqu	fst 1 1/4	:48 1:12 1:362 2:004	3↑ Stymie H 29k	Valenzuela I	128	*1.25	96-14	Klso128 2 1/4 Plyld114 hd Tutnkhmn110 hd — With complete authority 11
8Sep62-7Atl	fm 1 1/16 T	1:431	3↑ Alw 6000	Pierce D	113	*.40	93-05	Callthe Witness113 nk Art Market113 hd Windy Sands1131 1/2 — Tired 7
22Aug62-6Sar	fm 1 1/16 T	1:414	3↑ Alw 5000	Valenzuela I	124	*.25	97-03	Kelso1241 1/2 Callthe Witness1175 Fountain Hill1172 — Mild drive 7
14Jly62-8Mth	fst 1	:46 1:10 1:342 2:002	3↑ Monmouth H 109k	Shoemaker W	130	*.80	101-14	Carry Back1243 Kelso130 1/2 Beau Purple117 1/2 — In close turn 6
4Jly62-7Aqu	fst 1 1/8	:481 1:124 1:363 2:003	3↑ Suburban H 105k	Shoemaker W	132	*.65	100-08	BeauPurpl1152 1/2 Klso1323 1/2 Grwol1091 1/2 — Couldn't reach winner 4
16Jun62-3Bel	fst 1	:241 :472 1:131 1:353	3↑ Alw 7500	Shoemaker W	117	*.60	96-14	Kelso1172 1/2 Grwol1153 1/2 RosNt117 1/2 — Rated early,drew out easily 6
30May62-7Lrl	fm 1 1/16 T	:221 :44 1:08 1:333	3↑ Merryland H 111k	Shoemaker W	133	*.60	92-08	CarryBack1232 1/2 MerryRuler120 1/2 RullahRed1114 1/2 — Dull effort 9
11Nov61-7Lrl	fm 1 1/16 T	:483 2:013 2:521 3:004	3↑ D C Int'l 100k	Arcaro E	126	*.40	108-01	T.V.Lrk126 1/2 Klso1261 2 Prnupcl12610 — Made very sharp effort 8
21Oct61-7Aqu	fst 2	:494 2:35 3:004 3:254	3↑ J C Gold Cup 105k	Arcaro E	124	*.10	68-25	Kelso1245 Hillsborough124 8 Peace Isle12430 — Easily best 4
30Sep61-7Bel	fst 1 1/4	:461 1:10 1:342 2:00	3↑ Woodward 109k	Arcaro E	124	*.50	100-13	Kelso126 8 Divine Comedy126 1/2 Carry Back120 nk — Much the best 5
4Sep61-8AP	gd 1	:224 :452 1:093 1:343	3↑ Wash Park H 120k	Arcaro E	132	*.70	94-08	ChiefofChiefs112 4 3/4 TalentShow110 nk RunforNurse112 3 — Boxed 11
22Jly61-7Aqu	fst 1 1/8	:461 1:101 1:36 2:013	3↑ Brooklyn H 112k	Arcaro E	136	*.50	98-10	Klso1361 1/2 DvnComdy118 no Yorky122 hd — Under strong handling 10
4Jly61-7Aqu	fst 1 1/8	:481 1:221 1:372 2:02	3↑ Suburban H 111k	Arcaro E	133	*.60	96-13	Kelso135 nk NickelBoy112 nk TalentShow110 hd — Speed in reserve 10
17Jun61-7Bel	fst 1 1/8	:454 1:021 1:351 1:48	4↑ Whitney 56k	Arcaro E	130	*.45	96-12	[D]Our Hope111 hd Klso130 5 Reinzi114 hd — Roughed repeatedly 7
Placed first through disqualification								
30May61-7Aqu	fst 1	:23 :46 1:102 1:353	3↑ Metropolitan H 114k	Arcaro E	130	*1.05	90-16	Kelso130 nk AllHands1175 SweetWillim108 4 — Altered course,up 10
19May61-7Aqu	fst 7f	:23 :461 1:11 1:24	4↑ Alw 10000	Arcaro E	124	*.35	90-17	Kelso1241 1/2 Gyro115 nk LongGoneJohn121 1/2 — Drew out with ease 8
29Oct60-7Aqu	fst 1	:472 2:29 2:54 3:192	3↑ J C Gold Cup 109k	Arcaro E	119	1.19	114-16	Kelso1193 1/2 DonPoggio12410 BaldEagle12415 — Speed to spare 8
15Oct60-8Haw	my 1 1/4	:464 1:131 1:362 2:02	3↑ Haw Gold Cup H 144k	Arcaro E	117	*.20	86-21	Kelso1179 Heroshogala119 10 On-and-On1221 1/2 — Speed to spare 9
28Sep60-7Bel	fst 1 1/8	:471 3:722 2:012 2:404	Lawrence Realizatn 56k	Arcaro E	120	*.50	100-14	Kelso1204 1/2 Tompion1231 1/2 ToothandNal1165 1/2 — Speed in reserve 8
14Sep60-7Aqu	fst 1 1/8	:463 1:101 1:354 1:482	Discovery H 28k	Arcaro E	121	*1.20	102-14	Kelso1241 1/2 CarelsJohn1161 1/2 CountAmbr116 1/2 — Swerved,driving 8
3Sep60-7Aqu	gd 1	:223 :452 1:10 1:344	Jerome H 59k	Arcaro E	121	2.65	94-13	Kelso121 hd CarelessJohn1162 1/2 FourLan1192 1/2 — Long,hard drive 13
3Aug60-7Mth	fst 1	:224 :46 1:093 1:411	Choice 56k	Hartack W	114	3.90	93-18	Klso1147 CarelessJohn114 3/4 CountAmber1143 1/2 — Speed to spare 8
23Jly60-8AP	fst 1	:223 :452 1:103 1:361	Arl Classic 135k	Brooks S	117	3.90	81-13	T.V.Lark120 1/2 JohnWilliam1232 1/2 VenetianWay1231 — Dull try 12
16Jly60-5Aqu	fst 1	:23 :451 1:09 1:341	Alw 4500	Blum W	117	*1.30	97-10	Kelso1172 DoubleDly120 no AugustSun109 nk — As rider pleased 8
22Jun60-5Mth	fst 6f	:214 :45 1:10	Alw 4500	Hartack W	117	*1.00	92-12	Kelso1170 Burnt Clover1172 1/2 Gordian Knot1171 1/2 — Ridden out 8
Previously trained by J.M. Lee								
23Sep59-3Atl	fst 7f	:22 :442 1:093 1:23	@Alw 3600	Blum W	117	*1.90	87-11	WindySands1173 Klso1172 WeGuarantee1172 1/2 — Made good try 8
14Sep59-4Atl	fst 6f	:231 :462 1:112	@Alw 3400	Block J	117	4.40	86-18	DressUp1201 1/2 Kelso1171 3/4 DuskyRam117 nk — Rallied for placing 7
4Sep59-2Atl	gd 6f	:232 :471 1:134	@Md Sp Wt	Block J	120	6.00	76-23	Kelso1201 1/4 Crafty Master120 3/4 Adapt1201 — Under a hard drive 12

Past Performances of Great Horses of the 20th Century

Lady's Secret

gr. f. 1982, by Secretariat (Bold Ruler)–Great Lady M., by Icecapade
Own.– Mr. and Mrs. Eugene V. Klein
Br.– R.H. Spreen (Okla)
Tr.– D. Wayne Lukas

Lifetime record: 45 25 9 3 $3,021,425

10Aug87- 1Sar	sly	1⅛	:471 1:113 1:361 1:492	3↑ Alw 45000	2	0	-	-	-	-	McCarron CJ	117	*.30	--	Kamakura11511The Watcher122 2¼Jack of Clubs119 2½	Bolted	5
21Jly87- 8Mth	fst	1 1/16	:231 :462 1:11 1:432	3↑ ⒻAlw 25000	1	2	1½	13½	19	17	McCarron CJ	119	*.10	88-18	Lady'sSecret1197BriefRemarks115nkShaknBy115¾	Easy score	6
4Jly87-10Mth	fst	1 1/16	:231 :461 1:10 1:42	3↑ ⒻMolly Pitcher H-G2	3	2	21½	2½	2hd	22	McCarron CJ	125	*.30	93-10	ReelEasy1122Lady'sSecret125¾Cattonc117nk	Best of others	8
13Jun87- 8Mth	sly	6f	:222 :444 1:094	3↑ ⒻAlw 25000	5	1	2hd	1½	11	13½	Cordero A Jr	122	*.30	91-14	Lady'sSecret1223½Nick'sNag1156BriefRmrks1158	Ridden out	5
14Mar87-10GP	fst	1⅛	:462 1:11 1:361 1:484	3↑ Donn H-G2	2	1	12	43	618	632½	Day P	120	*.80	55-18	LittleBoldJohn111noSkipTrl1186WsTms1174½	Fin. after½	7
1Nov86- 5SA	fst	1¼	:461 1:10 1:344 2:011	3↑ ⒻBC Distaff-G1	5	1	14	14	14	12½	Day P	123	*.50	83-13	Lady's Secret1232½Fran's Valentine1232Outstandingly123¾		8
	Ridden out																
12Oct86- 8Bel	fst	1¼	:461 1:10 1:352 2:013	3↑ ⒻBeldame-G1	4	1	15	11	1½	1½	Day P	123	*.05	90-13	Lady's Secret123½Coup de Fusil1231¾Classy Cathy11823½		4
	Drifted,ridden out																
21Sep86- 8Bel	fst	1⅛	:454 1:093 1:341 1:464	3↑ ⒻRuffian H-G1	5	2	1½	13½	16	18	Day P	129	*.50	93-12	Lady's Secret1298Steal a Kiss1092¼Endear1196	Handily	6
6Sep86- 8Bel	fst	1	:231 :454 1:094 1:332	3↑ ⒻMaskette-G1	5	1	11	11½	14½	17	Day P	125	*.30	98-10	Lady's Secret1257Steal a Kiss1091¾Endear120no	Handily	6
30Aug86- 8Bel	fst	1⅛	:453 1:092 1:334 1:46	3↑ Woodward-G1	4	1	11½	12½	2hd	24¾	Cordero A Jr	121	1.40e	92-14	Precisionist1264¾Lady'sScrt1215½PrsonlFlg1105¾	2nd best	5
16Aug86- 9Mth	sly	1⅛	:464 1:103 1:353 1:484	3↑ Iselin H-G1	1	1	11½	1hd	1hd	33½	Day P	120	*1.20	86-16	Roo Art1172¼Precisionist1251¼Lady's Secret1206	Gave way	5
2Aug86- 8Sar	sly	1⅛	:463 1:104 1:363 1:494	3↑ Whitney H-G1	2	1	12½	13	12½	14½	Day P	119	*1.30e	86-22	Lady's Secret1194½Ends Well1163¼Fuzzy110nk	Ridden out	7
5Jly86- 9Mth	fst	1 1/16	:23 :46 1:091 1:411	3↑ ⒻMolly Pitcher H-G2	4	1	1½	1½	13½	16¼	Day P	126	*.20	99-13	Lady's Secret1266¼Chaldea1142¼Key Witness1121½	Easily	8
8Jun86- 8Bel	my	1⅛	:444 1:094 1:353 1:483	3↑ ⒻHempstead H-G1	4	2	1hd	1hd	22½	26	Day P	128	*.40	78-16	Endear1156Lady's Secret1281½Ride Sally12413	2nd best	5
26May86- 8Bel	fst	1	:232 :454 1:091 1:333	3↑ Metropolitan H-G1	4	1	2hd	1hd	1½	31¼	Day P	120	5.30	96-11	Garthorn1241¼LoveThatMac117noLady'sSecrt120nk	Held well	8
17May86- 8Bel	fst	1 1/16	:233 :461 1:101 1:414	3↑ ⒻShuvee H-G1	3	1	11	11	13	13½	Day P	126	*.70	93-15	Lady's Secret1263½Endear1156¼Ride Sally1251	Easy score	6
16Apr86- 9OP	fst	1 1/16	:231 :454 1:101 1:402	4↑ ⒻApple Blossom H-G1	4	1	13	1hd	2½	2nk	Velasquez J	127	*.40	99-16	LoveSmitten119nkLady'sSecret1276Sefa'sBeauty1226	Failed	7
23Feb86- 8SA	fst	1⅛	:462 1:10 1:343 1:47	4↑ ⒻS Margarita H-G1	1	1	11½	11	11½	12¾	Velasquez J	125	*1.60	94-11	Lady'sSecret1252¾Johnica1201¼DontstopThemusc1222	Easily	9
9Feb86- 8SA	fst	1⅛	:464 1:11 1:363 1:494	ⒻLa Canada-G1	3	1	1½	11½	11½	11¼	McCarron CJ	126	*.50	80-16	Lady'sSecret1261¼Shywing1194NorthSider1181¾	Hard ridden	6
18Jan86- 8SA	fst	1 1/16	:222 :452 1:093 1:414	ⒻEl Encino-G3	8	3	1½	13	12½	12	McCarron CJ	124	*.80	92-12	Ldy'sScrt1242Shywng1194ShrpAscnt119nk	Lugged into stretch	10
27Dec85- 8SA	fst	7f	:222 :45 1:093 1:222	ⒻLa Brea-G3	1	3	1hd	1½	2hd	2½	McCarron CJ	124	*.80	87-16	SavannahSlew119½Lady'sScret1243AmbraRidge1142½	Gamely	7
	Previously owned by E.V. Klein																
2Nov85- 5Aqu	fst	1¼	:464 1:112 1:364 2:02	3↑ ⒻBC Distaff-G1	1	1	14	11	21½	26¼	Velasquez J	119	*.40e	80-10	Life's Magic1236¼Lady's Secret1193Dontstop Themusic1231¼		7
	Ducked out start																
13Oct85- 8Bel	fst	1¼	:454 1:102 1:36 2:033	3↑ ⒻBeldame-G1	4	1	1½	12	13	12	Velasquez J	118	*.60	80-19	Lady'sSecret1182Isayso1232¾KamikazeRick1182¼	Ridden out	5
22Sep85- 8Bel	fst	1⅛	:462 1:094 1:343 1:472	3↑ ⒻRuffian H-G1	3	1	11½	14	15	14	Velasquez J	116	*.30e	90-17	Lady's Secret1164Isayso1152¼Sintrillium118hd	Ridden out	6
7Sep85- 8Bel	fst	1	:222 :444 1:091 1:344	3↑ ⒻMaskette-G1	6	1	1½	11	14	15½	Velasquez J	111	*1.00e	91-14	Lady's Secret1115½Dowery117noMrs. Revere117¾	Ridden out	8
9Aug85- 8Sar	fst	7f	:214 :441 1:091 1:223	3↑ ⒻBallerina-G2	4	3	21½	2hd	1½	1no	MacBeth D	117	*.90e	89-19	Lady'sSecret117noMrs.Revere1162¾SolarHalo116¾	Driving	9
1Aug85- 8Sar	gd	7f	:221 :444 1:09 1:213	ⒻTest-G2	9	1	42½	31½	1hd	12	Velasquez J	121	10.10	94-13	Lady'sScrt1212Mom'sCommand124nkMjstcFolly118½	Driving	10
6Jly85- 6Bel	fst	6f	:22 :451 1:111	3↑ ⒻThe Rose 54k	6	1	32	3nk	12	14¾	Velasquez J	116	*.40	86-20	Lady'sScrt1164¾FoolishIntentions115¾ProudClarioness115nk		6
	Ridden out																
22Jun85- 9Mth	fst	6f	:221 :443 1:093	3↑ ⒻRegret H 49k	6	1	11½	11½	12½	13½	Antley CW	114	*.40	92-16	Lady'sSecret1143½FurashFolly1182Nck'sNg1202½	Ridden out	6
26May85- 5Bel	fst	6f	:222 :444 1:09	ⒻBowl of Flowers 55k	6	1	1½	1hd	14	17	Velasquez J	121	*.50	97-13	Lady'sSecret1217RideSally114nkIndinRomnc1143	Ridden out	7
11May85- 8Bel	fst	7f	:22 :443 1:091 1:221	ⒻComely-G3	1	4	43	45	47½	411	Cordero A Jr	121	6.30	80-12	Mom'sCommnd1214½MajestcFolly1131¾ClocksScrt1214¾	Tired	9
28Apr85- 8Aqu	fst	6f	:222 :451 1:10	ⒻPrioress-G3	5	1	21	21½	21½	21¼	Velasquez J	118	*1.30	90-21	ClocksSecret1151¼Lady'sSecret1185RideSally1122	Gamely	8
16Apr85- 9OP	fst	6f	:214 :45 1:10	ⒻPrima Donna 76k	7	2	32½	3½	11½	15	Velasquez J	123	*.80	90-18	Lady'sSecret1235TakeMyPictur1232Lt.A.J.1121¾	Ridden out	9
23Feb85- 8GG	fst	6f	:213 :442 :573 1:10	ⒻVallejo 43k	1	3	1½	1½	1hd	21½	Baze RA	122	1.90	87-16	SavannahSlew1141½Lady'sScrt1226SprtdMdm1143½	Game try	7

Past Performances of Great Horses of the 20th Century

30Jan85- 8SA	fst 7f	:221 :444 1:094 1:232	ⒻS Ynez-G3	6 1	2hd	1hd	2hd	53¾	Valenzuela PA	122	7.40	79-17	Wising Up119¾Rascal Lass1222Reigning Countess119¾	Hung	9
12Jan85- 8BM	fst 6f	:222 :444 :572 1:101	Determine 44k	7 1	2½	1hd	2hd	2nk	Baze RA	115	*1.10	88-21	Bedside Promise113nkLady'sScrt1151½DSantaRosaPrince115no		8
	Gamely														
5Jan85- 8BM	fst 6f	:222 :45 :573 1:10	ⒻHail Hilarious 43k	5 3	31½	1hd	13	14	Baze RA	120	*.70	89-16	Lady's Secret1204Missadoon1125Bloomer Miss115no		7
	Bumped start,wide into str														
9Nov84- 9Hol	fst 6f	:221 :453 :58 1:111	ⒻMoccasin 61k	8 1	1hd	2½	1½	1½	McCarron CJ	120	*1.90	- -	Lady's Secret120½Neshia1131Lotta Blue1173	Driving	9
20Oct84- 8SA	fst 1 1/16	:224 :454 1:102 1:423	ⒻOak Leaf-G1	6 1	13	1½	36	516¼	Sibille R	115	7.10	72-13	FolkArt1174½Pirate'sGlow1156½WaywardPirate1153½	Tired	6
8Oct84- 8SA	fst 7f	:22 :443 1:101 1:233	ⒻAnoakia-G3	11 1	12½	13½	12	3hd	Black K	120	6.10e	82-16	WaywardPirate120hdPrt'sGlow117noLdy'sScrt1201¼	Weakened	11
8Aug84- 8Dmr	fst 6f	:22 :451 :58 1:111	ⒻJunior Miss 53k	3 1	2hd	1hd	22½	46	Valenzuela PA	122	3.00e	76-21	Doon's Baby1172½Fiesta Lady1173Trunk117½	Weakened	6
23Jly84- 3Hol	fst 6f	:214 :443 :572 1:11	ⒻⓇWavy Waves 46k	5 1	1½	12	12	11½	Valenzuela PA	117	2.20	82-18	Lady's Secret1171½Full o Wisdom115½Neshia1172¼	Driving	6
7Jly84- 8Hol	fst 6f	:213 :444 :571 1:10	ⒻLandaluce-G3	13 1	2hd	22½	25	49	Valenzuela PA	116	21.40e	78-18	WindowSeat1146½RaiseaProspctor1191FulloWsdom1141½	Tired	13
2Jly84- 8Bel	fst 5½f	:214 :454 :583 1:051	ⒻAstoria 75k	4 3	1hd	1hd	21	55½	Cordero A Jr	112	2.60	83-15	Faster Than Fast1103Something113½Queen Breeze1121½		9
	Pace between horses														
21May84- 4Bel	fst 5f	:221 :454 :584	ⒻMd Sp Wt	1 3	11½	11½	11½	11½•	Cordero A Jr	117	*1.40	93-09	DHLady'sScrt117DHBonnie's Axe1171½Launching Shot1172¼		8
	Drifted out														

Man o' War

ch. c. 1917, by Fair Play (Hastings)–Mahubah, by Rock Sand
Own.– S.D. Riddle
Br.– August Belmont (Ky)
Tr.– L. Feustel

Lifetime record: 21 20 1 0 $249,465

12Oct20- 4Knw	fst 1¼	:462 1:114 1:372 2:03 3↑	Ken Park Gold Cup 75k	2 1	12	15	16	17	Kummer C	120 w	*.05	132-03	Man o' War1207Sir Barton126	Never extended	2
18Sep20- 5HdG	fst 1 1/16	:23 :473 1:113 1:444	Potomac H 10k	4 1	11½	11	11½	11½	Kummer C	138 w	*.15	101-16	Man o' War1381½Wildair10815Blazes104.52	Easing late	4
11Sep20- 4Bel	fst 1½	:493 1:141 2:032 2:284 3↑	Jockey Club 6.8k	2 1	15	18	112	115	Kummer C	118 w	*.01	117-02	Man o' War11815Damask118	Under a pull	2
4Sep20- 4Bel	fst 1⅝	:474 1:382 2:033 2:404	Lawrence Realizatn 16k	2 1	120	130	150	1100	Kummer C	126 w	*.01	134-00	Man o' War126100Hoodwink116	Restrained at end	2
21Aug20- 4Sar	fst 1¼	:463 1:10 1:353 2:014	Travers 12k	1 1	12	14	14	12½	Schuttinger A	129 w	*.22	102-08	Mano'War1292½Upset1237JohnP.Grier115	Restrained in str	3
7Aug20- 4Sar	fst 1 3/16	:481 1:124 1:374 1:563	Miller 5.7k	2 1	11½	13	14	16	Sande E	131 w	*.03	97-09	Mano'War1316Donnacona1194KingAlbert114	Never extended	3
10Jly20- 4Aqu	fst 1⅛	:46 1:093 1:36 1:491	Dwyer 5.5k	1 1	1hd	1hd	1½	11½	Kummer C	126 w	*.20	101-08	Man o' War1261½John P. Grier108	Hard ridden,drew away	2
22Jun20- 4Jam	gd 1	:253 :49 1:141 1:413	Stuyvesant H 4.5k	1 1	14	17	18	18	Kummer C	135 w	*.01	86-13	Man o' War1358Yellow Hand103	Eased final ⅛	2
12Jun20- 4Bel	fst 1⅜	2:141	Belmont 9.2k	1 1	12	17	112	120	Kummer C	126 w	*.04	116-10	Man o' War12620Donnacona126	Taken up final 1/16	2
29May20- 4Bel	fst 1	:24 :471 1:11 1:354	Withers 5.8k	2 1	11½	12	12	12	Kummer C	118 w	*.14	104-10	Man o' War1182Wildair11812David Harum118	Won under pull	3
18May20- 4Pim	fst 1⅛	:473 1:122 1:381 1:513	Preakness 29k	7 1	11½	14	12	11½	Kummer C	126 w	*.80	97-10	Man o' War1261½Upset1225Wildair1145	Speed in reserve	9
13Sep19- 3Bel	fst 6f-Str	1:113	Futurity 31k	8 2	31½	1½	12	12½	Loftus J	127 w	*.50	85-21	Mano'War1272½JohnP.Grier1174Dominiqu122nk	Won easing up	10
30Aug19- 3Sar	sl 6f	:23 :47 1:13	Hopeful 29k	3 4	22	21	15	14	Loftus J	130 w	*.45	87-14	Man o' War1304Cleopatra1124Constancy1242	Easily	8
23Aug19- 3Sar	fst 6f	:223 :462 1:12	Grand Union Hotel 9.8k	2 3	1hd	13	13	11	Loftus J	130 w	*.55	92-08	Man o' War1301Upset1254Blazes122½	Eased final 16th	10
13Aug19- 4Sar	fst 6f	:231 :464 1:111	Sanford Memorial 4.9k	6 5	41½	32	31½	2½	Loftus J	130 w	*.55	95-09	Upst115½Mno'Wr1303GoldnBroom1302	Slow start,gaining	7
2Aug19- 3Sar	fst 6f	:23 :471 1:122	U S Hotel 9.8k	8 1	13	13	14	12	Loftus J	130 w	*.90	90-13	Man o' War1302Upset1151Homely1121	Eased final 16th	10
5Jly19- 3Aqu	fst 6f	:233 :472 1:13	Tremont 5.8k	2 2	11	11	11½	11	Loftus J	130 w	*.10	90-12	Man o' War1301Ralco11520Ace of Aces112	Never extended	3
23Jun19- 3Aqu	fst 5f	1:013	Hudson 3.4k	2 1	1½	11	11	11½	Loftus J	130 w	*.10e	83-12	Mano'War1301½VioletTip1094Shoal11512	Broke thru barrier	5
21Jun19- 3Jam	gd 5½f	:231 :473 1:001 1:063	Youthful 4.8k	4 3	11	12	14	12½	Loftus J	120 w	*.50	92-09	Mno'War1202½OnWtch1082LdyBrumml10510	Easing final 16th	4
9Jun19- 4Bel	sl 5½f-Str	1:053	Keene Mem 5.2k	3 2	2½	3¾	31	13	Loftus J	115 w	*.70	91-17	Man o' War1153On Watch115½Anniversary1154	Drew away	6
6Jun19- 6Bel	fst 5f-Str	:59	Md Sp Wt	7 1	2nk	2½	13	16	Loftus J	115 w	*.60	83-18	Man o' War1156Retrieve112½Neddam1154	Easily	7

Past Performances of Great Horses of the 20th Century

Nashua

b. c. 1952, by Nasrullah (Nearco)–Segula, by Johnstown **Lifetime record: 30 22 4 1 $1,288,565**

Own.–Leslie Combs II
Br.– Belair Stud Inc (Ky)
Tr.– J. Fitzsimmons

13Oct56- 6Bel	fst 2	:491 2:282 2:541 3:202	3 ↑ J C Gold Cup 54k	1	1	1½	2hd	11½	12¼	Arcaro E	124wb	*.75	102-09	Nashua1242¼Rily1191¾ThrdBrothr1194	Kept to strong drive	7
29Sep56- 7Bel	gd 1¼	:47 1:112 1:371 2:03	3 ↑ Woodward 80k	1	2	1hd	3nk	31½	22½	Arcaro E	126wb	*.30	82-12	Mister Gus1262½Nashua126½Jet Action12620	No excuse	4
14Jly56- 6Mth	my 1¼	:46 1:11 1:364 2:024	3 ↑ Monmouth H 114k	7	1	14	14	14	13½	Arcaro E	129wb	*.30	92-20	Nashua1293½Mr. First1105Mielleux1071	Speed in reserve	8
4Jly56- 7Bel	fst 1¼	:463 1:101 1:35 2:004	3 ↑ Suburban H 83k	4	2	2hd	2hd	2½	11¼	Arcaro E	128wb	*1.20	96-10	Nashua1281¼Dedicat1112¼Subhdr1125	Well rated,going away	8
30Jun56- 7Bel	fst 7f	:221 :452 1:102 1:231	3 ↑ Carter H 58k	3	6	44½	65	62¾	73½	Arcaro E	130 w	*1.10	90-12	Red Hannigan1141½Switch On119½Artismo111¾	Well up,hung	10
30May56- 7Bel	fst 1	:224 :451 1:094 1:35	3 ↑ Metropolitan H 55k	7	1	32½	42½	53	4¾	Arcaro E	130 w	*.65	98-09	Midaftrnoon111hdSwtchOn113½Fnd116nk	Came again too late	7
19May56- 7GS	fst 1⅛	:463 1:111 1:362 1:491	3 ↑ Camden H 33k	4	1	11	1½	11	12	Arcaro E	129 w	*.40	91-10	Nashua1292Fisherman1201½Mielleux1102	Very handy score	5
5May56- 7Jam	fst 1⅛	:49 1:13 1:38 1:503	3 ↑ Grey Lag H 55k	6	3	2hd	1hd	1hd	1hd	Atkinson T	128 w	*.95	93-17	Nashua128hdFind118hdFisherman1201¾	Almost fell at start	7
17Mar56- 8GP	fst 1¼	:47 1:113 1:36 2:003	3 ↑ Gulf Park H 112k	6	5	43½	53¼	56	57	Arcaro E	129 w	*.70	89-08	Sailor1191¾Mielleux1101Find116¾	Wide both turns,tired	7
18Feb56- 8Hia	fst 1¼	:463 1:104 1:353 2:02	3 ↑ Widener H 129k	9	3	41¾	2½	2hd	1hd	Arcaro E	127 w	*.40	95-11	Nashua127hdSocilOutcst121hdSlor119nk	Under strong drive	9
	Previously owned by Belair Stud															
15Oct55- 6Bel	sly 2	:494 2:321 2:583 3:244	3 ↑ J C Gold Cup 79k	3	2	1½	11	13½	15	Arcaro E	119 w	*.25	80-14	Nashua1195Thinking Cap11915Mark's Puzzle1198	Easy score	5
24Sep55- 6Bel	sly 1⅛	:451 1:101 1:36 1:491	3 ↑ Sysonby 106k	5	1	41½	3nk	22	31¾	Arcaro E	121 w	*.65	91-10	HighGun126hdJetActn1261¾Nshu1213½	Weakened when urged	5
31Aug55- 7Was	gd 1¼	:46 1:102 1:373 2:041	WP Match 100k	1	1	1½	11½	12	16½	Arcaro E	126 w	1.20	81-17	Nashua1266½Swaps126	Drew far out to handy score	2
16Jly55- 7AP	fst 1	:231 :453 1:093 1:351	Arl Classic 148k	2	2	22	24	21	1½	Arcaro E	126 w	*.30	96-10	Nashua126½Traffic Judge1201¼Impromptu1204	Under a drive	7
2Jly55- 0Aqu	fst 1¼	:493 1:134 1:382 2:034	Dwyer 55k	3	1	1½	11½	11½	15	Arcaro E	126 w	-	88-15	Nashua1265Saratoga12240Mainlander114	Easing up late	3
	Run as special event with no wagering															
11Jun55- 6Bel	fst 1½	:49 1:133 2:042 2:29	Belmont 119k	5	2	1hd	12½	16	19	Arcaro E	126 w	*.15	93-12	Nashua1269Blazing Count1265½Portersville1266	A romp	8
	Geldings not eligible															
28May55- 7Pim	fst 1 3/16	:471 1:11 1:353 1:543	Preakness 116k	5	4	42½	2hd	1hd	11	Arcaro E	126 w	*.30	106-08	Nashua1261Saratoga1267TrafficJudg126nk	Rated,mild drive	8
7May55- 7CD	fst 1¼	:472 1:122 1:37 2:014	Ky Derby 152k	5	3	31	2½	2½	21½	Arcaro E	126 w	*1.30	96-12	Swaps1261½Nashua1266½Summer Tan1264	Good bid,no excuse	10
23Apr55- 6Jam	fst 1⅛	:471 1:111 1:363 1:503	Wood Memorial 111k	4	2	21½	22	21½	1nk	Atkinson T	126 w	1.10	93-17	Nashua126nkSummer Tan12625Simmy1266	Sensational score	5
26Mar55- 7GP	sly 1⅛	:463 1:122 1:391 1:531	Fla Derby 148k	1	5	56½	22½	2½	1nk	Arcaro E	122 w	*.95	78-26	Nashua122nkBlueLem1132¼FirstCabin1131	Unruly,hard urged	9
26Feb55- 7Hia	fst 1⅛	:462 1:113 1:371 1:493	Flamingo 141k	2	2	1hd	1hd	1hd	11½	Arcaro E	122 w	*.70	88-12	Nashua1221½Saratoga1224½CupMan1227	Drifted out in drive	12
21Feb55- 0Hia	fst 1 1/16	:231 :47 1:114 1:441	Alw 7500	2	2	3nk	2hd	1½	11½	Arcaro E	126wb	-	94-11	Nshua1261½Munchausen1172HappyMemries1142½	Unruly late	4
	Special event run between 2nd and 3rd races - No wagering															
9Oct54- 6Bel	fst 6½f-W	:222 :451 1:092 1:153	Futurity 112k	6	4		21	1½	1hd	Arcaro E	122wb	*.65	94-06	Nshua122hdSummrTan122¾RoylCoinage1227	Held on gamely	7
	Geldings not eligible															
1Oct54- 6Bel	fst 6f-WC	:22 :442 1:081	Sp Wt 10000	4	2		4¾	2hd	11	Arcaro E	118wb	*1.05	100-00	Nashua1181Royal Coinage1185Pyrenees1181½	Clever score	7
21Sep54- 6Aqu	fst 6½f	:223 :451 1:092 1:16	Cowdin 30k	9	1	2hd	4¾	41½	21½	Arcaro E	124wb	*1.25	101-12	SummerTn1201½Nshua124¾Bunny'sBabe1201½	Mildly impeded	10
28Aug54- 6Sar	fst 6½f	:23 :464 1:111 1:174	Hopeful 78k	4	1	1½	1hd	11	1nk	Arcaro E	122wb	*.55e	96-18	Nashua122nkSummrTan1221½Pyrens1221½	Well rated,held on	8
21Aug54- 4Sar	fst 6f	:23 :463 :592 1:122	Grand Union Hotel 27k	5	2	23	1hd	12	11¾	Arcaro E	122 w	2.75e	86-17	Nashua1221¾Pyrens1152½ModlAc1143½	Won in clever fashion	6
19May54- 7GS	fst 5f	:221 :454 :583	Cherry Hill 20k	3	5	2½	22	21½	2nk	Higley J	119 w	3.80	98-13	RoyalNote122nkNashua1195Menolen1191½	Unruly all the way	11
12May54- 6Bel	fst 5f-WC	:221 :453 :58	Juvenile 15k	1	2		1hd	2½	1½	Arcaro E	117 w	3.00e	89-18	Nshua117½SummerTn1228Lugh1172	Scored under clever ride	8
5May54- 4Bel	fst 4½f-W	:222 :462 :523	©Md Sp Wt	14	9		81½	11½	13	Higley J	118 w	8.50e	86-14	Nashua1183Retract118½Danger Quest118no	Won in hand	21

Past Performances of Great Horses of the 20th Century

Native Dancer

gr. c. 1950, by Polynesian (Unbreakable)–Geisha, by Discovery
Own.– A.G. Vanderbilt
Br.– Alfred G. Vanderbilt (Ky)
Tr.– W.C. Winfrey

Lifetime record: 22 21 1 0 $785,240

16Aug54- 0Sar	sly 7f	:23^3 :47^2 1:12 1:24^4 3↑	Handicap 5025	2	3	22½	22	18	19	Guerin E	137	w	-	91-19	Native Dancer137^{9}First Glance119$^{4\frac12}$Gigantic107	Easily	3
15May54- 6Bel	fst 1	:23^1 :46 1:10^1 1:35^1 3↑	Metropolitan H 39k	3	8	77¾	57	23½	1nk	Guerin E	130	w	*.25	98-11	Native Dancer130^{nk}Straight Face117^{6}Jamie K.110^2	Just up	9
7May54- 6Bel	fst 6f	:22^4 :46^3 1:11^4 3↑	Alw 15000	4	3	42	31	12	11¼	Guerin E	126	w	*.15	90-15	Native Dancer126$^{1\frac14}$Laffango121^{nk}Impasse114^{nk}	Easily best	7
22Aug53- 7Was	fst 1⅛	:46^2 1:10^3 1:35^2 1:48^2	American Derby 112k	4	7	711	45½	41¾	12	Arcaro E	128	w	*.20e	99-11	NativeDancr128^{2}Landlocked120$^{1\frac14}$PrecousSton114^3	Drew out	8
15Aug53- 6Sar	fst 1¼	:49^1 1:14 1:39^3 2:05^3	Travers 27k	1	3	31	21½	11	15½	Guerin E	126	w	*.05	80-20	NativeDancer126$^{5\frac12}$Dictar120$^{2\frac12}$GuardianII114^1	Easily best	5
	Geldings not eligible																
18Jly53- 7AP	hy 1	:23^2 :47^1 1:11^4 1:38	Arl Classic 154k	4	6	67	34	13	19	Guerin E	126	w	*.70	82-25	NativeDancer126^{9}SirMango120^{hd}VanCrosby120^2	Easily best	8
4Jly53- 6Aqu	fst 1¼	:49^4 1:14 1:39^2 2:05^1	Dwyer 56k	3	4	33½	11½	12½	11¾	Guerin E	126	w	*.05	81-17	NativeDancer126$^{1\frac34}$[D]Dictar114^{2}GuardnII114^4	Much the best	5
13Jun53- 6Bel	fst 1½	:50^1 1:15 2:04^1 2:28^3	Belmont 118k	5	4	32½	2hd	1hd	1nk	Guerin E	126	w	*.45	95-11	NativeDancr126^{nk}JamieK.126^{10}RoylByGm126$^{4\frac12}$	Held gamely	6
	Geldings not eligible																
23May53- 7Pim	fst 1$\frac{3}{16}$	:47 1:11^4 1:38^2 1:57^4	Preakness 113k	4	3	33	2hd	1hd	1nk	Guerin E	126	w	*.20	91-19	NativeDancer126^{nk}JamieK.126^{6}RoyalBayGem126^2	Hard drive	7
16May53- 6Bel	fst 1	:23^4 :47^1 1:11^3 1:36^1	Withers 32k	3	2	2½	1½	12½	14	Guerin E	126	w	*.05	93-12	Native Dancer126^{4}Invigorator126$^{2\frac12}$Real Brother126	Easily	3
	Geldings not eligible																
2May53- 7CD	fst 1¼	:47^4 1:12^1 1:36^3 2:02	Ky Derby 118k	6	8	42½	42½	21½	2hd	Guerin E	126	w	*.70e	97-09	DarkStar126^{hd}NativeDancer126^{5}Invgortor126^2	Roughed,wide	11
25Apr53- 6Jam	fst 1⅛	:50 1:13^3 1:37^1 1:50^3	Wood Memorial 123k	4	2	31	2hd	1½	14½	Guerin E	126	w	*.10e	93-12	NativeDancer126$^{4\frac12}$TahitianKing126^{hd}Invigortor126^3	Easily	7
	Geldings not eligible																
18Apr53- 6Jam	fst 1$\frac{1}{16}$	:24^2 :49 1:13^4 1:44^1	Gotham (Div 1) 35k	8	4	62¾	41¼	2hd	12	Guerin E	120	w	*.15	91-10	NatveDancr120^{2}MagicLmp120^{3}Sckl'sSound120$^{1\frac14}$	Ridden out	9
22Oct52- 6Jam	fst 1$\frac{1}{16}$	:24^2 :48 1:12^3 1:44^1	©East View 56k	1	4	46	33	1½	11½	Guerin E	122	w	*.20	91-15	Native Dancer122$^{1\frac12}$Laffango122^{9}Teds Jeep122$^{1\frac12}$	Ridden out	6
	Geldings not eligible																
27Sep52- 6Bel	fst 6½f-W	:21^4 :44^2 1:08^2 1:14^2	Futurity 107k	8	6		54	2½	12¼	Guerin E	122	w	*.35	100-05	NativeDancer122$^{2\frac14}$TahitianKing122^{4}DarkStr122^3	Ridden out	10
	Geldings not eligible																
22Sep52- 5Bel	fst 6f-WC	:22 :44^3 1:09^3	Sp Wt 5000	6	6		53	12	11¼	Guerin E	118	w	*.40	93-07	NativeDancer118$^{1\frac14}$TahitianKing118$^{2\frac14}$Reprimnd118^{hd}	In hand	8
30Aug52- 6Sar	fst 6½f	:23^3 :48 1:12^3 1:18^4	Hopeful 62k	4	1	62¾	52½	2hd	12	Guerin E	122	w	*.25	91-19	Native Dancer122^{2}Tiger Skin122^{2}Platan122^1	Handily	7
23Aug52- 4Sar	fst 6f	:22^4 :46^2 1:11^1	Grand Union Hotel 20k	1	2	31	1½	11½	13½	Guerin E	126	w	*.55	92-17	NativeDancer126$^{3\frac12}$Laffango122$^{2\frac12}$TahitianKing122$^{5\frac12}$	In hand	5
16Aug52- 4Sar	sly 6f	:23^1 :46^4 1:13^1	Sar Spl 17k	4	2	42½	42	11	13½	Guerin E	122	w	*.70	82-22	NativeDancr122$^{3\frac12}$DocWalkr122^{4}SouthPont122$^{3\frac12}$	Ridden out	8
4Aug52- 6Sar	fst 5½f	:23^1 :47 :59^3 1:06	Flash 10k	6	4	31	31	1½	12¼	Guerin E	122	w	*.80	87-20	Native Dancer122$^{2\frac14}$Tiger Skin114^{2}Bradley122^{no}	Easily	7
23Apr52- 6Jam	fst 5f	:22^3 :46^3 :59^2	©Youthful 14k	4	2	21	2hd	13	16	Guerin E	117	w	*.90	93-19	NativeDancr117^{6}Tribe122$^{1\frac12}$[DH]Mr.Mdnght117^1	Much the best	12
19Apr52- 2Jam	fst 5f	:23 :47 :59^3	Md Sp Wt	9	7	42	42	1½	14½	Guerin E	118	w	*1.40	92-16	Native Dancer118$^{4\frac12}$Putney118^{nk}Khan118^{hd}	Drew out easily	9

Past Performances of Great Horses of the 20th Century

Personal Ensign

b. f. 1984, by Private Account (Damascus)–Grecian Banner, by Hoist the Flag
Own.– Ogden Phipps
Br.– Ogden Phipps (Ky)
Tr.– Claude McGaughey III

Lifetime record: 13 13 0 0 $1,679,880

5Nov88- 6CD	my $1\frac{1}{8}$	:47^{4} 1:12 1:38^{1} 1:52	3↑ ⒻBC Distaff-G1	6	6	$5^{8\frac{1}{2}}$	5^{8}	3^{4}	1no	Romero RP	123	*.50	82-20	Personal Ensign123^{no}Winning Colors$119^{\frac{1}{2}}$Goodbye Halo119^{5}	Tight early,just up	9
16Oct88- 8Bel	fst $1\frac{1}{4}$	:48^{1} 1:12 1:36^{2} 2:01^{1}	3↑ ⒻBeldame-G1	1	3	2^{2}	2^{hd}	1^{2}	$1^{5\frac{1}{2}}$	Romero RP	123	*.10	92-16	PersonlEnsign$123^{5\frac{1}{2}}$ClassicCrown$118^{\frac{1}{2}}$ShmSy118^{7}	Ridden out	5
10Sep88- 8Bel	fst 1	:22^{4} :45^{1} 1:09 1:34^{1}	3↑ ⒻMaskette-G1	2	3	3^{6}	2^{2}	2^{hd}	$1^{\frac{3}{4}}$	Romero RP	123	*.30	94-14	PersonalEnsgn$123^{\frac{3}{4}}$WinningColrs$118^{5\frac{1}{4}}$ShmSy$115^{11\frac{1}{4}}$	Driving	4
6Aug88- 8Sar	sly $1\frac{1}{8}$	:47^{2} 1:11^{3} 1:35^{3} 1:47^{4}	3↑ Whitney H-G1	3	3	3^{3}	2^{1}	1^{hd}	$1^{1\frac{1}{2}}$	Romero RP	117	*.80	96-12	PersonalEnsign$117^{1\frac{1}{2}}$Gulch124^{17}King'sSwan123	Brisk urging	3
4Jly88-10Mth	fst $1\frac{1}{16}$	:24 :47^{2} 1:10^{4} 1:41^{4}	3↑ ⒻMolly Pitcher H-G2	5	3	2^{3}	$2^{\frac{1}{2}}$	$1^{2\frac{1}{2}}$	1^{8}	Romero RP	125	*.40	96-14	Personal Ensign125^{8}Grecian Flight119^{7}Le L'Argent117^{1}	Bumped,forced wide	5
11Jun88- 7Bel	fst $1\frac{1}{8}$	:47^{1} 1:11^{2} 1:35^{3} 1:47^{3}	3↑ ⒻHempstead H-G1	5	3	$3^{1\frac{1}{2}}$	3^{1}	1^{4}	1^{7}	Romero RP	123	*.40	89-13	PersonlEnsgn123^{7}HomtwnQun109^{2}ClbbrGrl118^{nk}	Ridden out	5
15May88- 8Bel	fst $1\frac{1}{16}$	:23 :45^{3} 1:10 1:41^{3}	3↑ ⒻShuvee H-G1	5	3	3^{3}	2^{hd}	$1^{\frac{1}{2}}$	$1^{1\frac{3}{4}}$	Romero RP	121	*.70	94-15	Personal Ensign$121^{1\frac{3}{4}}$Clabber Girl$118^{3\frac{1}{4}}$Bishop's Delight$111^{2\frac{3}{4}}$	Driving	6
18Oct87- 8Bel	fst $1\frac{1}{4}$	:49^{3} 1:13^{4} 1:38^{2} 2:04^{2}	3↑ ⒻBeldame-G1	8	2	$2^{\frac{1}{2}}$	1^{3}	1^{4}	$1^{2\frac{1}{4}}$	Romero RP	118	1.30	76-23	PersnlEnsgn$118^{2\frac{1}{4}}$CoupdFusl$123^{2\frac{1}{2}}$SlntTurn$118^{3\frac{3}{4}}$	Drew clear	10
10Oct87- 5Bel	fst 1	:22^{3} :45^{4} 1:10^{2} 1:36^{3}	ⒻRare Perfume-G2	2	3	1^{1}	1^{5}	1^{5}	$1^{4\frac{3}{4}}$	Romero RP	115	*.80	82-22	PrsnlEnsign$115^{4\frac{3}{4}}$OneFromHevn$118^{3\frac{3}{4}}$KyBd$118^{1\frac{1}{2}}$	Ridden out	9
24Sep87- 5Bel	fst 1	:23^{3} :46^{4} 1:11^{3} 1:36^{1}	3↑ ⒻAlw 33000	5	2	$1^{2\frac{1}{2}}$	1^{3}	1^{5}	$1^{7\frac{3}{4}}$	Romero RP	113	*.20	84-20	PersonalEnsign$113^{7\frac{3}{4}}$WithaTwist117^{nk}RosaMay117^{6}	Handily	5
6Sep87- 5Bel	fst 7f	:23^{2} :46^{2} 1:10^{3} 1:23^{1}	3↑ ⒻAlw 31000	3	5	4^{3}	1^{hd}	$1^{1\frac{1}{2}}$	$1^{3\frac{3}{4}}$	Bailey JD	113	*.70	86-19	PersonalEnsign$113^{3\frac{3}{4}}$ChicShirine$113^{1\frac{1}{4}}$WithTwst$117^{\frac{1}{2}}$	Handily	6
13Oct86- 8Bel	fst 1	:23^{2} :46 1:10^{1} 1:36^{2}	ⒻFrizette-G1	2	2	$2^{\frac{1}{2}}$	2^{hd}	1^{hd}	1^{hd}	Romero RP	119	*.30	83-16	PersonalEnsign119^{hd}Collins$119^{5\frac{1}{2}}$FlyingKatuna119	Driving	3
28Sep86- 6Bel	my 7f	:23^{1} :46^{3} 1:10^{3} 1:22^{4}	ⒻMd Sp Wt	5	7	$2^{2\frac{1}{2}}$	$1^{1\frac{1}{2}}$	1^{7}	$1^{12\frac{3}{4}}$	Romero RP	117	*.90	88-15	Personal Ensign$117^{12\frac{3}{4}}$Graceful Darby$117^{2\frac{3}{4}}$Nastique$117^{1\frac{1}{2}}$	Hesitated start,clear	7

Ruffian

dkbbr. f. 1972, by Reviewer (Bold Ruler)–Shenanigans, by Native Dancer
Own.– Locust Hill Farm
Br.– Mr & Mrs Stuart S. Janney Jr (Ky)
Tr.– F.Y. Whiteley Jr

Lifetime record: 11 10 0 0 $313,429

6Jly75- 8Bel	fst $1\frac{1}{4}$	:44^{3} 1:08^{3} 1:35^{2} 2:02^{4}	Match Race 350k	1	1	-	-	-	-	Vasquez J	121	*.40	- -	Foolish Pleasure126	Broke down	2
21Jun75- 8Bel	fst $1\frac{1}{2}$	:49 1:13^{2} 2:03^{1} 2:27^{4}	ⒻC C A Oaks-G1	5	1	1^{4}	$1^{1\frac{1}{2}}$	1^{3}	$1^{2\frac{3}{4}}$	Vasquez J	121	*.05	81-12	Ruffn$121^{2\frac{3}{4}}$EqulChng121^{9}LtMLngr$121^{2\frac{1}{4}}$	Confidently ridden	7
31May75- 8Aqu	fst $1\frac{1}{8}$	:47^{3} 1:11^{3} 1:35^{3} 1:47^{4}	ⒻMother Goose-G1	6	1	$1^{1\frac{3}{4}}$	1^{2}	1^{8}	$1^{13\frac{1}{2}}$	Vasquez J	121	*.10	96-07	Rffian$121^{13\frac{1}{2}}$SweetOldGirl121^{2}SunandSnow$121^{2\frac{1}{2}}$	Easy score	7
10May75- 8Aqu	fst 1	:23^{2} :45^{3} 1:09^{3} 1:34^{2}	ⒻAcorn-G1	3	1	1^{1}	1^{3}	1^{7}	$1^{8\frac{1}{4}}$	Vasquez J	121	*.10	94-08	Ruffian$121^{8\frac{1}{4}}$Somethingregal121^{no}GallantTrial121^{1}	In hand	7
30Apr75- 8Aqu	fst 7f	:22^{4} :45 1:08^{4} 1:21^{1}	ⒻComely-G3	3	5	1^{1}	$1^{1\frac{1}{2}}$	1^{6}	$1^{7\frac{3}{4}}$	Vasquez J	113	*.05	95-16	Ruffian$113^{7\frac{3}{4}}$AuntJin$113^{2\frac{1}{2}}$PointnTm113^{2}	Slow start,handily	5
14Apr75- 8Aqu	fst 6f	:23 :45^{4} 1:09^{2}	ⒻAlw 20000	2	3	1^{1}	$1^{\frac{1}{2}}$	1^{2}	$1^{4\frac{3}{4}}$	Vasquez J	122	*.10	96-17	Ruffian$122^{4\frac{3}{4}}$SirIvor'sSorrow113^{hd}Channelette113^{2}	Easily	5
23Aug74- 8Sar	fst 6f	:22^{1} :44^{4} 1:08^{3}	ⒻSpinaway-G1	2	1	1^{2}	1^{3}	1^{7}	$1^{12\frac{3}{4}}$	Bracciale V Jr	120	*.20	97-10	Ruffian$120^{12\frac{3}{4}}$LaughingBridge$120^{1\frac{1}{2}}$ScottshMlody120^{5}	Easily	4
27Jly74- 8Mth	fst 6f	:21^{3} :44^{1} 1:09	ⒻSorority-G1	3	3	$1^{\frac{1}{2}}$	1^{hd}	$1^{\frac{1}{2}}$	$1^{2\frac{1}{4}}$	Vasquez J	119	*.30	95-15	Ruffian$119^{2\frac{1}{4}}$Hot n Nasty119^{22}Stream Across119^{4}	Driving	4
10Jly74- 8Aqu	fst $5\frac{1}{2}$f	:21^{4} :44^{2} :56^{2} 1:02^{4}	ⒻAstoria-G3	2	2	1^{1}	1^{3}	1^{6}	1^{9}	Bracciale V Jr	118	*.10	99-15	Ruffian118^{9}Laughing Bridge115^{12}Our Dancing Girl$115^{3\frac{1}{4}}$	Speed to spare	4
12Jun74- 8Bel	fst $5\frac{1}{2}$f	:22^{2} :45^{1} :57 1:03	ⒻFashion-G3	3	4	$1^{1\frac{1}{2}}$	$1^{1\frac{1}{2}}$	1^{4}	$1^{6\frac{3}{4}}$	Vasquez J	117	*.40	100-12	Ruffian$117^{6\frac{3}{4}}$Copernica117^{13}Jan Verzal117^{nk}	Ridden out	6
22May74- 3Bel	fst $5\frac{1}{2}$f	:22^{1} :45 :57 1:03	ⒻMd Sp Wt	9	8	1^{3}	1^{5}	1^{8}	1^{15}	Vasquez J	116	4.20	100-15	Ruffian116^{15}Suzest113^{5}Garden Quad$116^{\frac{1}{2}}$	Ridden out	10

Past Performances of Great Horses of the 20th Century

Seabiscuit — **b. c. 1933, by Hard Tack (Man o' War)–Swing On, by Whisk Broom II** — **Lifetime record: 89 33 15 13 $437,730**

Own.– C.S. Howard
Br.– Wheatley Stable (Ky)
Tr.– T. Smith

2Mar40- 6SA	fst	1¼	:471 1:111 1:36 2:011	3↑ S Anita H 121k	12	5	21	2hd	1hd	11½	Pollard J	130wb	*.70e	101-11	Seabiscuit1301½Kayak II1291Whichcee1141½		13
	Avoided trouble first turn																
24Feb40- 6SA	fst	1 1/16	:231 :464 1:111 1:422	3↑ S Antonio H 13k	10	5	2½	2½	1½	12½	Pollard J	124wb	*1.70e	100-07	Seabiscuit1242½Kayak II128½Viscounty1104	Much best	13
17Feb40- 6SA	fst	7f	:223 :453 1:103 1:232	3↑ San Carlos H 12k	1	2	94	85¼	69	66¾	Pollard J	127wb	*.80e	88-14	Specify1151¼Lassator105hdViscounty1093	Close quarters	11
9Feb40- 6SA	fst	7f	:224 :454 1:103 1:23	4↑ Handicap 2000	2	5	52¼	63¾	43¼	33	Pollard J	128wb	*1.00	94-13	Heelfly1181Sun Egret1152Seabiscuit1283	Close quarters	8
14Feb39- 6SA	fst	1	:223 :453 1:102 1:353	4↑ Alw 1900	1	3	2nk	23	23	22¼	Woolf G	128wb	*.20	99-06	Today1042¼Seabiscuit1286Marica113	Went lame	3
1Nov38- 6Pim	fst	1 3/16	:473 1:114 1:364 1:563	3↑ Pim Spl 15k	2	1	11	1no	1½	14	Woolf G	120wb	2.20	101-08	Seabiscuit1204War Admiral120	Driving,best	2
15Oct38- 5Lrl	fst	1	:231 :472 1:121 1:37	2↑ Laurel 10k	6	8	63½	41¼	21½	22½	Woolf G	126wsb	*.60	98-12	Jacola1022½Seabiscuit1263The Chief1164	Second best	12
28Sep38- 5HdG	fst	1⅛	:472 1:122 1:372 1:50	3↑ Havre de Grace H 11k	6	5	32½	2½	11	12½	Woolf G	128wb	*.55	99-16	Seabiscuit1282½Savage Beauty1031Menow1201½	Going away	8
20Sep38- 5Bel	my	1½	:49 1:14 2:051 2:31	3↑ Manhattan H 6k	4	1	52¾	53½	34¼	33	Woolf G	128wb	*1.20	85-12	Isolater108hdRegal Lily1083Seabiscuit12810	Forced wide	5
12Aug38- 5Dmr	fst	1⅛	:462 1:104 1:361 1:49	3↑ Match Race 25k	1	2	2hd	1hd	1hd	1no	Woolf G	130wb	-	124-02	Seabiscuit130noLigaroti115	Driving	2
16Jly38- 7Hol	fst	1¼	:471 1:112 1:373 2:034	3↑ Hol Gold Cup 55k	7	8	912	48	24	11½	Woolf G	133wb	*.70	- -	Seabiscuit1331½Specify109noWhichcee1145	Going away	10
4Jly38- 6AP	sl	1⅛	:484 1:143 1:41 1:541	3↑ Stars & Stripes H 12k	10	7	97¾	67	42½	23½	Woolf G	130wb	*.90	72-30	WarMinstrel1073½Seabiscut130½Arb'sArrow1114	Closed fast	10
16Apr38- 7BM	fst	1⅛	:474 1:114 1:37 1:49	3↑ Bay Meadows H 16k	7	2	21	2hd	11	13	Woolf G	133wb	*.20e	107-10	Seabiscuit1333Gosum1131¾Today112no	Going away	7
27Mar38- 8AC	fst	1⅛	:47 1:114 1:37 1:502	3↑ Agua Caliente H 13k	1	1	1½	11½	13	12	Rich'son N	130wb	*.30	97-13	Seabiscuit1302Gray Jack103hdLittle Nymph984½	Eased up	8
5Mar38- 6SA	fst	1¼	:461 1:111 1:364 2:013	3↑ S Anita H 126k	12	14	127½	1hd	1hd	2no	Woolf G	130wb	*1.90	103-12	Stagehand100noSeabisct1306Pmpoon1202	Impeded,game try	18
26Feb38- 6SA	fst	1⅛	:47 1:113 1:371 1:50	3↑ San Antonio H 9.2k	5	5	46	42½	3½	2no	Workman R	130wb	*.40e	94-12	Aneroid118noSeabiscuit1301½IndianBroom108hd	Just missed	13
11Nov37- 6Pim	fst	1⅝	:501 1:41 2:062 2:451	3↑ Bowie H 12k	8	3	52¾	41¼	1hd	2no	Pollard J	130wb	*1.25	107-11	Esposa115noSeabiscuit1301¼Burning Star1141	Game try	8
5Nov37- 5Pim	fst	1 3/16	:47 1:113 1:37 1:572	3↑ Riggs H 12k	11	4	55½	4¾	1½	1nk	Pollard J	130wb	*.40e	103-11	Seabiscuit130nkBurningStar114¾CaballroII116½	Hard drive	11
	Previously owned by Mrs C.S. Howard																
16Oct37- 5Lrl	fst	1	:24 :471 1:121 1:372	2↑ Laurel 9.6k	7	3	2hd	2nk	1hd	11½•	Pollard J	126wb	*.70	99-14	DH Seabiscuit126 DH Heelfly1141½Deliberator1161	Gamely	7
12Oct37- 5Jam	fst	1 1/16	:24 :48 1:124 1:444	3↑ Continental H 12k	2	1	1hd	1nk	12	15	Pollard J	130wb	*.80	89-20	Seabiscuit1305Caballero II1172Moon Side1121	Easily	12
11Sep37- 5Nar	sly	1 3/16	:473 1:12 1:38 1:57	3↑ Nar Spl H 33k	5	4	46½	21½	33½	32½	Pollard J	132wb	*.85	87-16	Calumet Dick1151Snark1171½Seabiscuit1324	Weakened	6
7Aug37- 5Suf	fst	1⅛	:47 1:11 1:36 1:49	3↑ Mass H 70k	3	3	22½	21	1nk	11	Pollard J	130wb	*1.00	102-06	Seabiscuit1301CaballeroII1081FairKnghtss1082½	Drove out	13
24Jly37- 5Emp	fst	1 1/16	:233 :472 1:113 1:441	3↑ Yonkers H 10k	2	2	22	1hd	11½	14	Pollard J	129wb	*1.00	102-12	Seabiscuit1294Jesting1083Corinto1093	Going away	6
10Jly37- 5Emp	fst	1 3/16	:48 1:12 1:382 1:583	3↑ Butler H 25k	1	2	1½	1½	11½	11½	Pollard J	126wb	*.90	98-08	Seabiscuit1261½Thorson1073Corinto1091	Driving,best	6
26Jun37- 5Aqu	fst	1⅛	:47 1:112 1:37 1:501	3↑ Brooklyn H 25k	1	1	11	1½	1hd	1no	Pollard J	122wb	3.20	90-14	Seabiscuit122noAneroid1225Memory Book1143	Hard drive	9
22May37- 7BM	fst	1 1/16	:24 :473 1:11 1:443	3↑ Bay Meadows H 11k	8	2	2nk	21	1½	11¼	Pollard J	127wb	*.10e	87-15	Seabiscuit1271¼Exhibit105noWatersplash1031	Going away	8
17Apr37- 6Tan	fst	1⅛	:452 1:103 1:36 1:484	3↑ Marchbank H 11k	7	1	15	12	14	13	Pollard J	124wb	*.40	94-08	Seabiscuit1243Grand Manitou110hdSobriety1095	Easily	7
6Mar37- 6SA	fst	1⅛	:463 1:11 1:361 1:484	3↑ S Juan Capistrano H 12k	2	2	21½	2hd	14	17	Pollard J	120wb	*1.50	103-08	Seabiscuit1207GrandManitou108¾SpecialAgent116nk	Easily	10
27Feb37- 6SA	gd	1¼	:454 1:104 1:364 2:024	3↑ S Anita H 125k	3	9	44½	41½	1hd	2no	Pollard J	114wb	6.40	97-13	Rosemont124noSeabiscuit1141Indian Broom1162½	Nosed out	18
20Feb37- 6SA	fst	1⅛	:464 1:11 1:372 1:501	3↑ San Antonio H 9.4k	11	14	128¾	129¼	98¾	53¾	Pollard J	115wb	2.30	92-11	Rosemnt122¾StarShadow106½SpecialAgent1171	Forced wide	16
9Feb37- 6SA	fst	7f	:224 :452 1:104 1:231	4↑ Handicap 1545	5	1	1½	11	1½	14½	Pollard J	112wb	3.20	96-13	Seabiscuit1124½Sir Emerson104nkTime Supply1185	Easily	6
12Dec36- 7BM	fst	1 3/16	:47 1:112 1:364 1:554	2↑ World's Fair H 11k	4	3	15	13	13	15	Pollard J	113wb	*1.10	- -	Seabiscuit1135Wildland1012½GiantKiller1071½	Easily best	7
28Nov36- 7BM	fst	1	:232 :464 1:112 1:36	2↑ Bay Bridge H 2.7k	6	8	51¾	22	1hd	15	Pollard J	116wb	*2.20	106-07	Seabiscuit1165Uppermost114½Velociter107nk	Eased up	8
31Oct36- 4Emp	fst	1⅛	:491 1:14 1:392 1:52	3↑ Yorktown H 6.5k	7	6	54	66½	33½	31¾	Pollard J	119wb	8.00	93-11	Thorson112nkPiccolo1071½Seabiscuit1193	Closed fast	8
24Oct36- 4Emp	fst	1 70	:233 :473 1:121 1:44	3↑ Scarsdale H 7.3k	2	7	84¾	88¾	63¾	1no	Pollard J	116wb	12.00e	90-13	Seabiscuit116noJesting112hdPiccolo105.53	Just up	11
17Oct36- 6RD	my	1 1/16	:26 :51 1:18 1:562	3↑ East Hills H 2.7k	4	2	22	24	23	32½	Pollard J	116wb	3.20	29-59	MuchoGusto1111½SafeandSound1031Sebscut1162½	Closed well	6
3Oct36- 5RD	fst	1 1/16	:232 :464 1:113 1:44	3↑ Western Hills H 2.8k	7	4	52¼	53½	43½	31½	Pollard J	116wb	4.90	92-16	Marynell100½Cristate1081Seabiscuit1161	Closed fast	8

Past Performances of Great Horses of the 20th Century

26Sep36-6Det	fst 1 1/16	:24^3 :48^3 1:13 1:44^2	3↑ Hendrie H 2.8k	2 2 2½ 1^1 1^2 1^4	Pollard J	115wb	2.10	98-12	Seabiscuit115^4 Cristate114^2½ Safe and Sound108^3	Easily 6
19Sep36-6Det	fst 1 1/16	:24^3 :48^3 1:13^3 1:46	3↑ De La Salle H 2.8k	7 1 1^1 3^1 6^3½ 6^3¾	Pollard J	115wb	*1.60	86-13	Cristate106^hd Professor Paul105^hd Paradisical109^1½	Quit 8
7Sep36-6Det	fst 1⅛	:47 1:12 1:38 1:50^4	3↑ Governor's H 5.6k	12 3 2^hd 2^hd 1½ 1^nk	Pollard J	109wb	4.90	96-13	Seabiscuit109^nk Professor Paul99^1½ Azucar112^3	Driving 12
2Sep36-6Det	sl 1 70	:24^3 :48^4 1:14 1:44	3↑ Handicap 1200	3 1 1^hd 4^1¼ 3^1 3½	Pollard J	114wb	3.90	89-18	ProfessorPaul104^no SafeandSound102^½ Seabsct114^2½	Impeded 8
22Aug36-6Det	fst 1 1/16	:24 :47 1:11^3 1:43^2	3↑ Motor City H 5.7k	3 1 3^3 7^8 6^5 4^4¼	Pollard J	110wb	13.20	99-08	Myrtlewood122^3 Professor Paul95^nk Cristate106^1	Tired 11
	Previously owned by Wheatley Stable; previously trained by J. Fitzsimmons									
10Aug36-6Sar	gd 1⅛	:48^2 1:13^2 1:40^1 1:54	3↑ Handicap 1070	1 1 1^2 1^2 1^3 1^4	Stout J	112wb	*.90	80-17	Seabiscuit112^4 Treford110	Easily 2
3Aug36-5Sar	fst 1	:24^2 :48^1 1:12^4 1:38^2	3↑ Mohawk Claiming 6k	1 1 1^1½ 1^1 1^3 1^6	Stout J	109wb	4.00	89-15	Seabiscuit109^6 Ann O'Ruley112^2 Balkan Land109^2	Easily 7
25Jly36-5Suf	fst 1⅛	:47^3 1:12^2 1:38^1 1:51^1	Miles Standish H 3k	1 2 2^4 3^1¾ 3^3½ 4^4¼	Kopel F	115wb	5.90	87-08	Kearsarge99^nk Tatterdemalion113.5^4 BrownTop109^no	Faltered 7
29Jun36-4Suf	fst 6f	:22^4 :45^3 1:11^4	Alw 1000	2 8 6^4¾ 6^2¾ 3^4 1^1½	Knott K	115wb	12.60	96-11	Seabiscuit115^1½ Deliberate115^1½ Liberal115^3	Handily 12
24Jun36-5Suf	sl 6f	:23^4 :48 1:13^4	Commonwealth H 3.2k	6 13 12^8 12^12 10^9¼ 10^10¾	Kopel F	115wb	29.40	75-21	PartySpirit107^nk Indomitable105^4 SpeedtoSpare114^½	Outrun 13
1Jun36-5Bel	fst 1 1/16	:24 :47^4 1:13 1:45	3↑ Handicap 1240	5 6 6^7¼ 6^5½ 6^5 6^6¼	Hanford I	112wb	*1.60e	80-16	Gallant Prince116^1½ Brown Twig114^hd Gillie114^nk	Stumbled 6
27May36-5Rkm	sly 1	:23^4 :47^3 1:13^2 1:41^1	New Hampshire H 4k	9 11 12^9 12^9½ 12^9 12^9½	Kopel F	116wb	8.40	71-16	Faust103^no Gallant Gay110.5^no Party Spirit111^2	Outrun 15
18May36-5Nar	fst 1 1/16	:23^4 :47^2 1:12^3 1:44^1	Alw 1200	7 1 1^1 1^hd 1½ 1^3	Kopel F	111wb	2.60	96-11	Seabiscuit111^3 Piccolo106^3 Swamp Angel111^3½	Easily 7
13May36-5Nar	fst 1 1/16	:23^4 :47^2 1:12^3 1:44^4	Providence H 3.8k	8 1 1^2½ 2^1 3^1¼ 4^2½	Kopel F	115wb	4.20	90-13	Tugboat Frank110^2 Piccolo108^no Gallant Gay109^½	No excuse 8
8May36-4Jam	fst 6f	:23^1 :47 1:12	Alw 1000	4 6 7^7 7^7¾ 5^3½ 4^2¾	Stout J	113wb	*2.40	89-14	Gleeman110^1½ Wha Hae113^1 Stubbs116^nk	Finished fast 7
23Apr36-4Jam	fst 6f	:23^3 :47^1 1:12^1	Handicap 1220	4 4 4^8 4^7½ 3^3½ 3^7	Hanford I	120wb	*.50	84-17	Goldeneye105^3 Chancer105^4 Seabiscuit120^3	No excuse 4
18Apr36-3Jam	fst 6f	:22^4 :46^2 1:12	Alw 1000	1 1 2^2 2^5 2^1½ 2^1½	Hanford I	105wb	5.00	90-13	Tintagel118^1½ Seabiscuit105^4 Hollyrood118^8	Good effort 5
11Nov35-6Pim	my 1 1/16	:24 :49^1 1:14^3 1:49^4	Walden H 11k	10 7 10^8¾ 10^12 9^15 6^6	Kopel F	108wb	14.45	65-27	Ned Reigh116^½ Challephen107^hd Wise Duke112^½	No excuse 10
26Oct35-5Nar	fst 6f	:22^3 :45^1 1:11^1	Pawtucket H 6k	4 4 4^3½ 4^4 4^3¾ 2½	Stout J	117wb	*1.85	95-10	Clocks111^½ Seabiscuit117^1½ Crossbow II121^1	Finished fast 5
23Oct35-5Emp	fst 5¾f	:23 :47 1:08^4	Ardsley H 3.7k	4 3 2^hd 2^hd 1^1 1^3	Kopel F	112wb	4.00	95-13	Seabiscuit112^3 Neap107^2 Wha Hae115^½	Easily 6
16Oct35-5Agm	fst 6f	:23^4 :46 1:11^2	Springfield H 2.8k	8 1 1^2 1^1½ 1^1 1^1	Stout J	109wb	8.00	--	Seabiscuit109^1 BrightPlumage117^hd Infidox117^1½	Ridden out 8
2Oct35-4Suf	fst 6f	:23^1 :46^2 1:12^1	Constitution H 9.2k	10 10 9^5½ 10^7 10^8¼ 10^10	Woolf G	115wb	21.90	84-08	Infidox110^nk Clocks110^nk Sparta109^½	Outrun 10
21Sep35-3Jam	fst 6f	:23^3 :46^4 1:12	Remsen H 4.7k	2 11 11^15 10^14 9^12 9^7¾	Horn F	112wb	7.00e	84-12	The Fighter122^no Teufel112^2 Postage Due124^1½	Off slowly 11
14Sep35-4HdG	fst 6f	:23^2 :47^4 1:13	Eastern Shore H 14k	6 7 8^5¼ 9^2½ 6^4½ 4^1½	Rosengarten C	112wb	38.50e	86-11	Postage Due117^½ Wise Duke115^no Maerial120^1	Forced wide 14
9Sep35-6Aqu	fst 6f	:23^3 :48 1:13^1	Alw 1000	4 4 1^1 1^1½ 1^2 1^3	Kopel F	115wb	12.00	88-13	Seabiscuit115^3 Count Morse109^5 Dark Wizard112^2	Easily 8
4Sep35-3Aqu	sly 6f	:23^2 :47^3 1:12^2	Alw 1000	5 3 4^6¾ 4^5½ 5^4½ 3^6	Kopel F	110wb	10.00	86-10	PhantomFox106^no Pullman114^6 Seabiscuit110^nk	Finished well 7
2Sep35-3Aqu	fst 6f	:24^1 :49 1:12	Babylon H 4.2k	5 6 5^11 6^7 6^7¾ 6^12	Horn F	112wb	1.50e	82-09	NedReigh116^no SpeedtoSpare115^no Granville114^5	No excuse 6
26Aug35-4Sar	fst 6f	:23 :47 1:12	Alw 1000	5 8 8^12 8^6¼ 6^6 6^8½	Horn F	112wb	25.00	83-10	BoldVenture115^1½ GrandSlam122^3 Valvctorn115^2	Dropped back 9
14Aug35-5Sar	gd 5½f	:23^1 :47^3 1:07^1	Alw 1000	11 13 13^13 13^9¼ 10^6½ 9^5¼	Gilbert J	112wb	6.00e	82-14	Maerial118^1 Lovely Girl104^2 Speed109^no	Off slowly 13
27Jly35-6Suf	fst 6f	:23^3 :46^3 1:12^2	Bay State 3.7k	4 6 3^1¼ 5^2¼ 3^2½ 4^3	Stout J	123wb	13.60	--	BlackHighbrow111^3 NouveauRiche108^no St.Lous108^no	Faltered 7
22Jly35-3Suf	fst 6f	:23^1 :45^4 1:11^2	Alw 1000	5 5 2^1 2½ 2^2½ 2^1½	Stout J	115wb	*1.70	--	Black Highbrow115^1½ Seabiscuit115^8 Nedvive112^½	Gamely 5
15Jly35-5Suf	fst 6f	:23^2 :47^2 1:13^1	Mayflower 3k	4 8 5^2¼ 4^2¼ 6^2½ 4^4	Horn F	123wb	15.00	--	Maerial123^2 Jair111^½ Tugboat Frank111^1½	No excuse 9
4Jly35-5Nar	fst 5f	:22^3 :46 :59^3	Old Colony 6.7k	3 4 4^2 4^5 4^4¾ 5^2½	Stout J	117wb	*1.40	101-07	BrightandEarly114^1 Swashbuckler114^½ Chllphn112^1	No excuse 6
26Jun35-5Nar	fst 5f	:22^3 :45^4 :59^3	Watch Hill Claiming 5k	6 5 2½ 1^1½ 1^1 1^2	Horn F	108wb	*1.70	104-08	Seabiscuit108^2 Infidox108^1 Zowie102^2	Easily 8
22Jun35-2Nar	fst 5f	:23^1 :46^4 1:00^3	Alw 1000	9 5 1½ 1^2 1^1½ 1^2	Stout J	110wb	*2.55	99-12	Seabiscuit110^2 Ned Reigh110^2½ Tugboat Frank115^1½	Easily 9
11Jun35-1Rkm	hy 5f	:23^4 :49 1:02	Md Sp Wt	3 8 1½ 2^1½ 2^4 2^6	Stout J	116wb	*.60	78-18	Jubilee Jim116^6 Seabiscuit116^2½ Sky Pirate116^2	Gamely 8
8Jun35-4Rkm	fst 5f	:23^1 :46^2 :59^4	Juvenile H 5.7k	2 8 7^4¼ 6^5 3^1¾ 3^1¼	Stout J	103wb	30.20	94-12	WinterSport105^1 PostageDue124^nk Seabiscut103^½	Good effort 12
1Jun35-1Rkm	fst 5f	:23 :46^1 1:01^1	Md Sp Wt	5 7 2^1 2^1½ 2^3 2^3	Stout J	116wb	7.75	85-14	Swashbuckler116^3 Seabiscuit116^1½ Sobriety116^3	Good effort 12
28May35-1Rkm	fst 5f	:23^2 :47^4 1:01^1	Md Sp Wt	2 11 9^8¼ 9^7¾ 3^4½ 4^2½	Stout J	116wb	*2.05	85-11	SandyMack116^1½ Browbeatn113^1 TugboatFrnk116^hd	Closed gap 11
21May35-2Rkm	fst 5f	:23^1 :47^3 1:00^4	Alw 800	7 9 7^6¼ 8^7½ 3^1¼ 3^nk	Stout J	106wb	9.85	90-13	Microbe114^nk BlackMistress111^no Seabiscuit106^1	Closed fast 9
4May35-1Jam	fst 5f	:23^3 :47^2 1:00^2	Md Sp Wt	2 2 5^7½ 5^5¼ 6^4½ 6^8	Burke JH	115wb	2.00e	83-11	Pullman115^1½ Knowing115^½ Royal Fox115^5	Shuffled 8
1May35-4Jam	fst 5f	:23^1 :47^3 1:01	Alw 1000	4 6 6^9¼ 5^6½ 5^3¾ 2½	Horn F	110wb	10.00	87-15	Galsac116^½ Seabiscuit110^no TransitLady110^no	Finished fast 6

Past Performances of Great Horses of the 20th Century

Previously trained by G. Tappen

Date	Track	Cond	Dist	Time1	Time2	Race	PP/Running	Jockey	Wt	Odds	Pos	Comment
25Apr35- 2HdG	fst 4½f	:232.473	:542			Clm 4000	5 2　51¼ 44½ 4½	Workman R	114wb	3.50	92-07	Cherry Stone115no Hiatus110hd Prosy113½ Finished fast 11
22Apr35- 2HdG	fst 4½f	:232.473	:542			Clm 2500	6 7　89¼ 47½ 33½	Peters M	116wb	11.95	89-07	Hiatus113½ Deliberate1143 Seabiscuit116½ Close quarters 13
13Apr35-4Bow	my 4f	:492				Md Sp Wt	8 7　712 66¾ 35½	Horn F	115wb	7.35	80-13	ParaguayTea1122½ PatseyBegone1123 Sebscut115½ Off slowly 9
10Apr35-4Bow	my 4f	:233	:492			Alw 800	9 10　911 97¾ 87¼	Horn F	110wb	30.35	79-15	VictoriousAnn112hd WinterSport115½ Ste.Louise1121 Outrun 12
4Apr35-1Bow	sl 4f	:24				⊚Md Sp Wt	1 1　58½ 35½ 21½	Horn F	115wb	3.80	83-15	Borsa115½ Seabiscuit1153 Green Mist1151 Finished gamely 8

Previously trained by V. Mara

8Mar35- 1Hia	fst 3f	:343				Alw 1000	12 10　63¼ 43½	Horn F	113wb	4.50f	--	VctorousAnn1102 WllwWood113hd TwoEdgd113½ Finished fast 14
5Mar35- 1Hia	fst 3f	:343				Alw 800	8 8　83¾ 85	Horn F	109wb	49.50	--	James City1191½ Grand Slam108nk Bright Light114hd Impeded 13
27Feb35- 1Hia	fst 3f	:341				Clm 2500	2 1　73½ 63	Horn F	108 w	11.35	--	Black Bess100no Transit110no Edri1051½ No excuse 11
22Jan35- 1Hia	fst 3f	:351				Clm 2500	10 6　53¾ 22	Stout J	110	9.50	--	ClappingJane1072½ Seabiscuit110hd Spart107nk Finished fast 12
19Jan35-1Hia	fst 3f	:343				Alw 1000	5 6　55¾ 44½	Stout J	110	16.85e	--	Wha Hae1131 Wise Duke1103 Blue Donna107½ Good effort 10

Seattle Slew

dkbbr. c. 1974, by Bold Reasoning (Boldnesian)–My Charmer, by Poker
Own.– Tayhill Stable
Br.– B.S. Castleman (Ky)
Tr.– Douglas Peterson
Lifetime record: 17 14 2 0 $1,208,726

Date	Track	Cond	Dist	Times	Race	PP/Running	Jockey	Wt	Odds	Pos	Comment
11Nov78- 8Aqu	fst 1⅛	:46 1:10 1:342 1:473	3↑		Stuyvesant H-G3	1 1　11½ 13 13 13¼	Cordero A Jr	134	*.10	98-12	SeattleSlew1343¼ JumpingHill1152¼ WisePhlp113½ Ridden out 5
14Oct78- 8Bel	sly 1⅛	:451 1:092 2:014 2:273	3↑		J C Gold Cup-G1	1 1　1hd 1hd 2½ 2no	Cordero A Jr	126	*.60	84-13	Exceller126no SeattleSlew126¼ GrtContrctor1264¾ Bore out 6
30Sep78- 8Bel	sly 1¼	:473 1:104 1:351 2:00	3↑		Woodward-G1	5 1　12 12½ 12½ 14	Cordero A Jr	126	*.30	109-12	SeattleSlew1264 Exceller126⁶ It'sFreezng126no Ridden out 5
16Sep78- 8Bel	fst 1⅛	:47 1:10 1:331 1:454	3↑		Marlboro Cup H-G1	4 1　12½ 12½ 13 13	Cordero A Jr	128	2.10	98-12	Seattle Slew1283 Affirmed1244 Nasty and Bold1184 Driving 6

Previously owned by Karen L. Taylor

5Sep78- 6Med	fst 1⅛	:46 1:094 1:35 1:48	3↑		Paterson H-G3	10 1　13½ 11½ 11½ 2nk	Cruguet J	128	*.20	93-13	Dr.Patches114nk SeattleSlew1282¼ It'sFrzng1125 Drifted in 10
12Aug78- 7Sar	sly 7f	:22 :44 1:091 1:213	3↑		Alw 25000	5 2　11 15 14 16	Cruguet J	119	*.10	97-18	SeattleSlew1196 ProudBirdie1153¼ CapitalIdea11516 Handily 5
14May78- 7Aqu	sly 7f	:224 :453 1:10 1:224	3↑		Alw 25000	3 3　2½ 11½ 17 18¼	Cruguet J	122	*.10	87-26	SeattleSlew1228¼ ProudArion1191¼ Capult'sSong1155 Handily 6

Previously trained by William Turner Jr

3Jly77- 8Hol	fst 1¼	:452 1:091 1:331 1:583			Swaps-G1	2 2　32 36 411 416	Cruguet J	126	*.20	82-11	J.O. Tobin1208 Affiliate117no Text1208 Steadied,bore in 7
11Jun77- 8Bel	my 1½	:481 1:14 2:032 2:293			Belmont-G1	5 1　1½ 14 13½ 14	Cruguet J	126	*.40	72-17	SeattleSlew1264 RunDstyRun1263² Sanhedrn1262¾ Handy score 8
21May77- 8Pim	fst 1 3⁄16	:453 1:094 1:344 1:542			Preakness-G1	8 2　1hd 2½ 13 11½	Cruguet J	126	*.40	98-10	Seattle Slew12614 Iron Constitution1262 Run Dusty Run1261¾ 9

Drew clear

7May77- 8CD	fst 1¼	:454 1:103 1:36 2:021			Ky Derby-G1	4 2　2hd 1hd 13 11¾	Cruguet J	126	*.50	86-12	SeattleSlew12613 RunDstyRn126nk Sanhdrn1263¼ Ridden out 15
23Apr77- 8Aqu	fst 1⅛	:474 1:121 1:363 1:493			Wood Memorial-G1	6 1　1hd 11½ 16 13¼	Cruguet J	126	*.10	87-13	Seattle Slew1263½ Sanhedrin126¾ Catalan126hd Handily 7
26Mar77- 9Hia	fst 1⅛	:451 1:09 1:34 1:472			Flamingo-G1	4 1　11½ 16 16 14	Cruguet J	122	*.20	95-15	SeattleSlew1224 Gboul122nk FortPrvl1224½ Speed in reserve 13
9Mar77- 9Hia	fst 7f	:221.44 1:08 1:203			Alw 7000	2 6　1hd 12 14 19	Cruguet J	117	*.10	102-10	SeattleSlw1179 WhitRammr1223½ SmashingNatv1192½ Easily 8
16Oct76- 7Bel	fst 1	:233.46 1:10 1:342			Champagne-G1	3 1　12 12 12 19¾	Cruguet J	122	*1.30	96-13	SeattleSlew1179 FortheMoment1227½ SltoRom1223 Easy score 10
5Oct76- 7Bel	fst 7f	:223.454 1:092 1:22			Alw 11000	1 8　11½ 11 13 13½	Cruguet J	122	*.40	92-13	SeattleSlew1223¼ CruiseonIn1196 Lancer'sPrld1174 Handily 8
20Sep76- 5Bel	fst 6f	:222.452 1:101			Md Sp Wt	8 10　1½ 12 15 15	Cruguet J	122	*2.60	91-12	Seattle Slew1225 Proud Arion122¾ Prince Andrew1222 Easily 12

Past Performances of Great Horses of the 20th Century

Secretariat

ch. c. 1970, by Bold Ruler (Nasrullah)–Somethingroyal, by Princequillo — **Lifetime record: 21 16 3 1 $1,316,808**

Own.– Meadow Stable
Br.– Meadow Stud Inc (Va)
Tr.– L. Laurin

28Oct73-8WO	fm 1⅝[T]	:47^2 1:37^3 2:41^4	3↑ Can Int'l-G2	12 2 2$^{1\frac{1}{2}}$ 1^5 1^{12} 1$^{6\frac{1}{2}}$	Maple E	117 b	*.20	96-04	Secretariat117$^{6\frac{1}{2}}$BigSpruce126$^{1\frac{1}{2}}$GoldenDon117$^{\frac{3}{4}}$	Ridden out	12
8Oct73-7Bel	fm 1½[T]	:47 1:11^3 2:00 2:24^4	3↑ Man o' War-G1	3 1 1^3 1$^{1\frac{1}{2}}$ 1^3 1^5	Turcotte R	121 b	*.50	103-01	Secretariat121^{5}Tentam126$^{7\frac{1}{2}}$Big Spruce126$^{\frac{1}{2}}$	Ridden out	7
29Sep73-7Bel	sly 1½	:50 1:13^2 2:01^4 2:25^4	3↑ Woodward-G1	5 2 2$^{\frac{1}{2}}$ 1^{hd} 2$^{1\frac{1}{2}}$ 2$^{4\frac{1}{2}}$	Turcotte R	119 b	*.30	86-15	ProveOut126$^{4\frac{1}{2}}$Secretariat119^{11}CougarII126$^{\frac{1}{2}}$	Best of rest	5
15Sep73-7Bel	fst 1⅛	:45^3 1:09^1 1:33 1:45^2	3↑ Marl Cup Inv'l H 250k	7 5 5$^{1\frac{1}{4}}$ 3$^{\frac{1}{2}}$ 1^2 1$^{3\frac{1}{2}}$	Turcotte R	124 b	*.40e	104-07	Secretariat124$^{3\frac{1}{2}}$Riva Ridge127^{2}Cougar II126$^{6\frac{1}{2}}$	Ridden out	7
4Aug73-7Sar	fst 1⅛	:47^4 1:11 1:36 1:49^1	3↑ Whitney H-G2	3 4 3^1 2$^{\frac{1}{2}}$ 2^{hd} 2^1	Turcotte R	119 b	*.10	94-15	Onion119^{1}Secretariat119$^{\frac{1}{2}}$Rule by Reason119^2	Weakened	5
30Jun73-8AP	fst 1⅛	:48 1:11^1 1:35 1:47	Invitational 125k	4 1 1^3 1$^{2\frac{1}{2}}$ 1^6 1^9	Turcotte R	126 b	*.05	99-17	Secretariat126^{9}My Gallant120^{nk}Our Native120^{17}	Easily	4
9Jun73-8Bel	fst 1½	:46^1 1:09^4 1:59 2:24	Belmont-G1	1 1 1^{hd} 1^{20} 1^{28} 1^{31}	Turcotte R	126 b	*.10	113-05	Secretariat126^{31}TwiceaPrince126$^{\frac{1}{2}}$MyGllnt126^{13}	Ridden out	5
19May73-8Pim	fst 1$\frac{3}{16}$	:48^1 1:11^2 1:35^3 1:54^2	Preakness-G1	3 4 1$^{\frac{1}{2}}$ 1$^{2\frac{1}{2}}$ 1$^{2\frac{1}{2}}$ 1$^{2\frac{1}{2}}$	Turcotte R	126 b	*.30	98-13	Secretariat126$^{2\frac{1}{2}}$Sham126^{8}Our Native126^1	Handily	6
	Daily Racing Form time 1:53 2/5										
5May73-9CD	fst 1¼	:47^2 1:11^4 1:36^1 1:59^2	Ky Derby-G1	10 11 6$^{9\frac{1}{2}}$ 2$^{\frac{1}{2}}$ 1$^{\frac{1}{2}}$ 1$^{2\frac{1}{2}}$	Turcotte R	126 b	*1.50e	103-10	Secretariat126$^{2\frac{1}{2}}$Sham126^{8}Our Native126$^{\frac{1}{2}}$	Handily	13
21Apr73-7Aqu	fst 1⅛	:48^1 1:12^1 1:36^4 1:49^4	Wood Memorial-G1	6 7 6^6 5$^{5\frac{1}{2}}$ 4$^{5\frac{1}{2}}$ 3^4	Turcotte R	126 b	*.30e	83-17	Angle Light126^{hd}Sham126^{4}Secretariat126$^{\frac{1}{2}}$	Wide,hung	8
7Apr73-7Aqu	fst 1	:23^1 :45^1 1:08^3 1:33^2	Gotham-G2	3 3 1^{hd} 1^2 1$^{\frac{1}{2}}$ 1^3	Turcotte R	126 b	*.10	100-08	Secretariat126^{3}ChampagneCharl117^{10}Flush117$^{2\frac{1}{2}}$	Ridden out	6
17Mar73-7Aqu	sly 7f	:22^1 :44^4 1:10 1:23^1	Bay Shore-G3	4 5 5^6 5^3 1^{hd} 1$^{4\frac{1}{2}}$	Turcotte R	126 b	*.20	85-17	Secretarit126$^{4\frac{1}{2}}$ChmpgnChrl118$^{2\frac{1}{2}}$Impcunous126^{no}	Mild drive	6
18Nov72-8GS	fst 1$\frac{1}{16}$	:24^1 :47^2 1:12 1:44^2	Garden State 298k	6 6 4$^{6\frac{1}{4}}$ 3^3 1$^{1\frac{1}{2}}$ 1$^{3\frac{1}{2}}$	Turcotte R	122 b	*.10e	83-23	Secretariat122$^{3\frac{1}{2}}$Angle Light122$^{\frac{1}{2}}$Step Nicely122$^{\frac{3}{4}}$	Handily	6
28Oct72-7Lrl	sly 1$\frac{1}{16}$	:22^4 :45^4 1:11^2 1:42^4	Lrl Futurity 133k	5 6 5^{10} 5^3 1^5 1^8	Turcotte R	122 b	*.10e	99-14	Secretariat122^{8}Stop the Music122^{8}Angle Light122^1	Easily	6
14Oct72-7Bel	fst 1	:22^4 :45^1 1:09^4 1:35	Champagne 146k	4 11 9$^{8\frac{1}{2}}$ 5$^{3\frac{1}{2}}$ 1$^{\frac{1}{2}}$ 1^2	Turcotte R	122 b	*.70e	97-12	[D]Secretariat122^{2}StoptheMusic122^{2}StepNicly122$^{1\frac{1}{2}}$	Bore in	12
	Disqualified and placed second										
16Sep72-7Bel	fst 6½f	:22^3 :45^3 1:10 1:16^2	Futurity 144k	4 5 6$^{5\frac{1}{2}}$ 5$^{3\frac{1}{2}}$ 1^2 1$^{1\frac{3}{4}}$	Turcotte R	122 b	*.20	98-09	Secretariat122$^{1\frac{3}{4}}$StoptheMusic122^{5}SwiftCourr122$^{2\frac{1}{2}}$	Handily	7
26Aug72-7Sar	fst 6½f	:22^4 :46^3 1:09^4 1:16^1	Hopeful 86k	8 8 9$^{6\frac{1}{2}}$ 1^{hd} 1^4 1^5	Turcotte R	121 b	*.30	97-12	Secretariat121^{5}FlighttoGlory121^{nk}StopthMusc121^2	Handily	9
16Aug72-7Sar	fst 6f	:22^4 :46^1 1:10	Sanford 27k	2 5 5^4 4^1 1$^{\frac{1}{2}}$ 1^3	Turcotte R	121 b	1.50	96-14	Secretariat121^{3}Lnd'sChf121^{6}NorthstrDncr121$^{3\frac{1}{2}}$	Ridden out	5
31Jly72-4Sar	fst 6f	:23^1 :46^2 1:10^4	Alw 9000	4 7 7$^{3\frac{3}{4}}$ 3$^{\frac{1}{2}}$ 1^{hd} 1$^{1\frac{1}{2}}$	Turcotte R	118 b	*.40	92-13	Secretariat118$^{1\frac{1}{2}}$Russ Miron118^{7}Joe Iz118$^{2\frac{1}{2}}$	Ridden out	7
15Jly72-4Aqu	fst 6f	:22^1 :45^2 1:10^3	[C]Md Sp Wt	8 11 6$^{6\frac{1}{2}}$ 4^3 1$^{\frac{1}{2}}$ 1^6	Feliciano P^5	113 b	*1.30	90-14	Secretariat113^{6}Master Achiever118$^{\frac{3}{4}}$Be on It118^4	Handily	11
4Jly72-2Aqu	fst 5½f	:22^2 :46^1 :58^4 1:05	[C]Md Sp Wt	2 11 10^7 10$^{8\frac{3}{4}}$ 7$^{5\frac{1}{2}}$ 4$^{1\frac{1}{4}}$	Feliciano P^5	113 b	*3.10	87-11	Herbull118^{nk}Master Achiever118^{1}Fleet 'n Royal118^{no}		12
	Impeded,rallied										

Shuvee

ch. f. 1966, by Nashua (Nasrullah)–Levee, by Hill Prince — **Lifetime record: 44 16 10 6 $890,445**

Own.– Mrs. Whitney Stone
Br.– W. Stone (Va)
Tr.– W.C. Freeman

30Oct71-7Aqu	fst 2	:48^2 2:30 2:55^2 3:20^2	3↑ J C Gold Cup 111k	6 4 2$^{\frac{1}{2}}$ 1$^{1\frac{1}{2}}$ 1^5 1^7	Velasquez J	121	*1.30	94-16	Shuvee121^{7}Paraje124^{2}Loud124^8	Ridden out	7
11Oct71-8Atl	gd 1$\frac{3}{16}$	:48^2 1:11^3 1:36^4 1:56^4	3↑ [F]Matchmaker 50k	6 5 4$^{5\frac{1}{2}}$ 5$^{6\frac{1}{2}}$ 3^1 4$^{\frac{3}{4}}$	Turcotte R	118	*1.30	91-12	Deceit113^{hd}Sea Saga114^{hd}Double Delta125$^{\frac{1}{2}}$	No excuse	8
2Oct71-7Bel	fst 1¼	:46^1 1:10 1:35 2:00^2	3↑ Woodward 113k	7 4 5^{10} 6^9 6^9 6^9	Turcotte R	123	3.70	89-13	[D]CougarII126^{5}WestCoastScout121^{nk}Tinajro121^{no}	No threat	10
11Sep71-7Bel	sly 1⅛	:45^3 1:09^3 1:35^1 1:48^3	3↑ [F]Beldame 82k	2 6 4$^{6\frac{1}{2}}$ 2^6 2^4 2$^{\frac{1}{2}}$	Baeza B	123	*.70	90-12	Double Delta123$^{\frac{1}{2}}$Shuvee123^{10}Cathy Honey123$^{1\frac{1}{2}}$	Second best	7
23Aug71-7Sar	fst 1⅛	:50 1:14^1 1:38^2 1:50^3	3↑ [F]Diana H 44k	5 3 3$^{1\frac{1}{2}}$ 2^1 2^1 1^{nk}	Turcotte R	128	*1.10	88-11	Shuvee128^{nk}Double Delta126$^{5\frac{1}{2}}$Cathy Honey116^{nk}	Hard drive	5
7Aug71-7Sar	fst 1⅛	:47^3 1:11^4 1:36^4 1:49^2	3↑ Whitney 60k	13 9 10$^{8\frac{1}{4}}$ 11$^{6\frac{1}{4}}$ 6^6 3^3	Turcotte R	116	*4.10	91-11	Protanto117^{hd}Peace Corps114^{3}Shuvee116^{nk}	Rallied wide	14
22May71-7Aqu	fst 1⅛	:47^1 1:12^2 1:37 1:49^3	3↑ [F]Top Flight H 53k	5 3 3$^{1\frac{1}{2}}$ 1$^{\frac{1}{2}}$ 1^1 1$^{\frac{3}{4}}$	Turcotte R	127	*.70e	88-17	Shuvee127$^{\frac{3}{4}}$Cathy Honey118$^{1\frac{1}{4}}$Office Queen127^7	Driving	5
28Apr71-7Aqu	fst 1	:23^2 :46^4 1:11^3 1:36^4	3↑ [F]Bed o' Roses H 32k	2 4 4$^{2\frac{1}{2}}$ 4^2 2$^{1\frac{1}{2}}$ 2^2	Turcotte R	127	*.60	81-23	Office Queen125^{2}Shuvee127^{3}Royal Fillet110$^{3\frac{1}{2}}$	Gamely	6
15Apr71-7Aqu	fst 6f	:23 :46^2 1:10^3	3↑ Alw 20000	6 1 5$^{3\frac{1}{2}}$ 6^7 6^8 2^5	Baeza B	116	*1.60e	85-25	SummerAir119^{5}Shuvee116^{nk}PrimeVenture121$^{1\frac{1}{2}}$	Finished well	9
31Oct70-7Aqu	fst 2	:50^3 2:30^2 2:55^4 3:21^3	3↑ J C Gold Cup 108k	4 1 1$^{\frac{1}{2}}$ 1^{hd} 1$^{2\frac{1}{2}}$ 1^2	Turcotte R	121	2.90	88-16	Shuvee121^{2}Loud119$^{1\frac{1}{4}}$Hydrologist124$^{3\frac{3}{4}}$	Mild urging	5

Past Performances of Great Horses of the 20th Century

3Oct70- 7Bel	fst 1¼	:462 1:101 1:353 2:014 3↑	Woodward 109k	2	4	46	41½	55½	57¾	Turcotte R	123		7.70	83-08	Personality121nk[DH]Hydrologst126[DH]Twogundn1264½	Hit rail	7
12Sep70- 7Bel	fst 1⅛	:454 1:10 1:351 1:48 3↑	Ⓕ Beldame 83k	2	2	25	23	11	11	Turcotte R	123		*1.30e	94-14	Shuvee1231Obeah1231¼Cold Comfort1182½	Brisk drive	7
24Aug70- 7Sar	sly 1⅛	:464 1:112 1:371 1:493 3↑	Ⓕ Diana H 49k	4	6	76¾	43	21	1no	Turcotte R	120		3.50	93-15	Shuvee120noDark Emerald1094Native Partner1121	Driving	12
8Jly70- 8Mth	fst 1 1/16	:232 :463 1:111 1:44 3↑	Ⓕ Molly Pitcher 44k	4	3	58¼	67½	66½	56	Baeza B	123		*.70	79-13	DoubleRipple112¾WhataDream1151Deb'sDarlng1144	No excuse	9
10Jun70- 7Bel	fst 7f	:222 :452 1:102 1:234 3↑	Ⓕ Vagrancy H 28k	2	4	511	611	611	510	Baeza B	123		2.00	78-15	Process Shot1272½Powder Mountain104¾Native Partner1106		6
	No response																
23May70- 7Aqu	fst 1⅛	:481 1:114 1:362 1:483 3↑	Ⓕ Top Flight H 57k	2	1	1hd	1½	1½	14	Baeza B	120		2.40	93-13	Shuvee1204Singing Rain1227Swiss Cheese110¾	Handily	10
2May70- 8Pim	fst 1 1/16	:233 :464 1:11 1:433 3↑	Ⓕ Gallorette H 32k	5	6	67	56½	27	28	Davidson J	122		*1.20	84-13	SingingRain1198Shuvee1223½MissFallRiver1091½	No excuse	7
25Apr70- 8Aqu	fst 1	:24 :464 1:11 1:352 3↑	Alw 15000	6	5	75¼	53	42	43¼	Davidson J	113		*3.30	87-18	GleamingSword1161¾ShiningSword1181½Bromtr120hd	No rally	9
8Apr70- 7Aqu	fst 7f	:23 :452 1:10 1:224 3↑	Ⓕ Distaff H 27k	2	5	510	512	613	615	Davidson J	123		7.50	72-20	ProcessShot1261¾TaWee1342DedctdtoSu115hd	Never a factor	6
27Nov69- 7Aqu	fst 1⅛	:492 1:134 1:381 1:50 3↑	Ⓕ Firenze H 56k	1	1	2½	42	21	2¾	Davidson J	122		*1.40	85-19	Amerigo Lady121¾Shuvee1221½Obeah120½	Finished willingly	8
11Nov69- 7Aqu	gd 1¼	:473 1:121 1:38 2:03 3↑	Ⓕ Ladies H 58k	7	3	612	43	3½	11¼	Davidson J	117		*2.80	81-22	Shuvee1171¼AmerigoLady1211¼Obeh1212½	Blocked,hard drive	11
1Nov69- 7Aqu	fst 7f	:221 :442 1:083 1:213 3↑	Vosburgh H 58k	3	10	119	1012	85½	61¾	Turcotte R	114		14.90	91-13	TaWee123hd[DH]PluckyLucky116[DH]RisingMarket120½	Late bid	11
13Sep69- 7Bel	fst 1⅛	:462 1:103 1:36 1:491 3↑	Ⓕ Beldame 81k	3	4	48½	46	37	36½	Davidson J	118		3.00	83-16	Gamely1233Amerigo Lady1233½Shuvee1182	Finished willing	5
30Aug69- 7Bel	fst 1⅛	:462 1:102 1:352 1:49	Ⓕ Gazelle H 53k	1	5	57	56½	47	36½	Davidson J	127		*1.10	84-12	Gallant Bloom1273½Pit Bunny1163Shuvee1271½	No excuse	5
9Aug69- 6Sar	gd 1¼	:483 1:131 1:392 2:062	Ⓕ Alabama 54k	2	4	46	31½	11½	14	Davidson J	124		*1.00	76-15	Shuvee1244PitBunny114½HailtoPatsy1182	Easily the best	5
26Jly69- 8Del	gd 1⅛	:464 1:122 1:384 1:511	Ⓕ Del Oaks 59k	7	5	68½	56½	411	417	Davidson J	121		1.60	64-23	[D]PitBunny1121¼GallantBloom12112WhitXmss1113¼	No excuse	7
12Jly69- 7Lib	fst 1 1/16	:231 :47 1:104 1:431	Ⓕ Cotillion H 55k	3	6	54¾	53¼	3½	1nk	Davidson J	124		*.40	- -	Shuvee124nkClass Is Out1133Secret Verdict1142	Just up	7
21Jun69- 7Bel	fst 1¼	:462 1:103 1:363 2:031	Ⓕ C C A Oaks 119k	4	5	511	44½	1hd	13	Davidson J	121		*.30	84-17	Shuvee1213Hail to Patsy1211½Secret Verdict1211½	Easily	7
31May69- 7Aqu	fst 1⅛	:474 1:123 1:38 1:501	Ⓕ Mother Goose 87k	1	4	511	55½	22	12½	Davidson J	121		*1.10	85-17	Shuvee1212½HailtoPatsy1212½RestlssTorndo1214	Ridden out	6
17May69- 7Aqu	fst 1	:223 :443 1:091 1:353	Ⓕ Acorn 59k	7	5	58½	36	2hd	1¾	Davidson J	121		*.80	89-14	Shuvee121¾Hail to Patsy1213Big Advance121nk	Mild drive	9
7May69- 7Aqu	fst 7f	:222 :451 1:092 1:223	Ⓕ Comely 28k	3	6	66	45	23	2hd	Davidson J	121		2.90	88-13	TaWee118hdShuvee1215HastyHitter118hd	Getting to winner	6
9Nov68- 8GS	sl 1 1/16	:23 :474 1:13 1:454	Ⓕ Gardenia 183k	5	7	52½	2hd	21½	21¼	Davidson J	119		*1.00	75-28	Gallant Bloom1191¼Shuvee11915Let's Be Gay119nk	Game try	7
26Oct68- 0Lrl	fst 1 1/16	:23 :463 1:123 1:444	Ⓕ Selima 108k	4	5	47	23½	2hd	1nk	Turcotte R	122		-	93-17	Shuvee122nkProcess Shot1196Queen's Double11940	Driving	5
	Exhibition race run between 7th and 8th races-No wagering.																
5Oct68- 7Bel	fst 1	:23 :463 1:112 1:37	Ⓕ Frizette 130k	7	8	99½	76	23	1nk	Davidson J	119		4.50e	89-13	Shuvee119nkGallant Bloom1193Dihela1194	Up final strides	11
23Sep68- 7Bel	fst 7f	:223 :46 1:104 1:241	Ⓕ Astarita (Div 2) 23k	3	6	56½	65½	74¾	31¼	Davidson J	112		10.80	85-17	Dihela1121Imbibe116nkShuvee1122	Found stride late	8
14Sep68- 4Aqu	fst 6f	:223 :461 1:114	Ⓕ Alw 7000	3	10	107½	97	64¼	21¼	Davidson J	119		*2.70	83-14	Gunite1081¼Shuvee119¾Plane119hd	In close,rallied	12
30Aug68- 6Aqu	fst 6f	:222 :46 1:112	Ⓕ Alw 12000	1	7	711	69½	25	23	Baeza B	114		6.40	83-20	Gallant Bloom1063Shuvee1143Prefer1161	Finished strongly	7
20Aug68- 5Sar	fst 6f	:221 :462 1:114	Ⓕ Md Sp Wt	13	11	98	98¼	2½	14	Baeza B	119		3.70	89-09	Shuvee1194Table D'Hote119½Ambranded1192½	Easily best	14
13Aug68- 5Sar	fst 5½f	:221 :454 :573 1:04	Ⓕ Md Sp Wt	4	7	87¼	1012	613	512	Gustines H	119		4.20	85-11	Ta Wee1196Drip Spring1192Socializing1192½	No mishap	12
3Aug68- 1Sar	fst 5½f	:224 :471 :592 1:054	Ⓕ Md Sp Wt	7	4	41½	52¾	31½	31½	Baeza B	119	b	*1.40	86-12	Pashamin119noElizabeth'sDancer1161½Shuvee1195	No mishap	10
25Jly68- 5Aqu	gd 5½f	:222 :462 :584 1:051	Ⓕ Md Sp Wt	8	8	63½	74¾	33½	23	Baeza B	119	b	*2.50	84-18	French Bread1193Shuvee1194Keep a Secret1191	Rallied	9
5Jun68- 4Bel	fst 5½f	:231 :47 :591 1:053	Ⓕ Md Sp Wt	9	8	52	52	43½	35¾	Davidson J	119	b	*1.70	87-15	Golden Or119¾Go to Bed1195Shuvee119¾	Raced wide late	10
22May68- 4Bel	fst 5½f	:23 :462 :584 1:052	Ⓕ Md Sp Wt	4	7	34	33	45	42¼	Davidson J	119		*2.50	92-14	Fillypasser119hdFoolish Miss119nkTudor Home1192	Hung	10
8May68- 4Aqu	fst 5f	:222 :461 :59	Ⓕ Md Sp Wt	5	8	87¾	69½	56½	47¾	Davidson J	119		*1.90	82-11	Gunite1194Miss Georgene119¾Most Welcome1193	No threat	10

Past Performances of Great Horses of the 20th Century

Skip Away — gr/ro. c. 1993, by Skip Trial (Bailjumper)–Ingot Way, by Diplomat Way — Lifetime record: 38 18 10 6 $9,616,360

Own.– Carolyn H. Hine
Br.– Anna Marie Barnhart (Fla)
Tr.– Hubert Hine

7Nov98-10CD	fst 1¼	:473 1:12 1:371 2:02	3↑ B C Classic-G1	6	3	21	4¾	63¼	64	Bailey JD	L 126	b	*1.90	91-07	AwesomeAgn126¾SlvrChrm126nkSwain126no	Pressed,empty	10
10Oct98-10Bel	sly 1¼	:462 1:093 1:341 2:003	3↑ JC Gold Cup-G1	4	1	2hd	22	34	310¼	Bailey JD	L 126	b	*.35	81-14	Wagon Limit1265½Gentlemen1264¾Skip Away1264		6
	Dueled outside,faded																
19Sep98- 9Bel	fst 1⅛	:452 1:09 1:341 1:474	3↑ Woodward-G1	2	2	1½	11	12	11¾	Bailey JD	L 126	b	*1.10	91-18	Skip Away1261¾Gentlemen1266RunningStag1269		5
	About his business																
30Aug98-11Mth	fst 1⅛	:463 1:10 1:344 1:471	3↑ P H Iselin H-G2	4	3	2hd	11	1hd	1no	Bailey JD	L 131	b	*.05	102-09	Skip Away131noStormin Fever1139Testafly1142¾	Driving	7
28Jun98- 7Hol	fst 1¼	:462 1:093 1:34 2:00	3↑ Hol Gold Cup-G1	2	1	11	1hd	11	11¾	Bailey JD	LB 124	b	*.40	95-05	Skip Away1241¾Puerto Madero1241Gentlemen1243		8
	Gamely kicked clear																
30May98- 9Suf	fst 1⅛	:462 1:101 1:344 1:471	3↑ Mass H-G3	1	1	12½	12	13½	14¼	Bailey JD	L 130	b	*.30	103-07	Skip Away1304¼Puerto Madero1164¾K.J.'s Appeal1134		5
	2 path,ridden out																
9May98- 7Pim	gd 1 3/16	:47 1:112 1:354 1:541	3↑ Pim Special H-G1	4	1	13	12½	13	13¼	Bailey JD	L 128	b	*.20	94-16	Skip Away1283¼Precocity115nkHot Brush113¾	Driving	5
28Feb98-10GP	fst 1¼	:463 1:101 1:351 2:031	3↑ Gulf Park H-G1	2	2	21	12½	13	12¼	Bailey JD	L 127	b	*.10	95-16	Skip Away1272¼Unruled1121¾Behrens1141¼	Driving,clear	6
7Feb98-10GP	fst 1⅛	:463 1:104 1:362 1:50	3↑ Donn H-G1	3	2	31½	1hd	13	12¾	Bailey JD	L 126	b	*.40	87-24	SkipAway1262¾Unruled112½SirBr113nk	3-wide bid,hand ride	10
8Nov97- 8Hol	fst 1¼	:461 1:093 1:334 1:59	3↑ B C Classic-G1	1	3	31	14	15	16	Smith ME	L 126	b	*1.80	102-06	Skip Away1266DeputyCommnder123¾[D]Whiskey Wisdom1263		9
	Much best,driving																
18Oct97- 9Bel	wf 1¼	:47 1:10 1:334 1:584	3↑ J C Gold Cup-G1	1	2	2½	11	16	16½	Bailey JD	L 126	b	1.45	103-04	Skip Away1266½Instant Friendship12610Wagon Limit121¾		7
	Contested pace,gamely																
20Sep97- 9Bel	fst 1⅛	:471 1:111 1:35 1:472	3↑ Woodward-G1	2	1	2hd	32½	33½	25½	Sellers SJ	L 126	b	1.35	87-15	FormalGold1265½SkpAwy126nkWll'sWy12640	Game,2nd best	5
23Aug97- 9Mth	fst 1 1/16	:224 :452 1:09 1:401	3↑ PH Iselin H-G2	1	4	44	32½	25	25¼	Sellers SJ	L 124	b	*.90	101-07	Formal Gold1215¼Skip Away1242½Distorted Humor1156		4
	3-wide bid,2nd best																
2Aug97- 8Sar	fst 1⅛	:47 1:104 1:352 1:481	3↑ Whitney H-G1	2	3	32½	31½	33	36½	Sellers SJ	L 125	b	*1.10	88-25	Will's Way117noFormal Gold1206½Skip Away1259½		6
	Lacked response																
4Jly97- 9Bel	fst 1¼	:472 1:12 1:371 2:021	3↑ Suburban H-G2	1	2	3½	31½	3½	11½	Sellers SJ	L 122	b	*1.00	86-23	Skip Away1221½Will's Way116¾Formal Gold12015		6
	Shuffled back ½ pl,awaited room turn,determinedly																
31May97-11Suf	fst 1⅛	:471 1:104 1:351 1:474	3↑ Mass H-G3	3	2	2½	1hd	1hd	1hd	Sellers SJ	L 119	b	*.70	104-01	SkpAwy119hdFormlGold1143½Wll'sWy1142¼	2 wide,long drive	6
10May97- 9Pim	fst 1 3/16	:463 1:10 1:343 1:53	3↑ Pim Spl H-G1	8	4	42½	32	21½	2½	Sellers SJ	L 119	b	3.30	101-17	Gentlemen122½Skip Away1196½Tejano Run1148		8
	Three wide both turns,gamely																
20Apr97- 7LS	fst 1	:232 :461 1:093 1:342	3↑ Texas Mile 250k	5	6	52½	43½	34	37½	Sellers SJ	L 11	b	*.60	--	Isitingood1233Spiritbound1164½Skip Away1162½		7
	5 wide first turn,empty drive																
1Mar97-10GP	fst 1¼	:46 1:104 1:354 2:021	3↑ Gulf Park H-G1	2	2	21	2hd	2hd	22¼	Sellers SJ	L 122	b	*.40	89-19	Mt. Sassafras1132¼Skip Away122nkTejano Run1142	Gamely	6
8Feb97-10GP	fst 1⅛	:47 1:104 1:35 1:472	3↑ Donn H-G1	7	2	21	21½	22	21¼	Sellers SJ	L 123	b	*.70	99-04	Formal Gold1131¼Skip Away1236Mecke120hd	Rallied 3 path	10
5Oct96-10Bel	fst 1¼	:473 1:112 1:354 2:003	3↑ J C Gold Cup-G1	4	2	2½	2½	11	1hd	Sellers SJ	L 121	b	5.80	94-10	Skip Away121hdCigar1262Louis Quatorze1211	Hard drive	6
15Sep96- 9WO	fst 1⅛	:464 1:103 1:36 1:49	WO Million-G1	1	5	55	53¼	1hd	14	Sellers SJ	L 126	b	*1.15	101-09	SkipAwy1264VictorCooley119noStephanotis1193½	Drew away	7
24Aug96- 7Sar	fst 1¼	:461 1:103 1:361 2:022	Travers-G1	3	4	32	31	31½	31¾	Santos JA	L 126	b	*1.45	95-03	Will's Way126¾Louis Quatorze1261Skip Away1263½		7
	In tight ¾ pl,wide turn																
4Aug96-10Mth	fst 1⅛	:461 1:094 1:342 1:473	Haskell Inv'l H-G1	2	4	43	3½	3½	11	Santos JA	L 124	b	*.60	103-01	Skip Away1241Dr. Caton1151Victory Speech1214½	Driving	7
23Jun96-14Tdn	fst 1⅛	:461 1:104 1:353 1:474	Ohio Derby-G2	10	5	52	1½	13	13½	Santos JA	LB 122	b	*.70	103-08	Skip Away1223½Victory Speech1189¼Clash by Night118nk		10
	Widened,brisk hand ride																
8Jun96- 9Bel	fst 1½	:464 1:104 2:02 2:284	Belmont-G1	13	6	2hd	11½	1½	21	Santos JA	L 126	b	8.00	89-13	Editor'sNote1261SkipAwy1264MyFlg1216	Long drive,gamely	14

Past Performances of Great Horses of the 20th Century

18May96-10Pim	fst 1 3/16	:461 1:094 1:342 1:532	Preakness-G1	11	2	22	21½	21½	23¼	Sellers SJ	L	126	b	3.30	98-10	Louis Quatorze1263¼Skip Away1263Editor's Note1262½		12
	Bid far turn,2nd best																	
4May96-8CD	fst 1¼	:46 1:103 1:35 2:01	Ky Derby-G1	16	5	64½	108¾	1319	1216¾	Sellers SJ	L	126	b	7.70	84-04	Grindstone126noCavonnr1263½PrncofThvs126nk	5 wide tired	19
13Apr96-9Kee	wf 1⅛	:462 1:101 1:344 1:471	Blue Grass-G2	5	2	1hd	1½	14½	16	Sellers SJ	L	121	b	4.60	98-10	Skip Away1216Louis Quatorze1211½Editor's Note1213		7
	Dueled,driving clear impressivey																	
16Mar96-10GP	fst 1⅛	:462 1:094 1:343 1:474	Florida Derby-G1	3	5	46½	46½	24	36¼	Sellers SJ	L	122	b	7.90	92-07	Unbridled's Song1225¾Editor's Note122½Skip Away1222¼		9
	Seven wide top stretch,weakened																	
10Feb96-8GP	fst 1 1/16	:233 :474 1:114 1:441	Alw 26000	4	5	31½	11	17	112	Sellers SJ	L	117	b	*1.10	87-12	Skip Away11712Hedge120noNatural Selection1201½		12
	Crowded,bumped turn,five wide final turn,driving																	
10Jan96-1GP	fst 1 1/16	:23 :463 1:114 1:454	Alw 26000	1	4	54	58	528	-	Bailey JD		117		*.40	- -	Blushing Jim1171½HedMinistr1171¼Night Runner1177¾		5
	Eased str in distress																	
25Nov95-7Bel	fst 1⅛	:471 1:114 1:373 1:501	Remsen-G2	1	5	42½	32	1hd	2nk	Bailey JD		112		2.30	89-09	Tropcool112nkSkpAwy1122CrftyFrnd1133	Yielded grudgingly	11
29Oct95-7Bel	fst 1	:223 :461 1:113 1:37	Cowdin-G2	7	3	31	2½	2hd	2no	Wilson R		122		5.30	78-19	Gator Dancer122noSkip Away1223In Contention1224¾		8
	Lost bob,gamely																	
6Oct95-9Med	fst 1⊗	:23 :463 1:104 1:371	World Appeal 40k	10	6	62½	34½	36	33¼	Wilson R		115		1.80	87-10	SpicyFact1153¼PlayItAgnStn117noSkpAwy1159	Even finish	10
16Aug95-5Mth	fst 1	:24 :474 1:13 1:39	Md Sp Wt	2	3	23	11½	19	112¼	Wilson R		118		*.80	83-17	SkpAwy11812ClashbyNight1187½DarnThatErc1134¼	Drew off	8
9Jly95-9Mth	fm 5f(T)	:22 :451 :572	Gilded Time 33k	4	7	77½	66½	45	21½	Marquez CH Jr		112		5.00	85-13	ColdSnap1181½SkipAway1121Cobb'sCreek1211¾	Closed well	7
16Jun95-5Mth	fst 5f	:22 :462 :584	Md Sp Wt	2	10	87½	79½	59	48¾	Marquez CH Jr		118		*.80e	81-18	ColdSnap1134¼Foolspruce1182BeauCoup1182½	Broke slowly	10

Spectacular Bid

gr. c. 1976, by Bold Bidder (Bold Ruler)–Spectacular, by Promised Land

Lifetime record: 30 26 2 1 $2,781,608

Own.– Hawksworth Farm

Br.– Mmes Gilmour & Jason (Ky)

Tr.– Grover G. Delp

20Sep80-0Bel	fst 1¼	:502 1:141 1:381 2:022	3↑ Woodward-G1	1	1	1	1	1	1	Shoemaker W	126		88-21	Spectacular Bid126	In hand	1
	Walkover,run between 7th and 8th race - Walkover,no wagering															
16Aug80-9Mth	fst 1⅛	:464 1:111 1:353 1:48	3↑ AL Haskell H-G1	5	7	65½	5¾	1½	11¾	Shoemaker W	132	*.10	95-15	SpectcularBd1321¾Glorious Song1171¼The Cool Virginian1124		8
	Ridden out															
19Jly80-8AP	fst 1⅛	:461 1:094 1:34 1:461	3↑ Wash Park-G3	4	4	44	2hd	14	110	Shoemaker W	130	*.05	103-17	SpectacularBid13010HoldYourTrcks1198Archtct1191½	Easily	6
8Jun80-8Hol	fst 1⅛	:45 1:084 1:331 1:454	3↑ Californian-G1	3	3	31½	11	16	14¼	Shoemaker W	130	*.05	103-05	SpectaculrBid1304¼PaintKng1153¾CroBmbno1188	Easy score	7
18May80-8Hol	fst 1 1/16	:223 :452 1:084 1:402	3↑ Mervyn LeRoy H-G2	1	5	42	2hd	13½	17	Shoemaker W	132	*.20	93-18	SpectaculrBd1327Peregrintor119¾Beau'sEgl1212	Ridden out	6
2Mar80-8SA	sly 1¼	:483 1:122 1:364 2:003	4↑ S Anita H-G1	5	2	22½	1hd	12½	15	Shoemaker W	130	*.30	90-18	SpctaclarBid1305FlyingPstr1238Beau'sEgl12214	Ridden out	5
3Feb80-8SA	fst 1¼	:443 1:082 1:324 1:574	C H Strub-G1	3	4	29	2hd	13	13¼	Shoemaker W	126	*.30	104-08	SpectacularBid1263¼FlyingPaster1219Vldz122½	Handy score	4
19Jan80-8SA	gd 1⅛	:462 1:11 1:353 1:48	San Fernando-G2	1	3	33½	1hd	1½	11½	Shoemaker W	126	*.05	89-19	SpectacularBid1261½FlyngPstr12615Rlunch12033	Drew clear	4
5Jan80-8SA	fst 7f	:221 :442 1:08 1:20	Malibu-G2	3	4	52½	41	1½	15	Shoemaker W	126	*.30	103-10	SpectacularBid1265FlyingPastr1231½Ros'sSvll117no	Easily	5
18Oct79-6Med	fst 1¼	:474 1:12 1:362 2:011	3↑ Med Cup H-G2	1	3	33	1½	11½	13	Shoemaker W	126	*.10	102-14	Spectacular Bid1263Smarten120hdValdez12111	Drew out	5
6Oct79-8Bel	fst 1½	:49 1:131 2:022 2:272	3↑ J C Gold Cup-G1	2	3	2½	31	2½	2¾	Shoemaker W	121	1.40	82-21	Affirmed126¾Spectacular Bid1213Coastal12131	Gamely	4
8Sep79-8Bel	fst 1⅛	:472 1:11 1:341 1:463	3↑ Marlboro Cup H-G1	5	3	1hd	1½	13	15	Shoemaker W	124	*.50	94-17	SpectacularBid1245GenrlAssmbly1201¼Costl122½	Ridden out	6
26Aug79-7Del	gd 1 1/16	:23 :463 1:111 1:413	Alw 18000	3	3	21½	16	112	117	Shoemaker W	122	*.05	101-14	SpectacularBd12217ArmadaStrik1127NotSoProud1126	Easily	5
9Jun79-8Bel	fst 1½	:473 1:111 2:022 2:283	Belmont-G1	3	2	2½	13	2½	33½	Franklin RJ	126	*.30	73-17	Coastal1263¼Golden Act126nkSpectacular Bid1269½	Tired	8
19May79-8Pim	gd 1 3/16	:464 1:103 1:35 1:541	Preakness-G1	2	4	45	1hd	16	15½	Franklin RJ	126	*.10	99-09	SpctacularBd1265½GoldenAct1264ScrnKng1261½	Ridden out	5
5May79-8CD	fst 1¼	:472 1:122 1:373 2:022	Ky Derby-G1	3	7	610	2hd	11½	12¾	Franklin RJ	126	*.60	85-14	SpectacularBid1262¾GnrlAssmbly1263GoldnAct1261¾	Driving	10

Past Performances of Great Horses of the 20th Century

26Apr79-7Kee	fst 1⅛	:463 1:103 1:361 1:50	Blue Grass-G1	4	4	1hd	12	15½	17	Franklin RJ	121		*.05	87-20	Spectacular Bid1217Lot o' Gold1218Bishop's Choice12110	Easily best	4
24Mar79-10Hia	fst 1⅛	:46 1:093 1:351 1:482	Flamingo-G1	8	3	1½	18	110	112	Franklin RJ	122		*.05	90-16	Spectacular Bid12212Strike the Min1183Sir Ivor Again122hd	Ridden out	8
6Mar79-11GP	fst 1⅛	:474 1:114 1:363 1:484	Florida Derby-G1	5	5	47½	3½	11½	14½	Franklin RJ	122		*.05	90-14	Spectacular Bid1224½Lot o' Gold122¾Fantasy 'n Reality1223	Four wide,clear	7
19Feb79-9GP	fst 1 1/16	:24 :472 1:104 1:411	Fountain of Youth-G3	2	3	1hd	13	14	18½	Franklin RJ	122		*.10	95-12	Spectacular Bid1228½Lot o'Gold1171Bishop's Choice1221	Ridden out	6
7Feb79-9GP	fst 7f	:224 :444 1:084 1:212	Hutcheson 28k	1	2	2hd	22	13	13¾	Franklin RJ	122		*.05	97-22	SpectcularBid1223¾Lot o' Gold1147½Northern Prospect1143½	In hand	4
11Nov78-8Key	fst 1 1/16	:224 :462 1:103 1:42	Heritage-G2	6	5	55	1hd	13	16	Franklin RJ	122		*.10	94-13	SpctacularBid1226SunWatcher112¾TerrfcSon117no	Handily	7
28Oct78-8Lrl	fst 1 1/16	:234 :464 1:11 1:413	Lrl Futurity-G1	2	1	11½	1½	14	18½	Franklin RJ	122		*.90	105-14	SpectacularBd1228½General Assembly12212Clever Trick1223½	Driving	4
19Oct78-6Med	fst 1 1/16	:232 :462 1:111 1:431	Young America-G1	5	3	2hd	2½	2hd	1nk	Velasquez J	122		*.30	95-14	SpectclrBid122nkStrikeYourColrs119hdInstrumntLanding1134	Driving	9
8Oct78-8Bel	fst 1	:231 :46 1:101 1:344	Champagne-G1	1	2	11	12½	14	12¾	Velasquez J	122		2.40	94-19	SpectclrBid1222¾GeneralAssembly1225½Crest of theWave122¾	Ridden out	6
23Sep78-8Atl	gd 7f	:22 :443 1:09 1:204	World's Playground-G3	3	3	1½	12	16	115	Franklin RJ	114		5.20	98-25	SpctaculrBid11415CrstofthWv1241¼GrotonHgh118½	Driving	7
20Aug78-9Del	fst 6f	:222 :46 :58 1:104	Dover 34k	2	4	43	53¾	44	22½	Franklin RJ	112		*1.00	88-13	StrikeYourColors1122½SpectacularBid1125½Spy Charger1221	2nd best	7
2Aug78-8Mth	sly 5½f	:224 :461 :59 1:044	Tyro (Div 2) 27k	6	8	816	812	610	46¾	Franklin RJ	118		*1.70	86-22	GrotonHigh1222½GreatBoon116nkOurGry1164	Very wide early	8
22Jly78-5Pim	fst 5½f	:223 :461 :581 1:041	Alw 6500	3	4	31	1hd	13	18	Franklin RJ5	115		*.30	100-17	SpectacularBid1158SilentNative1209DoublePrd1141	Driving	5
30Jun78-3Pim	fst 5½f	:223 :463 :582 1:043	Md Sp Wt	5	4	1½	11½	12½	13¼	Franklin RJ5	115		6.30	98-15	Spectacular Bid1153¼Strike Your Colors1204Instant Love1124	Drew out	11

Swaps

ch. c. 1952, by Khaled (Hyperion)–Iron Reward, by Beau Pere

Own.– R.C. Ellsworth

Br.– Rex C. Ellsworth (Cal)

Tr.– M.A. Tenney

Lifetime record: 25 19 2 2 $848,900

3Sep56-8Was	fst 1	:221 :441 1:074 1:332 3↑	Wash Park H 142k	5	3	22	1½	13	12	Shoemaker W	130	w	*.40	102-13	Swaps1302Summer Tan1152Sea o Erin1123	Well in hand late	6
25Aug56-8Was	fm 1 3/16 Ⓣ	:47 1:103 1:362 1:55 3↑	Arch Ward Mem H 54k	7	2	3½	2hd	31	76¼	Shoemaker W	130	w	*.30	92-02	Mahan114½SirTribal1161¾PrincMorv113hd	Well up,no excuse	8
25Jly56-7Hol	fst 1⅝	:463 1:361 2:003 2:381 3↑	Sunset H 110k	5	1	11½	11½	16	14¼	Shoemaker W	130	w	*.10	112-08	Swaps1304¼Honeys Alibi1081Blue Volt1083	Eased up late	9
14Jly56-8Hol	fst 1¼	:452 1:09 1:331 1:583 3↑	Hol Gold Cup H 162k	3	1	22	1hd	14	12	Shoemaker W	130	w	*.15	105-05	Swaps1302MisterGus1171¼Porterhouse1192¼	Eased at finish	7
4Jly56-8Hol	fst 1⅛	:462 1:092 1:34 1:464 3↑	American H 103k	3	3	34½	3nk	13	11¾	Shoemaker W	130	w	*.20	100-12	Swaps1301¾MstrGus1116BobbyBrocto1158	Eased final stages	5
23Jun56-7Hol	fst 1 1/16	:231 :46 1:09 1:39 3↑	Inglewood H 52k	5	3	21½	1hd	13	12¾	Shoemaker W	130	w	*.30	107-06	Swaps1302¾MisterGus1152BobbyBrocto1217	Eased final 16th	7
9Jun56-7Hol	fst 1	:222 :451 1:084 1:331 3↑	Argonaut H 52k	1	1	11	1½	12	11¼	Shoemaker W	128	w	*.20	108-07	Swaps1281¼Bobby Brocato1236Porterhouse1192¾	In hand	6
26May56-7Hol	fst 1 1/16	:23 :453 1:092 1:404 3↑	Californian 109k	6	4	21½	1½	13	2hd	Shoemaker W	127	w	*.35	98-11	Porterhse118hdSwaps1275MistrGus1181¾	Eased by mistake	6
14Apr56-7GP	fst 1 70	:23 :453 1:092 1:393 3↑	Broward H 25k	4	2	22	11½	13	12¼	Shoemaker W	130	w	*.30	105-09	Swaps1302¼Gldr1055OurGob114no	Never to a drive,eased up	8
17Feb56-7SA	fst 1 1/16	:224 :462 1:103 1:43 4↑	Handicap 15000	7	4	42	1hd	1hd	11¾	Shoemaker W	127	w	*.70	89-15	Swaps1271¾Bobby Brocato124nkArrogate1159	Strong finish	7
31Aug55-7Was	gd 1¼	:46 1:102 1:373 2:041	WP Match 100k	2	2	21	21½	22	26½	Shoemaker W	126	w	*.30	74-17	Nashua1266½Swaps126	Wide on stretch turn,tired,swerved	2
20Aug55-7Was	fm 1 3/16 Ⓣ	:472 1:114 1:354 1:543	American Derby 146k	5	1	11	11½	13	11	Shoemaker W	126	w	*.20	101-05	Swaps1261Traffic Judge1194Parador1131½	Very handy score	6
9Jly55-7Hol	fst 1¼	:463 1:102 1:344 2:003	Westerner 57k	1	1	11½	12	110	16	Shoemaker W	126	w	*.05	96-11	Swaps1266Fabulous Vegas1171Jean's Joe1203½	Eased up	5
11Jun55-7Hol	fst 1 1/16	:231 :46 1:10 1:402 3↑	Californian 109k	1	1	22	21	11	11¼	Erb D	115	w	*.65	103-06	Swaps1151¼Detrmine126½MistrGus1173	In hand throughout	6

Past Performances of Great Horses of the 20th Century

30May55- 6Hol	fst 1	:222 :452 1:101 1:35	©Will Rogers 27k	3 3 21½ 1hd 13 112	Shoemaker W	126	w	*.15e	100-07	Swaps12612Bequeath122noMr.Sullivan1183	Drew out in hand 6
7May55- 7CD	fst 1¼	:472 1:122 1:37 2:014	Ky Derby 152k	8 1 11 1½ 1½ 11½	Shoemaker W	126	w	2.80	98-12	Swps1261½Nshua1266½SummrTn1264	Drew clear when urged 10
30Apr55- 6CD	fst 6f	:23 :462 1:101	Alw 5000	1 3 12½ 12 14 18½	Shoemaker W	123	w	*.30	99-13	Swaps1238½TrimDestiny115¾Styrunnr1104½	Speed in reserve 5
19Feb55- 7SA	fst 1⅛	:454 1:103 1:37 1:50	SA Derby 137k	12 3 31 13 11 1½	Longden J	118	w	3.60e	91-14	Swaps118½Jean'sJoe1183½BlueRuler1183	Went wide,driving 14
19Jan55- 7SA	my 7f	:214 :45 1:103 1:24	San Vicente 22k	1 5 56½ 21 12 13½	Shoemaker W	116	w	4.40e	83-25	Swaps1163½Trentonian120hdJean'sJoe1146	Speed in reserve 8
30Dec54- 6SA	fst 6f	:221 :451 1:10	Alw 6000	5 5 2hd 21 2hd 1no	Shoemaker W	118	w	5.25	95-11	Swaps118noBeau Busher1131¾Battle Dance118½	Strong drive 12
8Jly54- 6Hol	fst 5½f	:221 :453 :581 1:044	©CS Howard 29k	1 5 63½ 65¼ 58 58¾	Burton J	118	w	9.95e	85-12	ColonlMack114¾Mr.Sullivan1221BackHo1181	Showed nothing 6
22Jun54- 7Hol	fst 5f	:221 :454 :582	©Haggin 24k	9 7 83¾ 73 31½ 32	Burton J	122	w	6.40e	92-13	Mr. Sullivan114½Back Hoe1221½Swaps1221¾	Good effort 10
10Jun54- 7Hol	fst 5f	:221 :46 :582	©June Juv 16k	5 5 42½ 32 1½ 12½	Burton J	116	w	4.70	94-10	Swaps1162½Trentonian1192Noir116nk	Drew out 7
3Jun54- 7Hol	fst 5f	:221 :452 :58	Westchester 16k	2 5 42½ 53½ 51¾ 32¼	Burton J	116	w	7.25	94-11	Back Hoe1191¼Trentonian1191Swaps116½	Failed to rally 7
20May54- 2Hol	fst 5f	:222 :454 :582	©Md Sp Wt	9 5 2hd 2hd 1hd 13	Burton J	120	w	12.60	94-12	Swaps1203Irish Cheer1203½Battle Dance1201½	Won handily 11

Tom Fool

b. c. 1949, by Menow (Pharamond II)–Gaga, by Bull Dog

Own.– Greentree Stable

Br.– Duval A. Headley (Ky)

Tr.– J.M. Gaver

Lifetime record: 30 21 7 1 $570,165

24Oct53- 7Pim	fst 1 3/16	:474 1:114 1:371 1:554	3↑ Pim Spl 50k	1 1 13 15 16 18	Atkinson T	126	w	-	101-20	Tom Fool1268Navy Page120noAlerted126	Much the best 3
	No wagering										
26Sep53- 6Bel	fst 1	:231 :461 1:11 1:364	3↑ Sysonby 54k	2 1 11 12½ 16 13	Atkinson T	126	w	-	90-15	Tom Fool1263Alerted126½Grecian Queen116	Under restraint 3
	No wagering										
8Aug53- 7Sar	fst 1¼	:49 1:13 1:382 2:052	3↑ Whitney 27k	1 2 22 12 14 13½	Atkinson T	126	w	-	81-20	Tom Fool1263½Combat Boots114	Very much the best 2
	No wagering										
4Aug53- 6Sar	fst 1	:232 :462 1:111 1:371	3↑ Wilson 16k	1 1 11 12½ 16 18	Atkinson T	126	w	-	91-17	Tom Fool1268Indian Land117	No competition here 2
	No wagering										
11Jly53- 6Aqu	fst 1¼	:483 1:132 1:38 2:042	3↑ Brooklyn H 56k	3 2 2hd 13½ 13 11½	Atkinson T	136	w	*.25	85-13	Tom Fool1361½Golden Gloves1107High Scud109no	Easing up 5
27Jun53- 6Aqu	fst 7f	:22 :443 1:092 1:22	3↑ Carter H 59k	5 5 56 45 21½ 12	Atkinson T	135	w	*.65	100-09	Tom Fool1352Squared Away1222¼Eatontown1131¼	Easily best 9
30May53- 6Bel	fst 1¼	:471 1:11 1:353 2:003	3↑ Suburban H 58k	1 1 13 13 11 1no	Atkinson T	128	w	*2.05	97-17	Tom Fool128noRoyal Vale1247Cold Command1142	Hard drive 7
23May53- 6Bel	gd 1	:223 :46 1:111 1:354	3↑ Metropolitan H 36k	3 2 22½ 1½ 11½ 1½	Atkinson T	130	w	*.50	95-13	Tom Fool130½Royal Vale1278½Intent1251½	Driving,bore in 7
19May53- 6Bel	fst 6f	:223 :462 1:113	3↑ Joe Palmer H 15k	4 3 21½ 2hd 12½ 11½	Atkinson T	130	w	*.70	91-27	Tom Fool1301½Tea-Maker1141½Dark Peter121¾	Eased up 7
25Apr53- 5Jam	fst 5½f	:23 :461 :582 1:041	3↑ Handicap 7560	1 1 33 33½ 2½ 12½	Atkinson T	128	w	*.95	97-12	Tom Fool1282½Do Report1162¼Earmarked1143	Ridden out 5
8Nov52- 6Jam	fst 1 3/16	:47 1:112 1:381 1:58	Empire City H 55k	4 1 1½ 1hd 1½ 1hd	Atkinson T	128	w	*.65	86-23	Tom Fool128hdMarcador1092Roaring Bull1051½	Hard drive 8
1Nov52- 6Jam	fst 1⅛	:484 1:13 1:374 1:501	3↑ Westchester H 56k	3 2 31 31 2½ 2no	Atkinson T	125	w	*1.75	95-18	Battlefield123noTomFool1251Alerted1251¼	Blocked,gaining 9
18Oct52- 6Jam	fst 1⅛	:471 1:11 1:354 1:492	3↑ Grey Lag H 60k	10 2 1hd 2hd 1hd 1no	Atkinson T	119	wb	*1.40e	99-16	Tom Fool119noBattlefield118nkAlerted1211¼	Hard drive 11
11Oct52- 6Jam	fst 1 3/16	:472 1:11 1:361 1:554	Roamer H 47k	7 5 42 31½ 21 22	Atkinson T	126	w	*.75	95-14	Quiet Step1112Tom Fool1261Risque Rouge105¾	No excuse 9
30Sep52- 6Bel	fst 1	:232 :463 1:114 1:362	3↑ Sysonby H 15k	7 3 31½ 3½ 12 11¼	Atkinson T	126	w	*1.10	92-18	Tom Fool1261¼Alerted1183Greek Ship1181¼	Easily 8
17Sep52- 6Bel	fst 1	:232 :471 1:122 1:37	Jerome H 24k	5 2 21½ 21½ 14 17	Atkinson T	120	w	2.80	89-26	Tom Fool1207Marcador111nkMark-Ye-Well1301½	Hard drive 10
16Aug52- 6Sar	sly 1¼	:493 1:144 1:401 2:072	Travers 23k	4 1 11 11½ 21 34	Atkinson T	114	w	*1.55	67-22	OneCount1263Armageddon1231TomFl114¾	Wide,weakened 8
	Geldings not eligible										
11Aug52- 6Sar	sl 1⅛	:482 1:13 1:383 1:532	Alw 5000	3 2 21 2½ 1hd 2no	Atkinson T	117	w	*.80	83-22	CountFlame117noTomFool117½GoldnGloves117½	Just missed 7
5Aug52- 6Sar	sly 1	:232 :47 1:123 1:392	3↑ Wilson 16k	1 3 37 22 12 14½	Atkinson T	106	w	*.25e	80-25	TomFool1064½NorthernStar1201ColonyDate1148	Drew clear 4
14Jly52- 6AP	fst 7f	:232 :452 1:10 1:223	Alw 6000	4 1 2hd 31 33½ 44	Atkinson T	124	w	*.90	93-11	High Scud118½Mark-Ye-Well118½Eljay1183	Weakened 5
26Jun52- 6Aqu	fst 6f	:223 :462 1:103	Rippey H 10k	3 4 41½ 52¾ 2hd 2hd	Atkinson T	126	w	*1.00	99-15	Hitex120hdTom Fool1262Duke Fanelli1022	Hung 8
19Apr52- 6Jam	fst 1⅛	:48 1:12 1:383 1:522	Wood Memorial 63k	2 1 2hd 22½ 1hd 2nk	Atkinson T	126	w	*1.65	84-16	Master Fiddle126nkTom Fool126½Pintor126½	Just failed 14

Past Performances of Great Horses of the 20th Century

7Apr52- 6Jam fst 6f :232 :464 1:121 Alw 10000 1 5 1½ 1hd 11 1nk Atkinson T 120 w *.80 86-20 Tom Fool120nkPrimate117nkCousin1202 Won cleverly 6
24Oct51- 6Jam sly 1 1/16 :242 :48 1:131 1:451 ©East View 53k 4 3 45½ 42 1hd 1nk Atkinson T 122 w *.65 86-15 Tom Fool122nkPut Out122nkRisque Rouge122¾ Hard drive 6
6Oct51- 6Bel fst 6½f-W :221 :451 1:101 1:171 Futurity 111k 7 4 41¼ 1nk 11¾ Atkinson T 122 w 5.75 86-14 Tom Fool1221¾Primate1221Jet's Date122hd Driving 10
Geldings not eligible
1Oct51- 5Bel fst 6f-WC :223 :45 1:092 Sp Wt 5000 3 1 31½ 31½ 24 Atkinson T 118 w *1.90 90-11 Hill Gail1184Tom Fool118nkBaybrook1182 Bothered early 16
1Sep51- 6Sar gd 6½f :233 :472 1:123 1:191 Hopeful 62k 2 4 31 1hd 1hd 21¼ Atkinson T 122 w *.75e 88-20 Cousin1221¼Tom Fool122nkHannibal12212 No excuse 6
25Aug51- 4Sar fst 6f :224 :463 1:114 Grand Union Hotel 21k 4 3 32 32 1hd 11 Atkinson T 122 w 2.05 89-16 Tom Fool1221Cousin126¾Jet Master1261¼ Driving 5
20Aug51- 6Sar fst 6f :231 :47 1:123 Sanford 11k 6 3 21 21 1½ 12¼ Atkinson T 113 w *.90 85-18 Tom Fool1132¼First Refusal1163½Secant1082½ Easily 8
13Aug51- 5Sar fst 5½f :232 :47 :593 1:062 ©Md Sp Wt 8 7 52 43½ 11 14 Atkinson T 118 w *2.00 85-17 Tom Fool1184Handsome Teddy1181Warpath1181 Easily 12

Twilight Tear

b. f. 1941, by Bull Lea (Bull Dog)–Lady Lark, by Blue Larkspur **Lifetime record: 24 18 2 2 $202,165**
Own.– Calumet Farm
Br.– Calumet Farm (Ky)
Tr.– B.A. Jones

28Aug45- 6Was fst 6f :221 :452 1:102 3↑ Alw 5000 3 1 21½ 24 47½ - Dodson D 117 w 1.80 -- FightingDon1103Occupy1165MyTetRambler1111½ Bled,eased 5
1Nov44- 7Pim fst 1⅜ :481 1:122 1:372 1:563 3↑ Pim Spl 25k 2 1 13 14 14 16 Dodson D 117 w *.65 99-12 Twilight Tear1176Devil Diver12610Megogo120 Galloping 3
21Oct44- 6Lrl my 1¼ :481 1:14 1:414 2:083 Maryland H 16k 4 1 11 23 46½ 415½ Dodson D 130 w *.15e 51-40 Dare Me1097Miss Keeneland1102½Aera1066 Quit badly 6
12Oct44- 6Lrl fst 1⅛ :472 1:123 1:40 1:531 3↑ ⒻQueen Isabella H 11k 4 1 16 16 15 15 Dodson D 126 w *.15e 82-23 Twilight Tear1265Good Morning1182Legend Bearer1083½ 8
Never extended
2Oct44- 5Bel fst 5½f-W :224 :452 1:032 3↑ ⒻHandicap 3480 3 1 2hd 1½ 12½ Arcaro E 126 w *.40e 97-08 Twilight Tear1262½Tellmenow118¾Cocopet1145 5
Bore out,impeded runner-up str
8Aug44- 6Bel fst 1¼ :471 1:112 1:372 2:033 ⒻAlabama 23k 1 1 1½ 11 11½ 2¾ Haas L 126 w *.05 81-14 Vienna114¾Twilight Tear1265Thread o' Gold1171¼ Faltered 4
22Jly44- 6Was fst 1¼ :48 1:12 1:372 2:033 Classic 79k 1 1 11 12 13 12 Haas L 114 w *.10e 92-08 TwlghtTr1142OldKntuck1194½Pnsv1265 Saved ground,handily 5
17Jly44- 3Was fst 1 :233 :471 1:112 1:361 Alw 5000 2 1 12 12 13 11¼ Haas L 117 w -e 97-11 Twilight Tear1171¼Pensive1222Appleknocker1101 Easily 4
Nonwagering event
6Jly44- 6Was fst 7f :23 :453 1:093 1:223 Skokie H 11k 5 2 11 12 13 11½ Haas L 121 w *.30e 103-10 TwilightTear1211½Sirde1142½ChallengM1065 Speed to spare 7
28Jun44- 6Was fst 6f :222 :453 1:103 ⒻPrincess Doreen 11k 1 2 21 22½ 2hd 11½ McCreary C 121 w *.40 98-09 TwilightTear1211½BellSong1106HrrtSu114nk Altered course 6
27May44- 6Bel gd 1⅜ :481 1:133 1:40 2:21 ⒻC C A Oaks 17k 1 1 12 13 13 14 McCreary C 121 w *.10 66-27 Twilight Tear1214Dare Me1213Plucky Maud1212 Easily 6
17May44- 6Bel fst 1 :233 :464 1:112 1:37 ⒻAcorn 14k 9 4 42 21 11½ 12½ McCreary C 121 w *.20 89-13 TwilightTear1212½Whirlabout1216Evrgt1211 Speed to spare 10
10May44- 6Pim fst 1 1/16 :234 :48 1:123 1:451 ⒻPim Oaks 18k 5 1 11½ 11 11½ 13 McCreary C 121 w *.30 92-19 Twilight Tear1213Plucky Maud1213Everget1215 In hand 5
3May44- 6Pim fst 6f :221 :453 1:113 Rennert H 7k 10 3 22 2½ 13 11½ McCreary C 118 w *.40e 95-17 TwilightTear1181½Glctc1083IdlGft112.52 As rider pleased 10
25Apr44- 6Pim sl 6f :224 :474 1:14 Alw 4000 3 2 2hd 11 1½ 11¼ McCreary C 117 w *.50e 83-35 TwilightTear1171¼GrampsImage1145Jmm1146Rated,drew away 5
17Mar44- 5TrP sly 6f :221 :453 1:122 ⒻAlw 1800 5 3 37 36½ 2¼ 13 McCreary C 118 w *.30 88-29 Twilight Tear1183Lassie Sue1201½Cuban Bomb1062 Handily 7
10Mar44- 6TrP fst 6f :23 :464 1:114 Alw 1800 7 1 11 11 14 12 McCreary C 117 w *.25 91-16 Twilight Tear1172Comenow1192½Surrogate122nk Easily 7
29Feb44- 6Hia fst 6f :23 :462 1:121 3↑ Leap Year H 5k 4 5 42¼ 3½ 31 32 Smith FA 101 w 9.00 86-23 Mettlesome1161Adulator1121Twilight Tear101hd Held well 8
8Nov43- 6Pim sly 1 70 :241 :49 1:153 1:472 ⒻAlw 5000 4 1 15 12 11 12¼ Thompson B 120 w *.50e 74-28 Twilight Tear1202¼Miss Keeneland1208Red Wonder11110 5
Speed in reserve
27Oct43- 6Pim my 1 1/16 :234 :481 1:14 1:482 ⒻSelima 24k 5 3 11 11½ 1nk 21 Thompson B 119 w *1.20e 75-27 MissKeeneland1111TwilightTear1191½Whrlbout1226 No match 8
20Oct43- 5Pim fst 1 70 :241 :49 1:143 1:454 ⒻAlw 2500 6 1 11½ 12 11 12 Thompson B 115 w *.40e 82-21 TwilightTear1152MissKenlnd1096MyMlch1061 Speed to spare 6
16Oct43- 7Pim sly 6f :23 :481 1:153 ⒻAlw 2500 1 4 1nk 2hd 2hd 32½ Smith FA 117 w *1.05e 72-21 Red Wonder111noCountess Wise1142½Twilight Tear117nk 8
Used in pace,lost ground
3Jly43- 6Was fst 6f :224 :464 1:131 ⒻArl Lassie 34k 3 6 22 22 13 12½ Jemas N 113 w *1.00e 85-14 TwilightTear1132½MissKeeneland1132MusicHall1104 Easily 15
25Jun43- 1Was fst 5½f :224 :473 1:003 1:073 ⒻMd Sp Wt 6 5 68½ 45 21 1¾ Eads W 115 w *1.60 87-17 Twilight Tear115¾Letmenow1151Durazna1153 12
Slow into stride,drawing clear

2003 RACING IN REVIEW

BY JAY PRIVMAN

One week after the Kentucky Derby, racing found itself the headline story around the country in newspapers, and on television and radio. The movies came next, with the summertime release of a fanciful tale of a runner from yesteryear. If Thoroughbred racing ever wanted to cross over and become part of the public's mainstream consciousness, it got its wish in 2003.

There was the right hand of Jose Santos being examined on ESPN and the nightly network newscasts as though it was behind the grassy knoll on the Zapruder film. There was jockey Gary Stevens in People magazine - named one of the 50 most beautiful people - and sitting alongside Jeff Bridges on the "Charlie Rose Show," discussing his acting debut in the film "Seabiscuit."

The stories were, strangely, connected. Everybody loves an underdog, present or past.

Santos was part of the feel-good story of the spring, the whirlwind Triple Crown quest of Funny Cide. The 3-year-old Funny Cide was foaled in New York, far from the breeding palaces of Kentucky. He was gelded, a fate that had never before befallen a winner of both the Derby and Preakness Stakes. He was owned by Sackatoga Stable, a group of workaday guys from upstate New York, most of whom had known each other since high school, and who arrived at the Triple Crown races in yellow school buses. And he was trained by Barclay Tagg, a veteran horseman who had never sought the spotlight, and whom the spotlight had never sought.

Strides away from the first dead-heat in Breeders Cup history, the inseparable finish of Johar (outside) and High Chaparral was among the highlights of the 20th Breeders Cup.

Funny Cide's notoriety exploded exponentially in the fortnight between the Derby and Preakness. A story in the Miami Herald, accompanied by an oblique still photo, insinuated that Santos might have carried an electrical buzzer in his right hand during the Derby. It was a titillating story for news outlets that usually shun racing. For 48 hours, Santos had his credibility unnecessarily questioned, since any cursory examination of the videotape of the stretch run, or any number of other still photos, would have found the story preposterous.

There was an emotional catharsis when Funny Cide won the Preakness. Santos's wife, Rita, and son, Jose Jr., cried tears of joy, believing the victory was vindication. By the time Funny Cide arrived at the Belmont Stakes, only five weeks after he burst into national consciousness, Funny Cide was the most popular horse in racing. More than 100,000 people braved a miserable deluge to watch his attempt for the Triple Crown in the Belmont.

More than 60 years ago, racing's most popular horse was Seabiscuit, who rose from obscurity to become a sports hero of the late-1930s. Seabiscuit enjoyed a renaissance two years ago with the publication of a best-selling book, and the subsequent movie proved a pleasant summertime diversion for those not troubled by factual inaccuracies. "Seabiscuit" did allow racing to achieve broad, popular appeal. It had ticket sales of more than $120 million, and was a red-hot item once released on DVD nearing the holidays. The film's impact on the sport was debatable. Attendance spiked in the summer at Del Mar and Saratoga, but declined in the fall at tracks nationwide. It did have at least one tangible impact, though. Many of the principals in "Seabiscuit," including impresario Steven Spielberg, bought a piece of the 3-year-old colt Atswhatimtalknbout, who finished fourth in the Derby.

It was a year of great anticipation, followed by severe letdowns. Funny Cide faltered in his bid to sweep the Triple Crown. Empire Maker won the Belmont, setting the stage for a showdown with Funny Cide the second half of the year, but they never met again. Mineshaft, the Horse of the Year and champion older horse, roared to three straight Grade 1 victories in New York, including the Jockey Club Gold Cup, but was retired before the Breeders' Cup. A number of other Eastern-based runners, including the winners of the Champagne Stakes and Lane's End Breeders' Futurity, failed to make the trip to Santa Anita for the Breeders' Cup. Candy Ride won Del Mar's Pacific Classic in the premier performance of the year, but he too could not answer the bell for the Breeders' Cup.

Others, though, displayed their brilliance all year. Jockey Jerry Bailey and trainer Bobby Frankel both set records for purse earnings. Frankel won a record 25 Grade 1 stakes races, and Bailey won a record 70 stakes. Both earned the Eclipse Award in their categories for the fourth straight year. For Bailey, it was his record seventh Eclipse Award overall. Frankel's primary client, the Juddmonte Farms of Prince Khalid Abdullah of Saudi Arabia, won the Eclipse Award for both owner and breeder because of Grade 1 wins earned by homebreds Empire Maker, Heat Haze, Sightseek, and Tates Creek. At Saratoga, trainer Todd Pletcher and jockey John Velazquez set meet records for victories. Trainer Richard Mandella had an outstanding year. He trained the year's champion 2-year-olds - the unbeaten filly Halfbridled, and the colt Action This Day. Those two were half of Mandella's record-setting four victories on Breeders' Cup Day. Jockey Patrick Valenzuela was the leading rider at all five major meetings in Southern California, a feat accomplished just once previously, in 1983 by Chris McCarron. Julie Krone finished second to Valenzuela at Del Mar, but her successful comeback made her the most popular racing figure on the West Coast. Russell Baze rode 400 winners for the 11th time in the last 12 years. Florida-based Eddie Castro won the Eclipse Award as champion apprentice jockey.

Those who displayed brilliance for years - champions Precisionist and Dance Smartly, the jockey Mike Smith, and the late trainer Sonny Hine - became the newest members of the Hall of Fame. Still on the outside looking in is trainer King Leatherbury, who won his 6,000th race.

Records were set at auction. A 2-year-old by Sea of Secrets, subsequently named Diamond Fury, sold for $2.7 million to owner Charles Fipke, who gave the colt to Bob Baffert. The mare Cash Run, in foal to Storm Cat, sold for $7.1 million. A weanling colt by Storm Cat sold for $2.4 million. Yearling sales at Saratoga in August and Keeneland in September also found the top of the market surprisingly robust.

Controversy was not in short supply. The strangest race of the year might have been the Arlington Million, in which Storming Home took a sharp, right-hand turn near the shadow of the wire and dislodged Stevens right into the path of the rest of the field. The budding movie star was spun about like a rag doll, and though he punctured a lung, he returned weeks later.

Owner Michael Gill and trainer Mark Shuman obliterated the Gulfstream Park record for wins in a season, but became pariahs because of their aggressive claiming tactics and questionable methods, most disturbing the amputation - by one of their veterinarians - of the damaged leg of a horse of theirs who had perished on the track.

The New York Racing Association was fined $3 million after a lengthy investigation by the state attorney general that focused on money laundering perpetrated by members of the mutuel department. In the midst of the investigation, NYRA president Terry Meyocks resigned. California had its woes, with dwindling attendance at Santa Anita and Hollywood Park and continued stress on trainers facing costly worker's compensation insurance rates. Fair Grounds declared bankruptcy after a ruling that it had underpaid horse owners, and Suffolk Downs canceled the Massachusetts Handicap for one year.

The three men - Glen DaSilva, Derrick Davis, and Chris Harn - who tried to hijack the Breeders' Cup Pick Six of 2002 were sentenced, though racing officials decried their punishment as lenient. Players continued to be frustrated by significant odds fluctuations after races had begun, a problem racing officials ascribed to dated software rather than nefarious gamblers. A controversial betting outfit in South Dakota, Racing Services, was found to be grossly arrears in paying state taxes, and owner Susan Bala was ousted. Jockey Norberto Arroyo found himself in prison for 39 days after being convicted of second-degree assault for a pool-hall fight. It was a brutal winter for him, and for Aqueduct, Oaklawn Park, and Turfway Park, all of which had numerous weather-related cancellations. An ice storm smacked Central Kentucky in February. Too cold, then too hot. A summer heat wave overload the East Coast electrical grid on Aug. 14, causing a massive power outage that impacted racetracks in the Northeast, and fires ringed Southern California the weekend of the Breeders' Cup.

Racing suffered numerous profound losses in 2003. Bill Shoemaker and the riding great whose record he broke, John Longden, both died. Laffit Pincay Jr., who passed Shoemaker to become the world's winningest rider, retired, as did another classy Hall of Famer, Eddie Delahoussaye.

In addition to Shoemaker and Longden, death claimed former jockeys Jimmy Nichols and Wayne Wright, trainers Sunshine Calvert, Gene Cilio, Charles Hadry, Harold Rose, Joe Trovato, and Barney Willis; owners and breeders William Bancroft, Zelda Cohen, Henryk de Kwiatkowski, Scott Dudley, John Franks, Ed Gaylord, Elmer and Harriet Heubeck, Jack Hoover, Kay Jeffords, William T. Pascoe III, Nathan Scherr, Farid Sefa, Joe Taylor, Jeanne Vance, Robert Walter, and Mary Lou Wootton; racetrack executives Joseph Carney, Marie Krantz, and Mervin Muniz; bloodstock agent Packy McMurry, longtime Calumet Farm employee Margaret Glass, racecaller Dick Riley, photographer Jerry Frutkoff, journalists Bob Adair, John Crittenden, John Harrell, Leon Rasmussen, Marvin Root, Vic Thornton, and Robert Via; and Harry "The Horse" Tendler, a long-time press aide in Maryland and then Florida.

Pincay and Delahoussaye were joined in retirement by Daily Racing Form executive columnist Joe Hirsch, steeplechase jockeys Arch Kingsley and Blythe Miller, and Claiborne Farm manager John Sosby, whose pitch-perfect drawl graces the Kentucky Derby Museum's moving video presentation.

A staggering number of top-class horses died, but the most heart-wrenching death apparently happened in 2002. Ferdinand, the 1986 Derby winner, was found by a dogged reporter based in Japan to have been callously slaughtered. The story echoed that of Exceller, who, ironically, also was trained by the late Charlie Whittingham. Belmont Stakes winner Temperence Hill, who had been at stud in Thailand, was reported dead, apparently having also died in 2002.

Spectacular Bid, whom Shoemaker said was the best horse he had ridden, died at age 27, 23 years after his sublime 1980 Horse of the Year campaign. Also passing were the mare Lady's Secret, the 1986 Horse of the Year, as well Derby winner Sunny's Halo, classic winners Aloma's Ruler, Creme Fraiche, and Little Current; the sires Allen's

Prospect, Anees, Answer Lively, Chester House, Desert Wine, Fly So Free, Notebook, Old Trieste, Proud Birdie, Sandpit, Shelter Half, Skywalker, and Smarten; and the mares Glorious Song, Kelley's Day, Maplejinsky, Ms. Eloise, Northern Sunset, Our Mims, Oustandingly, Stick to Beauty, Too Chic, Wayward Lass, Wild Applause, Wings of Grace, and Ubetshedid.

As for the racing, here's a look back at 2003, division-by-division.

3-YEAR-OLD MALES: Funny Cide grabbed the headlines, but Empire Maker bested him twice in three meetings. Empire Maker won the Wood Memorial, Funny Cide took the Derby, and Empire Maker won the Belmont. At year's end, Funny Cide was declared the division's champion. Even though Funny Cide failed to win the Belmont, there was a Triple Crown winner. Oh, Canada. Wando swept the Queen's

Plate, Prince of Wales and Breeders' Stakes. Peace Rules, the Derby runner-up, won the Blue Grass and Haskell Invitational. Strong Hope captured five straight races, including the Jim Dandy against Empire Maker. Ten Most Wanted finished second in the Belmont, then later won the Travers and Super Derby.

OLDER MALE: This was the deepest, most exciting division of the year. Mineshaft, the overwhelming winner as Horse of the Year with 209 of a possible 248 votes, blossomed after being repatriated from Great Britain. The son of A.P. Indy captured four Grade 1 races, won seven races overall, and never finished worse than second in nine starts for trainer Neil Howard and jockey Robby Albarado. Perfect Drift upset Mineshaft in the Stephen Foster, then beat Congaree in the Kentucky Jockey Club, but could only finish sixth in the Breeders'

Kentucky Derby winner Funny Cide gallops to win the Preakness by a near-record margin of nine and three-quarter lengths. The classic double would earn year-end honors for the gelding.

Cup Classic, when a victory might have made him Horse of the Year. Congaree was a throw-back to the hearty horses of yesteryear. He won five times, including Grade 1 races ranging from seven furlongs to 1 1/4 miles, while racing in California, Kentucky, and New York. Milwaukee Brew joined John Henry as the only two-time winners of the Santa Anita Handicap. Candy Ride, imported from Argentina, won all three of his starts, on both turf and dirt, to run his overall record to 6 for 6. Medaglia d'Oro was another who did not perform often, but who dazzled when he did. He won the Strub, the Oaklawn Handicap, and the Whitney, and finished second in the Pacific Classic and Breeders' Cup Classic. Pleasantly Perfect capped Mandella's singularly sensational Breeders' Cup Day with his late-running victory in the Classic. Fleetstreet Dancer braved a downpour to capture the Japan Cup Dirt.

OLDER FILLY OR MARE: Azeri dominated in the West, Sightseek in the East, but they never met. Azeri, the 2002 Horse of the Year, ran her winning streak to 11 for trainer Laura de Seroux before a dull effort in the Lady's Secret. Then all the backstage tension between de Seroux and owner Michael Paulson finally came to the fore. Azeri was sent to Kentucky with a tendon injury that de Seroux said should force her retirement. But two months later, Paulson said she had recovered. He put Azeri back in training and sent her to D. Wayne Lukas. Despite the drama, Azeri's on-track performance earned her the divisional championship by 123-107 over Sightseek. Sightseek lost her first three starts of the year in California, then won four straight Grade 1 races in Kentucky and New York before returning to California to fail at 3-5 in the Breeders' Cup Distaff. Sightseek was part of a one-two punch for Frankel, who also had Ruffian winner Wild Spirit. Adoration led from start to finish in the Distaff for a 40-1 surprise. Starrer was the best in the country early in the year - she beat Sightseek in the Santa Margarita for her second Grade 1 victory - but she never raced after March. Got Koko swept the La Canada Series.

3-YEAR-OLD FILLIES: The wealth was spread here. Composure won the Las Virgenes and Santa Anita Oaks, but never raced after March. Bird Town took the Kentucky Oaks and Acorn, but did not win a race the second half of the year. Island

Fashion was well beaten in the Kentucky Oaks, but later beat Bird Town in the Alabama, and closed out her season with a devastating victory in the La Brea. The Alabama ended a five-race winning streak for Spoken Fur, who captured the Mother Goose and Coaching Club American Oaks. Elloluv won the Ashland, and later was second in the Breeders' Cup Distaff, but she lost her two meetings against Composure. Buy The Sport pulled off a 48-1 shocker in the Gazelle. Mighty mite Lady Tak won the Fair Grounds Oaks, but showed her best asset with a powerful victory sprinting in the Test, in which she avenged Kentucky Oaks and Acorn losses to Bird Town. Six Perfections only ran once in this country, and only on turf, but she beat the boys in the Breeders' Cup Mile. That almost was enough to get her an Eclipse Award, but she lost narrowly to Bird Town in the closest vote of the year, 96-94.

MALE TURF HORSE: High Chaparral and Johar finished in the first dead-heat for win in Breeders' Cup history when they hit the wire in the Turf, just ahead of international superstar Falbrav. It was the best race on an outstanding Breeders' Cup card, and helped get High Chaparral his second straight divisional championship. Storming Home became best known for his frightening antics in the Arlington Million, but minded his manners in the Whittingham and Clement Hirsch. Sulamani, who backed into the Million victory, won the Turf Classic after bobbling noticeably on the final turn. Balto Star won the United Nations and the Red Smith, Phoenix Reach the Canadian International, and Denon took the Manhattan. The best middle-distance runners were old man Redattore (who won the Shoemaker Mile and San Gabriel), Perfect Soul (Shadwell Turf), Special Ring (Eddie Read), and Touch of the Blues (Atto Mile).

FEMALE TURF HORSE: Six Perfections (Mile) and Islington (Filly and Mare Turf) shipped over from Europe and were haughtily dismissive of the oppressive heat when scoring Breeders' Cup victories. Islington, benefiting greatly from the sympathy earned via her tough-luck Breeders' Cup loss in 2002, was named the division's champion. Heat Haze was the best American-based runner. She took the Beverly D. and the Matriarch, but was upset by Dimitrova in the Flower Bowl and Voodoo Dancer in the Diana. In addition to Heat Haze, Frankel won major races with Megahertz (Mabee/Ramona) and Tates Creek (Gamely and Yellow Ribbon). We did not see enough of Zimbabwe sensation Ipi Tombe, who beat the boys in the Dubai Duty Free, but was retired after winning Churchill's Locust Grove.

2-YEAR-OLD COLTS: Action This Day, the division's champion, rallied to win a Breeders' Cup Juvenile that was more notable for who did not show up. The winners of the Champagne (Birdstone), Lane's End Breeders' Futurity (Eurosilver), Norfolk (Ruler's Court), and Hopeful (Silver Wagon) all were kept out of the race, either because their connections wanted to point for a race six months later (the Derby) or because they did not want to travel to California, as though it involves flying by way of Mars on a rocketship. Chapel Royal was the early-season sensation, and Cuvee took over in the late summer, but both were beaten on Breeders' Cup Day. Lion Heart won the Hollywood Futurity to complete a 3-for-3 season, Cactus Ridge was unbeaten in four starts in the Midwest, Tapit was a powerful winner of the Laurel Futurity, and Sir Oscar dominated the stallion series in Florida.

2-YEAR-OLD FILLIES: Halfbridled was perfect in four starts, and received all but one Eclipse Award vote. She saved the best for last, overcoming the 14 post going 1 1/16 miles at Santa Anita in the Breeders' Cup Juvenile Fillies. She also captured the Del Mar Debutante and Oak Leaf for the team of Mandella and Krone. Ashado, second in the Breeders' Cup, won the Spinaway and Demoiselle for Pletcher, who also won the Matron with Marylebone. Hollywood Story was rewarded for chasing the very best all year when she won the Hollywood Starlet for her first victory.

SPRINTER: Aldebaran used his breathtaking late rush to capture the San Carlos, Met Mile, and Forego, but he found six furlongs too sharp, and was nowhere near the wickedly fast Cajun Beat when they hit the wire in the Breeders' Cup Sprint. Aldebaran's overall record stood out, however, and he was rewarded with the Eclipse Award. Congaree beat Aldebaran in the Carter in Congaree's lone race at less than one mile. Beau's Town was the king of the Midwest, then flashed his heels at Del Mar in the Bing Crosby. Ghostzapper finished furiously to take the Vosburgh. Avanzado won the Ancient Title and was second in the Dubai Golden Shaheen. The former claimer Shake You Down won five straight after moving to Scott Lake's barn, then finished third in the Breeders' Cup. Memories of Da Hoss came rushing back when Michael Dickinson brought A Huevo back from a four-year absence to win the De Francis Dash. Two of the all-time greats, Kona Gold and Xtra Heat, were retired, but not before adding stakes wins to their lengthy résumés.

STEEPLECHASER: McDynamo won three Grade 1 races, including the Colonial Cup and an overpowering 15 1/4-length victory in the Breeders' Cup Steeplechase, to reign supreme and receive the Eclipse Award.

The Year in Sales and Breeding

By Glenye Cain

The 2003 breeding season got off to a bad start in the country's primary nursery in central Kentucky, when the state's worst ice storm in 50 years hit the area on Feb. 16. That would have been the traditional start of the breeding season, but many roads and farms were damaged by fallen trees and had no power. For a community that had taken the brunt of the mysterious abortion-causing disease mare reproductive loss syndrome just a couple of years earlier, it seemed like a bad omen. But the year in breeding and sales generally got brighter from that inauspicious start.

Breeders and sale companies expected the full effects of MRLS, which hit hardest in 2001, to have some follow-on damage in 2003, the year that many of the aborted fetuses would have been yearlings. Indeed, those abortions reduced the 2003 yearling crop by about 23 percent. Keeneland even cited the disease's ravages when it canceled its July select sale, although the growing allure of the company's September auction seemed at least as blameworthy in the July sale's decline. As if MRLS was not worrying enough, the nation went to war in March and the U.S. economy was sluggish - none of which seemed to bode well for the sale of perishable luxury items.

The doom-and-gloomers had cause to nod knowingly when the nation's 2-year-old sales produced some early declines. But a juvenile sale-record colt at Barretts, $2.7 million Diamond Fury, was a good omen. As it happen, things did get better from there. The yearling market, whose uppermost tier had dropped sharply at in 2002, bounced back for high-end sellers in 2003, prompting some to muse that the decreased supply of horses might have whetted buyers' appetites. Fasig-Tipton's July yearling sale - the first of the season after Keeneland July's historic cancellation - saw across-the-board declines on its MRLS-abbreviated catalog, but they reversed the trend easily at Saratoga. That auction galloped to increases at every level of the market. Topped by a $2.7 million Unbridled half-brother to E Dubai that Satish Sanan bought, the sale increased its average price by 25 percent, its median by 33 percent, and its gross by 37 percent. Relieved sellers were clearly pleased: buybacks fell sharply from 29 percent to 21 percent.

The bull market rolled on to Keeneland September, which posted a 30-percent jump in gross, a 29-percent increase in average, and a 13-percent gain in median. The sale topper was similarly heady, a $3.8 million Gone West-Touch of Greatness filly bought by Sheikh Mohammed al Maktoum.

And Keeneland's fall breeding stock sales, too, enjoyed great buoyancy. After Fasig-Tipton's small 101-horse mixed auction saw declines in average and median, Keeneland fired a rocket that took even the auction house by surprise. The 11-day sale rang up enormous gains, including a $7.1 million record broodmare for Cash Run in foal to Storm Cat and a $2.4 million record weanling for a Storm Cat colt out of Spain. Gerry Dilger signed the ticket for the weanling, but Cash Run's buyer had a twist to it. The bidding duel that erupted over Cash Run was between Satish Sanan's Padua Stables and Coolmore Stud, who had been ownership partners in the mare. This meant each party was bidding with 50-cent dollars, a circumstance that deflated the record's aura, even though the hammer price was still $7.1 million in the books.

Overall, the auction increased its gross by 26 percent, average by 15 percent, and median by 14 percent, with only a small gain in buybacks from 20 percent to 22 percent.

The business year had turned out to be a pleasant surprise for breeders. For one breeder in particular - Khalid Abdullah's Juddmonte Farms - the racing year held some disappointments when homebred Empire Maker failed to win the Kentucky Derby. But even that story had some happy elements: the colt won the Belmont Stakes and he was part of a huge year otherwise for the operation, which cruised to Eclipse Awards as the year's top breeder and owner.

There was bad news in 2003. For a start, the 2002 Derby winner War Emblem, who had been sold for stud duty in Japan, turned out to have little interest in his new job. The farm that bought him, Shadai Stallion Station, said he refused to cover mares and filed an insurance claim on him. Far worse news also emerged from Japan in July when reporter Barbara Bayer discovered that 1986 Derby hero Ferdinand, who also stood in Japan, had been sent to a slaughterhouse there in 2002. That shocking revelation sparked formation of Old Friends, a Kentucky retirement farm for pensioned stallions, and also made stud owners consider putting return clauses in their overseas sale contracts.

There was sadness, too, over human losses in the Thoroughbred breeding world. Among those were Henryk De Kwiatkowski, viewed as Calumet Farm's savior in 1992 when he bought it for $17 million at a bankruptcy auction and vowed never to change a blade of grass, died in March; his family has so far stuck to his pledge and continued to operate the farm as 2003 ended. Linda Conley, famed around the international sales circuit as a longtime representative for Tattersalls, also died that month. Elmer Heubeck, one of the Florida breeding industry's founding father and owner of Quail Roost Farm in Ocala, died in May. And in December, two of the breeding world's legends also departed: Ewell Rice and Joe Taylor. Rice had worked his way up from exercise rider to farm management at Calumet Farm during its heydey in the 1940s and '50s. Taylor was the legendary former manager of Gainesway Farm, father of the founders of Taylor Made Farm, and an author whose book, Joe Taylor's Complete Guide to Breeding and Raising Racehorses, has become the standard for many aspiring breeders.

PROFILES OF TOP HORSES OF 2003

BY MIKE WATCHMAKER

2-Year-Old Colts and Geldings

Eurosilver

In a division where none of the leading members raced against each other, he made a winning move in the Lane's End Breeders' Futurity that is rarely successful at Keeneland, breaking from post 10 in a field of 11 going 1 1/16 miles, and making a bold run from well off the pace around the far turn to score by a widening 4 3/4 lengths...only loss in three starts came in his first start when second to entrymate Silver Wagon...two days after Silver Wagon

came back to win the Grade 1 Hopeful, he recorded his first victory in runaway fashion, and in time strong enough to earn a better Beyer Speed Figure than the Hopeful winner.

Birdstone

Half-brother to Kentucky Oaks and Acorn winner Bird Town wowed the Saratoga crowd when he won his first start by 12 1/2 lengths in time fast enough to earn a Beyer Figure of 99...was somewhat cold on the tote board at nearly 5-2 when he ran back in the Hopeful and came up empty in the final furlong after making a wide run into contention...made thorough amends by winning the Grade 1 Champagne, tracking a

slow pace and coming home fairly quickly to master early-season 2-year-old leader, the distance-challenged Chapel Royal, in a going-away score...his Champagne win is flattered when Read the Footnotes, who finished a distant sixth after winning his first two starts comfortably, rebounds to win both the Nashua and Remsen in decisive fashion.

Ruler's Court

It was hard to figure out what the fuss was about when he had to work hard to win at first asking as the 4-5 favorite and then was a soundly beaten third at 1-5 in the Hollywood Juvenile Championship, followed by an ineffective fourth in the Best Pal...then blinkers were added to his equipment, and what a difference they made...won the Norfolk by 14 laughing lengths, and though he demolished a weak field, his performance was of such quality that he earned a 102 Beyer Figure...probably would have been favored in the weakest Breeders' Cup Juvenile in Breeders' Cup history, but his connections passed, citing the fact that no Juvenile winner has gone on to win the Kentucky Derby...poor decision, as Ruler's Court came up with an injury that has put his racing career in jeopardy.

Tapit

A pure example of raw talent with giant potential...started only twice and beat little in both races, although the two who finished immediately behind him in his crushing maiden victory did come back to win their next starts...even though he ran strongly enough to earn a very respectable 98 Beyer Figure in his victory in the Laurel Futurity, his performance had to be seen to be totally appreciated...slow start, trapped in a box behind opponents, rank...he still ran away and hid upon his first glimpse of daylight in the stretch...trained by Michael Dickinson.

2-Year-Old Fillies

Halfbridled

Truly sensational winning all four of her starts by decisive margins, and totally dominant in her division...showed a devastating late kick winning her first start, made two moves winning the Grade 1 Del Mar Debutante, and made most of the pace when no one else wanted to winning the Oak Leaf, adding versatility to her list of many attributes...overcame post 14 and a short run to the first turn winning the Breeders' Cup Juvenile Fillies in faster time than Action This Day required to win the Breeders' Cup Juvenile at the same distance, lending weight to the belief that she was the best 2-year-old of either sex in 2003.

Ashado

Was the East coast version of Halfbridled for the first half of her campaign, winning her first three starts, albeit not with the same flash or in final times as strong as Halfbridled...her third victory, which came in the Grade 1 Spinaway, was actually her first attempt on a dry track...was without an excuse when a soundly beaten third in the Frizette but was game snaring second in the

maidens in early September, instead waiting for the Tempted in November, which she won convincingly...beaten a nose by Ashado in the Demoiselle but may have been best...was in tight on the rail much of the way, lost her action in upper stretch perhaps because of intimidation and fell back, but fought back with a resolve rarely seen in a young filly to fall a stride short.

Society Selection

Came from way back to win her first start going five furlongs at Saratoga and showed a lot of substance to win the Grade 1 Frizette Stakes in her next start...went into the Frizette off a near two-month layoff and was not only taking a huge jump in class, she was doing the same in terms of distance, stretching out to 1 1/16 miles...produced another potent late kick to catch Victory U. S. A., who was odds-on against Halfbridled in the Del Mar Debutante, and leave the accomplished Ashado back in third...clearly turned in an aberrational performance off the journey west in the Breeders' Cup Juvenile, checking on the first turn, trailing early and failing to get closer than 10th.

Breeders' Cup Juvenile Fillies, although she had a much easier trip than the victorious Halfbridled did...benefited from a brilliant ride by Jerry Bailey and flattered Halfbridled when she prevailed in the subsequent Demoiselle, but the fact that she almost squandered a clear stretch lead gave rise to questions involving her stamina.

La Reina

Impeccably bred daughter of A. P. Indy and Queena demonstrated a combination of talent and courage...was not rushed to the Breeders' Cup following a big victory over

3-Year-Old Colts and Geldings

Empire Maker

Enigmatic colt made no friends when he was retired early but showed flashes of real brilliance winning three Grade 1's and finishing second in three other stakes in six starts…became a force in the Florida Derby with blinkers on, winning by almost 10…toyed with Funny Cide in winning the Wood Memorial but finished second to that rival in the Kentucky Derby after missing a few critical days of training close to the race because of a foot bruise…stopped Funny

Cide's Triple Crown bid with a determined victory in the Belmont…his maddening tendency to lose focus and race in spots surfaced when he was denied at 1-5 in the Jim Dandy, a race that surprisingly turned out to be his last…he proved barely enough, there was plenty more he could have proven.

Funny Cide

Inexpensive New York-bred became everyone's Cinderella horse when he became the first gelding in 74 years to win the Kentucky Derby, turning back an Empire Maker who may have been a short horse because of missed training time…In the absence of Empire Maker, he romped over a dreadful field in the Preakness but was a soundly beaten third in the Belmont, a soundly beaten third in the Haskell, and a distant ninth when unsuitably spotted in the Breeders' Cup Classic…did win two-thirds of the Triple Crown, but when all is said and done, all two of his wins came over just a two-week period in May.

Ten Most Wanted

Became a popular wiseguy pick in the Kentucky Derby off a breakthrough victory in the Illinois Derby, but like so many before

him, he was uncharacteristically dull in the Derby…rebounded with a sharp second in the Belmont, giving Empire Maker all he could want, and a near miss in the Swaps when he ran against the grain of a rail bias…almost made everyone forget Empire Maker and Funny Cide when a very stylish winner of the Travers and was a more decisive winner of the Super Derby than his half-length win margin over Soto suggests…like the Derby, was a popular wiseguy pick in the Breeders' Cup Classic but seemed to lose interest after being walloped by Funny Cide going into the first turn.

Peace Rules

Totally overshadowed by barn mate Empire Maker but was only a head behind Empire Maker in their only meeting…Won the Louisiana Derby and Blue Grass in his first two starts of the year and tried to become the first horse in 20 years to win the Kentucky Derby off two preps…he finished third, just behind Empire Maker, but it was a big effort considering he contested a solid pace and was going a little bit farther than he prefers…came up completely empty in the Preakness, by far the worst effort on dirt in his career, but exacted revenge on Funny Cide in winning the Haskell, leaving him nine lengths back in third…out of his element at 1 1/4 miles in the Travers, which partly explains why the Breeders' Cup race he went for was the Mile…an unsuccessful choice, it turned out.

3-Year-Old Fillies

Composure

Started only twice before sustaining a career-ending injury in March but won both starts with a style not seen in her contemporaries throughout the rest of the year, and both victories came in Grade 1 races...no other 3-year-old filly won more than two Grade 1 events...overcame a poor start and a slow pace to win the Las Virgenes...in what turned out to be her career finale in the Santa Anita Oaks, she overcame a slow pace controlled in uncontested fashion by the

quality filly Elloluv, yet had an even easier time catching that opponent than she did in the Las Virgenes...at the time of her retirement, she was the best 3-year-old of either sex in trainer Bob Baffert's barn.

Elloluv

Proved to be a useful measuring stick of how good Composure was when just prior to losing close decisions to that opponent in the Las Virgenes and Santa Anita Oaks, she romped in the Santa Ynez, and then right after, galloped in the Grade 1 Ashland...sat out much of the spring and all of the summer after a speed duel fried her in the Kentucky Oaks...returned with two solid second-place finishes, first in the Lady's Secret (she was subsequently disqualified and placed fourth), in which she finished nearly two lengths ahead of Horse of the Year Azeri, and then in the Breeders' Cup Distaff...managed the best finish of any 3-year-old in the Distaff while going a distance (1 1/8 miles) that may be slightly beyond her best.

Bird Town

Emerged as one of the leaders of her division after consecutive victories in the Kentucky Oaks and the Acorn but jeopardized her position when she was unable to win again after the Acorn in June...even at 18-1, she was much the best in the Kentucky Oaks, winning by a widening 3 1/4 lengths despite stumbling badly at the start ...showed a lot of versatility to shorten up in distance from 1 1/8 miles to a mile in prevailing in the Acorn...seemed primed for a win in the Alabama after finishing second to Lady Tak in the Test but turned in the worst finish of her career, a distant fifth...easily second best to top older female Sightseek in the Beldame...was never even considered for the Breeders' Cup and was retired.

Spoken Fur

Returned immediate dividends after being purchased privately and turned over to trainer Bobby Frankel by winning the first two legs of the New York Racing Association's Triple Tiara for 3-year-old fillies but concluded her campaign with three consecutive losses...showed an explosive turn of foot into the stretch of the Tiara's new opener, the Mother Goose, blowing the race wide open...employed similar tactics winning the Coaching Club American Oaks, which proved judicious as she walked home toward the end of that grueling 1 1/2 miles...predictably came up empty in the new finale of the Tiara, the Alabama, finishing a distant third...still lacked her spark when third in the subsequent Gazelle and so undertook a turf experiment in the Queen Elizabeth II Challenge Cup in her final start, which proved unsuccessful.

Older Males

Mineshaft

He danced just about every dance but the last one, the Breeders' Cup Classic; was retired after winning the Jockey Club Gold Cup because of ongoing ankle issues...won over four different tracks in four states and won four Grade 1 events...it should have been five Grade 1 victories and wins over five different tracks but narrowly missed in the Stephen Foster after making a premature move...won three straight before the Foster and three straight after to conclude his career...burst onto the national scene winning the Pimlico Special on a sloppy track, but it was his overwhelming victories in the Suburban and Woodward that became the standards by which his peers were measured.

Medaglia d'Oro

Was the ranking older horse in the nation for the first part of 2003 on the basis of easy victories in the Strub and Oaklawn Handicap but was overtaken by Mineshaft's larger volume of accomplishment...his hard-fought victory in the Whitney, in which he proved

he could win in a big spot after being denied control of the early pace, enabled him to claim important scores in the East, West and the middle of the country...had no answer for Candy Ride in the Pacific Classic but probably regressed after that taxing effort in the Whitney, which followed a long layoff...turned in perhaps his most compelling performance in defeat in the Breeders' Cup Classic, a sharp second after contesting a strong pace.

Candy Ride

Undeniably talented, but this native of Argentina was still a bit of an unknown after a brief, albeit perfect three-race campaign...as he did in his native country, he went dirt to turf after his American debut and mastered a top-class turf miler in Special Ring in the American Handicap...Special Ring came back in his next start to win a Grade 1 event by five lengths...was 2-1 against Medaglia d'Oro's 3-5 on his return to dirt in the Pacific Classic but had little trouble overpowering him in the final furlong...was taken out of training, and thus consideration for the Breeders' Cup, in early September, disappointing those who wanted to see him confirm his big performance in the Pacific Classic.

Pleasantly Perfect

Was considered a prime contender for the 2002 Breeders' Cup Classic but was unable to perform in Illinois because of medication issues...Instead upset the 2003 Classic on his home court of Santa Anita...put on a late-season charge in October after being on the shelf much of the season following two sub-par performances early in the year to begin the campaign...earned his Breeders' Cup shot with a comeback victory in the Goodwood, and this closer certainly benefited in the Breeders' Cup from the Classic's strong and contested pace...nevertheless, he was the one good enough to capitalize in America's richest race.

Older Fillies and Mares

Sightseek

Despite a dismal fourth in the Breeders' Cup Distaff as the 3-5 favorite, she had the most accomplished season of any prominent older female...won four Grade 1's at distances from seven furlongs to 1 1/8 miles...set the standard for the division with an 11 1/2-length romp in the Go for Wand and rivaled that performance when, coming off a better than two-month layoff, she absolutely toyed with five other Grade 1 winners in the

Beldame...all four of her losses in 2003 occurred at Santa Anita, but the Distaff was the only time she finished worse than second there...the legitimacy of the Distaff is in question, anyway, with a 40-1 shot having won it, and with the first two finishers having come back to lose in their next starts.

Azeri

Defending Horse of the Year and older female champion undertook a campaign similar to her very rewarding 2002 campaign...she may have demonstrated her best right off the bat, as her repeat score in the Apple Blossom revealed the heart of a champion...the very capable Take Charge Lady seemed on her way to victory, but she caught her in the last jump, coming from off the pace, something she had been increasingly disinclined to do...mastered mainly modest opposition winning the Milady, Vanity and Clement Hirsch, and then was found wanting when the going got a lot tougher in the Lady's Secret, finishing a dull third...was reported to be sick afterward, and that, plus an apparent tendon injury,

precluded a defense of her title in the Breeders' Cup Distaff.

Wild Spirit

Seemed to surprise everyone when she mauled her field in the Shuvee at 10-1 in her first start outside her native Chile but was odds-on in her three subsequent starts...dominated the Delaware and Ruffian handicaps and was just a nose away from perfection in 2003, as that was the margin of her defeat in the Personal Ensign...that Personal Ensign effort may have been better than it looked, as her barn was in the midst of an uncharacteristic, brief, but very deep slump that may have been due to illness...slightly overshadowed by barn mate Sightseek...would have had to have been supplemented to the Breeders' Cup Distaff at a cost of $400,000 and was not.

Got Koko

Her obvious affinity for Santa Anita helped her to gain recognition on a national scale...swept the La Canada series at Santa Anita, which actually began in the last days of 2002, and bested Sightseek in the series finale, the La Canada...in September, she defeated Azeri, among others, in the Lady's Secret at Santa Anita, showing predictable improvement second start back off a layoff after finishing second to Azeri in the Clement Hirsch in her first start back...made little impression finishing a distant third in the Breeders' Cup Distaff despite it being over her favorite surface, but evidence suggests the form of that race is open to serious question.

Turf Males

Storming Home

Beaten favorite on a 99-degree day in the Breeders' Cup Turf, but that does not change the fact that he was the best turf horse in the nation the entire season…will forever be remembered for snatching defeat from the jaws of victory in the Arlington Million…was on his way to a daylight victory when, for some bizarre reason known only to him, he ducked out sharply nearing the wire…still hit the wire first before dumping his rider but was subsequently disqualified…showed no such misbehavior winning

the Jim Murray and Charlie Whittingham in his first two starts of the year, and first two North American starts, nor in the subsequent Clement Hirsch…his effort in the Hirsch was brilliant as he came home his last quarter mile in a 1 1/4 mile race in 22 seconds flat to best Johar, who came back to dead-heat for win in the Breeders' Cup Turf.

High Chaparral

As was the case in 2002, he made only one start in the United States in 2003 and required no more to achieve a high ranking…successfully defended his title in the Breeders' Cup Turf by dead-heating for win with Johar…interesting to note that when he won the 2002 Breeders' Cup Turf at Arlington, it was 46 degrees; when he shared the win with Johar at Santa Anita, it was one degree shy of 100…his Breeders' Cup performance quashed the notion that he wasn't quite as effective as a 4-year-old as he was as a 3-year-old in 2002.

Johar

Was the third leg in trainer Dick Mandella's unprecedented four-win day in the Breeders' Cup…signaled he was coming up to a big effort in the Breeders' Cup Turf when a narrowly beaten second in the Clement Hirsch by Storming Home after making all the pace in just his second start back off a long layoff…is much more effective coming from off the pace, which is what he did in the Breeders' Cup and in winning the San Marcos in January…sidelined after the San Marcos because of a fractured shoulder.

Falbrav

Like High Chaparral, made only one start in the United States and impressed in narrow defeat…rallied to take the lead in midstretch of the Breeders' Cup Turf only to come out on the short end of a three-way photo, beaten a head for all the money…it was a very commendable performance, since the 1 1/2 miles of the Turf was always considered to be beyond his range…under good racing conditions (unlike what Johar encountered in the Japan Cup), he came back to win the Hong Kong Cup, validating the form of the Breeders' Cup Turf.

Turf Fillies and Mares

Islington

In a division that lacked a United States-based standout, and in a division that has become essentially a one-race division, she won that one race, the Breeders' Cup Filly and Mare Turf...British-based filly was a deserving winner of the Filly and Mare Turf for several reasons: she overcame unusually hot Southern California weather, she overcame the tight turns of the Santa Anita turf course, and she was probably best in the 2002 Filly and Mare Turf but had to settle for third after steadying all over Arlington Park...also deserving because, just before her Breeders' Cup victory, she was beaten a neck by High Chaparral and a head by Falbrav, when third in the Irish Champion Stakes...High Chaparral and Falbrav came back to be first in a dead-heat and third beaten a head in the Breeders' Cup Turf, and were two of the best male horses in the world.

Six Perfections

Ran a tremendous race winning the Breeders' Cup Mile over 12 male opponents, many older than this then 3-year-old filly...like Islington, she overcame the heat

and tight turns...she also overcame her reluctance to load into the gate, and the disadvantageous 12 post with a short run to the first turn...quite likely very little between her and Islington, only the opinion that the field Islington defeated in the Filly and Mare Turf had more quality top to bottom than the Mile did, even though the Mile was open to males.

L'Ancresse

If Islington tops the rankings in this division, then L'Ancresse has to be somewhere near the top, as she was a surprisingly sharp second in the Breeders' Cup Filly and Mare Turf at odds of 46-1...seemed to be in the Filly and Mare Turf as a "rabbit" for stretch-running stablemate Yesterday but instead adopted the thankless role of prompting Bien Nicole's uncontested pace...nevertheless, after taking the lead in upper stretch, she gave the much more accomplished Islington all she could handle before finally bowing by a neck.

Yesterday

Finished third in the division's definitive race, the Breeders' Cup Filly and Mare Turf...as was the case with Islington, Six Perfection, and L'Ancresse, she made her only appearance in the United States on 2003 in the Breeders' Cup...came from way back to loom a threat for the win in mid-stretch but was unable to make headway in the final furlong...still managed to finish in front of such important American-based stakes winners as Heat Haze, Megahertz, Voodoo Dancer, and Tates Creek.

Sprinters

Congaree

Admirably versatile performer and Grade 1 winner from seven furlongs to 1 1/4 miles had only one sprint start, at least in a conventional sense, but it was a compelling one...shortened up in distance from the 1 1/4 miles of the Santa Anita Handicap, in which he was nailed in the last jump, to the seven furlongs of the Carter Handicap, and blew the race open into the stretch after making almost all the running...cruised to a

3 1/2-length score over Aldebaran, who had previously romped in the Grade 1 San Carlos, and who went on to record four other stakes victories, three in important sprint stakes...concluded his 5-year-old campaign by winning another Grade 1 event around one turn, a blowout score in the Cigar Mile, although most do not consider mile races, even one-turn mile races such as the Cigar, sprint events.

Aldebaran

Although he was soundly beaten by Congaree in the Carter, he compiled perhaps the best overall record in important sprint stakes...blew away his field in the Grade 1 San Carlos in his first start of the year and overwhelmed the Churchill Downs Handicap in similar fashion on the Kentucky Derby undercard...that was followed by a determined score in the Metropolitan Mile Handicap, which is often not considered a sprint even though it is a one-turn mile event but later won the Tom Fool and Forego handicaps...only sub-par sprint attempt came at an inopportune time, in the

Breeders' Cup Sprint, but did make progress to finish sixth after being last of 13 early in, amazingly, what was his first career attempt at a distance as short as six furlongs.

Shake You Down

For the majority of the year, was America's best horse at six furlongs, the distance that is most closely associated with American sprinting...claimed for $65,000 in March at Aqueduct after losing his third straight start to begin the year, he went on to win five straight, including the Bold Ruler, True North and Smile Sprint handicaps...was a creditable third in the Breeders' Cup Sprint after breaking last of 13 and rushing up to contest the pace...finished second at odds-on in the subsequent De Francis Dash but concluded his campaign in the final days of 2003 with another six-furlong stakes victory in the Gravesend at Aqueduct.

Cajun Beat

Emerged from obscurity after changing trainers in the middle of the year and engineered a 22-1 upset in what is often the definitive race in the division, the Breeders' Cup Sprint...encountered significant trouble when second in the Carry Back Stakes in his first start for his new barn, and then, in his next start two months later, he managed a breakthrough in terms of Beyer Speed Figures upsetting fellow 3-year-olds in the Kentucky Cup Sprint...was able to improve even more in the Breeders' Cup Sprint, being right with the pace from the outset, and capitalizing on either some of his more accomplished opponents' poor racing luck, or inexperience at the distance.

2003 OBITUARY OF THE TURF

OWNERS AND BREEDERS

Date	Name	Age	Location	Cause
Jan. 8	Harriet Jones	84	Louisville (KY)	
Jan. 18	William Bancroft	71		
Jan. 29	Philip Clements Jr.	78	Paris (KY)	
Feb. 3	Mary Lou Wootton	69		Cancer
Feb. 15	Bob Brummel	76	Grants Pass (OR)	
March 12	Scott Dudley	56	Florida	Cancer
March 13	Dan Jones	58	Arkansas	
March 17	H. de Kwiatkowski	79	Bahamas	Pneumonia
April 17	Farid Sefa	74	Lexington (KY)	Cancer
May 7	Robert Walter	86	Sebastopol (CA)	Leukemia
May 31	Giuseppe Sacchetti	57	Ontario	
Late June	William Pascoe III	87	Murrieta (CA)	
July 8	Kay Jeffords	80	New York City (NY)	Parkinson's
July 13	Jerome Torsney	75	New Jersey	
Late July	John Hoover	78	California	
Aug. 12	Hays Biggs	74	Arkansas	Cancer
Oct. 15	Jim Rasmussen	66	Iowa	Cancer
Oct. 16	Sam Longo	96	Arcadia (CA)	
Oct. 25	Dwight Sutherland	81	Kansas City (MO)	Brief illness
Dec. 15	Jeanne Vance	68	Manalapan (FL)	

TRAINERS

Date	Name	Age	Location	Cause
Jan. 5	Kevin Stucki	49	California	Leukemia
Jan. 6	Vance Longden	72	Oceanside (CA)	Cancer
Jan. 14	Barney Willis	84		
Jan. 21	John Shoemaker	90	Florida	
Jan. 29	Louis Bellocq	75	France	Long illness
Feb. 24	Charlie Hadry	72	Westminster (MD)	Cancer
Feb. 28	Joe Trovato	67		Natural causes
May 31	Robert Scetta	62		Heart Attack
June 12	Richard Shockey Jr.	81		
June 19	William Adams	67	Lexington (KY)	Long illness
Aug. 3	Pat Devereux Sr.	77	Lexington (KY)	Brief illness
Aug. 6	Robert J. Cagney	79	Oldsmar (FL)	
Late August	Charlie Reynolds	89	New York	
Sept. 8	Harold Rose	92	Miami (FL)	
Sept. 10	Lewis Wartchow	65	Oklahoma City (OK)	Heart failure
Nov. 22	Gene Cilio	74	Illinois	Cancer
Nov. 29	Mike Harte	57		Heart attack
Dec. 8	William Hickam	60	Collinsville (IL)	Self-inflicted gunshot

JOCKEYS

Date	Name	Age	Location	Cause
Feb. 14	John Longden	96	Banning (CA)	Natural
Feb. 27	Jimmy Nichols	74	Fort Worth (TX)	Kidney failure
March 12	Ruben Martinez Jr.	50	Houston (TX)	
March 11	Wayne Wright	86	Yerington (NV)	
April 17	Dale Long	64	Santa Rosa (CA)	
June 20	Chris Valovich	41	Phoenix (AZ)	Suicide
Oct. 12	Bill Shoemaker	72	San Marino (CA)	Natural
Nov. 11	Timmy Houlihan	21	Ireland	

OTHERS CONNECTED WITH THE TURF

Date	Name	Age	Location	Cause
Jan. 15	Frank Drea	69	Canada	Pneumonia
Jan. 20	Harold Rogers	64	Louisville (KY)	Brief illness
Jan. 24	Zelda Cohen	98	Baltimore (MD)	
Feb. 16	Mae DeVol	92		
Feb. 22	Marie Krantz	67	New Orleans (LA)	Long illness
March 9	Joseph Carney Jr.	70		Long Illness
March 31	Linda McGaughey	59	Lexington (KY)	Illness
April 1	John Harrell	37	Louisville (KY)	Stroke
March 24	Phil Norman	80	Ramona (CA)	
May 2	Gerry Howard	61	Phoenix (AZ)	Car accident
May 10	Jack Servis	73	Bensalem (PA)	
May 24	Joan O'Shea			
May 30	Victor Sanchez	25	Muskegon (MI)	Track accident
July 18	Robert Via	68	Charles Town (WV)	
Aug. 2	Margaret Glass	82	Lexington (KY)	
July 20	Marvin Sugarman	87	Roslyn Heights (NY)	
Aug. 10	Dick Riley	74	California	Cancer
Aug. 13	Melvin Calvert	93	Florida	
Aug. 15	Leon Rasmussen	88	Los Feliz (CA)	Cancer
Aug. 25	Mervin Muniz	60	New Orleans (LA)	Cancer
Aug. 28	Antonio Figueroa	32	Monmouth Park (NJ)	Stabbed
Nov. 7	Betty Ann Drago	40	New York	Heart attack
Nov. 30	Paul Meyocks	81	Florida	Alzheimer's
Dec. 2	Art Pedrgal Jr.	60		
Dec. 3	Raymond Beard	61	Kenner (LA)	
Dec. 12	Daryl Wells	81		Heart disease
Dec. 15	Ewell Rice	78	Lexington (KY)	
Dec. 19	Joe Taylor	79	Lexington (KY)	Car accident
Dec. 31	John Franks	78	Shreveport (LA)	Heart complications

HORSES

Date	Horse	Age	Location	Cause
Jan. 2	Old Trieste	8	Jonabell Farm (KY)	Laminitis
Jan. 12	Bosque Redondo	6	Chino Valley (CA)	Laminitis
Jan. 19	Little Current	32	Monroe (WA)	Colic
Jan. 21	Little Bold John	21	Weston Farm (MD)	Colic
Jan. 27	Teddy Drone	18	Imlaystown (NJ)	Laminitis
Jan. 27	Slewsbox	6	UC-Davis (CA)	Colic
Feb. 15	Claramount	19	Stallion Park (NY)	Ruptured aorta
Feb. 25	Skywalker	21	Stone Farm (KY)	Heart attack
March 4	Lady's Secret	21	Valley Creek Farm (CA)	Foaling
Feb. 28	Lead Kindly Light	20	Claiborne Farm (KY)	Foaling
March 31	Smarten	27	Northview (MD)	Intestinal blockage
April 5	Anees	6	Mill Ridge Farm (KY)	Pastern fracture
April 2	Wild Applause	22	Rood & Riddle (KY)	Foaling
May 6	Traitor	9	Ocala Jockey Club Farm (FL)	Fire
	Darn That Alarm	22		
	Faygo	11		
	Reality Road	11		
	Star of Valor	10		
Early May	Ridgewood Pearl	11	Ireland	Foaling
May 14	Danehill	17	Coolmore (Ire)	Hit head
May 27	El Sysco Kid	2	Kentucky	Colitis
June 3	Sunny's Halo	23	Double S (TX)	Euthanized
June 9	Spectacular Bid	27	Milfer Farm (NY)	Heart Atack
June 27	Stick to Beauty	30	Taylor Made Farm (KY)	Euthanized
June 28	Chester House	8	Lexington (KY)	Cancer
Late June	Wayward Lass	25	Contemp. Stallions (NY)	Heart attack
June 21	Aloma's Ruler	24	Illinois	Heart attack
Late July	Golden Nepi	3		After surgery
Summer 2003	Temperence Hill	26	Thailand	
Aug. 22	Too Chic	24	Middlebrook Farm (KY)	Old age
Aug. 25	Carson Hollow	4	Adena Springs (Canada)	Colic surgery
Aug. 27	Cyber Secret	3	Aqueduct (NY)	Not known
Sept. 3	Allen's Prospect	21	New Bolton (PA)	Surgery complications
Sept. 4	Sandpit	14	Lexington (KY)	Liver tumor
Sept. 27	A.P. Assay	9	Lane's End (KY)	Broke neck
Early Sept.	Benny the Dip	9	Rathbarry Stud (Ire)	Fractured knee
Oct. 9	Northern Sunset	26	Payson Stud (KY)	Stroke
Oct. 9	Creme Fraiche	21	Brushwood (PA)	Laminitis
Oct. 13	Sgt Pepper Feature	25	Kentucky Horse Park (KY)	Stomach rupture
Oct. 19	Tap the Admiral	5	Belmont Park (NY)	Bacterial infection
Oct. 21	Fly So Free	15	Three Chimneys Farm (KY)	Heart failure
October?	Teleprompter	23	England	Euthanized
Dec. 4	She's a Devil Due	5	Hill 'n' Dale Farm (KY)	Colic
Dec. 5	Maplejinsky	18	Three Chimneys Farm (KY)	Ruptured aorta
Dec. 9	Our Mims	29	Rood and Riddle (KY)	Colic
Dec. 24	Grand Lodge	11	Woodlands Stud (Aust.)	Euthanized

–Compiled by Ira Kaplan

Experimental Free Handicap Weights

Highweight 2-Year-Olds in Annual Experimentals

Year	Horse	Weight	Year	Horse	Weight
1933	First Minstrel	126	1982	Copelan	126
1935	Red Rain	126		Roving Boy	126
1936	Brooklyn	126	1983	Devil's Bag	128
1937	Menow	126	1984	Chief's Crown	126
1938	El Chico	126	1985	Ogygian	126
1939	Bimelech	130		Tasso	126
1940	Whirlaway	126		I'm Splendid (f)	123
1941	Alsab	130	1986	Capote	126
1942	Count Fleet	132		Brave Raj (f)	123
1943	Pukka Gin	126	1987	Forty Niner	126
1944	Pavot	126		Epitome (f)	123
	Free for All	126		All Over (f)	123
1945	Lord Boswell	126	1988	Easy Goer	126
1946	Cosmic Bomb	126		Open Mind (f)	123
	First Flight	126	1989	Rhythm	126
	Double Jay	126		Go for Wand (f)	123
1947	Citation	126	1990	Fly So Free	126
1948	Blue Peter	126		Meadow Star (f)	123
1949	Middleground	126	1991	Arazi	130
1950	Uncle Miltie	126		Pleasant Stage (f)	123
1951	Tom Fool	126	1992	Gilded Time	126
1952	Native Dancer	130		Eliza (f)	123
1953	Porterhouse	126	1993	Brocco	126
	Turn-to	126		Dehere	126
1954	Summer Tan	128		Phone Chatter (f)	123
1955	Career Boy	126	1994	Timber Country	126
1956	Barbizon	126		Flanders (f)	124
1957	Jewel's Reward	126	1995	Maria's Mon	126
1958	First Landing	126		Unbridled's Song	126
1959	Warfare	126		My Flag (f)	123
1960	Hail to Reason	126	1996	Boston Harbor	126
1961	Crimson Satan	126		Storm Song (f)	124
1962	Never Bend	126	1997	Favorite Trick	128
1963	Raise a Native	126		Countess Diana (f)	125
1964	Bold Lad	130	1998	Answer Lively	126
1965	Buckpasser	126		Silverbulletday (f)	123
1966	Successor	126	1999	Anees	126
1967	Vitriolic	126		Cash Run (f)	123
1968	Top Knight	126		Chilukki (f)	123
1969	Silent Screen	128		Surfside (f)	123
1970	Hoist the Flag	126	2000	Macho Uno	126
1971	Riva Ridge	126		Caressing (f)	123
1972	Secretariat	129	2001	Johannesburg	126
1973	Protagonist	126		Tempera	123
1974	Foolish Pleasure	127	2002	Vindication	126
1975	Honest Pleasure	126		Storm Flag Flying (f)	123
1976	Seattle Slew	126	2003	Action This Day	126
1977	Affirmed	126		Cuvee	126
1978	Spectacular Bid	126		Ruler's Court	126
1979	Rockhill Native	126		Halfbridled (f)	124
1980	Lord Avie	126			
1981	Deputy Minister	126			
	Timely Writer	126			

Experimental Handicap for 2–Year–Olds in 2003

Three colts were co-highweights among colts and geldings on the 2003 Experimental Handicap, the first time three males shared top billing since 1946, while an undefeated filly was rated pounds better than her peers and closer than usual to her male counterparts. Breeders' Cup Juvenile winner Action This Day, three-time stakes winner Cuvee and runaway Norfolk winner Ruler's Court were top rated among the males, while Breeders' Cup Juvenile Fillies winner Halfbridled received the highest weighting among fillies. The Experimental Free Handicap annually is published in Daily Racing Form and is compiled by a panel of racing secretaries based on 2-year-old form projected in a hypothetical 1 1/16-mile race on the dirt in the spring of their 3-year-old seasons.

Action This Day, Cuvee and Ruler's Court were each assigned 126 pounds, the standard weight for a leading 2-year-old colt or gelding, while Halfbridled was assigned 124 pounds, a pound higher than par for fillies. The last time the top filly was weighted within two pounds of the top colt was in 1996, when Storm Song received 124 pounds compared to Boston Harbor's 126 pounds.

The participating racing secretaries for the 2003 Experimental were Mike Lakow of NYRA, Frank Gabriel Jr. of Arlington Park and Tom Robbins of Del Mar Turf Club. A total of 88 colts and geldings were rated along with 78 fillies.

COLTS and GELDINGS

Wgt.	Horse	Color	Sire	State	Breeder
126	Action This Day	b	by Kris S.	KY	Jaime S. Carrion, Trustee
	Cuvee	ch	by Carson City	KY	Verne H. Winchell
	Ruler's Court	dk b/br	by Doneraile Court	KY	Douglas Arnold & Dr. Roy Sadovsky
124	Birdstone	b	by Grindstone	KY	Marylou Whitney Stables
123	Lion Heart	ch	by Tale of the Cat	KY	Sabine Stable
122	Eurosilver	dk b/br	by Unbridled's Song	KY	Buckram Oak Farm
121	Chapel Royal	dk b/br	by Montbrook	FL	Ocala Stud Farm
	Minister Eric	ch	by Old Trieste	KY	Diamond A Racing Corp.
120	Silver Wagon	gr/ro	by Wagon Limit	FL	Mr. & Mrs. Leverett S. Miller
119	Perfect Moon	b	by Malibu Moon	MD	Mr. & Mrs. Hugh J. O'Donovan
	Siphonizer	dk b/br	by Siphon (BRZ)	KY	Brereton C. Jones
118	Read the Footnotes	b	by Smoke Glacken	NY	Lawrence Goichman
117	The Cliff's Edge	dk b/br	by Gulch	KY	Stonerside Stable
116	Tiger Hunt	dk b/br	by Kris S.	KY	WinStar Farm, LLC
115	Cactus Ridge	b	by Hennessy	KY	Dream Walkin' Farms, Inc.
	Dashboard Drummer	dk b/br	by Alamocitos	OK	Bob Pogue & Paulette Pogue
	Limehouse	ch	by Grand Slam	FL	Cheryl A. Curtin
	Mr. Jester	dk b/br	by Silver Deputy	KY	G. Watts Humphrey Jr.
	Pomeroy	b	by Boundary	KY	Cherry Valley Farm LLC
	St Averil	dk b/br	by Saint Ballado	KY	Gunsmith Stables
114	Fire Slam	b	by Grand Slam	KY	Julie Jones Mogge
	Tapit	gr/ro	by Pulpit	KY	Oldenburg Farms, LLC
112	Castledale (IRE)	b	by Peintre Celebre	IRE	Gigginstown House Stud
	Second of June	dk b/br	by Louis Quatorze	FL	Lambholm & E. Felcher
	Value Plus	gr/ro	by Unbridled's Song	KY	Just the Beginning Farm
111	Capitano	ch	by Belong to Me	PA	Brushwood Stable
	Cooperation	b	by Halo's Image	FL	Louis A. Gurino

WGT	HORSE	COLOR	SIRE	STATE	BREEDER
	Dealer Choice (FR)	b	by Green Tune	FR	William Trichter
110	Master David	ch	by Grand Slam	KY	Hopewell Investments LLC, et al.
	Notorious Rogue	b	by Victory Gallop	KY	Mr. & Mrs. T. M. Foreman III
	Sir Oscar	dk b/br	by Halo's Image	FL	Oscar Novo
	That's an Outrage	b	by Quiet American	KY	Christopher L. Elser
	Timo	gr/ro	by El Prado (IRE)	KY	C.K. Woods Stables, Inc
109	Deputy Storm	b	by Forestry	KY	Lady Slipper Farm
	Heckle	gr/ro	by Hennessy	KY	Gaines-Gentry Thoroughbreds & Pacelco S.A.
	Smokume	ch	by Smoke Glacken	FL	Hobeau Farm Ltd.
108	Blairs Roarin Star	dk b/br	by Roar	KY	John J. Greely III
	First Money	dk b/br	by Lil's Lad	KY	Dreabon Copeland
	Joe Six Pack	b	by Silver Deputy	KY	Gainesway Thoroughbreds LTD
	Paddington	ch	by Saint Ballado	KY	Gulf Coast Farms Bloodstock, L.P.
	Stolen Time	ch	by Time Bandit	FL	Dr. K. K. Jayaraman & Dr. Vilasini Jayaraman
107	Artie Schiller	b	by El Prado (IRE)	KY	Haras Du Mezeray S.A.
	Blushing Indian	b	by Cherokee Run	KY	Thomas/Lakin/Kintz
	Commendation	gr/ro	by Capote	KY	William Schettine
	Excellent Band	b	by Dixieland Band	KY	Brereton C. Jones
	Gran Prospect	ch	by Crafty Prospector	KY	Foxfield
	Lightnin N Thunder	gr/ro	by Storm Cat	KY	WinStar Farm, LLC
	Military Mandate	b	by Perfect Mandate	CA	Joe Turner
	Wynn Dot Comma	ch	by Struggler (GB)	FL	T. Wynn Jolley & Harry Hoglander
106	Lucky Pulpit	ch	by Pulpit	KY	Mr. & Mrs. Larry Williams
	Quiet Cash	dk b/br	by Real Quiet	KY	Michael E. Pegram
	Skipaslew	ch	by Skip Away	VA	Morgan's Ford Farm & Skip Away, LLC
	Stalking Tiger	b	by Twin Spires	CA	Woolsey & Daehling
105	El Sysco Kid	ch	by Sea of Secrets	KY	Running Grey Stable Inc.
	Korbyn Gold	gr/ro	by Gold Case	KY	L. T. Smith Enterprises
	The Herc	b	by Lord Carson	KY	Paula Capestro
104	Charming Jim	gr/ro	by Silver Charm	KY	Mr. & Mrs. Robert Lewis
	Consecrate	gr/ro	by Silver Charm	KY	Ironwater Farms Joint Venture
	Polish Rifle	b	by Polish Numbers	MD	Mr. & Mrs. Charles McGinnes
	Proper Prado	gr/ro	by El Prado (IRE)	KY	Mrs. James Winn
	Tin Can Sailor	dk b/br	by Military	KY	Glencrest Farm LLC
103	Adage	ch	by Tale of the Cat	KY	Arthur B. Hancock III
	El Prado Rob	b	by El Prado (IRE)	KY	Mill Ridge Farm Ltd., Chandler, McGaughey & Jamm
	Flushing Meadows	b	by Grand Slam	KY	Liberation Farm & Oratis Thoroughbreds
	Ghost Mountain	dk b/br	by Silver Ghost	KY	Carolyn T. Groves
	Glittergem	b	by Glitterman	KY	Justice Farm, Greg Justice & Steve Justice
	Grand Score	b	by Grand Slam	KY	Group One & J. Mamakos
	Hasslefree	dk b/br	by Forestry	KY	Lynn B. Schiff

WGT	HORSE	COLOR	SIRE	STATE	BREEDER
	Hi Teck Man	ch	by Claudius	TX	Hassel R. Spraberry
	Imperialism	gr/ro	by Langfuhr	KY	Farnsworth Farms
	Milestone Victory	b	by Dynaformer	KY	Richard Kaster, Nathan Fox & Haller Stables Ltd.
	Oncearoundtwice	ch	by Prospector's Music	TX	Parrish Hill Farm, Seeligson Jr. & Bass
	Pro Prado	gr/ro	by El Prado (IRE)	KY	Mrs. James Winn
	Texas Deputy	ch	by Deputy Commander	TX	Stonerside Stable
	Voladero	ch	by Private Talk	FL	University of Florida Foundation
	West Virginia	dk b/br	by Tomorrows Cat	NY	D. & R.M. Zuckerman, as tenants by the Entireties
102	Acclimate	ch	by Forestry	KY	Aaron U. Jones & Marie D. Jones
	Afternoon Charlie	b	by Afternoon Deelites	TX	Phillip Robertson
	Boston Brahmin	b	by Boston Harbor	KY	Overbrook Farm
	Capejinsky	dk b/br	by Cape Town	KY	Cabotaba Partnership
	Cool Conductor	b	by Stravinsky	KY	Rio Claro Tbs. Inc., R. D. Hubbard & C. Sczesny
	Dave the Dude	dk b/br	by Swiss Yodeler	CA	Harrington & Vander Houwen & Vander Houwen
	Don'tsellmeshort	gr/ro	by Benchmark	CA	Mary H. Caldwell
	Grand Heritage	ch	by Grand Slam	KY	Foxfield
	Limit Free	dk b/br	by Mecke	FL	Suzanne Sharra Maxwell
	Terroplane (FR)	gr/ro	by Verglas (IRE)	FR	Patricia Beck
	There Goes Rocket	dk b/br	by Valid Expectations	TX	Ed Few
	Twice as Bad	gr/ro	by Stormy Atlantic	FL	Linda S. Rosenblatt

Fillies

Wgt.	Horse	Color	Sire	State	Breeder
124	Halfbridled	dk b/br	by Unbridled	KY	Wertheimer & Frere
120	Ashado	dk b/br	by Saint Ballado	KY	Aaron U. Jones & Marie D. Jones
119	La Reina	ch	by A.P. Indy	KY	Emory A. Hamilton
	Society Selection	b	by Coronado's Quest	KY	Marjorie Cowan & Irving Cowan
118	Be Gentle	dk b/br	by Tale of the Cat	VA	Mrs. Nellie M. Cox & Rose Retreat Farm
	Victory U. S. A.	ch	by Victory Gallop	KY	George Brunacini
117	Hollywood Story	dk b/br	by Wild Rush	KY	Vinery
	Tizdubai	b	by Cee's Tizzy	CA	Cee's Stable LLC
116	Class Above	dk b/br	by Quiet American	KY	Michael G. Marenchic MD
	Marylebone	gr/ro	by Unbridled's Song	KY	Runnymede Farm Inc., Clay & Clay Jr.
114	Lokoya	dk b/br	by Woodman	KY	North Wales Farm LLC
	Tarlow	dk b/br	by Stormin Fever	KY	Brereton C. Jones
113	Feline Story	b	by Tale of the Cat	KY	Eclipse Thoroughbreds Inc.
	Whoopi Cat	dk b/br	by Tale of the Cat	KY	Richard Giacopelli
111	Mambo Slew	dk b/br	by Kingmambo	KY	F.J.F.M., LLC
	Rahy Dolly	ch	by Rahy	KY	Thomas L. Nichols & Maxine Nichols

WGT	HORSE	COLOR	SIRE	STATE	BREEDER
110	Dr. Kathy	ch	by Polish Numbers	FL	Harold J. Plumley
	Maple Syrple	dk b/br	by American Chance	ON	Taylor Made Farm, Inc.
	Smokey Glacken	b	by Forestry	KY	Jayeff B Stables
109	America America	ch	by Mister Baileys (GB)	KY	GreenHill Farm LLC
	Dirty Diana	ch	by Flying Continental	CA	Stein Stable
	Dynaville	b	by Barkerville	KY	Richard Kaster & Nathan Fox
	Eye Dazzler	dk b/br	by Boundary	KY	Lee Lewis
	Lotta Kim	b	by Roar	KY	Dolphus C. Morrison
	Salty Romance	b	by Salt Lake	KY	Dr. & Mrs. Stuart E. Brown II & Mrs. Abbie S. Wood
	Spectacular Moon	dk b/br	by Migrating Moon	FL	Nancy Economy
	Unbridled Beauty	gr/ro	by Unbridled's Song	KY	Muirfield Ventures & Gainesway Thoroughbreds Ltd.
108	Richetta	b	by Polish Numbers	MD	Elk Manor Farm
107	Galloping Gal	dk b/br	by Victory Gallop	KY	Jackie D. Huckabay MD
	Stellar Jayne	gr/ro	by Wild Rush	KY	Wind Hill Farm
	Ticker Tape (GB)	b	by Royal Applause (GB)	GB	Car Colston Hall Stud
	Wacky Patty	dk b/br	by Formal Dinner	FL	D. W. Frazier MD & Suzanne Sharra Maxwell
	Zosima	dk b/br	by Capote	KY	Darley
106	Amorama (FR)	dk b/br	by Sri Pekan	FR	Jean Etienne Dubois
	Daydreaming	b	by A.P. Indy	KY	Ogden Mills Phipps
	Wind Flow	dk b/br	by Indian Charlie	KY	E&D Enterprises
105	Deb's Charm	gr/ro	by Silver Charm	KY	Russell West
	House of Fortune	dk b/br	by Free House	CA	John Treasure
	Please Take Me Out	dk b/br	by Take Me Out	KY	Robert Perez
	Sweet Jo Jo	dk b/br	by Grand Slam	FL	Mr. & Mrs. S. H. Rogers Jr.
	Winendynme	dk b/br	by Dynaformer	KY	Takao Zako
104	East Bay	b	by Stormin Fever	KY	Brereton C. Jones
	Everyday Angel	dk b/br	by Forestry	KY	N&P Horse Racing Venture, DD Speedmaster Venture, et al
	From Away	dk b/br	by Gulch	KY	Kilroy Thoroughbred Partnership
	Honey Ryder	gr/ro	by Lasting Approval	KY	Wimborne Farm, Inc.
	Rodeo Licious	ch	by Rodeo	NY	Glenn Brok
	Solar Fire	ch	by Stravinsky	KY	Denali Stud & S. D. Brilie
103	Bluegrass Sara	b	by Tabasco Cat	TX	Heiligbrodt Racing Stable
	Bobbie Use	b	by Not For Love	NY	Thomas/Lakin
	Chelsea's Pearl	b	by Chelsey Cat	NC	Nancy C. Shuford
	Ender's Sister	b	by A.P. Indy	KY	Green Lantern Stables, LLC
	Marina de Chavon	gr/ro	by Exploit	KY	Marvin Little Jr. & Ron McKee
	Quanah County	dk b/br	by Valid Expectations	TX	T. Winston Keng
	Questionable Past	dk b/br	by Petionville	KY	Pope McLean
	Shadow of Mine	dk b/br	by Belong to Me	KY	Thomas L. Nichols

WGT	HORSE	COLOR	SIRE	STATE	BREEDER
	Topango	b	by Distant View	KY	Ralph M. Evans & Lauren Evans
	Vous	b	by Wild Rush	FL	Adam Staple
	Yogi's Polar Bear	gr/ro	by Lucky Lionel	FL	Adena Springs
102	Baldomera	b	by Doneraile Court	KY	Hidden Lane Farms Inc.
	Cherish Destiny	gr/ro	by Grand Slam	KY	C. Bruce Hundley & Doug Arnold
	Cryptos' Best	b	by Cryptoclearance	KY	Bryan M. Carney & Philip Peinowitz
	For All Who Dream	b	by Eltish	FL	New Life Farm, Ltd.
	Hermione's Magic	b	by Forest Wildcat	KY	Big C Farm
	Homemaker	dk b/br	by Afternoon Deelites	KY	Brereton C. Jones
	Lucifer's Stone	b	by Horse Chestnut (SAF)	KY	Mega Stable
	Native Annie	b	by Manzotti	TX	Stonerside Stable
	Peace Symbol	dk b/br	by Dove Hunt	FL	Dr. Sandy Lynn Price
	Renaissance Lady	ch	by A.P. Indy	KY	Mr. & Mrs. Robert Lewis
	Sisti's Pride	dk b/br	by Forestry	KY	Aaron U. Jones & Marie D. Jones
	Taittinger Rose	dk b/br	by Menifee	KY	Mike G. Rutherford Sr.
	Turn to Lass	b	by Bright Launch	KY	Hurstland Farm, Inc.
	Vogue Girl	dk b/br	by Souvenir Copy	KY	Stan Stefanski & Ingrid Stefanski
101	Art Fan	b	by Lear Fan	KY	William Backer
	Platinum Princess	gr/ro	by Wolf Power (SAF)	KY	James M. Herbener Jr.
	Ride Her Out	ch	by Stormy Atlantic	FL	Cheryl A. Curtin
	Sister Star	dk b/br	by Langfuhr	KY	John C. Marker
	Stoic	dk b/br	by Forestry	KY	Lance K. Robinson
	Wild for Jeanne	gr/ro	by Wild Zone	KY	Sabine Stable

Thoroughbred Racing Hall of Fame
Mailing Address and Phone

National Museum of Racing and Hall of Fame
191 Union Avenue
Saratoga Springs, NY 12866-3566
Phone: (518) 584-0400
Fax: (518) 584-4574
Email: nmrinfo@racingmuseum.net Website: www.racingmuseum.org

Location and Directions

The National Museum of Racing and Hall of Fame is located in Saratoga Springs, New York, across from the historic Saratoga Race Course, the oldest operating track in the country.
To get to the National Museum of Racing and Hall of Fame, take exit 14 from I-87 (the Northway) to Saratoga Springs. Proceed 1 1/2 miles into town, taking Union Avenue. The Museum is located on the right hand side at the corner of Union Avenue and Ludlow Street.

Hours

Monday-Saturday — 10:00 a.m. to 4:00 p.m.
Sunday — 12.00 p.m. to 4:00 p.m.
During the Race Meet, the Museum is open daily from 9:00 a.m. to 5:00 p.m. The Museum is closed New Year's Day, Easter, Thanksgiving, and Christmas.

Admission Fees

$7.00 adults, $5.00 students and senior citizens; members and children under 5 are free. Group rates available; call (518) 584-0400, ext. 120.

Mission

The mission of the Official National Thoroughbred Racing Hall of Fame is to honor the achievements of those horses, jockeys, and trainers whose records and reputations have withstood the difficult test of time.

Brief History

The National Museum of Racing was incorporated in historic Saratoga Springs, New York, in 1950. In 1955 the Museum moved to its present site on Union Avenue, and the Hall of Fame was created to recognize and honor deserving horses, jockeys, and trainers.
Over the years the selection process and criteria have been fine-tuned, but the Hall of Fame remains devoted to the original three categories.
As of Hall of Fame Day 2003, members include 168 Thoroughbreds, 82 jockeys, and 77 trainers.

The Nomination and Induction Process

The Hall of Fame Nomination Committee

Each fall preceding the year of induction, the approximately 150 members of the Hall of Fame Voting Panel are asked to submit names of horses, jockeys and trainers who meet the criteria for nomination to the Hall of Fame. All of the names are submitted to the Nomination Committee, chaired by Edward L. Bowen (President, Grayson-Jockey Club Foundation). The nominating committee is currently comprised of the following members: Steven Crist (Daily Racing Form), Russ Harris (New York Daily News), Jay Hovdey (Daily Racing Form), Neil Milbert (Chicago Tribune), William Nack (Sports Illustrated), Ray Paulick (The Blood-Horse), Jay Privman (Daily Racing Form), Jennie Rees (The Louisville Courier-Journal), John Sparkman (The Thoroughbred Times), Clark Spencer (The Miami Herald), Michael Veitch (The Saratogian) and John T. von Stade (President, National Museum of Racing). The committee votes on the total ballot and the top three vote getters in each category are then submitted to the entire Voting Panel. The top vote getter in each category is then selected as the inductee.

The categories under consideration each year usually include Contemporary runners of both sexes, jockeys, and trainers. From time to time, additional selections to the Hall of Fame are made by the Historical Review Committee and the Steeplechase Committee. Candidates in these categories must meet the General Eligibility Criteria for consideration. The Historical Review Committee meets to consider if a jockey, trainer, or horse merits consideration for induction in the Hall of Fame, but would otherwise remain unrecognized. The Steeplechase Committee meets to consider if a steeplechase jockey, trainer, or horse merits consideration for induction to the Hall of Fame.

General Eligibility Criteria

To earn a place on the annual ballot, nominees must meet the following criteria:

1. Thoroughbreds become eligible when five calendar years have elapsed between their final racing year and their year of nomination;

2. Eligible Thoroughbreds are classified as Contemporary Male or Female if they have been retired between five and 25 years. Horses that have been retired for more than 25 years are considered by the Historical Review Committee;

3. Active jockeys become eligible after riding Thoroughbreds for 15 years (any interruptions in their careers for injury not being counted against them);

4. Active trainers become eligible after 25 years as licensed Thoroughbred trainers;

5. The 15- and 25-year requirements may be waived for retired jockeys and trainers, but a five-year waiting period is then observed before they become eligible. In cases of fragile health, the Hall of Fame Committee may request that the five-year waiting period be waived at the discretion of the Executive Committee.

The Final Vote

Brief biographies of the final nominees are incorporated on ballots and mailed to the Voting Committee. These men and women have the responsibility to elect one candidate from each category.

Each spring when the final votes have been tallied, the announcement of new inductees is made.

2003 Hall of Fame Inductees

Male Horse

PRECISIONIST

Chestnut colt foaled in 1981.

By Crozier - -Excellently, by Forli

Breeder: Fred W. Hooper

Owner: Fred W. Hooper

Trainers: Bill Donovan, Ross Fenstermaker, John Russell

RACE RECORD

YEAR	AGE	ST.	1ST	2ND	3RD	EARNED
1983	2	5	3	0	0	$74,050
1984	3	12	5	3	1	631,000
1985	4	9	4	3	0	1,106,100
1986	5	10	5	2	2	1,262,560
1988	7	10	3	2	1	411,688
Total		**46**	**20**	**10**	**4**	**$3,485,398**

A horse of tremendous versatility, Precisionist was honored with an Eclipse Award as champion sprinter of 1985, the year in which he won the Breeders' Cup Sprint, but he was capable of brilliance at a mile, showed himself thoroughly able to handle up to 10 furlongs against top company and even won the Hoist the Flag on the turf as a 2-year-old. The 1985 Breeders' Cup Sprint, the second of four Breeders' Cup appearances by Precisionist, was accomplished at the direct expense of 1986 Sprint winner and divisional champion, Smile, and, remarkably, came as Precisionist's first start since finishing second in the Hollywood Gold Cup over four months earlier. Among his other major accomplishments in a five-year career was a runaway victory in the then-Grade 1 Swaps in 1:59 4/5 as a 3-year-old, turning in one of the fastest miles in history in winning the 1985 Mervyn Le Roy Handicap in 1:32 4/5 and winning the 1986 Grade 1 Woodward in 1:46, defeating a field that included 1986 Horse of the Year Lady's Secret. After 1986, Precisionist entered stud but when he was unable to get his mares in foal, he returned for a final season in 1988.

Female Horse

DANCE SMARTLY

Dark bay/brown filly foaled in 1988.

By Danzig - Classy 'n Smart, by Smarten

Breeder: Sam-Son Farms

Owner: Sam-Son Farms

Trainer: James E. Day

RACE RECORD

YEAR	AGE	ST.	1ST	2ND	3RD	EARNED
1990	2	5	3	1	1	$206,634
1991	3	8	8	0	0	2,876,821
1992	4	4	1	1	2	180,380
Total		**17**	**12**	**2**	**3**	**$3,263,835**

One of Canada's greatest fillies, Dance Smartly was honored as champion 2-year-old filly in her native land and returned as a 3-year-old to go eight-for-eight, winning the Canadian Oaks, sweeping the Canadian Triple Crown with disdainful ease and concluding the season with a victory in the Breeders' Cup Distaff. In a relatively brief 4-year-old campaign, all in turf stakes, Dance Smartly won the Grade 1 Maturity against open company. She retired as North America's leading earning filly or mare. A daughter of a Canadian Oaks winner, Dance Smartly has already proved to be a classic producer herself, and was honored as Canada's broodmare of the year of 2001 after her offspring won back-to-back Queen's Plates in 2000 and 2001.

Jockey
MIKE SMITH
Riding Career: 1982-Present
Mounts: 25,944
Winners: 4,329
Winning Percentage: 17%

Achievements
* Rode winners of the Preakness, Breeders' Cup Classic, Distaff, Turf, Mile, Sprint, Juvenile
* Twice honored with an Eclipse Award as leading jockey (1993 and 1994).
* Rode a record 62 stakes winners in 1993, then broke his own record the following year with 67 stakes winners in 1994, including 20 Grade 1s.

Classic and Breeders' Cup Races Won
Preakness: Prairie Bayou
Breeders' Cup Classic: Skip Away
Breeders' Cup Distaff: Ajina, Azeri, Inside Information
Breeders' Cup Turf: Tikkanen
Breeders' Cup Mile: Lure (twice)
Breeders' Cup Sprint: Cherokee Run
Breeders' Cup Juvenile: Unbridled's Song, Vindication

Other Significant Mounts
Sky Beauty
Holy Bull
Heavenly Prize
Coronado's Quest
Devil His Due

Mike Smith was born on Aug. 10, 1965, in New Mexico and rode his first winner in June 1982 at Santa Fe Downs. By the early 1990s, he was riding a crescendo of success, mainly in the East, where he regularly rode for Shug McGaughey and other top stables. In 1993 and 1994, he won back-to-back Eclipse Awards, led all jockeys in winnings and set stakes-won records while riding champions like Horse of the Year Holy Bull, Sky Beauty and Heavenly Prize. Bad luck and accidents intervened and by 1999, Grade 1 victories became few and far between. Enjoying a revival after moving to California, Smith in recent years has been the regular rider of Horse of the Year Azeri.

Trainer
HUBERT "SONNY" HINE

Champions
Skip Away (1996 3-year-old colt, 1997 older horse, 1998 Horse of the Year and older horse), Guilty Conscience (1981 sprinter)

Major achievements
* Trained Skip Away, Horse of the Year of 1998, winner of the 1997 Breeders' Cup Classic and a champion in 1996 and 1997.
* Since 1976, Hine campaigned 46 stakes winners.

The tale of Hubert "Sonny" Hine is forever intertwined with the story of Hine and wife Carolyn's travels through the backstretches of America's racetracks, spiced by the exotic hints of Hine's past involvement with the FBI and CIA. Hine saddled his first winner in Maryland at Marlboro Race Course in 1948 and met Carolyn in 1961 and from the there, the Hines began their hard-fought climb to the pinnacle of American racing. Guilty Conscience, winner of the 1981 Vosburgh and subsequently voted champion sprinter, was one of Hine's early national stars, followed up in the mid-1980s by Skip Trial, and in the early 1990s by classic prospect Technology, but it would be Skip Away, a son of Skip Trial bought by Hine as a gift for Carolyn, that would become a career highlight. After beating Cigar in the 1996 Jockey Club Gold Cup en route to champion 3-year-old honors, Skip Away went on to be honored as the champion older male in both 1997 and 1998, earning Horse of the Year honors in the latter. Already battling cancer in his later years, Hine died of pneumonia in March 2000.

Horses

Horse	Year Elected	Year Foaled	Horse	Year Elected	Year Foaled
A.P. Indy	2000	1989	Exceller	1999	1973
Ack Ack	1986	1966	Exterminator	1957	1915
Affectionately	1989	1960	Fair Play	1956	1905
Affirmed	1980	1975	Fairmount	1985	1921
All Along	1990	1979	Fashion	1980	1837
Alsab	1976	1939	Firenze	1981	1884
Alydar	1989	1975	Flatterer	1994	1979
Alysheba	1993	1984	Foolish Pleasure	1995	1972
American Eclipse	1970	1814	Forego	1979	1970
Armed	1963	1941	Fort Marcy	1998	1964
Artful	1956	1902	Gallant Bloom	1977	1966
Arts and Letters	1994	1966	Gallant Fox	1957	1927
Assault	1964	1943	Gallant Man	1987	1954
Battleship	1969	1927	Gallorette	1962	1942
Bayakoa	1998	1984	Gamely	1980	1964
Bed o'Roses	1976	1947	Genuine Risk	1986	1977
Beldame	1956	1901	Go For Wand	1996	1987
Ben Brush	1955	1893	Good and Plenty	1956	1900
Bewitch	1977	1945	Granville	1997	1933
Bimelech	1990	1937	Grey Lag	1957	1918
Black Gold	1989	1921	Gun Bow	1999	1960
Black Helen	1991	1932	Hamburg	1986	1895
Blue Larkspur	1957	1926	Hanover	1955	1884
Bold 'n Determined	1997	1977	Henry of Navarre	1985	1891
Bold Ruler	1973	1954	Hill Prince	1991	1947
Bon Nouvel	1976	1960	Hindoo	1955	1878
Boston	1955	1833	Holy Bull	2001	1991
Broomstick	1956	1901	Imp	1965	1894
Buckpasser	1970	1963	Jay Trump	1971	1957
Busher	1964	1942	John Henry	1990	1975
Bushranger	1967	1930	Johnstown	1992	1936
Cafe Prince	1985	1970	Jolly Roger	1965	1922
Carry Back	1975	1958	Kelso	1967	1957
Cavalcade	1993	1931	Kentucky	1983	1861
Challedon	1977	1936	Kingston	1955	1884
Chris Evert	1988	1971	L'Escargot	1977	1963
Cicada	1967	1959	La Prevoyante	1995	1970
Cigar	2002	1990	Lady's Secret	1992	1982
Citation	1959	1945	Lexington	1955	1850
Coaltown	1983	1945	Longfellow	1971	1867
Colin	1956	1905	Luke Blackburn	1956	1877
Commando	1956	1898	Majestic Prince	1988	1966
Count Fleet	1961	1940	Man o ' War	1957	1917
Crusader	1995	1923	Maskette	2001	1906
Dahlia	1981	1970	Miesque	1999	1984
Damascus	1974	1964	Miss Woodford	1967	1880
Dance Smartly	2003	1988	Myrtlewood	1979	1932
Dark Mirage	1974	1965	Nashua	1965	1952
Davona Dale	1985	1976	Native Dancer	1963	1950
Desert Vixen	1979	1970	Native Diver	1978	1959
Devil Diver	1980	1939	Needles	2000	1953
Discovery	1969	1931	Neji	1966	1950
Domino	1955	1891	Northern Dancer	1976	1961
Dr. Fager	1971	1964	Oedipus	1978	1946
Easy Goer	1997	1986	Old Rosebud	1968	1911
Eight Thirty	1994	1936	Omaha	1965	1932
Elkridge	1966	1938	Pan Zareta	1972	1910
Emperor of Norfolk	1988	1885	Parole	1984	1873
Equipoise	1957	1928	Paseana	2001	1987

Horses

Horse	Year Elected	Year Foaled	Horse	Year Elected	Year Foaled
Personal Ensign	1993	1984	Spectacular Bid	1982	1976
Peter Pan	1956	1904	Stymie	1975	1941
Precisionist	2003	1981	Sun Beau	1996	1925
Princess Doreen	1982	1921	Sunday Silence	1996	1986
Princess Rooney	1991	1980	Susan's Girl	1976	1969
Real Delight	1987	1949	Swaps	1966	1952
Regret	1957	1912	Sword Dancer	1977	1956
Reigh Count	1978	1925	Sysonby	1956	1902
Riva Ridge	1998	1969	Ta Wee	1994	1966
Roamer	1981	1911	Ten Broeck	1982	1872
Roseben	1956	1901	Tim Tam	1985	1955
Round Table	1972	1954	Tom Fool	1960	1949
Ruffian	1976	1972	Top Flight	1966	1929
Ruthless	1975	1864	Tosmah	1984	1961
Salvator	1955	1886	Twenty Grand	1957	1928
Sarazen	1957	1921	Twilight Tear	1963	1941
Seabiscuit	1958	1933	Two Lea	1982	1946
Searching	1978	1952	War Admiral	1958	1934
Seattle Slew	1981	1974	Whirlaway	1959	1938
Secretariat	1974	1970	Whisk Broom II	1979	1907
Serena's Song	2002	1992	Winning Colors	2000	1985
Shuvee	1975	1966	Zaccio	1990	1976
Silver Spoon	1978	1956	Zev	1983	1920
Sir Archy	1955	1805			
Sir Barton	1957	1916			
Slew o' Gold	1992	1980			

Jockeys

Jockey	Year Inducted	Jockey	Year Inducted
John Adams	1965	Mack Garner	1969
Frank D. Adams	1970	Edward Garrison	1955
Joe Aitcheson , Jr	1978	Avelino Gomez	1982
G. Edward Arcaro	1958	Henry F. Griffin	1956
Ted F. Atkinson	1957	O. Eric Guerin	1972
Braulio Baeza	1976	William J. Hartack	1959
Jerry Bailey	1995	Sandy Hawley	1992
George Barbee	1996	Albert Johnson	1971
Caroll K. Bassett	1972	William J. Knapp	1969
Russell Baze	1999	Julie Krone	2000
Walter Blum	1987	Clarence Kummer	1972
George Bostwick	1968	Charles Kurtsinger	1967
Sam Boulmetis , Sr.	1973	John P. Loftus	1959
Steve Brooks	1963	John Eric Longden	1958
Don Brumfield	1996	Daniel A. Maher	1955
Thomas H. Burns	1983	J. Linus McAtee	1956
James H. Butwell	1984	Chris McCarron	1989
J. Dallett Byers	1967	Conn McCreary	1975
Steve Cauthen	1994	Rigan McKinney	1968
Frank Coltiletti	1970	James McLaughlin	1955
Angel Cordero , Jr.	1988	Walter Miller	1955
Robert H. Crawford	1973	Isaac B. Murphy	1955
Pat Day	1991	Ralph Neves	1960
Eddie Delahoussaye	1993	Joe Notter	1963
Lavelle Ensor	1962	Winfield O'Conner	1956
Laverne Fator	1955	Frank O'Neill	1956
Earlie Fires	2001	George M. Odom	1955
Jerry Fishback	1992	Ivan H. Parke	1978

Jockeys

Jockey	Year Inducted	Jockey	Year Inducted
Gilbert W. Patrick	1970	Gary Stevens	1997
Laffit Pincay Jr.	1975	James Stout	1968
Samuel Purdy	1970	Fred Taral	1955
John Reiff	1956	Bayard Tuckerman Jr.	1973
Alfred Robertson	1971	Ron Turcotte	1979
John L. Rotz	1983	Nash Turner	1955
Earl Sande	1955	Robert N. Ussery	1980
Carroll H. Shilling	1970	Jacinto Vasquez	1998
William Shoemaker	1958	Jorge Velasquez	1990
Willie Simms	1977	Jack Westrope	2002
Tod Sloan	1955	George M. Woolf	1955
Mike Smith	2003	Raymond Workman	1956
Alfred P. Smithwick	1973	Manuel Ycaza	1977

Trainers

Trainer	Year Inducted	Trainer	Year Inducted
Lazaro S. Barrera	1979	Horatio A. Luro	1980
H. Guy Bedwell	1971	John E. Madden	1983
Edward D. Brown	1984	James W. Maloney	1989
J. Elliott Burch	1980	Richard Mandella	2001
Preston M. Burch	1963	Frank Martin	1981
William P. Burch	1955	Ron McAnally	1990
Fred Burlew	1973	Henry McDaniel	1956
Frank E. Childs	1968	MacKenzie Miller	1987
Henry S. Clark	1982	William Molter	1960
W. Burling Cocks	1985	William I. Mott	1998
James P. Conway	1996	W. F. Mulholland	1967
Warren A. Croll , Jr.	1994	Edward A. Neloy	1983
Grover G. Delp	2002	John A. Nerud	1972
Neil D. Drysdale	2000	Burley Parke	1986
William Duke	1956	Angel Penna	1988
Louis Feustel	1964	Jacob Pincus	1988
James Fitzsimmons	1958	John W. Rogers	1955
Robert Frankel	1995	James G. Rowe Sr.	1955
John M. Gaver Sr.	1966	Flint S. Schulhofer	1992
Thomas J. Healey	1955	Jonathan Sheppard	1990
Samuel C. Hildreth	1955	Robert A. Smith	1976
Hubert "Sonny" Hine	2003	D. M. Smithwick	1971
Maximilian Hirsch	1959	Woodford Stephens	1976
William J. Hirsch	1982	Mesh Tenney	1991
Thomas Hitchcock	1973	Henry J. Thompson	1969
Hollie Hughes	1973	Harry Trotsek	1984
John J. Hyland	1956	Jack C. Van Berg	1985
Hirsch Jacobs	1958	Marion Van Berg	1970
H. Allen Jerkens	1975	Sylvester Veitch	1977
Philip G. Johnson	1997	R. W. Walden	1970
William R. Johnson	1986	Michael G. Walsh	1997
LeRoy Jolley	1987	Sherrill W. Ward	1978
Benjamin A. Jones	1958	Frank Whiteley Jr	1978
Horace A. Jones	1959	Charles Whittingham	1974
A. Jack Joyner	1955	Ansel Williamson	1998
Thomas J. Kelly	1993	G. Carey Winfrey	1975
Lucien Laurin	1977	William C. Winfrey	1971
J. Howard Lewis	1969		
D. Wayne Lukas	1999		

Richest Stakes Races in North America in 2003

Race Name	Date	Race	Winning Horse	Jockey		Track	Earnings	Purse
BCClasicG1	25-Oct-03	9	Pleasantly Perfect	Alex	Solis	Santa Anita	$2,080,000	$4,000,000
BCTurfG1	25-Oct-03	8	High Chaparral (Ire)	Michael	Kinane	Santa Anita	763,200	2,110,100
			Johar	Alex	Solis	Santa Anita	763,200	
BCDistafG1	25-Oct-03	2	Adoration	Patrick	Valenzuela	Santa Anita	1,040,000	2,000,000
CanIntnlG1	19-Oct-03	9	Phoenix Reach (Ire)	Martin	Dwyer	Woodbine	900,000	1,500,000
BCMileG1	25-Oct-03	4	Six Perfections (FR)	Jerry	Bailey	Santa Anita	780,000	1,500,000
BCJuvnlG1	25-Oct-03	7	Action This Day	David	Flores	Santa Anita	780,000	1,500,000
BCSprintG1	25-Oct-03	5	Cajun Beat	Cornelio	Velasquez	Santa Anita	613,600	1,180,000
KyDerbyG1	3-May-03	10	Funny Cide	Jose	Santos	Churchill Downs	800,200	1,100,200
BCF&MTrfG1	25-Oct-03	6	Islington (IRE)	Kieren	Fallon	Santa Anita	551,200	1,060,000
Breeders	9-Aug-03	8	Wando	Patrick	Husbands	Woodbine	*800,000	1,000,000
PreaknesG1	17-May-03	12	Funny Cide	Jose	Santos	Pimlico	650,000	1,000,000
ArlMillnG1	16-Aug-03	10	Sulamani (IRE)	David	Flores	Arlington Park	600,000	1,000,000
AttoMileG1	14-Sep-03	9	Touch of the Blues (Fr)	Kent	Desormeaux	Woodbine	600,000	1,000,000
BdGmgDltJk	5-Dec-03	8	Mr. Jester	Roman	Chapa	Delta Downs	600,000	1,000,000
BelmontG1	7-Jun-03	11	Empire Maker	Jerry	Bailey	Belmont	600,000	1,000,000
FlaDerbyG1	15-Mar-03	8	Empire Maker	Jerry	Bailey	Gulfstream Park	600,000	1,000,000
HsklInvHG1	3-Aug-03	11	Peace Rules	Edgar	Prado	Monmouth Park	600,000	1,000,000
JkyClbGCG1	27-Sep-03	10	Mineshaft	Robby	Albarado	Belmont	600,000	1,000,000
PacifcClG1	24-Aug-03	5	Candy Ride (ARG)	Julie	Krone	Del Mar	600,000	1,000,000
QueensPlt	22-Jun-03	9	Wando	Patrick	Husbands	Woodbine	600,000	1,000,000
SantaAnitHG1	1-Mar-03	9	Milwaukee Brew	Edgar	Prado	Santa Anita	600,000	1,000,000
TraversG1	23-Aug-03	11	Ten Most Wanted	Pat	Day	Saratoga	600,000	1,000,000
OclBrdSlCl	25-Jan-03	7	Best of the Rest	Eibar	Coa	Gulfstream Park	533,500	1,000,000
BCJuvFilG1	25-Oct-03	3	Halfbridled	Julie	Krone	Santa Anita	520,000	1,000,000
SFosterHG1	14-Jun-03	10	Perfect Drift	Pat	Day	Churchill Downs	531,030	856,500
BlueGrasG1	12-Apr-03	9	Peace Rules	Edgar	Prado	Keeneland	465,000	750,000
AlabamaG1	16-Aug-03	9	Island Fashion	John	Velazquez	Saratoga	450,000	750,000
AmercnOaks	5-Jul-03	5	Dimitrova	David	Flores	Hollywood Park	450,000	750,000
BeldameG1	4-Oct-03	9	Sightseek	Jerry	Bailey	Belmont	450,000	750,000
DelHG2~	20-Jul-03	10	Wild Spirit (CHI)	Jerry	Bailey	Delaware Park	450,000	750,000
EPTaylorG1	19-Oct-03	5	Volga (IRE)	Richard	Migliore	Woodbine	450,000	750,000
FlwrBllvG1	27-Sep-03	8	Dimitrova	Jerry	Bailey	Belmont	450,000	750,000
HawGldCHG2	28-Sep-03	9	Perfect Drift	Pat	Day	Hawthorne	450,000	750,000
HolGldCpG1	13-Jul-03	9	Congaree	Jerry	Bailey	Hollywood Park	450,000	750,000
LaDerbyG2	9-Mar-03	9	Peace Rules	Edgar	Prado	Fair Grounds	450,000	750,000
MtropltHG1	26-May-03	9	Aldebaran	Jerry	Bailey	Belmont	450,000	750,000
PaDerbyG3	1-Sep-03	11	Grand Hombre	Joe	Bravo	Philadelphia Park	450,000	750,000
SADerbyG1	5-Apr-03	6	Buddy Gil	Gary	Stevens	Santa Anita	450,000	750,000
TfClscIvG1	27-Sep-03	9	Sulamani (IRE)	Jerry	Bailey	Belmont	450,000	750,000
UntdNtnHG1	5-Jul-03	10	Balto Star	Jose	Velez, Jr.	Monmouth Park	450,000	750,000
WhitneyHG1	2-Aug-03	9	Medaglia d'Oro	Jerry	Bailey	Saratoga	450,000	750,000
WoodMemG1	12-Apr-03	8	Empire Maker	Jerry	Bailey	Aqueduct	450,000	750,000
VesslsDstf	25-Jan-03	5	Smok'n Frolic	Jerry	Bailey	Santa Anita	411,400	750,000
BeverlyDG1	16-Aug-03	8	Heat Haze (GB)	Jose	Valdivia, Jr.	Arlington Park	420,000	700,000
ExploBdHG2	23-Mar-03	8	Candid Glen	Elvis	Perrodin	Fair Grounds	390,000	650,000
PimSpclHG1	16-May-03	11	Mineshaft	Robby	Albarado	Pimlico	400,000	600,000
ShdwITfMG1	4-Oct-03	9	Perfect Soul (Ire)	Edgar	Prado	Keeneland	372,000	600,000
HolDerbyG1	30-Nov-03	9	Sweet Return (GB)	Julie	Krone	Hollywood Park	360,000	600,000
WVDerbyG3	9-Aug-03	8	Soto	Ramon	Dominguez	Mountaineer	360,000	600,000
ClarkHG2	28-Nov-03	11	Quest	Javier	Castellano	Churchill Downs	360,840	582,000

Race Name	Date	Race	Winning Horse	Jockey		Track	Earnings	Purse
KyOaksG1	2-May-03	10	Bird Town	Edgar	Prado	Churchill Downs	355,756	573,800
AshlandG1	5-Apr-03	8	Elloluv	Robby	Albarado	Keeneland	342,085	551,750
QEIICupG1	11-Oct-03	8	Film Maker	Edgar	Prado	Keeneland	310,000	500,000
SpinsterG1	5-Oct-03	8	Take Charge Lady	Edgar	Prado	Keeneland	310,000	500,000
WnStGlxyG2	5-Oct-03	6	Bien Nicole	Donald	Pettinger	Keeneland	310,000	500,000
AplBlsmHG1	5-Apr-03	8	Azeri	Mike	Smith	Oaklawn Park	300,000	500,000
ArkDerbyG2	12-Apr-03	9	Sir Cherokee	Terry	Thompson	Oaklawn Park	300,000	500,000
CCAOaksG1	19-Jul-03	9	Spoken Fur	Jerry	Bailey	Belmont	300,000	500,000
ChampagnG1	4-Oct-03	7	Birdstone	Jerry	Bailey	Belmont	300,000	500,000
DelOaksG3	19-Jul-03	8	Island Fashion	Ignacio	Puglisi	Delaware Park	300,000	500,000
DianaHG1	26-Jul-03	8	Voodoo Dancer	Corey	Nakatani	Saratoga	300,000	500,000
DonnHG1	22-Feb-03	11	Harlan's Holiday	John	Velazquez	Gulfstream Park	300,000	500,000
FrizetteG1	4-Oct-03	6	Society Selection	Ray	Ganpath	Belmont	300,000	500,000
GdwdBCHG2	4-Oct-03	5	Pleasantly Perfect	Alex	Solis	Santa Anita	300,000	500,000
IlnosDrby2	5-Apr-03	8	Ten Most Wanted	Pat	Day	Hawthorne	300,000	500,000
JimDandyG2	3-Aug-03	9	Strong Hope	John	Velazquez	Saratoga	300,000	500,000
LanesEndG2	22-Mar-03	10	New York Hero	Norberto	Arroyo, Jr.	Turfway Park	300,000	500,000
LbatWoOaks	8-Jun-03	9	Too Late Now	Robert	Landry	Woodbine	300,000	500,000
ManOWarG1	6-Sep-03	8	Lunar Sovereign	Richard	Migliore	Belmont	300,000	500,000
MatriarcG1	30-Nov-03	6	Heat Haze (GB)	John	Velazquez	Hollywood Park	300,000	500,000
NwOrlnsHG2	2-Mar-03	9	Mineshaft	Robby	Albarado	Fair Grounds	300,000	500,000
OaklawnHG2	5-Apr-03	11	Medaglia d'Oro	Jerry	Bailey	Oaklawn Park	300,000	500,000
PrncOWales	20-Jul-03	8	Wando	Patrick	Husbands	Fort Erie	300,000	500,000
SuburbnHG1	5-Jul-03	9	Mineshaft	Robby	Albarado	Belmont	300,000	500,000
SuperDbyG2	20-Sep-03	10	Ten Most Wanted	Pat	Day	Louisiana Downs	300,000	500,000
SwrdDncHG1	9-Aug-03	9	Whitmore's Conn	Jean-Luc	Samyn	Saratoga	300,000	500,000
VosburghG1	27-Sep-03	7	Ghostzapper	Javier	Castellano	Belmont	300,000	500,000
VrgniaDrby	12-Jul-03	10	Silver Tree	Edgar	Prado	Colonial Downs	300,000	500,000
WoodwardG1	6-Sep-03	9	Mineshaft	Robby	Albarado	Belmont	300,000	500,000
YlwRibbnG1	28-Sep-03	7	Tates Creek	Patrick	Valenzuela	Santa Anita	300,000	500,000
PrcsRnyHG2	12-Jul-03	11	Gold Mover	Jerry	Bailey	Calder Race Course	294,000	500,000
SmlSprtHG3	12-Jul-03	12	Shake You Down	Michael	Luzzi	Calder Race Course	294,000	500,000
LnStrDbyG3	10-May-03	8	Dynever	Edgar	Prado	Lone Star Park	277,500	500,000
WinStrDrby	30-Mar-03	9	Excessivepleasure	Pat	Day	Sunland Park	270,000	500,000
BarCTBATrf	25-Jan-03	2	Adminniestrator	David	Flores	Santa Anita	262,900	500,000
ShoeBCMG1	26-May-03	8	Redattore (BRZ)	Alex	Solis	Hollywood Park	225,000	475,000
WRTurfClG1	3-May-03	9	Honor in War	David	Flores	Churchill Downs	276,086	445,300
GamlyBCHG1	26-May-03	6	Tates Creek	Patrick	Valenzuela	Hollywood Park	263,400	439,000
IndnaDbyG3	4-Oct-03	9	Excessivepleasure	Jon	Court	Hoosier Park	247,080	411,800
AlcibiadG2	3-Oct-03	9	Be Gentle	Cornelio	Velasquez	Keeneland	248,000	400,000
LnsEndFtG2	4-Oct-03	6	Eurosilver	Javier	Castellano	Keeneland	248,000	400,000
CalfrninG2	14-Jun-03	8	Kudos	Alex	Solis	Hollywood Park	240,000	400,000
CtationHG2	29-Nov-03	9	Redattore (BRZ)	Julie	Krone	Hollywood Park	240,000	400,000
EdReadHG1	27-Jul-03	8	Special Ring	David	Flores	Del Mar	240,000	400,000
FKilroeHG2	1-Mar-03	8	Redattore (BRZ)	Alex	Solis	Santa Anita	240,000	400,000
FSMyDrGirl	11-Oct-03	10	Chatter Chatter	Jerry	Bailey	Calder Race Course	240,000	400,000
FSNReality	11-Oct-03	11	Sir Oscar	Julio	Garcia	Calder Race Course	240,000	400,000
JMurryMemH	10-May-03	7	Storming Home (GB)	Gary	Stevens	Hollywood Park	240,000	400,000
ManhttnHG1	7-Jun-03	10	Denon	Jerry	Bailey	Belmont	240,000	400,000
Mbe/RnaHG1	26-Jul-03	8	Megahertz (GB)	Alex	Solis	Del Mar	240,000	400,000
MedBCG2	3-Oct-03	8	Bowman's Band	Ramon	Dominguez	Meadowlands	240,000	400,000
PrsnlEnHG1	22-Aug-03	9	Passing Shot	Jose	Santos	Saratoga	240,000	400,000

Race Name	Date	Race	Winning Horse	Jockey		Track	Earnings	Purse
SecretarG1	16-Aug-03	11	Kicken Kris	Javier	Castellano	Arlington Park	240,000	400,000
SnJnCpoHG1	20-Apr-03	9	Passinetti	Brice	Blanc	Santa Anita	240,000	400,000
StrubG2	1-Feb-03	9	Medaglia d'Oro	Jerry	Bailey	Santa Anita	240,000	400,000
SwapsG2	13-Jul-03	6	During	Jerry	Bailey	Hollywood Park	240,000	400,000
WashPkHG2	19-Jul-03	9	Perfect Drift	Pat	Day	Arlington Park	240,000	400,000
HolFutG1	20-Dec-03	4	Lion Heart	Mike	Smith	Hollywood Park	225,600	382,000
ClmrLexG2	19-Apr-03	8	Scrimshaw	Edgar	Prado	Keeneland	225,479	363,675
HolStrltG1	21-Dec-03	9	Hollywood Story	Patrick	Valenzuela	Hollywood Park	209,700	355,500
KyCpClHG2	13-Sep-03	11	Perfect Drift	Pat	Day	Turfway Park	221,500	350,000
CarterHG1	12-Apr-03	9	Congaree	Gary	Stevens	Aqueduct	210,000	350,000
CigarMiHG1	29-Nov-03	9	Congaree	Jerry	Bailey	Aqueduct	210,000	350,000
CrnhsBCHG3	12-Jul-03	6	Tenpins	Robby	Albarado	Prairie Meadows	210,000	350,000
CWhtghmHG1	14-Jun-03	3	Storming Home (GB)	Gary	Stevens	Hollywood Park	210,000	350,000
FGOaksG2	8-Mar-03	9	Lady Tak	Donnie	Meche	Fair Grounds	210,000	350,000
KelsoBCHG2	4-Oct-03	8	Freefourinternet	Jose	Espinoza	Belmont	210,000	350,000
FrkFrmFMTf	25-Jan-03	9	Stay Forever	Jose	Santos	Gulfstream Park	192,500	350,000
KngEdBCHG2	15-Jun-03	8	Perfect Soul (Ire)	Robert	Landry	Woodbine	203,760	339,600
NiagrBCHG2	30-Aug-03	8	Strut the Stage	Todd	Kabel	Woodbine	202,320	337,200
FallCtyHG2	27-Nov-03	10	Lead Story	Calvin	Borel	Churchill Downs	207,204	334,200
BCDerbyG2	21-Sep-03	9	Roscoe Pito	Pedro	Alvarado	Hastings	198,750	331,250
ChneseCCG2	20-Jul-03	8	Strut the Stage	Todd	Kabel	Woodbine	198,540	330,900
CanadinHG2	14-Sep-03	6	Inish Glora	Todd	Kabel	Woodbine	197,400	329,000
NassauG2	1-Jun-03	8	Strait From Texas	Richard	Dos Ramos	Woodbine	166,920	328,200
FlrDLisHG2	14-Jun-03	9	You	Jerry	Bailey	Churchill Downs	203,298	327,900
LouvlBCHG2	2-May-03	8	You	Jerry	Bailey	Churchill Downs	201,810	325,500
InBCOaksG3	3-Oct-03	9	Awesome Humor	Robby	Albarado	Hoosier Park	184,140	306,900
OhioDrbyG2	21-Jun-03	14	Wild and Wicked	Shane	Sellers	Thistledown	180,000	306,300
CLHrschHG2	10-Aug-03	8	Azeri	Mike	Smith	Del Mar	180,000	300,000
DeFrncsMG1	15-Nov-03	10	A Huevo	Ramon	Dominguez	Laurel Park	180,000	300,000
DmrDerbyG2	6-Sep-03	8	Fairly Ransom	Alex	Solis	Del Mar	180,000	300,000
DmrOaksG1	24-Aug-03	9	Dessert	Corey	Nakatani	Del Mar	180,000	300,000
GPHG2	29-Mar-03	11	Hero's Tribute	Edgar	Prado	Gulfstream Park	180,000	300,000
LdyScBCHG2	28-Sep-03	6	Got Koko	Alex	Solis	Santa Anita	180,000	300,000
LSParkHG3	26-May-03	8	Pie N Burger	Jamie	Theriot	Lone Star Park	180,000	300,000
MPchrBCHG2	28-Jun-03	11	Summer Colony	Gary	Stevens	Monmouth Park	180,000	300,000
MthrGoosG1	28-Jun-03	9	Spoken Fur	Jerry	Bailey	Belmont	180,000	300,000
OkTrBCMIG2	5-Oct-03	8	Designed for Luck	Patrick	Valenzuela	Santa Anita	180,000	300,000
OPhippsHG1	21-Jun-03	9	Sightseek	Jerry	Bailey	Belmont	180,000	300,000
RuffianHG1	13-Sep-03	9	Wild Spirit (CHI)	Jerry	Bailey	Belmont	180,000	300,000
SAOaksG1	8-Mar-03	4	Composure	Jerry	Bailey	Santa Anita	180,000	300,000
SarBCHG2	16-Aug-03	7	Puzzlement	Jorge	Chavez	Saratoga	180,000	300,000
SMrgrtaHG1	9-Mar-03	8	Starrer	Patrick	Valenzuela	Santa Anita	180,000	300,000
CarryBckG3	12-Jul-03	10	Valid Video	Joe	Bravo	Calder Race Course	177,000	300,000
AzaleaBCG3	12-Jul-03	9	Ebony Breeze	Cornelio	Velasquez	Calder Race Course	176,000	300,000
TexsMileG3	26-Apr-03	9	Bluesthestandard	Martin	Pedroza	Lone Star Park	170,000	300,000
TrBndBCHG1	5-Jul-03	8	Joey Franco	Patrick	Valenzuela	Hollywood Park	150,000	300,000
FrckrBCHG2	5-Jul-03	9	Tap the Admiral	John	McKee	Churchill Downs	178,870	288,500
NearctcHG2	22-Jun-03	6	Soaring Free	Todd	Kabel	Woodbine	171,900	286,500
SummerG2	14-Sep-03	4	Bachelor Blues	Todd	Kabel	Woodbine	171,300	285,500
SeleneG1	19-May-03	8	Too Late Now	Robert	Landry	Woodbine	166,650	277,750
GreyBCG2	5-Oct-03	9	Smoocher	James	McAleney	Woodbine	166,350	277,250
PhoenxBCG3	3-Oct-03	7	Najran	Javier	Castellano	Keeneland	169,880	274,000

Race Name	Date	Race	Winning Horse	Jockey		Track	Earnings	Purse
CmwlthBCG2	13-Apr-03	8	Smooth Jazz	Edgar	Prado	Keeneland	169,725	273,750
SkyClscHG2	28-Sep-03	8	Bowman Mill	Brice	Blanc	Woodbine	163,050	271,750
MazarnBCG2	20-Sep-03	8	Dream About	Patrick	Husbands	Woodbine	160,950	268,250
WinStarOak	29-Mar-03	9	Island Fashion	Ignacio	Puglisi	Sunland Park	153,870	256,450
BeaumontG2	10-Apr-03	8	My Boston Gal	Pat	Day	Keeneland	155,000	250,000
AcornG1	6-Jun-03	10	Bird Town	Edgar	Prado	Belmont	150,000	250,000
AGleamHG2	13-Jul-03	4	Cee's Elegance	Victor	Espinoza	Hollywood Park	150,000	250,000
AmercnDbG2	20-Jul-03	8	Evolving Tactics (Ire)	Pat	Smullen	Arlington Park	150,000	250,000
ArlgtnHG3	26-Jul-03	9	Honor in War	David	Flores	Arlington Park	150,000	250,000
Aventura	5-Apr-03	11	Dynever	Edgar	Prado	Gulfstream Park	150,000	250,000
BalrinaHG1	24-Aug-03	9	Harmony Lodge	Richard	Migliore	Saratoga	150,000	250,000
BdGmgDltPr	5-Dec-03	6	Salty Romance	Mike	Smith	Delta Downs	150,000	250,000
BroklynHG2	14-Jun-03	9	Iron Deputy	Richard	Migliore	Belmont	150,000	250,000
CalCpClscH	8-Nov-03	9	Tizbud	Victor	Espinoza	Santa Anita	150,000	250,000
CLHirschG1	28-Sep-03	3	Storming Home (GB)	Gary	Stevens	Santa Anita	150,000	250,000
CoronatnFu	1-Nov-03	10	A Bit O'Gold	Jono	Jones	Woodbine	150,000	250,000
CotillnHG2	4-Oct-03	9	Fast Cookie	Nick	Santagata	Philadelphia Park	150,000	250,000
Cup&Saucer	11-Oct-03	8	Master William	Patrick	Husbands	Woodbine	150,000	250,000
DelMarHG2	31-Aug-03	8	Irish Warrior	Alex	Solis	Del Mar	150,000	250,000
DllasTfCpH	21-Jun-03	7	Patrol	Michael	Luzzi	Lone Star Park	150,000	250,000
DmrDebG1	30-Aug-03	8	Halfbridled	Julie	Krone	Del Mar	150,000	250,000
DmrFutG2	10-Sep-03	8	Siphonizer	Julie	Krone	Del Mar	150,000	250,000
EmpirClscH	18-Oct-03	10	Well Fancied	Edgar	Prado	Belmont	150,000	250,000
ForegoHG1	31-Aug-03	10	Aldebaran	Jerry	Bailey	Saratoga	150,000	250,000
GazelleHG1	6-Sep-03	7	Buy the Sport	Pat	Day	Belmont	150,000	250,000
GoFWandHG1	27-Jul-03	9	Sightseek	Jerry	Bailey	Saratoga	150,000	250,000
GrdCyBCHG1	7-Sep-03	9	Indy Five Hundred	Pat	Day	Belmont	150,000	250,000
HawDerbyG3	18-Oct-03	8	False Promises	Carlos	Marquez, Jr.	Hawthorne	150,000	250,000
HolTrfCpG1	22-Nov-03	8	Continuously	Alex	Solis	Hollywood Park	150,000	250,000
IowaDerby	5-Jul-03	6	Excessivepleasure	Jon	Court	Prairie Meadows	150,000	250,000
KentBCG3	20-Jul-03	5	Foufa's Warrior	Ramon	Dominguez	Delaware Park	150,000	250,000
LaBreaG1	27-Dec-03	7	Island Fashion	Kent	Desormeaux	Santa Anita	150,000	250,000
LRichrdsG3	14-Jun-03	11	Awesome Time	Anthony	Black	Delaware Park	150,000	250,000
MalibuG1	26-Dec-03	8	Southern Image	Victor	Espinoza	Santa Anita	150,000	250,000
NewYorkHG2	4-Jul-03	10	Snow Dance	Richard	Migliore	Belmont	150,000	250,000
NorfolkG2	5-Oct-03	10	Ruler's Court	Alex	Solis	Santa Anita	150,000	250,000
NtlJClbHG3	19-Apr-03	8	Fight for Ally	Eusebio	Razo, Jr.	Hawthorne	150,000	250,000
NYStlCbCwy	8-Jun-03	6	Bo Bo's Vice	Jorge	Chavez	Belmont	150,000	250,000
NYStStLbty	8-Jun-03	7	Beautiful America	Jose	Santos	Belmont	150,000	250,000
OakLeafG2	28-Sep-03	9	Halfbridled	Julie	Krone	Santa Anita	150,000	250,000
PrncssEliz	12-Oct-03	8	My Vintage Port	Jono	Jones	Woodbine	150,000	250,000
SanLsRyHG2	15-Mar-03	7	Champion Lodge (Ire)	Alex	Solis	Santa Anita	150,000	250,000
SixtySlHG3	26-Apr-03	8	Bare Necessities	Rene	Douglas	Hawthorne	150,000	250,000
SnAntnoHG2	2-Feb-03	8	Congaree	Jerry	Bailey	Santa Anita	150,000	250,000
SnDiegoHG2	3-Aug-03	8	Taste of Paradise	Victor	Espinoza	Del Mar	150,000	250,000
SnFelipeG2	16-Mar-03	5	Buddy Gil	Gary	Stevens	Santa Anita	150,000	250,000
SnowChief	26-Apr-03	4	Chief Planner	David	Flores	Hollywood Park	150,000	250,000
SntBrbrHG2	19-Apr-03	4	Megahertz (GB)	Alex	Solis	Santa Anita	150,000	250,000
TampaDbyG3	16-Mar-03	11	Region of Merit	Eibar	Coa	Tampa Bay Downs	150,000	250,000
TestG1	26-Jul-03	9	Lady Tak	Jerry	Bailey	Saratoga	150,000	250,000
VanityHG1	21-Jun-03	8	Azeri	Mike	Smith	Hollywood Park	150,000	250,000
WondrWhere	4-Aug-03	8	Alpha Saphire	Emile	Ramsammy	Woodbine	150,000	250,000

Race Name	Date	Race	Winning Horse	Jockey		Track	Earnings	Purse
FedExSprnt	25–Jan–03	4	Captain Squire	Alex	Solis	Santa Anita	137,500	250,000
JDeereOaks	25–Jan–03	3	Atlantic Ocean	David	Flores	Santa Anita	137,500	250,000
LgaMileHG3	24–Aug–03	8	Sky Jack	Russell	Baze	Emerald Downs	137,500	250,000
OcalStdDsh	25–Jan–03	8	Valid Video	Edgar	Prado	Gulfstream Park	137,500	250,000
PaduaFMSpr	25–Jan–03	6	Madame Pietra	Patrick	Valenzuela	Gulfstream Park	137,500	250,000
WVBrdrClsc	11–Oct–03	7	Cape Power	Anthony	Mawing	Charles Town	112,500	250,000
BisonCity	1–Jul–03	8	Brattothecore	Jake	Barton	Fort Erie	100,000	250,000
BisonCity	1–Jul–03	8	Seeking the Ring	Slade	Callaghan	Fort Erie	100,000	250,000
DmrBCHG2	1–Sep–03	8	Joey Franco	Patrick	Valenzuela	Del Mar	90,000	250,000
TrNthBCHG2	7–Jun–03	7	Shake You Down	Michael	Luzzi	Belmont	90,000	250,000
MaplLeafG3	1–Nov–03	8	One for Rose	Emile	Ramsammy	Woodbine	147,810	246,350
CDHG2	3–May–03	5	Aldebaran	Jerry	Bailey	Churchill Downs	144,956	233,800
RegretG3	14–Jun–03	8	Sand Springs	Mark	Guidry	Churchill Downs	143,220	231,000
GoldnRodG2	29–Nov–03	10	Be Gentle	John	McKee	Churchill Downs	142,600	230,000
NatalmaG3	6–Sep–03	8	Pink Champagne	Richard	Dos Ramos	Woodbine	106,200	227,000
DomDayHG3	1–Jul–03	8	Phantom Light	Todd	Kabel	Woodbine	135,600	226,000
CDDstafHG2	8–Nov–03	9	Lead Story	Calvin	Borel	Churchill Downs	139,748	225,400
ConlyBCTH	15–Feb–03	7	Candid Glen	Elvis	Perrodin	Sam Houston	133,800	223,000
GCHndriHG3	11–May–03	8	El Prado Essence	Patrick	Husbands	Woodbine	103,770	222,950
HmnaDstHG1	3–May–03	8	Sightseek	Jerry	Bailey	Churchill Downs	137,888	222,400
KyJCG2	29–Nov–03	11	The Cliff's Edge	Shane	Sellers	Churchill Downs	137,764	222,200
DncSmrtHG3	5–Jul–03	8	Madeira Mist (Ire)	Patrick	Husbands	Woodbine	103,050	221,750
JfrsnCupG3	7–Jun–03	9	Senor Swinger	Robby	Albarado	Churchill Downs	136,772	220,600
PtrGrBCHG2	29–Mar–03	8	Bluesthestandard	Mike	Smith	Santa Anita	72,000	220,000
SnFndoBCG2	11–Jan–03	8	Pass Rush	Corey	Nakatani	Santa Anita	131,760	219,600
StrStBCHG3	5–Jul–03	8	Ballingarry (IRE)	Rene	Douglas	Arlington Park	131,700	219,500
RylNrthHG3	2–Aug–03	8	Chopinina	Todd	Kabel	Woodbine	131,430	219,050
DuchessG3	9–Aug–03	5	Finally Here	Patrick	Husbands	Woodbine	100,350	217,250
HnymnBCHG2	7–Jun–03	8	Quero Quero	Tyler	Baze	Hollywood Park	130,170	216,950
CinmaBCHG3	29–Jun–03	8	Just Wonder (GB)	Kent	Desormeaux	Hollywood Park	98,730	214,550
JsAGmBCHG3	7–Jun–03	8	Mariensky	Jose	Santos	Belmont	128,700	214,500
BessarbHG3	16–Nov–03	8	Winter Garden	David	Clark	Woodbine	98,640	214,400
BlSpaBCHG3	23–Aug–03	8	Stylish	John	Velazquez	Saratoga	128,040	213,400
HolBCOakG2	14–Jun–03	6	Santa Catarina	Gary	Stevens	Hollywood Park	127,320	212,200
MladyBCHG1	24–May–03	8	Azeri	Mike	Smith	Hollywood Park	127,080	211,800
AnTtlBCHG1	5–Oct–03	7	Avanzado (ARG)	Tyler	Baze	Santa Anita	81,375	210,625
BelBCHG2	13–Sep–03	7	Della Francesca	Jorge	Chavez	Belmont	125,760	209,600
MGDCradle	1–Sep–03	12	Tiger Hunt	Larry	Melancon	River Downs	120,000	206,300
KyCpTrfHG3	20–Sep–03	14	Rochester	Eddie	Martin, Jr.	Kentucky Downs	124,000	200,000
MakrsMrkG2	11–Apr–03	8	Royal Spy	Robby	Albarado	Keeneland	124,000	200,000
4strdavHG2	23–Aug–03	9	Trademark (SAF)	Richard	Migliore	Saratoga	120,000	200,000
AGVndbtHG2	10–Aug–03	9	Private Horde	Jason	Lumpkins	Saratoga	120,000	200,000
AlAlngBCG3	12–Jul–03	9	Dress To Thrill (Ire)	Edgar	Prado	Colonial Downs	120,000	200,000
BCrsbBCHG2	26–Jul–03	6	Beau's Town	Patrick	Valenzuela	Del Mar	120,000	200,000
BevHilsHG2	28–Jun–03	8	Voodoo Dancer	Corey	Nakatani	Hollywood Park	120,000	200,000
BFrtcheHG2	22–Feb–03	10	Xtra Heat	Rick	Wilson	Laurel Park	120,000	200,000
BlkEySsnG2	16–May–03	10	Roar Emotion	John	Velazquez	Pimlico	120,000	200,000
BonnieMsG2	14–Mar–03	9	Ivanavinalot	John	Velazquez	Gulfstream Park	120,000	200,000
CalderOaks	11–Oct–03	9	Love Sting	Gary	Bain	Calder Race Course	120,000	200,000
CGRoseClsH	15–Nov–03	12	Best of the Rest	Eibar	Coa	Calder Race Course	120,000	200,000
CitgoDixG2	17–May–03	10	Dr. Brendler	Ramon	Dominguez	Pimlico	120,000	200,000
CrcDerbyG3	11–Oct–03	12	Stroll	Jerry	Bailey	Calder Race Course	120,000	200,000
CRodneyH	27–Sep–03	7	Private Lap	Anthony	Black	Delaware Park	120,000	200,000
DemoiselG2	29–Nov–03	7	Ashado	Jerry	Bailey	Aqueduct	120,000	200,000

Race Name	Date	Race	Winning Horse	Jockey		Track	Earnings	Purse
EHeubckDsH	15-Nov-03	11	Scapade	Julio	Garcia	Calder Race Course	120,000	200,000
EndineHG3	6-Sep-03	8	House Party	Jose	Santos	Delaware Park	120,000	200,000
FantasyG2	11-Apr-03	10	Ruby's Reception	Terry	Thompson	Oaklawn Park	120,000	200,000
FntnOYthG1	15-Feb-03	11	Trust N Luck	Cornelio	Velasquez	Gulfstream Park	120,000	200,000
FuturityG1	14-Sep-03	7	Cuvee	Jerry	Bailey	Belmont	120,000	200,000
GenGrgeHG2	22-Feb-03	9	My Cousin Matt	Ramon	Dominguez	Laurel Park	120,000	200,000
GothamG3	16-Mar-03	9	Alysweep	Richard	Migliore	Aqueduct	120,000	200,000
GPBCHG1	16-Feb-03	10	Man From Wicklow	Jerry	Bailey	Gulfstream Park	120,000	200,000
GrdeniaHG3	9-Aug-03	10	Bare Necessities	Rene	Douglas	Ellis Park	120,000	200,000
HopefulG1	30-Aug-03	8	Silver Wagon	Jerry	Bailey	Saratoga	120,000	200,000
IselnBCHG3	23-Aug-03	10	Tenpins	Robby	Albarado	Monmouth Park	120,000	200,000
JamaicaHG2	21-Sep-03	9	Stroll	Jerry	Bailey	Belmont	120,000	200,000
JBMoslyBCH	21-Jun-03	13	Peeping Tom	Shaun	Bridgmohan	Suffolk Downs	120,000	200,000
KngsBshpG1	23-Aug-03	10	Valid Video	Joe	Bravo	Saratoga	120,000	200,000
LaCanadaG2	8-Feb-03	6	Got Koko	Alex	Solis	Santa Anita	120,000	200,000
LaPvyteHG2	27-Dec-03	9	Volga (IRE)	Richard	Migliore	Calder Race Course	120,000	200,000
LATimesHG3	10-May-03	6	Hombre Rapido	Jose	Valdivia, Jr.	Hollywood Park	120,000	200,000
LsVrgnesG1	9-Feb-03	7	Composure	Jerry	Bailey	Santa Anita	120,000	200,000
MatronG1	14-Sep-03	6	Marylebone	Edgar	Prado	Belmont	120,000	200,000
Melair	26-Apr-03	9	Bartok's Blithe	Victor	Espinoza	Hollywood Park	120,000	200,000
NasauCBCG2	10-May-03	8	House Party	Jose	Santos	Belmont	120,000	200,000
NATCFut	30-Aug-03	6	Tym Beau	Jose	Caraballo	Delaware Park	120,000	200,000
NATCSorFut	30-Aug-03	8	From Away	Ramon	Dominguez	Delaware Park	120,000	200,000
OaklwnBCG3	15-Mar-03	10	Bien Nicole	Donald	Pettinger	Oaklawn Park	120,000	200,000
OrchidHG2	23-Mar-03	8	Tweedside	Rene	Douglas	Gulfstream Park	120,000	200,000
PalmrBCHG2	7-Sep-03	6	Spring Star (FR)	Alex	Solis	Del Mar	120,000	200,000
PanAmerHG2	22-Mar-03	10	Quest Star	Edgar	Prado	Gulfstream Park	120,000	200,000
PeterPanG2	24-May-03	8	Go Rockin' Robin	Shaun	Bridgmohan	Belmont	120,000	200,000
PrioressG1	4-Jul-03	9	House Party	Jose	Santos	Belmont	120,000	200,000
RampartHG2	1-Mar-03	10	Allamerican Bertie	John	Velazquez	Gulfstream Park	120,000	200,000
RcSclBCHG2	8-Mar-03	10	Tour of the Cat	Abad	Cabassa, Jr.	Gulfstream Park	120,000	200,000
RemsenG2	29-Nov-03	8	Read the Footnotes	Jerry	Bailey	Aqueduct	120,000	200,000
RvaRdgBCG2	7-Jun-03	9	Posse	Corey	Lanerie	Belmont	120,000	200,000
ShuveeHG2	17-May-03	8	Wild Spirit (CHI)	Javier	Castellano	Belmont	120,000	200,000
SLsObspHG2	15-Feb-03	7	The Tin Man	Mike	Smith	Santa Anita	120,000	200,000
SnCrlosHG1	2-Mar-03	7	Aldebaran	Jose	Valdivia, Jr.	Santa Anita	120,000	200,000
SnRafaelG2	1-Mar-03	7	Rojo Toro	Jerry	Bailey	Santa Anita	120,000	200,000
SntMncaHG1	25-Jan-03	8	Affluent	Alex	Solis	Santa Anita	120,000	200,000
SntMriaHG1	16-Feb-03	6	Starrer	Patrick	Valenzuela	Santa Anita	120,000	200,000
SpinawayG1	29-Aug-03	8	Ashado	Edgar	Prado	Saratoga	120,000	200,000
USA	26-May-03	7	Crowned King	Chandra	Rennie	Lone Star Park	120,000	200,000
WLMcKntHG2	27-Dec-03	11	Balto Star	John	Velazquez	Calder Race Course	120,000	200,000
WnStDstHG3	26-May-03	10	Eagle Lake	Gerard	Melancon	Lone Star Park	120,000	200,000
ElCamRIDG3	8-Mar-03	8	Ocean Terrace	Mike	Smith	Golden Gate Fields	110,000	200,000
MdMilClasc	11-Oct-03	11	Docent	Clinton	Potts	Laurel Park	110,000	200,000
SnFrnBCHG2	26-Apr-03	7	Ninebanks	Ronald	Warren, Jr.	Bay Meadows	110,000	200,000
ExlsrBCHG3	5-Apr-03	8	Classic Endeavor	Charles	Lopez	Aqueduct	90,000	200,000
MdBCHG3	17-May-03	4	Pioneer Boy	Jeremy	Rose	Pimlico	60,000	200,000
BMBCHG3	27-Sep-03	6	Mister Acpen (Chi)	Roberto	Gonzalez	Bay Meadows	55,000	200,000

* Earnings include $500,000 bonus

Snapshot Facts: There were 310 North American stakes worth $200,000 or more in 2003 of which 86 were worth $500,000 or more and 25 were worth $1 million or more.

Leading Money–Winning Horses in 2003

Horse	Age	Sex	Sts	1st	2d	3d	Won
Moon Ballad (IRE)	4	C	6	2	0	0	$3,719,798
Falbrav (IRE)	5	H	10	5	1	2	3,013,845
Sulamani (IRE)	4	C	6	3	1	0	2,603,842
Pleasantly Perfect	5	H	4	2	0	1	2,470,000
Mineshaft	4	C	9	7	2	0	2,209,686
Wando *	3	C	8	5	1	1	2,017,323
Medaglia d'Oro	4	C	5	3	2	0	1,990,000
Funny Cide	3	G	8	2	2	2	1,963,200
Empire Maker	3	C	6	3	3	0	1,936,200
Peace Rules	3	C	7	3	1	1	1,850,000
High Chaparral (IRE)	4	C	4	3	0	1	1,717,124
Harlan's Holiday	4	C	6	2	2	0	1,685,100
Congaree	5	H	9	5	2	0	1,608,000
Ten Most Wanted	3	C	10	4	2	1	1,544,860
Fleetstreet Dancer	5	G	10	1	4	2	1,519,026
Perfect Drift	4	G	8	5	0	0	1,505,388
Ipi Tombe (ZIM)	5	M	4	4	0	0	1,416,273
State City	4	C	8	2	0	1	1,292,469
Six Perfections (FR)	3	F	6	3	3	0	1,256,076
Sightseek	4	F	8	4	3	0	1,171,888
Adoration	4	F	5	2	1	1	1,160,750
Dynever	3	C	9	3	3	1	1,154,020
Island Fashion	3	F	10	4	1	0	1,112,970
Aldebaran	5	H	8	5	1	1	1,110,606
Heat Haze (GB)	4	F	7	4	1	1	1,101,460
Touch of the Blues (FR)	6	H	6	2	1	3	1,082,885
Dimitrova	3	F	7	4	1	1	1,042,970
Phoenix Reach (IRE)	3	C	4	3	0	1	1,035,526
Elloluv	3	F	8	2	3	0	978,775
Islington (IRE)	4	F	6	2	0	2	955,142
Johar	4	C	5	2	1	1	912,281
Balto Star	5	G	13	4	2	1	907,500
Redattore (BRZ)	8	H	8	5	0	2	864,147
Perfect Soul (IRE)	5	H	8	3	2	1	856,195
Halfbridled	2	F	4	4	0	0	849,400
Wild Spirit (CHI)	4	F	4	3	1	0	830,000
Shake You Down	5	G	13	7	2	2	829,160
Excessivepleasure	3	G	9	3	4	0	821,782
Cajun Beat	3	G	9	4	2	0	820,000
Action This Day	2	C	3	2	1	0	817,200
Azeri	5	M	5	4	1	0	817,080
Bird Town	3	F	8	3	4	0	815,976
Smok'n Frolic	4	F	11	3	3	1	776,856
Best of the Rest	8	H	6	3	2	0	753,500
Mobil	3	C	9	5	2	1	753,405
Milwaukee Brew	6	H	4	2	1	0	743,000
Paolini (GER)	6	H	4	0	2	1	742,300
Mr. Jester	2	C	6	4	2	0	730,800
Volga (IRE)	5	M	6	3	2	0	730,800
Candy Ride (ARG)	4	C	3	3	0	0	724,800
Take Charge Lady	4	F	7	2	3	0	720,026
Tates Creek	5	M	5	3	1	0	704,067
Soaring Free	4	G	8	5	1	0	699,200
Bien Nicole	5	M	10	4	2	1	690,540
Yesterday (IRE)	3	F	7	1	3	1	689,791
Got Koko	4	F	6	3	1	1	688,000
You	4	F	8	2	4	1	677,108
Lady Tak	3	F	9	4	3	0	675,350
Spoken Fur	3	F	10	5	1	3	670,630
Buddy Gil	3	G	6	3	0	0	668,730
Brian Boru (GB)	3	C	6	1	1	2	664,844
Polish Summer (GB)	6	H	7	1	3	0	661,904
Storming Home (GB)	5	H	5	3	0	0	650,000
Quest	4	C	11	2	4	3	637,860
Bluesthestandard	6	G	10	4	2	2	631,975
Honor in War	4	C	9	4	1	1	616,723
Ashado	2	F	6	4	1	1	610,800
Avanzado (ARG)	6	H	8	2	2	0	602,645
Grand Hombre	3	G	5	4	1	0	598,360
Kicken Kris	3	C	9	4	3	1	593,540
Strong Hope	3	C	7	5	0	1	582,360
Too Late Now	3	F	7	4	0	1	566,110
House Party	3	F	10	5	1	2	551,354
Candid Glen	6	G	8	2	0	0	543,300
Awesome Humor	3	F	7	2	4	0	539,835
Tigertail (FR)	4	F	8	0	2	1	535,164
Megahertz (GB)	4	F	7	2	1	3	534,480
Kudos	6	G	5	1	1	3	530,000
Sir Oscar	2	C	6	6	0	0	528,800
Oasis Dream (GB)	3	C	5	2	1	1	524,836
Be Gentle	2	F	7	4	1	0	523,078
Harmony Lodge	5	M	8	5	1	2	516,300
During	3	C	13	5	2	1	514,750
Musical Chimes	3	F	8	2	2	1	513,103
Tenpins	5	H	5	2	2	0	512,760
Casual Look	3	F	7	1	0	2	505,104
Sweet Return (GB)	3	C	9	2	2	2	500,360
Irish Warrior	5	H	10	2	3	4	500,300
Macaw (IRE)	4	G	9	0	4	1	496,500
Strut the Stage	5	H	4	2	1	0	485,085
Chapel Royal	2	C	6	3	2	1	484,755
Posse	3	C	11	5	1	1	478,426
One for Rose	4	F	10	6	2	0	476,377
Brass in Pocket	4	F	7	5	0	1	475,830
Valid Video	3	G	7	4	1	0	474,500
Soto	3	C	3	2	1	0	473,200
Winter Garden	3	F	9	6	1	2	470,826
Puzzlement	4	C	11	2	3	3	470,450
New York Hero	3	C	14	4	3	0	465,860
Gold Mover	5	M	6	2	2	2	462,480
Film Maker	3	F	9	4	2	2	457,220
Gimmeawink	3	C	14	6	3	0	456,880
Joey Franco	4	C	10	4	1	0	452,361
Sand Springs	3	F	7	4	1	0	451,390
Lead Story	4	F	11	3	1	1	449,062
Atlantic Ocean	3	F	9	2	3	1	443,430
The Tin Man	5	G	6	1	2	0	440,840
Volponi	5	H	8	0	5	2	438,256
King Robyn	3	G	11	8	1	0	436,990
Voodoo Dancer	5	M	4	2	0	1	432,364
Bowman's Band	5	H	9	3	3	1	432,240
Bare Necessities	4	F	8	4	0	3	431,175
Evening Attire	5	G	9	2	2	2	430,160
Peeping Tom	6	G	14	3	4	3	428,733
Denon	5	H	7	1	1	1	425,000
Roscoe Pito	3	G	9	6	1	2	424,566
Captain Squire	4	G	7	1	2	1	419,625
Freefourinternet	5	H	11	2	1	5	418,598
Private Horde	4	C	9	6	2	0	411,582
Lunar Sovereign	4	C	7	2	0	1	410,000
Century City (IRE)	4	C	9	2	0	2	409,392
Yell	3	F	9	3	1	1	408,527
Whitmore's Conn	5	H	6	2	0	1	404,236
Mezzo Soprano	3	F	8	3	1	2	401,920
Randaroo	3	F	10	4	4	0	401,500
Stroll	3	C	6	5	1	0	398,800
Cee's Elegance	6	M	6	2	1	0	398,600
Silver Tree	3	C	6	3	0	1	390,660
Minister Eric	2	C	5	1	2	1	387,920
Forever Grand	4	G	10	4	0	3	385,120
Refuse To Bend (IRE)	3	C	6	3	0	0	383,998
Chatter Chatter	2	F	7	3	2	1	383,470
Special Ring	6	G	5	1	2	0	383,000
Inamorato	3	C	7	2	0	4	382,078
L'Ancresse (IRE)	3	F	9	1	3	0	380,738
Ghostzapper	3	C	4	3	0	1	378,400
Pie N Burger	5	G	7	5	0	0	373,800

Horse	Age	Sex	Sts	1st	2d	3d	Won
Grey Memo	6	H	8	0	1	3	373,400
Ebony Breeze	3	F	8	4	1	2	365,887
Sir Cherokee	3	C	5	3	0	0	365,535
Passing Shot	4	F	10	3	2	2	362,637
Senor Swinger	3	C	11	3	0	2	361,290
Spice Island	4	F	13	6	3	1	361,286
Cuvee	2	C	6	4	0	1	360,704
Inish Glora	5	M	6	3	1	1	359,667
Fairly Ransom	3	C	6	2	2	1	358,819
Wild and Wicked	3	C	5	3	0	0	358,480
Hollywood Story	2	F	5	1	2	1	356,500
Perfect Moon	2	G	10	3	1	3	353,870
Scrimshaw	3	C	8	1	0	2	352,479
Beau's Town	5	G	6	4	1	0	351,800
Crafty Shaw	5	H	14	4	3	2	351,185
Tour of the Cat	5	G	9	3	2	2	351,070
My Vintage Port	2	F	6	3	2	1	351,051
Crowned King	3	C	13	3	0	3	351,000
Victory U. S. A.	2	F	6	2	1	2	350,370
Well Fancied	5	G	8	4	1	1	350,164
Private Lap	4	C	12	6	1	0	346,640
Trust N Luck	3	C	4	1	1	1	344,684
Santa Catarina	3	F	5	2	1	1	342,680
Raylene	3	F	10	6	2	0	339,687
Birdstone	2	C	3	2	0	0	339,000
Riskaverse	4	F	8	2	1	2	336,324
Aeneas	4	C	9	0	4	2	336,300
Dancewithavixen	3	F	11	8	2	0	335,921
Buy the Sport	3	F	7	2	0	1	334,521
Midas Eyes	3	C	6	2	2	1	333,788
Bowman Mill	5	H	5	1	2	0	327,682
Society Selection	2	F	3	2	0	0	327,000
Shoal Water	3	G	7	2	1	2	325,690
Mulligan the Great	4	G	8	4	1	3	322,396
Katdogawn (GB)	3	F	10	4	3	1	320,580
Winning Chance	4	F	8	3	4	0	317,435
Maiden Tower (GB)	3	F	6	3	2	0	316,824
State Shinto	7	H	8	1	1	0	315,701
Seeking the Ring	3	F	7	3	2	0	314,515
Champali	3	C	10	4	1	3	313,522
Valentine Dancer	3	F	14	5	3	2	312,846
Tiger Hunt	2	C	4	2	1	0	312,820
Walzerkoenigin	4	F	5	1	1	1	312,320
Lion Heart	2	C	3	3	0	0	310,800
Barbeau Ruckus	4	G	7	4	2	0	310,585
Ninebanks	5	G	9	3	2	1	310,400
Chris's Bad Boy	6	G	12	7	2	0	308,099
Hero's Tribute	5	H	6	2	1	0	307,660
Najran	4	C	7	2	1	1	305,700
Bright Sky (IRE)	4	F	6	1	1	2	303,832
Wake At Noon	6	H	10	3	1	1	303,671
Meridiana (GER)	3	F	5	2	0	0	303,478
Composure	3	F	2	2	0	0	300,000
Starrer	5	M	2	2	0	0	300,000
Phantom Light	4	C	6	3	0	0	299,610
No Comprende	5	G	10	2	3	1	298,700
America America	2	F	17	3	6	3	298,640
Quest Star	4	C	10	3	3	0	298,380
My Cousin Matt	4	G	6	1	1	1	297,500
She's Got the Beat	4	F	12	4	5	1	294,556
Don'tsellmeshort	2	C	8	4	2	1	294,395
Requete (GB)	4	C	6	2	2	0	294,300
Excess Summer	3	G	10	6	2	0	294,261
Continuously	4	C	8	3	1	1	293,200
Adminnistrator	6	G	3	1	0	1	292,900
D' Wildcat Speed	3	F	12	12	0	0	290,815
Docent	5	G	9	6	1	1	292,800
Eugene's Third Son	3	C	6	3	3	0	292,120
Highway Prospector	6	G	13	5	1	4	290,397
Passinetti	7	G	4	2	0	1	289,320
Willow Bunch	3	F	5	4	0	0	288,483
Summer Mis	4	F	8	6	0	0	286,495
Eurosilver	2	C	3	2	1	0	284,000
Danuta	3	F	4	2	1	0	280,000
Supah Blitz	3	C	10	2	2	2	278,000
Ciento	5	H	6	5	1	0	276,654
Green Team	4	G	13	5	5	1	276,103
Strait From Texas	4	F	9	3	3	0	275,936
Shine Again	6	M	7	2	5	0	275,620
Rouvres (FR)	4	C	7	1	3	1	274,020
Ladyecho	3	F	11	2	4	3	273,593
Tusayan	3	C	9	3	1	0	272,958
Stylish	5	M	6	3	0	1	270,955
Despreciado	3	C	10	6	1	1	270,418
Midway Road	3	C	5	1	1	2	270,146
Designed for Luck	6	G	4	3	0	0	267,735
Dublino	4	F	5	1	3	0	266,067
Bachelor Blues	2	C	8	2	3	0	265,406
Battlements	3	G	9	4	2	2	265,150
Tap the Admiral	5	H	6	2	0	1	265,046
Open Concert	4	G	12	3	6	0	264,801
Alysweep	3	R	8	3	2	0	263,680
Wiggins	3	C	7	5	0	1	263,444
Saarland	4	C	8	2	2	1	263,040
Traffic Chief	3	C	6	4	1	0	262,890
Pass Rush	4	C	9	1	3	1	261,865
Limehouse	2	C	6	3	0	2	260,435
Dr. Brendler	5	H	8	2	1	1	259,935
Dessert	3	F	6	3	1	1	259,560
Fire Slam	2	C	3	2	1	0	259,430
Foufa's Warrior	3	G	10	1	1	3	257,358
Gators N Bears	3	C	13	5	3	4	257,270
Summer Colony	5	M	5	1	1	0	256,500
Mystery Giver	5	G	10	2	2	1	256,260
Fast Cookie	3	F	8	4	0	2	255,787
Mariensky	4	F	7	3	0	0	255,300
The Cliff's Edge	2	C	5	3	1	0	255,258
Kabul	3	F	12	2	6	1	255,152
Royal Dalliance	6	M	13	3	3	2	252,064
McDynamo	6	G	3	3	0	0	252,025
Remind	3	C	8	3	4	0	251,420
Trademark (SAF)	7	G	9	2	1	1	251,143
Parose	9	G	9	3	1	2	250,177
Travelator	3	F	12	6	3	1	248,071
Norfolk Knight	4	G	14	5	3	0	245,939
Aggadan	4	C	11	3	2	2	243,230
Mandy's Gold	5	M	6	2	0	3	243,100
Hold That Tiger	3	C	5	0	1	0	242,746
Classic Endeavor	5	H	11	5	2	0	241,595
Olmodavor	4	C	4	1	2	0	241,080
Etoile Montante	3	F	7	3	1	1	240,719
Read the Footnotes	2	C	5	4	0	0	240,660
Better Talk Now	4	G	7	3	1	2	240,152
Eagle Lake	5	M	11	4	3	0	238,874
Champion Lodge (IRE)	6	G	4	2	0	1	238,638
Iron Deputy	4	C	5	2	0	1	238,620
Devious Boy (GB)	3	G	7	2	2	2	236,480
Kaieteur	4	C	6	0	1	2	235,449
Silver Bird	2	F	5	3	1	0	235,445
Twisted Wit	2	G	5	3	0	0	234,855
Labirinto	5	G	15	5	3	3	234,633
Go Rockin' Robin	3	C	11	3	1	2	233,446
French Charmer	4	G	7	5	0	0	232,800
Shawklit Mint	4	F	11	4	1	0	232,725
Smoocher	2	C	4	2	1	0	231,653
Crazy Ensign (ARG)	7	M	7	3	1	2	231,405
Fencelineneighbor	3	F	12	5	2	2	231,107
Shalini	4	F	9	3	1	1	230,159

Horse	Age	Sex	Sts	1st	2d	3d	Won
A Bit O'Gold	2	G	4	3	0	0	230,029
Region of Merit	3	C	6	3	0	0	229,986
Shiny Sheet	5	M	10	3	2	3	229,870
Bartok's Blithe	3	F	9	3	2	1	229,700
Savedbythelight	3	F	7	2	0	4	229,080
Buffythecenterfold	3	F	7	2	2	2	228,815
Cherokee's Boy	3	C	7	3	1	1	228,500
Ocean Silk	3	F	8	2	3	1	228,430
Mister Acpen (CHI)	5	H	8	2	1	1	228,200
Classic Stamp	3	F	8	3	2	2	228,054
Aud	3	F	11	4	2	0	228,045
Lacie Girl	4	F	11	4	6	0	227,990
Chopinina	5	M	5	1	1	0	227,070
Hennie's Song	3	F	5	5	0	0	226,800
One Only Knows	3	F	11	4	1	2	225,349
Winter Whiskey	2	G	6	3	0	2	225,093
Shemoveslikeaghost	3	F	6	3	2	0	224,510
Dream About	2	F	5	2	1	0	224,430
Vision in Flight	4	F	13	2	8	1	224,430
Booklet	4	C	2	0	1	0	224,000
Patton's Victory	5	G	13	6	0	2	223,501
Dancal (IRE)	5	M	9	3	2	0	223,011
Ivanavinalot	3	F	10	1	2	1	223,000
Taste of Paradise	4	C	7	2	0	0	222,910
Bo Bo's Vice	3	G	7	3	0	1	222,259
Quick Tip	5	M	11	2	3	1	221,582
Fantastic Day	3	G	11	5	3	1	221,456
Skeet	3	C	13	7	2	2	221,095
Patrol	4	C	5	2	0	0	220,930
Miss Crissy	3	F	8	1	3	2	220,687
Snow Dance	5	M	8	1	1	2	220,510
El Prado Essence	6	M	7	2	2	0	220,108
Sabiango (GER)	5	H	6	1	0	1	218,563
Scapade	3	F	9	3	2	3	218,440
Coach Jimi Lee	3	G	11	5	1	2	218,120
Spite the Devil	3	G	14	1	3	3	217,924
Warleigh	5	H	8	5	1	0	217,545
France (GB)	3	C	8	1	1	1	217,307
My Boston Gal	3	F	4	1	1	0	216,714
Continental Red	7	G	10	1	3	1	216,705
Dyna Da Wyna	3	F	9	5	0	0	216,517
Sky Mesa	3	C	3	0	1	1	216,500
Mysterious Affair	6	M	12	1	3	4	214,926
Western Pride	5	H	6	1	1	0	214,750
Eye of the Tiger	3	C	8	2	1	2	214,689
Denied	5	G	9	4	2	3	214,360
Hoh Buzzard (IRE)	3	F	10	4	1	2	214,178
Cyber Secret	3	F	5	3	1	0	214,107
Greattobeloved	3	F	8	5	1	1	213,639
Hanselina	3	F	9	3	3	0	213,180
Brancusi	3	C	6	1	1	1	212,580
Mountain General	5	G	6	2	3	0	212,580
Devon Rose	4	F	8	4	0	1	212,380
El Dorado Shooter	6	H	5	3	2	0	211,950
Kool Humor	3	G	11	4	1	3	211,800

Horse	Age	Sex	Sts	1st	2d	3d	Won
Alpha Saphire	3	F	8	2	1	1	211,470
Rock Again	3	C	5	2	2	1	211,320
Bold Roberta	5	M	14	3	3	3	211,198
False Promises	3	G	13	3	3	1	210,740
Icantgoforthat	4	F	12	2	1	4	210,724
Redoubled Miss	4	F	9	2	4	2	210,545
Devil Time	6	G	11	5	0	0	210,460
Spritely Walker	3	C	9	4	2	1	210,340
Colorful Tour	4	C	9	4	2	0	209,525
Betty's Wish	3	F	9	5	2	1	209,440
Atswhatimtalknbout	3	C	6	2	1	1	209,120
Lismore Knight	3	C	6	2	0	2	208,800
Love That Moon	4	G	15	5	2	1	208,265
Pat's Expectation	4	C	10	4	2	1	208,041
Puffer	4	G	10	3	5	2	207,654
My Pal Lana	3	F	10	3	2	3	207,224
Piensa Sonando (CHI)	5	H	9	1	2	1	206,773
Blind Ambition	5	M	6	3	2	0	206,640
Indy Five Hundred	3	F	7	2	1	0	206,400
Singletary	3	C	8	2	2	1	206,352
Christine's Outlaw	3	C	10	2	2	1	206,160
Fuse It	5	M	13	3	1	3	205,620
Grey Comet	3	C	5	2	2	1	205,080
Bossanova	3	C	7	3	1	1	204,906
Galloping Gal	2	F	5	3	1	0	204,884
Taiaslew	3	G	7	4	2	0	204,325
Ask the Lord	6	G	11	5	1	2	204,120
Spring Meadow	4	F	10	3	0	3	204,002
A Huevo	7	G	3	2	0	0	204,000
F J's Pace	8	G	13	5	1	1	203,840
Hard Buck (BRZ)	4	C	4	3	0	0	203,636
Proud Man	5	H	7	2	3	1	203,142
Southern Image	3	C	3	2	0	1	202,800
Political Attack	4	G	7	3	0	1	202,688
Changeintheweather	4	C	7	2	4	1	202,245
Julie's Prize	3	F	9	4	1	1	202,095
Sophia's Prince	4	G	9	3	3	1	201,998
The Name's Bond	3	C	9	5	1	0	201,850
Feline Story	2	F	6	3	1	0	201,780
Cappuchino	4	C	10	2	0	3	201,712
That Tat	5	G	9	5	2	1	201,700
Madame Pietra	6	M	3	2	0	0	201,580
Music's Storm	4	C	9	2	3	1	201,554
Daunting	5	G	11	5	1	0	201,405
Brown Eyed Beauty	4	F	10	4	4	2	201,350
Just Too Too	3	F	5	5	0	0	201,240
Sonic West	4	G	9	4	2	1	200,970
City Fire	3	F	10	5	1	0	200,549
Native Heir	5	G	10	4	3	1	200,280
Cloakof Vagueness	3	F	10	2	5	2	200,145

* Includes $500,000 bonus

Horses with at least one North American start and earnings of $200,000 or more in 2003.

There were 28 horses with earnings of at least $1 million.

Annual Leading Money Winners Since 1902

Year	Horse	Age	Strs	1st	2d	3d	Earnings	Year	Horse	Age	Strs	1st	2d	3d	Earnings
1902	Major Daingerfield	3	7	4	2	1	$57,685	1955	Nashua	3	12	10	1	1	752,550
1903	Africander	3	15	8	3	1	70,810	1956	Needles	3	8	4	2	0	445,850
1904	Delhi	3	10	6	2	0	75,225	1957	Round Table	3	22	15	1	3	600,383
1905	Sysonby	3	9	9	0	0	144,380	1958	Round Table	4	20	14	4	0	662,780
1906	Accountant	3	13	9	1	1	131,705	1959	Sword Dancer	3	13	8	4	0	537,004
1907	Colin	2	12	12	0	0	131,705	1960	Bally Ache	3	15	10	3	1	445,045
1908	Sir Martin	2	13	8	4	0	78,590	1961	Carry Back	3	16	9	1	3	565,349
1909	Joe Madden	3	15	5	9	1	44,905	1962	Never Bend	2	10	7	1	2	402,969
1910	Novelty	2	16	11	2	2	72,630	1963	Candy Spots	3	12	7	2	1	604,481
1911	Worth	2	13	10	1	0	16,645	1964	Gun Bow	4	16	8	4	2	580,100
1912	Star Charter	4	17	6	2	5	14,655	1965	Buckpasser	2	11	9	1	0	568,096
1913	Old Rosebud	2	14	12	2	0	19,057	1966	Buckpasser	3	14	13	1	0	669,078
1914	Roamer	3	16	12	1	2	29,105	1967	Damascus	3	16	12	3	1	817,941
1915	Borrow	7	9	4	1	1	20,195	1968	Forward Pass	3	13	7	2	0	546,674
1916	Campfire	2	9	6	2	0	49,735	1969	Arts and Letters	3	14	8	5	1	555,604
1917	Sun Briar	2	9	5	1	2	59,505	1970	Personality	3	18	8	2	1	444,049
1918	Eternal	2	8	6	1	0	56,173	1971	Riva Ridge	2	9	7	0	0	503,263
1919	Sir Barton	3	13	8	3	2	88,250	1972	Droll Role	4	19	7	3	4	471,633
1920	Man o' War	3	11	11	0	0	166,140	1973	Secretariat	3	12	9	2	1	860,404
1921	Morvich	2	11	11	0	0	115,234	1974	Chris Evert (f)	3	8	5	1	2	551,063
1922	Pillory	3	7	4	1	1	95,654	1975	Foolish Pleasure	3	11	5	4	1	716,278
1923	Zev	3	14	12	1	0	272,008	1976	Forego	6	8	6	1	1	401,701
1924	Sarazen	3	12	8	1	1	95,640	1977	Seattle Slew	3	7	6	0	0	641,370
1925	Pompey	2	10	7	2	0	121,630	1978	Affirmed	3	11	8	2	0	901,541
1926	Crusader	3	15	9	4	0	166,033	1979	Spectacular Bid	3	12	10	1	1	1,279,334
1927	Anita Peabody	2	7	6	0	1	111,905	1980	Temperance Hill	3	17	8	3	1	1,130,452
1928	High Strung	2	6	5	0	0	153,590	1981	John Henry	6	10	8	0	0	1,798,030
1929	Blue Larkspur	3	6	4	1	0	153,450	1982	*Perrault	5	8	4	1	2	1,197,400
1930	Gallant Fox	3	10	9	1	0	308,275	1983	*All Along (f)	4	7	4	1	1	2,138,963
1931	Gallant Flight	2	7	7	0	0	219,000	1984	Slew o' Gold	4	6	5	1	0	2,627,944
1932	Gusto	3	16	4	3	2	145,940	1985	Spend a Buck	3	7	5	1	1	3,552,704
1933	Singing Wood	2	9	3	2	2	88,050	1986	Snow Chief	3	9	6	1	1	1,875,200
1934	Cavalcade	3	7	6	1	0	111,235	1987	Alysheba	3	10	3	3	1	2,511,156
1935	Omaha	3	9	6	1	2	142,255	1988	Alysheba	4	9	7	1	0	3,808,600
1936	Granville	3	11	7	3	0	110,295	1989	Sunday Silence	3	9	7	2	0	4,578,454
1937	Seabiscuit	4	15	11	2	2	168,580	1990	Unbridled	3	11	4	3	2	3,718,149
1938	Stagehand	3	15	8	2	3	189,710	1991	Dance Smartly (f)	3	8	8	0	0	2,876,821
1939	Challedon	3	15	9	2	3	184,535	1992	A.P. Indy	3	7	5	0	1	2,622,560
1940	Bimelech	3	7	4	2	1	110,005	1993	Kotashaan	5	10	6	3	0	2,619,014
1941	Whirlaway	3	20	13	5	2	272,386	1994	Paradise Creek	5	11	8	2	1	2,620,283
1942	Shut Out	3	12	8	2	0	238,872	1995	Cigar	5	10	10	0	0	4,819,800
1943	Count Fleet	3	6	6	0	0	174,055	1996	Cigar	6	8	5	2	1	4,910,000
1944	Pavot	2	8	8	0	0	179,040	1997	Skip Away	4	11	4	5	2	4,089,000
1945	Busher	3	13	10	2	1	273,735	1998	Silver Charm	4	9	6	2	0	4,696,506
1946	Assault	3	15	8	2	3	424,195	1999	Almutawakel	4	5	1	1	1	3,290,000
1947	Armed	6	17	11	4	1	376,325	2000	Fantastic Light	4	9	3	2	1	4,524,423
1948	Citation	3	20	19	1	0	709,470	2001	Captain Steve	4	6	2	1	1	4,210,200
1949	Ponder	3	21	9	5	2	321,825	2002	Street Cry	4	4	3	1	0	4,323,777
1950	Noor	5	12	7	4	1	346,940	2003	Moon Ballad	4	6	2	0	0	3,719,798
1951	Counterpoint	3	15	7	2	1	250,525								
1952	Crafty Admiral	4	16	9	4	1	277,225								
1953	Native Dancer	3	10	9	1	0	513,425								
1954	Determine	3	15	10	3	2	328,700								

Leading Horses in 2003 – Races Won

Horse	Age	Sex	Sts	1st	2d	3d	Won
D' Wildcat Speed *	3	F	12	12	0	0	$290,815
Call Me Mr. Vain	9	G	20	11	4	0	62,162
Storming On Merit	4	F	12	10	0	0	108,643
Diplomatical	6	G	19	10	2	0	58,460
Nicole's Dream	3	F	17	9	2	1	176,040
Dr Arbatach *	4	C	13	9	1	1	127,296
Piccolo Honey	4	F	16	9	3	2	124,920
Padre Valeriano *	4	C	15	9	1	2	63,270
El Teide *	5	M	19	9	3	1	40,956
King Robyn	3	G	11	8	1	0	436,990
Dancewithavixen	3	F	11	8	2	0	335,921
Bensalem	6	G	12	8	0	4	161,066
Heat of the Moment	3	F	14	8	1	1	156,257
Ashagio	5	G	16	8	4	0	149,331
Boston Fox	3	G	13	8	3	0	146,740
Margarita's Garden	4	F	12	8	1	1	139,451
James	3	G	20	8	6	2	136,290
River Rammer	3	C	17	8	0	2	58,385
Proven Honor	3	F	16	8	1	1	57,930
Sr. Eddie B. *	5	H	21	8	5	4	56,241
Trumps Clown	9	G	13	8	4	0	54,170
La Murga *	3	F	13	8	2	1	51,107
Basinbob	6	G	10	8	0	0	50,146
Comprendido *	3	C	16	8	2	2	49,696
La Policlinica *	5	M	11	8	2	1	48,403
Watch Me Dazzle	5	G	15	8	4	2	39,497
Fergie's Showtime	7	G	17	8	3	3	34,821
Siward	5	G	13	8	2	2	34,768
Keoki Native	9	G	21	8	2	1	9,571
Mineshaft	4	C	9	7	2	0	2,209,686
Shake You Down	5	G	13	7	2	2	829,160
Chris's Bad Boy	6	G	12	7	2	0	308,099
Skeet	3	C	13	7	2	2	221,095
Price of Honour	3	G	13	7	3	2	191,327
Danceinthestreets	3	F	11	7	0	1	175,710
Fancy Buckles	3	F	9	7	2	0	165,968
Mum's Gold	4	F	11	7	1	1	158,630
This Cat's for You	3	C	13	7	3	1	158,581
Mister Fanucci *	2	C	8	7	1	0	136,105
Kylers Midge	4	F	13	7	0	0	133,000
Hirapour (IRE)	7	G	10	7	1	1	128,167
Quest for Truth	3	F	12	7	1	1	125,712
Rod	5	H	15	7	2	1	122,166
Irish Colony	3	G	14	7	2	0	104,255
Crypt de Chine	8	H	11	7	1	0	98,600
Landler	4	G	11	7	3	0	95,945
Unpeteable	6	G	15	7	3	2	85,709
Westmoreland Girl *	3	F	18	7	6	4	85,032
Trijonia	3	F	13	7	0	0	81,273
Shut Out Time	7	G	17	7	3	2	79,335
Hurricane Havoc	6	G	16	7	0	1	78,923
Title for Title	6	G	17	7	2	3	77,910
Monarquica	4	F	15	7	1	1	75,140
Birdie Putt	5	M	12	7	1	0	73,470
Iverson	4	C	15	7	2	4	71,280
Classy Report	4	F	16	7	2	1	70,833
Tomorrows Peach	3	F	14	7	1	1	69,984
Tan Campante (ARG)	4	F	14	7	2	1	67,768
Perty Number	5	M	13	7	6	0	65,404
Cooky Joe Fletcher	4	C	14	7	0	1	61,370
Sweep in Philly	3	F	12	7	1	2	60,310
Miss Fixed Income	3	F	11	7	1	0	58,160
Bright Diplomat	4	F	21	7	6	1	57,984
Smoke Till Dawn	4	G	18	7	2	0	56,170
El Diago	7	G	12	7	1	1	55,829
Erin G.	7	M	12	7	2	1	55,672
Shoot It	4	G	13	7	2	1	54,290
Kaoma *	3	F	13	7	3	1	54,166
Mi Amigo Cesar *	3	C	22	7	7	5	53,057
The Garbage Man	5	G	14	7	1	3	51,743
Reassess	4	C	14	7	3	2	48,210
Moe Greene	6	G	15	7	1	2	45,820
Soy de San Diego *	3	F	15	7	4	3	45,294
Sindbad the Sailor	5	G	10	7	2	0	44,980
Yariana *	3	F	17	7	4	2	44,886
Rainkona *	3	F	21	7	5	3	41,946
Oro Viejo *	4	C	23	7	4	1	41,668
United Cat *	3	C	13	7	2	1	40,567
Open Magnet *	4	C	18	7	2	5	39,441
Squadron Commander	6	G	22	7	4	2	38,934
I'm That Way *	3	C	18	7	4	4	38,154
High Springs *	3	C	20	7	5	1	37,816
Play in Vermont *	6	M	18	7	3	3	37,769
Caguanas *	6	H	16	7	4	3	37,292
Desert Wolf Girl	4	F	19	7	2	4	35,197
Rustridge Brix	7	G	19	7	1	3	34,455
John Paul	6	G	20	7	3	3	34,363
Apple Butter Annie	4	F	17	7	2	2	33,689
Hook	4	G	18	7	0	3	33,650
Diablo's Chronicle *	6	H	11	7	2	2	33,605
Prospecter's Gold *	3	C	25	7	3	2	33,440
Airship	5	G	14	7	1	3	33,350
Secretary to Angel *	3	F	15	7	1	0	32,490
El Aguilio	9	G	15	7	3	3	30,838
John the Broker	6	G	13	7	3	0	27,610
Pleasant Cloud	5	M	13	7	1	1	27,059
Count Them All	6	M	15	7	4	2	15,673
Theycallmecolonel	6	H	18	7	3	1	15,326
Alleged Feu	8	G	15	7	2	1	10,940
Sir Oscar	2	C	6	6	0	0	528,800
One for Rose	4	F	10	6	2	0	476,377
Winter Garden	3	F	9	6	1	2	470,826
Gimmeawink	3	C	14	6	3	0	456,880
Roscoe Pito	3	G	9	6	1	2	424,566
Private Horde	4	C	9	6	2	0	411,582
Spice Island	4	F	13	6	3	1	361,286
Private Lap	4	C	12	6	1	0	346,640
Raylene	3	F	10	6	2	0	339,687
Excess Summer	3	G	10	6	2	0	294,261
Docent	5	G	9	6	1	1	292,800
Summer Mis	4	F	8	6	0	0	286,495
Despreciado *	3	C	10	6	1	1	270,418
Travelator	3	F	12	6	3	1	248,071
Patton's Victory	5	G	13	6	0	2	223,501
Kedington	4	G	15	6	3	3	199,548
Ema Bovary (CHI)	4	F	7	6	0	0	184,340
Moscow Burning	3	F	9	6	1	0	179,565

Horse	Age	Sex	Sts	1st	2d	3d	Won
Expresso Bay	6	G	10	6	2	0	176,420
Leslie's Love	6	M	15	6	5	0	176,140
A Shaky Start	3	F	9	6	2	0	173,931
Ditch Digger (ARG)	8	G	13	6	0	2	172,440
Lost Appeal	5	M	13	6	3	1	161,145
Bulldog George	4	G	13	6	2	2	154,515
Lou's Expectation	4	G	9	6	2	1	148,740
Heroofthegame	7	G	15	6	0	6	145,160
Morning Merry	3	G	15	6	2	3	145,050
Elegant Mercedes	3	F	11	6	0	2	144,425
Distinct Vision	3	G	12	6	3	0	138,460
Andiroba *	3	F	9	6	1	0	137,186
Pelican Beach	5	G	10	6	2	1	136,780
Festive Lady	5	M	15	6	3	1	136,200
Que Facil Corazon	5	M	14	6	3	2	134,970
Donald's Pride	3	C	10	6	0	2	133,817
My Meow	5	M	11	6	1	1	125,380
Sharp Miss	3	F	13	6	0	1	123,572
Sombodyswatchnovme	4	G	10	6	2	0	120,700
Anstar (GB)	6	G	11	6	3	1	120,300
Shining Britely	5	M	15	6	6	0	112,886
In Season	6	G	16	6	1	3	111,921
College Honor	3	G	12	6	1	0	110,590
Nat and Julie	4	F	12	6	3	1	109,925
Feather Maraine	3	F	10	6	0	0	108,021
Scottish Warrior	4	G	18	6	5	4	104,632
W W Robin de Hood	5	G	13	6	7	0	102,920
Captain Holloway	4	C	15	6	4	1	102,632
Spooky Mulder	5	G	15	6	3	1	101,912
Don Piero *	6	H	10	6	3	0	101,407
Omar Alejandro *	2	C	7	6	1	0	101,060
Mi Jesuse *	4	C	13	6	4	1	99,275
No Secrets Here	3	F	17	6	3	1	97,914
News Report	3	G	15	6	0	4	95,770
No Peso No Dance	4	F	10	6	2	1	95,442
Another Ivory	5	M	13	6	3	1	95,130
Officer's Sword	5	G	12	6	1	2	93,120
Runawayfun	5	M	13	6	1	1	91,956
Foxy Captain	3	G	14	6	3	1	91,228
Sea Leon	5	H	12	6	2	0	91,030
Pleasant Company	4	G	14	6	2	1	90,805
Such a Flirt	3	F	12	6	1	1	88,306
Slot Happy	5	M	14	6	1	0	88,126
D C Storm	5	G	11	6	1	0	87,510
Ganendyl	3	F	15	6	3	0	85,550
Doug's Lad	4	G	17	6	2	4	83,838
Salty O'Rourke	6	G	12	6	1	1	83,071
Sir Shimmy	8	G	14	6	1	3	78,910
Prime Step	5	M	10	6	0	2	75,210
Forever in Love	5	M	10	6	2	0	75,132
Mi Abogada *	3	F	14	6	4	2	73,657
Imablazinbeauty	3	F	13	6	0	1	73,480
Nicole's Apollo	4	C	22	6	1	5	73,360
Aat Falt	5	M	14	6	3	1	73,215
Western Punch	3	F	15	6	1	2	72,656
Spouse	3	F	14	6	4	0	72,610
Barath	4	G	15	6	4	1	72,540
Loosecannonondeck	4	F	12	6	2	0	71,590
Slew Ann	6	M	11	6	1	0	71,172
Morethanastar	4	G	16	6	1	2	70,709
Fostress	3	F	16	6	3	2	70,190
Pockets	5	G	17	6	2	2	69,961
Forbidden King *	3	C	12	6	2	2	68,777
Fan the Flame	6	H	12	6	1	2	66,850
Saratoga Blues	4	C	16	6	0	2	65,810
Witch Revival	3	F	15	6	1	0	65,080
Kouri Jill	3	F	15	6	2	4	65,065
Lorraine's Secret	5	G	20	6	3	5	64,843
Fancy M. D.	4	G	14	6	0	2	64,780
Glory's Ace	8	G	12	6	1	0	64,600
Let's Behave	5	G	12	6	0	2	64,060
Slewzy Floozy	4	F	20	6	1	2	63,412
Kiss Me Jim	4	G	15	6	1	1	63,226
Candid Remark	5	G	14	6	2	1	62,292
At a Boy Luther	4	G	16	6	3	1	61,475
Tour of the Rose	6	M	21	6	3	2	61,308
Here Comes Justice	3	F	16	6	0	0	60,910
Norjet	4	C	13	6	1	2	59,967
Briartic Gold	6	G	14	6	2	1	59,248
Everwhat	5	G	14	6	0	3	58,953
El Master	8	G	15	6	3	0	58,912
Fully Packed	4	G	15	6	3	2	57,958
Tack Room Lady	4	F	13	6	0	1	57,580
Ghoastly Prize	5	G	13	6	2	1	56,927
Valid Fury	4	G	12	6	0	2	56,705
Friskys Show *	6	H	28	6	8	9	56,250
Pinky Floyd	4	G	13	6	2	1	56,133
Just Allen	5	H	12	6	0	2	56,107
Quiet Charm	4	F	15	6	1	1	55,972
Threewishesforme	5	G	14	6	2	3	55,836
Pembroke Hall	6	G	6	6	0	0	55,420
Copelan's Devilet	5	M	12	6	1	1	53,260
Street Band	4	F	8	6	0	0	52,260
Victory Pose	6	H	8	6	1	0	52,100
Excuse My French	5	G	11	6	3	1	51,905
Brennan D	5	M	20	6	2	1	51,615
Toast for Mr. Expo	5	G	14	6	3	0	51,174
Overnight Delivery	4	F	14	6	1	1	50,768
Bed Pro	3	F	16	6	1	2	50,507
Four Cards Too	4	G	14	6	2	1	50,491
Phone Prospector	7	G	13	6	3	1	50,261
Sum Reward	4	C	16	6	3	0	49,861
Stormy Approval *	3	F	20	6	3	5	49,266
Call Fiorello	8	G	12	6	1	1	49,135
Jethro Blue	5	G	9	6	0	1	48,918
Regal Again	5	G	9	6	0	0	48,450
Junket	7	G	10	6	2	0	47,723
Wandy's Pride *	5	M	20	6	3	3	47,256
Darned Bold	4	G	25	6	4	2	47,063
Going Round	4	G	12	6	0	2	46,815
Miss Dorado *	2	F	11	6	1	1	46,594
Mystic Appeal	4	G	14	6	0	1	46,275
Skeeman	5	G	20	6	4	3	45,892
Rightbyu	4	F	13	6	3	1	45,315
Stormy Sky	3	F	14	6	1	5	44,325
French Twist	5	M	15	6	3	3	43,414
Loot N Plunder	4	G	16	6	2	1	43,231
Brave Opponent	6	M	19	6	3	1	42,491

Horse	Age	Sex	Sts	1st	2d	3d	Won
Random Thoughts	3	F	13	6	1	1	42,378
Fanzoca	3	F	10	6	0	1	42,234
Green Speed	4	F	12	6	0	1	42,080
Golden Sunshine	3	F	17	6	1	0	41,801
Foggia	3	F	16	6	0	1	41,711
Seymour Moves	3	F	16	6	0	2	41,297
Hitchcock's Best	3	G	17	6	2	1	41,232
Bolognesa *	2	F	16	6	4	3	41,166
Sammy Jr. *	6	H	15	6	6	1	41,005
El Solitario *	8	H	12	6	4	1	40,983
Doctor Gutierrez *	4	C	26	6	3	5	39,912
Atlantis Crusader	4	G	9	6	1	0	39,900
Miss Ednarie *	4	F	18	6	2	3	39,594
Katovilla	5	G	18	6	2	2	39,555
Creating a Ruckus *	3	C	18	6	6	1	39,538
Pyrite in Flight	9	G	17	6	3	2	39,527
Garlic Country	4	G	9	6	0	2	39,475
Personal Memories	4	F	13	6	2	2	39,461
Max Force	3	C	16	6	1	1	39,147
Mexican Connection	6	M	16	6	0	2	38,380
Rag King	6	G	12	6	0	1	37,978
Miss Victory	4	F	13	6	2	2	37,557
Dyf	4	G	16	6	3	1	37,220
Isla Del Sol *	4	G	22	6	5	5	37,059
Tino *	4	C	18	6	4	1	36,898
Triangulo *	3	C	18	6	2	2	36,206
La Implosion *	8	M	18	6	1	7	36,028
Sozo	6	G	19	6	5	2	35,820
Blue Bandit *	3	C	15	6	1	3	35,745
Renacer Borincano *	4	C	17	6	4	2	35,010
Fast Departure	10	G	19	6	2	1	34,725
Bedford Road	3	G	10	6	1	1	34,453
Hopeful Intent *	4	C	21	6	4	1	34,084
Sooner Shine	5	G	20	6	2	3	33,955
Don't Ignore Her	6	M	12	6	0	1	33,920
Its Sylviesbag	4	C	20	6	2	1	33,870
El Carenero *	3	C	19	6	4	2	33,601
Without Bond	3	G	17	6	0	3	33,498
Vixen Running *	5	M	18	6	4	2	33,252
Panchita Villa	5	M	13	6	2	0	32,855
Platinum Profit *	4	F	21	6	6	3	32,442
Catch'em All	5	G	24	6	5	3	31,762
Bunny Slope	3	F	10	6	1	2	31,680
Explosive Gamble *	3	C	22	6	5	3	31,530
Miss Marigold	4	F	22	6	4	1	31,225
Sage Road	5	G	20	6	3	4	31,194
Basilisk	4	G	14	6	0	1	30,517
Doji Groom *	6	H	17	6	4	2	29,843
Quiet Syns	7	H	9	6	3	0	29,420
Beep Me	9	G	17	6	4	2	28,729
Special Motion	4	F	14	6	2	1	28,699
Red Hot Rocket	5	G	17	6	2	2	28,101
Revere *	7	H	24	6	3	2	28,098
J. Maria Voltage *	3	F	20	6	3	2	28,032
Old Man's Delite	7	H	15	6	2	1	27,952
Bonny Sweet *	6	H	12	6	2	1	26,346
Snowbound Native	3	H	12	6	3	2	25,038
Spanish Gypsy	4	F	10	6	3	0	24,785
I P O Dude	5	G	12	6	1	2	23,292
Belal	8	G	16	6	2	1	20,786
Double Time	5	G	11	6	2	0	20,120
Air Forbes Too	6	H	14	6	2	4	18,368
Firefall	7	G	14	6	0	0	17,805
Neil's Advice	3	C	13	6	2	2	17,279
City Parkway	4	G	17	6	2	2	16,006
Tickle Me Malmo	5	M	11	6	0	1	15,909
Sweet N Brassy	6	M	9	6	0	0	12,522
Abstract Image	5	M	12	6	1	2	12,450
Dixie Drifter	6	G	9	6	0	0	11,051
Revenue	8	G	16	6	2	3	10,339
Foxy Walker	7	G	16	6	0	2	8,428

* Raced exclusively in Puerto Rico. There were 306 horses that won six or more races in North America in 2003. Horse of the Year Mineshaft won seven of his nine outings.

Annual Leading Winner of Races Since 1975

Year	Horse	Age	St	1st	2d	3d	Earnings	Year	Horse	Age	St	1st	2d	3d	Earnings
1975	Gallant Bob	3	18	14	1	2	$273,388	1987	Navajo Family	6	17	12	1	1	31,107
1975	Up Alone	4	24	14	6	3	58,585	1988	Gene	5	24	16	3	2	54,590
1976	T.V. Vixen	3	16	13	2	0	315,424	1989	Just Like Lace	3	18	13	0	2	140,417
1976	Nickel C.	7	28	13	3	7	33,778	1989	Immunity	5	18	13	2	0	49,205
1977	Jiva Cool It	5	23	12	5	4	77,462	1990	Jilsie's Gigalo	6	26	17	5	1	78,885
1978	Albert the Consort	8	31	15	3	6	46,416	1991	The King's Sloop	3	24	14	2	2	114,128
1979	American Moon	5	19	12	0	0	28,782	1991	Sweet Sachet	5	21	14	0	1	65,615
1979	Little Chuck	7	25	12	1	1	18,050	1992	Speedy Crossing	5	18	14	1	0	38,591
1980	Sunny Lee	7	29	13	1	2	17,360	1993	Inspector Moomaw	6	19	12	1	3	52,209
1981	Antiquarian	6	27	13	5	5	38,196	1994	Belle's Ruckus	9	20	16	0	1	59,068
1982	Lunamor	4	24	13	2	1	86,916	1995	Bandit Bomber	4	13	11	0	0	104,275
1982	City Fair	4	23	13	4	1	46,420	1995	Time to Cope	4	18	11	2	0	91,740
1982	Rollar Ring	6	27	13	3	1	26,917	1996	Tragedy	5	24	11	7	2	111,172
1983	Expressive Dock	2	12	11	0	1	231,001	1996	Meine Empress	7	18	11	3	2	42,822
1983	Diamond Road	7	25	11	4	5	66,900	1997	Maybe Jack	4	23	13	1	4	137,220
1983	Navy Days	5	15	11	3	1	21,960	1998	Aunt Ping	4	23	11	6	3	131,993
1984	Paumatuck	4	34	13	7	4	56,568	1999	Ben's Quixote	5	19	10	3	0	88,919
1984	Rapid Robber	5	17	13	3	1	34,210	1999	Raise a Count	4	18	10	2	0	70,546
1985	Billy the Best	6	24	13	6	2	111,884	2000	Bricola	3	14	12	2	0	462,330
1985	Fastway Home	8	30	13	4	4	58,549	2000	Difficult Doll	4	26	12	1	4	83,900
1985	Olga M.	4	28	13	3	2	50,311	2000	Governors Ego	5	21	12	1	3	78,470
1986	Moxeytown	9	29	14	7	4	74,506	2001	La Mistica	4	16	13	3	0	180,176
1987	Chilcoton Blaze	7	15	12	0	1	221,810	2002	La Policlinica	4	15	12	3	0	71,222
1987	Power Rule	4	24	12	3	1	45,795	2003	D' Wildcat Speed	3	12	12	0	0	290,815
1987	Center Stage Anne	4	21	12	3	2	40,100								

Leading North American Stakes Earners in 2003

Horse	Stakes Starts	1st	2nd	3rds	Stakes Earnings
Pleasantly Perfect	4	2	0	1	$2,470,000
Mineshaft	9	7	2	0	2,209,686
Wando	8	5	1	1	*2,017,323
Medaglia d'Oro	5	3	2	0	1,990,000
Funny Cide	8	2	2	2	1,963,200
Empire Maker	6	3	3	0	1,936,200
Peace Rules	7	3	1	1	1,850,000
Congaree	9	5	2	0	1,608,000
Ten Most Wanted	9	3	2	1	1,514,860
Perfect Drift	7	4	0	0	1,464,795
Sightseek	8	4	3	0	1,171,888
Adoration	5	2	1	1	1,160,750
Dynever	7	2	2	1	1,127,500
Sulamani (IRE)	3	2	0	0	1,113,600
Aldebaran	8	5	1	1	1,110,606
Island Fashion	9	4	0	0	1,103,370
Heat Haze (GB)	7	4	1	1	1,101,460
Touch of the Blues (FR)	6	2	1	3	1,082,885
Elloluv	8	2	3	0	978,775
Dimitrova	4	2	1	0	950,000
Johar	4	2	1	1	912,281
Balto Star	13	4	2	1	907,500
Phoenix Reach (IRE)	1	1	0	0	900,000
Wild Spirit (CHI)	4	3	1	0	830,000
Redattore (BRZ)	7	4	0	2	822,147
Perfect Soul (IRE)	7	2	2	1	821,940
Excessivepleasure	9	3	4	0	821,782
Halfbridled	3	3	0	0	820,000
Azeri	5	4	1	0	817,080
Bird Town	7	3	3	0	809,516
Cajun Beat	7	3	1	0	785,600
Action This Day	1	1	0	0	780,000
Six Perfections (FR)	1	1	0	0	780,000
Smok'n Frolic	11	3	3	1	776,856
High Chaparral (IRE)	1	1	0	0	763,200
Best of the Rest	6	3	2	0	753,500
Mobil	9	5	2	1	753,405
Volga (IRE)	6	3	2	0	730,800
Take Charge Lady	7	2	3	0	720,026
Shake You Down	7	4	1	1	716,240
Mr. Jester	4	3	1	0	712,000
Milwaukee Brew	3	1	1	0	710,000
Tates Creek	5	3	1	0	704,067
Candy Ride (ARG)	2	2	0	0	690,000
Got Koko	6	3	1	1	688,000
You	8	2	4	1	677,108
Lady Tak	9	4	3	0	675,350
Buddy Gil	6	3	0	0	668,730
Bien Nicole	9	3	3	0	665,040
Storming Home (GB)	5	3	0	0	650,000
Soaring Free	6	3	1	0	610,100
Spoken Fur	5	2	0	2	590,000
Ashado	5	3	1	1	585,000
Quest	3	1	1	0	560,840
Bluesthestandard	8	2	2	2	558,775
House Party	10	5	1	2	551,354
Islington (IRE)	1	1	0	0	551,200
Honor in War	5	2	1	0	546,086
Candid Glen	7	2	0	0	543,300
Kicken Kris	5	2	2	1	542,000
Megahertz (GB)	7	2	1	3	534,480
Grand Hombre	2	1	1	0	532,360
Kudos	5	1	1	3	530,000
Harmony Lodge	8	5	1	2	516,300
Awesome Humor	5	1	4	0	514,220
Tenpins	5	2	2	0	512,760
Sir Oscar	5	5	0	0	510,000
Be Gentle	6	3	1	0	503,858
Strong Hope	3	2	0	1	500,000
Macaw (IRE)	8	0	4	1	496,500
Too Late Now	5	2	0	1	491,650
Strut the Stage	4	2	1	0	485,085
Sweet Return (GB)	5	2	1	1	480,180
Valid Video	7	4	1	0	474,500
Brass in Pocket	6	5	0	1	473,475
Gold Mover	6	2	2	2	462,480
Soto	2	1	1	0	460,000
Posse	10	4	1	1	459,226
Chapel Royal	5	2	2	1	458,955
Harlan's Holiday	4	1	1	0	457,500
Gimmeawink	14	6	3	0	456,880
Joey Franco	8	4	1	0	450,775
Atlantic Ocean	9	2	3	1	443,430
Irish Warrior	7	1	2	3	441,500
The Tin Man	6	1	2	0	440,840
During	9	3	1	1	440,190
Lead Story	8	3	1	0	439,702
Voodoo Dancer	4	2	0	1	432,364
Bare Necessities	8	4	0	3	431,175
Volponi	7	0	4	2	427,056
Denon	5	1	1	1	425,000
Puzzlement	8	1	0	3	420,050
Bowman's Band	7	2	2	0	416,540
Century City (IRE)	9	2	0	2	409,392
Roscoe Pito	7	5	1	0	409,082
Film Maker	5	2	1	1	405,200
Whitmore's Conn	5	2	0	1	402,496
Cee's Elegance	6	2	1	0	398,600
Freefourinternet	9	1	1	4	390,038
Yell	8	2	1	1	388,127
Forever Grand	10	4	0	3	385,120
Sand Springs	5	2	1	0	383,220
Special Ring	5	1	2	0	383,000
Lunar Sovereign	5	1	0	1	380,000
Randaroo	9	3	4	0	371,500
Private Horde	7	4	2	0	369,390
King Robyn	9	6	1	0	368,590
Peeping Tom	11	1	3	3	365,133
Ebony Breeze	7	4	1	2	362,622
Evening Attire	7	0	2	2	360,560
Stroll	4	4	0	0	360,000
Chatter Chatter	4	2	1	0	358,000
New York Hero	7	1	0	0	355,500
Scrimshaw	8	1	0	2	352,479
Beau's Town	6	4	1	0	351,800
Tour of the Cat	9	3	2	2	351,070
Crowned King	13	3	0	3	351,000
Pie N Burger	6	4	0	0	351,000
Minister Eric	2	0	2	0	350,000
Silver Tree	3	1	0	1	348,320
Senor Swinger	10	2	0	2	347,250
Hollywood Story	4	1	1	1	346,700
Trust N Luck	4	1	1	1	344,684
Raylene	10	6	2	0	339,687
Perfect Moon	6	2	1	3	336,710
Cuvee	5	3	0	1	335,829
Midas Eyes	6	2	2	1	333,788
Winter Garden	6	3	1	2	331,866
My Vintage Port	4	3	0	1	326,811
Aeneas	7	0	3	2	326,700
Fairly Ransom	4	1	2	0	325,860
Bowman Mill	4	1	1	0	323,282
Ghostzapper	2	1	0	0	322,000
Victory U.S.A.	5	1	1	2	320,970
Dancewithavixen	10	7	0	0	318,768
Sir Cherokee	3	1	0	0	312,000
Birdstone	2	1	0	0	312,000
Ninebanks	9	3	2	1	310,400
Champali	9	4	1	3	310,292
Santa Catarina	4	1	1	1	309,080

Horse	Stks Starts	1st	2nd	3rd	Stks Earnings	Horse	Stks Starts	1st	2nd	3rd	Stks Earnings
Najran	7	2	1	1	305,700	Cherokee's Boy	7	3	1	1	228,500
Riskaverse	7	1	1	2	301,524	The Cliff's Edge	4	2	1	0	228,258
Well Fancied	5	3	0	0	300,624	Lacie Girl	11	4	6	0	227,990
Society Selection	2	1	0	0	300,000	Mariensky	6	2	0	0	227,700
Composure	2	2	0	0	300,000	Highway Prospector	10	2	1	4	227,397
Starrer	2	2	0	0	300,000	Chopinina	5	1	1	0	227,070
Wild and Wicked	3	1	0	0	300,000	Designed for Luck	3	2	0	0	225,735
Wake At Noon	9	3	1	1	298,817	Booklet	2	0	1	0	224,000
Inish Glora	4	2	1	0	298,325	Mulligan the Great	5	2	1	2	223,077
Barbeau Ruckus	6	4	1	0	296,145	Ivanavinalot	10	1	2	1	223,000
Adminniestrator	3	1	0	1	292,900	Dr. Brendler	4	1	1	1	222,900
Buy the Sport	3	1	0	1	292,500	Miss Crissy	8	1	3	2	220,687
Fleetstreet Dancer	8	0	3	2	288,000	Snow Dance	8	1	1	2	220,510
Lion Heart	2	2	0	0	285,600	Hold That Tiger	2	0	1	0	220,000
Tiger Hunt	3	1	1	0	285,500	Captain Squire	6	1	2	0	219,625
Katdogawn (GB)	8	3	3	0	285,060	Shalini	7	3	1	0	219,525
Hero's Tribute	5	1	1	0	281,000	Savedbythelight	5	2	0	2	218,520
Seeking the Ring	5	2	1	0	279,665	My Boston Gal	4	1	1	0	216,714
Passing Shot	5	1	0	1	278,577	Continental Red	10	1	3	1	216,705
Private Lap	8	4	1	0	278,000	Sky Mesa	3	0	1	1	216,500
Shoal Water	5	1	1	1	275,280	Mandy's Gold	5	1	0	3	215,500
Ladyecho	11	2	4	3	273,593	Western Pride	6	1	1	0	214,750
Docent	8	5	1	1	272,280	Cyber Secret	5	3	1	0	214,107
Stylish	6	3	0	1	270,955	Mountain General	6	2	3	0	212,580
One for Rose	4	2	1	0	268,797	Better Talk Now	5	2	1	1	212,312
Dublino	5	1	3	0	266,067	Willow Bunch	2	2	0	0	212,205
Requete (GB)	5	1	2	0	260,700	L'Ancresse (IRE)	1	0	1	0	212,000
Supah Blitz	9	1	2	2	260,000	El Dorado Shooter	5	3	2	0	211,950
Don'tsellmeshort	6	3	1	1	259,195	Remind	6	1	4	0	210,620
Tusayan	4	3	0	0	258,870	Traffic Chief	4	2	1	0	208,890
Crafty Shaw	8	2	1	1	257,835	Devil Time	10	5	0	0	208,410
Spice Island	8	2	3	0	257,586	Walzerkoenigin	3	0	1	0	207,500
Foufa's Warrior	10	1	1	3	257,358	America America	8	1	2	2	207,375
Summer Colony	5	1	1	0	256,500	Iron Deputy	3	1	0	1	207,000
Ciento	5	4	1	0	253,314	Singletary	7	2	2	1	205,232
McDynamo	3	3	0	0	252,025	No Comprende	5	1	1	0	205,080
Pass Rush	8	1	2	1	251,265	Grey Comet	5	2	2	1	205,080
Phantom Light	3	2	0	0	251,190	Eagle Lake	7	3	2	0	204,454
Passinetti	2	1	0	0	249,000	Taiaslew	7	4	2	0	204,325
Eurosilver	1	1	0	0	248,000	Hard Buck (BRZ)	3	3	0	0	203,636
Strait From Texas	5	2	1	0	247,072	Avanzado (ARG)	7	2	1	0	202,645
Rouvres (FR)	6	0	3	1	246,420	Shemoveslikeaghost	5	2	2	0	202,310
Mystery Giver	8	2	1	1	246,060	Icantgoforthat	11	2	1	3	202,144
Shine Again	6	1	5	0	243,220	Cappuchino	10	2	0	3	201,712
Excess Summer	6	4	0	0	242,541	Madame Pietra	3	2	0	0	201,580
Wiggins	5	4	0	0	241,044	Fuse It	10	3	1	2	200,250
Olmodavor	3	1	2	0	240,000	Fire Slam	1	0	1	0	200,000
Alysweep	7	2	2	0	237,880	Musical Chimes	3	0	2	0	200,000
Quest Star	8	1	3	0	237,860	Eugene's Third Son	2	0	2	0	200,000
My Cousin Matt	5	1	1	1	237,500	Champion Lodge (IRE)	3	1	0	1	199,638
Continuously	5	1	1	1	235,000	Saarland	6	0	2	1	199,440
Limehouse	5	2	0	2	234,085	Bachelor Blues	4	1	1	0	198,850
Trademark (SAF)	4	2	1	0	233,240						
Falbrav (IRE)	1	0	0	1	233,200						
Devious Boy (GB)	5	2	2	0	230,580						
Tap the Admiral	5	1	0	1	230,246						
Midway Road	3	0	1	1	230,000						
Buffythecenterfold	7	2	2	2	228,815						

* Includes $500,000 bonus

Snapshot Facts: Two horses, Mineshaft and Dancewithavixen, tied with seven North American stakes victories in 2003

Top Money–Winning Turf Runners in North America in 2003

Horse	Sex	Age	St	1st	2d	3d	Earnings
Sulamani (IRE)	4	C	3	2	0	0	$1,113,600
Heat Haze (GB)	4	F	7	4	1	1	1,101,460
Touch of the Blues (FR)	6	H	6	2	1	3	1,082,885
Dimitrova	3	F	4	2	1	0	950,000
Johar	4	C	4	2	1	1	912,281
Phoenix Reach (IRE)	3	C	1	1	0	0	900,000
Wando	3	C	2	1	0	0	*860,000
Perfect Soul (IRE)	5	H	8	3	2	1	856,195
Redattore (BRZ)	8	H	7	5	0	1	846,147
Six Perfections (FR)	3	F	1	1	0	0	780,000
Balto Star	5	G	8	3	0	1	772,500
High Chaparral (IRE)	4	C	1	1	0	0	763,200
Volga (IRE)	5	M	6	3	2	0	730,800
Tates Creek	5	M	5	3	1	0	704,067
Storming Home (GB)	5	H	5	3	0	0	650,000
Honor in War	4	C	9	4	1	1	616,723
Soaring Free	4	G	6	3	1	0	610,100
Kicken Kris	3	C	8	4	3	1	593,200
Islington (IRE)	4	F	1	1	0	0	551,200
Bien Nicole	5	M	7	2	3	0	545,040
Candid Glen	6	G	8	2	0	0	543,300
Megahertz (GB)	4	F	7	2	1	3	534,480
Sweet Return (GB)	3	C	9	2	2	2	500,360
Irish Warrior	5	H	10	2	3	4	500,300
Macaw (IRE)	4	G	9	0	4	1	496,500
Strut the Stage	5	H	4	2	1	0	485,085
Film Maker	3	F	9	4	2	2	457,220
Sand Springs	3	F	7	4	1	0	451,390
The Tin Man	5	G	6	1	2	0	440,840
Voodoo Dancer	5	M	4	2	0	1	432,364
Denon	5	H	5	1	1	1	425,000
Lunar Sovereign	4	C	6	2	0	1	410,000
Century City (IRE)	4	C	8	2	0	2	405,000
Whitmore's Conn	5	H	6	2	0	1	404,236
Stroll	3	C	6	5	1	0	398,800
Silver Tree	3	C	5	3	0	1	390,320
Freefourinternet	5	H	9	1	1	4	383,090
Special Ring	6	G	5	1	2	0	383,000
Inish Glora	5	M	5	3	1	0	351,725
Riskaverse	4	F	8	2	1	2	336,324
Bowman Mill	5	H	5	1	2	0	327,682
Fairly Ransom	3	C	4	1	2	0	325,860
Katdogawn (GB)	3	F	10	4	3	1	320,580
Ninebanks	5	G	9	3	2	1	310,400
King Robyn	3	G	6	5	1	0	308,870
Quest Star	4	C	9	3	3	0	298,380
Spice Island	4	F	9	4	3	1	294,940
Senor Swinger	3	C	7	2	0	2	294,750
Requete (GB)	4	C	6	2	2	0	294,300
Continuously	4	C	8	3	1	1	293,200
Adminniestrator	6	G	3	1	0	1	292,900
Passinetti	7	G	4	2	0	1	289,320
Strait From Texas	4	F	9	3	3	0	275,936
Rouvres (FR)	4	C	7	1	3	1	274,020
Stylish	5	M	6	3	0	1	270,955
Designed for Luck	6	G	4	3	0	0	267,735
Dublino	4	F	5	1	3	0	266,067
Tap the Admiral	5	H	6	2	0	1	265,046
Tusayan	3	C	6	3	0	0	260,838
Dr. Brendler	5	H	8	2	1	1	259,935
Dessert	3	F	6	3	1	1	259,560
Mystery Giver	5	G	10	2	2	1	256,260
Mariensky	4	F	7	3	0	0	255,300
Remind	3	C	8	3	4	0	251,420
Better Talk Now	4	G	7	3	1	2	240,152
Champion Lodge (IRE)	6	G	4	2	0	1	238,638
Trademark (SAF)	7	G	4	2	1	0	233,240
Falbrav (IRE)	5	H	1	0	0	1	233,200
French Charmer	4	G	7	5	0	0	232,800
Crazy Ensign (ARG)	7	M	7	3	1	2	231,405
Devious Boy (GB)	3	G	4	2	2	0	230,580
Shalini	4	F	8	3	1	1	230,159
Mister Acpen (CHI)	5	H	7	2	1	1	228,200
Chopinina	5	M	5	1	1	0	227,070
Bachelor Blues	2	C	4	2	1	0	222,100
Quick Tip	5	M	11	2	3	1	221,582
Patrol	4	C	5	2	0	1	220,930
Snow Dance	5	M	8	1	1	2	220,510
Dyna Da Wyna	3	F	8	5	0	0	212,267
L'Ancresse (IRE)	3	F	1	0	1	0	212,000
Alpha Saphire	3	F	7	2	1	1	211,470
False Promises	3	G	9	3	3	1	210,320
Lismore Knight	3	C	6	2	0	2	208,800
Puffer	4	G	10	3	5	2	207,654
Walzerkoenigin	4	F	3	0	1	0	207,500
Mobil	3	C	3	2	0	1	207,478
Continental Red	7	G	9	1	3	1	206,705
Indy Five Hundred	3	F	5	2	1	0	206,400
Singletary	3	C	6	2	2	1	205,232
Hard Buck (BRZ)	4	C	3	3	0	0	203,636
Proud Man	5	H	7	2	3	1	203,142
Political Attack	4	G	7	3	0	1	202,688
Aud	3	F	8	3	2	0	201,675
Music's Storm	4	C	8	2	3	1	200,084
Musical Chimes	3	F	3	0	2	0	200,000
Madeira Mist (IRE)	4	F	7	2	3	1	198,950
Stay Forever	6	M	3	1	0	0	198,500
Roberta's Mango	4	F	9	4	1	0	198,053
Delta Princess	4	F	8	4	0	0	196,110
Belleski	4	F	7	4	1	1	195,059
Deeliteful Irving	5	H	3	1	1	0	195,000
Ballingarry (IRE)	4	C	5	1	0	1	194,700
Blind Ambition	5	M	5	3	1	0	193,380
Something Ventured	4	F	11	3	3	3	193,171
Noches De Rosa (CHI)	5	M	5	2	1	1	192,860
Magic Mission (GB)	5	M	8	1	2	1	190,980
Just Wonder (GB)	3	C	5	3	0	0	190,330
Man From Wicklow	6	G	3	1	2	0	190,000
Garden in the Rain (FR)	6	M	10	2	4	1	189,830
Dress To Thrill (IRE)	4	F	5	1	0	0	187,780
Slew Valley	6	H	8	0	1	3	186,880
Colorful Judgement	3	G	6	2	0	4	184,576
Valentine Dancer	3	F	7	3	1	2	183,966
Lady Bi Bi	4	F	9	4	1	1	183,720
Denied	5	G	6	4	1	1	183,200
Spring Star (FR)	4	F	5	2	0	3	182,313
Warleigh	5	H	6	4	1	0	181,760

Horse	Sex	Age	St	1st	2d	3d	Earnings
Quero Quero	3	F	5	2	2	0	181,170
Foufa's Warrior	3	G	5	1	0	1	180,758
Janeian (NZ)	5	M	12	4	3	3	180,510
Personal Legend	3	F	7	2	2	1	178,690
Kim Loves Bucky	6	G	8	2	0	0	177,940
Della Francesca	4	C	8	2	1	0	177,360
Expresso Bay	6	G	10	6	2	0	176,420
Quantum Merit	4	G	8	3	1	2	176,180
Wonder Again	4	F	6	1	1	1	176,075
Eagle Lake	5	M	6	3	1	0	175,480
Skeet	3	C	7	5	1	1	173,815
Lindsay Jean	5	M	6	3	1	1	173,125
Fencelineneighbor	3	F	8	3	1	1	172,892
Pertuisane (GB)	4	F	4	2	1	1	172,800
Miss Crissy	3	F	5	1	2	2	172,355
Runaway Dancer	4	G	7	3	0	0	172,170
Love Sting	3	F	9	4	3	0	171,590
Special Matter	5	G	9	1	2	1	169,660
Atlantic Ocean	3	F	4	0	2	1	169,390
Royal Spy	5	H	3	2	0	0	169,000
Moonshine Hall	3	C	9	3	2	1	168,001
Sea to See	5	G	11	1	2	3	166,325
Decarchy	6	H	7	0	2	1	166,209
Rock Slide	5	H	5	2	1	0	165,910
Moscow Burning	3	F	6	4	1	0	165,840
Shoal Water	3	G	3	1	1	0	165,280
Brian Boru (GB)	3	C	1	0	0	1	165,000
Rochester	7	G	8	1	2	1	164,757
Joe's Son Joey	5	H	6	3	1	1	163,186
Sharbayan (IRE)	5	G	5	4	0	0	162,601
Thunder Bullet	4	G	8	4	1	0	162,264
Heyahohowdy	4	F	5	2	1	0	161,995
Lennyfromalibu	4	G	5	2	0	1	161,766
Ocean Drive	3	F	6	2	1	0	159,356
Formal Miss	3	F	10	2	3	4	158,190
Evolving Tactics (IRE)	3	C	2	1	0	0	158,000
Gal O Gal	3	F	11	3	0	3	156,957
Dancal (IRE)	5	M	4	2	1	0	154,800
Timo	2	C	5	3	2	0	153,515
Lojo	4	F	9	3	3	1	152,810
Angel On the Wing	4	G	8	3	3	1	152,719
Love n' Kiss S.	5	M	8	3	2	0	152,558
Master William	2	C	2	1	0	0	151,500
All the Boys	6	G	4	2	2	0	151,400
San Dare	5	M	9	2	0	2	150,939
Just Too Too	3	F	3	3	0	0	150,840
Kiss the Devil	5	M	3	1	2	0	150,626
Paolini (GER)	6	H	1	0	1	0	150,000
Tigertail (FR)	4	F	1	0	1	0	150,000
Kaieteur	4	C	1	0	1	0	150,000
Crowned King	3	C	3	2	0	0	150,000
Ecstatic	4	C	13	2	5	3	148,400
Storybook Kid	5	G	11	4	1	3	148,300
Sarafan	6	G	5	2	1	1	145,299
Lilac Queen (GER)	5	M	5	3	0	0	144,858
Classic Stamp	3	F	2	2	0	0	142,740
Owsley	5	M	5	1	1	0	141,744
Sweet Stepper	4	C	11	4	2	1	140,760
Testify	6	G	10	2	2	2	139,975
Nicole's Dream	3	F	9	7	0	0	136,500
Last Tango (IRE)	5	M	10	4	1	3	136,360
Move Those Chains	4	C	8	4	1	2	136,020
Package Store	5	H	4	2	0	2	135,984
Puerto Banus	4	C	5	2	1	0	135,400
F J's Pace	8	G	9	4	1	0	133,740
Islander	8	H	9	4	2	1	133,340
Pink Champagne	2	F	2	2	0	0	132,000
Del Mar Show	6	H	7	1	1	1	131,698
Lost Appeal	5	M	8	3	3	1	131,485
Southern Oasis	5	M	6	3	1	0	131,400
Cruising Executive	3	F	6	2	0	0	131,037
My Sweet Tooch	3	F	5	2	0	2	130,525
Solitary Dancer	7	H	8	1	4	1	130,441
Trial by Jury	4	C	7	3	2	1	130,160
Sir Blitz	4	G	8	2	3	1	130,122
Commendation	2	C	4	3	0	0	130,010
Flirt With Fortune	3	C	9	2	4	2	129,164
No Jacket Required	6	G	11	4	2	0	128,654
Dedication (FR)	4	F	5	1	1	1	128,450
Makeup Artist	3	F	3	2	1	0	128,100
Hazen	5	M	13	5	2	1	127,850
Dressed for Action	3	F	3	1	1	0	127,700
Rowans Park	3	C	7	2	1	2	126,535
Oneexcessivenite	3	F	11	3	2	0	126,277
Forty Milito (ARG)	5	H	9	4	1	0	125,640
Love the Game	5	H	8	3	2	1	125,565
Byzantine	7	M	5	1	0	3	125,555
Tam's Terms	5	G	6	4	0	0	125,520
Al's Dearly Bred	6	G	7	3	2	0	125,300
Delmonico Cat	4	F	6	3	2	0	124,934
Carib Lady (IRE)	4	F	8	2	1	0	124,703
Tangier Sound	4	F	7	4	2	0	124,520
Gretchen's Star	8	G	7	2	2	0	124,275
Petrina Above	8	M	7	3	3	0	124,247
A Smile Per Mile	5	M	11	5	2	2	124,020
Betty's Wish	3	F	3	2	0	1	123,720
Fun House	4	F	8	2	3	2	123,340
Stanley Park	3	C	8	3	0	1	123,316
Clubay	5	M	6	2	2	1	122,775
Mr. Epperson	8	G	6	2	2	1	122,659
Hoh Buzzard (IRE)	3	F	3	1	0	0	122,403
Impolite	3	F	10	4	0	1	121,970
Repository	5	M	8	2	1	0	121,958
Californian (GB)	3	C	6	1	1	0	121,944
Five Schillings	7	R	11	5	1	1	121,240
War Zone	4	C	5	2	0	0	120,436
Magic Mecke	3	C	8	3	3	0	120,090
Nothing to Lose	3	C	2	2	0	0	120,000

The above list contains only the performance records of horses that raced on the grass in North America in 2003. It does not include earnings outside North America.

Leading Money–Winning Horses by Division in 2003

2-Year-Olds

Horse	Sex	St	1st	2d	3d	Earnings
Halfbridled	F	4	4	0	0	$849,400
Action This Day	C	3	2	1	0	817,200
Mr. Jester	C	6	4	2	0	730,800
Ashado	F	6	4	1	1	610,800
Sir Oscar	C	6	6	0	0	528,800
Be Gentle	F	7	4	1	0	523,078
Chapel Royal	C	6	3	2	1	484,755
Minister Eric	C	5	1	2	1	387,920
Chatter Chatter	F	7	3	2	1	383,470
Cuvee	C	6	4	0	1	360,704
Hollywood Story	F	5	1	2	1	356,500
Perfect Moon	G	10	3	1	3	353,870
My Vintage Port	F	6	3	2	0	351,051
Victory U. S. A.	F	6	2	1	2	350,370
Birdstone	C	3	2	0	0	339,000
Society Selection	F	3	2	0	0	327,000
Tiger Hunt	C	4	2	1	0	312,820
Lion Heart	C	3	3	0	0	310,800
America America	F	17	3	6	3	298,640
Don'tsellmeshort	C	8	4	2	1	294,395
Eurosilver	C	3	2	1	0	284,000
Bachelor Blues	C	8	2	3	0	265,406
Limehouse	C	6	3	0	2	260,435
Fire Slam	C	3	2	1	0	259,430
The Cliff's Edge	C	5	3	1	0	255,258
Read the Footnotes	C	5	4	0	0	240,660
Silver Bird	F	5	3	1	0	235,445
Twisted Wit	G	5	3	0	0	234,855
Smoocher	C	4	2	1	0	231,653
A Bit O'Gold	G	4	3	0	0	230,029
Winter Whiskey	G	6	3	0	2	225,093
Dream About	F	5	2	1	0	224,430
Galloping Gal	F	5	3	1	0	204,884
Feline Story	F	6	3	1	0	201,780
There Goes Rocket	C	6	4	1	1	199,500
Ruler's Court	C	4	2	0	1	197,700
Siphonizer	C	5	2	0	0	197,400
Blonde Executive	F	7	3	1	1	196,328
House of Fortune	F	5	3	0	1	195,944
Hay Lauren	F	8	4	2	0	190,290
Cactus Ridge	C	4	4	0	0	187,850
Wacky Patty	F	7	4	0	0	184,569
Salty Romance	F	3	2	0	1	178,440
From Away	F	4	2	1	0	177,860
West Virginia	C	5	3	0	1	172,405
Tym Beau	C	6	3	1	0	172,400
Richetta	F	6	4	0	1	168,110
Maple Syrple	F	3	2	1	0	166,260
Rocky Gulch	G	5	4	1	0	163,909
Copper Trail	G	4	2	1	1	162,170

2-Year-Old Fillies

Horse	St	1st	2d	3d	Earnings
Halfbridled	4	4	0	0	$849,400
Ashado	6	4	1	1	610,800
Be Gentle	7	4	1	0	523,078
Chatter Chatter	7	3	2	1	383,470
Hollywood Story	5	1	2	1	356,500
My Vintage Port	6	3	2	0	351,051
Victory U. S. A.	6	2	1	2	350,370
Society Selection	3	2	0	0	327,000
America America	17	3	6	3	298,640
Silver Bird	5	3	1	0	235,445
Dream About	5	2	1	0	224,430
Galloping Gal	5	3	1	0	204,884
Feline Story	6	3	1	0	201,780
Blonde Executive	7	3	1	1	196,328
House of Fortune	5	3	0	1	195,944
Hay Lauren	8	4	2	0	190,290
Wacky Patty	7	4	0	0	184,569
Salty Romance	3	2	0	1	178,440
From Away	4	2	1	0	177,860
Richetta	6	4	0	1	168,110
Maple Syrple	3	2	1	0	166,260
So Sweet a Cat	6	2	3	1	158,278
Ontheqt	4	2	2	0	156,940
Dirty Diana	5	2	2	0	153,397
Capeside Lady	4	3	0	0	149,940
Nashinda	2	2	0	0	148,635
Marylebone	3	2	0	0	147,000
La Grande Mamma	4	2	1	0	143,975
La Reina	4	2	2	0	142,420
Mother's Sacrifice	2	2	0	0	141,503

3-Year-Olds

Horse	Sex	St	1st	2d	3d	Earnings
Wando *	C	8	5	1	1	$2,017,323
Funny Cide	G	8	2	2	2	1,963,200
Empire Maker	C	6	3	3	0	1,936,200
Peace Rules	C	7	3	1	1	1,850,000
Ten Most Wanted	C	10	4	2	1	1,544,860
Six Perfections (FR)	F	6	3	3	0	1,256,076
Dynever	C	9	3	3	1	1,154,020
Island Fashion	F	10	4	1	0	1,112,970
Dimitrova	F	7	4	1	1	1,042,970
Phoenix Reach (IRE)	C	4	3	0	1	1,035,526
Elloluv	F	8	2	3	0	978,775
Excessivepleasure	G	9	3	4	0	821,782
Cajun Beat	G	9	4	2	0	820,000
Bird Town	F	8	3	4	0	815,976
Mobil	C	9	5	2	1	753,405
Yesterday (IRE)	F	7	1	3	1	689,791
Lady Tak	F	9	4	3	0	675,350
Spoken Fur	F	10	5	1	3	670,630
Buddy Gil	G	6	3	0	0	668,730
Brian Boru (GB)	C	6	1	1	2	664,844
Grand Hombre	G	5	4	1	0	598,360
Kicken Kris	C	9	4	3	1	593,540
Strong Hope	C	7	5	0	1	582,360
Too Late Now	F	7	4	0	1	566,110
House Party	F	10	5	1	2	551,354
Awesome Humor	F	7	2	4	0	539,835
Oasis Dream (GB)	C	5	2	1	1	524,836
During	C	13	5	2	1	514,750
Musical Chimes	F	8	2	2	1	513,103
Casual Look	F	7	1	0	2	505,104
Sweet Return (GB)	C	9	2	2	2	500,360
Posse	C	11	5	1	1	478,426
Valid Video	G	7	4	1	0	474,500
Soto	C	3	2	1	0	473,200
Winter Garden	F	9	6	1	2	470,826
New York Hero	C	14	4	3	0	465,860
Film Maker	F	9	4	2	2	457,220
Gimmeawink	F	14	6	3	0	456,880
Sand Springs	F	7	4	1	0	451,390
Atlantic Ocean	F	9	2	3	1	443,430
King Robyn	G	11	8	1	0	436,990
Roscoe Pito	G	9	6	1	2	424,566
Yell	F	9	3	1	1	408,527
Mezzo Soprano	F	8	3	1	2	401,920
Randaroo	F	10	4	4	0	401,500
Stroll	C	6	5	1	0	398,800
Silver Tree	C	6	3	0	1	390,660
Refuse To Bend (IRE)	C	6	3	0	0	383,998
Inamorato	C	7	2	0	4	382,078
L'Ancresse (IRE)	F	9	1	3	0	380,738

* Includes $500,000 bonus

3-Year-Old Fillies

Horse	St	1st	2d	3d	Earnings
Six Perfections (FR)	6	3	3	0	$1,256,076
Island Fashion	10	4	1	0	1,112,970
Dimitrova	7	4	1	1	1,042,970
Elloluv	8	2	3	0	978,775
Bird Town	8	3	4	0	815,976
Yesterday (IRE)	7	1	3	1	689,791
Lady Tak	9	4	3	0	675,350
Spoken Fur	10	5	1	3	670,630
Too Late Now	7	4	0	1	566,110
House Party	10	5	1	2	551,354
Awesome Humor	7	2	4	0	539,835
Musical Chimes	8	2	2	1	513,103
Casual Look	7	1	0	2	505,104
Winter Garden	9	6	1	2	470,826
Film Maker	9	4	2	2	457,220
Sand Springs	7	4	1	0	451,390
Atlantic Ocean	9	2	3	1	443,430
Yell	9	3	1	1	408,527
Mezzo Soprano	8	3	1	2	401,920
Randaroo	10	4	4	0	401,500
L'Ancresse (IRE)	9	1	3	0	380,738
Ebony Breeze	8	4	1	2	365,887
Santa Catarina	5	2	1	1	342,680
Raylene	10	6	2	0	339,687
Dancewithavixen	11	8	2	0	335,921
Buy the Sport	7	2	0	1	334,521
Katdogawn (GB)	10	4	3	1	320,580
Maiden Tower (GB)	6	3	2	0	316,824
Seeking the Ring	7	3	2	0	314,515
Valentine Dancer	14	5	3	2	312,846

4-Year-Olds

Horse	Sex	Starts	1st	2d	3d	Earnings
Moon Ballad (IRE)	C	6	2	0	0	$3,719,798
Sulamani (IRE)	C	6	3	1	0	2,603,842
Mineshaft	C	9	7	2	0	2,209,686
Medaglia d'Oro	C	5	3	2	0	1,990,000
High Chaparral (IRE)	C	4	3	0	1	1,717,124
Harlan's Holiday	C	6	2	2	0	1,685,100
Perfect Drift	G	8	5	0	0	1,505,388
State City	C	8	2	0	1	1,292,469
Sightseek	F	8	4	3	0	1,171,888
Adoration	F	5	2	1	1	1,160,750
Heat Haze (GB)	F	7	4	1	1	1,101,460
Islington (IRE)	F	6	2	0	2	955,142
Johar	C	5	2	1	1	912,281
Wild Spirit (CHI)	F	4	3	1	0	830,000
Smok'n Frolic	F	11	3	3	1	776,856
Candy Ride (ARG)	C	3	3	0	0	724,800
Take Charge Lady	F	7	2	3	0	720,026
Soaring Free	G	8	5	1	0	699,200
Got Koko	F	6	3	1	1	688,000
You	F	8	2	4	1	677,108
Quest	C	11	2	4	3	637,860
Honor in War	C	9	4	1	1	616,723
Tigertail (FR)	F	8	0	2	1	535,164
Megahertz (GB)	F	7	2	1	3	534,480
Macaw (IRE)	G	9	0	4	1	496,500
One for Rose	F	10	6	2	0	476,377
Brass in Pocket	F	7	5	0	1	475,830
Puzzlement	C	11	2	2	3	470,450
Joey Franco	C	10	4	1	0	452,361
Lead Story	F	11	3	1	1	449,062
Bare Necessities	F	8	4	0	3	431,175
Captain Squire	G	7	1	2	1	419,625
Private Horde	C	9	6	2	0	411,582
Lunar Sovereign	C	7	2	0	1	410,000
Century City (IRE)	C	9	2	0	2	409,392
Forever Grand	G	10	4	0	3	385,120
Passing Shot	F	10	3	2	2	362,637

Horse	Age	Sex	Starts	1st	2d	3d	Won
Spice Island	F	13	6	3	1		361,286
Private Lap	C	12	6	1	0		346,640
Riskaverse	F	8	2	1	2		336,324
Aeneas	C	9	0	4	2		336,300
Mulligan the Great	G	8	4	1	3		322,396
Winning Chance	F	8	3	4	0		317,435
Walzerkoenigin	F	5	1	1	1		312,320
Barbeau Ruckus	G	7	4	2	0		310,585
Najran	C	7	2	1	1		305,700
Bright Sky (IRE)	F	6	1	1	2		303,832
Phantom Light	C	6	3	0	0		299,610
Quest Star	C	10	3	3	0		298,380
My Cousin Matt	G	6	1	1	1		297,500

5-Year-Olds and Up

Horse	Age	Sex	St	1st	2d	3d	Earnings
Falbrav (IRE)	5	H	10	5	1	2	$3,013,845
Pleasantly Perfect	5	H	4	2	0	1	2,470,000
Congaree	5	H	9	5	2	0	1,608,000
Fleetstreet Dancer	5	G	10	1	4	2	1,519,026
Ipi Tombe (ZIM)	5	M	4	4	0	0	1,416,273
Aldebaran	5	H	8	5	1	1	1,110,606
Touch of the Blues (FR)	6	H	6	2	1	3	1,082,885
Balto Star	5	G	13	4	2	1	907,500
Redattore (BRZ)	8	H	8	5	0	2	864,147
Perfect Soul (IRE)	5	H	8	3	2	1	856,195
Shake You Down	5	G	13	7	2	2	829,160
Azeri	5	M	5	4	1	0	817,080
Best of the Rest	8	H	6	3	2	0	753,500
Milwaukee Brew	6	H	4	2	1	0	743,000
Paolini (GER)	6	H	4	0	2	1	742,300
Volga (IRE)	5	M	6	3	2	0	730,800
Tates Creek	5	M	5	3	1	0	704,067
Bien Nicole	5	M	10	4	3	0	690,540
Polish Summer (GB)	6	H	7	1	3	0	661,904
Storming Home (GB)	5	H	5	3	0	0	650,000
Bluesthestandard	6	G	10	4	2	2	631,975
Avanzado (ARG)	6	H	8	2	2	0	602,645
Candid Glen	6	G	8	2	0	0	543,300
Kudos	6	G	5	1	1	3	530,000
Harmony Lodge	5	M	8	5	1	2	516,300
Tenpins	5	H	5	2	2	0	512,760
Irish Warrior	5	H	10	2	3	4	500,300
Strut the Stage	5	H	4	2	1	0	485,085
Gold Mover	5	M	6	2	2	2	462,480
The Tin Man	5	G	6	1	2	0	440,840
Volponi	5	H	8	0	5	2	438,256
Voodoo Dancer	5	M	4	2	0	1	432,364
Bowman's Band	5	H	9	2	3	1	432,240
Evening Attire	5	G	9	2	2	2	430,160
Peeping Tom	6	G	14	3	4	3	428,733
Denon	5	H	7	1	1	1	425,000
Freefourinternet	5	H	11	2	1	5	418,598
Whitmore's Conn	5	H	6	2	0	1	404,236
Cee's Elegance	6	M	6	2	1	0	398,600
Special Ring	6	G	5	1	2	0	383,000
Pie N Burger	5	G	7	5	0	0	373,800
Grey Memo	6	H	8	0	1	3	373,400
Inish Glora	5	M	6	3	1	1	359,667
Beau's Town	5	G	6	4	1	0	351,800
Crafty Shaw	5	H	14	4	3	2	351,185
Tour of the Cat	5	G	9	3	2	2	351,070
Well Fancied	5	G	8	4	1	1	350,164
Bowman Mill	5	H	5	1	2	0	327,682
State Shinto	7	H	8	1	1	0	315,701
Ninebanks	5	G	9	3	2	1	310,400

Annual Leaders by Age
2-Year-Olds

Year	Horse	Earnings	Year	Horse	Earnings	Year	Horse	Earnings
1876	Leonard	$8,450	1919	Man o' War	83,325	1962	Never Bend	402,969
1877	Duke of Magenta	9,987	1920	Tryster	49,925	1963	Castle Forbes	237,690
1878	Harold	9,250	1921	Morvich	115,234	1964	Sadair	498,217
1879	Sensation	19,670	1922	Sally's Alley	94,847	1965	Buckpasser	568,096
1880	Spinaway	16,100	1923	St. James	89,385	1966	Successor	441,404
1881	Onondaga	17,690	1924	Master Charlie	95,525	1967	Vitriolic	429,896
1882	George Kinney	17,370	1925	Pompey	121,630	1968	Top Knight	325,954
1883	General Harding	16,635	1926	Fair Star	88,960	1969	Silent Screen	397,966
1884	Wanda	35,475	1927	Anita Peabody	111,905	1970	Limit to Reason	319,055
1885	Ban Fox	22,840	1928	High Strung	153,590	1971	Riva Ridge	503,263
1886	Tremont	39,135	1929	Whichone	136,455	1972	Secretariat	456,404
1887	Emperor of Norfolk	37,020	1930	Equipoise	156,835	1973	Protagonist	200,527
1888	Proctor Knott	69,780	1931	Top Flight	219,000	1974	L'Enjoleur	285,865
1889	Chaos	63,550	1932	Ladysman	111,435	1975	Honest Pleasure	370,227
1890	Potomac	78,460	1933	Singing Wood	88,050	1976	Royal Ski	309,704
1891	His Highness	106,900	1934	Chance Sun	83,985	1977	Affirmed	343,477
1892	Morello	55,260	1935	Tintagel	75,100	1978	Spectacular Bid	384.484
1893	Domino	170,890	1936	Pompoon	82,260	1979	Smart Angle	359,717
1894	The Butterflies	50,410	1937	Menow	65,825	1980	Lord Avie	439,240
1895	Requital	58,615	1938	El Chico	84,100	1981	Stalwart	528,595
1896	Ogden	58,855	1939	Bimelech	135,090	1982	Roving Boy	800,425
1897	L'Alouette	42,290	1940	Whirlaway	77,275	1983	Fali Time	748,829
1898	Jean Beraud	65,357	1941	Alsab	110,600	1984	Chief's Crown	920,890
1899	Mesmerist	49,152	1942	Occupation	192,355	1985	Snow Chief	935,740
1900	Commando	40,862	1943	Occupy	112,949	1986	Brave Raj	933,650
1901	Blue Girl	64,105	1944	Pavot	179,040	1987	Tejano	1,177,189
1902	Savable	46,100	1945	Star Pilot	165,385	1988	Open Mind	724,064
1903	Hamburg Belle	47,125	1946	Education	164,473	1989	Grand Canyon	1,019,540
1904	Artful	57,805	1947	Bewitch	213,675	1990	Best Pal	1,026,195
1905	Burgomaster	39,500	1948	Blue Peter	189,185	1991	Pleasant Stage	687,240
1906	Electioneer	53,701	1949	Bed o' Roses	199,200	1992	Mountain Cat	1,460,627
1907	Colin	131,007	1950	Battlefield	198,677	1993	Brocco	653,550
1908	Sir Martin	78,590	1951	Tom Fool	155,960	1994	Timber Country	928,590
1909	Sweep	41,323	1952	Native Dancer	230,495	1995	Golden Attraction	675,587
1910	Novelty	72,630	1953	Hasty Road	277,132	1996	Boston Harbor	1,928,605
1911	Worth	72,630	1954	Summer Tan	230,421	1997	Favorite Trick	1,231,998
1912	Helios	12,524	1955	Nail	239,930	1998	Silverbulletday	1,114,110
1913	Old Rosebud	19,057	1956	Greek Game	214,805	1999	Chilukki	762,723
1914	Regret	17,390	1957	Jewel's Reward	349,642	2000	Macho Uno	768,803
1915	Dominant	18,495	1958	First Landing	396,460	2001	Johannesburg	1,002,893
1916	Campfire	49,735	1959	Warfare	394,610	2002	Storm Flag Flying	967,000
1917	Sun Briar	59,505	1960	Hail to Reason	428,434	2003	Halfbridled	849,400
1918	Eternal	56,137	1961	Cicada	384,676			

2-Year-Old Fillies

Year	Horse	Earnings	Year	Horse	Earnings	Year	Horse	Earnings
1901	Blue Girl	$64,105	1917	Rosie o' Grady	9,800	1933	Mata Hari	55,364
1902	Eugenia Burch	23,330	1918	Elfin Queen	15,936	1934	Nellie Flag	57,240
1903	Hamburg Belle	47,125	1919	Miss Jemima	20,055	1935	Forever Yours	34,165
1904	Artful	57,805	1920	Step Lightly	40,471	1936	Apogee	35,940
1905	Perverse	23,990	1921	Startle	47,970	1937	Jacola	31,715
1906	Court Dress	31,094	1922	Sally's Alley	94,847	1938	Dinner Date	33,950
1907	Stamina	29,265	1923	Anna Marrone II	21,061	1939	Now What	36,245
1908	Maskette	53,140	1924	Mother Goose	72,775	1940	Valdina Myth	41,625
1909	Ocean Bound	12,545	1925	Taps	20,250	1941	Petrify	41,085
1910	Bashti	27,235	1926	Fair Star	88,960	1942	Askmenow	39,510
1911	Moisant	8,010	1927	Anita Peabody	111,905	1943	Bee Mac	44,900
1912	Gowell	7,812	1928	Current	50,501	1944	Busher	60,300
1913	Southern Maid	8,373	1929	Khara	34,017	1945	Beaugay	105,910
1914	Regret	17,390	1930	Baba Kenny	28,750	1946	First Flight	134,965
1915	Pleione	5,915	1931	Top Flight	219,000	1947	Bewitch	213,675
1916	America	7,064	1932	Swivel	71,755	1948	Alsab's Day	66,970

Year	Horse	Earnings	Year	Horse	Earnings	Year	Horse	Earnings
1949	Bed o' Roses	199,200	1968	Gallant Bloom	231,400	1987	Epitome	534,805
1950	Aunt Jinny	78,370	1969	Tudor Queen	150,004	1988	Open Mind	724,064
1951	Rose Jet	132,285	1970	Forward Gal	268,194	1989	Go for Wand	548,390
1952	Fulvous	111,375	1971	Numbered Account	446,594	1990	Meadow Star	992,250
1953	Queen Hopeful	169,534	1972	La Prevoyante	417,109	1991	Pleasant Stage	687,240
1954	High Voltage	167,825	1973	Talking Picture	158,939	1992	Eliza	808,000
1955	Nasrina	152,625	1974	Hot n Nasty	172,562	1993	Phone Chatter	753,500
1956	Leallah	129,240	1975	Optimistic Gal	356,477	1994	Flanders	805,000
1957	Idun	220,995	1976	Sensational	218,710	1995	Golden Attraction	675,587
1958	Quill	144,692	1977	L'Alezane	254,390	1996	Storm Song	898,205
1959	My Dear Girl	185,622	1978	Terlingua	271,596	1997	Countess Diana	1,019,785
1960	Bowl of Flowers	198,706	1979	Smart Angle	359,717	1998	Silverbulletday	1,114,110
1961	Cicada	384,676	1980	Heavenly Cause	269,819	1999	Chilukki	762,723
1962	Affectionately	216,357	1981	Skillful Joy	411,312	2000	Caressing	690,642
1963	Castle Forbes	237,690	1982	Fabulous Notion	378,368	2001	Tempera	670,240
1964	Queen Empress	319,262	1983	Althea	582,630	2002	Storm Flag Flying	967,000
1965	Moccasin	319,731	1984	Outstandingly	867,872	2003	Halfbridled	849,400
1966	Mira Femme	229,525	1985	Family Style	805,809			
1967	Queen of the Stage	289,275	1986	Brave Raj	933,650			

3-Year-Olds

Year	Horse	Earnings	Year	Horse	Earnings	Year	Horse	Earnings
1903	Africander	$70,810	1937	War Admiral	166,500	1971	Jim French	320,291
1904	Delhi	75,225	1938	Stagehand	189,710	1972	Riva Ridge	395,632
1905	Sysonby	144,380	1939	Challedon	184,535	1973	Secretariat	860,404
1906	Accountant	83,750	1940	Bimelech	110,005	1974	Chris Evert (f)	551,063
1907	Peter Pan	86,790	1941	Whirlaway	272,386	1975	Foolish Pleasure	716,278
1908	Fair Play	70,215	1942	Shut Out	238,972	1976	Bold Forbes	460,286
1909	Joe Madden	44,905	1943	Count Fleet	174,055	1977	Seattle Slew	641,370
1910	Sweep	22,625	1944	Twilight Tear (f)	165,555	1978	Affirmed	901,541
1911	Governor Grey	15,051	1945	Busher (f)	273,735	1979	Spectacular Bid	1,279,334
1912	The Manager	12,270	1946	Assault	424,195	1980	Temperence Hill	1,130,452
1913	Ten Point	12,840	1947	Phalanx	269,250	1981	Pleasant Colony	877,415
1914	Roamer	29,105	1948	Citation	709,470	1982	Gato Del Sol	588,779
1915	The Finn	17,985	1949	Ponder	321,825	1983	Sunny's Halo	1,011,962
1916	Dodge	26,410	1950	Hill Prince	314,265	1984	Gate Dancer	1,136,525
1917	Omar Khayyam	49,070	1951	Counterpoint	250,525	1985	Spend a Buck	3,552,704
1918	Johren	49,156	1952	Mark Ye-Well	268,745	1986	Snow Chief	1,875,200
1919	Sir Barton	88,250	1953	Native Dancer	513,425	1987	Alysheba	2,511,156
1920	Man o' War	166,140	1954	Determine	328,700	1988	Seeking the Gold	2,145,620
1921	Grey Lag	62,596	1955	Nashua	752,550	1989	Sunday Silence	4,578,454
1922	Pillory	95,651	1956	Needles	440,850	1990	Unbridled	3,718,149
1923	Zev	272,008	1957	Round Table	600,383	1991	Dance Smartly (f)	2,876,821
1924	Sarazen	95,610	1958	Tim Tam	467,200	1992	A.P. Indy	2,622,560
1925	American Flag	68,350	1959	Sword Dancer	537,004	1993	Sea Hero	2,484,190
1926	Crusader	166,033	1960	Bally Ache	455,045	1994	Concern	2,541,670
1927	Sir Harry	86,842	1961	Carry Back	565,349	1995	Thunder Gulch	2,644,080
1928	Victorian	126,750	1962	Jaipur	395,437	1996	Skip Away	2,699,280
1929	Blue Larkspur	153,450	1963	Candy Spots	604,481	1997	Silver Charm	1,638,750
1930	Gallant Fox	308,275	1964	Northern Dancer	490,171	1998	Victory Gallop	1,981,720
1931	Twenty Grand	218,545	1965	Tom Rolfe	444,901	1999	Cat Thief	3,020,500
1932	Gusto	145,940	1966	Buckpasser	669,078	2000	Tiznow	3,445,950
1933	Inlander	57,430	1967	Damascus	817,941	2001	Point Given	3,350,000
1934	Cavalcade	111,235	1968	Forward Pass	449,074	2002	War Emblem	3,455,000
1935	Omaha	142,255	1969	Arts and Letters	555,604	2003	Wando	2,017,323
1936	Granville	110,295	1970	Personality	444,049			

4-Year-Olds

Year	Horse	Earnings	Year	Horse	Earnings	Year	Horse	Earnings
1903	Waterboy	$50,775	1909	King James	38,253	1915	Hodge	16,928
1904	Irish Lad	29,150	1910	Olambala	22,815	1916	Ed Crump	16,351
1905	Beldame	26,850	1911	Follie Levy	9,324	1917	King Gorin	15,575
1906	Dandelion	26,850	1912	Star Charter	14,655	1918	Cudgel	33,826
1907	Nealon	44,890	1913	Rudolfo	14,450	1919	Exterminator	26,402
1908	Ballot	55,915	1914	Robert Bradley	10,345	1920	Citrus	25,193

Year	Horse	Earnings	Year	Horse	Earnings	Year	Horse	Earnings
1921	Yellow Hand	42,271	1949	Coaltown	276,125	1977	Crystal Water	564,627
1922	Firebrand	39,110	1950	Ponder	219,050	1978	Seattle Slew	473,006
1923	Rebuke	31,800	1951	County Delight	170,985	1979	Affirmed	1,148,800
1924	Spot Cash	46,420	1952	Crafty Admiral	277,225	1980	Spectacular Bid	1,117,790
1925	Princess Doreen (f)	69,220	1953	Tom Fool	256,355	1981	Eleven Stitched	644,125
1926	Peanuts	41,450	1954	Rejected	276,800	1982	Lemhi Gold	1,066,375
1927	Chance Play	86,800	1955	Helioscope	225,250	1983	All Along (f)	2,138,963
1928	Crystal Peanut	97,200	1956	Swaps	409,400	1984	Slew o' Gold	2,627,944
1929	Diavolo	87,190	1957	Pucker Up	229,235	1985	Gate Dancer	1,229,720
1930	Blue Larkspur	51,650	1958	Round Table	662,780	1986	Lady's Secret (f)	1,871,053
1931	Plucky Play	86,725	1959	Hillsdale	502,090	1987	Ferdinand	2,185,150
1932	Equipoise	101,375	1960	Dotted Swiss	296,900	1988	Alysheba	3,808,600
1933	Larranga	47,240	1961	Kelso	425,965	1989	Blushing John	1,232,030
1934	Clarify	15,115	1962	Carry Back	319,177	1990	Flying Continental	1,096,700
1935	Discovery	102,545	1963	Crimson Satan	383,355	1991	Farma Way	2,598,350
1936	Roman Soldier	42,145	1964	Gun Bow	580,100	1992	Fraise	1,534,720
1937	Seabiscuit	168,580	1965	Hill Rise	318,365	1993	Bertrando	2,217,800
1938	War Admiral	90,840	1966	Bold Bidder	360,092	1994	Cherokee Run	943,690
1939	Kayak II	170,875	1967	Pretense	431,850	1995	Northern Spur	1,265,000
1940	Eight Thirty	81,450	1968	Dr. Fager	460,110	1996	Singspiel	2,721,987
1941	Mioland	123,520	1969	Nodouble	454,240	1997	Skip Away	4,089,000
1942	Whirlaway	211.250	1970	Shuvee (f)	201,852	1998	Silver Charm	4,696,506
1943	Thumbs Up	97,100	1971	Twice Worthy	179,520	1999	Almutawakel	3,290,000
1944	Happy Issue	118,500	1972	Droll Role	471,633	2000	Fantastic Light	4,524,423
1945	Stymie	225,375	1973	Susan's Girl (f)	340,496	2001	Captain Steve	4,201,200
1946	Gallorette (f)	159,160	1974	Forego	545,086	2002	Street Cry	4,323,777
1947	Assault	181,925	1975	Snow Knight (f)	286,435	2003	Moon Ballad	3,719,798
1948	On Trust	196,950	1976	King Pellinore	463,390			

5-Year-Olds or Older

Year	Horse	Age	Erngs	Year	Horse	Age	Erngs	Year	Horse	Age	Erngs
1903	Land of Clover	5	$16,040	1937	Rosemont	5	97,525	1970	Fort Marcy	6	388,537
1904	Colonial Girl	5	49,635	1938	Seabiscuit	5	130,395	1971	Cougar II	7	416,022
1905	Proper	5	20,125	1939	Whichee	5	35,950	1972	Typecast	6	366,387
1906	Go Between	5	38,255	1940	Seabiscuit	7	96,850	1973	Cougar II	7	356,344
1907	Glorifier	5	21,800	1941	Big Pebble	5	159,437	1974	True Knight	5	359,495
1908	Dandelion	6	9,300	1942	Marriage	6	59,600	1975	Royal Glint	5	487,110
1909	Jack Atkin	5	10,820	1943	Marriage	7	88,875	1976	Forego	6	491,701
1910	Jack Atkin	6	15,965	1944	First Fiddle	5	124,105	1977	Forego	7	268,740
1911	Plate Glass	5	13,165	1945	First Fiddle	6	129,965	1978	Exceller	5	879,790
1912	High Private	6	12,046	1946	Armed	5	288,725	1979	Bowl Game	5	585,738
1913	Donald McDonal	7	16,080	1947	Armed	6	376,325	1980	John Henry	5	925,217
1914	Buckthorn	5	11,175	1948	Shannon II	7	211,610	1981	John Henry	6	1,798,030
1915	Borrow	7	20,195	1949	Donor	5	99,075	1982	Perrault	5	1,197,400
1916	Short Grass	8	16,395	1950	Noor	5	346,940	1983	Sangue (f)	5	764,600
1917	Old Rosebud	6	31,720	1951	Moonrush	5	221,050	1984	John Henry	9	2,336,650
1918	Roamer	7	21,950	1952	Two Lea		174,550	1985	Bounding Basque	5	678,360
1919	Midway	5	22,065	1953	Royal Vale	5	215,825	1986	Precisionist	5	1,262,560
1920	Exterminator	5	52,405	1954	Pet Bully	6	240,375	1987	Theatrical	5	2,235,500
1921	Exterminator	6	56,827	1955	Social Outcast	5	390,775	1988	Great Communicator	5	2,017,950
1922	Exterminator	7	71,075	1956	Bobby Brocato	5	298,800	1989	Steinlen	6	1,521,378
1923	Chacolet	5	73,970	1957	Dedicate	5	259,500	1990	Criminal Type	5	2,270,290
1924	Runstar	5	44,550	1958	Swoon's Son	5	201,700	1991	Black Tie Affair	5	2,483,540
1925	Atherstone	5	58,025	1959	Round Table	5	413,380	1992	Pleasant Tap	5	1,959,914
1926	Sarazen	5	42,970	1960	Bald Eagle	5	396,085	1993	Kotashaan	5	2,619,014
1927	Jolly Roger	5	63,075	1961	Whodunit	6	142,260	1994	Paradise Creek	5	2,620,283
1928	Jolly Roger	6	45,950	1962	Prove It	5	348,750	1995	Cigar	5	4,819,800
1929	Golden Prince	5	121,600	1963	Kelso	6	569,762	1996	Cigar	6	4,910,000
1930	Sun Beau	5	105,005	1964	Kelso	7	311,660	1997	Gentlemen	5	2,125,300
1931	Mike Hall	7	112,975	1965	Native Diver	6	241,650	1998	Swain	6	2,260,526
1932	Phar Lap	6	50,050	1966	Native Diver	7	205,750	1999	Daylami	5	3,488,217
1933	Equipoise	5	55,760	1967	Straight Deal	5	302,270	2000	Behrens	6	1,786,500
1934	Falreno	5	27,160	1968	Politely	5	317,473	2001	Fantastic Light	5	3,634,859
1935	Azucar	7	117,950	1969	Hawaii	5	279,280	2002	Sarafan	5	2,039,765
1936	Top Row	5	106,600					2003	Falbrav	5	3,013,845

Annual Leading Money Winning Stakes Performers

Year	Horse	Events Won	Stakes Earnings	Year	Horse	Events Won	Stakes Earnings
1930	Gallant Fox	9	$304,275	1967	Damascus	11	814,691
1931	Top Flight	7	219,000	1968	Forward Pass	7	546,674
1932	Gusto	3	145,190	1969	Arts and Letters	8	555,054
1933	Singing Wood	1	86,800	1970	Personality	5	427,549
1934	Cavalcade	5	110,535	1971	Riva Ridge	5	492,763
1935	Omaha	5	141,425	1972	Droll Role	6	462,973
1936	Granville	6	109,445	1973	Secretariat	9	860,404
1937	Seabiscuit	10	167,455	1974	Forego	8	545,086
1938	Stagehand	5	186,810	1975	Foolish Pleasure	4	706,678
1939	Challedon	9	184,535	1976	Forego	5	476,701
1940	Bimelech	4	110,005	1977	Seattle Slew	5	637,170
1941	Whirlaway	9	267,486	1978	Affirmed	7	885,041
1942	Shut Out	6	234,837	1979	Spectacular Bid	9	1,268,534
1943	Count Fleet	5	172,105	1980	Spectacular Bid	9	1,117,790
1944	Pavot	7	177,390	1981	John Henry	8	1,798,030
1945	Busher	9	277,235	1982	Perrault	4	1,197,400
1946	Assault	8	424,195	1983	All Along	3	1,813,630
1947	Armed	11	375,025	1984	Slew O' Gold	4	2,606,344
1948	Citation	17	703,620	1985	Spend A Buck	5	3,552,704
1949	Ponder	6	314,775	1986	Snow Chief	6	1,875,200
1950	Noor	6	343,190	1987	Alysheba	3	2,508,906
1951	Counterpoint	6	248,800	1988	Alysheba	7	3,808,600
1952	Crafty Admiral	6	269,250	1989	Sunday Silence	6	4,560,854
1953	Native Dancer	9	513,425	1990	Unbridled	3	3,704,049
1954	Determine	10	328,700	1991	Dance Smartly	8	2,876,821
1955	Nashua	9	747,675	1992	A. P. Indy	5	2,622,560
1956	Needles	4	438,850	1993	Kotashaan	6	2,619,014
1957	Round Table	12	593,883	1994	Concern	2	2,523,070
1958	Round Table	11	656,030	1995	Cigar	9	4,800,000
1959	Sword Dancer	6	531,479	1996	Skip Away	5	2,683,420
1960	Bally Ache	6	441,345	1997	Skip Away	4	4,089,000
1961	Carry Back	7	556,874	1998	Awesome Again	5	3,818,090
1962	Jaipur	6	395,437	1999	Cat Thief	2	3,020,500
1963	Candy Spots	6	598,981	2000	Fantastic Light	3	4,524,423
1964	Gun Bow	8	580,100	2001	Captain Steve	2	4,201,200
1965	Buckpasser	6	558,331	2002	War Emblem	4	3,428,000
1966	Buckpasser	12	662,553	2003	Pleasantly Perfect	2	2,470,000

All–Time Leading Money Earners ($1 million minimum)

Horse	Sex	Born	Sts	1st	2d	3d	Earnings
Cigar	H	1990	33	19	4	5	$9,999,815
Skip Away	H	1993	38	18	10	6	9,616,360
Fantastic Light	H	1996	25	12	5	3	8,486,957
Silver Charm	H	1994	24	12	7	2	6,944,369
Captain Steve	H	1997	25	9	3	7	6,828,356
Alysheba	H	1984	26	11	8	2	6,679,242
John Henry	G	1975	83	39	15	9	6,591,860
Tiznow	H	1997	15	8	4	2	6,427,830
Singspiel (IRE)	H	1992	20	9	8	0	5,952,825
Falbrav (IRE)	H	1998	26	13	5	5	5,825,517
Best Pal	G	1988	47	18	11	4	5,668,245
Taiki Blizzard	H	1991	23	6	8	2	5,523,549
High Chaparral (IRE)	C	1999	13	10	1	2	5,331,231
Street Cry (IRE)	H	1998	12	5	6	1	5,150,837
Jim and Tonic (FR)	G	1994	39	13	13	4	4,975,807
Sunday Silence	H	1986	14	9	5	0	4,968,554
Easy Goer	H	1986	20	14	5	1	4,873,770
Daylami (IRE)	H	1994	21	11	3	4	4,614,762
Behrens	H	1994	27	9	8	3	4,563,500
Unbridled	H	1987	24	8	6	6	4,489,475
Awesome Again	H	1994	12	9	0	2	4,374,590
Moon Ballad (IRE)	C	1999	14	5	3	1	4,364,791
Medaglia d'Oro	C	1999	15	7	6	0	4,254,720
Spend a Buck	H	1982	15	10	3	2	4,220,689
Pilsudski (IRE)	H	1992	22	10	6	2	4,080,297
Creme Fraiche	G	1982	64	17	12	13	4,024,727
Seeking the Pearl	M	1994	21	8	2	3	4,021,716
Point Given	H	1998	13	9	3	0	3,968,500
Cat Thief	H	1996	30	4	9	8	3,951,012
Devil His Due	H	1989	41	11	12	3	3,920,405
Sandpit (BRZ)	H	1989	40	14	11	6	3,812,597
Swain (IRE)	H	1992	22	10	4	6	3,797,566
Ferdinand	H	1983	29	8	9	6	3,777,978
Almutawakel (GB)	H	1995	19	4	4	1	3,643,021
Sulamani (IRE)	C	1999	12	7	2	0	3,640,845
Harlan's Holiday	C	1999	22	9	6	1	3,632,664
Gentlemen (ARG)	H	1992	24	13	4	2	3,608,558
Spain	M	1997	35	9	9	7	3,540,542
Slew o' Gold	H	1980	21	12	5	1	3,533,534
Victory Gallop	H	1995	17	9	5	1	3,505,895
War Emblem	C	1999	13	7	0	0	3,491,000
Precisionist	H	1981	46	20	10	4	3,485,398
Strike the Gold	H	1988	31	6	8	5	3,457,026
Lando (GER)	H	1990	24	10	3	1	3,438,727
Paradise Creek	H	1989	25	14	7	1	3,401,416
Snow Chief	H	1983	24	13	3	5	3,383,210
Chief Bearhart	H	1993	26	12	5	3	3,381,557
Cryptoclearance	H	1984	44	12	10	7	3,376,327
Black Tie Affair (IRE)	H	1986	45	18	9	6	3,370,694
Agnes World	H	1995	20	8	6	1	3,365,680
Sky Classic	H	1987	29	15	6	1	3,320,398
Paseana (ARG)	M	1987	36	19	10	2	3,317,427
Bet Twice	H	1984	26	10	6	4	3,308,599
Steinlen (GB)	H	1983	45	20	10	7	3,297,169
Serena's Song	M	1992	38	18	11	3	3,283,388
Real Quiet	H	1995	20	6	5	6	3,271,802
Awad	H	1990	70	14	10	11	3,270,131
Dance Smartly	M	1988	17	12	2	3	3,263,835
Sakhee	H	1997	14	8	3	1	3,253,253
Lemon Drop Kid	H	1996	24	10	3	3	3,245,370
Congaree	H	1998	23	12	2	4	3,241,400
Volponi	H	1998	31	7	12	5	3,187,232
Bertrando	H	1989	24	9	6	2	3,185,610
Caller One	G	1997	20	10	3	2	3,184,500
Free House	H	1994	22	9	5	3	3,178,971
Montjeu (IRE)	H	1996	16	11	2	0	3,178,177
Siphon (BRZ)	H	1991	25	12	6	2	3,136,428
Gulch	H	1984	32	13	8	4	3,095,521
Silverbulletday	M	1996	23	15	3	1	3,093,207
Concern	H	1991	30	7	7	11	3,079,350
Giant's Causeway	H	1997	13	9	4	0	3,078,989
Azeri	M	1998	16	14	2	0	3,044,820
Lady's Secret	M	1982	45	25	9	3	3,021,325
Albert the Great	H	1997	22	8	6	4	3,012,490
Alphabet Soup	H	1991	24	10	3	6	2,990,270
A.P. Indy	H	1989	11	8	0	1	2,979,815
Escena	M	1993	29	11	9	3	2,962,639
Pleasantly Perfect	H	1998	13	6	2	1	2,949,880
Theatrical (IRE)	H	1982	22	10	4	2	2,940,036
Hansel	H	1988	14	7	2	3	2,936,586
Sea Hero	H	1990	24	6	3	4	2,929,869
Great Communicator	H	1983	56	14	10	7	2,922,615
Thunder Gulch	H	1992	16	9	2	2	2,915,086
Farma Way	H	1987	23	8	5	1	2,897,175
Milwaukee Brew	H	1997	24	8	4	5	2,879,612
General Challenge	G	1996	21	9	3	1	2,877,178
With Approval	H	1986	23	13	5	1	2,863,540
Bayakoa (ARG)	M	1984	39	21	9	0	2,861,701
Rough Habit (NZ)	G	1986	66	28	16	7	2,861,579
Marquetry	H	1987	36	10	9	4	2,857,886
Budroyale	G	1993	52	17	12	2	2,840,810
Kotashaan (FR)	H	1988	22	10	5	2	2,812,114
Banshee Breeze	M	1995	18	10	5	2	2,784,798
Spectacular Bid	H	1976	30	26	2	1	2,781,608
Symboli Rudolf (JPN)	H	1981	16	13	1	1	2,764,980
Buck's Boy	G	1993	30	16	5	2	2,750,148
Beautiful Pleasure	M	1995	25	10	5	2	2,734,078
Forty Niner	H	1985	19	11	5	0	2,726,000
Pleasant Tap	H	1987	32	9	9	5	2,721,169
Lido Palace (CHI)	H	1997	23	11	7	2	2,705,865
Izvestia	H	1987	21	11	2	2	2,702,527
Manila	H	1983	18	12	5	0	2,692,799
Broad Brush	H	1983	27	14	5	5	2,656,793
With Anticipation	G	1995	47	15	9	7	2,654,563
Trinycarol (VEN)	M	1979	29	18	3	1	2,644,392
Fraise	H	1988	34	10	5	6	2,613,105
Flawlessly	M	1988	28	16	4	3	2,572,536
Dramatic Gold	G	1991	39	9	13	6	2,567,630
Sir Bear	G	1993	71	19	12	14	2,538,422
Let's Elope (NZ)	M	1987	26	11	0	5	2,528,902
Lure	H	1989	25	14	8	0	2,515,289
Gate Dancer	H	1981	28	7	8	7	2,501,705
Holy Bull	H	1991	16	13	0	0	2,481,760
Take Charge Lady	F	1999	22	11	7	0	2,480,377
Mecke	H	1992	40	12	7	9	2,470,550
Golden Pheasant	H	1986	22	7	4	3	2,453,958
Paolini (GER)	H	1997	23	4	6	4	2,453,469
Marlin	H	1993	26	9	3	5	2,448,880
Affirmed	H	1975	29	22	5	1	2,393,818
Sarafan	G	1997	36	9	9	4	2,390,271

Horse	Sex	Born	Sts	1st	2d	3d	Earnings
Xtra Heat	M	1998	35	26	5	2	2,389,635
Malek (CHI)	H	1993	23	10	7	2	2,382,623
Heritage of Gold	M	1995	28	16	2	4	2,381,762
Wando	C	2000	13	8	2	1	2,379,700
Criminal Type	H	1985	24	10	5	3	2,351,274
Tabasco Cat	H	1991	18	8	3	2	2,347,671
Quiet Resolve	G	1995	31	10	6	4	2,346,768
Bien Bien	H	1989	26	9	8	1	2,331,875
Fly So Free	H	1988	33	12	5	3	2,330,954
Silvano (GER)	H	1996	18	7	2	2	2,321,024
Triptych	M	1982	41	14	5	11	2,318,946
Star of Cozzene	H	1988	38	14	8	5	2,308,923
Seeking the Gold	H	1985	15	8	6	0	2,307,000
Soul of the Matter	H	1991	16	7	4	2	2,302,818
Kona Gold	G	1994	30	14	7	2	2,293,384
Skimming	H	1996	20	8	5	1	2,286,601
Affirmed Success	G	1994	42	17	10	6	2,285,315
Mineshaft	C	1999	18	10	3	1	2,283,402
Yankee Affair	H	1982	55	22	14	8	2,282,156
Prized	H	1986	17	9	2	3	2,262,555
Festin (ARG)	H	1986	24	9	4	4	2,256,295
Pine Bluff	H	1989	13	6	1	3	2,255,884
Life's Magic	M	1981	32	8	11	6	2,255,218
Galileo (IRE)	H	1998	8	6	1	0	2,245,373
Skywalker	H	1982	20	8	3	3	2,226,750
Waquoit	H	1983	30	19	4	3	2,225,360
Perfect Drift	G	1999	18	9	3	1	2,221,368
Wild Again	H	1980	28	8	7	4	2,204,829
Perfect Sting	M	1996	21	14	3	0	2,202,042
Proud Truth	H	1982	21	10	4	0	2,198,895
Golden Missile	H	1995	25	7	7	4	2,194,510
Safely Kept	M	1986	31	24	2	3	2,194,206
Chief's Crown	H	1982	21	12	3	3	2,191,168
Twilight Agenda	H	1986	32	13	5	4	2,174,529
Nostalgia's Star	H	1982	59	9	17	13	2,154,827
Kalanisi (IRE)	H	1996	11	6	4	1	2,148,836
Turkoman	H	1982	22	8	8	3	2,146,924
Caitano (GB)	H	1994	44	9	6	7	2,137,459
All Along (FR)	M	1979	21	9	4	2	2,125,828
Daliapour (IRE)	H	1996	26	7	3	3	2,123,763
Val's Prince	G	1992	52	13	12	5	2,118,785
You	F	1999	23	9	8	2	2,101,353
Funny Cide	G	2000	11	5	2	2	2,099,385
Say Florida Sandy	H	1994	98	33	17	12	2,085,408
Lost Code	H	1984	27	15	5	2	2,085,396
Sunshine Forever	H	1985	23	8	6	3	2,084,800
Hernando (FR)	H	1990	20	7	4	1	2,081,978
Majesty's Prince	H	1979	43	12	10	10	2,077,796
Miesque	M	1984	16	12	3	1	2,070,163
Peace Rules	C	2000	13	6	2	2	2,059,990
Louis Quatorze	H	1993	18	7	5	1	2,054,434
Coronado's Quest	H	1995	17	10	2	0	2,046,190
Charismatic	H	1996	17	5	2	4	2,038,064
Sharp Cat	M	1994	22	15	3	0	2,032,575
Risen Star	H	1985	11	8	2	1	2,029,845
Essence of Dubai	C	1999	13	5	1	2	2,001,058
Itsallgreektome	G	1987	29	8	10	2	1,994,618
Fusaichi Pegasus	H	1997	9	6	2	0	1,994,400
Empire Maker	C	2000	8	4	3	1	1,985,800
Arcangues	H	1988	19	6	2	2	1,981,423
Kelso	G	1957	63	39	12	2	1,977,896
Ladies Din	G	1995	37	12	6	6	1,966,754
Aptitude	H	1997	15	5	4	2	1,965,410
Guided Tour	G	1996	31	12	8	1	1,964,253
Little Bold John	G	1982	105	38	16	14	1,956,406
Evening Attire	G	1998	28	10	6	3	1,952,970
Balto Star	G	1998	33	11	6	2	1,952,946
Chester House	H	1995	21	6	4	4	1,944,545
Greinton (GB)	H	1981	22	10	8	0	1,943,605
Forego	G	1970	57	34	9	7	1,938,957
Estrapade	M	1980	30	12	5	5	1,937,142
Boston Harbor	H	1994	8	6	1	0	1,934,605
Pay the Butler	H	1984	40	5	5	5	1,934,140
Da Hoss	G	1992	20	12	5	2	1,931,558
King's Swan	H	1980	107	31	19	18	1,924,845
Java Gold	H	1984	15	9	3	1	1,908,832
Deputy Commander	H	1994	13	4	3	2	1,906,640
Jewel Princess	M	1992	29	13	4	7	1,904,060
Rock of Gibraltar (IRE)	C	1999	13	10	2	0	1,888,048
Royal Anthem	H	1995	12	6	3	1	1,876,876
High-Rise (IRE)	H	1995	13	5	2	2	1,871,726
Missionary Ridge (GB)	H	1987	42	8	5	8	1,864,498
Subotica (FR)	H	1988	15	6	4	1	1,856,255
Surfside	M	1997	15	8	3	2	1,852,987
Macho Uno	H	1998	14	6	1	3	1,851,803
Tinners Way	H	1990	27	7	6	4	1,846,546
Open Mind	M	1986	19	12	2	2	1,844,372
Summer Squall	H	1987	20	13	4	0	1,844,282
Hatoof	M	1989	21	9	4	1	1,841,070
Skip Trial	H	1982	38	16	7	2	1,837,451
Came Home	C	1999	12	9	0	0	1,835,940
Precocity	H	1994	33	9	7	5	1,835,798
Native Desert	G	1993	74	21	13	17	1,828,177
Heavenly Prize	M	1991	18	9	6	3	1,825,940
Ruhlmann	H	1985	27	10	3	4	1,824,154
Banks Hill (GB)	M	1998	15	5	5	3	1,824,008
Lu Ravi	M	1995	26	11	8	3	1,819,781
Flying Continental	H	1986	51	12	15	10	1,815,938
Beat Hollow (GB)	H	1997	12	7	2	2	1,814,481
Sea Cadet	H	1988	29	10	6	5	1,807,150
Mutafaweq	H	1996	19	7	1	3	1,800,800
Big Jag	G	1993	30	13	5	3	1,800,329
Redattore (BRZ)	H	1995	32	15	2	6	1,799,883
Quest for Fame (GB)	H	1987	19	5	4	4	1,790,417
Tout Charmant	M	1996	29	9	9	1	1,781,879
Unbridled Elaine	M	1998	11	6	2	1	1,770,740
El Senor	H	1984	44	12	7	5	1,769,215
Express Tour	H	1998	14	5	1	1	1,767,515
User Friendly (GB)	M	1989	16	8	1	2	1,764,938
Gander	G	1996	55	14	10	9	1,761,183
Miss Alleged	M	1987	15	5	4	3	1,757,342
Round Table	H	1954	66	43	8	5	1,749,869
Dear Doctor (FR)	H	1987	32	8	7	4	1,742,671
Aldebaran	H	1998	25	8	12	3	1,739,186
Denon	H	1998	21	6	4	3	1,739,156
In Excess (ire)	H	1987	25	11	2	3	1,736,733
Spinning World	H	1993	14	8	3	1	1,734,477
Grey Memo	H	1997	50	8	4	10	1,733,059
Good Journey	H	1996	16	7	5	3	1,733,058
Menifee	H	1996	11	5	4	1	1,732,000

Horse	Sex	Born	Sts	1st	2d	3d	Earnings
Hawksley Hill (IRE)	G	1993	46	14	12	6	1,730,922
Frisk Me Now	H	1994	36	12	5	6	1,727,707
Favorite Trick	H	1995	16	12	0	1	1,726,793
L'Carriere	G	1991	23	8	4	3	1,726,175
Monarchos	H	1998	10	4	1	3	1,720,830
Orientate	H	1998	19	10	3	0	1,716,950
Geri	H	1992	19	9	4	3	1,707,980
Goodbye Halo	M	1985	24	11	5	4	1,706,702
Urban Sea	M	1989	23	8	4	3	1,704,553
Yagli	H	1993	27	10	6	3	1,702,121
Proper Reality	H	1985	19	10	3	1	1,701,650
Flag Down	H	1990	43	11	11	8	1,699,711
Borgia (GER)	M	1994	22	6	7	2	1,697,771
Defensive Play	H	1987	26	6	4	5	1,688,631
Artax	H	1995	25	7	9	3	1,685,840
Forbidden Apple	H	1995	31	8	6	9	1,680,640
Pistols and Roses	H	1989	44	10	4	6	1,680,506
Touch Gold	H	1994	15	6	3	1	1,679,907
Personal Ensign	M	1984	13	13	0	0	1,679,880
Odalea (ARG)	M	1986	21	8	7	2	1,674,812
Fleetstreet Dancer	G	1998	23	5	7	2	1,674,806
Exceller	H	1973	33	15	5	6	1,674,587
Starine (FR)	M	1997	33	10	12	1	1,674,491
Snurge (IRE)	H	1987	30	7	10	5	1,674,441
Golden Apples (IRE)	M	1998	16	6	6	2	1,672,583
Opening Verse	H	1986	30	10	7	2	1,669,357
Simply Majestic	H	1984	44	18	4	7	1,667,713
Smile	H	1982	27	14	4	3	1,664,027
Running Stag	H	1994	40	7	11	2	1,663,227
Tranquility Lake	M	1995	27	11	7	3	1,662,390
Keeper Hill	M	1995	21	4	7	5	1,661,281
Include	H	1997	20	10	1	4	1,659,560
Strawberry Road (AUS)	H	1979	50	21	7	9	1,655,678
Touch of the Blues (FR)	H	1997	35	8	6	5	1,655,358
River Keen (IRE)	H	1992	42	11	5	5	1,642,385
Inside Information	M	1991	17	14	1	2	1,641,806
Fourstardave	G	1985	100	21	18	16	1,636,737
Colonial Affair	H	1990	20	7	4	3	1,635,228
Ibn Bey (GB)	H	1984	28	10	3	4	1,626,059
Golan (IRE)	H	1998	11	4	2	1	1,623,376
Desert Wine	H	1980	25	8	8	3	1,618,043
Kissin Kris	H	1990	35	4	8	5	1,616,936
Valley Crossing	H	1988	48	8	13	8	1,616,490
Sultry Song	H	1988	23	9	3	5	1,616,276
Northern Spur (IRE)	H	1991	15	6	4	3	1,614,425
Hawk Wing	C	1999	12	5	5	0	1,610,604
Dancethruthedawn	M	1998	16	7	2	3	1,609,643
Dare and Go	H	1991	22	7	7	5	1,608,972
Very Subtle	M	1984	29	12	6	4	1,608,360
Editor's Note	H	1993	31	6	4	3	1,601,394
Tikkanen	H	1991	17	4	2	3	1,599,335
Fourstars Allstar	H	1988	59	14	14	9	1,596,760
Rhythm	H	1987	20	6	3	4	1,592,532
Peaks and Valleys	H	1992	16	9	3	2	1,589,270
Swale	H	1981	14	9	2	2	1,583,660
Judge Angelucci	H	1983	22	10	4	2	1,582,535
Happyanunoit (NZ)	M	1995	21	9	6	2	1,582,118
Fastness (IRE)	H	1990	24	9	6	1	1,581,165
River Verdon (IRE)	G	1987	26	16	4	2	1,574,735
John's Call	G	1991	40	16	11	3	1,571,267
Temperence Hill	H	1977	31	11	4	2	1,567,650
Tight Spot	H	1987	21	12	3	1	1,566,100
Wake At Noon	H	1997	46	19	6	5	1,564,492
In the Wings (GB)	H	1986	11	7	1	0	1,562,335
Timber Country	H	1992	12	5	1	4	1,560,400
My Flag	M	1993	20	6	3	4	1,557,057
Fly Till Dawn	H	1986	27	10	5	4	1,556,525
Riboletta (BRZ)	M	1995	28	13	3	3	1,555,103
Ten Most Wanted	C	2000	11	4	3	1	1,553,460
Islington (IRE)	F	1999	15	6	0	4	1,553,043
Blushing John	H	1985	19	9	1	2	1,548,081
Brave Act (GB)	H	1994	27	13	6	2	1,546,269
Lively One	H	1985	36	9	7	5	1,544,100
Ballingarry (IRE)	C	1999	16	5	1	4	1,543,975
Annus Mirabilis (FR)	H	1992	30	9	7	6	1,541,938
Family Style	M	1983	35	10	8	7	1,537,118
Storming Home (GB)	H	1998	24	8	4	3	1,536,704
Perrault (GB)	H	1977	25	9	5	5	1,536,103
Formal Gold	H	1993	16	8	4	1	1,533,600
Cherokee Run	H	1990	28	13	5	5	1,531,818
Ipi Tombe (ZIM)	M	1998	14	12	2	0	1,529,799
Winning Colors	M	1985	19	8	3	1	1,526,837
Gold Mover	M	1998	31	13	9	5	1,523,010
Wekiva Springs	H	1991	21	10	4	2	1,512,575
Dispersal	H	1986	22	12	3	2	1,511,137
Hawkster	H	1986	23	6	3	4	1,510,942
Ecton Park	H	1996	23	6	4	6	1,503,825
Cardmania	G	1986	76	16	12	20	1,503,780
Music Merci	G	1986	35	12	7	4	1,500,710
Affluent	M	1998	23	8	5	4	1,497,651
Johar	C	1999	16	6	4	2	1,494,496
Polar Expedition	G	1991	49	20	5	7	1,491,071
Dahlia	M	1970	48	15	3	7	1,489,105
Dr Devious (IRE)	H	1989	15	6	4	0	1,484,230
Wilderness Song	M	1988	37	15	12	2	1,482,033
Mountain Cat	H	1990	11	6	2	0	1,478,901
Kooyonga (IRE)	M	1988	18	9	4	1	1,476,193
Mi Selecto	H	1985	40	9	7	9	1,475,762
Tates Creek	M	1998	17	11	3	0	1,471,674
Ski Paradise	M	1990	20	6	8	1	1,470,588
Dancing Spree	H	1985	35	10	6	9	1,470,484
Indian Skimmer	M	1984	16	10	1	3	1,469,299
Super Diamond	H	1980	37	16	5	5	1,469,233
Labeeb (GB)	H	1992	20	8	3	4	1,464,950
Buckpasser	H	1963	31	25	4	1	1,462,014
Halo America	M	1990	40	15	8	2	1,460,992
Carnegie (IRE)	H	1991	13	7	1	1	1,458,787
Raging Fever	M	1998	26	11	7	3	1,458,198
Regal Classic	H	1985	27	8	8	3	1,456,584
Olympio	H	1988	17	9	4	0	1,456,315
Equalize	H	1982	43	13	9	8	1,455,298
Six Perfections (FR)	F	2000	10	6	4	0	1,451,544
Prairie Bayou	G	1990	12	7	3	0	1,450,621
Soviet Line (IRE)	G	1990	48	16	8	6	1,450,130
Bet On Sunshine	G	1992	47	22	7	10	1,449,882
Summer Colony	M	1998	24	10	5	1	1,448,930
Memories of Silver	M	1993	19	9	3	5	1,448,715
Men's Exclusive	H	1993	47	11	16	4	1,447,928
Twice the Vice	M	1991	23	12	6	1	1,447,064
Meadow Star	M	1988	20	11	1	2	1,445,740

Horse	Sex	Born	Sts	1st	2d	3d	Earnings	Horse	Sex	Born	Sts	1st	2d	3d	Earnings
Adoration	F	1999	15	5	2	1	1,443,856	Tuzla (FR)	M	1994	26	12	6	1	1,332,587
Dream Well (FR)	H	1995	14	4	4	4	1,439,441	Hap	H	1996	20	10	2	2	1,329,210
Lil E. Tee	H	1989	13	7	4	1	1,437,506	Ajina	M	1994	17	7	3	2	1,327,915
Dancing Brave	H	1983	10	8	1	0	1,435,434	Lonesome Glory	G	1988	44	24	5	6	1,325,868
Sightseek	F	1999	13	8	4	0	1,433,866	Burning Roma	H	1998	28	11	4	5	1,324,037
Hollywood Wildcat	M	1990	21	12	3	3	1,432,160	Savinio	G	1990	48	11	11	8	1,321,860
Noverre	H	1998	21	5	7	4	1,429,344	Victor Cooley	G	1993	39	13	12	3	1,320,475
Falcon Flight (FR)	H	1996	20	5	2	3	1,428,849	Grecian Flight	M	1984	40	21	6	3	1,320,215
Tejano	H	1985	21	5	6	3	1,428,177	Unshaded	G	1997	20	6	3	3	1,318,492
Voodoo Dancer	M	1998	21	11	4	2	1,427,952	Lassigny	H	1991	28	8	2	5	1,318,371
Talloires	H	1990	28	5	8	3	1,423,949	Secretariat	H	1970	21	16	3	1	1,316,808
Silic (FR)	H	1995	15	8	2	0	1,422,299	Richman	H	1988	33	14	5	5	1,314,360
Slew of Damascus	G	1988	48	16	9	8	1,420,350	Alphabatim	H	1981	22	7	3	5	1,313,175
Surfers Paradise (NZ)	G	1987	57	17	5	0	1,419,964	Manistique	M	1995	15	11	1	1	1,311,800
Pebbles (GB)	M	1981	15	8	4	0	1,419,632	Unbridled's Song	H	1993	12	5	4	0	1,311,800
Imperial Gesture	F	1999	11	6	2	1	1,419,140	Concerto	H	1994	21	10	4	2	1,308,118
Outstandingly	M	1982	28	10	4	3	1,412,206	Tappiano	M	1984	34	17	2	4	1,305,522
Vanlandingham	H	1981	19	10	3	3	1,409,476	Littlebitlively	H	1994	33	10	9	5	1,303,343
Win	G	1980	44	14	10	3	1,408,980	Brown Bess	M	1982	36	16	8	6	1,300,920
Sayyedati (GB)	M	1990	22	6	5	3	1,408,616	Sacahuista	M	1984	21	6	7	2	1,298,842
Best of the Rest	H	1995	32	16	8	2	1,407,796	Lazy Lode (ARG)	H	1994	29	8	4	6	1,296,740
Cutlass Reality	H	1982	66	14	12	9	1,405,660	Misil	H	1988	36	14	8	3	1,296,417
Left Bank	H	1997	24	14	2	0	1,402,806	King Cugat	H	1997	16	7	7	1	1,293,782
Excellent Meeting	M	1996	20	8	5	3	1,402,396	Windsharp	M	1991	29	11	7	3	1,293,075
Lit de Justice	H	1990	36	10	8	6	1,397,649	Victory Speech	H	1993	27	9	2	5	1,289,020
Opera House (GB)	H	1988	18	8	4	3	1,397,456	Western Pride	H	1998	29	10	4	1	1,288,569
Timboroa (GB)	H	1996	25	10	3	3	1,397,228	Nashua	H	1952	30	22	4	1	1,288,565
Honor Glide	H	1994	38	11	5	2	1,397,187	Peteski	H	1990	11	7	2	1	1,287,866
Jostle	M	1997	20	8	5	2	1,389,932	Exchange	M	1988	30	15	7	4	1,287,795
Clever Trevor	G	1986	30	15	5	2	1,388,841	Carotene	M	1983	41	12	8	5	1,287,232
Mutamam (GB)	H	1995	21	11	2	1	1,388,410	Raintrap (GB)	H	1990	28	9	4	2	1,283,707
Apple Tree (FR)	H	1989	26	7	4	5	1,388,260	Silveyville	H	1978	56	19	11	8	1,282,880
Solar Splendor	G	1987	42	11	3	6	1,386,468	Farda Amiga	F	1999	8	4	1	0	1,282,302
Wild Rush	H	1994	16	8	0	3	1,386,302	Petite Ile (IRE)	M	1986	14	6	3	4	1,281,665
Mt. Sassafras	G	1992	47	8	7	14	1,382,985	Smok'n Frolic	F	1999	25	8	5	1	1,276,500
Go for Gin	H	1991	19	5	7	2	1,380,866	Saumarez (GB)	H	1987	9	5	1	0	1,275,719
Astra	M	1996	16	11	1	2	1,378,424	Althea	M	1981	15	8	4	0	1,275,255
Possibly Perfect	M	1990	18	11	2	4	1,377,634	Frankly Perfect	H	1985	22	6	6	4	1,272,957
Fran's Valentine	M	1982	34	13	4	5	1,375,465	Sangue (IRE)	M	1978	30	13	6	3	1,272,086
State City	C	1999	15	6	0	3	1,374,707	Shine Again	M	1997	34	14	10	7	1,271,840
Go for Wand	M	1987	13	10	2	0	1,373,338	Pleasant Breeze	G	1995	36	10	8	6	1,271,680
Trempolino	H	1984	11	4	3	3	1,369,233	Versailles Treaty	M	1988	20	9	9	2	1,271,154
Sunny Sunrise	G	1987	63	18	12	9	1,367,268	Soaring Softly	M	1995	16	9	1	3	1,270,433
Puerto Madero (CHI)	H	1994	24	11	3	2	1,361,626	Cozzene's Prince	G	1987	68	16	10	10	1,270,057
North East Bound	G	1996	45	12	7	2	1,357,148	Scott's Scoundrel	H	1992	50	22	4	8	1,270,052
Tank's Prospect	H	1982	14	5	2	2	1,355,645	Diplomatic Jet	H	1992	51	9	5	9	1,267,202
Rodrigo de Triano	H	1989	13	9	0	0	1,354,192	One Dreamer	M	1988	25	12	6	2	1,266,067
Track Barron	H	1981	21	12	3	1	1,353,674	Strut the Stage	H	1998	19	9	2	2	1,265,923
Different (ARG)	M	1992	19	9	3	5	1,349,802	Chief Honcho	H	1987	34	10	6	3	1,265,719
Rhythm Band	G	1996	18	5	2	2	1,349,066	Allez France	M	1970	21	13	3	1	1,262,801
Honor Medal	H	1981	87	19	13	19	1,347,073	Bienamado	H	1996	16	8	3	0	1,261,089
Groovy	H	1983	26	12	4	1	1,346,956	Personal Flag	H	1983	24	8	4	4	1,258,924
Ibero (ARG)	H	1987	34	10	7	4	1,345,199	Glitter Woman	M	1994	23	10	9	3	1,256,805
Princess Rooney	M	1980	21	17	2	1	1,343,339	Bounding Basque	H	1980	40	10	4	6	1,256,258
Ryafan	M	1994	10	7	1	0	1,342,142	Repent	C	1999	10	5	3	1	1,255,660
Gato Del Sol	H	1979	39	7	9	7	1,340,107	Gourmet Girl	M	1995	33	9	7	10	1,255,373
In the Groove (GB)	M	1987	21	7	4	4	1,336,783	Stephan's Odyssey	H	1982	16	6	4	1	1,255,328
Sky Beauty	M	1990	21	15	2	2	1,336,000	Wandesta (GB)	M	1991	21	7	3	5	1,255,145
Dixie Dot Com	H	1995	23	8	6	1	1,332,775	Cavonnier	G	1993	23	8	3	2	1,254,165
Halling	H	1991	18	12	1	0	1,332,651	Rubiano	H	1987	28	13	6	1	1,252,817

Horse	Sex	Born	Sts	1st	2d	3d	Earnings
Ancient Title	H	1970	57	24	11	9	1,252,791
Susan's Girl	M	1969	63	29	14	11	1,251,668
Peeping Tom	G	1997	41	12	7	7	1,251,016
Al Mamoon	H	1981	32	11	7	3	1,249,906
Sunny's Halo	H	1980	20	9	3	2	1,247,791
Friendly Lover	H	1988	66	22	13	12	1,247,670
Private Terms	H	1985	17	12	0	0	1,243,947
Irish Prize	G	1996	28	10	4	2	1,242,364
Desert Waves	G	1990	63	15	9	6	1,241,295
Carry Back	H	1958	62	21	11	11	1,241,165
Kudos	G	1997	24	7	5	4	1,238,935
Nuclear Debate	G	1995	52	11	8	10	1,234,054
Erins Isle (IRE)	H	1978	33	9	9	3	1,233,889
Dixie Union	H	1997	12	7	3	0	1,233,190
Lite Light	M	1988	26	8	4	4	1,231,596
Earl of Barking (IRE)	H	1990	37	9	3	10	1,230,519
Sheikh Albadou (GB)	H	1988	15	6	4	1	1,229,702
Housebuster	H	1987	22	15	3	1	1,229,696
Royal Heroine (IRE)	M	1980	21	10	4	2	1,229,449
Fit for a Queen	M	1986	51	13	14	9	1,226,429
Zoffany	H	1980	36	15	10	2	1,225,569
Dollar Bill	H	1998	22	4	5	5	1,225,546
Real Connection	M	1991	72	7	14	7	1,225,018
Grindstone	H	1993	6	3	2	0	1,224,510
Elloluv	F	2000	11	4	3	1	1,221,475
Classic Cat	H	1995	20	6	3	5	1,221,300
Subordination	H	1994	21	11	3	1	1,221,068
Irish Linnet	M	1988	62	19	16	10	1,220,180
Isitingood	H	1991	24	11	3	4	1,219,430
Gaily Magnum	G	1993	24	8	2	2	1,218,578
Jolie's Halo	H	1987	20	8	0	2	1,218,120
Foolish Pleasure	H	1972	26	16	4	3	1,216,705
Arazi	H	1989	14	9	1	1	1,212,351
Fieldy (IRE)	M	1983	54	19	9	8	1,212,168
Stalwars	H	1985	79	17	17	8	1,211,556
Leger Cat (ARG)	H	1986	53	16	5	7	1,211,402
Candid Glen	G	1997	38	10	9	6	1,210,130
Primal	G	1985	45	17	11	7	1,209,530
Ten Keys	H	1984	54	21	8	4	1,209,211
Seattle Slew	H	1974	17	14	2	0	1,208,726
Tasso	H	1983	23	9	4	4	1,207,884
Tomisue's Delight	M	1994	20	7	5	4	1,207,537
Dahar	H	1981	29	7	6	4	1,207,286
Lottsa Talc	G	1990	65	21	10	12	1,206,248
Thornfield	G	1994	19	6	1	3	1,206,074
Atticus	H	1992	18	7	3	1	1,205,933
Wallenda	H	1990	33	7	5	5	1,205,929
Volochine (IRE)	H	1991	45	8	12	9	1,205,580
Honour and Glory	H	1993	17	6	5	2	1,202,942
Kiridashi	H	1992	44	14	9	8	1,201,981
Chilukki	M	1997	17	11	3	0	1,201,828
License Fee	H	1995	43	16	7	6	1,200,416
Kostroma (IRE)	M	1986	26	12	2	3	1,200,088
Yavana's Pace (IRE)	G	1992	74	16	14	11	1,199,409
Nasr El Arab	H	1985	16	6	2	2	1,198,585
Dushyantor	H	1993	20	5	5	2	1,197,570
Frost King	H	1978	55	27	10	3	1,196,954
My Big Boy	G	1983	50	10	12	10	1,196,102
Anet	H	1994	19	8	5	0	1,189,873
Barathea (IRE)	H	1990	16	5	4	0	1,189,181
Val Royal (FR)	H	1996	12	7	2	0	1,186,687
Blazing Sword	G	1994	45	11	7	7	1,184,055
Heat Haze (GB)	F	1999	14	7	2	2	1,183,696
April Run (IRE)	M	1978	18	8	2	4	1,182,819
The Wicked North	H	1989	17	8	4	1	1,180,750
Ridgewood Pearl (GB)	M	1992	8	6	1	1	1,179,301
Damascus	H	1964	32	21	7	3	1,176,781
King Glorious	H	1986	9	8	1	0	1,175,650
Maxzene	M	1993	23	11	5	0	1,175,259
Cougar II	H	1966	50	20	7	17	1,172,625
Homebuilder	H	1984	60	11	11	17	1,172,153
Ezzoud (IRE)	H	1989	22	6	5	2	1,171,885
Sefa's Beauty	M	1979	52	25	7	8	1,171,628
Gorgeous	M	1986	14	8	4	1	1,171,370
Mystic Lady	M	1998	27	10	8	2	1,170,390
Cetewayo	H	1994	36	11	5	4	1,170,258
High Yield	H	1997	14	4	4	3	1,170,196
Cacoethes	H	1986	14	4	3	3	1,169,064
River Bay	H	1993	20	8	3	3	1,167,970
Tejano Run	H	1992	21	8	4	6	1,166,842
Slew City Slew	H	1984	42	11	10	6	1,166,296
Educated Risk	M	1990	23	11	6	4	1,163,717
Red Bullet	H	1997	14	6	2	2	1,161,920
Chorwon	G	1993	44	13	7	8	1,161,795
Luthier Fever	H	1991	25	6	5	6	1,160,852
Benburb	G	1989	22	7	2	4	1,159,949
Megahertz (GB)	F	1999	22	8	3	5	1,159,094
Bonapaw	G	1996	46	18	7	4	1,158,752
Kelly Kip	H	1994	31	15	3	4	1,157,142
Early Pioneer	G	1995	33	9	9	5	1,156,815
Empress Club (ARG)	M	1988	26	16	2	1	1,155,235
Videogenic	M	1982	73	20	9	10	1,154,360
Flying Pidgeon	H	1981	56	12	9	13	1,154,337
King's Theatre (IRE)	H	1991	19	5	3	4	1,154,329
Dynever	C	2000	9	3	3	1	1,154,020
Present Value	H	1984	42	15	5	3	1,153,853
Dernier Empereur	H	1990	30	8	5	4	1,152,425
Bourbon Belle	M	1995	40	16	11	5	1,152,223
Pine Tree Lane	M	1982	38	19	4	4	1,150,561
High Brite	H	1984	45	15	7	9	1,150,519
Lazy Slusan	M	1995	47	12	7	10	1,150,410
Nite Dreamer	H	1995	37	5	10	6	1,149,788
Sir Beaufort	H	1987	34	10	10	4	1,149,130
Graeme Hall	H	1997	22	7	7	1	1,147,441
Maltese Superb	M	1997	35	4	7	4	1,145,491
Island Whirl	H	1978	34	11	6	6	1,144,010
Volga (IRE)	M	1998	19	7	5	2	1,141,759
Drum Taps	H	1986	31	15	5	2	1,140,788
Bold Ruritana	M	1990	44	14	10	6	1,140,163
Richter Scale	H	1994	25	12	2	0	1,139,958
Swept Overboard	H	1997	20	8	5	3	1,137,767
Perfect Soul (IRE)	H	1998	15	6	3	1	1,136,215
Mr Purple	H	1992	21	6	3	5	1,133,538
Shantou	H	1993	14	6	2	4	1,132,399
Steady Power	G	1984	70	13	19	9	1,132,197
Helmsman	H	1992	22	6	7	3	1,132,142
Lemhi Gold	H	1978	22	8	4	1	1,131,355
War Chant	H	1997	7	5	1	0	1,130,600
Manndar (IRE)	H	1996	20	4	6	3	1,128,835
Western Playboy	H	1986	45	8	7	7	1,128,449

Horse	Sex	Born	Sts	1st	2d	3d	Earnings
Lashkari (GB)	H	1981	13	5	2	2	1,127,658
Flying Paster	H	1976	27	13	7	2	1,127,460
Strategic Choice	H	1991	33	5	5	5	1,126,735
North Sider	M	1982	36	15	7	5	1,126,400
On the Line	H	1984	37	14	7	2	1,125,810
Ela Athena (GB)	M	1996	17	3	7	2	1,125,252
Pleasant Variety	H	1984	58	8	10	11	1,123,783
Star Standard	H	1992	25	7	4	3	1,121,512
Tenpins	H	1998	16	9	2	2	1,121,449
Polish Navy	H	1984	12	7	1	3	1,118,076
Countess Diana	M	1995	14	7	2	0	1,117,185
Timarida (IRE)	M	1992	16	10	2	2	1,116,186
Sky Jack	G	1996	18	10	2	2	1,115,127
Temperate Sil	H	1984	19	6	2	1	1,113,775
Island Fashion	F	2000	10	4	1	0	1,112,970
Colonial Waters	M	1985	32	6	12	3	1,112,847
Not Surprising	G	1990	61	23	4	5	1,112,301
Squirtle Squirt	H	1998	16	8	4	0	1,112,220
Riva Ridge	H	1969	30	17	3	1	1,111,497
Single Empire (IRE)	H	1994	23	5	5	3	1,110,889
Top Corsage	M	1983	53	15	7	9	1,110,028
Fort Marcy	G	1964	75	21	18	14	1,109,791
Dispute	M	1990	19	9	4	4	1,106,907
Rainbows for Life	H	1988	36	15	5	3	1,105,926
The Very One	M	1975	71	22	12	9	1,104,623
Public Purse	H	1994	14	7	1	4	1,103,324
Celtic Arms (FR)	H	1991	23	5	2	3	1,102,806
Flute	M	1998	8	4	3	0	1,101,504
Elmhurst	G	1990	51	8	11	6	1,100,567
Recoup the Cash	G	1990	74	23	6	3	1,098,920
Track Robbery	M	1976	59	22	12	7	1,098,537
Hal's Hope	H	1997	33	9	5	3	1,098,422
Sabin	M	1980	25	18	0	2	1,098,341
Eliza	M	1990	12	5	2	2	1,095,316
Event of the Year	H	1995	9	5	2	1	1,095,200
Basquein	G	1991	37	13	10	2	1,094,767
Thirty Six Red	H	1987	20	4	3	5	1,094,310
Kazzia (GER)	F	1999	7	5	0	0	1,094,206
Mr Ross	G	1995	44	18	6	10	1,091,046
Fruits of Love	H	1995	23	5	3	5	1,089,543
Freedom Cry (GB)	H	1991	12	5	5	0	1,089,080
Mercedes Won	H	1986	52	12	7	12	1,087,435
Citation	H	1945	45	32	10	2	1,085,760
Judy's Red Shoes	M	1983	83	25	13	12	1,085,668
Clear Mandate	M	1992	31	10	6	4	1,085,588
Silver Goblin	G	1991	26	16	4	3	1,083,895
Regal Intention	H	1985	41	14	7	10	1,083,103
Prowl (AUS)	G	1995	22	5	2	2	1,082,344
Mandy's Gold	M	1998	24	11	4	6	1,081,744
Yes It's True	H	1996	22	11	2	3	1,080,700
Dave's Friend	H	1975	76	35	16	8	1,079,915
Tobougg (IRE)	H	1998	12	3	2	2	1,079,901
Dumaani	H	1991	26	7	3	3	1,079,098
De Roche	H	1986	28	5	8	7	1,078,200
Bien Nicole	M	1998	26	12	8	2	1,074,620
The Tin Man	G	1998	18	7	4	1	1,074,460
Silver Ending	H	1987	37	8	1	9	1,073,420
Hopeful Word	H	1981	43	18	12	3	1,073,051
Interco	H	1980	21	10	4	3	1,070,688
Corporate Report	H	1988	10	3	5	0	1,067,908
Mobil	C	2000	15	8	3	1	1,067,711
Taylor's Special	H	1981	41	21	7	2	1,065,805
Megan's Interco	G	1989	36	16	11	0	1,062,465
Afternoon Deelites	H	1992	12	7	3	0	1,061,193
Critical Eye	M	1997	38	14	4	3	1,060,984
Two Item Limit	M	1998	28	7	3	5	1,060,585
White Muzzle (GB)	H	1990	17	6	3	2	1,060,443
Mysterious Affair	M	1997	37	12	9	6	1,059,971
Beau Genius	H	1985	42	19	7	4	1,055,600
Kiss a Native	G	1997	30	12	4	2	1,054,817
Secret Status	M	1997	19	8	3	4	1,053,705
Colstar	M	1996	18	11	2	1	1,053,056
Tap to Music	H	1995	21	6	4	4	1,052,526
Capades	M	1986	27	11	9	2	1,051,006
Hodges Bay	G	1985	51	7	15	3	1,050,363
Alpride (IRE)	M	1991	26	11	4	4	1,048,270
Continental Red	G	1996	56	7	12	11	1,047,558
Thunder Rumble	H	1989	19	8	0	1	1,047,552
Dimitrova	F	2000	9	4	2	1	1,047,292
Salem Drive	M	1982	46	13	7	10	1,046,065
Morluc	H	1996	40	11	9	5	1,045,758
Kalookan Queen	M	1996	25	11	8	4	1,044,474
Echo Eddie	G	1997	28	10	7	3	1,044,354
Starrer	M	1998	20	6	5	3	1,043,033
Algenib (ARG)	H	1987	21	7	5	2	1,042,299
Mr. Epperson	G	1995	63	19	10	10	1,042,131
Fit to Fight	H	1979	26	14	3	3	1,042,075
Southjet	H	1983	30	5	7	2	1,040,483
Zoman	H	1987	24	7	5	3	1,040,372
Bolshoi Boy	G	1983	58	16	7	8	1,039,702
Silent Eskimo	M	1995	31	9	4	9	1,039,485
Jameela	M	1976	58	27	15	6	1,038,704
It's the One	H	1978	28	9	7	9	1,038,444
West by West	H	1989	30	10	3	7	1,038,123
Troyanos (BRZ)	H	1985	13	10	1	1	1,038,083
Vivace	M	1993	40	20	4	6	1,037,671
Phoenix Reach (IRE)	C	2000	5	3	1	1	1,037,276
Lite the Fuse	H	1991	21	9	4	6	1,036,882
A Fleets Dancer	H	1995	45	12	6	8	1,036,649
Urgent Request (IRE)	H	1990	25	7	4	1	1,035,339
Queen Alexandra	M	1982	46	19	8	5	1,034,144
Fali Time	H	1981	15	5	4	2	1,033,179
Bessarabian	M	1982	37	18	5	4	1,032,640
Vision and Verse	H	1996	21	4	3	5	1,030,330
Janet (GB)	M	1997	27	8	4	6	1,027,237
Native Diver	H	1959	81	37	7	12	1,026,500
More Than Ready	H	1997	17	7	4	1	1,026,229
Sure Shot Biscuit	G	1996	54	23	10	11	1,025,480
Del Mar Dennis	G	1990	26	10	1	4	1,023,373
Heatherten	M	1979	53	21	7	4	1,022,699
J J'sdream	M	1993	40	13	11	7	1,022,217
Hever Golf Rose (GB)	M	1991	66	17	11	10	1,020,328
Storm Song	M	1994	12	4	1	2	1,020,050
Grand Canyon	H	1987	8	4	3	0	1,019,540
Stephen Got Even	H	1996	11	5	1	1	1,019,200
Corwyn Bay (IRE)	H	1986	15	6	4	0	1,018,749
Urbane	M	1992	18	8	4	4	1,018,568
Riviera (FR)	H	1994	21	10	4	3	1,018,535
Super Moment	H	1977	47	10	8	5	1,017,940
Sewickley	H	1985	32	11	9	4	1,017,517

Horse	Sex	Born	Sts	1st	2d	3d	Earnings	Horse	Sex	Born	Sts	1st	2d	3d	Earnings
My Own Business (Ven)	H	1997	50	37	5	1	1,016,908	Kiri's Clown	H	1989	62	16	6	8	1,005,469
Spook Express (SAF)	M	1994	22	11	2	3	1,016,744	Rivlia	H	1982	41	9	2	8	1,005,041
Full Moon Madness	G	1995	39	15	6	10	1,015,885	Lost Mountain	H	1988	36	5	6	8	1,004,939
Captain Bodgit	H	1994	12	7	1	4	1,014,849	Royal Glint	H	1970	52	21	9	4	1,004,816
Johannesburg	C	1999	10	7	1	0	1,014,585	Glorious Song	M	1976	34	17	9	1	1,004,534
Letthebighossroll	G	1988	60	18	14	6	1,014,377	Fighting Fit	H	1979	49	14	7	8	1,004,174
Alwuhush	H	1985	22	5	4	7	1,012,423	Brocco	H	1991	8	4	2	0	1,003,550
Antespend	M	1993	24	10	4	2	1,011,954	Dr. Fager	H	1964	22	18	2	1	1,002,642
Roo Art	H	1982	27	10	4	5	1,011,723	Danzig Connection	H	1983	17	6	5	4	1,002,620
Miss Oceana	M	1981	19	11	6	1	1,010,385	Annoçonnor	M	1984	29	12	7	5	1,002,420
Forty Niner Days	G	1987	45	9	9	3	1,009,625	Forever Silver	H	1985	47	8	9	9	1,001,974
Kurofune Mystery	M	1990	21	6	5	4	1,009,342	Brian's Time	H	1985	21	5	2	6	1,001,269
Down the Aisle	H	1993	21	9	5	5	1,007,988	Riskaverse	F	1999	21	7	4	4	1,000,234
Dream Supreme	M	1997	16	9	2	2	1,007,680	Exbourne	H	1986	14	8	5	1	1,000,198
Clabber Girl	M	1983	39	8	12	6	1,006,261								

This section includes all horses with at least $1 million in career earnings
that had at least one start in North America. It includes any foreign earnings and bonus money
awarded for racing performance that was reported to *Daily Racing Form.*

Lifetime Leaders – Races Won

Kingston, a brown horse by Spendthrift - Kapanga, by Victorious, holds the record of most wins in North American racing. He won 89 of his 138 starts and was unplaced only four times in his racing career, which extended from 1886 to 1894.

Kingston was bred at James R. Keene's Spendthrift Stud, near Lexington, Ky. He was sold as a yearling to E.V. Snedeker and J.F. Cushman for $2,200. He raced as a 2-year-old in Snedeker's colors. In July 1887, he was purchased by the Dwyer brothers for $12,500 and raced in their red and blue silks until the parnership was dissolved in November 1890, when he was acquired by Michael F. Dwyer for $30,000. He raced for the latter until he retired, perfectly sound, in 1894. During his career, Kingston reigned as America's leading money winner for a time but was displaced from that spot prior to his retirement by Domino, who amassed more in just over three months as a 2-year-old in 1893 than had then-9-year-old Kingston in his entire career to that point.

Thoroughbreds on record who won the most number of races in North America during their careers are listed below:

Horse	YOB	Sts	1st	2d	3d	Won	Horse	YOB	Sts	1st	2d	3d	Won
Kingston	1884	138	89	33	12	$138,917	Seth's Hope	1924	327	62	51	50	74,341
Little Minch	1880	222	85	40	39	58,225	Imp	1894	171	62	35	29	70,119
King Crab	1885	310	85	63	52	55,682	Leochares	1910	175	62	47	28	68,867
Hiblaze	1935	396	78	72	51	31,597	Ed R.	1948	248	62	49	35	63,552
Tippity Witchet	1915	266	78	52	42	88,241	Vantime	1939	295	62	65	36	46,290
Pan Zareta	1910	151	76	31	21	39,082	Mucho Gusto	1932	216	61	32	36	101,880
Raceland	1885	130	70	25	12	116,391	Irene's Bob	1929	237	61	37	30	58,010
Badge	1885	167	70	47	27	73,253	Brandon Prince	1929	280	61	36	47	47,287
Care Free	1918	227	67	36	35	59,873	Shuchor	1936	261	61	49	36	33,607
Shot One	1941	360	65	65	68	29,982	Vantryst	1936	334	61	78	48	31,971
Worthowning	1935	333	63	61	64	41,760	Lewis A. D.	1947	212	60	50	27	65,482
Banquet	1887	166	62	42	23	118,535	George de Mar	1922	333	60	54	64	69,091

Horses with at least 40 wins in North America or Canada who raced in 1950 or later are listed below:

Horse	YOB	Sex	Sts	1st	2d	3d	Won	Horse	YOB	Sex	Sts	1st	2d	3d	Won
Hiblaze	1935	H	396	78	72	51	$31,597	Flyingphere	1961	G	213	48	41	25	85,683
Shot One	1941	G	360	65	65	68	29,982	Bill Pac	1951	H	272	48	42	37	73,374
Worthowning	1935	G	333	63	61	64	41,760	Waco Scamp	1950	H	226	48	33	21	64,647
Ed R.	1948	H	248	62	49	35	63,552	Youville	1939	G	275	48	28	49	51,326
Vantime	1939	G	295	62	65	36	46,290	See D.	1942	H	260	48	41	32	48,890
Shuchor	1936	G	261	61	49	36	33,607	Thos	1938	H	255	48	38	43	43,884
Vantryst	1936	H	334	61	78	48	31,971	Lexington Park	1967	G	209	47	35	29	357,861
Lewis A. D.	1947	H	212	60	50	27	65,482	Grand Wizard	1956	G	220	47	35	36	222,312
Charlie Boy	1955	H	241	58	45	35	207,642	Montana Winds	1967	H	191	47	29	15	202,535
Golden Arrow	1961	H	176	58	25	22	167,264	Maxwell G.	1961	H	234	47	52	37	181,420
Columcille	1948	H	182	57	30	30	89,665	Master Red	1950	G	217	47	44	23	109,684
End of Street	1963	H	202	57	40	30	67,686	Bee Lee Tee	1947	H	270	47	51	46	104,805
Tommy Whelan	1936	G	233	55	34	23	33,279	Aquanotte	1960	H	142	47	29	18	80,603
Argos	1937	G	215	54	40	27	37,507	Gary's Star	1954	H	210	47	37	23	72,105
Crying for More	1965	H	192	53	32	29	183,685	Annette G.	1951	M	237	47	47	25	68,932
Bee Golly	1942	M	183	53	34	26	54,544	Cain's Abel	1956	H	102	47	24	12	58,267
Post War Style	1941	M	179	53	26	23	52,600	Gourmet	1937	G	177	47	22	21	53,400
Port Conway Lane	1969	H	242	52	39	36	431,593	Pooch	1948	H	209	47	38	26	48,505
Agrarian-U	1942	G	236	52	36	34	199,345	Algasir	1946	G	165	46	39	24	210,250
Fleet Argo	1947	G	243	52	37	38	149,000	Amberope	1968	G	153	46	26	13	197,085
Billy Brier	1953	G	231	52	27	33	83,168	Perennial	1967	G	216	46	52	31	137,010
Float Away	1936	G	265	52	43	41	61,365	War Marshal	1953	H	227	46	33	41	120,259
Air Patrol	1941	H	146	51	33	17	163,100	Bold Scholar	1956	H	141	46	27	22	101,752
Sagely	1970	H	124	51	23	11	116,196	Legate	1949	H	260	46	39	57	99,915
Blenweed	1938	G	202	51	35	25	105,415	Silver Fir	1963	H	165	46	20	18	79,347
Dr. Johnson	1940	H	256	51	44	27	54,422	Nirgo	1955	G	273	46	39	33	63,987
Time to Bid	1975	H	179	50	33	35	241,247	Dakota Bill	1952	H	170	46	29	27	39,215
Big Devil	1963	H	237	50	42	34	222,715	Jilsie's Gigalo	1984	G	136	45	28	22	315,456
Go Lite	1960	H	211	50	28	27	96,938	Guy	1974	H	161	45	25	13	281,085
Brownskin	1946	H	224	50	41	36	77,913	Dot's Imp	1966	H	138	45	34	14	265,112
Misty Eye	1938	M	220	50	26	40	25,236	Dobi's Knight	1971	G	219	45	28	22	178,996
Candle Wood	1949	H	253	49	53	37	171,127	War Allies	1942	G	182	45	38	24	141,313
Ahba's Bull	1949	H	157	49	22	22	97,057	Sailawayin	1967	G	172	45	36	19	138,917
Imahead	1955	H	246	49	46	30	69,884	Tidy Sum	1943	H	149	45	21	23	116,271
Win Man	1985	G	178	48	38	23	416,316	Happy Monday	1965	H	157	45	22	15	115,008
Dot the T.	1972	H	261	48	33	31	227,033	Roman Spy	1951	H	229	45	26	23	106,462
Bayou Teche	1961	G	281	48	35	43	107,577	Acerullah	1970	H	219	44	33	39	186,214
Apple	1958	G	195	48	27	20	102,385	Vet's Boy	1950	H	177	44	22	20	122,230

Horse	Age	Sex	Sts	1st	2d	3d	Won
Title Gain	1958	G	171	44	21	24	106,086
Station Master	1968	H	185	44	28	36	95,496
Arrc Flash	1960	G	205	44	38	31	91,451
Ogham	1941	G	198	44	24	28	73,815
Navy	1936	H	202	44	34	21	65,345
Betty's Bobby	1937	G	224	44	30	29	60,655
Brown Pirate	1949	H	167	44	22	15	56,214
Irish Wash	1942	H	180	44	32	18	51,269
Javalina	1950	H	168	44	25	31	49,664
Half Nelson	1954	G	147	44	23	14	47,203
Slamming Slam	1948	G	201	44	30	24	44,465
Jack Rubens	1939	G	207	44	36	23	38,255
Prince A. A.	1950	G	192	44	30	33	34,495
Grand Lady	1937	M	287	44	47	54	27,406
Chronology	1935	G	301	44	41	46	14,632
Round Table	1954	H	66	43	8	5	1,749,869
Kintla's Folly	1972	G	130	43	25	21	397,761
Damage Control	1965	H	168	43	27	21	250,364
Alhambra Son	1964	H	160	43	17	16	244,032
Git	1967	H	203	43	44	34	191,423
Alexis	1942	G	253	43	56	45	183,404
Norman Prince	1974	H	161	43	37	15	169,947
Rob Bob	1957	H	261	43	31	38	166,716
Chrystal Gail	1973	M	137	43	25	20	154,910
Flying Hitch	1972	H	125	43	27	13	124,352
Fleet Charge	1952	G	226	43	32	27	115,192
Mister Snow Man	1959	G	310	43	37	36	104,074
Till's Jeff	1963	H	163	43	27	32	101,880
Quien Es	1938	G	126	43	26	16	89,136
Bolo Tie	1940	G	252	43	48	32	77,062
Lindsey-Jan	1965	H	208	43	36	27	68,958
Leaping Moose	1941	G	205	43	33	26	55,067
Vinum	1937	H	264	43	29	30	53,990
Golden Grip	1950	H	180	43	32	24	45,870
Happy's First	1954	H	250	43	32	34	42,985
Swear Off	1947	G	246	43	36	31	41,964
Brown Blizzard	1939	G	190	43	26	32	25,755
Michaelmas	1935	G	245	43	31	28	24,231
Opelika	1936	H	215	43	45	48	22,850
English Dancer	1967	G	172	42	41	21	208,239
Appease Not	1946	G	314	42	44	46	122,802
Missouri Brave	1972	H	137	42	22	12	116,717
Cheju	1962	G	185	42	28	23	114,040
Johnathen J. S.	1970	H	191	42	26	28	111,594
Sky Light	1955	H	176	42	30	25	111,577
Three Larks	1969	H	154	42	32	18	111,339
Bee's Little Man	1961	H	315	42	32	31	108,675
Turkson	1954	H	228	42	49	33	105,477
A Roman Dragon	1967	H	157	42	25	17	101,266
Cross Ring	1948	H	161	42	33	26	83,605
Halterman	1962	H	173	42	22	25	79,760
Phantom Heels	1942	H	206	42	28	23	73,642
Lawless Miss	1943	M	111	42	22	13	67,415
Ormazd	1952	G	118	42	20	8	63,677
Flyfosta	1951	H	178	42	26	20	56,864
Walloon	1941	G	243	42	40	35	56,320
Boss Bennie	1948	G	187	42	32	28	51,530
Free Valley	1943	H	89	42	18	7	37,695
Ready Standard	1947	H	245	42	25	27	35,401
Virden	1950	M	162	42	22	28	34,911
Copin	1937	G	323	42	40	53	27,926
Slaver	1941	G	252	42	47	32	26,357
Scotch Dot	1942	M	247	42	41	31	13,332
Armed	1941	G	81	42	20	10	817,475
Lancer's Pride	1974	G	217	41	28	32	294,903
Rose's Gem	1954	H	125	41	34	12	230,964
Victory Beauty	1956	H	184	41	18	28	223,716
Moxeytown	1977	H	116	41	20	19	216,652
Mandingo	1948	G	208	41	29	29	177,662
Flaming Folly	1970	G	207	41	34	24	164,410
Flying Weather	1943	H	226	41	43	31	145,164
Boca Ratony	1988	G	139	41	18	15	133,715
Ariel Beau	1967	H	229	41	34	26	118,183
Gerowa	1963	G	203	41	32	25	112,630
Mighty Master	1939	G	203	41	37	31	111,021
Diamond in the Sky	1968	G	203	41	37	26	110,482
Night Final	1960	H	238	41	32	26	107,537
Scholarship	1942	G	192	41	22	21	104,460
Loons Buster	1968	G	159	41	25	18	97,990
Air Flight	1948	H	261	41	43	44	95,870
Trico	1953	H	198	41	25	25	88,675
Hypostyle	1945	G	225	41	37	20	85,833
Navy Coach	1966	H	129	41	14	8	69,899
Bell's Range	1954	G	274	41	44	39	65,100
Prince Bonanza	1955	H	137	41	27	17	65,026
Prince Ivan	1956	H	164	41	28	23	62,198
Slipton Fell	1960	H	180	41	17	37	60,303
High Nail	1963	H	112	41	13	12	59,700
Mr. Edgor	1956	H	209	41	25	29	58,235
Little Welch	1955	H	220	41	44	32	55,884
Alfios	1940	G	204	41	27	25	54,390
Turntable	1938	G	278	41	33	32	53,920
Fort Garry	1943	G	173	41	27	18	50,052
Plitshon	1960	H	219	41	41	39	49,700
Cosmo Lea	1953	H	204	41	31	23	49,272
Port o' Fogo	1958	H	119	41	23	15	46,688
Heliolater	1952	H	201	41	26	38	43,632
Galafre	1949	H	153	41	31	16	27,246
Jubilo	1936	H	238	41	42	43	26,575
Soldiers Call	1936	G	226	41	37	23	25,370
Last Don B.	1987	G	104	40	31	18	471,461
Creme de La Fete	1976	G	151	40	27	16	460,350
Noble But Nasty	1981	G	200	40	44	27	325,588
Hereford Man	1978	H	165	40	29	21	308,286
Kiss and Run	1968	H	144	40	23	22	295,681
Sawmill Run	1988	G	160	40	30	9	253,744
Best Boy's Jade	1989	G	175	40	14	24	223,983
Navy Admiral	1962	H	194	40	37	34	219,303
Untangle	1970	G	229	40	45	27	179,819
Hi Billee	1948	G	172	40	38	25	160,520
Laran	1944	G	194	40	33	29	138,037
Wild Wink	1969	H	275	40	48	53	129,004
Beau Sock	1969	H	132	40	27	16	124,910
Toeless Tom	1968	G	197	40	32	19	118,243
Dobi Pay	1971	H	136	40	19	24	118,188
Our Holiday	1953	H	204	40	39	30	117,626
Conty Bay	1949	H	188	40	21	28	117,255
First Refusal	1949	H	209	40	36	33	106,720
Full Steam Ahead	1966	H	216	40	36	25	105,568
Seebit	1947	G	123	40	26	13	104,195
Sloop	1959	H	213	40	29	31	93,706
Family Trouble	1965	H	240	40	31	38	90,891
Traveler	1945	H	172	40	31	20	86,925
Dermagh	1957	G	222	40	40	31	79,252
One Only	1939	G	252	40	42	39	78,345
Hi-Sag	1953	H	158	40	23	17	71,752
Ducat	1951	G	205	40	32	17	70,031
Kantar Run	1938	G	265	40	37	39	67,070
Eagle Speed	1946	G	284	40	47	41	66,337
Layaway	1939	G	213	40	41	22	65,742
Andy Johnson	1951	G	160	40	16	16	63,658
Birchwood	1955	G	153	40	19	10	59,046
Austin Venn	1956	G	224	40	27	33	56,444
Crafty Charger	1966	G	163	40	15	21	50,074
Herby B. Good	1964	H	151	40	26	26	49,000
Naomi	1950	M	231	40	33	31	47,015
Miss Boston	1947	M	148	40	22	20	44,990
Firey Isle	1951	H	149	40	37	21	43,872
Bow to You	1945	H	108	40	14	14	42,080
Deep Current	1954	H	164	40	29	19	41,690
Mister Buckle	1957	G	160	40	24	21	36,170
Victory Play	1940	M	192	40	30	22	34,715
Copper Buster	1950	G	179	40	31	31	32,294
Salesman	1957	H	141	40	17	13	31,798
Khayyam's Kid	1942	G	212	40	35	30	26,755
Glenpool	1935	G	214	40	39	30	24,210
Whirling Dust	1947	H	196	40	25	25	21,320

Top Beyer Speed Figures

By Andrew Beyer

When Mineshaft won the Eclipse Award as the horse of the year for 2003, few devotees of speed figures could quarrel with the choice. The 4-year-old ran faster than many champions of recent years, and he was a paragon of consistency. Beginning with his victory in the New Orleans Handicap, he recorded Beyer Speed Figures of 116, 116, 118, 117, 115, 117 and 114. Each of these figures was better than the lifetime best race of the previous horse of the year, Azeri. Mineshaft was a running machine.

But he was only one of several exceptionally fast horses who raced in 2003. The outstanding single performance of the year was the victory of the Argentine import, Candy Ride, in the Pacific Classic at Del Mar. His figure of 123 equaled the best number earned in a distance race during the last seven years. Physical problems ended Candy Ride's campaign after the Pacific Classic and cost him a shot at a championship, but he was surely one of the best horses to compete in this country in recent years.

Congaree didn't win a championship, either, but he was a versatile and fast runner who recorded a figure of 120 in the Cigar Mile and Aqueduct and ran 116 or higher three other times at longer distances.

The year was a good one for sprinters, too. Aldebaran ran a 122 in his smashing victory in the Forego Handicap at Saratoga. Shake You Down recorded a 121 at Calder and Cajun Beat won the Breeders' Cup with a 120.

The Beyer Speed Figures were incorporated into *Daily Racing Form* past performances in 1992. Their principal purpose is to aid bettors in everyday handicapping by answering the question, "Who is faster than whom?" But by providing an objective measurement of horses' ability, the numbers also make possible the comparison of horses from different generations. (American breeders recognize the importance of such a measurement; advertisements for stallions now regularly cite the top Beyer Speed Figures that a racehorse has earned.)

During the 12 years the Beyer Speed Figures have been published, the most celebrated horses were Cigar, Holy Bull and Skip Away. But the top performer—from the standpoint of figures—was a horse who never earned a single championship or the acclaim he deserved: Formal Gold.

In 1997, as a 4-year-old, Formal Gold recorded Beyer Speed Figures of 126, 124 and 125 in consecutive races—three of the eight highest numbers from 1992 to 2003. This remarkable streak wasn't Formal Gold's only distinction; he had won his career debut with a figure of 112—the best ever earned by a first-time starter.

The fastest sprinter from 1992 through 2003 was Artax. Although he was an in-and-outer for much of his career, he recorded figures of 124, 123 and 123 in his championship season of 1999—three of the six best sprint numbers during the past decade.

We are often asked how horses of recent vintage compare with the stars of the past, and we wish we could offer a definitive answer. Our figures took their present form when we started compiling them in 1986 for an on-line data service, but in earlier years they were still in an evolutionary phase. Our figures of today aren't exactly comparable to our numbers in the "decade of champions"—the 1970s—when Secretariat, Seattle Slew, Affirmed and Spectacular Bid competed. I believe these great horses earned numbers that would have trounced the champions of today. When I attempted to improvise a figure of Secretariat's historic victory in the Belmont Stakes, I estimated that he earned a 139—probably the greatest race ever run.

2-year-olds, 1996

Beyer No.	Horse	Track	Date
108	THISNEARLYWASMINE	SA	10/23/1996
107	KELLY KIP	SAR	07/26/1996
106	IN EXCESSIVE BULL	SA	10/23/1996
104	KELLY KIP	BEL	06/21/1996
104	HOLZMEISTER	HAW	11/17/1996
103	IN C C'S HONOR	LRL	12/21/1996
102	DIXIE FLAG	AQU	11/24/1996
101	GOLD CASE	FG	12/30/1996
101	IN EXCESSIVE BULL	SA	10/05/1996
101	MUD ROUTE	HOL	02/15/1996
101	IN EXCESSIVE BULL	HOL	11/10/1996
101	ORDWAY	BEL	10/05/1996
101	CAPTAIN BODGIT	LRL	11/02/1996
100	BROAD DYNAMITE	DMR	07/24/1996
100	ARTHUR L.	CRC	12/14/1996
100	CONCERTO	LRL	11/02/1996
99	KING BUCK	DEL	09/17/1996
99	JULES	BEL	09/28/1996
99	TRAUFAST SLEW	CD	11/16/1996
99	ACCEPTABLE	WO	10/26/1996
99	BOSTON HARBOR	WO	10/26/1996

Boston Harbor was juvenile champion and winner of the Breeders' Cup Juvenile at Woodbine over Acceptable.

2-year-olds, 1997

Beyer No.	Horse	Track	Date
108	ORVILLE N WILBUR'S	HOL	11/07/1997
108	ORVILLE N WILBUR'S	HOL	12/11/1997
105	CORONADO'S QUEST	AQU	10/26/1997
103	RODEO	BEL	09/07/1997
102	GRAND SLAM	BEL	10/18/1997
102	REAL QUIET	HOL	12/14/1997
101	LIQUID GOLD	SA	12/28/1997
101	LIL'S LAD	BEL	10/18/1997
101	FAVORITE TRICK	HOL	11/08/1997
100	STAR OF BROADWAY	CD	11/28/1997
100	BOURBON BELLE	KEE	10/08/1997
100	UNREAL MADNESS	MED	12/05/1997
100	BOURBON BELLE	TP	12/06/1997
100	ALLEN'S OOP	HOL	11/15/1997
100	SOUVENIR COPY	SA	10/19/1997
100	ARTAX	HOL	12/14/1997
100	FAVORITE TRICK	KEE	10/18/1997
99	COUNTESS DIANA	SAR	07/23/1997
99	ALLEN'S OOP	HOL	12/11/1997
99	F J'S PACE	SA	10/30/1997
99	MISSION PARK	CD	11/02/1997
99	SWEETSOUTHERNSAINT	CRC	11/27/1997
99	SWEETSOUTHERNSAINT	CRC	12/13/1997

Favorite Trick was the unbeaten 2-year-old champion and 1997 Horse of the Year. Countess Diana was Juvenile Filly champion; Real Quiet went on to win the 1998 Kentucky Derby and Preakness, while Artax developed into the 1999 Sprint champ.

2-year-olds, 1998

Beyer No.	Horse	Track	Date
107	OLYMPIC CHARMER (F)	SA	12/28/1998
105	BET ME BEST	FG	12/12/1998
104	LONG DISTANCE (F)	AQU	11/15/1998
104	SILVERBULLETDAY (F)	CD	11/28/1998
103	SHAMROCK'S PICK	BEL	10/10/1998
103	BET ME BEST	LAD	11/07/1998
102	ARRESTED DREAMS (F)	FG	11/29/1998
102	SWEEP BACK	HOL	12/12/1998
101	LOVESME LEGEND (F)	PRM	09/06/1998
101	INCURABLE OPTIMIST	HOL	11/28/1998
101	SILVERBULLETDAY (F)	CD	11/07/1998
101	EXPLOIT	CD	11/28/1998
101	EXCELLENT MEETING (F)	HOL	12/13/1998
100	BET ME BEST	RET	09/25/1998
100	ANSWER LIVELY	LAD	10/03/1998
100	PRIME DIRECTIVE	SAR	08/19/1998
100	EXCELLENT MEETING (F)	CD	11/07/1998
98	MCKENDREE	PIM	06/12/1998
98	TACTICAL CAT	BEL	07/04/1998
98	PREMIER PROPERTY	SA	10/28/1998
98	SHUT OUT TIME	BEL	10/11/1998
98	EXCELLENT MEETING (F)	DMR	08/29/1998
98	EXPLOIT	CD	11/07/1998
98	VICAR	CD	11/28/1998

Silverbulletday won the Breeders' Cup Juvenile Fillies and was champion 2-year-old filly in 1998 as well as the 3-year-old filly champion in 1999. Answer Lively won the Breeders' Cup Juvenile and was champion 2-year-old in 1998, but none of the horses on this list won any of the 1999 Triple Crown races.

2-year-olds, 1999

Beyer No.	Horse	Track	Date
110	HOOK AND LADDER	HOL	11/28/1999
109	CHILUKKI (F)	CD	04/28/1999
106	FOREST CAMP	DMR	09/08/1999
105	MORE THAN READY	BEL	07/04/1999
105	MORE THAN READY	SAR	07/29/1999
105	CAPTAIN STEVE	CD	11/27/1999
104	PERSONAL FIRST	TP	12/26/1999
104	DIXIE UNION	SA	10/10/1999
103	LITTLEEXPECTATIONS	FG	11/27/1999
103	JOOPY DOOPY	SA	10/22/1999
103	FOREST CAMP	SA	10/10/1999
102	DIABLO'S ADDITION	BEL	06/04/1999
102	MORE THAN READY	BEL	06/04/1999
102	SWEPT OVERBOARD	SA	11/08/1999
102	B L'S APPEAL	CRC	10/23/1999
102	ORANGEMAN	SA	10/22/1999
102	ANEES	GP	11/06/1999
101	HERE'S ZEALOUS	SA	10/09/1999
101	HERE'S ZEALOUS	SA	10/22/1999
101	KISS A NATIVE	CRC	10/23/1999
101	CAPTAIN STEVE	HOL	12/18/1999

Anees won the Breeders' Cup Juvenile over Chief Seattle and was voted champion 2-year-old. Chilukki, the champion 2-year-old filly, won several graded stakes before finishing second to Cash Run in the Breeders' Cup Juvenile Fillies.

2-year-olds, 2000

Beyer No.	Horse	Track	Date
105	FLAME THROWER	SA	10/07/2000
105	STREET CRY	SA	10/07/2000
104	PROUD TOWER	SA	12/30/2000
103	FLAME THROWER	DMR	09/13/2000
103	STREET CRY	DMR	09/13/2000
101	RAGING FEVER (F)	SAR	08/14/2000
101	UNBRIDLED ELAINE (F)	CD	11/03/2000
101	POINT GIVEN	HOL	12/16/2000
101	PROUD TOWER	SA	10/28/2000
100	LASERSPORT	TP	12/09/2000
100	SILK CONCORDE (F)	CRC	08/26/2000
100	I'MADRIFTER	GG	12/26/2000
99	VALID FORBES (F)	CRC	08/05/2000
99	CINDY'S HERO (F)	DMR	09/02/2000
99	OMMADON	AQU	11/05/2000
99	MACHO UNO	CD	11/04/2000
99	POINT GIVEN	CD	11/04/2000
99	MILLENNIUM WIND	HOL	12/16/2000

Macho Uno won the Breeders' Cup Juvenile in a narrow decision over tough-trip Point Given, who came back to win the Hollywood Futurity over Millennium Wind.

2-year-olds, 2001

Beyer No.	Horse	Track	Date
108	CAME HOME	SAR	09/01/2001
107	ROMAN DANCER	SA	10/20/2001
107	WERBLIN	SA	12/26/2001
107	YOU (F)	SAR	08/13/2001
107	TEMPERA (F)	BEL	10/27/2001
106	CASHEL CASTLE	HOO	11/24/2001
106	OFFICER	DMR	08/15/2001
106	CASHIER'S DREAM (F)	SAR	08/13/2001
105	FOREST HEIRESS (F)	AQU	11/18/2001
105	CAME HOME	HOL	07/15/2001
104	IN HIGH GEAR	BEL	06/10/2001
104	MAYAKOVSKY	SAR	09/01/2001

Tempera, the eventual 2-year-old filly champ, earned the highest route figure with a 107 in the Breeders' Cup Juvenile Fillies, eight points higher than Johannesburg performance in the Juvenile.

2-year-olds, 2002

Beyer No.	Horse	Track	Date
110	TRUST N LUCK	CRC	12/14/2002
105	D'S BERTRANDO	GG	11/09/2002
104	RANDAROO	AQU	11/24/2002
103	LADY TAK (F)	CD	11/29/2002
103	SCRIMSHAW	SA	12/26/2002
103	ZAYED	SA	12/26/2002
103	POINT CLEAR (F)	SA	12/28/2002
103	FUNNY CIDE	BEL	09/29/2002
103	SKY MESA	KEE	08/31/2002
102	ZAVATA	BEL	06/29/2002
102	SIBERLAND	DMR	08/18/2002
102	WHYWHYWHY	BEL	09/15/2002

Trust N Luck's victory in the What a Pleasure at Calder was one of the top Beyer Figures on record for a 2-year-old. Sky Mesa was a fast juvenile, but was forced to scratch from the Breeders' Cup because of injury.

2-year-olds, 2003

Beyer No.	Horse	Track	Date
105	FOREST MUSIC (F)	LRL	10/08/2003
105	SMARTY JONES	PHA	11/22/2003
105	READ THE FOOTNOTES	AQU	11/29/2003
105	SILENT SIGHS (F)	SA	12/27/2003
103	CUVEE	SAR	08/13/2003
103	LION HEART	HOL	11/15/2003
103	JUDITHS WILD RUSH	WO	11/15/2003
103	WILDCAT SHOES	FG	12/28/2003
102	RULER'S COURT	SA	10/05/2003
101	CACTUS RIDGE	CBY	07/12/2003
101	CUVEE	BEL	09/14/2003
101	THE CLIFF'S EDGE	CD	11/2/2003

Cuvee won four of six starts but finished last in the Breeders' Cup Juvenile as the favorite. Many top 2-year-olds bypassed the Breeders' Cup, including Read the Footnotes, Lion Heart and Ruler's Court.

2-year-olds, 1996-2003

Beyer No.	Horse	Track	Date
110	TRUST N LUCK	CRC	12/14/2002
110	HOOK AND LADDER	HOL	11/28/1999
109	CHILUKKI (F)	CD	04/28/1999
108	ORVILLE N WILBUR'S	HOL	11/07/1997
108	ORVILLE N WILBUR'S	HOL	12/11/1997
108	THISNEARLYWASMINE	SA	10/23/1996
108	CAME HOME	SAR	09/01/2001
107	ROMAN DANCER	SA	10/20/2001
107	WERBLIN	SA	12/26/2001
107	YOU (F)	SAR	08/13/2001
107	TEMPERA (F)	BEL	10/27/2001
107	KELLY KIP	SAR	07/26/1996
107	OLYMPIC CHARMER (F)	SA	12/28/1998
106	FOREST CAMP	DMR	09/08/1999
106	CASHEL CASTLE	HOO	11/24/2001
106	OFFICER	DMR	08/15/2001
106	CASHIER'S DREAM (F)	SAR	08/13/2001

3-year-olds, 1996

Beyer No.	Horse	Track	Date
119	LOUIS QUATORZE	SAR	08/04/1996
119	WILL'S WAY	SAR	08/04/1996
118	HONOUR AND GLORY	SAR	08/08/1996
115	SKIP AWAY	BEL	10/05/1996
115	LOUIS QUATORZE	WO	10/26/1996
114	CAPOTE BELLE	BEL	06/23/1996
114	UNBRIDLED'S SONG	GP	03/16/1996
114	DEVIL'S HONOR	PHA	09/02/1996
114	WILL'S WAY	SAR	08/24/1996
113	ELUSIVE QUALITY	SAR	08/24/1996
113	HONOUR AND GLORY	SAR	08/24/1996
113	VALID ROMEO	CRC	09/28/1996
113	SKIP AWAY	KEE	04/13/1996
113	SKIP AWAY	MTH	08/04/1996
113	FORMAL GOLD	PHA	09/02/1996

113	LOUIS QUATORZE	SAR	08/24/1996
112	TANJA	BM	08/31/1996
112	MEN'S EXCLUSIVE	HOL	12/07/1996
112	FORMAL GOLD	MTH	06/12/1996
112	VALID EXPECTATIONS	AQU	11/03/1996
112	LOUIS QUATORZE	PIM	05/18/1996
112	LOUIS QUATORZE	BEL	10/05/1996
112	CAVONNIER	CD	05/04/1996
112	GRINDSTONE	CD	05/04/1996

Skip Away, winner of several Grade-1 stakes was voted top 3 year old despite not winning a Triple Crown event. Grindstone narrowly won the Kentucky Derby over Cavonnier; Louis Quatorze won the Preakness, Will's Way won the Travers and Editor's Note the Belmont Stakes.

3-year-olds, 1997

Beyer No.	Horse	Track	Date
120	KELLY KIP	SAR	08/23/1997
118	BEHRENS	MED	09/20/1997
118	CAPTAIN BODGIT	PIM	05/17/1997
118	FREE HOUSE	PIM	05/17/1997
118	SILVER CHARM	PIM	05/17/1997
117	SMOKE GLACKEN	MTH	06/28/1997
116	TOUCH GOLD	PIM	05/17/1997
115	FREE HOUSE	HOL	07/20/1997
115	CAPTAIN BODGIT	CD	05/03/1997
115	SILVER CHARM	CD	05/03/1997
114	SMOKE GLACKEN	BEL	06/07/1997
114	TOUCH GOLD	MTH	08/03/1997
114	FRISK ME NOW	PHA	09/01/1997
114	WILD RUSH	SPT	05/10/1997
113	PURPLE PASSION	LRL	12/13/1997
113	PARTNER'S HERO	MTH	08/23/1997
113	TALE OF THE CAT	SAR	08/23/1997
113	TATE	AQU	12/06/1997
112	HOLZMEISTER	HOL	05/26/1997
112	RICHTER SCALE	CD	04/26/1997

Silver Charm won the Kentucky Derby and Preakness and was second to Touch Gold in the Belmont Stakes. Captain Bodgit was second in the Derby and third behind Silver Charm and Free House in the Preakness. Silver Charm was voted champion 3-year-old. Smoke Glacken, champion sprinter.

3-year-olds, 1998

Beyer No.	Horse	Track	Date
121	ROCK AND ROLL	BEL	06/13/1998
119	RERAISE	TP	09/26/1998
116	LIMIT OUT	AQU	04/11/1998
116	CORONADO'S QUEST	AQU	04/11/1998
116	OLD TRIESTE	HOL	07/19/1998
116	RERAISE	HOL	07/04/1998
115	BANSHEE BREEZE	KEE	10/17/1998
114	GOOD AND TOUGH	BEL	06/14/1998
114	DICE DANCER	AQU	05/02/1998
114	EVENT OF THE YEAR	TP	03/29/1998
114	VICTORY GALLOP	CD	11/07/1998
113	MAJORBIGTIMESHEET	HOL	11/29/1998
113	THRILLIN DISCOVERY	CRC	11/28/1998
113	SISTER ACT	CD	11/14/1998

113	LIL'S LAD	GP	02/21/1998
113	CORONADO'S QUEST	CD	11/07/1998
112	RERAISE	CD	11/07/1998
112	PROSPEROUS BID	SA	01/18/1998
112	GOOD AND TOUGH	BEL	05/29/1998
112	INDIAN CHARLIE	SA	03/13/1998
112	MAZEL TRICK	HOL	11/14/1998
112	DICE DANCER	AQU	04/11/1998

Victory Gallop won the Belmont Stakes over Derby-Preakness winner Real Quiet, who was voted champion 3-year-old colt; Banshee Breeze was voted champion 3-year-old filly.

3-year-olds, 1999

Beyer No.	Horse	Track	Date
119	SUCCESSFUL APPEAL	TP	09/25/1999
119	GENERAL CHALLENGE	DMR	08/29/1999
118	YES IT'S TRUE	PIM	05/15/1999
118	GENERAL CHALLENGE	SA	10/16/1999
118	CAT THIEF	GP	11/06/1999
117	ECTON PARK	LAD	10/02/1999
116	FORESTRY	SAR	08/28/1999
115	TEXAS GLITTER	GP	01/03/1999
115	SILVERBULLETDAY (F)	SAR	08/21/1999
114	FORESTRY	GP	11/06/1999
114	SUCCESSFUL APPEAL	GP	11/06/1999
114	LOVE THAT RED	SA	10/30/1999
114	HIDDEN CITY	SAR	08/01/1999
114	DAVID	AQU	12/18/1999
114	STEPHEN GOT EVEN	BEL	09/18/1999
114	MENIFEE	LAD	10/02/1999
113	STRAVINSKY	GP	11/06/1999
113	FIVE STAR DAY	SAR	08/28/1999
112	KALOOKAN QUEEN (F)	SA	10/08/1999
112	ECTON PARK	SAR	08/08/1999

Charismatic, voted Horse of the Year, won the Kentucky Derby and Preakness and was third in the Belmont while injured. Lemon Drop Kid won the Belmont Stakes and the Travers. Cat Thief won the Breeders' Cup Classic.

3-Year-Olds, 2000

Beyer No.	Horse	Track	Date
121	CONCERNED MINISTER	FG	12/03/2000
119	TIZNOW	SA	10/15/2000
119	ALBERT THE GREAT	BEL	10/14/2000
118	CAPTAIN STEVE	SA	10/15/2000
117	CALLER ONE	TP	09/16/2000
116	CALLER ONE	CRC	07/15/2000
116	CALLER ONE	HOL	05/29/2000
116	SURFSIDE (F)	CD	11/24/2000
116	CAPTAIN STEVE	TP	09/16/2000
116	TIZNOW	CD	11/04/2000
116	GIANT'S CAUSEWAY	CD	11/04/2000
115	FOREST CAMP	DMR	09/09/2000
115	FUSAICHI PEGASUS	BEL	09/23/2000
115	TIZNOW	DMR	08/26/2000

Tiznow, 2000 Horse of the Year, scored his top figure in the Goodwood Handicap against older horses, then followed up with a victory in the Breeders' Cup Classic. Caller One was the top 3-year-old sprinter, with his best race coming in the Kentucky Cup Sprint.

3-Year-Olds, 2001

Beyer No.	Horse	Track	Date
120	XTRA HEAT	DEL	09/29/2001
119	SQUIRTLE SQUIRT	BEL	10/27/2001
118	XTRA HEAT	BEL	10/27/2001
117	XTRA HEAT	DEL	09/08/2001
117	SQUIRTLE SQUIRT	BEL	09/22/2001
117	POINT GIVEN	SAR	08/25/2001
116	MONARCHOS	CD	05/05/2001
116	MILAN	BEL	10/27/2001
114	HE'S A KNOCKOUT	LRL	11/22/2001
114	BURNING ROMA	DEL	06/172001
114	MILLENNIUM WIND	KEE	04/14/2001
114	POINT GIVEN	BEL	06/09/2001
113	XTRA HEAT	BEL	07/04/2001
113	XTRA HEAT	PIM	08/18/2001

Xtra Heat, a sprinting filly, turned in five of the top performances in the division. Her runner-up effort in the Breeders' Cup Sprint, in which she set a heavily pressured pace before succumbing to eventual sprint champion Squirtle Squirt, enabled her to win the 3-year-old filly title.

3-Year-Olds, 2002

Beyer No.	Horse	Track	Date
120	MEDAGLIA D'ORO	SAR	08/04/2002
116	CAME HOME	DMR	08/25/2002
114	WAR EMBLEM	CD	05/04/2002
113	THUNDERELLO	AP	10/26/2002
113	GYGISTAR	SAR	08/24/2002
113	MEDAGLIA D'ORO	SAR	08/24/2002
112	MIGHTY DAVID	HOL	06/10/2002
112	SAINT MARDEN	BEL	09/19/2002
112	IMPERIAL GESTURE (F)	BEL	09/07/2002
112	WAR EMBLEM	SPT	04/06/2002
112	WAR EMBLEM	MTH	08/04/2002
112	REPENT	SAR	08/24/2002

Medaglia d'Oro posted two of the fastest figures of the year in the Jim Dandy (120) and Travers (113) at Saratoga. War Emblem, who was named champion, won the Kentucky Derby off the highest-rated prep race, the Illinois Derby, in which he earned a 112 Beyer.

3-Year-Olds, 2003

Beyer No.	Horse	Track	Date
120	CAJUN BEAT	SA	10/25/2003
116	GHOSTZAPPER	BEL	09/27/2003
116	DYNEVER	SA	10/25/2003
115	KAFWAIN	SA	02/01/2003
114	FUNNY CIDE	PIM	05/17/2003
114	SOTO	MNR	08/09/2003
114	DYNEVER	MNR	08/09/2003
113	QUAIS	SAR	08/30/2003
113	CAJUN BEAT	TP	09/13/2003
112	ZAVATA	SAR	08/02/2003
112	TEN MOST WANTED	SAR	08/23/2003
111	EMPIRE MAKER	AQU	04/12/2003
111	POSSE	BEL	06/07/2003
111	MIDAS EYES	BEL	06/07/2003
111	WANDO	WO	06/22/2003
111	CLOCK STOPPER	TP	09/13/2003
111	COMIC TRUTH	RP	11/16/2003
111	STOCKHOLDER	AQU	11/27/2003

Champion Funny Cide's Preakness ranks among the fastest 3-year-old performances of 2003, but Breeders' Cup third Dynever is the only routing 3-year-old with two top-rated performances. Breeders' Cup Sprint winner Cajun Beat ranked among the best sprinters in the nation.

3-year-olds, 1996-2003

Beyer No.	Horse	Track	Date
121	CONCERNED MINISTER	FG	12/03/2000
121	ROCK AND ROLL	BEL	06/13/1998
120	CAJUN BEAT	SA	10/25/2003
120	MEDAGLIA D'ORO	SAR	08/04/2002
120	XTRA HEAT	DEL	09/29/2001
120	KELLY KIP	SAR	08/23/1997
119	TIZNOW	SA	10/15/2000
119	ALBERT THE GREAT	BEL	10/14/2000
119	SUCCESSFUL APPEAL	TP	09/25/1999
119	RERAISE	TP	09/26/1998
119	GENERAL CHALLENGE	DMR	08/29/1999
118	XTRA HEAT	BEL	10/27/2001
118	CAPTAIN STEVE	SA	10/15/2000
118	YES IT'S TRUE	PIM	05/15/1999
118	GENERAL CHALLENGE	SA	10/16/1999
118	BEHRENS	MED	09/20/1997
118	CAPTAIN BODGIT	PIM	05/17/1997
118	FREE HOUSE	PIM	05/17/1997
118	SILVER CHARM	PIM	05/17/1997

Sprints, 1996

Beyer No.	Horse	Track	Date
123	PROSPECT BAY	SAR	08/08/1996
118	HONOUR AND GLORY	SAR	08/08/1996
118	MEADOW MONSTER	LRL	02/19/1996
117	MEADOW MONSTER	GP	01/03/1996
117	LITE THE FUSE	LRL	07/20/1996
117	MEADOW MONSTER	LRL	07/20/1996
117	FOREST WILDCAT	PIM	09/15/1996
116	SPLENDID SPRINTER	AQU	01/06/1996
116	LITE THE FUSE	AQU	04/14/1996
116	BAGINONE	SA	04/06/1996
116	CONSTANT ESCORT	CRC	09/28/1996
116	SMART STRIKE	WO	07/07/1996
115	LORD CARSON	TP	09/15/1996
114	LIT DE JUSTICE	SA	01/07/1996
114	FT. STOCKTON	AP	08/25/1996
114	CAPOTE BELLE	BEL	06/23/1996
114	LORD CARSON	BEL	10/06/1996
114	WESTERN FAME	GP	02/16/1996
114	PAYING DUES	HOL	12/07/1996
114	FOREST WILDCAT	KEE	10/13/1996
114	LIT DE JUSTICE	WO	10/26/1996
114	ALPHABET SOUP	DMR	08/17/1996

Lit de Justice won the Breeders' Cup Sprint at Woodbine and was voted Eclipse Award sprint champion for 1996.

Sprint, 1997

Beyer No.	Horse	Track	Date
122	ELUSIVE QUALITY	GP	02/21/1997
120	KELLY KIP	SAR	08/23/1997
118	DISTORTED HUMOR	CD	06/04/1997
118	WILD ESCAPADE	CD	06/04/1997
118	UNBRIDLED'S SONG	GP	01/19/1997
117	MEN'S EXCLUSIVE	HOL	05/26/1997
117	SMOKE GLACKEN	MTH	06/28/1997
116	BUNKER HILL ROAD	OP	01/24/1997
115	APPEALING SKIER	GP	03/16/1997
115	PUNCH LINE	GP	03/16/1997
114	PUNCH LINE	GP	01/03/1997
114	ROYAL HAVEN	SAR	08/08/1997
114	SMOKE GLACKEN	BEL	06/07/1997
114	WILD ESCAPADE	CD	05/16/1997
114	BOLD CAPITAL	HOL	05/10/1997
114	BUSY LITTLE BEAVER	DMR	08/10/1997
113	WIRE ME COLLECT	BEL	10/12/1997
113	M J CLAIM	DEL	07/13/1997
113	WIRE ME COLLECT	LRL	11/23/1997
113	PURPLE PASSION	LRL	12/13/1997
113	PARTNER'S HERO	MTH	08/23/1997
113	WESTERN FAME	SUF	05/31/1997
113	VICTOR COOLEY	BEL	09/27/1997
113	FRISCO VIEW	GP	03/14/1997
113	TALE OF THE CAT	SAR	08/23/1997

Elmhurst, who did not make this list, won the Breeders' Cup Sprint. Smoke Glacken was voted Eclipse Award Champion.

Sprints, 1998

Beyer No.	Horse	Track	Date
123	ELUSIVE QUALITY	GP	02/05/1998
121	KELLY KIP	AQU	04/11/1998
120	AFFIRMED SUCCESS	SAR	09/07/1998
119	KELLY KIP	LRL	07/18/1998
119	RERAISE	TP	09/26/1998
119	AFFIRMED SUCCESS	BEL	09/26/1998
118	SON OF A PISTOL	DMR	07/26/1998
118	WAGON LIMIT	AQU	04/04/1998
118	WILD RUSH	BEL	05/25/1998
117	DISTORTED HUMOR	CD	05/02/1998
117	ORIGINATERDL GRAY	LRL	03/04/1998
116	RICHTER SCALE	BEL	06/06/1998
116	AMERICAN CHAMP	MED	11/07/1998
116	SON OF A PISTOL	SA	04/04/1998
116	AFFIRMED SUCCESS	SAR	08/06/1998
116	LIMIT OUT	AQU	04/11/1998
116	STORMIN FEVER	BEL	09/26/1998
116	DISTORTED HUMOR	KEE	04/11/1998
116	DREAM SCHEME	CD	11/14/1998
116	EL AMANTE	MTH	08/01/1998

Reraise won the Breeders' Cup Sprint and was voted champion sprinter.

Sprints, 1999

Beyer No.	Horse	Track	Date
124	ARTAX	GP	11/06/1999
123	ARTAX	BEL	10/16/1999
123	KONA GOLD	GP	11/06/1999
123	ARTAX	AQU	05/02/1999
121	LEXICON	DMR	08/08/1999
120	KELLY KIP	AQU	04/10/1999
120	LEXICON	SA	10/17/1999
120	INTIDAB	SAR	08/11/1999
119	SUCCESSFUL APPEAL	TP	09/25/1999
118	YES IT'S TRUE	PIM	05/15/1999
118	MAZEL TRICK	HOL	06/27/1999
117	CHRISTMAS BOY	DMR	07/25/1999
117	CHRISTMAS BOY	DMR	08/14/1999
117	REGAL THUNDER	DMR	08/14/1999
116	RICHTER SCALE	AQU	11/25/1999
116	ARTAX	SAR	08/11/1999
116	AFFIRMED SUCCESS	AQU	05/02/1999
116	GOOD AND TOUGH	GP	03/12/1999
116	BIG JAG	SA	03/06/1999
116	FORESTRY	SAR	08/28/1999

Sprint champion Artax broke Dr. Fager's track record for 7 furlongs at Aqueduct in May, Groovy's 6-furlong track record at Belmont Park in October and equaled Mr. Prospector's track record for six furlongs while winning the Breeders' Cup Sprint at Gulfstream Park in November.

Sprints, 2000

Beyer No.	Horse	Track	Date
119	KONA GOLD	SA	04/08/2000
118	KONA GOLD	DMR	07/29/2000
117	KONA GOLD	SA	10/14/2000
117	CALLER ONE	TP	09/16/2000
116	CALLER ONE	CRC	07/15/2000
116	LOVE THAT RED	DMR	07/29/2000
116	FIVE STAR DAY	KEE	10/14/2000
116	DELAWARE TOWNSHIP	MTH	08/27/2000
116	CALLER ONE	HOL	05/29/2000
116	CROWNING MEETING	EMD	09/10/2000
115	FORTY ONE CARATS	CRC	10/07/2000
115	FOREST CAMP	DMR	09/09/2000
115	BOURBON BELLE	SAR	08/02/2000
115	YANKEE VICTORY	BEL	05/29/2000
115	FUSAICHI PEGASUS	BEL	09/23/2000
115	LA FEMINN	GG	06/03/2000

Kona Gold dominated the sprint ranks in 2000 winning all but one start. He set a track and stakes record in winning the Breeders' Cup Sprint at Churchill Downs

Sprints, 2001

Beyer No.	Horse	Track	Date
121	SWEPT OVERBOARD	SA	10/06/2001
120	XTRA HEAT	DEL	09/29/2001
119	SQUIRTLE SQUIRT	BEL	10/27/2001
119	KONA GOLD	DMR	07/22/2001
119	BONAPAW	OP	04/12/2001

No.	Horse	Track	Date
119	EL CORREDOR	DMR	08/12/2001
118	XTRA HEAT	BEL	10/27/2001
118	EXPLICIT	GP	03/12/2001
118	LEFT BANK	BEL	09/22/2001
118	LEFT BANK	AQU	11/24/2001
117	CALLER ONE	BEL	10/27/2001
117	XTRA HEAT	DEL	09/08/2001
117	CALLER ONE	DMR	07/22/2001
117	CALLER ONE	HOL	05/27/2001
117	SQUIRTLE SQUIRT	BEL	09/22/2001

Squirtle Squirt defeated top 3-year-olds in the King's Bishop and ran second to top Grade 1 older horses in the Vosburgh before clinching the sprint title with a half-length victory over Xtra Heat in the Breeders' Cup Sprint.

Sprints, 2002

Beyer No.	Horse	Track	Date
122	SWEPT OVERBOARD	BEL	05/27/2002
121	LEFT BANK	BEL	07/04/2002
120	SLIDER	KEE	04/20/2002
120	CONGAREE	AQU	11/30/2002
117	SNOW RIDGE	SA	01/27/2002
116	BONAPAW	FG	01/12/2002
116	MOUNTAIN GENERAL	FG	11/28/2002
116	ORIENTATE	SAR	09/01/2002
115	ORIENTATE	CRC	07/15/2002
115	ORIENTATE	CD	06/29/2002
115	THERE'S ZEALOUS	AP	08/17/2002
115	REBA'S GOLD	SA	02/09/2002

Orientate came on late to dominate the division, but Swept Overboard, in the Metropolitan Mile, and Left Bank, in the Tom Fool, posted the biggest numbers of the year.

Sprints, 2003

Beyer No.	Horse	Track	Date
122	ALDEBARAN	SAR	08/31/2003
121	SHAKE YOU DOWN	CRC	07/12/2003
120	CAJUN BEAT	SA	10/25/2003
120	CONGAREE	AQU	11/29/2003
118	SHAKE YOU DOWN	AQU	04/11/2003
118	SHAKE YOU DOWN	AQU	04/26/2003
117	CAPTAIN SQUIRE	SA	01/25/2003
117	AVANZADO	SA	01/26/2003
117	SMOOTH JAZZ	KEE	04/13/2003
117	PRIVATE HORDE	SAR	08/10/2003
117	YANKEE GENTLEMAN	DMR	09/06/2003
116	CONGAREE	AQU	04/12/2003
116	TRUE DIRECTION	BEL	05/24/2003
116	BEAU'S TOWN	DMR	07/26/2003
116	GHOSTZAPPER	BEL	09/27/2003
116	TOUGH GAME	HOL	11/15/2003
116	SPOOKY MULDER	AQU	11/23/2003

Shake You Down, third in the Breeders' Cup Sprint, owned the three of the highest figures, but divisional champion Aldebaran rated highest of all with his Forego Handicap victory. Versatile Congaree had high figures at both short and long distances.

Sprints, 1992-2003

Beyer No.	Horse	Track	Date
124	ARTAX	GP	11/06/1999
123	ARTAX	BEL	10/16/1999
123	KONA GOLD	GP	11/06/1999
123	PROSPECT BAY	SAR	08/08/1996
123	ARTAX	AQU	05/02/1999
123	ELUSIVE QUALITY	GP	02/05/1998
122	ALDEBARAN	SAR	08/31/2003
122	SWEPT OVERBOARD	BEL	05/27/2002
122	ELUSIVE QUALITY	GP	02/21/1997
122	HOLY BULL	BEL	05/30/1994
121	SHAKE YOU DOWN	CRC	07/12/2003
121	LEFT BANK	BEL	07/04/2002
121	LEXICON	DMR	08/08/1999
121	KELLY KIP	AQU	04/11/1998
121	IMTOOCOOL	PIM	05/05/1995
121	SWEPT OVERBOARD	SA	10/06/2001
120	CAJUN BEAT	SA	10/25/2003
120	CONGAREE	AQU	11/29/2003
120	KELLY KIP	AQU	04/10/1999
120	XTRA HEAT	DEL	09/29/2001
120	LEXICON	SA	10/17/1999
120	INTIDAB	SAR	08/11/1999
120	LUCKY FOREVER	HOL	05/20/1995
120	KELLY KIP	SAR	08/23/1997
120	NOT SURPRISING	SAR	08/23/1995
120	AFFIRMED SUCCESS	SAR	09/07/1998

Races More Than 1 Mile, 1996

Beyer No.	Horse	Track	Date
120	KIRIDASHI	WO	08/17/1996
119	LOUIS QUATORZE	SAR	08/04/1996
119	WILL'S WAY	SAR	08/04/1996
118	GENTLEMEN	HOL	12/22/1996
117	CIGAR	AP	07/13/1996
117	CIGAR	GP	02/10/1996
117	SIPHON	HOL	06/30/1996
116	SIPHON	HOL	05/04/1996
116	CIGAR	BEL	09/14/1996
116	JEWEL PRINCESS	HOL	07/21/1996
116	GERI	OP	04/06/1996
116	DARE AND GO	DMR	08/10/1996
116	GERI	HOL	6/30/1996
116	L'CARRIERE	SAR	08/25/1996
115	ARRIVEDERCI BABY	GG	11/29/1996
115	DEL MAR DENNIS	HOL	05/04/1996
115	SMART STRIKE	MTH	08/25/1996
115	CIGAR	BEL	10/05/1996
115	SKIP AWAY	BEL	10/05/1996
115	RICHIE THE COACH	LRL	11/23/1996
115	ALPHABET SOUP	WO	10/26/1996
115	CIGAR	WO	10/26/1996
115	LOUIS QUATORZE	WO	10/26/1996

Cigar's 16-race winning streak that began in 1994 ended when he was defeated by Dare and Go in the 1996 Pacific Classic, at Del Mar, August 25. Cigar was voted Horse of the Year for the 2nd consecutive season.

Races More Than 1 Mile, 1997

Beyer No.	Horse	Track	Date
126	FORMAL GOLD	SAR	08/02/1997
126	WILL'S WAY	SAR	08/02/1997
126	GENTLEMEN	PIM	05/10/1997
125	FORMAL GOLD	BEL	09/20/1997
125	SKIP AWAY	PIM	05/10/1997
124	FORMAL GOLD	MTH	08/23/1997
123	TEJANO RUN	HIA	03/22/1997
122	FORMAL GOLD	SUF	05/31/1997
122	SKIP AWAY	SUF	05/31/1997
121	ORMSBY	AQU	04/26/1997
121	GENTLEMEN	DMR	08/09/1997
121	GENTLEMEN	HOL	06/29/1997
120	ORMSBY	AQU	04/05/1997
120	SKIP AWAY	HOL	11/08/1997
120	SIPHON	SA	03/02/1997
119	HIDDEN LAKE	BEL	06/28/1997
118	WHISKEY WISDOM	KEE	10/17/1997
118	BEHRENS	MED	09/20/1997
118	CAPTAIN BODGIT	PIM	05/17/1997
118	FREE HOUSE	PIM	05/17/1997
118	SILVER CHARM	PIM	05/17/1997
118	SKIP AWAY	BEL	07/04/1997
118	MT. SASSAFRAS	GP	03/01/1997

Many of the highest Beyer Figures since 1992 were scored by the top routers on this list. Skip Away won the Breeders' Cup Classic and was champion older horse.

Races More Than 1 Mile, 1999

Beyer No.	Horse	Track	Date
119	GENERAL CHALLENGE	DMR	08/29/1999
119	FREE HOUSE	SA	03/06/1999
118	MAZEL TRICK	DMR	08/07/1999
118	RUNNING STAG	BEL	06/12/1999
118	VICTORY GALLOP	CD	06/12/1999
118	OLD TRIESTE	HOL	05/29/1999
118	BUDROYALE	SA	10/16/1999
118	GENERAL CHALLENGE	SA	10/16/1999
118	CAT THIEF	GP	11/06/1999
118	EVENT OF THE YEAR	SA	03/06/1999
118	SILVER CHARM	SA	03/06/1999
117	ALMUTAWAKEL	BEL	09/18/1999
117	RIVER KEEN	BEL	09/18/1999
117	BEHRENS	OP	04/03/1999
117	BEHRENS	SUF	05/29/1999
117	RIVER KEEN	BEL	10/10/1999
117	ECTON PARK	LAD	10/02/1999
116	BEHRENS	SAR	08/01/1999
116	VICTORY GALLOP	SAR	08/01/1999
116	RUNNING STAG	SUF	05/29/1999
116	BUDROYALE	GP	11/06/1999
116	GOLDEN MISSILE	GP	11/06/1999
116	RUNNING STAG	SAR	08/29/1999

River Keen paired up 117 Beyers in his Woodward and Jockey Club Gold Cup victories, but ran poorly in the Breeders' Cup Classic, finishing 11th.

Races More Than 1 Mile, 1998

Beyer No.	Horse	Track	Date
123	SILVER CHARM	TP	09/26/1998
123	WILD RUSH	TP	09/26/1998
121	ROCK AND ROLL	BEL	06/13/1998
121	SKIP AWAY	SUF	05/30/1998
119	SKIP AWAY	BEL	09/19/1998
119	SHARP CAT	BEL	10/10/1998
119	MOSSFLOWER	BEL	06/20/1998
118	AWESOME AGAIN	CD	06/13/1998
118	SKIP AWAY	PIM	05/09/1998
117	FREE HOUSE	DMR	08/15/1998
117	SKIP AWAY	HOL	06/28/1998
116	CORONADO'S QUEST	AQU	04/11/1998
116	GENTLEMEN	BEL	09/19/1998
116	SILVER CHARM	CD	06/13/1998
116	OLD TRIESTE	HOL	07/19/1998
116	AWESOME AGAIN	CD	11/07/1998
115	FRISK ME NOW	HIA	03/21/1998
115	SIR BEAR	HIA	03/21/1998
115	BANSHEE BREEZE	KEE	10/17/1998
115	WAGON LIMIT	BEL	10/10/1998
115	SILVER CHARM	CD	11/07/1998
115	SWAIN	CD	11/07/1998

Awesome Again won the Breeders' Cup Classic, but Skip Away was voted Horse of the Year for several excellent performances.

Races More Than 1 Mile, 2000

Beyer No.	Horse	Track	Date
122	SKY JACK	SA	12/03/2000
121	CONCERNED MINISTER	FG	12/03/2000
120	STEPHEN GOT EVEN	GP	02/05/2000
119	GOLDEN MISSILE	GP	02/05/2000
119	TIZNOW	SA	10/15/2000
119	ALBERT THE GREAT	BEL	10/14/2000
118	CAPTAIN STEVE	SA	10/15/2000
118	LEMON DROP KID	SAR	08/06/2000
118	SKIMMING	DMR	08/26/2000
117	FORTY ONE CARATS	CRC	07/09/2000
117	RUNNING STAG	SUF	06/03/2000
117	GENERAL CHALLENGE	SA	03/04/2000
116	DIXIE DOT COM	SA	01/16/2000
116	HERITAGE OF GOLD (F)	CD	06/03/2000
116	GOLDEN MISSILE	CD	06/17/2000
116	SURFSIDE (F)	CD	11/24/2000
116	EUCHRE	SA	10/15/2000
116	CAPTAIN STEVE	TP	09/16/2000
116	TIZNOW	CD	11/04/2000
116	GIANT'S CAUSEWAY	CD	11/04/2000

Sky Jack and Concerned Minister individually came up big in relatively obscure races to score the two highest Beyer Figures of the season. Stephen Got Even rated a 120 in the Donn Handicap, but subsequently was injured and retired.

Races More Than 1 Mile, 2001

Beyer No.	Horse	Track	Date
123	APTITUDE	BEL	10/06/2001
119	ALBERT THE GREAT	BEL	07/01/2001
119	SKIMMING	DMR	08/19/2001
118	EUCHRE	PRM	07/07/2001
117	GUIDED TOUR	CD	06/16/2001
117	INCLUDE	SUF	06/02/2001
117	ALBERT THE GREAT	PIM	05/12/2001
117	INCLUDE	PIM	05/12/2001
117	GUIDED TOUR	AP	07/21/2001
117	TIZNOW	BEL	10/27/2001
117	SAKHEE	BEL	10/27/2001
117	TIZNOW	SA	03/03/2001
117	POINT GIVEN	SAR	08/25/2001
116	BROKEN VOW	GP	02/05/2001

Tiznow won his second straight Breeders' Cup Classic, defeating Arc winner Sakhee in a courageous performance. Aptitude, an also-ran in the Classic, scored the year's highest Beyer Figure with a stunning 10-length score in the Jockey Club Gold Cup.

Races More Than 1 Mile, 2002

Beyer No.	Horse	Track	Date
121	LEFT BANK	SAR	08/03/2002
120	MEDAGLIA D'ORO	SAR	08/04/2002
119	MIZZEN MAST	SA	02/02/2002
119	LIDO PALACE	SAR	08/03/2002
119	STREET CRY	SAR	08/03/2002
118	STREET CRY	CD	06/15/2002
118	MILWAUKEE BREW	SA	03/02/2002
116	PLEASANTLY PERFECT	SA	10/06/2002
116	MACHO UNO	SAR	08/03/2002
116	VOLPONI	AP	10/26/2002
116	CAME HOME	DMR	08/25/2002

Left Bank turned the rare trick of posting 120-plus Beyers going short and long. Volponi, winner of the Breeders' Cup Classic, scored 110-plus Beyers on both the dirt and turf.

Races More Than 1 Mile, 2003

Beyer No.	Horse	Track	Date
123	CANDY RIDE	DMR	08/24/2003
119	MEDAGLIA D'ORO	SA	02/01/2003
119	PLEASANTLY PERFECT	SA	10/25/2003
118	CONGAREE	SA	02/02/2003
118	MINESHAFT	PIM	05/16/2003
118	MEDAGLIA D'ORO	DMR	08/24/2003
117	PERFECT DRIFT	CD	06/14/2003
117	MINESHAFT	CD	06/14/2003
117	MINESHAFT	BEL	09/06/2003
117	MEDAGLIA D'ORO	SA	10/25/2003
116	MILWAUKEE BREW	SA	03/01/2003
116	CONGAREE	SA	03/01/2003
116	MINESHAFT	FG	03/02/2003
116	MINESHAFT	KEE	04/25/2003
116	CONGAREE	HOL	07/13/2003
116	DYNEVER	SA	10/25/2003

Champion Mineshaft turned in five of the fastest route performances of the year. Medaglia d'Oro and Congaree, who never faced Mineshaft, were among the others to record multiple fast times. The best figure of the season was turned in by Candy Ride, in defeating Medaglia d'Oro in the Pacific Classic.

Races More Than 1 Mile, 1992-2003

Beyer No.	Horse	Track	Date
126	FORMAL GOLD	SAR	08/02/1997
126	WILL'S WAY	SAR	08/02/1997
126	GENTLEMEN	PIM	05/10/1997
125	BERTRANDO	BEL	09/18/1993
125	FORMAL GOLD	BEL	09/20/1997
125	SKIP AWAY	PIM	05/10/1997
124	FORMAL GOLD	MTH	08/23/1997
123	CANDY RIDE	DMR	08/24/2003
123	APTITUDE	BEL	10/06/2001
123	TEJANO RUN	HIA	03/22/1997
123	SILVER CHARM	TP	09/26/1998
123	WILD RUSH	TP	09/26/1998
123	BEST PAL	SA	03/07/1992
122	SKY JACK	SA	12/03/2000
122	FORMAL GOLD	SUF	05/31/1997
122	SKIP AWAY	SUF	05/31/1997
121	LEFT BANK	SAR	08/03/2002
121	CONCERNED MINISTER	FG	12/03/2000
121	ROCK AND ROLL	BEL	06/13/1998
121	ORMSBY	AQU	04/26/1997
121	BEST PAL	OP	04/11/1992
121	CRAFTY CASH*	OP	04/11/1992
121	CIGAR	OP	04/15/1995
121	BEST PAL	SA	01/18/1992
121	SKIP AWAY	SUF	05/30/1998
121	GENTLEMEN	DMR	08/09/1997
121	GENTLEMEN	HOL	06/29/1997

The top three Beyer Speed Figures and seven of the top 10, were earned in 1997. Formal Gold earned three of the top 10 Beyer Figures himself.

Turf, 1996

Beyer No.	Horse	Track	Date
118	FASTNESS	DMR	08/04/1996
117	SMOOTH RUNNER	DMR	08/04/1996
115	SINGSPIEL	WO	09/29/1996
115	PILSUDSKI	WO	10/26/1996
114	DA HOSS	WO	10/26/1996
114	TALLOIRES	HOL	07/21/1996
113	SINGSPIEL	WO	10/26/1996
112	URGENT REQUEST	SA	10/05/1996
112	KIRIDASHI	WO	09/29/1996
112	FASTNESS	HOL	05/12/1996
112	AURIETTE	HOL	06/09/1996
112	SANDPIT	HOL	05/27/1996
112	BROADWAY FLYER	SAR	08/10/1996
111	SMOOTH RUNNER	BEL	07/04/1996
111	FASTNESS	HOL	06/16/1996
111	SPINNING WORLD	WO	10/26/1996
111	ALLIED FORCES	BEL	10/06/1996
111	THE VID	GP	01/06/1996
111	N B FORREST	MTH	08/04/1996
111	SANDPIT	ATL	06/22/1996
111	MECKE	AP	08/25/1996
111	DIPLOMATIC JET	BEL	06/08/1996
111	DIPLOMATIC JET	BEL	09/14/1996

111	DIPLOMATIC JET	BEL	10/05/1996
111	CHIEF BEARHART	WO	09/29/1996

Singspiel was second to European invader Pilsudski in the Breeders' Cup Turf at Woodbine and was voted champion turf horse of 1996.

Turf, 1997

Beyer

No.	Horse	Track	Date
115	ATTICUS	SA	03/01/1997
114	SPINNING WORLD	HOL	11/08/1997
113	RIVER FLYER	BM	02/15/1997
112	LUCKY COIN	BEL	09/20/1997
112	LUCKY COIN	BEL	10/18/1997
112	CHIEF BEARHART	WO	09/28/1997
111	ISITINGOOD	SA	02/05/1997
111	INFLUENT	ATL	06/28/1997
111	GERI	BEL	06/14/1997
111	CHIEF BEARHART	WO	10/19/1997
110	GERI	HOL	11/08/1997
110	EL ANGELO	BM	09/20/1997
110	OK BY ME	RKM	06/15/1997
110	CHIEF BEARHART	WO	06/14/1997
110	MEMORIES OF SILVER	AP	08/24/1997
110	INFLUENT	BEL	09/21/1997
110	CHIEF BEARHART	HOL	11/08/1997
109	ADVANCING STAR	HOL	11/28/1997
109	DECORATED HERO	HOL	11/08/1997
109	LUCKY COIN	HOL	11/08/1997
109	VIA LOMBARDIA	SA	02/05/1997
109	PINFLORON	SA	03/01/1997
109	DEVIL'S CUP	GP	01/25/1997
109	MAXZENE	AP	08/24/1997
109	VAL'S PRINCE	BEL	10/18/1997
109	BORGIA	HOL	11/08/1997
109	RIVER BAY	HOL	12/14/1997

Chief Bearhart won the Breeders' Cup Turf at Hollywood Park and was voted Eclipse Award champion. Atticus set a world record when he earned his 115 Beyer Figure over a blazingly fast turf course at Santa Anita.

Turf, 1998

Beyer

No.	Horse	Track	Date
114	JIM AND TONIC	WO	09/20/1998
114	LABEEB	WO	09/20/1998
113	DA HOSS	CD	11/07/1998
113	HAWKSLEY HILL	CD	11/07/1998
112	ELUSIVE QUALITY	BEL	07/04/1998
112	FANTASTIC FELLOW	HOL	04/26/1998
112	JOYEUX DANSEUR	CD	05/02/1998
112	JOYEUX DANSEUR	FG	02/07/1998
112	JOYEUX DANSEUR	FG	03/29/1998
112	BUCK'S BOY	BEL	10/10/1998
111	FLORISELLI	DMR	08/09/1998
111	LABEEB	HOL	06/14/1998
111	SUBORDINATION	BEL	09/26/1998
111	CHIEF BEARHART	BEL	06/06/1998

111	DAYLAMI	BEL	09/12/1998
110	FANTASTIC FELLOW	HOL	06/14/1998
110	JAUNATXO	FG	12/04/1998
110	BUCK'S BOY	CD	11/07/1998
110	ROYAL ANTHEM	WO	10/18/1998
109	HAWKSLEY HILL	GG	05/23/1998
109	FAVORITE TRICK	KEE	10/17/1998
109	HAWKSLEY HILL	BM	09/19/1998
109	WILD EVENT	CD	11/08/1998
109	FIJI	HOL	06/07/1998
109	VERGENNES	HOL	11/29/1998
109	BUCK'S BOY	BEL	09/12/1998
109	FLAG DOWN	GP	02/14/1998
109	LAZY LODE	HOL	12/12/1998

Da Hoss, winner of the 1996 Mile at Woodbine, scored his second victory in that Breeders' Cup race after missing the 1997 Mile and racing only once in 1998. Buck's Boy won the Breeders' Cup Turf and was voted champion turf horse..

Turf, 1999

Beyer

No.	Horse	Track	Date
118	DAYLAMI	GP	11/06/1999
113	BRAVE ACT	HOL	05/16/1999
113	ROYAL ANTHEM	GP	11/06/1999
112	CRYSTAL HEARTED	DMR	07/30/1999
112	TRANQUILITY LAKE	HOL	06/06/1999
111	HAWKSLEY HILL	SA	03/06/1999
111	LORD SMITH	SA	03/06/1999
111	SUPER QUERCUS	HOL	11/28/1999
110	MIDDLESEX DRIVE	BEL	10/16/1999
110	SILIC	GP	11/06/1999
110	GARBU	GP	03/13/1999
110	BUCK'S BOY	WO	09/10/1999
110	LAZY LODE	HOL	06/26/1999
110	VAL'S PRINCE	BEL	09/11/1999
110	YAGLI	GP	02/06/1999
110	BUCK'S BOY	GP	11/06/1999
110	LAZY LODE	HOL	12/04/1999
109	DOCKSIDER	GP	11/06/1999
109	LEND A HAND	GP	11/06/1999
109	TUZLA	GP	11/06/1999
109	LADIES DIN	HOL	06/13/1999
109	SILIC	HOL	06/13/1999
109	SILIC	SA	10/16/1999
109	HAWKSLEY HILL	WO	09/19/1999
109	QUIET RESOLVE	WO	09/19/1999
109	BRAVE ACT	HOL	11/27/1999
109	GARBU	CD	05/01/1999
109	HAWKSLEY HILL	CD	05/01/1999
109	WILD EVENT	CD	05/01/1999
109	HAPPYANUNOIT	KEE	10/15/1999
109	WILD EVENT	GP	02/06/1999
109	HONOR GLIDE	SAR	08/14/1999

European Horse of the Year, Daylami, owned by Dubai based Godolphin stables won the Breeders' Cup Turf and was voted champion turf horse in North America. Silic won the Breeders' Cup Mile.

Turf, 2000

Beyer No.	Horse	Track	Date
112	JOHN'S CALL	SAR	08/12/2000
110	SILIC	HOL	06/18/2000
110	FEDERAL TRIAL	GP	02/19/2000
110	CHESTER HOUSE	AP	08/19/2000
110	ROYAL ANTHEM	GP	02/12/2000
110	KALANISI	CD	11/04/2000
109	FULL MOON MADNESS	HOL	12/22/2000
109	TEXAS GLITTER	HOL	12/22/2000
109	FORBIDDEN APPLE	BEL	10/08/2000
109	LADIES DIN	HOL	06/18/2000
109	SPINDRIFT	AQU	05/06/2000
109	LADIES DIN	DMR	07/30/2000
109	TOUT CHARMANT	HOL	11/26/2000
109	TRANQUILITY LAKE	HOL	11/26/2000
109	BRAVE ACT	SA	01/01/2000
109	NATIVE DESERT	SA	01/01/2000
109	JOHN'S CALL	BEL	10/07/2000
109	JOHN'S CALL	CD	11/04/2000
109	QUIET RESOLVE	CD	11/04/2000
109	MUTAMAM	CD	11/04/2000

The 9-year-old John's Call recorded the highest figure of the year, going wire to wire to win the Sword Dancer at Saratoga. Many of the division's stars, including Silic, Chester House, and Royal Anthem, were derailed by injury.

Turf, 2001

Beyer No.	Horse	Track	Date
118	SILVANO	AP	08/18/2001
117	FANTASTIC LIGHT	BEL	10/27/2001
116	MILAN	BEL	10/27/2001
114	VAL ROYAL	BEL	10/27/2001
114	KING CUGAT	BEL	07/07/2001
113	SLEW VALLEY	BEL	07/07/2001
112	YARALINO	GG	02/04/2001
112	BANKS HILL	BEL	10/27/2001
111	SPEAK IN PASSING	HOL	11/23/2001
111	SWEPT OVERBOARD	HOL	11/23/2001
111	EL CIELO	SA	11/05/2001
111	EL CIELO	SA	01/04/2001

German-bred Silvano turned in a very impressive performance on a soggy Arlington turf course in the Million. Fantastic Light, who defeated many of the top turf horses in Europe, clinched a title in North America with a victory in the Breeders' Cup Turf over another European, the 3-year-old Milan.

Turf, 2002

Beyer No.	Horse	Track	Date
113	DOMEDRIVER	AP	10/26/2002
113	GOOD JOURNEY	AP	10/26/2002
111	ROCK OF GIBRALTAR	AP	10/26/2002
111	LADIES DIN	HOL	05/27/2002
111	BEAT HOLLOW	BEL	06/08/2002
111	HIGH CHAPARRAL	AP	10/26/2002
111	BALLINGARRY	WO	09/29/2002
110	BLU AIR FORCE	HOL	06/19/2002
110	VOLPONI	BEL	07/05/2002
110	SPECIAL RING	HOL	07/07/2002
110	DEL MAR SHOW	SAR	07/26/2002
110	WITH ANTICIPATION	MTH	07/06/2002

The Europeans dominated turf racing in North America once again, as Domedriver and High Chaparral took the Breeders' Cup Mile and Turf, respectively.

Turf, 2003

Beyer No.	Horse	Track	Date
112	STORMING HOME	HOL	05/10/2003
112	JOHAR	SA	10/25/2003
112	HIGH CHAPARRAL	SA	10/25/2003
112	FALBRAV	SA	10/25/2003
111	THE TIN MAN	SA	02/15/2003
111	REDATTORE	HOL	05/26/2003
111	SPECIAL RING	DMR	07/27/2003
110	HONOR IN WAR	CD	05/03/2003
110	BALTO STAR	MTH	07/05/2003
110	TRADEMARK	SAR	07/25/2003
110	LUNAR SOVEREIGN	BEL	09/06/2003
110	SULAMANI	BEL	09/27/2003

There was a four-way tie for the top figure in turf racing in 2003, shared in part by the dead-heat Breeders' Cup Turf winners, Johar and High Chaparral; Falbrav, who was beaten just a head in the Turf; and Storming Home.

Turf, 1992-2003

Beyer No.	Horse	Track	Date
118	FASTNESS	DMR	08/04/1996
118	DAYLAMI	GP	11/06/1999
118	SILVANO	AP	08/18/2001
117	FANTASTIC LIGHT	BEL	10/27/2001
117	MEGAN'S INTERCO	HOL	05/22/1994
117	SMOOTH RUNNER	DMR	08/04/1996
117	STAR OF COZZENE	ATL	06/27/1993
117	PARADISE CREEK	BEL	06/11/1994
117	STAR OF COZZENE	BEL	09/18/1993
116	MILAN	BEL	10/27/2001
116	STAR OF COZZENE	BEL	06/06/1993
115	ROTSALUCK	SA	11/05/1994
115	FURIOUSLY	HOL	05/22/1994
115	ATTICUS	SA	03/01/1997
115	LURE	ATL	06/27/1993
115	STAR OF COZZENE	AP	08/29/1993
115	SINGSPIEL	WO	09/29/1996
115	PILSUDSKI	WO	10/26/1996
114	PEMBROKE	HOL	07/15/1995
114	RIDGEWOOD PEARL	BEL	10/28/1995
114	SPINNING WORLD	HOL	11/08/1997
114	DA HOSS	WO	10/26/1996
114	JIM AND TONIC	WO	09/20/1998
114	LABEEB	WO	09/20/1998
114	AWAD	AP	08/27/1995
114	LURE	BEL	06/06/1993
114	PARADISE CREEK	LRL	10/15/1994
114	FREEDOM CRY	BEL	10/28/1995
114	NORTHERN SPUR	BEL	10/28/1995
114	TALLOIRES	HOL	07/21/1996

There was a very narrow spread of only four Beyer points among the top 30 Beyer Speed figures earned on the turf from 1992-2003.

GRADED STAKES

2003 GRADED STAKES CHARTS
PAST PERFORMANCES FOR GRADED STAKES WINNERS

Graded Stakes Chart Index

TENTH RACE
Calder
JANUARY 1, 2003

1⅛ MILES. (Turf)(1.44^{4}) 27th Running of THE TROPICAL PARK DERBY. Grade III. Purse $100,000 Guaranteed. THREE YEAR OLDS (FOALS OF 2000). By subscription of $100 each which shall accompany the nomination, $2,000 to pass the entry box, with $100,000 guaranteed. The owner of the winner to receive $60,000, $20,000 to second, $11,000 tothird, $6,000 to fourth and $3,000 to fifth. Weights: 122 lbs. Non-winners of $35,000 twice at a mile or over allowed 3 lbs.; $30,000 at a mile or over, 5 lbs.; $15,000 at a mile or over other than Maiden or Claiming, 7 lbs.; a race other than Maiden or Claiming, 10 lbs. Graded placed horses of equal weights preferred. A trophy will be presented to the winning Owner. This race will be limited to 12 Starters, with Also Eligibles. (High Weights Preferred). Supplemental Nominations due at time of entry with a fee of $3,000 to enter and start. Closed Wednesday, December 18, 2002 with 27 nominations.

Value of Race: $100,000 Winner $60,000; second $20,000; third $11,000; fourth $6,000; fifth $3,000. Mutuel Pool $276,147.00 Exacta Pool $242,316.00 Trifecta Pool $205,831.00 Superfecta Pool $67,787.00

Last Raced	Horse	M/Eqt.	A.Wt	PP	St	¼	½	¾	Str	Fin	Jockey	Odds $1
14Dec02 ^{9}Crc^{1}	Nothing To Lose	Lb	3 115	4	5	5^{hd}	6^{1}	$5^{\frac{1}{2}}$	$3^{\frac{1}{2}}$	$1^{1\frac{3}{4}}$	Bailey J D	1.80
30Nov02 ^{8}Crc^{1}	Millennium Storm	Lb	3 119	10	3	$2^{2\frac{1}{2}}$	$2^{1\frac{1}{2}}$	2^{1}	1^{hd}	2^{hd}	Velasquez C	13.80
7Dec02 ^{4}Hou^{2}	Supah Blitz	Lb	3 115	11	4	$3^{\frac{1}{2}}$	3^{hd}	4^{hd}	$2^{1\frac{1}{2}}$	$3^{\frac{3}{4}}$	Prado E S	4.60
5Nov02 ^{8}Pha^{2}	Flank Attack	Lb	3 114	5	9	12	$10^{\frac{1}{2}}$	$10^{2\frac{1}{2}}$	$8^{1\frac{1}{2}}$	4^{nk}	Santos J A	68.40
14Dec02 ^{9}Crc^{3}	Supervisor	Lb	3 112	7	11	11^{hd}	$11^{2\frac{1}{2}}$	9^{hd}	9^{1}	5no	Chavez J F	5.90
14Dec02 ^{11}Crc^{4}	White Cat	Lb	3 117	6	7	8^{1}	8^{hd}	$8^{\frac{1}{2}}$	7^{hd}	6^{nk}	Guidry M	27.80
16Nov02 ^{7}CD^{2}	Christmas Away	Lb	3 117	1	2	1^{hd}	1^{hd}	1^{hd}	$6^{\frac{1}{2}}$	7^{hd}	Velazquez J R	11.70
30Nov02 ^{5}Crc^{1}	Unbridels King	Lb	3 115	3	1	4^{1}	4^{hd}	$6^{\frac{1}{2}}$	5^{hd}	8^{5}	Cruz M R	10.70
14Dec02 ^{11}Crc^{3}	Super Frolic	Lb	3 119	2	6	$7^{1\frac{1}{2}}$	7^{1}	7^{1}	10^{5}	$9^{\frac{3}{4}}$	Coa E M	6.80
30Nov02 ^{8}Crc^{7}	Sea Pleasure	Lb	3 117	12	8	$6^{\frac{1}{2}}$	5^{1}	3^{hd}	4^{hd}	$10^{5\frac{1}{4}}$	Homeister R B Jr	20.50
30Nov02 ^{8}Crc^{9}	Newsbreak	Lb	3 117	8	12	10^{hd}	9^{1}	11^{6}	11^{11}	$11^{9\frac{1}{2}}$	Douglas R R	10.70
14Dec02 ^{9}Crc^{7}	Magic Ruby	Lb	3 112	9	10	$9^{1\frac{1}{2}}$	12	12	12	12	Garcia J A	174.60

OFF AT 4:21 Start Good. Won driving. Course good.
TIME :24, :48^{3}, 1:13^{1}, 1:38^{1}, 1:50^{2} (:24.19, :48.74, 1:13.23, 1:38.23, 1:50.45)

$2 Mutuel Prices:

4–NOTHING TO LOSE	5.60	4.20	3.00
10–MILLENNIUM STORM		10.20	5.80
11–SUPAH BLITZ			4.60

$2 EXACTA 4–10 PAID $60.40 $2 TRIFECTA 4–10–11 PAID $272.60 $2 SUPERFECTA 4–10–11–5 PAID $7,069.20

B. c, (Jan), by Sky Classic–Cherlindrea, by Clever Trick. Trainer Lukas D Wayne. Bred by Kenneth L Ramsey & Sarah K Ramsey (Ky).

NOTHING TO LOSE checked in traffic on the first turn, raced between horses for six furlongs, angled out on the turn, rallied between horses in midstretch then closed steadily to get up in the final seventy yards. MILLENNIUM STORM forced the pace from outside for six furlongs, gained a slim lead in upper stretch, battled into deep stretch and yielded grudgingly. SUPAH BLITZ never far back, rallied between horses leaving the turn, mad a run to challenge in midstretch then held well for a share. FLANK ATTACK steadied then was shuffled back in the early stages, raced well back while saving ground to the turn then rallied belatedly between horses. SUPERVISOR was outrun to the top of the stretch then improved his position with a mild late rally. WHITE CAT checked in traffic on the far turn, circled six wide into the stretch then lacked a strong closing bid. CHRISTMAS AWAY dueled along the rail to the top of the stretch and tired. UNBRIDELS KING settled in good position while saving ground, checked inside the winner on the far turn then failed to threaten thereafter. SUPER FROLIC steadied in traffic along the rail leaving the first turn then failed to mount a serious rally. SEA PLEASURE lodged a mild rally four wide on the turn then checked while tiring inside the furlong marker. NEWSBREAK never reached contention. MAGIC RUBY raced wide while always far back.

Owners— 1, Ramsey Kenneth L & Sarah K; 2, Barnett Gloria Proscia Nicholas & I; 3, Bee Bee Stables & Tortora Jacquelin; 4, Link O W; 5, Lundock Rodney G; 6, Cottrell Raymond H Sr; 7, Bowling Carl & Thompson Charles R; 8, Oxenberg Bea & Montanari Marion; 9, Stride Rite Racing Stable; 10, Lewis James R Jr; 11, Courtlandt Farms; 12, Marti Eduardo H

Trainers—1, Lukas D Wayne; 2, White William P; 3, Tortora Emanuel; 4, Durso Robert J; 5, Tortora Emanuel; 6, McPeek Kenneth G; 7, Byrne Patrick B; 8, Plesa Edward Jr; 9, Wolfson Milton W; 10, Tortora Emanuel; 11, Motion H Graham; 12, Corredor Enrique

Scratched— Don't Be Cruel (28Nov02 ^{3}AQU^{7}), Falcon Ten (7Nov02 ^{5}CRC^{3})

$2 Pick Three (3–2–4) Paid $189.80; Pick Three Pool $37,227.

SEVENTH RACE
Santa Anita
JANUARY 1, 2003

5½ FURLONGS. (1.01^{3}) 22nd Running of THE EL CONEJO HANDICAP. Grade III. Purse $100,000 Added. FOUR-YEAR-OLDS AND UPWARD. By subscription of $100 each to accompany the nomination or by supplementary nomination of $2,000 by Monday, December 22 $1,000 additional to start with $100,000 added. The added money and all fees to be divided 60% to the winner, 20% to second, 12% to third, 6% to fourth and 2% to fifth. Weights: Monday, December 23. NOMINATIONS CLOSED Thursday, December 19, 2002 with 18.

Value of Race: $108,800 Winner $65,280; second $21,760; third $13,056; fourth $6,528; fifth $2,176. Mutuel Pool $479,652.00 Exacta Pool $325,256.00 Quinella Pool $36,497.00 Trifecta Pool $342,863.00 Superfecta Pool $120,978.00

Last Raced	Horse	M/Eqt.	A.	Wt	PP	St	¼	⅜	Str	Fin	Jockey	Odds $1
26Oct02 $^{6}AP^{4}$	Kona Gold	LB	9	123	1	7	7	6^{hd}	4^{2}	1^{nk}	Solis A	1.30
7Sep02 $^{4}Dmr^{6}$	Radiata	LB	6	115	3	2	1^{hd}	1^{hd}	1^{hd}	$2^{3/4}$	Valenzuela P A	17.10
29Jun02 $^{9}CD^{3}$	No Armistice	LBb	6	116	5	1	3^{hd}	3^{hd}	3^{1}	3^{hd}	Flores D R	5.10
7Dec02 $^{8}Hol^{7}$	Mellow Fellow	LBbf	8	117	7	6	6^{hd}	7	7	$4^{2\frac{1}{2}}$	Pincay L Jr	6.90
21Nov02 $^{4}GG^{1}$	Our Magistrate	LB	5	111	4	4	2^{hd}	2^{1}	$2^{1/2}$	$5^{1/2}$	Martinez F F	19.90
16Nov02 $^{10}Lrl^{7}$	Avanzado-ARG	LB	6	117	6	5	$4^{1\frac{1}{2}}$	4^{1}	5^{hd}	6^{nk}	Baze T C	3.30
13Apr02 $^{7}Aqu^{1}$	Roman Dancer	LB	4	116	2	3	$5^{2\frac{1}{2}}$	$5^{2\frac{1}{2}}$	6^{hd}	7	Desormeaux K J	6.20

OFF AT 3:41 Start Good. Won driving. Track fast.
TIME :21^{2}, :44^{2}, :56^{2}, 1:02^{3} (:21.43, :44.47, :56.50, 1:02.63)

$2 Mutuel Prices:			
1-KONA GOLD	4.60	3.40	2.60
3-RADIATA		10.40	4.60
6-NO ARMISTICE			4.00

$1 EXACTA 1-3 PAID $21.60 $2 QUINELLA 1-3 PAID $28.60 $1 TRIFECTA 1-3-6 PAID $105.00 $1 SUPERFECTA 1-3-6-8 PAID $340.00

B. g, by Java Gold-Double Sunrise, by Slew o' Gold. Trainer Headley Bruce. Bred by Perez Carlos (Ky).

KONA GOLD chased the leaders inside then came off the rail on the backstretch, angled back in on the turn, rallied along the fence under urging in the stretch and proved narrowly best. RADIATA had good early speed and dueled inside rivals but a bit off the rail, inched away in deep stretch and continued gamely but could not hold off the winner. NO ARMISTICE prompted the pace three deep between horses on the backstretch, continued three wide on the turn and into the stretch and went willingly to the end. MELLOW FELLOW settled outside on the backstretch and turn, came wide into the stretch and finished well. OUR MAGISTRATE dueled for command between horses, fought back in the stretch but weakened late. AVANZADO (ARG) well placed forcing the pace four wide to the stretch, also weakened. ROMAN DANCER sent between horses to stalk the pace along the inside, swung out into the stretch and also weakened.

Owners— 1, Headley Molasky & Molasky; 2, Jones Aaron U & Marie D; 3, Hughes Bradley W; 4, Craig Sidney H & Jenny; 5, Plan B Stable; 6, Cees Stable; 7, Rodriguez Lorraine & Rod

Trainers—1, Headley Bruce; 2, Inda Eduardo; 3, Ellis Ronald W; 4, Spawr Bill; 5, Glatt Mark; 6, O'Neill Doug; 7, Paasch Christopher S

Scratched— Giovannetti (28Nov02 $^{7}GG^{1}$), Hombre Rapido (20Dec02 $^{7}HOL^{1}$)

$2 Daily Double (6-1) Paid $16.20; Daily Double Pool $36,365.
$1 Pick Three (7-6-1/4/9) Paid $52.30; Pick Three Pool $100,212.

NINTH RACE
Gulfstream
JANUARY 3, 2003

6 FURLONGS. (1.07^{4}) 23rd Running of THE SPECTACULAR BID. Grade III. Purse $100,000. 3-year-olds. By subscription of $100 each, which shall accompany the nomination, $1,000 to pass the entry box and $1,000 additional to start. Weight, 122 lbs. Non-winners of $50,000 twice, allowed 2 lbs. $40,000 once or $25,000 twice, 4 lbs. $35,000 once or two races other than maiden or claiming, 6 lbs. Horses finishing first, second or third in the Spectacular Bid Stakes will automatically be nominated to the Florida Derby.

Value of Race: $100,000 Winner $60,000; second $20,000; third $11,000; fourth $6,000; fifth $3,000. Mutuel Pool $412,752.00 Exacta Pool $324,820.00 Trifecta Pool $294,682.00 Superfecta Pool $101,758.00

Last Raced	Horse	M/Eqt.	A.	Wt	PP	St	¼	½	Str	Fin	Jockey	Odds $1
17Nov02 $^{8}Aqu^{3}$	First Blush		3	116	8	4	4^{hd}	$3^{1\frac{1}{2}}$	1^{hd}	$1^{1/2}$	Chavez J F	11.90
7Dec02 $^{8}Lrl^{1}$	Crafty Guy	L	3	120	7	3	1^{hd}	$1^{1/2}$	$2^{2\frac{1}{2}}$	$2^{3/4}$	Santos J A	3.40
25Oct02 $^{7}Aqu^{1}$	Silver Squire	L	3	120	5	9	9	9	6^{1}	3^{2}	Prado E S	2.30
23Nov02 $^{4}Hoo^{1}$	Coach Jimi Lee	L	3	120	6	1	3^{2}	4^{3}	$3^{1/2}$	$4^{3/4}$	Meier R	8.50
17Nov02 $^{8}Aqu^{1}$	Super Fuse	Lbf	3	120	3	7	$6^{1/2}$	6^{3}	4^{hd}	5^{2}	Gonzalez C V	2.00
18Nov02 $^{9}Crc^{1}$	Formal Charade	L	3	116	4	8	8^{4}	7^{1}	$7^{1/2}$	$6^{3/4}$	Bain G W	80.90
7Dec02 $^{4}Hou^{4}$	Hear No Evil	Lbf	3	120	2	6	5^{2}	5^{1}	8^{3}	$7^{5\frac{1}{4}}$	Guidry M	9.30
21Dec02 $^{4}Crc^{1}$	Laughing Luke	Lbf	3	116	9	2	7^{1}	$8^{1/2}$	9	$8^{5\frac{1}{2}}$	Cruz M R	39.40
13Oct02 $^{9}Bel^{4}$	Paris Adventure	Lb	3	116	1	5	2^{hd}	$2^{1/2}$	5^{hd}	9	Coa E M	73.40

OFF AT 4:55 Start Good For All But SILVER SQUIRE Won driving. Track good.
TIME :21^{3}, :44^{4}, :57^{2}, 1:10^{4} (:21.72, :44.86, :57.56, 1:10.97)

$2 Mutuel Prices:			
8-FIRST BLUSH	25.80	10.20	4.80
7-CRAFTY GUY		5.40	3.60
5-SILVER SQUIRE			3.40

$2 EXACTA 8-7 PAID $127.20 $2 TRIFECTA 8-7-5 PAID $691.60 $2 SUPERFECTA 8-7-5-6 PAID $4,489.20

Ch. c, (May), by French Deputy-Blushing Princess, by Crafty Prospector. Trainer Jerkens H Allen. Bred by Irving Cowan (Ky).

FIRST BLUSH settled just behind the early leaders, closed the gap while three wide leaving the turn, surged to the front in midstretch then edged away under strong left hand encouragement. CRAFTY GUY alternated for the early lead from outside, shook off PARIS ADVENTURE leaving the quarter pole, dug in when challenged by the winner in midstretch, fought gamely into deep stretch then yielded grudgingly. SILVER SQUIRE hit the side of the gate at the start, trailed to the turn, rallied slightly off the rail at the top of the stretch, split rivals while gaining in midstretch then finished fastest but could not get up. COACH JIMI LEE raced up close between horses, dropped back slightly on the far turn, saved ground approaching the stretch then continued on willingly. SUPER FUSE was reserved for a half, rallied four wide to reach contention in upper stretch then finished evenly. FORMAL CHARADE failed to mount a serious rally while saving ground. HEAR NO EVIL raced in the middle of the pack along the backstretch, angled out on the turn, advanced three wide into the stretch, altered course to the outside in upper stretch then lacked a strong closing bid. LAUGHING LUKE failed to threaten while five wide. PARIS ADVENTURE dueled along the rail for a half and gave way.

Owners— 1, Cowan Marjorie & Irving M; 2, M Gill; 3, Cherry Martin L; 4, Lee Battaglia & J P Divito; 5, C T Stable; 6, Fritz Theophilus; 7, Jacks or Better Farm Inc; 8, Heard Thomas H Jr; 9, Carroll Donald J

Trainers—1, Jerkens H Allen; 2, Robb John J; 3, Kimmel John C; 4, DiVito James P; 5, Ciardullo Richard Jr; 6, Ziadie Ralph; 7, Hatchett James; 8, Heard Thomas H Jr; 9, Hills Timothy A

$2 Pick Three (8-1-8) Paid $3,739.60; Pick Three Pool $42,097.
$2 Consolation Pick Three (8-4-8) Paid $1,161.80

EIGHTH RACE
Gulfstream
JANUARY 4, 2003

6 FURLONGS. (1.07^{4}) MR. PROSPECTOR H. Grade III. Purse $100,000 FOR THREE YEAR OLDS AND UPWARD. By subscription of $100 each, which shall accompany the nomination, $1,000 to pass the entry box and $1,000 additional to start, with $100,000 guaranteed. The owner of the winner to receive $60,000; $20,000 to second, $11,000 to third, $6,000 to fourth and $3,000 to fifth. Trophy to winning Owner. Closed Monday, December 23, 2002 with 13 Nominations.

Value of Race: $100,000 Winner $60,000; second $20,000; third $11,000; fourth $6,000; fifth $3,000. Mutuel Pool $343,554.00 Exacta Pool $295,436.00 Trifecta Pool $200,829.00 Superfecta Pool $56,229.00

Last Raced	Horse	M/Eqt.	A.	Wt	PP	St	¼	½	Str	Fin	Jockey	Odds $1
17Nov02 ^{5}CD^{2}	Baileys Edge	L	6	114	4	3	6	6	2^{2}	1^{nk}	Boulanger G	17.80
16Dec02 ^{7}Crc^{1}	Friendly Frolic	L f	4	114	6	1	$5^{2\frac{1}{2}}$	$5^{\frac{1}{2}}$	5^{1}	$2^{2\frac{1}{4}}$	Velasquez C H	22.10
28Nov02 ^{8}Aqu^{4}	Out of Fashion	L b	7	115	1	6	$4^{1\frac{1}{2}}$	3^{2}	3^{hd}	3^{1}	Prado E S	1.80
22Dec02 ^{10}Crc^{1}	Harmony Hall	L	4	112	5	4	3^{hd}	4^{1}	6	$4^{\frac{3}{4}}$	Velazquez J R	6.80
16Nov02 ^{9}Haw^{1}	Bet On Joe	L b	5	114	3	2	$1^{2\frac{1}{2}}$	$1^{2\frac{1}{2}}$	$1^{1\frac{1}{2}}$	$5^{4\frac{1}{2}}$	Coa E	4.90
7Dec02 ^{5}Hou^{5}	Day Trader	L b	4	114	2	5	2^{3}	$2^{1\frac{1}{2}}$	$4^{\frac{1}{2}}$	6	Day P	1.30

OFF AT 4:09 Start Good . Won driving. Track fast.
TIME :21^{2}, :44, :56^{4}, 1:09^{4} (:21.52, :44.18, :56.80, 1:09.95)

$2 Mutuel Prices:

4 – BAILEYS EDGE	37.60	13.60	5.00
6 – FRIENDLY FROLIC		16.80	5.40
1 – OUT OF FASHION			3.00

$2 EXACTA 4–6 PAID $305.60 $2 TRIFECTA 4–6–1 PAID $1,931.00
$2 SUPERFECTA 4–6–1–5 PAID $7,028.60

Dk. b or br. g, (May), by Mister Baileys–GB – Ocean's Edge , by Coastal . Trainer Margolis Stephen R. Bred by Dr Brian Davidson & George De Benedicty (Ky).

BAILEYS EDGE trailed for a half, rapidly gained along the rail entering the stretch, slipped through along the inside to gain the lead a sixteenth out then was fully extended to hold off FRIENDLY FROLIC in the final strides. FRIENDLY FROLIC was reserved for a half, circled five wide entering the stretch then closed steadily in the middle of the track but could not get up. OUT OF FASHION rushed up along the rail after breaking slowly, angled out while lodging a bid on the turn then finished evenly. HARMONY HALL gained a bit while four wide on the turn then lacked a strong closing response. BET ON JOE opened a clear lead along the backstretch, set a rapid pace slightly off the rail into midstretch then tired from his early efforts. DAY TRADER chased the pacesetter along the inside into upper stretch and gave way.

Owners– 1, Holm Thoroughbred Company; 2, Stride Rite Racing Stable Inc; 3, Gill Michael J; 4, Platt Joseph P Jr; 5, Castro John; 6, Overbrook Farm

Trainers– 1, Margolis Stephen R; 2, Wolfson Milton W; 3, Shuman Mark; 4, Alexander Frank A; 5, Standridge Steven W; 6, Lukas D Wayne

$2 Pick Three (8–9–4) Paid $765.20 ; Pick Three Pool $66,002 .

TENTH RACE
Gulfstream
JANUARY 4, 2003

1 MILE. (Turf)(1.32^{4}) 52nd Running of THE APPLETON HANDICAP. Grade II. Purse $150,000 Guaranteed. THREE YEAR OLDS AND UPWARD. By subscription of $150 each, which shall accompany the nomination, $1,500 to pass the entry box and $1,500 additional to start, with $150,000 guaranteed. The owner of the winner to receive $90,000; $30,000 to second, $16,500 to third, $9,000 to fourth and $4,500 to fifth. Weights: Friday, December 27, 2002. Starters to be named through the entry box by the usual time of closing. This race will be limited to 12 Starters, with Also Eligibles. (High Weights on the scale Preferred) In the event this stake race is taken off the turf, it may be subject to downgrading upon review by the Graded Stakes Committee.

Value of Race: $150,000 Winner $90,000; second $30,000; third $16,500; fourth $9,000; fifth $4,500. Mutuel Pool $402,860.00 Exacta Pool $317,860.00 Trifecta Pool $246,788.00 Superfecta Pool $79,340.00

Last Raced	Horse	M/Eqt.	A.	Wt	PP	St	¼	½	¾	Str	Fin	Jockey	Odds $1
24Nov02 ^{7}CD^{2}	Point Prince	L	4	115	9	8	$5^{1\frac{1}{2}}$	4^{hd}	$4^{1\frac{1}{2}}$	1^{hd}	$1^{1\frac{1}{4}}$	Cruz M R	29.30
7Dec02 ^{11}Crc^{1}	Krieger	Lb	5	115	2	1	$1^{1\frac{1}{2}}$	$1^{1\frac{1}{2}}$	1^{2}	$2^{2\frac{1}{2}}$	2^{nk}	Coa E M	2.20
3Nov02 ^{6}WO^{1}	Red Sea-GB	L	7	114	6	7	$4^{\frac{1}{2}}$	5^{1}	$6^{\frac{1}{2}}$	3^{2}	$3^{1\frac{3}{4}}$	Velasquez C	14.00
29Nov02 ^{8}CD^{1}	Bail Out The King	Lbf	5	114	1	9	9	9	9	$5^{1\frac{1}{2}}$	$4^{1\frac{1}{4}}$	Day P	5.80
16Nov02 ^{9}Crc^{4}	Marquette	Lf	7	115	5	6	8^{4}	$8^{4\frac{1}{2}}$	8^{3}	4^{hd}	5^{2}	Turner T G	39.90
7Dec02 ^{11}Crc^{5}	Autonomy-IRE	Lf	6	114	3	2	7^{3}	7^{3}	5^{hd}	$6^{1\frac{1}{2}}$	6^{nk}	Douglas R R	9.80
8Nov02 ^{8}Aqu^{5}	Good Boy Sam	Lb	6	114	4	5	6^{hd}	6^{hd}	7^{1}	$7^{1\frac{1}{2}}$	$7^{4\frac{3}{4}}$	Aguilar M	22.50
21Nov02 ^{8}Aqu^{1}	Balto Star	L	5	118	8	4	3^{3}	3^{3}	$3^{\frac{1}{2}}$	9	$8^{1\frac{1}{2}}$	Velazquez J R	1.80
2Nov02 ^{9}Aqu^{6}	North East Bound	L	7	116	7	3	$2^{1\frac{1}{2}}$	$2^{\frac{1}{2}}$	2^{hd}	8^{hd}	9	Velez J A Jr	8.00

OFF AT 5:02 Start Good. Won driving. Course good.
TIME :23^{2}, :47^{2}, 1:12^{1}, 1:37^{4} (:23.46, :47.43, 1:12.21, 1:37.84)

$2 Mutuel Prices:

13–POINT PRINCE	60.60	16.80	7.80
2–KRIEGER		4.00	3.80
9–RED SEA–GB			7.00

$2 EXACTA 13–2 PAID $273.40 $2 TRIFECTA 13–2–9 PAID $2,484.40 $2 SUPERFECTA 13–2–9–1 PAID $13,223.20

Dk. b. or br. g, by Youmadeyourpoint–Princess of Note, by Notebook. Trainer Romans Dale. Bred by Stanley M Ersoff (Fla).

POINT PRINCE was rated in good position while three wide along the backstretch, angled to the inside while gaining on the turn, overtook KRIEGER to gain the lead in midstretch then edged away under good handling. KRIEGER sprinted clear soon after the start, set the pace along the inside into upper stretch, relinquished the lead to the winner a furlong out then continued on willingly to hold for the place. RED SEA (GB) raced just inside the winner while saving ground to the turn then finished willingly to gain a share. BAIL OUT THE KING trailed to the top of the stretch then rallied belatedly along the inside. MARQUETTE failed to threaten while improving his position. AUTONOMY (IRE) failed to mount a serious rally while five wide leaving the turn. GOOD BOY SAM was never a factor. BALTO STAR stalked the leaders while four wide to the top of the stretch and gave way. NORTH EAST BOUND prompted the pace between horses for six furlongs and faltered.

Owners— 1, Team Valor Stables; 2, Stronach Stable; 3, R Attfield W Werner & Windhaven Far; 4, Ramsey Kenneth L & Sarah K; 5, Cavanaugh J R & Early Morning Farm; 6, Klatsky Brian; 7, D Soblick; 8, Anstu Stables; 9, Demarco Julian & Disano Richard J

Trainers—1, Romans Dale; 2, Orseno Joseph; 3, Attfield Roger L; 4, Romans Dale; 5, Root Richard R; 6, Oliver Philip J; 7, Sciacca Gary; 8, Pletcher Todd A; 9, Perry William W

Scratched— Illusionary (7Dec02 ^{11}CRC^{4}), Baptize (5Oct02 ^{7}BEL^{5}), Hail The Chief (29Nov02 ^{11}CD^{9}), Saint Verre (21Nov02 ^{8}AQU^{3}), Maumee (21Sep02 DR^{2})

$2 Pick Three (4–2–13) Paid $13,720.80; Pick Three Pool $42,878.

EIGHTH RACE
Santa Anita
JANUARY 4, 2003

$1\frac{1}{16}$ MILES. (1.39) SAN PASQUAL H. Grade II. Purse $150,000 FOR FOUR-YEAR-OLDS AND UPWARD. By subscription of $150 each to accompany the nomination or by supplementary nomination of $3,000 by Sunday, December 29. $1,500 additional to start, with $150,000 guaranteed, of which $90,000 to first, $30,000 to second, $18,000 to third, $6,000 to fourth and $3,000 to fifth. NOMINATIONS CLOSED Thursday, December 26, 2002 with 23.

Value of Race: $150,000 Winner $90,000; second $30,000; third $18,000; fourth $9,000; fifth $3,000. Mutuel Pool $578,018.00 Exacta Pool $360,526.00 Quinella Pool $38,451.00 Trifecta Pool $424,546.00 Superfecta Pool $167,232.00

Last Raced	Horse	M/Eqt.	A.	Wt	PP	St	¼	½	¾	Str	Fin	Jockey	Odds $1
30Nov02 9Aqu1	Congaree	LB	5	121	5	6	4^{1}	4^{1}	$3^{1\frac{1}{2}}$	$1^{1\frac{1}{2}}$	1^{6}	Bailey J D	0.80
6Apr02 8OP1	Kudos	LB b	6	119	1	2	$3^{\frac{1}{2}}$	3^{hd}	5^{hd}	$4^{\frac{1}{2}}$	2no	Solis A O	4.30
23Nov02 4Hol1	Hot Market	LB b	5	116	6	5	2^{1}	2^{1}	2^{hd}	$2^{\frac{1}{2}}$	$3^{1\frac{1}{4}}$	Desormeaux K J	10.80
14Dec02 9Hol1	PiensaSonando-Chi	LB	5	118	7	8	$8^{1\frac{1}{2}}$	8^{hd}	8^{1}	$7^{1\frac{1}{2}}$	$4^{\frac{1}{2}}$	Pincay L A Jr	6.50
13Dec02 6Hol2	Freedom Crest	LB	7	115	2	1	$1^{\frac{1}{2}}$	1^{hd}	1^{hd}	3^{2}	$5^{\frac{1}{2}}$	Valdivia J Jr	41.50
14Dec02 9Hol3	Nose The Trade-GB	LB	5	116	8	9	9	9	$7^{1\frac{1}{2}}$	5^{hd}	6^{hd}	Flores D R	18.80
6Oct02 7SA8	Kela	LB b	5	116	4	3	$5^{\frac{1}{2}}$	6^{1}	6^{1}	6^{1}	7^{3}	Nakatani C S	17.90
22Nov02 2Hol1	Cottage-Arg	LB	5	114	3	4	7^{hd}	7^{hd}	9	9	8^{1}	Smith M E	10.20
29Nov02 3GG3	Mercenary	LB b	5	113	9	7	6^{1}	$5^{\frac{1}{2}}$	$4^{\frac{1}{2}}$	$8^{1\frac{1}{2}}$	9	Espinoza V	28.80

OFF AT 4:12 Start Good. Won ridden out. Track fast.
TIME :23^{4}, :47^{3}, 1:11^{2}, 1:35, 1:41 (:23.92, :47.71, 1:11.50, 1:35.03, 1:41.04)

$2 Mutuel Prices:

6 – CONGAREE	3.60	2.80	2.60
1 – KUDOS		3.60	2.80
7 – HOT MARKET			4.40

$1 EXACTA 6–1 PAID $6.70 $2 QUINELLA 1–6 PAID $9.60
$1 TRIFECTA 6–1–7 PAID $34.20 $1 SUPERFECTA 6–1–7–8 PAID $75.60

Ch. h, (Apr), by Arazi – Mari's Sheba , by Mari's Book . Trainer Baffert Bob. Bred by Stonerside Stable Ltd (Ky).

CONGAREE bobbled a bit at the start, stalked outside a rival, bid three deep on the second turn, was floated out into the stretch, took command in upper stretch and drew off under a moderate hand ride. KUDOS saved ground stalking the pace, came out a bit in the stretch and just got the place. HOT MARKET prompted the pace outside a rival, took the lead leaving the second turn, drifted out onto the winner into the stretch, was no match for that one and just lost second. PIENSA SONANDO (CHI) chased between horses then off the rail, split rivals leaving the backstretch, angled in on the second turn and improved position in the stretch. FREEDOM CREST sped to the early lead, dueled inside, fought back on the second turn but weakened in the stretch. NOSE THE TRADE (GB) allowed to settle outside chasing the pace, went three deep on the turns and lacked the needed rally. KELA was in a good position chasing the leaders a bit off the rail, split horses on the second turn and also lacked the necessary response. COTTAGE (ARG) saved ground off the pace, came out on the second turn and into the stretch and was not a threat. MERCENARY chased four wide on the turns and outside on the backstretch and weakened in the stretch.

Owners– 1, Stonerside Stable LLC; 2, Moss Mr and Mrs Jerome S; 3, Harris Farms Inc and Antonsen Per; 4, Hunt Nelson B; 5, Nguyen Calvin and Tran Joey; 6, Tanaka Gary A; 7, Jones Aaron U and Marie D; 8, Farfellow Farms Ltd; 9, Beck Robert L

Trainers– 1, Baffert Bob; 2, Mandella Richard E; 3, Lewis Craig A; 4, McAnally Ronald L; 5, Perez Dagoberto L; 6, Puhich Michael; 7, Inda Eduardo; 8, Spawr William; 9, Canani Julio C

Scratched– Fleetstreet Dancer (14Dec02 9Hol2) , Euchre (14Dec02 9Hol7)

$2 Daily Double (9–6) Paid $114.20 ; Daily Double Pool $52,752 .
$1 Pick Three (3–9–4/6) Paid $312.90 ; Pick Three Pool $98,019 .

TENTH RACE
Gulfstream
JANUARY 5, 2003

$1\frac{1}{16}$ MILES. (Turf)(1.39^{1}) 19th Running of THE HONEY FOX HANDICAP. Grade III. Purse $100,000 Guaranteed. FOR FILLIES AND MARES, THREE YEARS OLD AND UPWARD. By subscription of $100 each, which shall accompany the nomination, $1,000 to pass the entry box and $1,000 additional to start, with $100,000 guaranteed. The owner of the winner to receive $60,000; $20,000 to second, $11,000 to third, $6,000 to fourth and $3,000 to fifth. Weights: Friday. December 27, 2002. Trophy to winning Owner. This race will be limited to 12 Starters, with Also Eligibles. (High Weights on the scale Preferred). In the event this stake race is taken off the turf, it may be subject to downgrading upon review by the Graded Stakes Committee Closed Monday, December 23, 2002 with 25 Nominations. (Rail at 0 feet).

Value of Race: $100,000 Winner $60,000; second $20,000; third $11,000; fourth $6,000; fifth $3,000. Mutuel Pool $388,429.00 Exacta Pool $313,270.00 Trifecta Pool $297,702.00 Superfecta Pool $109,466.00

Last Raced	Horse	M/Eqt.	A.	Wt	PP	St	¼	½	¾	Str	Fin	Jockey	Odds $1
23Nov02 8CD2	San Dare	L	5	115	7	10	10	10	9^{hd}	$7^{\frac{1}{2}}$	1^{hd}	Guidry M	11.60
8Sep02 6WO1	Calista-GB	L	5	118	9	9	8^{hd}	$9^{2\frac{1}{2}}$	$6^{1\frac{1}{2}}$	$6^{\frac{1}{2}}$	$2^{1\frac{1}{2}}$	Santos J A	4.40
15Dec02 7Crc3	Laurica	L	6	114	3	8	9^{1}	8^{hd}	10	8^{1}	3^{nk}	Prado E S	15.40
16Dec02 9Crc1	Remediate	Lf	6	114	1	7	7^{hd}	7^{1}	7^{hd}	5^{1}	4^{nk}	Velasquez C	44.00
7Dec02 8Crc1	Wander Mom	Lb	5	115	5	3	4^{hd}	3^{hd}	$5^{\frac{1}{2}}$	2^{hd}	5^{nk}	Coa E M	17.50
15Dec02 7Crc1	Amonita-GB	L	5	119	4	6	5^{hd}	4^{1}	3^{hd}	1^{hd}	$6^{2\frac{1}{4}}$	Bailey J D	1.40
15Dec02 7Crc2	Notable Craft	Lf	7	113	2	1	6^{1}	6^{hd}	4^{1}	10	$7^{1\frac{1}{4}}$	Homeister R B Jr	63.10
7Dec02 8Crc4	Abuela Esther-UR	L	6	114	8	2	3^{hd}	5^{hd}	$8^{1\frac{1}{2}}$	9^{1}	8^{nk}	Cruz M R	42.20
7Dec02 10Crc5	Mimi's Tizzy	L	6	115	10	5	2^{1}	2^{1}	2^{1}	3^{hd}	9^{nk}	Douglas R R	40.40
28Nov02 10CD1	Allamerican Bertie	L	4	116	6	4	1^{1}	1^{1}	1^{hd}	4^{hd}	10	Day P	2.20

OFF AT 5:03 Start Good. Won driving. Course firm.
TIME :24^{4}, :50^{2}, 1:15^{1}, 1:40^{1}, 1:46 (:24.99, :50.44, 1:15.26, 1:40.24, 1:46.19)

$2 Mutuel Prices:

7–SAN DARE	25.20	9.40	6.80
9–CALISTA–GB		5.60	4.80
3–LAURICA			8.20

$2 EXACTA 7–9 PAID $119.80 $2 TRIFECTA 7–9–3 PAID $1,210.00 $2 SUPERFECTA 7–9–3–1 PAID $12,630.60

B. m, by Dare and Go–San Empery, by Empery. Trainer Hiles Rick. Bred by Sidney Turner (Ky).

SAN DARE trailed to the turn, circled five wide into the stretch then closed strongly in the middle of the track to get up in the final strides. CALISTA (GB) reserved early, waited patiently for room on the turn, closed strong to gain a slim lead in deep stretch but couldn't hold the winner safe. LAURICA checked entering the backstretch, trailed on the turn, raced in traffic while gaining in midstretch then rallied belatedly. REMEDIATE saved ground to the turn, slipped through along the rail in upper stretch and finished willingly. WANDER MOM never far back, split horses to threaten in upper stretch and weakened late. AMONITA (GB) raced three wide to the turn and flattened out. NOTABLE CRAFT raced up close to the turn and faded. ABUELA ESTHER (URU) stalked three wide for six furlongs and tired. MIMI'S TIZZY was used for forcing the early pace. ALLAMERICAN BERTIE set the pace along the inside to the top of the stretch and gave way.

Owners— 1, D Mounts; 2, The Leigh Family Stable; 3, M-2 Stable; 4, Klatsky Brian; 5, Carrion Jaime S; 6, Haras du Mezeray; 7, Rosin Tim W; 8, Stud El Aguila; 9, Harold Williams; 10, Klein Richard Bertram & Elaine

Trainers— 1, Hiles Rick; 2, Clement Christophe; 3, Wolfson Martin D; 4, Oliver Philip J; 5, Plesa Edward Jr; 6, Clement Christophe; 7, Mongeon Kathy P; 8, Wolfson Martin D; 9, Wolfson Martin D; 10, Flint Steve

Scratched— Mystic Lady (7Dec02 6HOU2)

$2 Pick Three (1–7–7) Paid $453.60; Pick Three Pool $31,754.

THIRD RACE

Santa Anita
JANUARY 5, 2003

1¹⁄₁₆ MILES. (1.39) 36th Running of THE SANTA YSABEL. Grade III. Purse $100,000 added. FILLIES THREE YEARS OLD. By subscription of $100 each to accompany the nomination or by supplementary nomination of $2,000 by time of entry. $1,000 additional to start, with $100,000 added. The added money and all fees to be divided 60% to the winner, 20% to second, 12% to third, 6% to fourth and 2% to fifth. Weight, 120 lbs. Winners of a race of $200,000 to carry 3 lbs. additional. Non–winners of $55,000 at one mile or over, allowed 3 lbs. Of such a race any distance, 5 lbs. Of $20,000 at one mile or over or $30,000 any distance, 7 lbs. (Maiden and claiming races not considered). Closed Thursday, December 26 with 9 nominations.

Value of Race: $110,900 Winner $66,540; second $22,180; third $13,308; fourth $6,654; fifth $2,218. Mutuel Pool $370,354.00 Exacta Pool $205,947.00 Quinella Pool $26,228.00 Trifecta Pool $195,085.00

Last Raced	Horse	M/Eqt. A.Wt	PP	St	¼	½	¾	Str	Fin	Jockey	Odds $1
29Nov02 4Hol¹	Atlantic Ocean	LB 3 120	1	1	4²½	3½	3¹½	2²	1¾	Flores D R	1.50
26Oct02 4AP⁴	Sea Jewel	LBb 3 115	5	3	2¹	2¹½	2¹½	1½	2¹	Valenzuela P A	3.40
14Dec02 4Hol³	SummerWindDancer	LB 3 120	4	4	5¹	5¹	5²	3hd	3⁵	Solis A	1.80
7Dec02 5Hol⁴	Harbor Blues	LBb 3 113	3	2	1½	1hd	1hd	4⁴½	4⁵	Baze T C	a–11.20
23Nov02 4Hol¹	Dash For Money	LB 3 113	2	6	6	6	6	5⁴	5⁸	Espinoza V	6.30
7Dec02 5Hol¹	Shapes And Shadows	LB 3 116	6	5	3hd	4²	4¹½	6	6	Desormeaux K J	a–11.20

a–Coupled: Harbor Blues and Shapes And Shadows.

OFF AT 1:35 Start Good. Won driving. Track fast.

TIME :23¹, :47², 1:11³, 1:36³, 1:43¹ (:23.38, :47.57, 1:11.60, 1:36.70, 1:43.25)

$2 Mutuel Prices:	2–ATLANTIC OCEAN	5.00	3.40	2.20
	6–SEA JEWEL		4.40	2.20
	5–SUMMER WIND DANCER			2.10

$1 EXACTA 2–6 PAID $8.60 $2 QUINELLA 2–6 PAID $10.20 $1 TRIFECTA 2–6–5 PAID $15.90

Dk. b. or br. f, (Jan), by Stormy Atlantic–Super Chef, by Seattle Slew. Trainer Baffert Bob. Bred by Arthur I Appleton (Fla).

ATLANTIC OCEAN pulled her way around inside and steadied briefly into the first turn, stalked the dueling leaders from the rail, came out on the second turn, bid three deep into the stretch, gained the advantage outside the runner-up nearing the sixteenth pole and gamely prevailed under urging. SEA JEWEL pulled three deep early, prompted the pace outside a rival, took the lead into the stretch, fought back inside the winner through the drive and continued willingly to the wire. SUMMER WIND DANCER chased off the rail then outside a rival, began to advance under urging leaving the second turn, came out into the stretch, had the rider lose the whip in midstretch and was slowly gaining late. HARBOR BLUES sped to the early lead, angled in on the first turn and duele4d inside, dropped back into the stretch and weakened. DASH FOR MONEY off a bit slowly, came out from the rail on the first turn, angled back in on the backstretch and chased the pace, came out into the stretch and did not rally. SHAPES AND SHADOWS three deep into the first turn, stalked outside the winner then off the rail on the second turn, drifted out into the stretch and gave way.

Owners— 1, The Thoroughbred Corporation; 2, Moss Mr & Mrs Jerome S; 3, Vetter Wira & Wira; 4, Everest Stables; 5, Stronach Stable; 6, Everest Stables

Trainers— 1, Baffert Bob; 2, Shirreffs John; 3, Sahadi Jenine; 4, Canani Nick; 5, Frankel Robert; 6, Canani Nick

Scratched— Artist's Studio (19Dec02 1GG¹)

$2 Daily Double (6–2) Paid $13.20; Daily Double Pool $32,723.
$1 Pick Three (2–6–2/4) Paid $35.20; Pick Three Pool $119,879.

EIGHTH RACE

Aqueduct
JANUARY 11, 2003

1¹⁄₁₆ MILES. (Inner Dirt)(1.41) 28th Running of THE AFFECTIONATELY HANDICAP. Grade III. Purse $100,000. FILLIES AND MARES THREE YEARS OLD AND UPWARD. By subscription of $100 each, which should accompany the nomination; $500 to pass the entry box; $500 to start, with $100,000 added. The added money and all fees to be divided 60% to the winner, 20% to second, 11% to third, 6% to fourth and 3% to fifth. Trophies will be presented to the winning owner, trainer and jockey.Closed Saturday, December 28, 2002 with 16 Nominations.

Value of Race: $109,600 Winner $65,760; second $21,920; third $12,056; fourth $6,576; fifth $3,288. Mutuel Pool $432,014.00 Exacta Pool $341,178.00 Trifecta Pool $237,096.00

Last Raced	Horse	M/Eqt. A.Wt	PP	St	¼	½	¾	Str	Fin	Jockey	Odds $1
29Nov02 9Aqu²	Zonk	L 5 118	5	5	4½	3½	1¹	1⁸	1⁴	Lopez C C	2.00
21Dec02 8Aqu⁴	Wishful Splendor	L 4 112	7	6	6¹½	7	5³½	3⁴½	2nk	Castellano J J	15.60
27Dec02 8Aqu¹	Kiss A Miss	Lf 5 113	1	2	3³½	4⁵½	3³½	2½	3⁷¾	Samyn J L	5.10
14Dec02 8Lrl³	Shop Till You Drop	Lb 4 114	3	7	7	6½	4¹	5¹⁰	4⁸½	Vega H	9.70
8Dec02 7Aqu¹	Pocus Hocus	Lb 5 114	2	1	1¹½	1²	2¹½	4hd	5³½	Migliore R	3.45
15Nov02 8Aqu⁵	Persky–ARG	L 6 109	4	3	5²½	5½	6⁶	6¹⁰	6¹⁵¼	Chavez Luis	45.75
21Dec02 8Aqu³	With Ability	L 5 117	6	4	2⁵	2¹½	7	7	7	Gryder A T	2.70

OFF AT 3:53 Start Good. Won ridden out. Track fast.

TIME :22¹, :45⁴, 1:11², 1:37³, 1:44² (:22.34, :45.87, 1:11.42, 1:37.65, 1:44.58)

$2 Mutuel Prices:	7–ZONK	6.00	3.50	2.70
	9–WISHFUL SPLENDOR		10.80	4.60
	1–KISS A MISS			3.60

$2 EXACTA 7–9 PAID $73.00 $2 TRIFECTA 7–9–1 PAID $286.00

Ch. m, by Farma Way–In Concert, by Riverman. Trainer Servis John C. Bred by Vinery & Dale Nelson (Ky).

ZONK was urged along early, advanced outside into the second turn, drew away when asked and was ridden out to the wire, winning with something left. WISHFUL SPLENDOR was outrun early, rallied three wide on the second turn and finished well outside to earn the place award. KISS A MISS raced up early while in hand, put in a three wide run on the second turn and lacked a solid finishing kick. SHOP TILL YOU DROP had no response when roused. POCUS HOCUS was hustled up inside, set the pace along the inside and tired after the opening three quarters. PERSKY (ARG) raced inside and tired. WITH ABILITY was hustled outside, chased the pace and was finished after a half mile.

Owners— 1, Fox Hill Farms Inc; 2, Manganaro John H Jr; 3, Carpenito Noreen; 4, White Dewey & Karen; 5, Moore Susan & John; 6, Fernandez Floreano; 7, Evans Edward P

Trainers— 1, Servis John C; 2, Zito Nicholas J; 3, Johnson Philip G; 4, Fee John; 5, Jerkens James A; 6, Ortiz Juan; 7, Hennig Mark

Scratched— Ms. Rapunzel (13Dec02 8AQU¹), Forest Princess (27Dec02 8AQU⁴)

$2 Pick Six (2–4–3–2–3–7) 5
Correct Paid $688.00; Pick Six Pool $86,080; Carryover Pool $51,648.

EIGHTH RACE
Golden Gate
JANUARY 11, 2003

1¹⁄₁₆ MILES. (1.39²) 15th Running of THE GOLDEN GATE DERBY. Grade III. Purse $100,000. 3–year–olds. By subscription of $100 each to accompany the nomination or by supplementary nomination of $2,000 by time of entry. $500 to pass the entry box and $500 additional to start with $100,000 Guaranteed of which $55,000 to the winner, $20,000 to second, $15,000 to third, $7,500 to fourth and $2,500 to fifth. Weight 120 lbs; In the event this race overfills, first preference will be given to graded stakes winners; second preference to horses with the highest earnings at the time of entry. Atrophy will be presented to the owner of the winner. Closed Thursday, January 2, 2003 with 19 nominations.

Value of Race: $100,000 Winner $55,000; second $20,000; third $15,000; fourth $7,500; fifth $2,500. Mutuel Pool $287,970.00 Exacta Pool $179,966.00 Quinella Pool $21,526.00 Trifecta Pool $201,227.00 Superfecta Pool $81,021.00

Last Raced	Horse	M/Eqt. A.Wt	PP	St	¼	½	¾	Str	Fin	Jockey	Odds $1
20Dec02 7GG³	Standard Setter	LBb 3 120	1	1	12½	12½	11	1½	1nk	Gonzalez R M	17.40
28Dec02 1SA³	Ozzie Cat	LBb 3 120	5	4	3¹	3¹	2hd	2¹	2¹	Valdivia J Jr	1.70
19Dec02 2Hol²	Pine For Java	LBb 3 120	4	10	10	10	9½	7½	3¾	Alvarado F T	10.70
14Dec02 8GG¹	Spensive	LBb 3 120	9	6	5½	5²	5²	3²	4¾	Baze R A	1.90
14Dec02 8GG²	Always Remember	LB 3 120	10	7	7²	7hd	7½	6hd	5¹	Schvaneveldt C P	14.10
19Dec02 3GG²	Yozo	LB 3 120	7	8	9²	9²	10	9hd	6¾	Duran F	63.50
14Dec02 8GG⁵	Buddy Gil	LB 3 120	2	3	4²	4²	4¹	4²½	7²	Krigger K	7.70
15Dec02 8Hol⁵	Taliano	LBb 3 120	8	5	6⁴	6³½	6²	5hd	8½	Lopez A D	9.90
20Dec02 7GG²	Tactical Strike	LBb 3 120	6	9	8¹½	8²	8⁴	10	9²	Castro J M	23.10
14Dec02 8GG⁶	Quietly Quick	LBb 3 120	3	2	2¹	2²	3¹	8²	10	Miranda A	74.60

OFF AT 4:24 Start Good. Won driving. Track muddy.
TIME :22¹, :45², 1:10³, 1:36⁴, 1:43³ (:22.33, :45.42, 1:10.69, 1:36.83, 1:43.76)

$2 Mutuel Prices:

1–STANDARD SETTER	36.80	14.80	8.60
5–OZZIE CAT		3.80	3.00
4–PINE FOR JAVA			4.80

$1 EXACTA 1–5 PAID $78.90 $2 QUINELLA 1–5 PAID $50.60 $1 TRIFECTA 1–5–4 PAID $692.30 $1 SUPERFECTA 1–5–4–9 PAID $2,811.70

Ch. c, (Mar), by Benchmark–When and Where, by Siyah Kalem. Trainer Bonde Jeff. Bred by Phillip E Lebherz & Richard William Meister (Cal).

STANDARD SETTER broke on top and sprinted clear in the opening quarter despite strong restraint, remained well in hand to the second turn, turned back a brief bid from QUIETLY QUICK on the second turn then was quickly engaged by OZZIE CAT, met that rival's bid at the furlong pole and refused to yield. OZZIE CAT took a favorable striking position from the outside early, remained unhurried to the second turn, moved menacingly on the turn to be challenging for command in the upper stretch but could not get by. PINE FOR JAVA lagged well back in the early going, advanced inside ALWAYS REMEMBER on the second turn and into the stretch, dropped inside leaving the furlong pole and closed steadily. SPENSIVE was permitted to settle early in mid pack, offered his best bid three wide into the lane but lost much of his punch in the final furlong. ALWAYS REMEMBER was not asked for speed early while racing just off the rail, commenced his bid two wide on the second turn, loomed a factor in the upper stretch but lost his punch. YOZO was void of early speed, collected his stride entering the lane and closed steadily but too late. BUDDY GIL stalked the winner from the rail, advanced briefly into the second turn then fell back steadily. TALIANO settled early while wide, remained out on the second turn but did not rally. TACTICAL STRIKE broke slow and was outrun. QUIETLY QUICK prompted the pace two wide early, offered a brief bid on the second turn and stopped.

Owners— 1, Lebherz Philip & Meister Richard; 2, Overbrook Farm; 3, Carvajal Foltz & Pauma Vista Farm; 4, Watson & Weipman; 5, Miceli Gary Ratajczak Paul & Wiest; 6, Smolich Andy & Marilyn; 7, Billingsley Creek Ranch & Desperado; 8, Sample Joe & Lola; 9, Two J Racing Stable & Evan Trommer; 10, Everest Stables

Trainers—1, Bonde Jeff; 2, Lukas D Wayne; 3, Dominguez Caesar F; 4, Baffert Bob; 5, Sherman Art; 6, Specht Steve; 7, Jenda Charles J; 8, Van Berg Jack C; 9, Koriner Brian; 10, Knight Terry

Scratched— Rapier Dance (19Dec02 3GG¹).

$2 Daily Double (9–1) Paid $49.00; Daily Double Pool $20,113.
$1 Pick Three (11–9–1) Paid $419.00; Pick Three Pool $21,526.

TENTH RACE
Gulfstream
JANUARY 11, 2003

1$\frac{1}{16}$ MILES. (1.40¹) 13th Running of THE HAL'S HOPE HANDICAP (formerly The Creme Fraiche). Grade III. Purse $100,000 Guaranteed. THREE YEAR OLDS AND UPWARD. By subscription of $100 each, which shall accompany the nomination, $1,000 to pass the entry box and an additional $1,000 to start, with $100,000 guaranteed. The owner of the winner to recieve $60,000; $20,000 to second, $11,000 to third, $6,000 to fourth and $3,000 to fifth. Trophy to winning Owmer. ClosedMonday, December 30, 2002 with 24 Nominations.

Value of Race: $100,000 Winner $60,000; second $20,000; third $11,000; fourth $6,000; fifth $3,000. Mutuel Pool $503,061.00 Exacta Pool $347,978.00 Trifecta Pool $265,355.00 Superfecta Pool $80,468.00

Last Raced	Horse	M/Eqt.	A.Wt	PP	St	¼	½	¾	Str	Fin	Jockey	Odds $1
30Nov02 9Aqu6	Windsor Castle	L	5 115	4	8	8	7hd	73	51½	11½	Coa E M	4.70
21Nov02 8Aqu3	Saint Verre	L	5 114	6	7	71	8	62	21	2nk	Santos J A	9.50
29Nov02 11CD5	Najran	L	4 114	8	6	5½	2hd	1hd	1½	32¾	Day P	a-2.60
29Nov02 11CD3	Hero's Tribute	L	5 115	2	2	4hd	4hd	4hd	4½	43	Prado E S	2.00
29Nov02 11CD8	American Style	L	4 114	3	3	61	61½	31	61½	5nk	Bailey J D	a-2.60
29Nov02 11CD9	Hail The Chief-GB	L	6 116	5	4	1hd	1½	2½	3hd	6no	Chavez J F	3.60
26Nov02 8CD3	Dream Run	L	5 114	7	5	3½	51½	5hd	74	77¾	Velasquez C	19.40
11Nov02 8CD1	Speed Hunter	L	4 115	1	1	2½	3hd	8	8	8	Guidry M	22.00

a–Coupled: Najran and American Style.

OFF AT 5:05 Start Good. Won driving. Track fast.
TIME :23¹, :46³, 1:10², 1:36, 1:42¹ (:23.31, :46.70, 1:10.53, 1:36.17, 1:42.33)

$2 Mutuel Prices:

4–WINDSOR CASTLE	11.40	6.00	4.00
6–SAINT VERRE		11.40	5.40
1A–NAJRAN (a–entry)			3.00

$2 EXACTA 4–6 PAID $116.60 $2 TRIFECTA 4–6–1 PAID $422.40 $2 SUPERFECTA 4–6–1–3 PAID $1,219.20

B. h, by Lord Carson–Frigidette, by It's Freezing. Trainer Alexander Frank A. Bred by Windwoods Farm (Ky).

WINDSOR CASTLE outrun early, swung to the outside for the stretch run, rallied to take over at the sixteenth pole and won going away. SAINT VERRE unhurried early, rallied four wide around the far turn and closed to be up for the place while being outfinished. NAJRAN stalked the pace, moved to gain a slim lead outside HAIL THE CHIEF on the far turn, then weakened in the drive and was just edged for the place. HERO'S TRIBUTE well placed racing along the rail, was steadied along when blocked on the far turn and into the stretch, then had no response when clear. AMERICAN STYLE rated off the pace, made a run three wide to join the leaders on the far turn, then tired in the drive. HAIL THE CHIEF (GB) set the pace, moved to the inside when SPEED HUNTER dropped back entering the far turn, continued on well into the stretch and gave way. DREAM RUN chased the leaders into the far turn and faltered. SPEED HUNTER raced with the pace along the inside, then steadied when caught in tight entering the far turn and faded.

Owners— 1, Dogwood Stable; 2, J Allen; 3, Buckram Oak Farm; 4, Oxley John C; 5, Buckram Oak Farm; 6, Crane Peter M; 7, J D Murphy; 8, Mansell Stables

Trainers—1, Alexander Frank A; 2, Jerkens H Allen; 3, Zito Nicholas P; 4, Ward John T Jr; 5, Zito Nicholas P; 6, O'Callaghan Niall M; 7, McGee Paul J; 8, Walden W Elliott

$2 Pick Three (4–6–4) Paid $568.40; Pick Three Pool $48,678.

THIRD RACE
Santa Anita
JANUARY 11, 2003

1⅛ MILES. (Turf) (1.43⁴) SAN GORGONIO H. Grade II. Purse $150,000 FOR FILLIES AND MARES FOUR YEARS OLD AND UPWARD. By subscription of $150 each to accompany the nomination or by supplementary nomination of $3,000 by Sunday, January 5. $500 to pass the entry box and $1,000 additional to start, with $150,000 guaranteed, of which $90,000 to first, $30,000 to second, $18,000 to third, $9,000 to fourth, and $3,000 to fifth. NOMINATIONS CLOSED Thursday, January 2, 2003 with 16 (Rail at 8 Feet). (Rail at 8 feet).

Value of Race: $150,000 Winner $90,000; second $30,000; third $18,000; fourth $9,000; fifth $3,000. Mutuel Pool $475,778.00 Exacta Pool $293,976.00 Quinella Pool $30,999.00 Trifecta Pool $330,581.00

Last Raced	Horse	M/Eqt.	A. Wt	PP	St	¼	½	¾	Str	Fin	Jockey	Odds $1
3Nov02 8SA1	Tates Creek	LB	5 121	3	1	2½	2½	21	1hd	1¾	Valenzuela P A	0.90
12Oct02 7Kee6	Megahertz-GB	LB	4 117	4	6	62	5hd	5½	31½	2½	Solis A O	3.20
21Dec02 5Hol5	Double Cat	LB	5 114	5	2	1½	11	1hd	21½	31½	Smith M E	25.50
30Nov02 7GG7	Crazy Ensign-Arg	LB b	7 117	6	3	31½	32	31	51	4½	Pincay L A Jr	15.40
21Dec02 5Hol4	Alozaina-Ire	LB	4 116	2	4	42½	41½	4½	4hd	5½	Flores D R	9.60
1Dec02 4Hol3	Magic Mission-GB	LB	5 113	7	5	5hd	62	62	61½	64	Espinoza V	3.60
21Dec02 5Hol8	Miss Gazon-Ire	LB	5 112	1	7	7	7	7	7	7	Krone J A	31.70

OFF AT 1:32 Start Good . Won driving. Course firm.
TIME :24³, :49, 1:12⁴, 1:35⁴, 1:46⁴ (:24.79, :49.01, 1:12.84, 1:35.87, 1:46.91)

$2 Mutuel Prices:

3 – TATES CREEK	3.80	2.40	2.20
4 – MEGAHERTZ–GB		3.00	2.40
5 – DOUBLE CAT			4.00

$1 EXACTA 3–4 PAID $5.40 $2 QUINELLA 3–4 PAID $6.60
$1 TRIFECTA 3–4–5 PAID $53.80

Ch. m, (Jan), by Rahy – Viviana , by Nureyev . Trainer Frankel Robert. Bred by Juddmonte Farms (Ky).

TATES CREEK pulled a bit while prompting the early pace, stalked a bit off the rail into and on the first turn, bid outside DOUBLE CAT on the backstretch and second turn, took a short lead nearing midstretch, inched away then held under some urging. MEGAHERTZ (GB) broke in and bumped the winner, saved ground off the early pace, moved up outside a rival leaving the backstretch, continued between foes on the second turn, waited a bit leaving that bend, came out in the stretch and finished well. DOUBLE CAT took a short early lead between horses, inched away and angled in approaching the first turn, set a pressured pace inside, fought back along the rail through the stretch but could not quite match the top pair late. CRAZY ENSIGN (ARG) close up forcing or stalking the pace outside, bid three deep on the second turn and into the stretch and was outfinished. ALOZAINA (IRE) pulled her way along inside stalking the pace, steadied in tight leaving the second turn, was blocked off heels from the quarter to eighth poles, then could not summon the needed late response. MAGIC MISSION (GB) chased outside a rival, went three deep on the second turn and four wide into the stretch and could not summon the necessary response. MISS GAZON (IRE) broke slowly, saved ground off the pace, came out into the stretch and did not rally.

Owners– 1, Juddmonte Farms Inc; 2, Bello Michael; 3, Cowan Marjorie and Irving M; 4, El Faruk Stable; 5, Zetcher Arnold; 6, Al Maktoum Sheik Maktoum b; 7, Tucker Jeffrey

Trainers– 1, Frankel Robert J; 2, Frankel Robert J; 3, Drysdale Neil D; 4, Mandella Richard E; 5, McAnally Ronald L; 6, Drysdale Neil D; 7, Morrison John

$2 Daily Double (5–3) Paid $30.60 ; Daily Double Pool $35,625 .
$1 Pick Three (7–5–3) Paid $299.30 ; Pick Three Pool $117,022 .

EIGHTH RACE
Santa Anita
JANUARY 11, 2003

$1\frac{1}{16}$ MILES. (1.39) SAN FERNANDO BREEDERS' CUP S. Grade II. Purse $200,000 (includes $100,000 BC – Breeders' Cup) FOR FOUR-YEAR-OLDS. (Includes $100,000 from Breeders' Cup Fund for Cup nominees only) By subscription of $200 each to accompany the nomination or by supplementary nomination of $4,000 by time of entry. $2,000 additional to start. Breeders' Cup fund moniesalso correspondingly divided provided a Breeders' Cup nominee has finished in an awarded position. Any Breeders' Cup fund monies not awarded will revert to the fund. 122 lbs. Non-winners of $100,000 twice at one mile or over in 2002–2003 allowed 2 lbs.;of such a race in 2002–2003 or $60,000 any distance since December 25, 4lbs.; of a race of $50,000 since July 1, 6 lbs. NOMINATIONS CLOSED Thursday, January 2, 2003 with 18.

Value of Race: $219,600 Winner $131,760; second $43,920; third $26,352; fourth $13,176; fifth $4,392. Mutuel Pool $566,086.00 Exacta Pool $318,239.00 Quinella Pool $35,225.00 Trifecta Pool $324,587.00 Superfecta Pool $118,987.00

Last Raced	Horse	M/Eqt.	A.	Wt	PP	St	¼	½	¾	Str	Fin	Jockey	Odds $1
7Dec02 ^{8}Hou^{2}	Pass Rush	LB b	4	116	8	5	3^{2}	3^{hd}	2^{hd}	$1^{1\frac{1}{2}}$	$1^{3\frac{1}{2}}$	Nakatani C S	3.60
20Dec02 ^{3}Hol^{2}	Tracemark	LB b	4	116	4	2	5^{2}	5^{hd}	$5^{\frac{1}{2}}$	5^{hd}	$2^{\frac{1}{2}}$	Desormeaux K J	4.30
14Nov02 ^{4}Hol^{1}	Tizbud	LB	4	116	3	3	2^{1}	2^{1}	$3^{\frac{1}{2}}$	$3^{\frac{1}{2}}$	3^{nk}	Espinoza V	3.00
11Dec02 ^{3}Hol^{1}	Rushin' to Altar	LB	4	116	6	8	$7^{\frac{1}{2}}$	8	7^{2}	4^{2}	$4^{\frac{1}{2}}$	Solis A O	4.30
1Dec02 ^{8}Hol^{8}	Century City-Ire	LB b	4	118	7	6	$6^{4\frac{1}{2}}$	$6^{4\frac{1}{2}}$	6^{1}	6^{3}	5^{4}	Pincay L A Jr	6.30
1Jan03 ^{5}SA^{2}	Groom On the Run	LB bf	4	116	1	4	8	7^{hd}	8	7^{1}	$6^{1\frac{1}{2}}$	Krone J A	23.50
1Dec02 ^{8}Hol^{2}	Mananan McLir	LB	4	120	5	7	4^{hd}	4^{2}	$1^{\frac{1}{2}}$	2^{hd}	$7^{12\frac{1}{2}}$	Valenzuela P A	6.50
29Dec02 ^{3}SA^{8}	Traditional	LB b	4	116	2	1	1^{1}	1^{1}	$4^{2\frac{1}{2}}$	8	8	Flores D R	26.80

OFF AT 4:10 Start Good . Won driving. Track fast.

TIME :23, :46^{2}, 1:10^{1}, 1:35^{3}, 1:42^{1} (:23.04, :46.54, 1:10.32, 1:35.61, 1:42.37)

$2 Mutuel Prices:

8 – PASS RUSH	9.20	5.40	3.60
4 – TRACEMARK		5.20	3.40
3 – TIZBUD			3.00

$1 EXACTA 8–4 PAID $18.90 $2 QUINELLA 4–8 PAID $22.60
$1 TRIFECTA 8–4–3 PAID $85.30 $1 SUPERFECTA 8–4–3–6 PAID $220.30

Ch. h, (Apr), by Crown Ambassador – Profitable Knight , by Knight . Trainer Byrne Patrick B. Bred by Swifty Farms Inc (Ind).

PASS RUSH stalked the pace outside, bid four wide into and on the second turn, took a short lead three deep into the stretch and pulled clear under urging. TRACEMARK bobbled slightly at the start, chased outside, came four wide into the stretch and gained the place late. TIZBUD had speed outside a rival early then stalked off the rail, bid three deep between horses into the second turn, continued outside a foe leaving that turn, could not match the winner, drifted in late and lost second. RUSHIN' TO ALTAR off a bit slowly, settled outside a rival, split horses three deep into the stretch and put in a late bid. CENTURY CITY (IRE) wide into the first turn, chased off the rail, angled in on the second turn, came out into the stretch and could not offer the necessary late response. GROOM ON THE RUN saved ground off the pace, swung out into the stretch and did not rally. MANANAN MCLIR stalked the pace inside, bid along the rail to gain a short lead on the second turn but weakened in the stretch. TRADITIONAL bumped lightly with TIZBUD at the start, sped to the early lead, drifted out a bit into the first turn, set the pace just off the rail, dueled between horses into the second turn, dropped back leaving that bend and had little left.

Owners– 1, Tabor Michael B; 2, McGrath Edward T; 3, Cees Stable LLC; 4, Vogel Arthur; 5, Kitchwa Stables and Nichols Thomas L; 6, Robison J Kirk and Judy; 7, Horizon Stable Jarvis and Margolis et al; 8, Lewis Robert B and Beverly J

Trainers– 1, Byrne Patrick B; 2, Dollase Craig; 3, Sadler John W; 4, McAnally Ronald L; 5, Greely C Beau; 6, Greenman Dean; 7, Dollase Wallace A; 8, Lukas D Wayne

$2 Daily Double (5–8) Paid $108.00 ; Daily Double Pool $53,723 .
$1 Pick Three (2–5–8) Paid $657.80 ; Pick Three Pool $93,131 .

TENTH RACE
Gulfstream
JANUARY 12, 2003

6 FURLONGS. (1.07^{4}) 23rd Running of THE FIRST LADY HANDICAP. Grade III. Purse $100,000 FOR FILLIES AND MARES, THREE YEARS OLD AND UPWARD. By subscription of $100 each, which shall accompany the nomination, $1,000 to pass the entry box and $1,000 additional to start, with $100,000 guaranteed. The owner of the winner to receive $60,000; $20,000 to second, $11,000 to third, $6,000 to fourth and $3,000 to fifth. Trophy to winning Owner. Closed Tuesday, December 31, 2002 with 14 Nominations. (Rail at 20 feet).

Value of Race: $100,000 Winner $60,000; second $20,000; third $11,000; fourth $6,000; fifth $3,000. Mutuel Pool $307,547.00 Exacta Pool $233,879.00 Trifecta Pool $186,802.00 Superfecta Pool $62,110.00

Last Raced	Horse	M/Eqt.	A.	Wt	PP	St	¼	½	Str	Fin	Jockey	Odds $1
26Oct02 ^{1}AP^{5}	Harmony Lodge	L	5	113	7	5	5^{2}	1^{hd}	1^{1}	$1^{1\frac{3}{4}}$	Velazquez J R	6.80
29Dec02 ^{11}Crc^{2}	Fly Me Crazy	Lb	5	114	4	7	6^{2}	$5^{2\frac{1}{2}}$	$4^{1\frac{1}{2}}$	$2^{1\frac{3}{4}}$	Santos J A	7.50
21Jly02 ^{7}Del^{2}	Haunted Lass	L	4	114	5	3	3^{1}	2^{hd}	$2^{1\frac{1}{2}}$	$3^{3\frac{1}{2}}$	Guidry M	21.40
28Nov02 ^{7}Aqu^{4}	Preferred Option	L	4	113	3	4	7	7	5^{1}	4^{1}	Chavez J F	3.90
29Dec02 ^{11}Crc^{1}	Forest Heiress	L	4	119	2	6	1^{hd}	3^{1}	$3^{2\frac{1}{2}}$	$5^{1\frac{1}{4}}$	Bailey J D	0.90
7Sep02 ^{8}Del^{4}	Bruanna	Lb	5	113	6	2	4^{1}	$4^{1\frac{1}{2}}$	6^{4}	$6^{9\frac{1}{4}}$	Prado E S	7.90
7Dec02 ^{10}Crc^{7}	Interest Only	Lf	5	113	1	1	2^{hd}	6^{hd}	7	7	Day P	14.90

OFF AT 5:04 Start Good. Won driving. Track fast.

TIME :21^{4}, :44^{4}, :57, 1:10^{1} (:21.88, :44.89, :57.17, 1:10.31)

$2 Mutuel Prices:

8–HARMONY LODGE	15.60	10.20	6.60
5–FLY ME CRAZY		8.80	5.60
6–HAUNTED LASS			6.80

$2 EXACTA 8–5 PAID $129.00 $2 TRIFECTA 8–5–6 PAID $1,015.20 $2 SUPERFECTA 8–5–6–4 PAID $5,175.80

Ch. m, by Hennessy–Win Crafty Lady, by Crafty Prospector. Trainer Pletcher Todd A. Bred by Sabine Stables (Ky).

HARMONY LODGE rated off the pace, rallied four wide to take over at the quarter pole, then edged away through the stretch under pressure. FLY ME CRAZY unhurried after breaking slowly, swung out for the stretch run and rallied to be up for the place. HAUNTED LASS raced with the pace three wide on the turn, continued on well into the stretch and weakened. PREFERRED OPTION trailed after being steadied from tight quarters in the early going, then passed tired rivals in the drive without threatening. FOREST HEIRESS vied for the lead outside INTEREST ONLY, moved to the inside when that rival dropped back on the turn, then gave way in the drive. BRUANNA chased the leaders four wide to midway of the turn and faltered. INTEREST ONLY vied for the lead along the inside into the turn and faded.

Owners— 1, Melnyk Eugene & Laura; 2, Gill Michael J; 3, Iwin99; 4, Shields Joseph V Jr; 5, Stonerside Stable; 6, Murphy John D & Old Coach Farm; 7, Klein Richard Bertram & Elaine

Trainers—1, Pletcher Todd A; 2, Shuman Mark; 3, Iwinski Allen; 4, Jerkens H Allen; 5, Mott William I; 6, Gorham Michael E; 7, Flint Steve

Scratched— Chispiski (7Dec02 ^{10}CRC^{1})

$2 Pick Three (10–5–8) Paid $1,837.40; Pick Three Pool $34,452.

SEVENTH RACE
Santa Anita
JANUARY 12, 2003

6 FURLONGS. (1.07^1) 46th Running of THE SAN MIGUEL. Grade III. Purse $100,000 FOR THREE-YEAR-OLDS. By subscription of $100 each to accompany the nomination. The added money and all fees to be divided 60% to the winner, 20% tosecond, 12% to third, 6% to fourth and 2% to fifth. 121 lbs. Non-winners of a race of $50,000 or two of $30,000 allowed 3 lbs.; of a race of $35,000 since July 23 or $25,000 at any time, 5 lbs.; of a race other than Maiden of Claiming, 7 lbs. (Claiming races not considered). NOMINATIONS CLOSED Thursday, January 2, 2003 with 8. SUPPLEMENTAL NOMINATION FEE OF $2000: JIMMY O.

Value of Race: $107,800 Winner $64,680; second $21,560; third $12,936; fourth $6,468; fifth $2,156. Mutuel Pool $365,309.00 Exacta Pool $197,825.00 Quinella Pool $25,854.00 Trifecta Pool $163,781.00

Last Raced	Horse	M/Eqt.	A.Wt	PP	St	¼	½	Str	Fin	Jockey	Odds $1
25Oct02 ^{5}AP^3	Omega Code	**LB**	3 121	1	3	3^{hd}	2^{hd}	1^{hd}	1^1	Pedroza M A	1.80
7Dec02 ^{4}Hou^6	Only The Best	**LB**	3 121	5	2	1^1	1^1	2^2	2^5	Valenzuela P A	*1.80
21Dec02 ^{8}TuP^2	Jimmy O	**LB**b	3 118	2	5	$4^{1\frac{1}{2}}$	3^1	3^3	3^6	Espinoza V	7.20
28Sep02 ^{9}AP^8	Echeverria	**LB**b	3 116	4	1	5	5	4^{hd}	4^8	Flores D R	5.60
22Dec02 ^{6}Hol^1	Bossanova	**LB**b	3 115	3	4	2^{hd}	$4^{1\frac{1}{2}}$	5	5	Solis A	3.70

***—Actual Betting Favorite.**

OFF AT 3:41 Start Good. Won driving. Track fast.
TIME :21^1, :44, :56^1, 1:08^3 (:21.38, :44.12, :56.33, 1:08.65)

$2 Mutuel Prices:

1–OMEGA CODE	5.60	3.00	2.40
6–ONLY THE BEST		3.00	2.20
2–JIMMY O			2.60

$1 EXACTA 1–6 PAID $7.80 $2 QUINELLA 1–6 PAID $6.20 $1 TRIFECTA 1–6–2 PAID $20.20

B. c, (Feb), by Elusive Quality–Tin Oaks, by Deputy Minister. Trainer Ward Wesley A. Bred by Sally J Andersen (Fla).

OMEGA CODE stalked inside then came out from a bit of a tight spot on the backstretch, tracked the leader between horses, angled out into the stretch, put a head in front in midstretch and inched away under steady handling. ONLY THE BEST sped to the early lead, angled in and set the pace a bit off the rail, fought back when challenged in the stretch but could not match the winner late while clearly second best. JIMMY O settled a bit off the rail then went up three deep to stalk the pace, came out into the stretch, then drifted in through the drive and held third. ECHEVERRIA chased off the inside on the backstretch and turn and lacked a response in the stretch. BOSSANOVA pulled his way along outside the winner early, angled in on the backstretch and stalked inside, began to drop back some leaving the turn, then gave way in the stretch.

Owners— 1, Butler Moore & Ward; 2, Toffel Mr & Mrs Alvin E; 3, Anderson Anderson & Meadowbrook Far; 4, Pegram Michael E; 5, Rodriguez Lorraine & Rod

Trainers—1, Ward Wesley A; 2, Lynch Brian A; 3, La Croix David; 4, Baffert Bob; 5, Paasch Christopher S

Scratched— Red Apache (23Nov02 ^{7}HOL^2)

$2 Daily Double (10–1) Paid $50.80; Daily Double Pool $26,734.
$1 Pick Three (5–10–1) Paid $747.70; Pick Three Pool $79,623.

EIGHTH RACE
Aqueduct
JANUARY 18, 2003

1$\frac{1}{16}$ MILES. (Inner Dirt)(1.41) 84th Running of THE AQUEDUCT HANDICAP. Grade III. Purse $100,000. THREE YEAR OLDS AND UPWARD. By subscription of $100 each, which should accompany the nomination; $500 to pass the entry box; $500 to start, with $100,000 added. The added money and all fees to be divided 60% to the winner, 20% to second, 11% to third, 6% to fourth and 3% to fifth. Trophies will be presented to he winning owner, trainer and jockey. Closed Saturday, January 4,2002 with 14 Nominations.

Value of Race: $107,400 Winner $64,440; second $21,480; third $11,814; fourth $6,444; fifth $3,222. Mutuel Pool $405,020.00 Exacta Pool $324,430.00

Last Raced	Horse	M/Eqt.	A.Wt	PP	St	¼	½	¾	Str	Fin	Jockey	Odds $1
7Dec02 ^{8}Aqu^1	Snake Mountain	L	5 120	4	5	4^{hd}	4^{hd}	2^{hd}	1^7	$1^{7\frac{1}{2}}$	Luzzi M J	a-0.35
18Dec02 ^{8}Aqu^1	Ground Storm	Lb	7 117	5	4	5	5	$4^{4\frac{1}{2}}$	2^{hd}	$2^{2\frac{1}{4}}$	Castellano J J	2.60
7Dec02 ^{8}Aqu^3	Cat's At Home	Lb	6 114	2	1	$2^{2\frac{1}{2}}$	$2^{\frac{1}{2}}$	$3^{\frac{1}{2}}$	$3^{5\frac{1}{2}}$	3^9	Gryder A T	7.20
27Nov02 ^{7}Aqu^7	Mr. Determined	Lbf	4 109	3	3	$3^{\frac{1}{2}}$	3^{hd}	5	5	$4^{5\frac{3}{4}}$	Chavez Luis	22.10
29Nov02 ^{8}Aqu^1	Voodoo	Lb	5 115	1	2	$1^{4\frac{1}{2}}$	$1^{1\frac{1}{2}}$	1^1	$4^{2\frac{1}{2}}$	5	Migliore R	a-0.35

a–Coupled: Snake Mountain and Voodoo.

OFF AT 3:53 Start Good. Won ridden out. Track fast.
TIME :23^2, :47^4, 1:12^1, 1:37^3, 1:44 (:23.56, :47.96, 1:12.33, 1:37.68, 1:44.17)

$2 Mutuel Prices:

1A–SNAKE MOUNTAIN (a–entry)	2.70	2.10	—
5–GROUND STORM		2.10	—
3–CAT'S AT HOME		—	—

$2 EXACTA 1–5 PAID $4.60

Ch. h, by A.P. Indy–Coup de Genie, by Mr. Prospector. Trainer Jerkens James A. Bred by Flaxman Holdings Ltd (Ky).

SNAKE MOUNTAIN was rated along on the rail, advanced inside on the second turn, split rivals turning for home, drew away when asked and was ridden out to the wire. GROUND STORM was three wide on the first turn, rallied four wide on the second turn and was along from the outside to get the place award. CAT'S AT HOME was bumped at the start, raced close up from the outside, advanced three wide on the second turn and had no response when roused. MR. DETERMINED was bumped at the start, raced inside and had no rally. VOODOO was bumped at the start, was hustled out to a clear lead, set the pace along the inside and tired in the stretch.

Owners— 1, Berkshire Stud et al; 2, Centennial Farms; 3, Evans Edward P; 4, Demola Dorothy; 5, Moore Susan & John

Trainers—1, Jerkens James A; 2, Mott William I; 3, Hennig Mark; 4, Demola Richard; 5, Jerkens James A

Scratched— Tempest Fugit (18Dec02 ^{8}AQU^3), My Man Ryan (18Dec02 ^{8}AQU^2)

$2 Pick Six (4–1–1–6–5–1) 6 Correct Paid $1,267.00; Pick Six Pool $204,245. $2 Pick Six (4–1–1–6–5–1) 5 Correct Paid $13.00

TENTH RACE

Gulfstream

JANUARY 18, 2003

1¹⁄₁₆ MILES. (1.40¹) 14th Running of THE HOLY BULL. Grade III. Purse $100,000. 3-year-olds. By subscription of $100 each, which shall accompany the nomination, $1,000 to pass the entry box and $1,000 additional to start, with $100,000 guaranteed. The owner of the winner to receive $60,000; $20,000 to second, $11,000 to third, $6,000 to fourth and $3,000 to fifth. Weight, 122 lbs. Non-winners of $50,000 at a mile or over, allowed, 2 lbs. $50,000 at any distance or $35,000 at a mile or over, 4 lbs. $30,000 at any distance or $25,000 at a mile or over, 6 lbs. Horses finishing first, second or third in the Holy Bull Stakes will automatically be nominated to the Florida Derby. Closed Wednesday, January 8 with 10 nominations. Early Bird Florida Derby Nominations closed, November 13 with 117.

Value of Race: $100,000 Winner $60,000; second $20,000; third $11,000; fourth $6,000; fifth $3,000. Mutuel Pool $763,016.00 Exacta Pool $582,630.00 Trifecta Pool $471,987.00 Superfecta Pool $152,044.00

Last Raced	Horse	M/Eqt. A.Wt	PP	St	¼	½	¾	Str	Fin	Jockey	Odds $1
17Nov02 8CD2	Offlee Wild	L 3 116	9	5	3½	3½	31	2½	1hd	Guidry M	27.40
30Nov02 6Aqu1	Powerful Touch	L 3 116	4	1	2½	2½	22½	1½	23	Chavez J F	9.40
30Nov02 8Aqu2	Bham	Lb 3 118	3	4	1½	1½	1½	33	32½	Velazquez J R	2.70
1Jan03 10Crc5	Supervisor	Lb 3 116	10	10	13	13	13	7hd	41	Boulanger G	25.70
19Oct02 5Bel1	Funny Cide	L 3 122	13	12	71	41	41	4hd	51¾	Santos J A	5.30
23Nov02 4Hoo6	Boston Park	Lb 3 116	11	6	6hd	7½	7½	5½	6nk	Douglas R R	62.10
14Dec02 11Crc2	Patriotic Flame	Lb 3 116	2	2	8½	82	81½	81½	7½	Velasquez C	14.10
14Dec02 11Crc5	Seek Gold	L 3 118	7	7	5hd	6½	61	62½	81¼	Coa E M	56.10
1Jan03 10Crc7	Christmas Away	L 3 118	5	13	124	125	12½	11½	92¼	Day P	16.00
8Nov02 3Aqu1	Spite The Devil	3 118	12	11	9½	114	9½	10½	102	Bailey J D	14.90
24Nov02 8CD1	Not For Profit	Lb 3 118	6	9	10½	10½	112½	13	11nk	Prado E S	46.90
1Jan03 10Crc4	Flank Attack	Lb 3 116	8	8	114	9hd	10½	12½	12½	Velez R I	101.60
2Nov02 8Aqu1	Added Edge	3 122	1	3	4½	5½	5hd	9½	13	Husbands P	1.80

OFF AT 5:11 Start Good. Won driving. Track fast.

TIME :23², 1:11², 1:36², 1:43 (:23.52, :47.31, 1:11.43, 1:36.46, 1:43.00)

$2 Mutuel Prices:

9–OFFLEE WILD	56.80	21.60	8.80
4–POWERFUL TOUCH		11.60	6.60
3–BHAM			3.80

$2 EXACTA 9–4 PAID $496.00 $2 TRIFECTA 9–4–3 PAID $2,889.60 $2 SUPERFECTA 9–4–3–ALL PAID $2,886.80

Dk. b. or br. c, (Apr), by Wild Again–Alvear, by Seattle Slew. Trainer Smith Thomas V. Bred by Dorothy A Matz (Ky).

OFFLEE WILD stalked the pace three wide, rallied to gain a slim lead inside the eighth pole, then was fully extended to prevail. POWERFUL TOUCH pressed the pace outside BHAM, moved to gain a slim lead at the top of the stretch, responded when headed by OFFLEE WILD inside the eighth pole and continued on gamely while being edged to the wire. BHAM set the pace under pressure along the inside, continued on well to midstretch and weakened. SUPERVISOR outrun early, swung to the outside for the stretch run and closed with a belated rally. FUNNY CIDE hit the gate at the start, was caught out five wide around the first turn, chased the pace four wide into the stretch and tired. BOSTON PARK allowed to settle, raced three wide on the far turn and lacked a late response. PATRIOTIC FLAME reserved early, saved ground into the stretch and failed to rally. SEEK GOLD raced in striking position off the rail, then was steadied in traffic on the far turn and faltered. CHRISTMAS AWAY off slowly, was never a factor. SPITE THE DEVIL failed to menace after breaking awkwardly. NOT FOR PROFIT saved ground to no avail. FLANK ATTACK was outrun while racing four wide. ADDED EDGE chased the leaders along the rail into the far turn and faded.

Owners— 1, Azalea Stables LLC; 2, Stronach Stable; 3, Starlight Stable LLC & Barbara Curt; 4, Lundock Rodney G; 5, Sackatoga Stable; 6, Overbrook Farm; 7, Kinsman Stable; 8, Lapenta Robert V; 9, Bowling Carl & Thompson Charles R; 10, Hardwicke Stable; 11, Ramsey Kenneth L & Sarah K; 12, Link O W; 13, Team Valor & Robert J Wilson.

Trainers— 1, Smith Thomas V; 2, McPeek Kenneth G; 3, Pletcher Todd A; 4, Tortora Emanuel; 5, Tagg Barclay; 6, Lukas D Wayne; 7, Tortora Emanuel; 8, Zito Nicholas P; 9, Byrne Patrick B; 10, Jerkens H Allen; 11, McPeek Kenneth G; 12, Durso Robert J; 13, Casse Mark

$2 Pick Three (1–5–9) Paid $529.00; Pick Three Pool $58,854.

SEVENTH RACE

Santa Anita

JANUARY 18, 2003

1 1/16 MILES. (1.39) SANTA CATALINA S. Grade II. Purse $150,000 FOR THREE-YEAR-OLDS. By subscription of $150 each to accompany the nomination or by supplementary nomination of $3,000 by time of entry. $1,500 additional to start, with $150,000 guaranteed of which $90,000 to first, $30,000 to second, $18,000 to third, $9,000 to fourth and $3,000 to fifth. 120 lbs. Winners of a race of $200,000 to carry 3 lbs. additional; non-winners of $55,000 at one mile or over allowed 3 lbs.; of such a race any distance, 5 lbs.; of $20,000 at one mile or over or$30,000 at any distance, 7 lbs. (Maiden and Claiming races not considered.) NOMINATIONS CLOSED Thursday, January 9, 2003 with 22.

Value of Race: $150,000 Winner $90,000; second $30,000; third $18,000; fourth $9,000; fifth $3,000. Mutuel Pool $731,898.00 Exacta Pool $433,034.00 Quinella Pool $42,272.00 Trifecta Pool $425,417.00 Superfecta Pool $157,627.00

Last Raced	Horse	M/Eqt.	A.	Wt	PP	St	1/4	1/2	3/4	Str	Fin	Jockey	Odds $1
21Dec02 8Hol2	Domestic Dispute	L B	3	113	8	7	68	612	42½	22	13	Flores D R	2.90
17Nov02 7Hol1	Our Bobby V.	L B	3	113	4	3	11	11½	11	1hd	23½	Pincay L A Jr	5.60
26Dec02 3SA1	Scrimshaw	L B b	3	115	6	5	2½	2hd	2½	34	34	Solis A O	1.90
7Dec02 4Hou1	Crackup	L B b	3	120	2	1	3½	4hd	610	65	4hd	Baze T	3.60
23Oct02 2Kee1	Storm Gulch	b	3	113	7	6	4hd	51	5½	5hd	52	Farina T	36.90
28Dec02 1SA4	Hell Cat	L B	3	113	1	2	74½	7	7	7	61	Pedroza M A	23.20
28Dec02 3SA2	Singletary	L B	3	113	3	4	51½	31	31	41	7	Valenzuela P A	9.70
28Dec02 1SA1	Robledo	L B	3	115	5	8	8	—	—	—	—	Krone J A	13.60

OFF AT 3:37 Start Good . Won driving. Track fast.

TIME :23, :462, 1:101, 1:353, 1:421 (:23.08, :46.57, 1:10.35, 1:35.64, 1:42.20)

$2 Mutuel Prices:

10 – DOMESTIC DISPUTE	7.80	4.00	2.60
4 – OUR BOBBY V.		5.80	3.40
6 – SCRIMSHAW			2.80

$1 EXACTA 10–4 PAID $25.30 $2 QUINELLA 4–10 PAID $27.40
$1 TRIFECTA 10–4–6 PAID $72.20 $1 SUPERFECTA 10–4–6–2 PAID $198.70

Ch. c, (Mar), by Unbridled's Song – Majestical Moment , by Magesterial . Trainer Baffert Bob. Bred by Gary Garber (Ky).

DOMESTIC DISPUTE settled off the rail, split rivals into the second turn, bid three deep into the stretch, collared the runner-up past the eighth pole, drifted in and pulled clear under some urging. OUR BOBBY V. bumped at the start, sped to the early lead, set the pace a bit off the rail, responded between horses into the second turn, inched away and angled in leaving that turn, could not match the winner in the final furlong but held second. SCRIMSHAW broke in and bumped a rival, stalked three deep, continued off the rail into the stretch and bested the others. CRACKUP saved ground stalking the pace, dropped back into the second turn, came a bit off the rail in the stretch and edged a foe for fourth. STORM GULCH four wide into the first turn, chased three deep on the backstretch and second turn, drifted inward and was in tight off heels in midstretch while the rider lost the whip, then weakened. HELL CAT allowed to settle inside, saved ground off the pace, came out in the stretch and was outrun. SINGLETARY pulled his way along between horses and was in a bit tight into the first turn, stalked between foes, bid inside into the second turn, dropped back on that bend and weakened. ROBLEDO bumped between foes at the start, clipped heels in the initial strides, was pulled up on the first turn and was vanned off.

Owners– 1, Garber Gary M; 2, Verratti Kathleen and Robert; 3, Lewis Robert B and Beverly J; 4, Fulton Stan E; 5, Tabor Michael B; 6, Bradford Joe C; 7, Little Red Feather Racing; 8, Push Push Stable

Trainers– 1, Baffert Bob; 2, Spawr William; 3, Lukas D Wayne; 4, Becerra Rafael; 5, Biancone Patrick L; 6, Carava Jack; 7, Chatlos Donald Jr; 8, Cerin Vladimir

Scratched– Judge Swiss (26Dec02 5SA 3) , Nation Wide News (26Dec02 6SA 1)

$2 Daily Double (3–10) Paid $55.20 ; Daily Double Pool $52,795 .
$1 Pick Three (9–3–10) Paid $164.90 ; Pick Three Pool $115,137 .

TENTH RACE
Gulfstream
JANUARY 19, 2003

1⅜ MILES. (Turf)(2.10^{3}) 8th Running of THE MAC DIARMIDA HANDICAP. Grade III. Purse $100,000 Guaranteed. FOR THREE YEAR OLDS AND UPWARD. By subscription of $100 each, which shall accompany the nomination, $1,000 to pass the entry box and $1,000 additional to start, with $100,000 guaranteed. The owner of the winner to receive $60,000; $20,000 to second, $11,000 to third, $6,000 to fourth and $3,000 to fifth. Trophy to winning owner. This race will be limited to 12 Starters, with Also Eligibles. (High Weights on the scale Preferred.) In the event this stake is taken off the turf, it may be subject to downgrading upon review of the Graded Stakes Committee. Closed Wednesday, January 8, 2003 with 31 Nominations. (Rail at 0 feet).

Value of Race: $100,000 Winner $60,000; second $20,000; third $11,000; fourth $6,000; fifth $3,000. Mutuel Pool $442,522.00 Exacta Pool $326,400.00 Trifecta Pool $259,372.00 Superfecta Pool $92,500.00

Last Raced	Horse	M/Eqt.	A.Wt	PP	¼	½	¾	1	Str	Fin	Jockey	Odds $1
28Dec02 ^{11}Crc^{11}	Riddlesdown-IRE	L	6 113	4	$1^{1\frac{1}{2}}$	1^{2}	1^{4}	1^{3}	$1^{2\frac{1}{2}}$	$1^{1\frac{1}{2}}$	Velez R I	29.80
28Dec02 ^{11}Crc^{9}	Macaw-IR	L	4 114	3	6^{1}	$6^{\frac{1}{2}}$	$7^{\frac{1}{2}}$	$6^{1\frac{1}{2}}$	2^{hd}	$2^{1\frac{3}{4}}$	Santos J A	8.10
28Dec02 ^{11}Crc^{8}	Just Listen	Lb	7 113	7	3^{2}	3^{1}	$5^{1\frac{1}{2}}$	5^{hd}	$4^{1\frac{1}{2}}$	3^{nk}	Homeister R B Jr	37.90
28Dec02 ^{11}Crc^{6}	Williams News	L	8 118	12	$10^{1\frac{1}{2}}$	$9^{1\frac{1}{2}}$	$9^{1\frac{1}{2}}$	$7^{\frac{1}{2}}$	5^{2}	4^{nk}	Husbands P	16.00
28Dec02 ^{11}Crc^{4}	Gritty Sandie	Lbf	7 114	11	12	11^{1}	11^{2}	9^{1}	6^{1}	5^{nk}	Bailey J D	7.50
28Dec02 ^{11}Crc^{3}	Rochester	L	7 117	9	$4^{\frac{1}{2}}$	$4^{\frac{1}{2}}$	$3^{\frac{1}{2}}$	2^{hd}	$3^{1\frac{1}{2}}$	$6^{1\frac{3}{4}}$	Day P	3.00
28Dec02 ^{11}Crc^{7}	Whata Brainstorm	L	6 114	5	$5^{\frac{1}{2}}$	$10^{\frac{1}{2}}$	10^{hd}	12	$8^{1\frac{1}{2}}$	$7^{1\frac{1}{4}}$	Chavez J F	9.50
28Dec02 ^{11}Crc^{5}	DH Whitmore's Conn	Lb	5 114	1	8^{hd}	5^{hd}	$4^{\frac{1}{2}}$	$8^{1\frac{1}{2}}$	7^{hd}	8	Prado E S	2.70
28Dec02 ^{11}Crc^{12}	DH Mr. Pleasentfar-BRZ	L	6 114	2	11^{1}	12	12	$11^{\frac{1}{2}}$	9^{2}	$8^{2\frac{1}{2}}$	Martin C W	93.00
7Dec02 ^{7}Hou^{6}	Quiet Ruler	L	5 113	6	9^{2}	$8^{1\frac{1}{2}}$	$8^{1\frac{1}{2}}$	10^{1}	$10^{\frac{1}{2}}$	10^{1}	Velazquez J R	12.70
28Dec02 ^{11}Crc^{2}	Serial Bride	Lb	6 115	10	7^{1}	7^{1}	6^{hd}	$4^{\frac{1}{2}}$	11^{2}	$11^{5\frac{3}{4}}$	Coa E M	6.80
4Jan03 ^{10}GP^{5}	Marquette	Lf	7 114	8	$2^{\frac{1}{2}}$	$2^{\frac{1}{2}}$	2^{1}	3^{1}	12	12	Turner T G	52.00

DH—Dead Heat.

OFF AT 5:09 Start Good. Won driving. Course firm.
TIME :25^{1}, :49^{4}, 1:14^{4}, 1:39, 2:03, 2:14^{3} (:25.31, :49.80, 1:14.98, 1:39.07, 2:03.08, 2:14.75)

$2 Mutuel Prices:				
	4–RIDDLESDOWN–IRE	61.60	32.00	22.40
	3–MACAW–IR		10.80	8.60
	7–JUST LISTEN			21.80

$2 EXACTA 4–3 PAID $607.80 $2 TRIFECTA 4–3–7 PAID $10,515.00 $1 SUPERFECTA 4–3–7–12 PAID $69,375.00

Ch. h, by Common Grounds–Neat Dish, by Stalwart. Trainer O'Callaghan Niall M. Bred by McLoughlin John (Ire).

RIDDLESDOWN (IRE) sprinted clear in the early stages, set a moderate pace while racing uncontested on the lead for a mile, maintained a clear advantage into midstretch then held off the runner-up under brisk urging. MACAW (IRE) raced in good position along the inside for a good part of the way, angled between horses leaving the turn and finished willingly for the place. JUST LISTEN raced up close along the inside for a mile, was shuffled back a bit on the turn then finished willingly along the rail. WILLIAMS NEWS raced well back to the turn, advanced four wide into the stretch then closed late in the middle of the track. GRITTY SANDIE was outrun to the turn then rallied belatedly. ROCHESTER chased the leaders while three wide to the top of the stretch and weakened. WHATA BRAINSTORM checked in tight during the early stages, raced in traffic while well back on the turn then failed to threaten while improving his position. WHITMORE'S CONN failed to mount a serious rally. MR. PLEASENTFAR (BRZ) was never a factor. QUIET RULER raced in traffic on the turn then lacked a strong closing bid. SERIAL BRIDE raced wide and tired. MARQUETTE raced up close between horses to the turn then gave way.

Owners— 1, Tanaka Gary A; 2, Melillo George & Sandra; 3, Guez Marie Romaine & Guez D; 4, On Target Racing Stable; 5, Kimmel Caesar P & Nicholson Ronald; 6, Augustin Stable; 7, Eaton John & Laymon Steve; 8, Shanley Michael & Lynn; 9, Raising Dust Stable; 10, Sarf Randy J & Old Brookside Farm; 11, Runnin Horse Farm Inc; 12, Cavanaugh J R & Early Morning Farm

Trainers—1, O'Callaghan Niall M; 2, Tagg Barclay; 3, Catanese Joseph C III; 4, Vivian David A; 5, Toner James J; 6, Sheppard Jonathan E; 7, Picou James E; 8, Schulhofer Randy; 9, Malek Raja; 10, Bates Larry; 11, Pointer Norman R; 12, Root Richard R

Scratched— Maumee (5Jan03 ^{7}GP^{1}), Zloty (8Jan03 ^{9}GP^{3})

$2 Pick Three (1–3–4) Paid $2,717.20; Pick Three Pool $40,758.

SEVENTH RACE

Santa Anita

JANUARY 19, 2003

1 1/16 MILES. (1.39) 39th Running of THE EL ENCINO. Grade II. Purse $150,000. FILLIES FOUR YEARS OLD. By subscription of $150 each to accompany the nomination or by supplementary nomination of $3,000 by time of entry, $1,500 additional to start, with $150,000 guaranteed, of which $90,000 to first, $30,000 to second, $18,000 to third, $9,000 to fourth and $3,000 to fifth. Weight, 122 lbs. Non-winners of $100,000 twice at one mile or over in 2002-2003, allowed 3 lbs. Of such a race in 2002-2003 or $60,000 any distance since October 1, 5 lbs. Of $35,000 at any distance at anytime, 7 lbs. (Maiden and claiming races not considered). Closed Thursday, January 9 with 12 nominations.

Value of Race: $150,000 Winner $90,000; second $30,000; third $18,000; fourth $9,000; fifth $3,000.   Mutuel Pool $487,591.00 Exacta Pool $250,014.00   Quinella Pool $29,502.00 Trifecta Pool $255,536.00 Superfecta Pool $100,178.00

Last Raced	Horse	M/Eqt. A.Wt	PP	St	1/4	1/2	3/4	Str	Fin	Jockey	Odds $1
28Dec02 7SA1	Got Koko	LBb 4 119	7	7	6hd	5½	33	1½	11½	Solis A	3.20
28Dec02 7SA4	Bella Bellucci	LB 4 117	2	3	51	6hd	5hd	42½	23	Smith M E	2.30
9Nov02 9CD2	Bare Necessities	LB 4 119	6	4	4½	4hd	2hd	2hd	3no	Valdivia J Jr	4.10
31Dec02 8SA9	Adoration	LB 4 119	3	2	32½	31	1½	31½	44	Valenzuela P A	9.70
6Dec02 7Hol1	Ile De France	LB 4 115	8	8	8	7½	41	51½	52	Krone J A	19.20
16Nov02 9CD2	Glia	LB 4 119	5	6	7½	8	71½	62½	64½	Espinoza V	2.80
18Dec02 7Hol1	Ponche De Leona	LB 4 117	1	1	1hd	2½	61	7	7	Martinez F F	40.80
28Dec02 7SA10	Ms Louisett	LB 4 117	4	5	21½	1hd	8	—	—	Desormeaux K J	40.40

Ms Louisett:Pulled up;

OFF AT 3:37 Start Good. Won driving. Track fast.

TIME :23, :462, 1:102, 1:353, 1:421 (:23.13, :46.54, 1:10.57, 1:35.74, 1:42.25)

$2 Mutuel Prices:	7-GOT KOKO	8.40	4.00	2.80
	2-BELLA BELLUCCI		4.00	2.80
	6-BARE NECESSITIES			3.00

$1 EXACTA 7-2 PAID $17.60 $2 QUINELLA 2-7 PAID $15.00 $1 TRIFECTA 7-2-6 PAID $57.30 $1 SUPERFECTA 7-2-6-3 PAID $223.90

B. f, by Signal Tap–Baby North, by Northern Baby. Trainer Headley Bruce. Bred by Eileen H Hartis (Tex).

GOT KOKO four wide into the first turn, chased outside, launched a bid five wide leaving the backstretch, battled three deep on the second turn, gained a short lead in upper stretch and pulled clear under urging. BELLA BELLUCCI came off the rail leaving the first turn, went between horses on the backstretch, advanced outside on the second turn and three deep into the stretch and finished well for second. BARE NECESSITIES stalked outside, split rivals four wide with a move on the backstretch, battled between horses on the second turn and in the stretch and just held third. ADORATION prompted the early pace three deep then stalked off the rail, took a short lead three wide leaving the backstretch, angled in and dueled inside on the second turn and in the stretch and weakened in the final furlong. ILE DE FRANCE pulled her way between rivals early, moved up on the backstretch, went three deep into the second turn, angled in some and weakened. GLIA chased a bit off the rail, moved up inside on the backstretch, went outside a rival on the second turn and lacked a further response. PONCHE DE LEONA had good early speed and dueled inside, dropped back leaving the backstretch and weakened. MS LOUISETT bobbled and bumped with ADORATION at the start, dueled between horses then outside a rival, was between those again on the backstretch, fell back, was pulled up on the second turn but walked off.

Owners— 1, Headley & Leung; 2, Tabor Michael B; 3, Iron County Farms Inc; 4, Amerman Racing Stables; 5, T N T Stud; 6, Flaxman Holdings Ltd; 7, Eastern Sky Unlimited Trust & Cono; 8, McGrath Edward T

Trainers—1, Headley Bruce; 2, Drysdale Neil; 3, Dollase Wallace; 4, Hofmans David; 5, Mandella Richard; 6, Frankel Robert; 7, Paasch Christopher S; 8, Dollase Craig

Scratched— Theresa's Year (3Jan03 7SA2)

$2 Daily Double (9–7) Paid $100.80; Daily Double Pool $34,155.
$1 Pick Three (5–9–7) Paid $154.90; Pick Three Pool $87,148.

THIRD RACE

Santa Anita

JANUARY 20, 2003

7 FURLONGS. (1.20) 52nd Running of THE SANTA YNEZ. Grade II. Purse $150,000. Fillies, 3-year-olds. By subscription of $150 each to accompany the nomination or by supplementary nomination of $3,000 by time of entry. $1,500 additional to start, with $150,000 guaranteed, of which $90,000 to first, $30,000 to second, $18,000 to third, $9,000 to fourth and $3,000 to fifth. Weight, 121 lbs. Winners of $50,000 twice to carry an additional 2 lbs. Non-winners of two races of $40,000 or one of $60,000 at any time, allowed 3 lbs. Of two of $20,000 or one of $30,000 at anytime, 5 lbs. Of a race of $20,000, 7 lbs. Closed Thursday, January 9 with 10 nominations.

Value of Race: $150,000 Winner $90,000; second $30,000; third $18,000; fourth $9,000; fifth $3,000.   Mutuel Pool $341,630.00 Exacta Pool $194,997.00   Quinella Pool $19,474.00 Trifecta Pool $136,541.00

Last Raced	Horse	M/Eqt. A.Wt	PP	St	1/4	1/2	Str	Fin	Jockey	Odds $1
14Dec02 4Hol1	Elloluv	LB 3 121	5	2	31½	3½	11	12½	Valenzuela P A	1.80
14Dec02 4Hol4	Watching You	LB 3 116	4	3	41	42½	21½	28	Desormeaux K J	3.60
31Dec02 7SA1	Himalayan	LB 3 116	1	1	2hd	1hd	34	32	Nakatani C S	7.30
16Nov02 9Hol1	Puxa Saco	LB 3 121	2	5	5	2hd	410	425	Smith M E	1.30
6Dec02 5Hol1	No Love Song	LBb 3 116	3	4	1½	5	5	5	Pedroza M A	11.80

OFF AT 1:32 Start Good. Won driving. Track fast.

TIME :222, :451, 1:10, 1:23 (:22.41, :45.23, 1:10.01, 1:23.03)

$2 Mutuel Prices:	5-ELLOLUV	5.60	3.80	2.10
	4-WATCHING YOU		3.80	2.80
	1-HIMALAYAN			3.20

$1 EXACTA 5-4 PAID $11.30 $2 QUINELLA 4-5 PAID $14.60 $1 TRIFECTA 5-4-1 PAID $43.00

B. f, (Feb), by Gilded Time–Currency Quest, by Cryptoclearance. Trainer Dollase Craig. Bred by North Wales LLC (Ky).

ELLOLUV prompted the pace outside on the backstretch and four wide into the turn, dueled three deep on the bend, took a short lead between horses into the stretch, drifted in through the drive but pulled clear under urging. WATCHING YOU pulled her way along off the rail then outside stalking the pace, bid five wide leaving the backstretch and four wide on the turn, was three deep into the stretch and second best. HIMALAYAN had good early speed and dueled a bit off the rail, battled between foes into and on the turn, regained the inside nearing the stretch and weakened but held third. PUXA SACO settled toward the inside, moved up along the rail with a bid leaving the backstretch, dueled inside on the turn, dropped back leaving the bend and also weakened. NO LOVE SONG sent between horses to duel for the lead, fell back approaching the turn, gave way readily and was eased but crossed the wire.

Owners— 1, Reddam John P; 2, Hughes Bradley W; 3, West Mary E; 4, Rowan Richard; 5, Orseno or Patitucci

Trainers—1, Dollase Craig; 2, Stute Warren; 3, West Ted H; 4, Sahadi Jenine; 5, Ward Wesley A

Scratched— Buttertart (27Dec02 7SA4)

$2 Daily Double (11–5) Paid $21.60; Daily Double Pool $22,725.
$1 Pick Three (6–11–5) Paid $134.30; Pick Three Pool $91,704.

EIGHTH RACE
Santa Anita
JANUARY 20, 2003

1¼ MILES. (Turf)(1.57^{2}) 51st Running of THE SAN MARCOS. Grade II. Purse $150,000. 4-year-olds and upward. By subscription of $150 each to accompany the nomination or by supplementary nomination of $3,000 by time of entry. $1,500 additional to start, with $150,000 guaranteed, of which $90,000 to first, $30,000 to second, $18,000 to third, $9,000 to fourth and $3,000 to fifth. Weight, 122 lbs. Non-winners of $200,000 or $90,000 twice at a mile or over since July 1, allowed 3 lbs. Non-winners of $90,000 at a mile or over since July 1, 5 lbs. Of such a race since January 15, 7 lbs. Closed Thursday, January 9 with 18 nominations. (Rail at 15 feet).

Value of Race: $150,000 Winner $90,000; second $30,000; third $18,000; fourth $9,000; fifth $3,000. Mutuel Pool $430,183.00 Exacta Pool $228,344.00 Quinella Pool $26,727.00 Trifecta Pool $234,888.00 Superfecta Pool $101,234.00

Last Raced	Horse	M/Eqt.	A.	Wt	PP	¼	½	¾	1	Str	Fin	Jockey	Odds $1
1Dec02 ^{8}Hol^{1}	Johar	LB	4	120	6	7	7	7	5^{1}	4$^{2\frac{1}{2}}$	1^{hd}	Solis A	2.30
26Oct02 ^{9}AP^{4}	The Tin Man	LB	5	122	3	2$^{1\frac{1}{2}}$	2^{2}	2$^{1\frac{1}{2}}$	2$^{1\frac{1}{2}}$	2$^{1\frac{1}{2}}$	2no	Smith M E	1.80
29Dec02 ^{8}SA^{1}	Grammarian	LB	5	122	1	1^{1}	1^{1}	1$^{\frac{1}{2}}$	1$^{\frac{1}{2}}$	1$^{\frac{1}{2}}$	3$^{\frac{1}{2}}$	Valdivia J Jr	3.60
8Dec02 ^{4}Hol^{1}	Harrisand-FR	LB	5	115	4	4^{1}	4^{1}	3^{hd}	3$^{1\frac{1}{2}}$	3^{1}	4$^{2\frac{1}{2}}$	Valenzuela P A	5.00
8Dec02 ^{4}Hol^{2}	National Anthem-GB	LB	7	115	5	5$^{\frac{1}{2}}$	5$^{\frac{1}{2}}$	5$^{\frac{1}{2}}$	7	5^{1}	5$^{2\frac{1}{2}}$	Flores D R	33.00
14Sep02 ^{6}Bel^{4}	El Gran Papa	LB	6	116	2	6^{1}	6$^{\frac{1}{2}}$	6^{hd}	6$^{\frac{1}{2}}$	6^{hd}	6^{nk}	Pincay L Jr	11.00
15Dec02 ^{5}Hol^{1}	T. H. Lear	LB	5	115	7	3$^{\frac{1}{2}}$	3^{1}	4^{1}	4^{hd}	7	7	Espinoza V	26.90

OFF AT 4:08 Start Good. Won driving. Course firm.
TIME :23^{1}, :46^{3}, 1:10^{4}, 1:34, 1:57^{4} (:23.28, :46.77, 1:10.80, 1:34.14, 1:57.92)

$2 Mutuel Prices:

8-JOHAR	6.60	2.80	2.40
3-THE TIN MAN		3.00	2.40
1-GRAMMARIAN			2.80

$1 EXACTA 8-3 PAID $8.30 $2 QUINELLA 3-8 PAID $6.60 $1 TRIFECTA 8-3-1 PAID $18.80 $1 SUPERFECTA 8-3-1-4 PAID $33.00

B. c, by Gone West-Windsharp, by Lear Fan. Trainer Mandella Richard. Bred by The Thoroughbred Corporation (Ky).

JOHAR settled outside a rival, went between horses leaving the backstretch and on the second turn, waited a bit for room leaving that bend, came out in upper stretch and rallied gamely under left handed urging to get up four wide at the wire. THE TIN MAN stalked the early pace off the rail, bid outside the pacesetter and dueled for command, fought back in the stretch and continued gamely between foes late. GRAMMARIAN broke out a bit, took the early lead off the rail in the stretch the first time, angled in for the clubhouse turn, set a pressured pace inside, also fought back through a long, hard drive and continued gamely to the end. HARRISAND (FR) saved ground stalking the pace, came out into the stretch and went willingly between foes three deep late. NATIONAL ANTHEM (GB) allowed to settle outside a rival chasing the pace, went three deep leaving the backstretch and on the second turn, came four wide into the stretch and lacked the needed rally. EL GRAN PAPA squeezed at the start, saved ground chasing the leaders and could not offer the necessary response. T. H. LEAR pulled his way along while wide on the hill and in the stretch the first time, angled in and stalked outside a rival, came three deep into the stretch, was momentarily crowded behind the winner in upper stretch, then weakened.

Owners— 1, The Thoroughbred Corporation; 2, Todd Aury & Ralph E; 3, Pacific Heritage Farm; 4, Gann Edmund A; 5, Duchossois Richard L; 6, Oakcliff Stable; 7, Marin & Sears

Trainers—1, Mandella Richard; 2, Mandella Richard; 3, Greely C Beau; 4, Frankel Robert; 5, McAnally Ronald; 6, Frankel Robert; 7, O'Neill Doug

Scratched— Night Patrol (29Dec02 ^{8}SA^{9}), Hataab (24Nov02 ^{7}HOL^{1})

$2 Daily Double (7-8) Paid $93.60; Daily Double Pool $35,841.
$1 Pick Three (8-7-8) Paid $110.80; Pick Three Pool $68,321.

EIGHTH RACE
Santa Anita
JANUARY 25, 2003

7 FURLONGS. (1.20) 46th Running of THE SANTA MONICA HANDICAP. Grade I. Purse $200,000 FOR FILLIES AND MARES FOUR YEARS OLD AND UPWARD. By subscription of $200 each to accompany the nomination or by supplementary nomination of $4,000 by Sunday, January 20. $2,000 additional to start, with $200,000 guaranteed, of which $120,000 to first, $40,000 to second, $24,000 to third, $12,000 to fourth and $4,000 to fifth. Weights Tuesday, January 21.NOMINATIONS CLOSED Thursday, January 16, 2003 with 14.

Value of Race: $200,000 Winner $120,000; second $40,000; third $24,000; fourth $12,000; fifth $4,000. Mutuel Pool $747,792.00 Exacta Pool $424,066.00 Quinella Pool $44,749.00 Trifecta Pool $501,113.00

Last Raced	Horse	M/Eqt.	A.	Wt	PP	St	¼	½	Str	Fin	Jockey	Odds $1
1Dec02 ^{4}Hol^{5}	Affluent	LB	5	119	4	2	6^{hd}	7	3$^{1\frac{1}{2}}$	1$^{\frac{1}{2}}$	Solis A	2.50
29Nov02 ^{9}Aqu^{1}	Sightseek	LB	4	115	5	6	4^{hd}	3$^{\frac{1}{2}}$	1^{1}	2$^{1\frac{1}{2}}$	Bailey J D	0.70
15Dec02 ^{7}Hol^{4}	Secret Of Mecca	LBf	5	110	3	7	7	6^{1}	2^{hd}	3^{3}	Krone J A	31.40
21Dec02 ^{3}Hol^{1}	Whoopddoo	LB	5	113	7	4	3^{hd}	4$^{\frac{1}{2}}$	5^{4}	4^{5}	Espinoza V	11.00
3Jan03 ^{7}SA^{3}	Kitty On The Track	LBb	6	117	1	1	1$^{\frac{1}{2}}$	1^{hd}	4^{hd}	5^{9}	Pincay L Jr	5.60
23Jun02 ^{2}Hol^{3}	Reine Des Neiges	LB	4	115	2	5	5^{8}	5$^{3\frac{1}{2}}$	6$^{2\frac{1}{2}}$	6^{10}	Flores D R	23.60
23Nov02 ^{1}Hol^{1}	Live Free Or Die	LBb	4	115	6	3	2^{1}	2^{hd}	7	7	Puglisi I L	57.50

OFF AT 3:40 Start Good. Won driving. Track fast.
TIME :22, :44^{3}, 1:09^{2}, 1:22 (:22.13, :44.66, 1:09.45, 1:22.17)

$2 Mutuel Prices:

4-AFFLUENT	7.00	2.80	2.10
5-SIGHTSEEK		2.40	2.10
3-SECRET OF MECCA			2.40

$1 EXACTA 4-5 PAID $6.30 $2 QUINELLA 4-5 PAID $4.00 $1 TRIFECTA 4-5-3 PAID $41.50

Ch. m, by Affirmed-Trinity Place, by Strawberry Road*Aus. Trainer McAnally Ronald. Bred by Janis R Whitham (Ky).

AFFLUENT settled off the inside, moved up off the rail on the turn and three deep into the stretch, found room between horses in upper stretch, rallied to the front past the eighth pole and gamely prevailed under urging. SIGHTSEEK chased between horses on the backstretch, bid three deep into the turn, took a short lead outside a rival leaving the bend, inched away in upper stretch and continued willingly but could not quite match the winner. SECRET OF MECCA a bit slow to begin, settled outside the winner then off the rail, bid five wide on the turn and four wide into the stretch and bested the others. WHOOPDDOO stalked outside on the backstretch, bid four wide into the turn and three deep into the stretch and weakened some. KITTY ON THE TRACK sped to the early lead, dueled inside to the stretch and weakened. REINE DES NEIGES stalked a bit off the rail then inside on the turn, fell back some leaving the turn, was in a bit tight in upper stretch and also weakened. LIVE FREE OR DIE forced the pace outside a rival then between horses into and on the turn, dropped back approaching the stretch, steadied in tight when the winner went past in upper stretch and had little left.

Owners— 1, Whitham Janis R; 2, Juddmonte Farms Inc; 3, Henton Hitbound Stable & Turrell; 4, Garber Diane; 5, Craig Halo Farms & Magerman; 6, Ballantyne Lynn & Welty W R; 7, J B K Stable & Litt

Trainers—1, McAnally Ronald; 2, Frankel Robert; 3, Cardenas Ruben; 4, Baffert Bob; 5, Sise Clifford Jr; 6, Sise Clifford Jr; 7, Litt Joshua M

$2 Daily Double (5-4) Paid $55.00; Daily Double Pool $47,469.
$1 Pick Three (2-5-4) Paid $372.30; Pick Three Pool $118,941.

NINTH RACE
Fair Grounds
JANUARY 25, 2003

1 MILE. (1.35^{4}) 60th Running of THE LECOMTE. Grade III. Purse $100,000 For Three Year Olds. By subscription of $100 each (Louisiana Derby early bird nominees automatically subscribed); $500 to enter; $500 additional to start. $100,000 Guaranteed of which $60,000 to the winner; $20,000 to second; $11,000to third; $6,000 to fourth; $3,000 to fifth. Weight: 122 lbs. Non-winners of $36,000 allowed 3 lbs.; $25,000, 5 lbs.; $20,000, 8 lbs. (Maiden and claiming races not considered). Starters to be named through the entry box by the usual time of closing. Closed Wednesday, January15, 2003, with 138 nominations. This race will start and finish at the 1/16 pole. THE OWNER OF THE WINNER TO RECEIVE A TROPHY.

Value of Race: $100,000 Winner $60,000; second $20,000; third $11,000; fourth $6,000; fifth $3,000. Mutuel Pool $390,459.00 Exacta Pool $309,329.00 Quinella Pool $24,576.00 Trifecta Pool $248,854.00 Superfecta Pool $65,273.00

Last Raced	Horse	M/Eqt.	A.	Wt	PP	St	¼	½	¾	Str	Fin	Jockey	Odds $1
29Dec02 ^{9}FG^{1}	Saintly Look	L	3	122	11	1	2^{2}	2$^{2\frac{1}{2}}$	2$^{1\frac{1}{2}}$	1^{hd}	1$^{2\frac{3}{4}}$	Sellers S J	4.30
28Dec02 ^{9}Hou^{1}	Call Me Lefty	Lb	3	122	5	3	1^{hd}	1^{hd}	1^{hd}	2^{1}	2$^{\frac{1}{2}}$	Leblanc K P	12.10
21Dec02 ^{9}DeD^{4}	Winning Fans	L	3	114	8	7	6^{1}	5$^{1\frac{1}{2}}$	4$^{1\frac{1}{2}}$	3^{hd}	3$^{\frac{1}{2}}$	Jacinto J	108.70
13Jan03 ^{10}FG^{1}	Defrere's Vixen	L	3	118	9	9	8^{3}	8^{3}	8^{2}	5$^{\frac{1}{2}}$	4^{hd}	Meche D J	12.00
11Jan03 ^{9}FG^{4}	Zydeco Affair	Lb	3	122	4	5	7$^{1\frac{1}{2}}$	6^{hd}	6^{hd}	6^{1}	5^{hd}	Albarado R J	19.00
7Dec02 ^{4}Hou^{7}	Catalissa	L	3	119	1	4	4$^{1\frac{1}{2}}$	4$^{\frac{1}{2}}$	5$^{\frac{1}{2}}$	7$^{2\frac{1}{2}}$	6no	Lovato F Jr	17.80
26Oct02 ^{8}AP^{11}	Lone Star Sky	L	3	122	6	2	3^{1}	3^{hd}	3^{hd}	4$^{1\frac{1}{2}}$	7$^{1\frac{3}{4}}$	Borel C H	4.00
29Dec02 ^{9}FG^{3}	Crowned King	L	3	118	7	10	9^{hd}	9^{hd}	9^{1}	8^{2}	8$^{3\frac{1}{4}}$	Martin E M Jr	22.90
25Oct02 ^{8}Kee^{1}	Rapid Proof	Lb	3	122	2	6	11	11	11	10^{8}	9^{1}	Melancon L	46.20
30Nov02 ^{11}CD^{3}	Most Feared	Lb	3	122	10	8	5^{1}	7^{1}	7^{1}	9^{1}	10$^{23\frac{1}{2}}$	Guidry M	1.70
16Nov02 ^{9}Hou^{1}	Leo's Last Hurrahy	Lb	3	122	3	11	10$^{2\frac{1}{2}}$	10^{5}	10^{4}	11	11	Melancon G	6.40

OFF AT 4:25 Start Good. Won driving. Track fast.
TIME :23^{3}, :46^{4}, 1:11^{4}, 1:37^{3} (:23.71, :46.85, 1:11.84, 1:37.62)

$2 Mutuel Prices:

11–SAINTLY LOOK	10.60	5.80	5.80
5–CALL ME LEFTY		11.60	6.60
8–WINNING FANS			24.40

$2 EXACTA 11–5 PAID $135.20 $2 QUINELLA 5–11 PAID $79.40 $2 TRIFECTA 11–5–8 PAID $4,911.40 $2 SUPERFECTA 11–5–8–9 PAID $24,477.20

Dk. b. or br. c, (Mar), by Saint Ballado–Sensational Eyes, by Roman Majesty. Trainer Stewart Dallas. Bred by William A Carl (Ky).

SAINTLY LOOK stalked CALL ME LEFTY from early on, gained the edge approaching the drive and proved clearly best. CALL ME LEFTY drifted in a bit after the start, was straightened, moved to the lead entering the first turn, set a pressured pace, got headed and then lasted for second. WINNING FANS between foes early, ranged up nearing the drive and hung. DEFRERE'S VIXEN back early, rallied gamely between foes. ZYDECO AFFAIR drifted in a bit in the early going, settled until the second turn, swung out and then did not have enough late. CATALISSA saved ground and had no rally. LONE STAR SKY forwardly placed three wide, had no final kick. CROWNED KING devoid speed, circled foes for the drive and hung. RAPID PROOF steadied between foes early, was outrun. MOST FEARED raced wide and faded. LEO'S LAST HURRAHY lugged in after the start bumping with RAPID PROOF, then was not a factor.

Owners— 1, Carl William A; 2, Christine S Moore Family Lmt Partne; 3, Cuadra Valedor Inc Gonzalo Fernande; 4, Oleson Jack A; 5, Beard David; 6, Stonerside Stable; 7, New Walter L; 8, McKeever Billy C Jr; 9, Morrison Dolphus; 10, Durant Tom R; 11, Murphy Kenneth W

Trainers—1, Stewart Dallas; 2, Morgan Tommie T; 3, Flores Ramon; 4, Asmussen Steven M; 5, Robideaux Larry R Jr; 6, Stidham Michael; 7, Amoss Thomas; 8, McKeever Billy C Jr; 9, Wiggins Hal R; 10, Werner Ronny; 11, Young Bob

$2 Pick Three (4–5–11) Paid $137.20; Pick Three Pool $16,578.

SEVENTH RACE
Santa Anita
JANUARY 26, 2003

6 FURLONGS. (1.07^{1}) 51st Running of THE PALOS VERDES HANDICAP. Grade II. Purse $150,000. By subscription of $150 each to accompany the nomination. $1,500 additional to start, with $150,000 guaranteed, of which $90,000 to first, $30,000 to second, $18,000 to third, $9,000 to fourth and $3,000 to fifth. Closed Thursday, January 16 with 16 nominations.

Value of Race: $150,000 Winner $90,000; second $30,000; third $18,000; fourth $6,000 each. Mutuel Pool $464,395.00 Exacta Pool $284,365.00 Quinella Pool $29,055.00 Trifecta Pool $293,924.00

Last Raced	Horse	M/Eqt.	A.	Wt	PP	St	¼	½	Str	Fin	Jockey	Odds $1
1Jan03 ^{7}SA^{6}	Avanzado-ARG	LBbf	6	116	5	1	1$^{\frac{1}{2}}$	1^{2}	1$^{2\frac{1}{2}}$	1$^{4\frac{1}{2}}$	Baze T C	6.50
1Jan03 ^{7}SA^{4}	Mellow Fellow	LBbf	8	117	4	6	6	6	6	2$^{\frac{1}{2}}$	Pincay L Jr	7.10
26Oct02 ^{6}AP^{7}	Disturbingthepeace	LBb	5	120	1	5	2^{1}	2^{1}	2$^{\frac{1}{2}}$	3^{nk}	Espinoza V	2.40
1Jan03 ^{7}SA^{2}	DH Radiata	LB	6	115	2	3	3^{hd}	4$^{1\frac{1}{2}}$	4^{1}	4	Krone J A	9.50
16Nov02 ^{10}Lrl^{1}	DH D'wildcat	LBb	5	120	6	2	4^{3}	5^{3}	5$^{1\frac{1}{2}}$	4$^{\frac{1}{2}}$	Valenzuela P A	6.60
1Jan03 ^{7}SA^{1}	Kona Gold	LB	9	124	3	4	5^{4}	3$^{\frac{1}{2}}$	3^{1}	6	Solis A	1.40

DH—Dead Heat.

OFF AT 2:05 Start Good. Won driving. Track fast.
TIME :21^{2}, :43^{4}, :55^{2}, 1:07^{4} (:21.52, :43.81, :55.58, 1:07.85)

$2 Mutuel Prices:

5–AVANZADO–ARG	15.00	7.20	5.20
4–MELLOW FELLOW		5.60	4.00
1–DISTURBINGTHEPEACE			3.40

$1 EXACTA 5–4 PAID $59.10 $2 QUINELLA 4–5 PAID $57.40 $1 TRIFECTA 5–4–1 PAID $269.90

Ch. h, by Luhuk–Avian Eden, by Storm Bird. Trainer O'Neill Doug. Bred by Haras La Quebrada (Arg).

AVANZADO (ARG) sprinted to the early lead off the rail, dueled between horses then outside a rival leaving the backstretch and into the turn, kicked clear and angled in on the turn and proved best under urging. MELLOW FELLOW off a bit slowly, was unhurried off the rail on the backstretch and turn, came a bit wide into the stretch and just got the place. DISTURBINGTHEPEACE a bit slow to begin, was sent up inside to vie for command, had the winner slip away on the turn, came out into the stretch and weakened some but just held third. RADIATA pulled his way along between horses to force or stalk the pace on the backstretch, continued outside a rival on the turn, came three deep into the stretch and split horses at the wire to share fourth place. D'WILDCAT close up stalking the pace three deep on the backstretch, continued outside on the turn and weakened. KONA GOLD settled off the rail, moved up inside leaving the turn, remained along the rail in the stretch and lacked the needed late response.

Owners— 1, Cees Stable; 2, Craig Sidney H & Jenny; 3, Herrick Racing LLC Milch & Milch; 4, Jones Aaron U & Marie D; 5, Fog City Stables or Windfields Farm; 6, Headley Molasky & Molasky

Trainers—1, O'Neill Doug; 2, Spawr Bill; 3, Vienna Darrell; 4, Inda Eduardo; 5, Hess R B Jr; 6, Headley Bruce

Scratched— Echo Eddie (25Jan03 ^{4}SA^{4}), Hombre Rapido (12Jan03 ^{3}SA^{1})

$2 Daily Double (9–5) Paid $48.00; Daily Double Pool $36,975.
$1 Pick Three (7–9–5) Paid $78.50; Pick Three Pool $60,610.

FIFTH RACE
Golden Gate
FEBRUARY 1, 2003

1 1/16 MILES. (Turf Chute)(1.41^1) 24th Running of THE BROWN BESS HANDICAP. Grade III. Purse $100,000. Fillies and mares, 4-year-olds and upward. By subscription of $100 each to accompany the nomination or by supplementary nomination of $2,000 by Sunday, January 26. $500 to pass the entry box and $500 additional to start, with $100,000 guaranteed of which $55,000 to the winner, $20,000 to second, $15,000 to third $7,500 to fourth and $2,500 to fifth. 4-year-olds, allowed 1 lb. Closed Thursday, January 23 with 24 nominations. (If deemed inadvisable by management to run this race over the turf, it will be contested at 1 1/16 miles on the main track). Rail at 0 feet.

Value of Race: $100,000 Winner $55,000; second $20,000; third $15,000; fourth $7,500; fifth $2,500. Mutuel Pool $330,657.00 Exacta Pool $184,884.00 Quinella Pool $21,224.00 Trifecta Pool $199,505.00 Superfecta Pool $65,895.00

Last Raced	Horse	M/Eqt.	A.Wt	PP	St	¼	½	¾	Str	Fin	Jockey	Odds $1
30Nov02 7GG2	Lindsay Jean	LB	5 116	2	1	2 1½	2 2	2 2	1 2½	1 1½	Schvaneveldt C P	6.70
2Jan03 7SA3	Bush Triumph	LBb	5 116	7	7	8 2	7 ½	4 ½	3 ½	2 no	Alvarado F T	3.60
11Jan03 3SA4	Crazy Ensign-ARG	LBb	7 118	1	3	4 1	4 1½	5 2	4 1	3 1½	Baze R A	2.00
19Jan03 2SA3	Janeian-NZ	LB	5 116	8	5	3 1	3 ½	3 ½	5 1½	4 1	Castro J M	22.70
4Jan03 8FG1	Naturally Wild	LB	6 116	6	6	5 hd	5 hd	6 ½	6 1½	5 1	Warren R J Jr	14.30
20Jan03 2GG1	Neon Queen	LB	5 115	9	2	1 3	1 2	1 hd	2 hd	6 1½	Duran F	42.00
11Jan03 3SA3	Double Cat	LB	5 117	3	4	6 1½	6 hd	8 2	7 2	7 1	Steiner J J	3.40
15Jan03 7SA6	Canasita-GB	LBb	5 118	5	9	9	9	9	8 hd	8 2	Baze G	25.50
20Nov02 1Hol2	L'Emeraude-FR	LB	5 117	4	8	7 ½	8 3	7 1½	9	9	Garcia M S	7.80

OFF AT 2:25 Start Good. Won driving. Course yielding.
TIME :23^1, :47^4, 1:12^2, 1:37^3, 1:44^1 (:23.33, :47.94, 1:12.55, 1:37.71, 1:44.35)

$2 Mutuel Prices:				
	2-LINDSAY JEAN	15.40	8.60	4.20
	7-BUSH TRIUMPH		5.00	3.00
	1-CRAZY ENSIGN-ARG			2.80

$1 EXACTA 2-7 PAID $37.30 $2 QUINELLA 2-7 PAID $44.40 $1 TRIFECTA 2-7-1 PAID $161.90 $1 SUPERFECTA 2-7-1-8 PAID $2,022.90

B. m, by Saint Ballado-Colony Bay, by Pleasant Colony. Trainer Sherman Art. Bred by Robert Lothenbach (Fla).

LINDSAY JEAN broke alertly then took back off the pacesetting NEON QUEEN, tracked that rival to the second turn, challenged two wide leaving the three eighths, forged to the front and drew clear in the upper stretch then held driving. BUSH TRIUMPH was permitted to settle early from the outside, remained out while advanced into the second turn, came three wide to the stretch to loom a bold factor but lost some of her punch late. CRAZY ENSIGN (ARG) was never too far back from the inside, commenced her bid two wide into the second turn, dropped to the rail for the turn, appeared to brush with JANEIAN entering the lane, quickly recovered but finished with only a mild rally. JANEIAN (NZ) stalked the pace three wide from the outset, was caught in tight between horses entering the lane, appeared to brush CRAZY ENSIGN then had no real response. NATURALLY WILD was unhurried early, raced three wide throughout and failed to rally. NEON QUEEN sprinted clear leaving the chute to set all of the pace to the second turn, dueled with the winner from the rail to the upper stretch and slackened. DOUBLE CAT raced unhurried in traffic early, was shuffled back on the backstretch, tried to rally three wide on the second turn but came up empty. CANASITA (GB) lagged to the stretch and failed to mount a closing response. L'EMERAUDE (FR) settled early from the inside, remained inside and offered an early bid to the second turn then faded steadily.

Owners— 1, Moss Mr & Mrs Jerome S; 2, Fishelberg Mr & Mrs Leonard; 3, El Faruk Stable; 4, Belmonte Kadner Shapiro et al; 5, Imagination Stable & Rancho San Mig; 6, A J Tony Segale & David Taylor Jr; 7, Cowan Marjorie & Irving M; 8, Couturier Florent; 9, Amerman Racing Stables

Trainers—1, Sherman Art; 2, Mitchell Mike; 3, Mandella Richard; 4, Stein Roger M; 5, Sumja Brent; 6, Ward Wesley A; 7, Drysdale Neil 8, Drysdale Neil; 9, Frankel Robert

$2 Daily Double (5-2) Paid $140.80; Daily Double Pool $18,762.
$1 Pick Three (3-5-2) Paid $273.00; Pick Three Pool $28,053.

TENTH RACE
Gulfstream
FEBRUARY 1, 2003

1 1/16 MILES. (Turf Chute)(1.39) 18th Running of THE HERECOMESTHEBRIDE. Grade III. Purse $100,000. Fillies, 3-year-olds. By subscription of $100 each, which shall accompany the nomination, $1,000 to pass the entry box and $1,000 additional to start, with $100,000 guaranteed. The owner of the winner will receive $60,000; $20,000 to second, $11,000 to third, $6,000 to fourth and $3,000 to fifth. Weights: 121 lbs. Non-winners of $50,000 at a mile or over allowed on the turf, allowed 2 lbs.; $40,000 at any distance or $30,000 at a mile or over, 4 lbs. $24,000 at any distance or $18,000 at a mile or over, 6 lbs. Trophy to winning Owner. In the event this stake race is taken off the turf, it may be subject to downgrading upon review by the Graded Stake Committee. Closed Wednesday, January 22, 2003 with 23 Nominations. (Rail at 0 feet).

Value of Race: $100,000 Winner $60,000; second $20,000; third $11,000; fourth $6,000; fifth $3,000. Mutuel Pool $555,540.00 Exacta Pool $428,921.00 Trifecta Pool $341,873.00 Superfecta Pool $109,349.00

Last Raced	Horse	M/Eqt.	A.Wt	PP	St	¼	½	¾	Str	Fin	Jockey	Odds $1
22Jan03 10GP1	Gal O Gal	L	3 117	1	6	8	8	8	3 1½	1 ½	Decarlo C P	3.30
20Oct02 4Crc1	Formal Miss	L	3 117	2	4	2 1½	2 2½	2 1½	1 hd	2 2	Gonzalez C V	11.60
1Jan03 6Crc2	Devil At The Wire	Lb	3 117	5	5	3 hd	3 hd	5 ½	5 hd	3 no	Guidry M	3.00
1Jan03 6Crc3	Askforaraise	L	3 115	4	2	4 hd	5 hd	3 hd	6 2	4 1	Suckie M C	8.90
14Dec02 10Crc6	Bolaro	L	3 119	7	3	1 1½	1 ½	1 ½	2 1	5 nk	Douglas R R	27.90
1Jan03 7Crc1	Storm Clipper	L	3 115	3	1	5 1	4 ½	4 ½	4 ½	6 ½	Velasquez C	13.20
10Jan03 7GP1	Barboura-FR	L	3 117	6	8	7 1½	7 2	7 hd	7 3½	7 5¼	Velazquez J R	10.50
1Jan03 6Crc1	Sweettrickydancer	L	3 121	8	7	6 hd	6 1½	6 ½	8	8	Coa E M	2.00

OFF AT 5:14 Start Good. Won driving. Course firm.
TIME :24^2, :49, 1:12^3, 1:36^2, 1:42^1 (:24.40, :49.01, 1:12.60, 1:36.56, 1:42.38)

$2 Mutuel Prices:				
	2-GAL O GAL	8.60	5.20	3.60
	3-FORMAL MISS		11.20	7.00
	6-DEVIL AT THE WIRE			3.00

$2 EXACTA 2-3 PAID $88.00 $2 TRIFECTA 2-3-6 PAID $341.60 $1 SUPERFECTA 2-3-6-5 PAID $672.20

B. f, (Mar), by Manlove-Barnard Gal, by Harvard Man. Trainer Blengs Vincent L. Bred by Hugel Max (Fla).

GAL O GAL outrun early, rallied along the hedge, slipped through to gain the lead inside the eighth pole and was fully extended to prevail. FORMAL MISS stalked the pace, rallied to gain a slim lead in the stretch, then held on well while being edged to the wire. DEVIL AT THE WIRE tracked the pace off the hedge, eased out for the drive and didn't do enough late while closing to be up for the show. ASKFORARAISE steadied along in traffic on the first turn, made a run three wide to loom a threat on the far turn, then didn't do enough late. BOLARO set the pace along the inside to midstretch, then gave way. STORM CLIPPER rank and steadied in the early going, raced in striking position while saving ground, came off the rail for the stretch run and lacked a late response. BARBOURA (FR) off slowly, was not a factor. SWEETTRICKYDANCER allowed to settle, raced in striking position four wide around the far turn, then tired.

Owners— 1, Hugel Max; 2, Elite Racing Partners & Fornaro N e; 3, S & M Taulbee D Banks B Griggs & Te; 4, J Damico & Stenaj Stable; 5, Marshall Edward E; 6, Three Friends Stable; 7, Amerman Racing Stables; 8, La Colmena Racing Stable

Trainers—1, Blengs Vincent L; 2, Maxwell Paul M; 3, McPeek Kenneth G; 4, Edwards Oliver S; 5, Sobol Alan; 6, Tagg Barclay; 7, Hennig Mark; 8, Garcia Rodolfo

Scratched— City Fire (17Jan03 8GP1), Holiday Runner (11Jan03 10TAM4), All My Yesterdays (31Dec02 4TAM1)

$2 Pick Three (10-10-2) Paid $288.80; Pick Three Pool $45,690.

FOURTH RACE
Santa Anita
FEBRUARY 1, 2003

7 FURLONGS. (1.20) 62nd Running of THE SAN VICENTE. Grade II. Purse $150,000 Guaranteed. THREE-YEAR-OLDS. By subscription of $150 each to accompany the nomination or by supplementary nomination of $3,000 by time of entry. $1,500 additional to start, with $150,000 guaranteed, of which $90,000 to first, $30,000 to second, $18,000 to third, $9,000 to fourth, and $3,000 to fifth. 123 lbs. Non-winners of two races of $60,000 allowed 3 lbs., of one of $60,000 at any time, 5 lbs.; of a race of $40,000 since December 25 or two races of $25,000 at any time, 7 lbs. (Maiden and Claiming races not considered).NOMINATIONS CLOSED Thursday, January 23, 2003 with 16.

Value of Race: $150,000 Winner $90,000; second $30,000; third $18,000; fourth $9,000; fifth $3,000. Mutuel Pool $774,830.00 Exacta Pool $318,176.00 Quinella Pool $35,603.00 Trifecta Pool $258,692.00

Last Raced	Horse	M/Eqt.	A.Wt	PP	St	1/4	1/2	Str	Fin	Jockey	Odds $1
21Dec02 ^{8}Hol^{2}	Kafwain	LBb	3 123	5	2	5	$4^{\frac{1}{2}}$	$1^{2\frac{1}{2}}$	$1^{4\frac{1}{2}}$	Espinoza V	0.80
29Dec02 ^{10}Sun^{1}	Sum Trick	LB	3 120	1	1	$1^{\frac{1}{2}}$	1^{hd}	$2^{1\frac{1}{2}}$	$2^{1\frac{1}{2}}$	Baze T C	19.10
26Dec02 ^{9}SA^{1}	Southern Image	LB	3 117	3	5	2^{hd}	3^{1}	3^{4}	3^{6}	Nakatani C S	2.50
18Dec02 ^{4}Hol^{1}	Runnin' On Nitro	LB	3 116	2	4	$3^{1\frac{1}{2}}$	$2^{\frac{1}{2}}$	5	$4^{2\frac{1}{2}}$	Krone J A	2.60
5Oct02 ^{5}SA^{5}	Mr. Technique	LBb	3 117	4	3	$4^{\frac{1}{2}}$	5	4^{hd}	5	Desormeaux K J	32.80

OFF AT 1:38 Start Good. Won ridden out. Track fast.
TIME :22, :44, 1:08, 1:21 (:22.13, :44.12, 1:08.10, 1:21.12)

$2 Mutuel Prices:				
	6–KAFWAIN	3.60	2.60	2.10
	1–SUM TRICK		7.00	2.10
	3–SOUTHERN IMAGE			2.10

$1 EXACTA 6–1 PAID $13.10 $2 QUINELLA 1–6 PAID $22.20 $1 TRIFECTA 6–1–3 PAID $31.30

Dk. b. or br. c, (Feb), by Cherokee Run–Swazi's Moment, by Moment of Hope. Trainer Baffert Bob. Bred by Dr & Mrs R Smiser West (Ky).

KAFWAIN stalked the dueling leaders outside, moved up boldly four wide on the turn, took command three deep approaching the stretch and drew clear under a brisk hand ride while being shown the whip and drifting in. SUM TRICK sped to the early lead off the rail, dueled between horses on the backstretch and into the turn, angled in leaving the bend, was no match for the winner in the stretch but held second. SOUTHERN IMAGE off a bit slowly, pulled his way between horses early, dueled three deep and weakened in the stretch. RUNNIN' ON NITRO bobbled slightly and was off a bit slowly, pulled inside to stalk the early pace, bid along the rail and dueled for the lead, dropped back on the turn and had little left for the stretch. MR. TECHNIQUE stalked the pace off the rail, was roused leaving the backstretch, angled in some on the turn and gave way.

Owners— 1, The Thoroughbred Corporation; 2, Fulton Stan E; 3, Blahut Stables; 4, Brewer Haagsma & Ward; 5, Vreeland James R
Trainers—1, Baffert Bob; 2, Becerra Rafael; 3, Machowsky Michael; 4, Ward Wesley A; 5, Bonde Jeff
Scratched— Storm Gulch (18Jan03 ^{7}SA^{5})

$2 Daily Double (5–6) Paid $8.80; Daily Double Pool $42,602.
$1 Pick Three (4–5–5/6) Paid $20.00; Pick Three Pool $74,172.

NINTH RACE
Santa Anita
FEBRUARY 1, 2003

1⅛ MILES. (1.45^{4}) 56th Running of THE STRUB. Grade II. Purse $400,000 Guaranteed. FOUR-YEAR-OLDS. By subscription of $400 each to accompany the nomination. Supplementary nominations may be made at time of entry, by payment of $8,000. All horses shall pay $1,000 to pass the entry box and $3,000 additional to start, with $400,000 guaranteed, of which $240,000 guaranteed to the winner, $80,000 to second, $48,000 to third, $24,000 to fourth and $8,000 to fifth; Weight: 123 lbs. Non-winners of $200,000 twice or $300,000 once at one mile or over since May 1, 2002 allowed 2 lbs.; of such a race of $200,000 since then or $100,000 any distance since December 25, 2002, 4 lbs.; of $100,000 at one mile or over in 2002–2003 or $60,000 any distance since July 1, 2002, 6 lbs. NOMINATIONS CLOSED Thursday, January 23, 2003 with 12.

Value of Race: $400,000 Winner $240,000; second $80,000; third $48,000; fourth $24,000; fifth $8,000. Mutuel Pool $663,157.00 Exacta Pool $404,502.00 Quinella Pool $34,438.00 Trifecta Pool $446,627.00

Last Raced	Horse	M/Eqt.	A.Wt	PP	St	1/4	1/2	3/4	Str	Fin	Jockey	Odds $1
26Oct02 ^{10}AP^{2}	Medaglia d'Oro	LB	4 123	6	5	1^{1}	1^{1}	1^{3}	1^{5}	1^{7}	Bailey J D	0.40
13Dec02 ^{6}Hol^{1}	Olmodavor	LBb	4 117	1	2	5^{1}	5^{2}	4^{hd}	3^{3}	$2^{\frac{1}{2}}$	Solis A	4.30
11Jan03 ^{8}SA^{2}	Tracemark	LBb	4 117	4	1	3^{hd}	2^{1}	$2^{1\frac{1}{2}}$	$2^{1\frac{1}{2}}$	3^{7}	Desormeaux K J	18.30
4Jan03 ^{5}SA^{2}	Easy Grades	LB	4 117	3	6	6	6	$5^{1\frac{1}{2}}$	5^{6}	4^{2}	Krone J A	17.10
11Jan03 ^{8}SA^{1}	Pass Rush	LBb	4 121	5	4	4^{4}	4^{2}	3^{1}	$4^{\frac{1}{2}}$	5^{22}	Nakatani C S	6.30
15Jan03 ^{2}SA^{3}	Castle Gandolfo	LBf	4 117	2	3	2^{hd}	3^{hd}	6	6	6	Smith M E	16.90

OFF AT 4:16 Start Good. Won ridden out. Track fast.
TIME :22^{4}, :45^{4}, 1:09^{4}, 1:34^{4}, 1:48 (:22.91, :45.96, 1:09.98, 1:34.87, 1:48.04)

$2 Mutuel Prices:				
	6–MEDAGLIA D'ORO	2.80	2.20	2.10
	1–OLMODAVOR		3.20	2.10
	4–TRACEMARK			2.10

$1 EXACTA 6–1 PAID $4.30 $2 QUINELLA 1–6 PAID $6.00 $1 TRIFECTA 6–1–4 PAID $20.00

Dk. b. or br. c, by El Prado*Ire–Cappucino Bay, by Bailjumper. Trainer Frankel Robert. Bred by Albert Bell & Joyce Bell (Ky).

MEDAGLIA D'ORO sped to the early lead, angled to the inside in the run to the first turn, set all the pace along the rail, kicked clear into the second turn, was pushed along some to widen in the stretch and drew off under a moderate hand ride. OLMODAVOR saved ground off the pace, split horses into the second turn, angled back in and just got up for second along the rail. TRACEMARK stalked between horses on the first turn then a bit off the rail, was no match for the winner and just lost the place. EASY GRADES settled outside a rival then off the rail on the backstretch, went three deep into and out of the second turn and did not rally. PASS RUSH tracked the winner three deep on the first turn then outside a rival, dropped back on the second turn and weakened. CASTLE GANDOLFO stalked along the inside, fell back approaching the second turn, came out into the stretch, then drifted to the outside while being eased in the final furlong.

Owners— 1, Gann Edmund A; 2, Wertheimer Farm; 3, McGrath Edward T; 4, Desperado Stables; 5, Tabor Michael B; 6, Reddam John P
Trainers—1, Frankel Robert; 2, Mandella Richard; 3, Dollase Craig; 4, West Ted H; 5, Byrne Patrick B; 6, Dollase Craig

$2 Daily Double (13–6) Paid $6.00; Daily Double Pool $68,930.
$1 Pick Three (9–13–6) Paid $69.40; Pick Three Pool $81,927.

EIGHTH RACE

Santa Anita

FEBRUARY 2, 2003

1⅛ MILES. (1.45⁴) 65th Running of THE SAN ANTONIO HANDICAP. Grade II. Purse $250,000. FOUR-YEAR-OLDS AND UPWARD. By subscription of $250 each to accompany the nomination. $2,500 additional to start, with $250,000 guaranteed, of which $150,000 to first, $50,000 to second, $30,000 to third, $15,000 to fourth and $5,000 to fifth. Closed Thursday, January 23 with 12 nominations.

Value of Race: $250,000 Winner $150,000; second $50,000; third $30,000; fourth $15,000; fifth $5,000. Mutuel Pool $889,361.00 Exacta Pool $337,409.00   Quinella Pool $34,388.00 Trifecta Pool $416,513.00

Last Raced	Horse	M/Eqt. A.Wt	PP	St	¼	½	¾	Str	Fin	Jockey	Odds $1
4Jan03 8SA¹	Congaree	LB	5 123	1	2	2½	2½	2½	12¼	12¼	Bailey J D	0.50
26Oct02 10AP³	Milwaukee Brew	LBb	6 120	5	6	6	4hd	31	2hd	21	Prado E S	4.90
6Oct02 7SA¹	Pleasantly Perfect	LBb	5 117	6	5	5hd	5hd	4hd	3½	35	Solis A	3.10
4Jan03 8SA⁴	Piensa Sonando-CH	LB	5 117	3	4	4hd	6	6	5hd	4nk	Pincay L Jr	17.80
4Jan03 8SA⁸	Cottage-ARG	LB	5 114	4	3	31	31	5hd	6	52½	Smith M E	53.30
14Dec02 9Hol²	Fleetstreet Dancer	LBb	5 112	2	1	1½	12	1½	42½	6	Baze T C	25.90

OFF AT 4:10 Start Good. Won driving. Track fast.

TIME :23¹, :46², 1:10¹, 1:35, 1:47³ (:23.25, :46.53, 1:10.32, 1:35.06, 1:47.60)

$2 Mutuel Prices:

1-CONGAREE	3.00	2.40	2.10
5-MILWAUKEE BREW		3.20	2.10
6-PLEASANTLY PERFECT			2.10

$1 EXACTA 1-5 PAID $4.50 $2 QUINELLA 1-5 PAID $7.40 $1 TRIFECTA 1-5-6 PAID $7.60

Ch. h, by Arazi–Mari's Sheba, by Mari's Book. Trainer Baffert Bob. Bred by Stonerside Stable Ltd (Ky).

CONGAREE pulled his way between horses to force the pace into the first turn, stalked a bit off the rail, bid outside the pacesetter into the second turn, took the lead into the stretch and drew clear under a couple cracks of the whip and steady handling. MILWAUKEE BREW four wide into the first turn, stalked outside, bid three deep into the second turn and four wide again into the stretch and was second best. PLEASANTLY PERFECT settled outside a rival early, chased between horses, came three deep into the stretch and picked up the show. PIENSA SONANDO (CHI) angled in and saved ground in good position, went around the pacesetter past midstretch and lacked the needed response. COTTAGE (ARG) prompted the pace three deep into the first turn, stalked between horses on the backstretch, continued outside on the second turn, angled in some nearing the stretch and weakened. FLEETSTREET DANCER sped into the early lead inside, shook loose leaving the first turn, dueled inside the winner on the second turn and weakened in the stretch.

Owners— 1, Stonerside Stable; 2, Stronach Stable; 3, Diamond A Racing Corporation; 4, Hunt Nelson B; 5, Farfellow Farms Ltd; 6, Leatherman Lee & Ty

Trainers—1, Baffert Bob; 2, Frankel Robert; 3, Mandella Richard; 4, McAnally Ronald; 5, Spawr Bill; 6, O'Neill Doug

$2 Daily Double (7–1) Paid $24.20; Daily Double Pool $59,592.
$1 Pick Three (9–7–1) Paid $81.50; Pick Three Pool $115,399.

EIGHTH RACE
Gulfstream
FEBRUARY 8, 2003

1⅜ MILES. (Turf)(2.10^{3}) 15th Running of THE VERY ONE HANDICAP. Grade III. Purse $100,000 Guaranteed. FILLIES AND MARES, THREE YEAR OLDS AND UPWARD. By subscription of $100 each shall accompany the nomination, $1,000 to pass the entry box and $1,000 additional to start, with $100,000 guaranteed. The owner of the winner to receive $60,000, $20,000 to second, $11,000 to third, $6,000 to fourth and $3,000 to fifth. Trophy to winning Owner. This race will be limited to 12 Starters, with Also Eligibles. (High Weights on the scale Preferred) In the event this stake is taken off the turf,it may be subject to downgrading upon review by the Graded Stakes Committee. Closed Wednesday, January 29, 2003 with 26 Nominations. (Rail at 0 Feet).

Value of Race: $100,000 Winner $60,000; second $20,000; third $11,000; fourth $6,000; fifth $3,000. Mutuel Pool $665,799.00 Exacta Pool $535,721.00 Trifecta Pool $396,096.00 Superfecta Pool $112,226.00

Last Raced	Horse	M/Eqt.	A.Wt	PP	¼	½	¾	1	Str	Fin	Jockey	Odds $1
5Jan03 $^{10}GP^{1}$	San Dare	L	5 116	11	$10^{2\frac{1}{2}}$	10^{2}	$10^{1\frac{1}{2}}$	12	$6^{1\frac{1}{2}}$	$1^{2\frac{1}{4}}$	Guidry M	6.00
28Dec02 $^{8}Crc^{3}$	Tweedside	Lf	5 115	9	5^{hd}	$5^{1\frac{1}{2}}$	$3^{\frac{1}{2}}$	1^{hd}	$1^{1\frac{1}{2}}$	$2^{\frac{1}{2}}$	Velazquez J R	4.20
21Dec02 $^{7}Crc^{5}$	Hi Tech Honeycomb	Lb	4 113	1	$7^{1\frac{1}{2}}$	6^{hd}	6^{hd}	$6^{\frac{1}{2}}$	$4^{1\frac{1}{2}}$	$3^{\frac{1}{2}}$	Prado E S	12.90
28Dec02 $^{8}Crc^{6}$	Queue	Lbf	6 115	5	$11^{1\frac{1}{2}}$	12	12	11^{1}	9^{hd}	4^{1}	Douglas R R	24.40
28Dec02 $^{8}Crc^{8}$	Uriah-GE		4 114	8	12	11^{hd}	11^{hd}	10^{hd}	8^{hd}	5^{nk}	Bailey J D	2.60
23Nov02 $^{8}CD^{4}$	Lady Linda	Lb	5 114	6	4^{hd}	4^{hd}	5^{1}	$3^{\frac{1}{2}}$	2^{hd}	$6^{1\frac{1}{2}}$	Coa E M	34.80
28Dec02 $^{8}Crc^{1}$	New Economy	L	5 115	7	6^{hd}	$7^{1\frac{1}{2}}$	$7^{1\frac{1}{2}}$	7^{hd}	5^{hd}	$7^{\frac{3}{4}}$	Homeister R B Jr	8.60
9Nov02 $^{9}Aqu^{6}$	Decencia-ARG	L	6 113	10	$9^{1\frac{1}{2}}$	$8^{\frac{1}{2}}$	9^{2}	9^{1}	10^{2}	8^{nk}	Decarlo C P	59.80
30Dec02 $^{11}Crc^{6}$	Reina Blanca-GB	L	5 111	12	2^{hd}	3^{1}	2^{1}	2^{1}	3^{hd}	$9^{1\frac{3}{4}}$	Day P	37.50
25Jan03 $^{9}GP^{6}$	Jennasietta	Lb	5 114	4	$8^{\frac{1}{2}}$	$9^{2\frac{1}{2}}$	8^{hd}	$8^{\frac{1}{2}}$	7^{hd}	$10^{1\frac{1}{4}}$	Velasquez C	12.70
16Nov02 $^{8}Aqu^{11}$	Moon Queen-IR	L	5 117	2	3^{1}	2^{hd}	$4^{\frac{1}{2}}$	5^{hd}	11^{hd}	11^{1}	Santos J A	4.10
20Jan03 $^{8}GP^{5}$	Chez Cherie-GB	Lf	6 111	3	1^{hd}	1^{1}	1^{hd}	$4^{\frac{1}{2}}$	12	12	Chavez J F	59.80

OFF AT 4:11 Start Good. Won driving. Course firm.

TIME :24^{2}, :48^{1}, 1:13^{1}, 1:38, 2:02, 2:13^{3} (:24.55, :48.23, 1:13.34, 1:38.00, 2:02.14, 2:13.76)

$2 Mutuel Prices:

11–SAN DARE	14.00	6.00	4.60
9–TWEEDSIDE		4.80	4.20
1–HI TECH HONEYCOMB			9.80

$2 EXACTA 11–9 PAID $72.80 $2 TRIFECTA 11–9–1 PAID $914.00 $1 SUPERFECTA 11–9–1–5 PAID $4,676.00

B. m, by Dare and Go–San Empery, by Empery. Trainer Hiles Rick. Bred by Sidney Turner (Ky).

SAN DARE taken in hand for a mile, circled rivals five wide on the final turn, rallied to catch TWEEDSIDE at the sixteenth pole and won going away. TWEEDSIDE tracked the pace three wide, rallied to gain the lead entering the final turn, edged clear in midstretch but couldn't match strides with the winner late while holding the place. HI TECH HONEYCOMB rated off the pace, advanced into contention while working her way through traffic in the stretch, angled to the inside and closed for the show. QUEUE outrun for a mile, saved ground to nearing the stretch, swung out for the drive and closed with a belated rally. URIAH (GER) unhurried after breaking slowly, was caught in traffic on the far turn, then improved her position in the drive without threatening. LADY LINDA tracked the pace, made a run four wide to on the far turn to reach the attending position in the stretch, then weakened. NEW ECONOMY reserved in striking position off the pace, lacked a late response. DECENCIA (ARG) allowed to settle, was racing four wide when steadied from tight quarters soon after entering the final turn and failed to rally. REINA BLANCA (GB) contested the pace outside CHEZ CHERIE, continued to contest the pace with TWEEDSIDE around the final turn and into the stretch, then tired. JENNASIETTA steadied in behind HI TECH HONEYCOMB on the first turn, came out to race three wide on the final turn and faltered. MOON QUEEN (IRE) with the pace along the hedge, was steadied entering the clubhouse turn, remained in contention into the final turn and gave way. CHEZ CHERIE (GB) contested the pace racing just off the hedge, was steadied when caught along the hedge entering the final turn and faded.

Owners— 1, D Mounts; 2, Melnyk Eugene & Laura; 3, Select Stable; 4, Robins Gerald & Weiss Jay; 5, Tanaka Gary A; 6, Domino Stud of Lexington Inc; 7, R S Evans; 8, Mack Earle I; 9, Gaillardia Racing; 10, Acclaimed Racing Stable; 11, J Allen; 12, New Phoenix Stb & Hidaway Farms

Trainers—1, Hiles Rick; 2, Pletcher Todd A; 3, McPeek Kenneth G; 4, Blengs Vincent L; 5, Mott William I; 6, Eppler Mary E; 7, Motion H Graham; 8, Kimmel John C; 9, Pletcher Todd A; 10, Ziadie Ralph; 11, Clement Christophe; 12, de Brevedent Bertrand

Scratched— Beyond The Waves (11Jan03 $^{8}GP^{2}$)

$2 Pick Three (1–2–11) Paid $753.20; Pick Three Pool $69,212.

SIXTH RACE
Santa Anita
FEBRUARY 8, 2003

1⅛ MILES. (1.45^{4}) 29th Running of THE LA CANADA. Grade II. Purse $200,000. Fillies, 4–year–olds. By subscription of $200 each to accompany the nomination or by supplementary nomination of $4,000 by time of entry. $2,000 additional to start, with $200,000 guaranteed, of which $120,000 to first, $40,000 to second, $24,000 to third, $12,000 to fourth and $4,000 to fifth. Weight, 121 lbs. Non–winners of $100,000 twice at one mile or over in 2002–2003 or $90,000 once at a mile or over in 2003, allowed 3 lbs. Of such a race of $60,000 in 2002–2003, 5 lbs. Of such a race of $40,000 or $60,000 any distance at any time, 7 lbs. Closed Thursday, January 30 with 8 nominations.

Value of Race: $200,000 Winner $120,000; second $40,000; third $24,000; fourth $12,000; fifth $4,000. Mutuel Pool $681,443.00 Exacta Pool $389,735.00 Quinella Pool $39,236.00

Last Raced	Horse	M/Eqt.	A.Wt	PP	St	¼	½	¾	Str	Fin	Jockey	Odds $1
19Jan03 $^{7}SA^{1}$	Got Koko	LBb	4 121	5	4	4^{hd}	3^{hd}	$3^{\frac{1}{2}}$	$3^{1\frac{1}{2}}$	$1^{\frac{3}{4}}$	Solis A	2.10
25Jan03 $^{8}SA^{2}$	Sightseek	LB	4 118	1	3	$1^{\frac{1}{2}}$	1^{hd}	1^{hd}	$1^{\frac{1}{2}}$	$2^{1\frac{1}{2}}$	Valenzuela P A	0.90
19Jan03 $^{7}SA^{2}$	Bella Bellucci	LB	4 118	4	2	$2^{1\frac{1}{2}}$	$2^{1\frac{1}{2}}$	2^{1}	$2^{\frac{1}{2}}$	3^{3}	Smith M E	3.00
19Jan03 $^{7}SA^{3}$	Bare Necessities	LB	4 118	3	1	3^{hd}	4^{hd}	4^{hd}	4^{10}	4^{17}	Valdivia J Jr	15.30
17Jan03 $^{7}SA^{2}$	Revenante	LB	4 116	2	5	5	5	5	5	5	Flores D R	24.40

OFF AT 3:06 Start Good. Won driving. Track fast.

TIME :23, :46^{3}, 1:10^{4}, 1:35^{3}, 1:48^{2} (:23.03, :46.67, 1:10.95, 1:35.69, 1:48.41)

$2 Mutuel Prices:

5–GOT KOKO	6.20	2.60	2.10
1–SIGHTSEEK		2.40	2.10
4–BELLA BELLUCCI			2.10

$1 EXACTA 5–1 PAID $6.20 $2 QUINELLA 1–5 PAID $4.60

B. f, by Signal Tap–Baby North, by Northern Baby. Trainer Headley Bruce. Bred by Eileen H Hartis (Tex).

GOT KOKO four wide early, stalked the pace three deep, came four wide again into the stretch, brushed with BELLA BELUCCI past midstretch but closed determinedly under urging to prove best. SIGHTSEEK took the early lead under a long hold, set a pressured pace a bit off the rail, fought back gamely through a long, hard drive and continued willingly to the wire. BELLA BELLUCCI between horses early, prompted the pace outside SIGHTSEEK, fought back between horses again in the stretch, was brushed by the winner past midstretch and weakened some but held third. BARE NECESSITIES close up stalking the pace between horses then off the rail on the second turn, came three deep into the stretch, angled inward in upper stretch and weakened. REVENANTE angled in and pulled her way along tracking the leaders inside, dropped back on the second turn and gave way.

Owners— 1, Headley & Leung; 2, Juddmonte Farms Inc; 3, Tabor Michael B; 4, Iron County Farms Inc; 5, Red Baron's Barn

Trainers—1, Headley Bruce; 2, Frankel Robert; 3, Drysdale Neil; 4, Dollase Wallace; 5, Vienna Darrell

$2 Daily Double (8–5) Paid $33.60; Daily Double Pool $45,295.
$1 Pick Three (7–8–5) Paid $82.10; Pick Three Pool $119,970.

TENTH RACE

Gulfstream

FEBRUARY 8, 2003

1 1/16 MILES. (1.40[1]) 13th Running of THE SABIN HANDICAP. Grade III. Purse $100,000 Guaranteed. FILLIES AND MARES, THREE YEARS OLD AND UPWARD. By subscription of $100 each, which shall accompany the nomination, $1,000 to pass the entry box and $1,000 additional to start, with $100,000 guaranteed. The owner of the winner to receive $60,000; $20,000 to second, $11,000 to third, $6,000 to fourth and $3,000 to fifth. Trophy to winning Owner. Closed Wednesday, January 29, 2003 with 18 Nominations.

Value of Race: $100,000 Winner $60,000; second $20,000; third $11,000; fourth $6,000; fifth $3,000. Mutuel Pool $549,439.00 Exacta Pool $480,612.00 Trifecta Pool $399,161.00 Superfecta Pool $124,120.00

Last Raced	Horse	M/Eqt. A.Wt	PP	St	1/4	1/2	3/4	Str	Fin	Jockey	Odds $1
5Jan03 10GP10	Allamerican Bertie	L 4 120	9	7	1hd	11 1/2	11 1/2	13	15 1/2	Bailey J D	1.10
28Dec02 9Crc2	Small Promises	Lb 5 112	6	3	22	31 1/2	31 1/2	21 1/2	2hd	Chavez J F	a-9.70
28Dec02 9Crc3	Redoubled Miss	Lbf 4 114	4	4	41 1/2	51 1/2	4hd	41 1/2	31	Velasquez C	33.20
28Dec02 9Crc5	Tuff Chick	L 5 115	7	11	104	9hd	94	61	41 1/2	Douglas R R	a-9.70
20Jan03 9GP6	Mystic Lady	L 5 115	11	8	52	4hd	51 1/2	5hd	5nk	Guidry M	12.50
28Nov02 10CD3	Softly	Lb 5 116	8	10	7hd	71 1/2	71/2	71 1/2	61 1/2	Coa E M	5.60
20Jan03 9GP2	Vespers	L 5 113	10	9	6hd	6hd	6hd	83 1/2	7nk	Velazquez J R	13.20
14Sep02 11TP5	Happily Unbridled	Lbf 5 114	5	6	3hd	2 1/2	2hd	3hd	87 1/2	Day P	20.80
20Jan03 9GP1	Tonight's Wager	L 5 115	3	2	94	108	82	93	92 1/2	Prado E S	5.20
20Jan03 9GP4	Stormy Frolic	Lb 4 114	2	5	11	11	11	11	10 3/4	Santos J A	11.60
28Dec02 9Crc7	Sara's Success	Lb 5 115	1	1	83	81 1/2	101	10hd11		Velez J A Jr	60.20

a-Coupled: Small Promises and Tuff Chick.

OFF AT 5:11 Start Good. Won driving. Track fast.

TIME :23, :46 3/4, 1:11 1, 1:36 1, 1:42 2 (:23.16, :46.75, 1:11.38, 1:36.20, 1:42.49)

$2 Mutuel Prices:	8–ALLAMERICAN BERTIE	4.20	3.20	2.80
	1–SMALL PROMISES (a–entry)		8.20	4.80
	5–REDOUBLED MISS			11.00

$2 EXACTA 8–1 PAID $27.80 $2 TRIFECTA 8–1–5 PAID $313.80 $1 SUPERFECTA 8–1–5–10 PAID $2,164.80

B. f, by Quiet American–Clever Bertie, by Timeless Native. Trainer Flint Steve. Bred by Bert Klein (Ky).

ALLAMERICAN BERTIE outran SMALL PROMISES for the lead around the first turn, made the pace off the rail into the stretch, then increased her margin to the wire under urging. SMALL PROMISES chased the winner along the rail into the stretch, then was no match for that rival while just saving the place. REDOUBLED MISS rated in striking position racing off the rail, eased out for the stretch run and closed to just miss the place. TUFF CHICK outrun early, saved ground and passed tired rivals without threatening. MYSTIC LADY tracked the pace three wide into the stretch and lacked a late response. SOFTLY failed to menace. VESPERS reserved early, raced three wide on the far turn and lacked a rally. HAPPILY UNBRIDLED chased the pace into the stretch and tired. TONIGHT'S WAGER unhurried early, raced four wide on the far turn and failed to be a factor. STORMY FROLIC steadied from tight quarters racing into the first turn and was outrun. SARA'S SUCCESS was through early.

Owners— 1, Klein Richard Bertram & Elaine; 2, Kinghaven Farms & Attfield Roger; 3, Centaur Farms Inc; 4, C Allard; 5, Lewis Lee; 6, Tafel James B; 7, Janney III Stuart S; 8, WinStar Farm; 9, E R Stud; 10, Stride Rite Racing Stable; 11, Thorobeam Farm

Trainers—1, Flint Steve; 2, Attfield Roger L; 3, Spatz Ronald B; 4, Attfield Roger L; 5, Hennig Mark; 6, Nafzger Carl A; 7, McGaughey Claude III; 8, Walden W Elliott; 9, Mott William I; 10, Wolfson Milton W; 11, Plesa Edward Jr

$2 Pick Three (11–3–8) Paid $295.80; Pick Three Pool $81,729.

NINTH RACE

Fair Grounds

FEBRUARY 9, 2003

1 1/16 MILES. (1.42) WHIRLAWAY H. Grade III. Purse $125,000 A Handicap For Four Year Olds and Upward. By subscription of $100 each; $600 to enter; $600 additional to start. $125,000 Guaranteed of which $75,000 to the winner; $25,000 to second; $13,750 to third; $7,500 to fourth; $3,750 to fifth. Starters to be named through the entry box by the usual time of closing. THE OWNER OF THE WINNER TO RECEIVE A TROPHY. Closed Thursday, January 30, 2003, with 22 nominations.

Value of Race: $125,000 Winner $75,000; second $25,000; third $13,750; fourth $7,500; fifth $3,750. Mutuel Pool $321,783.00 Exacta Pool $217,726.00 Quinella Pool $19,573.00 Trifecta Pool $191,566.00 Superfecta Pool $53,573.00

Last Raced	Horse	M/Eqt. A.Wt	PP	St	1/4	1/2	3/4	Str	Fin	Jockey	Odds $1
4Jan03 10GP8	Balto Star	L 5 118	4	1	2hd	31 1/2	2hd	11	12 1/2	Martin E M Jr	2.50
19Jan03 9FG1	Mineshaft	4 116	7	6	51 1/2	4hd	52 1/2	42 1/2	2 3/4	Albarado R	2.70
12Jan03 9FG6	Bonapaw	L f 7 115	2	3	15	14	12	21 1/2	33 1/2	Martinez W	6.00
2Jan03 9FG5	Easyfromthegitgo	L 4 116	8	8	71	71	71	5hd	41	Lanerie C J	8.40
19Jan03 9FG3	Discreet Hero	L 5 115	5	2	4hd	52	41	3hd	51	Sellers S J	6.20
2Jan03 9FG1	Connected	L bf 6 114	1	4	8	8	8	61	6nk	Melancon L	3.50
19Jan03 9FG4	Fighting Indians	L 4 117	3	5	32	2hd	31 1/2	75	78	Bourque C C	41.30
4Jan03 9GP1	Deferred Comp	L 5 116	6	7	61 1/2	63	62 1/2	8	8	Lovato F Jr	35.60

OFF AT 4:24 Start Good. Won ridden out. Track fast.

TIME :24, :47 4, 1:12 4, 1:37 2, 1:43 3 (:24.03, :47.88, 1:12.98, 1:37.40, 1:43.74)

$2 Mutuel Prices:	4–BALTO STAR	7.00	4.00	3.80
	7–MINESHAFT		3.60	2.80
	2–BONAPAW			4.60

$2 EXACTA 4–7 PAID $24.40 $2 QUINELLA 4–7 PAID $11.00 $2 TRIFECTA 4–7–2 PAID $104.60 $2 SUPERFECTA 4–7–2–9 PAID $443.00

Dk. b or br. g, (Mar), by Glitterman – Miss Livi , by Devil's Bag . Trainer Pletcher Todd A. Bred by Anstu Stables Inc (Ky).

BALTO STAR broke alertly, was confidently handled while within striking distance, moved up outside BONAPAW in upper stretch, took over command and drew out while ridden out. MINESHAFT reserved until nearing the drive, split foes turning for home, responded to pressure and got up for second. BONAPAW got clear early, remained clear until the drive, was overtaken approaching mid stretch and missed second late. EASYFROMTHEGITGO allowed to settle, rallied mid track and could make little impact. DISCREET HERO forwardly placed while three wide, was asked for run nearing the drive and then gave way inside the final furlong. CONNECTED trailed until the drive and was not a factor. FIGHTING INDIANS saved ground and faded. DEFERRED COMP crossed to the rail and was always outrun.

Owners– 1, Anstu Stables Inc; 2, Farish William S Elkins Jr James A and Webber Jr W Temple; 3, Richard James and Dennis; 4, Cassels James Zollars Bob and Parra Ro; 5, Hughes B Wayne; 6, Alexander Helen C and Helen K; 7, C B Racing Inc and Calkins Linne and Nancy; 8, Galli Charles

Trainers– 1, Pletcher Todd A; 2, Howard Neil J; 3, Miller Norman C III; 4, Asmussen Steven M; 5, Stall Albert M Jr; 6, Carroll David M; 7, Bettis Charles L; 8, Reinstedler Anthony L

Scratched– Lord Jim (ARG) (31Dec02 5SA 2)

$2 Pick Three (5–4–4) Paid $95.80 ; Pick Three Pool $15,852 .

TENTH RACE

Gulfstream

FEBRUARY 9, 2003

6½ FURLONGS. (1.15) 14th Running of THE DEPUTY MINISTER HANDICAP. Grade III. Purse $100,000. THREE YEAR OLDS AND UPWARD. By subscription of $100 each, which shall accompany the nomination, $1,000 to pass the entry and $1,000 additional to start, with $100,000 guaranteed. The owner of the winner to receive $60,000; second $20,000 to second, $11,000 to third, $6,000 to fourth and $3,000 to fifth. Trophy to winning Owner. Closed Wednesday, January 29 with 22 nominations.

Value of Race: $100,000 Winner $60,000; second $11,000; third $6,000; fifth $3,000.   Mutuel Pool $426,139.00 Exacta Pool $356,083.00   Trifecta Pool $298,403.00 Superfecta Pool $96,298.00

Last Raced	Horse	M/Eqt. A.Wt	PP	St	¼	½	Str	Fin	Jockey	Odds $1
22Jan03 9GP2	Native Heir	Lb 5 114	6	2	11½	12	12½	14½	Velasquez C	9.40
26Nov02 8CD2	Binthebest	Lbf 6 115	7	7	76	75	3hd	21½	Douglas R R	15.30
22Dec02 10Crc2	Fire And Glory	L 4 114	3	8	8	8	61	3¾	Boulanger G	51.60
5Jan03 9GP1	Deer Lake	L 4 112	1	1	21	21	21½	4¾	Chavez J F	5.70
24Aug02 9Sar1	Gygistar	L 4 120	2	4	3½	31½	51½	5no	Velazquez J R	0.80
24Nov02 9CD1	Elite Mercedes	L 6 115	5	5	54	51½	41½	61¾	Day P	7.00
19Jan03 9GP4	Greatness	4 113	4	3	41½	41½	8	71¼	Prado E S	6.00
19Jan03 9GP1	Maybry's Boy	4 114	8	6	63	62	7hd	8	Santos J A	27.90

OFF AT 5:10 Start Good. Won driving. Track fast.

TIME :212, :432, 1:082, 1:15 (:21.41, :43.54, 1:08.40, 1:15.17)

$2 Mutuel Prices:

8–NATIVE HEIR	20.80	10.60	6.80
9–BINTHEBEST		12.20	6.80
4–FIRE AND GLORY			11.00

$2 EXACTA 8–9 PAID $166.80 $2 TRIFECTA 8–9–4 PAID $6,304.20 $1 SUPERFECTA 8–9–4–2 PAID $9,027.90

B. h, by Makin–Mary Had A Lot, by Double Zeus. Trainer Shuman Mark. Bred by Young Spencer F (Va).

NATIVE HEIR quickly moved to the fore, made the pace along the inside into the stretch, then increased his margin to the wire under urging. BINTHEBEST unhurried early, rallied off the rail to gain the place while no threat to the winner. FIRE AND GLORY outrun early, saved ground into the stretch and closed to be up for the show. DEER LAKE chased the pace off the rail into the stretch and weakened. GYGISTAR chased the pace three wide into the stretch and tired. ELITE MERCEDES well placed while saving ground into the stretch, lacked a rally. GREATNESS raced four wide on the turn and faltered. MAYBRY'S BOY was no factor while racing five wide.

Owners— 1, M Gill; 2, J B Tafel Et Al; 3, Dover Lane Stables & Nutmeg Stables; 4, Amerman Racing Stables; 5, Evans Edward P; 6, WinStar Farm; 7, Marilyn & E Seltzer & Stronach Stab; 8, R C Hill Stable

Trainers—1, Shuman Mark; 2, Nafzger Carl A; 3, Gambolati Cam; 4, McGee Paul J; 5, Hennig Mark; 6, Walden W Elliott; 7, Jerkens H Allen; 8, Weaver George

Scratched— Najran (11Jan03 10GP3), Harmony Hall (4Jan03 8GP4)

$2 Pick Three (3–9–8) Paid $1,806.00; Pick Three Pool $45,154.

SEVENTH RACE

Santa Anita

FEBRUARY 9, 2003

1 MILE. (1.332) 21st Running of THE LAS VIRGENES. Grade I. Purse $200,000 FOR FILLIES THREE YEARS OLD. By subscription of $200 each to accompany the nomination. $2,000 additional to start, with $200,000 guaranteed, of which $120,000 to first, $40,000 to second, $24,000 to third, $12,000 to fourth and $4,000 to fifth. 122 lbs. Non–winners of $70,000 twice or $50,000 three times allowed 2 lbs.; of $50,000 twice since December 25 or one of $70,000 at any time, 4 lbs.; of a race of $50,000 since December 25 or two of $30,000 at any time, 6 lbs. (Maiden and claiming races not considered). NOMINATIONS CLOSED Thursday, January 30, 2003 with 11.

Value of Race: $200,000 Winner $120,000; second $40,000; third $24,000; fourth $12,000; fifth $4,000. Mutuel Pool $755,139.00 Exacta Pool $308,859.00   Quinella Pool $42,313.00 Trifecta Pool $291,333.00

Last Raced	Horse	M/Eqt. A.Wt	PP	St	¼	½	¾	Str	Fin	Jockey	Odds $1
14Dec02 4Hol2	Composure	LB 3 120	5	6	41	51	32	2½	1nk	Bailey J D	0.80
20Jan03 3SA1	Elloluv	LB 3 122	3	1	1½	1hd	11½	11½	23	Valenzuela P A	1.30
20Jan03 3SA2	Watching You	LB 3 116	4	4	31	21	2hd	34½	38	Solis A	11.20
20Jan03 3SA4	Puxa Saco	LB 3 118	1	2	6	6	54	43	49	Smith M E	11.20
28Dec02 3GG1	Maddie's Charm	LBb 3 116	6	3	5hd	4hd	4hd	52½	5½	Espinoza V	25.60
30Oct02 New7	Favola–GB	LB 3 116	2	5	2½	3hd	6	6	6	Krone J A	29.50

OFF AT 3:37 Start Good For All But COMPOSURE Won driving. Track fast.

TIME :241, :474, 1:114, 1:233, 1:36 (:24.28, :47.81, 1:11.86, 1:23.67, 1:36.13)

$2 Mutuel Prices:

5–COMPOSURE	3.60	2.20	2.10
3–ELLOLUV		2.20	2.10
4–WATCHING YOU			2.10

$1 EXACTA 5–3 PAID $2.90 $2 QUINELLA 3–5 PAID $2.60 $1 TRIFECTA 5–3–4 PAID $7.70

B. f, (Apr), by Touch Gold–Party Cited, by Alleged. Trainer Baffert Bob. Bred by Rancho San Peasea S A (Ky).

COMPOSURE stumbled at the start, stalked between horses on the first turn then a bit off the rail, angled in leaving the second turn, altered path outside in midstretch and determinedly wore down ELLOLUV late under urging late. ELLOLUV sped to the early lead, dueled between horses on the first turn, set a pressured pace a bit off the rail, inched away leaving the second turn, drifted inward in midstretch and held on well but was edged late. WATCHING YOU forced the pace three deep then outside the runner–up to the stretch, was no match for the top pair but clearly best of the rest. PUXA SACO came off the rail and went three deep on the first turn, stalked off the rail thereafter to the stretch and weakened. MADDIE'S CHARM was in a good position stalking the pace four wide but gave way in the stretch. FAVOLA (GB) off a bit slowly, pulled her way up to prompt the pace inside on the first turn, stalked along the rail on the backstretch, dropped back on the second turn and also gave way.

Owners— 1, Lewis Robert B & Beverly J; 2, Reddam John P; 3, Hughes Bradley W; 4, Rowan Richard; 5, Alki Roma Racing & Retzer; 6, Wilson David W & Holly F

Trainers—1, Baffert Bob; 2, Dollase Craig; 3, Stute Warren; 4, Sahadi Jenine; 5, Bonde Jeff; 6, Cerin Vladimir

---

$2 Daily Double (2–5) Paid $64.40; Daily Double Pool $36,223.
$1 Pick Three (4–2–5) Paid $189.90; Pick Three Pool $104,222.

NINTH RACE
Gulfstream
FEBRUARY 14, 2003

7 FURLONGS. (1.20) 25th Running of THE SHIRLEY JONES HANDICAP. Grade III. Purse $100,000 Guaranteed. FILLIES AND MARES, THREE YEAR OLDS AND UPWARD. By subscription of $100 each, which shall accompany the nomination, $1,000 to pass the entry box and $1,000 additional to start, with $100,000 guaranteed. The owner of the winner to receive $60,000; $20,000 to second, $11,000 to third, $6,000 to fourth and $3,000 to fifth. Closed Wednesday, February 5, 2003 with 18 Nominations. Trophy to winning Owner.

Value of Race: $100,000 Winner $60,000; second $20,000; third $11,000; fourth $6,000; fifth $3,000. Mutuel Pool $309,521.00 Exacta Pool $181,906.00 Trifecta Pool $141,956.00 Superfecta Pool $47,093.00

Last Raced	Horse	M/Eqt.	A.Wt	PP	St	¼	½	Str	Fin	Jockey	Odds $1
12Jan03 ^{10}GP^{1}	Harmony Lodge	L	5 114	2	1	2^{1}	1^{hd}	1^{3}	1^{3}	Velazquez J R	4.70
26Oct02 ^{1}AP^{1}	Gold Mover	L	5 117	1	2	$4^{2\frac{1}{2}}$	4^{2}	3^{1}	$2^{\frac{1}{2}}$	Bailey J D	0.50
14Oct02 ^{8}Bel^{2}	Nonsuch Bay	L	4 117	4	6	6	5^{1}	4^{2}	$3^{2\frac{3}{4}}$	Chavez J F	6.90
12Jan03 ^{10}GP^{5}	Forest Heiress	L	4 116	6	4	1^{hd}	$2^{1\frac{1}{2}}$	2^{hd}	$4^{4\frac{3}{4}}$	Day P	5.10
3Feb03 ^{8}GP^{3}	Preferred Option	L	4 114	3	3	3^{hd}	3^{1}	$5^{2\frac{1}{2}}$	5^{1}	Santos J A	32.90
7Dec02 ^{10}Crc^{3}	Away	L	6 115	5	5	5^{1}	6	6	6	Prado E S	26.90

OFF AT 4:54 Start Good. Won driving. Track fast.
TIME :22^{2}, :44^{3}, 1:09^{1}, 1:22^{1} (:22.49, :44.68, 1:09.21, 1:22.35)

$2 Mutuel Prices:

2–HARMONY LODGE	11.40	3.40	2.10
1–GOLD MOVER		2.20	2.10
4–NONSUCH BAY			2.10

$2 EXACTA 2–1 PAID $21.00 $2 TRIFECTA 2–1–4 PAID $57.20 $1 SUPERFECTA 2–1–4–6 PAID $74.50

Ch. m, by Hennessy–Win Crafty Lady, by Crafty Prospector. Trainer Pletcher Todd A. Bred by Sabine Stables (Ky).

HARMONY LODGE vied for the lead along the inside to the quarter pole, opened a clear lead in early stretch and maintained her advantage to the wire under steady urging. GOLD MOVER tracked the pace along the inside around the turn, then couldn't gain on the winner late while closing to be up for the place. NONSUCH BAY unhurried after bumping AWAY at the start, angled out for the stretch run and closed to gain the show. FOREST HEIRESS bumped with AWAY at the start, vied for the lead outside HARMONY LODGE to the quarter pole, then tired in the drive. PREFERRED OPTION chased the pace three wide around the turn and faltered. AWAY was outrun after being jostled between rivals at the start.

Owners— 1, Melnyk Eugene & Laura; 2, Evans Edward P; 3, Platt Joseph P Jr; 4, Stonerside Stable; 5, Shields Joseph V Jr; 6, Clay Robert N

Trainers—1, Pletcher Todd A; 2, Hennig Mark; 3, Alexander Frank A; 4, Mott William I; 5, Jerkens H Allen; 6, Kimmel John C

$2 Pick Three (5–10–2) Paid $710.40; Pick Three Pool $35,522.

NINTH RACE
Fair Grounds
FEBRUARY 15, 2003

1$\frac{1}{16}$ MILES. (1.42) 22nd Running of THE SILVERBULLETDAY. Grade II. Purse $150,000. Fillies, 3–year–olds. By subscription of $100 each; $750 to enter; $750 additional to start. $150,000 of which $90,000 to the winner; $30,000 to second; $16,500 to third; $9,000 to fourth; $4,500 to fifth. Weight, 122 lbs. Non–winners of $36,000, allowed 3 lbs. $25,000, 5 lbs. (Maiden and claiming races not considered.) Two races other than maiden or claiming since November 16, 8 lbs. $15,000 other than maiden or claiming since December 16, 10 lbs. Closed Wednesday, February 15 with 15 nominations.

Value of Race: $150,000 Winner $90,000; second $30,000; third $16,500; fourth $9,000; fifth $4,500. Mutuel Pool $307,091.00 Exacta Pool $207,938.00 Quinella Pool $16,424.00 Trifecta Pool $165,548.00 Superfecta Pool $43,366.00

Last Raced	Horse	M/Eqt.	A.Wt	PP	St	¼	½	¾	Str	Fin	Jockey	Odds $1
26Jan03 ^{8}FG^{8}	Belle Of Perintown	L	3 122	5	4	$2^{1\frac{1}{2}}$	$2^{1\frac{1}{2}}$	$2^{1\frac{1}{2}}$	$1^{2\frac{1}{2}}$	$1^{8\frac{1}{4}}$	Borel C H	10.20
26Jan03 ^{4}FG^{6}	Afternoon Dreams	L	3 112	6	5	$5^{1\frac{1}{2}}$	5^{1}	4^{2}	$3^{1\frac{1}{2}}$	$2^{1\frac{1}{2}}$	Martinez W	a-2.90
4Jan03 ^{4}FG^{1}	Rebridled Dreams	L	3 117	4	2	$1^{1\frac{1}{2}}$	$1^{\frac{1}{2}}$	$1^{\frac{1}{2}}$	2^{2}	3^{nk}	Martin E M Jr	a-2.90
20Dec02 ^{9}DeD^{2}	Souris	L	3 122	1	1	8	8	8	4^{1}	$4^{1\frac{1}{2}}$	Lanerie C J	2.90
26Jan03 ^{8}FG^{2}	Allspice	Lb	3 122	3	6	6^{hd}	6^{hd}	5^{1}	6^{5}	$5^{1\frac{1}{4}}$	Albarado R J	1.40
18Jan03 ^{10}TP^{1}	Golden Marlin	L	3 119	7	7	$4^{\frac{1}{2}}$	3^{hd}	3^{1}	$5^{1\frac{1}{2}}$	$6^{8\frac{3}{4}}$	Sellers S J	5.20
18Jan03 ^{5}FG^{2}	Arrival Time	L	3 116	2	3	3^{hd}	4^{hd}	7^{1}	$7^{2\frac{1}{2}}$	7^{4}	Lovato F Jr	28.70
26Jan03 ^{8}FG^{5}	Cheryl's Myth	Lb	3 122	8	8	7^{3}	7^{6}	6^{1}	8	8	Meche L J	71.20

a–Coupled: Afternoon Dreams and Rebridled Dreams.

OFF AT 4:20 Start Good. Won easily. Track fast.
TIME :23^{2}, :46^{4}, 1:12^{2}, 1:37^{2}, 1:44^{2} (:23.41, :46.92, 1:12.51, 1:37.54, 1:44.48)

$2 Mutuel Prices:

5–BELLE OF PERINTOWN	22.40	9.00	5.60
1A–AFTERNOON DREAMS (a–entry)		4.20	6.00
1–REBRIDLED DREAMS (a–entry)		4.20	6.00

$2 EXACTA 5–1 PAID $122.40 $2 QUINELLA 1–5 PAID $49.20 $2 TRIFECTA 5–1–2 PAID $392.80 $2 SUPERFECTA 5–1–2–4 PAID $891.00

B. f, (Jan), by Dehere–Hot Match, by Mr. Prospector. Trainer Kenneally Eddie. Bred by Bradley Wayne Hughes (Ky).

BELLE OF PERINTOWN bumped with AFTERNOON DREAMS leaving the gate, recovered, moved up to race reserved off REBRIDLED DREAMS from early on, collared that one before a half, gained the edge before the furlong marker and then drew out while winning easily. AFTERNOON DREAMS bumped with BEELE OF PERINTOWN leaving the gate, settled early, raced between foes until the second turn, raced along the rail around the turn, continued inside for the drive, was switched out inside the furlong marker and finished gamely for second. REBRIDLED DREAMS got clear early, responded when collared down the backstretch, was displaced before mid stretch and then held on for third. SOURIS reserved along the rail, continued inside while trailing, eased out around the second turn, closed gamely. ALLSPICE restrained off the rail until before the second turn, was asked around the turn while continuing outside and had no response. GOLDEN MARLIN four wide early, was unhurried while three wide, ranged up around the turn and then faded once turning for home. ARRIVAL TIME saved ground and faded. CHERYL'S MYTH wide early, was not a factor.

Owners— 1, Mahler Kenneth & Schloss Jamie; 2, Coast To Coast Racing Fund; 3, Coast To Coast Racing Fund; 4, Hunt Nelson B; 5, Tafel James B; 6, Estate Of J Famularo & William D Gl; 7, Winchell Family Trust; 8, Schaffrick William C

Trainers—1, Kenneally Eddie; 2, Calhoun William Bret; 3, Calhoun William Bret; 4, Asmussen Steven M; 5, Cilio Gene A; 6, Foley Gregory D; 7, Asmussen Steven M; 8, Kassen David C

$2 Pick Three (6–6–5) Paid $571.40; Pick Three Pool $15,619.

NINTH RACE
Gulfstream
FEBRUARY 15, 2003

7 FURLONGS. (1.20) 50th Running of THE HUTCHESON. Grade II. Purse $150,000 Guaranteed. THREE YEAR OLDS. By subscription of $150 each, which shall accompany the nomination, $1,500 to pass the entry box and $1,500 additional to start, with $150,000 guaranteed. The owner of the winner to recieve $90,000; $30,000 to second, $16,500 to third, $9,000 to fourth and $4,500 to fifth. Weight: 122 lbs. Non-winners of $50,000 once, allowed 2 lbs,; $40,000 once anytime or $30,000 in 2003, 4 lbs.; $25,000 once or two races other than Maiden or Claiming, 6 lbs. Horses finishing first, second or third in the Hutcheson Stakes will automatically be nominated to the Florida Derby. Trophy to winning Owner. Closed Wednesday, February 5, 2003 with 6 Nominations. Early Bird Florida Darby Nominations closed, Wednesday November 13, 2002 with 117.

Value of Race: $150,000 Winner $90,000; second $30,000; third $16,500; fourth $9,000; fifth $4,500. Mutuel Pool $861,151.00 Exacta Pool $664,175.00 Trifecta Pool $423,954.00 Superfecta Pool $139,622.00

Last Raced	Horse	M/Eqt.	A.Wt	PP	St	¼	½	Str	Fin	Jockey	Odds $1
4Jan03 ^{5}GP^{1}	Lion Tamer	L	3 118	4	5	$2\frac{1}{2}$	2^{1}	$1\frac{1}{2}$	1^{6}	Velazquez J R	1.30
11Jan03 ^{5}GP^{1}	Strength Within	L	3 116	6	1	6	$5\frac{1}{2}$	$3\frac{1}{2}$	$2\frac{3}{4}$	Fires E	10.20
3Jan03 ^{9}GP^{2}	Crafty Guy	L	3 122	3	2	$1\frac{1}{2}$	1^{1}	2^{3}	$3^{3\frac{3}{4}}$	Santos J A	8.80
18Jan03 ^{7}SA^{3}	Scrimshaw	Lb	3 118	5	6	3^{1}	3^{1}	$4^{1\frac{1}{2}}$	$4^{1\frac{3}{4}}$	Bailey J D	2.00
3Jan03 ^{9}GP^{1}	First Blush		3 122	2	3	$5\frac{1}{2}$	4^{hd}	5^{12}	$5^{29\frac{3}{4}}$	Chavez J F	7.30
26Jan03 ^{8}GP^{1}	Cajun Beat	L	3 116	1	4	$4\frac{1}{2}$	6	6	6	Boulanger G	7.60

OFF AT 4:40 Start Good. Won driving. Track fast.
TIME :22, :44^{1}, 1:09^{1}, 1:22^{3} (:22.18, :44.29, 1:09.22, 1:22.60)

$2 Mutuel Prices:

4–LION TAMER	4.60	3.40	2.60
6–STRENGTH WITHIN		6.80	3.80
3–CRAFTY GUY			4.00

$2 EXACTA 4–6 PAID $36.00 $2 TRIFECTA 4–6–3 PAID $217.20 $1 SUPERFECTA 4–6–3–5 PAID $303.30

Ch. c, (Feb), by Will's Way–Tippecanoe Creek, by Olympio. Trainer Pletcher Todd A. Bred by Paul Smith (Ky).

LION TAMER off slowly, moved up quickly to stalk the pace, rallied to catch CRAFTY GUY at the top of the stretch, then drew off under steady pressure. STRENGTH WITHIN unhurried early, raced four wide around the turn and closed to wear down CRAFTY GUY for the place while no match for the winner. CRAFTY GUY fractious in the gate, quickly moved to the fore, made the pace along the inside to the top of the stretch, continued on well to inside the eighth pole and gave way. SCRIMSHAW a bit fractious in the gate, broke slowly, tracked the pace three wide into the stretch and tired. FIRST BLUSH rated in striking position off the pace while a bit hard to handle, faltered in the drive. CAJUN BEAT steadied in behind FIRST BLUSH in the chute, showed early foot along the inside, then steadied inside FIRST BLUSH again approaching the quarter pole, faded and eased in the final eighth.

Owners— 1, M Tabor; 2, Glen Hill Farm; 3, M Gill; 4, Lewis Robert B & Beverly J; 5, Cowan Marjorie & Irving M; 6, Sanan Satish & Iracane John & Josep

Trainers—1, Pletcher Todd A; 2, Proctor Thomas F; 3, Robb John J; 4, Lukas D Wayne; 5, Jerkens H Allen; 6, Gambolati Cam

$2 Pick Three (4–1–4) Paid $671.60; Pick Three Pool $77,250.

ELEVENTH RACE
Gulfstream
FEBRUARY 15, 2003

$1\frac{1}{16}$ MILES. (1.40^{1}) 57th Running of THE FOUNTAIN OF YOUTH. Grade I. Purse $200,000 Guaranteed. THREE YEAR OLDS. By subscription of $200 each which shall accompany the nomination, $2,000 to pass the entry box and $2,000 additional to start. The owner of the winner to recieve $120,000; $40,000 to second, $22,000 to third, $12,000 to fourth and $6,000 to fifth. Weight: 122 lbs. Non–winners of $75,000 once at a mile or over, allowed, 2 lbs.; $50,000 once at any distance or $30,000 at a mile or over, 4 lbs.; $30,000 at any distance or $24,000 twice at a mile orover, 6 lbs. Horses finishing first, second or third in the Fountain of Youth Stakes will automatically be nominated to the Florida Derby. Closed Wednesday, February 5, 2003 with 7 Nominations. Early Bird Florida Derby nominations closed, November 13, 2002 with 117.

Value of Race: $200,000 Winner $120,000; second $40,000; third $22,000; fourth $12,000; fifth $6,000. Mutuel Pool $1,139,824.0 Exacta Pool $733,162.00 Trifecta Pool $598,581.00 Superfecta Pool $165,299.00

Last Raced	Horse	M/Eqt.	A.Wt	PP	St	¼	½	¾	Str	Fin	Jockey	Odds $1
14Dec02 ^{11}Crc^{1}	Trust N Luck	L	3 122	6	5	1^{2}	$1^{1\frac{1}{2}}$	$1^{1\frac{1}{2}}$	1^{4}	$1^{5\frac{1}{4}}$	Velasquez C	4.90
25Jan03 ^{8}GP^{3}	Supah Blitz	Lb	3 120	1	3	$5\frac{1}{2}$	$4\frac{1}{2}$	4^{hd}	2^{1}	$2^{2\frac{1}{4}}$	Homeister R B Jr	33.90
18Jan03 ^{5}GP^{1}	Midway Cat	Lb	3 116	4	4	2^{hd}	$2^{1\frac{1}{2}}$	$2\frac{1}{2}$	3^{1}	3^{hd}	Chavez J F	6.40
18Jan03 ^{10}GP^{1}	Offlee Wild	L	3 120	8	8	$4\frac{1}{2}$	5^{hd}	5^{7}	$4^{1\frac{1}{2}}$	$4^{3\frac{3}{4}}$	Guidry M	3.80
26Oct02 ^{8}AP^{10}	Whywhywhy	L	3 122	5	6	3^{hd}	3^{1}	$3\frac{1}{2}$	5^{8}	$5^{12\frac{3}{4}}$	Prado E S	3.80
31Jan03 ^{8}GP^{2}	Ten Cents A Shine	L	3 116	2	1	$6\frac{1}{2}$	$6^{1\frac{1}{2}}$	8	8	$6\frac{3}{4}$	Bailey J D	2.50
11Jan03 ^{9}GP^{1}	Conservation	L	3 116	7	7	8	8	$7\frac{1}{2}$	6^{hd}	$7^{2\frac{1}{4}}$	Santos J A	15.10
11Jan03 ^{8}GG^{2}	Ozzie Cat	Lb	3 118	3	2	$7\frac{1}{2}$	$7^{1\frac{1}{2}}$	6^{hd}	7^{4}	8	Day P	10.80

OFF AT 5:40 Start Good. Won driving. Track fast.
TIME :23^{3}, :46^{3}, 1:10^{4}, 1:36^{2}, 1:43^{1} (:23.61, :46.68, 1:10.99, 1:36.49, 1:43.33)

$2 Mutuel Prices:

6–TRUST N LUCK	11.80	7.20	5.00
1–SUPAH BLITZ		25.00	9.60
4–MIDWAY CAT			5.60

$2 EXACTA 6–1 PAID $209.40 $2 TRIFECTA 6–1–4 PAID $1,236.60 $1 SUPERFECTA 6–1–4–9 PAID $2,883.10

Ch. c, (Apr), by Montbrook–Bold Burst, by Dahar. Trainer Ziadie Ralph. Bred by Edward Wiest & Ashley Wiest (Fla).

TRUST N LUCK outran MIDWAY CAT to the first turn, moved to the inside after clearing that rival, was well handled while making the pace along the inside into the stretch, then drew away when set down for the drive. SUPAH BLITZ reserved racing along the rail, advanced to loom a threat leaving the far turn, then was no match for the winner while gaining the place. MIDWAY CAT was steadied and angled outside the leader soon after entering the first turn, chased the pace off the rail into the stretch and tired. OFFLEE WILD reserved off the pace, raced in striking position four wide around the far turn, then had no response when set down for the drive. WHYWHYWHY chased the leaders three wide, made a run to loom a threat entering the stretch, then faltered. TEN CENTS A SHINE was never a factor. CONSERVATION raced four wide throughout while being outrun. OZZIE CAT saved ground into the far turn and faded.

Owners— 1, Robsham Einar P; 2, Bee Bee Stables & Tortora Jacquelin; 3, B M H Stable; 4, Azalea Stables; 5, F Ouaki & Patrick L Biancone Racing; 6, Ramsey Kenneth L & Sarah K; 7, Bohemia Stable; 8, Overbrook Farm

Trainers—1, Ziadie Ralph; 2, Tortora Emanuel; 3, Hiles Rick; 4, Smith Thomas V; 5, Biancone Patrick L; 6, McPeek Kenneth G; 7, Tagg Barclay; 8, Lukas D Wayne

Scratched— Seek Gold (18Jan03 ^{10}GP^{8})

$2 Pick Three (4–5–6) Paid $111.20; Pick Three Pool $139,622.

SEVENTH RACE
Santa Anita
FEBRUARY 15, 2003

1½ MILES. (Turf)(2.22^4) 36th Running of THE SAN LUIS OBISPO HANDICAP. Grade II. Purse $200,000. FOUR-YEAR-OLDS AND UPWARD. By subscription of $200 each to accompany the nomination or by supplementary nomination of $4,000 by Sunday, February 9. $2,000 additional to start, with $200,000 guaranteed,of which $120,000 to first, $40,000 to second, $24,000 to third, $12,000 to fourth and $4,000 to fifth. Closed Thursday, February 6 with 14 nominations. (Rail at 24 Feet). (Start on backstretch.)

Value of Race: $200,000 Winner $120,000; second $40,000; third $24,000; fourth $12,000; fifth $4,000. Mutuel Pool $519,160.00 Exacta Pool $315,670.00 Quinella Pool $31,076.00 Trifecta Pool $300,831.00

Last Raced	Horse	M/Eqt.	A.	Wt	PP	¼	½	1	1¼	Str	Fin	Jockey	Odds $1
20Jan03 ^{8}SA^2	The Tin Man	LB	5	121	1	1^{1½}	1^{1½}	1^{1½}	1^{2½}	1^8	1^{9½}	Smith M E	0.50
25Jan03 ^{2}SA^4	Special Matter	LBb	5	113	5	4^3	4^4	3^{1½}	3^3	3^{2½}	2^{1½}	Baze T C	9.20
20Jan03 ^{8}SA^4	Harrisand-FR	LB	5	116	2	3^1	2^{hd}	2^{1½}	2^2	2^{hd}	3^{½}	Valenzuela P A	3.30
25Jan03 ^{2}SA^7	Lucky Molar	LBb	8	114	3	5	5	5	4^6	4^{15}	4^{24}	Krone J A	17.00
25Jan03 ^{7}GP^8	Continental Red	LB	7	118	4	2^{hd}	3^2	4^{½}	5	5	5	Pincay L Jr	5.60

OFF AT 3:36 Start Good. Won ridden out. Course yielding.
TIME :26, :51, 1:15^3, 1:41, 2:05^4, 2:31^1 (:26.03, :51.10, 1:15.60, 1:41.14, 2:05.96, 2:31.22)

$2 Mutuel Prices:				
	2–THE TIN MAN	3.00	2.40	2.10
	7–SPECIAL MATTER		4.00	2.20
	3–HARRISAND–FR			2.20

$1 EXACTA 2–7 PAID $7.20 $2 QUINELLA 2–7 PAID $11.40 $1 TRIFECTA 2–7–3 PAID $19.10

Dk. b. or br. g, by Affirmed–Lizzie Rolfe, by Tom Rolfe. Trainer Mandella Richard. Bred by Ralph Todd & Aury Todd (Ky).

THE TIN MAN took the early lead and set the pace inside under good rating, kicked away on the final turn and drew off in the stretch under a tap of the whip and a brisk hand ride, then was under a hold late. SPECIAL MATTER three deep early, chased off the rail, angled in on the second turn, came out a bit on the last turn, went around a rival into the stretch and was second best. HARRISAND (FR) stalked the winner along the inside, came out a bit into the stretch and just held third. LUCKY MOLAR unhurried and angled in early, saved ground off the pace, went outside a rival leaving the backstretch, came out some in the stretch and was edged for the show. CONTINENTAL RED was in a good position stalking outside a rival, fell back some on the second turn, dropped back again on the backstretch, angled in for the final turn, gave way readily and was eased in the stretch.

Owners— 1, Todd Aury & Ralph E; 2, Elder McClintock & McClintock et al; 3, Gann Edmund A; 4, Englander Richard A; 5, Fitzpatrick Sharon M

Trainers—1, Mandella Richard; 2, Becerra Rafael; 3, Frankel Robert; 4, Mullins Jeff; 5, Jory Ian P D

Scratched— Hannibal Lad (16Jan03 ^{7}SA^1), Royal Gem (1Dec02 ^{8}HOL^3)

$2 Daily Double (2–2) Paid $10.20; Daily Double Pool $34,628.
$1 Pick Three (8–2–1/2/4) Paid $32.60; Pick Three Pool $89,082.

NINTH RACE
Fair Grounds
FEBRUARY 16, 2003

1$\frac{1}{16}$ MILES. (1.42) 15th Running of THE RISEN STAR. Grade III. Purse $150,000. Three Year Olds. By subscription of $100 each (Louisiana Derby early bird nominees automatically subscribed). $750 to enter; $750 additional to start. $150,000 guaranteed of which $90,000 to the winner; $30,000 to second; $16,500 to third; $9,000 to fourth; $4,500 to fifth. Weight, 122 lbs. Non-winners of $36,000, allowed 3 lbs. $25,000, 5 lbs. $20,000, 8 lbs. (Maiden and claiming races not considered). The owner of the winner to recieve a trophy. Closed Thursday, February 6, with 9 nominations plus 129 early bird nominations.

Value of Race: $150,000 Winner $90,000; second $30,000; third $16,500; fourth $9,000; fifth $4,500. Mutuel Pool $524,369.00 Exacta Pool $345,677.00 Quinella Pool $27,250.00 Trifecta Pool $297,965.00 Superfecta Pool $104,289.00

Last Raced	Horse	M/Eqt.	A.	Wt	PP	St	¼	½	¾	Str	Fin	Jockey	Odds $1
23Jan03 ^{7}FG^1	Badge Of Silver	L	3	116	10	1	2^{1½}	2^{2½}	1^{hd}	1^3	1^{10}	Albarado R J	2.90
25Jan03 ^{9}FG^7	Lone Star Sky	L	3	122	5	3	3^{hd}	3^{hd}	3^1	2^{2½}	2^{¾}	Borel C H	9.20
25Jan03 ^{9}FG^4	Defrere's Vixen	L	3	114	8	8	7^3	6^{hd}	5^{2½}	4^{½}	3^{½}	Lanerie C J	16.30
11Jan03 ^{9}FG^1	Prince Alphie	Lbf	3	122	4	11	9^1	8^1	6^3	5^{2½}	4^7	Melancon L	30.00
25Jan03 ^{9}FG^1	Saintly Look	L	3	122	1	2	1^1	1^{hd}	2^3	3^{1½}	5^{¾}	Sellers S J	3.20
25Jan03 ^{9}FG^{11}	Leo's Last Hurrahy	Lb	3	122	2	5	5^{hd}	5^1	4^{1½}	6^6	6^{¾}	Melancon G	61.10
4Jan03 ^{3}GP^1	Indy Dancer	L	3	117	12	12	12	11^{hd}	12	9^1	7^5	Velazquez J R	2.30
11Jan03 ^{9}FG^2	Canaan Land	Lb	3	114	9	4	11^{2½}	12	10^1	7^1	8^{7½}	Martin E M Jr	38.00
17Jan03 ^{9}FG^1	Seattle Hoofer	L	3	116	3	6	8^1	9^{1½}	9^2	10^3	9^{4¾}	Lovato F Jr	6.00
25Jan03 ^{9}FG^8	Crowned King	L	3	117	7	7	6^{hd}	7^2	7^2	8^1	10^1	Leblanc K P	140.20
25Jan03 ^{8}FG^1	Gentlemen J J	Lb	3	114	6	10	10^{hd}	10^1	11^{3½}	11^5	11^{13½}	Perrodin E J	99.50
1Feb03 ^{10}SA^1	Deep Shadow	Lb	3	115	11	9	4^{1½}	4^{1½}	8^{hd}	12	12	Smith M E	30.60

OFF AT 4:32 Start Good. Won ridden out. Track fast.
TIME :23^3, :47^2, 1:12, 1:36^3, 1:42^4 (:23.71, :47.42, 1:12.10, 1:36.68, 1:42.99)

$2 Mutuel Prices:				
	11–BADGE OF SILVER	7.80	5.40	4.80
	6–LONE STAR SKY		8.80	6.20
	9–DEFRERE'S VIXEN			8.00

$2 EXACTA 11–6 PAID $65.20 $2 QUINELLA 6–11 PAID $43.00 $2 TRIFECTA 11–6–9 PAID $516.00 $2 SUPERFECTA 11–6–9–5 PAID $10,424.60

Dk. b. or br. c, (Mar), by Silver Deputy–Silveroo, by Silver Hawk. Trainer Werner Ronny. Bred by Liberation Farm & Oratis T'breds & Trackside Farm (Ky).

BADGE OF SILVER reserved just outside SAINTLY LOOK, bid under restraint completing a half, gained the edge before the drive, was roused turning for home and drew away while ridden out. LONE STAR SKY raced close up while in hand, was put to pressure midway around the second turn, angled out for the drive and while no match for the winner held second. DEFRERE'S VIXEN allowed to settle off the rail, was asked around the second turn and rallied gamely. PRINCE ALPHIE moved to the rail early, advanced down the backstretch, split foes entering the turn, moved out and could make little impact. SAINTLY LOOK held the early lead, was headed nearing the drive and faded. LEO'S LAST HURRAHY inside until the drive, was not a threat. INDY DANCER wide early, angled to the rail down the backstretch, advanced and then was not a factor. CANAAN LAND wide early, was devoid speed until the second turn, split foes to advance but was outrun. SEATTLE HOOFER showed little. CROWNED KING between foes early, faded. GENTLEMEN J J was always back. DEEP SHADOW forwardly placed off the rail for a half, stopped.

Owners— 1, Ramsey Kenneth L & Sarah K; 2, New Walter L; 3, Oleson Jack A; 4, Schettine William C; 5, Carl William A; 6, Murphy Kenneth W; 7, Wertheimer Farm; 8, Alane Inc; 9, Stonerside Stable; 10, McKeever Billy C Jr; 11, Rancha Fresa Inc; 12, Fog City Stable

Trainers—1, Werner Ronny; 2, Amoss Thomas; 3, Asmussen Steven M; 4, Carroll Josie; 5, Stewart Dallas; 6, Young Bob; 7, Pletcher Todd A; 8, Stidham Michael; 9, Stidham Michael; 10, McKeever Billy C Jr; 11, Leggio Andrew Jr; 12, Lukas D Wayne

Scratched— Gohalo (17Jan03 ^{9}FG^3)

$2 Pick Three (4–3–11) Paid $118.80; Pick Three Pool $27,828.

TENTH RACE
Gulfstream
FEBRUARY 16, 2003

1⅜ MILES. (Turf)(2.10^{3}) 18th Running of THE GULFSTREAM PARK BREEDERS' CUP HANDICAP. Grade I. Purse $200,000 (includes $100,000 BC – Breeders' Cup) FOR THREE YEAR OLDS AND UPWARD. (Includes $100,000 from Breeders' Cup Fund for Cup nominees only) By subscription of $200 each, which shall accompany the nomination, $1,500 to pass the entry box and $1,500 additional to start. Weights: Monday, February 10,2003. This race will not be divided. The field will be limited to 12 Starters. If more than 12 entries pass the entry box, the starters will be determined at the time with preference given to Breeders' Cup Nominees only of equal racing quality or weight assignment (respective of sex and weight for age). Trophy to winning Owner given by Breeders' Cup, Ltd. (High Weights on the scale Preferred.) In the event this stake is taken off the turf, it may be subject to downgrading upon review by the Graded Stakes Committee. Closed Friday, February 7, 2003 with 28 Nominations. (Rail at 0 Feet).

Value of Race: $194,000 Winner $120,000; second $40,000; third $22,000; fourth $6,000; fifth $6,000. Mutuel Pool $507,209.00 Exacta Pool $381,128.00 Trifecta Pool $312,824.00 Superfecta Pool $108,523.00

Last Raced	Horse	M/Eqt.	A.	Wt	PP	¼	½	¾	1	Str	Fin	Jockey	Odds $1
28Dec02 ^{11}Crc^{1}	Man From Wicklow	Lb	6	119	7	4^{hd}	5^{2}	$5^{1\frac{1}{2}}$	4^{hd}	3^{1}	$1^{4\frac{3}{4}}$	Bailey J D	1.60
19Jan03 ^{10}GP^{3}	Just Listen	Lb	7	113	6	6^{hd}	6^{1}	$6^{\frac{1}{2}}$	6^{hd}	$4^{\frac{1}{2}}$	$2^{\frac{1}{2}}$	Homeister R B Jr	30.10
24Jan03 ^{9}GP^{2}	Sardaukar-GB	L	7	114	5	8^{hd}	9^{2}	$9^{3\frac{1}{2}}$	$9^{1\frac{1}{2}}$	6^{hd}	3^{1}	Santos J A	11.70
19Jan03 ^{10}GP^{1}	Riddlesdown-IRE	L	6	115	1	$1^{2\frac{1}{2}}$	$1^{1\frac{1}{2}}$	$1^{1\frac{1}{2}}$	$1^{1\frac{1}{2}}$	1^{hd}	4^{nk}	Velez R I	a-4.20
12Jan03 ^{9}GP^{2}	Stokosky		7	114	2	$2^{1\frac{1}{2}}$	2^{hd}	2^{2}	$2^{1\frac{1}{2}}$	2^{hd}	$5^{\frac{3}{4}}$	Prado E S	a-4.20
12Jan03 ^{9}GP^{1}	Della Francesca	b	4	115	9	3^{1}	$4^{3\frac{1}{2}}$	$4^{\frac{1}{2}}$	5^{2}	5^{1}	$6^{\frac{3}{4}}$	Chavez J F	8.90
19Jan03 ^{10}GP^{7}	Whata Brainstorm	Lb	6	114	3	5^{1}	$3^{\frac{1}{2}}$	3^{3}	3^{3}	7^{1}	$7^{\frac{1}{2}}$	Boulanger G	15.60
19Jan03 ^{10}GP^{6}	Rochester	L	7	115	8	$7^{1\frac{1}{2}}$	7^{hd}	7^{hd}	7^{2}	$8^{1\frac{1}{2}}$	$8^{1\frac{1}{4}}$	Day P	7.80
19Jan03 ^{10}GP^{4}	Williams News	L	8	117	10	$9^{\frac{1}{2}}$	$8^{\frac{1}{2}}$	8^{1}	$8^{\frac{1}{2}}$	9^{hd}	$9^{\frac{3}{4}}$	Husbands P	12.00
23Nov02 ^{8}Hol^{10}	Cetewayo	Lb	9	117	4	10	10	10	10	10	10	Velasquez C	5.70

a–Coupled: Riddlesdown–IRE and Stokosky.

OFF AT 5:11 Start Good. Won driving. Course firm.
TIME :24^{2}, :48^{1}, 1:12^{1}, 1:35^{3}, 2:00, 2:11^{3} (:24.49, :48.37, 1:12.30, 1:35.68, 2:00.01, 2:11.62)

$2 Mutuel Prices:				
	6–MAN FROM WICKLOW	5.20	3.80	2.80
	5–JUST LISTEN		18.60	9.00
	2B–SARDAUKAR–GB			6.20

$2 EXACTA 6–5 PAID $99.60 $2 TRIFECTA 6–5–2 PAID $839.40 $1 SUPERFECTA 6–5–2–1 PAID $1,427.90

Dk. b. or br. g, by Turkoman–Star of Wicklow, by Fast Play. Trainer Violette Richard A Jr. Bred by Cavanaugh J R (Fla).

MAN FROM WICKLOW rated in striking position off the pace into the stretch the final time, angled outside the leaders and rallied to gain command just past the eighth pole, then drew away under urging. JUST LISTEN steadied in traffic on the first turn, was reserved into the stretch, angled to the inside and rallied along the hedge to be up for the place. SARDAUKAR (GB) reserved along the inside for more than a mile, angled to the outside for the drive and closed to gain the show. RIDDLESDOWN (IRE) quickly moved to the fore, made the pace along the hedge to midstretch and gave way. STOKOSKY stalked the pace, made a run to reach even terms for command in midstretch, then tired. DELLA FRANCESCA taken in hand to track the pace, angled to the hedge on the backstretch, raced in contention into the stretch and lacked a late response. WHATA BRAINSTORM tracked the leaders three wide to nearing the stretch the final time and faltered. ROCHESTER was never a factor. WILLIAMS NEWS was outrun. CETEWAYO trailed.

Owners— 1, Violette Richard A Jr; 2, Guez Marie Romaine & Guez D; 3, M Gill; 4, Tanaka Gary A; 5, Tanaka Gary A; 6, Ol Memorial Stable & Dell Ridge Far; 7, Eaton John & Laymon Steve; 8, Augustin Stable; 9, On Target Racing Stable; 10, Chandler Dr John A

Trainers—1, Violette Richard A Jr; 2, Catanese Joseph C III; 3, Shuman Mark; 4, O'Callaghan Niall M; 5, Mott William I; 6, O'Callaghan Niall M; 7, Picou James E; 8, Sheppard Jonathan E; 9, Vivian David A; 10, Dickinson Michael W

Scratched— Roger E (31Jan03 ^{9}GP^{1}), Saint Verre (11Jan03 ^{10}GP^{2}), Aeneas (15Feb03 ^{7}GP^{2})

$2 Pick Three (3–2–6/7/11) Paid $196.20; Pick Three Pool $58,672.

SIXTH RACE
Santa Anita
FEBRUARY 16, 2003

1$\frac{1}{16}$ MILES. (1.39) 61st Running of THE SANTA MARIA HANDICAP. Grade I. Purse $200,000 FOR FILLIES AND MARES FOUR YEARS OLD AND UPWARD. By subscription of $200 each to accompany the nomination. $2,000 additional to start, with $200,000 guaranteed, of which $120,000 to first, $40,000 to second, $24,00 to third, $12,000 to fourth and $4,000 to fifth. NOMINATIONS CLOSED Thursday, February 6, 2003 with 11.

Value of Race: $200,000 Winner $120,000; second $40,000; third $24,000; fourth $12,000; fifth $4,000. Mutuel Pool $445,694.00 Exacta Pool $308,409.00 Quinella Pool $32,478.00

Last Raced	Horse	M/Eqt.	A.	Wt	PP	St	¼	½	¾	Str	Fin	Jockey	Odds $1
15Dec02 ^{7}Hol^{1}	Starrer	LBb	5	119	1	1	2^{hd}	$3^{1\frac{1}{2}}$	$1^{\frac{1}{2}}$	$1^{1\frac{1}{2}}$	$1^{4\frac{1}{2}}$	Valenzuela P A	1.10
28Dec02 ^{7}SA^{5}	You	LB	4	118	5	4	$3^{2\frac{1}{2}}$	$2^{\frac{1}{2}}$	4^{12}	2^{hd}	$2^{\frac{1}{2}}$	Desormeaux K J	1.30
15Jan03 ^{7}SA^{2}	Rhiana	LB	6	112	3	5	4^{7}	4^{12}	3^{hd}	3^{3}	3^{7}	Krone J A	15.60
15Jan03 ^{7}SA^{1}	Printemps-CHI	LB	6	118	2	2	5	5	5	5	4^{1}	Pincay L Jr	3.80
15Jan03 ^{7}SA^{5}	Se Me Acabo-CH	LBb	5	116	4	3	1^{hd}	1^{1}	2^{hd}	4^{6}	5	Stevens G L	37.90

OFF AT 3:06 Start Good. Won driving. Track good.
TIME :23, :46^{1}, 1:10^{4}, 1:36^{1}, 1:42^{3} (:23.02, :46.37, 1:10.90, 1:36.38, 1:42.75)

$2 Mutuel Prices:				
	1–STARRER	4.20	2.40	2.10
	5–YOU		2.60	2.10
	3–RHIANA			2.10

$1 EXACTA 1–5 PAID $4.70 $2 QUINELLA 1–5 PAID $4.00

Dk. b. or br. m, by Dynaformer–To the Hunt, by Relaunch. Trainer Shirreffs John. Bred by Wind Hill Farm (Ky).

STARRER pulled her way up inside to press the pace on the first turn, stalked under restraint on the backstretch, bid again inside and took a short lead on the second turn, inched away in upper stretch then kicked clear under urging. YOU went up three deep on the first turn to challenge, stalked outside the winner on the backstretch, re-bid three wide between horses on the second turn, continued between foes into the stretch, could not match the winner but gamely held second. RHIANA chased off the rail, bid four wide on the second turn and three deep into the stretch and was edged for the place. PRINTEMPS (CHI) angled in and lagged back inside, came out in the stretch and failed to menace. SE ME ACABO (CHI) sent between horses to the early lead, dueled between foes on the first turn, inched away again on the backstretch, battled briefly between rivals on the second turn, dropped back, angled in approaching the stretch and weakened.

Owners— 1, Krikorian George; 2, Gann Edmund A; 3, Ernst Allegra & John; 4, Amerman Racing Stables; 5, Zarour Marcel

Trainers—1, Shirreffs John; 2, Frankel Robert; 3, Hendricks Dan L; 4, McAnally Ronald; 5, Inda Eduardo

$2 Daily Double (6–1) Paid $12.40; Daily Double Pool $24,008.
$1 Pick Three (2–5/6–1) Paid $9.40; Pick Three Pool $72,490.

SEVENTH RACE

Santa Anita

FEBRUARY 17, 2003

1 MILE. (Turf)(1.31⁴) 16th Running of THE BUENA VISTA HANDICAP. Grade II. Purse $150,000. Fillies and mares, 4–year–olds and upward. By subscription of $150 each to accompany the nomination. $1,500 additional to start, with $150,000 guaranteed, with $90,000 to first, $30,000 to second, $18,000 to third, $9,000 to fourth, and $3,000 to fifth. Closed Thursday, February 6 with 20 nominations. (Rail at 24 Feet).

Value of Race: $150,000 Winner $90,000; second $30,000; third $18,000; fourth $9,000; fifth $3,000. Mutuel Pool $428,597.00 Exacta Pool $242,356.00 Quinella Pool $27,224.00 Trifecta Pool $223,477.00 Superfecta Pool $79,198.00

Last Raced	Horse	M/Eqt. A.Wt	PP	St	¼	½	¾	Str	Fin	Jockey	Odds $1
11Dec02 7Hol¹	Final Destination-NZ	LB	5 115	2	2	3½	3½	3hd	2¹	1½	Espinoza V	1.90
29Jan03 3SA¹	GardenintheRain-FR	LB	6 115	4	3	4¹	4¹	4¹½	4¹½	2²½	Valdivia J Jr	1.60
29Jan03 7SA²	Embassy Belle-IR	LB	5 116	3	5	5¹½	5hd	5½	5½	3hd	Stevens G L	3.30
31Dec02 8SA¹²	Repository	LB	5 116	6	4	2²½	2²	2¹½	1hd	4²	Pincay L Jr	16.30
29Jan03 7SA⁶	I'm The Business-NZ	LB	6 116	5	6	6	6	6	6	5⁶	Desormeaux K J	9.40
24Jun02 8Cnl⁵	Walts Wharf	LB	5 110	1	1	1¹½	1¹	1½	3hd	6	Krone J A	9.80

OFF AT 3:38 Start Good. Won driving. Course good.

TIME :23⁴, :47², 1:11⁴, 1:23⁴, 1:35⁴ (:23.84, :47.42, 1:11.84, 1:23.87, 1:35.99)

$2 Mutuel Prices:

4–FINAL DESTINATION–NZ	5.80	3.00	2.60
6–GARDEN IN THE RAIN–FR		2.40	2.20
5–EMBASSY BELLE–IR			2.80

$1 EXACTA 4–6 PAID $6.30 $2 QUINELLA 4–6 PAID $6.80 $1 TRIFECTA 4–6–5 PAID $14.60 $1 SUPERFECTA 4–6–5–8 PAID $71.80

Dk. b. or br. m, by O'Reilly*NZ–Logical Lady*NZ, by Sound Reason. Trainer Frankel Robert. Bred by Setchell P (NZ).

FINAL DESTINATION (NZ) saved ground stalking the pace, came out three deep into the stretch, gained the lead just past the eighth pole, inched away and held under urging. GARDEN IN THE RAIN (FR) stalked the pace outside the winner, swung four wide into the stretch and continued willingly to the wire. EMBASSY BELLE (IRE) saved ground chasing the pace, came out into the stretch and just got the show. REPOSITORY pulled her way along three deep early, stalked off the rail, bid outside the pacesetter leaving the second turn, took a short lead in upper stretch, could not match the top pair and just lost third. I'M THE BUSINESS (NZ) angled to the inside after a bit of a slow beginning, came out leaving the first turn, chased outside a rival, went three deep into the stretch and lacked the needed rally. WALTS WHARF sped to the early lead, set the pace along the inside, dueled from the rail on the second turn but weakened in the stretch.

Owners— 1, Gann Edmund A; 2, Englander Richard A; 3, Rooney June; 4, Rafter L Stables; 5, Doll Kadner Shapiro et al; 6, Henton Hitbound Stable & Turrell

Trainers—1, Frankel Robert; 2, Mullins Jeff; 3, Cecil B D A; 4, Lukas D Wayne; 5, Stein Roger M; 6, Cardenas Ruben

Scratched— Rhiana (16Feb03 6SA³), Sea Of Showers (17Jan03 7SA¹), Sentimental Value (18Dec02 7HOL³)

$2 Daily Double (2–4) Paid $67.60; Daily Double Pool $24,251.
$1 Pick Three (5–2–4) Paid $105.40; Pick Three Pool $78,892.

NINTH RACE
Gulfstream
FEBRUARY 21, 2003

1⅛ MILES. (Turf) PALM BEACH S. Grade III. Purse $100,000 FOR THREE YEAR OLDS. By subscription of $100 each, which shall accompany the nomination, $1,000 to pass the entry box and $1,000 additional to start, with $100,000 guaranteed. Weight: 122 lbs. Non-winners of $50,000 at a mile or over on the turf, allowed,2 lbs.; $40,000 at any distance or $30,000 at a mile or over, 4 lbs.; $24,000 at any distance or $18,000 at a mile or over, 6 lbs. This race will be limited to 12 Starters, with Also Eligibles. (High Weights Prferred) (Total lifetime earnings will be used to determine the order of preference of horses with equal weight.) In the event this stake is taken off the turf, it may be subject to downgrading upon review by the Graded Stakes Committee. Closed February 12, 2003 with 31 Nominations. (Rail at 0 Feet).

Value of Race: $100,000 Winner $60,000; second $20,000; third $11,000; fourth $6,000; fifth $3,000. Mutuel Pool $500,738.00 Exacta Pool $429,017.00 Trifecta Pool $362,118.00 Superfecta Pool $122,381.00

Last Raced	Horse	M/Eqt.	A.	Wt	PP	St	¼	½	¾	Str	Fin	Jockey	Odds $1
1Jan03 ^{10}Crc^{1}	Nothing to Lose	L b	3	122	10	11	10^{1}	$10\frac{1}{2}$	8^{1}	6^{hd}	$1\frac{1}{2}$	Bailey J D	1.60
26Jan03 ^{9}GP^{2}	White Cat	L b	3	118	5	6	7^{hd}	4^{1}	3^{1}	$1\frac{1}{2}$	$2\frac{1}{2}$	Prado E S	5.60
30Nov02 ^{6}Hol^{5}	Imitation	L	3	118	4	2	8^{2}	$7^{1\frac{1}{2}}$	6^{1}	3^{hd}	$3\frac{3}{4}$	Santos J A	6.00
26Jan03 ^{9}GP^{7}	Unbridels King	L b	3	116	1	10	11^{2}	9^{hd}	11^{2}	9^{3}	$4^{1\frac{1}{2}}$	Coa E	21.80
26Jan03 ^{9}GP^{1}	Hypnotist	L bf	3	120	3	1	9^{1}	8^{hd}	$9^{1\frac{1}{2}}$	$7\frac{1}{2}$	5^{2}	Velasquez C H	8.80
26Jan03 ^{9}GP^{3}	Private Gold	L b	3	120	7	3	2^{hd}	1^{hd}	$2\frac{1}{2}$	$2^{1\frac{1}{2}}$	6^{hd}	Day P	3.90
30Jan03 ^{9}GP^{1}	Purely Classic	L	3	118	6	5	3^{1}	3^{hd}	4^{hd}	$5^{1\frac{1}{2}}$	$7\frac{3}{4}$	Velazquez J R	12.40
26Jan03 ^{9}GP^{5}	Sea Pleasure	L b	3	118	2	7	4^{hd}	6^{hd}	7^{hd}	8^{2}	$8^{2\frac{1}{4}}$	Cruz M R	74.00
30Jan03 ^{9}GP^{3}	Aventura Place		3	116	11	12	12	12	$10\frac{1}{2}$	10^{2}	$9\frac{1}{2}$	DeCarlo C P	58.20
26Jan03 ^{9}GP^{9}	Millennium Storm	L b	3	122	8	4	1^{hd}	$2^{1\frac{1}{2}}$	1^{hd}	4^{hd}	$10^{2\frac{3}{4}}$	Guidry M	30.60
24Jan03 ^{7}GP^{2}	Title Contender	L b	3	120	9	8	5^{hd}	$5\frac{1}{2}$	$5\frac{1}{2}$	11^{6}	$11^{9\frac{3}{4}}$	Chavez J F	53.30
4Jan03 ^{4}Tam^{1}	Shining Rock	L	3	116	12	9	6^{hd}	11^{2}	12	12	12	Homeister R B Jr	126.60

OFF AT 4:54 Start Good. Won driving. Course firm.

TIME :23^{3}, :47^{2}, 1:11^{4}, 1:36^{1}, 1:48^{1} (:23.73, :47.57, 1:11.84, 1:36.20, 1:48.28)

$2 Mutuel Prices:

11 – NOTHING TO LOSE	5.20	3.40	2.80
5 – WHITE CAT		6.20	4.40
4 – IMITATION			5.00

$2 EXACTA 11–5 PAID $29.60 $2 TRIFECTA 11–5–4 PAID $156.60
$1 SUPERFECTA 11–5–4–1 PAID $717.00

B. c, (Jan), by Sky Classic – Cherlindrea , by Clever Trick . Trainer Lukas D Wayne. Bred by Kenneth L Ramsey & Sarah K Ramsey (Ky).

NOTHING TO LOSE unhurried early, raced three wide on the far turn, angled outside the leaders for the drive and rallied to be up in the final strides. WHITE CAT tracked the pace, rallied three wide on the far turn to take over in the stretch and continued on with good courage while unable to resist the winner late. IMITATION steadied in the early going, raced three wide on the far turn, angled out for the stretch run and finished willingly. UNBRIDELS KING outrun early, angled wide in early stretch and closed with a belated rally. HYPNOTIST steadied in the early going and again on the backstretch, moved into contention between horses in the stretch, then lacked the needed late response. PRIVATE GOLD vied for the lead along the hedge to midstretch, then gave way. PURELY CLASSIC well placed while saving ground into the stretch, weakened. SEA PLEASURE rated off the pace, was blocked leaving the far turn and into the stretch, checked and failed to threaten. AVENTURA PLACE failed to menace after being outrun early. MILLENNIUM STORM vied for the lead outside PRIVATE GOLD into the stretch and faltered. TITLE CONTENDER tracked the pace, raced four wide on the far turn and faltered. SHINING ROCK was through early.

Owners– 1, Ramsey Kenneth L and Sarah K; 2, Cottrell Raymond H Sr; 3, Calumet Farm; 4, Oxenberg Bea and Montanari Marion; 5, Dogwood Stable; 6, Mountain Top Racing and Lewis Beverly and Bob; 7, Khaled Saud b; 8, Lewis James R Jr; 9, Vegso Peter; 10, Barnett Gloria Proscia Nicholas and Ise R; 11, Team Canonie Stable and Hough Stanley M; 12, Fernung Brent

Trainers– 1, Lukas D Wayne; 2, McPeek Kenneth G; 3, Clement Christophe; 4, Plesa Edward Jr; 5, Tagg Barclay; 6, Byrne Patrick B; 7, Pletcher Todd A; 8, Tortora Emanuel; 9, Mott William I; 10, White William P; 11, Hough Stanley M; 12, O'Connell Kathleen

Scratched– One Colony (26Jan03 ^{9}GP ^{11})

$2 Pick Three (6–4–11) Paid $523.20 ; Pick Three Pool $37,936 .

ELEVENTH RACE
Gulfstream
FEBRUARY 22, 2003

1⅛ MILES. (1.46²) 45th Running of THE DONN HANDICAP. Grade I. Purse $500,000 Guaranteed. THREE YEAR OLDS AND UPWARD. By subscription of $500 each, will shall accompany the nomination, $3,000 to pass the entry box and $3,000 additional to start, with $500,000 guaranteed. The owner of the winner to receive $300,000, $95,000 to second, $50,000 to third, $30,000 to fourth, $15,000 to fifth and 10,000 to sixth. Closed Wednesday, February 19, 2003 with 20 Nominations. Trophy to winning Owner.

Value of Race: $500,000 Winner $300,000; second $95,000; third $50,000; fourth $30,000; fifth $15,000; sixth $10,000. Mutuel Pool $959,789.00 Exacta Pool $682,903.00 Trifecta Pool $554,652.00 Superfecta Pool $172,523.00

Last Raced	Horse	M/Eqt.	A.	Wt	PP	St	¼	½	¾	Str	Fin	Jockey	Odds $1
2Feb03 ^{4}GP^{1}	Harlan's Holiday	L	4	120	11	6	$5^{1\frac{1}{2}}$	$4^{\frac{1}{2}}$	3^{1}	$1^{\frac{1}{2}}$	$1^{2\frac{1}{2}}$	Velazquez J R	2.20
11Jan03 ^{10}GP^{4}	Hero's Tribute	L	5	114	2	3	2^{hd}	2^{1}	$2^{1\frac{1}{2}}$	2^{hd}	$2^{1\frac{1}{2}}$	Prado F S	4.10
25Jan03 ^{10}GP^{2}	Puzzlement	Lb	4	114	8	11	11	10^{hd}	10^{1}	$5^{2\frac{1}{2}}$	3^{nk}	Velasquez C	18.80
10Jan03 ^{9}GP^{1}	Keats	L	5	111	3	2	1^{3}	1^{3}	1^{hd}	$3^{3\frac{1}{2}}$	$4^{\frac{1}{2}}$	Chavez J F	10.90
25Jan03 ^{10}GP^{1}	Blue Burner	Lb	4	114	6	9	$10^{1\frac{1}{2}}$	11	11	$8^{\frac{1}{2}}$	5^{1}	Bailey J D	8.50
11Jan03 ^{10}GP^{1}	Windsor Castle	L	5	116	4	4	9^{2}	$9^{2\frac{1}{2}}$	7^{hd}	6^{hd}	$6^{\frac{1}{2}}$	Coa E M	4.70
25Jan03 ^{7}GP^{5}	Free Of Love	Lb	5	113	7	7	4^{hd}	$5^{1\frac{1}{2}}$	$4^{1\frac{1}{2}}$	4^{hd}	$7^{4\frac{1}{4}}$	Day P	32.70
2Feb03 ^{4}GP^{3}	Mr. John	Lb	5	114	1	1	3^{1}	3^{hd}	6^{3}	$7^{1\frac{1}{2}}$	$8^{2\frac{1}{2}}$	Guidry M	11.00
2Feb03 ^{4}GP^{2}	Bonus Pack	Lb	5	115	10	10	6^{hd}	6^{2}	5^{1}	$9^{2\frac{1}{2}}$	9^{4}	Fires E	12.50
11Jan03 ^{10}GP^{2}	Saint Verre	L	5	114	5	5	$7^{\frac{1}{2}}$	$7^{1\frac{1}{2}}$	$8^{1\frac{1}{2}}$	11	$10^{\frac{1}{2}}$	Santos J A	14.40
2Feb03 ^{4}GP^{4}	Request For Parole	L	4	115	9	8	8^{1}	8^{2}	9^{hd}	10^{2}	11	Cruz M R	69.60

OFF AT 5:41 Start Good. Won driving. Track fast.

TIME $:23^{2}$, $:46^{3}$, $1:10^{2}$, $1:35^{3}$, 1:49 (:23.46, :46.61, 1:10.59, 1:35.77, 1:49.17)

$2 Mutuel Prices:			
11–HARLAN'S HOLIDAY	6.40	4.00	3.20
2–HERO'S TRIBUTE		4.20	3.40
8–PUZZLEMENT			6.40

$2 EXACTA 11–2 PAID $35.00 $2 TRIFECTA 11–2–8 PAID $427.00 $1 SUPERFECTA 11–2–8–3 PAID $1,990.60

B. c, by Harlan–Christmas in Aiken, by Affirmed. Trainer Pletcher Todd A. Bred by Double D Farm Corp (Ohio).

HARLAN'S HOLIDAY hustled from the gate to get position, tracked the leaders three wide, rallied to gain command in early stretch and drew clear under steady pressure. HERO'S TRIBUTE hit the gate at the start, stalked the pace off the rail, rallied to gain a brief lead leaving the far turn, then continued on with good courage to prove second best while unable to match strides with the winner in the final eighth. PUZZLEMENT outrun after breaking slowly, saved ground while advancing into the stretch, eased out and closed to be up for the show. KEATS sprinted to a clear lead along the inside, made the pace to nearing the stretch, then weakened in the drive. BLUE BURNER unhurried after being steadied outside SAINT VERRE at the start, angled wide in the stretch run and closed with a belated rally. WINDSOR CASTLE steadied when caught in tight inside SAINT VERRE racing into the first turn, hit the rail soon after, swung out for the stretch run and failed to rally. FREE OF LOVE raced in striking position into the stretch and tired. MR. JOHN chased the pace along the inside to the far turn and faltered. BONUS PACK rated off the pace while racing four wide, had no response when asked leaving the far turn. SAINT VERRE rank when taken in hand after the start, steadied and put WINDSOR CASTLE in tight entering the first turn, then was not a factor. REQUEST FOR PAROLE raced four wide on the far turn while being outrun.

Owners— 1, Starlight Stable; 2, Oxley John C; 3, Shields Joseph V Jr; 4, Pabst Henry E; 5, Kinsman Stable; 6, Dogwood Stable; 7, Aprilante Anthony J & Evans Ralph M; 8, Van Meter II Thomas M & Lowenbaum M; 9, Glen Hill Farm; 10, Allen Joseph; 11, Knighton Jeri & Sam

Trainers—1, Pletcher Todd A; 2, Ward John T Jr; 3, Jerkens H Allen; 4, O'Callaghan Niall M; 5, Mott William I; 6, Alexander Frank A; 7, Violette Richard A Jr; 8, Walden W Elliott; 9, Proctor Thomas F; 10, Jerkens H Allen; 11, Hough Stanley M

$2 Pick Three (5–5–11) Paid $613.00; Pick Three Pool $76,252.

TENTH RACE
Laurel
FEBRUARY 22, 2003

7 FURLONGS. (1.21²) BARBARA FRITCHIE H. Grade II. Purse $200,000 A HANDICAP FOR FILLIES AND MARES, THREE-YEARS-OLD AND UPWARD. By free subscription. $1500 to pass the entry box. $1500 additional to start with $200,000 Guaranteed, of which 60% to the winner, 20% to second, 11% to third, 6% to fourth, and 3% to fifth. Supplemental nominations of $2000 each will be accepted by Saturday, February 8, 2003 with all other fees due as noted. Weights Sunday, February 9, 2003. Field will be limited to fourteen starters with preference to high weights on the scale. Starters to benamed through the entry box by the usual time of closing. Closed Wednesday, January 29, 2003 with 21 nominations.

Value of Race: $200,000 Winner $120,000; second $40,000; third $22,000; fourth $12,000; fifth $6,000. Mutuel Pool $397,123.00 Exacta Pool $281,079.00 Trifecta Pool $219,792.00

Last Raced	Horse	M/Eqt.	A.	Wt	PP	St	¼	½	Str	Fin	Jockey	Odds $1
18Jan03 ^{8}Lrl^{1}	Xtra Heat	L	5	125	3	*	*	*	*	$1^{1\frac{3}{4}}$	Wilson R	1.00
26Oct02 ^{6}AP^{13}	Carson Hollow	L f	4	119	2	*	*	*	*	$2^{1\frac{1}{4}}$	Desormeaux K J	1.90
18Dec02 ^{8}Lrl^{1}	Spelling	L bf	4	113	7	*	*	*	*	3^{hd}	Santana J Z	9.80
11Jan03 ^{8}Aqu^{1}	Zonk	L f	5	117	5	*	*	*	*	$4^{\frac{1}{2}}$	Elliott S	3.10
25Jan03 ^{6}GP^{4}	Fly Me Crazy	L b	5	114	4	*	*	*	*	$5^{1\frac{1}{4}}$	Rose J	24.00
25Jan03 ^{8}Lrl^{3}	Pass the Virtue	L f	4	115	6	*	*	*	*	$6^{22\frac{1}{2}}$	Delgado A	54.40
21Dec02 ^{7}Crc^{7}	Heyahohowdy	L bf	4	116	1	*	*	*	*	7	Potts C L	98.50

OFF AT 4:48 Start Good . Won driving. Track sloppy.

TIME $:22^{4}$, $:45^{2}$, $1:10^{3}$, $1:24^{3}$ (:22.97, :45.57, 1:10.61, 1:24.76)

$2 Mutuel Prices:			
3 – XTRA HEAT	4.00	2.60	2.10
2 – CARSON HOLLOW		3.00	2.10
8 – SPELLING			2.10

$2 EXACTA 3–2 PAID $12.20 $2 TRIFECTA 3–2–8 PAID $37.00

B. m, (Mar), by Dixieland Heat – Begin , by Hatchet Man . Trainer Salzman John E. Bred by P McLean Sr P McLean Jr M McLean &P Feringa Jr et al (Ky).

XTRA HEAT prompted the pace outside of CARSON HOLLOW down the backstretch, surged to a clear lead approaching the three furlong marker, widened her advantage in upper stretch then held sway under a drive. CARSON HOLLOW sped to the early lead along the rail, was overtaken into the far turn, chased the winner around the turn then battled back gamely along the inside to be clear for the place. SPELLING raced off the rail and finished willingly between rivals. ZONK chased the pace four wide on the turn then flattened out late. FLY ME CRAZY came five wide for the drive and had a belated gain. PASS THE VIRTUE raced very wide in the stretch and failed to threaten. HEYAHOHOWDY chased the pace for a half mile while saving ground then retreated. Points of call omitted due to dense fog.

Owners– 1, Classic Star Stable LLC; 2, Stronach Stables and Hemlock Hills Farm; 3, Augustin Stable; 4, Fox Hill Farms Inc; 5, Gill Michael J; 6, Christiansen Susan L; 7, S V G B Stable

Trainers– 1, Salzman John E Sr; 2, Dutrow Richard E Jr; 3, Campitelli Francis P; 4, Servis John C; 5, Shuman Mark; 6, Glazier Leslie G; 7, Pizzurro Peter

Scratched– Saskya (01Feb03 ^{8}Aqu^{4})

$2 Pick Three (2/7–4–3/5) Paid $43.60 ; Pick Three Pool $24,723 .

NINTH RACE
Laurel
FEBRUARY 22, 2003

7 FURLONGS. (1.21^{2}) GENERAL GEORGE H. Grade II. Purse $200,000 A HANDICAP FOR THREE-YEAR-OLDS AND UPWARD. By free subscription. $1500 to pass the entry box. $1500 additional to start. Supplemental nominations of $2000 each will be accepted by Saturday, February 8, 2003 with all other fees due as noted. Weights Sunday, February 9, 2003. Field will be limited to fourteen starters with preference to high weights on the scale. Starters to be named through the entry box by the usual time of closing. Closed Wednesday, January 29, 2003 with 38 nominations.

Value of Race: $200,000 Winner $120,000; second $40,000; third $22,000; fourth $12,000; fifth $6,000. Mutuel Pool $377,956.00 Exacta Pool $306,533.00 Superfecta Pool $52,679.00 Trifecta Pool $216,862.00

Last Raced	Horse	M/Eqt.	A.	Wt	PP	St	¼	½	Str	Fin	Jockey	Odds $1
26Dec02 ^{8}SA^{6}	My Cousin Matt	L f	4	113	4	*	5^{1}	4^{hd}	1^{hd}	1^{3}	Dominguez R A	4.00
9Feb03 ^{8}Aqu^{1}	Peeping Tom	L bf	6	114	1	*	$3^{\frac{1}{2}}$	3^{2}	2^{hd}	$2^{1\frac{1}{4}}$	Pino M G	7.00
26Jan03 ^{7}SA^{3}	Disturbingthepeace	L b	5	118	7	*	$2^{1\frac{1}{2}}$	1^{hd}	3^{4}	3^{nk}	Fogelsonger R	3.80
11Jan03 ^{6}Aqu^{1}	American Century	L b	5	111	6	*	8^{2}	7^{1}	4^{hd}	$4^{1\frac{3}{4}}$	Rose J	23.60
19Jan03 ^{8}Aqu^{2}	Resolve	L bf	5	113	3	*	6^{1}	5^{1}	5^{1}	$5^{\frac{1}{2}}$	Luzzi M J	5.20
20Jan03 ^{8}Lrl^{2}	Griffinite	L b	5	113	10	*	$10^{2\frac{1}{2}}$	9^{2}	7^{1}	6^{2}	Vega H	21.90
20Jan03 ^{8}Lrl^{1}	Shake the Dice	L b	5	116	11	*	7^{hd}	8^{2}	8^{3}	$7^{2\frac{3}{4}}$	Potts C L	8.70
28Dec02 ^{8}Lrl^{5}	Deer Run	L bf	6	114	8	*	9^{hd}	10^{1}	9^{hd}	$8^{1\frac{1}{4}}$	Acosta J D	32.30
26Jan03 ^{7}SA^{4}	D'wildcat	L b	5	118	5	*	1^{1}	$2^{1\frac{1}{2}}$	$6^{1\frac{1}{2}}$	9^{2}	Desormeaux K J	2.70
16Jan03 ^{6}Lrl^{5}	Stormin Oedy	L	6	113	9	*	11	11	10^{3}	$10^{7\frac{1}{4}}$	Petro N J	136.80
22Jan03 ^{9}GP^{3}	Dream Run	L	5	116	2	*	$4^{\frac{1}{2}}$	$6^{\frac{1}{2}}$	11	11	Johnston M T	26.10

OFF AT 4:22 Start Good. Won driving. Track sloppy.

TIME :22^{2}, :46^{1}, 1:09^{3}, 1:22 (:22.50, :46.34, 1:09.79, 1:22.12)

$2 Mutuel Prices:				
	4 – MY COUSIN MATT	10.00	5.60	4.40
	1 – PEEPING TOM		7.60	5.60
	7 – DISTURBINGTHEPEACE			3.80

$2 EXACTA 4–1 PAID $66.80 $1 SUPERFECTA 4–1–7–6 PAID $3,911.40
$2 TRIFECTA 4–1–7 PAID $311.60

Dk. b or br. g, (Jan), by Matty G – Conquistamiss, by Conquistador Cielo. Trainer Lake Scott A. Bred by Donald Marino (Fla).

MY COUSIN MATT, forwardly placed off the rail, rallied strongly four wide into the lane, surged to command in mid stretch and drew clear under a drive. PEEPING TOM, well placed off of a disputed pace, lodged a three wide bid leaving the three furlong marker, dueled into the stretch, finished gamely but was no match. DISTURBINGTHEPEACE lodged a two wide bid into the turn, dueled outside of D'WILDCAT leaving the three eighths pole, was joined by PEEPING TOM soon after, continued a presence to mid stretch then faded in the final sixteenth of a mile. AMERICAN CENTURY settled off the pace and off the rail, continued wide for the drive and finished with interest. RESOLVE saved ground most of the trip and went evenly. GRIFFINITE, sluggish early towards the inside, passed tiring rivals. SHAKE THE DICE raced wide and failed to threaten. DEER RUN was outrun. D'WILDCAT broke alertly, set the pace along the inside, was joined by DISTURBUINGTHEPEACE nearing the turn, dueled inside of that one past the three furlong marker then gave way entering the stretch. STORMIN OEDY was never a factor. DREAM RUN raced within range towards the inside for a half mile then dropped back. The start call was omitted due to foggy conditions.

Owners– 1, Englander Richard A; 2, Flatbird Stable; 3, Milch David S and Rita and Herrick Racing; 4, Peachtree Stable; 5, Valente Roddy Abbruzzese Jared and Baron Robert J; 6, Paraneck Stable; 7, Cole Robert L Jr; 8, Harris William R; 9, Fog City Stables and Windfields Farm; 10, Cunningham Timothy; 11, Murphy John D Sr

Trainers– 1, Lake Scott A; 2, Reynolds Patrick L; 3, Vienna Darrell; 4, Klesaris Steve B; 5, Levine Bruce N; 6, Preciado Guadalupe; 7, Lake Scott A; 8, Grove Christopher W; 9, Hess Robert B Jr; 10, Petro Michael P; 11, McGee Paul J

Scratched– Kela (04Jan03 ^{8}SA ^{7})

NINTH RACE
Oaklawn
FEBRUARY 22, 2003

$1\frac{1}{16}$ MILES. (1.40^{1}) ESSEX H. Grade III. Purse $100,000 FOUR-YEAR-OLDS AND UPWARD. Weights to be announced Sunday, February 16. In Handicap Stakes starting preference will be given to highweights. Starters to be named through the entry box by the usual time of closing. The owner of the winner to receive a trophy. Nominations closed Friday, February 14, 2003 with 24 nominees.

Value of Race: $100,000 Winner $60,000; second $20,000; third $10,000; fourth $6,000; fifth $4,000. Mutuel Pool $260,668.00 Exacta Pool $200,188.00 Trifecta Pool $203,092.00

Last Raced	Horse	M/Eqt.	A.	Wt	PP	St	¼	½	¾	Str	Fin	Jockey	Odds $1
1Feb03 ^{5}OP^{1}	Colorful Tour	L	4	116	3	4	2^{1}	2^{hd}	$5^{1\frac{1}{2}}$	3^{2}	$1^{1\frac{1}{2}}$	Quinonez L S	5.10
18Jan03 ^{8}Hou^{3}	Ask the Lord	L f	6	118	8	6	$8^{3\frac{1}{2}}$	8^{6}	$4^{\frac{1}{2}}$	1^{hd}	2no	Theriot J	8.20
1Feb03 ^{7}TuP^{7}	Premeditation	L	4	117	10	5	6^{hd}	5^{2}	$1^{\frac{1}{2}}$	2^{hd}	$3^{1\frac{3}{4}}$	Bourque C C	12.50
8Feb03 ^{1}OP^{1}	Crafty Shaw	L	5	120	2	9	7^{1}	6^{hd}	8^{2}	4^{hd}	$4^{2\frac{1}{2}}$	Lopez J	0.60
5Feb03 ^{8}OP^{5}	Makors Mark	L	6	114	1	1	$1^{1\frac{1}{2}}$	$1^{1\frac{1}{2}}$	3^{hd}	6^{2}	$5^{\frac{1}{2}}$	Kuntzweiler G	27.80
11Jan03 ^{10}Sun^{3}	Big Numbers	L b	6	115	7	2	5^{hd}	$7^{1\frac{1}{2}}$	6^{1}	5^{1}	6^{1}	Court J K	13.40
8Feb03 ^{1}OP^{2}	Dust On the Bottle	L b	8	115	5	8	$9^{4\frac{1}{2}}$	$9^{4\frac{1}{2}}$	9^{5}	9^{2}	$7^{1\frac{1}{2}}$	Castellano A Jr	21.30
28Nov02 ^{8}CD^{1}	Bright Sea	L	4	115	6	7	$3^{\frac{1}{2}}$	4^{hd}	$7^{1\frac{1}{2}}$	8^{hd}	8^{nk}	Murphy G	29.70
15Feb03 ^{7}Hou^{11}	Maysville Slew	L f	7	115	4	10	10	10	10	10	$9^{1\frac{3}{4}}$	Thompson T J	14.60
18Jan03 ^{8}Hou^{10}	Rare Cure	L b	5	117	9	3	$4^{1\frac{1}{2}}$	$3^{1\frac{1}{2}}$	2^{1}	7^{2}	10	Lovato A J	55.40

OFF AT 4:59 Start Good. Won driving. Track muddy.

TIME :23^{3}, :47^{4}, 1:13^{4}, 1:40^{1}, 1:46^{3} (:23.64, :47.87, 1:13.90, 1:40.26, 1:46.62)

$2 Mutuel Prices:				
	3 – COLORFUL TOUR	12.20	5.20	5.40
	8 – ASK THE LORD		8.20	4.80
	10 – PREMEDITATION			7.20

$2 EXACTA 3–8 PAID $104.20 $2 TRIFECTA 3–8–10 PAID $1,154.20

Ch. h, (Feb), by Tour d'Or – For You and Me, by For Love and Glory. Trainer Hickey P Noel. Bred by Irish Acres Farm (Ill).

COLORFUL TOUR closest to the early leader, lost position into the far turn, continued under patient handling into the stretch, set down a furlong out, burst clear to finished willingly. ASK THE LORD unhurried early, advanced into a forward position four wide in the second turn, showed the way past the furlong marker, dug in for the place while unable to match the winner late. PREMEDITATION settled off the pace, ranged up three wide to take the advantage, outfinished for the place. CRAFTY SHAW off bit slow, took up along the rail into the first turn, settled inside, moved out five wide turning for home, left with too much to do. MAKORS MARK broke on top, clear for a half, weakened when displaced in the second turn. BIG NUMBERS went evenly in lacking a late bid. DUST ON THE BOTTLE lacked speed, managed only a small rally. BRIGHT SEA forwardly placed for a half, weakened. MAYSVILLE SLEW last away, showed little. RARE CURE pressed the pace for six furlongs, gave way.

Owners– 1, Irish Acres Farm; 2, Gaffney Peter and Madison Stewart M; 3, Clifton William L Jr; 4, Cella Charles J; 5, McMurry L L; 6, Cassels James and Zollars Bob; 7, Hild Sharon L; 8, Spence James C; 9, Trout C R; 10, Dyson Larry

Trainers– 1, Hickey P Noel; 2, Stall Albert M Jr; 3, Leach William F; 4, Vestal Peter M; 5, Forster Grant T; 6, Asmussen Steven M; 7, Hild Glenn L; 8, Nicks Morris G; 9, Trout C R; 10, Petalino Joseph

---

$2 Pick Three (5–1–3) Paid $361.60 ; Pick Three Pool $19,919.

EIGHTH RACE
Santa Anita
FEBRUARY 22, 2003

6 FURLONGS. (1.07¹) 51st Running of THE LAS FLORES HANDICAP. Grade III. Purse $125,000 added. FILLIES AND MARES FOUR YEARS OLD AND UPWARD. By subscription of $125 each to accompany the nomination or by supplementary nomination of $2,500 by Sunday, February 16 and $1,250 additional to start, with $125,000 added. The added money and all fees to be divided 60% to first, 20% to second, 12% to third, 6% to fourth and 2% to fifth. Closed Thursday, February 13 with 14 nominations.

Value of Race: $135,500 Winner $81,300; second $27,100; third $12,195 each; fifth $2,710. Mutuel Pool $626,707.00 Exacta Pool $392,264.00 Quinella Pool $42,041.00 Trifecta Pool $411,173.00

Last Raced	Horse	M/Eqt.	A.Wt	PP	St	1/4	1/2	Str	Fin	Jockey	Odds $1
28Dec02 7SA2	Spring Meadow	LB	4 117	5	1	4½	4½	3hd	1nk	Nakatani C S	2.60
29Jan03 7SA3	Brisquette	LB	5 116	6	6	7	6½	5½	21½	Solis A	7.10
18May02 3Hol1	DH September Secret	LB	4 116	1	7	2hd	2hd	11	3	Valenzuela P A	4.80
8Dec02 8Hol3	DH Wild Tickle	LB	5 117	4	4	62½	7	61	3½	Pincay L Jr	24.90
16Jan03 5SA1	Mon Ange	LB	5 116	2	5	5hd	52½	42½	55	Flores D R	2.80
14Jly02 9Hol2	Secret Liaison	LB	5 117	7	3	31	1hd	2hd	63	Smith M E	3.40
25Jan03 6GP2	Shameful	LB	4 115	3	2	1hd	31½	7	7	Espinoza V	10.10

DH—Dead Heat.

OFF AT 4:11 Start Good. Won driving. Track fast.
TIME :21¹, :43⁴, :56², 1:10¹ (:21.25, :43.81, :56.57, 1:10.20)

$2 Mutuel Prices:

5-SPRING MEADOW	7.20	4.00	2.60
6-BRISQUETTE		6.20	3.60
1-DH SEPTEMBER SECRET			2.60
4-DH WILD TICKLE			3.40

$1 EXACTA 5–6 PAID $23.80 $2 QUINELLA 5–6 PAID $23.40 $1 TRIFECTA 5–6–1 PAID $56.90 $1 TRIFECTA 5–6–4 PAID $96.20

Ch. f, by Meadowlake–Go for It Lady, by Mr. Prospector. Trainer Hess R B Jr. Bred by John T L Jones Jr & Ashford Stud (Ky).

SPRING MEADOW stalked the pace between horses on the backstretch and outside a rival on the turn, came four wide into the stretch, rallied to the lead past midstretch, inched away in deep stretch and held gamely under urging. BRISQUETTE unhurried off the rail on the backstretch, went outside a foe on the turn, followed the winner's path into the stretch and closed willingly to just miss. SEPTEMBER SECRET broke in and bobbled at the start, went up inside to duel for the lead, came a bit off the rail into the stretch, inched away in midstretch, drifted inward nearing the sixteenth pole, could not match the top pair but held for a share of third. WILD TICKLE close up stalking between horses early, steadied when squeezed back past the half mile pole, angled in for the turn, angled out in the stretch and came back on late. MON ANGE bobbled at the start, stalked a bit off the rail, split rivals in upper stretch, angled inward, lacked room in tight off heels in deep stretch, came out and could not offer the needed late response. SECRET LIAISON stalked four wide early then bid three deep and dueled leaving the backstretch and on the turn and into the stretch but weakened in the final furlong. SHAMEFUL had good early speed and dueled outside a rival then between horses to the stretch and also weakened.

Owners— 1, Fog City Stable; 2, Sarkowsky & Wygod; 3, Lo Hi Stable; 4, Bell Richard A; 5, The Merv Griffin Ranch Co; 6, Desperado Stables; 7, Earnhardt III Hal J

Trainers—1, Hess R B Jr; 2, Mandella Richard; 3, Machowsky Michael; 4, Blincoe Thomas H; 5, Matlow Richard P; 6, West Ted H; 7, Baffert Bob

$2 Daily Double (8–5) Paid $83.80; Daily Double Pool $56,182.
$1 Pick Three (2/3–8–5) Paid $169.90; Pick Three Pool $77,496.

NINTH RACE
Gulfstream
FEBRUARY 23, 2003

1 1/16 MILES. (1.40¹) 16th Running of THE DAVONA DALE. Grade II. Purse $150,000. FILLIES, THREE YEARS OLD. By subscription of $100 each, which shall accompany the nomination, $1,500 to pass the entry box and $1,500 additional to start. Weight: 121 lbs. Non-winners of $50,000 once at a mile or over, allowed 2 lbs. $40,000 once at any distance or $30,000 at a mile or over, 4 lbs. $25,000 once at any distance or $20,000 at a mile or over, 6 lbs. Closed Wednesday February 12 with 15 nominations.

Value of Race: $150,000 Winner $90,000; second $30,000; third $16,500; fourth $9,000; fifth $4,500. Mutuel Pool $436,400.00 Exacta Pool $259,458.00 Trifecta Pool $132,233.00 Superfecta Pool $43,407.00

Last Raced	Horse	M/Eqt.	A.Wt	PP	St	1/4	1/2	3/4	Str	Fin	Jockey	Odds $1
16Jan03 9GP1	Yell	L	3 117	4	4	3hd	3hd	32½	11½	16	Velazquez J R	5.20
25Jan03 3SA2	Ivanavinalot	Lf	3 121	3	1	12	11½	1½	24	25¾	Cruz M R	1.90
3Feb03 9GP5	Gold Player	Lb	3 115	5	5	5	5	5	5	33	Bailey J D	13.10
5Feb03 8GP1	Perfect Story	L	3 117	1	2	21½	21½	21	32½	46¼	Prado E S	3.50
30Nov02 9CD1	My Boston Gal	L	3 121	2	3	42½	42	45	41	5	Borel C H	1.50

OFF AT 4:40 Start Good. Won driving. Track fast.
TIME :23, :47¹, 1:12, 1:38¹, 1:44⁴ (:23.13, :47.28, 1:12.08, 1:38.24, 1:44.96)

$2 Mutuel Prices:

5-YELL	12.40	4.40	2.40
4-IVANAVINALOT		3.00	2.10
6-GOLD PLAYER			2.40

$2 EXACTA 5–4 PAID $38.20 $2 TRIFECTA 5–4–6 PAID $266.20 $1 SUPERFECTA 5–4–6–2 PAID $250.40

Dk. b. or br. f, (Apr), by A.P. Indy–Wild Applause, by Northern Dancer. Trainer McGaughey Claude III. Bred by Claiborne Farm & Mrs Adele Dilschneider (Ky).

YELL stalked the pace three wide, rallied to catch IVANAVINALOT at the top of the stretch, then drew off under pressure. IVANAVINALOT quickly moved to the fore, made the pace along the inside to the top of the stretch, then couldn't stay with winner while clearly second best. GOLD PLAYER outrun early, angled out for the stretch run and passed tired rivals for the show. PERFECT STORY chased the pace off the rail, made a run at the leader midway of the far turn, then faltered. MY BOSTON GAL saved ground and faded.

Owners— 1, Claiborne Farm & Dilschneider Adele; 2, Campbell Gilbert G; 3, Evans Edward P; 4, Oxley John C; 5, C Porter R Bloch & P Milner

Trainers—1, McGaughey Claude III; 2, O'Connell Kathleen; 3, Hennig Mark; 4, Ward John T Jr; 5, Nafzger Carl A

Scratched— Smokey Blue (24Jan03 1SA1)

$2 Pick Three (1–2–5) Paid $46.80; Pick Three Pool $49,675.

EIGHTH RACE

Santa Anita

FEBRUARY 23, 2003

ABOUT 6½ FURLONGS. (Turf)(1.11²) 36th Running of THE BALDWIN. Grade III. Purse $100,000 added. THREE–YEAR–OLDS. By subscription of $100 each to accompany the nomination or by supplementary nomination of $2,000 by time of entry. $250 to pass the entry box and $750 additional to start. Weight, 122 lbs. Non–winners of a race of $60,000, allowed 3 lbs. Of a race of $40,000 since December 25, 5 lbs. Of a race other than maiden or claiming since then or $25,000 at any time, 8 lbs. (Maiden and claiming races not considered). Closed Thursday, February 13 with 33 nominations. (Rail at 0 feet hill, 8 Feet stretch).

Value of Race: $114,550 Winner $68,730; second $22,910; third $13,746; fourth $6,873; fifth $2,291. Mutuel Pool $550,755.00 Exacta Pool $306,393.00 Quinella Pool $33,991.00 Trifecta Pool $319,872.00 Superfecta Pool $122,254.00

Last Raced	Horse	M/Eqt.	A.Wt	PP	St	¼	½	Str	Fin	Jockey	Odds $1
11Jan03 8GG7	Buddy Gil	LB	3 117	8	2	5¹	5hd	2hd	1²	Stevens G L	26.70
23Jan03 7SA1	King Robyn	LBb	3 116	4	4	1hd	1¹	12½	2⁴	Solis A	9.30
9Feb03 6SA1	Flirt With Fortune	LB	3 116	2	11	1¹	9hd	7½	3¹	Nakatani C S	5.10
24Jan03 7SA1	Apalachian Thunder	LBb	3 117	5	8	4½	3hd	3²	4hd	Espinoza V	2.60
21Dec02 8Hol5	Roll Hennessy Roll	LBb	3 122	10	10	10³½	10hd	9³	5no	Baze T C	4.20
12Jan03 7SA3	Jimmy O	LBb	3 117	6	6	6hd	7hd	8½	6²	Smith M E	24.10
2Nov02 3SA2	Excessive Barb	LB	3 117	7	1	3½	4½	4½	7¹	Desormeaux K J	14.70
30Jan03 2GG1	Zayed	LBb	3 117	9	3	9⁴	6²½	6¹	8⁴	Pincay L Jr	7.70
12Jan03 7SA2	Only The Best	LB	3 122	3	7	2¹½	2hd	5hd	9³	Valenzuela P A	6.50
23Jan03 7SA6	Echeverria	LBb	3 114	1	9	7½	11	11	10no	Krone J A	52.70
12Oct02 Yor5	Love Is Blind–IR	LB	3 114	11	5	8¹	8³	10¹	11	Pedroza M A	16.80

OFF AT 4:09 Start Good. Won driving. Course firm.
TIME :21⁴, :43², 1:06², 1:12³ (:21.83, :43.51, 1:06.55, 1:12.56)

$2 Mutuel Prices:

9–BUDDY GIL	55.40	22.80	12.40
5–KING ROBYN		11.00	7.40
3–FLIRT WITH FORTUNE			4.80

$1 EXACTA 9–5 PAID $239.50 $2 QUINELLA 5–9 PAID $224.20 $1 TRIFECTA 9–5–3 PAID $2,201.00 $1 SUPERFECTA 9–5–3–6 PAID $32,527.70

B. g, (Feb), by Eastern Echo–Really Rising, by For Really. Trainer Mullins Jeff. Bred by Billingsley Creek Ranch (Ky).

BUDDY GIL chased three deep early then outside a rival, came out five wide into the stretch and rallied while drifting in under some urging to collar the leader in deep stretch and pulled clear. KING ROBYN had good early speed and dueled outside a rival, inched away on the hill, kicked clear into the stretch but could not hold off the winner. FLIRT WITH FORTUNE steadied when bumped and shut off at the start, settled off the rail then angled in down the hill, split rivals in the stretch and gained the show late. APALACHIAN THUNDER stalked toward the inside then between horses down the hill, continued a bit off the rail in the stretch and lost third late. ROLL HENNESSY ROLL stumbled then took up just after the start, settled off the rail, came five wide into the stretch and improved position. JIMMY O pulled his way toward horses then outside a rival, continued off the rail leaving the hill, came out into the stretch and lacked the needed rally. EXCESSIVE BARB had good early speed then stalked three wide or outside a rival, came four wide into the stretch and weakened. ZAYED chased between horses then angled in on the hill, came out in the stretch and lacked the needed response. ONLY THE BEST broke in onto a rival, dueled inside then stalked along the rail and weakened in the stretch. ECHEVERRIA saved ground chasing the pace, dropped back on the hill, came out into the stretch and had little left. LOVE IS BLIND (IRE) was in a good striking position chasing four wide down the hill, dropped back into the stretch and weakened.

Owners— 1, Desperado Stbs Inc Mcfadden Merrill; 2, Cornejo Racing Inc; 3, Chapman Carolyn M; 4, Dizney Donald R; 5, Fulton Stan E; 6, Anderson Anderson & Meadowbrook Far; 7, Brown Rubin; 8, Leung Moore & Ward; 9, Toffel Mr & Mrs Alvin E; 10, Bienstock Parks Winner et al; 11, Jim Ford Inc & Pearson

Trainers— 1, Mullins Jeff; 2, Mullins Jeff; 3, Chapman James K; 4, Baffert Bob; 5, Becerra Rafael; 6, La Croix David; 7, Lewis Craig A; 8, Ward Wesley A; 9, Lynch Brian A; 10, Gallagher Patrick; 11, Cassidy James

Scratched— Sailinwithcaptain (26Dec02 5SA5), Bossanova (12Jan03 7SA5), Steelaninch (26Oct02 DNR5)

$2 Daily Double (10–9) Paid $483.80; Daily Double Pool $56,694.
$1 Pick Three (6–10–9) Paid $1,847.40; Pick Three Pool $87,950.

TENTH RACE

Gulfstream

MARCH 1, 2003

1⅛ MILES. (1.46²) 24th Running of THE RAMPART HANDICAP. Grade II. Purse $200,000. FILLIES AND MARES, THREE YEARS OLD AND UPWARD. By subscription of $200 each, which shall accompany the nomination, $2,000 to pass the entry box and $2,000 additional to start, with $200,000 guaranteed. The owner of the winner to recieve $120,000, $40,000 to second, $22,000 to third, $12,000 to fourth and $6,000 to fifth. Trophy to winning Owner. Closed Wednesday, February 19 with 14 nominations.

Value of Race: $200,000 Winner $120,000; second $40,000; third $22,000; fourth $12,000; fifth $6,000. Mutuel Pool $816,895.00 Exacta Pool $302,495.00 Trifecta Pool $277,125.00 Superfecta Pool $104,041.00

Last Raced	Horse	M/Eqt. A.Wt	PP	St	¼	½	¾	Str	Fin	Jockey	Odds $1
8Feb03 10GP1	Allamerican Bertie	L	4 122	6	1	1²	11½	12½	14½	17¾	Velazquez J R	0.40
25Jan03 5SA1	Smok'n Frolic	L	4 118	4	3	2½	21½	2½	2³	26¼	Santos J A	2.80
8Feb03 10GP6	Softly	Lb	5 115	1	2	31½	31½	3³	32½	33¼	Coa E M	7.50
8Feb03 10GP4	Tuff Chick	L	5 113	3	6	6	6	5²	53½	4½	Nunez E O	36.90
8Feb03 10GP3	Redoubled Miss	Lbf	4 113	5	4	4¹	4²	4¹	4½	56½	Velasquez C	22.40
29Jun02 10Mth4	Southern Fiction	Lb	5 113	2	5	5¹	5¹	6	6	6	Douglas R R	42.80

OFF AT 5:14 Start Good. Won driving. Track fast.

TIME :23⁴, :47¹, 1:10², 1:35¹, 1:47⁴ (:23.85, :47.26, 1:10.59, 1:35.21, 1:47.92)

$2 Mutuel Prices:

6–ALLAMERICAN BERTIE	2.80	2.10	2.10
4–SMOK'N FROLIC		2.20	2.10
1–SOFTLY			2.10

$1 EXACTA 6–4 PAID $3.00 $1 TRIFECTA 6–4–1 PAID $5.80 $1 SUPERFECTA 6–4–1–3 PAID $18.10

B. f, by Quiet American–Clever Bertie, by Timeless Native. Trainer Flint Steve. Bred by Bert Klein (Ky).

ALLAMERICAN BERTIE quickly sprinted to a clear lead, was well handled while making the pace into the stretch, then drew off under a strong hand ride. SMOK'N FROLIC chased the winner off the rail into the stretch but was no match for the winner while clearly second best. SOFTLY tracked the leaders along the inside into the stretch and tired. TUFF CHICK saved ground and failed to be a factor. REDOUBLED MISS allowed to settle, raced in striking position off the rail into the far turn and faltered. SOUTHERN FICTION showed little.

Owners— 1, Klein Richard Bertram & Elaine; 2, Dogwood Stable; 3, Tafel James B; 4, C Allard; 5, Centaur Farms Inc; 6, Humphrey G W Jr

Trainers— 1, Flint Steve; 2, Pletcher Todd A; 3, Nafzger Carl A; 4, Attfield Roger L; 5, Spatz Ronald B; 6, Oliver Victoria

---

$1 Pick Three (2–3–6) Paid $9.10; Pick Three Pool $53,720.

SEVENTH RACE

Santa Anita

MARCH 1, 2003

1 MILE. (1.33²) 23rd Running of THE SAN RAFAEL. Grade II. Purse $200,000 Guaranteed. THREE–YEAR–OLDS. By subscription of $200 each to accompany the nomination or by supplementary nomination of $4,000 by time of entry. $2,000 additional to start. Early bird nominees to the 2003 Santa Anita Derby (Closing Date Monday, December 9, 2002) are automatically eligible to the San Rafael Stakes with all fees waived. Weight: 121 lbs. Non–winners of $70,000 at one mile or once allowed 3 lbs.; of a race of $40,000 at any distance, 6 lbs. Early nominations closed December 9 with 149. Closed Thursday, February 20, 2003 with 3.

Value of Race: $200,000 Winner $120,000; second $40,000; third $24,000; fourth $12,000; fifth $4,000. Mutuel Pool $905,185.00 Exacta Pool $510,937.00 Quinella Pool $49,982.00 Trifecta Pool $490,075.00 Superfecta Pool $137,734.00

Last Raced	Horse	M/Eqt. A.Wt	PP	St	¼	½	¾	Str	Fin	Jockey	Odds $1
17Nov02 8CD1	Rojo Toro	LBb	3 115	6	4	31½	1½	1hd	11½	1¹	Bailey J D	2.10
7Feb03 7SA3	Spensive	LBb	3 118	3	3	6²	6²	64½	3hd	22½	Espinoza V	5.00
20Jly02 8Hol1	Crowned Dancer	LBb	3 118	7	5	5hd	4¹	5½	5¹	31½	Solis A	17.10
18Jan03 7SA2	Our Bobby V.	LB	3 116	1	1	1¹	2¹	21½	21½	4no	Flores D R	2.80
1Feb03 4SA2	Sum Trick	LB	3 118	2	2	2hd	3hd	3¹	4hd	52½	Baze T C	3.10
31Jan03 4SA1	Just Wonder–GB	LB	3 116	5	7	4hd	51½	41½	6⁵	6½	Desormeaux K J	6.60
16Feb03 3SA5	Iron Lad–IR	LB	3 115	4	6	7	7	7	7	7	Smith M E	65.30

OFF AT 3:12 Start Good. Won driving. Track fast.

TIME :22², :45¹, 1:09², 1:22², 1:35⁴ (:22.54, :45.33, 1:09.45, 1:22.47, 1:35.89)

$2 Mutuel Prices:

8–ROJO TORO	6.20	3.40	3.00
3–SPENSIVE		4.80	3.40
9–CROWNED DANCER			5.40

$1 EXACTA 8–3 PAID $13.10 $2 QUINELLA 3–8 PAID $16.20 $1 TRIFECTA 8–3–9 PAID $120.40 $1 SUPERFECTA 8–3–9–1 PAID $238.90

Ch. c, (Feb), by Mountain Cat–Pinta, by Carson City. Trainer Baffert Bob. Bred by Haras El Aguila SA (Fla).

ROJO TORO pulled his way up three deep on the first turn, dueled outside a rival on the backstretch and second turn, inched away in the stretch and held on gamely under urging. SPENSIVE angled in and pulled a bit stalking the pace toward the inside, went outside a rival on the second turn and four wide into the stretch, lugged in the drive but continued willingly to the wire. CROWNED DANCER a bit wide into the first turn, stalked outside on the backstretch and three deep on the second turn, was between horses in midstretch, could not match either of the top pair but bested the rest. OUR BOBBY V. sped to the early lead inside, dueled along the rail on the backstretch and second turn and weakened in the final furlong. SUM TRICK tracked the pace a bit off the rail then between horses into the stretch and lacked the needed response. JUST WONDER (GB) settled outside then chased between horses, continued toward the inside leaving the backstretch and on the second turn and weakened. IRON LAD (IRE) allowed to settle off the pace, came out from the rail into the backstretch, trailed off the inside and was outrun.

Owners— 1, Earnhardt III Hal J; 2, Watson & Weipman; 3, Eastern Sky Unlimited Trust & Cono; 4, Verratti Kathleen & Robert; 5, Fulton Stan E; 6, Hubbard Naify Vistas LLC Et Al; 7, Jim Ford Inc & Pearson

Trainers— 1, Baffert Bob; 2, Baffert Bob; 3, Paasch Christopher S; 4, Spawr Bill; 5, Becerra Rafael; 6, De Seroux Laura; 7, Cassidy James

Scratched— Peace Rules (28Dec02 3SA1), Indian Express (27Oct02 REM1)

$2 Daily Double (6–8) Paid $79.80; Daily Double Pool $49,683.
$1 Pick Three (9–6–5/6/8) Paid $502.20; Pick Three Pool $137,179.

EIGHTH RACE

Santa Anita

MARCH 1, 2003

1 MILE. (Turf)(1.31⁴) 3rd Running of THE FRANK E. KILROE MILE HANDICAP. Grade II. Purse $400,000 Guaranteed. FOUR–YEAR–OLDS AND UPWARD. By subscription of $400 each to accompany the nomination or by supplementary nomination of $8,000 by Saturday, February 22. $4,000 additional to start, with $400,000 guaranteed, of which $240,000 to first, $80,000 to second, $48,000 to third, $24,000 to fourth, and $8,000 to fifth. Closed Saturday, February 15, 2003 with 16 nominations. (Rail at 0 Feet).

Value of Race: $400,000 Winner $240,000; second $80,000; third $48,000; fourth $24,000; fifth $8,000. Mutuel Pool $1,045,949.0 Exacta Pool $592,220.00 Quinella Pool $55,903.00 Trifecta Pool $586,990.00 Superfecta Pool $186,769.00

Last Raced	Horse	M/Eqt.	A.Wt	PP	St	¼	½	¾	Str	Fin	Jockey	Odds $1
8Feb03 ³SA¹	Redattore-BRZ	LB	8 120	8	3	1ʰᵈ	1½	1ʰᵈ	1ʰᵈ	1¹	Solis A	5.20
30Nov02 ⁸Hol¹	Good Journey	LB	7 124	7	4	6ʰᵈ	7½	5½	5½	2²	Day P	1.20
25Jan03 ⁹SA⁴	Decarchy	LBb	6 118	6	9	8¹	8²	8¹½	8³	3ⁿᵏ	Valenzuela P A	6.90
1Feb03 ⁷TuP¹	Century City-IR	LBb	4 116	4	5	4ʰᵈ	3ʰᵈ	4²	4½	4ⁿᵏ	Stevens G L	22.20
16Jan03 ²SA¹	Cayoke-FR	LBb	6 116	3	1	2¹	2¹	2¹½	2²	5ⁿᵏ	Flores D R	9.60
15Oct99 RED¹⁰	Night Life-IR	LB	7 114	11	10	10ʰᵈ	9ʰᵈ	9ʰᵈ	7ʰᵈ	6¹	Espinoza V	a–14.00
8Feb03 ⁸GG¹	Seinne-CH	LB	6 116	10	11	11	11	11	9¹½	7ⁿᵒ	Nakatani C S	25.50
25Jan03 ²SA²	Music's Storm	LB	4 116	1	2	3ʰᵈ	5¹½	3ʰᵈ	3ʰᵈ	8½	Desormeaux K J	15.30
2Nov02 New¹	Smirk-GB	LB	5 117	2	6	7¹½	6ʰᵈ	7½	6¹½	9¹½	Prado E S	7.20
21Feb03 ⁷SA²	Kachamandi-CH	LB	6 114	5	7	9²	10²½	10¹½	10¹	10⁵	Bailey J D	30.40
25Jan03 ⁹SA¹	Alyzig	LB	6 113	9	8	5²½	4ʰᵈ	6¹	11	11	Krone J A	a–14.00

a–Coupled: Night Life–IR and Alyzig.

OFF AT 3:46 Start Good. Won driving. Course good.

TIME :23⁴, :47², 1:11¹, 1:23¹, 1:34⁴ (:23.84, :47.57, 1:11.36, 1:23.33, 1:34.94)

$2 Mutuel Prices:

10–REDATTORE–BRZ	12.40	4.40	3.20
9–GOOD JOURNEY		3.00	2.60
7–DECARCHY			3.60

$1 EXACTA 10–9 PAID $14.70 $2 QUINELLA 9–10 PAID $11.80 $1 TRIFECTA 10–9–7 PAID $63.20 $1 SUPERFECTA 10–9–7–5 PAID $709.90

B. h, by Roi Normand–Political Intrigue, by Deputy Minister. Trainer Mandella Richard. Bred by Haras Santa Ana do Rio Grande (Brz).

REDATTORE (BRZ) angled in and dueled outside a rival to midstretch, kicked clear under urging and held on gamely. GOOD JOURNEY between horses early, chased outside a rival, went between foes again on the second turn, came out off heels in upper stretch and finished well. DECARCHY pulled a bit outside rivals early, went three deep on the first turn then chased off the rail, continued outside on the second turn and three wide into the stretch, came out in upper stretch and just got the show. CENTURY CITY (IRE) also pulled early, stalked between horses, came out some in the stretch and was edged for third. CAYOKE (FR) angled in and prompted the pace inside the winner to midstretch, then weakened but lost the show late. NIGHT LIFE (FR) angled in and saved ground off the pace, came out leaving the second turn, lacked room off heels into the stretch, split rivals in midstretch and finished with some interest. SEINNE (CHI) unhurried outside a rival for six furlongs, swung out into the stretch and improved position. MUSIC'S STORM pulled his way along inside to stalk the pace, continued a bit off the rail on the backstretch and second turn, waited briefly behind rivals leaving that turn and lacked the needed response. SMIRK (GB) saved ground chasing the pace, continued inside throughout and could not offer the necessary rally. KACHAMANDI (CHI) angled in and settled early, went outside a rival on the backstretch, found the rail again on the second turn and failed to menace. ALYZIG bobbled at the start, raced wide early then stalked three deep, came four wide into the stretch and weakened.

Owners— 1, Taunay Luis A; 2, Flaxman Holdings Ltd Jarvis McDonal; 3, Juddmonte Farms Inc; 4, Kitchwa Stables & Nichols Thomas L; 5, House Michael; 6, Taub Steve; 7, Hunt Nelson B; 8, Jones Aaron U & Marie D; 9, Tabor Michael B; 10, Miraleste Inc Nakkashian & Roberts; 11, Taub Steve

Trainers—1, Mandella Richard; 2, Dollase Wallace; 3, Frankel Robert; 4, Greely C Beau; 5, Canani Julio C; 6, Mulhall Kristin; 7, McAnally Ronald; 8, Inda Eduardo; 9, Elsworth David C; 10, Abrams Barry; 11, Mulhall Kristin

Scratched— Western Pride (11May02 KRN¹¹), Star Life (25Jan03 ⁹SA²)

$2 Daily Double (8–10) Paid $34.80; Daily Double Pool $83,993.
$1 Pick Three (6–5/6/8–10) Paid $253.50; Pick Three Pool $161,340.

NINTH RACE

Santa Anita

MARCH 1, 2003

1¼ MILES. (1.57⁴) 66th Running of THE SANTA ANITA HANDICAP. Grade I. Purse $1,000,000 Guaranteed. FOUR-YEAR-OLDS AND UPWARD. By subscription of $100 each to accompany the nomination or by supplementary nomination of $20,000 by Saturday, February 22. $2,500 to pass the entry box and $7,500 to start with $1,000,000guaranteed, of which $600,000 to first, $200,000 to second, $120,000 to third, $60,000 to fourth and $20,000 to fifth. Weights Sunday, February 23. No horse shall be assigned more than 126 lbs. Closed Saturday, February 15, 2003 with 21 nominations.

Value of Race: $1,000,000 Winner $600,000; second $200,000; third $120,000; fourth $60,000; fifth $20,000. Mutuel Pool $1,134,038.0 Exacta Pool $551,643.00 Quinella Pool $44,059.00 Trifecta Pool $624,660.00

Last Raced	Horse	M/Eqt. A.Wt	PP	¼	½	¾	1	Str	Fin	Jockey	Odds $1
2Feb03 8SA2	Milwaukee Brew	LBb 6 119	6	2hd	3½	32½	21½	22	1hd	Prado E S	3.80
2Feb03 8SA1	Congaree	LB 5 124	5	31	2½	2½	1½	1hd	24½	Bailey J D	0.60
4Jan03 8SA2	Kudos	LBb 6 117	4	4½	4hd	4½	3hd	31½	31½	Krone J A	8.80
2Feb03 8SA3	Pleasantly Perfect	LBb 5 116	3	6	6	6	5½	4hd	41	Solis A	3.70
2Feb03 8SA4	Piensa Sonando-CH	LB 5 116	2	5½	51	51½	41½	510	512½	Stevens G L	30.40
12Feb03 2SA1	Trompolino-CH	LBb 5 112	1	11	1½	1hd	1hd	6	6	Baze T C	35.60

OFF AT 4:18 Start Good. Won driving. Track fast.

TIME :23¹, :46³, 1:11¹, 1:35², 1:59⁴ (:23.28, :46.70, 1:11.24, 1:35.52, 1:59.80)

$2 Mutuel Prices:

7–MILWAUKEE BREW	9.60	3.00	2.10
6–CONGAREE		2.40	2.10
5–KUDOS			2.10

$1 EXACTA 7–6 PAID $9.70 $2 QUINELLA 6–7 PAID $5.60 $1 TRIFECTA 7–6–5 PAID $31.80

B. h, by Wild Again–Ask Anita, by Wolf Power*SAf. Trainer Frankel Robert. Bred by Robert Spiegel (Ky).

MILWAUKEE BREW close up outside early, went up three deep to prompt the pace on the first turn and backstretch, battled outside CONGAREE on the second turn and into the stretch, got a head in front past midstretch and held on gamely under urging. CONGAREE stalked early, bid between horses into the first turn and dueled for command, took a short lead into the second turn, angled in and battled inside the winner, fought back gamely through a long hard drive and continued willingly to the wire. KUDOS pulled between horses early, came out into the first turn, chased outside, went three deep into the stretch and picked up the show. PLEASANTLY PERFECT also between horses early, chased outside or off the rail, continued alongside a rival into the stretch and lacked the needed rally. PIENSA SONANDO (CHI) chased inside then a bit off the rail, split horses on the second turn, angled in and could not offer the necessary response. TROMPOLINO (CHI) sped to the early lead, set a pressured pace inside, dropped back on the second turn, drifted out in the stretch and gave way.

Owners— 1, Stronach Stable; 2, Stonerside Stable; 3, Moss Mr & Mrs Jerome S; 4, Diamond A Racing Corporation; 5, Hunt Nelson B; 6, Wayside Corp

Trainers—1, Frankel Robert; 2, Baffert Bob; 3, Mandella Richard; 4, Mandella Richard; 5, McAnally Ronald; 6, Mandella Gary

Scratched— Sligo Bay (8Feb03 8GG2)

$2 Daily Double (10–7) Paid $73.60; Daily Double Pool $88,689.
$1 Pick Three (5/6/8–10–7) Paid $92.40; Pick Three Pool $247,480.

TENTH RACE

Gulfstream

MARCH 2, 2003

1⅛ MILES. (Turf Chute)(1.46²) 54th Running of THE SUWANNEE RIVER HANDICAP. Grade III. Purse $100,000 FOR FILLIES AND MARES, THREE YEAR OLDS AND UPWARD. By subscription of $100 each, which shall accompany the nomination, $1,000 to pass the entry box and $1,000 additional to start, with $100,000 guaranteed. For each of the winner to receive $60,000; $20,000 to second, $11,000 to third, $6,000 to fourth and $3,000 to fifth. Trophy to winning Owner. In the event this stake is taken off the turf, it may be subject to downgrading upon review of the Graded Stakes Committee. Closed Wednesday, February 19,2003 with 41 Nominations. (Rail at 0 feet).

Value of Race: $100,000 Winner $60,000; second $20,000; third $11,000; fourth $6,000; fifth $3,000. Mutuel Pool $491,309.00 Exacta Pool $356,089.00 Trifecta Pool $308,821.00 Superfecta Pool $109,983.00

Last Raced	Horse	M/Eqt. A.Wt	PP	St	¼	½	¾	Str	Fin	Jockey	Odds $1
5Jan03 10GP6	Amonita-GB	L 5 117	5	3	2¹	21½	22	1hd	12½	Samyn J L	5.40
9Feb03 9GP1	What A Price	L 5 114	2	2	41	41	41	3hd	2no	Velasquez C	17.20
5Jan03 10GP2	Calista-GB	L 5 118	4	4	3½	3½	31	42	3nk	Velazquez J R	1.50
25Jan03 9GP1	Stay Forever	Lb 6 117	9	7	7²½	7²	7³	6¹½	4¾	Santos J A	2.70
8Feb03 8GP3	Hi Tech Honeycomb	Lb 4 114	3	5	6hd	6¹½	6hd	5½	5²	Cruz M R	15.20
19Dec02 6Aqu4	Sparkling Ava	Lf 4 114	8	1	1¹	11	11	21½	6no	Boulanger G	64.80
8Feb03 8GP4	Queue	Lbf 6 114	1	8	9	8¹	9	71	71¼	Douglas R R	19.30
2Feb03 9GP2	Peanut Gallery	Lb 6 113	6	6	5¹½	5¹½	5²	8¹½	8nk	Chavez J F	20.60
15Jan03 9GP1	Party Queen	L 4 114	7	9	8hd	9	8hd	9	9	Guidry M	6.20

OFF AT 5:10 Start Good. Won driving. Course firm.

TIME :24², :49³, 1:13¹, 1:36², 1:47⁴ (:24.57, :49.62, 1:13.31, 1:36.59, 1:47.90)

$2 Mutuel Prices:

5–AMONITA–GB	12.80	7.00	4.40
2–WHAT A PRICE		15.00	5.60
4–CALISTA–GB			2.40

$1 EXACTA 5–2 PAID $78.80 $1 TRIFECTA 5–2–4 PAID $266.20 $1 SUPERFECTA 5–2–4–9 PAID $1,071.20

Dk. b. or br. m, by Anabaa–Spectacular Joke, by Spectacular Bid. Trainer Clement Christophe. Bred by Ship Commodities International (GB).

AMONITA (GB) steadied in behind SPARKLING AVA racing into the first turn, stalked that rival into the stretch, rallied to take over at the eighth pole and drew clear under pressure. WHAT A PRICE steadied along the inside in the early going, tracked the pace along the hedge into the stretch and closed to be up for the place while unable to stay with the winner. CALISTA (GB) chased the pace off the hedge into the stretch and lacked a late response. STAY FOREVER unhurried early, angled to the outside at the top of the stretch and closed with a mild response. HI TECH HONEYCOMB allowed to settle, saved ground into the stretch, eased out and couldn't gain late. SPARKLING AVA set the pace along the hedge to midstretch and tired. QUEUE was outrun. PEANUT GALLERY rated off the pace, raced three wide on the far turn and faltered. PARTY QUEEN outrun early, lacked a rally.

Owners— 1, Haras du Mezeray; 2, Hale Kay; 3, The Leigh Family Stable; 4, Santa Cruz Ranch Inc; 5, Select Stable; 6, Schwartz Barry K; 7, Robins Gerald & Weiss Jay; 8, Pokoik Lee; 9, Humphrey G W Jr

Trainers— 1, Clement Christophe; 2, Hale Robert A; 3, Clement Christophe; 4, Wolfson Martin D; 5, McPeek Kenneth G; 6, Plesa Edward Jr; 7, Blengs Vincent L; 8, Sciacca Gary; 9, Oliver Victoria

---

$1 Pick Three (1–5–5) Paid $30.30; Pick Three Pool $52,298.

NINTH RACE
Fair Grounds
MARCH 2, 2003

1⅛ MILES. (1.48) 76th Running of THE NEW ORLEANS HANDICAP. Grade II. Purse $500,000 A Handicap for Four Year Olds and Upward. By subscription of $100 each; $3,000 to pass the entry box; $3,000 additional to start. $500,000 Guaranteed of which $300,000 to the winner; $100,000 to second; $55,000 to third; $30,000 to fourth; $15,000 to fifth. THE OWNER OF THE WINNER TO RECEIVE A TROPHY. Closed Thursday, February 20, 2003, with 21 nominations.

Value of Race: $500,000 Winner $300,000; second $100,000; third $55,000; fourth $30,000; fifth $15,000. Mutuel Pool $641,122.00 Exacta Pool $409,578.00 Quinella Pool $29,697.00 Trifecta Pool $356,747.00 Superfecta Pool $108,650.00

Last Raced	Horse	M/Eqt.	A.Wt	PP	St	¼	½	¾	Str	Fin	Jockey	Odds $1
9Feb03 ^{9}FG^{2}	Mineshaft	L	4 115	6	1	2^{1}	2^{1}	1^{hd}	$1^{1\frac{1}{2}}$	$1^{3\frac{1}{2}}$	Albarado R J	5.00
1Feb03 ^{9}SA^{2}	Olmodavor	Lb	4 117	7	7	$5^{1\frac{1}{2}}$	$5^{\frac{1}{2}}$	4^{hd}	2^{2}	$2^{2\frac{1}{2}}$	Solis A	6.80
31Jan03 ^{9}GP^{2}	Strive	Lb	4 114	2	9	$6^{\frac{1}{2}}$	6^{1}	$5^{1\frac{1}{2}}$	5^{3}	$3^{1\frac{1}{2}}$	Bailey J D	10.10
25Jan03 ^{7}GP^{2}	Booklet	L	4 117	8	4	4^{hd}	3^{1}	3^{1}	$3^{\frac{1}{2}}$	$4^{1\frac{1}{4}}$	Day P	6.30
19Jan03 ^{9}FG^{2}	Learned	Lb	5 116	11	10	11	11	11	$7^{1\frac{1}{2}}$	$5^{2\frac{1}{2}}$	Borel C H	9.50
25Jan03 ^{7}GP^{1}	Best of the Rest	L	8 118	1	3	3^{hd}	$4^{\frac{1}{2}}$	6^{1}	$6^{\frac{1}{2}}$	$6^{\frac{1}{2}}$	Coa E M	5.10
18Jan03 ^{8}Hou^{1}	Valhol	L	7 117	4	2	7^{hd}	$10^{1\frac{1}{2}}$	8^{1}	$8^{3\frac{1}{2}}$	$7^{3\frac{1}{4}}$	Meche D J	24.90
9Feb03 ^{9}FG^{3}	Bonapaw	Lf	7 113	5	5	$1^{1\frac{1}{2}}$	$1^{2\frac{1}{2}}$	2^{2}	4^{1}	8^{2}	Martinez W	34.80
9Feb03 ^{9}FG^{1}	Balto Star	L	5 120	3	8	9^{1}	7^{1}	$7^{1\frac{1}{2}}$	9^{hd}	$9^{\frac{1}{2}}$	Martin E M Jr	3.40
26Dec02 ^{8}SA^{11}	Sunday Break-JP	Lf	4 115	9	11	$10^{3\frac{1}{2}}$	8^{hd}	9^{hd}	10^{4}	$10^{8\frac{3}{4}}$	Prado E S	8.90
1Feb03 ^{9}SA^{3}	Tracemark	Lb	4 116	10	6	8^{1}	9^{hd}	$10^{1\frac{1}{2}}$	11	11	Sellers S J	25.70

OFF AT 4:34 Start Good For All But SUNDAY BREAK (JPN) Won driving. Track fast.
TIME :23^{4}, :47^{4}, 1:12^{1}, 1:36^{2}, 1:48^{4} (:23.87, :47.90, 1:12.35, 1:36.58, 1:48.92)

$2 Mutuel Prices:				
	6–MINESHAFT	12.00	6.00	3.80
	7–OLMODAVOR		7.80	5.40
	2–STRIVE			7.20

$2 EXACTA 6–7 PAID $82.80 $2 QUINELLA 6–7 PAID $48.40 $2 TRIFECTA 6–7–2 PAID $759.00 $2 SUPERFECTA 6–7–2–8 PAID $4,527.00

Dk. b. or br. c, by A.P. Indy–Prospectors Delite, by Mr. Prospector. Trainer Howard Neil J. Bred by W. S. Farish, James Elkins & W. T. Webber Jr. (Ky).

MINESHAFT broke alertly, settled off BONAPAW until entering the second turn, bid outside that one midway around the turn, took over the lead and proved best while kept to the task. OLMODAVOR three wide early, was restrained between foes down the backstretch, rallied around the second turn, came four wide turning for home and while no match for the winner was best of the rest. STRIVE raced inside until the drive, angled out turning for home and closed mildly. BOOKLET settled off the rail while within striking distance, continued outside until the second turn, moved in a bit, rallied nearing the drive and then could make little impact. LEARNED trailed until the second turn, saved ground around the turn, was steered out for the drive and then did not have enough late. BEST OF THE REST eased off the rail just after the start, raced between foes while up close and then faded. VALHOL restrained early, was outrun. BONAPAW got clear quickly, was collared midway around the second turn and then faltered inside the final furlong. BALTO STAR eased out early around the first turn, raced wide down the backstretch and then was never dangerous. SUNDAY BREAK (JPN) fractious before the start, hopped at the break, raced wide early and then was never a factor. TRACEMARK wide early, moved inward before the second turn and then was no real threat.

Owners— 1, Farish William S Elkins James A & W; 2, Wertheimer Farm; 3, Wygod Mr & Mrs Martin J; 4, Oxley John C; 5, Midway Farm; 6, Oxenberg Beatrice; 7, Jackson James D; 8, Richard James & Dennis; 9, Anstu Stables; 10, Maeda Koji; 11, McGrath Edward T

Trainers—1, Howard Neil J; 2, Mandella Richard; 3, Mott William I; 4, Ward John T Jr; 5, Barnett Bobby C; 6, Plesa Edward Jr; 7, Keen Dallas E; 8, Miller Norman C III; 9, Pletcher Todd A; 10, Drysdale Neil; 11, Sauque Alex

$2 Pick Three (1–8–6) Paid $179.00; Pick Three Pool $23,887.

SEVENTH RACE
Santa Anita
MARCH 2, 2003

7 FURLONGS. (1.20) 65th Running of THE SAN CARLOS HANDICAP. Grade I. Purse $200,000. FOUR-YEAR-OLDS AND UPWARD. By subscription of $200 each to accompany the nomination. $2,000 additional to start, with $200,000 guaranteed, of which $120,000 to first, $40,000 to second, $24,000 to third, $12,000 to fourth and $4,000 to fifth. Closed Thursday, February 20 with 17 nominations.

Value of Race: $200,000 Winner $120,000; second $40,000; third $24,000; fourth $12,000; fifth $4,000. Mutuel Pool $604,058.00 Exacta Pool $309,028.00 Quinella Pool $34,503.00 Trifecta Pool $325,352.00

Last Raced	Horse	M/Eqt.	A.Wt	PP	St	¼	½	Str	Fin	Jockey	Odds $1
30Nov02 ^{9}Aqu^{2}	Aldebaran	LB	5 116	6	2	5^{8}	5^{10}	1^{hd}	1^{5}	Valdivia J Jr	2.40
30Nov02 ^{9}Aqu^{3}	Crafty C. T.	L	5 116	1	5	$3^{1\frac{1}{2}}$	$3^{\frac{1}{2}}$	$2^{\frac{1}{2}}$	$2^{\frac{1}{2}}$	Valenzuela P A	1.10
25Jan03 ^{7}GP^{3}	Grey Memo	LB	6 116	3	6	6	6	6	3^{3}	Stevens G L	9.30
26Jan03 ^{7}SA^{2}	Mellow Fellow	LBbf	8 116	2	1	1^{hd}	1^{hd}	$3^{\frac{1}{2}}$	4^{1}	Flores D R	15.80
1Feb03 ^{3}SA^{2}	Shah Jehan	LBb	4 114	4	4	4^{8}	4^{4}	$5^{3\frac{1}{2}}$	$5^{\frac{1}{2}}$	Smith M E	40.80
25Jan03 ^{1}SA^{1}	Total Limit	LB	4 113	5	3	$2^{\frac{1}{2}}$	2^{hd}	4^{hd}	6	Espinoza V	2.80

OFF AT 3:38 Start Good. Won driving. Track fast.
TIME :22^{2}, :44^{3}, 1:09^{1}, 1:21^{2} (:22.41, :44.72, 1:09.38, 1:21.53)

$2 Mutuel Prices:

7–ALDEBARAN	6.80	3.00	2.40
2–CRAFTY C. T.		2.60	2.20
4–GREY MEMO			2.80

$1 EXACTA 7–2 PAID $7.10 $2 QUINELLA 2–7 PAID $5.20 $1 TRIFECTA 7–2–4 PAID $24.10

B. h, by Mr. Prospector–Chimes of Freedom, by Private Account. Trainer Frankel Robert. Bred by Flaxman Holdings Ltd (Ky).

ALDEBARAN unhurried well off the rail on the backstretch, advanced off the fence on the turn, swung five wide into the stretch, surged to the front outside in midstretch and drew clear while drifting in under energetic handling. CRAFTY C. T. broke inward, went up inside to duel for command, fought back on the turn and to midstretch, then was no match for the winner but held second. GREY MEMO lagged back off the rail without early speed, angled out into the stretch and rallied but was edged for the place. MELLOW FELLOW had good early speed and dueled between horses to midstretch, then weakened. SHAH JEHAN forced or stalked the pace four wide to the stretch, was briefly between foes in midstretch and also weakened. TOTAL LIMIT vied for the lead three deep between horses, fought back into the stretch but weakened in the final eighth of a mile.

Owners— 1, Flaxman Holdings Ltd; 2, C T Grether Inc; 3, Manzani Ridgeley Farm & Sarno; 4, Craig Sidney H & Jenny; 5, Helzer James E; 6, Sarkowsky Herman

Trainers—1, Frankel Robert; 2, Zucker Howard L; 3, Stute Warren; 4, Spawr Bill; 5, Lukas D Wayne; 6, Mandella Gary

Scratched— Roman Dancer (1Jan03 ^{7}SA^{7})

$2 Daily Double (4–7) Paid $503.00; Daily Double Pool $39,439.
$1 Pick Three (9–4–7) Paid $4,172.20; Pick Three Pool $88,860.
$2 Consolation Daily Double (4–1) Paid $67.20

NINTH RACE
Fair Grounds
MARCH 8, 2003

1$\frac{1}{16}$ MILES. (1.42) 38th Running of THE FAIR GROUNDS OAKS. Grade II. Purse $350,000 For Three Year Old Fillies. By subscription of $100 each; $2,000 to enter; $2,000 additional to start. $350,000 Guaranteed of which $210,000 to the winner; $70,000 to second; $38,500 to third; $21,000 to fourth; and $10,500 to fifth .Weight: 121 lbs. THE OWNER OF THE WINNER TO RECEIVE A TROPHY. Closed Thursday, February 27, 2003, with 15 nominations.

Value of Race: $350,000 Winner $210,000; second $70,000; third $38,500; fourth $21,000; fifth $10,500. Mutuel Pool $496,019.00 Exacta Pool $256,148.00 Quinella Pool $17,794.00 Trifecta Pool $176,089.00

Last Raced	Horse	M/Eqt.	A.Wt	PP	St	¼	½	¾	Str	Fin	Jockey	Odds $1
26Jan03 ^{8}FG^{1}	Lady Tak	L	3 121	4	2	4^{1}	4^{1}	$3^{\frac{1}{2}}$	1^{1}	$1^{3\frac{1}{2}}$	Meche D J	1.10
25Jan03 ^{3}SA^{1}	Atlantic Ocean	L	3 121	5	4	2^{1}	2^{1}	$2^{1\frac{1}{2}}$	3^{2}	$2^{2\frac{1}{4}}$	Flores D R	1.60
15Feb03 ^{9}FG^{1}	Belle Of Perintown	L	3 121	2	5	3^{1}	$3^{\frac{1}{2}}$	$4^{1\frac{1}{2}}$	$4^{2\frac{1}{2}}$	$3^{\frac{3}{4}}$	Borel C H	2.80
15Feb03 ^{9}FG^{3}	Rebridled Dreams	L	3 121	3	1	$1^{1\frac{1}{2}}$	$1^{1\frac{1}{2}}$	1^{1}	$2^{\frac{1}{2}}$	$4^{5\frac{1}{2}}$	Martinez W	a-23.20
9Feb03 ^{7}FG^{1}	Lovely Sage	Lb	3 121	6	6	6	5^{hd}	5^{1}	5^{2}	$5^{4\frac{3}{4}}$	Lanerie C J	18.60
15Feb03 ^{9}FG^{2}	Afternoon Dreams	L	3 121	1	3	5^{1}	6	6	6	6	Martin E M Jr	a-23.20

a–Coupled: Rebridled Dreams and Afternoon Dreams.

OFF AT 4:30 Start Good. Won ridden out. Track fast.
TIME :24^{1}, :48, 1:13, 1:37^{3}, 1:44^{1} (:24.24, :48.17, 1:13.04, 1:37.78, 1:44.36)

$2 Mutuel Prices:

3–LADY TAK	4.20	2.60	2.10
4–ATLANTIC OCEAN		2.40	2.10
2–BELLE OF PERINTOWN			2.10

$2 EXACTA 3–4 PAID $9.00 $2 QUINELLA 3–4 PAID $4.20 $2 TRIFECTA 3–4–2 PAID $14.20

Ch. f, (Apr), by Mutakddim–Star of My Eye, by Lucky North. Trainer Asmussen Steven M. Bred by John Franks (Fla).

LADY TAK restrained from early on while settling just outside BELLE OF PERINTOWN, bid three wide nearing the drive, took over before the final furlong and drew out while ridden out. ATLANTIC OCEAN stalked AFTERNOON DREAMS while just off the rail, ranged up when asked before mid stretch and then while no match for the winner was second best. BELLE OF PERINTOWN veered out into REBRIDLED DREAMS at the break, was straightened, eased to the rail while unhurried, continued inside until nearing the drive, angled out four wide and then hung. REBRIDLED DREAMS bumped with BELLE OF PERINTOWN at the break, got clear early, remained clear until upper stretch, got overtaken and faded late. LOVELY SAGE off last, settled off the rail and then was no real threat. AFTERNOON DREAMS saved ground and was outrun.

Owners— 1, Heiligbrodt Racing Stable; 2, The Thoroughbred Corporation; 3, Mahler Kenneth & Schloss Jamie; 4, Coast To Coast Racing Fund; 5, Devenport Roger J; 6, Coast To Coast Racing Fund

Trainers—1, Asmussen Steven M; 2, Baffert Bob; 3, Kenneally Eddie; 4, Calhoun William Bret; 5, Amoss Thomas; 6, Calhoun William Bret

---

$2 Pick Three (7–6–3) Paid $398.20; Pick Three Pool $22,310.

EIGHTH RACE
Golden Gate
MARCH 8, 2003

$1\frac{1}{16}$ MILES. (1.39^{2}) 22nd Running of THE EL CAMINO REAL DERBY. Grade III. Purse $200,000 Guaranteed. FOR THREE-YEAR-OLDS. By subscription of $200 each to accompany the nomination or by supplementary nomination of $4,000 by time of entry. $1,000 to pass the entry box and $1,000 additional to start with $200,000 Guaranteed, of which $110,000 to the winner, $40,000 to second, $30,000 to third, $15,000 to fourth and $5,000 to fifth. Weight 120 lbs. Non-winners of $75,000 at one mile or over allowed 3 lbs.;$50,000, 5 lbs.(Maiden, claiming and starter races not considered). Starters to be named through the entry box by the closing time of entries. A trophy will be presented to the owner of the winner. High weights preferred. NOMINATIONS CLOSED THURSDAY, FEBRUARY 27, 2003.

Value of Race: $200,000 Winner $110,000; second $40,000; third $30,000; fourth $15,000; fifth $5,000. Mutuel Pool $498,282.00 Exacta Pool $287,838.00 Quinella Pool $27,328.00 Trifecta Pool $319,160.00 Superfecta Pool $116,006.00

Last Raced	Horse	M/Eqt.	A.Wt	PP	St	¼	½	¾	Str	Fin	Jockey	Odds $1
16Feb03 ^{3}SA^{1}	Ocean Terrace	**LB**	3 115	9	6	3^{1}	2^{1}	2^{2}	1^{1}	$1^{1\frac{1}{2}}$	Smith M E	4.80
9Feb03 ^{8}GG^{1}	Ministers Wild Cat	**LB**	3 117	10	2	$5^{\frac{1}{2}}$	4^{1}	3^{hd}	3^{1}	2no	Desormeaux K J	1.30
7Feb03 ^{7}SA^{4}	Ten Most Wanted	**LB**	3 115	2	4	2^{1}	$3^{\frac{1}{2}}$	4^{2}	4^{3}	3^{1}	Day P	3.30
9Feb03 ^{8}GG^{2}	Winning Stripes	**LB**b	3 115	6	7	7^{2}	7^{1}	7^{4}	$5^{1\frac{1}{2}}$	$4^{2\frac{1}{2}}$	Baze R A	11.30
30Jan03 ^{2}GG^{2}	Onebadshark	**LB**	3 116	1	1	$1^{\frac{1}{2}}$	$1^{\frac{1}{2}}$	1^{1}	$2^{\frac{1}{2}}$	$5^{1\frac{1}{2}}$	Warren R J Jr	58.80
18Jan03 ^{7}SA^{4}	Crackup	**LB**b	3 120	8	3	$6^{3\frac{1}{2}}$	6^{4}	$6^{1\frac{1}{2}}$	6^{hd}	6^{1}	Baze T C	5.30
15Feb03 ^{11}GP^{8}	Ozzie Cat	**LB**b	3 115	3	5	$4^{\frac{1}{2}}$	5^{2}	5^{1}	7^{2}	$7^{\frac{1}{2}}$	Valdivia J Jr	13.80
1Feb03 ^{4}SA^{5}	Mr. Technique	**LB**b	3 117	4	8	8^{hd}	$8^{\frac{1}{2}}$	9^{2}	8^{2}	8^{2}	Alvarado F T	70.70
7Feb03 ^{4}GG^{1}	Frisco Johnny	**LB**bf	3 115	7	9	10	9^{1}	8^{hd}	9^{2}	9^{2}	Duran F	84.10
21Feb03 ^{4}GG^{1}	Allwood	**LB**	3 115	5	10	9^{1}	10	10	10	10	Rollins C J	110.60

OFF AT 4:23 Start Good. Won driving. Track fast.
TIME :22^{3}, :45^{2}, 1:09^{2}, 1:35^{2}, 1:42^{1} (:22.73, :45.47, 1:09.47, 1:35.41, 1:42.26)

$2 Mutuel Prices:				
	9-OCEAN TERRACE	11.60	4.20	3.40
	10-MINISTERS WILD CAT		3.20	2.60
	2-TEN MOST WANTED			3.20

$1 EXACTA 9-10 PAID $13.00 $2 QUINELLA 9-10 PAID $10.20 $1 TRIFECTA 9-10-2 PAID $59.00 $1 SUPERFECTA 9-10-2-6 PAID $160.70

Ch. c, (Feb), by Saint Ballado-Crystal River, by Black Tie Affair*Ire. Trainer Hess R B Jr. Bred by Damara Farm (Ky).

OCEAN TERRACE was off a step slow but quickly gained his stride and raced up three wide into the first turn to stalk the pace, moved nearest the pacesetter after a half mile, challenged into the lane, forged to the front a furlong out and held driving. MINISTERS WILD CAT broke alertly but took back just off the pace while forced four wide to the backstretch, remained close up and under a snug hold into the second turn, advanced three wide to loom a bold factor in the upper stretch, but lugged in at mid stretch and lost his punch. TEN MOST WANTED was never too far back while racing just off the rail, remained in contention and two wide on the second turn then finished steadily but lacked the needed response. WINNING STRIPES took back at the start and raced unhurried to the half commenced his bid from just off the rail on the second turn, shifted out at the quarter pole to circle horses four wide to the stretch then closed best but too late. ONEBADSHARK was quickly in front to the set the pace from the rail and well in hand, continued on the lead into the lane, resisted the winner briefly then slackened. CRACKUP was permitted to settle early, saved ground on the second turn but did not rally. OZZIE CAT was well placed early from just off the rail, tried to rally while three wide on the second turn but lacked the needed response. MR. TECHNIQUE saved ground early and was never a factor. FRISCO JOHNNY showed little. ALLWOOD had no speed.

Owners— 1, Fog City Stable; 2, Cowan Marjorie & Irving M; 3, Chisholm Horizon Stable & Jarvis et; 4, Robinson Shustek & Stanley et al; 5, E-Racing Com; 6, Fulton Stan E; 7, Overbrook Farm; 8, Vreeland James R; 9, Haynes Kevin & Staudacher David; 10, Franks John

Trainers—1, Hess R B Jr; 2, Drysdale Neil; 3, Dollase Wallace; 4, Morey William J Jr; 5, Koriner Brian; 6, Becerra Rafael; 7, Lukas D Wayne; 8, Bonde Jeff; 9, Sumja Brent; 10, Hollendorfer Jerry

$2 Daily Double (11-9) Paid $21.80; Daily Double Pool $17,522.
$1 Pick Three (4/10/12-11-9) Paid $30.20; Pick Three Pool $47,882.

TENTH RACE
Gulfstream
MARCH 8, 2003

7 FURLONGS. (1.20) 25th Running of THE RICHTER SCALE BREEDERS' CUP HANDICAP. Grade II. Purse $200,000. (includes $100,000 Breeders' Cup). 3-year-olds and upward. (Includes $100,000 from the Breeders' Cup Fund for cup nominees only). By subscription of $200 each which shall accompany the nomination, $1,500 to pass the entry box and $1,500 additional to start, with $100,000 guaranteed. The host association monies to be divided 60% to the owner of the winner, 20% to second, 11% to third, 6% to fourth and 3% to fifth. Closed Wednesday, February 26 with 16 nominations. (Formerly run as The Gulfstream Park Breeders' Cup Sprint Championship.)

Value of Race: $200,000 Winner $120,000; second $40,000; third $22,000; fourth $12,000; fifth $6,000. Mutuel Pool $683,960.00 Exacta Pool $452,929.00 Trifecta Pool $386,365.00 Superfecta Pool $127,152.00

Last Raced	Horse	M/Eqt.	A.Wt	PP	St	¼	½	Str	Fin	Jockey	Odds $1
15Feb03 ^{10}Tam^{2}	Tour Of The Cat	**L**f	5 116	2	4	4^{4}	3^{hd}	$1^{\frac{1}{2}}$	1^{hd}	Cabassa A Jr	9.60
15Feb03 ^{10}Tam^{1}	Burning Roma	**L**	5 116	6	3	$2^{\frac{1}{2}}$	$2^{\frac{1}{2}}$	2^{2}	$2^{1\frac{1}{4}}$	Coa E M	2.80
16Feb03 ^{9}GP^{1}	Highway Prospector	**L**b	6 114	5	5	6^{5}	6^{4}	$5^{1\frac{1}{2}}$	3^{nk}	Santos J A	a-0.70
9Feb03 ^{10}GP^{3}	Fire And Glory	**L**	4 114	1	8	7^{3}	7^{4}	$6^{1\frac{1}{2}}$	4^{2}	Boulanger G	58.20
28Nov02 ^{8}Aqu^{8}	Smooth Jazz	**L**	4 114	7	2	$3^{1\frac{1}{2}}$	4^{4}	$3^{\frac{1}{2}}$	5^{2}	Prado E S	5.60
9Feb03 ^{10}GP^{2}	Binthebest	**L**bf	6 114	4	6	5^{1}	5^{3}	7^{3}	6^{nk}	Douglas R R	10.60
9Feb03 ^{10}GP^{1}	Native Heir	**L**b	5 116	3	1	$1^{\frac{1}{2}}$	1^{1}	4^{hd}	$7^{4\frac{1}{4}}$	Velasquez C	a-0.70
16Feb03 ^{9}GP^{8}	Ticket To Freedom	**L**	6 115	8	7	8	8	8	8	Velez J A Jr	63.00

a-Coupled: Highway Prospector and Native Heir.

OFF AT 5:11 Start Good. Won driving. Track fast.
TIME :22^{1}, :44^{2}, 1:08^{2}, 1:21 (:22.32, :44.41, 1:08.43, 1:21.15)

$2 Mutuel Prices:				
	3-TOUR OF THE CAT	21.20	10.80	2.60
	5-BURNING ROMA		5.40	2.20
	1A-HIGHWAY PROSPECTOR (a-entry)			2.10

$1 EXACTA 3-5 PAID $39.30 $1 TRIFECTA 3-5-1 PAID $77.40 $1 SUPERFECTA 3-5-1-2 PAID $627.30

B. h, by Tour d'Or-Tune in to the Cat, by Tunerup. Trainer Mora Myra. Bred by C V S Sales Company (Fla).

TOUR OF THE CAT chased the pace along the rail, slipped through to reach even terms for command at the top of the stretch, then dueled with BURNING ROMA to the wire and prevailed. BURNING ROMA prompted the pace three wide, moved up to reach even terms for command at the top of the stretch, dueled with TOUR OF THE CAT and continued on gamely while being edged to the wire. HIGHWAY PROSPECTOR unhurried early, rallied along the rail to be up for the show. FIRE AND GLORY outrun early, angled outside the leaders for the drive and closed with a belated rally to just miss the show. SMOOTH JAZZ chased the pace, angled out leaving the turn and weakened. BINTHEBEST raced three wide around the turn and lacked a rally. NATIVE HEIR showed speed off the rail to the top of the stretch and faltered. TICKET TO FREEDOM was always outrun.

Owners— 1, Double G Stable; 2, H Queen; 3, M Gill; 4, Dover Lane Stables & Nutmeg Stables; 5, M Tabor; 6, Tafel James B et al; 7, M Gill; 8, Double B & S Inc

Trainers—1, Mora Myra; 2, Giglio Heather A; 3, Shuman Mark; 4, Gambolati Cam; 5, Pletcher Todd A; 6, Nafzger Carl A; 7, Shuman Mark; 8, Perry William W

$1 Pick Three (8-1-3) Paid $954.40; Pick Three Pool $66,808.

FOURTH RACE
Santa Anita
MARCH 8, 2003

$1\frac{1}{16}$ MILES. (1.39) 64th Running of THE SANTA ANITA OAKS. Grade I. Purse $300,000. Fillies, 3-year-olds. By subscription of $300 each to accompany the nomination or by supplementary nomination of $6,000 by time of entry. $3,000 additional to start, with $300,000 guaranteed, of which $180,000 to first, $60,000 to second, $36,000 to third, $18,000 to fourth and $6,000 to fifth. Weight, 117 lbs. Closed Thursday, February 27 with 8 nominations.

Value of Race: $300,000 Winner $180,000; second $60,000; third $36,000; fourth $18,000; fifth $6,000. Mutuel Pool $1,218,387.0 Exacta Pool $471,592.00 Quinella Pool $47,555.00

Last Raced	Horse	M/Eqt.	A.Wt	PP	St	¼	½	¾	Str	Fin	Jockey	Odds $1
9Feb03 7SA1	Composure	LB	3 117	1	3	$4^{2\frac12}$	3^1	3^5	1^{hd}	$1^{\frac34}$	Bailey J D	0.40
9Feb03 7SA2	Elloluv	LB	3 117	4	1	1^1	$1^{\frac12}$	$1^{\frac12}$	$2^{2\frac12}$	$2^{4\frac12}$	Valenzuela P A	1.60
12Feb03 3SA1	Go For Glamour	LB	3 117	5	4	$2^{\frac12}$	2^{hd}	2^{hd}	3^5	$3^{7\frac12}$	Stevens G L	10.40
1Feb03 8TuP1	Harbor Blues	LBb	3 117	3	2	3^{hd}	4^4	$4^{4\frac12}$	$4^{2\frac12}$	4^9	Puglisi I L	43.30
15Feb03 8SA1	Long Term Wish	LB	3 117	2	5	5	5	5	5	5	Solis A	31.10

OFF AT 2:01 Start Good. Won driving. Track fast.
TIME $:24^2$, $:48^2$, $1:11^4$, $1:36^2$, $1:43^1$ (:24.59, :48.57, 1:11.80, 1:36.44, 1:43.34)

$2 Mutuel Prices:

1-COMPOSURE	2.80	2.10	2.10
4-ELLOLUV		2.10	2.10
5-GO FOR GLAMOUR			2.10

$1 EXACTA 1-4 PAID $1.80 $2 QUINELLA 1-4 PAID $2.20

B. f, (Apr), by Touch Gold-Party Cited, by Alleged. Trainer Baffert Bob. Bred by Rancho San Peasea S A (Ky).

COMPOSURE taken off the rail early, stalked outside a rival then three deep on the first turn, bid three wide on the backstretch, dueled for command, took a short lead outside ELLOLUV under strong handling in upper stretch and gamely prevailed under a crack of the whip and good handling late. ELLOLUV took the early lead and angled in, set a pressured pace inside, fought back along the rail through a long, hard drive and continued willingly to the wire. GO FOR GLAMOUR stalked the early pace off the rail, bid between horses on the backstretch and dueled for the lead, dropped back nearing the stretch and weakened but held third. HARBOR BLUES close up stalking the pace along the inside, came out on the second turn and weakened. LONG TERM WISH allowed to settle inside, saved ground off the pace and was outrun.

Owners— 1, Lewis Robert B & Beverly J; 2, Reddam John P; 3, Columbine Stable; 4, Everest Stables; 5, Golden Eagle Farm

Trainers—1, Baffert Bob; 2, Dollase Craig; 3, Greely C Beau; 4, Canani Nick; 5, Dominguez Caesar F

$2 Daily Double (1-1) Paid $5.40; Daily Double Pool $39,380.
$1 Pick Three (4-1/4/5/7-1) Paid $6.40; Pick Three Pool $89,263.

NINTH RACE
Fair Grounds
MARCH 9, 2003

$1\frac{1}{16}$ MILES. (1.42) 91st Running of THE LOUISIANA DERBY. Grade II. Purse $750,000 For Three Year Olds. (Foals of 2000)(A $1 Million Dollar Bonus to the Winner of the Louisiana Derby that goes on to win the 2003 Kentucky Derby). The guaranteed purse will be divided as follows: $450,000 to first; $150,000 to second;$82,500 to third; $45,000 to fourth; $22,500 to fifth. Weight: Colts and Geldings, 122 lbs.; Fillies, 117 lbs. THE OWNER OF THE WINNER TO RECEIVE A TROPHY. Closed Friday, February 28, 2003, with 132 nominations.

Value of Race: $750,000 Winner $450,000; second $150,000; third $82,500; fourth $45,000; fifth $22,500. Mutuel Pool $938,511.00 Exacta Pool $547,749.00 Quinella Pool $43,757.00 Trifecta Pool $524,764.00 Superfecta Pool $202,854.00

Last Raced	Horse	M/Eqt.	A.Wt	PP	St	¼	½	¾	Str	Fin	Jockey	Odds $1
28Dec02 3SA1	Peace Rules	L	3 122	9	4	2^1	$2^{\frac12}$	$2^{\frac12}$	1^1	$1^{2\frac14}$	Prado E S	9.40
1Feb03 4SA1	Kafwain	Lb	3 122	5	3	$5^{\frac12}$	5^1	4^{hd}	3^1	2^1	Espinoza V	1.40
18Jan03 10GP5	Funny Cide	L	3 122	2	6	1^1	$1^{1\frac12}$	$1^{\frac12}$	4^2	$3^{\frac12}$	Santos J A	6.10
16Feb03 9FG2	Lone Star Sky	L	3 122	3	1	6^1	$6^{\frac12}$	$7^{1\frac12}$	6^2	$4^{1\frac14}$	Borel C H	14.30
16Feb03 9FG3	Defrere's Vixen	L	3 122	4	2	$3^{\frac12}$	$4^{1\frac12}$	5^3	5^2	$5^{\frac34}$	Meche D J	58.10
16Feb03 9FG1	Badge Of Silver	L	3 122	10	5	4^1	3^1	3^2	$2^{1\frac12}$	$6^{4\frac12}$	Albarado R J	1.20
25Jan03 9FG3	Winning Fans	L	3 122	7	10	10	7^{hd}	6^2	7^5	7^{11}	Jacinto J	127.80
16Feb03 9FG4	Prince Alphie	Lbf	3 122	6	9	$7^{1\frac12}$	8^3	8^3	8^{10}	$8^{20\frac14}$	Melancon L	99.30
23Feb03 8FG2	Gohalo	L	3 122	1	7	9^1	9^{hd}	10	9^8	9	Meche L J	187.80
13Feb03 9FG1	Commander's Affair	Lb	3 122	8	8	8^{hd}	10	9^5	10	—	Melancon G	87.00

Commander's Affair:Distanced;

OFF AT 4:29 Start Good. Won driving. Track fast.
TIME $:23^2$, $:46^3$, $1:10^3$, $1:35^4$, $1:42^3$ (:23.51, :46.74, 1:10.60, 1:35.86, 1:42.67)

$2 Mutuel Prices:

9-PEACE RULES	20.80	6.20	4.60
5-KAFWAIN		3.20	2.60
2-FUNNY CIDE			4.00

$2 EXACTA 9-5 PAID $58.80 $2 QUINELLA 5-9 PAID $27.40 $2 TRIFECTA 9-5-2 PAID $276.00 $2 SUPERFECTA 9-5-2-3 PAID $1,455.80

Ch. c, (Apr), by Jules-Hold to Fashion, by Hold Your Peace. Trainer Frankel Robert. Bred by Newchance Farm (Fla).

PEACE RULES close up, was restrained off FUNNY CIDE, eased up outside that one nearing the second turn, took over inside BADE OF SILVER nearing the furlong marker and increased his margin while kept to the task. KAFWAIN between foes early, settled off the rail down the backstretch, moved up four wide around the second turn, finished gamely but did not have enough late. FUNNY CIDE sprinted clear early, set the pace until the second turn, was collared midway around the turn, dropped back a bit then came again for the show from the inside. LONE STAR SKY saved ground until the drive, was steered out after turning for home and could make little impact. DEFRERE'S VIXEN raced inside until the drive, swung out for the drive and then lacked a finish. BADGE OF SILVER settled off the leaders while three wide, moved up around the second turn, gained the edge turning for home, got headed and flattened out inside the final sixteenth. WINNING FANS brushed with PRINCE ALPHIE, was devoid speed, advanced between foes down the backstretch and then could make little impact. PRINCE ALPHIE drifted out at the break to brush with PRINCE ALPHIE, settled while in reserve, raced wide down the backstretch and then stopped. GOHALO raced along the rail early and then dropped back. COMMANDER'S AFFAIR never dangerous, was distanced.

Owners— 1, Gann Edmund A; 2, The Thoroughbred Corporation; 3, Sackatoga Stable Jackson Knowlton; 4, New Walter L; 5, Heiligbrodt Racing Stable; 6, Ramsey Kenneth L & Sarah K; 7, Cuadra Valedor; 8, Schettine William C; 9, Shepard Robert H; 10, Martin Racing Stable & Massey Betty

Trainers—1, Frankel Robert; 2, Baffert Bob; 3, Tagg Barclay; 4, Amoss Thomas; 5, Asmussen Steven M; 6, Werner Ronny; 7, Martinez Eleuterio Jr; 8, Carroll Josie; 9, Bailey Isaac L; 10, Calhoun William Bret

$2 Pick Three (4-5-9) Paid $2,343.40; Pick Three Pool $28,121.

NINTH RACE

Gulfstream

MARCH 9, 2003

1¹⁄₁₆ MILES. (Turf Chute)(1.39) 37th Running of THE CANADIAN TURF HANDICAP. Grade III. Purse $100,000. THREE YEAR OLDS AND UPWARD. By subscription of $100 each, which shall accompany the nomination, $1,000 to pass the entry box and $1,000 additional to start, with $100,000 guaranteed. The owner of the winner to receive $60,000; $20,000 to second, $11,000 to third, $6,000 to fourth and $3,000 to fifth. Trophy to winning owner. In the event this stake is taken off the turf, it may be subject to downgrading upon review of the Graded Stakes Committee. Closed Wednesday, February 26 with 38 nominations. (Rail at 0 feet).

Value of Race: $100,000 Winner $60,000; second $20,000; third $11,000; fourth $6,000; fifth $3,000. Mutuel Pool $522,090.00 Exacta Pool $340,296.00   Trifecta Pool $271,750.00 Superfecta Pool $86,795.00

Last Raced	Horse	M/Eqt. A.Wt	PP	St	¼	½	¾	Str	Fin	Jockey	Odds $1
24Jan03 ⁹GP³	Political Attack	Lb 4 114	4	2	2⁵	2²	2¹½	1¹	1½	Guidry M	9.20
25Jan03 ²SA⁵	Miesque's Approval	L 4 116	5	3	3¹	3¹	3½	2ʰᵈ	2¹	Bailey J D	1.10
10Feb03 ⁹GP³	Strategic Partner	Lb 5 114	2	5	5¹	4ʰᵈ	4¹	3¹½	3²	Velazquez J R	4.90
16Feb03 ¹⁰GP³	Sardaukar-GB	L 7 114	1	6	6ʰᵈ	6¹½	6²	6¹½	4ⁿᵏ	Velasquez C	4.80
10Feb03 ⁹GP¹	French Charmer	Lb 4 114	3	7	4¹	5¹	5¹	5ʰᵈ	5ʰᵈ	Coa E M	6.70
15Feb03 ¹⁰Tam³	First Lieutenant	Lf 6 113	7	4	7	7	7	7	6⁴¼	Day P	9.20
17Feb03 ⁹GP²	Rakoon	Lf 5 114	6	1	1¹	1²	1ʰᵈ	4½	7	Aguilar M	24.00

OFF AT 4:40 Start Good. Won driving. Course firm.

TIME :23⁴, :47⁴, 1:11, 1:34², 1:40² (:23.84, :47.85, 1:11.02, 1:34.57, 1:40.43)

$2 Mutuel Prices:	5–POLITICAL ATTACK	20.40	8.40	6.40
	7–MIESQUE'S APPROVAL		3.20	2.40
	3–STRATEGIC PARTNER			3.60

$1 EXACTA 5–7 PAID $31.90 $1 TRIFECTA 5–7–3 PAID $134.20 $1
SUPERFECTA 5–7–3–2 PAID $327.10

B. c, by Hawk Attack–Cope's Light, by Copelan. Trainer Matz Michael R. Bred by Brereton C Jones (Ky).

POLITICAL ATTACK chased the pace after being outrun for the lead, rallied to take over leaving the far turn, then was fully extended to hold off MIESQUE'S APPROVAL. The latter, tracked the leaders off the hedge, eased outside POLITICAL ATTACK for the drive, rallied to reach that rival inside the eighth pole but didn't do enough late. STRATEGIC PARTNER rated off the pace, came around RAKOON and angled in to make run at the leaders in midstretch but couldn't sustain his bid. SARDAUKAR (GB) allowed to settle, saved ground into the stretch and lacked a late response. FRENCH CHARMER reserved early, raced in contention three wide into the stretch and failed to rally. FIRST LIEUTENANT was outrun. RAKOON outran POLITICAL ATTACK to get the lead, opened a clear advantage while angling over to the hedge, made the pace to nearing the stretch and faltered.

Owners— 1, Dixon Fitz E Jr; 2, Live Oak Plantation; 3, Lewis Lee; 4, M Gill; 5, Double S Stable; 6, Humphrey G W Jr; 7, Lenci Anthony
Trainers—1, Matz Michael R; 2, Mott William I; 3, Hennig Mark; 4, Shuman Mark; 5, Benson Harry; 6, Oliver Philip J; 7, Lopez Robert E
Scratched— Regency Park (16Feb03 ⁵GP¹), Saint Verre (22Feb03 ¹¹GP¹⁰)

$1 Pick Three (6–1–5) Paid $779.70; Pick Three Pool $54,582.

EIGHTH RACE

Santa Anita

MARCH 9, 2003

1⅛ MILES. (1.45⁴) 66th Running of THE SANTA MARGARITA HANDICAP. Grade I. Purse $300,000 fOR FILLIES AND MARES FOUR YEARS OLD AND UPWARD. By invitation, with no nomination or starting fees. The winner to receive $180,000, with $60,000 to second, $36,000 to third, $18,000 to fourth and $6,000 to fifth.

Value of Race: $300,000 Winner $180,000; second $60,000; third $36,000; fourth $18,000; fifth $6,000. Mutuel Pool $568,063.00 Exacta Pool $270,158.00   Quinella Pool $31,580.00 Trifecta Pool $226,016.00

Last Raced	Horse	M/Eqt. A.Wt	PP	St	¼	½	¾	Str	Fin	Jockey	Odds $1
16Feb03 ⁶SA¹	Starrer	LBb 5 121	5	5	2¹	2²½	2¹½	1ʰᵈ	1²	Valenzuela P A	1.60
8Feb03 ⁶SA²	Sightseek	LB 4 116	4	3	1¹	1¹	1¹½	2¹½	2³	Valdivia J Jr	2.50
8Feb03 ⁶SA³	Bella Bellucci	LB 4 116	3	4	4⁴	3¹	3⁴	3²½	3⁵	Stevens G L	5.30
8Feb03 ⁶SA¹	Got Koko	LBb 4 120	1	2	3½	4⁸	4⁶	4⁴½	4²	Solis A	2.00
16Feb03 ⁶SA⁴	Printemps-CHI	LB 6 116	2	1	5	5	5	5	5	Flores D R	25.30

OFF AT 4:09 Start Good. Won driving. Track fast.

TIME :23², :47, 1:10³, 1:35³, 1:48¹ (:23.58, :47.16, 1:10.64, 1:35.62, 1:48.20)

$2 Mutuel Prices:	5–STARRER	5.20	3.00	3.40
	4–SIGHTSEEK		3.60	4.00
	3–BELLA BELLUCCI			4.20

$1 EXACTA 5–4 PAID $8.70 $2 QUINELLA 4–5 PAID $11.20 $1 TRIFECTA
5–4–3 PAID $33.60

Dk. b. or br. m, by Dynaformer–To the Hunt, by Relaunch. Trainer Shirreffs John. Bred by Wind Hill Farm (Ky).

STARRER pulled her way along early, stalked off the rail, bid outside SIGHTSEEK into the stretch, gained the advantage nearing midstretch and gamely inched clear late under urging. SIGHTSEEK took the early lead and angled in, set the pace inside, fought back inside the stretch but could not match that one late. BELLA BELLUCCI stalked outside a rival then off the rail, bid three deep into the stretch but could make no impact on the top pair in the final furlong. GOT KOKO saved ground chasing the pace, came out into the stretch and lacked a further response. PRINTEMPS (CHI) angled to the inside when unhurried early, trailed a bit off the rail on the backstretch and second turn and was outrun.

Owners— 1, Krikorian George; 2, Juddmonte Farms Inc; 3, Tabor Michael B; 4, Headley & Leung; 5, Amerman Racing Stables
Trainers—1, Shirreffs John; 2, Frankel Robert; 3, Drysdale Neil; 4, Headley Bruce; 5, McAnally Ronald
Scratched— Affluent (25Jan03 ⁸SA¹)

$2 Daily Double (6–5) Paid $12.00; Daily Double Pool $54,378.
$1 Pick Three (6–6–5/6) Paid $44.90; Pick Three Pool $74,923.

SEVENTH RACE
Gulfstream
MARCH 14, 2003

7 FURLONGS. (1.20) 23rd Running of THE STONERSIDE FORWARD GAL. Grade III. Purse $100,000 Guaranteed. FILLIES, THREE YEAR OLDS. By subscription of $100 each, which shall accompany the nomination, $1,000 to pass the entry box and $1,000 additional to start, with $100,000 guaranteed. The owner of the winner to receive $60,000; $20,000 to second, $11,000 to third, $6,000 to fourth and $3,000 to fifth. Weight: 121 lbs. Non-winners of $50,000 once allowed, 2 lbs.; $40,000 once anytime or $30,000 in 2003, 4 lbs.; $25,000 once or two races other than Maiden of Claiming, 6 lbs. Trophy to winning Owner. Closed Wednesday, March 5, 2003 with 19 Nominations.

Value of Race: $100,000 Winner $60,000; second $20,000; third $11,000; fourth $6,000; fifth $3,000. Mutuel Pool $318,252.00 Exacta Pool $229,505.00 Trifecta Pool $164,324.00 Superfecta Pool $46,588.00

Last Raced	Horse	M/Eqt.	A.Wt	PP	St	¼	½	Str	Fin	Jockey	Odds $1
7Dec02 3Hou2	Midnight Cry	L	3 117	1	5	$5^{2\frac{1}{2}}$	4^2	1^1	$1^{2\frac{3}{4}}$	Prado E S	4.60
5Feb03 8GP2	Final Round	L	3 117	7	8	8	8	5^{hd}	$2^{\frac{3}{4}}$	Day P	6.10
2Feb03 10GP2	Chimichurri	L	3 121	3	4	1^{hd}	2^1	2^1	$3^{\frac{1}{2}}$	Velazquez J R	3.60
2Feb03 10GP1	House Party		3 121	4	2	6^9	6^8	4^1	$4^{1\frac{3}{4}}$	Santos J A	2.80
22Feb03 10GP1	Bella Lauren	Lb	3 115	6	7	7^{hd}	7^{hd}	6^4	$5^{5\frac{3}{4}}$	Guidry M	24.60
6Feb03 8GP1	Fast Cookie		3 117	2	6	$3^{1\frac{1}{2}}$	1^1	$3^{1\frac{1}{2}}$	$6^{6\frac{3}{4}}$	Bailey J D	*2.80
2Feb03 10GP3	Glorious Miss	L	3 117	8	1	4^{hd}	5^{hd}	$7^{1\frac{1}{2}}$	7^2	Coa E M	27.50
17Jan03 8GP1	City Fire	Lb	3 117	5	3	2^{hd}	3^{hd}	8	8	Velasquez C	17.80

***—Actual Betting Favorite.**

OFF AT 3:53 Start Good For All But FINAL ROUND Won driving. Track fast.
TIME $:22, :44^2, 1:09^2, 1:22^2$ (:22.08, :44.42, 1:09.40, 1:22.55)

$2 Mutuel Prices:

1-MIDNIGHT CRY	11.20	6.40	3.80
7-FINAL ROUND		6.00	3.80
3-CHIMICHURRI			3.00

$1 EXACTA 1-7 PAID $41.70 $1 TRIFECTA 1-7-3 PAID $226.10 $1 SUPERFECTA 1-7-3-4 PAID $698.80

Ch. f, (May), by Smart Strike-Mythical Dancer, by Sovereign Dancer. Trainer McPeek Kenneth G. Bred by Runnymede Farm Inc & Peter J Callahan (Ky).

MIDNIGHT CRY well placed while well in hand along the inside, angled three wide just past midway of the turn, rallied to take over in early stretch and drew clear under pressure. FINAL ROUND trailed after stumbling badly at the start, angled out for the stretch run and closed well for the place. CHIMICHURRI showed speed off the rail, was outmoved by FAST COOKIE racing into the turn, came on again to reach near even terms for command entering the stretch but was outfinished. HOUSE PARTY reserved early, swung out for the stretch run and failed to rally. BELLA LAUREN off slowly, failed to menace. FAST COOKIE outran CHIMICHURRI to gain the lead down the backstretch, showed speed along the inside to the top of the stretch and tired. GLORIOUS MISS showed early foot, raced four wide on the turn and faltered. CITY FIRE showed brief speed, raced three wide on the turn and faded.

Owners— 1, Barrister Hall Stable; 2, Humphrey G W Jr; 3, Peachtree Stable; 4, Shields Joseph V Jr; 5, Tortora Jacqueline & Emanuel; 6, Stonerside Stable; 7, Buckram Oak Farm; 8, M Gill

Trainers—1, McPeek Kenneth G; 2, Arnold George R II; 3, Pletcher Todd A; 4, Jerkens H Allen; 5, Tortora Emanuel; 6, Mott William I; 7, Zito Nicholas P; 8, Shuman Mark

$1 Pick Three (2-1-1) Paid $90.70; Pick Three Pool $45,938.

NINTH RACE
Gulfstream
MARCH 14, 2003

1⅛ MILES. (1.46^2) 33rd Running of THE BONNIE MISS. Grade II. Purse $200,000 Guaranteed. FILLIES, THREE YEARS OLD. By subscription of $200 each, which shall accompany the nomination, $2,000 to pass the entry box and $2,000 additional to start, with $200,000 guaranteed. The owner of the winner to receive $120,000, $40,000 to second, $22,000 to third, $12,000 to fourth and $6,000 to fifth. Weight: 122 lbs. Non-winners of $50,000 twice at a mile or over, allowed 2 lbs.; $50,000 once at a mile or over lifetime or $35,000 at any distance in 2003, 4 lbs.; $30,000 at any distance or$25,000 at amile or over, 6 lbs. Trophy to winning Owner. Closed Wednesday, March 5, 2003 with 17 Nominations.

Value of Race: $200,000 Winner $120,000; second $40,000; third $22,000; fourth $12,000; fifth $6,000. Mutuel Pool $437,742.00 Exacta Pool $257,282.00 Trifecta Pool $201,116.00 Superfecta Pool $73,597.00

Last Raced	Horse	M/Eqt.	A.Wt	PP	St	¼	½	¾	Str	Fin	Jockey	Odds $1
23Feb03 9GP2	Ivanavinalot	Lf	3 122	7	6	$2^{1\frac{1}{2}}$	2^2	2^1	2^1	$1^{1\frac{3}{4}}$	Velazquez J R	1.00
23Feb03 9GP5	My Boston Gal	L	3 120	3	2	$1^{1\frac{1}{2}}$	1^1	1^1	$1^{\frac{1}{2}}$	$2^{3\frac{1}{4}}$	Day P	3.20
3Feb03 9GP1	Holiday Lady	L	3 118	2	4	$6^{3\frac{1}{2}}$	5^3	5^5	4^3	3^1	Coa E M	9.70
23Feb03 9GP3	Gold Player	Lb	3 116	6	7	5^1	6^3	6^1	6^3	4^{nk}	Guidry M	43.60
23Feb03 5GP3	Westerly Breeze	L	3 120	4	3	3^{hd}	4^6	4^4	3^1	$5^{2\frac{3}{4}}$	Douglas R R	10.90
3Feb03 9GP4	Tarnished Halo	L	3 116	1	1	7	7	7	$5^{\frac{1}{2}}$	$6^{9\frac{1}{2}}$	Santos J A	47.70
23Feb03 8GP1	Spin Control	L	3 116	5	5	4^5	3^{hd}	$3^{\frac{1}{2}}$	7	7	Prado E S	3.20

OFF AT 4:55 Start Good For All But HOLIDAY LADY Won driving. Track fast.
TIME $:23^1, :47^1, 1:11^4, 1:37^3, 1:50^3$ (:23.32, :47.29, 1:11.93, 1:37.74, 1:50.72)

$2 Mutuel Prices:

8-IVANAVINALOT	4.00	2.60	2.10
4-MY BOSTON GAL		3.40	2.10
3-HOLIDAY LADY			2.20

$1 EXACTA 8-4 PAID $6.80 $1 TRIFECTA 8-4-3 PAID $22.70 $1 SUPERFECTA 8-4-3-7 PAID $118.70

Dk. b. or br. f, (Mar), by West Acre-Beaty Sark, by Deputy Minister. Trainer O'Connell Kathleen. Bred by Gilbert G Campbell (Fla).

IVANAVINALOT stalked the pace off the rail, rallied under pressure to catch MY BOSTON GAL at the sixteenth pole and edged away. MY BOSTON GAL quickly moved to the fore, made the pace along the inside to the sixteenth pole, then couldn't stay with the winner while clearly second best. HOLIDAY LADY unhurried after stumbling at the start, moved into contention on the far turn, swung out for the stretch run and had no late response. GOLD PLAYER failed to menace. WESTERLY BREEZE rated in striking position while saving ground, made a run along the inside to loom a threat in midstretch, then tired. TARNISHED HALO saved ground and failed to be a factor. SPIN CONTROL chased the leaders three wide into the far turn and faded.

Owners— 1, Campbell Gilbert G; 2, Porter C Bloch R & Milner P; 3, Farmer Tracy; 4, Evans Edward P; 5, Miles A S Jr; 6, Snowden Diane & Guy B; 7, R S Evans

Trainers—1, O'Connell Kathleen; 2, Nafzger Carl A; 3, Zito Nicholas P; 4, Hennig Mark; 5, Nafzger Carl A; 6, Reinstedler Anthony; 7, Motion H Graham

Scratched— Ebony Breeze (1Feb03 10TAM1)

$1 Pick Three (1-6/8-8) Paid $57.90; Pick Three Pool $29,971.

EIGHTH RACE
Aqueduct
MARCH 15, 2003

6 FURLONGS. (1.07^4) TOBOGGAN H. Grade III. Purse $100,000 INNER DIRT. (Up to $19,400 NYSBFOA) A HANDICAP FOR THREE YEAR OLDS AND UPWARD. By subscription of $100 each, which should accompany the nomination; $500 to pass the entry box; $500 to start, with $100,000 added. The added money and all fees to be divided60% to the winner, 20% to second, 11% to third, 6% to fourth and 3% to fifth. Trophies will be presented to the winning owner, trainer and jockey. Closed Saturday, March 1, 2003 with 26 Nominations.

Value of Race: $109,100 Winner $65,460; second $21,820; third $12,001; fourth $6,546; fifth $3,273. Mutuel Pool $382,120.00 Exacta Pool $302,661.00 Trifecta Pool $197,177.00

Last Raced	Horse	M/Eqt.	A.	Wt	PP	St	¼	½	Str	Fin	Jockey	Odds $1
26Feb03 8Aqu3	Affirmed Success	L	9	118	2	5	3½	2hd	2½	11	Migliore R	1.75
22Feb03 9Lrl2	Peeping Tom	L bf	6	117	3	2	4½	41½	32½	2¾	Bridgmohan S	4.00
26Feb03 8Aqu1	Captain Red	L bf	6	115	6	1	13	13	1½	3nk	McKee J	4.00
29Dec02 9Aqu1	Multiple Choice	L b	5	119	4	3	53½	53½	4hd	41¾	Carrero V	4.20
26Feb03 8Aqu2	Gold I. D.	L	4	113	1	4	21½	3hd	55	51¾	Castellano J	4.80
9Feb03 8Aqu3	Judge's Case	L b	6	113	5	6	6	6	6	6	Luzzi M J	24.25

OFF AT 4:24 Start Good . Won driving. Track fast.
TIME :21^4, :44^1, :56^1, 1:09 (:21.93, :44.22, :56.32, 1:09.09)

$2 Mutuel Prices:			
3 – AFFIRMED SUCCESS	5.50	3.40	2.40
4 – PEEPING TOM		3.70	2.60
7 – CAPTAIN RED			2.50

$2 EXACTA 3–4 PAID $17.80 $2 TRIFECTA 3–4–7 PAID $54.00

B. g, (Apr), by Affirmed – Towering Success , by Irish Tower . Trainer Schosberg Richard. Bred by Albert Fried Jr (Ky).

AFFIRMED SUCCESS showed good speed while in hand, raced three wide, dug in gamely when roused for the drive, reached the front inside the eighth pole and drew clear under a drive. PEEPING TOM stumbled at the start, was hustled up inside, put in a run on the rail nearing the stretch and finished gamely while in tight quarters in deep stretch. CAPTAIN RED quickly opened a clear lead, was angled over to the rail, set the pace and weakened along the inside in the final furlong. MULTIPLE CHOICE was outrun early, raced three wide and finished well outside. GOLD I. D. chased the pace along the inside and tired after a half mile. JUDGE'S CASE dropped back early, raced inside and lacked a rally. A claim of foul against the winner by the rider of the second place finisher, alleging interference in deep stretch, was not allowed.

Owners– 1, Fried Albert Jr; 2, Flatbird Stable; 3, Pyliotis Anthony; 4, Blum Peter E; 5, Mendel Bruce; 6, Pompa Paul P Jr

Trainers– 1, Schosberg Richard E; 2, Reynolds Patrick L; 3, Synnefias Dimitrios K; 4, Jerkens James A; 5, Bazeos Peter; 6, Araya Rene A

Scratched– The Deputy Is Home (20Feb03 7Lrl2)

EIGHTH RACE
Gulfstream
MARCH 15, 2003

1⅛ MILES. (1.46^2) 52nd Running of THE FLORIDA DERBY. Grade I. Purse $1,000,000 Guaranteed. THREE YEAR OLDS. By subscription of $3,000 each, which shall accompany the nomination, $6,000 to pass the entry box and $6,000 additional to start. The owner of the winner to receive $600,000; $190,000 to second, $100,000 to third, $60,000 to fourth, $30,000 to fifth and $20,000 to sixth. WEIGHT: 122 lbs. Horses finishing first, second or third in the Spectacular Bid Stakes, Holy Bull Stakes, Hutcheson Stakes, and/or the Fountain of Youth Stakes, will automatically be nominated to the Florida Derby. Early bird nominations to the Florida Derby series closed on Wednesday, November 13, 2002 with 117 nominations at a fee of $595. Closed Wednesday, March 5, 2003 with 5 Nominations at a fee of $3,000.

Value of Race: $1,000,000 Winner $600,000; second $190,000; third $100,000; fourth $60,000; fifth $30,000; sixth $20,000. Mutuel Pool $2,028,691.0 Exacta Pool $1,165,994.0 Trifecta Pool $976,428.00 Superfecta Pool $297,508.00

Last Raced	Horse	M/Eqt.	A.	Wt	PP	St	¼	½	¾	Str	Fin	Jockey	Odds $1
7Feb03 7SA2	Empire Maker	Lb	3	122	6	4	42½	3hd	21	1½	19¾	Bailey J D	2.10
15Feb03 11GP1	Trust N Luck	L	3	122	1	1	11	11½	11	25	2½	Velasquez C	1.00
16Feb03 9FG7	Indy Dancer	L	3	122	4	7	7	7	7	4½	32½	Velazquez J R	11.10
15Feb03 11GP2	Supah Blitz	Lb	3	122	2	2	616	616	68	33	47½	Homeister R B Jr	15.70
31Jan03 8GP1	Senor Swinger	L	3	122	5	5	5½	53½	42½	53	512	Prado E S	6.70
22Feb03 7GP2	Formal Attire	Lb	3	122	7	6	3hd	43	31	6	6	Coa E M	46.70
15Feb03 11GP3	Midway Cat	Lb	3	122	3	3	21½	2hd	52	—	—	Chavez J F	12.10

Midway Cat:Fell;

OFF AT 4:22 Start Good. Won driving. Track fast.
TIME :22^4, :46^1, 1:10^3, 1:36, 1:49 (:22.86, :46.35, 1:10.73, 1:36.14, 1:49.05)

$2 Mutuel Prices:			
6–EMPIRE MAKER	6.20	2.80	2.40
1–TRUST N LUCK		2.40	2.10
4–INDY DANCER			3.20

$1 EXACTA 6–1 PAID $7.00 $1 TRIFECTA 6–1–4 PAID $34.00 $1 SUPERFECTA 6–1–4–2 PAID $119.60

Dk. b. or br. c, (Apr), by Unbridled–Toussaud, by El Gran Senor. Trainer Frankel Robert. Bred by Juddmonte Farms Inc (Ky).

EMPIRE MAKER angled to the inside entering the first turn, tracked the leader into the far turn, eased outside that rival and rallied to take over at the eighth pole, then drew off while being put to the whip twice left handed. TRUST N LUCK quickly moved to the fore, made the pace along the inside into the stretch, then was no match for the winner while saving the place. INDY DANCER far back after being steadied in behind MIDWAY CAT at the start, swung out for the stretch run and finished willingly for the show. SUPAH BLITZ unhurried early, advanced along the inside to reach contention in the stretch but had no further response. SENOR SWINGER allowed to settle, raced four wide on the far turn and faltered. FORMAL ATTIRE chased the pace three wide into the far turn, then faded. MIDWAY CAT broke to the outside, chased the pace off the rail to the far turn, then was tiring when he broke down and fell leaving the far turn.

Owners— 1, Juddmonte Farms Inc; 2, Robsham Einar P; 3, Wertheimer Farm; 4, Bee Bee Stables & Tortora Jacquelin; 5, Golden Barry & Ackerman Robert Jr; 6, Flying Zee Stable; 7, B M H Stable

Trainers—1, Frankel Robert; 2, Ziadie Ralph; 3, Pletcher Todd A; 4, Tortora Emanuel; 5, Goldfine Mickey A; 6, Serpe Philip M; 7, Hiles Rick

---

$1 Pick Three (6–2–6) Paid $65.60; Pick Three Pool $129,055.

ELEVENTH RACE
Gulfstream
MARCH 15, 2003

7 FURLONGS. (1.20) 18th Running of THE SWALE. Grade III. Purse $150,000 Guaranteed. THREE YEAR OLDS. By subscription of $150 each, which shall accompany the nomination, $1,500 to pass the entry box and $1,500 additional to start, with $150,000 guaranteed. The owner of the winner to receive $90,000; $30,000 to second, $16,500 to third, $9,000 to fourth and $4,500 to fifth. Weights; 122 lbs. Non-winners of $50,000 twice allowed, 2 lbs.; $50,000 once anytime or $30,000 twice in 2003, 4 lbs.; $30,000 in 2003 or two races other than Maiden or Claiming, 6 lbs. Trophy to the winning Owner. Closed Wednesday, March 5, 2003 with 16 Nominations.

Value of Race: $150,000 Winner $90,000; second $30,000; third $16,500; fourth $9,000; fifth $4,500. Mutuel Pool $771,473.00 Exacta Pool $512,732.00 Trifecta Pool $405,591.00 Superfecta Pool $135,300.00

Last Raced	Horse	M/Eqt.	A.Wt	PP	St	¼	½	Str	Fin	Jockey	Odds $1
17Aug02 9Crc1	Midas Eyes	L	3 116	6	6	2½	1½	16	19¼	Bailey J D	4.30
10Feb03 7FG1	Posse	L	3 120	3	1	5hd	4hd	32	24½	Meche D J	3.30
15Feb03 11GP5	Whywhywhy	Lb	3 122	8	3	4hd	31½	2½	32¼	Prado E S	1.40
15Feb03 5GP1	Massive	L	3 116	5	5	1½	21	4hd	41¼	Day P	9.00
31Jan03 8GP3	Roaring Fever	Lb	3 116	1	2	3½	64	62½	5hd	Coa E M	25.80
15Feb03 9GP5	First Blush		3 120	4	4	62	51	53	64	Velasquez C	10.50
11Jan03 6GP4	Eagle Eyrie	L	3 116	2	8	8	8	7hd	7½	Guidry M	99.90
15Feb03 11GP7	Conservation	Lb	3 116	7	7	72½	71	8	8	Santos J A	7.60

OFF AT 5:46 Start Good For All But MIDAS EYES Won driving. Track fast.
TIME :21 4, :44 1, 1:08 2, 1:21 (:21.96, :44.33, 1:08.50, 1:21.06)

$2 Mutuel Prices:

6–MIDAS EYES	10.60	5.60	2.80
3–POSSE		4.80	2.80
8–WHYWHYWHY			2.40

$1 EXACTA 6–3 PAID $25.20 $1 TRIFECTA 6–3–8 PAID $67.80 $1 SUPERFECTA 6–3–8–5 PAID $205.40

B. c, (Apr), by Touch Gold–Bayou Plans, by Bayou Hebert. Trainer Frankel Robert. Bred by Jacks or Better Farm Inc (Fla).

MIDAS EYES stumbled at the start, prompted the pace outside MASSIVE, moved to take over from that rival after entering the turn, then drew off when set down for the drive. POSSE rated between horses, angled out for the drive and closed to prove second best. WHYWHYWHY chased the pace three wide into the stretch, then gave way. MASSIVE set the pace along the inside into the turn, continued on well to nearing the stretch and faltered. ROARING FEVER showed early foot along the inside and tired. FIRST BLUSH was no factor while racing three wide. EAGLE EYRIE was outrun. CONSERVATION showed little.

Owners— 1, E A Gann; 2, Heiligbrodt Racing Stable; 3, F Ouaki & P L Biancone Racing; 4, Jacks or Better Farm Inc; 5, Evans Edward P; 6, Cowan Marjorie & Irving M; 7, Dizney Donald R; 8, Bohemia Stable

Trainers—1, Frankel Robert; 2, Asmussen Steven M; 3, Biancone Patrick L; 4, Hatchett James; 5, Hennig Mark; 6, Jerkens H Allen; 7, Zito Nicholas P; 8, Tagg Barclay

$1 Pick Three (6–4–6) Paid $111.40; Pick Three Pool $62,813.

TENTH RACE
Oaklawn
MARCH 15, 2003

$1\frac{1}{16}$ MILES. (1.40 1) 17th Running of THE OAKLAWN BREEDERS' CUP. Grade III. Purse $200,000 (includes $100,000 BC – Breeders' Cup). FILLIES AND MARES, THREE-YEAR-OLDS AND UPWARD. (Includes $100,000 from Breeder's Cup Fund for Cup nominees only). Supplementary nominations may be made by closing time of entries at a fee of $10,000 which qualifies to start with $100,000 guaranteed. Weights: Three-year-olds, 114 lbs. Older, 122 lbs. Non-winners of $60,000 twice at a mile or over since September 16, 2002, allowed 3 lbs. $50,000 once at a mile or over since October 15, 2002 5 lbs. $30,000 at a mile or over in 2002, 7 lbs. $25,000 at any distance in 2003, 9 lbs. This race will not be divided. Preference will be given in the following order: Breeders' Cup nominees only of equal racing quality or weight assignment (Respective of sex and weight for age).

Value of Race: $200,000 Winner $120,000; second $40,000; third $20,000; fourth $12,000; fifth $8,000. Mutuel Pool $349,881.00 Exacta Pool $224,201.00 Trifecta Pool $227,713.00

Last Raced	Horse	M/Eqt.	A.Wt	PP	St	¼	½	¾	Str	Fin	Jockey	Odds $1
23Nov02 8CD3	Bien Nicole	L	5 122	8	6	51	31	2½	2hd	11¼	Pettinger D R	8.00
15Feb03 9OP1	Red n'Gold	L	5 117	7	2	21	2hd	1hd	1hd	2¾	Thompson T J	9.70
24Feb03 4GP1	Mandy's Gold	Lf	5 117	3	1	1½	1½	31½	3½	31	Douglas R R	0.40
15Feb03 9OP2	Reason To Talk	Lf	4 117	2	3	41	5½	5hd	45	41¼	Lopez J	15.10
22Feb03 9FG3	Took Out	L	4 114	9	8	9	9	9	5½	54¾	Kuntzweiler G	a-42.00
15Feb03 1OP1	Lotta Rhythm	L	4 117	5	5	71	86	81	9	6nk	Court J K	30.90
2Mar03 9OP7	Due To Win Again	Lb	5 117	4	4	3hd	63	62½	61½	7nk	Castellano A Jr	a-42.00
9Feb03 1OP1	Cherylville Slew	L	4 115	6	7	84½	7½	73½	7½	85¼	Quinonez L S	46.40
25Jan03 8SA3	Secret Of Mecca	Lf	5 113	1	9	61½	4½	4hd	8hd	9	Garcia M S	4.10

a–Coupled: Took Out and Due To Win Again.

OFF AT 5:42 Start Good. Won driving. Track fast.
TIME :24 1, :48 2, 1:13, 1:37 4, 1:44 (:24.31, :48.56, 1:13.07, 1:37.89, 1:44.19)

$2 Mutuel Prices:

8–BIEN NICOLE	18.00	7.00	2.40
7–RED N'GOLD		7.40	2.40
4–MANDY'S GOLD			2.20

$2 EXACTA 8–7 PAID $117.80 $2 TRIFECTA 8–7–4 PAID $278.80

Ch. m, by Bien Bien–Dana Nicole, by Flying Paster. Trainer Von Hemel Donnie K. Bred by The Richter Family Trust (Ky).

BIEN NICOLE four wide when off the pace in the first turn, ranged up on the outside to challenge in the second turn, professional through stretch, edged clear in game fashion. RED N'GOLD pressured the early leader off the rail, vied between foes when challenging in the second bend, slight advantage past the furlong marker, could not match strides late. MANDY'S GOLD broke cleanly, set a soft pace along the inside, took a bad step entering the far turn, had little left the final furlong. REASON TO TALK tracked the pace inside, angled out sharply with a quarter remaining to be four wide, lodged a bid soon after widest of all, hung. TOOK OUT trailed early, improved position into the stretch, made little impact. LOTTA RHYTHM lacked a significant late response. DUE TO WIN AGAIN forwardly placed, backed up. CHERYLVILLE SLEW remained back throughout. SECRET OF MECCA off a step slow, within striking distance on the outside into the far turn, fanned five wide entering the stretch, faded.

Owners— 1, Richter Kristine & John; 2, English Kenneth D & Braun Alan; 3, Steeplechase Farm John A Gorham; 4, K & K Racing Stable; 5, Scarberry Howard & Penny; 6, Morrison Dolphus; 7, Scarberry Howard & Penny; 8, Trout C R; 9, Mike Henton & Toby Turrell

Trainers—1, Von Hemel Donnie K; 2, Holthus Robert E; 3, Gorham Michael E; 4, Vance David R; 5, Scarberry Howard; 6, Wiggins Hal R 7, Scarberry Howard; 8, Trout C R; 9, Cardenas Ruben

$2 Pick Three (5–5–8) Paid $242.60; Pick Three Pool $17,969.

SEVENTH RACE
Santa Anita
MARCH 15, 2003

1½ MILES. (Turf)(2.22^{4}) 52nd Running of THE SAN LUIS REY HANDICAP. Grade II. Purse $250,000. FOUR-YEAR-OLDS AND UPWARD. By subscription of $250 each to accompany the nomination or by supplementary nomination of $5,000 by Sunday, March 9. $2,500 additional to start. Weights Tuesday, March 11. Highweights preferred. Closed Thursday, March 6 with 17 nominations. (Rail at 15 Feet).

Value of Race: $250,000 Winner $150,000; second $50,000; third $30,000; fourth $15,000; fifth $5,000. Mutuel Pool $568,623.00 Exacta Pool $302,264.00 Quinella Pool $30,603.00 Trifecta Pool $291,930.00 Superfecta Pool $96,224.00

Last Raced	Horse	M/Eqt.	A.Wt	PP	¼	½	1	1¼	Str	Fin	Jockey	Odds $1
20Feb03 ^{5}SA^{5}	Champion Lodge-IR	LB	6 116	2	4^{1}	5^{1}	$5^{1\frac{1}{2}}$	$4^{\frac{1}{2}}$	$2^{3\frac{1}{2}}$	1^{6}	Solis A	7.10
15Feb03 ^{7}SA^{2}	Special Matter	LBb	5 113	1	1^{1}	$1^{\frac{1}{2}}$	1^{1}	$1^{2\frac{1}{2}}$	$1^{\frac{1}{2}}$	2^{1}	Baze T C	4.10
25Jan03 ^{2}SA^{1}	Adminniestrator	LB	6 116	3	7	7	7	$5^{\frac{1}{2}}$	$4^{1\frac{1}{2}}$	3^{3}	Flores D R	3.50
8Jan03 ^{5}SA^{2}	Bonaguil	LB	6 112	6	6^{hd}	$6^{\frac{1}{2}}$	6^{hd}	6^{2}	6^{15}	4^{1}	Farina Tony	30.60
20Feb03 ^{5}SA^{2}	Sumitas-GER	LB	7 115	4	$2^{\frac{1}{2}}$	$3^{\frac{1}{2}}$	3^{1}	$2^{\frac{1}{2}}$	3^{hd}	$5^{\frac{1}{2}}$	Valenzuela P A	3.10
15Dec02 ST^{14}	Delta Form-AU	LB	7 117	7	5^{1}	$4^{\frac{1}{2}}$	4^{hd}	3^{hd}	$5^{\frac{1}{2}}$	6^{30}	Smith M E	2.30
4Dec02 ^{5}Hol^{1}	Tenaja Trail	LB	4 113	5	3^{hd}	$2^{\frac{1}{2}}$	$2^{\frac{1}{2}}$	7	7	7	Almeida G F	11.90

OFF AT 3:38 Start Good. Won driving. Course yielding.
TIME $:24^{4}$, $:50^{1}$, $1:15^{4}$, $1:41^{3}$, $2:06^{4}$, $2:33^{2}$ (:24.89, :50.32, 1:15.86, 1:41.65, 2:06.98, 2:33.48)

$2 Mutuel Prices:				
	2-CHAMPION LODGE-IR	16.20	7.20	4.40
	1-SPECIAL MATTER		6.40	4.00
	3-ADMINNIESTRATOR			3.40

$1 EXACTA 2-1 PAID $45.40 $2 QUINELLA 1-2 PAID $46.20 $1 TRIFECTA 2-1-3 PAID $155.10 $1 SUPERFECTA 2-1-3-8 PAID $1,669.60

B. g, by Sri Pekan-Legit*Ire, by Runnett*GB. Trainer Shulman Sanford. Bred by Whitehead Mrs A (Ire).

CHAMPION LODGE (IRE) content to settle off the pace while saving ground, rousing nearing the three eighths marker, spilt foes, then whittled the gap on pacesetter, collared that foe inside the eighth marker and powered clear under urging. SPECIAL MATTER quickly stepped to the front, dictated the pace into the stretch, dug in when challenged, could not match the winner in the drive but gamely held second. ADMINNIESTRATOR lagged back from the inside and saved ground, moved up from along the rail into the final bend, awaited room, came off the fence into the stretch and gained the show. BONAGUIL unhurried while between rivals early and outside ADMINNIESTRATOR, commenced a rally nearing the final turn, caught three wide on that bend and four wide into the stretch and failed to menace. SUMITAS (GER) stalked the pacesetter from along the fence into the third turn, continued inside but weakened. DELTA FORM (AUS) content to stalk the pace while outside the eventual winner, remained off the rail, then three wide entering the stretch and lacked any late response. TENAJA TRAIL tugged his way into a prominent position, remained close up nearing the final turn and off the rail, dropped back on that bend and gave way readily. RACE STARTED ON MAIN COURSE.

Owners— 1, Charles Ronald L & Clear Valley Sta; 2, Elder McClintock & McClintock et al; 3, Nierenberg Nico; 4, Red Baron's Barn; 5, Tanaka Gary A; 6, Team Valor Stables; 7, Cobra Farm Inc

Trainers—1, Shulman Sanford; 2, Becerra Rafael; 3, Gallagher Patrick; 4, Vienna Darrell; 5, Frankel Robert; 6, Sahadi Jenine; 7, Young Steven W

Scratched— Requete (20Feb03 ^{5}SA^{1}), Night Patrol (1Feb03 ^{7}TUP^{9}), Blue Steller (29Dec02 ^{8}SA^{4})

$2 Daily Double (11-2) Paid $453.20; Daily Double Pool $25,840.
$1 Pick Three (4-11-2) Paid $648.10; Pick Three Pool $70,641.

NINTH RACE
Aqueduct
MARCH 16, 2003

1 MILE 70 YARDS. (Inner Dirt)(1.38^{4}) 51st Running of THE GOTHAM. Grade III. Purse $200,000. (Up to $34,800 NYSBFOA). THREE YEAR OLDS. By subscription of $200 each, which should accompany the nomination; $1,000 to pass the entry box; $1,000 to start. The purse to be divided 60% to the winner, 20% to second, 11% to third, 6% to fourth and 3% to fifth. 123 lbs. Non-winners of $150,000; or $45,000 twice other than restricted stakes allowed 3 lbs.; $50,000; or $30,000 in 2003, 5 lbs.; three races other than maiden or claiming, 7 lbs. Trophies will be presented to the winning owner, trainer and jockey. Closed Saturday, March 1, 2003 with 53 Nominations.

Value of Race: $200,000 Winner $120,000; second $40,000; third $22,000; fourth $12,000; fifth $6,000. Mutuel Pool $580,712.00 Exacta Pool $428,062.00 Trifecta Pool $318,164.00

Last Raced	Horse	M/Eqt.	A.Wt	PP	St	¼	½	¾	Str	Fin	Jockey	Odds $1
22Feb03 ^{8}Aqu^{6}	Alysweep	Lbf	3 120	3	2	1^{1}	$1^{1\frac{1}{2}}$	$1^{1\frac{1}{2}}$	$1^{5\frac{1}{2}}$	$1^{4\frac{1}{4}}$	Migliore R	9.50
1Mar03 ^{10}TP^{3}	Grey Comet	L	3 120	2	1	$4^{\frac{1}{2}}$	4^{2}	$3^{1\frac{1}{2}}$	2^{3}	$2^{1\frac{1}{2}}$	Gryder A T	4.00
15Feb03 ^{3}GP^{2}	Spite The Devil		3 116	5	3	$7^{2\frac{1}{2}}$	7^{3}	6^{hd}	$4^{\frac{1}{2}}$	3^{nk}	Luzzi M J	5.00
22Feb03 ^{10}Tam^{5}	Colita	L	3 116	8	8	8^{3}	8^{3}	7^{hd}	5^{hd}	4^{1}	Bridgmohan S X	2.80
8Feb03 ^{8}Aqu^{5}	Torre And Zim	L	3 116	6	6	2^{hd}	3^{hd}	$2^{\frac{1}{2}}$	$3^{\frac{1}{2}}$	$5^{1\frac{3}{4}}$	Arroyo N Jr	8.20
8Feb03 ^{9}Lrl^{1}	Gimmeawink	L	3 120	9	9	$6^{\frac{1}{2}}$	$5^{1\frac{1}{2}}$	$5^{1\frac{1}{2}}$	$6^{3\frac{1}{2}}$	6^{5}	Black A S	4.10
1Mar03 ^{6}Aqu^{1}	Max Forever	Lb	3 116	7	7	$3^{1\frac{1}{2}}$	2^{hd}	4^{1}	7^{hd}	7^{1}	Castellano J J	12.80
22Feb03 ^{8}Aqu^{3}	Mustbinthefrontrow	L	3 116	4	4	$5^{\frac{1}{2}}$	6^{hd}	$8^{2\frac{1}{2}}$	8^{6}	$8^{11\frac{1}{2}}$	Fogelsonger R	42.75
19Feb03 ^{6}Aqu^{1}	Midnight Charlie	Lbf	3 116	1	5	9	9	9	9	9	Castillo H Jr	21.50

OFF AT 4:50 Start Good. Won driving. Track fast.
TIME $:23^{4}$, $:47^{3}$, $1:11^{4}$, $1:36^{2}$, $1:40^{3}$ (:23.80, :47.69, 1:11.89, 1:36.48, 1:40.60)

$2 Mutuel Prices:				
	3-ALYSWEEP	21.00	9.30	7.30
	2-GREY COMET		5.10	3.40
	5-SPITE THE DEVIL			5.00

$2 EXACTA 3-2 PAID $88.00 $2 TRIFECTA 3-2-5 PAID $513.00

Ch. r, (Mar), by End Sweep-Chronicler, by Alysheba. Trainer Reynolds Patrick L. Bred by M G G Holdings (Fla).

ALYSWEEP came away running, quickly showed in front, controlled the pace along the inside while in hand, responded when set down entering the stretch, drew away and remained well clear under a steady drive. GREY COMET was rated along inside, saved ground, angled out into the stretch and finished gamely but could not get near the winner. SPITE THE DEVIL was rated inside, raced on the rail while in hand, responded when asked for run, angled out in deep stretch and finished well. COLITA was outrun early outside, advanced four wide on the second turn and offered a mild rally outside. TORRE AND ZIM raced with the pace while between rivals, took a run at the winner midway on the second turn, could not get to that rival and faded in the stretch. GIMMEAWINK was rated outside, raced three wide and had no response when roused. MAX FOREVER raced with the pace while three wide and tired after the opening three quarters. MUSTBINTHEFRONTROW raced close up while between rivals and tired after a half mile. MIDNIGHT CHARLIE dropped back after the start, raced inside and tired in the stretch.

Owners— 1, Doneson Mark & Dubb Michael; 2, Star Track Farms; 3, Hardwicke Stable; 4, Team Valor Stables Alvarez Mercedes; 5, Goldfarb Sanford Hemlock Hills Rose; 6, Wienkowitz Walter; 7, Dweck Raymond; 8, Borislow Daniel M; 9, Papandrea Vincent

Trainers—1, Reynolds Patrick L; 2, Contessa Gary C; 3, Jerkens H Allen; 4, Morales Carlos J; 5, Dutrow Richard E Jr; 6, Ritchey Tim F; 7, Perkins Ben W Jr; 8, Scanlan John F; 9, Gyarmati Leah

Scratched— New York Hero (27Feb03 ^{8}AQU^{2}), Cherokee's Boy (1Mar03 ^{8}LRL^{1})

THIRD RACE

Golden Gate

MARCH 16, 2003

1⅛ MILES. (Turf)(1.47^{3}) 57th Running of THE GOLDEN GATE BREEDERS' CUP HANDICAP. Grade III. Purse $150,000 (includes $50,000 BC – Breeders' Cup) A HANDICAP FOR THREE-YEAR-OLDS AND UPWARD. (Includes $50,000 from Breeders' Cup for Cup nominees only) By subscription of $100 each to accompany the nomination or by supplementary nomination of $2,000 by Noon, Sunday, March 9, 2003. $500 to pass the entry box and $500 additional to start with. The host association's Guaranteed monies to be divided 55% to the winner, 20% to second, 15% to third, 7.5% to fourth and 2.5% to fifth. Breeders' Cup monies also correspondingly divided providing a Breeders' Cup nominee has finished in an awarded position. Any Breeders' Cup Fund monies not awarded will revert back to the Fund. A trophy will be presented to the owner of the winner by Breeders' Cup Ltd. Closed Thursday, March 6, 2003 with 16 nominations.

Value of Race: $136,250 Winner $82,500; second $20,000; third $22,500; fourth $11,250. Mutuel Pool $141,621.00 Exacta Pool $86,939.00 Quinella Pool $10,217.00

Last Raced	Horse	M/Eqt.	A.Wt	PP	St	¼	½	¾	Str	Fin	Jockey	Odds $1
25Jan03 ^{2}SA^{10}	Ninebanks	LBb	5 116	4	1	$2^{3\frac{1}{2}}$	$2^{3\frac{1}{2}}$	2^{3}	2^{5}	1no	Warren R J Jr	2.60
8Feb03 ^{8}GG^{3}	Surprise Halo	LB	5 115	1	3	1^{1}	1^{1}	$1^{\frac{1}{2}}$	1^{hd}	$2^{6\frac{1}{2}}$	Alvarado F T	1.60
1Dec02 ^{8}Hol^{3}	Royal Gem	LBb	4 118	2	4	4	4	3^{hd}	$3^{\frac{1}{2}}$	3^{2}	Baze R A	1.10
23Feb03 ^{4}GG^{3}	Capt. Fly Hook	LB	6 114	3	2	3^{2}	3^{hd}	4	4	4	Castro J M	15.00

OFF AT 1:48 Start Good. Won driving. Course yielding.

TIME :24^{2}, :49^{4}, 1:13^{1}, 1:37^{3}, 1:50 (:24.54, :49.86, 1:13.21, 1:37.71, 1:50.07)

$2 Mutuel Prices:			
4–NINEBANKS	7.20	3.80	—
1–SURPRISE HALO		2.60	—
2–ROYAL GEM		—	—

$1 EXACTA 4–1 PAID $7.30 $2 QUINELLA 1–4 PAID $7.20

B. g, by Smokester–Nataka, by With Approval. Trainer Hollendorfer Jerry. Bred by Trudy McCaffery & John Toffan (Cal).

NINEBANKS pressed the pace for six furlongs, was asked for more on the second turn, raced up to engage SURPRISE HALO a furlong out, took a short lead to deep stretch then battled gamely late to hold. SURPRISE HALO set the pace while under constant pressure to the second turn, responded to urging to mid stretch, was headed by the winner in deep stretch but was fighting back gamely late and just missed. ROYAL GEM had no speed, was asked once on the second turn, lugged inward at the five sixteenths with the rider getting the whip caught in the reins while trying to switch, was pulled out to clear CAPT. FLY HOOK then finished evenly in the drive. CAPT. FLY HOOK was allowed to settle, saved ground on the second turn but lacked a closing response.

Owners— 1, Abruzzo Peter; 2, Karp Lawrence M & Ward Dennis; 3, Blatz Pamela & Smith Helen; 4, Aiello Ratzi Anderson Carol & Jerry

Trainers—1, Hollendorfer Jerry; 2, Ward Wesley A; 3, Frankel Robert; 4, Buckridge Gloria

$2 Daily Double (1–4) Paid $17.40; Daily Double Pool $8,903.
$1 Pick Three (5–1–4) Paid $67.40; Pick Three Pool $30,662.

FIFTH RACE

Santa Anita

MARCH 16, 2003

1$\frac{1}{16}$ MILES. (1.39) 66th Running of THE SAN FELIPE. Grade II. Purse $250,000. 3-year-olds. By subscription of $250 each to accompany the nomination. $2,500 additional to start. Early bird nominees to the 2003 Santa Anita Derby (Closing Date Monday, December 9, 2002) are automatically eligible to the San Felipe Stakes with all fees waived. Closed with 150. 122 lbs. Non-winners of $60,000 twice at one mile or over at any time or one such race since December 25 allowed 3 lbs.; of $50,000 at any distance, 6 lbs.

Value of Race: $250,000 Winner $150,000; second $50,000; third $30,000; fourth $15,000; fifth $5,000. Mutuel Pool $946,793.00 Exacta Pool $488,792.00 Quinella Pool $49,138.00 Trifecta Pool $502,960.00 Superfecta Pool $177,895.00

Last Raced	Horse	M/Eqt.	A.Wt	PP	St	¼	½	¾	Str	Fin	Jockey	Odds $1
23Feb03 ^{8}SA^{1}	Buddy Gil	LB	3 119	5	4	5^{1}	6^{hd}	$5^{1\frac{1}{2}}$	4^{1}	1no	Stevens G L	9.80
20Feb03 ^{2}SA^{1}	Atswhatimtalknbout	LB	3 116	7	10	10	10	7^{hd}	6^{5}	$2^{\frac{3}{4}}$	Flores D R	3.20
15Feb03 ^{4}SA^{1}	Brancusi	LB	3 116	8	6	2^{hd}	$3^{\frac{1}{2}}$	3^{1}	$1^{\frac{1}{2}}$	$3^{1\frac{1}{4}}$	Farina Tony	48.90
28Feb03 ^{5}SA^{3}	Logician	LBb	3 117	10	9	6^{hd}	2^{hd}	2^{hd}	3^{hd}	4^{1}	Desormeaux K J	86.20
18Jan03 ^{7}SA^{1}	Domestic Dispute	LB	3 122	6	7	$8^{1\frac{1}{2}}$	$8^{1\frac{1}{2}}$	$4^{\frac{1}{2}}$	$5^{\frac{1}{2}}$	5no	Bailey J D	2.00
1Feb03 ^{6}TuP^{2}	Siberland	LB	3 119	4	3	$1^{\frac{1}{2}}$	$1^{\frac{1}{2}}$	$1^{1\frac{1}{2}}$	$2^{\frac{1}{2}}$	$6^{9\frac{1}{2}}$	Baze T C	10.60
7Feb03 ^{7}SA^{1}	Man Among Men	LBb	3 116	1	5	9^{2}	$9^{1\frac{1}{2}}$	9^{2}	7^{1}	7^{1}	Solis A	2.60
15Feb03 ^{11}GP^{6}	Ten Cents A Shine	LB	3 116	9	8	$7^{\frac{1}{2}}$	$4^{\frac{1}{2}}$	6^{hd}	8^{hd}	8^{4}	Valenzuela P A	11.70
23Feb03 ^{8}SA^{3}	Flirt With Fortune	LB	3 116	2	2	$3^{\frac{1}{2}}$	$5^{\frac{1}{2}}$	10	9^{3}	9^{4}	Nakatani C S	36.60
20Feb03 ^{2}SA^{3}	Buckland Manor	LB	3 116	3	1	4^{hd}	$7^{1\frac{1}{2}}$	$8^{\frac{1}{2}}$	10	10	Smith M E	36.50

OFF AT 2:42 Start Good. Won driving. Track good.

TIME :22^{4}, :46^{2}, 1:10^{4}, 1:36^{4}, 1:43^{3} (:22.88, :46.57, 1:10.84, 1:36.88, 1:43.64)

$2 Mutuel Prices:			
5–BUDDY GIL	21.60	7.20	5.20
7–ATSWHATIMTALKNBOUT		4.60	4.00
8–BRANCUSI			13.20

$1 EXACTA 5–7 PAID $49.80 $2 QUINELLA 5–7 PAID $46.20 $1 TRIFECTA 5–7–8 PAID $1,475.90 $1 SUPERFECTA 5–7–8–10 PAID $17,749.40

B. g, (Feb), by Eastern Echo–Really Rising, by For Really. Trainer Mullins Jeff. Bred by Billingsley Creek Ranch (Ky).

BUDDY GIL content to settle off the leaders from between rivals, moved up a bit around the second turn, blocked and lacked room behind a wall of rivals in upper stretch, finally found room inside the eighth marker, surged under right hand pressure to reach the front and barely held. ATSWHATIMTALKNBOUT taken in hand leaving the gate and chased from off the fence, launched a rally early on the final bend, swung out and advanced five wide entering the stretch and closed furiously from far outside to narrowly miss. BRANCUSI angled to the rail and forced the pace in the middle stages, bid between rivals into the lane, gained lead and edged away past eighth marker but was overhauled in final strides. LOGICIAN caught five wide into the initial turn, forced the pace outside foe, challenged three deep entering the stretch but gave ground grudgingly late in the drive. DOMESTIC DISPUTE chased while securing the rail into the backstretch, came back out on the final bend, caught four wide into the stretch and lacked the necessary late response. SIBERLAND stepped to the front, set a pressured pace from just off the rail, resisted when challenged approaching the stretch and but weakened over the final sixteenth. MAN AMONG MEN chased the leaders while saving ground, came out and raced three wide around the second turn and improved placing late. TEN CENTS A SHINE caught a bit tight into the initial turn, advanced four wide departing that bend, continued three wide and weakened. FLIRT WITH FORTUNE prominent from along the inside into the backstretch, continued within striking position but had little left for the drive. BUCKLAND MANOR settled off the leaders from along the rail, raced inside the eventual winner into and early on the second turn, then gave way readily.

Owners— 1, Desperado Stabless McFadden Merrill; 2, Hughes & Biscuit Stables LLC; 3, Tabor Michael B; 4, Reddam John P; 5, Garber Gary M; 6, Weir Dennis E; 7, Gamel Hubbard Sczesny Et Al; 8, Ramsey Kenneth L & Sarah K; 9, Chapman Carolyn M; 10, McCaffery Trudy & Toffan John A

Trainers—1, Mullins Jeff; 2, Ellis Ronald W; 3, Biancone Patrick L; 4, Dollase Craig; 5, Baffert Bob; 6, Lewis Kevin; 7, Mandella Gary; 8, Lukas D Wayne; 9, Chapman James K; 10, Gonzalez J Paco

$2 Daily Double (6–5) Paid $88.60; Daily Double Pool $38,376.
$1 Pick Three (3/7–6–5) Paid $97.90; Pick Three Pool $109,833.

NINTH RACE
Oaklawn
MARCH 16, 2003

1 1/16 MILES. (1.40^{1}) 44th Running of THE RAZORBACK HANDICAP. Grade III. Purse $100,000. FOUR-YEAR-OLDS AND UPWARD. Weights to be announced Sunday, March 9. In Handicap Stakes starting preference will be given to highweights. Starters to be named through the entry box by the usual time of closing. The owner of the winner to receive a trophy. Nominations closed Friday, March 7 with 22 nominations.

Value of Race: $100,000 Winner $60,000; second $20,000; third $10,000; fourth $6,000; fifth $4,000. Mutuel Pool $273,718.00 Exacta Pool $185,609.00 Trifecta Pool $203,510.00

Last Raced	Horse	M/Eqt.	A.Wt	PP	St	¼	½	¾	Str	Fin	Jockey	Odds $1
22Feb03 9OP1	Colorful Tour	L	4 118	3	1	1½	1½	1hd	11½	1nk	Quinonez L S	1.90
22Feb03 9OP4	Crafty Shaw	L	5 119	2	7	53½	53½	31½	3hd	2hd	Lopez J	1.20
2Feb03 9OP1	Windward Passage	L	4 118	7	3	4½	3½	4hd	4½	31	Meche D J	3.60
1Feb03 8FG1	Colonial Colony	L	5 115	4	5	61½	7	5hd	63	4nk	Johnson J M	34.00
4Mar03 9FG6	Gold Tango	L	4 112	6	4	31	4½	62	5½	5no	Thompson T J	27.00
22Feb03 9OP5	Makors Mark	L	6 118	5	2	22½	22	2hd	2hd	62½	Baze G	9.70
7Mar03 9OP3	Dust On the Bottle	Lb	8 113	1	6	7	6hd	7	7	7	Doocy T T	21.50

OFF AT 5:11 Start Good. Won driving. Track fast.
TIME :23^{2}, :47, 1:11^{4}, 1:37, 1:43^{2} (:23.47, :47.18, 1:11.88, 1:37.10, 1:43.53)

$2 Mutuel Prices:				
	4-COLORFUL TOUR	5.80	2.80	2.40
	3-CRAFTY SHAW		2.60	2.20
	8-WINDWARD PASSAGE			2.60

$2 EXACTA 4-3 PAID $13.20 $2 TRIFECTA 4-3-8 PAID $33.60

Ch. c, by Tour d'Or–For You and Me, by For Love and Glory. Trainer Hickey P Noel. Bred by Irish Acres Farm (Ill).

COLORFUL TOUR broke on top, set a moderate pace toward the inside, set down for the drive, long, determined drive, not to be denied. CRAFTY SHAW slow to settle, ranged up on the outside to challenge in the second turn, failed to sustain that effort fully entering the stretch, drifted slightly, dug in for the place. WINDWARD PASSAGE tracked the leader into the second turn toward the inside, waited for room a late in that bend and into the stretch, moved out to make a hole nearing the furlong marker bumping GOLD TANGO, finished well while missing the place. FOLLOWING A CLAIM OF FOUL BY THE RIDER OF GOLD TANGO AGAINST WINDWARD PASSAGE FOR INTERFERENCE THROUGH THE STRETCH, THE RESULT WAS ALLOWED TO STAND. COLONIAL COLONY lacked speed, came five wide into the stretch, some late gain midtrack. GOLD TANGO within striking distance, bumped and put in tight by WINDWARD PASSAGE approaching the furlong marker, finished evenly. MAKORS MARK pressured the leader, weakened the final furlongs. DUST ON THE BOTTLE never a serious factor.

Owners— 1, Irish Acres Farm; 2, Cella Charles J; 3, Team Valor Stables; 4, Lakeside Farms; 5, Franks John; 6, Ll McMurry; 7, Hild Sharon L

Trainers—1, Hickey P Noel; 2, Vestal Peter M; 3, Asmussen Steven M; 4, Bindner Walter M Jr; 5, Barnett Bobby C; 6, Forster Grant T; 7, Hild Glenn L

Scratched— Slider (22Feb03 7OP1)

$2 Pick Three (2-10-4) Paid $768.80; Pick Three Pool $12,166.

ELEVENTH RACE
Tampa Bay
MARCH 16, 2003

1 1/16 MILES. (1.43^{2}) 23rd Running of THE TAMPA BAY DERBY. Grade III. Purse $250,000 Guaranteed. FOR THREE YEARS OLD. By subscription of $150 each which should accompany the nomination. $1,500 to pass the entry box. $1,500 additional to start with $200,000 Guaranteed. With 60% to the winner, 20% to second, 10% to third, 5% to fourth, 3% to fifth and 2% to sixth. Weight: 123 lbs. Non-winners of $60,000 allowed 3 lbs.; $30,000 once or $15,000 twice 5 lbs. $15,000 once or $7,500 twice, 7 lbs. (Maiden and Claiming races not considered). Starters and riders to be named through the entry box Thursday, March 13, 2003. SUPPLEMENTARY NOMINATIONS OF $7,500 EACH, WHICH INCLUDE ENTRY AND STARTING FEES, CLOSED THURSDAY, MARCH 13, 2003. Closed Saturday, March 1, 2003 with 38 nominations.

Value of Race: $250,000 Winner $150,000; second $50,000; third $25,000; fourth $12,500; fifth $7,500; sixth $5,000. Mutuel Pool $295,333.00 Exacta Pool $186,360.00 Trifecta Pool $159,593.00 Superfecta Pool $51,160.00

Last Raced	Horse	M/Eqt.	A.Wt	PP	St	¼	½	¾	Str	Fin	Jockey	Odds $1
15Feb03 3GP1	Region Of Merit	L	3 120	8	2	31½	31	2hd	2½	1¾	Coa E M	1.60
15Feb03 10GP1	Aristocat	L	3 118	6	3	41	4½	5½	5½	2nk	Velazquez J R	1.90
18Jan03 10Tam2	Hear No Evil	Lbf	3 123	7	1	12	12½	12	11	31¾	Cruz M R	34.60
22Feb03 10Tam1	White Buck	Lb	3 118	3	7	76	6½	42	32	4hd	Velez R I	27.40
15Feb03 9GP2	Strength Within	L	3 116	4	4	5hd	76	6½	63½	52	Guidry M	2.60
15Feb03 9GP6	Cajun Beat	L	3 118	2	5	21	21	3½	42	61¼	Boulanger G	10.70
27Feb03 4Tam1	Fast Eddie D	Lb	3 116	1	8	8	8	8	72	77¾	Ramirez M R	43.50
8Feb03 9GP1	Popular Groom		3 118	5	6	6hd	5½	78	8	8	Judice J C	13.00

OFF AT 5:21 Start Good. Won driving. Track fast.
TIME :23^{1}, :47, 1:11^{3}, 1:37^{3}, 1:44^{3} (:23.33, :47.06, 1:11.68, 1:37.64, 1:44.61)

$2 Mutuel Prices:				
	9-REGION OF MERIT	5.20	3.00	2.40
	6-ARISTOCAT		3.00	2.80
	7-HEAR NO EVIL			5.60

$2 EXACTA 9-6 PAID $12.20 $2 TRIFECTA 9-6-7 PAID $127.60 $2 SUPERFECTA 9-6-7-3 PAID $773.60

Ch. c, (Feb), by Touch Gold–Innocently Astray, by Gone West. Trainer Clement Christophe. Bred by Louie J Roussel III (Ky).

REGION OF MERIT stalked the leader from the outset while four wide, rallied out of the second turn to go after HEAR NO EVIL, gained a short lead from that one inside the final furlong then held ARISTOCRAT safe under steady handling. ARISTOCAT also stalked the leaders into the second turn, dropped back a bit through that turn then angled out five wide, brushing STRENGTH WITHIN in the process and finished willingly but too late. HEAR NO EVIL broke sharp, set a moderate pace under good handling then just hung late. WHITE BUCK made an inside middle move to be within striking distance a furlong out but was outfinished late. STRENGTH WITHIN was shuffled back early, made a four wide middle move but failed to respond to pressure. CAJUN BEAT chased for six furlongs then gave way. FAST EDDIE D bore in at the break and was no factor. POPULAR GROOM failed to menace.

Owners— 1, Calumet Farm; 2, Tabor Michael B; 3, Jacks or Better Farm Inc; 4, Paradise Olga; 5, Glen Hill Farm; 6, Satish Sanan & Joe & John Iracane; 7, Alnwick James; 8, Firestone Bertram R

Trainers—1, Clement Christophe; 2, Pletcher Todd A; 3, Decker Kenneth; 4, Paradise Jerry P; 5, Proctor Thomas F; 6, Gambolati Cam; 7, Gibson Linda M; 8, Mott William I

Scratched— Freedom Lane (22Feb03 10TAM2)

$2 Daily Double (6-9) Paid $43.00; Daily Double Pool $9,583.

TWELFTH RACE
Tampa Bay
MARCH 16, 2003

$1\frac{1}{16}$ MILES. (1.43^{2}) 41st Running of THE FLORIDA OAKS. Grade III. Purse $150,000 Guaranteed. FOR FILLIES THREE YEARS OLD. By subscription of $100 each which should accompany the nomination. $700 to pass the entry box. $700 additional to start. With 60% to the winner, 20% to second, 10% to third, 5% to fourth, 3% to fifth and 2% to sixth. Weight: 122 lbs. Non-winners of $50,000 allowed 2 lbs.; $25,000 once or $15,000 twice 4 lbs. $15,000 once or $7,500 twice, 6 lbs. (Maiden and Claiming races not considered). Closed Saturday, March 1, 2003 with 25 nominations. SUPPLEMENTAL NOMINATION FEE OF $5000: JUDGING LADY.

Value of Race: $150,000 Winner $90,000; second $30,000; third $15,000; fourth $7,500; fifth $4,500; sixth $3,000. Mutuel Pool $135,996.00 Exacta Pool $71,011.00 Quinella Pool $4,195.00 Trifecta Pool $66,590.00 Superfecta Pool $20,482.00

Last Raced	Horse	M/Eqt.	A.	Wt	PP	St	¼	½	¾	Str	Fin	Jockey	Odds $1
1Feb03 ^{10}Tam^{1}	Ebony Breeze	L	3	120	2	3	$1^{\frac{1}{2}}$	$2^{1\frac{1}{2}}$	2^{1}	2^{1}	$1^{\frac{1}{2}}$	Guidry M	0.30
22Feb03 ^{6}Tam^{3}	Dakota Light	Lb	3	122	1	1	$3^{\frac{1}{2}}$	4^{2}	4^{2}	$3^{\frac{1}{2}}$	2^{hd}	Coa E M	5.50
22Feb03 ^{6}Tam^{2}	Crimson And Roses	L	3	116	3	2	2^{2}	1^{hd}	1^{hd}	1^{hd}	3^{5}	Velez R I	4.80
5Feb03 ^{8}GP^{3}	Never Fail		3	118	6	6	6	5^{hd}	5^{2}	5^{5}	$4^{\frac{1}{2}}$	Cruz M R	8.60
6Feb03 ^{8}Tam^{1}	Judging Lady	L	3	116	5	4	$4^{2\frac{1}{2}}$	3^{hd}	3^{1}	4^{3}	5^{hd}	Castanon J L	25.40
5Mar03 ^{4}GP^{2}	Groomeroma	Lb	3	116	4	5	$5^{\frac{1}{2}}$	6	6	6	6	Ferrer J C	44.20

OFF AT 5:49 Start Good. Won driving. Track fast.
TIME :24, :48^{4}, 1:13^{3}, 1:38^{3}, 1:45^{1} (:24.01, :48.91, 1:13.67, 1:38.71, 1:45.20)

$2 Mutuel Prices:

2–EBONY BREEZE	2.60	2.20	2.10
1–DAKOTA LIGHT		3.40	2.10
3–CRIMSON AND ROSES			2.10

$2 EXACTA 2–1 PAID $8.40 $2 QUINELLA 1–2 PAID $7.60 $2 TRIFECTA 2–1–3 PAID $16.80 $2 SUPERFECTA 2–1–3–6 PAID $26.80

B. f, (Jan), by Belong to Me–Valid Carnauba, by Valid Appeal. Trainer Mott William I. Bred by Kinsman Farm (Ky).

EBONY BREEZE dueled for the lead inside from the outset, gamely resisted CRIMSON AND ROSES past the furlong marker then after gaining a short lead inside the final furlong, dug in to turn back DAKOTA LIGHT late. DAKOTA LIGHT was boxed inside from the three eighths pole to upper stretch, angled out leaving the furlong marker then finished gamely but too late. CRIMSON AND ROSES dueled two wide to the final 40 yards before just hanging late. NEVER FAIL passed tiring rivals. JUDGING LADY stalked the early pace outside, bid three wide out of the second turn to pose a threat a furlong out but weakened late. GROOMEROMA showed little.

Owners— 1, Kinsman Stable; 2, J D Farms; 3, Jacks or Better Farm Inc; 4, Bracken Micki; 5, J & J Investments; 6, Punches Dennis G
Trainers—1, Mott William I; 2, Brownlee David R; 3, Decker Kenneth; 4, Bracken James E; 5, Michael James A; 6, Hurtak Daniel C
Scratched— Ivanavinalot (14Mar03 ^{9}GP^{1})

$2 Daily Double (9–2) Paid $6.60; Daily Double Pool $29,512.
$2 Pick Three (6–9–2) Paid $91.20; Pick Three Pool $18,495.

TENTH RACE
Gulfstream
MARCH 22, 2003

ABOUT 1½ MILES. (Turf)(2.26^{1}) 42nd Running of THE PAN AMERICAN HANDICAP. Grade II. Purse $200,000 Guaranteed. THREE YEAR OLDS AND UPWARD. By subscription of $200 each, which shall accompany the nomination, $2,000 to pass the entry box and $2,000 additional to start, with $200,000 guaranteed. The owner of the winner to receive $120,000; $40,000 to second, $22,000 to third, $12,000 to fourth and $6,000 to fifth. Trophy to winning Owner. In the event this stake is taken off the turf, it may be subject to downgrading upon review of the Graded Stakes Committee. Closed Wednesday, March 12, 2003 with 20 Nominations. (Rail at 10 feet).

Value of Race: $200,000 Winner $120,000; second $40,000; third $22,000; fourth $12,000; fifth $6,000. Mutuel Pool $512,523.00 Exacta Pool $375,673.00 Trifecta Pool $315,647.00 Superfecta Pool $105,490.00

Last Raced	Horse	M/Eqt.	A.	Wt	PP	¼	½	1	1¼	Str	Fin	Jockey	Odds $1
9Feb03 ^{6}GP^{1}	Quest Star	Lb	4	113	3	$1^{\frac{1}{2}}$	$1^{1\frac{1}{2}}$	$1^{1\frac{1}{2}}$	1^{1}	$1^{2\frac{1}{2}}$	$1^{1\frac{3}{4}}$	Prado E S	4.90
16Feb03 ^{10}GP^{1}	Man From Wicklow	Lb	6	122	6	6^{1}	6^{hd}	7^{2}	$4^{1\frac{1}{2}}$	3^{hd}	2^{1}	Bailey J D	0.60
1Mar03 ^{8}GP^{1}	Reduit-GB	L	5	114	4	9	9	9	9	$6^{1\frac{1}{2}}$	3no	Guidry M	13.10
4Mar03 ^{9}FG^{4}	Whata Brainstorm	L	6	114	8	3^{1}	3^{hd}	3^{1}	$2^{1\frac{1}{2}}$	$2^{\frac{1}{2}}$	4^{nk}	Boulanger G	24.90
19Jan03 ^{10}GP^{2}	Macaw-IR	L	4	116	9	7^{hd}	$7^{2\frac{1}{2}}$	$6^{\frac{1}{2}}$	5^{1}	5^{1}	$5^{2\frac{1}{4}}$	Santos J A	6.10
17Feb03 ^{9}GP^{4}	Mr. Livingston	Lf	6	114	5	$2^{1\frac{1}{2}}$	2^{2}	2^{hd}	3^{hd}	$4^{2\frac{1}{2}}$	$6^{1\frac{1}{4}}$	Velasquez C	16.40
28Feb03 ^{10}GP^{1}	North Of Six	Lb	4	113	1	4^{hd}	$4^{1\frac{1}{2}}$	4^{1}	$7^{\frac{1}{2}}$	7^{2}	$7^{4\frac{1}{4}}$	Toribio Aurelio Jr	53.70
16Feb03 ^{10}GP^{2}	Just Listen	Lb	7	114	2	$5^{\frac{1}{2}}$	$5^{1\frac{1}{2}}$	5^{hd}	$6^{\frac{1}{2}}$	9	8^{nk}	Homeister R B Jr	19.70
13Feb03 ^{9}GP^{1}	Mr. Pleasentfar-BRZ	L	6	114	7	8^{2}	8^{1}	$8^{1\frac{1}{2}}$	8^{hd}	8^{hd}	9	Velez R I	31.10

OFF AT 5:12 Start Good. Won driving. Course firm.
TIME :24^{4}, :50, 1:15, 1:40^{2}, 2:04^{1}, 2:28^{2} (:24.98, :50.05, 1:15.15, 1:40.56, 2:04.35, 2:28.45)

$2 Mutuel Prices:

3–QUEST STAR	11.80	3.40	3.00
7–MAN FROM WICKLOW		2.20	2.20
4–REDUIT–GB			4.80

$1 EXACTA 3–7 PAID $13.10 $1 TRIFECTA 3–7–4 PAID $73.80 $1 SUPERFECTA 3–7–4–9 PAID $719.20

Dk. b. or br. c, by Broad Brush–Tinaca, by Manila. Trainer Walden W Elliott. Bred by John Messara (Ky).

QUEST STAR quickly moved to the fore, made the pace along the rail into the stretch and was fully extended to prevail. MAN FROM WICKLOW rated off the pace, made a run three wide on the final turn to reach contention, then didn't do enough late while up for the place. REDUIT (GB) outrun for more than a mile, angled wide in early stretch and rallied to be up for the show, then was vanned off after the finish. WHATA BRAINSTORM stalked the pace off the rail to nearing the stretch, weakened and was just edged for the show. MACAW (IRE) unhurried for a mile, steadied in tight quarters entering the final turn, then gained some ground in the drive without threatening. MR. LIVINGSTON chased the winner for more than a mile and tired. NORTH OF SIX well placed while saving ground, steadied entering the final turn and faltered. JUST LISTEN steadied in the early going, raced three wide and faded. MR. PLEASENTFAR (BRZ) showed little.

Owners— 1, Mansell Stables; 2, Violette Richard A Jr; 3, Thomas Soo; 4, Eaton John & Laymon Steve; 5, Melillo George & Sandra; 6, Palmer Teresa & David; 7, Fish Steven W & Bukowiecki Chris; 8, Guez Marie Romaine & Guez D; 9, Dubb Michael
Trainers—1, Walden W Elliott; 2, Violette Richard A Jr; 3, Skiffington Thomas J; 4, Picou James E; 5, Tagg Barclay; 6, Kaplan William A; 7, Bukowiecki Chris; 8, Catanese Joseph C III; 9, Reynolds Patrick L
Scratched— Generous Rosi (1Mar03 ^{4}GP^{1}), Serial Bride (19Jan03 ^{10}GP^{11})

$1 Pick Three (2/4/5/11–5–3) Paid $19.70; Pick Three Pool $41,636.

NINTH RACE
Aqueduct
MARCH 22, 2003

7 FURLONGS. (1.20) 11th Running of THE CICADA. Grade III. Purse $100,000 (Up to $19,400 NYSBFOA). FILLIES, THREE YEARS OLD. By subscription of $100 each, which should accompany the nomination; $500 to pass the entry box; $500 to start, with $100,000 added. The added money and all fees to be divided 60% to the winner, 20% tosecond, 11% to third, 6% to fourth and 3% to fifth. Weight 122 lbs. Non–winners of $35,000 in 2003 other than restricted stake allowed 2 lbs.; three races other than maiden or claiming, 4 lbs.; two races other than maiden or claiming, 6 lbs. Trophies will be presented to the winning owner, trainer and jockey. Closed Saturday, March 8, 2003 with 23 Nominations.

Value of Race: $108,300 Winner $64,980; second $21,660; third $11,913; fourth $6,498; fifth $3,249. Mutuel Pool $389,481.00 Exacta Pool $293,337.00 Trifecta Pool $212,861.00

Last Raced	Horse	M/Eqt.	A.	Wt	PP	St	¼	½	Str	Fin	Jockey	Odds $1
1Mar03 ^{8}Aqu^{4}	Cyber Secret	L	3	122	2	4	$2^{2\frac{1}{2}}$	$2^{1\frac{1}{2}}$	1^{5}	$1^{4\frac{1}{2}}$	Bridgmohan S X	4.50
30Nov02 ^{7}Aqu^{1}	Roar Emotion	L	3	116	1	6	4^{hd}	$4^{\frac{1}{2}}$	$2^{2\frac{1}{2}}$	$2^{1\frac{3}{4}}$	Migliore R	0.80
1Feb03 ^{9}Lrl^{1}	Boxer Girl	L	3	118	3	5	5^{hd}	6	$3^{\frac{1}{2}}$	3^{4}	Castillo O O	4.00
15Feb03 ^{8}Aqu^{1}	Ladyecho	L	3	122	4	3	6	$5^{\frac{1}{2}}$	$4^{4\frac{1}{2}}$	$4^{4\frac{3}{4}}$	Elliott S	9.40
28Feb03 ^{7}Aqu^{1}	Southern Smoke	L	3	116	6	1	3^{hd}	3^{hd}	$5^{2\frac{1}{2}}$	$5^{14\frac{1}{4}}$	Toribio A R	23.90
5Mar03 ^{5}Aqu^{3}	Leniently	Lb	3	116	5	2	$1^{2\frac{1}{2}}$	$1^{\frac{1}{2}}$	6	6	Castellano J J	9.60

OFF AT 4:49 Start Good. Won driving. Track fast.
TIME :22, :44^{4}, 1:09^{3}, 1:22^{2} (:22.06, :44.80, 1:09.71, 1:22.55)

$2 Mutuel Prices:

2–CYBER SECRET	11.00	3.70	2.40
1–ROAR EMOTION		2.70	2.20
3–BOXER GIRL			2.40

$2 EXACTA 2–1 PAID $24.80 $2 TRIFECTA 2–1–3 PAID $58.00

B. f, (Mar), by Cyberspace–Merry Maudie, by Maudlin. Trainer Dutrow Richard E Jr. Bred by Earl Pierport & Teresa Pierport (Fla).

CYBER SECRET raced close up inside while in hand, advanced outside on the turn, drew clear when roused entering the stretch and remained well clear under a drive. ROAR EMOTION was hustled along inside, came three wide approaching the stretch and finished well but could not get to the winner. BOXER GIRL was hustled along early, raced inside and lacked a rally. LADYECHO was outrun early, raced four wide and had no response when roused. SOUTHERN SMOKE was hustled along while between rivals, raced three wide and tired in the stretch. LENIENTLY quickly opened a clear lead, set the pace for a half mile and tired.

Owners— 1, Goldfarb Sanford & Irwin & Team Jul; 2, Allen Joseph; 3, Sarah S Farish; 4, Polin Charlotte C; 5, Presidential Path Stable & Gallo Ri; 6, Iavarone Michael

Trainers—1, Dutrow Richard E Jr; 2, Martin Carlos F; 3, Zwiesler Michael; 4, Servis John C; 5, Breen Kelly J; 6, Martin Gregory F

NINTH RACE
Santa Anita
MARCH 22, 2003

1⅛ MILES. (Turf)(1.43^{4}) 36th Running of THE SANTA ANA HANDICAP. Grade II. Purse $150,000 Guaranteed. FILLIES AND MARES FOUR YEARS OLD AND UPWARD. By subscription of $150 each to accompany the nomination or by supplementary nomination by Sunday, March 16. $500 to pass the entry box and $1,000 additional to start, of which $150,000 guaranteed, with $90,000 to first, $30,000 to second, $18,000 to third, $9,000 to fourth, $3,000 to fifth. Weights Tuesday, March 18. High weights preferred. Starters to be named through the entry box by the closing time of entries. A trophy will be presented to the owner of the winner. NOMINATIONS CLOSED Thursday, March 13, 2003 with EIGHTEEN (18) (Rail at 0 Feet).

Value of Race: $150,000 Winner $90,000; second $30,000; third $18,000; fourth $9,000; fifth $3,000. Mutuel Pool $499,651.00 Exacta Pool $282,610.00 Quinella Pool $27,304.00 Trifecta Pool $301,745.00 Superfecta Pool $133,359.00

Last Raced	Horse	M/Eqt.	A.	Wt	PP	St	¼	½	¾	Str	Fin	Jockey	Odds $1
31Jan03 ^{7}SA^{1}	Noches de Rosa-CH	LBb	5	115	7	6	$1^{1\frac{1}{2}}$	$1^{1\frac{1}{2}}$	1^{1}	1^{1}	$1^{\frac{1}{2}}$	Smith M E	13.00
17Feb03 ^{7}SA^{2}	GardenintheRain-FR	LB	6	116	1	4	5^{1}	6^{hd}	7^{hd}	5^{hd}	2^{nk}	Stevens G L	2.70
11Jan03 ^{3}SA^{2}	Megahertz-GB	LB	4	117	6	2	7^{hd}	7^{1}	$6^{1\frac{1}{2}}$	$3^{\frac{1}{2}}$	3^{1}	Solis A	1.00
11Jan03 ^{3}SA^{6}	Magic Mission-GB	LB	5	116	4	5	4^{hd}	4^{1}	$2^{\frac{1}{2}}$	$2^{\frac{1}{2}}$	4^{1}	Nakatani C S	8.50
2Mar03 ^{4}SA^{4}	Dancing-GB	LB	4	112	2	3	2^{1}	2^{hd}	3^{1}	$4^{1\frac{1}{2}}$	$5^{1\frac{1}{2}}$	Farina Tony	78.60
19Jan03 ^{7}SA^{6}	Glia	LB	4	114	5	1	3^{hd}	$3^{\frac{1}{2}}$	$5^{\frac{1}{2}}$	6^{3}	$6^{\frac{1}{2}}$	Valdivia J Jr	6.10
31Jan03 ^{7}SA^{2}	Snowflake-IR	LB	5	116	3	8	8	8	8	$7^{2\frac{1}{2}}$	7^{5}	Flores D R	13.40
2Mar03 ^{4}SA^{2}	Splendeur-FR	LB	4	113	8	7	$6^{\frac{1}{2}}$	5^{hd}	4^{hd}	8	8	Espinoza V	39.50

OFF AT 4:37 Start Good. Won driving. Course firm.
TIME :24^{4}, :50^{1}, 1:13^{3}, 1:37, 1:48^{1} (:24.94, :50.22, 1:13.76, 1:37.14, 1:48.31)

$2 Mutuel Prices:

7–NOCHES DE ROSA–CH	28.00	12.40	4.00
1–GARDEN IN THE RAIN–FR		4.20	2.40
6–MEGAHERTZ–GB			2.20

$1 EXACTA 7–1 PAID $54.80 $2 QUINELLA 1–7 PAID $49.00 $1 TRIFECTA 7–1–6 PAID $126.90 $1 SUPERFECTA 7–1–6–4 PAID $598.00

Dk. b. or br. m, by Stagecraft*GB–Night Girl*Chi, by Noble Fighter. Trainer Mandella Richard. Bred by Haras Don Alberto (Chi).

NOCHES DE ROSA (CHI) stepped to the front and allowed to dictate the pace while setting leisurely fractions, responded when roused entering the stretch and stubbornly held under strong handling. GARDEN IN THE RAIN (FR) content to settle along the rail, lacked room leaving the backstretch and forced to drop back early on the second turn, swung out for room into the stretch, advanced four wide and closed furiously from outside. MEGAHERTZ (GB) chased from between rivals, was in tight and forced to steady passing the three eighths marker, quickly recovered and advanced four wide into the lane, menacingly loomed passing the sixteenth marker but lost placing in final yards. MAGIC MISSION (GB) broke in, tracked the pacesetter while two and three wide to the stretch, then gave ground grudgingly in the drive. DANCING (GB) broke out, led the second pack into and around the initial turn, continued inside and remained prominent into the stretch but weakened slightly late in the drive. GLIA reserved from between foes in the early stages, dropped back slightly entering the final bend, raced inside stablemate around that turn and weakened. SNOWFLAKE (IRE) was crowded at the start, settled along the rail and saved ground to the second turn, angled out and failed to threaten. SPLENDEUR (FR) settled from the outside, raced three wide around both turns, dropped back nearing the stretch and gave way readily.

Owners— 1, Diamond A Racing Corporation; 2, Englander Richard A; 3, Bello Michael; 4, Al Maktoum Sheik Maktoum b; 5, Baker Howard J; 6, Flaxman Holdings Ltd; 7, Stonerside Stable; 8, Fisher Derrick

Trainers—1, Mandella Richard; 2, Mullins Jeff; 3, Frankel Robert; 4, Drysdale Neil; 5, Sahadi Jenine; 6, Frankel Robert; 7, McAnally Ronald; 8, Jory Ian P D

$2 Daily Double (5–7) Paid $222.80; Daily Double Pool $43,434.
$1 Pick Three (5–5–7) Paid $513.00; Pick Three Pool $88,062.

TENTH RACE
Turfway Park
MARCH 22, 2003

1⅛ MILES. (1.46^3) 22nd Running of THE LANE'S END. Grade II. Purse $500,000 FOR THREE-YEAR-OLDS. Colts and Geldings, 121 lbs.; Fillies, 116 lbs. By subscription of $300, $2,500 to enter and $2,500 additional to start. Supplementary nominations may be made at time of entry Thursday, March 20, 2003 by payment of $30,000 each (includes entry and starting fees).$500,000 Guaranteed. Monies to be divided: $300,000 to the owner of the winner; $100,000 to second; $50,000 to third; $25,000 to fourth; $15,000 to fifth and $10,000 to sixth.

Value of Race: $500,000 Winner $300,000; second $100,000; third $50,000; fourth $25,000; fifth $15,000; sixth $10,000. Mutuel Pool $692,389.00 Exacta Pool $387,216.00 Trifecta Pool $378,435.00 Superfecta Pool $118,231.00

Last Raced	Horse	M/Eqt.	A.Wt	PP	St	¼	½	¾	Str	Fin	Jockey	Odds $1
27Feb03 ^{8}Aqu^2	New York Hero	Lb	3 121	6	4	$2^{1\frac{1}{2}}$	2^2	$2^{1\frac{1}{2}}$	1^{hd}	1^{nk}	Arroyo N Jr	14.70
22Feb03 ^{7}GP^1	Eugene's Third Son	Lb	3 121	8	3	$4^{\frac{1}{2}}$	$3^{\frac{1}{2}}$	4^1	$2^{\frac{1}{2}}$	$2^{2\frac{1}{4}}$	Day P	7.30
1Mar03 ^{10}TP^1	Champali	L	3 121	2	2	3^{hd}	4^{hd}	3^{hd}	3^2	3^{hd}	Lumpkins J	2.80
15Feb03 ^{9}GP^1	Lion Tamer	L	3 121	9	8	8^4	5^{hd}	5^3	$4^{1\frac{1}{2}}$	$4^{8\frac{3}{4}}$	Velazquez J R	0.80
16Feb03 ^{9}FG^5	Saintly Look	L	3 121	1	1	$1^{\frac{1}{2}}$	$1^{\frac{1}{2}}$	1^{hd}	5^5	$5^{\frac{3}{4}}$	Sellers S J	7.20
20Feb03 ^{9}FG^3	Lots Of Sizzle	Lb	3 121	3	7	5^1	$7^{\frac{1}{2}}$	7^1	6^5	$6^{10\frac{1}{4}}$	Rivera L Jr	66.20
1Mar03 ^{10}TP^2	Chicken Soup Kid	Lb	3 121	7	6	6^{hd}	6^2	$6^{\frac{1}{2}}$	7^6	$7^{8\frac{3}{4}}$	Peck B D	36.10
1Mar03 ^{10}TP^5	Wendlar	b	3 121	5	9	9	9	9	9	$8^{2\frac{1}{4}}$	Ouzts P W	146.10
8Mar03 ^{8}GG^7	Ozzie Cat	Lb	3 121	4	5	7^{hd}	8^6	8^{12}	$8^{2\frac{1}{2}}$	9	Pedroza M A	17.80

OFF AT 4:42 Start Good For All But CHAMPALI Won driving. Track fast.
TIME :22^4, :46^3, 1:11, 1:37, 1:50^3 (:22.98, :46.60, 1:11.11, 1:37.13, 1:50.68)

$2 Mutuel Prices:

6–NEW YORK HERO	31.40	15.20	6.80
8–EUGENE'S THIRD SON		7.80	4.40
2–CHAMPALI			3.00

$2 EXACTA 6–8 PAID $226.40 $2 TRIFECTA 6–8–2 PAID $983.80 $2 SUPERFECTA 6–8–2–9 PAID $2,794.40

Dk. b. or br. c, (Mar), by Partner's Hero–Nin Two, by John Alden. Trainer Pedersen Jennifer. Bred by Dark Hollow Farm & William Beatson (Md).

NEW YORK HERO pressed the early pace from the three path, challenged after a half, gained a short lead in upper stretch, responded willingly when challenged by EUGENE'S THIRD SON in midstretch and outfinished that one while drifting out steadily the final sixteenth. EUGENE'S THIRD SON within striking distance from the start three wide, advanced four wide into the stretch, challenged with a furlong to go and could not quite get to NEW YORK HERO while carried out by that one in the final sixteenth. CHAMPALI stumbled at the start, recovered to be close up, saved ground on the second turn and into the stretch, challenged inside the top pair with a furlong to go but weakened. LION TAMER outsprinted early, moved to within striking distance four wide on the first turn, moved in a bit around the second turn, angled out in upper stretch but hung. SAINTLY LOOK vied for the lead along the inside, came off the rail after a half, held on well to midstretch and tired. LOTS OF SIZZLE reserved along the inside, tired. CHICKEN SOUP KID five wide on the first turn when within striking distance, moved in to the four path on the second turn and faded in the final quarter. WENDLAR outrun early, was no factor. OZZIE CAT recovered awkwardly when bumped after the start, raced within striking distance early three wide and gave way.

Owners— 1, Paraneck Stable; 2, Serengatti Stable Richard Nip; 3, Lloyd Madison Farms IV; 4, Tabor Michael B; 5, Carl William A; 6, Everest Stables; 7, Nash Robert D; 8, Crowder Mike; 9, Overbrook Farm

Trainers—1, Pedersen Jennifer; 2, Byrne Patrick B; 3, Foley Gregory D; 4, Pletcher Todd A; 5, Stewart Dallas; 6, Keen Dallas E; 7, Flint Bernard S; 8, Crowder Michael; 9, Lukas D Wayne

---

$2 Daily Double (8–6) Paid $142.80; Daily Double Pool $34,569.
$2 Pick Three (5–8–6) Paid $823.40; Pick Three Pool $51,537.
$2 Pick Four (7–5–8–6) Paid $1,369.60; Pick Four Pool $33,365.
$2 Pick Six (6–7–7–5–8–6) 5
Correct Paid $77.60; Pick Six Pool $6,176; Carryover Pool $3,612.

NINTH RACE
Aqueduct
MARCH 23, 2003

1⅛ MILES. (1.47) 29th Running of THE NEXT MOVE HANDICAP. Grade III. Purse $100,000 (Up to $19,400 NYSBFOA). FILLIES AND MARES THREE YEARS OLD AND UPWARD. By subscription of $100 each, which should accompany the nomination; $500 to pass the entry box; $500 to start, with $100,000 added. The added money and all fees to be divided 60% to the winner, 20% to second, 11% to third, 6% to fourth and 3% to fifth. Trophies will be presented to the winning owner, trainer and jockey. Closed Saturday, March 8, 2003 with 15 Nominations

Value of Race: $108,000 Winner $64,800; second $21,600; third $11,880; fourth $6,480; fifth $3,240. Mutuel Pool $317,100.00 Exacta Pool $269,416.00 Trifecta Pool $195,370.00

Last Raced	Horse	M/Eqt.	A.Wt	PP	St	¼	½	¾	Str	Fin	Jockey	Odds $1
1Mar03 ^{10}GP^2	Smok'n Frolic	L	4 120	4	1	$1^{\frac{1}{2}}$	1^{hd}	$1^{\frac{1}{2}}$	1^3	$1^{2\frac{1}{4}}$	Velazquez J R	0.90
19Feb03 ^{8}Aqu^1	Ellie's Moment	L	5 116	2	6	6	$5^{\frac{1}{2}}$	5^5	$2^{\frac{1}{2}}$	$2^{3\frac{3}{4}}$	Bridgmohan S X	2.60
22Feb03 ^{8}Lrl^1	Pupil	Lbf	4 113	3	3	$3^{\frac{1}{2}}$	$3^{\frac{1}{2}}$	$3^{2\frac{1}{2}}$	$3^{2\frac{1}{2}}$	3^1	Elliott S	5.40
31Jan03 ^{8}Aqu^3	Kiss A Miss	Lf	5 113	6	2	$4^{\frac{1}{2}}$	$4^{1\frac{1}{2}}$	4^{hd}	$5^{5\frac{1}{2}}$	$4^{2\frac{3}{4}}$	Samyn J L	17.10
13Feb03 ^{5}Pen^1	Run for Joy	L	7 114	5	4	$2^{1\frac{1}{2}}$	$2^{\frac{1}{2}}$	$2^{\frac{1}{2}}$	$4^{\frac{1}{2}}$	$5^{8\frac{1}{4}}$	Bocachica O	8.30
9Feb03 ^{5}Aqu^2	Database	L	4 111	1	5	5^{hd}	6	6	6	6	Castellano J J	21.30

OFF AT 4:48 Start Good. Won driving. Track fast.
TIME :24^1, :47^3, 1:10^4, 1:35^4, 1:49 (:24.22, :47.65, 1:10.89, 1:35.90, 1:49.11)

$2 Mutuel Prices:

5–SMOK'N FROLIC	3.80	2.40	2.10
2–ELLIE'S MOMENT		2.90	2.10
3–PUPIL			2.10

$2 EXACTA 5–2 PAID $7.20 $2 TRIFECTA 5–2–3 PAID $19.20

Gr/ro f, by Smoke Glacken–Cherokyfrolicflash, by Green Dancer. Trainer Pletcher Todd A. Bred by Cherokee Farms Inc (Fla).

SMOK'N FROLIC quickly showed in front, dictated the pace along the inside while in hand, responded when set down in upper stretch and drew clear under a drive. ELLIE'S MOMENT was outrun along the inside early, advanced inside on the second turn, came wide into the stretch and finished gamely outside. PUPIL raced close up inside early, angled out on the backstretch, chased the pace while three wide, lugged in in the stretch and tired in the final furlong. KISS A MISS raced close up while wide and had no response when roused. RUN FOR JOY pressed the pace from the outside and tired in the stretch. DATABASE was outrun early, raced inside and tired in the stretch.

Owners— 1, Dogwood Stable; 2, Phillips Joan G & John W; 3, Fox Hill Farms Inc; 4, Carpenito Noreen; 5, Fral Eric; 6, Janney III Stuart S
Trainers—1, Pletcher Todd A; 2, Toner James J; 3, Servis John C; 4, Johnson Philip G; 5, McCaslin John S; 6, McGaughey Claude III
Scratched— Ms. Rapunzel (31Jan03 ^{8}AQU^5)

EIGHTH RACE
Fair Grounds
MARCH 23, 2003

ABOUT 1⅛ MILES. (Turf)(1.46^{4}) 12th Running of THE EXPLOSIVE BID HANDICAP. Grade II. Purse $650,000 A Handicap For Four Year Olds and Upward. By subscription of $100 each; $4,000 to enter; $4,000 additional to start. $650,000 Guaranteed of which $390,000 to the winner; $130,000 to second; $71,500 to third; $39,000 to fourth; $19,500 to fifth. THE OWNER OF THE WINNER TO RECEIVE A TROPHY. Closed Thursday, March 13, 2003, with 21 nominations.

Value of Race: $650,000 Winner $390,000; second $130,000; third $71,500; fourth $39,000; fifth $19,500. Mutuel Pool $492,662.00 Exacta Pool $322,154.00 Quinella Pool $24,593.00 Trifecta Pool $289,242.00 Superfecta Pool $101,091.00

Last Raced	Horse	M/Eqt.	A.	Wt	PP	St	¼	½	¾	Str	Fin	Jockey	Odds $1
15Feb03 ^{7}Hou^{1}	Candid Glen	L	6	114	4	5	7^{2}	$5^{1/2}$	4^{hd}	1^{hd}	1^{nk}	Perrodin E J	84.10
17Feb03 ^{9}GP^{1}	Rouvres-FR	L	4	115	3	7	4^{1}	$4^{1 1/2}$	$5^{1 1/2}$	2^{1}	2no	Bailey J D	1.30
15Feb03 ^{7}Hou^{4}	Freefourinternet	Lb	5	115	6	6	6^{hd}	7^{hd}	7^{1}	$4^{2 1/2}$	3no	Sellers S J	61.70
1Mar03 ^{8}SA^{7}	Seinne-CHI	L	6	116	9	11	11	11	11	5^{1}	$4^{2 1/2}$	Borel C H	9.80
1Feb03 ^{9}FG^{1}	Mystery Giver	L	5	116	5	9	$9^{1/2}$	10^{5}	9^{2}	$3^{1/2}$	5^{nk}	Albarado R J	4.70
20Feb03 ^{5}SA^{1}	Requete-GB	L	4	112	11	2	3^{1}	3^{2}	3^{1}	6^{1}	$6^{3/4}$	Day P	4.20
8Mar03 ^{10}FG^{1}	Run To Victory	L	4	115	2	8	$10^{3 1/2}$	9^{1}	8^{hd}	7^{2}	$7^{3/4}$	Melancon G	17.50
4Mar03 ^{9}FG^{1}	Even The Score	Lb	5	113	7	4	5^{hd}	6^{3}	6^{hd}	$10^{3 1/2}$	$8^{2 1/4}$	Lanerie C J	20.70
1Mar03 ^{8}SA^{4}	Century City-IR	L	4	116	10	1	2^{hd}	$2^{1/2}$	$2^{1/2}$	$9^{1/2}$	9^{2}	Valdivia J Jr	8.90
16Feb03 ^{10}GP^{6}	Della Francesca	Lb	4	113	8	3	$1^{1/2}$	$1^{1/2}$	1^{1}	$8^{1/2}$	10^{2}	Melancon L	25.70
17Aug02 ^{11}AP^{7}	Orchard Park	L	4	115	1	10	$8^{1 1/2}$	$8^{1 1/2}$	10^{4}	11	11	Velasquez C	14.30

OFF AT 4:04 Start Good. Won driving. Course firm.

TIME :24, :48^{2}, 1:12^{2}, 1:38, 1:51 (:24.07, :48.42, 1:12.52, 1:38.18, 1:51.15)

$2 Mutuel Prices:				
	4-CANDID GLEN	170.20	33.00	14.80
	3-ROUVRES-FR		3.60	2.80
	6-FREEFOURINTERNET			14.00

$2 EXACTA 4-3 PAID $524.20 $2 QUINELLA 3-4 PAID $124.40 $2 TRIFECTA 4-3-6 PAID $6,573.60 $2 SUPERFECTA 4-3-6-9 PAID $75,818.20

Dk. b. or br. g, by El Gran Senor–Candid Moments, by Pirate's Bounty. Trainer Leggio Andrew Jr. Bred by W Kenan Rand Jr (Ky).

CANDID GLEN between foes early, gained the rail before the first turn, continued inside while unhurried, moved up around the second turn, eased out to take over outside DELLA FRANCESCA before mid stretch, gained the edge and proved best under a drive. ROUVRES (FR) reserved along the inside early, eased outside for the run down the backstretch, continued outside while advancing around the second turn, swung out six wide turning for home, loomed boldly a furlong out but was out kicked to the wire. FREEFOURINTERNET reserved early, raced inside around the second turn, eased out for the drive, angled back to the rail, finished big but missed. SEINNE (CHI) trailed until the drive, swung out ten wide for the drive and was gaining late. MYSTERY GIVER inside early, moved out to race wide down the backstretch, continued outside to circle foes nearing the drive, loomed a threat and then weakened. REQUETE (GB) raced close up while three wide until upper stretch and tired. RUN TO VICTORY devoid speed, split foes but was no real threat. EVEN THE SCORE close up, faded. CENTURY CITY (IRE) forced the pace until before the drive and stopped. DELLA FRANCESCA crossed to the rail, set the pace until turning for home and emptied out. ORCHARD PARK was always outrun.

Owners— 1, Warren Glen C; 2, Head Alec; 3, Equirace Com; 4, Hunt Nelson B; 5, Team Block; 6, Juddmonte Farms Inc; 7, Jayeff B Stables; 8, Vanderhyde Thomas; 9, Kitchwa Stables & Tom Nichols John; 10, Ol Memorial Stable & Dell Ridge Far; 11, Vegso Peter

Trainers—1, Leggio Andrew Jr; 2, Clement Christophe; 3, Simon Charles; 4, McAnally Ronald; 5, Scherer Richard R; 6, Frankel Robert; 7, Badgett William Jr; 8, Stewart Dallas; 9, Greely C Beau; 10, O'Callaghan Niall M; 11, Mott William I

$2 Pick Three (6-5-4) Paid $1,930.00; Pick Three Pool $14,154. $2 Pick Six (8-4-3-6-5-4) 5 Correct Paid $576.00; Pick Six Pool $2,560; Carryover Pool $2,471.

EIGHTH RACE
Gulfstream
MARCH 23, 2003

1½ MILES. (2.27^{3}) 40th Running of THE ORCHID HANDICAP. Grade II. Purse $200,000 Guaranteed. FOR FILLIES AND MARES, THREE YEARS OLD AND UPWARD. By subscription of $200 each, which shall accompany the nomination, $2,000 to pass the entry box and $2,000 additional to start, with $200,000 guaranteed. The owner of the winner to receive $120,000; $40,000 to second, $22,000 to third, $12,000 to fourth and $6,000 to fifth. Trophy to winning Owner. In the event this stake is taken off the turf, it may be subject to downgrading upon review of the Graded Stakes Committee. Closed Wednesday, March 12, 2003 with 15 Nominations. (Rail at 10 feet). (ORIGINALLY SCHEDULED FOR TURF.)

Value of Race: $200,000 Winner $120,000; second $40,000; third $22,000; fourth $12,000; fifth $6,000. Mutuel Pool $329,707.00 Exacta Pool $251,943.00 Trifecta Pool $210,235.00 Superfecta Pool $66,050.00

Last Raced	Horse	M/Eqt.	A.	Wt	PP	¼	½	1	1¼	Str	Fin	Jockey	Odds $1
8Feb03 ^{8}GP^{2}	Tweedside	Lf	5	116	4	2^{2}	$2^{1 1/2}$	2^{hd}	$1^{2 1/2}$	1^{4}	$1^{5 1/2}$	Douglas R R	1.20
8Feb03 ^{8}GP^{1}	San Dare	L	5	119	6	$5^{1/2}$	5^{4}	5^{9}	$3^{1 1/2}$	$2^{2 1/2}$	2^{5}	Guidry M	2.20
2Mar03 ^{10}GP^{5}	Hi Tech Honeycomb	Lb	4	115	5	4^{2}	4^{2}	4^{hd}	2^{1}	3^{2}	$3^{4 1/4}$	Cruz M R	8.10
23Feb03 ^{10}GP^{1}	Spice Island	Lb	4	113	3	3^{hd}	3^{hd}	$3^{1/2}$	5^{3}	$4^{1/2}$	$4^{3/4}$	Coa E M	10.80
6Mar03 ^{8}GP^{2}	Flying Marlin	L	4	111	7	6^{2}	6^{2}	6^{8}	6^{15}	5^{5}	$5^{14 1/2}$	Nunez E O	23.60
9Feb03 ^{9}GP^{5}	Amelia	L	5	113	1	$1^{2 1/2}$	1^{5}	1^{2}	4^{1}	6^{7}	$6^{10 1/2}$	Boulanger G	7.70
2Mar03 ^{10}GP^{7}	Queue	Lbf	6	113	2	7	7	7	7	7	7	Decarlo C P	14.10

OFF AT 4:10 Start Good. Won driving. Track sloppy.

TIME :24^{1}, :48^{2}, 1:14, 1:40, 2:06^{1}, 2:32^{1} (:24.39, :48.54, 1:14.04, 1:40.18, 2:06.21, 2:32.36)

$2 Mutuel Prices:				
	5-TWEEDSIDE	4.40	2.60	2.20
	7-SAN DARE		3.00	2.40
	6-HI TECH HONEYCOMB			3.20

$1 EXACTA 5-7 PAID $5.70 $1 TRIFECTA 5-7-6 PAID $17.00 $1 SUPERFECTA 5-7-6-4 PAID $62.40

B. m, by Thunder Gulch–Twitchet, by Roberto. Trainer Pletcher Todd A. Bred by Dr & Mrs R S West & Mr & Mrs Mackenzie Miller (Ky).

TWEEDSIDE stalked the pace off the rail, moved to gain command from AMELIA on the final turn and drew away under urging. SAN DARE reserved after hitting the gate at the start, raced off the rail, split rivals while rallying on the far turn and closed to prove second best while unable to stay with the winner. HI TECH HONEYCOMB rated off the pace, made a run three wide on the final turn to reach the attending position, then tired in the drive. SPICE ISLAND chased the pace along the inside into the stretch and faltered. FLYING MARLIN was not a factor. AMELIA quickly sprinted to a clear lead, made the pace along the inside into the final turn and faded. QUEUE trailed.

Owners— 1, Melnyk Eugene & Laura; 2, D Mounts; 3, Select Stable; 4, Butenhoff Kim; 5, Jones Frank L Jr; 6, Alexander Helen C Groves Helen K &; 7, Robins Gerald & Weiss Jay

Trainers—1, Pletcher Todd A; 2, Hiles Rick; 3, McPeek Kenneth G; 4, Pregman John S Jr; 5, Romans Dale; 6, McGaughey Claude III; 7, Blengs Vincent L

Scratched— Crooked Wood (12Feb03 ^{9}GP^{1}), Stay Forever (2Mar03 ^{10}GP^{4})

$1 Pick Three (5-2/3-3/5/8) Paid $19.70; Pick Three Pool $41,724.

NINTH RACE   7 FURLONGS. (1.20) 49th Running of THE DISTAFF BREEDERS' CUP HANDICAP. Grade II. Purse

Aqueduct

MARCH 29, 2003

$150,000 (includes $50,000 BC – Breeders' Cup Fund). (Up to $19,400 NYSBFOA). FILLIES AND MARES THREE YEARS OLD AND UPWARD. By subscription of $100 each, which should accompany the nomination $500 to pass the entry box; $500 to start. Any Breeders' Cup fund monies not awarded will revert back to the Fund. Closed Saturday, March 15, 2003 with 19 Nominations.

Value of Race: $152,400 Winner $94,740; second $31,580; third $11,869; fourth $9,474; fifth $4,737. Mutuel Pool $594,856.00 Exacta Pool $343,762.00 Trifecta Pool $252,387.00

Last Raced	Horse	M/Eqt. A.Wt	PP	St	$\frac{1}{4}$	$\frac{1}{2}$	Str	Fin	Jockey	Odds $1
22Feb03 10Lrl2	Carson Hollow	Lf 4 120	4	3	1$\frac{1}{2}$	1hd	1$\frac{1}{2}$	11$\frac{1}{2}$	Luzzi M J	0.50
26Oct02 5Aqu3	Raging Fever	L 5 118	1	5	2^2	2$3\frac{1}{2}$	2^6	2$1\frac{3}{4}$	Gryder A T	2.15
9Mar03 9Aqu4	Bonefide Reason	L 5 112	3	6	6	6	4$2\frac{1}{2}$	3$3\frac{1}{2}$	Castellano J J	25.25
19Dec02 8Aqu5	Outstanding Info	Lb 5 116	6	1	5$1\frac{1}{2}$	5$\frac{1}{2}$	3hd	4$3\frac{3}{4}$	Caraballo J C	20.50
9Mar03 9Aqu6	A. P. Andie	L 5 113	2	4	3$5\frac{1}{2}$	3$4\frac{1}{2}$	5	5	Arroyo N Jr	25.50
9Mar03 9Aqu1	Saskya	Lf 5 112	5	2	4$2\frac{1}{2}$	4$2\frac{1}{2}$	—	—	Bridgmohan S X	13.30

Saskya:Broke Down;

OFF AT 4:53 Start Good. Won driving. Track fast.

TIME :22, :44^2, 1:08^4, 1:22^2 (:22.09, :44.49, 1:08.81, 1:22.42)

$2 Mutuel Prices:

4–CARSON HOLLOW	3.00	2.10	2.10
1–RAGING FEVER		2.30	2.10
3–BONEFIDE REASON			2.10

$2 EXACTA 4–1 PAID $5.00 $2 TRIFECTA 4–1–3 PAID $22.00

B. f, by Carson City–Lizeality, by Hold Your Peace. Trainer Dutrow Richard E Jr. Bred by Patricia Staskowski Purdy (NY).

CARSON HOLLOW quickly showed in front, set the pace along the inside, responded when joined from the outside by RAGING FEVER on the turn, dug in determinedly in the stretch and drew clear from that rival late, driving. RAGING FEVER showed good speed while in hand, tried the winner from the outside on the turn, could not get by that rival and continued on to hold the place. BONEFIDE REASON was outrun early, raced inside and finished gamely. OUTSTANDING INFO was outrun early outside, was steadied to avoid a fallen rival entering the stretch and lacked a rally. A. P. ANDIE chased the pace along the inside and tired in the stretch. SASKYA broke down entering the stretch. There was a general Stewards' inquiry before the result was declared official.

Owners– 1, Stronach Stables & Hemlock Hills Fa; 2, Evans Edward P; 3, Sunny Meadow Farm; 4, Generazio Patricia A; 5, Garafolo Bruce; 6, Berkshire Stud & Oak Cliff Stable

Trainers–1, Dutrow Richard E Jr; 2, Hennig Mark; 3, Friedman Mitchell; 4, Generazio Frank Jr; 5, Servis Jason; 6, Bush Thomas M

SEVENTH RACE   1 MILE. (1.33) 52nd Running of THE BERKELEY HANDICAP. Grade III. Purse $100,000. 3–year–olds

Golden Gate

MARCH 29, 2003

and upward. By subscription of $100 each to accompany the nomination or by supplementary nomination of $2,000 by Noon, Sunday, March 23, 2003. $500 to pass the entry box and $500 to additional to start,with $100,000 Guaranteed of which $55,000 to the winner, $20,000 to second, $15,000 to third, $7,500 to fourth and $2,500 to fifth. A trophy will be presented to the owner of the winner. High weights preferred. Closed Thursday, March 20, 2003 with 20 nominations.

Value of Race: $100,000 Winner $55,000; second $20,000; third $15,000; fourth $7,500; fifth $2,500. Mutuel Pool $311,973.00 Exacta Pool $179,091.00 Quinella Pool $17,958.00 Trifecta Pool $226,781.00

Last Raced	Horse	M/Eqt. A.Wt	PP	St	$\frac{1}{4}$	$\frac{1}{2}$	$\frac{3}{4}$	Str	Fin	Jockey	Odds $1
1Mar03 8GG3	I'madrifter	LB 5 115	4	1	1$1\frac{1}{2}$	11	12	13$\frac{1}{2}$	12$\frac{1}{2}$	Gonzalez R M	10.00
4Aug02 8Dmr7	Palmeiro	LBb 5 117	2	2	2$1\frac{1}{2}$	2$1\frac{1}{2}$	22	2$1$	2$1\frac{1}{4}$	Rollins C J	6.90
8Mar03 9SA5	Skip To The Stone	LBb 5 116	3	6	3$1$	3hd	3hd	33	33	Alvarado F T	10.10
5Mar03 4GG1	Rhetoric Express	LB 4 115	1	3	4hd	4$\frac{1}{2}$	4$1\frac{1}{2}$	42	4$2\frac{1}{2}$	Schvaneveldt C P	7.80
8Mar03 9SA4	Cottage-ARG	LBb 5 115	6	5	6	6	6	5$\frac{1}{2}$	51	Duran F	3.40
1Mar03 8GG1	Halo Cat	LBbf 5 117	5	4	5$\frac{1}{2}$	5hd	5hd	6	6	Baze R A	0.80

OFF AT 3:56 Start Good. Won driving. Track fast.

TIME :22, :44^3, 1:08^3, 1:21^2, 1:35 (:22.03, :44.71, 1:08.66, 1:21.54, 1:35.13)

$2 Mutuel Prices:

5–I'MADRIFTER	22.00	10.40	28.20
3–PALMEIRO		7.60	23.80
4–SKIP TO THE STONE			26.40

$1 EXACTA 5–3 PAID $98.50 $2 QUINELLA 3–5 PAID $82.00 $1 TRIFECTA 5–3–4 PAID $672.90

Dk. b. or br. h, by Slewdledo–Exploded's Girl, by Exploded. Trainer Specht Steve. Bred by Paulson Bros Ranch & Roy Dane (Wash).

I'MADRIFTER was quick from the gate to gain a clear early lead despite heavy pressure PALMEIRO from the inside, was in hand once on the backstretch and maintained the advantage under his own courage, responded in the lane while shortening stride but had enough in reserve to win driving. PALMEIRO was sent hard inside the winner into the first turn but could not reach him, pressured him to the second turn, but could only make minor impact in the very late stages. SKIP TO THE STONE was permitted to settle within striking distance early, raced two wide to the stretch but lacked the needed response. RHETORIC EXPRESS was well placed from the rail for six furlongs but had no closing rally. COTTAGE (ARG) lagged early while racing outside a four horse spread to the backstretch, remained out on the second turn but did not respond. HALO CAT took back in the early stages and raced just inside COTTAGE to the second turn then had nothing to offer when the real test came.

Owners– 1, O'Neill Daniel; 2, Moss Mr & Mrs Jerome S; 3, Greystone Racing Stable & Loverso V; 4, Doug ONeill Tony Scott or Aron Well; 5, Farfellow Farms Ltd; 6, Rancho San Miguel Abruzzo Peter & F

Trainers–1, Specht Steve; 2, Sadler John W; 3, Baffert Bob; 4, O'Neill Doug; 5, Spawr Bill; 6, Hollendorfer Jerry

Scratched– Western Pride (11May02 KRN11).

$2 Daily Double (7–5) Paid $247.40; Daily Double Pool $13,642.
$1 Pick Three (3–7–5) Paid $180.20; Pick Three Pool $22,576.

ELEVENTH RACE Gulfstream MARCH 29, 2003

1¼ MILES. (1.59) 58th Running of THE GULFSTREAM PARK HANDICAP. Grade II. Purse $300,000 FOR THREE YEAR OLDS AND UPWARD. By subscription of $200 each, which shall accompany the nomination, $3,000 to pass the entry box and $3,000 additional to start, with $300,000 guaranteed. The owner of the winner to receive $180,000; $60,000 to second, $33,000 to third, $18,000 to fourth and $9,000 to fifth. Trophy to winning Owner. Closed Wednesday, March 19,2003 with 19 Nominations.

Value of Race: $300,000 Winner $180,000; second $60,000; third $33,000; fourth $18,000; fifth $9,000. Mutuel Pool $632,419.00 Exacta Pool $393,034.00 Trifecta Pool $322,914.00 Superfecta Pool $106,233.00

Last Raced	Horse	M/Eqt.	A.Wt	PP	¼	½	¾	1	Str	Fin	Jockey	Odds $1
22Feb03 ^{11}GP^{2}	Hero's Tribute	L	5 115	4	2^{1}	2^{hd}	2^{hd}	1^{hd}	$1^{2\frac{1}{2}}$	1^{4}	Prado E S	1.80
15Feb03 ^{7}GP^{2}	Aeneas	L	4 115	7	6^{3}	6^{hd}	7^{3}	$2^{\frac{1}{2}}$	2^{3}	2^{1}	Douglas R R	54.00
22Feb03 ^{11}GP^{3}	Puzzlement	Lb	4 114	2	5^{hd}	$5^{2\frac{1}{2}}$	5^{1}	$3^{\frac{1}{2}}$	$3^{1\frac{1}{2}}$	$3^{1\frac{1}{2}}$	Velasquez C	4.20
2Mar03 ^{9}FG^{3}	Strive	Lb	4 114	3	8	8	8	$6^{1\frac{1}{2}}$	4^{1}	4^{2}	Bailey J D	5.10
22Feb03 ^{11}GP^{9}	Bonus Pack	Lb	5 115	1	$3^{1\frac{1}{2}}$	$3^{2\frac{1}{2}}$	3^{4}	$5^{\frac{1}{2}}$	5^{hd}	$5^{1\frac{3}{4}}$	Castanon J L	5.10
1Mar03 ^{4}GP^{1}	Generous Rosi-GB	L	8 114	8	$1^{2\frac{1}{2}}$	1^{4}	$1^{\frac{1}{2}}$	4^{1}	$6^{2\frac{1}{2}}$	6^{4}	Guidry M	7.80
2Mar03 ^{9}FG^{5}	Learned	Lb	5 115	5	7^{1}	$7^{1\frac{1}{2}}$	6^{hd}	8	$7^{1\frac{1}{2}}$	$7^{1\frac{3}{4}}$	Borel C H	20.80
22Feb03 ^{11}GP^{6}	Windsor Castle	L	5 115	6	4^{1}	4^{hd}	4^{hd}	$7^{1\frac{1}{2}}$	8	8	Coa E M	6.60

OFF AT 5:43 Start Good. Won driving. Track fast.
TIME :23^{4}, :48, 1:12^{3}, 1:38, 2:04^{1} (:23.80, :48.07, 1:12.73, 1:38.07, 2:04.24)

$2 Mutuel Prices:

5–HERO'S TRIBUTE	5.60	3.40	2.80
8–AENEAS		23.00	10.20
3–PUZZLEMENT			4.00

$1 EXACTA 5–8 PAID $77.80 $1 TRIFECTA 5–8–3 PAID $282.90 $1 SUPERFECTA 5–8–3–4 PAID $1,154.70

Dk. b. or br. h, by Sea Hero–Eastern Dawn, by Damascus. Trainer Ward John T Jr. Bred by Dr & Mrs R Smiser West & Mr & Mrs M Miller (Ky).

HERO'S TRIBUTE settled behind the early pacesetter, closed the gap leaving the backstretch, rallied between horses to gain a slim lead approaching the stretch, extended his advantage in upper stretch then drew off under steady right hand urging. AENEAS was unhurried for six furlongs, circled four wide on the turn then outfinished PUZZLEMENT for the place. PUZZLEMENT settled in good position, rallied between horses to threaten approaching the quarter pole but couldn't sustain his bid. STRIVE raced well back after being squeezed a bit at the start, circled four wide on the turn then improved his position with a mild late rally. BONUS PACK raced in close contention along the inside for a mile and lacked a strong closing bid. GENEROUS ROSI (GB) sprinted clear in the early stages, set the pace along the inside to the turn and gave way. LEARNED failed to mount a serious rally. WINDSOR CASTLE raced within striking distance to the far turn and gave way.

Owners— 1, Oxley John C; 2, Pavlish Patricia; 3, Shields Joseph V Jr; 4, Wygod Mr & Mrs Martin J; 5, Glen Hill Farm; 6, Addison Racing Ltd; 7, Midway Farm; 8, Dogwood Stable

Trainers—1, Ward John T Jr; 2, Wolfson Martin D; 3, Jerkens H Allen; 4, Mott William I; 5, Proctor Thomas F; 6, O'Callaghan Niall M; 7, Barnett Bobby C; 8, Alexander Frank A

Scratched— The Judge Sez Who (25Jan03 ^{7}GP^{4})

$1 Pick Three (3–1–5) Paid $85.50; Pick Three Pool $35,194.

EIGHTH RACE Santa Anita MARCH 29, 2003

6½ FURLONGS. (1.13^{3}) POTRERO GRANDE BREEDERS' CUP H. Grade II. Purse $200,000 (includes $100,000 BC – Breeders' Cup) FOR FOUR-YEAR-OLDS AND UPWARD. (Includes $100,000 from Breeders' Cup Fund for Cup nominees only) By subscription of $200 each, which shall accompany the nomination or by supplementary nomination of $4,000 by Sunday, March 23. $2,000 additional to start. Breeders' Cup Fund monies also correspondingly divided provided a Breeder's Cup nominee has finished in an awarded position. Any Breeders' Cup Fund monies not awarded will revert to the fund. NOMINATIONS CLOSED Thursday, March 20, 2003 with 10. SUPPLEMENTAL NOMINATION FEE OF $4,000: BLUESTHESTANDARD.

Value of Race: $134,000 Winner $72,000; second $24,000; third $26,400; fourth $7,200; fifth $4,400. Mutuel Pool $483,739.00 Exacta Pool $278,041.00 Quinella Pool $26,700.00 Trifecta Pool $278,007.00

Last Raced	Horse	M/Eqt.	A.	Wt	PP	St	¼	½	Str	Fin	Jockey	Odds $1
12Mar03 ^{6}SA^{1}	Bluesthestandard	LB f	6	115	7	5	3^{1}	1^{hd}	1^{hd}	1^{2}	Smith M E	2.20
1Mar03 ^{3}SA^{5}	Joey Franco	LB	4	116	5	4	$4^{1\frac{1}{2}}$	2^{hd}	2^{2}	$2^{\frac{1}{2}}$	Stevens G L	24.90
26Jan03 ^{7}SA^{6}	Kona Gold	LB	9	121	6	6	6^{1}	$5^{\frac{1}{2}}$	$3^{2\frac{1}{2}}$	$3^{5\frac{1}{2}}$	Nakatani C S	1.50
22Feb03 ^{3}GG^{4}	Debonair Joe	LB	4	118	1	7	7	6^{3}	$4^{\frac{1}{2}}$	$4^{1\frac{1}{2}}$	Valenzuela P A	a- 5.40
22Feb03 ^{9}Lrl^{9}	D'wildcat	LB b	5	118	4	2	5^{hd}	7	6^{8}	5^{6}	Espinoza V	4.70
1Mar03 ^{3}SA^{1}	F J's Pace	LB bf	8	117	3	1	2^{1}	$3^{1\frac{1}{2}}$	$5^{1\frac{1}{2}}$	6^{6}	Flores D R	7.50
15Mar03 ^{2}SA^{1}	Martel	LB bf	6	109	2	3	1^{1}	$4^{1\frac{1}{2}}$	7	7	Garcia M S	a- 5.40

a–Coupled: Debonair Joe and Martel.

OFF AT 4:08 Start Good . Won driving. Track fast.
TIME :21^{2}, :44, 1:08^{2}, 1:14^{4} (:21.48, :44.19, 1:08.47, 1:14.86)

$2 Mutuel Prices:

6 – BLUESTHESTANDARD	6.40	4.00	2.80
4 – JOEY FRANCO		15.60	4.80
5 – KONA GOLD			2.80

$1 EXACTA 6–4 PAID $44.60 $2 QUINELLA 4–6 PAID $63.00 $1 TRIFECTA 6–4–5 PAID $135.30

B. g, (Apr), by American Standard – Bob's Blue , by Bob's Dusty . Trainer West Ted H. Bred by Terry Brown (Ga).

BLUESTHESTANDARD stalked outside on the backstretch, moved up outside on the turn, took a short lead three deep, battled outside a rival into the stretch and until deep stretch, then inched clear under left handed urging while drifting out late. JOEY FRANCO between horses early, angled in and saved ground stalking the pace, bid along the rail on the turn and through the stretch, could not match the winner late but held second. KONA GOLD chased outside then off the rail on the turn, came a bit wide into the stretch and just missed the place. DEBONAIR JOE settled inside, went around a rival into the turn, came out into the stretch and lacked the needed rally. D'WILDCAT between horses early, angled in and saved ground chasing the pace, dropped back on the turn, came out in the stretch and could not offer the necessary response. F J'S PACE forced the pace outside a rival early then stalked that one off the rail, bid between horses on the turn, dropped back approaching the stretch and weakened. MARTEL sent to the early lead, set the pace a bit off the rail, dropped back between foes nearing midway on the turn and gave way.

Owners– 1, Sengara Jeffrey; 2, Frankel Jerry; 3, Headley Aase Molasky Irwin and Molasky Andrew; 4, Ristad-Lidgett Lynne; 5, Fog City Stables and Windfields Farm; 6, Ren-Mar Thoroughbreds; 7, Ristad-Lidgett Lynne

Trainers– 1, West Ted H; 2, Vienna Darrell; 3, Headley Bruce; 4, Silva Juan P; 5, Hess Robert B Jr; 6, O'Neill Doug; 7, Silva Juan P

$2 Daily Double (3–6) Paid $16.00 ; Daily Double Pool $37,250 .
$1 Pick Three (9–3–6) Paid $61.20 ; Pick Three Pool $111,535 .

EIGHTH RACE

Keeneland

APRIL 4, 2003

1 MILE. (Turf)(1.33³) 15th Running of THE TRANSYLVANIA. Grade III. Purse $100,000 Guaranteed. Three year olds. By subscription of $100 each, which should accompany the nomination; $1,000 to enter and start with $100,000 guaranteed, of which $62,000 to the owner of the winner, $20,000 to second, $10,000 to third, $5,000 to fourth and $3,000 tofifth. Weight 123 lbs. Non–winners of $45,000 twice at a mile or over on the turf allowed 3 lbs.; $45,000 at a mile or over on the turf, 5 lbs.; $30,000 twice at a mile or over, 7 lbs. Starters to be named through the entry box by the usual time of closing. A gold julep cup will be presented to the owner of the winner. Closed Wednesday, March 26, 2003 with 26 nominations. Keeneland Course.

Value of Race: $100,000 Winner $62,000; second $20,000; third $10,000; fourth $5,000; fifth $3,000. Mutuel Pool $353,821.00 Exacta Pool $248,228.00 Quinella Pool $9,657.00 Trifecta Pool $211,302.00 Superfecta Pool $60,998.00

Last Raced	Horse	M/Eqt. A.Wt	PP	St	¼	½	¾	Str	Fin	Jockey	Odds $1
21Feb03 9GP²	White Cat	Lb 3 116	3	1	44½	44	31½	2½	1hd	Sellers S J	3.50
14Mar03 7SA³	Deep Shadow	Lb 3 118	7	4	31½	2½	21½	11½	2¹	Desormeaux K J	6.90
12Mar03 8GP⁴	Christmas Away	Lb 3 116	1	3	5¹	61½	6¹	5²	3nk	Day P	22.20
9Mar03 11GP¹	Remind	Lb 3 116	6	9	8²	51½	4hd	42½	42¾	Bailey J D	1.10
12Mar03 8GP⁷	Strizzi	L 3 116	9	6	6½	7½	8¹	6²	52¼	Santos J A	17.20
21Feb03 9GP⁵	Hypnotist	Lbf 3 120	2	2	1²	11½	1hd	3¹	6½	Guidry M	6.90
25Jan03 9FG⁹	Rapid Proof	Lb 3 120	4	5	7½	8²	7hd	86	7no	Borel C H	7.80
3Mar03 8FG⁴	Larry B	L 3 116	5	8	9	9	9	7hd	814¼	Meche L J	51.30
22Mar03 10TP⁷	Chicken Soup Kid	Lb 3 116	8	7	2hd	33	53	9	9	Peck B D	28.50

OFF AT 4:46 Start Good. Won driving. Course firm.

TIME :22⁴, :46, 1:10³, 1:22³, 1:34⁴ (:22.83, :46.01, 1:10.68, 1:22.76, 1:34.98)

$2 Mutuel Prices:	3–WHITE CAT	9.00	5.60	5.00
	7–DEEP SHADOW		7.40	7.40
	1–CHRISTMAS AWAY			9.20

$2 EXACTA 3–7 PAID $68.20 $2 QUINELLA 3–7 PAID $38.20 $2 TRIFECTA 3–7–1 PAID $797.80 $2 SUPERFECTA 3–7–1–6 PAID $2,600.40

Ch. c, (Mar), by Mountain Cat–Our Friend Terry, by Cox's Ridge. Trainer McPeek Kenneth G. Bred by Stillmeadow Farm LLC & Dr. Steve Conboy (Ky).

WHITE CAT, away well, was eased back inside soon after to follow the leaders under light rating, angled out to advance four wide into the stretch, reached the front at the sixteenth pole, then proved gamely best. DEEP SHADOW, well placed always while tracking the pace three or four wide, was put to a drive at the three-furlong marker, took over when straightened into the stretch, gained a clear lead, lost it to the winner a sixteenth out and held on stubbornly the remainder. CHRISTMAS AWAY, unhurried early and three or four wide, came out six abreast for the drive and finished with good energy. REMIND, bumped at the start and forced out, was outrun for a half, reached contention in behind rivals four wide on the far turn, continued four or five wide into the stretch and slowly was gaining late. STRIZZI, outrun for six furlongs and four or five wide, moved out farther on the course for the stretch run and offered a minor gain. HYPNOTIST gained the lead inside early, edged clear, showed the way to the stretch and weakened thereafter. RAPID PROOF, outrun to the stretch while racing near the inside, came out four wide for the drive and failed to offer a closing account. LARRY B drifted out at the start bumping REMIND, was outrun to the stretch, came out eight wide for the drive but never fired. CHICKEN SOUP KID moved up four wide early to chase the pace and tired approaching the stretch.

Owners— 1, Cottrell Raymond H Sr; 2, Fog City Stable; 3, Bowling Carl & Thompson Charles R; 4, Claiborne Farm; 5, Stronach Stable; 6, Dogwood Stable; 7, Morrison Dolphus; 8, Bielfeldt Larry D; 9, Nash Robert D

Trainers— 1, McPeek Kenneth G; 2, Lukas D Wayne; 3, Byrne Patrick B; 4, Mott William I; 5, Pierce Malcolm; 6, Tagg Barclay; 7, Wiggins Hal R; 8, Kassen David C; 9, Flint Bernard S

$2 Pick Three (8–2–3) Paid $535.60; Pick Three Pool $32,737.
$1 Pick Six (5–1–1/3/7–8–2–3) 5
Correct Paid $549.40; Pick Six Pool $5,427; Carryover Pool $3,296.

EIGHTH RACE

Aqueduct

APRIL 5, 2003

1⅛ MILES. (1.47) 91st Running of THE EXCELSIOR BREEDERS' CUP HANDICAP. Grade III. Purse $200,000 (includes $50,000 BC – Breeders' Cup) (Up to $29,100 NYSBFOA) A HANDICAP FOR THREE YEAR OLDS AND UPWARD. (Plus $50,000 Breeders' Cup Fund for Cup nominees only). By subscription of $150 each, which should accompany the nomination; $750 to pass the entry box; $750 to start. The NYRA purse to be divided 60% to the winner, 20% to second, 11% to third, 6% to fourth and 3% to fifth. Breeders' Cup Fund monies also correspondingly divided, provided a Breeders' Cup nominee has finished in an award position. Any Breeders' Cup Fund monies not awarded will revert back to the Fund. Trophy to the winning ownergiven by the Breeders' Cup Ltd. The New York Racing Association will present trophies to the winning trainer and jockey. Closed Saturday, March 22, 2003 with 25 Nominations.

Value of Race: $170,000 Winner $90,000; second $40,000; third $22,000; fourth $12,000; fifth $6,000. Mutuel Pool $463,178.00 Exacta Pool $405,833.00

Last Raced	Horse	M/Eqt. A.Wt	PP	St	¼	½	¾	Str	Fin	Jockey	Odds $1
16Mar03 7Aqu²	Classic Endeavor	Lf 5 113	1	1	11½	12½	1½	1²	1½	Lopez C C	3.45
2Mar03 9FG⁹	Balto Star	L 5 119	4	2	42¹	41	3hd	2½	2¾	Castellano J J	2.80
23Feb03 9Lrl¹	Tempest Fugit	Lf 6 114	2	4	3hd	3½	41½	3²	3¾	Gryder A T	8.20
16Mar03 7Aqu¹	Snake Mountain	L 5 122	3	5	5	5	5	4hd	43¾	Luzzi M J	1.10
22Feb03 11GP¹⁰	Saint Verre	L 5 114	5	3	2½	2½	2¹	5	5	Arroyo N Jr	8.50

OFF AT 4:21 Start Good. Won driving. Track fast.

TIME :23, :46², 1:10², 1:35, 1:48 (:23.11, :46.41, 1:10.45, 1:35.03, 1:48.10)

$2 Mutuel Prices:	1–CLASSIC ENDEAVOR	8.90	4.80	5.10
	5–BALTO STAR		4.70	4.10
	2–TEMPEST FUGIT			7.20

$2 EXACTA 1–5 PAID $42.80

Dk. b. or br. h, by Silver Buck–Bold Juana, by John Alden. Trainer Schwartz Scott M. Bred by Diane H Flowers (Fla).

CLASSIC ENDEAVOR quickly opened a clear lead, set the pace along the inside, dug in determinedly when set down in upper stretch and prevailed under a drive. BALTO STAR was rated along outside, rallied three wide on the second turn, was carried out entering the stretch, came in leaving the eighth pole and finished gamely from the outside. TEMPEST FUGIT was rated along inside, found room inside in the stretch and finished well. SNAKE MOUNTAIN was outrun early, came wide for the drive and finished well outside. SAINT VERRE prompted the pace from the outside, drifted out entering the stretch, was steadied between rivals in the drive and tired in the final furlong.

Owners— 1, Schwartz Herbert T & Carol A; 2, Anstu Stables; 3, Drazin Dennis A; 4, Berkshire Stud et al; 5, Allen Joseph

Trainers— 1, Schwartz Scott M; 2, Pletcher Todd A; 3, Servis Jason; 4, Jerkens James A; 5, Jerkens H Allen

Scratched— Iwin (21Mar03 6AQU⁴)

EIGHTH RACE
Hawthorne
APRIL 5, 2003

1⅛ MILES. (1.46^{3}) 46th Running of THE ILLINOIS DERBY. Grade II. Purse $500,000 Guaranteed. FOR THREE YEAR OLDS. By subscription of $100 each Early Bird nomination made by February 5, 2003, or $500 each, which shall accompany the nomination made by March 19, 2003, $2,500 to pass entry box, $2,500 additional to start. Weight 122 lbs. Winners of $100,000 at a mile or over in 2003 to carry 2 lbs. Non-winners of $75,000 at a mile or over in 2003 allowed, 2 lbs.; such a race at anytime, 4 lbs.; of $50,000 at a mile or over at any time, 6 lbs.; of $30,000 at a mile or over at any time, 8 lbs. (Maiden & claiming races not considered.) Unnominated entries may be supplemented at time of entry on April 2, 2003 accompanied by $10,000 fee includes entry and starting fees and is only refundable if entry is excluded. Early Closing – February 5, 2003 ($100 Fee) closed with 135. Late Closing – March 19, 2003. SUPPLEMENTAL NOMINATION FEE OF $500: RUNNIN' ON NITRO.

Value of Race: $500,000 Winner $300,000; second $100,000; third $55,000; fourth $30,000; fifth $15,000. Mutuel Pool $820,757.00 Exacta Pool $492,181.00 Trifecta Pool $430,437.00 Superfecta Pool $111,401.00

Last Raced	Horse	M/Eqt.	A.Wt	PP	St	¼	½	¾	Str	Fin	Jockey	Odds $1
8Mar03 ^{8}GG^{3}	Ten Most Wanted	L	3 114	2	7	7^{3}	$6^{1/2}$	5^{1}	2^{4}	1^{4}	Day P	2.30
16Mar03 ^{5}Aqu^{2}	Fund Of Funds	Lb	3 114	3	1	2^{hd}	$3^{1\,1/2}$	$3^{1\,1/2}$	$1^{1\,1/2}$	2^{8}	Bridgmohan S X	21.20
1Mar03 ^{8}Lrl^{2}	Foufa's Warrior	Lbf	3 118	1	10	10	8^{2}	7^{5}	5^{3}	$3^{3/4}$	Vega H	33.20
9Mar03 ^{9}FG^{4}	Lone Star Sky	L	3 120	10	6	$6^{1\,1/2}$	5^{hd}	6^{7}	$4^{1\,1/2}$	$4^{1/2}$	Borel C H	2.90
1Mar03 ^{8}Lrl^{1}	Cherokee's Boy	Lb	3 116	7	5	5^{2}	$4^{1\,1/2}$	$4^{1/2}$	$3^{1/2}$	$5^{10\,1/2}$	Fogelsonger R	9.30
18Mar03 ^{4}Haw^{1}	Lx Commander	Lb	3 114	4	2	1^{1}	$1^{1/2}$	$2^{1\,1/2}$	7^{6}	6no	Emigh C A	13.70
16Mar03 ^{9}Aqu^{1}	Alysweep	Lbf	3 124	9	4	$3^{1\,1/2}$	2^{1}	1^{hd}	$6^{2\,1/2}$	$7^{7\,3/4}$	Migliore R	3.40
1Mar03 ^{6}GP^{1}	Runnin' On Nitro	L	3 114	6	9	9^{hd}	$9^{1/2}$	9^{7}	8^{8}	$8^{15\,3/4}$	Lumpkins J	4.70
18Mar03 ^{4}Haw^{2}	Blackinton	Lb	3 114	5	3	$4^{1/2}$	7^{4}	$8^{1/2}$	9^{4}	9^{2}	Cadman Z	84.40
7Mar03 ^{4}Haw^{2}	Brian Dude	L	3 114	8	8	$8^{1\,1/2}$	10	10	10	10	Baird E T	88.20

OFF AT 4:27 Start Good For All But FOUFA'S WARRIOR Won driving. Track fast.
TIME :23, :46^{3}, 1:11^{3}, 1:38^{2}, 1:51^{2} (:23.03, :46.73, 1:11.72, 1:38.59, 1:51.47)

$2 Mutuel Prices:

2–TEN MOST WANTED	6.60	4.00	3.20
3–FUND OF FUNDS		15.40	10.80
1–FOUFA'S WARRIOR			8.20

$2 EXACTA 2–3 PAID $108.60 $2 TRIFECTA 2–3–1 PAID $820.40 $2 SUPERFECTA 2–3–1–10 PAID $3,978.60

Dk. b. or br. c, (Feb), by Deputy Commander–Wanted Again, by Criminal Type. Trainer Dollase Wallace. Bred by Jim H Plemmons (Ky).

TEN MOST WANTED was void of early speed while saving ground, moved up steadily inside, had to wait for room in upper stretch, angled out near the furlong marker, rallied to the lead in the final furlong and drew off while under urging. FUND OF FUNDS established good position behind the leaders and along the rail, came three wide into the stretch, rallied to a clear lead in the stretch then could not go with the winner late. FOUFA'S WARRIOR hopped at the start and lacked speed, angled out in the stretch and rallied belatedly for minor awards. LONE STAR SKY raced near the middle of the field while off the rail and failed to reach a contending position. CHEROKEE'S BOY broke inward, raced just outside near the middle of the field, made a mild bid in the stretch and faltered. LX COMMANDER set the pace from the inside while pressed but tired in the drive. ALYSWEEP pressed the pace from just outside and also tired. RUNNIN' ON NITRO was shuffled back then stumbled just after the start and was always outrun. BLACKINTON raced close up outside and dropped back steadily. BRIAN DUDE was never close.

Owners— 1, James Chisholm Michael Jarvis & Hor; 2, Klaravich Stables Seth A Klarman; 3, Bender Sondra D; 4, New Walter L; 5, Z W P Stable Foard Wilgis; 6, Ed Wright Miles Childers & Ltb Inc; 7, Doneson Mark & Dubb Michael; 8, Brewer Haagsma & Ward; 9, Cumberland Paul; 10, Wexler Racing Stables

Trainers—1, Dollase Wallace; 2, Violette Richard A Jr; 3, Murray Lawrence E; 4, Amoss Thomas; 5, Capuano Gary; 6, Flint Bernard S; 7, Reynolds Patrick L; 8, Ward Wesley A; 9, Boyce Michele; 10, Vinci Charles J

$2 Pick Four (6–5–5–2) Paid $154.80; Pick Four Pool $7,018. $2 Pick Six (2/4–1–6–5–5–2) 5 Correct Paid $29.00; Pick Six Pool $1,544; Carryover Pool $874.

ELEVENTH RACE
Oaklawn
APRIL 5, 2003

1⅛ MILES. (1.46^{3}) 57th Running of THE OAKLAWN HANDICAP. Grade II. Purse $500,000 FOUR-YEAR-OLDS AND UPWARD. Weights to be announced Thursday, March 27. In Handicap Stakes starting preference will be given to highweights. Starters to be named through the entry box by the usual time of closing. Nominations closed Thursday, March 20, 2003 with 20 nominees.

Value of Race: $500,000 Winner $300,000; second $100,000; third $50,000; fourth $30,000; fifth $20,000. Mutuel Pool $1,886,104.0 Exacta Pool $384,805.00 Trifecta Pool $217,306.00

Last Raced	Horse	M/Eqt.	A.Wt	PP	St	¼	½	¾	Str	Fin	Jockey	Odds $1
1Feb03 ^{9}SA^{1}	Medaglia d'Oro	L	4 122	1	1	1^{1}	$1^{1/2}$	$1^{1/2}$	$1^{1\,1/2}$	$1^{2\,3/4}$	Bailey J D	0.10
22Mar03 ^{9}OP^{1}	Slider	Lb	5 112	4	2	2^{2}	$2^{1\,1/2}$	$2^{1/2}$	$2^{3\,1/2}$	2^{hd}	Marquez C H Jr	17.20
1Mar03 ^{9}SA^{3}	Kudos	Lb	6 117	5	5	5	5	5	$3^{1\,1/2}$	3^{4}	Solis A	3.70
16Mar03 ^{9}OP^{2}	Crafty Shaw	L	5 114	3	4	$3^{2\,1/2}$	3^{3}	$3^{3\,1/2}$	5	4^{2}	Lopez J	13.90
16Mar03 ^{9}OP^{5}	Gold Tango	L	4 111	2	3	4^{2}	$4^{3\,1/2}$	$4^{2\,1/2}$	$4^{1/2}$	5	Thompson T J	40.70

OFF AT 6:06 Start Good. Won driving. Track fast.
TIME :23^{3}, :47^{4}, 1:12, 1:35^{4}, 1:47^{3} (:23.76, :47.84, 1:12.00, 1:35.99, 1:47.66)

$2 Mutuel Prices:

1–MEDAGLIA D'ORO	2.20	2.20	2.20
4–SLIDER		3.80	2.20
5–KUDOS			2.20

$2 EXACTA 1–4 PAID $15.60 $2 TRIFECTA 1–4–5 PAID $31.20

Dk. b. or br. c, by El Prado*Ire–Cappucino Bay, by Bailjumper. Trainer Frankel Robert. Bred by Albert Bell & Joyce Bell (Ky).

MEDAGLIA D'ORO broke well, set a comfortable pace just off the inside, shook off SLIDER nearing the furlong marker, roused one time, came home full of run. SLIDER pressed the winner outside that one early well in hand, tried that same rival turning for home, no match, narrowly held the place. KUDOS last away, trailed well back, began to move a bit when asked midway on the second turn off the rail, roused soon after, finished willingly to be rapidly getting to the runner up. CRAFTY SHAW settled behind the top two, lodged a mild bid three wide in the second turn, failed to sustain that bid in the drive. GOLD TANGO off the early pace, no impact in the drive.

Owners— 1, Gann Edmund A; 2, Hays Billy; 3, Moss Mr & Mrs Jerome S; 4, Cella Charles J; 5, Franks John

Trainers—1, Frankel Robert; 2, Woodard Joe; 3, Mandella Richard; 4, Vestal Peter M; 5, Barnett Bobby C

$2 Daily Double (6–1) Paid $2.40; Daily Double Pool $64,154.
$2 Pick Three (4–4–1) Paid $24.60; Pick Three Pool $41,357.

EIGHTH RACE
Oaklawn
APRIL 5, 2003

1 1/16 MILES. (1.40^{1}) 38th Running of THE APPLE BLOSSOM HANDICAP. Grade I. Purse $500,000 FILLIES AND MARES, FOUR-YEAR-OLDS AND UPWARD. Weights to be announced Friday, March 28. In Handicap Stakes starting preference will be given to highweights. Starters to be named through the entry box by the usual time of closing. Nominations closed Thursday, March 20, 2003 with 14 nominees.

Value of Race: $500,000 Winner $300,000; second $100,000; third $50,000; fourth $30,000; fifth $20,000. Mutuel Pool $1,168,549.0 Exacta Pool $417,203.00 Trifecta Pool $422,386.00

Last Raced	Horse	M/Eqt.	A.Wt	PP	St	¼	½	¾	Str	Fin	Jockey	Odds $1
26Oct02 3AP1	Azeri	L	5 123	6	4	31½	43	2hd	21	1hd	Smith M E	0.40
7Dec02 6Hou1	Take Charge Lady	L	4 118	5	2	11½	11	1½	11½	23¼	Sellers S J	3.80
15Mar03 10OP3	Mandy's Gold	Lf	5 116	7	1	2½	31	33	33	32	Douglas R R	17.30
25Jan03 8SA1	Affluent	L	5 117	2	3	5½	51½	51½	43½	41¾	Solis A	4.20
7Mar03 2SA4	Rhiana	L	6 112	3	5	63	63½	64	5½	52¼	Marquez C H Jr	58.40
15Mar03 10OP1	Bien Nicole	L	5 115	4	6	42½	2hd	42½	62½	6nk	Pettinger D R	17.30
15Mar03 10OP5	Took Out	L	4 113	1	7	7	7	7	7	7	Castellano A Jr	96.70

OFF AT 4:42 Start Good. Won driving. Track fast.
TIME :24^{1}, :48^{3}, 1:12^{1}, 1:36^{3}, 1:43 (:24.33, :48.70, 1:12.38, 1:36.69, 1:43.00)

$2 Mutuel Prices:

6-AZERI	2.80	2.20	2.20
5-TAKE CHARGE LADY		2.80	2.20
7-MANDY'S GOLD			2.20

$2 EXACTA 6-5 PAID $8.20 $2 TRIFECTA 6-5-7 PAID $47.40

Ch. m, by Jade Hunter-Zodiac Miss*Aus, by Ahonoora. Trainer De Seroux Laura. Bred by Allen E Paulson (Ky).

AZERI forwardly placed, restrained toward the inside opening quarter, moved out and advanced four wide to join the fray into a quick third quarter, lost ground to the winner into the stretch, roused with a furlong remaining and finished with good courage to be up in the final strides. TAKE CHARGE LADY broke sharp, set a soft set of early fractions, continued to show the way into the second turn closest to the inside, shook clear when straightened for home, could not contain the winner while remaining clear of the others. MANDY'S GOLD prompted the early pace, vied between foes into the second turn, fell back turning for home, moved to the inside, finished best of the rest. AFFLUENT turned in an even effort off the inside. RHIANA fractious in the gate, four wide into the stretch, lacked a late response. BIEN NICOLE stalked, lodged a mild bid three wide onto the backstretch, gave way from between foes into the second turn. TOOK OUT last away, trailed throughout off the inside.

Owners— 1, Allen E Paulson Living Trust; 2, Select Stable; 3, Steeplechase Farm; 4, Whitham Janis R; 5, Ernst Allegra & John; 6, Richter Kristine & John; 7, Scarberry Howard & Penny

Trainers—1, De Seroux Laura; 2, McPeek Kenneth G; 3, Gorham Michael E; 4, McAnally Ronald; 5, Hendricks Dan L; 6, Von Hemel Donnie K; 7, Scarberry Howard

$2 Pick Three (1-7-6) Paid $31.40; Pick Three Pool $18,354.
$2 Classix (1-7-3-1-7-6) Paid $713.20; Classix Pool $13,244.
$2 Classix (1-7-3-1-7-6) Paid $14.20

EIGHTH RACE
Keeneland
APRIL 5, 2003

1 1/16 MILES. (1.40^{4}) 66th Running of THE ASHLAND. Grade I. Purse $500,000 Added. Fillies, three years old. By subscription of $250 each, which should accompany the nomination; $5,000 to enter and start, with $500,000 added, of which 62% of all monies to the owner of the winner, 20% to second, 10% to third, 5% to fourth and 3% to fifth. Weight: 123 lbs. Non-winners of $60,000 twice at a mile or over allowed 3 lbs.; $60,000 at a mile or over, 5 lbs.; $30,000 twice at any distance, 7 lbs. Starters to named through the entry box by the usual time of closing. A gold julep cup will be presented to the owner of the winner. A silver julep cup will be presented to the winning trainer and jockey. No supplementary nominations. Closed Wednesday, February 19, 2003 with 67 nominations.

Value of Race: $551,750 Winner $342,085; second $110,350; third $55,175; fourth $27,588; fifth $16,552. Mutuel Pool $701,927.00 Exacta Pool $349,510.00 Quinella Pool $14,507.00 Trifecta Pool $295,840.00 Superfecta Pool $89,025.00

Last Raced	Horse	M/Eqt.	A.Wt	PP	St	¼	½	¾	Str	Fin	Jockey	Odds $1
8Mar03 4SA2	Elloluv	L	3 120	5	3	11	11	1½	12	13¾	Albarado R J	2.10
8Mar03 9FG1	Lady Tak	Lf	3 123	2	1	4½	3hd	3hd	21½	2¾	Lanerie C J	1.30
14Mar03 9GP3	Holiday Lady	L	3 116	7	2	2½	21	21½	33½	35	Santos J A	28.50
23Feb03 9GP1	Yell	L	3 120	1	5	5½	52	53½	41	4½	Velazquez J R	2.30
15Feb03 9FG5	Allspice	Lb	3 116	6	4	3½	42	41½	58	510½	Court J K	52.20
22Mar03 8TP3	Unbridled Femme	Lb	3 116	3	6	7	7	64	66	68	Peck B D	65.50
14Mar03 9GP1	Ivanavinalot	Lf	3 123	4	7	61½	6hd	7	7	7	Guidry M	10.70

OFF AT 4:47 Start Good. Won driving. Track fast.
TIME :24^{3}, :48^{3}, 1:12^{2}, 1:37^{1}, 1:43^{2} (:24.63, :48.72, 1:12.56, 1:37.26, 1:43.58)

$2 Mutuel Prices:

5-ELLOLUV	6.20	2.80	2.20
2-LADY TAK		3.00	2.40
7-HOLIDAY LADY			4.00

$2 EXACTA 5-2 PAID $18.40 $2 QUINELLA 2-5 PAID $7.40 $2 TRIFECTA 5-2-7 PAID $170.00 $2 SUPERFECTA 5-2-7-1 PAID $337.60

B. f, (Feb), by Gilded Time-Currency Quest, by Cryptoclearance. Trainer Dollase Craig. Bred by North Wales LLC (Ky).

ELLOLUV drifted in at the start bumping IVANAVINALOT, continued inward to gain the lead approaching the first turn, went along under careful handling, turned back a challenge from HOLIDAY LADY midway on the second turn, settled into the stretch with a clear advantage, then increased her lead under mild hand encouragement. LADY TAK broke in front, was eased back to be well placed along the inside, appeared full of run approaching the end of the backstretch while in behind the leaders, eased out three abreast on the second turn, made a mild run outside the leaders entering the stretch but couldn't seriously menace as second best. HOLIDAY LADY moved up soon after the start to stalk ELLOLUV three or four wide under light rating, moved menacingly after that one approaching the three-eighths pole, continued forwardly to the stretch and weakened gradually. YELL settled along the inside early, moved out between rivals four or five on the backstretch, raced within easy striking distance to the stretch but came up empty. ALLSPICE, nicely placed while tracking the leaders under light restraint four wide, weakened soon after going six furlongs. UNBRIDLED FEMME bobbled while breaking sluggishly to the inside, was checked, raced within striking distance for six furlongs and tired. IVANAVINALOT, away sluggishly and forced in by the winner, was checked sharply, raced in contention four or five wide to the far turn and faded.

Owners— 1, Reddam J P; 2, Heiligbrodt Racing Stable; 3, Farmer Tracy; 4, Claiborne Farm & Dilschneider Adele; 5, Tafel James B; 6, Duzee Stable Duane Ducharme & Jerry; 7, Campbell Gilbert G

Trainers—1, Dollase Craig; 2, Asmussen Steven M; 3, Zito Nicholas P; 4, McGaughey Claude III; 5, Cilio Gene A; 6, Pate David E; 7, O'Connell Kathleen

$2 Pick Three (5-3-5) Paid $101.80; Pick Three Pool $42,344. $1 Pick Six (4-1-8-5-3-5) 5 Correct Paid $134.80; Pick Six Pool $11,991; Carryover Pool $10,581.

FOURTH RACE
Santa Anita
APRIL 5, 2003

ABOUT 6½ FURLONGS. (Turf) (1.11^{2}) LAS CIENEGAS H. Grade III. Purse $100,000 FOR FILLIES AND MARES FOUR YEARS OLD AND UPWARD. By subscription of $100 each to accompany the nomination or by supplementary nomination of $2,000 by Sunday, March 30. $1,000 additional to start, with $100,000 added. The added money and all fees to be divided 60% to the winner, 20% to second, 12% to third, 6% to fourth and 2% to fifth. **NOMINATIONS CLOSED** Thursday, March 27, 2003 with 20 (Rail at 0 Feet hill & stretch).

Value of Race: $110,000 Winner $66,000; second $22,000; third $13,200; fourth $6,600; fifth $2,200. **Mutuel Pool** $738,692.00 **Exacta Pool** $403,526.00 **Quinella Pool** $42,819.00 **Trifecta Pool** $395,777.00 **Superfecta Pool** $123,227.00

Last Raced	Horse	M/Eqt.	A.	Wt	PP	St	¼	½	Str	Fin	Jockey	Odds $1
27Dec02 ^{3}SA^{1}	Heat Haze-GB	LB	4	114	7	6	8	8	$4^{\frac{1}{2}}$	1^{3}	Valdivia J Jr	2.80
16Mar03 ^{3}SA^{3}	Icantgoforthat	LB b	4	114	5	2	$1^{\frac{1}{2}}$	$1^{1\frac{1}{2}}$	$1^{1\frac{1}{2}}$	2^{hd}	Baze T	42.30
12Mar03 ^{7}SA^{3}	Paga-Arg	LB	6	116	3	3	3^{2}	3^{1}	$2^{\frac{1}{2}}$	3^{1}	Flores D R	2.50
8Feb03 ^{8}TuP^{1}	Secret Garden-Ire	LB	4	116	1	4	4^{hd}	$5^{\frac{1}{2}}$	3^{2}	4^{1}	Johnston M T	15.60
17Feb03 ^{7}SA^{3}	Embassy Belle-Ire	LB	5	116	6	7	7^{hd}	$7^{\frac{1}{2}}$	$6^{1\frac{1}{2}}$	5^{nk}	Stevens G L	5.00
17Feb03 ^{7}SA^{5}	I'm theBusiness-NZ	LB	6	115	4	5	6^{1}	$6^{1\frac{1}{2}}$	$7^{\frac{1}{2}}$	$6^{\frac{1}{2}}$	Espinoza V	16.40
12Mar03 ^{7}SA^{2}	Brocky'sDream-Aus	LB b	5	118	2	8	5^{1}	4^{hd}	5^{hd}	$7^{5\frac{1}{2}}$	Nakatani C S	6.20
12Mar03 ^{7}SA^{1}	Repository	LB	5	116	8	1	2^{1}	$2^{\frac{1}{2}}$	8	8	Valenzuela P A	4.00

OFF AT 1:34 Start Good . Won driving. Course firm.

TIME :22, $:44^{2}$, $1:07^{1}$, 1:13 (:22.09, :44.56, 1:07.35, 1:13.11)

$2 Mutuel Prices:				
	7 – HEAT HAZE–GB	7.60	5.00	4.00
	5 – ICANTGOFORTHAT		27.60	9.60
	3 – PAGA–ARG			3.60

$1 EXACTA 7–5 PAID $123.60 $2 QUINELLA 5–7 PAID $173.40
$1 TRIFECTA 7–5–3 PAID $514.50 $1 SUPERFECTA 7–5–3–1 PAID $3,278.60

Dk. b or br. m, (Mar), by Green Desert – Hasili-Ire , by Kahyasi . Trainer Frankel Robert. Bred by Juddmonte Farms (GB).

HEAT HAZE (GB) cut the corner at the right hand curve then angled in and settled outside a rival, came out on the dirt crossing and five wide into the stretch and rallied under some urging to win clear. ICANTGOFORTHAT had good early speed off the rail and dueled inside a rival, inched away and angled in leaving the hill, could not hold off the winner and just saved the place. PAGA (ARG) saved ground stalking the leaders, came a bit off the rail in the stretch and just missed second. SECRET GARDEN (IRE) pulled her way along inside to track the pace down the hill, came out on the dirt and four wide into the stretch and could not offer the necessary late kick. EMBASSY BELLE (IRE) angled in after the right hand curve and chased inside, remained along the rail in the stretch and improved position. I'M THE BUSINESS (NZ) was in a good position chasing three deep then four wide leaving the hill, came six wide into the stretch and did not rally. BROCKY'S DREAM (AUS) off a bit slowly, chased between horses then outside a rival, came out on the dirt and wide into the stretch and weakened. REPOSITORY cut the corner at the right hand curve then dueled outside the runner-up, stalked alongside a foe leaving the hill, dropped back between horses into the stretch and also weakened.

Owners– 1, Juddmonte Farms Inc; 2, Broberg Andy and Knapp Steve; 3, Hubbard R D and Allred Edward C; 4, Sangster Robert E; 5, Rooney June; 6, Doll Ken Kadner Marshall Shapiro Barry et al; 7, Burns Mike and Kolbe Al; 8, Rafter L Stables

Trainers– 1, Frankel Robert J; 2, Knapp Steve; 3, Mandella Richard E; 4, Bray Simon; 5, Cecil Ben D; 6, Stein Roger M; 7, Carno Louis R; 8, Lukas D Wayne

$1 Pick Three (4–9–7) Paid $39.40 ; Pick Three Pool $95,002 .
$2 Daily Double (9–7) Paid $33.60 ; Daily Double Pool $30,207 .

TENTH RACE
Santa Anita
APRIL 5, 2003

1⅛ MILES. (1.45^{4}) SAN BERNARDINO H. Grade III. Purse $150,000 FOR FOUR-YEAR-OLDS AND UPWARD. By subscription fo $150 each to accompany the nomination or by supplementary nomination of $3,000 by Sunday, March 30. $1,500 additional to start, with $150,000 guaranteed, of which $90,000 to first, $30,000 to second, $18,000 to third, $9,000 to fourth and $3,000 to fifth. **NOMINATIONS CLOSED** Thursday, March 27, 2003 with 18.

Value of Race: $150,000 Winner $90,000; second $30,000; third $18,000; fourth $9,000; fifth $3,000. **Mutuel Pool** $570,302.00 **Exacta Pool** $296,743.00 **Quinella Pool** $32,699.00 **Trifecta Pool** $300,055.00 **Superfecta Pool** $112,956.00

Last Raced	Horse	M/Eqt.	A.	Wt	PP	St	¼	½	¾	Str	Fin	Jockey	Odds $1
11May02 ^{8}Sin^{11}	Western Pride	LB	5	116	8	6	2^{1}	2^{1}	2^{1}	1^{1}	1^{nk}	Valenzuela P A	4.00
22Mar03 ^{8}SA^{1}	Total Impact-Chi	LB	5	113	6	7	$4^{\frac{1}{2}}$	$3^{\frac{1}{2}}$	$3^{1\frac{1}{2}}$	2^{2}	2^{1}	Espinoza V	10.60
1Mar03 ^{8}GG^{2}	Fleetstreet Dancer	LB b	5	112	5	5	$5^{1\frac{1}{2}}$	5^{1}	$5^{2\frac{1}{2}}$	$3^{1\frac{1}{2}}$	$3^{2\frac{1}{2}}$	Baze T	9.30
1Mar03 ^{9}SA^{5}	PiensaSonando-Chi	LB	5	116	7	8	8	8	8	$6^{\frac{1}{2}}$	4^{3}	Flores D R	4.40
22Mar03 ^{8}SA^{4}	Tracemark	LB b	4	117	3	2	3^{hd}	$4^{1\frac{1}{2}}$	4^{hd}	$5^{1\frac{1}{2}}$	$5^{1\frac{1}{2}}$	Desormeaux K J	33.00
8Mar03 ^{9}SA^{1}	Kela	LB	5	116	1	4	7^{6}	7^{10}	$6^{1\frac{1}{2}}$	7^{8}	$6^{4\frac{1}{2}}$	Garcia M S	3.70
21Mar03 ^{7}SA^{4}	Lord Jim-Arg	LB f	6	116	4	1	$1^{\frac{1}{2}}$	1^{1}	$1^{\frac{1}{2}}$	4^{hd}	7^{10}	Stevens G L	18.70
5Jan02 ^{8}SA^{1}	Wooden Phone	LB b	6	119	2	3	$6^{2\frac{1}{2}}$	6^{hd}	$7^{4\frac{1}{2}}$	8	8	Nakatani C S	2.00

OFF AT 4:54 Start Good . Won driving. Track fast.

TIME $:22^{4}$, $:46^{2}$, $1:10^{2}$, $1:35^{1}$, $1:48^{2}$ (:22.91, :46.57, 1:10.50, 1:35.29, 1:48.56)

$2 Mutuel Prices:				
	8 – WESTERN PRIDE	10.00	5.60	5.00
	6 – TOTAL IMPACT–CHI		9.20	8.40
	5 – FLEETSTREET DANCER			6.60

$1 EXACTA 8–6 PAID $50.00 $2 QUINELLA 6–8 PAID $64.20
$1 TRIFECTA 8–6–5 PAID $386.20 $1 SUPERFECTA 8–6–5–7 PAID $1,408.70

Dk. b or br. h, (May), by Way West-Fr – Strongerthanpride , by Proud Birdie . Trainer Chapman James K. Bred by C Bowling & C Thompson (Fla).

WESTERN PRIDE forced or stalked the pace outside a rival, took command on the second turn, inched away off the rail and held on gamely under urging. TOTAL IMPACT (CHI) stalked three deep then outside on the backstretch and second turn, bid into the stretch, continued willingly but could not get by the winner. FLEETSTREET DANCER chased between horses or outside a rival, came three deep into the stretch and bested the others. PIENSA SONANDO (CHI) angled in and saved ground off the pace, went around a rival past midstretch and improved position. TRACEMARK stalked a bit off the rail, swung out into the stretch and weakened. KELA came off the rail early, chased outside, went four wide into the second turn, angled in some and did not rally. LORD JIM (ARG) sped to a slim early lead, set a pressured pace a bit off the rail, angled in for the second turn, dropped back leaving that bend and weakened. WOODEN PHONE saved ground stalking the pace, also dropped back on the second turn and gave way.

Owners– 1, Chapman Carolyn and McArthur Theresa; 2, Al Kabeer Sultan Mohammed Saud and Bridport S A; 3, Leatherman Lee and Ty; 4, Hunt Nelson B; 5, McGrath Edward T; 6, Jones Aaron U and Marie D; 7, Tanaka Gary A; 8, Durant Tom Helzer Marilyn and James E

Trainers– 1, Chapman James K; 2, De Seroux Laura; 3, O'Neill Doug; 4, McAnally Ronald L; 5, Sauque Alex; 6, Barrera Larry S; 7, Gaines Carla; 8, Baffert Bob

$1 Pick Three (2–7–8) Paid $2,043.70 ; Pick Three Pool $97,297 .
$2 Daily Double (7–8) Paid $92.20 ; Daily Double Pool $51,040 .
$1 Place Pick All (9–OF–10) Paid $8,144.10 ; Place Pick All Pool $51,016 .

SIXTH RACE
Santa Anita
APRIL 5, 2003

1⅛ MILES. (1.45⁴) SANTA ANITA DERBY Grade I. Purse $750,000 FOR THREE-YEAR-OLDS. By subscription of $250 each to accompany the nomination (Early Bird) on or before December 9, 2002. Early Bird nominees to the Santa Anita Derby are automatically eligible to both the San Rafael and San Felipe Stakes with nominationand starting fees waived to those two stakes. Late nominations close Thursday, March 13, 2003 by payment of $2,500 each. Supplementary nominations are due at time of entry, by payment of $15,000. All horses shall pay $7,500 to start,with $750,000 guaranteed, of which $450,000 to first, $150,000 to second, $90,000 to third, $45,000 to fourth and $15,000 to fifth. 122 lbs. 149 early noms, 2 late.

Value of Race: $750,000 Winner $450,000; second $150,000; third $90,000; fourth $45,000; fifth $15,000. Mutuel Pool $2,151,087.00 Exacta Pool $1,073,685.00 Quinella Pool $85,480.00 Trifecta Pool $1,193,283.00

Last Raced	Horse	M/Eqt. A. Wt	PP	St	¼	½	¾	Str	Fin	Jockey	Odds $1
16Mar03 5SA1	Buddy Gil	LB 3 122	4	4	6³	63½	5⁴	1½	1hd	Stevens G L	6.30
22Mar03 6SA4	Indian Express	LB 3 122	2	1	2¹	2²	1hd	2²	22¼	Baze T	35.80
9Mar03 9FG10	Kafwain	LB b 3 122	7	5	5²	4½	41½	4½	31¼	Valenzuela P A	1.70
16Mar03 5SA2	Atswhatimtlknbout	LB 3 122	5	9	8hd	8³	6¹	515	4²	Flores D R	1.50
16Mar03 5SA5	Domestic Dispute	LB 3 122	9	7	4hd	3¹	3hd	3hd	523	Nakatani C S	10.30
16Mar03 5SA4	Logician	LB b 3 122	8	6	7hd	7hd	7hd	6¹	6²	Valdivia J Jr	45.40
16Mar03 5SA9	Flirt With Fortune	LB 3 122	6	8	9	9	9	8³	7¹	Pedroza M A	128.10
1Mar03 7SA7	Iron Lad-Ire	LB f 3 122	3	3	3hd	51½	8⁶	7½	816	Johnston M T	134.70
8Mar03 8GG1	Ocean Terrace	LB 3 122	1	2	1hd	1hd	2¹	9	9	Desormeaux K J	6.00

OFF AT 2:47 Start Good. Won driving. Track fast.
TIME :22², :45⁴, 1:10, 1:36, 1:49¹ (:22.58, :45.82, 1:10.16, 1:36.14, 1:49.36)

$2 Mutuel Prices:			
4 – BUDDY GIL	14.60	5.80	3.80
2 – INDIAN EXPRESS		21.60	7.80
8 – KAFWAIN			3.20

$1 EXACTA 4-2 PAID $141.80 $2 QUINELLA 2-4 PAID $141.80
$1 TRIFECTA 4-2-8 PAID $568.90

B. g, (Feb), by Eastern Echo – Really Rising, by For Really. Trainer Mullins Jeff. Bred by Billingsley Creek Ranch (Ky).
    BUDDY GIL settled a bit off the rail then outside a rival leaving the backstretch, moved up on the second turn, bid three deep into the stretch, gained a short advantage in upper stretch and held on gamely under urging. INDIAN EXPRESS dueled outside a rival, put a head in front into the second turn, continued inside on that bend, fought back along the rail through a long, hard drive and continued gamely to the wire. KAFWAIN stalked between horses then off the rail or outside a rival, continued toward the inside into the second turn, waited briefly then split rivals on that turn, came out for room into the stretch and bested the others. ATSWHATIMTALKNBOUT bobbled at the start, angled in and saved ground off the pace, moved up inside leaving the backstretch, came out into the second turn and four wide into the stretch and could not offer the necessary late kick. DOMESTIC DISPUTE stalked the pace outside, bid three deep on the second turn then outside the runner-up, was between horses into the stretch and weakened. LOGICIAN pulled some early, chased three deep on the first turn and outside on the backstretch, dropped back leaving the second turn, was floated well wide into the stretch, gave way and was eased. FLIRT WITH FORTUNE broke awkwardly, pulled his way along off the rail then drifted out into the first turn, went between horses on that bend then chased a bit on the rail, angled in on the second turn and also was eased late. IRON LAD (IRE) angled in on the first turn and saved ground stalking the pace, fell back on the second turn, came out into the stretch and gave way, then was not persevered with in the lane. OCEAN TERRACE had good early speed and dueled inside, dropped back when headed into the second turn, drifted wide into the stretch, gave way and was eased through the stretch.
    Owners– 1, Desperado Stables Inc McFadden Donnie and Merrill Stables et al; 2, Chess Phil; 3, The Thoroughbred Corporation; 4, Hughes B Wayne and Biscuit Stables LLC; 5, Garber Gary M; 6, Reddam J Paul; 7, Chapman Carolyn M; 8, Cuchna John R Jim Ford Inc and Pearson Daron; 9, Fog City Stable
    Trainers– 1, Mullins Jeff; 2, Baffert Bob; 3, Baffert Bob; 4, Ellis Ronald W; 5, Baffert Bob; 6, Dollase Craig; 7, Chapman James K; 8, Cassidy James M; 9, Hess Robert B Jr
    Scratched– Ministers Wild Cat (08Mar03 8GG 2)

$1 Pick Three (7-4-4) Paid $67.80 ; Pick Three Pool $165,756 .
$1 Pick Three (3-2-4 (NTRA)) Paid $57.70 ; Pick Three Pool $615,621 .
$2 Daily Double (4-4) Paid $31.60 ; Daily Double Pool $75,339 .

EIGHTH RACE
Keeneland
APRIL 6, 2003

7 FURLONGS. (1.20^{1}) 66th Running of THE LAFAYETTE. Grade III. Purse $100,000 Added. For three year olds. By subscription of $100 each, which should accompany the nomination; $1,000 to enter and start with $100,000 added, of which 62% of all monies to the owner of the winner, 20% to second, 10% to third, 5% to fourth and 3% to fifth. Weight 123 lbs. Non-winners of $60,000 twice allowed 3 lbs.; $45,000 twice, 5 lbs.; $30,000 twice, 7 lbs. Starters to be named through the entry box by the usual time of closing. A gold julep cup will be presented to the owner of the winner. Nominations closed Wednesday, March 26, 2003 with 19 nominations.

Value of Race: $107,900 Winner $66,898; second $21,580; third $10,790; fourth $5,395; fifth $3,237. Mutuel Pool $357,672.00 Exacta Pool $209,548.00 Quinella Pool $9,546.00 Trifecta Pool $139,067.00 Superfecta Pool $33,909.00

Last Raced	Horse	M/Eqt.	A.	Wt	PP	St	¼	½	Str	Fin	Jockey	Odds $1
15Mar03 ^{11}GP^{2}	Posse	L	3	118	2	5	5^{5}	$4^{3\frac{1}{2}}$	2^{hd}	$1^{2\frac{1}{4}}$	Lanerie C J	2.00
23Feb03 ^{8}SA^{5}	Roll Hennessy Roll	Lb	3	118	4	3	$3^{2\frac{1}{2}}$	2^{1}	1^{hd}	$2^{2\frac{1}{4}}$	Sellers S J	2.20
12Jan03 ^{7}SA^{5}	Bossanova	Lb	3	116	6	1	1^{1}	$1^{1\frac{1}{2}}$	3^{3}	$3^{2\frac{1}{4}}$	Bailey J D	12.40
15Mar03 ^{11}GP^{3}	Whywhywhy	Lb	3	123	3	6	6	6	4^{hd}	$4^{2\frac{1}{2}}$	Farina Tony	5.80
14Mar03 ^{8}FG^{1}	Battle Won	L	3	116	1	4	2^{1}	$3^{1\frac{1}{2}}$	5^{4}	$5^{5\frac{3}{4}}$	Martinez W	3.60
22Mar03 ^{7}TP^{1}	Quick Draw	L	3	116	5	2	$4^{\frac{1}{2}}$	$5^{\frac{1}{2}}$	6	6	Day P	6.80

OFF AT 4:45 Start Good For All But WHYWHYWHY Won driving. Track fast.
TIME :21^{3}, :44^{2}, 1:09^{4}, 1:23 (:21.68, :44.42, 1:09.99, 1:23.14)

$2 Mutuel Prices:			
2–POSSE	6.00	3.60	3.20
4–ROLL HENNESSY ROLL		3.40	3.20
6–BOSSANOVA			4.00

$2 EXACTA 2–4 PAID $21.60 $2 QUINELLA 2–4 PAID $11.00 $2 TRIFECTA 2–4–6 PAID $218.80 $2 SUPERFECTA 2–4–6–3 PAID $617.20

B. c, (Feb), by Silver Deputy–Raska, by Rahy. Trainer Asmussen Steven M. Bred by Robert E Low & Lawana L Low (Ky).

POSSE drifted in slightly at the start, settled in behind foes, came out four wide while entering the upper stretch, reached the front leaving the furlong grounds and drove clear under mild hand urging. ROLL HENNESSY ROLL stalked the pace early while four wide, gained a brief, slim lead in the upper stretch, then wasn't a match for POSSE in the final furlong. BOSSANOVA gained the lead at the start, worked his way inward, made the pace two or three wide into the upper stretch and weakened. WHYWHYWHY broke in the air to trail, raced near the inside to the stretch, came out to make a mild run three or four wide approaching the final furlong but couldn't continue. BATTLE WON drifted in a bit at the break, moved up inside to force the pace, held on well until approaching the stretch and faltered. QUICK DRAW, four wide most of the way, tired upon going a half.

Owners— 1, Heiligbrodt Racing Stable; 2, Fulton Stan E; 3, Rodriguez Lorraine & Rod; 4, Fabian Ouaki & Patrick L Biancone E; 5, Lazy Lane Farms Inc; 6, Overbrook Farm

Trainers—1, Asmussen Steven M; 2, Becerra Rafael; 3, Paasch Christopher S; 4, Biancone Patrick L; 5, Brothers Frank L; 6, Lukas D Wayne

$2 Pick Three (3–3–2) Paid $246.60; Pick Three Pool $33,967.
$1 Pick Six (8–1–3/7–3–3–2) 5 Correct Paid $28.00; Pick Six Pool $21,858. $1 Pick Six (8–1–3/7–3–3–2) 6 Correct Paid $2,651.10

SEVENTH RACE
Santa Anita
APRIL 6, 2003

1⅛ MILES. (Turf) (1.43^{4}) ARCADIA H. Grade II. Purse $150,000 FOR FOUR-YEAR-OLDS AND UPWARD. By subscription of $150 each to accompany the nomination. $1,500 additional to start, with $150,000 guaranteed, of which $90,000 to first, $30,000 to second, $18,000 to third, $9,000 to fourth and $3,000 to fifth. NOMINATIONS CLOSED Thursday, March 27, 2003 with 18 (Rail at 0 Feet).

Value of Race: $150,000 Winner $90,000; second $30,000; third $18,000; fourth $9,000; fifth $3,000. Mutuel Pool $586,234.00 Exacta Pool $358,761.00 Quinella Pool $38,701.00 Trifecta Pool $373,808.00 Superfecta Pool $147,517.00

Last Raced	Horse	M/Eqt.	A.	Wt	PP	St	¼	½	¾	Str	Fin	Jockey	Odds $1
23Mar03 ^{8}FG^{9}	Century City-Ire	LB b	4	114	5	2	$4^{\frac{1}{2}}$	4^{hd}	4^{2}	4^{hd}	1^{nk}	Valdivia J Jr	19.90
8Mar03 ^{9}SA^{3}	Gondolieri-Chi	LB b	4	116	6	1	$1^{2\frac{1}{2}}$	$1^{2\frac{1}{2}}$	1^{hd}	2^{2}	2^{hd}	Solis A O	3.90
2Mar03 ^{9}FG^{10}	Sunday Break-Jpn	LB b	4	117	7	3	2^{1}	2^{1}	2^{2}	1^{hd}	$3^{\frac{1}{2}}$	Nakatani C S	12.90
19Mar03 ^{6}SA^{1}	Passinetti	LB	7	111	9	5	3^{1}	3^{1}	3^{hd}	3^{hd}	4^{1}	Baze T	16.00
1Mar03 ^{8}SA^{6}	Night Life-FR	LB	6	113	2	7	7^{hd}	8^{2}	$8^{2\frac{1}{2}}$	$6^{2\frac{1}{2}}$	$5^{\frac{1}{2}}$	Espinoza V	8.10
6Mar03 ^{3}SA^{2}	Mananan McLir	LB	4	114	4	4	6^{1}	$7^{\frac{1}{2}}$	6^{1}	$5^{\frac{1}{2}}$	6^{1}	Smith M E	15.00
26Oct02 ^{9}AP^{7}	Ballingarry-Ire	LB	4	120	3	8	5^{1}	5^{1}	5^{hd}	$7^{\frac{1}{2}}$	7^{nk}	Desormeaux K J	1.60
15Mar03 ^{7}SA^{6}	Delta Form-Aus	LB	7	116	1	6	9	9	9	$8^{1\frac{1}{2}}$	$8^{1\frac{1}{2}}$	Stevens G L	10.10
15Feb03 ^{7}SA^{3}	Harrisand-FR	LB	5	115	8	9	8^{2}	6^{hd}	7^{hd}	9	9	Valenzuela P A	5.10

OFF AT 3:37 Start Good . Won driving. Course firm.
TIME :24^{4}, :49^{3}, 1:13^{1}, 1:36^{1}, 1:47^{4} (:24.97, :49.75, 1:13.36, 1:36.39, 1:47.84)

$2 Mutuel Prices:			
5 – CENTURY CITY-IRE	41.80	15.80	8.80
6 – GONDOLIERI-CHI		5.80	4.60
7 – SUNDAY BREAK-JPN			8.80

$1 EXACTA 5–6 PAID $117.80 $2 QUINELLA 5–6 PAID $113.00
$1 TRIFECTA 5–6–7 PAID $1,332.00 $1 SUPERFECTA 5–6–7–9 PAID $19,624.60

B. h, (Feb), by Danzig – Alywow , by Alysheba . Trainer Greely C Beau. Bred by Kilcarn Stud (Ire).

CENTURY CITY (IRE) angled in early and saved ground stalking the pace, came out leaving the second turn and into the stretch and rallied gamely under urging to get up three deep late. GONDOLIERI (CHI) took the early lead and angled in, set the pace inside, dueled along the rail on the second turn and into the stretch, fought back along the inside through a long drive and continued gamely to the wire. SUNDAY BREAK (JPN) angled in and stalked toward the inside, bid outside the runner-up and dueled leaving the backstretch and on the second turn, put a head in front in midstretch, also went on willingly between foes but was outgamed. PASSINETTI pulled his way along to stalk the pace outside a rival, bid three deep into the stretch and was outfinished. NIGHT LIFE (FR) also pulled between horses early, angled in on the second turn, bid inside in the stretch but was blocked off heels and steadied late. MANANAN MCLIR pulled inside under a hold and steadied early, saved ground chasing the pace, came out into the stretch and could not offer the needed late kick. BALLINGARRY (IRE) off a bit slowly, chased between horses then outside a rival, came three deep into the stretch and also lacked the necessary rally. DELTA FORM (AUS) unhurried a bit off the rail, angled in on the second turn, came out some into the stretch and was not a threat. HARRISAND (FR) broke slowly, chased three deep to the stretch and lacked a further response.

Owners– 1, Kitchwa Stables and Nichols Thomas L; 2, Hunt Nelson B; 3, Maeda Koji; 4, Tanaka Gary A; 5, Taub Steve; 6, Horizon Stable Jarvis and Margolis et al; 7, Port Trust Naify Marsha and San Gabriel Investments; 8, Team Valor Stables LLC; 9, Gann Edmund A

Trainers– 1, Greely C Beau; 2, McAnally Ronald L; 3, Drysdale Neil D; 4, Cecil Ben D; 5, Mulhall Kristin; 6, Dollase Wallace A; 7, De Seroux Laura; 8, Sahadi Jenine; 9, Frankel Robert J

$2 Daily Double (7–5) Paid $150.80 ; Daily Double Pool $56,316 .
$1 Pick Three (9–7–5) Paid $225.50 ; Pick Three Pool $130,540 .

NINTH RACE
Oaklawn
APRIL 9, 2003

$1\frac{1}{16}$ MILES. (1.40^{1}) 1st Running of THE FIFTH SEASON. Grade III Purse $100,000 FOUR-YEAR-OLDS AND UPWARD. Weights: 122 lbs. Non-winners of $35,000 since November 9 allowed 3 lbs.; $25,000 since January 9, 5 lbs.; $18,000 since February 9, 2003, 7 lbs. (Maiden and Claiming races not considered). In Allowance Stakes starting preference will be given to horses that have accumulated the highest earnings, excluding money won in restricted races. Starters to be named through the entry box by the usual time of closing. Nominations closed Thursday, March 20, 2003 with 29 nominees.

Value of Race: $100,000 Winner $60,000; second $20,000; third $10,000; fourth $6,000; fifth $4,000. Mutuel Pool $188,572.00 Exacta Pool $129,534.00 Trifecta Pool $129,136.00

Last Raced	Horse	M/Eqt.	A.	Wt	PP	St	¼	½	¾	Str	Fin	Jockey	Odds $1
16Mar03 ^{5}OP^{1}	Patton's Victory	Lb	5	117	4	2	$1^{1\frac{1}{2}}$	$1^{2\frac{1}{2}}$	1^{3}	1^{3}	1^{1}	Birzer A E	12.30
16Mar03 ^{9}OP^{1}	Colorful Tour	L	4	122	7	3	4^{1}	3^{hd}	3^{hd}	$2^{\frac{1}{2}}$	$2^{3\frac{1}{4}}$	Quinonez L S	2.90
16Mar03 ^{9}OP^{6}	Makors Mark	L	6	118	5	1	$2^{1\frac{1}{2}}$	2^{1}	$2^{\frac{1}{2}}$	3^{3}	$3^{\frac{3}{4}}$	Baze G	17.80
23Mar03 ^{8}DeD^{3}	Ask The Lord	Lf	6	118	6	4	6^{1}	$5^{\frac{1}{2}}$	4^{2}	$4^{\frac{1}{2}}$	$4^{\frac{1}{2}}$	Theriot H J II	4.00
29Mar03 ^{8}OP^{2}	Winning Connection	Lbf	7	115	2	5	5^{1}	7	7	6^{4}	$5^{1\frac{3}{4}}$	Castellano A Jr	33.20
16Mar03 ^{9}OP^{3}	Windward Passage	L	4	115	1	7	7	6^{1}	$5^{\frac{1}{2}}$	5^{1}	$6^{6\frac{1}{4}}$	Marquez C H Jr	1.40
20Mar03 ^{9}OP^{1}	Drewman	Lbf	5	117	3	6	3^{hd}	$4^{\frac{1}{2}}$	6^{3}	7	7	Court J K	4.10

OFF AT 5:11 Start Good. Won driving. Track fast.
TIME :23^{3}, :47^{3}, 1:12, 1:36^{4}, 1:43^{1} (:23.68, :47.65, 1:12.13, 1:36.92, 1:43.26)

$2 Mutuel Prices:

4-PATTON'S VICTORY	26.60	9.40	5.60
7-COLORFUL TOUR		4.80	4.00
5-MAKORS MARK			10.20

$2 EXACTA 4-7 PAID $101.60 $2 TRIFECTA 4-7-5 PAID $1,299.40

Dk. b. or br. g, by Patton–Tri Skipping, by Skip Trial. Trainer Roberts Stanley W. Bred by Brereton C Jones (Ky).

PATTON'S VICTORY got loose up front, clear and comfortable pace, continued to relax through the second turn, had enough left. COLORFUL TOUR a bit slow to settle while under restraint early, roused off the inside for the drive, slow gain on the winner late. MAKORS MARK raced closest to the winner, was called on for some run turning for home, lacked the necessary late muster, held the show. ASK THE LORD raced off the pace and the inside, moved a bit closer into the far turn, went evenly in the drive while four wide into the lane. WINNING CONNECTION lacked a late bid. WINDWARD PASSAGE last away, trailed early, came up empty for the drive well out in the strip. DREWMAN bit tight in traffic first turn, steadily faded.

Owners— 1, Highway 1 Racing Stable; 2, Irish Acres Farm; 3, Ll McMurry; 4, Gaffney Peter & Madison Stewart M; 5, Hays Billy; 6, Team Valor Stables; 7, Williams Family Partnership

Trainers—1, Roberts Stanley W; 2, Hickey P Noel; 3, Forster Grant T; 4, Stall Albert M Jr; 5, Woodard Joe; 6, Asmussen Steven M; 7, Williams Harold

$2 Pick Three (5-2-4) Paid $302.40; Pick Three Pool $14,932.

EIGHTH RACE
Keeneland
APRIL 10, 2003

ABOUT 7 FURLONGS. (1.24^{3}) 18th Running of THE STONERSIDE BEAUMONT. Grade II. Purse $250,000 Guaranteed. Fillies, three year olds. By subscription of $250 each, which should accompany the nomination; $2,500 to enter and start with $250,000 guaranteed, of which $155,000 to the owner of the winner, $50,000 to second, $25,000 to third, $12,500 to fourth and $7,500 to fifth. Weight 123 lbs. Non-winners of a Grade I allowed 3 lbs.; Grade II, 5 lbs.; a sweepstakes, 7 lbs. Starters to be named through the entry box by the usual time of closing. A gold julep cup will be presented to the owner of the winner. Closed Wednesday, March 26, 2003 with 31 nominations. Beard Course.

Value of Race: $250,000 Winner $155,000; second $50,000; third $25,000; fourth $12,500; fifth $7,500. Mutuel Pool $276,856.00 Exacta Pool $216,752.00 Quinella Pool $8,463.00 Trifecta Pool $167,084.00 Superfecta Pool $42,805.00

Last Raced	Horse	M/Eqt.	A.	Wt	PP	St	¼	½	Str	Fin	Jockey	Odds $1
14Mar03 ^{9}GP^{2}	My Boston Gal	L	3	120	3	7	5^{1}	3^{hd}	1^{hd}	$1^{1\frac{1}{4}}$	Day P	2.70
23Feb03 ^{5}GP^{1}	Bird Town	L	3	118	7	1	$2^{\frac{1}{2}}$	$1^{1\frac{1}{2}}$	2^{4}	$2^{4\frac{3}{4}}$	Coa E M	3.30
14Mar03 ^{7}GP^{1}	Midnight Cry	L	3	118	9	4	4^{hd}	$4^{1\frac{1}{2}}$	$3^{2\frac{1}{2}}$	3^{4}	Prado E S	5.20
14Mar03 ^{7}GP^{3}	Chimichurri	L	3	118	1	5	$6^{2\frac{1}{2}}$	6^{1}	4^{2}	$4^{3\frac{1}{2}}$	Velazquez J R	10.40
22Mar03 ^{8}TP^{2}	Adopted Daughter	Lf	3	118	5	2	$8^{1\frac{1}{2}}$	7^{hd}	5^{3}	$5^{5\frac{1}{2}}$	Albarado R J	6.80
1Mar03 ^{8}Aqu^{1}	Elegant Designer	L	3	118	6	9	9	9	6^{6}	$6^{12\frac{1}{4}}$	Pino M G	9.30
2Nov02 ^{7}CD^{1}	Vibs	Lb	3	116	8	3	$3^{1\frac{1}{2}}$	2^{hd}	7^{1}	$7^{5\frac{1}{4}}$	Santos J A	35.10
23Feb03 ^{9}GP^{4}	Perfect Story	L	3	117	4	8	7^{1}	$8^{1\frac{1}{2}}$	8^{3}	$8^{24\frac{1}{2}}$	Desormeaux K J	7.10
14Mar03 ^{8}GP^{1}	Wild Light	L	3	116	2	6	1^{hd}	$5^{\frac{1}{2}}$	9	9	Bailey J D	13.60

OFF AT 4:46 Start Good. Won driving. Track muddy.
TIME :21^{4}, :44^{2}, 1:09^{4}, 1:26^{4} (:21.91, :44.46, 1:09.91, 1:26.87)

$2 Mutuel Prices:

3-MY BOSTON GAL	7.40	4.60	3.20
7-BIRD TOWN		3.60	3.20
9-MIDNIGHT CRY			3.40

$2 EXACTA 3-7 PAID $36.00 $2 QUINELLA 3-7 PAID $19.80 $2 TRIFECTA 3-7-9 PAID $110.00 $2 SUPERFECTA 3-7-9-1 PAID $559.20

B. f, (Feb), by Boston Harbor–Western League, by Forty Niner. Trainer Nafzger Carl A. Bred by Overbrook Farm (Ky).

MY BOSTON GAL settled in behind the dueling leaders early, moved boldly from between horses midway on the turn, reached the front three or four wide while dueling outside of BIRD TOWN approaching the final furlong, then, despite attempting to lug in slightly leaving the sixteenth pole, edged clear late under hand urging. BIRD TOWN broke in front, dueled from between foes, was headed for a stride from the inside by WILD LIGHT right at the quarter-mile call, regained the advantage, opened a clear lead on the turn, was engaged by the winner in the upper stretch, lost the edge to that one and continued on to easily best the others. MIDNIGHT CRY, well placed from early on while tracking the leaders four or five wide, moved with the winner while outside that one approaching the stretch, then was empty when straightened for the drive. CHIMICHURRI, within striking distance while in behind the leaders early, eased out between foes three furlong out to make a run four or five wide, continued in contention into the stretch but flattened out. ADOPTED DAUGHTER moved out seven or eight wide on the backstretch while outsprinted, angled near the inside entering the turn, raced between foes into the stretch but failed to rally. ELEGANT DESIGNER, off slowly, raced four or five wide throughout and failed to reach contention. VIBS broke inward while bobbling lightly, moved up soon after to force the pace three abreast, held on well for a half and weakened thereafter. PERFECT STORY, four or five wide, failed to menace. WILD LIGHT was sent up inside to contest the pace early, stuck her head in front just before going a quarter, lost the advantage to BIRD TOWN, faded upon going a half and wasn't persevered with at the end when hopelessly beaten.

Owners— 1, C Porter R Bloch & P Milner; 2, Marylou Whitney Stable; 3, Barrister Hall Stables; 4, Peachtree Stable; 5, Ramsey Kenneth L & Sarah K; 6, Sherman Michael H; 7, Tarp Mike; 8, Oxley John C; 9, Zuckerman Roberta M

Trainers—1, Nafzger Carl A; 2, Zito Nicholas P; 3, McPeek Kenneth G; 4, Pletcher Todd A; 5, Werner Ronny; 6, Dutrow Anthony W; 7, Romans Dale; 8, Ward John T Jr; 9, Pletcher Todd A

$2 Pick Three (3-2-3) Paid $116.00; Pick Three Pool $30,517. $1 Pick Six (7-5-1-3-2-3) 5 Correct Paid $34.80; Pick Six Pool $7,227. $1 Pick Six (7-5-1-3-2-3) 6 Correct Paid $2,288.20

TENTH RACE
Oaklawn
APRIL 10, 2003

6 FURLONGS. (1.07^{4}) 30th Running of THE COUNT FLEET SPRINT HANDICAP. Grade III. Purse $150,000 FOUR-YEAR-OLDS AND UPWARD.

Value of Race: $150,000 Winner $90,000; second $30,000; third $15,000; fourth $9,000; fifth $6,000. Mutuel Pool $621,752.00 Exacta Pool $154,608.00 Trifecta Pool $125,445.00

Last Raced	Horse	M/Eqt.	A.	Wt	PP	St	¼	½	Str	Fin	Jockey	Odds $1
16Mar03 9FG1	Beau's Town	L	5	122	2	2	21½	1hd	1^{1}	1½	Theriot H J II	0.40
23Mar03 9OP1	Honor Me	Lbf	5	116	5	3	32½	33½	22½	2^{4}	Trader R R	12.80
23Mar03 9OP3	Sand Ridge	L	8	114	6	4	55½	53½	4½	3½	Shino K A	8.90
23Mar03 9OP2	Chindi	L	9	114	4	6	6	6	6	41¾	Marquez C H Jr	4.20
23Mar03 9OP5	Cojet	Lf	4	116	1	1	1^{2}	21½	3^{1}	5¾	Court J K	9.20
23Mar03 9OP6	Big Bad George	L	6	113	3	5	4½	4^{1}	51½	6	Thompson T J	24.10

OFF AT 5:45 Start Good. Won driving. Track fast.
TIME :22^{1}, :45^{1}, :57, 1:09 (:22.26, :45.33, :57.16, 1:09.01)

$2 Mutuel Prices:			
2-BEAU'S TOWN	2.80	2.40	2.20
5-HONOR ME		4.20	2.20
6-SAND RIDGE			2.20

$2 EXACTA 2-5 PAID $12.20 $2 TRIFECTA 2-5-6 PAID $53.00

Ch. h, by Beau Genius-Frio Town, by Kerosene. Trainer Norman Cole. Bred by Bryant H Prentice III (Ark).

BEAU'S TOWN sat off the early leader in hand, moved on that one when asked in the turn, gained control with a quarter remaining, responded when challenged from the outside soon after, not to be denied while fully extended. HONOR ME rated early, began to move toward the front with the winner in the turn, tried that rival from the outside turning for home, could not get by. SAND RIDGE raced off the pace and the inside, set down for the drive, no match for the top two while prevailing for the show. CHINDI fell back to trail after the start, swung to the outside exiting the turn, failed to fire. COJET broke on top, sprinted clear toward the inside, faltered when headed by the winner late in the turn. BIG BAD GEORGE gave way after a half.

Owners— 1, Coast To Coast Racing Fund & Hulkew; 2, Highway 1 Racing Stable; 3, Thunderhead Farms; 4, Cresran; 5, Estate of Dan Jones; 6, Hines James T Jr

Trainers—1, Norman Cole; 2, Roberts Stanley W; 3, Von Hemel Don; 4, Hobby Steve; 5, Holthus Robert E; 6, Holthus Robert E

$2 Pick Three (8-5-2) Paid $302.20; Pick Three Pool $26,214.

EIGHTH RACE
Keeneland
APRIL 11, 2003

1 MILE. (Turf)(1.33^{3}) 15th Running of THE MAKER'S MARK MILE. Grade II. Purse $200,000 Guaranteed. Four year olds and upward. By subscription of $200 each, which should accompany the nomination; $2,000 to enter and start with $200,000 guaranteed, of which $124,000 to the owner of the winner, $40,000 to second, $20,000 to third, $10,000 to fourth and $6,000 to fifth. Weight 123 lbs. Non-winners of Grade I or II stakes on the turf since October 3, allowed 3 lbs.; $60,000 twice on the turf since August 1, 5 lbs.; $45,000 twice on the turf since July 1, 7 lbs. Starters to be named through the entry box by usual time of closing. A gold julep cup will be presented to the owner of the winner. Closed Wednesday, April 2, 2003 with 38 nominations. HAGGIN COURSE.

Value of Race: $200,000 Winner $124,000; second $40,000; third $20,000; fourth $10,000; fifth $6,000. Mutuel Pool $419,108.00 Exacta Pool $327,838.00 Quinella Pool $14,532.00 Trifecta Pool $270,658.00 Superfecta Pool $90,900.00

Last Raced	Horse	M/Eqt.	A.	Wt	PP	St	¼	½	¾	Str	Fin	Jockey	Odds $1
1Feb03 9FG6	Royal Spy	L	5	118	3	2	23½	1½	11½	12½	11¼	Albarado R J	11.60
9Mar03 9GP2	Miesque's Approval	L	4	118	5	5	51½	5^{1}	4hd	2½	21¾	Bailey J D	4.20
26Oct02 5AP10	Touch of the Blues-FR	L	6	117	9	6	3½	41½	3hd	3^{4}	31½	Desormeaux K J	3.20
3Feb02 Val1	Mister Acpen-CH	Lb	5	116	6	7	9	9	7½	6^{1}	42¼	Sellers S J	29.30
3Mar03 9GP1	Statement	L	5	116	8	4	71½	6½	8^{3}	7^{2}	5nk	Coa E M	5.70
1Mar03 8SA3	Decarchy	Lb	6	116	7	8	6hd	7^{1}	61½	5½	6^{2}	Prado E S	1.90
22Mar03 8GP9	Private Son	L	5	116	2	1	4^{1}	3hd	51½	4hd	71½	Velasquez C	31.70
9Mar03 9GP1	Political Attack	Lb	4	116	4	9	8hd	8^{1}	9	9	82¼	Guidry M	8.90
20Mar03 7FG1	Angel On The Wing	L	4	116	1	3	1^{1}	25½	2^{1}	8^{2}	9	Lovato F Jr	27.00

OFF AT 4:45 Start Good For All But POLITICAL ATTACK Won driving. Course firm.
TIME :23^{3}, :46^{3}, 1:11^{2}, 1:23^{2}, 1:35^{4} (:23.60, :46.69, 1:11.49, 1:23.45, 1:35.82)

$2 Mutuel Prices:			
3-ROYAL SPY	25.20	11.60	6.00
5-MIESQUE'S APPROVAL		5.20	3.80
9-TOUCH OF THE BLUES-FR			3.60

$2 EXACTA 3-5 PAID $140.40 $2 QUINELLA 3-5 PAID $62.80 $2 TRIFECTA 3-5-9 PAID $749.40 $2 SUPERFECTA 3-5-9-6 PAID $14,725.80

B. h, by Peteski-Caro's Beauty, by Caro*Ire. Trainer Amoss Thomas. Bred by Dr K K Jayaraman & Dr V Devi Jayaraman (Fla).

ROYAL SPY went up soon after the break to press front-running ANGEL ON THE WING under light rating, raced three or four wide, took over from that one just prior to going a half while within himself, opened a clear lead when called upon in the upper stretch, then held sway under energetic handling. MIESQUE'S APPROVAL, bumped at the start but never far back, was six wide on the backstretch under light restraint, edged in a bit while advancing on the second turn, loomed prominently outside the winner through the drive but wasn't good enough. TOUCH OF THE BLUES (FR) gained a forward position early while maneuvering in between foes, began to edge closer leaving the backstretch, moved menacingly between horses into the upper stretch but lacked the needed late response. MISTER ACPEN (CHI), unhurried for a half while in hand four or five wide, continued in that position on the course approaching the stretch, then offered a mild gain. STATEMENT settled between foes early while three or four wide, continued behind rivals around the far turn and into the stretch and improved position while unable to menace four wide. DECARCHY, in contention from the outset and five or six wide to the stretch, moved out farther on the course for the drive but failed to respond. PRIVATE SON, nicely placed near the inside from early on, worked his way out four or five wide when entering the stretch but flattened out the last eighth. POLITICAL ATTACK stumbled at the start and came out bumping MIESQUE'S APPROVAL, was unhurried inside, saved ground for six furlongs, swung out eight wide for the drive but failed to respond. ANGEL ON THE WING gained the lead inside early, showed the way for a half, surrendered the advantage to the winner, continued forwardly to the stretch and faded.

Owners— 1, Jayaraman Kalarikkal K & Vilasini D; 2, Live Oak Plantation; 3, Gainsborough Farm Inc; 4, The Thoroughbred Corporation; 5, The Thoroughbred Corporation; 6, Juddmonte Farms Inc; 7, Starlex Farm; 8, Erdenheim Farm; 9, Sam-Son Farms

Trainers—1, Amoss Thomas; 2, Mott William I; 3, Drysdale Neil; 4, Mulhall Kristin; 5, Kimmel John C; 6, Frankel Robert; 7, Schu Sally S; 8, Matz Michael R; 9, Frostad Mark

Scratched— Music's Storm (1Mar03 8SA8)

$2 Pick Three (3-4-3) Paid $173.00; Pick Three Pool $39,095. $1 Pick Six (2-4-8-3-4-3) 5 Correct Paid $544.50; Pick Six Pool $8,067; Carryover Pool $4,900.

TENTH RACE
Oaklawn
APRIL 11, 2003

1 1/16 MILES. (1.40¹) 31st Running of THE FANTASY. Grade II. Purse $200,000. Fillies, Three Years Old. By subscription of $100 each which shall accompany the nomination, original nominators paying $2,000 to pass the entry box and $2,000 additional to start. Supplementary nominations may be made by closing time of entires at a fee of $10,000 which qualifies to start, with $200,000 guaranteed of which $120,000 to owner of the winner, $40,000 to second, $20,000 to third, $12,000 to fourth and $8,000 to fifth. Weight, 121 lbs, Non-winners of a sweepstakes, allowed 4 lbs. The owner of the winner to receive a trophy.

Value of Race: $200,000 Winner $120,000; second $40,000; third $20,000; fourth $12,000; fifth $8,000. Mutuel Pool $374,744.00 Exacta Pool $185,026.00 Trifecta Pool $152,846.00

Last Raced	Horse	M/Eqt.	A.Wt	PP	St	¼	½	¾	Str	Fin	Jockey	Odds $1
8Mar03 10OP2	Ruby's Reception	L	3 121	2	5	6	6	53½	1½	12¼	Thompson T J	4.70
8Mar03 4SA4	Harbor Blues	Lb	3 121	1	3	1½	1hd	1hd	3hd	21	Theriot H J II	19.00
8Mar03 4SA3	Go For Glamour	L	3 117	3	2	2hd	21	31½	42½	3½	Solis A	1.70
8Mar03 10OP1	My Trusty Cat	Lbf	3 121	5	1	33	33½	2hd	2hd	42	Pettinger D R	1.30
14Mar03 9GP5	Westerly Breeze	L	3 121	6	6	51	52	4½	53½	53½	Court J K	8.40
8Mar03 5OP1	Kristina's Wish	L	3 117	4	4	42½	41	6	6	6	Marquez C H Jr	12.90

OFF AT 5:56 Start Good. Won driving. Track fast.
TIME :22⁴, :45⁴, 1:11, 1:37⁴, 1:44³ (:22.82, :45.94, 1:11.10, 1:37.92, 1:44.61)

$2 Mutuel Prices:

2-RUBY'S RECEPTION	11.40	5.00	3.20
1-HARBOR BLUES		16.40	7.20
3-GO FOR GLAMOUR			2.20

$2 EXACTA 2-1 PAID $127.20 $2 TRIFECTA 2-1-3 PAID $419.20

Gr/ro f, (Jan), by Rubiano-Court Reception, by A.P. Indy. Trainer Jones J Larry. Bred by Avalon Farm (Ky).

RUBY'S RECEPTION void of early foot, began to move after a half well off the inside, advanced five wide in the second turn, put a head in front from the outside nearing the furlong marker, edged clear under steady handling. HARBOR BLUES narrowly set the pace early inside, briefly headed backstretch, quickly regained the advantage into the second turn, gave ground grudgingly to the winner while comfortably holding the place. GO FOR GLAMOUR bumped at the start, vied between foes, briefly put a head in front after a half, lost the advantage then did not have enough left in the drive. MY TRUSTY CAT prompted the pace three wide for six furlongs, weakened through the stretch. WESTERLY BREEZE settled early, moved out a bit behind horses four wide turning for home, came up empty. KRISTINA'S WISH within striking distance, gave way after a half.

Owners— 1, Oasis Racing Stable et al; 2, Everest Stables; 3, Columbine Stable; 4, Pollard Carl F; 5, Miles A S Jr; 6, Jer-Mar Stable
Trainers—1, Jones J Larry; 2, Canani Nick; 3, Greely C Beau; 4, Vance David R; 5, Nafzger Carl A; 6, Robertson Hugh H

$2 Pick Three (3-3-2) Paid $387.40; Pick Three Pool $28,692.

SEVENTH RACE
Aqueduct
APRIL 12, 2003

7 FURLONGS. (1.20) 43rd Running of THE BAY SHORE. Grade III. Purse $150,000. (Up to $29,100 NYSBFOA). THREE YEAR OLDS. By subscription of $150 each, which should accompany the nomination; $750 to pass the entry box; $750 to start. The purse to be divided 60% to the winner, 20% to second, 11% to third, 6% to fourth and 3% to fifth. 123 lbs. Non-winners of $100,000; or $50,000 twice allowed 3 lbs.; $60,000; or $35,000 in 2003 5 lbs.; $30,000; or three races other than maiden or claiming, 7 lbs. Trophies will be presented to the winning owner, trainer and jockey. Closed Saturday,March 29, 2003 with 28 Nominations.

Value of Race: $150,000 Winner $90,000; second $30,000; third $16,500; fourth $9,000; fifth $4,500. Mutuel Pool $737,391.00 Exacta Pool $625,767.00 Trifecta Pool $441,679.00

Last Raced	Horse	M/Eqt.	A.Wt	PP	St	¼	½	Str	Fin	Jockey	Odds $1
22Mar03 9GP1	Halo Homewrecker		3 116	6	4	42½	32½	22½	11	Velazquez J R	3.80
23Mar03 5Aqu1	Don Six	L	3 116	7	5	1½	1½	11	25¼	Gryder A T	4.00
23Mar03 7Aqu2	Stanislavsky	L	3 116	1	11	95½	86	4½	3¾	Santos J A	33.50
12Mar03 8Aqu1	Fifth Of Hennessy	Lb	3 116	9	3	8½	4hd	33½	41¾	Nelson D	72.75
22Mar03 7Aqu1	Infinite Justice	Lf	3 120	10	1	6hd	61½	52½	5¾	Bridgmohan S X	38.75
16Mar03 9Aqu9	Midnight Charlie	Lbf	3 116	8	6	11	108	6½	64¾	Castillo H Jr	50.75
12Mar03 4SA1	During	Lb	3 118	3	8	3½	5hd	7hd	72	Stevens G L	2.00
23Mar03 8Lrl1	Deadline	Lbf	3 118	4	7	5hd	7½	86	89¼	Wilson R	24.75
23Mar03 8Lrl8	Second In Command	L	3 120	11	2	2hd	2½	9	9	Samyn J L	19.30
12Mar03 4SA3	Special Rate	L	3 116	5	10	71½	92	—	—	Bailey J D	5.20
23Mar03 8Lrl2	Gators N Bears	Lbf	3 116	2	9	10½	11	—	—	Migliore R	9.50

Gators N Bears:Eased;Special Rate:Eased;

OFF AT 3:46 Start Good. Won driving. Track muddy.
TIME :21⁴, :44³, 1:10, 1:23 (:21.88, :44.68, 1:10.12, 1:23.19)

$2 Mutuel Prices:

6-HALO HOMEWRECKER	9.60	5.00	4.60
7-DON SIX		5.60	5.70
1-STANISLAVSKY			12.60

$2 EXACTA 6-7 PAID $42.40 $2 TRIFECTA 6-7-1 PAID $681.00

B. c, (Apr), by Southern Halo-Marital Spook, by Silver Ghost. Trainer Hennig Mark. Bred by Edward P Evans (Va).

HALO HOMEWRECKER raced close up outside, rallied three wide on the turn, responded when roused and gradually drew clear under a drive. DON SIX quickly showed in front, set the pace along the inside, drew clear in upper stretch and dug in gamely along the inside to the finish. STANISLAVSKY was outrun early, advanced inside on the turn, swung wide into the stretch and finished well outside. FIFTH OF HENNESSY was outrun early, put in a four wide run on the turn and weakened in the final furlong. INFINITE JUSTICE was hustled outside, raced three wide, was bumped on the turn and lacked a rally. MIDNIGHT CHARLIE was outrun early, came wide for the drive and had no rally. DURING chased the pace along the inside and was finished after a half mile. DEADLINE raced close up while between rivals, was bumped on the turn, was steadied, dropped back, came wide and tired. SECOND IN COMMAND pressed the pace from the outside and tired in the stretch. SPECIAL RATE had trouble with the footing, dropped back on the turn and was eased in the stretch. GATORS N BEARS lost his action along the inside on the backstretch, was taken up, dropped back and was eased soon thereafter.

Owners— 1, Evans Edward P; 2, Generazio Patricia A; 3, Cohn Seymour; 4, Christian Mills Stable; 5, Behringer Edward C & Murray Thomas; 6, Papandrea Vincent; 7, McIngvale James; 8, Newell John; 9, Golden Richard L; 10, Juddmonte Farms Inc; 11, Nechamkin II Leo S
Trainers—1, Hennig Mark; 2, Generazio Frank Jr; 3, Hertler John O; 4, Quick Patrick J; 5, Bush Thomas M; 6, Gyarmati Leah; 7, Baffert Bob; 8, Salzman John E; 9, Rice Linda; 10, Frankel Robert; 11, Nechamkin Leo S II

$2 Daily Double (3-6) Paid $25.40; Daily Double Pool $135,905.
$2 Pick Three (3-3-6) Paid $115.50; Pick Three Pool $68,393.

EIGHTH RACE
Aqueduct
APRIL 12, 2003

1⅛ MILES. (1.47) 79th Running of THE WOOD MEMORIAL. Grade I. Purse $750,000. (Up to $65,500 NYSBFOA). THREE YEAR OLDS. By subscription of $750 each, which should accompany the nomination; $3,500 to pass the entry box; $4,000 to start. The purse to be divided 60% to the winner, 20% to second, 11% to third, 6% to fourth and 3% to fifth. 123 lbs. Trophies will be presented to the winning owner, trainer and jockey. A bonus of $100,000 (which will follow the horse) to the trainer of the horse which wins both The Wood Memorial and The Kentucky Derby. Closed Saturday, March 29th, 2003 with 27 Nominations.

Value of Race: $750,000 Winner $450,000; second $150,000; third $82,500; fourth $45,000; fifth $22,500. Mutuel Pool $1,680,035.0 Exacta Pool $1,032,527.0 Trifecta Pool $770,804.00 Superfecta Pool $173,179.00

Last Raced	Horse	M/Eqt.	A.	Wt	PP	St	¼	½	¾	Str	Fin	Jockey	Odds $1
15Mar03 ^{8}GP^{1}	Empire Maker	Lb	3	123	8	3	$3^{\frac{1}{2}}$	$3^{2\frac{1}{2}}$	$3^{3\frac{1}{2}}$	1^{hd}	$1^{\frac{1}{2}}$	Bailey J D	0.55
9Mar03 ^{9}FG^{3}	Funny Cide	L	3	123	4	5	2^{1}	$2^{\frac{1}{2}}$	$2^{\frac{1}{2}}$	2^{6}	$2^{7\frac{1}{2}}$	Santos J A	5.20
28Mar03 ^{8}Aqu^{1}	Kissin Saint	Lf	3	123	3	2	$5^{1\frac{1}{2}}$	5^{hd}	5^{hd}	4^{1}	3^{1}	Migliore R	16.00
22Mar03 ^{10}TP^{1}	New York Hero	Lbf	3	123	1	1	$1^{1\frac{1}{2}}$	$1^{1\frac{1}{2}}$	1^{1}	3^{2}	4^{nk}	Arroyo N Jr	8.90
15Mar03 ^{8}GP^{5}	Senor Swinger	L	3	123	5	6	$6^{2\frac{1}{2}}$	6^{6}	6^{7}	5^{6}	$5^{5\frac{3}{4}}$	Stevens G L	17.30
15Mar03 ^{8}GP^{3}	Indy Dancer	Lb	3	123	6	8	8	8	8	$7^{5\frac{1}{2}}$	$6^{4\frac{1}{2}}$	Velazquez J R	8.90
29Mar03 ^{8}Lrl^{1}	Sky Soldier	L	3	123	7	7	$4^{3\frac{1}{2}}$	$4^{2\frac{1}{2}}$	4^{2}	6^{1}	$7^{4\frac{3}{4}}$	Madrigal R Jr	22.20
16Mar03 ^{9}Aqu^{3}	Spite The Devil		3	123	2	4	$7^{5\frac{1}{2}}$	$7^{3\frac{1}{2}}$	$7^{\frac{1}{2}}$	8	8	Luzzi M J	57.75

OFF AT 4:15 Start Good. Won driving. Track muddy.
TIME :23^{2}, :47^{1}, 1:11, 1:35^{4}, 1:48^{3} (:23.50, :47.21, 1:11.19, 1:35.91, 1:48.70)

$2 Mutuel Prices:

8–EMPIRE MAKER	3.10	2.50	2.10
4–FUNNY CIDE		4.40	2.10
3–KISSIN SAINT			2.10

$2 EXACTA 8–4 PAID $11.40 $2 TRIFECTA 8–4–3 PAID $83.50 $2 SUPERFECTA 8–4–3–1 PAID $242.00

Dk. b. or br. c, (Apr), by Unbridled–Toussaud, by El Gran Senor. Trainer Frankel Robert. Bred by Juddmonte Farms Inc (Ky).

EMPIRE MAKER came away quickly and raced close up while three wide, advanced three wide on the far turn, moved to the front under confident handling approaching the eighth pole and was kept alert with a couple of under hand slaps from the right side while drifting in slightly nearing the finish. FUNNY CIDE was bumped after the start, raced with the pace while in hand, advanced with the winner approaching the stretch and dug in gamely on the rail in the drive. KISSIN SAINT was bumped after the break, was taken to the inside, raced on the rail, put in a run along the inside on the second turn and had little left for the drive. NEW YORK HERO came out after the start, was hustled to the front, set the pace along the inside and gave way in upper stretch. SENOR SWINGER was bumped after the start, dropped back early, raced three wide on the second turn and had no response when roused. INDY DANCER was outrun early, came wide into the stretch and had no rally. SKY SOLDIER was bumped after the start, was steadied entering the first turn, chased the pace along the inside and tired after three quarters. SPITE THE DEVIL raced inside and tired.

Owners— 1, Juddmonte Farms Inc; 2, Sackatoga Stable; 3, Karches Peter F & Rankowitz Michael; 4, Paraneck Stable; 5, Lewis Robert B & Beverly J; 6, Wertheimer Farm; 7, Vickers Arthur E; 8, Hardwicke Stable

Trainers—1, Frankel Robert; 2, Tagg Barclay; 3, Lewis Lisa L; 4, Pedersen Jennifer; 5, Baffert Bob; 6, Pletcher Todd A; 7, Beattie Todd M; 8, Jerkens H Allen

$2 Pick Three (3–6–8) Paid $41.40; Pick Three Pool $107,103.

NINTH RACE
Aqueduct
APRIL 12, 2003

7 FURLONGS. (1.20) 103rd Running of THE CARTER HANDICAP. Grade I. Purse $350,000. (Up to $45,900 NYSBFOA). THREE YEAR OLDS AND UPWARD. By subscription of $350 each, which should accompany the nomination; $1,500 to pass the entry box; $2,000 to start. The purse to be divided 60% to the winner, 20% to second, 11% to third,6% to fourth and 3% to fifth. Trophies will be presented to the winning owner, trainer and jockey. Closed Saturday, March 29, 2003 with 20 Nominations.

Value of Race: $350,000 Winner $210,000; second $70,000; third $38,500; fourth $21,000; fifth $10,500. Mutuel Pool $818,660.00 Exacta Pool $654,343.00

Last Raced	Horse	M/Eqt.	A.	Wt	PP	St	¼	½	Str	Fin	Jockey	Odds $1
1Mar03 ^{9}SA^{2}	Congaree	L	5	122	2	4	$2^{1\frac{1}{2}}$	$1^{\frac{1}{2}}$	1^{5}	$1^{3\frac{1}{2}}$	Stevens G L	0.80
2Mar03 ^{7}SA^{1}	Aldebaran	L	5	118	5	1	5	5	$3^{2\frac{1}{2}}$	$2^{1\frac{1}{4}}$	Bailey J D	2.15
15Mar03 ^{8}Aqu^{2}	Peeping Tom	Lbf	6	114	1	5	4^{7}	3^{hd}	2^{hd}	$3^{3\frac{3}{4}}$	Bridgmohan S X	10.10
2Mar03 ^{8}Aqu^{1}	Papua	Lbf	4	114	4	3	3^{hd}	$4^{3\frac{1}{2}}$	$4^{\frac{1}{2}}$	$4^{6\frac{1}{4}}$	Santos J A	26.50
15Mar03 ^{8}Aqu^{1}	Affirmed Success	L	9	117	3	2	1^{hd}	$2^{2\frac{1}{2}}$	5	5	Migliore R	4.60

OFF AT 4:49 Start Good. Won driving. Track muddy.
TIME :22^{4}, :45^{2}, 1:09^{1}, 1:21^{2} (:22.90, :45.51, 1:09.36, 1:21.48)

$2 Mutuel Prices:

2–CONGAREE	3.60	2.30	2.10
5–ALDEBARAN		2.50	2.10
1–PEEPING TOM			2.10

$2 EXACTA 2–5 PAID $7.10

Ch. h, by Arazi–Mari's Sheba, by Mari's Book. Trainer Baffert Bob. Bred by Stonerside Stable Ltd (Ky).

CONGAREE argued the pace along the inside, drew clear when roused and remained well clear while being kept to the task to the wire. ALDEBARAN was outrun early, rallied inside nearing the stretch and finished gamely on the rail. PEEPING TOM chased the pace along the inside, came wide into the stretch and lacked a rally. PAPUA chased the pace from the outside and had no response when roused. AFFIRMED SUCCESS contested the pace from the outside and tired in the stretch.

Owners— 1, Stonerside Stable; 2, Flaxman Stable; 3, Flatbird Stable; 4, Schwartz Barry K; 5, Fried Albert Jr

Trainers—1, Baffert Bob; 2, Frankel Robert; 3, Reynolds Patrick L; 4, Hushion Michael E; 5, Schosberg Richard

$2 Daily Double (8–2) Paid $5.40; Daily Double Pool $163,816.

SEVENTH RACE

Keeneland

APRIL 12, 2003

5½ FURLONGS. (Turf)(1.01³) 7th Running of THE SHAKERTOWN. Grade III. Purse $100,000 Added. Three year olds and upward. By subscription of $100 each, which should accompany the nomination; $1,000 to enter and start. Weights: Three year olds, 116 lbs.; older 123 lbs. Non-winners of $45,000 twice on the turf since October 1 allowed 3 lbs.; a sweepstakes on the turf in 2002-2003, 5 lbs. The maximum number of starters for the Shakertown will be limited to ten with two also eligibles. In the event that more than ten pass the entry box, the ten starters will be determined at that time with preference given by condition eligibility, beginning with graded stakes winners. Same owner entry cannot start to the exclusion of a single entry. Starters to be named through the entry box by the usual time of closing. Closed April 2, 2003 with 37 nominations. HAGGIN COURSE.

Value of Race: $113,700 Winner $70,494; second $22,740; third $11,370; fourth $5,685; fifth $3,411. Mutuel Pool $452,424.00 Exacta Pool $317,795.00 Quinella Pool $13,777.00 Trifecta Pool $245,022.00 Superfecta Pool $67,406.00

Last Raced	Horse	M/Eqt. A.Wt	PP	St	¼	⅜	Str	Fin	Jockey	Odds $1
20Mar03 9FG1	No Jacket Required	L	6 118	7	5	9½	10	8³	1nk	Blanc B	12.40
15Feb03 9Hou1	Testify	L	6 120	1	10	10	8hd	5½	2hd	Albarado R J	3.30
28Nov02 3CD1	Abderian-IRE	Lf	6 120	2	7	4½	4½	3²	3nk	Prado E S	1.90
22Mar03 3GP2	Medal Play-ARG	L	6 118	10	8	8½	9²	7hd	4hd	Velasquez C	15.50
13Nov02 6CD10	Airbourne Command	Lf	8 118	8	3	5¹	5²	4¹	5½	Day P	20.60
21Mar03 8GP7	Fiscally Speaking	Lf	4 118	9	4	7¹½	6½	6¹	6¹¼	Desormeaux K J	10.90
29Nov02 8Hol5	Mighty Beau	L	4 118	5	6	2hd	1hd	1½	7½	Smith M E	4.10
11Mar03 11Tam2	Shades Of Sunny	Lb	5 118	6	2	3³	3¹	2hd	8⁷	Lumpkins J	38.40
26Oct02 4Kee1	Bananas	Lf	4 118	4	9	6½	7¹	10	9¹¼	Martinez W	22.80
15Nov02 7Lrl4	Ghostly Numbers	L	5 120	3	1	1hd	2½	9³	10	Melancon L	8.80

OFF AT 4:15 Start Good. Won driving. Course firm.

TIME :21², :44³, :57, 1:03¹ (:21.52, :44.67, :57.02, 1:03.25)

$2 Mutuel Prices:

7–NO JACKET REQUIRED	26.80	10.80	5.60
1–TESTIFY		5.40	3.40
2–ABDERIAN-IRE			3.00

$2 EXACTA 7–1 PAID $164.00 $2 QUINELLA 1–7 PAID $72.80 $2 TRIFECTA 7–1–2 PAID $467.40 $2 SUPERFECTA 7–1–2–10 PAID $7,279.80

B. g, by Jolie's Halo–Island Spirit, by Shahrastani. Trainer Amoss Thomas. Bred by Richard S Kaster (Ky).

NO JACKET REQUIRED bobbled lightly soon after the start, was unhurried while angling near the inside, raced behind rivals to the stretch, split horses four or five wide in the final furlong and closed relentlessly to prevail. TESTIFY, outrun from the start, saved ground to the stretch, circled foes nine or 10 wide in the upper stretch, gained about even terms in the late going but wasn't quite good enough. ABDERIAN (IRE), never far back while racing near the inside, lacked room for a stride at the three-sixteenths, moved down along the rail, reached the front between calls in the final furlong, then failed to last. MEDAL PLAY (ARG), outrun to the stretch while in behind horses, moved with the winner while inside that one three or four wide in the final furlong and was going well at the end. AIRBOURNE COMMAND, within easy striking distance while three or four wide, could gain only slightly when the test came. FISCALLY SPEAKING, within striking distance while in behind horses, four or five wide to the stretch, continued in that position on the course but couldn't muster the needed response. MIGHTY BEAU went up at once to vie for the lead from between rivals, stuck a head in front approaching the stretch, held on well into the final furlong and faltered. SHADES OF SUNNY forced the pace from early on while three abreast, reached the front briefly between calls leaving the eighth pole but faltered. BANANAS faded leaving the turn. GHOSTLY NUMBERS gained a slim lead near the inside early, dueled with MIGHTY BEAU and SHADES OF SUNNY and gave way leaving the turn.

Owners— 1, Webber Temple W Jr; 2, Robert S Mitchell Trust; 3, Englander Richard A; 4, Johnston Mrs S K Jr; 5, Saland Richard; 6, Whitham Janis R; 7, Mc Stables Michael Cloonan; 8, Furlong Kenyon G; 9, Campbell Alex G Jr; 10, Ghost Breeding Stables Michael J Tr

Trainers— 1, Amoss Thomas; 2, Morse Randy L; 3, Feliciano Ben M Jr; 4, Simon Charles; 5, Saland Richard; 6, Nafzger Carl A; 7, Morse Randy L; 8, Furlong Kenyon G; 9, Lopresti Charles; 10, Trombetta Michael J

Scratched— Bully Bully (17Mar03 8FG2).

$2 Pick Three (6/10–1–7) Paid $426.60; Pick Three Pool $51,878.

NINTH RACE

Keeneland

APRIL 12, 2003

1⅛ MILES. (1.46⁴) 79th Running of THE TOYOTA BLUE GRASS. Grade I. Purse $750,000 Guaranteed. Three year olds. By subscription of $375 each, which should accompany the nomination; $7,500 to enter and start, with $750,000 guaranteed, of which $465,000 to the owner of the winner, $150,000 to second, $75,000 to third, $37,500 to fourth and $22,500 to fifth. Weights: Colts and geldings, 123 lbs.; Fillies, 118 lbs. Starters to be named through the entry box by the usual time of closing. A gold julep cup will be presented to the owner of the winner. A silver julep cup will be presented to the winning trainer and jockey. No supplementary nominations. Closed Wednesday, February 19, 2003 with 141 nominations.

Value of Race: $750,000 Winner $465,000; second $150,000; third $75,000; fourth $37,500; fifth $22,500.   Mutuel Pool $1,520,905.0 Exacta Pool $887,065.00   Quinella Pool $32,360.00   Trifecta Pool $724,501.00   Superfecta Pool $215,378.00

Last Raced	Horse	M/Eqt. A.Wt	PP	St	¼	½	¾	Str	Fin	Jockey	Odds $1
9Mar03 9FG1	Peace Rules	L	3 123	2	3	11½	11½	11	11	13½	Prado E S	0.60
16Mar03 5SA3	Brancusi	L	3 123	8	5	2½	21	21½	23	24½	Farina Tony	8.20
15Feb03 11GP4	Offlee Wild	L	3 123	3	1	41½	4½	3hd	33½	310½	Day P	5.80
1Mar03 7SA3	Crowned Dancer	Lb	3 123	4	6	51	62½	52	43	42½	Desormeaux K J	23.40
22Mar03 9TP2	Acceptable Venture	Lb	3 123	1	4	9	9	81	51	513	Perret C	67.60
22Mar03 10TP4	Lion Tamer	L	3 123	7	9	61	51½	42½	63	6½	Velasquez C	5.70
22Mar03 10TP6	Lots Of Sizzle	Lb	3 123	9	7	3½	3½	64½	74	79	Lumpkins J	130.40
16Mar03 5SA8	Ten Cents A Shine	L	3 123	6	8	8hd	81½	71½	89	88	Smith M E	16.80
22Mar03 10OP2	Great Notion	Lf	3 123	5	2	72	7½	9	9	9	Melancon L	15.90

OFF AT 5:16 Start Good. Won driving. Track fast.

TIME :23², :47, 1:11¹, 1:37⁴, 1:51³ (:23.40, :47.10, 1:11.33, 1:37.80, 1:51.73)

$2 Mutuel Prices:

2–PEACE RULES	3.20	2.40	2.10
9–BRANCUSI		5.00	3.00
3–OFFLEE WILD			2.40

$2 EXACTA 2–9 PAID $20.20 $2 QUINELLA 2–9 PAID $14.80 $2 TRIFECTA 2–9–3 PAID $71.00 $2 SUPERFECTA 2–9–3–5 PAID $375.40

Ch. c, (Apr), by Jules–Hold to Fashion, by Hold Your Peace. Trainer Frankel Robert. Bred by Newchance Farm (Fla).

PEACE RULES moved to the fore near the inside approaching the first turn while rating kindly, went along under careful handling, turned back a bid from BRANCUSI leaving the three furlong marker, then expanded his advantage in the drive under six, well-spaced right-handed strokes of the whip. BRANCUSI angled in approaching the first turn while gaining a forward position, tightened it up on GREAT NOTION which forced that one to check nearing the first turn, edged up outside PEACE RULES to press the pace four wide, was asked for his best leaving the eight-eighths pole, then couldn't sustain the needed momentum while clearly second best. OFFLEE WILD exchanged bumps approaching the first turn with CROWNED DANCER when that one was forced in by GREAT NOTION, settled inside within easy striking distance, saved ground to the stretch, came out five wide when straightened for the drive, was empty the last eighth but much the best of the others. CROWNED DANCER, in tight between rivals approaching the first turn, exchanged bumps first with GREAT NOTION, then bounced inward bumping with OFFLEE WILD, moved inside on the backstretch, saved ground into the stretch, angled five wide for the drive but couldn't menace. ACCEPTABLE VENTURE, outrun into the backstretch while in behind horses, moved out five or six wide and never seriously menaced while improving position. LION TAMER worked his way in behind rivals approaching the first turn, came out jolting GREAT NOTION at the seven furlong marker, settled to race under light rating between foes four wide, continued four wide in a striking position to the final quarter and was finished. LOTS OF SIZZLE raced in contention five wide for six furlongs and faded. TEN CENTS A SHINE, six wide on the first turn, moved in behind horses on the backstretch and was through after three-quarters. GREAT NOTION, checked approaching the first turn behind BRANCUSI and forced in when that one angled in, exchanged bumps with CROWNED DANCER while placing that one in tight, was jolted soundly at the seven furlong marker by LION TAMER and was through soon after. A foul claim lodged by the rider of CROWNED DANCER against BRANCUSI for alleged interference entering the first turn was disallowed. Because of camera malfunction, the order of finish was confirmed by the placing judges. The margins were determined by the Equibase field crew.

Owners— 1, Gann Edmund A; 2, Tabor Michael B; 3, Azalea Stable Lansdon Robbins III; 4, Charles Cono & Victory Racing LLC B; 5, Richard Kaster Nathan & Richard Fox; 6, Tabor Michael B; 7, Everest Stables; 8, Ramsey Kenneth L & Sarah K; 9, Silverton Hills Farm

Trainers— 1, Frankel Robert; 2, Biancone Patrick L; 3, Smith Thomas V; 4, Paasch Christopher S; 5, Romans Dale; 6, Pletcher Todd A; 7, Keen Dallas E; 8, Lukas D Wayne; 9, Miller Darrin

Scratched— Badge Of Silver (9Mar03 9FG6)

$2 Daily Double (2–2) Paid $20.00; Daily Double Pool $48,880.
$2 Pick Three (7–2–2/4) Paid $443.80; Pick Three Pool $67,945.
$1 Pick Four (1–7–2–2/4) Paid $1,128.40; Pick Four Pool $61,297.

NINTH RACE

Oaklawn

APRIL 12, 2003

1⅛ MILES. (1.46³) 67th Running of THE ARKANSAS DERBY. Grade II. Purse $500,000. THREE–YEAR–OLDS. Weights: Colts and geldings, 122 lbs. Fillies 117 lbs. Non–winners of a sweepstakes, allowed 4 lbs.

Value of Race: $500,000 Winner $300,000; second $100,000; third $50,000; fourth $30,000; fifth $20,000. Mutuel Pool $1,413,782.0 Exacta Pool $905,264.00 Trifecta Pool $696,125.00 Superfecta Pool $191,976.00

Last Raced	Horse	M/Eqt. A.Wt	PP	St	¼	½	¾	Str	Fin	Jockey	Odds $1
22Mar03 10OP4	Sir Cherokee	L	3 118	5	12	12	12	9½	22½	11¾	Thompson T J	55.60
22Mar03 10TP2	Eugene's Third Son	L b	3 118	12	1	2½	22	1hd	13½	26½	Sellers S J	6.40
15Mar03 10GP1	Christine's Outlaw	L f	3 118	4	2	31	41½	3½	33½	31	Guidry M	10.50
16Mar03 11Tam1	Region Of Merit	L	3 122	7	4	41	3½	4½	4½	4¾	Coa E M	5.50
22Mar03 10OP1	Crowned King	L	3 122	2	9	10½	10²½	116	62½	53¾	Rennie C R	33.00
22Mar03 10OP3	Comic Truth	L b	3 122	8	8	7hd	7¹½	62½	53	61	Theriot H J II	27.70
28Mar03 7GP1	Saint Liam	L	3 118	11	11	95	94	8hd	8hd	71¾	Court J K	73.00
16Mar03 11Tam2	Aristocat	L b	3 118	9	5	5½	5½	101	9hd	81	Douglas R R	6.70
9Mar03 9FG5	Defrere's Vixen	L	3 118	3	7	6hd	8hd	7hd	108	91½	Meche D J	6.80
16Mar03 5SA7	Man Among Men	L b	3 122	10	6	8hd	6hd	51½	7hd	108¾	Solis A	2.60
6Mar03 9TP4	Sell To Survive	L b	3 118	1	10	115½	112½	12	114½	116¾	Marquez C H Jr	101.00
9Mar03 8DeD1	Cat Genius	L b	3 122	6	3	11½	12	22½	12	12	Borel C H	4.10

OFF AT 4:47 Start Good. Won driving. Track fast.

TIME :21⁴, :45², 1:09⁴, 1:35⁴, 1:48¹ (:21.93, :45.42, 1:09.98, 1:35.94, 1:48.39)

$2 Mutuel Prices:

5–SIR CHEROKEE	113.20	33.60	13.20
12–EUGENE'S THIRD SON		8.00	5.20
4–CHRISTINE'S OUTLAW			9.80

$2 EXACTA 5–12 PAID $1,054.00 $2 TRIFECTA 5–12–4 PAID $17,458.20
$2 SUPERFECTA 5–12–4–7 PAID $101,107.20

B. c, (Feb), by Cherokee Run–La Cucina*Ire, by Last Tycoon*Ire. Trainer Tomlinson Michael A. Bred by Domino Stud of Lexington LLC (Ky).

SIR CHEROKEE last away, trailed, circled the field six wide in the second turn, kicked down the leader inside the furlong grounds, continued willingly to the wire, well clear. EUGENE'S THIRD SON closest to the leader, collared that one far turn from the outside, quickly clear into the stretch, proved no match for the winner, well clear of the others. CHRISTINE'S OUTLAW evenly paced, finished best of the others while off the inside. REGION OF MERIT also within striking distance off the inside, lacked a final kick. CROWNED KING void of early foot, lacked room in traffic late in the second turn, bumped, finished willingly when clear. COMIC TRUTH in traffic most of the way, lacked a late kick. SAINT LIAM four wide out of the final turn, no late gain. ARISTOCAT settled off the pace, also came up empty for the drive. DEFRERE'S VIXEN was never involved toward the inside. MAN AMONG MEN four wide in the first turn, advanced middle half mile, gave way when the real running started. SELL TO SURVIVE was never close. CAT GENIUS set a very quick pace and stopped before six furlongs.

Owners— 1, Domino Stud of Lexington Inc; 2, Serengeti Stable; 3, R C Hill Stables Randy Hill; 4, Calumet Farm Mrs B De Kwiatkowski; 5, McKeever Racing Stable; 6, Jayaraman Kalarikkal K & Vilasini D; 7, Warren Mr & Mrs William K Jr; 8, Tabor Michael B; 9, Heiligbrodt Racing Stable; 10, R D Hubbard Et Al; 11, Langford Michael; 12, Parker John R

Trainers—1, Tomlinson Michael A; 2, Byrne Patrick B; 3, Weaver George; 4, Clement Christophe; 5, McKeever Billy C Jr; 6, Norman Cole; 7, Reinstedler Anthony; 8, Pletcher Todd A; 9, Asmussen Steven M; 10, Mandella Gary; 11, Morse Randy L; 12, Amoss Thomas

$2 Pick Three (3–6–5) Paid $4,581.00; Pick Three Pool $28,994.

SIXTH RACE

Keeneland

APRIL 13, 2003

$1\frac{1}{16}$ MILES. (Turf)(1.40^1) 15th Running of THE JENNY WILEY. Grade III. Purse $100,000 For fillies and mares four years old and upward. By subscription of $100 each, which should accompany the nomination; $1,000 to enter and start. Weight 123 lbs. Non–winners of Grade I or II stakes on the turf since September 1 allowed 3 lbs.; $60,000 twice on the turf since August 1, 5 lbs.; $45,000 twice on turf since July 4, 7 lbs. Max number of starters for the Jenny Wiley will be limited to 10 with 2 also eligibles. In the event that more than 10 fillies or mares pass the entry box, 10 starters determined at time with preference given to graded stakes winners, then highest turf earnings in 2002–2003. Same owner entry cannot start to the exclusion of a single entry. Starters to be named through entry box by usual time of closing. Closed April 2, 2003 with 33 nominations.

Value of Race: $113,300 Winner $70,246; second $22,660; third $11,330; fourth $5,665; fifth $3,399. Mutuel Pool $433,795.00 Exacta Pool $290,951.00 Quinella Pool $14,395.00 Trifecta Pool $241,818.00 Superfecta Pool $71,496.00

Last Raced	Horse	M/Eqt. A.Wt	PP	St	$\frac{1}{4}$	$\frac{1}{2}$	$\frac{3}{4}$	Str	Fin	Jockey	Odds $1
17Jan03 7SA1	Sea Of Showers	L	4 116	2	10	8^{hd}	9^1_2	9^2	6^3	11^1_4	Bailey J D	2.10
22Mar03 9SA4	Magic Mission–GB	Lb	5 116	1	3	5^1_2	6^1_2	5^1_2	3^1	2^{nk}	Prado E S	6.50
1Mar03 9FG3	Snow Dance	L	5 116	10	6	4^1	5^1	7^{hd}	4^{hd}	3^{hd}	Santos J A	3.90
2Mar03 10GP1	Amonita–GB	L	5 116	4	5	3^1_2	3^{hd}	3^1	2^{hd}	4^1_2	Samyn J L	3.90
12Mar03 7SA7	Sentimental Value	Lb	4 117	6	1	2^1_2	2^1	1^2	1^1	5^3_4	Desormeaux K J	19.40
1Mar03 9FG1	Quick Tip	L	5 120	8	8	9^2_1	8^1_2	6^{hd}	5^{hd}	6^2	Albarado R J	6.50
1Mar03 9FG2	Histoire Sainte–FR	L	7 116	3	4	7^1_2	7^1_2	8^{hd}	7^1_2	7^1	Sellers S J	13.60
2Mar03 10GP9	Party Queen	Lf	4 116	7	9	10	10	10	10	8^2_4	Guidry M	26.30
14Mar03 6GP2	Cozy Island	Lf	5 116	9	7	6^1	4^{hd}	4^1_2	9^1	9^1_2	Peck B D	37.40
15Mar03 9GP4	Ever With You	Lb	5 116	5	2	12^1_2	1^1	2^1	8^{hd}	10	Borel C H	46.30

OFF AT 3:45 Start Good. Won driving. Course firm.

TIME :23³, :48, 1:12, 1:36, 1:41⁴ (:23.64, :48.08, 1:12.03, 1:36.02, 1:41.89)

$2 Mutuel Prices:

2–SEA OF SHOWERS	6.20	3.80	3.00
1–MAGIC MISSION–GB		6.60	4.00
10–SNOW DANCE			3.40

$2 EXACTA 2–1 PAID $43.20 $2 QUINELLA 1–2 PAID $19.00 $2 TRIFECTA 2–1–10 PAID $208.40 $2 SUPERFECTA 2–1–10–4 PAID $548.80

B. f, by Seattle Slew–Chimes of Freedom, by Private Account. Trainer Frankel Robert. Bred by Flaxman Holdings Ltd (Ky).

SEA OF SHOWERS outrun into the backstretch, raced in behind horses, moved out to secure room seven wide upon entering the upper stretch and was under brisk urging to edge clear late. MAGIC MISSION (GB), never far back, raced near the inside, eased out to make her run from between foes three or four wide for the final furlong, gained even terms for the lead at the sixteenth pole, then wasn't good enough. SNOW DANCE, within easy striking distance while following the leaders four or five wide, was a bit wider for the drive and gained only slightly in the final stages. AMONITA (GB), rated in behind the leaders from early on, angled out three or four wide on the far turn, loomed prominently for the drive but was empty late. SENTIMENTAL VALUE drifted out at the start putting PARTY QUEEN in a bit tight, moved up soon after to press front-running EVER WITH YOU, took over leaving the backstretch, opened a clear advantage, made the pace into the final furlong and faltered. QUICK TIP drifted in at the start tightening it up on PARTY QUEEN, was unhurried, moved in behind horses, reached contention near the inside in the upper stretch but lacked a further account. HISTOIRE SAINTE (FR), five wide on the far turn, lacked a rally. PARTY QUEEN, squeezed back in tight quarters soon after the start, wasn't a factor and six wide much of the way. COZY ISLAND tracked the pace four or five wide for six furlongs and weakened gradually. EVER WITH YOU gained the lead early, moved near the inside while drawing clear, made the pace to the end of the backstretch, lost the edge to SENTIMENTAL VALUE and tired upon going six furlongs.

Owners— 1, Flaxman Holdings Ltd; 2, Gainsborough Farm Inc; 3, Oxley John C; 4, Haras Du Mezeray Charles Henri De M; 5, The Thoroughbred Corporation; 6, Farish William S; 7, Tanaka Gary A; 8, Humphrey G W Jr; 9, Marylou Whitney Stable; 10, Wimborne Farms

Trainers—1, Frankel Robert; 2, Drysdale Neil; 3, Ward John T Jr; 4, Clement Christophe; 5, Mulhall Kristin; 6, Howard Neil J; 7, Asmussen Steven M; 8, Oliver Victoria; 9, Gothard Akiko; 10, Perkins Diane

Scratched— Crystal Sea (15Mar03 9GP5), Sunset Skies (9Mar03 9TP9)

$2 Pick Three (4–3–2/11/12) Paid $480.40; Pick Three Pool $71,175.

EIGHTH RACE
Keeneland
APRIL 13, 2003

7 FURLONGS. (1.20^{1}) 17th Running of THE COMMONWEALTH BREEDERS' CUP. Grade II. Purse $250,000 (includes $100,000 BC – Breeders' Cup) For three year olds and upward. (Includes $100,000 from Breeders' Cup Fund for Cup Nominees only). By subscription of $250 each, which should accompany the nomination, $2,500 to enter and start with $150,000 added and an additional $100,000 from the Breeders' Cup Fund for Cup eligibles only. Breeders' Cup Fund monies also correspondingly divided providing a Breeders' Cup nominee has finished in an awarded position. Any Breeders' Cup monies not awarded will revert back to the fund. Weights: Three year olds, 116 lbs.; Older 124 lbs. Non-winners of a Grade I stakes since October 25 allowed 2 lbs.; a Grade II since September 1, 4 lbs.; $45,000 twice since July 4, 6 lbs. Starters to be named through the entry box by the usual time of closing. Closed April 2, 2003 with 25 nominations.

Value of Race: $273,750 Winner $169,725; second $54,750; third $27,375; fourth $13,688; fifth $8,212. Mutuel Pool $453,391.00 Exacta Pool $306,626.00 Quinella Pool $11,069.00 Trifecta Pool $246,004.00 Superfecta Pool $67,235.00

Last Raced	Horse	M/Eqt.	A.Wt	PP	St	¼	½	Str	Fin	Jockey	Odds $1
8Mar03 ^{10}GP^{5}	Smooth Jazz	Lf	4 118	1	1	$1^{\frac{1}{2}}$	1^{1}	1^{2}	1^{3}	Prado E S	7.00
2Mar03 ^{7}SA^{2}	Crafty C. T.	L	5 118	6	3	$5^{2\frac{1}{2}}$	3^{hd}	$2^{1\frac{1}{2}}$	$2^{6\frac{1}{4}}$	Bailey J D	0.90
15Mar03 ^{8}Aqu^{4}	Multiple Choice	Lb	5 120	2	4	$2^{\frac{1}{2}}$	2^{1}	$3^{4\frac{1}{2}}$	$3^{3\frac{3}{4}}$	Sellers S J	4.50
8Mar03 ^{10}GP^{6}	Binthebest	Lbf	6 118	3	7	7	7	4^{4}	$4^{6\frac{3}{4}}$	Santos J A	35.40
23Feb03 ^{9}FG^{2}	Speed Hunter	L	4 118	7	2	6^{6}	6^{1}	6^{5}	$5^{5\frac{1}{2}}$	Day P	14.90
1Jan03 ^{7}SA^{7}	Roman Dancer	L	4 118	5	5	4^{hd}	5^{3}	5^{hd}	6^{9}	Desormeaux K J	15.80
11Jan03 ^{10}GP^{3}	Najran	L	4 118	4	6	$3^{1\frac{1}{2}}$	4^{2}	7	7	Coa E M	3.60

OFF AT 4:46 Start Good For All But NAJRAN Won driving. Track fast.
TIME :22, :44^{4}, 1:09^{2}, 1:21^{3} (:22.12, :44.94, 1:09.53, 1:21.73)

$2 Mutuel Prices:			
1–SMOOTH JAZZ	16.00	5.20	3.40
6–CRAFTY C. T.		2.60	2.20
2–MULTIPLE CHOICE			2.80

$2 EXACTA 1–6 PAID $44.20 $2 QUINELLA 1–6 PAID $14.80 $2 TRIFECTA 1–6–2 PAID $123.40 $2 SUPERFECTA 1–6–2–3 PAID $1,057.40

Dk. b. or br. c, by Storm Boot–Blushing Issue, by Blushing John. Trainer Pletcher Todd A. Bred by San Gabriel Investment & T F Van Meter (Ky).

SMOOTH JAZZ moved to the fore near the inside soon after the start, went along under careful handling, then expanded his advantage late under mild encouragement. CRAFTY C. T., never far back, worked his way in behind the leaders approaching the end of the backstretch, saved ground to the stretch, came out three wide for the drive, loomed just off the winner but couldn't offer a challenge as second best. MULTIPLE CHOICE attended the pace early while between rivals, continued in closest attendance to SMOOTH JAZZ while outside that one to the stretch and weakened. BINTHEBEST, outrun to the stretch while near the inside, came out five wide for the drive, made a mild bid to reach contention at the furlong grounds but lacked a further account. SPEED HUNTER, five or six wide, wasn't a factor. ROMAN DANCER broke open the doors of his starting stall prior to the start but was in the hands of the assistant starter and couldn't escape. During the running, ROMAN DANCER leaned in at the break and bumped NAJRAN, raced close up early while five wide, fell back concluding the backstretch and weakened gradually. NAJRAN also popped the doors of the gate open prior to the start and immediately was grabbed by the assistant starter. During the running, NAJRAN broke in the air, was bumped by ROMAN DANCER, went up soon after to force the pace three abreast and tired upon going a half.

Owners— 1, Tabor Michael B; 2, C T Grether Inc C T Grether; 3, Blum Peter E; 4, Tafel James B et al; 5, Mansell Stables; 6, Rodriguez Lorraine & Rod; 7, Buckram Oak Farm

Trainers—1, Pletcher Todd A; 2, Zucker Howard L; 3, Jerkens James A; 4, Nafzger Carl A; 5, Walden W Elliott; 6, Paasch Christopher S; 7, Zito Nicholas P

$2 Pick Three (2/11/12–8–1) Paid $637.60; Pick Three Pool $44,871.
$1 Pick Six (1–4–3–2/11/12–8–1) 4
Correct Paid $158.40; Pick Six Pool $7,043; Carryover Pool $4,278.

EIGHTH RACE
Aqueduct
APRIL 18, 2003

1 MILE. (1.32^{2}) 54th Running of THE COMELY. Grade III. Purse $100,000. (Up to $19,400 NYSBFOA). FILLIES, THREE YEARS OLD. By subscription of $100 each, which should accompany the nomination; $500 to pass the entry box; $500 to start, with $100,000 added. The added money and all fees to be divided 60% to the winner, 20% tosecond, 11% to third, 6% to fourth and 3% to fifth. 122 lbs. Non-winners of $60,000 other than restricted stake; or $30,000 twice in 2003 allowed 2 lbs.; $30,000 at a mile or over in 2003, 4 lbs.; $30,000; or three races other than maiden or claiming, 6 lbs. Trophies will be presented to the winning owner, trainer and jockey. Closed Saturday, April 5, 2003 with 24 Nominations.

Value of Race: $107,900 Winner $64,740; second $21,580; third $11,869; fourth $6,474; fifth $3,237. Mutuel Pool $1,658,527.0 Exacta Pool $400,561.00

Last Raced	Horse	M/Eqt.	A.Wt	PP	St	¼	½	¾	Str	Fin	Jockey	Odds $1
22Mar03 ^{9}Aqu^{1}	Cyber Secret	L	3 122	2	3	1^{1}	$1^{1\frac{1}{2}}$	$1^{2\frac{1}{2}}$	1^{7}	$1^{5\frac{1}{2}}$	Bridgmohan S X	3.50
26Oct02 ^{4}AP^{1}	Storm Flag Flying	L	3 122	1	4	3^{7}	2^{hd}	$3^{4\frac{1}{2}}$	$2^{\frac{1}{2}}$	2^{3}	Velazquez J R	0.25
3Apr03 ^{5}Aqu^{1}	Bonay	Lb	3 116	5	1	2^{hd}	3^{8}	2^{hd}	$3^{3\frac{1}{2}}$	$3^{2\frac{1}{4}}$	Coa E M	14.70
21Mar03 ^{5}Aqu^{2}	Glorious Jenna	L	3 116	4	5	5	5	5	5	4no	Luzzi M J	42.50
10Apr03 ^{5}Aqu^{4}	Xtra Heart	Lbf	3 116	3	2	$4^{2\frac{1}{2}}$	4^{5}	$4^{2\frac{1}{2}}$	4^{2}	5	Arroyo N Jr	13.00

OFF AT 4:21 Start Good. Won driving. Track fast.
TIME :23^{1}, :45^{1}, 1:10, 1:35^{4} (:23.22, :45.35, 1:10.12, 1:35.97)

$2 Mutuel Prices:			
2–CYBER SECRET	9.00	2.10	2.10
1–STORM FLAG FLYING		2.10	2.10
5–BONAY			2.10

$2 EXACTA 2–1 PAID $15.00

B. f, (Mar), by Cyberspace–Merry Maudie, by Maudlin. Trainer Dutrow Richard E Jr. Bred by Earl Pierport & Teresa Pierport (Fla).

CYBER SECRET quickly opened a clear lead, set the pace along the inside, drew away when roused and remained well clear under a drive. STORM FLAG FLYING was hustled along early, chased the pace, could not get to the winner in the stretch and stayed on to earn the place award. BONAY chased the pace while three wide and tired in the stretch. GLORIOUS JENNA was outrun early and had no response when roused. XTRA HEART was outrun early, came wide into the stretch and had no rally.

Owners— 1, Goldfarb Sanford & Irwin & Team Jul; 2, Phipps Ogden Mills et al; 3, Centaur Farms Inc; 4, Iracane Joseph A; 5, Paraneck Stable

Trainers—1, Dutrow Richard E Jr; 2, McGaughey Claude III; 3, Schulhofer Randy; 4, Pletcher Todd A; 5, Pedersen Jennifer

Scratched— Belong To Sea (30Mar03 ^{3}AQU^{1})

NINTH RACE
Aqueduct
APRIL 19, 2003

1 MILE. (1.32^{2}) 47th Running of THE BED O' ROSES BREEDERS' CUP HANDICAP. Grade III. Purse $150,000 (includes $50,000 BC – Breeders' Cup). (Up to $19,400 NYSBFOA). FILLIES AND MARES THREE YEARS OLD AND UPWARD. By subscription of $100 each, which should accompany the nomination; $500 to pass the entry box; $500 to start, with $100,000 added and an additional $50,000 from the Breeders' Cup Fund for Cup nominees only. The NYRA added money and all fees to be divided 60% to the winner, 20% to second, 11% to third, 6% to fourth and 3% to fifth. Breeders' Cup Fund monies also correspondingly divided, provided a Breeders' Cup nominee has finished in an award position. Weights Sunday, April 13. Closed Saturday, April 5, 2003 with 16 Nominations.

Value of Race: $155,100 Winner $93,960; second $31,320; third $17,226; fourth $9,396; fifth $3,198. Mutuel Pool $528,816.00 Exacta Pool $418,967.00

Last Raced	Horse	M/Eqt.	A.Wt	PP	St	¼	½	¾	Str	Fin	Jockey	Odds $1
29Mar03 ^{9}Aqu^{2}	Raging Fever	L	5 119	5	1	1^{2}	$1^{2\frac{1}{2}}$	$1^{\frac{1}{2}}$	$1^{1\frac{1}{2}}$	$1^{\frac{1}{2}}$	Gryder A T	0.90
23Mar03 ^{9}Aqu^{1}	Smok'n Frolic	L	4 120	2	3	$2^{1\frac{1}{2}}$	$2^{1\frac{1}{2}}$	$2^{4\frac{1}{2}}$	$2^{3\frac{1}{2}}$	$2^{3\frac{1}{4}}$	Velazquez J R	2.25
4Apr03 ^{8}GP^{1}	Nonsuch Bay	L	4 117	1	5	$4^{2\frac{1}{2}}$	4^{3}	$4^{5\frac{1}{2}}$	$3^{2\frac{1}{2}}$	$3^{1\frac{3}{4}}$	Coa E M	3.40
10Mar03 ^{8}GP^{2}	Alchemilla	L	4 112	4	2	$3^{2\frac{1}{2}}$	$3^{5\frac{1}{2}}$	3^{hd}	$4^{3\frac{1}{2}}$	$4^{3\frac{1}{2}}$	Bridgmohan S X	15.50
29Mar03 ^{9}Aqu^{3}	Bonefide Reason	L	5 114	3	4	5	5	5	5	5	Santos J A	16.40

OFF AT 4:52 Start Good. Won driving. Track fast.
TIME :23^{3}, :47, 1:10^{3}, 1:34^{4} (:23.78, :47.05, 1:10.62, 1:34.86)

$2 Mutuel Prices:				
	5–RAGING FEVER	3.80	2.40	2.10
	2–SMOK'N FROLIC		2.60	2.10
	1–NONSUCH BAY			2.10

$2 EXACTA 5–2 PAID $8.00

Dk. b. or br. m, by Storm Cat–Pennant Fever, by Seattle Slew. Trainer Hennig Mark. Bred by Edward P Evans (Ky).

RAGING FEVER quickly showed in front, controlled the pace while in hand, turned back a run from SMOK'N FROLIC turning for home, drew clear then dug in gamely on the rail and held off that rival under a steady drive. SMOK'N FROLIC raced close up early while in hand, took a run at the winner nearing the stretch then came again gamely in deep stretch. NONSUCH BAY was outrun early, advanced inside on the turn, angled out in upper stretch and finished gamely. ALCHEMILLA chased the pace from the outside and tired in the stretch. BONEFIDE REASON was outrun early, raced inside and had no response when roused.

Owners— 1, Evans Edward P; 2, Dogwood Stable; 3, Thorn Stable; 4, Alexander Helen C Groves Helen K &; 5, Sunny Meadow Farm

Trainers—1, Hennig Mark; 2, Pletcher Todd A; 3, Alexander Frank A; 4, McGaughey Claude III; 5, Friedman Mitchell

---

EIGHTH RACE
Hawthorne
APRIL 19, 2003

1⅛ MILES. (1.46^{3}) 17th Running of THE NATIONAL JOCKEY CLUB HANDICAP. Grade III. Purse $250,000 A HANDICAP FOR THREE–YEAR–OLDS AND UPWARD. By subscription of $100 each, which shall accompany the nomination, $1,500 to pass the entry box, $1,500 additional to start. Nominations closed Wednesday, April 9, 2003 with 21.

Value of Race: $250,000 Winner $150,000; second $50,000; third $27,500; fourth $15,000; fifth $7,500. Mutuel Pool $210,960.00 Exacta Pool $122,562.00 Trifecta Pool $114,477.00 Superfecta Pool $33,535.00

Last Raced	Horse	M/Eqt.	A.Wt	PP	St	¼	½	¾	Str	Fin	Jockey	Odds $1
5Apr03 ^{6}Haw^{1}	Fight For Ally	Lb	6 116	2	2	2^{1}	$2^{1\frac{1}{2}}$	$2^{3\frac{1}{2}}$	$1^{1\frac{1}{2}}$	1^{nk}	Razo E Jr	7.90
16Mar03 ^{9}OP^{4}	Colonial Colony	L	5 114	1	5	4^{hd}	4^{1}	3^{hd}	4^{7}	2no	Martinez W	8.40
23Mar03 ^{8}DeD^{2}	Parrott Bay	Lb	6 115	5	3	3^{1}	3^{1}	$4^{2\frac{1}{2}}$	3^{hd}	$3^{4\frac{1}{4}}$	Sterling L J Jr	18.40
22Mar03 ^{3}GP^{3}	Keats	Lf	5 114	4	1	$1^{\frac{1}{2}}$	1^{2}	$1^{\frac{1}{2}}$	$2^{1\frac{1}{2}}$	$4^{6\frac{3}{4}}$	Melancon L	2.10
5Apr03 ^{6}Haw^{3}	Fourth Floor	Lb	5 111	8	6	7^{1}	7^{1}	7^{2}	5^{4}	$5^{9\frac{3}{4}}$	Vitek J J	51.40
15Mar03 ^{12}GP^{2}	Regency Park	L	4 114	3	8	$5^{\frac{1}{2}}$	5^{1}	$6^{1\frac{1}{2}}$	6^{3}	$6^{10\frac{1}{2}}$	Decarlo C P	3.20
9Apr03 ^{9}OP^{2}	Colorful Tour	L	4 119	7	4	6^{1}	$6^{2\frac{1}{2}}$	5^{1}	7^{5}	7^{10}	Bourque C C	2.60
22Mar03 ^{9}OP^{2}	Mc Mahon	Lb	5 114	6	7	8	8	8	8	8	St Julien M	9.30

OFF AT 4:29 Start Good. Won driving. Track fast.
TIME :24^{1}, :47^{4}, 1:12^{2}, 1:38^{4}, 1:53^{2} (:24.38, :47.91, 1:12.52, 1:38.96, 1:53.46)

$2 Mutuel Prices:				
	2–FIGHT FOR ALLY	17.80	10.60	7.60
	1–COLONIAL COLONY		7.00	5.20
	6–PARROTT BAY			7.60

$2 EXACTA 2–1 PAID $112.40 $2 TRIFECTA 2–1–6 PAID $2,173.60 $2 SUPERFECTA 2–1–6–5 PAID $10,007.00

Dk. b. or br. g, by Fit to Fight–Colonial Ally, by Pleasant Colony. Trainer Catalano Wayne M. Bred by Justice Farm (Ind).

FIGHT FOR ALLY raced close up inside, angled out for the drive, rallied to a clear lead then was fully extended to hold off his challengers. COLONIAL COLONY was allowed to settle along the rail near the middle of the field, came out for the drive, gained late and did not miss by much. PARROTT BAY raced just outside of COLONIAL COLONY, rallied with that one in the stretch and also narrowly missed. KEATS set the pace inside, took clear command on the backstretch but weakened thereafter. FOURTH FLOOR failed to reach a contending position. REGENCY PARK was never a factor. COLORFUL TOUR always outrun in a dull effort. MC MAHON trailed throughout.

Owners— 1, Calabrese Frank C; 2, Lakeside Farms; 3, Hoffman Kenneth E; 4, Pabst Henry E; 5, Cook Tim; 6, Melnyk Eugene & Laura; 7, Irish Acres Farm; 8, Cherrywood Racing Stables II

Trainers—1, Catalano Wayne M; 2, Bindner Walter M Jr; 3, Hoffman Kenneth E; 4, O'Callaghan Niall M; 5, Goodridge Ronald O; 6, Pletcher Todd A; 7, Hickey P Noel; 8, Boyce Michele

Scratched— Fighting Indians (5Apr03 ^{6}HAW^{2}), Deferred Comp (15Mar03 ^{10}TP^{2})

$2 Pick Three (2–4–2) Paid $675.20; Pick Three Pool $7,204. $2 Pick Six (5–5–4–2–4–2) 3 Correct Paid $38.80; Pick Six Pool $9,564; Carryover Pool $22,498.

EIGHTH RACE

Keeneland

APRIL 19, 2003

1$\frac{1}{16}$ MILES. (1.40⁴) 22nd Running of THE COOLMORE LEXINGTON. Grade II. Purse $325,000 For three year olds. By subscription of $325 each, which should accompany the nomination; $3,250 to enter and start with $325,000 added, of which 62% of all monies to the owner of the winner, 20% to second, 10% to third, 5% to fourth and 3% to fifth. Weight: 123 lbs. Non–winners of $60,000 twice at a mile or over allowed, 3 lbs.; $45,000 twice at a mile or over, 5 lbs.; $30,000 twice at a mile or over, 7 lbs. Starters to be named through the entry box by the usual time of closing. A gold julep cup will be presented to the owner of the winner. Closed Wednesday, April 9, 2003 with 39 nominations.

Value of Race: $363,675 Winner $225,479; second $72,735; third $36,367; fourth $18,184; fifth $10,910.   Mutuel Pool $1,058,826.0 Exacta Pool $566,705.00 Quinella Pool $23,502.00 Trifecta Pool $463,363.00 Superfecta Pool $130,104.00

Last Raced	Horse	M/Eqt. A.Wt	PP	St	$\frac{1}{4}$	$\frac{1}{2}$	$\frac{3}{4}$	Str	Fin	Jockey	Odds $1
15Feb03 9GP4	Scrimshaw	Lb	3 116	1	2	2hd	3hd	3½	1½	13	Prado E S	6.30
22Mar03 6SA3	Eye Of The Tiger	L	3 116	3	7	7	51	56	3hd	2nk	Albarado R J	7.90
5Apr03 6SA5	Domestic Dispute	L	3 116	5	6	6½	7	4hd	42½	3nk	Bailey J D	3.70
15Mar03 8GP2	Trust N Luck	L	3 123	7	4	11½	11	11½	21½	45¾	Velasquez C	2.30
8Mar03 6GG2	Ministers Wild Cat	L	3 116	2	3	3hd	21	2½	510	511½	Espinoza V	2.10
25Jan03 9FG10	Most Feared	Lbf	3 118	4	1	4½	4hd	68	6	6	Guidry M	20.60
5Apr03 6SA9	Ocean Terrace	L	3 116	6	5	52	6hd	7	—	—	Sellers S J	12.50

Ocean Terrace: Eased;

OFF AT 4:45 Start Good. Won driving. Track fast.

TIME :23, :47, 1:11³, 1:38³, 1:45² (:23.06, :47.08, 1:11.78, 1:38.66, 1:45.47)

$2 Mutuel Prices:	1–SCRIMSHAW	14.60	6.20	3.40
	3–EYE OF THE TIGER		8.80	5.00
	5–DOMESTIC DISPUTE			3.40

$2 EXACTA 1–3 PAID $87.40 $2 QUINELLA 1–3 PAID $55.80 $2 TRIFECTA 1–3–5 PAID $320.20 $2 SUPERFECTA 1–3–5–8 PAID $1,368.60

Dk. b. or br. c, (Apr), by Gulch–Rogue Girl, by Sham. Trainer Lukas D Wayne. Bred by Stefanski Stan & Ingrid (Ky).

SCRIMSHAW bobbled at the start while breaking outward, was checked lightly approaching the first turn behind TRUST N LUCK when bumped by MINISTERS WILD CAT, settled nicely under a rating hold upon entering the backstretch, went along under patient handling while saving ground, moved smoothly three wide entering the stretch, took over approaching the final furlong, was roused three times with the whip on the left side, then, after the rider switched his stick to the right side, was struck four more times to move well clear. EYE OF THE TIGER, off a bit sluggish and bumped soon after by MINISTERS WILD CAT from the inside then from the outside by MOST FEARED, was checked and eased back toward the inside, raced three wide, moved between rivals approaching the stretch, was outside the winner four wide for the drive but couldn't threaten. DOMESTIC DISPUTE, within striking distance and four or five wide most of the way, moved with SCRIMSHAW while outside that one approaching the stretch but couldn't sustain the needed momentum. TRUST N LUCK brushed the side of the gate at the start, moved up quickly to vie for the lead, gained the inside by the first turn, made the pace to the stretch and weakened. MINISTERS WILD CAT came out bumping EYE OF THE TIGER soon after the start, was bumped by MOST FEARED and steadied when forced in on SCRIMSHAW approaching the first turn, recovered to press front-running TRUST N LUCK, raced close up until approaching the stretch while between rivals and tired. MOST FEARED leaned in soon after the start bumping EYE OF THE TIGER, came in again bumping MINISTERS WILD CAT, forcing that one into SCRIMSHAW approaching the first turn, raced four or five in a striking position for four furlongs and weakened thereafter. OCEAN TERRACE drifted out slightly at the start, raced in contention for a half while six wide, gave way soon after and was eased when hopelessly beaten.

Owners— 1, Lewis Robert B & Beverly J; 2, Gunther John D; 3, Garber Gary M; 4, Robsham Einar P; 5, Cowan Marjorie & Irving M; 6, Durant Tom R; 7, Fog City Stable.

Trainers— 1, Lukas D Wayne; 2, Hollendorfer Jerry; 3, Baffert Bob; 4, Ziadie Ralph; 5, Drysdale Neil; 6, Werner Ronny; 7, Hess R B Jr

Scratched— Champali (22Mar03 10TP3)

$2 Pick Three (7/11/12–4/5/11/12–1) Paid $185.40; Pick Three Pool $76,348.
$1 Pick Six (1/5–3–8–7/11/12–4/5/11/12–1) 5
Correct Paid $335.70; Pick Six Pool Carryover Pool $7,050.

NINTH RACE

Pimlico

APRIL 19, 2003

1$\frac{1}{8}$ MILES. (1.47¹) 18th Running of THE BALTIMORE BREEDERS' CUP HANDICAP. Grade III. Purse $125,000 (includes $50,000 BC – Breeders' Cup) A HANDICAP FOR THREE–YEAR–OLDS AND UPWARD. (Includes $50,000 from Breeders' Cup Fund for Cup nominees only). By subscription of $50 each which should accompany the nomination, $350 to pass the entry box, $350 additional to start. Supplemental nominations of $750 each will be accepted by Saturday, April 12, 2003 with all other fees due as noted. Weights Sunday, April 13, 2003. Preference will be given to Breeders' Cup nominees only of equal racing quality or high weight assignment (respective of sex and weight for age). Closed Wednesday, March 26, 2003.

Value of Race: $112,000 Winner $75,000; second $15,000; third $13,750; fourth $4,500; fifth $3,750.   Mutuel Pool $110,852.00 Exacta Pool $81,754.00   Trifecta Pool $53,240.00 Superfecta Pool $11,642.00

Last Raced	Horse	M/Eqt. A.Wt	PP	St	$\frac{1}{4}$	$\frac{1}{2}$	$\frac{3}{4}$	Str	Fin	Jockey	Odds $1
15Mar03 8Lrl1	P Day	Lf	8 118	3	5	4½	4hd	41	12	12¾	Fogelsonger R	3.30
15Feb03 7GP1	Changeintheweather	Lb	4 114	4	2	35	34	3½	44	2hd	Dominguez R A	1.80
15Mar03 8Lrl5	Full Brush	Lbf	8 115	7	4	62	6½	63	2½	31	Potts C L	12.30
21Mar03 8Aqu1	Private Lap	L	4 113	5	3	22½	21	22	31½	43¼	Alvarado R Jr	3.90
27Mar03 9Lrl1	Hay Getoutofmyway	Lbf	4 114	2	6	51½	54	5hd	52	5hd	Pino M G	13.80
15Mar03 8Lrl2	Lyracist	Lb	7 116	6	7	7	7	7	62½	66½	Petro N J	4.30
15Mar03 8Lrl7	First Amendment	Lb	6 115	1	1	12	12½	11½	7	7	Wilson R	8.00

OFF AT 5:06 Start Good. Won driving. Track fast.

TIME :23², :47¹, 1:11², 1:36², 1:48⁴ (:23.50, :47.23, 1:11.50, 1:36.45, 1:48.94)

$2 Mutuel Prices:	3–P DAY	8.60	3.80	3.60
	4–CHANGEINTHEWEATHER		3.60	3.40
	7–FULL BRUSH			6.40

$2 EXACTA 3–4 PAID $31.00 $2 TRIFECTA 3–4–7 PAID $181.60 $1 SUPERFECTA 3–4–7–5 PAID $332.40

Dk. b. or br. h, by Private Terms–Gilded Connection, by Gilded Age. Trainer Hadry Charles J. Bred by Hadry Charles H (Md).

P DAY, unhurried early, advanced three wide into the stretch, took command in upper stretch and drew off under rousing. CHANGEINTHEWEATHER, two wide the far turn, was taken to the rail in midstretch and rallied. FULL BRUSH lacked speed, raced wide entering the stretch and failed to sustain his bid. PRIVATE LAP pressed the pace two wide, bid for the lead in upper stretch and gave way. HAY GETOUTOFMYWAY saved ground, swung five wide at the head of the stretch and was no factor. LYRACIST, outrun, swung wide entering the stretch. FIRST AMENDMENT set the pace near the rail and stopped.

Owners— 1, Russo Adam; 2, Pin Oak Stable; 3, Bailey Morris; 4, Preferred Pals Stable; 5, Knight Larry E Sr; 6, Cunningham Timothy; 7, Gill Michael J

Trainers— 1, Hadry Charles J; 2, Motion H Graham; 3, Gaudet Edmond D; 4, Iwinski Allen; 5, Campitelli Francis P; 6, Petro Michael P; 7, Robb John J

$2 Pick Four (6–1/5/7–3–3) Paid $197.20; Pick Four Pool $19,509.

FOURTH RACE

Santa Anita
APRIL 19, 2003

1¼ MILES. (Turf)(1.57²) 55th Running of THE SANTA BARBARA HANDICAP. Grade II. Purse $250,000. FILLIES AND MARES FOUR YEARS OLD AND UPWARD. By subscription of $250 each to accompany the nomination or by supplementary nomination of $5,000 by Sunday, April 13. $2,500 additonal to start, with $250,000 guaranteed, of which $150,000 to first, $50,000 to second, $30,000 to third, $15,000 to fourth and $5,000 to fifth. Weights Tuesday, April 15. Closed Thursday, April 10 with 14 nominations. (Rail at 0 Feet).

Value of Race: $250,000 Winner $150,000; second $50,000; third $30,000; fourth $15,000; fifth $5,000. Mutuel Pool $508,522.00 Exacta Pool $246,407.00 Quinella Pool $29,013.00 Trifecta Pool $167,209.00

Last Raced	Horse	M/Eqt. A.Wt	PP	¼	½	¾	1	Str	Fin	Jockey	Odds $1
22Mar03 9SA3	Megahertz-GB	LB	4 117	5 5	5	5	5	2hd	1¾	Solis A	1.30
1Mar03 1SA1	Trekking	LB	4 111	2	11½	11½	11½	11	11	2½	Baze T C	4.90
22Mar03 9SA1	Noches de Rosa-CH	LBb	5 117	1	42	41½	41½	4hd	5	3hd	Smith M E	4.50
13Oct02 GAV2	Notting Hill-BR	LB	4 115	4	2½	2hd	2½	2½	3½	4¾	Valenzuela P A	9.60
22Mar03 9SA2	GardenintheRain-FR	LB	6 116	3	3²	3²	3½	3¹	4¹	5	Stevens G L	2.10

OFF AT 2:02 Start Good. Won driving. Course firm.
TIME :24², :48¹, 1:12², 1:36¹, 2:00 (:24.49, :48.22, 1:12.47, 1:36.29, 2:00.08)

$2 Mutuel Prices:	5–MEGAHERTZ–GB	4.60	3.00	2.20
	2–TREKKING		5.20	3.00
	1–NOCHES DE ROSA–CH			2.80

$1 EXACTA 5–2 PAID $10.80 $2 QUINELLA 2–5 PAID $13.20 $1 TRIFECTA
5–2–1 PAID $33.10

Ch. f, by Pivotal*GB–Heavenly Ray, by Rahy. Trainer Frankel Robert. Bred by Cheveley Park Stud Ltd (GB).

MEGAHERTZ (GB) angled in and saved ground chasing the pace, came off the rail on the second turn, split horses in upper stretch, gained the lead past the eighth pole and gamely prevailed under energetic handling. TREKKING took the early lead and was well rated on the advantage along the inside, fought back when challenged in the stretch and continued willingly to the wire. NOCHES de ROSA (CHI) chased a bit off the rail, went three deep into and on the second turn and into the stretch and finished willingly for third. NOTTING HILL (BRZ) close up stalking the pace outside a rival to the stretch, could not summon the necessary late response and was edged for the show late. GARDEN IN THE RAIN (FR) angled in and saved ground stalking the leader to the stretch and weakened.

Owners— 1, Bello Michael; 2, Juddmonte Farms Inc; 3, Diamond A Racing Corporation; 4, Green Lantern Stables & Barber G; 5, Englander Richard A

Trainers—1, Frankel Robert; 2, Frankel Robert; 3, Mandella Richard; 4, Sahadi Jenine; 5, Mullins Jeff

Scratched— Medinaceli (11Apr03 2SA4)

$2 Daily Double (3–5) Paid $9.00; Daily Double Pool $38,876.
$1 Pick Three (4–3–5/6) Paid $14.00; Pick Three Pool $79,442.

EIGHTH RACE

Santa Anita
APRIL 19, 2003

ABOUT 6½ FURLONGS. (Turf)(1.11²) 36th Running of THE SAN SIMEON HANDICAP. Grade III. Purse $125,000 added. FOUR–YEAR–OLDS AND UPWARD. By subscription of $125 each to accompany the nomination or by supplementary nomination of $2,500 by Sunday, April 13. $1,250 additional to start, with $125,000 added. The added money and all fees to be divided 60% to the winner, 20% to second, 12% to third, 6% to fourth, 2% to fifth. Weights: Tuesday, April 15. Closed Thursday, April 10 with 20 nominations. (Rail at 0 Feet).

Value of Race: $137,500 Winner $82,500; second $27,500; third $16,500; fourth $8,250; fifth $2,750. Mutuel Pool $605,517.00 Exacta Pool $359,812.00 Quinella Pool $42,690.00 Trifecta Pool $358,421.00 Superfecta Pool $122,522.00

Last Raced	Horse	M/Eqt. A.Wt	PP	St	¼	½	Str	Fin	Jockey	Odds $1
4Jan02 7SA1	Speak In Passing	LB	6 118	3	6	51½	41	4½	1½	Flores D R	2.40
23Mar03 7SA1	Spinelessjellyfish	LBb	7 115	6	4	72	72	5²½	2½	Garcia M S	6.50
21Feb03 7SA9	Rocky Bar	LB	5 116	4	3	12½	11	1hd	3¹	Stevens G L	5.20
6Mar03 7SA1	Thunder Bullet	LB	4 116	8	2	2hd	2hd	2hd	4¹	Solis A	2.00
28Mar03 7SA2	Ecstatic	LBb	4 117	7	1	3¹	3¹	3½	5no	Nakatani C S	12.10
20Mar03 5SA3	Los Solano-GB	LB	6 115	5	8	8	8	8	6¹½	Valdivia J Jr	8.50
3Apr03 7SA5	Canny Fly-AU	LB	6 114	2	7	6²	6hd	6¹	7³	Smith M E	17.90
13Sep02 10FpX5	Line Rider	LB	4 115	1	5	4½	51½	71½	8	Valenzuela P A	29.70

OFF AT 4:08 Start Good. Won driving. Course firm.
TIME :21³, :43², 1:06³, 1:12⁴ (:21.64, :43.43, 1:06.67, 1:12.87)

$2 Mutuel Prices:	3–SPEAK IN PASSING	6.80	4.00	3.40
	6–SPINELESSJELLYFISH		5.80	3.80
	4–ROCKY BAR			4.20

$1 EXACTA 3–6 PAID $20.40 $2 QUINELLA 3–6 PAID $27.40 $1 TRIFECTA
3–6–4 PAID $107.00 $1 SUPERFECTA 3–6–4–8 PAID $262.80

B. h, by Danzig–Diese, by Diesis*GB. Trainer Frankel Robert. Bred by Juddmonte Farms (Ky).

SPEAK IN PASSING stalked off the rail then outside on the hill, came four wide into the stretch, bid five wide in midstretch and gamely prevailed. SPINELESSJELLYFISH cut the corner at the right hand curve then angled in down the hill, bid along the rail in the stretch and continued willingly to the wire. ROCKY BAR quickly sprinted clear, set the pace off the rail, drifted out into the stretch, was fought back between foes in midstretch and also went on well to the end. THUNDER BULLET pulled early, cut the corner at the right hand curve then stalked three deep, continued outside a rival, came four wide into the stretch, bid between horses in midstretch and was outfinished. ECSTATIC stalked between horses then a bit off the rail down the hill, split rivals with a bid in midstretch but also was outfinished. LOS SOLANO (GB) unhurried and angled in on the hill, swung out crossing the dirt and found his best stride late. CANNY FLY (AUS) angled right early and chased outside, came four wide into the stretch and lacked the needed rally. LINE RIDER close up stalking the pace inside, dropped back some leaving the hill, came out into the stretch and weakened.

Owners— 1, Juddmonte Farms Inc; 2, Cardiff Stud Farm; 3, Triple AAA Ranch; 4, Bone Robert D; 5, The Thoroughbred Corporation; 6, Fanning Kohn & Villa Vista Stable; 7, Blackmon Fast Lane Farms & Hudnut e; 8, Lionheart Thoroughbreds Jablonski T

Trainers—1, Frankel Robert; 2, Sahadi Jenine; 3, Mullins Jeff; 4, Mullins Jeff; 5, Baffert Bob; 6, Fanning Jerry; 7, Lynch Brian A; 8, Machowsky Michael

$2 Daily Double (9–3) Paid $59.80; Daily Double Pool $48,600.
$1 Pick Three (2–9–3) Paid $123.30; Pick Three Pool $126,897.

NINTH RACE
Gulfstream
APRIL 20, 2003

$1\frac{1}{16}$ MILES. (1.40^{1}) 16th Running of THE SKIP AWAY HANDICAP. Grade III. Purse $100,000. THREE YEAR OLDS AND UPWARD. By subscription of $100 each, which shall accompany the nomination, $1,000 to pass the entry box and $1,000 additional to start, with $100,000 guaranteed. The owner of the winner to receive $60,000; $20,000 to second, $11,000 to third, $6,000 to fourth and $3,000 to fifth. Closed Wednesday, April 9 with 13 nominations.

Value of Race: $100,000 Winner $60,000; second $20,000; third $11,000; fourth $6,000; fifth $3,000. Mutuel Pool $166,250.00 Exacta Pool $107,692.00 Trifecta Pool $58,377.00 Superfecta Pool $27,535.00

Last Raced	Horse	M/Eqt.	A.Wt	PP	St	¼	½	¾	Str	Fin	Jockey	Odds $1
2Mar03 ^{9}FG^{6}	Best of the Rest	L	8 121	4	1	2^{hd}	3^{5}	3^{6}	2^{hd}	$1\frac{1}{2}$	Coa E M	1.50
8Mar03 ^{7}GP^{1}	Consistency	Lb	4 114	1	4	$3^{2\frac{1}{2}}$	$2\frac{1}{2}$	$2\frac{1}{2}$	3^{7}	$2\frac{1}{2}$	Guidry M	1.70
21Mar03 ^{9}GP^{4}	Roger E	L	4 114	3	3	$1^{3\frac{1}{2}}$	$1^{2\frac{1}{2}}$	1^{2}	1^{2}	$3^{9\frac{3}{4}}$	Velasquez C	3.90
25Jan03 ^{7}GP^{4}	The Judge Sez Who	L	4 119	5	5	5	5	4^{hd}	4^{3}	$4^{6\frac{1}{4}}$	Homeister R B Jr	4.80
21Mar03 ^{9}GP^{3}	Dancing Guy	Lbf	8 114	2	2	4^{hd}	4^{hd}	5	5	5	Ferrer J C	20.70

OFF AT 4:50 Start Good. Won driving. Track fast.
TIME :23^{3}, :46^{4}, 1:10^{4}, 1:36, 1:42^{3} (:23.77, :46.98, 1:10.96, 1:36.17, 1:42.72)

$2 Mutuel Prices:

5–BEST OF THE REST	5.00	2.60	2.20
2–CONSISTENCY		3.20	2.40
4–ROGER E			2.60

$1 EXACTA 5–2 PAID $7.00 $1 TRIFECTA 5–2–4 PAID $18.20 $1 SUPERFECTA 5–2–4–6 PAID $21.90

Gr/ro h, by Skip Trial–Obstinacy, by Valid Appeal. Trainer Plesa Edward Jr. Bred by Oxenberg Bea (Fla).

BEST OF THE REST stalked the pace, raced three wide on the far turn, then rallied under pressure to gain the lead just inside the seventy yard pole and held CONSISTENCY safe. The latter, stalked the pace off the rail into the stretch and wore down ROGER E for the place while being edged to the wire by the winner. ROGER E sprinted to a clear lead along the inside, made the pace to just past the seventy yard pole and gave way. THE JUDGE SEZ WHO failed to menace after being outrun early. DANCING GUY was not a factor.

Owners— 1, Oxenberg Beatrice; 2, Glen Hill Farm; 3, M Gill; 4, Sez Who Racing; 5, Green Newcomb
Trainers—1, Plesa Edward Jr; 2, Proctor Thomas F; 3, Shuman Mark; 4, Wolfson Milton W; 5, Green Newcomb
Scratched— Catlike Move (8Mar03 ^{7}GP^{3})

$1 Pick Three (1–10–5) Paid $253.80; Pick Three Pool $20,627.

NINTH RACE
Santa Anita
APRIL 20, 2003

ABOUT 1¾ MILES. (Turf)(2.42^{4}) 64th Running of THE SAN JUAN CAPISTRANO HANDICAP. Grade I. Purse $400,000 FOR FOUR-YEAR-OLDS AND UPWARD. By invitation, with no nomination or starting fees. The winner to receive $240,000, with $80,000 to second, $48,000 to third, $24,000 to fourth and $8,000 to fifth. Invitations and weights to be published Sunday, April 13, 2003. (Rail at 0 Feet hill & stretch).

Value of Race: $400,000 Winner $240,000; second $80,000; third $48,000; fourth $24,000; fifth $8,000. Mutuel Pool $507,262.00 Exacta Pool $234,601.00 Quinella Pool $28,837.00 Trifecta Pool $278,722.00 Superfecta Pool $131,506.00

Last Raced	Horse	M/Eqt.	A.Wt	PP	½	1	1¼	1½	Str	Fin	Jockey	Odds $1
6Apr03 ^{7}SA^{4}	Passinetti	LB	7 111	4	$4\frac{1}{2}$	$4^{1\frac{1}{2}}$	4^{1}	$5^{2\frac{1}{2}}$	3^{hd}	$1\frac{1}{2}$	Blanc B	11.10
2Mar03 ^{1}SA^{1}	All The Boys	LBf	6 115	3	$2^{1\frac{1}{2}}$	2^{3}	2^{2}	2^{2}	1^{1}	$2\frac{3}{4}$	Valenzuela P A	11.70
15Mar03 ^{7}SA^{1}	Champion Lodge-IR	LB	6 117	2	6^{1}	5^{hd}	$7\frac{1}{2}$	$3\frac{1}{2}$	4^{2}	$3\frac{3}{4}$	Solis A	1.20
2Apr03 ^{7}SA^{1}	Nazirali-IR	LB	6 116	1	9	9	9	6^{1}	$5\frac{1}{2}$	$4\frac{1}{2}$	Valdivia J Jr	4.70
23Feb03 ^{5}SA^{1}	Timber Cruiser	LB	4 111	8	1^{3}	1^{1}	1^{2}	1^{hd}	$2^{1\frac{1}{2}}$	5^{1}	Garcia M S	14.50
6Apr03 ^{7}SA^{8}	Delta Form-AU	LB	7 115	5	3^{1}	$3^{1\frac{1}{2}}$	3^{1}	4^{hd}	$6^{1\frac{1}{2}}$	6no	Almeida G F	10.90
15Mar03 ^{7}SA^{2}	Special Matter	LBb	5 113	7	5^{1}	6^{2}	5^{1}	$7^{3\frac{1}{2}}$	7^{5}	7^{13}	Baze T C	7.30
15Mar03 ^{7}SA^{3}	Adminniestrator	LB	6 116	6	$7^{1\frac{1}{2}}$	7^{1}	6^{hd}	8^{1}	8^{4}	8^{8}	Flores D R	6.70
30Mar03 ^{7}SA^{6}	Noble Kinsman	LBb	5 110	9	8^{hd}	$8\frac{1}{2}$	8^{1}	9	9	9	Martinez F F	71.80

OFF AT 4:39 Start Good. Won driving. Course firm.
TIME :48^{2}, 1:13^{1}, 1:38^{3}, 2:06, 2:27^{3}, 2:46^{4} (:48.51, 1:13.37, 1:38.64, 2:06.18, 2:27.72, 2:46.97)

$2 Mutuel Prices:

4–PASSINETTI	24.20	10.00	5.40
3–ALL THE BOYS		11.80	4.40
2–CHAMPION LODGE–IR			3.00

$1 EXACTA 4–3 PAID $104.20 $2 QUINELLA 3–4 PAID $162.00 $1 TRIFECTA 4–3–2 PAID $543.90 $1 SUPERFECTA 4–3–2–1 PAID $1,749.40

B. g, by Slew o' Gold–Cloelia, by Lyphard. Trainer Cecil B D A. Bred by Katom Ltd & Kilboy Estates (Ky).

PASSINETTI angled in and saved ground chasing the pace, went between horses on the final turn, came three deep into the stretch and rallied under urging to get up late. ALL THE BOYS pulled some while stalking the leader a bit off the rail, bid outside that one on the final turn, took the lead into the stretch, inched away but could not hold off the winner. CHAMPION LODGE (IRE) saved ground chasing the pace, came out into the stretch, split horses in midstretch and finished well. NAZIRALI (IRE) saved ground off the early pace, went between horses on the backstretch, continued a bit off the rail on the final turn, came out in the stretch and finished with some interest. TIMBER CRUISER took a clear early lead and angled in on the hill, went the opening quarter mile in :24.04, set the pace along the inside, dueled inside the runner-up on the last turn but weakened in the stretch. DELTA FORM (AUS) between horses early, chased outside a rival or a bit off the rail, went three deep leaving the final turn and four wide into the stretch and lacked the needed rally. SPECIAL MATTER chased outside a rival, split horses three deep approaching the last turn, came three wide into the stretch and also could not offer the necessary late kick. ADMINNIESTRATOR allowed to settle outside a rival, went four wide between foes into the final turn, angled in leaving that bend and weakened. NOBLE KINSMAN unhurried three deep early, went five wide into the last turn, dropped back, angled in approaching the stretch and gave way.

Owners— 1, Tanaka Gary A; 2, Jpf Investments I; 3, Charles Ronald L & Clear Valley Sta; 4, House Michael; 5, Jones Aaron U & Marie D; 6, Team Valor Stables; 7, Elder McClintock & McClintock et al; 8, Nierenberg Nico; 9, Gomez Ronald
Trainers—1, Cecil B D A; 2, Aguirre Paul G; 3, Shulman Sanford; 4, Canani Julio C; 5, Barrera Larry; 6, Sahadi Jenine; 7, Becerra Rafael; 8, Gallagher Patrick; 9, Baker D Wayne

$2 Daily Double (7–4) Paid $638.40; Daily Double Pool $27,597.
$1 Pick Three (7/8–7–4) Paid $936.60; Pick Three Pool $70,405.

EIGHTH RACE
Keeneland
APRIL 23, 2003

1½ MILES. (Turf)(2.27^{2}) 18th Running of THE ELKHORN. Grade III. Purse $150,000 Guaranteed. Four year olds and upward. By subscription of $150 each, which should accompany the nomination; $1,500 to enter and start. Weight: 123 lbs. Non-winners of $60,000 twice over ten furlongs on the turf since October 3 allowed 3 lbs.; $45,000 twice over nine furlongs on the turf since August 1, 5 lbs.; $60,000 over nine furlongs on the turf in 2003, 7 lbs. The maximum number of starters for the Elkhorn will be limited to ten with two also eligibles. In the event that more than ten pass the entry box, theten starters will be determined at that time with preference give to graded stakes winners, then highest turf earnings in 2002–2003. Closed Wednesday, April 16, 2003 with 28 nominations. Haggin Course.

Value of Race: $150,000 Winner $93,000; second $30,000; third $15,000; fourth $7,500; fifth $4,500. Mutuel Pool $378,203.00 Exacta Pool $285,662.00 Quinella Pool $15,539.00 Trifecta Pool $244,568.00 Superfecta Pool $77,073.00

Last Raced	Horse	M/Eqt.	A.Wt	PP	¼	½	1	1¼	Str	Fin	Jockey	Odds $1
6Oct02 ^{4}Kee^{6}	Kim Loves Bucky	L	6 117	7	4^{1}	4^{1}	3^{hd}	3^{2}	$2^{1\frac{1}{2}}$	$1^{\frac{1}{2}}$	Desormeaux K J	11.90
22Mar03 ^{10}GP^{2}	Man From Wicklow	Lb	6 123	9	$5^{\frac{1}{2}}$	$5^{\frac{1}{2}}$	2^{2}	$2^{1\frac{1}{2}}$	1^{1}	2no	Bailey J D	1.40
16Feb03 ^{10}GP^{9}	Williams News	L	8 116	5	$6^{\frac{1}{2}}$	$6^{1\frac{1}{2}}$	7^{1}	6^{1}	4^{hd}	$3^{1\frac{1}{4}}$	Blanc B	18.60
19Jan03 ^{10}GP^{5}	Gritty Sandie	Lbf	7 116	4	8^{hd}	8^{hd}	$9^{2\frac{1}{2}}$	8^{3}	6^{hd}	$4^{1\frac{3}{4}}$	Velasquez C	24.70
23Mar03 ^{8}FG^{5}	Mystery Giver	L	5 116	3	10	10	10	7^{hd}	7^{2}	5^{hd}	Albarado R J	7.90
16Feb03 ^{10}GP^{8}	Rochester	L	7 120	8	$7^{\frac{1}{2}}$	7^{hd}	6^{1}	4^{hd}	5^{hd}	6^{nk}	Guidry M	9.00
23Mar03 ^{8}FG^{1}	Candid Glen	L	6 116	6	$2^{\frac{1}{2}}$	2^{hd}	$4^{1\frac{1}{2}}$	5^{1}	3^{1}	$7^{6\frac{1}{2}}$	Perrodin E J	13.70
22Mar03 ^{10}GP^{1}	Quest Star	Lb	4 118	1	$1^{1\frac{1}{2}}$	$1^{1\frac{1}{2}}$	$1^{\frac{1}{2}}$	1^{hd}	8^{6}	$8^{3\frac{1}{4}}$	Prado E S	2.40
31Mar03 ^{9}FG^{3}	Full Of Wonder	Lbf	5 116	10	9^{1}	9^{3}	$8^{\frac{1}{2}}$	$9^{1\frac{1}{2}}$	9^{4}	$9^{5\frac{3}{4}}$	Lovato F Jr	26.10
5Apr03 ^{4}Kee^{5}	Muntej-GB	Lb	6 116	2	$3^{1\frac{1}{2}}$	$3^{1\frac{1}{2}}$	5^{hd}	10	10	10	Borel C H	61.40

OFF AT 4:48 Start Good. Won driving. Course firm.

TIME :25^{4}, :51^{2}, 1:16^{4}, 1:40^{4}, 2:05^{1}, 2:29^{1} (:25.97, :51.54, 1:16.94, 1:40.98, 2:05.34, 2:29.39)

$2 Mutuel Prices:

7–KIM LOVES BUCKY	25.80	8.80	6.40
9–MAN FROM WICKLOW		3.20	2.60
5–WILLIAMS NEWS			9.20

$2 EXACTA 7–9 PAID $84.20 $2 QUINELLA 7–9 PAID $41.00 $2 TRIFECTA 7–9–5 PAID $1,445.80 $2 SUPERFECTA 7–9–5–4 PAID $13,873.00

B. g, by Green Dancer–Moondust Mink, by Great Above. Trainer Glenney John. Bred by Dr & Mrs John Glenney (Ky).

KIM LOVES BUCKY, in hand from early on while tracking the leaders three or four wide, advanced from that position on the course approaching the stretch, then closed determinedly under stout left-handed urging to wear down MAN FROM WICKLOW. The latter, never far back four wide, moved after front-running QUEST STAR after five furlongs, reached the front in the upper stretch, briefly was clear but couldn't contain the winner's surge. WILLIAMS NEWS, in contention from the outset while racing in behind horses, saved ground until the final quarter, eased out six wide for the drive and was going well at the end. GRITTY SANDIE settled near the inside early, reached contention approaching the stretch as the field tightened, came out seven or eight wide for the drive and offered a minor gain. MYSTERY GIVER angled near the inside early, was unhurried, circled foes nine wide into the stretch but couldn't offer a serious threat. ROCHESTER, rated along five wide early, made a bid from that position concluding the final turn, then flattened out the last eighth. CANDID GLEN tracked the pace four wide from early on, dropped back a bit after seven furlong, continued within easy striking distance while between rivals into the final furlong and faltered. QUEST STAR gained the lead near the inside early, made the pace until the stretch and tired. FULL OF WONDER, five or six wide, never threatened. MUNTEJ (GB), rated near the inside early, was finished after a mile.

Owners— 1, Glenney Kim; 2, Violette Richard A Jr; 3, On Target Racing Stable; 4, Kimmel Caesar P & Nicholson Ronald; 5, Team Block; 6, Augustin Stable; 7, Warren Glen C; 8, Mansell Stables; 9, Sam-Son Farms; 10, McLaughlin David et al

Trainers—1, Glenney John; 2, Violette Richard A Jr; 3, Stall Albert M Jr; 4, Toner James J; 5, Block Chris M; 6, Sheppard Jonathan E; 7, Leggio Andrew Jr; 8, Walden W Elliott; 9, Frostad Mark; 10, Attfield Roger L

Scratched— Macaw (22Mar03 ^{10}GP^{5}), Dr. Brendler (5Apr03 ^{4}KEE^{1})

$2 Pick Three (6–7/8–7) Paid $243.20; Pick Three Pool $32,435.
$1 Pick Six (1/4–8–4–6–7/8–7) 5
Correct Paid $372.20; Pick Six Pool $7,353; Carryover Pool $11,517.

EIGHTH RACE

Keeneland

APRIL 24, 2003

1½ MILES. (Turf)(2.27²) 42nd Running of THE BEWITCH. Grade III. Purse $100,000 Added. Fillies and mares four years old and upward. By subscription of $100 each, which should accompany the nomination; $1,000 to enter and start with $100,000 added, of which 62% to the owner of the winner, 20% to second, 10%, to third, 5%, to fourth and 3% to fifth. Weight: 123 lbs. Non–winners of $60,000 twice over nine furlongs on the turf since October 3 allowed 3 lbs.; $45,000 twice over nine furlongs on the turf since August 1, 5 lbs.; $45,000 over nine furlongs on the turf in 2003, 7 lbs. Starters to be named through the entry box by the usual time of closing. A gold julep cup will be presented to the owner of the winner. Closed Wednesday, April 16, 2003 with 21 nominations. HAGGIN COURSE.

Value of Race: $112,100 Winner $69,503; second $22,420; third $11,210; fourth $5,605; fifth $1,681 each. Mutuel Pool $430,690.00 Exacta Pool $290,748.00 Quinella Pool $13,670.00 Trifecta Pool $249,997.00 Superfecta Pool $89,159.00

Last Raced	Horse	M/Eqt.	A.Wt	PP	¼	½	1	1¼	Str	Fin	Jockey	Odds $1
6Apr03 4Kee1	Lilac Queen-GE	L	5 116	7	6hd	71½	61½	2hd	12	14	Bailey J D	0.70
12Feb03 9GP2	Beyond The Waves	L	6 116	5	5½	6½	71½	61	3hd	2hd	Day P	24.00
23Mar03 8GP2	San Dare	L	5 118	2	81	9½	10	10	8½	3hd	Guidry M	3.50
22Mar03 9SA5	Dancing-GB	L	4 116	4	32	4½	5½	71½	4½	4hd	Farina Tony	39.40
8Feb03 8GP7	DH New Economy	L	5 116	3	10	10	92	8½	6hd	5	Albarado R J	8.30
5Mar03 8GP1	DH Something Ventured	Lb	4 116	6	22½	2½	31½	1hd	21½	51	Velasquez C	33.20
22Mar03 9SA8	Splendeur-FR	L	4 116	10	72	51	4hd	41	51	72½	Blanc B	58.70
16Nov02 8Aqu2	Sunstone-GB	Lb	5 116	8	93	8hd	8hd	92	97	81½	Bridgmohan S X	11.50
23Mar03 8GP3	Hi Tech Honeycomb	Lb	4 116	9	1½	11	1hd	31	7hd	910¼	Sellers S J	23.00
18Apr03 7Kee2	Daisyago	L	4 116	1	4hd	3hd	2hd	51	10	10	Desormeaux K J	17.50

DH—Dead Heat.

OFF AT 4:47 Start Good. Won driving. Course firm.

TIME :25¹, :50², 1:15³, 1:41, 2:05³, 2:29³ (:25.30, :50.53, 1:15.60, 1:41.06, 2:05.76, 2:29.70)

$2 Mutuel Prices:

7–LILAC QUEEN–GE	3.40	2.60	2.20
5–BEYOND THE WAVES		10.00	4.20
2–SAN DARE			2.60

$2 EXACTA 7–5 PAID $50.80 $2 QUINELLA 5–7 PAID $29.60 $2 TRIFECTA 7–5–2 PAID $140.20 $2 SUPERFECTA 7–5–2–4 PAID $1,805.40

Dk. b. or br. m, by Law Society–Lilac Dance*GB, by Fabulous Dancer. Trainer Frankel Robert. Bred by Gestut Zoppenbroich (Ger).

LILAC QUEEN (GER), between horses early while unhurried, moved up four or five wide while continuing under wraps approaching the final turn, commenced a sweeping five wide run nearing the stretch, took over when straightened for the drive, moved clear at the furlong grounds, then widened a bit thereafter under hand urging. BEYOND THE WAVES, never far back while racing in behind rivals three wide, followed the winner from the outside six abreast into the stretch and outgamed SAN DARE for second while unable to menace LILAC QUEEN (GER). SAN DARE, eased back near the inside early, moved out five or six wide on the backstretch, circled nine or 10 wide into the stretch and was slowly gaining late. DANCING (GB), forwardly placed from early on while near the inside between rivals, angled to the rail for the drive, loomed a solid threat but failed to respond. NEW ECONOMY, reserved near the inside soon after the start, saved ground while edging closer on the final turn, came out between rivals five or six wide for the drive and failed to offer a late response while dead heating for fifth with SOMETHING VENTURED. The latter stalked front-running HI TECH HONEYMOON from early on, challenged just before going a mile, gained a slim, brief lead a quarter-mile out, then weakened in the drive to finish on even terms with NEW ECONOMY. SPLENDEUR (FR) settled in a striking position four or five wide, continued in contention to the stretch and flattened out. SUNSTONE (GB), reluctant to load into the gate, raced three or four wide while unable to outrun early, reached contention a quarter-mile out, came out nine wide for the drive and failed to offer a late response. HI TECH HONEYCOMB gained the lead early, maneuvered near the inside, made the pace for nearly 10 furlongs while dueling much of the way and faltered. DAISYAGO, well placed under light rating from early on, made a solid bid from the rail upon going a mile but wea kened approaching the stretch.

Owners— 1, Tanaka Gary A; 2, Augustin Stable; 3, Mounts David G; 4, Baker Howard J; 5, Evans Robert J; 6, John McLane & Irwin Weimer; 7, Fisher Derrick; 8, Georgica Stable Peter Minikes; 9, Select Stable; 10, Glenney John & Kim

Trainers— 1, Frankel Robert; 2, Sheppard Jonathan E; 3, Hiles Rick; 4, Wigginton Jesse N; 5, Motion H Graham; 6, Pletcher Todd A; 7, Jory Ian P D; 8, Barbara Robert; 9, McPeek Kenneth G; 10, Glenney John

$2 Pick Three (4–1–7) Paid $128.00; Pick Three Pool $31,066. $1 Pick Six (5–2–4–4–1–7) 5 Correct Paid $90.20; Pick Six Pool $20,945. $1 Pick Six (5–2–4–4–1–7) 6 Correct Paid $24,241.60

THIRD RACE
Hollywood
APRIL 25, 2003

$1\frac{1}{16}$ MILES. (1.40) 30th Running of THE HAWTHORNE HANDICAP. Grade III. Purse $100,000 Added. FILLIES AND MARES THREE-YEARS-OLD AND UPWARD. By subscription of $100 each on or before Wednesday, April 16. $1,000 additional to start, with $100,000 added. The added money and all fees to be divided 60% to the winner, 20% to second, 12% to third, 6% to fourth and 2% to fifth. Nominations closed Wednesday April 16 with 14.

Value of Race: $103,292 Winner $63,240; second $21,080; third $12,648; fourth $6,324. Mutuel Pool $171,367.00 Exacta Pool $99,305.00 Quinella Pool $10,268.00 Trifecta Pool $46,531.00

Last Raced	Horse	M/Eqt.	A.Wt	PP	St	¼	½	¾	Str	Fin	Jockey	Odds $1
5Apr03 6BM8	Keys To The Heart	LB	4 115	3	1	21	22	1hd	12	1½	Valdivia J Jr	17.50
5Apr03 8OP5	Rhiana	LB	6 116	1	4	4	4	3hd	3hd	2hd	Flores D R	2.40
30Mar03 8SA4	[D]Se Me Acabo-CH	LBb	5 112	4	3	11	1hd	21½	21	33½	Martinez F F	4.10
30Mar03 8SA2	Alexine-ARG	LB	7 117	2	2	31	3hd	4	4	4	Nakatani C S	0.50

[D]-Se Me Acabo-CH disqualified and placed 4th.

OFF AT 8:02 Start Good. Won driving. Track fast.
TIME :24[1], :48[1], 1:12, 1:36[2], 1:42[4] (:24.32, :48.28, 1:12.08, 1:36.50, 1:42.97)

$2 Mutuel Prices:

5-KEYS TO THE HEART	37.00	12.60	—
1-RHIANA		6.00	—
4-ALEXINE-ARG		—	—

$1 EXACTA 5-1 PAID $57.60 $2 QUINELLA 1-5 PAID $33.00 $1 TRIFECTA 5-1-4 PAID $72.10

Dk. b. or br. f, by Wild Again-Gold Shadow, by Mr. Prospector. Trainer Greely C Beau. Bred by Thomas L Nichols (Ky).

KEYS TO THE HEART angled in on the first turn then came out into the backstretch, prompted the pace outside a rival, took a short lead on the second turn, kicked clear in the stretch and held on gamely between foes late under urging. RHIANA came off the rail on the first turn, stalked outside a rival, angled out into the stretch and closed gamely three deep on the line. SE ME ACABO (CHI) had speed outside then angled in on the first turn, dueled inside, came out in midstretch, angled back to the inside in deep stretch and re-bid along the rail. ALEXINE (ARG) angled in and saved ground stalking the pace, inched forward past midstretch but steadied sharply off heels and could not recover. Following a stewards' inquiry, SE ME ACABO was disqualified and placed fourth for interference in deep stretch.

Owners— 1, Nichols Thomas L; 2, Ernst Allegra & John; 3, Zarour Marcel; 4, Hubbard R D Masterson Robert Rio Cl
Trainers—1, Greely C Beau; 2, Hendricks Dan L; 3, Inda Eduardo; 4, Mandella Richard
Scratched— Styler (30Mar03 1SA1), Meguial (30Mar03 8SA7)

$2 Daily Double (5-5) Paid $225.80; Daily Double Pool $14,855.
$1 Pick Three (2-5-5) Paid $1,071.40; Pick Three Pool $95,304.

NINTH RACE
Keeneland
APRIL 25, 2003

1⅛ MILES. (1.46[4]) 73rd Running of THE BEN ALI. Grade III. Purse $100,000 Added. Four year olds and upward. By subscription of $100 each, which should accompany the nomination; $1,000 to enter and start. Weight: 123 lbs. Non-winners of $60,000 twice over a mile since September 1 allowed 3 lbs.; $60,000 over a mile in 2003, 5 lbs.; $45,000 twice over a mile since September 1, 7 lbs. A gold julep cup will be presented to the owner of the winner. Closed Wednesday, April 16, 2003 with 23 nominations.

Value of Race: $106,991 Winner $68,386; second $22,060; third $11,030; fourth $5,515. Mutuel Pool $254,968.00 Exacta Pool $328,029.00 Trifecta Pool $130,178.00

Last Raced	Horse	M/Eqt.	A.Wt	PP	St	¼	½	¾	Str	Fin	Jockey	Odds $1
2Mar03 9FG1	Mineshaft	L	4 120	1	2	36	37	21	12½	19	Albarado R J	0.30
6Apr03 7Kee4	American Style	L	4 116	2	1	21½	22	33½	33	21¼	Bailey J D	3.90
15Mar03 6GG1	Metatron	Lf	4 116	3	3	11	11	1hd	2hd	31¾	Desormeaux K J	8.20
11Apr03 9Kee5	X Country	Lb	5 116	4	4	4	4	4	4	4	Zuniga J E	7.90

OFF AT 5:20 Start Good. Won driving. Track fast.
TIME :24, :47[4], 1:12, 1:36[2], 1:48[2] (:24.04, :47.99, 1:12.07, 1:36.50, 1:48.52)

$2 Mutuel Prices:

2-MINESHAFT	2.60	—	—
3-AMERICAN STYLE		—	—
5-METATRON		—	—

$2 EXACTA 2-3 PAID $5.60 $2 TRIFECTA 2-3-5 PAID $11.20

Dk. b. or br. c, by A.P. Indy-Prospectors Delite, by Mr. Prospector. Trainer Howard Neil J. Bred by W. S. Farish, James Elkins & W. T. Webber Jr. (Ky).

MINESHAFT, lightly bumped at the start by AMERICAN STYLE, was taken in hand and positioned near the inside, eased out four wide while continuing under rating on the backstretch, moved steadily four abreast to challenge upon going six furlongs, reached the front a quarter-mile out, edged clear soon after, then won going away under hand urging as much the best. AMERICAN STYLE leaned in at the break bumping lightly with the winner, went up soon after to press front-running METATRON three or four wide, continued forwardly to the stretch, angled outside of MINESHAFT for the drive but couldn't menace as second best. METATRON moved to the front early, made the pace from the three path, was joined by the winner from the outside upon going six furlongs, held on well until the stretch and tired. X COUNTRY angled inside soon after the start, saved ground to the stretch, swung out five or six wide for the drive but was empty.

Owners— 1, Farish William S Elkins James A & W; 2, Buckram Oak Farm; 3, Coyote Creek Stable Marie & Brian B; 4, Maier George E
Trainers—1, Howard Neil J; 2, Zito Nicholas P; 3, Hollendorfer Jerry; 4, Fuchs Jack
Scratched— Malmaison (13Feb03 9GP7), Crafty Shaw (5Apr03 11OP4), Horrible Evening (15Mar03 10TP4), El Gran Papa (6Apr03 7KEE2)

$2 Daily Double (1-2) Paid $12.40; Daily Double Pool $30,972.
$2 Pick Three (1-1-1/2/4/7/8) Paid $223.20; Pick Three Pool $47,379.
$1 Pick Four (2-1-1-1/2/4/7/8) Paid $1,323.30; Pick Four Pool $43,983.

EIGHTH RACE
Aqueduct
APRIL 26, 2003

1 MILE. (1.32²) 27th Running of THE FORT MARCY HANDICAP. Purse $100,000. (Up to $19,400 NYSBFOA). THREE YEAR OLDS AND UPWARD. By subscription of $100 each, which should accompany the nomination; $500 to pass the entry box; $500 to start, with $100,000 added. The added money and all fees to be divided 60% to the winner, 20% to second, 11% to third, 6% to fourth and 3% to fifth. Trophies will be presented to the winning owner, trainer and jockey. The New York Racing Association reserves the right to transfer this race to the Main Track. In the event that this race is taken off the turf, it may be subject to downgrading upon review by the Graded Stakes Committee. Closed Saturday, April 12, 2003 with 50 Nominations. (ORIGINALLY SCHEDULED FOR TURF AT ONE MILE AND ONE SIXTEENTH).

Value of Race: $117,500 Winner $70,500; second $23,500; third $12,925; fourth $7,050; fifth $3,525. Mutuel Pool $371,270.00 Exacta Pool $263,810.00 Trifecta Pool $152,672.00

Last Raced	Horse	M/Eqt.	A.Wt	PP	St	¼	½	¾	Str	Fin	Jockey	Odds $1
5Apr03 ^{8}Aqu^{5}	Saint Verre	L	5 117	1	4	$1^{\frac12}$	1^{1}	1^{5}	1^{8}	$1^{8\frac12}$	Espinoza J L	6.40
29Mar03 ^{11}GP^{8}	Windsor Castle	L	5 119	5	3	$4^{\frac12}$	5^{3}	2^{hd}	$2^{2\frac12}$	2^{1}	Coa E M	7.50
26Mar03 ^{5}Aqu^{2}	Judge's Case	Lb	6 115	8	2	$6^{1\frac12}$	$6^{\frac12}$	$7^{3\frac12}$	4^{hd}	$3^{1\frac34}$	Luzzi M J	f-12.60
29Mar03 ^{11}GP^{3}	Puzzlement	Lb	4 118	2	8	8	7^{2}	$5^{\frac12}$	6^{hd}	4^{2}	Arroyo N Jr	2.60
24Mar03 ^{9}FG^{6}	Devine Wind	Lf	7 112	3	6	$5^{1\frac12}$	4^{hd}	6^{1}	5^{hd}	$5^{\frac34}$	Castellano J J	34.50
10Mar03 ^{7}GP^{1}	Global Quest	Lb	4 113	4	7	$7^{3\frac12}$	8	8	8	$6^{\frac34}$	Velazquez J R	6.50
6Apr03 ^{8}Aqu^{1}	Onthedeanslist	L	4 117	7	1	2^{1}	$2^{\frac12}$	3^{hd}	3^{hd}	7^{nk}	Gryder A T	9.60
5Apr03 ^{8}Aqu^{1}	Classic Endeavor	Lf	5 118	6	5	$3^{\frac12}$	$3^{1\frac12}$	$4^{\frac12}$	$7^{2\frac12}$	8	Prado E S	2.25

f-Mutuel Field: Judge's Case.

OFF AT 4:21 Start Good. Won driving. Track sloppy.
TIME :23^{1}, :46, 1:09^{4}, 1:33^{3} (:23.34, :46.17, 1:09.96, 1:33.77)

$2 Mutuel Prices:				
	5-SAINT VERRE	14.80	7.60	5.50
	13-WINDSOR CASTLE		8.50	6.00
	17-JUDGE'S CASE (f-field)			4.80

$2 EXACTA 5-13 PAID $86.50 $2 TRIFECTA 5-13-17 PAID $786.00

B. h, by Saint Ballado-Margot Verre, by Tom Rolfe. Trainer Jerkens H Allen. Bred by Georgelina Gonzalez (Fla).

SAINT VERRE quickly showed in front, set the pace while in hand, drew away turning for home and was kept to a drive to the wire. WINDSOR CASTLE raced close up early, advanced inside on the turn and rallied to earn the place prize. JUDGE'S CASE was unhurried early on, raced inside and lacked a rally. PUZZLEMENT was outrun early, raced five wide and had no response when roused. DEVINE WIND chased the pace along the inside and tired in the stretch. GLOBAL QUEST was outrun early, came wide into the stretch and had no rally. ONTHEDEANSLIST chased the pace for three quarters and tired. CLASSIC ENDEAVOR was hustled along o''tside, chased the pace while four wide and tired in the stretch.

Owners— 1, Allen Joseph; 2, Do vood Stable; 3, Goldfarb Sanford & Team Julep Stabl; 4, Shields Joseph V Jr; 5, Englander Richard A; 6, Acquavalla William & Phipps Ogo n M; 7, Team Valor Stables; 8, Schwartz Herbert T & Carol A

Trainers—1, Jerkens H Allen; 2, ‚lexander Frank A; 3, Klesaris Steve; 4, Jerkens H Allen; 5, Hansen Scott; 6, McGaughey Claude III; 7, Terranova John P II; 8, Schwartz Scott M

Scratched— Run To Victory (23Mar03 ^{8}FG^{7}), Bowman's Band (11Apr03 ^{9}KEE^{3}), Shaanmer (22Sep02 LCH^{2}), Regal Sanction (27Mar03 ^{7}AQU^{1}), Haggs Castle (28Dec02 ^{9}AQU^{4}), Patrol (22Mar03 ^{8}GP^{1}), Statement (11Apr03 ^{8}KEE^{5}), Irish Colonial (12Oct02 ^{9}BEL^{2}), Union Place (2Mar03 ^{8}GP^{1})

SEVENTH RACE
Bay Meadows
APRIL 26, 2003

1 MILE. (Turf)(1.34³) 54th Running of THE SAN FRANCISCO BREEDERS' CUP MILE HANDICAP. Grade II. Purse $200,000 Guaranteed (includes $50,000 BC - Breeders' Cup) THREE-YEAR-OLDS AND UPWARD. (Includes $50,000 from Breeders' Cup Fund for Cup nominees only). By subscription of $150 each to accompany the nomination or by supplementary nomination of $3,000 by Noon Sunday, April 20, 2003. $750 to pass the entry box and $750 additional to start with$150,000 Guaranteed and an additional $50,000 from Breeders' Cup Fund for Breeders' Cup eligibles only. Closed Thursday, April 17, 2003 with 16 nominations.(If deemed inadvisable by management to run this race on the turf course, it will be run on the main track at One Mile) Rail at 25 feet.

Value of Race: $177,500 Winner $110,000; second $30,000; third $22,500; fourth $11,250; fifth $3,750. Mutuel Pool $239,505.00 Exacta Pool $144,933.00 Quinella Pool $14,929.00 Trifecta Pool $168,789.00 Superfecta Pool $58,196.00

Last Raced	Horse	M/Eqt.	A.Wt	PP	St	¼	½	¾	Str	Fin	Jockey	Odds $1
16Mar03 ^{3}GG^{1}	Ninebanks	LBb	5 117	3	5	$3^{1\frac12}$	3^{2}	$2^{\frac12}$	1^{1}	1no	Warren R J Jr	4.60
30Nov02 ^{8}Hol^{5}	Nicobar-GB	LB	6 116	2	3	$6^{1\frac12}$	6^{1}	5^{hd}	4^{1}	2^{1}	Alvarado F T	7.20
20Jan03 ^{8}SA^{5}	National Anthem-GB	LB	7 116	5	8	8	8	7^{hd}	$5^{\frac12}$	3^{1}	Lopez A D	33.00
27May02 ^{8}Hol^{1}	Ladies Din	LBb	8 120	1	4	7^{2}	7^{2}	6^{3}	$3^{\frac12}$	4^{nk}	Baze R A	0.70
6Apr03 ^{8}BM^{1}	Bit Of Luck-GB	LB	4 116	6	1	2^{2}	2^{1}	3^{1}	$2^{\frac12}$	5^{2}	Rollins C J	9.30
16Mar03 ^{3}GG^{2}	Surprise Halo	LB	5 116	8	7	5^{1}	$5^{1\frac12}$	$4^{\frac12}$	$6^{1\frac12}$	6^{1}	Castro J M	15.60
6Apr03 ^{8}BM^{2}	Wolfwithintegrity	LBb	6 114	7	6	$4^{\frac12}$	4^{hd}	8	7^{hd}	7^{8}	Schvaneveldt C P	23.20
29Mar03 ^{7}GG^{1}	I'madrifter	LB	5 115	4	2	$1^{1\frac12}$	1^{2}	1^{hd}	8	8	Gonzalez R M	9.00

OFF AT 4:23 Start Good. Won driving. Course yielding.
TIME :23^{2}, :47^{3}, 1:12^{1}, 1:24^{3}, 1:37^{1} (:23.52, :47.64, 1:12.20, 1:24.66, 1:37.20)

$2 Mutuel Prices:				
	3-NINEBANKS	11.20	5.00	4.40
	2-NICOBAR-GB		7.20	5.00
	5-NATIONAL ANTHEM-GB			8.20

$1 EXACTA 3-2 PAID $30.90 $2 QUINELLA 2-3 PAID $31.40 $1 TRIFECTA 3-2-5 PAID $371.10 $1 SUPERFECTA 3-2-5-1 PAID $1,935.50

B. g, by Smokester-Nataka, by With Approval. Trainer Hollendorfer Jerry. Bred by Trudy McCaffery & John Toffan (Cal).

NINEBANKS broke cleanly and tracked the pace from the rail from the outset, waited patiently on the second turn then got through inside I'MADRIFTER to gain command in the upper stretch while coming off the rail, responded gamely and held off NICOBAR in the finals strides. NICOBAR (GB) raced unhurried early but always within striking distance, saved ground on the second turn and followed the winner into the stretch, got up inside that rival in mid stretch to challenge for command but could not get by. NATIONAL ANTHEM (GB) was permitted to lag to the second turn then offered a steady rally from the inside and was gaining at the wire. LADIES DIN was not asked for speed early while just off the rail, eased to the outside for the second turn, offered a menacing bid while circling rivals five wide to the stretch, loomed a bold factor in mid stretch but flattened out late. BIT OF LUCK (GB) prompted the pace from the outset, offered his best bid three wide at the quarter pole and slackened in the lane. SURPRISE HALO was permitted to settle early while three wide, was fanned four wide and between horses on the second turn while offering his bid then lost much of his punch in the final furlong. WOLFWITHINTEGRITY was well placed early from off the rail but failed to respond in the lane. I'MADRIFTER set the pace from off the rail for six furlongs and gave out.

Owners— 1, Abruzzo Peter; 2, Zetcher Arnold; 3, R L Duchossios; 4, Lanni J Terrence & Schiappa Bernard; 5, Wilson David W & Holly F; 6, Karp Lawrence M & Ward Dennis; 7, E A Ranches; 8, O'Neill Daniel

Trainers—1, Hollendorfer Jerry; 2, McAnally Ronald; 3, McAnally Ronald; 4, Monteleone Frank J; 5, Cerin Vladimir; 6, Ward Wesley A; 7, Vienna Darrell; 8, Specht Steve

---

$2 Daily Double (4-3) Paid $45.00; Daily Double Pool $12,460.
$1 Pick Three (4-4-3) Paid $224.80; Pick Three Pool $31,264.

NINTH RACE
Churchill
APRIL 26, 2003

1 MILE. (1.33^{2}) 79th Running of THE DERBY TRIAL. Grade III. Purse $150,000 FOR THREE-YEAR-OLDS. By subscription of $150 each on or before April 12, 2003 or by Supplementary Nomination of $7,500 at the time of entry. $750 to pass the entry box; $750 additional to start, with $150,000 added of which 62% of all monies to the owner of the winner, 20% to second, 10% to third, 5% to fourth and 3% to fifth. Weight 122 lbs. Non-winners of $50,000 allowed 2 lbs.; three races other than maiden or claiming, 4 lbs.; two races other than maiden or claiming, 6 lbs.; a race other than maiden or claiming, 8 lbs. Starters to be named through the entry box at the usual time of closing. All supplementary nominations will be required to pay entry and starting fees if they participate. Trophy to winning owner.

Value of Race: $167,400 Winner $103,788; second $33,480; third $16,740; fourth $8,370; fifth $5,022. Mutuel Pool $1,367,897.0 Exacta Pool $418,484.00 Trifecta Pool $335,151.00 Superfecta Pool $114,127.00

Last Raced	Horse	M/Eqt.	A.	Wt	PP	St	¼	½	¾	Str	Fin	Jockey	Odds $1
15Mar03 11GP1	Midas Eyes	L	3	122	3	5	1hd	11½	12½	12½	12½	Bailey J D	0.30
22Mar03 10TP3	Champali	L	3	122	5	3	21	31½	2½	25½	213¼	Day P	2.80
12Apr03 8Kee1	Desert Warrior	Lb	3	118	1	1	4hd	21½	31	43½	3nk	Velasquez C	11.30
27Mar03 8TP1	Miner Moss	Lb	3	118	2	6	6	6	6	51	41	Zuniga J E	73.00
22Mar03 9TP1	Private Gold	Lb	3	122	4	2	52	4hd	43½	3½	53	Sellers S J	15.50
5Apr03 10OP1	Unbridled America	L	3	116	6	4	3hd	5hd	51½	6	6	Albarado R J	20.60

OFF AT 4:47 Start Good. Won driving. Track fast.
TIME :22^{4}, :46, 1:10^{4}, 1:23^{1}, 1:36^{1} (:22.85, :46.10, 1:10.98, 1:23.29, 1:36.22)

$2 Mutuel Prices:

3–MIDAS EYES	2.60	2.10	2.10
5–CHAMPALI		2.10	2.10
1–DESERT WARRIOR			2.10

$2 EXACTA 3-5 PAID $4.40 $2 TRIFECTA 3-5-1 PAID $15.40 $1 SUPERFECTA 3-5-1-2 PAID $45.00

B. c, (Apr), by Touch Gold-Bayou Plans, by Bayou Hebert. Trainer Frankel Robert. Bred by Jacks or Better Farm Inc (Fla).

MIDAS EYES drifted in at the start bumping with MINER MOSS, gained a slight lead while racing inside of CHAMPALI under light restraint, edged clear soon after the opening quarter, was put to energetic hand urging entering the upper stretch, received one slap of the whip on the right side soon after, then continued under hand encouragement the remainder. CHAMPALI, in a bit tight after the start when lightly bumped from both sides, went up soon after four wide to track MIDAS EYES, raced within easy striking distance while outside that one into the stretch, couldn't produce the needed response but was superior to the others. DESERT WARRIOR came out at the start bumping MINER MOSS, settled behind horses, moved up between foes soon after the opening quarter, remained prominent into the stretch but flattened out in the drive. MINER MOSS, bumped from both sides after the start, settled inside, saved ground to the stretch, came out four wide for the drive, improved position but couldn't menace. PRIVATE GOLD came out at the break lightly bumping with CHAMPALI, raced in behind the leaders three or four wide on the backstretch, angled near the inside on the turn, continued in that manner the remainder but was empty. UNBRIDLED AMERICA leaned in bumping CHAMPALI at the start, followed the leaders within striking distance to the stretch and tired.

Owners— 1, Gann Edmund A; 2, Lloyd Madison Farms IV; 3, Overbrook Farm; 4, Brown Tim & Hickman Kenneth G; 5, Mountain Top Racing & Bob & Beverly; 6, Estate of Dan Jones

Trainers—1, Frankel Robert; 2, Foley Gregory D; 3, Lukas D Wayne; 4, Hickman Kenneth G; 5, Byrne Patrick B; 6, Holthus Robert E

$1 Pick Three (2-10-3) Paid $35.70; Pick Three Pool $66,396.

EIGHTH RACE
Hawthorne
APRIL 26, 2003

1⅛ MILES. (1.46^{3}) 28th Running of THE SIXTY SAILS HANDICAP. Grade III. Purse $250,000 Guaranteed. FILLIES AND MARES, THREE-YEARS-OLD AND UPWARD. By subscription of $100 each, which shall accompany the nomination, $1,500 to pass the entry box, $1,500 additional to start. Nominations closed Wednesday, April 26, 2003 with 22.

Value of Race: $250,000 Winner $150,000; second $50,000; third $27,500; fourth $15,000; fifth $7,500. Mutuel Pool $254,225.00 Exacta Pool $191,484.00 Trifecta Pool $184,121.00 Superfecta Pool $64,279.00

Last Raced	Horse	M/Eqt.	A.	Wt	PP	St	¼	½	¾	Str	Fin	Jockey	Odds $1
30Mar03 8SA1	Bare Necessities	L	4	118	2	3	31	4hd	31	1½	12½	Douglas R R	0.60
4Apr03 7Kee1	Jaramar Rain	L	4	114	5	1	11½	11	1½	2hd	2nk	Decarlo C P	29.30
29Mar03 6Haw3	Lakenheath	L	5	114	7	2	2hd	31½	2½	32	34¾	Emigh C A	17.50
23Mar03 9Aqu2	Ellie's Moment	Lb	5	115	6	6	62½	5hd	53	43	45	Bridgmohan S X	2.30
6Apr03 10OP1	Mckinney	L	5	115	4	8	7hd	8½	6½	64	53¼	Marquez C H Jr	10.00
29Mar03 6Haw1	Curious Conundrum	Lb	5	116	3	4	4hd	2½	4hd	51	63¾	Razo E Jr	13.00
4Apr03 8GP2	Lead Story	L	4	113	1	7	8½	71	7hd	73	72½	Vitek J J	31.70
29Mar03 6Haw2	Barney's Mistress	Lbf	5	115	8	9	9	9	9	87	824	Silva C H	76.40
10Mar03 8GP7	Katy Kat	L	5	117	9	5	5½	62	8½	9	9	Sibille R	44.70

OFF AT 4:35 Start Good. Won driving. Track fast.
TIME :24^{2}, :49, 1:14, 1:39^{3}, 1:52^{4} (:24.52, :49.16, 1:14.18, 1:39.76, 1:52.84)

$2 Mutuel Prices:

2–BARE NECESSITIES	3.20	2.80	2.40
5–JARAMAR RAIN		12.20	8.00
7–LAKENHEATH			6.20

$2 EXACTA 2-5 PAID $55.00 $2 TRIFECTA 2-5-7 PAID $411.40 $2 SUPERFECTA 2-5-7-6 PAID $1,320.80

Gr/ro f, by Silver Deputy-Shrewd Vixen, by Spectacular Bid. Trainer Dollase Wallace. Bred by Iron County Farms Inc (Ky).

BARE NECESSITIES was allowed to settle close up along the rail, got through inside turning for home, took the lead in the stretch and drew off while kept to her task. JARAMAR RAIN sprinted to a clear lead and dropped to the inside, set the balance of the pace, came out just a bit entering the stretch then could not match strides with the winner through the lane. LAKENHEATH raced in good position just off the rail, remained close up to the stretch then drifted out badly and lacked a winning bid. ELLIE'S MOMENT raced off the rail near the middle of the field and made a run to contention in the stretch but flattened out late. MCKINNEY was void of early speed then improved her position without threatening. CURIOUS CONUNDRUM raced close up just outside but tired in the drive. LEAD STORY lacked speed and was never a factor. BARNEY'S MISTRESS was always outrun. KATY KAT dropped back steadily.

Owners— 1, Iron County Farms Inc; 2, Humphrey G W Jr; 3, James B Tafel; 4, Phillips Joan G & John W; 5, Hunt Nelson B; 6, My Jo Lee Stable II; 7, A Stevens Miles Jr; 8, Abt Martin Derybowski Greg & Hat Tr; 9, Moore Donna Saylor Paul & Voss Gene

Trainers—1, Dollase Wallace; 2, Arnold George R II; 3, Cilio Gene A; 4, Toner James J; 5, Asmussen Steven M; 6, Brajczewski Eugene F; 7, Nafzger Carl A; 8, Poulos Dee; 9, O'Callaghan Niall M

$2 Pick Three (1-4-2) Paid $308.40; Pick Three Pool $5,964. $2 Pick Six (1-4-2-1-4-2) 4 Correct Paid $52.60; Pick Six Pool $1,124; Carryover Pool $632.

NINTH RACE

Lone Star

APRIL 26, 2003

1 MILE. (1.34²) 7th Running of THE TEXAS MILE. Grade III. Purse $300,000 (Plus Up To $7,500 From ATBOIA) FOR THREE YEARS OLD AND UPWARD. No nomination fee. $2,250 to pass the entry box and an additional $2,250 to start. If less than 10 horses start, the purse money not distributed will revert to the winning owner. Weights: Three Year Olds, 114 lbs. Older, 123 lbs. Non–winners of $90,000 at a mile or over in 2003 allowed 3 lbs.; $60,000 since November 1, 2002, 5 lbs.; $30,000 in 2003, 7 lbs.; $30,000 in 2002–2003, 10 lbs. Maiden and Claiming races not considered in weight allowances. Total earnings in 2002–2003 will be used in determining the order of preference of horses assigned equal weights. The field will be limited to twelve starters. NOMINATIONS CLOSE WEDNESDAY, APRIL 16, 2003.

Value of Race: $300,000 Winner $170,000; second $55,000; third $30,250; fourth $16,500; fifth $8,250; sixth $5,000; seventh $5,000; eighth $5,000; ninth $5,000. Mutuel Pool $323,312.00 Exacta Pool $201,869.00 Quinella Pool $14,934.00 Trifecta Pool $197,076.00 Superfecta Pool $72,665.00

Last Raced	Horse	M/Eqt.	A.Wt	PP	St	¼	½	¾	Str	Fin	Jockey	Odds $1
29Mar03 ⁸SA¹	Bluesthestandard	L	6 120	9	3	2²	2½	2¹	1²	1⁴	Pedroza M A	1.50
16Mar03 ⁹FG³	Bonapaw	Lf	7 116	7	4	3hd	4¹	3hd	3¹½	2nk	Melancon G	5.30
4Apr03 ⁹LS¹	Compendium	Lbf	5 116	5	2	1¹½	1²½	1½	2¹½	3½	Lambert C T	16.60
29Mar03 ⁸OP¹	Private Emblem	L	4 116	2	5	5hd	5hd	5hd	4½	4nk	Lanerie C J	1.90
4Apr03 ⁹LS²	Maysville Slew	Lf	7 116	8	9	9	9	9	8⁵	5hd	Perrodin E J	41.30
15Feb03 ⁷Hou³	Dynameaux	L	5 114	1	8	7½	7½	6hd	6hd	6no	Chapa R	31.90
23Mar03 ⁸DeD⁴	Seainsky	Lb	4 116	3	6	6¹½	6½	7¹½	7²	7¹	Martin E M Jr	8.10
2Mar03 ⁷DeD²	Oak Hall	Lb	7 118	4	1	4²	3½	4¹	5½	8⁷	Leblanc K P	11.40
4Apr03 ⁹LS⁵	Unrullah Bull	L	6 118	6	7	8¹½	8²½	8¹½	9	9	Theriot H J II	28.80

OFF AT 5:19 Start Good. Won ridden out. Track fast.

TIME :23⁴, :47, 1:10⁴, 1:23, 1:35³ (:23.93, :47.09, 1:10.95, 1:23.11, 1:35.68)

$2 Mutuel Prices:

9–BLUESTHESTANDARD	5.00	3.40	3.00
7–BONAPAW		5.60	4.40
5–COMPENDIUM			6.60

$2 EXACTA 9–7 PAID $41.60 $2 QUINELLA 7–9 PAID $25.00 $2 TRIFECTA 9–7–5 PAID $235.40 $2 SUPERFECTA 9–7–5–2 PAID $681.20

Dk. b. or br. g, by American Standard–Bob's Blue, by Bob's Dusty. Trainer West Ted H. Bred by Terry Brown (Ga).

BLUESTHESTANDARD was hustled from the start, angled over entering the first turn, tracked the pace set by COMPENDIUM, ranged up nearing the quarter pole, gained the lead at the top of the stretch, and drew away while ridden out. BONAPAW was rank on the first turn, settled off the pace on the backstretch, made a mild bid entering the stretch, and finished willingly to get the place. COMPENDIUM was well rated while setting the clear pace, lost the lead at the top of the stretch, and gradually gave way. PRIVATE EMBLEM saved ground throughout, raced unhurried in mid pack, roused with five-sixteenths to run, and lacked the needed response. MAYSVILLE SLEW was caught four wide entering the first turn, trailed the field into the stretch, and improved position without threatening. DYNAMEAUX raced well back in the field, went four wide on the final turn, and failed to threaten. SEAINSKY settled in mid pack, roused leaving the far turn, and failed to rally. OAK HALL was well placed into the stretch, but came up empty. UNRULLAH BULL raced four wide on both turns, and was outrun.

Owners— 1, Sengara Jeffrey; 2, Dennis Richard; 3, Ackerley Brothers Farm; 4, Cassels James & Zollars Bob; 5, Trout C R; 6, Wolff George & Munn ONeal; 7, Gullett Jack L; 8, Ortego Ena; 9, Donnan Jim & Theresa

Trainers— 1, West Ted H; 2, Miller Norman C III; 3, Asmussen Steven M; 4, Asmussen Steven M; 5, Trout C R; 6, Pish Danny; 7, Hawley Wesley; 8, Bourgeois Keith; 9, Norman Cole

$2 Pick Three (8–4–9) Paid $112.40; Pick Three Pool $8,772.

EIGHTH RACE

Hollywood

APRIL 27, 2003

1 MILE. (Turf)(1.32³) 42nd Running of THE WILSHIRE HANDICAP. Grade III. Purse $100,000 added. Fillies and mares, 3–year–olds and upward. By subscription of $100 each on or before Wednesday, April. $1,000 additional to start, with $100,000 added. The added money and all fees to be divided 60% to the winner, 20% to second, 12% tothird, 6% to fourth and 2% to fifth. Rail at zero. Closed with 20 nominations.

Value of Race: $111,000 Winner $66,600; second $22,200; third $13,320; fourth $6,660; fifth $2,220. Mutuel Pool $393,848.00 Exacta Pool $205,245.00 Quinella Pool $23,322.00 Trifecta Pool $235,506.00 Superfecta Pool $99,991.00

Last Raced	Horse	M/Eqt.	A.Wt	PP	St	¼	½	¾	Str	Fin	Jockey	Odds $1
26Oct02 7AP¹⁰	Dublino	LB	4 120	6	9	6½	5½	3hd	1½	12½	Desormeaux K J	a-2.90
7Mar03 2SA¹	Southern Oasis	LB	5 116	2	4	2¹½	2¹	2¹½	2hd	2¹	Solis A	7.10
17Feb03 7SA¹	Final Destination-NZ	LB	5 118	3	8	7½	8hd	8½	6½	3½	Espinoza V	1.40
23Nov02 CAU¹	Damaschino-AU	LB	5 117	9	6	8½	7¹	7²½	4½	4¹½	Nakatani C S	10.60
30Mar03 8SA⁸	Coney Kitty-IR	LB	5 112	1	5	1hd	1½	1½	3¹½	5nk	Lopez C C	31.20
26Oct02 7AP⁹	Turtle Bow-FR	LB	4 121	5	2	4¹	4hd	4½	5¹	6²	Baze T C	3.30
5Apr03 6BM⁴	Little Treasure-FR	LB	4 118	4	3	3½	3½	5¹	7²	7¹	Valenzuela P A	a-2.90
2Mar03 4SA¹	Melody Blue-FR	LBb	4 115	8	7	9	9	9	9	8¹	Johnston M T	58.10
20Mar03 7SA¹	Rhythm Of Life-GB	LB	4 115	7	1	5hd	6½	6hd	8hd	9	Valdivia J Jr	24.90

a–Coupled: Dublino and Little Treasure–FR.

OFF AT 4:54 Start Good. Won driving. Course firm.

TIME :23, :46², 1:10¹, 1:33³ (:23.05, :46.56, 1:10.32, 1:33.62)

$2 Mutuel Prices:	1A–DUBLINO (a–entry)	7.80	4.60	2.40
	3–SOUTHERN OASIS	7.00	3.00
	4–FINAL DESTINATION–NZ	2.20

$1 EXACTA 1–3 PAID $20.90 $2 QUINELLA 1–3 PAID $21.60 $1 TRIFECTA 1–3–4 PAID $53.80 $1 SUPERFECTA 1–3–4–8 PAID $317.90

Dk. b. or br. f, by Lear Fan–Tuscoga, by Theatrical*Ire. Trainer De Seroux Laura. Bred by Arthur B Hancock III (Ky).

DUBLINO chased between horses, moved up into the second turn, bid three deep into the stretch, gained the lead nearing midstretch and pulled clear under some urging and good handling. SOUTHERN OASIS forced the early pace between horses then outside a rival, battled between foes again into the stretch and to midstretch, could not match the winner but held second. FINAL DESTINATION (NZ) pulled her way up into a bit of a tight spot into the first turn, saved ground chasing the pace, steadied, bumped with a rival and hit the inner rail after passing a shadow midway through the second turn to fall back, came out in the stretch and just got the show. DAMASCHINO (AUS) pulled her way along three deep on the first turn and steadied into the backstretch, moved up between horses approaching the second turn, angled in a bit on that bend, went outside a rival into the stretch and was edged for third. CONEY KITTY (IRE) had speed off the rail then angled in and dueled inside, fought back on the second turn but weakened in the final furlong. TURTLE BOW (FR) angled in and stalked the pace inside to the stretch and lacked the needed response. LITTLE TREASURE (FR) pressed the early pace three deep, took back,stalked outside, went three wide into and on the second turn and weakened. MELODY BLUE (FR) steadied off heels into the first turn, settled outside a rival, steadied off heels again and was bumped midway on the second turn and did not rally. RHYTHM OF LIFE (GB) stalked three deep then four wide on the second turn and weakened.

Owners— 1, Geringer Klein Naify Et Al; 2, Whitham Janis R; 3, Gann Edmund A; 4, Newton R B; 5, Humphrey Steven & Seelbinder G A; 6, Crichton Andrew; 7, Port Trust Naify & San Gabriel Inve; 8, Wertheimer Farm; 9, Blue Melinda or Club Med

Trainers— 1, De Seroux Laura; 2, McAnally Ronald; 3, Frankel Robert; 4, Drysdale Neil; 5, Hofmans David; 6, De Seroux Laura; 7, De Seroux Laura; 8, Mandella Richard; 9, Cassidy James

$2 Daily Double (9–1) Paid $51.00; Daily Double Pool $32,327.
$1 Pick Three (13–9–1) Paid $245.30; Pick Three Pool $75,313.

NINTH RACE
Churchill
MAY 1, 2003

7 FURLONGS. (1.20^{2}) 48th Running of THE LA TROIENNE. Grade III. Purse $100,000 Addded. FILLIES, THREE YEARS OLD. By subscription of $100 each on or before April 12, 2003 or by Supplementary Nomination of $5,000 at the time of entry. $500 to pass the entry box; $500 additional to start. Weight 122 lbs. Non–winners of $50,000 allowed 2 lbs.; three races other than maiden or claiming, 4 lbs.; two races other than maiden or claiming, 6 lbs.; arace other than maiden or claiming, 8 lbs. Closed Saturday, April 12, 2003 with 53 nominations.

Value of Race: $111,800 Winner $69,316; second $22,360; third $11,180; fourth $5,590; fifth $3,354. Mutuel Pool $477,415.00 Exacta Pool $386,185.00 Trifecta Pool $269,036.00 Superfecta Pool $54,169.00

Last Raced	Horse	M/Eqt.	A.Wt	PP	St	¼	½	Str	Fin	Jockey	Odds $1
14Mar03 ^{7}GP^{2}	Final Round	L	3 116	2	6	6	5^{hd}	$3^{1\frac{1}{2}}$	1^{1}	Bailey J D	1.20
8Mar03 ^{9}FG^{5}	Lovely Sage	Lb	3 116	3	4	$5^{1\frac{1}{2}}$	$4^{\frac{1}{2}}$	2^{hd}	$2^{1\frac{1}{4}}$	Borel C H	6.20
11Apr03 ^{6}Kee^{1}	Fast Cookie	b	3 118	5	2	$4^{\frac{1}{2}}$	3^{1}	1^{1}	3^{2}	Velasquez C	8.00
6Apr03 ^{5}Kee^{1}	Real Bear	L	3 114	1	5	$3^{\frac{1}{2}}$	6	5^{3}	$4^{6\frac{1}{4}}$	Melancon L	9.90
6Apr03 ^{6}Tam^{1}	Just Bill Me	L	3 120	4	3	$1^{\frac{1}{2}}$	1^{hd}	6	5^{nk}	Albarado R J	6.70
11Apr03 ^{5}Kee^{1}	Crow Jane	L	3 116	6	1	2^{1}	$2^{\frac{1}{2}}$	4^{hd}	6	Lovato F Jr	2.60

OFF AT 4:50 Start Good. Won driving. Track fast.
TIME :22^{2}, :45^{1}, 1:09^{3}, 1:22 (:22.55, :45.24, 1:09.74, 1:22.13)

$2 Mutuel Prices:

2–FINAL ROUND	4.40	2.80	2.60
3–LOVELY SAGE		5.00	3.80
6–FAST COOKIE			3.20

$2 EXACTA 2–3 PAID $21.80 $2 TRIFECTA 2–3–6 PAID $97.40 $1 SUPERFECTA 2–3–6–1 PAID $160.80

B. f, (Mar), by Storm Cat–Profit Column, by Private Account. Trainer Arnold George R II. Bred by Dinwiddie Farm Limited Partnership (Ky).

FINAL ROUND, lightly bumped at the start by LOVELY SAGE when that one leaned in, settled in hand near the inside, eased out three or four wide nearing the end of the backstretch, continued in that manner until the final quarter, came out five wide to rally, leaned in and brushed twice in the final furlong with FAST COOKIE and proved best under strong handling. LOVELY SAGE leaned in at the break bumping lightly with the winner, moved to the rail to race under rating, made a bold run into the stretch, came through close quarters in the final furlong and was second best in a good try. FAST COOKIE drifted out at the start, quickly recovered to track the leaders four or five wide, took over in the upper stretch, was brushed by the winner in the final furlong and weakened while swerving in and out a bit in the late going. REAL BEAR, well placed early, was checked in tight quarters between foes at the five-eighths pole, continued in contention behind rivals four wide into the lane and couldn't produce a late response. JUST BILL ME gained the advantage early, dueled with CROW JANE until the final quarter and faltered CROW JANE drifted out at the start, was straightened and sent up soon after to press the pace, stuck a head in front between calls leaving the turn but tired soon after.

Owners— 1, Humphrey G W Jr; 2, Devenport Roger J; 3, Stonerside Stable; 4, Durant Tom R; 5, Franks John & Hollendorfer Jerry; 6, Totier Creek Farm

Trainers—1, Arnold George R II; 2, Amoss Thomas; 3, Mott William I; 4, Werner Ronny; 5, Hollendorfer Jerry; 6, Thornbury Jeffrey D

Scratched— Stellar (30Apr03 ^{8}CD^{3})

$1 Pick Three (10–1/4/5/7–2/4) Paid $87.90; Pick Three Pool $56,892.

EIGHTH RACE
Churchill
MAY 2, 2003

$1\frac{1}{16}$ MILES. (1.41^{3}) 18th Running of THE LOUISVILLE BREEDERS' CUP HANDICAP. Grade II. Purse $300,000 Added (includes $100,000 BC – Breeders' Cup) FILLIES AND MARES, THREE YEARS OLD AND UPWARD. (Includes $100,000 from the Breeders' Cup Fund for Cup Nominees Only). By subscription of $300 each on or before April 12, 2003 or by Supplementary Nomination of $15,000 each by the closing ofentries on Friday, April, 25, 2003. $1,500 to pass the entry box; $1,500 additional to start, with $200,000 added. The host association's added monies to be divided 62% to the owner of the winner, 20% to second, 10% to third, 5% to fourth and 3% to fifth.Breeders' Cup Fund monies also correspondingly divided providing a Breeders' Cup nominee has finished in an awarded position. Weights to be announced Saturday, April 26. Starters to be named through the entry box at the usual time of closing. Closed Saturday, April 12, 2003, with 30 nominations.

Value of Race: $325,500 Winner $201,810; second $65,100; third $32,550; fourth $16,275; fifth $9,765. Mutuel Pool $955,799.00 Exacta Pool $759,288.00 Trifecta Pool $343,460.00

Last Raced	Horse	M/Eqt.	A.Wt	PP	St	¼	½	¾	Str	Fin	Jockey	Odds $1
16Feb03 ^{6}SA^{2}	You	L	4 118	2	1	$1^{\frac{1}{2}}$	2^{3}	$2^{5\frac{1}{2}}$	$1^{2\frac{1}{2}}$	$1^{7\frac{3}{4}}$	Bailey J D	0.30
5Apr03 ^{7}Kee^{1}	Fly Borboleta	Lbf	4 111	3	3	2^{2}	1^{hd}	1^{hd}	$2^{4\frac{1}{2}}$	2^{1}	Melancon L	12.40
16Apr03 ^{8}Kee^{4}	Seven Four Seven	L	5 113	5	2	5	5	$3^{2\frac{1}{2}}$	3^{4}	$3^{9\frac{3}{4}}$	Peck B D	7.50
6Apr03 ^{10}OP^{2}	Majority Whip	L	5 112	4	5	4^{hd}	3^{hd}	$4^{3\frac{1}{2}}$	4^{7}	$4^{20\frac{1}{4}}$	Day P	6.30
6Apr03 ^{10}OP^{3}	Red n'Gold	L	5 114	1	4	3^{hd}	4^{hd}	5	5	5	Prado E S	9.50

OFF AT 3:55 Start Good. Won driving. Track fast.
TIME :23^{1}, :45^{4}, 1:10, 1:36^{1}, 1:43^{1} (:23.34, :45.90, 1:10.03, 1:36.34, 1:43.21)

$2 Mutuel Prices:

2–YOU	2.60	2.20	—
3–FLY BORBOLETA		4.40	—
5–SEVEN FOUR SEVEN		—	—

$2 EXACTA 2–3 PAID $18.40 $2 TRIFECTA 2–3–5 PAID $73.40

Dk. b. or br. f, by You and I–Our Dani, by Homebuilder. Trainer Frankel Robert. Bred by Dolphus C Morrison (Ky).

YOU moved to the fore near the inside early, went along under careful rating while shadowed by FLY BORBOLETA, alternated for the lead with that one on the backstretch and far turn, took over for good just prior to going six furlongs, was roused with the whip right-handed eight times between the three-sixteenth and sixteenth pole while drawing off, then continued under solid hand urging as much the best. FLY BORBOLETA moved right up outside YOU approaching the first turn to force the pace, headed that one on the backstretch, alternated for the advantage as those two drew well clear on the far turn, then couldn't keep pace in the drive. SEVEN FOUR SEVEN tracked the dueling leaders four or five wide most of the way and was unable to menace in the drive while superior to the others. MAJORITY WHIP, lightly rated between foes to the far turn, continued near the inside and weakened. RED N'GOLD, in contention near the inside from the start, remained within striking distance to the end of the backstretch, weakened gradually and wasn't persevered with in the late going when hopelessly beaten.

Owners— 1, Gann Edmund A; 2, Thomas F Van Meter II & WinStar Far; 3, Pollock Sam B; 4, WinStar Farm; 5, English Kenneth D & Braun Alan

Trainers—1, Frankel Robert; 2, Walden W Elliott; 3, Flint Bernard S; 4, Walden W Elliott; 5, Holthus Robert E

Scratched— Take Charge Lady (5Apr03 ^{8}OP^{2})

$1 Pick Three (5–10–2/6) Paid $342.60; Pick Three Pool $131,128.

SEVENTH RACE

Churchill

MAY 2, 2003

5 FURLONGS. (Turf)(.55³) 9th Running of THE AEGON TURF SPRINT. Grade III. Purse $100,000 Added. THREE–YEAR–OLDS AND UPWARD. By subscription of $100 each on or before April 12, 2003 or by Supplementary Nomination of $5,000 at time of entry. $500 to pass the entry box; $500 additional to start, with $100,000 added of which 62% of all monies to the owner of the winner, 20% to second, 10% to third, 5% to fourth and 3% to fifth. Three–year–olds, 115 lbs.; Older, 122 lbs. Non–winners of $50,000 on the turf in 2002–2003 allowed 2 lbs.; a sweepstakes on the turf in 2002–2003, 4 lbs.; $30,000 on the turf since July 4, 6 lbs.; three races other than maiden, claiming or starter on the turf, 8 lbs. Starters to be named through the entry box at the usual time of closing. Closed Saturday, April 12, 2003, with 43 nominations.

Value of Race: $115,300 Winner $71,486; second $23,060; third $11,530; fourth $5,765; fifth $3,459.   Mutuel Pool $1,372,667.0 Exacta Pool $950,778.00 Trifecta Pool $746,889.00 Superfecta Pool $115,632.00

Last Raced	Horse	M/Eqt. A.Wt	PP	St	$\frac{1}{16}$	$\frac{3}{8}$	Str	Fin	Jockey	Odds $1
12Apr03 7Kee⁶	Fiscally Speaking	Lf	4 114	11	7	5½	5²	5²	1hd	Court J K	47.40
4Jly02 10CD²	Morluc	L	7 122	10	3	3hd	4½	4²	2¹	Sellers S J	a–3.10
12Apr03 7Kee²	Testify	L	6 122	7	10	7³	7³	7½	3no	Albarado R J	6.30
12Apr03 7Kee⁷	Mighty Beau	L	4 114	4	1	1¹	1hd	1½	4nk	Prado E S	a–3.10
28Mar03 7SA³	Nuclear Debate	L	8 122	9	9	10²	9⁶	8³	5hd	Stevens G L	6.00
12Apr03 7Kee⁵	Airbourne Command	Lf	8 116	3	4	6³	6⁴	6²	6¾	Velazquez J R	37.70
12Apr03 7Kee³	Abderian–IRE	Lf	6 122	1	5	4½	3hd	3hd	7hd	Bailey J D	4.30
12Apr03 9GP¹	Bop	Lf	6 120	6	2	2³	2²	2hd	8²½	Valenzuela P A	2.70
27Oct02 6AP⁴	Red Lightning	L	5 122	2	6	8²½	8hd	9³	9⁴	Borel C H	52.20
5Apr03 12Beu¹	Devil Time	Lb	6 120	5	11	11	11	11	10no	Day P	14.20
12Apr03 7Kee¹	No Jacket Required	L	6 122	8	8	9²	10³½	10⁴	11	Blanc B	10.70

a–Coupled: Morluc and Mighty Beau.

OFF AT 3:08 Start Good. Won driving. Course firm.

TIME :21³, :44¹, :56 (:21.67, :44.22, :56.01)

$2 Mutuel Prices:

10–FISCALLY SPEAKING	96.80	33.20	12.20
1A–MORLUC (a–entry)		6.00	3.80
7–TESTIFY			3.80

$2 EXACTA 10–1 PAID $519.00 $2 TRIFECTA 10–1–7 PAID $3,804.80 $1 SUPERFECTA 10–1–7–9 PAID $9,011.30

Ch. g, by Belong to Me–Tuesday Evening, by Nodouble. Trainer Nafzger Carl A. Bred by Janis R Whitham (Ky).

FISCALLY SPEAKING, bobbled at the start, raced within easy striking distance, worked his way in four wide by the end of the backstretch, was put to a drive approaching the five–sixteenths pole, came six abreast for the drive, then closed relentlessly under strong handling to be along in time. MORLUC, well placed from early on while near the inside between foes, moved with the winner while inside that one into the upper stretch, gained a brief, slight advantage between calls in the final sixteenth but was outfinished. TESTIFY, settled front wide while within striking distance, moved out six or seven wide for the drive and was going well in the late stages. MIGHTY BEAU moved to the fore early, made the pace two or three wide, managed a slim lead into the final furlong and weakened. NUCLEAR DEBATE, sluggish to begin, angled in to race four wide, was outsprinted to the stretch, came out nine or 10 wide for the drive and was gaining late. AIRBOURNE COMMAND settled in behind rivals three wide, came out seven wide for the stretch run and offered a mild gain. ABDERIAN (IRE), well placed inside from the beginning, made a bid along the rail leaving the eighth pole, was forced to check in tight quarters leaving the sixteenth pole and was finished. BOP went up outside front–running MIGHTY BEAU early to force the pace four wide, battled on about even terms into the final furlong and weakened thereafter. RED LIGHTNING, reserved inside early, swung out seven or eight wide for the drive but failed to rally. DEVIL TIME, sluggish to start, was outrun. NO JACKET REQUIRED was done early.

Owners— 1, Whitham Janis R; 2, M C Stable; 3, Robert S Mitchell Trust; 4, M C Stable & Carolan Anthony; 5, Herrick Racing; 6, Saland Richard; 7, Englander Richard A; 8, Folly Quarter Stable; 9, Maas Phillip S; 10, Anderson Brad; 11, Webber Temple W Jr

Trainers—1, Nafzger Carl A; 2, Morse Randy L; 3, Morse Randy L; 4, Morse Randy L; 5, Vienna Darrell; 6, Saland Richard; 7, Poe John; 8, Trombetta Michael J; 9, Thornbury Jeffrey D; 10, Carroll David; 11, Amoss Thomas

---

$1 Pick Three (7–5–10) Paid $767.70; Pick Three Pool $178,002.

NINTH RACE
Churchill
MAY 2, 2003

$1\frac{1}{16}$ MILES. (Turf)(1.40^{4}) 12th Running of THE CROWN ROYAL AMERICAN TURF. Grade III. Purse $100,000 Added. THREE-YEAR-OLDS. By subscription of $100 each on or before April 12, 2003. $500 to pass the entry box; $500 additional to start, with $100,000 added of which 62% of all monies to the owner of the winner, 20% to second, 10% to third, 5% to fourth and 3% to fifth. Weight 123 lbs. Non-winners of a sweepstakes on the turf allowed 2 lbs.; three races other than maiden or claiming, 4 lbs.; two races other than maiden or claiming, 6 lbs.; a race other than maiden or claiming, 8 lbs. The maximum number of starters for the Crown Royal American Turf will be limited to twelve. If more than twelve entries pass the entry box preference will be given to high weights, however two horses having common ties through ownership cannot start to the exclusion of a single interest. SUPPLEMENTAL NOMINATION OF $5,000: TORRE AND ZIM.

Value of Race: $121,400 Winner $75,268; second $24,280; third $12,140; fourth $6,070; fifth $3,642. Mutuel Pool $1,497,265.0 Exacta Pool $1,009,825.0 Trifecta Pool $790,478.00 Superfecta Pool $221,194.00

Last Raced	Horse	M/Eqt.	A.Wt	PP	St	¼	½	¾	Str	Fin	Jockey	Odds $1
12Apr03 ^{8}Aqu^{5}	Senor Swinger	Lf	3 117	3	1	$7^{3\frac{1}{2}}$	7^{2}	$8^{2\frac{1}{2}}$	5^{1}	$1^{2\frac{1}{2}}$	Day P	3.10
4Apr03 ^{8}Kee^{4}	Remind	L	3 117	6	5	2^{1}	1^{hd}	1^{hd}	1^{1}	2^{1}	Bailey J D	2.10
5Apr03 ^{8}Haw^{3}	Foufa's Warrior	Lb	3 117	8	10	10	10	10	9^{6}	$3^{\frac{1}{2}}$	Vega H	11.40
17Apr03 ^{8}Kee^{2}	Rapid Proof	Lb	3 123	7	6	4^{1}	$3^{\frac{1}{2}}$	3^{1}	2^{2}	4^{nk}	Albarado R J	11.70
5Apr03 ^{9}LS^{8}	Marsh	L	3 117	4	8	8^{4}	8^{1}	$7^{\frac{1}{2}}$	6^{2}	5no	Solis A	26.40
17Apr03 ^{8}Kee^{5}	Hot Hand	Lb	3 117	5	4	3^{hd}	$5^{2\frac{1}{2}}$	5^{5}	3^{hd}	6no	Velasquez C	18.10
3Apr03 ^{7}GP^{1}	Imitation	L	3 117	2	2	5^{1}	4^{hd}	4^{hd}	$4^{\frac{1}{2}}$	$7^{1\frac{1}{4}}$	Santos J A	6.40
17Apr03 ^{8}Kee^{1}	Californian-GB	L	3 123	9	9	$9^{1\frac{1}{2}}$	9^{2}	9^{3}	8^{1}	$8^{3\frac{3}{4}}$	Desormeaux K J	3.90
5Apr03 ^{8}Haw^{6}	Lx Commander	Lb	3 119	1	3	1^{hd}	2^{1}	$2^{\frac{1}{2}}$	7^{2}	$9^{7\frac{1}{4}}$	Meche L J	35.80
26Apr03 ^{7}Aqu^{5}	Torre And Zim	L	3 117	10	7	6^{1}	$6^{2\frac{1}{2}}$	6^{hd}	10	10	Velazquez J R	36.80

OFF AT 4:51 Start Good For All But FOUFA'S WARRIOR Won driving. Course firm.
TIME :23^{1}, :46^{4}, 1:10^{2}, 1:35^{1}, 1:41^{1} (:23.31, :46.95, 1:10.50, 1:35.27, 1:41.38)

$2 Mutuel Prices:			
3–SENOR SWINGER	8.20	4.20	3.20
6–REMIND		3.60	3.00
10–FOUFA'S WARRIOR			4.80

$2 EXACTA 3–6 PAID $26.00 $2 TRIFECTA 3–6–10 PAID $255.60 $1 SUPERFECTA 3–6–10–9 PAID $857.20

Gr/ro c, (Apr), by El Prado*Ire–Smooth Swinger, by Kris S.. Trainer Baffert Bob. Bred by Bob Ackerman (Ky).

SENOR SWINGER, reserved in behind the leaders from early on four wide, was patiently ridden, eased out six wide leaving the second turn, was roused eight times with the whip on the right side, struck seven more times after the rider changed to his left-hand, once more when Day switched back to the right and drove clear late. REMIND went up early to contest the pace from between horses, battled with LX COMMANDER while outside that one, raced heads apart into the stretch, briefly was clear about the three-sixteenths pole and wasn't a match for SENOR SWINGER late. FOUFA'S WARRIOR broke in the air to immediately trail, was allowed to settle and angled in to race four wide, was outrun to the stretch, circled foes 10 wide and was going well at the end. RAPID PROOF, full of run and positioned outside the dueling leaders from early on five wide, loomed menacingly between foes for the last eighth and flattened out. MARSH, unhurried from early on while racing near the inside, saved ground to the stretch, eased out five wide for the drive but could gain only slightly at the end. HOT HAND, bobbled sharply, quickly recovered, raced close up between foes, was checked lightly between rivals approaching the first turn, loomed a solid threat leaving the furlong grounds but came up empty. IMITATION, taken in hand soon after the break and eased in behind the dueling leaders, saved ground until the stretch, came out to make a run between foes four wide leaving the eighth pole but weakened when the test came. CALIFORNIAN (GB) angled in early, was unhurried three or four wide for six furlongs, came out seven abreast concluding the second turn but failed to offer a closing account. LX COMMANDER moved up near the inside early to duel with REMIND for the lead, lost the edge to that one soon after a quarter, continued to battle inside REMIND on even terms until the final quarter and weakened steadily when straightened for the drive. TORRE AND ZIM worked his way in behind horses four wide by the first turn, raced in that manner within easy striking distance for six furlongs, came out six wide for the drive, then drifted out while tiring.

Owners— 1, Lewis Robert B & Beverly J; 2, Claiborne Farm; 3, Bender Sondra D; 4, Morrison Dolphus; 5, Heiligbrodt Racing Stable; 6, Overbrook Farm; 7, Calumet Farm Trust UDeed Of Henryk; 8, Steve Taub & Neil Papiano; 9, Childers Miles L T B Inc & Wright E; 10, Goldfarb Sanford J

Trainers—1, Baffert Bob; 2, Mott William I; 3, Murray Lawrence E; 4, Wiggins Hal R; 5, Asmussen Steven M; 6, Lukas D Wayne; 7, Clement Christophe; 8, Mulhall Kristin; 9, Flint Bernard S; 10, Dutrow Richard E Jr

Scratched— White Cat (4Apr03 ^{8}KEE^{1}), Ontario (12Apr03 ^{8}KEE^{7}), Color Me Gone (17Apr03 ^{8}KEE^{3}), Rahy Vision (9Apr03 ^{7}SA^{3}), Moonshine Hall (3Apr03 ^{7}GP^{2})

$1 Pick Three (10–2/6–3) Paid $329.60; Pick Three Pool $109,883.

TENTH RACE
Churchill
MAY 2, 2003

1⅛ MILES. (1.47^{1}) 129th Running of THE KENTUCKY OAKS. Grade I. Purse $500,000 Added. FILLIES, THREE YEARS OLD. By subscription of $100 each on or before February 15, 2003 or by Supplementary Nomination of $25,000 at time of entry. $2,500 to pass the entry box; $2,500 additional to start with $500,000 added of which 62% of all monies to the owner of the winner, 20% to second, 10% to third, 5% to fourth and 3% to fifth. Weight 121 lbs. Starters to be named through the entry box Tuesday, April 29, 2003, at the usual time of closing. Closed Saturday, February 15, 2003 with 138 nominations.

Value of Race: $573,800 Winner $355,756; second $114,760; third $57,380; fourth $28,690; fifth $17,214. Mutuel Pool $3,029,055.0 Exacta Pool $1,802,859.0 Trifecta Pool $1,524,155.0 Superfecta Pool $432,459.00

Last Raced	Horse	M/Eqt.	A.Wt	PP	St	¼	½	¾	Str	Fin	Jockey	Odds $1
10Apr03 8Kee2	Bird Town	L	3 121	5	11	8^{1}	$8^{2\frac{1}{2}}$	7^{3}	$4^{1\frac{1}{2}}$	$1^{3\frac{1}{4}}$	Prado E S	18.20
12Mar03 2SA1	Santa Catarina	L	3 121	11	9	$7^{\frac{1}{2}}$	$7^{1\frac{1}{2}}$	3^{1}	1^{hd}	2^{hd}	Stevens G L	5.90
5Apr03 8Kee4	Yell	L	3 121	6	7	6^{1}	6^{1}	$5^{\frac{1}{2}}$	$5^{1\frac{1}{2}}$	$3^{\frac{3}{4}}$	Velazquez J R	6.80
5Apr03 8Kee1	Elloluv	L	3 121	1	5	$1^{\frac{1}{2}}$	1^{1}	1^{hd}	2^{hd}	$4^{2\frac{1}{2}}$	Albarado R J	2.70
10Apr03 8Kee1	My Boston Gal	L	3 121	2	6	3^{1}	$3^{\frac{1}{2}}$	$4^{\frac{1}{2}}$	6^{4}	$5^{1\frac{1}{4}}$	Day P	5.80
5Apr03 8Kee2	Lady Tak	L	3 121	7	2	$5^{\frac{1}{2}}$	$4^{\frac{1}{2}}$	2^{1}	3^{hd}	$6^{2\frac{3}{4}}$	Bailey J D	2.60
29Mar03 9Sun1	Island Fashion	Lb	3 121	12	4	$4^{1\frac{1}{2}}$	5^{1}	6^{1}	7^{3}	$7^{2\frac{3}{4}}$	Valenzuela P A	21.70
5Apr03 8Kee3	Holiday Lady	L	3 121	4	1	10^{hd}	9^{hd}	10^{7}	8^{7}	$8^{11\frac{1}{2}}$	Santos J A	30.60
8Mar03 9FG2	Atlantic Ocean	L	3 121	8	10	$11^{3\frac{1}{2}}$	10^{4}	9^{1}	9^{6}	$9^{3\frac{1}{2}}$	Flores D R	19.30
11Apr03 6Kee4	In Case Of Wind	L	3 121	10	12	12	12	11^{1}	$10^{\frac{1}{2}}$	10^{2}	Borel C H	79.00
18Apr03 6Kee1	Tempus Fugit	L	3 121	9	3	2^{2}	$2^{\frac{1}{2}}$	8^{hd}	$11^{2\frac{1}{2}}$	$11^{5\frac{1}{4}}$	Sellers S J	46.10
11Apr03 10OP3	Go For Glamour	L	3 121	3	8	9^{hd}	11^{3}	12	12	12	Solis A	49.20

OFF AT 5:45 Start Good For All But BIRD TOWN Won driving. Track fast.
TIME :23, :46, 1:10, 1:35^{3}, 1:48^{3} (:23.09, :46.08, 1:10.15, 1:35.67, 1:48.64)

$2 Mutuel Prices:				
	5–BIRD TOWN	38.40	14.20	9.20
	11–SANTA CATARINA		8.60	6.20
	6–YELL			6.00

$2 EXACTA 5–11 PAID $332.20 $2 TRIFECTA 5–11–6 PAID $2,202.60 $1 SUPERFECTA 5–11–6–1 PAID $8,543.70

B. f, (Apr), by Cape Town–Dear Birdie, by Storm Bird. Trainer Zito Nicholas P. Bred by Marylou Whitney Stables (Ky).

BIRD TOWN stumbled in her initial stride, settled and was taken in hand after the first few jumps, raced three or four wide, commenced her rally leaving the three furlong marker, split foes approaching the final quarter, maneuvered out five or six wide when straightened into the stretch, brushed for a stride with SANTA CATARINA approaching the final sixteenth and drove clear soon after under strong left-handed encouragement. SANTA CATARINA, well in hand while following the leaders five wide around the first turn and into the backstretch, edged closer approaching the far turn, made a bold run through the upper stretch to gain a slight, brief lead at the furlong grounds, brushed for a stride with LADY TAK, came out for a stride brushing with the winner, then couldn't match strides with BIRD TOWN late while gamely saving second. YELL, appeared to be bumped approaching the first turn by LADY TAK and forced in slightly on GO FOR GLAMOUR, was sharply checked for a stride soon after, settled within easy striking distance three or four wide, advanced between foes around the far turn, came out from behind rivals five wide in the final furlong and finished with good courage. ELLOLUV gained a narrow advantage near the inside early, went along under careful handling while dueling with TEMPUS FUGIT, shook off that one, continued to battle on even terms for the lead while inside LADY TAK and SANTA CATARINA into the upper stretch, then gradually weakened the last eighth. MY BOSTON GAL, rated forwardly in behind the leaders from the outset, inched closer approaching the final quarter, worked her way out five wide in deep stretch but was empty. LADY TAK leaned in approaching the first turn and appeared to force YELL in a bit, was never far back while between foes three wide under light rating, made a bold run to reach the front briefly at the three-sixteenths pole, exchanged brushes first with ELLOLUV soon after, again with SANTA CATARINA and weakened thereafter. ISLAND FASHION worked her way in five wide early to stalk the leaders, remained prominent to the stretch and flattened out. HOLIDAY LADY, steadied behind rivals approaching the first turn while near the inside, saved ground into the stretch, moved out four wide but failed to rally. ATLANTIC OCEAN, four or five wide, failed to menace. IN CASE OF WIND never reached contention. TEMPUS FUGIT moved up early to press front-running ELLOLUV three wide, held on well until the end of the backstretch and faded. GO FOR GLAMOUR, steadied along the inside approaching the first turn, never was prominent.

Owners— 1, Marylou Whitney Stable; 2, Lewis Robert B & Beverly J; 3, Claiborne Farm & Dilschneider Adele; 4, Reddam J P; 5, J Chester Porter Randy Bloch & Phil; 6, Heiligbrodt Racing Stable; 7, Everest Stables; 8, Farmer Tracy; 9, The Thoroughbred Corporation; 10, Stone Karen & James C; 11, Briland Farm & David Gray Rob & Sta; 12, Columbine Stable

Trainers—1, Zito Nicholas P; 2, Baffert Bob; 3, McGaughey Claude III; 4, Dollase Craig; 5, Nafzger Carl A; 6, Asmussen Steven M; 7, Canani Nick; 8, Zito Nicholas P; 9, Baffert Bob; 10, Million William N; 11, McPeek Kenneth G; 12, Greely C Beau

---

$1 Daily Double (3–5) Paid $89.20; Daily Double Pool $186,585.
$1 P 3 (2/6–3–5) Paid $131.00; P 3 Pool $304,563.
$1 P 4 (10–2/6–3–5) Paid $10,724.40; P 4 Pool $569,320. $1 Pick Six (7–5–10–2/6–3–5) 5 Correct Paid $665.00; Pick Six Pool $85,391; Carryover Pool $67,479.

EIGHTH RACE
Aqueduct
MAY 3, 2003

1 1/16 MILES. (Turf)(1.40^{4}) 26th Running of THE BEAUGAY HANDICAP. Grade III. Purse $100,000. (Up to $19,400 NYSBFOA). FILLIES AND MARES, THREE YEARS OLD AND UPWARD. By subscription of $100 each, which should accompany the nomination; $500 to pass the entry box: $500 to start, with $100,000 added. The added money and all fees to be divided 60% to the winner, 20% to second, 11% to third, 6% to fourth and 3% to fifth. Trophies will be presented to the winning owner, trainer and jockey. The New York Racing Association reserves the right to transfer this race to the Main Track. In the event that this race is taken off the turf, it may be subject to downgrading upon review by the Graded Stakes Committee. Closed Saturday, April 19, 2003 with 34 Nominations.

Value of Race: $112,400 Winner $67,440; second $22,480; third $12,364; fourth $6,744; fifth $3,372. Mutuel Pool $863,512.00 Exacta Pool $814,410.00 Trifecta Pool $687,265.00

Last Raced	Horse	M/Eqt.	A.Wt	PP	St	1/4	1/2	3/4	Str	Fin	Jockey	Odds $1
14Mar03 6GP1	Delta Princess	L	4 113	6	6	6 2½	7½	7hd	2½	1½	Luzzi M J	7.50
12Oct02 7Kee5	Wonder Again	L	4 118	5	1	3½	4½	4hd	1hd	2¾	Velazquez J R	2.90
3Nov02 8SA2	Voodoo Dancer	L	5 120	8	3	5hd	5½	5hd	4hd	3 2¾	Samyn J L	0.80
26Oct02 7AP12	Owsley	L	5 118	7	5	4 2	3½	3½	5 1½	4 1¼	Castellano J J	7.10
19Dec02 8Aqu4	Cozzy Corner	L	5 113	1	7	1 1½	1½	1½	3hd	5hd	Arroyo N Jr	31.25
2Mar03 10GP8	Peanut Gallery	Lb	6 113	2	2	8 1½	6hd	6 1½	6 1½	6½	Bravo J	41.50
31Jan03 7SA6	Miss Gazon-IR	Lf	5 114	4	9	9	9	9	8 5	7½	Carr D	65.25
1Mar03 9FG5	Dynamic Lady	Lb	4 114	3	8	7 1½	8 3	8 1½	7hd	8 5¾	Gryder A T	35.75
2Apr03 8GP1	She's Vested	Lbf	4 114	9	4	2½	2½	2hd	9	9	Migliore R	40.00

OFF AT 4:30 Start Good. Won driving. Course firm.
TIME :23^{1}, :48^{1}, 1:12^{4}, 1:36^{3}, 1:42^{1} (:23.37, :48.32, 1:12.85, 1:36.68, 1:42.36)

$2 Mutuel Prices:				
	6–DELTA PRINCESS	17.00	6.80	2.80
	5–WONDER AGAIN		4.80	2.50
	8–VOODOO DANCER			2.20

$2 EXACTA 6–5 PAID $80.00 $2 TRIFECTA 6–5–8 PAID $169.50

Dk. b. or br. f, by A.P. Indy–Lyphard's Delta, by Lyphard. Trainer Mott William I. Bred by Palides Investments N V Inc (Ky).

DELTA PRINCESS was rated along inside, saved ground, rallied turning for home, slipped through inside in upper stretch, dug in gamely on the rail and reported under a drive. WONDER AGAIN raced close up inside while well in hand, came wide entering the stretch and finished gamely while between rivals in the drive. VOODOO DANCER was rated along between rivals, rallied four wide into the stretch and finished gamely outside. OWSLEY raced with the pace while three wide and weakened in the final furlong. COZZY CORNER quickly showed in front, set the pace along the inside and tired in the final furlong. PEANUT GALLERY was outrun early, advanced outside on the backstretch, put in a four wide run on the second turn and faded outside in the stretch. MISS GAZON (IRE) was outrun early, came wide into the stretch and lacked a rally. DYNAMIC LADY was outrun early, raced inside and had no response when roused. SHE'S VESTED pressed the pace while between rivals and tired after three quarters.

Owners— 1, Khaled Saud b; 2, Phillips Joan G & John W; 3, Green Hills Farm; 4, Hancock III Arthur B; 5, Fox Ridge Farm Inc; 6, Pokoik Lee; 7, Tucker Jeffrey; 8, C K Woods Stable; 9, Graffeo Joseph F

Trainers—1, Mott William I; 2, Toner James J; 3, Clement Christophe; 4, Schulhofer Randy; 5, Kelly Patrick J; 6, Sciacca Gary; 7, Morrison John; 8, Badgett William Jr; 9, DiMauro Stephen L

Scratched— Message Red (28Mar03 7AQU1), Vespers (16Mar03 6GP1), Annatoga (2Apr03 4AQU1)

$2 Pick Three (3–3–6) Paid $531.00; Pick Three Pool $89,665.

NINTH RACE
Aqueduct
MAY 3, 2003

1 MILE. (1.32^{2}) 124th Running of THE WITHERS. Grade III. Purse $150,000. (Up to $20,100 NYSBFOA). THREE YEAR OLDS. By subscription of $150 each, which should accompany the nomination; $750 to pass the entry box; $750 to start. The purse to be divided 60% to the winner, 20% to second, 11% to third, 6% to fourth and 3% to fifth. 123 lbs. Non–winners of $60,000 in 2003 other than restricted stake allowed 3 lbs.; $45,000; or three races other than maiden or claiming, 5 lbs.; $30,000; or two races other than maiden or claiming, 7 lbs. Trophies will be presented to the inning owner, trainer and jockey. Closed Saturday, April 19, 2003 with 29 Nominations.

Value of Race: $150,000 Winner $90,000; second $30,000; third $16,500; fourth $9,000; fifth $4,500. Mutuel Pool $924,892.00 Exacta Pool $623,393.00 Trifecta Pool $479,846.00

Last Raced	Horse	M/Eqt.	A.Wt	PP	St	1/4	1/2	3/4	Str	Fin	Jockey	Odds $1
12Apr03 8Aqu8	Spite The Devil	b	3 116	5	4	7 4½	7 4½	6 2½	4hd	1nk	Chavez Luis	16.90
5Apr03 8Haw7	Alysweep	Lf	3 123	3	5	5hd	6½	5 1½	2hd	2 1	Migliore R	4.90
12Apr03 7Aqu3	Stanislavsky	L	3 116	8	2	6 2	4 1	2½	3 1½	3hd	Samyn J L	11.20
12Apr03 7Aqu2	Don Six	L	3 116	6	3	1½	1hd	1hd	1½	4 2¾	Gryder A T	4.60
12Apr03 8Aqu4	New York Hero	Lb	3 123	1	6	3 1½	2 1½	3½	5hd	5½	Castellano J J	3.50
12Apr03 7Aqu1	Halo Homewrecker		3 123	2	7	2hd	3hd	4hd	6 3½	6 1¾	Velazquez J R	1.50
16Mar03 5Aqu1	Atfirst Blush	Lb	3 118	4	8	8	8	7 6	7 10	7 17¾	Castillo H Jr	38.00
12Apr03 5Aqu1	Awesome Time	Lb	3 116	7	1	4½	5hd	8	8	8	Arroyo N Jr	26.75

OFF AT 5:01 Start Good. Won driving. Track fast.
TIME :22^{3}, :45, 1:09^{3}, 1:35^{4} (:22.68, :45.00, 1:09.69, 1:35.89)

$2 Mutuel Prices:				
	5–SPITE THE DEVIL	35.80	12.20	6.50
	3–ALYSWEEP		6.10	4.30
	8–STANISLAVSKY			5.10

$2 EXACTA 5–3 PAID $155.00 $2 TRIFECTA 5–3–8 PAID $1,442.00

Dk. b. or br. c, (Mar), by Devil His Due–Samantha D, by Cryptoclearance. Trainer Jerkens H Allen. Bred by Elisabeth R. Jerkens (NY).

SPITE THE DEVIL stumbled at the start, was bumped, was outrun early, advanced inside on the turn, angled out in upper stretch, finished determinedly outside and was up late, driving. ALYSWEEP raced close up early, rallied four wide approaching the stretch, reached the front between calls in deep stretch and was caught nearing the wire. STANISLAVSKY showed good speed from the outside, rallied three wide on the turn and dug in gamely in the stretch. DON SIX was bumped at the start, set the pace while in hand and stayed on gamely to the finish. NEW YORK HERO was bumped soundly at the start, argued the pace along the inside and faded in the stretch. HALO HOMEWRECKER was bumped soundly at the start, raced close up while between rivals and lacked a rally while between rivals in the stretch. ATFIRST BLUSH was outrun early, came wide into the stretch and had no rally. AWESOME TIME stumbled at the start, raced wide and tired.

Owners— 1, Hardwicke Stable; 2, Doneson Mark & Dubb Michael; 3, Cohn Seymour; 4, Generazio Patricia A; 5, Paraneck Stable; 6, Evans Edward P; 7, Streicher Judson L; 8, Lapenta Robert V

Trainers—1, Jerkens H Allen; 2, Reynolds Patrick L; 3, Hertler John O; 4, Generazio Frank Jr; 5, Pedersen Jennifer; 6, Hennig Mark; 7, Russo Sal; 8, Zito Nicholas P

FIFTH RACE

Churchill

MAY 3, 2003

7 FURLONGS. (1.20²) 69th Running of THE CHURCHILL DOWNS HANDICAP. Grade II. Purse $200,000 Added. FOUR-YEAR-OLDS AND UPWARD. By subscription of $200 each on or before April 12, 2003 or by Supplementary Nomination of $10,000 each by the closing of entries Friday, April 25, 2003. $1,000 to pass the entry box; $1,000 additional to start, with $200,000 added of which 62% of all monies to the owner of the winner, 20% to second, 10% to third, 5% to fourth and 3% to fifth. Weights to be announced though the entry box at the usual time of closing. Closed Saturday, April 12, 2003 with 44 nominations.

Value of Race: $233,800 Winner $144,956; second $46,760; third $23,380; fourth $11,690; fifth $7,014.   Mutuel Pool $2,098,265.0 Exacta Pool $1,690,623.0 Trifecta Pool $1,243,632.0 Superfecta Pool $293,799.00

Last Raced	Horse	M/Eqt.	A.Wt	PP	St	¼	½	Str	Fin	Jockey	Odds $1
12Apr03 ⁹Aqu²	Aldebaran	L	5 120	5	10	11⁶	9½	3½	12½	Bailey J D	1.30
1Feb03 ⁹SA⁵	Pass Rush	Lb	4 117	3	3	4¹½	4½	4½	2ⁿᵏ	Farina Tony	10.10
22Mar03 ⁴GG⁶	Cappuchino	Lbf	4 115	6	7	3¹	5½	2½	3ʰᵈ	Coa E M	79.70
12Apr03 ⁹Aqu³	Peeping Tom	Lbf	6 116	1	11	7ʰᵈ	8¹½	7¹½	4ⁿᵏ	Bridgmohan S X	5.10
12Apr03 ⁹GP⁶	Lord Abounding	Lb	4 114	11	1	2ʰᵈ	11½	11½	5²½	Guidry M	6.80
13Apr03 ⁸Kee⁴	Binthebest	Lbf	6 114	8	8	10¹	10½	6¹½	6²	Albarado R J	27.50
19Nov02 ⁸CD⁴	Twilight Road	L	6 116	9	6	1½	2½	5½	7ʰᵈ	Desormeaux K J	20.50
10Apr03 ⁷SA¹	R. Baggio	Lb	5 115	4	9	12	12	11¹½	8ʰᵈ	Sellers S J	36.00
8Jun02 ¹⁰Bel⁵	Proud Citizen	L	4 119	12	2	5½	3¹½	8½	9ʰᵈ	Velasquez C	6.60
16Mar03 ⁹FG²	Mountain General	Lb	5 118	10	5	9²½	11⁶	10¹	10¹¾	Meche L J	13.80
5Apr03 ⁹GP²	Swift Replica	L	4 112	2	12	8¹	7¹	9½	11¹¾	Lumpkins J	49.30
29Mar03 ⁸SA⁵	D'wildcat	Lb	5 117	7	4	6³	6½	12	12	Solis A	21.00

OFF AT 1:28 Start Good. Won driving. Track fast.
TIME :22², :45, 1:09³, 1:21⁴ (:22.48, :45.17, 1:09.69, 1:21.80)

$2 Mutuel Prices:

6–ALDEBARAN		4.60	3.20	2.60
4–PASS RUSH			7.20	5.00
7–CAPPUCHINO				13.60

$2 EXACTA 6–4 PAID $39.20 $2 TRIFECTA 6–4–7 PAID $1,685.80 $1 SUPERFECTA 6–4–7–1 PAID $4,249.50

B. h, by Mr. Prospector–Chimes of Freedom, by Private Account. Trainer Frankel Robert. Bred by Flaxman Holdings Ltd (Ky).

ALDEBARAN was outrun while between horses along the backstretch, swung seven wide for clear sailing while launching his bid at the top of the stretch, charged to the front while coming in slightly in mid stretch then drew off under steady left hand encouragement. PASS RUSH steadied in tight between horses along the backstretch, moved out nearing the far turn, rallied between horses while four wide entering the stretch, checked slightly in mid stretch then closed steadily to edge CAPPUCHINO for the place. A claim of foul lodged by the rider and trainer of PASS RUSH against the winner for interference in the stretch was disallowed. CAPPUCHINO steadied along the rail behind horses at the half mile pole, saved ground through the turn, rallied along the inside to threaten in upper stretch then held well for a share. PEEPING TOM was reserved for a half, altered course to the middle of the track while gaining in upper stretch then rallied belatedly. LORD ABOUNDING pressed the early pace from outside, accelerated to the front opening a clear advantage on the far turn, continued on the front into mid stretch then weakened from his early efforts. BINTHEBEST raced well back while saving ground to the top of the stretch then closed late along the inside. TWILIGHT ROAD set or forced the pace along the inside into upper stretch and steadily tired thereafter. R. BAGGIO never reached contention. PROUD CITIZEN stalked four wide along the backstretch, lodged a mild rally on the turn then flattened out. MOUNTAIN GENERAL failed to menace while eight wide on the turn. SWIFT REPLICA raced five wide after breaking slowly. D'WILDCAT gave way before going a half.

Owners— 1, Flaxman Holdings Ltd; 2, Tabor Michael B; 3, Hollendorfer Jerry & Todaro George; 4, Flatbird Stable Louis C Milazzo; 5, Bridle Path Stables Eugene Conese; 6, Tafel James B et al; 7, Donamire Farm; 8, Lewkowitz Frank; 9, Baker Robert C Cornstein David & Ma; 10, Asmussen Keith A; 11, Mario & Karen Zacco; 12, Fog City Stable & Windfields Farm

Trainers—1, Frankel Robert; 2, Byrne Patrick B; 3, Hollendorfer Jerry; 4, Reynolds Patrick L; 5, Plesa Edward Jr; 6, Nafzger Carl A; 7, McGee Paul J; 8, Kruljac J Eric; 9, Lukas D Wayne; 10, Asmussen Steven M; 11, Zacco Mario T; 12, Hess R B Jr

Scratched— Wiseman's Ferry (21Mar03 ⁹GP²)

$1 Pick Three (5–4/10–2/6) Paid $44.40; Pick Three Pool $164,902.

SEVENTH RACE
Churchill
MAY 3, 2003

1 MILE. (Turf)(1.33^3) 14th Running of THE CITGO DISTAFF TURF MILE. Grade III. Purse $100,000 Added. FILLIES AND MARES, THREE YEARS OLD AND UPWARD. By subscription of $100 each on or before April 12, 2003 or by Supplementary Nomination of $5,000 at time of entry. $500 to pass the entry box; $500 additional to start with $100,000 added of which 62% of all monies to the owner of the winner, 20% to second, 10% to third, 5 % to fourth and 3% to fifth. Three-year-olds, 115 lbs.; Older, 123 lbs. Non-winners of $60,000 on the turf in 2003 allowed 2 lbs.; a sweepstakes on the turf in 2002–2003, 4 lbs.; $30,000 twice on the turf since July 4, 6 lbs.; $18,000 twice on the turf in 2002–2003, 8 lbs. Closed Saturday, April 12, 2003 with 55 nominations.

Value of Race: $117,000 Winner $72,540; second $23,400; third $11,700; fourth $5,850; fifth $3,510. Mutuel Pool $2,765,011.0 Exacta Pool $1,879,094.0 Trifecta Pool $1,365,477.0 Superfecta Pool $336,030.00

Last Raced	Horse	M/Eqt.	A.Wt	PP	St	¼	½	¾	Str	Fin	Jockey	Odds $1
5Apr03 ^{4}SA^1	Heat Haze-GB	L	4 123	4	11	11	11	$9^{2\frac{1}{2}}$	3^{hd}	$1^{1\frac{1}{2}}$	Valdivia J Jr	2.40
13Apr03 ^{6}Kee^6	Quick Tip	L	5 123	10	7	$7^{1\frac{1}{2}}$	7^{hd}	3^{hd}	1^{hd}	$2^{\frac{3}{4}}$	Albarado R J	6.30
13Apr03 ^{6}Kee^5	Sentimental Value	Lb	4 121	7	9	$10^{2\frac{1}{2}}$	9^1	10^2	4^1	$3^{1\frac{1}{4}}$	Desormeaux K J	8.50
16Mar03 ^{10}Tam^2	Dedication-FR	L	4 121	5	5	9^{hd}	8^1	6^{hd}	5^{hd}	$4^{\frac{3}{4}}$	Bailey J D	2.10
1Mar03 ^{9}FG^9	Bag Of Stars	Lbf	5 117	2	4	2^1	$2^{1\frac{1}{2}}$	$2^{1\frac{1}{2}}$	$2^{1\frac{1}{2}}$	5^2	Sellers S J	52.80
6Apr03 ^{9}Tam^4	Maliziosa	L	4 121	6	10	8^{hd}	$10^{\frac{1}{2}}$	11	10^{hd}	6no	Valenzuela P A	9.30
16Mar03 ^{10}Tam^9	Presumed Innocent	Lb	6 121	1	2	$1^{2\frac{1}{2}}$	1^3	1^1	$6^{\frac{1}{2}}$	7^{hd}	Solis A	48.40
16Apr03 ^{8}Kee^2	Salty Farma	Lbf	5 117	8	8	5^{hd}	6^{hd}	$8^{1\frac{1}{2}}$	7^{hd}	$8^{\frac{3}{4}}$	Meche L J	21.80
12Apr03 ^{10}Kee^5	Pina Colada-GB	L	4 121	3	1	6^{hd}	$5^{\frac{1}{2}}$	5^{hd}	8^1	$9^{1\frac{1}{4}}$	Prado E S	20.70
2Feb03 ^{9}GP^5	Mimi's Tizzy	Lf	6 115	9	3	3^1	3^{hd}	7^{hd}	9^2	$10^{1\frac{1}{4}}$	Borel C H	51.70
16Mar03 ^{10}Tam^1	Strait From Texas	L	4 123	11	6	$4^{\frac{1}{2}}$	$4^{\frac{1}{2}}$	4^1	11	11	Day P	8.90

OFF AT 3:14 Start Good. Won driving. Course firm.
TIME :23^2, :46^2, 1:10^4, 1:22^2, 1:33^4 (:23.57, :46.59, 1:10.80, 1:22.51, 1:33.96)

$2 Mutuel Prices:				
	4–HEAT HAZE–GB	6.80	4.20	3.60
	11–QUICK TIP		6.20	4.60
	8–SENTIMENTAL VALUE			5.80

$2 EXACTA 4–11 PAID $39.00 $2 TRIFECTA 4–11–8 PAID $314.60 $1 SUPERFECTA 4–11–8–5 PAID $340.60

B. f, by Green Desert–Hasili*Ire, by Kahyasi*ire. Trainer Frankel Robert. Bred by Juddmonte Farms (GB).

HEAT HAZE (GB), reserved soon after the start and angled near the inside, went along under patient handling, raced three or four wide from the backstretch until approaching the final quarter, came out eight wide for the drive and drove clear late under steady handling. QUICK TIP, well placed from early on while four or five wide, made a bold run to reach the front approaching the final furlong but couldn't race with the winner late while saving second. SENTIMENTAL VALUE, bumped at the start by MALIZIOSA when that one came out, settled four wide between foes, moved out seven wide to secure room when making his run approaching the stretch, was inside the winner on even terms with that one entering the final furlong but couldn't sustain the needed momentum. DEDICATION (FR), in hand early while racing in behind the leaders, saved ground for nearly six furlongs, worked his way out nine wide at the furlong grounds and offered a mild gain. BAG OF STARS, nicely placed inside front-running PRESUMED INNOCENT early, eased out three wide on the backstretch, made a menacing run into the upper stretch, leaned in and bumped PRESUMED INNOCENT when putting a head in front, then flattened out late. MALIZIOSA came out while breaking sluggishly and bumped the side of the gate, continued out to bump SENTIMENTAL VALUE, moved in soon after to race three wide, continued in that manner to the stretch, worked his way out 10 wide when straightened for the drive but lacked a serious response while improving position. PRESUMED INNOCENT moved to the fore near the inside early, kicked clear on the first turn, expanded her advantage briefly on the far turn, showed the way into the stretch and faltered. SALTY FARMA gained a forward position between rivals three or four wide early, continued in a striking position to the stretch and came up empty. PINA COLADA (GB), well placed near the inside to the stretch, weakened thereafter. M IMI'S TIZZY edged in early to track the pace four wide, remained prominent to the end of the backstretch and gradually weakened. STRAIT FROM TEXAS followed the leaders five wide until approaching the stretch and faded in the drive.

Owners— 1, Juddmonte Farms Inc; 2, Farish William S; 3, The Thoroughbred Corporation; 4, Head Ghislaine; 5, Merrill R Scherer George Rose & Ken; 6, Haras Santa Maria de Araras; 7, McKee Stables; 8, Weaver Edward & Bielfeldt Larry; 9, Team Valor & Gary Barber Barry Irwi; 10, Williams Frances G; 11, Michael James A

Trainers—1, Frankel Robert; 2, Howard Neil J; 3, Mulhall Kristin; 4, Clement Christophe; 5, Scherer Merrill R; 6, Mott William I; 7, Simon Charles; 8, Kassen David C; 9, Romans Dale; 10, Williams Harold; 11, Maker Michael J

Scratched— Love Talkin (19Apr03 ^{6}KEE^5), Madame Cerito (9Apr03 ^{9}KEE^1), Red n'Gold (2May03 ^{8}CD^5), Stylish (16Mar03 ^{10}TAM^3)

$1 Pick Three (2/6–3–4) Paid $57.30; Pick Three Pool $277,212.

EIGHTH RACE

Churchill

MAY 3, 2003

7 FURLONGS. (1.20²) 17th Running of THE HUMANA DISTAFF HANDICAP. Grade I. Purse $200,000 Added. FILLIES AND MARES, FOUR YEARS OLD AND UPWARD. By subscription of $200 each on or before April 12, 2003 or by Supplementary Nomination of $10,000 each by the closing of entries Friday, April 25, 2003. $1,000 to pass the entry box; $1,000 additional to start, with $200,000 added of which 62% of all monies to the owner of the winner, 20% to second, 10% to third, 5% to fourth and 3% to fifth. Weights to be announced Saturday, April 26. Starters to be named through the entry box at the usual time of closing. Closed Saturday, April 12, 2003 with 32 nominations.

Value of Race: $222,400 Winner $137,888; second $44,480; third $22,240; fourth $11,120; fifth $6,672. Mutuel Pool $2,667,363.0 Exacta Pool $2,011,018.0 Trifecta Pool $1,504,242.0 Superfecta Pool $384,740.00

Last Raced	Horse	M/Eqt.	A.Wt	PP	St	¼	½	Str	Fin	Jockey	Odds $1
9Mar03 ⁸SA²	Sightseek	L	4 116	2	5	5¹	5½	1½	14½	Bailey J D	0.80
16Mar03 ¹⁰GP¹	Gold Mover	L	5 119	1	2	4ʰᵈ	4ʰᵈ	4²	2ʰᵈ	Prado E S	3.00
15Mar03 ⁹FG²	Miss Lodi	L	4 114	4	7	2ʰᵈ	2½	2¹½	32¼	Albarado R J	9.00
31Dec02 ¹⁰Crc¹	Slews Final Answer	L	4 114	6	8	3ʰᵈ	3½	3¹	4³	Velasquez C	13.00
9Apr03 ⁸Kee⁴	Spring Meadow	L	4 117	3	6	8	7¹	6³	5²	Stevens G L	25.40
9Apr03 ⁸Kee²	Flaxen Flyer	Lb	4 116	5	1	1¹	1½	5¹	62¼	Desormeaux K J	38.60
19Mar03 ⁹GP¹	Sixtyone Margaux		4 113	8	4	6ʰᵈ	6¹	7³	73½	Day P	13.30
11Sep02 ³Dmr¹	Palmarola-ARG	Lbf	6 116	7	3	7½	8	8	8	Solis A	10.10

OFF AT 4:00 Start Good. Won driving. Track fast.

TIME :22², :45², 1:10, 1:22 (:22.56, :45.54, 1:10.02, 1:22.12)

$2 Mutuel Prices:

2–SIGHTSEEK	3.60	2.60	2.40
1–GOLD MOVER		3.20	2.80
4–MISS LODI			3.20

$2 EXACTA 2–1 PAID $8.60 $2 TRIFECTA 2–1–4 PAID $29.60 $1
SUPERFECTA 2–1–4–6 PAID $50.40

Ch. f, by Distant View–Viviana, by Nureyev. Trainer Frankel Robert. Bred by Juddmonte Farms, Inc. (Ky).

SIGHTSEEK, rated in behind the leaders from early on, raced between foes three wide on the backstretch, continued in that manner around the turn and into the stretch, split horses three wide about the three-sixteenths pole, then drew off under steady right-handed urging. GOLD MOVER, never far back and saving ground into the stretch, worked her way out five wide for the final furlong and outgamed MISS LODI for second while no threat to SIGHTSEEK. MISS LODI leaned in at the break bumping with SPRING MEADOW, went up soon after to press front-running FLAXEN FLYER three or four wide, gained a narrow advantage between calls in the upper stretch but gradually weakened soon after. SLEWS FINAL ANSWER stalked the pace four wide from early on, moved on about even terms for the lead when five wide in the upper stretch but flattened out the last eighth. SPRING MEADOW, bumped at the start, raced four wide early, edged close to the inside on the turn, swung out four or five wide for the drive but failed to rally. FLAXEN FLYER gained the lead early, raced two wide, showed the way until the final quarter and faltered. SIXTYONE MARGAUX, seven wide on the backstretch, continued off the inside and was done upon gong a half. PALMAROLA (ARG), running in two front bar shoes, raced between rivals six wide early, then tired on the turn.

Owners— 1, Juddmonte Farms Inc; 2, Evans Edward P; 3, Colton Richard C & Mast Thoroughbre; 4, Live Oak Plantation; 5, Fog City Stable; 6, Gus Goldsmith & Kerri Long; 7, Rutherford Mike G; 8, A Preston J Preston & D Sutherland

Trainers—1, Frankel Robert; 2, Hennig Mark; 3, Amoss Thomas; 4, Mott William I; 5, Hess R B Jr; 6, Hicks Denette L; 7, Mott William I; 8, Mandella Richard

---

$1 Pick Three (3–4–2) Paid $54.00; Pick Three Pool $346,415.

NINTH RACE
Churchill
MAY 3, 2003

1⅛ MILES. (Turf)(1.46^{1}) 17th Running of THE WOODFORD RESERVE TURF CLASSIC. Grade I. Purse $400,000 Added. THREE-YEAR-OLDS AND UPWARD. By subscription of $100 each on or before February 15, 2003 or by Supplementary Nomination of $20,000 at time of entry. $2,000 to pass the entry box; $2,000 additional to start with $400,000 added of which 62% of all monies to the owner of the winner, 20% to second, 10% to third, 5% to fourth and 3% to fifth. Three-year-olds, 115 lbs.; Older, 123 lbs. Non-winners of $200,000 at a mile or over since August 1 allowed 3 lbs.; $100,000 at a mile or over since June 30, 5 lbs.; $46,500 twice at a mile or over in 2002-2003, 7 lbs.; $46,500 at a mile or over in 2003, 9 lbs. Starters to be named through the entry box Wednesday, April 30, 2003 at the usual time of closing. Closed Saturday, February 15, 2003 with 113 nominations.

Value of Race: $445,300 Winner $276,086; second $89,060; third $44,530; fourth $22,265; fifth $13,359. Mutuel Pool $2,955,393.0 Exacta Pool $1,959,436.0 Trifecta Pool $1,462,274.0 Superfecta Pool $361,727.00

Last Raced	Horse	M/Eqt.	A.Wt	PP	St	¼	½	¾	Str	Fin	Jockey	Odds $1
17Apr03 ^{6}Kee^{1}	Honor In War	L	4 116	8	1	3^{hd}	4^{2}	4^{1}	1^{1}	$1^{1\frac{1}{4}}$	Flores D R	24.30
23Mar03 ^{8}FG^{6}	Requete-GB	L	4 116	1	8	8	7^{hd}	7^{1}	$4^{2\frac{1}{2}}$	$2^{\frac{3}{4}}$	Prado E S	5.50
22Mar03 ^{8}GP^{1}	Patrol	L	4 114	4	2	$1^{\frac{1}{2}}$	1^{1}	$1^{\frac{1}{2}}$	2^{3}	$3^{\frac{1}{2}}$	Velasquez C	7.40
11Apr03 ^{9}Kee^{1}	Perfect Drift	L	4 123	5	6	5^{hd}	$5^{\frac{1}{2}}$	5^{1}	3^{hd}	$4^{1\frac{1}{4}}$	Desormeaux K J	5.80
26Oct02 ^{9}AP^{2}	With Anticipation	Lb	8 123	3	3	7^{1}	8	8	$5^{\frac{1}{2}}$	$5^{2\frac{1}{4}}$	Day P	2.10
6Apr03 ^{7}SA^{1}	Century City-IR	Lb	4 118	7	7	6^{1}	$6^{1\frac{1}{2}}$	6^{2}	7^{5}	6^{4}	Valdivia J Jr	7.40
23Mar03 ^{8}FG^{2}	Rouvres-FR	L	4 114	2	4	4^{5}	2^{1}	$2^{\frac{1}{2}}$	$6^{\frac{1}{2}}$	$7^{5\frac{1}{4}}$	Bailey J D	2.60
19Apr03 ^{7}Kee^{5}	Even The Score	Lb	5 115	6	5	$2^{2\frac{1}{2}}$	$3^{\frac{1}{2}}$	3^{1}	8	8	Sellers S J	31.90

OFF AT 4:53 Start Good. Won driving. Course firm.
TIME :24^{1}, :47^{4}, 1:11^{1}, 1:34^{4}, 1:46^{3} (:24.22, :47.84, 1:11.33, 1:34.85, 1:46.67)

$2 Mutuel Prices:				
	9-HONOR IN WAR	50.60	17.00	7.80
	1-REQUETE-GB		8.80	5.80
	5-PATROL			6.40

$2 EXACTA 9-1 PAID $462.40 $2 TRIFECTA 9-1-5 PAID $3,313.00 $1 SUPERFECTA 9-1-5-6 PAID $11,719.90

Ch. c, by Lord At War*Arg-Catumbella, by Diesis*GB. Trainer McGee Paul J. Bred by Mill Ridge Farm Ltd & W Lazy T Ltd (Ky).

HONOR IN WAR hopped slightly at the start while breaking alertly, gained a forward position three or four wide under light rating, was between foes on the backstretch, moved closer to the inside on the far turn while losing a bit of position, followed front-running PATROL into the stretch, eased outside that one three or four wide when straightened for the drive, reached the front leaving the three-sixteenths pole, then was under steady left-handed urging the remainder. REQUETE (GB), bumped at the break and forced in a bit by ROUVRES (FR), settled three wide, continued in that manner around the far turn, was close to the hedge in the upper stretch, angled between horses three wide late and was going well as second best. PATROL gained the lead early, raced two or three wide under restraint, made the pace into the upper stretch and grudgingly weakened. PERFECT DRIFT, well placed while lightly rated in behind horses to the stretch, maneuvered out five wide for the drive, loomed a solid threat for the last eighth and came up empty. WITH ANTICIPATION settled inside early, was unhurried to the far turn, reached contention as the field tightened, came out eight wide for the drive and lacked a closing bid. CENTURY CITY (IRE) tracked the leaders five wide until approaching the final quarter, angled wider for the drive but lacked a closing response. ROUVRES (FR) drifted in at the start bumping REQUETTE (GB), was rated along in behind front-running PATROL soon after, edged up outside that one on the far turn, continued forwardly to the stretch and flattened out. EVEN THE SCORE went up soon after the start to track front-running PATROL, continued forwardly to the far turn and weakened thereafter.

Owners— 1, 3rd Turn Stables; 2, Juddmonte Farms Inc; 3, Claiborne Farm; 4, Stonecrest Farm; 5, Augustin Stable; 6, Tom Nichols & Kitchwa Stables John; 7, Head Alec; 8, Vanderhyde Thomas

Trainers—1, McGee Paul J; 2, Frankel Robert; 3, Mott William I; 4, Johnson Murray W; 5, Sheppard Jonathan E; 6, Greely C Beau; 7, Clement Christophe; 8, Stewart Dallas

Scratched— Epicentre (13Apr03 ^{9}KEE^{1})

$1 Pick Three (4-2-9) Paid $325.80; Pick Three Pool $257,075.

TENTH RACE
Churchill
MAY 3, 2003

1¼ MILES. (1.592) 129th Running of THE KENTUCKY DERBY. Grade I. Purse $1,000,000 Guaranteed. THREE-YEAR-OLDS. $15,000 to pass the entry box and $15,000 additional to start. Supplemental nominations may be made upon payment of $150,000 and in accordance with the rules set forth. All fees, including supplemental nominations, in excess of $500,000 in the aggregate shall be paid to the winner. The winner shall receive $700,000, second place shall receive $170,000, third place shall receive $85,000 and fourth place shall receive $45,000. Starters shall be named through the entry box on Wednesday, April 30, 2003. Colts and Geldings shall each carry a weight of one hundred twenty-six (126) pounds; Fillies shall each carry one hundred twenty-one (121) pounds. Closed with 446 nominations and 8 late nominations.

Value of Race: $1,100,200 Winner $800,200; second $170,000; third $85,000; fourth $45,000. Mutuel Pool $36,610,341. Exacta Pool $17,429,596. Trifecta Pool $19,040,971. Superfecta Pool $4,908,214.0 Pool $516,906.00 Pool $391,002.00 Pool $222,261.00

Last Raced	Horse	M/Eqt.	A.Wt	PP	¼	½	¾	1	Str	Fin	Jockey	Odds $1
12Apr03 8Aqu2	Funny Cide	L	3 126	5	4½	3½	31½	21	1hd	11¾	Santos J A	12.80
12Apr03 8Aqu1	Empire Maker	Lb	3 126	11	8½	82½	81½	31½	31½	2hd	Bailey J D	2.50
12Apr03 9Kee1	Peace Rules	L	3 126	4	21½	21½	21½	1½	2½	3hd	Prado E S	6.30
5Apr03 6SA4	Atswhatimtalknbout	Lb	3 126	3	101½	122	112	10½	5½	42¾	Flores D R	8.90
19Apr03 8Kee2	Eye Of The Tiger	L	3 126	12	3hd	41½	4½	41	42½	51	Coa E M	41.50
5Apr03 6SA1	Buddy Gil	L	3 126	7	13hd	132½	134	111	6½	6¾	Stevens G L	7.20
29Mar03 NAS4	Outta Here	L	3 126	14	151½	14hd	16	153	141½	71	Desormeaux K J	39.70
12Apr03 9Kee8	Ten Cents A Shine	L	3 126	13	16	16	15½	143½	111	8nk	Borel C H	37.20
5Apr03 8Haw1	Ten Most Wanted	L	3 126	15	121½	10½	101½	9½	10½	91¾	Day P	6.60
19Apr03 8Kee3	Domestic Dispute	L	3 126	10	7½	71	5hd	7hd	7½	101	Solis A	44.00
19Apr03 8Kee1	Scrimshaw	Lb	3 126	16	5½	6½	7hd	8hd	8½	111	Velasquez C	16.50
12Apr03 9Kee3	Offlee Wild	L	3 126	6	111½	111½	91½	6½	91	125½	Albarado R J	29.90
5Apr03 11GP2	Supah Blitz	Lb	3 126	1	92½	9½	122½	13hd	121	131¾	Homeister R B Jr	43.10
5Apr03 6SA2	Indian Express	L	3 126	8	6½	5hd	6hd	12hd	152½	141¼	Baze T C	10.80
5Apr03 8Haw4	Lone Star Sky	L	3 126	9	141½	151	14½	16	16	151	Sellers S J	52.10
12Apr03 9Kee2	Brancusi	L	3 126	2	1½	1½	1hd	5hd	131½	16	Farina Tony	29.30

OFF AT 6:08 Start Good. Won driving. Track fast.
TIME :223, :461, 1:102, 1:353, 2:01 (:22.78, :46.23, 1:10.48, 1:35.75, 2:01.19)

$2 Mutuel Prices:			
6-FUNNY CIDE	27.60	12.40	8.20
12-EMPIRE MAKER		5.80	4.40
5-PEACE RULES			6.00

$2 EXACTA 6-12 PAID $97.00 $2 TRIFECTA 6-12-5 PAID $664.80 $1 SUPERFECTA 6-12-5-4 PAID $2,795.80 $2 POOL 1 PAID $188.00 $2 POOL 2 PAID $120.80 $2 POOL 3 PAID $107.40

Ch. g, (Apr), by Distorted Humor-Belle's Good Cide, by Slewacide. Trainer Tagg Barclay. Bred by Win Star Farm LLC (NY).

FUNNY CIDE came out bumping with OFFLEE WILD for several strides just after the start, gained a forward position four wide while under a rating hold when under the wire for the first time, edged nearer the inside to draft in behind front-running BRANCUSI and PEACE RULES, eased outside of PEACE RULES when that one took over approaching the end of the backstretch, inched to challenge that one approaching the final quarter, reached the front when straightened for the drive, opened a clear advantage leaving the furlong grounds after being roused sharply on the right side, then, after the rider switched the whip to his left hand and again back to his right, gamely maintained his advantage. EMPIRE MAKER, away in good order and six or seven wide during the early stages while under light restraint, continued five wide on the backstretch and into the far turn, advanced steadily five wide leaving the three-eighths pole, loomed boldly outside FUNNY CIDE through the drive and wasn't good enough. PEACE RULES broke sharply to briefly lead, surrendered the advantage to BRANCUSI from the inside, raced well out in the track the opening eighth, edged in three wide to battle heads apart with that one into the first turn while full of run, assumed the advantage just after going six furlongs, opened a clear lead on the far turn, was displaced on the lead by the winner when straightened into the stretch and continued with good courage to save third position. ATSWHATIMTALKNBOUT, bumped at the start by BRANCUSI and forced out slightly, quickly recovered, was taken in hand to the inside, saved ground for a mile, came out for the drive to make a run between rivals seven wide and was going well at the end. EYE OF THE TIGER gradually worked his way in four wide by the first turn to track the leaders under light rating, leaned in lightly bumping with BRANCUSI approaching the stretch, continued in a challenging position into the lan e but flattened out. BUDDY GIL, slightly sluggish at the break and bumped soon after by OFFLEE WILD when that one was forced out by FUNNY CIDE, settled three or four wide, reached contention nearing the final quarter, moved near the rail for the drive and improved position while unable to seriously menace. OUTTA HERE, eight or nine wide early, was checked slightly and able to angle in behind rivals while losing position entering the first turn, raced four or five wide while outrun to the stretch, came to the extreme outside to be 12 wide for the final furlong and offered mild gain. TEN CENTS A SHINE, reserved after the start and maneuvered towards the inside, raced three or four wide while outrun for seven furlongs, eased out to make a run 10 wide into the stretch and offered a mild gain. TEN MOST WANTED, bumped after the start by SCRIMSHAW, was checked during the opening furlong, settled six wide, continued off the inside, reached contention as the field tightened approaching the stretch but failed to offer a closing response. DOMESTIC DISPUTE, within striking distance while five or six wide, remained in contention into the upper stretch while five wide between rivals but was empty when the test came. SCRIMSHAW drifted in at the start bumping with TEN MOST WANTED, tracked the leaders four or five wide, was asked for his best three furlongs out while between foes but flattened out in the drive. OFFLEE WILD, bumped for several strides soon after the start by FUNNY CIDE, reserved between foes, three or four wide to the end of the backstretch, moved to contention midway with a burst of speed between calls on the far turn, came out five or six wide for the drive but couldn't sustain the needed momentum. SUPAH BLITZ came out brushing BRANCUSI after the start, saved ground, was checked lightly soon after passing the wire the first time and failed to menace. INDIAN EXPRESS, rank early and steadied repeatedly when ca ught between rivals approaching the first turn, raced in contention to the end of the backstretch and weakened thereafter. LONE STAR SKY, steadied and shuffled nearing the first turn, failed to reach contention. BRANCUSI came out brushing with ATSWHATIMTALKINBOUT soon after the start, moved to the fore near the inside, held a slight advantage while battling inside of PEACE RULES to the end of the backstretch, lost the edge to that one, continued forwardly to the stretch and faded. SIR CHEROKEE was declared from the race on Friday morning due to an injury to his right hind ankle. Because of the scratch, the number one post position in the starting gate was left unoccupied. Post positions do not correspond to actual gate position. The horses in the auxiliary gate were OUTTA HERE, TEN MOST WANTED and SCRIMSHAW.

Owners— 1, Sackatoga Stable Jackson W Knowlton; 2, Juddmonte Farms Inc; 3, Gann Edmund A; 4, B Wayne Hughes & Biscuit Stables LL; 5, Gunther John D; 6, Desperado Stables; 7, William Currin & Al Eisman; 8, Ramsey Kenneth L & Sarah K; 9, James Chisholm Michael Jarvis & J P; 10, David Bienstock & Chuck Winner; 11, Lewis Robert B & Beverly J; 12, Azalea Stables LLC Lansdon B Robbin; 13, Bee Bee Stables & Jacqueline Tortor; 14, Chess Phil & Sheva; 15, New Walter L; 16, Tabor Michael B

Trainers—1, Tagg Barclay; 2, Frankel Robert; 3, Frankel Robert; 4, Ellis Ronald W; 5, Hollendorfer Jerry; 6, Mullins Jeff; 7, Currin William L; 8, Lukas D Wayne; 9, Dollase Wallace; 10, Gallagher Patrick; 11, Lukas D Wayne; 12, Smith Thomas V; 13, Tortora Emanuel; 14, Baffert Bob; 15, Amoss Thomas; 16, Biancone Patrick L

Scratched— Sir Cherokee (12Apr03 9OP1)

$1 Daily Double (9-6) Paid $425.90; Daily Double Pool $429,666.
$2 Daily Double (OAKS/DERBY 5-6) Paid $421.80; Daily Double Pool $1,231,072.
$1 Pick Three (2-9-6) Paid $1,042.50; Pick Three Pool $629,374.
$1 Pick Four (4-2-9-6) Paid $7,017.50; Pick Four Pool $1,533,459.
$2 Pick Six (2/6-3-4-2-9-6) 5
Correct Paid $808.80; Pick Six Pool $635,072. $2 Pick Six (2/6-3-4-2-9-6) 6
Correct Paid $453,285.40

EIGHTH RACE

Hollywood
MAY 4, 2003

7 FURLONGS. (1.19⁴) 41st Running of THE RAILBIRD. Grade III. Purse $100,000 added. Fillies, 3-year-olds. By subscription of $100 each on or before Wednesday, April 23. $1,000 additional to start, with $100,000 added. The added money and all fees to be divided 60% to the winner, 20% to second,12% to third,6% to fourth and 2% to fifth. Weight, 123 lbs. Non-winners of $90,000, allowed 3 lbs. A race of $60,000 since December 25, 5 lbs. Two races other than claiming or starter 8 lbs. Such a race 10 lbs. Closed April 23 with 12 nominations.

Value of Race: $107,200 Winner $64,320; second $21,440; third $12,864; fourth $6,432; fifth $2,144. Mutuel Pool $366,826.00 Exacta Pool $272,313.00 Quinella Pool $28,264.00

Last Raced	Horse	M/Eqt. A.Wt	PP	St	¼	½	Str	Fin	Jockey	Odds $1
23Mar03 ³SA¹	Buffythecenterfold	LB	3 123	5	3	3³	3²	1½	1¹	Espinoza V	a-0.40
12Mar03 ²SA²	Honest Answer	LB	3 117	2	2	1½	1½	2³	2²	Nakatani C S	9.50
6Apr03 ⁴SA²	Dash For Money	LBb	3 115	4	4	4½	4½	4½	3½	Solis A	a-0.40
29Mar03 ⁹Sun⁴	Himalayan	LB	3 118	6	1	2½	2½	3¹	4½	Pedroza M A	4.90
7Apr03 ⁹TuP³	Hostility	LB	3 118	1	5	5¹	5ʰᵈ	6	5½	Garcia M S	26.90
13Apr03 ⁸B M²	Lucky Sabre	LB	3 118	3	6	6	6	5²½	6	Flores D R	3.90

a-Coupled: Buffythecenterfold and Dash For Money.

OFF AT 4:57 Start Good. Won driving. Track fast.
TIME :22², :45³, 1:09³, 1:22² (:22.47, :45.64, 1:09.71, 1:22.54)

$2 Mutuel Prices:

1A –BUFFYTHECNTRFLD (a)	2.80	2.10	2.10
3 –HONEST ANSWER		3.40	2.10
1 –DASH FOR MONEY (a)	2.80	2.10	2.10

$1 EXACTA 1-3 PAID $6.80 $2 QUINELLA 1-3 PAID $9.80

B. f, (Mar), by Capote–Augusta Springs, by Nijinsky II. Trainer Stute Melvin F. Bred by Overbrook Farm (Ky).

BUFFYTHECENTERFOLD stalked the pace off the rail on the backstretch and turn, ranged up three deep into the stretch to gain the lead, ducked in when shown the whip right handed past midstretch but gamely prevailed under good handling. HONEST ANSWER had good early speed and dueled inside, fought back in the stretch, steadied slightly when a bit crowded by the winner past midstretch and could not match that one late. DASH FOR MONEY bumped at the start, chased off the rail, angled in some on the turn, came out into the stretch and bested the rest. HIMALAYAN angled in and dueled outside the runner-up to the stretch and weakened. HOSTILITY off a bit slowly, settled just off the rail then outside a rival, came out for the stretch and did not rally. LUCKY SABRE broke out and bumped a rival in a slow start, angled in and saved ground off the pace, remained inside and failed to menace.

Owners— 1, Brian Allen A & Stronach Stables; 2, The Thoroughbred Corporation; 3, Stronach Stable; 4, Sengara Jeffrey; 5, Strader Scott & Hannahs Gerald & Gu; 6, Abruzzo Peter Franks John & Hollend

Trainers— 1, Stute Melvin F; 2, Baffert Bob; 3, Frankel Robert; 4, West Ted H; 5, Cardenas Ruben; 6, Hollendorfer Jerry

---

$2 Daily Double (4–1) Paid $7.60; Daily Double Pool $33,485.
$1 Pick Three (9–4–1) Paid $45.60; Pick Three Pool $54,432.

EIGHTH RACE

Belmont
MAY 7, 2003

1 MILE. (1.32¹) 75th Running of THE WESTCHESTER HANDICAP. Grade III. Purse $100,000 (Up to $19,400 NYSBFOA) A HANDICAP FOR THREE YEAR OLDS AND UPWARD. By subscription of $100 each, which should accompany the nomination; $500 to pass the entry box; $500 to start, with $100,000 added. The added money and all fees to be divided 60% to the winner, 20% to second, 11% to third, 6% to fourth and 3% to fifth. Trophies will be presented to the winning owner, trainer and jockey. Closed Saturday, April 26, 2003 with 27 Nominations.

Value of Race: $109,700 Winner $65,820; second $21,940; third $12,067; fourth $6,582; fifth $3,291. Mutuel Pool $441,972.00 Exacta Pool $385,126.00 Trifecta Pool $294,317.00

Last Raced	Horse	M/Eqt. A.Wt	PP	St	¼	½	¾	Str	Fin	Jockey	Odds $1
13Apr03 ⁸Kee⁷	Najran	L	4 113	1	2	12½	13½	15½	18	14½	Prado E S	5.40
11Apr03 ⁷Aqu¹	Saarland	Lbf	4 114	4	7	7	7	5ʰᵈ	3½	2³	Velazquez J R	1.35
23Apr03 ⁸Aqu¹	Justification	L	6 113	3	4	5½	5¹	6²	5ʰᵈ	3½	Luzzi M J	12.60
21Mar03 ⁹GP¹	Gander	Lb	7 116	2	5	6²	6ʰᵈ	7	7	4ʰᵈ	Migliore R	4.00
27Mar03 ⁷Aqu¹	Regal Sanction	L	4 114	6	1	2½	2ʰᵈ	2¹½	2ʰᵈ	5¹¼	Santos J A	16.50
11Apr03 ⁹Kee³	Bowman's Band	L	5 116	5	3	4¹½	4²	3½	4¹	6²	Bailey J D	4.40
5Apr03 ⁶GP¹	Saint Appeal	L	4 113	7	6	3ʰᵈ	3³½	4ʰᵈ	6ʰᵈ	7	Chavez J F	13.20

OFF AT 4:41 Start Good. Won driving. Track fast.
TIME :22³, :44³, 1:07³, 1:32¹ (:22.65, :44.67, 1:07.76, 1:32.24) New Track Record

New Track Record

$2 Mutuel Prices:

1 –NAJRAN	12.80	4.70	3.20
4 –SAARLAND		3.10	2.40
3 –JUSTIFICATION			4.50

$2 EXACTA 1-4 PAID $37.40 $2 TRIFECTA 1-4-3 PAID $255.50

Gr/ro c, by Runaway Groom–Line Command, by Capote. Trainer Zito Nicholas P. Bred by France Weiner & Irv Weiner (Ky).

NAJRAN quickly sprinted clear, set the pace while away from the inner railing, widened on the turn, drew away entering the stretch and remained well clear while being shown the whip through the stretch. SAARLAND was outrun early, rallied five wide approaching the stretch and finished gamely to earn the place award. JUSTIFICATION was hustled along early, raced four wide on the turn and lacked a rally. GANDER was outrun early, came wide entering the stretch and had no rally. REGAL SANCTION was hustled from the gate, chased the pace along the inside and tired in the stretch. BOWMAN'S BAND was urged along early, chased the pace while three wide on the turn, angled to the inside for the drive and tired in the stretch. SAINT APPEAL stumbled at the start, hit the gate, was hustled outside, chased the pace and tired after three quarters.

Owners— 1, Buckram Oak Farm; 2, Phipps Cynthia; 3, Shields Joseph V Jr; 4, Gatsas Thoroughbreds; 5, Moore Susan & John; 6, Schwartz Martin S; 7, Stronach Stable

Trainers— 1, Zito Nicholas P; 2, McGaughey Claude III; 3, Jerkens H Allen; 4, Terranova John P II; 5, Jerkens James A; 6, Matz Michael R; 7, Jolley Leroy

SIXTH RACE
Belmont
MAY 10, 2003

6 FURLONGS. (1.07^{3}) 28th Running of THE BOLD RULER HANDICAP. Grade III. Purse $100,000. (Up to $19,400 NYSBFOA). THREE YEAR OLDS AND UPWARD. By subscription of $100 each, which should accompany the nomination; $500 to pass the entry box; $500 to start, with $100,000 added. The added money and all fees to be divided 60% to the winner, 20% to second, 11% to third, 6% to fourth and 3% to fifth. Trophies will be presented to the winning owner, trainer and jockey. Closed Saturday, April 26, 2003 with 14 Nominations.

Value of Race: $108,400 Winner $65,040; second $21,680; third $11,924; fourth $6,504; fifth $3,252. Mutuel Pool $687,854.00 Exacta Pool $562,855.00 Trifecta Pool $388,018.00

Last Raced	Horse	M/Eqt.	A.	Wt	PP	St	¼	½	Str	Fin	Jockey	Odds $1
26Apr03 ^{5}Aqu^{1}	Shake You Down	Lbf	5	115	7	1	$1^{1\frac{1}{2}}$	$1^{1\frac{1}{2}}$	$1^{\frac{1}{2}}$	1^{1}	Luzzi M J	1.80
3Apr03 ^{8}Aqu^{2}	Here's Zealous	L	6	114	3	2	2^{hd}	2^{2}	$2^{3\frac{1}{2}}$	$2^{3\frac{1}{4}}$	Velazquez J R	4.50
3May03 ^{5}CD^{4}	Peeping Tom	Lb	6	117	1	3	$5^{\frac{1}{2}}$	4^{hd}	$3^{\frac{1}{2}}$	$3^{\frac{3}{4}}$	Bridgmohan S X	2.95
3Apr03 ^{8}Aqu^{3}	Well Fancied	L	5	113	5	6	$6^{1\frac{1}{2}}$	$6^{1\frac{1}{2}}$	$6^{2\frac{1}{2}}$	$4^{1\frac{3}{4}}$	Castellano J J	11.40
3Apr03 ^{8}Aqu^{1}	Say Florida Sandy	Lf	9	116	6	4	$3^{1\frac{1}{2}}$	3^{hd}	4^{hd}	5^{nk}	Santos J A	7.30
3Apr03 ^{8}GP^{1}	Pinch Hitter	L	4	114	2	5	4^{hd}	$5^{2\frac{1}{2}}$	$5^{\frac{1}{2}}$	6^{nk}	Coa E M	33.00
13Apr03 ^{8}Kee^{3}	Multiple Choice	Lb	5	117	4	7	7	7	7	7	Carrero V	5.80

OFF AT 3:41 Start Good. Won driving. Track fast.
TIME :22, :44^{3}, :56^{1}, 1:08^{2} (:22.14, :44.65, :56.25, 1:08.47)

$2 Mutuel Prices:

7–SHAKE YOU DOWN	5.60	3.70	2.60
3–HERE'S ZEALOUS		4.80	2.80
1–PEEPING TOM			2.60

$2 EXACTA 7–3 PAID $29.60 $2 TRIFECTA 7–3–1 PAID $64.00

Ch. h, by Montbrook–Mauvin Gway, by Rajab. Trainer Lake Scott A. Bred by Ocala Stud Farm (Fla).

SHAKE YOU DOWN was hustled to the front, set the pace while in hand, turned back a bid from HERE'S ZEALOUS in upper stretch and was clear under the wire, driving. HERE'S ZEALOUS showed good speed along the inside, tried the winner nearing the eighth pole, could not by that rival and continued on gamely to the finish. PEEPING TOM was hustled up inside, chased the pace and lacked a rally. WELL FANCIED was outrun early, raced four wide and offered a mild rally outside. SAY FLORIDA SANDY chased the pace while three wide and tired in the stretch. PINCH HITTER was hustled along while between rivals and had no response when roused. MULTIPLE CHOICE broke slowly, was outrun early, came wide into the stretch and had no rally.

Owners— 1, Cole Robert L Jr; 2, Jay Em Ess Stable; 3, Flatbird Stable; 4, Goldfarb Sanford Hoffman Stewart &; 5, Rotella John; 6, Gatsas Thoroughbreds; 7, Blum Peter E

Trainers—1, Lake Scott A; 2, Dutrow Richard E Jr; 3, Reynolds Patrick L; 4, Dutrow Richard E Jr; 5, Cuadra Victor; 6, Terranova John P II; 7, Jerkens James A

$2 Pick Three (4–9–7) Paid $458.50; Pick Three Pool $101,800.

EIGHTH RACE
Belmont
MAY 10, 2003

7 FURLONGS. (1.20) 8th Running of THE NASSAU COUNTY BREEDERS' CUP. Grade II. Purse $200,000. (includes $50,000 BC – Breeders' Cup) (Up to $20,100 NYSBFOA). FILLIES, THREE YEARS OLD. By subscription of $150 each, which should accompany the nomination; $750 to pass the entry box; $750 to start. Breeders' Cup fund monies also correspondingly divided provided a Breeders' Cup nominee has finished in an award position. Any Breeders' Cup monies not awarded will revert back to the fund.122 lbs. Non–winners of $60,000 other than restricted stake since October 1 allowed 2 lbs.; $45,000 other than restricted stake, 4 lbs.; $30,000; or three races other than maiden or claiming, 6 lbs. Trophy to winning owner given by Breeders' Cup Ltd. The New York Racing Association will present trophies to the winning trainer and jockey. Closed Saturday, April 26, 2003 with 19 nominations.

Value of Race: $184,000 Winner $120,000; second $30,000; third $22,000; fourth $12,000. Mutuel Pool $403,843.00 Exacta Pool $397,937.00

Last Raced	Horse	M/Eqt.	A.	Wt	PP	St	¼	½	Str	Fin	Jockey	Odds $1
26Apr03 ^{7}Del^{1}	House Party		3	122	4	4	4	4	$1^{\frac{1}{2}}$	1^{3}	Santos J A	2.25
18Apr03 ^{8}Aqu^{1}	Cyber Secret	L	3	122	2	2	$1^{\frac{1}{2}}$	$1^{\frac{1}{2}}$	$2^{1\frac{1}{2}}$	$2^{\frac{1}{2}}$	Bridgmohan S X	0.65
19Apr03 ^{7}Aqu^{1}	City Sister	L	3	116	3	3	$3^{\frac{1}{2}}$	2^{hd}	3^{1}	3^{5}	Coa E M	6.40
10Apr03 ^{5}Aqu^{1}	Uphill Skier	L	3	118	1	1	$2^{\frac{1}{2}}$	$3^{\frac{1}{2}}$	4	4	Luzzi M J	7.30

OFF AT 4:46 Start Good. Won driving. Track fast.
TIME :22^{4}, :46^{3}, 1:11, 1:23^{1} (:22.94, :46.62, 1:11.04, 1:23.28)

$2 Mutuel Prices:

4–HOUSE PARTY	6.50	2.30	—
2–CYBER SECRET		2.10	—
3–CITY SISTER		—	—

$2 EXACTA 4–2 PAID $9.90

Gr/ro f, (Apr), by French Deputy–Bill Back, by Relaunch. Trainer Jerkens H Allen. Bred by J V Shields Jr (Fla).

HOUSE PARTY raced close up between rivals while under wraps, found room in upper stretch, drew clear and widened when roused. CYBER SECRET set the pace while in hand, was no match for the winner in the stretch and continued on to save the place. CITY SISTER raced with the pace while three wide and drifted out in the stretch. UPHILL SKIER raced with the pace along the inside and tired in the final furlong.

Owners— 1, Shields Joseph V Jr; 2, Goldfarb Sanford & Irwin & Team Jul; 3, Evans Edward P; 4, New Farm

Trainers—1, Jerkens H Allen; 2, Dutrow Richard E Jr; 3, Hennig Mark; 4, Perkins Ben W Jr

Scratched— Randaroo (13Apr03 ^{8}PIM^{2})

SIXTH RACE

Hollywood

MAY 10, 2003

6 FURLONGS. (1.07²) 51st Running of THE LOS ANGELES TIMES HANDICAP. Grade III. Purse $200,000. 3-year-olds and upward. By subscription of $200 each on or before April 30. $2,000 additional to start, with $120,000 to the winner, $40,000 to second, $24,000 to third, $12,000 to fourth and $3000 to fifth. Weights Sunday, May 4. Closed with 17 nominations.

Value of Race: $200,000 Winner $120,000; second $40,000; third $24,000; fourth $12,000; fifth $4,000. Mutuel Pool $577,289.00 Exacta Pool $332,201.00 Quinella Pool $35,067.00 Trifecta Pool $324,857.00 Superfecta Pool $106,116.00

Last Raced	Horse	M/Eqt. A.Wt	PP	St	¼	½	Str	Fin	Jockey	Odds $1
19Mar03 ⁷SA⁴	Hombre Rapido	LBb 6 116	8	1	1¹	1¹	1¹½	1¹	Valdivia J Jr	6.50
5Apr03 ⁸SA¹	Publication	LBb 4 116	4	6	8	8	6¹	2¹	Flores D R	6.10
8Mar03 ⁸TuP¹	Giovannetti	LB 4 116	6	3	2½	2½	2hd	3hd	Valenzuela P A	12.80
30Mar03 CYO¹³	Disturbingthepeace	LBb 5 120	1	5	4½	4¹	4hd	4no	Espinoza V	a-1.10
30Mar03 CYO¹⁷	Echo Eddie	LBb 6 117	7	2	3³½	3¹½	3¹	5¹½	Stevens G L	a-1.10
19Mar03 ⁷SA²	Golden Hare	LB 4 115	2	7	7²½	7¹½	7½	6no	Smith M E	7.00
24Apr03 ⁵Hol¹	Do Whats Right	LBbf 4 108	5	4	5¹	5³	5²½	7²	Martinez F F	7.50
19Mar03 ⁷SA¹	Men's Exclusive	LB 10 117	3	8	6½	6½	8	8	Solis A	6.30

a–Coupled: Disturbingthepeace and Echo Eddie.

OFF AT 3:56 Start Good. Won driving. Track fast.

TIME :21², :43², :55⁴, 1:08² (:21.51, :43.43, :55.80, 1:08.49)

$2 Mutuel Prices:

8–HOMBRE RAPIDO	15.00	8.80	5.60
5–PUBLICATION		8.00	6.40
7–GIOVANNETTI			7.80

$1 EXACTA 8–5 PAID $51.90 $2 QUINELLA 5–8 PAID $50.00 $1 TRIFECTA 8–5–7 PAID $592.00 $1 SUPERFECTA 8–5–7–1 PAID $1,598.10

B. g, by Falstaff–Tengo Prisa, by Relaunch. Trainer Sadler John W. Bred by Granja Vista Del Rio (Ky).

HOMBRE RAPIDO quickly sped to the front, angled in on the backstretch and set the pace a bit off the rail, inched away in the stretch and held on gamely under left handed urging. PUBLICATION unhurried off the rail on the backstretch, angled to the fence approaching the turn, moved up inside in the stretch, split horses in deep stretch and closed fast. GIOVANNETTI well placed stalking the winner off the rail to the stretch, could not summon the needed late response and just held third. DISTURBINGTHEPEACE was in a good position tracking the pace along the inside, remained on the rail in the stretch and also lacked the necessary late kick. ECHO EDDIE close up stalking the winner outside on the backstretch and turn, came four wide into the stretch and did not rally. GOLDEN HARE between horses early, chased inside, came out into the stretch and was not a threat. DO WHATS RIGHT chased three deep then outside a rival, split horses in midstretch but could make no impact in the final furlong. MEN'S EXCLUSIVE settled between horses then outside a rival, came three deep into the stretch and lacked a further response.

Owners— 1, Granja Vista Del Rio Stable; 2, Mercedes Stables; 3, Schiappa Bernard C; 4, Milch David S & Rita & Herrick Raci; 5, Milch David S & Rita; 6, Dream Walkin Farms Inc; 7, Chan Norissa & Marin Manny; 8, Reed Hartsel E

Trainers— 1, Sadler John W; 2, Cerin Vladimir; 3, Monteleone Frank J; 4, Vienna Darrell; 5, Vienna Darrell; 6, Mandella Richard; 7, O'Neill Doug; 8, Ward Wesley A

Scratched— Medecis (26Dec02 ⁷SA⁷), Laffit (27Apr03 ⁷EMD⁶)

$2 Daily Double (9–8) Paid $64.80; Daily Double Pool $32,772.
$1 Pick Three (9–9–8) Paid $139.40; Pick Three Pool $91,744.

EIGHTH RACE

Hollywood

MAY 10, 2003

1 1/16 MILES. (1.40) 24th Running of THE MERVYN LEROY HANDICAP. Grade II. Purse $150,000. 3–year–olds and upward. By subscription of $150 each on or before Wednesday, April 30. $1,500 additional to start, with $90,000 to the winner, $30,000 to second, $18,000 to third, $9,000 to fourth and $3,000 to fifth. Weights Sunday, May 4. Closed with 17 nominations.

Value of Race: $150,000 Winner $90,000; second $30,000; third $18,000; fourth $9,000; fifth $3,000.   Mutuel Pool $468,804.00 Exacta Pool $257,296.00   Quinella Pool $26,700.00 Trifecta Pool $250,935.00 Superfecta Pool $92,866.00

Last Raced	Horse	M/Eqt. A.Wt	PP	St	1/4	1/2	3/4	Str	Fin	Jockey	Odds $1
5Apr03 10SA2	Total Impact-CH	LB	5 114	4	5	3$\frac{1}{2}$	32	21	12	12	Smith M E	2.30
5Apr03 10SA3	Fleetstreet Dancer	LBb	5 114	6	3	5$\frac{1}{2}$	5hd	52	31	24	Baze T C	8.40
5Apr03 10SA4	Piensa Sonando-CH	LB	5 115	5	8	8	8	8	8	31	Solis A	6.40
6Apr03 7SA3	Sunday Break-JP	LBb	4 117	8	4	6hd	6$\frac{1}{2}$	3$\frac{1}{2}$	2hd	4$\frac{1}{2}$	Stevens G L	3.00
5Apr03 10SA8	Wooden Phone	LBb	6 118	1	2	1hd	21	4hd	5$\frac{1}{2}$	5$\frac{3}{2}$	Nakatani C S	8.00
15Jun02 9Hol8	Lethal Instrument	LB	7 116	2	6	41	4hd	6$\frac{1}{2}$	61	62	Flores D R	a–9.60
12Mar03 6SA2	Bring Home Thegold	LB	5 114	7	7	78	712	78	71	72$\frac{1}{2}$	Espinoza V	a–9.60
29Mar03 7GG2	Palmeiro	LBb	5 115	3	1	22$\frac{1}{2}$	1hd	1$\frac{1}{2}$	42$\frac{1}{2}$	8	Valenzuela P A	4.00

a–Coupled: Lethal Instrument and Bring Home Thegold.

OFF AT 4:56 Start Good. Won driving. Track fast.

TIME :23, :45^3, 1:09^2, 1:34^2, 1:40^4 (:23.00, :45.63, 1:09.41, 1:34.55, 1:40.88)

$2 Mutuel Prices:

4–TOTAL IMPACT–CH	6.60 3.60 2.80	
7–FLEETSTREET DANCER	7.00 4.40	
5–PIENSA SONANDO–CH	4.40	

$1 EXACTA 4–7 PAID $18.20 $2 QUINELLA 4–7 PAID $25.00 $1 TRIFECTA 4–7–5 PAID $73.60 $1 SUPERFECTA 4–7–5–8 PAID $210.50

Ch. h, by Stuka–Pebbles*Chi, by Manos de Piedra. Trainer De Seroux Laura. Bred by Haras Don Alberto (Chi).

TOTAL IMPACT (CHI) stalked the pace off the rail, bid outside on the second turn, gained the lead alongside a foe leaving that bend and pulled clear under urging. FLEETSTREET DANCER pulled his way along wide into the first turn, stalked outside a rival then between horses into the second turn, continued outside a foe nearing the stretch, bid toward the inside in the drive and was clearly second best. PIENSA SONANDO (CHI) allowed to lag back along the inside to the stretch, swung out in upper stretch and gained the show late. SUNDAY BREAK (JPN) four wide into the first turn, chased outside, moved up three deep with a bid on the second turn and into the stretch but could not sustain the bid in the lane and lost third late. WOODEN PHONE had good early speed and dueled inside, dropped back on the second turn, had the rider lose the whip into the stretch and weakened. LETHAL INSTRUMENT saved ground in a good position chasing the pace, came out a bit into the stretch and weakened. BRING HOME THEGOLD allowed to settle toward the inside, came out on the second turn and four wide into the stretch and did not rally. PALMEIRO dueled outside a rival, inched away from that one on the second turn, battled inside the winner leaving that bend and into the stretch and had little left.

Owners— 1, Al Kabeer Sultan Mohammed Saud & Br; 2, Leatherman Lee & Ty; 3, Hunt Nelson B; 4, Maeda Koji; 5, Durant Tom Helzer Marilyn & James E; 6, Craig Sidney H & Jenny; 7, Craig Sidney H & Jenny; 8, Moss Mr & Mrs Jerome S

Trainers—1, De Seroux Laura; 2, O'Neill Doug; 3, McAnally Ronald; 4, Drysdale Neil; 5, Baffert Bob; 6, Shirreffs John; 7, Shirreffs John; 8, Sadler John W

Scratched— Shacane (20Oct02 8HST1)

$2 Daily Double (1–4) Paid $23.00; Daily Double Pool $40,914.
$1 Pick Three (8–1–4/6) Paid $112.10; Pick Three Pool $130,725.

EIGHTH RACE
Lone Star
MAY 10, 2003

1⅛ MILES. (1.49^{3}) 7th Running of THE LONE STAR DERBY. Grade III. Purse $500,000 (Plus Up To $7,500 From ATBOIA). 3-year-olds. No nomination fee. $3,000 to pass the entry box and an additional $3,000 to start. Weight: Colts and Geldings, 122 lbs. Fillies, 117 lbs. Starters to benamed through the entry box by the usual time of closing. In allowance stakes starting preference will be given to horses that have accumulated the highest earnings at the time of entry. Closed Wednesday, April 30 with 53 nominations.

Value of Race: $500,000 Winner $277,500; second $92,500; third $50,875; fourth $27,750; fifth $13,875; sixth $7,500; seventh $7,500; eighth $7,500; ninth $7,500; tenth $7,500. Mutuel Pool $513,157.00 Exacta Pool $236,749.00 Quinella Pool $13,533.00 Trifecta Pool $221,289.00 Superfecta Pool $82,852.00

Last Raced	Horse	M/Eqt.	A.Wt	PP	St	¼	½	¾	Str	Fin	Jockey	Odds $1
5Apr03 11GP1	Dynever	L	3 122	4	5	8½	61½	61	5½	11½	Prado E S	0.30
19Apr03 8Kee6	Most Feared	Lb	3 122	7	1	41½	3hd	4hd	31½	21	Sellers S J	18.90
5Apr03 9LS3	Commander's Affair	L	3 122	10	6	1½	22	1hd	2hd	31½	Melancon G	44.80
12Apr03 9OP5	Crowned King	L	3 122	2	10	12	12	9hd	7hd	4no	Rennie C R	26.00
12Apr03 4BM1	Mr. Technique	Lb	3 122	9	12	3hd	41½	31½	1½	5½	Gonzalez R M	13.10
12Apr03 9OP9	Defrere's Vixen	L	3 122	3	2	102	7hd	7½	93	6½	Martin E M Jr	9.20
12Apr03 9Kee4	Crowned Dancer	Lb	3 122	8	7	5½	5½	51½	6hd	7nk	Perrodin E J	12.20
10Apr03 6LS1	On The Border	L	3 122	11	9	7hd	91	81	8hd	8¾	Beasley J A	40.10
12Apr03 7OP1	Mauk Four	Lb	3 122	12	3	21½	1hd	2½	4½	9½	Theriot H J II	18.70
23Mar03 7FG3	Grendel	Lb	3 122	5	8	9½	111½	10½	106	10 13¼	Melancon L	25.30
5Apr03 9LS2	Leo's Last Hurrahy	Lb	3 122	6	4	6hd	8½	113	114	117¼	Cogburn K L	54.00
5Apr03 9LS4	Gentlemen J J	L	3 122	1	11	11hd	10hd	12	12	12	Walker B J Jr	97.90

OFF AT 5:14 Start Good. Won driving. Track fast.
TIME :23^{2}, :47^{2}, 1:11^{3}, 1:37^{3}, 1:50^{2} (:23.41, :47.43, 1:11.77, 1:37.70, 1:50.43)

$2 Mutuel Prices:

5-DYNEVER	2.60	2.40	2.10
8-MOST FEARED		7.00	2.10
11-COMMANDER'S AFFAIR			2.10

$2 EXACTA 5–8 PAID $33.20 $2 QUINELLA 5–8 PAID $26.40 $2 TRIFECTA 5–8–11 PAID $633.40 $2 SUPERFECTA 5–8–11–3 PAID $3,883.60

Dk. b. or br. c, (Mar), by Dynaformer–Flamboyance, by Zilzal. Trainer Clement Christophe. Bred by Catherine Wills (Ky).

DYNEVER jostled at the start, settled off the pace while between rivals, was blocked from the quarter pole to the eighth pole, shifted to the outside for racing room, and quickly accelerated and closed very fast under right hand urging. MOST FEARED was under some restraint entering the first turn, stalked the pace down the backstretch, was blocked behind horses from the quarter pole to the eighth pole, split rivals and bumped with COMMANDER'S AFFAIR, then couldn't go with the winner late, but earned the place in a good effort. COMMANDER'S AFFAIR was bumped after the start, crossed over to set the joint pace, held a short lead passing the quarter pole, bumped with MOST FEARED near the furlong marker, battled resolutely in the final furlong, and gave way very grudgingly late. CROWNED KING moved off the rail to race four wide on the first turn, settled well back in the field, saved ground on the final turn, tried to force his way out entering the stretch and bumped with DEFRERE'S VIXEN, then finished willingly in the stretch without the needed winning response. MR. TECHNIQUE was bumped after the start, tracked the pace from a good position, ranged up leaving the backstretch, made a bid passing the quarter pole, led the field into the final furlong, but gave way thereafter. DEFRERE'S VIXEN was jostled in the hindquarters after the start, settled while saving ground, was bumped at the top of the stretch, and lacked the needed rally. CROWNED DANCER was well placed through the backstretch, ranged up while four wide on the turn, raced in good striking position entering the stretch, but came up empty. ON THE BORDER was bumped after the start, raced four wide on both turns, and had nothing left. MAUK FOUR quickly crossed over after the start, set the joint pace along the rail, vied into the final furlong, and weakened. GRENDEL broke inward and bumped a rival, steadied passing the seven furlong marker, raced four wide on both turns, and failed to threaten. LEO'S LAST HURRAHY raced between rivals on the first turn, dropped out on the final turn, and was outrun. GENTLEMEN J J raced well back in the field, and was always outrun.

Owners— 1, Wills Catherine & Karches Peter; 2, Durant Tom R; 3, Martin Racing Stable & Massey Betty; 4, McKeever Racing Stable; 5, Vreeland James R; 6, Heiligbrodt Racing Stable; 7, Charles Cono & Victory Racing LLC; 8, Nelson James E; 9, R & Wygley Partnership Sr; 10, Hughes B W; 11, Murphy Kenneth W; 12, Rancha Fresa Inc

Trainers—1, Clement Christophe; 2, Werner Ronny; 3, Calhoun William Bret; 4, McKeever Billy C Jr; 5, Bonde Jeff; 6, Asmussen Steven M; 7, Paasch Christopher S; 8, Asmussen Steven M; 9, Cart Jerry D; 10, Stall Albert M Jr; 11, Young Bob; 12, Leggio Andrew Jr

Scratched— Desert Spirit (8Feb03 LIN1)

$2 Pick Three (4–9–1/5) Paid $63.20; Pick Three Pool $15,271.

EIGHTH RACE
Belmont
MAY 11, 2003

6 FURLONGS. (1.07^{3}) 20th Running of THE GENUINE RISK HANDICAP. Grade II. Purse $150,000. (Up to $29,100 NYSBFOA). FILLIES AND MARES THREE YEARS OLD AND UPWARD. By subscription of $150 each, which should accompany the nomination; $750 to pass the entry box and $750 to start. The purse to be divided 60% to the winner, 20% to second, 11% to third, 6% to fourth and 3% to fifth. Trophies will be presented to the winning owner, trainer and jockey. Closed Saturday, April 26, with 15 Nominations.

Value of Race: $145,500 Winner $90,000; second $30,000; third $16,500; fourth $9,000. Mutuel Pool $376,197.00 Exacta Pool $297,300.00

Last Raced	Horse	M/Eqt.	A.Wt	PP	St	¼	½	Str	Fin	Jockey	Odds $1
19Apr03 4Aqu1	Shine Again	L	6 119	2	—	4	4	1hd	14	Samyn J L	2.10
29Mar03 9Aqu1	Carson Hollow	L	4 122	4	—	1½	1½	22	21¼	Velazquez J R	0.65
16Mar03 10GP2	Harmony Lodge	L	5 116	1	—	2hd	2hd	32½	36¼	Prado E S	7.00
11Apr03 7Kee1	September Secret	Lf	4 116	3	—	31½	31	4	4	Coa E M	7.00

OFF AT 4:47 Start Good. Won driving. Track fast.
TIME :21^{4}, :44^{2}, :56^{2}, 1:09 (:21.82, :44.58, :56.55, 1:09.19)

$2 Mutuel Prices:

2-SHINE AGAIN	6.20	2.10	—
4-CARSON HOLLOW		2.10	—
1-HARMONY LODGE		—	—

$2 EXACTA 2–4 PAID $11.00

Dk. b. or br. m, by Wild Again–Shiner, by Two Punch. Trainer Jerkens H Allen. Bred by Mrs Richard C duPont (Md).

SHINE AGAIN raced close up early while in hand, responded when roused and was going away late, driving. CARSON HOLLOW showed in front soon after the start, set the pace while between rivals, had no answer for the winner and continued on to hold the place. HARMONY LODGE raced with the pace along the inside and dug in stubbornly through the stretch. SEPTEMBER SECRET raced with the pace while three wide and tired in the stretch.

Owners— 1, Bohemia Stable; 2, Stronach Stables & Hemlock Hills Fa; 3, Melnyk Eugene & Laura; 4, Michael MacHowsky

Trainers—1, Jerkens H Allen; 2, Dutrow Richard E Jr; 3, Pletcher Todd A; 4, Machowsky Michael

Scratched— A New Twist (9Apr03 8KEE1)

EIGHTH RACE
Pimlico
MAY 15, 2003

6 FURLONGS. (1.09) 18th Running of THE MISS PREAKNESS. Grade III. Purse $100,000 Guaranteed. FILLIES, THREE-YEARS-OLD. By free subscription. $500 to pass the entry box, $500 additional to start. Supplemental nominations of $1,000 each will be accepted by the usual time of entry with all other fees due as noted. Weight 122 lbs. Non-winners of a race of $50,000, allowed, 3 lbs.; a race of $30,000, 5 lbs.; a race of $15,000, 7 lbs. (Maiden and Claiming races not considered in estimating allowances). Preference to starters with highest career earnings. Horses may be placed on the also eligible list. Closed Sunday, May 4, 2003.

Value of Race: $100,000 Winner $60,000; second $20,000; third $11,000; fourth $6,000; fifth $3,000. Mutuel Pool $152,323.00 Exacta Pool $133,524.00 Trifecta Pool $73,043.00

Last Raced	Horse	M/Eqt.	A.Wt	PP	St	¼	½	Str	Fin	Jockey	Odds $1
30Mar03 ^{3}Aqu^{1}	Belong To Sea	Lf	3 117	5	2	2^{1}	2^{1}	1^{2}	1^{hd}	Castellano J J	4.70
10Apr03 ^{8}Kee^{4}	Chimichurri	L	3 122	2	5	5	4^{hd}	4^{1}	$2\frac{3}{4}$	Dominguez R A	3.70
12Apr03 ^{9}Pim^{1}	Forever Partners	L	3 119	1	3	3^{4}	3^{5}	2^{hd}	$3^{2\frac{1}{4}}$	Pino M G	0.90
26Apr03 ^{7}Del^{2}	Ladyecho	L	3 119	3	4	4^{1}	5	5	$4\frac{1}{2}$	Castillo O O	17.10
19Apr03 ^{4}Pim^{1}	Pompamento	L	3 115	4	1	$1^{2\frac{1}{2}}$	$1\frac{1}{2}$	$3^{2\frac{1}{2}}$	5	Fogelsonger R	2.50

OFF AT 4:34 Start Good. Won driving. Track fast.
TIME :23, :45^{4}, :58, 1:11 (:23.17, :45.85, :58.00, 1:11.10)

$2 Mutuel Prices:

6–BELONG TO SEA	11.40	5.00	2.10
2–CHIMICHURRI		4.40	2.10
1–FOREVER PARTNERS			2.10

$2 EXACTA 6–2 PAID $47.60 $2 TRIFECTA 6–2–1 PAID $91.20

B. f, (Apr), by Belong to Me–Windansea, by Conquistador Cielo. Trainer Lewis Lisa L. Bred by Domino Stud of Lexington LLC (Ky).

BELONG TO SEA tracked the pace three wide, was pushed along a bit mid way on the turn, lodged a bid approaching the quarter pole, moved clear nearing mid stretch, dug in gamely under left handed pressure and prevailed. CHIMICHURRI , unhurried early while saving ground, picked up some momentum along the inside into the lane, swung out six wide leaving the furlong marker, closed gamely and simply ran out of ground. FOREVER PARTNERS was steadied along inside through the first quarter of a mile, angled out near the three and a half furlong marker, moved up four wide into the lane but was outfinished in the final furlong. LADYECHO , outrun early, raced seven wide in the drive and had a belated gain. POMPAMENTO , fractious in the starting gate, quickly went clear, set a brisk pace along the inside, was joined by the winner into the lane, battled to mid stretch then succumbed.

Owners— 1, S C Duncker J Amling & A Quartucci; 2, Peachtree Stable; 3, Skeedattle Associates; 4, Polin Charlotte C; 5, Crown Valley Stable

Trainers—1, Lewis Lisa L; 2, Pletcher Todd A; 3, Dutrow Anthony W; 4, Servis John C; 5, Capuano Dale

Scratched— Awesome Humor (14May03 ^{8}CD^{4}), Hour Of Justice (5Apr03 ^{8}WO^{2})

EIGHTH RACE
Pimlico
MAY 16, 2003

$1\frac{1}{16}$ MILES. (1.40^{4}) 12th Running of THE PIMLICO BREEDERS' CUP DISTAFF HANDICAP. Grade III. Purse $150,000 Guaranteed (includes $50,000 BC – Breeders' Cup) FILLIES AND MARES, THREE-YEAR-OLD AND UPWARD. (Includes $50,000 from Breeders' Cup Fund for Cup nominees only). By subscription of $50 each which should accompany the nomination, $500 to pass the entry box, $500 additional to start, with $100,000 Guaranteed. Breeders' Cup Fund monies also correspondingly divided provided a Breeders' Cup Nominee has finished in an awarded position. A 2004 breeding season will be awarded to the first finishers. Stallions for the year 2004 breeding season: (Golden Missile, Wild Rush, Alphabet Soup.) Supplemental nominations of $1000 each will be accepted by Friday, May 9, 2003 with all other fees due as noted. Weights Friday, May 9, 2003.

Value of Race: $145,500 Winner $90,000; second $30,000; third $16,500; fourth $9,000.

Last Raced	Horse	M/Eqt.	A.Wt	PP	St	¼	½	¾	Str	Fin	Jockey	Odds $1
5Apr03 ^{8}OP^{3}	Mandy's Gold	Lf	5 117	1	2	3^{1}	3^{1}	4	$3^{2\frac{1}{2}}$	1^{nk}	Bailey J D	0.80
26Oct02 ^{3}AP^{8}	Summer Colony	L	5 121	4	4	4	4	$3\frac{1}{2}$	1^{hd}	$2^{3\frac{3}{4}}$	Velazquez J R	1.60
26Apr03 ^{5}Crc^{1}	Stormy Frolic	Lb	4 114	3	3	$2\frac{1}{2}$	2^{1}	1^{1}	2^{2}	$3^{1\frac{1}{2}}$	Santos J A	3.40
4Apr03 ^{8}GP^{6}	Dance The Slew	Lb	5 112	2	1	1^{1}	$1\frac{1}{2}$	$2\frac{1}{2}$	4	4	Rose J	13.30

OFF AT 4:14 Start Good. Won driving. Track sloppy.
TIME :23^{3}, :47^{3}, 1:12^{3}, 1:39^{3}, 1:46^{1} (:23.76, :47.71, 1:12.72, 1:39.78, 1:46.32)

$2 Mutuel Prices:

2–MANDY'S GOLD	3.60	2.20	—
6–SUMMER COLONY		2.40	—
5–STORMY FROLIC		—	—

Ch. m, by Gilded Time–Manduria, by Aloma's Ruler. Trainer Gorham Michael E. Bred by Audley Farm Inc (Va).

MANDY'S GOLD , forwardly placed towards the inside, moved up between rivals into the lane, swung out for room leaving the furlong marker, drifted out a bit, closed determinedly when straightened under right handed pressure and wore down SUMMER COLONY in the final jumps. SUMMER COLONY broke a step slow, was urged along three wide down the backstretch while in striking position, moved closer leaving the far turn, took command nearing the furlong marker, came in a bit brushing STORMY FROLIC edged away some a sixteenth out then just failed to last. STORMY FROLIC prompted the pace outside of DANCE THE SLEW, took over around the far turn, went clear after six furlongs, was collared by SUMMER COLONY in upper stretch, was brushed by that one leaving the eighth pole then weakened late. DANCE THE SLEW broke sharply, set the pace along the inside, took pressure down the backstretch, dueled briefly leaving the far turn then gave way in upper stretch.

Owners— 1, Steeplechase Farm; 2, Evans Edward P; 3, Stride Rite Racing Stable; 4, Gill Michael J

Trainers—1, Gorham Michael E; 2, Hennig Mark; 3, Wolfson Milton W; 4, Shuman Mark

Scratched— Smok'n Frolic (19Apr03 ^{9}AQU^{2}), You'll Be Happy (19Mar03 ^{10}GP^{1}), Kiss A Miss (23Mar03 ^{9}AQU^{4})

TENTH RACE

Pimlico

MAY 16, 2003

1⅛ MILES. (1.47¹) 79th Running of THE BLACK–EYED SUSAN. Grade II. Purse $200,000 Guaranteed. FILLIES, THREE–YEARS–OLD. By free subscription. $1000 to pass the entry box, $1000 additional to start, with $200,000 Guaranteed. Supplemental nominations of $2000 each will be accepted by the usual time of entry with all other fees due as noted. Weight 122 lbs. Non–winners of $60,000 at one mile or over allowed, 3 lbs.; $40,000 at one mile or over, 5 lbs.; $20,000 at one mile or over 7 lbs. (Maiden and Claiming races not considered in estimating allowances). Preference to starters with highest career earnings. Horses may be placed on the also eligible list. Starters to be named through the entry box by the usual time of closing. Trophy to the owner of the winner. Closed Sunday, May 4, 2003.

Value of Race: $200,000 Winner $120,000; second $40,000; third $22,000; fourth $12,000; fifth $6,000. Mutuel Pool $574,836.00 Exacta Pool $419,135.00 Trifecta Pool $332,516.00 Superfecta Pool $107,082.00

Last Raced	Horse	M/Eqt. A.Wt	PP	St	¼	½	¾	Str	Fin	Jockey	Odds $1
22Mar03 9Aqu²	Roar Emotion	L	3 122	1	1	1¹½	1¹½	1hd	1⁵	1½	Velazquez J R	3.40
22Mar03 8TP⁶	Fircroft	Lb	3 119	7	8	7¹	7¹½	6¹½	3⁵	2⁸½	Day P	13.40
2May03 10CD²	Santa Catarina	L	3 117	6	5	4hd	4²	2⁴½	2¹½	3⁵¾	Stevens G L	0.80
5Apr03 8Kee⁷	Ivanavinalot	Lf	3 122	4	4	2½	2hd	3²	4¹½	4nk	Prado E S	2.80
18Apr03 8Aqu¹	Xtra Heart	Lb	3 117	8	7	8	8	8	7²½	5hd	Valenzuela P A	40.90
26Apr03 8Pim¹	Grace Bay	Lb	3 119	5	6	6¹½	5hd	5³	5½	6¹	Dominguez R A	11.10
6May03 7Del⁷	Blushing Valleys	Lb	3 115	3	1	3¹	3½	4hd	6²	7⁹¾	Wilson R	57.40
26Apr03 7Del⁶	Lets Just Do It	Lbf	3 115	2	3	5¹	6²½	7¹	8	8	Pindell M D	70.50

OFF AT 5:14 Start Good. Won driving. Track sloppy.

TIME :23¹, :47³, 1:12¹, 1:38¹, 1:52¹ (:23.20, :47.71, 1:12.23, 1:38.21, 1:52.33)

$2 Mutuel Prices:	2–ROAR EMOTION	8.80	5.40	2.80
	9–FIRCROFT		11.60	3.20
	8–SANTA CATARINA			2.10

$2 EXACTA 2–9 PAID $109.80 $2 TRIFECTA 2–9–8 PAID $249.60 $1 SUPERFECTA 2–9–8–5 PAID $247.60

Dk. b. or br. f, (Mar), by Roar–Emotional Outburst, by Capote. Trainer Martin Carlos F. Bred by Brenda Jones (Ky).

ROAR EMOTION broke alertly, set a rated pace in the two path, took pressure from SANTA CATARINA from the far turn to the quarter pole, opened up when put to stout right handed pressure in upper stretch then had enough to hold off the late charging FIRCROFT. FIRCROFT was unhurried early while racing off the inside, picked up some momentum three wide leaving the three furlong marker, advanced between rivals into the lane, angled to the rail, closed stoutly and was steadily getting to the winner. SANTA CATARINA rated close up while four wide, moved up in hand approaching the far turn, pressed the winner while under stiff pressure leaving the five sixteenths pole, remained a presence to the head of the lane but weakened through the final furlong. IVANAVINALOT stalked the winner while three wide, was put to urging near the far turn, had no response and faded. XTRA HEART broke outward, lacked speed, raced between horses late and never threatened. GRACE BAY raced in mid pack down the backstretch, circled five wide into the lane and weakened. BLUSHING VALLEYS stalked the pace while saving ground and tired leaving the three furlong marker. LETS JUST DO IT saved ground, raced close up for a half mile then faltered.

Owners— 1, Allen Joseph; 2, Humphrey G W Jr; 3, Lewis Robert B & Beverly J; 4, Campbell Gilbert G; 5, Paraneck Stable; 6, Newby Steven T; 7, Taylor Kenneth & McCutcheon David; 8, Casey John A

Trainers—1, Martin Carlos F; 2, Arnold George R II; 3, Baffert Bob; 4, O'Connell Kathleen; 5, Pedersen Jennifer; 6, Capuano Dale; 7, Salzman John E; 8, Casey James M

Scratched— Austin's Mom (2May03 3CD¹), Holiday Lady (2May03 10CD⁸)

$2 Pick Three (2/3/4–1/2/3/4/5/11/12/13/14–2) Paid $43.20; Pick Three Pool $66,638.
$2 Perfect Six (2 VS 5–WINNER 2) Paid $4.00; Perfect Six Pool $8,549.

ELEVENTH RACE
Pimlico
MAY 16, 2003

$1\frac{3}{16}$ MILES. (1.52^2) 37th Running of THE PIMLICO SPECIAL HANDICAP. Grade I. Purse $600,000 Guaranteed. FOUR-YEAR-OLDS AND UPWARD. By subscription of $500 each which should accompany the nomination. All horses shall pay $6,000 to pass the entry box and $6,000 additional to start. Weights, Friday, May 9, 2003. Preference to starters with high weights on the scale. Horses not drawn into the body of the race will be placed on the also eligible list in order of preference as specified herein. In the event of a scratch in the race prior to the official scratch time, horses onthe also eligible list will draw in to the race based upon their order of preference. Excluded horses shall be refunded all entry fee payments. Starters to be named through the entry box by the usual time of closing. Closed Sunday, May 4, 2003.

Value of Race: $600,000 Winner $400,000; second $100,000; third $50,000; fourth $30,000; fifth $20,000. Mutuel Pool $755,288.00 Exacta Pool $554,136.00 Trifecta Pool $433,321.00 Superfecta Pool $133,752.00

Last Raced	Horse	M/Eqt.	A.Wt	PP	St	¼	½	¾	Str	Fin	Jockey	Odds $1
25Apr03 ^{9}Kee^1	Mineshaft	L	4 121	3	5	$4^{2\frac{1}{2}}$	$4^{4\frac{1}{2}}$	$2^{2\frac{1}{2}}$	$1^{1\frac{1}{2}}$	$1^{3\frac{3}{4}}$	Albarado R J	1.30
5Apr03 ^{10}SA^1	Western Pride	L	5 116	8	3	$2^{1\frac{1}{2}}$	$2^{2\frac{1}{2}}$	1^1	2^5	2^{hd}	Valenzuela P A	3.40
26Apr03 ^{8}Aqu^3	Judge's Case	Lb	6 113	6	7	7^3	$7^{2\frac{1}{2}}$	$7^{\frac{1}{2}}$	$4^{2\frac{1}{2}}$	$3^{1\frac{3}{4}}$	Dominguez R A	41.90
19Apr03 ^{8}Haw^2	Colonial Colony	Lf	5 113	4	8	8^4	8^4	$5^{\frac{1}{2}}$	3^{hd}	4^1	Martinez W	86.00
26Apr03 ^{8}Aqu^4	Puzzlement	Lb	4 114	1	9	9	9	9	5^6	5^{13}	Bailey J D	12.50
5Apr03 ^{8}Aqu^4	Snake Mountain	L	5 120	5	6	6^2	$5^{\frac{1}{2}}$	6^1	6^2	$6^{5\frac{1}{2}}$	Santos J A	10.10
29Mar03 ^{11}GP^2	Aeneas	L	4 114	9	2	5^{hd}	6^2	8^2	$7^{1\frac{1}{2}}$	$7^{3\frac{1}{4}}$	Douglas R R	53.20
29Mar03 ^{11}GP^1	Hero's Tribute	L	5 116	7	1	3^{hd}	3^{hd}	4^3	$8^{3\frac{1}{2}}$	$8^{2\frac{1}{2}}$	Prado E S	3.80
5Apr03 ^{8}Aqu^2	Balto Star	L	5 118	2	4	$1^{\frac{1}{2}}$	1^{hd}	3^{hd}	9	9	Velazquez J R	5.70

OFF AT 5:50 Start Good. Won driving. Track sloppy.
TIME :23, :46^3, 1:11, 1:36^2, 1:56 (:23.09, :46.79, 1:11.12, 1:36.40, 1:56.16)

$2 Mutuel Prices:

3-MINESHAFT	4.60	3.00	2.80
8-WESTERN PRIDE		4.00	3.80
6-JUDGE'S CASE			4.40

$2 EXACTA 3-8 PAID $18.40 $2 TRIFECTA 3-8-6 PAID $361.20 $1 SUPERFECTA 3-8-6-4 PAID $2,546.40

Dk. b. or br. c, by A.P. Indy-Prospectors Delite, by Mr. Prospector. Trainer Howard Neil J. Bred by W. S. Farish, James Elkins & W. T. Webber Jr. (Ky).

MINESHAFT stalked the pace near the rail, eased out three wide leaving the backstretch, bid for the lead outside WESTERN PRIDE leaving the far turn and steadily pulled away through the stretch while kept to his business. WESTERN PRIDE prompted the pace outside BALTO STAR, opened a clear lead leaving the backstretch, dueled with the winner to midstretch then faded. JUDGE'S CASE lacked speed, raced two wide between horses near the three eighths pole, swung wide in midstretch and closed gamely. COLONIAL COLONY saved ground to the far turn, split foes two wide midway on the bend and flattened out. PUZZLEMENT , sluggish early, awaited room near the three eighths pole, split rivals two wide midway on the turn, angled inside in midstretch and lacked the necessary late response. SNAKE MOUNTAIN saved ground the first turn, drifted very wide leaving the far turn and weakened. AENEAS circled horses on the far turn, was carried to the six path entering the stretch and weakened. HERO'S TRIBUTE , difficult to load into the starting gate, lost ground both turns, chased the pace and gave way. BALTO STAR , sent to the front, set the pace and dropped back leaving the three eighths pole.

Owners— 1, W Farish T Webber & J Elkins; 2, Chapman Carolyn & McArthur Theresa; 3, Sanford Goldfarb L Roche & J Puglis; 4, Lakeside Farm Ltd; 5, Shields Joseph V Jr; 6, Berkshire Stud et al; 7, Pavlish Patricia; 8, Oxley John C; 9, Anstu Stables

Trainers—1, Howard Neil J; 2, Chapman James K; 3, Klesaris Steve; 4, Bindner Walter M Jr; 5, Jerkens H Allen; 6, Jerkens James A; 7, Wolfson Martin D; 8, Ward John T Jr; 9, Pletcher Todd A

$2 Daily Double (2-3) Paid $31.20; Daily Double Pool $96,504.
$2 Perfect Six (2 VS 7- WINNER 7) Paid $3.00; Perfect Six Pool $12,804.

EIGHTH RACE
Belmont
MAY 17, 2003

1 MILE. (1.32^1) 28th Running of THE SHUVEE HANDICAP. Grade II. Purse $200,000 (Up to $34,800 NYSBFOA). FILLIES AND MARES THREE YEARS OLD AND UPWARD. By subscription of $200 each, which should accompany the nomination; $1,000 to pass the entry box and $1,000 to start. The purse to be divided 60% to the winner, 20% to second, 11% to third, 6%to fourth and 3% to fifth. Trophies will be presented to the winning owner, trainer and jockey. Closed Saturday, May 3, 2003 with 18 Nominations.

Value of Race: $200,000 Winner $120,000; second $40,000; third $22,000; fourth $12,000; fifth $6,000. Mutuel Pool $792,201.00 Exacta Pool $614,549.00 Trifecta Pool $417,301.00

Last Raced	Horse	M/Eqt.	A.Wt	PP	St	¼	½	¾	Str	Fin	Jockey	Odds $1
14Dec02 HC^2	Wild Spirit-CH		4 115	3	4	$3^{\frac{1}{2}}$	3^{hd}	3^{hd}	1^{hd}	$1^{3\frac{1}{2}}$	Castellano J J	10.20
19Apr03 ^{9}Aqu^2	Smok'n Frolic	L	4 119	2	2	$2^{\frac{1}{2}}$	$2^{\frac{1}{2}}$	$2^{1\frac{1}{2}}$	$2^{\frac{1}{2}}$	$2^{1\frac{1}{4}}$	Velazquez J R	3.10
2May03 ^{8}CD^1	You	L	4 120	1	3	1^2	$1^{\frac{1}{2}}$	1^{hd}	3^6	$3^{4\frac{1}{4}}$	Bridgmohan S X	1.45
16Apr03 ^{6}Aqu^2	Princess Dixie	Lb	4 112	6	5	6	6	6	$5^{5\frac{1}{2}}$	4^1	Arroyo N Jr	32.00
19Apr03 ^{9}Aqu^3	Nonsuch Bay	L	4 115	5	1	$5^{\frac{1}{2}}$	5^{hd}	5^1	$4^{1\frac{1}{2}}$	$5^{9\frac{1}{2}}$	Coa E M	5.10
19Apr03 ^{9}Aqu^1	Raging Fever	L	5 119	4	6	$4^{2\frac{1}{2}}$	$4^{4\frac{1}{2}}$	$4^{1\frac{1}{2}}$	6	6	Gryder A T	3.25

OFF AT 4:48 Start Good For All But RAGING FEVER Won driving. Track fast.
TIME :22^4, :45^2, 1:09^2, 1:34^2 (:22.92, :45.43, 1:09.50, 1:34.51)

$2 Mutuel Prices:

3-WILD SPIRIT-CH	22.40	8.50	3.70
2-SMOK'N FROLIC		4.20	2.40
1-YOU			2.30

$2 EXACTA 3-2 PAID $78.50 $2 TRIFECTA 3-2-1 PAID $209.50

Dk. b. or br. f, by Hussonet-Wild Princess, by Wild Again. Trainer Frankel Robert. Bred by Haras Sumaya (Chi).

WILD SPIRIT (CHI) raced close up inside while well in hand, angled to the outside entering the stretch, responded when roused in upper stretch and drew away late, driving. SMOK'N FROLIC pressed the pace from the outside, earned a short advantage between calls in upper stretch and dug in gamely to the finish. YOU was hustled to the front, set the pace along the inside and tired in the final furlong. PRINCESS DIXIE was outrun early, raced inside and had no rally. NONSUCH BAY was outrun early, came wide into the stretch and had no response when roused. RAGING FEVER broke in the air, chased the pace while three wide and tired in the stretch.

Owners— 1, Sumaya Us Stable; 2, Dogwood Stable; 3, Gann Edmund A; 4, Edwards James F; 5, Thorn Stable; 6, Evans Edward P

Trainers—1, Frankel Robert; 2, Pletcher Todd A; 3, Frankel Robert; 4, Bond Harold James; 5, Alexander Frank A; 6, Hennig Mark

NINTH RACE   1¹⁄₁₆ MILES. (1.41³) 29th Running of THE DOGWOOD. Grade III. Purse $100,000 Added. FILLIES, THREE YEARS OLD. By subscription of $100 each on or before May 6, 2003 or by Supplementary Nomination of $5,000 at time of entry. $500 to pass the entry box; $500 additional to start. Weight 122 lbs. Non-winners of $50,000 twice at a mile or over and twice 2 lbs.; $50,000 at a mile or over, 4 lbs.; three races at a mile or over other than maiden or claiming, 6 lbs.; two races at a mile or over other than maiden or claiming, 8 lbs. Closed Tuesday, May 6, 2003 with 20 nominations.

Churchill
MAY 17, 2003

Value of Race: $109,000 Winner $67,580; second $21,800; third $10,900; fourth $5,450; fifth $3,270.   Mutuel Pool $512,943.00 Exacta Pool $370,273.00   Trifecta Pool $271,760.00 Superfecta Pool $59,342.00

Last Raced	Horse	M/Eqt. A.Wt	PP	St	¼	½	¾	Str	Fin	Jockey	Odds $1
18Apr03 9Kee⁴	Golden Marlin	L	3 115	7	5	1½	1½	11½	1hd	11	Sellers S J	3.80
24Apr03 5Kee¹	Double Scoop	Lf	3 114	2	3	31½	31½	21	24	22½	Borel C H	2.30
9May03 9CD⁵	Throne	Lb	3 114	1	6	7	7	6¹	6¹²	31½	Guidry M	32.20
11Apr03 10OP⁴	My Trusty Cat	Lbf	3 120	5	7	6¹²	4½	4hd	32	43	Meche L J	3.10
2May03 2CD³	Westerly Breeze	Lb	3 120	4	1	5¹	51½	59	42	59½	Court J K	6.60
13Apr03 4Kee²	Wildcat Queen	L	3 114	3	2	2¹	2¹	31½	5hd	611	Melancon L	2.90
29Mar03 8TP¹	Risky Kitten	L	3 114	6	4	4hd	69	7	7	7	Troilo W D	27.80

OFF AT 5:32 Start Good. Won driving. Track sloppy.

TIME :234, :48, 1:124, 1:39, 1:454 (:23.81, :48.09, 1:12.90, 1:39.03, 1:45.96)

$2 Mutuel Prices:

7–GOLDEN MARLIN	9.60	4.60	3.80
2–DOUBLE SCOOP		4.00	3.60
1–THRONE			6.60

$2 EXACTA 7–2 PAID $32.40 $2 TRIFECTA 7–2–1 PAID $357.20 $1 SUPERFECTA 7–2–1–5 PAID $828.70

B. f, (Feb), by Marlin–Golden Reality, by Unreal Zeal. Trainer Foley Gregory D. Bred by Timothy Thornton (Ky).

GOLDEN MARLIN gained a narrow lead early, edged in to show the way under a long rating hold three or four wide, was headed for several strides leaving the half-mile marker from the inside by WILDCAT QUEEN, regained the advantage when asked for a bit more, moved clear approaching the stretch, turned back another challenge leaving the furlong grounds from the outside by DOUBLE SCOOP, then, after the rider switched the whip from his right to left hand, continued under pressure to prevail in a game effort. DOUBLE SCOOP, in hand inside early, eased out three or four wide on the first turn, was patiently handled, made a bold run outside the winner approaching the final furlong, gained almost even terms, then wasn't good enough. THRONE, badly outrun for a half and five wide on the backstretch, edged nearer the inside on the far turn, continued three or four wide into the stretch and was going well at the end. MY TRUSTY CAT settled in a contending position behind the leaders early, saved ground until the final quarter, came out five wide for the drive, loomed a threat for the last eighth but flattened out. WESTERLY BREEZE, lightly rated in behind horses three wide to the far turn while within easy striking distance, came out five wide for the drive but was empty the last eighth. WILDCAT QUEEN, close up inside the winner from early on, inched to challenge nearing the end of the backstretch, headed GOLDEN MARLIN for several strides, lost the edge back to that one, then faded upon going six furlongs. RISKY KITTEN was finished leaving the backstretch.

Owners— 1, Estate of Joe Famularo & Glass W D; 2, Humphrey G Watts & Louise I Jr; 3, Blackwood Don; 4, Pollard Carl F; 5, Miles A S Jr; 6, Thomas Van Meter & Michael Ryan; 7, Wilkinson Charles

Trainers— 1, Foley Gregory D; 2, Arnold George R II; 3, Barnett Bobby C; 4, Vance David R; 5, Nafzger Carl A; 6, Walden W Elliott; 7, Wilkinson Jack R III

$1 Pick Three (3/5–2/3/5/8/11/12/13–7) Paid $24.60; Pick Three Pool $31,492.

THIRD RACE   1 MILE. (Turf)(1.32³) 35th Running of THE SENORITA. Grade III. Purse $100,000 Added. FILLIES THREE–YEARS–OLD. By subscription of $100 each on or before Wednesday, May 7, or by supplementary nomination of $5,000 each by closing time of entries, closed with 1. $1,000 additional to start, with $100,000 added. The added money and all fees to be divided 60% to the winner, 20% to second, 12% to third, 6% to fourth and 2% to fifth. Weight 123 lbs. Non-winners of $100,000 at a mile or over allowed 2 lbs.; such a race of $50,000 allowed 4 lbs.; non–winners of two races other than claiming or starter at a mile or over allowed 6 lbs.; such a race allowed 8 lbs. Nominations closed May 7 with 15. One supplemental nominee: Makeup Artist.

Hollywood
MAY 17, 2003

Value of Race: $113,500 Winner $68,100; second $22,700; third $13,620; fourth $6,810; fifth $2,270.   Mutuel Pool $518,696.00 Exacta Pool $290,785.00   Quinella Pool $31,139.00 Trifecta Pool $330,267.00

Last Raced	Horse	M/Eqt. A.Wt	PP	St	¼	½	¾	Str	Fin	Jockey	Odds $1
13Apr03 3SA²	Makeup Artist	LB	3 117	4	6	6²	6²	4½	21½	11½	Espinoza V	1.00
29Sep02 MSB¹	Rutters Renegade–IR	LB	3 117	2	7	7	7	6²	6⁸	2½	Solis A	5.40
13Apr03 3SA³	Shapes And Shadows	LBb	3 117	3	1	2¹	2¹	2¹	1hd	3¹	Valdivia J Jr	5.80
13Apr03 3SA⁵	Major Idea	LB	3 121	5	5	5½	5½	51½	41	42½	Nakatani C S	2.50
5Oct02 New²	Little Malvern–GB	LB	3 115	1	4	3hd	3hd	3hd	5hd	5no	Smith M E	14.10
12Apr03 4SA¹	Bartok's Beau	LBb	3 115	7	3	11½	1½	1hd	3hd	611	Puglisi I L	39.30
27Apr03 3Hol⁴	Deja	LBb	3 119	6	2	41½	4½	7	7	7	Flores D R	32.30

OFF AT 2:27 Start Good. Won driving. Course firm.

TIME :24³, :49, 1:13¹, 1:36² (:24.72, :49.09, 1:13.25, 1:36.54)

$2 Mutuel Prices:

4–MAKEUP ARTIST	4.00	2.60	2.20
2–RUTTERS RENEGADE–IR		4.00	3.00
3–SHAPES AND SHADOWS			3.00

$1 EXACTA 4–2 PAID $10.00 $2 QUINELLA 2–4 PAID $13.80 $1 TRIFECTA 4–2–3 PAID $35.30

B. f, (May), by Dynaformer–Deux Anes*GB, by Longleat. Trainer Shirreffs John. Bred by Mike H Sloan (Ky).

MAKEUP ARTIST pulled her way along outside a rival chasing the early pace, went four wide on the second turn, continued three deep leaving that bend and into the stretch, gained a short lead past the eighth pole and proved best under some urging. RUTTERS RENEGADE (IRE) off a bit slowly, saved ground off the pace, swung out into the stretch and picked up the place late. SHAPES AND SHADOWS stalked the leader a bit off the rail, bid alongside that one leaving the backstretch and on the second turn, put a head in front into the stretch, fought back inside the winner in midstretch, could not match that one and was edged late for second. MAJOR IDEA stalked the pace outside a foe, was in a bit tight between horses into the second turn, steadied between rivals leaving that bend and could not offer the necessary late response. LITTLE MALVERN (GB) saved ground stalking the leader, was in a bit tight into the second turn, waited some leaving that bend, came out off heels in deep stretch and also lacked the needed rally. BARTOK'S BEAU sped to the early lead, angled in on the first turn, set a pressured pace inside, fought back along the rail on the second turn and into the stretch but weakened in the final furlong. DEJA tracked the leader outside a rival, went three deep between foes into the second turn, dropped back on that turn and weakened. A claim of foul by the rider of MAJOR IDEA against the winner for alleged interference on the second turn was not allowed by the stewards, who ruled the videotape failed to substantiate the claim.

Owners— 1, Krikorian George; 2, Class Racing Stable A & R Stables L; 3, Everest Stables; 4, The Thoroughbred Corporation; 5, Cuchna John John Richard Jim Ford I; 6, 5C Racing Stable; 7, Steven D Kenly

Trainers— 1, Shirreffs John; 2, Mandella Gary; 3, Canani Nick; 4, Drysdale Neil; 5, Cassidy James; 6, Gutierrez Jorge; 7, McFarlane Dan L

$2 Daily Double (4–4) Paid $40.80; Daily Double Pool $26,543.
$1 Pick Three (2–4–4) Paid $237.00; Pick Three Pool $117,892.

FOURTH RACE
Pimlico
MAY 17, 2003

6 FURLONGS. (1.09) 17th Running of THE MARYLAND BREEDERS' CUP HANDICAP. Grade III. Purse $200,000 Guaranteed (includes $100,000 BC – Breeders' Cup). THREE-YEAR-OLDS AND UPWARD. (Includes $100,000 from Breeders' Cup Fund for Cup nominees only) By subscription of $50 each, which should accompany the nomination, $500 to pass the entry box, $500 additional to start. Weights May 11, 2003. This race will not be divided. Preference to Breeders' Cup nominees only of equal racing quality or weight assignment (respective of sex and weight forage). Closed May 4, 2003. Supplementary nomination fee of $1000: THE DEPUTY IS HOME.

Value of Race: $120,000 Winner $60,000; second $20,000; third $17,000 each; fifth $6,000. Mutuel Pool $411,036.00 Exacta Pool $353,911.00 Trifecta Pool $175,577.00 Superfecta Pool $49,374.00

Last Raced	Horse	M/Eqt.	A.Wt	PP	St	¼	½	Str	Fin	Jockey	Odds $1
12Apr03 8Pim2	Pioneer Boy	L	5 113	4	6	1hd	12½	14	11½	Rose J	a-0.70
12Apr03 8Pim3	Sassy Hound	Lb	6 113	2	7	4½	4hd	31	21½	Dominguez R A	3.30
5Apr03 6GP2	DH Tasty Caberneigh	Lbf	5 114	1	3	2½	31½	2½	3	Prado E S	a-0.70
5Apr03 9GP1	DH Highway Prospector	Lb	6 115	6	2	7	7	51½	32¾	Santos J A	a-0.70
25Apr03 8Aqu2	Clergy	L	4 112	3	5	64	62	61	5nk	Day P	7.00
26Apr03 7CD4	Shah Jehan	Lb	4 115	7	1	31	2hd	42½	63	Stevens G L	14.90
3May03 9Pim4	The Deputy Is Home	L	5 113	5	4	5hd	52	7	7	Chavez J F	3.10

DH—Dead Heat.
a–Coupled: Pioneer Boy and Tasty Caberneigh and Highway Prospector.

OFF AT 12:00 Start Good. Won driving. Track muddy.
TIME :23 3, :46 1, :57 4, 1:10 1 (:23.60, :46.24, :57.86, 1:10.35)

$2 Mutuel Prices:

1A–PIONEER BOY (a)	3.40	2.20	2.10
3–SASSY HOUND		3.00	2.10
1–DH TASTYCABRNEIGH (a)	3.40	2.20	2.10
1X–DH HIGHWAYPRSPCTR (a)	3.40	2.20	2.10

$2 EXACTA 1–3 PAID $9.60 $2 TRIFECTA 1–3–4 PAID $30.40 $1 SUPERFECTA 1–3–4–6 PAID $43.50

B. g, by Pioneering–Jovial Wings, by Northern Jove. Trainer Robb John J. Bred by Ruth C Brightbill (Tex).

PIONEER BOY broke a step slow, was rushed to the front soon after, shook clear into the turn while under urging and two wide, opened up in mid stretch then held sway under constant pressure. SASSY HOUND angled off the rail into the turn, rated close up, rallied between rivals leaving mid stretch and finished gamely. TASTY CABERNEIGH forced the issue along the rail to the half mile marker, dropped back a bit on the turn, chased the winner into lane but lacked a solid stretch response. HIGHWAY PROSPECTOR was outrun early while saving ground, continued inside into the lane, swung out in mid stretch and found his best too late. CLERGY , close up between rivals into the turn, dropped back some leaving the three furlong marker, entered the stretch three wide but lacked the needed response. SHAH JEHAN tracked the pace three wide, was pushed along on the turn, remained a presence to upper stretch then gradually gave way. THE DEPUTY IS HOME lost ground four to five wide, was put to pressure nearing the quarter pole then weakened in upper stretch.

Owners— 1, Gill Michael J; 2, Roth Toby; 3, Gill Michael J; 4, Gill Michael J; 5, Dilschneider Adele B; 6, Helzer James E; 7, Borislow Daniel M

Trainers—1, Robb John J; 2, Feliciano Ben M Jr; 3, Shuman Mark; 4, Shuman Mark; 5, McGaughey Claude III; 6, Lukas D Wayne; 7, Scanlan John F

Scratched— Crossing Point (3May03 9MNR1)

$2 Daily Double (1–1) Paid $5.60; Daily Double Pool $37,748.
$2 P 3 (7–1/9–1/2) Paid $30.00; P 3 Pool $54,380.
$2 (3 VS 5– WINNER 3) Paid $3.60; Matchup Pool $12,847.

TENTH RACE
Pimlico
MAY 17, 2003

1⅛ MILES. (Turf)(1.47) 102nd Running of THE CITGO DIXIE. Grade II. Purse $200,000 Guaranteed. THREE-YEAR-OLDS AND UPWARD. By subscription of $100. $950 to pass the entry box, $950 additional to start. Supplemental nominations of $2000 each will be accepted by the usual time of entry with all other fees due as noted. Weights: Three-Year-olds, 114 lbs.; Older 122 lbs.; Non-winners of $100,000 at one mile or over in 2003, allowed 3 lbs.; $60,000 at one mile or over in 2003, allowed, 5lbs. (Maiden and claiming races not considered in estimating allowances). Preference to starters with highest earnings in 2002-03. Horses may be placed on the also eligible list. Closed Sunday, May 4, 2003.

Value of Race: $200,000 Winner $120,000; second $40,000; third $22,000; fourth $12,000; fifth $6,000. Mutuel Pool $887,351.00 Exacta Pool $681,859.00 Trifecta Pool $433,763.00 Superfecta Pool $114,922.00

Last Raced	Horse	M/Eqt.	A.Wt	PP	St	¼	½	¾	Str	Fin	Jockey	Odds $1
5Apr03 4Kee1	Dr. Brendler	L	5 117	6	6	6	6	5½	1½	1½	Dominguez R A	18.70
13Apr03 7Kee1	Perfect Soul-IR	Lb	5 117	4	3	21	22½	22	2hd	23½	Prado E S	1.70
3May03 9Pim5	Sardaukar-GB	L	7 117	1	5	51½	51	6	46	3no	Rose J	18.60
19Apr03 7Kee1	Del Mar Show	L	6 117	3	1	11	1½	1½	32½	410¼	Bailey J D	0.90
13Apr03 7Kee4	Loup Masque-FR	L	4 117	5	4	31	3hd	3hd	53	52	Santos J A	7.80
9Mar03 9GP3	Strategic Partner	Lb	5 117	2	2	41½	41½	4½	6	6	Migliore R	7.10

OFF AT 4:20 Start Good. Won driving. Course soft.
TIME :27 1, :53 1, 1:18 3, 1:44 2, 1:57 3 (:27.30, :53.21, 1:18.66, 1:44.56, 1:57.78)

$2 Mutuel Prices:

10–DR. BRENDLER	39.40	10.40	5.00
8–PERFECT SOUL–IR		4.00	3.20
4–SARDAUKAR–GB			5.20

$2 EXACTA 10–8 PAID $127.80 $2 TRIFECTA 10–8–4 PAID $947.20 $1 SUPERFECTA 10–8–4–7 PAID $853.20

B. h, by Distant View–Lady of Vision*Ire, by Vision. Trainer Motion H Graham. Bred by O'Toole Francis J (Md).

DR. BRENDLER settled off the rail, commenced a wide run leaving the far turn, rallied four wide into the stretch, moved to command a furlong out then was fully extended to prevail. PERFECT SOUL (IRE) prompted the pace two wide, drew on even terms approaching the stretch, dueled briefly, was overtaken by the winner nearing the furlong marker then continued gamely inside of that one to the wire. SARDAUKAR (GB) was allowed to settle towards the inside, angled out leaving the three furlong marker, came four wide for the drive and finished willingly. DEL MAR SHOW cleared early, set a slow pace along the inside, dueled from the head of the lane to the eighth pole then surrendered. LOUP MASQUE (FR) stalked the pace while off the rail and tired in upper stretch. STRATEGIC PARTNER saved ground in a forward position for six furlongs then retreated.

Owners— 1, O'Toole Francis J; 2, Fipke Charles E; 3, Gill Michael J; 4, Allen E Paulson Living Trust; 5, Lael Stables; 6, Lewis Lee

Trainers—1, Motion H Graham; 2, Attfield Roger L; 3, Shuman Mark; 4, Mott William I; 5, Clement Christophe; 6, Hennig Mark

Scratched— Statement (11Apr03 8KEE5), Sarafan (15Dec02 ST4), Dr. Kashnikow (19Apr03 7KEE9), Blue Steller (21Mar03 7SA1)

$2 Daily Double (4–10) Paid $194.00; Daily Double Pool $58,585.
$2 Pick Three (14–4–10) Paid $1,480.40; Pick Three Pool $111,662.

SEVENTH RACE
Pimlico
MAY 17, 2003

$1\frac{1}{16}$ MILES. (Turf)(1.40^{1}) 52nd Running of THE GALLORETTE HANDICAP. Grade III. Purse $100,000 Guaranteed. FILLIES AND MARES, THREE-YEARS-OLD AND UPWARD. By subscription of $100. $450 to pass the entry box, $450 additional to start. Supplemental nominations of $1000 each will be accepted by Saturday, May 10, 2003 with all other fees due as noted. Weights Sunday, May 11, 2003. Preference to starters high weights on the scale. Horses may be placed on the also eligible list. Closed Sunday, May 4, 2003.

Value of Race: $100,000 Winner $60,000; second $20,000; third $11,000; fourth $6,000; fifth $3,000. Mutuel Pool $726,934.00 Exacta Pool $575,867.00 Trifecta Pool $371,951.00 Superfecta Pool $88,810.00

Last Raced	Horse	M/Eqt.	A.Wt	PP	St	¼	½	¾	Str	Fin	Jockey	Odds $1
6Apr03 ^{4}Kee^{4}	Carib Lady-IR	L	4 116	3	7	4^{hd}	$5^{2\frac{1}{2}}$	3^{hd}	$2^{\frac{1}{2}}$	1^{nk}	Valenzuela P A	6.20
18Apr03 ^{7}Kee^{1}	Affirmed Dancer	L	4 113	5	1	2^{hd}	$4^{\frac{1}{2}}$	6^{1}	$4^{2\frac{1}{2}}$	$2^{\frac{3}{4}}$	Day P	3.10
23Nov02 ^{8}CD^{6}	Lady Of The Future	L	5 114	7	2	6^{1}	6^{1}	4^{3}	3^{2}	$3^{2\frac{1}{4}}$	Fogelsonger R	13.10
30Apr03 ^{7}Pim^{1}	Lady Linda	Lb	5 114	6	3	$1^{2\frac{1}{2}}$	1^{1}	1^{hd}	1^{hd}	$4^{4\frac{1}{4}}$	Albarado R J	5.30
16Mar03 ^{6}GP^{1}	Vespers	L	5 115	4	6	7	7	7	$5^{\frac{1}{2}}$	$5^{5\frac{1}{2}}$	Santos J A	4.30
12Apr03 ^{10}Kee^{1}	Saranac Lake	L	4 115	1	5	3^{2}	$2^{\frac{1}{2}}$	2^{2}	6^{8}	$6^{5\frac{1}{2}}$	Bailey J D	1.50
30Apr03 ^{7}Pim^{5}	Guitar	L	6 114	2	4	$5^{2\frac{1}{2}}$	$3^{\frac{1}{2}}$	5^{hd}	7	7	Jurado E M	36.50

OFF AT 2:07 Start Good. Won driving. Course soft.
TIME :24^{4}, :51^{1}, 1:17^{1}, 1:43^{4}, 1:50^{3} (:24.93, :51.23, 1:17.20, 1:43.95, 1:50.69)

$2 Mutuel Prices:

5-CARIB LADY-IR	14.40	6.20	4.40
7-AFFIRMED DANCER		4.60	3.20
14-LADY OF THE FUTURE			4.60

$2 EXACTA 5-7 PAID $64.00 $2 TRIFECTA 5-7-14 PAID $681.80 $1 SUPERFECTA 5-7-14-13 PAID $942.00

B. f, by Sadler's Wells-Belle Passe*Ire, by Be My Guest. Trainer Pletcher Todd A. Bred by O'Brien D P (Ire).

CARIB LADY (IRE) stalked the pace two wide, awaited room leaving the far turn, split foes in upper stretch and prevailed in a hard drive. AFFIRMED DANCER saved ground while unhurried, swung to the four path in upper stretch, switched to her left lead near the sixteenth pole and rallied. LADY OF THE FUTURE lacked speed, raced wide around the far turn and flattened out between horses. LADY LINDA , quickly clear, set the pace along the rail and weakened. VESPERS lacked speed, circled the far turn and failed to rally. SARANAC LAKE , unhurried early, pressed the pace two wide, drifted out in upper stretch and dropped back. GUITAR , a forward factor four wide, dropped back.

Owners— 1, Gaillardia Racing; 2, Farmer Tracy; 3, Pearson Max H; 4, Domino Stud of Lexington Inc; 5, Janney III Stuart S; 6, Firestone Diane & B R; 7, Elamri Hassan

Trainers—1, Pletcher Todd A; 2, Kimmel John C; 3, Greene Thomas M; 4, Eppler Mary E; 5, McGaughey Claude III; 6, Mott William I; 7, Elamri Hassan

Scratched— Media Access (9Nov02 ^{9}AQU^{9}), You'll Be Happy (19Mar03 ^{10}GP^{1}), Katzen (21Sep02 ^{8}DEL^{1}), Riskaverse (26Oct02 ^{7}AP^{7}), Morena Park (9Feb03 ^{9}GP^{4}), Guillotine (30Apr03 ^{7}PIM^{3}), La Belle Simone (17Apr03 ^{9}KEE^{2})

$2 Daily Double (7-5) Paid $106.60; Daily Double Pool $57,962.
$2 Pick Three (2-7-5) Paid $1,068.80; Pick Three Pool $87,808.
$2 Pick Four (1/2-2-7-5) Paid $1,832.40; Pick Four Pool $250,376.
$2 (3 VS 5- WINNER 5) Paid $5.80; Matchup Pool $15,723.

ELEVENTH RACE
Pimlico
MAY 17, 2003

1⅛ MILES. (1.47^{1}) 17th Running of THE WILLIAM DONALD SCHAEFER HANDICAP. Grade III. Purse $100,000 Guaranteed. THREE-YEAR-OLDS AND UPWARD. By free subscription. $500 to pass the entry box, $500 to start. Supplementalnominations of $1000 each will be accepted by Saturday, May 10, 2003 with all other fees due as noted. Weights Sunday, May 11, 2003. Preference to starters with high weights on the scale. Horses may be placed on the also eligible list. Closed Sunday, May 4, 2003.

Value of Race: $100,000 Winner $60,000; second $20,000; third $11,000; fourth $6,000; fifth $3,000. Mutuel Pool $1,176,330.0 Exacta Pool $892,178.00 Trifecta Pool $659,033.00 Superfecta Pool $164,342.00

Last Raced	Horse	M/Eqt.	A.Wt	PP	St	¼	½	¾	Str	Fin	Jockey	Odds $1
26Apr03 ^{8}Aqu^{2}	Windsor Castle	L	5 117	7	1	$4^{\frac{1}{2}}$	$4^{\frac{1}{2}}$	4^{hd}	$1^{2\frac{1}{2}}$	$1^{1\frac{3}{4}}$	Santos J A	4.70
19Apr03 ^{9}Pim^{2}	Changeintheweather	Lb	4 113	2	5	2^{hd}	2^{hd}	3^{1}	$3^{\frac{1}{2}}$	$2^{1\frac{3}{4}}$	Prado E S	6.20
5Apr03 ^{8}Aqu^{3}	Tempest Fugit	Lf	6 116	3	3	$3^{2\frac{1}{2}}$	3^{3}	$2^{\frac{1}{2}}$	2^{1}	3^{1}	Caraballo J C	4.50
19Apr03 ^{9}Pim^{1}	P Day	Lf	8 116	4	4	$5^{3\frac{1}{2}}$	5^{4}	5^{3}	4^{2}	$4^{\frac{3}{4}}$	Fogelsonger R	3.60
15Mar03 ^{8}Lrl^{4}	Pickupspeed	Lb	6 113	6	8	7^{hd}	7^{1}	8	6^{3}	5^{1}	Karamanos H A	22.60
3May03 ^{9}Pim^{6}	Full Brush	Lbf	8 113	1	6	$6^{1\frac{1}{2}}$	6^{1}	$6^{\frac{1}{2}}$	5^{hd}	$6^{7\frac{1}{4}}$	Dominguez R A	15.80
29Mar03 ^{11}GP^{4}	Strive	Lb	4 115	8	7	8	8	7^{hd}	$7^{3\frac{1}{2}}$	$7^{9\frac{1}{2}}$	Bailey J D	2.50
20Apr03 ^{9}GP^{3}	Roger E	L	4 113	5	2	$1^{1\frac{1}{2}}$	1^{1}	$1^{\frac{1}{2}}$	8	8	Rose J	7.00

OFF AT 5:05 Start Good. Won driving. Track good.
TIME :24, :48^{1}, 1:12^{4}, 1:37^{2}, 1:50 (:24.16, :48.37, 1:12.81, 1:37.59, 1:50.08)

$2 Mutuel Prices:

8-WINDSOR CASTLE	11.40	6.00	4.00
2-CHANGEINTHEWEATHER		7.20	4.60
4-TEMPEST FUGIT			4.00

$2 EXACTA 8-2 PAID $70.60 $2 TRIFECTA 8-2-4 PAID $413.20 $1 SUPERFECTA 8-2-4-5 PAID $726.30

B. h, by Lord Carson-Frigidette, by It's Freezing. Trainer Alexander Frank A. Bred by Windwoods Farm (Ky).

WINDSOR CASTLE stalked the pace, circled the far turn, raced four wide in upper stretch, opened up in midstretch and prevailed under brisk urging. CHANGEINTHEWEATHER , two wide entering the backstretch, was in close quarters midway on the far turn, angled to the rail in upper stretch and rallied gamely. TEMPEST FUGIT , steadied in tight quarters about a furlong into the race, prompted the pace outside ROGE E, had a three wide bid for the lead at the head of the stretch and weakened in the drive. P DAY saved ground to the far turn, swung very wide in upper stretch and was no threat. PICKUPSPEED lacked speed, raced near the rail through the stretch and passed tired ones. FULL BRUSH , two wide entering the stretch, swung to the six path in midstretch and failed to rally. STRIVE , outrun, raced wide around the far turn in a dull showing. ROGER E , sent to the front, set the pace along the rail and stopped.

Owners— 1, Dogwood Stable; 2, Pin Oak Stable; 3, Drazin Dennis A; 4, Russo Adam; 5, Bender Sondra D; 6, Bailey Morris; 7, Wygod Mr & Mrs Martin J; 8, Gill Michael J

Trainers—1, Alexander Frank A; 2, Motion H Graham; 3, Servis Jason; 4, Hadry Charles J; 5, Murray Lawrence E; 6, Gaudet Edmond D; 7, Mott William I; 8, Shuman Mark

Scratched— Seattle Glory (19Apr03 ^{5}GP^{1})

$2 Daily Double (10-8) Paid $301.60; Daily Double Pool $52,906.
$2 (5 VS 9- WINNER 5) Paid $3.00; Matchup Pool $19,982.

TWELFTH RACE
Pimlico
MAY 17, 2003

$1\frac{3}{16}$ MILES. (1.52^{2}) 128th Running of THE PREAKNESS. Grade I. Purse $1,000,000 Guaranteed. THREE-YEAR-OLDS. $10,000 to pass the entry box, starters to pay $10,000 additional. Supplemental nominations may be made in accordance with the rules, upon payment of $100,000. 65% of the purse to the winner, 20% to second, 10% to third, and 5% to fourth. Weight 126 pounds for colts and geldings, 121 pounds for fillies. A replica of the Woodlawn Vase will be presented to the winning owner to remain his or her personal property. Closed Sunday, May 4, 2003.

Value of Race: $1,000,000 Winner $650,000; second $200,000; third $100,000; fourth $50,000. Mutuel Pool $14,711,833. Exacta Pool $9,205,919.0 Trifecta Pool $11,041,055. Superfecta Pool $3,198,747.0

Last Raced	Horse	M/Eqt.	A.Wt	PP	St	¼	½	¾	Str	Fin	Jockey	Odds $1
3May03 ^{10}CD^{1}	Funny Cide	L	3 126	9	6	3^{1}	2^{1}	$2^{1\frac{1}{2}}$	1^{5}	$1^{9\frac{3}{4}}$	Santos J A	1.90
24Apr03 ^{7}Kee^{1}	Midway Road	L	3 126	6	7	7^{2}	$5^{1\frac{1}{2}}$	$3^{\frac{1}{2}}$	4^{3}	$2^{\frac{3}{4}}$	Albarado R J	20.00
3May03 ^{10}CD^{11}	Scrimshaw	Lb	3 126	2	3	1^{hd}	$3^{1\frac{1}{2}}$	4^{1}	2^{hd}	3no	Stevens G L	a-4.90
3May03 ^{10}CD^{3}	Peace Rules	L	3 126	7	2	2^{2}	1^{1}	$1^{\frac{1}{2}}$	3^{1}	4^{2}	Prado E S	2.40
2May03 ^{9}CD^{1}	Senor Swinger	Lf	3 126	10	10	10	10	10	6^{hd}	5^{hd}	Day P	a-4.90
3May03 ^{9}Aqu^{5}	New York Hero	Lbf	3 126	8	5	5^{hd}	$6^{1\frac{1}{2}}$	6^{1}	$5^{3\frac{1}{2}}$	$6^{3\frac{1}{4}}$	Chavez J F	19.60
2May03 ^{9}CD^{3}	Foufa's Warrior	Lbf	3 126	3	9	$9^{4\frac{1}{2}}$	8^{hd}	7^{3}	7^{hd}	$7^{1\frac{1}{4}}$	Dominguez R A	22.40
19Apr03 ^{8}Pim^{1}	Cherokee's Boy	Lb	3 126	1	4	$4^{1\frac{1}{2}}$	$4^{\frac{1}{2}}$	5^{2}	8^{3}	$8^{5\frac{3}{4}}$	Fogelsonger R	9.70
3May03 ^{10}CD^{8}	Ten Cents A Shine	L	3 126	5	8	8^{hd}	$9^{4\frac{1}{2}}$	$8^{2\frac{1}{2}}$	$9^{3\frac{1}{2}}$	9^{1}	Bailey J D	8.50
12Apr03 ^{8}Aqu^{3}	Kissin Saint	L	3 126	4	1	$6^{1\frac{1}{2}}$	$7^{2\frac{1}{2}}$	9^{hd}	10	10	Migliore R	10.20

a-Coupled: Scrimshaw and Senor Swinger.

OFF AT 6:14 Start Good. Won driving. Track good.
TIME :23^{1}, :47, 1:11^{3}, 1:36^{2}, 1:55^{3} (:23.37, :47.14, 1:11.62, 1:36.42, 1:55.61)

$2 Mutuel Prices:

9–FUNNY CIDE	5.80	4.60	3.40
6–MIDWAY ROAD		15.40	9.00
1–SCRIMSHAW (a–entry)			4.00

$2 EXACTA 9–6 PAID $120.60 $2 TRIFECTA 9–6–1 PAID $684.20 $1 SUPERFECTA 9–6–1–7 PAID $792.20

Ch. g, (Apr), by Distorted Humor–Belle's Good Cide, by Slewacide. Trainer Tagg Barclay. Bred by Win Star Farm LLC (NY).

FUNNY CIDE was brushed slightly by NEW YORK HERO at the start, moved up three wide approaching the first turn, stalked the pace while well in hand along the backstretch, launched a rally three wide leaving the far turn, closed the gap midway on the turn, accelerated to the front nearing the quarter pole, opened a commanding lead under right hand urging in midstretch, extended his advantage when struck with the left hand a sixteenth out then drew off under a vigorous hand ride. MIDWAY ROAD broke inward bumping with TEN CENTS A SHINE at the start, was unhurried along the rail through the opening half mile, made a sharp move inside the winner at the half mile pole, saved ground while racing just behind the leader leaving the turn, battled along the inside in midstretch, was brushed by PEACE RULES with a sixteenth remaining then outfinished SCRIMSHAW for the place. SCRIMSHAW moved up along the rail to gain a brief advantage in the early stages, relinquished the lead to PEACE RULES midway on the first turn, moved out along the backstretch, raced within striking distance while three wide on the turn, closed the gap in upper stretch, came in a bit under right hand urging to bump twice with PEACE RULES a sixteenth out then continued on willingly to gain a share. PEACE RULES battled for the early lead from outside, opened a clear advantage leaving the seven-eighths pole, was rated on the front while slightly off the rail along the backstretch, maintained a clear advantage to the turn, relinquished control to the winner approaching the quarter pole, remained a factor into midstretch, was bumped twice while in tight quarters between horses at the sixteenth pole then weakened from his early efforts. SENOR SWINGER trailed for a good portion of the trip, circled five wide entering the stretch then improved his position with a belated rally in the middle of the track. NEW YORK HERO broke outward brushing slightly with the winner at the start, raced in the middle of the pack while five wide for a half, angled to the rail on the far turn, raced within striking distance to the top of the stretch then faded in the drive. FOUFA'S WARRIOR broke in the air a bit then was pinched back at the start, saved ground while well back for six furlongs, angled three wide leaving the turn then lacked a strong closing bid. CHEROKEE'S BOY up close while saving ground for five furlongs, angled out on the far turn, circled five wide into the stretch then lacked a further response. TEN CENTS A SHINE was brushed by MIDWAY ROAD at the start, checked and altered course to the outside while rank approaching the first turn then never reached contention and was not abused while well back through the stretch. KISSIN SAINT bobbled at the start, raced three wide along the backstretch and lacked the needed response when called upon.

Owners— 1, Sackatoga Stable; 2, Farish William S; 3, Lewis Robert B & Beverly J; 4, Gann Edmund A; 5, Lewis Robert B & Beverly J; 6, Paraneck Stable; 7, Bender Sondra D; 8, Z W P Stable; 9, Ramsey Kenneth L & Sarah K; 10, Karches Peter F & Rankowitz Michael

Trainers—1, Tagg Barclay; 2, Howard Neil J; 3, Lukas D Wayne; 4, Frankel Robert; 5, Baffert Bob; 6, Pedersen Jennifer; 7, Murray Lawrence E; 8, Capuano Gary; 9, Lukas D Wayne; 10, Lewis Lisa L

$2 Daily Double (8–9) Paid $30.40; Daily Double Pool $287,996.
$2 Daily Double (SPECIAL/PREAKNESS(3–9)) Paid $18.80; Daily Double Pool $254,970 $2 P 3 (10–8–9) Paid $652.40; P 3 Pool $271,515.
$2 P 4 (4–10–8–9) Paid $4,987.40; P 4 Pool $846,702.
$2 (7 VS 9–WINNER 9) Paid $3.80; Head to Head Pool $36,175.

EIGHTH RACE
Belmont
MAY 24, 2003

1⅛ MILES. (1.45^{2}) 50th Running of THE PETER PAN. Grade II. Purse $200,000. (Up to $34,800 NYSBFOA). THREE YEAR OLDS. By subscription of $200 each, which should accompany the nomination; $1,000 to pass the entry box and $1,000 to start. The purse to be divided 60% to the winner, 20% to second, 11% to third, 6% to fourth and 3% to fifth. 123 lbs. Non-winners of $100,000 at a mile or over in 2003 allowed 2 lbs.; $50,000 other than restricted stake at a mile or over, or $30,000 twice at a mile or over 4 lbs.; $50,000, or three races other than maiden or claiming, 6 lbs.; two races other than maiden or claiming, 8 lbs. Trophies will be presented to the winning owner, trainer and jockey. Closed Saturday, May 10, 2003 with 33 Nominations.

Value of Race: $200,000 Winner $120,000; second $40,000; third $22,000; fourth $12,000; fifth $6,000. Mutuel Pool $649,572.00 Exacta Pool $476,811.00 Trifecta Pool $348,945.00

Last Raced	Horse	M/Eqt.	A.Wt	PP	St	¼	½	¾	Str	Fin	Jockey	Odds $1
2May03 ^{7}Aqu^{1}	Go Rockin' Robin	Lb	3 117	3	4	5^{7}	4^{hd}	$3^{1\frac{1}{2}}$	1^{1}	1^{6}	Bridgmohan S X	13.00
3May03 ^{9}Aqu^{2}	Alysweep	Lf	3 123	4	2	1^{hd}	$1\frac{1}{2}$	1^{hd}	2^{6}	$2\frac{3}{4}$	Bailey J D	2.75
27Apr03 ^{7}Crc^{1}	Supervisor	Lb	3 115	5	3	6	6	6	$4^{2\frac{1}{2}}$	3^{2}	Santos J A	24.00
3May03 ^{9}Aqu^{1}	Spite The Devil	b	3 121	6	1	$4\frac{1}{2}$	5^{8}	$4^{1\frac{1}{2}}$	$3\frac{1}{2}$	$4^{7\frac{1}{4}}$	Castellano J J	6.90
12Apr03 ^{10}Aqu^{1}	Nacheezmo	L	3 115	1	6	3^{hd}	3^{hd}	5^{5}	6	$5^{1\frac{1}{4}}$	Velazquez J R	1.20
12Apr03 ^{9}OP^{3}	Christine's Outlaw	Lf	3 115	2	5	2^{1}	2^{1}	2^{hd}	5^{1}	6	Coa E M	3.80

OFF AT 4:45 Start Good For All But NACHEEZMO Won driving. Track sloppy.
TIME :22^{3}, :44^{4}, 1:08^{4}, 1:34^{4}, 1:48^{2} (:22.69, :44.98, 1:08.91, 1:34.93, 1:48.47)

$2 Mutuel Prices:

3-GO ROCKIN' ROBIN	28.00	8.60	4.70
4-ALYSWEEP		4.00	3.20
5-SUPERVISOR			6.80

$2 EXACTA 3-4 PAID $104.00 $2 TRIFECTA 3-4-5 PAID $649.00

Dk. b. or br. c, (Mar), by Distorted Humor-Flag Support, by Personal Flag. Trainer Schwartz Scott M. Bred by WinStar Farm LLC & McMahon Thoroughbreds (NY).

GO ROCKIN' ROBIN raced close up outside while under wraps, advanced three wide on the turn, responded when roused entering the stretch, drew clear and widened while under a drive to the wire. ALYSWEEP contested the pace from the outside and stayed on to hold the place position. SUPERVISOR was outrun early, came wide into the stretch and was going well outside late. SPITE THE DEVIL was hustled along outside, raced wide and tired in the stretch. NACHEEZMO hit the gate at the start, ducked to the inside, was steadied then was hustled up inside, chased the pace for three quarters and tired. CHRISTINE'S OUTLAW contested the pace along the inside and tired in the stretch.

Owners— 1, Schwartz Herbert T & Carol A; 2, Doneson Mark & Dubb Michael; 3, Lundock Rodney G; 4, Hardwicke Stable; 5, Johnson Ted J & Kim; 6, R C Hill Stable

Trainers—1, Schwartz Scott M; 2, Reynolds Patrick L; 3, Rice Linda; 4, Jerkens H Allen; 5, Bond Harold James; 6, Weaver George

---

SEVENTH RACE
Bay Meadows
MAY 24, 2003

ABOUT 1⅛ MILES. (Turf)(1.45^{1}) 30th Running of the YERBA BUENA BREEDERS' CUP HANDICAP. Grade III. Purse $150,000 (includes $50,000 Breeders' Cup). Fillies and mares, 3-year-olds and upward. (125 feet short of 1 1/8 miles). By subscription of $100 each to accompany the nomination or by supplementary nomination of $2,000 by Noon Sunday, May 18. $500 to pass the entry box and $500 additional to start with $100,000 Guaranteed. Closed May 15 with 21 nominations. (If deemed inadvisable by management to run this race on the turf, it will be contested at 1 1/8 miles on the main track). Rail at 0 feet.

Value of Race: $107,500 Winner $55,000; second $20,000; third $22,500; fourth $7,500; fifth $2,500. Mutuel Pool $309,084.00 Exacta Pool $165,196.00 Quinella Pool $16,814.00 Trifecta Pool $194,362.00 Superfecta Pool $66,125.00

Last Raced	Horse	M/Eqt.	A.Wt	PP	St	¼	½	¾	Str	Fin	Jockey	Odds $1
2May03 ^{7}Hol^{2}	Chiming-IR	LB	5 116	2	4	4^{1}	3^{1}	3^{hd}	2^{1}	$1^{3\frac{1}{2}}$	Nakatani C S	4.00
19Apr03 ^{4}SA^{3}	Noches de Rosa-CH	LBb	5 119	1	7	7	7	7	$4\frac{1}{2}$	2^{3}	Almeida G F	3.20
5Apr03 ^{6}BM^{1}	Lindsay Jean	LB	5 118	7	2	2^{1}	2^{1}	$2^{1\frac{1}{2}}$	$1\frac{1}{2}$	$3^{2\frac{1}{4}}$	Schvaneveldt C P	5.10
27Apr03 ^{8}Hol^{6}	Turtle Bow-FR	LB	4 119	4	3	3^{hd}	5^{hd}	4^{hd}	$5^{2\frac{1}{2}}$	$4\frac{1}{2}$	Baze R A	1.50
19Apr03 ^{4}SA^{4}	Notting Hill-BR	LBf	4 116	6	1	1^{2}	1^{2}	1^{1}	3^{3}	5^{1}	Rollins C J	7.70
22Mar03 ^{9}SA^{7}	Snowflake-IR	LB	5 116	3	5	$5\frac{1}{2}$	4^{hd}	$5^{1\frac{1}{2}}$	6^{1}	$6^{2\frac{1}{2}}$	Alvarado F T	20.80
7May03 ^{7}Hol^{3}	Miss Pitz-GB	LB	5 115	5	6	6^{1}	6^{1}	6^{hd}	7	7	Atkinson P	25.40

OFF AT 4:13 Start Good. Won driving. Course firm.
TIME :24^{3}, :48^{1}, 1:11^{3}, 1:36, 1:45^{2} (:24.65, :48.37, 1:11.73, 1:36.08, 1:45.41)

$2 Mutuel Prices:

2-CHIMING-IR	10.00	4.60	3.20
1-NOCHES DE ROSA-CH		3.80	2.80
8-LINDSAY JEAN			3.00

$1 EXACTA 2-1 PAID $16.90 $2 QUINELLA 1-2 PAID $15.80 $1 TRIFECTA 2-1-8 PAID $87.10 $1 SUPERFECTA 2-1-8-4 PAID $199.10

B. m, by Danehill-Strutting*Ire, by Ela-Mana-Mou*Ire. Trainer Frankel Robert. Bred by Waters Mrs C A (Ire).

CHIMING (IRE) broke cleanly and tracked the pace well in hand, remained unhurried to the second turn, came off the rail nearing the quarter pole to enter the lane directly behind LINDSAY JEAN, shifted outside that rival approaching the furlong pole to challenge, quickly drew clear and extended her advantage driving. NOCHES DE ROSA (CHI) raced unhurried to the three eighths, angled three wide at mid turn and seemed to lose some of her momentum into the stretch, caught hold again leaving the furlong pole and closed willingly but was never a threat to the winner. LINDSAY JEAN prompted the pace early well in hand, advanced to challenge nearing the quarter pole from the outside, forged to the front once in the stretch, drew clear briefly but had little left for the drive. TURTLE BOW (FR) raced within easy striking distance from between horses to the second turn then failed to respond. NOTTING HILL (BRZ) set all of the pace from the inside to the head of the lane and gave way. SNOWFLAKE (IRE) tracked the pace three wide and outside TURTLE BOW to the second turn then had no rally. MISS PITZ (GB) was never a factor.

Owners— 1, Castleton Lyons; 2, Diamond A Racing Corporation; 3, Moss Mr & Mrs Jerome S; 4, Crichton Andrew; 5, Green Lantern Stables & Barber Gary; 6, Stonerside Stable; 7, Charles Ronald L & Clear Valley Sta

Trainers—1, Frankel Robert; 2, Mandella Richard; 3, Sherman Art; 4, De Seroux Laura; 5, Sahadi Jenine; 6, McAnally Ronald; 7, Shulman Sanford

---

$2 Daily Double (4-2) Paid $40.80; Daily Double Pool $14,255.
$1 Pick Three (3-4-2) Paid $169.20; Pick Three Pool $16,331.

NINTH RACE

Churchill

MAY 24, 2003

1$\frac{1}{16}$ MILES. (Turf)(1.40⁴) 27th Running of THE EARLY TIMES MINT JULEP HANDICAP. Grade III. Purse $150,000 added. Fillies and mares, 4–year–olds and upward. By subscription of $150 each on or before May 10 or by supplementary nomination of $7,500 each by the closing of entries Friday, May 16, 2003. $750 to pass the entry box; $750 additional to start, with $150,000 added of which 62% of all monies to the owner of the winner, 20% to second, 10 % to third, 5% to fourth and 3% to fifth. Weights to be announced Saturday, May 17. If the race is moved to the main track after the time of closing, a horse may be scratched for any reason at any time up to fifteen minutes prior to post time for the race preceding this race or thereafter with a valid physical reason and approved by the stewards. (If this race is taken off the turf it will be downgraded one grade level for this running only in accordance with American Graded Stakes Committee policy).

Value of Race: $168,300 Winner $104,346; second $33,660; third $16,830; fourth $8,415; fifth $5,049. Mutuel Pool $609,500.00 Exacta Pool $464,194.00 Trifecta Pool $403,738.00 Superfecta Pool $138,648.00

Last Raced	Horse	M/Eqt. A.Wt	PP	St	$\frac{1}{4}$	$\frac{1}{2}$	$\frac{3}{4}$	Str	Fin	Jockey	Odds $1
23Apr03 6Kee²	Kiss The Devil	Lb	5 115	4	3	2$1\frac{1}{2}$	2$2\frac{1}{2}$	2³	1²	1nk	Meche L J	13.80
3May03 7CD²	Quick Tip	L	5 119	9	2	6²	5$\frac{1}{2}$	4²	2hd	2¹	Albarado R J	1.60
26Apr03 5Crc⁴	Cellars Shiraz	Lbf	4 120	8	8	5¹	3$\frac{1}{2}$	3¹	3³	3¹	Day P	7.10
16Mar03 10Tam³	Stylish	Lb	5 117	5	7	8$\frac{1}{2}$	9	9	7$3\frac{1}{2}$	4¹	Velasquez C	5.40
24Apr03 8Kee³	San Dare	L	5 119	6	9	9	8$1\frac{1}{2}$	5²	4¹	5$1\frac{1}{2}$	Guidry M	3.60
30Apr03 6CD¹	Guana-FR	L	4 114	7	6	7¹	7hd	6hd	6hd	6$6\frac{1}{2}$	Melancon L	11.90
7May03 8CD¹	Salzurita-ARG	L	5 112	3	4	3¹	4¹	7$\frac{1}{2}$	9	7nk	Blanc B	21.30
1May03 7CD²	Crystal Sea	L	6 114	2	1	1$\frac{1}{2}$	1¹	1$\frac{1}{2}$	5hd	8¹	Borel C H	9.80
14Dec02 8Lrl⁷	Desert Gold	L	4 113	1	5	4hd	6$1\frac{1}{2}$	8²	8$\frac{1}{2}$	9	Sellers S J	21.30

OFF AT 5:33 Start Good. Won driving. Course firm.

TIME :23², :47¹, 1:11¹, 1:35², 1:41³ (:23.52, :47.32, 1:11.33, 1:35.49, 1:41.73)

$2 Mutuel Prices:

4–KISS THE DEVIL	29.60	11.80	6.40
9–QUICK TIP		3.40	2.80
8–CELLARS SHIRAZ			4.40

$2 EXACTA 4–9 PAID $88.00 $2 TRIFECTA 4–9–8 PAID $575.60 $1 SUPERFECTA 4–9–8–5 PAID $1,497.30

Dk. b. or br. m, by Kris S.–Devil's Nell, by Devil's Bag. Trainer Vance David R. Bred by Domino Stud Of Lexington (Ky).

KISS THE DEVIL went up soon after the start to press front-running CRYSTAL SEA under light rating three or four wide, took over from that one entering the upper stretch, was roused twice on the left nearing the final furlong, then gamely held sway under hand urging. QUICK TIP drifted in at the start bumping CELLARS SHIRAZ and was straightened, settled four wide while never far back, was asked for her best leaving the five-sixteenths pole and was slowly reducing the winner's advantage at the end. CELLARS SHIRAZ, bumped at the start, raced under light rating with easy striking distance while also four wide, loomed boldly between foes for the final furlong but gained only slightly. STYLISH, in a bit tight after the start and checked, settled three or four wide, was outrun for six furlongs while continuing in behind horses, came out between foes five or six wide for the drive and offered a mild gain. SAN DARE, sluggish to start and squeezed back in tight quarters, was unhurried, reached contention five wide entering the far turn, commenced her bid three furlongs out, continued six wide into the lane and failed to gain in the last eighth. GUANA (FR) drifted in at the start bumping SAN DARE, raced between foes three or four wide, continued four wide into the stretch and failed to rally. SALZURITA (ARG) settled in behind horses early but weakened gradually after five furlongs. CRYSTAL SEA gained the lead early, raced near the hedge, made the pace for six furlongs and weakened thereafter. DESERT GOLD tired after leaving the backstretch.

Owners— 1, Pollard Carl F; 2, Farish William S; 3, Bitterroot Racing Stable Robert Wal; 4, The Thoroughbred Corporation; 5, Mounts David G; 6, Vanmeter II Thomas F Hendrickson D; 7, Korkames David; 8, Foster Dennis E; 9, Stonerside Stable

Trainers—1, Vance David R; 2, Howard Neil J; 3, Cesare William; 4, Mott William I; 5, Hiles Rick; 6, Walden W Elliott; 7, Murty Wayne; 8, McGee Paul J; 9, Byrne Patrick B

$1 Pick Three (3–5–4) Paid $318.90: Pick Three Pool $44.890.

EIGHTH RACE

Hollywood

MAY 24, 2003

1$\frac{1}{16}$ MILES. (1.40) 52nd Running of THE MILADY BREEDERS' CUP HANDICAP. Grade I. Purse $200,000 added. (includes $50,000 Breeders' Cup). Fillies and mares, 3–year–olds and upward. By subscription of $200 each on or before Wednesday, May 14. $1,500 additional to start, with $150,000 added. Weight assigned on the scale. Closed with 14 nominations.

Value of Race: $211,800 Winner $127,080; second $42,360; third $25,416; fourth $12,708; fifth $4,236. Mutuel Pool $1,946,195.0 Exacta Pool $304,116.00 Quinella Pool $21,555.00 Trifecta Pool $314,325.00

Last Raced	Horse	M/Eqt. A.Wt	PP	St	$\frac{1}{4}$	$\frac{1}{2}$	$\frac{3}{4}$	Str	Fin	Jockey	Odds $1
5Apr03 8OP¹	Azeri	LB	5 125	4	2	2$4\frac{1}{2}$	1¹	1$2\frac{1}{2}$	1$2\frac{1}{2}$	1³	Smith M E	0.20
24Apr03 7Hol¹	Enjoy	LB	4 114	1	6	6	6	6	2$\frac{1}{2}$	2³	Espinoza V	9.80
24Apr03 7Hol³	Tropical Blossom	LBb	5 111	2	5	3$\frac{1}{2}$	3hd	2hd	3hd	3¹	Garcia M S	53.00
25Apr03 3Hol¹	Keys To The Heart	LB	4 115	6	3	5$4\frac{1}{2}$	55	4$2\frac{1}{2}$	42	44	Valdivia J Jr	26.90
5Apr03 8OP⁴	Affluent	LB	5 117	5	4	4$1\frac{1}{2}$	42	3$1\frac{1}{2}$	55	5¹⁷	Stevens G L	4.80
27Apr03 8Hol⁴	Damaschino-AU	LB	5 116	3	1	1hd	2$2\frac{1}{2}$	5hd	6	6	Valenzuela P A	15.30

OFF AT 4:57 Start Good. Won driving. Track fast.

TIME :23, :46¹, 1:10, 1:35², 1:41⁴ (:23.08, :46.23, 1:10.13, 1:35.49, 1:41.87)

$2 Mutuel Prices:

4–AZERI	2.40	2.10	2.10
1–ENJOY		2.40	2.10
2–TROPICAL BLOSSOM			2.10

$1 EXACTA 4–1 PAID $4.80 $2 QUINELLA 1–4 PAID $8.60 $1 TRIFECTA 4–1–2 PAID $63.50

Ch. m, by Jade Hunter–Zodiac Miss*Aus, by Ahonoora. Trainer De Seroux Laura. Bred by Allen E Paulson (Ky).

AZERI had speed between horses then dueled outside a rival on the first turn, tugged her way to the front early on the backstretch, inched away, set the pace a bit off the rail, responded when rivals loomed nearing the second turn and kicked clear again, then proved best under some left handed urging and steady handling late. ENJOY settled inside then a bit off the rail, moved up three deep on the second turn and four wide into the stretch and was clearly second best. TROPICAL BLOSSOM stalked the pace toward the inside, moved up along the rail leaving the second turn, continued just off the inside on the second turn and between horses in midstretch and bested the others. KEYS TO THE HEART settled three deep into the first turn, angled in on the backstretch, advanced inside on the second turn but could not offer the needed late response. AFFLUENT chased outside a rival, moved up three deep and bid outside the winner leaving the backstretch, dropped back outside a foe on the second turn and weakened. DAMASCHINO (AUS) had good early speed and dueled inside the winner, stalked that one toward the inside on the backstretch, fell back on the second turn and gave way.

Owners— 1, Allen E Paulson Living Trust; 2, Greely III John J; 3, Wygod Mr & Mrs Martin J; 4, Nichols Thomas L; 5, Whitham Janis R; 6, Newton R B

Trainers— 1, De Seroux Laura; 2, Greely C Beau; 3, Canani Julio C; 4, Greely C Beau; 5, McAnally Ronald; 6, Drysdale Neil

$2 Daily Double (7–4) Paid $13.60; Daily Double Pool $42,751.
$1 Pick Three (1–7–4) Paid $75.70; Pick Three Pool $82,229.

EIGHTH RACE
Hollywood
MAY 25, 2003

1 MILE. (Turf)(1.32^{3}) 63rd Running of THE WILL ROGERS. Grade III. Purse $100,000 added. 3-year-olds. By subscription of $100 each on or before Wednesday, May 14, or by supplementary nomination of $5,000 each by closing time of entries. $1,000 additional to start. Weight, 123 lbs. Non-winners of $100,000 at a mile or over, allowed 2 lbs. Such a race of $50,000, 4 lbs. Non-winners of two races other than claiming or starter at a mile or over, 6 lbs. Such a race, 8 lbs. Closed Wedensday, May 14 with 16 nominations. Supplementary nominee: PRIVATE CHEF. Rail at 15 feet.

Value of Race: $112,600 Winner $67,560; second $22,520; third $13,512; fourth $6,756; fifth $2,252. Mutuel Pool $446,318.00 Exacta Pool $232,497.00 Quinella Pool $19,699.00 Trifecta Pool $239,294.00

Last Raced	Horse	M/Eqt.	A.Wt	PP	St	¼	½	¾	Str	Fin	Jockey	Odds $1
16Feb03 2SA1	Private Chef	LBb	3 115	6	6	6	6	51½	32½	1¾	Espinoza V	6.00
25Apr03 8Hol2	Banshee King	LBb	3 115	3	2	11	11	11½	12	21¼	Baze T C	6.30
12Apr03 7SA2	Singletary	LB	3 117	1	3	21½	21½	22	21	33	Valenzuela P A	0.40
3May03 7Hol6	American Fury	LB	3 116	2	4	5½	5hd	6	6	4½	Enriquez I D	33.70
10May03 8BM2	Rapier Dance	LBb	3 119	4	5	32	3hd	4hd	5hd	5no	Nakatani C S	9.90
26Apr03 4Hol8	Winning Stripes	LBb	3 119	5	1	41	42½	3½	4hd	6	Solis A	10.00

OFF AT 4:56 Start Good. Won driving. Course firm.
TIME :24^{1}, :48^{2}, 1:12^{1}, 1:35^{2} (:24.24, :48.42, 1:12.35, 1:35.57)

$2 Mutuel Prices:

6–PRIVATE CHEF	14.00	7.00	2.10
3–BANSHEE KING		7.00	2.10
1–SINGLETARY			2.10

$1 EXACTA 6–3 PAID $44.80 $2 QUINELLA 3–6 PAID $43.80 $1 TRIFECTA 6–3–1 PAID $76.10

B. g, (Feb), by Partner's Hero–Mississippi Lights, by Majestic Light. Trainer Shirreffs John. Bred by Candyland Farm (Md).

PRIVATE CHEF angled in and settled a bit off the rail then outside a rival on the backstretch, advanced three deep on the second turn and into the stretch and rallied determinedly under urging to get up in the late stages. BANSHEE KING sped to the early lead, angled in on the first turn and set the pace inside, responded when challenged into the second turn, slipped away again and held on well but was caught late. SINGLETARY pulled his way along inside then stalked a bit off the rail, bid outside the leader into the second turn, continued to track that one just off the inside, came out some in the stretch, was in a bit tight off heels late and was outfinished. AMERICAN FURY saved ground chasing the pace, came out into the stretch and lacked the needed rally. RAPIER DANCE stalked the pace outside a rival, was between horses into the stretch and weakened. WINNING STRIPES chased outside a rival then angled in on the backstretch, stalked along the rail and also weakened.

Owners— 1, Moss Mr & Mrs Jerome S; 2, Deberdt Bruno & Jmj Racing Stables; 3, Little Red Feather Racing; 4, Ingalls Jim L; 5, Abruzzo Hollendorfer & Litt; 6, Robinson Ken Shustek Mike & Stanley

Trainers—1, Shirreffs John; 2, O'Neill Doug; 3, Chatlos Donald Jr; 4, Kenney Martin; 5, Hollendorfer Jerry; 6, Morey William J Jr

$2 Daily Double (5–6) Paid $117.60; Daily Double Pool $33,057.
$1 Pick Three (2–5–6) Paid $193.50; Pick Three Pool $25,888.

NINTH RACE
Belmont
MAY 26, 2003

1 MILE. (1.32^{1}) 110th Running of THE METROPOLITAN HANDICAP. Grade I. Purse $750,000. (Up to $35,500 NYSBFOA). THREE YEAR OLDS AND UPWARD. By subscription of $750 each, which should accompany the nomination; $3,500 to pass the entry box and $4,000 to start. The purse to be divided 60% to the winner, 20% to second, 11% to third, 6% to fourth and 3% to fifth. Trophies will be presented to the winning owner, trainer and jockey. Closed Saturday, May 10, 2003 with 18 Nominations.

Value of Race: $750,000 Winner $450,000; second $150,000; third $82,500; fourth $45,000; fifth $22,500. Mutuel Pool $832,881.00 Exacta Pool $624,969.00 Trifecta Pool $506,430.00 Superfecta Pool $142,814.00

Last Raced	Horse	M/Eqt.	A.Wt	PP	St	¼	½	¾	Str	Fin	Jockey	Odds $1
3May03 5CD1	Aldebaran	L	5 119	6	5	72	74½	53	11½	1nk	Bailey J D	4.40
7May03 8Bel2	Saarland	Lbf	4 114	1	8	8	8	710	2hd	23	Velazquez J R	8.20
10May03 6Bel3	Peeping Tom	Lbf	6 114	2	7	5hd	53½	4hd	3½	33¾	Bridgmohan S X	31.00
3May03 5CD9	Proud Citizen	L	4 116	4	2	43	3½	3hd	5½	4hd	Chavez J F	18.10
7May03 8Bel3	Justification	L	6 113	8	1	66	63	6hd	722	52¼	Castellano J J	42.00
12Apr03 9Aqu1	Congaree	L	5 124	7	4	2hd	21½	1hd	41½	62¾	Stevens G L	0.80
7May03 8Bel1	Najran	L	4 116	3	3	1½	1hd	21½	6hd	724¼	Prado E S	4.10
26Apr03 8WO1	Wake At Noon	Lbf	6 115	5	6	31½	4½	8	8	8	Ramsammy E	50.75

OFF AT 5:16 Start Good. Won driving. Track sloppy.
TIME :22^{1}, :44^{2}, 1:08^{3}, 1:34 (:22.23, :44.48, 1:08.60, 1:34.15)

$2 Mutuel Prices:

6–ALDEBARAN	10.80	5.50	5.70
1–SAARLAND		7.50	8.40
2–PEEPING TOM			17.60

$2 EXACTA 6–1 PAID $63.00 $2 TRIFECTA 6–1–2 PAID $686.00 $2 SUPERFECTA 6–1–2–4 PAID $6,491.00

B. h, by Mr. Prospector–Chimes of Freedom, by Private Account. Trainer Frankel Robert. Bred by Flaxman Holdings Ltd (Ky).

ALDEBARAN was bumped at the start, dropped back early, advanced four wide on the turn, swung wide into the stretch, drew clear when roused, was straightened away while attempting to duck out when confronted by SAARLAND in deep stretch, dug in and prevailed over that rival after a hard drive. SAARLAND was unhurried while outrun early, advanced inside on the turn, came wide entering the stretch and finished fast from the outside. PEEPING TOM was urged along early on, rallied inside on the turn, came wide into the stretch and weakened in the final furlong. PROUD CITIZEN raced close up outside, put in a three wide run on the turn and had little left for the stretch drive. JUSTIFICATION was hustled along outside, jumped puddles on the backstretch, raced four wide and had no rally. CONGAREE bobbled at the start, was bumped after the start, contested the pace from the outside, earned a short lead turning for home and tired in the drive. NAJRAN was hustled to the front, set the pace under constant pressure and tired after three quarters. WAKE AT NOON was bumped at the start then was rushed up inside, argued the pace and was finished after the first half mile.

Owners— 1, Flaxman Stable; 2, Phipps Cynthia; 3, Flatbird Stable; 4, Baker Robert C Cornstein David & Ma; 5, Shields Joseph V Jr; 6, Stonerside Stable; 7, Buckram Oak Farm; 8, Schickedanz Bruno

Trainers—1, Frankel Robert; 2, McGaughey Claude III; 3, Reynolds Patrick L; 4, Lukas D Wayne; 5, Jerkens H Allen; 6, Baffert Bob; 7, Zito Nicholas P; 8, Katryan Abraham R

EIGHTH RACE

Bay Meadows
MAY 26, 2003

1 1/16 MILES. (1.38²) 36th Running of THE SEABISCUIT HANDICAP. Grade III. Purse $100,000. (Formerly run as the All American Handicap) 3-year-olds and upward. By subscription of $100 each to accompany the nomination or by supplementary nomination of $2,000 by Noon Sunday, May 18. $500 to pass the entry box and $500 additional to start with $100,000 Guaranteed of which $55,000 to the winner, $20,000 to second, $15,000 to third, $7,500 to fourth and $2,500 to fifth. Closed Thursday, May 15 with 15 nominations.

Value of Race: $100,000 Winner $55,000; second $20,000; third $15,000; fourth $7,500; fifth $2,500. Mutuel Pool $235,907.00 Exacta Pool $129,145.00 Quinella Pool $13,480.00 Trifecta Pool $151,278.00

Last Raced	Horse	M/Eqt. A.Wt	PP	St	1/4	1/2	3/4	Str	Fin	Jockey	Odds $1
23Nov02 NAK⁹	Reba's Gold	LBb 6 118	3	3	4³	4³½	4⁶	1³	1⁸	Rollins C J	2.00
27Apr03 7TuP¹	Free Corona	LB 5 116	6	5	6	5¹	5²½	5³	2no	Ziegler M G	5.20
3May03 8Hol²	Truly A Judge	LBb 5 117	4	4	3³	2½	2hd	3hd	3¾	Puglisi I L	3.30
26Apr03 7BM⁸	I'madrifter	LB 5 116	1	2	1¹	1¹½	1¹½	2²	4¹	Gonzalez R M	4.60
26Apr03 4Hol³	Tiz A Coup	LB 3 111	5	6	5¹	6	6	6	5hd	Rivera J L Jr	20.50
25Apr03 9Kee³	Metatron	LBf 4 116	2	1	2hd	3³	3½	4²	6	Baze R A	3.10

OFF AT 4:52 Start Good. Won handily. Track fast.
TIME :22¹, :45, 1:09⁴, 1:35, 1:41³ (:22.29, :45.16, 1:09.85, 1:35.14, 1:41.63)

$2 Mutuel Prices:

4-REBA'S GOLD	6.00	3.60	2.60
7-FREE CORONA		4.80	3.00
5-TRULY A JUDGE			2.60

$1 EXACTA 4-7 PAID $14.50 $2 QUINELLA 4-7 PAID $17.60 $1 TRIFECTA 4-7-5 PAID $44.20

B. h, by Slew o' Gold-Lovely Reba, by Herat. Trainer Hendricks Dan L. Bred by Mereworth Farm (Ky).

REBA'S GOLD took back off the leaders early but was always within striking distance, offered a quick move four wide on the second turn to take command once in the stretch then drew off at will without being asked for his best. FREE CORONA lagged well back to the second turn, came four wide to the stretch and finished gamely but passed mainly tiring horses. TRULY A JUDGE prompted IMADRIFTER from the outside to the stretch but lacked the needed response. I'MADRIFTER set the pace from just off the rail to the stretch and shortened stride. TIZ A COUP lagged early and failed to reach serious contention. METATRON stalked the pace from the inside but came up empty in the lane.

Owners— 1, Creston Farms; 2, Krieg III Karl C; 3, Aidekman Alan Ailshie Gaylord & Har; 4, O'Neill Daniel; 5, Irvin Betty & Robert G; 6, Coyote Creek Racing Stable
Trainers—1, Hendricks Dan L; 2, Schenk Kathy; 3, Bernstein David; 4, Specht Steve; 5, Severinsen Allen; 6, Hollendorfer Jerry
Scratched— Bonus Pay Day (26Apr03 8HOL²)

$2 Daily Double (7-4) Paid $89.40; Daily Double Pool $8,182.
$1 Pick Three (6-7-4) Paid $308.30; Pick Three Pool $19,703.

NINTH RACE

Churchill
MAY 26, 2003

5½ FURLONGS. (1.02²) 16th Running of THE KENTUCKY BREEDERS' CUP. Grade III. Purse $150,000. (includes $50,000 BC – Breeders' Cup) FOR TWO-YEAR-OLDS. ($50,000 from Breeders' Cup Fund for Cup nominees only.) By subscription of $150 each on or before May 10, 2003 or by supplementary nomination of $7,500 at time of entry. $750 to pass the entry box; $750 additional to start, with $100,000 added and an additional $50,000 from the Breeders' Cup Fund for Cup nominees only. The host associations' added monies to be divided 62% to the owner of the winner, 20% to second, 10% to third, 5% to fourth and 3% to fifth. Breeders' Cup Fund monies also correspondingly divided providing a Breeders' Cup nominee has finished in an awarded position. Any Breeders' Cup Fund monies not awarded will revert back to the Fund. Colts and Geldings, 121 lbs. Fillies, 118 lbs. Non-winners of a sweepstakes, allowed 2 lbs. A race other than maiden or claiming, 4 lbs. A race other than claiming, 6 lbs. Starters named through the entry box at the usual time of closing. All supplementary nominations will be required to pay entry and starting fees if they participate. Closed Saturday, May 18 with 18 nominations. Trophy to winning owner given by Breeders' Cup Ltd.

Value of Race: $174,200 Winner $109,554; second $35,340; third $17,670; fourth $6,335; fifth $5,301. Mutuel Pool $407,253.00 Exacta Pool $340,346.00 Trifecta Pool $253,816.00 Superfecta Pool $82,074.00

Last Raced	Horse	M/Eqt. A.Wt	PP	St	1/4	3/8	Str	Fin	Jockey	Odds $1
2May03 1CD¹	Cuvee	L 2 117	6	6	3¹½	1¹½	1³½	1⁸¼	Meche L J	0.60
14May03 4CD¹	First Money	L 2 117	4	2	1hd	2¹	2³½	2⁶	Albarado R J	5.30
27Apr03 1CD¹	Exploit Lad	Lb 2 117	2	1	2¼	4³	4²	3⁴	Lumpkins J	14.10
17May03 1CD¹	Toin And Boin	L 2 117	5	3	4hd	3hd	3¹	4no	Perret C	3.00
12May03 1RD¹	Another Freddy	f 2 117	3	4	6	5¹	5³	5⁶¾	Solomon N G	23.30
10May03 6AP¹	Voladero	Lb 2 117	1	5	5³	6	6	6	Velasquez C	11.00

OFF AT 5:36 Start Good. Won driving. Track fast.
TIME :22², :46, :58, 1:04² (:22.46, :46.01, :58.05, 1:04.45)

$2 Mutuel Prices:

6-CUVEE	3.20	2.40	2.20
4-FIRST MONEY		3.40	2.60
2-EXPLOIT LAD			3.40

$2 EXACTA 6-4 PAID $13.00 $2 TRIFECTA 6-4-2 PAID $57.20 $1 SUPERFECTA 6-4-2-5 PAID $69.10

Ch. c, (Mar), by Carson City-Christmas Star, by Star de Naskra. Trainer Asmussen Steven M. Bred by (Ky).

CUVEE hopped while failing to break alertly, moved up to force the pace three abreast, took over on the turn, drew clear, then won going away under hand urging as much the best. FIRST MONEY drifted in at the break bumping ANOTHER FREDDY, gained a slim lead while dueling outside of EXPLOIT LAD, lost the edge to the winner approaching the stretch and continued on as second best. EXPLOIT LAD drifted out at the start bumping ANOTHER FREDDY, vied for the lead inside to the turn and couldn't keep pace. TOIN AND BOIN ran off briefly prior to reaching the starting gate, then was reluctant and a bit difficult to load. TOIN AND BOIN broke awkwardly, raced three or four wide and weakened in the drive. ANOTHER FREDDY, bumped soundly from both sides at the start and steadied when squeezed back, raced three or four wide around the turn and failed to threaten. VOLADERO saved ground throughout and failed to menace.

Owners— 1, Winchell Thoroughbreds; 2, Copeland Dreabon; 3, Jones Frank L Jr; 4, Fayard Keith; 5, Nemann Fred A; 6, Lewis Robert B & Beverly J
Trainers—1, Asmussen Steven M; 2, Flint Bernard S; 3, Romans Dale; 4, Werner Ronny; 5, Nemann Kris; 6, Lukas D Wayne

$1 Pick Three (6-11-6) Paid $34.50: Pick Three Pool $49,625.

ELEVENTH RACE
Calder
MAY 26, 2003

$1\frac{1}{16}$ MILES. (1.42^{2}) 29th Running of THE MEMORIAL DAY HANDICAP. Grade III. Purse $100,000 FOR THREE YEAR OLDS AND UPWARD. By subscription of $100 each which shall accompany the nomination, $1,000 to pass the entry box and an additional $1,000 to start – with $100,000 guaranteed. The owner of the winner to receive $60,000,$20,000 to second, $11,000 to third, $6,000 to fourth and $3,000 to fifth. A trophy will be presented to the winning Owner. Closed Saturday, May 17, 2003 with (8) nominations.

Value of Race: $100,000 Winner $60,000; second $20,000; third $11,000; fourth $6,000; fifth $3,000. Mutuel Pool $110,124.00 Exacta Pool $111,268.00 Trifecta Pool $82,944.00 Superfecta Pool $31,060.00

Last Raced	Horse	M/Eqt.	A.Wt	PP	St	¼	½	¾	Str	Fin	Jockey	Odds $1
3May03 ^{7}Crc^{4}	Dancing Guy	Lbf	8 113	6	6	7	6^{hd}	6^{hd}	4^{hd}	1^{nk}	Velez R I	10.00
2May03 ^{2}Crc^{2}	Shotgun Fire	L	5 110	2	3	4^{hd}	$4\frac{1}{2}$	$3\frac{1}{2}$	2^{2}	$2^{2\frac{1}{4}}$	Garcia J A	15.90
3May03 ^{7}Crc^{1}	High Ideal	Lb	5 113	1	2	1^{1}	1^{1}	1^{1}	1^{hd}	$3^{1\frac{1}{4}}$	Castanon J L	1.00
3May03 ^{7}Crc^{3}	Sebastian Light	Lb	4 113	7	7	$3^{1\frac{1}{2}}$	$2^{1\frac{1}{2}}$	2^{hd}	5^{2}	4^{1}	Aguilar M	62.00
3May03 ^{7}Crc^{2}	Lavender's Lad	Lf	5 115	3	1	2^{hd}	$3\frac{1}{2}$	4^{1}	3^{hd}	$5^{8\frac{1}{4}}$	Toscano P R	6.00
19Apr03 ^{8}Haw^{3}	Parrott Bay	Lb	6 114	4	4	5^{3}	$5^{3\frac{1}{2}}$	5^{1}	7	$6^{1\frac{1}{4}}$	Homeister R B Jr	3.50
25Apr03 ^{5}Crc^{1}	Mr. Livingston	Lf	6 114	5	5	$6^{1\frac{1}{2}}$	7	7	$6^{1\frac{1}{2}}$	7	Cruz M R	3.90

OFF AT 5:25 Start Good. Won driving. Track fast.
TIME :23^{4}, :47^{3}, 1:12, 1:38^{3}, 1:45^{2} (:23.87, :47.65, 1:12.02, 1:38.71, 1:45.56)

$2 Mutuel Prices:				
	6–DANCING GUY	22.00	7.60	4.00
	2–SHOTGUN FIRE		10.80	4.40
	1–HIGH IDEAL			2.80

$2 EXACTA 6–2 PAID $283.40 $2 TRIFECTA 6–2–1 PAID $742.80 $2 SUPERFECTA 6–2–1–7 PAID $6,478.20

Gr. g, by Robyn Dancer–Dancing Myrrh, by Gold and Myrrh. Trainer Green Newcomb. Bred by Farnsworth Farms (Fla).

DANCING GUY outrun early, swung to the outside for the stretch run and rallied under pressure to be just up at the wire. SHOTGUN FIRE tracked the pace along the inside, eased outside HIGH IDEAL for the stretch run, rallied to gain the lead from that rival inside the eighth pole, then just failed to last. HIGH IDEAL set the pace along the inside to midstretch and gave way. SEBASTIAN LIGHT prompted the pace from the outside into the stretch and weakened. LAVENDER'S LAD well placed from the outset, angled three wide on the far turn, then tired in the drive. PARROTT BAY reserved off the pace, raced four wide on the far turn and faltered. MR. LIVINGSTON turned in a dull effort.

Owners— 1, Green Newcomb; 2, Cherry Martin L; 3, Brodkin Judith; 4, Jerry G Bozzo Trust; 5, Lucky Lavender Stable; 6, Hoffman Kenneth E; 7, Palmer Teresa & David

Trainers—1, Green Newcomb; 2, Wolfson Martin D; 3, Wolfson Martin D; 4, Bozzo Jerry; 5, White William P; 6, Hoffman Kenneth E; 7, Kaplan William A

$2 Pick Three (2–2–6) Paid $2,542.40; Pick Three Pool $6,691.

SIXTH RACE
Hollywood
MAY 26, 2003

1⅛ MILES. (Turf Chute)(1.44^{3}) 37th Running of THE GAMELY BREEDERS' CUP HANDICAP. Grade I. Purse $350,000 added (includes $100,000 Breeders' Cup). Fillies and mares, 3-year-olds and upward. ($100,000 from Breeders' Cup Fund for Cup nominees only). By subscription of $500 each on or before February 8 which should accompany the nomination. To remain eligible the following payment must be made; $1,500 on or before April 25. Late nominations for horses not previously nominated or not remaining eligible, may be made on or before May 21 by payment of $10,000, which should accompany the nomination, of which $8,000 is refundable if the nominee is entered and does not draw into the body of the race or if the nominee is not entered and a veterinarian certificate is produced indicating the horse is unfit to run. Nominees to pay $2,500 to enter and an additional $3,000 to start, with $250,000 added. Breeders' Cup monies also correspondingly divided providing a Breeders' Cup nominee has finished in an awarded position. Weights: May 18. Late nominee weights: May 22. Closed Friday, February 28 with 19 nominations. Rail at zero. Supplemental nomination: TATES CREEK.

Value of Race: $421,000 Winner $263,400; second $87,800; third $40,680; fourth $20,340; fifth $8,780. Mutuel Pool $599,954.00 Exacta Pool $323,043.00 Quinella Pool $31,488.00 Trifecta Pool $290,320.00

Last Raced	Horse	M/Eqt.	A.Wt	PP	St	¼	½	¾	Str	Fin	Jockey	Odds $1
11Jan03 ^{3}SA^{1}	Tates Creek	LB	5 122	6	2	3^{1}	$3^{1\frac{1}{2}}$	3^{1}	$2\frac{1}{2}$	1^{1}	Valenzuela P A	3.50
27Apr03 ^{8}Hol^{1}	Dublino	LB	4 122	4	4	5^{6}	4^{hd}	$5^{1\frac{1}{2}}$	4^{2}	$2\frac{1}{2}$	Desormeaux K J	1.50
19Apr03 ^{4}SA^{1}	Megahertz-GB	LB	4 118	1	6	6	6	6	$5^{1\frac{1}{2}}$	$3\frac{1}{2}$	Solis A	6.00
2Nov02 SI^{1}	Miss Terrible-ARG	LB	4 117	3	1	$1^{1\frac{1}{2}}$	1^{1}	1^{1}	1^{1}	4^{2}	Flores D R	5.10
1Dec02 ^{4}Hol^{1}	Dress To Thrill-IR	LB	4 122	5	5	2^{1}	2^{1}	$2\frac{1}{2}$	3^{hd}	$5^{4\frac{1}{2}}$	Santos J A	3.30
3May03 ^{7}CD^{3}	Sentimental Value	LBb	4 113	2	3	4^{hd}	5^{3}	4^{1}	6	6	Espinoza V	22.40

OFF AT 4:02 Start Good. Won driving. Course firm.
TIME :24, :48^{2}, 1:12, 1:35^{1}, 1:46^{4} (:24.09, :48.45, 1:12.14, 1:35.29, 1:46.97)

$2 Mutuel Prices:				
	6–TATES CREEK	9.00	3.40	2.60
	4–DUBLINO		2.80	2.40
	1–MEGAHERTZ–GB			3.20

$1 EXACTA 6–4 PAID $12.50 $2 QUINELLA 4–6 PAID $10.60 $1 TRIFECTA 6–4–1 PAID $29.00

Ch. m, by Rahy–Viviana, by Nureyev. Trainer Frankel Robert. Bred by Juddmonte Farms (Ky).

TATES CREEK pulled a bit and angled in early, stalked just off the rail on the backstretch then outside a rival, came three deep into the stretch, rallied to the front under urging past the eighth pole, then drifted in while pulling clear and held gamely. DUBLINO allowed to settle outside a rival chasing the pace, came four wide into the stretch and finished well but could not catch the winner. MEGAHERTZ (GB) unhurried inside to the second turn, swung out into the stretch and also closed gamely. MISS TERRIBLE (ARG) sped to the early lead and angled in, set the pace inside, held on gamely until just past midstretch and weakened late. DRESS TO THRILL (IRE) pulled a bit early, stalked outside a rival then off the rail, loomed a threat into the second turn, continued just off the inside and weakened in the final furlong. SENTIMENTAL VALUE saved ground chasing the pace, dropped back on the second turn and weakened in the stretch.

Owners— 1, Juddmonte Farms Inc; 2, Geringer Robert Klein Michael & Nai; 3, Bello Michael; 4, Carol & Charles Hammersmith; 5, Moyglare Stud Farm Ltd; 6, The Thoroughbred Corporation

Trainers—1, Frankel Robert; 2, De Seroux Laura; 3, Frankel Robert; 4, Frankel Robert; 5, Clement Christophe; 6, Mulhall Kristin

$2 Daily Double (4–6) Paid $76.00; Daily Double Pool $46,359.
$1 Pick Three (7–4–6) Paid $154.40; Pick Three Pool $88,992.

SEVENTH RACE

Hollywood

MAY 26, 2003

7 FURLONGS. (1.19⁴) 10th Running of THE LAZARO BARRERA MEMORIAL. Grade II. Purse $150,000. THREE YEAR OLDS. By subscription of $150 each on or before Wednesday, May 14 or by supplementary nomination of $7,500 each by closing time of entries. $1,500 additional to start, with $90,000 to the winner, $30,000 to second, $18,000 to third, $9,000 to fourth and $3,000 to fifth. Weight, 123 lbs. Non–winners of $60,000, allowed 3 lbs. A race of $40,000 since December 25, 5 lbs. Non–winners of two races other than maiden, claiming or starter, 8 lbs.; Of such a race, 10 lbs. Closed Wedensday, May 14 with 20 nominations.

Value of Race: $150,000 Winner $90,000; second $30,000; third $18,000; fourth $9,000; fifth $3,000. Mutuel Pool $573,199.00 Exacta Pool $369,781.00 Quinella Pool $33,692.00 Trifecta Pool $348,439.00 Superfecta Pool $135,055.00

Last Raced	Horse	M/Eqt. A.Wt	PP	St	¼	½	Str	Fin	Jockey	Odds $1
2Apr03 ⁴SA³	Blazonry	LB	3 115	2	9	9	7ʰᵈ	21½	12½	Smith M E	4.70
25Apr03 ⁸Hol⁴	Fly To The Wire	LB	3 116	6	7	8½	82½	52	2⅓	Desormeaux K J	18.10
23Apr03 ⁷Hol²	Jimmy O	LBb	3 115	4	5	4ʰᵈ	4ʰᵈ	41	31	Garcia M S	37.80
2May03 ⁴Hol⁵	Truckle Feature	LBb	3 116	3	8	5½	31	3ʰᵈ	41	Flores D R	21.10
23Apr03 ⁷Hol¹	King Robyn	LB	3 120	7	2	2¹	1ʰᵈ	1ʰᵈ	53½	Solis A	1.80
3May03 ⁷Hol¹	Martinblestme	LBb	3 118	9	3	6ʰᵈ	62	6½	6ʰᵈ	Nakatani C S	7.60
12Apr03 ⁷SA⁶	Our Bobby V.	LB	3 115	1	4	1ʰᵈ	2½	71	73	Baze T C	16.80
26Apr03 ⁴Hol²	Excessivepleasure	LBb	3 123	8	1	3½	5ʰᵈ	88	8¹³	Valenzuela P A	4.10
5Apr03 ⁸Haw⁸	Runnin' On Nitro	LBb	3 115	5	6	7²	9	9	9	Santos J A	4.80

OFF AT 4:33 Start Good. Won driving. Track fast.
TIME :21³, :44, 1:09, 1:22 (:21.62, :44.11, 1:09.01, 1:22.19)

$2 Mutuel Prices:	2–BLAZONRY	11.40	6.80	5.20
	7–FLY TO THE WIRE		15.00	8.40
	5–JIMMY O			10.80

$1 EXACTA 2–7 PAID $63.40 $2 QUINELLA 2–7 PAID $126.80 $1 TRIFECTA 2–7–5 PAID $1,154.00 $1 SUPERFECTA 2–7–5–3 PAID $15,400.10

B. c, (Feb), by Hennessy–Altair, by Alydar. Trainer Walsh Kathy. Bred by Sanford R Robertson (Ky).

BLAZONRY broke slowly, settled off the rail then outside a rival, launched a bid three deep into the turn, came six wide into the stretch, rallied to the lead while drifting in under left handed urging then pulled clear. FLY TO THE WIRE angled in and saved ground off the pace, came out in upper stretch, then split horses late for second. JIMMY O stalked the pace off the rail, waited off heels through much of the turn, came out three deep between horses into the stretch, could not match the winner in the drive and lost the place late. TRUCKLE FEATURE a bit slow to begin, moved up inside on the backstretch, bid along the rail in a bit tight into the turn, dueled inside on the bend and weakened in the stretch. KING ROBYN had good early speed and dueled outside a rival, battled on a short lead three deep on the turn, angled in a bit and inched away into the stretch but weakened in the final furlong. MARTINBLESTME chased outside on the backstretch and four wide on the turn, came five wide into the stretch and lacked the needed response. OUR BOBBY V. went up inside but a bit off the rail to duel for command, battled between horses on the turn, dropped back into the stretch and weakened. EXCESSIVEPLEASURE close up stalking outside on the backstretch and between foes into the turn, steadied when squeezed while four wide into the stretch and fell back. RUNNIN' ON NITRO chased between horses then dropped back off the rail leaving the backstretch and gave way.

Owners— 1, Robertson Sanford R; 2, Flying A Farms & Jack & Gloria Kram; 3, Anderson Gene & Dr Kevin & Meadowbr; 4, McIngvale James; 5, Cornejo Racing Inc; 6, Henn Terry & Dawn; 7, Verratti Kathleen & Robert; 8, Leatherman Ty & Leroy & Sutalo Gene; 9, Brewer Ron Haagsma John & Ward Wesl

Trainers—1, Walsh Kathy; 2, Bacorn Herbert L; 3, La Croix David; 4, Baffert Bob; 5, Mullins Jeff; 6, Baffert Bob; 7, Spawr Bill; 8, O'Neill Doug; 9, Ward Wesley A

Scratched— Roll Hennessy Roll (6Apr03 ⁸KEE²), Desert Spirit (8Feb03 LIN¹), Ministers Wild Cat (19Apr03 ⁸KEE⁵)

$2 Daily Double (6–2) Paid $63.40; Daily Double Pool $49,924.
$1 Pick Three (4–6–2) Paid $232.70; Pick Three Pool $136,179.

EIGHTH RACE

Hollywood

MAY 26, 2003

1 MILE. (Turf)(1.32³) 60th Running of THE SHOEMAKER BREEDERS' CUP MILE. Grade I. Purse $350,000 added (includes $100,000 Breeders' Cup). 3–year–olds and upward. ($100,000 from Breeders' Cup Fund for Cup nominees only). By subscription of $500 each on or before Friday, February 28 which should accompany the nomination. To remain eligible the following payment must be made; $1,500 on or before April 25. Late nominations, for horses not previously nominated or not remaining eligible, may be made on or before May 21 by payment of $10,000, which should accompany the nomination, of which $8,000 is refundable if the nominee is entered and does not draw into the body of the race or if the nominee is not entered and a veterinarian certificate is produced indicating the horse is unfit to run. All nominees to pay $2,500 to enter and an additional $3,000 to start with $250,000 added. Breeders' Cup monies also correspondingly divided provided a Breeders' Cup nominee has finished in an awarded position. Any Breeders' Cup monies not awarded will revert to the fund. Weights: 3–year–olds, 113 lbs. Older 124 lbs. Closed Friday February 28 with 43 nominations.–April 25 with 16 nominations. Rail at zero. Supplemental nominations: WAR ZONE, NICOBAR and CENTURY CITY.

Value of Race: $415,000 Winner $225,000; second $95,000; third $57,000; fourth $28,500; fifth $9,500. Mutuel Pool $638,511.00 Exacta Pool $371,461.00 Quinella Pool $35,269.00 Trifecta Pool $342,262.00 Superfecta Pool $125,629.00

Last Raced	Horse	M/Eqt. A.Wt	PP	St	1/4	1/2	3/4	Str	Fin	Jockey	Odds $1
1Mar03 8SA1	Redattore–BRZ	LB	8 124	9	2	2$1\frac{1}{2}$	2$1$	2$1\frac{1}{2}$	2$2\frac{1}{2}$	1$\frac{3}{4}$	Solis A	2.20
2Aug02 7Dmr1	Special Ring	LBb	6 124	8	3	1$2$	1$3\frac{1}{2}$	1$2$	1$1$	2$3$	Valdivia J Jr	3.20
11Apr03 8Kee3	TouchotheBlues–FR	LB	6 124	4	7	9	9	8$\frac{1}{2}$	5$2\frac{1}{2}$	3$2$	Desormeaux K J	10.10
26Dec02 7SA7	Medecis–GB	LB	4 124	2	8	6$1\frac{1}{2}$	5$1$	4$3$	3$1$	4$1\frac{1}{2}$	Smith M E	9.80
28Mar03 7SA1	War Zone	LB	4 124	5	9	8$2$	7hd	7hd	6$\frac{1}{2}$	5no	Flores D R	5.20
26Apr03 7BM4	Ladies Din	LBb	8 124	3	5	3hd	3hd	3$\frac{1}{2}$	4$2$	6$2\frac{1}{2}$	Valenzuela P A	3.90
3May03 9CD6	Century City–IR	LBb	4 124	6	6	4hd	4$1$	6$1\frac{1}{2}$	8hd	7hd	Espinoza V	18.70
26Apr03 7BM2	Nicobar–GB	LB	6 124	7	4	7$\frac{1}{2}$	8$4\frac{1}{2}$	9	9	8$2\frac{1}{2}$	Alvarado F T	29.70
16May02 9CD4	Tijiyr–IRE	LBf	7 124	1	1	5$2$	6$2\frac{1}{2}$	5$\frac{1}{2}$	7$1\frac{1}{2}$	9	Nakatani C S	78.10

OFF AT 5:03 Start Good. Won driving. Course firm.

TIME :24, :46³, 1:09¹, 1:33¹ (:24.09, :46.68, 1:09.39, 1:33.37)

$2 Mutuel Prices:

9–REDATTORE–BRZ	6.40	4.20	3.40
8–SPECIAL RING		4.40	3.60
4–TOUCH OF THE BLUES–FR			5.20

$1 EXACTA 9–8 PAID $13.60 $2 QUINELLA 8–9 PAID $13.40 $1 TRIFECTA 9–8–4 PAID $92.60 $1 SUPERFECTA 9–8–4–2 PAID $835.60

B. h, by Roi Normand–Political Intrigue, by Deputy Minister. Trainer Mandella Richard. Bred by Haras Santa Ana do Rio Grande (Brz).

REDATTORE (BRZ) angled in and stalked the leader a bit off the rail, came out into the stretch, bid alongside that rival past midstretch, gained a short lead under urging in deep stretch and gamely prevailed. SPECIAL RING broke in a bit, sprinted to the front and angled in, set the pace along the inside, fought back when challenged in the stretch and also continued gamely to the wire but could not quite match the winner late. TOUCH OF THE BLUES (FR) a bit crowded early, angled in and saved ground off the pace, got through inside into the stretch, came out approaching midstretch and finished well for third. MEDECIS (GB) squeezed at the start, chased inside then outside a rival on the backstretch, continued inside on the second turn and lacked the needed response. WAR ZONE off a bit slowly, settled just off the rail, came out some in the stretch and also lacked the necessary rally. LADIES DIN pulled his way between horses into the first turn, stalked off the rail then outside the winner early on the second turn and weakened in the stretch. CENTURY CITY (IRE) also pulled some between horses into the first turn, stalked three deep then outside on the backstretch, dropped back on the second turn and also weakened. NICOBAR (GB) four wide into the first turn, chased outside, came three deep into the stretch and did not rally. TIJIYR (IRE) broke outward, saved ground chasing the pace, came out into the stretch and had little left.

Owners— 1, Taunay Luis A; 2, Prestonwood Farm LLC; 3, Al Maktoum Sheik Maktoum b; 4, Wertheimer Farm; 5, Juddmonte Farms Inc; 6, Lanni J Terrence & Schiappa Bernard; 7, Kitchwa Stables & Nichols Thomas L; 8, Zetcher Arnold; 9, Tanaka Gary A

Trainers—1, Mandella Richard; 2, Canani Julio C; 3, Drysdale Neil; 4, Mandella Richard; 5, Frankel Robert; 6, Monteleone Frank J; 7, Greely C Beau; 8, McAnally Ronald; 9, Burke Donald J II

$2 Daily Double (2–9) Paid $55.20; Daily Double Pool $47,342.
$1 Pick Three (6–2–9) Paid $143.80; Pick Three Pool $175,745.

EIGHTH RACE
Lone Star
MAY 26, 2003

1 1/16 MILES. (1.40^{2}) 7th Running of THE LONE STAR PARK HANDICAP. Grade III. Purse $300,000 Guaranteed. (Plus Up To $7,500 From ATBOIA) A HANDICAP FOR THREE YEAR OLDS AND UPWARD. No nomination fee. $2,250 to pass the entry box and an additional $2,250 to start with $300,000 guaranteed of which $180,000 to the owner of the winner, $60,000 to second, $33,000 to third, $18,000 to fourth and $9,000 to fifth. Weights: Sunday, May 18, 2003. Starters to be named through the entry box by the usual time of closing. High weights preferred. The field will be limited to fourteen starters. Horses not drawing a starting position in the gate will receive a refund of the entry fee. A suitable award will be presented to the winning owner. NOMINATIONS CLOSED WEDNESDAY, MAY 14, 2003.

Value of Race: $300,000 Winner $180,000; second $46,500 each; fourth $18,000; fifth $9,000. Mutuel Pool $314,230.00 Exacta Pool $215,497.00 Quinella Pool $18,720.00 Trifecta Pool $191,832.00 Superfecta Pool $62,822.00

Last Raced	Horse	M/Eqt.	A.	Wt	PP	St	¼	½	¾	Str	Fin	Jockey	Odds $1
9May03 ^{7}LS^{1}	Pie N Burger	Lb	5	117	5	3	2½	1^{hd}	1^{1}	1^{2}	12¾	Theriot H J II	6.50
26Apr03 ^{9}LS^{5}	DH Maysville Slew	Lf	7	114	2	7	7^{5}	6^{1}	6^{2}	6^{2}	2	Perrodin E J	36.60
26Apr03 ^{9}LS^{1}	DH Bluesthestandard	L	6	120	8	1	4^{4}	42½	2½	21½	21½	Pedroza M A	1.50
26Apr03 ^{9}LS^{4}	Private Emblem	Lf	4	115	4	5	5^{2}	5^{3}	5^{3}	5½	4^{nk}	Lanerie C J	a-4.20
3May03 ^{5}CD^{2}	Pass Rush	Lb	4	118	6	2	3^{1}	31½	4½	3½	5^{nk}	Day P	1.70
17Apr03 ^{9}LS^{1}	Where's The Ring	Lb	4	113	1	4	1^{hd}	21½	3½	4½	6^{2}	Pettinger D R	9.20
7May03 ^{8}LS^{1}	Fifty Stars	Lf	5	116	7	6	8	8	7^{1}	7^{4}	79½	Sellers S J	a-4.20
26Apr03 ^{9}Fon^{1}	Dusty Spike	L	4	117	3	8	6½	7^{5}	8	8	8	Kretzer K D	45.90

DH—Dead Heat.
a–Coupled: Private Emblem and Fifty Stars.

OFF AT 5:17 Start Good. Won driving. Track fast.
TIME :22^{4}, :46, 1:10^{1}, 1:35^{2}, 1:42 (:22.85, :46.00, 1:10.26, 1:35.56, 1:42.03)

$2 Mutuel Prices:				
	5–PIE N BURGER	15.00	4.40	3.40
	3–DH MAYSVILLE SLEW		6.80	6.00
	7–DH BLUESTHESTANDARD		2.40	2.80

$2 EXACTA 5–3 PAID $166.40 $2 EXACTA 5–7 PAID $28.40 $2 QUINELLA 3–5 PAID $81.80 $2 QUINELLA 5–7 PAID $12.40 $2 TRIFECTA 5–3–7 PAID $864.80 $2 TRIFECTA 5–7–3 PAID $306.60 $2 SUPERFECTA 5–3–7–1 PAID $1,681.80 $2 SUPERFECTA 5–7–3–1 PAID $889.40

Ch. g, by Twining–Abarca, by Topsider. Trainer Norman Cole. Bred by Helen C Alexander (Ky).

PIE N BURGER contested the pace on the outside, inched away passing the three-eighths pole, responded well when set down in upper stretch, edged clear into the final furlong, and held well under strong left hand urging. MAYSVILLE SLEW was unhurried while saving ground, roused on the final turn, and finished willingly to share the place award. BLUESTHESTANDARD pulled hard early, was taken back behind the leaders entering the first turn, continued to pull on that turn, settled a bit and eased outside of PASS RUSH midway down the backstretch, ranged up four wide with three furlongs to run, was just behind the winner through upper stretch, but proved no match for that rival in the final furlong, and weakened to finish on even terms for second. PRIVATE EMBLEM settled into stride, advanced while in hand on the final turn, was floated five wide by PASS RUSH entering the stretch, and lacked the needed rally. PASS RUSH contested the pace four wide on the first turn, was well placed tracking the pace on the backstretch, roused passing the quarter pole, came four wide entering the stretch, and lacked the needed rally. WHERE'S THE RING contested the pace on the inside, vied into the far turn, and faded steadily. FIFTY STARS dropped well behind the field, and never reached contention. DUSTY SPIKE raced four wide on the final turn, and was always outrun.

Owners— 1, Kagele Bros Inc & James A Bailey; 2, Trout C R; 3, Sengara Jeffrey; 4, Cassels James & Zollars Bob; 5, Tabor Michael B; 6, Pin Oak Stable; 7, Cassels James & Zollars Bob; 8, Deiter Raymond W

Trainers—1, Norman Cole; 2, Trout C R; 3, West Ted H; 4, Asmussen Steven M; 5, Byrne Patrick B; 6, Von Hemel Donnie K; 7, Asmussen Steven M; 8, Lee Mark

$2 Pick Three (3–4–5) Paid $704.00; Pick Three Pool $13,613.

TENTH RACE
Monmouth
MAY 26, 2003

1 1/16 MILES. (1.40^{1}) 59th Running of THE JERSEY DERBY. Purse $100,000 FOR THREE-YEAR-OLDS. By subscription of $100 each, which should accompany the nomination. $1,500 to enter. The winner to receive $60,000; $20,000 to second; $11,000 to third; $6,000 to fourth; $3,000 to fifth. Weight: 122 lbs. Non-winners of $60,000 at a mile or over on the turf allowed 3 lbs.; $45,000 at a mile or over or $60,000, 5 lbs.; a sweepstakes anytime, 7 lbs.; $20,000 at a mile or over, 10 lbs. (Maiden, Claiming and Starter races not considered.) Starters to be named through the entrybox by the usual time of closing. This race will not be divided. Graded stakes winners, placed, stakes winners then highweights preferred. Lifetime earnings will break all ties. Supplementary nominations may be made at time of entry by payment of a fee of $5,000 each, which includes all fees. The Owner of the Winner to Receive a Trophy. NOMINATIONS CLOSED Monday, May 12, 2003 with 29.(ORIGINALLY SCHEDULED FOR TURF.)

Value of Race: $100,000 Winner $60,000; second $20,000; third $11,000; fourth $6,000; fifth $3,000. Mutuel Pool $123,249.00 Exacta Pool $118,757.00

Last Raced	Horse	M/Eqt.	A.	Wt	PP	St	¼	½	¾	Str	Fin	Jockey	Odds $1
1May03 ^{6}Aqu^{4}	Happy Trails	Lb	3	114	2	3	5^{5}	5^{4}	41½	3^{2}	12¼	Toribio A R	a-1.90
7May03 ^{2}Bel^{1}	Stone Canyon	L	3	114	4	5	3^{hd}	3½	3½	2^{hd}	2¾	Luzzi M J	0.50
11May03 ^{8}Del^{1}	Angelic Aura	Lb	3	115	3	2	2^{1}	2½	1^{hd}	1^{hd}	35½	Gryder A T	a-1.90
23Apr03 ^{7}GP^{4}	Flank Attack	Lb	3	114	1	1	4^{hd}	4^{hd}	5^{3}	5^{6}	42¼	King E L Jr	10.20
9May03 ^{5}Bel^{2}	Shoalihs Tale	Lb	3	114	6	4	11½	1½	2^{hd}	4½	5^{13}	Lopez C C	8.40
16Apr03 ^{9}GP^{5}	Wesman	L	3	114	5	6	6	6	6	6	6	Bravo J	22.00

a–Coupled: Happy Trails and Angelic Aura.

OFF AT 4:57 Start Good. Won driving. Track sloppy.
TIME :23^{3}, :47^{4}, 1:12^{4}, 1:38^{4}, 1:45^{2} (:23.74, :47.88, 1:12.85, 1:38.97, 1:45.40)

$2 Mutuel Prices:				
	1–HAPPY TRAILS (a–entry)	5.80	2.20	2.60
	4–STONE CANYON		2.10	2.10
	1A–ANGELIC AURA (a–entry)	5.80	2.20	2.60

$2 EXACTA 1–4 PAID $8.80

Dk. b. or br. c, (Mar), by Peaks and Valleys–Part With Pride, by Executive Pride*Ire. Trainer Klesaris Steve. Bred by Paula E Parsons (Ky).

HAPPY TRAILS rated close from the three path while in tight quarters, was blocked when making his bid on the final turn, found an opening entering the stretch, dueled gamely and edged clear the final sixteenth. STONE CANYON rated close in the four path, dueled from the top of the stretch and outfinished through the final sixteenth. ANGELIC AURA rated close in the three path, assumed the lead nearing the final turn, dueled between horses from the top of the stretch and weakened the final sixteenth. FLANK ATTACK kept close to the early pace inside, eased out leaving the quarter pole then proved empty in the drive. SHOALIHS TALE rated the pace inside, was tested saving ground through the final turn then dropped out of it approaching the eighth pole. WESMAN never factored.

Owners— 1, Goldfarb Sanford J; 2, Lewis Lee; 3, Goldfarb Sanford & Klesaris Steve; 4, Link O W; 5, Our Canterbury Stables; 6, Shining Armor Stable

Trainers—1, Klesaris Steve; 2, Hennig Mark; 3, Klesaris Steve; 4, Durso Robert J; 5, Contessa Gary C; 6, Oliver Philip J

Scratched— Hogan's Spirit (27Apr03 ^{8}PIM^{4}), Empire Maker (3May03 ^{10}CD^{2})

TENTH RACE
Lone Star
MAY 26, 2003

1 MILE. (Turf)(1.332) 5th Running of THE WINSTAR DISTAFF HANDICAP. Grade III. Purse $200,000 Guaranteed. (Plus Up To $7,500 From ATBOIA) A HANDICAP FOR FILLIES AND MARES, THREE YEARS OLD AND UPWARD. No nomination fee. $1,500 to pass the entry box and an additional $1,500 to start with $200,000 guaranteed of which $120,000 to the owner of the winner, $40,000 to second, $22,000 to third, $12,000 to fourth and $6,000 to fifth. Weights: Sunday, May 18, 2003. Starters to be named through the entry box by the usual time of closing. High weights preferred. The field will be limited to twelve starters. Horses not drawing a starting position in the gate will receive a refund of the entry fee. A suitable award will be presented to the winning owner. NOMINATIONS CLOSED WEDNESDAY, MAY 14, 2003.

Value of Race: $200,000 Winner $120,000; second $40,000; third $22,000; fourth $12,000; fifth $6,000. Mutuel Pool $235,980.00 Exacta Pool $170,786.00 Quinella Pool $12,948.00 Trifecta Pool $156,745.00 Superfecta Pool $55,928.00

Last Raced	Horse	M/Eqt.	A.Wt	PP	St	¼	½	¾	Str	Fin	Jockey	Odds $1
2May03 7LS2	Eagle Lake	Lb	5 116	3	1	12½	14	12	13	12¼	Melancon G	8.00
27Apr03 8Hol7	Little Treasure-FR	L	4 117	6	2	21	2½	2½	22½	2¾	Sellers S J	7.30
13Apr03 6Kee2	Magic Mission-GB	Lb	5 116	4	8	71½	72	71	6½	31½	Day P	2.70
11May03 8LS1	Academic Angel	L	4 115	5	4	4hd	5½	51	3hd	41¾	Lanerie C J	32.60
27Apr03 9LS3	Strawbailey	Lb	5 115	2	7	9	9	9	84	51	Berry M C	69.60
2May03 7LS1	Bien Nicole	L	5 118	9	9	64	65	63	71	6hd	Pettinger D R	2.30
2May03 7LS3	Cherylville Slew	Lf	4 115	7	6	5hd	4½	4½	51	7nk	Perrodin E J	23.70
19Apr03 4SA5	Garden in the Rain-FR	L	6 116	8	5	31	3hd	3½	41	86¾	Guidry M	3.10
29Jan03 3SA4	Adalgisa	L	4 115	1	3	81½	81	82	9	9	Borel C H	9.20

OFF AT 6:18 Start Good. Won driving. Course soft.
TIME :24, :492, 1:154, 1:291, 1:43 (:24.04, :49.48, 1:15.85, 1:29.33, 1:43.02)

$2 Mutuel Prices:

3–EAGLE LAKE	18.00	8.60	4.80
6–LITTLE TREASURE–FR		8.60	4.80
4–MAGIC MISSION–GB			3.20

$2 EXACTA 3–6 PAID $149.60 $2 QUINELLA 3–6 PAID $88.00 $2 TRIFECTA 3–6–4 PAID $816.20 $2 SUPERFECTA 3–6–4–5 PAID $10,486.40

Dk. b. or br. m, by Desert Royalty–Great Notrariety, by Great Above. Trainer Norman Cole. Bred by Norman Patricia & Robert (Tex).

EAGLE LAKE brushed with MAGIC MISSION after the start, went straight to the lead, set the pace while well rated, responded well throughout, and maintained a safe advantage under mild hand urging. LITTLE TREASURE (FR) followed behind the solo leader, moved into striking range entering the stretch, but was no match while able to hold the place. MAGIC MISSION (GB) brushed with EAGLE LAKE after the start, dropped well back in the field, remained well back into the stretch, and finished well but reached her best stride too late. ACADEMIC ANGEL was reserved in the front half of the field, vied between horses entering the stretch, and finished evenly. STRAWBAILEY trailed the field into the stretch, and passed tired rivals. BIEN NICOLE was caught four wide on the first turn, settled in the back half of the field, and showed little in a dull effort. CHERYLVILLE SLEW advanced along the rail with a half mile to run, was within striking range entering the stretch, but faded. GARDEN IN THE RAIN (FR) raced towards the front of the field, ranged up on the final turn, but came up empty. ADALGISA raced four wide on the final turn, and was always outrun.

Owners— 1, Turf Express Inc; 2, Port Trust Marsha Naify & San Gabri; 3, Gainsborough Farm Inc; 4, Asmussen Cash; 5, Crooked Creek Stables; 6, Richter Kristine & John; 7, Trout C R; 8, Englander Richard A; 9, Coast To Coast Racing Fund

Trainers—1, Norman Cole; 2, De Seroux Laura; 3, Drysdale Neil; 4, Asmussen Steven M; 5, Offolter Joe S; 6, Von Hemel Donnie K; 7, Trout C R; 8, Mullins Jeff; 9, Canani Julio C

$2 Pick Three (5–6–3) Paid $750.80; Pick Three Pool $28,533.
$2 Pick Four (4–5–6–3) Paid $16,757.40; Pick Four Pool $49,287.

EIGHTH RACE
Belmont
MAY 31, 2003

1⅜ MILES. (Inner Turf)(2.101) 45th Running of THE SHEEPSHEAD BAY HANDICAP. Grade II. Purse $150,000. (Up to $29,100 NYSBFOA). FILLIES AND MARES THREE YEARS OLD AND UPWARD. By subscription of $150 each, which should accompany the nomination; $750 to pass the entry box and $750 to start. The purse to be divided 60% to the winner,20% to second, 11% to third, 6% to fourth and 3% to fifth. Trophies will be presented to the winning owner, trainer and jockey. The New York Racing Association reserves the right to transfer this race to the Main Track. In the event that this race is taken off the turf, it may be subject to downgrading upon review by the Graded Stakes Committee. Closed Saturday, May 17, 2003 with 28 Nominations.

Value of Race: $150,000 Winner $90,000; second $30,000; third $16,500; fourth $9,000; fifth $4,500. Mutuel Pool $676,249.00 Exacta Pool $608,078.00 Trifecta Pool $510,979.00

Last Raced	Horse	M/Eqt.	A.Wt	PP	¼	½	¾	1	Str	Fin	Jockey	Odds $1
4May03 7Aqu1	Mariensky	L	4 114	3	72½	6½	6hd	55½	1½	18¼	Velazquez J R	13.70
3May03 8Aqu4	Owsley	L	5 119	8	21	2½	21½	2½	22½	24¾	Prado E S	3.80
23Apr03 9Kee1	Silent Crystal		4 112	1	1½	1½	1½	1hd	4½	31¾	Luzzi M J	28.50
15May03 8Bel4	Sunstone-GB	Lb	5 113	4	3hd	52½	3hd	4½	520	45¾	Castellano J J	24.25
24Apr03 8Kee1	Lilac Queen-GE	Lf	5 119	6	8	8	7½	31½	31	516½	Bailey J D	0.70
13Apr03 6Kee3	Snow Dance	L	5 116	7	6hd	72½	8	712	64½	68¾	Santos J A	5.00
15May03 8Bel2	Peanut Gallery	Lb	6 113	2	5½	4hd	4½	63½	7	7	Chavez J F	17.10
15May03 8Bel1	Primetimevalentine	b	4 115	5	4½	31½	5hd	8	—	—	Migliore R	41.00

Primetimevalentine:Eased;

OFF AT 4:48 Start Good. Won driving. Course soft.
TIME :253, :524, 1:203, 1:472, 2:144, 2:28 (:25.67, :52.90, 1:20.70, 1:47.50, 2:14.83, 2:28.19)

$2 Mutuel Prices:

3–MARIENSKY	29.40	11.40	8.80
9–OWSLEY		5.50	4.70
1–SILENT CRYSTAL			11.80

$2 EXACTA 3–9 PAID $122.50 $2 TRIFECTA 3–9–1 PAID $1,688.00

B. f, by Gulch–Julie La Rousse*Ire, by Lomond. Trainer Clement Christophe. Bred by Calumet Farm (Ky).

MARIENSKY, bumped shortly after the start, was rated along early, advanced outside on the second turn, rallied three wide turning for home, accelerated quickly when put to the whip and drew away through the final furlong, driving. OWSLEY prompted the pace from the outside, could not stay with the winner in the stretch and continued on to be best of the others. SILENT CRYSTAL set the pace along the inside while well in hand and tired along the inside in the stretch. SUNSTONE (GB) was rated along between rivals, advanced on the second turn and tired in the stretch. LILAC QUEEN (GER) was outrun early, advanced outside on the backstretch, put in a three wide move to reach the leaders on the second turn and faltered in the final furlong. SNOW DANCE was rated along early, raced inside and had no response when roused. PEANUT GALLERY bobbled leaving the gate, was bumped after the start, raced close up for three quarters and tired. PRIMETIMEVALENTINE raced close up while wide, dropped back entering the second turn and was eased in the stretch.

Owners— 1, Waterville Lake Stable; 2, Hancock III Arthur B; 3, Greenbaum Robert; 4, Georgica Stable; 5, Tanaka Gary A; 6, Oxley John C; 7, Pokoik Lee; 8, Low Lawana L & Robert E

Trainers—1, Clement Christophe; 2, Schulhofer Randy; 3, Mott William I; 4, Barbara Robert; 5, Frankel Robert; 6, Ward John T Jr; 7, Sciacca Gary; 8, Peitz Daniel C

Scratched— Decencia (23Apr03 6KEE3), Message Red (7May03 6BEL1), Call An Audible (18May03 3BEL2)

NINTH RACE
Churchill
MAY 31, 2003

1⅜ MILES. (Turf)(2.13) 66th Running of THE LOUISVILLE HANDICAP. Grade III. Purse $100,000 added. THREE-YEAR-OLDS AND UPWARD. By subscription of $100 each on or before May 17, $500 to pass the entry box; $500 additional to start. Weights to be announced May 24. If the race is moved to the main track after the time of closing, a horse may be scratched for any reason at any time up to 15 minutes prior to post time for the race preceding this race or there after with a valid physical reason and approved by the stewards. The entry fee shall be refunded for scratches made in compliance with the above conditions. Starters to be named through the entry box at the usual time of closing. Closed Saturday, May 17 with 35 nominations. (If this race is taken off the turf it will be downgraded one grade level for this running only in accordance with American Graded Stakes Committee policy.).

Value of Race: $112,000 Winner $69,440; second $22,400; third $11,200; fourth $5,600; fifth $3,360. Mutuel Pool $485,101.00 Exacta Pool $358,400.00 Trifecta Pool $278,571.00 Superfecta Pool $77,882.00

Last Raced	Horse	M/Eqt.	A.	Wt	PP	¼	½	¾	1	Str	Fin	Jockey	Odds $1
10May03 ^{7}Hol^{5}	Kim Loves Bucky	L	6	117	2	2^{1}	$2^{1\frac{1}{2}}$	2^{3}	$2^{4\frac{1}{2}}$	1^{hd}	$1^{\frac{1}{2}}$	Sellers S J	4.20
23Apr03 ^{8}Kee^{6}	Rochester	L	7	117	4	7^{3}	7^{1}	7^{1}	6^{1}	$4^{1\frac{1}{2}}$	$2^{1\frac{1}{2}}$	Day P	5.80
19Apr03 ^{7}Kee^{9}	Dr. Kashnikow	L	6	117	3	3^{hd}	5^{2}	$5^{2\frac{1}{2}}$	5^{hd}	5^{4}	$3^{\frac{1}{2}}$	Guidry M	4.70
11May03 ^{9}CD^{2}	Roxinho-BR	Lbf	5	115	8	5^{4}	4^{3}	$4^{2\frac{1}{2}}$	4^{3}	3^{hd}	$4^{1\frac{1}{4}}$	Albarado R J	6.00
11May03 ^{9}CD^{1}	Quest Star	Lb	4	117	7	1^{1}	1^{1}	1^{hd}	1^{hd}	2^{2}	$5^{1\frac{3}{4}}$	Melancon L	2.70
23Apr03 ^{8}Kee^{3}	Williams News	Lf	8	115	5	8	8	8	$7^{2\frac{1}{2}}$	6^{hd}	$6^{\frac{1}{2}}$	Blanc B	4.60
3May03 ^{7}LS^{2}	Skate Away	L	4	113	1	$6^{1\frac{1}{2}}$	6^{3}	6^{2}	8	$7^{\frac{1}{2}}$	$7^{4\frac{3}{4}}$	Borel C H	16.60
11May03 ^{9}CD^{7}	Red Mountain	Lb	6	114	6	4^{hd}	3^{4}	$3^{2\frac{1}{2}}$	$3^{\frac{1}{2}}$	8	8	Court J K	26.50

OFF AT 5:32 Start Good For All But WILLIAMS NEWS Won driving. Course firm.
TIME :25^{3}, :48^{4}, 1:13^{3}, 1:37^{3}, 2:01^{4}, 2:14 (:25.72, :48.97, 1:13.62, 1:37.61, 2:01.87, 2:14.09)

$2 Mutuel Prices:

3-KIM LOVES BUCKY	10.40	6.40	4.80
5-ROCHESTER		6.40	4.60
4-DR. KASHNIKOW			4.60

$2 EXACTA 3-5 PAID $54.00 $2 TRIFECTA 3-5-4 PAID $269.00 $1 SUPERFECTA 3-5-4-9 PAID $1,051.40

B. g, by Green Dancer-Moondust Mink, by Great Above. Trainer Glenney John. Bred by Dr & Mrs John Glenney (Ky).

KIM LOVES BUCKY, in front briefly after the start, surrendered the advantage to QUEST STAR, raced outside that one four wide while well in hand, battled heads apart before taking over nearing the final furlong, opened a clear lead between calls, then gamely held off ROCHESTER under strong handling. ROCHESTER, unhurried early, raced in hand three wide, edged closer entering the final turn while between foes, angled five wide for the drive, loomed prominently but wasn't quite good enough. DR. KASHNIKOW, never far back while racing near the inside, was asked for more entering the final turn, continued between rivals three or four wide into the stretch and finished willingly. ROXINHO (BRZ), within easy striking distance while tracking the leaders five wide most of the way, was empty the last eighth. QUEST STAR moved up to gain the lead before going a furlong, worked his way in near the hedge, accomplished a modest opening quarter while dueling inside of KIM LOVES BUCKY, battled with that one into the final furlong and faltered. WILLIAMS NEWS stumbled badly at the start, nearly unseated the rider, was unhurried and outrun to the final turn, came out five or six wide for the drive but never menaced. SKATE AWAY, reserved inside early, saved ground until the final quarter, circled foes seven wide but failed to rally. RED MOUNTAIN stalked the leaders four or five wide for a mile and weakened thereafter.

Owners— 1, Glenney Kim; 2, Augustin Stable; 3, Erdenheim Farm; 4, Fox Gregory J & Mack Earle I; 5, Mansell Stables; 6, On Target Racing Stable; 7, Robinson J M; 8, Morrison Dolphus

Trainers—1, Glenney John; 2, Sheppard Jonathan E; 3, Fisher John R S; 4, Fox Jamie; 5, Walden W Elliott; 6, Stall Albert M Jr; 7, Trosclair Jeff; 8, Wiggins Hal R

Scratched— Dr. Brendler (17May03 ^{10}PIM^{1})

$1 Pick Three (7/13/14-4-3) Paid $1,060.80; Pick Three Pool $40,602.

SEVENTH RACE
Belmont
JUNE 6, 2003

5 FURLONGS. (.55^{3}) 103rd Running of THE FLASH. Grade III. Purse $100,000 Added (Up to $19,400 NYSBFOA) TWO YEAR OLDS. By subscription of $100 each, which should accompany the nomination; $500 to pass the entry box; $500 to start with $100,000 added. The added money and all fees to be divided 60% to the winner, 20% to second, 11% to third, 6% to fourth and 3% to fifth. 118 lbs. Non-winners of $40,000 allowed 2 lbs.; a race other than maiden or claiming, 4 lbs. Trophies will be presented to the winning owner, trainer and jockey. Closed Saturday, May 24, 2003 with 14 Nominations.

Value of Race: $103,400 Winner $63,955; second $21,322; third $11,727; fourth $6,396. Mutuel Pool $384,129.00 Exacta Pool $370,179.00

Last Raced	Horse	M/Eqt.	A.	Wt	PP	St	3/16	⅜	Str	Fin	Jockey	Odds $1
15May03 ^{2}Bel^{1}	Chapel Royal	L	2	114	3	2	2^{7}	$1^{\frac{1}{2}}$	$1^{1\frac{1}{2}}$	$1^{5\frac{1}{4}}$	Velazquez J R	0.30
24Apr03 ^{2}Kee^{1}	Hasslefree		2	114	2	1	1^{hd}	2^{6}	2^{8}	$2^{2\frac{1}{4}}$	Bailey J D	2.60
1May03 ^{3}Aqu^{1}	Juventus	Lf	2	114	1	3	4	3^{hd}	3^{2}	$3^{4\frac{1}{4}}$	Castellano J J	9.80
16May03 ^{4}CT^{1}	Mighty Awesome	L	2	115	4	4	$3^{2\frac{1}{2}}$	4	4	4	Sanchez J	22.80

OFF AT 4:10 Start Good. Won ridden out. Track fast.
TIME :21^{4}, :44^{2}, :57 (:21.80, :44.55, :57.02)

$2 Mutuel Prices:

1A-CHAPEL ROYAL	2.60	2.10	—
3-HASSLEFREE		2.10	—
2-JUVENTUS		—	—

$2 EXACTA 1-3 PAID $3.60

Dk. b. or br. c, (Mar), by Montbrook-Cut Class Leanne, by Cutlass. Trainer Pletcher Todd A. Bred by Ocala Stud Farm (Fla).

CHAPEL ROYAL argued the pace from the outside, drew clear when asked for run entering the stretch and widened under a hand ride. HASSLEFREE argued the pace along the inside, proved no match for the winner in the stretch but was clearly best of the other two. JUVENTUS raced inside and had no rally. MIGHTY AWESOME had no response when roused.

Owners— 1, Smith Derrick & Tabor Michael; 2, Lewis Robert B & Beverly J; 3, Aldie Germania Farms Inc; 4, McKee John D

Trainers—1, Pletcher Todd A; 2, Lukas D Wayne; 3, Tullock Timothy Jr; 4, McKee John D

Scratched— Korsakoff (3May03 ^{6}CD^{6}), Exploit Lad (26May03 ^{9}CD^{3})

$2 Daily Double (1-1) Paid $18.20; Daily Double Pool $100,371.
$2 Pick Three (2-1-1) Paid $360.50; Pick Three Pool $67,325.

TENTH RACE
Belmont
JUNE 6, 2003

1 MILE. (1.32^1) 73rd Running of THE ACORN. Grade I. Purse $250,000 (Up to $38,500 NYSBFOA) FILLIES THREE YEARS OLD. By subscription of $250 each, which should accompany the nomination; $1,250 to pass the entry box and $1,250 to start. The purse to be divided 60% to the winner, 20% to second, 11% to third, 6% to fourth and 3% to fifth. 121 lbs. Trophies will be presented to the winning owner, trainer and jockey. Closed Saturday, May 24, 2003 with 19 Nominations.

Value of Race: $250,000 Winner $150,000; second $50,000; third $27,500; fourth $15,000; fifth $7,500. Mutuel Pool $851,874.00 Exacta Pool $659,752.00 Trifecta Pool $541,442.00

Last Raced	Horse	M/Eqt.	A.Wt	PP	St	¼	½	¾	Str	Fin	Jockey	Odds $1
2May03 ^{10}CD^1	Bird Town	L	3 121	7	1	2½	1^{hd}	1½	1^1	1^{hd}	Prado E S	2.65
2May03 ^{10}CD^6	Lady Tak	L	3 121	2	5	5½	6^{hd}	4^{hd}	2^{hd}	2^1	Bailey J D	2.80
1May03 ^{9}CD^1	Final Round	L	3 121	6	3	6^{hd}	4^{hd}	3^{1½}	3^{2½}	3^{3¼}	Stevens G L	16.40
10May03 ^{8}Bel^1	House Party		3 121	5	6	7	5^{hd}	5^{2½}	4½	4^{5¼}	Santos J A	7.10
13Apr03 ^{8}Pim^2	Randaroo	Lf	3 121	4	2	1^{hd}	2½	2½	5^7	5^{1½}	Chavez J F	14.50
18Apr03 ^{8}Aqu^2	Storm Flag Flying	L	3 121	1	4	4^{hd}	7	7	7	6¾	Velazquez J R	1.70
2May03 ^{5}Aqu^1	Kitty Knight	L	3 121	3	7	3^{hd}	3^1	6^{2½}	6^2	7	Samyn J L	48.25

OFF AT 5:42 Start Good. Won driving. Track fast.
TIME :23^2, :46^1, 1:10^2, 1:35^1 (:23.41, :46.35, 1:10.40, 1:35.29)

$2 Mutuel Prices:

7–BIRD TOWN	7.30	3.40	2.60
2–LADY TAK		4.30	3.40
6–FINAL ROUND			5.00

$2 EXACTA 7–2 PAID $23.80 $2 TRIFECTA 7–2–6 PAID $162.50

B. f, (Apr), by Cape Town–Dear Birdie, by Storm Bird. Trainer Zito Nicholas P. Bred by Marylou Whitney Stables (Ky).

BIRD TOWN argued the pace from the outside while well in hand, responded when roused, dug in gamely while drifting out in the stretch and prevailed after a long drive. LADY TAK was unhurried early on, advanced three wide nearing the stretch and finished gamely outside but could not get to the winner. FINAL ROUND raced in hand outside early, rallied four wide on the turn and finished gamely while being crowded a bit in deep stretch. HOUSE PARTY bobbled at the start, raced close up along the inside, came wide into the stretch and lacked a rally. RANDAROO argued the pace along the inside and tired in the stretch. STORM FLAG FLYING raced close up while between rivals and had no response when roused. KITTY KNIGHT raced with the pace while three wide and tired in the stretch.

Owners— 1, Marylou Whitney Stable; 2, Heiligbrodt Racing Stable; 3, Humphrey G W Jr; 4, Shields Joseph V Jr; 5, Allen Joseph; 6, Phipps Ogden Mills et al; 7, Bohemia Stable

Trainers—1, Zito Nicholas P; 2, Asmussen Steven M; 3, Arnold George R II; 4, Jerkens H Allen; 5, Dutrow Anthony W; 6, McGaughey Claude III; 7, Jerkens H Allen

---

$2 Daily Double (11–7) Paid $21.20; Daily Double Pool $333,182.
$2 Pick Three (6–11–7) Paid $3,344.00; Pick Three Pool $149,409.
2 Pick Four (1–6–11–7) Paid $3,308.00; Pick Four Pool $280,081. $2 Pick Six (2–1–1–6–11–7) 6 Corre Paid $119,429.00; Pick Six Pool $167,896. $2 Pick Six (2–1–1–6–11–7) 5 Correct Paid $684.00

Belmont Park Attendance: Unavailable Mutuel Pool: $1,914,518.00 ITW Mutuel Pool: $3,457,259.00 ISW Mutuel Pool: $8,474,177.00

SEVENTH RACE
Belmont
JUNE 7, 2003

6 FURLONGS. (1.07^3) 25th Running of THE TRUE NORTH BREEDERS' CUP HANDICAP. Grade II. Purse $250,000 (includes $100,000 BC – Breeders' Cup) (Up To $29,100 NYSBFOA) THREE YEAR OLDS AND UPWARD. (Includes $100,000 from the Breeders' Cup Fund for Cup Nominees Only). By subscription of $150 each, which should accompany the nomination; $750 to pass the entry box and $750 to start. The NYRA purse to be divided 60% to the winner, 20% to second, 11% to third, 6% to fourth and 3%to fifth. Breeders' Cup fund monies correspondingly divided providing a Breeders' Cup nominee has finished in an award position. Any Breeders' Cup fund monies not awarded will revert back to the fund. Closed Saturday , May 24, 2003 with 21 Nominations.

Value of Race: $190,000 Winner $90,000; second $50,000; third $27,500; fourth $15,000; fifth $7,500. Mutuel Pool $1,570,871.0 Exacta Pool $1,234,985.0 Trifecta Pool $580,105.00

Last Raced	Horse	M/Eqt.	A.Wt	PP	St	¼	½	Str	Fin	Jockey	Odds $1
10May03 ^{6}Bel^1	Shake You Down	Lbf	5 118	6	4	2^3	1½	1^{2½}	1^{nk}	Luzzi M J	0.85
17May03 ^{4}Pim^4	Highway Prospector	Lb	6 115	2	3	6	5½	2^3	2^{4½}	Santos J A	a-3.35
24May03 ^{6}Bel^3	Vodka	L	6 114	5	5	5^{2½}	6	4^{hd}	3¾	Castillo H Jr	18.60
10May03 ^{6}Hol^3	Giovannetti	L	4 115	4	1	1^{hd}	2^{2½}	3^{1½}	4^{2¾}	Stevens G L	8.80
29Mar03 NAS^1	State City	L	4 121	1	6	4^{2½}	4^{hd}	6	5^2	Bailey J D	2.90
17May03 ^{4}Pim^1	Pioneer Boy	L	5 115	3	2	3^{5½}	3^2	5½	6	Wilson R	a-3.35

a–Coupled: Highway Prospector and Pioneer Boy.

OFF AT 3:53 Start Good. Won driving. Track sloppy.
TIME :21^2, :44, :56^1, 1:09^2 (:21.52, :44.05, :56.23, 1:09.59)

$2 Mutuel Prices:

6–SHAKE YOU DOWN	3.70	2.60	2.20
1–HIGHWAY PROSPECTOR (a-entry)		2.90	2.20
5–VODKA			2.60

$2 EXACTA 6–1 PAID $7.70 $2 TRIFECTA 6–1–5 PAID $40.40

Ch. g, by Montbrook–Mauvin Gway, by Rajab. Trainer Lake Scott A. Bred by Ocala Stud Farm (Fla).

SHAKE YOU DOWN was hustled up outside, dueled with GIOVANNETTI for a half mile, put away that rival, drew clear then dug in and held off HIGHWAY PROSPECTOR under a drive. HIGHWAY PROSPECTOR was outrun early, rallied on the rail nearing the stretch and finished gamely inside. VODKA was outrun early, raced four wide and offered a mild rally outside. GIOVANNETTI dueled with the winner along the inside and tired in the stretch. STATE CITY was outrun early, raced inside and had no response when roused. PIONEER BOY was hustled from the gate, chased the pace from the outside and tired after a half mile.

Owners— 1, Cole Robert L Jr; 2, Gill Michael J; 3, Gerrity Joseph W Jr; 4, Schiappa Bernard C; 5, Godolphin Racing Inc; 6, Gill Michael J

Trainers—1, Lake Scott A; 2, Shuman Mark; 3, Hertler John O; 4, Monteleone Frank J; 5, Suroor Saeed bin; 6, Robb John J

Scratched— Here's Zealous (10May03 ^{6}BEL^2)

$2 Pick Three (2–5–6) Paid $36.00; Pick Three Pool $194,134.

EIGHTH RACE
Belmont
JUNE 7, 2003

1 MILE. (Turf)(1.31^{3}) 10th Running of THE JUST A GAME BREEDERS' CUP HANDICAP. Grade III. Purse $200,000 Added (includes $100,000 BC – Breeders' Cup). (Up To $19,400 NYSBFOA) FILLIES AND MARES THREE YEARS OLD AND UPWARD. (Includes $100,000 from the Breeders' Cup Fund for Cup Nominees Only). By subscription of $100 each, which should accompany the nomination; $500 to pass the entry box; $500 to start, with $100,000 added. The NYRA Purse to be divided 60% to the winner, 20% to second, 11% to third, 6% to fourth and 3% to fifth. Breeders' Cup fund monies also correspondingly divided provided a Breeders' Cup nominee has finished in an award position. The New York Racing Association reserves the right to transfer this race to the Main Track. Closed Saturday, May 24, 2003 with 45 Nominations.

Value of Race: $214,500 Winner $128,700; second $42,900; third $23,595; fourth $12,870; fifth $6,435. Mutuel Pool $1,511,218.0 Exacta Pool $1,177,227.0 Trifecta Pool $839,253.00

Last Raced	Horse	M/Eqt.	A.Wt	PP	St	¼	½	¾	Str	Fin	Jockey	Odds $1
31May03 ^{8}Bel^{1}	Mariensky	L	4 116	7	6	8	7^{6}	3^{hd}	1^{hd}	1^{2}	Santos J A	3.05
18May03 ^{7}Bel^{1}	Riskaverse	L	4 119	8	1	$5^{\frac{1}{2}}$	5^{2}	2^{hd}	$2^{2\frac{1}{2}}$	2^{hd}	Velazquez J R	3.20
3May03 ^{8}Aqu^{2}	Wonder Again	L	4 119	3	4	$6^{3\frac{1}{2}}$	$6^{\frac{1}{2}}$	5^{hd}	$4^{2\frac{1}{2}}$	$3^{6\frac{1}{4}}$	Prado E S	2.65
3May03 ^{8}Aqu^{1}	Delta Princess	L	4 117	6	5	$4^{\frac{1}{2}}$	4^{hd}	$4^{\frac{1}{2}}$	$3^{\frac{1}{2}}$	$4^{2\frac{3}{4}}$	Luzzi M J	8.10
18May03 ^{7}Bel^{2}	Love N' Kiss S.	L	5 114	1	8	$2^{\frac{1}{2}}$	2^{hd}	6^{8}	$5^{3\frac{1}{2}}$	5^{7}	Day P	7.40
17May03 ^{7}Pim^{1}	Carib Lady-IR	L	4 115	4	7	$7^{\frac{1}{2}}$	8	8	7^{6}	$6^{13\frac{1}{2}}$	Bailey J D	8.40
16Mar03 ^{10}Tam^{5}	Silver Rail	L	6 113	5	3	3^{2}	$3^{\frac{1}{2}}$	$7^{3\frac{1}{2}}$	8	$7^{1\frac{1}{2}}$	Coa E M	32.25
16May03 ^{9}Pim^{6}	Repository	L	5 114	2	2	1^{6}	1^{7}	$1^{\frac{1}{2}}$	6^{7}	8	Stevens G L	20.60

OFF AT 4:33 Start Good. Won driving. Course soft.
TIME :24^{1}, :49^{1}, 1:16^{1}, 1:43^{1} (:24.33, :49.25, 1:16.28, 1:43.28)

$2 Mutuel Prices:

2B–MARIENSKY	8.10	4.50	3.30
1A–RISKAVERSE		4.30	3.00
5–WONDER AGAIN			2.90

$2 EXACTA 2–1 PAID $27.20 $2 TRIFECTA 2–1–5 PAID $63.50

B. f, by Gulch–Julie La Rousse*Ire, by Lomond. Trainer Clement Christophe. Bred by Calumet Farm (Ky).

MARIENSKY was unhurried while outrun early, advanced outside leaving the backstretch, swept four wide approaching the stretch, caught RISKAVERSE nearing the eighth pole and drew clear under a drive. RISKAVERSE was unhurried outside early, put in a three wide run approaching the stretch, led between calls in upper stretch, could not handle the winner in the final furlong and continued on to hold the place. WONDER AGAIN was rated along inside, rallied inside nearing the stretch, was caught in traffic along the inside turning for home and finished gamely once clear. DELTA PRINCESS raced in hand along the inside early, put in a run along the inside on the turn and tired in the stretch. LOVE N' KISS S. chased the pace along the inside and lacked a rally. CARIB LADY (IRE) had no response when roused. SILVER RAIL chased the pace from the outside and tired. REPOSITORY quickly opened a clear lead, set the pace for three quarters and tired.

Owners— 1, Waterville Lake Stable; 2, Fox Ridge Farm Inc; 3, Phillips Joan G & John W; 4, Khaled Saud b; 5, Lael Stables; 6, Gaillardia Racing; 7, Quadracci Betty; 8, Bonham Mary L

Trainers—1, Clement Christophe; 2, Kelly Patrick J; 3, Toner James J; 4, Mott William I; 5, Clement Christophe; 6, Pletcher Todd A; 7, Rice Linda; 8, Lukas D Wayne

Scratched— Cozzy Corner (3May03 ^{8}AQU^{5}), Voodoo Dancer (3May03 ^{8}AQU^{3}), Lady Of The Future (17May03 ^{7}PIM^{3}), Quick Blue (16May03 ^{9}PIM^{4}), Smok'n Frolic (17May03 ^{8}BEL^{2}), Raging Fever (17May03 ^{8}BEL^{6}), Vespers (17May03 ^{7}PIM^{5})

$2 Pick Three (5–6–2) Paid $31.80; Pick Three Pool $228,617.

NINTH RACE
Belmont
JUNE 7, 2003

7 FURLONGS. (1.20) 19th Running of THE RIVA RIDGE BREEDERS' CUP. Grade II. Purse $200,000. (includes $50,000 BC – Breeders' Cup) (Up To $29,100 NYSBFOA). THREE YEAR OLDS. (Includes $50,000 from the Breeders' Cup Fund for Cup Nominees Only). By subscription of $150 each, which should accompany the nomination; $750 to pass the entry box and $750 to start. The NYRA purse to be divided 60% to the winner, 20% to second, 11% to third, 6% to fourth and 3% to fifth. 123 lbs. Non–winners of $60,000 other than restricted stake in 2003 or $45,000 twice in 2003 allowed 2 lbs.; $50,000 other than restricted stake, 4 lbs.; $35,000, or three races other than maiden or claiming, 6 lbs.; two races other than maiden or claiming, 8 lbs.

Value of Race: $200,000 Winner $120,000; second $40,000; third $22,000; fourth $12,000; fifth $6,000. Mutuel Pool $2,032,846.0 Exacta Pool $1,686,759.0 Trifecta Pool $1,317,424.0

Last Raced	Horse	M/Eqt.	A.Wt	PP	St	¼	½	Str	Fin	Jockey	Odds $1
10May03 ^{9}CD^{1}	Posse	L	3 123	5	6	$7^{\frac{1}{2}}$	$7^{3\frac{1}{2}}$	$2^{\frac{1}{2}}$	1no	Lanerie C J	3.15
26Apr03 ^{9}CD^{1}	Midas Eyes	L	3 123	3	3	2^{2}	$2^{4\frac{1}{2}}$	$1^{1\frac{1}{2}}$	$2^{6\frac{1}{4}}$	Bailey J D	0.80
3May03 ^{9}Aqu^{6}	Halo Homewrecker	L	3 123	8	1	6^{5}	5^{2}	$4^{3\frac{1}{2}}$	3^{hd}	Stevens G L	7.40
17May03 ^{6}Bel^{1}	Bishop Court Hill	L	3 115	2	4	$1^{\frac{1}{2}}$	$1^{\frac{1}{2}}$	$3^{2\frac{1}{2}}$	$4^{2\frac{3}{4}}$	Velazquez J R	19.60
15May03 ^{5}Bel^{1}	Midnight Charlie	Lf	3 117	4	2	$4^{\frac{1}{2}}$	6^{2}	6^{8}	$5^{3\frac{1}{4}}$	Castillo H Jr	28.50
24May03 ^{8}Bel^{2}	Alysweep	Lf	3 123	7	5	$5^{1\frac{1}{2}}$	$4^{\frac{1}{2}}$	5^{hd}	$6^{10\frac{1}{2}}$	Chavez J F	9.20
27Apr03 ^{9}CD^{1}	Battle Won	Lb	3 117	1	8	3^{1}	3^{hd}	$7^{\frac{1}{2}}$	7^{hd}	Martinez W	17.90
17May03 ^{6}Pim^{4}	Epic	Lbf	3 115	6	7	8	8	8	8	Luzzi M J	44.75

OFF AT 5:15 Start Good. Won driving. Track sloppy.
TIME :22^{1}, :44^{3}, 1:08^{4}, 1:22 (:22.27, :44.60, 1:08.99, 1:22.03)

$2 Mutuel Prices:

5–POSSE	8.30	3.00	2.50
3–MIDAS EYES		2.50	2.30
8–HALO HOMEWRECKER			3.00

$2 EXACTA 5–3 PAID $15.60 $2 TRIFECTA 5–3–8 PAID $52.00

B. c, (Feb), by Silver Deputy–Raska, by Rahy. Trainer Asmussen Steven M. Bred by Robert E Low & Lawana L Low (Ky).

POSSE was outrun early, advanced inside on the turn, came wide into the stretch, dug in resolutely outside and prevailed after a long drive. MIDAS EYES pressed the pace from the outside, drew clear in the stretch then dug in and fought it out gamely to the wire, just missing. HALO HOMEWRECKER was unhurried outside early, put in a four wide run approaching the stretch and had little left for the drive. BISHOP COURT HILL was hustled to the front, set the pace along the inside and tired in the final furlong. MIDNIGHT CHARLIE was hustled outside, raced wide and had no response when roused. ALYSWEEP was hustled from the gate, chased the pace while wide and tired in the stretch. BATTLE WON chased the pace along the inside and tired after a half mile. EPIC broke slowly and was outrun.

Owners— 1, Heiligbrodt Racing Stable; 2, Gann Edmund A; 3, Evans Edward P; 4, Melnyk Eugene & Laura; 5, Papandrea Vincent; 6, Doneson Mark & Dubb Michael; 7, Lazy Lane Farms Inc; 8, Jay Em Ess Stable

Trainers—1, Asmussen Steven M; 2, Frankel Robert; 3, Hennig Mark; 4, Pletcher Todd A; 5, Gyarmati Leah; 6, Reynolds Patrick L; 7, Brothers Frank L; 8, Dutrow Richard E Jr

$2 Daily Double (2–5) Paid $39.00; Daily Double Pool $187,915.
$2 Pick Three (6–2–5) Paid $54.00; Pick Three Pool $318,020.

TENTH RACE
Belmont
JUNE 7, 2003

1¼ MILES. (Inner Turf)(1.573) 102nd Running of THE MANHATTAN HANDICAP. Grade I. Purse $400,000. (Up To $49,600 NYSBFOA). THREE YEAR OLDS AND UPWARD. By subscription of $400 each, which should accompany the nomination; $2,000 to pass the entry box and $2,000 to start. The purse to be divided 60% to the winner, 20% to second, 11% to third, 6% to fourth and 3% to fifth. The New York Racing Association reserves the right to transfer this race to the Main Track. In the event that this race is taken off the turf, it may be subject to downgrading upon review by the Graded Stakes Committee. Closed Saturday, May 24, 2003 with 40 Nominations.

Value of Race: $400,000 Winner $240,000; second $80,000; third $44,000; fourth $24,000; fifth $12,000. Mutuel Pool $2,165,517.0 Exacta Pool $1,643,900.0 Trifecta Pool $1,272,584.0

Last Raced	Horse	M/Eqt.	A.	Wt	PP	¼	½	¾	1	Str	Fin	Jockey	Odds $1
10May03 7Hol2	Denon	L	5	122	9	6hd	72½	61	31	13	1½	Bailey J D	2.15
3May03 9CD2	Requete-GB	L	4	116	2	72	6hd	51	5hd	4½	21¼	Prado E S	6.00
17May03 10Pim1	Dr. Brendler	L	5	116	5	92½	91½	81	8½	62½	31	Stevens G L	22.30
24Apr03 6Kee6	Macaw-IR	Lbf	4	114	8	10	10	91½	912	8½	4hd	Bridgmohan S X	45.75
30Mar03 Lch9	Caesarion-IR	L	4	115	3	4hd	3hd	2½	2hd	2hd	5¾	Migliore R	23.30
3May03 9CD1	Honor In War	L	4	117	10	21	21	41	6hd	5hd	6hd	Flores D R	8.90
25May03 8Bel1	Irish Colonial	L	4	114	7	12½	12½	11	1hd	3½	7¾	Castellano J J	10.20
2May03 8Aqu2	Shaanmer-IR	L	4	116	4	51½	42	3hd	4hd	71½	81½	Santos J A	3.90
23Apr03 8Kee4	Gritty Sandie	Lbf	7	113	6	8½	8½	7hd	71½	922	916½	Samyn J L	34.50
3May03 9CD5	With Anticipation	Lb	8	122	1	3hd	5hd	10	10	10	10	Day P	4.50

OFF AT 5:55 Start Good. Won driving. Course soft.
TIME :261, :534, 1:203, 1:472, 2:14 (:26.29, :53.87, 1:20.76, 1:47.53, 2:14.16)

$2 Mutuel Prices:

10–DENON	6.30	4.20	3.10
2–REQUETE–GB		6.40	4.90
6–DR. BRENDLER			7.10

$2 EXACTA 10–2 PAID $33.80 $2 TRIFECTA 10–2–6 PAID $427.50

B. h, by Pleasant Colony–Aviance*Ire, by Northfields. Trainer Frankel Robert. Bred by Flaxman Holdings Ltd (Ky).

DENON was rated along outside, rallied four wide approaching the stretch, drew clear then dug in gamely and held off REQUETE under a drive. REQUETE (GB) was rated along between rivals, responded when roused turning for home and finished gamely outside. DR. BRENDLER was outrun early, rallied four wide on the second turn and finished well outside. MACAW (IRE) was outrun early, came wide for the drive and was going well late. CAESARION (IRE) raced with the pace from the outside and weakened in the final furlong. HONOR IN WAR raced close up inside, saved ground and lacked a rally. IRISH COLONIAL was hustled to the front, set the pace along the inside and tired in the final furlong. SHAANMER (IRE) raced close up while three wide and had no response when roused. GRITTY SANDIE broke slowly, raced inside and tired. WITH ANTICIPATION dropped back after the opening half mile and tired.

Owners— 1, Gann Edmund A & Flaxman Stable; 2, Juddmonte Farms Inc; 3, O'Toole Francis J; 4, Melillo George & Sandra; 5, Tanaka Gary A; 6, Third Turn Stable; 7, Blue Sky Farm & Martin Fred; 8, de Rothschild Edouard; 9, Kimmel Caesar P & Nicholson Ronald; 10, Augustin Stable

Trainers—1, Frankel Robert; 2, Frankel Robert; 3, Motion H Graham; 4, Tagg Barclay; 5, De Roualle Jean; 6, McGee Paul J; 7, Schulhofer Randy; 8, Clement Christophe; 9, Toner James J; 10, Sheppard Jonathan E

Scratched— Patrol (3May03 9CD3), Evening Attire (23Nov02 8AQU1), State Shinto (29Mar03 NAS5), Judge's Case (16May03 11PIM3), Short Hair (6Jun03 8BEL7)

THIRD RACE
Bay Meadows
JUNE 7, 2003

6 FURLONGS. (1.071) 18th Running of THE BAY MEADOWS BREEDERS' CUP SPRINT. Grade III. Purse $150,000 Guaranteed (includes $50,000 BC – Breeders' Cup) THREE-YEAR-OLDS AND UPWARD. ($50,000 from Breeders' Cup Fund for Cup nominees only). By subscription of $100 each to accompany the nomination or by supplementary nomination of $2,000 by Noon Sunday, June 1, 2003. $500 to pass the entry box and $500 additional to start with $100,000 Guaranteed. The host association's Guaranteed monies to be divided 55% to the winner 20% to second 15% to third 7.5% to fourth and 2.5% to fifth. Breeders' Cup Fund Monies also correspondingly divided providing a Breeders' Cup nominee has finished in an awarded position. Any Breeders' Cup fund monies not awarded will revert back to the Fund. A trophy will be presented to the owner of the winner by Breeders' Cup Ltd. Closed May29, 2003 with 11 nominations.

Value of Race: $142,500 Winner $82,500; second $30,000; third $15,000; fourth $11,250; fifth $3,750. Mutuel Pool $194,980.00 Exacta Pool $94,761.00 Quinella Pool $10,280.00 Trifecta Pool $115,798.00

Last Raced	Horse	M/Eqt.	A.	Wt	PP	St	¼	½	Str	Fin	Jockey	Odds $1
18May03 2BM1	El Dorado Shooter	LB	6	120	6	1	11	12	14	14¾	Schvaneveldt C P	2.30
19Apr03 3BM2	Halo Cat	LBbf	5	118	2	5	52½	4hd	31	21¼	Baze R A	2.20
18May03 2BM2	Radar Contact	LB	7	116	1	4	6	6	52	31½	Lopez A D	22.60
2May03 4Hol1	Taste Of Paradise	LB	4	116	5	2	3hd	3hd	42	4½	Rollins C J	5.20
19Apr03 3BM1	Presidio Heights	LB	5	119	3	6	22½	23	22	55½	Gonzalez R M	2.00
24May02 3BM1	How Bout Jose	LB	6	115	4	3	4hd	53½	6	6	Warren R J Jr	23.70

OFF AT 2:08 Start Good. Won driving. Track fast.
TIME :213, :432, :553, 1:083 (:21.73, :43.58, :55.60, 1:08.61)

$2 Mutuel Prices:

6–EL DORADO SHOOTER	6.60	3.40	2.60
2–HALO CAT		3.00	2.40
1–RADAR CONTACT			3.40

$1 EXACTA 6–2 PAID $9.40 $2 QUINELLA 2–6 PAID $9.80 $1 TRIFECTA 6–2–1 PAID $52.90

Ch. g, by Man From Eldorado–Maui Lyphear J.*Undefi, by Lypheor*GB. Trainer Delima Clifford. Bred by Clifford DeLima (Cal).

EL DORADO SHOOTER was quickly clear, set all the pace to the stretch, edged clear to mid stretch then was under steady pressure to the wire. HALO CAT was bumped by PRESIDIO HEIGHTS at the start, recovered and chased the pace to the turn, saved ground to the stretch then made a late run to be a non-threatening second. RADAR CONTACT had no speed, saved ground to the stretch then gradually picked off rivals to the line. TASTE OF PARADISE tracked the leaders to the turn, raced three wide to the stretch but had little to offer in the drive. PRESIDIO HEIGHTS broke a step slow then came in slightly and bumped HALO CAT, was hustled out of the chute and raced up to press the pace to the turn, remained a factor to upper stretch then weakened. HOW BOUT JOSE was allowed to settle, raced between rivals on the turn but gave out in the drive.

Owners— 1, DeLima Barbara; 2, Rancho San Miguel Abruzzo Peter & F; 3, G & N Thoroughbreds; 4, Keith Abrahams & David Bloom; 5, Zellerbach William J; 6, Smith Cindy A

Trainers—1, Delima Clifford; 2, Hollendorfer Jerry; 3, Ross Larry; 4, Sadler John W; 5, Sherman Art; 6, Hollendorfer Jerry

---

$2 Daily Double (1–6) Paid $19.60; Daily Double Pool $6,137.
$1 Pick Three (6–1–6) Paid $19.90; Pick Three Pool $31,081.

ELEVENTH RACE
Belmont
JUNE 7, 2003

1½ MILES. (2.24) 135th Running of THE BELMONT. Grade I. Purse $1,000,000 (Up To $72,000 NYSBFOA). THREE YEAR OLDS. By subscription of $600 each to accompany the nomination if made on or before January 18, 2003, or $6,000 if made on or before March 29 2003, $10,000 to pass the entry box and $10,000 additional to start. At any time prior to the closing time of entries, horses may be nominated to The Belmont Stakes upon payment of a supplementary fee of $100,000 to The New York Racing Association Inc. The Purse to be divided 60% to the winner, 20% to second, 11% to third, 6% to fourth and 3% to fifth. Colts and Geldings, 126 lbs.; Fillies, 121 lbs. Starters to be named at the closing time of entries. The Belmont field will be limited to sixteen (16) starters.

Value of Race: $1,000,000 Winner $600,000; second $200,000; third $110,000; fourth $60,000; fifth $30,000. Mutuel Pool $21,283,153. Exacta Pool $11,308,960. Trifecta Pool $12,485,369.

Last Raced	Horse	M/Eqt.	A.Wt	PP	¼	½	1	1¼	Str	Fin	Jockey	Odds $1
3May03 $^{10}CD^{2}$	Empire Maker	Lb	3 126	1	3^{2}	2^{1}	$2^{1\frac{1}{2}}$	1^{1}	$1^{1\frac{1}{2}}$	$1^{\frac{3}{4}}$	Bailey J D	2.00
3May03 $^{10}CD^{9}$	Ten Most Wanted	Lf	3 126	6	$4^{\frac{1}{2}}$	5^{5}	4^{hd}	3^{4}	$2^{1\frac{1}{2}}$	$2^{4\frac{1}{4}}$	Day P	9.70
17May03 $^{12}Pim^{1}$	Funny Cide	L	3 126	4	1^{1}	1^{1}	1^{hd}	2^{1}	3^{5}	$3^{5\frac{1}{4}}$	Santos J A	1.00
10May03 $^{8}LS^{1}$	Dynever	L	3 126	5	5^{4}	4^{hd}	5^{7}	4^{3}	4^{10}	$4^{15\frac{1}{4}}$	Prado E S	8.50
24May03 $^{8}Bel^{3}$	Supervisor	Lb	3 126	2	6	6	6	6	5^{1}	$5^{4\frac{1}{2}}$	Velazquez J R	14.80
17May03 $^{12}Pim^{3}$	Scrimshaw	Lb	3 126	3	$2^{1\frac{1}{2}}$	3^{1}	3^{hd}	5^{4}	6	6	Stevens G L	11.00

OFF AT 6:40 Start Good. Won driving. Track sloppy.
TIME $:23^{4}$, $:48^{3}$, $1:13^{2}$, 1:38, $2:02^{3}$, $2:28^{1}$ (:23.85, :48.70, 1:13.51, 1:38.05, 2:02.62, 2:28.26)

$2 Mutuel Prices:

1–EMPIRE MAKER	6.00	3.70	2.80
6–TEN MOST WANTED		5.80	3.20
4–FUNNY CIDE			2.70

$2 EXACTA 1–6 PAID $44.00 $2 TRIFECTA 1–6–4 PAID $67.50

Dk. b. or br. c, (Apr), by Unbridled–Toussaud, by El Gran Senor. Trainer Frankel Robert. Bred by Juddmonte Farms Inc (Ky).

EMPIRE MAKER was taken to the outside approaching the first turn, stalked the pace while four wide along the backstretch, edged closer on the far turn, drew along side FUNNY CIDE to challenge at the three-eighths pole, surged to the front midway on the turn, shook off FUNNY CIDE to gain a clear advantage leaving the quarter pole, dug in when threatened in upper stretch, drifted out when struck left handed with the whip nearing the eighth pole then turned back TEN MOST WANTED through the final sixteenth of a mile. TEN MOST WANTED brushed with DYNEVER at the start, was strung out five wide on the first turn, continued wide while just behind the leaders along the backstretch, closed the gap a bit on the turn, launched a rally five wide entering the stretch, made a run outside the winner to threaten in deep stretch, but could not get up. FUNNY CIDE broke outward slightly at the start, rushed up to gain the early advantage on the first turn, set the pace well off the rail while in hand along the backstretch, led to the far turn, relinquished the lead to the winner at the three-sixteenths pole, battled along the inside to the top of the stretch then weakened from his early efforts. DYNEVER brushed with TEN MOST WANTED at the start, settled just off the pace while between horses for a mile, raced within striking distance to the turn then came up empty in the stretch. SUPERVISOR never reached contention after breaking a step slowly while racing wide throughout. SCRIMSHAW moved up along the rail to contest the early pace, raced close up along the inside for a mile, dropped back on the turn, drifted very wide at the quarter pole then gave way.

Owners— 1, Juddmonte Farms Inc; 2, J P Reddam M Jarvis J Chisholm K Sm; 3, Sackatoga Stable; 4, Peter F Karches & Catherine Wills; 5, Lundock Rodney G; 6, Lewis Robert B & Beverly J

Trainers—1, Frankel Robert; 2, Dollase Wallace; 3, Tagg Barclay; 4, Clement Christophe; 5, Rice Linda; 6, Lukas D Wayne

---

$2 Daily Double (10–1) Paid $16.00; Daily Double Pool $513,341.
$2 Daily Double (7–1(ACORN/BELMONT)) Paid $20.20; Daily Double Pool $569,982.
$2 Pick Three (5–10–1) Paid $84.00; Pick Three Pool $496,621.
$2 Pick Four (2–5–10–1) Paid $271.00; Pick Four Pool $1,205,886.
$2 Pick Six (5–6–2–5–10–1) 6
Correct Paid $900.00; Pick Six Pool $1,298,118. $2 Pick Six (5–6–2–5–10–1) 5
Correct Paid $24.20

FOURTH RACE
Hollywood
JUNE 7, 2003

6 FURLONGS. (1.07^{2}) 7th Running of THE DESERT STORMER HANDICAP. Grade III. Purse $100,000 added. FILLIES AND MARES THREE YEARS OLD AND UPWARD. By subscription of $100 each on or before Thursday, May 29. $1,000 additional to start, with $100,000 added. The added money and all fees to be divided 60% to the winner, 20% to second, 12% to third, 6% to fourth and 2% to fifth. Closed Thursday, May 29 with 8 nominations.

Value of Race: $106,800 Winner $64,080; second $21,360; third $12,816; fourth $6,408; fifth $2,136. Mutuel Pool $515,883.00 Exacta Pool $257,184.00 Quinella Pool $26,634.00 Trifecta Pool $228,008.00

Last Raced	Horse	M/Eqt.	A.Wt	PP	St	¼	½	Str	Fin	Jockey	Odds $1
25Jan03 $^{6}GP^{1}$	Madame Pietra	LB	6 121	2	6	6	$5^{1\frac{1}{2}}$	$3^{\frac{1}{2}}$	$1^{\frac{3}{4}}$	Valenzuela P A	6.10
15May03 $^{2}BM^{1}$	Bear Fan	LB	4 116	6	2	$3^{2\frac{1}{2}}$	2^{hd}	$1^{\frac{1}{2}}$	2^{3}	Bourque C C	3.30
26Apr03 $^{1}Hol^{2}$	Jetinto Houston	LB	4 116	3	1	1^{hd}	$1^{\frac{1}{2}}$	2^{2}	3no	Smith M E	2.10
26Mar03 $^{2}SA^{2}$	Wild Tickle	LB	5 116	1	5	$5^{1\frac{1}{2}}$	$4^{\frac{1}{2}}$	5^{3}	4^{2}	Baze T C	24.00
3May03 $^{8}CD^{8}$	Palmarola-ARG	LBb	6 116	4	4	4^{hd}	6	6	5^{1}	Solis A	3.00
26Apr03 $^{1}Hol^{1}$	Cee's Elegance	LB	6 120	5	3	2^{hd}	3^{3}	$4^{1\frac{1}{2}}$	6	Espinoza V	3.90

OFF AT 2:57 Start Good. Won driving. Track fast.
TIME $:21^{3}$, $:43^{3}$, $:56^{1}$, $1:09^{3}$ (:21.79, :43.75, :56.39, 1:09.71)

$2 Mutuel Prices:

2–MADAME PIETRA	14.20	5.80	3.60
6–BEAR FAN		4.40	3.20
3–JETINTO HOUSTON			2.80

$1 EXACTA 2–6 PAID $32.10 $2 QUINELLA 2–6 PAID $23.80 $1 TRIFECTA 2–6–3 PAID $118.10

Dk. b. or br. m, by Roy–Missy White Oak, by Baederwood. Trainer Zucker Howard L. Bred by Curtis G Mikkelsen & Patricia J Horth (Fla).

MADAME PIETRA settled a bit off the rail, moved up outside a rival leaving the turn, came out in the stretch and closed willingly under urging to wear down the runner-up. BEAR FAN broke out a bit, was four wide early then dueled three deep on the backstretch and turn, took a short lead in upper stretch, inched away past midstretch but could not hold off the winner. JETINTO HOUSTON went up inside to duel for command, battled along the rail on the turn, fought back in midstretch, weakened late and just held third. WILD TICKLE saved ground chasing the pace, came out in upper stretch and just missed the show. PALMAROLA (ARG) between horses early, chased off the rail, dropped back on the turn and weakened. CEE'S ELEGANCE vied for command between horses on the backstretch and turn, fell back into the stretch and also weakened.

Owners— 1, C T Grether Inc; 2, Fan & Ward; 3, Team Valor Stables & Barber Gary; 4, Bell Richard A; 5, Prestonwood Farm & Sutherland; 6, Cees Stable

Trainers—1, Zucker Howard L; 2, Ward Wesley A; 3, Sahadi Jenine; 4, Blincoe Thomas H; 5, Mandella Richard; 6, O'Neill Doug

---

$2 Daily Double (7–2) Paid $66.80; Daily Double Pool $35,713.
$1 Pick Three (5–7–2) Paid $139.00; Pick Three Pool $84,813.

NINTH RACE	1⅛ MILES. (Turf)(1.46¹) 26th Running of THE JEFFERSON CUP. Grade III. Purse $200,000 Added.	
Churchill	THREE–YEAR–OLDS. By subscription of $200 each on or before May 24, 2003 or by Supplementary Nomination of $10,000 at time of entry. $1,000 to pass entry box; $1,000 additional to start, with $200,000	
JUNE 7, 2003	added. Weight 122 lbs. Non–winners of $50,000 twice on the turf allowed 2 lbs.; a sweepstakes on the turf, 4 lbs.; two races at a mile or over other than maiden or claiming, 6 lbs.; a raceother than claiming on the turf, 8 lbs. If race is moved to main track after time of closing, a horse may be scratched for any reason at any time up to 15 minutes prior to post time for race preceding this race or thereafter with valid physical reason and approved by the stewards. Entry fee shall be refunded for scratches made in compliance with the above conditions. Closed May 24, 2003 with 33 nominations. (If this race is taken off the turf it will be downgraded one grade level for this running only in accordance with American Graded Stakes Committee policy).	

Value of Race: $220,600 Winner $136,772; second $44,120; third $22,060; fourth $11,030; fifth $6,618. Mutuel Pool $573,077.00 Exacta Pool $425,292.00 Trifecta Pool $365,437.00 Superfecta Pool $85,459.00

Last Raced	Horse	M/Eqt. A.Wt	PP	St	¼	½	¾	Str	Fin	Jockey	Odds $1
17May03 ¹²Pim⁵	Senor Swinger	L	3 120	7	5	6³	6²½	4ʰᵈ	1¹	1⁵½	Albarado R J	0.70
2May03 ⁹CD²	Remind	L	3 116	5	6	2½	2³	2¹½	2½	2ⁿᵒ	Velasquez C	5.90
2May03 ⁹CD⁴	Rapid Proof	Lb	3 120	1	1	7	7	6¹½	3ʰᵈ	3½	Guidry M	13.30
11May03 ⁷CD¹	Moonshine Hall	L	3 116	3	7	5²½	4²½	5³½	5²	4¹¾	Peck B D	28.70
17May03 ¹²Pim⁷	Foufa's Warrior	Lbf	3 114	2	2	3²½	3²½	3²½	6¹⁸	5²	Karamanos H A	5.60
8May03 ⁷CD¹	Shake The Bank	Lb	3 116	6	4	1³½	1⁶	1⁵½	4ʰᵈ	6¹9½	Lopez J	22.10
7May03 ⁷Bel¹	Willard Straight	L	3 116	4	3	4ʰᵈ	5ʰᵈ	7	7	7	Sellers S J	4.70

OFF AT 5:41 Start Good. Won driving. Course firm.
TIME :23¹, :46², 1:10⁴, 1:35⁴, 1:47² (:23.25, :46.48, 1:10.96, 1:35.84, 1:47.54)

$2 Mutuel Prices:

7–SENOR SWINGER	3.40	2.60	2.20
5–REMIND		4.00	2.80
1–RAPID PROOF			4.00

$2 EXACTA 7–5 PAID $14.60 $2 TRIFECTA 7–5–1 PAID $64.60 $1
SUPERFECTA 7–5–1–3 PAID $147.20

Gr/ro c, (Apr), by El Prado*Ire–Smooth Swinger, by Kris S.. Trainer Baffert Bob. Bred by Bob Ackerman (Ky).

SENOR SWINGER, reserved early and angled in behind horses three wide, was confidently ridden, edged closer nearing the final quarter, was put to a drive a quarter-mile out, swung out five wide when straightened for the drive, was roused twice with the whip sharply on the right side, then, after the jockey switched the stick to his left hand, widened late under hand urging. REMIND stalked front-running SHAKE THE BANK form early on, inched after that one entering the far turn, was with the winner while inside that one in the upper stretch and couldn't match strides while fully extended to save second position. RAPID PROOF, away in front, was taken in hand along the inside, saved ground throughout, made a menacing run along the hedge into the final furlong but couldn't sustain the needed momentum. MOONSHINE HALL broke in at the start bumping with FOUFA'S WARRIOR, followed the leaders four or five wide to the stretch, came wider for the drive but failed to rally. FOUFA'S WARRIOR came out bumping with MOONSHINE HALL at the start, eased out on the backstretch to race four wide, raced in contention to the stretch and flattened out in the drive. SHAKE THE BANK sprinted clear, raced three wide while showing the way to the stretch and tired. WILLARD STRAIGHT tired leaving the backstretch and wasn't persevered with at the end when hopelessly beaten.

Owners— 1, Lewis Robert B & Beverly J; 2, Claiborne Farm; 3, Morrison Dolphus; 4, Melnyk Eugene & Laura; 5, Bender Sondra D; 6, Silverton Hills Farm; 7, Goichman Lawrence
Trainers— 1, Baffert Bob; 2, Mott William I; 3, Wiggins Hal R; 4, Reinstedler Anthony; 5, Murray Lawrence E; 6, Miller Darrin; 7, Pletcher Todd A

$1 Pick Three (1–2–7) Paid $43.40; Pick Three Pool $27,156.

EIGHTH RACE
Hollywood
JUNE 7, 2003

1⅛ MILES. (Turf Chute)(1.44^3) 52nd Running of THE HONEYMOON BREEDERS' CUP HANDICAP. Grade II. Purse $200,000 added (includes $50,000 BC – Breeders' Cup). FILLIES THREE-YEARS-OLD. By subscription of $150 each. $1,500 additional to start, with $150,000 added and an additional $50,000 from the Breeders' Cup Fund for Cup nominees only. The host association's added money and all fees to be divided 60% to the winner, 20% to second, 12% to third, 6% to fourth and 2% to fifth. Breeders' Cup monies correspondingly divided. Breeders'.Cup monies not awarded revert to the fund. Closed Thursday, May 29 with 13 nominations. Rail zero.

Value of Race: $215,950 Winner $130,170; second $43,390; third $26,034; fourth $13,017; fifth $3,339. Mutuel Pool $622,666.00 Exacta Pool $336,211.00 Quinella Pool $30,875.00 Trifecta Pool $349,153.00 Superfecta Pool $137,910.00

Last Raced	Horse	M/Eqt.	A.Wt	PP	St	¼	½	¾	Str	Fin	Jockey	Odds $1
11May03 ^{8}Hol^1	Quero Quero	LB	3 113	10	7	4^1	4^1	5^{hd}	$5^{1\frac{1}{2}}$	1^{nk}	Baze T C	10.30
2May03 ^{10}CD^9	Atlantic Ocean	LB	3 121	5	5	3^1	$3^{2\frac{1}{2}}$	3^1	2^{hd}	$2^{1\frac{1}{2}}$	Valenzuela P A	a-1.80
8May03 ^{7}Hol^2	Sharpbill-GB	LBb	3 113	6	4	2^{hd}	$2^{\frac{1}{2}}$	2^{hd}	3^{hd}	$3^{\frac{1}{2}}$	Garcia M S	25.70
17May03 ^{3}Hol^3	Shapes And Shadows	LBb	3 116	1	1	1^1	1^1	1^1	$1^{1\frac{1}{2}}$	4^1	Johnston M T	20.70
25Oct02 ^{7}SA^1	Gotdream-FR	LB	3 117	3	2	$5^{\frac{1}{2}}$	$5^{\frac{1}{2}}$	6^1	6^1	5no	Valdivia J Jr	4.60
17May03 ^{3}Hol^4	Major Idea	LB	3 118	8	6	6^1	$6^{1\frac{1}{2}}$	$4^{\frac{1}{2}}$	$4^{\frac{1}{2}}$	6^1	Nakatani C S	a-1.80
17May03 ^{3}Hol^2	Rutters Renegade-IR	LB	3 116	4	10	10	10	9^{hd}	9^4	$7^{\frac{1}{2}}$	Solis A	5.80
26Apr03 ^{9}Hol^1	Bartok's Blithe	LB	3 116	2	3	7^{hd}	9^1	$8^{\frac{1}{2}}$	7^1	8^{nk}	Espinoza V	8.80
13Apr03 ^{3}SA^1	Star Vega-GB	LB	3 118	7	9	$9^{1\frac{1}{2}}$	7^{hd}	$7^{1\frac{1}{2}}$	8^{hd}	9^6	Smith M E	b-3.30
11May03 ^{4}Hol^5	Lady's Mantle-IR	LB	3 114	9	8	$8^{\frac{1}{2}}$	8^1	10	10	10	Enriquez I D	b-3.30

a–Coupled: Atlantic Ocean and Major Idea.
b–Coupled: Star Vega-GB and Lady's Mantle-IR.

OFF AT 5:44 Start Good. Won driving. Course firm.
TIME :24^4, :49^4, 1:14, 1:37^2, 1:49^1 (:24.89, :49.88, 1:14.19, 1:37.49, 1:49.34)

$2 Mutuel Prices:

9–QUERO QUERO	22.60	7.80	5.80
1–ATLANTIC OCEAN (a–entry)		3.40	2.80
7–SHARPBILL–GB			9.80

$1 EXACTA 9–1 PAID $36.20 $2 QUINELLA 1–9 PAID $26.80 $1 TRIFECTA 9–1–7 PAID $514.10 $1 SUPERFECTA 9–1–7–3 PAID $4,786.00

B. f, (Mar), by Royal Academy–Big Dreams, by Great Above. Trainer Lobo Paulo H. Bred by John R Gaines Thoroughbreds & Pacelco SA (Ky).

QUERO QUERO four wide leaving the chute, angled in and chased outside a rival then between horses on the second turn, came out into the stretch and closed gamely under some left handed urging and strong handling to get up late. ATLANTIC OCEAN angled in and pulled her way up inside to stalk the pace, steadied briefly midway on the second turn, awaited room on that bend, came out into the stretch, bid between foes past midstretch to put a head in front in deep stretch but could not hold off the winner. SHARPBILL (GB) stalked the pace outside the runner-up came out into the stretch and finished with interest to best the rest. SHAPES AND SHADOWS sped to the early lead, set the pace inside, inched away nearing midstretch, fought back in deep stretch but was overtaken. GOTDREAM (FR) angled in and saved ground chasing the pace, came out into the stretch and was outfinished. MAJOR IDEA pulled early, chased outside a rival then three deep into and on the second turn, came four wide into the stretch and could not summon the necessary late response. RUTTERS RENEGADE (IRE) off a bit slowly, angled in and saved ground off the pace, split rivals on the second turn, swung four wide into the stretch and lacked the needed rally. BARTOK'S BLITHE angled in and chased along the inside,came out into the stretch and did not rally. STAR VEGA (GB) pulled early, chased outside a rival then between horses on the backstretch, went three deep on the second turn and was not a threat. LADY'S MANTLE (IRE) also pulled her way along early, chased outside then three deep on the backstretch, continued off the rail on the second turn, angled in some into the stretch and weakened.

Owners— 1, Old Friends Inc; 2, The Thoroughbred Corporation; 3, Wilson David W & Holly F; 4, Everest Stables; 5, Amerman Racing Stables; 6, The Thoroughbred Corporation; 7, Class Racing Stable A & R Stables L; 8, 5C Racing Stable; 9, Cuchna John R Jim Ford Inc & Pearso; 10, Cuchna John R Jim Ford Inc & Pearso

Trainers—1, Lobo Paulo H; 2, Baffert Bob; 3, Cerin Vladimir; 4, Canani Nick; 5, Frankel Robert; 6, Drysdale Neil; 7, Mandella Gary; 8, Gutierrez Jorge; 9, Cassidy James; 10, Cassidy James

Scratched— Cherokee's Disco (2May03 ^{7}HOL^5)

$2 Daily Double (3–9) Paid $69.20; Daily Double Pool $46,342.
$1 Pick Three (4–3/6–9) Paid $563.60; Pick Three Pool $70,612.

EIGHTH RACE
Belmont
JUNE 8, 2003

6½ FURLONGS. (1.14^2) 53rd Running of THE VAGRANCY HANDICAP. Grade II. Purse $150,000. (Up to $29,100 NYSBFOA). FILLIES AND MARES THREE YEARS OLD AND UPWARD. By subscription of $150 each, which should accompany the nomination; $750 to pass the entry box; $750 to start. The purse to be divided 60% to the winner, 20% to second,11% to third, 6% to fourth and 3% to fifth. Trophies will be presented to the winning owner, trainer and jockey. Closed Saturday, May 24, 2003 with 16 Nominations.

Value of Race: $136,500 Winner $90,000; second $30,000; third $16,500.

Last Raced	Horse	M/Eqt.	A.Wt	PP	St	¼	½	Str	Fin	Jockey	Odds $1
22May03 ^{8}Bel^1	Shawklit Mint	L	4 115	2	1	1^2	$1^{1\frac{1}{2}}$	$1^{2\frac{1}{2}}$	$1^{1\frac{3}{4}}$	Migliore R	4.30
11May03 ^{8}Bel^1	Shine Again	L	6 121	1	3	3	3	2^2	$2^{3\frac{1}{4}}$	Samyn J L	0.70
3May03 ^{8}CD^2	Gold Mover	L	5 118	3	2	$2^{\frac{1}{2}}$	2^{hd}	3	3	Bailey J D	1.45

OFF AT 4:46 Start Good. Won driving. Track muddy.
TIME :22^4, :45^4, 1:09^1, 1:15^1 (:22.96, :45.92, 1:09.20, 1:15.38)

$2 Mutuel Prices:

5–SHAWKLIT MINT	10.60	—	—
2–SHINE AGAIN		—	—
1A–GOLD MOVER		—	—

Dk. b. or br. f, by Air Forbes Won–Shawklit Delight, by Pine Bluff. Trainer Reynolds Patrick L. Bred by Treasure Hill Farm Inc (NY).

SHAWKLIT MINT broke running, quickly opened a clear lead, set the pace, responded when roused and remained clear under a drive. SHINE AGAIN raced close up inside, came wide into the stretch and finished gamely outside. GOLD MOVER raced close up outside and had no response when roused.

Owners— 1, Flatbird Stable; 2, Bohemia Stable; 3, Evans Edward P

Trainers—1, Reynolds Patrick L; 2, Jerkens H Allen; 3, Hennig Mark

Scratched— Raging Fever (17May03 ^{8}BEL^6), Fly Me Crazy (26May03 ^{9}PHA^5), Harmony Lodge (11May03 ^{8}BEL^3), Slews Final Answer (3May03 ^{8}CD^4), Bonefide Reason (22May03 ^{8}BEL^2)

EIGHTH RACE
Arlington
JUNE 14, 2003

7 FURLONGS. (1.20^2) 17th Running of THE CHICAGO BREEDERS' CUP HANDICAP. Grade III. Purse $175,000 (includes $75,000 BC - Breeders' Cup) A HANDICAP FOR FILLIES AND MARES, THREE-YEARS-OLD AND UPWARD. (Includes $75,000 from Breeders' Cup Fund for Cup nominees only). By subscription of $125 each, which should accompany the nomination. Original nominees to pay $750 to pass the entry box and an additional $750 to start. Breeders' Cup Fund monies correspondingly divided providing a Breeders' Cup nominee has finished in an awarded position. Any Breeders' Cup Fund Monies not awarded will revert back to the Fund. WEIGHTS: June 8, 2003. This event will not be divided, the field will be limited to fourteen starters. Preference will be given to Breeders' Cup Nominees only of equal racing quality or weight assignment (respective of sex and weight-for-age) Total earnings in 2003 will be used to determine the order of preference of horses assigned equal weight (on the scale).

Value of Race: $145,750 Winner $69,450; second $38,150; third $20,982; fourth $11,445; fifth $5,723. Mutuel Pool $266,701.00 Exacta Pool $183,730.00 Trifecta Pool $165,107.00 Superfecta Pool $44,787.00

Last Raced	Horse	M/Eqt.	A.Wt	PP	St	¼	½	Str	Fin	Jockey	Odds $1
15May03 ^{7}CD^1	For Rubies	L	4 116	3	7	2^{hd}	2^2	1^{hd}	1^3	Perret C	7.20
17May03 ^{8}Bel^6	Raging Fever	L	5 120	1	3	1^1	1^{hd}	2^6	2^4	Gryder A T	1.00
25May03 ^{8}AP^2	Oglala Sue	L	5 113	5	6	6^2	6^3	5^3	$3^{1\frac{1}{2}}$	Emigh C A	35.20
25May03 ^{8}AP^1	Summer Mis	Lb	4 115	8	1	5^4	3^{hd}	3^{hd}	$4^{\frac{1}{2}}$	Sterling L J Jr	14.50
3May03 ^{8}CD^3	Miss Lodi	L	4 115	6	5	3^{hd}	$5^{1\frac{1}{2}}$	6^{hd}	5^{nk}	Razo E Jr	2.10
29Mar03 ^{6}Haw^4	Ifyouprefersilver	L	4 116	7	2	4^{hd}	4^3	4^2	6^7	Lovato F Jr	12.00
5Apr03 ^{10}Sun^1	Cielo Girl	L	4 115	2	8	8	8	7^{hd}	$7^{\frac{3}{4}}$	Douglas R R	10.60
27May03 ^{9}Mnr^2	Abundantly Blessed	L	4 114	4	4	7^{hd}	7^2	8	8	St Julien M	48.60

OFF AT 5:09 Start Good. Won driving. Track fast.
TIME :22^3, :45^1, 1:10^2, 1:24^1 (:22.62, :45.27, 1:10.46, 1:24.21)

$2 Mutuel Prices:

3-FOR RUBIES	16.40	4.60	3.80
1-RAGING FEVER		3.00	2.60
6-OGLALA SUE			5.80

$2 EXACTA 3-1 PAID $47.60 $2 TRIFECTA 3-1-6 PAID $478.00 $2 SUPERFECTA 3-1-6-9 PAID $2,313.80

B. f, by Not For Love-Eliza Donner, by Oh Say. Trainer Whiting Lynn S. Bred by Sharon Maloney (Md).

FOR RUBIES was guided to a good prompting position just to the outside of RAGING FEVER, inched closer to challenge that one on the turn, took a short lead in the stretch and drew off under steady urging. RAGING FEVER quickly went out to the lead from the inside, made the pace for a half mile, surrendered grudgingly in the stretch and continued gamely to be clearly second best. OGLALA SUE was void of early speed while racing just outside, came to the middle of the track for the drive and belatedly gained minor awards. SUMMER MIS raced off the rail near the middle of the field, rallied outside on the turn to loom a threat but weakened in the run to the wire. MISS LODI raced close up off the rail in the early going but weakened. IFYOUPREFERSILVER raced near the middle of the field but weakened late. CIELO GIRL showed no speed and was always outrun. ABUNDANTLY BLESSED also failed to make an impression.

Owners— 1, Choctaw Racing Stable; 2, Evans Edward P; 3, Bluestem Farm Inc; 4, R Otto Stables; 5, Richard C Colton & Mast Thoroughbre; 6, Tanaka Gary A; 7, Parra Rosendo G; 8, Ligon Tom G

Trainers—1, Whiting Lynn S; 2, Hennig Mark; 3, Robertson Hugh H; 4, Mitchell Anthony; 5, Amoss Thomas; 6, Stidham Michael; 7, Asmussen Steven M; 8, Hamm Timothy

Scratched— See How She Runs (26May03 ^{4}LS^1)

$1 Pick Three (6-5-3) Paid $161.40; Pick Three Pool $9,258.

SEVENTH RACE
Belmont
JUNE 14, 2003

1⅛ MILES. (1.45^2) 29th Running of THE HILL PRINCE. Purse $100,000. (Up to $19,400 NYSBFOA). THREE YEAR OLDS. By subscription of $100 each, which should accompany the nomination; $500 to pass the entry box; $500 to start with $100,000 added. 122 lbs. Non-winners of $35,000 twice on the turf allowed 2 lbs.; $45,000 at a mile or over; or $35,000 at a mile or over in 2003, 4 lbs.; $30,000, or two races at a mile or over, 6 lbs.; two races, 8 lbs. (Maiden, Claiming and Restricted races not considered in allowances). The New York Racing Association reserves the right to transfer this race to the Main Track. In the event that this race is taken off the turf, it may be subject to downgrading upon review by the Graded Stakes Committee. Closed Saturday, May 31, 2003 with 41 Nominations. (ORIGINALLY SCHEDULED FOR TURF.)

Value of Race: $113,100 Winner $67,860; second $22,620; third $12,441; fourth $6,786; fifth $3,393. Mutuel Pool $448,431.00 Exacta Pool $388,661.00 Trifecta Pool $240,927.00

Last Raced	Horse	M/Eqt.	A.Wt	PP	St	¼	½	¾	Str	Fin	Jockey	Odds $1
26May03 ^{10}Mth^1	Happy Trails	Lb	3 120	4	3	6	6	5^1	$3^{\frac{1}{2}}$	$1^{1\frac{1}{4}}$	Bridgmohan S X	11.10
31May03 ^{5}Bel^1	Traffic Chief	Lf	3 114	6	1	3^1	$4^{\frac{1}{2}}$	$3^{\frac{1}{2}}$	1^1	2^4	Santos J A	1.70
29May03 ^{6}Bel^1	Chilly Rooster		3 114	3	4	$2^{\frac{1}{2}}$	$2^{1\frac{1}{2}}$	1^{hd}	2^{hd}	$3^{\frac{1}{2}}$	Espinoza J L	2.85
12Apr03 ^{9}OP^4	Region Of Merit	L	3 120	5	2	$4^{\frac{1}{2}}$	3^{hd}	4^3	4^3	4^5	Arroyo N Jr	1.90
30Mar03 ^{9}GP^1	Charge	L	3 120	1	5	1^{hd}	$1^{\frac{1}{2}}$	2^1	5^{10}	$5^{9\frac{1}{2}}$	Coa E M	12.40
25May03 ^{7}Bel^1	Elusive Gentleman	L	3 118	2	6	5^7	5^7	6	6	6	Castellano J J	25.25

OFF AT 4:06 Start Good. Won driving. Track good.
TIME :23, :46^1, 1:11^2, 1:36^4, 1:50 (:23.05, :46.39, 1:11.42, 1:36.83, 1:50.13)

$2 Mutuel Prices:

9-HAPPY TRAILS	24.20	7.00	4.20
12-TRAFFIC CHIEF		3.60	2.80
6-CHILLY ROOSTER			3.00

$2 EXACTA 9-12 PAID $74.00 $2 TRIFECTA 9-12-6 PAID $258.00

Dk. b. or br. c, (Mar), by Peaks and Valleys-Part With Pride, by Executive Pride*Ire. Trainer Klesaris Steve. Bred by Paula E Parsons (Ky).

HAPPY TRAILS was outrun early, rallied inside nearing the stretch, came wide for the drive and was along late from the outside, driving. TRAFFIC CHIEF raced close up outside, rallied three wide on the turn, drew clear in the stretch then dug in gamely but could not withstand the winner. CHILLY ROOSTER contested the pace from the outside and tired in the final furlong. REGION OF MERIT raced close up along the inside and had no response when roused. CHARGE contested the pace along the inside and tired in the stretch. ELUSIVE GENTLEMAN tired after an inside trip.

Owners— 1, Goldfarb Sanford & Team Julep Stabl; 2, Schwartz Barry K; 3, Hobeau Farm; 4, Kennelot Stables Ltd; 5, Whitney Wheelock; 6, Marylou Whitney Stable

Trainers—1, Klesaris Steve; 2, Hushion Michael E; 3, Jerkens H Allen; 4, Clement Christophe; 5, McGaughey Claude III; 6, Zito Nicholas P

Scratched— Urban King (12Apr03 ^{7}SA^3), Lismore Knight (17May03 ^{7}BEL^1), Silver Tree (23Apr03 ^{9}GP^1), Hypnotist (17Apr03 ^{8}KEE^8), Kicken Kris (4Apr03 ^{5}GP^1), Christine's Outlaw (24May03 ^{8}BEL^6)

$2 Daily Double (9-9) Paid $30.60; Daily Double Pool $118,938.
$2 Pick Three (12-9-9) Paid $147.50; Pick Three Pool $110,122.

NINTH RACE
Belmont
JUNE 14, 2003

1⅛ MILES. (1.45^{2}) 115th Running of THE BROOKLYN HANDICAP. Grade II. Purse $250,000. (Up to $38,500 NYSBFOA). THREE YEAR OLDS AND UPWARD. By subscription of $250 each, which should accompany the nomination; $1,250 to pass the entry box and $1,250 to start. The purse to be divided 60% to the winner, 20% to second, 11% to third, 6% to fourth and 3% to fifth. Trophies will be presented to the winning owner, trainer and jockey. Closed Saturday, May 31, 2003 with 28 Nominations.

Value of Race: $250,000 Winner $150,000; second $50,000; third $27,500; fourth $15,000; fifth $7,500. Mutuel Pool $781,971.00 Exacta Pool $593,782.00

Last Raced	Horse	M/Eqt.	A.Wt	PP	St	¼	½	¾	Str	Fin	Jockey	Odds $1
4May03 ^{4}Aqu^{1}	Iron Deputy	L	4 114	2	4	$1^{\frac{1}{2}}$	$1^{\frac{1}{2}}$	$1^{1\frac{1}{2}}$	1^{2}	$1^{2\frac{1}{2}}$	Migliore R	6.60
9May03 ^{8}Bel^{2}	Volponi	Lf	5 122	3	2	$3^{\frac{1}{2}}$	3^{1}	2^{hd}	$2^{2\frac{1}{2}}$	2^{3}	Santos J A	3.70
26May03 ^{9}Bel^{2}	Saarland	Lbf	4 115	5	1	2^{1}	2^{hd}	$3^{2\frac{1}{2}}$	$3^{2\frac{1}{2}}$	$3^{2\frac{1}{2}}$	Prado E S	3.20
23Nov02 ^{8}Aqu^{1}	Evening Attire	Lb	5 122	4	3	5	5	5	4^{6}	$4^{6\frac{1}{2}}$	Bridgmohan S X	2.95
29Mar03 NAS^{2}	Harlan's Holiday	L	4 122	1	5	4^{5}	4^{3}	4^{hd}	5	5	Velazquez J R	2.00

OFF AT 5:20 Start Good. Won driving. Track sloppy.
TIME :23^{2}, :46^{4}, 1:10, 1:35, 1:47^{4} (:23.46, :46.84, 1:10.03, 1:35.07, 1:47.84)

$2 Mutuel Prices:

2–IRON DEPUTY	15.20	8.20	3.60
3–VOLPONI		4.80	3.10
6–SAARLAND			2.80

$2 EXACTA 2–3 PAID $61.00

B. c, by Silver Deputy–Femme De Fer*Fr, by Iron Duke. Trainer Jerkens James A. Bred by Jose Soriano (Ky).

IRON DEPUTY was hustled to the front, set the pace while in hand, drew clear when asked, dug in gamely in the stretch and remained clear under a steady drive. VOLPONI came away well, raced close up inside, rallied inside nearing the stretch, angled out in upper stretch and finished gamely. SAARLAND raced with the pace while three wide and had no response when roused. EVENING ATTIRE was outrun early, put in a run along the inside on the turn and had little left for the stretch drive. HARLAN'S HOLIDAY broke slowly, was urged along outside, raced four wide and tired in the stretch. DUE TO A SEVERE ELECTRICAL THUNDERSTORM, THIS RACE WAS HAND-TIMED.

Owners— 1, Moore Susan & John; 2, Amherst Stable & Spruce Pond Stable; 3, Phipps Cynthia; 4, Grant Mary & Joseph & Kelly Thomas; 5, Starlight Stable

Trainers—1, Jerkens James A; 2, Johnson Philip G; 3, McGaughey Claude III; 4, Kelly Patrick J; 5, Pletcher Todd A

Scratched— El Gran Papa (1May03 ^{8}CD^{1})

$2 Daily Double (1–2) Paid $67.00; Daily Double Pool $255,942. $2 Pick Three (2–2–9) (NTRA SUMMER PICK 3)) Paid $2,043.00; Pick Three Pool $344, $2 Pick Four (9–9–1–2) Paid $988.00; Pick Four Pool $238,671. $2 Pick Six (6–12–9–9–1–2) 5 Correct Paid $6,319.00; Pick Six Pool $94,794; Carryover Pool $56,876. $2 Consolation Pick Three (9–1–2) Paid $571.00; Consolation Pick Three Pool $103

Belmont Park Attendance: N/A Total Mutual Pool: N/A

NINTH RACE
Churchill
JUNE 14, 2003

1⅛ MILES. (1.47^{1}) 29th Running of THE FLEUR DE LIS HANDICAP. Grade II. Purse $300,000 Added. FILLIES AND MARES, THREE YEARS OLD AND UPWARD. By subscription of $300 each on or before May 31, 2003 or by Supplementary Nomination of $15,000 each by the closing of entries Friday, June 6, 2003. $1,500 to pass the entry box; $1,500 additional to start, with $300,000 added of which 62% of all monies to the owner of the winner, 20% to second, 10% to third, 5% to fourth and 3% to fifth. Weights to be announced Saturday, June 7. Starters to be named through the entry box at the usual time of closing. Closed Saturday, May 31, 2003 with 28 nominations. Trophy to winning owner.

Value of Race: $327,900 Winner $203,298; second $65,580; third $32,790; fourth $16,395; fifth $9,837. Mutuel Pool $381,534.00 Exacta Pool $280,467.00 Trifecta Pool $198,379.00 Superfecta Pool $49,642.00

Last Raced	Horse	M/Eqt.	A.Wt	PP	St	¼	½	¾	Str	Fin	Jockey	Odds $1
17May03 ^{8}Bel^{3}	You	L	4 119	2	3	$2^{1\frac{1}{2}}$	$2^{1\frac{1}{2}}$	2^{2}	1^{2}	$1^{3\frac{3}{4}}$	Bailey J D	0.50
30Mar03 ^{8}SA^{3}	Printemps-CHI	L	6 114	5	1	5^{2}	6	6	$4^{2\frac{1}{2}}$	2^{nk}	Borel C H	6.10
17May03 ^{8}Bel^{5}	Nonsuch Bay	L	4 114	6	6	6	$5^{\frac{1}{2}}$	$5^{\frac{1}{2}}$	3^{2}	3^{hd}	Guidry M	9.00
25May03 ^{9}CD^{1}	So Much More	L	4 114	3	2	$1^{1\frac{1}{2}}$	1^{1}	$1^{\frac{1}{2}}$	$2^{\frac{1}{2}}$	$4^{10\frac{1}{4}}$	Day P	8.70
11May03 ^{6}CD^{1}	Charmed Gift	Lf	4 112	4	5	$4^{6\frac{1}{2}}$	$4^{6\frac{1}{2}}$	3^{1}	5^{5}	$5^{7\frac{1}{4}}$	Albarado R J	7.50
25May03 ^{9}CD^{2}	Minister's Baby	L	5 115	1	4	3^{hd}	$3^{\frac{1}{2}}$	$4^{5\frac{1}{2}}$	6	6	Sellers S J	10.30

OFF AT 5:13 Start Good. Won driving. Track fast.
TIME :24, :48, 1:11^{4}, 1:36^{3}, 1:49 (:24.00, :48.00, 1:11.94, 1:36.67, 1:49.12)

$2 Mutuel Prices:

2–YOU	3.00	2.20	2.10
5–PRINTEMPS–CHI		3.40	2.40
7–NONSUCH BAY			2.60

$2 EXACTA 2–5 PAID $14.20 $2 TRIFECTA 2–5–7 PAID $51.40 $1 SUPERFECTA 2–5–7–3 PAID $85.30

Dk. b. or br. f, by You and I–Our Dani, by Homebuilder. Trainer Frankel Robert. Bred by Dolphus C Morrison (Ky).

YOU, close up from the outset, eased outside of SO MUCH MORE entering the first turn when that one dropped inside, tracked SO MUCH MORE three or four wide under light restraint, inched after that one approaching the final quarter, reached the front entering the upper stretch, was roused sharply twice on the right side, then, after the rider switched the stick to his left hand, three more times while increasing her advantage. PRINTEMPS (CHI), unhurried for six furlongs and four or five wide, circled horses eight wide into the stretch and couldn't threaten YOU while gamely earning second. NONSUCH BAY, also outrun for six furlongs while three wide, came out six abreast into the stretch, loomed a solid threat for the last eighth but couldn't sustain the needed momentum. SO MUCH MORE gained the lead early, moved near the inside approaching the first turn, showed the way two or three wide on the backstretch, lost the advantage to YOU entering the upper stretch, then weakened grudgingly. CHARMED GIFT hopped while ducking in at the start, followed the leaders within easy striking distance four wide to the stretch and flattened out. MINISTER'S BABY, well placed while saving ground until nearing the stretch, weakened thereafter.

Owners— 1, Gann Edmund A; 2, Amerman Racing Stables; 3, Platt Joseph P Jr; 4, Schettine William C; 5, Kilroy Mrs William S; 6, Lucky Seven Stable

Trainers—1, Frankel Robert; 2, McAnally Ronald; 3, Alexander Frank A; 4, O'Callaghan Niall M; 5, Howard Neil J; 6, McPeek Kenneth G

Scratched— Missing Miss (1Jun03 ^{6}CD^{2})

$1 Pick Three (3–6–2/6) Paid $17.50; Pick Three Pool $47,297.

EIGHTH RACE

Churchill

JUNE 14, 2003

1⅛ MILES. (Turf)(1.46¹) 34th Running of THE REGRET. Grade III. Purse $200,000 Added. FILLIES, THREE YEARS OLD. By subscription of $200 each on or before May 31, 2003 or by Supplementary Nomination of $10,000 at time of entry. $1,000 to pass the entry box; $1,000 additional to start, with $200,000 added of which 62% of all monies to the owner of the winner, 20% to second, 10% to third, 5% to fourth and 3% to fifth. Weight, 122 lbs. Non– winners of $50,000 twice on the turf allowed, 2 lbs.; a sweepstakes on the turf, 4 lbs.; two races at a mile or over other than maiden or claiming, 6 lbs.; a race other than claiming on the turf, 8 lbs. If the race is moved to the main track after the time of closing, a horse may be scratched for any reason at any time up to fifteen (15) minutes prior to post time for the race preceding this race or thereafter with a valid physical reason and approved by the stewards. The entry fee shall be refunded for scratches made in compliance with the above conditions. Starters to be named through the entry box at the usual time of closing. Closed Saturday, May 31, 2003 with 35 nominations. Trophy to winning owner. (If this race is taken off the turf it will be downgraded one grade level for this running only in accordance with American Graded Stakes Committee policy).

Value of Race: $231,000 Winner $143,220; second $46,200; third $23,100; fourth $11,550; fifth $6,930. Mutuel Pool $561,089.00 Exacta Pool $424,301.00   Trifecta Pool $330,883.00 Superfecta Pool $107,381.00

Last Raced	Horse	M/Eqt. A.Wt	PP	St	¼	½	¾	Str	Fin	Jockey	Odds $1
21May03 7CD¹	Sand Springs	L	3 118	6	5	1¹	1²	1¹½	1¹½	1³	Guidry M	4.90
10May03 ¹⁰CD¹	Personal Legend	Lb	3 116	8	9	8¹	9hd	7hd	3hd	2½	Bailey J D	2.50
21May03 7CD³	Achnasheen	L	3 116	7	12	12	11hd	11½	7²	3hd	Velasquez C	11.10
21May03 7CD⁶	Unbridled Femme	Lb	3 114	12	1	5½	4½	4½	5¹	4½	McKee J	24.50
18May03 7CD¹	Dyna Da Wyna	Lf	3 116	11	2	3¹	3¹	3¹	2¹½	5¹¾	Sellers S J	26.70
17May03 9CD¹	Golden Marlin	L	3 114	4	6	4hd	5¹½	6hd	6²	6hd	Day P	8.40
21May03 7CD²	Keiai Sakura	Lb	3 116	2	3	2hd	2²	2¹	4hd	7³	Albarado R J	10.90
26May03 8CD¹	Aud	L	3 116	10	11	10½	10¹½	9²	8²	8¹	Peck B D	10.70
2May03 5CD¹	Forest Shadows	L	3 120	5	10	11¹½	12	10½	10hd	9¹½	Melancon L	3.30
13May03 8Mnr¹	Violet Eyed Diva	L	3 116	3	7	7½	6hd	12	11⁷	10½	Bejarano R	78.50
18May03 7CD³	Radiantly	L	3 114	1	4	9hd	8hd	5hd	9hd	11¹½	Lumpkins J	38.50
13Oct02 Mil¹²	Bakewell Tart-IR	L	3 120	9	8	6¹	7¹½	8hd	12	12	Meche L J	25.70

OFF AT 4:46 Start Good For All But SAND SPRINGS Won driving. Course firm.
TIME :23², :47¹, 1:11⁴, 1:36², 1:48³ (:23.42, :47.25, 1:11.85, 1:36.44, 1:48.78)

$2 Mutuel Prices:

6–SAND SPRINGS	11.80	5.40	4.40
8–PERSONAL LEGEND		4.40	3.60
7–ACHNASHEEN			5.80

$2 EXACTA 6–8 PAID $61.80 $2 TRIFECTA 6–8–7 PAID $493.00 $1
SUPERFECTA 6–8–7–12 PAID $3,953.50

Dk. b. or br. f, (May), by Dynaformer–Lovely Martha, by Storm Bird. Trainer Reinstedler Anthony. Bred by Willmott Stables Inc (Ky).

SAND SPRINGS stumbled at the start, quickly recovered to gain the lead, raced four wide, went along under careful handling, opened a clear advantage on the backstretch, made the balance of the pace and increased his margin late under vigorous hand urging. PERSONAL LEGEND, unhurried for a half, was rated in behind horses four or five wide, continued between foes four wide into the lane, loomed a threat outside the winner in the drive but wasn't good enough. ACHNASHEEN, unhurried early after breaking a bit awkwardly, raced three or four wide to the stretch, worked her way out six or seven wide when straightened for the drive and offered a mild gain. UNBRIDLED FEMME angled in early to stalk the pace five wide, raced within easy striking distance into the final furlong and failed to offer a closing account. DYNA DA WYNA also maneuvered in early to race four or five wide while tracking the pace, angled to the rail on the far turn, loomed menacingly inside the winner leaving the furlong grounds but flattened out. GOLDEN MARLIN moved inside early, remained near the hedge for the drive but lacked a response. KEIAI SAKURA moved up inside the winner early to contest the pace, eased out four wide on the backstretch, was asked for her best at the five-sixteenths pole but weakened when straightened into the lane. AUD, unhurried early, made a mild bid six wide between calls on the far turn and failed to continue. FOREST SHADOWS, checked off horse's heels approaching the first turn, failed to menace. VIOLET EYED DIVA raced in contention inside to the far turn and was empty in the drive. RADIANTLY, rank along the inside and steadied approaching the first turn, was done approaching the stretch. BAKEWELL TART (IRE) faded approaching the stretch.

Owners– 1, Willmott Stables; 2, Gann Edmund A; 3, Sterling Stud; 4, Duzee Stable Ducharme D & Szczepans; 5, WinStar Farm; 6, Estate of Joe Famularo & Glass W D; 7, Kameda Morihiro; 8, Willmott Stables; 9, Phillips Racing Partnership & Pam G; 10, Davidovich Andrew; 11, McKee Stables; 12, Andrew J Smith & Morton Fink

Trainers–1, Reinstedler Anthony; 2, Frankel Robert; 3, Shirota Mitch; 4, Pate David E; 5, Walden W Elliott; 6, Foley Gregory D; 7, Gothard Akiko; 8, Reinstedler Anthony; 9, Stall Albert M Jr; 10, Davidovich Andrew; 11, Romans Dale; 12, O'Callaghan Niall M

$1 Pick Three (7–3–6) Paid $47.10; Pick Three Pool $64,955.

TENTH RACE
Churchill
JUNE 14, 2003

1⅛ MILES. (1.47^{1}) 22nd Running of THE STEPHEN FOSTER HANDICAP. Grade I. Purse $750,000 Added. THREE-YEAR-OLDS AND UPWARD. By subscription of $750 each on or before May 31, 2003 or by Supplementary Nomination of $37,500 each by the closing of entries Saturday, June 7, 2003. $3,750 to pass the entry box; $3,750 additional to start, with $750,000 added of which 62% of all monies to the owner of the winner, 20% to second, 10% to third, 5% to fourth and 3% to fifth. Weights to be announced Sunday, June 8. The maximum number of starters for the Stephen Foster will be limited to fourteen (14). If more than fourteen (14) entries pass the entry box preference will be given to highweights with consideration to age, however two horses having common ties through ownership cannot start to the exclusion of a single interest. Any horse excluded from running because of the aforementioned preference shall be refunded the entry fee and supplementary nomination fee if applicable. Starters to be named through the entry box at the usual time of closing. All supplementary nominations will be required to pay entry and starting fees if they participate. Closed Saturday, May 31, 2003 with 32 nominations Trophy to winnng owner.

Value of Race: $856,500 Winner $531,030; second $171,300; third $85,650; fourth $42,825; fifth $25,695. Mutuel Pool $854,032.00 Exacta Pool $617,253.00 Trifecta Pool $494,474.00 Superfecta Pool $172,142.00

Last Raced	Horse	M/Eqt.	A.Wt	PP	St	¼	½	¾	Str	Fin	Jockey	Odds $1
3May03 ^{9}CD^{4}	Perfect Drift	L	4 115	7	4	4^{1}	4^{1}	5^{1}	$2^{3\frac{1}{2}}$	1^{hd}	Day P	6.80
16May03 ^{11}Pim^{1}	Mineshaft	L	4 123	10	2	5^{1}	$5^{2\frac{1}{2}}$	$1^{1\frac{1}{2}}$	1^{1}	$2^{9\frac{1}{2}}$	Albarado R J	0.70
26May03 ^{9}Bel^{1}	Aldebaran	L	5 120	6	3	$6^{1\frac{1}{2}}$	$6^{\frac{1}{2}}$	$6^{1\frac{1}{2}}$	$5^{1\frac{1}{2}}$	$3^{\frac{1}{2}}$	Bailey J D	3.20
1May03 ^{8}CD^{3}	Crafty Shaw	L	5 113	2	6	$1^{\frac{1}{2}}$	$1^{\frac{1}{2}}$	$2^{\frac{1}{2}}$	3^{2}	$4^{\frac{3}{4}}$	Borel C H	30.70
16May03 ^{11}Pim^{4}	Colonial Colony	Lf	5 112	1	7	$7^{\frac{1}{2}}$	$7^{2\frac{1}{2}}$	7^{3}	4^{hd}	5^{2}	Martinez W	64.10
1May03 ^{6}CD^{1}	Unbridled Vision	Lb	5 111	5	10	8^{2}	$8^{\frac{1}{2}}$	8^{4}	6^{hd}	$6^{1\frac{3}{4}}$	Melancon L	39.90
10May03 ^{8}AP^{3}	Woodmoon	Lbf	5 110	4	9	10	10	10	8^{2}	$7^{1\frac{1}{4}}$	McKee J	60.30
26May03 ^{9}Bel^{4}	Proud Citizen	L	4 115	9	1	$3^{\frac{1}{2}}$	$3^{\frac{1}{2}}$	3^{hd}	7^{2}	$8^{5\frac{1}{4}}$	Velasquez C	11.50
10May03 ^{8}AP^{1}	Full Mandate	Lb	4 113	3	8	$9^{\frac{1}{2}}$	$9^{1\frac{1}{2}}$	9^{hd}	10	$9^{1\frac{1}{2}}$	Meche L J	51.50
17May03 ^{7}CD^{1}	Consistency	Lb	4 114	8	5	$2^{\frac{1}{2}}$	$2^{1\frac{1}{2}}$	$4^{\frac{1}{2}}$	9^{1}	10	Guidry M	13.50

OFF AT 5:45 Start Good. Won driving. Track fast.
TIME :23^{2}, :46^{4}, 1:10^{2}, 1:35, 1:47^{2} (:23.48, :46.80, 1:10.45, 1:35.10, 1:47.55)

$2 Mutuel Prices:

9–PERFECT DRIFT	15.60	4.40	2.40
12–MINESHAFT		2.60	2.10
8–ALDEBARAN			2.20

$2 EXACTA 9–12 PAID $48.80 $2 TRIFECTA 9–12–8 PAID $117.40 $1 SUPERFECTA 9–12–8–4 PAID $636.60

B. g, by Dynaformer–Nice Gal, by Naskra. Trainer Johnson Murray W. Bred by Reed William & Stonecrest Farm (Ky).

PERFECT DRIFT, bumped at the start by CONSISTENCY when that one leaned in, settled nicely in behind the leaders three wide under light restraint, eased out five wide leaving the three furlong marker to commence his rally, caught front-running MINESHAFT a sixteenth out, gained a slight advantage, then outgamed that one the remainder under strong handling. MINESHAFT leaned in bumping lightly at the start with PROUD CITIZEN, gained a position five or six wide while in hand, accelerated suddenly leaving the backstretch to take over when asked to pick up the pace, settled into the stretch with a clear advantage, was headed by the winner at the sixteenth pole and held on stubbornly the remainder as easily second best. ALDEBARAN, within easy striking distance while four or five wide, followed PERFECT DRIFT from the outside into the stretch but couldn't threaten in the drive while improving position. CRAFTY SHAW moved to the fore inside, showed the way until the end of the backstretch, lost the edge to the winner, continued forwardly into the upper stretch and weakened. COLONIAL COLONY settled inside early, swung out six wide leaving the quarter-mile ground, loomed a factor into the final furlong but flattened out. UNBRIDLED VISION, a bit sluggish at the break, raced four or five wide to the stretch, was between foes and lacked late response. WOODMOON, outrun to the stretch, came out nine wide for the drive and improved position while unable to menace. PROUD CITIZEN, bumped lightly at the start, stalked the pace four wide, remained a factor into the upper stretch and weakened. FULL MANDATE raced near the inside most of the way and was outrun. CONSISTENCY bobbled lightly at the start and leaned in bumping the winner, moved up soon after to press front-running CRAFTY SHAW three or four wide, held on well for nearly six furlongs and tired..

Owners— 1, Stonecrest Farm; 2, Farish William S Elkins James A & W; 3, Flaxman Holdings Ltd; 4, Cella Charles J; 5, Lakeside Farms; 6, Lunsford Bruce; 7, Pabst Henry E; 8, Baker Robert C Cornstein David & Ma; 9, Fog City Stable & Padua Stable; 10, Glen Hill Farm

Trainers—1, Johnson Murray W; 2, Howard Neil J; 3, Frankel Robert; 4, Vestal Peter M; 5, Bindner Walter M Jr; 6, Mott William I; 7, O'Callaghan Niall M; 8, Lukas D Wayne; 9, Asmussen Steven M; 10, Proctor Thomas F

Scratched— Bonus Pack (1Jun03 ^{9}CD^{2}), Slider (1May03 ^{8}CD^{2})

$1 Pick Three (6–2/6–9) Paid $110.90; Pick Three Pool $77,790.
$1 Pick Four (3–6–2/6–9) Paid $234.80; Pick Four Pool $285,827.
$2 Pick Six (1–7–3–6–2/6–9) 5
Correct Paid $96.20; Pick Six Pool $18,076. $2 Pick Six (1–7–3–6–2/6–9) 6
Correct Paid $10,981.00

ELEVENTH RACE 1¹⁄₁₆ MILES. (1.41²) 52nd Running of THE LEONARD RICHARDS. Grade III. Purse $250,000.

Delaware
JUNE 14, 2003

3-year-olds. By subscription of $200 each, which shall accompany the nomination; $750 to enter and $1,000 to start. Supplemental nominations of $2,500 will be accepted at time of entry and shall include all fees.$250,000 Guaranteed, of which $150,000 to the winner, $50,000 to second, $27,500 to third, $15,000 to fourth and $7,500 to fifth. Weight: 122 lbs. Non-winners of $90,000 at a mile or over in 2003, allowed 3 lbs. $60,000 twice at a mile or over in 2003, 5 lbs. One such race 7 lbs. (Maiden and claiming races not considered). Closing Saturday, May 31.

Value of Race: $250,000 Winner $150,000; second $50,000; third $27,500; fourth $15,000; fifth $7,500. Mutuel Pool $192,079.00 Exacta Pool $128,922.00 Trifecta Pool $76,014.00 Superfecta Pool $17,431.00

Last Raced	Horse	M/Eqt. A.Wt	PP	St	¼	½	¾	Str	Fin	Jockey	Odds $1
3May03 9Aqu8	Awesome Time	L	3 115	1	4	3½	31	1hd	1hd	1no	Black A S	20.30
24May03 8Bel6	Christine's Outlaw	Lf	3 115	7	5	4hd	4hd	2hd	2½	2¾	Dominguez R A	9.90
17May03 12Pim8	Cherokee's Boy	Lb	3 122	8	1	7½	6½	4½	3³	34½	Fogelsonger R	5.00
24May03 8Bel1	Go Rockin' Robin	Lb	3 122	2	6	5¹	5hd	5½	4hd	4½	Luzzi M J	1.50
24May03 7Del2	Gimmeawink	L	3 115	3	7	6½	8	7hd	5hd	510	Madrigal R Jr	9.10
24May03 7Del4	Ironton	Lb	3 115	4	2	1hd	1hd	32½	610	68¼	Petro N J	40.80
24May03 7Del1	Don Six	L	3 115	6	8	8	7hd	8	7¹½	76	Caraballo J C	4.30
17May03 12Pim6	New York Hero	Lbf	3 122	5	3	2¹	2¹	6½	8	8	Castillo L A	3.90

OFF AT 5:30 Start Good. Won driving. Track fast.

TIME :22³, :46, 1:10³, 1:37, 1:43¹ (:22.77, :46.07, 1:10.73, 1:37.17, 1:43.26)

$2 Mutuel Prices:

2–AWESOME TIME	42.60	19.20	7.00
10–CHRISTINE'S OUTLAW		11.60	5.80
11–CHEROKEE'S BOY			4.00

$2 EXACTA 2–10 PAID $463.00 $2 TRIFECTA 2–10–11 PAID $3,081.60 $1
SUPERFECTA 2–10–11–3 PAID $6,490.10

B. c, (Feb), by Awesome Again–Slew Boyera, by Seattle Slew. Trainer Zito Nicholas P. Bred by FJFM LLC (Ky).

AWESOME TIME moved up to engage for the lead leaving the backstretch then was put to a hard drive to outfinish CHRISTINE'S OUTLAW and narrowly prevail. CHRISTINE'S OUTLAW moved up menacingly completing six furlongs to challenge for the lead then fought it out gamely to the end. CHEROKEE'S BOY moved closer leaving the far turn then lacked the needed closing response while under strong handling to best the others. GO ROCKIN' ROBIN raced within easy striking distance but lacked the needed rally. GIMMEAWINK failed to menace. IRONTON saved ground disputing the pace and weakened in the drive. DON SIX failed to threaten. NEW YORK HERO disputed the pace two abreast and tired.

Owners— 1, Lapenta Robert V; 2, R C Hill Stable; 3, Z W P Stable; 4, Herbert & Carol Schwartz; 5, Wienkowitz Walter; 6, Cunningham Timothy; 7, Generazio Patricia A; 8, Paraneck Stable

Trainers—1, Zito Nicholas P; 2, Weaver George; 3, Capuano Gary; 4, Schwartz Scott M; 5, Ritchey Tim F; 6, Petro Michael P; 7, Generazio Frank Jr; 8, Pedersen Jennifer

Scratched— Gang (17May03 5PIM1), Region Of Merit (12Apr03 9OP4), Mt. Carson (17May03 6PIM1), Lone Star Sky (26May03 7LS6)

$2 Daily Double (3–2) Paid $388.60; Daily Double Pool $7,198.
$2 Pick Three (2–3–2) Paid $3,042.60; Pick Three Pool $4,057.

Delaware Park Attendance: 6,882 Mutuel Pool: $338,229.00 F Mutuel Pool: $1,702,694.00

THIRD RACE 1¼ MILES. (Turf)(1.57³) 35th Running of THE CHARLES WHITTINGHAM HANDICAP. Grade I.

Hollywood
JUNE 14, 2003

Purse $350,000. 3-year-olds and upward. By subscription of $350 each on or before Wednesday, June 4 or by supplementary nomination of $17,500 each by Saturday, June 7. $1,750 additional to pass the entry box and $1,750 additional to start, with $210,000 to the winner, $70,000 to second, $42,000 to third, $21,000 to fourth and $7,000 to fifth. Closed June 4 with nine nominations. Rail at zero.

Value of Race: $350,000 Winner $210,000; second $70,000; third $42,000; fourth $21,000; fifth $7,000. Mutuel Pool $636,426.00 Exacta Pool $357,603.00 Quinella Pool $25,946.00

Last Raced	Horse	M/Eqt. A.Wt	PP	¼	½	¾	1	Str	Fin	Jockey	Odds $1
10May03 7Hol1	Storming Home-GB	LBbf	5 124	5	5¹	52½	5³	5³	2½	1¾	Stevens G L	0.30
21May03 7Hol1	Mister Acpen-CH	LBb	5 115	2	24½	25	2hd	2¹	31½	2½	Espinoza V	8.40
21May03 7Hol4	Cagney-BRZ	LBb	6 114	3	6	6	6	6	5hd	3¹	Smith M E	a-7.20
5Apr03 11Sun1	Night Patrol	LBb	7 114	1	11½	12	1½	11½	1hd	42	Baze T C	26.20
21Mar03 7SA1	Blue Steller-IR	LB	5 116	6	4¹	41	4hd	4hd	41	5½	Valenzuela P A	4.20
21May03 7Hol2	Gigli-BR	LB	5 115	4	3²	32½	3hd	3½	6	6	Solis A	a-7.20

a-Coupled: Cagney-BRZ and Gigli-BR.

OFF AT 2:24 Start Good. Won driving. Course firm.

TIME :24³, :48⁴, 1:13², 1:36¹, 2:00³ (:24.78, :48.91, 1:13.46, 1:36.25, 2:00.66)

$2 Mutuel Prices:

4–STORMING HOME–GB	2.60	2.20	2.10
3–MISTER ACPEN–CH		4.00	2.10
1–CAGNEY–BRZ (a-entry)			2.10

$1 EXACTA 4-3 PAID $5.90 $2 QUINELLA 3-4 PAID $9.80

B. h, by Machiavellian–Try To Catch Me, by Shareef Dancer. Trainer Drysdale Neil. Bred by Gainsborough Stud Management Ltd (GB).

STORMING HOME (GB) angled in and settled outside a rival early, bid five wide leaving the backstretch, stalked outside on the second turn, came four wide into the stretch, gained the lead three deep past midstretch and gamely prevailed under urging. MISTER ACPEN (CHI) pulled his way along to stalk the leader a bit off the rail, bid between horses leaving the backstretch, tracked a bit off the rail on the second turn, bid again between foes in the stretch and continued willingly to the wire. CAGNEY (BRZ) off a bit slowly, saved ground off the pace, came out on the second turn and three deep into the stretch and closed gamely. NIGHT PATROL took the early lead and set the pace inside, turned back bids leaving the backstretch to inch away again on the second turn, fought back a bit off the rail in the stretch but weakened some late. BLUE STELLER (IRE) pulled a bit while chasing inside, bid four wide between horses leaving the backstretch, fell back and angled in on the second turn, bid along the rail in the stretch but was outfinished. GIGLI (BRZ) saved ground off the early pace, went up three deep between horses leaving the backstretch, continued three wide into the stretch and weakened.

Owners— 1, Al Maktoum Sheik Maktoum b; 2, Noctis Stable Papiano Neil & Taub S; 3, T N T Stud; 4, Everest Stables; 5, Amerman Racing Stables; 6, T N T Stud

Trainers—1, Drysdale Neil; 2, Mulhall Kristin; 3, Mandella Richard; 4, Canani Nick; 5, Frankel Robert; 6, Mandella Richard

$2 Daily Double (1–4) Paid $6.40; Daily Double Pool $23,807.
$1 Pick Three (4–1–4) Paid $15.30; Pick Three Pool $113,864.

SIXTH RACE

Hollywood
JUNE 14, 2003

1¹⁄₁₆ MILES. (1.40) 58th Running of THE HOLLYWOOD BREEDERS' CUP OAKS. Grade II. Purse $200,000 added (includes $50,000 Breeders' Cup Fund). Fillies, 3–year–olds. By subscription of $200 each on or before Wednesday, June 4, or by supplementary nomination of $10,000 each by closing time of entries. $2,000 additional to start, with $150,000 added. Weight 123 lbs. Non–winners of $300,000 at a mile or over, allowed 2 lbs. Non–winners of $120,000 twice at a mile or over, 4 lbs. Such a race of $90,000, 6 lbs. Non–winners of two races other than maiden, claiming or starter at a mile or over, 8 lbs. One such race 10 lbs. Closed June 4 with 11 nominations.

Value of Race: $206,200 Winner $127,320; second $42,440; third $19,464; fourth $12,732; fifth $4,244. Mutuel Pool $508,606.00 Exacta Pool $300,927.00 Quinella Pool $27,154.00 Trifecta Pool $247,728.00

Last Raced	Horse	M/Eqt. A.Wt	PP	St	¼	½	¾	Str	Fin	Jockey	Odds $1
16May03 ¹⁰Pim³	Santa Catarina	LB	3 116	1	3	5	4½	44½	1½	1⁴	Stevens G L	0.80
4May03 ⁸Hol¹	Buffythecenterfold	LB	3 113	2	2	33	2hd	21	2²	2⁵	Espinoza V	3.70
26Apr03 ⁹Hol²	Princess V.	LB	3 114	4	1	11	12½	12	35	36	Valdivia J Jr	3.50
24May03 ⁸LS¹	Miss Bridget Jones	LB	3 114	5	4	2¹	3⁵	3½	46	41⁴	Smith M E	4.90
11Apr03 ¹⁰OP²	Harbor Blues	LBb	3 115	3	5	42½	5	5	5	5	Valenzuela P A	20.50

OFF AT 3:56 Start Good For All But HARBOR BLUES Won driving. Track fast.
TIME :23¹, :45⁴, 1:09², 1:35, 1:41³ (:23.32, :45.99, 1:09.52, 1:35.10, 1:41.62)

$2 Mutuel Prices:

2–SANTA CATARINA	3.60	2.40	2.10
1A–BUFFYTHECENTERFOLD		3.00	2.20
5–PRINCESS V.			2.20

$1 EXACTA 2–1 PAID $4.60 $2 QUINELLA 1–2 PAID $5.20 $1 TRIFECTA 2–1–5 PAID $10.50

B. f, (Feb), by Unbridled–Purrfectly, by Storm Cat. Trainer Baffert Bob. Bred by Dinwiddie Farm (Ky).

SANTA CATARINA settled inside then came off the rail on the backstretch, moved up outside a rival, continued outside on the second turn, bid three deep into the stretch, gained the lead in upper stretch and pulled clear under left handed urging and steady handling late. BUFFYTHECENTERFOLD stalked the leader along the inside, bid between horses into the stretch, drifted in past midstretch, could not match the winner but was clearly second best. PRINCESS V. sped to the early lead, angled in on the first turn and set the pace inside, dueled along the rail in upper stretch, then weakened but held third. MISS BRIDGET JONES pulled her way along a bit wide into the first turn, stalked off the rail then outside the runner–up, dropped back on the second turn and had little left for the stretch. HARBOR BLUES stumbled at the start, settled a bit off the rail chasing the pace, came out into the stretch and gave way.

Owners— 1, Lewis Robert B & Beverly J; 2, Brian Allen A & Stronach Stables; 3, Porter Ken V; 4, Geringer Naify & Vistas LLC; 5, Everest Stables
Trainers—1, Baffert Bob; 2, Stute Melvin F; 3, French Neil; 4, De Seroux Laura; 5, Canani Nick
Scratched— Cinema Paradisa (25May03 ¹BM¹), Dash For Money (4May03 ⁸HOL³), Ela Ela (26Apr03 ⁹HOL¹⁰)

$2 Daily Double (5–2) Paid $35.60; Daily Double Pool $34,729.
$1 Pick Three (3/4–5–2/3/6) Paid $40.50; Pick Three Pool $79,807.

EIGHTH RACE

Hollywood
JUNE 14, 2003

1¹⁄₈ MILES. (1.45¹) 50th Running of THE CALIFORNIAN. Grade II. Purse $400,000. By subscription of $400 each on or before Wednesday, June 4, or by supplementary nomination of $20,000 each by closing time of entries. With $2,000 to pass the entry box and an additional $2,000 to start, with $240,000 to the winner, $80,000 to second, $48,000 to third, $24,000 to fourth and $8,000 to fifth. Weights: 3–year–olds, 112 lbs. Older, 126 lbs. Non–winners of $220,000 three times since October 1 or four such races since February 1, 2002, allowed 2 lbs. Two such races since October 1 or three such races since February 1, 2002, 4 lbs. One such race since October 1 or two such races since February 1, 2002, 6 lbs. $75,000 twice at a mile or over since October 1 or three such races since February 1, 2002 or such a race of $110,000 in 2003, 8 lbs. Such a race of $55,000 since December 1, 2002, 10 lbs. Closed June 4 with 15 nominations.

Value of Race: $400,000 Winner $240,000; second $80,000; third $48,000; fourth $24,000; fifth $8,000. Mutuel Pool $506,895.00 Exacta Pool $293,248.00 Quinella Pool $26,008.00 Trifecta Pool $316,209.00

Last Raced	Horse	M/Eqt. A.Wt	PP	St	¼	½	¾	Str	Fin	Jockey	Odds $1
5Apr03 ¹¹OP³	Kudos	LBb	6 116	1	6	6½	7	7	41½	1½	Solis A	1.90
10May03 ⁸Hol³	Piensa Sonando–CH	LBb	5 118	4	7	7	5½	3hd	32½	21½	Stevens G L	a–5.20
26May03 ⁸BM¹	Reba's Gold	LBb	6 118	3	1	2hd	2hd	42½	2hd	31½	Flores D R	8.30
3May03 ⁸Hol¹	Gondolieri–CH	LBb	4 118	2	2	41½	4½	2½	1hd	42½	Alvarado F T	a–5.30
10May03 ⁸Hol²	Fleetstreet Dancer	LBb	5 116	7	5	5³	62½	6³	5½	5²	Baze T C	10.50
16May03 ¹¹Pim²	Western Pride	LB	5 118	5	3	11	1¹	1½	6⁵	6⁴	Valenzuela P A	1.20
10May03 ⁸Hol⁵	Wooden Phone	LBb	6 116	6	4	3²	32½	5hd	7	7	Nakatani C S	17.70

a–Coupled: Piensa Sonando–CH and Gondolieri–CH.

OFF AT 4:54 Start Good. Won driving. Track fast.
TIME :23¹, :46³, 1:10³, 1:35, 1:47⁴ (:23.32, :46.76, 1:10.65, 1:35.08, 1:47.91)

$2 Mutuel Prices:

2–KUDOS	5.80	3.40	4.60
1A–PIENSA SONANDO–CH (a–entry)		4.80	5.20
3–REBA'S GOLD			7.40

$1 EXACTA 2–1 PAID $14.00 $2 QUINELLA 1–2 PAID $15.80 $1 TRIFECTA 2–1–3 PAID $64.60

B. g, by Kris S.–Souq, by Damascus. Trainer Mandella Richard. Bred by Mr & Mrs J S Moss (Ky).

KUDOS unhurried inside then a bit off the rail, swung out into the stretch and closed gamely under left handed urging to be along in time. PIENSA SONANDO (CHI) settled outside a rival, advanced four wide on the backstretch and into the second turn, dueled three deep into the stretch, put a head in front in deep stretch but could not hold off the winner. REBA'S GOLD stalked the early pace off the rail then angled in on the first turn, bid inside into and on the second turn and into the stretch, gained a short lead past the eighth pole and held third. GONDOLIERI (CHI) pulled his way along inside and steadied off heels into the first turn and again on that bend, bid three deep between horses leaving the backstretch, dueled between foes into the stretch, briefly led in midstretch but weakened. FLEETSTREET DANCER pulled his way along off the rail early, angled in on the backstretch, went around a rival on the second turn, found the rail into the stretch and lacked the needed rally. WESTERN PRIDE had speed three deep while pulling a bit, angled in on the lead, set the pace off the rail, dueled between horses on the second turn, took up sharply between foes leaving that bend and weakened. WOODEN PHONE stalked off the rail then outside a rival, dropped back and angled in on the second turn and had little left. The stewards conducted an inquiry into the incident leaving the second turn but made no change when they found the videotape failed to establish responsibility for the trouble.

Owners— 1, Moss Mr & Mrs Jerome S; 2, Hunt Nelson B; 3, Creston Farms; 4, Hunt Nelson B; 5, Leatherman Lee & Ty; 6, Chapman Carolyn & McArthur Theresa; 7, Durant Tom Helzer Marilyn & James E
Trainers—1, Mandella Richard; 2, McAnally Ronald; 3, Hendricks Dan L; 4, McAnally Ronald; 5, O'Neill Doug; 6, Chapman James K; 7, Baffert Bob
Scratched— Calkins Road (2Nov02 ⁸SA¹)

$2 Daily Double (6–2) Paid $90.00; Daily Double Pool $29,775.
$1 Pick Three (2/3/6–6–2) Paid $91.90; Pick Three Pool $125,515.

TENTH RACE

Monmouth

JUNE 14, 2003

1¹⁄₁₆ MILES. (1.40¹) 56th Running of THE OCEANPORT HANDICAP. Grade III. Purse $100,000. 3-year-olds and upward. By subscription of $100 each, which should accompany the nomination. $1,500 to enter. The winner to receive $60,000; $20,000 to second; $11,000 to third; $6,000 to fourth; $3,000 to fifth. Weights Sunday, June 8. This race will not be divided. Starters to be named through the entry box by the usual time of closing. High weights preferred. Nominations closed Saturday, May 31. (Rail at 0 Feet). (ORIGINALLY SCHEDULED FOR TURF.)

Value of Race: $100,000 Winner $60,000; second $20,000; third $11,000; fourth $6,000; fifth $3,000. Mutuel Pool $142,777.00 Exacta Pool $126,555.00 Trifecta Pool $77,255.00

Last Raced	Horse	M/Eqt. A.Wt	PP	St	¼	½	¾	Str	Fin	Jockey	Odds $1
24May03 ¹⁰Mth³	Runspastum	Lb 6 113	5	6	6	5¹½	4½	3⁴	1¹¾	Pimentel J	9.20
16May03 ¹¹Pim⁹	Balto Star	Lf 5 119	1	1	2hd	2hd	2²½	1hd	2¹	Velez J A Jr	2.00
24May03 ¹⁰Mth²	Saint Verre	L 5 118	2	2	1½	1½	1½	2½	35½	Lopez C C	2.60
6Jun03 ⁸Bel¹	Short Hair	L 4 114	6	5	5hd	6	6	5⁸	42¾	King E L Jr	f–26.40
5Apr03 ⁹GP⁴	Burning Roma	L 5 119	4	4	43½	43½	3¹	4¹	517¼	Bravo J	1.50
9Mar03 ¹⁰GP⁹	Private Ryan	Lf 6 114	3	3	35	34½	54	6	6	Rose J	12.00

f–Mutuel Field: Short Hair.

OFF AT 5:05 Start Good. Won driving. Track fast.

TIME :22⁴, :45¹, 1:09³, 1:35³, 1:42¹ (:22.80, :45.32, 1:09.76, 1:35.79, 1:42.31)

$2 Mutuel Prices:	11–RUNSPASTUM	20.40	7.20	4.00
	3–BALTO STAR		3.60	3.00
	5–SAINT VERRE			3.60

$2 EXACTA 11–3 PAID $107.00 $2 TRIFECTA 11–3–5 PAID $291.80

B. h, by Woodman–Erandel, by Danzig. Trainer Goldberg Alan E. Bred by Calumet Farm (Ky).

RUNSPASTUM raced unhurriedly inside, rallied angling three wide around the pacesetters leaving the final turn, advanced steadily to take the lead a sixteenth out then drew clear the final seventy yards. BALTO STAR rated close in the three path, contested the final turn, dueled gamely with a short lead to the sixteenth pole and was outfinished from there. SAINT VERRE rated the pace just off the rail, dueled gamely from the top of the stretch then yielded the final sixteenth. SHORT HAIR, unhurriedly, made a mild inside bid through the final turn and finished evenly off the rail. BURNING ROMA kept off the pace in mid track, bid five wide into the final turn then came up empty in the drive. PRIVATE RYAN rated close in the four path then faded through the final turn.

Owners— 1, Jayeff B Stables; 2, Anstu Stables; 3, Allen Joseph; 4, Pompa Paul P Jr; 5, Queen Harold L; 6, Gill Michael J

Trainers— 1, Goldberg Alan E; 2, Pletcher Todd A; 3, Jerkens H Allen; 4, Araya Rene A; 5, Giglio Heather A; 6, Shuman Mark

Scratched— French Charmer (10Apr03 ⁷GP¹), Sardaukar (17May03 ¹⁰PIM3), Tam's Terms (3May03 ⁹PIM¹), Strategic Partner (17May03 ¹⁰PIM⁶), Political Attack (11Apr03 ⁸KEE⁸), Autonomy (19Apr03 ⁷KEE⁴), Union One (4May03 ⁸AQU³), Patrol (3May03 ⁹CD³), Trademark (10Apr03 NAS⁴).

$2 Pick Three (2–1–11) Paid $182.60; Pick Three Pool $5,483.

NINTH RACE

Belmont

JUNE 21, 2003

1¹⁄₁₆ MILES. (1.39²) 35th Running of THE OGDEN PHIPPS HANDICAP. Grade I. Purse $300,000. (Up to $42,200 NYSBFOA). FILLIES AND MARES THREE YEARS OLD AND UPWARD. By subscription of $300 each, which should accompany the nomination; $1,500 to pass the entry box and $1,500 to start. The purse to be divided 60% to the winner, 20% to second, 11% to third, 6% to fourth and 3% to fifth. Trophies will be presented to the winning owner, trainer and jockey. Closed Saturday, June 7, 2003 with 18 Nominations.

Value of Race: $300,000 Winner $180,000; second $60,000; third $33,000; fourth $18,000; fifth $9,000. Mutuel Pool $628,608.00 Exacta Pool $509,844.00

Last Raced	Horse	M/Eqt. A.Wt	PP	St	¼	½	¾	Str	Fin	Jockey	Odds $1
3May03 ⁸CD¹	Sightseek	L 4 114	2	4	22½	2½	2¹	11½	1⁵	Bailey J D	1.05
5Apr03 ⁸OP²	Take Charge Lady	L 4 119	3	2	1½	1½	1hd	23½	2⁵	Prado E S	1.65
16May03 ⁸Pim¹	Mandy's Gold	Lf 5 118	1	5	4⁷	4⁷	46	34½	31¾	Migliore R	6.80
17May03 ⁸Bel²	Smok'n Frolic	L 4 118	5	1	35	33½	3½	4³	41¾	Velazquez J R	5.90
30May03 ⁸Bel¹	Lady Liberty	L 4 114	4	3	5	5	5	5	5	Santos J A	24.00

OFF AT 5:12 Start Good. Won driving. Track sloppy.

TIME :22², :45¹, 1:09¹, 1:34¹, 1:40⁴ (:22.52, :45.30, 1:09.35, 1:34.34, 1:40.89)

$2 Mutuel Prices:	2–SIGHTSEEK	4.10	2.60	2.10
	3–TAKE CHARGE LADY		2.40	2.10
	1–MANDY'S GOLD			2.10

$2 EXACTA 2–3 PAID $9.00

Ch. f, by Distant View–Viviana, by Nureyev. Trainer Frankel Robert. Bred by Juddmonte Farms, Inc. (Ky).

SIGHTSEEK showed good speed along the inside, was angled out on the backstretch, pressed TAKE CHARGE LADY from the outside, responded when roused turning for home and drew clear under a drive. TAKE CHARGE LADY set the pace along the inside while in hand, could not stay with the winner in upper stretch and continued on to be clearly best of the others. MANDY'S GOLD was outrun early, put in a run along the inside on the turn, angled out in upper stretch and had little left for the drive. SMOK'N FROLIC raced with the pace while three wide and tired in the stretch. LADY LIBERTY dropped back early, raced inside and had no rally.

Owners— 1, Juddmonte Farms Inc; 2, Select Stable; 3, Steeplechase Farm; 4, Dogwood Stable; 5, Janney III Stuart S

Trainers— 1, Frankel Robert; 2, McPeek Kenneth G; 3, Gorham Michael E; 4, Pletcher Todd A; 5, McGaughey Claude III

$2 Daily Double (6–2) Paid $8.50; Daily Double Pool $223,499.
$2 Pick Three (6–6–2) Paid $72.00; Pick Three Pool $135,795.
$2 Pick Four (5–6–6–2) Paid $605.00; Pick Four Pool $203,446.
$2 Pick Six (6–6–5–6–6–2) 6
Correct Paid $2,148.00; Pick Six Pool $93,110. $2 Pick Six (6–6–5–6–6–2) 5
Correct Paid $29.60

Belmont Park Attendance: N/A Total Mutual Pool: N/A

NINTH RACE
Churchill
JUNE 21, 2003

6½ FURLONGS. (1.14^{1}) 15th Running of THE ARISTIDES HANDICAP. Grade III. Purse $100,000 Added. THREE-YEAR-OLDS AND UPWARD. By subscription of $100 each on or before June 7, 2003 or by Supplementary Nomination of $5,000 each by the closing of entries Friday, June 13, 2003. $500 to pass the entry box; $500 additional to start, with $100,000 added of which 62% of all monies to the owner of the winner, 20% to second, 10% to third, 5% to fourth and 3% to fifth. Weights to be announced Saturday, June 14. Starters to be named through the entry box at the usual time of closing. Closed Saturday, June 7, 2003 with 20 nominations. Trophy to winning owner.

Value of Race: $109,000 Winner $67,580; second $21,800; third $10,900; fourth $5,450; fifth $3,270. Mutuel Pool $417,646.00 Exacta Pool $272,298.00 Trifecta Pool $218,970.00 Superfecta Pool $53,596.00

Last Raced	Horse	M/Eqt.	A.	Wt	PP	St	¼	½	Str	Fin	Jockey	Odds $1
3May03 $^{5}CD^{10}$	Mountain General	Lb	5	116	2	7	7	$6\frac{1}{2}$	6^{3}	1^{hd}	Lanerie C J	10.20
10Apr03 $^{10}OP^{1}$	Beau's Town	L	5	123	3	2	$2^{1\frac{1}{2}}$	$2^{\frac{1}{2}}$	$1^{\frac{1}{2}}$	2^{nk}	Theriot H J II	1.60
26May03 $^{8}LS^{5}$	Pass Rush	Lb	4	118	1	4	4^{1}	4^{1}	3^{hd}	$3^{\frac{3}{4}}$	Melancon L	3.80
23May03 $^{9}CD^{2}$	Strength And Honor	L	4	114	4	3	1^{hd}	1^{hd}	$2^{1\frac{1}{2}}$	$4^{\frac{1}{2}}$	Velasquez C	3.20
23May03 $^{9}CD^{1}$	Twilight Road	L	6	116	6	5	5^{4}	5^{1}	4^{hd}	$5^{1\frac{1}{4}}$	Day P	5.20
1May03 $^{8}CD^{2}$	Slider	Lb	5	113	7	1	3^{hd}	3^{1}	5^{hd}	$6^{4\frac{1}{4}}$	Court J K	12.00
3May03 $^{4}CD^{1}$	Trion Georgia	Lf	5	114	5	6	6^{hd}	7	7	7	Borel C H	18.90

OFF AT 5:32 Start Good. Won driving. Track fast.
TIME :22^{4}, :45^{4}, 1:09^{3}, 1:16 (:22.94, :45.83, 1:09.73, 1:16.01)

$2 Mutuel Prices:

2-MOUNTAIN GENERAL	22.40	7.60	4.40
3-BEAU'S TOWN		3.40	2.80
1-PASS RUSH			3.20

$2 EXACTA 2-3 PAID $64.20 $2 TRIFECTA 2-3-1 PAID $298.20 $1 SUPERFECTA 2-3-1-4 PAID $602.90

Dk. b. or br. g, by Mountain Cat-Tulira, by General Assembly. Trainer Asmussen Steven M. Bred by Curtis Green (Ky).

MOUNTAIN GENERAL settled near the inside early, was three wide around the turn, came five wide to find an opening in the upper stretch, was steadied at the three-sixteenths pole and bumped with TWILIGHT ROAD, angled to the rail in the final sixteenth and closed determinedly under pressure to be along in time. BEAU'S TOWN contested the pace at once while inside of STRENGTH AND HONOR, alternated for the advantage with that one, gained the edge at the furlong grounds, then held on stubbornly only to be outfinished. PASS RUSH, well placed near the inside from the beginning, edged closer approaching the stretch, lacked room at the three-sixteenths pole, came out between foes four wide, bumped lightly with SLIDER, was going well at the end but wasn't good enough. STRENGTH AND HONOR went up early to battle for the lead outside of BEAU'S TOWN, alternated for the lead with that one, battled gamely into the final furlong and weakened grudgingly. TWILIGHT ROAD, never far back while racing in behind horses three or four wide, was asked for his best entering the upper stretch, leaned in tightening it up on the winner leaving the three-sixteenths pole, then couldn't produce a final account. SLIDER angled in a bit early to track the dueling leaders four wide, raced within easy striking distance into the final furlong, was bumped lightly by PASS RUSH when that one advanced between foes, then flattened out late. TRION GEORGIA raced six wide on the backstretch and much of the way, lacked a closing account.

Owners— 1, Asmussen Keith A; 2, David Hulkewicz & Coast To Coast Ra; 3, Tabor Michael B; 4, Requiem Racing; 5, Donamire Farm; 6, Hays Billy; 7, Bohanon Pat & Jim

Trainers—1, Asmussen Steven M; 2, Norman Cole; 3, Byrne Patrick B; 4, Simon Charles; 5, McGee Paul J; 6, Woodard Joe; 7, O'Connor Robert R II

$1 Pick Three (4-4-2) Paid $611.60; Pick Three Pool $45,308.

EIGHTH RACE
Hollywood
JUNE 21, 2003

1⅛ MILES. (1.45^{1}) 62nd Running of THE VANITY HANDICAP. Grade I. Purse $250,000. FILLIES AND MARES THREE YEARS OLD AND UPWARD. By subscription of $250 each on or before Wednesday, June 11 or by supplementary nomination of $12,500 each by 3:00 pm Saturday, June 14. $1,000 to pass the entry box and an additional $1,500 to start. Closed Wedensday June 11 with 10 nominations. (NO SHOW WAGERING.)

Value of Race: $250,000 Winner $150,000; second $50,000; third $30,000; fourth $15,000; fifth $5,000. Mutuel Pool $1,145,573.0 Exacta Pool $311,401.00 Quinella Pool $23,556.00 Trifecta Pool $344,169.00

Last Raced	Horse	M/Eqt.	A.	Wt	PP	St	¼	½	¾	Str	Fin	Jockey	Odds $1
24May03 $^{8}Hol^{1}$	Azeri	LB	5	127	6	3	2^{1}	1^{hd}	2^{2}	1^{1}	1^{2}	Smith M E	0.30
22May03 $^{7}Hol^{1}$	Sister Girl Blues	LBf	4	111	3	4	$1^{\frac{1}{2}}$	2^{1}	1^{hd}	2^{2}	$2^{\frac{1}{2}}$	Almeida G F	12.40
26Apr03 $^{8}Haw^{1}$	Bare Necessities	LB	4	118	5	6	4^{hd}	$3^{\frac{1}{2}}$	$3^{1\frac{1}{2}}$	$3^{2\frac{1}{2}}$	$3^{4\frac{1}{2}}$	Solis A	a-2.70
24May03 $^{8}Hol^{3}$	Tropical Blossom	LBb	5	110	1	1	3^{1}	$5^{1\frac{1}{2}}$	5^{4}	4^{3}	4^{6}	Baze T C	34.80
24May03 $^{8}Hol^{4}$	Keys To The Heart	LB	4	115	4	5	5^{1}	4^{hd}	$4^{\frac{1}{2}}$	5^{2}	5^{1}	Valdivia J Jr	49.90
25May03 $^{6}Hol^{6}$	Meguial-ARG	LB	4	110	7	2	7	7	7	6^{5}	6^{10}	Martinez F F	37.30
29May03 $^{2}Hol^{5}$	American Czarina	LBb	5	112	2	7	$6^{2\frac{1}{2}}$	6^{6}	$6^{2\frac{1}{2}}$	7	7	Espinoza V	a-2.70

a-Coupled: Bare Necessities and American Czarina.

OFF AT 4:54 Start Good. Won driving. Track fast.
TIME :23^{4}, :47^{1}, 1:10^{3}, 1:35^{1}, 1:48^{2} (:23.86, :47.31, 1:10.66, 1:35.32, 1:48.48)

$2 Mutuel Prices:

5-AZERI	2.60	2.10	—
3-SISTER GIRL BLUES		2.10	—
1A-BARE NECESSITIES (a-entry)		—	—

$1 EXACTA 5-3 PAID $6.30 $2 QUINELLA 3-5 PAID $11.00 $1 TRIFECTA 5-3-1 PAID $10.00

Ch. m, by Jade Hunter-Zodiac Miss*Aus, by Ahonoora. Trainer De Seroux Laura. Bred by Allen E Paulson (Ky).

AZERI bumped after the start, pulled her way up alongside SISTER GIRL BLUES to press the pace, alternated in front outside that one while dueling for the lead, regained the advantage into the stretch and inched away under some urging and good handling. SISTER GIRL BLUES sped between horses to the early lead, angled in and dueled inside the winner, fought back on the second turn and into the stretch, could not match that one but gamely held second. BARE NECESSITIES bumped between horses after the start, stalked three deep then off the rail on the second turn and was edged for the place. TROPICAL BLOSSOM pulled early and was in tight off heels on the first turn, stalked inside, dropped back some on the second turn and lacked a further response. KEYS TO THE HEART bumped after the start, chased off the rail then between horses, continued outside a rival on the second turn and weakened. MEGUIAL (ARG) pulled hard when off the rail into the first turn, angled in on the backstretch, came out into the stretch and did not rally. AMERICAN CZARINA brushed the gate at the start, chased inside then off the rail, dropped back on the second turn, gave way and was not persevered with late.

Owners— 1, Allen E Paulson Living Trust; 2, Everest Stables; 3, Iron County Farms Inc; 4, Wygod Mr & Mrs Martin J; 5, Nichols Thomas L; 6, David J Lanzman Racing Stable; 7, Conway Horizon Stable Iron County F

Trainers—1, De Seroux Laura; 2, Knight Terry; 3, Dollase Wallace; 4, Canani Julio C; 5, Greely C Beau; 6, O'Neill Doug; 7, Dollase Wallace

$2 Daily Double (2-5) Paid $37.00; Daily Double Pool $41,916.
$1 Pick Three (1-2-5) Paid $92.30; Pick Three Pool $83,498.

FOURTEENTH RACE

Thistledown
JUNE 21, 2003

1⅛ MILES. (1.47²) 69th Running of THE OHIO DERBY. Grade II. Purse $300,000 (plus $6,300 OTF – Ohio Thoroughbred Fund) FOR THREE-YEAR-OLDS. By subscription of $300 by Monday June 9, 2003, Supplementary nominations accepted to the Ohio Derby of $10,000 due Tuesday June 17, 2003,$ 2,000 to enter and $1,000 additional to start. Weight: 124 lbs. Non-Winners of $100,000 twice at a mile or over in 2003 allowed 3 lbs; of $100,000 at a mile or over in 2003; 6 lbs; of $100,000 at any distance 9 lbs; of $50,000 at any distance 12 lbs. (Maiden, Claiming, Optional or Starter not considered in weight allowances) The Ohio Derby will be limited to fourteen starters, in the event more than fourteen entries pass the entry box by 10:30 A. M. EST, June 18, 2003, preference will be given to those horses having accumulated the highest lifetime earnings at the time of closing entries.

Value of Race: $300,000 Winner $180,000; second $60,000; third $30,000; fourth $15,000; fifth $9,000; sixth $6,000. Mutuel Pool $362,961.00
Exacta Pool $211,448.00   Trifecta Pool $193,057.00 Superfecta Pool $70,267.00

Last Raced	Horse	M/Eqt. A.Wt	PP	St	¼	½	¾	Str	Fin	Jockey	Odds $1
25May03 2CD1	Wild And Wicked	3 114	6	5	2¹	2¹	2¹	2⁴	13¼	Sellers S J	1.10
31May03 6RD1	Hackendiffy	L 3 112	3	2	11½	12½	1½	1hd	22½	Rowland M F	15.60
17May03 12Pim2	Midway Road	L 3 114	2	4	5hd	5½	4¹	3¹	32¼	Albarado R J	1.30
26May03 7LS1	Crowned King	L 3 121	4	3	4hd	66	51½	4½	4no	Rennie C R	13.40
30May03 7Bel1	Private City	3 112	1	1	3½	31½	3½	5²	56	Samyn J L	5.30
26May03 7LS4	On The Border	L 3 113	5	6	65	4½	6¹⁰	6¹²	617¾	Meche L J	25.70
31May03 9Mnr1	Miss Karry Thenews	L 3 112	7	7	7	7	7	7	7	Garcia F	70.20

OFF AT 5:30 Start Good. Won ridden out. Track fast.
TIME :23⁴, :48³, 1:13, 1:37³, 1:50 (:23.98, :48.62, 1:13.04, 1:37.70, 1:50.08)

$2 Mutuel Prices:

6-WILD AND WICKED	4.20	3.60	2.20
3-HACKENDIFFY		7.20	2.60
2-MIDWAY ROAD			2.10

$2 EXACTA 6-3 PAID $65.40 $2 TRIFECTA 6-3-2 PAID $134.40 $2
SUPERFECTA 6-3-2-4 PAID $668.00

Dk. b. or br. c, (Jan), by Wild Again–Wicked Witchcraft, by Good Behaving. Trainer McPeek Kenneth G. Bred by Mr & Mrs Robert David Randal (Ky).

WILD AND WICKED went up to chased the pacesetting HACKENDIFFY soon after the start while to his outside, drew to his flank on the middle of the second turn, gave a length and one-half then came on again to gain the advantage inside the eighth pole then drew clear under a brisk hand ride. HACKENDIFFY hit the side of the gate at the start, made the lead a few jumps thereafter, sprinted to a clear lead, made the pace to the eighth pole while setting sift fractions, could not handle the winner but was clearly second best. MIDWAY ROAD checked hard on the first turn, while behind PRIVATE CITY and in a box, was allowed to settle, offered a bid on the second turn then finished evenly. CROWNED KING close up around the first, gave up some ground down the backstretch, came on again on the second turn then faded. PRIVATE CITY close up, offered a mild bid on the second turn then flattened out. ON THE BORDER was through after a half. MISS KARRY THENEWS trailed throughout.

Owners— 1, Randal Mr & Mrs R David; 2, Eigel David; 3, Farish William S; 4, McKeever Racing Stable; 5, Bohemia Stable; 6, Nelson James E; 7, Price Kathleen A
Trainers—1, McPeek Kenneth G; 2, Flint Bernard S; 3, Howard Neil J; 4, McKeever Billy C Jr; 5, Jerkens H Allen; 6, Asmussen Steven M; 7, Price Kathleen A

THIRD RACE

Hollywood
JUNE 22, 2003

1¹⁄₁₆ MILES. (1.40) 25th Running of THE AFFIRMED HANDICAP. Grade III. Purse $100,000 added. 3-year-olds. By subscription of $100 each on or before Wednesday, June 11 or by supplementary nomination of $5,000 each by Saturday, June 14. $1,000 additional to start. Closed June 11 with 12 nominations.

Value of Race: $103,096 Winner $63,120; second $21,040; third $12,624; fourth $6,312. Mutuel Pool $362,705.00 Exacta Pool $231,053.00
Quinella Pool $19,522.00

Last Raced	Horse	M/Eqt. A.Wt	PP	St	¼	½	¾	Str	Fin	Jockey	Odds $1
3May03 10CD5	Eye Of The Tiger	LB 3 119	4	3	3¹½	35	35	11½	14½	Solis A	0.90
19Apr03 8Kee5	Ministers Wild Cat	LB 3 118	1	4	1²	11½	11	2²	2nk	Espinoza V	2.20
4Jun03 7Ho16	Bullistic	LBb 3 115	2	1	22½	2²	2½	33	31½	Valenzuela P A	7.50
3May03 10CD7	Outta Here	LB 3 119	3	2	4	4	4	4	4	Baze T C	3.00

OFF AT 2:24 Start Good. Won driving. Track fast.
TIME :23², :47, 1:10⁴, 1:35⁴, 1:42¹ (:23.56, :47.07, 1:10.91, 1:35.90, 1:42.30)

$2 Mutuel Prices:

4-EYE OF THE TIGER	3.80	2.40	—
1-MINISTERS WILD CAT		2.80	—
2-BULLISTIC			—

$1 EXACTA 4-1 PAID $3.70 $2 QUINELLA 1-4 PAID $5.20

B. c, (Apr), by American Chance–Dial a Trick, by Phone Trick. Trainer Hollendorfer Jerry. Bred by John D Gunther (Ky).

EYE OF THE TIGER chased off the rail on the first turn and backstretch, angled in and bid inside on the second turn, took a short lead nearing the quarter pole, came a bit off the rail into the stretch, kicked clear under urging and was under steady handling late. MINISTERS WILD CAT off a bit awkwardly, sped to the early lead, set the pace inside, came a bit off the rail into the second turn, shook off BULLISTIC then battled inside the winner leaving that turn, was no match for the latter in the stretch and just held second. BULLISTIC stalked the pace off the rail, bid outside the runner-up into the second turn, fell back some on that bend, went three deep into the stretch and was coming back on at MINISTERS WILD CAT late. OUTTA HERE angled in and saved ground off the pace, came out in midstretch and was not a threat.

Owners— 1, Gunther John D; 2, Cowan Marjorie & Irving M; 3, Moss Mr & Mrs Jerome S; 4, Currin William L & Eisman Alvin
Trainers—1, Hollendorfer Jerry; 2, Drysdale Neil; 3, Shirreffs John; 4, Currin William L

$2 Daily Double (1–4) Paid $59.20; Daily Double Pool $26,940.
$1 Pick Three (1–1–4) Paid $105.60; Pick Three Pool $117,405.

EIGHTH RACE

Arlington

JUNE 28, 2003

1 1/16 MILES. (Turf)(1.41) 69th Running of THE ARLINGTON CLASSIC. Grade II. Purse $175,000. 3-year-olds. By subscription of $300 each horse (Early) April 2, 2003, $500 each horse (Late) on June 11, 2003. Fee to accompany the nomination. A Supplementary Nomination of $7,000 may be made on June 25, 2003, which includes entry and starting fees. Original nominees to pay $1,250 to pass entry box and $1,250 additional to start, with $175,000 Guaranteed. Weight, 126 lbs. Non-winners of $100,000 twice at 1 mile or over in 2003, allowed 3 lbs. $55,000 twice at 1 mile or over in 2003, 5 lbs. $55,000 once at a mile or over in 2003, 7 lbs. $40,000 at a mile or over anytime, 10 lbs.

Value of Race: $175,000 Winner $105,000; second $35,000; third $19,250; fourth $10,500; fifth $5,250. Mutuel Pool $503,137.00 Exacta Pool $334,151.00 Trifecta Pool $260,302.00 Superfecta Pool $66,112.00

Last Raced	Horse	M/Eqt.	A.Wt	PP	St	1/4	1/2	3/4	Str	Fin	Jockey	Odds $1
17May03 7Bel1	Lismore Knight	L	3 119	2	3	2hd	41	4 1/2	3 1/2	1 3/4	Douglas R R	2.20
7Jun03 9CD2	Remind	L	3 116	6	2	1 1/2	12	11	1 1/2	2 1/2	Velasquez C	2.60
25May03 Cur2	Good Day Too-IR		3 116	3	5	3hd	3 1/2	2hd	22	31 1/2	Bourque C C	7.00
8Jun03 8AP5	Scottago	L	3 116	8	8	95	96	910	86	4no	Marquez C H Jr	36.60
7Jun03 9CD3	Rapid Proof	Lb	3 119	10	9	83	81 1/2	71	7hd	5 1/4	Borel C H	11.00
31May03 7CD6	Ontario	L	3 116	4	4	76	6hd	61	5 1/2	6 3/4	Sibille R	28.50
8Jun03 8AP4	Distinguishable	Lb	3 116	7	1	4 1/2	2hd	3 1/2	4 1/2	7nk	Lopez U A	95.60
8Jun03 8AP3	Herculated	L	3 116	9	7	5 1/2	51	54	6 1/2	88 1/2	Lovato F Jr	17.50
26May03 7LS10	Lone Star Deputy	L	3 121	1	6	6hd	74	8 1/2	910	94	Laviolette B S	64.70
11May03 Leo1	European-IR	L	3 116	5	10	10	10	10	10	10	Sellers S J	2.60

OFF AT 4:28 Start Good For All But EUROPEAN (IRE). Won driving. Course firm.

TIME :241, :484, 1:123, 1:362, 1:423 (:24.32, :48.86, 1:12.60, 1:36.58, 1:42.73)

$2 Mutuel Prices:

2-LISMORE KNIGHT	6.40	3.00	2.60
6-REMIND		3.60	2.80
3-GOOD DAY TOO-IR			3.20

$2 EXACTA 2-6 PAID $21.20 $2 TRIFECTA 2-6-3 PAID $107.60 $2 SUPERFECTA 2-6-3-8 PAID $1,101.80

B. c, (Jan), by Woodman-Lismore Lady, by Ogygian. Trainer Pletcher Todd A. Bred by Bon Marche Wallace (Ky).

LISMORE KNIGHT raced close up along the rail while tracking the leaders, angled out for the stretch run, accelerated in the final furlong and was along in the closing strides. REMIND sprinted to a clear early lead, settled in along the rail with the advantage, turned back a bid from GOOD DAY TOO (IRE) in the stretch then just failed to last in a game effort. GOOD DAY TOO (IRE) raced close up between rivals made a run for the lead in the stretch but could not finish with the top two. SCOTTAGO was void of early speed just outside then finished well with a belated bid that fell short. RAPID PROOF lacked speed and improved his position without threatening. ONTARIO failed to reach a contending position and was not a factor. DISTINGUISHABLE raced close up off the rail and tired in the final eighth. HERCULATED raced near the middle of the field and gave way. LONE STAR DEPUTY saved ground near the middle of the track but tired. EUROPEAN (IRE) proved very difficult to load, broke slowly and trailed throughout.

Owners— 1, J J Pletcher; 2, Claiborne Farm; 3, Gilbert Ross S; 4, Jer-Mar Stable; 5, Morrison Dolphus; 6, Pabst Henry E; 7, Inman Virginia; 8, Oak Crest Farm; 9, Coast To Coast Racing Fund; 10, Team Valor Stables.

Trainers—1, Pletcher Todd A; 2, Mott William I; 3, Stack Tommy; 4, Robertson Hugh H; 5, Wiggins Hal R; 6, O'Callaghan Niall M; 7, Livesay Charlie; 8, Stidham Michael; 9, Calhoun William Bret; 10, Walden W Elliott.

$1 Pick Three (6-10-2) Paid $40.00; Pick Three Pool $12,763.

SEVENTH RACE

Belmont

JUNE 28, 2003

5 1/2 FURLONGS. (1.022) 111th Running of THE TREMONT. Grade III. Purse $100,000. (Up to $19,400 NYSBFOA). TWO YEAR OLDS. By subscription of $100 each, which should accompany the nomination; $500 to pass the entry box; $500 to start with $100,000 added. The added money and all fees to be divided 60% to the winner, 20% to second, 11% to third, 6% to fourth and 3% to fifth. 118 lbs. Non-winners of $35,000 allowed 2 lbs.; a race other than maiden or claiming, 4 lbs. Trophies will be presented to the winning owner, trainer and jockey. Closed Saturday, June 14, 2003 with 27 Nominations.

Value of Race: $110,200 Winner $66,120; second $22,040; third $12,122; fourth $6,612; fifth $3,306. Mutuel Pool $586,400.00 Exacta Pool $528,752.00 Trifecta Pool $399,504.00

Last Raced	Horse	M/Eqt.	A.Wt	PP	St	1/4	3/8	Str	Fin	Jockey	Odds $1
3May03 6CD4	Heckle	L	2 114	6	4	1 1/2	1 1/2	16	13 1/4	Velazquez J R	2.95
31May03 6CD1	Adage		2 114	3	2	5 1/2	63 1/2	33 1/2	21	Prado E S	9.00
6Jun03 7Bel2	Hasslefree		2 114	1	1	2hd	31 1/2	21 1/2	36 1/4	Santos J A	11.10
23May03 3Bel1	Pretty Wild Again	L	2 114	5	3	42 1/2	42 1/2	4 1/2	43 1/2	Chavez J F	3.35
3May03 6CD6	Korsakoff	L	2 114	2	6	62 1/2	5hd	63 1/2	51 1/2	Coa E M	34.25
24May03 1CD1	Best To Be King	L	2 114	7	7	32 1/2	2hd	52 1/2	61 1/2	Bailey J D	1.20
8Jun03 5Pim1	Snow Eagle	L	2 114	4	5	7	7	7	7	Wilson R	37.25

OFF AT 4:12 Start Good. Won driving. Track fast.

TIME :221, :453, :574, 1:043 (:22.24, :45.64, :57.96, 1:04.70)

$2 Mutuel Prices:

1A-HECKLE	7.90	4.90	3.70
4-ADAGE		8.30	5.10
2-HASSLEFREE			5.30

$2 EXACTA 1-4 PAID $61.50 $2 TRIFECTA 1-4-2 PAID $285.00

Gr/ro c, (Jan), by Hennessy-Bid Me Adieu, by Spectacular Bid. Trainer Pletcher Todd A. Bred by Gaines-Gentry Thoroughbreds & Orpendale (Ky).

HECKLE flashed good speed from the outside, soon opened a clear lead, drew away when roused and remained well clear under a drive. ADAGE was bumped after the start, raced inside and finished gamely on the rail. HASSLEFREE was bumped after the start, chased the pace along the inside and weakened in the stretch. PRETTY WILD AGAIN was steadied while between rivals entering the turn, chased the pace while three wide and tired in the stretch. KORSAKOFF was pinched back at the start, raced wide and tired in the stretch. BEST TO BE KING was hustled outside, chased the pace and was finished early. SNOW EAGLE dropped back early and was outrun.

Owners— 1, Dogwood Stable; 2, Overbrook Farm William T Young & Ar; 3, Lewis Robert B & Beverly J; 4, Robsham Einar P; 5, Tabor Michael B; 6, Oak Cliff Stable; 7, Gill Michael J

Trainers—1, Pletcher Todd A; 2, Lukas D Wayne; 3, Lukas D Wayne; 4, Hough Stanley M; 5, Pletcher Todd A; 6, Asmussen Steven M; 7, Robb John J

Scratched— Limehouse (3May03 6CD1)

$2 Daily Double (2-1) Paid $72.50; Daily Double Pool $112,288.
$2 Pick Three (11-2-1) Paid $681.00; Pick Three Pool $101,267.

NINTH RACE
Belmont
JUNE 28, 2003

1⅛ MILES. (1.45²) 47th Running of THE MOTHER GOOSE. Grade I. First Leg of The Triple Tiara. Purse $300,000. (Up to $42,200 NYSBFOA). FILLIES, THREE YEARS OLD. By subscription of $300 each, which should accompany the nomination; $1,500 to pass the entry box and $1,500 to start. Weight 121 lbs. A $2,000,000 bonus will be awarded to the owner of the filly which wins all three legs of the Triple Tiara (The Mother Goose, The Coaching Club American Oaksand The Alabama).Closed Saturday, June 14, 2003 with 22 Nominations.

Value of Race: $300,000 Winner $180,000; second $60,000; third $33,000; fourth $18,000; fifth $9,000. Mutuel Pool $689,457.00 Exacta Pool $439,600.00 Trifecta Pool $309,879.00

Last Raced	Horse	M/Eqt.	A.Wt	PP	St	¼	½	¾	Str	Fin	Jockey	Odds $1
21May03 $^{8}CD^{1}$	Spoken Fur	L	3 121	4	2	4^{hd}	4^{hd}	3^{1}	1^{8}	$1^{5\frac{1}{4}}$	Bailey J D	4.50
2May03 $^{10}CD^{3}$	Yell	L	3 121	3	5	3^{hd}	3^{hd}	$4^{\frac{1}{2}}$	$3^{2\frac{1}{2}}$	$2^{\frac{3}{4}}$	Velazquez J R	1.45
6Jun03 $^{10}Bel^{3}$	Final Round	L	3 121	1	6	6	6	6	$2^{\frac{1}{2}}$	$3^{8\frac{1}{4}}$	Prado E S	2.90
15Jun03 $^{8}Bel^{2}$	Virgin Voyage	Lb	3 121	2	4	5^{2}	5^{2}	2^{hd}	$4^{\frac{1}{2}}$	$4^{5\frac{1}{4}}$	Chavez J F	37.25
16May03 $^{10}Pim^{1}$	Roar Emotion	L	3 121	6	1	1^{hd}	1^{hd}	1^{hd}	5^{8}	$5^{5\frac{1}{2}}$	Santos J A	3.20
12Jun03 $^{8}Bel^{1}$	Rhumb Line	L	3 121	5	3	$2^{1\frac{1}{2}}$	$2^{1\frac{1}{2}}$	5^{hd}	6	6	Coa E M	15.10

OFF AT 5:15 Start Good. Won ridden out. Track fast.
TIME :23, :46^{2}, 1:11^{3}, 1:37, 1:50^{2} (:23.07, :46.54, 1:11.63, 1:37.10, 1:50.41)

$2 Mutuel Prices:

4–SPOKEN FUR	11.00	4.20	2.60
3–YELL		2.80	2.20
1–FINAL ROUND			2.40

$2 EXACTA 4–3 PAID $32.80 $2 TRIFECTA 4–3–1 PAID $72.50

Gr/ro f, (Mar), by Notebook–Siberian Fur, by Siberian Express. Trainer Frankel Robert. Bred by (Fla).

SPOKEN FUR was rated along early, advanced three wide on the turn, drew away when asked and was wrapped in the final yards. YELL raced in hand while between rivals, came wide into the stretch and finished well outside. FINAL ROUND was outrun early, rallied four wide on the turn and weakened in the final furlong. VIRGIN VOYAGE pressed the pace from the inside and tired in the stretch. ROAR EMOTION ducked out at the start but quickly showed in front, set the pace while between rivals and tired in the stretch. RHUMB LINE pressed the pace while three wide and tired after three quarters.

Owners— 1, Amerman Racing Stables; 2, Claiborne Farm & Dilschneider Adele; 3, Humphrey G W Jr; 4, Paraneck Stable; 5, Allen Joseph; 6, Thorn Stable

Trainers—1, Frankel Robert; 2, McGaughey Claude III; 3, Arnold George R II; 4, Pedersen Jennifer; 5, Martin Carlos F; 6, Alexander Frank A

$2 Daily Double (3–4) Paid $25.20; Daily Double Pool $174,344.
$2 Pick Three (1–3–4) Paid $91.50; Pick Three Pool $174,432.
$2 Pick Four (2–1–3–4) Paid $491.00; Pick Four Pool $260,062.
$2 Pick Six (5–11–2–1–3–4) 6
Correct Paid $106,584.00; Pick Six Pool $519,356. $2 Pick Six (5–11–2–1–3–4) 5
Correct Paid $504.00

NINTH RACE
Churchill
JUNE 28, 2003

1⅛ MILES. (Turf)(1.46¹) LOCUST GROVE H.. Grade III. Purse $150,000 A HANDICAP FOR FILLIES AND MARES, THREE YEARS OLD AND UPWARD. By subscription of $150 each on or before June 14, 2003 or by Supplementary Nomination of $7,500 each by the close of entries Friday, June 20, 2003. $750 to pass the entry box;$750 additional to start, with $150,000 added of which 62% of all monies to the owner of the winner, 20% to second, 10% to third, 5% to fourth and 3% to fifth. The entry fee shall be refunded for scratches made in compliance with the above conditions. Starters to be named through the entry box at the usual time of closing. Closed Saturday, June 14, 2003. Trophy to winning owner.

Value of Race: $164,400 Winner $101,928; second $32,880; third $16,440; fourth $8,220; fifth $4,932. Mutuel Pool $412,849.00 Exacta Pool $231,691.00 Trifecta Pool $143,046.00

Last Raced	Horse	M/Eqt.	A.Wt	PP	St	¼	½	¾	Str	Fin	Jockey	Odds $1
29Mar03 NAS^{1}	Ipi Tombe-ZIM	L	5 123	1	5	$3^{2\frac{1}{2}}$	$3^{1\frac{1}{2}}$	$3^{\frac{1}{2}}$	$2^{1\frac{1}{2}}$	$1^{\frac{1}{2}}$	Day P	0.40
24May03 $^{9}CD^{1}$	Kiss The Devil	Lb	5 116	5	2	$1^{1\frac{1}{2}}$	1^{2}	$1^{\frac{1}{2}}$	$1^{1\frac{1}{2}}$	$2^{\frac{1}{2}}$	Meche L J	6.60
24May03 $^{9}CD^{2}$	Quick Tip	L	5 117	3	3	$4^{1\frac{1}{2}}$	$4^{2\frac{1}{2}}$	4^{4}	$3^{1\frac{1}{2}}$	$3^{1\frac{1}{2}}$	Albarado R J	3.20
24May03 $^{9}CD^{5}$	San Dare	L	5 117	2	4	5	5	5	5	4^{4}	Guidry M	11.30
15Jun03 $^{8}Cby^{3}$	Voodoo Lady	L	4 112	4	1	$2^{2\frac{1}{2}}$	$2^{\frac{1}{2}}$	2^{3}	$4^{1\frac{1}{2}}$	5	Melancon L	24.70

OFF AT 5:32 Start Good. Won driving. Course firm.
TIME :24^{1}, :47^{4}, 1:11^{2}, 1:35^{1}, 1:47^{3} (:24.24, :47.81, 1:11.40, 1:35.26, 1:47.70)

$2 Mutuel Prices:

1–IPI TOMBE–	2.80	2.10	—
6–KISS THE DEVIL		2.10	—
4–QUICK TIP		—	—

$2 EXACTA 1–6 PAID $9.40 $2 TRIFECTA 1–6–4 PAID $17.20

B. m, by Manshood*GB–Carnet de Danse*GB, by Dance In Time. Trainer Walden W Elliott. Bred by Moor P J (Zim).

IPI TOMBE (ZIM) hesitated at the start to trail, quickly recovered to gain a contending position three wide during the opening quarter, raced near the inside in hand on the backstretch, eased out three wide to rally from between foes into the stretch, reached the front a sixteenth out when put to a light hand ride, then finished under her own power. KISS THE DEVIL went up early to force the pace outside of VOODOO LADY, took over from that one before going a quarter, angled near the inside, shook off a challenge from VOODOO LADY entering the stretch, managed a clear lead into the final furlong but wasn't a match for the winner late. QUICK TIP settled near the inside early, moved four or five wide on the far turn, loomed prominently outside the leaders through the drive and wasn't good enough. SAN DARE, outrun and unhurried while three wide for six furlongs, worked her way out four or five wide in the last eighth and lacked a serious response. VOODOO LADY gained the lead at the start, lost the edge to KISS THE DEVIL, eased outside that one on the far turn, challenged approaching the final quarter but flattened out in the drive. Show and superfecta wagering on this race was canceled when the field was reduced to five wagering interests.

Owners— 1, Davenport Team Valor Winstar Farm &; 2, Pollard Carl F; 3, Farish William S; 4, Mounts David G; 5, WinStar Farm

Trainers—1, Walden W Elliott; 2, Vance David R; 3, Howard Neil J; 4, Hiles Rick; 5, Walden W Elliott

Scratched— Honorable Cat (7Jun03 $^{8}CD^{2}$)

$1 Pick Three (4–6–1/2) Paid $40.20; Pick Three Pool $34,846.

EIGHTH RACE

Hollywood

JUNE 28, 2003

1¼ MILES. (Turf)(1.57³) 38th Running of THE BEVERLY HILLS HANDICAP. Grade II. Purse $200,000 Guaranteed. FILLIES AND MARES THREE YEARS OLD AND UPWARD. By subscription of $200 each on or before Wednesday, June 18 or by supplementary nomination of $10,000 each by 3:00 pm Saturday, June 21. $2,000 additional to start. Nominations closed June 18 with 13. Rail at zero.

Value of Race: $200,000 Winner $120,000; second $40,000; third $24,000; fourth $12,000; fifth $4,000.   Mutuel Pool $576,053.00 Exacta Pool $239,962.00 Quinella Pool $21,171.00 Trifecta Pool $195,990.00

Last Raced	Horse	M/Eqt. A.Wt	PP	¼	½	¾	1	Str	Fin	Jockey	Odds $1
3May03 8Aqu³	Voodoo Dancer	LB	5 120	5	4¹	4½	4½	32½	2hd	1¾	Nakatani C S	2.60
26May03 6Hol²	Dublino	LB	4 122	1	3¹	3¹	2hd	21½	11½	22½	Espinoza V	1.00
26May03 6Hol³	Megahertz-GB	LB	4 117	4	5	5	5	43	47	31	Solis A	1.90
24May03 8Hol⁶	Damaschino-AU	LB	5 113	2	1²	13½	17	13	32½	47	Almeida G F	16.30
17May03 5Hol⁴	Se Vera-CH	LB	5 112	3	2½	2hd	31	5	5	5	Baze T C	39.80

OFF AT 4:54 Start Good. Won driving. Course firm.

TIME :26, :50², 1:13⁴, 1:36⁴, 2:00⁴ (:26.05, :50.49, 1:13.86, 1:36.92, 2:00.80)

$2 Mutuel Prices:	6–VOODOO DANCER	7.20	3.20	2.10
	1–DUBLINO		2.40	2.10
	5–MEGAHERTZ–GB			2.10

$1 EXACTA 6–1 PAID $7.90 $2 QUINELLA 1–6 PAID $5.60 $1 TRIFECTA
6–1–5 PAID $11.00

B. m, by Kingmambo–Zuri, by Danzig. Trainer Clement Christophe. Bred by Lazy E Ranch Inc (Ky).

VOODOO DANCER chased outside a rival then off the rail on the second turn, came three deep into the stretch and closed gamely to wear down DUBLINO under strong handling. DUBLINO saved ground chasing the leader, moved up inside on the second turn, came out into the stretch, took the lead outside a foe approaching midstretch, inched away but could not hold off the winner. MEGAHERTZ (GB) settled off the pace inside, moved up some along the rail on the second turn, came out in the stretch and picked up the show late. DAMASCHINO (AUS) pulled her way to the early lead, set a slow pace along the inside and weakened in the final furlong but lost third late. SE VERA (CHI) was in a good position tracking the leader outside a rival, dropped back on the second turn, angled in some into the stretch and weakened.

Owners— 1, Green Hills Farm; 2, Geringer Robert Klein Michael & Nai; 3, Bello Michael; 4, Newton R B; 5, Hunt Nelson B
Trainers— 1, Clement Christophe; 2, De Seroux Laura; 3, Frankel Robert; 4, Drysdale Neil; 5, McAnally Ronald
Scratched— Tates Creek (26May03 6HOL¹)

$2 Daily Double (1–6) Paid $15.80; Daily Double Pool $40,661.
$1 Pick Three (4–1–6) Paid $103.10; Pick Three Pool $87,856.

ELEVENTH RACE

Monmouth

JUNE 28, 2003

1⅛ MILES. (1.46⁴) 58th Running of THE MOLLY PITCHER BREEDERS' CUP HANDICAP. Grade II. Purse $300,000 A HANDICAP FOR FILLIES AND MARES, THREE YEARS OLD AND UPWARD. (Includes $100,000 from the Breeders' Cup Fund for Cup nominees only). By subscription of $250 each, which should accompany the nomination. $3,500 to enter. Field will be limited to 14 starters. If more than 14 entries pass the entry box, preference will be given to Breeders' Cup nominees only of equal racing quality or weight assignment. Weights 5:00 P.M.,Sunday, June 22. NOMINATIONS CLOSED Saturday, June 14, 2003 with TWENTY ONE (21).

Value of Race: $291,000 Winner $180,000; second $60,000; third $33,000; fourth $18,000.   Mutuel Pool $221,140.00 Exacta Pool $211,337.00

Last Raced	Horse	M/Eqt. A.Wt	PP	St	¼	½	¾	Str	Fin	Jockey	Odds $1
16May03 8Pim²	Summer Colony	L	5 120	1	1	4	4	31½	1½	13	Stevens G L	0.40
7Jun03 6Bel²	She's Got The Beat	Lf	4 112	2	2	2hd	32	4	4	2½	Samyn J L	5.00
7Jun03 6Bel⁴	Call An Audible	L	4 110	3	4	34½	2½	2½	31½	3½	Bravo J	9.90
7Jun03 6Bel¹	Alchemilla	L	4 113	4	3	11½	1½	1hd	2hd	4	Bridgmohan S X	2.90

OFF AT 5:44 Start Good. Won driving. Track fast.

TIME :23⁴, :48², 1:13, 1:38³, 1:51⁴ (:23.90, :48.51, 1:13.05, 1:38.62, 1:51.83)

$2 Mutuel Prices:	1–SUMMER COLONY	2.80	2.10	—
	2–SHE'S GOT THE BEAT		2.10	—
	3–CALL AN AUDIBLE		—	—

$2 EXACTA 1–2 PAID $7.00

Dk. b. or br. m, by Summer Squall–Probable Colony, by Pleasant Colony. Trainer Hennig Mark. Bred by Edward P Evans (Ky).

SUMMER COLONY broke in some then allowed to settle, moved outside on the backstretch, advanced three deep to challenge for the lead approaching the quarter pole, bumped lightly with a rival at the head of the stretch then finished steadily and was edging away late. SHE'S GOT THE BEAT under restraint early while along the inside, moved out after dropping back some on the final turn then finished well for the place. CALL AN AUDIBLE close up early from the outside, lodged a bid on the final turn and raced head and head for command while between foes, bumped lightly with a rival at the top of the lane then weakened through the late stages. ALCHEMILLA drew clear after the opening sixteenth and angled inside, was rated on the early pace, saved ground and responded when challenged in earnest then weakened in the drive.

Owners— 1, Evans Edward P; 2, Walsh Elizabeth; 3, Amerman John W; 4, Alexander Helen C & Helen K
Trainers—1, Hennig Mark; 2, Johnson Philip G; 3, Hennig Mark; 4, McGaughey Claude III
Scratched— Enjoy (24May03 8HOL²)

$2 Daily Double (10–1) Paid $13.20; Daily Double Pool $16,955.
$2 Pick Three (4–2–1 (NTRA)) Paid $65.50; Pick Three Pool $413,957.
$2 Pick Three (2–10–1) Paid $36.40; Pick Three Pool $9,883

Monmouth Park Attendance: 10,667 Mutuel Pool: $1,018,236.00 F Mutuel Pool: $2,898,207.00

EIGHTH RACE
Arlington
JUNE 29, 2003

1 MILE. (1.32^{1}) 12th Running of THE HANSHIN CUP HANDICAP. Grade III. Purse $100,000 A HANDICAP FOR THREE-YEAR-OLDS AND UPWARD. By subscription of $75 each, which should accompany the nomination. A Supplementary Nomination of $4,000 may be made on Saturday, June 21, 2003, which includes entry and starting fees. Original nominees to pay $750 to pass the entry box and an additional $750 to start. WEIGHTS: Sunday, June 22, 2003.This event will be limited to fourteen starters. Preference will be Highweights (on the scale). Total earnings in 2003 will be used to determine the order of preference of horses assigned equal weight (on the scale). Failure to draw into this race at time of entry cancels all fees with the exception of the nominating fee(s). Two (2) horses having common ties ownership cannot start to the exclusion of a single ownership interest.

Value of Race: $100,000 Winner $60,000; second $20,000; third $11,000; fourth $6,000; fifth $3,000. Mutuel Pool $170,836.00 Exacta Pool $123,197.00 Trifecta Pool $105,912.00 Superfecta Pool $26,376.00

Last Raced	Horse	M/Eqt.	A.	Wt	PP	St	¼	½	¾	Str	Fin	Jockey	Odds $1
7Jun03 ^{8}AP^{1}	Apt To Be	Lb	6	117	3	2	2^{1}	2^{1}	2^{3}	$1^{1\frac{1}{2}}$	1^{7}	Razo E Jr	3.90
31May03 ^{8}CD^{6}	There's Zealous	Lbf	5	116	2	4	1^{1}	$1^{1\frac{1}{2}}$	1^{1}	2^{4}	2^{hd}	Sibille R	6.60
1Jun03 ^{8}AP^{3}	San Pedro	Lf	5	116	5	1	7	7	6^{4}	6^{7}	3^{nk}	Fires E	11.50
9Apr03 ^{9}OP^{4}	Ask The Lord	Lf	6	117	7	3	$3^{\frac{1}{2}}$	3^{hd}	4^{4}	$5^{\frac{1}{2}}$	4^{1}	Laviolette B S	8.70
1Jun03 ^{9}CD^{2}	Bonus Pack	Lb	5	117	6	5	5^{3}	4^{3}	$3^{1\frac{1}{2}}$	3^{3}	$5^{1\frac{1}{4}}$	Douglas R R	2.00
17May03 ^{7}AP^{1}	Bright Valour	Lf	7	116	1	7	6^{1}	5^{1}	$5^{\frac{1}{2}}$	4^{hd}	6^{5}	Emigh C A	3.70
1Jun03 ^{9}CD^{1}	R. Baggio	Lb	5	117	4	6	4^{hd}	$6^{1\frac{1}{2}}$	7	7	7	Kuntzweiler G	5.50

OFF AT 4:39 Start Good. Won driving. Track fast.
TIME :23^{2}, :45^{3}, 1:09, 1:21^{2}, 1:34^{2} (:23.49, :45.61, 1:09.01, 1:21.52, 1:34.40)

$2 Mutuel Prices:

4–APT TO BE	9.80	4.80	4.20
3–THERE'S ZEALOUS		7.60	7.60
1–SAN PEDRO			6.80

$2 EXACTA 4–3 PAID $99.80 $2 TRIFECTA 4–3–1 PAID $718.80 $2 SUPERFECTA 4–3–1–7 PAID $3,290.60

B. g, by Rahy–Lets Do Lunch, by Royal Roberto. Trainer Block Chris M. Bred by Hill 'N Dale Farm (Ky).

APT TO BE settled in to a good stalking position just outside, moved to the leader turning for home, took command in the stretch and drew off under urging. THERE'S ZEALOUS sprinted to the early lead inside, set all of the pace from the rail then could not go with the winner in the drive and just saved the place. SAN PEDRO was void of early speed, angled out for the drive and rallied belatedly for minor awards. ASK THE LORD raced close up off the rail and weakened. BONUS PACK moved up steadily to the turn then faltered in late stretch. BRIGHT VALOUR was never a factor. R. BAGGIO was through early.

Owners— 1, Duchossois Richard L; 2, Jay Em Ess Stable; 3, Rudolph Richard F; 4, Stewart M Madison & Peter Gaffney; 5, Glen Hill Farm; 6, Lamarque Ronnie; 7, Lewkowitz Frank

Trainers—1, Block Chris M; 2, McGee Paul J; 3, Broussard Joseph E; 4, Stall Albert M Jr; 5, Proctor Thomas F; 6, Roussel Louie J III; 7, Kruljac J Eric

Scratched— Castlewood (4Jun03 ^{8}AP^{1}), Stormy Impact (7Jun03 ^{8}AP^{3})

$1 Pick Three (8–6–4) Paid $97.70; Pick Three Pool $9,513.

EIGHTH RACE
Hollywood
JUNE 29, 2003

1⅛ MILES. (Turf Chute)(1.44^{3}) 57th Running of THE CINEMA BREEDERS' CUP HANDICAP. Grade III. Purse $200,000 added (includes $50,000 Breeders' Cup). 3-year-olds. By subscription of $150 each on or before Wednesday, June 18. $1,500 additional to start. Rail at 15 feet.

Value of Race: $184,550 Winner $98,730; second $42,910; third $25,746; fourth $12,873; fifth $4,291. Mutuel Pool $472,739.00 Exacta Pool $251,299.00 Quinella Pool $26,757.00 Trifecta Pool $297,043.00 Superfecta Pool $117,936.00

Last Raced	Horse	M/Eqt.	A.	Wt	PP	St	¼	½	¾	Str	Fin	Jockey	Odds $1
10May03 ^{8}BM^{1}	Just Wonder-GB	LB	3	117	7	8	8	8	8	1^{2}	$1^{\frac{3}{4}}$	Desormeaux K J	3.40
14Mar03 ^{7}SA^{6}	Bis Repetitas	LB	3	115	2	5	5^{hd}	5^{1}	4^{hd}	$3^{\frac{1}{2}}$	2^{4}	Valdivia J Jr	9.20
22May03 ^{6}Hol^{1}	Slew City Citadel	LB	3	115	1	2	2^{1}	2^{1}	1^{hd}	2^{1}	3^{1}	Valenzuela P A	8.40
25May03 ^{8}Hol^{1}	Private Chef	LBb	3	117	5	4	$6^{1\frac{1}{2}}$	$6^{1\frac{1}{2}}$	6^{hd}	6^{1}	4^{1}	Espinoza V	1.20
4Jun03 ^{3}Hol^{2}	Devote	LBb	3	115	3	6	$7^{1\frac{1}{2}}$	$7^{1\frac{1}{2}}$	$7^{1\frac{1}{2}}$	5^{1}	5^{1}	Flores D R	32.50
11Jun03 ^{5}Hol^{4}	Royal Place	LB	3	113	4	1	3^{hd}	3^{hd}	3^{1}	4^{hd}	$6^{4\frac{1}{2}}$	Almeida G F	34.10
11Jun03 ^{5}Hol^{2}	Helms Deep-GB	LB	3	117	6	3	1^{hd}	1^{hd}	2^{1}	$7^{1\frac{1}{2}}$	$7^{2\frac{1}{2}}$	Nakatani C S	12.50
4Jun03 ^{7}Hol^{1}	Ender's Shadow	LBb	3	116	8	7	$4^{2\frac{1}{2}}$	4^{2}	5^{1}	8	8	Solis A	4.90

OFF AT 5:03 Start Good. Won driving. Course firm.
TIME :23, :46^{2}, 1:10, 1:35, 1:47^{2} (:23.11, :46.44, 1:10.06, 1:35.02, 1:47.41)

$2 Mutuel Prices:

7–JUST WONDER–GB	8.80	4.40	4.00
2–BIS REPETITAS		8.00	6.20
1–SLEW CITY CITADEL			5.80

$1 EXACTA 7–2 PAID $34.20 $2 QUINELLA 2–7 PAID $43.60 $1 TRIFECTA 7–2–1 PAID $206.50 $1 SUPERFECTA 7–2–1–5 PAID $517.20

B. c, (Mar), by Hernando*Fr–Just Fly, by Capote. Trainer De Seroux Laura. Bred by Bingen Lutz & Feldman Gerd (GB).

JUST WONDER (GB) unhurried and angled in early, came a bit off the rail leaving the backstretch, circled four wide on the second turn, swept to the front, kicked clear and held under urging. BIS REPETITAS saved ground stalking the pace, came out leaving the second turn and three deep into the stretch and went willingly to the wire. SLEW CITY CITADEL dueled inside, inched away leaving the second turn, came a bit off the rail in the stretch and held third. PRIVATE CHEF pulled early, chased outside a rival, went between horses on the second turn then waited and was shuffled back, came out into the stretch, was boxed in between and behind rivals in midstretch, came out again and finished with interest too late. DEVOTE saved ground chasing the pace, moved up inside into the stretch but lacked the needed late kick. ROYAL PLACE stalked the pace between horses then a bit off the rail, bid three deep leaving the second turn but weakened in the stretch. HELMS DEEP (GB) had good early speed and dueled outside a rival, was between horses leaving the second turn, dropped back and also weakened. ENDER'S SHADOW was in a good position stalking the pace three deep, fell back on the second turn and had little left for the stretch.

Owners— 1, Naify Sugarman & Vistas et al; 2, Gann Edmund A; 3, Taylor Finney Karen & Mickey; 4, Moss Mr & Mrs Jerome S; 5, McIngvale James; 6, Anderson Gene & Dr Kevin & Meadowbr; 7, Williamson Warren B; 8, Green Lantern Stables

Trainers—1, De Seroux Laura; 2, Frankel Robert; 3, French Neil; 4, Shirreffs John; 5, Baffert Bob; 6, La Croix David; 7, Gaines Carla; 8, Sahadi Jenine

$2 Daily Double (5–7) Paid $129.20; Daily Double Pool $37,339.
$1 Pick Three (3/6–5–7) Paid $240.80; Pick Three Pool $91,735.

EIGHTH RACE
Belmont
JULY 4, 2003

7 FURLONGS. (1.20) 29th Running of THE TOM FOOL HANDICAP. Grade II. Purse $150,000. (Up to $29,100 NYSBFOA). THREE YEAR OLDS AND UPWARD. By subscription of $150 each, which should accompany the nomination; $750 to pass the entry box and $750 to start. The purse to be divided 60% to the winner, 20% to second, 11% to third, 6% to fourth and 3% to fifth. Trophies will be presented to the winning owner, trainer and jockey. Closed Saturday, June 21, 2003 with 19 Nominations.

Value of Race: $150,000 Winner $90,000; second $30,000; third $16,500; fourth $9,000; fifth $4,500. Mutuel Pool $763,844.00 Exacta Pool $565,719.00 Trifecta Pool $462,320.00

Last Raced	Horse	M/Eqt.	A.Wt	PP	St	¼	½	Str	Fin	Jockey	Odds $1
14Jun03 10CD3	Aldebaran	Lf	5 122	4	6	7	7	$2^{1\frac{1}{2}}$	1^{2}	Bailey J D	0.95
21Jun03 13Suf1	Peeping Tom	Lbf	6 117	7	7	5^{hd}	$5^{\frac{1}{2}}$	3^{hd}	$2^{2\frac{1}{2}}$	Bridgmohan S X	8.20
7Jun03 7Bel5	State City	L	4 118	5	2	$4^{1\frac{1}{2}}$	$4^{2\frac{1}{2}}$	$4^{1\frac{1}{2}}$	$3^{3\frac{3}{4}}$	Chavez J F	13.50
26May03 9Bel7	Najran	L	4 116	1	3	$3^{2\frac{1}{2}}$	3^{hd}	$5^{2\frac{1}{2}}$	$4^{\frac{1}{2}}$	Prado E S	3.55
18Jan03 8Aqu5	Voodoo	Lb	5 114	6	1	$1^{2\frac{1}{2}}$	$1^{5\frac{1}{2}}$	$1^{\frac{1}{2}}$	5^{3}	Velazquez J R	18.90
12Jun03 5Bel1	Northern Rock-JP	Lb	5 114	3	4	$2^{\frac{1}{2}}$	2^{3}	6^{6}	$6^{6\frac{1}{4}}$	Migliore R	4.00
7Jun03 7Bel3	Vodka	L	6 113	2	5	6^{6}	6^{hd}	7	7	Castillo H Jr	58.75

OFF AT 4:41 Start Good. Won driving. Track fast.
TIME $:22^{2}$, $:44^{4}$, $1:09^{3}$, $1:22^{2}$ (:22.44, :44.83, 1:09.79, 1:22.54)

$2 Mutuel Prices:				
	5–ALDEBARAN	3.90	2.50	2.10
	8–PEEPING TOM		4.60	2.80
	6–STATE CITY			3.50

$2 EXACTA 5–8 PAID $16.00 $2 TRIFECTA 5–8–6 PAID $110.00

B. h, by Mr. Prospector–Chimes of Freedom, by Private Account. Trainer Frankel Robert. Bred by Flaxman Holdings Ltd (Ky).

ALDEBARAN was outrun early, split rivals while advancing on the turn, angled to the inside entering the stretch, finished gamely on the rail and was going away late under a drive. PEEPING TOM was outrun early, raced four wide, responded when roused and finished gamely outside to earn the place award. STATE CITY was hustled along outside, chased the pace while three wide and lacked a rally. NAJRAN chased the pace along the inside and tired in the final furlong. VOODOO quickly opened a clear lead, set the pace along the inside and faltered in the final furlong. NORTHERN ROCK (JPN) chased the pace from the outside and tired in the stretch. VODKA was outrun early along the inside, came wide into the stretch and tired.

Owners— 1, Flaxman Stable; 2, Flatbird Stable; 3, Godolphin Racing Inc; 4, Buckram Oak Farm; 5, Moore Susan & John; 6, Al Maktoum Mohammed b; 7, Gerrity Joseph W Jr

Trainers—1, Frankel Robert; 2, Reynolds Patrick L; 3, Albertrani Thomas; 4, Zito Nicholas P; 5, Jerkens James A; 6, McLaughlin Kiaran P; 7, Hertler John O

Scratched— Ginzano (13Jun03 8BEL3)

$2 Pick Three (1–2–5) Paid $125.50; Pick Three Pool $114,989.

NINTH RACE
Belmont
JULY 4, 2003

6 FURLONGS. (1.07³) 56th Running of THE PRIORESS. Grade I. Purse $200,000. (Up to $34,800 NYSBFOA). FILLIES, THREE YEARS OLD. By subscription of $200 each, which should accompany the nomination; $1,000 to pass the entry box and $1,000 to start. The purse to be divided 60% to the winner, 20% to second, 11% to third, 6% to fourth and 3% to fifth. 121 lbs. Non-winners of $60,000 twice allowed 2 lbs.; $60,000; or $45,000 in 2003, 4 lbs.; $30,000 or two races, 6 lbs. (Maiden, claiming, starter, restricted and restricted stake races not considered in allowances.) Trophies will be presented to the winning owner, trainer and jockey Closed Saturday, June 21,2003 with 24 Nominations.

Value of Race: $200,000 Winner $120,000; second $40,000; third $22,000; fourth $12,000; fifth $6,000. Mutuel Pool $644,422.00 Exacta Pool $486,224.00 Trifecta Pool $369,849.00

Last Raced	Horse	M/Eqt.	A.Wt	PP	St	¼	½	Str	Fin	Jockey	Odds $1
6Jun03 10Bel4	House Party		3 121	2	6	$7^{\frac{1}{2}}$	6^{2}	$2^{\frac{1}{2}}$	$1^{3\frac{1}{4}}$	Santos J A	2.10
15May03 8Pim2	Chimichurri	Lf	3 119	1	5	8	7^{5}	6^{5}	$2^{\frac{1}{2}}$	Velazquez J R	9.60
14Jun03 6Hol3	Princess V.	L	3 115	5	4	1^{1}	1^{hd}	$1^{\frac{1}{2}}$	$3^{\frac{1}{2}}$	Bailey J D	3.15
6Jun03 10Bel5	Randaroo	Lf	3 119	7	3	2^{hd}	$4^{1\frac{1}{2}}$	$5^{1\frac{1}{2}}$	$4^{1\frac{3}{4}}$	Prado E S	8.30
31May03 7AP1	In Secure	Lf	3 119	3	7	6^{3}	$3^{1\frac{1}{2}}$	3^{hd}	$5^{3\frac{1}{2}}$	Chavez J F	13.10
15May03 8Pim1	Belong To Sea	Lf	3 119	8	2	$3^{1\frac{1}{2}}$	$2^{\frac{1}{2}}$	4^{hd}	$6^{2\frac{1}{2}}$	Castellano J J	13.90
7Jun03 13Bel3	Sensibly Chic	Lbf	3 115	4	1	$5^{2\frac{1}{2}}$	8	$7^{\frac{1}{2}}$	$7^{8\frac{1}{2}}$	Bridgmohan S X	48.75
11Jun03 8Mth1	Wild Snitch	L	3 119	6	8	4^{hd}	$5^{\frac{1}{2}}$	8	8	Coa E M	3.10

OFF AT 5:13 Start Good. Won driving. Track fast.
TIME $:21^{4}$, $:44^{3}$, $:56^{4}$, $1:09^{2}$ (:21.94, :44.71, :56.97, 1:09.45)

$2 Mutuel Prices:				
	2–HOUSE PARTY	6.20	3.60	2.60
	1–CHIMICHURRI		8.10	4.40
	5–PRINCESS V.			3.00

$2 EXACTA 2–1 PAID $37.60 $2 TRIFECTA 2–1–5 PAID $110.50

Gr/ro f, (Apr), by French Deputy–Bill Back, by Relaunch. Trainer Jerkens H Allen. Bred by J V Shields Jr (Fla).

HOUSE PARTY was outrun early, advanced inside on the turn, swung wide entering the stretch, responded when roused and drew away late under a drive. CHIMICHURRI was outrun early along the inside, altered course to the outside in upper stretch and finished gamely to earn the place prize. PRINCESS V. was hustled to the front, set the pace along the inside and weakened in the final furlong. RANDAROO stumbled at the start, was bumped after the start, chased the pace from the outside and faded late. IN SECURE was hustled up inside, put in a run on the rail nearing the stretch, was forced to be taken up when in tight quarters entering the stretch and dropped back. BELONG TO SEA chased the pace while three wide and tired in the final furlong. SENSIBLY CHIC raced wide and tired in the stretch. WILD SNITCH was bumped at the start, stumbled after the start, was steadied on the backstretch, chased the pace while four wide and tired in the stretch. There was a Stewards' inquiry into the incident on the turn before the result was declared official.

Owners— 1, Shields Joseph V Jr; 2, Peachtree Stable; 3, Kenneth Porter; 4, Allen Joseph; 5, Louie Roussel III & Ronnie Lamarque; 6, Amling Jeffery Duncker C Steven Qua; 7, Nervitt Lois S; 8, New Farm

Trainers—1, Jerkens H Allen; 2, Pletcher Todd A; 3, French Neil; 4, Dutrow Anthony W; 5, Roussel Louie J III; 6, Lewis Lisa L; 7, Ribaudo Robert J; 8, Perkins Ben W Jr

---

$2 Daily Double (5–2) Paid $14.60; Daily Double Pool $147,040.
$2 Pick Three (2–5–2) Paid $71.50; Pick Three Pool $126,174.

TENTH RACE
Belmont
JULY 4, 2003

1¼ MILES. (Inner Turf)(1.57³) 60th Running of THE NEW YORK HANDICAP. Grade II. Purse $250,000. (Up to $38,500 NYSBFOA). FILLIES AND MARES THREE YEARS OLD AND UPWARD. By subscription of $250 each, which should accompany the nomination; $1,250 to pass the entry box and $1,250 to start. The purse to be divided 60% to the winner, 20% to second, 11% to third, 6%to fourth and 3% to fifth. Trophies will be presented to the winning owner, trainer and jockey. The New York Racing Association reserves the right to transfer this race to the Main Track. In the event that this race is taken off the turf, it may be subject to downgrading upon review by the Graded Stakes Committee. Closed Saturday, June 21, 2003 with 35 Nominations.

Value of Race: $250,000 Winner $150,000; second $50,000; third $27,500; fourth $15,000; fifth $7,500. Mutuel Pool $704,295.00 Exacta Pool $406,023.00 Trifecta Pool $297,819.00

Last Raced	Horse	M/Eqt.	A.Wt	PP	¼	½	¾	1	Str	Fin	Jockey	Odds $1
31May03 8Bel6	Snow Dance	L	5 116	4	2½	2½	2hd	21½	12½	11	Migliore R	27.00
29May03 2Hol1	Pertuisane-GB	Lb	4 115	1	5½	5½	5½	5½	4½	2¾	Prado E S	a-0.75
7Jun03 8Bel2	Riskaverse	L	4 119	7	4½	4½	4½	3hd	2hd	33¼	Velazquez J R	3.60
31May03 8Bel2	Owsley	L	5 117	3	3½	3½	3½	41	55	41	Samyn J L	11.20
19Apr03 4SA2	Trekking	L	4 113	2	11½	12½	11½	1hd	3hd	5nk	Coa E M	a-0.75
7Jun03 8Bel1	Mariensky	L	4 117	6	72	73	73	73	6½	6¾	Santos J A	2.85
31May03 8Bel4	Sunstone-GB	Lb	5 112	8	8	8	8	8	8	7hd	Luzzi M J	67.50
31May03 8Bel5	Lilac Queen-GE	Lf	5 117	5	6½	61½	61½	61	71	8	Bailey J D	a-0.75

a-Coupled: Pertuisane-GB and Trekking and Lilac Queen-GE.

OFF AT 5:45 Start Good. Won driving. Course firm.
TIME :23⁴, :49¹, 1:13¹, 1:36⁴, 1:59³ (:23.92, :49.28, 1:13.23, 1:36.89, 1:59.63)

$2 Mutuel Prices:

3-SNOW DANCE	56.00	9.10	2.10
1-PERTUISANE-GB (a-entry)		2.50	2.10
6-RISKAVERSE			2.10

$2 EXACTA 3-1 PAID $127.00 $2 TRIFECTA 3-1-6 PAID $328.50

Gr/ro m, by Forest Wildcat-Northern Pageant, by Spectacular Bid. Trainer Ward John T Jr. Bred by Aspiration Stable (Ky).

SNOW DANCE raced with the pace from the outside while in hand, responded when roused turning for home, drew clear and remained clear under a drive. PERTUISANE (GB) was rated along inside, saved ground, angled out entering the stretch and finished gamely outside. RISKAVERSE was rated along outside, rallied three wide on the second turn and stayed on gamely to the wire. OWSLEY raced close up inside while in hand and lacked a rally. TREKKING quickly showed in front, set the pace along the inside and tired in the final furlong. MARIENSKY was outrun early, raced inside and had no response when roused. SUNSTONE (GB) dropped back early and had no rally. LILAC QUEEN (GER) was rated along early, came wide into the stretch and had no rally.

Owners— 1, Oxley John C; 2, Robert J Frankel Louis Lazzinnaro N; 3, Fox Ridge Farm Inc; 4, Hancock III Arthur B; 5, Juddmonte Farms Inc; 6, Waterville Lake Stable; 7, Georgica Stable; 8, Tanaka Gary A

Trainers—1, Ward John T Jr; 2, Frankel Robert; 3, Kelly Patrick J; 4, Schulhofer Randy; 5, Frankel Robert; 6, Clement Christophe; 7, Barbara Robert; 8, Frankel Robert

Scratched— Sixty Seconds (5Oct02 FLE14)

TENTH RACE
Churchill
JULY 4, 2003

5½ FURLONGS. (1.02²) 103rd Running of THE DEBTUTANTE. Grade III. Purse $100,000 added. FILLIES, TWO YEARS OLD. By subscription of $100 each on or before June 21, 2003 or by Supplementary Nomination of $5,000 at time of entry. $500 to pass the entry box; $500 additional to start, with $100,000 added of which 62% of all monies to the owner of the winner, 20% to second, 10% to third, 5% to fourth and 3% to fifth. Weight, 121 lbs. Non-winners of a sweepstakes, allowed 2 lbs. A race other than maiden or claiming, 4 lbs. A race other than claiming, 6 lbs. Starters to be named through the entry box at the usual time of closing. Closed Saturday June 21 with 24 nominations. Trophy to winning owner.

Value of Race: $110,900 Winner $68,758; second $22,180; third $11,090; fourth $5,545; fifth $3,327. Mutuel Pool $284,721.00 Exacta Pool $184,105.00 Trifecta Pool $168,467.00 Superfecta Pool $56,191.00

Last Raced	Horse	M/Eqt.	A.Wt	PP	St	¼	⅜	Str	Fin	Jockey	Odds $1
11May03 3CD1	Be Gentle		2 117	4	1	1hd	1½	11½	11¼	Velasquez C	1.80
5Jun03 7Bel2	Renaissance Lady		2 117	8	6	74	62½	3hd	24½	Day P	1.70
30May03 1LS1	Sweet Jo Jo	L	2 117	2	3	21½	3½	2½	32½	Meche L J	3.50
15Jun03 6CD1	Secret Romance	L	2 117	7	8	4½	2hd	42	4no	Albarado R J	24.70
15Jun03 1AP1	Lady's Room	Lb	2 117	6	4	3hd	4½	5½	51¼	Lovato F Jr	15.20
8Jun03 2CD2	In Rome	Lb	2 115	5	7	5½	5hd	64	62¼	Bejarano R	27.90
1Jun03 5CD1	Cryptos' Best	Lb	2 117	1	2	61½	75	71½	73¼	Court J K	8.00
6Jun03 1RD1	Go Grace Go	Lb	2 117	3	5	8	8	8	8	McKee J	94.00

OFF AT 5:58 Start Good. Won driving. Track fast.
TIME :22, :45¹, :57², 1:03⁴ (:22.00, :45.26, :57.54, 1:03.96)

$2 Mutuel Prices:

5-BE GENTLE	5.60	2.60	2.40
9-RENAISSANCE LADY		2.60	2.20
2-SWEET JO JO			2.60

$2 EXACTA 5-9 PAID $14.00 $2 TRIFECTA 5-9-2 PAID $42.20 $1 SUPERFECTA 5-9-2-8 PAID $81.70

Dk. b. or br. f, (May), by Tale of the Cat-Gentlelilstar, by Risen Star. Trainer Lukas D Wayne. Bred by Mrs Nellie M Cox & Rose Retreat Farm (Va).

BE GENTLE gained a slim lead early while between foes three abreast, battled with SWEET JO JO from the inside and SECRET ROMACE from the outside, edged clear into the upper stretch, then maintained her advantage under intermittent left-handed encouragement. RENAISSANCE LADY, seven or eight wide during the early going, edged in around the turn, raced five wide into the stretch, had aim at the winner through the drive but couldn't offer the needed response while clearly superior to the others. SWEET JO JO contested the pace inside the winner from early on, raced close up into the final furlong and weakened. SECRET ROMANCE forced the pace four or five wide, was asked for her best concluding the turn but flattened out when straightened for the drive. LADY'S ROOM, in contention between foes four wide to the stretch, weakened thereafter. IN ROME, near the inside between foes, moved closer to the inside entering the stretch but tired. CRYPTOS' BEST, close up inside early, lost position on the turn, swung out five wide for the drive and was empty. GO GRACE GO raced four wide and was outrun.

Owners— 1, Van Meter II Thomas F; 2, Lewis Robert B & Beverly J; 3, Grunwald Racing; 4, Kaster Nancy & Richard & Ricker Sco; 5, Estrorace Racing; 6, Pollard Carl F; 7, Shepard Robert H; 8, Collins Charles V

Trainers—1, Lukas D Wayne; 2, Lukas D Wayne; 3, Asmussen Steven M; 4, Romans Dale; 5, Maker Rebecca; 6, Vance David R; 7, Thompson Mark E; 8, Adams Darrel K

Scratched— Thesmellofhoney (13Jun03 9CD2)

$1 Pick Three (3-3-5) Paid $311.60; Pick Three Pool $33,084.

FOURTH RACE
Hollywood
JULY 4, 2003

6 FURLONGS. (1.07²) 59th Running of THE LANDALUCE. Grade III. Purse $100,000 Added. FILLIES TWO–YEARS–OLD. By subscription of $100 each on or before Wednesday, June 25, or by supplementary nomination of $5,000 each by closing time of entries.$1,000 additional to start, with $100,000 added. The added money and all fees to be divided 60% to the winner, 20% to second, 12% to third, 6% to fourth and 2% to fifth. Weight 119 lbs. Non–winners of a sweepstakes allowed 3 lbs. Maidens allowed 5 lbs. Closed June 25 with 10 nominations.

Value of Race: $100,300 Winner $60,180; second $20,060; third $12,036; fourth $6,018; fifth $2,006. Mutuel Pool $362,402.00 Exacta Pool $180,974.00 Quinella Pool $22,048.00 Trifecta Pool $188,271.00

Last Raced	Horse	M/Eqt. A.Wt	PP	St	¼	½	Str	Fin	Jockey	Odds $1
8Jun03 7Hol⁴	Wacky Patty	LBb	2 119	6	1	2¹½	2¹½	1½	1¹	Valdivia J Jr	1.90
12Jun03 4Hol¹	Cherish Destiny	LBb	2 116	3	2	1ʰᵈ	1ʰᵈ	2²½	25	Baze T C	7.90
11Jun03 3B M¹	Platinum Princess	LBb	2 116	4	6	4½	3½	31½	3¹	Flores D R	2.10
5Jun03 4Hol¹	Alpenwald	LB	2 116	1	5	3ʰᵈ	4²	4²	4¹	Solis A	2.80
8Jun03 7Hol³	Outrageous Oyster	LB	2 116	2	4	5³	5³	5²½	5⁶	Smith M E	12.50
12Jun03 4Hol⁴	Silver Hawk Lady	LB	2 116	5	3	6	6	6	6	Stevens G L	10.60

OFF AT 2:54 Start Good For All But PLATINUM PRINCESS Won driving. Track fast.
TIME :22, :44³, :57¹, 1:10¹ (:22.07, :44.67, :57.24, 1:10.28)

$2 Mutuel Prices:

6–WACKY PATTY	5.80	3.40	2.60
3–CHERISH DESTINY		6.80	3.20
4–PLATINUM PRINCESS			2.60

$1 EXACTA 6–3 PAID $18.00 $2 QUINELLA 3–6 PAID $21.00 $1 TRIFECTA 6–3–4 PAID $53.80

Dk. b. or br. f, (Feb), by Formal Dinner–As a Day in June, by Fly So Free. Trainer Chapman James K. Bred by Frazier D W & Maxwell Suzanne Sharra (Fla).

WACKY PATTY angled in and dueled outside the runner–up, brushed with that one in upper stretch, took a short lead and inched away late under urging. CHERISH DESTINY had good early speed and dueled inside, brushed with the winner in upper stretch, fought back along the rail but could not quite match strides late. PLATINUM PRINCESS bobbled slightly then hopped in a slow start, went up three deep to stalk the pace, continued outside on the turn and held third. ALPENWALD was in a good position stalking the leaders along the inside but weakened in the stretch. OUTRAGEOUS OYSTER broke in a bit, stalked between horses on the backstretch and into the turn, steadied approaching midway on the bend, continued off the inside into the stretch and also weakened. SILVER HAWK LADY unhurried off the inside on the backstretch and turn, failed to menace and was outrun.

Owners— 1, Chapman James K; 2, David J Lanzman Racing Stable; 3, Vreeland James R; 4, Steinmann Heinz; 5, 5C Racing LLC; 6, Rubio Miguel

Trainers—1, Chapman James K; 2, O'Neill Doug; 3, Bonde Jeff; 4, Harrington Mike; 5, Gutierrez Jorge; 6, Garcia Juan

$2 Daily Double (5–6) Paid $7.80; Daily Double Pool $21,100.
$1 Pick Three (3–5–6) Paid $66.30; Pick Three Pool $66,168.

SEVENTH RACE
Hollywood
JULY 4, 2003

1⅛ MILES. (Turf)(1.44³) 64th Running of THE AMERICAN HANDICAP. Grade II. Purse $150,000 Guaranteed. THREE–YEAR–OLDS AND UPWARD. By subscription of $150 each on or before Wednesday, June 25 or by supplementary nomination of $7,500 each by noon Friday, June 27. $1,500 additional to start, with $90,000 to the winner, $30,000 to second, $18,000 to third, $9,000 to fourth and $3,000 to fifth. Closed June 25 with 23 nominations.Rail at 15 feet.

Value of Race: $150,000 Winner $90,000; second $30,000; third $18,000; fourth $9,000; fifth $3,000. Mutuel Pool $424,915.00 Exacta Pool $231,135.00 Quinella Pool $21,348.00 Trifecta Pool $191,927.00

Last Raced	Horse	M/Eqt. A.Wt	PP	St	¼	½	¾	Str	Fin	Jockey	Odds $1
7Jun03 7Hol¹	Candy Ride–ARG	LB	4 120	5	3	2²	2¹½	2¹½	2²½	1¾	Stevens G L	1.00
26May03 8Hol²	Special Ring	LBb	6 118	3	2	1½	1ʰᵈ	1½	1ʰᵈ	2²	Flores D R	2.00
13Jun03 5Hol¹	Irish Warrior	LB	5 116	2	4	4ʰᵈ	4ʰᵈ	4ʰᵈ	3ʰᵈ	3¹	Solis A	4.40
10May03 8Hol⁴	Sunday Break–JP	LBb	4 117	4	5	5	5	5	4²½	4²½	Nakatani C S	7.10
15Jun03 4B M²	Ninebanks	LBb	5 115	1	1	3½	3ʰᵈ	3ʰᵈ	5	5	Warren R J Jr	14.30

OFF AT 4:27 Start Good. Won driving. Course firm.
TIME :24, :47⁴, 1:11, 1:34¹, 1:46¹ (:24.04, :47.91, 1:11.02, 1:34.23, 1:46.20)

$2 Mutuel Prices:

7–CANDY RIDE–ARG	4.00	2.60	2.10
5–SPECIAL RING		3.00	2.10
3–IRISH WARRIOR			2.10

$1 EXACTA 7–5 PAID $3.80 $2 QUINELLA 5–7 PAID $4.80 $1 TRIFECTA 7–5–3 PAID $10.20

B. c, by Ride The Rails–Candy Girl*Arg, by Candy Stripes. Trainer McAnally Ronald. Bred by Haras Abolengo (Arg).

CANDY RIDE (ARG) three deep in the chute, prompted the pace outside SPECIAL RING most of the way, fought back alongside that one through a long, hard drive and gamely prevailed under a couple cracks of the whip and good handling. SPECIAL RING had speed between horses in the chute then angled in, set the pace inside, inched away from the winner leaving the first turn, responded when challenged again, also fought back through a stiff drive but could not quite match that one late. IRISH WARRIOR was in a good position stalking the top pair between horses to the stretch and settled for the show. SUNDAY BREAK (JPN) well placed tracking the pace three deep to the stretch, was outfinished for third. NINEBANKS close up stalking the leaders inside, was shuffled back into the stretch and weakened.

Owners— 1, Craig Sidney H & Jenny; 2, Prestonwood Farm Inc; 3, Coleman Dasaro & Thompson et al; 4, Maeda Koji; 5, Abruzzo Peter

Trainers—1, McAnally Ronald; 2, Canani Julio C; 3, Dollase Wallace; 4, Drysdale Neil; 5, Hollendorfer Jerry

Scratched— Californian (2May03 9CD⁸), Tijiyr (13Jun03 5HOL⁵)

$2 Daily Double (1–7) Paid $10.80; Daily Double Pool $35,656.
$1 Pick Three (10–1–2/4/7) Paid $307.30; Pick Three Pool $78,561.

TENTH RACE
Monmouth
JULY 4, 2003

6 FURLONGS. (1.07^{4}) 13th Running of THE JERSEY SHORE BREEDERS' CUP. Grade III. Purse $100,000 (includes $25,000 BC – Breeders' Cup) FOR THREE-YEAR-OLDS. (Includes $25,000 from Breeders' Cup Fund for Cup nominees only). By subscription of $100 each, which should accompany the nomination, $1,500 to pass the entry box with $100,000 guaranteed which includes $25,000 from the Breeders' Cup Fund for Cup nominees only. Breeders' Cup Fund money also correspondingly divided providing a Breeders' Cup nominee has finished in an awarded position. Any Breeders' Cup Fund moneynot awarded reverts to the fund. Weight: 122 lbs. Non-winners of $60,000 in 2003, allowed 3 lbs. $45,000 in 2003, 5 lbs.; $45,000, 7 lbs. A sweepstakes or two races other than maiden or claiming, 9 lbs. The owner of the winner to receive a trophy presented by Breeders' Cup Ltd. Closed Saturday, June 21 with 27 nominations.

Value of Race: $97,250 Winner $60,000; second $20,000; third $8,250; fourth $6,000; fifth $3,000. Mutuel Pool $114,699.00 Exacta Pool $79,400.00 Trifecta Pool $44,199.00

Last Raced	Horse	M/Eqt.	A.	Wt	PP	St	¼	½	Str	Fin	Jockey	Odds $1
14Jun03 ^{8}Mth^{1}	Gators N Bears	Lbf	3	115	4	2	2½	1^{3}	14½	1½	Lopez C C	7.30
17May03 ^{6}Pim^{1}	Mt. Carson	Lf	3	122	3	5	6	6	2½	28¼	Dominguez R A	1.60
14Jun03 ^{11}Del^{7}	Don Six	L	3	115	1	6	4^{1}	4^{hd}	3^{hd}	32¼	Toribio A R	4.60
7Jun03 ^{9}Bel^{4}	Bishop Court Hill	L	3	113	6	3	5½	3½	42½	46¼	Bravo J	*1.60
17May03 ^{6}Pim^{3}	Only The Best	Lf	3	117	2	1	1^{hd}	2^{hd}	5^{4}	5^{8}	Alvarado R Jr	8.10
21Jun03 ^{7}Cnl^{3}	Love Sam	Lb	3	115	5	4	3^{hd}	5½	6	6	Teator P A	25.20

***—Actual Betting Favorite.**

OFF AT 5:17 Start Good. Won driving. Track fast.
TIME :21^{4}, :44^{1}, :56^{4}, 1:09^{4} (:21.80, :44.35, :56.81, 1:09.80)

$2 Mutuel Prices:				
	5–GATORS N BEARS	16.60	6.20	3.20
	3–MT. CARSON		3.00	2.40
	1–DON SIX			3.20

$2 EXACTA 5–3 PAID $47.00 $2 TRIFECTA 5–3–1 PAID $141.60

B. c, (Feb), by Stormy Atlantic–I'll Be Along, by Notebook. Trainer Nechamkin Leo S II. Bred by Robert W Camac (NJ).

GATORS N BEARS stayed with a fast pace in the three path, moved clear off the rail through the turn then persevered under steady handling. MT. CARSON rated back in the three path, lacked room steadying into the turn, angled to the outside through the turn, rallied from the top of the stretch and finished well. DON SIX was a step slow on the break, rated close to the pace off the rail, bid between horses at the quarter pole, dueled the upper stretch then languished the final furlong. BISHOP COURT HILL kept close to the front from the outside, bid widest on the turn, entered the stretch in the four path but had nothing left for the drive. ONLY THE BEST set a fast pace just off the rail, dropped back into the turn and was through for the drive. LOVE SAM kept up with a fast pace toward the outside, gave chase through the turn then gave way the final quarter.

Owners— 1, Nechamkin II Leo S; 2, Reynolds David P; 3, Generazio Frank Jr; 4, Melnyk Eugene & Laura; 5, Mr & Mrs Alvin E Toffel; 6, Giddy-Up Go Stables

Trainers—1, Nechamkin Leo S II; 2, Jenkins Rodney; 3, Generazio Frank Jr; 4, Pletcher Todd A; 5, Lynch Brian A; 6, Begley Earl P Jr

Scratched— Midnight Charlie (7Jun03 ^{9}BEL^{5})

$2 Pick Three (4–9–5) Paid $383.60; Pick Three Pool $12,793.

EIGHTH RACE
Arlington
JULY 5, 2003

1½ MILES. (Turf)(2.27^{2}) 75th Running of THE STARS AND STRIPES BREEDERS' CUP TURF HANDICAP. Grade III. Purse $200,000 (includes $75,000 BC – Breeders' Cup). THREE-YEAR-OLDS AND UPWARD.(Includes $75,000 from the Breeders' Cup fund for Cup nominees only). By subscription of $150 each, which should accompany the nomination. 2003 Million Nominees Free Nomination. Original nominees to pay $1,000 to pass the entry box and an additional $1,000 to start, with $125,000 added by Arlington Park. The $125,000 added by Arlington Park. Breeders' Cup Fund monies also correspondingly divided providing a Breeders' Cup nominee has finished in an awarded position. Any Breeders' Cup Fund monies not awarded will revert back to the fund. WEIGHTS: June 29, 2003. This event will not be divided, the field will be limited to fourteen starters. Preference will be given to Breeders' Cup Nominees only of equal racing quality or weight assignment (respective of sex and weight-for-age). Total Earnings in 2003 will be used to determine the order of preference of horses assigned equal weight (on the scale).

Value of Race: $219,200 Winner $131,520; second $43,840; third $24,112; fourth $13,152; fifth $6,576. Mutuel Pool $331,064.00 Exacta Pool $211,544.00 Trifecta Pool $204,212.00 Superfecta Pool $59,643.00

Last Raced	Horse	M/Eqt.	A.	Wt	PP	¼	½	1	1¼	Str	Fin	Jockey	Odds $1
10May03 ^{7}Hol^{3}	Ballingarry-IR	L	4	121	1	5½	5½	4^{hd}	41½	21½	1½	Douglas R R	0.60
7Jun03 ^{10}Bel^{3}	Dr. Brendler	L	5	118	3	7^{2}	71½	7^{2}	5^{hd}	4^{2}	22½	Bourque C C	2.70
7Jun03 ^{2}Bel^{1}	Jack's Own Time	L	4	112	2	6^{2}	61½	6^{hd}	7½	5^{1}	3¾	Molina Tommy	18.70
28Dec02 ^{9}FG^{5}	Extra Check	Lbf	4	116	6	1^{1}	1^{1}	1½	1½	1^{hd}	41½	Fires E	22.10
31May03 ^{9}CD^{6}	Williams News	Lf	8	117	5	9	9	8^{hd}	8^{hd}	6½	5¾	St Julien M	8.40
13Jun03 ^{8}AP^{1}	Private Son	L	5	116	7	3^{hd}	4^{1}	5^{2}	3½	3^{hd}	6^{1}	Razo E Jr	12.10
21Jun03 ^{9}AP^{4}	Ivan Jay Perry	L	7	115	9	8^{hd}	8^{1}	9	9	7½	71¼	Emigh C A	40.30
21Jun03 ^{9}AP^{3}	Scooter Roach	L	4	115	4	2^{1}	3½	3½	6^{hd}	8^{hd}	8¾	Campbell J M	59.60
5Jun03 ^{8}AP^{1}	North Of Six	Lb	4	116	8	4^{2}	2½	2^{3}	2^{1}	9	9	Lovato F Jr	31.70

OFF AT 4:41 Start Good. Won driving. Course good.
TIME :24^{3}, :49^{4}, 1:15^{1}, 1:39^{2}, 2:04, 2:28^{1} (:24.78, :49.88, 1:15.26, 1:39.54, 2:04.16, 2:28.30)

$2 Mutuel Prices:				
	1–BALLINGARRY–IR	3.20	2.40	2.20
	3–DR. BRENDLER		2.80	2.40
	2–JACK'S OWN TIME			3.80

$2 EXACTA 1–3 PAID $8.20 $2 TRIFECTA 1–3–2 PAID $63.80 $2 SUPERFECTA 1–3–2–6 PAID $434.20

B. c, by Sadler's Wells–Flamenco Wave, by Desert Wine. Trainer De Seroux Laura. Bred by Orpendale (Ire).

BALLINGARRY (IRE) was allowed to settle along the inside near the middle of the field, raced in that position to the stretch, split horses in upper stretch, rallied to the lead and held sway at the wire. DR. BRENDLER was void of early speed along the rail, followed BALLINGARRY (IRE) through the hole in the stretch and rallied late but could not get to the winner and settled for the place. JACK'S OWN TIME settled in just outside near the middle of the field, rallied when asked for his best in the lane and belatedly gained minor awards. EXTRA CHECK broke to the lead, set all of the pace to the stretch while pressed then weakened in the final furlong. WILLIAMS NEWS lacked speed then improved his position from the outside without threatening. PRIVATE SON raced close up to the stretch while just outside then tired in the final eighth. IVAN JAY PERRY was always outrun. SCOOTER ROACH raced close up just outside and tired. NORTH OF SIX pressed the pace from just outside and tired.

Owners— 1, Port Trust Naify & San Gabriel Inve; 2, Frances J OToole; 3, J G & J W Phillips P Gartin & R Nic; 4, Three King Stable; 5, On Target Racing Stable; 6, Starlex Farm; 7, Sawatske Steve; 8, Cumberland Paul; 9, Fish Steven W & Bukowiecki Chris

Trainers—1, De Seroux Laura; 2, Motion H Graham; 3, Toner James J; 4, Stidham Michael; 5, Stall Albert M Jr; 6, Schu Sally S; 7, Vanier Harvey L; 8, Boyce Michele; 9, Bukowiecki Chris

$1 Pick Three (3–6–1) Paid $197.40; Pick Three Pool $13,692.

NINTH RACE
Belmont
JULY 5, 2003

1¼ MILES. (1.58^{1}) 117th Running of THE SUBURBAN HANDICAP. Grade I. Purse $500,000. (Up to $57,000 NYSBFOA). THREE YEAR OLDS AND UPWARD. By subscription of $500 each, which should accompany the nomination; $2,500 to pass the entry box and $2,500 to start. The purse to be divided 60% to the winner, 20% to second, 11% to third, 6% to fourth and 3% to fifth. Weights Sunday, June 29 Starters to be name at the closing time of entries. Trophies will be presented to the winning owner, trainer and jockey.

Value of Race: $500,000 Winner $300,000; second $100,000; third $55,000; fourth $30,000; fifth $15,000. Mutuel Pool $1,094,957.0 Exacta Pool $748,549.00 Trifecta Pool $627,923.00

Last Raced	Horse	M/Eqt.	A.Wt	PP	¼	½	¾	1	Str	Fin	Jockey	Odds $1
14Jun03 ^{10}CD^{2}	Mineshaft	L	4 121	1	$2^{1/2}$	$2^{1/2}$	$2^{1 1/2}$	1^{hd}	$1^{1/2}$	$1^{2 1/4}$	Albarado R J	0.75
14Jun03 ^{9}Bel^{2}	Volponi	Lb	5 121	5	4^{6}	$4^{5 1/2}$	$3^{1/2}$	$2^{2 1/2}$	2^{6}	2^{4}	Santos J A	2.40
29Nov02 ^{11}CD^{6}	Dollar Bill	L	5 115	7	5^{hd}	6^{1}	6^{5}	3^{2}	3^{3}	$3^{2 1/4}$	Castellano J J	9.80
12Jun03 ^{5}Bel^{2}	Puzzlement	Lb	4 113	6	$6^{1 1/2}$	5^{hd}	$5^{1/2}$	$4^{1/2}$	4^{2}	$4^{3/4}$	Chavez J F	33.25
14Jun03 ^{9}Bel^{4}	Evening Attire	Lb	5 120	4	7^{hd}	8	7^{hd}	$7^{1 1/2}$	$5^{3 1/2}$	$5^{7 1/2}$	Bridgmohan S X	7.40
21Jun03 ^{7}Bel^{1}	Nothing Flat	L	4 113	8	8	$7^{1/2}$	8	8	8	$6^{1 1/2}$	Coa E M	65.50
16May03 ^{11}Pim^{8}	Hero's Tribute	L	5 115	3	$3^{1 1/2}$	3^{1}	$4^{3 1/2}$	6^{1}	$7^{1/2}$	7^{3}	Samyn J L	22.90
9Jun03 ^{7}Del^{2}	Judge's Case	Lb	6 113	2	$1^{2 1/2}$	$1^{1 1/2}$	$1^{1/2}$	$5^{1 1/2}$	6^{hd}	8	Luzzi M J	85.25

OFF AT 5:13 Start Good. Won ridden out. Track fast.
TIME :24^{2}, :48^{3}, 1:12^{3}, 1:37, 2:01^{2} (:24.43, :48.67, 1:12.68, 1:37.11, 2:01.57)

$2 Mutuel Prices:			
1–MINESHAFT	3.50	2.40	2.10
6–VOLPONI		2.60	2.10
8–DOLLAR BILL			2.40

$2 EXACTA 1–6 PAID $7.20 $2 TRIFECTA 1–6–8 PAID $29.00

Dk. b. or br. c, by A.P. Indy–Prospectors Delite, by Mr. Prospector. Trainer Howard Neil J. Bred by W. S. Farish, James Elkins & W. T. Webber Jr. (Ky).

MINESHAFT showed good speed and raced with the pace while well in hand, cruised to the front on the second turn, turned back a bid from VOLPONI at the top of the stretch, drew clear when shaken up nearing the eighth pole and was ridden out to the wire. VOLPONI raced close up along the inside, advanced on the second turn, angled out, rallied three wide, tried the winner turning for home, could not get by that rival and stayed on gamely to be clearly best of the others. DOLLAR BILL was outrun early, put in a four wide run on the second turn and had little left for the stretch drive. PUZZLEMENT was outrun early, put in a run along the inside on the second turn and tired in the stretch. EVENING ATTIRE was outrun early, raced inside and had no response when roused. NOTHING FLAT dropped back early, raced outside and had no rally. HERO'S TRIBUTE raced with the pace while three wide and came up empty when asked. JUDGE'S CASE quickly showed in front, set the pace for three quarters and tired.

Owners— 1, Farish William S Elkins James A & W; 2, Amherst Stable & Spruce Pond Stable; 3, West Gary L & Mary E; 4, Shields Joseph V Jr; 5, Grant Mary & Joseph & Kelly Thomas; 6, Condren William J & Sherman Michael; 7, Oxley John C; 8, Sanford Goldfarb Lawrence Roche & P

Trainers—1, Howard Neil J; 2, Johnson Philip G; 3, Frankel Robert; 4, Jerkens H Allen; 5, Kelly Patrick J; 6, Zito Nicholas P; 7, Ward John T Jr; 8, Klesaris Steve

Scratched— Harlan's Holiday (14Jun03 ^{9}BEL^{5})

$2 Daily Double (7–1) Paid $15.20; Daily Double Pool $151,399.
$2 Pick Three (2–7–1) Paid $25.00; Pick Three Pool $126,888.

EIGHTH RACE
Belmont
JULY 5, 2003

1 MILE. (Turf)(1.31^{3}) 19th Running of THE POKER HANDICAP. Grade III. Purse $100,000. (Up to $19,400 NYSBFOA). THREE YEAR OLDS AND UPWARD. By subscription of $100 each, which should accompany the nomination; $500 to pass the entry box; $500 to start with $100,000 added. The added money and all fees to be divided 60% to the winner, 20% to second, 11% to third, 6% to fourth and 3% to fifth. Trophies will be presented to the winning owner, trainer and jockey. The New York Racing Association reserves the right to transfer this race to the Main Track. In the event that this race is taken off the turf, it may be subject to downgrading upon review by the Graded Stakes Committee. Closed Saturday, June 21, 2003 with 52 Nominations.

Value of Race: $116,200 Winner $69,720; second $23,240; third $12,782; fourth $6,972; fifth $3,486. Mutuel Pool $607,095.00 Exacta Pool $470,844.00 Trifecta Pool $316,912.00

Last Raced	Horse	M/Eqt.	A.Wt	PP	St	¼	½	¾	Str	Fin	Jockey	Odds $1
26May03 ^{8}Hol^{5}	War Zone	L	4 117	6	11	$8\frac{1}{2}$	8^{1}	$3\frac{1}{2}$	$3^{2\frac{1}{2}}$	$1\frac{1}{2}$	Castellano J J	2.45
10Apr03 NAS^{4}	Trademark-	L	7 114	2	3	$5\frac{1}{2}$	$4\frac{1}{2}$	$2^{1\frac{1}{2}}$	2^{hd}	$2\frac{1}{2}$	Coa E M	13.80
14Jun03 ^{10}Mth^{3}	Saint Verre	L	5 112	7	1	$1\frac{1}{2}$	$1\frac{1}{2}$	1^{1}	$1\frac{1}{2}$	$3^{1\frac{1}{4}}$	Espinoza J L	5.20
7Jun03 ^{5}Bel^{2}	Proud Man	Lb	5 114	8	10	7^{2}	$7\frac{1}{2}$	6^{hd}	$4^{2\frac{1}{2}}$	4^{2}	Chavez J F	a-8.90
6Jun03 ^{8}Bel^{5}	Pinky Pizwaanski	L	5 112	1	7	$10^{2\frac{1}{2}}$	10^{3}	8^{hd}	$6\frac{1}{2}$	$5^{1\frac{3}{4}}$	Bridgmohan S X	30.00
21May03 ^{8}Bel^{9}	Mystic Salse-GB	L	4 113	3	6	$6\frac{1}{2}$	5^{hd}	5^{hd}	5^{hd}	6^{nk}	Samyn J L	a-8.90
15Feb03 ^{7}Hou^{9}	Green Fee	L	7 117	9	9	11	11	$10\frac{1}{2}$	$8^{1\frac{1}{2}}$	7no	Santos J A	6.70
29Nov02 ^{8}CD^{5}	Aslaaf	Lb	5 115	10	8	9^{hd}	$9^{1\frac{1}{2}}$	7^{hd}	$7\frac{1}{2}$	8^{4}	Albarado R J	25.25
29Mar03 NAS^{5}	Equerry	L	5 115	4	4	3^{hd}	2^{hd}	4^{hd}	9^{6}	9^{6}	Luzzi M J	6.90
7Nov02 ^{8}Aqu^{6}	Artax Too	Lb	4 113	5	5	$4^{1\frac{1}{2}}$	$6^{1\frac{1}{2}}$	11	$10\frac{1}{2}$	10^{nk}	Rojas R I	51.00
22Sep02 ^{9}Bel^{1}	Finality	L	4 116	11	2	2^{hd}	$3\frac{1}{2}$	9^{hd}	11	11	Velazquez J R	3.85

a–Coupled: Proud Man and Mystic Salse–GB.

OFF AT 4:40 Start Good. Won driving. Course firm.
TIME :23^{4}, :46^{1}, 1:09^{2}, 1:32^{4} (:23.86, :46.36, 1:09.48, 1:32.81)

$2 Mutuel Prices:			
7–WAR ZONE	6.90	4.50	3.10
4–TRADEMARK–		11.20	8.00
8–SAINT VERRE			4.60

$2 EXACTA 7–4 PAID $75.50 $2 TRIFECTA 7–4–8 PAID $422.50

B. c, by Danzig–Proflare, by Mr. Prospector. Trainer Frankel Robert. Bred by Juddmonte Farms Inc (Ky).

WAR ZONE was rated along early, rallied inside on the turn, came wide into the stretch, finished stoutly and was along late from the outside, driving. TRADEMARK (SAF) raced close up inside, came wide into the stretch and dug in gamely while between rivals in the drive. SAINT VERRE quickly showed in front, set the pace and dug in gamely along the inside in the stretch. PROUD MAN was rated along outside, raced wide and finished gamely outside. PINKY PIZWAANSKI was outrun early, came wide into the stretch and was going well late outside. MYSTIC SALSE (GB) was rated along early, raced inside and lacked a rally. GREEN FEE was outrun early, came widest nearing the stretch and finished well outside. ASLAAF was outrun early, put in a three wide run on the turn and faded in the stretch. EQUERRY raced close up early and tired in the stretch. ARTAX TOO tired after a half mile. FINALITY chased the pace while three wide and tired in the stretch.

Owners— 1, Juddmonte Farms Inc; 2, Al Maktoum Mohammed b; 3, Allen Joseph; 4, Double R Stable Kaufman Robert & We; 5, Houyhnhnm Stable; 6, Kaufman Robert & Iselin James H; 7, Low Lawana L & Robert E; 8, Al Maktoum Sheik Maktoum b; 9, Godolphin Racing Inc; 10, Paraneck Stable; 11, Dogwood Stable

Trainers—1, Frankel Robert; 2, McLaughlin Kiaran P; 3, Jerkens H Allen; 4, Clement Christophe; 5, Turner William H Jr; 6, Reinacher Robert Jr; 7, Peitz Daniel C; 8, McLaughlin Kiaran P; 9, Albertrani Thomas; 10, Pedersen Jennifer; 11, Pletcher Todd A

Scratched— Windsor Castle (7Jun03 ^{7}DEL^{4}), Regal Sanction (6Jun03 ^{8}BEL^{2})

$2 Pick Three (1–2–7) Paid $188.00; Pick Three Pool $87,511.

TENTH RACE
Monmouth
JULY 5, 2003

1⅜ MILES. (Turf)(2.12^{3}) 49th Running of THE UNITED NATIONS HANDICAP. Grade I. Purse $750,000. THREE–YEAR–OLDS AND UPWARD. By subscription of $500 each, which should accompany the nomination and $7,500 to pass the entry box. The winning owner to receive $450,000, $150,000 to second, $80,000 to third, $42,500 to fourth, $20,000 to fifth and $7,500 to sixth. (Should this race be taken off the turf it will be run at one mile and one–quarter on the main track). The owner of the winner to receive a trophy. Closed Saturday, June 21 with 29 nominations.

Value of Race: $750,000 Winner $450,000; second $150,000; third $80,000; fourth $42,500; fifth $20,000; sixth $7,500. Mutuel Pool $490,083.00 Exacta Pool $303,070.00 Trifecta Pool $212,390.00

Last Raced	Horse	M/Eqt.	A.Wt	PP	¼	½	¾	1	Str	Fin	Jockey	Odds $1
14Jun03 ^{10}Mth^{2}	Balto Star	L	5 117	1	1^{1}	1^{1}	1^{1}	1^{1}	1^{hd}	$1\frac{1}{2}$	Velez J A Jr	37.00
10May03 ^{7}Hol^{7}	The Tin Man	L	5 121	2	$2^{1\frac{1}{2}}$	$2^{1\frac{1}{2}}$	2^{1}	2^{1}	2^{1}	2no	Smith M E	5.90
21May03 ^{8}Bel^{1}	Lunar Sovereign	L	4 112	4	6^{hd}	$6\frac{1}{2}$	6^{hd}	$6\frac{1}{2}$	3^{hd}	3^{nk}	Migliore R	7.60
7Jun03 ^{10}Bel^{2}	Requete-GB	L	4 115	3	7	7	7	7	5^{hd}	4^{hd}	Prado E S	2.50
7Jun03 ^{10}Bel^{1}	Denon	L	5 122	5	4^{hd}	4^{hd}	4^{hd}	4^{hd}	4^{1}	$5^{2\frac{1}{2}}$	Bailey J D	1.20
31May03 ^{9}CD^{1}	Kim Loves Bucky	L	6 115	7	$5\frac{1}{2}$	5^{1}	$3\frac{1}{2}$	3^{hd}	6^{1}	6^{hd}	Sellers S J	20.40
7Jun03 ^{10}Bel^{10}	With Anticipation	Lb	8 120	6	$3\frac{1}{2}$	$3\frac{1}{2}$	$5^{1\frac{1}{2}}$	5^{1}	7	7	Day P	6.20

OFF AT 5:21 Start Good. Won driving. Course firm.
TIME :24^{2}, :48^{3}, 1:14, 1:37^{3}, 2:12^{3} (:24.57, :48.79, 1:14.15, 1:37.66, 2:12.78)
(New Course Record)

$2 Mutuel Prices:			
1–BALTO STAR	76.00	28.40	15.00
2–THE TIN MAN		8.20	8.00
4–LUNAR SOVEREIGN			8.60

$2 EXACTA 1–2 PAID $422.80 $2 TRIFECTA 1–2–4 PAID $2,819.20

Dk. b. or br. g, by Glitterman–Miss Livi, by Devil's Bag. Trainer Pletcher Todd A. Bred by Anstu Stables Inc (Ky).

BALTO STAR firmly rated the pace inside then responded gamely to stretch pressure and held well just off the rail. THE TIN MAN rated close off the rail, took aim in midstretch, held well in place but needed more. LUNAR SOVEREIGN, unhurriedly while not far back, bid angling widest on the final turn, closed to late stretch and finished well. REQUETE (GB), unhurriedly inside, lacked room on the rail from the quarter pole to midstretch, was eased out through late stretch and finished well when clear. DENON rated just off the pace inside, remained close through the stretch and finished evenly. KIM LOVES BUCKY rated close toward the outside, was five wide on the final turn, brushed lightly with With Anticipation entering the stretch then faded. WITH ANTICIPATION rated just off the pace in the three path, ran evenly through the final turn, brushed lightly with Kim Loves Bucky entering the stretch then showed no stretch response.

Owners— 1, Anstu Stables; 2, Aury & Ralph E Todd; 3, Al Maktoum Sheikh Rashid b; 4, Juddmonte Farms Inc; 5, Flaxman Holdings Ltd & Edmund A Gan; 6, Glenney Kim; 7, Augustin Stable

Trainers—1, Pletcher Todd A; 2, Mandella Richard; 3, McLaughlin Kiaran P; 4, Frankel Robert; 5, Frankel Robert; 6, Glenney John; 7, Sheppard Jonathan E

$2 Pick Three (9–6–1) Paid $1,003.60; Pick Three Pool $24,091.

NINTH RACE
Churchill
JULY 5, 2003

1 MILE. (Turf)(1.33^3) 14th Running of THE FIRECRACKER BREEDERS' CUP HANDICAP. Grade II. Purse $250,000 Added (Includes $75,000 BC – Breeders' Cup) THREE-YEAR-OLDS AND UPWARD. (Includes $75,000 from the Breeders' Cup Fund for Cup Nominees Only). By subscription of $250 each on or before June 21, 2003 or by Supplementary Nomination of $12,500 each by the closing of entries Friday, June 27, 2003. $1,250 to pass the entry box; $1,250 additional to start, with $175,000 added and an additional $75,000 from the Breeders' Cup Fund for Cup Nominees only. The host association's added monies to be divided 62% to the owner of the winner, 20% to second, 10% to third, 5% to fourth and 3% to fifth. Breeders' Cup Fund monies also correspondingly divided providing a Breeders' Cup nominee has finished in an awarded position. Weights to be announced Saturday, June 28. If the race is moved to the main track after the time of closing, a horse may be scratched for any reason at any time up to 15 minutes prior to post time for the race preceding this race or thereafter with a valid physical reason and approved by the stewards. Closed Saturday, June 21, 2003 with 64.

Value of Race: $288,500 Winner $178,870; second $57,700; third $28,850; fourth $14,425; fifth $8,655. Mutuel Pool $475,508.00 Exacta Pool $338,325.00 Trifecta Pool $280,416.00 Superfecta Pool $68,185.00

Last Raced	Horse	M/Eqt.	A.Wt	PP	St	¼	½	¾	Str	Fin	Jockey	Odds $1
15Jun03 ^{8}WO^{4}	Tap The Admiral	L	5 115	4	8	7^{5}	7^{5}	6^{hd}	$2\frac{1}{2}$	$1^{1\frac{1}{4}}$	McKee J	7.20
7Jun03 ^{5}CD^{3}	Freefourinternet	L	5 114	1	5	8^{hd}	9	$8^{2\frac{1}{2}}$	$6\frac{1}{2}$	$2\frac{1}{2}$	Blanc B	7.60
15Jun03 ^{8}AP^{3}	Package Store	Lf	5 114	3	6	$2^{2\frac{1}{2}}$	$2\frac{1}{2}$	1^{hd}	1^{1}	$3^{1\frac{1}{2}}$	Velasquez C	2.30
31May03 ^{8}CD^{2}	Classic Par	L	5 112	8	3	$5\frac{1}{2}$	$6^{1\frac{1}{2}}$	5^{1}	4^{2}	4^{3}	Meche L J	11.70
21Jun03 ^{9}CD^{3}	Pass Rush	Lb	4 115	6	2	$1\frac{1}{2}$	$1^{1\frac{1}{2}}$	$2^{1\frac{1}{2}}$	3^{hd}	$5\frac{3}{4}$	Melancon L	5.20
20Jun03 ^{8}CD^{2}	Cat Tracker	L	5 111	9	4	6^{1}	$4\frac{1}{2}$	4^{hd}	5^{hd}	6^{1}	Court J K	24.90
15Jun03 ^{8}AP^{1}	Rock Slide	L	5 117	7	1	$3\frac{1}{2}$	$3\frac{1}{2}$	3^{hd}	$7^{1\frac{1}{2}}$	7no	Martinez W	2.70
15Jun03 ^{8}AP^{5}	Al's Dearly Bred	Lb	6 114	5	9	9	$8\frac{1}{2}$	9	9	$8\frac{3}{4}$	Perret C	20.40
8Jun03 ^{8}CD^{1}	Entitlement	L	4 113	2	7	4^{2}	5^{hd}	7^{4}	$8^{2\frac{1}{2}}$	9	Borel C H	14.10

OFF AT 5:26 Start Good. Won driving. Course firm.
TIME :23^4, :47, 1:10^3, 1:23, 1:35^2 (:23.88, :47.19, 1:10.60, 1:23.10, 1:35.48)

$2 Mutuel Prices:

4–TAP THE ADMIRAL	16.40	8.20	6.00
1–FREEFOURINTERNET		10.60	5.60
3–PACKAGE STORE			3.00

$2 EXACTA 4–1 PAID $141.80 $2 TRIFECTA 4–1–3 PAID $441.40 $1 SUPERFECTA 4–1–3–8 PAID $3,068.30

Ch. h, by Pleasant Tap–Polish Buck, by Polish Navy. Trainer Carroll Del W II. Bred by Highland Farms Inc (Ky).

TAP THE ADMIRAL broke in front, settled near the inside, moved out five or six wide concluding the second turn, caught PACKAGE STORE nearing the sixteenth pole and drove clear late under strong handling. FREEFOURINTERNET, outrun for a half while saving ground, remained near the inside while edging closer approaching the stretch, worked his way out eight wide at the furlong grounds and was going well at the end. PACKAGE STORE, close up inside early, eased outside of front-running PASS RUSH on the backstretch, inched to a slight edge just before going six furlongs, showed the way into the final furlong and faltered. CLASSIC PAR tracked the pace four wide early, angled in behind foes nearing the far turn, swung out again to be four or five wide for the last eighth and lacked a further account. PASS RUSH hopped at the start, recovered quickly to gain the lead, raced near the inside, was headed by PACKAGE STORE nearing the final quarter and weakened thereafter. CAT TRACKER, within easy striking distance although five wide, flattened out the last eighth. ROCK SLIDE tracked the pace four wide to the stretch and faltered when straightened for the drive. AL'S DEARLY BRED, four or five wide most of the trip, never was a factor. ENTITLEMENT settled inside, raced in a striking position to the stretch and weakened.

Owners— 1, Ettinger Stanley; 2, Estrorace Stable; 3, Eutrophia Farm; 4, Centaur Farms Inc; 5, Tabor Michael B; 6, WinStar Farm; 7, Farish William S Elkins James A & W; 8, Castro John; 9, Jones Brereton C

Trainers—1, Carroll Del W II; 2, Scott Joan; 3, Bindner Walter M Jr; 4, Scherer Merrill R; 5, Byrne Patrick B; 6, Walden W Elliott; 7, Howard Neil J; 8, Robertson Hugh H; 9, Hennig John K

$1 Pick Three (8–2/3/6–4) Paid $231.50; Pick Three Pool $37,441.

SEVENTH RACE

Hollywood
JULY 5, 2003

1 MILE. (Turf)(1.32³) 6th Running of THE ROYAL HEROINE. Grade III. Purse $100,000 Added. FILLIES AND MARES THREE–YEAR–OLDS AND UPWARD. By subscription of $100 each on or before Wednesday, June 25 or by supplementary nomination of $5,000 each by closing time of entries. $1,000 additional to start, with $100,000 added, of which 60% to the winner, 20% to second, 12% to third, 6% to fourth and 2% to fifth. Three year olds 114 lbs. Older 123 lbs. Non–winners of $60,000 at a mile or over in 2003 allowed 2 lbs. Such a race in 2002 allowed 4 lbs. Non–winners of two races other than maiden, claiming or starter at a mile over in 2003 allowed 6 lbs. Such a race in 2003 allowed 8 lbs. Starters to be named through the entry box by closing time of entries. Rail at 0 Feet.

Value of Race: $112,200 Winner $67,320; second $22,440; third $13,464; fourth $6,732; fifth $2,244. Mutuel Pool $610,651.00 Exacta Pool $362,320.00 Quinella Pool $35,879.00 Trifecta Pool $367,917.00 Superfecta Pool $115,378.00

Last Raced	Horse	M/Eqt. A.Wt	PP	St	¼	½	¾	Str	Fin	Jockey	Odds $1
26May03 ¹⁰LS³	Magic Mission-GB	LBb 5 115	8	7	8¹½	8²	8²	3hd	1hd	Nakatani C S	6.30
26May03 ¹⁰LS²	Little Treasure-FR	LB 4 121	2	3	1¹	1hd	1hd	1¹	2²	Desormeaux K J	9.60
29May03 7Hol¹	Belleski	LB 4 115	5	1	4¹	4½	6¹	5¹½	3¹½	Espinoza V	a-2.30
13Oct02 Lch⁹	Chercheuse	LB 5 116	1	8	7¹	5½	5½	4½	4nk	Flores D R	14.70
15Jan03 7SA³	Angel Gift	LB 5 115	6	2	2¹	2¹	2hd	2hd	5hd	Valdivia J Jr	21.20
2Jan03 7SA⁶	Innit-IR	LB 5 115	3	9	9	9	9	9	6½	Baze T C	60.10
27Apr03 8Hol²	Southern Oasis	LB 5 119	4	6	5hd	7¹½	7½	7½	7¹	Solis A	1.80
24May03 7BM³	Lindsay Jean	LB 5 119	7	5	6½	6hd	4hd	6hd	8⁴	Schvaneveldt C P	a-2.30
7May03 7Hol¹	Polygreen-FR	LB 4 117	9	4	3hd	3hd	3¹½	8¹	9	Stevens G L	4.60

a–Coupled: Belleski and Lindsay Jean.

OFF AT 3:51 Start Good. Won driving. Course firm.
TIME :23³, :47², 1:10⁴, 1:34¹ (:23.73, :47.57, 1:10.99, 1:34.25)

$2 Mutuel Prices:

7–MAGIC MISSION–GB	14.60	8.40	4.80
3–LITTLE TREASURE–FR		10.40	6.20
1–BELLESKI (a–entry)			3.60

$1 EXACTA 7–3 PAID $65.20 $2 QUINELLA 3–7 PAID $72.00 $1 TRIFECTA 7–3–1 PAID $281.20 $1 SUPERFECTA 7–3–1–2 PAID $2,631.20

B. m, by Machiavellian–Dream Ticket, by Danzig. Trainer Drysdale Neil. Bred by Gainsborough Stud Management Ltd (GB).

MAGIC MISSION (GB) settled outside a rival then off the rail, went four wide on the second turn and five wide into the stretch, drifted in through the drive, bid outside and wore down the runner-up under strong handling. LITTLE TREASURE (FR) sped to the early lead, dueled inside on the backstretch and second turn, inched away again in the stretch, fought back along the rail and continued gamely to the wire. BELLESKI stalked inside but a bit off the rail, continued between horses into and on the second turn, waited a bit into the stretch, split rivals in midstretch and picked up the show. CHERCHEUSE saved ground chasing the pace, moved up inside leaving the backstretch and on the second turn, continued along the rail and lacked the needed late kick. ANGEL GIFT stalked off the rail then bid outside a rival and dueled for the lead, battled between horses on the second turn and into the stretch and weakened. INNIT (IRE) threw her head in the early going, angled in and settled off the rail then inside, came out in midstretch and was not a threat. SOUTHERN OASIS pulled her way between horses to stalk the pace, was boxed in on the second turn and blocked until past midstretch and could not recover. LINDSAY JEAN rank early, stalked outside, went four wide on the second turn and into the stretch and weakened. POLYGREEN (FR) three deep into the first turn, stalked outside, bid three wide into and on the second turn, dropped back in the stretch and had little left.

Owners— 1, Al Maktoum Sheik Maktoum b; 2, Port Trust Naify Marsha & San Gabri; 3, Moss Mr & Mrs Jerome S; 4, Darley Stud Management Inc; 5, Delahoussaye Enterprises Strauss &; 6, Duchossois Richard L; 7, Whitham Janis R; 8, Moss Mr & Mrs Jerome S; 9, Wertheimer Farm

Trainers— 1, Drysdale Neil; 2, De Seroux Laura; 3, Sadler John W; 4, Harty Eoin; 5, Gallagher Patrick; 6, McAnally Ronald; 7, McAnally Ronald; 8, Sherman Art; 9, Mandella Richard

$2 Daily Double (1–7) Paid $59.00; Daily Double Pool $32,076.
$1 Pick Three (10–1–7) Paid $155.60; Pick Three Pool $123,036.

EIGHTH RACE
Hollywood
JULY 5, 2003

7 FURLONGS. (1.19⁴) 52nd Running of THE TRIPLE BEND BREEDERS' CUP INVITATIONAL HANDICAP. Grade I. Purse $300,000 Guaranteed (includes $50,000 BC – Breeders' Cup). AN INVITATIONAL HANDICAP FOR THREE YEAR OLDS AND UPWARD. (Includes $50,000 from the Breeders' Cup Fund for Cup Nominees Only). No Nominating or Starting Fees. With $250,000 guaranteed, and an additional $50,000 from the Breeders' Cup Fund for Breeders' Cup nominees only. The host association's money to be divided 60% to the winner, 20% to second, 12% to third, 6% to fourth and 2% to fifth.

Value of Race: $300,000 Winner $180,000; second $60,000; third $36,000; fourth $18,000; fifth $6,000. Mutuel Pool $631,405.00 Exacta Pool $379,326.00 Quinella Pool $39,523.00 Trifecta Pool $363,238.00 Superfecta Pool $141,685.00

Last Raced	Horse	M/Eqt.	A.Wt	PP	St	¼	½	Str	Fin	Jockey	Odds $1
31May03 8Hol1	Joey Franco	LB	4 118	9	3	3hd	3hd	11	1hd	Valenzuela P A	2.50
31May03 8Hol3	Publication	LBb	4 116	5	4	8½	7½	52½	21½	Desormeaux K J	8.70
26May03 8LS3	[D]Bluesthestandard	LB	6 117	8	1	41	42½	21½	33½	Pedroza M A	3.90
7Jun03 7Hol2	Primerica	LB	5 113	2	7	53½	53½	4hd	42	Espinoza V	8.90
31May03 8Hol2	Kela	LBb	5 115	3	6	71½	82½	6½	5½	Nakatani C S	12.80
29Mar03 NAS2	Avanzado-ARG	LBbf	6 118	1	5	1hd	1½	31	64	Baze T C	2.40
31May03 8Hol5	Cappuchino	LBbf	4 112	4	2	21	21	73½	74½	Garcia M S	39.50
4Jun03 5Hol3	Geronimo-CH	LBb	4 115	6	9	9	9	82	810	Valdivia J Jr	45.50
29Mar03 NAS4	Cayoke-FR	LBb	6 116	7	8	61½	63	9	9	Flores D R	9.70

[D]-Bluesthestandard disqualified and placed 6th.

OFF AT 4:21 Start Good. Won driving. Track fast.
TIME :21⁴, :44², 1:08², 1:21² (:21.97, :44.40, 1:08.58, 1:21.56)

$2 Mutuel Prices:

10–JOEY FRANCO	7.00	4.40	3.20
5–PUBLICATION		7.40	4.40
2–PRIMERICA			5.60

$1 EXACTA 10–5 PAID $21.10 $2 QUINELLA 5–10 PAID $24.60 $1 TRIFECTA 10–5–2 PAID $96.40 $1 SUPERFECTA 10–5–2–3 PAID $796.40

Dk. b. or br. c, by Avenue of Flags–Susan Powter, by Native Prospector. Trainer Vienna Darrell. Bred by Jerry Frankel (Cal).

JOEY FRANCO stalked the pace outside, ranged up three deep leaving the turn, gained command into the stretch, inched away and drifted in a bit in midstretch, kicked clear, drifted out but held under urging. PUBLICATION angled in and saved ground off the pace, rode the rail on the turn, split horses past midstretch, then came out and closed with a rush to just miss. BLUESTHESTANDARD stalked off the rail, bid between horses leaving the turn, drifted inward in midstretch and could not match the top pair. PRIMERICA saved ground chasing the pace, came out on the turn and four wide into the stretch and lacked the needed rally. KELA allowed to settle a bit off the rail then outside a rival on the turn, came out into the stretch and was not a threat. AVANZADO (ARG) had good early speed and dueled inside, inched away between calls on the turn, fought back leaving the bend, began to weaken in upper stretch, steadied when crowded in midstretch and dropped back. CAPPUCHINO prompted the pace outside a rival, began to fall back some leaving the turn, steadied nearing the quarter pole, lugged out into the stretch and had little left. GERONIMO (CHI) bobbled at the start, settled between horses then outside a rival, angled in on the turn and was outrun. CAYOKE (FR) squeezed at the start, chased off the rail, dropped back on the turn, came a bit wide into the stretch and gave way, then did not return to be unsaddled and was vanned off. Following a stewards' inquiry, BLUESTHESTANDARD was disqualified and placed sixth for interference midstretch. A claim of foul by the rider of the runner-up against the winner for alleged interference in deep stretch was not allowed by the stewards, who ruled the latter was clear when he drifted out.

Owners— 1, Frankel Jerry; 2, Mercedes Stables; 3, Sengara Jeffrey; 4, Jess L Miller Trust; 5, Jones Aaron U & Marie D; 6, Cees Stable; 7, Hollendorfer Litt & Todaro; 8, JMJ Racing Stable; 9, House Michael

Trainers—1, Vienna Darrell; 2, Cerin Vladimir; 3, West Ted H; 4, Dollase Wallace; 5, Barrera Larry; 6, O'Neill Doug; 7, Hollendorfer Jerry; 8, O'Neill Doug; 9, Canani Julio C

Scratched— Medecis (26May03 8HOL4)

$2 Daily Double (7–10) Paid $73.40; Daily Double Pool $47,815.
$1 Pick Three (1–7–10) Paid $107.80; Pick Three Pool $108,361.

TENTH RACE
Belmont
JULY 6, 2003

1 1/16 MILES. (1.39²) 86th Running of THE DWYER. Grade II. Purse $150,000. (Up to $29,100 NYSBFOA). THREE YEAR OLDS. By subscription of $150 each, which should accompany the nomination; $750 to pass the entry box and $750 to start. Weight 123 lbs. Non-winners of $200,000 at a mile or over in 2003 allowed 2 lbs. $60,000 at a mile or over in 2003; or $40,000 twice in 2003, 4 lbs.; $50,000; or $30,000 twice at a mile or over, 6 lbs. $30,000, or three races, 8 lbs. (Maiden, claiming, starter, restricted or restricted stake races not considered in allowances.) Closed Saturday, June 21, 2003 with 28 Nominations.

Value of Race: $150,000 Winner $90,000; second $30,000; third $16,500; fourth $9,000; fifth $4,500. Mutuel Pool $598,480.00 Exacta Pool $424,658.00 Trifecta Pool $315,955.00

Last Raced	Horse	M/Eqt.	A.Wt	PP	St	¼	½	¾	Str	Fin	Jockey	Odds $1
7Jun03 4Bel1	Strong Hope	L	3 115	3	3	1½	11	11½	12½	1nk	Velazquez J R	2.50
22Jun03 7Bel1	Nacheezmo	L	3 115	2	7	7	52	44½	23½	23	Chavez J F	9.00
5Oct02 9Kee1	Sky Mesa	L	3 119	6	4	34½	2½	2½	33½	35¼	Prado E S	1.55
21Jun03 14Tdn5	Private City		3 115	1	6	51	61½	62	42½	42	Samyn J L	27.00
17May03 9Pim1	Best Minister	L	3 121	4	5	6hd	7	7	56	56¼	Santos J A	5.60
14Jun03 11Del4	Go Rockin' Robin	Lb	3 121	5	2	45½	43½	5½	67	615	Bridgmohan S X	15.30
18Jun03 4Bel1	Albaaz	L	3 115	7	1	21½	37	32½	7	7	Migliore R	5.90

OFF AT 5:44 Start Good. Won driving. Track fast.
TIME :23¹, :45³, 1:09³, 1:35, 1:41³ (:23.33, :45.73, 1:09.60, 1:35.01, 1:41.76)

$2 Mutuel Prices:

4–STRONG HOPE	7.00	4.20	2.70
2–NACHEEZMO		7.60	4.10
7–SKY MESA			2.50

$2 EXACTA 4–2 PAID $42.40 $2 TRIFECTA 4–2–7 PAID $176.50

B. c, (Feb), by Grand Slam–Shining Through, by Deputy Minister. Trainer Pletcher Todd A. Bred by Trackside Farm GA Seelbinder & Liberation Farm (Ky).

STRONG HOPE showed good speed along the inside, took charge after leaving the chute, set the pace, drew clear, responded when roused, dug in gamely on the rail and held off NACHEEZMO under a drive. NACHEEZMO was outrun early on, advanced inside on the turn, angled out for the drive and was coming fast from the outside at the finish. SKY MESA showed good speed while in hand, chased the winner from the outside and stayed on gamely in the stretch. PRIVATE CITY was outrun early, put in a four wide run on the turn and had nothing left for the stretch drive. BEST MINISTER was outrun early, raced inside and had no response when roused. GO ROCKIN' ROBIN had no response when roused. ALBAAZ chased the pace while three wide and tired after the opening three quarters.

Owners— 1, Melnyk Eugene & Laura; 2, Johnson Ted J & Kim; 3, Oxley John C; 4, Bohemia Stable; 5, Phillips Joan G & John W; 6, Schwartz Herbert T & Carol A; 7, Shadwell Stable

Trainers—1, Pletcher Todd A; 2, Bond Harold James; 3, Ward John T Jr; 4, Jerkens H Allen; 5, McPeek Kenneth G; 6, Schwartz Scott M; 7, McLaughlin Kiaran P

Scratched— Colita (21May03 7BEL1)

TENTH RACE	6 FURLONGS. (1.07³) 102nd Running of THE BASHFORD MANOR. Grade III. Purse $150,000 added.
Churchill	TWO YEARS OLD. By subscription of $150 each on or before June 21 or by Supplementary Nomination of $7,500 at time of entry. $750 to pass the entry box; $750 additional to start, with $150,000 added of which
JULY 6, 2003	62% of all monies to the owner of the winner, 20% to second, 10% to third, 5% to fourth and 3% to fifth. Colts and geldings, 121 lbs. Fillies, 118 lbs. Non–winners of a sweepstakes, allowed 2 lbs. A race other than maiden or claiming, 4 lbs. A race other than claiming, 6 lbs. Starters to be named through the entry box at the usual time of closing. Closed Saturday, June 21 with 25 nominations.

Value of Race: $162,750 Winner $100,905; second $32,550; third $16,275; fourth $8,138; fifth $4,882. Mutuel Pool $310,973.00 Exacta Pool $216,670.00 Trifecta Pool $176,106.00 Superfecta Pool $53,155.00

Last Raced	Horse	M/Eqt. A.Wt	PP	St	¼	½	Str	Fin	Jockey	Odds $1
3May03 6CD1	Limehouse	L	2 121	2	5	4hd	31	32	14½	Albarado R J	3.00
26May03 9CD2	First Money	L	2 117	4	4	2½	21	1½	22	Butler D P	42.40
26May03 9CD1	Cuvee	L	2 121	1	6	3hd	54½	45	3no	Meche L J	0.50
14Jun03 1CD1	Bustin' Out	L	2 117	3	3	11	1½	2½	45	Velasquez C	4.90
14Jun03 4CD2	Exploit Lad	Lb	2 117	5	2	6	6	51	511	Sellers S J	37.30
7Jun03 8LS1	Next Bandit	L	2 121	6	1	52½	41	6	6	Martin E M Jr	11.10

OFF AT 5:57 Start Good. Won driving. Track fast.
TIME :21¹, :44³, :57², 1:10³ (:21.24, :44.69, :57.44, 1:10.62)

$2 Mutuel Prices:

2–LIMEHOUSE	8.00	4.20	2.10
4–FIRST MONEY		14.00	2.10
1–CUVEE			2.10

$2 EXACTA 2–4 PAID $190.40 $2 TRIFECTA 2–4–1 PAID $353.40 $1
SUPERFECTA 2–4–1–3 PAID $518.70

Ch. c, (Feb), by Grand Slam–Dixieland Blues, by Dixieland Band. Trainer Pletcher Todd A. Bred by (Fla).

LIMEHOUSE, bumped at the start by BUSTIN' OUT and forced in on CUVEE, was in tight at the half-mile ground, continued inside, eased out four wide entering the upper stretch, took over approaching the sixteenth pole and drove well clear. FIRST MONEY bobbled at the start, moved up soon after to press front-running BUSTIN' OUT, took over from that one in the upper stretch but wasn't a match for LIMEHOUSE late. CUVEE, bumped at the start and forced in, raced inside, was steadied in tight quarters and appeared to graze the inner railing leaving the half-mile ground, was checked for several more strides, continued inside until the stretch, swung out four or five wide for the drive and improved his position. BUSTIN' OUT drifted in at the start bumping the winner, forced LIMEHOUSE in on CUVEE, gained the lead, raced near the inside, moved closer to the rail leaving the backstretch, made the pace into the stretch and weakened. EXPLOIT LAD, four or five wide throughout, wasn't a serious factor. NEXT BANDIT drifted out at the start, angled in to followed the pace four or five wide and tired entering the stretch.

Owners– 1, Dogwood Stable; 2, Copeland Dreabon; 3, Winchell Thoroughbreds; 4, Overbrook Farm; 5, Jones Frank L Jr; 6, Coast To Coast Racing Fund
Trainers– 1, Pletcher Todd A; 2, Flint Bernard S; 3, Asmussen Steven M; 4, Lukas D Wayne; 5, Romans Dale; 6, Calhoun William Bret

---

$1 Pick Three (8–2/4/6/8–2) Paid $145.10; Pick Three Pool $34,767.

TENTH RACE	1⅜ MILES. (Turf)(2.11) 46th Running of THE BOWLING GREEN HANDICAP. Grade II. Purse
Belmont	$150,000. (Up to $29,100 NYSBFOA).THREE YEAR OLDS AND UPWARD. By subscription of $150 each, which should accompany the nomination; $750 to pass the entry box and $750 to start. The New York
JULY 12, 2003	Racing Association reserves the right to transfer this race to the Main Track. In the event that this race is taken off the turf, it may be subject to downgrading upon review by the Graded Stakes Committee. Closed Saturday, June 28, 2003 with 30 Nominations.

Value of Race: $150,000 Winner $90,000; second $30,000; third $16,500; fourth $9,000; fifth $4,500. Mutuel Pool $611,371.00 Exacta Pool $465,184.00 Trifecta Pool $342,145.00

Last Raced	Horse	M/Eqt. A.Wt	PP	¼	½	¾	1	Str	Fin	Jockey	Odds $1
25Jun03 8Bel5	Whitmore's Conn	Lb	5 116	1	9	8hd	7hd	7½	4hd	1½	Samyn J L	11.80
31May03 9CD5	Quest Star	Lb	4 117	2	3½	4½	3hd	3hd	2hd	2nk	Velazquez J R	5.70
7Jun03 10Bel4	Macaw–IR	Lbf	4 116	9	5½	51½	5½	5hd	51½	3¾	Bridgmohan S X	5.40
25Jun03 8Bel6	Slew Valley	L	6 114	5	21	21	21	21½	1hd	4¾	Fragoso P	21.80
25Jun03 8Bel1	State Shinto	Lb	7 116	4	1½	1hd	1hd	1hd	32½	52¼	Migliore R	1.00
7Jun03 10Bel9	Gritty Sandie	Lbf	7 115	8	8hd	9	9	9	74½	65½	Santos J A	13.80
26Oct02 6Kee1	Esperence	L	6 113	3	6hd	72	82½	8½	8½	71½	Espinoza J L	39.50
17Apr03 Lch7	Thompson Rouge–IR	L	4 115	6	4½	3hd	4½	41½	9	815	Gryder A T	6.40
25Jun03 8Bel7	Dawn Of The Condor	Lb	6 114	7	72½	6½	62	62½	6hd	9	Farina Tony	61.50

OFF AT 5:43 Start Good. Won driving. Course good.
TIME :25³, :51¹, 1:15¹, 1:39, 2:03², 2:15⁴ (:25.61, :51.28, 1:15.26, 1:39.13, 2:03.52, 2:15.92)

$2 Mutuel Prices:

1–WHITMORE'S CONN	25.60	11.60	6.70
2–QUEST STAR		7.50	4.90
10–MACAW–IR			3.80

$2 EXACTA 1–2 PAID $129.00 $2 TRIFECTA 1–2–10 PAID $918.00

Dk. b. or br. h, by Kris S.–Albonita, by Deputed Testamony. Trainer Schulhofer Randy. Bred by Bud Wolf & Joe D'Agostino (NY).

WHITMORE'S CONN was outrun early, advanced outside on the second turn, came four wide into the stretch, dug in gamely outside and was up in the final yards, driving. QUEST STAR raced close up inside while in hand, angled out into the stretch, reached the front leaving the eighth pole and dug in gamely to the wire. MACAW (IRE) was rated along outside, rallied three wide approaching the stretch and finished gamely outside. SLEW VALLEY prompted the pace from the outside and stayed on stubbornly through the stretch. STATE SHINTO set the pace along the inside and weakened in the final furlong. GRITTY SANDIE was outrun early, advanced four wide on the second turn and offered a mild rally outside. ESPERENCE raced inside, saved ground and had no response when roused. THOMPSON ROUGE (IRE) raced close up outside, was three wide on the second turn and tired in the stretch. DAWN OF THE CONDOR raced inside and tired.

Owners– 1, Shanley Michael & Lynn; 2, Mansell Stables; 3, Melillo George & Sandra; 4, Rich Meadow Farm; 5, Al Maktoum Mohammed b; 6, Kimmel Caesar P & Nicholson Ronald; 7, Niall J Brennan & Mary Ryan; 8, Abdullah Saeed Almaddah; 9, David Soblick & Piety Hill Stable
Trainers– 1, Schulhofer Randy; 2, Walden W Elliott; 3, Tagg Barclay; 4, Sciacca Gary; 5, McLaughlin Kiaran P; 6, Toner James J; 7, Brennan Niall J; 8, Mott William I; 9, Sciacca Gary
Scratched– Epicentre (21May03 8BEL2)

NINTH RACE
Colonial
JULY 12, 2003

1⅛ MILES. (Turf)(1.47^{2}) 15th Running of THE ALL ALONG BREEDERS' CUP. Grade III. Purse $200,000 (includes $50,000 BC – Breeders' Cup) FILLIES AND MARES, THREE-YEARS-OLD AND UPWARD. (Includes $50,000 from the Breeders' Cup Fund for Cup nominees only). By subscription of $100 each which should accompany the nomination. $950 to pass the entry box. $950 additional to start with $150,000 Guaranteed. The Host Association's added monies to be divided, of which 60% to the winner, 20% to second, 11% to third, 6% to fourth, and 3% to fifth. Breeders' Cup Fund monies also correspondingly divided provided a Breeders' Cup Nominee has finished in an awarded position. Any Breeders' Cup Fund money not awarded will revert back to the fund. Supplemental nominations of $1500 each will be accepted by the usual time of entry with all other fees due as noted. Weights Three-year-olds 117., Older 122 lbs. Non-winners of two races of $50,000 at one mile or over since April 1 2003, allowed 3 lbs.; of such since then, 5 lbs. (Maiden and claiming races not considered in estimating allowances).

Value of Race: $190,000 Winner $120,000; second $30,000; third $22,000; fourth $12,000; fifth $6,000. Mutuel Pool $141,834.00 Exacta Pool $96,357.00 Trifecta Pool $69,067.00 Superfecta Pool $17,774.00

Last Raced	Horse	M/Eqt.	A.Wt	PP	St	¼	½	¾	Str	Fin	Jockey	Odds $1
26May03 ^{6}Hol^{5}	Dress To Thrill-IR	L	4 117	4	3	$1^{1\frac{1}{2}}$	$1^{1\frac{1}{2}}$	1^{1}	$1^{\frac{1}{2}}$	$1^{\frac{1}{2}}$	Prado E S	0.60
22Jun03 ^{10}Cnl^{1}	Lady Linda	Lb	5 117	8	9	8^{2}	7^{3}	6^{2}	3^{1}	2^{1}	Fogelsonger R	10.80
17May03 ^{7}Pim^{3}	Lady Of The Future	L	5 117	7	8	7^{hd}	8^{hd}	8^{1}	6^{1}	3^{1}	Rose J	12.30
7Jun03 ^{8}Bel^{6}	Carib Lady-IR	L	4 119	9	7	$5^{3\frac{1}{2}}$	4^{1}	4^{2}	4^{hd}	4^{nk}	Castellano J J	11.90
18May03 ^{7}Bel^{3}	Golden Corona	Lf	5 117	5	4	$2^{\frac{1}{2}}$	$2^{\frac{1}{2}}$	2^{1}	2^{1}	$5^{\frac{1}{2}}$	Pino M G	9.70
6Jun03 ^{9}Bel^{3}	Bail Bond		6 117	3	2	6^{2}	$6^{\frac{1}{2}}$	7^{hd}	7^{3}	6^{hd}	Jurado E M	45.80
31May03 ^{8}Bel^{3}	Silent Crystal		4 117	1	6	3^{1}	3^{1}	$3^{\frac{1}{2}}$	$5^{\frac{1}{2}}$	7^{1}	Day P	4.10
22Jun03 ^{10}Cnl^{4}	Cruise Along	Lb	5 117	6	1	9	9	9	$8^{2\frac{1}{2}}$	$8^{2\frac{3}{4}}$	Karamanos H A	23.00
20Jun03 ^{8}Cnl^{2}	Class Yankee	Lbf	5 117	2	5	$4^{1\frac{1}{2}}$	$5^{1\frac{1}{2}}$	5^{hd}	9	9	Boucher R	55.60

OFF AT 5:04 Start Good. Won driving. Course firm.
TIME :25, :49, 1:12^{1}, 1:36^{3}, 1:49 (:25.04, :49.17, 1:12.38, 1:36.70, 1:49.16)

$2 Mutuel Prices:				
	5–DRESS TO THRILL–IR	3.20	2.80	2.40
	9–LADY LINDA		5.80	4.00
	8–LADY OF THE FUTURE			4.40

$2 EXACTA 5–9 PAID $22.00 $2 TRIFECTA 5–9–8 PAID $114.80 $1 SUPERFECTA 5–9–8–10 PAID $294.90

B. f, by Danehill–Trusted Partner, by Affirmed. Trainer Clement Christophe. Bred by Moyglare Stud Farm Ltd (Ire).

DRESS TO THRILL (IRE) broke through the starting gate and ran off about an eighth of a mile without her rider before the race, set the pace in the two path, drifted out badly in midstretch and lasted under stout urging. LADY LINDA stumbled when bumped by CARIB LADY soon after the start, raced five wide entering the stretch, was floated out in midstretch and closed gamely. LADY OF THE FUTURE lacked speed, raced in the six path entering the stretch, was floated out inside the eighth and closed gamely. CARIB LADY (IRE) drifted in leaving the starting gate, stalked the pace, eased out four wide at the head of the stretch and finished willingly between horses. GOLDEN CORONA pressed the pace outside the winner, lost momentum when floated out in midstretch and weakened. BAIL BOND lacked speed and passed tired ones. SILENT CRYSTAL saved ground chasing the pace and weakened the final furlong. CRUISE ALONG , outrun, raced wide the far turn. CLASS YANKEE stalked the pace, saved ground around the far turn and weakened.

Owners— 1, Moyglare Stud Farm Ltd; 2, Domino Stud of Lexington Inc; 3, Pearson Max H; 4, Galardia Racing; 5, Stronach Stable; 6, Meadow Patricia E; 7, Greenbaum Robert; 8, Bender Sondra D; 9, Mede Cahaba Stable & Stud

Trainers—1, Clement Christophe; 2, Eppler Mary E; 3, Greene Thomas M; 4, Pletcher Todd A; 5, Nixon Justin; 6, Meadow Patricia E; 7, Mott William I; 8, Murray Lawrence E; 9, Boucher Lilith

Scratched— New Economy (24Apr03 ^{8}KEE^{5}), Brandala (11Jly03 ^{8}BEL^{5})

TENTH RACE
Calder
JULY 12, 2003

6 FURLONGS. (1.08^{4}) 29th Running of THE CARRY BACK. Grade III. Purse $300,000. THREE YEAR OLDS. By subscription of $300 each which shall accompany the nomination, $1,500 to pass the entry box and an additional $1,500 to start. Weight, 122 lbs. Non-winners of $50,000 twice, allowed 3 lbs. Once, 5 lbs. $25,000, 7 lbs. $20,000 or two races other than maiden or claiming, 10 lbs. Closed Saturday, June 28 with 19 nominations.

Value of Race: $300,000 Winner $177,000; second $60,000; third $33,000; fourth $18,000; fifth $9,000; sixth $3,000. Mutuel Pool $476,892.00 Exacta Pool $326,141.00 Trifecta Pool $216,966.00 Superfecta Pool $64,502.00

Last Raced	Horse	M/Eqt.	A.Wt	PP	St	¼	½	Str	Fin	Jockey	Odds $1
24May03 ^{7}Mth^{2}	Valid Video	L	3 122	9	2	$6^{1\frac{1}{2}}$	$3^{1\frac{1}{2}}$	1^{1}	$1^{2\frac{1}{2}}$	Bravo J	8.80
14Jun03 ^{2}CD^{2}	Cajun Beat	Lb	3 117	3	3	4^{hd}	4^{1}	3^{3}	$2^{1\frac{1}{4}}$	Boulanger G	26.90
17Mar03 ^{2}OTC^{2}	Super Fuse	Lb	3 117	8	6	8^{2}	$7^{\frac{1}{2}}$	$6^{\frac{1}{2}}$	3^{nk}	Valenzuela P A	6.50
18Jun03 ^{7}Hol^{1}	King Robyn	L	3 117	10	1	2^{1}	1^{hd}	$2^{\frac{1}{2}}$	$4^{1\frac{3}{4}}$	Solis A	2.70
15Jun03 ^{6}AP^{1}	Coach Jimi Lee	L	3 122	7	5	5^{hd}	5^{2}	4^{hd}	5^{3}	St Julien M	5.70
16Jun03 ^{4}Crc^{3}	Lawbook	Lf	3 119	4	10	9^{4}	8^{2}	7^{3}	$6^{\frac{1}{2}}$	Velasquez C	27.70
7Jun03 ^{9}Bel^{3}	Halo Homewrecker	L	3 119	2	8	7^{1}	6^{1}	5^{1}	$7^{8\frac{3}{4}}$	Bailey J D	2.30
18Jun03 ^{7}Hol^{5}	Roll Hennessy Roll	Lb	3 119	1	9	3^{hd}	9^{3}	9^{3}	$8^{5\frac{1}{2}}$	Espinoza V	5.60
5Dec02 ^{3}Crc^{2}	Sweet Devil	L	3 113	6	7	10	10	10	$9^{3\frac{1}{2}}$	Aguilar M	162.80
16Jun03 ^{4}Crc^{1}	Awesome Of Course	L	3 117	5	4	1^{1}	2^{hd}	8^{3}	10	Cruz M R	24.20

OFF AT 4:55 Start Good. Won driving. Track fast.
TIME :21^{3}, :44^{3}, :57, 1:10 (:21.66, :44.60, :57.03, 1:10.15)

$2 Mutuel Prices:				
	10–VALID VIDEO	19.60	10.60	7.80
	4–CAJUN BEAT		20.40	8.80
	9–SUPER FUSE			5.40

$2 EXACTA 10–4 PAID $303.60 $2 TRIFECTA 10–4–9 PAID $2,043.60 $2 SUPERFECTA 10–4–9–11 PAID $10,463.60

Dk. b. or br. g, (Mar), by Valid Wager–Miss Video, by Star Gallant. Trainer Manning Dennis J. Bred by Casey Seaman (Fla).

VALID VIDEO rated off the pace, rallied three wide around the turn to take over at the top of the stretch, then edged away under urging. CAJUN BEAT steadied in the early going, tracked the pace, eased out for the drive and closed to gain the place while unable to stay with the winner. SUPER FUSE allowed to settle, swung out for the stretch run and closed to be up for the show. KING ROBYN chased the pace, moved up to vie for the lead outside AWESOME OF COURSE around the turn and to the top of the stretch, then weakened. COACH JIMI LEE reserved in striking position off the pace, lacked a late response. LAWBOOK failed to menace. HALO HOMEWRECKER checked when caught in tight early, saved ground into the stretch and tired. ROLL HENNESSY ROLL broke slowly, moved up quickly to chase the pace along the rail, checked from tight quarters on the turn and faltered. SWEET DEVIL showed little. AWESOME OF COURSE showed speed along the rail, vied with KING ROBYN around the turn, then faded in the drive.

Owners— 1, M Fehsenfeld; 2, Sanan Satish & Iracane John & Josep; 3, Alpha One Stable; 4, Cornejo Racing Inc; 5, Battaglia Lee & Divito James P; 6, Heard Thomas H Jr; 7, Evans Edward P; 8, Fulton Stan E; 9, Zacco Karon & Mario; 10, Jacks or Better Farm Inc

Trainers—1, Manning Dennis J; 2, Margolis Stephen R; 3, Ciardullo Richard Jr; 4, Mullins Jeff; 5, DiVito James P; 6, Heard Thomas H Jr; 7, Hennig Mark; 8, Becerra Rafael; 9, Zacco Mario T; 10, Hatchett James

Scratched— Savoy Special (7Jun03 ^{3}BEL^{1})

NINTH RACE
Calder
JULY 12, 2003

6 FURLONGS. (1.08^{4}) 29th Running of THE AZALEA BREEDERS' CUP. Grade III. Purse $300,000 (includes $75,000 BC). FILLIES, THREE YEARS OLD. (Includes $75,000 from the Breeders' Cup Fund for Cup nominees only). By subscription of $300 each which should accompany the nomination, $1,500 to pass the entry box and an additional $1,500 to start. Breeders' Cup Fund monies also correspondingly divided providing a Breeders' Cup nominee has finished in an awarded position. Any Breeders' Cup Fund monies not awarded will revert back to the fund. Weight: 121 lbs. Non–winners of $50,000 twice, allowed 3 lbs. Once, 5 lbs.; $25,000, 7 lbs.; $20,000 or two races other than maiden or claiming, 9 lbs. Supplemental nominee: FABULOUS BRUSH.

Value of Race: $291,525 Winner $176,025; second $60,000; third $24,750; fourth $18,000; fifth $9,000; sixth $3,750. Mutuel Pool $400,412.00 Exacta Pool $302,739.00 Trifecta Pool $230,403.00 Superfecta Pool $76,254.00

Last Raced	Horse	M/Eqt.	A.Wt	PP	St	¼	½	Str	Fin	Jockey	Odds $1
21May03 ^{7}CD^{4}	Ebony Breeze	L	3 118	1	13	4^{hd}	$2^{1\frac{1}{2}}$	2^{4}	$1^{4\frac{1}{4}}$	Velasquez C	9.10
8Jun03 ^{10}Crc^{1}	Storm Flag	Lf	3 116	4	6	1^{1}	$1^{1\frac{1}{2}}$	1^{hd}	$2^{2\frac{3}{4}}$	Boulanger G	2.30
13Jun03 ^{8}Crc^{1}	Crafty Brat	Lf	3 116	2	11	10^{hd}	$9^{\frac{1}{2}}$	$5^{1\frac{1}{2}}$	$3^{2\frac{3}{4}}$	Cruz M R	14.60
17May03 ^{4}CD^{2}	Littlemiss Sparkle	Lf	3 116	9	8	6^{1}	6^{1}	3^{hd}	$4^{\frac{1}{2}}$	Luzzi M J	11.80
14Jun03 ^{12}Crc^{2}	Crimson And Roses	L	3 114	5	10	13	11^{1}	7^{1}	5^{1}	Nunez E O	38.60
14Jun03 ^{6}Hol^{2}	Buffythecenterfold	L	3 121	6	12	12^{1}	$8^{\frac{1}{2}}$	$8^{\frac{1}{2}}$	$6^{\frac{3}{4}}$	Espinoza V	1.90
29Jun03 ^{7}Crc^{1}	Silver Lace	L	3 113	8	5	11^{hd}	13	$9^{\frac{1}{2}}$	7^{hd}	Coa E M	28.40
13Jun03 ^{8}Crc^{3}	All The Honor	Lb	3 115	3	7	5^{1}	4^{hd}	4^{1}	$8^{1\frac{1}{4}}$	Toscano P R	a-30.90
29Jun03 ^{9}CD^{3}	Fabulous Brush	Lf	3 118	10	4	$3^{\frac{1}{2}}$	3^{hd}	6^{hd}	$9^{\frac{1}{2}}$	Valenzuela P A	43.30
13Jun03 ^{8}Crc^{5}	Lady Stars	L	3 112	12	1	$7^{\frac{1}{2}}$	7^{1}	10^{3}	$10^{6\frac{1}{4}}$	Garcia J A	142.00
27Jun03 ^{10}Crc^{3}	Master Prospect	L	3 112	11	3	9^{1}	$10^{1\frac{1}{2}}$	11^{3}	$11^{4\frac{1}{2}}$	Velez R I	242.20
19Jun03 ^{6}CD^{1}	Angela's Love	L	3 114	13	2	2^{hd}	5^{1}	12^{3}	12^{5}	Bailey J D	3.70
22Jun03 ^{1}Crc^{1}	Big League Lady	L	3 112	7	9	8^{1}	$12^{\frac{1}{2}}$	13	13	Chavez J F	a-30.90

a–Coupled: All The Honor and Big League Lady.

OFF AT 4:25 Start Good. Won driving. Track fast.
TIME :21^{2}, :44^{4}, :57^{2}, 1:10^{4} (:21.59, :44.81, :57.56, 1:10.82)

$2 Mutuel Prices:				
	2–EBONY BREEZE	20.20	7.20	5.40
	4–STORM FLAG		4.00	3.40
	3–CRAFTY BRAT			5.40

$2 EXACTA 2–4 PAID $93.40 $2 TRIFECTA 2–4–3 PAID $675.40 $2 SUPERFECTA 2–4–3–8 PAID $3,838.80

B. f, (Jan), by Belong to Me–Valid Carnauba, by Valid Appeal. Trainer Mott William I. Bred by Kinsman Farm (Ky).

EBONY BREEZE tracked the pace off the rail, rallied to catch STORM FLAG just inside the eighth pole and drew clear under pressure. STORM FLAG set the pace along the inside into the stretch, then was no match for the winner while proving second best. CRAFTY BRAT unhurried early, saved ground into the stretch, eased out and closed to be up for the show. LITTLEMISS SPARKLE raced in striking position into the stretch and tired. CRIMSON AND ROSES outrun after bumping hard with BUFFYTHECENTERFOLD at the start, angled out in the stretch and improved her position. BUFFYTHECENTERFOLD jammed back at the start, raced six wide on the turn and passed tired rivals. SILVER LACE bumped hard with BIG LEAGUE LADY at the start and failed to menace. ALL THE HONOR tracked the pace along the inside, steadied entering the turn, remained in contention into the stretch and tired. FABULOUS BRUSH chased the pace three wide around the turn and gave way. LADY STARS reserved off the pace, raced four wide on the turn and faltered. MASTER PROSPECT raced five wide on the turn and was not a factor. ANGELA'S LOVE showed brief speed, raced four wide on the turn and faded. BIG LEAGUE LADY was through early after being knocked into BUFFYTHECENTERFOLD at the start.

Owners— 1, Kinsman Stable; 2, Raffa Joseph W; 3, Calascibetta Inc & Cheeks W et al; 4, Rising Graph Stable; 5, Jacks or Better Farm Inc; 6, A A Brian & Stronach Stables; 7, Mount Joy Stables; 8, Thorobeam Farm; 9, Jayaraman Kalarikkal K & Vilasini D; 10, Track Ho Farms; 11, Bishop Chester A; 12, Poston Bill & Vicki; 13, Thorobeam Farm

Trainers—1, Mott William I; 2, Root Richard R; 3, Calascibetta Joseph; 4, Whiting Lynn S; 5, Hatchett James; 6, Stute Melvin F; 7, Stutts Bennie F Jr; 8, Plesa Edward Jr; 9, Daly Patrick J; 10, Towne Steve; 11, Simpson Willoughby; 12, Romans Dale; 13, Plesa Edward Jr

$2 Pick Three (3–7–2) Paid $2,773.00; Pick Three Pool $47,434.

ELEVENTH RACE
Calder
JULY 12, 2003

6 FURLONGS. (1.08^{4}) 19th Running of THE PRINCESS ROONEY HANDICAP. Grade II. Purse $500,000. FILLIES AND MARES, THREE YEARS OLD AND UPWARD. By subscription of $500 each which shall accompany the nomination, $2,000 to pass the entry box and an additional $2,000 to start. Closed Saturday, June 28 with 19 nominations.

Value of Race: $500,000 Winner $294,000; second $100,000; third $55,000; fourth $30,000; fifth $15,000; sixth $6,000. Mutuel Pool $397,461.00 Exacta Pool $277,822.00 Trifecta Pool $211,236.00 Superfecta Pool $68,305.00

Last Raced	Horse	M/Eqt.	A.	Wt	PP	St	¼	½	Str	Fin	Jockey	Odds $1
8Jun03 ^{8}Bel^{3}	Gold Mover	L	5	118	3	5	2^{1}	2^{1}	$2^{\frac{1}{2}}$	1no	Bailey J D	1.50
22Jun03 ^{9}Crc^{2}	Vision In Flight	L	4	113	8	2	$5^{\frac{1}{2}}$	4^{hd}	3^{hd}	$2^{4\frac{1}{4}}$	Boulanger G	64.70
22Jun03 ^{3}WO^{1}	Harmony Lodge	L	5	116	2	4	$1^{\frac{1}{2}}$	$1^{1\frac{1}{2}}$	$1^{\frac{1}{2}}$	3^{hd}	Coa E M	3.30
14Jun03 ^{8}AP^{5}	Miss Lodi	L	4	116	1	8	$4^{1\frac{1}{2}}$	3^{1}	$4^{2\frac{1}{2}}$	4no	Valenzuela P A	9.10
14Jun03 ^{9}Mth^{1}	Slews Final Answer	L	4	113	4	6	6^{hd}	7^{2}	$5^{2\frac{1}{2}}$	$5^{5\frac{1}{4}}$	Luzzi M J	5.30
25Jan03 ^{6}GP^{3}	Chispiski	Lbf	4	114	7	1	$3^{\frac{1}{2}}$	5^{1}	6^{1}	$6^{\frac{3}{4}}$	Garcia J A	24.20
8Jun03 ^{8}Bel^{1}	Shawklit Mint	L	4	116	5	3	$7^{1\frac{1}{2}}$	8	8	$7^{1\frac{3}{4}}$	Velasquez C	4.10
14Jun03 ^{8}AP^{1}	For Rubies	L	4	115	6	7	8	6^{1}	$7^{\frac{1}{2}}$	8	Perret C	10.40

OFF AT 5:25 Start Good For All But FOR RUBIES Won driving. Track fast.
TIME :21^{2}, :44^{2}, :57^{3}, 1:11^{1} (:21.47, :44.56, :57.71, 1:11.31)

$2 Mutuel Prices:

3–GOLD MOVER	5.00	3.00	2.40
8–VISION IN FLIGHT		24.00	7.00
2–HARMONY LODGE			3.20

$2 EXACTA 3–8 PAID $154.80 $2 TRIFECTA 3–8–2 PAID $623.00 $2 SUPERFECTA 3–8–2–1 PAID $2,624.20

Ch. m, by Gold Fever–Intentional Move, by Tentam. Trainer Hennig Mark. Bred by Edward P Evans (Ky).

GOLD MOVER stalked the pace, moved to gain a slim lead inside the eighth pole, then responded when challenged by VISION IN FLIGHT at the seventy yard pole and was all out to edge that rival to the wire. VISION IN FLIGHT rated off the pace, angled outside the leaders for the drive, rallied to catch GOLD MOVER at the seventy yard pole, then just missed. HARMONY LODGE set the pace along the inside, came off the rail for the stretch run and gave way. MISS LODI chased the pace along the rail, made a run to loom a threat in midstretch, then tired. SLEWS FINAL ANSWER reserved off the pace, saved ground around the turn and lacked a rally. CHISPISKI chased the leaders three wide to midway of the turn and faltered. SHAWKLIT MINT was never a factor. FOR RUBIES was outrun after breaking poorly.

Owners— 1, Evans Edward P; 2, Cherry Martin L; 3, Melnyk Eugene & Laura; 4, R C Colton & Mast Thoroughbreds Jr; 5, Live Oak Plantation; 6, Brazil Stable; 7, Flatbird Stable; 8, Choctaw Racing Stable

Trainers—1, Hennig Mark; 2, Wolfson Martin D; 3, Pletcher Todd A; 4, Amoss Thomas; 5, Mott William I; 6, Spatz Ronald B; 7, Reynolds Patrick L; 8, Whiting Lynn S

$2 Pick Three (2–10–3) Paid $537.60; Pick Three Pool $70,032.

TWELFTH RACE
Calder
JULY 12, 2003

6 FURLONGS. (1.08^{4}) 21st Running of THE SMILE SPRINT HANDICAP. Grade III. Purse $500,000, THREE YEAR OLDS AND UPWARD. By subscription of $500 each which shall accompany the nomination, $2,000 to pass the entry box and an additional $2,000 to start. Closed Saturday, June 28 with 22 nominations.

Value of Race: $500,000 Winner $294,000; second $100,000; third $55,000; fourth $30,000; fifth $15,000; sixth $6,000. Mutuel Pool $437,349.00 Exacta Pool $294,070.00 Trifecta Pool $205,378.00 Superfecta Pool $77,275.00

Last Raced	Horse	M/Eqt.	A.	Wt	PP	St	¼	½	Str	Fin	Jockey	Odds $1
7Jun03 ^{7}Bel^{1}	Shake You Down	Lbf	5	119	13	1	3^{2}	$2^{4\frac{1}{2}}$	1^{4}	$1^{8\frac{1}{4}}$	Luzzi M J	2.80
21Jun03 ^{8}PrM^{2}	Private Horde	Lbf	4	113	11	11	$9^{\frac{1}{2}}$	7^{1}	4^{hd}	$2^{\frac{3}{4}}$	Lumpkins J	24.80
21Jun03 ^{13}Suf^{2}	My Cousin Matt	Lf	4	116	3	5	6^{1}	5^{2}	3^{1}	$3^{\frac{1}{2}}$	Dominguez R A	3.40
7Jun03 ^{12}Crc^{1}	Built Up	L	5	114	7	8	5^{1}	$6^{\frac{1}{2}}$	5^{2}	4^{hd}	Aguilar M	40.30
10May03 ^{6}Bel^{2}	Here's Zealous	L	6	114	2	3	$1^{1\frac{1}{2}}$	1^{hd}	$2^{2\frac{1}{2}}$	$5^{\frac{3}{4}}$	Velasquez C	4.90
14Jun03 ^{3}Crc^{3}	Tour Of The Cat	Lf	5	114	12	2	7^{hd}	$8^{1\frac{1}{2}}$	$7^{\frac{1}{2}}$	6^{1}	Cabassa A Jr	13.70
21Jun03 ^{1}Crc^{1}	Juggernaut	Lb	4	114	4	10	11^{3}	$9^{\frac{1}{2}}$	$8^{\frac{1}{2}}$	7^{nk}	Bailey J D	12.50
7Jun03 ^{12}Crc^{2}	Lord Abounding	Lb	4	112	1	12	12^{5}	12^{3}	$10^{3\frac{1}{2}}$	$8^{1\frac{1}{4}}$	Chavez J F	13.50
4Jun03 ^{5}Hol^{1}	Echo Eddie	Lb	6	116	5	6	$4^{1\frac{1}{2}}$	4^{1}	$6^{\frac{1}{2}}$	9^{5}	Valenzuela P A	3.50
14Jun03 ^{3}Crc^{1}	Swift Replica	L	4	113	6	7	2^{hd}	3^{hd}	$9^{1\frac{1}{2}}$	10^{3}	Boulanger G	60.30
21Jun03 ^{12}Crc^{1}	Hear No Evil	Lbf	3	113	10	9	10^{hd}	$10^{\frac{1}{2}}$	11^{hd}	$11^{1\frac{1}{2}}$	Nunez E O	54.60
28Jun03 ^{11}Crc^{1}	Demeteor	L	4	110	9	4	8^{1}	11^{2}	12^{5}	$12^{8\frac{3}{4}}$	Homeister R B Jr	36.50
8Nov02 ^{7}Hol^{4}	Bills Paid	Lb	5	110	8	13	13	13	13	13	Garcia J A	76.60

OFF AT 5:56 Start Good For All But BILLS PAID Won driving. Track fast.
TIME :21^{1}, :43^{4}, :56^{2}, 1:10 (:21.24, :43.83, :56.51, 1:10.03)

$2 Mutuel Prices:

13–SHAKE YOU DOWN	7.60	6.00	3.40
11–PRIVATE HORDE		14.80	6.40
3–MY COUSIN MATT			3.20

$2 EXACTA 13–11 PAID $117.80 $2 TRIFECTA 13–11–3 PAID $534.40 $2 SUPERFECTA 13–11–3–7 PAID $10,256.40

Ch. g, by Montbrook–Mauvin Gway, by Rajab. Trainer Lake Scott A. Bred by Ocala Stud Farm (Fla).

SHAKE YOU DOWN chased the pace, rallied to take over leaving the turn and drew off under a strong hand ride. PRIVATE HORDE allowed to settle, raced four wide on the turn, angled in at the top of the stretch and closed to be up for the place. MY COUSIN MATT reserved early, advanced between rivals on the turn, angled out for the drive and gained the show. BUILT UP rated off the pace, raced three wide on the turn and lacked a late response. HERE'S ZEALOUS set the pace along the inside to nearing the stretch and gave way. TOUR OF THE CAT raced three wide on the turn and lacked a rally. JUGGERNAUT steadied from tight quarters early and failed to menace. LORD ABOUNDING was never a factor. ECHO EDDIE chased the leaders three wide into the stretch and tired. SWIFT REPLICA chased the pace along the inside and faltered. HEAR NO EVIL was outrun. DEMETEOR was through early. BILLS PAID trailed after breaking in the air.

Owners— 1, Cole Robert L Jr; 2, Tucker Billy R; 3, Englander Richard A; 4, Susi Raymond; 5, Jay Em Ess Stable; 6, Double G Stable; 7, Ellison Siobhan P & McMakin Nelson; 8, Bridle Path Racing Stable; 9, Milch David S & Rita; 10, Zacco Karon & Mario; 11, Jacks or Better Farm Inc; 12, Hoffman Kenneth E; 13, J G Vachon

Trainers—1, Lake Scott A; 2, Cain Joe; 3, Lake Scott A; 4, Alonso Enrique; 5, Dutrow Richard E Jr; 6, Mora Myra; 7, Pilotti Larry; 8, Plesa Edward Jr; 9, Vienna Darrell; 10, Zacco Mario T; 11, Hatchett James; 12, Hoffman Kenneth E; 13, Mendoza Jesus

$1 Pick Five (7–2–10–3–13) 5 Correct Paid $11,260.40; Pick Five Pool $528,266.

NINTH RACE
Monmouth
JULY 12, 2003

$1\frac{1}{16}$ MILES. (1.40^1) 68th Running of THE LONG BRANCH BREEDERS' CUP. Purse $100,000 (includes $25,000 BC – Breeders' Cup) THREE–YEAR–OLDS. (Includes $25,000 from Breeders' Cup Fund for Cup nominees only). By subscription of $100 each, which should accompany the nomination. $1,500 to enter. Field will be limited to 14 Starters. If more than 14 entries pass the entry box, preference will be given to Breeders' Cup nominees only of equal racing quality or weight assignment. Weight, 122 lbs. Non–winners of $60,000 at a mile or over in 2003 allowed, 2 lbs.; $45,000 at a mile or over in 2003, 4 lbs.; a sweepstakes at a mile or over in 2003, 6 lbs.; a sweepstakes anytime, 8 lbs.; two races other than Maiden or Claiming, 10 lbs. Supplementary nominations may be made at time of entry by payment of a fee of $5,000 each which includes entry and starting fees. NOMINATIONS CLOSED Saturday, June 28, 2003.

Value of Race: $100,000 Winner $60,000; second $20,000; third $11,000; fourth $6,000; fifth $3,000. Mutuel Pool $148,245.00 Exacta Pool $110,099.00 Trifecta Pool $59,881.00

Last Raced	Horse	M/Eqt.	A.	Wt	PP	St	¼	½	¾	Str	Fin	Jockey	Odds $1
15Jun03 ^{9}Mth^4	Max Forever	L	3	113	3	1	3^1	2^{hd}	$3^{1\frac{1}{2}}$	2^{hd}	1^{hd}	Ferrer J C	11.50
14Jun03 ^{11}Del^2	Christine's Outlaw	Lbf	3	115	5	4	2^{hd}	3^1	2^{hd}	1^{hd}	$2^{2\frac{1}{4}}$	Velez J A Jr	0.90
22Jun03 ^{7}Bel^2	Chilly Rooster		3	112	6	6	$1^{1\frac{1}{2}}$	$1^{\frac{1}{2}}$	1^{hd}	$3^{3\frac{1}{2}}$	3^{hd}	Carrero V	3.20
23Jun03 ^{7}Del^3	Ashmore	Lb	3	114	2	5	$4^{\frac{1}{2}}$	4^{hd}	4^{hd}	4^{hd}	$4^{1\frac{3}{4}}$	Toribio A R	8.60
22Jun03 ^{5}Mth^3	In Hand	L	3	113	4	2	6	6	6	5^3	$5^{7\frac{3}{4}}$	Pimentel J	37.70
14Jun03 ^{5}Bel^1	Newfoundland	Lb	3	112	1	3	5^2	5^3	$5^{2\frac{1}{2}}$	6	6	Lopez C C	3.20

OFF AT 4:49 Start Good. Won driving. Track fast.
TIME :23^4, :48, 1:11^3, 1:36^4, 1:43^2 (:23.91, :48.12, 1:11.70, 1:36.99, 1:43.56)

$2 Mutuel Prices:				
	3–MAX FOREVER	25.00	6.80	2.60
	5–CHRISTINE'S OUTLAW		2.80	2.10
	6–CHILLY ROOSTER			2.40

$2 EXACTA 3–5 PAID $64.60 $2 TRIFECTA 3–5–6 PAID $327.80

Dk. b. or br. c, (Feb), by Montbrook–Jiffener, by Derby Wish. Trainer Perkins Ben W Jr. Bred by John Franks (Fla).

MAX FOREVER steadied off heels entering the clubhouse turn, continued to be steadied along rounding the initial bend and into the backstretch while down along the inside, was sent to the front between calls approaching the half mile pole, saved ground into the stretch while contesting the lead then responded gamely to prevail. CHRISTINE'S OUTLAW close up early from the outside, raced three deep on the final turn while challenging for command, reached the front a furlong out then continued on gamely. CHILLY ROOSTER angled over entering the clubhouse turn, set the early pace from the two path, responded when displaced approaching the half mile pole, raced between rivals into the far turn and regained the advantage, continued between foes and drifted out some while tiring through the late stages. ASHMORE well placed early, raced off the rail on the final turn while inside a rival then was gaining late outside. IN HAND trailed while not far back, saved ground and advanced some into midstretch then lacked the needed late response. NEWFOUNDLAND raced out in the strip on the final turn and flattened out in upper stretch.

Owners— 1, Dweck Raymond & Dorothy; 2, R C Hill Stables; 3, Hobeau Farm; 4, Ryan Daniel M; 5, Shining Armor Stable & Humphrey G W; 6, Sumaya Us Stables

Trainers—1, Perkins Ben W Jr; 2, Weaver George; 3, Jerkens H Allen; 4, Pino Michael V; 5, Oliver Philip J; 6, Pletcher Todd A

$2 Pick Three (3–7–3) Paid $4,208.40; Pick Three Pool $14,028.

SIXTH RACE
Prairie Mdw
JULY 12, 2003

$1\frac{1}{8}$ MILES. (1.46^3) PRAIRIE MEADOWS CORNHUSKER BREEDERS' CUP H. Grade III. Purse $350,000 (includes $50,000 BC – Breeders' Cup) A HANDICAP FOR THREE–YEAR–OLDS AND UPWARD. (Includes $50,000 from Breeders' Cup Fund for Cup nominees only). No nomination fee. $2,000 to pass the entry box on Tuesday, July 8. $3,000 additional to start on Saturday, July 12. Weights; Friday, July 4. Therace will not be divided. Preference will be given in the following order: Breeders' Cup nominees only of equal racing quality or weight assignment (respective of sex and weight for age). The winning owner will receive a trophy from Breeders' Cup Limited. Closed Monday June 23, 2003 with thirty–six (36) nominations.

Value of Race: $350,000 Winner $210,000; second $70,000; third $35,000; fourth $17,500; fifth $10,500; sixth $7,000. Mutuel Pool $52,026.00 Exacta Pool $18,720.00 Quinella Pool $3,661.00 Trifecta Pool $18,325.00

Last Raced	Horse	M/Eqt.	A.	Wt	PP	St	¼	½	¾	Str	Fin	Jockey	Odds $1
29Nov02 ^{11}CD^4	Tenpins	LB	5	118	5	1	$3^{2\frac{1}{2}}$	$3^{1\frac{1}{2}}$	$1^{\frac{1}{2}}$	$1^{\frac{1}{2}}$	1^2	Albarado R	1.30
7Jun03 ^{7}Del^1	Bowman's Band	LB	5	116	1	5	6	6	5^1	2^4	$2^{5\frac{1}{2}}$	Guidry M	2.70
14Jun03 ^{10}CD^7	Woodmoon	LB b	5	116	6	6	5^2	4^1	3^{hd}	3^2	$3^{4\frac{3}{4}}$	Sibille R	6.70
25May03 ^{8}PrM^1	Patton's Victory	LB b	5	116	3	3	$2^{1\frac{1}{2}}$	2^{hd}	2^{hd}	4^1	4^2	Birzer A	6.90
21Jun03 ^{9}AP^5	Colorful Tour	LB	4	115	4	2	1^{hd}	$1^{\frac{1}{2}}$	$4^{\frac{1}{2}}$	$5^{\frac{1}{2}}$	$5^{\frac{1}{2}}$	Quinonez L S	16.10
21Jun03 ^{9}CD^6	Slider	LB b	5	115	2	4	$4^{\frac{1}{2}}$	$5^{\frac{1}{2}}$	6	6	6	Marquez C H Jr	4.60

OFF AT 8:50 Start Good . Won driving. Track fast.
TIME :22^2, :46^2, 1:10^1, 1:35^3, 1:48^1 (:22.44, :46.42, 1:10.37, 1:35.75, 1:48.39)

$2 Mutuel Prices:				
	7 – TENPINS	4.60	3.40	2.80
	1 – BOWMAN'S BAND		3.20	2.40
	8 – WOODMOON			2.80

$2 EXACTA 7–1 PAID $12.60 $2 QUINELLA 1–7 PAID $7.00
$2 TRIFECTA 7–1–8 PAID $48.40

Ch. h, (Mar), by Smart Strike – Maid's Broom , by Deputy Minister . Trainer Winfree Donald R. Bred by Joseph Vitello (Mich).

TENPINS pressed the pace racing three wide in front of the stands the first time, took back into a stalking position around the first turn, moved up again to challenge three deep on the backstretch, got the best of his pace rivals entering the second turn but was immediately joined on his outside by both WOODMOON and BOWMAN'S BAND, dueled inside those rivals around the bend, drifted out a bit entering the lane, continued to vie inside the runner up to midstretch before drawing clear late under steady handling. BOWMAN'S BAND was unhurried trailing the field around the first turn, moved a bit closer while racing well in hand and in the five path up the backstretch, made a quick four wide move entering the second turn, dueled three wide around the bend and briefly stuck a head in front approaching the stretch, continued to duel outside of the winner to the final furlong, proved no match late but easily bested the rest. WOODMOON settled off the early pacesetters, moved up quickly while three wide entering the second turn, dueled from between the top pair around the turn, was floated out a bit by the winner entering the stretch and weakened through the drive. PATTON'S VICTORY dueled along the rail to the second turn before tiring. COLORFUL TOUR dueled from the two path to the second turn, tired thereafter. SLIDER settled along the rail early, raced just off the dueling leaders on the backstretch, was shuffled back a bit to trail the compact field entering the second turn, angled out three wide entering the bend, remained within range to the stretch before giving way.

Owners– 1, Vitello Joseph V; 2, Schwartz Martin S; 3, Pabst Henry E; 4, Hwy 1 Racing Stable LLC; 5, Irish Acres Farm; 6, Hays Billy

Trainers– 1, Winfree Donald R; 2, Matz Michael R; 3, O'Callaghan Niall M; 4, Roberts Stanley W; 5, Hickey P Noel; 6, Woodard Joe

Scratched– Northwest Hill (04Jul03 ^{5}PrM^1) , Vito Corleone (14Jun03 ^{8}Cby^5)

NINTH RACE

Belmont

JULY 13, 2003

1¼ MILES. (Inner Turf)(1.57³) 39th Running of THE LEXINGTON. Grade III. Purse $150,000. (Up to $29,100 NYSBFOA). THREE YEAR OLDS. By subscription of $150 each, which should accompany the nomination; $750 to pass the entry box and $750 to start. 122 lbs. Non–winners of $45,000 over a mile on the turf in 2003 allowed 2 lbs.; $30,000 twice over a mile, 4 lbs.; $30,000 over a mile, or three races 6 lbs.; two races at a mile or over, 8 lbs. (Maiden, claiming, starter, restricted races not considered in allowances.)Trophies will be presented to the winning owner, trainer and jockey. The New York Racing Association reserves the right to transfer this race to the Main Track. In the event this race is taken off the turf it may be subject to a downgrade by the Graded Stakes Committee. Closed Saturday, June 28, 2003 with 27 Nominations.

Value of Race: $150,000 Winner $90,000; second $30,000; third $16,500; fourth $9,000; fifth $4,500. Mutuel Pool $507,021.00 Exacta Pool $389,609.00 Trifecta Pool $278,343.00

Last Raced	Horse	M/Eqt. A.Wt	PP	¼	½	¾	1	Str	Fin	Jockey	Odds $1
8Jun03 ⁵Bel¹	Sharp Impact	Lb	3 114	6	1²	11½	11	1²	11	1½	Migliore R	4.00
31May03 ⁷CD¹	Hidden Truth	L	3 118	3	4½	4½	51½	42½	2ʰᵈ	2²	Albarado R J	2.40
12Apr03 ⁷SA³	Urban King-IR	L	3 114	1	2½	2ʰᵈ	2½	2ʰᵈ	31½	3¾	Prado E S	0.90
7Jun03 ¹¹Bel⁵	Supervisor	Lb	3 114	5	51½	53½	6	5ʰᵈ	5⁶	4²	Santos J A	10.90
3May03 ⁵Aqu⁹	Vettriano-IR	Lb	3 114	2	6	6	4ʰᵈ	31½	41½	53½	Samyn J L	38.50
28Jun03 ¹²Bel⁶	Deputy Lad	Lb	3 114	4	31½	31½	33½	6	6	6	Gryder A T	23.30

OFF AT 5:10 Start Good. Won driving. Course firm.

TIME :24³, :50¹, 1:14⁴, 1:38³, 2:02³ (:24.62, :50.38, 1:14.93, 1:38.74, 2:02.62)

$2 Mutuel Prices:	7–SHARP IMPACT	10.00	5.90	2.30
	4–HIDDEN TRUTH		4.70	2.20
	1–URBAN KING-IR			2.10

$2 EXACTA 7–4 PAID $28.20 $2 TRIFECTA 7–4–1 PAID $49.40

Dk. b. or br. c, (Mar), by Siphon*Brz–Fast and Early, by Carson City. Trainer McLaughlin Kiaran P. Bred by Airdrie Stud (Ky).

SHARP IMPACT quickly showed in front, controlled the pace while well in hand, dug in gamely when roused in upper stretch and held off HIDDEN TRUTH under a drive. HIDDEN TRUTH was rated along early, angled out and rallied three wide approaching the stretch, responded when roused and finished gamely but could not get to the winner. URBAN KING (IRE) raced with the pace while well in hand and stayed on well through the stretch. SUPERVISOR was rated along early, raced inside, angled out in upper stretch and lacked a rally. VETTRIANO (IRE) was rated along early, put in a run along the inside on the second turn and had little left for the stretch drive. DEPUTY LAD raced close up while three wide and tired in the stretch.

Owners— 1, Al Maktoum Mohammed b; 2, Farish William S & Webber W Temple; 3, Amerman Racing Stables; 4, Lundock Rodney G; 5, Tucker Jeffrey; 6, Stengel Cindy & Ron

Trainers—1, McLaughlin Kiaran P; 2, Howard Neil J; 3, Frankel Robert; 4, Rice Linda; 5, Morrison John; 6, McPeek Kenneth G

Scratched— Coalition (18Jun03 ⁴BEL²)

FOURTH RACE

Hollywood

JULY 13, 2003

7 FURLONGS. (1.19⁴) 49th Running of THE A GLEAM INVITATIONAL HANDICAP. Grade II. Purse $250,000 Guaranteed. FILLIES AND MARES THREE YEARS OLD AND UPWARD. By Invitation with no Nominating or Starting Fees. The owner of the winner to receive $150,000, with $50,000 to second, $30,000 to third, $15,000 to fourth and $5,000 to fifth.

Value of Race: $250,000 Winner $150,000; second $50,000; third $30,000; fourth $15,000; fifth $5,000. Mutuel Pool $534,010.00 Exacta Pool $241,492.00 Quinella Pool $24,484.00 Trifecta Pool $176,980.00

Last Raced	Horse	M/Eqt. A.Wt	PP	St	¼	½	Str	Fin	Jockey	Odds $1
7Jun03 ⁴Hol⁶	Cee's Elegance	LB	6 116	3	2	3½	2½	1½	11½	Espinoza V	9.70
14Jun03 ⁹CD¹	You	LB	4 121	1	4	4⁸	4½	3ʰᵈ	2ⁿᵒ	Bailey J D	1.20
24May03 ⁸Hol⁵	Affluent	LB	5 119	4	3	5	5	42½	3²	Stevens G L	1.50
7Jun03 ⁴Hol²	Bear Fan	LB	4 116	2	5	12½	11½	2³	45½	Flores D R	3.40
7Jun03 ⁴Hol⁴	Wild Tickle	LB	5 113	5	1	2¹	3¹	5	5	Day P	32.30

OFF AT 2:24 Start Good. Won driving. Track fast.

TIME :22, :44³, 1:08³, 1:21² (:22.12, :44.62, 1:08.69, 1:21.47)

$2 Mutuel Prices:	4–CEE'S ELEGANCE	21.40	6.20	2.40
	1–YOU		3.00	2.10
	5–AFFLUENT			2.10

$1 EXACTA 4–1 PAID $27.00 $2 QUINELLA 1–4 PAID $16.20 $1 TRIFECTA 4–1–5 PAID $59.70

Gr/ro m, by Cee's Tizzy–Elegant Beauty, by Norcliffe. Trainer O'Neill Doug. Bred by Cecilia P Straub–Rubens (Cal).

CEE'S ELEGANCE stalked outside a rival on the backstretch and turn, bid outside BEAR FAN into the stretch, gained the advantage in upper stretch and proved best under a strong hand ride. YOU a bit slow to begin, stalked the leader inside, came out into the stretch, split horses in late stretch, could not catch the winner but gamely edged a foe for second. AFFLUENT dropped back early and raced unhurried off the rail on the backstretch and turn, came three deep into the stretch and finished well but was edged for the place. BEAR FAN off a step slowly, sprinted up toward the inside to gain the lead, set the pace along the rail, dueled inside the winner into the stretch but weakened in the final furlong. WILD TICKLE sped to the early lead then stalked a bit off the rail, was outside the runner-up leaving the turn and had little left for the stretch.

Owners— 1, Cees Stable; 2, Gann Edmund A; 3, Whitham Janis R; 4, Fan & Ward; 5, Bell Richard A

Trainers—1, O'Neill Doug; 2, Frankel Robert; 3, McAnally Ronald; 4, Ward Wesley A; 5, Blincoe Thomas H

Scratched— Brisquette (20Jun03 ⁷HOL³)

$2 Daily Double (2–4) Paid $156.80; Daily Double Pool $44,004.
$1 Pick Three (5–2–4) Paid $632.40; Pick Three Pool $87,158.

SIXTH RACE
Hollywood
JULY 13, 2003

1⅛ MILES. (1.45¹) 30th Running of THE SWAPS. Grade II. Purse $400,000 Guaranteed. THREE YEAR OLDS. By subscription of $400 each, on or before Wednesday, July 2,2003, which shall accompany the nomination. A supplementary nomination of $15,000 may be made at the time of entry. All horses (including supplements) to pay $2,000 to pass the entry box, and $2,000 additional to start. Weight 124 lbs. Winners of $250,000 at a mile or over three times in 2003, 2 lbs additional. Non–winners of two such races in 2003 allowed 2 lbs. Such a race in 2003 4 lbs. Such a race of $100,000 in 2002–03 allowed 6 lbs. Such a race of $50,000 in 2002–03 allowed 8 lbs. Non–winners of three races other than maiden or claiming allowed 10 lbs, two such races allowed 12 lbs.

Value of Race: $400,000 Winner $240,000; second $80,000; third $36,000 each; fifth $8,000.   Mutuel Pool $726,808.00 Exacta Pool $378,116.00   Quinella Pool $36,313.00 Trifecta Pool $341,894.00

Last Raced	Horse	M/Eqt. A.Wt	PP	St	¼	½	¾	Str	Fin	Jockey	Odds $1
14Jun03 7CD3	During	LBb	3 115	4	2	1¹	1¹	1¹	3³	1hd	Bailey J D	8.20
7Jun03 11Bel2	Ten Most Wanted	LB	3 122	1	6	6	6	4½	1hd	2¾	Day P	a-0.60
22Jun03 3Hol1	DH Eye Of The Tiger	LB	3 118	5	5	2½	2¹½	2¹	2hd	3	Solis A	1.90
22Jun03 3Hol4	DH Outta Here	LB	3 120	6	4	4¹	3hd	3hd	42	34½	Baze T C	16.10
22Jun03 3Hol3	Bullistic	LBb	3 115	3	3	5¹½	5¹	6	5hd	53½	Valenzuela P A	11.90
5Apr03 6SA6	Logician	LBb	3 116	2	1	3½	4hd	5½	6	6	Nakatani C S	a-0.60

DH—Dead Heat.
a–Coupled: Ten Most Wanted and Logician.

OFF AT 3:36 Start Good. Won driving. Track fast.
TIME :24, :48, 1:11³, 1:36², 1:49¹ (:24.09, :48.18, 1:11.74, 1:36.50, 1:49.38)

$2 Mutuel Prices:

4–DURING	18.40	4.40	2.10
1–TEN MOST WANTED (a–entry)		2.40	2.10
5–DH EYE OF THE TIGER			2.10
6–DH OUTTA HERE			2.10

$1 EXACTA 4–1 PAID $18.80 $2 QUINELLA 1–4 PAID $11.40 $1 TRIFECTA 4–1–5 PAID $17.00 $1 TRIFECTA 4–1–6 PAID $38.60

Dk. b. or br. c, (Feb), by Cherokee Run–Blading Saddle, by Blade. Trainer Baffert Bob. Bred by Gulf States Racing Stables II (Ky).

DURING took the early lead and angled in, set the pace inside, turned back bids from EYE OF THE TIGER twice on the backstretch, fought back along the rail when headed into the stretch, regained the advantage in deep stretch and gamely prevailed under urging. TEN MOST WANTED came off the rail on the first turn, launched a bid four wide leaving the backstretch and into the second turn, put a head in front three deep into the stretch and continued willingly through a stiff drive but was outgamed. EYE OF THE TIGER stalked the pace outside a rival then a bit off the rail, bid outside the winner twice on the backstretch, bid again between horses into the stretch and also continued on with good courage between foes to the wire. OUTTA HERE four wide early, stalked three deep then between horses leaving the backstretch and on the second turn, steadied off heels midway on that turn, angled out in upper stretch and came back on four wide on the line to share the show. BULLISTIC stalked off the rail then between horses, waited a bit between foes midway on the second turn and weakened in the stretch. LOGICIAN close up stalking the winner along the inside, dropped back some on the second turn and also weakened.

Owners— 1, McIngvale James; 2, Chisholm Jarvis Reddam Et Al; 3, Gunther John D; 4, Currin William L & Eisman Alvin; 5, Moss Mr & Mrs Jerome S; 6, Reddam J P

Trainers—1, Baffert Bob; 2, Dollase Wallace; 3, Hollendorfer Jerry; 4, Currin William L; 5, Shirreffs John; 6, Dollase Craig
Scratched— Blazonry (26May03 7HOL¹)

$2 Daily Double (2–4) Paid $160.00; Daily Double Pool $52,266.
$1 Pick Three (4–2–4) Paid $590.30; Pick Three Pool $114,643.

NINTH RACE
Hollywood
JULY 13, 2003

1¼ MILES. (1.58²) 64th Running of THE HOLLYWOOD GOLD CUP. Grade I. Purse $750,000 Guaranteed. THREE YEAR OLDS AND UPWARD. By subscription of $1,000 each on or before Wednesday, July 2, 2003 which should accompany the nomination. Supplementary nominations may be made at time of entry by payment of $20,000 each. All nominees to pay $3,750 to enter and an additional $3,750 to start. Gross Purse $750,000 of which $450,000 to be paid to the winner, $150,000 to second, $90,000 to third, $45,000 to fourth and $15,000 to fifth. Weight: Older, 124 lbs.; 3–Year–Olds, 112 lbs.

Value of Race: $750,000 Winner $450,000; second $150,000; third $90,000; fourth $45,000; fifth $15,000.   Mutuel Pool $783,958.00 Exacta Pool $407,082.00   Quinella Pool $35,066.00 Trifecta Pool $438,431.00

Last Raced	Horse	M/Eqt. A.Wt	PP	¼	½	¾	1	Str	Fin	Jockey	Odds $1
26May03 9Bel6	Congaree	LB	5 124	4	3¹	3½	1½	1¹½	12½	13	Bailey J D	1.20
14Jun03 9Bel5	Harlan's Holiday	LB	4 124	6	46	4¹²	3¹½	2¹½	22	22	Velazquez J R	3.90
14Jun03 8Hol1	Kudos	LBb	6 124	3	6¹	6¹	5hd	4¹	3¹½	31	Solis A	2.80
14Jun03 8Hol2	Piensa Sonando-CH	LBb	5 124	7	7	7	7	53½	54½	42	Stevens G L	5.70
14Jun03 8Hol6	Western Pride	LB	5 124	5	2½	2¹	21	32½	41	512	Valdivia J Jr	13.10
24May03 6Hol3	Rodion-ARG	LB	5 124	1	5¹	5½	6hd	64	6¹²	622	Flores D R	58.10
7Jun03 10Pha1	Golden Ticket	LB	5 124	2	1¹	1¹	410	7	7	7	Valenzuela P A	21.50

OFF AT 5:47 Start Good. Won driving. Track fast.
TIME :22⁴, :45³, 1:09², 1:34¹, 2:00² (:22.93, :45.71, 1:09.52, 1:34.29, 2:00.48)

$2 Mutuel Prices:

4–CONGAREE	4.40	3.00	2.20
6–HARLAN'S HOLIDAY		4.20	2.60
3–KUDOS			2.40

$1 EXACTA 4–6 PAID $8.50 $2 QUINELLA 4–6 PAID $10.80 $1 TRIFECTA 4–6–3 PAID $17.20

Ch. h, by Arazi–Mari's Sheba, by Mari's Book. Trainer Baffert Bob. Bred by Stonerside Stable Ltd (Ky).

CONGAREE angled in and stalked the pace inside, went to the front along the rail on the backstretch, dueled inside, inched away into the second turn, kicked clear and held under urging. HARLAN'S HOLIDAY stalked the pace off the rail then outside CONGAREE early on the backstretch, continued outside WESTERN PRIDE midway on the second turn, remained off the inside into the stretch and went willingly to the end but could not catch the winner. KUDOS unhurried off the rail then between horses on the backstretch, split rivals early on the second turn, came out into the stretch and rallied for third. PIENSA SONANDO (CHI) allowed to settle off the rail then three deep on the backstretch, continued outside KUDOS on the second turn, came a bit wide into the stretch and lacked the needed rally. WESTERN PRIDE stalked the pace outside then off the rail, bid three deep on the backstretch, dueled outside the winner, stalked on the second turn and weakened. RODION (ARG) saved ground without early speed, came out a bit into the stretch, then drifted back in and was outrun. GOLDEN TICKET sped to the early lead off the rail, set the pace a bit off the fence, dropped back between foes midway on the backstretch, angled in on the second turn, gave way and was not urged in the lane.

Owners— 1, Stonerside Stable; 2, Starlight Stables I LLC; 3, Moss Mr & Mrs Jerome S; 4, Hunt Nelson B; 5, Chapman Carolyn & McArthur Theresa; 6, Florida Equine Research Inc & Herri; 7, Holsinger Glenn

Trainers—1, Baffert Bob; 2, Pletcher Todd A; 3, Mandella Richard; 4, McAnally Ronald; 5, Chapman James K; 6, Vienna Darrell; 7, Sise Clifford Jr

$2 Daily Double (8–4) Paid $23.60; Daily Double Pool $52,119.
$1 Pick Three (4–8–4) Paid $44.50; Pick Three Pool $119,625.

NINTH RACE
Arlington
JULY 19, 2003

$1\frac{1}{16}$ MILES. (1.55) 73rd Running of THE WASHINGTON PARK HANDICAP. Grade II. Purse $400,000 Guaranteed. A HANDICAP FOR THREE-YEAR-OLDS AND UPWARD. By subscription of $300 each, which should accompany the nomination. A Supplementary Nomination of $14,000 may be made on Saturday, July 12, 2003, which includes entry and starting fees. Original nominees to pay $3,000 to pass the entry box and an additional $3,000 to start, with $400,000 Guaranteed, of which $240,000 to the winner; $80,000 to second; $44,000 to third; $24,000 to fourth and $12,000 to fifth. WEIGHTS: Sunday, July 13, 2003. Total Earnings in 2003 will be used to determine the order of preference of horses assigned equal weight (on the scale). Failure to draw into this race at time of entry cancels all fees with the exception of the nominating fee(s). Trophy to the owner of the winner.

Value of Race: $400,000 Winner $240,000; second $80,000; third $44,000; fourth $24,000; fifth $12,000. Mutuel Pool $344,849.00 Exacta Pool $234,012.00 Trifecta Pool $133,308.00

Last Raced	Horse	M/Eqt.	A.Wt	PP	St	¼	½	¾	Str	Fin	Jockey	Odds $1
14Jun03 ^{10}CD^{1}	Perfect Drift	L	4 120	5	5	$4^{1\frac{1}{2}}$	4^{3}	3^{1}	1^{hd}	1^{5}	Day P	0.60
16May03 ^{11}Pim^{7}	Aeneas	L	4 115	1	2	5	5	5	$3^{1\frac{1}{2}}$	$2^{1\frac{1}{4}}$	Boulanger G	31.00
27Jun03 ^{9}CD^{1}	Flatter	Lf	4 114	4	4	2^{1}	2^{2}	$2^{1\frac{1}{2}}$	2^{1}	$3^{5\frac{1}{2}}$	Perret C	4.20
14Jun03 ^{9}Bel^{1}	Iron Deputy	L	4 117	3	1	1^{1}	$1^{\frac{1}{2}}$	1^{hd}	$4^{2\frac{1}{2}}$	4^{hd}	Migliore R	2.20
1Jly03 ^{8}WO^{1}	Phantom Light	Lb	4 116	2	3	$3^{\frac{1}{2}}$	3^{hd}	4^{2}	5	5	Douglas R R	11.50

OFF AT 5:12 Start Good. Won ridden out. Track fast.
TIME :24^{3}, :48, 1:10^{4}, 1:36, 1:55^{2} (:24.73, :48.03, 1:10.93, 1:36.03, 1:55.49)

$2 Mutuel Prices:

5-PERFECT DRIFT	3.20	2.80	2.10
1-AENEAS		9.40	2.80
4-FLATTER			2.40

$2 EXACTA 5-1 PAID $34.60 $2 TRIFECTA 5-1-4 PAID $138.40

B. g, by Dynaformer-Nice Gal, by Naskra. Trainer Johnson Murray W. Bred by Reed William & Stonecrest Farm (Ky).

PERFECT DRIFT was allowed to settle just outside while not far back, began to move up on the final turn, reached near even terms for the lead entering the stretch then drew off in the final furlong under a brisk hand ride. AENEAS was void of early speed while trailing to the stretch, angled to the middle of the track for the drive, rallied in the stretch and gained the place late but proved no threat to the winner. FLATTER stumbled at the start, pressed the pace of IRON DEPUTY while just outside that one, was even for the lead between horses turning for home but could not go with the winner and lost the place in the final yards. IRON DEPUTY broke to the lead and was guided to the rail, set all of the pace with pressure to his outside then had no response when challenged turning for home. PHANTOM LIGHT race close up to the inside but gave way after a half mile.

Owners— 1, Stonecrest Farm; 2, Ed H Pavlish & Patricia Pavlish; 3, Adele Dilschneider & Claiborne Farm; 4, Moore Susan & John; 5, Stronach Stables B & E & A Stronach

Trainers—1, Johnson Murray W; 2, Wolfson Martin D; 3, Penrod Steven C; 4, Jerkens James A; 5, Vella Daniel J

$1 Pick Three (3/4/10-2-5) Paid $27.50; Pick Three Pool $14,300.

NINTH RACE
Belmont
JULY 19, 2003

1½ MILES. (2.24) 87th Running of THE COACHING CLUB AMERICAN OAKS. Grade I. Purse $500,000. (Up to $57,000 NYSBFOA). SECOND LEG OF TRIPLE TIARA. FILLIES, THREE YEARS OLD. By subscription of $500 each, which should accompany the nomination; $2,500 to pass the entry box and $2,500 to start. The purse to be divided 60% to the winner, 20% to second, 11% to third, 6% to fourth and 3% to fifth. 121 lbs. Trophies will be presented to the winning owner, trainer and jockey. A $2,000,000 bonus will be awarded the the owner of the filly which wins all three legs of the Triple Tiara (The Mother Goose, The Coaching Club American Oaks and The Alabama). Closed Saturday, July 5, 2003 with 17 Nominations.

Value of Race: $500,000 Winner $300,000; second $100,000; third $55,000; fourth $30,000; fifth $15,000. Mutuel Pool $683,919.00 Exacta Pool $436,089.00 Trifecta Pool $399,241.00

Last Raced	Horse	M/Eqt.	A.Wt	PP	¼	½	1	1¼	Str	Fin	Jockey	Odds $1
28Jun03 ^{9}Bel^{1}	Spoken Fur	L	3 121	7	4^{6}	$4^{5\frac{1}{2}}$	$2^{3\frac{1}{2}}$	$1^{2\frac{1}{2}}$	1^{8}	$1^{3\frac{1}{2}}$	Bailey J D	0.90
15Jun03 ^{8}Bel^{4}	Fircroft	Lbf	3 121	4	7	7	4^{hd}	$3^{1\frac{1}{2}}$	$2^{\frac{1}{2}}$	$2^{2\frac{1}{2}}$	Samyn J L	17.60
15Jun03 ^{8}Bel^{1}	Savedbythelight	Lb	3 121	2	$6^{1\frac{1}{2}}$	$6^{1\frac{1}{2}}$	$6^{1\frac{1}{2}}$	4^{8}	4^{22}	$3^{4\frac{1}{4}}$	Santos J A	6.90
28Jun03 ^{9}Bel^{2}	Yell	L	3 121	3	3^{2}	$3^{2\frac{1}{2}}$	$1^{\frac{1}{2}}$	$2^{2\frac{1}{2}}$	$3^{1\frac{1}{2}}$	$4^{29\frac{1}{4}}$	Velazquez J R	1.55
15Jun03 ^{8}Bel^{3}	Little Bonnet	Lf	3 121	6	5^{3}	5^{6}	3^{hd}	5	5	5	Prado E S	23.20
7Jun03 ^{8}Hol^{4}	Shapes And Shadows	Lb	3 121	5	1^{hd}	$1^{2\frac{1}{2}}$	$5^{1\frac{1}{2}}$	—	—	—	Coa E M	36.50
19Jun03 ^{10}CD^{1}	Skipamiss	Lb	3 121	1	2^{2}	2^{hd}	7	—	—	—	Bridgmohan S X	54.00

Shapes And Shadows:Eased;Skipamiss:Eased;

OFF AT 5:19 Start Good. Won ridden out. Track fast.
TIME :22^{4}, :46^{2}, 1:11^{3}, 1:37^{2}, 2:03^{3}, 2:31 (:22.92, :46.59, 1:11.72, 1:37.50, 2:03.69, 2:31.02)

$2 Mutuel Prices:

7-SPOKEN FUR	3.80	2.90	2.20
4-FIRCROFT		8.30	6.00
2-SAVEDBYTHELIGHT			4.40

$2 EXACTA 7-4 PAID $42.00 $2 TRIFECTA 7-4-2 PAID $154.00

Gr/ro f, (Mar), by Notebook-Siberian Fur, by Siberian Express. Trainer Frankel Robert. Bred by (Fla).

SPOKEN FUR raced in hand early, was angled to the inside entering the first turn, advanced outside approaching the second turn, drew clear nearing the stretch, widened in upper stretch and remained well clear under a hand ride. FIRCROFT was outrun early, advanced inside on the second turn, came wide into the stretch and finished gamely outside but could not get to the winner. SAVEDBYTHELIGHT was rated along inside, put in a three wide run on the second turn and had little left for the stretch drive. YELL raced close up early while in hand, moved with the winner on the backstretch, could not stay with that rival approaching the stretch and tired in the drive. LITTLE BONNET jumped shadows along the inside nearing the first turn, was checked hard as the winner went by in front of her entering the first turn then raced wide and tired in the stretch. SHAPES AND SHADOWS stumbled at the start, quickly showed in front, set the pace for three quarters, stopped and was eased when hopelessly beaten. SKIPAMISS was hard-used inside for a half mile, stopped and was eased on the second turn.

Owners— 1, Amerman Racing Stables LLC; 2, Humphrey G W Jr; 3, Mack Earle I; 4, Claiborne Farm & Dilschneider Adele; 5, Ackerley Brothers Farm; 6, Nielsen Jeffrey L; 7, Equirace Com LLC

Trainers—1, Frankel Robert; 2, Arnold George R II; 3, Violette Richard A Jr; 4, McGaughey Claude III; 5, Pletcher Todd A; 6, Canani Nick; 7, Scott Joan

EIGHTH RACE
Delaware
JULY 19, 2003

$1\frac{1}{16}$ MILES. (1.41^{2}) 52nd Running of THE DELAWARE OAKS. Grade III. Purse $500,000 FOR FILLIES THREE YEARS OLD. By subscription of $400 each, which shall accompany the nomination; $1,500 to enter and $2,000 to start. Supplemental nominations of $5,000 will be accepted at time of entry which shall include all fees. Weight;122 lbs. Non-winners of $120,000 at a mile or over in 2003 allowed 3 lbs.,$90,000 at a mile or over in 2003, 5 lbs,;$45,000 at a mile or over in 2003, 7 lbs (Maiden,claiming and starter races not considered). Field limited to 14 starters. Preference to horses that have accumulated the highest total earnings. Closing Saturday, July 5, 2003.

Value of Race: $500,000 Winner $300,000; second $100,000; third $55,000; fourth $30,000; fifth $15,000. Mutuel Pool $186,885.00 Exacta Pool $100,511.00 Trifecta Pool $55,344.00 Superfecta Pool $7,663.00

Last Raced	Horse	M/Eqt.	A.Wt	PP	St	¼	½	¾	Str	Fin	Jockey	Odds $1
2May03 ^{10}CD^{7}	Island Fashion	Lb	3 122	2	1	1^{hd}	$2^{2\frac{1}{2}}$	$1^{1\frac{1}{2}}$	1^{4}	$1^{6\frac{1}{2}}$	Puglisi I L	9.10
6Jun03 ^{8}AP^{1}	Awesome Humor	L	3 115	1	8	4^{hd}	$3^{1\frac{1}{2}}$	$3^{2\frac{1}{2}}$	2^{3}	$2^{4\frac{1}{4}}$	Albarado R J	1.00
28Jun03 ^{7}Del^{2}	Ladyecho	L	3 115	6	4	$3^{\frac{1}{2}}$	4^{2}	4^{2}	3^{1}	3^{nk}	Castillo O O	14.70
28Jun03 ^{7}Del^{4}	Mt. Kobla	L	3 115	9	5	7^{3}	$7^{1\frac{1}{2}}$	$6^{\frac{1}{2}}$	$4^{\frac{1}{2}}$	4^{hd}	Dominguez R A	23.30
22Jun03 ^{9}CD^{1}	Meet Me At Midnite	L	3 115	4	7	8	8	$7^{1\frac{1}{2}}$	6^{1}	$5^{4\frac{3}{4}}$	Guidry M	10.00
19Jun03 ^{8}AP^{1}	Sue's Good News	L	3 117	3	2	$5^{\frac{1}{2}}$	$5^{1\frac{1}{2}}$	5^{hd}	7^{3}	$6^{1\frac{1}{4}}$	Doocy T T	3.20
4Jly03 ^{6}PrM^{1}	Wildwood Royal	Lb	3 117	5	3	2^{3}	1^{hd}	$2^{1\frac{1}{2}}$	5^{hd}	$7^{4\frac{3}{4}}$	Sukie D G	10.10
28Jun03 ^{9}Bel^{4}	Virgin Voyage	Lb	3 115	8	6	$6^{3\frac{1}{2}}$	6^{3}	8	8	8	Chavez J F	10.10
20Jun03 ^{8}Bel^{1}	Cherokee Lite	L	3 115	7	9	—	—	—	—	—	Castellano J J	–

Cherokee Lite:Lost rider;

OFF AT 4:26 Start Good For All But CHEROKEE LITE Won driving. Track fast.
TIME :23^{1}, :46^{3}, 1:11^{2}, 1:38, 1:44^{4} (:23.35, :46.73, 1:11.41, 1:38.14, 1:44.95)

$2 Mutuel Prices:				
	2–ISLAND FASHION	20.20	5.60	4.40
	1–AWESOME HUMOR		3.00	2.40
	7–LADYECHO			3.80

$2 EXACTA 2–1 PAID $51.20 $2 TRIFECTA 2–1–7 PAID $377.20 $1 SUPERFECTA 2–1–7–10 PAID $957.80

Gr/ro f, (Mar), by Petionville–Danzigs Fashion, by A Native Danzig. Trainer Canani Nick. Bred by Everest Stables Inc (Ky).

ISLAND FASHION broke sharp and saved ground vying for the lead with WILDWOOD ROYAL, shook loose to open a clear lead after six furlongs then was kept to her task through the stretch. AWESOME HUMOR broke in a tangle, made a run after six furlongs then was clearly no threat to the winner and finished second best. LADYECHO raced within easy striking distance but could gain little on the top two. MT. KOBLA was unhurried early, made a run leaving the far turn then made no further gain. MEET ME AT MIDNITE was unhurried early then failed to threaten when called upon. SUE'S GOOD NEWS, forwardly placed, flattened out in the drive. WILDWOOD ROYAL broke alertly to vie two wide with the winner to the far turn then tired. VIRGIN VOYAGE tired. CHEROKEE LITE was fractious in the gate prior to the start, then the rider was not mounted at the break thus was left in the starting gate and CHEROKEE LITE was declared a non-starter following a stewards inquiry. Wagers on her were ordered refunded and a consolation daily double was paid.

Owners— 1, Everest Stables; 2, Winstar Farm; 3, Polin Charlotte C; 4, Evans Edward P; 5, B M H Stable; 6, Cresran LLC; 7, Stiritz William; 8, Paraneck Stable; 9, Double C Stables

Trainers—1, Canani Nick; 2, Walden W Elliott; 3, Servis John C; 4, Hennig Mark; 5, Hiles Rick; 6, Hobby Steve; 7, Zook Jimmy; 8, Pedersen Jennifer; 9, Zito Nicholas P

Scratched— Hennie's Song (28Jun03 ^{7}DEL^{1})

$2 Daily Double (6–2) Paid $134.00; Daily Double Pool $15,617.
$2 Pick Three (1–6–2) Paid $3,212.20; Pick Three Pool $8,566.
$2 Consolation Daily Double (6–8) Paid $18.80

FOURTH RACE
Hollywood
JULY 19, 2003

6 FURLONGS. (1.07^{2}) 64th Running of THE HOLLYWOOD JUVENILE CHAMPIONSHIP. Grade III. Purse $100,000 Added. TWO YEAR OLDS. By subscription of $100 each on or before Wednesday, July 9. $1,000 additional to start, with $100,000 added. The added money and all fees to be divided 60% to the winner, 20% to second, 12% to third, 6% to fourth and 2% to fifth. Weight 120 lbs. Non-winners of a sweepstakes allowed 3 lbs. Maidens allowed 5 lbs. A trophy will be presented to the winning owner. Closed July 9 with 10 nominations.

Value of Race: $102,500 Winner $61,500; second $20,500; third $12,300; fourth $6,150; fifth $2,050. Mutuel Pool $1,117,929.0 Exacta Pool $287,863.00 Quinella Pool $22,829.00

Last Raced	Horse	M/Eqt.	A.Wt	PP	St	¼	½	Str	Fin	Jockey	Odds $1
21Jun03 ^{4}Hol^{2}	Perfect Moon	LB	2 117	2	5	$4^{2\frac{1}{2}}$	2^{hd}	2^{1}	$1^{2\frac{1}{2}}$	Valenzuela P A	3.00
21Jun03 ^{4}Hol^{6}	Blairs Roarin Star	LB	2 117	1	4	$1^{1\frac{1}{2}}$	$1^{1\frac{1}{2}}$	1^{1}	2^{3}	Baze T C	15.90
11Jun03 ^{4}Hol^{1}	Ruler's Court	LB	2 117	5	3	3^{1}	$3^{2\frac{1}{2}}$	3^{4}	3^{3}	Flores D R	0.20
21Jun03 ^{4}Hol^{3}	Dave The Dude	LBb	2 117	4	1	5	5	5	4^{3}	Espinoza V	12.50
21Jun03 ^{4}Hol^{5}	Tricky Flash Flood	LBb	2 117	3	2	2^{hd}	$4^{1\frac{1}{2}}$	4^{hd}	5	Martinez F F	38.90

OFF AT 2:55 Start Good. Won driving. Track fast.
TIME :22^{1}, :44^{3}, :57^{1}, 1:10^{1} (:22.23, :44.75, :57.36, 1:10.39)

$2 Mutuel Prices:				
	2–PERFECT MOON	8.00	4.40	2.10
	1–BLAIRS ROARIN STAR		10.00	2.10
	5–RULER'S COURT			2.10

$1 EXACTA 2–1 PAID $43.00 $2 QUINELLA 1–2 PAID $39.00

B. g, (Mar), by Malibu Moon–Perfectly, by Parfaitement. Trainer Stute Melvin F. Bred by Mr & Mrs Hugh J O'Donovan (Md).

PERFECT MOON stalked a bit off the rail then along the inside, came out some on the turn and again into the stretch, drifted in and brushed the runner-up under right handed pressure nearing the sixteenth pole but pulled clear. BLAIRS ROARIN STAR quickly sped to the front, set the pace inside, was brushed by the winner past midstretch and could not match that one thereafter. RULER'S COURT bumped at the start, stalked the leader three deep to the stretch, drifted out some late and came up empty in the final furlong. DAVE THE DUDE broke out and bumped a foe, trailed off the rail, came wide into the stretch and did not rally. TRICKY FLASH FLOOD stalked off the inside then between horses, steadied in tight midway on the turn, dropped back off the rail and weakened. The stewards conducted an inquiry into the stretch run of the top pair but made no change when they ruled the light contact between those two did not alter the original order of finish. A claim of foul by the rider of the runner-up against the winner was not allowed for the same reason.

Owners— 1, Stute Annabelle & The Hat Ranch; 2, David J Lanzman Racing Stable; 3, Darley Stud Management LLC; 4, Harrington & Vanderhouwen; 5, Sides Clay R

Trainers—1, Stute Melvin F; 2, O'Neill Doug; 3, Harty Eoin; 4, Harrington Mike; 5, Sides Robert C

$2 Daily Double (7–2) Paid $63.80; Daily Double Pool $26,259.
$1 Pick Three (4–7–2) Paid $2,001.40; Pick Three Pool $67,701.

TENTH RACE Monmouth JULY 19, 2003

$1\frac{1}{16}$ MILES. (Turf Chute)(1.39^3) 33rd Running of THE EATONTOWN HANDICAP. Grade III. Purse $100,000 A HANDICAP FOR FILLIES AND MARES, THREE YEARS OLD AND UPWARD. By subscription of $100 each, which should accompany the nomination. $1,500 to enter. The winner to receive $60,000; $20,000 to second; $11,000 to third; $6,000 to fourth and $3,000 to fifth. Weights 5:00 P.M. Sunday, July 12 This race will not be divided. Starters to be named through the entry box by the usual time of closing. Highweights preferred. The owner of the winner to receive a trophy. NOMINATIONS CLOSED Saturday, July 5, 2003 with THIRTY TWO (32) (Rail at 10 Feet)

Value of Race: $100,000 Winner $60,000; second $20,000; third $11,000; fourth $6,000; fifth $3,000. Mutuel Pool $169,689.00 Exacta Pool $118,751.00 Trifecta Pool $75,712.00

Last Raced	Horse	M/Eqt.	A.Wt	PP	St	¼	½	¾	Str	Fin	Jockey	Odds $1
15Jun03 ^{8}Cby^1	Stylish	Lb	5 118	7	3	6^{1}	6^{1}	$6^{1\frac{1}{2}}$	4^{hd}	1^{nk}	Castillo H Jr	2.00
29Jun03 ^{10}Bel^1	Something Ventured	Lb	4 117	3	5	$3^{\frac{1}{2}}$	3^{1}	2^{hd}	1^{hd}	$2^{\frac{1}{2}}$	Velez J A Jr	4.70
19Jun03 ^{9}CD^1	Sweet Deimos-GB	L	4 113	6	9	8^{hd}	7^{hd}	7^{1}	6^{1}	3^{hd}	Pimentel J	11.00
7Jun03 ^{8}Bel^5	Love N' Kiss S.	L	5 114	5	4	$4^{\frac{1}{2}}$	4^{hd}	$3^{1\frac{1}{2}}$	2^{hd}	4no	Cruz C	3.90
29Jun03 ^{9}Mth^1	Southern Fiction	Lb	5 117	4	7	$5^{\frac{1}{2}}$	$5^{\frac{1}{2}}$	5^{hd}	$5^{1\frac{1}{2}}$	$5^{2\frac{1}{2}}$	Bravo J	4.00
29Jun03 ^{9}Mth^2	Cocktailsandreams	L	6 114	8	6	7^{hd}	8^{hd}	9	$7^{2\frac{1}{2}}$	$6^{2\frac{3}{4}}$	Toribio A R	36.00
15Jun03 ^{5}Crc^1	Win's Fair Lady	Lb	4 115	1	1	$2^{6\frac{1}{2}}$	1^{2}	$1^{1\frac{1}{2}}$	3^{hd}	$7^{1\frac{1}{2}}$	Homeister R B Jr	9.00
29Jun03 ^{9}Mth^3	Caught Out	L	5 115	9	8	9	9	8^{hd}	8^{5}	$8^{12\frac{1}{4}}$	King E L Jr	15.00
25Jun03 ^{5}Mth^2	La Tizona	Lb	5 113	2	2	1^{hd}	2^{5}	4^{hd}	9	9	Ferrer J C	32.40

OFF AT 5:23 Start Good. Won driving. Course soft.

TIME :22^1, :46, 1:10^2, 1:35^2, 1:41^3 (:22.35, :46.05, 1:10.50, 1:35.46, 1:41.69)

$2 Mutuel Prices:			
8–STYLISH	6.00	4.00	3.20
4–SOMETHING VENTURED		4.00	2.80
7–SWEET DEIMOS–GB			6.20

$2 EXACTA 8–4 PAID $31.20 $2 TRIFECTA 8–4–7 PAID $238.00

B. m, by Thunder Gulch–Miss Lenora, by Theatrical*Ire. Trainer Mott William I. Bred by Allen E Paulson (Ky).

STYLISH, unhurriedly toward mid track, started her bid through the final turn then endured a long stretch drive, getting up the final yards. SOMETHING VENTURED exchanged light contact with Southern Fiction at the break, stayed off the pace off the rail, bid in the three path on the final turn, dueled gamely with a short lead from the furlong pole but was outfinished in the last yards. SWEET DEIMOS (GB), unhurriedly off the rail, was steadied lacking room in midstretch, eased out when able and closed, finishing well. LOVE N' KISS S. rated off the pace in mid track, bid five wide on the final turn, dueled through the stretch but was outgamed in a crowded finish. SOUTHERN FICTION exchanged light contact with Something Ventured at the start, was roughed leaving the chute, raced unhurriedly off the rail, bid through the final turn, eased out for room in the upper stretch, came back to the inside late and finished evenly. COCKTAILSANDREAMS raced unhurriedly in mid track, eased out entering the stretch and made a mild bid toward the outside. WIN'S FAIR LADY rated a clear lead inside, dueled on the rail through the upper stretch then weakened the final furlong. CAUGHT OUT raced well back toward the outside, angled in entering the stretch and offered no rally. LA TIZONA kept up with the early pace in the three path then faded through the final turn.

Owners— 1, The Thoroughbred Corporation; 2, McLane John & Weimer Irv; 3, Higgins Joseph; 4, Lael Stables; 5, Humphrey G W Jr; 6, Generazio Patricia A; 7, Sabine Stable; 8, Farish William S; 9, Gill Michael J

Trainers—1, Mott William I; 2, Pletcher Todd A; 3, Carroll David; 4, Clement Christophe; 5, Oliver Victoria; 6, Generazio Frank Jr; 7, Standridge Steve W; 8, Zwiesler Michael; 9, Vazquez Gamaliel

Scratched— Maresha (29Jun03 ^{9}MTH^5)

$2 Pick Three (8–7–8) Paid $109.60; Pick Three Pool $7,819.

EIGHTH RACE Arlington JULY 20, 2003

$1\frac{3}{16}$ MILES. (Turf)(1.53^1) 91st Running of THE AMERICAN DERBY. Grade II. Purse $250,000 FOR THREE-YEAR-OLDS. By subscription of $300 each horse (Early) Wednesday, April 2, 2003, $600 each horse (Late Nomination) on Wednesday, July 2, 2003. Fee to accompany the nomination. A Supplementary Nomination of $10,000 may be made on Thursday, July 17, 2003, which includes entry and starting fees. Original Nominees to pay $2,000 to pass the entry box and $2,000 additional to start. WEIGHT: 126 lbs. Non-winners of $100,000 twice at one mile or over in 2003, allowed 3 lbs.; $55,000 twice at one mile or over in 2003, 5 lbs.; $55,000 once at one mile or over in 2003, 7 lbs.; $40,000 at one mile or over at anytime, 10 lbs. (Maiden and Claiming races not considered.) This event will be limited to fourteen (14) starters ([7] Non-North American starters and [7] North American starters). Preference will be given in the following order: (1st) (A) Grade/Group I Turf winners in 2003 – (B) Grade/Group I winners on Dirt; (2nd) (A) Grade/Group II Turf winners in 2003 – (B) Grade/Group II winners on Dirt; (3rd) (A) Grade/Group III Turf winners in 2003 – (B) Grade/Group III winners on Dirt. (Total Earnings in 2003).

Value of Race: $250,000 Winner $150,000; second $50,000; third $27,500; fourth $15,000; fifth $7,500. Mutuel Pool $190,111.00 Exacta Pool $96,388.00 Trifecta Pool $75,054.00

Last Raced	Horse	M/Eqt.	A.Wt	PP	St	¼	½	¾	Str	Fin	Jockey	Odds $1
19Jun03 Asc^3	Evolving Tactics-IR	L	3 117	5	2	$2^{2\frac{1}{2}}$	2^{2}	$2^{1\frac{1}{2}}$	2^{1}	1^{nk}	Smullen P J	1.00
2May03 ^{9}CD^8	Californian-GB	L	3 121	4	5	3^{5}	3^{3}	4^{2}	3^{1}	$2^{2\frac{3}{4}}$	Desormeaux K J	2.00
28Jun03 ^{8}AP^4	Scottago	L	3 116	2	4	$4^{\frac{1}{2}}$	5	$3^{\frac{1}{2}}$	4^{4}	$3^{1\frac{1}{2}}$	Marquez C H Jr	8.80
22Jun03 ^{7}LS^1	Gato Gato Gato	Lb	3 116	3	1	$1^{2\frac{1}{2}}$	1^{2}	1^{1}	$1^{\frac{1}{2}}$	$4^{1\frac{3}{4}}$	Emigh C A	11.30
28Jun03 ^{8}AP^5	Rapid Proof	Lb	3 119	1	3	5	$4^{\frac{1}{2}}$	5	5	5	Borel C H	3.90

OFF AT 4:21 Start Good. Won driving. Course good.

TIME :25, :51, 1:17, 1:41^2, 1:59 (:25.11, :51.08, 1:17.16, 1:41.48, 1:59.04)

$2 Mutuel Prices:			
7–EVOLVING TACTICS–IR	4.00	2.80	2.20
5–CALIFORNIAN–GB		3.00	2.40
3–SCOTTAGO			2.60

$2 EXACTA 7–5 PAID $9.20 $2 TRIFECTA 7–5–3 PAID $30.00

B. c, (Mar), by Machiavellian–Token Gesture*Ire, by Alzao. Trainer Weld Dermot K. Bred by Moyglare Stud Farm Ltd (Ire).

EVOLVING TACTICS (IRE) stalked the pace of GATO GATO GATO while just off the rail, was asked to pick it up turning for home, rallied to the lead in the stretch then was fully extended to hold off CALIFORNIAN (GB) at the wire. CALIFORNIAN (GB) was allowed to settle along the rail near the middle of the field, angled out a bit in the stretch, finished willingly and did not miss by much. SCOTTAGO was void of speed while just outside, began moving up on the final bend and rallied late for minor awards while no danger to the top two. GATO GATO GATO veered out a bit at the break, quickly made an uncontested lead, set all of the pace from the inside on a clear lead then weakened in the drive. RAPID PROOF was void of speed and trailed throughout. (Race run in lane 1, rail at 0).

Owners— 1, Moyglare Stud Farm Ltd; 2, Stephen Taub & Neil Papiano & Nocti; 3, Jer-Mar Stable LLC; 4, Everest Stables; 5, Morrison Dolphus

Trainers—1, Weld Dermot K; 2, Mulhall Kristin; 3, Robertson Hugh H; 4, Keen Dallas E; 5, Wiggins Hal R

Scratched— Bim's Baby Bun (25Jun03 ^{8}CD^1), G. W.'s Skippie (26May03 ^{7}LS^5)

$1 Pick Three (6–1–1/6/7) Paid $81.10; Pick Three Pool $14,927.

FIFTH RACE
Delaware
JULY 20, 2003

1⅛ MILES. (Turf)(1.47^{2}) 49th Running of THE KENT BREEDERS' CUP. Grade III. Purse $250,000 (includes $100,000 Breeders' Cup Fund). 3–year–olds. By subscription of $200 each, which shall accompany the nomination; $1,000 to enter and $1,250 to start. Supplemental nominations of $3,000 will be accepted at time of entry which shall include all fees. Weight, 122 lbs. Non–winners of $120,000 at a mile or over in 2003, allowed 3 lbs. $90,000 at a mile or over in 2003, 5 lbs.; $45,000 at a mile or over in 2003, 7 lbs. (Maiden, claiming and starter races not considered). Nominations Closed Saturday, July 5. Supplemental nomination: MONKEY JUNIOR and PIKE PLACE GOLD.

Value of Race: $250,000 Winner $150,000; second $50,000; third $27,500; fourth $15,000; fifth $7,500. Mutuel Pool $178,031.00 Exacta Pool $152,487.00 Trifecta Pool $116,095.00

Last Raced	Horse	M/Eqt.	A.Wt	PP	St	¼	½	¾	Str	Fin	Jockey	Odds $1
7Jun03 9CD5	Foufa's Warrior	Lbf	3 115	3	5	6^{2}	$6^{3\frac{1}{2}}$	$5^{2\frac{1}{2}}$	$4^{\frac{1}{2}}$	$1^{1\frac{1}{4}}$	Dominguez R A	4.40
28Jun03 8AP2	Remind	L	3 115	6	2	3^{1}	3^{2}	2^{1}	1^{1}	$2^{\frac{1}{2}}$	Bailey J D	2.10
28Jun03 8AP1	Lismore Knight	L	3 119	7	3	4^{1}	4^{2}	$4^{2\frac{1}{2}}$	3^{1}	$3^{3\frac{1}{4}}$	Velazquez J R	1.20
23Jun03 7Del1	Gimmeawink	L	3 117	5	1	1^{1}	$1^{2\frac{1}{2}}$	1^{1}	$2^{1\frac{1}{2}}$	4^{nk}	Madrigal R Jr	11.90
1Jly03 8Del1	Pike Place Gold	Lf	3 115	4	4	2^{2}	$2^{1\frac{1}{2}}$	$3^{\frac{1}{2}}$	$5^{2\frac{1}{2}}$	5^{1}	Castillo O O	18.80
28Jun03 4Del1	Kings Course	L	3 115	2	6	7	7	7	7	6^{nk}	Caraballo J C	8.30
21Jun03 3Bel1	Monkey Junior	L	3 115	1	7	5^{1}	$5^{2\frac{1}{2}}$	$6^{\frac{1}{2}}$	$6^{\frac{1}{2}}$	7	Black A S	38.40

OFF AT 2:52 Start Good. Won driving. Course firm.
TIME :24, :46^{2}, 1:09^{4}, 1:34^{4}, 1:47^{2} (:24.09, :46.49, 1:09.84, 1:34.85, 1:47.44)
(New Course Record)

$2 Mutuel Prices:				
	4–FOUFA'S WARRIOR	10.80	6.20	2.40
	7–REMIND		4.80	2.20
	8–LISMORE KNIGHT			2.10

$2 EXACTA 4–7 PAID $33.60 $2 TRIFECTA 4–7–8 PAID $58.00

Ch. g, (May), by Jade Hunter–Foufa, by Storm Bird. Trainer Murray Lawrence E. Bred by Sondra Bender & Howard M Bender (Md).

FOUFA'S WARRIOR was unhurried for five furlongs, made a strong three wide middle move then fanned four wide out of the final turn and responded to strong handling to wear down the leaders leaving the furlong grounds. REMIND raced close up from the outset,bid outside GIMMEAWINK after six furlongs, drew clear a furlong out but hung late while saving the place. LISMORE KNIGHT bid three wide out of the second turn, posed a threat in the furlong grounds but was then outfinished by the top two. GIMMEAWINK set a very fast pace to upper stretch then gave way. PIKE PLACE GOLD was well placed inside to the stretch then weakened. KINGS COURSE failed to menace. MONKEY JUNIOR was through early. The portable inner rail was set at zero feet. The final time of 1:47.44 establishes a new track record for a mile and an eighth on the turf.

Owners— 1, Bender Sondra D; 2, Claiborne Farm; 3, J Pletcher & Barry W Simon; 4, Wienkowitz Walter; 5, Courtlandt Farms; 6, Winchell Thoroughbreds LLC; 7, Joseph Graffeo

Trainers—1, Murray Lawrence E; 2, Mott William I; 3, Pletcher Todd A; 4, Ritchey Tim F; 5, Motion H Graham; 6, Dickinson Michael W; 7, DiMauro Stephen L

Scratched— Elusive Gentleman (14Jun03 7BEL6)

$2 Daily Double (1–4) Paid $290.80; Daily Double Pool $15,084.
$2 Pick Three (5–1–4) Paid $17,622.00; Pick Three Pool $11,748.

TENTH RACE
Delaware
JULY 20, 2003

1¼ MILES. (1.59^{4}) 66th Running of THE DELAWARE HANDICAP. Grade II. Purse $750,000. Fillies and mares, 3–year–olds and upward. By subscription of $600 each, which shall accompany the nomination; $3,000 to enter and $4,000 to start. $750,000 Guaranteed, of which $450,000 to the winner, $150,000 to second, $82,500 to third, $45,000 to fourth and $22,500 to fifth. Weights :Saturday,July 12. Starters to pass the entry box by the usual time of closing. Nominations closed Saturday, July 5.

Value of Race: $750,000 Winner $450,000; second $150,000; third $82,500; fourth $45,000; fifth $22,500. Mutuel Pool $430,799.00 Exacta Pool $282,805.00 Trifecta Pool $222,573.00 Superfecta Pool $67,404.00

Last Raced	Horse	M/Eqt.	A.Wt	PP	¼	½	¾	1	Str	Fin	Jockey	Odds $1
17May03 8Bel1	Wild Spirit-CH		4 117	2	4^{1}	$4^{\frac{1}{2}}$	$2^{\frac{1}{2}}$	2^{1}	1^{2}	1^{6}	Bailey J D	0.80
21Jun03 9Bel2	Take Charge Lady	L	4 120	3	1^{hd}	$1^{\frac{1}{2}}$	1^{hd}	1^{hd}	2^{3}	$2^{2\frac{3}{4}}$	Sellers S J	4.30
21Jun03 7Del2	Shiny Sheet	Lb	5 112	6	$5^{\frac{1}{2}}$	5^{hd}	6^{1}	4^{hd}	4^{1}	$3^{\frac{1}{2}}$	Rose J	62.40
21Jun03 7Del1	Devon Rose	L	4 116	7	$3^{\frac{1}{2}}$	$3^{\frac{1}{2}}$	$5^{\frac{1}{2}}$	3^{2}	3^{1}	$4^{1\frac{1}{2}}$	Dominguez R A	12.10
21Jun03 9Bel3	Mandy's Gold	Lf	5 117	5	2^{1}	$2^{\frac{1}{2}}$	$3^{1\frac{1}{2}}$	5^{1}	$5^{3\frac{1}{2}}$	$5^{5\frac{1}{4}}$	Black A S	12.80
28Jun03 11Mth1	Summer Colony	L	5 122	8	$7^{\frac{1}{2}}$	$6^{\frac{1}{2}}$	7^{2}	$6^{\frac{1}{2}}$	$6^{2\frac{1}{2}}$	6^{3}	Velazquez J R	2.60
22Jun03 7Del1	Jaramar Rain	L	4 115	4	$6^{\frac{1}{2}}$	7^{1}	4^{hd}	7^{1}	$7^{\frac{1}{2}}$	7^{nk}	Madrigal R Jr	43.80
22Jun03 8Bel5	French Hideaway	L	4 113	1	8	8	8	8	8	8	Decarlo C P	87.90

OFF AT 5:43 Start Good For All But SUMMER COLONY. Won ridden out. Track fast.
TIME :24^{2}, :49^{2}, 1:13^{4}, 1:38^{2}, 2:02^{4} (:24.42, :49.41, 1:13.95, 1:38.50, 2:02.95)

$2 Mutuel Prices:				
	2–WILD SPIRIT–CH	3.60	2.60	2.20
	3–TAKE CHARGE LADY		3.80	3.40
	6–SHINY SHEET			7.20

$2 EXACTA 2–3 PAID $14.20 $2 TRIFECTA 2–3–6 PAID $207.20 $1 SUPERFECTA 2–3–6–7 PAID $537.70

Dk. b. or br. f, by Hussonet–Wild Princess, by Wild Again. Trainer Frankel Robert. Bred by Haras Sumaya (Chi).

WILD SPIRIT (CHI) was under a snug hold while rated just off the lead through the opening five furlongs, split horses on the backstretch to press the pace while still in hand, shook off TAKE CHARG LADY shown the whip out of the second turn to gain a clear lead, had her rider lose his whip as he attempted to switch from a right to left handed whip passing the furlong marker then drew off under a vigorous hand ride. TAKE CHARGE LADY broke sharp, was well rated setting a slow pace for a mile but couldn't stay with the winner's rally out of the second turn but was clearly best of the rest. SHINY SHEET made an inside middle move to the stretch but failed to sustain that rally. DEVON ROSE stalked the leaders three wide, attempted to collar the leaders outside after seven furlongs but gave way in the drive. MANDY'S GOLD pressed the leader while off the inner rail to the second turn then weakened. SUMMER COLONY moved her head at the start to be off behind the field, moved up outside to prompt the pace for a half then faded. JARAMAR RAIN was well placed inside to the second turn then faded. FRENCH HIDEAWAY trailed.

Owners— 1, Sumaya Us Stables; 2, Select Stable; 3, Rathbun Mrs Henry T; 4, Englander Richard A; 5, Steeplechase Farm; 6, Evans Edward P; 7, Humphrey G W Jr; 8, Anstu Stables

Trainers—1, Frankel Robert; 2, McPeek Kenneth G; 3, Hadry Charles J; 4, Iwinski Allen; 5, Gorham Michael E; 6, Hennig Mark; 7, Arnold George R II; 8, Moloney James J

$2 Daily Double (7–2) Paid $177.20; Daily Double Pool $29,213.
$2 Pick Three (9/10–7–2) Paid $181.60; Pick Three Pool $16,106.

SEVENTH RACE
Hollywood
JULY 20, 2003

1½ MILES. (Turf)(2.23^{2}) 62nd Running of THE SUNSET HANDICAP. Grade II. Purse $150,000. 3-year-olds and upward. By subscription of $150 each on or before Wednesday, July 9. $500 additional to pass the entry box, and $1,000 additional to start, with $90,000 to the winner, $30,000 to second, $18,000 to third, $9,000 to fourth and $3,000 to fifth. Closed with 19 nominations. (Rail at zero.)

Value of Race: $150,000 Winner $90,000; second $30,000; third $18,000; fourth $9,000; fifth $3,000. Mutuel Pool $503,938.00 Exacta Pool $271,501.00 Quinella Pool $31,525.00 Trifecta Pool $292,292.00 Superfecta Pool $116,361.00

Last Raced	Horse	M/Eqt.	A.	Wt	PP	¼	½	1	1¼	Str	Fin	Jockey	Odds $1
22Jun03 ^{8}Hol^{2}	Puerto Banus	LBb	4	113	2	7^{1}	6^{hd}	5^{1}	3^{hd}	$3^{2\frac{1}{2}}$	$1^{\frac{1}{2}}$	Espinoza V	11.90
14Jun03 ^{3}Hol^{3}	Cagney-BRZ	LBb	6	116	4	$5^{1\frac{1}{2}}$	4^{hd}	$4^{1\frac{1}{2}}$	$2^{1\frac{1}{2}}$	1^{1}	$2^{1\frac{1}{2}}$	Smith M E	2.30
15Jun03 ^{8}Hol^{1}	Continental Red	LB	7	116	6	$3^{1\frac{1}{2}}$	$3^{1\frac{1}{2}}$	3^{hd}	$4^{\frac{1}{2}}$	4^{3}	$3^{\frac{1}{2}}$	Valenzuela P A	2.00
22Jun03 ^{8}Hol^{1}	Asong For Billy	LBf	4	113	3	2^{2}	$2^{3\frac{1}{2}}$	2^{hd}	1^{hd}	2^{hd}	$4^{3\frac{1}{2}}$	Almeida G F	5.30
22Jun03 ^{8}Hol^{4}	Nazirali-IRE	LB	6	116	8	$6^{\frac{1}{2}}$	7^{2}	7^{1}	7^{3}	$5^{\frac{1}{2}}$	5^{3}	Flores D R	5.30
8Jun03 ^{8}Hol^{1}	Stormin' Heaven	LBb	5	115	5	8	8	8	$6^{1\frac{1}{2}}$	6^{3}	$6^{1\frac{1}{2}}$	Valdivia J Jr	18.00
5Jun03 ^{7}Hol^{1}	Tifonica-ARG	LB	5	109	1	4^{hd}	5^{1}	6^{hd}	8	7^{2}	$7^{12\frac{1}{2}}$	Baze T C	38.70
14Jun03 ^{3}Hol^{4}	Night Patrol	LBb	7	114	7	$1^{1\frac{1}{2}}$	1^{6}	$1^{1\frac{1}{2}}$	5^{1}	8	8	Krone J A	10.60

OFF AT 4:24 Start Good. Won driving. Course firm.
TIME :25, :48^{3}, 1:13^{3}, 1:39^{3}, 2:03, 2:26^{4} (:25.07, :48.71, 1:13.68, 1:39.65, 2:03.02, 2:26.95)

$2 Mutuel Prices:

3–PUERTO BANUS	25.80	11.60	4.40
5–CAGNEY–BRZ		4.80	2.40
7–CONTINENTAL RED			2.40

$1 EXACTA 3–5 PAID $49.80 $2 QUINELLA 3–5 PAID $43.20 $1 TRIFECTA 3–5–7 PAID $142.00 $1 SUPERFECTA 3–5–7–4 PAID $649.50

Ch. c, by Supremo–Drina, by Regal and Royal. Trainer Mulhall Kristin. Bred by The Thoroughbred Corporation (Ky).

PUERTO BANUS settled toward the inside then between horses on the backstretch, moved up three deep on the third turn, came out into the stretch and rallied under urging to get up. CAGNEY (BRZ) chased outside a rival early, advanced three deep on the backstretch, bid three wide on the final turn then outside a rival leaving than bend, took the lead into the stretch, inched away in midstretch but could not hold off the winner. CONTINENTAL RED also chased outside a rival then off the rail leaving the backstretch and on the last turn, came out in the stretch and edged a foe for the show. ASONG FOR BILLY took the early lead then stalked inside on the first turn, saved ground chasing the leader, bid between horses into the third turn, dueled inside the runner-up leaving that bend, weakened some in the final furlong but lost third late. NAZIRALI (IRE) three deep into the first turn, settled outside a rival or off the rail and improved position in the stretch. STORMIN' HEAVEN unhurried and angled in a bit off the rail early, came out into the stretch and lacked the needed rally. TIFONICA (ARG) saved ground in midpack, dropped back on the final turn, came out in the stretch and had no further response. NIGHT PATROL took the lead outside a rival on the first turn, opened up in the stretch the first time, offered little resistance when challenged on the last turn, dropped back fast and gave way.

Owners— 1, Noctis Stable Papiano Neil & Taub S; 2, T N T Stud; 3, Fitzpatrick Sharon M; 4, Wongs Stable; 5, House Michael; 6, Fog City Stable; 7, Currin William L & Eisman Alvin; 8, Everest Stables

Trainers—1, Mulhall Kristin; 2, Mandella Richard; 3, Jory Ian P D; 4, Aguirre Paul G; 5, Canani Julio C; 6, Hess R B Jr; 7, Currin William L; 8, Canani Nick

Scratched— Nates Colony (8Jun03 ^{8}ALB^{3})

$2 Daily Double (4–3) Paid $93.80; Daily Double Pool $39,314.
$1 Pick Three (3–4–3) Paid $277.40; Pick Three Pool $91,080.

NINTH RACE
Saratoga
JULY 23, 2003

6 FURLONGS. (1.08) 86th Running of THE SCHUYLERVILLE. Grade II. Purse $150,000 (Up to $21,100 NYSBFOA). FILLIES, TWO YEARS OLD. By subscription of $150 each, which should accompany the nomination; $750 to pass the entry box; $750 to start. The purse to be divided 60% to the winner, 20% to second, 11% to third, 6% to fourth and 3%to fifth. 122 lbs. Non-winners of $40,000 allowed 2 lbs.; a race other than maiden or claiming, 4 lbs.; a race other than claiming, 6 lbs. Trophies will be presented to the winning owner, trainer and jockey. Closed Saturday, July 12, 2003 with 21 Nominations.

Value of Race: $150,000 Winner $90,000; second $30,000; third $16,500; fourth $9,000; fifth $4,500. Mutuel Pool $584,135.00 Exacta Pool $469,060.00 Trifecta Pool $314,709.00

Last Raced	Horse	M/Eqt.	A.	Wt	PP	St	¼	½	Str	Fin	Jockey	Odds $1
18Jun03 ^{3}Bel^{1}	Ashado	L	2	118	6	5	$4^{\frac{1}{2}}$	$2^{2\frac{1}{2}}$	$1^{1\frac{1}{2}}$	1^{3}	Prado E S	2.55
28Jun03 ^{8}WO^{1}	Maple Syrple	L	2	122	7	1	2^{hd}	$3^{\frac{1}{2}}$	2^{hd}	$2^{2\frac{1}{2}}$	Husbands P	6.50
25Jun03 ^{5}Bel^{1}	Hermione's Magic	L	2	118	4	3	$1^{\frac{1}{2}}$	1^{hd}	$3^{1\frac{1}{2}}$	3^{1}	Velazquez J R	2.65
29Jun03 ^{9}Bel^{1}	Feline Story	L	2	122	2	4	3^{hd}	$4^{2\frac{1}{2}}$	4^{6}	$4^{5\frac{1}{4}}$	Chavez J F	3.00
4Jly03 ^{10}CD^{1}	Be Gentle	L	2	122	1	7	$6^{2\frac{1}{2}}$	5^{hd}	$5^{\frac{1}{2}}$	$5^{\frac{3}{4}}$	Velasquez C	5.10
4Jly03 ^{10}CD^{4}	Secret Romance	L	2	118	3	6	7	7	$6^{\frac{1}{2}}$	$6^{3\frac{1}{4}}$	Albarado R J	40.75
2Jly03 ^{5}CD^{1}	Goodies Galore	L	2	118	5	2	5^{hd}	$6^{1\frac{1}{2}}$	7	7	Day P	20.40

OFF AT 5:19 Start Good. Won driving. Track sloppy.
TIME :22, :45^{2}, :58^{2}, 1:12 (:22.09, :45.51, :58.40, 1:12.12)

$2 Mutuel Prices:

7–ASHADO	7.10	4.70	3.10
8–MAPLE SYRPLE		6.60	3.40
5–HERMIONE'S MAGIC			3.20

$2 EXACTA 7–8 PAID $55.00 $2 TRIFECTA 7–8–5 PAID $205.00

Dk. b. or br. f, (Feb), by Saint Ballado–Goulash, by Mari's Book. Trainer Pletcher Todd A. Bred by Aaron U Jones & Marie D Jones (Ky).

ASHADO trailed briefly while in hand during the early stages, moved up from outside along the backstretch, made a sharp move while three wide to take the lead on the turn, extended her advantage after shaking off HERMIONE'S MAGIC in upper stretch then drew off under steady left hand urging. MAPLE SYRPLE settled just off the pace between horses, launched a rally three wide leaving the turn then finished willingly to clearly best the others. HERMIONE'S MAGIC dueled outside FELINE STORY along the backstretch, opened a clear advantage on the far turn, relinquished the lead to the winner approaching the stretch, remained a factor into midstretch then weakened from her early efforts. FELINE STORY battled for the early lead along the rail, dropped back a bit on the turn, swung out in upper stretch then lacked a strong closing bid. BE GENTLE broke inward a bit at the start, rushed up along the inside, steadied sharply in traffic at the half mile pole,angled five wide at the quarter pole then lacked a further response. SECRET ROMANCE steadied sharply in traffic along the backstretch and failed to threaten thereafter. GOODIES GALORE raced wide wide to the top of the stretch and tired.

Owners— 1, Starlight Stables Saylor Paul & Mar; 2, Team Valor Stable & Robert J Wilson; 3, Edgewood Farm; 4, Robsham Einar P; 5, Van Meter II Thomas F; 6, Kaster Nancy & Richard & Ricker; 7, Heiligbrodt Racing Stable

Trainers—1, Pletcher Todd A; 2, Casse Mark; 3, Pletcher Todd A; 4, Hough Stanley M; 5, Lukas D Wayne; 6, Romans Dale; 7, Asmussen Steven M

Scratched— Bikini Wiggle (5Jun03 ^{7}BEL^{3})

EIGHTH RACE
Saratoga
JULY 24, 2003

6 FURLONGS. (1.08) 90th Running of THE SANFORD. Grade II. Purse $150,000 (Up to $21,100 NYSBFOA). TWO YEAR OLDS. By subscription of $150 each, which should accompany the nomination; $750 to pass the entry box; $750 to start. The purse to be divided 60% to the winner, 20% to second, 11% to third, 6% to fourth and 3% to fifth. 122 lbs. Non–winners of $40,000 allowed 2 lbs.; a race other than maiden or claiming, 4 lbs.; a race other than claiming, 6 lbs. Trophies will be presented to the winning owner, trainer and jockey. Closed Saturday, July 12, 2003 with 23 Nominations.

Value of Race: $150,000 Winner $90,000; second $30,000; third $16,500; fourth $9,000; fifth $4,500. Mutuel Pool $474,959.00 Exacta Pool $364,268.00 Trifecta Pool $257,246.00

Last Raced	Horse	M/Eqt.	A.	Wt	PP	St	¼	½	Str	Fin	Jockey	Odds $1
6Jun03 ^{7}Bel^{1}	Chapel Royal	L	2	122	2	4	$4\frac{1}{2}$	3^{3}	1^{2}	$1^{5\frac{3}{4}}$	Velazquez J R	1.00
7Jun03 ^{1}CD^{1}	Blushing Indian	L	2	118	1	7	$6^{1\frac{1}{2}}$	$5^{2\frac{1}{2}}$	$4^{2\frac{1}{2}}$	$2^{3\frac{1}{2}}$	Albarado R J	19.20
22Jun03 ^{6}Hol^{1}	Flushing Meadows	L	2	118	7	3	2^{hd}	1^{hd}	2^{hd}	$3^{1\frac{1}{4}}$	Flores D R	7.90
5Jly03 ^{3}Bel^{1}	Boston Brahmin	Lb	2	118	6	2	$1\frac{1}{2}$	$2^{1\frac{1}{2}}$	3^{1}	$4\frac{1}{2}$	Velasquez C	a-4.70
28Jun03 ^{7}Bel^{2}	Adage	L	2	118	3	1	7	6^{hd}	6^{12}	$5\frac{3}{4}$	Prado E S	a-4.70
28Jun03 ^{7}Bel^{4}	Pretty Wild Again	L	2	118	4	5	5^{6}	4^{1}	$5^{2\frac{1}{2}}$	$6^{21\frac{1}{4}}$	Chavez J F	8.30
28Jun03 ^{7}Bel^{1}	Heckle	L	2	122	5	6	$3\frac{1}{2}$	7	7	7	Bailey J D	3.30

a–Coupled: Boston Brahmin and Adage.

OFF AT 4:48 Start Good. Won ridden out. Track sloppy.
TIME :21^{2}, :44^{4}, :57^{2}, 1:10^{3} (:21.59, :44.97, :57.55, 1:10.74)

$2 Mutuel Prices:

3–CHAPEL ROYAL	4.00	3.30	2.50
2–BLUSHING INDIAN		11.00	5.00
6–FLUSHING MEADOWS			4.60

$2 EXACTA 3–2 PAID $63.00 $2 TRIFECTA 3–2–6 PAID $326.00

Dk. b. or br. c, (Mar), by Montbrook–Cut Class Leanne, by Cutlass. Trainer Pletcher Todd A. Bred by Ocala Stud Farm (Fla).

CHAPEL ROYAL, well placed in the early stages, tucked in behind the leaders while saving ground for a half, swung out to launch his bid at the op of the stretch, accelerated to the front in upper stretch, opening a clear advantage despite jumping puddles nearing the furlong marker, extended his lead while jumping again in deep stretch then drew off while being ridden out. BLUSHING INDIAN was unhurried along the backstretch, rallied along the inside leaving the turn, drifted out leaving the eighth pole then finished with good energy in the middle of the track to clearly best the others. FLUSHING MEADOWS moved up from outside to contest the early pace, battled heads apart in the two path through the turn, relinquished the lead to the winner in upper stretch then weakened from his early efforts. BOSTON BRAHMIN set or forced the pace along the rail into upper stretch and steadily tired thereafter. ADAGE drifted to the outside while appearing to have trouble handling the track along the backstretch and was never close thereafter. PRETTY WILD AGAIN, reserved early, raced in traffic while between horses on the far turn then lacked the needed response when called upon. HECKLE stumbled at the start, rushed up from outside to contest the early pace then gave way on the turn.

Owners— 1, Smith Derrick & Tabor Michael; 2, Pacella William Rizza Joseph & Schw; 3, Al Maktoum Mohammed b; 4, Overbrook Farm; 5, Overbrook Farm & Hancock III A B; 6, Robsham Einar P; 7, Dogwood Stable

Trainers—1, Pletcher Todd A; 2, Romans Dale; 3, Harty Eoin; 4, Lukas D Wayne; 5, Lukas D Wayne; 6, Hough Stanley M; 7, Pletcher Todd A

EIGHTH RACE
Saratoga
JULY 25, 2003

1⅛ MILES. (Inner Turf)(1.46^{1}) 45th Running of THE BERNARD BARUCH HANDICAP. Grade II. Purse $150,000. (Up to $21,100 NYSBFOA). THREE YEAR OLDS AND UPWARD. By subscription of $150 each, which should accompany the nomination; $750 to pass the entry box, $750 to start. The purse to be divided 60% to the winner, 20% to second, 11% to third, 6% to fourth and 3% to fifth. . Trophies will be presented to the winning owner, trainer and jockey. The New York Racing Association reserves the right to transfer this race to the Main Track. In the event that this race is taken off the turf, it may be subject to downgrading upon review by the Graded Stakes Committee. Closed Saturday, July 12, 2003 with 47 Nominations.

Value of Race: $150,000 Winner $90,000; second $30,000; third $16,500; fourth $9,000; fifth $4,500. Mutuel Pool $589,929.00 Exacta Pool $465,743.00 Trifecta Pool $318,309.00

Last Raced	Horse	M/Eqt.	A.	Wt	PP	St	¼	½	¾	Str	Fin	Jockey	Odds $1
5Jly03 ^{8}Bel^{2}	Trademark-	L	7	114	6	5	$4\frac{1}{2}$	4^{2}	$4\frac{1}{2}$	$1\frac{1}{2}$	$1^{4\frac{3}{4}}$	Migliore R	6.60
3May03 ^{9}CD^{7}	Rouvres-FR	L	4	116	7	6	5^{3}	$5^{1\frac{1}{2}}$	$5\frac{1}{2}$	3^{hd}	2^{nk}	Nakatani C S	3.15
12Jly03 ^{10}Bel^{4}	Slew Valley	L	6	113	5	7	7	7	7	$5\frac{1}{2}$	$3^{1\frac{1}{2}}$	Chavez J F	12.00
5Jly03 ^{9}CD^{1}	Tap The Admiral	L	5	116	4	4	$6^{1\frac{1}{2}}$	6^{5}	6^{7}	4^{3}	4^{hd}	Samyn J L	4.50
15Jun03 ^{8}WO^{3}	Del Mar Show	L	6	118	1	2	1^{hd}	1^{hd}	$1\frac{1}{2}$	$2^{1\frac{1}{2}}$	5^{7}	Bailey J D	2.65
13Jly03 ^{8}Mth^{9}	Union Place	L	4	114	3	1	$2\frac{1}{2}$	$2\frac{1}{2}$	$2\frac{1}{2}$	7	$6\frac{1}{2}$	Coa E M	34.50
21Jun03 ^{7}LS^{1}	Patrol	L	4	118	2	3	$3^{2\frac{1}{2}}$	$3\frac{1}{2}$	3^{hd}	$6^{2\frac{1}{2}}$	7	Luzzi M J	3.25

OFF AT 4:47 Start Good. Won driving. Course yielding.
TIME :23^{1}, :47^{1}, 1:11^{2}, 1:36^{4}, 1:49 (:23.35, :47.39, 1:11.49, 1:36.85, 1:49.06)

$2 Mutuel Prices:

1A–TRADEMARK–	15.20	7.30	5.10
10–ROUVRES–FR		4.40	3.60
8–SLEW VALLEY			6.50

$2 EXACTA 1–10 PAID $69.50 $2 TRIFECTA 1–10–8 PAID $458.50

B. g, by Goldmark*SAf–Popular*SAf, by Elliodor*Fr. Trainer McLaughlin Kiaran P. Bred by D Cohen and Sons (Pty) Ltd (SAf).

TRADEMARK (SAF) settled in good position in the early stages, tucked in behind the leaders while saving ground along the backstretch, waited patiently for room while continuing to save ground through the turn, angled between horses for clear sailing at the top of the stretch, charged past DEL MAR SHOW to gain command a furlong out then drew away with authority under strong right hand encouragement. ROUVRES (FR), in hand early, was unhurried for six furlongs, launched a rally between horses on the turn, brushed with TAP THE ADMIRAL while in a bit tight in upper stretch, took up chase after the winner in midstretch but was no match for that one while holding for the place. SLEW VALLEY, outrun early, trailed while saving ground to the turn, angled out entering the stretch then rallied belatedly in the middle of the track. TAP THE ADMIRAL was unhurried for six furlongs, rapidly gained to reach contention on the turn, circled five wide to threaten entering the stretch then flattened out. DEL MAR SHOW rushed up along the rail to gain the early advantage, set a rapid pace while being pressured along the backstretch, continued on the front while saving ground into upper stretch, relinquished the lead to the winner in midstretch then weakened. UNION PLACE moved up from outside to contest the early pace, pressed the pace outside DEL MAR SHOW to the top of the stretch then checked in traffic while giving way in upper stretch. PATROL, taken in hand soon after the start, was rank while under a snug hold leaving the first turn, stalked the leaders while three wide along the backstretch, remained a factor to the turn and steadily tired thereafter.

Owners— 1, Al Maktoum Mohammed b; 2, Head Alec; 3, Rich Meadow Farm; 4, Pont Street Stable; 5, Allen E Paulson Living Trust M Paul; 6, Sorokolit William A Sr; 7, Claiborne Farm

Trainers—1, McLaughlin Kiaran P; 2, Clement Christophe; 3, Sciacca Gary; 4, Carroll Del W II; 5, Mott William I; 6, Schulhofer Randy; 7, Mott William I

Scratched— Millennium Dragon (4Jly03 ^{7}BEL^{1}), Saint Verre (5Jly03 ^{8}BEL^{3}), Rock Slide (5Jly03 ^{9}CD^{7}), El Gran Papa (28Jun03 ^{4}BEL^{2})

SEVENTH RACE
Arlington
JULY 26, 2003

$1\frac{3}{16}$ MILES. (Turf)(1.53^{1}) 47th Running of THE MODESTY HANDICAP. Grade III. Purse $150,000. FILLIES AND MARES, THREE-YEARS-OLD AND UPWARD. By subscription of $100 each, which should accompany the nomination. A Supplementary Nomination of $6,000 may be made on Saturday, July 19, 2003, which includes entry and starting fees. 2003 Beverly D. Nominees Free Nomination. Original nominees to pay $1,000 to pass the entry box and an additional $1,000 to start. Weights: Sunday, July 20, 2003. This event will be limited to fourteen (14) starters. Preference will be Highweights (on the scale). Total Earnings in 2003 will be used to determine the order of preference of horses assigned equal weight (on the scale). Failure to draw into this race at time of entry cancels all fees with the exception of the nominating fee(s). Two (2) horses having common ties through ownership cannot start to the exclusion of a single ownership interest. In the event this Stakes race is taken off the turf, it may be subject to downgrading upon review by the Graded Stakes Committee.

Value of Race: $150,000 Winner $90,000; second $30,000; third $16,500; fourth $9,000; fifth $4,500. Mutuel Pool $333,227.00 Exacta Pool $187,191.00 Trifecta Pool $152,059.00 Superfecta Pool $41,415.00

Last Raced	Horse	M/Eqt.	A.Wt	PP	St	¼	½	¾	Str	Fin	Jockey	Odds $1
4Jly03 ^{10}Bel^{4}	Owsley	L	5 120	2	4	5^{1}	5^{4}	$3\frac{1}{2}$	1^{hd}	1^{1}	Douglas R R	1.30
28Jun03 ^{10}LaD^{1}	Bien Nicole	L	5 119	4	2	$1\frac{1}{2}$	1^{hd}	1^{1}	$2^{1\frac{1}{2}}$	2^{4}	Pettinger D R	1.60
2Jly03 ^{8}AP^{1}	Beret	L	4 115	7	7	$6\frac{1}{2}$	6^{4}	6^{8}	4^{8}	3^{3}	Emigh C A	6.60
28Jun03 ^{6}CD^{1}	Flager-ARG	L	4 115	5	5	2^{1}	2^{3}	$2^{1\frac{1}{2}}$	3^{2}	4^{8}	Albarado R J	3.70
15Jun03 ^{8}Cby^{7}	Curious Conundrum	Lb	5 116	1	1	7	7	7	$6\frac{1}{2}$	5^{4}	Marquez C H Jr	40.70
24Jun03 ^{4}Mnr^{1}	Eyes The Duchess	L	4 115	6	6	4^{1}	4^{hd}	$5^{1\frac{1}{2}}$	7	$6^{5\frac{1}{2}}$	Spieth S	53.50
27Apr02 ^{8}CD^{7}	Moonlady-GER	L	6 116	3	3	$3\frac{1}{2}$	$3^{1\frac{1}{2}}$	4^{2}	5^{hd}	7	Sibille R	46.70

OFF AT 4:09 Start Good. Won driving. Course firm.
TIME :23^{3}, :47^{3}, 1:11^{3}, 1:36^{3}, 1:55 (:23.70, :47.71, 1:11.71, 1:36.63, 1:55.06)

$2 Mutuel Prices:			
2-OWSLEY	4.60	2.40	2.10
4-BIEN NICOLE		2.40	2.10
7-BERET			2.20

$2 EXACTA 2-4 PAID $8.80 $2 TRIFECTA 2-4-7 PAID $18.00 $2 SUPERFECTA 2-4-7-5 PAID $38.20

Dk. b. or br. m, by Harlan-Insipid, by Sham. Trainer Schulhofer Randy. Bred by Arthur B Hancock III (Ky).

OWSLEY established good position along the rail near the middle of the field, eased off the inside on the final turn, came three wide into the stretch, took the lead a furlong out and held sway under urging. BIEN NICOLE quickly made the lead and move to the inside, set all of the pace inside, could not resist the winner but continued gamely in a good effort. BERET was void of early foot, while off the rail, came out widest for the drive and rallied belatedly for minor awards. FLAGER (ARG) pressed the pace from just outside, remained prominent to upper stretch then tired in the drive. CURIOUS CONUNDRUM lacked speed and showed little. EYES THE DUCHESS raced just outside near the middle of the field and gave way. MOONLADY (GER) stalked the leaders from the inside but gave way on the final turn. (Race run in lane 5, rail at 0).

Owners— 1, Hancock III Arthur B; 2, Richter Kristine & John; 3, Vanier Nancy A & Williamson Lyda; 4, Stony Oak Farm LLC; 5, My Jo Lee Stable II; 6, Buckerine Stable R Blevins & R Bren; 7, Tanaka Gary A

Trainers—1, Schulhofer Randy; 2, Von Hemel Donnie K; 3, Vanier Harvey L; 4, Barnett Bobby C; 5, Brajczewski Eugene F; 6, King Gary M; 7, Burke Donald J II

$1 Pick Three (1-5-2) Paid $31.40; Pick Three Pool $20,737.

NINTH RACE
Arlington
JULY 26, 2003

1¼ MILES. (Turf)(1.58^{3}) 68th Running of THE ARLINGTON HANDICAP. Grade III. Purse $250,000. THREE-YEAR-OLDS AND UPWARD. By subscription of $200 each, which should accompany the nomination. A Supplementary Nomination of $10,000 may be made on Saturday, July 19, 2003, which includes entry and starting fees. 2003 Million Nominees Free Nomination. Original nominees to pay $2,000 to pass the entry box and an additional $2,000 to start. Weights: Sunday, July 20, 2003. This event will be limited to fourteen (14) starters. Preference will be Highweights (on the scale). Total Earnings in 2003 will be used to determine the order of preference of horses assigned equal weight (on the scale). Failure to draw into this race at time of entry cancels all fees with the exception of the nominating fee(s). Two (2) horses having common ties through ownership cannot start to the exclusion of a single ownership interest. In the event this Stakes race is taken off the turf, it may be subject to downgrading upon review by the Graded Stakes Committee.

Value of Race: $250,000 Winner $150,000; second $50,000; third $27,500; fourth $15,000; fifth $7,500. Mutuel Pool $478,247.00 Exacta Pool $309,249.00 Trifecta Pool $266,568.00 Superfecta Pool $87,443.00

Last Raced	Horse	M/Eqt.	A.Wt	PP	¼	½	¾	1	Str	Fin	Jockey	Odds $1
7Jun03 ^{10}Bel^{6}	Honor In War	L	4 120	10	$7^{2\frac{1}{2}}$	$7^{1\frac{1}{2}}$	$5\frac{1}{2}$	1^{hd}	1^{hd}	1^{nk}	Flores D R	1.60
29Jun03 ^{7}Del^{1}	Better Talk Now	L	4 115	1	9^{1}	$9^{2\frac{1}{2}}$	$8\frac{1}{2}$	8^{3}	3^{2}	$2\frac{3}{4}$	Douglas R R	9.90
21Jun03 ^{9}AP^{2}	Mystery Giver	L	5 118	3	8^{2}	8^{hd}	7^{hd}	6^{hd}	$4\frac{1}{2}$	3^{nk}	Albarado R J	6.00
2Jly03 ^{6}CD^{2}	Della Francesca	Lb	4 114	2	2^{1}	2^{5}	2^{4}	2^{hd}	$2^{2\frac{1}{2}}$	$4\frac{1}{2}$	Melancon L	16.20
21Jun03 ^{9}AP^{1}	Act Of War	Lbf	5 116	4	10	10	10	10	7^{1}	$5^{4\frac{1}{2}}$	Bourque C C	10.10
7Jun03 ^{10}Bel^{8}	Shaanmer-IR	L	4 117	5	$5\frac{1}{2}$	$5\frac{1}{2}$	6^{1}	7^{hd}	8^{1}	6^{2}	Blanc B	2.20
13Jun03 ^{5}Hol^{5}	Tijiyr-IRE	Lf	7 117	9	6^{hd}	6^{hd}	9^{4}	9^{5}	$9\frac{1}{2}$	7^{nk}	Sibille R	40.90
21Jun03 ^{7}LS^{4}	Candid Glen	L	6 118	7	$3\frac{1}{2}$	$3\frac{1}{2}$	$3\frac{1}{2}$	$5^{1\frac{1}{2}}$	$6\frac{1}{2}$	8^{4}	Perrodin E J	19.20
5Jly03 ^{8}AP^{4}	Extra Check	Lbf	4 116	6	1^{1}	$1\frac{1}{2}$	1^{hd}	3^{1}	10	9^{4}	Fires E	21.30
6Jly03 ^{9}CD^{1}	Gretchen's Star	Lf	8 116	8	$4^{1\frac{1}{2}}$	4^{1}	4^{1}	$4\frac{1}{2}$	$5\frac{1}{2}$	10	Razo E Jr	31.80

OFF AT 5:12 Start Good. Won driving. Course firm.
TIME :25, :49^{1}, 1:14, 1:38^{3}, 2:02^{3} (:25.04, :49.35, 1:14.05, 1:38.66, 2:02.71)

$2 Mutuel Prices:			
11-HONOR IN WAR	5.20	3.60	2.60
1-BETTER TALK NOW		8.40	5.20
4-MYSTERY GIVER			3.80

$2 EXACTA 11-1 PAID $43.40 $2 TRIFECTA 11-1-4 PAID $169.00 $2 SUPERFECTA 11-1-4-2 PAID $1,047.60

Ch. c, by Lord At War*Arg-Catumbella, by Diesis*GB. Trainer McGee Paul J. Bred by Mill Ridge Farm Ltd & W Lazy T Ltd (Ky).

HONOR IN WAR was allowed to settle three wide near the middle of the field, began moving up on the final turn, took a short lead turning for home then was fully extended to last. BETTER TALK NOW was void of early speed while along the rail, angled out four wide turning for home, gained steadily through the stretch and did not miss by much. MYSTERY GIVER also lacked early speed, went to the middle of the course for the drive and belatedly rallied for minor awards. DELLA FRANCESCA went up to press the pace from just outside, remained prominent to the furlong marker and weakened a bit. ACT OF WAR trailed to the stretch then gained in the drive. SHAANMER (IRE) was never a factor. TIJIYR (IRE) was squeezed at the start and was always outrun. CANDID GLEN raced close up just outside and tired. EXTRA CHECK was bumped at the start, set the pace from the inside while pressed and tired. GRETCHEN'S STAR raced close up off the rail and remained prominent to the stretch but tired. (Race run in lane 5, rail at 0).

Owners— 1, 3rd Turn Stables LLC William Wolfor; 2, Bushwood Racing Partners; 3, Team Block; 4, Ol Memorial Stable Rick Pitino & De; 5, RNR Breeders; 6, de Rothschild Edouard; 7, Tanaka Gary A; 8, Warren Glen C; 9, Three King Stable; 10, Isbell Ron Jr

Trainers—1, McGee Paul J; 2, Motion H Graham; 3, Block Chris M; 4, O'Callaghan Niall M; 5, Cilio Gene A; 6, Clement Christophe; 7, Burke Donald J II; 8, Leggio Andrew Jr; 9, Stidham Michael; 10, Isbell Ron Jr

Scratched— Drewman (22Jun03 ^{8}CD^{1})

$1 Pick Three (2-1/4-3/11) Paid $30.70; Pick Three Pool $17,829.

SIXTH RACE
Del Mar
JULY 26, 2003

6 FURLONGS. (1.07^{3}) 58th Running of THE BING CROSBY BREEDERS' CUP HANDICAP. Grade II. Purse $200,000 (includes $50,000 BC – Breeders' Cup). THREE-YEAR-OLDS AND UPWARD. By subscription of $100 each, which shall accompany the nomination, or by supplementary nomination of $1,500 each by Sunday, July 20, $1,000 additional to start, $150,000 and an additional $50,000 from Breeders' Cup Fund for Cup nominees only. The host association's monies to be divided 60% to the winner; 20% to second; 12% to third; 6% to fourth and 2% to fifth. Breeders' Cup Fund monies also correspondingly divided, provided a Breeders' Cup nominee has finished in an awarded position. Any unearned Breeders' Cup Fund monies will revert to the Fund. Weights Monday, July 21. The starters will be determined at entry time with preference given to Breeders' Cup nominees only of equal racing quality or weight assignment (respective of sex and weight for age). Starters to be named through the entry box Thursday, July 24, by the closing time of entries. A trophy will be presented to the owner of the winner. Closed Thursday, July 17 with 18 nominations.

Value of Race: $191,000 Winner $120,000; second $40,000; third $18,000; fourth $9,000; fifth $4,000. Mutuel Pool $692,110.00 Exacta Pool $361,870.00 Quinella Pool $36,647.00 Trifecta Pool $327,651.00 Superfecta Pool $111,779.00

Last Raced	Horse	M/Eqt.	A.	Wt	PP	St	¼	½	Str	Fin	Jockey	Odds $1
21Jun03 ^{9}CD^{2}	Beau's Town	LB	5	119	9	2	2^{1}	1^{hd}	$1^{1\frac{1}{2}}$	$1^{1\frac{1}{2}}$	Valenzuela P A	5.10
29Mar03 NAS^{3}	Captain Squire	LB	4	117	7	3	4^{1}	3^{1}	$2^{1\frac{1}{2}}$	2^{nk}	Stevens G L	2.10
5Jly03 ^{8}Hol^{3}	Bluesthestandard	LB	6	117	3	4	$5^{\frac{1}{2}}$	$5^{\frac{1}{2}}$	3^{hd}	3^{2}	Pedroza M A	9.90
5Jly03 ^{8}Hol^{6}	Avanzado-ARG	LBbf	6	117	4	5	3^{hd}	$4^{\frac{1}{2}}$	4^{3}	4^{1}	Baze T C	6.00
29Mar03 ^{8}SA^{3}	Kona Gold	LB	9	119	5	7	9	7^{hd}	5^{hd}	$5^{2\frac{1}{2}}$	Solis A	3.50
10May03 ^{6}Hol^{4}	Disturbingthepeace	LB	5	118	6	6	$7^{2\frac{1}{2}}$	$6^{2\frac{1}{2}}$	$6^{\frac{1}{2}}$	$6^{10\frac{1}{2}}$	Espinoza V	7.10
26May03 ^{8}Hol^{4}	Medecis-GB	LB	4	115	1	9	6^{hd}	$8^{3\frac{1}{2}}$	$8^{2\frac{1}{2}}$	7^{nk}	Smith M E	15.00
12Jly03 ^{8}Hol^{5}	No Armistice	LBb	6	115	2	8	8^{hd}	9	9	$8^{7\frac{1}{2}}$	Valdivia J Jr	27.50
28Jun03 ^{11}Pln^{9}	Giovannetti	LB	4	117	8	1	$1^{\frac{1}{2}}$	2^{1}	$7^{3\frac{1}{2}}$	9	Desormeaux K J	34.70

OFF AT 4:36 Start Good. Won driving. Track fast.
TIME :21^{4}, :44, :55^{3}, 1:07^{4} (:21.87, :44.10, :55.70, 1:07.96)

$2 Mutuel Prices:

9–BEAU'S TOWN	12.20	5.60	3.80
7–CAPTAIN SQUIRE		3.80	3.00
3–BLUESTHESTANDARD			4.00

$1 EXACTA 9–7 PAID $22.20 $2 QUINELLA 7–9 PAID $19.80 $1 TRIFECTA 9–7–3 PAID $133.20 $1 SUPERFECTA 9–7–3–4 PAID $607.30

Ch. g, by Beau Genius–Frio Town, by Kerosene. Trainer Norman Cole. Bred by Bryant H Prentice III (Ark).

BEAU'S TOWN angled in and dueled outside a rival, kicked clear into the stretch, drifted in under right handed urging and held on gamely. CAPTAIN SQUIRE wide early, stalked outside a rival, came three deep into the stretch, also drifted in, could not catch the winner but saved the place. BLUESTHESTANDARD bobbled slightly at the start, chased between horses then off the rail on the turn, also came three deep into the stretch, drifted in some and just missed second. AVANZADO (ARG) angled in and stalked the dueling leaders inside, came out into the stretch, split rivals in midstretch and lacked the needed late kick. KONA GOLD unhurried outside a rival on the backstretch, inched forward while ridden along on the turn, came out in the stretch and also could not offer the necessary late response. DISTURBINGTHEPEACE between horses early, chased outside on the backstretch and three deep on the turn, came four wide into the stretch and did not rally. MEDECIS (GB) off a bit slowly, saved ground chasing the pace and gave way. NO ARMISTICE unhurried a bit off the rail on the backstretch and turn, failed to menace. GIOVANNETTI angled in and dueled inside the winner, dropped back into the stretch and had nothing left.

Owners— 1, Beck & Hulkewicz; 2, Bone Robert D & Diener Jeffrey S; 3, Sengara Jeffrey; 4, Cees Stable LLC; 5, Headley Aase Molasky Irwin & Molask; 6, Milch David S & Rita & Herrick Raci; 7, Wertheimer Farm; 8, Hughes B W; 9, Schiappa Bernard C

Trainers—1, Norman Cole; 2, Mullins Jeff; 3, West Ted H; 4, O'Neill Doug; 5, Headley Bruce; 6, Vienna Darrell; 7, Mandella Richard; 8, Ellis Ronald W; 9, Monteleone Frank J

$2 Daily Double (2–9) Paid $1,015.60; Daily Double Pool $47,720.
$1 Pick Three (5–2–9) Paid $2,903.00; Pick Three Pool $130,931.

NINTH RACE
Monmouth
JULY 26, 2003

1 MILE. (1.33^{4}) 56th Running of THE SALVATOR MILE HANDICAP. Grade III. Purse $100,000 A HANDICAP FOR THREE YEAR OLDS AND UPWARD. By subscription of $100 each, which should accompany the nomination. $1,500 to enter. The winner to receive $60,000; $20,000 to second; $11,000 to third; $6,000 to fourth; $3,000 to fifth. Weights 5:00P.M. Saturday, July 19 Starters to be named through the entry box by the usual time of closing. Highweights preferred. The owner of the winner to receive a trophy. NOMINATIONS CLOSED Saturday, July 12, 2003 with TWENTY EIGHT (28).

Value of Race: $100,000 Winner $60,000; second $20,000; third $11,000; fourth $6,000; fifth $3,000. Mutuel Pool $137,127.00 Exacta Pool $96,273.00 Trifecta Pool $59,991.00

Last Raced	Horse	M/Eqt.	A.	Wt	PP	St	¼	½	¾	Str	Fin	Jockey	Odds $1
26Jun03 ^{8}Mth^{4}	Vinemeister	L	4	114	3	3	$2^{1\frac{1}{2}}$	2^{1}	1^{hd}	1^{2}	$1^{\frac{3}{4}}$	Velez J A Jr	14.10
4Jly03 ^{8}Mth^{1}	Jersey Giant	Lb	4	117	1	2	3^{hd}	3^{hd}	$3^{\frac{1}{2}}$	2^{hd}	2^{2}	Pimentel J	2.80
21Jun03 ^{13}Suf^{4}	Highway Prospector	Lb	6	113	6	4	$5^{2\frac{1}{2}}$	$5^{\frac{1}{2}}$	5^{hd}	$4^{2\frac{1}{2}}$	$3^{\frac{1}{2}}$	Lopez C C	4.40
5Jly03 ^{8}Suf^{1}	Dhaffir-CH	Lf	7	113	4	1	1^{2}	1^{1}	2^{1}	$3^{2\frac{1}{2}}$	$4^{4\frac{1}{4}}$	Piermarini T	21.10
12Jly03 ^{6}PrM^{2}	Bowman's Band	L	5	116	2	5	$4^{\frac{1}{2}}$	$4^{1\frac{1}{2}}$	4^{1}	$5^{2\frac{1}{2}}$	5^{6}	Bravo J	1.00
4Jly03 ^{8}Mth^{2}	Sea of Tranquility	L	7	115	5	6	6	6	6	6	6	Ferrer J C	5.30

OFF AT 4:43 Start Good. Won driving. Track fast.
TIME :23^{4}, :47^{1}, 1:11^{1}, 1:35^{4} (:23.98, :47.29, 1:11.24, 1:35.89)

$2 Mutuel Prices:

4–VINEMEISTER	30.20	14.60	6.40
2–JERSEY GIANT		5.40	3.40
7–HIGHWAY PROSPECTOR			4.40

$2 EXACTA 4–2 PAID $90.40 $2 TRIFECTA 4–2–7 PAID $882.20

Dk. b. or br. c, by Williamstown–Fairway Jet, by Pleasant Colony. Trainer Seewald Alan. Bred by Nestor Camino (Ky).

VINEMEISTER stalked the early issue, moved to the front approaching the quarter pole, drew clear in upper stretch then held off JERSEY GIANT through the late stages. JERSEY GIANT close up early while saving ground, eased out nearing the top of the lane and finished gamely. HIGHWAY PROSPECTOR never far back, saved ground turning for home, eased out and was gaining some late. DHAFFIR (CHI) posted the early fractions, saved ground and weakened in the drive. BOWMAN'S BAND stumbled leaving the gate then well placed outside a rival, came up empty when asked on the final turn. SEA OF TRANQUILITY trailed while not far back, raced outside turning for home and lacked a response.

Owners— 1, Travin Stables; 2, Kligman Joel A; 3, Gill Michael J; 4, Henry Barry & David Barry; 5, Schwartz Martin S; 6, Triple M Farm

Trainers—1, Seewald Alan; 2, Ryerson James T; 3, Shuman Mark; 4, Angevine Pamela J; 5, Matz Michael R; 6, Paulus Richard E

Scratched— Pinky Pizwaanski (5Jly03 ^{8}BEL^{5})

$2 Pick Three (1–7–4) Paid $408.60; Pick Three Pool $13,079.

EIGHTH RACE
Del Mar
JULY 26, 2003

1⅛ MILES. (Turf)(1.46^{3}) 46th Running of THE JOHN C. MABEE HANDICAP. Grade I. Purse $400,000. FILLIES AND MARES,THREE-YEAR-OLDS AND UPWARD. By subscription of $400 each, which shall accompany the nomination, or by supplementary nomination of $4,000 each by Sunday, July 20, $4,000 additional to start, with $400,000 Guaranteed, of which $240,000 to first, $80,000 to second, $48,000 to third, $24,000 to fourth and $8,000 to fifth. Weight: Monday, July 21. Highweights preferred. A trophy will be presented to the owner of the winner. Closed Thursday, July 17 with 11 nominations. (Rail at 0 feet.)

Value of Race: $400,001 Winner $240,000; second $50,667 each; fifth $8,000. Mutuel Pool $627,129.00 Exacta Pool $268,986.00 Quinella Pool $33,003.00 Trifecta Pool $216,781.00

Last Raced	Horse	M/Eqt.	A.Wt	PP	St	¼	½	¾	Str	Fin	Jockey	Odds $1
28Jun03 8Hol3	Megahertz-GB	LB	4 116	3	4	5	5	5	5	$1^{\frac{1}{2}}$	Solis A	8.20
26May03 6Hol1	DH Tates Creek	LB	5 123	1	2	$2^{\frac{1}{2}}$	2^{1}	$2^{\frac{1}{2}}$	$1^{1\frac{1}{2}}$	2	Valenzuela P A	1.10
28Jun03 8Hol2	DH Dublino	LB	4 121	2	5	$4^{\frac{1}{2}}$	$4^{\frac{1}{2}}$	$4^{\frac{1}{2}}$	$4^{\frac{1}{2}}$	2	Desormeaux K J	3.40
1Dec02 4Hol2	DH Golden Apples-IR	LB	5 122	5	3	3^{1}	3^{1}	3^{1}	$3^{\frac{1}{2}}$	2^{2}	Stevens G L	1.90
12Jun03 7Hol1	Voz de Colegiala-CH	LB	4 114	4	1	1^{1}	$1^{\frac{1}{2}}$	1^{hd}	2^{hd}	5	Krone J A	17.10

DH—Dead Heat.

OFF AT 5:36 Start Good. Won driving. Course firm.
TIME :25, :50^{1}, 1:14^{4}, 1:37^{3}, 1:49 (:25.15, :50.20, 1:14.92, 1:37.76, 1:49.09)

$2 Mutuel Prices:

3–MEGAHERTZ-GB	18.40	2.10	2.10
1–DH TATES CREEK		2.10	2.10
2–DH DUBLINO		2.10	2.10
5–DH GOLDEN APPLES-IR		2.10	2.10

$1 EXACTA 3–1 PAID $7.60 $1 EXACTA 3–2 PAID $10.10 $1 EXACTA 3–5 PAID $11.70 $2 QUINELLA 1–3 PAID $5.20 $2 QUINELLA 2–3 PAID $8.40 $2 QUINELLA 3–5 PAID $8.60 $1 TRIFECTA 3–1–2 PAID $7.40 $1 TRIFECTA 3–1–5 PAID $11.80 $1 TRIFECTA 3–2–1 PAID $9.20 $1 TRIFECTA 3–2–5 PAID $19.70 $1 TRIFECTA 3–5–1 PAID $13.60 $1 TRIFECTA 3–5–2 PAID $20.70

Ch. f, by Pivotal*GB–Heavenly Ray, by Rahy. Trainer Frankel Robert. Bred by Cheveley Park Stud Ltd (GB).

MEGAHERTZ (GB) stalked the pace outside a rival, swung three deep into the stretch, rallied gamely four wide under urging through the drive to get up late. TATES CREEK stalked a bit off the rail, bid between horses on the backstretch, took a short lead in the second turn, inched away, drifted in under urging in midstretch and held on well but was caught late and shared the place. DUBLINO saved ground tracking the pace, came off the rail on the second turn, rallied between horses through the final furlong and also went willingly to the wire. GOLDEN APPLES (IRE) stalked the early leader outside, bid three deep on the backstretch and second turn and also continued gamely between rivals to the end. VOZ DE COLEGIALA (CHI) took the early lead and set the pace inside, dueled along the rail, fought back on the second turn, was in a bit tight inside rail in midstretch and weakened.

Owners— 1, Bello Michael; 2, Juddmonte Farms Inc; 3, Geringer Robert Klein Michael & Nai; 4, Tanaka Gary A; 5, Hunt Nelson B
Trainers—1, Frankel Robert; 2, Frankel Robert; 3, De Seroux Laura; 4, Cecil B D A; 5, McAnally Ronald
Scratched— Magic Mission (5Jly03 7HOL1)

$2 Daily Double (8–3) Paid $126.20; Daily Double Pool $44,273.
$1 Pick Three (9–8–3) Paid $614.70; Pick Three Pool $143,260.

NINTH RACE
Saratoga
JULY 26, 2003

7 FURLONGS. (1.20^{3}) 78th Running of THE TEST. Grade I. Purse $250,000. (Up to $28,500 NYSBFOA). FILLIES, THREE YEARS OLD. By subscription of $250 each, which should accompany the nomination; $1,250 to pass the entry box, $1,250 to start. 122 lbs. Non-winners of $50,000 twice in 2003 allowed 2 lbs.; $50,000 in 2003 or $40,000 twice since September 1, 4 lbs.; $50,000; or three races other than maiden or claiming, 6 lbs. (Restricted races not considered in allowances.) Closed Saturday, July 12, 2003 with 34 nominations.

Value of Race: $250,000 Winner $150,000; second $50,000; third $27,500; fourth $15,000; fifth $7,500. Mutuel Pool $950,771.00 Exacta Pool $642,678.00 Trifecta Pool $481,897.00

Last Raced	Horse	M/Eqt.	A.Wt	PP	St	¼	½	Str	Fin	Jockey	Odds $1
6Jun03 10Bel2	Lady Tak	L	3 122	2	3	$2^{\frac{1}{2}}$	$2^{\frac{1}{2}}$	$1^{5\frac{1}{2}}$	$1^{4\frac{1}{2}}$	Bailey J D	2.00
6Jun03 10Bel1	Bird Town	L	3 122	7	1	$3^{\frac{1}{2}}$	$3^{2\frac{1}{2}}$	2^{2}	$2^{1\frac{1}{2}}$	Prado E S	1.75
4Jly03 9Bel1	House Party		3 122	6	4	$6^{1\frac{1}{2}}$	5^{hd}	3^{hd}	$3^{1\frac{3}{4}}$	Santos J A	3.60
28Jun03 9Bel3	Final Round	L	3 120	4	6	5^{hd}	$6^{3\frac{1}{2}}$	$5^{4\frac{1}{2}}$	4^{hd}	Day P	7.40
4Jly03 4CD1	Molto Vita	L	3 116	3	5	$1^{\frac{1}{2}}$	1^{hd}	$4^{\frac{1}{2}}$	$5^{1\frac{3}{4}}$	Coa E M	37.25
25Jun03 9CD1	Halory Leigh	L	3 116	1	7	7	7	$6^{\frac{1}{2}}$	6^{1}	Sellers S J	21.10
4Jly03 9Bel2	Chimichurri	Lf	3 118	5	2	$4^{\frac{1}{2}}$	4^{hd}	7	7	Velazquez J R	15.10

OFF AT 5:47 Start Good. Won driving. Track fast.
TIME :22^{3}, :45^{1}, 1:08^{1}, 1:20^{4} (:22.66, :45.27, 1:08.39, 1:20.83)

$2 Mutuel Prices:

2–LADY TAK	6.00	2.90	2.30
8–BIRD TOWN		3.00	2.30
6–HOUSE PARTY			2.70

$2 EXACTA 2–8 PAID $14.40 $2 TRIFECTA 2–8–6 PAID $32.20

Ch. f, (Apr), by Mutakddim–Star of My Eye, by Lucky North. Trainer Asmussen Steven M. Bred by John Franks (Fla).

LADY TAK moved up along the inside to contest the early pace while in hand, surged to the front along the rail leaving the five-sixteenths pole, shook off BIRD TOWN and MOLTO VITA entering the stretch, opened a commanding lead in midstretch then held sway under a vigorous hand ride. BIRD TOWN eased back just outside the early leaders, stalked the pace three wide for a half, took up chase after the winner leaving the turn but was no match for that one while holding well for the place. HOUSE PARTY was unhurried though the opening quarter, raced in traffic between horses going into the far turn, angled four wide to get clear at the top of the stretch, lodged a mild rally to reach contention in upper stretch but couldn't sustain her bid. FINAL ROUND was reserved for a half, lodged a mild rally along the rail in upper stretch then lacked a strong closing response. MOLTO VITA stumbled at the start, rushed up to gain the early advantage, set the pace under pressure to the turn then gave way. HALORY LEIGH never reached contention after breaking a bit slowly. CHIMICHURRI raced within striking distance while five wide the entire way and faded in the stretch.

Owners— 1, Heiligbrodt Racing Stable; 2, Marylou Whitney Stable; 3, Shields Joseph V Jr; 4, Humphrey G W Jr; 5, Gunther John D; 6, Gerald Crawford; 7, Peachtree Stable
Trainers—1, Asmussen Steven M; 2, Zito Nicholas P; 3, Jerkens H Allen; 4, Arnold George R II; 5, Stewart Dallas; 6, Romans Dale; 7, Pletcher Todd A
Scratched— Country Romance (29Jun03 9CD1)

EIGHTH RACE

Saratoga

JULY 26, 2003

1⅛ MILES. (Turf)(1.45²) 65th Running of THE DIANA HANDICAP. Grade I. Purse $500,000. (Up to $36,000 NYSBFOA). FILLIES AND MARES THREE YEARS OLD AND UPWARD. By subscription of $500 each, which should accompany the nomination; $2,500 to pass the entry box, $2,500 to start. The New York Racing Association reserves the right to transfer this race to the Main Track. In the event that this race is taken off the turf, it may be subject to downgrading upon review by the Graded Stakes Committee. Closed Saturday, July 12, 2003 with 26 Nominations.

Value of Race: $500,000 Winner $300,000; second $100,000; third $55,000; fourth $30,000; fifth $15,000. Mutuel Pool $1,128,855.0 Exacta Pool $773,212.00 Trifecta Pool $532,209.00

Last Raced	Horse	M/Eqt. A.Wt	PP	St	¼	½	¾	Str	Fin	Jockey	Odds $1
28Jun03 8Hol¹	Voodoo Dancer	L 5 120	3	1	6½	7²½	7²½	1hd	1nk	Nakatani C S	2.60
3May03 7CD¹	Heat Haze-GB	L 4 118	1	2	7³½	6½	5hd	2hd	2¹¾	Bailey J D	a-1.45
4Jly03 10Bel²	Pertuisane-GB	Lb 4 115	6	7	4½	4hd	4hd	6¹½	3¾	Castellano J J	a-1.45
4Jly03 10Bel³	Riskaverse	L 4 118	8	5	3hd	3½	3½	4hd	4hd	Velazquez J R	9.40
7Jun03 8Bel³	Wonder Again	L 4 118	5	3	2½	2hd	2½	3½	5½	Prado E S	3.85
28Jun03 9CD³	Quick Tip	L 5 116	7	6	5½	5½	6¹	8	6no	Day P	25.00
4Jly03 10Bel¹	Snow Dance	L 5 117	2	8	8	8	8	7hd	7¹¾	Migliore R	9.40
5Jly03 9Pha¹	Delta Princess	L 4 116	4	4	1¹	1½	1½	5¹	8	Luzzi M J	22.10

a–Coupled: Heat Haze–GB and Pertuisane–GB.

OFF AT 5:15 Start Good For All But SNOW DANCE Won driving. Course firm.

TIME :24, :49, 1:13, 1:36³, 1:47⁴ (:24.15, :49.10, 1:13.15, 1:36.64, 1:47.98)

$2 Mutuel Prices:	2B –VOODOO DANCER	7.20	3.00	2.70
	1–HEAT HAZE–GB (a–entry)		2.70	2.80
	1A–PERTUISANE–GB (a–entry)		2.70	2.80

$2 EXACTA 2–1 PAID $17.60 $2 TRIFECTA 2–1–7 PAID $2 6–1–2 PAID $19.00

B. m, by Kingmambo–Zuri, by Danzig. Trainer Clement Christophe. Bred by Lazy E Ranch Inc (Ky).

VOODOO DANCER raced well back for six furlongs, launched a rally from outside on the turn, circled six wide entering the stretch, made a strong move to gain a slim advantage in midstretch then prevailed in a long drive. HEAT HAZE (GB) was unhurried for a half, gradually worked her way forward from outside on the turn, made a run four wide to reach contention in upper stretch, drew on even terms with the leaders a furlong out, battled gamely inside the winner into deep stretch and yielded grudgingly. PERTUISANE (GB) was rated just off the pace in the early stages, raced in good position while saving ground along the backstretch, edged closer on the turn, steadied in traffic while behind a wall of horses in upper stretch then finished well after getting clear to gain a share. RISKAVERSE moved up from outside to contest the early pace, stalked the leaders while three wide along the backstretch, raced in close contention between horses to the top of the stretch then finished evenly. WONDER AGAIN forced the pace between horses for seven furlongs, battled heads apart for the lead in upper stretch then weakened in the final eighth. QUICK TIP raced in hand between horses to the turn and lacked the needed response when called upon. SNOW DANCE broke in the air at the start and was grabbed by the assistant start, came out well behind the field, rushed up to the turn, circled six wide into the stretch and lacked a strong closing bid. DELTA PRINCESS set the pace under pressure along the inside to the top of the stretch and gave way.

Owners— 1, Green Hills Farm; 2, Juddmonte Farms Inc; 3, Frankel Robert Lazzinaro Louis & Pa; 4, Fox Ridge Farm Inc; 5, Phillips Joan G & John W; 6, Farish William S; 7, Oxley John C; 8, Khaled Saud b

Trainers—1, Clement Christophe; 2, Frankel Robert; 3, Frankel Robert; 4, Kelly Patrick J; 5, Toner James J; 6, Howard Neil J; 7, Ward John T Jr; 8, Mott William I

Scratched— Mariensky (4Jly03 10BEL6)

$2 Pick Three (6–5–2) Paid $29.60; Pick Three Pool $155,231.

NINTH RACE

Saratoga

JULY 27, 2003

1⅛ MILES. (1.47) 50th Running of THE GO FOR WAND HANDICAP. Grade I. Purse $250,000. (Up to $28,500 NYSBFOA). FILLIES AND MARES THREE YEARS OLD AND UPWARD. By subscription of $250 each, which should accompany the nomination; $1,250 to pass the entry box, $1,250 to start. The purse to be divided 60% to the winner, 20% to second, 11% to third, 6% to fourth and 3% to fifth. Trophies will be presented to the winning owner, trainer and jockey. Closed Saturday, July 12, 2003 with 24 Nominations.

Value of Race: $250,000 Winner $150,000; second $50,000; third $27,500; fourth $15,000; fifth $7,500. Mutuel Pool $1,495,391.0 Exacta Pool $491,250.00 Trifecta Pool $357,774.00

Last Raced	Horse	M/Eqt. A.Wt	PP	St	¼	½	¾	Str	Fin	Jockey	Odds $1
21Jun03 9Bel¹	Sightseek	L 4 121	5	4	3²½	2½	2¹½	1⁸	1¹¹½	Bailey J D	0.15
28Jun03 11Mth²	She's Got The Beat	Lf 4 112	6	6	4½	4³½	3½	2½	2⁵	Samyn J L	20.90
14Jun03 9CD³	Nonsuch Bay	L 4 113	4	3	6	5hd	5⁷	3hd	3⁴	Coa E M	10.40
9Jly03 7Mth²	Miss Linda-ARG	L 6 116	3	2	1¹½	1¹½	1½	4³	4½	Migliore R	9.50
9Apr03 8Kee³	Forest Secrets	L 5 115	1	1	2hd	3²	4²	5⁸	5¹⁴	Prado E S	22.10
28Jun03 5AP²	Happily Unbridled	Lbf 5 112	2	5	5¹	6	6	6	6	Day P	27.75

OFF AT 5:23 Start Good. Won ridden out. Track fast.

TIME :25, :49¹, 1:13², 1:38, 1:50⁴ (:25.06, :49.25, 1:13.55, 1:38.07, 1:50.92)

$2 Mutuel Prices:	5–SIGHTSEEK	2.30	2.10	2.10
	7–SHE'S GOT THE BEAT		2.90	2.10
	4–NONSUCH BAY			2.10

$2 EXACTA 5–7 PAID $15.20 $2 TRIFECTA 5–7–4 PAID $29.40

Ch. f, by Distant View–Viviana, by Nureyev. Trainer Frankel Robert. Bred by Juddmonte Farms, Inc. (Ky).

SIGHTSEEK moved up from outside in the early stages, stalked a slow pace while three wide along the backstretch, launched a rally leaving the turn, took charge in upper stretch then drew off to a lengthy score while being ridden out. SHE'S GOT THE BEAT was rated in the middle of the pack for a half, closed the gap while three wide to the turn, lodged a mild bid at the top of the stretch but was no match for the winner. NONSUCH BAY trailed for nearly a half, rapidly closed the gap while four wide to reach contention approaching the quarter pole but couldn't sustain her bid. MISS LINDA (ARG) took the lead soon after the start, set a moderate pace for six furlongs then gave way. FOREST SECRETS raced in close contention along the inside, angled wide entering the stretch and lacked strong closing response. HAPPILY UNBRIDLED trailed for most of the way.

Owners— 1, Juddmonte Farms Inc; 2, Walsh Elizabeth; 3, Thorn Stable; 4, Ackerley Brothers Farm; 5, Oxley Debby M; 6, Winstar Farm

Trainers—1, Frankel Robert; 2, Johnson Philip G; 3, Alexander Frank A; 4, Kimmel John C; 5, Ward John T Jr; 6, Walden W Elliott

Scratched— Call An Audible (28Jun03 11MTH3)

EIGHTH RACE

Del Mar

JULY 27, 2003

1⅛ MILES. (Turf)(1.45⁴) 30th Running of THE EDDIE READ HANDICAP. Grade I. Purse $400,000. THREE–YEAR–OLDS AND UPWARD. By subscription of $400 each, which shall accompany the nomination, or by supplementary nomination of $4,000 by Sunday, July 20, $1,000 to pass the entry box and $3,000 additional to start, with $400,000 Guaranteed, of which $240,000 to first, $80,000 to second, $48,000 to third, $24,000 to fourth and $8,000 to fifth. Weights Monday, July 21. Highweights preferred. Starters to be named through the entry box Friday, July 25, by the closing time of entries. A trophy will be presented to the owner of the winner. Closed Thursday, July 17 with 12 nominations. Rail at 0 feet.

Value of Race: $400,000 Winner $240,000; second $80,000; third $48,000; fourth $24,000; fifth $8,000. Mutuel Pool $533,947.00 Exacta Pool $286,403.00 Quinella Pool $31,364.00 Trifecta Pool $261,281.00

Last Raced	Horse	M/Eqt. A.Wt	PP	St	¼	½	¾	Str	Fin	Jockey	Odds $1
4Jly03 7Hol²	Special Ring	LBb 6 117	4	1	1¹	1¹	1¹½	1²	1⁵	Flores D R	3.10
13Jun03 5Hol²	Decarchy	LB 6 117	5	3	4¹	4¹½	4ʰᵈ	3ʰᵈ	2ⁿᵏ	Desormeaux K J	4.20
4Jly03 7Hol³	Irish Warrior	LB 5 114	6	5	5ʰᵈ	5ʰᵈ	5½	4ʰᵈ	3ʰᵈ	Krone J A	8.30
23Aug02 7Dmr³	Fateful Dream	LBb 6 115	1	6	6	6	6	5ʰᵈ	4ⁿᵒ	Valenzuela P A	10.00
14Jun03 3Hol²	Mister Acpen–CH	LB 5 115	2	4	2ʰᵈ	2½	3½	6	5ⁿᵒ	Espinoza V	6.50
26May03 8Hol¹	Redattore–BRZ	LB 8 121	3	2	3¹½	3¹½	2ʰᵈ	2¹	6	Solis A	1.30

OFF AT 5:36 Start Good. Won driving. Course firm.

TIME :23⁴, :47², 1:11, 1:34², 1:45⁴ (:23.90, :47.46, 1:11.03, 1:34.43, 1:45.87)

(New Course Record)

$2 Mutuel Prices:

4–SPECIAL RING	8.20	4.40	4.00
5–DECARCHY		4.80	4.40
6–IRISH WARRIOR			3.80

$1 EXACTA 4–5 PAID $23.90 $2 QUINELLA 4–5 PAID $23.60 $1 TRIFECTA 4–5–6 PAID $107.80

B. g, by Nureyev–Ring Beaune, by Bering*GB. Trainer Canani Julio C. Bred by Wertheimer & Frere (Ky).

SPECIAL RING quickly stepped to the front, carved out fractions while under a snug hold early, came out slightly around the initial turn, resisted when challenged on the second bend, then responded very willingly when roused passing eighth marker and accelerated away under brisk handling and only shown the stick. DECARCHY content to chase pacesetter from off the rail, between foes leaving the backstretch, loomed three deep nearing the stretch and gamely gained the place while four deep at the wire. IRISH WARRIOR lagged back and outside FATEFUL DREAM in early stages, caught three deep nearing the backstretch, four wide around the final bend and finished willingly while five deep at the wire. FATEFUL DREAM settled inside early, came out slightly entering the backstretch, was between rivals on the second turn and through the drive and just missed the show while three deep hitting the wire. MISTER ACPEN (CHI) prominent early along the fence and inside REDATTORE, dropped back a bit on the second turn, continued inside and finished willingly. REDATTORE (BRZ) stalked the pacesetter from outside foe early, inched closer to the winner and loomed late on the final bend, could not go with that rival through the drive and lost placing late.

Owners— 1, Prestonwood Farm LLC; 2, Juddmonte Farms Inc; 3, Coleman Dasaro & Thompson et al; 4, Gann Edmund A; 5, Noctis Stable Papiano Neil & Taub S; 6, Taunay Luis A

Trainers— 1, Canani Julio C; 2, Frankel Robert; 3, Dollase Wallace; 4, Frankel Robert; 5, Mulhall Kristin; 6, Mandella Richard

---

$2 Daily Double (3–4) Paid $183.40; Daily Double Pool $43,349.
$1 Pick Three (8–3–4) Paid $919.70; Pick Three Pool $88,725.

EIGHTH RACE
Saratoga
JULY 28, 2003

$1\frac{1}{16}$ MILES. (Turf)(1.38^{4}) 7th Running of THE LAKE GEORGE. Grade III. Purse $100,000. (Up to $19,400 NYSBFOA). FILLIES, THREE YEARS OLD. By subscription of $100 each, which should accompany the nomination; $500 to pass the entry box; $500 to start, with $100,000 added. The added money and all fees to be divided 60% to the winner, 20% to second, 11% to third, 6% to fourth and 3% to fifth. 122 lbs. Non-winners of a graded sweepstake on the turf in 2003 allowed 3 lbs.; $45,000 on the turf, 5 lbs.; two races, 7 lbs. (Maiden, claiming, starter or restricted races not considered in allowances).Trophies will be presented to the winning owner, trainer and jockey. The New York Racing Association reserves the right to transfer this race to the main track.

Value of Race: $114,500 Winner $68,700; second $22,900; third $12,595; fourth $6,870; fifth $3,435. Mutuel Pool $506,337.00 Exacta Pool $458,139.00 Trifecta Pool $336,257.00

Last Raced	Horse	M/Eqt.	A.Wt	PP	St	¼	½	¾	Str	Fin	Jockey	Odds $1
6Jly03 ^{10}Mth^{2}	Film Maker	Lb	3 115	4	3	5^{1}	$5\frac{1}{2}$	$6^{2\frac{1}{2}}$	$5^{2\frac{1}{2}}$	$1^{2\frac{1}{2}}$	Prado E S	9.00
2Jly03 ^{8}Bel^{1}	Ocean Drive	L	3 119	11	10	$4\frac{1}{2}$	$4^{1\frac{1}{2}}$	$3\frac{1}{2}$	2^{hd}	$2\frac{3}{4}$	Bailey J D	1.20
5Jly03 ^{5}Hol^{13}	Gal O Gal	L	3 122	9	8	8^{1}	8^{hd}	$5\frac{1}{2}$	6^{hd}	$3\frac{1}{2}$	Velazquez J R	9.60
6Jly03 ^{10}Mth^{1}	Impolite	L	3 117	1	1	$1^{4\frac{1}{2}}$	$1^{5\frac{1}{2}}$	1^{2}	$1\frac{1}{2}$	4^{nk}	Ferrer J C	13.80
6Jly03 ^{5}AP^{3}	U K Trick	Lb	3 117	6	5	$3^{1\frac{1}{2}}$	3^{hd}	4^{hd}	$3\frac{1}{2}$	$5\frac{1}{2}$	Sellers S J	25.00
2Jly03 ^{8}Bel^{2}	Beautiful America	Lf	3 117	8	7	$2\frac{1}{2}$	$2^{1\frac{1}{2}}$	$2\frac{1}{2}$	4^{hd}	6^{nk}	Santos J A	8.10
30May03 ^{8}Bel^{7}	Indy Five Hundred	L	3 115	10	11	10^{12}	10^{15}	$9^{2\frac{1}{2}}$	10	7^{hd}	Day P	32.25
15Jun03 ^{8}Bel^{5}	Snowdrops-GB	L	3 115	2	2	9^{hd}	9^{2}	10^{20}	$8^{1\frac{1}{2}}$	8^{nk}	Guidry M	7.10
6Jly03 ^{5}AP^{1}	Aud	L	3 117	7	6	6^{hd}	$6\frac{1}{2}$	$8^{1\frac{1}{2}}$	7^{hd}	$9^{1\frac{3}{4}}$	Luzzi M J	14.20
2Jly03 ^{8}Bel^{3}	Broadway Lady	L	3 115	5	4	$7\frac{1}{2}$	7^{hd}	$7\frac{1}{2}$	$9\frac{1}{2}$	10	Velasquez C	21.80
2Jly03 ^{8}Bel^{4}	Mariakel	L	3 115	3	9	11	11	11	—	—	Chavez J F	24.25

Mariakel:Distanced;

OFF AT 4:47 Start Good. Won driving. Course firm.
TIME :24, :48^{1}, 1:12^{1}, 1:35^{4}, 1:41^{4} (:24.18, :48.23, 1:12.21, 1:35.99, 1:41.80)

$2 Mutuel Prices:			
4–FILM MAKER	20.00	5.30	4.60
12–OCEAN DRIVE		2.80	2.50
10–GAL O GAL			5.40

$2 EXACTA 4–12 PAID $57.00 $2 TRIFECTA 4–12–10 PAID $288.50

Dk. b. or br. f, (Mar), by Dynaformer–Miss Du Bois, by Mr. Prospector. Trainer Motion H Graham. Bred by TAC Holdings Inc (Ky).

FILM MAKER raced in the middle of the pack along the backstretch, waited patiently for room while in traffic between horses on the turn, split rivals to get clear in upper stretch then unleashed a strong late run to win going away. OCEAN DRIVE settled just behind the early leaders, was in hand while well placed along the backstretch, ranged up three wide on the turn, made a run to challenge inside the furlong marker but couldn't stay with the winner through the final sixteenth. GAL O GAL steadied while being bothered entering the backstretch, raced well back for five furlongs while five wide, continued wide advancing into the stretch then rallied belatedly in the middle of the track. IMPOLITE sprinted clear soon after the start, raced uncontested on the lead for five furlongs, continued on the front into midstretch then weakened from her early efforts. U K TRICK raced in close contention along the inside for six furlongs, lodged a mild rally along the rail in upper stretch but couldn't sustain her bid. BEAUTIFUL AMERICA settled just behind the pacesetter to the turn, closed the gap to threaten in upper stretch then flattened out. INDY FIVE HUNDRED outrun for seven furlongs, swung eight wide entering the stretch then rallied belatedly. SNOWDROPS (GB) checked along the inside on the first turn, failed to threaten while saving ground. AUD lodged a mild rally four wide on the turn and flattened out. BROADWAY LADY steadied between horses on the first turn, failed to mount a serious rally. MARIAKEL was pinched back at the start, dropped back early, and was never close thereafter.

Owners— 1, Adam Donald A; 2, Baskin Bonnie & Sy; 3, Hugel Max; 4, Noble Ray; 5, Rising Graph Stable & Richard A Stu; 6, Broman Mary R & Chester Sr; 7, Georgica Stable; 8, Geoffrey Howard-Spinks; 9, Willmott Stables; 10, Punk William J & Dileo Philip Jr; 11, Crown Stable & John Zoldac

Trainers—1, Motion H Graham; 2, Pletcher Todd A; 3, Blengs Vincent L; 4, Rice Linda; 5, Stall Albert M Jr; 6, Hernandez Ramon M; 7, Barbara Robert; 8, Clement Christophe; 9, Reinstedler Anthony; 10, O'Brien Keith; 11, Martin Carlos F

Scratched— Kitty Knight (9Jly03 ^{8}BEL^{2}), Andover Lady (26Jun03 ^{7}BEL^{2}), Double Scoop (21Jun03 ^{10}MTH^{3})

EIGHTH RACE
Saratoga
AUGUST 1, 2003

6 FURLONGS. (1.08) 12th Running of THE HONORABLE MISS HANDICAP. Grade III. Purse $100,000 Added (Up to $19,400 NYSBFOA) FILLIES AND MARES THREE YEARS OLD AND UPWARD. By subscription of $100 each which should accompany the nomination; $500 to pass the entry box; $500 to start, with $100,000 added. The added money and all fees to be divided 60% to the winner,20% to second, 11% to third, 6% to fourth and 3% to fifth. Trophies will be presented to the winning owner, trainer and jockey. Closed Saturday, July 19, 2003 with 16 Nominations.

Value of Race: $107,600 Winner $64,560; second $21,520; third $11,836; fourth $6,456; fifth $3,228. Mutuel Pool $634,333.00 Exacta Pool $509,451.00 Trifecta Pool $314,870.00

Last Raced	Horse	M/Eqt.	A.Wt	PP	St	¼	½	Str	Fin	Jockey	Odds $1
27Jun03 ^{9}Bel^{2}	Willa On The Move	L	4 114	6	6	6	4^{hd}	3^{hd}	$1\frac{1}{2}$	Prado E S	2.50
8Jun03 ^{8}Bel^{2}	Shine Again	L	6 120	5	4	$2\frac{1}{2}$	$2^{1\frac{1}{2}}$	2^{hd}	2no	Samyn J L	1.65
21Jun03 ^{9}Bel^{4}	Smok'n Frolic	L	4 117	2	3	$5\frac{1}{2}$	$5^{2\frac{1}{2}}$	5^{10}	3^{1}	Velazquez J R	7.80
16Jly03 ^{8}Bel^{3}	Redhead Riot	Lbf	4 113	3	2	$1\frac{1}{2}$	$1\frac{1}{2}$	$1\frac{1}{2}$	$4^{1\frac{3}{4}}$	Castellano J J	21.40
14Jun03 ^{8}AP^{2}	Raging Fever	Lf	5 118	1	5	$3^{1\frac{1}{2}}$	3^{hd}	$4\frac{1}{2}$	$5^{10\frac{1}{2}}$	Bailey J D	4.70
12Jly03 ^{11}Crc^{7}	Shawklit Mint	L	4 115	4	1	$4^{1\frac{1}{2}}$	6	6	6	Migliore R	4.80

OFF AT 4:47 Start Good. Won driving. Track sloppy.
TIME :22^{1}, :45^{2}, :57^{2}, 1:09^{4} (:22.28, :45.40, :57.41, 1:09.92)

$2 Mutuel Prices:			
6–WILLA ON THE MOVE	7.00	3.70	2.90
5–SHINE AGAIN		2.90	2.20
2–SMOK'N FROLIC			3.00

$2 EXACTA 6–5 PAID $18.40 $2 TRIFECTA 6–5–2 PAID $62.00

Ch. f, by Two Punch–Willa Joe*Ire, by El Gran Senor. Trainer Dutrow Anthony W. Bred by Robert L Quinichett (Md).

WILLA ON THE MOVE was outrun early, rallied three wide on the turn, responded when roused, finished strongly from the outside and was along in time, driving. SHINE AGAIN came away well, pressed the pace from the outside and dug in gamely through the stretch. SMOK'N FROLIC was outrun early inside, split rivals approaching the stretch, responded when roused and finished gamely while between rivals in the stretch. REDHEAD RIOT was hustled to the front, set the pace and weakened in the final furlong. RAGING FEVER raced close up inside, chased the pace around the turn and lacked a rally. SHAWKLIT MINT was hard ridden from the outside, had no response and tired in the stretch.

Owners— 1, Angelos Peter G; 2, Bohemia Stable; 3, Dogwood Stable; 4, Fostock Ann S; 5, Evans Edward P; 6, Flatbird Stable

Trainers—1, Dutrow Anthony W; 2, Jerkens H Allen; 3, Pletcher Todd A; 4, LaFavers Laurie; 5, Hennig Mark; 6, Reynolds Patrick L

EIGHTH RACE
Del Mar
AUGUST 2, 2003

1 MILE. (Turf)(1.32^3) 35th Running of THE SAN CLEMENTE HANDICAP. Grade II. Purse $150,000. FILLIES, THREE-YEAR-OLDS. By subscription of $150 each, which shall accompany the nomination, or by supplementary nomination of $1,500 each by Sunday, July 27, $500 to pass the entry box and $1,000 additional to start. Weights Monday, July 28. Highweights preferred. Starters to be named through the entry box Thursday, July 31, by the closing time of entries. Closed Thursday, July 24 with 15 nominations. (Rail at 7 feet).

Value of Race: $150,000 Winner $90,000; second $30,000; third $18,000; fourth $9,000; fifth $3,000. Mutuel Pool $708,664.00 Exacta Pool $379,206.00 Quinella Pool $43,338.00 Trifecta Pool $360,907.00 Superfecta Pool $139,008.00

Last Raced	Horse	M/Eqt.	A.Wt	PP	St	¼	½	¾	Str	Fin	Jockey	Odds $1
6Jly03 ^{8}Hol^2	Katdogawn-GB	**LB**	3 116	1	3	$5^{2\frac{1}{2}}$	$4^{\frac{1}{2}}$	4^1	4^3	1^2	Krone J A	a-5.10
5Jly03 ^{5}Hol^3	Atlantic Ocean	**LB**	3 120	2	1	3^1	3^1	$3^{1\frac{1}{2}}$	1^1	2^2	Valenzuela P A	1.20
12Jly03 ^{9}Crc^6	Buffythecenterfold	**LB**b	3 118	7	4	2^1	$2^{\frac{1}{2}}$	$2^{\frac{1}{2}}$	2^{hd}	$3^{\frac{1}{2}}$	Espinoza V	9.10
5Jly03 ^{5}Hol^9	Star Vega-GB	**LB**	3 116	8	9	8^3	8^3	$8^{3\frac{1}{2}}$	$6^{1\frac{1}{2}}$	4^{nk}	Smith M E	a-5.10
6Jly03 ^{8}Hol^4	Fencelineneighbor	**LB**b	3 115	9	6	4^{hd}	$5^{1\frac{1}{2}}$	$5^{1\frac{1}{2}}$	5^1	5no	Valdivia J Jr	28.30
6Jly03 ^{8}Hol^3	Valentine Dancer	**LB**b	3 117	5	2	$1^{\frac{1}{2}}$	1^{hd}	1^{hd}	3^{hd}	6^2	Desormeaux K J	4.50
5Jly03 ^{5}Hol^{12}	WelcmMillenm-FR	**LB**	3 118	6	7	$7^{1\frac{1}{2}}$	$7^{2\frac{1}{2}}$	7^2	7^{hd}	7^2	Solis A	8.30
28Jun03 NAN^1	Cellamare-FR	**LB**	3 116	3	5	6^1	6^{hd}	6^1	8^5	8^4	Flores D R	17.30
1May03 Mil^1	Bukat Timah-GB	**B**	3 116	4	8	9	9	9	9	9	Nakatani C S	8.20

a-Coupled: Katdogawn-GB and Star Vega-GB.

OFF AT 5:38 Start Good. Won driving. Course firm.
TIME :22^3, :46^3, 1:10^2, 1:22, 1:33^3 (:22.79, :46.62, 1:10.45, 1:22.09, 1:33.62)

$2 Mutuel Prices:

1-KATDOGAWN-GB (a-entry)	12.20	4.60	3.60
2-ATLANTIC OCEAN		3.00	2.80
7-BUFFYTHECENTERFOLD			4.80

$1 EXACTA 1-2 PAID $13.50 $2 QUINELLA 1-2 PAID $10.60 $1 TRIFECTA 1-2-7 PAID $95.60 $1 SUPERFECTA 1-2-7-8 PAID $834.20

B. f, (Feb), by Bahhare-Trempkate, by Trempolino. Trainer Cassidy James. Bred by Gibson Fleming Mrs W H (GB).

KATDOGAWN (GB) saved ground stalking the pace, swung out into the stretch, rallied to the lead under energetic handling in late stretch and pulled clear. ATLANTIC OCEAN pulled her way along inside early, came out leaving the first turn, bid three deep on the backstretch and second turn, took a short lead into the stretch, inched away but could not match the winner while clearly second best. BUFFYTHECENTERFOLD three deep early, pressed the pace outside a rival then between horses on the backstretch and second turn, could not match strides with the top pair in the final furlong but held third. STAR VEGA (GB) saved ground off the pace, came out nearing midstretch and put in a late bid at third between foes. FENCELINENEIGHBOR four wide early, stalked three deep then outside a rival, came out into the stretch and also put in a late bid at a minor award. VALENTINE DANCER between foes early, angled in and dueled inside, fought back on the second turn but weakened in the stretch. WELCOME MILLENIUM (FR) allowed to settle off the rail then outside a rival, came out into the stretch and did not rally. CELLAMARE (FR) angled in and saved ground chasing the leaders, came out a bit into the stretch and lacked a further response. BUKAT TIMAH (GB) allowed to settle off the pace along the inside, saved ground throughout and was outrun.

Owners— 1, Cuchna John R Jim Ford Inc & Pearso; 2, The Thoroughbred Corporation; 3, Brian Allen A & Stronach Stables; 4, Cuchna John R Jim Ford Inc & Pearso; 5, Frank Bertolino; 6, Kirkwood Al & Saundra S; 7, Zetcher Arnold; 8, Lanni Schiappa & Torre; 9, Tanaka Gary A

Trainers—1, Cassidy James; 2, Baffert Bob; 3, Stute Melvin F; 4, Cassidy James; 5, Machowsky Michael; 6, Lewis Craig A; 7, McAnally Ronald; 8, Monteleone Frank J; 9, Bary Pascal F

$2 Daily Double (4-1) Paid $37.20; Daily Double Pool $46,604.
$1 Pick Three (8-4/5-1) Paid $116.70; Pick Three Pool $129,867.

EIGHTH RACE
Saratoga
AUGUST 2, 2003

6 FURLONGS. (1.08) 11th Running of THE AMSTERDAM. Grade II. Purse $150,000 (Up to $21,100 NYSBFOA) THREE YEAR OLDS. By subscription of $150 each, which should accompany the nomination; $750 to pass the entry box; $750 to start. The purse to be divided 60% to the winner, 20% to second, 11% to third, 6% to fourth and 3% to fifth. 123 lbs. Non-winners of a graded sweepstakes in 2003 allowed 2 lbs.; $45,000 since October 1, 4 lbs.; three races, 6 lbs.; two races, 8 lbs. (maiden, claiming, and restricted races not considered in allowances). Trophies will be presented to the winning owner, trainer and jockey. Closed Saturday, July 19, 2003 with 20 Nominations.

Value of Race: $150,000 Winner $90,000; second $30,000; third $16,500; fourth $9,000; fifth $4,500. Mutuel Pool $1,089,886.0 Exacta Pool $869,705.00 Trifecta Pool $550,528.00

Last Raced	Horse	M/Eqt.	A.Wt	PP	St	¼	½	Str	Fin	Jockey	Odds $1
26Jun03 ^{8}Mth^1	Zavata		3 119	3	4	$2^{1\frac{1}{2}}$	2^{hd}	$1^{2\frac{1}{2}}$	$1^{5\frac{1}{4}}$	Bailey J D	3.15
12Apr03 ^{9}Kee^9	Great Notion	L	3 121	4	7	$3^{1\frac{1}{2}}$	4^2	3^{hd}	$2^{\frac{1}{2}}$	Day P	21.20
19Apr03 ^{8}Kee^4	Trust N Luck	L	3 123	6	1	1^{hd}	1^{hd}	$2^{1\frac{1}{2}}$	3^{nk}	Velasquez C	6.50
7Jun03 ^{9}Bel^1	Posse	L	3 123	2	3	7	$6^{1\frac{1}{2}}$	4^{hd}	$4^{1\frac{3}{4}}$	Lanerie C J	1.05
10Jly03 ^{5}Bel^3	First Blush	b	3 123	5	2	5^{hd}	$3^{\frac{1}{2}}$	5^2	$5^{1\frac{1}{2}}$	Chavez J F	15.00
7Jun03 ^{11}Bel^6	Scrimshaw	Lb	3 123	1	5	$4^{\frac{1}{2}}$	$5^{\frac{1}{2}}$	$6^{3\frac{1}{2}}$	$6^{4\frac{1}{4}}$	Prado E S	5.60
12Jly03 ^{10}Crc^3	Super Fuse	Lbf	3 121	7	6	$6^{1\frac{1}{2}}$	7	7	7	Santos J A	15.80

OFF AT 5:10 Start Good. Won driving. Track fast.
TIME :22, :44^3, :56^2, 1:08^3 (:22.00, :44.79, :56.49, 1:08.64)

$2 Mutuel Prices:

3-ZAVATA	8.30	4.70	4.30
4-GREAT NOTION		12.80	6.80
6-TRUST N LUCK			6.00

$2 EXACTA 3-4 PAID $127.00 $2 TRIFECTA 3-4-6 PAID $719.00

B. c, (Feb), by Phone Trick-Pert Lady, by Cox's Ridge. Trainer Biancone Patrick L. Bred by Mill Ridge Farm Ltd Jamm Ltd & Dr John A Chandler (Ky).

ZAVATA moved up along the rail to contest the early pace, forced the pace along the inside through the turn, battled heads apart approaching the quarter pole, surged to the front at the top of the stretch, extended his lead in midstretch then drew away under strong right hand encouragement. GREAT NOTION broke a bit slowly, moved up rapidly from outside along the backstretch, raced just behind the dueling leaders while three wide between horses on the turn, brushed with FIRST BLUSH in upper stretch then outfinished TRUST N LUCK for the place. TRUST N LUCK away alertly, rushed up from outside to gain a slim early advantage, set a rapid pace under steady pressure to the top of the stretch, relinquished the lead to the winner in upper stretch then weakened from his early efforts. POSSE was taken in hand soon after the start, trailed along the backstretch, closed the gap a bit while four wide on the turn, angled out entering the stretch then lacked a strong closing bid. FIRST BLUSH was unhurried early, made a strong run while four wide to threaten approaching the quarter pole but couldn't sustain his bid. SCRIMSHAW was hustled up along the rail, chased the leaders along the inside for a half and steadily tired thereafter. SUPER FUSE away a bit slowly, failed to mount a serious rally while four wide.

Owners— 1, Tabor Michael B; 2, Tom Hamilton & Bonnie Hamilton; 3, Robsham Einar P; 4, Heiligbrodt Stables & Vinery Stable; 5, Cowan Marjorie & Irving M; 6, Lewis Robert B & Beverly J; 7, Alpha One Stable

Trainers—1, Biancone Patrick L; 2, Miller Darrin; 3, Ziadie Ralph; 4, Asmussen Steven M; 5, Jerkens H Allen; 6, Lukas D Wayne; 7, Ciardullo Richard Jr

$2 Pick Three (6-2-3) Paid $36.60; Pick Three Pool $153,346.

NINTH RACE
Saratoga
AUGUST 2, 2003

1⅛ MILES. (1.47) 76th Running of THE WHITNEY HANDICAP. Grade I. Purse $750,000 (Up to $39,000 NYSBFOA) THREE YEAR OLDS AND UPWARD. By subscription of $750 each, which should accompany the nomination; $3,500 to pass the entry box, $4,000 to start. The purse to be divided 60% to the winner, 20% to second, 11% to third,6% to fourth and 3% to fifth. Trophies will be presented to the winning owner, trainer and jockey. Closed Saturday, July 19th, 2003 with 16 Nominations.

Value of Race: $750,000 Winner $450,000; second $150,000; third $82,500; fourth $45,000; fifth $22,500. Mutuel Pool $1,482,454.0 Exacta Pool $1,041,570.0 Trifecta Pool $804,651.00

Last Raced	Horse	M/Eqt.	A.Wt	PP	St	¼	½	¾	Str	Fin	Jockey	Odds $1
5Apr03 11OP1	Medaglia d'Oro	L	4 123	5	2	2½	21	21½	1½	11	Bailey J D	0.80
5Jly03 9Bel2	Volponi	Lb	5 120	6	7	41½	42½	43	2½	21¼	Santos J A	2.90
23Jly03 8Sar1	Evening Attire	Lb	5 118	4	6	66	66	5hd	4hd	3nk	Guidry M	8.90
24Jly03 5Sar1	Puzzlement	Lb	4 112	1	5	7	7	7	6hd	4½	Chavez J F	21.70
4Jly03 8Bel6	Northern Rock-JP	Lb	5 114	3	1	1½	11½	1hd	31½	5¾	Migliore R	28.00
14Jun03 9Bel3	Saarland	Lbf	4 113	2	4	52½	5hd	62	51½	62¼	Velazquez J R	7.40
6Jly03 4CD1	Proud Citizen	L	4 114	7	3	31½	3½	3½	7	7	Prado E S	15.80

OFF AT 5:44 Start Good. Won driving. Track fast.
TIME :23^{2}, :46^{4}, 1:10^{2}, 1:34^{4}, 1:47^{3} (:23.53, :46.81, 1:10.47, 1:34.83, 1:47.69)

$2 Mutuel Prices:

5–MEDAGLIA D'ORO	3.60	2.50	2.30
7–VOLPONI		2.80	2.40
4–EVENING ATTIRE			3.20

$2 EXACTA 5–7 PAID $8.10 $2 TRIFECTA 5–7–4 PAID $30.00

Dk. b. or br. c, by El Prado*Ire–Cappucino Bay, by Bailjumper. Trainer Frankel Robert. Bred by Albert Bell & Joyce Bell (Ky).

MEDAGLIA D'ORO moved up from outside to contest the early pace, settled in good position while just behind the leader entering the backstretch, stalked NORTHERN ROCK from outside for seven furlongs, made a run outside that one to challenge in upper stretch, surged to the front nearing the furlong marker then turned back VOLPONI under steady right hand urging. VOLPONI came away slowly after turning his head sideways at the start,angled to the inside leaving the first turn, raced in close contention while saving ground along the backstretch, raced just to the inside of PROUD CITIZEN approaching the far turn, waited patiently for room midway on the turn, angled three wide for clear sailing at the top of the stretch, made a run outside the winner to threaten in upper stretch, but couldn't gain on that one through the final eighth. EVENING ATTIRE was unhurried for six furlongs while slightly off the rail, launched a rally between horses leaving the turn then finished willingly to gain a share. PUZZLEMENT devoid of early speed, trailed along the backstretch, raced well back to the turn, circled five wide into the stretch then rallied belatedly in the middle of the track. NORTHERN ROCK (JPN) rushed up along the rail to gain the early advantage, set the pace under pressure along the backstretch, continued on the front while saving ground to the turn, dug in when challenged leaving the quarter pole, fought gamely into midstretch then weakened from his early efforts. SAARLAND was rated well off the pace while saving ground along the backstretch, edged a bit closer along the inside on the turn, made a run along the rail to reach contention in upper stretch but couldn't sustain his bid. PROUD CITIZEN was rated just outside the early leaders, stalked the pace while three wide to the far turn then steadily tired thereafter.

Owners— 1, Gann Edmund A; 2, Amherst Stable & Spruce Pond Stable; 3, Grant Mary & Joseph & Kelly Thomas; 4, Shields Joseph V Jr; 5, Darley Stable; 6, Phipps Cynthia; 7, Baker Robert C Cornstein David & Ma

Trainers—1, Frankel Robert; 2, Johnson Philip G; 3, Kelly Patrick J; 4, Jerkens H Allen; 5, McLaughlin Kiaran P; 6, McGaughey Claude III; 7, Lukas D Wayne

Scratched— Harlan's Holiday (13Jly03 9HOL2)

ELEVENTH RACE
Monmouth
AUGUST 3, 2003

1⅛ MILES. (1.46^{4}) 36th Running of THE HASKELL INVITATIONAL HANDICAP. Grade I. Purse $1,000,000. THREE–YEAR–OLDS. By invitation only, with no nomination, entry or starting fees. The owner of the winner to receive $600,000, $200,000 to second,$100,000 to third, $60,000 to fourth, $30,000 to fifth and $10,000 to sixth. Weights 5:00 P.M. Friday, July 18. Monmouth Park reserves the right to assign or reassign weight to any horse after the release of weights. A bonus of $25,000 per race will be given to both the owner and trainer of any horse that has won a leg of the triple crown and starts in the Haskell. Starters to be named through the entry box on Thursday July 31. Closed Sunday, July 20 with 25 nominations.

Value of Race: $1,000,000 Winner $600,000; second $200,000; third $100,000; fourth $60,000; fifth $30,000; sixth $10,000. Mutuel Pool $1,744,213.0 Exacta Pool $1,029,203.0 Trifecta Pool $728,484.00 Superfecta Pool $157,176.00

Last Raced	Horse	M/Eqt.	A.Wt	PP	St	¼	½	¾	Str	Fin	Jockey	Odds $1
17May03 12Pim4	Peace Rules	L	3 121	1	2	11½	11½	11½	13	11¾	Prado E S	2.30
6Jly03 10Bel3	Sky Mesa	L	3 118	2	7	3hd	42	3½	23	27¼	Albarado R J	4.30
7Jun03 11Bel3	Funny Cide	L	3 123	5	4	51½	5½	5hd	4hd	31	Santos J A	1.00
21Jun03 14Tdn1	Wild And Wicked		3 118	3	1	2½	31	42	31½	42½	Sellers S J	4.90
12Jly03 9Mth1	Max Forever	L	3 115	4	5	7	7	6hd	54	54½	Ferrer J C	47.40
5Jly03 9LS1	Kool Humor	Lb	3 115	6	3	6½	6hd	7	7	61	Martin E M Jr	47.40
5Jly03 6PrM1	Excessivepleasure	Lb	3 117	7	6	4½	2hd	21	62	7	Court J K	31.00

OFF AT 5:45 Start Good For All But EXCESSIVEPLEASURE Won driving. Track fast.
TIME :23^{1}, :47, 1:10^{4}, 1:36, 1:49^{1} (:23.29, :47.06, 1:10.86, 1:36.18, 1:49.32)

$2 Mutuel Prices:

1–PEACE RULES	6.60	3.80	2.10
2–SKY MESA		4.40	2.10
5–FUNNY CIDE			2.10

$2 EXACTA 1–2 PAID $28.20 $2 TRIFECTA 1–2–5 PAID $54.40 $1 SUPERFECTA 1–2–5–3 PAID $61.20

Ch. c, (Apr), by Jules–Hold to Fashion, by Hold Your Peace. Trainer Frankel Robert. Bred by Newchance Farm (Fla).

PEACE RULES taken off the inside through the early stages, set the early pace away from the rail, showed the way to the lane and widened then responded well and held SKY MESA safe through the closing stages. SKY MESA well placed early while saving ground, raced just off the inside and lodged a bid nearing the top of the lane then finished well while cutting into the winners margin through the final yards. FUNNY CIDE in close briefly early, raced between rivals into the far turn, was outside into the lane and offered a mild bid. WILD AND WICKED stalked early, lost some position into the far turn, lodged a bid outside on the final turn then weakened in the drive. MAX FOREVER in close briefly early, trailed while not far back, saved ground and lacked a rally. KOOL HUMOR broke inward some, raced outside throughout and lacked the needed response. EXCESSIVEPLEASURE stumbled at the start, stalked early from the outside, dropped back from between rivals turning for home and faded through the lane.

Owners— 1, Gann Edmund A; 2, Oxley John C; 3, Sackatoga Stable; 4, Randal Mr & Mrs R David; 5, Dweck Raymond & Dorothy; 6, Durant Tom R; 7, Leatherman Lee & Ty

Trainers—1, Frankel Robert; 2, Ward John T Jr; 3, Tagg Barclay; 4, McPeek Kenneth G; 5, Perkins Ben W Jr; 6, Bruner Jack A; 7, O'Neill Doug

---

$2 Pick Three (2–12–1) Paid $386.20; Pick Three Pool $67,486.

EIGHTH RACE
Del Mar
AUGUST 3, 2003

$1\frac{1}{16}$ MILES. (1.40) 62nd Running of THE SAN DIEGO HANDICAP. Grade II. Purse $250,000 A HANDICAP FOR THREE-YEAR-OLDS AND UPWARD. By subscription of $250 each, which shall accompany the nomination, or by supplementary nomination of $2,500 each by Sunday, July 27, $2,500 additional to start, with $250,000 Guaranteed, of which $150,000 to first, $50,000 to second, $30,000 to third, $15,000 to fourth and $5,000 to fifth. Weights Monday, July 28. A trophy will be presented to the owner of the winner. Nominations closed Thursday, July 24, 2003 with 17.

Value of Race: $250,000 Winner $150,000; second $50,000; third $30,000; fourth $15,000; fifth $5,000. Mutuel Pool $602,680.00 Exacta Pool $303,435.00 Quinella Pool $33,213.00 Trifecta Pool $285,779.00 Superfecta Pool $105,032.00

Last Raced	Horse	M/Eqt.	A.Wt	PP	St	¼	½	¾	Str	Fin	Jockey	Odds $1
12Jly03 ^{6}Hol^{4}	Taste Of Paradise	LB	4 113	8	2	$1^{1/2}$	$1^{1/2}$	1^{1}	1^{3}	$1^{3/4}$	Espinoza V	37.40
14Jun03 ^{8}Hol^{4}	Gondolieri-CH	LBb	4 117	2	4	$6^{1\,1/2}$	$6^{1\,1/2}$	5^{2}	$3^{2\,1/2}$	2^{nk}	Alvarado F T	5.00
14Jun03 ^{8}Hol^{3}	Reba's Gold	LBb	6 116	1	5	7^{2}	$7^{4\,1/2}$	$6^{1\,1/2}$	2^{hd}	$3^{6\,1/2}$	Flores D R	3.00
28Jun03 ^{4}CD^{1}	Danthebluegrassman	LB	4 116	7	6	$4^{1/2}$	3^{1}	$2^{1/2}$	$5^{1/2}$	4^{2}	Smith M E	5.40
10Jly03 ^{2}Hol^{1}	Bayou The Moon	LB	5 116	3	7	8	8	8	$6^{1\,1/2}$	$5^{1\,1/2}$	Solis A	10.30
5Jly03 ^{6}Hol^{2}	Legendary Weave	LBb	5 113	5	3	$5^{2\,1/2}$	5^{2}	4^{hd}	7^{2}	6^{4}	Pedroza M A	12.50
13Jly03 ^{9}Hol^{5}	Western Pride	LB	5 118	6	8	2^{hd}	2^{hd}	7^{1}	8	7^{1}	Valdivia J Jr	6.10
5Jly03 ^{8}Hol^{1}	Joey Franco	LB	4 117	4	1	3^{1}	4^{3}	3^{1}	4^{1}	8	Valenzuela P A	2.40

OFF AT 5:37 Start Good. Won driving. Track fast.
TIME :22^{4}, :45^{3}, 1:10, 1:35^{3}, 1:42^{3} (:22.81, :45.79, 1:10.07, 1:35.71, 1:42.62)

$2 Mutuel Prices:

11–TASTE OF PARADISE	76.80	20.80	6.60
3–GONDOLIERI–CH		6.40	4.20
1–REBA'S GOLD			3.00

$1 EXACTA 11–3 PAID $418.30 $2 QUINELLA 3–11 PAID $285.00 $1 TRIFECTA 11–3–1 PAID $2,092.70 $1 SUPERFECTA 11–3–1–9 PAID $9,315.10

Dk. b. or br. c, by Conquistador Cielo–Tastetheteardrops, by What Luck. Trainer Sadler John W. Bred by Abrahams & Snukal & Bloom (Ky).

TASTE OF PARADISE had speed five wide then angled in approaching and into the first turn, set a pressured pace a bit off the rail, inched away on the second turn, kicked clear and held under urging. GONDOLIERI (CHI) pulled early and was in a bit tight into the first turn, chased a bit off the inside then moved up into the second turn, waited off heels leaving that bend, got through inside into the stretch and finished with interest. REBA'S GOLD settled a bit off the inside, moved up outside on the second turn and five wide into the stretch and closed willingly. DANTHEBLUEGRASSMAN five wide into the first turn, prompted the pace three deep on the backstretch, dropped back some leaving the second turn and weakened. BAYOU THE MOON unhurried along the inside early, remained on the rail and improved position in the stretch. LEGENDARY WEAVE in a bit tight off heels into the first turn, chased outside then off the rail, came three deep into the stretch and weakened. WESTERN PRIDE a half step slow into stride, went up four wide into the first turn, dueled between horses, dropped back into the second turn and weakened. JOEY FRANCO pulled early, was steadied in tight into and leaving the first turn, stalked inside, came out into the stretch and had little left.

Owners— 1, Abrahams Keith & Bloom Paul; 2, Hunt Nelson B; 3, Creston Farms; 4, Pegram Michael E; 5, Hubbard R D & Allred Edward C; 6, Fritz Norm & Lake Forest Stable; 7, Chapman Carolyn & McArthur Theresa; 8, Frankel Jerry

Trainers—1, Sadler John W; 2, McAnally Ronald; 3, Hendricks Dan L; 4, Baffert Bob; 5, Mandella Richard; 6, Carava Jack; 7, Chapman James K; 8, Vienna Darrell

Scratched— Primerica (5Jly03 ^{8}HOL^{4}), Daunting (19Jly03 ^{9}CBY^{1}), Publication (5Jly03 ^{8}HOL^{2})

$2 Daily Double (4–11) Paid $173.40; Daily Double Pool $46,952.
$1 Pick Three (7–4–11) Paid $1,027.00; Pick Three Pool $90,066.
$2 Consolation Daily Double (4–2) Paid $3.20

NINTH RACE
Saratoga
AUGUST 3, 2003

$1\frac{1}{8}$ MILES. (1.47) 40th Running of THE JIM DANDY. Grade II. Purse $500,000 (Up to $36,000 NYSBFOA) FOR THREE YEAR OLDS. By subscription of $500 each, which should accompany the nomination; $2,500 to pass the entry box, $2,500 to start. The purse to be divided 60% to the winner, 20% to second, 11% to third, 6% to fourth and 3% to fifth. 123 lbs. Non–winners of a Grade I in 2003 allowed 2 lbs.; a Grade II over a mile in 2003, 4 lbs.; a Graded Sweepstakes at a mile or over, 6 lbs.; $40,000 at a mile or over or three races other than maiden or claiming, 8 lbs. Trophies will be presented to the winning owner, trainer and jockey. Closed Saturday, July 19, 2003 with 23 Nominations.

Value of Race: $500,000 Winner $300,000; second $100,000; third $55,000; fourth $30,000; fifth $15,000. Mutuel Pool $1,747,485.0 Exacta Pool $970,247.00 Trifecta Pool $754,716.00

Last Raced	Horse	M/Eqt.	A.Wt	PP	St	¼	½	¾	Str	Fin	Jockey	Odds $1
6Jly03 ^{10}Bel^{1}	Strong Hope	L	3 121	1	2	$1^{1/2}$	$1^{1\,1/2}$	$1^{1/2}$	1^{2}	1^{nk}	Velazquez J R	6.70
7Jun03 ^{11}Bel^{1}	Empire Maker	Lb	3 123	5	4	5^{3}	$5^{4\,1/2}$	5^{5}	$2^{1\,1/2}$	$2^{2\,1/2}$	Bailey J D	0.30
10Jly03 ^{8}Bel^{1}	Congrats	L	3 115	4	6	6	6	6	3^{hd}	3^{1}	Luzzi M J	30.50
2Jly03 ^{7}Bel^{1}	Tafaseel	Lb	3 115	2	5	$3^{2\,1/2}$	$4^{4\,1/2}$	$2^{2\,1/2}$	$4^{2\,1/2}$	$4^{2\,3/4}$	Migliore R	9.90
6Jly03 ^{10}Bel^{2}	Nacheezmo	L	3 115	6	3	$4^{1/2}$	3^{hd}	4^{hd}	5^{6}	$5^{4\,1/2}$	Chavez J F	8.50
13Jly03 ^{6}Hol^{1}	During	Lb	3 121	3	1	$2^{2\,1/2}$	$2^{1/2}$	$3^{1/2}$	6	6	Day P	23.60

OFF AT 5:26 Start Good. Won driving. Track fast.
TIME :23^{3}, :47, 1:10^{3}, 1:35, 1:48 (:23.66, :47.17, 1:10.63, 1:35.01, 1:48.10)

$2 Mutuel Prices:

1–STRONG HOPE	15.40	3.30	2.10
6–EMPIRE MAKER		2.30	2.10
5–CONGRATS			2.10

$2 EXACTA 1–6 PAID $27.40 $2 TRIFECTA 1–6–5 PAID $168.50

B. c, (Feb), by Grand Slam–Shining Through, by Deputy Minister. Trainer Pletcher Todd A. Bred by Trackside Farm GA Seelbinder & Liberation Farm (Ky).

STRONG HOPE came away well and moved to the front along the inside entering the first turn, dictated the pace while in hand, put away DURING leaving the backstretch, turned back a bid from TAFASEEL midway on the second turn, drew clear into the stretch, took a clear lead past the eighth pole then dug in resolutely and held off EMPIRE MAKER to the wire. EMPIRE MAKER was unhurried while outrun early, advanced three wide on the second turn, dug in determinedly in the stretch and finished gamely outside. CONGRATS was outrun early, angled out and rallied four wide nearing the stretch and finished well outside. TAFASEEL was rated along inside, angled out and advanced three wide into the second turn, tried the winner passing the three- eighths pole, could not get by that rival and faded in the drive. NACHEEZMO was rated outside on the first turn, angled in, making a run along the rail on the backstretch, tired entering the second turn and was vanned off after the finish. DURING attended the pace from the outside while in hand, could not stay with the winner leaving the backstretch and tired after the opening three quarters.

Owners— 1, Melnyk Eugene & Laura; 2, Juddmonte Farms Inc; 3, Claiborne Farm & Dilschneider Adele; 4, Shadwell Stable; 5, Johnson Ted J & Kim; 6, McIngvale James

Trainers—1, Pletcher Todd A; 2, Frankel Robert; 3, McGaughey Claude III; 4, McLaughlin Kiaran P; 5, Bond Harold James; 6, Baffert Bob

Scratched— Awesome Time (14Jun03 ^{11}DEL^{1})

EIGHTH RACE
Saratoga
AUGUST 4, 2003

1⅛ MILES. (Inner Turf)(1.46^{1}) 19th Running of THE NATIONAL MUSEUM OF RACING HALL OF FAME HANDICAP. Grade II. Purse $150,000. (Up to $21,100 NYSBFOA) FOR THREE YEAR OLDS. By subscription of $150 each, which should accompany the nomination; $750 to pass the entry box, $750 to start. 122 lbs.; Non-winners of a graded sweepstake on the turf in 2003 allowed 3 lbs.; $45,000 on the turf, 5 lbs., two races, 7 lbs. (maiden, claiming, starter or restricted races not considered in allowances). Trophies will be presented to the winning owner, trainer and jockey. The New York Racing Association reserves the right to transfer this race to the Main Track. In the event that this race is taken off the turf, it may be subject to downgrading upon review by the Graded Stakes Committee. Closed Saturday, July 19, 2003 with 46 Nominations.

Value of Race: $150,000 Winner $90,000; second $30,000; third $16,500; fourth $9,000; fifth $4,500. Mutuel Pool $591,716.00 Exacta Pool $505,899.00 Trifecta Pool $404,767.00

Last Raced	Horse	M/Eqt.	A.Wt	PP	St	¼	½	¾	Str	Fin	Jockey	Odds $1
5Jly03 ^{8}Mth^{1}	Stroll	L	3 117	9	4	2½	21½	22½	14½	14	Bailey J D	2.65
13Jly03 ^{9}Bel^{3}	Urban King-IR	L	3 115	8	10	9^{5}	8^{hd}	9^{6}	4^{hd}	21¼	Prado E S	4.90
6Jly03 ^{11}Bel^{1}	Saint Stephen	L	3 115	5	3	5½	5½	41½	5^{2}	3¾	Coa E M	a-5.00
1Jly03 ^{7}Del^{3}	Hypnotist	Lbf	3 119	2	2	4^{hd}	3½	3½	2^{hd}	43¼	Samyn J L	37.00
17May03 ^{12}Pim^{10}	Kissin Saint	Lbf	3 117	7	6	6^{2}	61½	6^{hd}	62½	5^{nk}	Santos J A	a-5.00
19Jly03 ^{10}ElP^{1}	G P Fleet	L	3 115	3	9	7^{hd}	7^{hd}	7^{hd}	7½	61¾	Velazquez J R	14.50
13Jly03 ^{9}Bel^{1}	Sharp Impact	Lb	3 122	1	1	1^{hd}	1½	1½	3½	7½	Migliore R	7.30
13Jly03 ^{9}Bel^{4}	Supervisor	Lb	3 115	6	8	105½	105½	104½	10^{10}	8no	Chavez J F	38.00
13Jly03 ^{9}Bel^{2}	Hidden Truth	L	3 117	4	7	8^{2}	9^{6}	8^{hd}	8½	9½	Albarado R J	3.40
5Jly03 ^{6}PrM^{2}	Saint Liam	L	3 115	10	5	3^{hd}	41½	5^{hd}	91½	1010¼	Day P	11.90
18Jun03 ^{4}Bel^{2}	Coalition	Lb	3 115	11	11	11	11	11	11	11	Sellers S J	55.75

a-Coupled: Saint Stephen and Kissin Saint.

OFF AT 4:48 Start Good. Won driving. Course yielding.
TIME :23^{2}, :48^{1}, 1:12^{4}, 1:37^{1}, 1:49^{1} (:23.55, :48.27, 1:12.80, 1:37.31, 1:49.34)

$2 Mutuel Prices:

8-STROLL	7.30	3.70	2.90
7-URBAN KING-IR		5.90	4.10
1-SAINT STEPHEN (a-entry)			3.80

$2 EXACTA 8-7 PAID $34.80 $2 TRIFECTA 8-7-1 PAID $146.50

Dk. b. or br. c, (Apr), by Pulpit-Maid for Walking*GB, by Prince Sabo. Trainer Mott William I. Bred by Claiborne Farm (Ky).

STROLL moved up rapidly to contest the early pace, stalked the leader while well in hand along the backstretch, edged closer leaving the turn, charged to the front at the three-sixteenths pole, quickly opened a comfortable advantage in midstretch then drew off with authority under steady left hand encouragement. URBAN KING (IRE) raced well back along the inside for six furlongs, continued to saved ground while rallying on the turn, slipped through along the rail in midstretch then finished well along the inside to gain the place. SAINT STEPHEN was rated just off the pace while saving ground, closed the gap a bit on the turn, angled out approaching the stretch then finished willingly from outside to gain a share. HYPNOTIST was taken in hand along the rail on the first turn, angled out along the backstretch, raced just behind the leaders to the top of the stretch then finished evenly. KISSIN SAINT raced in the middle of the pack while in hand along the backstretch, lodged a mild rally while four wide on the turn but couldn't sustain his bid. G P FLEET checked slightly in tight between horses in the early stages, was unhurried while racing well off the rail on the backstretch, advanced four wide on the turn then lacked a strong closing bid. SHARP IMPACT rushed up to gain the early advantage, set an honest pace along the rail for six furlongs, relinquished the lead to the winner turning for home then steadily tired thereafter. SUPERVISOR raced far back while saving ground, angled to the middle of the track in upper stretch and lacked a strong closing bid. HIDDEN TRUTH failed to mount a serious rally while five wide throughout. SAINT LIAM chased the leaders while three wide for six furlongs and gave way. COALITION trailed throughout.

Owners— 1, Claiborne Farm; 2, Amerman Racing Stables LLC; 3, Karches Peter F & Harris Charles E; 4, Dogwood Stable; 5, Karches Peter F & Rankowitz Michael; 6, Klein Richard Bertram & Elaine; 7, Darley Stable; 8, Lundock Rodney G; 9, Farish William S & Webber W Temple; 10, William K Warren & Suzanne Warren; 11, Literary Lion Farm

Trainers—1, Mott William I; 2, Frankel Robert; 3, Clement Christophe; 4, Tagg Barclay; 5, Lewis Lisa L; 6, Flint Steve; 7, McLaughlin Kiaran P; 8, Rice Linda; 9, Howard Neil J; 10, Reinstedler Anthony; 11, O'Brien Leo

Scratched— Colita (21May03 ^{7}BEL^{1}), Awesome Time (14Jun03 ^{11}DEL^{1}), Christine's Outlaw (12Jly03 ^{9}MTH^{2})

EIGHTH RACE
Arlington
AUGUST 9, 2003

1⅛ MILES. (1.46^1) 24th Running of THE SINGAPORE PLATE. Grade III. Purse $100,000 FOR FILLIES, THREE-YEARS-OLD. By subscription of $75 each, which should accompany the nomination. A Supplementary Nomination of $4,000 may be made on Wednesday, August 6, 2003, which includes entry and starting fees. Original nominees to pay $750 to pass the entry box and an additional $750 to start. WEIGHT: 122 lbs. Non-winners of $50,000 once at one mile or over in 2003, allowed 2 lbs.; $40,000 once or $25,000 twice at one mile or over in 2003, 4 lbs.; a sweepstakes at one mile or over in 2002-2003 or $20,000 twice at one mile or over in 2003, 6 lbs. (Maiden and Claiming races not considered.) This event will be limited to fourteen (14) starters. Preference will be winners of Graded/Group Stakes (in order of I-II-III), next preference, Highest Total Earnings in 2003. Failure to draw into this race at time of entry cancels all fees with the exception of the nominating fee(s). Two (2) horses having common ties through ownership cannot start to the exclusion of a single ownership interest.

Value of Race: $100,000 Winner $60,000; second $20,000; third $11,000; fourth $6,000; fifth $3,000. Mutuel Pool $210,930.00 Exacta Pool $134,573.00 Trifecta Pool $111,369.00 Superfecta Pool $26,661.00

Last Raced	Horse	M/Eqt.	A.Wt	PP	St	¼	½	¾	Str	Fin	Jockey	Odds $1
19Jly03 8Del6	Sue's Good News	Lf	3 120	4	7	6^{1½}	6^{½}	6^{1½}	3^{1}	1^{1¼}	Doocy T T	2.40
19Jly03 4AP1	Keeping The Gold	L	3 122	8	5	5^{½}	4^{½}	4^{1}	1^{½}	2^{7}	Razo E Jr	4.40
19Jly03 8Del5	Meet Me At Midnite	L	3 118	1	9	8^{hd}	8^{½}	7^{hd}	6^{½}	3no	Marquez C H Jr	5.40
21Jun03 4AP2	Julie's Prize	Lbf	3 122	6	1	2^{½}	2^{½}	2^{hd}	4^{½}	4^{1½}	Sterling L J Jr	8.00
14Jun03 12Crc1	Splasha	Lb	3 122	5	8	9	9	8^{½}	8^{2½}	5^{½}	Lovato F Jr	10.60
15Jly03 9Mnr1	Lil Scout	L	3 117	7	6	3^{1½}	3^{1}	3^{1}	5^{3}	6^{½}	St Julien M	6.90
19Jly03 8Del7	Wildwood Royal	Lbf	3 122	2	4	1^{1}	1^{½}	1^{hd}	2^{hd}	7^{¾}	Baird E T	8.20
4Jly03 6PrM2	Golden Reputashn	L	3 116	3	3	4^{hd}	5^{½}	9	7^{2}	8^{9}	Emigh C A	8.20
5Jly03 8CD4	Austin's Mom	L	3 116	9	2	7^{½}	7^{1}	5^{1}	9	9	Sibille R	24.70

OFF AT 4:40 Start Good. Won driving. Track fast.
TIME :24^1, :48^4, 1:13^3, 1:38^3, 1:50^2 (:24.27, :48.98, 1:13.79, 1:38.61, 1:50.53)

$2 Mutuel Prices:

4-SUE'S GOOD NEWS	6.80	3.60	3.20
8-KEEPING THE GOLD		4.20	3.40
1-MEET ME AT MIDNITE			4.40

$2 EXACTA 4-8 PAID $28.60 $2 TRIFECTA 4-8-1 PAID $114.60 $2 SUPERFECTA 4-8-1-6 PAID $325.00

Ch. f, (Apr), by Woodman-Montera, by Easy Goer. Trainer Hobby Steve. Bred by Twilite Farms Inc (Ky).

SUE'S GOOD NEWS raced between foes near the middle of the field, angled out for the drive, rallied late and was along in the closing yards. KEEPING THE GOLD was five wide on the first turn, raced close up off the rail, rallied to a short lead in the stretch then could not hold off the winner. MEET ME AT MIDNITE lacked speed, angled out and rallied belatedly for minor awards. JULIE'S PRIZE pressed the pace from just outside and tired. SPLASHA lacked speed and improved her position. LIL SCOUT was four wide on the first turn, raced close up three wide and gave way. WILDWOOD ROYAL set the pace from the inside while pressed and tired. GOLDEN REPUTASHN was through after a half. AUSTIN'S MOM was six wide on the first turn, made a bid on the final turn and faltered.

Owners— 1, Cresran LLC; 2, Fedro Tom & Brommer Darrell & Sadie; 3, B M H Stable; 4, Richard Otto Stables; 5, Gibson Douglas P; 6, Horned Owl Stable Amy Hunter Et Al; 7, Stiritz William; 8, Ashby Thoroughbreds; 9, Friedman Len Nilsen Jan & Keifetz B

Trainers—1, Hobby Steve; 2, Block Chris M; 3, Hiles Rick; 4, Mitchell Anthony; 5, Vivian David A; 6, Smith Austin; 7, Zook Jimmy; 8, Von Hemel Don; 9, O'Callaghan Niall M

$1 Pick Three (2-5-4) Paid $921.50; Pick Three Pool $19,659.

EIGHTH RACE
Del Mar
AUGUST 9, 2003

6½ FURLONGS. (1.13^3) 35th Running of THE SORRENTO. Grade II. Purse $150,000. FILLIES, TWO-YEAR-OLDS. (FOALS OF 2001.) By subscription of $150 each, which shall accompany the nomination, or by supplementary nomination of $1,500 each by closing time of entries, $1,500 additional to start, with $150,000 Guaranteed, of which $90,000 to first, $30,000 to second, $18,000 to third, $9,000 to fourth and $3,000 to fifth. Weight, 122 lbs. Non-winners of $50,000, 2 lbs. Of $25,000 other than maiden or claiming, 4 lbs, Of a race other than claiming, 6 lbs. Closed Thursday, July 31 with 13 nominations.

Value of Race: $150,000 Winner $90,000; second $30,000; third $18,000; fourth $9,000; fifth $3,000. Mutuel Pool $566,104.00 Exacta Pool $286,736.00 Quinella Pool $39,577.00 Trifecta Pool $266,077.00 Superfecta Pool $113,592.00

Last Raced	Horse	M/Eqt.	A.Wt	PP	St	¼	½	Str	Fin	Jockey	Odds $1
6Jly03 7Hol1	Tizdubai	LB	2 118	7	1	2^{½}	2^{2½}	2^{5}	1^{4}	Flores D R	2.00
25Jly03 7Dmr1	Dirty Diana	LBb	2 122	8	2	1^{2½}	1^{3}	1^{1½}	2^{4½}	Smith M E	1.10
17Jly03 1Hol1	Solar Fire	LB	2 118	2	7	7^{2}	6^{2½}	4^{1½}	3^{½}	Stevens G L	28.60
17Apr03 1SA1	Wind Flow	LBb	2 118	6	3	3^{2½}	3^{hd}	3^{hd}	4^{3}	Krone J A	11.90
16Jly03 1Hol1	Madam Bahri	LBb	2 116	4	4	5^{3½}	5^{hd}	5^{3}	5^{1}	Solis A	48.20
4Jly03 4Hol2	Cherish Destiny	LBb	2 118	1	8	8	7^{1½}	8	6no	Baze T C	7.50
26Jly03 9Dmr6	Fabulous Bonus	LB	2 116	5	6	6^{hd}	8	7^{hd}	7^{11}	Martinez F F	57.70
10Jly03 4Hol1	Absolute Nectar	LBb	2 116	3	5	4^{1½}	4^{6}	6^{hd}	8	Valenzuela P A	7.10

OFF AT 5:36 Start Good For All But CHERISH DESTINY, ABSOLUTE NECTAR Won driving. Track fast.
TIME :22, :44^1, 1:10^1, 1:17 (:22.09, :44.35, 1:10.35, 1:17.15)

$2 Mutuel Prices:

7-TIZDUBAI	6.00	3.00	2.80
8-DIRTY DIANA		2.60	2.40
2-SOLAR FIRE			4.20

$1 EXACTA 7-8 PAID $6.50 $2 QUINELLA 7-8 PAID $4.80 $1 TRIFECTA 7-8-2 PAID $74.30 $1 SUPERFECTA 7-8-2-6 PAID $321.50

B. f, (Jan), by Cee's Tizzy-Cee's Song, by Seattle Song. Trainer Harty Eoin. Bred by Cee's Stable LLC (Cal).

TIZDUBAI stalked the pace outside a rival on the backstretch, angled in on the turn, came out into the stretch, rallied to the front under some urging a sixteenth out and pulled clear. DIRTY DIANA quickly sped to a clear lead, set the pace a bit off the rail, continued just off the inside in the stretch, could not match the winner late but was clearly second best. SOLAR FIRE off a bit awkwardly and a bit crowded at the break, steadied when forced inward in the early going, chased a bit off the rail, moved up outside a rival on the turn, came out some and edged a rival for third. WIND FLOW angled in and stalked the pace inside, fell back some on the turn and was edged for the show, then was unsaddled a pole from the wire but walked off. MADAM BAHRI chased a bit off the rail on the backstretch and inside on the turn and lacked a further response. CHERISH DESTINY stumbled at the start then steadied in the opening strides when forced inward, saved ground off the pace, went three deep into the turn and did not rally. FABULOUS BONUS chased outside a rival on the backstretch, dropped back on the turn and failed to menace. ABSOLUTE NECTAR bobbled at the start then veered inward, went up inside on the backstretch, came out on the turn and three deep into the stretch and gave way.

Owners— 1, Darley Stud Management LLC; 2, Watson & Weitman Performances LLC; 3, Chaiken Family Trust & Green Lanter; 4, Walski Peter A & Walski Barbara; 5, Running K Stable; 6, David J Lanzman Racing Stable; 7, Gomez Ronald; 8, Soares Michael & Suarez Pablo

Trainers—1, Harty Eoin; 2, Baffert Bob; 3, Sahadi Jenine; 4, Dominguez Caesar F; 5, Dominguez Caesar F; 6, O'Neill Doug; 7, Baker D Wayne; 8, O'Neill Doug

$2 Daily Double (5-7) Paid $20.20; Daily Double Pool $40,400.
$1 Pick Three (4-5-7) Paid $121.70; Pick Three Pool $133,210.

TENTH RACE

Ellis Park

AUGUST 9, 2003

1⅛ MILES. (1.47³) 22nd Running of THE GARDENIA HANDICAP. Grade III. Purse $200,000 A HANDICAP FOR FILLIES AND MARES THREE-YEARS-OLD AND UPWARD. By subscription of $200 each to accompany the nomination, $1,000 to pass the entry box and $1,000 additional to start. Supplementary nominations may be made by 12:00 PM Friday, August 1, 2003 by payment of $7,500 (includes entry and starting fees). $200,000 guaranteed. The Association's money to be divided: $120,000 to winner, $40,000 to second, $22,000 to third, $12,000 to fourth and $6,000 to fifth. Weights to be announced Saturday, August 2,2003. Starters to be named through the entry box by the usual time of closing. This field will be limited to twelve starters. Preference to start will be given to those horses having been assigned the highest weights (scale considered).

Value of Race: $200,000 Winner $120,000; second $40,000; third $22,000; fourth $12,000; fifth $6,000.   Mutuel Pool $313,606.00 Exacta Pool $221,809.00   Trifecta Pool $229,490.00 Superfecta Pool $82,372.00

Last Raced	Horse	M/Eqt. A.Wt	PP	St	¼	½	¾	Str	Fin	Jockey	Odds $1
21Jun03 8Hol3	Bare Necessities	L 4 119	9	6	6²	6³½	6²½	11½	15¼	Douglas R R	0.40
28Jun03 5AP1	Desert Gold	L 4 114	1	2	3¹	3¹	4hd	2½	22¾	Bejarano R	9.80
11Jly03 6PrM2	So Much More	L 4 115	2	1	2½	2hd	1½	3²½	3hd	Melancon L	9.80
12Jly03 10ElP1	Lead Story	L 4 115	5	9	9	9	8¹½	45	48½	Borel C H	7.20
5Jly03 5Hol7	Achnasheen	L 3 109	6	8	8¹½	8¹	9	6²	55¼	Butler D P	26.80
19Jly03 12Crc1	Stormy Frolic	Lb 4 114	7	5	5³	5¹½	3hd	51	6²½	Velez R I	30.00
6Jun03 8AP2	Lakenheath	L 5 114	4	4	4hd	4hd	5¹½	83	7½	Court J K	8.20
12Jly03 10ElP6	Reason To Talk	Lbf 4 113	8	7	76½	78	72	7½	8¹²	Coa E D	49.50
29Jun03 8LS1	Peaceful Place	Lb 4 113	3	3	13½	11	2hd	9	9	Martinez J R Jr	72.90

OFF AT 5:28 Start Good. Won driving. Track fast.

TIME :22⁴, :46², 1:11³, 1:37², 1:50 (:22.91, :46.53, 1:11.78, 1:37.52, 1:50.09)

$2 Mutuel Prices:

9–BARE NECESSITIES	2.80	2.40	2.10
1–DESERT GOLD		5.20	2.10
2–SO MUCH MORE			2.10

$2 EXACTA 9–1 PAID $16.60 $2 TRIFECTA 9–1–2 PAID $54.40 $1 SUPERFECTA 9–1–2–5 PAID $69.10

Gr/ro f, by Silver Deputy–Shrewd Vixen, by Spectacular Bid. Trainer Dollase Wallace. Bred by Iron County Farms Inc (Ky).

BARE NECESSITIES quickly settled in hand four or five wide, raced in behind the leaders on the backstretch, edged closer while within herself on the far turn, split foes four wide a quarter-mile out, quickly gained command when straightened for the drive, was roused right-handed, then, after the rider switched the whip to the left side, drew off as much the best. DESERT GOLD, nicely placed along the inside from the outset, saved ground for six furlongs, moved out between foes three wide while rallying, was just inside the winner on even terms entering the stretch but couldn't match strides in the drive as second best. SO MUCH MORE tracked front-running PEACEFUL PLACE from early on three or four wide, inched to a narrow lead on the far turn but weakened upon entering the stretch. LEAD STORY, reserved early and angled inside, reached contention upon going six furlongs, came out between horses five wide into the stretch to make a run but was empty the last eighth. ACHNASHEEN, outrun for six furlongs, was bumped in tight quarter while between foes at the quarter-mile ground and never threatened while improving position late. STORMY FROLIC stalked the leaders five wide to the stretch and flattened out. LAKENHEATH, never far back while four wide, leaned in bumping lightly with ACHNASHEEN a quarter-mile out and was finished soon after. REASON TO TALK, three wide while outrun to the far turn, never seriously menaced. PEACEFUL PLACE sprinted clear near the inside, showed the way for nearly six furlongs and gave way readily soon after.

Owners— 1, Iron County Farms Inc; 2, Stonerside Stable LLC; 3, Schettine William C; 4, Miles A S Jr; 5, Sterling Stud; 6, Stride Rite Racing Stable; 7, Tafel James B; 8, K & K Racing Stable LLC; 9, Everest Stables

Trainers— 1, Dollase Wallace; 2, Byrne Patrick B; 3, O'Callaghan Niall M; 4, Nafzger Carl A; 5, Shirota Mitch; 6, Wolfson Milton W; 7, Cilio Gene A; 8, Vance David R; 9, Keen Dallas E

$1 Pick Three (4–4–9) Paid $34.30; Pick Three Pool $12,189.

TENTH RACE

Monmouth

AUGUST 9, 2003

6 FURLONGS. (1.07⁴) 69th Running of THE SAPLING. Grade III. Purse $100,000 TWO YEAR-OLDS. By subscription of $100 each which should accompany the nomination. $1,500 to enter. The winner to receive $60,000; $20,000 to second; $11,000 to third; $6,000 to fourth and $3,000 to fifth. Weight: 120 lbs. Maidens allowed 5lbs. Starters to be named through the entry box by the usual time of closing. Supplementary nominations may be made at time of entry by payment of a fee of $7,500 each which includes entry and starting fees. The owner of the winner to receive a trophy. NOMINATIONS CLOSED Saturday, July 26, 2003 with TWENTY FIVE (25).

Value of Race: $100,000 Winner $60,000; second $20,000; third $11,000; fourth $6,000; fifth $3,000.   Mutuel Pool $230,678.00 Exacta Pool $154,233.00   Trifecta Pool $85,549.00

Last Raced	Horse	M/Eqt. A.Wt	PP	St	¼	½	Str	Fin	Jockey	Odds $1
27Jun03 8PrM1	Dashboard Drummer	L 2 120	1	6	5½	42	3²	12½	Ferrer J C	4.40
20Jly03 3Mth1	Deputy Storm	Lb 2 120	5	2	11	11½	12	2½	Bravo J	0.70
5Jly03 8Crc2	Charming Jim	L 2 120	7	3	2hd	23	22	32	Coa E M	3.90
11Jly03 5Mth1	Limit Free	L 2 120	2	5	69	69	4hd	44½	Cruz C	a–9.90
6Jly03 10CD4	Bustin' Out	Lb 2 120	4	4	33	31	53½	53½	King E L Jr	6.40
7Jly03 1Pha1	Johnny Tornado	2 120	3	7	7	7	7	6¹	Estrada E A	32.60
20Jly03 2Mth1	Stringtown Wonder	Lb 2 120	6	1	4³½	5¹	64	7	Lopez C C	a–9.90

a–Coupled: Limit Free and Stringtown Wonder.

OFF AT 5:06 Start Good. Won driving. Track sloppy.

TIME :21¹, :43⁴, :56³, 1:10⁴ (:21.31, :43.82, :56.76, 1:10.84)

$2 Mutuel Prices:

2–DASHBOARD DRUMMER	10.80	3.60	2.10
5–DEPUTY STORM		2.40	2.10
6–CHARMING JIM			2.10

$2 EXACTA 2–5 PAID $25.00 $2 TRIFECTA 2–5–6 PAID $46.00

Dk. b. or br. g, (Apr), by Alamocitos–Groovin Moment, by Magic Moment II*Fr. Trainer Iwinski Allen. Bred by (Okla).

DASHBOARD DRUMMER, briefly unsettled at the start, rated back inside, started his drive angling out through the turn, was widest turning for home, sustained a long drive drifting out through the stretch and drew clear the final yards. DEPUTY STORM rated a fast pace just off the rail, was under pressure drifting out through the stretch then outfinished the final seventy yards. CHARMING JIM chased the pace from the four path, closed to the pacesetter in late stretch but ran out of ground. LIMIT FREE showed no speed in mid track, accelerated drifting inward through the stretch but leveled out the final sixteenth. BUSTIN' OUT chased the pace, dropped back off the rail down the turn and was empty for the drive. JOHNNY TORNADO dropped well back showing no speed and never factored. STRINGTOWN WONDER chased the early pace from the outside, angled in saving ground for the turn then weakened.

Owners— 1, Double S & Preferred Pals Stables &; 2, Spence James C; 3, Carrion Jaime S; 4, Fehsenfeld Mack; 5, Overbrook Farm; 6, Patton Joanne; 7, Fehsenfeld Mack

Trainers— 1, Iwinski Allen; 2, Pletcher Todd A; 3, Plesa Edward Jr; 4, Manning Dennis J; 5, Lukas D Wayne; 6, Seeger Robert J; 7, Manning Dennis J

$2 Pick Three (8–11–2) Paid $772.40; Pick Three Pool $9,785.

EIGHTH RACE

Mountaineer

AUGUST 9, 2003

1⅛ MILES. (1.46¹) 31st Running of THE WEST VIRGINIA DERBY. Grade III. Purse $600,000 FOR THREE YEAR OLDS. No Nomination Fee. $750 to pass the entry box. $2,000 additional to start. WEIGHT 122 lbs. Winners of Two Grade I races at a Mile or Over in 2003.3 lbs. Additional; Non–winners of a Grade I race at a Mile or Over in 2003. Allowed 3 lbs.; Non–winners of a Grade II race at a Mile or Over in 2003.5 lbs.; Non–winners of a Grade III race at a Mile or Over in 2003. 7 lbs.; Non–winners of $150,000 at a Mile or Over in 2003. 9 lbs.; Non–winners of a Sweepstakes at a Mile or Over in 2003. 11 lbs. THIS RACE WILL NOT BE DIVIDED. This race is limited to Twelve Starters, with Four Also Eligibles. In the event more than Twelve entries pass through the entry box, the Starters will be determined with first preference given to the Highest Grade Winners, and second preference given to those that have accumulated the highest total earnings at the close of entries.

Value of Race: $600,000 Winner $360,000; second $120,000; third $60,000; fourth $30,000; fifth $18,000; sixth $12,000. **Mutuel Pool** $414,178.00 Perfecta Pool $235,125.00 Trifecta Pool $175,767.00

Last Raced	Horse	M/Eqt. A.Wt	PP	St	¼	½	¾	Str	Fin	Jockey	Odds $1
19Jly03 8Pha¹	Soto	LBf 3 111	3	4	2²	2²	1 1	2⁶	1nk	Dominguez R A	2.20
7Jun03 11Bel⁴	Dynever	LB 3 117	1	3	5½	4²	2³	1hd	25½	Prado E S	1.20
21May03 7Bel¹	Colita	LBb 3 111	7	7	7²	5 1	3²	3hd	31½	Santos J A	5.10
26Jly03 1Crc¹	Supah Blitz	LBb 3 113	9	6	9	8²	4½	4⁶	42½	Velasquez C	7.10
12Jly03 8WO¹	Mobil	LB 3 117	4	8	8 1	7hd	6 1	5 12	59¼	Chavez J F	7.70
11Jly03 7Hol³	Coax Kid	LB 3 111	6	9	6²	3½	7 7	6½	63½	Lumpkins J	38.00
5Jly03 11Tdn¹	Cat Singer	LBf 3 113	2	1	1 1	1hd	5 1	7 13	710¾	Rosario H L Jr	46.60
29Jly03 4Mnr⁷	Miss Karry Thenews	LB 3 112	5	2	3hd	9	812	820	821	Krigger K	212.30
6Jun03 8Mnr⁸	Dr. E. Claire	LB 3 113	8	5	4hd	6³	9	9	9	Salguero S C	253.20

OFF AT 5:21 Start Good For All But COAX KID Won driving. Track fast.

TIME :23³, :47², 1:10⁴, 1:34³, 1:46¹ (:23.66, :47.45, 1:10.80, 1:34.60, 1:46.29)

New Track Record

$2 Mutuel Prices:

5–SOTO	6.40	3.40	2.60
1–DYNEVER		2.80	2.40
10–COLITA			2.80

$2 PERFECTA 5–1 PAID $14.80 $2 TRIFECTA 5–1–10 PAID $51.40

Ch. c, (Feb), by Dehere–Subtle Fragrance, by Crafty Prospector. Trainer Dickinson Michael W. Bred by Domino Stud of Lexington LLC (Ky).

SOTO used to contest the early pace, went head and head with CAT SINGER to the 1/2 mile pole, wrested a short lead on final turn, hooked entering the stretch by DYNEVER, battled back on the inside to prevail determinedly . DYNEVER never far back, content to track the pace for a 1/2 mile, angled out and prompted to strong move nearing the 1/4 pole, hooked SOTO as the pair reached upper stretch, went in tandem late, ceded in final strides . COLITA unhurried at the start, edged steadily closer to the 1/4 pole, couldn't go with top pair, was extended to hold off others . SUPAH BLITZ dropped back early, varied little to the 1/2, gave a mild rally passing tired rivals on final turn, continued with an even response through the stretch . MOBIL stumbled at the start, tried to mount a move leaving the backstretch, proved no menace under a drive . COAX KID reared up as the starting gate opened, was rushed 5 wide into the first turn, hustled to leaders nearing the 1/2 mile pole, flattened out on second turn and gave way . CAT SINGER showed early speed, contested on the inside of SOTO for a 1/2 mile, came up empty into final turn, put away at the head of the stretch . MISS KARRY THENEWS was rushed for brief contention, gave way soon after entering the backstretch . DR. E. CLAIRE sent along while losing ground, wilted after a 1/2 mile .

Owners— 1, Galopp LLC; 2, Wills Catherine & Karches Peter; 3, Team Valor Stables LLC; 4, Bee Bee Stables J Bush & Jacqueline; 5, Gus Schickedanz; 6, Royce Jaime; 7, Sugar Joe & Daniels Eugene Jr; 8, Kathleen Price; 9, Thornton Thomas L

Trainers—1, Dickinson Michael W; 2, Clement Christophe; 3, Pletcher Todd A; 4, Tortora Emanuel; 5, Keogh Michael; 6, O'Neill Doug; 7, Palacios Luis A; 8, Price Kathleen A; 9, Thornton Nancy

Scratched— Outta Here (13Jly03 6HOL⁴), During (3Aug03 9SAR⁶), Lone Star Sky (14Jun03 7CD²)

$2 Pick Three (9–1–5) Paid $323.40; Pick Three Pool $24,589.

NINTH RACE
Saratoga
AUGUST 9, 2003

1½ MILES. (Inner Turf)(2.23^{1}) 29th Running of THE SWORD DANCER INVITATIONAL HANDICAP. Grade I. Purse $500,000. (Up to $36,000 NYSBFOA). THREE YEAR OLDS AND UPWARD. By invitation only with no subscription, entry or starting fees. The purse to be divided 60% to the owner of the winner, 20% to second, 11% to third, 6% to fourth and 3% to fifth. Trophies will be presented to the winning owner, trainer and jockey. The New York Racing Association reserves the right to transfer this race to the Main Track. In the event that this race it taken off the turf, it may be subject to downgrading upon review by the Graded Stakes Committee.

Value of Race: $500,000 Winner $300,000; second $100,000; third $55,000; fourth $30,000; fifth $15,000. Mutuel Pool $1,348,563.0 Exacta Pool $944,592.00 Trifecta Pool $679,858.00 Superfecta Pool $162,395.00

Last Raced	Horse	M/Eqt.	A.Wt	PP	¼	½	1	1¼	Str	Fin	Jockey	Odds $1
12Jly03 10Bel1	Whitmore's Conn	Lb	5 115	5	9 1	9½	11	10hd	3hd	11¼	Samyn J L	24.75
12Jly03 10Bel3	Macaw-IR	Lbf	4 114	10	7hd	7hd	83½	9½	63½	2nk	Bridgmohan S X	15.30
25Jly03 8Sar3	Slew Valley	L	6 114	7	5½	5 1	7hd	4hd	21½	3¾	Castellano J J	59.75
5Jly03 10Mth5	Denon	L	5 122	11	8 2	83½	6½	1½	1½	4 1	Bailey J D	2.15
5Jly03 8AP2	Dr. Brendler	L	5 116	3	10hd	11	10½	7½	5hd	5no	Guidry M	12.40
20Jly03 7Hol1	Puerto Banus	Lb	4 115	2	11	101½	9 1	8hd	4hd	67¾	Espinoza V	18.20
5Jly03 10Mth6	Kim Loves Bucky	L	6 115	6	21½	2 1	21½	6hd	81½	7hd	Sellers S J	20.80
5Jly03 10Mth3	Lunar Sovereign	L	4 114	4	4½	4½	3hd	5 1	73½	86¼	Migliore R	4.00
5Jly03 8AP1	Ballingarry-IR	L	4 119	8	3½	3hd	4½	11	10hd	9½	Velazquez J R	4.00
5Jly03 5Hol8	Meridiana-GE		3 109	9	6 1	6 1	5hd	3½	9½	10nk	Demuro M	56.75
5Jly03 10Mth1	Balto Star	L	5 119	1	1½	1½	1½	2 1	11	11	Velez J A Jr	5.70

OFF AT 5:40 Start Good. Won driving. Course good.

TIME :24^{2}, :49, 1:13, 1:37^{4}, 2:03^{1}, 2:28 (:24.54, :49.16, 1:13.12, 1:37.81, 2:03.24, 2:28.14)

$2 Mutuel Prices:			
6–WHITMORE'S CONN	51.50	22.60	13.80
11–MACAW–IR		14.00	8.10
8–SLEW VALLEY			16.80

$2 EXACTA 6–11 PAID $511.00 $2 TRIFECTA 6–11–8 PAID $13,969.00 $2 SUPERFECTA 6–11–8–13 PAID $40,598.00

Dk. b. or br. h, by Kris S.–Albonita, by Deputed Testamony. Trainer Schulhofer Randy. Bred by Bud Wolf & Joe D'Agostino (NY).

WHITMORE'S CONN dropped back soon after the start, raced in the back of the pack for a good portion of the way, angled to the outside leaving the far turn, circled seven wide at the top of the stretch, unleashed a strong late run in the middle of the track to challenge inside the furlong marker then edged clear under strong right hand encouragement. MACAW (IRE) was unhurried for six furlongs while saving ground, closed the gap midway on the turn, raced in traffic while trapped along the rail approaching the stretch, swung five wide for room at the top of the stretch, split horses while gaining in midstretch then finished willingly to edge SLEW VALLEY for the place. SLEW VALLEY was outrun early, moved up between horses along the backstretch, raced in the middle of the pack to the far turn, rallied four wide to reach contention in upper stretch, surged past DENON to gain a slim lead inside the furlong marker, battled into deep stretch and yielded late. DENON was unhurried while well back for six furlongs, was strung out six wide along the backstretch, made a strong run while four wide to take the lead on the turn, continued on the front into midstretch then weakened under pressure in the final eighth. DR. BRENDLER was outrun early while saving ground, raced just inside the winner along the backstretch, moved out on the far turn, advanced six wide into the stretch then rallied mildly, PUERTO BANUS raced far back to the turn then failed to threaten while improving his position. KIM LOVES BUCKY prompted the pace from outside to the far turn and steadily tired thereafter. LUNAR SOVEREIGN raced in close contention along the inside for a mile, dropped back on the turn then lacked a further response. BALLINGARRY (IRE) raced up close while three wide for a mile and gave way. MERIDIANA (GER) raced in the middle of the pack while five wide for a mile, lodged a mild rally inside DENON on the turn and gave way. BALTO STAR set the pace along the inside to the turn and faltered.

Owners— 1, Shanley Michael & Lynn; 2, Melillo George & Sandra; 3, Rich Meadow Farm; 4, Gann Edmund A & Flaxman Stable; 5, O'Toole Francis J; 6, Steve Taub Neil Papiano & Michael M; 7, Glenney Kim; 8, Darley Stable; 9, Sidney L Port Marsha Naify Laura De; 10, Klaus Hofmann; 11, Anstu Stables

Trainers—1, Schulhofer Randy; 2, Tagg Barclay; 3, Sciacca Gary; 4, Frankel Robert; 5, Motion H Graham; 6, Mulhall Kristin; 7, Glenney John; 8, McLaughlin Kiaran P; 9, De Seroux Laura; 10, Blume Hans; 11, Pletcher Todd A

Scratched— With Anticipation (5Jly03 10MTH7), Mariensky (4Jly03 10BEL6), Quest Star (12Jly03 10BEL2), State Shinto (12Jly03 10BEL5)

EIGHTH RACE
Del Mar
AUGUST 10, 2003

1$\frac{1}{16}$ MILES. (1.40) 33rd Running of THE CLEMENT L. HIRSCH HANDICAP. Grade II. Purse $300,000. FILLIES AND MARES, THREE-YEAR-OLDS AND UPWARD. By subscription of $300 each, which shall accompany the nomination, or by supplementary nomination of $3,000 each by Sunday, August 3, $3,000 additional to start. Weights: Monday August 4. Closed Thursday July 31 with 8 nominations.

Value of Race: $300,000 Winner $180,000; second $60,000; third $36,000; fourth $18,000; fifth $6,000. Mutuel Pool $1,009,490.0 Exacta Pool $445,454.00 Quinella Pool $44,331.00

Last Raced	Horse	M/Eqt.	A.Wt	PP	St	¼	½	¾	Str	Fin	Jockey	Odds $1
21Jun03 8Hol1	Azeri	LB	5 127	1	1	1 1	1½	11½	12½	13¼	Smith M E	0.30
9Mar03 8SA4	Got Koko	LBb	4 118	2	2	3 1	3hd	2hd	2hd	2hd	Solis A	4.20
21Jun03 8Hol4	Tropical Blossom	LBb	5 108	4	5	4 2	5	3½	32½	34½	Krone J A	18.90
21Jun03 8Hol2	Sister Girl Blues	LBf	4 109	3	3	2½	2 1	4½	41½	4 5	McKee J	5.60
5Jly03 7Hol5	Angel Gift	LB	5 114	5	4	5	4hd	5	5	5	Valdivia J Jr	24.50

OFF AT 5:42 Start Good. Won handily. Track fast.

TIME :23^{1}, :47, 1:11, 1:35^{3}, 1:42 (:23.34, :47.09, 1:11.04, 1:35.65, 1:42.12)

$2 Mutuel Prices:			
1–AZERI	2.60	2.10	—
2–GOT KOKO		2.10	—
4–TROPICAL BLOSSOM		—	—

$1 EXACTA 1–2 PAID $2.70 $2 QUINELLA 1–2 PAID $4.20

Ch. m, by Jade Hunter–Zodiac Miss*Aus, by Ahonoora. Trainer De Seroux Laura. Bred by Allen E Paulson (Ky).

AZERI a bit washy at the gate, bobbled slightly in the opening stride, sped to the early lead, set the pace a bit off the rail, turned back a bid on the backstretch, inched away on the second turn, was pushed along some to open up in early stretch and drew clear in hand. GOT KOKO also bobbled slightly at the start, raced close up stalking the winner inside, came out into the stretch, was not a match for that one in the drive but gamely held second. TROPICAL BLOSSOM stalked outside a rival then between horses on the backstretch and second turn, came out into the stretch and was edged for the place. SISTER GIRL BLUES stalked the early pace off the rail, bid outside the winner on the backstretch, dropped back three deep between horses on the second turn, angled in some into the stretch and weakened. ANGEL GIFT three deep early, angled in on the first turn, came out and stalked three deep on the backstretch and four wide on the second turn and also weakened.

Owners— 1, Allen E Paulson Living Trust; 2, Headley Aase & Leung Paul; 3, Wygod Mr & Mrs Martin J; 4, Everest Stables; 5, Delahoussaye Enterprises Strauss Ri

Trainers—1, De Seroux Laura; 2, Headley Bruce; 3, Canani Julio C; 4, Knight Terry; 5, Gallagher Patrick

---

$2 Daily Double (5–1) Paid $8.20; Daily Double Pool $47,840.
$1 Pick Three (2–5–1) Paid $26.60; Pick Three Pool $96,452.

NINTH RACE
Saratoga
AUGUST 10, 2003

6 FURLONGS. (1.08) 19th Running of THE ALFRED G. VANDERBILT HANDICAP. Grade II. Purse $200,000. (Up to $24,800 NYSBFOA). THREE YEAR OLDS AND UPWARD. By subscription of $200 each, which should accompany the nomination; $1,000 to pass the entry box, $1,000 to start. The purse to be divided 60% to the winner, 20% to second, 11% to third, 6% to fourth and 3% to fifth. Trophies will be presented to the winning owner, trainer and jockey. Closed Saturday, July 26, 2003 with 17 Nominations.

Value of Race: $200,000 Winner $120,000; second $40,000; third $22,000; fourth $12,000; fifth $6,000. Mutuel Pool $707,446.00 Exacta Pool $519,172.00 Trifecta Pool $194,229.00

Last Raced	Horse	M/Eqt.	A.	Wt	PP	St	¼	½	Str	Fin	Jockey	Odds $1
12Jly03 ^{12}Crc^{2}	Private Horde	Lbf	4	115	5	4	$3^{1\frac{1}{2}}$	3^{3}	2^{hd}	1^{5}	Lumpkins J	10.00
21Jun03 ^{9}CD^{1}	Mountain General	Lb	5	118	1	3	5	5	4^{hd}	2^{hd}	Day P	6.70
12Jly03 ^{9}Bel^{1}	Mike's Classic	Lb	4	114	4	2	$2^{2\frac{1}{2}}$	2^{2}	1^{hd}	3^{nk}	Ganpath R	3.50
12Jly03 ^{12}Crc^{1}	Shake You Down	Lbf	5	123	2	1	1^{hd}	1^{hd}	$3^{5\frac{1}{2}}$	4^{4}	Luzzi M J	0.55
4Jly03 ^{8}Bel^{3}	State City	L	4	117	3	5	4^{5}	$4^{2\frac{1}{2}}$	5	5	Chavez J F	9.90

OFF AT 5:59 Start Good. Won driving. Track sloppy.
TIME :22, :44^{3}, :56^{3}, 1:09 (:22.18, :44.72, :56.76, 1:09.18)

$2 Mutuel Prices:

7–PRIVATE HORDE	22.00	7.40	12.80
2–MOUNTAIN GENERAL		7.00	12.40
6–MIKE'S CLASSIC			9.70

$2 EXACTA 7–2 PAID $127.00 $2 TRIFECTA 7–2–6 PAID $363.00

B. c, by Brunswick–Manila Rose, by Manila. Trainer Cain Joe. Bred by Billy Tucker (Ky).

PRIVATE HORDE settled in good position behind the dueling leaders, launched a rally from outside on the turn, angled four wide entering the stretch, closed the gap to challenge in midstretch, surged to the front leaving the furlong marker, then edged away under good handling. MOUNTAIN GENERAL trailed along the backstretch, angled four wide while gaining at the quarter pole then closed strongly in the middle of the pack to nip MIKE'S CLASSIC for the place. MIKE'S CLASSIC rushed up from outside to contest the early pace, dueled heads apart outside the winner into upper stretch, gained a brief lead a furlong out then weakened in the final sixteenth. SHAKE YOU DOWN battled heads apart along the rail for five furlongs and weakened from his early efforts. STATE CITY saved ground to the top of the stretch and lacked a strong closing bid.

Owners— 1, Tucker Billy R; 2, Asmussen Keith A; 3, Middletown Stables; 4, Cole Robert L Jr; 5, Godolphin Racing Inc

Trainers—1, Cain Joe; 2, Asmussen Steven M; 3, Jerkens H Allen; 4, Lake Scott A; 5, Albertrani Thomas

Scratched— Najran (4Jly03 ^{8}BEL^{4}), Sunray Spirit (17Jly03 ^{8}BEL^{1})

EIGHTH RACE
Saratoga
AUGUST 11, 2003

6½ FURLONGS. (1.14^{2}) 88th Running of THE ADIRONDACK. Grade II. Purse $150,000. (Up to $21,200 NYSBFOA). FILLIES, TWO YEAR OLDS. By subscription of $150 each, which should accompany the nomination; $750 to pass the entry box, $750 to start. The purse to be divided 60% to the winner, 20% to second, 11% to third, 6% to fourth and 3%to fifth. 122 lbs. Non–winners of $60,000; or $35,000 twice allowed 2 lbs.; two races, 4 lbs.; a race, 6 lbs. (maiden and claiming races not considered). Trophies will be presented to the winning owner, trainer and jockey. Closed Saturday, July 26, 2003 with 23 Nominations.

Value of Race: $150,000 Winner $90,000; second $30,000; third $16,500; fourth $9,000; fifth $4,500. Mutuel Pool $514,507.00 Exacta Pool $439,156.00 Trifecta Pool $366,044.00

Last Raced	Horse	M/Eqt.	A.	Wt	PP	St	¼	½	Str	Fin	Jockey	Odds $1
11Jly03 ^{3}Bel^{1}	Whoopi Cat		2	116	5	3	$3^{1\frac{1}{2}}$	$2^{\frac{1}{2}}$	2^{2}	$1^{1\frac{1}{4}}$	Prado E S	1.35
29Jun03 ^{9}Bel^{2}	Unbridled Beauty	L	2	116	4	2	$1^{\frac{1}{2}}$	$1^{\frac{1}{2}}$	1^{hd}	$2^{3\frac{3}{4}}$	Bailey J D	2.50
20Jly03 ^{6}Mth^{1}	Eye Dazzler	L	2	116	2	4	$2^{\frac{1}{2}}$	4^{2}	3^{hd}	$3^{\frac{1}{2}}$	Coa E M	15.20
4Jly03 ^{6}Bel^{1}	Lokoya	L	2	116	3	5	4^{hd}	$3^{\frac{1}{2}}$	$4^{4\frac{1}{2}}$	$4^{8\frac{3}{4}}$	Velazquez J R	2.45
24Jly03 ^{4}Sar^{1}	Wild Berry	L	2	116	1	7	5^{8}	5^{6}	5^{10}	$5^{7\frac{1}{4}}$	Velasquez C	13.90
2Jly03 ^{3}Bel^{1}	Pierian Spring		2	116	6	1	$6^{\frac{1}{2}}$	$6^{1\frac{1}{2}}$	$6^{1\frac{1}{2}}$	$6^{3\frac{1}{4}}$	Albarado R J	51.00
17Jly03 ^{4}Bel^{3}	Earthquake Ride	L	2	116	7	6	7	7	7	7	Castellano J J	40.25

OFF AT 4:47 Start Good. Won driving. Track muddy.
TIME :21^{1}, :44^{3}, 1:10^{3}, 1:17^{2} (:21.37, :44.79, 1:10.67, 1:17.51)

$2 Mutuel Prices:

5–WHOOPI CAT	4.70	2.80	2.50
4–UNBRIDLED BEAUTY		3.10	2.70
2–EYE DAZZLER			4.40

$2 EXACTA 5–4 PAID $13.00 $2 TRIFECTA 5–4–2 PAID $51.50

Dk. b. or br. f, (Feb), by Tale of the Cat–Whoopi*NZ, by Sky Filou*NZ. Trainer Biancone Patrick L. Bred by Richard Giacopelli (Ky).

WHOOPI CAT bobbled at the start, moved up quickly outside, rallied three wide approaching the stretch, dug in resolutely when roused and was clear under the wire, driving. UNBRIDLED BEAUTY broke to the inside, was bumped after the start, was hustled up to get the lead, set a strong pace and dug in gamely in the stretch. EYE DAZZLER was bumped after the start, showed good speed along the inside, chased the pace and weakened on the rail in the final furlong. LOKOYA was bumped at the start, was hustled outside, put in a four wide run nearing the stretch and drifted in while tiring in the stretch. WILD BERRY was hustled from the gate, chased the pace along the inside, came wide into the stretch and tired. PIERIAN SPRING was hustled from the gate but had no response and tired in the stretch. EARTHQUAKE RIDE dropped back early, raced wide throughout and tired.

Owners— 1, Smith Derrick & Tabor Michael; 2, Lewis Robert B & Beverly J; 3, Lewis Lee; 4, Scatuorchio James T; 5, Steeplechase Farm; 6, Old Brookside Farm & Acqua Nova Sta; 7, S J Bee Stable

Trainers—1, Biancone Patrick L; 2, Lukas D Wayne; 3, Hennig Mark; 4, Pletcher Todd A; 5, Gorham Michael E; 6, Mueller Russell; 7, Orseno Joseph

EIGHTH RACE
Saratoga
AUGUST 13, 2003

6½ FURLONGS. (1.14^{2}) 101st Running of THE SARATOGA SPECIAL. Grade II. Purse $150,000 (Up to $21,100 NYSBFOA) FOR TWO YEAR OLDS. By subscription of $150 each, which should accompany the nomination; $750 to pass the entry box, $750 to start. The purse to be divided 60% to the winner, 20% to second, 11% to third, 6% to fourth and 3% to fifth. 122 lbs. Non-winners of $60,000; or $35,000 twice allowed 2 lbs.; two races, 4 lbs.; a race, 6 lbs. (maiden and claiming races not considered). Trophies will be presented to the winning owner, trainer and jockey. Closed Saturday, August 2, 2003 with 21 Nominations.

Value of Race: $150,000 Winner $90,000; second $30,000; third $16,500; fourth $9,000; fifth $4,500. Mutuel Pool $666,581.00 Exacta Pool $507,084.00 Trifecta Pool $337,232.00

Last Raced	Horse	M/Eqt.	A.Wt	PP	St	¼	½	Str	Fin	Jockey	Odds $1
6Jly03 ^{10}CD^{3}	Cuvee	L	2 122	7	1	1^{1}	1^{1}	1^{6}	$1^{7\frac{1}{2}}$	Bailey J D	2.75
10Jly03 ^{3}Mth^{1}	Pomeroy		2 118	8	2	3^{1}	$2^{2\frac{1}{2}}$	2^{3}	$2^{2\frac{3}{4}}$	Prado E S	1.70
6Jly03 ^{10}CD^{1}	Limehouse	L	2 122	2	6	$5^{2\frac{1}{2}}$	5^{6}	3^{6}	$3^{4\frac{1}{2}}$	Albarado R J	3.00
23Jly03 ^{4}Sar^{1}	El Prado Rob	L	2 116	3	5	8	7^{7}	$5^{\frac{1}{2}}$	$4^{6\frac{1}{2}}$	Day P	17.80
12Jly03 ^{5}Bel^{1}	Tequesta		2 116	5	8	$7^{1\frac{1}{2}}$	$6^{1\frac{1}{2}}$	$6^{1\frac{1}{2}}$	5^{4}	Migliore R	14.20
24Jly03 ^{8}Sar^{4}	Boston Brahmin	Lb	2 116	4	3	2^{hd}	3^{hd}	4^{hd}	$6^{3\frac{3}{4}}$	Velasquez C	a-8.20
20Jly03 ^{8}ElP^{1}	Toin And Boin	L	2 118	1	4	$4^{1\frac{1}{2}}$	4^{hd}	7^{15}	7^{16}	Perret C	17.40
9Jly03 ^{3}Bel^{1}	Desert Patrol	Lb	2 116	6	7	6^{hd}	8	8	8	Velazquez J R	a-8.20

a-Coupled: Boston Brahmin and Desert Patrol.

OFF AT 4:49 Start Good. Won ridden out. Track sloppy.
TIME :21^{1}, :44^{2}, 1:09^{1}, 1:15^{4} (:21.28, :44.51, 1:09.33, 1:15.97)

$2 Mutuel Prices:

6-CUVEE	7.50	3.50	2.60
7-POMEROY		3.30	2.20
3-LIMEHOUSE			2.50

$2 EXACTA 6-7 PAID $21.60 $2 TRIFECTA 6-7-3 PAID $52.50

Ch. c, (Mar), by Carson City-Christmas Star, by Star de Naskra. Trainer Asmussen Steven M. Bred by (Ky).

CUVEE sprinted clear soon after the start, maintained a clear advantage going into the far turn, set a rapid pace under his own power to the top of the stretch, opened a commanding lead in midstretch then drew off under a vigorous hand ride. POMEROY rushed up from outside, chased the winner while three wide into upper stretch but was no match for that rival while clearly best of the others. LIMEHOUSE settled in the middle of the pack along the backstretch, split rivals while making a strong run to reach contention approaching the quarter pole but couldn't sustain his bid. EL PRADO ROB lunged in the air a bit at the start, raced well back for a half, swung wide on the turn then failed to threat while improving his position. TEQUESTA took up after being bumped and pinched back at the start and was never close thereafter. BOSTON BRAHMIN broke outward at the start, rushed up along the rail, chased the winner along the inside to the top of the stretch and tired. TOIN AND BOIN raced just off the early pace, angled five wide on the turn then tired. DESERT PATROL broke inward then stumbled after bumping with TEQUESTA at the start, was never a factor.

Owners— 1, Ron Winchell; 2, Smith Derrick & Tabor Michael; 3, Dogwood Stable; 4, Lapenta Robert V; 5, Drazin Dennis & Kimmel John C; 6, Overbrook Farm; 7, Fayard Keith; 8, Overbrook Farm

Trainers—1, Asmussen Steven M; 2, Biancone Patrick L; 3, Pletcher Todd A; 4, Zito Nicholas P; 5, Kimmel John C; 6, Lukas D Wayne; 7, Werner Ronny; 8, Lukas D Wayne

---

EIGHTH RACE
Arlington
AUGUST 16, 2003

1$\frac{3}{16}$ MILES. (Turf)(1.53^{1}) 14th Running of THE BEVERLY D. Grade I. Purse $700,000 Guaranteed. FILLIES AND MARES, THREE-YEARS-OLD AND UPWARD. By subscription of $300 if made on or before May 14, 2003, with fee to accompany the nomination. Late nomination of $1,500 (each horse) on July 23, 2003. All Beverly D. nominees will automatically be nominated to the 2003 running of the Modesty Handicap with the nomination fee being waived. Supplementary Nomination of $20,000 may be made by August 8, 2003, which includes entry and starting fees. (A refund of $18,000 will be made to any Supplementary Nominee that fails to make the starting field or upon production of a veterinarian certificate indicating that the horse is not fit to run.) Nominees of May 14 and July 23 to pay $5,000 to pass the entry box and $5,000 to start. WEIGHT-FOR-AGE: NORTHERN HEMISPHERE: Three-Year-Old Fillies, 117 lbs.; Older, 123 lbs.; SOUTHERN HEMISPHERE: Three-Year-Old Fillies, 111 lbs.; Four-Year-Old Fillies, 118 lbs.; Older, 123 lbs. This event will be limited to fourteen (14) starters ([7] Non-North American starters and [7] North American starters). (If the management considers it inadvisable to run this race on the turf course, it will be run on the main track at One Mile and Three Sixteenths).

Value of Race: $700,000 Winner $420,000; second $140,000; third $70,000; fourth $35,000; fifth $21,000; sixth $14,000. Mutuel Pool $833,524.00 Exacta Pool $448,888.00 Trifecta Pool $321,050.00 Superfecta Pool $78,837.00

Last Raced	Horse	M/Eqt.	A.Wt	PP	St	¼	½	¾	Str	Fin	Jockey	Odds $1
26Jly03 ^{8}Sar^{2}	Heat Haze-GB	L	4 123	2	7	7	7	7	5^{hd}	$1^{1\frac{1}{4}}$	Valdivia J Jr	1.70
26Jly03 ^{7}AP^{2}	Bien Nicole	L	5 123	3	3	$1^{1\frac{1}{2}}$	$1^{2\frac{1}{2}}$	$1^{\frac{1}{2}}$	$1^{1\frac{1}{2}}$	$2^{\frac{1}{2}}$	Pettinger D R	20.90
26Jly03 ^{8}Sar^{4}	Riskaverse	L	4 123	5	2	$3^{\frac{1}{2}}$	3^{1}	$3^{\frac{1}{2}}$	$4^{1\frac{1}{2}}$	$3^{1\frac{1}{2}}$	Day P	7.10
9Jly03 New^{3}	Walzerkoenigin	L	4 123	6	6	$5^{\frac{1}{2}}$	$6^{1\frac{1}{2}}$	$5^{\frac{1}{2}}$	3^{hd}	$4^{\frac{3}{4}}$	Suborics A	12.20
26Jly03 ^{8}Dmr^{3}	Dublino	L	4 123	4	4	$2^{\frac{1}{2}}$	2^{1}	$2^{\frac{1}{2}}$	$2^{\frac{1}{2}}$	$5^{\frac{3}{4}}$	Desormeaux K J	2.30
12Jly03 ^{9}Cnl^{1}	Dress To Thrill-IR	L	4 123	7	5	$6^{1\frac{1}{2}}$	$5^{\frac{1}{2}}$	6^{1}	$6^{\frac{1}{2}}$	$6^{3\frac{3}{4}}$	Smullen P J	4.40
26Jly03 ^{7}AP^{1}	Owsley	L	5 123	1	1	$4^{\frac{1}{2}}$	4^{hd}	4^{hd}	7	7	Douglas R R	7.30

OFF AT 4:10 Start Good. Won driving. Course good.
TIME :25, :49^{3}, 1:13^{3}, 1:38, 1:55^{4} (:25.04, :49.78, 1:13.68, 1:38.04, 1:55.94)

$2 Mutuel Prices:

3-HEAT HAZE-GB	5.40	3.80	2.80
4-BIEN NICOLE		12.80	5.60
6-RISKAVERSE			4.20

$2 EXACTA 3-4 PAID $107.00 $2 TRIFECTA 3-4-6 PAID $391.40 $2 SUPERFECTA 3-4-6-7 PAID $3,369.80

B. f, by Green Desert-Hasili*Ire, by Kahyasi*Ire. Trainer Frankel Robert. Bred by Juddmonte Farms (GB).

HEAT HAZE (GB) was taken in hand soon after the start, raced well back while saving ground along the backstretch, edged a bit closer along the rail leaving the far turn, was blocked behind a wall of horses while gaining on the turn, waited patiently for room approaching the quarter pole, angled out entering the stretch, split horses to get clear in upper stretch then unleashed a strong late run to win going away. BIEN NICOLE sprinted clear soon after the start, set the pace along the inside entering the backstretch, extended her lead midway down the backstretch, raced uncontested on the front to the turn, maintained a slim advantage into upper stretch, relinquished the lead to the winner inside the furlong marker then continued on well to best the others. RISKAVERSE moved up three wide going into the first turn, raced in closed contention from outside along the backstretch, launched a rally three wide on the far turn, gradually gained while four wide to threaten at the top of the stretch, took up chase after the leader in midstretch then lacked a strong closing bid. WALZERKOENIGIN in hand early, raced in traffic between horses on the first turn, was under a snug hold between horses along the backstretch, edged closer in traffic between horses on the turn, rallied along the rail to threat in upper stretch but couldn't sustain her bid. DUBLINO stalked the pace between horses along the backstretch, moved up outside BIEN NICOLE to challenge leaving the far turn, battled just behind the leader into upper stretch and weakened in the final eighth. DRESS TO THRILL (IRE) reserved early, moved up four wide to reach contention along the backstretch, raced within striking distance while wide to the turn and gave way. OWSLEY raced in the middle of the pack while saving ground the entire way and faltered in the stretch.

Owners— 1, Juddmonte Farms Inc; 2, Richter Kristine & John; 3, Fox Ridge Farm Inc; 4, Gestut Schlenderhan; 5, Robert Geringer Michael Klein & Nai; 6, Moyglare Stud Farm Ltd; 7, Hancock III Arthur B

Trainers—1, Frankel Robert; 2, Von Hemel Donnie K; 3, Kelly Patrick J; 4, Schiergen Peter; 5, De Seroux Laura; 6, Clement Christophe 7, Schulhofer Randy

Scratched— Tates Creek (26Jly03 ^{8}DMR^{2})

TENTH RACE

Arlington
AUGUST 16, 2003

1¼ MILES. (Turf)(1.58³) 21st Running of THE ARLINGTON MILLION. Grade I. Purse $1,000,000 Guaranteed. THREE–YEAR–OLDS AND UPWARD. WEIGHT–FOR–AGE. By subscription of $500 each horse on May 14, 2003. Fee to accompany the nomination. Late nomination of $2,000 on July 23, 2003. All Million nominees will automatically be nominated to the 2003 running of the Stars and Stripes Breeders' Cup Turf and the Arlington Handicap with the nomination fee being waived. Owners and/or trainers of nominated horses will be required to contact officials of Arlington Park or officials of the International Racing Bureau to pre–enter their horses on August 8, 2003, at a fee of $5,000, which will only be refundable on production of a veterinary certificate indicating that the horse is unfit to run or fails to draw into the starting field; $10,000 additional to start. WEIGHT–FOR–AGE: NORTHERN HEMISPHERE: Three year olds, 120 lbs.; Fillies, 117 lbs.; Four year olds and upwards, 126 lbs.; Fillies and mares, 123 lbs.; SOUTHERN HEMISPHERE: Three year olds, 115 lbs.; Fillies, 111 lbs.; Four year olds, 122 lbs.; Fillies, Four year olds, 118 lbs.; Older, 126 lbs.; Mares, 123 lbs. (If the management considers it inadvisable to run this race on the turf course, it will be run on the main track at One Mile and a Quarter).

Value of Race: $1,000,000 Winner $600,000; second $150,000 each; fourth $50,000; fifth $30,000; sixth $20,000.   Mutuel Pool $1,588,651.0
Exacta Pool $847,279.00 Trifecta Pool $759,698.00 Superfecta Pool $216,680.00

Last Raced	Horse	M/Eqt. A.Wt	PP	¼	½	¾	1	Str	Fin	Jockey	Odds $1
14Jun03 ³Hol¹	ⒹStorming Home–GB Lb	5 126	4	11½	12¹	10½	41½	3²	1½	Stevens G L	2.40
26Jly03 Asc²	Sulamani–IR	L	4 126	1	9¹	7²	6ʰᵈ	5¹	4ʰᵈ	2ʰᵈ	Flores D R	2.80
18Jun03 Asc⁸	ⒹⒽPaolini–GE	6 126	3	12²	11½ 11½	11½	5¹	3	Suborics A	17.50
5Jly03 San³	ⒹⒽKaieteur	L	4 126	9	7¹	9½	9²	8²	6½	3ⁿᵏ	Douglas R R	37.40
20Jly03 ⁸WO²	Perfect Soul–IR	Lb	5 126	5	8ʰᵈ	4ʰᵈ	5½	6¹	1ʰᵈ	51¾	Nakatani C S	16.60
5Jly03 ¹⁰Mth²	The Tin Man	L	5 126	10	3ʰᵈ	2½	2¹	21½	2ʰᵈ	6ⁿᵏ	Smith M E	5.90
23Jly03 VHY¹	Vangelis	L	4 126	2	4½	6ʰᵈ	7½	9²	9⁴	7½	Soumillon C	54.30
19Jly03 ⁹AP¹	Perfect Drift	L	4 126	6	2¹½	3½	3½	3ʰᵈ	7ʰᵈ	8ⁿᵏ	Day P	3.80
26Jly03 ⁹AP¹	Honor In War	L	4 126	11	10²	10½	13	13	13	93½	Valdivia J Jr	13.70
28Jun03 HBG⁶	Tripat–IR		4 126	12	13	13	12²	12²	10ʰᵈ103		Kinane M J	100.40
1Jun03 CHY⁴	Touch Of Land–FR	L	3 120	8	5½	5²	4¹	7¹	11² 11²	Smullen P J	69.50
12Jly03 Asc²	Beauchamp Pilot–GB L	5 126	7	12½	11½ 11	1½	8½ 12¹⁵	Ahern E		89.00
5Jly03 San⁴	Olden Times–GB	L	5 126	13	6½	8ʰᵈ 8²	10½	12¹	13	Desormeaux K J	20.50

Ⓓ–Storming Home–GB disqualified and placed 4th.
ⒹⒽ–Dead Heat.

OFF AT 5:18 Start Good. Won driving. Course good.
TIME :24¹, :49, 1:13², 1:37³, 2:02¹ (:24.22, :49.11, 1:13.43, 1:37.77, 2:02.29)

$2 Mutuel Prices:

1–SULAMANI–IR	7.60	5.20	4.40
3–ⒹⒽPAOLINI–GE		7.20	9.40
9–ⒹⒽKAIETEUR		12.00	13.00

$2 EXACTA 1–3 PAID $53.00 $2 EXACTA 1–9 PAID $98.40 $2 TRIFECTA
1–3–9 PAID $811.80 $2 TRIFECTA 1–9–3 PAID $1,019.00 $2 SUPERFECTA
1–3–9–4 PAID $3,316.60 $2 SUPERFECTA 1–9–3–4 PAID $3,693.20

B. c, by Hernando*Fr–Sould Dream, by Alleged. Trainer Suroor Saeed bin. Bred by Niarchos Family (Ire).

STORMING HOME (GB) far back early, moved up from outside along the backstretch, rapidly gained while circling four wide on the turn, rallied between horses to challenge in upper stretch, charged to the front inside the furlong marker, began to edge away in deep stretch, then ducked out sharply nearing the wire and unseated his rider just after the finish. SULAMANI (IRE) broke outward at the start was outrun for six furlongs while saving ground, angled out on the turn, circled seven wide into the stretch then unleashed a strong late run in the middle of the track but could not get up while being bothered by the winner in the closing strides. PAOLINI (GER) steadied while being pinched back at the start, saved ground while far back along the backstretch, moved between horses on the turn, angled five wide entering the stretch, rallied strongly through the lane then took up between horses in the final strides. KAIETEUR was unhurried early, raced well back while four wide along the backstretch, launched a rally from well inside SULAMANI while six wide leaving the turn, battled inside that one into deep stretch then steadied while being bothered in the final strides. PERFECT SOUL (IRE) angled in on the first turn, moved up between horses along the backstretch, closed the gap from outside on the turn, circled five wide while threatening in upper stretch, surged to the front a furlong out then yielded grudgingly. THE TIN MAN forced the pace from outside along the backstretch, made a run to challenge at the quarter pole then tired from his early efforts. VANGELIS steadied in tight at the start, rushed up early, dropped back along the backstretch and failed to threaten thereafter. PERFECT DRIFT raced up close along the rail to the top of the stretch and tired. HONOR IN WAR never reached contention while five wide. TRIPAT (IRE) was never a factor while wide throughout. TOUCH OF LAND (FR) raced up close between ho rses for a mile and faded. BEAUCHAMP PILOT (GB) was used up setting the early pace. OLDEN TIMES (GB) failed to mount a serious rally. Following a stewards inquiry along with claims of foul by the riders of PAOLINI and KAITEUR, STORMING HOME was disqualified from first and placed fourth for interference in deep stretch. (Race run in lane 5, rail at 0).

Owners— 1, Gainsborough Farm LLC; 2, Godolphin Racing Inc William T Bish; 3, Ritcher Mrs Carde Ostemann; 4, Mrs Susan McCarthy; 5, Fipke Charles E; 6, Todd Aury & Ralph E; 7, 6 C Racing Ltd Andreas Putsch; 8, Stonecrest Farm; 9, 3rd Turn Stables LLC; 10, SNC Ecurie Jean-Louis Bouchard; 11, Tanaka Gary A; 12, Penser Eric; 13, H R H Prince A A Faisal

Trainers—1, Drysdale Neil; 2, Suroor Saeed bin; 3, Wohler Andreas; 4, Meehan Brian; 5, Attfield Roger L; 6, Mandella Richard; 7, Dupre Alain D; 8, Johnson Murray W; 9, McGee Paul J; 10, Gibson Richard; 11, Pantall Henri-Alex; 12, Butler Gerard A; 13, Dunlop John L

ELEVENTH RACE

Arlington
AUGUST 16, 2003

1¼ MILES. (Turf)(1.58³) 27th Running of THE SECRETARIAT. Grade I. Purse $400,000 Guaranteed. THREE–YEAR–OLDS. By subscription of $300 each horse (early) April 2, 2003, $800 each horse (Late Nomination) on July 30, 2003. Fee to accompany the nomination. A Supplementary Nomination of $14,000 may be made on August 13, 2003, which includes entry and starting fees. Original Nominees to pay $3,000 to pass the entry box and $3,000 additional to start. WEIGHT: 126 lbs. Non–winners of $100,000 twice at one mile or over in 2003, allowed 3 lbs.; $55,000 twice at one mile or over in 2003, 5 lbs.; $55,000 once at one mile or over in 2003, 7 lbs.; $40,000 at one mile or over at anytime, 10 lbs. (Maiden and Claiming races not considered.) This event will be limited to 14 starters ([7] Non–North American starters and [7] North American starters). (If the management considers it inadvisable to run this race on the turf course, it will be run on the main track at One Mile and a Quarter).

Value of Race: $400,000 Winner $240,000; second $80,000; third $40,000; fourth $20,000; fifth $12,000; sixth $8,000. Mutuel Pool $648,392.00 Exacta Pool $384,325.00   Trifecta Pool $306,850.00 Superfecta Pool $88,181.00

Last Raced	Horse	M/Eqt.	A.Wt	PP	¼	½	¾	1	Str	Fin	Jockey	Odds $1
12Jly03 10Cnl2	Kicken Kris	L	3 116	6	3hd	3hd	3½	3¹½	11½	13½	Castellano J J	15.00
18Jly03 New1	Joe Bear–IR	L	3 116	10	10¹½	8½	9½	8¹	2²	2²	Flores D R	20.00
20Jly03 5Del3	Lismore Knight	L	3 121	1	4¹	4¹	4hd	4½	3¹	3nk	Douglas R R	4.90
12Jly03 Cur3	France–GB	L	3 116	4	8hd	9¹	8hd	7¹	5hd	4nk	Kinane M J	3.20
20Jly03 5Del1	Foufa's Warrior	Lbf	3 121	2	7½	7hd	6½	11	6³	5¾	Dominguez R A	6.90
20Jly03 8AP1	Evolving Tactics–IR	Lb	3 121	3	5½	6¹	10¹½	9¹	4hd	6²½	Smullen P J	8.10
2Aug03 8Cby2	Native Hawk		3 116	9	1²	11½	1½	1½	7¹	7¾	Nolan P M	69.40
20Jly03 8AP2	Californian–GB	L	3 121	5	11	11	11	10½	85	84	Day P	8.80
12Jly03 10Cnl3	King's Drama–IR	L	3 116	7	6¹	5½	5hd	6hd	9¹	9¾	Smith M E	10.40
29Jun03 8Hol1	Just Wonder–GB	L	3 123	8	9¹½	10¹	7½	5hd	105	107	Desormeaux K J	3.10
20Jly03 8AP4	Gato Gato Gato	Lb	3 116	11	2¹	2¹½	2¹	2hd 11	11		Emigh C A	72.00

OFF AT 6:05 Start Good. Won driving. Course good.
TIME :24¹, :49¹, 1:14, 1:38⁴, 2:02² (:24.24, :49.31, 1:14.19, 1:38.87, 2:02.53)

$2 Mutuel Prices:

7–KICKEN KRIS	32.00	13.00	7.60
11–JOE BEAR–IR		16.40	8.00
1–LISMORE KNIGHT			5.00

$2 EXACTA 7–11 PAID $414.20 $2 TRIFECTA 7–11–1 PAID $3,711.80 $2
SUPERFECTA 7–11–1–4 PAID $26,426.00

B. c, (Mar), by Kris S.–Kicken Grass, by Jade Hunter. Trainer Matz Michael R. Bred by Valerie Naify (Ky).

KICKEN KRIS moved up from outside going into the first turn, stalked the pace while three wide along the backstretch, swung out midway on the turn, rallied three wide to challenge at the top of the stretch, accelerated to the front in upper stretch, opened a clear advantage a furlong out, then drew away under steady right hand encouragement. JOE BEAR (IRE) was outrun early, raced well back for six furlongs, made a strong move along the rail at the half mile pole, steadied while lacking room approaching the far turn, saved while rallying on the turn, waited behind a wall of horses nearing the quarter pole, slipped through along the rail in upper stretch then finished strongly along the inside but couldn't threaten the winner. LISMORE KNIGHT settled in good position while saving ground into the backstretch, raced just behind the leaders while close up to the turn, launched rally along the fence entering the stretch but couldn't sustain his bid. FRANCE (GB) was reserved for five furlongs, gained a bit between horses on the far turn, lodged a mild rally five wide nearing the quarter pole then lacked a strong closing response. FOUFA'S WARRIOR was shuffled back entering the backstretch, checked in traffic on the far turn then failed to threaten while improving his position. EVOLVING TACTICS (IRE) raced in the middle of the pack for six furlongs, lodged a bid between horses on the turn then flattened out. NATIVE HAWK set the pace along the rail to the top of the stretch and faltered. CALIFORNIAN (GB) was never a factor. KING'S DRAMA (IRE) raced within striking distance between horses while five wide for a mile and faltered. JUST WONDER (GB) failed to menace while racing wide. GATO GATO GATO forced the pace between horses to the top of the stretch and gave way. (Race run in lane 5, rail at 0).

Owners— 1, Brushwood Stable; 2, Christopher Ransom; 3, J J Pletcher & Barry Simon; 4, Tabor Michael & Magnier Mrs John; 5, Bender Sondra D; 6, Moyglare Stud Farm Ltd; 7, Rice Brett; 8, Stephen Taub & Neil Papiano & Nocti; 9, Tanaka Gary A; 10, Naify Sugarman & Vistas LLC et al; 11, Everest Stables

Trainers—1, Matz Michael R; 2, Mitchell Philip; 3, Pletcher Todd A; 4, O'Brien Aidan P; 5, Murray Lawrence E; 6, Weld Dermot K; 7, Cheeks Kitty; 8, Mulhall Kristin; 9, Collet Robert; 10, De Seroux Laura; 11, Keen Dallas E

Scratched— Bis Repetitas (29Jun03 8HOL2)

$2 Daily Double (1–7) Paid $126.20; Daily Double Pool $79,936.
$1 Pick Three (1/9/10/11–1–7) Paid $291.70; Pick Three Pool $82,473.
$2 Pick Four (2/3–1/9/10/11–1–7) Paid $1,752.80; Pick Four Pool
$632,183.

EIGHTH RACE
Del Mar
AUGUST 16, 2003

$1\frac{1}{16}$ MILES. (Turf)(1.40) 63rd Running of the LA JOLLA HANDICAP. Grade III. Purse $150,000 FOR THREE-YEAR OLDS. By subscription of $150 each, which shall accompany the nomination, or by supplementary nomination of $1,500 each by Sunday, August 10, $500 additional to pass the entry box and $1000 additional to start, with $150,000 Guaranteed, of which $90,000 to first, $30,000 to second, $18,000 to third, $9,000 to fourth and $3,000 to fifth. Nominations closed Thursday, August 7, 2003 with 11. Rail at zero.

Value of Race: $150,000 Winner $90,000; second $30,000; third $18,000; fourth $9,000; fifth $3,000. Mutuel Pool $617,021.00 Exacta Pool $322,955.00 Quinella Pool $39,129.00 Trifecta Pool $311,771.00

Last Raced	Horse	M/Eqt.	A.Wt	PP	St	¼	½	¾	Str	Fin	Jockey	Odds $1
23Jly03 ^{5}Dmr^{2}	Singletary	LB	3 118	6	2	1^{hd}	$1^{1\frac{1}{2}}$	$1^{2\frac{1}{2}}$	1^{3}	$1^{\frac{1}{2}}$	Valenzuela P A	6.80
23Jly03 ^{8}Dmr^{1}	Devious Boy-GB	LB	3 117	7	7	4^{1}	4^{1}	5^{2}	3^{1}	$2^{\frac{1}{2}}$	Krone J A	11.90
12Jly03 ^{10}Cnl^{4}	Senor Swinger	LB	3 120	3	5	7	7	7	6^{1}	$3^{\frac{1}{2}}$	Alvarado F T	1.40
23Jly03 ^{8}Dmr^{2}	Fairly Ransom	LB	3 117	1	6	6^{3}	6^{3}	6^{2}	$4^{1\frac{1}{2}}$	4^{2}	Solis A	2.90
23Jly03 ^{5}Dmr^{1}	Sweet Return-GB	LB	3 117	5	3	$3^{2\frac{1}{2}}$	3^{3}	3^{1}	2^{hd}	$5^{\frac{1}{2}}$	Baze R A	7.90
23Jly03 ^{8}Dmr^{3}	Stanley Park	LBb	3 117	2	4	5^{2}	5^{2}	4^{hd}	5^{hd}	$6^{4\frac{1}{2}}$	Almeida G F	13.50
22Jun03 ^{3}Hol^{2}	Ministers Wild Cat	LB	3 117	4	1	2^{1}	$2^{\frac{1}{2}}$	2^{hd}	7	7	Espinoza V	6.40

OFF AT 5:36 Start Good. Won driving. Course firm.
TIME :23^{3}, :47^{1}, 1:10^{3}, 1:34^{1}, 1:40^{1} (:23.70, :47.34, 1:10.67, 1:34.32, 1:40.39)

$2 Mutuel Prices:				
	6-SINGLETARY	15.60	7.40	3.60
	7-DEVIOUS BOY-GB		9.40	3.60
	3-SENOR SWINGER			2.60

$1 EXACTA 6-7 PAID $68.70 $2 QUINELLA 6-7 PAID $77.80 $1 TRIFECTA 6-7-3 PAID $259.70

B. c, (May), by Sultry Song-Joiski's Star, by Star de Naskra. Trainer Chatlos Donald Jr. Bred by Disler Farms Ltd (Ky).

SINGLETARY had speed three deep early then outside a rival into the first turn, inched away and angled in on the backstretch, kicked clear on the second turn and held gamely under urging. DEVIOUS BOY (GB) off a bit slowly, chased off the rail, angled in some on the second turn, split rivals into the stretch and closed gamely. SENOR SWINGER unhurried outside a rival then a bit off the rail, angled in on the backstretch, came out a bit in upper stretch, split horses in midstretch and rallied along the rail. FAIRLY RANSOM saved ground off the pace, came out on the second turn and four wide into the stretch and finished well. SWEET RETURN (GB) pulled his way between horses early then stalked outside a rival, continued between horses past midstretch and weakened. STANLEY PARK saved ground off the pace, came out on the second turn and three deep into the stretch and lacked the needed rally. MINISTERS WILD CAT pulled his way up inside to press the early pace, stalked the winner a bit off the rail on the backstretch, found the fence again on the second turn, weakened in the stretch and was not urged in the final furlong.

Owners— 1, Little Red Feather Racing; 2, Vreeland James R; 3, Lewis Robert B & Beverly J; 4, Zetcher Arnold; 5, Red Oak Stable; 6, Moss Mr & Mrs Jerome S; 7, Cowan Marjorie & Irving M

Trainers—1, Chatlos Donald Jr; 2, Walsh Kathy; 3, Baffert Bob; 4, McAnally Ronald; 5, McAnally Ronald; 6, Shirreffs John; 7, Drysdale Neil

$2 Daily Double (9-6) Paid $52.60; Daily Double Pool $48,376.
$1 Pick Three (4-2/8/9-6) Paid $561.60; Pick Three Pool $103,428.

SEVENTH RACE
Saratoga
AUGUST 16, 2003

1¼ MILES. (2.00) SARATOGA BREEDERS' CUP H.. Grade II. Purse $300,000 (includes $100,000 BC – Breeders' Cup) (Up to $24,800 NYSBFOA) A HANDICAP FOR THREE YEAR OLDS AND UPWARD. (Includes $100,000 from Breeders' Cup Fund for Cup nonminees only). By subscription of $200 each, which should accompany the nomination; $1,000 to pass the entry box; $1,000 to start. The Breeders' Cup fund monies also correspondingly divided providing a Breeders' Cup nominee has finished in an awarded position. Any Breeders' Cup monies not awarded will revert back to the fund. Closed Saturday, August 2, 2003 with 30 Nominations.

Value of Race: $294,000 Winner $180,000; second $60,000; third $33,000; fourth $12,000; fifth $9,000. Mutuel Pool $1,201,203.0 Exacta Pool $835,844.00 Trifecta Pool $625,761.00

Last Raced	Horse	M/Eqt.	A.Wt	PP	¼	½	¾	1	Str	Fin	Jockey	Odds $1
2Aug03 ^{9}Sar^{4}	Puzzlement	Lb	4 113	2	8	8	6^{hd}	$4^{2\frac{1}{2}}$	1^{hd}	$1^{3\frac{1}{4}}$	Chavez J F	6.90
2Aug03 ^{9}Sar^{2}	Volponi	Lb	5 122	3	$2^{\frac{1}{2}}$	2^{1}	2^{1}	$2^{1\frac{1}{2}}$	$2^{1\frac{1}{2}}$	$2^{1\frac{3}{4}}$	Bailey J D	0.90
19Jly03 ^{9}AP^{4}	Iron Deputy	L	4 115	7	$3^{2\frac{1}{2}}$	3^{2}	3^{1}	3^{1}	$3^{2\frac{1}{2}}$	$3^{4\frac{1}{4}}$	Santos J A	12.70
1Jly03 ^{8}WO^{4}	No Comprende	Lb	5 112	4	$6^{2\frac{1}{2}}$	$6^{2\frac{1}{2}}$	7^{hd}	5^{hd}	$5^{1\frac{1}{2}}$	4no	Luzzi M J	69.50
5Jly03 ^{9}Bel^{6}	Nothing Flat	L	4 114	1	$7^{2\frac{1}{2}}$	7^{hd}	8	7^{1}	$6^{\frac{1}{2}}$	$5^{2\frac{3}{4}}$	Velasquez C	70.50
23Jly03 ^{2}Sar^{1}	Blue Boat	L	4 114	8	$1^{\frac{1}{2}}$	1^{hd}	$1^{1\frac{1}{2}}$	1^{hd}	$4^{1\frac{1}{2}}$	$6^{2\frac{1}{4}}$	Prado E S	8.70
12Jly03 ^{10}Bel^{5}	State Shinto	Lb	7 115	6	$5^{2\frac{1}{2}}$	$5^{3\frac{1}{2}}$	4^{hd}	$6^{\frac{1}{2}}$	$7^{2\frac{1}{2}}$	$7^{2\frac{1}{2}}$	Migliore R	34.50
13Jly03 ^{9}Hol^{2}	Harlan's Holiday	L	4 121	5	$4^{1\frac{1}{2}}$	$4^{\frac{1}{2}}$	$5^{2\frac{1}{2}}$	8	8	8	Velazquez J R	2.55

OFF AT 4:33 Start Good. Won driving. Track fast.
TIME :23^{4}, :48, 1:11^{4}, 1:37, 2:03^{2} (:23.98, :48.10, 1:11.89, 1:37.09, 2:03.54)

$2 Mutuel Prices:				
	2-PUZZLEMENT	15.80	4.60	3.20
	3-VOLPONI		2.50	2.10
	7-IRON DEPUTY			3.80

$2 EXACTA 2-3 PAID $34.40 $2 TRIFECTA 2-3-7 PAID $208.50

B. c, by Pine Bluff-Taine, by Sir Ivor. Trainer Jerkens H Allen. Bred by J V Shields Jr (Fla).

PUZZLEMENT was unhurried while trailing for five furlongs, saved ground leaving the backstretch, rapidly gained between horses on the turn, angled inside IRON DEPUTY when that one drifted in a bit at the quarter pole, slipped through along the rail to challenge at the three-sixteenths pole, surged to the front in midstretch then edged away under intermittent right hand urging. VOLPONI moved to the outside in the early stages, was strung out four wide on the first turn, stalked the pace while well out in the track along the backstretch, made his move to challenge midway on the turn, gained a slim advantage just inside the quarter pole, battled into midstretch but couldn't stay with the winner through the final eighth. IRON DEPUTY bumped at the start, was carried five wide on the first turn, continued wide while just outside the leaders along the backstretch, angled in on the turn, remained a factor into upper stretch then drifted out while tiring in the stretch. NO COMPRENDE raced well back for five furlongs, gained a bit while three wide on the turn then ducked out while racing erratically in upper stretch. NOTHING FLAT failed to mount a serious rally while wide throughout. BLUE BOAT bumped at the start, rushed up to gain the early advantage while wide into the first turn, drifted out while setting the pace along the backstretch, led to the turn, bumped with VOLPONI after relinquishing the lead at the quarter pole then faltered. STATE SHINTO bumped at the start, raced wide while in the middle of the pack, saved ground while gaining on the turn, then steadied in tight along the rail the quarter pole and failed to threaten thereafter. HARLAN'S HOLIDAY steadied inside VOLPONI soon after the start, angled to the rail in the early stages, raced in good position along the inside to the far turn and gave way.

Owners— 1, Shields Joseph V Jr; 2, Amherst Stable & Spruce Pond Stable; 3, Moore Susan & John; 4, Dennis Brown & Debby Brown; 5, Condren William J & Sherman Michael; 6, Juddmonte Farms Inc; 7, Darley Stable; 8, Starlight Stable LLC

Trainers—1, Jerkens H Allen; 2, Johnson Philip G; 3, Jerkens James A; 4, Smith James J; 5, Zito Nicholas P; 6, Frankel Robert; 7, McLaughlin Kiaran P; 8, Pletcher Todd A

$2 Daily Double (5-2) Paid $50.00; Daily Double Pool $174,100.
$2 Pick Three (4-5-2) Paid $120.50; Pick Three Pool $134,774.

NINTH RACE
Saratoga
AUGUST 16, 2003

1¼ MILES. (2.00) ALABAMA S.. Grade I. Purse $750,000 (Up to $39,000 NYSBFOA) FOR FILLIES THREE YEARS OLD. By subscription of $750 each, which should accompany the nomination; $3,500 to pass the entry box, $4,000 to start. A special permanent trophy will be presented to the owner of the winner of The Alabama if the filly also wins The Mother Goose and The Coaching Club American Oaks. A $2,000,000 bonus will be awarded to the owner of the filly which wins all three legs of the Triple Tiara. Closed Saturday, August 2, 2003 with 15 Nominations.

Value of Race: $750,000 Winner $450,000; second $150,000; third $82,500; fourth $45,000; fifth $22,500. Mutuel Pool $1,184,364.0 Exacta Pool $678,793.00 Trifecta Pool $476,064.00

Last Raced	Horse	M/Eqt.	A.Wt	PP	¼	½	¾	1	Str	Fin	Jockey	Odds $1
19Jly03 ^{8}Del^1	Island Fashion	Lb	3 121	1	2½	2^{2½}	1½	1^2	1^6	1^6	Velazquez J R	8.30
19Jly03 ^{8}Del^2	Awesome Humor	L	3 121	6	1^{1½}	1½	2^{1½}	3^2	2^{hd}	2^1	Albarado R J	15.50
19Jly03 ^{9}Bel^1	Spoken Fur	L	3 121	2	4^2	4^3	4^6	4^{hd}	3^{1½}	3^{1¼}	Bailey J D	0.85
26Jly03 ^{9}Sar^6	Halory Leigh	L	3 121	3	5^3	5^{2½}	5^{5½}	5^7	4^{hd}	4^{2¾}	Velasquez C	47.75
26Jly03 ^{9}Sar^2	Bird Town	L	3 121	5	3^{1½}	3^2	3^{2½}	2½	5^7	5^{6¼}	Prado E S	1.60
19Jly03 ^{9}Bel^2	Fircroft	Lb	3 121	4	6	6	6	6	6	6	Samyn J L	15.30

OFF AT 5:44 Start Good. Won driving. Track fast.
TIME :23^4, :48^2, 1:12^4, 1:37^4, 2:05 (:23.84, :48.41, 1:12.91, 1:37.95, 2:05.08)

$2 Mutuel Prices:				
	1–ISLAND FASHION	18.60	8.80	2.30
	6–AWESOME HUMOR		12.20	2.40
	2–SPOKEN FUR			2.10

$2 EXACTA 1–6 PAID $175.50 $2 TRIFECTA 1–6–2 PAID $464.50

Gr/ro f, (Mar), by Petionville–Danzigs Fashion, by A Native Danzig. Trainer Tagg Barclay. Bred by Everest Stables Inc (Ky).

ISLAND FASHION moved up in hand going into the first turn, stalked the pace from outside along the backstretch, edged closer on the far turn, took command approaching the five-sixteenths pole, shook loose leaving the turn, opened a comfortable advantage in upper stretch then drew away under steady right hand urging. AWESOME HUMOR exchanged bumps with BIRD TOWN soon after the start and nearing the first turn, took the lead in the early stages, set the pace under pressure along the inside on the backstretch, continued on the front to the far turn, relinquished the lead to the winner midway on the turn, raced just behind that one into upper stretch then outfinished SPOKEN FUR for the place. SPOKEN FUR was strung out four wide on the first turn, angled in approaching the backstretch, was unhurried for six furlongs while racing out from the fence, angled back to the inside on the far turn, rallied along the rail to reach contention in upper stretch but couldn't sustain her bid. HALORY LEIGH was taken in hand soon after the start, raced well back for a half, circled six wide on the turn then lacked a strong closing response. BIRD TOWN exchanged bumps then was eased back on the first turn, raced up close while three wide to the far turn, lodged a mild bid nearing the quarter pole then faltered. FIRCROFT fractious in the gate prior to the start was never a factor.

Owners— 1, Nielsen Jeffrey L; 2, WinStar Farm LLC; 3, Amerman Racing Stables LLC; 4, Jerry Crawford Matt Gannon & Charli; 5, Marylou Whitney Stables; 6, Humphrey G W Jr

Trainers—1, Tagg Barclay; 2, Walden W Elliott; 3, Frankel Robert; 4, Romans Dale; 5, Zito Nicholas P; 6, Arnold George R II

SECOND RACE
Del Mar
AUGUST 17, 2003

6½ FURLONGS. (1.13^3) 33rd Running of the BEST PAL STAKES.. Grade II. Purse $150,000 FOR TWO-YEAR-OLDS. By subscription of $150 each, which shall accompany the nomination, or by supplementary nomination of $1,500 each by closing time of entries, $1,500 additional to start, with $150,000 Guaranteed, of which $90,000 to first, $30,000 to second, $18,000 to third, $9,000 to fourth and $3,000 to fifth. Weight 122 lbs.; Non-winners of $50,000, 2 lbs.; of a race of $25,000 other than maiden or claiming, 4 lbs.; of a race other than claiming, 6 lbs. Nominations closed Thursday, August 7, 2003 with 15.

Value of Race: $150,000 Winner $90,000; second $30,000; third $18,000; fourth $9,000; fifth $3,000. Mutuel Pool $570,498.00 Exacta Pool $334,231.00 Quinella Pool $34,881.00 Trifecta Pool $305,587.00 Superfecta Pool $104,791.00

Last Raced	Horse	M/Eqt.	A.Wt	PP	St	¼	½	Str	Fin	Jockey	Odds $1
19Jly03 ^{4}Hol^1	Perfect Moon	LB	2 122	9	2	4^{hd}	3^1	3^{1½}	1^{1¼}	Valenzuela P A	3.70
5Jly03 ^{3}Hol^1	Capitano	LBb	2 118	10	4	3^1	2^2	1^{hd}	2^{1¼}	Valdivia J Jr	10.70
30Jly03 ^{7}Dmr^3	Military Mandate	LB	2 118	7	3	1½	1½	2^1	3^1	Solis A	19.00
19Jly03 ^{4}Hol^3	Ruler's Court	LB	2 118	8	1	8^1	5^{hd}	4^{hd}	4^{hd}	Flores D R	2.10
2Aug03 ^{6}Dmr^1	Siphonizer	LB	2 118	3	7	6^{hd}	6^{hd}	5^4	5^{5½}	Krone J A	1.80
25Jly03 ^{5}Dmr^1	Rush Into Heaven	LB	2 116	5	5	2^{hd}	4^1	6^{1½}	6^{2½}	Puglisi I L	17.30
30Jly03 ^{7}Dmr^4	Badgett's Mandate	LBb	2 118	6	8	7^{hd}	8^4	7^3	7^{2½}	Desormeaux K J	43.80
2Jun03 ^{4}PrM^1	Last Time In Town	LBb	2 118	4	9	10	10	8^2	8^6	Smith M E	22.90
28Jly03 ^{3}Dmr^1	Feb Eleven	LB	2 116	1	10	9^5	9^1	10	9^3	Garcia M S	71.50
26Jly03 ^{3}Dmr^1	Wild Babe	LB	2 118	2	6	5^1	7^2	9½	10	Espinoza V	32.00

OFF AT 2:32 Start Good. Won driving. Track fast.
TIME :22, :44^4, 1:10^1, 1:16^4 (:22.17, :44.92, 1:10.26, 1:16.90)

$2 Mutuel Prices:				
	10–PERFECT MOON	9.40	4.40	3.40
	11–CAPITANO		7.60	5.20
	8–MILITARY MANDATE			7.00

$1 EXACTA 10–11 PAID $42.30 $2 QUINELLA 10–11 PAID $48.00 $1 TRIFECTA 10–11–8 PAID $386.50 $1 SUPERFECTA 10–11–8–9 PAID $1,115.20

B. g, (Mar), by Malibu Moon–Perfectly, by Parfaitement. Trainer Stute Melvin F. Bred by Mr & Mrs Hugh J O'Donovan (Md).

PERFECT MOON wide between horses early, stalked three deep on the backstretch and turn, continued off the rail into the stretch, rallied to the front outside foes under left handed urging a sixteenth out and proved best while drifting out some. CAPITANO had good early speed and pressed the pace four wide then outside a rival leaving the backstretch and on the turn, gained a slim advantage in midstretch, fought back between horses in deep stretch, could not match the winner late but held second. MILITARY MANDATE sped to the early lead between horses, angled in and dueled inside on the turn and in the stretch, also fought back along the rail in the drive and bested the others. RULER'S COURT between horses early, stalked outside on the backstretch and three deep on the turn, came out into the stretch and lacked the needed response. SIPHONIZER also between horses early, stalked a bit off the rail, split horses leaving the turn, came out into the stretch, angled back in some behind rivals in midstretch and also could not summon the necessary late kick. RUSH INTO HEAVEN dueled between horses on the backstretch, stalked a bit off the rail on the turn and weakened in the stretch. BADGETT'S MANDATE chased between foes on the backstretch and most of the turn, came four wide into the stretch and did not rally. LAST TIME IN TOWN settled off the rail without early speed, came out in the stretch and was not a threat. FEB ELEVEN off a bit slowly, saved ground off the pace, came out into the stretch and was not a factor. WILD BABE went up inside to prompt the pace, dropped back on the turn and gave way.

Owners— 1, Stute Annabelle & The Hat Ranch; 2, Meguerditchian Mr & Mrs; 3, Turner Joe L; 4, Darley Stud Management LLC; 5, Hughes B W; 6, Wood Jason; 7, S L U Inc; 8, Fog City Stable; 9, Thomas Paula & Thomas Racing; 10, Williams Mr & Mrs Larry D

Trainers—1, Stute Melvin F; 2, Bell Thomas R II; 3, Hollendorfer Jerry; 4, Harty Eoin; 5, Mandella Richard; 6, Aguirre Paul G; 7, Warren Donald; 8, Mullins Jeff; 9, Stute Warren; 10, Dutton Jerry

Scratched— Blairs Roarin Star (19Jly03 ^{4}HOL^2)

$2 Daily Double (2–10) Paid $31.40; Daily Double Pool $153,289.

EIGHTH RACE
Del Mar
AUGUST 17, 2003

7 FURLONGS. (1.20) 18th Running of the PAT O'BRIEN HANDICAP.. Grade II. Purse $150,000 FOR THREE-YEAR-OLDS AND UPWARD. By subscription of $150 each, which shall accompany the nomination, or by supplementary nomination of $1,500 each by Sunday, August 10, $1,500 additional to start, with $150,000 Guaranteed, of which $90,000 to first, $30,000 to second, $18,000 to third, $9,000 to fourth and $3,000 to fifth. Nominations closed Thursday, August 7, 2003 with 17.

Value of Race: $150,000 Winner $90,000; second $30,000; third $18,000; fourth $9,000; fifth $3,000. Mutuel Pool $641,889.00 Exacta Pool $338,970.00 Quinella Pool $40,195.00 Trifecta Pool $352,352.00 Superfecta Pool $143,615.00

Last Raced	Horse	M/Eqt. A.Wt	PP	St	¼	½	Str	Fin	Jockey	Odds $1
26Jly03 6Dmr6	Disturbingthepeace	LB 5 116	1	5	4½	1hd	12½	12	Espinoza V	6.20
3Jly03 7Hol1	Rushin' To Altar	LBf 4 117	3	9	10	81	21	24½	Nakatani C S	8.10
12Jly03 8Hol1	Full Moon Madness	LBb 8 119	9	2	2hd	52½	61	3½	Valdivia J Jr	7.90
12Jly03 6Hol2	Tough Game	LBb 4 117	5	7	53½	31½	4hd	4nk	Desormeaux K J	11.10
12Jly03 6Hol1	Ditch Digger-ARG	LBf 8 115	10	3	3hd	42	5½	51	Smith M E	16.40
5Jly03 8Hol5	Kela	LBb 5 115	4	6	8hd	7hd	72	6½	Valenzuela P A	13.40
26Jly03 6Dmr3	Bluesthestandard	LB 6 117	7	4	1½	2hd	31½	7hd	Solis A	1.50
12Jly03 8Hol2	Sea To See	LBb 5 113	2	10	9hd	10	10	8½	Martinez F F	43.50
3Aug03 8Dmr4	Danthebluegrassman	LB 4 116	6	8	74	92	91	91	Flores D R	6.20
19Jly03 7Cby2	Debonair Joe	LB 4 115	8	1	61	61½	81½	10	Krone J A	17.70

OFF AT 5:36 Start Good. Won driving. Track fast.
TIME :221, :44, 1:081, 1:212 (:22.20, :44.00, 1:08.35, 1:21.53)

$2 Mutuel Prices:

1–DISTURBINGTHEPEACE	14.40	7.60	5.40
3–RUSHIN' TO ALTAR		7.40	5.40
10–FULL MOON MADNESS			5.20

$1 EXACTA 1–3 PAID $50.40 $2 QUINELLA 1–3 PAID $48.40 $1 TRIFECTA 1–3–10 PAID $654.00 $1 SUPERFECTA 1–3–10–5 PAID $4,408.90

B. g, by Bold Badgett–Regal Riot, by Sovereign Dancer. Trainer Vienna Darrell. Bred by Old English Rancho & Patsy McKuen (Cal).

DISTURBINGTHEPEACE went up inside to duel for command, put a head in front nearing the turn, inched away into the stretch and won clear under urging. RUSHIN' TO ALTAR settled outside on the backstretch, moved up between horses on the turn and along the inside into the stretch and was clearly second best. FULL MOON MADNESS forced the early pace between horses then dropped back into the turn, came four wide into the stretch and edged foes late for third. TOUGH GAME off a bit awkwardly, stalked off the rail then went up five wide leaving the backstretch, prompted the pace three deep on the turn and weakened in the stretch. DITCH DIGGER (ARG) pressed the early pace four wide then stalked outside on the turn, came four wide into the stretch and also weakened. KELA allowed to settle off the rail then between horses, angled in on the turn and lacked the needed rally. BLUESTHESTANDARD had good early speed and dueled between horses on the backstretch and turn but weakened in the stretch. SEA TO SEE off a bit slowly, saved ground off the pace, came on out the turn and into the stretch and did not rally. DANTHEBLUEGRASSMAN wide early, chased outside or off the rail, came a bit wide into the stretch and failed to menace. DEBONAIR JOE was in a good position stalking the pace off the rail on the backstretch and turn, weakened.

Owners— 1, Milch David S & Rita & Herrick Raci; 2, Vogel Arthur; 3, Corey Family Trust; 4, Noctis Stable Papiano Neil & Taub S; 5, Acker Lindo & Meguiar; 6, Larry S Barrera Lessee; 7, Sengara Jeffrey; 8, Soares Michael & Suarez Pablo; 9, Pegram Michael E; 10, Ristad-Lidgett Lynne

Trainers—1, Vienna Darrell; 2, McAnally Ronald; 3, Marshall Robert W; 4, Mulhall Kristin; 5, Spawr Bill; 6, Barrera Larry; 7, West Ted H; 8, O'Neill Doug; 10, Ledezma Sergio

Scratched— Grey Memo (26Apr03 8HOL7)

$2 Daily Double (3–1) Paid $87.80; Daily Double Pool $51,923.
$1 Pick Three (1/2/3/7/9–3–1) Paid $164.60; Pick Three Pool $95,904.

TENTH RACE
Monmouth
AUGUST 17, 2003

1⅛ MILES. (Turf)(1.46^{1}) MATCHMAKER H.. Grade III. Purse $100,000 FOR FILLIES AND MARES, THREE YEARS OLD AND UPWARD. By subscription of $100 each, which should accompany the nomination. $1,500 to enter. The winner to receive $60,000; $20,000 to second; $11,000 to third; $6,000 to fourth; $3,000 to fifth. Highweights preferred. Weights 5:00 P.M., Saturday, August 9.The owner of the Winner to Receive a Trophy. NOMINATIONS CLOSED Saturday, August 2, 2003 with TWENTY FIVE (25).

Value of Race: $100,000 Winner $60,000; second $20,000; third $11,000; fourth $6,000; fifth $3,000. Mutuel Pool $151,852.00 Exacta Pool $133,139.00 Trifecta Pool $85,761.00

Last Raced	Horse	M/Eqt.	A.Wt	PP	St	¼	½	¾	Str	Fin	Jockey	Odds $1
7Dec02 ^{8}Crc^{7}	Volga-IR	L	5 116	9	9	10	$9\frac{1}{2}$	$9\frac{1}{2}$	4^{hd}	$11\frac{3}{4}$	Bravo J	2.50
19Jly03 ^{10}Mth^{2}	Something Ventured	Lb	4 117	8	8	4^{1}	3^{1}	4^{2}	3^{hd}	$2\frac{3}{4}$	Velez J A Jr	3.40
19Jly03 ^{10}Mth^{6}	Cocktailsandreams	L	6 115	3	2	$5\frac{1}{2}$	5^{1}	3^{hd}	$11\frac{1}{2}$	3no	King E L Jr	31.70
12Jly03 ^{9}Cnl^{2}	Lady Linda	Lb	5 115	1	7	7^{1}	6^{hd}	$5\frac{1}{2}$	$51\frac{1}{2}$	4^{hd}	Karamanos H A	3.30
27Jly03 ^{10}Mth^{1}	Twilights Prayer	L	5 113	5	4	$2\frac{1}{2}$	$24\frac{1}{2}$	$22\frac{1}{2}$	$21\frac{1}{2}$	$53\frac{1}{2}$	Beckner D V	26.70
31Jly03 ^{8}Mth^{1}	France Soir-CH	L	5 112	7	5	6^{hd}	7^{1}	$8\frac{1}{2}$	$81\frac{1}{2}$	6^{1}	Bracho R A	38.20
12Jly03 ^{9}Cnl^{8}	Cruise Along	Lb	5 113	10	10	$9\frac{1}{2}$	10	$7\frac{1}{2}$	7^{hd}	7^{2}	Pimentel J	20.40
19Jly03 ^{10}Mth^{5}	Southern Fiction	Lbf	5 115	2	6	8^{hd}	8^{hd}	10	10	$83\frac{1}{4}$	Toribio A R	7.90
17May03 ^{7}Pim^{2}	Affirmed Dancer	L	4 114	4	3	3^{hd}	$4\frac{1}{2}$	6^{hd}	$9\frac{1}{2}$	9^{3}	Blanc B	4.00
31Jly03 ^{8}Mth^{6}	Katie Kreitz	Lf	4 114	6	1	1^{3}	$12\frac{1}{2}$	$12\frac{1}{2}$	6^{hd}	10	Clemente A V	53.90

OFF AT 5:12 Start Good. Won driving. Course good.

TIME :23^{3}, :47^{4}, 1:11^{3}, 1:36^{1}, 1:48^{1} (:23.67, :47.94, 1:11.69, 1:36.20, 1:48.22)

$2 Mutuel Prices:				
	1–VOLGA–IR	7.00	4.20	3.60
	10–SOMETHING VENTURED		4.20	4.00
	4–COCKTAILSANDREAMS			9.60

$2 EXACTA 1–10 PAID $27.40 $2 TRIFECTA 1–10–4 PAID $494.60 $2 9–7–12 PAID $47.40

Dk. b. or br. m, by Caerleon–Verveine, by Lear Fan. Trainer Clement Christophe. Bred by Allez France Stables Ltd (Ire).

VOLGA (IRE) angled to the inside rating well back, was behind a wall of horses leaving the quarter pole, angled to the outside making her bid at the top of the stretch, advanced steadily and was clear the final yards. SOMETHING VENTURED rated off the pace in mid track, made her bid from the top of the stretch and advanced to place in the final yards. COCKTAILSANDREAMS, unhurriedly in mid track, advanced off the rail entering the final turn, drew clear into the stretch but was outfinished through the final sixteenth. LADY LINDA was boxed in on the rail the opening turn, raced unhurriedly just off the rail, bid angling to the outside on the final turn then closed well to late stretch. TWILIGHTS PRAYER rated off the pace inside, made a bid three wide on the final turn then faltered in the drive. FRANCE SOIR (CHI) rated back toward the outside, came through the final turn in mid track and finished evenly. CRUISE ALONG raced unhurriedly outside and offered no rally. SOUTHERN FICTION, unhurriedly in the three path, angled out through the final turn then didn't rally. AFFIRMED DANCER rated off the pace inside, bid off the rail through the final turn, was checked on the heels of the tiring pacesetter entering the stretch and gave way from there. KATIE KREITZ set a clear pace inside and had nothing left for the stretch.

Owners— 1, Allen Joseph; 2, McLane John & Weimer Irv; 3, Generazio Patricia A; 4, Domino Stud LLC; 5, Sheerin Matthew; 6, Masterson Robert E; 7, Bender Sondra D; 8, Humphrey G W Jr; 9, Farmer Tracy; 10, Deckert Robert & Deckert Robert Jr

Trainers—1, Clement Christophe; 2, Pletcher Todd A; 3, Generazio Frank Jr; 4, Eppler Mary E; 5, Contessa Gary C; 6, Goldberg Alan E; 7, Murray Lawrence E; 8, Oliver Victoria; 9, Kimmel John C; 10, Farro Patricia

Scratched— Lady Of The Future (19Jly03 ^{7}DEL^{3}), Sixty Seconds (11Jly03 ^{8}BEL^{1}), City Fire (27Jly03 ^{9}MTH^{1})

$2 Pick Three (9–7–1) Paid $224.20; Pick Three Pool $11,097.

NINTH RACE

Saratoga

AUGUST 17, 2003

1⅛ MILES. (Turf)(1.45²) LAKE PLACID H.. Grade II. Purse $150,000 MELLON TURF. (Up to $21,100 NYSBFOA) A HANDICAP FOR FILLIES THREE YEARS OLD. By subscription of $150 each, which should accompany the nomination; $750 to pass the entry box; $750 to start. The purse to be divided 60% to the winner, 20% to second, 11% to third, 6% to fourth and 3% to fifth. Trophies will be presented to the winning owner, trainer and jockey. The New York Racing Association reserves the right to transfer this race to the Main Track. In the event that this race is taken off the turf, it maybe subject to downgrading upon review by the Graded Stakes Committee. Closed Saturday, August 2, 2003 with 33 Nominations.

Value of Race: $150,000 Winner $90,000; second $30,000; third $16,500; fourth $9,000; fifth $4,500.   Mutuel Pool $844,465.00 Exacta Pool $705,884.00   Trifecta Pool $580,583.00

Last Raced	Horse	M/Eqt.	A.Wt	PP	St	¼	½	¾	Str	Fin	Jockey	Odds $1
5Jly03 5Hol²	Sand Springs	L	3 121	9	9	1¹	1⁶	15½	1²	1¾	Guidry M	1.35
28Jly03 8Sar⁷	Indy Five Hundred	L	3 114	4	7	10	10	10	4³	2no	Day P	15.70
28Jly03 8Sar¹	Film Maker	Lb	3 119	2	2	3hd	4½	32½	2½	33½	Prado E S	3.00
19Jly03 9Bel⁶	Shapes And Shadows	Lb	3 117	8	4	4½	3½	22½	3½	4½	Samyn J L	17.40
28Jly03 8Sar³	Gal O Gal	L	3 119	6	6	8hd	8½	7hd	6½	5¹	Velazquez J R	6.30
19Jly03 9Bel³	Savedbythelight	Lb	3 114	1	1	5hd	6²	6²	5¹	61¾	Migliore R	6.70
2Aug03 7Del¹	Broad Hopes	L	3 114	5	5	7¹	71½	5½	7²	7½	Velasquez C	25.25
26Jun03 7Bel¹	Noisette	b	3 115	7	8	9³	92½	8½	915	8²	Luzzi M J	25.25
17Jly03 7Mth¹	Danse de Sable	L	3 115	10	10	6²	5½	4½	81½	9¹⁶	Farina Tony	38.75
9Jly03 8Bel⁵	Brusque	L	3 114	3	3	22½	2hd	9¹	10	10	Espinoza J L	57.00

OFF AT 5:26 Start Good. Won driving. Course firm.
TIME :23¹, :46², 1:10², 1:36, 1:49 (:23.26, :46.41, 1:10.51, 1:36.01, 1:49.03)

$2 Mutuel Prices:

10–SAND SPRINGS	4.70	3.50	2.50
4–INDY FIVE HUNDRED		9.50	4.50
2–FILM MAKER			2.50

$2 EXACTA 10–4 PAID $61.50 $2 TRIFECTA 10–4–2 PAID $174.00

Dk. b. or br. f, (May), by Dynaformer–Lovely Martha, by Storm Bird. Trainer Reinstedler Anthony. Bred by Willmott Stables Inc (Ky).

SAND SPRINGS sprinted clear soon after the start, opened a wide gap before going a half, set a rapid pace while racing uncontested on the lead to the turn, maintained a comfortable advantage into upper stretch then was fully extended to hold off INDY FIVE HUNDRED in the closing strides. INDY FIVE HUNDRED was bounced around between horses then pinched back soon after the start, trailed while racing far back for seven furlongs, saved ground while finding her best stride rallying into the stretch then finished strongly along the rail to relish FILM MAKER for the place. FILM MAKER raced up close along the inside for a half, moved around BRUSQUE on the far turn, launched a rally four wide at the quarter pole and finished willingly from outside to gain the place. SHAPES AND SHADOWS settled in good position while saving ground, took up chase after the winner on the far turn, closed the gap along the inside to threaten in upper stretch but couldn't sustain her bid. GAL O GAL was outrun for six furlongs, rallied a bit along the inside on the turn, angled out entering the stretch, steadied in tight between horses at the three-sixteenths pole then failed to threaten thereafter. SAVEDBYTHELIGHT was rated in the middle of the pack along the rail, worked her way forward while saving ground on the turn, angled out in upper stretch then finished evenly between horses. BROAD HOPES bumped in tight soon after the start, was unhurried for a half, closed the gap while five wide on the turn, made a run to reach contention entering the stretch then flattened out. NOISETTE failed to mount a serious rally while five wide leaving the turn. DANSE DE SABLE broke outward at the start, raced just off the pace while four wide to the turn then steadily tired thereafter. BRUSQUE was bumped in tight soon after the start, chased the winner to the far turn and gave way.

Owners— 1, Willmott Stables; 2, Georgica Stable; 3, Adam Donald A; 4, Nielsen Jeffrey L; 5, Hugel Max; 6, Mack Earle I; 7, Augustin Stable; 8, Haras Santa Maria de Araras; 9, Fab Oak Stable; 10, Lael Stables
Trainers—1, Reinstedler Anthony; 2, Barbara Robert; 3, Motion H Graham; 4, Tagg Barclay; 5, Blengs Vincent L; 6, Violette Richard A Jr; 7, Sheppard Jonathan E; 8, Mott William I; 9, Biancone Patrick L; 10, Tagg Barclay
Scratched— Rhumb Line (28Jun03 9BEL⁶), A Queen's Smile (16Aug03 9LRL²)

NINTH RACE

Saratoga

AUGUST 22, 2003

1¼ MILES. (2.00) 56th Running of THE PERSONAL ENSIGN HANDICAP. Grade I. Purse $400,000. (Up to $33,600 NYSBFOA). FILLIES AND MARES THREE YEARS OLD AND UPWARD. By subscription of $400 each, which should accompany the nomination; $2,000 to pass the entry box and $2,000 to start. The purse to be divided 60% to the winner, 20% to second, 11% to third, 6% to fourth and 3% to fifth. Trophies will be presented to the winning owner, trainer and jockey. Closed Saturday, August 9, 2003 with 12 Nominations.

Value of Race: $400,000 Winner $240,000; second $80,000; third $44,000; fourth $24,000; fifth $12,000.   Mutuel Pool $1,804,584.0 Exacta Pool $552,659.00   Trifecta Pool $239,374.00

Last Raced	Horse	M/Eqt.	A.Wt	PP	¼	½	¾	1	Str	Fin	Jockey	Odds $1
30Jly03 8Sar¹	Passing Shot	L	4 114	4	2½	21½	2½	2¹	21½	1no	Santos J A	11.30
20Jly03 10Del¹	Wild Spirit–CH	L	4 122	1	3hd	3hd	3½	3hd	11	26¼	Bailey J D	0.20
27Jly03 9Sar⁴	Miss Linda–ARG	L	6 114	3	1½	11	11	1hd	31½	32½	Migliore R	17.90
20Jly03 10Del⁶	Summer Colony	L	5 120	2	5	5	5	42½	45	45	Prado E S	6.50
30Jly03 8Sar²	Golden Sonata	Lb	4 110	5	4½	41½	4½	5	5	5	Day P	14.90

OFF AT 5:32 Start Good. Won driving. Track fast.
TIME :24⁴, :49³, 1:14¹, 1:38², 2:03¹ (:24.96, :49.74, 1:14.31, 1:38.54, 2:03.33)

$2 Mutuel Prices:

4–PASSING SHOT	24.60	2.90	2.10
1–WILD SPIRIT–CH		2.10	2.10
3–MISS LINDA–ARG			2.10

$2 EXACTA 4–1 PAID $43.60 $2 TRIFECTA 4–1–3 PAID $206.00

Dk. b. or br. f, by A.P. Indy–Aucilla, by Relaunch. Trainer Jerkens H Allen. Bred by J V Shields Jr (Ky).

PASSING SHOT moved up from outside to contest the early pace, stalked the leader along the backstretch, kept WILD SPIRIT (CHI) pinned in along the rail while racing heads apart outside that one on the turn, was carried out a bit at the top of the stretch, fought back gamely to challenge in deep stretch then prevailed by a bob of a head. WILD SPIRIT (CHI) settled just behind the leaders leaving the first turn, was well in hand along the backstretch, was trapped along the inside through the turn, steadied briefly while waiting patiently for room at the quarter pole, charged through along the rail to gain a clear advantage in upper stretch, maintained a clear lead approaching the sixteenth pole, battled into deep stretch and yielded grudgingly. MISS LINDA (ARG) sprinted clear in the early stages, set a moderate pace along the rail to the turn, drifted out a bit at the top of the stretch then weakened under pressure through the final eighth. SUMMER COLONY stumbled then brushed with WILD SPIRIT (CHI) at the start, was raced between horses for about five furlongs, lodged a brief rally three wide to reach contention on the turn but couldn't sustain her bid. GOLDEN SONATA raced within striking distance while four wide to the turn and steadily tired thereafter.

Owners— 1, Shields Joseph V Jr; 2, Sumaya Us Stables; 3, Ackerley Brothers Farm; 4, Evans Edward P; 5, Spence James C
Trainers—1, Jerkens H Allen; 2, Frankel Robert; 3, Kimmel John C; 4, Hennig Mark; 5, Mott William I

EIGHTH RACE
Del Mar
AUGUST 23, 2003

6½ FURLONGS. (1.13^{3}) 32nd Running of THE RANCHO BERNARDO HANDICAP. Grade III. Purse $150,000. FILLIES AND MARES, THREE-YEAR-OLDS AND UPWARD. By subscription of $150 each, which shall accompany the nomination, or by supplementary nomination of $1,500 each by Sunday, August 17, $1,500 additional to start, with $150,000 Guaranteed, of which $90,000 to first, $30,000 to second, $18,000 to third, $9,000 to fourth and $3,000 to fifth. Closed Thursday, August 14 with 16 nominations.

Value of Race: $150,000 Winner $90,000; second $30,000; third $18,000; fourth $9,000; fifth $3,000. Mutuel Pool $582,440.00 Exacta Pool $315,660.00 Quinella Pool $38,584.00 Trifecta Pool $289,701.00 Superfecta Pool $120,662.00

Last Raced	Horse	M/Eqt.	A.Wt	PP	St	¼	½	Str	Fin	Jockey	Odds $1
6Aug03 ^{6}Dmr^{1}	Secret Liaison	LB	5 116	8	1	$1^{\frac{1}{2}}$	1^{1}	$1^{2\frac{1}{2}}$	1^{4}	Nakatani C S	3.70
12Jly03 ^{10}Sol^{1}	Lacie Girl	LB	4 116	5	6	6^{hd}	5^{hd}	$3^{\frac{1}{2}}$	2^{1}	Baze R A	5.20
20Jly03 ^{9}Del^{3}	Spring Meadow	LB	4 117	3	7	$7^{2\frac{1}{2}}$	6^{3}	$5^{1\frac{1}{2}}$	3^{hd}	Krone J A	8.90
13Jly03 ^{4}Hol^{1}	Cee's Elegance	LB	6 119	1	5	4^{hd}	3^{hd}	4^{1}	4^{1}	Espinoza V	2.30
6Aug03 ^{6}Dmr^{4}	Fancee Bargain	LBf	7 115	2	8	8	7^{hd}	7^{6}	$5^{1\frac{1}{2}}$	Alvarado F T	50.40
7Jun03 ^{4}Hol^{1}	Madame Pietra	LB	6 122	4	3	$5^{1\frac{1}{2}}$	$2^{\frac{1}{2}}$	2^{hd}	6^{hd}	Valenzuela P A	2.60
12Jly03 ^{10}Sol^{4}	Jetinto Houston	LB	4 116	7	4	3^{1}	$4^{1\frac{1}{2}}$	6^{2}	7^{10}	Smith M E	16.00
28Jly03 ^{7}Dmr^{2}	Ragin T Rex	LB	4 112	6	2	2^{hd}	8	8	8	Garcia M S	16.10

OFF AT 5:36 Start Good. Won driving. Track fast.
TIME :22^{2}, :45, 1:09, 1:15^{2} (:22.46, :45.03, 1:09.04, 1:15.53)

$2 Mutuel Prices:				
	9–SECRET LIAISON	9.40	5.40	4.60
	6–LACIE GIRL		6.00	4.00
	3–SPRING MEADOW			5.00

$1 EXACTA 9–6 PAID $24.60 $2 QUINELLA 6–9 PAID $29.80 $1 TRIFECTA 9–6–3 PAID $188.10 $1 SUPERFECTA 9–6–3–1 PAID $972.80

B. m, by Housebuster–Pennant Winner, by Crafty Prospector. Trainer West Ted H. Bred by Needham/ Betz Thoroughbreds Liberation Farm & Elia (Ky).

SECRET LIAISON had good early speed and angled in, dueled inside on the backstretch, inched away a bit off the rail on the turn, then drew clear in the stretch under energetic handling. LACIE GIRL chased outside on the backstretch and turn, came four wide into the stretch and gained the place. SPRING MEADOW between horses early, chased off the rail, split horses in midstretch and gained third. CEE'S ELEGANCE saved ground stalking the pace, waited briefly along the rail on the turn but lacked the needed late response. FANCEE BARGAIN allowed to settle inside, saved ground on the turn and into the stretch and improved position. MADAME PIETRA chased outside a rival then between horses into and on the turn and weakened in the stretch. JETINTO HOUSTON forced the pace three deep then stalked four wide, continued three wide on the turn and weakened. RAGIN T REX went up between horses to press the pace, stalked between horses leaving the backstretch, dropped back on the turn and gave way.

Owners— 1, Desperado Stables; 2, Marta Racing Ventures & Hollendorfe; 3, Fog City Stable; 4, Cees Stable LLC; 5, G & G Stables; 6, C T Grether Inc; 7, Team Valor Stables LLC & Barber Gar; 8, Thomas Paula & Thomas Racing

Trainers—1, West Ted H; 2, Hollendorfer Jerry; 3, Hess R B Jr; 4, O'Neill Doug; 5, Sherman Art; 6, Zucker Howard L; 7, Sahadi Jenine; 8, Stute Warren

Scratched— Coconut Girl (10Aug03 ^{3}DMR^{1})

$2 Daily Double (9–9) Paid $153.80; Daily Double Pool $39,822.
$1 Pick Three (4/8–9–9) Paid $126.30; Pick Three Pool $82,959.

TENTH RACE
Monmouth
AUGUST 23, 2003

1⅛ MILES. (1.46^{4}) 68th Running of THE PHILIP H. ISELIN BREEDERS' CUP HANDICAP. Grade III. Purse $200,000 (includes $100,000 BC – Breeders' Cup) A HANDICAP FOR THREE-YEAR-OLDS AND UPWARD. ($100,000 from Breeders' Cup Fund for Cup nominees only). By subscription of $200 each, which should accompany the nomination. $2,500 to enter. Breeders' Cup Fund money also corresponingly divided providing a Breeders' Cup nominee has finished in an awarded position.Any Breeders' Cup Fund money not awarded reverts to the fund. Field will be limited to 14 starters. If more than 14 entries pass the entry box, preference will be given to Breeders' Cup nominees only of equal weight assignment. Weights 5:00 P.M., August 16, 2003,Supplementary nominations may be made by 12;00 p.m., August 16 2003, by payment of a fee of $7,500 each which includes all fees. NOMINATIONS CLOSED Saturday, August 9, 2003 with 29.

Value of Race: $189,000 Winner $120,000; second $40,000; third $11,000; fourth $12,000; fifth $6,000. Mutuel Pool $249,307.00 Exacta Pool $180,258.00 Trifecta Pool $135,687.00

Last Raced	Horse	M/Eqt.	A.Wt	PP	St	¼	½	¾	Str	Fin	Jockey	Odds $1
12Jly03 ^{6}PrM^{1}	Tenpins	Lf	5 119	4	2	2^{hd}	1^{hd}	1^{hd}	$1^{\frac{1}{2}}$	1^{1}	Albarado R J	1.00
19Jly03 ^{9}AP^{2}	Aeneas	L	4 114	3	3	6^{1}	6^{hd}	$6^{2\frac{1}{2}}$	3^{hd}	2no	Boulanger G	9.30
26Jly03 ^{9}Mth^{2}	Jersey Giant	Lb	4 115	7	5	5^{1}	3^{hd}	3^{hd}	$2^{\frac{1}{2}}$	$3^{2\frac{1}{4}}$	Pimentel J	14.70
20Jly03 ^{8}Bel^{3}	Sherpa Guide	Lf	5 114	5	6	4^{hd}	$5^{1\frac{1}{2}}$	$5^{\frac{1}{2}}$	4^{5}	$4^{\frac{3}{4}}$	Lopez C C	61.40
9Aug03 ^{7}Del^{4}	Country Be Gold	L	6 112	8	9	8^{hd}	9	9	$5^{\frac{1}{2}}$	$5^{6\frac{1}{2}}$	Beckner D V	45.60
2Aug03 ^{9}Sar^{6}	Saarland	Lb	4 117	6	7	$7^{\frac{1}{2}}$	$8^{3\frac{1}{2}}$	7^{1}	7^{2}	$6^{\frac{1}{2}}$	Coa E M	1.80
19Jly03 ^{9}Del^{1}	Private Lap	L	4 115	2	1	$1^{\frac{1}{2}}$	2^{1}	$2^{\frac{1}{2}}$	8^{8}	$7^{1\frac{3}{4}}$	Toribio A R	10.90
19Jly03 ^{9}Del^{3}	Runspastum	Lb	6 114	9	8	9	$7^{\frac{1}{2}}$	$4^{\frac{1}{2}}$	6^{hd}	8^{18}	Ferrer J C	25.80
26Jly03 ^{9}Mth^{1}	Vinemeister	L	4 114	1	4	$3^{\frac{1}{2}}$	4^{hd}	8^{1}	9	9	Velez J A Jr	16.20

OFF AT 5:09 Start Good. Won driving. Track fast.
TIME :23^{1}, :48, 1:12^{1}, 1:37^{2}, 1:50^{1} (:23.39, :48.07, 1:12.22, 1:37.46, 1:50.35)

$2 Mutuel Prices:				
	4–TENPINS	4.00	2.80	2.20
	3–AENEAS		5.00	3.60
	7–JERSEY GIANT			3.60

$2 EXACTA 4–3 PAID $32.40 $2 TRIFECTA 4–3–7 PAID $178.60

Ch. h, by Smart Strike–Maid's Broom, by Deputy Minister. Trainer Winfree Donald R. Bred by Joseph Vitello (Mich).

TENPINS assumed the lead approaching the five eighths pole, rated the pace just off the rail, was under pressure into the final turn, dueled gamely with a short lead through the stretch and edged clear the last sixteenth. AENEAS rated off the pace in mid track, made his bid angling widest on the final turn, sustained a long stretch drive and was just up getting the bob for place. JERSEY GIANT rated off the pace in the four path, bid three wide through the final turn, dueled close on the heels of the winner, relented the final sixteenth then was outfinished for place under the wire. SHERPA GUIDE rated close off the rail, lacked room leaving the quarter pole, bid on the rail then faded the final sixteenth. COUNTRY BE GOLD broke a step slow, raced unhurriedly, started his drive off the rail on the final turn, eased out for the stretch run and finished well. SAARLAND rated off the pace mid track, bid through the final turn but came up empty outside. PRIVATE LAP set the early pace inside, dropped back into the final turn and was through for the drive. RUNSPASTUM, unhurriedly outside, advanced five wide through the final turn then gave way from the quarter pole. VINEMEISTER was kept close to the early pace but gave way after five eighths.

Owners— 1, Vitello Joseph V; 2, Ed & Patricia Pavlish; 3, Kligman Joel A; 4, Berkshire Stud; 5, Seinfeld Barry & Dodson Elizabeth K; 6, Phipps Cynthia; 7, Puglisi Stables; 8, Jayeff B Stables; 9, Travin Stables

Trainers—1, Winfree Donald R; 2, Wolfson Martin D; 3, Ryerson James T; 4, Bush Thomas M; 5, Nobles Reynaldo H; 6, McGaughey Claude III; 7, Klesaris Steve; 8, Goldberg Alan E; 9, Seewald Alan

$2 Pick Three (7–8–4) Paid $108.00; Pick Three Pool $12,619.

EIGHTH RACE

Saratoga

AUGUST 23, 2003

1$\frac{1}{16}$ MILES. (Inner Turf)(1.39^4) 15th Running of THE BALLSTON SPA BREEDERS' CUP HANDICAP. Grade III. Purse $200,000. (Includes $100,000 BC – Breeders' Cup plus up to $19,400 NYSBFOA). FILLIES AND MARES THREE YEARS OLD AND UPWARD. ($100,000 from the Breeders' Cup Fund for Cup nominees only.) By subscription of $100 each, which should accompany the nomination; $500 to pass the entry box; $500 to start. Any Breeders' Cup fund monies not awarded will revert back to the Fund. In the event the Ballston Spa Breeders' Cup overfills, preference will be given to highweight fillies or mares (weight for age considered). Breeders' Cup nominees given first preference only in equal weight situations. Trophies will be presented to the winning trainer and jockey. The New York Racing Association reserves the right to transfer this race to the Main Track. In the event that this race is taken off the turf, it may be subject to downgrading upon review by the Graded Stakes Committee. Closed Saturday, August 9, 2003 with 44 Nominations.

Value of Race: $200,000 Winner $120,000; second $40,000; third $22,000; fourth $12,000; fifth $6,000. Mutuel Pool $1,282,517.0 Exacta Pool $995,080.00 Trifecta Pool $709,526.00

Last Raced	Horse	M/Eqt. A.Wt	PP	St	¼	½	¾	Str	Fin	Jockey	Odds $1
19Jly03 ^{10}Mth^1	Stylish	Lb	5 116	3	2	4$\frac{1}{2}$	4^1	4$\frac{1}{2}$	3^1	1$\frac{1}{2}$	Velazquez J R	8.70
26Jly03 ^{8}Sar^7	Snow Dance	L	5 117	6	9	5^{hd}	5$\frac{1}{2}$	5^{hd}	4$\frac{1}{2}$	2^1	Migliore R	5.00
11Jly03 ^{8}Bel^2	Cozzy Corner	L	5 112	4	3	1$\frac{1}{2}$	1^1	1^{hd}	2^{hd}	3^{hd}	Chavez J F	45.75
19Jly03 ^{10}Mth^4	Love N' Kiss S.	L	5 115	9	8	3$^2_\frac{1}{2}$	2$\frac{1}{2}$	2$1\frac{1}{2}$	1^{hd}	4$\frac{1}{2}$	Solis A	22.60
26Jly03 ^{8}Sar^6	Quick Tip	L	5 115	7	7	8$\frac{1}{2}$	7$\frac{1}{2}$	7^{hd}	7^{hd}	5$1\frac{1}{4}$	Day P	8.80
27Jly03 ^{8}Sar^2	Lentil	Lb	4 114	1	1	2^{hd}	3$1\frac{1}{2}$	3$\frac{1}{2}$	5^2	6^{nk}	Espinoza J L	53.00
3Aug03 ^{8}Sar^2	Vespers	L	5 114	8	6	9	9	9	6^{hd}	7$1\frac{1}{2}$	Santos J A	23.00
26Jly03 ^{8}Sar^5	Wonder Again	L	4 117	5	4	6$1\frac{1}{2}$	6$\frac{1}{2}$	6^2	8^6	8$3\frac{1}{2}$	Prado E S	3.20
13Apr03 ^{6}Kee^1	Sea Of Showers	L	4 117	2	5	7^{hd}	8$\frac{1}{2}$	8$1\frac{1}{2}$	9	9	Bailey J D	1.30

OFF AT 4:33 Start Good. Won driving. Course firm.

TIME :23^2, :47^1, 1:11, 1:35, 1:41 (:23.56, :47.36, 1:11.17, 1:35.01, 1:41.03)

$2 Mutuel Prices:

3–STYLISH	....	19.40	8.00	5.50
6–SNOW DANCE	....		5.60	4.80
4–COZZY CORNER	....			13.20

$2 EXACTA 3–6 PAID $104.00 $2 TRIFECTA 3–6–4 PAID $2,981.00

B. m, by Thunder Gulch–Miss Lenora, by Theatrical*Ire. Trainer Mott William I. Bred by Allen E Paulson (Ky).

STYLISH raced close up inside, angled out and was hard ridden from the outside on the second turn, dug in determinedly under steady pressure in the stretch and prevailed after a long, hard drive. SNOW DANCE broke in the air and was away behind the field then moved up inside, saved ground while in hand, came wide into the stretch and finished gamely outside. COZZY CORNER was hustled up to get the lead, set the pace while in hand, responded when set down for the drive and stayed on stubbornly along the inside in the stretch. LOVE N' KISS S. raced close up inside, rallied three wide approaching the eighth pole and weakened in the final furlong. QUICK TIP was unhurried while outrun early, advanced nearing the stretch, angled out for the drive and finished well outside. LENTIL raced with the pace along the inside and tired in the final furlong. VESPERS was outrun early, put in a run along the inside turning for home and lacked a solid finishing kick. WONDER AGAIN was rated along outside, came wide for the drive and had no response when roused. SEA OF SHOWERS was outrun early, raced three wide, took an awkward step in upper stretch and tired.

Owners— 1, Estate of Ahmed Bin Salman; 2, Oxley John C; 3, Fox Ridge Farm Inc; 4, Lael Stables; 5, Farish William S; 6, Lerman Roy S; 7, Janney III Stuart S; 8, Phillips Joan G & John W; 9, Flaxman Stable

Trainers—1, Mott William I; 2, Ward John T Jr; 3, Kelly Patrick J; 4, Clement Christophe; 5, Howard Neil J; 6, Lerman Roy S; 7, McGaughey Claude III; 8, Toner James J; 9, Frankel Robert

Scratched— Nonsuch Bay (27Jly03 ^{9}SAR^3)

NINTH RACE
Saratoga
AUGUST 23, 2003

$1\frac{1}{16}$ MILES. (Turf)(1.38^{4}) 19th Running of THE FOURSTARDAVE HANDICAP. Grade II. Purse $200,000. (Up to $24,800 NYSBFOA). THREE YEAR OLDS AND UPWARD. By subscription of $200 each, which should accompany the nomination; $1,000 to pass the entry box and $1,000 to start. The New York Racing Association reserves the right to transfer this race to the Main Track. In the event that this race is taken off the turf, it may be subject to downgrading upon review by the Graded Stakes Committee. Closed Saturday, August 9, 2003 with 42 Nominations.

Value of Race: $200,000 Winner $120,000; second $40,000; third $22,000; fourth $12,000; fifth $6,000. Mutuel Pool $1,238,357.0 Exacta Pool $1,071,608.0 Trifecta Pool $720,002.00

Last Raced	Horse	M/Eqt.	A.	Wt	PP	St	¼	½	¾	Str	Fin	Jockey	Odds $1
25Jly03 ^{8}Sar^{1}	Trademark-	L	7	118	5	3	$4^{1\frac{1}{2}}$	$4^{\frac{1}{2}}$	$4^{1\frac{1}{2}}$	1^{hd}	1^{2}	Migliore R	2.90
12Jly03 ^{10}Bel^{2}	Quest Star	Lb	4	116	1	1	$1^{\frac{1}{2}}$	1^{hd}	$1^{\frac{1}{2}}$	2^{2}	$2^{1\frac{1}{4}}$	Prado E S	9.20
25Jly03 ^{8}Sar^{4}	Tap The Admiral	L	5	115	4	9	$10^{\frac{1}{2}}$	$10^{1\frac{1}{2}}$	8^{2}	$4^{4\frac{1}{2}}$	3^{1}	Luzzi M J	15.10
11Apr03 ^{8}Kee^{8}	Political Attack	Lb	4	115	9	6	3^{hd}	$2^{\frac{1}{2}}$	2^{1}	3^{hd}	$4^{3\frac{1}{4}}$	Guidry M	41.25
25Jly03 ^{8}Sar^{2}	Rouvres-FR	L	4	115	8	8	11	11	$9^{2\frac{1}{2}}$	8^{hd}	$5^{\frac{1}{2}}$	Solis A	7.60
25Jly03 ^{8}Sar^{7}	Patrol	L	4	117	10	11	$6^{\frac{1}{2}}$	3^{1}	3^{hd}	5^{1}	$6^{\frac{1}{2}}$	Bailey J D	5.30
25Jly03 ^{8}Sar^{6}	Union Place	L	4	112	2	2	2^{1}	5^{hd}	$10^{3\frac{1}{2}}$	$9^{\frac{1}{2}}$	$7^{\frac{1}{2}}$	Chavez J F	48.00
2Aug03 ^{9}Lrl^{2}	Rock Slide	L	5	115	11	10	5^{hd}	$6^{\frac{1}{2}}$	6^{hd}	$7^{\frac{1}{2}}$	$8^{1\frac{1}{4}}$	Day P	22.20
5Jly03 ^{8}Bel^{1}	War Zone	L	4	119	3	7	$9^{1\frac{1}{2}}$	9^{hd}	$7^{\frac{1}{2}}$	10^{12}	9^{hd}	Castellano J J	3.75
7Aug03 ^{7}Lrl^{1}	Tam's Terms	L	5	115	6	4	$7^{1\frac{1}{2}}$	7^{1}	$5^{\frac{1}{2}}$	6^{hd}	$10^{12\frac{1}{4}}$	Karamanos H A	14.10
8Aug03 ^{8}Sar^{1}	Finality	L	4	116	7	5	8^{hd}	8^{hd}	11	11	11	Velazquez J R	7.90

OFF AT 5:10 Start Good. Won driving. Course firm.
TIME :22^{4}, :46, 1:09^{3}, 1:33^{1}, 1:39^{1} (:22.84, :46.08, 1:09.61, 1:33.23, 1:39.29)

$2 Mutuel Prices:				
	5–TRADEMARK–	7.80	4.40	3.70
	1–QUEST STAR		9.20	6.80
	4–TAP THE ADMIRAL			8.00

$2 EXACTA 5–1 PAID $73.00 $2 TRIFECTA 5–1–4 PAID $629.00

B. g, by Goldmark*SAf–Popular*SAf, by Elliodor*Fr. Trainer McLaughlin Kiaran P. Bred by D Cohen and Sons (Pty) Ltd (SAf).

TRADEMARK (SAF) was taken in hand entering the backstretch, raced in good position while tucked in along the rail for six furlongs, edged a bit closer leaving the turn, angled out in upper stretch, charged to the front inside the furlong marker then drew clear under a vigorous hand ride. QUEST STAR outsprinted rivals for the early lead, set a brisk pace along the inside along the backstretch, dug in when challenged on the turn, fought gamely into upper stretch, relinquished the lead to the winner in midstretch then continued on well to hold the place. TAP THE ADMIRAL broke in the air at the start, raced far back for five furlongs, closed the gap while saving ground on the turn then finished willingly along the inside to gain a share. POLITICAL ATTACK pressed the pace between horses to the top of the stretch and weakened from his early efforts. ROUVRES (FR) dropped back soon after the start, steadied behind a wall of horses on the first turn, trailed to the far turn, swerved out at the quarter pole, circled seven wide into the stretch then failed to threaten while improving his position. PATROL broke a bit slowly, made a strong move midway down the backstretch, chased three wide to the turn and steadily tired thereafter. UNION PLACE raced up close through a brisk pace for a half and faltered. ROCK SLIDE raced in the middle of the pack while four wide to the turn and tired. WAR ZONE was outrun for a half, rallied five wide to reach contention on the turn and flattened out. TAM'S TERMS steadied along the inside entering the backstretch, raced in traffic to the far turn and tired. FINALITY checked between horses on the first turn, was never a factor.

Owners— 1, Darley Stable; 2, Mansell Stables LLC; 3, Pont Street Stable; 4, Erdenheim Farm; 5, Head Alec; 6, Claiborne Farm; 7, Sorokolit William A Sr; 8, Farish William S Elkins James A & W; 9, Juddmonte Farms Inc; 10, Bender Sondra D; 11, Dogwood Stable

Trainers—1, McLaughlin Kiaran P; 2, Walden W Elliott; 3, Carroll Del W II; 4, Matz Michael R; 5, Clement Christophe; 6, Mott William I; 7, Schulhofer Randy; 8, Howard Neil J; 9, Frankel Robert; 10, Murray Lawrence E; 11, Pletcher Todd A

Scratched— Evening Attire (2Aug03 ^{9}SAR^{3})

$2 Pick Three (12–3–5) Paid $1,260.00; Pick Three Pool $205,075.

TENTH RACE
Saratoga
AUGUST 23, 2003

7 FURLONGS. (1.20^3) 20th Running of THE KING'S BISHOP. Grade I. Purse $200,000. (Up to $24,800 NYSBFOA). THREE YEAR OLDS. By subscription of $200 each, which should accompany the nomination; $1,000 to pass the entry box, $1,000 to start. 123 lbs. Non-winners of a Grade I or Grade II since March 1, allowed 2 lbs.; a Graded Sweepstakes, 4 lbs.; $50,000, or three races, 6 lbs. (Maiden, Claiming, Starter, Restricted or Restricted Stake not considered). Closed Saturday, August 9, 2003 with 29 Nominations.

Value of Race: $200,000 Winner $120,000; second $40,000; third $22,000; fourth $12,000; fifth $6,000. Mutuel Pool $1,684,327.0 Exacta Pool $1,297,782.0 Trifecta Pool $924,433.00

Last Raced	Horse	M/Eqt.	A.Wt	PP	St	¼	½	Str	Fin	Jockey	Odds $1
12Jly03 ^{10}Crc^1	Valid Video	L	3 121	2	8	4^2	$4\frac{1}{2}$	$3^{3\frac{1}{2}}$	1^{nk}	Bravo J	7.80
2Aug03 ^{8}Sar^2	Great Notion	Lf	3 117	1	13	$1^{1\frac{1}{2}}$	$1^{2\frac{1}{2}}$	$1^{1\frac{1}{2}}$	2^{nk}	Day P	16.70
26Jly03 ^{7}Sar^1	Ghostzapper	Lb	3 117	9	5	10^{hd}	$8\frac{1}{2}$	8^6	$3^{1\frac{3}{4}}$	Castellano J J	6.30
3Aug03 ^{9}Sar^6	During	Lb	3 123	10	2	2^1	$2^{1\frac{1}{2}}$	2^{hd}	$4^{1\frac{1}{4}}$	Velasquez C	31.50
2Aug03 ^{8}Sar^4	Posse	L	3 123	3	10	$12^{3\frac{1}{2}}$	11^3	$7\frac{1}{2}$	5^{nk}	Lanerie C J	6.90
13Jly03 ^{6}Hol^3	Eye Of The Tiger	L	3 121	11	9	$9^{3\frac{1}{2}}$	$7^{2\frac{1}{2}}$	6^{hd}	$6^{3\frac{3}{4}}$	Solis A	7.00
12Jly03 ^{9}Mth^2	Christine's Outlaw	Lbf	3 117	13	1	3^{hd}	$3\frac{1}{2}$	4^{hd}	7^{hd}	Velazquez J R	26.75
2Aug03 ^{8}Sar^1	Zavata		3 123	8	4	5^{hd}	$5^{3\frac{1}{2}}$	5^{hd}	8^1	Bailey J D	1.25
10Aug03 ^{7}Sar^3	Private City	Lb	3 117	4	11	11^3	12^5	10^3	$9^{2\frac{3}{4}}$	Santos J A	57.25
2Aug03 ^{8}Sar^6	Scrimshaw	Lb	3 123	6	6	$7^{2\frac{1}{2}}$	$9^{1\frac{1}{2}}$	9^{hd}	$10^{2\frac{1}{2}}$	Chavez J F	20.40
10Jly03 ^{5}Bel^1	Midnight Charlie	Lf	3 119	7	12	13	13	12^8	11^1	Castillo H Jr	87.50
12Jly03 ^{10}Crc^7	Halo Homewrecker	Lb	3 121	5	7	$6\frac{1}{2}$	6^{hd}	11^2	$12^{7\frac{1}{2}}$	Migliore R	54.50
14Jun03 ^{11}Del^1	Awesome Time	L	3 121	12	3	$8\frac{1}{2}$	10^{hd}	13	13	Prado E S	72.00

OFF AT 5:46 Start Good. Won driving. Track fast.
TIME :21^3, :43^3, 1:08^3, 1:22 (:21.76, :43.79, 1:08.67, 1:22.14)

$2 Mutuel Prices:

2–VALID VIDEO	17.60	9.80	7.30
1–GREAT NOTION		14.60	10.20
9–GHOSTZAPPER			5.40

$2 EXACTA 2–1 PAID $197.00 $2 TRIFECTA 2–1–9 PAID $1,436.00

Dk. b. or br. g, (Mar), by Valid Wager–Miss Video, by Star Gallant. Trainer Manning Dennis J. Bred by Casey Seaman (Fla).

VALID VIDEO settled in good position along the backstretch, steadily gained while saving ground on the turn, closed the gap in upper stretch, steadied along the rail then altered course to the outside in midstretch, finished determinedly to get up in the final strides. GREAT NOTION rushed up along the rail after breaking a bit slowly, set a rapid pace for a half, extended his lead in upper stretch, fought gamely into deep stretch and yielded grudgingly. GHOSTZAPPER dropped back while racing well off the rail along the backstretch, launched a rally from outside on the turn, circled six wide into the stretch then finished fastest in the middle of the track but could not get up. DURING pressed the pace while three wide to the top of the stretch, battled into midstretch then weakened under pressure in the final eighth. POSSE lagged far behind along the backstretch, closed the gap between horses while five wide at the top of the stretch then rallied belatedly while racing erratically through the lane. EYE OF THE TIGER was outrun for a half, advanced four wide between horses entering the stretch then failed to threaten while improving his position. CHRISTINE'S OUTLAW stalked three wide for a half and tired. ZAVATA was taken in hand in the early stages, raced just off the pace while five wide to the turn then lacked the needed response when called upon. PRIVATE CITY outrun for a half, circled seven wide on the turn then lugged in while tiring in upper stretch. SCRIMSHAW bumped at the start, was never a factor. MIDNIGHT CHARLIE was outrun while racing wide. HALO HOMEWRECKER, bumped at the start, saved ground to no avail. AWESOME TIME showed only brief speed.

Owners— 1, Fehsenfeld Mack; 2, Hamilton Tommy & Bonnie; 3, Stronach Stable; 4, McIngvale James; 5, Heiligbrodt Stables & Vinery Stable; 6, Gunther John D; 7, R C Hill Stable; 8, Tabor Michael B; 9, Bohemia Stable; 10, Lewis Robert B & Beverly J; 11, Papandrea Vincent; 12, Evans Edward P; 13, Lapenta Robert V

Trainers—1, Manning Dennis J; 2, Miller Darrin; 3, Frankel Robert; 4, Baffert Bob; 5, Asmussen Steven M; 6, Hollendorfer Jerry; 7, Weaver George; 8, Biancone Patrick L; 9, Jerkens H Allen; 10, Lukas D Wayne; 11, Gyarmati Leah; 12, Hennig Mark; 13, Zito Nicholas P

ELEVENTH RACE   1¼ MILES. (2.00) 134th Running of THE TRAVERS. Grade I. Purse $1,000,000. (Up to $72,000 NYSBFOA). THREE YEAR OLDS. By subscription of $1,000 each, which should accompany the nomination; $5,000 to pass the entry box, $5,000 to start. Weights at 126 lbs. Closed Saturday, August 9th, 2003 with 18 Nominations.

Saratoga

AUGUST 23, 2003

Value of Race: $1,000,000 Winner $600,000; second $200,000; third $110,000; fourth $60,000; fifth $30,000. Mutuel Pool $3,246,367.0 Exacta Pool $1,860,759.0 Trifecta Pool $1,295,476.0

Last Raced	Horse	M/Eqt. A.Wt	PP	¼	½	¾	1	Str	Fin	Jockey	Odds $1
13Jly03 6Hol2	Ten Most Wanted	Lb 3 126	4	54½	45½	48	1hd	1½	14½	Day P	2.75
3Aug03 11Mth1	Peace Rules	L 3 126	3	22	24½	21½	2½	25½	210	Bailey J D	2.30
3Aug03 9Sar1	Strong Hope	L 3 126	2	1hd	1hd	1½	36	35	3¾	Velazquez J R	4.40
3Aug03 11Mth4	Wild And Wicked	L 3 126	5	6	6	6	6	4hd	43¼	Sellers S J	16.90
3Aug03 9Sar3	Congrats	Lb 3 126	1	4½	57	55½	52½	52½	52	Luzzi M J	13.20
3Aug03 11Mth2	Sky Mesa	L 3 126	6	3½	3½	3hd	4hd	6	6	Prado E S	2.50

OFF AT 6:28 Start Good. Won driving. Track fast.

TIME :23², :46¹, 1:09⁴, 1:35², 2:02 (:23.55, :46.36, 1:09.98, 1:35.46, 2:02.14)

$2 Mutuel Prices:

4–TEN MOST WANTED	7.50	3.40	2.80
1–PEACE RULES		3.80	2.80
3–STRONG HOPE			3.10

$2 EXACTA 4–1 PAID $27.00 $2 TRIFECTA 4–1–3 PAID $76.00

Dk. b. or br. c, (Feb), by Deputy Commander–Wanted Again, by Criminal Type. Trainer Dollase Wallace. Bred by Jim H Plemmons (Ky).

TEN MOST WANTED broke inward brushing with PEACE RULES at the start, bumped with CONGRATS going info the first turn, settled in good position entering the backstretch, raced in hand while tucked in behind the leaders for six furlongs, angled out leaving the three-eighths pole, closed the gap to challenge on the turn, drew on even terms with PEACE RULES in upper stretch, surged to the front approaching the furlong marker then drew off under a vigorous hand ride. PEACE RULES rushed up from outside to contest the early, dueled through brisk fractions along the backstretch, fought heads apart along the rail to the top of the stretch, hung in gamely info midstretch, but couldn't stay with the winner through the final eighth. STRONG HOPE moved up along the rail to gain a slim early advantage, set the pace under pressure along the inside to the turn, dropped back leaving the quarter pole and gradually tired thereafter. WILD AND WICKED trailed to the top of the stretch and failed to threaten while improving his position. CONGRATS steadied after bumping with PEACE RULES on and hitting the rail on the first turn and failed to seriously threaten thereafter. SKY MESA broke awkwardly, moved quickly into contention while three wide on the first turn, raced just outside the leaders along the backstretch, was put to the whip nearing the far turn, then gave way after going seven furlongs.

Owners— 1, J Paul Reddam Michael Jarvis James; 2, Gann Edmund A; 3, Melnyk Eugene & Laura; 4, Robert David Randal & Mrs Robert Da; 5, Claiborne Farm & Dilschneider Adele; 6, Oxley John C

Trainers—1, Dollase Wallace; 2, Frankel Robert; 3, Pletcher Todd A; 4, McPeek Kenneth G; 5, McGaughey Claude III; 6, Ward John T Jr

Scratched— Empire Maker (3Aug03 9SAR²), Funny Cide (3Aug03 11MTH³).

$2 Pick Three (5–2–4) Paid $303.50; Pick Three Pool $371,739.
$2 Pick Four (3–5–2–4) Paid $3,606.00; Pick Four Pool $1,488,479.
$2 Pick Six (6–12–3–5–2–4) 6
Correct Paid $128,675.00; Pick Six Pool $541,466. $2 Pick Six (6–12–3–5–2–4) 5
Correct Paid $914.00

FIFTH RACE   1¼ MILES. (1.59) 13th Running of THE PACIFIC CLASSIC. Grade I. Purse $1,000,000. 3–year–olds and upward. By subscription of $200 each to accompany the nomination. All horses shall pay $2,500 to pass the entry box and $7,500 additional to start, with $1,000,000 Guaranteed with $600,000 to the winner, $200,000 to second, $120,000 to third, $60,000 to fourth and $20,000 to fifth. Weights, 3–year–olds, 117 lbs. Older, 124 lbs. Closed Thursday, August 14 with 14 nominators.

Del Mar

AUGUST 24, 2003

Value of Race: $980,000 Winner $600,000; second $200,000; third $120,000; fourth $60,000.   Mutuel Pool $1,074,261.0 Exacta Pool $437,601.00 Quinella Pool $52,634.00

Last Raced	Horse	M/Eqt. A.Wt	PP	¼	½	¾	1	Str	Fin	Jockey	Odds $1
4Jly03 7Hol1	Candy Ride–ARG	LB 4 124	3	2½	2²	21	2⁴	11	13¼	Krone J A	2.20
2Aug03 9Sar1	Medaglia d'Oro	LB 4 124	2	1½	11	1½	1hd	26	27	Bailey J D	0.60
26Jly03 7Dmr2	Fleetstreet Dancer	LBbf 5 124	1	3½	31½	4	31	32	32	Baze T C	24.90
3Aug03 1Mth1	Milwaukee Brew	LBb 6 124	4	4	4	3½	4	4	4	Prado E S	3.10

OFF AT 2:45 Start Good. Won driving. Track fast.

TIME :23², :46⁴, 1:10⁴, 1:34³, 1:59 (:23.40, :46.82, 1:10.95, 1:34.78, 1:59.11)

(New Track Record)

$2 Mutuel Prices:

3–CANDY RIDE–ARG	6.40	2.80	—
2–MEDAGLIA D'ORO		2.20	—
1–FLEETSTREET DANCER			—

$1 EXACTA 3–2 PAID $6.20 $2 QUINELLA 2–3 PAID $5.60

B. c, by Ride The Rails–Candy Girl*Arg, by Candy Stripes. Trainer McAnally Ronald. Bred by Haras Abolengo (Arg).

CANDY RIDE (ARG) bobbled at the start, pulled under a hold while lugging in a bit in the stretch the first time, prompted the pace outside the runner-up, took command into the stretch, inched away in midstretch and drew clear under good handling. MEDAGLIA D'ORO set the early lead and angled in, set a pressured pace inside a rating mild, inched away briefly leaving the first turn, fought back inside the winner on the second turn and into the stretch but could not match that one in the final furlong while clearly second best. FLEETSTREET DANCER pulled a bit stalking the early pace inside, inched forward leaving the backstretch, came out into the stretch and weakened. MILWAUKEE BREW broke out a bit, stalked off the rail, went up outside FLEETSTREET DANCER leaving the backstretch and three deep into the second turn, dropped back on that turn and had nothing left. NEW TRACK RECORD.

Owners— 1, Craig Sidney H & Jenny; 2, Gann Edmund A; 3, Leatherman Lee & Ty; 4, Stronach Stable

Trainers—1, McAnally Ronald; 2, Frankel Robert; 3, O'Neill Doug; 4, Frankel Robert

Scratched— Kudos (13Jly03 9HOL³).

$2 Daily Double (9–3) Paid $18.00; Daily Double Pool $44,152.
$1 Pick Three (1–9–3) Paid $26.50; Pick Three Pool $126,390.

NINTH RACE
Del Mar
AUGUST 24, 2003

1⅛ MILES. (Turf)(1.45^{4}) 47th Running of THE DEL MAR OAKS. Grade I. Purse $300,000 Guaranteed. FILLIES, THREE-YEAR-OLDS. By subscription of $300 each, which shall accompany the nomination, or by supplementary nomination of $3,000 each by closing time of entries, with $1,000 to pass the entry box and $2,000 additional to start, with $300,000 guaranteed, of which $180,000 to first, $60,000 to second, $36,000 to third, $18,000 to fourth and $6,000 to fifth. Weight 122 lbs. First preference will be given to graded or group stakes winners. Second preference will be given to fillies which have finished second or third in graded or group stakes. Total non-claiming purse earnings will determine the order of preference for fillies of equal status. Nominations closed Thursday, August 14, 2003 with 17. (Rail at 7 feet).

Value of Race: $300,000 Winner $180,000; second $60,000; third $36,000; fourth $18,000; fifth $6,000. Mutuel Pool $609,948.00 Exacta Pool $293,971.00 Quinella Pool $37,083.00 Trifecta Pool $257,165.00

Last Raced	Horse	M/Eqt.	A.Wt	PP	St	¼	½	¾	Str	Fin	Jockey	Odds $1
4Aug03 ^{7}Dmr^{1}	Dessert	LB	3 122	4	1	$1^{1\frac{1}{2}}$	$1^{1\frac{1}{2}}$	$1^{\frac{1}{2}}$	1^{1}	1^{nk}	Nakatani C S	b-2.50
4Aug03 ^{4}Dmr^{1}	Solar Echo	LB	3 122	7	3	3^{1}	$3^{\frac{1}{2}}$	4^{hd}	$3^{\frac{1}{2}}$	2^{1}	Flores D R	3.10
5Jly03 ^{5}Hol^{5}	Personal Legend	LBb	3 122	3	5	6^{2}	6^{3}	6^{1}	5^{hd}	3no	Bailey J D	4.70
2Aug03 Goo^{6}	Cassis	LB	3 122	6	4	$4^{\frac{1}{2}}$	5^{1}	$5^{1\frac{1}{2}}$	4^{1}	$4^{\frac{1}{2}}$	Desormeaux K J	4.60
2Aug03 ^{8}Dmr^{2}	Atlantic Ocean	LB	3 122	5	2	2^{1}	$2^{1\frac{1}{2}}$	$2^{1\frac{1}{2}}$	$2^{1\frac{1}{2}}$	$5^{2\frac{1}{2}}$	Valenzuela P A	b-2.50
2Aug03 ^{8}Dmr^{4}	Star Vega-GB	LB	3 122	1	6	5^{1}	4^{1}	3^{hd}	6^{3}	$6^{1\frac{1}{2}}$	Smith M E	a-2.80
2Aug03 ^{8}Dmr^{1}	Katdogawn-GB	LB	3 122	2	8	8	8	$7^{\frac{1}{2}}$	7^{2}	7^{4}	Krone J A	a-2.80
10Aug03 Dea^{3}	Well Done My Love-GER	LBb	3 122	8	7	7^{1}	7^{hd}	8	8	8	Solis A	17.90

a-Coupled: Star Vega-GB and Katdogawn-GB.
b-Coupled: Dessert and Atlantic Ocean.

OFF AT 5:00 Start Good. Won driving. Course firm.
TIME :23^{1}, :47^{2}, 1:11^{4}, 1:35^{1}, 1:47 (:23.31, :47.45, 1:11.90, 1:35.29, 1:47.04)

$2 Mutuel Prices:

2-DESSERT (b-entry)	7.00	3.60	2.40
5-SOLAR ECHO		4.20	3.20
3-PERSONAL LEGEND			3.00

$1 EXACTA 2-5 PAID $15.70 $2 QUINELLA 2-5 PAID $15.60 $1 TRIFECTA 2-5-3 PAID $79.10

Dk. b. or br. f, (Feb), by Storm Cat-Windsharp, by Lear Fan. Trainer Mandella Richard. Bred by The Thoroughbred Corporation (Ky).

DESSERT sped to the early lead and angled in, set the pace inside, responded when challenged on the second turn, kicked clear again past the eighth pole and held gamely under urging. SOLAR ECHO broke out a bit, stalked outside a rival then between horses into the second turn, continued just off the rail leaving that bend, came out in the stretch and bumped with CASSIS, then finished well to just miss. PERSONAL LEGEND chased inside then outside a rival leaving the second turn, came out in the stretch and rallied late for third. CASSIS stalked outside a rival or off the rail, went three deep on the second turn and into the stretch, bumped with the runner-up in midstretch and continued willingly between foes at the wire. ATLANTIC OCEAN stalked the winner off the rail, bid outside that one on the second turn and into the stretch but weakened in the final furlong. STAR VEGA (GB) was in a good position chasing the pace along the inside, remained on the rail and lacked the needed response. KATDOGAWN (GB) unhurried inside then outside a rival, came out some in the stretch and lacked a rally, then was not urged late. WELL DONE MY LOVE (GER) angled in and saved ground off the pace and did not rally.

Owners— 1, The Thoroughbred Corporation; 2, Whitham Janis R; 3, Gann Edmund A; 4, Robertson Sanford R; 5, The Thoroughbred Corporation; 6, Cuchna John R Jim Ford Inc & Pearso; 7, Cuchna John R Jim Ford Inc & Pearso; 8, Peacock Cecil N

Trainers—1, Mandella Richard; 2, McAnally Ronald; 3, Frankel Robert; 4, Noseda Jeremy; 5, Baffert Bob; 6, Cassidy James; 7, Cassidy James; 8, Hendricks Dan L

$2 Daily Double (7-2) Paid $38.80; Daily Double Pool $47,686.
$1 Pick Three (7-7-2) Paid $53.90; Pick Three Pool $121,484.

NINTH RACE
Saratoga
AUGUST 24, 2003

7 FURLONGS. (1.20^{3}) 25th Running of THE BALLERINA HANDICAP. Grade I. Purse $250,000 (Up to $38,500 NYSBFOA) FILLIES AND MARES THREE YEARS OLD AND UPWARD. By subscription of $250 each, which should accompany the nomination; $1,250 to pass the entry box, $1,250 to start. The purse to be divided 60% to the winner, 20% to second, 11% to third, 6% to fourth and 3% to fifth. Trophies will be presented to the winning owner, trainer and jockey. Closed Saturday, August 9, 2003 with 20 Nominations.

Value of Race: $250,000 Winner $150,000; second $50,000; third $27,500; fourth $15,000; fifth $7,500. Mutuel Pool $889,118.00 Exacta Pool $654,528.00 Trifecta Pool $455,422.00

Last Raced	Horse	M/Eqt.	A.Wt	PP	St	¼	½	Str	Fin	Jockey	Odds $1
12Jly03 ^{11}Crc^{3}	Harmony Lodge	L	5 115	8	1	$1^{\frac{1}{2}}$	1^{hd}	$1^{1\frac{1}{2}}$	1no	Migliore R	12.90
1Aug03 ^{8}Sar^{2}	Shine Again	L	6 120	5	5	$4^{\frac{1}{2}}$	$4^{1\frac{1}{2}}$	$3^{\frac{1}{2}}$	2^{2}	Santos J A	2.60
12Jly03 ^{11}Crc^{1}	Gold Mover	L	5 118	6	3	2^{hd}	3^{1}	4^{hd}	3^{hd}	Coa E M	a-8.70
19Jly03 ^{9}Bel^{4}	Yell	L	3 113	1	6	6^{hd}	6^{hd}	6^{5}	4no	Day P	12.60
1Aug03 ^{8}Sar^{1}	Willa On The Move	L	4 116	2	7	8	$5^{1\frac{1}{2}}$	5^{2}	5^{hd}	Albarado R J	3.65
3Aug03 ^{7}Sar^{1}	Stellar	L	3 110	4	2	3^{1}	$2^{\frac{1}{2}}$	2^{hd}	$6^{3\frac{1}{4}}$	Farina Tony	a-8.70
13Jly03 ^{4}Hol^{2}	You	L	4 120	7	4	5^{hd}	7^{hd}	$7^{2\frac{1}{2}}$	$7^{2\frac{1}{4}}$	Castellano J J	3.75
1Aug03 ^{8}Sar^{3}	Smok'n Frolic	L	4 117	3	8	$7^{\frac{1}{2}}$	8	8	8	Velazquez J R	3.65

a-Coupled: Gold Mover and Stellar.

OFF AT 5:24 Start Good. Won driving. Track fast.
TIME :22^{3}, :45, 1:09, 1:22^{1} (:22.70, :45.06, 1:09.03, 1:22.23)

$2 Mutuel Prices:

7-HARMONY LODGE	27.80	11.40	5.60
5-SHINE AGAIN		4.10	3.00
1A-GOLD MOVER (a-entry)			4.20

$2 EXACTA 7-5 PAID $110.50 $2 TRIFECTA 7-5-1 PAID $506.00

Ch. m, by Hennessy-Win Crafty Lady, by Crafty Prospector. Trainer Pletcher Todd A. Bred by Sabine Stables (Ky).

HARMONY LODGE quickly showed in front, set the pace while in hand, drew clear when roused then dug in gamely and held on, driving. SHINE AGAIN was taken in hand after the start, was steadied on the backstretch, raced four wide, responded when roused, finished gamely outside and just missed. GOLD MOVER raced with the pace while in hand between rivals and finished well. YELL raced in hand along the inside, advanced nearing the stretch, altered course to the outside in the stretch and finished gamely. WILLA ON THE MOVE was steadied while between rivals on the backstretch, put in a run along the inside on the turn and finished well. STELLAR argued the pace along the inside and gave ground grudgingly on the rail in the drive. YOU was outrun early, raced five wide and had no response when roused. SMOK'N FROLIC was rated along while six wide and had no rally.

Owners— 1, Melnyk Eugene & Laura; 2, Bohemia Stable; 3, Evans Edward P; 4, Claiborne Farm & Dilschneider Adele; 5, Angelos Peter G; 6, Tabor Michael & Evans Edward P; 7, Gann Edmund A; 8, Dogwood Stable

Trainers—1, Pletcher Todd A; 2, Jerkens H Allen; 3, Hennig Mark; 4, McGaughey Claude III; 5, Dutrow Anthony W; 6, Biancone Patrick L; 7, Frankel Robert; 8, Pletcher Todd A

EIGHTH RACE

Emerald

AUGUST 24, 2003

1 MILE. (1.33¹) 68th Running of THE LONGACRES MILE HANDICAP. Grade III. Purse $250,000. By subscription of $250 each, which shall accompany the nomination, $1,250 to enter, $1,250 additional to start with $137,500 guaranteed to the owner of the winner, $50,000 to second, $37,500 to third, $18,750 to fourth and $6,250 to fifth. Weights Saturday, August 16. Closed August 10 with 30 nominations.

Value of Race: $250,000 Winner $137,500; second $50,000; third $37,500; fourth $18,750; fifth $6,250. Mutuel Pool $323,355.00 Exacta Pool $148,646.00 Trifecta Pool $155,870.00 Superfecta Pool $54,299.00

Last Raced	Horse	M/Eqt. A.Wt	PP	St	¼	½	¾	Str	Fin	Jockey	Odds $1
5Jly03 ⁶Hol¹	Sky Jack	LBb 7 123	3	2	1ʰᵈ 2¹	1ʰᵈ	1⁵	16¼	Baze R A	1.50
27Jly03 ⁷EmD¹	Poker Brad	LB 5 116	8	7	9² 8¹	6ʰᵈ	2ʰᵈ 2²	Russell B R	6.40
4Aug03 ⁹Hst¹	Lord Nelson	LBf 6 116	4	9	6ʰᵈ 7²	8½	3½ 3²¾	Fuentes F P	24.20
27Jly03 ⁷EmD³	Alfurune	LBbf 5 117	6	4	8ʰᵈ 9ʰᵈ	9ʰᵈ	5ʰᵈ 4ʰᵈ	Gutierrez J M	11.60
27Jly03 ⁷EmD²	Moonlight Meeting	LBf 8 116	9	10	10 10	10	6½ 5²¾	Baze G	15.60
3Aug03 ⁹EmD²	Salt Grinder	LBbf 4 114	7	5	5ʰᵈ 5½	4¹	4¹ 6³¼	Mitchell G V	35.00
3Aug03 ⁹EmD⁵	Total Limit	LB 4 116	2	8	4¹ 4¹	7¹	9½ 7¹	Saito S T	14.00
27Jly03 ⁷EmD⁴	Sabertooth	LBbf 5 116	5	3	3¹ 3½	31½	7½ 8½	Krigger K	33.40
3Aug03 ⁸Dmr²	Gondolieri-CH	LBb 4 121	10	6	7³ 6¹	5½	10 9³¼	Alvarado F T	2.00
3Aug03 ⁹EmD¹	Handy N Bold	LBbf 8 115	1	1	2¹½ 1ʰᵈ	2ʰᵈ	8ʰᵈ10	Wilson D H	32.30

OFF AT 4:49 Start Good For All But LORD NELSON Won ridden out. Track fast.

TIME :22¹, :44², 1:08¹, 1:20², 1:33 (:22.20, :44.40, 1:08.20, 1:20.40, 1:33.00))

(New Track Record)

$2 Mutuel Prices:

3–SKY JACK	5.00	3.40	3.00
8–POKER BRAD		5.20	4.60
4–LORD NELSON			8.60

$1 EXACTA 3–8 PAID $16.60 $1 TRIFECTA 3–8–4 PAID $185.00 $1
SUPERFECTA 3–8–4–6 PAID $863.20

Gr/ro g, by Jaklin Klugman–Sky Captive, by Skywalker. Trainer O'Neill Doug. Bred by Lambert Rene & Margie (Cal).

SKY JACK vied for the lead with HANDY N BOLD racing in hand while two-wide, disposed of that one nearing the stretch and increased his advantage through the stretch in a record breaking performance. POKER BRAD unhurried early, came four-wide into the stretch, angled further out while splitting rivals during the drive, then had his rider lose the whip nearing the eighth pole and finished well to prove second best. LORD NELSON hopped in the air at the start to get away slightly behind his field, then was reserved off the early pace, came six-wide into the stretch to offer his bid, but was unable to improve his position late. ALFURUNE dropped back early, saved ground to the stretch, angled out to come between horses during the drive, steadied in tight nearing the eighth pole and finished willingly when clear. MOONLIGHT MEETING was three-wide early, came seven-wide into the stretch and failed to seriously threaten. SALT GRINDER forwardly placed from the outset, moved up four-wide to offered a bid nearing the quarter pole and then flattened out during the drive. TOTAL LIMIT saved ground to the stretch stalking the pace, swung out for the drive, but lacked a response when called upon. SABERTOOTH forced the pace for six furlongs while racing three-wide, came out slightly nearing the eighth pole and tired. GONDOLIERI (CHI) was prominently placed for six furlongs while racing three-wide, but came up empty when put to pressure. HANDY N BOLD was hard used dueling for the lead from the inside and stopped after six furlongs.

Owners— 1, Ren-Mar Thoroughbreds; 2, Quadrun Farm LLC; 3, Bennett Mr & Mrs R J; 4, Savario Farm Garrison L & Jewett De; 5, Beal Richard T; 6, Homestretch Farm; 7, Sarkowsky Herman; 8, Sparling Robert & Bruce; 9, Hunt Nelson B; 10, Orr Doris M

Trainers— 1, O'Neill Doug; 2, McCanna Tim; 3, Condilenios Dino; 4, Doutrich David K; 5, Ross Sharon; 6, Penney Jim; 7, Forster Grant T; 8, Penney Jim; 9, McAnally Ronald; 10, Essex Charles

---

$2 Daily Double (OAKS–MILE 9–3) Paid $8.60; Daily Double Pool $7,376.
$1 Pick Three (7–9–3) Paid $399.60; Pick Three Pool $9,234.
$2 Perfect Six (6 VS. 8 (WINNER 8)) Paid $3.60; Perfect Six Pool $5,183.

EIGHTH RACE
Saratoga
AUGUST 25, 2003

1⅜ MILES. (Inner Turf)(2.12) 8th Running of THE GLENS FALLS HANDICAP. Grade III. Purse $100,000. (Up to $19,400 NYSBFOA) A HANDICAP FOR FILLIES AND MARES THREE YEARS OLD AND UPWARD. By subscription of $100 each, which should accompany the nomination; $500 to pass the entry box, $500 to start, with $100,000 added. The added money and all fees to be divided 60% to the winner, 20% to second, 11% to third, 6% to fourth and 3% to fifth. Trophies will be presented to the winning owner, trainer and jockey. The New York Racing Association reserves the right to transfer this race to the Main Track. In the event that this race is taken off the turf, it may be subject to downgrading upon review by the Graded Stakes Committee. Closed Saturday, August 9, 2003 with 36 Nominations.

Value of Race: $113,100 Winner $67,860; second $22,620; third $12,441; fourth $6,786; fifth $3,393. Mutuel Pool $501,461.00 Exacta Pool $481,425.00 Trifecta Pool $389,395.00

Last Raced	Horse	M/Eqt.	A.Wt	PP	¼	½	¾	1	Str	Fin	Jockey	Odds $1
11Jly03 8Bel1	Sixty Seconds-NZ	L	5 115	7	51½	4½	5½	4½	2hd	1hd	Santos J A	3.25
19Jly03 7Del4	Primetimevalentine	b	4 113	9	83	82½	85½	87	4hd	2nk	Coa E M	8.30
19Jly03 7Del1	Alternate	Lb	4 116	8	2½	21½	36	22½	1½	3¾	Castillo O O	8.70
13Aug03 7Sar5	Sunstone-GB	Lb	5 112	2	61½	6hd	73½	75½	51½	4nk	Castellano J J	25.75
19Jly03 7Del3	Lady Of The Future	L	5 114	6	9	9	9	9	82½	5½	Guidry M	13.80
15Aug03 5Sar1	Dynamic Lisa	L	4 112	5	32½	33	2½	31½	31	62½	Day P	4.40
4Jly03 10Bel6	Mariensky	L	4 119	1	4hd	51	4hd	5hd	6hd	71	Velazquez J R	2.20
29Jun03 5Bel1	Cozie Advantage	Lb	4 114	3	73	76	6½	6½	9	86¼	Albarado R J	26.75
29Jun03 5Bel2	Midnight Angel-GE	L	4 115	4	1½	1½	1hd	11½	7½	9	Migliore R	10.70

OFF AT 4:47 Start Good. Won driving. Course firm.
TIME :24^{3}, :48^{4}, 1:13^{3}, 1:37, 2:01^{2}, 2:13^{4} (:24.60, :48.95, 1:13.69, 1:37.05, 2:01.59, 2:13.96)

$2 Mutuel Prices:

8–SIXTY SECONDS–NZ	8.50	4.70	3.70
10–PRIMETIMEVALENTINE		6.70	5.60
9–ALTERNATE			5.90

$2 EXACTA 8–10 PAID $68.50 $2 TRIFECTA 8–10–9 PAID $361.50

Dk. b. or br. m, by Centaine*Aus–Fifteen Reasons*NZ, by Sound Reason. Trainer Clement Christophe. Bred by T E Parae Trust (NZ).

SIXTY SECONDS (NZ) in hand early, was rated in good position while slightly off the rail along the backstretch, launched a rally between horses on the turn, closed the gap in upper stretch, made a run to challenge in midstretch, surged to the front inside the furlong marker, battled into deep stretch and was all out to hold off PRIMETIMEVALENTINE in the final strides. PRIMETIMEVALENTINE raced well back for seven furlongs, rapidly gained from outside on the turn, circled six wide into the stretch, unleashed a strong late run in the middle of the track to draw on nearly even terms with the winner then lost the bob. ALTERNATE stalked he pace from outside, raced in close contention while three wide along the backstretch, chased the leader to the then, gained a slim advantage entering the stretch, battled into deep stretch and yielded grudgingly. SUNSTONE (GB) was unhurried for seven furlongs while saving ground, angled between horses on the turn, swung four wide entering the stretch then improved her position with a late run between horses. LADY OF THE FUTURE trailed for a good portion of the way while saving ground, swung to the middle of the track at the top of the stretch then rallied belatedly. DYNAMIC LISA was under a snug hold between horses, steadied slightly while up close nearing the far turn, fought gamely into midstretch then weakened. MARIENSKY was rated just inside the winner to the far turn, steadied along the rail on the turn then lacked a strong closing bid. COZIE ADVANTAGE raced in the middle of the pack between horses, angled five wide while gaining a bit at the quarter pole then flattened out. MIDNIGHT ANGEL (GER) set the pace under pressure to the top of the stretch and gave way.

Owners— 1, The Leigh Family Stable; 2, Low Lawana L & Robert E; 3, Pin Oak Stable; 4, Georgica Stable; 5, Pearson Max H; 6, Schwartz Herbert T & Carol A; 7, Waterville Lake Stable; 8, Red Oak Stable; 9, Newsells Park Stud

Trainers—1, Clement Christophe; 2, Peitz Daniel C; 3, Motion H Graham; 4, Barbara Robert; 5, Greene Thomas M; 6, Schwartz Scott M 7, Clement Christophe; 8, Kimmel John C; 9, Clement Christophe

Scratched— Trekking (4Jly03 10BEL5), Ellie's Quest (27Jly03 8SAR7), Belles Lettres (16Aug03 8SAR11), Fly Borboleta (12Jly03 10ELP7)

EIGHTH RACE
Saratoga
AUGUST 29, 2003

7 FURLONGS. (1.20^{3}) 112th Running of THE SPINAWAY. Grade I. Purse $200,000. (Up to $34,800 NYSBFOA). FILLIES, TWO YEARS OLD. By subscription of $200 each, which should accompany the nomination; $1,000 to pass the entry box, $1,000 to start. The purse to be divided 60% to the winner, 20% to second, 11% to third, 6% to fourth and 3% to fifth. 121 lbs. Trophies will be presented to the winning owner, trainer and jockey. Closed Saturday, August 16, 2003 with 27 Nominations.

Value of Race: $200,000 Winner $120,000; second $40,000; third $22,000; fourth $12,000; fifth $6,000. Mutuel Pool $753,187.00 Exacta Pool $585,244.00 Trifecta Pool $381,888.00

Last Raced	Horse	M/Eqt.	A.Wt	PP	St	¼	½	Str	Fin	Jockey	Odds $1
23Jly03 9Sar1	Ashado	L	2 121	2	3	2½	1hd	1½	11¼	Prado E S	3.10
23Jly03 9Sar5	Be Gentle	L	2 121	3	4	3½	31	25½	28¼	Velasquez C	10.50
27Jly03 5Sar1	Daydreaming		2 121	4	5	51½	58	4hd	31¾	Velazquez J R	1.25
11Aug03 8Sar2	Unbridled Beauty	L	2 121	6	1	4hd	4hd	3hd	4½	Bailey J D	2.50
30Jly03 5Sar1	Dixie Waltz	L	2 121	1	6	1hd	2½	515	529½	Day P	12.30
30Jly03 5Sar2	Stoic	L	2 121	5	2	6	6	6	6	Luzzi M J	24.75

OFF AT 4:48 Start Good For All But DAYDREAMING Won driving. Track fast.
TIME :22^{2}, :45^{2}, 1:10^{3}, 1:24 (:22.46, :45.52, 1:10.64, 1:24.08)

$2 Mutuel Prices:

3–ASHADO	8.20	4.80	2.80
4–BE GENTLE		8.20	3.30
6–DAYDREAMING			2.40

$2 EXACTA 3–4 PAID $63.50 $2 TRIFECTA 3–4–6 PAID $140.00

Dk. b. or br. f, (Feb), by Saint Ballado–Goulash, by Mari's Book. Trainer Pletcher Todd A. Bred by Aaron U Jones & Marie D Jones (Ky).

ASHADO bumped with DIXIE WALTZ at the start, rushed up between horses to contest the early pace, surged to the front on the turn, battled gamely into midstretch then edged clear under brisk urging. BE GENTLE stalked the pace while three wide along the backstretch, made a run from outside to challenge on the turn, battled outside the winner into midstretch but couldn't stay with that one through the final eighth. DAYDREAMING stumbled badly at the start, moved up along the inside on the backstretch, waited patiently for room while saving ground on the turn, angled out to get clear at the top of the stretch then lacked a strong closing bid. UNBRIDLED BEAUTY raced within striking distance from outside along the backstretch, ranged up four wide to threaten on the turn turn faded in the stretch. DIXIE WALTZ bumped at the start, rushed up along the rail to gain a slim early advantage, dueled along the rail to the turn and steadily tired thereafter. STOIC broke awkwardly then trailed throughout and was eased late.

Owners— 1, Starlight Stables Saylor Paul & Mar; 2, Van Meter II Thomas F; 3, Phipps Ogden M; 4, Lewis Robert B & Beverly J; 5, Conway Dee & Family Stable; 6, Jay Em Ess Stable

Trainers—1, Pletcher Todd A; 2, Lukas D Wayne; 3, McGaughey Claude III; 4, Lukas D Wayne; 5, Zito Nicholas P; 6, Dutrow Richard E Jr

Scratched— America America (13Aug03 SAL2), Charming Humor (24Jly03 6SAR3)

EIGHTH RACE
Del Mar
AUGUST 30, 2003

7 FURLONGS. (1.20) 53rd Running of THE DEL MAR DEBUTANTE. Grade I. Purse $250,000 FILLIES, TWO YEAR OLDS (FOALS OF 2001) BY SUBSCRIPTION OF $250 EACH, ON OR BEFORE JUNE 6, 2003. FOR HORSES NOT NOMINATED, SUPPLEMENTARY NOMINATIONS OF $10,000 EACH WILL CLOSE AT THE TIME OF ENTRY, THURSDAY, AUGUST 28. All horses shall pay $500 to pass the entry box and $2,000 additional to start, with $250,000 Guaranteed, of which $150,000 to first, $50,000 to second, $30,000 to third, $15,000 to fourth and $5,000 to fifth. Weight, 122 lbs.; Non-winners of $50,000 twice, allowed 2 lbs. Of such a race, 4 lbs. Of $25,000 other than maiden of claiming, 6 lbs. Of a race other than claiming, 8 lbs. Closed Friday, June 6 with 139 nominations.

Value of Race: $250,000 Winner $150,000; second $50,000; third $30,000; fourth $15,000; fifth $5,000. Mutuel Pool $771,254.00 Exacta Pool $311,863.00 Quinella Pool $48,500.00 Trifecta Pool $301,806.00

Last Raced	Horse	M/Eqt.	A.Wt	PP	St	¼	½	Str	Fin	Jockey	Odds $1
27Jly03 3Dmr1	Halfbridled	LB	2 116	1	4	$4^{\frac12}$	$2^{1\frac12}$	$1^{1\frac12}$	1^{5}	Krone J A	1.60
3Aug03 5Dmr2	Hollywood Story	LB	2 115	5	2	3^{1}	4^{2}	4^{6}	2no	Valenzuela P A	8.50
3Aug03 5Dmr1	Victory U. S. A.	LB	2 116	6	3	2^{hd}	3^{hd}	$3^{\frac12}$	$3^{1\frac12}$	Smith M E	0.60
9Aug03 8Dmr4	Wind Flow	LBb	2 117	3	1	1^{1}	1^{hd}	2^{1}	4^{10}	Nakatani C S	36.00
13Jly03 3Hol1	Shadow Of Mine	LB	2 116	4	6	5^{hd}	6	5^{1}	5^{2}	Valdivia J Jr	55.80
9Aug03 8Dmr3	Solar Fire	LB	2 116	2	5	6	5^{hd}	6	6	Espinoza V	16.30

OFF AT 5:36 Start Good. Won driving. Track fast.
TIME :22^{4}, :45^{1}, 1:09^{3}, 1:22^{1} (:22.87, :45.32, 1:09.75, 1:22.20)

$2 Mutuel Prices:

1–HALFBRIDLED	5.20	3.80	2.10
5–HOLLYWOOD STORY		5.60	2.10
6–VICTORY U. S. A.			2.10

$1 EXACTA 1–5 PAID $17.00 $2 QUINELLA 1–5 PAID $24.80 $1 TRIFECTA 1–5–6 PAID $24.70

Dk. b. or br. f, (Feb), by Unbridled–Half Queen, by Deputy Minister. Trainer Mandella Richard. Bred by Frere & Wertheimer (Ky).

HALFBRIDLED stalked the pace inside, bid along the rail into the turn, let WIND FLOW inch away then re-bid inside leaving the turn, took the lead nearing the stretch, came a bit off the fence in the lane and drew clear under urging. HOLLYWOOD STORY stalked off the rail then between horses briefly leaving the backstretch, continued close up just off the inside on the turn, angled to the rail leaving the bend, remained inside, could not match the winner but was game for second. VICTORY U. S. A. was in a good position tracking the pace outside on the backstretch and turn, bid three deep leaving the turn and was edged for the place. WIND FLOW drifted out while taking the early lead, set the pace off the rail, dueled outside the winner into the turn, slipped away between calls on the turn, fought back between horses into the stretch but weakened in the final furlong. SHADOW OF MINE stalked three deep then outside a rival leaving the backstretch and on the turn and weakened. SOLAR FIRE chased between horses then along the inside and also weakened.

Owners— 1, Wertheimer Farm; 2, Krikorian George; 3, Van Meter II Thomas F; 4, Walski Peter A & Walski Barbara; 5, Nichols Thomas L; 6, Barber Chaiken Trust Green Lantern

Trainers—1, Mandella Richard; 2, Shirreffs John; 3, Baffert Bob; 4, Dominguez Caesar F; 5, Greely C Beau; 6, Sahadi Jenine

$2 Daily Double (6–1) Paid $20.80; Daily Double Pool $51,630.
$1 Pick Three (6–6–1) Paid $49.20; Pick Three Pool $84,844.

TENTH RACE
Monmouth
AUGUST 30, 2003

6 FURLONGS. (1.07^{4}) 49th Running of THE SORORITY. Grade III. Purse $100,000. FILLIES, TWO YEARS OLD. By subscription of $100 each, which should accompany the nomination and $1,500 to pass the entry box. The winning owner to receive $60,000, $20,000 to second, $11,000 to third, $6,000 to fourth and $3,000 to fifth. Weight: 119 lbs. Maidens allowed 5 lbs. The owner of the winner to receive a trophy. Closed Saturday, August 16, 2003 with 25 nominations. .

Value of Race: $100,000 Winner $60,000; second $20,000; third $11,000; fourth $6,000; fifth $3,000. Mutuel Pool $174,344.00 Exacta Pool $137,873.00 Trifecta Pool $104,920.00

Last Raced	Horse	M/Eqt.	A.Wt	PP	St	¼	½	Str	Fin	Jockey	Odds $1
23Jly03 9Sar4	Feline Story	L	2 119	3	6	$4^{\frac12}$	$1^{\frac12}$	$1^{3\frac12}$	$1^{5\frac34}$	Ferrer J C	1.40
3Aug03 8Mth3	Whirlwind Charlott	Lb	2 119	5	4	$5^{\frac12}$	$4^{\frac12}$	2^{hd}	$2^{1\frac14}$	Pimentel J	18.20
30Jly03 2Sar1	Stand On Top	L	2 119	6	5	7^{hd}	$6^{\frac12}$	5^{hd}	$3^{2\frac12}$	Cruz C	10.30
3Aug03 8Mth2	Fashion Girl	L	2 119	2	3	1^{hd}	$5^{2\frac12}$	3^{1}	$4^{\frac34}$	King E L Jr	6.10
7Aug03 6Lrl1	Private Gayla	f	2 119	8	2	8	8	$7^{1\frac12}$	$5^{5\frac12}$	Castellano A Jr	7.10
3Aug03 8Mth1	Standswithafist	Lb	2 119	7	1	2^{hd}	$2^{\frac12}$	$4^{\frac12}$	$6^{2\frac12}$	Carrero V	19.80
6Aug03 5Del1	Foolishly	L	2 119	1	8	3^{1}	3^{hd}	$6^{1\frac12}$	7^{1}	Lopez C C	21.90
7Aug03 4Sar1	Capeside Lady	L	2 119	4	7	$6^{2\frac12}$	7^{1}	8	8	Velez J A Jr	2.30

OFF AT 5:09 Start Good. Won driving. Track wet fast.
TIME :21^{4}, :45^{2}, :57^{4}, 1:10^{4} (:21.98, :45.48, :57.97, 1:10.93)

$2 Mutuel Prices:

4–FELINE STORY	4.80	4.40	3.00
6–WHIRLWIND CHARLOTT		12.40	6.20
7–STAND ON TOP			4.80

$2 EXACTA 4–6 PAID $67.60 $2 TRIFECTA 4–6–7 PAID $507.60

B. f, (Apr), by Tale of the Cat–Shappy, by Really Secret. Trainer Hough Stanley M. Bred by Eclipse Thoroughbreds Inc (Ky).

FELINE STORY chased the pace about four wide, moved to a short lead in mid turn, drew clear entering the stretch and widened slightly under steady handling. WHIRLWIND CHARLOTT rated off the pace in mid track, came through the turn five wide then dueled through the stretch finishing evenly in place. STAND ON TOP showed no speed off the rail, eased out entering the stretch and finished evenly mid track. FASHION GIRL set a pressured pace in the three path, contested the turn between horses then dropped back weakening in the drive. PRIVATE GAYLA showed no speed in the three path then drifted out leveling off. STANDSWITHAFIST hustled along with the early pace toward the outside, contested three wide on the turn then weakened. FOOLISHLY pressured the pace from the inside after a slow start, contested the turn while saving ground then weakened. CAPESIDE LADY chased the pace toward the outside then tired.

Owners— 1, Robsham Einar P; 2, Classic Star Stable LLC; 3, John C Jayko & William McNeary; 4, Overbrook Farm; 5, Fowler Paul L Jr; 6, Pompa Paul P Jr; 7, Fox Hill Farms Inc; 8, So Madcapt Stable

Trainers—1, Hough Stanley M; 2, Dowd John F; 3, Pompay Terri; 4, Lukas D Wayne; 5, Capuano Gary; 6, Araya Rene A; 7, Servis John C; 8, Pletcher Todd A

Scratched— Ms. Trick Or Treat (11Jly03 3LS1)

$2 Pick Three (6–3–4) Paid $39.40; Pick Three Pool $8,915.

EIGHTH RACE
Saratoga
AUGUST 30, 2003

7 FURLONGS. (1.20^{3}) 99th Running of THE HOPEFUL. Grade I. Purse $200,000. (Up to $34,800 NYSBFOA). TWO YEAR OLDS. By subscription of $200 each, which should accompany the nomination; $1,000 to pass the entry box, $1,000 to start. The purse to be divided 60% to the winner, 20% to second, 11% to third, 6% to fourth and 3% to fifth. 122 lbs. Trophies will be presented to the winning owner, trainer and jockey. Closed Saturday, August 16, 2003 with 30 Nominations.

Value of Race: $200,000 Winner $120,000; second $40,000; third $22,000; fourth $12,000; fifth $6,000. Mutuel Pool $1,194,817.0 Exacta Pool $830,738.00 Trifecta Pool $660,789.00

Last Raced	Horse	M/Eqt.	A.	Wt	PP	St	¼	½	Str	Fin	Jockey	Odds $1
8Aug03 ^{4}Sar^{1}	Silver Wagon	L	2	122	5	4	7	6^{hd}	$2\frac{1}{2}$	1^{4}	Bailey J D	12.50
24Jly03 ^{8}Sar^{1}	Chapel Royal	L	2	122	7	5	4^{1}	3^{hd}	$1\frac{1}{2}$	$2^{1\frac{1}{2}}$	Velazquez J R	0.65
26Jly03 ^{5}Sar^{1}	Notorious Rogue	L	2	122	1	7	5^{hd}	7	6^{7}	3^{1}	Coa E M	40.75
2Aug03 ^{4}Sar^{1}	Birdstone	L	2	122	6	1	6^{hd}	5^{hd}	3^{hd}	4^{2}	Prado E S	2.30
13Aug03 ^{8}Sar^{3}	Limehouse	L	2	122	4	2	$3\frac{1}{2}$	2^{hd}	5^{hd}	5^{hd}	Albarado R J	10.30
31Jly03 ^{6}Sar^{1}	Hasslefree	Lb	2	122	3	3	2^{hd}	1^{hd}	4^{hd}	6^{9}	Velasquez C	26.75
13Aug03 ^{8}Sar^{8}	Desert Patrol	Lb	2	122	2	6	1^{hd}	4^{1}	7	7	Day P	27.00

OFF AT 4:46 Start Good. Won driving. Track fast.
TIME :22^{2}, :45^{2}, 1:10^{2}, 1:23^{2} (:22.47, :45.49, 1:10.49, 1:23.47)

$2 Mutuel Prices:

5–SILVER WAGON	27.00	5.00	2.60
8–CHAPEL ROYAL		2.50	2.10
2–NOTORIOUS ROGUE			3.30

$2 EXACTA 5–8 PAID $64.00 $2 TRIFECTA 5–8–2 PAID $629.00

Gr/ro c, (Mar), by Wagon Limit–So Ritzy, by Darn That Alarm. Trainer Ziadie Ralph. Bred by Mr & Mrs Leverett S Miller (Fla).

SILVER WAGON was unhurried while between rivals in the early stages, trailed to the far turn, worked his way forward on the turn, waited patiently while behind a wall of horses approaching the quarter pole, split rivals to get clear at the three-sixteenths pole, made a run to challenge in midstretch, surged past CHAPEL ROYAL to take control inside the furlong marker then drifted out a bit under left hand encouragement while drawing off in the late stages. CHAPEL ROYAL stalked the pace from outside along the backstretch, closed the gap while four wide to challenge midway on the turn, surged to the front approaching the top of the stretch, battled heads apart with the winner leaving the furlong marker but was no match for that one while holding well for the place. NOTORIOUS ROGUE raced well back for a half after breaking slowly, closed the gap to reach contention while behind the leaders on the turn, angled out for room in upper stretch, followed the winner while rallying in midstretch then finished willingly while drifting out in the late stages to gain a share. BIRDSTONE hit the side of the gate at the start, was unhurried along the backstretch, launched a rally from outside on the turn, circled five wide to reach contention at the top of the stretch then lacked a strong closing response. LIMEHOUSE forced the pace between horses through the opening quarter, battled heads apart for the lead on the turn, remained a factor into upper stretch then bumped with HASSLEFREE while tiring in midstretch. HASSLEFREE alternated for the lead between horses into upper stretch and tired from his early efforts. DESERT PATROL rushed up along the rail after breaking a bit slowly, set or forced the pace to the top of the stretch and gave way.

Owners— 1, Buckram Oak Farm; 2, Smith Derrick & Tabor Michael; 3, Lewis Lee; 4, Marylou Whitney Stables; 5, Dogwood Stable; 6, Lewis Robert B & Beverly J; 7, Overbrook Farm

Trainers—1, Ziadie Ralph; 2, Pletcher Todd A; 3, Hennig Mark; 4, Zito Nicholas P; 5, Pletcher Todd A; 6, Lukas D Wayne; 7, Lukas D Wayne

Scratched— Golden Tones (30Jly03 ^{4}SAR^{1}), Saratoga Episode (14Aug03 ^{4}SAR^{1})

$2 Pick Three (8–4–5) Paid $2,377.00; Pick Three Pool $142,679.

TENTH RACE
Saratoga
AUGUST 31, 2003

7 FURLONGS. (1.20^{3}) 24th Running of THE FOREGO HANDICAP. Grade I. Purse $250,000. (Up to $38,500 NYSBFOA). THREE YEAR OLDS AND UPWARD. By subscription of $250 each, which should accompany the nomination; $1,250 to pass the entry box, $1,250 to start. The purse to be divided 60% to the winner, 20% to second, 11% to third, 6% to fourth and 3% to fifth. Closed Saturday, August 16, 2003 with 21 nominations. Trophies will be presented to the winning owner, trainer and jockey.

Value of Race: $250,000 Winner $150,000; second $50,000; third $27,500; fourth $15,000; fifth $7,500. Mutuel Pool $949,078.00 Exacta Pool $647,391.00 Trifecta Pool $502,136.00

Last Raced	Horse	M/Eqt.	A.	Wt	PP	St	¼	½	Str	Fin	Jockey	Odds $1
4Jly03 ^{8}Bel^{1}	Aldebaran	Lf	5	123	4	7	7	5^{hd}	$1\frac{1}{2}$	$1^{4\frac{3}{4}}$	Bailey J D	1.60
4Jly03 ^{8}Bel^{4}	Najran	L	4	114	7	2	$1\frac{1}{2}$	$1\frac{1}{2}$	$2^{4\frac{1}{2}}$	$2^{1\frac{1}{4}}$	Castellano J J	12.80
25Jly03 ^{3}Sar^{1}	Gygistar	L	4	119	1	5	5^{hd}	4^{2}	3^{hd}	$3^{6\frac{3}{4}}$	Day P	1.85
26Jly03 ^{7}Del^{1}	Sing Me Back Home	Lb	5	113	5	1	3^{1}	3^{2}	$4^{2\frac{1}{2}}$	4^{4}	Rose J	26.50
12Jly03 ^{12}Crc^{3}	My Cousin Matt	Lf	4	115	2	6	$4\frac{1}{2}$	7	$6\frac{1}{2}$	$5^{1\frac{1}{4}}$	Velazquez J R	7.00
2Aug03 ^{9}Sar^{7}	Proud Citizen	L	4	114	3	3	6^{6}	$6\frac{1}{2}$	7	6^{3}	Prado E S	7.40
10Aug03 ^{9}Sar^{3}	Mike's Classic	Lb	4	113	6	4	$2^{1\frac{1}{2}}$	$2^{2\frac{1}{2}}$	$5^{1\frac{1}{2}}$	7	Ganpath R	11.20

OFF AT 5:53 Start Good. Won driving. Track fast.
TIME :22, :44^{1}, 1:08^{3}, 1:21^{1} (:22.11, :44.29, 1:08.67, 1:21.26)

$2 Mutuel Prices:

4–ALDEBARAN	5.20	2.90	2.10
7–NAJRAN		8.90	3.20
1–GYGISTAR			2.40

$2 EXACTA 4–7 PAID $53.00 $2 TRIFECTA 4–7–1 PAID $137.00

B. h, by Mr. Prospector–Chimes of Freedom, by Private Account. Trainer Frankel Robert. Bred by Flaxman Holdings Ltd (Ky).

ALDEBARAN was outrun early, advanced on the rail on the turn, found a clear path along the inside turning for home, came on through and drew away under a drive. NAJRAN quickly showed in front, set the pace under pressure from MIKE'S CLASSIC, put away that rival into the stretch but had little left to resist the winner and continued on to hold safe the place. GYGISTAR was in hand along the inside early, angled out and came four wide approaching the stretch and lacked a rally. SING ME BACK HOME was hustled away from the gate, chased the pace, came three wide nearing the stretch and tired in the drive. MY COUSIN MATT raced close up early, had no response when roused and tired. PROUD CITIZEN was in hand early, raced three wide on the turn and tired in the stretch. MIKE'S CLASSIC pressed the pace from the outside and tired in the stretch.

Owners— 1, Flaxman Stable; 2, Buckram Oak Farm; 3, Evans Edward P; 4, Wachtel Stable & Double S Stable; 5, Englander Richard A; 6, Baker Robert C Cornstein David & Ma; 7, Middletown Stables

Trainers—1, Frankel Robert; 2, Zito Nicholas P; 3, Hennig Mark; 4, Iwinski Allen; 5, Lake Scott A; 6, Lukas D Wayne; 7, Jerkens H Allen

EIGHTH RACE
Del Mar
AUGUST 31, 2003

1⅜ MILES. (Turf)(2.12) 64th Running of THE DEL MAR HANDICAP. Grade II. Purse $250,000. THREE–YEAR–OLDS AND UPWARD. By subscription of $250 each, which shall accompany the nomination, or by supplementary nomination of $2,500 by Sunday, August 24, $2,500 additional to start, with $250,000 guaranteed, of which $150,000 to first, $50,000 to second, $30,000 to third, $15,000 to fourth and $5,000 to fifth. Closed Thursday, August 21 with 59 nominations. (Rail at 14 feet).

Value of Race: $250,000 Winner $150,000; second $50,000; third $30,000; fourth $15,000; fifth $5,000. Mutuel Pool $599,238.00 Exacta Pool $315,636.00 Quinella Pool $38,227.00 Trifecta Pool $301,837.00 Superfecta Pool $108,803.00

Last Raced	Horse	M/Eqt. A.Wt	PP	¼	½	¾	1	Str	Fin	Jockey	Odds $1
27Jly03 8Dmr3	Irish Warrior	LB	5 116	4	5²	5hd	6½	72	3¹	1hd	Solis A	3.10
20Jly03 7Hol3	Continental Red	LB	7 117	3	3¹	3½	3³	3²½	1¹	2½	Krone J A	10.00
28Jly03 1Dmr1	Continuously	LB	4 114	9	8¹	7¹	7½	6hd	4²½	3¹	Valdivia J Jr	11.20
9Aug03 9Sar9	Ballingarry-IR	LB	4 119	8	9	9	9	9	5hd	4no	Smith M E	5.70
6Aug03 7Dmr2	Mont Saint Michl-CH	LB	5 114	5	7hd	8½	8½	8½	6½	5½	Flores D R	13.90
27Jly03 8Dmr5	Mister Acpen-CH	LBb	5 116	1	1¹½	1¹	1¹	1hd	2¹½	6³	Espinoza V	2.60
9Aug03 9Sar7	Kim Loves Bucky	LB	6 116	7	6¹	6¹½	5hd	4¹	7¹½	7¹	Valenzuela P A	7.00
15Aug03 7Dmr1	Like A Hero	LBb	4 114	6	4³	4²½	4¹	5¹	84	87	Baze T C	14.40
6Aug03 7Dmr1	Bonus Pack	LBb	5 117	2	2¹½	2¹	2¹	2¹½	9	9	Nakatani C S	10.70

OFF AT 5:47 Start Good. Won driving. Course firm.
TIME :23¹, :47², 1:12, 1:35³, 1:59⁴, 2:12¹ (:23.35, :47.40, 1:12.09, 1:35.71, 1:59.87, 2:12.28)

$2 Mutuel Prices:

4–IRISH WARRIOR	8.20	4.40	3.60
3–CONTINENTAL RED		8.80	5.80
9–CONTINUOUSLY			7.00

$1 EXACTA 4–3 PAID $38.70 $2 QUINELLA 3–4 PAID $39.80 $1 TRIFECTA 4–3–9 PAID $370.60 $1 SUPERFECTA 4–3–9–8 PAID $2,554.30

Ch. h, by Irish River*Fr–Spiritofpocahontas, by Alleged. Trainer Dollase Wallace. Bred by Robert B Berger (Ky).

IRISH WARRIOR chased off the rail then outside a rival, went three deep on the final turn and four wide into the stretch, rallied under urging to engage the runner-up in deep stretch and gamely prevailed. CONTINENTAL RED angled in on the first turn and stalked inside, came out leaving the backstretch, bid three deep on the last turn, took a short lead into the stretch, inched away, fought back gamely through the final furlong and continued willingly to the wire. CONTINUOUSLY chased outside a rival or off the rail, angled in some into the third turn, came out three deep into the stretch, rallied between horses in midstretch and finished well. BALLINGARRY (IRE) settled outside a rival then off the rail, came out into the stretch and found his best stride late. MONT SAINT MICHEL (CHI) angled in and chased inside, came a bit off the rail into the stretch, steadied briefly in upper stretch and was outfinished. MISTER ACPEN (CHI) took the early lead, set the pace inside, dueled along the rail on the final turn and weakened in the stretch. KIM LOVES BUCKY angled in and saved ground chasing the pace, moved up on the backstretch and final turn, clipped heels in upper stretch and fell back. LIKE A HERO chased off the rail then outside a rival, went between horses on the final turn, came four wide into the stretch and weakened. BONUS PACK between horses early, stalked a bit off the rail, bid outside the pacesetter then between horses on the last turn, dropped back into the stretch and weakened.

Owners— 1, Coleman Dasaro & Thompson et al; 2, Fitzpatrick Sharon M; 3, Khaled Saud b; 4, Port Trust Trust Naify Marsha & San Gabri; 5, Amerman Racing Stables LLC; 6, Noctis Stable Papiano Neil & Taub S; 7, Gardens Glen Racing Stable; 8, Columbine Stable; 9, Glen Hill Farm

Trainers— 1, Dollase Wallace; 2, Jory Ian P D; 3, Frankel Robert; 4, De Seroux Laura; 5, Frankel Robert; 6, Mulhall Kristin; 7, Glenney John; 8, Greely C Beau; 9, Proctor Thomas F

Scratched— Bonaguil (25Jly03 6DMR9).

$2 Daily Double (5–4) Paid $133.80; Daily Double Pool $36,641.
$1 Pick Three (4–5–4) Paid $241.00; Pick Three Pool $117,770.

EIGHTH RACE
Arlington
SEPTEMBER 1, 2003

1⅛ MILES. (1.46¹) 67th Running of THE ARLINGTON MATRON HANDICAP. Grade III. Purse $150,000. Fillies and mares, 3–year–olds and upward. By subscription of $100 each, which should accompany the nomination. A Supplementary Nomination of $6,000 may be made on Saturday, August 23, which includes entry and starting fees. Original nominees to pay $1,000 to pass the entry box and an additional $1,000 to start. Weights: Sunday, August 24.

Value of Race: $150,000 Winner $90,000; second $30,000; third $16,500; fourth $9,000; fifth $4,500. Mutuel Pool $511,751.00 Exacta Pool $125,339.00 Trifecta Pool $108,347.00 Superfecta Pool $33,912.00

Last Raced	Horse	M/Eqt. A.Wt	PP	St	¼	½	¾	Str	Fin	Jockey	Odds $1
20Jly03 10Del2	Take Charge Lady	L	4 123	6	1	2¹½	2¹	1¹	1⁸	1¹⁰½	Sellers S J	0.30
9Aug03 10ElP7	Lakenheath	L	5 116	4	3	4¹	4¹	3hd	47	2¹¾	Emigh C A	9.20
10Aug03 8AP1	To The Queen	L	4 117	2	5	58	5¹⁰	58	2hd	3nk	Bourque C C	4.10
12Jly03 10ElP7	Fly Borboleta	Lb	4 116	1	4	12	11	2¹	3hd	4¹¾	Lanerie C J	23.90
9Aug03 10ElP4	Lead Story	L	4 116	3	6	6	6	6	53	52¹	Marquez C H Jr	8.30
24May03 8AP7	Salty Farma	Lbf	5 116	5	2	3¹½	3hd	4hd	6	6	Razo E Jr	20.40

OFF AT 4:39 Start Good. Won handily. Track muddy.
TIME :24, :48, 1:12², 1:37¹, 1:50 (:24.14, :48.02, 1:12.40, 1:37.20, 1:50.19)

$2 Mutuel Prices:

7–TAKE CHARGE LADY	2.60	2.20	2.10
5–LAKENHEATH		4.20	2.10
2–TO THE QUEEN			2.10

$2 EXACTA 7–5 PAID $11.20 $2 TRIFECTA 7–5–2 PAID $30.20 $2 SUPERFECTA 7–5–2–1 PAID $86.60

B. f, by Dehere–Felicita, by Rubiano. Trainer McPeek Kenneth G. Bred by William Schettine (Ky).

TAKE CHARGE LADY was allowed to stalk the pace from just off the rail, took over on the final turn, steadily widened her margin and won as her rider pleased. LAKENHEATH raced off the rail near the middle of the field, rallied in the stretch and gained the place while no danger to the top one. TO THE QUEEN lacked speed, angled out for the drive and rallied closest to the winner in the stretch but lost the place in the late going. FLY BORBOLETA set the pace from the inside and weakened. LEAD STORY was always outrun. SALTY FARMA raced close up off the rail and tired.

Owners— 1, Select Stable; 2, Tafel James B; 3, Dapple Stable; 4, Thomas Van Meter II & Winstar Farm; 5, Miles A S Jr; 6, Weaver Edward & Bielfeldt Larry

Trainers— 1, McPeek Kenneth G; 2, Cilio Gene A; 3, Mott William I; 4, Walden W Elliott; 5, Nafzger Carl A; 6, Kassen David C

Scratched— Summer Mis (26Jly03 6AP1).

$1 Pick Three (8–3–7) Paid $64.10; Pick Three Pool $21,481.

FIFTH RACE
Calder
SEPTEMBER 1, 2003

1 MILE. (1.36^{1}) 17th Running of THE MIAMI MILE BREEDERS' CUP HANDICAP. Grade III. Purse $150,000 (includes $75,000 Breeders' Cup). 3-year-olds. By subscription of $150 each which should accompany the nomination, $1,000 to pass the entry box and an additional $1,000 to start – with $75,000 Guaranteed and an additional $75,000 from the Breeders' Cup for Cup nominees only. The host association's monies to be divided $45,000 to the owner of the winner, $15,000 to second, $8,250 to third, $4,500 to fourth and $2,250 to fifth. This race will not be divided. Preference will be given in the following order: High Weights will be preferred under the following conditions – Breeders' Cup Nominees will be preferred over non-Breeders' Cup Nominees assigned equal weights. This race will be limited to 12 Starters, with Also Eligibles. Closed Saturday, August 16 with 25 nominations. (ORIGINALLY SCHEDULED FOR TURF.)

Value of Race: $150,000 Winner $90,000; second $30,000; third $16,500; fourth $9,000; fifth $4,500. Mutuel Pool $149,494.00 Exacta Pool $156,583.00 Trifecta Pool $121,403.00 Superfecta Pool $34,796.00

Last Raced	Horse	M/Eqt.	A.	Wt	PP	St	¼	½	¾	Str	Fin	Jockey	Odds $1
12Jly03 ^{12}Crc^{6}	Tour Of The Cat	Lf	5	115	4	2	$1^{\frac12}$	$1^{\frac12}$	1^{hd}	$1^{2\frac12}$	$1^{2\frac12}$	Cabassa A Jr	3.30
11Jly03 ^{9}Crc^{1}	Last Stand	Lb	4	113	1	1	2^{hd}	$3^{\frac12}$	$3^{1\frac12}$	3^{1}	2^{hd}	Castanon J L	11.50
16Aug03 ^{6}Crc^{3}	Lavender's Lad	L	5	114	2	3	4^{hd}	$5^{2\frac12}$	4^{hd}	5^{4}	$3^{\frac34}$	Aguilar M	9.40
9Aug03 ^{8}Mnr^{4}	Supah Blitz	Lb	3	118	9	9	$9^{2\frac12}$	7^{hd}	$6^{2\frac12}$	4^{hd}	4^{2}	Velasquez C	0.90
12Jly03 ^{12}Crc^{11}	Hear No Evil	Lb	3	115	6	4	$3^{2\frac12}$	$2^{\frac12}$	$2^{2\frac12}$	2^{hd}	$5^{4\frac14}$	Nunez E O	15.10
13Jly03 ^{8}Crc^{3}	Longford Arms	Lb	4	114	10	10	10	10	$9^{1\frac12}$	6^{hd}	$6^{1\frac34}$	Boulanger G	23.00
13Jly03 ^{8}Crc^{4}	Dustys Birthday	Lb	4	115	3	8	6^{hd}	6^{hd}	$7^{\frac12}$	9^{5}	7^{nk}	Delgado J J	72.70
13Jly03 ^{8}Crc^{2}	Shotgun Fire	L	5	115	7	5	5^{3}	$4^{\frac12}$	5^{hd}	7^{1}	8^{1}	Garcia J A	17.40
4Jly03 ^{12}Crc^{1}	Tammany Star	L	4	113	5	6	8^{hd}	$9^{\frac12}$	10	8^{hd}	$9^{13\frac34}$	Teator P A	49.40
25Jly03 ^{5}Crc^{1}	Mr. Livingston	Lf	6	114	8	7	$7^{1\frac12}$	$8^{2\frac12}$	8^{1}	10	10	Cruz M R	8.20

OFF AT 2:17 Start Good. Won driving. Track good.
TIME :24, :47^{2}, 1:12, 1:38^{3} (:24.12, :47.59, 1:12.06, 1:38.65)

$2 Mutuel Prices:

4–TOUR OF THE CAT	8.60	5.20	3.80
1–LAST STAND		10.00	5.40
2–LAVENDER'S LAD			5.20

$2 EXACTA 4–1 PAID $102.40 $2 TRIFECTA 4–1–2 PAID $510.80 $2 SUPERFECTA 4–1–2–12 PAID $4,233.40

B. g, by Tour d'Or–Tune in to the Cat, by Tunerup. Trainer Mora Myra. Bred by C V S Sales Company (Fla).

TOUR OF THE CAT set the pace along the inside, eased out for the stretch run and drew clear under urging. LAST STAND stalked the pace along the inside into the stretch, then couldn't gain on the winner late while saving the place. LAVENDER'S LAD tracked the pace, angled outside the leaders in the stretch and closed with a mild response to just miss the place. SUPAH BLITZ unhurried early, advanced three wide around the far turn to reach contention, then flattened out. HEAR NO EVIL prompted the pace outside TOUR OF THE CAT, made a run at that rival on the far turn and into the stretch, then gave way. LONGFORD ARMS outrun early, failed to menace. DUSTYS BIRTHDAY tired from good position. SHOTGUN FIRE raced in striking position to nearing the stretch and faltered. TAMMANY STAR was outrun. MR. LIVINGSTON raced four wide on the far turn and faded.

Owners— 1, Double G Stables LLC; 2, Fawkes Racing Inc; 3, Lucky Lavender Stable; 4, Bee Bee Stables & Tortora Jacquelin; 5, Jacks or Better Farm Inc; 6, Three G Stable; 7, Curry Diane & Gentry Lloyd; 8, Cherry Martin L; 9, Robinson J M; 10, Palmer Teresa & David

Trainers—1, Mora Myra; 2, Fawkes David; 3, White William P; 4, Tortora Emanuel; 5, Hatchett James; 6, Olivares Luis; 7, Nazareth John A; 8, Wolfson Martin D; 9, Gomez Frank; 10, Kaplan William A

Scratched— Unite's Big Red (2Sep02 ^{5}CRC^{4}), Stauch (25Jly03 ^{5}CRC^{9}), Stormy Roman (25Jly03 ^{5}CRC^{2}), Win's Fair Lady (19Jly03 ^{10}MTH^{7}), Callthesheriff (12Jly03 ^{8}CRC^{2}), Cellars Merlot (25Jly03 ^{5}CRC^{3}), True Love's Secret (10Aug03 ^{4}CRC^{1})

$2 Pick Three (1–6–4) Paid $180.00; Pick Three Pool $16,713.

EIGHTH RACE
Del Mar
SEPTEMBER 1, 2003

1 MILE. (1.33^{1}) 17th Running of THE DEL MAR BREEDERS' CUP HANDICAP. Grade II. Purse $250,000 (includes $100,000 BC – Breeders' Cup) FOR THREE-YEAR-OLDS AND UPWARD. ($100,000 from Breeders' Cup Fund for Cup nominees only). By subscription of $150 each, which shall accompany the nomination, or by supplementary nomination of $2,500 each by Sunday, August 24, $1,500 additional to start, with $150,000 and an additional $100,000 from the Breeders' Cup Fund for Cup nominees only. The host association's monies to be divided 60% to the winner, 20% to second, 12% to third, 6% to fourth and 2% to fifth. Breeders' Cup monies also correspondingly divided, provided a Breeders' Cup nominee has finished inan awarded position. Any Breeders' Cup Fund monies not awarded will revert to the Fund. Nominations closed Thursday, August 21, 2003 with 11.

Value of Race: $178,000 Winner $90,000; second $50,000; third $18,000; fourth $15,000; fifth $5,000. Mutuel Pool $614,802.00 Exacta Pool $319,313.00 Quinella Pool $34,840.00 Trifecta Pool $299,349.00

Last Raced	Horse	M/Eqt.	A.	Wt	PP	St	¼	½	¾	Str	Fin	Jockey	Odds $1
3Aug03 ^{8}Dmr^{8}	Joey Franco	LB	4	116	6	1	4^{1}	4^{2}	$2^{2\frac12}$	$1^{1\frac12}$	1^{2}	Valenzuela P A	4.80
3Aug03 ^{8}Dmr^{3}	Reba's Gold	LBb	6	116	3	3	5^{hd}	5^{hd}	$4^{1\frac12}$	3^{3}	$2^{1\frac12}$	Flores D R	5.20
26Apr03 ^{8}Hol^{7}	Grey Memo	LB	6	117	7	7	7	7	7	6^{2}	$3^{\frac12}$	Desormeaux K J	6.50
3Aug03 ^{8}Dmr^{1}	Taste Of Paradise	LB	4	115	4	2	$3^{1\frac12}$	3^{hd}	1^{hd}	$2^{1\frac12}$	4^{3}	Espinoza V	9.60
3Aug03 ^{7}Dmr^{1}	Seattle Shamus	LB	4	111	1	4	1^{1}	$1^{\frac12}$	$3^{\frac12}$	4^{hd}	5^{2}	Krone J A	16.70
26Jly03 ^{6}Dmr^{2}	Captain Squire	LB	4	116	2	5	2^{hd}	2^{hd}	5^{2}	$5^{\frac12}$	6^{1}	Solis A	1.20
26Jly03 ^{7}Dmr^{3}	Crafty C. T.	LB	5	115	5	6	6^{10}	6^{12}	6^{3}	7	7	Smith M E	7.10

OFF AT 5:38 Start Good. Won driving. Track fast.
TIME :21^{4}, :45^{1}, 1:09^{2}, 1:22^{1}, 1:35^{3} (:21.96, :45.37, 1:09.59, 1:22.25, 1:35.70)

$2 Mutuel Prices:

6–JOEY FRANCO	11.60	5.00	4.20
3–REBA'S GOLD		5.20	3.60
7–GREY MEMO			4.60

$1 EXACTA 6–3 PAID $33.70 $2 QUINELLA 3–6 PAID $29.80 $1 TRIFECTA 6–3–7 PAID $197.90

Dk. b. or br. c, by Avenue of Flags–Susan Powter, by Native Prospector. Trainer Vienna Darrell. Bred by Jerry Frankel (Cal).

JOEY FRANCO stalked the early pace off the rail, bid three deep leaving the backstretch and into the second turn, battled outside TASTE OF PARADISE on that turn, took a short lead into the stretch, inched clear in midstretch, then drifted in under right handed urging but proved best. REBA'S GOLD chased inside then a bit off the rail, moved up outside on the second turn and three deep into the stretch and continued willingly to be second best. GREY MEMO allowed to lag back and angled in early, continued inside to the second turn, came out leaving that bend and in the stretch and finished well to gain third late. TASTE OF PARADISE four wide early, stalked outside a rival, bid between horses on the backstretch and into the second turn, angled in and dueled inside the winner, could not match that one in the stretch and lost the show late. SEATTLE SHAMUS sped to the early lead and came a bit off the rail, dueled between foes leaving the backstretch, dropped back on the second turn and weakened. CAPTAIN SQUIRE stalked the pace inside, was in tight early on the second turn and also dropped back and weakened. CRAFTY C. T. chased off the rail then outside on the backstretch and second turn, came a bit wide into the stretch and had little left.

Owners— 1, Frankel Jerry; 2, Creston Farms; 3, Manzani Ridgeley Farm & Sarno; 4, Abrahams Keith & Bloom Paul; 5, Karen & Mickey Taylor LLC & Finney; 6, Bone Robert D & Diener Jeffrey S; 7, C T Grether Inc

Trainers—1, Vienna Darrell; 2, Hendricks Dan L; 3, Stute Warren; 4, Sadler John W; 5, French Neil; 6, Mullins Jeff; 7, Zucker Howard L

$2 Daily Double (3–6) Paid $502.00; Daily Double Pool $43,404.
$1 Pick Three (5–3–6) Paid $2,122.20; Pick Three Pool $119,646.

ELEVENTH RACE
Philadelphia
SEPTEMBER 1, 2003

1⅛ MILES. (1.47) 25th Running of THE PENNSYLVANIA DERBY. Grade III. Purse $750,000 FOR THREE YEAR OLDS. By subscription of $500 each which should accompany the nomination, $800 to pass the entry box, $1,200 additional to start. The winner to receive $450,000 with $150,000 to second, $82,500 to third, $45,000 to fourth, $22,500 to fifth. Weight 122 lbs. Non-winners of $60,000 at a mile or over in 2003 allowed 3 lbs.; of a sweepstakes at a mile or over in 2003, 5 lbs.; of three races at a mile or over other than maiden or claiming in 2003, 8 lbs. This race will not be divided. A field of14 horses will be drawn with the preference given to those horses with the highest total earnings at the time of the draw. Starters to be named through the entry box by the usual time of closing on Friday, August 29, 2003. Trophies will be presented to the winning owner, trainer and jockey. Nominations closed Tuesday, August 19, 2003 with 25.

Value of Race: $750,000 Winner $450,000; second $150,000; third $82,500; fourth $45,000; fifth $22,500. Mutuel Pool $388,415.00 Exacta Pool $259,916.00 Trifecta Pool $189,543.00 Superfecta Pool $55,231.00

Last Raced	Horse	M/Eqt.	A.Wt	PP	St	¼	½	¾	Str	Fin	Jockey	Odds $1
25Jly03 ^{8}Mth^{1}	Grand Hombre	L	3 114	5	6	6^{hd}	7^{hd}	3^{hd}	1^{1}	$1^{5\frac{1}{4}}$	Bravo J	5.70
9Aug03 ^{9}Pha^{1}	Gimmeawink	L	3 122	10	3	$2^{1\frac{1}{2}}$	$2^{1\frac{1}{2}}$	1^{2}	2^{4}	2^{2}	Madrigal R Jr	29.00
19Aug03 ^{8}Pha^{2}	Ashmore	Lb	3 114	8	5	7^{2}	4^{hd}	5^{hd}	3^{hd}	3^{nk}	Rose J	36.10
23Aug03 ^{10}Sar^{7}	Christine's Outlaw	Lbf	3 114	2	2	3^{hd}	3^{2}	2^{hd}	4^{2}	$4^{3\frac{3}{4}}$	Black A S	28.00
19Aug03 ^{8}Pha^{1}	Toccet	Lb	3 119	1	1	4^{hd}	$5^{\frac{1}{2}}$	$7^{\frac{1}{2}}$	6^{4}	$5^{\frac{3}{4}}$	Chavez J F	2.50
9Aug03 ^{8}Mnr^{2}	Dynever	L	3 122	7	9	9^{3}	9^{4}	6^{2}	5^{2}	$6^{3\frac{1}{4}}$	Prado E S	1.50
9Aug03 ^{9}Pha^{2}	Valleyman	Lbf	3 114	3	10	10	10	10	$7^{\frac{1}{2}}$	$7^{1\frac{1}{2}}$	Rocco J	65.20
3Aug03 ^{9}Sar^{4}	Tafaseel	Lb	3 114	4	8	$8^{\frac{1}{2}}$	$8^{\frac{1}{2}}$	9^{3}	9^{1}	$8^{1\frac{1}{2}}$	Migliore R	6.00
3May03 ^{10}CD^{10}	Domestic Dispute	L	3 122	9	4	5^{1}	$6^{\frac{1}{2}}$	8^{2}	8^{1}	$9^{4\frac{3}{4}}$	Nakatani C S	8.20
3Aug03 ^{11}Mth^{5}	Max Forever	L	3 122	6	7	$1^{\frac{1}{2}}$	1^{hd}	$4^{\frac{1}{2}}$	10	10	Ferrer J C	52.60

OFF AT 5:15 Start Good. Won driving. Track sloppy.
TIME :22^{3}, :46^{3}, 1:10^{4}, 1:36^{1}, 1:49 (:22.72, :46.64, 1:10.92, 1:36.25, 1:49.03)

$2 Mutuel Prices:				
	5–GRAND HOMBRE	13.40	7.20	5.60
	10–GIMMEAWINK		17.60	10.60
	8–ASHMORE			11.80

$2 EXACTA 5–10 PAID $251.80 $2 TRIFECTA 5–10–8 PAID $3,845.80 $1 SUPERFECTA 5–10–8–2 PAID $38,661.70

Dk. b. or br. c, (Apr), by Grand Slam–Santona*Chi, by Winning. Trainer Manning Dennis J. Bred by (Ky).

GRAND HOMBRE was allowed to settle early, advanced on the second turn, eased out four wide past the quarter pole, drew off in the stretch to prove much the best, driving. GIMMEAWINK pressed the early pace and made a three wide bid to draw clear on the second turn, proved to be no match for the winner in the final furlong while being second best. ASHMORE was reserved early, advanced while five wide on the second turn, flattened out in the drive while getting up for the show. CHRISTINE'S OUTLAW was well placed early, made a three wide bid on the far turn, but was empty in the drive, missed show. TOCCET was rated early, came three wide into the stretch, but offered no response. DYNEVER was squeezed back at the start, made a six wide move on the second turn, but tired in the drive. VALLEYMAN lacked a serious rally. TAFASEEL was not a factor. DOMESTIC DISPUTE chased the early pace and tired. MAX FOREVER vied for the lead for a half mile and gave way.

Owners— 1, Mack Earle I; 2, Wienkowitz Walter; 3, Ryan Daniel M; 4, R C Hill Stables; 5, Borislow Daniel M; 6, Wills Catherine & Karches Peter; 7, Trin-Brook Stables; 8, Shadwell Stable; 9, David Bienstock & Charles Winner; 10, Dweck Raymond & Dorothy

Trainers—1, Manning Dennis J; 2, Ritchey Tim F; 3, Pino Michael V; 4, Weaver George; 5, Scanlan John F; 6, Clement Christophe; 7, St Lewis Uriah; 8, McLaughlin Kiaran P; 9, Gallagher Patrick; 10, Perkins Ben W Jr

---

$2 Daily Double (8–5) Paid $42.00; Daily Double Pool $25,031.
$2 Pick Three (12–8/10–5) Paid $445.00; Pick Three Pool $28,565.

TENTH RACE
Saratoga
SEPTEMBER 1, 2003

1$\frac{3}{16}$ MILES. (Turf)(1.51^{3}) 96th Running of THE SARANAC HANDICAP. Grade III. Purse $100,000. (Up to $19,400 NYSBFOA). THREE YEAR OLDS. By subscription of $100 each, which should accompany the nomination; $500 to pass the entry box; $500 to start, with $100,000 added. The added money and all fees to be divided 60% to the winner, 20% to second, 11% to third, 6% to fourth and 3% to fifth. Weights Wednesday, August 27. Starters to be named at the closing time of entries. Trophies will be presented to the winning owner, trainer and jockey. The New York Racing Association reserves the right to transfer this race to the Main Track. In the event that this race is taken off the turf, it may be subject to downgrading upon review by the Graded Stakes Committee. Closed, Saturday, August 16, 2003 with 26 Nominations.

Value of Race: $108,800 Winner $65,280; second $21,760; third $11,968; fourth $6,528; fifth $3,264. Mutuel Pool $601,034.00 Exacta Pool $456,919.00 Trifecta Pool $181,548.00

Last Raced	Horse	M/Eqt.	A.Wt	PP	St	¼	½	¾	Str	Fin	Jockey	Odds $1
9Aug03 ^{8}WO^{2}	Shoal Water	L	3 116	6	3	$2^{2\frac{1}{2}}$	$2^{1\frac{1}{2}}$	$2^{1\frac{1}{2}}$	2^{2}	$1^{2\frac{1}{4}}$	Velazquez J R	1.15
4Aug03 ^{8}Sar^{2}	Urban King-IR	L	3 115	1	5	6	6	$4^{\frac{1}{2}}$	$3^{1\frac{1}{2}}$	2^{hd}	Bailey J D	1.80
4Aug03 ^{8}Sar^{7}	Sharp Impact	Lb	3 116	3	1	$1^{\frac{1}{2}}$	$1^{1\frac{1}{2}}$	1^{hd}	$1^{\frac{1}{2}}$	$3^{1\frac{1}{2}}$	Coa E M	a-3.95
9Aug03 ^{7}Sar^{2}	Five Eighty Four	L	3 114	5	6	$4^{\frac{1}{2}}$	4^{1}	$5^{2\frac{1}{2}}$	4^{hd}	$4^{1\frac{1}{2}}$	Bridgmohan S X	7.80
14Aug03 ^{8}Sar^{7}	Regal Bear	Lb	3 114	2	4	$5^{2\frac{1}{2}}$	$5^{\frac{1}{2}}$	6	6	5^{nk}	Luzzi M J	28.50
9Aug03 ^{7}Sar^{1}	Burchfield	Lb	3 114	4	2	3^{1}	3^{hd}	3^{hd}	$5^{2\frac{1}{2}}$	6	Day P	a-3.95

a–Coupled: Sharp Impact and Burchfield.

OFF AT 5:48 Start Good. Won driving. Course good.
TIME :23^{2}, :48, 1:12^{4}, 1:36^{4}, 1:55^{2} (:23.45, :48.17, 1:12.85, 1:36.93, 1:55.43)

$2 Mutuel Prices:				
	5–SHOAL WATER	4.30	2.50	2.20
	2–URBAN KING-IR		2.70	2.20
	1–SHARP IMPACT (a-entry)			2.40

$2 EXACTA 5–2 PAID $9.20 $2 TRIFECTA 5–2–1 PAID $15.20

B. g, (Feb), by Smart Strike–Puffin Island, by Pleasant Colony. Trainer Frostad Mark. Bred by Sam-Son Farm (Ont–C).

SHOAL WATER prompted the pace from the outside, dug in resolutely when roused for the drive and was clear under the line, driving. URBAN KING (IRE) was outrun early, rallied three wide on the second turn and finished gamely outside to get the place award. SHARP IMPACT quickly showed in front, set the pace along the inside and weakened in the final furlong. FIVE EIGHTY FOUR was rated along between rivals and had no response when roused. REGAL BEAR was outrun early, raced inside and lacked a rally. BURCHFIELD was rated along inside, saved ground and tired in the stretch.

Owners— 1, Sam-Son Farms; 2, Amerman Racing Stables LLC; 3, Darley Stable; 4, Evans Ralph M & Rapaport H Lewis; 5, Smollin Barbara; 6, Darley Stable

Trainers—1, Frostad Mark; 2, Frankel Robert; 3, McLaughlin Kiaran P; 4, Violette Richard A Jr; 5, Ziadie Ralph; 6, Albertrani Thomas

Scratched— Newfoundland (9Aug03 ^{8}SAR^{2})

SEVENTH RACE
Belmont
SEPTEMBER 6, 2003

1⅛ MILES. (1.45^{2}) 108th Running of THE GAZELLE HANDICAP. Grade I. Purse $250,000. (Up to $38,500 NYSBFOA). FILLIES, THREE YEARS OLD. By subscription of $250 each, which should accompany the nomination; $1,250 to pass the entry box and $1,250 to start. The purse to be divided 60% to the winner, 20% to second, 11% to third,6% to fourth and 3% to fifth. Trophies will be presented to the winning owner, trainer and jockey. Closed Saturday, August 23, 2003 with 21 Nominations.

Value of Race: $250,000 Winner $150,000; second $50,000; third $27,500; fourth $15,000; fifth $7,500. Mutuel Pool $751,446.00 Exacta Pool $598,274.00 Trifecta Pool $472,014.00

Last Raced	Horse	M/Eqt.	A.	Wt	PP	St	¼	½	¾	Str	Fin	Jockey	Odds $1
9Jly03 New^{5}	Buy The Sport	L	3	113	6	4	2^{1}	3^{1}	$3^{\frac{1}{2}}$	3^{3}	$1^{\frac{1}{2}}$	Day P	48.00
26Jly03 ^{9}Sar^{1}	Lady Tak	L	3	121	8	2	4^{hd}	$4^{\frac{1}{2}}$	1^{hd}	$1^{3\frac{1}{2}}$	2no	Bailey J D	0.95
16Aug03 ^{9}Sar^{3}	Spoken Fur	L	3	121	1	8	$7^{\frac{1}{2}}$	$5^{\frac{1}{2}}$	4^{3}	$2^{1\frac{1}{2}}$	$3^{8\frac{1}{4}}$	Velasquez C	4.30
16Aug03 ^{9}Sar^{1}	Island Fashion	Lb	3	122	3	6	$3^{\frac{1}{2}}$	2^{hd}	$2^{1\frac{1}{2}}$	4^{9}	4^{11}	Velazquez J R	3.15
8Aug03 ^{5}Sar^{2}	Holiday Lady	Lb	3	113	4	7	8	8	8	6^{3}	5^{1}	Castellano J J	62.00
24Aug03 ^{9}Sar^{6}	Stellar	L	3	113	7	1	6^{hd}	6^{hd}	6^{3}	5^{4}	$6^{3\frac{3}{4}}$	Farina Tony	37.50
25Jly03 ^{7}Sar^{1}	Alchemist	L	3	114	5	5	5^{1}	7^{2}	7^{2}	7^{1}	$7^{5\frac{3}{4}}$	Prado E S	10.60
20Jun03 ^{8}Bel^{2}	Danuta	Lb	3	114	2	3	$1^{\frac{1}{2}}$	$1^{\frac{1}{2}}$	5^{hd}	8	8	Chavez J F	11.90

OFF AT 4:10 Start Good. Won driving. Track fast.

TIME :22^{4}, :45^{2}, 1:09^{3}, 1:34^{4}, 1:48^{2} (:22.92, :45.55, 1:09.69, 1:34.96, 1:48.57)

$2 Mutuel Prices:				
	6–BUY THE SPORT	98.00	16.80	6.40
	8–LADY TAK		3.20	2.60
	1–SPOKEN FUR			3.30

$2 EXACTA 6–8 PAID $287.50 $2 TRIFECTA 6–8–1 PAID $1,220.00

Dk. b. or br. f, (Apr), by Devil's Bag–Final Accord, by D'Accord. Trainer Meehan Brian. Bred by Patricia Calandro (NY).

BUY THE SPORT alternated for the early lead between horses, eased back a bit before going a half, settled just off the pace while three wide to the turn, swung four wide to launch her bid leaving the quarter pole then closed steadily in the middle of the track to get up in the final twenty yards. LADY TAK settled in good position while well off the rail along the backstretch, worked her way forward from outside on the far turn, charged to the front while four wide on the turn, extended her advantage in upper stretch, continued on the front into deep stretch then yielded grudgingly. SPOKEN FUR was reserved for five furlongs while saving ground, angled out on the far turn, circled five wide advancing into the stretch, closed the gap to threaten in midstretch then narrowly missed for the place. ISLAND FASHION raced just behind the pacesetter along the backstretch, lodged a mild bid between horses on the turn but couldn't sustain her rally. HOLIDAY LADY was bumped slightly in the early stages, angled wide along the backstretch, continued wide to the top of the stretch and failed to threaten while improving her position. STELLAR failed to mount a serious rally while four wide. ALCHEMIST up close early, dropped back before going a half then failed to menace while racing wide. DANUTA rushed up along the rail to gain the early advantage, set the pace along the inside to the turn then steadied sharply while giving way near the quarter pole.

Owners— 1, Georgica Stable; 2, Heiligbrodt Racing Stable; 3, Amerman Racing Stables LLC; 4, Nielsen Jeffrey L; 5, Farmer Tracy; 6, Tabor Michael & Evans Edward P; 7, Alexander Helen C Groves Helen K &; 8, Godolphin Racing Inc

Trainers—1, Meehan Brian; 2, Asmussen Steven M; 3, Frankel Robert; 4, Tagg Barclay; 5, Zito Nicholas P; 6, Biancone Patrick L; 7, McGaughey Claude III; 8, Albertrani Thomas

---

$2 Daily Double (7–6) Paid $212.50; Daily Double Pool $132,308.
$2 Pick Three (1–7–6) Paid $364.00; Pick Three Pool $115,854.

NINTH RACE
Belmont
SEPTEMBER 6, 2003

1⅛ MILES. (1.45^{2}) 50th Running of THE WOODWARD. Grade I. Purse $500,000. (Up to $57,000 NYSBFOA). THREE YEAR OLDS AND UPWARD AT WEIGHT FOR AGE. By subscription of $500 each, which should accompany the nomination; $2,500 to pass the entry box and $2,500 to start. The purse to be divided 60% to the winner, 20% to second, 11%to third, 6% to fourth and 3% to fifth. Weights for age. Three year olds, 122 lbs.; older, 126 lbs. The estate of Mrs. William Woodward, Sr. to add the Woodard Challenge Cup, to be won three times, not necessarily consecutively, by the same owner before becoming his or her property. The owner of the winner will also receive a trophy for permanent possession and trophies will be presented to the winning trainer and jockey. Closed Saturday, August 23, 2003 with 20 nominations.

Value of Race: $500,000 Winner $300,000; second $100,000; third $55,000; fourth $30,000; fifth $15,000. Mutuel Pool $2,295,322.0 Exacta Pool $483,278.00 Trifecta Pool $210,414.00

Last Raced	Horse	M/Eqt.	A.	Wt	PP	St	¼	½	¾	Str	Fin	Jockey	Odds $1
5Jly03 ^{9}Bel^{1}	Mineshaft	L	4	126	2	4	4^{3}	$4^{2\frac{1}{2}}$	$3^{1\frac{1}{2}}$	$1^{2\frac{1}{2}}$	$1^{4\frac{1}{4}}$	Albarado R J	0.30
5Jly03 San^{9}	Hold That Tiger	L	3	122	5	3	3^{3}	3^{2}	$2^{1\frac{1}{2}}$	2^{4}	$2^{4\frac{3}{4}}$	Prado E S	8.50
16Aug03 ^{7}Sar^{1}	Puzzlement	Lb	4	126	1	5	5	5	5	$3^{1\frac{1}{2}}$	$3^{11\frac{1}{4}}$	Chavez J F	6.90
15Aug03 ^{7}Sar^{1}	Northern Rock-JP	Lb	5	126	3	1	$2^{\frac{1}{2}}$	$1^{\frac{1}{2}}$	$1^{\frac{1}{2}}$	4^{10}	4^{4}	Migliore R	9.00
9Aug03 ^{8}Sar^{1}	Thompson Rouge-IR	L	4	126	4	2	1^{hd}	2^{hd}	$4^{1\frac{1}{2}}$	5	5	Bailey J D	13.10

OFF AT 5:12 Start Good. Won driving. Track fast.

TIME :23^{4}, :47^{2}, 1:11^{1}, 1:34^{2}, 1:46^{1} (:23.89, :47.40, 1:11.25, 1:34.51, 1:46.21)

$2 Mutuel Prices:				
	2–MINESHAFT	2.60	2.10	2.10
	5–HOLD THAT TIGER		3.20	2.10
	1–PUZZLEMENT			2.10

$2 EXACTA 2–5 PAID $13.60 $2 TRIFECTA 2–5–1 PAID $32.20

Dk. b. or br. c, by A.P. Indy–Prospectors Delite, by Mr. Prospector. Trainer Howard Neil J. Bred by W. S. Farish, James Elkins & W. T. Webber Jr. (Ky).

MINESHAFT tucked in behind the early leaders, raced well in hand along the backstretch, moved to the outside on the far turn, rapidly closed the gap while four wide on the turn, made a run to challenge leaving the quarter pole, shook off HOLD THAT TIGER to get clear approaching the furlong marker then drew away under a vigorous hand ride. HOLD THAT TIGER stalked the pace while three wide along the backstretch, launched a rally between horses on the turn, fought heads apart inside the winner into upper stretch but couldn't stay with that one through the final eighth. PUZZLEMENT was outrun while trailing to the far turn, gained a bit in the three path leaving the turn then failed to threaten while improving his position. NORTHERN ROCK (JPN) stumbled at the start, moved up to gain the early advantage, set the pace in hand to the far turn, continued on the front to the turn then steadily tired thereafter. THOMPSON ROUGE (IRE) dueled between horses along the backstretch, pressed the pace from outside to the turn and gave way.

Owners— 1, Farish William S Elkins James A & W; 2, Tabor Michael & Magnier Mrs John; 3, Shields Joseph V Jr; 4, Darley Stable; 5, Almaddah Abdullah S

Trainers—1, Howard Neil J; 2, O'Brien Aidan P; 3, Jerkens H Allen; 4, McLaughlin Kiaran P; 5, Mott William I

EIGHTH RACE

Belmont

SEPTEMBER 6, 2003

1⅜ MILES. (Turf)(2.11) 45th Running of THE MAN O' WAR. Grade I. Purse $500,000. (Up to $57,000 NYSBFOA). THREE YEAR OLDS AND UPWARD AT WEIGHT FOR AGE. By subscription of $500 each, which should accompany the nomination; $2,500 to pass the entry box and $2,500 to start. The purse to be divided 60% to the winner, 20% to second, 11% to third, 6% to fourth and 3% to fifth. Weight for age. Three year olds, 121 lbs.; older, 126 lbs. The New York Racing Association reserves the right to transfer this race to the Main Track. In the event that this race is taken off the turf, it may be subject to downgrading upon review by the Graded Stakes Committee. Closed Saturday, August 23, 2003 with 28 Nominations.

Value of Race: $500,000 Winner $300,000; second $100,000; third $55,000; fourth $30,000; fifth $15,000.   Mutuel Pool $854,938.00 Exacta Pool $577,373.00   Trifecta Pool $426,816.00

Last Raced	Horse	M/Eqt. A.Wt	PP	¼	½	¾	1	Str	Fin	Jockey	Odds $1
9Aug03 9Sar8	Lunar Sovereign	L	4 126	3	5¹	5½	5½	5²½	1³	12¾	Migliore R	10.00
9Aug03 9Sar3	Slew Valley	L	6 126	5	3¹	3¹	3½	3½	4²	2nk	Castellano J J	17.10
9Aug03 9Sar4	Denon	L	5 126	8	4½	4²	4¹½	4¹½	3½	3¹¼	Bailey J D	1.40
9Aug03 9Sar11	Balto Star	L	5 126	7	1¹	1¹	1¹	1¹	2¹	4¹	Velazquez J R	a-4.70
16Aug03 6Mth1	Deeliteful Irving	Lf	5 126	1	7½	7½	7hd	6hd	5½	5¹¼	Velasquez C	a-4.70
9Aug03 9Sar2	Macaw-IR	Lbf	4 126	2	8	8	8	8	7½	6½	Bridgmohan S X	6.80
9Aug03 9Sar1	Whitmore's Conn	Lb	5 126	4	6½	6½	6½	7hd	8	7¹	Day P	5.80
17Aug03 Leo2	Carpanetto-IR	L	3 121	6	2hd	2½	2¹	2¹	6¹½	8	Prado E S	5.50

a–Coupled: Balto Star and Deeliteful Irving.

OFF AT 4:41 Start Good. Won driving. Course yielding.

TIME :25⁴, :51⁴, 1:17¹, 1:42, 2:05³, 2:17⁴ (:25.97, :51.81, 1:17.34, 1:42.00, 2:05.79, 2:17.99)

$2 Mutuel Prices:	3–LUNAR SOVEREIGN	22.00	12.80	5.50
	5–SLEW VALLEY		17.60	6.70
	7–DENON			2.80

$2 EXACTA 3–5 PAID $221.50 $2 TRIFECTA 3–5–7 PAID $901.00

Dk. b. or br. c, by Cobra King–January Moon, by Apalachee. Trainer McLaughlin Kiaran P. Bred by Cobra Farm Inc. (Ky).

LUNAR SOVEREIGN was unhurried early, raced in good position along the backstretch, swung out on the turn, unleashed a strong move while circling five wide to take command in upper stretch then drew away under steady left hand encouragement. SLEW VALLEY raced in close contention along the inside for six furlongs, edged closer while saving ground on the turn, angled out to launch his bid in upper stretch then outfinished DENON for the place. DENON was rated just off the pace while three wide along the backstretch, made a run from outside to reach contention at the top of the stretch, lodged a mild bid in midstretch but couldn't sustain his rally. BALTO STAR sprinted clear in the early stages, set the pace along the inside to the top of the stretch then weakened from his early efforts. DEELITEFUL IRVING fractious in the gate prior to the start, steadied along the inside nearing the first turn, raced well back while saving ground to the turn, angled four wide entering the stretch then rallied mildly in the middle of the track. MACAW (IRE) raced well back between horses for six furlongs, checked slightly on the far turn then lacked a strong closing bid. WHITMORE'S CONN was outrun for six furlongs, raced well back while three wide to the turn then lacked the needed response when called upon. CARPANETTO (IRE) pressed the pace from outside to the quarter pole and gave way.

Owners— 1, Darley Stable; 2, Rich Meadow Farm; 3, Gann Edmund A & Flaxman Stable; 4, Anstu Stables; 5, Anstu Stables; 6, Melillo George & Sandra; 7, Shanley Michael & Lynn; 8, Tabor Michael & Magnier Mrs John

Trainers—1, McLaughlin Kiaran P; 2, Sciacca Gary; 3, Frankel Robert; 4, Pletcher Todd A; 5, Dickinson Michael W; 6, Tagg Barclay; 7, Schulhofer Randy; 8, O'Brien Aidan P

Scratched— Evening Attire (25Aug03 7SAR1)

$2 Pick Three (7–6–3) Paid $1,863.00; Pick Three Pool $96,926.

EIGHTH RACE

Delaware

SEPTEMBER 6, 2003

6 FURLONGS. (1.08) 20th Running of THE ENDINE HANDICAP. Grade III. Purse $200,000 Guaranteed. FILLIES AND MARES THREE YEARS OLD AND UPWARD. By subscription of $175 each which shall accompany the nomination; $800 to enter and $800 to start. $200,000 Guaranteed of which $120,000 to the winner, $40,000 to second, $22,000 to third, $12,000 to fourth and $6,000 to fifth. Weights Saturday August 30.Starters to pass the entry box by the usual time of closing. Field limited to 14 starters. Preference to horses with the high weights on the scale. Trophy to the winner. Closing Saturday, August 23, 2003.

Value of Race: $200,000 Winner $120,000; second $40,000; third $22,000; fourth $12,000; fifth $6,000.   Mutuel Pool $131,171.00 Exacta Pool $120,989.00   Trifecta Pool $74,851.00 Superfecta Pool $14,829.00

Last Raced	Horse	M/Eqt.	A.Wt	PP	St	1/4	1/2	Str	Fin	Jockey	Odds $1
26Jly03 9Sar3	House Party		3 117	2	7	$5\frac{1}{2}$	42	2hd	11	Santos J A	0.80
3Aug03 11Crc2	Vision In Flight	L	4 114	3	4	32	$31\frac{1}{2}$	1hd	$24\frac{1}{2}$	Boulanger G	9.90
3Aug03 5Mth1	Mooji Moo	L	4 115	4	1	$22\frac{1}{2}$	1hd	$31\frac{1}{2}$	$32\frac{3}{4}$	Toribio A R	10.20
9Aug03 2Mnr3	Haunted Lass	L	4 116	1	2	1hd	$21\frac{1}{2}$	44	41	Rose J	11.00
20Jly03 9Del1	Lights On	Lb	4 114	8	6	73	$6\frac{1}{2}$	54	54	Dominguez R A	18.50
16Aug03 7Del3	Outstanding Info	Lb	5 115	5	5	8	8	73	6no	Caraballo J C	43.20
10Aug03 8Pha1	Bernie's Gold	Lf	5 115	7	3	$62\frac{1}{2}$	74	$6\frac{1}{2}$	$75\frac{1}{4}$	Prado A J	47.00
1Jan03 9Aqu1	Wilzada	Lb	4 117	6	8	4hd	51	8	8	Pino M G	2.30

OFF AT 3:58 Start Good. Won driving. Track fast.

TIME :214, :442, :563, 1:081 (:21.99, :44.46, :56.61, 1:08.35)

$2 Mutuel Prices:

4–HOUSE PARTY	3.60	2.80	2.10
6–VISION IN FLIGHT		5.00	3.60
7–MOOJI MOO			3.00

$2 EXACTA 4–6 PAID $18.20 $2 TRIFECTA 4–6–7 PAID $79.80 $2 SUPERFECTA 4–6–7–1 PAID $119.50

Gr/ro f, (Apr), by French Deputy–Bill Back, by Relaunch. Trainer Jerkens H Allen. Bred by J V Shields Jr (Fla).

HOUSE PARTY moved closer leaving the turn then closed with good energy outside rivals and ran down the leader to edge away late. VISION IN FLIGHT was well placed close to the pace, went after the leaders in midstretch then was not quite good enough for the winner. MOOJI MOO dueled for the lead two wide from the outset and faded the final furlong. HAUNTED LASS broke sharp, saved ground disputing the pace and weakened in the final furlong. LIGHTS ON failed to threaten. OUTSTANDING INFO showed little. BERNIE'S GOLD was outrun. WILZADA broke in a tangle, showed early speed then tired.

Owners— 1, Shields Joseph V Jr; 2, Cherry Martin L; 3, Deckert Robert & Deckert Robert Jr; 4, Iwin99; 5, Jayeff B Stables; 6, Generazio Patricia A; 7, Mamone Raymond; 8, Beatson William P Jr

Trainers—1, Jerkens H Allen; 2, Wolfson Martin D; 3, Hills Timothy A; 4, Iwinski Allen; 5, Goldberg Alan E; 6, Generazio Frank Jr; 7, Correnti Anthony; 8, Dutrow Anthony W

Scratched— Lilah (18Aug03 5SAR2), Mandy's Gold (20Jly03 10DEL5), Vicki Vallencourt (10Aug03 9ELP1), Bronze Abe (16Aug03 8LRL1), Forest Heiress (3Aug03 5MTH4), Margarita's Garden (16Aug03 7DEL5)

$2 Daily Double (4–4) Paid $10.40; Daily Double Pool $11,450.
$2 Pick Three (8–4–2/3/4/5/9/14) Paid $90.00; Pick Three Pool
$5,643.

EIGHTH RACE
Del Mar
SEPTEMBER 6, 2003

1⅛ MILES. (Turf)(1.45⁴) 59th Running of THE DEL MAR DERBY. Grade II. Purse $300,000 Guaranteed. THREE-YEAR-OLDS. By subscription of $300 each, which shall accompany the nomination, or by supplementary nomination of $3,000 each by closing time of entries, $1,000 to pass the entry box and $2,000 additional to start, with $300,000 Guaranteed, of which $180,000 to first, $60,000 to second, $36,000 to third, $18,000 to fourth and $6,000 to fifth. Weight 122 lbs. Nominations closed Thursday, August 28, 2003 with 14. (Rail at 0 feet.)

Value of Race: $300,000 Winner $180,000; second $60,000; third $36,000; fourth $18,000; fifth $6,000. Mutuel Pool $735,284.00 Exacta Pool $339,575.00 Quinella Pool $38,286.00 Trifecta Pool $346,001.00 Superfecta Pool $137,825.00

Last Raced	Horse	M/Eqt. A.Wt	PP	St	¼	½	¾	Str	Fin	Jockey	Odds $1
16Aug03 8Dmr4	Fairly Ransom	LB	3 122	4	2	4½	3hd	3½	2½	11¼	Solis A	4.50
16Aug03 8Dmr2	Devious Boy-GB	LB	3 122	8	4	3½	42	41½	31½	2no	Krone J A	4.80
16Aug03 8Dmr5	Sweet Return-GB	LB	3 122	9	5	5½	5hd	5½	5½	3½	Stevens G L	20.80
16Aug03 8Dmr3	Senor Swinger	LB	3 122	1	7	8½	7hd	6hd	61	4½	Valdivia J Jr	1.90
16Aug03 8Dmr1	Singletary	LB	3 122	5	1	1½	1½	1½	11	52	Valenzuela P A	4.30
11Aug03 3Dmr1	Middleweight	LBb	3 122	7	3	21	21	4hd	6½		Flores D R	26.40
21Aug03 1Dmr1	Bis Repetitas	LB	3 122	2	6	6hd	9	9	72	7½	Nakatani C S	8.60
21Aug03 1Dmr2	Outta Here	LB	3 122	6	8	71	61½	72	9	81	Baze T C	9.70
23Jly03 8Dmr6	Puma-IR	LBf	3 122	3	9	9	81	8hd	81	9	Smith M E	45.90

OFF AT 5:39 Start Good. Won driving. Course firm.
TIME :23², :47², 1:11, 1:34³, 1:46² (:23.42, :47.51, 1:11.18, 1:34.73, 1:46.45)

$2 Mutuel Prices:
5-FAIRLY RANSOM	11.00	5.60	4.40
9-DEVIOUS BOY-GB		5.60	4.20
10-SWEET RETURN-GB			8.40

$1 EXACTA 5-9 PAID $27.50 $2 QUINELLA 5-9 PAID $28.80 $1 TRIFECTA 5-9-10 PAID $380.40 $1 SUPERFECTA 5-9-10-1 PAID $1,089.20

Gr/ro c, (Jan), by Red Ransom-Fairly Grey*Fr, by Linamix*Fr. Trainer McAnally Ronald. Bred by Lagardere Jean-Luc (Ky).

FAIRLY RANSOM pulled his way along and angled in early to stalk the pace, came out into the stretch, gained a short advantage between horses past midstretch and gamely prevailed under some urging. DEVIOUS BOY (GB) prompted the early pace three deep then stalked outside a rival, bid three wide into the stretch, could not match the winner late but held second. SWEET RETURN (GB) angled in outside a rival then found the rail on the first turn, chased inside, came out into the stretch, split rivals in deep stretch and finished with interest. SENOR SWINGER came off the inside into the first turn, chased between horses, moved up some outside leaving the second turn, came three deep into the stretch and was outfinished for a minor award. SINGLETARY took the early lead and angled in, set a pressured pace inside, inched away on the second turn, came a bit off the rail into the stretch, held on well until past midstretch and weakened late. MIDDLEWEIGHT between horses early, prompted the pace outside SINGLETARY, stalked outside the winner on the second turn and weakened in the stretch. BIS REPETITAS saved ground off the pace, bid inside in the stretch but could not summon the needed late kick. OUTTA HERE a bit wide into the first turn, chased outside a rival, came four wide into the stretch and weakened. PUMA (IRE) off a bit slowly and slightly crowded at the start, settled three deep then outside a foe on the second turn and did not rally.

Owners— 1, Zetcher Arnold; 2, Vreeland James R; 3, Red Oak Stable; 4, Lewis Robert B & Beverly J; 5, Little Red Feather Racing; 6, Hughes B W; 7, Gann Edmund A; 8, Currin William L & Eisman Alvin; 9, Lionheart Thoroughbreds Surfside Eq

Trainers—1, McAnally Ronald; 2, Walsh Kathy; 3, McAnally Ronald; 4, Baffert Bob; 5, Chatlos Donald Jr; 6, Mandella Richard; 7, Frankel Robert; 8, Currin William L; 9, Machowsky Michael

Scratched— Californian (16Aug03 11AP8)

$2 Daily Double (4-5) Paid $52.00; Daily Double Pool $40,300.
$1 Pick Three (5/9-4-5) Paid $29.30; Pick Three Pool $128,359.

SIXTH RACE
Del Mar
SEPTEMBER 7, 2003

1¹⁄₁₆ MILES. (Turf)(1.39⁴) 50th Running of THE PALOMAR BREEDERS' CUP HANDICAP. Grade II. Purse $200,000 (includes $50,000 BC – Breeders' Cup) A HANDICAP FOR FILLIES AND MARES THREE YEAR-OLDS AND UPWARD. (Includes $50,000 from Breeders' Cup Fund for Cup nominees only). By subscription of $150 each, which shall accompany the nomination, or by supplementary nomination of $1,500 each by Sunday, August 31. $500 to pass the entry box and $1,000 additional to start. Weights Monday, September 1. The field will be limited to 10 starters. High weights preferred. If more than10 entries pass the entry box, the starters will be determined at the time of entry with preference given to Breeders' Cup nominees of equal racing quality or weight assignment (respective of age). A trophy will be presented to the owner of the winner. Rail at zero. Closed with 13 nominations.

Value of Race: $191,000 Winner $120,000; second $40,000; third $18,000; fourth $9,000; fifth $4,000. Mutuel Pool $460,899.00 Exacta Pool $281,010.00 Quinella Pool $39,648.00

Last Raced	Horse	M/Eqt. A.Wt	PP	St	¼	½	¾	Str	Fin	Jockey	Odds $1
13Aug03 7Dmr3	Spring Star-FR	LB	4 116	3	4	11	11½	11½	1½	1nk	Solis A	1.50
5Jly03 7Hol1	Magic Mission-GB	LBb	5 117	4	1	5	5	3½	21	2no	Nakatani C S	2.50
26May03 10LS8	GardenintheRain-FR	LB	6 114	1	3	41	4½	42	32	33	Krone J A	2.00
22Aug03 6Dmr1	Esmay-AU	LB	4 112	2	2	21	21½	2hd	42½	44	Almeida G F	11.20
25Apr03 3Hol2	Rhiana	LB	6 115	5	5	3½	3hd	5	5	5	Valenzuela P A	9.50

OFF AT 4:38 Start Good. Won driving. Course firm.
TIME :24³, :48², 1:11⁴, 1:34⁴, 1:40³ (:24.64, :48.45, 1:11.81, 1:34.95, 1:40.78)

$2 Mutuel Prices:
3-SPRING STAR-FR	5.00	2.80	2.20
4-MAGIC MISSION-GB		3.00	2.20
1-GARDEN IN THE RAIN-FR			2.40

$1 EXACTA 3-4 PAID $6.40 $2 QUINELLA 3-4 PAID $6.60

B. f, by Danehill-L'Irlandaise, by Irish River*Fr. Trainer Mandella Richard. Bred by Wertheimer & Frere (Fr.).

SPRING STAR (FR) took the early lead and angled in, set the pace toward the inside, came a bit off the rail past midstretch and held on gamely holding horses late under urging. MAGIC MISSION (GB) chased outside a rival or off the rail, went up three deep on the backstretch and second turn, bid outside the winner in the stretch and continued willingly but could not get by. GARDEN IN THE RAIN (FR) saved ground stalking the pace, awaited room from midstretch until sixteenth pole, got through inside in deep stretch and continued gamely to the wire. ESMAY (AUS) stalked inside then between horses on the second turn and into the stretch and lacked the needed response. RHIANA chased outside a rival then between horses on the backstretch, continued off the rail on the second turn and weakened. A claim of foul by the rider of the runner-up against the winner for alleged interference in the stretch was not allowed by the stewards, who ruled the videotape failed to substantiate the claim.

Owners— 1, Wertheimer Farm; 2, Al Maktoum Sheik Maktoum b; 3, Englander Richard A; 4, Burns Mike & Kolbe Al; 5, Ernst Allegra & John

Trainers—1, Mandella Richard; 2, Drysdale Neil; 3, Mullins Jeff; 4, Carno Louis R; 5, Hendricks Dan L

$2 Daily Double (3-3) Paid $104.20; Daily Double Pool $35,319.
$1 Pick Three (1-3-3) Paid $67.50: Pick Three Pool $73,684.

NINTH RACE
Belmont
SEPTEMBER 7, 2003

1⅛ MILES. (Inner Turf)(1.45^{3}) 25th Running of THE GARDEN CITY BREEDERS' CUP HANDICAP. Grade I. Purse $250,000. (includes $100,000 BC – Breeders' Cup). (Up to $38,500 NYSBFOA). FILLIES, THREE YEAR OLDS. By subscription of $150 each, which should accompany the nomination; $750 to pass the entry box; $750 additional to start. Breeders' Cup Fund monies also correspondingly divided provided a Breeders' Cup nominee has finished in an awarded position. Any Breeders' Cup Fund monies not awarded will revert back to the Fund. In the event the Garden City Breeders' Cup overfills, preference will be given to Breeders' Cup nominees only of equal racing quality or weight assignment. Starters to be named at the closing of entries. The New York Racing Association reserves the right to transfer this race to the Main Track. In the event that this race is taken off the turf, it may be subject to downgrading upon review by the Graded Stakes Committee. Closed August 23, 2003 with 35 Nominations.

Value of Race: $244,000 Winner $150,000; second $50,000; third $27,500; fourth $9,000; fifth $7,500. Mutuel Pool $573,283.00 Exacta Pool $413,566.00 Trifecta Pool $363,621.00

Last Raced	Horse	M/Eqt.	A.Wt	PP	St	¼	½	¾	Str	Fin	Jockey	Odds $1
17Aug03 ^{9}Sar^{2}	Indy Five Hundred	L	3 113	6	7	8	8	8	$3^{1\frac{1}{2}}$	1^{4}	Day P	7.90
5Jly03 ^{5}Hol^{1}	Dimitrova	L	3 122	3	6	$4^{\frac{1}{2}}$	4^{hd}	$4^{\frac{1}{2}}$	$1^{1\frac{1}{2}}$	$2^{2\frac{1}{4}}$	Bailey J D	0.75
3Aug03 Dea^{7}	Campsie Fells-UAE	L	3 116	8	4	$5^{1\frac{1}{2}}$	5^{2}	3^{hd}	$2^{\frac{1}{2}}$	3^{1}	Flores D R	28.00
9Aug03 Dea^{2}	Baie-FR		3 119	7	2	6^{hd}	$6^{\frac{1}{2}}$	$6^{1\frac{1}{2}}$	5^{4}	4^{hd}	Santos J A	13.00
3Aug03 Dea^{4}	Acago		3 120	4	3	3^{2}	$2^{\frac{1}{2}}$	$2^{1\frac{1}{2}}$	4^{2}	$5^{3\frac{1}{2}}$	Peslier O	6.70
31Jly03 ^{7}Sar^{1}	Andover Lady	L	3 114	1	8	7^{1}	7^{2}	7^{1}	$6^{\frac{1}{2}}$	$6^{1\frac{1}{2}}$	Prado E S	15.80
17Aug03 ^{9}Sar^{1}	Sand Springs	L	3 120	2	5	1^{2}	$1^{1\frac{1}{2}}$	1^{1}	7^{24}	7^{27}	Guidry M	4.60
4Jly03 ^{9}LS^{1}	Petionville Indeed	Lb	3 116	5	1	$2^{\frac{1}{2}}$	$3^{2\frac{1}{2}}$	5^{1}	8	8	Beasley J A	49.25

OFF AT 5:15 Start Good For All But INDY FIVE HUNDRED Won driving. Course good.
TIME :23^{2}, :46^{4}, 1:11^{3}, 1:36^{2}, 1:48^{2} (:23.50, :46.83, 1:11.60, 1:36.48, 1:48.44)

$2 Mutuel Prices:				
	8–INDY FIVE HUNDRED	17.80	4.70	3.80
	5–DIMITROVA		2.80	2.40
	11–CAMPSIE FELLS–UAE			6.90

$2 EXACTA 8–5 PAID $44.80 $2 TRIFECTA 8–5–11 PAID $534.00

Ch. f, (Feb), by A.P. Indy–Lyphard's Delta, by Lyphard. Trainer Barbara Robert. Bred by Palides Investments N V Inc (Ky).

INDY FIVE HUNDRED was unhurried for six furlongs after breaking in the air at the start, split rivals on the far turn, worked her way forward in the three path on the turn, swung out in upper stretch then unleashed a strong late run from outside to win going away. DIMITROVA settled in good position while saving ground, angled between horses to launch her bid at the quarter pole, charged to the front in upper stretch, maintained a clear lead inside the furlong marker but couldn't withstand the winner's late charge. CAMPSIE FELLS (UAE) was reserved while racing in the middle of the pack for five furlongs, split rivals while gaining on the turn, made a run to threaten in upper stretch but couldn't sustain her bid. BAIE (FR) raced well back along the backstretch, closed the gap along the inside on the turn and lacked a strong finishing bid. ACAGO pressed the pace along the rail to the turn and steadily tired thereafter. ANDOVER LADY failed to mount a serious rally while saving ground. SAND SPRINGS sprinted clear in the early stages, set the pace in the three path to the turn then drifted wide while giving way at the top of the stretch. PETIONVILLE INDEED chased the leaders while three wide for seven furlongs and gave way.

Owners— 1, Georgica Stable; 2, Higgins Joseph; 3, Darley Stable; 4, Six C Stable; 5, Wertheimer Farm; 6, Farmer Tracy; 7, Willmott Stables; 8, Nielsen Jeffrey L

Trainers—1, Barbara Robert; 2, Weld Dermot K; 3, Pantall Henri-Alex; 4, Rohaut Francois; 5, Head-Maarek Christiane; 6, Kimmel John C; 7, Reinstedler Anthony; 8, Keen Dallas E

Scratched— Ocean Drive (28Jly03 ^{8}SAR^{2}), Spoken Fur (6Sep03 ^{7}BEL^{3}), Sarie Marais (16Aug03 ^{10}MTH^{2}), Alchemist (6Sep03 ^{7}BEL^{7})

EIGHTH RACE
Del Mar
SEPTEMBER 10, 2003

7 FURLONGS. (1.20) 56th Running of THE DEL MAR FUTURITY. Grade II. Purse $250,000 FOR TWO YEAR OLDS (FOALS OF 2001) By subscription of $250 each if made on or before June 6, 2003, the fee to accompany the nomination. All horses shall pay $500 to pass the entry box and $2,000 additional to start, with $250,000 Guaranteed, of which $150,000 to first, $50,000 to second, $30,000 to third, $15,000 to fourth and $5,000 to fifth. Weights: colts and geldings, 122 lbs.; fillies, 119 lbs. Non–winners of $50,000 twice allowed 2 lbs.; of such a race, 4 lbs. of $25,000 other than maiden or claiming, 6 lbs.; of a race other than claiming, 8 lbs. Nominations closed Friday, June 6, 2003 with 211.

Value of Race: $250,000 Winner $150,000; second $50,000; third $30,000; fourth $15,000; fifth $5,000. Mutuel Pool $518,434.00 Exacta Pool $283,314.00 Quinella Pool $35,483.00

Last Raced	Horse	M/Eqt.	A.Wt	PP	St	¼	½	Str	Fin	Jockey	Odds $1
17Aug03 ^{2}Dmr^{5}	Siphonizer	LB	2 116	1	4	3^{1}	$2^{\frac{1}{2}}$	1^{1}	$1^{\frac{1}{2}}$	Krone J A	5.40
24Aug03 ^{2}Dmr^{1}	Minister Eric	LB	2 116	2	3	2^{hd}	4^{hd}	3^{hd}	2^{2}	Solis A	7.60
17Aug03 ^{2}Dmr^{1}	Perfect Moon	LB	2 122	5	2	5	5	4^{hd}	3^{nk}	Valenzuela P A	2.80
17Aug03 ^{6}Dmr^{1}	Cooperation	LBb	2 116	3	5	$4^{\frac{1}{2}}$	3^{2}	$2^{1\frac{1}{2}}$	4^{8}	Bailey J D	*2.00
18Aug03 ^{2}Dmr^{1}	Gulf Of Mexico	LB	2 116	4	1	1^{1}	1^{hd}	5	5	Flores D R	2.00

***—Actual Betting Favorite.**

OFF AT 5:40 Start Good. Won driving. Track fast.
TIME :22^{1}, :44^{2}, 1:09^{2}, 1:23 (:22.26, :44.51, 1:09.42, 1:23.10)

$2 Mutuel Prices:				
	1–SIPHONIZER	12.80	5.40	3.20
	2–MINISTER ERIC		6.00	3.40
	5–PERFECT MOON			2.80

$1 EXACTA 1–2 PAID $29.80 $2 QUINELLA 1–2 PAID $30.60

Dk. b. or br. c, (Mar), by Siphon*Brz–Thesky'sthelimit, by Northern Prospect. Trainer Mandella Richard. Bred by Brereton C Jones (Ky).

SIPHONIZER a bit awkwardly into stride, went up inside to press the pace, put a head in front past midway on the turn, inched away under urging in midstretch, then drifted out late under left handed pressure but held gamely. MINISTER ERIC stalked between horses then a bit off the rail, angled out into the stretch and finished well while being floated out some at the wire. PERFECT MOON chased off the rail then outside a rival, came four wide into the stretch and edged a foe for third late. COOPERATION went up outside to stalk the pace, bid three deep into and on the turn and into the stretch, then weakened in the final furlong and just lost the show. GULF OF MEXICO sped to the early lead off the rail, dueled between horses into and on the turn and into the stretch, then weakened.

Owners— 1, Hughes B W; 2, Diamond A Racing Corporation; 3, Jaime Royce; 4, McIngvale James; 5, Darley Stud Management LLC

Trainers—1, Mandella Richard; 2, Mandella Richard; 3, O'Neill Doug; 4, Baffert Bob; 5, Harty Eoin

---

$2 Daily Double (7–1) Paid $257.80; Daily Double Pool $41,347.
$1 Pick Three (1–7–1) Paid $389.10; Pick Three Pool $98,965.

EIGHTH RACE
Arlington
SEPTEMBER 13, 2003

1⅛ MILES. (Turf)(1.472) 40th Running of THE PUCKER UP. Grade III. Purse $175,000 Guaranteed. FILLIES, THREE–YEARS–OLD. By subscription of $125 each, which should accompany the nomination. Nominees to pay $1,250 to pass the entry box and an additional $1,250 to start, with $175,000 Guaranteed, of which $105,000 to the winner; $35,000 to second; $19,250 to third; $10,500 to fourth and $5,250 to fifth. WEIGHT: 122 lbs. Non–winners of $65,000 once at one mile or over or $40,000 twice at one mile or over in 2003, allowed 2 lbs.; $50,000 once or $30,000 twice at one mile or over in 2003, 4 lbs.; a sweepstakes at one mile or over in 2002–2003 or $35,000 once at one mile or over in 2003, 6 lbs. Perference will be winners of Graded/Group Stakes (in order of I–II–III), next preference, Highest Total Earnings in 2003.

Value of Race: $175,000 Winner $105,000; second $35,000; third $19,250; fourth $10,500; fifth $5,250. Mutuel Pool $344,832.00 Exacta Pool $237,673.00 Trifecta Pool $208,446.00 Superfecta Pool $63,408.00

Last Raced	Horse	M/Eqt.	A.Wt	PP	St	¼	½	¾	Str	Fin	Jockey	Odds $1
28Jly03 8Sar9	Aud	L	3 118	1	2	71	8½	7½	5½	11¾	Peck B D	15.00
23Aug03 6AP2	Hail Hillary	L	3 116	11	5	21	2½	21½	1½	2no	Juarez A J Jr	41.70
9Aug03 8AP4	Julie's Prize	Lbf	3 120	12	10	111½	12	12	81	3½	Sterling L J Jr	54.00
24Aug03 Dea2	Hoh Buzzard-IR	Lb	3 118	5	4	31	3½	41½	41	4nk	Stevens G L	1.40
9Aug03 8AP2	Keeping The Gold	L	3 120	3	7	8½	91	10½	61	5no	Razo E Jr	20.20
21Aug03 TIP1	Plume Rouge-GB	L	3 116	9	6	51	4½	3½	3hd	6¾	McDonogh Daragh P	10.70
9Aug03 8AP1	Sue's Good News	Lf	3 122	4	1	4hd	5½	5½	7½	7½	Doocy T T	6.20
9Aug03 8AP3	Meet Me At Midnite	L	3 116	10	9	91½	6½	62	91½	8½	Douglas R R	30.40
23Aug03 6AP1	Cat's Cat	Lb	3 118	7	3	11	11	1hd	21	91¼	Lovato F Jr	13.60
9Aug03 10EIP5	Achnasheen	L	3 116	6	11	12	11½	11½	103	102¾	Johnson J M	15.30
16Aug03 8Sar1	With Certainty	Lb	3 116	8	8	6½	72	9hd	117	118	Blanc B	13.00
16Aug03 10Mth2	Sarie Marais	L	3 116	2	12	101½	10½	81	12	12	Velez J A Jr	4.10

OFF AT 4:44 Start Good For All But SARIE MARAIS Won driving. Course yielding.
TIME :234, :483, 1:12, 1:364, 1:49 (:23.99, :48.64, 1:12.12, 1:36.86, 1:49.16)

$2 Mutuel Prices:				
	1–AUD	32.00	15.80	9.80
	11–HAIL HILLARY		27.40	13.60
	12–JULIE'S PRIZE			14.20

$2 EXACTA 1–11 PAID $787.20 $2 TRIFECTA 1–11–12 PAID $31,266.80 $2 SUPERFECTA 1–11–12–5 PAID $47,556.00

Dk. b. or br. f, (Feb), by Wild Again–Gail's Brush, by Broad Brush. Trainer Reinstedler Anthony. Bred by Willmott Stable (Ky).

AUD lacked speed along the inside, angled out turning for home, rallied in the stretch and won going away. HAIL HILLARY pressed the pace from just outside, rallied to a short lead in the stretch then could not hold off the winner in the drive. JULIE'S PRIZE was void of early speed off the rail and rallied belatedly for a share. HOH BUZZARD (IRE) raced close up inside, was boxed in in upper stretch then lacked a rally when clear. KEEPING THE GOLD raced near the middle of the field, dropped back then improved her position. PLUME ROUGE (GB) gained steadily to the stretch and faltered late. SUE'S GOOD NEWS raced close up but weakened. MEET ME AT MIDNITE was never a factor. CAT'S CAT set a pressured pace from the inside and tired. ACHNASHEEN was always outrun. WITH CERTAINTY raced near the middle of the field and gave way. SARIE MARAIS broke in the air and was always outrun. (Race run in lane 4, rail at 0).

Owners— 1, Willmott Stables; 2, Slavin Larry; 3, Richard Otto Stables; 4, Tanaka Gary A; 5, Fedro Tom & Brommer Darrell & Sadie; 6, Skymarc Farms Lady OReilly; 7, Cresran LLC; 8, B M H Stable; 9, Frankel Jerry; 10, Sterling Stud; 11, Shapiro Robert; 12, Chandler Dr John A

Trainers—1, Reinstedler Anthony; 2, Kassen David C; 3, Mitchell Anthony; 4, Bell Michael H; 5, Block Chris M; 6, Prendergast Kevin; 7, Hobby Steve; 8, Hiles Rick; 9, Stidham Michael; 10, Shirota Mitch; 11, Walden W Elliott; 12, Dickinson Michael W

$1 Pick Three (3/4/6/7/9/10–10–1) Paid $242.90; Pick Three Pool $19,112.

SIXTH RACE
Belmont
SEPTEMBER 13, 2003

6 FURLONGS. (1.073) 9th Running of THE FLORAL PARK HANDICAP. Grade III. Purse $100,000 (Up to $19,400 NYSBFOA) A HANDICAP FOR FILLIES AND MARES THREE YEARS OLD AND UPWARD. By subscription of $100 each, which should accompany the nomination; $500 to pass the entry box; $500 to start, with $100,000 added. The added money and all fees to be divided 60% to the winner, 20% to second, 11% to third 6% to fourth and 3% to fifth. Trophies will be presented to the winning owner, trainer and jockey. Closed Saturday, August 30, 2003 with 20 Nominations.

Value of Race: $108,500 Winner $65,100; second $21,700; third $11,935; fourth $6,510; fifth $3,255. Mutuel Pool $519,394.00 Exacta Pool $410,573.00 Trifecta Pool $251,820.00

Last Raced	Horse	M/Eqt.	A.Wt	PP	St	¼	½	Str	Fin	Jockey	Odds $1
7Aug03 8Sar1	Bauhauser-ARG	L	5 115	6	6	31½	1½	12½	1¾	Migliore R	5.60
24Aug03 9Sar2	Shine Again	L	6 120	3	4	4hd	4½	3hd	22¼	Santos J A	0.55
18Aug03 5Sar1	Literary Light	L	4 113	2	3	2hd	32	44½	31¼	Velazquez J R	18.50
3Aug03 5Mth4	Forest Heiress	L	4 115	4	2	1hd	2½	2hd	42	Coa E M	9.60
18Aug03 5Sar3	Raging Fever	L	5 117	5	5	51½	54½	56	53¼	Bailey J D	5.70
18Aug03 5Sar2	Lilah	L	6 110	1	1	6	6	6	6	Uske S	10.30

OFF AT 3:36 Start Good. Won driving. Track fast.
TIME :22, :45, :571, 1:104 (:22.13, :45.02, :57.36, 1:10.84)

$2 Mutuel Prices:				
	6–BAUHAUSER–ARG	13.20	3.20	2.10
	4–SHINE AGAIN		2.20	2.10
	3–LITERARY LIGHT			2.10

$2 EXACTA 6–4 PAID $27.80 $2 TRIFECTA 6–4–3 PAID $151.50

Gr/ro m, by Numerous–Barbaloot, by Relaunch. Trainer Asmussen Steven M. Bred by Haras Los Cerros de Loma Verde (Arg).

BAUHAUSER (ARG) was hustled up outside after a sluggish break, argued the pace while three wide, drew clear when roused in upper stretch then dug in gamely and held off SHINE AGAIN under a drive. SHINE AGAIN was urged along to stay close early, came wide entering the stretch and finished gamely outside. LITERARY LIGHT contested the pace along the inside and weakened on the rail in the final furlong. FOREST HEIRESS contested the pace while between rivals and tired in the stretch. RAGING FEVER was unhurried early on, raced four wide and had no response when roused. LILAH was hustled along inside and tired in the stretch.

Owners— 1, Heiligbrodt Racing Stable & Jones J; 2, Bohemia Stable; 3, Two Kings Stable; 4, Stonerside Stable LLC; 5, Evans Edward P; 6, Hobeau Farm

Trainers—1, Asmussen Steven M; 2, Jerkens H Allen; 3, Schosberg Richard; 4, Mott William I; 5, Hennig Mark; 6, Jerkens H Allen
Scratched— Gold Mover (24Aug03 9SAR3)

$2 Pick Three (7–3–6) Paid $870.00; Pick Three Pool $70,862.

SEVENTH RACE
Belmont
SEPTEMBER 13, 2003

1⅛ MILES. (Inner Turf)(1.45^{3}) 18th Running of THE BELMONT BREEDERS' CUP HANDICAP. Grade II. Purse $200,000 (includes $100,000 BC – Breeders' Cup) (Up to $19,400 NYSBFOA) A HANDICAP FOR THREE YEAR OLDS AND UPWARD. (Plus $100,000 from the Breeders' Cup Fund for Cup nominees only). By subscription of $100 each, which should accompany the nomination; $500 to pass the entry box; $500 additional to start. Weights Sunday, September 7. The New York Racing Association reserves the right to transfer this race to the Main Track. In the event that this race is taken off the turf, it may be subject to downgrading upon review by the Graded Stakes Committee. Closed Saturday, August 30, 2003 with 26 Nominations.

Value of Race: $209,600 Winner $125,760; second $41,920; third $23,056; fourth $12,576; fifth $6,288. Mutuel Pool $569,165.00 Exacta Pool $483,919.00 Trifecta Pool $365,156.00

Last Raced	Horse	M/Eqt.	A.	Wt	PP	St	¼	½	¾	Str	Fin	Jockey	Odds $1
26Jly03 9AP4	Della Francesca	Lb	4	114	1	7	5hd	5hd	51	31½	11½	Chavez J F	16.30
23Aug03 9Sar5	Rouvres-FR	L	4	116	5	3	3½	3½	32	2½	2nk	Nakatani C S	3.20
16Aug03 7Sar2	Volponi	Lb	5	119	3	2	22½	23	1½	1hd	3½	Velazquez J R	0.75
16Aug03 7Sar7	State Shinto	Lb	7	115	2	4	1hd	1½	21½	42½	41¾	Migliore R	5.90
23Aug03 9Sar4	Political Attack	Lb	4	114	6	6	4½	42	4hd	5½	51¼	Guidry M	10.20
3Aug03 10Mth1	Eltawaasul	Lf	7	114	7	1	62	65½	7	6½	63¾	Martin E M Jr	24.25
17Aug03 7Sar2	Dawn Of The Condor	Lb	6	112	4	5	7	7	6hd	7	7	Castellano J J	34.50

OFF AT 4:08 Start Good. Won driving. Course firm.
TIME :25^{1}, :48^{3}, 1:11^{3}, 1:35^{2}, 1:47^{2} (:25.29, :48.62, 1:11.71, 1:35.58, 1:47.48)

$2 Mutuel Prices:				
	1–DELLA FRANCESCA	34.60	14.80	2.80
	5–ROUVRES–FR		5.40	2.30
	3–VOLPONI			2.10

$2 EXACTA 1–5 PAID $154.00 $2 TRIFECTA 1–5–3 PAID $323.50

B. c, by Danzig–La Affirmed, by Affirmed. Trainer O'Callaghan Niall M. Bred by Brushwood Stable (Pa).

DELLA FRANCESCA was rated along inside, advanced inside on the second turn, came wide entering the stretch, dug in gamely when set down for the drive, reached the front leaving the eighth pole and was clear under the line, driving. ROUVRES (FR) raced close up inside while well in hand, saved ground, angled out for the drive, gained the lead between calls inside the eighth pole and stayed on well to earn the place award. VOLPONI argued the pace from the outside while in hand, drew clear midway on the second turn, dug in stubbornly along the inside in the stretch and weakened in the final furlong. STATE SHINTO argued the pace along the inside, dropped back on the second turn then stayed on stubbornly through the stretch. POLITICAL ATTACK hit the gate at the start, was steadied after the start, raced three wide on both turns and had no response when roused. ELTAWAASUL was in hand early, raced inside into the stretch and had no response when roused. DAWN OF THE CONDOR was outrun early, put in a four wide run on the second turn and tired in the stretch.

Owners— 1, Ol Memorial Stable; 2, Head Alec; 3, Amherst Stable & Spruce Pond Stable; 4, Darley Stable; 5, Erdenheim Farm; 6, Connors Christopher G; 7, Soblick David

Trainers—1, O'Callaghan Niall M; 2, Clement Christophe; 3, Johnson Philip G; 4, McLaughlin Kiaran P; 5, Matz Michael R; 6, Hubley Mark; 7, Sciacca Gary

Scratched— Sohaib (30Aug03 7SAR4)

$2 Daily Double (6–1) Paid $172.00; Daily Double Pool $129,591.
$2 Pick Three (3–6–1) Paid $1,053.00; Pick Three Pool $115,919.

EIGHTH RACE
Belmont
SEPTEMBER 13, 2003

1 MILE. (1.32^{1}) 134th Running of THE JEROME HANDICAP. Grade II. Purse $150,000 (Up to $29,100 NYSBFOA) A HANDICAP FOR THREE YEAR OLDS. By subscription of $150 each, which should accompany the nomination; $750 to pass the entry box and $750 to start. The purse to be divided 60% to the winner, 20% to second, 11% to third, 6% to fourth and 3% to fifth. Trophies will be presented to the winning owner, trainer and jockey. Closed Saturday, August 30, 2003 with 33 Nominations.

Value of Race: $150,000 Winner $90,000; second $30,000; third $16,500; fourth $9,000; fifth $4,500. Mutuel Pool $608,945.00 Exacta Pool $529,106.00 Trifecta Pool $406,394.00

Last Raced	Horse	M/Eqt.	A.	Wt	PP	St	¼	½	¾	Str	Fin	Jockey	Odds $1
23Aug03 10Sar4	During	Lb	3	118	7	1	3½	3½	1½	11½	1¾	Santos J A	6.60
1Sep03 11Pha8	Tafaseel	Lb	3	114	2	7	4hd	51	41½	2hd	24¾	Migliore R	6.30
23Aug03 6Sar1	Pretty Wild	L	3	116	1	8	1hd	1hd	2hd	35½	31¼	Bailey J D	1.20
24Aug03 8Sar1	Inamorato	Lb	3	114	6	4	71½	4½	53½	42	42½	Chavez J F	4.60
20Aug03 7Lrl1	Your Bluffing	Lb	3	113	9	3	8½	8hd	74½	6½	5¾	Luzzi M J	57.75
17Aug03 3Sar1	Roses In May	L	3	113	4	6	61½	61½	6½	78	64¾	Velazquez J R	6.00
25Aug03 8Del1	Distinct Vision	Lb	3	114	3	5	2½	2½	31	5hd	74¾	Martin E M Jr	29.25
24Jly03 5Sar4	Gigawatt	Lb	3	115	8	2	5hd	71½	8½	81	85¾	Guidry M	30.25
14Jun03 7Bel4	Region Of Merit	L	3	118	5	9	9	9	9	9	9	Nakatani C S	23.70

OFF AT 4:40 Start Good. Won driving. Track fast.
TIME :22^{2}, :45, 1:09^{3}, 1:36^{1} (:22.58, :45.04, 1:09.68, 1:36.32)

$2 Mutuel Prices:				
	7–DURING	15.20	6.90	4.00
	2–TAFASEEL		7.30	4.10
	1–PRETTY WILD			2.50

$2 EXACTA 7–2 PAID $92.50 $2 TRIFECTA 7–2–1 PAID $333.50

Dk. b. or br. c, (Feb), by Cherokee Run–Blading Saddle, by Blade. Trainer Baffert Bob. Bred by Gulf States Racing Stables II (Ky).

DURING showed good speed from the outside while in hand, advanced three wide approaching the stretch, drew clear when roused then dug in determinedly and held on under a drive. TAFASEEL was urged along inside to stay close, responded when roused on the turn, came wide into the stretch and finished gamely outside but could not get by the winner. PRETTY WILD hit the gate at the start but quickly showed in front, set the pace under constant pressure and weakened on the rail in the final furlong. INAMORATO was hustled up outside after the start, put in a four wide run entering the turn, raced four wide around the turn and had no response in the stretch. YOUR BLUFFING was outrun early, raced inside and had no response when roused. ROSES IN MAY raced close up outside, chased the pace while three wide and tired in the stretch. DISTINCT VISION pressed the pace while between rivals and tired after the opening three quarters. GIGAWATT raced close up while four wide and tired after a half mile. REGION OF MERIT was outrun early, raced inside and tired.

Owners— 1, McIngvale James; 2, Shadwell Stable; 3, Robsham Einar P; 4, Godolphin Racing Inc; 5, Trombetta Michael; 6, Ramsey Kenneth L & Sarah K; 7, Stuart Grant; 8, Stonerside Stable LLC; 9, Kennelot Stables Ltd

Trainers—1, Baffert Bob; 2, McLaughlin Kiaran P; 3, Hough Stanley M; 4, Albertrani Thomas; 5, Trombetta Michael J; 6, Romans Dale; 7, Pino Michael V; 8, Casse Mark; 9, Clement Christophe

$2 Pick Three (6–1–7) Paid $1,666.00; Pick Three Pool $118,864.

NINTH RACE
Belmont
SEPTEMBER 13, 2003

$1\frac{1}{16}$ MILES. (1.39^2) 28th Running of THE RUFFIAN HANDICAP. Grade I. Purse $300,000 (Up to $42,200 NYSBFOA) A HANDICAP FOR FILLIES AND MARES THREE YEARS OLD AND UPWARD. By subscription of $300 each, which should accompany the nomination; $1,500 to pass the entry box and $1,500 to start. The purse to be divided 60% to the winner, 20% to second, 11% to third, 6%to fourth and 3% to fifth. Trophies will be presented to the winning owner, trainer and jockey. Closed Saturday, August 30, 2003 with 22 Nominations.

Value of Race: $300,000 Winner $180,000; second $60,000; third $33,000; fourth $18,000; fifth $9,000. Mutuel Pool $776,946.00 Exacta Pool $416,285.00 Trifecta Pool $287,453.00

Last Raced	Horse	M/Eqt.	A.Wt	PP	St	¼	½	¾	Str	Fin	Jockey	Odds $1
22Aug03 ^{9}Sar^2	Wild Spirit-CH	L	4 121	1	6	5^{6}	5^{6}	$3^{\frac{1}{2}}$	1^{2}	$1^{3\frac{1}{2}}$	Bailey J D	0.55
24Aug03 ^{9}Sar^7	You	L	4 118	3	5	$1^{1\frac{1}{2}}$	1^{1}	1^{hd}	2^{5}	2^{5}	Coa E M	4.30
22Aug03 ^{9}Sar^1	Passing Shot	L	4 115	4	1	3^{2}	$3^{\frac{1}{2}}$	2^{hd}	3^{6}	$3^{5\frac{1}{2}}$	Santos J A	6.40
20Jly03 ^{10}Del^4	Devon Rose	L	4 115	2	2	$2^{\frac{1}{2}}$	$2^{\frac{1}{2}}$	4^{1}	4^{hd}	4^{1}	Chavez J F	14.50
21Aug03 ^{3}Sar^1	She's Got The Beat	L	4 113	6	3	4^{hd}	4^{hd}	$5^{2\frac{1}{2}}$	$5^{\frac{1}{2}}$	$5^{4\frac{1}{4}}$	Velazquez J R	8.60
27Jly03 ^{9}Sar^3	Nonsuch Bay	L	4 113	5	4	6	6	6	6	6	Guidry M	19.60

OFF AT 5:12 Start Good. Won ridden out. Track fast.
TIME :23, :45^4, 1:10, 1:34^3, 1:41^1 (:23.11, :45.90, 1:10.10, 1:34.67, 1:41.23)

$2 Mutuel Prices:

1–WILD SPIRIT–CH	3.10	2.30	2.10
3–YOU		3.10	2.10
4–PASSING SHOT			2.10

$2 EXACTA 1–3 PAID $8.70 $2 TRIFECTA 1–3–4 PAID $22.80

Dk. b. or br. f, by Hussonet–Wild Princess, by Wild Again. Trainer Frankel Robert. Bred by Haras Sumaya (Chi).

WILD SPIRIT (CHI) was taken to the outside soon after the start, advanced five wide on the turn, took over when shaken up turning for home, drew clear under confident handling and was taken in hand nearing the wire, winning with something left. YOU was hustled to the front, set the pace while removed from the inner railing, proved no match for the winner in the stretch but was clearly best of the others. PASSING SHOT raced close up outside while in hand, moved four wide just inside the winner on the turn, could not stay with that rival nearing the stretch and faded in the drive. DEVON ROSE showed good speed while in hand, chased the pace while between rivals and tired after three quarters. SHE'S GOT THE BEAT raced close up while in hand, put in a run along the inside nearing the stretch and tired on the rail in the drive. NONSUCH BAY was outrun early, came wide into the stretch and had no response when roused.

Owners— 1, Sumaya Us Stables; 2, Gann Edmund A; 3, Shields Joseph V Jr; 4, Englander Richard A; 5, Walsh Elizabeth; 6, Thorn Stable
Trainers—1, Frankel Robert; 2, Frankel Robert; 3, Jerkens H Allen; 4, Iwinski Allen; 5, Johnson Philip G; 6, Alexander Frank A

TENTH RACE
Turfway Park
SEPTEMBER 13, 2003

$1\frac{1}{16}$ MILES. (1.40^3) 10th Running of THE KENTUCKY CUP JUVENILE. Grade III. Purse $100,000. 2-year-olds. By subscription of $100, $500 to enter and $500 additional to start. Supplementary nominations may be made at the time of entry Thursday, September 11, 2003 by payment of $5,000 each (includes all fees). Weight: 120 lbs. Non-winners of a Graded Stake allowed 2 lbs.; of a non-graded stake, 4 lbs.; of two races other than claiming, 6 lbs.; a race other than claiming, 8 lbs. This race will be limited to twelve (12) starters with no also-eligible list. Preference to start will be given in the following order: Graded/Group Stakes Winners (in order I–II–III). Stakes winners, then highest total earnings. Subscription fee may be paid with the subscription or paid at a later date when invoiced. Closed Wednesday, September 3,2003 with 35 nominations.

Value of Race: $100,000 Winner $62,000; second $20,000; third $10,000; fourth $5,000; fifth $3,000. Mutuel Pool $261,509.00 Exacta Pool $185,877.00 Trifecta Pool $160,660.00 Superfecta Pool $47,183.00

Last Raced	Horse	M/Eqt.	A.Wt	PP	St	¼	½	¾	Str	Fin	Jockey	Odds $1
13Aug03 ^{8}Sar^2	[D]Pomeroy		2 116	2	1	$2^{1\frac{1}{2}}$	$2^{1\frac{1}{2}}$	$1^{\frac{1}{2}}$	1^{2}	1no	Prado E S	0.70
10Aug03 ^{10}LaD^1	Mr. Jester	L	2 118	6	6	5^{1}	5^{hd}	$4^{2\frac{1}{2}}$	$3^{\frac{1}{2}}$	$2^{1\frac{1}{4}}$	Bejarano R	20.60
24Aug03 ^{2}Sar^1	The Cliff's Edge	L	2 114	7	8	$7^{1\frac{1}{2}}$	6^{6}	3^{2}	2^{2}	$3^{\frac{3}{4}}$	Sellers S J	3.50
17Aug03 ^{9}ElP^2	Proper Prado	L	2 114	8	5	8	7^{hd}	7^{8}	4^{1}	$4^{4\frac{3}{4}}$	McKee J	5.30
23Aug03 ^{7}AP^1	Bogangles	L	2 114	5	3	4^{3}	$3^{\frac{1}{2}}$	5^{3}	5^{1}	$5^{7\frac{1}{4}}$	Borel C H	14.00
9Aug03 ^{10}Mth^5	Bustin' Out	Lb	2 114	4	4	$1^{2\frac{1}{2}}$	$1^{1\frac{1}{2}}$	2^{hd}	6^{15}	$6^{16\frac{1}{4}}$	Albarado R J	15.00
22Aug03 ^{4}ElP^1	Ravadon	Lb	2 114	1	7	$6^{\frac{1}{2}}$	8	8	8	7^{15}	Butler D P	87.20
30Jly03 ^{4}Sar^1	Golden Tones	L	2 114	3	2	$3^{\frac{1}{2}}$	4^{3}	6^{hd}	$7^{1\frac{1}{2}}$	8	Velasquez C	9.90

[D]–Pomeroy disqualified and placed 3rd.

OFF AT 5:18 Start Good For All But THE CLIFF'S EDGE Won driving. Track fast.
TIME :23^1, :47, 1:11^4, 1:39^3, 1:46^3 (:23.22, :47.12, 1:11.99, 1:39.72, 1:46.61)

$2 Mutuel Prices:

6–MR. JESTER	43.20	12.20	4.00
7–THE CLIFF'S EDGE		5.20	2.80
2–POMEROY			2.20

$2 EXACTA 6–7 PAID $228.00 $2 TRIFECTA 6–7–2 PAID $885.60 $2 SUPERFECTA 6–7–2–8 PAID $2,944.20

Dk. b. or br. c, (Apr), by Silver Deputy–Future Pretense, by Fappiano. Trainer Wren Steve. Bred by G Watts Humphrey Jr (Ky).

POMEROY closest to the pace while off the inside, challenged after a half, gained a short lead entering the second turn, swerved out in upper stretch, opened a clear lead soon after then lasted when tiring late. MR. JESTER reserved early three wide,made a bold middle move in company with THE CLIFF'S EDGE, could not keep pace with that one with three furlongs to go, drifted five wide approaching the stretch, angled in a bit, bumped with PROPER PRADE in midstretch then finished willingly inside POMEROY to just miss. THE CLIFF'S EDGE broke in the air, was outrun early, made a bold five wide move into the second turn, made a run at the leaders midway through that turn, steadied when POMEROY swerved out in upper stretch, then held on gamely to the finish. PROPER PRADO outrun early three wide, advanced off the inside on the second turn, came out four wide approaching the stretch, bumped with MR. JESTER in midstretch then rallied willingly late. BOGANGLES four wide on the first turn when within striking distance, weakened in the final quarter. BUSTIN' OUT bumped with GOLDEN TONES at the start, sprinted clear, set the pace near the inside and gave way in the drive. RAVADON unhurried early along the inside, was no factor. GOLDEN TONES bumped at the start, was forwardly placed, stopped after five furlongs and was vanned off. Following a foul claim by the rider of THE CLIFF'S EDGE against the rider of the winner, POMEROY was disqualified and placed third for interference in the stretch.

Owners— 1, Smith Derrick & Tabor Michael; 2, Kaaren J Biggs; 3, Lapenta Robert V; 4, Winn Mrs James A; 5, Mahler Ken; 6, Overbrook Farm; 7, Strandwitz Peter; 8, Lewis Robert B & Beverly J
Trainers—1, Biancone Patrick L; 2, Wren Steve; 3, Zito Nicholas P; 4, Holthus Robert E; 5, Kenneally Eddie; 6, Lukas D Wayne; 7, Baker James E; 8, Lukas D Wayne
Scratched— Ruler's Court (17Aug03 ^{2}DMR^4)

$1 Daily Double (6–6) Paid $38.40; Daily Double Pool $10,790.
$2 Pick Three (1–6–6) Paid $715.80; Pick Three Pool $15,604.
$2 Pick Four (6–1–6–6) Paid $5,913.80; Pick Four Pool $22,746.

ELEVENTH RACE
Turfway Park
SEPTEMBER 13, 2003

1⅛ MILES. (1.46^{3}) 10th Running of THE KENTUCKY CUP CLASSIC HANDICAP. Grade II. Purse $350,000 (includes $150,000 KTDF – KY TB Devt Fund). 3-year-olds and upward. By subscription of $200, $1,750 to enter and $1,750 additional to start. Supplementary nominations may be made by the closing of entries Saturday, September 6, 2003 by payment of $20,000 each (includes all fees). Weights to be announced Sunday, September 7, 2003 by 5:00 PM. This race will be limited to twelve (12) starters with no also-eligible list. Preference to start will be given to those horses having been assigned the highest weight (scale considered). Total 2003 earnings will be used in determining order of preference for horses assigned equal weights (scale considered). Subscription fee may be paid with the subscription or paid at a later date when invoiced. Closed Wednesday, September 3, 2003 with 19 nominations.

Value of Race: $350,000 Winner $221,500; second $70,000; third $35,000; fourth $17,500; fifth $6,000. Mutuel Pool $256,193.00 Exacta Pool $106,068.00 Trifecta Pool $66,301.00

Last Raced	Horse	M/Eqt.	A.	Wt	PP	St	¼	½	¾	Str	Fin	Jockey	Odds $1
16Aug03 $^{10}AP^{8}$	Perfect Drift	L	4	120	3	2	3^{1}	$3^{3\frac{1}{2}}$	2^{1}	2^{4}	1^{1}	Day P	1.40
13Jly03 $^{9}Hol^{1}$	Congaree	L	5	124	4	1	$1^{\frac{1}{2}}$	1^{1}	1^{hd}	1^{hd}	2^{4}	Prado E S	0.50
25Aug03 $^{7}Sar^{2}$	Crafty Shaw	L	5	115	2	3	2^{2}	$2^{\frac{1}{2}}$	3^{2}	$3^{\frac{1}{2}}$	$3^{\frac{1}{2}}$	Sellers S J	9.50
10Aug03 $^{8}Sar^{1}$	Even The Score	Lb	5	115	1	5	4^{2}	$4^{\frac{1}{2}}$	$4^{1\frac{1}{2}}$	$4^{1\frac{1}{2}}$	$4^{1\frac{1}{4}}$	Albarado R J	27.10
9Aug03 $^{7}Mnr^{2}$	M B Sea	Lb	4	114	5	4	5	5	5	5	5	Velasquez C	33.20

OFF AT 5:45 Start Good. Won ridden out. Track fast.
TIME :24^{1}, :48^{1}, 1:11^{4}, 1:37, 1:50^{2} (:24.31, :48.35, 1:11.84, 1:37.15, 1:50.43)

$2 Mutuel Prices:				
	3–PERFECT DRIFT	4.80	2.10	—
	4–CONGAREE		2.10	—
	2–CRAFTY SHAW		—	—

$2 EXACTA 3–4 PAID $6.00 $2 TRIFECTA 3–4–2 PAID $13.60

B. g, by Dynaformer–Nice Gal, by Naskra. Trainer Johnson Murray W. Bred by Reed William & Stonecrest Farm (Ky).

PERFECT DRIFT reserved early when forwardly placed and outside the two leaders, moved closer before a half, engaged CONGAREE on his own courage with three furlongs to go, continued on his own initiative while outside CONGAREE to the final furlong, edged off when ridden just a bit near the sixteenth marker and was eased up a bit in the closing yards. CONGAREE bobbled slightly at the start, recovered quickly, set the pace outside CRAFTY SHAW while in hand, responded willingly when engaged by the winner with three furlongs to go, battled that one to the sixteenth marker and held on gamely late. CRAFTY SHAW prompted the pace from the inside, continued on when the top pair picked up the pace on the second turn, held on well to the stretch and tired. EVEN THE SCORE awkward at the start, was reserved early, made a mild gain four wide on the second turn but was no real threat. M B SEA outrun early, raced five wide into the second turn then went evenly in the stretch.

Owners— 1, Stonecrest Farm; 2, Stonerside Stable LLC; 3, Cella Charles J; 4, Vanderhyde Thomas; 5, Bruder Michael J

Trainers—1, Johnson Murray W; 2, Baffert Bob; 3, Vestal Peter M; 4, Stewart Dallas; 5, Romans Dale

$1 Daily Double (6–3) Paid $134.00; Daily Double Pool $9,463.
$2 Pick Three (6–6–3) Paid $379.00; Pick Three Pool $39,603.

TWELFTH RACE
Turfway Park
SEPTEMBER 13, 2003

1$\frac{1}{16}$ MILES. (1.40^{3}) 16th Running of THE TURFWAY BREEDERS' CUP S.. Grade III. Purse $175,000 (includes $75,000 BC – Breeders' Cup). Fillies and mares, 3-year-olds and upward. (Plus $75,000 from the Breeders' Cup fund for Cup nominees only.) By subscription of $100, $500 to enter and $500 additional to start. Supplementary nominations may be made at the time of entry Thursday, September 11, 2003 by payment of $8,750 each (includes all fees). Weights: Three-Year-Olds; 118 lbs.; Older; 122 lbs. Non-winners of a Graded Stake at a mile or over in 2003 allowed 2 lbs.; Non-winners of a Non-Grade Stake at a mile or over in 2003, 4 lbs.; $30,000 at a mile or over in 2003, 6 lbs. This race will be limited to twelve (12) starters with no also-eligible list. Preference to start will be given in the following order: Graded/Group Stakes Winners (in order I–II–III). Stakes winners, then highest total earnings in 2003.

Value of Race: $175,000 Winner $108,500; second $35,000; third $17,500; fourth $8,750; fifth $5,250. Mutuel Pool $216,439.00 Exacta Pool $148,664.00 Trifecta Pool $134,361.00 Superfecta Pool $43,214.00

Last Raced	Horse	M/Eqt.	A.	Wt	PP	St	¼	½	¾	Str	Fin	Jockey	Odds $1
24Aug03 $^{9}Sar^{8}$	Smok'n Frolic	L	4	122	8	4	$3^{\frac{1}{2}}$	1^{hd}	1^{1}	1^{3}	$1^{3\frac{1}{2}}$	Prado E S	1.80
16Aug03 $^{9}Sar^{2}$	Awesome Humor	L	3	112	2	2	4^{1}	5^{2}	$4^{\frac{1}{2}}$	2^{2}	$2^{2\frac{1}{2}}$	Albarado R J	2.10
9Aug03 $^{10}EIP^{3}$	So Much More	L	4	118	5	3	2^{1}	$3^{1\frac{1}{2}}$	$5^{2\frac{1}{2}}$	$5^{1\frac{1}{2}}$	$3^{1\frac{3}{4}}$	Borel C H	6.60
13Aug03 $^{6}AP^{1}$	Hi Tech Honeycomb	Lb	4	116	9	7	$8^{2\frac{1}{2}}$	8^{8}	$6^{2\frac{1}{2}}$	6^{7}	$4^{1\frac{1}{4}}$	D'Amico A J	18.70
19Jly03 $^{10}Mth^{7}$	Win's Fair Lady	Lb	4	120	6	8	$6^{1\frac{1}{2}}$	$4^{1\frac{1}{2}}$	3^{1}	$4^{\frac{1}{2}}$	$5^{3\frac{1}{4}}$	Bejarano R	20.20
23Aug03 $^{7}Sar^{1}$	Country Romance	Lb	3	114	4	1	$1^{\frac{1}{2}}$	2^{hd}	$2^{\frac{1}{2}}$	$3^{\frac{1}{2}}$	6^{6}	Day P	3.60
30Aug03 $^{9}EIP^{1}$	Reason To Talk	Lbf	4	120	1	5	$7^{2\frac{1}{2}}$	7^{hd}	8^{15}	$7^{\frac{1}{2}}$	$7^{6\frac{1}{4}}$	Court J K	13.50
12Jly03 $^{10}EIP^{9}$	Red n'Gold	L	5	120	3	6	5^{hd}	$6^{2\frac{1}{2}}$	7^{3}	8^{15}	$8^{13\frac{1}{2}}$	McKee J	42.90
29Aug03 $^{8}AP^{4}$	Barney's Mistress	bf	5	116	7	9	9	9	9	9	9	Sellers S J	99.50

OFF AT 6:14 Start Good. Won driving. Track fast.
TIME :24, :47^{3}, 1:12, 1:38^{1}, 1:44^{4} (:24.09, :47.71, 1:12.09, 1:38.28, 1:44.98)

$2 Mutuel Prices:				
	9–SMOK'N FROLIC	5.60	3.00	2.80
	2–AWESOME HUMOR		2.80	2.40
	5–SO MUCH MORE			3.40

$2 EXACTA 9–2 PAID $17.00 $2 TRIFECTA 9–2–5 PAID $56.00 $2 SUPERFECTA 9–2–5–10 PAID $381.60

Gr/ro f, by Smoke Glacken–Cherokyfrolicflash, by Green Dancer. Trainer Pletcher Todd A. Bred by Cherokee Farms Inc (Fla).

SMOK'N FROLIC prompted the pace three wide, challenged before a half, gained command on the second turn when ready and drew clear under steady urging. AWESOME HUMOR forwardly placed early inside, angled out on the backstretch, raced five wide with three furlongs to go when making a mild bid then held on gamely to be second best while no threat to the winner. SO MUCH MORE pressed the pace off the inside, dropped back a bit on the second turn then went evenly in the drive. HI TECH HONEYCOMB outrun early in the three path, improved her position while no threat. WIN'S FAIR LADY within striking distance three wide, raced in the four path on the second turn and tired in the stretch. COUNTRY ROMANCE vied for the lead along the inside, held on well to the stretch and tired. REASON TO TALK was no threat. RED N'GOLD within striking distance, held on well for six furlongs and faded. BARNEY'S MISTRESS was outrun.

Owners— 1, Dogwood Stable; 2, WinStar Farm LLC; 3, Schettine William C; 4, Select Stable; 5, Sabine Stable Joseph Greeley; 6, Overbrook Farm; 7, K & K Racing Stable LLC; 8, English Kenneth D & Braun Alan; 9, Hat Trick Racing Stable Nick Polydo

Trainers—1, Pletcher Todd A; 2, Walden W Elliott; 3, O'Callaghan Niall M; 4, McPeek Kenneth G; 5, Standridge Steve W; 6, Lukas D Wayne; 7, Vance David R; 8, Holthus Robert E; 9, Poulos Dee

Scratched— Desert Gold (9Aug03 $^{10}ELP^{2}$)

$1 Daily Double (3–9) Paid $10.00; Daily Double Pool $8,764.
$2 Pick Three (6–3–9) Paid $554.00; Pick Three Pool $25,191.

THIRTEENTH RACE
Turfway Park
SEPTEMBER 13, 2003

6 FURLONGS. (1.08¹) 10th Running of THE KENTUCKY CUP SPRINT. Grade III. Purse $100,000. 3-year-olds. By subscription of $100, $500 to enter and $500 additional to start. Supplementary nominations may be made at the time of entry Thursday, September 11, 2003 by payment of $5,000 each (includes all fees). Weight: 122 lbs. Non-winners of a Sweepstake since April 3 allowed 3 lbs.; non-winners of $30,000 twice in 2003 6 lbs. This race will be limited to twelve (12) starters with no also-eligible list. Preference to start will be given in the following order: Graded/Group Stakes Winners (in order I-II-III). Stakes winners, then highest total earnings in 2003. Subscription fee may be paid with the subscription or paid at a later date when invoiced. Closed Wednesday, September 3, 2003 with 27 nominations.

Value of Race: $100,000 Winner $62,000; second $20,000; third $10,000; fourth $5,000; fifth $3,000. Mutuel Pool $341,597.00 Exacta Pool $216,972.00 Trifecta Pool $177,970.00 Superfecta Pool $57,962.00

Last Raced	Horse	M/Eqt.	A.Wt	PP	St	¼	½	Str	Fin	Jockey	Odds $1
12Jly03 10Crc2	Cajun Beat	Lb	3 122	5	3	2½	1hd	12½	1¾	Velasquez C	7.60
16Aug03 4Sar1	Clock Stopper	Lb	3 116	6	11	91½	64	4½	23½	Albarado R J	3.00
5Jly03 6PrM4	Champali	L	3 122	10	1	53	4hd	3hd	32½	Day P	2.30
1Sep03 9Sar4	Ozzie Cat	Lb	3 116	2	9	101	11	9½	4no	Borel C H	70.10
1Aug03 11LaD1	Gold Storm	Lb	3 116	9	6	4hd	53	5½	5no	Berry M C	13.60
12Apr03 9OP6	Comic Truth	Lb	3 116	11	10	11	91	81½	6nk	Bejarano R	74.30
16Aug03 5AP2	Fifteen Rounds	L	3 122	3	5	6½	7½	71½	7hd	Lasala J	30.70
31Aug03 9ElP1	Skeet	L	3 119	7	7	31	3½	2hd	82¼	McKee J	33.30
3May03 10CD12	Offlee Wild	L	3 116	8	2	72	81½	10hd	9½	Court J K	6.70
16Aug03 5AP1	Coach Jimi Lee	L	3 122	1	8	8½	10½	11	10¾	Sellers S J	5.00
10May03 9CD4	Cat Genius	Lb	3 116	4	4	11	21½	62	11	Prado E S	9.30

OFF AT 6:41 Start Good. Won driving. Track fast.
TIME :21², :44¹, :56³, 1:09² (:21.49, :44.22, :56.74, 1:09.54)

$2 Mutuel Prices:

6-CAJUN BEAT	17.20	7.20	3.60
7-CLOCK STOPPER		4.20	3.00
11-CHAMPALI			2.80

$2 EXACTA 6-7 PAID $58.20 $2 TRIFECTA 6-7-11 PAID $262.80 $2 SUPERFECTA 6-7-11-2 PAID $6,028.00

Dk. b. or br. g, (Mar), by Grand Slam-Beckys Shirt, by Cure the Blues. Trainer Margolis Stephen R. Bred by John T L Jones Jr & H Smoot Fahlgren (Ky).

CAJUN BEAT closest to the pace in the three path, challenged on the turn, drew clear into the stretch then lasted late. CLOCK STOPPER outrun early, advanced three wide on the turn, steadied in upper stretch when blocked, split horses with a furlong to go and closed well late. CHAMPALI forwardly placed six wide, held on well in the stretch. OZZIE CAT outrun early, angled out four wide with three furlongs to go then made a good late bid. GOLD STORM forwardly placed four wide, lacked a late bid. COMIC TRUTH outrun early, was five wide with three furlongs to go and finished well. FIFTEEN ROUNDS within striking distance, saved ground on the turn and had nothing left in the stretch. SKEET in tight early, prompted the pace four wide and tired. OFFLEE WILD within striking distance early in the three path, faded. COACH JIMI LEE was no threat. CAT GENIUS set the early pace out in the strip, angled in to the two path on the turn and faded in the drive.

Owners— 1, Padua Stable Satish K Sanan John &; 2, Overbrook Farm; 3, Lloyd Madison Farms IV LLC; 4, Overbrook Farm; 5, Keith McKinney & Jack Sweesy; 6, Jayaraman Kalarikkal K & Vilasini D; 7, Emerald Ridge Farm Christine K Jank; 8, Fly Racing LLC; 9, Azalea Stables LLC; 10, Lee Battaglia & James P DiVito; 11, Parker John R

Trainers—1, Margolis Stephen R; 2, Stewart Dallas; 3, Foley Gregory D; 4, Lukas D Wayne; 5, Cascio C W Bubba; 6, Daly Patrick J; 7, Janks Christine K; 8, Holthus Robert E; 9, Smith Thomas V; 10, DiVito James P; 11, Amoss Thomas

Scratched— Salty Genius (31Aug03 10ELP1)

$1 Daily Double (9-6) Paid $29.20; Daily Double Pool $25,921.
$2 Pick Three (3-9-6) Paid $122.60; Pick Three Pool $32,773.
$2 Pick Four (6-3-9-6) Paid $3,512.80; Pick Four Pool $56,297.

SEVENTH RACE
Belmont
SEPTEMBER 14, 2003

1 MILE. (1.32¹) 114th Running of THE FUTURITY. Grade I. Purse $200,000. (Up to $34,800 NYSBFOA). TWO YEAR OLDS. By subscription of $200 each, which should accompany the nomination; $1,000 to pass the entry box and $1,000 to start. The purse to be divided 60% to the winner, 20% to second, 11% to third, 6% to fourth and 3% to fifth. 120 lbs. Trophies will be presented to the winning owner, trainer and jockey. Closed Saturday, August 30, 2003 with 32 nominations.

Value of Race: $200,000 Winner $120,000; second $40,000; third $22,000; fourth $12,000; fifth $6,000. Mutuel Pool $562,208.00 Exacta Pool $365,437.00 Trifecta Pool $262,442.00

Last Raced	Horse	M/Eqt.	A.Wt	PP	St	¼	½	¾	Str	Fin	Jockey	Odds $1
13Aug03 8Sar1	Cuvee	L	2 120	3	3	21½	21½	11½	16	18¼	Bailey J D	1.30
26Jly03 3Sar1	Value Plus	L	2 120	5	6	51½	31½	22½	212	25¼	Velazquez J R	1.90
13Aug03 8Sar4	El Prado Rob	L	2 120	4	4	4hd	53	53	4½	37¼	Castellano J J	42.75
30Aug03 6Del2	Tabacchi	Lb	2 120	6	2	3hd	42½	43½	53½	42¼	Bravo J	7.60
22Aug03 5Sar1	Flushing Meadows	L	2 120	1	1	1½	1hd	33½	3½	52	Flores D R	11.40
23Aug03 Cur2	Tumblebrutus	L	2 120	2	5	6	6	6	6	6	Prado E S	4.90

OFF AT 4:21 Start Good. Won driving. Track fast.
TIME :23, :45², 1:10, 1:35³ (:23.04, :45.56, 1:10.03, 1:35.75)

$2 Mutuel Prices:

4-CUVEE	4.60	2.80	2.10
6-VALUE PLUS		2.80	2.10
5-EL PRADO ROB			2.30

$2 EXACTA 4-6 PAID $10.40 $2 TRIFECTA 4-6-5 PAID $65.00

Ch. c, (Mar), by Carson City-Christmas Star, by Star de Naskra. Trainer Asmussen Steven M. Bred by Winchell Verne H (Ky).

CUVEE pressed the pace from the outside while in hand, took over nearing the stretch, drew clear when asked and widened his margin under a drive. VALUE PLUS hit the gate at the start, was away slowly, dropped back early, rallied three wide on the turn, could not stay with the winner in the stretch but was well clear of the others. EL PRADO ROB was outrun early, raced inside and lacked a rally while on the rail in the stretch. TABACCHI was rated along between rivals, raced four wide on the turn and had no response when roused. FLUSHING MEADOWS broke well, quickly showed in front, set the pace and tired after the opening three quarters. TUMBLEBRUTUS was rank at the post, came away awkwardly, dropped back along the inside and trailed.

Owners— 1, Ron Winchell & Spendthrift Farm; 2, Jones Aaron U & Marie D; 3, Lapenta Robert V; 4, Joel Sokol & Deborah Sokol; 5, Darley Stable; 6, Tabor Michael & Magnier Mrs John

Trainers—1, Asmussen Steven M; 2, Pletcher Todd A; 3, Zito Nicholas P; 4, Pompay Terri; 5, Harty Eoin; 6, O'Brien Aidan P

Scratched— Distressed Debt (23Aug03 2SAR1)

$2 Daily Double (5-4) Paid $38.60; Daily Double Pool $124,623.
$2 Pick Three (3-5-4) Paid $252.50; Pick Three Pool $96,904.

SIXTH RACE
Belmont
SEPTEMBER 14, 2003

1 MILE. (1.32^{1}) 97th Running of THE MATRON. Grade I. Purse $200,000 (Up to $34,800 NYSBFOA). FILLIES, TWO YEARS OLD. By subscription of $200 each, which should accompany the nomination; $1,000 to pass the entry box and $1,000 to start. The purse to be divided 60% to the winner, 20% to second, 11% to third, 6% to fourth and 3% to fifth. 119 lbs. Trophies will be presented to the winning owner, trainer and jockey. Closed Saturday, August 30, 2003 with 21 Nominations.

Value of Race: $200,000 Winner $120,000; second $40,000; third $22,000; fourth $12,000; fifth $6,000. Mutuel Pool $505,307.00 Exacta Pool $432,047.00 Trifecta Pool $340,184.00

Last Raced	Horse	M/Eqt.	A.Wt	PP	St	¼	½	¾	Str	Fin	Jockey	Odds $1
31Jly03 ^{3}Sar^{1}	Marylebone	L	2 119	5	5	5½	5^{3}	4^{hd}	2½	1no	Prado E S	7.00
11Aug03 ^{8}Sar^{4}	Lokoya	L	2 119	4	4	1½	2^{hd}	1^{hd}	1^{hd}	$2^{5\frac{3}{4}}$	Velazquez J R	2.40
11Aug03 ^{8}Sar^{3}	Eye Dazzler	L	2 119	8	1	2^{hd}	1^{hd}	3^{1}	$3^{2\frac{1}{2}}$	$3^{1\frac{3}{4}}$	Flores D R	5.40
30Aug03 ^{10}Mth^{1}	Feline Story	L	2 119	3	3	4½	4^{hd}	5^{7}	5^{15}	$4^{1\frac{1}{2}}$	Castellano J J	2.35
22Aug03 ^{4}Sar^{1}	Sisti's Pride	L	2 119	7	2	3½	3^{2}	2^{hd}	4^{2}	$5^{14\frac{1}{2}}$	Bailey J D	4.80
7Aug03 ^{2}Sar^{1}	Funny Honey	L	2 119	6	6	6½	$6^{4\frac{1}{2}}$	$7^{1\frac{1}{2}}$	7^{1}	$6^{2\frac{1}{2}}$	Migliore R	15.80
30Aug03 ^{6}Sar^{5}	Charming Humor		2 119	2	8	8	8	6½	$6^{1\frac{1}{2}}$	7½	Gryder A T	59.00
30Aug03 ^{10}Mth^{3}	Stand On Top	L	2 119	1	7	7^{8}	$7^{2\frac{1}{2}}$	8	8	8	Velasquez C	20.80

OFF AT 3:48 Start Good. Won driving. Track fast.
TIME :22^{2}, :45^{1}, 1:10^{3}, 1:38 (:22.49, :45.27, 1:10.70, 1:38.02)

$2 Mutuel Prices:

5-MARYLEBONE	16.00	7.50	4.30
4-LOKOYA		4.60	3.20
8-EYE DAZZLER			4.20

$2 EXACTA 5-4 PAID $64.00 $2 TRIFECTA 5-4-8 PAID $315.00

Gr/ro f, (Feb), by Unbridled's Song–Desert Queen, by Wavering Monarch. Trainer Pletcher Todd A. Bred by Runnymede Farm Inc Catesby W Clay & W Clay Jr (Ky).

MARYLEBONE raced in hand while between rivals early, was three wide on the turn, was steadied behind EYE DAZZLER midway on the turn, rallied four wide approaching the stretch, dug in determinedly outside and got the nod after a prolonged drive. LOKOYA showed good speed along the inside, contested the pace every step of the way and fought back gamely on the rail through the stretch, just missing. EYE DAZZLER contested the pace while three wide, was steadied after jumping a wet spot in the track midway on the turn, continued on gamely to the eighth pole and faded in the final furlong. FELINE STORY was hustled along inside, chased the pace, came wide into the stretch and tired in the drive. SISTI'S PRIDE showed good speed while between rivals, contested the pace into the stretch and tired in the final furlong. FUNNY HONEY raced close up while three wide, chased the pace for a half mile and tired. CHARMING HUMOR was outrun early, raced inside and had no response when roused. STAND ON TOP was hustled along inside, stayed close for a half mile and tired.

Owners— 1, Tabor Michael B; 2, Scatuorchio James T; 3, Lewis Lee; 4, Robsham Einar P; 5, Jones Aaron U & Marie D; 6, Sovereign Stable & Gatsas Stables; 7, Windmill Manor Farm & Schonefeld Ka; 8, Jayko John C

Trainers—1, Pletcher Todd A; 2, Pletcher Todd A; 3, Hennig Mark; 4, Hough Stanley M; 5, Pletcher Todd A; 6, Terranova John P II; 7, Jolley Leroy; 8, Pompay Terri

$2 Pick Three (1-3-5) Paid $1,230.00; Pick Three Pool $76,265.

NINTH RACE
Belmont
SEPTEMBER 20, 2003

1 MILE. (Turf)(1.31^{3}) 15th Running of THE NOBLE DAMSEL HANDICAP. Grade III. Purse $150,000. (Up to $21,100 NYSBFOA). FILLIES AND MARES THREE YEARS OLD AND UPWARD. By subscription of $150 each, which should accompany the nomination; $750 to pass the entry box; $750 to start. The purse to be divided 60% to the winner, 20% to second, 11% to third, 6% to fourth and 3% to fifth. Trophies will be presented to the winning owner, trainer and jockey. The New York Racing Association reserves the right to transfer this race to the Main Track. In the event that this race is taken off the turf, it may be subject to downgrading upon review by the Graded Stakes Committee. Closed Saturday, September 6, 2003 with 35 Nominations.

Value of Race: $150,000 Winner $90,000; second $30,000; third $16,500; fourth $9,000; fifth $4,500. Mutuel Pool $649,825.00 Exacta Pool $516,778.00 Trifecta Pool $383,420.00

Last Raced	Horse	M/Eqt.	A.Wt	PP	St	¼	½	¾	Str	Fin	Jockey	Odds $1
23Aug03 ^{8}Sar^{8}	Wonder Again	L	4 117	11	8	8^{1}	8½	5½	3^{hd}	1^{nk}	Prado E S	6.10
3Aug03 ^{8}Sar^{1}	Dancal-IR	L	5 114	3	10	5^{hd}	6½	6^{hd}	4^{3}	2^{nk}	Castellano J J	5.10
17Aug03 ^{10}Mth^{2}	Something Ventured	Lb	4 115	7	5	7^{1}	$7^{2\frac{1}{2}}$	4½	1^{hd}	$3^{1\frac{3}{4}}$	Velazquez J R	6.40
3May03 ^{7}CD^{4}	Dedication-FR	L	4 117	1	9	6^{2}	3^{hd}	$2^{1\frac{1}{2}}$	$2^{1\frac{1}{2}}$	$4^{2\frac{3}{4}}$	Bailey J D	1.85
23Aug03 ^{8}Sar^{1}	Stylish	Lb	5 118	5	6	10^{hd}	11	11	7^{6}	5^{nk}	Castillo H Jr	7.00
13Aug03 ^{7}Sar^{2}	Sky Cover	L	5 112	4	7	11	10½	10^{1}	6^{hd}	6^{nk}	Luzzi M J	57.25
11Sep03 ^{7}Bel^{6}	Cozzy Corner	L	5 112	8	11	$9^{3\frac{1}{2}}$	9^{1}	9^{hd}	$5^{1\frac{1}{2}}$	$7^{4\frac{1}{4}}$	Chavez Luis	34.50
26Jly03 ^{8}Sar^{8}	Delta Princess	L	4 115	9	4	3½	4^{hd}	3^{hd}	8½	8½	Migliore R	7.30
20Aug03 ^{7}Sar^{4}	Pioneer Inn	L	5 112	2	3	2½	2½	7^{hd}	$9^{1\frac{1}{2}}$	$9^{1\frac{1}{4}}$	Bridgmohan S X	80.25
25Aug03 ^{8}Sar^{6}	Dynamic Lisa	L	4 111	10	1	4^{hd}	$5^{1\frac{1}{2}}$	$8^{2\frac{1}{2}}$	10^{2}	$10^{3\frac{3}{4}}$	Chavez J F	14.70
23Aug03 ^{8}Sar^{6}	Lentil	Lb	4 110	6	2	$1^{5\frac{1}{2}}$	$1^{1\frac{1}{2}}$	1½	11	11	Espinoza J L	73.75

OFF AT 5:12 Start Good. Won driving. Course firm.
TIME :22^{2}, :45^{2}, 1:09, 1:33 (:22.46, :45.49, 1:09.17, 1:33.07)

$2 Mutuel Prices:

11-WONDER AGAIN	14.20	7.40	5.60
3-DANCAL-IR		7.50	4.90
7-SOMETHING VENTURED			4.20

$2 EXACTA 11-3 PAID $89.50 $2 TRIFECTA 11-3-7 PAID $515.00

B. f, by Silver Hawk–Ameriflora, by Danzig. Trainer Toner James J. Bred by Phillips Racing Partnership & John Phillips (Ky).

WONDER AGAIN was rated along early, advanced inside on the turn, angled out for the drive, dug in gamely when roused and prevailed under a drive. DANCAL (IRE) raced close up inside while in hand, came wide entering the stretch and finished gamely outside. SOMETHING VENTURED was unhurried outside, rallied five wide on the turn and dug in gamely through the stretch. DEDICATION (FR) raced with the pace along the inside and weakened in the final furlong. STYLISH was outrun early, came wide into the stretch and offered a mild rally outside. SKY COVER was outrun early, angled out entering the stretch and finished well. COZZY CORNER was pinched back at the start, was outrun early, raced inside and lacked a rally. DELTA PRINCESS chased the pace while three wide and tired after three quarters. PIONEER INN chased the pace while between rivals and tired in the stretch. DYNAMIC LISA chased the pace while four wide and tired. LENTIL was hustled to the front, set the pace for three quarters and tired.

Owners— 1, Phillips Joan G & John W; 2, Aronstam Marlon; 3, Wiemer Irvin & McLane John; 4, Head Ghislaine; 5, Estate of Ahmed Bin Salman; 6, Picwynn Stables; 7, Fox Ridge Farm Inc; 8, Khaled Saud b; 9, Besinger Greg; 10, Schwartz Herbert T & Carol A; 11, Lerman Roy S

Trainers—1, Toner James J; 2, Pletcher Todd A; 3, Pletcher Todd A; 4, Clement Christophe; 5, Mott William I; 6, Dupps Kristina; 7, Kelly Patrick J; 8, Mott William I; 9, Ritvo Timothy; 10, Schwartz Scott M; 11, Lerman Roy S

Scratched— Artist Johanna (5Sep03 ^{7}BEL^{2})

FOURTEENTH RACE 1½ MILES. (Turf)(2.27³) 6th Running of THE KENTUCKY CUP TURF HANDICAP. Grade III. Purse $200,000 A HANDICAP FOR THREE YEAR OLDS AND UPWARD. By subscription of $200, $1,000 to enter and an additional $1,000 to start. Supplementary nominations may be made on September 13, 2003 by payment of $10,000 each (includes all fees). Weights to be announced Sunday, September 14, 2003 by 5:00 P.M. Nominations closed September 11, 2003 with 34 nominations.

Ky Downs
SEPTEMBER 20, 2003

Value of Race: $200,000 Winner $124,000; second $40,000; third $20,000; fourth $10,000; fifth $6,000. Mutuel Pool $172,209.00 Exacta Pool $119,502.00 Trifecta Pool $88,978.00 Superfecta Pool $22,688.00

Last Raced	Horse	M/Eqt.A.Wt	PP	¼	½	1	1¼	Str	Fin	Jockey	Odds $1
24Aug03 ³Sar³	D Art Variety-BR	Lb	5 111	3	4½	4²	2½	2hd	1hd	1hd	Bejarano R	13.70
20Jly03 ⁷Del²	Rochester	L	7 116	1	61	6hd	7hd	4hd	31	2½	Martin E M Jr	4.90
23Aug03 ⁹Sar²	Quest Star	Lb	4 116	2	2¹	2¹	3½	1½	2hd	3nk	Albarado R J	2.50
30Aug03 ⁸AP³	Act of War	Lbf	5 116	6	7½	7²	4hd	6hd	4hd	41	Bourque C C	7.40
30Aug03 ⁸WO⁷	Cetewayo	L	9 115	8	5½	51	5hd	71	5hd	53½	Blanc B	7.60
31Aug03 ⁸Dmr²	Continental Red	L	7 117	5	3hd	3½	61	3hd	6hd	61	Court J K	3.00
31Aug03 ⁸Dmr⁷	Kim Loves Bucky	L	6 116	4	8	8	8	8	7hd	73½	Sellers S J	4.60
31Aug03 ⁸Dmr⁹	Bonus Pack	Lb	5 114	7	1½	13½	14	5hd	8	8	McKee J	27.00

D–Art Variety-BR disqualified and placed 3rd.

OFF AT 4:52 Start Good. Won driving. Course firm.
TIME :50¹, 1:14, 1:38², 2:04³, 2:31¹ (:50.34, 1:14.10, 1:38.56, 2:04.72, 2:31.39)

$2 Mutuel Prices:

1–ROCHESTER	11.80	4.80	3.60
2–QUEST STAR		4.20	3.00
3–ART VARIETY–BR			4.60

$2 EXACTA 1–2 PAID $44.60 $2 TRIFECTA 1–2–3 PAID $393.20 $2 SUPERFECTA 1–2–3–6 PAID $3,932.40

B. g, by Green Dancer–Central City*GB, by Midyan. Trainer Sheppard Jonathan E. Bred by Strawbridge George Jr (Pa).

ART VARIETY (BRZ), reserved near the inside soon after the start, went along under careful handling, continued inside while advancing into the stretch, battled on even terms with QUEST STAR, then, while drifting out in the final yards and bumping with that one, prevailed under pressure. ROCHESTER, never far back, raced in behind horses early, rallied five or six wide into to the stretch, loomed menacingly through the drive and wasn't quite good enough when bumped approaching the wire by QUEST STAR when that one was forced out by ART VARIETY (BRZ). QUEST STAR, rated along the inside early, edged closer upon going a mile, moved boldly five wide nearing the stretch, gained a slim lead, was joined from the inside by ART VARIETY (BRZ) in the upper stretch and wasn't good enough at the end when bumped by ART VARIETY (BRZ) in the final yards and forced out on ROCHESTER. ACT OF WAR, within easy striking distance, made a run between foes four or five wide into the final furlong and couldn't sustain the needed momentum. CETEWAYO, in a striking position five or six wide much of the way, lacked a final response. CONTINENTAL RED, well placed to the stretch, was empty in the drive. KIM LOVES BUCKY never threatened. BONUS PACK gained the lead early, raced five wide, drew off after six furlongs, made the pace until approaching the stretch and tired. THE RIDERS OF ROCHESTER AND QUEST STAR LODGED FOUL CLAIMS AGAINST ART VARIETY (BRZ) FOR ALLEGED INTERFERENCE NEARING THE WIRE. FOLLOWING A REVIEW OF THE VIDEO TAPE REPLAYS, STEWARDS DISQUALIFIED ART VARIETY (BRZ) AND PLACED HIM THIRD. ALL RACES AT KENTUCKY DOWNS ARE HAND TIMED. MISSING FRACTIONAL TIME WAS UNAVAILABLE.

Owners— 1, Team Victory II Rick Pitino et al; 2, Augustin Stable; 3, Mansell Stables LLC; 4, R n R Breeders L Roseman & G Rintel; 5, Chandler Dr John A; 6, Fitzpatrick Sharon M; 7, Gardens Glen Racing Stable John & K; 8, Glen Hill Farm
Trainers— 1, McPeek Kenneth G; 2, Sheppard Jonathan E; 3, Walden W Elliott; 4, Cilio Gene A; 5, Dickinson Michael W; 6, Jory Ian P D; 7, Glenney John; 8, Proctor Thomas F

$2 Pick Three (5–4–1) Paid $227.60; Pick Three Pool $18,535.

TENTH RACE 1⅛ MILES. (1.48) 24th Running of THE SUPER DERBY XXIV. Grade II. Purse $500,000 (includes $1,900 Other Sources) FOR THREE YEAR OLDS. Weights: Colts and Geldings – 124 lbs.; Fillies – 121 lbs.

La. Downs
SEPTEMBER 20, 2003

Value of Race: $500,000 Winner $300,000; second $100,000; third $50,000; fourth $25,000; fifth $15,000; sixth $10,000. Mutuel Pool $1,372,070.00 Exacta Pool $341,859.00 Quinella Pool $33,411.00 Trifecta Pool $289,313.00 Superfecta Pool $100,563.00

Last Raced	Horse	M/Eqt.A.Wt	PP	St	¼	½	¾	Str	Fin	Jockey	Odds $1
23Aug03 ¹¹Sar¹	Ten Most Wanted	Lb	3 124	1	6	3hd	4½	31	2²½	1½	Day P	0.50
9Aug03 ⁸Mnr¹	Soto	Lf	3 124	4	4	4½	3²½	2½	2hd	2⁵¼	Dominguez R A	1.20
30Aug03 ¹¹LaD³	Crowned King	L	3 124	5	5	6	5hd	6	5⁶	31	Rennie C R	33.30
30Aug03 ¹¹LaD¹	Kool Humor	Lb	3 124	3	3	2¹	11½	1hd	33	4½	Clark K D	22.60
30Aug03 ¹¹LaD²	Zydeco Affair	Lb	3 124	6	2	5hd	6	4½	4hd	5⁹¾	Melancon G	37.00
30Aug03 ¹¹LaD⁴	Taxicat	Lf	3 124	2	1	1hd	2¹	5½	6	6	Jacinto J	63.50

OFF AT 5:08 Start Good. Won driving. Track fast.
TIME :24², :49³, 1:13³, 1:37⁴, 1:50³ (:24.41, :49.64, 1:13.64, 1:37.92, 1:50.77)

$2 Mutuel Prices:

1–TEN MOST WANTED	3.00	2.10	2.10
4–SOTO		2.10	2.10
5–CROWNED KING			2.10

$2 EXACTA 1–4 PAID $4.20 $2 QUINELLA 1–4 PAID $2.20 $2 TRIFECTA 1–4–5 PAID $13.40 $2 SUPERFECTA 1–4–5–3 PAID $26.80

Dk. b. or br. c, (Feb), by Deputy Commander–Wanted Again, by Criminal Type. Trainer Dollase Wallace. Bred by Jim H Plemmons (Ky).

TEN MOST WANTED last away, tracked the early pace toward the inside, moved well off the rail backstretch, ranged up to challenge four wide turning for home, edging clear late under steady handling. SOTO stalked the two leaders off the inside, moved to the fore in the second turn, showed the way into the stretch, proved stubborn until late. CROWNED KING lacked speed, moved toward the rail to save ground into the stretch, bothered, checked nearing the furlong marker, recovered, moved out, up for show. KOOL HUMOR dueled early off the inside, gained sole possession of the lead late backstretch, dueled with the runner up through the second turn, was tiring when he came in nearing the furlong grounds bothering CROWNED KING, continued to weaken. ZYDECO AFFAIR lacked speed, came five wide out of the final turn, came up empty for the drive. TAXICAT dueled early closest to the inside, fell back before a half, well beaten.

Owners— 1, J Reddam M Jarvis J Chisholm et al; 2, Galopp LLC Georg Karin & Corinna vo; 3, McKeever Racing Stable LLC; 4, Durant Tom R; 5, Beard David; 6, Giesse Carl & Block Lou
Trainers— 1, Dollase Wallace; 2, Dickinson Michael W; 3, McKeever Billy C Jr; 4, Bruner Jack A; 5, Robideaux Larry R Jr; 6, Giesse Carl

$2 Pick Three (10–1/8–1) Paid $20.00; Pick Three Pool $22,122.

NINTH RACE

Belmont

SEPTEMBER 21, 2003

1⅛ MILES. (Inner Turf)(1.45³) 54th Running of THE JAMAICA HANDICAP. Grade II. Purse $200,000. (Up to $34,800 NYSBFOA). THREE YEAR OLDS. By subscription of $200 each, which should accompany the nomination; $1,000 to pass the entry box and $1,000 to start. The purse to be divided 60% to the winner, 20% to second, 11% to third, 6% to fourth and 3% to fifth. Trophies will be presented to the winning owner, trainer and jockey. The New York Racing Association reserves the right to transfer this race to the Main Track. In the event that this race is taken off the turf, it may be subject to downgrading upon review by the Graded Stakes Committee. Closed Saturday, September 6, 2003 with 37 Nominations.

Value of Race: $200,000 Winner $120,000; second $40,000; third $22,000; fourth $12,000; fifth $6,000. Mutuel Pool $532,043.00 Exacta Pool $364,977.00 Trifecta Pool $287,897.00

Last Raced	Horse	M/Eqt. A.Wt	PP	St	¼	½	¾	Str	Fin	Jockey	Odds $1
4Aug03 ⁸Sar¹	Stroll	L	3 121	3	3	2hd 4½	4½	11	12	Bailey J D	1.40
16Aug03 ¹¹AP¹	Kicken Kris	L	3 121	6	6	41½ 3½	31	2½	2no	Castellano J J	3.10
16Aug03 ¹¹AP²	Joe Bear–IR	L	3 117	1	7	66 5½	52½ 32½	32½	Prado E S	4.20
20Aug03 ³WO¹	Stone Cat	Lb	3 114	2	4	5hd 66	63	61	43¾	Santos J A	17.10
14Aug03 ⁸Sar⁵	Y. V. Five	L	3 112	4	1	7 7	7	7	51½	Fragoso P	72.00
16Aug03 ¹¹AP³	Lismore Knight	L	3 119	5	2	3½ 2½	2hd 5hd	65	Velazquez J R	5.10
1Sep03 ¹⁰Sar³	Sharp Impact	Lb	3 116	7	5	1½ 1½	1hd 4hd	7	Migliore R	10.70

OFF AT 5:12 Start Good. Won driving. Course firm.

TIME :24, :47¹, 1:10⁴, 1:34², 1:46 (:24.17, :47.34, 1:10.94, 1:34.57, 1:46.02)

$2 Mutuel Prices:

3–STROLL	4.80	2.80	2.30
7–KICKEN KRIS		3.60	2.80
1–JOE BEAR–IR			2.80

$2 EXACTA 3–7 PAID $14.60 $2 TRIFECTA 3–7–1 PAID $36.40

Dk. b. or br. c, (Apr), by Pulpit–Maid for Walking*GB, by Prince Sabo. Trainer Mott William I. Bred by Claiborne Farm (Ky).

STROLL raced close up inside while well in hand, saved ground, got through on the rail in the stretch and drew clear under a drive. KICKEN KRIS raced close up outside, was four wide on the first turn, rallied three wide on the second turn, dug in gamely in the stretch and got the nod for the place prize. JOE BEAR (IRE) raced close up outside while in hand, rallied wide into the stretch and finished gamely outside. STONE CAT was rated along inside, angled out in upper stretch then drifted in in deep stretch and lacked a rally. Y. V. FIVE was outrun early, came wide into the stretch and had no rally. LISMORE KNIGHT pressed the pace while three wide and tired in the final furlong. SHARP IMPACT quickly showed in front, set the pace while in hand and tired in the stretch.

Owners— 1, Claiborne Farm; 2, Brushwood Stable; 3, Ransom Christopher; 4, Live Oak Plantation & Stonerside St; 5, Llorente Enrique Lauria Jesus & Amp; 6, Pletcher J J & Simon Barry; 7, Darley Stable

Trainers—1, Mott William I; 2, Matz Michael R; 3, Mitchell Philip; 4, Pierce Malcolm; 5, Morales Carlos J; 6, Pletcher Todd A; 7, McLaughlin Kiaran P

Scratched— Fortune Writers (25Aug03 ⁹SAR¹), Sircharlesschnabel (1Sep03 ⁸SAR¹), Colita (9Aug03 ⁸MNR³)

SEVENTH RACE

Arlington

SEPTEMBER 27, 2003

1 MILE. (1.32¹) 39th Running of THE ARLINGTON–WASHINGTON FUTURITY. Grade III. Purse $150,000 FOR TWO–YEAR–OLDS. By subscription of $100 each horse, which should accompany the nomination. A Supplementary Nomination of $6,000 may be made on Wednesday, September 24, 2003, which includes entry and starting fees. Original nominees to pay $1,000 to pass the entry box and an additional $1,000 to start. WEIGHT: 122 lbs.; Fillies, 119 lbs. Non–winners of $50,000 once, allowed 3 lbs.; $35,000 once or a race other than Maiden or Claiming, 5 lbs. This event will be limited to fourteen starters. Preference will be to winners of Graded/Group Stakes (in order of I–II–III), next preference, Highest Lifetime Earnings. Failure to draw into this race at time of entry cancels all fees with the exception of the nominating fee(s).

Value of Race: $150,000 Winner $90,000; second $30,000; third $16,500; fourth $9,000; fifth $4,500. Mutuel Pool $560,044.00 Exacta Pool $153,899.00 Trifecta Pool $126,372.00 Superfecta Pool $40,822.00

Last Raced	Horse	M/Eqt. A.Wt	PP	St	¼	½	¾	Str	Fin	Jockey	Odds $1
17Aug03 ⁹EIP¹	Cactus Ridge	L	2 122	3	4	11 11	1½	12½	13	Martin E M Jr	0.20
16Aug03 ⁴AP¹	Glittergem	L	2 117	5	3	31 3½	31	44	2nk	Day P	6.50
1Sep03 ¹²RD⁴	Texas Deputy	L	2 119	1	5	4½ 41	4hd 2hd	3no	Douglas R R	14.90
6Sep03 ⁸AP¹	Korbyn Gold	L	2 119	4	2	2½ 2½	2hd 3hd	45¾	Lanerie C J	7.50
20Aug03 ³AP¹	Orphan Brigade	Lf	2 119	6	1	53 53	5½	51½	52¾	Sibille R	39.10
23Aug03 ⁷EIP¹	Night Charger	L	2 117	2	6	6 6	6	6	6	Sellers S J	14.10

OFF AT 4:09 Start Good For All But NIGHT CHARGER. CACTUS RIDGE Won ridden out. Track fast.

TIME :23, :45³, 1:10², 1:22⁴, 1:35² (:23.03, :45.73, 1:10.44, 1:22.82, 1:35.44)

$2 Mutuel Prices:

3–CACTUS RIDGE	2.40	2.10	2.10
5–GLITTERGEM		2.80	2.10
1–TEXAS DEPUTY			2.10

$2 EXACTA 3–5 PAID $9.40 $2 TRIFECTA 3–5–1 PAID $42.60 $2 SUPERFECTA 3–5–1–4 PAID $72.00

B. c, (Apr), by Hennessy–Double Park*Fr, by Lycius. Trainer Calhoun William Bret. Bred by Dream Walkin Farms Inc (Ky).

CACTUS RIDGE bobbled at the start, recovered nicely to set a pressured pace from the inside, drew off when roused in the stretch and finished under moderate urging. GLITTERGEM settled in good striking position while off the rail, rallied in the stretch and gained the place while no danger to the top one. TEXAS DEPUTY saved ground near the middle of the field, moved up inside in the stretch then could not reach the winner and lost the place late. KORBYN GOLD pressed the pace of the winner from just outside but could not go with that one in the drive and weakened. ORPHAN BRIGADE lacked speed, came four wide into the stretch but lacked a rally. NIGHT CHARGER stumbled badly at the start and trailed throughout.

Owners— 1, Dream Walkin Farms Inc; 2, Grum Janelle D; 3, Stonerside Stable LLC; 4, Heiligbrodt Racing Stable; 5, L W Z Racing Stable; 6, R Durham Racing LLC Randall Durham

Trainers—1, Calhoun William Bret; 2, Wiggins Hal R; 3, Flint Bernard S; 4, Asmussen Steven M; 5, McGee Paul J; 6, Byrne Patrick B

$1 Pick Three (3/6–8/10/11/13–3) Paid $11.90; Pick Three Pool $17,389.

NINTH RACE
Arlington
SEPTEMBER 27, 2003

1 MILE. (1.32^{1}) 71st Running of THE ARLINGTON-WASHINGTON LASSIE. Grade III Purse $100,000 FOR FILLIES, TWO-YEARS-OLD. By subscription of $75 each, which should accompany the nomination. A Supplementary Nomination of $4,000 may be made on September 24, 2003, which includes entry and starting fees. Original nominees to pay $750 to pass the entry box and an additional $750 to start. WEIGHT: 121 lbs. Non-winners of $50,000 once, allowed 3 lbs.; $35,000 once or a race other than Maiden or Claiming, 5 lbs. This event will be limited to 14 starters. Preference will be to winners of Graded/Group Stakes (in order of I-II-III), next preference, Highest Lifetime Earnings. Failure to draw into this race at time of entry cancels all fees with the exception of the nominating fee(s). Two (2) horses having common ties through ownership cannot start to the exclusion ofa single ownership interest.

Value of Race: $100,000 Winner $60,000; second $20,000; third $11,000; fourth $6,000; fifth $3,000. Mutuel Pool $325,432.00 Exacta Pool $235,567.00 Trifecta Pool $227,604.00 Superfecta Pool $84,189.00

Last Raced	Horse	M/Eqt.	A.Wt	PP	St	¼	½	¾	Str	Fin	Jockey	Odds $1
17Aug03 ^{4}AP^{1}	Zosima	L	2 118	5	4	2^{hd}	3^{1}	3^{1}	$2^{1\frac{1}{2}}$	1^{1}	Day P	2.70
11Aug03 ^{4}Sar^{1}	Everyday Angel	L	2 116	7	3	1^{1}	1^{1}	1^{1}	1^{2}	$2^{3\frac{1}{2}}$	Sellers S J	0.70
5Sep03 ^{4}LaD^{1}	Cryptos' Best	Lb	2 118	8	1	3^{1}	2^{1}	2^{1}	$3^{2\frac{1}{2}}$	3^{1}	Martin E M Jr	21.40
5Sep03 ^{8}AP^{3}	Lovely Afternoon	L	2 116	6	7	6^{1}	8^{hd}	7^{3}	$5^{\frac{1}{2}}$	$4^{2\frac{1}{4}}$	Sterling L J Jr	87.10
30Aug03 ^{8}Ret^{3}	Blondz Away	L	2 116	2	10	$7^{\frac{1}{2}}$	7^{hd}	$6^{\frac{1}{2}}$	$4^{\frac{1}{2}}$	$5^{\frac{3}{4}}$	Lanerie C J	29.60
12Sep03 ^{3}AP^{1}	Journey Fever		2 116	9	5	5^{hd}	4^{1}	4^{1}	6^{1}	$6^{6\frac{1}{2}}$	Juarez A J Jr	47.60
27Aug03 ^{4}AP^{1}	Anapest	L	2 116	4	6	$9^{\frac{1}{2}}$	$9^{1\frac{1}{2}}$	9^{hd}	8^{2}	$7^{\frac{3}{4}}$	Emigh C A	13.50
30Aug03 ^{7}AP^{1}	Bad Kitty	L	2 116	3	2	$4^{\frac{1}{2}}$	6^{hd}	5^{hd}	7^{3}	$8^{2\frac{1}{2}}$	Douglas R R	11.30
31Aug03 ^{9}EmD^{1}	Sala De Oro	L	2 118	10	9	$8^{\frac{1}{2}}$	5^{hd}	10	10	9^{2}	Baze G	10.60
1Sep03 ^{3}AP^{3}	Indian Jewel	Lb	2 116	1	8	10	10	8^{hd}	9^{hd}	10	Lovato F Jr	53.90

OFF AT 5:12 Start Good. Won driving. Track fast.
TIME :23, :45^{4}, 1:10^{1}, 1:22^{4}, 1:36 (:23.00, :45.97, 1:10.22, 1:22.84, 1:36.02)

$2 Mutuel Prices:

6-ZOSIMA	7.40	2.80	2.80
8-EVERYDAY ANGEL		2.60	2.40
9-CRYPTOS' BEST			4.40

$2 EXACTA 6-8 PAID $19.00 $2 TRIFECTA 6-8-9 PAID $141.60 $2 SUPERFECTA 6-8-9-7 PAID $1,618.00

Dk. b. or br. f, (May), by Capote-Grafin, by Miswaki. Trainer Harty Eoin. Bred by Darley (Ky).

ZOSIMA raced close up inside, angled out in the stretch, rallied late and was along in time. EVERYDAY ANGEL set the pace from the inside, took a clear lead in the stretch then could not hold off the winner. CRYPTOS' BEST stalked the pace from just outside but lacked a winning bid. LOVELY AFTERNOON lacked speed and improved her position. BLONDZ AWAY was bothered at the start, lacked speed, made a bid in the stretch and flattened out. JOURNEY FEVER raced close up off the rail and weakened. ANAPEST lacked speed and showed little. BAD KITTY gave way in the drive. SALA DE ORO made a mild bid on the backstretch but faltered. INDIAN JEWEL was outrun.

Owners— 1, Darley Stud Management LLC; 2, Nip Richard; 3, Shepard Robert H; 4, Richard Otto Stables; 5, Richey & Strode Stables LLC; 6, Carroll Justin & Stefanie; 7, Glander Richard H; 8, Ashby Thoroughbreds; 9, Ten Broeck Farm Inc David Mowat; 10, Russell L Reineman Stable

Trainers—1, Harty Eoin; 2, Byrne Patrick B; 3, Thompson Mark L; 4, Mitchell Anthony; 5, Desormeaux J Keith; 6, Vanier Harvey L; 7, Ebert Dennis W; 8, Robertson Hugh H; 9, Forster Grant T; 10, Mitchell Anthony

Scratched— Rebel Lil (5Sep03 ^{8}AP^{8})

$1 Pick Three (3-1-6) Paid $42.80; Pick Three Pool $22,811.

SEVENTH RACE
Belmont
SEPTEMBER 27, 2003

6½ FURLONGS. (1.14^{2}) 64th Running of THE VOSBURGH. Grade I. Purse $500,000 (Up to $57,000 NYSBFOA). THREE YEAR OLDS AND UPWARD. By subscription of $500 each, which should accompany the nomination; $2,500 to pass the entry box and $2,500 to start. The purse to be divided 60% to the winner, 20% to second, 11% to third, 6% to fourth and 3% to fifth. Three year olds, 123 lbs.; older, 126 lbs. Trophies will be presented to the winning owner, trainer and jockey. Closed Saturday, September 13, 2003 with 28 Nominations.

Value of Race: $500,000 Winner $300,000; second $100,000; third $55,000; fourth $30,000; fifth $15,000. Mutuel Pool $850,499.00 Exacta Pool $623,038.00 Trifecta Pool $424,247.00 Superfecta Pool $78,024.00

Last Raced	Horse	M/Eqt.	A.Wt	PP	St	¼	½	Str	Fin	Jockey	Odds $1
23Aug03 ^{10}Sar^{3}	Ghostzapper	Lb	3 123	2	10	10	7^{3}	3^{hd}	$1^{6\frac{1}{2}}$	Castellano J J	3.10
1Sep03 ^{9}Tim^{3}	Aggadan	Lf	4 126	10	2	3^{hd}	3^{hd}	1^{hd}	$2^{1\frac{1}{4}}$	Nakatani C S	63.25
23Aug03 ^{10}Sar^{5}	Posse	L	3 123	5	4	$5^{\frac{1}{2}}$	$5^{3\frac{1}{2}}$	6^{6}	$3^{1\frac{3}{4}}$	Bailey J D	4.70
31Aug03 ^{10}Sar^{3}	Gygistar	L	4 126	1	3	$4^{2\frac{1}{2}}$	4^{1}	4^{hd}	4^{1}	Velazquez J R	1.60
31Aug03 ^{10}Sar^{5}	My Cousin Matt	Lf	4 126	9	1	$2^{2\frac{1}{2}}$	$2^{1\frac{1}{2}}$	$5^{\frac{1}{2}}$	5^{1}	Dunkelberger T L	26.25
17Aug03 ^{8}Sar^{1}	Voodoo	Lb	5 126	3	5	$1^{\frac{1}{2}}$	$1^{2\frac{1}{2}}$	2^{hd}	$6^{\frac{1}{2}}$	Chavez J F	7.90
16Aug03 ^{9}Pha^{1}	Highway Prospector	Lb	6 126	7	9	$9^{1\frac{1}{2}}$	10	$7^{2\frac{1}{2}}$	$7^{3\frac{3}{4}}$	Santos J A	31.25
11Sep03 ^{8}Bel^{2}	Papua	Lbf	4 126	8	7	7^{hd}	$8^{\frac{1}{2}}$	$8^{4\frac{1}{2}}$	8^{7}	Prado E S	45.25
10Aug03 ^{5}AP^{1}	Ajedrez-ARG	L	4 126	6	6	$6^{2\frac{1}{2}}$	6^{1}	9^{5}	9^{nk}	Razo E Jr	15.20
4Jly03 ^{8}Bel^{2}	Peeping Tom	Lbf	6 126	4	8	$8^{3\frac{1}{2}}$	9^{hd}	10	10	Bridgmohan S X	10.30

OFF AT 4:09 Start Good. Won driving. Track fast.
TIME :21^{4}, :44^{1}, 1:08^{3}, 1:14^{3} (:21.89, :44.26, 1:08.75, 1:14.72)

$2 Mutuel Prices:

3-GHOSTZAPPER	8.20	5.50	4.00
11-AGGADAN		42.00	16.80
6-POSSE			5.00

$2 EXACTA 3-11 PAID $380.50 $2 TRIFECTA 3-11-6 PAID $2,121.00 $2 SUPERFECTA 3-11-6-1 PAID $5,088.00

B. c, (Apr), by Awesome Again-Baby Zip, by Relaunch. Trainer Frankel Robert. Bred by Adena Springs (Ky).

GHOSTZAPPER was outrun early, raced outside, put in a quick four wide move nearing the stretch, reached the front leaving the eighth pole and drew away under a drive. AGGADAN raced close up outside, rallied three wide entering the stretch, gained a short lead at the eighth pole, had no answer for the winner and dug in to hold the place. POSSE raced within striking distance along the inside, split rivals approaching the stretch, lacked room while in traffic in upper stretch and altered course to the outside. GYGISTAR stumbled at the start, raced close up inside and was bumped along the rail in the stretch. MY COUSIN MATT pressed the pace from the outside and tired in the final furlong. VOODOO was hustled to the front, set the pace along the inside and was bumped while tiring in the stretch. HIGHWAY PROSPECTOR was outrun early, raced three wide and had no response when roused. PAPUA dropped back early, raced between rivals and tired in the stretch. AJEDREZ (ARG) was hustled outside, chased the pace for a half mile and tired. PEEPING TOM was outrun early, raced inside and tired.

Owners— 1, Stronach Stable; 2, Goldfarb Sanford Rosenfeld Neil Fle; 3, Heiligbrodt Stables & Vinery Stable; 4, Evans Edward P; 5, Englander Richard A; 6, Moore Susan & John; 7, Gill Michael J; 8, Schwartz Barry K; 9, Calabrese Frank C; 10, Flatbird Stable

Trainers—1, Frankel Robert; 2, Dutrow Richard E Jr; 3, Asmussen Steven M; 4, Hennig Mark; 5, Lake Scott A; 6, Jerkens James A; 7, Shuman Mark; 8, Hushion Michael E; 9, Catalano Wayne M; 10, Reynolds Patrick L

Scratched— Proud Citizen (31Aug03 ^{10}SAR^{6})

$2 Daily Double (8-3) Paid $26.40; Daily Double Pool $154,485.
$2 Pick Three (1-8-3) Paid $77.00; Pick Three Pool $110,409.

EIGHTH RACE
Belmont
SEPTEMBER 27, 2003

1¼ MILES. (Inner Turf)(1.57^{3}) 26th Running of THE FLOWER BOWL INVITATIONAL. Grade I. Purse $750,000. (Up to $65,500 NYSBFOA). FILLIES AND MARES THREE YEARS OLD AND UPWARD. By invitation only with no subscription fees. The purse to be divided 60% to the winner, 20% to second, 11% to third, 6% to fourth and 3% to fifth. Three year olds, 118lbs.; older, 123 lbs. Non-winners of a Grade 1 since April 1, 2003 allowed 3 lbs.; a Grade 1 since October 1, 2002, or a Grade 2 since April 1, 2003, 5 lbs. Trophies will be presented to the winning owner, trainer and jockey. The New York Racing Association reserves the right to transfer this race to the Main Track. In the event that this race is taken off the turf, it may be subject to downgrading upon review by the Graded Stakes Committee.

Value of Race: $750,000 Winner $450,000; second $150,000; third $82,500; fourth $45,000; fifth $22,500. Mutuel Pool $903,796.00 Exacta Pool $630,328.00 Trifecta Pool $449,423.00

Last Raced	Horse	M/Eqt.	A.Wt	PP	¼	½	¾	1	Str	Fin	Jockey	Odds $1
7Sep03 ^{9}Bel^{2}	Dimitrova	L	3 114	5	$5^{3\frac{1}{2}}$	$5^{3\frac{1}{2}}$	$5^{\frac{1}{2}}$	$5^{1\frac{1}{2}}$	$3^{\frac{1}{2}}$	1^{1}	Bailey J D	3.70
16Aug03 ^{8}AP^{4}	Walzerkoenigin	L	4 120	2	$4^{2\frac{1}{2}}$	3^{hd}	3^{hd}	$3^{\frac{1}{2}}$	2^{hd}	2no	Prado E S	16.50
16Aug03 ^{8}AP^{1}	Heat Haze-GB	L	4 123	7	7	7	7	$6^{\frac{1}{2}}$	$5^{\frac{1}{2}}$	$3^{1\frac{1}{4}}$	Valdivia J Jr	0.85
16Aug03 ^{8}AP^{6}	Dress To Thrill-IR	L	4 120	3	2^{hd}	2^{2}	$2^{1\frac{1}{2}}$	$1^{\frac{1}{2}}$	1^{hd}	4^{nk}	Nakatani C S	10.10
16Aug03 ^{8}AP^{3}	Riskaverse	L	4 120	1	3^{hd}	$4^{1\frac{1}{2}}$	$4^{1\frac{1}{2}}$	4^{hd}	$4^{1\frac{1}{2}}$	$5^{\frac{3}{4}}$	Velazquez J R	6.60
25Aug03 ^{8}Sar^{2}	Primetimevalentine	b	4 118	4	$6^{1\frac{1}{2}}$	$6^{\frac{1}{2}}$	$6^{\frac{1}{2}}$	7	7	6^{3}	Santos J A	27.50
23Aug03 ^{8}Sar^{2}	Snow Dance	L	5 120	6	$1^{\frac{1}{2}}$	$1^{1\frac{1}{2}}$	1^{1}	2^{1}	6^{1}	7	Migliore R	9.00

OFF AT 4:42 Start Good. Won driving. Course firm.
TIME :25^{2}, :49^{4}, 1:14^{4}, 1:39, 2:02^{3} (:25.55, :49.86, 1:14.99, 1:39.02, 2:02.74)

$2 Mutuel Prices:

5-DIMITROVA	9.40	5.70	2.40
3-WALZERKOENIGIN		13.60	3.00
7-HEAT HAZE-GB			2.10

$2 EXACTA 5-3 PAID $106.50 $2 TRIFECTA 5-3-7 PAID $230.00

B. f, (May), by Swain*Ire-The Caretaker*Ire, by Caerleon. Trainer Weld Dermot K. Bred by Muirfield Ventures (Ky).

DIMITROVA raced in hand outside while well in hand, advanced on the second turn, came wide into the stretch, responded when roused and was clear under the wire, driving. WALZERKOENIGIN raced with the pace from the outside while in hand, rallied three wide approaching the stretch and dug in gamely to the finish. HEAT HAZE (GB) was outrun early, advanced three wide on the second turn and finished gamely outside. DRESS TO THRILL (IRE) prompted the pace from the outside, earned a short lead turning for home and gave ground grudgingly through the stretch. RISKAVERSE raced close up inside, saved ground and lacked a rally while on the rail in the stretch. PRIMETIMEVALENTINE was rated along early, raced inside and stayed on well in the stretch. SNOW DANCE bobbled at the start but quickly showed in front, set the pace along the inside and tired in the stretch.

Owners— 1, Higgins Joseph; 2, Baroness Karin Von Ullmann; 3, Juddmonte Farms Inc; 4, Moyglare Stud Farm Ltd; 5, Fox Ridge Farm Inc; 6, Low Lawana L & Robert E; 7, Oxley John C

Trainers—1, Weld Dermot K; 2, Schiergen Peter; 3, Frankel Robert; 4, Clement Christophe; 5, Kelly Patrick J; 6, Peitz Daniel C; 7, Ward John T Jr

Scratched— Sixty Seconds (25Aug03 ^{8}SAR^{1})

$2 Pick Three (8-3-5) Paid $184.00; Pick Three Pool $142,655.

NINTH RACE
Belmont
SEPTEMBER 27, 2003

1½ MILES. (Turf)(2.24^{1}) 27th Running of THE TURF CLASSIC INVITATIONAL. Grade I. Purse $750,000. (Up to $65,500 NYSBFOA). THREE YEAR OLDS AND UPWARD AT WEIGHT FOR AGE. By invitation only with no subscription fees. The purse to be divided 60% to the winner, 20% to second, 11% to third, 6% to fourth and 3% to fifth. Three year olds, 120 lbs.; older, 126 lbs. Fillies and Mares allowed 3 lbs. Trophies will be presented to the winning owner, trainer and jockey. The New York Racing Association reserves the right to transfer this race to the Main Track. In the event that this race is taken off the turf, it may be subject to downgrading upon review by the Graded Stakes Committee.

Value of Race: $750,000 Winner $450,000; second $150,000; third $82,500; fourth $45,000; fifth $22,500. Mutuel Pool $761,791.00 Exacta Pool $532,988.00 Trifecta Pool $359,090.00

Last Raced	Horse	M/Eqt.	A.Wt	PP	¼	½	1	1¼	Str	Fin	Jockey	Odds $1
16Aug03 ^{10}AP^{2}	Sulamani-IR	L	4 126	7	7	7	7	$6^{1\frac{1}{2}}$	$2^{\frac{1}{2}}$	$1^{2\frac{3}{4}}$	Bailey J D	0.75
6Sep03 ^{8}Bel^{5}	Deeliteful Irving	Lf	5 126	6	6^{hd}	$6^{\frac{1}{2}}$	$6^{\frac{1}{2}}$	5^{hd}	4^{hd}	$2^{\frac{3}{4}}$	Bravo J	a-6.50
6Sep03 ^{8}Bel^{4}	Balto Star	L	5 126	3	$1^{\frac{1}{2}}$	$1^{1\frac{1}{2}}$	$1^{\frac{1}{2}}$	$1^{1\frac{1}{2}}$	$1^{\frac{1}{2}}$	$3^{\frac{1}{2}}$	Prado E S	a-6.50
17Aug03 KOL^{4}	Sabiango-GE	L	5 126	5	$5^{\frac{1}{2}}$	5^{hd}	5^{hd}	$4^{\frac{1}{2}}$	5^{2}	$4^{1\frac{1}{2}}$	Flores D R	20.20
31Aug03 Dea^{1}	Polish Summer-GB		6 126	1	4^{hd}	$4^{\frac{1}{2}}$	$4^{\frac{1}{2}}$	2^{hd}	3^{hd}	5^{2}	Velazquez J R	6.10
6Sep03 ^{8}Bel^{2}	Slew Valley	L	6 126	2	$2^{1\frac{1}{2}}$	$2^{1\frac{1}{2}}$	$2^{\frac{1}{2}}$	3^{hd}	6^{10}	$6^{19\frac{1}{4}}$	Castellano J J	14.20
6Sep03 ^{8}Bel^{1}	Lunar Sovereign	L	4 126	4	$3^{\frac{1}{2}}$	3^{hd}	3^{hd}	7	7	7	Migliore R	3.60

a-Coupled: Deeliteful Irving and Balto Star.

OFF AT 5:13 Start Good. Won driving. Course firm.
TIME :25^{2}, :50^{1}, 1:14^{3}, 1:38, 2:02^{1}, 2:27^{2} (:25.46, :50.29, 1:14.69, 1:38.16, 2:02.29, 2:27.51)

$2 Mutuel Prices:

6-SULAMANI-IR	3.50	2.70	2.30
1A-DEELITEFUL IRVING (a-entry)		4.30	4.60
1-BALTO STAR (a-entry)		4.30	4.60

$2 EXACTA 6-1 PAID $19.80 $2 TRIFECTA 6-1-5 PAID $99.50

B. c, by Hernando*Fr-Soul Dream, by Alleged. Trainer Suroor Saeed bin. Bred by Niarchos Family (Ire).

SULAMANI (IRE) was taken back and raced in hand early on, advanced three wide on the second turn, stumbled badly after appearing to clip heels approaching the stretch, recovered quickly, caught the leaders leaving the eighth pole, drew clear after one left handed strike from the whip and was in hand and not fully extended under the wire. DEELITEFUL IRVING was rated along early, raced inside, was caught in traffic along the inside in upper stretch, got through on the rail inside the eighth pole and finished gamely. BALTO STAR soon showed in front, set the pace along the inside, drew clear into the stretch and stayed on gamely to the finish. SABIANGO (GER) was rated along outside, put in a four wide run on the second turn and weakened in deep stretch. POLISH SUMMER (GB) raced close up inside while well in hand, saved ground and came up empty when called on. SLEW VALLEY prompted the pace from the outside and tired in the stretch. LUNAR SOVEREIGN raced with the pace while three wide and tired in the stretch.

Owners— 1, Godolphin Racing Inc; 2, Anstu Stables; 3, Anstu Stables; 4, Jacobs Andreas; 5, Juddmonte Farms Inc; 6, Rich Meadow Farm; 7, Darley Stable

Trainers—1, Suroor Saeed bin; 2, Dickinson Michael W; 3, Pletcher Todd A; 4, Wohler Andreas; 5, Fabre Andre; 6, Sciacca Gary; 7, McLaughlin Kiaran P

TENTH RACE
Belmont
SEPTEMBER 27, 2003

1¼ MILES. (1.58¹) 85th Running of THE JOCKEY CLUB GOLD CUP. Grade I. Purse $1,000,000. (Up to $72,000 NYSBFOA). THREE YEAR OLDS AND UPWARD AT WEIGHT FOR AGE. By subscription of $1,000 each, which should accompany the nomination; $5,000 to pass the entry box and $5,000 to start. The purse to be divided 60% to the winner, 20% to second, 11% to third, 6% to fourth and 3% to fifth. Weight for age. Three year olds, 121 lbs., older, 126 lbs. The New York Racing Association will present a Gold Cup to the winning owner and trophies to the winning trainer and jockey. Closed Saturday, September 13th, 2003 with 16 Nominations.

Value of Race: $1,000,000 Winner $600,000; second $200,000; third $110,000; fourth $60,000; fifth $30,000. Mutuel Pool $1,130,629.0 Exacta Pool $525,649.00 Trifecta Pool $275,449.00

Last Raced	Horse	M/Eqt.	A.Wt	PP	¼	½	¾	1	Str	Fin	Jockey	Odds $1
6Sep03 9Bel1	Mineshaft	L	4 126	3	37	38	2hd	11½	15	14¼	Albarado R J	0.40
27Aug03 8Sar1	Quest	L	4 126	1	1½	1½	1½	26	27	22¾	Prado E S	22.10
25Aug03 7Sar1	Evening Attire	Lb	5 126	4	5	5	5	5	32½	36½	Guidry M	7.30
13Sep03 7Bel4	State Shinto	Lb	7 126	5	44½	41½	45	41½	46	49¼	Migliore R	43.25
6Sep03 Leo5	Moon Ballad-IR	L	4 126	2	22½	21½	37	31½	5	5	Bailey J D	2.70

OFF AT 5:45 Start Good. Won ridden out. Track fast.
TIME :24, :47³, 1:11, 1:34⁴, 2:00¹ (:24.08, :47.73, 1:11.05, 1:34.91, 2:00.25)

$2 Mutuel Prices:

3–MINESHAFT	2.80	2.10	—
1–QUEST		2.10	—
4–EVENING ATTIRE		—	—

$2 EXACTA 3–1 PAID $18.60 $2 TRIFECTA 3–1–4 PAID $34.80

Dk. b. or br. c, by A.P. Indy–Prospectors Delite, by Mr. Prospector. Trainer Howard Neil J. Bred by W. S. Farish, James Elkins & W. T. Webber Jr. (Ky).

MINESHAFT came away well and raced close up outside early while well in hand, moved to the leaders three wide leaving the backstretch, took over from QUEST approaching the stretch, drew clear, opened up when shaken up in upper stretch and remained comfortably clear under a confident hand ride. QUEST was hustled directly to the front, set the pace under pressure from MOON BALLAD, put away that rival leaving the backstretch but was confronted immediately by the winner, kept up with that rival into the stretch, could not stay with MINESHAFT in the drive and continued on gamely to be second best. EVENING ATTIRE was outrun early, was put to the task on the second turn, came wide into the stretch and finished well outside. STATE SHINTO was outrun early, raced inside and had no response when roused on the second turn. MOON BALLAD (IRE) pressed the pace from the outside and was finished after the opening three quarters.

Owners— 1, Farish William S Elkins James A & W; 2, Hancock III Arthur B & Healy Gerald; 3, Grant Mary & Joseph & Kelly Thomas; 4, Darley Stable; 5, Godolphin Racing Inc

Trainers—1, Howard Neil J; 2, Zito Nicholas P; 3, Kelly Patrick J; 4, McLaughlin Kiaran P; 5, Suroor Saeed bin

---

$2 Daily Double (6–3) Paid $4.80; Daily Double Pool $139,589.
$2 Pick Three (5–6–3) Paid $32.40; Pick Three Pool $188,509.
$2 Pick Four (3–5–6–3) Paid $122.50; Pick Four Pool $891,276.
$2 Pick Six (1–8–3–5–6–3) 6
Correct Paid $1,793.00; Pick Six Pool $368,914. $2 Pick Six (1–8–3–5–6–3) 5
Correct Paid $27.80

SIXTH RACE
Bay Meadows
SEPTEMBER 27, 2003

ABOUT 1⅛ MILES. (Turf)(1.45¹) 28th Running of THE BAY MEADOWS BREEDERS' CUP HANDICAP. Grade III. Purse $200,000 (includes $100,000 BC – Breeders') HREE-YEAR-OLDS AND UPWARD. (Includes $100,000 from Breeders' Cup Fund for Cup nominees only). By subscription of $100 each to accompany the nomination or by supplementary nominations of $2,000 by Noon September 21, 2003. $500 to pass the entry box and $500 additional to start. Any Breeders' Cup Fund monies not awarded will revert back to the Fund. Weights, Sunday, September 21, 2003. This race will not be divided. The starters will be determined at that time with preference given to Breeders' Cup nominees only of equal racing quality or weight assignment (respective of sex and weight for age). Preference to Non–Breeders' Cup nominees follow the same stipulation. NOMINATIONS CLOSE THURSDAY, SEPTEMBER 18, 2003.

Value of Race: $142,500 Winner $55,000; second $40,000; third $30,000; fourth $15,000; fifth $2,500. Mutuel Pool $312,463.00 Exacta Pool $210,340.00 Quinella Pool $15,944.00 Trifecta Pool $205,547.00 Superfecta Pool $69,710.00

Last Raced	Horse	M/Eqt.	A.Wt	PP	St	¼	½	¾	Str	Fin	Jockey	Odds $1
31Aug03 8Dmr6	Mister Acpen-CH	LBb	5 116	6	1	12½	12	12	12	11¼	Gonzalez R M	4.30
22Aug03 2Dmr2	Fateful Dream	LBb	6 117	7	6	7½	6hd	51	31½	2no	Valenzuela P A	1.50
1Sep03 8BM1	Ninebanks	LBb	5 118	3	4	5½	3hd	41½	22½	35	Warren R J Jr	4.10
31Aug03 8Dmr8	Like A Hero	LBb	4 115	5	9	81	8hd	7½	6hd	4nk	Espinoza V	8.80
1Sep03 8BM2	Surprise Halo	LB	5 115	2	5	6hd	7½	81	41	5no	Castro J M	7.90
25Aug03 7Dmr1	Runaway Dancer	LB	4 116	4	10	10	10	10	10	6¾	Rollins C J	17.80
1Sep03 8BM4	Aly Bubba	LB	4 114	8	3	3½	4hd	6hd	7½	7¾	Morris R	51.60
5Jly03 6Hol7	Calkins Road	LBb	4 116	9	7	4hd	910	910	81	82½	Baze R A	30.90
24Aug03 8EmD2	Poker Brad	LB	5 114	10	8	96	51½	3½	51	93	Lumpkins J	21.80
6Aug03 7Dmr5	Lily's Lad	LBb	6 115	1	2	21½	22	2hd	92½	10	Smith M E	19.50

OFF AT 3:52 Start Good. Won driving. Course firm.
TIME :23, :47⁴, 1:12², 1:37¹, 1:46⁴ (:23.06, :47.99, 1:12.47, 1:37.25, 1:46.94)

$2 Mutuel Prices:

6–MISTER ACPEN–CH	10.60	4.20	2.80
7–FATEFUL DREAM		3.20	2.60
3–NINEBANKS			2.60

$1 EXACTA 6–7 PAID $19.00 $2 QUINELLA 6–7 PAID $15.80 $1 TRIFECTA 6–7–3 PAID $61.30 $1 SUPERFECTA 6–7–3–5 PAID $219.90

Dk. b. or br. h, by Golden Voyager–Gruta Azul*Chi, by Semenenko. Trainer Mulhall Kristin. Bred by Haras Matancilla (Chi).

MISTER ACPEN (CHI) was quickly in front to set all of the pace under fine rating, was never seriously challenged to the stretch, responded and held driving. FATEFUL DREAM settled early in heavy traffic to the 2nd turn, came two wide into the stretch, shifted out and was closing late. NINEBANKS was well placed early, saved ground throughout, loomed a factor at the head of the lane but lacked the needed response. LIKE A HERO was caught behind heavy traffic into the first turn, raced up into tight quarter three wide entering the backstretch then remained between horses, dropped inside for the drive and finished steadily. SURPRISE HALO raced unhurried early, saved ground throughout but did not threaten. RUNAWAY DANCER was void of any early speed then closed steadily but too late from the inside in the final quarter. ALY BUBBA was forwardly placed three wide early, was fanned four wide on the second turn and had no response. CALKINS ROAD was forced wide into the first turn while taking back off the pace, remained widest on the second turn and did not rally. POKER BRAD stalked the pace four wide early and was through after six furlongs. LILY'S LAD prompted the pace from the rail and gave out.

Owners— 1, Noctis Stable Papiano Neil & Taub S; 2, Gann Edmund A; 3, Abruzzo Peter; 4, Columbine Stable; 5, Karp Lawrence M & Ward Dennis; 6, R L Stables; 7, Daehling Ives Marek et al; 8, Mr & Mrs Thomas Shapiro; 9, Quadrun Farm LLC; 10, Moss Mr & Mrs Jerome S

Trainers—1, Mulhall Kristin; 2, Frankel Robert; 3, Hollendorfer Jerry; 4, Greely C Beau; 5, Ward Wesley A; 6, Hendricks Dan L; 7, Evans Holly; 8, Shirreffs John; 9, McCanna Tim; 10, Shirreffs John

---

$2 Daily Double (9–6) Paid $67.00; Daily Double Pool $10,557.
$1 Pick Three (8–9–6) Paid $194.90; Pick Three Pool $21,493.

NINTH RACE

Pimlico

SEPTEMBER 27, 2003

1$\frac{1}{16}$ MILES. (Turf)(1.40[1]) 21st Running of THE MARTHA WAHINGTON BREEDERS' CUP. Grade III. Purse $150,000 (includes $50,000 BC – Breeders' Cup) FOR FILLIES, THREE–YEARS–OLD. (Includes $50,000 from Breeders' Cup Fund for Cup nominees only). By subscription of $100 each which should accompany the nomination. $500 to pass the entry box. $500 additional to start with $100,000 Guaranteed, Supplemental nominations of $1,500 each will be accepted by the usual time of closing with all other fees due as noted. Breeders' Cup Fund monies, divided provding a Breeders' Cup Nominee has finished in an awarded position. Any Breeders' Cup Fund monies not awarded will revert back to the fund. Weight 122 lbs. Non–winners of a Sweepstakesat a mile or over in 2003, allowed 3 lbs.; $30,000 twice at a mile or over in 2003, 5 lbs.; once 7 lbs. (Maiden and claiming races not considered in estimating allowances). Horses may be placed on the also eligible lists.

Value of Race: $147,000 Winner $90,000; second $30,000; third $16,500; fourth $6,000; fifth $4,500.   Mutuel Pool $117,201.00 Exacta Pool $73,966.00   Trifecta Pool $52,597.00 Superfecta Pool $11,803.00

Last Raced	Horse	M/Eqt. A.Wt	PP	St	$\frac{1}{4}$	$\frac{1}{2}$	$\frac{3}{4}$	Str	Fin	Jockey	Odds $1
2Aug03 Dea[6]	Derrianne	L 3 122	3	5	3[1]	3[1]	3[2]	2[1]	11$\frac{1}{4}$	Blanc B	1.60
25Aug03 3Sar[1]	Chic Joy	L 3 115	4	1	4[2]	43$\frac{1}{2}$	4$\frac{1}{2}$	3[1]	2[2]	Monterrey R	9.50
27Aug03 7Sar[4]	Twining And Dining	L 3 115	5	2	5[2]	5$\frac{1}{2}$	51$\frac{1}{2}$	5$\frac{1}{2}$	3nk	Castellano A Jr	27.30
17Aug03 9Sar[5]	Gal O Gal	L 3 122	6	6	7	7	63$\frac{1}{2}$	66	41$\frac{1}{2}$	Jurado E M	2.50
12Jly03 8Del[2]	Little Miss Pamela	L 3 122	2	3	2[5]	2[3]	2[5]	1hd	52$\frac{1}{2}$	Santana J Z	9.30
6Sep03 9Pim[4]	A Queen's Smile	Lbf 3 115	7	7	6hd	6hd	7	7	62$\frac{1}{2}$	Verge M E	12.40
13Sep03 9Mth[1]	Impolite	L 3 122	1	4	12$\frac{1}{2}$	12	1hd	4hd	7	Wilson R	2.70

OFF AT 4:59 Start Good. Won driving. Course good.

TIME :23[1], :48[1], 1:13[1], 1:39[4], 1:46[2] (:23.32, :48.22, 1:13.38, 1:39.89, 1:46.53)

$2 Mutuel Prices:

7–DERRIANNE	5.20	3.40	3.80
9–CHIC JOY		6.20	4.00
10–TWINING AND DINING			5.80

$2 EXACTA 7–9 PAID $48.00 $2 TRIFECTA 7–9–10 PAID $290.20 $1
SUPERFECTA 7–9–10–11 PAID $438.10

Gr/ro f, (Feb), by Cozzene–Stormy Gal, by Storm Cat. Trainer Clement Christophe. Bred by Warren W Rosenthal (Ky).

DERRIANNE stalked the pace, eased out four wide entering the stretch, closed and drew clear while drifting out. CHIC JOY raced very wide in the stretch and rallied. TWINING AND DINING lacked speed, raced in the two path in the stretch and rallied mildly. GAL O GAL raced wide in the stretch and passed tired ones. LITTLE MISS PAMELA prompted the pace outside IMPOLITE, gained a three wide lead entering the stretch and gave way the final furlong. A QUEEN'S SMILE raced along the rail to the stretch and was outrun. IMPOLITE set the pace near the rail and stopped.

Owners— 1, Waterville Lake Stable; 2, Groves Helen K; 3, C D & G Stable; 4, Hugel Max; 5, Salomone Mark E; 6, Cornacchia Joseph M; 7, Noble Ray

Trainers—1, Clement Christophe; 2, Matz Michael E; 3, Klesaris Robert P; 4, Blengs Vincent L; 5, Trimmer Richard K; 6, Boniface Kevin C; 7, Rice Linda

Scratched— Coquettish (6Sep03 9PIM[2]), Randaroo (23Aug03 6MTH[2]), Feisty Bull (16Aug03 10MTH[1]), Sarie Marais (13Sep03 8AP[12]), Nault (4Sep03 7PIM[1]), City Fire (1Sep03 10PHA[1]), Ladyecho (1Sep03 10PHA[3])

NINTH RACE

Turfway Park

SEPTEMBER 27, 2003

1 MILE. (1.34) 54th Running of THE TURFWAY PARK FALL CHAMPIONSHIP. Grade III. Purse $100,000 FOR THREE–YEAR–OLDS AND UPWARD. By subscription of $100, $500 to enter and $500 additional to start. Supplementary nominations may be made at the time of entry Thursday, September 25, 2003 by payment of $5,000 each (includes all fees). Monies to be divided 62% to the owner of the winner, 20% to second, 10% to third, 5% to fourth and 3% to fifth. Weights:Three–year–olds 118 lbs.; older 122 lbs. Non–winners of a Graded Stake at a mile or over since May 15 allowed 3 lbs.; non–winners of a non–graded stake at a mile or over in 2003, 5 lbs.; 30,000 twice at a mile or over in 2002–2003, 7 lbs.

Value of Race: $100,000 Winner $62,000; second $20,000; third $10,000; fourth $5,000; fifth $3,000.   Mutuel Pool $120,902.00 Exacta Pool $113,636.00   Trifecta Pool $101,009.00 Superfecta Pool $36,347.00

Last Raced	Horse	M/Eqt. A.Wt	PP	St	$\frac{1}{4}$	$\frac{1}{2}$	$\frac{3}{4}$	Str	Fin	Jockey	Odds $1
13Sep03 11TP[3]	Crafty Shaw	L 5 117	2	2	1hd	1$\frac{1}{2}$	11$\frac{1}{2}$	12	12$\frac{1}{4}$	Perret C	0.60
10Aug03 7Sar[1]	Cat Tracker	L 5 117	8	4	41$\frac{1}{2}$	3hd	3hd	2$\frac{1}{2}$	2$\frac{3}{4}$	Melancon L	12.00
23Aug03 8Sar[3]	Cappuchino	Lbf 4 119	5	6	5[3]	41	42$\frac{1}{2}$	33	32$\frac{3}{4}$	Court J K	7.60
24Aug03 8Sar[3]	Bold Truth	L 4 115	3	5	6hd	7hd	8	51	42$\frac{1}{2}$	McKee J	8.60
23Aug03 9EIP[2]	Trion Georgia	Lf 5 115	7	3	2$\frac{1}{2}$	21$\frac{1}{2}$	21	4$\frac{1}{2}$	5hd	Borel C H	9.00
16Aug03 7AP[1]	Ask The Lord	L 6 119	6	7	8	6$\frac{1}{2}$	6hd	6$\frac{1}{2}$	6hd	Bourque C C	6.50
5Sep03 9TP[4]	Sea of Tranquility	L 7 119	4	8	72$\frac{1}{2}$	8	7hd	8	73$\frac{1}{2}$	Burningham J	19.70
1Jan03 9TP[7]	Dayton Flyer	Lf 5 115	1	1	3hd	53	5$\frac{1}{2}$	71	8	Thompson T J	47.90

OFF AT 4:50 Start Good. Won driving. Track fast.

TIME :22[4], :46[1], 1:11, 1:23[4], 1:36[4] (:22.85, :46.21, 1:11.15, 1:23.89, 1:36.89)

$2 Mutuel Prices:

2–CRAFTY SHAW	3.20	2.60	2.10
8–CAT TRACKER		5.60	2.80
5–CAPPUCHINO			2.40

$2 EXACTA 2–8 PAID $19.20 $2 TRIFECTA 2–8–5 PAID $95.40 $2
SUPERFECTA 2–8–5–3 PAID $438.40

Ch. h, by Crafty Prospector–Her She Shawklit, by Air Forbes Won. Trainer Vestal Peter M. Bred by Lance K Robinson (Ky).

CRAFTY SHAW vied for the early lead between rivals, took over after a half, stayed out in the three path on the second turn while controlling the pace then stayed clear under steady urging. CAT TRACKER prompted the early pace four wide, dropped back a bit before a half, raced in the five path on the second turn and held on gamely for the place. CAPPUCHINO behind the leaders three wide, stayed on well to midstretch and lacked a closing bid. BOLD TRUTH reserved three wide, angled out four wide late on the second turn and had little left late. TRION GEORGIA forced the early pace three wide, moved out a bit for the second turn and tired in the drive. ASK THE LORD outrun early in the three path, moved out to be six wide with a quarter mile to go and was no real threat. SEA OF TRANQUILITY unhurried off the inside, could not menace. DAYTON FLYER prompted the pace along the inside and gave way.

Owners— 1, Cella Charles J; 2, WinStar Farm LLC; 3, Litt & Todaro Hollendorfer; 4, Oxley John C; 5, Bohanon Pat & Jim; 6, Peter Gaffney & Stewart M Madison; 7, Triple M Farm; 8, Hays Billy

Trainers—1, Vestal Peter M; 2, Walden W Elliott; 3, Hollendorfer Jerry; 4, Ward John T Jr; 5, O'Connor Robert R II; 6, Stall Albert M Jr; 7, Paulus Richard E; 8, Woodard Joe

---

$2 Pick Three (1–8–2) Paid $86.80; Pick Three Pool $6,636.

NINTH RACE
Hawthorne
SEPTEMBER 28, 2003

1¼ MILES. (1.58^{4}) 67th Running of THE HAWTHORNE GOLD CUP HANDICAP. Grade II. Purse $750,000 $750,000 Guaranteed. A HANDICAP FOR THREE-YEAR-OLDS AND UPWARD. By subscription of $100 each, which shall accompany the nomination, $2,500 to pass the entry box, $2,500 additional to start. With $750,000 Guaranteed, of which 60 percent to the winner, 20 percent to second, 11 percent to third, 6 percent to fourth, 3 percent to fifth. Nominations closed Wednesday, September 17, 2003 with 18.

Value of Race: $750,000 Winner $450,000; second $150,000; third $82,500; fourth $45,000; fifth $22,500. Mutuel Pool $853,657.00 Exacta Pool $191,564.00 Trifecta Pool $172,074.00 Superfecta Pool $59,168.00

Last Raced	Horse	M/Eqt.	A.	Wt	PP	¼	½	¾	1	Str	Fin	Jockey	Odds $1
13Sep03 ^{11}TP^{1}	Perfect Drift	L	4	122	6	$2^{1\frac{1}{2}}$	2^{1}	2^{2}	1^{hd}	1^{hd}	$1^{1\frac{3}{4}}$	Day P	0.40
23Aug03 ^{10}Mth^{1}	Tenpins	Lf	5	119	3	$1^{1\frac{1}{2}}$	1^{1}	$1^{\frac{1}{2}}$	$2^{\frac{1}{2}}$	$2^{\frac{1}{2}}$	$2^{\frac{1}{2}}$	Albarado R J	1.80
23Aug03 ^{10}Mth^{2}	Aeneas	L	4	114	2	4^{1}	$3^{1\frac{1}{2}}$	$3^{1\frac{1}{2}}$	$3^{2\frac{1}{2}}$	$3^{3\frac{1}{2}}$	3^{6}	Boulanger G	9.50
16Aug03 ^{7}Sar^{4}	No Comprende	Lb	5	115	4	5^{4}	$5^{3\frac{1}{2}}$	$5^{2\frac{1}{2}}$	4^{4}	4^{4}	$4^{9\frac{3}{4}}$	Marquez C H Jr	49.80
7Sep03 ^{8}AP^{1}	Scooter Roach	L	4	111	5	3^{hd}	4^{hd}	$4^{\frac{1}{2}}$	$5^{2\frac{1}{2}}$	$5^{1\frac{1}{2}}$	$5^{4\frac{1}{4}}$	Campbell J M	63.80
16Aug03 ^{7}AP^{2}	San Pedro	Lbf	5	116	1	6	6	6	6	6	6	Fires E	34.30

OFF AT 4:58 Start Good. Won ridden out. Track fast.
TIME :24^{2}, :49^{3}, 1:13^{3}, 1:39, 2:03^{3} (:24.50, :49.64, 1:13.71, 1:39.02, 2:03.63)

$2 Mutuel Prices:			
6-PERFECT DRIFT	2.80	2.10	2.10
3-TENPINS		2.10	2.10
2-AENEAS			2.10

$2 EXACTA 6-3 PAID $4.40 $2 TRIFECTA 6-3-2 PAID $6.40 $2 SUPERFECTA 6-3-2-4 PAID $19.60

B. g, by Dynaformer–Nice Gal, by Naskra. Trainer Johnson Murray W. Bred by Reed William & Stonecrest Farm (Ky).

PERFECT DRIFT moved up well off the rail to put pressure on TENPINS, continued to prompt the issue to the far turn, put a head in front turning for home, continued to battle with TENPINS to the furlong marker then edged clear under vigorous hand urging. TENPINS quickly established the early lead while kept away from the inside, continued setting a pressured pace to the final turn, battled gamely with PERFECT DRIFT to inside the furlong marker then succumbed in the final sixteenth. AENEAS was allowed to settle in while not far back, gained ground to challenge outside the top two entering the stretch and still loomed a threat a furlong out but could not get by the top two. NO COMPRENDE was void of speed while off the rail and never reached a contending position. SCOOTER ROACH was near the middle of the field while not far back early but was never a serious factor. SAN PEDRO trailed throughout.

Owners— 1, Stonecrest Farm; 2, Vitello Joseph V; 3, Pavlish Patricia; 4, Clarity Stables; 5, Win IV LLC; 6, Rudolph Richard F
Trainers—1, Johnson Murray W; 2, Winfree Donald R; 3, Wolfson Martin D; 4, Smith James J; 5, Boyce Michele; 6, Broussard Joseph E

$2 Daily Double (5–6) Paid $119.20; Daily Double Pool $20,350.
$2 Pick Three (1–5–6) Paid $302.20; Pick Three Pool $10,277.

THIRD RACE
Santa Anita
SEPTEMBER 28, 2003

1¼ MILES. (Turf)(1.57^{2}) 35th Running of THE CLEMENT L. HIRSCH MEMORIAL TURF CHAMPIONSHIP. Grade I. Purse $250,000. THREE-YEAR-OLDS AND UPWARD. By subscription of $250 each if made on or before September 4, 2003 or by supplementary nomination of $5,000 by September 26 or at time of entry. All horses shall pay $2,500 to start. Three-Year-Olds: 119 lbs. Older: 124 lbs. Starters to be named through the entry box by the closing time of entries. This race will not be divided. If the number of entries exceeds fourteen (14), preference will be determined in the following order: First preference will be given to graded or group stakes winners in 2003. Second preference will be given to those horses with highest total earnings in 2003. Entry and supplementary fees will be refunded to all horses which fail to draw into this race.

Value of Race: $245,000 Winner $150,000; second $50,000; third $30,000; fourth $15,000. Mutuel Pool $412,698.00 Exacta Pool $191,716.00 Quinella Pool $18,444.00

Last Raced	Horse	M/Eqt.	A.	Wt	PP	¼	½	¾	1	Str	Fin	Jockey	Odds $1
16Aug03 ^{10}AP^{1}	Storming Home-GB	LBbf	5	124	2	4	4	4	3^{1}	$2^{\frac{1}{2}}$	$1^{\frac{1}{2}}$	Stevens G L	0.30
22Aug03 ^{2}Dmr^{3}	Johar	LB	4	124	1	1^{2}	1^{2}	1^{2}	1^{1}	1^{2}	$2^{1\frac{1}{4}}$	Solis A	3.00
31Aug03 ^{8}Dmr^{1}	Irish Warrior	LB	5	124	4	$3^{2\frac{1}{2}}$	$3^{1\frac{1}{2}}$	$3^{\frac{1}{2}}$	4	4	$3^{1\frac{1}{2}}$	Krone J A	5.80
31Aug03 ^{8}Dmr^{3}	Continuously	LB	4	124	3	2^{2}	2^{2}	2^{3}	$2^{1\frac{1}{2}}$	3^{1}	4	Valdivia J Jr	12.50

OFF AT 1:37 Start Good. Won driving. Course firm.
TIME :25^{2}, :50^{3}, 1:15^{2}, 1:39, 2:01^{3} (:25.46, :50.78, 1:15.55, 1:39.12, 2:01.64)

$2 Mutuel Prices:			
3-STORMING HOME-GB	2.60	2.10	—
2-JOHAR		2.10	—
5-IRISH WARRIOR		—	—

$1 EXACTA 3-2 PAID $2.40 $2 QUINELLA 2-3 PAID $3.80

B. h, by Machiavellian–Try To Catch Me, by Shareef Dancer. Trainer Drysdale Neil. Bred by Gainsborough Stud Management Ltd (GB).

STORMING HOME (GB) chased a bit off the rail then outside a rival leaving he backstretch and on the second turn, came three deep into the stretch and rallied under some urging to wear down the runner-up. JOHAR took the early lead and set the pace inside under a long hold, held on well through the drive but could not quite match the winner late. IRISH WARRIOR hopped slightly onto the dirt crossing when three deep, angled in and chased inside or a bit off the rail, came out in the stretch and went on willingly for the show. CONTINUOUSLY pulled his way along between horses leaving the hill, angled in and stalked the pace a bit off the rail to the stretch and lacked the needed late response.

Owners— 1, Al Maktoum Sheik Maktoum b; 2, The Thoroughbred Corporation; 3, Coleman Dasaro & Thompson et al; 4, Khaled Saud b
Trainers—1, Drysdale Neil; 2, Mandella Richard; 3, Dollase Wallace; 4, Frankel Robert
Scratched— Mont Saint Michel (31Aug03 ^{8}DMR^{5})

$2 Daily Double (1–3) Paid $4.20; Daily Double Pool $19,727.
$1 Pick Three (5–1/7/8–1/3) Paid $5.10; Pick Three Pool $104,652.

SIXTH RACE

Santa Anita
SEPTEMBER 28, 2003

1$\frac{1}{16}$ MILES. (1.39) 11th Running of THE LADY'S SECRET BREEDERS' CUP HANDICAP. Grade II. Purse $300,000 (includes $50,000 BC – Breeders' Cup) FILLIES AND MARES, THREE YEARS OLD AND UPWARD. (Includes $50,000 from Breeders' Cup Fund for Cup nominees only). By subscription of $150 each if made on or before September 4, 2003 or by supplementary nomination of $6,000 by September 22, 2003. All horses shall pay $3,000 to start. Breeders' Cup Fund monies also correspondingly divided provided a Breeders' Cup nominee has finished in an awarded position. Any Breeders' Cup Fund monies not awarded will revert back to the Fund. Weights: September 23. The starters will be determined at entry time with preference given to Breeders' Cup nominees only of equal racing quality or weight assignment (respective of sex and weight for age.) Starters to be named through the entry box by the closing time of entries. A trophy will be presented to the owner of the winner.

Value of Race: $300,000 Winner $180,000; second $60,000; third $36,000; fourth $18,000; fifth $6,000. Mutuel Pool $694,925.00 Exacta Pool $283,583.00 Quinella Pool $22,899.00 Trifecta Pool $310,989.00

Last Raced	Horse	M/Eqt. A.Wt	PP	St	$\frac{1}{4}$	$\frac{1}{2}$	$\frac{3}{4}$	Str	Fin	Jockey	Odds $1
10Aug03 8Dmr2	Got Koko	LBb	4 118	2 3	6	6	6	4$1\frac{1}{2}$	1$\frac{1}{2}$	Solis A	5.00
2May03 10CD4	[D]Elloluv	LB	3 116	6 4	3hd	3$\frac{1}{2}$	31	1$\frac{1}{2}$	2$1\frac{3}{4}$	Nakatani C S	6.30
10Aug03 8Dmr1	Azeri	LB	5 128	5 6	5$2\frac{1}{2}$	5$4$	52	3hd	31	Smith M E	0.20
4Sep03 6Dmr1	Adoration	LBb	4 115	3 1	2$2$	2$1\frac{1}{2}$	22	2$1\frac{1}{2}$	4$3\frac{1}{2}$	Valenzuela P A	25.20
10Aug03 8Dmr3	Tropical Blossom	LBb	5 108	4 5	41	41	4$\frac{1}{2}$	5$2\frac{1}{2}$	5$12\frac{1}{2}$	Krone J A	22.80
4Sep03 6Dmr2	Royally Chosen	LB	5 115	1 2	1$1\frac{1}{2}$	1$\frac{1}{2}$	1hd	6	6	Flores D R	34.00

[D]–Elloluv disqualified and placed 4th.

OFF AT 3:15 Start Good. Won driving. Track fast.
TIME :23², :47¹, 1:11¹, 1:36¹, 1:42⁴ (:23.46, :47.23, 1:11.29, 1:36.32, 1:42.92)

$2 Mutuel Prices:

2–GOT KOKO	12.00	2.10	—
5–AZERI		2.10	—
3–ADORATION			—

$1 EXACTA 2–5 PAID $11.60 $2 QUINELLA 2–5 PAID $5.00 $1 TRIFECTA 2–5–3 PAID $57.30

B. f, by Signal Tap–Baby North, by Northern Baby. Trainer Headley Bruce. Bred by Eileen H Hartis (Tex).

GOT KOKO unhurried a bit off the rail early, came out on the second turn and four wide into the stretch and closed gamely under left handed urging to get up late. ELLOLUV stalked the pace outside a rival, bid three deep into the stretch, gained the advantage in upper stretch, drifted inward passing the sixteenth pole and could not hold off the winner. AZERI a bit slow into stride, chased outside a rival then off the rail, came three wide into the stretch and could not offer the necessary late response. ADORATION pulled early, stalked off the rail on the first turn then pressed the pace outside a rival, took a short lead nearing the quarter pole, battled a bit off the fence in midstretch, steadied off heels in deep stretch and weakened. TROPICAL BLOSSOM angled in and saved ground stalking the pace, came out a bit leaving the second turn, went around the early pacesetter into the stretch and did not rally. ROYALLY CHOSEN sped to the early lead, dueled inside on the backstretch and second turn but weakened once headed and had little left for the stretch. Following a stewards' inquiry, ELLOLUV was disqualified and placed fourth for interference in deep stretch.

Owners— 1, Headley Aase & Leung Paul; 2, Reddam J P; 3, Allen E Paulson Living Trust; 4, Amerman Racing Stables LLC; 5, Wygod Mr & Mrs Martin J; 6, Abruzzo Peter Johnston Vincent et a

Trainers—1, Headley Bruce; 2, Dollase Craig; 3, De Seroux Laura; 4, Hofmans David; 5, Canani Julio C; 6, Headley Bruce

$2 Daily Double (2–2) Paid $28.60; Daily Double Pool $27,856.
$1 Pick Three (5–2–2) Paid $199.00; Pick Three Pool $77,555.

NINTH RACE

Santa Anita
SEPTEMBER 28, 2003

1$\frac{1}{16}$ MILES. (1.39) 35th Running of THE OAK LEAF. Grade II. Purse $250,000 FOR FILLIES, TWO YEARS OLD. By subscription of $250 each if made on or before Thursday, September 4, 2003 or by supplementary nomination of $5,000 by Friday, September 26 or at time of entry. All horses shall pay $2,500 to start, with $250,000 guaranteed of which $150,000 to the winner, $50,000 to second, $30,000 to third, $15,000 to fourth and $5,000 to fifth. Weight: 119 lbs. Starters to be named through the entry box by the closing time of entries. Those horses with the highest earnings at time of entry will be preferred. A trophy will be presented to the owner of the winner.

Value of Race: $250,000 Winner $150,000; second $50,000; third $30,000; fourth $15,000; fifth $5,000. Mutuel Pool $726,895.00 Exacta Pool $229,730.00 Quinella Pool $19,937.00 Trifecta Pool $274,186.00

Last Raced	Horse	M/Eqt. A.Wt	PP	St	$\frac{1}{4}$	$\frac{1}{2}$	$\frac{3}{4}$	Str	Fin	Jockey	Odds $1
30Aug03 8Dmr1	Halfbridled	LB	2 119	4 4	1$1\frac{1}{2}$	2$1\frac{1}{2}$	11	12	1$4\frac{1}{2}$	Krone J A	0.30
16Aug03 2Dmr1	Tarlow	LB	2 119	7 7	3$1\frac{1}{2}$	1$\frac{1}{2}$	2¹	2$1\frac{1}{2}$	2$\frac{1}{2}$	Smith M E	8.00
30Aug03 8Dmr2	Hollywood Story	LB	2 119	6 6	6²	6⁵	4$1\frac{1}{2}$	3³	3$6\frac{1}{2}$	Valenzuela P A	6.40
30Aug03 8Dmr5	Shadow Of Mine	LB	2 119	2 3	7	7	7	6	4³	Solis A	62.90
4Sep03 5Dmr1	Lovely Rafaela	LBb	2 119	1 2	5¹	5¹	6$3\frac{1}{2}$	5hd	5²	Espinoza V	16.60
24Aug03 7Dmr1	Daddy's Princess	LB	2 119	3 5	2$\frac{1}{2}$	3$\frac{1}{2}$	3$\frac{1}{2}$	4hd	6	Flores D R	27.00
13Sep03 9TP2	Renaissance Lady	LB	2 119	5 1	4hd	4hd	5hd	—	—	Stevens G L	13.40

Renaissance Lady:Pulled up;

OFF AT 4:50 Start Good. Won driving. Track fast.
TIME :24, :48, 1:12², 1:37, 1:43³ (:24.02, :48.09, 1:12.56, 1:37.11, 1:43.72)

$2 Mutuel Prices:

4–HALFBRIDLED	2.60	2.20	2.10
7–TARLOW		3.40	2.10
6–HOLLYWOOD STORY			2.10

$1 EXACTA 4–7 PAID $4.20 $2 QUINELLA 4–7 PAID $6.80 $1 TRIFECTA 4–7–6 PAID $11.10

Dk. b. or br. f, (Feb), by Unbridled–Half Queen, by Deputy Minister. Trainer Mandella Richard. Bred by Frere & Wertheimer (Ky).

HALFBRIDLED took the early lead between horses and angled in, surrendered the advantage on the backstretch, regained command and inched away in hand midway on the second turn, responded when the runner-up loomed again nearing the stretch, kicked clear again under urging in the drive and was under steady handling late. TARLOW broke out and a bit slowly, advanced three deep on the first turn to challenge the winner, gained a lead on the backstretch, battled alongside the winner, bid again under some urging leaving the second turn but could not match strides in the stretch but saved second. HOLLYWOOD STORY off a bit slowly, settled off the inside, split horses on the second turn, bid inside in the stretch and was edged for the place. SHADOW OF MINE unhurried along the inside for more than six furlongs, came out in the stretch and bested the others. LOVELY RAFAELA saved ground stalking the pace, swung out into the stretch and weakened. DADDY'S PRINCESS stalked a bit off the rail, bid between horses leaving the backstretch, continued inside leaving the second turn and also weakened. RENAISSANCE LADY stalked outside a rival, bid three or four wide leaving the backstretch, dropped back, drifted out when being pulled up leaving the second turn and was walking off.

Owners— 1, Wertheimer Farm; 2, Moss Mr & Mrs Jerome S; 3, Krikorian George; 4, Nichols Thomas L; 5, T N T Stud; 6, Broguiere Ray Morrison Alan & Venne; 7, Lewis Robert B & Beverly J

Trainers—1, Mandella Richard; 2, Shirreffs John; 3, Shirreffs John; 4, Greely C Beau; 5, Mandella Richard; 6, Sise Clifford Jr; 7, Lukas D Wayne

$2 Daily Double (10–4) Paid $10.80; Daily Double Pool $28,205.
$1 Pick Three (3–10–4) Paid $14.10; Pick Three Pool $73,641.

SEVENTH RACE

Santa Anita

SEPTEMBER 28, 2003

1¼ MILES. (Turf)(1.57²) 27th Running of THE YELLOW RIBBON. Grade I. Purse $500,000. FILLIES AND MARES, THREE YEARS OLD AND UPWARD. By subscription of $500 each if made on or before Thursday, September 4, 2003 or by supplementary nomination of $10,000 by Friday, September 26. All horses shall pay $5,000 to start with $500,000 guaranteed, of which $300,000 to the winner, $100,000 to second, $60,000 to third, $30,000 to fourth and $10,000 to fifth. Three–Year–Olds: 118 lbs. Older: 123 lbs. Starters to be named through the entry box by the closing time of entries. This race will not be divided. If the number exceeds fourteen (14), preference will be determined in the following order: First preference will be given to graded or group winners in 2003. Second preference will be given to those horses with the highest total earnings in 2003. A trophy will be presented to the winning owner. Supplemental nomintion of $10,000: CELLAMARE (FR).

Value of Race: $500,000 Winner $300,000; second $100,000; third $60,000; fourth $30,000; fifth $10,000. Mutuel Pool $519,329.00 Exacta Pool $296,988.00 Quinella Pool $27,668.00 Trifecta Pool $321,066.00

Last Raced	Horse	M/Eqt. A.Wt	PP	¼	½	¾	1	Str	Fin	Jockey	Odds $1
26Jly03 8Dmr²	Tates Creek	LB	5 123	2	3¹	4¹½	3hd	3hd	2¹	1¾	Valenzuela P A	0.90
3Aug03 Dea¹⁰	Musical Chimes		3 118	3	7½	7²½	7⁵	6²½	6⁴	2nk	Stevens G L	a–3.30
29Aug03 7Dmr¹	Crazy Ensign–ARG	LBb	7 123	7	2¹	2¹	2¹	2¹½	1½	3¹¼	Solis A	4.00
7Sep03 6Dmr²	Magic Mission–GB	LBb	5 123	4	6¹½	5hd	5½	5¹½	5¹	4³½	Nakatani C S	a–3.30
6Sep03 2Dmr¹	Red Rioja–IR	LB	4 123	1	8	8	8	8	7¹	5no	Krone J A	15.60
28Aug03 7Dmr¹	Adalgisa	LB	4 123	8	5½	3½	4²½	4¹	4hd	6¹½	Flores D R	25.50
24Aug03 9Dmr⁴	Cassis	LB	3 118	6	1¹	1¹	1¹½	1½	3hd	7⁵	Smith M E	6.30
13Sep03 7BM¹	Cellamare–FR	LB	3 118	5	4hd	6¹½	6¹	7²	8	8	Valdivia J Jr	67.80

a–Coupled: Musical Chimes and Magic Mission–GB.

OFF AT 3:50 Start Good. Won driving. Course firm.
TIME :26, :50¹, 1:14⁴, 1:37⁴, 2:00³ (:26.06, :50.37, 1:14.90, 1:37.95, 2:00.77)

$2 Mutuel Prices:

3–TATES CREEK	3.80	2.40	2.10
1–MUSICAL CHIMES (a–entry)		3.00	2.20
6–CRAZY ENSIGN–ARG			2.40

$1 EXACTA 3–1 PAID $5.70 $2 QUINELLA 1–3 PAID $6.80 $1 TRIFECTA 3–1–6 PAID $11.50

Ch. m, by Rahy–Viviana, by Nureyev. Trainer Frankel Robert. Bred by Juddmonte Farms (Ky).

TATES CREEK saved ground stalking the pace, awaited room off heels when blocked on the second turn and into the stretch, bulled through between horses in midstretch, gained the lead and held gamely under urging. MUSICAL CHIMES settled a bit off the rail after breaking slowly, came out into the stretch and closed willingly to gain the place at the wire. CRAZY ENSIGN (ARG) a bit wide on the dirt crossing, stalked the pace off the rail, bid outside a foe leaving the second turn, gained the advantage in upper stretch, battled three deep in midstretch, could not quite match the winner and lost second late. MAGIC MISSION (GB) a bit slow to begin, angled in and saved ground chasing the pace, came out into the stretch, angled back inward and was outfinished. RED RIOJA (IRE) unhurried inside for a mile, came out in upper stretch and improved position. ADALGISA pulled her way along outside early, stalked alongside a rival, went three deep into the stretch and weakened in the final furlong. CASSIS took the early lead and angled in, set the pace inside, battled along the rail leaving the second turn and into the stretch, steadied in tight when the winner went by in midstretch and also weakened. CELLAMARE (FR) hopped onto the dirt crossing, pulled her way along between horses chasing the early pace, continued outside a rival on the backstretch, angled in on the second turn and had little left in the stretch. The stewards conducted an inquiry into the incident between the winner and CASSIS in midstretch but made no change when they ruled the original order of finished was not affected.

Owners– 1, Juddmonte Farms Inc; 2, Al Maktoum Sheik Maktoum b; 3, El Faruk Stable; 4, Al Maktoum Sheik Maktoum b; 5, Sanderson Dr Karen; 6, Barnett Mike Beck Robert & Hulkewic; 7, Robertson Sanford R; 8, Lanni J Terrence Schiappa Bernard & Trainers–1, Frankel Robert; 2, Fabre Andre; 3, Mandella Richard; 4, Drysdale Neil; 5, Cecil B D A; 6, Canani Julio C; 7, Walsh Kathy; 8, Monteleone Frank J

$2 Daily Double (2–3) Paid $35.60; Daily Double Pool $43,046.
$1 Pick Three (2–2–3) Paid $64.00; Pick Three Pool $95,991.

NINTH RACE
Hoosier Park
OCTOBER 3, 2003

1$\frac{1}{16}$ MILES. (1.41) 6th Running of THE INDIANA BREEDERS' CUP OAKS. Grade III. Purse $300,000 (includes $50,000 BC – Breeders' Cup) FOR FILLIES,THREE YEARS OLD. (Includes $50,000 from Breeders' Cup Fund for Cup nominees only). Weight 121 lbs. Non Winners of $50,000 at one mile or over in 2003, 3 lbs.;of $30,000 at such a distance in 2003 5 lbs.;of three races other than maiden or claiming 7 lbs.;of two such races 9 lbs.

Value of Race: $306,900 Winner $184,140; second $61,380; third $33,759; fourth $18,414; fifth $9,207. Mutuel Pool $95,132.00 Exacta Pool $73,038.00 Trifecta Pool $66,669.00 Superfecta Pool $19,403.00

Last Raced	Horse	M/Eqt.	A.Wt	PP	St	¼	½	¾	Str	Fin	Jockey	Odds $1
13Sep03 12TP2	Awesome Humor	LB	3 116	4	2	41½	31½	1½	14	1¾	Albarado R J	1.30
20Aug03 6Sar2	Cloakof Vagueness	LB	3 114	3	9	8½	72	5½	31½	23¼	Prado E S	6.60
12Sep03 6PrM1	Shot Gun Favorite	LB	3 118	10	10	91½	10	6½	43	3nk	Blanc B	14.20
23Aug03 7Sar4	Double Scoop	LBf	3 114	6	5	51½	55	42	2hd	48	Day P	4.00
1Sep03 10Pha2	Souris	LBb	3 116	9	8	10	9hd	82	54	52¾	Lanerie C J	14.40
13Sep03 8AP7	Sue's Good News	LBf	3 121	2	6	71	6hd	93	63	67¼	Doocy T T	7.60
14Jun03 6Hol5	Harbor Blues	LBb	3 118	7	4	2hd	4hd	71½	85	73¼	Puglisi I L	36.60
23Aug03 9EmD1	Youcan'ttakeme	LBbf	3 121	5	1	1hd	1½	2hd	71	87¼	Baze G	5.70
25Sep03 9TP4	Saratoga Humor	LBf	3 114	1	3	62	81	10	10	92¾	Mojica O	77.70
13Sep03 6AP4	Star Of Atticus	LB	3 114	8	7	3½	21½	31	94	10	Sellers S J	27.10

OFF AT 9:51 Start Good. Won driving. Track muddy.
TIME :23, :46^{3}, 1:11^{4}, 1:38^{4}, 1:45^{3} (:23.04, :46.69, 1:11.97, 1:38.86, 1:45.75)

$2 Mutuel Prices:			
6–AWESOME HUMOR	4.60	2.80	2.80
4–CLOAKOF VAGUENESS		5.40	4.60
12–SHOT GUN FAVORITE			7.40

$2 EXACTA 6–4 PAID $26.20 $2 TRIFECTA 6–4–12 PAID $212.60 $2 SUPERFECTA 6–4–12–8 PAID $761.40

Dk. b. or br. f, (Feb), by Distorted Humor–Horns Gray, by Pass the Tab. Trainer Walden W Elliott. Bred by Dr Naveed Chowhan (Ky).

AWESOME HUMOR broke alertly and attended the pace along the inside through the first turn, was eased outside rivals heading up the backstretch to bid three wide into the far turn, showed in front nearing the stretch and opened a clear lead coming to the furlong marker then was drifting out late from lefthanded whip to hold CLOAKOF VAGUENESS safe late. CLOAKOF VAGUENESS settled out from the rail through the first turn, moved up outside to rally five wide into the stretch and went willingly to be cutting the winner's margin late. SHOT GUN FAVORITE was off the early pace while outside rivals, moved up through the far turn to fan six wide into the stretch then could not produce the needed late effort. DOUBLE SCOOP was never far back stalking the pace three wide, moved to challenge into the stretch and show nearest the winner coming to the furlong marker but lacked the needed late response. SOURIS tucked in on the first turn to save ground racing two to three wide, moved along the inside through the far turn with her bid but could not sustain the effort. SUE'S GOOD NEWS was outside going to the far turn, lost considerable ground when hung seven wide turning for home and tired. HARBOR BLUES contested the early pace from between rivals, settled back and floated four wide on the far turn and tired. YOUCAN'TTAKEME had a short lead making the pace from along the inside to the far turn, went with the winner when challenged to late in the far turn and tired. SARATOGA HUMOR tracked the pace from along the inside for a half mile and tired. STAR OF ATTICUS forced the pace from three wide to the far turn and tired from between rivals through that bend.

Owners— 1, WinStar Farm LLC; 2, Duncker C S; 3, Steve Stan Stables; 4, Humphrey G W Jr; 5, Hunt Nelson B; 6, Cresran LLC; 7, Everest Stables; 8, Sarkowsky Herman; 9, Baker William A; 10, Tomillo Doris

Trainers—1, Walden W Elliott; 2, Huffman William G; 3, McPeek Kenneth G; 4, Arnold George R II; 5, Asmussen Steven M; 6, Hobby Steve; 7, Knight Terry; 8, Forster Grant T; 9, Cain Joe; 10, Barnett Bobby C

Scratched— Golden Marlin (14Sep03 9TP1), My Trusty Cat (1Sep03 10PHA5)

$2 Pick Three (3–3/4/6/12–2/5/6) Paid $47.60; Pick Three Pool $5,946.

EIGHTH RACE
Meadowlands
OCTOBER 3, 2003

1⅛ MILES. (1.45^{2}) 27th Running of THE MEADOWLANDS BREEDERS' CUP. Grade II. Purse $400,000 (includes $100,000 BC – Breeders' Cup) FOR THREE YEAR OLDS AND UPWARD. (Includes $100,000 from Breeders' Cup Fund for Cup nominees only) By subscription of $300 each which should accompany the nomination. $2,000 to enter, $2,000 to start. Field will be limited to 14 starters. If more than 14 entries pass the entry box, preference will be given to Breeders' Cup nominees only of equal weight assignment. Weight;Three year olds, 120 lbs; Older 123 lbs, Non winners of $100,000 at a mile or over since October,15 2002 allowed 2 lbs; $75,000 at a mile or over in 2003 4 lbs. Supplementary nominations may be made at time of entry by payment of a fee of $10,000 which includes all fees. NOMINATIONS CLOSED September 20, 2003 with 29.

Value of Race: $400,000 Winner $240,000; second $80,000; third $44,000; fourth $24,000; fifth $12,000. Mutuel Pool $193,550.00 Exacta Pool $146,964.00 Trifecta Pool $91,091.00

Last Raced	Horse	M/Eqt.	A.Wt	PP	St	¼	½	¾	Str	Fin	Jockey	Odds $1
26Jly03 9Mth5	Bowman's Band	L	5 119	4	4	2hd	2½	21½	11	1¾	Dominguez R A	12.30
1Sep03 11Pha6	Dynever	L	3 120	5	6	6	6	3½	2hd	23	Nakatani C S	1.80
30Aug03 8Mth1	[D]Unforgettable Max	L	3 116	3	3	11½	11	11	34	3nk	Ferrer J C	17.20
13Sep03 7Bel3	Volponi	Lb	5 123	2	2	5½	5½	4hd	43½	48½	Velazquez J R	0.90
25Aug03 7Sar3	Regal Sanction	L	4 119	1	1	3½	41	5hd	6	5½	Santos J A	6.10
13Sep03 3Mth1	Jersey Giant	Lb	4 119	6	5	41	3hd	6	5hd	6	Pimentel J	11.60

[D]–Unforgettable Max disqualified and placed 4th.

OFF AT 10:24 Start Good. Won driving. Track fast.
TIME :23^{3}, :46^{4}, 1:10, 1:34^{1}, 1:46^{4} (:23.76, :46.99, 1:10.15, 1:34.30, 1:46.84)

$2 Mutuel Prices:			
4–BOWMAN'S BAND	26.60	8.60	2.80
5–DYNEVER		4.60	2.40
2–VOLPONI			2.10

$2 EXACTA 4–5 PAID $102.60 $2 TRIFECTA 4–5–2 PAID $193.80

Ch. h, by Dixieland Band–Hometown Queen, by Pleasant Colony. Trainer Jerkens H Allen. Bred by John W Rooker (Ky).

BOWMAN'S BAND rated close about three wide, moved alongside the pacesetter nearing the quarter pole, dueled through the upper stretch, was clear approaching the eighth pole then held well with steady handling. DYNEVER raced unhurriedly while not far back outside, made his bid nearing the final turn, had aim entering the stretch then finished evenly in the chase. UNFORGETTABLE MAX angled in just after the break, rated the pace off the rail, was challenged leaving the quarter pole, dueled through the upper stretch but wearied the final furlong. VOLPONI was pinched back early, rated off the pace, bid toward the outside on the final turn then finished evenly. REGAL SANCTION broke somewhat awkwardly, rated just off the pace inside, gave chase nearing the final turn then was through for the drive. JERSEY GIANT rated off the early pace outside then showed no response in mid track on the final turn.

Owners— 1, Schwartz Martin S; 2, Wills Catherine & Karches Peter; 3, Dweck Raymond & Dorothy; 4, Amherst Stable & Spruce Pond Stable; 5, Moore Susan & John; 6, Kligman Joel A

Trainers—1, Jerkens H Allen; 2, Clement Christophe; 3, Perkins Ben W Jr; 4, Johnson Philip G; 5, Jerkens James A; 6, Ryerson James T

SEVENTH RACE

Keeneland

OCTOBER 3, 2003

6 FURLONGS. (1.07³) 151st Running of THE PHOENIX BREEDERS' CUP. Grade III. Purse $250,000 Added (includes $100,000 BC – Breeders' Cup) THREE YEAR OLDS AND UPWARD. (Includes $100,000 from Breeders' Cup Fund for Cup nominees only). By subscription of $250 each which should accompany the nomination; $2,500 to enter and start. Keeneland Association added monies and all fees to be divided 62% to the owner of the winner, 20% to second, 10% to third, 5% to fourth and 3% to fifth. Breeders' Cup fund monies also correspondingly divided providing a Breeders' Cup nominee has finished in an awarded position. Weight; Three–year–olds, 122 lbs.; Older, 124lbs. Non–winners of a Grade I or II in 2003 allowed 2 lbs.; Grade III or $60,000 in 2003, 4 lbs; $45,000 twice in 2003, 6 lbs. Breeders' Cup nominees given first preference only in equal quality situations.

Value of Race: $264,000 Winner $169,880; second $54,800; third $17,400; fourth $13,700; fifth $8,220. Mutuel Pool $458,638.00 Exacta Pool $261,962.00 Quinella Pool $15,054.00 Trifecta Pool $112,288.00 Superfecta Pool $54,637.00

Last Raced	Horse	M/Eqt.	A.Wt	PP	St	¼	½	Str	Fin	Jockey	Odds $1
31Aug03 ¹⁰Sar²	Najran	L	4 122	7	1	3½	3³	2¹	1¹¹⁄₂	Castellano J J	6.00
27Aug03 ⁸AP¹	Ethan Man	L	4 118	5	3	2hd	2hd	1½	2²	Douglas R R	14.50
1Sep03 ¹⁰Mth²	Take Achance On Me	Lbf	5 118	6	2	1hd	1hd	3³½	3²¾	Velasquez C	66.40
26Jly03 ¹⁰EIP¹	Dubai Sheikh	Lf	4 122	8	7	8	8	7½	4½	Albarado R J	31.10
23Aug03 ⁹AP¹	Out Of My Way	Lb	6 122	1	6	7³	7²	5½	5½	Bourque C C	7.90
23Aug03 ¹⁰Sar²	Great Notion	Lf	3 116	2	8	6½	6¹½	4hd	6³¾	Day P	2.30
21Jun03 ⁹CD⁴	Strength And Honor	L	4 118	3	5	5¹½	4½	6hd	7¹½	Prado E S	16.10
26Jly03 ⁶Dmr¹	Beau's Town	Lf	5 124	4	4	4¹	5¹	8	8	Valenzuela P A	1.10

OFF AT 4:15 Start Good For All But BEAU'S TOWN Won driving. Track fast.

TIME :21⁴, :44³, :56, 1:08¹ (:21.86, :44.61, :56.06, 1:08.32)

$2 Mutuel Prices:

7–NAJRAN	14.00	5.60	7.20
5–ETHAN MAN		9.00	9.00
6–TAKE ACHANCE ON ME			12.80

$1 EXACTA 7–5 PAID $85.00 $1 QUINELLA 5–7 PAID $85.40 $1 TRIFECTA 7–5–6 PAID $1,791.50 $1 SUPERFECTA 7–5–6–8 PAID $22,127.90

Gr/ro c, by Runaway Groom–Line Command, by Capote. Trainer Zito Nicholas P. Bred by France Weiner & Irv Weiner (Ky).

NAJRAN forced the pace from early on, raced four wide on the backstretch while under light restraint, came a bit wider when entering the stretch, was angled back in three wide when going after front-running ETHAN MAN and drove clear late under steady right-handed encouragement. ETHAN MAN went up inside early to contest the pace, battled with TAKE ACHANCE ON ME and NAJRAN, gained the advantage in the upper stretch, then couldn't handle the winner late as second best. TAKE ACHANCE ON ME gained a slim lead from between foes just before going a quarter, battled on about even terms with the top two into the stretch and weakened. DUBAI SHEIKH, outrun for a half and five wide, worked his way out seven wide at the furlong ground and bested the others while not a threat. OUT OF MY WAY, bumped during the opening sixteenth and taken up when nearly forced into the inner railing, made a mild run from between foes three or four wide into the last eighth but failed to sustain the needed momentum. GREAT NOTION, forced to steady and squeezed back in tight quarters soon after the start, settled near the inside, moved five or six wide into the stretch but flattened out at the end. STRENGTH AND HONOR, bumped at the start by BEAU'S TOWN and forced in on OUT OF MY WAY soon after, raced in contention three or four wide to the lane and weakened. BEAU'S TOWN stumbled at the start, drifted in soon after bumping STRENGTH AND HONOR, forced that one in on OUT OF MY WAY, raced near the inside and was finished upon going a half.

Owners— 1, Buckram Oak Farm; 2, West Point Thoroughbreds LLC; 3, Dale & Joan Everett; 4, Ramsey Kenneth L & Sarah K; 5, Crown's Way Farm Cappas P & Founder; 6, Silverton Hill Farm LLC Bonnie & To; 7, Requiem Racing LLC; 8, Coast To Coast Racing Fund LLC Robe

Trainers—1, Zito Nicholas P; 2, Byrne Patrick B; 3, Aguirre Anthony; 4, Romans Dale; 5, Cilio Gene A; 6, Miller Darrin; 7, Simon Charles; 8, Norman Cole

$1 Pick Three (2–2–7) Paid $194.50; Pick Three Pool $47,068.
$1 Pick Four (8–2–2–7) Paid $400.90; Pick Four Pool $26,233.

NINTH RACE
Keeneland
OCTOBER 3, 2003

$1\frac{1}{16}$ MILES. (1.40^{4}) 52nd Running of THE DARLEY ALCIBIADES. Grade II. Purse $400,000 Guaranteed. FILLIES, TWO YEARS OLD. By subscription of $400 each which should accompany the nomination, $4,000 to enter and start; with $400,000 guaranteed, of which $248,000 to the owner of the winner, $80,000 to second, $40,000 to third, $20,000 to fourth and$12,000 to fifth. Weight; 118 lbs. Starters to be named through the entry box by usual time of closing. A gold julep cup will be presented to the owner of the winner. The owner of the winner will receive a complimentary 2004 nomination to Street Cry. The breeder of the winner will receive a complimentary 2004 nomination to E Dubai. The first four finishers in the Darley Alcibiades are automatically made eligible for the Ashland Stakes of 2004 as to nomination fees.

Value of Race: $400,000 Winner $248,000; second $80,000; third $40,000; fourth $20,000; fifth $12,000. Mutuel Pool $330,516.00 Exacta Pool $189,236.00 Quinella Pool $9,756.00 Trifecta Pool $151,369.00 Superfecta Pool $34,842.00

Last Raced	Horse	M/Eqt.	A.Wt	PP	St	¼	½	¾	Str	Fin	Jockey	Odds $1
29Aug03 ^{8}Sar^{2}	Be Gentle	L	2 118	2	3	1^{1}	$1^{\frac{1}{2}}$	1^{1}	1^{3}	$1^{5\frac{1}{2}}$	Velasquez C	1.50
15Sep03 ^{3}KD^{1}	Galloping Gal	L	2 118	4	7	7	7	7	$3^{2\frac{1}{2}}$	$2^{3\frac{1}{2}}$	Blanc B	14.80
9Aug03 ^{4}Sar^{1}	Deb's Charm	L	2 118	7	5	5^{hd}	4^{hd}	3^{hd}	$2^{1\frac{1}{2}}$	3^{1}	Albarado R J	3.40
13Sep03 ^{9}TP^{3}	Sweet Jo Jo	L	2 118	1	4	3^{hd}	5^{hd}	$5^{1\frac{1}{2}}$	4^{3}	4^{5}	Lanerie C J	10.30
30Aug03 ^{10}Mth^{2}	Whirlwind Charlott	Lb	2 118	5	2	$2^{\frac{1}{2}}$	2^{1}	$2^{\frac{1}{2}}$	5^{5}	$5^{9\frac{1}{4}}$	Prado E S	22.30
30Aug03 ^{12}RD^{1}	In Rome	Lb	2 118	3	6	4^{hd}	$6^{5\frac{1}{2}}$	$6^{1\frac{1}{2}}$	6^{3}	6^{5}	Day P	21.10
14Sep03 ^{6}Bel^{2}	Lokoya	L	2 118	6	1	6^{5}	3^{hd}	$4^{\frac{1}{2}}$	7	7	Velazquez J R	1.90

OFF AT 5:16 Start Good. Won driving. Track fast.
TIME :23, :47^{2}, 1:12^{1}, 1:38^{4}, 1:45^{2} (:23.10, :47.50, 1:12.35, 1:38.93, 1:45.51)

$2 Mutuel Prices:

2–BE GENTLE	5.00	3.60	3.00
4–GALLOPING GAL		8.20	5.00
7–DEB'S CHARM			3.80

$1 EXACTA 2–4 PAID $41.70 $2 QUINELLA 2–4 PAID $59.60 $1 TRIFECTA 2–4–7 PAID $185.30 $1 SUPERFECTA 2–4–7–1 PAID $940.70

Dk. b. or br. f, (May), by Tale of the Cat–Gentlelilstar, by Risen Star. Trainer Lukas D Wayne. Bred by Mrs Nellie M Cox & Rose Retreat Farm (Va).

BE GENTLE moved to the fore near the inside approaching the first turn, relaxed nicely while controlling the pace from the two path, opened a clear advantage when asked a bit approaching the stretch, then increased her lead under solid hand encouragement. GALLOPING GAL, a bit sluggish to start and outrun three wide to the far turn, was put to a drive, came out five wide approaching the stretch and couldn't threaten BE GENTLE while superior to the others. DEB'S CHARM, fanned five or six wide approaching the first turn, continued five wide within easy striking distance from the backstretch on, was just off the winner entering the stretch but came up empty. SWEET JO JO, never far back and racing near the inside from the outset, remained inside for the drive but couldn't offer a closing account. WHIRLWIND CHARLOTT went up early to press the winner three or four wide, held on well for six furlongs and weakened. IN ROME, in a striking position while racing between rivals three or four wide for six furlongs, weakened thereafter. LOKOYA, well placed between rivals four wide for three-quarters, tired soon after.

Owners— 1, Van Meter II Thomas F; 2, Carl William A; 3, Francello Robert; 4, Grunwald Racing LLC; 5, Classic Star Stable LLC David Plumm; 6, Pollard Carl F; 7, Scatuorchio James T

Trainers—1, Lukas D Wayne; 2, McPeek Kenneth G; 3, McPeek Kenneth G; 4, Asmussen Steven M; 5, Dowd John F; 6, Vance David R; 7, Pletcher Todd A

$1 Daily Double (1–2) Paid $12.50; Daily Double Pool $24,777.
$1 Pick Three (7–1–2) Paid $87.60; Pick Three Pool $47,587.
$1 Pick Four (2–7–1–2) Paid $542.70; Pick Four Pool $62,316.

SIXTH RACE
Belmont
OCTOBER 4, 2003

$1\frac{1}{16}$ MILES. (1.39^{2}) 56th Running of THE FRIZETTE. Grade I. Purse $500,000. (Up to $57,000 NYSBFOA). FILLIES, TWO YEARS OLD. By subscription of $500 each, which should accompany the nomination; $2,500 to pass the entry box and $2,500 to start. The purse to be divided 60% to the winner, 20% to second, 11% to third, 6% to fourth and 3% to fifth. 120 lbs. Trophies will be presented to the winning owner, trainer and jockey. Closed Saturday, September 20, 2003 with 16 nominations.

Value of Race: $500,000 Winner $300,000; second $100,000; third $55,000; fourth $30,000; fifth $15,000. Mutuel Pool $678,785.00 Exacta Pool $519,988.00 Trifecta Pool $376,995.00 Superfecta Pool $115,566.00

Last Raced	Horse	M/Eqt.	A.Wt	PP	St	¼	½	¾	Str	Fin	Jockey	Odds $1
18Aug03 ^{2}Sar^{1}	Society Selection		2 120	8	3	8	7^{hd}	7^{5}	$2^{1\frac{1}{2}}$	$1^{1\frac{1}{4}}$	Ganpath R	8.20
30Aug03 ^{8}Dmr^{3}	Victory U. S. A.	L	2 120	4	2	2^{1}	$2^{\frac{1}{2}}$	1^{hd}	$1^{1\frac{1}{2}}$	$2^{2\frac{3}{4}}$	Bailey J D	2.65
29Aug03 ^{8}Sar^{1}	Ashado	L	2 120	3	4	$3^{\frac{1}{2}}$	4^{hd}	4^{hd}	3^{5}	$3^{6\frac{3}{4}}$	Santos J A	2.80
29Aug03 ^{8}Sar^{3}	Daydreaming	L	2 120	7	8	7^{hd}	6^{2}	$6^{1\frac{1}{2}}$	$5^{2\frac{1}{2}}$	4^{nk}	Velazquez J R	1.95
24Sep03 ^{7}Del^{1}	Little Andrea	Lf	2 120	5	1	$5^{1\frac{1}{2}}$	3^{1}	$3^{1\frac{1}{2}}$	4^{2}	$5^{2\frac{1}{2}}$	Dominguez R A	23.60
14Sep03 ^{6}Bel^{3}	Eye Dazzler	L	2 120	2	5	4^{hd}	$5^{\frac{1}{2}}$	5^{hd}	$6^{4\frac{1}{2}}$	$6^{10\frac{1}{2}}$	Nakatani C S	25.00
11Sep03 ^{4}Bel^{1}	Please Take Me Out		2 120	1	6	$1^{\frac{1}{2}}$	$1^{\frac{1}{2}}$	2^{hd}	$7^{4\frac{1}{2}}$	$7^{\frac{1}{2}}$	Gryder A T	69.50
14Sep03 ^{6}Bel^{1}	Marylebone	L	2 120	6	7	6^{hd}	8	8	8	8	Luzzi M J	9.50

OFF AT 3:44 Start Good. Won driving. Track fast.
TIME :23^{1}, :47^{1}, 1:12^{1}, 1:37^{2}, 1:43^{4} (:23.30, :47.21, 1:12.32, 1:37.57, 1:43.95)

$2 Mutuel Prices:

8–SOCIETY SELECTION	18.40	8.50	4.80
4–VICTORY U. S. A.		4.40	3.00
3–ASHADO			3.00

$2 EXACTA 8–4 PAID $74.50 $2 TRIFECTA 8–4–3 PAID $316.50 $2 SUPERFECTA 8–4–3–7 PAID $564.00

B. f, (Apr), by Coronado's Quest–Love That Jazz, by Dixieland Band. Trainer Jerkens H Allen. Bred by Marjorie Cowan & Irving Cowan (Ky).

SOCIETY SELECTION was unhurried while outrun early, advanced inside on the turn, angled out and came between rivals turning for home, finished determinedly outside and was clear under the line, driving. VICTORY U. S. A. argued the pace while between rivals, earned a short lead approaching the stretch, drew clear when roused and dug in gamely to the finish. ASHADO chased the pace while between rivals and stayed on well through the stretch. DAYDREAMING raced three wide while in hand and had no response when roused. LITTLE ANDREA contested the pace while three wide and tired in the stretch. EYE DAZZLER raced close up along the inside and tired in the stretch. PLEASE TAKE ME OUT was hustled to the front, set the pace along the inside and tired after three quarters. MARYLEBONE was outrun early and tired.

Owners— 1, Cowan Marjorie & Irving M; 2, Van Meter II Thomas F; 3, Starlight Stables Saylor Paul & Mar; 4, Phipps Ogden M; 5, Rickman William M; 6, Lewis Lee; 7, Perez Robert; 8, Tabor Michael B

Trainers—1, Jerkens H Allen; 2, Baffert Bob; 3, Pletcher Todd A; 4, McGaughey Claude III; 5, Dickinson Michael W; 6, Hennig Mark; 7, Callejas Alfredo; 8, Pletcher Todd A

$2 Pick Three (2–1–8) Paid $4,127.00; Pick Three Pool $68,093.

SEVENTH RACE
Belmont
OCTOBER 4, 2003

1 1/16 MILES. (1.39^2) 132nd Running of THE CHAMPAGNE. Grade I. Purse $500,000. (Up to $57,000 NYSBFOA). TWO YEAR OLDS. By subscription of $500 each, which should accompany the nomination; $2,500 to pass the entry box and $2,500 to start. 122 lbs. The New York Racing Association to add The Champagne Challenge Cup, to be won three times, not necessarily consecutively, by the same owner before becoming his or her property. The owner of the winner will also receive a trophy for permanent possession and trophies will be presented to the winning trainer and jockey. The winning horse will receive a free nomination to the 2004 Triple Crown. The winning horse will receive a free nomination to the Triple Crown. Closed Saturday, September 20,2003 with 31 nominations.

Value of Race: $500,000 Winner $300,000; second $100,000; third $55,000; fourth $30,000; fifth $15,000. Mutuel Pool $694,525.00 Exacta Pool $500,163.00 Trifecta Pool $355,054.00

Last Raced	Horse	M/Eqt.	A.Wt	PP	St	¼	½	¾	Str	Fin	Jockey	Odds $1
30Aug03 8Sar4	Birdstone	L	2 122	3	4	42½	3½	22	1hd	12½	Bailey J D	2.25
30Aug03 8Sar2	Chapel Royal	L	2 122	7	2	1hd	1½	1½	28	26¾	Velazquez J R	1.55
9Aug03 10Mth1	Dashboard Drummer	L	2 122	5	3	32	42½	41½	34½	32	Espinoza J L	15.20
13Sep03 8Del1	Paddington	Lf	2 122	2	5	53½	55	51	4hd	41½	Dominguez R A	7.60
30Aug03 8Sar3	Notorious Rogue	L	2 122	1	7	61½	63½	66	610	52¼	Nakatani C S	10.40
7Sep03 6Bel1	Read The Footnotes	L	2 122	6	1	21	2½	3hd	51	611¾	Santos J A	4.10
14Sep03 9Mth4	Midnight Express	f	2 122	4	6	7	7	7	7	7	Fragoso P	80.25

OFF AT 4:15 Start Good. Won driving. Track fast.
TIME :23^4, :48^1, 1:13^3, 1:37^4, 1:44 (:23.90, :48.33, 1:13.75, 1:37.84, 1:44.05)

$2 Mutuel Prices:				
	4–BIRDSTONE	6.50	3.00	2.90
	8–CHAPEL ROYAL		2.80	2.60
	6–DASHBOARD DRUMMER			4.40

$2 EXACTA 4–8 PAID $16.80 $2 TRIFECTA 4–8–6 PAID $113.00

B. c, (May), by Grindstone–Dear Birdie, by Storm Bird. Trainer Zito Nicholas P. Bred by Marylou Whitney Stable (Ky).

BIRDSTONE raced close up early while in hand advanced three wide on the turn, responded when roused and was going away late. CHAPEL ROYAL set the pace while in hand and weakened along the inside in the final furlong. DASHBOARD DRUMMER raced close up along the inside while in hand, came wide for the drive and lacked a rally. PADDINGTON was hustled along early, put in a three wide move on the turn and tired in the stretch. NOTORIOUS ROGUE was outrun early, put in a four wide run nearing the stretch and tired in the drive. READ THE FOOTNOTES pressed the pace from the inside and tired after the opening three quarters. MIDNIGHT EXPRESS was outrun early, raced inside and tired.

Owners— 1, Marylou Whitney Stables; 2, Smith Derrick & Tabor Michael; 3, Double S Stable Preferred Pals Stab; 4, Gallop U Stable; 5, Lewis Lee; 6, Klaravich Stables; 7, Birnbaum Joseph

Trainers—1, Zito Nicholas P; 2, Pletcher Todd A; 3, Iwinski Allen; 4, Dickinson Michael W; 5, Hennig Mark; 6, Violette Richard A Jr; 7, Thompson Glenn R

Scratched— Motivus

$2 Daily Double (8–4) Paid $89.00; Daily Double Pool $135,972.
$2 Pick Three (1–8–4) Paid $266.00; Pick Three Pool $118,046.

EIGHTH RACE
Belmont
OCTOBER 4, 2003

1 MILE. (Turf)(1.31^3) 23rd Running of THE KELSO BREEDERS' CUP HANDICAP. Grade II. Purse $350,000. (includes $100,000 BC – Breeders' Cup). (Up to $38,500 NYSBFOA). THREE YEAR OLDS AND UPWARD. By subscription of $250 each, which should accompany the nomination; $1,250 to pass the entry box and $1,250 to start. Breeders' Cup monies also correspondingly divided provided a Breeders' Cup nominee has finished in an award position. Any Breeders' Cup fund monies not awarded will revert back to the fund. In the event. The Kelso Breeders' Cup overfills, preference will be given to Breeders' Cup nominees only of equal racing quality or weight assignment. (Weight for age and sex allowance considered). The New York Racing Association reserves the right to transfer this race to the Main Track. In the event that this race is taken off the turf, it may be subject to downgrading upon review by the Graded Stakes Committee.

Value of Race: $347,000 Winner $210,000; second $70,000; third $38,500; fourth $21,000; fifth $7,500. Mutuel Pool $734,547.00 Exacta Pool $577,906.00 Trifecta Pool $446,293.00

Last Raced	Horse	M/Eqt.	A.Wt	PP	St	¼	½	¾	Str	Fin	Jockey	Odds $1
14Sep03 9WO7	Freefourinternet	L	5 113	7	10	10	10	10	3hd	1no	Espinoza J L	20.60
9Aug03 4Mnr1	Proud Man	Lb	5 114	10	6	9½	92½	7½	7½	21	Bailey J D	5.20
13Sep03 7Bel2	Rouvres-FR	L	4 115	8	7	6½	6hd	4hd	4hd	31¼	Nakatani C S	3.05
27Jly03 8Dmr2	Decarchy	L	6 118	1	9	7hd	8½	9hd	81½	4no	Santos J A	2.45
17Sep03 8Bel1	Millennium Dragon-GB	L	4 113	2	5	52½	4½	5hd	6hd	51½	Velazquez J R	4.40
23Aug03 10Mth8	Runspastum	Lb	6 112	5	8	81½	72½	8½	10	6nk	Luzzi M J	57.25
12Oct02 8Crc1	Pay The Preacher	L	5 114	6	1	31	31½	1hd	2hd	7nk	Dominguez R A	10.50
31Aug03 10Mth2	North East Bound	Lb	7 115	4	2	1½	1½	3½	5hd	8no	Velez J A Jr	39.25
14Sep03 8AP3	Mercenary	L	5 114	3	3	2hd	2hd	2½	1hd	9no	Smith A E	59.50
25Jly03 8Sar5	Del Mar Show	L	6 116	9	4	4hd	51	61½	9½	10	Pimentel J	9.30

OFF AT 4:48 Start Good. Won driving. Course firm.
TIME :24, :47^1, 1:10^3, 1:34^3 (:24.12, :47.34, 1:10.69, 1:34.73)

$2 Mutuel Prices:				
	7–FREEFOURINTERNET	43.20	16.40	8.30
	11–PROUD MAN		6.70	4.40
	9–ROUVRES-FR			3.40

$2 EXACTA 7–11 PAID $245.50 $2 TRIFECTA 7–11–9 PAID $1,282.00

B. h, by Tabasco Cat–Dixie Chimes, by Dixieland Band. Trainer Scott Joan. Bred by Evans Edward P (Ky).

FREEFOURINTERNET was bumped at the start, dropped back early, circled widest approaching the stretch, reached the front inside the eighth pole then dug in gamely and held on under a drive. PROUD MAN was outrun early, rallied inside into the stretch, split rivals and finished gamely, just missing. ROUVRES (FR) raced close up inside, rallied inside turning for home and was outfinished. DECARCHY was rated along early, raced inside and finished well in traffic. MILLENNIUM DRAGON (GB) raced close up in hand, rallied four wide approaching the stretch and weakened in the final furlong. RUNSPASTUM was outrun early, raced inside and lacked a rally. PAY THE PREACHER contested the pace while three wide and tired in the final furlong. NORTH EAST BOUND contested the pace along the inside and gave way in the stretch. MERCENARY contested the pace while between rivals and tired in the final furlong. DEL MAR SHOW chased the pace while four wide and tired.

Owners— 1, Equirace Com LLC; 2, Double R Stable Kaufman Robert & We; 3, Head Alec; 4, Juddmonte Farms Inc; 5, Darley Stable; 6, Jayeff B Stables; 7, Dickinson Michael W; 8, Demarco Julian & Disano Richard J; 9, Beck Robert L; 10, Allen E Paulson Living Trust

Trainers—1, Scott Joan; 2, Clement Christophe; 3, Clement Christophe; 4, Frankel Robert; 5, McLaughlin Kiaran P; 6, Goldberg Alan E; 7, Dickinson Michael W; 8, Perry William W; 9, Asmussen Steven M; 10, Mott William I

Scratched— Political Attack (13Sep03 7BEL5)

$2 Pick Three (8–4–7) Paid $1,148.00; Pick Three Pool $117,928.

NINTH RACE
Belmont
OCTOBER 4, 2003

1⅛ MILES. (1.45^2) 66th Running of THE BELDAME. Grade I. Purse $750,000 (Up to $65,500 NYSBFOA). FILLIES AND MARES THREE YEARS OLD AND UPWARD AT WEIGHT FOR AGE. By subscription of $750 each, which should accompany the nomination; $3,500 to pass the entry box and $4,000 to start. The purse to be divided 60% to the winner, 20% to second, 11% to third, 6% to fourth and 3% to fifth. Weight for age. Three-year-olds. 120 lbs.; older, 123 lbs. Mrs. John E. Cowdin has donated a perpetual cup to be held by the owner of the winner for one year. Trophies will be presented to the winning owner, trainer and jockey. Closed Saturday, September 20, 2003 with 16 nominations.

Value of Race: $750,000 Winner $450,000; second $150,000; third $82,500; fourth $45,000; fifth $22,500. Mutuel Pool $918,794.00 Exacta Pool $495,187.00 Trifecta Pool $400,786.00

Last Raced	Horse	M/Eqt.	A.	Wt	PP	St	¼	½	¾	Str	Fin	Jockey	Odds $1
27Jly03 ^{9}Sar^{1}	Sightseek	L	4	123	2	5	5^{1}	$5^{1\frac{1}{2}}$	3^{hd}	$1^{2\frac{1}{2}}$	$1^{4\frac{1}{2}}$	Bailey J D	0.30
16Aug03 ^{9}Sar^{5}	Bird Town	L	3	120	5	2	$1^{\frac{1}{2}}$	$1^{\frac{1}{2}}$	1^{hd}	2^{6}	$2^{4\frac{3}{4}}$	Gryder A T	11.20
6Sep03 ^{7}Bel^{1}	Buy The Sport	L	3	120	1	6	4^{hd}	$4^{\frac{1}{2}}$	4^{hd}	$3^{\frac{1}{2}}$	$3^{\frac{3}{4}}$	Nakatani C S	7.30
13Sep03 ^{12}TP^{1}	Smok'n Frolic	Lb	4	123	6	1	$2^{\frac{1}{2}}$	$2^{1\frac{1}{2}}$	2^{hd}	$4^{2\frac{1}{2}}$	$4^{3\frac{1}{4}}$	Dominguez R A	17.00
22Aug03 ^{9}Sar^{4}	Summer Colony	L	5	123	3	7	7	7	7	6^{1}	5no	Fragoso P	28.50
6Sep03 ^{7}Bel^{4}	Island Fashion	Lb	3	120	7	4	$3^{\frac{1}{2}}$	$3^{\frac{1}{2}}$	5^{5}	5^{hd}	$6^{6\frac{1}{2}}$	Velazquez J R	13.10
13Sep03 ^{9}Bel^{3}	Passing Shot	L	4	123	4	3	6^{3}	$6^{2\frac{1}{2}}$	$6^{\frac{1}{2}}$	7	7	Santos J A	18.10

OFF AT 5:20 Start Good. Won ridden out. Track fast.

TIME :24^2, :47^4, 1:12^2, 1:36^3, 1:49^1 (:24.52, :47.91, 1:12.44, 1:36.73, 1:49.27)

$2 Mutuel Prices:				
	2-SIGHTSEEK	2.60	2.20	2.10
	5-BIRD TOWN		4.00	2.10
	1-BUY THE SPORT			2.10

$2 EXACTA 2-5 PAID $11.20 $2 TRIFECTA 2-5-1 PAID $37.60

Ch. f, by Distant View-Viviana, by Nureyev. Trainer Frankel Robert. Bred by Juddmonte Farms, Inc. (Ky).

SIGHTSEEK raced in hand outside early, advanced four wide on the turn, collared BIRD TOWN turning for home, drew clear from that rival when asked and widened with speed to spare. BIRD TOWN quickly showed in front, set the pace along the inside, had no answer for the winner but was clearly best of the others. BUY THE SPORT raced close up inside and lacked a rally. SMOK'N FROLIC pressed the pace from the outside and tired in the stretch. SUMMER COLONY was outrun early, raced inside and had no response when roused. ISLAND FASHION chased the pace while three wide and tired. PASSING SHOT had no rally.

Owners— 1, Juddmonte Farms Inc; 2, Marylou Whitney Stables; 3, Georgica Stable Stephan Mack & Star; 4, Dogwood Stable; 5, Evans Edward P; 6, Nielsen Jeffrey L; 7, Shields Joseph V Jr

Trainers—1, Frankel Robert; 2, Zito Nicholas P; 3, Barbara Robert; 4, Pletcher Todd A; 5, Hennig Mark; 6, Tagg Barclay; 7, Jerkens H Allen

Scratched— Misty Sixes (6Sep03 ^{9}MTH^{1})

NINTH RACE
Hoosier Park
OCTOBER 4, 2003

1$\frac{1}{16}$ MILES. (1.41) 9th Running of THE INDIANA DERBY. Grade III. Purse $400,000. THREE YEAR OLDS. By subscription of $100 each which shall accompany the nomination, $400 to pass the entry box and $500 additional to start. Weight 124 lbs. Fillies,121 lbs.Non-winners of $50,000 at a mile over in 2003 allowed 3 lbs; of $30,000 at any distance in 2003, 5 lbs; three races other than maiden or claiming 7 lbs; two such races 9 lbs. NOTE: This stake will be limited to twelve starters. If more than twelve horses pass the entry box, preference will be (1)High weights (2) Highest Lifetime earnings. Two horses having common ties through ownership cannot start to the exclusion of a single interest.

Value of Race: $411,800 Winner $247,080; second $82,360; third $45,298; fourth $24,708; fifth $12,354. Mutuel Pool $148,470.00 Exacta Pool $87,029.00 Trifecta Pool $75,317.00 Superfecta Pool $25,007.00

Last Raced	Horse	M/Eqt.	A.	Wt	PP	St	¼	½	¾	Str	Fin	Jockey	Odds $1
3Aug03 ^{11}Mth^{7}	Excessivepleasure	LBb	3	124	2	1	1^{1}	$1^{\frac{1}{2}}$	1^{hd}	$1^{\frac{1}{2}}$	1^{1}	Court J K	10.10
1Sep03 ^{11}Pha^{1}	Grand Hombre	LB	3	124	8	8	7^{2}	6^{2}	6^{2}	3^{hd}	$2^{1\frac{1}{4}}$	Prado E S	1.10
14Sep03 ^{9}WO^{4}	Wando	LBf	3	124	6	5	$3^{\frac{1}{2}}$	3^{3}	2^{2}	2^{3}	$3^{1\frac{1}{4}}$	Husbands P	2.30
13Sep03 ^{13}TP^{6}	Comic Truth	LBb	3	119	1	7	8	8	8	$6^{\frac{1}{2}}$	$4^{1\frac{1}{4}}$	Bejarano R	30.80
13Sep03 ^{6}PrM^{1}	Wiggins	LB	3	124	7	4	5^{1}	$4^{\frac{1}{2}}$	$3^{\frac{1}{2}}$	4^{3}	$5^{2\frac{1}{4}}$	Razo E Jr	6.90
1Sep03 ^{11}Pha^{3}	Ashmore	LBb	3	117	4	3	$6^{\frac{1}{2}}$	7^{3}	$7^{\frac{1}{2}}$	5^{1}	$6^{1\frac{3}{4}}$	Rose J	17.00
13Sep03 ^{13}TP^{9}	Offlee Wild	LB	3	124	5	6	$4^{\frac{1}{2}}$	$5^{\frac{1}{2}}$	$5^{1\frac{1}{2}}$	7^{5}	7^{7}	Borel C H	11.20
1Sep03 ^{11}Pha^{4}	Christine's Outlaw	LBb	3	115	3	2	$2^{1\frac{1}{2}}$	2^{hd}	4^{1}	8	8	Bridgmohan S X	12.60

OFF AT 9:52 Start Good. Won driving. Track fast.

TIME :22^3, :46^2, 1:10^3, 1:36^2, 1:43^2 (:22.64, :46.45, 1:10.60, 1:36.41, 1:43.48)

$2 Mutuel Prices:				
	2-EXCESSIVEPLEASURE	22.20	5.20	2.80
	11-GRAND HOMBRE		2.60	2.40
	9-WANDO			2.60

$2 EXACTA 2-11 PAID $77.20 $2 TRIFECTA 2-11-9 PAID $191.60 $2 SUPERFECTA 2-11-9-1 PAID $3,569.00

Dk. b. or br. g, (Apr), by In Excess*Ire-Pleasing, by Falstaff. Trainer O'Neill Doug. Bred by Cypress Farms 1991 & Vessels Stallion Farm LLC (Cal).

EXCESSIVEPLEASURE broke alertly and moved clear into the first turn, made the pace along the inside, was challenged heading up the backstretch and responded well to repel his challengers, kicked clear leaving the eighth marker then held GRAND HOMBRE safe late under steady handling. GRAND HOMBRE settled in about three wide to track the pace, moved four wide through the far turn to rally into the stretch, responded when set down and was getting to the winner late. WANDO was close up to the pace racing three wide, moved to challenge in late backstretch to have aim at the winner, matched strides to midstretch but could not sustain the effort in the final furlong. COMIC TRUTH lacked early speed while well out from the rail, rallied four wide through the far turn to come six wide into the stretch and closed willingly. WIGGINS stalked the pace outside, made a four wide bid on the far turn to loom a threat approaching the stretch but could not continue the effort. ASHMORE stalked the pace racing three wide, angled in through the far turn and moved up inside the lane but lacked the needed late response. OFFLEE WILD tucked inside going to the first turn to save ground, stalked the pace in good striking position but weakened into the stretch. CHRISTINE'S OUTLAW tracked the pace racing just outside the winner, moved to bid between rivals heading up the backstretch, dropped back on the far turn and tired in the lane.

Owners— 1, Lee & Ty Leatherman; 2, Darley Stable Sheikh Mohammed; 3, Schickedanz Gustav; 4, Jayaraman Kalarikkal K & Vilasini D; 5, W Pacella J Rizza & R Schwed; 6, Ryan Daniel M; 7, Azalea Stables Lansdon Robbins; 8, R C Hill Stable

Trainers—1, O'Neill Doug; 2, Albertrani Thomas; 3, Keogh Michael; 4, Daly Patrick J; 5, Granitz Anthony J; 6, Pino Michael V; 7, Smith Thomas V; 8, Weaver George

Scratched— Hackendiffy (13Sep03 ^{6}KD^{9}), Shawklit Man (16Aug03 ^{5}AP^{3}), Roses In May (13Sep03 ^{8}BEL^{6})

$2 Pick Three (4/9-5-2) Paid $152.60; Pick Three Pool $10,705.

SIXTH RACE
Keeneland
OCTOBER 4, 2003

$1\frac{1}{16}$ MILES. (1.40^{4}) 90th Running of THE LANE'S END BREEDERS' FUTURITY. Grade II. Purse $400,000 Guaranteed. TWO YEARS OLD. By subscription of $400 each which should accompany the nomination; $4,000 to enter and start; with $400,000 guaranteed, of which $248,000 to the owner of the winner, $80,000 to second, $40,000 to third, $20,000 to fourth and $12,000 to fifth. Weight; Fillies, 118 lbs.; Colts and Geldings, 121 lbs. Starters to be named through the entry box by usual time of closing. A gold julep cup will be presented to the owner of the winner. The first four finishers in the Lane's End Breeders' Futurity are automatically made eligible for the Toyota Blue Grass Stakes of 2004 as to nomination fees.

Value of Race: $400,000 Winner $248,000; second $80,000; third $40,000; fourth $20,000; fifth $12,000. Mutuel Pool $655,023.00 Exacta Pool $429,127.00 Quinella Pool $16,100.00 Trifecta Pool $318,823.00 Superfecta Pool $79,453.00

Last Raced	Horse	M/Eqt.	A.Wt	PP	St	¼	½	¾	Str	Fin	Jockey	Odds $1
1Sep03 ^{3}Sar^{1}	Eurosilver	L	2 121	10	8	6^{1}	7^{4}	$5^{1\frac{1}{2}}$	$1^{\frac{1}{2}}$	$1^{4\frac{3}{4}}$	Castellano J J	11.90
1Sep03 ^{12}RD^{1}	Tiger Hunt	L	2 121	1	7	8^{2}	8^{1}	8^{hd}	5^{1}	2no	Melancon L	12.40
30Aug03 ^{8}Sar^{5}	Limehouse	L	2 121	2	1	7^{7}	$5^{\frac{1}{2}}$	$3^{2\frac{1}{2}}$	$4^{1\frac{1}{2}}$	3^{1}	Albarado R J	13.10
14Sep03 ^{7}Bel^{2}	Value Plus	L	2 121	3	2	3^{hd}	2^{hd}	2^{2}	2^{1}	4no	Valenzuela P A	2.20
14Sep03 ^{4}WO^{2}	Victory Light	Lb	2 121	11	9	9^{6}	9^{5}	7^{2}	$6^{1\frac{1}{2}}$	$5^{\frac{1}{2}}$	Day P	7.60
13Sep03 ^{10}TP^{3}	The Cliff's Edge	L	2 121	7	11	10^{2}	11	9^{3}	7^{4}	$6^{1\frac{1}{2}}$	Sellers S J	8.50
10Sep03 ^{8}Dmr^{4}	Cooperation	L	2 121	4	5	1^{1}	1^{1}	1^{hd}	3^{hd}	$7^{4\frac{1}{4}}$	Flores D R	12.50
4Sep03 ^{9}TP^{1}	War Image	L	2 121	6	10	11	10^{hd}	$10^{\frac{1}{2}}$	8^{15}	$8^{27\frac{3}{4}}$	Chavez J F	39.70
23Aug03 ^{2}Sar^{1}	Distressed Debt	L	2 121	9	3	$2^{\frac{1}{2}}$	$3^{\frac{1}{2}}$	$6^{1\frac{1}{2}}$	10^{5}	$9^{3\frac{1}{2}}$	Bridgmohan S X	25.00
7Sep03 ^{10}LaD^{1}	Mass Media	Lbf	2 121	8	4	$5^{\frac{1}{2}}$	4^{hd}	$4^{\frac{1}{2}}$	9^{hd}	$10^{13\frac{1}{4}}$	Prado E S	2.40
30Aug03 ^{8}Sar^{7}	Desert Patrol	Lb	2 121	5	6	$4^{1\frac{1}{2}}$	$6^{1\frac{1}{2}}$	11	11	11	Velasquez C	81.40

OFF AT 3:57 Start Good. Won driving. Track fast.
TIME :22^{4}, :46^{2}, 1:10^{2}, 1:36^{3}, 1:43^{2} (:22.92, :46.53, 1:10.46, 1:36.66, 1:43.42)

$2 Mutuel Prices:

10–EUROSILVER	25.80	12.00	9.20
1–TIGER HUNT		10.80	7.60
2–LIMEHOUSE			8.80

$1 EXACTA 10–1 PAID $145.10 $2 QUINELLA 1–10 PAID $213.60 $1 TRIFECTA 10–1–2 PAID $2,369.20 $1 SUPERFECTA 10–1–2–3 PAID $10,726.10

Dk. b. or br. c, (Feb), by Unbridled's Song–Russian Tango, by Nijinsky II. Trainer Zito Nicholas P. Bred by Buckram Oak Farm (Ky).

EUROSILVER reserved early when within striking distance, accelerated quickly after six furlongs when asked, caught the leader approaching the furlong marker and drew off under steady handling. TIGER HUNT outrun early, advanced in traffic on the second turn, angled out a bit for the drive, split rivals in deep stretch and was up for the place. LIMEHOUSE within striking distance along the inside, angled out entering the stretch for room but had no late bid. VALUE PLUS steadied from inside the leader late on the first turn, recovered, challenged outside that one after five furlongs, gained a short lead approaching the stretch but tired in the final furlong. VICTORY LIGHT outrun early when unhurried, made a good four wide middle move but could not sustain the bid. THE CLIFF'S EDGE carried in at the start, was far back when reserved, launched his rally after six furlongs, made a good gain thereafter but went evenly late. COOPERATION set the early pace near the inside, moved to the rail for the second turn, held on well to the furlong marker and tired. WAR IMAGE carried in at the start, was outrun early and was no factor. DISTRESSED DEBT came in a bit entering the first turn placing MASS MEDIA in tight, pressed the early pace four wide, held on well to the final quarter and tired. MASS MEDIA cane in a bit early, drifted wide after steadying entering the first turn, recovered to race within striking distance, moved in to the three path for the second turn and stopped. DESERT PATROL forwardly placed three wide, stopped badly.

Owners— 1, Buckram Oak Farm; 2, Team Valor Stables LLC; 3, Dogwood Stable; 4, Jones Aaron U & Marie D; 5, WinStar Farm LLC; 6, La Penta Robert V; 7, McIngvale James; 8, Equest Racing Stable LLC; 9, Klaravich Stables Seth Klarman; 10, Gary L & Mary E West; 11, Overbrook Farm

Trainers—1, Zito Nicholas P; 2, Walden W Elliott; 3, Pletcher Todd A; 4, Pletcher Todd A; 5, Walden W Elliott; 6, Zito Nicholas P; 7, Baffert Bob; 8, Maker Michael J; 9, Violette Richard A Jr; 10, Norman Cole; 11, Lukas D Wayne

$1 Pick Three (6–5–10) Paid $595.20; Pick Three Pool $47,034.

NINTH RACE
Philadelphia
OCTOBER 4, 2003

$1\frac{1}{16}$ MILES. (1.40^{4}) 34th Running of THE COTILLION HANDICAP. Grade II. Purse $250,000 FOR FILLIES THREE YEARS OLD. By subscription of $250 each which should accompany the nomination, $600 to pass the entry box, $800 additional to start, with $250,000 guaranteed. The winner to receive $150,000 with $50,000 to second, $27,500 to third, $15,000 to fourth and $7,500 to fifth. Weights: Saturday, September 27, 2003. Starters to be named through the entry box by the usual time of closing, on Tuesday, September 30, 2003. (Highweights preferred). Trophy will be presented to the winning owner, trainer and jockey. Nominations closed Tuesday, September 23, 2003 with 16.

Value of Race: $250,000 Winner $150,000; second $50,000; third $27,500; fourth $15,000; fifth $7,500. Mutuel Pool $43,835.00 Exacta Pool $31,099.00 Trifecta Pool $14,706.00

Last Raced	Horse	M/Eqt.	A.Wt	PP	St	¼	½	¾	Str	Fin	Jockey	Odds $1
1Sep03 ^{5}Sar^{1}	Fast Cookie	Lb	3 116	5	5	4^{hd}	$3^{1\frac{1}{2}}$	$2^{\frac{1}{2}}$	$1^{\frac{1}{2}}$	$1^{3\frac{3}{4}}$	Santagata N	2.70
1Sep03 ^{10}Pha^{3}	Ladyecho	L	3 116	1	2	2^{1}	2^{1}	$1^{\frac{1}{2}}$	2^{8}	2^{8}	Elliott S	6.50
17Aug03 ^{9}Sar^{6}	Savedbythelight	Lb	3 117	3	4	3^{hd}	5	5	3^{hd}	$3^{4\frac{1}{4}}$	Vega H	2.90
23Aug03 ^{7}Sar^{5}	Chimichurri	Lf	3 116	2	3	5	4^{hd}	4^{hd}	5	$4^{1\frac{3}{4}}$	Flores J L	7.00
1Sep03 ^{10}Pha^{1}	City Fire	Lb	3 118	4	1	1^{1}	$1^{\frac{1}{2}}$	$3^{3\frac{1}{2}}$	4^{hd}	5	Rocco J	1.30

OFF AT 4:21 Start Good. Won driving. Track fast.
TIME :24, :47^{4}, 1:12^{1}, 1:38^{4}, 1:45^{4} (:24.08, :47.94, 1:12.22, 1:38.85, 1:45.83)

$2 Mutuel Prices:

9–FAST COOKIE	7.40	3.80	4.20
3–LADYECHO		4.80	4.60
6–SAVEDBYTHELIGHT			3.60

$2 EXACTA 9–3 PAID $49.00 $2 TRIFECTA 9–3–6 PAID $108.20

B. f, (Mar), by Deputy Minister–Fleet Lady, by Avenue of Flags. Trainer Mott William I. Bred by Stonerside Stable LLC (Ky).

FAST COOKIE was rated early while four wide, made a four wide bid on the second turn, drew off in the final furlong to prove best under a drive. LADYECHO prompted the early pace and made a three wide bid on the second turn, but could not go with the winner late, second best. SAVEDBYTHELIGHT lacked a rally while besting the rest. CHIMICHURRI chased the early pace on the inside but offered no response. CITY FIRE gave way after six furlongs.

Owners— 1, Stonerside Stable LLC; 2, Polin Charlotte C; 3, Mack Earle I; 4, Peachtree Stable; 5, Gill Michael J

Trainers—1, Mott William I; 2, Servis John C; 3, Violette Richard A Jr; 4, Pletcher Todd A; 5, Shuman Mark

Scratched— Ain't Talkin (6Sep03 ^{6}PIM^{1}), Island Fashion (6Sep03 ^{7}BEL^{4}), Double Scoop (3Oct03 ^{9}HOO^{4}), Fircroft (16Aug03 ^{9}SAR^{6}), Danuta (6Sep03 ^{7}BEL^{8})

$2 Daily Double (3–9) Paid $264.80; Daily Double Pool $6,356.
$1 Pick Three (4–3–9) Paid $2,364.30; Pick Three Pool $3,195.
$2 Consolation Daily Double (3–1) Paid $36.00

SEVENTH RACE
Keeneland
OCTOBER 4, 2003

1½ MILES. (Turf)(2.27^{2}) 9th Running of The SYCAMORE BREEDERS' CUP. Grade III. Purse $150,000 Added (includes $50,000 BC – Breeders' Cup) FOR THREE YEAR OLDS AND UPWARD. (Includes $50,000 from Breeders' Cup Fund for Cup nominees only) By subscription of $150 each, which should accompany the nomination; $1,500 to enter and start. Weight; Three year olds, 121 lbs.; Older, 125 lbs. Non-winners of Grade I or II race over ten furlongs on the turf in 2003 allowed 3 lbs.; a grade III or Listed race at ten furlongs or more in 2002–2003, 5 lbs. The maximum number of starters for the Sycamore Breeders' Cup will be limited to ten. In the event that more than ten horses pass the entry box, the ten starters will be determined at that time with preference to nominees that are long graded stakes winners, long or intermediate stakes winners, then highest turf earnings over nine furlongs in 2003. Breeders'Cup nominees receive first preference only in equal quality situations. HAGGIN COURSE.

Value of Race: $138,200 Winner $73,904; second $33,840; third $16,920; fourth $8,460; fifth $5,076. Mutuel Pool $512,887.00 Exacta Pool $327,258.00 Quinella Pool $13,775.00 Trifecta Pool $252,520.00 Superfecta Pool $67,165.00

Last Raced	Horse	M/Eqt.	A.	Wt	PP	¼	½	1	1¼	Str	Fin	Jockey	Odds $1
30Aug03 ^{8}AP^{1}	Sharbayan-IR	Lb	5	120	2	$4^{2\frac{1}{2}}$	$4^{2\frac{1}{2}}$	$5^{3\frac{1}{2}}$	$3^{\frac{1}{2}}$	$1^{\frac{1}{2}}$	$1^{1\frac{3}{4}}$	Day P	2.90
20Sep03 ^{14}KD^{5}	Cetewayo	Lb	9	122	4	7^{1}	$9^{\frac{1}{2}}$	9^{2}	9^{1}	6^{2}	$2^{\frac{1}{2}}$	Blanc B	12.10
20Jly03 ^{8}WO^{5}	Deputy Strike	L	5	120	1	$6^{1\frac{1}{2}}$	$6^{\frac{1}{2}}$	8^{2}	6^{2}	3^{hd}	$3^{1\frac{1}{4}}$	Migliore R	22.30
30Aug03 ^{8}WO^{5}	Portcullis	L	4	120	6	5^{hd}	5^{hd}	6^{hd}	5^{2}	4^{hd}	$4^{1\frac{3}{4}}$	Kabel T K	21.10
30Aug03 ^{8}WO^{2}	Revved Up	L	5	120	7	$2^{1\frac{1}{2}}$	2^{1}	2^{hd}	4^{2}	$5^{\frac{1}{2}}$	$5^{2\frac{1}{4}}$	Prado E S	2.40
20Sep03 ^{14}KD^{7}	Kim Loves Bucky	L	6	122	8	$3^{1\frac{1}{2}}$	$3^{\frac{1}{2}}$	4^{1}	$1^{\frac{1}{2}}$	2^{1}	6no	Valenzuela P A	13.30
20Sep03 ^{14}KD^{2}	Rochester	L	7	122	9	$9^{\frac{1}{2}}$	10	10	10	8^{2}	$7^{5\frac{1}{2}}$	Martin E M Jr	6.90
10Sep03 ^{6}Bel^{2}	Blazing Fury	Lb	5	120	5	8^{2}	7^{hd}	$7^{2\frac{1}{2}}$	8^{hd}	9^{9}	8^{2}	Castellano J J	5.80
30Aug03 ^{8}WO^{3}	Better Talk Now	Lb	4	120	10	10	8^{1}	1^{1}	$2^{\frac{1}{2}}$	7^{hd}	$9^{19\frac{3}{4}}$	Douglas R R	9.50
16Feb03 ^{10}GP^{4}	Riddlesdown-IRE	L	6	122	3	$1^{\frac{1}{2}}$	$1^{2\frac{1}{2}}$	3^{hd}	7^{1}	10	10	Chavez J F	18.10

OFF AT 4:27 Start Good. Won driving. Course firm.

TIME :24^{4}, :50^{2}, 1:15^{4}, 1:39^{4}, 2:04^{4}, 2:29^{2} (:24.92, :50.47, 1:15.87, 1:39.89, 2:04.99, 2:29.55)

$2 Mutuel Prices:				
	2–SHARBAYAN–IR	7.80	4.60	3.20
	4–CETEWAYO		11.20	7.00
	1–DEPUTY STRIKE			8.80

$1 EXACTA 2–4 PAID $43.90 $2 QUINELLA 2–4 PAID $51.00 $1 TRIFECTA 2–4–1 PAID $643.20 $1 SUPERFECTA 2–4–1–6 PAID $1,360.90

B. g, by Doyoun*Ire–Sharbata*Ire, by Kahyasi*Ire. Trainer Dollase Wallace. Bred by HH the Aga Khan's Studs SC (Ire).

SHARBAYAN (IRE), rated in behind the leaders from early on, went along under patient handling, came out five wide for the drive, reached the front approaching the final furlong, then increased his advantage late under steady hand urging. CETEWAYO, unhurried for a mile, raced three or four wide, made a bold bid from between horses three or four wide in the final furlong and wasn't good enough. DEPUTY STRIKE settled near the inside, raced within easy striking distance, angled seven wide into the stretch but was empty the last sixteenth. PORTCULLIS, within easy striking distance and four wide, came a bit wider nearing the stretch, remained a threat between foes into the final furlong but lacked a further account. REVVED UP stalked front-running RIDDLESDOWN (IRE) from the start while three wide, moved to challenge between foes nearing the end of the backstretch, continued prominently into the stretch and flattened out. KIM LOVES BUCKY, well placed from early on while lightly rated three or four wide, gained the advantage approaching the final quarter, lost it to the winner nearing the eighth pole and weakened gradually thereafter. ROCHESTER, reserved early and angled inside, was outrun to the stretch, circled foes 10 wide and improved position while not a serious threat. BLAZING FURY raced three or four wide early, moved closer to the inside upon going a mile and failed to rally. BETTER TALK NOW settled early, moved out five wide soon after going a half, rushed to the lead approaching the end of the backstretch and was finished when straightened into the stretch. RIDDLESDOWN (IRE) gained the lead near the inside early, drew clear, made the pace for nearly a mile, then gave way readily on the far turn.

Owners— 1, Iron County Farms Inc George Middle; 2, Chandler Dr John A; 3, West Point Thoroughbreds LLC Terren; 4, Sam-Son Farms Mrs Elizabeth Samuel; 5, Live Oak Plantation; 6, Glenney John & Kim; 7, Augustin Stable; 8, Kimmel Caesar P & Nicholson Ronald; 9, Johnson Brent Barth Karl & Dwyer Ch; 10, Tanaka Gary A

Trainers—1, Dollase Wallace; 2, Dickinson Michael W; 3, McLaughlin Kiaran P; 4, Frostad Mark; 5, Clement Christophe; 6, Glenney John; 7, Sheppard Jonathan E; 8, Toner James J; 9, Motion H Graham; 10, O'Callaghan Niall M

Scratched— Dontbotherknocking (1Sep03 ^{9}CBY^{1}), Puffer (17Sep03 ^{2}WO^{3})

$1 Pick Three (5–10–2) Paid $184.60; Pick Three Pool $64,064.
$1 Pick Four (6–5–10–2) Paid $1,595.60; Pick Four Pool $33,489.

NINTH RACE

Keeneland

OCTOBER 4, 2003

1 MILE. (Turf)(1.33³) 18th Running of THE SHADWELL TURF MILE. Grade I. Purse $600,000 Guaranteed. THREE YEAR OLDS AND UPWARD. By subscription of $600 each, which should accompany the nomination; $6,000 to enter and start, with $600,000 guaranteed, of which $372,000 to the owner of the winner, $120,000 to second, $60,000 to third, $30,000 to fourth and $18,000 to fifth. Weight; Three year olds, 123 lbs.; Older, 126 lbs. Starters to be named through the entry box by the usual time of closing. A gold julep cup will be presented to the owner of the winner. Haggin Course.

Value of Race: $600,000 Winner $372,000; second $120,000; third $60,000; fourth $30,000; fifth $18,000. Mutuel Pool $628,994.00 Exacta Pool $360,793.00 Quinella Pool $15,849.00 Trifecta Pool $292,118.00 Superfecta Pool $83,771.00

Last Raced	Horse	M/Eqt. A.Wt	PP	St	¼	½	¾	Str	Fin	Jockey	Odds $1
14Sep03 9WO³	Perfect Soul-IR	Lb	5 126	3	2	6½	6²	7½	5¹½	1¾	Prado E S	6.50
16Aug03 10AP⁹	Honor In War	L	4 126	7	9	8¹	7hd	4hd	1hd	2½	Flores D R	9.90
14Sep03 9WO¹	Touch of the Blues-FR	L	6 126	4	5	9³	9²½	6½	3hd	3¹¼	Desormeaux K J	4.10
14Sep03 9WO²	Soaring Free	L	4 126	6	1	2³	2²	1¹	2½	4¹	Kabel T K	5.20
2Aug03 5Dmr²	Inesperado-FR	L	4 126	2	3	7¹	8²	3hd	4¹½	5¹½	Valenzuela P A	4.00
23Aug03 9Sar¹	Trademark-	L	7 126	1	4	4½	5¹	2½	6⁵	6²¾	Migliore R	2.50
13Sep03 7Bel¹	Della Francesca	Lb	4 126	8	10	10	10	10	8¹½	7²¼	Chavez J F	20.50
13Sep03 6KD¹	Naraingang-BR	L	5 126	9	7	3½	3½	5hd	7½	8³¾	Blanc B	56.10
29Aug03 7Sar¹	Stage Call-IR	Lb	4 126	5	8	5¹½	4hd	8²	9¹⁷	9	Day P	19.70
20Sep03 6KD¹	Fredericktown	L	4 126	10	6	14½	13½	9¹½	10	—	Bejarano R	67.30

Fredericktown:Distanced;

OFF AT 5:30 Start Good. Won driving. Course firm.

TIME :23, :46¹, 1:11⁴, 1:23⁴, 1:36 (:23.06, :46.35, 1:11.80, 1:23.86, 1:36.01)

$2 Mutuel Prices:

3-PERFECT SOUL-IR	15.00	7.20	4.40
7-HONOR IN WAR		9.00	6.00
4-TOUCH OF THE BLUES-FR			3.20

$1 EXACTA 3-7 PAID $72.10 $2 QUINELLA 3-7 PAID $85.00 $1 TRIFECTA 3-7-4 PAID $339.90 $1 SUPERFECTA 3-7-4-6 PAID $1,130.90

B. h, by Sadler's Wells-Ball Chairman, by Secretariat. Trainer Attfield Roger L. Bred by Fipke Charles E (Ire).

PERFECT SOUL (IRE), unhurried early and positioned near the inside between foes, continued in that manner until the stretch, worked his way out from behind a wall of horses to be six or seven wide when straightened for the drive and was hard ridden to be along in time. HONOR IN WAR, in hand early, but five or six wide much of the way, advanced steadily to reach the front approaching the final furlong, then failed to repel the winner's surge. TOUCH OF THE BLUES (FR), unhurried and also five wide much of the way, came wider approaching the stretch, made a bold run to loom solidly inside the winner for the last eighth but couldn't sustain the needed momentum. SOARING FREE, forwardly placed the start and racing inside of front-running FREDERICKTOWN, took over from that one on the far turn, made the pace into the stretch and weakened gradually. INESPERADO (FR) settled near the inside early, moved menacingly from the rail into the upper stretch but flattened out soon after. TRADEMARK (SAF), well placed inside from early on, eased out three or four wide when put to a drive at the five-sixteenths pole and weakened when straightened for the drive. DELLA FRANCESCA, outrun to the stretch, failed to menace while improving position. NARAINGANG (BRZ) raced in a striking position four wide between foes until nearing the stretch and tired. STAGE CALL (IRE) tracked the pace five wide until nearing the stretch and tired. FREDERICKTOWN rushed to the front soon after the start, opened a clear advantage while five wide, made the pace for five furlongs, gave way readily soon after and was distanced.

Owners— 1, Fipke Charles E; 2, 3rd Turn Stables LLC; 3, Gainsborough Farm Inc Maktoum al Ma; 4, Sam-Son Farms Mrs Elizabeth Samuel; 5, 3 Plus U Stable Audrey & Charles Ke; 6, Darley Stable Mohammed Al Maktoum; 7, Ol Memorial Stable Dell Ridge Farm; 8, Team Victory II; 9, WinStar Farm LLC Gaines-Gentry & Ni; 10, Silverton Hill Farm LLC Bonnie & To

Trainers— 1, Attfield Roger L; 2, McGee Paul J; 3, Drysdale Neil; 4, Frostad Mark; 5, Frankel Robert; 6, McLaughlin Kiaran P; 7, O'Callaghan Niall M; 8, McPeek Kenneth G; 9, Walden W Elliott; 10, Miller Darrin

---

$1 Daily Double (5-3) Paid $64.30; Daily Double Pool $31,480.
$1 Pick Three (2-5-3) Paid $437.80; Pick Three Pool $62,035.
$1 Pick Four (10-2-5-3) Paid $4,496.50; Pick Four Pool $66,615.

EIGHTH RACE
Pimlico
OCTOBER 4, 2003

6 FURLONGS. (1.09) 24th Running of THE SAFELY KEPT BREEDERS' CUP. Grade III. Purse $150,000 (includes $50,000 BC – Breeders' Cup) FOR FILLIES, THREE-YEARS-OLD. (Includes $50,000 from Breeders' Cup for Cup nominees only) By subscription of $100 each which should accompany the nomination. $750 to pass the entry box. $750 additional to start with $100,000 Guaranteed,and an additional $50,000 from the Breeders' Cup Fund. The Host Association's guaranteed monies to be divided 60% of all monies to the winner, 20% to second, 11% to third, 6% to fourth, and 3% to fifth. Weight 122 lbs. Non-winnersof $50,000 twice, allowed 3 lbs.; once, 5 lbs.; $25,000 once, 7 lbs. (Maiden and claiming races not considered in estimating allowances). Preference to Breeders' Cup nominees only of equal racing quality or starters with highest career earnings. Trophy presented to the owner of the winner.

Value of Race: $150,000 Winner $90,000; second $30,000; third $16,500; fourth $9,000; fifth $4,500. Mutuel Pool $120,474.00 Exacta Pool $99,737.00 Trifecta Pool $77,834.00

Last Raced	Horse	M/Eqt.	A.Wt	PP	St	¼	½	Str	Fin	Jockey	Odds $1
23Aug03 6Mth2	Randaroo	L	3 119	4	3	3hd	31½	2½	1¾	Castillo H Jr	9.70
13Sep03 9Mth7	Follow Me Home	Lb	3 117	7	1	12	11½	12	22¼	Monterrey R	32.90
5Sep03 8Pim1	Awesome Charm	Lf	3 115	8	2	61	4hd	52½	3nk	Santana J Z	29.80
23Aug03 7Sar2	She's Zealous	Lf	3 117	6	4	4½	2½	31½	4hd	Rojas R I	5.00
23Aug03 11LaD1	Holy Bubbette	L	3 117	2	5	2hd	52	41½	5¾	Karamanos H A	1.40
23Aug03 6Mth1	Elegant Designer	L	3 122	3	8	8	8	7hd	62¾	Pino M G	5.30
6Sep03 6Bel1	Flawless Diamond	L	3 117	1	7	51	7½	8	72¾	Wilson R	2.40
13Sep03 9Mth8	Home Run Hitter	Lb	3 117	5	6	74	62½	6hd	8	Klinger C O	22.50

OFF AT 4:34 Start Good. Won driving. Track fast.
TIME :22¹, :45, :57², 1:10² (:22.31, :45.04, :57.47, 1:10.54)

$2 Mutuel Prices:

4-RANDAROO	21.40	9.40	7.60
7-FOLLOW ME HOME		20.00	10.20
8-AWESOME CHARM			14.60

$2 EXACTA 4-7 PAID $413.60 $2 TRIFECTA 4-7-8 PAID $3,985.60

B. f, (Feb), by Gold Case-Validated, by Valid Appeal. Trainer McLaughlin Kiaran P. Bred by Dennis Drazin (Ky).

RANDAROO , between rivals nearing the half mile marker, stalked the pace two wide on the turn, eased out wider leaving the eighth pole, closed determinedly under pressure, struck the top leaving the sixteenth marker and was edging away at the finish. FOLLOW ME HOME was hustled to the front, set a brisk pace, raced off the rail in the lane, was collared a sixteenth out and gave way grudgingly. AWESOME CHARM , five wide approaching the half mile marker, chased the pace four wide on the turn and finished willingly. SHE'S ZEALOUS , four wide early, advanced three wide approaching the quarter pole to loom boldly, gave way grudgingly and was edged for the show. HOLY BUBBETTE chased the pace along the inside under urging and came up empty in the final furlong. ELEGANT DESIGNER , three wide on the turn, swung seven to eight wide in the drive and finished with interest. FLAWLESS DIAMOND saved ground, was shuffled back a bit nearing the turn, dropped back on the turn and failed to recover. HOME RUN HITTER was checked on the heels of rivals entering the turn, raced wide on the turn and failed to threaten.

Owners— 1, Allen Joseph; 2, Braunsdorf Robert & Levine Robert; 3, Matchmaker Farm LLC; 4, Jay Em Ess Stable; 5, Elam Katherine; 6, Sherman Michael H; 7, Padua Stables; 8, Muldoon J & D Zanella M & Reed C

Trainers—1, McLaughlin Kiaran P; 2, Levine Robert L; 3, Roadcap Jerrell E; 4, Dutrow Richard E Jr; 5, Amoss Thomas; 6, Dutrow Anthony W; 7, Pletcher Todd A; 8, Feliciano Ben M Jr

$2 Pick Three (2-7-4) Paid $1,425.20; Pick Three Pool $4,799.

FOURTH RACE
Santa Anita
OCTOBER 4, 2003

1⅛ MILES. (Turf)(1.43⁴) 34th Running of THE OAK TREE DERBY. Grade II. Purse $150,000 FOR THREE YEAR OLDS. BY SUBSCRIPTION OF $150 if made on or before Thursday September 4. All horses to pay $1500 to start with $150,000 guaranteed. 122 lbs. Non winners of $100,000 twice at a mile or over in 2003 allowed 2 lbs., of such a race in 20003, 4 lbs. Closed with 28 nominations. Rail at zero.

Value of Race: $150,000 Winner $90,000; second $30,000; third $18,000; fourth $9,000; fifth $3,000. Mutuel Pool $462,253.00 Exacta Pool $227,553.00 Quinella Pool $29,578.00 Trifecta Pool $180,084.00

Last Raced	Horse	M/Eqt.	A.Wt	PP	St	¼	½	¾	Str	Fin	Jockey	Odds $1
6Sep03 8Dmr2	Devious Boy-GB	LB	3 118	4	2	21	21½	21	1½	1hd	Krone J A	1.10
6Sep03 8Dmr3	Sweet Return-GB	LB	3 118	5	3	3½	41½	41	31	2nk	Stevens G L	2.80
1Sep03 10Sar2	Urban King-IR	LB	3 118	1	5	5	5	5	4hd	31½	Valdivia J Jr	3.10
1Sep03 11Pha9	Domestic Dispute	LB	3 118	2	1	11	12	1½	21	4hd	Solis A	8.00
16Aug03 11AP8	Californian-GB	LB	3 118	3	4	4hd	3½	3½	5	5	Espinoza V	8.50

OFF AT 2:13 Start Good. Won driving. Course firm.
TIME :25², :49⁴, 1:14¹, 1:37¹, 1:48⁴ (:25.48, :49.96, 1:14.32, 1:37.39, 1:48.82)

$2 Mutuel Prices:

5-DEVIOUS BOY-GB	4.20	2.40	2.10
6-SWEET RETURN-GB		3.00	2.10
1-URBAN KING-IR			2.20

$1 EXACTA 5-6 PAID $4.50 $2 QUINELLA 5-6 PAID $4.80 $1 TRIFECTA 5-6-1 PAID $8.90

B. g, (Feb), by Dr Devious*Ire-Oh Hebe*Ire, by Night Shift. Trainer Walsh Kathy. Bred by Van Straubeenzee Mrs C F & Gibson Fleming A (GB).

DEVIOUS BOY (GB) angled in and stalked the pace a bit off the rail, bid outside the pacesetter leaving the backstretch, put a head in front nearing the stretch and held on gamely between foes under urging. SWEET RETURN (GB) between horses early, angled in and stalked the pace inside, came off the rail on the second turn, bid outside in the stretch and continued gamely to the wire to just miss. URBAN KING (IRE) broke a bit slowly and bobbled slightly in the opening strides, saved ground chasing the pace, came out some on the second turn, split rivals in deep stretch then bid inside and went willingly to the end. DOMESTIC DISPUTE took the early lead and set a slow pace under a rating hold inside, fought back on the second turn and through the stretch but weakened some late. CALIFORNIAN (GB) three deep into the first turn, stalked outside a rival, bid three wide into the stretch but could not quite summon the needed late kick.

Owners— 1, Vreeland James R; 2, Red Oak Stable; 3, Amerman Racing Stables LLC; 4, Bienstock Dave & Winner Charles; 5, Noctis Stable Papiano Neil & Taub S

Trainers—1, Walsh Kathy; 2, McAnally Ronald; 3, Frankel Robert; 4, Gallagher Patrick; 5, Mulhall Kristin

Scratched— Blue Blood Boot (21Sep03 3BM1)

$2 Daily Double (5-5) Paid $9.00; Daily Double Pool $25,047.
$1 Pick Three (7-2/5-4/5) Paid $60.40; Pick Three Pool $54,905.

FIFTH RACE
Santa Anita
OCTOBER 4, 2003

1⅛ MILES. (1.45⁴) 22nd Running of THE GOODWOOD BREEDERS' CUP HANDICAP. Grade II. Purse $500,000 (includes $100,000 BC – Breeders' Cup) FOR THREE-YEAR-OLDS AND UPWARD. (Includes $100,000 from Breeders' Cup Fund for Cup nominees only). By subscription of $400 each if made on or before September 4, 2003 or by supplementary nomination of $10,000 by September 26. All horses shall pay $4,000 additional to start. Breeders' Cup Fund monies also correspondingly divided provided a Breeders' Cup nominee has finished in an awarded position. Any Breeders' Cup Fund monies not awarded will revert to the Fund. Closed with 17 nominations.

Value of Race: $482,000 Winner $300,000; second $100,000; third $48,000; fourth $24,000; fifth $10,000. Mutuel Pool $614,764.00 Exacta Pool $334,610.00 Quinella Pool $33,401.00 Trifecta Pool $318,607.00 Superfecta Pool $92,600.00

Last Raced	Horse	M/Eqt.	A.Wt	PP	St	¼	½	¾	Str	Fin	Jockey	Odds $1
1Mar03 9SA4	Pleasantly Perfect	LBb	5 116	2	4	6hd	6hd	41½	3½	1½	Solis A	1.40
24Aug03 5Dmr3	Fleetstreet Dancer	LBbf	5 113	7	7	74½	75	74	41	21¼	Baze T C	6.80
6Sep03 4Dmr5	Star Cross-ARG	LB	6 110	5	5	21	4hd	5hd	51½	33	Fogelsonger R	29.40
1Sep03 8Dmr1	Joey Franco	LB	4 117	3	3	51½	3hd	31	1hd	4½	Espinoza V	4.50
1Sep03 8Dmr4	Taste Of Paradise	LB	4 114	4	2	1½	1½	1hd	21½	52½	Valdivia J Jr	20.00
1Sep03 8Dmr2	Reba's Gold	LBb	6 115	1	1	3hd	51	6hd	61	61½	Smith M E	6.80
1Sep03 8Dmr3	Grey Memo	LB	6 116	6	8	8	8	8	8	7no	Stevens G L	9.00
1Sep03 11Pha5	Toccet	LBbf	3 113	8	6	4hd	21½	2hd	72	8	Krone J A	4.90

OFF AT 2:48 Start Good. Won driving. Track fast.
TIME :24¹, :48², 1:11⁴, 1:36, 1:48¹ (:24.25, :48.53, 1:11.83, 1:36.10, 1:48.37)

$2 Mutuel Prices:

2-PLEASANTLY PERFECT	4.80	3.20	2.80
7-FLEETSTREET DANCER		5.00	3.60
5-STAR CROSS-ARG			7.80

$1 EXACTA 2-7 PAID $12.00 $2 QUINELLA 2-7 PAID $18.60 $1 TRIFECTA 2-7-5 PAID $210.30 $1 SUPERFECTA 2-7-5-3 PAID $1,026.50

B. h, by Pleasant Colony-Regal State, by Affirmed. Trainer Mandella Richard. Bred by Clovelly Farms (Ky).

PLEASANTLY PERFECT settled a bit off the rail, was briefly in a bit tight off heels leaving the first turn, came out on the backstretch and moved up five wide, continued off the rail on the second turn and four wide into the stretch, rallied to the front between horses nearing the sixteenth pole and gamely prevailed under urging. FLEETSTREET DANCER chased three deep on the first turn, moved up six wide on the backstretch, remained outside on the second turn and five wide into the stretch and closed willingly. STAR CROSS (ARG) between foes early, prompted the pace outside a rival then stalked between foes, dropped back leaving the backstretch, lugged out some into the stretch, angled out behind rivals in midstretch and came back on for third. JOEY FRANCO pulled his way between horses and was in a bit tight leaving the first turn, bid three deep leaving the backstretch and outside a rival into the stretch, put a head in front nearing midstretch but weakened late. TASTE OF PARADISE took the early lead and angled in, set a pressured pace a bit off the rail, fought back into the stretch, had the rider lose the whip in midstretch and weakened. REBA'S GOLD saved ground stalking the pace and weakened in the stretch. GREY MEMO settled off the rail without early speed, came out into the stretch and did not rally. TOCCET pulled his way along outside stalking the early pace, tugged his way up three deep to force the pace on the backstretch, continued between foes into and on the second turn, dropped back into the stretch and had little left.

Owners— 1, Diamond A Racing Corporation; 2, Leatherman Lee & Ty; 3, E A Ranches; 4, Frankel Jerry; 5, Abrahams Keith & Bloom Paul; 6, Creston Farms; 7, Manzani Ridgeley Farm & Sarno; 8, Borislow Daniel M

Trainers—1, Mandella Richard; 2, O'Neill Doug; 3, Vienna Darrell; 4, Vienna Darrell; 5, Sadler John W; 6, Hendricks Dan L; 7, Stute Warren; 8, Scanlan John F

$2 Daily Double (5-2) Paid $13.40; Daily Double Pool $44,851.
$1 Pick Three (2/5-4/5-2) Paid $12.20; Pick Three Pool $76,031.
$2 Pick Six (10-7-4/5-2-3-2) 6
;orrect Paid $71,438.80; Pick Six Pool $352,785. $2 Pick Six ((NTRA NATIONAL PICK-6) 10-7-4/) Correct Paid $218.40

NINTH RACE
Belmont
OCTOBER 5, 2003

6½ FURLONGS. (1.14²) 10th Running of THE GALLANT BLOOM HANDICAP. Grade II. Purse $150,000.(Up to $29,100 NYSBFOA). FILLIES AND MARES THREE YEARS OLD AND UPWARD. By subscription of $150 each, which should accompany the nomination; $750 to pass the entry box and $750 to start. The purse to be divided 60% to the winner, 20% to second, 11% to third, 6% to fourth and 3% to fifth. Trophies will be presented to the winning owner, trainer and jockey. Closed Saturday, September 20, 2003 with 24 Nominations

Value of Race: $150,000 Winner $90,000; second $30,000; third $16,500; fourth $9,000; fifth $4,500. Mutuel Pool $343,513.00 Exacta Pool $252,751.00 Trifecta Pool $208,990.00

Last Raced	Horse	M/Eqt.	A.Wt	PP	St	¼	½	Str	Fin	Jockey	Odds $1
24Aug03 9Sar1	Harmony Lodge	L	5 117	2	1	1hd	1½	12½	1½	Migliore R	2.05
6Sep03 8Del1	House Party		3 116	6	6	6	6	2hd	2hd	Santos J A	0.75
7Aug03 8Sar2	Slews Final Answer	L	4 112	3	4	31	2½	32½	36	Bridgmohan S X	7.20
7Aug03 8Sar3	Alchemilla	L	4 111	4	5	5hd	5hd	4hd	41¾	Velazquez J R	10.40
1Sep03 9Pha5	Belle Artiste	L	5 111	1	2	4hd	4hd	56	55	Chavez J F	29.50
13Sep03 6Bel3	Literary Light	L	4 111	5	3	2hd	3½	6	6	Castellano J J	39.75

OFF AT 5:12 Start Good. Won driving. Track fast.
TIME :23³, :46⁴, 1:10, 1:16¹ (:23.68, :46.82, 1:10.07, 1:16.20)

$2 Mutuel Prices:

2-HARMONY LODGE	6.10	2.50	2.10
6-HOUSE PARTY		2.20	2.10
3-SLEWS FINAL ANSWER			2.10

$2 EXACTA 2-6 PAID $11.40 $2 TRIFECTA 2-6-3 PAID $32.00

Ch. m, by Hennessy-Win Crafty Lady, by Crafty Prospector. Trainer Pletcher Todd A. Bred by Sabine Stables (Ky).

HARMONY LODGE broke running, set the pace along the inside, drew clear coming off the turn, took a clear lead into deep stretch then dug in determinedly and held on, driving. HOUSE PARTY was unhurried outside, raced three wide, responded when roused and finished gamely outside. SLEWS FINAL ANSWER pressed the pace while between rivals, dropped back a bit turning for home then came again gamely in deep stretch. ALCHEMILLA raced close up while between rivals and had no response when roused. BELLE ARTISTE raced close up inside and tired in the stretch. LITERARY LIGHT chased the pace while three wide and tired after a half mile.

Owners— 1, Melnyk Eugene & Laura; 2, Shields Joseph V Jr; 3, Live Oak Plantation; 4, Alexander Helen C Groves Helen K &; 5, Peace John H; 6, Two Kings Stable

Trainers—1, Pletcher Todd A; 2, Jerkens H Allen; 3, Mott William I; 4, McGaughey Claude III; 5, Weaver George; 6, Schosberg Richard

SIXTH RACE
Keeneland
OCTOBER 5, 2003

$1\frac{3}{16}$ MILES. (Turf)(1.53^{4}) 6th Running of THE WINSTAR GALAXY. Grade II. Purse $500,000 FOR FILLIES AND MARES, THREE YEARS OLD AND UPWARD. By subscription of $500 each which should accompany the nomination. $5,000 to enter and start. Weight; Three-year-old fillies, 122 lbs.; Older fillies and mares, 125 lbs. Non-winners of a Grade or Group I on the Turf in 2003 allowed 2 lbs.; a Grade or Group II over a mile on the turf in 2003, 4 lbs.; a Grade or Group III over a mile on the turf in 2003 or $60,000 twice over a mile on the turf in 2002–2003, 6 lbs. Starters to be named through the entry box by usual time of closing. A gold julep cup will be presented to the owner of the winner.

Value of Race: $500,000 Winner $310,000; second $100,000; third $50,000; fourth $25,000; fifth $15,000. Mutuel Pool $271,546.00 Exacta Pool $143,602.00 Quinella Pool $8,766.00 Trifecta Pool $100,071.00 Superfecta Pool $24,944.00

Last Raced	Horse	M/Eqt.	A.Wt	PP	St	¼	½	¾	Str	Fin	Jockey	Odds $1
16Aug03 $^{8}AP^{2}$	Bien Nicole	L	5 121	1	4	1^{6}	1^{11}	1^{11}	1^{6}	$1^{7\frac{1}{4}}$	Pettinger D R	1.50
2Aug03 Goo^{7}	Approach-GB	L	3 116	2	6	$5^{\frac{1}{2}}$	$4^{2\frac{1}{2}}$	4^{2}	$4^{1\frac{1}{2}}$	$2^{1\frac{1}{4}}$	Bailey J D	6.50
24Apr03 $^{8}Kee^{5}$	New Economy	L	5 121	6	3	6	$5^{\frac{1}{2}}$	5^{hd}	$5^{1\frac{1}{2}}$	$3^{1\frac{1}{4}}$	Douglas R R	28.90
20Sep03 $^{9}Bel^{1}$	Wonder Again	L	4 121	4	1	3^{1}	$2^{1\frac{1}{2}}$	2^{hd}	3^{1}	4^{1}	Prado E S	2.70
14Sep03 $^{6}WO^{2}$	Volga-IR	L	5 121	5	2	4^{1}	$3^{1\frac{1}{2}}$	3^{2}	2^{3}	5^{1}	Nakatani C S	2.90
20Sep03 $^{12}KD^{1}$	Apasionata Sonata	Lf	5 119	3	5	2^{hd}	6	6	6	6	Bejarano R	8.50

OFF AT 3:45 Start Good. Won driving. Course firm.
TIME :25, :48^{4}, 1:12^{4}, 1:38, 1:55^{4} (:25.11, :48.86, 1:12.93, 1:38.17, 1:55.87)

$2 Mutuel Prices:			
1–BIEN NICOLE	5.00	3.40	2.40
2–APPROACH–GB		6.60	3.60
6–NEW ECONOMY			3.80

$2 EXACTA 1–2 PAID $36.00 $2 QUINELLA 1–2 PAID $23.00 $2 TRIFECTA 1–2–6 PAID $254.40 $2 SUPERFECTA 1–2–6–4 PAID $962.00

Ch. m, by Bien Bien–Dana Nicole, by Flying Paster. Trainer Von Hemel Donnie K. Bred by The Richter Family Trust (Ky).

BIEN NICOLE opened a clear lead before traveling a furlong, drew off when appearing full of run after a moderate opening quarter, pulled the rider to a commanding advantage on the backstretch, then coasted to victory under mild hand urging. APPROACH (GB), a bit sluggish to start, settled inside, moved three wide on the backstretch and around the far turn, was between foes four wide for the drive and improved position while no threat to the winner. NEW ECONOMY, outrun early, moved near the inside, continued near the rail while advancing into the stretch and improved position while unable to menace. WONDER AGAIN chased the winner four or five wide and was empty in the drive. VOLGA (IRE) tracked BIEN NICOLE three or four wide into the stretch and flattened out. APASIONATA SONATA was done on the far turn.

Owners— 1, Richter Kristine & John; 2, Faisel Salman; 3, Evans Robert S; 4, Phillips Joan G & John W; 5, Allen Joseph; 6, Seitz Frederick J

Trainers—1, Von Hemel Donnie K; 2, Prescott Sir Mark; 3, Motion H Graham; 4, Toner James J; 5, Clement Christophe; 6, Ward John T Jr

$2 Pick Three (4/9/11–2/6–1) Paid $53.80; Pick Three Pool $30,071.

EIGHTH RACE
Keeneland
OCTOBER 5, 2003

$1\frac{1}{8}$ MILES. (1.46^{4}) 48th Running of THE OVERBROOK SPINSTER. Grade I. Purse $500,000 FOR FILLIES AND MARES, THREE YEARS OLD AND UPWARD. By subscription of $500 each, which should accompany the nomination; $5,000 to enter and start, with $500,000 guaranteed, of which $310,000 to the owner of the winner, $100,000 to second, $50,000 to third, $25,000 to fourth and $15,000 to fifth. Weight; Three year olds, 120 lbs.; Older, 123 lbs. Starters to be named through the entry box by the usual time of closing. A gold julep cup will be presented to the owner of the winner. A silver julep cup will be presented to the winning trainer and jockey.

Value of Race: $500,000 Winner $310,000; second $100,000; third $50,000; fourth $25,000; fifth $15,000. Mutuel Pool $466,373.00 Exacta Pool $157,241.00 Quinella Pool $5,088.00 Trifecta Pool $145,181.00 Superfecta Pool $37,172.00

Last Raced	Horse	M/Eqt.	A.Wt	PP	St	¼	½	¾	Str	Fin	Jockey	Odds $1
1Sep03 $^{8}AP^{1}$	Take Charge Lady	L	4 123	4	1	$3^{1\frac{1}{2}}$	$3^{3\frac{1}{2}}$	2^{hd}	$1^{1\frac{1}{2}}$	1^{hd}	Prado E S	0.50
13Sep03 $^{9}Bel^{2}$	You	L	4 123	2	4	$2^{1\frac{1}{2}}$	$2^{\frac{1}{2}}$	1^{hd}	2^{2}	2^{4}	Bailey J D	2.00
22Aug03 $^{9}Sar^{3}$	Miss Linda-ARG	L	6 123	1	3	$1^{1\frac{1}{2}}$	$1^{\frac{1}{2}}$	$3^{4\frac{1}{2}}$	$3^{3\frac{1}{2}}$	$3^{\frac{3}{4}}$	Guidry M	20.90
4Sep03 $^{6}Dmr^{4}$	Printemps-CHI	L	6 123	3	6	6	6	6	$5^{3\frac{1}{2}}$	$4^{6\frac{1}{4}}$	Nakatani C S	14.40
9Aug03 $^{10}ElP^{2}$	Desert Gold	L	4 123	6	2	$4^{5\frac{1}{2}}$	4^{7}	4^{10}	$4^{2\frac{1}{2}}$	$5^{4\frac{3}{4}}$	Day P	9.50
13Sep03 $^{12}TP^{7}$	Reason To Talk	Lbf	4 123	5	5	5^{3}	$5^{3\frac{1}{2}}$	$5^{\frac{1}{2}}$	6	6	Thompson T J	69.50

OFF AT 4:45 Start Good. Won driving. Track fast.
TIME :23^{1}, :47, 1:10^{3}, 1:35^{4}, 1:49^{2} (:23.24, :47.09, 1:10.61, 1:35.96, 1:49.57)

$2 Mutuel Prices:			
4–TAKE CHARGE LADY	3.00	2.10	2.10
2–YOU		2.20	2.10
1–MISS LINDA–ARG			2.10

$2 EXACTA 4–2 PAID $4.80 $2 QUINELLA 2–4 PAID $2.60 $2 TRIFECTA 4–2–1 PAID $25.80 $2 SUPERFECTA 4–2–1–3 PAID $45.80

B. f, by Dehere–Felicita, by Rubiano. Trainer McPeek Kenneth G. Bred by William Schettine (Ky).

TAKE CHARGE LADY, lightly rated while tracking the leaders from early on, inched to challenge midway on the far turn, gained the advantage soon after going six furlongs, opened a clear lead in the upper stretch, then was hard ridden to hold YOU safe. YOU drifted in at the start bumping MISS LINDA (ARG), settled quickly to press that one three wide, put a head in front just before going three-quarters, surrendered the advantage to TAKE CHARGE LADY soon after, fell back in the upper stretch, then, during the late going, was coming back along the inside in game try. MISS LINDA (ARG), bumped at the break by YOU, gained the lead near the inside, made the pace for nearly six furlongs and weakened gradually. PRINTEMPS (CHI), outrun three or four wide for six furlongs, continued four wide into the stretch and offered a mild gain while not a serious threat. DESERT GOLD stalked the pace four or five wide to the stretch and flattened out. REASON TO TALK angled near the inside soon after the start but failed to menace.

Owners— 1, Select Stable; 2, Gann Edmund A; 3, Ackerley Brothers Farm; 4, Amerman Racing Stables Mr & Mrs Joh; 5, Stonerside Stable LLC; 6, K & K Racing Stable LLC

Trainers—1, McPeek Kenneth G; 2, Frankel Robert; 3, Kimmel John C; 4, McAnally Ronald; 5, Byrne Patrick B; 6, Vance David R

$2 Pick Three (1–6/7/9–4) Paid $17.80; Pick Three Pool $29,517.

SEVENTH RACE

Santa Anita
OCTOBER 5, 2003

6 FURLONGS. (1.071) 19th Running of THE ANCIENT TITLE BREEDERS' CUP HANDICAP. Grade I. Purse $200,000 (includes $75,000 BC – Breeders' Cup) FOR THREE-YEAR-OLDS AND UPWARD. (Includes $75,000 from Breeders' Cup Fund for Cup nominees only.) By subscription of $125 each if made on or before Thursday, September 4, 2003 or by supplementary nomination of $4,000 by Friday, September 26. All horses shall pay $1,250 to start. Breeders' Cup Fund monies also correspondingly divided provided a Breeders' Cup nominee has finished in an awarded position. Any Breeders' Cup Fund monies not awarded will revert to the Fund. Closed September 4 with 23 nominations.

Value of Race: $156,625 Winner $81,375; second $42,125; third $16,275; fourth $12,637; fifth $4,213. Mutuel Pool $497,891.00 Exacta Pool $265,976.00 Quinella Pool $25,825.00 Trifecta Pool $261,269.00

Last Raced	Horse	M/Eqt. A.Wt	PP	St	1/4	1/2	Str	Fin	Jockey	Odds $1
6Sep03 4Dmr2	Avanzado-ARG	LBf	6 116	4	1	1hd	1½	11	11½	Baze T C	8.80
1Sep03 8Dmr6	Captain Squire	LBb	4 117	6	2	22½	21½	21	2hd	Solis A	2.00
17Aug03 8Dmr7	Bluesthestandard	LB	6 115	5	3	3hd	41	3hd	31½	Smith M E	7.00
6Sep03 4Dmr1	Yankee Gentleman	LB	4 114	1	6	51	55	4hd	4½	Krone J A	1.20
23Aug03 10Sar8	Zavata	B	3 116	3	4	42	3hd	54½	54	Stevens G L	7.30
31Aug03 10Sar6	Proud Citizen	LBb	4 116	2	5	6	6	6	6	Flores D R	17.70

OFF AT 3:35 Start Good. Won driving. Track fast.
TIME :212, :432, :552, 1:08 (:21.54, :43.58, :55.42, 1:08.12)

$2 Mutuel Prices:

4–AVANZADO–ARG	19.60	6.40	3.80
6–CAPTAIN SQUIRE		3.40	2.80
5–BLUESTHESTANDARD			3.40

$1 EXACTA 4–6 PAID $35.40 $2 QUINELLA 4–6 PAID $25.00 $1 TRIFECTA 4–6–5 PAID $127.40

Ch. h, by Luhuk–Avian Eden, by Storm Bird. Trainer O'Neill Doug. Bred by Haras La Quebrada (Arg).

AVANZADO (ARG) had good early speed off the rail, dueled inside a foe but a bit off the fence, angled in on the turn, inched away in midstretch and held gamely under urging. CAPTAIN SQUIRE went up outside the winner to vie for command until nearing midstretch, then could not match that one and just held second. BLUESTHESTANDARD stalked outside a rival on the backstretch and turn, came three deep into the stretch and just missed the place. YANKEE GENTLEMAN chased inside on the backstretch, came a bit off the rail nearing the turn, moved up four wide into the stretch but failed to sustain the bid in the drive. ZAVATA well placed stalking the dueling leaders inside to the stretch, came out a bit and lacked the needed response. PROUD CITIZEN allowed to settle outside a rival, dropped back off the rail approaching the turn and did not rally.

Owners— 1, Cees Stable LLC; 2, Bone Robert D & Diener Jeffrey S; 3, Sengara Jeffrey; 4, Wygod Mr & Mrs Martin J; 5, Tabor Michael B; 6, Baker Cornstein & Mack

Trainers— 1, O'Neill Doug; 2, Mullins Jeff; 3, West Ted H; 4, Shirreffs John; 5, Biancone Patrick L; 6, Lukas D Wayne

$2 Daily Double (6–4) Paid $184.20; Daily Double Pool $26,776.
$1 Pick Three (6–6–4) Paid $348.20; Pick Three Pool $78,958.

EIGHTH RACE

Santa Anita
OCTOBER 5, 2003

1 MILE. (Turf)(1.314) 18th Running of THE OAK TREE BREEDERS' CUP MILE. Grade II. Purse $300,000 (includes $50,000 BC – Breeders' Cup) FOR THREE YEAR OLDS AND UPWARD. (Includes $50,000 from Breeders' Cup fund for Breeders' Cup nominees only.) By subscription of $250 each if made on or before September 4 or by supplementary nomination of $5000 by October 3. All horses to pay $2500 to start. Breeders' Cup monies to be correspondingly divided. Three year olds 119 lbs., older 123 lbs. Non winners of two races of $100,000 at one mile or over in 2003 allowed 2 lbs., of such a race in 2003, 4 lbs. Closed September 4 with 27 nominations. 1 supplement, CENTURY CITY.

Value of Race: $300,000 Winner $180,000; second $60,000; third $36,000; fourth $18,000; fifth $6,000. Mutuel Pool $511,992.00 Exacta Pool $276,091.00 Quinella Pool $27,538.00 Trifecta Pool $302,688.00 Superfecta Pool $133,653.00

Last Raced	Horse	M/Eqt. A.Wt	PP	St	1/4	1/2	3/4	Str	Fin	Jockey	Odds $1
10Sep03 3Dmr1	Designed For Luck	LBb	6 119	2	2	21	21½	21½	12	1½	Valenzuela P A	3.90
14Sep03 9WO8	Sarafan	LB	6 119	1	3	71	71	51	2hd	21½	Espinoza V	8.70
26May03 8Hol7	Century City-IR	LBb	4 119	6	7	6½	61½	71½	71½	3nk	Valdivia J Jr	30.50
28Sep97 2YD4	Special Ring	LBb	10 121	5	1	51½	52	6hd	6hd	42	Flores D R	0.70
26Jly03 6Dmr7	Medecis-GB	LB	4 119	3	5	4½	41	31	41	5½	Smith M E	14.40
18Aug03 7Dmr3	Mountain Rage	LBb	4 119	7	8	8	8	8	8	6½	Stevens G L	22.20
10Sep03 3Dmr2	Green Line-GB	LB	4 119	4	4	31	3hd	41½	5hd	7hd	Krone J A	10.70
14Mar03 5SA1	Apache Wings	LB	5 119	8	6	12	13	1½	31½	8	Baze T C	10.60

OFF AT 4:13 Start Good. Won driving. Course firm.
TIME :223, :454, 1:091, 1:204, 1:323 (:22.79, :45.86, 1:09.30, 1:20.87, 1:32.61)

$2 Mutuel Prices:

2–DESIGNED FOR LUCK	9.80	4.60	4.20
1–SARAFAN		7.00	7.40
6–CENTURY CITY–IR			15.80

$1 EXACTA 2–1 PAID $33.30 $2 QUINELLA 1–2 PAID $33.40 $1 TRIFECTA 2–1–6 PAID $541.70 $1 SUPERFECTA 2–1–6–5 PAID $2,269.80

Ch. g, by Rahy–Fantastic Look, by Green Dancer. Trainer Cerin Vladimir. Bred by Mabee Mr & Mrs John C (Ky).

DESIGNED FOR LUCK stalked the pace along the inside, bid outside the leader leaving the second turn, took a short advantage into the stretch, kicked clear along the inside and held under urging. SARAFAN saved ground off the pace, moved up on the second turn, came out in upper stretch and finished well. CENTURY CITY (IRE) settled outside a rival then a bit off the rail, went between horses on the second turn, split rivals past midstretch and edged a foe for third. SPECIAL RING chased outside a foe then three deep on the second turn, came four wide into the stretch and just missed the show. MEDECIS (GB) saved ground stalking the pace, came out into the stretch and could not offer the necessary late response. MOUNTAIN RAGE unhurried outside a rival then off the rail, angled in on the second turn and lacked the needed rally. GREEN LINE (GB) reluctant to load, stalked outside a rival, came three deep into the stretch and weakened. APACHE WINGS took the early lead and angled in, set the pace, dueled along the rail on the second turn but weakened in the stretch.

Owners— 1, Wilson David W & Holly F; 2, Tanaka Gary A; 3, Kitchwa Stables & Nichols Thomas L; 4, Prestonwood Farm LLC; 5, Wertheimer Farm LLC; 6, Baffert & Jacobs; 7, Harlequin Ranches & Duggan Emily; 8, Henton Hitbound Stable & Turrell

Trainers— 1, Cerin Vladimir; 2, Drysdale Neil; 3, Greely C Beau; 4, Canani Julio C; 5, Mandella Richard; 6, Baffert Bob; 7, Gallagher Patrick; 8, Breuer Denise E

Scratched— Special Ring (27Jly03 8DMR1)

$2 Daily Double (4–2) Paid $104.00; Daily Double Pool $52,522.
$1 Pick Three (6–4–2) Paid $535.00; Pick Three Pool $82,449.

TENTH RACE

Santa Anita

OCTOBER 5, 2003

1$\frac{1}{16}$ MILES. (1.39) 34th Running of THE NORFOLK. Grade II. Purse $250,000 FOR TWO-YEAR-OLDS. By subscription of $250 each if made on or before Thursday, September 4, 2003 or by supplementary nomination of $5,000 by Thursday, October 3 or at time of entry. All horses to pay $2,500 to start. Weight: 120 lbs. Closed September 4 with 38 nominations.

Value of Race: $250,000 Winner $150,000; second $50,000; third $30,000; fourth $15,000; fifth $5,000. Mutuel Pool $418,545.00 Exacta Pool $242,380.00 Quinella Pool $26,585.00 Trifecta Pool $260,219.00 Superfecta Pool $147,314.00

Last Raced	Horse	M/Eqt. A.Wt	PP	St	$\frac{1}{4}$	$\frac{1}{2}$	$\frac{3}{4}$	Str	Fin	Jockey	Odds $1
17Aug03 2Dmr4	Ruler's Court	LBb	2 120	7	2	2$\frac{1}{2}$	2^1	1^1	1^8	1^{14}	Solis A	4.90
17Aug03 2Dmr2	Capitano	LBb	2 120	5	4	3^{hd}	3^{hd}	3$\frac{1}{2}$	2^{hd}	2^1	Valdivia J Jr	11.20
10Sep03 8Dmr3	Perfect Moon	LB	2 120	6	7	6^1	6^1	5$\frac{1}{2}$	4$\frac{1}{2}$	3$3\frac{1}{2}$	Espinoza V	7.60
10Sep03 8Dmr1	Siphonizer	LB	2 120	4	1	5^{hd}	5$\frac{1}{2}$	4^{hd}	3^{hd}	4no	Krone J A	3.50
30Aug03 3Dmr1	Consecrate	LBb	2 120	3	8	8^4	7$\frac{1}{2}$	6$2\frac{1}{2}$	5^2	5$1\frac{1}{2}$	Valenzuela P A	a-2.20
27Aug03 2Dmr1	Mambo Train	LBb	2 120	9	9	9	9	7$\frac{1}{2}$	6$2\frac{1}{2}$	6$\frac{3}{4}$	Fogelsonger R	33.30
18Aug03 5Dmr1	Lucky Pulpit	LBb	2 120	1	6	4$1\frac{1}{2}$	8$4\frac{1}{2}$	9	8	7^{10}	Baze T C	24.70
5Sep03 2Dmr1	Coldntight	LBb	2 120	8	5	1^1	1$\frac{1}{2}$	2^1	7^3	8	Flores D R	3.50
6Sep03 6Dmr1	Odds On	LBb	2 120	2	3	7^1	4^1	8^8	—	—	Stevens G L	a-2.20

Odds On:Eased;

a-Coupled: Consecrate and Odds On.

OFF AT 5:31 Start Good. Won ridden out. Track fast.

TIME :22^2, :45^3, 1:10^1, 1:34^3, 1:41^1 (:22.54, :45.79, 1:10.22, 1:34.74, 1:41.27)

$2 Mutuel Prices:

6-RULER'S COURT	11.80	7.20	5.00
4-CAPITANO		10.60	6.80
5-PERFECT MOON			4.60

$1 EXACTA 6-4 PAID $52.30 $2 QUINELLA 4-6 PAID $65.40 $1 TRIFECTA 6-4-5 PAID $278.00 $1 SUPERFECTA 6-4-5-3 PAID $1,656.10

Dk. b. or br. c, (Apr), by Doneraile Court-Future Guest, by Copelan. Trainer Harty Eoin. Bred by Douglas Arnold & Roy Sadovsky (Ky).

RULER'S COURT five wide into the first turn, advanced four wide on that bend, bid outside a rival on the backstretch, took command on the second turn, kicked clear leaving that turn and drew off under a steady hand ride. CAPITANO stalked between horses then outside a rival, continued off the rail into and on the second turn, was no match for the winner but held second. PERFECT MOON steadied in tight four wide between foes into the first turn, chased outside, continued four wide on the second turn and into the stretch and bested the others. SIPHONIZER chased between horses then three deep on the second turn and into the stretch and lacked a further response. CONSECRATE pulled his way along off the rail early, chased off the inside, went outside a rival on the second turn and improved position. MAMBO TRAIN broke outward, blew the first turn, raced well wide throughout and was not a factor. LUCKY PULPIT saved ground stalking the pace, dropped back on the backstretch and weakened. COLDNTIGHT sped to the early lead, dueled inside on the backstretch and until nearing midway on the second turn, dropped back fast once headed, gave way and was eased late. ODDS ON pulled his way along inside early, tugged the rider between horses on the backstretch to stalk the pace, stopped and drifted out on the second turn, also was eased in upper stretch and walked off.

Owners— 1, Darley Stud Management LLC; 2, Meguerditchian Mr & Mrs; 3, Jaime Royce; 4, Hughes B W; 5, McIngvale James; 6, Everest Stables; 7, Williams Mr & Mrs Larry D; 8, Pegram Michael E; 9, McIngvale James

Trainers— 1, Harty Eoin; 2, Bell Thomas R II; 3, O'Neill Doug; 4, Mandella Richard; 5, Baffert Bob; 6, Polanco Marcelo; 7, Sise Clifford Jr; 8, Baffert Bob; 9, Baffert Bob

$2 Daily Double (8-6) Paid $45.60; Daily Double Pool $106,577.
$1 Pick Three (2-8-6) Paid $130.60; Pick Three Pool $164,361.
$1 Pick Four (4-2-8-6) Paid $2,322.90; Pick Four Pool $320,123.
$2 Pick Six (6-6-4-2-8-6) 5
Correct Paid $4,881.60; Pick Six Pool $285,404; Carryover Pool
$159,466. $1 Place Pick All (9-OF-10) Paid $2,864.80; Place Pick
All Pool $28,713.

Santa Anita Park Attendance: 11,932 Mutuel Pool: $2,866,614.00 ITW Mutuel Pool: $3,437,832.00 ISW Mutuel Pool: $4,696,607.00

NINTH RACE

Keeneland

OCTOBER 10, 2003

7 FURLONGS. (1.20¹) 5th Running of THE RAVEN RUN. Grade III. Purse $150,000 FOR FILLIES, THREE YEARS OLD. By subscription of $150 each, which should accompany the nomination; $1,500 to enter and start, with $150,000 added, of which 62% of all monies to the owner of the winner, 20% to second, 10% to third, 5% to fourth and 3% to fifth. Weight; 123 lbs. Non-winners of a Graded or Group stakes allowed 3 lbs.; a sweepstakes allowed 6 lbs. Starters to be named through the entry box by the usual time of closing. A gold julep cup will be presented to the owner of the winner.

Value of Race: $174,450 Winner $108,159; second $34,890; third $17,445; fourth $8,723; fifth $5,233. Mutuel Pool $375,177.00 Exacta Pool $243,882.00 Quinella Pool $12,128.00 Trifecta Pool $209,406.00 Superfecta Pool $66,001.00

Last Raced	Horse	M/Eqt.	A.Wt	PP	St	¼	½	Str	Fin	Jockey	Odds $1
24Aug03 9Sar⁴	Yell	L	3 123	9	9	9¹	9¹	3³	1²½	Day P	1.50
23Aug03 7Sar³	Ebony Breeze	L	3 123	10	8	7hd	5hd	2hd	2¾	Velasquez C	4.80
18Sep03 8Bel²	Tina Bull	L	3 117	7	6	2½	1hd	1½	3no	Lanerie C J	6.70
12Sep03 6PrM³	Halory Leigh	L	3 117	3	10	12	117	4¹	4³½	Perret C	9.70
1Sep03 10Pha⁵	My Trusty Cat	Lbf	3 120	4	11	10hd	10hd	72	54½	Thompson T J	49.60
18Sep03 8Bel¹	Molto Vita	L	3 117	6	7	6½	7½	6hd	62¾	Guidry M	17.10
14Sep03 9TP¹	Golden Marlin	L	3 123	11	2	8¹	8hd	8²	74	Bejarano R	15.20
17Sep03 7Del²	Holiday Runner	Lf	3 120	12	1	5½	6½	10²	8½¹	Lopez J	68.00
13Sep03 12TP⁶	Country Romance	Lb	3 120	1	12	3hd	3½	5hd	9³½	Albarado R J	3.80
13Sep03 7BM³	Hippogator	Lb	3 117	8	5	1hd	2¹½	9½	10hd	Douglas R R	83.50
30Aug03 7EIP³	Westerly Breeze	Lbf	3 123	2	4	4½	42½¹	11³	11½	Court J K	42.30
24May03 8LS¹¹	Valid Pulpit	Lbf	3 120	5	3	11½	12	12	12	McKee J	136.10

OFF AT 5:16 Start Good For All But COUNTRY ROMANCE. Won driving. Track fast.

TIME :21⁴, :44¹, 1:09², 1:21³ (:21.88, :44.29, 1:09.51, 1:21.75)

$2 Mutuel Prices:			
9–YELL	5.00	3.40	2.80
10–EBONY BREEZE		4.60	4.20
7–TINA BULL			4.00

$2 EXACTA 9–10 PAID $21.80 $2 QUINELLA 9–10 PAID $13.60 $2 TRIFECTA 9–10–7 PAID $127.40 $2 SUPERFECTA 9–10–7–3 PAID $752.80

Dk. b. or br. f, (Apr), by A.P. Indy–Wild Applause, by Northern Dancer. Trainer McGaughey Claude III. Bred by Claiborne Farm & Mrs Adele Dilschneider (Ky).

YELL settled three or four wide early, advanced between rivals approaching the stretch, angled out five wide for the drive, then responded to brisk left-handed urging to draw clear late. EBONY BREEZE, never far back, made a bold run four or five wide leaving the turn, moved with YELL while inside that one nearing the final furlong and couldn't match strides late as second best. TINA BULL moved up inside of front-running HIPPOGATOR early to vie for the lead, gained the advantage just before going a half, opened a clear margin in the upper stretch, then weakened leaving the furlong grounds. HALORY LEIGH, outrun three wide for a half, moved closer between foes nearing the final quarter, split rivals leaving the quarter-mile ground three wide, was checked when briefly lacking room, eased out five wide and was slowly gaining at the end. MY TRUSTY CAT, outrun to the stretch, was six wide at the quarter-mile and worked his way between rivals through the final furlong and improved position while not a serious threat. MOLTO VITA, between foes four wide on the backstretch, moved near the inside at the quarter-mile marker, was within striking distance into the final furlong but failed to respond. GOLDEN MARLIN, six or seven wide throughout, failed to rally. HOLIDAY RUNNER worked her way in early to stalk the pace five wide and weakened approaching the stretch. COUNTRY ROMANCE dwelt at the start, rushed up inside, raced forwardly for five furlongs and tired. HIPPOGATOR gained a narrow lead early, dueled with TINA BULL for a half and gradually weakened. WESTERLY BREEZE, well placed three or four wide, was put to a drive leaving the three-eighths pole but was finished when straightened for the drive. VALID PULPIT was outrun.

Owners— 1, Claiborne Farm Mrs A B Hancock & Ad; 2, Kinsman Stable; 3, Cecil Robert D; 4, Crawford Jerry Gannon Matt & Grask; 5, Pollard Carl F; 6, Gunther John D; 7, Estate of Joe Famularo & Glass Will; 8, S J B Stable Trust Stephen J Barber; 9, Overbrook Farm; 10, Bob Blanchard Tom Maser & George To; 11, Miles A S Jr; 12, Baker Stephen R

Trainers— 1, McGaughey Claude III; 2, Mott William I; 3, Asmussen Steven M; 4, Romans Dale; 5, Vance David R; 6, Stewart Dallas; 7, Foley Gregory D; 8, Ritchey Tim F; 9, Lukas D Wayne; 10, Hollendorfer Jerry; 11, Nafzger Carl A; 12, Frederick Edward

Scratched— Fabulous Brush (13Sep03 6AP²)

$2 Daily Double (1–9) Paid $27.40; Daily Double Pool $33,556.
$2 Pick Three (4–1–9/13) Paid $146.40; Pick Three Pool $42,412.
$2 Pick Four (2–4–1–9/13) Paid $4,556.60; Pick Four Pool $42,192.

NINTH RACE
Belmont
OCTOBER 11, 2003

1½ MILES. (Turf)(2.241) LAWRENCE REALIZATION H.. Grade III. Purse $150,000 WIDENER TURF. (Up to $29,100 NYSBFOA) A HANDICAP FOR THREE YEAR OLDS. By subscription of $150 each, which should accompany the nomination; $750 to pass the entry box and $750 to start. The purse to be divided 60% to the winner, 20% to second, 11% to third, 6% to fourth and 3% to fifth. Trophies will be presented to the winning owner, trainer and jockey. The New York Racing Association reserves the right to transfer this race to the Main Track. In the event that this race is taken off the turf, it may be subject to downgrading upon review by the Graded Stakes Committee. Closed Saturday, September 27, 2003 with 26 Nominations.

Value of Race: $150,000 Winner $90,000; second $30,000; third $16,500; fourth $9,000; fifth $4,500. Mutuel Pool $504,175.00 Exacta Pool $408,633.00 Trifecta Pool $351,145.00

Last Raced	Horse	M/Eqt.	A.Wt	PP	¼	½	1	1¼	Str	Fin	Jockey	Odds $1
21Sep03 9Bel2	Kicken Kris	L	3 121	4	2hd	2½	21½	1hd	12½	1¾	Castellano J J	0.55
20Aug03 9Sar1	Rowans Park	L	3 115	7	42½	41	3hd	31½	21½	2¾	Gryder A T	10.30
25Aug03 9Sar1	Fortune Writers	L	3 113	8	53½	52½	6½	4hd	3½	34¼	Bridgmohan S X	17.70
30Aug03 9Sar1	Go Deputy	L	3 115	3	7hd	71½	51½	51½	51½	42¾	Arroyo N Jr	6.60
20Sep03 10Bel1	Devils Peak	L	3 114	5	62½	61½	74½	65	66	51	Castillo H Jr	40.50
19Sep03 7Bel2	Carrier	Lb	3 113	2	12½	12½	1hd	22	42½	64¼	Chavez J F	28.25
20Aug03 9Sar2	Saint Stephen	L	3 115	1	31½	3½	4½	74½	73½	73½	Migliore R	4.40
12Sep03 6Bel5	Dark Whisper	Lb	3 115	6	8	8	8	8	8	8	Espinoza J L	45.25

OFF AT 5:17 Start Good. Won driving. Course firm.

TIME :241, :501, 1:144, 1:39, 2:031, 2:274 (:24.39, :50.25, 1:14.85, 1:39.02, 2:03.24, 2:27.98)

$2 Mutuel Prices:				
	4–KICKEN KRIS	3.10	2.40	2.10
	8–ROWANS PARK		5.20	2.60
	9–FORTUNE WRITERS			2.90

$2 EXACTA 4–8 PAID $18.80 $2 TRIFECTA 4–8–9 PAID $123.00

B. c, (Mar), by Kris S.–Kicken Grass, by Jade Hunter. Trainer Matz Michael R. Bred by Valerie Naify (Ky).

KICKEN KRIS raced with the pace while in hand, drew clear when roused and held sway under a drive. ROWANS PARK was rated along outside, raced three wide and finished gamely. FORTUNE WRITERS raced in hand early, came wide into the stretch and finished gamely. GO DEPUTY was outrun early, raced wide and lacked a rally. DEVILS PEAK had no response when roused. CARRIER set the pace along the inside and tired in the stretch. SAINT STEPHEN was rated along inside and tired. DARK WHISPER had no rally.

Owners— 1, Brushwood Stable; 2, Melnyk Eugene & Laura; 3, Nicholson Patricia E & Ronald; 4, Wertheimer Farm LLC; 5, Bader Peter & Kantor Bernard; 6, O'Connor John M; 7, Karches Peter F & Harris Charles E; 8, Wieczorek John L

Trainers—1, Matz Michael R; 2, Reinstedler Anthony; 3, Toner James J; 4, Pletcher Todd A; 5, Clement Christophe; 6, Lukas D Wayne; 7, Clement Christophe; 8, Bond Harold James

Scratched— Ramillus (6Sep03 10BEL1)

EIGHTH RACE
Calder
OCTOBER 11, 2003

1 1/16 MILES. (1.422) SPEND A BUCK H.. Grade III. Purse $100,000 FOR THREE YEAR OLDS AND UPWARD. By subscription of $100 each which shall accompany the nomination, $1,000 to pass the entry box and an additional $1,000 to start. Closed Saturday, September 27, 2003 with (12) nominations.

Value of Race: $100,000 Winner $60,000; second $20,000; third $11,000; fourth $6,000; fifth $3,000. Mutuel Pool $143,345.00 Exacta Pool $151,435.00 Trifecta Pool $120,898.00 Superfecta Pool $43,940.00

Last Raced	Horse	M/Eqt.	A.Wt	PP	St	¼	½	¾	Str	Fin	Jockey	Odds $1
1Sep03 5Crc1	Tour Of The Cat	Lf	5 116	5	1	11½	11	11	11½	11	Cabassa A Jr	1.90
20Apr03 9GP1	Best of the Rest	L	8 122	6	6	2½	21	21	2½	21	Bailey J D	0.80
27Sep03 10Crc6	Dancing Guy	Lbf	8 116	1	2	3½	4½	3hd	32	33	Velez R I	11.10
26Aug03 7Crc1	Patriotic Flame	Lb	3 114	7	7	41	3hd	4hd	4hd	4nk	Cruz M R	19.30
27Sep03 10Crc5	Lavender's Lad	L	5 113	2	4	6½	72½	63	52½	52¼	Toribio Aurelio Jr	12.70
11Sep03 7Crc1	R. Associate	Lbf	3 112	8	8	5½	5hd	51½	65	610¼	Homeister R B Jr	11.60
1Sep03 5Crc6	Longford Arms	Lb	4 112	3	5	8	8	8	74	720½	Garcia J A	24.80
13Jly03 8Crc5	Sebastian Light	Lb	4 114	4	3	73	61	71	8	8	Aguilar M	88.90

OFF AT 3:55 Start Good. Won driving. Track fast.

TIME :25, :494, 1:141, 1:393, 1:461 (:25.00, :49.84, 1:14.29, 1:39.67, 1:46.30)

$2 Mutuel Prices:				
	5–TOUR OF THE CAT	5.80	2.40	2.10
	6–BEST OF THE REST		2.20	2.10
	1–DANCING GUY			2.20

$2 EXACTA 5–6 PAID $12.80 $2 TRIFECTA 5–6–1 PAID $57.40 $2 SUPERFECTA 5–6–1–7 PAID $268.40

B. g, by Tour d'Or–Tune in to the Cat, by Tunerup. Trainer Mora Myra. Bred by C V S Sales Company (Fla).

TOUR OF THE CAT set the pace along the inside into the stretch, then was fully extended to prevail. BEST OF THE REST stalked the winner off the rail into the stretch, then couldn't gain on that rival late while holding the place. DANCING GUY tracked the leaders along the rail into the stretch, then lacked the needed late response. PATRIOTIC FLAME tracked the pace, raced three wide on the far turn and weakened. LAVENDER'S LAD bumped with LONGFORD ARMS at the start and failed to menace. R. ASSOCIATE rated off the pace, raced four wide on the far turn and tired. LONGFORD ARMS was outrun after being bumped and squeezed back from between rivals at the start. SEBASTIAN LIGHT bumped with LONGFORD ARMS at the start, then was steadied from tight quarters entering the first turn and failed to be a factor.

Owners— 1, Double G Stables LLC; 2, Oxenberg Beatrice; 3, Green Newcomb; 4, Kinsman Stable; 5, Lucky Lavender Stable; 6, A Kales Company; 7, Three G Stable; 8, Jerry G Bozzo Trust

Trainers—1, Mora Myra; 2, Plesa Edward Jr; 3, Green Newcomb; 4, Tortora Emanuel; 5, White William P; 6, Tortora Emanuel; 7, Olivares Luis; 8, Bozzo Jerry

---

$2 Pick Three (9–5–5) Paid $112.00; Pick Three Pool $23,909.

TWELFTH RACE

Calder

OCTOBER 11, 2003

1⅛ MILES. (Turf)(1.44⁴) CALDER DERBY. Grade III. Purse $200,000 FOR THREE YEAR OLDS. By subscription of $200 each which shall accompany the nomination, $2,000 to pass the entry box and an additional $2,000 to start. Weight: 122 lbs. Non-winners of a Sweepstakes of $75,000 at a mile or over allowed 3 lbs.; non-winners of a Sweepstakes of $50,000 at a mile or over, 5 lbs.; $25,000 other than Maiden or Claiming at a mile or over on the turf, 7 lbs.; non-winners of a race other than Maiden or Claiming at a mile or over, allowed 9 lbs. Graded placed horses at equal weights preferred. Closed Saturday, September 27, 2003 with (25)nominations.

Value of Race: $200,000 Winner $120,000; second $40,000; third $22,000; fourth $12,000; fifth $6,000. Mutuel Pool $561,394.00 Exacta Pool $151,829.00 Trifecta Pool $126,587.00 Superfecta Pool $54,597.00

Last Raced	Horse	M/Eqt. A.Wt	PP	St	¼	½	¾	Str	Fin	Jockey	Odds $1
21Sep03 9Bel1	Stroll	L 3 122	7	7	6¹	5hd	1hd	1²½	1³¾	Bailey J D	0.20
27Sep03 2Crc1	Certifiably Crazy	Lbf 3 115	2	2	1½	1¹	2¹½	2³½	2²¾	Hernandez C A	17.50
19Sep03 9Crc1	Super Frolic	Lb 3 119	4	9	9	7hd	6¹	4¹½	3²½	Boulanger G	20.50
6Sep03 5Crc8	He'sanoactor	Lb 3 115	5	8	8hd	9	9	6²	4hd	Toscano P R	19.70
11Jly03 9Crc5	Unbridels King	Lb 3 115	9	4	3½	3½	3¹½	3½	5²½	Garcia J A	35.60
6Sep03 5Crc4	Sea Pleasure	Lb 3 119	8	6	5½	6²	4hd	5¹	6nk	Castro E	8.10
8Aug03 5Crc6	King Cassia	Lb 3 115	1	3	4hd	4hd	8hd	9	7nk	Teator P A	63.10
17Sep03 6Suf1	Boston Fox	Lbf 3 115	3	5	7¹	8¹½	7½	8²	8³	Ferrer J C	10.60
6Sep03 5Crc2	Me My Mine	Lb 3 113	6	1	2hd	2½	5¹	7¹	9	Nunez E O	58.60

OFF AT 5:56 Start Good For All But HE'SANOACTOR Won handily. Course firm.

TIME :23⁴, :47⁴, 1:11², 1:35⁴, 1:48¹ (:23.83, :47.94, 1:11.45, 1:35.91, 1:48.39)

$2 Mutuel Prices:

10-STROLL	2.40	2.10	2.10
3-CERTIFIABLY CRAZY		4.40	2.10
5-SUPER FROLIC			2.10

$2 EXACTA 10-3 PAID $14.80 $2 TRIFECTA 10-3-5 PAID $119.00 $2 SUPERFECTA 10-3-5-6 PAID $669.80

Dk. b. or br. c, (Apr), by Pulpit-Maid for Walking*GB, by Prince Sabo. Trainer Mott William I. Bred by Claiborne Farm (Ky).

STROLL rated in between horses, steadied to avoid running up on rivals on the first turn, rallied along the hedge to take over racing down the backstretch, then drew clear while winning with something left. CERTIFIABLY CRAZY set the pace off the hedge, then was no match for the winner in the drive while proving second best. SUPER FROLIC outrun after being steadied in the early going, raced three wide on the far turn and closed to gain the show. HE'SANOACTOR stumbled at the start, steadied in the early going and again on the first turn, then passed tired rivals in the drive. UNBRIDELS KING chased the leaders three wide into the stretch and tired. SEA PLEASURE raced in striking position into the far turn and faltered. KING CASSIA was through after a half mile. BOSTON FOX was outrun. ME MY MINE chased the pace along the hedge into the far turn and faded.

Owners— 1, Claiborne Farm; 2, Alesso Al; 3, Stride Rite Racing Stable; 4, Van Worp Judson; 5, Oxenberg Bea & Montanari Marion; 6, Lewis James R Jr; 7, Weiss Richard M; 8, McDonnell Francis C; 9, Jacks or Better Farm Inc

Trainers—1, Mott William I; 2, Wilensky Herman; 3, Wolfson Milton W; 4, Croft Barry; 5, Plesa Edward Jr; 6, Tortora Emanuel; 7, Fawkes David; 8, Handy George R; 9, Hatchett James

Scratched— R. Associate (11Sep03 7CRC1), Patriotic Flame (26Aug03 7CRC1), Regal Bear (1Sep03 10SAR5).

$2 Pick Three (5-9-10) Paid $9.20; Pick Three Pool $37,017.
$1 Pick Four (7-5-9-10) Paid $173.00; Pick Four Pool $122,075.

EIGHTH RACE
Keeneland
OCTOBER 11, 2003

1⅛ MILES. (Turf)(1.45^{4}) 20th Running of THE QUEEN ELIZABETH II CHALLENGE CUP. Grade I. Purse $500,000 FOR FILLIES, THREE YEARS OLD. By invitation with no nomination or starting fee. The owner of the winner to receive $310,000, with $100,000 to second, $50,000 to third, $25,000 to fourth and $15,000 to fifth. Weight 121 lbs. The Keeneland Association will invite a representative field of ten fillies to compete. The field will be drawn by the usual time of closing. A gold julep cup will be presented to the owner of the winner. A silver julep cup will be presented to the winning trainer and jockey. HAGGIN COURSE.

Value of Race: $500,000 Winner $310,000; second $100,000; third $50,000; fourth $25,000; fifth $15,000. Mutuel Pool $598,239.00 Exacta Pool $369,221.00 Quinella Pool $12,793.00 Trifecta Pool $305,634.00 Superfecta Pool $77,245.00

Last Raced	Horse	M/Eqt.	A.Wt	PP	St	¼	½	¾	Str	Fin	Jockey	Odds $1
17Aug03 ^{9}Sar^{3}	Film Maker	Lb	3 121	9	4	4^{hd}	4^{1}	$4^{1\frac{1}{2}}$	$3^{\frac{1}{2}}$	1no	Prado E S	11.60
1Jun03 CHY^{1}	Maiden Tower-GB		3 121	3	3	1^{1}	$1^{1\frac{1}{2}}$	1^{2}	$1^{1\frac{1}{2}}$	$2^{\frac{3}{4}}$	Flores D R	4.10
14Sep03 Lch^{8}	Casual Look	L	3 121	7	9	10	$9^{\frac{1}{2}}$	9^{1}	$6^{2\frac{1}{2}}$	$3^{\frac{3}{4}}$	Albarado R J	6.90
28Jly03 ^{8}Sar^{2}	Ocean Drive	L	3 121	10	6	$2^{\frac{1}{2}}$	2^{hd}	3^{2}	2^{hd}	$4^{\frac{3}{4}}$	Velazquez J R	9.00
7Sep03 ^{9}Bel^{3}	Campsie Fells-UAE	L	3 121	4	7	$3^{\frac{1}{2}}$	$5^{\frac{1}{2}}$	$5^{\frac{1}{2}}$	5^{hd}	5^{1}	Blanc B	22.10
13Sep03 ^{8}AP^{1}	Aud	L	3 121	6	8	$9^{\frac{1}{2}}$	10	10	$8^{1\frac{1}{2}}$	$6^{1\frac{1}{2}}$	Peck B D	44.20
6Sep03 ^{7}Bel^{3}	Spoken Fur	L	3 121	1	2	7^{1}	$8^{1\frac{1}{2}}$	$8^{\frac{1}{2}}$	7^{hd}	7no	Velasquez C	7.80
24Aug03 ^{9}Dmr^{3}	Personal Legend	Lb	3 121	2	1	$8^{1\frac{1}{2}}$	7^{hd}	$7^{\frac{1}{2}}$	10	8^{hd}	Santos J A	9.20
7Sep03 ^{9}Bel^{7}	Sand Springs	L	3 121	5	10	6^{hd}	$3^{1\frac{1}{2}}$	2^{hd}	4^{hd}	$9^{2\frac{1}{2}}$	Guidry M	10.20
7Sep03 ^{9}Bel^{1}	Indy Five Hundred	L	3 121	8	5	5^{hd}	$6^{\frac{1}{2}}$	$6^{\frac{1}{2}}$	9^{hd}	10	Day P	2.00

OFF AT 4:46 Start Good For All But SAND SPRINGS Won driving. Course firm.
TIME :23^{3}, :47^{3}, 1:11^{3}, 1:35^{4}, 1:47^{4} (:23.62, :47.74, 1:11.61, 1:35.84, 1:47.82)

$2 Mutuel Prices:

9–FILM MAKER	25.20	10.00	6.40
3–MAIDEN TOWER–GB		6.60	4.80
7–CASUAL LOOK			4.80

$2 EXACTA 9–3 PAID $168.80 $2 QUINELLA 3–9 PAID $92.40 $2 TRIFECTA 9–3–7 PAID $1,655.80 $2 SUPERFECTA 9–3–7–10 PAID $13,904.00

Dk. b. or br. f, (Mar), by Dynaformer–Miss Du Bois, by Mr. Prospector. Trainer Motion H Graham. Bred by TAC Holdings Inc (Ky).

FILM MAKER, in hand while racing three or four wide from early on within easy striking distance, continued four wide into the stretch, drifted in when soundly roused right handed in the final furlong, bumped with MAIDEN TOWER (GB) in the final sixteenth, bumped twice more with that one in deep stretch and was up in the final nod. MAIDEN TOWER (GB) came out at the start bumping CAMPSIE FELLS (UAE), moved to the fore coming to the wire for the first time, went along under careful handling while racing in the three path, opened a clear advantage entering the far turn, remained clear into the final furlong, was bumped entering the final sixteenth by FILM MAKER when that one leaned in, came out under left-handed whipping and bumped twice more with that one and was outfinished in the last lunge. CASUAL LOOK, outrun to the far turn, raced in behind horses four wide, split foes five wide in the final furlong and was going well at the end. OCEAN DRIVE, close up from the outset, was maneuvered in behind of front-running MAIDEN TOWER (UAE) on the backstretch, dropped inside that one when straightened for the drive and was empty late. CAMPSIE FELLS (UAE), bumped from both sides at the start, raced within easy striking distance while near the inside to the stretch, came out six wide for the drive and failed to respond at the end. AUD, outrun until the stretch and four wide, worked her way out seven wide for the drive but lacked a serious late response. SPOKEN FUR, unhurried and racing near the inside into the stretch, eased out three wide but failed to rally. PERSONAL LEGEND, in behind horses for six furlongs, moved out seven or eight wide for the stretch run but never menaced. SAND SPRINGS stumbled at the start, ducked in bumping CAMPSIE FELLS (UAE), was never far back, moved up to press the pace leaving the backstretch, raced forwardly into the stretch and faltered. INDY FIVE HUNDRED raced in contentio n four or five wide to the stretch and tired. Stewards posted the inquiry sign involving the stretch run. No action was taken.

Owners— 1, Courtlandt Farms; 2, Darley Stable Mohammed Al Maktoum; 3, Farish William S; 4, Baskin Bonnie & Sy; 5, Darley Stable Mohammed Al Maktoum; 6, Willmott Stables; 7, Amerman Racing Stables Mr & Mrs Joh; 8, Gann Edmund A; 9, Willmott Stables; 10, Georgica Stable

Trainers—1, Motion H Graham; 2, Pantall Henri-Alex; 3, Balding Andrew; 4, Pletcher Todd A; 5, Clement Christophe; 6, Reinstedler Anthony; 7, Frankel Robert; 8, Frankel Robert; 9, Reinstedler Anthony; 10, Barbara Robert

$2 Pick Three (4–4–9) Paid $3,385.20; Pick Three Pool $45,974.

EIGHTH RACE
Santa Anita
OCTOBER 11, 2003

ABOUT 6½ FURLONGS. (Turf)(1.11^{2}) 35th Running of THE SEN. KEN MADDY HANDICAP. Grade III. Purse $100,000 FOR FILLIES AND MARES, THREE YEARS OLD AND UPWARD. By subscription of $100 each if made on or before Thursday, October 2 or by supplementary nomination of $2,000 by Sunday, October 5. All horses shall pay $1,000 to start, with $100,000 added. The added monies and all fees to be divided 60% to the winner, 20% to second, 12% to third, 6% to fourth and 2% to fifth. Closed October 2 with 20 nominations. (Rail at 8 feet, hill zero).

Value of Race: $112,000 Winner $67,200; second $22,400; third $13,440; fourth $6,720; fifth $2,240. Mutuel Pool $519,709.00 Exacta Pool $282,069.00 Quinella Pool $33,177.00 Trifecta Pool $284,174.00 Superfecta Pool $116,260.00

Last Raced	Horse	M/Eqt.	A.	Wt	PP	St	¼	½	Str	Fin	Jockey	Odds $1
13Aug03 ^{7}Dmr^{2}	Belleski	LB	4	117	8	1	5^{2}	5^{1}	$4^{1\frac{1}{2}}$	1^{2}	Espinoza V	1.90
2Aug03 ^{8}Dmr^{3}	Buffythecenterfold	LBb	3	116	2	6	$4^{2\frac{1}{2}}$	2^{1}	$2^{\frac{1}{2}}$	2^{1}	Solis A	a-3.70
19Sep03 ^{10}Fpx^{3}	Icantgoforthat	LBb	4	115	3	3	1^{1}	1^{1}	$1^{1\frac{1}{2}}$	3^{1}	Baze T C	39.00
28Aug03 ^{7}Dmr^{2}	Carbon Copy-GB	LB	5	116	7	8	8^{hd}	8^{hd}	6^{1}	4no	Stevens G L	5.80
29Aug03 ^{6}Dmr^{1}	Cee's Valley Girl	LBb	4	113	1	5	2^{hd}	$4^{1\frac{1}{2}}$	$3^{1\frac{1}{2}}$	$5^{\frac{1}{2}}$	Smith M E	11.70
1Aug03 ^{7}Dmr^{6}	Gabriellina Giof-GB	LBb	5	114	10	2	9^{2}	$9^{2\frac{1}{2}}$	5^{hd}	6^{1}	Pedroza M A	39.50
1Aug03 ^{7}Dmr^{1}	Roberta's Mango	LB	4	118	6	7	6^{hd}	6^{hd}	8^{hd}	7^{1}	Nakatani C S	3.70
20Aug03 ^{7}Sar^{7}	Dreamers Glory	LB	4	113	5	10	$7^{1\frac{1}{2}}$	$7^{1\frac{1}{2}}$	9^{2}	$8^{\frac{1}{2}}$	Valdivia J Jr	a-3.70
10Sep03 ^{6}Dmr^{8}	Brocky's Dream-AU	LBb	5	113	9	9	10	10	10	9no	Almeida G F	39.60
5Apr03 ^{4}SA^{3}	Paga-ARG	LB	6	115	4	4	3^{hd}	3^{hd}	7^{hd}	10	Krone J A	7.00

a-Coupled: Buffythecenterfold and Dreamers Glory.

OFF AT 4:11 Start Good. Won driving. Course firm.
TIME :21^{3}, :43^{2}, 1:06^{2}, 1:12^{1} (:21.76, :43.56, 1:06.56, 1:12.37)

$2 Mutuel Prices:

8-BELLESKI	5.80	3.80	2.80
1-BUFFYTHECENTERFOLD (a-entry)		5.00	3.40
3-ICANTGOFORTHAT			8.00

$1 EXACTA 8-1 PAID $14.40 $2 QUINELLA 1-8 PAID $14.60 $1 TRIFECTA 8-1-3 PAID $166.70 $1 SUPERFECTA 8-1-3-7 PAID $1,307.00

B. f, by Polish Numbers-Rangoon Belle, by Alysheba. Trainer Sadler John W. Bred by Camball & Duignan & Garvin (Ky).

BELLESKI chased outside down the hill, came out three deep into the stretch and rallied under some urging to prove best. BUFFYTHECENTERFOLD stalked between horses then a bit off the rail, bid between foes in deep stretch and held second. ICANTGOFORTHAT sped to the early lead, angled in leaving the hill, held on well until late stretch but was overtaken. CARBON COPY (GB) chased outside down the hill, came three deep into the stretch and found her best stride late. CEE'S VALLEY GIRL well placed stalking the pace along the inside to the stretch, weakened. GABRIELLINA GIOF (GB) pulled her way between horses early, angled in down the hill, remained inside in the stretch and could not offer the necessary late kick. ROBERTA'S MANGO chased outside a rival, came four wide into the stretch and did not rally. DREAMERS GLORY squeezed at the start, moved up inside to chase the pace, came out into the stretch and lacked the needed response. BROCKY'S DREAM (AUS) unhurried off the rail to the stretch, came out in midstretch and was not a threat. PAGA (ARG) broke through the gate prior to the start, came out at the break, stalked three deep then outside a rival and weakened in the stretch. Rail on hill at zero.

Owners— 1, Moss Mr & Mrs Jerome S; 2, Brian Allen A & Stronach Stables; 3, Broberg Andy & Knapp Palmer; 4, Red Baron's Barn LLC; 5, Wright Robert J; 6, Zetcher Arnold; 7, Lucky Ladies Stable LLC; 8, Stronach Stable; 9, Burns Mike & Kolbe Al; 10, Hubbard R D & Allred Edward C

Trainers—1, Sadler John W; 2, Stute Melvin F; 3, Knapp Steve; 4, Vienna Darrell; 5, Polanco Marcelo; 6, McAnally Ronald; 7, Canani Julio C; 8, Frankel Robert; 9, Carno Louis R; 10, Mandella Richard

Scratched— Swiss Lake (20Aug03 ^{7}DMR^{2}), Charm A Song (28Aug03 ^{4}DMR^{1}), Magarita Midnight (26Sep03 ^{8}AP^{2})

$2 Daily Double (5-8) Paid $61.60; Daily Double Pool $40,203.
$1 Pick Three (9-5-6/8/10) Paid $442.80; Pick Three Pool $77,669.

TENTH RACE
Belmont
OCTOBER 12, 2003

6½ FURLONGS. (1.14^{2}) ASTARITA S.. Grade II. Purse $150,000 (Up to $21,900 NYSBFOA) FOR FILLIES TWO YEARS OLD. By subscription of $150 each, which should accompany the nomination; $750 to pass the entry box; $750 to start. 120 lbs. Non-winners of $50,000 other than restricted allowed 3 lbs. Closed Saturday, September 27, 2003 with 23 Nominations.

Value of Race: $150,000 Winner $90,000; second $30,000; third $16,500; fourth $9,000; fifth $4,500. Mutuel Pool $394,572.00 Exacta Pool $316,384.00 Trifecta Pool $286,494.00

Last Raced	Horse	M/Eqt.	A.	Wt	PP	St	¼	½	Str	Fin	Jockey	Odds $1
13Sep03 ^{2}Pim^{1}	Spectacular Moon	L	2	117	8	1	8^{hd}	6^{5}	4^{6}	1^{nk}	Chavez J F	28.00
14Sep03 ^{6}Bel^{4}	Feline Story	L	2	120	6	5	$5^{3\frac{1}{2}}$	5^{6}	2^{3}	$2^{1\frac{1}{4}}$	Prado E S	3.25
21Sep03 ^{9}Mth^{1}	Smokey Glacken	L	2	117	1	7	4^{1}	$3^{\frac{1}{2}}$	1^{hd}	3^{13}	Santos J A	4.20
30Aug03 ^{2}PrM^{1}	Lovethatlegend	L	2	117	2	3	1^{hd}	4^{hd}	$5^{\frac{1}{2}}$	$4^{2\frac{1}{4}}$	Migliore R	8.80
21Aug03 ^{8}Sar^{1}	Ana's Lady Bird	L	2	117	4	6	2^{hd}	1^{hd}	3^{hd}	$5^{\frac{1}{2}}$	Bailey J D	1.40
18Sep03 ^{6}Bel^{1}	Forty Moves	L	2	117	9	2	$3^{\frac{1}{2}}$	$2^{1\frac{1}{2}}$	6^{6}	$6^{\frac{1}{2}}$	Fragoso P	26.00
21Sep03 ^{6}Bel^{1}	Freeroll	L	2	117	5	8	9	8^{3}	$7^{2\frac{1}{2}}$	$7^{5\frac{1}{4}}$	Castellano J J	14.00
1Sep03 ^{11}Mth^{1}	Cosmic Wish	L	2	117	7	4	6^{2}	$7^{\frac{1}{2}}$	8^{6}	$8^{3\frac{1}{4}}$	Clemente Alfredo	20.40
8Sep03 ^{8}Del^{1}	Ms. Trick Or Treat	Lb	2	117	3	9	$7^{5\frac{1}{2}}$	9	9	9	Velazquez J R	23.40

OFF AT 5:30 Start Good. Won driving. Track sloppy.
TIME :21^{2}, :44^{2}, 1:10^{2}, 1:17 (:21.55, :44.47, 1:10.48, 1:17.16)

$2 Mutuel Prices:

8-SPECTACULAR MOON	58.00	17.40	8.90
6-FELINE STORY		4.50	3.30
1-SMOKEY GLACKEN			4.10

$2 EXACTA 8-6 PAID $284.00 $2 TRIFECTA 8-6-1 PAID $1,665.00

Dk. b. or br. f, (Mar), by Migrating Moon-Doctor Danielle, by Spectacular Bid. Trainer Alecci John V. Bred by (Fla).

SPECTACULAR MOON ducked in at the start, was bumped, dropped back early, raced wide, finished determinedly from the far outside and was along in the final strides. FELINE STORY was bumped after the start, raced close up early, rallied four wide nearing the stretch, reached the front inside the eighth pole and dug in gamely but could not resist the winner. SMOKEY GLACKEN raced close up inside early, angled out and rallied wide approaching the stretch, earned a short lead in upper stretch and weakened in the final furlong. LOVETHATLEGEND contested the pace along the inside and tired in the stretch. ANA'S LADY BIRD contested the pace while between rivals and tired in the stretch. FORTY MOVES contested the pace while three wide and tired. FREEROLL was bumped after the start, stumbled, dropped back early, raced inside and had no rally. COSMIC WISH was bumped after the start, raced inside and tired. MS. TRICK OR TREAT drifted out entering the turn, raced wide thereafter and tired.

Owners— 1, Alecci John V; 2, Robsham Einar P; 3, Moore Susan & John; 4, Karches Peter F; 5, Oceanfront Properties & Asmussen Ke; 6, Evans Edward P; 7, Brodsky Alan; 8, Pavlish Patricia; 9, Joseph Boff Steven Oyer & Angela Le

Trainers—1, Alecci John V; 2, Hough Stanley M; 3, Jerkens James A; 4, Lewis Lisa L; 5, Asmussen Steven M; 6, Hennig Mark; 7, Hennig Mark; 8, Sobol Alan; 9, DeMasi Kathleen A

EIGHTH RACE
Keeneland
OCTOBER 12, 2003

6 FURLONGS. (1.07^{3}) THOROUGHBRED CLUB OF AMERICA S.. Grade III. Purse $125,000 FOR FILLIES AND MARES, THREE YEARS OLD AND UPWARD. By subscription of $125 each which should accompany the nomination; $1,250 to enter and start. Weight; Three year old fillies, 122 lbs., Older, 124 lbs. Non-winners of a Graded stakes in 2003 allowed 2 lbs.; a sweepstakes in 2003, 4 lbs.; $30,000 twice in 2003, 6 lbs. A gold julep cup and a Thoroughbred Club of America trophy will be presented to the winning owner.

Value of Race: $125,000 Winner $77,500; second $25,000; third $12,500; fourth $6,250; fifth $3,750. Mutuel Pool $295,413.00 Exacta Pool $200,643.00 Quinella Pool $10,180.00 Trifecta Pool $165,173.00 Superfecta Pool $53,920.00

Last Raced	Horse	M/Eqt.	A.Wt	PP	St	¼	½	Str	Fin	Jockey	Odds $1
19Sep03 8AP1	Summer Mis	Lb	4 122	7	4	3½	32½	31	1hd	Douglas R R	11.90
6Sep03 9TP1	Don't Countess Out		4 122	6	3	2½	2hd	1hd	2no	Thompson T J	7.50
6Sep03 9TP3	Born To Dance	Lbf	4 122	2	1	6hd	61½	52	3nk	Day P	8.00
13Sep03 6Bel1	Bauhauser-ARG	L	5 124	1	2	1hd	1hd	2hd	42½	Lanerie C J	1.60
16Aug03 3AP1	Savorthetime	L	4 122	9	6	7½	51	42	5½	Albarado R J	5.40
27Sep03 8Mth3	Bruanna	Lb	5 122	10	9	10	10	71	61¾	Velasquez C	39.30
30Aug03 7ElP1	Jodys Deelite	L	3 116	5	8	9½	9hd	8½	7½	Melancon L	56.60
12Jly03 10LaD1	Distinctive Code	Lb	4 122	8	5	41	41	62	8½	Sellers S J	8.30
6Sep03 9TP4	Vicki Vallencourt	L	4 122	4	10	81½	82½	9hd	93½	Bejarano R	4.50
18Sep03 9TP1	Crow Jane	L	3 116	3	7	5hd	7hd	10	10	Lovato F Jr	36.40

OFF AT 4:46 Start Good For All But DISTINCTIVE CODE Won driving. Track fast.
TIME :21^{2}, :44^{2}, :56^{3}, 1:09^{3} (:21.48, :44.44, :56.74, 1:09.77)

$2 Mutuel Prices:

8–SUMMER MIS	25.80	10.80	6.40
7–DON'T COUNTESS OUT		7.80	4.20
3–BORN TO DANCE			4.80

$2 EXACTA 8–7 PAID $206.80 $2 QUINELLA 7–8 PAID $73.60 $2 TRIFECTA 8–7–3 PAID $1,682.80 $2 SUPERFECTA 8–7–3–2 PAID $5,823.20

Dk. b. or br. f, by Summer Squall–Julie Mis, by Miswaki. Trainer Mitchell Anthony. Bred by R Otto Stables Inc (Ill).

SUMMER MIS forced the pace from early on while three abreast, came a bit wider into the lane, closed determinedly to reach the front in the final 20 yards, then gamely held sway. DON'T COUNTESS OUT attended the pace from between rivals from early on, gained a slim advantage approaching the final furlong, was headed by the winner in the final sixteenth and held on stubbornly the remainder. BORN TO DANCE, close up between foes early, was eased back in behind the dueling leaders on the backstretch, saved ground into the final furlong, altered course outside five wide leaving the sixteenth pole and finished with good energy. BAUHAUSER (ARG), moved up along the inside to gain a narrow lead early, battled with DON'T COUNTESSOUT and SUMMER MISS, managed a slight edge into the stretch and grudgingly weakened. SAVORTHETIME, never far back and five or six wide most of the way, was checked off BORN TO DANCE'S heels while tiring in the final sixteenth. BRUANNA, nine wide on the backstretch while outrun, moved near the inside on the turn, continued near the rail into the stretch and improved position. JODYS DEELITE was outrun. DISTINCTIVE CODE stumbled at the start, recovered to race in contention five wide to the lane and tired. VICKI VALLENCOURT, in a bit tight early and outrun four wide for a half, came out 10 wide for the drive and never fired. CROW JANE, three or four wide, weakened on the turn.

Owners— 1, Richard Otto Stables; 2, Southern Pride Stable LLC; 3, Parra Rosendo G; 4, Heiligbrodt Racing Stable L William; 5, Robertson Brenda & Phillip; 6, Old Coach Farm Michael E Gorham & J; 7, Rutherford Mike G; 8, Courtney Billie; 9, Rashinski Ron & Ricki; 10, Totier Creek Farm

Trainers—1, Mitchell Anthony; 2, Jones J Larry; 3, Jackson James R; 4, Asmussen Steven M; 5, Stall Albert M Jr; 6, Gorham Michael E; 7, Stewart Dallas; 8, Robideaux Larry R Jr; 9, Kenneally Eddie; 10, Thornbury Jeffrey D

Scratched— Knock Twice (24Aug03 5ELP3)

$2 Pick Three (5/6/7/8–9–8) Paid $472.20; Pick Three Pool $29,737.

NINTH RACE
Belmont
OCTOBER 13, 2003

1⅛ MILES. (Inner Turf)(1.45^{3}) PEBBLES H.. Grade III. Purse $100,000 INNER TURF. (Up to $19,400 NYSBFOA) A HANDICAP FOR FILLIES THREE YEARS OLD. By subscription of $100 each, which should accompany the nomination; $500 to pass the entry box; $500 to start, with $100,000 added. The added money and all fees to be divided 60% to the winner, 20% to second, 11% to third, 6% to fourth and 3% to fifth. Trophies will be presented to the winning owner, trainer and jockey. The New York Racing Association reserves the right to transfer this race to the Main Track. In the event that this race is taken off the turf, it may be subject to downgrading upon review by the Graded Stakes Committee. Closed Saturday, September 27, 2003 with 33 Nominations.

Value of Race: $110,300 Winner $66,180; second $22,060; third $12,133; fourth $6,618; fifth $3,309. Mutuel Pool $369,975.00 Exacta Pool $322,529.00 Trifecta Pool $309,727.00

Last Raced	Horse	M/Eqt.	A.Wt	PP	St	¼	½	¾	Str	Fin	Jockey	Odds $1
24Sep03 8Bel1	Betty's Wish	L	3 116	7	5	3½	3½	31½	13½	13¾	Velazquez J R	0.80
31Aug03 9Sar2	Mystery Itself	L	3 112	5	3	62½	5½	51	2½	21	Castellano J J	28.00
7Sep03 9Bel6	Andover Lady	L	3 114	2	6	7	7	6½	4½	3½	Prado E S	3.55
21Sep03 5Bel2	Harmonist	L	3 113	3	1	4½	4½	4hd	3hd	41¾	Espinoza J L	15.30
24Sep03 8Bel2	Where We Left Off-GB	L	3 114	1	7	5hd	6hd	7	615	5¾	Santos J A	3.80
21Sep03 5Bel6	Boom Bah Yay	Lb	3 112	6	2	21½	21	2½	52	618	Luzzi M J	44.75
27Sep03 9Pim5	Little Miss Pamela	L	3 115	4	4	1hd	1½	1hd	7	7	Migliore R	13.40

OFF AT 5:12 Start Good. Won driving. Course good.
TIME :24^{3}, :49^{1}, 1:14^{4}, 1:39^{1}, 1:51 (:24.64, :49.22, 1:14.80, 1:39.26, 1:51.00)

$2 Mutuel Prices:

7–BETTY'S WISH	3.60	3.10	2.10
5–MYSTERY ITSELF		12.00	3.60
2–ANDOVER LADY			2.40

$2 EXACTA 7–5 PAID $50.00 $2 TRIFECTA 7–5–2 PAID $187.00

Ch. f, (Apr), by Gold Case–Holy Land Band, by Dixieland Band. Trainer Frankel Robert. Bred by Dr Donald S Dreyfuss (Fla).

BETTY'S WISH was rated along outside, raced three wide on both turns, responded when roused and drew clear under a drive. MYSTERY ITSELF was rated outside, raced three wide on both turns and finished gamely to earn the place award. ANDOVER LADY was rated along early, put in a four wide run on the second turn and had little left for the stretch drive. HARMONIST was rated along early, raced inside and had no rally. WHERE WE LEFT OFF (GB) was rated along early, raced inside and had no response when roused. BOOM BAH YAY prompted the pace from the outside and tired in the stretch. LITTLE MISS PAMELA set the pace along the inside for three quarters and tired.

Owners— 1, Gann Edmund A; 2, Lael Stables; 3, Farmer Tracy; 4, Pont Street Stable; 5, Moyglare Stud Farm Ltd; 6, Dogwood Stable; 7, Salomone Mark E

Trainers—1, Frankel Robert; 2, Matz Michael R; 3, Kimmel John C; 4, Carroll Del W II; 5, Clement Christophe; 6, Orseno Joseph; 7, Trimmer Richard K

Scratched— Devotion Unbridled (24Sep03 2BEL1), Beauty On Duty (1Aug03 3SAR1)

SEVENTH RACE
Meadowlands
OCTOBER 17, 2003

$1\frac{1}{16}$ MILES. (Turf)(1.39^{2}) VIOLET H.. Grade III. Purse $150,000 A HANDICAP FOR FILLIES AND MARES, THREE YEARS OLD AND UPWARD. By subscription of $100 each, which should accompany the nomination and $2,000 to pass the entry box. The owner of the winner to receive $90,000, $30,000 to second, $16,500 to third,$9,000 to fourth and $4,500 to fifth. The winning owner, trainer and jockey to receive a trophy. Closed Friday, October 3, 2003 with 35 nominations. NOMINATIONS CLOSED Friday, October 3, 2003 with THIRTY FOUR (34) (Rail at 0 Feet).

Value of Race: $150,000 Winner $90,000; second $30,000; third $16,500; fourth $9,000; fifth $4,500. Mutuel Pool $94,027.00 Exacta Pool $75,837.00 Trifecta Pool $57,558.00

Last Raced	Horse	M/Eqt.	A.	Wt	PP	St	¼	½	¾	Str	Fin	Jockey	Odds $1
20Sep03 ^{9}Bel^{2}	Dancal-IR	L	5	116	6	3	1^{hd}	1^{1}	$1^{\frac{1}{2}}$	1^{2}	1^{2}	Castellano J J	1.80
6Sep03 ^{9}Del^{1}	Madeira Mist-IR	L	4	116	8	2	$4^{\frac{1}{2}}$	$2^{\frac{1}{2}}$	$2^{\frac{1}{2}}$	$2^{1\frac{1}{2}}$	$2^{1\frac{3}{4}}$	Prado E S	3.70
20Sep03 ^{9}Bel^{3}	Something Ventured	Lb	4	116	5	7	$5^{\frac{1}{2}}$	$5^{\frac{1}{2}}$	$3^{1\frac{1}{2}}$	$3^{\frac{1}{2}}$	$3^{\frac{3}{4}}$	Velazquez J R	2.90
20Sep03 ^{9}Bel^{8}	Delta Princess	L	4	115	3	4	3^{hd}	4^{hd}	4^{hd}	$4^{\frac{1}{2}}$	$4^{\frac{3}{4}}$	Luzzi M J	3.60
30Aug03 ^{8}Pha^{1}	Caught In The Rain	L	4	114	4	6	7^{2}	6^{hd}	$5^{1\frac{1}{2}}$	$5^{\frac{1}{2}}$	5^{hd}	King E L Jr	13.60
6Sep03 ^{9}Pim^{1}	Cruise Along	Lb	5	116	7	8	8	8	$7^{1\frac{1}{2}}$	6^{1}	6^{3}	Karamanos H A	21.40
27Sep03 ^{9}Mth^{2}	Nault	L	3	112	1	5	6^{hd}	7^{1}	$6^{\frac{1}{2}}$	7^{4}	$7^{4\frac{3}{4}}$	Bridgmohan S X	60.30
6Sep03 ^{9}Mth^{3}	Cocktailsandreams	L	6	115	2	1	$2^{\frac{1}{2}}$	3^{hd}	8	8	8	Velez J A Jr	18.00

OFF AT 9:53 Start Good. Won driving. Course good.
TIME :24^{4}, :49^{3}, 1:13^{4}, 1:37^{2}, 1:43^{3} (:24.88, :49.79, 1:13.80, 1:37.59, 1:43.69)

$2 Mutuel Prices:				
	7–DANCAL–IR	5.60	3.60	2.40
	9–MADEIRA MIST–IR		5.00	2.80
	5–SOMETHING VENTURED			2.40

$2 EXACTA 7–9 PAID $25.20 $2 TRIFECTA 7–9–5 PAID $55.80

B. m, by Mujadil–Majesty's Nurse*Ire, by Indian King. Trainer Pletcher Todd A. Bred by Kavanagh Eddie (Ire).

DANCAL (IRE) set a comfortable pace racing just off the rail, drew clear when roused in upper stretch and was kept clear under right hand urging. MADEIRA MIST (IRE) raced three wide early on, then pressed the pace outside of DANCAL (IRE) and stayed on gamely to earn the place award. SOMETHING VENTURED stalked outside, bid three wide midway on the far turn and finished evenly. DELTA PRINCESS raced close up between rivals, angled over to the inside on the second turn and lacked a rally in the lane. CAUGHT IN THE RAIN rated outside a rival and had no rally. CRUISE ALONG trailed the field, came four wide into the lane and failed to sustain a bid. NAULT saved ground, angled out three wide approaching the stretch and failed to respond. COCKTAILSANDREAMS was well rated inside and dropped back on the far turn.

Owners— 1, Aronstam Marlon; 2, Skymarc Farm Inc; 3, Wiemer Irvin & McLane John; 4, Khaled Saud b; 5, Heiligbrodt Racing Stable & New Wal; 6, Bender Sondra D; 7, Gill Michael J; 8, Generazio Patricia A

Trainers—1, Pletcher Todd A; 2, Clement Christophe; 3, Pletcher Todd A; 4, Mott William I; 5, Preciado Guadalupe; 6, Murray Lawrence E; 7, Shuman Mark; 8, Generazio Frank Jr

Scratched— Vespers (11Sep03 ^{7}BEL^{2})

$2 Pick Three (1–5–7) Paid $333.40; Pick Three Pool $10,229.

EIGHTH RACE
Hawthorne
OCTOBER 18, 2003

1⅛ MILES. (Turf)(1.44^{3}) HAWTHORNE DERBY. Grade III. Purse $250,000 FOR THREE-YEAR-OLDS. By subscription of $100 each, which shall accompany the nomination, $1,500 to pass the entry box, $1,500 additional to start. With $250,000 Guaranteed, of which 60 percent to the winner, 20 percent to second, 11 percent to third, 6 percent to fourth, 3 percent to fifth. Weight 122 lbs. Non-winners of $100,000 at a mile or over in 2003 allowed, 3 lbs.; of $55,000 at a mile or over in 2003, 5 lbs.; of $55,000 at a mile or over anytime, 7 lbs.; of $25,000 or $15,000twice at a mile or over in 2003, 9 lbs.; of $20,000 at a mile or over at any time, 11 lbs.Nominations closed Wednesday, October 8, 2003 with 29.

Value of Race: $250,000 Winner $150,000; second $50,000; third $27,500; fourth $15,000; fifth $7,500. Mutuel Pool $251,652.00 Exacta Pool $149,903.00 Trifecta Pool $121,167.00 Superfecta Pool $35,514.00

Last Raced	Horse	M/Eqt.	A.	Wt	PP	St	¼	½	¾	Str	Fin	Jockey	Odds $1
20Sep03 ^{9}AP^{1}	False Promises	L	3	115	2	9	9^{hd}	7^{hd}	6^{hd}	$4^{\frac{1}{2}}$	1^{1}	Marquez C H Jr	7.50
7Sep03 ^{6}AP^{1}	Megoman	Lb	3	115	9	7	$7^{\frac{1}{2}}$	5^{hd}	5^{1}	1^{2}	2^{1}	Perez E E	7.40
20Sep03 ^{8}GLD^{2}	Beau Classic	Lbf	3	113	3	3	$2^{\frac{1}{2}}$	$2^{1\frac{1}{2}}$	2^{1}	2^{1}	3^{nk}	Martinez Luis	85.10
4Oct03 ^{10}Haw^{4}	Scottago	L	3	116	7	11	11	10^{hd}	9^{hd}	$6^{1\frac{1}{2}}$	4no	Razo E Jr	19.30
21Sep03 ^{9}Bel^{6}	Lismore Knight	L	3	122	1	6	4^{hd}	4^{1}	$4^{\frac{1}{2}}$	$3^{\frac{1}{2}}$	5^{hd}	Arroyo N Jr	1.50
13Sep03 ^{6}Pim^{3}	Foufa's Warrior	Lbf	3	122	11	10	5^{1}	8^{1}	$10^{\frac{1}{2}}$	5^{hd}	$6^{\frac{1}{2}}$	Rose J	5.10
27Sep03 ^{11}Bel^{1}	Sir Walter Rahy	L	3	115	10	1	10^{2}	11	8^{1}	$7^{\frac{1}{2}}$	$7^{2\frac{1}{4}}$	Emigh C A	6.40
20Sep03 ^{5}LaD^{2}	Gentlemen J J	Lb	3	118	4	8	6^{hd}	6^{1}	$7^{\frac{1}{2}}$	8^{2}	$8^{2\frac{1}{4}}$	Martin E M Jr	7.50
13Sep03 ^{10}AP^{3}	Buzzle Ways	L	3	115	6	5	$3^{\frac{1}{2}}$	$3^{\frac{1}{2}}$	3^{hd}	9^{7}	$9^{9\frac{3}{4}}$	Laviolette B S	100.20
20Sep03 ^{8}GLD^{4}	Akatsakat	L	3	115	8	4	8^{hd}	9^{1}	11	10	10	Molina Tommy	90.50
21Sep03 ^{3}BM^{1}	Blue Blood Boot	L	3	115	5	2	$1^{\frac{1}{2}}$	$1^{\frac{1}{2}}$	$1^{\frac{1}{2}}$	—	—	Sterling L J Jr	10.40

OFF AT 4:28 Start Good. Won driving. Course firm.
TIME :23^{2}, :47^{2}, 1:11^{4}, 1:36, 1:48^{2} (:23.43, :47.55, 1:11.82, 1:36.14, 1:48.48)

$2 Mutuel Prices:				
	2–FALSE PROMISES	17.00	7.00	5.60
	9–MEGOMAN		7.20	4.40
	3–BEAU CLASSIC			28.40

$2 EXACTA 2–9 PAID $122.80 $2 TRIFECTA 2–9–3 PAID $5,048.60 $2 SUPERFECTA 2–9–3–ALL PAID $17,757.00

B. g, (Mar), by Jules–Stormy Divorce, by Storm Bird. Trainer Granitz Anthony J. Bred by Arther I Appleton (Fla).

FALSE PROMISES was void of early speed while saving ground, rallied in the stretch, split horses late and prevailed. MEGOMAN raced off the rail near the middle of the field, rallied out in the course to a clear lead then could not hold off the winner. BEAU CLASSIC pressed the pace from just outside and held on well in the drive. SCOTTAGO lacked speed and gained belatedly. LISMORE KNIGHT raced close up inside but lacked a winning bid. FOUFA'S WARRIOR lacked speed and made a bid in the stretch but flattened out. SIR WALTER RAHY never reached a contending position. GENTLEMEN J J was never a factor. BUZZLE WAYS raced close up off the rail and gave way. AKATSAKAT was always outrun. BLUE BLOOD BOOT set the pace from the inside then ducked through the rail in upper stretch.

Owners— 1, Maracich David; 2, Three Diamonds Stable; 3, Carlesimo John; 4, Jer-Mar Stable LLC; 5, Pletcher J J & Simon Barry; 6, Bender Sondra D; 7, Ronald A Nicholson & Caesar P Nicho; 8, Rancha Fresa Inc; 9, Orion Stables; 10, Mast Thouroughbreds LLC; 11, Everest Stables

Trainers—1, Granitz Anthony J; 2, Bettis Charles L; 3, Miller Robert M; 4, Robertson Hugh H; 5, Pletcher Todd A; 6, Murray Lawrence E; 7, Toner James J; 8, Leggio Andrew Jr; 9, McCoy James B; 10, Gorham Robert M; 11, Knight Terry

$2 Pick Three (2–12–2) Paid $2,992.80; Pick Three Pool $7,981.
$2 Pick Six (6–1/6–9–2–12–2) 4
Correct Paid $39.00; Pick Six Pool $2,201; Carryover Pool $11,304.

NINTH RACE
Keeneland
OCTOBER 18, 2003

$1\frac{1}{16}$ MILES. (Turf)(1.40^{1}) VALLEY VIEW S.. Grade III. Purse $100,000 FOR FILLIES, THREE YEARS OLD. By subscription of $100 each which should accompany the nomination; $1,000 to enter and start with $100,000 added, of which 62% of all monies to the owner of the winner, 20% to second, 10% to third, 5% to fourth and 3% to fifth. Weight; 123 lbs. Non-winners of a Graded or Group stakes on the turf allowed 4 lbs.; a sweepstakes, 7 lbs. The maximum number of starters for the Valley View will be limited to ten. In the event that more than ten fillies pass the entry box, the ten starters will be determined at the time with preference given to those nominees by condition eligibility. Starters to be named through the entry box by the usual time of closing. A gold julep cup will be presented to the owner of the winner. HAGGIN COURSE.

Value of Race: $112,900 Winner $69,998; second $22,580; third $11,290; fourth $5,645; fifth $3,387. Mutuel Pool $350,936.00 Exacta Pool $195,133.00 Quinella Pool $7,761.00 Trifecta Pool $172,153.00 Superfecta Pool $55,315.00

Last Raced	Horse	M/Eqt.	A.Wt	PP	St	¼	½	¾	Str	Fin	Jockey	Odds $1
20Sep03 9LaD1	Dyna Da Wyna	Lf	3 119	6	1	$3^{\frac12}$	3^{hd}	$3^{\frac12}$	2^{3}	$1^{\frac34}$	Day P	3.50
8Oct03 9Kee1	Mexican Moonlight	L	3 116	7	7	$4^{\frac12}$	2^{1}	$2^{1\frac12}$	$1^{\frac12}$	2^{3}	Lanerie C J	24.30
27Sep03 9Pim1	Derrianne	L	3 123	4	10	8^{1}	6^{hd}	7^{3}	3^{hd}	$3^{\frac12}$	Blanc B	2.20
13Sep03 8AP3	Julie's Prize	Lb	3 119	2	3	10	10	$8^{2\frac12}$	6^{2}	$4^{2\frac12}$	Albarado R J	4.30
24Aug03 8WO1	Shaconage	Lb	3 119	5	4	6^{hd}	7^{1}	6^{hd}	5^{hd}	$5^{4\frac14}$	Velasquez C	4.50
19Sep03 4AP1	Final Discount	L	3 116	3	2	5^{1}	$4^{\frac12}$	$5^{\frac12}$	7^{hd}	$6^{\frac34}$	Fires E	17.70
27Sep03 9Mth1	Feisty Bull	L	3 119	9	5	1^{hd}	$1^{\frac12}$	1^{hd}	$4^{\frac12}$	7^{1}	Sellers S J	8.70
9Aug03 8AP6	Lil Scout	L	3 116	1	9	$9^{2\frac12}$	9^{hd}	$4^{\frac12}$	$8^{4\frac12}$	$8^{3\frac34}$	McKee J	45.70
23Aug03 6AP7	Ruby's Reception	Lb	3 119	8	6	2^{3}	5^{1}	9^{hd}	$9^{1\frac12}$	9^{1}	Thompson T J	21.50
3Oct03 9Hoo8	Youcan'ttakeme	Lbf	3 119	10	8	7^{2}	$8^{1\frac12}$	10	10	10	Baze G	29.90

OFF AT 5:17 Start Good For All But DERRIANNE Won driving. Course firm.
TIME :23^{2}, :48^{1}, 1:13^{2}, 1:37^{1}, 1:43^{2} (:23.56, :48.39, 1:13.42, 1:37.33, 1:43.54)

$2 Mutuel Prices:				
	6–DYNA DA WYNA	9.00	5.60	3.40
	7–MEXICAN MOONLIGHT		17.80	6.60
	4–DERRIANNE			3.40

$2 EXACTA 6–7 PAID $117.00 $2 QUINELLA 6–7 PAID $89.80 $2 TRIFECTA 6–7–4 PAID $660.80 $2 SUPERFECTA 6–7–4–2 PAID $2,560.20

Gr/ro f, (May), by Doc's Leader–Dyna Peak, by Dynaformer. Trainer Walden W Elliott. Bred by Alan M Klein (Ky).

DYNA DA WYNA, nicely placed while racing in hand between foes four wide from early on, was patiently handled around the far turn, continued four wide into the stretch, was lightly roused at the furlong grounds and continued under energetic handling to wear down MEXICAN MOONLIGHT in the late going. MEXICAN MOONLIGHT followed the leaders five wide, inched to the front briefly leaving the backstretch while dueling outside of FEISTY BULL, was displaced on the lead by that one nearing the stretch, came again to take over, then failed to hold the winner safe. DERRIANNE lunged in the air at the start, bumped the side of the gate, settled inside, moved up steadily between horses four wide approaching the end of the backstretch, continued between rivals four wide into the final furlong and couldn't gain on the top two. JULIE'S PRIZE, reserved inside early, eased out four wide upon going a half, continued behind a wall of horses until the final quarter, swung out seven wide and offered a minor gain. SHACONAGE, within striking distance throughout while four or five wide, was empty the last eighth. FINAL DISCOUNT, well placed near the inside from the outset, continued within easy striking distance two or three wide into the stretch and flattened out. FEISTY BULL vied for the lead early while four or five wide, dueled outside of RUBY'S RECEPTION, managed a slight lead, was headed briefly entering the far turn between calls by MEXICAN MOONLIGHT, regained a slight edge, then faltered in the drive. LIL SCOUT broke to the inside in a tangle, was steadied, raced four wide into the backstretch, came out seven wide soon after, then never challenged. RUBY'S RECEPTION contested the pace inside of FEISTY BULL for nearly a half and gradually weakened. YOUCAN'TTAKEME, in contention five wide for a half, was steadied and swung out from behind horses at the three-eighths pole and finished thereafter.

Owners— 1, WinStar Farm LLC; 2, Pass Taggart Racing J T Pass & Patr; 3, Waterville Lake Stable; 4, Richard Otto Stables; 5, Sterling Stud; 6, Glen Hill Farm; 7, Feiss Daniel J; 8, Horned Owl Stable; 9, Oasis Racing Stable LLC; 10, Sarkowsky Herman

Trainers—1, Walden W Elliott; 2, Murphy Paul H; 3, Clement Christophe; 4, Mitchell Anthony; 5, Shirota Mitch; 6, Proctor Thomas F; 7, Rogers J Michael; 8, Smith Austin; 9, Jones J Larry; 10, Forster Grant T

Scratched— Snowdrops (28Jly03 8SAR8)

$2 Daily Double (2–6) Paid $92.00; Daily Double Pool $31,235.
$2 Pick Three (1–2–6) Paid $183.20; Pick Three Pool $42,867.
$2 Pick Four (2–1–2–6) Paid $4,874.80; Pick Four Pool $57,174.

FIFTH RACE

Santa Anita

OCTOBER 24, 2003

ABOUT 6½ FURLONGS. (Turf)(1.11²) MORVICH H.. Grade III. Purse $100,000 FOR THREE–YEAR–OLDS AND UPWARD. By subscription of $100 each if made on or before Thursday, October 16 or by supplementary nomination of $2,000 by Saturday, October 18. All horses shall pay $1,000 to start, with $100,000 added. The added monies and all fees to be divided 60% to the winner, 20% to second, 12% to third, 6% to fourth, and 2% to fifth. Nominations closed October 16 with 18. (Rail at 15 feet, zero on hill).

Value of Race: $110,800 Winner $66,480; second $22,160; third $13,296; fourth $6,648; fifth $2,216.   Mutuel Pool $559,094.00 Exacta Pool $342,733.00   Quinella Pool $33,389.00 Trifecta Pool $304,391.00 Superfecta Pool $107,002.00

Last Raced	Horse	M/Eqt. A.Wt	PP	St	¼	½	Str	Fin	Jockey	Odds $1
12Sep03 ¹¹Fpx¹	King Robyn	LB	3 117	3	3	11	11	1½	1hd	Solis A	2.60
5Oct03 ⁸SA⁵	Medecis–GB	LB	4 116	6	4	7³½	7¹½	3¹	2¾	Stevens G L	7.40
20Oct03 ⁷SA²	Geronimo–CH	LBb	4 115	1	7	5¹½	4hd	4½	3hd	Valenzuela P A	10.30
30Oct03 ⁶SA¹	Thunder Bullet	LBf	4 116	5	2	3¹½	2¹	2¹½	4½	Krone J A	3.80
23Aug03 ⁹Sar⁹	War Zone	LB	4 118	7	8	8hd	8hd	6²	5¹	Bailey J D	3.50
5Oct03 ⁸SA⁸	Apache Wings	LB	5 115	4	5	2hd	3¹	5¹	6²	Baze T C	10.00
5Oct03 ²SA¹	Gallant–GB	LB	6 113	2	6	4½	6¹½	7hd	7¹	Fogelsonger R	32.90
2Aug03 ⁵Dmr⁹	Van Rouge	LB	4 116	8	9	9	9	8½	8⁵	Flores D R	32.80
1Dec02 ⁸Hol⁴	Rock Opera	LB	4 118	9	1	6¹½	5½	9	9	Smith M E	6.90

OFF AT 3:07 Start Good. Won driving. Course firm.

TIME :21⁴, :43⁴, 1:06⁴, 1:13¹ (:21.91, :43.82, 1:06.85, 1:13.22)

$2 Mutuel Prices:

3–KING ROBYN	7.20	4.00	3.40
6–MEDECIS–GB		7.00	4.60
1–GERONIMO–CH			5.20

$1 EXACTA 3–6 PAID $30.20 $2 QUINELLA 3–6 PAID $38.40 $1 TRIFECTA 3–6–1 PAID $262.60 $1 SUPERFECTA 3–6–1–5 PAID $783.50

B. g, (Mar), by Robyn Dancer–Queen's Family, by New Prospect. Trainer Mullins Jeff. Bred by Farnsworth Farms (Fla).

KING ROBYN sped to the early lead, angled in and set the pace inside, responded when challenged in the stretch, shook off the bid of THUNDER BULLET in deep stretch and held on gamely under urging. MEDECIS (GB) pulled his way along and angled in on the hill, chased inside, came out in midstretch and surged late between foes. GERONIMO (CHI) chased inside, came out between foes leaving the hill, angled three deep into the stretch and put in a late bid. THUNDER BULLET stalked outside a rival then a bit off the rail, bid outside the winner in the stretch and was outfinished. WAR ZONE settled off the rail then angled in on the hill, came out in the stretch and rallied between horses. APACHE WINGS pulled a bit early, angled in and stalked inside, steadied behind the runner–up in midstretch and was outkicked late. GALLANT (GB) chased between horses down the hill, came out in the stretch and weakened. VAN ROUGE unhurried outside a rival down the hill, came out four wide into the stretch and did not rally. ROCK OPERA balked at the gate, stalked the winner three deep then four wide leaving the hill, came five wide into the stretch, drifted in some and weakened. Rail on hill at zero.

Owners— 1, Cornejo Racing Inc; 2, Wertheimer Farm LLC; 3, Buster William C Hays & Surfside Eq; 4, Bone Robert D; 5, Juddmonte Farms Inc; 6, Henton Hitbound Stable & Turrell; 7, Fisher Derrick; 8, Moss Mr & Mrs Jerome S; 9, Hidden Meadow Farm LLC

Trainers— 1, Mullins Jeff; 2, Mandella Richard; 3, Machowsky Michael; 4, Mullins Jeff; 5, Frankel Robert; 6, Breuer Denise E; 7, Jory Ian P D; 8, Shirreffs John; 9, Sise Clifford Jr

$2 Daily Double (1–3) Paid $36.40; Daily Double Pool $37,217.
$1 Pick Three (4–1–3) Paid $73.40; Pick Three Pool $95,271.

EIGHTH RACE

Santa Anita
OCTOBER 24, 2003

1½ MILES. (Turf)(2.22⁴) CARLETON F. BURKE H.. Grade III. Purse $125,000 FOR THREE-YEAR-OLDS AND UPWARD. By subscription of $125 each if made on or before Thursday, October 16 or by supplementary nomination of $2,500 by Saturday, October 18. All horses shall pay $1,250 to start with $125,000 added. The added monies and all fees to be divided 60% to the winner, 20% to second, 12% to third, 6% to fourth and 2% to fifth. Nominations closed October 16 with 24. (Rail at 15 feet).

Value of Race: $139,250 Winner $83,550; second $27,850; third $16,710; fourth $8,355; fifth $2,785. Mutuel Pool $580,830.00 Exacta Pool $300,851.00 Quinella Pool $26,874.00 Trifecta Pool $257,302.00 Superfecta Pool $113,375.00

Last Raced	Horse	M/Eqt.	A.Wt	PP	¼	½	1	1¼	Str	Fin	Jockey	Odds $1
27Sep03 ⁶BM⁶	Runaway Dancer	LB	4 112	1	9	9	9	9	8²	1ⁿᵏ	Smith M E	38.10
14Sep03 TAB¹	Labirinto	LB	5 116	9	7ʰᵈ	8½	8²½	4ʰᵈ	4½	2ⁿᵏ	Saint-Martin E	4.70
6Sep03 ⁸Dmr⁴	Senor Swinger	LB	3 114	4	4¹	3¹	3ʰᵈ	3¹	2ʰᵈ	3¹	Bailey J D	3.40
20Sep03 ¹⁴KD⁶	Continental Red	LB	7 116	7	1½	2½	2¹	2ʰᵈ	3¹	4ⁿᵏ	Krone J A	6.50
20Sep03 NBY²	Researched-IR	B	4 118	3	6½	5¹	5½	5ʰᵈ	5½	5ⁿᵏ	Fallon Kieren	4.50
23Aug03 ⁵Sar³	Epicentre	LB	4 115	6	5ʰᵈ	6½	6¹	8²½	7ʰᵈ	6¹½	Prado E S	a-3.90
10Sep03 ⁶Bel⁸	Staging Post	LB	5 115	2	8½	7¹	7ʰᵈ	7¹	6¹½	7¹	Valenzuela P A	a-3.90
28Sep03 ³SA⁴	Continuously	LB	4 114	5	2¹	1½	1²	1½	1½	8²½	Valdivia J Jr	5.90
8Oct03 ⁷SA¹	Special Matter	LBb	5 115	8	3ʰᵈ	4ʰᵈ	4½	6ʰᵈ	9	9	Baze T C	9.00

a-Coupled: Epicentre and Staging Post.

OFF AT 4:41 Start Good. Won driving. Course firm.

TIME :25³, :50³, 1:15⁴, 1:39⁴, 2:04³, 2:28¹ (:25.71, :50.75, 1:15.81, 1:39.85, 2:04.62, 2:28.38)

$2 Mutuel Prices:

2–RUNAWAY DANCER	78.20	25.80	14.00
9–LABIRINTO		7.00	4.60
4–SENOR SWINGER			3.60

$1 EXACTA 2-9 PAID $283.10 $2 QUINELLA 2-9 PAID $197.60 $1 TRIFECTA 2-9-4 PAID $1,833.70 $1 SUPERFECTA 2-9-4-6 PAID $6,980.10

Gr/ro g, by Runaway Groom–Salsa Dancer, by Dahar. Trainer Hendricks Dan L. Bred by Graber Reyla (Ky).

RUNAWAY DANCER dropped back inside early, saved ground off the pace, came out in upper stretch and again in midstretch gained willingly under urging to get up late. LABIRINTO off a bit slowly, chased outside a rival, went three deep on the second turn and four wide into the stretch and rallied gamely. SENOR SWINGER stalked the pace inside, came out into the stretch, bid between horses, took a short lead in deep stretch but was caught late. CONTINENTAL RED battled outside a rival early, stalked outside a foe, came three deep into the stretch, bid outside then between horses in the final furlong and continued willingly to the wire. RESEARCHED (IRE) pulled early, stalked inside then between horses on the backstretch and second turn, came out into the stretch, was in a bit tight between horses past midstretch and was outfinished. EPICENTRE off a bit slowly, pulled early, settled outside a rival, was blocked off heels in midstretch, swung out and finished with interest. STAGING POST saved ground chasing the pace, was boxed in along the rail in midstretch and lacked the needed response when clear. CONTINUOUSLY dueled inside then kicked clear and set the pace along the rail, fought back in midstretch but weakened some late. SPECIAL MATTER was in a good position stalking outside a rival, went three deep on the second turn, dropped back leaving that bend and also weakened.

Owners— 1, RL Stables; 2, Jean Pierre Mio; 3, Lewis Robert B & Beverly J; 4, Fitzpatrick Sharon M; 5, Tanaka Gary A; 6, Juddmonte Farms Inc; 7, Juddmonte Farms Inc; 8, Khaled Saud S; 9, Elder Nancy & McClintock Janice & G

Trainers— 1, Hendricks Dan L; 2, Collet Rodolphe; 3, Baffert Bob; 4, Jory Ian P D; 5, Stoute Michael R; 6, Frankel Robert; 7, Frankel Robert; 8, Frankel Robert; 9, Becerra Rafael

Scratched— Mountain Rage (5Oct03 ⁸SA⁶)

$2 Daily Double (2-2) Paid $423.20; Daily Double Pool $34,861.
$1 Pick Three (5-2-2) Paid $778.60; Pick Three Pool $71,212.
$2 Consolation Daily Double (2-7) Paid $13.00

FOURTH RACE

Belmont

OCTOBER 25, 2003

7 FURLONGS. (1.20) FIRST FLIGHT H.. Grade II. Purse $150,000 (Up to $29,100 NYSBFOA) A HANDICAP FOR FILLIES AND MARES THREE YEARS OLD AND UPWARD. By subscription of $150 each, which should accompany the nomination; $750 to pass the entry box; $750 to start. The purse to be divided 60% to the winner, 20% to second,11% to third, 6% to fourth and 3% to fifth. Trophies will be presented to the winning owner, trainer and jockey. Closed Saturday, October 11, 2003 with 19 nominations.

Value of Race: $150,000 Winner $90,000; second $30,000; third $16,500; fourth $9,000; fifth $4,500. Mutuel Pool $394,592.00 Exacta Pool $393,457.00 Quinella Pool $24,457.00 Trifecta Pool $296,197.00

Last Raced	Horse	M/Eqt. A.Wt	PP	St	1/4	1/2	Str	Fin	Jockey	Odds $1
40ct03 8Pim1	Randaroo	L	3 115	3	2	1$\frac{1}{2}$	1hd	15	1nk	Castillo H Jr	4.60
13Sep03 6Bel2	Shine Again	L	6 121	1	5	5$1\frac{1}{2}$	4$\frac{1}{2}$	2hd	2$1\frac{1}{4}$	Migliore R	0.50
18Aug03 5Sar5	Zawzooth	L	4 113	4	7	7$2\frac{1}{2}$	8	4hd	3$\frac{1}{2}$	Chavez J F	11.40
110ct03 7Med1	Drexel Monorail	L	4 114	5	8	8	7 3	3$\frac{1}{2}$	4$2\frac{3}{4}$	Dominguez R A	18.50
7May03 6Bel1	Message Red		4 114	7	6	6$\frac{1}{2}$	5hd	5hd	5$2\frac{1}{2}$	Castellano J J	8.40
40ct03 8Pim2	Follow Me Home	Lb	3 112	6	3	2hd	2$1\frac{1}{2}$	66	6$3\frac{3}{4}$	Pimentel J	16.30
60ct03 7Del3	Wish It Were	Lb	4 113	8	1	4$\frac{1}{2}$	3hd	715	71$7\frac{3}{4}$	Bridgmohan S X	46.75
22Aug98 4Sar7	Mousse Glacee-FR	b	9 111	2	4	3hd	61	8	8	Arroyo N Jr	53.00

OFF AT 12:30 Start Good. Won gamely. Track fast.

TIME :22², :45³, 1:10², 1:23³ (:22.45, :45.64, 1:10.42, 1:23.65)

$2 Mutuel Prices:

3–RANDAROO	11.20	3.40	2.40
1–SHINE AGAIN		2.30	2.10
4–ZAWZOOTH			2.60

$2 EXACTA 3–1 PAID $18.80 $2 QUINELLA 1–3 PAID $6.00 $2 TRIFECTA 3–1–4 PAID $129.00

B. f, (Feb), by Gold Case–Validated, by Valid Appeal. Trainer McLaughlin Kiaran P. Bred by Dennis Drazin (Ky).

RANDAROO quickly showed in front, set the pace, drew clear when roused then dug in gamely and held on, driving. SHINE AGAIN raced close up inside, early, came wide into the stretch and finished gamely outside. ZAWZOOTH was outrun early, came wide for the drive and finished gamely outside. DREXEL MONORAIL was outrun early, raced inside and finished well on the rail. MESSAGE RED raced three wide and had no response when roused. FOLLOW ME HOME pressed the pace while three wide and tired in the stretch. WISH IT WERE chased the pace while three wide and tired in the stretch. MOUSSE GLACEE (CHI) tired after showing brief speed.

Owners— 1, Allen Joseph; 2, Bohemia Stable; 3, Starlight Stable LLC; 4, Singer Craig B; 5, Robbins Lansdon B; 6, Braunsdorf Robert & Levine Robert; 7, Mascera Gregory; 8, Edition Farm

Trainers— 1, McLaughlin Kiaran P; 2, Jerkens H Allen; 3, Pletcher Todd A; 4, Klesaris Steve; 5, Jerkens James A; 6, Levine Bruce N; 7, Hills Timothy A; 8, Penna Angel Jr

Scratched— Mousse Glacee (10Apr03 HC8)

$2 Pick Three (6–3–3) Paid $204.00; Pick Three Pool $61,661.

FIFTH RACE

Belmont

OCTOBER 25, 2003

7 FURLONGS. (1.20) SPORT PAGE H.. Grade III. Purse $100,000 (Up to $19,400 NYSBFOA) A HANDICAP FOR THREE YEAR OLDS AND UPWARD. By subscription of $100 each, which should accompany the nomination; $500 to pass the entry box; $500 to start, with $100,000 added. The added money and all fees to be divided 60% to the winner, 20% to second, 11% to third, 6% to fourth and 3% to fifth. Trophies will be presented to the winning owner, trainer and jockey. Closed Saturday, October 11, 2003 with 32 nominations.

Value of Race: $112,700 Winner $67,620; second $22,540; third $12,397; fourth $6,762; fifth $3,381. Mutuel Pool $562,011.00 Exacta Pool $539,547.00 Trifecta Pool $350,255.00 Superfecta Pool $80,825.00

Last Raced	Horse	M/Eqt. A.Wt	PP	St	1/4	1/2	Str	Fin	Jockey	Odds $1
27Sep03 7Bel6	Voodoo	Lb	5 114	7	4	2hd	21	14$\frac{1}{2}$	12$\frac{1}{2}$	Chavez J F	4.30
30ct03 8Med1	Bowman's Band	L	5 120	2	9	6$5\frac{1}{2}$	63	21	2$\frac{1}{2}$	Dominguez R A	1.35
27Sep03 7Bel7	Highway Prospector	Lb	6 114	1	8	3hd	5hd	3$3\frac{1}{2}$	3$3\frac{1}{2}$	Bridgmohan S X	10.40
11Sep03 8Bel5	Speed Hunter	L	4 112	6	5	7$1\frac{1}{2}$	7$2\frac{1}{2}$	4$\frac{1}{2}$	42$\frac{1}{2}$	Arroyo N Jr	8.90
10Aug03 9Sar5	State City	L	4 118	9	6	5$\frac{1}{2}$	5$2\frac{1}{2}$	5$2\frac{1}{2}$	51$\frac{3}{4}$	Gryder A T	8.40
11Sep03 8Bel4	Pinch Hitter	L	4 111	5	3	9	9	82	6nk	Cotto P L Jr	48.50
25Sep03 8Bel5	Turn Back The Time	Lf	5 111	8	7	8$1\frac{1}{2}$	8$3\frac{1}{2}$	6$2\frac{1}{2}$	78	Fragoso P	55.00
30ct03 5Med1	Outstander	L	4 116	3	1	4hd	4hd	7hd	82$\frac{1}{2}$	Santana J Z	12.10
25Sep03 8Bel1	Bishop Court Hill	L	3 112	4	2	11	1hd	9	9	Migliore R	5.80

OFF AT 1:01 Start Good. Won driving. Track fast.

TIME :22³, :45², 1:09³, 1:22 (:22.75, :45.59, 1:09.71, 1:22.18)

$2 Mutuel Prices:

8–VOODOO	10.60	4.20	3.30
2–BOWMAN'S BAND		3.00	2.50
1–HIGHWAY PROSPECTOR			3.60

$2 EXACTA 8–2 PAID $28.00 $2 TRIFECTA 8–2–1 PAID $151.00 $2 SUPERFECTA 8–2–1–6 PAID $620.00

Ch. g, by Petionville–Slide Show, by Slewacide. Trainer Jerkens James A. Bred by Everest Stables Inc (Ky).

VOODOO raced with the pace while three wide, responded when roused, drew clear and remained clear under a drive. BOWMAN'S BAND raced in hand early, split rivals on the turn and finished gamely outside. HIGHWAY PROSPECTOR raced with the pace along the inside and finished gamely on the rail. SPEED HUNTER was outrun early, raced wide and offered a mild rally outside. STATE CITY chased the pace while three wide and tired in the stretch. PINCH HITTER had no rally. TURN BACK THE TIME had no response when roused. OUTSTANDER raced close up while between rivals and tired. BISHOP COURT HILL quickly showed in front, set the pace for a half mile and tired.

Owners— 1, Moore Susan & John; 2, Schwartz Martin S; 3, Gill Michael J; 4, Sullivan Lane Stable Vincent Scuder; 5, Godolphin Racing Inc; 6, Gatsas Thoroughbreds LLC; 7, Cotran Camille; 8, Schuler Edward F; 9, Melnyk Eugene & Laura

Trainers— 1, Jerkens James A; 2, Jerkens H Allen; 3, Shuman Mark; 4, Dutrow Richard E Jr; 5, Albertrani Thomas; 6, Terranova John P II; 7, LaFavers Laurie; 8, Jenkins Rodney; 9, Pletcher Todd A

Scratched— Aggadan (27Sep03 7BEL2)

$2 Daily Double (3–8) Paid $82.00; Daily Double Pool $157,816.
$2 Pick Three (3–3–8) Paid $459.50; Pick Three Pool $113,100.
$2 Pick Four (6–3–3–8) Paid $3,524.00; Pick Four Pool $108,089.

Belmont Park Attendance: Unavailable Mutuel Pool: $613,368.00 ITW Mutuel Pool: $1,518,543.00 ISW Mutuel Pool: $3,855,189.00

FOURTH RACE
Keeneland
OCTOBER 25, 2003

1 1/16 MILES. (1.46⁴) FAYETTE S.. Grade III. Purse $150,000 FOR THREE YEARS OLD AND UPWARD. By supscription of $150 each, which should accompany the nomination; $1,500 to enter and start, with $150,000 added, of which 62% of all monies to the owner of the winner, 20% to second, 10% to third, 5% to fourth and 3% to fifth. Weight; Three year old, 122 lbs., Older, 125 lbs. Non–winners of a Grade I stakes over a mile in 2003 allowed 2 lbs.; a Grade II stakes over a mile in 2003 allowed 4 lbs.; a Grade III stakes at a mile or over in 2003, 6 lbs. Starters to be named through the entry box by the usual time of closing. A gold julep cup will be presented to the owner of the winner.

Value of Race: $163,800 Winner $101,556; second $32,760; third $12,285 each; fifth $4,914. Mutuel Pool $508,513.00 Exacta Pool $356,285.00 Quinella Pool $14,884.00 Trifecta Pool $299,020.00 Superfecta Pool $88,239.00

Last Raced	Horse	M/Eqt. A.Wt	PP	St	1/4	1/2	3/4	Str	Fin	Jockey	Odds $1
4Oct03 7Del²	M B Sea	Lb 4 119	7	3	4hd	41½	31½	11	11	Perret C	34.70
28Sep03 9Haw²	Tenpins	Lf 5 121	5	1	21½	21	21	2hd	22½	Albarado R J	1.10
27Sep03 7Del²	DH Changeintheweather	Lb 4 119	2	4	3hd	3hd	41½	5hd	3	Castillo O O	16.60
27Sep03 6Bel¹	DH Seattle Fitz-ARG	L 4 119	3	6	61½	5hd	61	61	3hd	Borel C H	2.90
23Sep03 9Mnr¹	Sonic West	Lf 4 119	4	5	51½	63	5½	4hd	5nk	Bejarano R	17.20
4Oct03 7Del¹	Country Be Gold	L 6 119	6	7	7	7	7	7	6no	Alvarado R Jr	17.90
27Sep03 10Bel²	Quest	L 4 119	1	2	1½	1hd	1hd	32	7	Sellers S J	2.40

DH—Dead Heat.

OFF AT 2:10 Start Good. Won driving. Track fast.
TIME :25², :50¹, 1:14³, 1:38³, 1:50¹ (:25.40, :50.20, 1:14.65, 1:38.66, 1:50.30)

$2 Mutuel Prices:

7—M B SEA	71.40	13.40	4.20
5—TENPINS		3.00	2.40
2—DH CHANGEINTHEWEATHER			2.60
3—DH SEATTLE FITZ–ARG			2.60

$2 EXACTA 7–5 PAID $236.80 $2 QUINELLA 5–7 PAID $57.80 $2 TRIFECTA 7–5–2 PAID $828.80 $2 TRIFECTA 7–5–3 PAID $542.00 $2 SUPERFECTA 7–5–2–3 PAID $3,573.20 $2 SUPERFECTA 7–5–3–2 PAID $2,464.80

Dk. b. or br. c, by Alphabet Soup–Sea Ditty, by Afleet. Trainer Romans Dale. Bred by Adena Springs (Ky).

M B SEA, never far back, leaned in and exchanged bumps with SONIC WEST approaching the first turn, moved four wide entering the backstretch to track the dueling leaders, inched to challenge approaching the stretch, was bumped for a stride about the three-sixteenths pole by TENPINS when that one came out slightly, took over, drifted out for a stride under left-handed whipping at the furlong grounds, then continued under pressure to prevail. TENPINS went up to vie for the lead early while outside of QUEST, battled on near even terms with that one, put a head in front for a stride or two entering the lane, came out and bumped with the winner, then couldn't sustain the needed momentum as second best. CHANGEINTHEWEATHER, well placed in behind rivals from early on, raced within easy striking distance, angled between horses four wide about mid-stretch and offered only a minor gain while dead heating for third with SEATTLE FITZ (ARG). The latter brushed the side of the gate while breaking a bit sluggishly, settled three wide early, continued in behind horses entering the stretch, split foes three wide in the final furlong and finished on even terms with CHANGEINTHEWEATHER. SONIC WEST, between horses early, came out and exchanged bumps with M B SEA nearing the first turn, raced four or five wide, angled six wide to offer a mild bid into the final furlong but failed to continue. COUNTRY BE GOLD, outrun four wide to the far turn, made a mild run and angled seven wide into the stretch but was empty the last eighth. QUEST gained a slight edge inside early, dueled with TENPINS through moderate fractions and faltered in the drive.

Owners— 1, Bruder Michael J; 2, Vitello Joseph V; 3, Pin Oak Stable LLC; 4, West Point Thoroughbreds LLC; 5, Stone Spire LLC; 6, S A Partnership Barry Sienfeld; 7, Hancock III Arthur B & Healy Gerald

Trainers—1, Romans Dale; 2, Winfree Donald R; 3, Motion H Graham; 4, McLaughlin Kiaran P; 5, Van Berg Thomas L; 6, Nobles Reynaldo H; 7, Zito Nicholas P

$2 Daily Double (9–7) Paid $445.40; Daily Double Pool $59,403.
$2 Pick Three (4–9–7) Paid $5,810.80; Pick Three Pool $43,044.
$2 Pick Four (8–4–9–7) Paid $22,833.20; Pick Four Pool $70,473.

Keeneland Attendance: Unavailable Mutuel Pool: $531,743.00 ITW Mutuel Pool: $262,526.00 ISW Mutuel Pool: $3,392,299.00

SECOND RACE

Santa Anita

OCTOBER 25, 2003

1⅛ MILES. (1.45⁴) BREEDERS' CUP DISTAFF Grade I. Purse $2,000,000 FOR FILLIES AND MARES, THREE–YEAR–OLDS AND UPWARD. Northern Hemisphere three–year–olds, 119 lbs.; Older, 123 lbs.; Southern Hemisphere three–year–olds, 114 lbs.; Older, 123 lbs. $20,000 to pre–enter, with guaranteed $2 million purse including nominator awards (plus net supplementary fees, if any), of which 52% of all monies to the owner of the winner, 20% to second, 11% to third, 5.7% to fourth and 3% to fifth; plus stallion nominator awards of 2.6% of all monies to the winner, 1% to second and 0.55% to third and foal nominator awards of 2.6% of all monies to the winner, 1% to second and 0.55% to third. Closed with 8 pre–entries.

Value of Race: $1,834,000 Winner $1,040,000; second $400,000; third $220,000; fourth $114,000; fifth $60,000. Mutuel Pool $3,187,260.00 Exacta Pool $2,002,945.00 Trifecta Pool $1,464,573.00 Superfecta Pool $369,942.00 Head2Head Pool $45,817.00

Last Raced	Horse	M/Eqt.	A.	Wt	PP	St	¼	½	¾	Str	Fin	Jockey	Odds $1
28Sep03 6SA3	Adoration	LB	4	123	2	1	1¹	1¹	11½	1²	14½	Valenzuela P A	40.70
28Sep03 6SA4	Elloluv	LB	3	119	6	4	3½	2hd	2hd	21½	22½	Nakatani C S	8.80
28Sep03 6SA1	Got Koko	LB b	4	123	7	5	5¹	51½	5hd	41½	33½	Solis A O	4.00
4Oct03 9Bel1	Sightseek	LB	4	123	5	6	6hd	6½	61½	5hd	4½	Bailey J D	0.60
4Oct03 9Bel3	Buy the Sport	L	3	119	4	7	7	7	7	7	52½	Velazquez J R	35.20
5Oct03 8Kee1	Take Charge Lady	LB	4	123	1	3	2hd	3½	41	61½	6½	Prado E S	6.80
6Sep03 7Bel2	Lady Tak	LB	3	119	3	2	4hd	41	3hd	31½	7	Day P	10.70

OFF AT 10:21 Start Good. Won driving. Track fast.

TIME :23¹, :47, 1:11, 1:35⁴, 1:49 (:23.28, :47.08, 1:11.10, 1:35.89, 1:49.17)

	2 – ADORATION	83.40	33.40	25.80
$2 Mutuel Prices:	6 – ELLOLUV		9.20	12.20
	7 – GOT KOKO			6.80

$1 EXACTA 2–6 PAID $238.40 $1 TRIFECTA 2–6–7 PAID $1,017.40
$1 SUPERFECTA 2–6–7–5 PAID $1,981.70
$2 HEAD2HEAD 1VS.6; WINNER 6 PAID $3.20

B. f, (Apr), by Honor Grades – Sewing Lady, by Key to the Mint. Trainer Hofmans David. Bred by Lucy G Bassett (Ky).

ADORATION sped to the early lead and angled in, set all the pace inside, kicked clear into the second turn and held on gamely under urging. ELLOLUV broke in a bit, raced close up stalking the pace three deep then outside a rival leaving the second turn, drifted in through the stretch and was second best. GOT KOKO four wide into the first turn, chased outside, went three deep on the second turn and into the stretch and picked up the show. SIGHTSEEK a bit crowded at the start, pulled her way between horses into the first turn, chased outside a rival, came out into the second turn and four wide into the stretch and lacked the needed rally. BUY THE SPORT squeezed a bit at the start, angled in and saved ground off the pace, came out into the stretch and was not a threat. TAKE CHARGE LADY saved ground stalking the pace, dropped back on the second turn and weakened. LADY TAK broke out a bit, pulled her way between horses stalking the pace, angled in on the second turn and also weakened.

Owners– 1, Amerman Racing Stables LLC; 2, Reddam J Paul; 3, Aase Headley & Paul Leung; 4, Juddmonte Farms Inc; 5, Georgica Stable Stephen Mack & Andrew Rosen; 6, Select Stable; 7, Heiligbrodt Racing Stable

Trainers– 1, Hofmans David E; 2, Dollase Craig; 3, Headley Bruce; 4, Frankel Robert J; 5, Barbara Robert; 6, McPeek Kenneth G; 7, Asmussen Steven M

$2 Daily Double (7–2) Paid $572.40 ; Daily Double Pool $342,171.

THIRD RACE

Santa Anita

OCTOBER 25, 2003

1 1/16 MILES. (1.39) BREEDERS' CUP JUVENILE FILLIES Grade I. Purse $1,000,000 FOR FILLIES, TWO YEARS OLD. Weight, 119 lbs. $10,000 to pre-enter, $20,000 to enter, with guaranteed $1 million purse including nominator awards (plus Net Supplementary Fees, if any), of which 52% of all monies to the owner of the winner, 20% to second, 11% to third, 5.7% to fourth and 3% to fifth; plus stallion nominator awards of 2.6% of all monies to the winner, 1% to second and 0.55% to third and foal nominator awards of 2.6% of all monies to the winner, 1% to second and 0.55% to third. Closed with 14 pre-entries.

Value of Race: $917,000 Winner $520,000; second $200,000; third $110,000; fourth $57,000; fifth $30,000. Mutuel Pool $3,864,099.00 Exacta Pool $2,814,363.00 Trifecta Pool $2,210,836.00 Superfecta Pool $570,359.00 Head2Head Pool $28,962.00

Last Raced	Horse	M/Eqt.	A. Wt	PP	St	1/4	1/2	3/4	Str	Fin	Jockey	Odds $1
28Sep03 9SA1	Halfbridled	LB	2 119	14	6	7$\frac{1}{2}$	5hd	3hd	1$\frac{1}{2}$	12$\frac{1}{2}$	Krone J A	2.30
4Oct03 6Bel3	Ashado	LB	2 119	5	3	3$\frac{1}{2}$	3hd	4hd	36	2nk	Velazquez J R	13.30
4Oct03 6Bel2	Victory U. S. A.	LB	2 119	8	5	21	2$\frac{1}{2}$	1$\frac{1}{2}$	21	39$\frac{1}{4}$	Bailey J D	7.80
28Sep03 9SA3	Hollywood Story	LB b	2 119	3	4	5hd	8$2\frac{1}{2}$	7hd	4$1\frac{1}{2}$	4$1\frac{3}{4}$	Valenzuela P A	21.20
27Sep03 9AP1	Zosima	LB	2 119	11	11	4$\frac{1}{2}$	12$\frac{1}{2}$	91	8hd	51	Day P	24.20
20Sep03 11Fpx1	Dixie High	LB	2 119	1	1	9hd	101	102	6$\frac{1}{2}$	6$1\frac{1}{2}$	Espinoza V	50.00
13Sep03 9TP1	Class Above	LB b	2 119	7	10	10hd	7$\frac{1}{2}$	61	5hd	7$\frac{1}{2}$	Flores D R	4.30
28Sep03 8LaD1	Vino Tinto	LB	2 119	10	7	61	4hd	8$1\frac{1}{2}$	92	8$\frac{1}{2}$	Fogelsonger R	89.70
28Sep03 9SA2	Tarlow	LB	2 119	12	12	8hd	61	5$\frac{1}{2}$	7hd	91	Smith M E	31.20
4Oct03 6Bel1	Society Selection	B	2 119	6	13	14	14	13^8	10^3	104	Ganpath R	4.10
30Oct03 9Kee1	Be Gentle	LB	2 119	13	9	12^1	9$\frac{1}{2}$	11hd	11hd	11$\frac{1}{2}$	Velasquez C H	37.30
28Sep03 9SA4	Shadow of Mine	LB b	2 119	2	14	13hd	11hd	12hd	12^{10}	12^{11}	Valdivia J Jr	116.90
28Sep03 9SA7	Renaissance Lady	LB b	2 119	9	8	11$1\frac{1}{2}$	13$\frac{1}{2}$	14	136	13$8\frac{1}{2}$	Baze T	61.10
8Oct03 4Lrl1	Forest Music	LB	2 119	4	2	11$\frac{1}{2}$	11	2$\frac{1}{2}$	14	14	Prado E S	7.10

OFF AT 10:58 Start Good. Won driving. Track fast.

TIME :22^4, :46^4, 1:10^4, 1:36, 1:42^3 (:22.88, :46.82, 1:10.84, 1:36.14, 1:42.75)

$2 Mutuel Prices:				
14 – HALFBRIDLED	6.60	4.80	3.40
5 – ASHADO		11.60	7.20
8 – VICTORY U. S. A.			4.80

$1 EXACTA 14-5 PAID $63.00 $1 TRIFECTA 14-5-8 PAID $343.10
$1 SUPERFECTA 14-5-8-3 PAID $2,995.10
$2 HEAD2HEAD 8VS.12;WINNER8 PAID $3.20

Dk. b or br. f, (Feb), by Unbridled – Half Queen , by Deputy Minister . Trainer Mandella Richard. Bred by Wertheimer & Frere (Ky).

HALFBRIDLED moved up from outside in the early stages, raced in the middle of the pack while four wide along the backstretch, edged closer from outside on the turn, accelerated to the front in upper stretch, opened a clear advantage inside the furlong marker then drew off under steady left hand encouragement. ASHADO settled in good position along the backstretch, saved ground while racing just behind the leaders through the turn, angled three wide for clear sailing leaving the quarter pole, then outfinished VICTORY U. S. A. for the place. VICTORY U. S. A. stalked the pace from outside in the early stages, made a run to challenge on the turn, surged to the front midway on the turn, relinquished the lead to the winner in upper stretch then weakened under pressure in the final eighth. HOLLYWOOD STORY steadied between horses while being bumped on the first turn, raced well back while saving ground along the backstretch, closed the gap a bit on the turn then improved her position with a mild late rally. ZOSIMA was bumped off stride soon after the start, steadied in traffic on the first turn, was outrun along the backstretch, swung six wide on the turn then failed to threaten while improving her position. DIXIE HIGH failed to mount a serious rally while saving ground. CLASS ABOVE steadied between horses on the first turn, raced in the middle of the pack to the turn, circled seven wide into the stretch and lacked a strong closing bid. VINO TINTO raced up close while four wide for a half and tired. TARLOW bumped with BE GENTLE after stumbling at the start, raced within striking distance while five wide to the turn and lacked a further response. SOCIETY SELECTION steadied in traffic on the first turn then never reached contention. BE GENTLE raced wide throughout after being bumped at the start. SHADOW OF MINE steadied in traffic on the first turn and failed to menace thereafter. RENAISSANCE LADY caught in traffic on the first turn, was outrun. FOREST MUSIC rushed up to gain the early lead, set the pace for half then gave way.

Owners– 1, Wertheimer Farm LLC; 2, Starlight Stables LLC Paul H Saylor & Johns Martin; 3, Van Meter Thomas F II; 4, Krikorian George; 5, Darley Stable; 6, Peeples William R; 7, Padua Stables; 8, Triple B Farms; 9, Moss Mr and Mrs Jerome S; 10, Cowan Marjorie and Irving M; 11, Van Meter Thomas F II; 12, Nichols Thomas L; 13, Lewis Robert B and Beverly J; 14, Gill Michael J

Trainers– 1, Mandella Richard E; 2, Pletcher Todd A; 3, Baffert Bob; 4, Shirreffs John A; 5, Harty Eoin G; 6, Kitchingman Adam; 7, Baffert Bob; 8, Hines Nicholas J; 9, Shirreffs John A; 10, Jerkens H Allen; 11, Lukas D Wayne; 12, Greely C Beau; 13, Lukas D Wayne; 14, Shuman Mark

$2 Daily Double (2–14) Paid $830.40 ; Daily Double Pool $445,880 .
$2 Pick Three (7–2–14) Paid $2,675.90 ; Pick Three Pool $382,185 .

FOURTH RACE
Santa Anita
OCTOBER 25, 2003

1 MILE. (Turf) (1.31^{4}) NETJETS BREEDERS' CUP MILE Grade I. Purse $1,500,000 FOR THREE-YEAR-OLDS AND UPWARD. Northern Hemisphere Three-Year-Olds, 122 lbs.; Older, 126 lbs. Southern Hemisphere Three-Year-Olds, 119 lbs.; Older, 126 lbs. All Fillies and Mares allowed 3 lbs. $15,000 to pre-enter, $30,000 to enter, with guaranteed $1.5 million purse including nominator awards (plus Net Supplementary Fees, if any), of which 52% of all monies to the owner of the winner, 20% to second, 11% to third, 5.7% to fourth and 3% to fifth; plus stallion nominator awards of 2.6% of all monies to the winner, 1% to second and 0.55% to third and foal nominator awards of 2.6% of all monies to the winner, 1% to second and 0.55% to third. Closed with 17 pre-entries.

Value of Race: $1,375,500 Winner $780,000; second $300,000; third $165,000; fourth $85,500; fifth $45,000. Mutuel Pool $4,236,378.00 Exacta Pool $3,018,953.00 Trifecta Pool $2,348,195.00 Superfecta Pool $638,977.00 Head2Head Pool $39,398.00

Last Raced	Horse	M/Eqt.	A.	Wt	PP	St	¼	½	¾	Str	Fin	Jockey	Odds $1
17Aug03 DEA^{1}	Six Perfections-FR	B	3	119	12	11	$8^{2½}$	8^{1}	7^{1}	$4^{½}$	$1^{¾}$	Bailey J D	5.30
4Oct03 ^{9}Kee^{3}	TouchoftheBlus-FR	LB	6	126	8	9	$12^{1½}$	12^{2}	$11^{1½}$	3^{hd}	2^{nk}	Desormeaux K J	11.90
5Oct03 ^{8}SA^{3}	Century City-Ire	LB b	4	126	7	7	10^{hd}	$11^{1½}$	$10^{1½}$	8^{1}	$3^{1¼}$	Valdivia J Jr	39.00
28Sep03 ^{3}SA^{3}	Irish Warrior	LB	5	126	10	10	13	13	13	7^{hd}	4^{1}	Solis A O	32.90
4Oct03 ^{9}Kee^{4}	Soaring Free	LB	4	126	3	3	2^{hd}	$3^{2½}$	$3^{½}$	1^{hd}	5^{hd}	Velazquez J R	22.20
4Oct03 ^{8}Bel^{1}	Freefourinternet	LB	5	126	6	8	9^{hd}	10^{hd}	9^{1}	9^{hd}	$6^{1½}$	Espinoza J L	57.10
5Oct03 ^{8}SA^{1}	Designed for Luck	LB b	6	126	2	1	3^{2}	2^{hd}	1^{hd}	2^{2}	7^{nk}	Valenzuela P A	5.30
5Oct03 ^{8}SA^{4}	Special Ring	LB b	6	126	5	6	6^{1}	7^{1}	$8^{1½}$	$11^{½}$	8^{1}	Flores D R	5.10
4Oct03 ^{9}Kee^{1}	Perfect Soul-Ire	LB b	5	126	13	12	7^{hd}	6^{hd}	$6^{½}$	5^{hd}	$9^{1½}$	Santos J A	16.40
6Sep03 HAY^{2}	Oasis Dream-GB	B	3	122	9	4	5^{1}	4^{hd}	5^{1}	$6^{½}$	10^{1}	Hughes R	8.70
7Sep03 LCH^{11}	Refuse To Bend-Ire	B	3	122	4	13	4^{1}	$5^{½}$	$4^{½}$	10^{hd}	$11^{2½}$	Smullen P	9.70
4Oct03 ^{8}Bel^{4}	Decarchy	LB	6	126	11	5	11^{3}	9^{1}	12^{hd}	13	$12^{4½}$	Smith M E	51.60
23Aug03 ^{11}Sar^{2}	Peace Rules	LB	3	122	1	2	1^{1}	1^{hd}	2^{1}	12^{2}	13	Prado E S	3.10

OFF AT 11:40 Start Good. Won driving. Course firm.

TIME :22^{1}, :45^{2}, 1:09^{2}, 1:21^{4}, 1:33^{4} (:22.28, :45.40, 1:09.41, 1:21.86, 1:33.86)

$2 Mutuel Prices:				
	13 – SIX PERFECTIONS-FR	12.60	7.00	4.80
	9 – TOUCH OF THE BLUES-FR		9.80	6.80
	8 – CENTURY CITY-IRE			15.60

$1 EXACTA 13–9 PAID $76.80 $1 TRIFECTA 13–9–8 PAID $2,628.70
$1 SUPERFECTA 13–9–8–11 PAID $39,233.10
$2 HEAD2HEAD 1VS.6;WINNER6 PAID $3.80

Blk. f, (Feb), by Celtic Swing-GB – Yogya, by Riverman. Trainer Bary Pascal F. Bred by Famille Niarchos (Fr).

SIX PERFECTIONS (FR) reluctant to load, chased between horses, came three deep into the stretch, rallied between rivals in deep stretch to gain the lead and proved best under urging. TOUCH OF THE BLUES (FR) unhurried off the rail early, went up three deep on the second turn and four wide into the stretch and finished well. CENTURY CITY (IRE) settled between horses, came out in upper stretch, split rivals with a bid in midstretch then rallied toward the inside. IRISH WARRIOR allowed to settle off the rail, circled six wide into the stretch and closed willingly. SOARING FREE stalked outside a rival, bid three deep on the second turn and into the stretch, gained a short advantage nearing midstretch but was overtaken. FREEFOURINTERNET angled in and saved ground, swung out off heels into the stretch, was in tight between foes in midstretch and could not offer the needed late kick. DESIGNED FOR LUCK had speed outside a rival then stalked a bit off the rail, bid between horses on the backstretch and second turn, took a short lead leaving that bend but weakened in the final furlong. SPECIAL RING angled in and saved ground chasing the pace, was in a bit tight in upper stretch then steadied hard off heels in midstretch and lacked the needed rally. PERFECT SOUL (IRE) was in a good position stalking the pace three deep to the stretch and lacked a further response. OASIS DREAM (GB) pulled his way along early, angled in and chased between horses and weakened in the stretch. REFUSE TO BEND (IRE) broke slowly, was rank along the inside early, saved ground stalking the pace and weakened in the stretch. DECARCHY settled three deep on the first turn and backstretch, came five wide into the stretch and did not rally. PEACE RULES sped to the early lead, set a pressured pace inside, dropped back in upper stretch and gave way.

Owners– 1, Flaxman Holdings Ltd; 2, Al Maktoum Sheik Maktoum b; 3, Kitchwa Stables and Nichols Thomas L; 4, John Coleman George Dasaro James Thomson et al; 5, Sam-Son Farms; 6, EquiraceCom LLC; 7, Wilson David W and Holly F; 8, Prestonwood Farm LLC; 9, Fipke Charles E; 10, Juddmonte Farms Inc; 11, Moyglare Stud Farm Ltd Lessee; 12, JMJ Racing Stables LLC & Magali Ventures; 13, Gann Edmund A

Trainers– 1, Bary Pascal F; 2, Drysdale Neil D; 3, Greely C Beau; 4, Dollase Wallace A; 5, Frostad Mark R; 6, Scott Joan; 7, Cerin Vladimir; 8, Canani Julio C; 9, Attfield Roger L; 10, Gosden John H; 11, Weld Dermot K; 12, O'Neill Doug; 13, Frankel Robert J

Scratched– Sarafan (05Oct03 ^{8}SA ^{2})

$2 Daily Double (14–13) Paid $48.00; Daily Double Pool $233,517.
$1 Pick Three (2–14–13) Paid $2,112.70; Pick Three Pool $1,037,573.

FIFTH RACE
Santa Anita
OCTOBER 25, 2003

6 FURLONGS. (1.07^{1}) BREEDERS' CUP SPRINT Grade I. Purse $1,000,000 FOR THREE-YEAR-OLDS AND UPWARD. Northern Hemisphere Three-Year-Olds, 123 lbs.; Older, 126 lbs.; Southern Hemisphere Three-Year-Olds, 121 lbs.; Older, 126 lbs. All Fillies and Mares allowed 3 lbs. $10,000 to pre-enter, $20,000 to enter, with guaranteed $1million purse including nominator awards (plus Net Supplementary Fees, if any), of which 52% of all monies to the owner of the winner, 20% to second, 11% to third, 5.7% to fourth and 3% to fifth; plus stallion nominator awards of 2.6% of all monies to thewinner, 1% to second and 0.55% to third and foal nominator awards of 2.6% of all monies to the winner, 1% to second and 0.55% to third. Closed with 15 pre-entries.

Value of Race: $1,082,060 Winner $613,600; second $236,000; third $129,800; fourth $67,260; fifth $35,400. Mutuel Pool $4,217,299.00 Exacta Pool $3,149,760.00 Trifecta Pool $2,515,148.00 Superfecta Pool $702,384.00 Head2Head Pool $36,955.00

Last Raced	Horse	M/Eqt.	A.	Wt	PP	St	¼	½	Str	Fin	Jockey	Odds $1
13Sep03 ^{13}TP^{1}	Cajun Beat	LB b	3	123	11	2	3^{1}	1^{hd}	$1^{1\frac{1}{2}}$	$1^{2\frac{1}{4}}$	Velasquez C H	22.80
5Oct03 ^{7}SA^{3}	Bluesthestandard	LB	6	126	8	9	$10^{\frac{1}{2}}$	$7^{1\frac{1}{2}}$	$3^{1\frac{1}{2}}$	2^{2}	Smith M E	13.70
11Sep03 ^{8}Bel^{1}	Shake You Down	LB bf	5	126	2	13	$2^{\frac{1}{2}}$	2^{1}	$2^{\frac{1}{2}}$	$3^{\frac{1}{2}}$	Luzzi M J	3.50
27Sep03 ^{7}Bel^{3}	Posse	LB	3	123	3	10	11^{1}	$9^{\frac{1}{2}}$	$8^{1\frac{1}{2}}$	4^{nk}	Day P	23.50
5Oct03 ^{7}SA^{4}	Yankee Gentleman	LB	4	126	12	3	5^{hd}	3^{hd}	$4^{1\frac{1}{2}}$	$5^{\frac{1}{2}}$	Valenzuela P A	10.80
31Aug03 ^{10}Sar^{1}	Aldebaran	LB	5	126	6	12	13	12^{2}	9^{2}	$6^{2\frac{1}{4}}$	Bailey J D	2.10
5Oct03 ^{7}SA^{2}	Captain Squire	LB	4	123	13	1	6^{1}	$5^{\frac{1}{2}}$	$5^{\frac{1}{2}}$	$7^{1\frac{1}{2}}$	Solis A O	13.50
7Jun03 ^{9}Bel^{2}	Midas Eyes	LB	3	123	5	8	4^{hd}	6^{2}	7^{2}	8^{2}	Velazquez J R	8.30
20Sep03 ^{13}TP^{1}	Private Horde	LB bf	4	126	9	11	12^{5}	13	12^{3}	$9^{\frac{1}{2}}$	Lumpkins J P	29.20
3Oct03 ^{7}Kee^{2}	Ethan Man	LB	4	126	7	7	7^{hd}	8^{hd}	11^{2}	10^{1}	Douglas R R	23.30
3Oct03 ^{7}Kee^{6}	Great Notion	LB f	3	123	10	4	9^{2}	10^{hd}	$10^{\frac{1}{2}}$	11no	Baze T	57.10
5Oct03 ^{7}SA^{5}	Zavata	B	3	123	1	5	1^{hd}	4^{1}	6^{hd}	$12^{3\frac{1}{2}}$	Stevens G L	28.40
23Aug03 ^{10}Sar^{1}	Valid Video	LB	3	123	4	6	8^{1}	11^{hd}	13	13	Prado E S	8.10

OFF AT 12:14 Start Good . Won driving. Track fast.

TIME :21, :43^{1}, :55, 1:07^{4} (:21.02, :43.32, :55.07, 1:07.95)

$2 Mutuel Prices:

11 – CAJUN BEAT	47.60	19.80	11.20
8 – BLUESTHESTANDARD		12.60	8.00
2 – SHAKE YOU DOWN			5.00

$1 EXACTA 11–8 PAID $380.10 $1 TRIFECTA 11–8–2 PAID $2,151.70
$1 SUPERFECTA 11–8–2–3 PAID $31,146.80
$2 HEAD2HEAD 4VS.13;WINNER13 PAID $3.40

Dk. b or br. g, (Mar), by Grand Slam – Beckys Shirt , by Cure the Blues . Trainer Margolis Stephen R. Bred by John T L Jones Jr & H Smoot Fahlgren (Ky).

CAJUN BEAT stalked the leaders while four wide along the backstretch, made a run to challenge at the quarter pole, drifted out after opening a clear advantage in upper stretch then drew away under steady right hand urging. BLUESTHESTANDARD dropped back before going a quarter, raced well back for three furlongs, split rivals while launching his bid on the turn then finished well along the inside to best the others. SHAKE YOU DOWN rushed up between horses after breaking slowly, dueled outside ZAVATA to the top of the stretch then weakened from his early efforts. POSSE steadied between horses along the backstretch, raced well back for a half, swung six wide entering the stretch then rallied belatedly in the middle of the track. YANKEE GENTLEMAN chased the leaders while five wide for a half and weakened. ALDEBARAN dropped well back along the backstretch, raced far back into upper stretch then rallied belatedly between horses. CAPTAIN SQUIRE raced in the middle of the pack while five wide to the turn and steadily tired thereafter. MIDAS EYES was bumped while between horses along the backstretch, raced within striking distance to the top of the stretch and lacked a strong closing bid. PRIVATE HORDE was shuffled back between horses at the half mile pole, circled six wide on the turn then finished evenly. ETHAN MAN checked between horses at the half mile pole, advanced five wide on the turn and faded in the stretch then pulled up in distress and was vanned off. GREAT NOTION steadied in traffic along the backstretch, circled six wide on the turn then lacked a further response. ZAVATA dueled along the rail for a half and gave way. VALID VIDEO saved ground to the turn and faltered.

Owners– 1, Padua Stable John Iracane & Joseph Iracane; 2, Sengara Jeffrey; 3, Cole Robert L Jr; 4, Heiligbrodt Racing Stable & Vinery Stables; 5, Wygod Mr and Mrs Martin J; 6, Flaxman Holdings Ltd; 7, Robert D Bone & Jeffrey S Diener; 8, Gann Edmund A; 9, Tucker Billy R; 10, West Point Thoroughbreds LLC; 11, Silverton Hill Farm LLC; 12, Tabor Michael B; 13, Fehsenfeld Mac

Trainers– 1, Margolis Stephen R; 2, West Ted H; 3, Lake Scott A; 4, Asmussen Steven M; 5, Shirreffs John A; 6, Frankel Robert J; 7, Mullins Jeff; 8, Frankel Robert J; 9, Cain S Joseph; 10, Byrne Patrick B; 11, Miller Darrin; 12, Biancone Patrick L; 13, Manning Dennis J

$2 Daily Double (13–11) Paid $323.00 ; Daily Double Pool $241,517 .
$1 Pick Three (14–13–11) Paid $658.30 ; Pick Three Pool $914,696 .

SIXTH RACE
Santa Anita
OCTOBER 25, 2003

1¼ **MILES. (Turf) (1.57²) BREEDERS' CUP FILLY & MARE TURF Grade I. Purse $1,000,000 FOR FILLIES AND MARES, THREE-YEAR-OLDS AND UPWARD.** Northern Hemisphere Three-Year-Olds, 118 lbs.; Older, 123 lbs. Southern Hemisphere Three-Year-Olds, 113 lbs. Older, 123 lbs. $10,000 to pre-enter, $20,000 to enter, with guaranteed $1 million purse including nominator awards (plus Net Supplementary Fees, if any), of which 52% of all monies to the owner of the winner, 20% to second, 11% to third, 5.7% to fourth and 3% to fifth; plus stallion nominator awards of 2.6% of all monies to the winner, 1% to second and 0.55% to third and foal nominator awards of 2.6% of all monies to the winner, 1% to second and 0.55% to third. Closed with 14 pre-entries.

Value of Race: $972,020 Winner $551,200; second $212,000; third $116,600; fourth $60,420; fifth $31,800. Mutuel Pool $4,545,443.00 Exacta Pool $3,193,917.00 Trifecta Pool $2,543,090.00 Superfecta Pool $707,873.00 Head2Head Pool $31,654.00

Last Raced	Horse	M/Eqt.	A.	Wt	PP	¼	½	¾	1	Str	Fin	Jockey	Odds $1
6Sep03 7Leo³	Islington-Ire	B	4	123	4	5¹	5½	6½	6¹½	2¹½	1nk	Fallon K	2.90
12Oct03 Cur¹	L'Ancresse-Ire	B	3	118	11	3¹½	2¹½	2¹½	2¹	1hd	2²½	Prado E S	46.50
5Oct03 LCH²	Yesterday-Ire	B	3	118	2	10²	10¹½	10¹½	7hd	3hd	3no	Kinane M J	14.70
27Sep03 8Bel³	Heat Haze-GB	LB	4	123	3	11hd	11⁶	11⁷	10²	6½	4¾	Bailey J D	7.00
26Jly03 8Dmr¹	Megahertz-GB	LB	4	123	9	12	12	12	11³	10⁸	5¹½	Solis A O	16.10
27Sep03 8Bel⁵	Riskaverse	LB	4	123	8	4hd	4¹½	3½	3hd	4½	6hd	Velazquez J R	45.50
26Jly03 8Sar¹	Voodoo Dancer	LB	5	123	7	7hd	9²	9¹	5hd	9hd	7¹	Nakatani C S	8.90
28Sep03 7SA¹	Tates Creek	LB	5	123	1	6hd	7¹	7¹	9¹½	7hd	8½	Valenzuela P A	4.70
5Oct03 6Kee¹	Bien Nicole	LB	5	123	12	1¹½	1⁵	1⁸	1⁵	5¹½	9no	Pettinger D R	16.20
14Sep03 7LCH¹	Mezzo Soprano	B	3	118	5	8hd	8hd	8hd	4¹	8hd	10¹⁵	Dettori L	18.30
28Sep03 7SA²	Musical Chimes	B b	3	118	6	2hd	3hd	4¹	8hd	11¹½	11⁴½	Stevens G L	4.60
27Sep03 8Bel¹	Dimitrova	LB	3	118	10	9¹½	6½	5hd	12	12	12	Smullen P	11.70

OFF AT 12:51 Start Good. Won driving. Course firm.

TIME :23⁴, :46³, 1:10², 1:35¹, 1:59 (:23.82, :46.73, 1:10.52, 1:35.31, 1:59.13)

4 – ISLINGTON–IRE	7.80	6.00	4.20
11 – L'ANCRESSE–IRE		32.60	13.00
2 – YESTERDAY–IRE			7.80

$2 Mutuel Prices:

$1 EXACTA 4–11 PAID $212.40 $1 TRIFECTA 4–11–2 PAID $1,589.50
$1 SUPERFECTA 4–11–2–3 PAID $18,834.10
$2 HEAD2HEAD 1VS.4; WINNER4 PAID $3.20

B. f, (Feb), by Sadler's Wells – Hellenic , by Darshaan–GB . Trainer Stoute Sir Michael R. Bred by Ballymacoll Stud Farm Ltd (Ire).

ISLINGTON (IRE) pulled early, chased between horses then off the rail leaving the second turn, came out into the stretch, gained a short advantage outside the runner-up past the eighth pole and gamely prevailed under urging. L'ANCRESSE (IRE) stalked outside a rival then a bit off the rail, bid outside the pacesetter and took command nearing the stretch, fought back inside the winner through the final furlong and continued gamely to the wire. YESTERDAY (IRE) saved ground off the pace, moved up outside a rival on the second turn, split horses in the stretch and finished well for third. HEAT HAZE (GB) shuffled back down the hill, saved ground off the pace, came out on the second turn and three deep into the stretch, then rallied between foes and just missed the show. MEGAHERTZ (GB) unhurried early, angled in and lagged back inside, came out on the second turn and into the stretch and found her best stride late. RISKAVERSE was in a good position stalking the pace three deep to the stretch and lacked the needed late response. VOODOO DANCER chased between horses and was in a bit tight into the first turn, continued outside leaving the backstretch, went three and five wide on the second turn and five wide into the stretch and lacked the needed rally. TATES CREEK saved ground chasing the pace, split horses in the stretch, was in a bit tight past midstretch and also lacked the necessary response, then did not return to be unsaddled and was vanned off. BIEN NICOLE wide down the hill and crossing the dirt, took the lead and angled in, opened up on the clubhouse turn, began to come back to the field on the second turn, offered little resistance when challenged and weakened. MEZZO SOPRANO bumped at the start and away a bit slowly, pulled between foes early, chased outside, came four wide into the stretch and did not rally. MUSICAL CHIMES close up while rank inside early, saved ground chasing the pace, fell back some on the second turn, took up when in tight into the stretch and gave way. DIMITROVA well placed chasing the pace three deep, dropped back on the second turn and also gave way.

Owners– 1, Estate of the Late Lord Weinstock; 2, Tabor Michael and Magnier Mrs John; 3, Mrs John Magnier & Mrs Richard Henry; 4, Juddmonte Farms Inc; 5, Bello Michael; 6, Fox Ridge Farm Inc; 7, Green Hills Farm; 8, Juddmonte Farms Inc; 9, Richter Kristine and John; 10, Godolphin Racing Inc; 11, Al Maktoum Sheik Maktoum b; 12, Higgins Joseph

Trainers– 1, Stoute Sir Michael R; 2, O'Brien Aidan P; 3, O'Brien Aidan P; 4, Frankel Robert J; 5, Frankel Robert J; 6, Kelly Patrick J; 7, Clement Christophe; 8, Frankel Robert J; 9, Von Hemel Donnie K; 10, bin Suroor Saeed; 11, Drysdale Neil D; 12, Weld Dermot K

$2 Daily Double (11–4) Paid $218.00 ; Daily Double Pool $212,664 .
$1 Pick Three (13–11–4) Paid $627.80 ; Pick Three Pool $799,230 .

SEVENTH RACE

Santa Anita

OCTOBER 25, 2003

1 1/16 MILES. (1.39) BESSEMER TRUST BREEDERS' CUP JUVENILE Grade I. Purse $1,500,000 FOR COLTS AND GELDINGS, TWO YEARS OLD. Weight: 122 lbs.; $15,000 to pre–enter, $30,000 to enter, with guaranteed $1.5 million purse including nominator awards (plus Net Supplementary Fees, if any), of which 52% of all monies to the owner of the winner, 20% to second, 11% to third, 5.7% to fourth and 3% to fifth; plus stallion nominator awards of 2.6% of all monies to the winner, 1% to second and 0.55% to third and foal nominator awards of 2.6% of all monies to the winner, 1% to second and 0.55% to third. Closed with 15 pre–entries.

Value of Race: $1,375,500 Winner $780,000; second $300,000; third $165,000; fourth $85,500; fifth $45,000. Mutuel Pool $3,929,734.00 Exacta Pool $2,315,166.00 Trifecta Pool $2,846,786.00 Superfecta Pool $662,941.00 Head2Head Pool $34,555.00

Last Raced	Horse	M/Eqt. A. Wt	PP	St	1/4	1/2	3/4	Str	Fin	Jockey	Odds $1
28Sep03 1SA1	Action This Day	LB	2 122	2	12	12	12	102	32	12 1/4	Flores D R	26.80
10Sep03 8Dmr2	Minister Eric	LB	2 122	7	8	10 1/2 9 1/2	51	2hd	25	Solis A O	8.70
4Oct03 7Bel2	Chapel Royal	LB	2 122	10	7	3 1/2	2hd	11	11 1/2	3no	Velazquez J R	5.70
4Oct03 6Kee2	Tiger Hunt	LB	2 122	6	10	114	113 1/2 111 1/2 62 1/2	41 1/2	Day P	4.40
5Oct03 10SA5	Consecrate	LB b	2 122	4	3	5hd	51	2hd	43	5 3/4	Valenzuela P A	27.50
5Oct03 10SA2	Capitano	LB b	2 122	9	5	63 1/2 82 1/2	4hd	51 1/2	67	Valdivia J Jr	34.30
12Oct03 6SA1	That's an Outrage	LB b	2 122	3	11	82	71	6 1/2	81 1/2	71 1/2	Espinoza V	47.00
12Oct03 Cur2	Relaxed Gesture–Ire	B	2 122	11	9	9 1/2	102	12	105	81	Smullen P	20.00
10ct03 4SA1	Race for Glory	LB	2 122	1	1	2 1/2	3hd	7 1/2	71	94	Velasquez C H	6.20
5Oct03 10SA4	Siphonizer	LB	2 122	8	4	7hd	62	9hd	91	107	Krone J A	22.60
5Oct03 10SA6	Mambo Train	LB b	2 122	5	2	1hd	1hd	81 1/2	112	1128	Prado E S	42.40
14Sep03 7Bel1	Cuvee	LB	2 122	12	6	41	41	31 1/2	12	12	Bailey J D	1.60

OFF AT 1:25 Start Good. Won driving. Track fast.

TIME :221, :45, 1:094, 1:37, 1:433 (:22.31, :45.17, 1:09.80, 1:37.00, 1:43.62)

$2 Mutuel Prices:	2 – ACTION THIS DAY	55.60	19.20	11.00
	7 – MINISTER ERIC		8.80	7.20
	10 – CHAPEL ROYAL			5.60

$1 EXACTA 2–7 PAID $188.40 $1 TRIFECTA 2–7–10 PAID $2,245.40
$1 SUPERFECTA 2–7–10–6 PAID $9,123.40
$2 HEAD2HEAD 6VS.10; WINNER 10 PAID $3.20

B. c, (Feb), by Kris S. – Najecam , by Trempolino . Trainer Mandella Richard. Bred by Jaime S Carrion Trustee (Ky).

ACTION THIS DAY trailed while racing far back long the backstretch, launched a rally leaving the turn, split rivals while gaining just inside his stablemate on the turn, advanced four wide into the stretch, charged to the front nearing the sixteenth pole then drew away under intermittent right hand urging. MINISTER ERIC was unhurried for five furlongs while saving ground, angled out midway on the turn, closed the gap while four wide approaching the quarter pole then finished well to clearly best the others. CHAPEL ROYAL moved up from outside to contest the early pace, forced the pace while three wide along the backstretch, accelerated to the front at the three–eighths pole, opened a clear advantage midway on the turn, maintained a clear lead into midstretch and weakened under pressure in the final eighth. TIGER HUNT raced far back to the turn then failed to threaten while improving his position. CONSECRATE steadied along the inside on the first turn, moved up along the backstretch, split horses while making a threatening move on the turn, but couldn't sustain his bid. CAPITANO was reserved for a half while four wide, lodged a mild rally from outside on the turn and flattened out. THAT'S AN OUTRAGE failed to mount a serious rally. RELAXED GESTURE (IRE) never reached contention. RACE FOR GLORY dueled heads apart along the inside for a half, dropped back on the far turn and steadily tired thereafter. SIPHONIZER raced in traffic going into the first turn, settled in the middle of the pack while four wide for six furlongs and lacked a further response. MAMBO TRAIN rushed up between horses, dueled heads apart along the backstretch and gave way on the far turn. CUVEE stalked the leaders while four wide for five furlongs, remained a factor to the turn and faltered.

Owners– 1, Hughes B Wayne; 2, Diamond A Racing Corporation; 3, Smith Derrick and Tabor Michael; 4, Team Valor Stables LLC; 5, McIngvale James; 6, Meguerditchian Mr and Mrs; 7, Bull Stick Stables LLC & Mercedes Stables LLC; 8, Moyglare Stud Farm Ltd; 9, Lewis Robert B and Beverly J; 10, Hughes B Wayne; 11, Everest Stables Inc; 12, Winchell Thoroughbreds LLC & Spendthrift Farm

Trainers– 1, Mandella Richard E; 2, Mandella Richard E; 3, Pletcher Todd A; 4, Walden W Elliott; 5, Baffert Bob; 6, Bell Thomas R II; 7, Puhich Michael; 8, Weld Dermot K; 9, Lukas D Wayne; 10, Mandella Richard E; 11, Polanco Marcelo; 12, Asmussen Steven M

$2 Daily Double (4–2) Paid $293.20 ; Daily Double Pool $223,551.
$1 Pick Three (11–4–2) Paid $2,220.60 ; Pick Three Pool $687,180.

EIGHTH RACE
Santa Anita
OCTOBER 25, 2003

1½ MILES. (Turf) (2.22⁴) JOHN DEERE BREEDERS' CUP TURF Grade I. Purse $2,000,000 FOR THREE-YEAR-OLDS AND UPWARD. Northern Hemisphere Three-Year-Olds, 121 lbs.; Older, 126 lbs.; Southern Hemisphere Three-Year-Olds, 116 lbs.; Older, 125 lbs. All Fillies and Mares allowed 3 lbs. $20,000 to pre-enter, $40,000 to enter, with guaranteed $2million purse including nominator awards (plus Net Supplementary Fees, if any), of which 52% of all monies to the owner of the winner, 20% to second, 11% to third, 5.7% to fourth and 3% to fifth; plus stallion nominator awards of 2.6% of all monies to the winner, 1% to second and 0.55% to third and foal nominator awards of 2.6% of all monies to the winner, 1% to second and 0.55% to third. Closed with 12 pre-entries.

Value of Race: $1,944,040 Winner $763,200; Winner $763,200; third $233,200; fourth $120,840; fifth $63,600. Mutuel Pool $4,987,342.00 Exacta Pool $2,972,721.00 Trifecta Pool $2,414,746.00 Superfecta Pool $749,886.00 Head2Head Pool $115,131.00

Last Raced	Horse	M/Eqt.	A.	Wt	PP	¼	½	1	1¼	Str	Fin	Jockey	Odds $1
5Oct03 ⁹LCH³	DH High Chaparral-Ire	LB	4	126	3	5¹	5¹½	3hd	3½	3²	1	Kinane M J	4.90
28Sep03 ³SA²	DH Johar	LB	4	126	9	9	9	9	7⁶	4¹½	1hd	Solis A O	14.20
27Sep03 ¹⁰ASC¹	Falbrav-Ire	B	5	126	8	4hd	3hd	4¹	2¹	1½	3⁵½	Holland D	3.60
16Aug03 ¹⁰AP⁶	The Tin Man	LB	5	126	7	2¹	2¹	2¹	1¹	2¹½	4¾	Smith M E	14.30
27Sep03 ⁹Bel¹	Sulamani-Ire	LB	4	126	4	7hd	7hd	7½	6¹	6hd	5¹¾	Dettori L	3.10
5Oct03 ¹⁰LCH³	Bright Sky-Ire	B	4	123	2	8¹½	6hd	6¹	5½	7¹⁰	6¹	Boeuf D	22.60
28Sep03 ³SA¹	Storming Home-GB	LB bf	5	126	5	6hd	8²½	5¹	4¹½	5hd	7¹⁴	Stevens G L	2.00
4Oct03 ⁵SA⁸	Toccet	LB b	3	121	1	3¹	4½	8¹	9	9	8¹½	Baze R A	47.30
27Sep03 ⁹Bel³	Balto Star	LB	5	126	6	1½	1½	1hd	8¹	8hd	9	Velazquez J R	24.10

DH-Dead Heat.

OFF AT 1:58 Start Good. Won driving. Course firm.
TIME :25, :48³, 1:11², 1:35³, 2:00, 2:24¹ (:25.12, :48.73, 1:11.42, 1:35.76, 2:00.04, 2:24.24)

$2 Mutuel Prices:

3 - DH HIGH CHAPARRAL-IRE............	6.40	6.20	3.80
9 - DH JOHAR.............................	13.60	9.00	5.40
8 - FALBRAV-IRE.......................			4.20

$1 EXACTA 3-9 PAID $36.30 $1 EXACTA 9-3 PAID $44.40
$1 TRIFECTA 3-9-8 PAID $180.20 $1 TRIFECTA 9-3-8 PAID $248.30
$1 SUPERFECTA 3-9-8-7 PAID $1,116.90 $1 SUPERFECTA 9-3-8-7 PAID $1,905.80
$2 HEAD2HEAD 4VS.5; WINNER 4 PAID $3.20

High Chaparral-Ire —B. c, (Mar), by Sadler's Wells – Kasora , by Darshaan-GB . Trainer O'Brien Aidan P. Bred by S Coughlan (Ire).
Johar —B. c, (Feb), by Gone West – Windsharp , by Lear Fan . Trainer Mandella Richard. Bred by The Thoroughbred Corporation (Ky).

HIGH CHAPARRAL (IRE) stalked between horses then along the inside, split rivals into the second turn, came out into the stretch and rallied gamely while between foes late under urging to share the win. JOHAR unhurried and angled in a bit off the rail early, moved up outside on the second turn, came five wide into the stretch and closed willingly three deep on the line. FALBRAV (IRE) stalked three deep or outside a rival, bid outside the leader leaving the second turn, took a short advantage into the stretch, inched away past midstretch and held on gamely inside the top pair but was edged late. THE TIN MAN prompted the pace outside a rival, took command on the second turn, angled in, fought back inside in midstretch but weakened. SULAMANI (IRE) squeezed a bit in the opening strides, chased between horses, was in tight and clipped heels into the clubhouse turn, chased outside on the backstretch, came four wide into the stretch and lacked the needed rally. BRIGHT SKY (IRE) pulled along the inside early, was in tight between horses into the first turn, chased between foes, split rivals into the second turn, continued toward the inside and weakened. STORMING HOME (GB) squeezed a bit in the early stages, was in a good position chasing three and four wide to the stretch and lacked the necessary response. TOCCET pulled a bit early, raced close up stalking the pace inside, dropped back on the backstretch, came outside a rival into the stretch and gave way. BALTO STAR took the early lead and set a pressured pace inside, steadied while dropping back into the second turn and also gave way. Rail at zero on hill.

Owners— 1, Tabor Michael and Magnier Mrs John; 2, The Thoroughbred Corporation; 3, Scuderia Rencati SRL & Teruya Yoshida; 4, Todd Aury and Ralph E; 5, Godolphin Racing Inc; 6, Ecurie Wildenstein; 7, Al Maktoum Sheik Maktoum b; 8, Borislow Daniel M; 9, Anstu Stables Inc

Trainers— 1, O'Brien Aidan P; 2, Mandella Richard E; 3, Cumani Luca M; 4, Mandella Richard E; 5, bin Suroor Saeed; 6, Lellouche Elie; 7, Drysdale Neil D; 8, Scanlan John F; 9, Pletcher Todd A

$2 Daily Double (2-3) Paid $259.40 ; Daily Double Pool $220,540 .
$2 Daily Double (2-9) Paid $370.00 .
$1 Pick Three (4-2-3) Paid $379.50 ; Pick Three Pool $574,827 .
$1 Pick Three (4-2-9) Paid $1,046.60 .

NINTH RACE
Santa Anita
OCTOBER 25, 2003

1¼ MILES. (1.57⁴) BREEDERS' CUP CLASSIC Grade I. Purse $4,000,000 FOR THREE-YEAR-OLDS AND UPWARD. Northern Hemisphere Three-Year-Olds, 121 lbs.; Older, 126 lbs.; Southern Hemisphere Three-Year-Olds, 116 lbs.; Older, 126 lbs. All Fillies and Mares allowed 3 lbs. $40,000 to pre-enter, $80,000 to enter, with guaranteed $4million purse including nominator awards (plus Net Supplementary Fees, if any), of which 52% of all monies to the owner of the winner, 20% to second, 11% to third, 5.7% to fourth and 3% to fifth; plus stallion nominator awards of 2.6% of all monies to thewinner, 1% to second and 0.55% to third and foal nominator awards of 2.6% of all monies to the winner, 1% to second and 0.55% to third. Closed with 13 pre-entries.

Value of Race: $3,668,000 Winner $2,080,000; second $800,000; third $440,000; fourth $228,000; fifth $120,000. Mutuel Pool $7,437,398.00 Exacta Pool $4,339,747.00 Trifecta Pool $3,856,615.00 Superfecta Pool $1,210,941.00 Head2Head Pool $14,267.00

Last Raced	Horse	M/Eqt.	A.	Wt	PP	¼	½	¾	1	Str	Fin	Jockey	Odds $1
4Oct03 5SA1	Pleasantly Perfect	LB b	5	126	2	8½	82½	7½	52	32	11½	Solis A O	14.20
24Aug03 5Dmr2	Medaglia d'Oro	LB	4	126	8	1hd	1hd	21½	21½	21½	2¾	Bailey J D	2.60
3Oct03 8Med2	Dynever	LB	3	121	6	93	92	91½	61	4hd	3nk	Nakatani C S	15.20
13Sep03 11TP2	Congaree	LB	5	126	9	22	21	1½	1½	1hd	45	Valenzuela P A	6.30
6Sep03 9Bel2	Hold That Tiger	LB	3	121	5	32	31	33	32	51½	52¼	Prado E S	8.50
28Sep03 9Haw1	Perfect Drift	LB	4	126	7	4hd	6½	5hd	41	66	62	Stevens G L	5.70
27Sep03 10Bel3	Evening Attire	LB b	5	126	1	10	10	10	10	7hd	72½	Velazquez J R	24.90
20Sep03 10LaD1	Ten Most Wanted	LB b	3	121	10	75	72	82½	92	9hd	8½	Day P	4.10
3Aug03 11Mth3	Funny Cide	LB	3	121	4	51	51½	62	72	10	95	Krone J A	8.70
3Oct03 8Med3	Volponi	LB b	5	126	3	6hd	4hd	4hd	81½	8hd	10	Santos J A	16.70

OFF AT 2:40 Start Good. Won driving. Track fast.

TIME :22³, :46¹, 1:10¹, 1:34¹, 1:59⁴ (:22.79, :46.35, 1:10.32, 1:34.32, 1:59.88)

$2 Mutuel Prices:			
2 – PLEASANTLY PERFECT	30.40	9.60	6.60
8 – MEDAGLIA D'ORO		4.40	3.60
6 – DYNEVER			7.40

$1 EXACTA 2-8 PAID $70.00 $1 TRIFECTA 2-8-6 PAID $831.00
$1 SUPERFECTA 2-8-6-9 PAID $4,931.40
$2 HEAD2HEAD 3VS.4;WINNER4 PAID $3.40

B. h, (Apr), by Pleasant Colony – Regal State, by Affirmed. Trainer Mandella Richard. Bred by Clovelly Farms (Ky).

PLEASANTLY PERFECT was eased back soon after the start, was unhurried along the backstretch, gradually worked his way forward on the far turn, closed the gap between horses to reach contention on the turn, angled four wide nearing the quarter pole, made a run to challenge a sixteenth out then wore down MEDAGLIA D'ORO in the final seventy yards. MEDAGLIA D'ORO was in tight when bumped by CONGAREE at the start, rushed up along the inside to contest the early pace, forced the issue inside CONGAREE for a mile, edged closer nearing the quarter pole, surged to the front in midstretch, fought gamely into deep stretch then yielded grudgingly. DYNEVER trailed early after being bumped and pinched back at the start, raced far back for six furlongs, worked his way forward on the turn, angled four wide approaching the quarter pole then rallied belatedly to gain a share. CONGAREE broke inward causing crowding at the start, rushed up from outside, set the pace under pressure outside MEDAGLIA D'ORO along the backstretch, maintained a slim advantage through the turn, fought heads apart leaving the furlong marker then weakened from his early efforts. HOLD THAT TIGER was bumped a bit at the start, stalked the pace while three wide for seven furlongs, dropped back on the turn and steadily tired thereafter. PERFECT DRIFT was carried wide by FUNNY CIDE on the first turn, raced within striking distance from outside to the turn and lacked a further response. EVENING ATTIRE never reached contention. TEN MOST WANTED checked after being carried out on the first turn then angled to the inside, failed to mount a serious rally. FUNNY CIDE drifted out on the first turn, raced just off the pace while four wide for seven furlongs and faltered. VOLPONI failed to mount a serious rally while saving ground.

Owners– 1, Diamond A Racing Corporation; 2, Gann Edmund A; 3, Wills Catherine and Karches Peter; 4, Stonerside Stable LLC; 5, Tabor Michael and Magnier Mrs John; 6, Stonecrest Farm; 7, Mr & Mrs Joseph M Grant & Thomas J Kelly; 8, J Paul Reddam Michael Jarvis & James Chisholm Et Al; 9, Sackatoga Stable; 10, Amherst Stable and Spruce Pond Stable

Trainers– 1, Mandella Richard E; 2, Frankel Robert J; 3, Clement Christophe; 4, Baffert Bob; 5, O'Brien Aidan P; 6, Johnson Murray W; 7, Kelly Patrick J; 8, Dollase Wallace A; 9, Tagg Barclay; 10, Johnson Philip G

$2 Daily Double (9–2) Paid $157.20.
$2 Daily Double (3–2) Paid $85.00; Daily Double Pool $828,103.
$1 Pick Three (2–9–2) Paid $1,966.30.
$1 Pick Three (2–3–2) Paid $1,017.70; Pick Three Pool $808,208.
$2 Pick Six (13–11–4–2–3/9–2) 6 Correct Paid $2,687,611.60.
$2 Pick Six (13–11–4–2–3/9–2) 5 Correct Paid $18,663.80; Pick Six Pool $4,489,454.
$1 Pick Four (4–2–3/9–2) Paid $9,801.90; Pick Four Pool $1,289,407.

NINTH RACE
Churchill
OCTOBER 26, 2003

7½ FURLONGS. (1.28) ACK ACK H.. Grade III. Purse $150,000 A HANDICAP FOR THREE-YEAR-OLDS AND UPWARD. By subscription of $150 each on or before October 15, 2003 or by supplementary nomination of $7,500 each by 12:00 noon (local time) Monday, October 20, 2003. $750 to pass the entry box; $750 additional to start. Weights to be announced Tuesday, October 21.

Value of Race: $165,450 Winner $102,579; second $33,090; third $16,545; fourth $8,273; fifth $4,963. Mutuel Pool $239,734.00 Exacta Pool $160,004.00 Trifecta Pool $125,558.00 Superfecta Pool $34,983.00

Last Raced	Horse	M/Eqt.	A.Wt	PP	St	¼	½	Str	Fin	Jockey	Odds $1
27Sep03 9TP3	Cappuchino	Lbf	4 117	7	1	$2^{1\frac{1}{2}}$	2^{4}	1^{1}	1^{2}	Court J K	8.00
5Jly03 9CD5	Pass Rush	Lb	4 116	3	2	1^{hd}	1^{hd}	$2^{2\frac{1}{2}}$	2^{1}	Day P	2.20
10Sep03 8AP1	Twilight Road	Lf	6 116	2	5	5^{6}	4^{hd}	$4^{3\frac{1}{2}}$	3^{2}	Albarado R J	10.00
23Aug03 9ElP4	Woodmoon	Lbf	5 114	1	7	6^{2}	$6^{1\frac{1}{2}}$	5^{hd}	$4^{\frac{1}{2}}$	Guidry M	19.20
27Sep03 9TP2	Cat Tracker	L	5 116	4	4	$3^{\frac{1}{2}}$	$3^{1\frac{1}{2}}$	3^{1}	$5^{4\frac{3}{4}}$	Melancon L	6.20
3Oct03 7Kee4	Dubai Sheikh	Lf	4 117	5	6	7	7	6^{5}	$6^{23\frac{1}{2}}$	Velasquez C	4.50
21Sep03 8AP1	Apt To Be	Lb	6 120	6	3	$4^{\frac{1}{2}}$	$5^{6\frac{1}{2}}$	7	7	Razo E Jr	*2.20

***—Actual Betting Favorite.**

OFF AT 4:38 Start Good. Won driving. Track sloppy.
TIME :22^{4}, :45^{2}, 1:10^{3}, 1:31^{3} (:22.83, :45.41, 1:10.79, 1:31.66)

$2 Mutuel Prices:			
7-CAPPUCHINO	18.00	6.60	4.40
3-PASS RUSH		4.00	3.00
2-TWILIGHT ROAD			4.40

$2 EXACTA 7-3 PAID $68.80 $2 TRIFECTA 7-3-2 PAID $415.80 $2 SUPERFECTA 7-3-2-1 PAID $2,464.00

B. c, by Capote-Tara Roma, by Lyphard. Trainer Hollendorfer Jerry. Bred by Emory A Hamilton (Ky).

CAPPUCHINO went up early to contest the pace outside of PASS RUSH four wide, battled on even terms with that one, stuck a head in front at the quarter-mile ground, was sharply roused left-handed at the eighth pole, then, after the rider switched the whip to the right side, continued under pressure to the wire. PASS RUSH gained a narrow advantage inside early, battled with the winner while inside that one to the final furlong and couldn't keep pace as second best. TWILIGHT ROAD, within easy striking distance while racing near the inside to the stretch, angled out six or seven wide for the drive and offered a mild gain. WOODMOON, outsprinted for a half and four wide around the turn, continued four wide into the lane but gained only slightly at the end. CAT TRACKER, well placed three or four wide from early on, made a serious run between calls outside the top two into the upper stretch but flattened out late. DUBAI SHEIKH, outrun four wide on the backstretch, edged in on the turn but was never a factor. APT TO BE, five wide, faded after a half and wasn't persevered with in the late going.

Owners— 1, H Litt G Todaro & Jerry Hollendorfe; 2, Tabor Michael B; 3, Donamire Farm; 4, Pabst Henry E; 5, WinStar Farm LLC; 6, Ramsey Kenneth L & Sarah K; 7, Duchossois Richard L

Trainers—1, Hollendorfer Jerry; 2, Byrne Patrick B; 3, McGee Paul J; 4, O'Callaghan Niall M; 5, Walden W Elliott; 6, Romans Dale; 7, Block Chris M

$2 Pick Three (2-11-7) Paid $967.00; Pick Three Pool $23,283.

EIGHTH RACE
Aqueduct
OCTOBER 29, 2003

1⅛ MILES. (1.47) DISCOVERY H.. Grade III. Purse $100,000 (Up to $19,400 NYSBFOA) A HANDICAP FOR THREE YEAR OLDS. By subscription of $100 each, which should accompany the nomination; $500 to pass the entry box; $500 to start, with $100,000 added. The added money and all fees to be divided 60% to the winner, 20% to second, 11% to third, 6% to fourth and 3% to fifth. The owner of the winner to receive the Walter J. Salmon Challenge Trophy presented by the family of late Walter J. Salmon, to be retained for one year. A trophy will be presented to the winning owner for permanent possession, and trophies will be presented to the winning trainer and jockey. Closed Saturday, October 18, 2003 with 23 Nominations.

Value of Race: $111,800 Winner $67,080; second $22,360; third $12,298; fourth $6,708; fifth $3,354. Mutuel Pool $319,264.00 Exacta Pool $259,610.00 Trifecta Pool $188,484.00

Last Raced	Horse	M/Eqt.	A.Wt	PP	St	¼	½	¾	Str	Fin	Jockey	Odds $1
13Sep03 8Bel1	During	Lb	3 120	2	1	2^{hd}	$2^{\frac{1}{2}}$	2^{3}	$2^{5\frac{1}{2}}$	1no	Santos J A	5.20
3Oct03 8Med3	Unforgettable Max	L	3 114	6	3	3^{3}	$3^{2\frac{1}{2}}$	1^{hd}	1^{hd}	$2^{1\frac{3}{4}}$	Castellano J J	9.50
13Sep03 8Bel4	Inamorato	Lb	3 114	7	6	$5^{\frac{1}{2}}$	4^{hd}	$3^{\frac{1}{2}}$	$3^{1\frac{1}{2}}$	$3^{4\frac{1}{4}}$	Chavez J F	9.60
2Oct03 8Bel1	Congrats	L	3 116	1	2	$4^{\frac{1}{2}}$	$5^{\frac{1}{2}}$	4^{hd}	$4^{1\frac{1}{2}}$	4^{nk}	Prado E S	2.60
9Oct03 6Bel1	Newfoundland	Lb	3 117	4	8	$6^{\frac{1}{2}}$	$6^{2\frac{1}{2}}$	$7^{3\frac{1}{2}}$	6^{15}	5no	Velazquez J R	3.75
9Oct03 6Bel2	Conservation	L	3 114	3	5	$7^{\frac{1}{2}}$	7^{hd}	6^{hd}	$5^{\frac{1}{2}}$	$6^{23\frac{1}{2}}$	Espinoza J L	22.40
28Sep03 7Bel1	Colita	Lb	3 116	5	7	8	8	8	7	7	Migliore R	3.00
21Sep03 9Bel7	Sharp Impact	Lb	3 114	8	4	$1^{1\frac{1}{2}}$	$1^{\frac{1}{2}}$	$5^{1\frac{1}{2}}$	—	—	Gryder A T	24.50

Sharp Impact:Eased;

OFF AT 3:45 Start Good. Won driving. Track muddy.
TIME :23^{3}, :47, 1:11^{2}, 1:37^{2}, 1:51 (:23.72, :47.00, 1:11.41, 1:37.44, 1:51.18)

$2 Mutuel Prices:			
3-DURING	12.40	7.50	4.40
8-UNFORGETTABLE MAX		10.00	6.70
9-INAMORATO			7.10

$2 EXACTA 3-8 PAID $122.50 $2 TRIFECTA 3-8-9 PAID $951.00

Dk. b. or br. c, (Feb), by Cherokee Run-Blading Saddle, by Blade. Trainer Baffert Bob. Bred by Gulf States Racing Stables II (Ky).

DURING raced with the pace while in hand, dug in gamely when roused and prevailed after a long drive. UNFORGETTABLE MAX raced with the pace while three wide and stayed on gamely outside. INAMORATO was unhurried early on, rallied three wide on the second turn and finished gamely outside. CONGRATS raced between rivals early, advanced inside on the second turn, came wide for the drive and lacked a rally. NEWFOUNDLAND was outrun early, raced inside and had no response when roused. CONSERVATION was outrun early, came wide for the drive and had no rally. COLITA was outrun early, had no response when roused and tired. SHARP IMPACT was hustled to the front, set the pace, stopped after three quarters and was eased in the stretch.

Owners— 1, McIngvale James; 2, Dweck Raymond; 3, Godolphin Racing Inc; 4, Claiborne Farm & Dilschneider Adele; 5, Sumaya Us Stables; 6, Bohemia Stable; 7, Team Valor Stables Alvarez Mercedes; 8, Darley Stable

Trainers—1, Baffert Bob; 2, Perkins Ben W Jr; 3, Albertrani Thomas; 4, McGaughey Claude III; 5, Pletcher Todd A; 6, Tagg Barclay; 7, Pletcher Todd A; 8, McLaughlin Kiaran P

Scratched— Private City (19Oct03 8BEL2), Chilly Rooster (16Oct03 8BEL2), New York Hero (19Oct03 8BEL1)

EIGHTH RACE
Aqueduct
NOVEMBER 1, 2003

1⅛ MILES. (Turf)(1.47) KNICKERBOCKER H.. Grade II. Purse $150,000 (Up to $29,100 NYSBFOA) A HANDICAP FOR THREE YEAR OLDS AND UPWARD. By subscription of $150 each, which should accompany the nomination; $750 to pass the entry box; $750 to start. The purse to be divided 60% to the winner, 20% to second, 11% to third, 6% to fourth and 3% to fifth. Trophies will be presented to the winning owner, trainer and jockey. The New York Racing Association reserves the right to transfer this race to the Main Track. In the event that this race is taken off the turf, it may be subject to downgrading upon review by the Graded Stakes Committee. Closed Saturday, October 18, 2003 with 30 Nominations.

Value of Race: $150,000 Winner $90,000; second $30,000; third $16,500; fourth $9,000; fifth $4,500. Mutuel Pool $717,658.00 Exacta Pool $595,491.00 Trifecta Pool $416,134.00

Last Raced	Horse	M/Eqt.	A.	Wt	PP	St	¼	½	¾	Str	Fin	Jockey	Odds $1
4Oct03 7Kee9	Better Talk Now	Lbf	4	116	1	8	6hd	5hd	5½	33½	1½	Prado E S	6.80
4Oct03 8Bel10	Del Mar Show	L	6	116	4	4	4½	3½	3hd	21	2nk	Bailey J D	7.20
4Oct03 8Bel5	Millennium Dragon-GB	L	4	115	7	1	1½	11½	12	1½	32¾	Migliore R	10.80
3Oct03 8Bel1	Request For Parole	L	4	114	10	3	5½	6½	72	61	4¾	Bridgmohan S X	15.90
20Sep03 14KD3	Quest Star	Lb	4	118	5	6	7½	81½	82½	5½	5no	Velazquez J R	1.95
4Oct03 7Kee3	Deputy Strike	L	5	113	2	11	112½	11½	12	7hd	6nk	Arroyo N Jr	15.80
3Oct03 7Med1	Tam's Terms	L	5	114	11	5	3hd	42½	42	41½	71	Karamanos H A	11.40
27Sep03 9Bel6	Slew Valley	L	6	118	12	9	82½	72	6hd	91½	8nk	Castellano J J	8.50
3Oct03 8Bel3	Dawn Of The Condor	Lb	6	113	6	10	9hd	103½	9hd	8½	9¾	Luzzi M J	38.25
16Aug03 Dea5	Tau Ceti-GB	Lb	4	116	3	12	12	12	11½	10hd	103¼	Gryder A T	22.50
18Oct03 9Bel1	Quiet Ruler	L	5	114	9	2	2½	21	2½	12	11¾	Hampshire J F Jr	18.70
4Oct03 7Kee8	Blazing Fury	Lb	5	114	8	7	102	9hd	102	11hd	12	Santos J A	13.30

OFF AT 3:41 Start Good. Won driving. Course good.
TIME :24^3, :50, 1:14, 1:38^1, 1:50^2 (:24.78, :50.00, 1:14.04, 1:38.37, 1:50.53)

$2 Mutuel Prices:

1–BETTER TALK NOW	15.60	8.60	7.20
4–DEL MAR SHOW		9.10	6.50
7–MILLENNIUM DRAGON–GB			9.60

$2 EXACTA 1–4 PAID $117.00 $2 TRIFECTA 1–4–7 PAID $848.00

B. g, by Talkin Man–Bendita, by Baldski. Trainer Motion H Graham. Bred by Wimborne Farm Inc (Ky).

BETTER TALK NOW was rated along inside, saved ground, altered course to the outside in upper stretch, dug in gamely when roused and was up in time, driving. DEL MAR SHOW raced close up inside while in hand, angled out into the stretch and finished gamely while between rivals in the drive. MILLENNIUM DRAGON (GB) quickly showed in front, set the pace while in hand and dug in gamely along the inside in the stretch. REQUEST FOR PAROLE was rated along between rivals, was steadied while lacking room entering the stretch then finished gamely outside. QUEST STAR was rated along inside, altered course in the stretch and was going well late. DEPUTY STRIKE was outrun early, raced inside, was steadied in traffic in upper stretch and finished well inside. TAM'S TERMS chased the pace while three wide and weakened in the final furlong. SLEW VALLEY was rated along outside, raced wide throughout, was steadied entering the stretch and lacked a rally. DAWN OF THE CONDOR was outrun early, raced inside and had no response when roused. TAU CETI (GB) was outrun early, came wide into the stretch and had no rally. QUIET RULER chased the pace from the outside and tired in the stretch. BLAZING FURY was outrun early, raced wide and had no response when roused.

Owners— 1, Bushwood Stables; 2, Allen E Paulson Living Trust; 3, Darley Stable; 4, Knighton Jeri & Sam; 5, Mansell Stables LLC; 6, West Point Stable & Moss Maggi; 7, Bender Sondra D; 8, Rich Meadow Farm; 9, Soblick David; 10, Flaxman Stable; 11, Sarf Randy J & Old Brookside Farm; 12, Kimmel Caesar P & Nicholson Ronald

Trainers—1, Motion H Graham; 2, Mott William I; 3, McLaughlin Kiaran P; 4, Hough Stanley M; 5, Walden W Elliott; 6, McLaughlin Kiaran P; 7, Murray Lawrence E; 8, Sciacca Gary; 9, Sciacca Gary; 10, Lewis Lisa L; 11, Mueller Russell; 12, Toner James J

Scratched— Move Those Chains (11Oct03 9LRL1), Willard Straight (2Oct03 7BEL1)

$2 Pick Three (9–2–1) Paid $409.50; Pick Three Pool $76,482.

NINTH RACE
Aqueduct
NOVEMBER 1, 2003

1⅛ MILES. (1.47) TURNBACK THE ALARM H.. Grade III. Purse $100,000 (Up to $19,400 NYSBFOA) A HANDICAP FOR FILLIES AND MARES THREE YEARS OLD AND UPWARD. By subscription of $100 each, which should accompany the nomination; $500 to pass the entry box; $500 to start, with $100,000 added. The added money and all fees to be divided 60% to the winner, 20% to second, 11% to third, 6% to fourth and 3% to fifth. Trophies will be presented to the winning owner, trainer and jockey. Closed Saturday, October 18, 2003 with 15 Nominations.

Value of Race: $107,500 Winner $64,500; second $21,500; third $11,825; fourth $6,450; fifth $3,225. Mutuel Pool $389,810.00 Exacta Pool $276,233.00 Trifecta Pool $167,971.00

Last Raced	Horse	M/Eqt.	A.	Wt	PP	St	¼	½	¾	Str	Fin	Jockey	Odds $1
11Oct03 7Med2	Pocus Hocus	Lb	5	114	4	3	2½	2½	1hd	16	15¼	Santos J A	12.10
13Sep03 9Bel6	Nonsuch Bay	L	4	115	6	5	6	6	6	2hd	21½	Bailey J D	3.70
5Oct03 8Kee3	Miss Linda-ARG	L	6	118	1	2	1½	1½	2½	34½	31	Migliore R	2.65
19Sep03 8Bel3	Lady Liberty	L	4	114	3	4	52½	53	51½	4hd	46	Prado E S	12.90
6Sep03 9Mth1	Misty Sixes	L	5	114	5	6	3½	3hd	3½	515	529¾	Bridgmohan S X	4.10
18Oct03 6Bel2	She's Got The Beat	L	4	114	2	1	42½	4½	42½	6	6	Velazquez J R	1.95

OFF AT 4:06 Start Good. Won driving. Track fast.
TIME :24^2, :49, 1:13^3, 1:38, 1:50^3 (:24.51, :49.11, 1:13.78, 1:38.02, 1:50.67)

$2 Mutuel Prices:

4–POCUS HOCUS	26.20	9.30	4.30
6–NONSUCH BAY		4.70	3.80
1–MISS LINDA–ARG			3.60

$2 EXACTA 4–6 PAID $116.50 $2 TRIFECTA 4–6–1 PAID $439.50

Gr/ro m, by Quiet American–Cadabra Abra, by Al Hattab. Trainer Jerkens James A. Bred by David Allen (Ky).

POCUS HOCUS raced with the pace while between rivals under wraps, drew away when roused and was kept to a drive to the wire. NONSUCH BAY was outrun early, advanced inside on the second turn and finished well to earn the place prize. MISS LINDA (ARG) set the pace along the inside, could not stay with the winner turning for home and tired in the final furlong. LADY LIBERTY raced in hand along the inside early, came wide for the drive and lacked a rally. MISTY SIXES raced with the pace while three wide and tired in the stretch. SHE'S GOT THE BEAT raced close up inside, was steadied on the first turn, was pulled up in the stretch and was vanned off.

Owners— 1, Moore Susan & John; 2, Thorn Stable; 3, Ackerley Brothers Farm; 4, Janney III Stuart S; 5, Puglisi Stables; 6, Walsh Elizabeth

Trainers—1, Jerkens James A; 2, Alexander Frank A; 3, Kimmel John C; 4, McGaughey Claude III; 5, Klesaris Steve; 6, Johnson Philip G

EIGHTH RACE
Bay Meadows
NOVEMBER 1, 2003

1⅛ MILES. (Turf)(1.47^{4}) BAY MEADOWS DERBY. Grade III. Purse $100,000 FOR THREE-YEAR-OLDS. By subscription of $100 each to accompany the nomination or by supplementary nomination of $2,000 by Noon, Sunday, October 26, 2003. $500 to pass the entry box and $500 additional to start with $100,000 Guaranteed of which $55,000 to the winner, $20,000 to second, $15,000 to third, $7,500 to fourth and $2,500 to fifth. Weights, Sunday, October 26, 2003. Starters to be named through the entry box by the closing time of entries. A trophy will be presented to the owner of the winner. High weights preferred. NOMINATIONS CLOSE THURSDAY, OCTOBER 23, 2003.(If transferred to the main track the distance will be 1 1/18 miles) Rail at 25 feet.

Value of Race: $100,000 Winner $55,000; second $20,000; third $15,000; fourth $7,500; fifth $2,500. Mutuel Pool $291,452.00 Exacta Pool $155,954.00 Quinella Pool $15,645.00 Trifecta Pool $180,483.00 Superfecta Pool $72,715.00

Last Raced	Horse	M/Eqt.	A.Wt	PP	St	¼	½	¾	Str	Fin	Jockey	Odds $1
8Oct03 $^{7}SA^{6}$	Stanley Park	LBb	3 116	3	6	7^{2}	$6^{1\frac{1}{2}}$	$5^{\frac{1}{2}}$	$2^{\frac{1}{2}}$	$1^{2\frac{1}{2}}$	Saint-Martin E	7.40
6Sep03 $^{8}Dmr^{7}$	Bis Repetitas	LB	3 118	6	7	5^{hd}	$5^{2\frac{1}{2}}$	3^{hd}	1^{hd}	$2^{1\frac{1}{4}}$	Valdivia J Jr	2.00
20Oct03 $^{4}SA^{1}$	Kewen	LB	3 116	8	3	2^{2}	$2^{2\frac{1}{2}}$	2^{3}	3^{4}	$3^{1\frac{1}{4}}$	Baze R A	2.50
24Aug03 $^{10}Mth^{6}$	Sigint	LB	3 116	7	4	$6^{1\frac{1}{2}}$	$7^{1\frac{1}{2}}$	$7^{2\frac{1}{2}}$	$5^{2\frac{1}{2}}$	4^{6}	Alvarado F T	12.70
4Oct03 $^{6}SA^{1}$	Eyad-IR	LB	3 114	1	2	1^{1}	1^{hd}	$1^{\frac{1}{2}}$	4^{1}	5^{1}	Gonzalez R M	7.70
1Sep03 $^{9}EmD^{2}$	Condotierri	LBb	3 114	5	8	8	8	8	8	6^{1}	Schvaneveldt C P	24.50
21Sep03 $^{3}BM^{2}$	Winning Stripes	LB	3 116	4	1	3^{hd}	4^{hd}	$6^{2\frac{1}{2}}$	7^{2}	$7^{\frac{1}{2}}$	Rollins C J	25.60
28Sep03 $^{5}BM^{1}$	Mediator	LB	3 115	2	5	$4^{\frac{1}{2}}$	3^{2}	$4^{2\frac{1}{2}}$	$6^{1\frac{1}{2}}$	8	Warren R J Jr	4.30

OFF AT 4:23 Start Good. Won handily. Course firm.
TIME :23, :48, 1:11, $1:36^{4}$, $1:48^{4}$ (:23.07, :48.05, 1:11.16, 1:36.81, 1:48.97)

$2 Mutuel Prices:

3-STANLEY PARK	16.80	6.60	3.60
6-BIS REPETITAS		3.80	2.80
8-KEWEN			3.00

$1 EXACTA 3-6 PAID $27.50 $2 QUINELLA 3-6 PAID $22.40 $1 TRIFECTA 3-6-8 PAID $82.70 $1 SUPERFECTA 3-6-8-7 PAID $381.80

Ch. c, (Mar), by Swain*Ire–Tricky Bird, by Storm Bird. Trainer Shirreffs John. Bred by Fred Seitz (Ky).

STANLEY PARK was taken in hand early and raced unhurried from the inside, moved off the rail gradually once on the backstretch while gaining on the leaders, offered a quick bid while circling those rivals four wide to the stretch, got to terms at the furlong pole and drove clear while not necessarily being asked for his best. BIS REPETITAS sat just off the leaders early while three wide, remained three wide on the second turn to offer his bid, gained a brief lead at the furlong pole but could not match strides with the winner. KEWEN dueled outside EYAD to the stretch, disposed of that rival but was quickly engaged by BIS REPETITAS, resisted briefly but slackened in the final furlong. SIGINT raced unhurried while four wide to the backstretch, remained out on the second turn and closed a mild gap late. EYAD (IRE) set the pace from the rail to the stretch and gave out. CONDOTIERRI trailed to the stretch then passed tiring horses. WINNING STRIPES stalked the pace two wide to the stretch and came up empty. MEDIATOR was well placed from the rail to the second turn then had little left.

Owners— 1, Moss Mr & Mrs Jerome S; 2, Gann Edmund A; 3, Grossman Jack & Oliver Hal; 4, Parra Rosendo G; 5, Visionary Racing & Robert A Wiles; 6, September House Pavalunas Redd et a; 7, Robinson Ken Shustek Mike & Stanley; 8, The Thoroughbred Corporation

Trainers—1, Shirreffs John; 2, Frankel Robert; 3, Mandella Gary; 4, Cerin Vladimir; 5, Mulhall Kristin; 6, Roberts Craig; 7, Morey William J Jr; 8, Drysdale Neil

$2 Daily Double (9-3) Paid $48.00; Daily Double Pool $19,386.
$1 Pick Three (7-9-3) Paid $82.50; Pick Three Pool $22,443.

EIGHTH RACE
Hawthorne
NOVEMBER 1, 2003

1 MILE. (Turf)(1.33^{2}) ROBERT F. CAREY MEMORIAL H.. Grade III. Purse $150,000 A HANDICAP FOR THREE YEAR OLDS AND UPWARD. By subscription of $100 each, which shall accompany the nomination, $1,000 to pass the entry box, $1,000 additional to start. With $150,000 Guaranteed, of which 60 percent to the winner, 20 percent to second, 11 percent to third, 6 percent to fourth; 3 percent to fifth. Nominations closed Wednesday, October 22, 2003 with 30.

Value of Race: $150,000 Winner $90,000; second $30,000; third $16,500; fourth $9,000; fifth $4,500. Mutuel Pool $255,596.00 Exacta Pool $151,332.00 Trifecta Pool $145,934.00 Superfecta Pool $45,088.00

Last Raced	Horse	M/Eqt.	A.Wt	PP	St	¼	½	¾	Str	Fin	Jockey	Odds $1
12Oct03 $^{7}Kee^{2}$	Mystery Giver	L	5 120	1	6	8	8	8	4^{2}	$1^{\frac{1}{2}}$	Marquez C H Jr	1.90
12Oct03 $^{8}Haw^{2}$	Al's Dearly Bred	Lb	6 118	3	5	7^{4}	6^{hd}	7^{hd}	$6^{1\frac{1}{2}}$	$2^{\frac{3}{4}}$	Martin E M Jr	3.60
24Oct03 $^{7}Haw^{2}$	Major Rhythm	L	4 116	8	3	4^{1}	5^{hd}	$6^{1\frac{1}{2}}$	1^{hd}	$3^{\frac{1}{2}}$	Fires E	20.70
4Oct03 $^{8}Bel^{9}$	Mercenary	L	5 116	6	4	6^{hd}	7^{2}	$5^{\frac{1}{2}}$	3^{hd}	$4^{3\frac{1}{4}}$	Razo E Jr	9.60
3Oct03 $^{8}Kee^{1}$	Desert Dancer-ARG	L	5 114	4	7	3^{hd}	$3^{\frac{1}{2}}$	2^{1}	2^{hd}	$5^{1\frac{3}{4}}$	Melancon L	5.90
12Oct03 $^{8}Haw^{1}$	Mc Mahon	Lbf	5 115	2	2	2^{2}	$2^{\frac{1}{2}}$	$4^{\frac{1}{2}}$	5^{hd}	$6^{3\frac{1}{4}}$	Meier R	5.10
5Oct03 $^{4}Kee^{2}$	Moonshine Hall	L	3 112	5	8	$5^{1\frac{1}{2}}$	$4^{1\frac{1}{2}}$	3^{hd}	7^{1}	7^{6}	Peck B D	4.30
8Oct03 $^{5}Haw^{3}$	Canaverous	Lb	4 116	7	1	$1^{1\frac{1}{2}}$	1^{hd}	$1^{\frac{1}{2}}$	8	8	Compton P	53.70

OFF AT 4:28 Start Good. Won driving. Course firm.
TIME $:23^{4}$, $:47^{1}$, $1:11^{1}$, 1:23, $1:34^{3}$ (:23.94, :47.25, 1:11.24, 1:23.16, 1:34.70)

$2 Mutuel Prices:

2-MYSTERY GIVER	5.80	3.40	2.60
4-AL'S DEARLY BRED		4.00	3.20
11-MAJOR RHYTHM			7.00

$2 EXACTA 2-4 PAID $22.40 $2 TRIFECTA 2-4-11 PAID $238.40 $2 SUPERFECTA 2-4-11-8 PAID $1,123.80

B. g, by Dynaformer–Ioya, by Naskra. Trainer Block Chris M. Bred by David Block & Patricia Block (Ill).

MYSTERY GIVER trailed to the stretch, came out six wide for the drive, rallied through the lane and prevailed under steady handling. AL'S DEARLY BRED lacked speed inside, was pointed between horses when a rival came out, split foes late and rallied but missed. MAJOR RHYTHM raced off the rail near the middle of the field, rallied to a short lead in the stretch then could not finish with the top two. MERCENARY was void of early speed, angled out and challenged in the stretch but was outfinished. DESERT DANCER (ARG) raced close up but tired in the final furlong. MC MAHON raced close up inside and also tired. MOONSHINE HALL raced near the middle of the field and made a bid on the final turn but faltered. CANAVEROUS set the pace from just off the rail and tired.

Owners— 1, Team Block; 2, Castro John; 3, Messino James M; 4, Coast To Coast Racing Fund LLC; 5, WinStar Farm LLC; 6, Cherrywood Racing Stables II; 7, Melnyk Eugene & Laura; 8, Crossley Norman L & Pam

Trainers—1, Block Chris M; 2, Robertson Hugh H; 3, Beam Edward; 4, Calhoun William Bret; 5, Walden W Elliott; 6, Boyce Michele; 7, Reinstedler Anthony; 8, Bader Mark S

Scratched— Generals Sword (12Oct03 $^{8}HAW^{8}$), Beau Classic (18Oct03 $^{8}HAW^{3}$), Burning Roma (3Oct03 $^{7}MED^{2}$)

$2 Pick Three (11-4-2/6) Paid $341.80; Pick Three Pool $8,890.
$2 Pick Six (3-3-2-11-4-1/2/6/9) 6 Correct Paid $5,337.80; Pick Six Pool $2,196.

EIGHTH RACE
Aqueduct
NOVEMBER 2, 2003

1 MILE. (1.32^{2}) NASHUA S.. Grade III. Purse $100,000 (Up to $19,400 NYSBFOA) FOR TWO YEAR OLDS. By subscription of $100 each, which should accompany the nomination; $500 to pass the entry box; $500 to start, with $100,000 added. The added money and all fees to be divided 60% to the winner, 20% to second, 11% to third, 6% to fourth and 3% to fifth. 122 lbs. Non-winners of $50,000 allowed 2 lbs.; $30,000, 4 lbs.; a race other than maiden or claiming 6 lbs. Trophies will be presented to the winning owner, trainer and jockey. Closed Saturday, October 18, 2003 with 31 nominations.

Value of Race: $113,100 Winner $67,860; second $22,620; third $12,441; fourth $6,786; fifth $3,393. Mutuel Pool $411,952.00 Exacta Pool $361,398.00 Trifecta Pool $300,438.00

Last Raced	Horse	M/Eqt.	A.Wt	PP	St	¼	½	¾	Str	Fin	Jockey	Odds $1
4Oct03 ^{7}Bel^{6}	Read The Footnotes	L	2 118	1	6	$1\frac{1}{2}$	$1\frac{1}{2}$	1^{hd}	1^{2}	$1^{2\frac{1}{4}}$	Bailey J D	2.90
4Oct03 ^{7}Bel^{4}	Paddington	Lbf	2 120	5	1	$2^{2\frac{1}{2}}$	2^{5}	2^{7}	2^{10}	$2^{6\frac{1}{2}}$	Dominguez R A	6.50
12Oct03 ^{4}Bel^{1}	Who Is Chris G.	L	2 116	9	4	8	8	$4^{2\frac{1}{2}}$	4^{6}	$3^{3\frac{1}{4}}$	Luzzi M J	41.50
24Sep03 ^{6}Bel^{1}	Big Booster	L	2 116	3	8	$6\frac{1}{2}$	$3^{2\frac{1}{2}}$	3^{5}	3^{3}	$4^{1\frac{3}{4}}$	Migliore R	27.75
11Oct03 ^{7}Del^{2}	Tsuzomin	L	2 118	2	7	3^{hd}	$4^{1\frac{1}{2}}$	6^{2}	$5\frac{1}{2}$	$5^{1\frac{1}{2}}$	Munar L H	67.50
13Sep03 ^{5}Bel^{1}	Good Reward	L	2 116	6	2	4^{hd}	5^{hd}	5^{hd}	$6^{2\frac{1}{2}}$	$6^{3\frac{1}{4}}$	Prado E S	18.70
26Sep03 ^{3}Bel^{3}	Charismatic Rob	L	2 116	7	3	$7\frac{1}{2}$	6^{hd}	$7^{2\frac{1}{2}}$	7^{5}	7^{10}	Castellano J J	12.50
28Aug03 Lin^{1}	Motivus	L	2 118	8	5	5^{hd}	7^{hd}	8	8	8	Arroyo N Jr	30.50
4Oct03 ^{6}Kee^{4}	Value Plus	L	2 116	4	9	—	—	—	—	—	Velazquez J R	0.80

Value Plus:Lost rider;

OFF AT 3:45 Start Good For All But VALUE PLUS Won driving. Track fast.
TIME :23^{2}, :46^{1}, 1:10^{2}, 1:36^{2} (:23.48, :46.28, 1:10.40, 1:36.48)

$2 Mutuel Prices:				
	1–READ THE FOOTNOTES	7.80	5.20	3.80
	5–PADDINGTON		7.30	6.70
	11–WHO IS CHRIS G.			11.40

$2 EXACTA 1–5 PAID $46.80 $2 TRIFECTA 1–5–11 PAID $1,085.00

B. c, (Apr), by Smoke Glacken–Baydon Belle, by Al Nasr*Fr. Trainer Violette Richard A Jr. Bred by Lawrence Goichman (NY).

READ THE FOOTNOTES was hustled to the front, set the pace along the inside, dug in gamely when roused and drew clear under a drive. PADDINGTON pressed the pace from the outside, could not get by the winner in the stretch but was clearly best of the others. WHO IS CHRIS G. was outrun early, advanced outside and offered a mild rally in the stretch. BIG BOOSTER was hustled from the gate, chased the pace along the inside and tired in the stretch. TSUZOMIN raced close up inside and tired after a half mile. GOOD REWARD was hustled along between rivals and had no response when roused. CHARISMATIC ROB was outrun early, raced inside and tired in the stretch. MOTIVUS raced three wide and tired. VALUE PLUS stumbled badly at the start, unseating his rider. Following a Stewards' inquiry into the start of the race, the result was declared official.

Owners— 1, Klaravich Stables; 2, Gallop U Stable; 3, C D & G Stable; 4, Broman Mary R & Chester Sr; 5, Asbell Joseph E; 6, Phipps Ogden Mills et al; 7, Sabine Stable & Kelly Robert; 8, Double R Stable New Phoenix Stable; 9, Jones Aaron U & Marie D

Trainers—1, Violette Richard A Jr; 2, Dickinson Michael W; 3, Klesaris Robert P; 4, Kimmel John C; 5, Aristone Philip T; 6, McGaughey Claude III; 7, Barbara Robert; 8, Clement Christophe; 9, Pletcher Todd A

Scratched— China Coast (11Oct03 ^{4}BEL^{1}), War Fever (4Oct03 ^{3}BEL^{1})

NINTH RACE
Churchill
NOVEMBER 2, 2003

1 MILE. (1.33^{2}) IROQUIOS S.. Grade III. Purse $100,000 FOR TWO YEARS OLD. By subscripton of $100 each on or before October 15, 2003 or by supplementary nomination of $5,000 each by the time of closing Friday, October 31, 2003. $500 to pass the entry box; $500 additional to start, with $100,000 added of which 62% of all monies to the owner of the winner, 20% to second, 10% to third, 5% to fourth and 3% to fifth. Weight 121 lbs. Non-winners of a sweepstakes allowed 2 lbs.; two races other than claiming, 4 lbs.; a race other than claiming 6 lbs. Starters to be named through the entry box by the usual time of closing. Trophy to winning owner.

Value of Race: $113,700 Winner $70,494; second $22,740; third $11,370; fourth $5,685; fifth $3,411. Mutuel Pool $387,120.00 Exacta Pool $282,752.00 Trifecta Pool $255,056.00 Superfecta Pool $89,484.00

Last Raced	Horse	M/Eqt.	A.Wt	PP	St	¼	½	¾	Str	Fin	Jockey	Odds $1
4Oct03 ^{6}Kee^{6}	The Cliff's Edge	L	2 117	2	9	$8^{1\frac{1}{2}}$	5^{3}	$3^{1\frac{1}{2}}$	1^{4}	$1^{7\frac{3}{4}}$	Sellers S J	*2.20
27Sep03 ^{7}AP^{4}	Korbyn Gold	L	2 121	4	4	$4^{\frac{1}{2}}$	4^{1}	$4^{2\frac{1}{2}}$	$2^{\frac{1}{2}}$	$2^{\frac{1}{2}}$	Velasquez C	7.00
9Oct03 ^{5}Kee^{1}	Grand Score	L	2 117	7	7	$6^{2\frac{1}{2}}$	$7^{1\frac{1}{2}}$	5^{2}	$4^{1\frac{1}{2}}$	$3^{1\frac{1}{4}}$	Day P	2.20
4Oct03 ^{8}Kee^{1}	Pro Prado	L	2 119	6	6	$7^{\frac{1}{2}}$	$6^{\frac{1}{2}}$	$7^{\frac{1}{2}}$	$5^{\frac{1}{2}}$	$4^{\frac{3}{4}}$	McKee J	4.00
1Sep03 ^{12}RD^{3}	Blushing Indian	L	2 117	9	2	2^{1}	$2^{1\frac{1}{2}}$	1^{hd}	3^{1}	$5^{8\frac{3}{4}}$	Perret C	5.10
4Oct03 ^{6}Kee^{8}	War Image	L	2 119	3	1	1^{1}	1^{1}	$2^{\frac{1}{2}}$	6^{3}	6^{2}	Butler D P	33.00
25Sep03 ^{7}TP^{1}	Mutachi		2 117	8	8	9	8^{2}	8^{15}	7^{2}	$7^{1\frac{1}{4}}$	Melancon L	45.80
12Oct03 ^{9}Haw^{1}	Five Card Monty	L	2 117	1	5	$5^{\frac{1}{2}}$	3^{hd}	6^{1}	8^{20}	8	Court J K	42.80
4Oct03 ^{11}Beu^{2}	Affirmlode	L	2 117	5	3	3^{hd}	9	9	9	—	Borel C H	81.60

Affirmlode:Distanced;
***—Actual Betting Favorite.**

OFF AT 4:40 Start Good For All But PRO PRADO Won driving. Track fast.
TIME :22^{2}, :45, 1:10, 1:22^{2}, 1:35^{2} (:22.57, :45.12, 1:10.07, 1:22.56, 1:35.57)

$2 Mutuel Prices:				
	2-THE CLIFF'S EDGE	6.40	3.60	2.80
	4-KORBYN GOLD		6.20	3.60
	8-GRAND SCORE			2.80

$2 EXACTA 2-4 PAID $42.40 $2 TRIFECTA 2-4-8 PAID $155.80 $2 SUPERFECTA 2-4-8-7 PAID $352.60

Dk. b. or br. c, (Apr), by Gulch-Zigember, by Danzig. Trainer Zito Nicholas P. Bred by Stonerside Stable LLC (Ky).

THE CLIFF'S EDGE a bit sluggish early, made a quick move when angling out after three furlongs, advanced four wide to the leaders approaching the stretch, took over once in the stretch and drew off under steady urging. KORBYN GOLD forwardly placed from the start while off the inside, moved closest to the winner with a furlong to go, could not menace that one while holding sway for the place. GRAND SCORE bumped and forced out at the start, was reserved early, raced five wide on the turn then lacked the needed late bid. PRO PRADO stumbled at the start, was bumped and forced out recovering, raced within striking distance early while between rivals and improved his position late. BLUSHING INDIAN pressed the pace in the three path, challenged the leader in earnest on the turn, gained a short lead with a quarter mile to go but gave way in the drive. WAR IMAGE set the pace while kept off the inside, held on well to the stretch and tired. MUTACHI bumped and forced out at the start, steadied over BLUSHING INDIAN's heels, was reserved, raced five wide into the turn and was no threat. FIVE CARD MONTY well placed early, raced near the rail on the turn when within easy striking distance but faded in the drive. AFFIRMLODE drifted out at the start carrying outer rivals out, flashed speed, stopped badly and was outdistanced.

Owners— 1, La Penta Robert V; 2, Heiligbrodt Racing Stable; 3, Oxley John C; 4, Winn Mrs James A; 5, Pacella William Rizza Joseph & Schw; 6, Equest Racing Stable LLC; 7, Sterling Stud; 8, Orr James W Jr; 9, Horn H R

Trainers—1, Zito Nicholas P; 2, Asmussen Steven M; 3, Ward John T Jr; 4, Holthus Robert E; 5, Romans Dale; 6, Maker Michael J; 7, Shirota Mitch; 8, Irwin Robert D; 9, Horn Ray

Scratched— Wings On Springs (15Oct03 ^{2}KEE^{1}), Texas Deputy (27Sep03 ^{7}AP^{3})

$2 Pick Three (4-3/5-2/6/10) Paid $61.00; Pick Three Pool $31,730.

EIGHTH RACE
Aqueduct
NOVEMBER 4, 2003

1 MILE. (1.32^{2}) TEMPTED S.. Grade III. Purse $100,000 (Up to $19,400 NYSBFOA) FOR FILLIES TWO YEARS OLD. By subscription of $100 each, which should accompany the nomination; $500 to pass the entry box; $500 to start, with $100,000 added. The added money and all fees to be divided 60% to the winner, 20% to second, 11% to third, 6% to fourth and 3% to fifth. 121 lbs. Non-winners of $50,000 allowed 2 lbs.; $30,000, 4 lbs.; a race other than maiden or claiming, 6 lbs. Trophies will be presented to the winning owner, trainer, and jockey. Closed Saturday,October 18, 2003 with 27 Nominations.

Value of Race: $110,700 Winner $66,420; second $22,140; third $12,177; fourth $6,642; fifth $3,321. Mutuel Pool $272,908.00 Exacta Pool $265,415.00 Trifecta Pool $197,499.00

Last Raced	Horse	M/Eqt.	A.Wt	PP	St	¼	½	¾	Str	Fin	Jockey	Odds $1
6Sep03 ^{5}Bel^{1}	La Reina	L	2 115	1	8	2^{hd}	1^{hd}	$2^{1\frac{1}{2}}$	1^{hd}	1^{3}	Velazquez J R	1.05
4Oct03 ^{6}Bel^{6}	Eye Dazzler	L	2 115	8	2	5^{hd}	5^{hd}	$1^{\frac{1}{2}}$	2^{5}	$2^{5\frac{1}{2}}$	Fragoso P	2.55
6Oct03 ^{8}Del^{2}	Sisti's Pride	L	2 115	2	7	$4^{\frac{1}{2}}$	4^{hd}	$4^{2\frac{1}{2}}$	$3^{3\frac{1}{2}}$	3^{2}	Prado E S	8.30
28Sep03 ^{8}Bel^{2}	Fait Accompli	Lf	2 115	5	5	$6^{\frac{1}{2}}$	6^{1}	$6^{\frac{1}{2}}$	$4^{\frac{1}{2}}$	$4^{1\frac{3}{4}}$	Gryder A T	39.75
4Oct03 ^{5}Kee^{1}	Ellieonthemarch	L	2 119	6	3	8	8	$5^{\frac{1}{2}}$	$5^{\frac{1}{2}}$	$5^{4\frac{3}{4}}$	Bridgmohan S X	5.50
16Oct03 ^{3}Med^{1}	Fond	L	2 115	7	1	$3^{\frac{1}{2}}$	3^{1}	$3^{\frac{1}{2}}$	6^{10}	$6^{18\frac{3}{4}}$	Carrero V	55.25
21Sep03 ^{9}Mth^{2}	Baba Gonzo	Lf	2 117	4	4	1^{hd}	$2^{\frac{1}{2}}$	7^{6}	7^{6}	7^{4}	Clemente Alfredo	26.25
5Oct03 ^{3}Bel^{1}	Main Stream	L	2 115	3	6	$7^{1\frac{1}{2}}$	$7^{\frac{1}{2}}$	8	8	8	Migliore R	15.30

OFF AT 3:45 Start Good. Won driving. Track fast.
TIME :23^{2}, :46^{3}, 1:11^{1}, 1:36 (:23.50, :46.73, 1:11.38, 1:36.15)

$2 Mutuel Prices:				
	1-LA REINA	4.10	2.50	2.10
	8-EYE DAZZLER		3.20	2.40
	2-SISTI'S PRIDE			2.90

$2 EXACTA 1-8 PAID $12.20 $2 TRIFECTA 1-8-2 PAID $48.00

Ch. f, (Feb), by A.P. Indy-Queena, by Mr. Prospector. Trainer McGaughey Claude III. Bred by Emory A Hamilton (Ky).

LA REINA was hustled up inside, contested the pace, dug in gamely when roused in upper stretch and was going away late on the rail, driving. EYE DAZZLER raced close up outside while in hand, put in a four wide run approaching the stretch but could not handle the winner while clearly best of the others. SISTI'S PRIDE stumbled at the start, raced close up inside while in hand and had no response when roused. FAIT ACCOMPLI was rated along between rivals, came wide for the drive and had no rally. ELLIEONTHEMARCH was outrun early, raced wide and had no rally. FOND contested the pace while three wide and tired in the stretch. BABA GONZO contested the pace while between rivals and tired. MAIN STREAM raced inside and tired.

Owners— 1, Hamilton Emory A; 2, Lewis Lee; 3, Jones Aaron U & Marie D; 4, Berkshire Stud; 5, West Point Stable; 6, Dogwood Stable; 7, Edward Marshall; 8, Evans Robert S

Trainers—1, McGaughey Claude III; 2, Hennig Mark; 3, Pletcher Todd A; 4, Bush Thomas M; 5, Violette Richard A Jr; 6, Weaver George; 7, Sobol Alan; 8, Schulhofer Randy

NINTH RACE
Aqueduct
NOVEMBER 8, 2003

$1\frac{1}{16}$ MILES. (Turf)(1.40^{4}) ATHENIA H.. Grade III. Purse $100,000 TURF. (Up to $19,400 NYSBFOA) A HANDICAP FOR FILLIES AND MARES THREE YEARS OLD AND UPWARD. By subscription of $100 each, which should accompany the nomination; $500 to pass the entry box; $500 to start, with $100,000 added. The added money and all fees to be divided 60% to the winner, 20% to second, 11% to third, 6% to fourth and 3% to fifth. Trophies will be presented to the winning owner, trainer and jockey. The New York Racing Association reserves the right to transfer this race to the Main Track. In the event that this race is taken off the turf, it may be subject to downgrading by the Graded Stakes Committee. Closed Saturday, October 25, 2003 with 40 Nominations.

Value of Race: $113,000 Winner $67,800; second $22,600; third $12,430; fourth $6,780; fifth $3,390. Mutuel Pool $401,469.00 Exacta Pool $355,102.00 Trifecta Pool $251,337.00

Last Raced	Horse	M/Eqt.	A.Wt	PP	St	¼	½	¾	Str	Fin	Jockey	Odds $1
17Oct03 ^{7}Med^{5}	Caught In The Rain	L	4 115	6	8	7^{3}	$7^{2\frac{1}{2}}$	7^{3}	$5^{1\frac{1}{2}}$	1no	Migliore R	14.80
22Oct03 ^{8}Bel^{1}	Lojo	L	4 114	5	2	$4^{\frac{1}{2}}$	3^{hd}	$4^{1\frac{1}{2}}$	2^{hd}	2no	Bridgmohan S X	5.00
22Oct03 ^{8}Bel^{3}	Coney Kitty-IR	Lf	5 113	8	7	5^{1}	$5^{2\frac{1}{2}}$	5^{hd}	3^{hd}	$3^{\frac{1}{2}}$	Castellano J J	8.00
17Oct03 ^{7}Med^{3}	Something Ventured	Lb	4 116	1	5	$2^{\frac{1}{2}}$	$1^{\frac{1}{2}}$	1^{hd}	1^{hd}	4^{3}	Velazquez J R	2.10
18Oct03 ^{7}Bel^{2}	Brandala		5 113	2	6	8	8	8	8	5^{nk}	Espinoza J L	20.70
17Oct03 ^{7}Med^{2}	Madeira Mist-IR	L	4 117	7	3	$3^{\frac{1}{2}}$	4^{1}	3^{hd}	7^{1}	6^{1}	Prado E S	2.65
22Oct03 ^{8}Bel^{5}	Affirmed Dancer	L	4 113	4	1	1^{hd}	2^{1}	2^{1}	$4^{\frac{1}{2}}$	$7^{\frac{3}{4}}$	Chavez J F	9.60
18Oct03 ^{7}Bel^{1}	Lady Bi Bi	L	4 114	3	4	6^{2}	6^{hd}	6^{hd}	6^{hd}	8	Arroyo N Jr	10.30

OFF AT 4:06 Start Good. Won driving. Course soft.
TIME :25, :51, 1:16^{2}, 1:40^{4}, 1:47 (:25.00, :51.00, 1:16.45, 1:40.96, 1:47.05)

$2 Mutuel Prices:

8–CAUGHT IN THE RAIN	31.60	15.20	10.40
7–LOJO		6.60	5.40
10–CONEY KITTY–IR			6.60

$2 EXACTA 8–7 PAID $188.00 $2 TRIFECTA 8–7–10 PAID $1,545.00

Dk. b. or br. f, by Petionville–Jinger Feathers, by Fred Astaire. Trainer Preciado Guadalupe. Bred by Casino Royale Farms Inc (Pa).

CAUGHT IN THE RAIN was outrun early, rallied five wide on the second turn, finished determinedly outside and up in the final strides. LOJO raced close up inside while in hand, saved ground, got through inside in the stretch, dug in gamely inside and just missed. CONEY KITTY (IRE) was rated along early, rallied four wide on the second turn and dug in gamely to the wire. SOMETHING VENTURED argued the pace along the inside and stayed on gamely in the stretch. BRANDALA was outrun early, came wide into the stretch and finished well outside. MADEIRA MIST (IRE) raced close up while three wide and had no response when roused. AFFIRMED DANCER argued the pace from the outside and tired in the stretch. LADY BI BI was rated along inside and had no rally.

Owners— 1, Heiligbrodt Racing Stable & New Wal; 2, Durocher Lawrence & Hampshire Farm; 3, Betz William J Humphrey Steve & See; 4, Wiemer Irvin & McLane John; 5, Sorin Stables; 6, Skymarc Farm Inc; 7, Farmer Tracy; 8, Tri County Stables

Trainers—1, Preciado Guadalupe; 2, Hills Timothy A; 3, Toner James J; 4, Pletcher Todd A; 5, Walsh Thomas M; 6, Clement Christophe; 7, Kimmel John C; 8, Hertler John O

Scratched— Delta Princess (17Oct03 ^{7}MED^{4}), Artist Johanna (11Oct03 ^{7}MED^{3}), Drexel Monorail (25Oct03 ^{4}BEL^{4}), Misty Sixes (1Nov03 ^{9}AQU^{5}), Wishful Splendor (17Oct03 ^{5}MED^{2}), Cozzy Corner (22Oct03 ^{8}BEL^{7})

NINTH RACE
Churchill
NOVEMBER 8, 2003

1 MILE. (1.33^{2}) CHURCHILL DOWNS DISTAFF H.. Grade II. Purse $200,000 A HANDICAP FOR FILLIES AND MARES, THREE-YEAR-OLDS AND UPWARD. By subscription of $200 each on or before October 25, 2003 or by supplementary nomination of $10,000 each by the close of entries on Friday, October 31, 2003. $1,000 to pass the entry box; $1,000 additional to start, with $200,000 added of which 62% of all monies to the owner of the winner, 20% to second, 10% to third, 5% to fourth and 3% to fifth. Weights to be announced Saturday, November 1. Starters to be named through the entry box by the usual time of closing. Trophy to winning owner.

Value of Race: $225,400 Winner $139,748; second $45,080; third $22,540; fourth $11,270; fifth $6,762. Mutuel Pool $421,398.00 Exacta Pool $341,872.00 Trifecta Pool $294,594.00 Superfecta Pool $102,425.00

Last Raced	Horse	M/Eqt.	A.Wt	PP	St	¼	½	¾	Str	Fin	Jockey	Odds $1
24Oct03 ^{7}Kee^{3}	Lead Story	L	4 114	7	10	10	10	8^{1}	3^{hd}	$1^{\frac{1}{2}}$	Borel C H	35.80
3Oct03 ^{9}Hoo^{1}	Awesome Humor	L	3 118	4	3	2^{hd}	$2^{\frac{1}{2}}$	$3^{3\frac{1}{2}}$	1^{1}	$2^{1\frac{1}{4}}$	Melancon L	3.60
12Oct03 ^{8}Kee^{3}	Born To Dance	Lb	4 113	1	1	$1^{\frac{1}{2}}$	1^{3}	2^{hd}	$2^{\frac{1}{2}}$	$3^{3\frac{1}{4}}$	Bejarano R	21.80
10Oct03 ^{9}Kee^{5}	My Trusty Cat	Lbf	3 113	3	7	$7^{\frac{1}{2}}$	6^{hd}	4^{1}	5^{3}	$4^{1\frac{1}{2}}$	Thompson T J	18.00
18Oct03 ^{3}BM^{2}	Rhiana	L	6 116	10	5	5^{1}	5^{1}	6^{hd}	6^{hd}	5^{nk}	Blanc B	38.00
10Oct03 ^{9}Kee^{1}	Yell	L	3 116	8	8	8^{hd}	$8^{\frac{1}{2}}$	7^{3}	7^{2}	$6^{\frac{1}{2}}$	Day P	0.80
10Aug03 ^{9}ElP^{2}	Meteor Miracle	L	4 113	2	2	4^{hd}	3^{hd}	1^{hd}	$4^{2\frac{1}{2}}$	$7^{5\frac{3}{4}}$	McKee J	18.10
24Oct03 ^{3}Kee^{1}	Mayo On The Side	Lbf	4 115	9	4	$3^{1\frac{1}{2}}$	4^{2}	5^{2}	8^{2}	$8^{\frac{3}{4}}$	Butler D P	5.20
30Sep03 ^{9}Mnr^{1}	Salzurita-ARG	L	5 116	6	9	$9^{5\frac{1}{2}}$	$7^{1\frac{1}{2}}$	9^{3}	$9^{2\frac{1}{2}}$	9^{8}	Velasquez C	17.90
1Sep03 ^{8}AP^{2}	Lakenheath	L	5 116	5	6	6^{1}	$9^{2\frac{1}{2}}$	10	10	10	Lanerie C J	30.30

OFF AT 4:40 Start Good. Won driving. Track fast.
TIME :23, :45^{4}, 1:11, 1:23^{2}, 1:36^{2} (:23.09, :45.88, 1:11.00, 1:23.58, 1:36.55)

$2 Mutuel Prices:

7–LEAD STORY	73.60	25.00	16.40
4–AWESOME HUMOR		5.60	4.40
1–BORN TO DANCE			10.40

$2 EXACTA 7–4 PAID $394.00 $2 TRIFECTA 7–4–1 PAID $4,299.40 $2 SUPERFECTA 7–4–1–3 PAID $41,482.00

Ch. f, by Editor's Note–Gwenjinsky, by Seattle Dancer. Trainer Nafzger Carl A. Bred by Cabotaba Partnership (Ky).

LEAD STORY, reserved soon after the start and maneuvered near the inside, saved ground into the lane, was alertly angled out four or five wide when an opening appeared leaving the eighth pole, then closed determinedly under strong left-handed urging to prevail. AWESOME HUMOR, lightly rated early while tracking front-running BORN TO DANCE four wide, inched to challenge approaching the stretch, took over when straightened for the drive, gained a slight advantage, then failed to contain the winner's surge. BORN TO DANCE gained the lead inside early, moved clear before going a half, was headed a quarter-mile out by METEOR MIRACLE, then held on stubbornly the remainder. MY TRUSTY CAT, never far back, eased out to make a bid five or six wide into the final furlong but failed to continue. RHIANA, within easy striking distance to the stretch while four or five wide, was empty in the drive. YELL, unhurried early and five wide on the backstretch and turn, came out eight abreast for the drive and failed to menace. METEOR MIRACLE, well placed in behind horses from the outset, moved three or four wide approaching the final quarter, stuck her head in front, then faltered when straightened for the drive. MAYO ON THE SIDE raced in a striking position five wide for six furlongs and tired. SALZURITA (ARG) failed to menace. LAKENHEATH was finished early.

Owners— 1, Miles A S Jr; 2, WinStar Farm LLC; 3, Parra Rosendo G; 4, Pollard Carl F; 5, Dell Ridge Farm; 6, Claiborne Farm & Dilschneider Adele; 7, Hoskins George A; 8, Lothenbach Stables; 9, Korkames David; 10, James B Tafel LLC

Trainers—1, Nafzger Carl A; 2, Walden W Elliott; 3, Jackson James R; 4, Vance David R; 5, Hendricks Dan L; 6, McGaughey Claude III; 7, Carroll David; 8, Nafzger Carl A; 9, Murty Wayne; 10, Cilio Gene A

$2 Pick Three (4/11–3/13–7) Paid $1,074.40; Pick Three Pool $35,818.

EIGHTH RACE
Aqueduct
NOVEMBER 11, 2003

1⅛ MILES. (1.47) STUYVESANT H.. Grade III. Purse $100,000 (Up to $19,400 NYSBFOA) A HANDICAP FOR THREE YEAR OLDS AND UPWARD. By subscription of $100 each, which should accompany the nomination; $500 to pass the entry box; $500 to start, with $100,000 added. The added money and all fees to be divided 60% to the winner, 20% to second, 11% to third, 6% to fourth and 3% to fifth. Trophies will be presented to the winning owner, trainer and jockey. Closed Saturday, October 25, 2003 with 23 Nominations.

Value of Race: $110,300 Winner $66,180; second $22,060; third $12,133; fourth $6,618; fifth $3,309. Mutuel Pool $374,329.00 Exacta Pool $326,594.00 Trifecta Pool $235,430.00

Last Raced	Horse	M/Eqt.	A.	Wt	PP	St	¼	½	¾	Str	Fin	Jockey	Odds $1
11Oct03 11Lrl2	Presidentialaffair	L	4	115	4	1	1 1½	1 ½	1 ½	1 3½	1 nk	Migliore R	7.00
2Oct03 8Bel2	Thunder Blitz	L	5	114	6	3	4 ½	3 ½	3 3	2 hd	2 ½	Prado E S	5.10
18Oct03 10Bel2	Gander	L	7	115	5	7	2 1½	2 ½	2 ½	3 5	3 4	Gryder A T	6.80
5Oct03 7Bel2	Almuhathir	L	5	115	1	2	3 hd	4 ½	6 ½	4 3½	4 2¾	Castillo H Jr	9.00
5Oct03 7Bel4	El Gran Papa	Lf	6	113	2	8	8	8	8	5 ½	5 ½	Chavez J F	26.75
5Oct03 7Bel1	Saarland	Lbf	4	116	8	6	5 ½	5 ½	7 2	7 hd	6 ½	Velazquez J R	1.30
24Oct03 8Bel2	Justification	L	6	114	3	4	6 1	6 ½	4 hd	8	7 2¼	Bridgmohan S X	15.40
11Oct03 11Lrl1	Docent	Lbf	5	117	7	5	7 5½	7 3½	5 hd	6 hd	8	Potts C L	6.90

OFF AT 3:44 Start Good. Won driving. Track fast.

TIME :24^2, :48^2, 1:12, 1:37^1, 1:50^4 (:24.42, :48.45, 1:12.09, 1:37.21, 1:50.86)

$2 Mutuel Prices:				
	4–PRESIDENTIALAFFAIR	16.00	8.00	6.00
	6–THUNDER BLITZ		6.90	5.00
	5–GANDER			4.00

$2 EXACTA 4–6 PAID $107.50 $2 TRIFECTA 4–6–5 PAID $630.00

B. g, by Not For Love–Quite Amazing, by Bear Hunt. Trainer Ciresa Martin E. Bred by Will Run Farm (Pa).

PRESIDENTIALAFFAIR quickly showed in front, set the pace along the inside, drew clear when roused in upper stretch then dug in gamely and held on, driving. THUNDER BLITZ prompted the pace from the outside, dropped back in upper stretch then came again outside nearing the finish. GANDER prompted the pace while between rivals, dropped back in upper stretch then came again on the rail nearing the wire. ALMUHATHIR raced close up inside, altered course to the outside in the stretch and lacked a rally. EL GRAN PAPA was outrun early, raced five wide on the second turn and had no rally. SAARLAND raced four wide on the first turn, three wide on the second turn and had no response when roused. JUSTIFICATION raced between rivals and had no response when roused. DOCENT raced three wide on the first turn, four wide on the second turn and had no response when roused.

Owners— 1, Vincent Papandrea & Edward Ciresa; 2, Stronach Stable; 3, Gatsas Thoroughbreds LLC; 4, Shadwell Stable; 5, Oak Cliff Stable; 6, Phipps Cynthia; 7, Shields Joseph V Jr; 8, Daney Arlene R

Trainers—1, Ciresa Martin E; 2, Dutrow Richard E Jr; 3, Terranova John P II; 4, Peitz Daniel C; 5, Bush Thomas M; 6, McGaughey Claude III; 7, Jerkens H Allen; 8, Ritchey Tim F

EIGHTH RACE
Aqueduct
NOVEMBER 15, 2003

1½ MILES. (Turf)(2.27) LONG ISLAND H.. Grade II. Purse $150,000 TURF. (Up to $29,100 NYSBFOA) A HANDICAP FOR FILLIES AND MARES THREE YEARS OLD AND UPWARD. By subscription of $150 each, which should accompany the nomination; $750 to pass the entry box; $750 to start. The purse to be divided 60% to the winner, 20% to second, 11% to third, 6% to fourth and 3% to fifth. Trophies will be presented to the winning owner, trainer and jockey. The New York Racing Association reserves the right to transfer this race to the Main Track. In the event that this race is taken off the turf, it may be subject to downgrading by the Graded Stakes Committee. Closed Saturday, November 1, 2003 with 28 Nominations.

Value of Race: $150,000 Winner $90,000; second $30,000; third $16,500; fourth $9,000; fifth $4,500. Mutuel Pool $618,526.00 Exacta Pool $533,843.00 Trifecta Pool $372,945.00

Last Raced	Horse	M/Eqt.	A.	Wt	PP	¼	½	1	1¼	Str	Fin	Jockey	Odds $1
19Oct03 8Kee1	Spice Island	Lb	4	117	7	5 ½	5 3	3 ½	3 1	3 ½	1 1¼	Carrero V	7.00
19Oct03 5WO1	Volga-IR	L	5	120	10	3 ½	3 1½	2 1	1 hd	1 1½	2 2¾	Migliore R	2.10
1Oct03 8Bel2	Banyu Dewi-GE	Lf	4	114	9	2 2½	1 ½	1 1	2 2½	2 ½	3 ½	Krone J A	4.50
25Aug03 8Sar7	Mariensky	L	4	116	4	4 1½	4 ½	5 2½	4 ½	4 5	4 2¼	Castellano J J	3.70
4Oct03 Lch6	Mandela-GE		3	113	2	11	11	8 3	5 2	5 3½	5 4	Espinoza J L	a-12.80
25Oct03 9Lrl1	Lady Of The Future	L	5	114	11	8 hd	9 hd	11	8 3	8 7	6 ¾	Castillo O O	42.50
27Sep03 8Bel6	Primetimevalentine	Lb	4	115	3	7 2	6 hd	6 hd	7 ½	6 ½	7 1	Gryder A T	16.60
7Sep03 4AP2	Boana-GE	L	5	114	5	10 1½	10 2	7 hd	6 1½	7 ½	8 6½	Smith A E	a-12.80
24Oct03 7Bel2	D'Ohana-ARG	L	5	114	6	9 2	8 ½	10 hd	9 ½	9 3	9 1¾	Castillo H Jr	61.00
9Aug03 9Sar10	Meridiana-GE	L	3	113	1	6 hd	7 2½	9 1	11	10 1	10 1¾	Arroyo N Jr	13.50
5Oct03 6Kee2	Approach-GB	L	3	113	8	1 hd	2 ½	4 ½	10 2	11	11	Bridgmohan S X	10.00

a–Coupled: Mandela–GE and Boana–GE.

OFF AT 3:45 Start Good. Won driving. Course yielding.

TIME :26, :52, 1:17^2, 1:43, 2:08^2, 2:32^2 (:26.02, :52.07, 1:17.56, 1:43.19, 2:08.48, 2:32.58)

$2 Mutuel Prices:				
	7–SPICE ISLAND	16.00	5.90	4.00
	10–VOLGA–IR		4.00	2.90
	9–BANYU DEWI–GE			3.50

$2 EXACTA 7–10 PAID $62.00 $2 TRIFECTA 7–10–9 PAID $243.00

Dk. b. or br. f, by Tabasco Cat–Crown of Sheba, by Alysheba. Trainer Pregman John S Jr. Bred by Cranford Stud (Ky).

SPICE ISLAND raced close up outside while in hand, advanced three wide on the final turn, responded when roused and drew clear late under a drive. VOLGA (IRE) raced with the pace from the outside, drew clear when roused in upper stretch and stayed on well but could not resist the winner. BANYU DEWI (GER) made the pace while well in hand and weakened in the final furlong. MARIENSKY raced close up inside, saved ground and stayed on well on the rail. MANDELA (GER) was outrun early, put in a three wide run on the final turn and had nothing left for the drive. LADY OF THE FUTURE was outrun early and had no rally. PRIMETIMEVALENTINE had no response when roused. BOANA (GER) was outrun early and had no rally. D'OHANA (ARG) had no response when roused. MERIDIANA (GER) raced inside and tired. APPROACH (GB) raced with the pace along the inside and tired in the stretch.

Owners— 1, Denlea Park Ltd; 2, Allen Joseph; 3, Team Valor Stables LLC; 4, Waterville Lake Stable; 5, Tanaka Gary A; 6, Pearson Max H; 7, Low Lawana L & Robert E; 8, Tanaka Gary A; 9, Hubbard R D Machado Linneao & Sczes; 10, Kelly Jon & Sarah; 11, Faisal Salman

Trainers—1, Pregman John S Jr; 2, McLaughlin Kiaran P; 3, Matz Michael R; 4, Clement Christophe; 5, Suerland Ralf; 6, Greene Thomas M; 7, Peitz Daniel C; 8, Asmussen Steven M; 9, Hennig Mark; 10, Clement Christophe; 11, Motion H Graham

Scratched— Itnab (11Oct03 ASC1)

NINTH RACE
Churchill
NOVEMBER 15, 2003

$1\frac{1}{8}$ MILES. (Turf)(1.40^{4}) MRS. REVERE S.. Grade II. Purse $150,000 FOR FILLIES, THREE YEARS OLD. By subscription of $150 each on or before November 1, 2003 or by supplementary nomination of $7,500 each by the time of closing Thursday, November 13, 2003. $750 to pass the entry box; $750 additional to start, with $150,000 added of which 62% of all monies to the owner of the winner, 20% to second, 10% to third, 5% to fourth and 3% to fifth. Weights 122 lbs. Non-winners of $50,000 twice allowed 2 lbs.; a sweepstakes on the turf, 4 lbs.; three races other than maiden or claiming, 6 lbs.; two races other than maiden or claiming, 8 lbs. The maximum number of starters for the Mrs. Revere will be limited to twelve (12).

Value of Race: $175,650 Winner $108,903; second $35,130; third $17,565; fourth $8,783; fifth $5,269. Mutuel Pool $527,896.00 Exacta Pool $394,941.00 Trifecta Pool $337,433.00 Superfecta Pool $111,398.00

Last Raced	Horse	M/Eqt.	A.Wt	PP	St	¼	½	¾	Str	Fin	Jockey	Odds $1
13Sep03 ^{8}AP^{4}	Hoh Buzzard-IR	Lb	3 120	2	3	2^{1}	2^{3}	1^{hd}	$1^{1\frac{1}{2}}$	1^{nk}	Fogelsonger R	7.40
11Oct03 ^{8}Kee^{6}	Aud	L	3 120	1	7	10^{1}	10^{hd}	8^{hd}	5^{2}	2^{2}	Peck B D	6.80
16Oct03 ^{6}Kee^{1}	Gamble To Victory	L	3 116	6	1	4^{1}	$4^{\frac{1}{2}}$	3^{hd}	2^{hd}	$3^{\frac{1}{2}}$	Bejarano R	65.50
20Sep03 ^{9}LaD^{2}	Tiva's Little Sis	Lb	3 120	8	10	$9^{1\frac{1}{2}}$	$8^{\frac{1}{2}}$	$6^{\frac{1}{2}}$	6^{2}	4^{2}	Lanerie C J	50.00
11Oct03 ^{8}Kee^{3}	Casual Look	L	3 120	7	11	$11^{3\frac{1}{2}}$	11^{5}	9^{4}	8^{1}	5^{hd}	Day P	1.50
11Oct03 ^{8}Kee^{4}	Ocean Drive	L	3 122	4	9	5^{hd}	5^{2}	5^{1}	4^{hd}	$6^{\frac{3}{4}}$	Douglas R R	5.00
6Sep03 ^{9}TP^{5}	Keiai Sakura	Lb	3 118	3	8	1^{hd}	1^{hd}	2^{2}	$3^{\frac{1}{2}}$	$7^{\frac{3}{4}}$	McKee J	44.00
11Oct03 ^{8}Kee^{1}	Film Maker	Lb	3 122	11	5	$6^{1\frac{1}{2}}$	6^{1}	$7^{\frac{1}{2}}$	9^{4}	8^{nk}	Velasquez C	4.00
11Oct03 ^{7}Lrl^{1}	Hail Hillary	L	3 120	10	4	$3^{1\frac{1}{2}}$	3^{3}	4^{1}	$7^{\frac{1}{2}}$	$9^{5\frac{1}{4}}$	Perret C	12.90
18Oct03 ^{9}Kee^{5}	Shaconage	Lb	3 120	9	12	12	12	$11^{\frac{1}{2}}$	$11^{3\frac{1}{2}}$	10^{nk}	Johnson J M	55.50
11Oct03 ^{9}Crc^{4}	Petionville Indeed	Lb	3 120	5	2	7^{hd}	7^{hd}	10^{1}	$10^{\frac{1}{2}}$	$11^{5\frac{1}{2}}$	Court J K	76.90
1Nov03 ^{10}Aqu^{1}	Pattiano	Lb	3 114	12	6	$8^{\frac{1}{2}}$	$9^{\frac{1}{2}}$	12	12	12	Borel C H	40.60

OFF AT 4:40 Start Good. Won driving. Course yielding.
TIME :23^{3}, :47^{4}, 1:13, 1:38^{3}, 1:45 (:23.67, :47.87, 1:13.05, 1:38.62, 1:45.01)

$2 Mutuel Prices:

2–HOH BUZZARD–IR	16.80	7.80	5.80
1–AUD		7.00	6.20
7–GAMBLE TO VICTORY			19.80

$2 EXACTA 2–1 PAID $93.80 $2 TRIFECTA 2–1–7 PAID $2,954.80 $2 SUPERFECTA 2–1–7–9 PAID $45,116.00

Dk. b. or br. f, (Mar), by Alhaarth*Ire–Indian Express*GB, by Indian Ridge*Ire. Trainer Cecil B D A. Bred by Hodgkins R (Ire).

HOH BUZZARD (IRE) moved up along the inside early to vie for the lead, raced under light rating while dueling with KEIAI SAKURA, gained a slight edge entering the far turn when asked a bit, kicked clear into the upper stretch while coming out five wide, then gamely withstood AUD in the late going. AUD, unhurried for a half, raced in behind horses four wide, continued four wide into the lane, angled inside in the final sixteenth and was gaining late. GAMBLE TO VICTORY, always well placed while tracking the pace three or four wide, angled five wide for the drive, was just off the winner for the final furlong and came up empty. TIVA'S LITTLE SIS, unhurried early, raced near the inside between horses three or four wide, swung out seven wide for the drive and offered a mild gain. CASUAL LOOK, outrun to the far turn, advanced six wide, moved eight abreast into the stretch and could gain only slightly in the late stages. OCEAN DRIVE, well placed near the inside from early on, loomed prominently from the rail for the last eighth and flattened out. KEIAI SAKURA gained a slight edge early while four wide, dueled with the winner, battled close up to the stretch and weakened. FILM MAKER raced in contention to the lane while four or five wide and weakened. HAIL HILLARY followed the leaders within easy striking distance four or five wide into the upper stretch and faltered. SHACONAGE was outrun. PETIONVILLE INDEED tired after five furlongs. PATTIANO faded on the far turn.

Owners— 1, Tanaka Gary A; 2, Willmott Stables; 3, Van Den Broeck Herman; 4, Parra Rosendo G; 5, Farish William S; 6, Baskin Bonnie & Sy; 7, Kameda Morihiro; 8, Courtlandt Farms; 9, Slavin Larry; 10, Sterling Stud; 11, Everest Stables; 12, Miller Kelly A

Trainers—1, Cecil B D A; 2, Reinstedler Anthony; 3, Pellegrini Ronald; 4, Asmussen Steven M; 5, Howard Neil J; 6, Pletcher Todd A; 7, Gothard Akiko; 8, Motion H Graham; 9, Kassen David C; 10, Shirota Mitch; 11, Keen Dallas E; 12, Dupps Kristina

Scratched— Dyna Da Wyna (18Oct03 ^{9}KEE^{1})

$2 Pick Three (1–3–2) Paid $502.20; Pick Three Pool $33,796.

SEVENTH RACE
Hollywood
NOVEMBER 15, 2003

7 FURLONGS. (1.19^{4}) JACK DANIEL'S HOLLYWOOD PREVUE S. Grade III. Purse $100,000 FOR TWO-YEAR-OLDS. By subscription of $100 each, on or before Wednesday, November 5, or by supplementary nomination of $5,000 each by closing time of entries. $1,000 additional to start, with $60,000 to the winner, $20,000 to second, $12,000 to third, $6,000 to fourth and $2,000 to fifth. 122 lbs. Non-winners of $60,000 or $45,000 twice allowed 3 lbs. ; $45,000 or two races other than maiden or claiming, 5 lbs. ; of a sweepstakes of any value, 7 lbs. ; of a race other than maiden or claiming , 9 lbs. Starters to be named through the entry box by closing time of entries. Total earnings in 2003 will be used in determining the order of presence of horses assigned equal weights. All fees for entrants that fail to draw into this race will be cancelled. A trophy will be presented to the owner of the winner. No fees to any horse originally nominated to the 2003 Hollywood Futurity. (Does not include supplementary nomination). Closed with 10 Nominations.

Value of Race: $100,000 Winner $60,000; second $20,000; third $12,000; fourth $6,000; fifth $2,000. Mutuel Pool $304,566.00 Exacta Pool $199,288.00 Quinella Pool $16,068.00 Trifecta Pool $118,269.00

Last Raced	Horse	M/Eqt.	A. Wt	PP	St	¼	½	Str	Fin	Jockey	Odds $1
24Oct03 ^{6}SA^{1}	Lion Heart		2 114	4	1	$1^{1\frac{1}{2}}$	$1^{\frac{1}{2}}$	$1^{1\frac{1}{2}}$	1^{6}	Smith M E	0.50
18Oct03 ^{8}SA^{4}	Cooperation	LB b	2 116	5	2	3^{3}	3^{1}	3^{1}	2no	Solis A O	a- 2.20
18Oct03 ^{8}SA^{2}	Voladero	LB b	2 113	3	3	2^{hd}	2^{1}	2^{3}	3^{4}	Espinoza V	4.50
25Oct03 ^{7}SA^{5}	Consecrate	LB b	2 116	1	5	4^{hd}	4^{1}	4^{8}	4^{13}	Flores D R	a- 2.20
18Oct03 ^{8}SA^{3}	Longgonetrevorsen	LB	2 115	2	4	5	5	5	5	Valenzuela P A	13.80

a–Coupled: Cooperation and Consecrate.

OFF AT 3:38 Start Good . Won ridden out. Track fast.
TIME :22^{1}, :44^{3}, 1:08^{1}, 1:20^{3} (:22.28, :44.71, 1:08.34, 1:20.63)

$2 Mutuel Prices:

5 – LION HEART	3.00	2.20	—
1A– COOPERATION(a–entry)		2.20	—
4 – VOLADERO		—	—

$1 EXACTA 5–1 PAID $2.50 $2 QUINELLA 1–5 PAID $3.20 $1 TRIFECTA 5–1–4 PAID $3.50

Ch. c, (Jan), by Tale of the Cat – Satin Sunrise , by Mr. Leader . Trainer Biancone Patrick L. Bred by Sabine Stable (Ky).

LION HEART quickly sprinted to the lead off the rail, responded when challenged leaving the backstretch, kicked clear again on the turn, drifted out a bit into the stretch but drew off under a moderate hand ride. COOPERATION stalked outside a rival then off the rail, came out a bit in the stretch and just got the place. VOLADERO stalked a bit off the rail then bid inside the winner leaving the backstretch, angled in some on the turn, was no match for that rival in the lane and just lost second. CONSECRATE a bit slow into stride, saved ground throughout chasing the pace and had no response in the stretch. LONGGONETREVORSEAN allowed to settle outside a rival, dropped back off the rail on the turn, came out in the stretch and gave way.

Owners– 1, Smith Derrick and Tabor Michael; 2, McIngvale James; 3, Lewis Robert B and Beverly J; 4, McIngvale James; 5, Powell Ernest J

Trainers– 1, Biancone Patrick L; 2, Baffert Bob; 3, Lukas D Wayne; 4, Baffert Bob; 5, Mayberry Summer

Scratched– Cosmic Glitter (31Oct03 ^{3}SA ^{1}) , Skipaslew (19Oct03 ^{3}BM ^{3})

$2 Daily Double (7–5) Paid $9.60 ; Daily Double Pool $27,538 .
$1 Pick Three (5–7–2/5/6) Paid $35.00 ; Pick Three Pool $95,790 .

SIXTH RACE
Laurel
NOVEMBER 15, 2003

1¹⁄₁₆ MILES. (1.41⁴) LAUREL FUTURITY Grade III. Purse $100,000 FOR TWO–YEAR–OLDS. Free subscription. $500 to pass the entry box. $500 additional to start. Supplemental nominations of $1000 each will be accepted by the usual time of entry with all other fees due as noted. Weight 122 lbs. Fillies, allowed 3 lbs., Maidens allowed 5 lbs. Preference to starters with highest career earnings. Horses may be placed on the also–eligible list. Closed Wednesday, November 5, 2003 with 27 nominations.

Value of Race: $100,000 Winner $60,000; second $20,000; third $11,000; fourth $6,000; fifth $3,000. Mutuel Pool $220,899.00 Exacta Pool $177,266.00 Superfecta Pool $40,853.00 Trifecta Pool $137,385.00

Last Raced	Horse	M/Eqt.	A.	Wt	PP	St	¼	½	¾	Str	Fin	Jockey	Odds $1
19Oct03 ⁶Del¹	Tapit	L f	2	122	1	6	4³	4¹	4⁴	1hd	14¾	Dominguez R A	1.00
11Oct03 ⁵Lrl¹	Polish Rifle	L	2	122	4	7	5¹½	5³	3½	3½	2½	Pino M G	2.50
25Oct03 ²Kee¹	Ghost Mountain	L b	2	122	6	1	3½	2hd	1½	2²	3¹½	Prado E S	3.30
17Oct03 ⁶Lrl¹	Acclimate	L f	2	122	2	3	1hd	1¹	2¹	4⁴½	4²½	Chavez J F	26.10
11Oct03 ⁷Del¹	Capejinsky	L	2	122	5	4	7	7	7	6⁸	5nk	Valdes R A	7.10
26Oct03 ⁸Del¹	Charismatic Caller	L f	2	122	7	5	6¹	6¹	6hd	5¹½	6¹⁴¾	Alvarado R Jr	30.10
11Oct03 ⁷Del⁵	Tym Beau	L f	2	122	3	2	2¹	3½	5hd	7	7	Rose J	50.30

OFF AT 2:58 Start Good . Won handily. Track fast.

TIME :24, :48¹, 1:12⁴, 1:37², 1:43⁴ (:24.19, :48.31, 1:12.83, 1:37.54, 1:43.81)

$2 Mutuel Prices:	1 – TAPIT	4.00	2.60	2.10
	4 – POLISH RIFLE		3.00	2.10
	6 – GHOST MOUNTAIN			2.20

$2 EXACTA 1–4 PAID $9.80 $1 SUPERFECTA 1–4–6–2 PAID $64.50
$2 TRIFECTA 1–4–6 PAID $28.80

Gr/ro. c, (Feb), by Pulpit – Tap Your Heels , by Unbridled . Trainer Dickinson Michael W. Bred by Oldenburg Farms LLC (Ky).

TAPIT broke a bit in the air, quickly accelerated to contention along the inside, checked on heels when a bit rank entering the backstretch, awaited room inside under rating to the three furlong marker, angled out mid way on the final turn, found room between rivals leaving the three sixteenths marker, surged to command a furlong out, drew off impressively and won handily. POLISH RIFLE broke a step slow, angled out three to four wide around the first turn, advanced wide under rating into the far turn, loomed a major presence nearing the lane, continued willingly to gain the place but was no match for the winner. GHOST MOUNTAIN broke on top, stalked the pace three wide under rating, moved to command leaving the three furlong pole, edged clear into the lane, was overtaken by the winner in mid stretch then weakened a bit in the final sixteenth. ACCLIMATE set a pressured pace along the inside, was overtaken around the final turn, forced the issue into the lane, angled out leaving the eighth pole and kept trying to the finish. CAPEJINSKY had a wide trip and failed to respond. CHARISMATIC CALLER saved ground, was put to urging into the far turn, swung out in the drive but lacked a rally. TYM BEAU prompted the pace two wide and tired leaving the three furlong marker.

Owners– 1, Winchell Thoroughbreds LLC; 2, Helligbrodt RacingStoneride Stable LLC; 3, La Penta Robert V; 4, Miller David I; 5, John D Murphy; 6, Charles F Burnside & Finish Line Stable; 7, Papan Charles J

Trainers– 1, Dickinson Michael W; 2, Dutrow Anthony W; 3, Zito Nicholas P; 4, Testerman Valora A; 5, Gorham Michael E; 6, Lake Scott A; 7, Hershbell Lynnett A

Scratched– Who Is Chris G. (02Nov03 ⁸Aqu³)

EIGHTH RACE
Laurel
NOVEMBER 15, 2003

1¹⁄₈ MILES. (1.47³) ANNE ARUNDEL S. Grade III. Purse $100,000 FOR FILLIES, THREE–YEARS–OLD. Free subscription. $500 to pass the entry box. $500 additional to start. Supplemental nominations of $1000 each will be accepted by the usual time of entry with all other fees due as noted. Weight 122 lbs. Non–winners of a race of $50,000 at one mile or over, allowed 3 lbs.; $30,000 twice at one mile or over, 5 lbs.; once, 7 lbs. (Maiden and claiming races not considered in estimating allowances). Preference to starters with highest career earnings. Horses may be placed on the also–eligible list. Closed Wednesday, November 5, 2003 with 20 nominations.

Value of Race: $100,000 Winner $60,000; second $20,000; third $11,000; fourth $6,000; fifth $3,000. Mutuel Pool $160,230.00 Exacta Pool $114,023.00 Superfecta Pool $23,676.00 Trifecta Pool $86,618.00

Last Raced	Horse	M/Eqt.	A.	Wt	PP	St	¼	½	¾	Str	Fin	Jockey	Odds $1
25Oct03 ⁶Del²	Smooth Maneuvers	L f	3	115	1	2	1²	1½	1hd	12½	12½	Pino M G	8.90
25Oct03 ⁸Med¹	Devotion Unbridled	L	3	117	6	6	4¹½	5²	3hd	2¹½	2nk	Prado E S	0.70
8Oct03 ⁵Bel²	Alchemist	L	3	117	2	1	3½	3hd	4³	3½	3hd	Dominguez R A	3.40
10Oct03 ⁸Bel¹	Retroactive	L	3	117	7	7	7	6½	6hd	5¹⁰	44¼	Luzzi M J	7.20
4Oct03 ⁹Pha⁵	City Fire	L b	3	122	3	3	2²½	2¹	2²	4½	5¹⁰¾	Castellano A Jr	a– 4.40
17Oct03 ⁷Med⁷	Nault	L f	3	115	4	4	5½	7	7	6⁵	6⁸¼	Rosenthal M E	a– 4.40
1Nov03 ¹⁰Med³	Smart N Classy	L f	3	115	5	5	6hd	4½	5hd	7	7	Santana J Z	61.70

a–Coupled: City Fire and Nault.

OFF AT 3:52 Start Good . Won driving. Track fast.

TIME :24², :49³, 1:14³, 1:39, 1:51² (:24.54, :49.65, 1:14.60, 1:39.01, 1:51.56)

$2 Mutuel Prices:	2 – SMOOTH MANEUVERS	19.80	5.60	3.80
	7 – DEVOTION UNBRIDLED		2.60	2.40
	4 – ALCHEMIST			3.00

$2 EXACTA 2–7 PAID $42.40 $1 SUPERFECTA 2–7–4–8 PAID $279.00
$2 TRIFECTA 2–7–4 PAID $119.60

Dk. b or br. f, (Apr), by Grindstone – Aerobatics , by Caro–Ire . Trainer Pino Michael V. Bred by J D Squires (Ky).

SMOOTH MANEUVERS advanced along the inside into the first turn to take command, set a rated but pressured pace down the backstretch, shook clear nearing the lane, was set down in upper stretch and held sway under a drive. DEVOTION UNBRIDLED angled to the rail mid way around the first turn, prompted the pace under rating, eased out for room in upper stretch, finished gamely but could not gain in the final furlong. ALCHEMIST broke alertly, stalked the pace between rivals, circled four wide into the lane, finished willingly and was edged for the place. RETROACTIVE was lightly steadied on the heels of rivals early on in the first turn, settled down the backstretch, advanced between rivals leaving the three furlong marker, angled to the rail mid stretch and finished with good energy. CITY FIRE prompted the pace two wide and weakened nearing mid stretch. NAULT saved ground down the backstretch and failed to menace. SMART N CLASSY advanced three wide nearing the half mile marker, was put to pressure around the far turn and faltered after six furlongs.

Owners– 1, Nick Sanna Stables LLC; 2, Live Oak Plantation; 3, Alexander Helen C; 4, Humphrey Jr G Watts and Louise I; 5, Gill Michael J; 6, Gill Michael J; 7, Roseland Farm Stable

Trainers– 1, Pino Michael V; 2, Mott William I; 3, McGaughey III Claude R; 4, Arnold George R II; 5, Shuman Mark; 6, Shuman Mark; 7, Tammaro John J III

Scratched– Valley of the Gods (02Nov03 ⁷Del³) , Starship Daydream (02Nov03 ⁸Lrl¹) , River Cruise (11Oct03 ⁶Lrl¹)

$2 Pick Three (1/8–1–2) Paid $179.40 ; Pick Three Pool $19,588 .

TENTH RACE
Laurel
NOVEMBER 15, 2003

6 FURLONGS. (1.07⁴) FRANK J. DE FRANCIS MEMORIAL DASH S. Grade I. Purse $300,000 FOR THREE-YEAR-OLDS AND UPWARD. Free subscription. $3000 to pass the entry box.$3000 additional to start. Supplemental nominations at a fee of $10,000 each will be accepted by the usual time of entry with all other fees due as noted. Weights Three-year-olds 122 lbs., Older 126 lbs. Non-winners of $100,000 twice in 2003 allowed 3 lbs.; once, 5 lbs.; $60,000 twice in 2003, 7 lbs. Preference to starters with highest career earnings in 2002-2003. Horses may be placed on the also-eligible list. Closed Wednesday ,November 5, 2003 with 26 nominations.

Value of Race: $300,000 Winner $180,000; second $60,000; third $33,000; fourth $18,000; fifth $9,000. Mutuel Pool $385,264.00 Exacta Pool $297,137.00 Superfecta Pool $69,526.00 Trifecta Pool $213,517.00

Last Raced	Horse	M/Eqt. A. Wt	PP	St	1/4	1/2	Str	Fin	Jockey	Odds $1
21Sep03 7Del1	A Huevo	L f 7 119	3	10	10	81½	4hd	11¾	Dominguez R A	9.30
25Oct03 5SA3	Shake You Down	L bf 5 123	6	5	21½	22	1hd	2no	Luzzi M J	0.80
18Oct03 9Lrl1	Gators N Bears	L bf 3 115	4	6	3hd	31½	3hd	3½	Wilson R	5.40
9Oct03 8Bel1	Way to the Top	L f 5 119	5	8	7½	41	52	42	Rose J	19.70
27Sep03 7Bel2	Aggadan	L 4 119	7	1	5½	5hd	72½	5nk	Prado E S	6.50
25Oct03 5Bel8	Outstander	L 4 119	1	7	83	9hd	86	6nk	Santana J Z	41.60
31Oct03 8Lrl1	Boston Common	L 4 119	9	2	6hd	71	6hd	72½	Chavez J F	8.40
11Oct03 10Lrl2	Crossing Point	L f 6 119	2	4	11	1hd	21½	89¼	Pino M G	13.70
31Oct03 8Lrl2	Take AchanceOnMe	L bf 5 119	8	3	41½	6hd	915	9	Johnston M T	64.70
25Oct03 5Bel3	HighwayProspector	L b 6 119	10	9	92	10	10	—	Castellano A Jr	22.60

OFF AT 4:49 Start Good. Won ridden out. Track fast.

TIME :21⁴, :44², :56³, 1:08⁴ (:21.88, :44.47, :56.69, 1:08.90)

$2 Mutuel Prices:

3 – A HUEVO	20.60	6.00	3.00
6 – SHAKE YOU DOWN		2.80	2.10
4 – GATORS N BEARS			2.60

$2 EXACTA 3-6 PAID $67.00 $1 SUPERFECTA 3-6-4-5 PAID $1,518.30
$2 TRIFECTA 3-6-4 PAID $281.20

B. g, (May), by Cool Joe – Verabald , by Baldski . Trainer Dickinson Michael W. Bred by D Lopez (WV).

A HUEVO , pinched at the break, was unhurried early, circled the turn five wide, closed sharply when put to some hand urging leaving the three sixteenths marker, struck the top leaving the sixteenth marker and drew clear with something in reserve. SHAKE YOU DOWN bobbled at the break, quickly recovered and was sent up to prompt the pace two wide, moved to a short lead in mid stretch and finished gamely to save the place. GATORS N BEARS chased the pace, came three wide for the drive, lodged a bid leaving the furlong marker, finished well and just missed second. WAY TO THE TOP was hustled up between rivals nearing turn, advanced inside into the lane, angled out approaching the eighth pole but lacked the needed response inside of rivals. AGGADAN chased the leaders two wide on the turn, angled to the inside nearing the stretch but came up empty in the final furlong. OUTSTANDER saved ground while unhurried, swung out five wide for the drive and had belated interest. BOSTON COMMON lost ground four wide in an even effort. CROSSING POINT had speed to clear, set a rapid pace along the inside, dueled inside of SHAKE YOU DOWN past the furlong marker then succumbed in the final sixteenth. TAKE ACHANCE ON ME , fractious in the gate, chased the pace three wide and weakened nearing the quarter pole. HIGHWAY PROSPECTOR raced wide, was pulled up in upper stretch and walked off.

Owners– 1, Hopkins Mark S; 2, Cole Robert L Jr; 3, Nechamkin II Leo S; 4, Valente Roddy J; 5, Goldfarb Sanford J; 6, Manning Paul J and Schuler Edward F; 7, Englander Richard A; 8, Clark Nancy and Heyman Fred; 9, Ben Dover Stable; 10, Gill Michael J

Trainers– 1, Dickinson Michael W; 2, Lake Scott A; 3, Nechamkin Leo S II; 4, Levine Bruce N; 5, Dutrow Richard E Jr; 6, Jenkins Rodney; 7, Pino Michael V; 8, Feliciano Benjamin M Jr; 9, Aguirre Anthony; 10, Shuman Mark

$2 Pick Three (2–5–3) Paid $832.80 ; Pick Three Pool $19,630 .
$2 Pick Four (1–2–5–3) Paid $4,276.20 ; Pick Four Pool $29,834 .
$2 Daily Double (5–3) Paid $56.00 ; Daily Double Pool $36,558 .

Laurel Park Attendance: Unavailable Mutuel Pool: $.00

EIGHTH RACE
Remington
NOVEMBER 16, 2003

1⅛ MILES. (1.48) OKLAHOMA DERBY Grade III. Purse $150,000 (plus $1,700 OBP – Oklahoma Bred Pgm) FOR THREE-YEAR-OLDS. No nomination fee . $750 to enter and $750 additional to start. The added money and all fees to be divided 60% to the winner, 20% to second, 11% to third, 6% to fourth and 3% to fifth. Weight: Colts and Geldings, 124 lbs.; Fillies, 119 lbs. Non-winners of $100,000 twice at one mile or over in 2003 allowed, 3 lbs.; $100,000 once at a mile or over in 2003, 6 lbs.; $50,000 at a mile or over in 2003, 9 lbs.; $50,000 at any distance in 2002–2003, 12 lbs. Trophy to winning owner, trainer and jockey. NOMINATIONS CLOSED Thursday, November 6, 2003 with TWENTY FOUR (24).

Value of Race: $159,000 Winner $95,400; second $31,800; third $17,490; fourth $9,540; fifth $4,770. Mutuel Pool $65,158.00 Exacta Pool $44,459.00 Quinella Pool $4,879.00 Trifecta Pool $57,405.00

Last Raced	Horse	M/Eqt. A. Wt	PP	St	1/4	1/2	3/4	Str	Fin	Jockey	Odds $1
4Oct03 9Hoo4	Comic Truth	LB b 3 115	1	2	31	33	37	15	110	Berry M C	2.50
4Oct03 9Hoo1	Excessivepleasure	LB b 3 124	3	1	11½	11½	1½	23	22¼	Pettinger D R	0.90
1Nov03 9Wds3	Morning Merry	LB 3 112	5	6	6	6	53	46	32½	Eads J R	15.40
20Sep03 10LaD4	Kool Humor	LB b 3 115	2	4	2hd	21½	2½	34	46¾	Clark K D	4.40
26Oct03 1RP4	Tap Tap	LB 3 116	4	3	56	55	41½	515	544¾	Cogburn K L	5.80
1Nov03 8Wds2	Grayglen	LB b 3 116	6	5	4½	41	6	6	6	Landeros B C	45.40

OFF AT 4:38 Start Good. Won ridden out. Track fast.

TIME :23², :47², 1:11², 1:36³, 1:49² (:23.47, :47.45, 1:11.45, 1:36.68, 1:49.59)

$2 Mutuel Prices:

1 – COMIC TRUTH	7.00	2.80	2.10
3 – EXCESSIVEPLEASURE		2.20	2.10
5 – MORNING MERRY			2.10

$2 EXACTA 1-3 PAID $14.40 $2 QUINELLA 1-3 PAID $5.20
$2 TRIFECTA 1-3-5 PAID $75.00

Ch. c, (Feb), by Proudest Romeo – Comic Wish , by Lyphard's Ridge . Trainer Daly Patrick J. Bred by Dr K K Jayaraman & & Dr Vilasini D Jayaraman (Fla).

COMIC TRUTH stalked the early pace inside, remained in a forward position up the backstretch, inched closer entering the second turn, took command entering the stretch and drew off under light urging. EXCESSIVEPLEASURE broke well to gain the early advantage, held a clear margin up the backstretch, remained forward entering the second turn but could not keep pace. MORNING MERRY outrun early, advanced outside up the backstretch, responded when sat down for the drive but could only gain the show. KOOL HUMOR forced the early pace inside and weakened. TAP TAP up close from between foes but had no late response. GRAYGLEN was finished after a half.

Owners– 1, Jayaraman Kalarikkal K and Vilasini D; 2, Leatherman Lee and Ty; 3, Orion Stables; 4, Durant Tom R; 5, Richter Kristine and John; 6, Christensen Al

Trainers– 1, Daly Patrick J; 2, O'Neill Doug; 3, McCoy James B; 4, Bruner Jack A; 5, Von Hemel Donnie K; 6, Christensen Al

---

$2 Daily Double (10–1) Paid $73.80 ; Daily Double Pool $3,882 .

NINTH RACE
Churchill
NOVEMBER 16, 2003

1⅛ MILES. (Turf)(1.46^{1}) RIVER CITY H.. Grade III. Purse $150,000 A HANDICAP FOR THREE-YEARS-OLD AND UPWARD. By subscription of $150 each on or before November 1, 2003 or by supplementary nomination of $7,500 each by the closing of entries Friday, November 7, 2003. $750 to pass the entry box; $750 additional to start, with $150,000 added of which 62% of all monies to the owner of the winner, 20% to second, 10% to third, 5% to fourth and 3% to fifth. Weights to be announced Saturday, November 8. The maximum number of starters for the River City Handicap will be limited to twelve (12). If more than twelve (12) entries pass the entry box preference will be given to highweights, however two horses having common ties through ownership cannot start to the exclusion of a single interest. Any horse excluded from running because of the aforementioned preference shall be refunded the entry fee and supplementary nomination fee if applicable. If the race is moved to the main track after the time of closing, a horse may be scratched for any reason at any time up to fifteen (15) minutes prior to post time for the race preceding this race or thereafter with a valid physical reason and approved by the stewards. The entry fee and supplementary nomination fee, if applicable, shall be refunded for scratches made in compliance with t

Value of Race: $172,800 Winner $107,136; second $34,560; third $17,280; fourth $8,640; fifth $5,184. Mutuel Pool $437,507.00 Exacta Pool $294,885.00 Trifecta Pool $259,168.00 Superfecta Pool $85,221.00

Last Raced	Horse	M/Eqt.	A.	Wt	PP	St	¼	½	¾	Str	Fin	Jockey	Odds $1
20Sep03 ^{9}KD^{1}	Hard Buck-BR	L	4	118	2	4	3^{hd}	$3^{1\frac{1}{2}}$	$3^{\frac{1}{2}}$	$2^{2\frac{1}{2}}$	$1^{\frac{1}{2}}$	Blanc B	11.60
18Oct03 ^{10}LaD^{1}	Warleigh	L	5	117	3	2	1^{1}	$1^{1\frac{1}{2}}$	$1^{1\frac{1}{2}}$	1^{1}	2^{1}	Lanerie C J	2.50
11Oct03 ^{9}Bel^{2}	Rowans Park	L	3	114	7	8	8^{1}	$8^{\frac{1}{2}}$	7^{hd}	$5^{\frac{1}{2}}$	3^{1}	McKee J	11.00
12Oct03 ^{7}Kee^{1}	Gretchen's Star	Lf	8	115	4	3	$6^{\frac{1}{2}}$	6^{1}	$6^{1\frac{1}{2}}$	$4^{1\frac{1}{2}}$	$4^{\frac{3}{4}}$	Borel C H	14.50
4Oct03 ^{7}Kee^{1}	Sharbayan-IR	Lb	5	119	1	5	$9^{\frac{1}{2}}$	$9^{1\frac{1}{2}}$	8^{1}	6^{hd}	5^{hd}	Day P	1.90
20Sep03 ^{14}KD^{4}	Act Of War	Lb	5	115	5	6	$5^{\frac{1}{2}}$	4^{hd}	5^{hd}	3^{hd}	$6^{4\frac{1}{2}}$	Bourque C C	18.10
3Oct03 ^{8}Kee^{5}	Bud's Magic	Lb	5	113	6	7	10	10	10	9^{hd}	7^{nk}	Douglas R R	73.70
4Oct03 ^{9}Kee^{7}	Della Francesca	Lb	4	116	9	10	$4^{\frac{1}{2}}$	5^{3}	$4^{\frac{1}{2}}$	$7^{\frac{1}{2}}$	8no	Chavez J F	5.20
18Oct03 ^{8}Haw^{1}	False Promises	L	3	116	8	9	7^{hd}	$7^{\frac{1}{2}}$	$9^{1\frac{1}{2}}$	10	$9^{2\frac{1}{4}}$	Marquez C H Jr	14.50
18Oct03 ^{7}Kee^{2}	Foster's Landing	L	5	113	10	1	$2^{\frac{1}{2}}$	$2^{\frac{1}{2}}$	2^{hd}	8^{2}	10	Perret C	17.70

OFF AT 4:40 Start Good. Won driving. Course yielding.
TIME :24^{3}, :49^{2}, 1:14^{2}, 1:39^{1}, 1:51^{3} (:24.68, :49.58, 1:14.56, 1:39.36, 1:51.60)

$2 Mutuel Prices:

2-HARD BUCK-BR	25.20	10.20	7.60
4-WARLEIGH		4.60	4.20
9-ROWANS PARK			6.20

$2 EXACTA 2-4 PAID $90.20 $2 TRIFECTA 2-4-9 PAID $1,179.20 $2 SUPERFECTA 2-4-9-6 PAID $6,902.80

B. c, by Spend a Buck–Social Secret*GB, by Secreto. Trainer McPeek Kenneth G. Bred by Haras Old Friends (Brz).

HARD BUCK (BRZ), lightly rated early while racing inside of front-running WARLEIGH, was put to a drive approaching the final quarter, then responded to steady encouragement to wear down WARLEIGH in the late going after being brushed lightly by that one. WARLEIGH gained the lead early, raced in the three path, made the pace into deep stretch, and, while leaning in late and brushing the winner, couldn't last in a game try. ROWANS PARK, bumped at the start, was unhurried, raced in behind rivals four wide, came out between foes eight wide when straightened for the drive and was gaining late. GRETCHEN'S STAR, within easy striking distance from the start, followed the leaders five wide, moved out farther on the course for the drive but lacked a final response. SHARBAYAN (IRE), outrun for a half, moved between horses entering the far turn, came out nine wide for the stretch run and improved position while unable to offer a serious late bid. ACT OF WAR, nicely placed between rivals three or four wide to the lane, remained between horses four wide for the final furlong, loomed a solid threat but flattened out. BUD'S MAGIC, bumped at the start, raced five wide to the far turn, angled in behind horses but never threatened. DELLA FRANCESCA, bumped at the start by FOSTER'S LANDING, bobbled and was forced in on FALLS PROMISES, raced in contention five wide until approaching the stretch and weakened. FALSE PROMISES, bumped at the break and forced in, raced five wide into the first turn and weakened gradually. FOSTER'S LANDING ducked in at the start on DELLA FRANCESCA, maneuvered in soon after to press front-running WALEIGH, held on well until approaching the stretch and tired.

Owners— 1, Team Victory I Jose Carlos Carneval; 2, Parra Rosendo G; 3, Melnyk Eugene & Laura; 4, Isbell Ron Jr; 5, Iron County Farms Inc & Miller Trus; 6, RNR Breeders; 7, Barrett Partners LLC; 8, Ol Memorial Stable Dell Ridge Farm; 9, Maracich David; 10, McKee Stables

Trainers—1, McPeek Kenneth G; 2, Asmussen Steven M; 3, Reinstedler Anthony; 4, Isbell Ron Jr; 5, Dollase Wallace; 6, Cilio Gene A; 7, Million William N; 8, O'Callaghan Niall M; 9, Granitz Anthony J; 10, Romans Dale

Scratched— Dr. Kashnikow (22Oct03 ^{8}KEE^{2}), Better Talk Now (1Nov03 ^{8}AQU^{1}), Lacer (25Oct03 ^{10}HAW^{5})

$2 Pick Three (9-1-2) Paid $176.40; Pick Three Pool $33,543.

EIGHTH RACE
Aqueduct
NOVEMBER 22, 2003

$1\frac{3}{8}$ MILES. (Turf)(2.14^{1}) RED SMITH H.. Grade II. Purse $150,000 TURF. (Up to $29,100 NYSBFOA) A HANDICAP FOR THREE YEAR OLDS AND UPWARD. By subscription of $150 each, which should accompany the nomination; $750 to pass the entry box; $750 to start. The purse to be divided 60% to the winner, 20% to second, 11% to third, 6% to fourth and 3% to fifth. Trophies will be presented to the winning owner, trainer and jockey. The New York Racing Association reserves the right to transfer this race to the Main Track. In the event that this race is taken off the turf, it may be subject to downgrading upon review by the Graded Stakes Committee. Closed Saturday, November 8th, 2003 with 46 Nominations.

Value of Race: $150,000 Winner $90,000; second $30,000; third $16,500; fourth $9,000; fifth $4,500. Mutuel Pool $626,239.00 Exacta Pool $466,453.00 Trifecta Pool $333,262.00

Last Raced	Horse	M/Eqt.	A.	Wt	PP	¼	½	¾	1	Str	Fin	Jockey	Odds $1
25Oct03 ^{8}SA^{9}	Balto Star	L	5	120	6	1^{hd}	$1^{\frac{1}{2}}$	$1^{\frac{1}{2}}$	$1^{1\frac{1}{2}}$	1^{8}	$1^{3\frac{1}{4}}$	Velazquez J R	4.90
19Oct03 ^{9}WO^{2}	Macaw-IR	Lbf	4	118	5	$8^{2\frac{1}{2}}$	$7^{3\frac{1}{2}}$	7^{6}	$7^{2\frac{1}{2}}$	$6^{1\frac{1}{2}}$	2^{nk}	Bridgmohan S X	2.45
4Oct03 ^{7}Kee^{2}	Cetewayo	Lb	9	116	10	11	11	11	10^{5}	4^{hd}	$3^{3\frac{1}{2}}$	Santos J A	3.85
25Oct03 ^{4}Med^{4}	Final Prophecy	L	4	114	1	$7^{\frac{1}{2}}$	$9^{2\frac{1}{2}}$	10^{2}	11	$8^{\frac{1}{2}}$	4^{hd}	Lopez C C	90.75
9Nov03 ^{8}Aqu^{4}	Haggs Castle	bf	5	112	3	$10^{3\frac{1}{2}}$	10^{6}	9^{hd}	$8^{1\frac{1}{2}}$	$7^{\frac{1}{2}}$	$5^{\frac{1}{2}}$	Carrero V	18.30
1Nov03 ^{8}Aqu^{6}	Deputy Strike	L	5	115	7	$6^{1\frac{1}{2}}$	6^{hd}	6^{hd}	$6^{3\frac{1}{2}}$	5^{hd}	6^{hd}	Migliore R	6.80
4Oct03 ^{7}Kee^{5}	Revved Up	L	5	118	4	5^{3}	$5^{1\frac{1}{2}}$	$5^{3\frac{1}{2}}$	5^{3}	$3^{\frac{1}{2}}$	$7^{1\frac{3}{4}}$	Prado E S	4.40
31Oct03 ^{4}Med^{1}	He Flies	L	5	113	8	$4^{1\frac{1}{2}}$	$4^{3\frac{1}{2}}$	$4^{\frac{1}{2}}$	4^{1}	$2^{\frac{1}{2}}$	$8^{\frac{3}{4}}$	Pimentel J	52.25
1Nov03 ^{8}Aqu^{9}	Dawn Of The Condor	Lb	6	112	9	$9^{3\frac{1}{2}}$	8^{hd}	$8^{\frac{1}{2}}$	$9^{\frac{1}{2}}$	10^{10}	$9^{2\frac{1}{4}}$	Fragoso P	41.75
1Nov03 ^{8}Aqu^{11}	Quiet Ruler	L	5	114	2	$3^{\frac{1}{2}}$	$3^{3\frac{1}{2}}$	3^{5}	2^{hd}	9^{hd}	$10^{13\frac{1}{4}}$	Hampshire J F Jr	17.10
2Oct03 ^{7}Bel^{7}	Tripat-IR	L	4	113	11	2^{2}	$2^{\frac{1}{2}}$	$2^{\frac{1}{2}}$	$3^{\frac{1}{2}}$	11	11	Luzzi M J	30.50

OFF AT 3:45 Start Good. Won driving. Course soft.

TIME :24^{3}, :49^{3}, 1:15, 1:39^{3}, 2:05^{2}, 2:18^{4} (:24.73, :49.77, 1:15.10, 1:39.62, 2:05.56, 2:18.86)

$2 Mutuel Prices:

7–BALTO STAR	11.80	5.90	3.50
5–MACAW-IR		3.90	2.70
11–CETEWAYO			3.10

$2 EXACTA 7–5 PAID $46.00 $2 TRIFECTA 7–5–11 PAID $134.50

Dk. b. or br. g, by Glitterman–Miss Livi, by Devil's Bag. Trainer Pletcher Todd A. Bred by Anstu Stables Inc (Ky).

BALTO STAR quickly showed in front, made the pace along the inside while in hand, drew away when roused in upper stretch and remained well clear under a drive. MACAW (IRE) was rated along early, came wide for the drive and finished gamely outside. CETEWAYO was outrun early, rallied three wide on the final turn, angled to the inside in upper stretch and finished gamely. FINAL PROPHECY was outrun early, saved ground and finished well inside. HAGGS CASTLE was outrun early and was going well late. DEPUTY STRIKE was rated along outside, put in a three wide run on the final turn and had little left for the stretch drive. REVVED UP was rated along early and had no response when roused. HE FLIES raced close up while in hand and came up empty when asked. DAWN OF THE CONDOR had no rally. QUIET RULER raced with the pace while in hand, put in a three wide run on the last turn and tired in the stretch. TRIPAT (IRE) raced close up outside for three quarters and tired.

Owners— 1, Anstu Stables; 2, Melillo George & Sandra; 3, Chandler Dr John A; 4, Howes Jean & Dale; 5, Confort John & Weiss Albert; 6, West Point Stable; 7, Live Oak Plantation; 8, Our Blue Streaks Stables; 9, Soblick David; 10, Sarf Randy J & Old Brookside Farm; 11, Bouchard Ecurie J

Trainers—1, Pletcher Todd A; 2, Tagg Barclay; 3, Dickinson Michael W; 4, Cibelli Jane; 5, Jerkens James A; 6, McLaughlin Kiaran P; 7, Clement Christophe; 8, Schettino Dominick A; 9, Sciacca Gary; 10, Mueller Russell; 11, Clement Christophe

Scratched— Royal Regalia (20Oct03 ^{8}DEL^{1}), Peekskill (7Nov03 ^{7}AQU^{1}), Evening Attire (25Oct03 ^{9}SA^{7}), Snake Mountain (24Oct03 ^{8}BEL^{1} Private Lap (8Nov03 ^{7}DEL^{1})

NINTH RACE

Churchill

NOVEMBER 22, 2003

1⅛ MILES. (Turf)(1.46¹) CARDINAL H.. Grade III. Purse $150,000 A HANDICAP FOR FILLIES AND MARES, THREE-YEARS-OLD AND UPWARD. By subscription of $150 each on or before November 8, 2003 or by supplementary nomination of $7,500 each by the closing of entries Friday, November 14, 2003. $750 to pass the entry box; $750 additional to start. Weights to be announced November 15. The maximum number of starters for the Cardinal Handicap will be limited to 12. If more than 12 entries pass the entry box preference will be given to highweights, however two horses having common ties through ownership cannot start to the exclusion of a single interest. Any horse excluded from running because of the aforementioned preference shall be refunded the entry fee and supplementary nomination fee if applicable.

Value of Race: $175,200 Winner $108,624; second $35,040; third $17,520; fourth $8,760; fifth $5,256. Mutuel Pool $613,220.00 Exacta Pool $470,058.00 Trifecta Pool $380,720.00 Superfecta Pool $127,775.00

Last Raced	Horse	M/Eqt. A.Wt	PP	St	¼	½	¾	Str	Fin	Jockey	Odds $1
25Oct03 6SA6	Riskaverse	L	4 118	1	3	4 1½	4 1½	4 1½	2 2½	1 ¾	Velasquez C	2.70
25Oct03 6SA9	Bien Nicole	L	5 120	11	6	1hd	1 2	1 1½	1 1	2 4	Pettinger D R	2.00
14Sep03 8B M1	Firth Of Lorne-IR	L	4 116	2	8	7 1	6 1½	8 2	4hd	3 1	Johnston M T	8.50
19Oct03 8Kee3	Peacefally-IR	L	4 112	3	7	6hd	5hd	5hd	5hd	4no	Melancon L	36.70
18Oct03 9Kee1	Dyna Da Wyna	Lf	3 115	6	1	2 1½	2 ½	3 ½	3 ½	5no	Day P	6.20
11Oct03 8Haw2	Delmonico Cat	L	4 115	10	5	5hd	7 1	6 ½	7 2	6 1½	Lanerie C J	17.60
11Oct03 8Haw1	Janeian-NZ	L	5 117	7	4	3 1	3hd	2hd	6hd	7nk	Martin E M Jr	11.30
31Oct03 9CD3	San Dare	L	5 115	4	10	11 4	11 2½	9 ½	10 3	8no	Martinez W	24.70
31Oct03 9CD1	Quick Tip	L	5 116	12	12	9 1½	9 1	7hd	9 1	9 1½	Sellers S J	8.20
29Oct03 9CD1	Dick's Chick	L	4 114	9	9	8 ½	8 1	10 4	8hd10 4¾		Bejarano R	52.10
11Oct03 8Haw3	Delicatessa	Lf	4 114	5	2	10hd10 ½	12	11 3	11 2½		Thompson T J	89.10
19Oct03 8Kee6	Golden Rhythm	L	5 114	8	11	12	12	11 ½	12	12	Borel C H	97.00

OFF AT 4:40 Start Good For All But PEACEFALLY (IRE) Won driving. Course firm.

TIME :24¹, :49¹, 1:13⁴, 1:38¹, 1:50² (:24.34, :49.29, 1:13.98, 1:38.34, 1:50.53)

$2 Mutuel Prices:

1–RISKAVERSE		7.40	3.60	2.80
11–BIEN NICOLE			3.60	3.00
2–FIRTH OF LORNE–IR				4.40

$2 EXACTA 1–11 PAID $19.40 $2 TRIFECTA 1–11–2 PAID $161.40 $2
SUPERFECTA 1–11–2–3 PAID $2,299.80

Dk. b. or br. f, by Dynaformer–The Bink, by Seeking the Gold. Trainer Kelly Patrick J. Bred by Fox Ridge Farm Inc (Ky).

RISKAVERSE, well placed from early on while racing inside under a rating hold, eased outside of front-running BIEN NICOLE entering the upper stretch to be four wide, caught that one a sixteenth out and was hard ridden the remainder. BIEN NICOLE worked her way in early while dueling outside of DYNA DA WYNA, put a head in front just before going a quarter, made the pace three wide, drew clear on the first turn, showed the way into the final furlong and couldn't contain the winner's surge. FIRTH OF LORNE (IRE), well placed into the stretch, remained in behind the top two three wide for the drive and failed to offer a late response. PEACEFALLY (IRE) stumbled at the start, quickly recovered, raced within easy striking distance near the inside between rivals, continued prominently four or five wide into the final furlong and failed to respond. DYNA DA WYNA vied for the lead inside of pacesetting BIEN NICOLE during the opening quarter, eased outside that one four wide on the backstretch, posed a solid threat into the final furlong and flattened out. DELMONICO CAT, never far back, tracked the pace five wide, came wider into the stretch and couldn't produce a closing bid. JANEIAN (NZ) followed the leaders in a striking position four wide from the first turn on, remained a threat into the upper stretch and was empty. SAN DARE, outrun to the stretch while four wide, angled seven wide into the upper stretch and failed to fire. QUICK TIP lunged in at the start and bumped the side of the gate, settled five or six wide, reached contention nearing the final quarter as the field tightened but was empty when straightened into the stretch. DICK'S CHICK tired after a half. DELICATESSA was outrun. GOLDEN RHYTHM, outrun from the start, raced four wide early, eased out six wide on the backstretch, came 10 abreast into the stretch and never menaced.

Owners— 1, Fox Ridge Farm Inc Peter G Schiff; 2, Richter Kristine & John; 3, Darley Stable; 4, Van Meter II Thomas F Bradley Peter; 5, WinStar Farm LLC; 6, Wygod Mr & Mrs Martin J; 7, Greg L England; 8, Mounts David G; 9, Farish William S; 10, McGinn Dave; 11, Inman Barr H; 12, Sandstone Racing Stable Partnership

Trainers— 1, Kelly Patrick J; 2, Von Hemel Donnie K; 3, Harty Eoin; 4, Walden W Elliott; 5, Walden W Elliott; 6, Mott William I; 7, Calhoun William Bret; 8, Hiles Rick; 9, Howard Neil J; 10, Shapoff Alan W; 11, Livesay Charlie; 12, Murphy Paul H

Scratched— Synergistic (19Oct03 6KEE1)

$2 Pick Three (1–1/6/9–1) Paid $109.60; Pick Three Pool $39,794.

EIGHTH RACE
Hollywood
NOVEMBER 22, 2003

1½ MILES. (Turf) (2.232) HOLLYWOOD TURF CUP S. Grade I. Purse $250,000 FOR THREE-YEAR-OLDS AND UPWARD. By subscription of $250 each, on or before November 12. $1,250 to pass the entry box and $1,250 additional to start , with $150,000 to the winner, $50,000 to second, $30,000 to third, $15,000 to fourth and $5,000 to fifth.Three-year-olds 122 lbs. Older 126 lbs. Trophies will be presented to the winning owner and trainer. Nominations Closed, Wednesday, November 12th, 2003 with 17.

Value of Race: $250,000third $30,000; Winner $150,000; second $50,000; fourth $15,000; fifth $5,000. Mutuel Pool $530,406.00 Exacta Pool $269,448.00 Quinella Pool $25,713.00 Trifecta Pool $245,823.00 Superfecta Pool $87,547.00

Last Raced	Horse	M/Eqt.	A.	Wt	PP	¼	½	1	1¼	Str	Fin	Jockey	Odds $1
24Oct03 8SA6	[D]Epicentre	LB	4	126	3	3½	31½	32	21½	22½	1no	Nakatani C S	a- 2.60
24Oct03 8SA8	Continuously	LB	4	126	5	61½	62½	64	61½	3hd	2hd	Solis A O	6.20
19Oct03 9WO4	Bowman Mill	LB	5	126	6	11½	12	12	11½	1hd	3½	Flores D R	2.00
24Oct03 8SA1	Runaway Dancer	LB	4	126	7	7	7	7	7	52	42½	Krone J A	5.10
24Oct03 8SA7	Staging Post	LB	5	126	2	41	4hd	51	3hd	41	53	Valenzuela P A	a- 2.60
8Oct03 7SA5	Hatif-Brz	LB	4	126	1	21½	21	2hd	51	7	61	Baze T	31.90
24Oct03 8SA2	Labirinto	LB	5	126	4	5½	51	4½	4½	61	7	Smith M E	3.00

[D] – Epicentre disqualified and placed 3rd
a–Coupled: Epicentre and Staging Post.

OFF AT 4:11 Start Good . Won driving. Course firm.
TIME :261, :513, 1:164, 1:412, 2:052, 2:29 (:26.37, :51.76, 1:16.96, 1:41.58, 2:05.43, 2:29.01)

$2 Mutuel Prices:				
	5 – CONTINUOUSLY	14.40	6.40	3.60
	6 – BOWMAN MILL		3.80	2.60
	1A– EPICENTRE(a–entry)			2.60

$1 EXACTA 5–6 PAID $22.70 $2 QUINELLA 5–6 PAID $19.60
$1 TRIFECTA 5–6–1 PAID $70.60 $1 SUPERFECTA 5–6–1–8 PAID $173.80

B. c, (Jan), by Diesis-GB – Play On and On , by Stop the Music . Trainer Frankel Robert. Bred by Palides Investments N V Inc (Ky).

EPICENTRE stalked the pace outside a rival, split horses into the stretch, lugged in and bumped BOWMAN MILL in midstretch, battled outside that one through the final furlong and gamely prevailed between foes late. CONTINUOUSLY threw his head at the start, angled in and chased inside, came out on the final turn and three deep into the stretch and closed willingly. BOWMAN MILL took the lead outside a rival on the first turn, angled in and set a slow pace under a long hold along the inside, was bumped in midstretch, fought back through a long drive and continued gamely to the wire. RUNAWAY DANCER unhurried and angled in off the rail early, chased just off the fence, came out on the third turn and five wide into the stretch and finished fast. STAGING POST stalked the pace along the inside, waited briefly then split horses on the final turn and again into the stretch but could not offer the necessary late response. HATIF (BRZ) took the early lead then stalked along the inside, steadied in tight midway on the final turn, then weakened. LABIRINTO flipped in the paddock, was a half step slow to begin then chased outside a rival, went three deep on the last turn and weakened in the drive. Following a stewards' inquiry, EPICENTRE was disqualified and placed third for interference in the stretch. A claim of foul by the rider of HATIF against EPICENTRE for alleged interference on the last turn was not allowed by the stewards, who ruled the incident was minor and did not alter the original order of finish.

Owners– 1, Juddmonte Farms Inc; 2, Khaled Saud b; 3, Chandler Dr John A; 4, RL Stables; 5, Juddmonte Farms Inc; 6, Belmont Stable and Old Friends Inc; 7, Mio Jean P

Trainers– 1, Frankel Robert J; 2, Frankel Robert J; 3, Dickinson Michael W; 4, Hendricks Dan L; 5, Frankel Robert J; 6, Lobo Paulo H; 7, Collet Rodolphe

Scratched– Superiority (06Nov03 6SA 1) , Hataab (13Nov03 3Hol5)

$2 Daily Double (9–5) Paid $145.20 ; Daily Double Pool $32,128 .
$1 Pick Three (10–9–5) Paid $806.10 ; Pick Three Pool $61,605 .

EIGHTH RACE
Aqueduct
NOVEMBER 23, 2003

6 FURLONGS. (1.072) VALLEY STREAM S.. Grade III. Purse $100,000 (Up to $19,400 NYSBFOA) FOR FILLIES TWO YEARS OLD. By subscription of $100 each, which should accompany the nomination; $500 to pass the entry box; $500 to start, with $100,000 added. The added money and all fees to be divided 60% to the winner, 20% to second, 11% to third, 6% to fourth and 3% to fifth. 122 lbs. Non-winners of $40,000 allowed 2 lbs.; two races other than maiden or claiming, 4 lbs.; a race other than maiden or claiming 6 lbs. Trophies will be presented to the winning owner, trainer and jockey. Closed Saturday, November 8, 2003 with 32 Nominations.

Value of Race: $112,200 Winner $67,320; second $22,440; third $12,342; fourth $6,732; fifth $3,366. Mutuel Pool $386,231.00 Exacta Pool $335,633.00 Trifecta Pool $275,406.00

Last Raced	Horse	M/Eqt.	A.Wt	PP	St	¼	½	Str	Fin	Jockey	Odds $1
12Oct03 10Bel3	Smokey Glacken	L	2 118	1	5	1½	11½	15½	13¾	Santos J A	2.50
26Oct03 8Pha1	Baldomera	Lb	2 118	6	8	81½	75½	52½	2½	Vega H	33.00
31Oct03 8Aqu1	Stoic	L	2 118	4	4	55½	43½	31½	31	Castellano J J	5.80
5Nov03 7Del1	Royal Magician	L	2 118	2	9	9	82½	72½	41½	Migliore R	31.25
25Oct03 3SA14	Forest Music	Lb	2 116	9	6	3hd	2hd	2hd	51¾	Prado E S	1.00
1Nov03 8Del5	Lady Beelzebub	L	2 118	8	1	2½	31½	4½	62¼	Chavez J F	56.25
28Sep03 8Bel5	Wild Berry	L	2 118	3	7	62	5hd	6hd	72	Luzzi M J	19.70
31Oct03 8Aqu4	Hermione's Magic	Lb	2 116	7	2	42½	6½	83½	83¾	Velazquez J R	8.40
30Aug03 10Mth6	Standswithafist	L	2 116	5	3	75	9	9	9	Carrero V	106.75

OFF AT 3:44 Start Good. Won driving. Track fast.
TIME :213, :45, :572, 1:11 (:21.79, :45.04, :57.55, 1:11.18)

$2 Mutuel Prices:				
	1–SMOKEY GLACKEN	7.00	4.50	3.10
	6–BALDOMERA		17.00	7.00
	4–STOIC			3.40

$2 EXACTA 1–6 PAID $89.00 $2 TRIFECTA 1–6–4 PAID $326.50

B. f, (Mar), by Forestry–Majesty's Crown, by Magesterial. Trainer Jerkens James A. Bred by Jayeff 'B' Stables (Ky).

SMOKEY GLACKEN stumbled at the start but was hustled up inside, set the pace along the rail, drew clear into the stretch, widened when roused and was kept to a drive to the wire. BALDOMERA was outrun early, raced four wide and finished gamely outside to earn the place award. STOIC raced close up inside early, angled out for the drive and was outfinished. ROYAL MAGICIAN was bumped at the start, was steadied after the start, dropped back early and finished well. FOREST MUSIC chased the pace while three wide and tired in the stretch. LADY BEELZEBUB chased the pace while between rivals and tired after a half mile. WILD BERRY was bumped at the start, raced inside and had no response when roused. HERMIONE'S MAGIC stumbled at the start, raced close up inside and was finished early. STANDSWITHAFIST raced inside and tired.

Owners— 1, Moore Susan & John; 2, Hidden Lane Farms Inc; 3, Jay Em Ess Stable; 4, Win & Place Stable; 5, Gill Michael J; 6, Bonnell Sandra W; 7, Steeplechase Farm; 8, Edgewood Farm; 9, Pompa Paul P Jr

Trainers—1, Jerkens James A; 2, Preciado Guadalupe; 3, Dutrow Richard E Jr; 4, Dutrow Anthony W; 5, Shuman Mark; 6, Dullea Francis M; 7, Gorham Michael E; 8, Pletcher Todd A; 9, Araya Rene A

EIGHTH RACE
Aqueduct
NOVEMBER 27, 2003

6 FURLONGS. (1.07^{2}) FALL HIGHWEIGHT H.. Grade III. Purse $100,000 (Up to $19,400 NYSBFOA) A HANDICAP FOR THREE YEAR OLDS AND UPWARD. By subscription of $100 each, which should accompany the nomination; $500 to pass the entry box; $500 to start, with $100,000 added. The added money and all fees to be divided 60% to the winner, 20% to second, 11% to third, 6% to fourth and 3% to fifth. Trophies will be presented to the winning owner, trainer and jockey. Closed Saturday, November 15, 2003 with 18 Nominations.

Value of Race: $108,300 Winner $64,980; second $21,660; third $11,913; fourth $6,498; fifth $3,249. Mutuel Pool $330,292.00 Exacta Pool $249,199.00 Trifecta Pool $159,918.00

Last Raced	Horse	M/Eqt.	A.	Wt	PP	St	¼	½	Str	Fin	Jockey	Odds $1
8Nov03 ^{7}Aqu^{1}	Bossanova	Lb	3	128	2	3	1^{1}	$1^{1\frac{1}{2}}$	$1^{2\frac{1}{2}}$	$1^{\frac{1}{2}}$	Prado E S	1.70
7Nov03 ^{8}Aqu^{1}	Papua	Lbf	4	132	3	2	$4^{\frac{1}{2}}$	$3^{\frac{1}{2}}$	2^{hd}	$2^{\frac{3}{4}}$	Migliore R	5.40
8Nov03 ^{8}Aqu^{1}	Savoy Special	L	3	127	5	4	$2^{1\frac{1}{2}}$	2^{2}	3^{3}	$3^{2\frac{3}{4}}$	Velazquez J R	3.45
25Oct03 ^{5}Bel^{4}	Speed Hunter	L	4	130	6	1	3^{hd}	$4^{1\frac{1}{2}}$	4^{hd}	$4^{\frac{1}{2}}$	Castellano J J	7.50
1Nov03 ^{7}Med^{1}	Peeping Tom	Lbf	6	138	1	6	6	5^{hd}	5^{6}	5^{7}	Bridgmohan S X	3.15
7Nov03 ^{8}Aqu^{3}	Vodka	L	6	128	4	5	$5^{1\frac{1}{2}}$	6	6	6	Santos J A	15.40

OFF AT 2:11 Start Good. Won driving. Track fast.
TIME :22^{4}, :45^{4}, :57^{3}, 1:10 (:22.88, :45.80, :57.60, 1:10.06)

$2 Mutuel Prices:

2–BOSSANOVA	5.40	3.60	2.50
3–PAPUA		5.20	2.80
6–SAVOY SPECIAL			2.50

$2 EXACTA 2–3 PAID $29.20 $2 TRIFECTA 2–3–6 PAID $77.50

Dk. b. or br. c, (Apr), by Pine Bluff–Street Tappin, by Housebuster. Trainer Bond Harold James. Bred by Kent Wiechert & Katy Wiechert (NY).

BOSSANOVA quickly showed in front, set the pace along the inside, drew clear nearing the stretch, dug in gamely when roused and held on under a drive. PAPUA raced close up early, rallied inside turning for home and finished gamely. SAVOY SPECIAL stumbled at the start, was bumped then was hustled up outside, chased the pace and dug in gamely in the stretch. SPEED HUNTER was bumped at the start, raced with the pace while three wide and lacked a rally. PEEPING TOM was outrun early, came wide for the drive and had no rally. VODKA raced three wide and tired in the stretch.

Owners— 1, Rodriguez Lorraine & Rod; 2, Schwartz Barry K; 3, Scatuorchio James T; 4, Sullivan Lane Stable Scuderi Vincen; 5, Flatbird Stable; 6, Gerrity Joseph W Jr

Trainers—1, Bond Harold James; 2, Hushion Michael E; 3, Pletcher Todd A; 4, Dutrow Richard E Jr; 5, Reynolds Patrick L; 6, Hertler John O

Scratched— Sam Lord's Castle (1Nov03 ^{7}CD^{1})

TENTH RACE
Churchill
NOVEMBER 27, 2003

1⅛ MILES. (1.47^{1}) FALLS CITY H. Grade II. Purse $300,000 A HANDICAP FOR FILLIES AND MARES, THREE-YEARS-OLD AND UPWARD. By subscription of $300 each on or before November 15, 2003 or by supplementary nomination of $15,000 each by the closing of entries Friday, November 21, 2003. $1,500 to pass the entry box; $1,500 additional to start, with $300,000 added of which 62% of all monies to the owner of the winner, 20% to second, 10% to third, 5% to fourth and 3% to fifth. Weights to be announced Saturday, November 22. Starters to be named through the entry box bytheusual time of closing. Closed Saturday, November 15, 2003 with 19 nominations. Trophy to winning owner.

Value of Race: $334,200 Winner $207,204; second $66,840; third $33,420; fourth $16,710; fifth $10,026. Mutuel Pool $234,087.00 Exacta Pool $152,765.00 Trifecta Pool $145,548.00 Superfecta Pool $54,380.00

Last Raced	Horse	M/Eqt.	A.	Wt	PP	St	¼	½	¾	Str	Fin	Jockey	Odds $1
8Nov03 ^{9}CD^{1}	Lead Story	L	4	116	4	7	7^{1}	$7^{4\frac{1}{2}}$	5^{hd}	1^{hd}	$1^{6\frac{1}{2}}$	Borel C H	10.10
8Nov03 ^{9}CD^{8}	Mayo On the Side	L bf	4	114	1	2	$1^{1\frac{1}{2}}$	$1^{1\frac{1}{2}}$	1^{2}	$2^{5\frac{1}{2}}$	2^{6}	Butler D P	20.50
15Nov03 ^{8}Haw^{2}	Cloakof Vagueness	L	3	114	5	8	8^{6}	8^{2}	$8^{\frac{1}{2}}$	4^{1}	$3^{6\frac{1}{2}}$	McKee J	5.30
1Nov03 ^{9}Aqu^{5}	Misty Sixes	L	5	114	6	4	2^{hd}	4^{3}	4^{2}	$5^{2\frac{1}{2}}$	4no	Blanc B	25.80
25Oct03 ^{2}SA^{6}	Take Charge Lady	L	4	123	7	1	$3^{\frac{1}{2}}$	2^{hd}	$2^{\frac{1}{2}}$	3^{2}	$5^{3\frac{3}{4}}$	D'Amico A J	0.60
30Oct03 ^{3}Aqu^{2}	Fircroft	L	3	112	2	6	$6^{4\frac{1}{2}}$	5^{hd}	$6^{\frac{1}{2}}$	$6^{1\frac{1}{2}}$	6^{3}	Melancon L	6.20
9Nov03 ^{4}CD^{3}	SweetwaterPromise	L b	4	111	3	9	9	9	9	8^{2}	$7^{4\frac{1}{2}}$	Bejarano R	68.70
9Nov03 ^{4}CD^{1}	Golden Marlin	L	3	114	8	3	4^{2}	$3^{\frac{1}{2}}$	$3^{2\frac{1}{2}}$	7^{2}	$8^{3\frac{1}{2}}$	Perret C	13.10
8Nov03 ^{9}CD^{5}	Rhiana	L f	6	114	9	5	5^{2}	6^{4}	7^{4}	9	9	Velasquez C H	35.80

OFF AT 3:53 Start Good For All But SWEETWATER PROMISE. Won driving. Track sloppy.
TIME :23^{3}, :47^{4}, 1:12^{3}, 1:38^{2}, 1:51^{1} (:23.79, :47.86, 1:12.61, 1:38.48, 1:51.23)

$2 Mutuel Prices:

4 – LEAD STORY	22.20	10.00	7.60
1 – MAYO ON THE SIDE		17.20	10.00
6 – CLOAKOF VAGUENESS			6.00

$2 EXACTA 4–1 PAID $219.20 $2 TRIFECTA 4–1–6 PAID $1,295.40
$2 SUPERFECTA 4–1–6–7 PAID $14,682.60

Ch. f, (Apr), by Editor's Note – Gwenjinsky , by Seattle Dancer . Trainer Nafzger Carl A. Bred by Cabotaba Partnership (Ky).

LEAD STORY, reserved near the inside soon after the start, went along under patient handling, remained next to the inner rail when advancing on the far turn and and into the stretch, reached the front a furlong out when sharply roused, then increased her advantage under energetic hand urging. MAYO ON THE SIDE was hustled early to gain the lead, raced three wide, managed a clear margin into the stretch but wasn't a match for the winner in the drive while superior to the others. CLOAKOF VAGUENESS settled three wide early, was unhurried for six furlongs, remained near the inside entering the lane and improved position while no threat to the top two. MISTY SIXES moved in behind front-running MAYO ON THE SIDE early, raced in contention to the final quarter, came out four or five wide and was empty. TAKE CHARGE LADY stalked the pace from early on while between rivals three or four wide, was asked for her best when in closest attendance to the pacesetter leaving the three-eighth pole, angled five wide for the drive and flattened out. FIRCROFT settled four wide and failed to rally. SWEETWATER PROMISE broke in the air, then stumbled when landing, was gathered up and never menaced. GOLDEN MARLIN stalked the pace four or five wide for nearly seven furlongs and faded. RHIANA in contention four or five wide for six furlongs, weakened thereafter.

Owners– 1, Miles A Stevens Jr; 2, Lothenbach Stables Inc; 3, Duncker C Steven; 4, Puglisi Stables Jeff Puglisi; 5, Select Stable; 6, Humphrey G Watts Jr; 7, Parra Rosendo G; 8, Estate of Joe Famularo and Glass William D; 9, Dell Ridge Farm

Trainers– 1, Nafzger Carl A; 2, Nafzger Carl A; 3, Huffman William G; 4, Klesaris Steve B; 5, McPeek Kenneth G; 6, Arnold George R II; 7, Jackson James R; 8, Foley Gregory D; 9, Kenneally Eddie

Scratched– Awesome Humor (08Nov03 ^{9}CD ^{2})

$2 Pick Three (3/4/5–3/7/8/10–4) Paid $160.00 ; Pick Three Pool $25,401 .

SEVENTH RACE
Hollywood
NOVEMBER 27, 2003

6 FURLONGS. (1.07^{2}) VERNON O UNDERWOOD S. Grade III. Purse $100,000 FOR THREE-YEAR-OLDS AND UPWARD. By subscription of $100 each, on or before November 19. $1,000 additional to start, with $60,000 to the winner, $20,000 to second, $12,000 to third, $6,000 to fourth and $2,000 to fifth. Three-year-olds 120 lbs. Older 122lbs. Winners of two races of $60,000 in 2003, 2 lbs additional. Non-winners of two races of $45,000 since April 20 allowed 2 lbs. ; of three races of $25,000 or a race of $45,000 in 2003, 4 lbs. ; of $35,000 twice in 2003, 6 lbs. ; of $35,000 or two races of $20,000 in 2003, 8 lbs. (Claiming races not considered) A trophy will be presented to the owner of the winner. Nominations Closed Wednesday, November 19th, 2003 with 9.

Value of Race: $100,000 Winner $60,000; second $20,000; third $12,000; fourth $6,000; fifth $2,000. Mutuel Pool $296,079.00 Exacta Pool $145,630.00 Quinella Pool $16,277.00 Trifecta Pool $154,471.00

Last Raced	Horse	M/Eqt.	A.	Wt	PP	St	¼	½	Str	Fin	Jockey	Odds $1
3Oct03 ^{6}SA^{4}	Watchem Smokey	LB	3	112	2	6	4^{hd}	4^{3}	3^{1½}	1^{1}	Krone J A	3.70
26Oct03 ^{4}SA^{1}	Our New Recruit	LB	4	114	3	5	2^{hd}	2^{1½}	1^{1}	2^{1½}	Smith M E	a- 3.30
21Jun03 ^{6}Hol^{1}	Hasty Kris	LB b	6	116	4	1	5^{5}	5^{2}	5^{1½}	3no	Desormeaux K J	a- 3.30
8Nov03 ^{6}SA^{6}	Ride and Shine	LB	6	115	6	2	6	6	6	4^{1}	Puglisi I	21.80
5Oct03 ^{7}SA^{1}	Avanzado-Arg	LB f	6	124	1	4	1^{½}	1^{hd}	2^{½}	5^{3}	Baze T	0.70
26Oct03 ^{4}SA^{2}	Omega Code	LB	3	118	5	3	3^{3½}	3^{1}	4^{1}	6	Valenzuela P A	7.70

a-Coupled: Our New Recruit and Hasty Kris.

OFF AT 2:07 Start Good . Won driving. Track fast.
TIME :21^{4}, :44^{1}, :56, 1:08^{4} (:21.82, :44.22, :56.17, 1:08.93)

$2 Mutuel Prices:

4 – WATCHEM SMOKEY	9.40	4.40	5.00
1 – OUR NEW RECRUIT(a–entry)		3.40	3.60
1A– HASTY KRIS(a–entry)		3.40	3.60

$1 EXACTA 4–1 PAID $12.80 $2 QUINELLA 1–4 PAID $14.40
$1 TRIFECTA 4–1–6 PAID $64.80

B. g, (Feb), by Alphabet Soup – Karon's Dream , by Geiger Counter . Trainer Frankel Robert. Bred by Barbara R Smicklas & John E Smicklas (Okla).

WATCHEM SMOKEY saved ground chasing the pace, came out in upper stretch and again in midstretch, rallied to the front in deep stretch and proved best under strong handling. OUR NEW RECRUIT went up between horses to duel for command, battled outside a rival leaving the turn, put a head in front into the stretch, inched away while drifting out some in midstretch but could not hold off the winner. HASTY KRIS allowed to settle off the rail chasing the pace, angled inward in upper stretch and gained the show late. RIDE AND SHINE unhurried off the inside on the backstretch, angled in some on the turn, came out in the stretch and just missed third. AVANZADO (ARG) had good early speed and dueled inside, came a bit off the rail into the stretch and weakened in the final furlong while between foes nearing the wire. OMEGA CODE dueled three deep on the backstretch and most of the turn, dropped back nearing the quarter pole and also weakened.

Owners– 1, Gann Edmund A; 2, C R K Stable; 3, C R K Stable; 4, Bisharat Souheil and Raed; 5, Cees Stable LLC; 6, Team Valor Stables Margaux Farm and Ward Wesley

Trainers– 1, Frankel Robert J; 2, Sadler John W; 3, Sadler John W; 4, Stute Gary; 5, O'Neill Doug; 6, Ward Wesley A

Scratched– Fonz's (26May03 ^{9}Hol^{2})

$2 Daily Double (7–4) Paid $30.40 ; Daily Double Pool $20,010 .
$1 Pick Three (7–7–4) Paid $334.10 ; Pick Three Pool $38,516 .

NINTH RACE
Aqueduct
NOVEMBER 28, 2003

1 MILE. (1.32^{2}) TOP FLIGHT H.. Grade II. Purse $150,000 (Up to $29,100 NYSBFOA) A HANDICAP FOR FILLIES AND MARES THREE YEARS OLD AND UPWARD. By subscription of $150 each, which should accompany the nomination; $750 to pass the entry box; $750 to start. The purse to be divided 60% to the winner, 20% to second,11% to third, 6% to fourth and 3% to fifth. Trophies will be presented to the winning owner, trainer and jockey. Closed Saturday, November 15, 2003 with 25 nominations.

Value of Race: $150,000 Winner $90,000; second $30,000; third $16,500; fourth $9,000; fifth $4,500. Mutuel Pool $516,088.00 Exacta Pool $431,112.00 Trifecta Pool $305,922.00

Last Raced	Horse	M/Eqt.	A.	Wt	PP	St	¼	½	¾	Str	Fin	Jockey	Odds $1
25Oct03 ^{4}Bel^{1}	Randaroo	L	3	116	10	1	2^{½}	2^{1½}	1^{hd}	1^{½}	1^{2}	Castillo H Jr	9.20
11Oct03 ^{7}Kee^{1}	Beauty Halo-ARG	L	4	115	8	4	1^{½}	1^{½}	2^{3}	2^{7}	2^{3¼}	Migliore R	11.10
1Nov03 ^{9}Aqu^{1}	Pocus Hocus	Lb	5	116	5	11	8^{½}	8^{½}	6^{1½}	5^{hd}	3^{nk}	Luzzi M J	7.30
8Nov03 ^{9}Aqu^{1}	Caught In The Rain	Lf	4	112	11	3	10^{2}	9^{½}	7^{½}	6^{½}	4^{¾}	Molina V H	50.75
18Oct03 ^{6}Bel^{5}	Shawklit Mint	L	4	114	1	8	3^{1}	3^{hd}	4^{2}	3^{1½}	5^{3}	Arroyo N Jr	21.50
25Oct03 ^{4}Bel^{3}	Zawzooth	L	4	113	4	12	11^{1½}	11^{3}	9^{½}	9^{1}	6^{1¾}	Velazquez J R	4.70
6Nov03 ^{8}Aqu^{4}	Lights On	Lbf	4	113	7	6	7^{5}	6^{hd}	8^{2½}	8^{hd}	7no	Pimentel J	116.25
15Nov03 ^{7}Aqu^{3}	Sabre Of Silver	Lb	5	111	2	10	12	12	11^{2½}	10^{5½}	8no	Fragoso P	78.25
25Oct03 ^{4}Bel^{4}	Drexel Monorail	L	4	114	3	7	4^{hd}	5^{2½}	5^{½}	7^{1½}	9^{1½}	Lopez C C	25.25
11Oct03 ^{8}Lrl^{1}	Willa On The Move	L	4	116	9	5	5^{hd}	4^{hd}	3^{½}	4^{hd}	10^{3½}	Prado E S	1.20
15Nov03 ^{7}Aqu^{1}	Artist Johanna-ARG	L	5	113	6	9	9^{1½}	10^{2½}	10^{2}	11^{1}	11^{1¼}	Bridgmohan S X	26.00
13Nov03 ^{9}CD^{1}	Miss Lodi	L	4	116	12	2	6^{1½}	7^{2½}	12	12	12	Gryder A T	11.20

OFF AT 3:39 Start Good. Won driving. Track fast.
TIME :23^{1}, :46^{2}, 1:10^{3}, 1:36^{2} (:23.39, :46.48, 1:10.79, 1:36.49)

$2 Mutuel Prices:

10–RANDAROO	20.40	10.40	6.50
8–BEAUTY HALO–ARG		14.00	7.50
5–POCUS HOCUS			5.40

$2 EXACTA 10–8 PAID $187.00 $2 TRIFECTA 10–8–5 PAID $1,461.00

B. f, (Feb), by Gold Case–Validated, by Valid Appeal. Trainer McLaughlin Kiaran P. Bred by Dennis Drazin (Ky).

RANDAROO pressed the pace from the outside, dug in gamely when roused for the drive and drew clear late, driving. BEAUTY HALO (ARG) set the pace along the inside and dug in gamely on the rail in the stretch. POCUS HOCUS was pinched back at the start, was bumped and steadied, then put in a run along the inside on the turn and finished gamely. CAUGHT IN THE RAIN was outrun early, came wide for the drive and finished well outside. SHAWKLIT MINT was bumped after the start, was hustled up inside, chased the pace and lacked a rally. ZAWZOOTH was pinched back after the start, clipped heels, stumbled, dropped back early and had no rally. LIGHTS ON bobbled at the start, ducked to the inside, was bumped and lugged in while tiring in the stretch. SABRE OF SILVER was bumped after the start, was outrun early, raced inside and had no rally. DREXEL MONORAIL was bumped after the start, chased the pace while between rivals and tired in the stretch. WILLA ON THE MOVE chased the pace while three wide and had no response when roused. ARTIST JOHANNA (ARG) was pinched back at the start, was bumped and steadied then raced five wide and tired. MISS LODI raced three wide and tired.

Owners— 1, Allen Joseph; 2, WinStar Farm LLC; 3, Moore Susan & John; 4, Heiligbrodt Racing Stable & New Wal; 5, Flatbird Stable; 6, Starlight Stable LLC; 7, Jayeff B Stables; 8, Lucy Grace Stables; 9, Singer Craig B; 10, Angelos Peter G; 11, Thorn Stable; 12, Richard C Colton & Henry Mast Jr

Trainers— 1, McLaughlin Kiaran P; 2, Walden W Elliott; 3, Jerkens James A; 4, Preciado Guadalupe; 5, Reynolds Patrick L; 6, Pletcher Todd A; 7, Goldberg Alan E; 8, Ortiz Paulino O; 9, Klesaris Steve; 10, Dutrow Anthony W; 11, Alexander Frank A; 12, Amoss Thomas

ELEVENTH RACE
Churchill
NOVEMBER 28, 2003

1⅛ MILES. (1.47^{1}) CLARK H.. Grade II. Purse $500,000 A HANDICAP FOR THREE-YEAR-OLDS AND UPWARD. By subscripton of $500 each on or before November 15, 2003 or by supplementary nomination of $25,000 each by the closing of entries Friday, November 21, 2003. $2,500 to pass the entry box; $2,500 additional to start, with $500,000 added of which 62% of all monies to the owner of the winner, 20% to second, 10% to third, 5% to fourth and 3% to fifth. Weights to be announced Saturday, November 22. Starters to be named through the entry box by the usual time of closing. Nominations closed Saturday, November 15, 2003 with 24 nominations. Trophy to winning owner.

Value of Race: $582,000 Winner $360,840; second $116,400; third $58,200; fourth $29,100; fifth $17,460. Mutuel Pool $626,862.00 Exacta Pool $468,727.00 Trifecta Pool $379,519.00 Superfecta Pool $119,021.00

Last Raced	Horse	M/Eqt.	A.	Wt	PP	St	¼	½	¾	Str	Fin	Jockey	Odds $1
25Oct03 ^{9}SA^{7}	[D]Evening Attire	Lb	5	118	7	14	7^{1}	$7^{\frac{1}{2}}$	3^{hd}	$1^{\frac{1}{2}}$	1no	Velasquez C	2.40
25Oct03 ^{4}Kee^{7}	Quest	L	4	114	8	6	$8^{\frac{1}{2}}$	$9^{4\frac{1}{2}}$	7^{hd}	$2^{1\frac{1}{2}}$	$2^{3\frac{1}{4}}$	Castellano J J	17.40
28Sep03 ^{9}Haw^{3}	Aeneas	L	4	114	10	7	$10^{2\frac{1}{2}}$	10^{2}	10^{3}	$4^{\frac{1}{2}}$	$3^{1\frac{1}{4}}$	Boulanger G	19.00
25Oct03 ^{4}Kee^{4}	Seattle Fitz-ARG	L	4	114	1	4	$3^{1\frac{1}{2}}$	$3^{1\frac{1}{2}}$	$5^{\frac{1}{2}}$	3^{hd}	4^{nk}	McKee J	6.10
4Oct03 ^{14}Beu^{1}	Devil Time	L	6	114	5	10	$12^{\frac{1}{2}}$	$11^{2\frac{1}{2}}$	11^{4}	6^{1}	$5^{\frac{3}{4}}$	Troilo W D	28.10
1Nov03 ^{8}Aqu^{4}	Request For Parole	L	4	114	2	11	11^{hd}	$12^{3\frac{1}{2}}$	13	8^{2}	$6^{\frac{1}{2}}$	Borel C H	40.40
25Oct03 ^{4}Kee^{1}	M B Sea	Lb	4	116	11	8	$9^{3\frac{1}{2}}$	8^{hd}	9^{1}	7^{1}	$7^{\frac{1}{2}}$	Perret C	11.20
15Nov03 ^{9}Mnr^{1}	Sonic West	Lf	4	114	4	9	13	13	12^{1}	$10^{\frac{1}{2}}$	$8^{\frac{1}{2}}$	Bejarano R	53.50
1Nov03 ^{8}Aqu^{5}	Quest Star	Lb	4	115	3	5	5^{1}	5^{1}	8^{1}	9^{1}	$9^{1\frac{3}{4}}$	Melancon L	41.00
15Nov03 ^{8}Hoo^{7}	Cappuchino	Lbf	4	116	6	1	$1^{1\frac{1}{2}}$	$1^{\frac{1}{2}}$	$1^{\frac{1}{2}}$	5^{1}	10^{2}	Thompson T J	59.80
15Nov03 ^{8}Hoo^{1}	Crafty Shaw	L	5	117	13	3	6^{2}	$6^{\frac{1}{2}}$	$6^{\frac{1}{2}}$	12^{9}	11^{hd}	Sellers S J	14.50
25Oct03 ^{4}Kee^{2}	Tenpins	Lf	5	119	12	13	4^{hd}	4^{hd}	$4^{\frac{1}{2}}$	11^{hd}	12	Lanerie C J	3.60
29Oct03 ^{8}Aqu^{1}	During	Lb	3	117	9	2	2^{hd}	$2^{\frac{1}{2}}$	$2^{\frac{1}{2}}$	13	—	Santos J A	5.20
8Nov03 ^{7}Del^{1}	Private Lap	L	4	114	14	12	—	—	—	—	—	Blanc B	43.60

During:Eased;Private Lap:Pulled up;
[D]–Evening Attire disqualified and placed 2nd.

OFF AT 4:29 Start Good For All But TENPINS Won driving. Track sloppy.
TIME :23^{4}, :48^{1}, 1:13, 1:38^{4}, 1:52^{2} (:23.99, :48.36, 1:13.18, 1:38.98, 1:52.42)

$2 Mutuel Prices:

8–QUEST	36.80	15.00	10.00
7–EVENING ATTIRE		4.80	3.80
10–AENEAS			8.40

$2 EXACTA 8–7 PAID $159.00 $2 TRIFECTA 8–7–10 PAID $1,675.20 $2 SUPERFECTA 8–7–10–1 PAID $13,772.40

Ch. c, by Seeking the Gold–Starlore, by Spectacular Bid. Trainer Zito Nicholas P. Bred by Arthur B Hancock III & Gerald F Healy (Ky).

EVENING ATTIRE, lightly rated early while tracking the leaders four or five wide, inched to challenge nearing the five-sixteenths pole, gained a narrow advantage, drifted out steadily in the final furlong bumping several times with QUEST and lasted. QUEST, within striking distance while in behind rivals, moved five or six wide on the far turn while edging closer, engaged EVENING ATTIRE approaching the final furlong, was carried out steadily in the last eighth when bumped repeatedly by that one and missed. AENEAS, outrun for nearly six furlongs, unleashed a sudden moved seven abreast nearing the final quarter, came wider when the leaders drifted out in the final furlong but was empty late. SEATTLE FITZ (ARG), well placed in behind the leaders from the beginning, angled four or five wide for the drive, was a bold factor inside the top two when they drifted out in the final furlong but came up empty. DEVIL TIME, outrun while racing in behind rivals to the far turn, came out to make a sweeping move 10 wide entering the stretch, reached contention at the furlong grounds but couldn't sustain the needed momentum. REQUEST FOR PAROLE, unhurried inside from early on, made a bid from the rail upon entering the upper stretch and could gain only slightly in the final furlong. M B SEA worked his way inside on the backstretch, was along the rail entering the upper stretch, eased out five wide for the last eighth but failed to muster a closing account. SONIC WEST, outrun four wide for seven furlongs, came out 10 wide for the drive and improved position while unable to menace. QUEST STAR settled in behind the leaders, raced in contention near the inside between foes for seven furlongs and was empty when straightened into the stretch. CAPPUCHINO gained the lead early, raced in the three path, managed a narrow advantage until approaching the stretch and tired. CRAFTY SHAW, used a bit early to gain a position five wide, was finished nearing the stretch. TENPINS broke in the air, recovered to gain a forward position four or five wide, was asked for his best three furlongs out, remained a factor between rivals until the final quarter and tired. DURING angled in early to press front-running CAPPUCHINO, was put to a full drive midway on the far turn, couldn't keep pace, gave way and was eased very late when hopeless beaten. PRIVATE LAP drifted out when restrained soon after the start, continued very wide and was pulled up nearing the first turn. Following a foul claim lodged by the rider of QUEST against EVENING ATTIRE and his rider for alleged interference in the stretch, stewards disqualified EVENING ATTIRE and placed him second.

Owners— 1, Mary & Joseph Grant & Thomas J Kell; 2, Hancock III Arthur B & Healy Gerald; 3, Pavlish Patricia; 4, West Point Thoroughbreds LLC; 5, Anderson Brad; 6, Knighton Jeri & Sam; 7, Bruder Michael J; 8, Stone Spire LLC; 9, Mansell Stables LLC; 10, Hollendorfer Litt & Todaro; 11, Cella Charles J; 12, Vitello Joseph V; 13, McIngvale James; 14, Puglisi Stables Jeff Puglisi

Trainers—1, Kelly Patrick J; 2, Zito Nicholas P; 3, Wolfson Martin D; 4, McLaughlin Kiaran P; 5, Carroll David; 6, Margolis Stephen R; 7, Romans Dale; 8, Van Berg Thomas L; 9, Walden W Elliott; 10, Hollendorfer Jerry; 11, Vestal Peter M; 12, Winfree Donald R; 13, Baffert Bob; 14, Klesaris Steve

$2 Pick Three (12–3–8) Paid $1,897.20; Pick Three Pool $43,161.

FIFTH RACE
Hollywood
NOVEMBER 28, 2003

1 MILE. (Turf) (1.32³) MIESQUE S. Grade III. Purse $100,000 FOR FILLIES TWO-YEARS-OLD. By subscription of $100 each on or before Friday, November 19, or by supplementary nomination of $5,000 each by closing time of entries. All nominees to pay $500 to enter and an additional $1,000 to start. Gross purse $100,000of which $60,000 to be paid to the winner, $20,000 to second, $12,000 to third, $6,000 to fourth and $2,000 to fifth. 121 lbs. Non-winners of $60,000 at one mile or over allowed 3 lbs.; non winners of two races other than claiming at one mile or over,5 lbs.; a race other than claiming, 7 lbs. Hollywood Park reserves the right not to divide this race. Should this race not be divided and the number of entries exceed the starting gate capacity, first preference will be given to horses with the highest total earnings. Second preference will be given to those horses with the highest total earnings. Entry fees will be refunded to all horses which fail to draw into this race. A trophy will be presented to the winning owner.
Closed with 20 Nominations.

Value of Race: $100,000 Winner $60,000; second $20,000; third $12,000; fourth $6,000; fifth $1,000. Mutuel Pool $502,791.00 Exacta Pool $344,781.00 Quinella Pool $32,455.00 Trifecta Pool $327,587.00 Superfecta Pool $103,480.00

Last Raced	Horse	M/Eqt. A. Wt	PP	St	¼	½	¾	Str	Fin	Jockey	Odds $1
18Oct03 6SA1	Mambo Slew	2 116	4	4	3hd	2hd	2½	1½	11½	Smith M E	3.30
25Oct03 NBY3	Ticker Tape-GB	B	2 116	5	11	11	11	103	8hd	2½	Krone J A	4.70
7Nov03 1SA1	Winendynme	LB	2 116	2	5	43½	48	42½	22	3no	Valenzuela P A	3.90
21Oct03 DEA7	Amorama-FR	B	2 116	11	8	104	106	8hd	94	4½	Flores D R	8.30
6Nov03 2SA1	DH Cousineau	LB	2 116	7	9	51	5½	5hd	4hd	5	Desormeaux K J	3.60
25Oct03 3SA12	DH Shadow of Mine	LB b	2 116	10	7	71	6hd	71½	61	5½	Valdivia J Jr	14.60
18Oct03 6SA3	Vencedora Amiga	LB	2 114	3	3	6hd	8hd	92	7hd	73	Baze T	32.90
2Nov03 3BM2	Secret Corsage	LB	2 116	8	2	22	31½	31	51	85	Pedroza M A	17.90
2Nov03 3BM1	Very Vegas	LB f	2 116	9	1	15	15	11	3hd	9½	Fogelsonger R	11.30
29Sep03 HAM10	Letsimpress-Ire	B	2 116	1	10	8hd	92	61	105	105	Almeida G F	65.00
7Nov03 1SA3	Madam Bahri	LB b	2 116	6	6	9½	71	11	11	11	Nuesch D C	80.40

DH-Dead Heat.

OFF AT 2:38 Start Good. Won driving. Course firm.
TIME :23², :47, 1:11², 1:36 (:23.54, :47.01, 1:11.51, 1:36.17)

$2 Mutuel Prices:

4 – MAMBO SLEW	8.60	4.80	3.20
5 – TICKER TAPE-GB		6.00	3.80
2 – WINENDYNME			3.60

$1 EXACTA 4–5 PAID $23.30 $2 QUINELLA 4–5 PAID $21.60
$1 TRIFECTA 4–5–2 PAID $68.00 $1 SUPERFECTA 4–5–2–11 PAID $352.90

Dk. b or br. f, (Apr), by Kingmambo – Slew Boyera, by Seattle Slew. Trainer Biancone Patrick L. Bred by FJFM LLC (Ky).

MAMBO SLEW stalked the pace outside a rival, bid between horses into the stretch, gained a short lead, inched clear and held under left handed urging. TICKER TAPE (GB) unhurried off the rail early, angled in and saved ground off the pace, swung three deep into the stretch and finished fast outside. WINENDYNME chased inside, came out on the second turn, bid three deep into the stretch and outside the winner in midstretch and just held third. AMORAMA (FR) three deep into the first turn, settled outside, came three wide into the stretch and found her best stride late. COUSINEAU squeezed a bit at the start, chased between foes then outside a rival, came out into the stretch and also went between foes at the wire to share fifth place. SHADOW OF MINE allowed to settle three deep on the first turn, chased outside, came a bit wide into the stretch and was outfinished. VENCEDORA AMIGA was in a good position stalking the pace inside, came a bit off the rail into the stretch and lacked the needed rally. SECRET CORSAGE pulled hard while stalking the early pace off the rail, angled in some on the backstretch, found the rail on the second turn, was between horses in midstretch and weakened. VERY VEGAS sped to the early lead, set the pace along the inside, dueled from the rail into the stretch, then weakened. LETSIMPRESS (IRE) saved ground off the pace, split rivals into the second turn, continued inside on that bend and did not rally. MADAM BAHRI rank between horses early, chased outside, went four wide leaving the backstretch, angled in some on the second turn and gave way.

Owners– 1, Manganaro Frank; 2, Jim Ford Inc or Pearson or Sweesy; 3, Sahadi Fred N; 4, Woodside Farm LLC; 5, Reddam J Paul; 6, Nichols Thomas L; 7, Old Friends Inc and Winner Silk Inc; 8, Abruzzo Peter Franks John and Hollendorfer Jerry; 9, Everest Stables Inc; 10, Jamgotchian Jerry; 11, Running K Stable

Trainers– 1, Biancone Patrick L; 2, Cassidy James M; 3, Sahadi Jenine; 4, Zilber Maurice; 5, Dollase Craig; 6, Greely C Beau; 7, Lobo Paulo H; 8, Hollendorfer Jerry; 9, Knight Terry; 10, Cassidy James M; 11, Dominguez Caesar F

$2 Daily Double (6–4) Paid $16.20; Daily Double Pool $32,764.
$1 Pick Three (2–6–4) Paid $161.00; Pick Three Pool $78,905.

NINTH RACE
Hollywood
NOVEMBER 28, 2003

5$\frac{1}{2}$ FURLONGS. (Turf) (1.00^{2}) HOLLYWOOD TURF EXPRESS H. Grade III. Purse $150,000 A HANDICAP FOR THREE-YEAR-OLDS AND UPWARD. By subscription of $150 each on or before Wednesday, November 19 or by supplementary nomination of $7,500 each by 3:00 pm Friday, November 21. All nominees to pay $1,000 to enter and an additional $1,000 to start. Gross purse $150,000 of which $90,000 to be paid to the winner, $30,000 to second, $18,000 to third, $9,000 to fourth and $3,000 to fifth. Weights Saturday, November 22. Starters to be named through the entry box by closing time of entries. HollywoodPark reserves the right not to divide this race. Should this race not be divided and the number of entries exceed twelve (12), highweights on the weight scale will be preferred. Total earnings in 2003 will used in determining the order of preference ofhorses assigned equal weights on the scale. Entry fees will be refunded to all horses which fail to draw into this race. A trophy will be presented to the winning owner. Closed with 26 Nominations.

Value of Race: $150,000 Winner $90,000; second $30,000; third $18,000; fourth $9,000; fifth $3,000. Mutuel Pool $426,067.00 Exacta Pool $266,779.00 Quinella Pool $25,555.00 Trifecta Pool $295,094.00 Superfecta Pool $120,620.00

Last Raced	Horse	M/Eqt.	A.	Wt	PP	St	¼	⅜	Str	Fin	Jockey	Odds $1
24Oct03 ^{5}SA^{1}	King Robyn	LB	3	120	3	2	1^{hd}	$1\frac{1}{2}$	1^{1}	$1\frac{1}{2}$	Baze T	0.90
24Oct03 ^{5}SA^{3}	Geronimo-Chi	LB b	4	116	4	6	$6^{1\frac{1}{2}}$	3^{hd}	$2\frac{1}{2}$	2^{1}	Valenzuela P A	6.10
2Oct03 ^{7}SA^{1}	Golden Arrow	LB b	4	115	6	3	2^{1}	2^{2}	3^{2}	3^{1}	Desormeaux K J	5.60
19Jly03 NBY^{9}	NeedwoodBlde-GB	LB	5	115	9	8	9	9	$8\frac{1}{2}$	4no	Krone J A	8.90
28Jun03 ^{11}SI^{3}	Volterromo-Arg	LB	5	114	7	5	7^{1}	$7^{1\frac{1}{2}}$	5^{hd}	$5\frac{1}{2}$	Valdivia J Jr	32.50
16Nov03 ^{4}Hol^{2}	Forty Milito-Arg	LB	5	114	1	7	8^{2}	8^{hd}	$6\frac{1}{2}$	6^{nk}	Smith M E	28.80
7Nov03 ^{4}SA^{1}	Lydgate	LB	3	115	8	1	4^{hd}	4^{hd}	4^{1}	$7\frac{1}{2}$	Flores D R	21.80
24Oct03 ^{5}SA^{6}	Apache Wings	LB	5	114	5	9	5^{hd}	6^{hd}	9	$8^{2\frac{1}{2}}$	Martinez F F	16.00
8Nov03 ^{6}SA^{5}	Full Moon Madness	LB b	8	119	2	4	$3\frac{1}{2}$	$5^{2\frac{1}{2}}$	7^{1}	9	Fogelsonger R	7.30

OFF AT 4:42 Start Good . Won driving. Course firm.
TIME :22^{2}, :44^{1}, :55^{4}, 1:02 (:22.45, :44.33, :55.88, 1:02.08)

$2 Mutuel Prices:				
	3 – KING ROBYN	3.80	2.80	2.40
	4 – GERONIMO-CHI		4.40	3.20
	6 – GOLDEN ARROW			3.20

$1 EXACTA 3-4 PAID $8.60 $2 QUINELLA 3-4 PAID $11.60
$1 TRIFECTA 3-4-6 PAID $27.70 $1 SUPERFECTA 3-4-6-9 PAID $80.30

B. g, (Mar), by Robyn Dancer – Queen's Family , by New Prospect . Trainer Mullins Jeff. Bred by Farnsworth Farms (Fla).

KING ROBYN had speed between horses then dueled inside a rival but a bit off the rail, inched away into the stretch and held gamely under a strong hand ride. GERONIMO (CHI) was in a good position chasing the pace between horses to the stretch, bid along the rail late and continued gamely. GOLDEN ARROW between horses early, forced the pace outside the winner to the stretch, weakened some but held third. NEEDWOOD BLADE (GB) dropped back and angled in on the backstretch, went outside a rival on the turn and three deep into the stretch, had the rider lose the whip nearing midstretch but finished with some interest. VOLTERROMO (ARG) stalked outside on the backstretch, angled in on the turn and had a mild bid in the stretch. FORTY MILITO (ARG) saved ground chasing the pace, came out into the stretch and lacked the needed rally. LYDGATE close up four wide early, stalked three deep on the backstretch and turn and weakened in the drive. APACHE WINGS broke out and was crowded, was sent between foes on the backstretch, steadied off heels into the turn, came three deep into the stretch and weakened. FULL MOON MADNESS close up stalking the pace inside on the backstretch and turn, weakened in the stretch.

Owners– 1, Cornejo Racing Inc; 2, Buster Jr William C Hays and Surfside Equine et al; 3, Al Maktoum Sheik Maktoum b; 4, Vreeland James R; 5, Cees Stable LLC; 6, Gerson Racing Nobu Inc Vaughn et al; 7, Darley Stable; 8, Henton Hitbound Stable and Turrell; 9, R-Two Angels Stable Inc

Trainers– 1, Mullins Jeff; 2, Machowsky Michael; 3, Drysdale Neil D; 4, Walsh Kathy; 5, O'Neill Doug; 6, Mitchell Mike R; 7, Harty Eoin G; 8, Breuer Denise E; 9, Marshall Robert W

$2 Daily Double (3–3) Paid $12.60 ; Daily Double Pool $37,482 .
$1 Pick Three (1/6/7–3–3) Paid $11.70 ; Pick Three Pool $66,491 .

SEVENTH RACE
Aqueduct
NOVEMBER 29, 2003

1$\frac{1}{8}$ MILES. (1.47) DEMOISELLE S.. Grade II. Purse $200,000 (Up to $34,800 NYSBFOA) FOR FILLIES TWO YEARS OLD. By subscription of $200 each, which should accompany the nomination; $1,000 to pass the entry box; $1,000 to start. The purse to be divided 60% to the winner, 20% to second, 11% to third, 6% to fourth and 3% to fifth. 121 lbs. Non-winners of $60,000 at a mile or over other than restricted allowed 2 lbs.; $35,000 at a mile or over, 4 lbs.; two races other than maiden or claiming, 6 lbs. Trophies will be presented to the winning owner, trainer and jockey. Closed Saturday, November 15, 2003 with 19 nominations.

Value of Race: $200,000 Winner $120,000; second $40,000; third $22,000; fourth $12,000; fifth $6,000. Mutuel Pool $514,453.00 Exacta Pool $466,629.00 Trifecta Pool $352,213.00

Last Raced	Horse	M/Eqt.	A.	Wt	PP	St	¼	½	¾	Str	Fin	Jockey	Odds $1
25Oct03 ^{3}SA^{2}	Ashado	L	2	117	5	2	$3^{2\frac{1}{2}}$	$3\frac{1}{2}$	1^{hd}	$1\frac{1}{2}$	1no	Bailey J D	0.55
4Nov03 ^{8}Aqu^{1}	La Reina	L	2	121	2	1	$2\frac{1}{2}$	$2\frac{1}{2}$	$2^{2\frac{1}{2}}$	2^{2}	$2\frac{1}{2}$	Velazquez J R	1.90
17Oct03 ^{9}Med^{1}	Dr. Kathy	L	2	115	1	4	$4^{4\frac{1}{2}}$	$4^{1\frac{1}{2}}$	4^{2}	$3^{3\frac{1}{2}}$	3^{10}	Bridgmohan S X	45.00
26Oct03 ^{6}Del^{1}	Shamoiselle	Lbf	2	115	4	7	7	6^{hd}	$6^{3\frac{1}{2}}$	6^{7}	$4\frac{3}{4}$	Dominguez R A	69.75
26Oct03 ^{8}Bel^{1}	Please Take Me Out		2	119	6	3	1^{hd}	$1\frac{1}{2}$	$3\frac{1}{2}$	$4^{5\frac{1}{2}}$	$5^{1\frac{1}{2}}$	Gryder A T	53.25
17Oct03 ^{9}Med^{3}	Run Cat Run	L	2	115	7	6	$6^{5\frac{1}{2}}$	7	7	5^{hd}	$6^{7\frac{1}{4}}$	Santos J A	25.00
15Nov03 ^{5}Lrl^{2}	Taittinger Rose	L	2	115	3	5	$5\frac{1}{2}$	5^{5}	5^{5}	7	7	Prado E S	9.20

OFF AT 2:42 Start Good. Won driving. Track fast.
TIME :23^{1}, :47, 1:12, 1:38^{2}, 1:52^{4} (:23.33, :47.05, 1:12.03, 1:38.58, 1:52.88)

$2 Mutuel Prices:				
	5–ASHADO	3.10	2.20	2.10
	2–LA REINA		2.30	2.10
	1–DR. KATHY			2.10

$2 EXACTA 5–2 PAID $4.60 $2 TRIFECTA 5–2–1 PAID $33.40

Dk. b. or br. f, (Feb), by Saint Ballado–Goulash, by Mari's Book. Trainer Pletcher Todd A. Bred by Aaron U Jones & Marie D Jones (Ky).

ASHADO argued the pace while three wide, responded when roused, drew clear inside the eighth pole then dug in resolutely and got the nod after a furious finish. LA REINA contested the pace while between rivals, dug in along the inside in the stretch and came again on the rail late, just missing. DR. KATHY raced close up along the inside early, rallied three wide approaching the stretch and finished gamely outside. SHAMOISELLE was outrun early, raced inside and had no response when roused. PLEASE TAKE ME OUT was hustled to the front, set the pace along the inside and tired in the stretch. RUN CAT RUN was outrun early, came wide into the stretch and had no rally. TAITTINGER ROSE was hustled along outside, chased the pace while three wide and tired in the stretch.

Owners— 1, Starlight Stables LLC Saylor Paul &; 2, Hamilton Emory A; 3, Roman Lawrence P; 4, Hidden Lane Farms Inc; 5, Perez Robert; 6, Heiligbrodt Racing Stable & Team Va; 7, Rutherford Mike G

Trainers—1, Pletcher Todd A; 2, McGaughey Claude III; 3, Dutrow Richard E Jr; 4, Preciado Guadalupe; 5, Callejas Alfredo; 6, Terranova John P II; 7, Mott William I

$2 Daily Double (4–5) Paid $7.20; Daily Double Pool $117,016.
$2 Pick Three (11–4–5) Paid $23.80; Pick Three Pool $79,534.

EIGHTH RACE
Aqueduct
NOVEMBER 29, 2003

1⅛ MILES. (1.47) REMSEN S.. Grade II. Purse $200,000 (Up to $34,800 NYSBFOA) FOR TWO YEAR OLDS. By subscription of $200 each, which should accompany the nomination; $1,000 to pass the entry box; $1,000 to start. The purse to be divided 60% to the winner, 20% to second, 11% to third, 6% to fourth and 3% to fifth. 122 lbs. Non-winners of $60,000 at a mile or over other than restricted allowed 2 lbs.; $35,000 at a mile or over, 4 lbs.; two races, other than maiden or claiming, 6 lbs. Trophies will be presented to the winning owner, trainer and jockey. Closed Saturday, November 15, 2003 with 27 Nominations.

Value of Race: $200,000 Winner $120,000; second $40,000; third $22,000; fourth $12,000; fifth $6,000. Mutuel Pool $566,090.00 Exacta Pool $484,857.00 Trifecta Pool $340,507.00

Last Raced	Horse	M/Eqt.	A.Wt	PP	St	¼	½	¾	Str	Fin	Jockey	Odds $1
2Nov03 ^{8}Aqu^{1}	Read The Footnotes	L	2 122	9	2	2^{hd}	2^{2}	1^{hd}	1^{6}	$1^{3\frac{3}{4}}$	Bailey J D	2.00
16Sep03 THI^{1}	Master David	L	2 116	8	7	6^{2}	$6^{3\frac{1}{2}}$	$5^{1\frac{1}{2}}$	2^{7}	$2^{10\frac{3}{4}}$	Santos J A	12.00
9Nov03 ^{7}Aqu^{1}	West Virginia	L	2 116	7	1	1^{1}	$1^{\frac{1}{2}}$	$2^{2\frac{1}{2}}$	3^{hd}	$3^{\frac{3}{4}}$	Bridgmohan S X	10.10
19Oct03 ^{9}Bel^{2}	Artie Schiller	L	2 116	3	8	9^{hd}	$8^{2\frac{1}{2}}$	$6^{\frac{1}{2}}$	4^{hd}	$4^{1\frac{1}{2}}$	Migliore R	4.40
2Nov03 ^{8}Aqu^{4}	Big Booster	L	2 116	1	4	$3^{\frac{1}{2}}$	$3^{\frac{1}{2}}$	4^{1}	6^{3}	$5^{\frac{3}{4}}$	Arroyo N Jr	80.00
18Oct03 ^{3}Kee^{1}	El Prado Rob	L	2 116	5	3	5^{hd}	4^{hd}	$3^{\frac{1}{2}}$	5^{3}	$6^{1\frac{1}{4}}$	Prado E S	3.10
11Nov03 ^{6}Aqu^{1}	Mustanfar	L	2 116	4	9	8^{2}	9^{7}	$9^{1\frac{1}{2}}$	7^{hd}	7no	Gryder A T	64.50
9Nov03 ^{7}Aqu^{3}	Pa Pa Da		2 116	11	11	4^{hd}	$5^{1\frac{1}{2}}$	$8^{\frac{1}{2}}$	$9^{\frac{1}{2}}$	8^{3}	Velazquez J R	7.60
2Nov03 ^{8}Aqu^{3}	Who Is Chris G.	L	2 116	6	6	$10^{\frac{1}{2}}$	10^{hd}	$10^{1\frac{1}{2}}$	10^{8}	$9^{1\frac{1}{4}}$	Dominguez R A	35.75
19Oct03 ^{9}Bel^{3}	Milestone Victory	L	2 116	2	5	$7^{2\frac{1}{2}}$	7^{hd}	$7^{5\frac{1}{2}}$	$8^{\frac{1}{2}}$	$10^{15\frac{3}{4}}$	Castellano J J	19.50
16Nov03 ^{8}Aqu^{4}	Tap Day	L	2 116	10	10	11	11	11	11	11	Luzzi M J	40.50

OFF AT 3:10 Start Good. Won driving. Track fast.
TIME :24^{1}, :48^{1}, 1:12^{1}, 1:37^{3}, 1:50^{3} (:24.36, :48.24, 1:12.29, 1:37.75, 1:50.62)

$2 Mutuel Prices:				
	9–READ THE FOOTNOTES	6.00	4.20	3.10
	8–MASTER DAVID		10.60	6.70
	7–WEST VIRGINIA			6.00

$2 EXACTA 9–8 PAID $72.00 $2 TRIFECTA 9–8–7 PAID $447.00

B. c, (Apr), by Smoke Glacken–Baydon Belle, by Al Nasr*Fr. Trainer Violette Richard A Jr. Bred by Lawrence Goichman (NY).

READ THE FOOTNOTES argued the pace from the outside, took over after three quarters, drew away when roused and was kept to the task to the finish. MASTER DAVID raced close up while in hand between rivals, rallied three wide approaching the stretch and finished gamely but could not get to the winner while easily best of the others. WEST VIRGINIA quickly showed in front, set the pace along the inside, could not stay with the winner on the second turn and tired in the stretch. ARTIE SCHILLER was bumped after the start, was rated along inside, came wide nearing the stretch and had no rally. BIG BOOSTER chased the pace along the inside and tired after the opening three quarters. EL PRADO ROB bobbled at the start, was bumped, raced close up inside early and tired in the stretch. MUSTANFAR was bumped after the start, was outrun along the inside early and tired in the stretch. PA PA DA chased the pace while four wide and tired after a half mile. WHO IS CHRIS G. dropped back early, raced inside and tired. MILESTONE VICTORY raced inside, had no response when roused and tired. TAP DAY dropped back after the start and trailed throughout.

Owners— 1, Klaravich Stables; 2, Georgica Stable Mack Stephan & Star; 3, Zuckerman Donald S & Roberta Mary; 4, Timber Bay Farm & Walsh Mrs Thomas; 5, Broman Mary R & Chester Sr; 6, La Penta Robert V; 7, Shadwell Stable; 8, Behrendt Theresa E & John T; 9, C D & G Stable; 10, TYB Stable; 11, Evans Edward P

Trainers—1, Violette Richard A Jr; 2, Meehan Brian; 3, Pletcher Todd A; 4, Jerkens James A; 5, Kimmel John C; 6, Zito Nicholas P; 7, McLaughlin Kiaran P; 8, Donk David; 9, Klesaris Robert P; 10, Brennan Niall J; 11, Hennig Mark

$2 Pick Three (4–5–9) Paid $20.20; Pick Three Pool $83,802.

NINTH RACE
Aqueduct
NOVEMBER 29, 2003

1 MILE. (1.32^{2}) CIGAR MILE H.. Grade I. Purse $350,000 (Up to $45,900 NYSBFOA) A HANDICAP FOR THREE YEAR OLDS AND UPWARD. By subscription of $350 each, which should accompany the nomination; $1,500 to pass the entry box; $2,000 to start. The purse to be divided 60% to the winner, 20% to second, 11% to third,6% to fourth and 3% to fifth. Trophies will be presented to the winning owner, trainer and jockey. Closed Saturday, November 15, 2003 with 19 nominations.

Value of Race: $350,000 Winner $210,000; second $70,000; third $38,500; fourth $21,000; fifth $10,500. Mutuel Pool $569,161.00 Exacta Pool $458,656.00 Trifecta Pool $347,308.00

Last Raced	Horse	M/Eqt.	A.Wt	PP	St	¼	½	¾	Str	Fin	Jockey	Odds $1
25Oct03 ^{9}SA^{4}	Congaree	L	5 124	2	6	$3^{\frac{1}{2}}$	2^{hd}	2^{2}	$1^{1\frac{1}{2}}$	$1^{5\frac{1}{4}}$	Bailey J D	0.60
25Oct03 ^{5}SA^{8}	Midas Eyes	L	3 115	1	7	2^{hd}	$1^{\frac{1}{2}}$	1^{hd}	2^{6}	2^{3}	Velazquez J R	4.70
15Nov03 ^{7}Lrl^{2}	Toccet	Lb	3 115	4	5	$4^{\frac{1}{2}}$	$4^{\frac{1}{2}}$	$3^{2\frac{1}{2}}$	3^{2}	3^{1}	Luzzi M J	26.50
25Oct03 ^{5}Bel^{2}	Bowman's Band	L	5 118	7	2	$6^{\frac{1}{2}}$	$5^{\frac{1}{2}}$	$5^{\frac{1}{2}}$	$4^{\frac{1}{2}}$	$4^{3\frac{1}{2}}$	Dominguez R A	5.10
18Oct03 ^{10}Bel^{1}	Well Fancied	L	5 115	5	3	$1^{\frac{1}{2}}$	$3^{1\frac{1}{2}}$	$4^{\frac{1}{2}}$	$5^{\frac{1}{2}}$	$5^{\frac{3}{4}}$	Prado E S	13.20
2Nov03 ^{7}Aqu^{1}	New York Hero	Lb	3 113	3	4	7	7	7	$6^{\frac{1}{2}}$	$6^{\frac{1}{2}}$	Castellano J J	30.75
25Oct03 ^{5}Bel^{1}	Voodoo	Lb	5 116	6	1	$5^{\frac{1}{2}}$	$6^{\frac{1}{2}}$	$6^{\frac{1}{2}}$	7	7	Santos J A	12.20

OFF AT 3:38 Start Good. Won driving. Track fast.
TIME :22^{4}, :44^{2}, 1:08^{3}, 1:34^{1} (:22.86, :44.56, 1:08.79, 1:34.30)

$2 Mutuel Prices:				
	2–CONGAREE	3.20	2.60	2.20
	1–MIDAS EYES		4.60	3.50
	5–TOCCET			5.60

$2 EXACTA 2–1 PAID $12.00 $2 TRIFECTA 2–1–5 PAID $74.00

Ch. h, by Arazi–Mari's Sheba, by Mari's Book. Trainer Baffert Bob. Bred by Stonerside Stable Ltd (Ky).

CONGAREE came away in good order, raced with the pace while between rivals, responded when roused in upper stretch and drew away under a drive. MIDAS EYES was hustled up inside, argued the pace along the rail, proved no match for the winner and stayed on to be clearly best of the others. TOCCET was hustled along outside, chased the pace while four wide and faded in the stretch. BOWMAN'S BAND was bumped after the start, was outrun early, raced wide throughout and had no response when roused. WELL FANCIED chased the pace while three wide and tired after three quarters. NEW YORK HERO was outrun early, raced inside and had no response when roused. VOODOO was bumped after the start, raced between rivals and tired.

Owners— 1, Stonerside Stable LLC; 2, Gann Edmund A; 3, Borislow Daniel M; 4, Schwartz Martin S; 5, Goldfarb Sanford Hoffman Stewart &; 6, Paraneck Stable; 7, Moore Susan & John

Trainers—1, Baffert Bob; 2, Frankel Robert; 3, Scanlan John F; 4, Jerkens H Allen; 5, Dutrow Richard E Jr; 6, Pedersen Jennifer; 7, Jerkens James A

Scratched— Newfoundland (29Oct03 ^{8}AQU^{5})

TENTH RACE
Churchill
NOVEMBER 29, 2003

$1\frac{1}{16}$ MILES. (1.41^3) GOLDEN ROD S.. Grade II. Purse $200,000 FOR FILLIES, TWO YEARS OLD. By subscription of $200 each on or before November 15, 2003 or by supplementary nomination of $10,000 each by the time of closing Thursday, November 27, 2003. $1,000 to pass the entry box; $1,000 additional to start. Weight 122 lbs. Non-winners of a sweepstakes at a mile or over allowed 2 lbs; two races other than maiden or claiming 4 lbs; a race other than maiden or claiming 6 lbs. Starters to be named through the entry box by the usual time of closing. Closed Saturday, November 15, 2003 with 30 nominations. The Golden Rod Stakes winner will automatically be nominated to the 2004 Kentucky Oaks, as far as nomination fee.

Value of Race: $230,000 Winner $142,600; second $46,000; third $23,000; fourth $11,500; fifth $6,900. Mutuel Pool $523,823.00 Exacta Pool $400,383.00 Trifecta Pool $293,588.00 Superfecta Pool $86,277.00

Last Raced	Horse	M/Eqt.	A.Wt	PP	St	¼	½	¾	Str	Fin	Jockey	Odds $1
25Oct03 ^{3}SA^{11}	Be Gentle	L	2 122	9	4	$1^{1\frac{1}{2}}$	1^{1}	$1^{\frac{1}{2}}$	$1^{\frac{1}{2}}$	1^{1}	McKee J	2.00
8Nov03 ^{5}CD^{2}	Lotta Kim	L	2 116	3	2	2^{2}	$2^{\frac{1}{2}}$	$2^{\frac{1}{2}}$	$2^{\frac{1}{2}}$	2^{hd}	Thompson T J	5.10
6Nov03 ^{10}CD^{1}	Dynaville	L	2 116	10	8	$7^{1\frac{1}{2}}$	6^{1}	$4^{\frac{1}{2}}$	$3^{1\frac{1}{2}}$	3^{5}	Perret C	62.80
23Oct03 ^{8}Kee^{1}	Galloping Gal	Lb	2 122	2	10	11	11	11	6^{hd}	$4^{\frac{1}{2}}$	Blanc B	5.80
11Nov03 ^{10}CD^{1}	Lenatareese	L	2 116	4	1	3^{1}	$3^{\frac{1}{2}}$	3^{1}	$4^{1\frac{1}{2}}$	$5^{1\frac{3}{4}}$	Lanerie C J	34.60
9Nov03 ^{6}CD^{2}	Jinny's Gold	L	2 116	6	6	5^{hd}	5^{2}	5^{1}	5^{hd}	6^{hd}	Fox T L	32.30
8Nov03 ^{5}CD^{1}	Sheer Luck		2 118	7	11	9^{2}	9^{1}	7^{1}	$7^{2\frac{1}{2}}$	$7^{3\frac{3}{4}}$	Borel C H	3.60
1Nov03 ^{9}CD^{1}	Stellar Jayne	L	2 122	11	9	$10^{1\frac{1}{2}}$	10^{2}	10^{hd}	$8^{1\frac{1}{2}}$	$8^{1\frac{3}{4}}$	Velasquez C	4.50
30Oct03 ^{10}CD^{1}	Birthday Song	Lf	2 116	1	3	4^{1}	4^{hd}	6^{2}	9^{2}	$9^{1\frac{3}{4}}$	Castanon J L	21.00
1Nov03 ^{9}CD^{3}	Sister Star	Lb	2 116	5	7	8^{2}	$7^{\frac{1}{2}}$	$8^{\frac{1}{2}}$	10^{1}	$10^{2\frac{1}{2}}$	Melancon L	51.40
7Nov03 ^{1}CD^{1}	Twilight Gallop	L	2 116	8	5	$6^{1\frac{1}{2}}$	8^{1}	9^{hd}	11	11	Bejarano R	38.70

OFF AT 4:07 Start Good. Won driving. Track fast.
TIME :24, :48^4, 1:13^2, 1:39^1, 1:45^4 (:24.11, :48.92, 1:13.55, 1:39.20, 1:45.91)

$2 Mutuel Prices:			
10–BE GENTLE	6.00	3.80	3.80
4–LOTTA KIM		6.40	5.60
11–DYNAVILLE			14.40

$2 EXACTA 10–4 PAID $35.00 $2 TRIFECTA 10–4–11 PAID $1,339.60 $2 SUPERFECTA 10–4–11–2 PAID $7,356.20

Dk. b. or br. f, (May), by Tale of the Cat–Gentlelilstar, by Risen Star. Trainer Lukas D Wayne. Bred by Mrs Nellie M Cox & Rose Retreat Farm (Va).

BE GENTLE sprinted clear and was angled to the inside on the first turn, set the pace near the rail, responded willingly when challenged by LOTTA KIM on the second turn and proved best under pressure. LOTTA KIM closest to the winner while outside that one, made an earnest bit midway through the second turn and held on gamely in the drive. DYNAVILLE within striking distance from the outset, moved between rivals on the second turn, came to the inside for the drive and finished with good courage while lacking room late. GALLOPING GAL outrun early along the inside, angled out after a half, came out five wide leaving the second turn and improved her position while no real threat. LENATAREESE forwardly placed three wide, moved to challenge the top pair on the second turn, held on well to the furlong marker and tired. JINNY'S GOLD angled in a bit when within striking distance, saved ground on the second turn when moving closer, then tired in the final furlong. SHEER LUCK outrun early, raced in the two path around the second turn and was no threat. STELLAR JAYNE outsprinted early three wide, angled in, saved ground on the second turn and was no factor. BIRTHDAY SONG close up along the inside, steadied midway through the first turn, recovered, angled outside on the backstretch, raced four wide on the second turn and faded. SISTER STAR was no factor. TWILIGHT GALLOP forwardly placed three wide, was carried six wide entering the stretch and gave way.

Owners— 1, Van Meter II Thomas F; 2, Morrison Dolphus; 3, Fox Nathan & Kaster Richard; 4, Carl William A; 5, Anderson Brad; 6, Nancy R & Richard S Kaster & Freder; 7, Farish William S; 8, Spendthrift Farm LLC Kidder Chuck C; 9, Schaffrick William C; 10, Marker John C & Julie; 11, Courtney Mr & Mrs E Thompson & Tell

Trainers—1, Lukas D Wayne; 2, Wiggins Hal R; 3, Romans Dale; 4, McPeek Kenneth G; 5, Carroll David; 6, Romans Dale; 7, Howard Neil J; 8, Lukas D Wayne; 9, Kassen David C; 10, McPeek Kenneth G; 11, Amoss Thomas

Scratched— Penny's Fortune (23Oct03 ^{8}KEE^{4})

$2 Pick Three (5–3/4/6/11/12/13–3/10) Paid $132.20; Pick Three Pool $58,713.

ELEVENTH RACE 1¹⁄₁₆ MILES. (1.41³) KENTUCKY JOCKEY CLUB S.. Grade II. Purse $200,000 FOR TWO YEAR OLDS.

Churchill

NOVEMBER 29, 2003

By subscription of $200 each on or before November 15, 2003 or by supplementary nomination of $10,000 each by the time of closing Thursday, November 27, 2003. $1,000 to pass the entry box; $1,000 additional to start. Weight 122 lbs. Non–winners of a sweepstakes at a mile or over allowed 2 lbs.; two races other than maiden or claiming 4 lbs.; a race other than maiden or claiming 6 lbs. Starters to be named through the entry box by the usual time of closing. Closed Saturday, November 15, 2003 with 31 nominations. The Kentucky Jockey Club Stakes winner will automatically be nominated to the 2004 Visa Triple Crown, as far as nomination fee.

Value of Race: $222,200 Winner $137,764; second $44,440; third $22,220; fourth $11,110; fifth $6,666.   Mutuel Pool $482,542.00 Exacta Pool $397,513.00   Trifecta Pool $365,639.00 Superfecta Pool $117,784.00

Last Raced	Horse	M/Eqt. A.Wt	PP	St	¼	½	¾	Str	Fin	Jockey	Odds $1
2Nov03 ⁹CD¹	The Cliff's Edge	L	2 122	7	8	8	3ʰᵈ	1ʰᵈ	11½	1¾	Sellers S J	0.90
9Nov03 ⁹CD²	Gran Prospect	f	2 116	3	7	6ʰᵈ	6½	4ʰᵈ	21½	21¾	Perret C	21.60
9Nov03 ⁹CD¹	Proper Prado	Lb	2 118	6	6	7½	7¹½	74	31½	33¾	McKee J	15.20
24Oct03 ⁸Kee¹	Commendation	L	2 122	1	4	3½	51½	5ʰᵈ	4ʰᵈ	4½	Velasquez C	7.00
8Nov03 ⁶CD¹	Mach Speed	Lb	2 116	4	1	4¹½	4ʰᵈ	61	52	57¼	Borel C H	1.60
9Nov03 ⁹CD⁵	Saltire	Lb	2 116	8	2	1½	1½	21	66	65	Melancon L	55.40
9Nov03 ⁹CD⁴	Jamian	Lb	2 116	5	5	5ʰᵈ	8	8	73	710¾	Peck B D	66.30
9Nov03 ⁹CD³	Trust Me	L	2 116	2	3	2½	21	3ʰᵈ	8	8	Thompson T J	34.20

OFF AT 4:33 Start Good. Won driving. Track fast.

TIME :24¹, :48², 1:13, 1:38³, 1:45² (:24.23, :48.44, 1:13.07, 1:38.75, 1:45.50)

$2 Mutuel Prices:

7–THE CLIFF'S EDGE	3.80	2.60	2.20
3–GRAN PROSPECT		7.40	3.60
6–PROPER PRADO			3.20

$2 EXACTA 7–3 PAID $33.40 $2 TRIFECTA 7–3–6 PAID $134.40 $2
SUPERFECTA 7–3–6–1 PAID $398.20

Dk. b. or br. c, (Apr), by Gulch–Zigember, by Danzig. Trainer Zito Nicholas P. Bred by Stonerside Stable LLC (Ky).

THE CLIFF'S EDGE outsprinted early four wide, made a quick move to a forward position before a half, challenged when ready on the second turn, took over in upper stretch then lasted late. GRAN PROSPECT reserved along the inside, angled out to advance four wide approaching the stretch and rallied willingly to be steadily gaining on the winner late. PROPER PRADO unhurried early off the inside, angled out four wide to advance on the second turn, drifted in in the upper stretch, brushed with MACH SPEED, then lacked a late bid. COMMENDATION close up along the inside, tired in the drive. MACH SPEED forwardly placed three wide, steadied approaching the stretch when in tight, was brushed in upper stretch then tired. SALTIRE sprinted clear, set the pace near the inside, held on well to the stretch and tired. JAMIAN steadied late on the first turn behind a rival, dropped back then could not menace. TRUST ME closest to the pace while off the inside, steadied in traffic late on the second turn and stopped.

Owners— 1, La Penta Robert V; 2, Carey Thomas M; 3, Winn Mrs James A; 4, Courtlandt Farms; 5, Overbrook Farm; 6, Atkins Clinton C & Susan A; 7, Ducharme Stables; 8, Pollard Carl F

Trainers—1, Zito Nicholas P; 2, Vestal Peter M; 3, Holthus Robert E; 4, Motion H Graham; 5, Stewart Dallas; 6, Lukas D Wayne; 7, Pate David E; 8, Vance David R

$2 Pick Three (3/4/6/11/12/13–3/10–7) Paid $36.60; Pick Three Pool $47,273.

FIFTH RACE

Hollywood

NOVEMBER 29, 2003

1 MILE. (Turf)(1.32³) GENEROUS S.. Grade III. Purse $100,000 FOR TWO-YEAR-OLDS. By subscription of $100 each on or before Wednesday, November 19, or by supplementary nomination of $5,000 each by closing time of entries. All nominees to pay $500 to enter and an additional $1,000 to start. Gross purse $100,000 of which $60,000 to be paid to the winner, $20,000 to second, $12,000 to third, $6,000 to fourth and $2,000 to fifth. 121 lbs. Non-winners of $60,000 at one mile or over allowed 3 lbs.; non winners of two races other than claiming at one mile or over, 5 lbs.; a race other than claiming, 7 lbs. Entry fees will be refunded to all horses which fail to draw into this race. A trophy will be presented to the winning owner.

Value of Race: $100,000 Winner $60,000; second $20,000; third $12,000; fourth $6,000; fifth $2,000. Mutuel Pool $565,489.00 Exacta Pool $363,908.00 Quinella Pool $34,405.00 Trifecta Pool $342,782.00 Superfecta Pool $124,192.00

Last Raced	Horse	M/Eqt. A.Wt	PP	St	1/4	1/2	3/4	Str	Fin	Jockey	Odds $1
14Sep03 Cur1	Castledale-IR	LB 2 116	1	8	4hd	42	31	11	1no	Krone J A	3.70
15Oct03 BLB2	Dealer Choice-FR	LB 2 116	3	10	91	5hd	51½	2hd	22	Flores D R	2.20
1Nov03 8SA2	Lucky Pulpit	LBbf 2 116	6	11	5hd	31	21½	3hd	33	Valenzuela P A	5.50
19Sep03 Stc1	Terroplane-FR	LB 2 116	7	12	10½	10½	91	8½	4½	Desormeaux K J	4.10
8Nov03 10SA5	Tricky Flash Flood	LBb 2 120	11	5	11	11½	1hd	43	5½	Boag G L	135.50
1Nov03 8SA7	General Moody	LB 2 116	8	2	11hd	111½	102	94	6hd	Fogelsonger R	36.80
24Oct03 8Kee7	Atten Hut	LBf 2 116	4	3	31	6hd	61	51½	7no	Krigger K	101.90
26Oct03 6SA1	Borrego	LBb 2 116	10	7	61½	71	7hd	7hd	81	Valdivia J Jr	6.50
1Nov03 8SA1	Rush Into Heaven	LB 2 116	9	1	7hd	9½	81½	6hd	93	Puglisi I L	17.50
8Nov03 10SA2	Black Horse Money	LB 2 114	5	9	12	12	112½	102	102½	Baze T C	26.10
1Nov03 8SA4	Presumption	LB 2 115	2	4	2hd	2½	4hd	118	1110	Steiner J J	77.70
25Oct03 7SA11	Mambo Train	LB 2 116	12	6	8hd	8hd	12	12	12	Saint-Martin E	25.90

OFF AT 2:36 Start Good. Won driving. Course firm.

TIME :24¹, :47³, 1:11², 1:35² (:24.25, :47.75, 1:11.47, 1:35.43)

$2 Mutuel Prices:

1-CASTLEDALE-IR	9.40	5.20	3.80
3-DEALER CHOICE-FR		3.80	2.80
6-LUCKY PULPIT			3.80

$1 EXACTA 1-3 PAID $13.40 $2 QUINELLA 1-3 PAID $11.60 $1 TRIFECTA 1-3-6 PAID $61.10 $1 SUPERFECTA 1-3-6-7 PAID $151.10

B. c, (Apr), by Peintre Celebre–Louju, by Silver Hawk. Trainer Mullins Jeff. Bred by Gigginstown House Stud (Ire).

CASTLEDALE (IRE) stalked the pace inside, came out on the second turn, bid three deep into the stretch, gained the lead, inched away and just held under urging. DEALER CHOICE (FR) a bit slow to begin, saved ground chasing the pace, came out on the second turn and into the stretch and finished well to just miss. LUCKY PULPIT rank between foes and steadied on the first turn, stalked three deep, bid outside a rival on the second turn, put a head in front in upper stretch but could not match the top pair while best of the rest. TERROPLANE (FR) off a bit slowly, was forced out into the first turn, went four wide leaving that bend, moved up between horses into and on the second turn, was blocked off heels into the stretch and in tight in midstretch but rallied between foes. TRICKY FLASH FLOOD sped to the early lead and angled in, shook off a bid early on the backstretch, inched away again, dueled inside on the second turn and into the stretch and weakened. GENERAL MOODY between horses early, steadied in tight on the first turn, angled in on the backstretch, came out on the second turn and four wide into the stretch and improved position. ATTEN HUT stalked outside a rival then between horses or off the rail, continued just off the inside on the second turn, came out in the stretch and lacked the needed response. BORREGO five wide into the first turn, chased outside, came four wide into the stretch and did not rally. RUSH INTO HEAVEN four wide into the first turn, chased between horses, angled in on the second turn and also lacked the needed response. BLACK HORSE MONEY drifted out into the first turn, angled in and settled inside, came out into the stretch and failed to menace. PRESUMPTION pulled his way along to stalk inside then a bit off the rail, bid outside the leader into the backstretch, tracked between foes approaching the second turn, dropped back on that bend and weakened. MAMBO TRAIN six wide i nto the first turn, chased outside then four wide into the second turn, drifted out and dropped back on that bend and gave way.

Owners— 1, Lyons & Knee; 2, Amerman Racing Stables LLC; 3, Williams Mr & Mrs Larry D; 4, Bienstock Papiano & Winner; 5, Sides Clay R; 6, Mack Earle I & Anstu Stables; 7, Shepard Robert H; 8, Kelly Ralls & Foster LLC Scott Et A; 9, Wood Jason; 10, Royce S Jaime Racing Stable & O'Nei; 11, Barber Don & DeLima Jose; 12, Everest Stables

Trainers—1, Mullins Jeff; 2, Frankel Robert; 3, Sise Clifford Jr; 4, Drysdale Neil; 5, Sides Robert C; 6, Baffert Bob; 7, Chew Matthew; 8, Greely C Beau; 9, Aguirre Paul G; 10, O'Neill Doug; 11, DeLima Jose E; 12, Polanco Marcelo

$2 Daily Double (4–1) Paid $37.60; Daily Double Pool $35,057.
$1 Pick Three (1/2–4–1) Paid $48.30; Pick Three Pool $78,483.

NINTH RACE

Hollywood

NOVEMBER 29, 2003

1 1/16 MILES. (Turf)(1.38³) CITATION H.. Grade II. Purse $400,000 A HANDICAP FOR THREE-YEAR-OLD AND UPWARD. By subscription of $500 each on or before Friday, August 15, 2003 which should accompany the nomination. (No sustaining payments) All Nominees to pay $2,500 to enter and an additional $2,500 to start. Gross purse $400,000 of which $240,000 to be paid to the winner, $80,000 to second, $48,000 to third, $24,000 to fourth and $8,000 to fifth. Weights Sunday, November 23. Starters to be named through the entry box by closing time of entries. Hollywood Park reserves the right not to divide this race. Should this race not be divided and the number of entries exceed the starting gate capacity, high weights on the scale will be preferred. Total earnings in 2003 will be used.

Value of Race: $400,000 Winner $240,000; second $80,000; third $48,000; fourth $24,000; fifth $8,000. Mutuel Pool $433,225.00 Exacta Pool $230,657.00 Quinella Pool $25,868.00 Trifecta Pool $256,280.00

Last Raced	Horse	M/Eqt.	A.Wt	PP	St	¼	½	¾	Str	Fin	Jockey	Odds $1
25Oct03 11SA³	Redattore-BRZ	LB	8 120	6	2	3½	3¹	3hd	1½	1⅜	Krone J A	2.70
25Oct03 4SA⁴	Irish Warrior	LB	5 117	3	6	6	6	6	2hd	2²½	Flores D R	1.20
27Sep03 6BM¹	Mister Acpen-CH	LBb	5 116	4	3	2½	2¹	2¹	3¹	3nk	Valenzuela P A	2.90
7Nov03 7SA⁵	Green Line-GB	LB	4 114	1	5	4²½	4⁴	4¹	5½	4¹	Valdivia J Jr	20.70
29Oct03 5SA⁴	Nicobar-GB	LB	6 114	5	4	5¹½	5½	5½	6	5⁴½	Fogelsonger R	30.90
25Oct03 5SA⁷	Captain Squire	LB	4 115	2	1	1²	1¹½	1hd	4hd	6	Baze T C	6.30

OFF AT 4:36 Start Good. Won driving. Course firm.

TIME :23³, :47², 1:11¹, 1:34³, 1:40³ (:23.60, :47.41, 1:11.23, 1:34.77, 1:40.74)

$2 Mutuel Prices:

6–REDATTORE–BRZ	7.40	3.00	2.20
3–IRISH WARRIOR		2.40	2.10
4–MISTER ACPEN–CH			2.20

$1 EXACTA 6–3 PAID $8.20 $2 QUINELLA 3–6 PAID $5.40 $1 TRIFECTA 6–3–4 PAID $19.90

B. h, by Roi Normand–Political Intrigue, by Deputy Minister. Trainer Mandella Richard. Bred by Haras Santa Ana do Rio Grande (Brz).

REDATTORE (BRZ) stalked the leader outside a rival, bid three deep leaving the backstretch, fell back a bit on the second turn, re-bid three wide into the stretch, lugged in a bit while taking the lead nearing midstretch, then drifted in and held gamely under energetic handling. IRISH WARRIOR unhurried and angled in a bit off the rail early, went outside a rival on the backstretch and into the second turn, swung five wide into the stretch, bid four wide in midstretch and continued willingly but could not get by the winner. MISTER ACPEN (CHI) pulled his way along to stalk the pace a bit off the rail, bid between horses leaving the backstretch and outside a rival on the second turn, battled between foes again into the stretch and until past midstretch, could not match the top pair late and just held third. GREEN LINE (GB) pulled a bit early, stalked inside, came off the rail for room and split horses in midstretch and just missed the show. NICOBAR (GB) settled outside a rival then toward the inside, came out on the second turn and four wide into the stretch and could not summon the necessary late kick. CAPTAIN SQUIRE sped to the early lead, set the pace inside, dueled on the rail into and on the second turn and until nearing midstretch and weakened.

Owners— 1, Taunay Luis A; 2, Coleman John Dasaro George Thompson; 3, Noctis Stable Papiano Neil & Taub S; 4, Harlequin Ranches & Conroy Ian; 5, Zetcher Arnold; 6, Bone Robert D & Diener Jeffrey S

Trainers— 1, Mandella Richard; 2, Dollase Wallace; 3, Mulhall Kristin; 4, Gallagher Patrick; 5, McAnally Ronald; 6, Mullins Jeff

---

$2 Daily Double (2–6) Paid $32.60; Daily Double Pool $42,489.
$1 Pick Three (8–2–6) Paid $110.50; Pick Three Pool $69,806.

SIXTH RACE

Hollywood

NOVEMBER 30, 2003

1 MILE. (Turf)(1.32³) MATRIARCH S.. Grade I. Purse $500,000 FOR FILLIES AND MARES THREE–YEAR–OLD AND UPWARD. By subscription of $600 each on or before Friday, August 15, 2003 which should accompany the nomination. (No sustaining payments) Late nominations, for horses not previously nominated, may be made on or before Wednesday, October 8, 2003 by payment of $3,000, which should accompany the nomination. Late nominations, for horses not previously nominated, may be made on or before Wednesday, November 19, 2003 by payment of $15,000, which should accompany the nomination, of which $13,000 is refundable if the nominee is entered and does not draw into the body of the race or if the nominee is not entered and a veterinarian certificate is produced indicating the horse is unfit to run. All nominees to pay $3,000 to enter and an additional $3,000 to start. Gross purse $500,000 of which $300,000 to be paid to the winner, $100,000 to second, $60,000 to third, $30,000 to fourth and 10,000 to fifth. Three year olds 120 lbs. Older 123 lbs. Starters to be named throughthe entry box by closing time of entries. This race will not be divided. If the number of entries exceed fourteen (14), first preference will be given to graded or group stakes winners in 2003.

Value of Race: $500,000 Winner $300,000; second $100,000; third $60,000; fourth $30,000; fifth $10,000.   Mutuel Pool $657,522.00 Exacta Pool $400,793.00   Quinella Pool $33,873.00 Trifecta Pool $385,689.00 Superfecta Pool $176,315.00

Last Raced	Horse	M/Eqt. A.Wt	PP	St	¼	½	¾	Str	Fin	Jockey	Odds $1
25Oct03 6SA⁴	Heat Haze-GB	LB	4 123	11	14	14	14	14	9½	1nk	Velazquez J R	4.30
25Oct03 6SA¹¹	Musical Chimes	LB	3 120	7	3	10½	10²	10hd	6hd	2no	Prado E S	5.50
13Oct03 7Bel¹	Dedication-FR	LB	4 123	6	10	8hd	7hd	7½	3hd	3½	Nakatani C S	23.50
4Oct03 9Bel⁶	Island Fashion	LBb	3 120	8	12	11hd	11hd	12¹	8hd	4½	Puglisi I L	87.20
7Sep03 9Bel⁵	Acago	LBb	3 120	4	11	12²	12½	11½	7¹	5¹½	Krone J A	7.80
28Sep03 7SA⁴	Magic Mission-GB	LBb	5 123	12	6	7hd	8¹	8¹	5½	6hd	Desormeaux K J	26.00
9Nov03 8SA²	Garden in the Rain-FR	LB	6 123	2	8	6¹	6¹	6hd 11½	7½	Baze T C	28.60
19Oct03 5WO⁴	Mer de Corail-IR		4 123	13	13	13½	13²	13hd 12¹	8¹½	Smith M E	69.40
14Sep03 9WO⁵	Chopinina	LBb	5 123	5	2	1¹	1¹	1¹	1¹	9¹½	Dos Ramos R A	38.10
17Oct03 7Med¹	Dancal-IR	LB	5 123	3	9	9½	9½	9½	13²½ 10¹	Castellano J J	22.10
12Oct03 Lch¹	Etoile Montante	B	3 120	1	4	4¹	4hd	4hd	2½ 11²	Bailey J D	2.30
27Sep03 8Bel⁴	Dress To Thrill-IR	LB	4 123	10	5	5½	5¹	5½ 10¹ 12³	Valenzuela P A	15.50
11Oct03 8Kee²	Maiden Tower-GB	LB	3 120	9	1	3hd	3½	2hd 4hd 13²	Flores D R	6.00
11Oct03 8SA¹	Belleski	LB	4 123	14	7	2½	2hd	3½ 14	14	Espinoza V	40.60

OFF AT 3:19 Start Good. Won driving. Course firm.

TIME :23², :46⁴, 1:10², 1:34² (:23.45, :46.85, 1:10.44, 1:34.43)

$2 Mutuel Prices:

11–HEAT HAZE–GB	10.60	6.00	3.80
7–MUSICAL CHIMES		6.40	4.40
6–DEDICATION–FR			10.20

$1 EXACTA 11–7 PAID $29.40 $2 QUINELLA 7–11 PAID $26.00 $1 TRIFECTA 11–7–6 PAID $646.70 $1 SUPERFECTA 11–7–6–8 PAID $46,911.50

B. f, by Green Desert–Hasili*Ire, by Kahyasi*Ire. Trainer Frankel Robert. Bred by Juddmonte Farms (GB).

HEAT HAZE (GB) broke slowly, angled in and saved ground off the pace, moved up some inside leaving the second turn, came out into the stretch, split foes in midstretch and closed gamely under urging to get up late. MUSICAL CHIMES angled in and chased off the rail, swung four wide into the stretch, rallied to the front past midstretch but was caught late. DEDICATION (FR) between horses early, angled in and stalked inside, was blocked off heels into the stretch, got through in midstretch and finished well inside. ISLAND FASHION angled in and settled outside a rival, came out on the second turn and five wide into the stretch and closed willingly. ACAGO pulled early, angled in and steadied on the first turn, saved ground, moved up inside leaving the second turn, waited off heels then got through inside in the stretch and finished with interest. MAGIC MISSION (GB) four wide into the first turn, chased outside, came four wide again into the stretch and lacked the needed response. GARDEN IN THE RAIN (FR) between horses early, chased inside, went between foes again into and on the second turn, came three deep into the stretch, was in tight off heels in midstretch and could not offer the necessary rally. MER DE CORAIL (IRE) broke slowly, angled in and settled a bit off the rail, came out on the second turn and six wide into the stretch and found her best stride late. CHOPININA sped to the early lead and angled in, set the pace inside, held on well to midstretch then weakened. DANCAL (IRE) between horses early, chased outside a rival then three deep on the second turn, came five wide into the stretch and did not rally. ETOILE MONTANTE stalked inside, came out into the stretch, bid outside the leader in upper stretch, lugged in and steadied off that one's heels nearing the eighth pole and weakened. DRESS TO THRILL (IRE) four wide into the first turn, chased outside, bid four wide leaving the second t urn and into the stretch and weakened. MAIDEN TOWER (GB) pulled her way along early, stalked between foes to the stretch, steadied when squeezed back past the eighth pole and also weakened. BELLESKI close up four wide early, stalked three deep then between horses leaving the second turn, angled in and had little left for the stretch.

Owners– 1, Juddmonte Farms Inc; 2, Al Maktoum Sheik Maktoum b; 3, Head Mrs Alec; 4, Everest Stables; 5, Wertheimer Farm LLC; 6, Al Maktoum Sheik Maktoum b; 7, Englander Richard A; 8, Magnier Susan; 9, Knob Hill Stable; 10, Aronstam Marlon; 11, Juddmonte Farms Inc; 12, Moyglare Stud Farm Ltd; 13, Darley Stable; 14, Moss Mr & Mrs Jerome S

Trainers– 1, Frankel Robert; 2, Drysdale Neil; 3, Clement Christophe; 4, Polanco Marcelo; 5, Mandella Richard; 6, Drysdale Neil; 7, Mullins Jeff; 8, Hammond John; 9, Fehr John Alec; 10, Pletcher Todd A; 11, Head-Maarek Christiane; 12, Clement Christophe; 13, Harty Eoin; 14, Sadler John W

$2 Daily Double (8–11) Paid $32.40; Daily Double Pool $46,900.
$1 Pick Three (5–8–11) Paid $50.30; Pick Three Pool $110,675.

NINTH RACE

Hollywood

NOVEMBER 30, 2003

1¼ MILES. (Turf)(1.57³) HOLLYWOOD DERBY. Grade I. Purse $600,000 FOR THREE-YEAR-OLDS. By subscription of $700 each on or before Friday, August 15, 2003 which should accompany the nomination. (No sustaining payments) Late nominations , for horses not previously nominated, may be made on or before Wednesday, October8, 2003 by payment of $3,500 each, which should accompany the nomination. Late nominations, for horses not previously nominated, may be made on or before Wednesday, November 19, 2003 by payment of $15,000 each, which should accompany the nomination, of which $13,000 is refundable if the nominee is entered and does not draw into the body of the race or if nominee is not entered and a veterinarian certificate is produced indicating the horse is unfit to run. All nominees to pay $3,500 to enter and an additional $3,500 to start. Gross purse $600,000 of which $360,000 to be paid to the winner, $120,000 to second, $72,000 to third, $36,000 to fourth and $12,000 to fifth. Weight 122 lbs. Starters to be named through the entry box by the closing time of entries. This race will not be divided. If the number of entries exceeds fourteen (14), first preference will be given to graded or group stakes winners in 2003.

Value of Race: $600,000 Winner $360,000; second $120,000; third $72,000; fourth $36,000; fifth $12,000. Mutuel Pool $641,123.00 Exacta Pool $352,843.00 Quinella Pool $33,653.00 Trifecta Pool $372,536.00 Superfecta Pool $186,673.00

Last Raced	Horse	M/Eqt.	A.Wt	PP	¼	½	¾	1	Str	Fin	Jockey	Odds $1
4Oct03 4SA²	Sweet Return-GB	LB	3 122	8	1hd	11	1½	1½	11½	1½	Krone J A	16.70
6Sep03 8Dmr¹	Fairly Ransom	LB	3 122	13	9hd	111	12½	101½	81½	2½	Solis A	4.80
11Oct03 9Bel¹	Kicken Kris	LB	3 122	9	4hd	4hd	2hd	2hd	41	3hd	Castellano J J	3.00
12Jly03 10Cnl¹	Silver Tree	B	3 122	3	21½	31½	4hd	4hd	2hd	4no	Prado E S	5.70
1Nov03 8BM²	Bis Repetitas	LB	3 122	5	61	61	61	5hd	7hd	5½	Espinoza V	37.30
4Oct03 4SA³	Urban King-IR	LB	3 122	10	12¹	12½	13	13	111	6no	Valenzuela P A	11.20
16Oct03 LYP¹	Sign Of The Wolf-GB	B	3 122	11	3hd	2½	31	31½	3hd	7hd	Blanc B	39.80
1Nov03 8BM¹	Stanley Park	LBb	3 122	1	111½	10hd	11hd	11½	10hd	8no	Saint-Martin E	13.10
4Oct03 4SA⁵	Californian-GB	LB	3 122	7	13	13	8hd	81½	5hd	9no	Desormeaux K J	62.40
22Jun03 Lch⁶	Alberto Giacometti-IRB		3 122	4	81½	71	71	7hd	6hd	10½	Valdivia J Jr	9.00
16Nov03 7Aqu¹	Willard Straight	LB	3 122	2	51½	51	5hd	61	9hd	111	Velazquez J R	49.20
24Oct03 8SA³	Senor Swinger	LB	3 122	12	7hd	91	10hd	12½	121	121	Bailey J D	4.00
11Oct03 9Bel³	Fortune Writers	LB	3 122	6	10hd	8hd	91½	91½	13	13	Fogelsonger R	38.90

OFF AT 4:54 Start Good. Won driving. Course firm.

TIME :25¹, :51, 1:17², 1:41, 2:04¹ (:25.35, :51.04, 1:17.49, 1:41.00, 2:04.27)

$2 Mutuel Prices:

8-SWEET RETURN-GB	35.40	11.80	5.40
14-FAIRLY RANSOM		5.40	3.80
9-KICKEN KRIS			3.40

$1 EXACTA 8-14 PAID $95.50 $2 QUINELLA 8-14 PAID $76.60 $1 TRIFECTA 8-14-9 PAID $478.00 $1 SUPERFECTA 8-14-9-3 PAID $3,920.20

Ch. c, (Mar), by Elmaamul-Sweet Revival*GB, by Claude Monet. Trainer McAnally Ronald. Bred by Tateson C S (GB).

SWEET RETURN (GB) sped to the early lead and angled in, set the pace inside, turned back bids into the stretch to inch clear and held gamely under urging. FAIRLY RANSOM pulled his way along four wide into the first turn, chased three deep, came four wide into the stretch and closed gamely. KICKEN KRIS angled in and stalked outside a rival, bid three deep on the backstretch and second turn, dropped back a bit into the stretch but finished with interest. SILVER TREE pulled his way along to stalk the pace inside, came a bit off the rail past midstretch and was outfinished. BIS REPETITAS also pulled early, chased outside, went up four wide on the second turn and into the stretch and also was outfinished. URBAN KING (IRE) angled in outside rivals in the chute, chased off the rail, came four wide into the stretch and found his best stride late. SIGN OF THE WOLF (GB) angled in and stalked outside a rival, bid between horses on the backstretch and second turn and weakened in the stretch. STANLEY PARK saved ground off the pace, came out into the stretch, steadied when blocked off heels in midstretch and could not recover. CALIFORNIAN (GB) between horses early, clipped heels and steadied leaving the chute, angled in and saved ground, moved up inside, awaited room in midstretch and finished with some interest when clear. ALBERTO GIACOMETTI (IRE) pulled his way between horses, stalked between foes or off the rail, continued between rivals on the second turn, was in a bit tight in midstretch and weakened. WILLARD STRAIGHT stalked inside then a bit off the rail, went between horses into and on the second turn and also weakened. SENOR SWINGER angled in and chased outside a rival, went between horses leaving the backstretch, came out into the stretch, steadied in tight off heels in midstretch and lacked the needed response. FORTUNE WRITERS off a bit slowly and squeezed, chased between foes then outside, went three deep on the second turn and had little left for the stretch.

Owners— 1, Red Oak Stable; 2, Zetcher Arnold; 3, Brushwood Stable; 4, Vegso Peter; 5, Gann Edmund A; 6, Amerman Racing Stables LLC; 7, Berend Van Dalsfen; 8, Moss Mr & Mrs Jerome S; 9, Noctis Stable Papiano Neil & Taub S; 10, Port Sidney L & Trust 720270; 11, Goichman Lawrence; 12, Lewis Robert B & Beverly J; 13, Patricia & Ronald Nicholson

Trainers— 1, McAnally Ronald; 2, McAnally Ronald; 3, Matz Michael R; 4, Mott William I; 5, Frankel Robert; 6, Frankel Robert; 7, Rohaut Francois; 8, Shirreffs John; 9, Mulhall Kristin; 10, De Seroux Laura; 11, Pletcher Todd A; 12, Baffert Bob; 13, Toner James J

Scratched— Sigint (1Nov03 8BM⁴)

$2 Daily Double (7-8) Paid $189.20; Daily Double Pool $51,368.
$1 Pick Three (5-7-8) Paid $299.10; Pick Three Pool $103,448.

NINTH RACE
Calder
DECEMBER 6, 2003

$1\frac{1}{8}$ MILES. (Turf) (1.44^{4}) MY CHARMER H. Grade III. Purse $100,000 FOR FILLIES AND MARES, THREE YEARS OLD AND UPWARD. By subscription of $100 each which shall accompany the nomination, $1,000 to pass the entry box and an additional $1,000 to start – with $100,000 guaranteed. The owner of the winner to receive $60,000, $20,000 to second, $11,000 to third, $6,000 to fourth and $3,000 to fifth. A trophy will be presented to the winning Owner. This race will be limited to 12 Starters, with Also Eligibles. (High Weights Preferred). (1) Supplemental Nomination with a fee of $3,000 to enter and start. Closed Saturday, November 22, 2003 with (28) nominations. Supplemental Nomination: IVANAVINALOT.

Value of Race: $100,000 Winner $60,000; second $20,000; third $11,000; fourth $6,000; fifth $3,000. Mutuel Pool $338,096.00 Exacta Pool $276,326.00 Trifecta Pool $210,183.00 Superfecta Pool $70,456.00

Last Raced	Horse	M/Eqt.		A.	Wt	PP	St	¼	½	¾	Str	Fin	Jockey	Odds $1
19Oct03 ^{5}WO^{8}	New Economy	L		5	115	9	5	$7^{2\frac{1}{2}}$	$6^{\frac{1}{2}}$	$6^{1\frac{1}{2}}$	$4^{2\frac{1}{2}}$	$1^{\frac{1}{2}}$	Homeister R B Jr	7.40
8Nov03 ^{9}Aqu^{4}	SomethingVentured	L	b	4	116	10	6	$4^{2\frac{1}{2}}$	$4^{2\frac{1}{2}}$	$3^{\frac{1}{2}}$	2^{1}	$2^{2\frac{1}{2}}$	Douglas R R	2.20
8Nov03 ^{5}Crc^{9}	Ivanavinalot	L	f	3	113	1	1	1^{2}	$1^{1\frac{1}{2}}$	$1^{1\frac{1}{2}}$	1^{2}	$3^{\frac{3}{4}}$	Scocca D	27.10
18Oct03 ^{5}Crc^{2}	Lost Appeal	L	b	5	115	5	9	$10^{1\frac{1}{2}}$	$11^{1\frac{1}{2}}$	9^{1}	5^{1}	$4^{2\frac{3}{4}}$	Nunez E O	4.10
11Oct03 ^{9}Crc^{1}	Love Sting	L	b	3	114	3	2	3^{hd}	2^{hd}	$2^{1\frac{1}{2}}$	3^{hd}	$5^{\frac{3}{4}}$	Bain G W	7.90
25Aug03 ^{6}Sar^{1}	DameSylvieguilhem	L	b	4	112	12	10	12	12	12	9^{1}	6^{nk}	Arroyo N Jr	11.20
1Nov03 ^{9}Crc^{1}	Hermans Honor	L	b	4	115	7	4	2^{1}	$3^{1\frac{1}{2}}$	$4^{2\frac{1}{2}}$	$7^{2\frac{1}{2}}$	$7^{1\frac{1}{2}}$	Aguilar M	29.60
7Sep03 ^{8}WO^{2}	Carib Lady-Ire	L		4	115	8	8	8^{hd}	10^{hd}	$11^{\frac{1}{2}}$	12	8^{nk}	Blanc B	8.80
22Nov03 ^{9}Crc^{7}	Light Dancer	L	bf	5	114	4	3	6^{hd}	$5^{2\frac{1}{2}}$	5^{3}	$6^{\frac{1}{2}}$	$9^{\frac{3}{4}}$	Toribio A Jr	39.60
15Nov03 ^{11}Crc^{4}	Sierra Lady	L	bf	4	114	2	7	5^{hd}	7^{3}	10^{1}	$10^{\frac{1}{2}}$	$10^{\frac{3}{4}}$	Hernandez C A	a- 3.90
2Mar03 ^{10}GP^{4}	Stay Forever	L	b	6	116	11	11	11^{hd}	9^{1}	$7^{1\frac{1}{2}}$	8^{hd}	11^{hd}	Cruz M R	a- 3.90
15Nov03 ^{11}Crc^{6}	Ms Brookski	L	b	4	115	6	12	$9^{1\frac{1}{2}}$	$8^{1\frac{1}{2}}$	$8^{\frac{1}{2}}$	$11^{\frac{1}{2}}$	12	Toscano P R	89.10

a–Coupled: Sierra Lady and Stay Forever.

OFF AT 3:59 Start Good . Won driving. Course firm.

TIME :23^{3}, :47^{2}, 1:11, 1:35, 1:46^{4} (:23.67, :47.40, 1:11.17, 1:35.16, 1:46.97)

$2 Mutuel Prices:				
	9 – NEW ECONOMY	16.80	7.60	6.80
	10 – SOMETHING VENTURED		4.60	3.60
	2 – IVANAVINALOT			13.60

$2 EXACTA 9–10 PAID $61.60 $2 TRIFECTA 9–10–2 PAID $1,496.80
$2 SUPERFECTA 9–10–2–5 PAID $6,857.60

B. m, (Feb), by Red Ransom – Sunyata , by Proud Truth . Trainer Motion H Graham. Bred by R S Evans (Ky).

NEW ECONOMY rated off the pace, raced three wide on the far turn, then rallied under pressure to be up late. SOMETHING VENTURED tracked the pace off the hedge, rallied to gain a slim lead nearing the sixteenth pole but couldn't resist the winner late. IVANAVINALOT quickly moved to the fore, made the pace along the hedge to inside the eighth pole and weakened. LOST APPEAL unhurried early, advanced into contention three wide on the far turn but didn't do enough late. LOVE STING chased the pacesetter off the hedge into the stretch and gave way. DAME SYLVIEGUILHEM outrun after being checked along the inside on the first turn, passed tired rivals in the drive. HERMANS HONOR chased the pace into the far turn and tired. CARIB LADY (IRE) failed to menace. LIGHT DANCER reserved racing along the hedge, faltered in the drive. SIERRA LADY saved ground and faded. STAY FOREVER was outrun. MS BROOKSKI hopped at the start and was never a factor.

Owners– 1, R S Evans; 2, Wiemer Irvin and McLane John; 3, Campbell Gilbert G; 4, Poston Bill and Vicki; 5, Emerald Pastures Corp Inc; 6, Live Oak Plantation; 7, Federico J and Pincaro J; 8, Gaillardia Racing LLC; 9, Loewenstein Harvey J Criollo Barbara and Bluestar Stable; 10, Santa Cruz Ranch Inc; 11, Santa Cruz Ranch Inc; 12, Tanaka Gary A

Trainers– 1, Motion H Graham; 2, Pletcher Todd A; 3, O'Connell Kathleen; 4, Edwards Oliver; 5, Hayford Jennifer A; 6, Mott William I; 7, Alonso Enrique; 8, Casse Mark E; 9, Criollo Manuel; 10, Rizo Juan P; 11, Wolfson Martin D; 12, Combest Reed M

Scratched– Diadella (19Oct03 ^{5}WO ^{10}) , Pillow Talk (04Oct03 ^{5}Bel^{3}) , Tasso Run (01Nov03 ^{5}Crc^{3}) , Victory Snit (24Oct03 ^{2}Crc^{5}) , Shouldn't We All (01Nov03 ^{8}Med^{6})

$2 Pick Three (2–2–9) Paid $1,273.60 ; Pick Three Pool $40,225 .

ELEVENTH RACE
Calder
DECEMBER 6, 2003

$1\frac{1}{8}$ MILES. (Turf) (1.44^4) TROPICAL TURF H. Grade III. Purse $100,000 FOR THREE YEAR OLDS AND UPWARD. By subscription of $100 each which shall accompany the nomination, $1,000 to pass the entry box and an additional $1,000 to start. This race will be limited to 12 Starters, with Also Eligibles. (High Weights Preferred). (1)Supplemental Nomination with a fee of $3,000 to enter and start. Closed Saturday, November 22, 2003 with (23) nominations. Supplemental Nomination: PAH.

Value of Race: $100,000 Winner $60,000; second $20,000; third $11,000; fourth $6,000; fifth $3,000. Mutuel Pool $332,811.00 Exacta Pool $262,542.00 Trifecta Pool $200,978.00 Superfecta Pool $68,501.00

Last Raced	Horse	M/Eqt.	A.	Wt	PP	St	¼	½	¾	Str	Fin	Jockey	Odds $1
18Oct03 ^{8}Del^1	Political Attack	L b	4	116	8	5	4^1	3^{hd}	3^1	1^{hd}	$1^{1\frac{1}{2}}$	Douglas R R	6.80
1Nov03 ^{8}Aqu^3	MillnnumDrgon-GB	L	4	116	2	3	2^1	$2^{1\frac{1}{2}}$	2^{hd}	$2^{1\frac{1}{2}}$	2no	Cruz M R	3.30
16Nov03 ^{9}Aqu^1	Sforza-FR	L	4	115	1	4	5^{hd}	6^1	5^{hd}	3^2	3^{nk}	Karamanos H	33.50
1Nov03 ^{8}Aqu^2	Del Mar Show	L	6	117	6	8	11^3	11^3	$11^{1\frac{1}{2}}$	6^{hd}	$4^{\frac{3}{4}}$	Coa E	2.60
20Sep03 ^{8}Bel^8	Statement	L	5	115	11	9	8^{hd}	7^{hd}	8^{hd}	$4^{\frac{1}{2}}$	$5^{2\frac{3}{4}}$	Velez J A Jr	22.80
18Oct03 ^{8}Del^2	Estio-Chi	L f	7	113	5	11	10^{hd}	$10^{\frac{1}{2}}$	$10^{1\frac{1}{2}}$	$5^{1\frac{1}{2}}$	$6^{1\frac{1}{4}}$	Bravo J	25.80
18Oct03 ^{5}Crc^6	Just Listen	L b	7	113	10	12	12	12	12	$9^{\frac{1}{2}}$	$7^{2\frac{1}{4}}$	Velez R I	54.30
18Oct03 ^{5}Crc^1	French Charmer	L b	4	118	9	7	6^1	$5^{\frac{1}{2}}$	6^1	$7^{2\frac{1}{2}}$	8no	DeCarlo C P	3.70
18Oct03 ^{5}Crc^5	Mr. Livingston	L f	6	113	3	1	$3^{\frac{1}{2}}$	4^1	4^{hd}	8^1	9^1	Garcia J A	17.40
18Oct03 ^{9}Bel^9	Irish Colonial	L	4	113	4	6	$7^{\frac{1}{2}}$	$8^{\frac{1}{2}}$	$7^{\frac{1}{2}}$	10^3	$10^{8\frac{1}{2}}$	Arroyo N Jr	6.70
18Oct03 ^{5}Crc^7	Serial Bride	L	6	113	12	10	$9^{\frac{1}{2}}$	$9^{\frac{1}{2}}$	9^{hd}	11^5	$11^{10\frac{1}{4}}$	Castro E	21.60
18Oct03 ^{7}Kee^6	Last Stand	L b	4	114	7	2	$1^{2\frac{1}{2}}$	1^4	1^2	12	12	Boulanger G	43.10

OFF AT 4:53 Start Good For All But SFORZA (FR). Won driving. Course firm.
TIME $:22^2$, $:45^1$, 1:09, 1:34, $1:45^4$ (:22.58, :45.37, 1:09.11, 1:34.00, 1:45.81)

$2 Mutuel Prices:				
	8 – **POLITICAL ATTACK**	15.60	8.00	5.80
	2 – **MILLENNIUM DRAGON–GB**		7.20	5.20
	1 – **SFORZA–FR**			12.80

$2 EXACTA 8–2 PAID $80.20 $2 TRIFECTA 8–2–1 PAID $1,639.20
$2 SUPERFECTA 8–2–1–6 PAID $7,143.60

B. g, (Mar), by Hawk Attack – Cope's Light, by Copelan. Trainer Matz Michael R. Bred by Brereton C Jones (Ky).

POLITICAL ATTACK tracked the pace, rallied to take over in early stretch, then edged away under urging. MILLENNIUM DRAGON (GB) chased the pace, moved to gain a slim lead on the far turn, then couldn't stay with the winner in the drive while just saving the place. SFORZA (FR) rated off the pace after stumbling at the start, advanced between horses on the far turn to loom a threat in midstretch but couldn't gain on the winner late while closing to just miss the place. DEL MAR SHOW unhurried early, angled out for the stretch run and closed with a belated rally. STATEMENT reserved early, advanced four wide around the far turn to reach contention, then had no late response. ESTIO (CHI) steadied in the early going, then steadied again nearing the end of the backstretch, rallied between horses to reach contention in the stretch and flattened out. JUST LISTEN outrun after breaking slowly, swung wide for the stretch run and failed to threaten. FRENCH CHARMER allowed to settle, raced in striking position four wide around the far turn and tired. MR. LIVINGSTON up close racing along the hedge, checked in behind the tiring LAST STAND approaching the quarter pole and faltered. IRISH COLONIAL was saving ground when steadied entering the far turn, then checked in behind MR. LIVINGSTON nearing the quarter pole and faded. SERIAL BRIDE was outrun while racing four wide. LAST STAND sprinted to a clear lead racing along the hedge, made the pace into the far turn and stopped.

Owners– 1, Erdenheim Farm; 2, Darley Stud Management LLC; 3, Eaton John and Laymon Steve; 4, Allen E Paulson Living Trust; 5, The Thoroughbred Corporation; 6, M Fehsenfeld; 7, Guez Marie Romaine and Guez D; 8, Double S Stable Avanzino Kenneth and Sullivan Joseph; 9, Palmer Teresa and David; 10, F Martin & H Nolan; 11, Runnin Horse Farm Inc; 12, Fawkes Racing Inc

Trainers– 1, Matz Michael R; 2, McLaughlin Kiaran P; 3, Picou James E; 4, Mott William I; 5, Kimmel John C; 6, Manning Dennis J; 7, Catanese Joseph C III; 8, Benson Harry; 9, Kaplan William A; 10, Schulhofer Randy; 11, Pointer Norman R; 12, Fawkes David

Scratched– Pah (29Nov03 ^{10}Crc^1), Tammany Star (27Oct03 ^{7}Crc^8)

EIGHTH RACE
Hollywood
DECEMBER 6, 2003

$1\frac{1}{8}$ MILES. (1.45^1) NATIVE DIVER H. Grade III. Purse $100,000 A HANDICAP FOR THREE-YEAR-OLDS AND UPWARD. By subscription of $100 each, on or before November 26. $1,000 additional to start, with $60,000 to the winner, $20,000 to second, $12,000 to third, $6,000 to fourth and $2,000 to fifth. A trophy will be presented to the owner of the winner. Nominations Closed Wednesday, November 26th, 2003 with 15.

Value of Race: $100,000 Winner $60,000; second $20,000; third $12,000; fourth $6,000; fifth $2,000. Mutuel Pool $376,149.00 Exacta Pool $208,092.00 Quinella Pool $25,422.00 Trifecta Pool $172,212.00 Superfecta Pool $62,915.00

Last Raced	Horse	M/Eqt.	A.	Wt	PP	St	¼	½	¾	Str	Fin	Jockey	Odds $1
26Oct03 ^{4}SA^5	Olmodavor	LB	4	117	2	5	5	5	5	$2^{\frac{1}{2}}$	$1^{\frac{1}{2}}$	Solis A O	1.20
25Oct03 ^{11}SA^7	Nose The Trade-GB	LB	5	115	5	4	1^1	1^{hd}	$1^{\frac{1}{2}}$	1^3	$2^{1\frac{1}{2}}$	Valenzuela P A	4.30
25Oct03 ^{11}SA^2	Chinkapin	LB b	7	118	3	2	4^3	4^1	4^1	4^{hd}	3^1	Nakatani C S	4.00
19Nov03 ^{7}Hol^1	Legendary Weave	LB b	5	114	1	1	2^1	3^7	3^4	5	4^2	Pedroza M A	11.10
10May03 ^{8}Hol^1	Total Impact-Chi	LB	5	118	4	3	$3^{2\frac{1}{2}}$	2^2	2^2	3^{hd}	5	Smith M E	2.60

OFF AT 4:07 Start Good. Won driving. Track fast.
TIME $:23^1$, $:46^3$, $1:10^3$, $1:35^4$, 1:49 (:23.35, :46.63, 1:10.61, 1:35.93, 1:49.16)

$2 Mutuel Prices:				
	2 – **OLMODAVOR**	4.40	2.80	2.40
	8 – **NOSE THE TRADE–GB**		3.80	2.40
	4 – **CHINKAPIN**			2.60

$1 EXACTA 2–8 PAID $7.80 $2 QUINELLA 2–8 PAID $10.40
$1 TRIFECTA 2–8–4 PAID $16.30 $1 SUPERFECTA 2–8–4–1 PAID $45.80

B. c, (Apr), by A.P. Indy – Corrazona, by El Gran Senor. Trainer Mandella Richard. Bred by Wertheimer et Frere (Ky).

OLMODAVOR settled inside then a bit off the rail, went outside a rival leaving the backstretch and on the second turn, split horses into the stretch and in midstretch, then rallied determinedly under urging while drifting out some late to get up. NOSE THE TRADE (GB) had good early speed three deep then outside a rival on the first turn, inched away on that bend, angled in a bit off the rail on the backstretch, dueled inside, kicked clear nearing the stretch and held on well but was caught late. CHINKAPIN angled in and saved ground off the pace, came a bit off the rail in the stretch and continued willingly for third. LEGENDARY WEAVE sent inside to duel for the lead, relinquished control on the first turn, came off the rail into the backstretch, bid between foes early on the backstretch then stalked off the inside, came three deep into the stretch, was four wide in midstretch and could not offer the necessary late response. TOTAL IMPACT (CHI) pulled hard between horses early then took back on the first turn, went up three deep on the backstretch, dueled outside the runner-up until nearing the stretch and weakened.

Owners– 1, Wertheimer Farm LLC; 2, Tanaka Gary A; 3, Belmonte Vanburger and Vaughn et al; 4, Fritz Norm and Lake Forest Stable; 5, Al Kabeer Sultan Mohammed Saud and Bridport S A

Trainers– 1, Mandella Richard E; 2, Frankel Robert J; 3, Mitchell Mike R; 4, Carava Jack; 5, De Seroux Laura

Scratched– Gift of the Eagle (21Aug03 ^{3}Dmr^1), Tenaja Trail (15Mar03 ^{7}SA ^{7}), Buckland Manor (23Oct03 ^{7}SA ^{1})

$2 Daily Double (8–2) Paid $20.60; Daily Double Pool $34,931.
$1 Pick Three (5–8–2/3/6/7) Paid $62.10; Pick Three Pool $58,412.

EIGHTH RACE
Hollywood
DECEMBER 7, 2003

$1\frac{1}{16}$ MILES. (1.40) BAYAKOA H. Grade II. Purse $150,000 A HANDICAP FOR FILLIES AND MARES THREE -YEAR-OLDS AND UPWARD. By subscription of $150 each, on or before November 26. Closed with 10. $1,500 additional to start, with $90,000 to the winner, $30,000 to second, $18,000 to third, $9,000 to fourth and $3,000 to fifth. A trophy will be presented to the owner of the winner.

Value of Race: $150,000 Winner $90,000; second $30,000; third $18,000; fourth $9,000; fifth $3,000. Mutuel Pool $345,628.00 Exacta Pool $207,205.00 Quinella Pool $24,943.00 Trifecta Pool $229,892.00 Superfecta Pool $106,247.00

Last Raced	Horse	M/Eqt.	A.	Wt	PP	St	¼	½	¾	Str	Fin	Jockey	Odds $1
13Nov03 ^{5}Hol^{4}	Star Parade-Arg	LB	4	112	2	2	$1^{1\frac{1}{2}}$	1^{2}	$1^{1\frac{1}{2}}$	1^{1}	$1^{3\frac{1}{4}}$	Espinoza V	12.20
25Oct03 ^{2}SA^{1}	Adoration	LB	4	121	5	4	3^{1}	2^{hd}	2^{1}	$2^{2\frac{1}{2}}$	2^{4}	Valenzuela P A	1.40
9Aug03 ^{10}ElP^{1}	Bare Necessities	LB	4	119	6	6	5^{5}	5^{7}	$5^{4\frac{1}{2}}$	$3^{1\frac{1}{2}}$	3^{3}	Douglas R R	0.90
18Oct03 ^{3}BM^{1}	Angel Gift	LB	5	114	1	1	$4^{\frac{1}{2}}$	4^{hd}	3^{hd}	$5^{2\frac{1}{2}}$	4^{4}	Valdivia J Jr	8.60
21Jun03 ^{8}Hol^{5}	Keys to the Heart	LB	4	113	3	5	2^{1}	3^{1}	$4^{\frac{1}{2}}$	4^{hd}	5^{1}	Krone J A	14.20
18Oct03 ^{6}Bel^{7}	Sparkling Ava	LB b	4	114	4	3	6	6	6	6	6	Pedroza M A	66.60

OFF AT 4:06 Start Good . Won driving. Track fast.

TIME :23, :46, 1:09^{4}, 1:34^{3}, 1:41 (:23.17, :46.15, 1:09.99, 1:34.72, 1:41.02)

$2 Mutuel Prices:

4 – STAR PARADE-ARG	26.40	7.40	3.00
7 – ADORATION		3.80	2.20
8 – BARE NECESSITIES			2.20

$1 EXACTA 4–7 PAID $37.40 $2 QUINELLA 4–7 PAID $25.20
$1 TRIFECTA 4–7–8 PAID $76.20 $1 SUPERFECTA 4–7–8–2 PAID $210.90

Dk. b or br. f, (Oct), by Parade Marshal – Clerical Etoile-Arg , by The Watcher . Trainer Vienna Darrell. Bred by Firmamento (Arg).

STAR PARADE (ARG) sprinted to the early lead and angled in some, set the pace a bit off the rail, responded when rivals loomed into the second turn and again when the runner-up bid in the stretch and pulled clear under urging, then was under steady handling late. ADORATION bobbled at the start, stalked three deep then off the rail on the second turn and into the stretch, appeared a threat behind the winner in midstretch but could not match that one while clearly second best. BARE NECESSITIES four wide into the first turn, stalked outside a rival on the backstretch and three deep on the second turn and into the stretch and picked up the show. ANGEL GIFT saved ground close up stalking the pace, fell back some leaving the second turn and weakened. KEYS TO THE HEART tracked the winner off the rail then between horses on the backstretch and second turn and also weakened. SPARKLING AVA rank between horses early, took up and bore out into the first turn, chased off the rail and did not rally.

Owners– 1, McClure J Doug; 2, Amerman Racing Stables LLC; 3, Iron County Farms Inc; 4, Delahoussaye Enterprises Strauss Richard C and Williford Roberta; 5, Nichols Thomas L; 6, Schwartz Barry K

Trainers– 1, Vienna Darrell; 2, Hofmans David E; 3, Dollase Wallace A; 4, Gallagher Patrick; 5, Greely C Beau; 6, Inda Eduardo

Scratched– Summer Wind Dancer (08Nov03 ^{4}SA ^{2}) , Southern Oasis (13Aug03 ^{7}Dmr^{7})

$2 Daily Double (12–4) Paid $295.00 ; Daily Double Pool $35,861 .
$1 Pick Three (7–12–4) Paid $1,562.60 ; Pick Three Pool $78,309 .

EIGHTH RACE
Aqueduct
DECEMBER 13, 2003

$1\frac{3}{16}$ MILES. (1.54^{2}) QUEENS COUNTY H. Grade III. Purse $100,000 INNER DIRT. (Up to $19,400 NYSBFOA) A HANDICAP FOR THREE YEAR OLDS AND UPWARD. By subscription of $100 each, which should accompany the nomination; $500 to pass the entry box; $500 to start. Closed Saturday, November 22, 2003 with 23 nominations.

Value of Race: $108,300 Winner $64,980; second $21,660; third $10,830; fourth $5,415; fifth $3,249; sixth $2,166. Mutuel Pool $502,826.00 Exacta Pool $397,815.00 Trifecta Pool $252,408.00

Last Raced	Horse	M/Eqt.	A.	Wt	PP	St	¼	½	¾	Str	Fin	Jockey	Odds $1
11Nov03 ^{8}Aqu^{2}	Thunder Blitz	L	5	114	4	3	3^{1}	$2^{\frac{1}{2}}$	$2^{\frac{1}{2}}$	$1^{\frac{1}{2}}$	$1^{1\frac{1}{2}}$	Chavez J F	4.90
28Nov03 ^{11}CD^{2}	Evening Attire	L b	5	123	2	5	4^{hd}	4^{hd}	$3^{\frac{1}{2}}$	3^{hd}	2^{hd}	Bridgmohan S	1.10
28Nov03 ^{11}CD^{4}	Seattle Fitz-Arg	L	4	115	1	1	$2^{\frac{1}{2}}$	$3^{\frac{1}{2}}$	$4^{2\frac{1}{2}}$	$2^{\frac{1}{2}}$	$3^{3\frac{1}{4}}$	Migliore R	3.40
29Oct03 ^{8}Aqu^{2}	Unforgettable Max	L	3	113	6	2	1^{1}	1^{1}	1^{hd}	4^{5}	4^{4}	Castellano J	5.10
25Oct03 ^{4}Kee^{6}	Country Be Gold	L	6	114	5	6	6	6	6	5^{5}	$5^{3\frac{3}{4}}$	Santos J A	10.40
7Nov03 ^{7}Aqu^{2}	Nothing Flat	L	4	112	3	4	5^{5}	5^{4}	5^{2}	6	6	Arroyo N Jr	22.10

OFF AT 3:44 Start Good . Won driving. Track fast.

TIME :24^{2}, :49, 1:13^{2}, 1:37^{4}, 1:55^{4} (:24.46, :49.05, 1:13.43, 1:37.80, 1:55.90)

$2 Mutuel Prices:

4 – THUNDER BLITZ	11.80	3.80	2.80
2 – EVENING ATTIRE		2.70	2.20
1 – SEATTLE FITZ-ARG			3.00

$2 EXACTA 4–2 PAID $28.60 $2 TRIFECTA 4–2–1 PAID $88.50

Gr/ro. h, (May), by Holy Bull – Rasant , by Assert-Ire . Trainer Dutrow Richard E Jr. Bred by Adena Springs (Ky).

THUNDER BLITZ stalked the pace racing off the rail, bid two wide nearing the quarter pole, responded when roused and edged away in the final furlong under urging. EVENING ATTIRE rated off the pace, raced three wide in striking position on the backside, rallied four wide into the lane and closed gamely to earn the place award. SEATTLE FITZ (ARG) rated inside, angled out three wide at the quarter pole and was outfinished for second. UNFORGETTABLE MAX angled over to the rail to set the pace entering the clubhouse turn and tired in final furlong. COUNTRY BE GOLD stumbled at the start and did not factor after that. NOTHING FLAT raced three wide and faded.

Owners– 1, Stronach Stable; 2, Grant Mary and Joseph and Kelly Thomas J; 3, West Point Stable; 4, Dweck Raymond; 5, Seinfeld Barry and Dodson Elizabeth K; 6, Condren William J and Sherman Michael H

Trainers– 1, Dutrow Richard E Jr; 2, Kelly Patrick J; 3, McLaughlin Kiaran P; 4, Perkins Benjamin W Jr; 5, Kappes Steven W; 6, Zito Nicholas P

TENTH RACE
Calder
DECEMBER 13, 2003

7 FURLONGS. (1.21^{4}) CHAPOSA SPRINGS H. Grade III. Purse $100,000 FOR FILLIES AND MARES, THREE YEARS OLD AND UPWARD. By subscription of $100 each which shall accompany the nomination, $1,000 to pass the entry box and an additional $1,000 to start. Closed Saturday, November 29, 2003 with (18) nominations.

Value of Race: $100,000 Winner $60,000; second $20,000; third $11,000; fourth $6,000; fifth $3,000. Mutuel Pool $400,728.00 Exacta Pool $329,607.00 Trifecta Pool $239,873.00 Superfecta Pool $80,749.00

Last Raced	Horse	M/Eqt.	A.	Wt	PP	St	¼	½	Str	Fin	Jockey	Odds $1
15Nov03 ^{11}Crc^{7}	Barbara O'Brien	L	4	114	7	5	$2^{1\frac{1}{2}}$	2^{hd}	1^{3}	$1^{5\frac{1}{4}}$	Coa E	5.60
5Nov03 ^{9}CD^{2}	Holy Bubbette	L	3	114	6	11	5^{hd}	$4^{2\frac{1}{2}}$	$2^{\frac{1}{2}}$	2^{1}	Bailey J D	3.00
11Oct03 ^{7}Crc^{1}	Splasha	L b	3	114	8	10	11^{8}	$10^{\frac{1}{2}}$	5^{3}	3^{3}	Aguilar M	11.40
1Nov03 ^{9}Crc^{7}	Honeymooner	L f	4	112	2	7	$4^{\frac{1}{2}}$	6^{3}	$4^{\frac{1}{2}}$	4^{1}	Homeister R B Jr	31.10
18Nov03 ^{9}Mnr^{4}	FortyMarinesc-Arg	L b	5	114	3	12	12	12	$7^{1\frac{1}{2}}$	5^{hd}	Boulanger G	101.30
22Nov03 ^{9}Crc^{1}	Chispiski	L bf	4	122	1	6	$1^{1\frac{1}{2}}$	$1^{1\frac{1}{2}}$	3^{3}	$6^{3\frac{1}{4}}$	Garcia J A	4.70
15Nov03 ^{9}CD^{7}	Keiai Sakura	L b	3	113	4	9	7^{1}	7^{hd}	$8^{1\frac{1}{2}}$	$7^{\frac{1}{2}}$	Blanc B	10.00
22Nov03 ^{9}Crc^{2}	Belle Artiste	L	5	116	11	4	$9^{1\frac{1}{2}}$	$9^{1\frac{1}{2}}$	10^{3}	$8^{\frac{1}{2}}$	DeCarlo C P	11.40
9Nov03 ^{3}Aqu^{1}	Elegant Mercedes	L f	3	115	5	8	$6^{\frac{1}{2}}$	5^{hd}	9^{1}	$9^{1\frac{1}{2}}$	Douglas R R	3.80
11Oct03 ^{7}Crc^{4}	Win's Fair Lady	L b	4	113	10	3	3^{hd}	$3^{1\frac{1}{2}}$	6^{1}	$10^{4\frac{3}{4}}$	Bravo J	9.20
15Nov03 ^{11}Crc^{8}	Crimson and Roses	L	3	114	9	2	$8^{\frac{1}{2}}$	8^{hd}	11^{5}	$11^{12\frac{1}{4}}$	Velasquez C H	36.90
22Nov03 ^{9}Crc^{4}	Crafty Brat	L f	3	114	12	1	$10^{\frac{1}{2}}$	11^{6}	12	12	Cruz M R	37.60

OFF AT 4:32 Start Good . Won driving. Track fast.

TIME :22, :44^{4}, 1:10^{2}, 1:23^{2} (:22.02, :44.83, 1:10.41, 1:23.51)

$2 Mutuel Prices:				
	7 – BARBARA O'BRIEN	13.20	5.60	4.40
	6 – HOLY BUBBETTE		4.60	3.80
	8 – SPLASHA			5.60

$2 EXACTA 7–6 PAID $68.40 $2 TRIFECTA 7–6–8 PAID $572.20
$2 SUPERFECTA 7–6–8–2 PAID $9,824.40

B. f, (Jan), by Eltish – Brandy O'Brien , by Desert Wine . Trainer Benson Harry. Bred by Marty Hershe & Galloping Acres Farm (Fla).

BARBARA O'BRIEN never far back, rallied three wide to the turn, charged to the front in upper stretch then drew off while being kept to the task. HOLY BUBBETTE settled early, rallied along the inside on the turn and. SPLASHA raced far back to the turn and rallied belatedly. HONEYMOONER saved ground to the turn and lacked a strong closing bid. FORTY MARINESCA (ARG) checked at the start and failed to threaten thereafter. CHISPISKI was used up setting the early pace. KEIAI SAKURA failed to mount a serious rally. BELLE ARTISTE was never a factor. ELEGANT MERCEDES raced in the middle of the pack four wide for a half and tired. WIN'S FAIR LADY chased three wide to the turn and faltered. CRIMSON AND ROSES never reached contention. CRAFTY BRAT was outrun.

Owners– 1, Double S Stable Avanzino Kenneth and Wachtel Ed et al; 2, Elam Katherine; 3, Gibson Douglas P; 4, Paul Derek K; 5, Nolan Howard C Jr; 6, Brazil Stable; 7, Kameda Morihiro; 8, Peace John H; 9, Sullivan Lane Stable V Scuderi & T Williams; 10, Sabine Stable; 11, Jacks or Better Farm Inc; 12, Calascibetta Inc and Cheeks W et al

Trainers– 1, Benson Harry; 2, Amoss Thomas M; 3, Vivian David A; 4, Green N; 5, Root Richard R; 6, Spatz Ronald B; 7, Gothard Akiko M; 8, Weaver George; 9, Dutrow Richard E Jr; 10, Standridge Steven W; 11, Hatchett James; 12, Calascibetta Joseph G

$2 Pick Three (2–4–7) Paid $606.60 ; Pick Three Pool $33,129 .

EIGHTH RACE
Aqueduct
DECEMBER 20, 2003

1¼ MILES. (2.01^{2}) LADIES H. Grade III. Purse $100,000 INNER DIRT. (Up to $19,400 NYSBFOA) A HANDICAP FOR FILLIES AND MARES THREE YEARS OLD AND UPWARD. By subscription of $100 each, which should accompany the nomination; $500 to pass the entry box; $500 to start, with $100,000 added. The added money and all fees to be divided 60% to the winner, 20% to second, 10% to third, 5% to fourth, 3% to fifth and 2% divided equally among the remaining starters. Starters to be named at the closing time of entries. A trophy will be presented to the winning owner. Closed Saturday, December 6, 2003 with 16 Nominations.

Value of Race: $112,100 Winner $67,260; second $22,420; third $11,210; fourth $5,605; fifth $3,363; sixth $449; seventh $449; eighth $449; ninth $449; tenth $446. Mutuel Pool $547,717.00 Exacta Pool $454,153.00 Trifecta Pool $321,286.00

Last Raced	Horse	M/Eqt.	A.	Wt	PP	¼	½	¾	1	Str	Fin	Jockey	Odds $1
26Nov03 ^{7}Aqu^{3}	Savedbythelight	L b	3	115	7	$2^{\frac{1}{2}}$	$2^{\frac{1}{2}}$	2^{1}	2^{1}	$1^{2\frac{1}{2}}$	1^{3}	Migliore R	4.50
30Nov03 ^{8}Aqu^{1}	Queen's Triomphe	L	4	113	1	$4^{\frac{1}{2}}$	4^{1}	3^{1}	3^{hd}	2^{1}	2^{hd}	Espinoza J L	9.40
15Nov03 ^{8}Lrl^{4}	Retroactive	L	3	113	3	$7^{\frac{1}{2}}$	$7^{\frac{1}{2}}$	7^{1}	5^{hd}	$5^{\frac{1}{2}}$	3^{1}	Castellano J	3.45
8Nov03 ^{4}Haw^{1}	Julie's Prize	L b	3	113	10	6^{1}	$6^{\frac{1}{2}}$	8^{1}	6^{2}	3^{hd}	$4^{\frac{1}{2}}$	Bridgmohan S	4.70
28Nov03 ^{9}Aqu^{4}	Caught in the Rain	L f	4	113	4	$8^{\frac{1}{2}}$	8^{2}	6^{hd}	$4^{1\frac{1}{2}}$	$4^{\frac{1}{2}}$	$5^{2\frac{1}{2}}$	Molina V H	2.90
15Nov03 ^{7}Aqu^{5}	Consort Music	L	4	113	2	10	9^{hd}	9^{3}	7^{2}	7^{8}	6^{5}	Pimentel J	104.50
15Nov03 ^{8}Lrl^{5}	City Fire	L b	3	114	9	$1^{\frac{1}{2}}$	$1^{\frac{1}{2}}$	$1^{\frac{1}{2}}$	1^{hd}	6^{2}	$7^{7\frac{1}{2}}$	Luzzi M J	11.60
1Nov03 ^{9}Aqu^{4}	Lady Liberty	L	4	114	5	5^{1}	5^{1}	$4^{\frac{1}{2}}$	8^{6}	8^{8}	$8^{9\frac{3}{4}}$	Arroyo N Jr	16.50
19Sep03 ^{8}Bel^{2}	Call an Audible	L	4	114	8	3^{hd}	3^{hd}	5^{hd}	9^{4}	9^{6}	$9^{15\frac{3}{4}}$	Gryder A T	14.60
19Oct03 ^{8}Kee^{7}	Kabylia-Ire	L b	5	114	6	9^{2}	10	10	10	10	10	Castillo H Jr	40.50

OFF AT 3:49 Start Good . Won driving. Track fast.

TIME :25^{3}, :51, 1:15^{4}, 1:41^{1}, 2:05^{4} (:25.73, :51.08, 1:15.84, 1:41.25, 2:05.99)

$2 Mutuel Prices:				
	8 – SAVEDBYTHELIGHT	11.00	6.00	4.00
	1 – QUEEN'S TRIOMPHE		9.00	5.80
	3 – RETROACTIVE			3.40

$2 EXACTA 8–1 PAID $107.00 $2 TRIFECTA 8–1–3 PAID $377.00

Dk. b or br. f, (Mar), by Saint Ballado – Wild Royal , by Wild Again . Trainer Violette Richard A Jr. Bred by R C Durr & George Budig (Ky).

SAVEDBYTHELIGHT pressed the pace racing outside of CITY FIRE, moved alongside that one to challenge at the quarter pole and drew clear, driving. QUEEN'S TRIOMPHE was well placed on the inside, split rivals in the three path in upper stretch and closed gamely to earn the place award. RETROACTIVE saved ground racing off the pace, came through between rivals in the stretch and closed well inside. JULIE'S PRIZE raced three wide in the early stages, rallied five wide into the lane and failed to sustain that bid. CAUGHT IN THE RAIN raced off the rail, made a four wide move on the far turn and flattened out. CONSORT MUSIC saved ground and failed to respond. CITY FIRE rated the pace on the rail and faltered in the stretch. LADY LIBERTY raced between rivals and tired. CALL AN AUDIBLE rated three wide and tired. KABYLIA (IRE) was squeezed at the start and outrun.

Owners– 1, Mack Earle I; 2, Kelly Gregory W and Stephen P; 3, Humphrey Jr G Watts and Louise I; 4, Otto Richard F; 5, Heiligbrodt Racing Stable and New Walter L; 6, Evans Edward P; 7, Gill Michael J; 8, Janney Stuart S III; 9, Amerman Racing Stables LLC; 10, Agnew Dan J

Trainers– 1, Violette Richard A Jr; 2, Bush Thomas M; 3, McGaughey III Claude R; 4, Mitchell Anthony; 5, Preciado Guadalupe; 6, Hennig Mark A; 7, Shuman Mark; 8, McGaughey III Claude R; 9, Hennig Mark A; 10, Lukas D Wayne

Scratched– Sabre of Silver (28Nov03 ^{9}Aqu^{8})

NINTH RACE
Hollywood
DECEMBER 20, 2003

1$\frac{1}{16}$ MILES. (Turf) (1.38³) DAHLIA H. Grade II. Purse $150,000 A HANDICAP FOR FILLIES AND MARES THREE-YEARS-OLD AND UPWARD. By subscription of $150 each, on or before December 10. Closed with 24. $1,500 additional to start, with $90,000 to the winner, $30,000 to second, $18,000 to third, $9,000 to fourth and $3,000to fifth. A trophy will be presented to the owner of the winner. Nominations closed with 24.

Value of Race: $150,000 Winner $90,000; second $30,000; third $18,000; fourth $9,000; fifth $3,000. Mutuel Pool $521,257.00 Exacta Pool $292,339.00 Quinella Pool $26,207.00 Trifecta Pool $314,539.00 Superfecta Pool $137,298.00

Last Raced	Horse	M/Eqt. A. Wt	PP	St	¼	½	¾	Str	Fin	Jockey	Odds $1
23Nov03 8Hol²	Katdogawn-GB	LB 3 116	8	10	9⁴	8½	82½	6ʰᵈ	1ⁿᵒ	Smith M E	7.90
15Nov03 8Hol¹	Personal Legend	LB b 3 115	9	7	7¹½	7¹	7ʰᵈ	7¹	2¹½	Solis A O	a- 0.90
13Oct03 9Bel¹	Betty's Wish	LB 3 117	3	3	4¹	4ʰᵈ	5ʰᵈ	5¹	3½	Nakatani C S	a- 0.90
8Nov03 3SA¹	Moscow Burning	LB 3 114	4	2	3ʰᵈ	3ʰᵈ	4½	2ʰᵈ	4¹	Valdivia J Jr	13.10
15Nov03 9CD¹	Hoh Buzzard-Ire	LB b 3 117	10	1	1ʰᵈ	1½	1½	11½	51½	Baze T	8.40
8Nov03 5SA¹	Blind Ambition	LB f 5 116	6	6	8ʰᵈ	9⁴	9¹	91½	6½	Stevens G L	3.60
23Nov03 8Hol⁵	Valdoura-FR	LB b 3 112	2	5	62½	6½	61½	8¹	7¹	Espinoza V	46.60
15Oct03 2SA⁴	VozDeColegiala-Chi	LB 4 113	1	4	2¹½	2²	2¹	4ʰᵈ	8ⁿᵏ	Ramsammy E	24.50
9Nov03 8SA⁶	Innit-Ire	LB b 5 114	7	8	10	10	10	10	9½	Pedroza M A	52.00
27Nov03 3Hol³	Adalgisa	LB 4 115	5	9	5ʰᵈ	51½	3¹	3¹	10	Valenzuela P A	9.40

a-Coupled: Personal Legend and Betty's Wish.

OFF AT 4:36 Start Good . Won driving. Course firm.

TIME :23⁴, :47², 1:11, 1:35⁴, 1:41² (:23.96, :47.41, 1:11.16, 1:35.83, 1:41.52)

$2 Mutuel Prices:

8 – KATDOGAWN–GB	17.80	5.20	5.40
1A– PERSONAL LEGEND(a–entry)		2.60	2.60
1– BETTY'S WISH(a–entry)		2.60	2.60

$1 EXACTA 8–1 PAID $22.80 $2 QUINELLA 1–8 PAID $14.80
$1 TRIFECTA 8–1–4 PAID $147.10 $1 SUPERFECTA 8–1–4–9 PAID $622.50

B. f, (Feb), by Bahhare – Trempkate , by Trempolino . Trainer Cassidy James. Bred by Mrs W H Gibson Fleming (GB).

KATDOGAWN (GB) off a bit slowly, angled in and settled a bit off the rail, came out some leaving the second turn, awaited room behind rivals into the stretch, came out, rallied under urging between foes in midstretch to gain a short lead in deep stretch and held gamely. PERSONAL LEGEND chased outside a rival, came three deep into the stretch and closed willingly but could not quite get by the winner. BETTY'S WISH pulled between horses early then stalked inside, waited behind rivals leaving the second turn, split horses twice in the stretch and finished well. MOSCOW BURNING three deep early, stalked the pace outside a rival then between horses on the second turn, continued between foes in the stretch and was outfinished. HOH BUZZARD (IRE) angled in and dueled outside a rival, inched away in the stretch and held on well but weakened late. BLIND AMBITION pulled her way along inside early, came out on the second turn and three deep into the stretch, then rallied between foes. VALDOURA (FR) stalked the pace inside, came out on the second turn and four wide into the stretch and weakened. VOZ DE COLEGIALA (CHI) went up inside to duel for the lead to the stretch and also weakened. INNIT (IRE) threw her head and steadied between horses after the start, angled in and saved ground off the pace and lacked the needed rally. ADALGISA pulled her way along to stalk the pace outside a rival, went three deep leaving the second turn and into the stretch and weakened.

Owners– 1, Cuchna John R Jim Ford Inc and Pearson Daron; 2, Gann Edmund A; 3, Gann Edmund A; 4, Mariani or Nentwig or Van Kempen; 5, Tanaka Gary A; 6, Harris Farms Inc and Bowers-Lepore Racing; 7, Fogelson Gayle D and Stathatos Damon; 8, Hunt Nelson B; 9, Duchossois Richard L; 10, Beck Robert L

Trainers– 1, Cassidy James M; 2, Frankel Robert J; 3, Frankel Robert J; 4, Cassidy James M; 5, Cecil Ben D; 6, Jones Martin F; 7, Whittingham Michael C; 8, McAnally Ronald L; 9, McAnally Ronald L; 10, Canani Julio C

Scratched– Atlantic Ocean (24Aug03 9Dmr⁵)

$2 Daily Double (8–8) Paid $229.20 ; Daily Double Pool $38,489 .
$1 Pick Three (1–8–8) Paid $423.70 ; Pick Three Pool $81,221 .

FOURTH RACE
Hollywood
DECEMBER 20, 2003

1$\frac{1}{16}$ MILES. (1.40) HOLLYWOOD FUTURITY Grade I. Purse $200,000 (plus $10,000 Other Sources) FOR TWO YEAR OLDS (FOALS OF 2001). By subscription of $250 each on or before Friday, May 16, 2003. Fee to accompany subscription. To remain eligible the following payment must be made: $500 each on or before Wednesday, July 9, 2003. Original nominees topay $2,500 to pass the entry box and an additional $2,500 to start. Supplementary nominations may be made at time of entry by a payment of $10,000 each which qualifies to enter and an additional $10,000 to start. Horses made eligible to the futurity by way of supplemental nominations are not eligible to receive nominator awards. Any nominator awards not paid from the gross purse of the futurity will be added back into the gross purse of the futurity. Nominations closed with 224 May 16th. 142 sustaining nominations July 9. 2 supplementary nominations: ST AVERIL and THAT'S AN OUTRAGE.

Value of Race: $376,000 Winner $225,600; second $75,200; third $45,120; fourth $22,560; fifth $7,520. Mutuel Pool $530,534.00 Exacta Pool $388,214.00 Quinella Pool $31,907.00

Last Raced	Horse	M/Eqt. A. Wt	PP	St	¼	½	¾	Str	Fin	Jockey	Odds $1
15Nov03 7Hol¹	Lion Heart	2 121	4	2	1²	12½	1¹	11½	13½	Smith M E	0.50
9Nov03 6SA¹	St Averil	LB b 2 121	2	1	22½	2½	3²	2ʰᵈ	2¹	Baze T	2.90
25Oct03 7SA⁷	That's an Outrage	LB b 2 121	3	5	4½	4²	2ʰᵈ	3²	3½	Stevens G L	17.40
26Nov03 5Hol¹	Quiet Cash	LB b 2 121	5	4	5	5	42½	41½	42½	Flores D R	9.80
7Dec03 2Hol¹	Saint Afleet	LB b 2 121	1	3	32½	3ʰᵈ	5	5	5	Solis A O	6.00

OFF AT 2:05 Start Good . Won ridden out. Track fast.

TIME :23¹, :46², 1:10³, 1:36, 1:42⁴ (:23.28, :46.56, 1:10.65, 1:36.04, 1:42.80)

$2 Mutuel Prices:

4 – LION HEART	3.00	2.20	2.10
2 – ST AVERIL		2.60	2.10
3 – THAT'S AN OUTRAGE			2.10

$1 EXACTA 4–2 PAID $2.50 $2 QUINELLA 2–4 PAID $3.60

Ch. c, (Jan), by Tale of the Cat – Satin Sunrise , by Mr. Leader . Trainer Biancone Patrick L. Bred by Sabine Stable (Ky).

LION HEART pulled a bit while taking the early lead off the rail, angled in and set the pace a bit off the fence under a snug hold, responded when rivals loomed leaving the backstretch and on the second turn, inched away again and drew clear under a moderate hand ride. ST AVERIL stalked the winner inside then a bit off the rail, continued outside a rival leaving the backstretch and on the second turn, came out a bit into the stretch, was no match for the winner but held game for second. THAT'S AN OUTRAGE chased off the rail then angled in, moved up leaving the backstretch to loom a threat along the rail on the second turn, then lacked the needed response in the stretch but held third. QUIET CASH chased off the rail early, angled in leaving the backstretch, came out into the stretch and was edged for the show. SAINT AFLEET broke inward, stalked inside then a bit off the rail, went outside a rival on the backstretch, dropped back on the second turn and weakened.

Owners– 1, Smith Derrick and Tabor Michael; 2, Fulton Stan E; 3, Bull Stick Stables LLC and Mercedes Stables LLC; 4, Pegram Michael E; 5, Waranch Ronald C

Trainers– 1, Biancone Patrick L; 2, Becerra Rafael; 3, Puhich Michael; 4, Baffert Bob; 5, Dollase Craig

---

$2 Daily Double (5–4) Paid $11.20 ; Daily Double Pool $47,910 .
$1 Pick Three (1–5–4) Paid $34.70 ; Pick Three Pool $81,512 .

EIGHTH RACE

Aqueduct

DECEMBER 21, 2003

6 FURLONGS. (1.07⁴) GRAVESEND H. Grade III. Purse $100,000 INNER DIRT. (Up to $19,400 NYSBFOA) A HANDICAP FOR THREE YEAR OLDS AND UPWARD. By subscription of $100 each, which should accompany the nomination; $500 to pass the entry box; $500 to start, with $100,000 added. The added money and all fees to be divided 60% to the winner, 20% to second, 10% to third, 5% to fourth, 3% to fifth and 2% divided equally among the remaining starters. A trophy will be presented to the winning owner. Closed Saturday, December 6, 2003 with 20 Nominations.

Value of Race: $109,000 Winner $65,400; second $21,800; third $10,900; fourth $5,450; fifth $3,270; sixth $1,090; seventh $1,090. Mutuel Pool $390,151.00 Exacta Pool $393,540.00 Trifecta Pool $307,807.00

Last Raced	Horse	M/Eqt. A. Wt	PP	St	¼	½	Str	Fin	Jockey	Odds $1
15Nov03 10Lrl2	Shake You Down	L bf 5 124	4	2	1hd	11	12	12¼	Luzzi M J	0.90
15Nov03 10Lrl4	Way to the Top	L f 5 114	1	3	2½	2hd	21	21¾	Arroyo N Jr	6.20
15Nov03 10Lrl3	Gators N Bears	L bf 3 115	3	4	4½	51	5hd	3¾	Wilson R	5.30
27Nov03 8Aqu5	Peeping Tom	L bf 6 116	7	6	64	63	4hd	4½	Bridgmohan S	8.70
27Nov03 8Aqu2	Papua	L bf 4 115	6	5	52	4hd	63	51½	Migliore R	5.10
29Nov03 6Aqu2	Black Silk-GB	L f 7 111	5	1	3½	31	3½	62½	Fragoso P	60.75
11Nov03 8Aqu1	Presidentialaffair	L 4 116	2	7	7	7	7	7	Gryder A T	14.00

OFF AT 3:44 Start Good . Won driving. Track fast.

TIME :22³, :45¹, :57, 1:09² (:22.64, :45.37, :57.13, 1:09.55)

$2 Mutuel Prices:			
4 – SHAKE YOU DOWN	3.80	2.50	2.30
1 – WAY TO THE TOP		5.10	3.10
3 – GATORS N BEARS			2.90

$2 EXACTA 4–1 PAID $14.60 $2 TRIFECTA 4–1–3 PAID $45.40

Ch. g, (Apr), by Montbrook – Mauvin Gway , by Rajab . Trainer Lake Scott A. Bred by Ocala Stud Farm (Fla).

SHAKE YOU DOWN set the pace in the two path down the backside, angled over to the rail on the turn, drew clear in upper stretch and maintained the edge under steady hand urging. WAY TO THE TOP vied inside, dropped back a bit entering the turn and then dug in gamely to earn the place award. GATORS N BEARS raced close up on the inside, angled out for the drive and closed gamely outside for third. PEEPING TOM raced off the pace, rallied up the rail and was outfinished. PAPUA stalked three wide and lacked a sufficient rally. BLACK SILK (GB) chased two wide and tired. PRESIDENTIALAFFAIR was off slowly and outrun.

Owners– 1, Cole Robert L Jr; 2, Valente Roddy J; 3, Nechamkin II Leo S; 4, Flatbird Stable; 5, Schwartz Barry K; 6, Fustok Salah M; 7, Ciresa Edward and Papapandrea Vincent

Trainers– 1, Lake Scott A; 2, Levine Bruce N; 3, Nechamkin Leo S II; 4, Reynolds Patrick L; 5, Hushion Michael E; 6, Lafavers Laurie; 7, Ciresa Martin E

NINTH RACE

Hollywood

DECEMBER 21, 2003

1¹⁄₁₆ MILES. (1.40) HOLLYWOOD STARLET S. Grade I. Purse $200,000 (plus $10,000 Other Sources) FOR FILLIES TWO YEARS OLD (FOALS OF 2001). By subscription of $250 each on or before Friday, May 16, 2003. Fee to accompany subscription. To remain eligible the following payment must be made: $500 on or before July 9, 2003. Original nominees to pay $2,500 to pass entry box and an additional $2,500 to start. A total of $10,000 in nominator awards will be distributed: Horses made eligible to the Starlet by way of supplementary nominations are not eligible to receive nominator awards. Any nominator awards not paid will be added back into the gross purse of the Starlet. Closed with 170 original nominations. Closed with 106 sustaining nominations on July 9. Supplemental Nominations of $10,000: HOUSE OF FORTUNE, RAHY DOLLY.

Value of Race: $349,500 Winner $209,700; second $41,940; third $41,940; fourth $20,970; fifth $6,990. Mutuel Pool $441,483.00 Exacta Pool $255,219.00 Quinella Pool $22,187.00 Trifecta Pool $299,407.00

Last Raced	Horse	M/Eqt. A. Wt	PP	St	¼	½	¾	Str	Fin	Jockey	Odds $1
25Oct03 3SA4	Hollywood Story	LB b 2 120	4	5	6	6	3hd	23	12¾	Valenzuela P A	6.30
9Nov03 1SA1	Rahy Dolly	LB b 2 120	6	3	11½	1hd	13	11	24½	Valdivia J Jr	3.30
8Nov03 7SA1	House of Fortune	LB 2 120	2	4	2½	3hd	2hd	3hd	34	Solis A O	4.10
16Nov03 3Hol1	Victory U. S. A.	LB 2 120	1	2	33	51½	44	48	49½	Flores D R	0.90
19Nov03 1Hol1	Rings and Things	2 120	5	6	53	41	6	52	510	Smith M E	13.90
25Oct03 3SA6	Dixie High	LB 2 120	3	1	4hd	2½	5½	6	6	Desormeaux K J	27.40

OFF AT 4:38 Start Good . Won driving. Track fast.

TIME :23, :46³, 1:10⁴, 1:36¹, 1:42⁴ (:23.06, :46.78, 1:10.89, 1:36.32, 1:42.87)

$2 Mutuel Prices:			
4 – HOLLYWOOD STORY	14.60	5.60	4.40
6 – RAHY DOLLY		5.80	6.00
2 – HOUSE OF FORTUNE			3.80

$1 EXACTA 4–6 PAID $38.80 $2 QUINELLA 4–6 PAID $28.80
$1 TRIFECTA 4–6–2 PAID $127.10

Dk. b or br. f, (Mar), by Wild Rush – Wife for Life , by Dynaformer . Trainer Shirreffs John. Bred by Vinery (Ky).

HOLLYWOOD STORY chased inside then a bit off the rail, split horses into the second turn, bid three deep then shifted inward entering the stretch, collared the runner-up inside the eighth pole and pulled clear under left handed urging. RAHY DOLLY had good early speed three deep, inched away and angled to the inside leaving the first turn, responded when rivals bid on the backstretch, kicked clear again on the second turn, could not hold off the winner but was clearly second best. HOUSE OF FORTUNE pulled her way between horses early then stalked outside a rival, bid between foes on the backstretch, continued between rivals on the second turn, steadied in tight behind the winner into the stretch and saved the show. VICTORY U. S. A. close up stalking the pace inside, came out in upper stretch and weakened. RINGS AND THINGS chased outside, moved up boldly four wide on the backstretch, dropped back into the second turn, angled in some leaving that turn and gave way. DIXIE HIGH chased off the rail, split horses three deep with a quick move forward on the backstretch, fell back into the second turn, drifted out some and had nothing left. The stewards conducted an inquiry into the run into the stretch but made no change when they ruled the trouble to HOUSE OF FORTUNE did not affect the original order of finish.

Owners– 1, Krikorian George; 2, Fulton Stan E; 3, Zetcher Arnold; 4, Van Meter Thomas F II; 5, Andrew Farm and Tabor Michael; 6, Peeples William R

Trainers– 1, Shirreffs John A; 2, Becerra Rafael; 3, McAnally Ronald L; 4, Baffert Bob; 5, Biancone Patrick L; 6, Kitchingman Adam

$2 Daily Double (5–4) Paid $55.20 ; Daily Double Pool $39,657 .
$1 Pick Three (9–5/9–4) Paid $286.70 ; Pick Three Pool $84,049 .

EIGHTH RACE
Santa Anita
DECEMBER 26, 2003

7 FURLONGS. (1.20) MALIBU S. Grade I. Purse $250,000 FOR THREE-YEAR-OLDS. (Foals of 2000). By subscription of $200 each to accompany the nomination or by supplementary nomination of $4,000 by time of entry. $1000 to pass the entry box and $1,500 additional to start, with $250,000 guaranteed, of which $150,000 to first, $50,000 to second, $30,000 to third, $15,000 to fourth and $5,000 to fifth. 123 lbs. Non-winners of $200,000 twice in 2003 allowed 2 lbs.; of such a race in 2003, 4 lbs.; of $100,000 in 2003 or $60,000 since September 25, 6 lbs.; of $60,000 in 2003 or $30,000 since September 25, 8 lbs. (Claiming races not considered). Starters to be named through the entry box by the closing time of entries. A trophy will be presented to the owner of the winner. Closed with 24 Nominations.

Value of Race: $250,000 Winner $150,000; second $50,000; third $30,000; fourth $15,000; fifth $5,000. Mutuel Pool $932,565.00 Exacta Pool $497,050.00 Quinella Pool $46,906.00 Trifecta Pool $500,491.00 Superfecta Pool $185,750.00

Last Raced	Horse	M/Eqt. A. Wt	PP	St	¼	½	Str	Fin	Jockey	Odds $1
2Aug03 7Dmr1	Southern Image	LB 3 115	10	7	3hd	51	32	1hd	Espinoza V	13.70
7Dec03 7Hol1	Marino Marini	LB 3 115	4	4	21½	21½	11	21	Baze T	33.90
29Nov03 9Aqu2	Midas Eyes	LB 3 119	1	9	1hd	1½	21½	33	Velazquez J R	a- 1.10
23Aug03 10Sar6	Eye of the Tiger	LB 3 117	8	8	5½	3½	41	4nk	Pedroza M A	24.00
27Nov03 7Hol1	Watchem Smokey	LB 3 119	2	10	7½	61½	71½	5½	Valenzuela P A	a- 1.10
4Oct03 4SA4	Domestic Dispute	LB 3 117	5	11	10½	9hd	81½	6½	Solis A O	42.40
27Nov03 9FG1	Posse	LB 3 119	9	3	114	103	6½	72	Lanerie C J	6.80
26May03 7Hol1	Blazonry	LB 3 117	3	12	12	12	91½	81½	Smith M E	10.30
3May03 10CD6	Buddy Gil	LB 3 121	6	6	61	4hd	5hd	92	Stevens G L	3.50
11Nov03 7Hol1	Special Rate	LB 3 117	8	5	93	82	102½	102½	Valdivia J Jr	43.20
29Nov03 9Aqu3	Toccet	LB b 3 115	11	1	8½	112	111	113½	Chavez J F	20.00
25Oct03 5SA12	Zavata	B b 3 117	12	2	4hd	7hd	12	12	Desormeaux K J	16.50

a-Coupled: Midas Eyes and Watchem Smokey.

OFF AT 3:54 Start Good . Won driving. Track fast.

TIME :222, :45, 1:091, 1:223 (:22.55, :45.08, 1:09.36, 1:22.65)

$2 Mutuel Prices:	10 – SOUTHERN IMAGE	29.40	13.00	5.60
	4 – MARINO MARINI		26.00	9.00
	1 – MIDAS EYES (a-entry)			2.80

$1 EXACTA 10-4 PAID $522.70 $2 QUINELLA 4-10 PAID $400.40
$1 TRIFECTA 10-4-1 PAID $2,007.40 $1 SUPERFECTA 10-4-1-7 PAID $13,478.60

Dk. b or br. c, (Apr), by Halo's Image – Pleasant Dixie, by Dixieland Band . Trainer Machowsky Michael. Bred by Arthur I Appleton (Fla).

SOUTHERN IMAGE stalked between horses on the backstretch and four wide into the turn, continued outside on the bend and three deep into the stretch and rallied under left handed urging to get up at the wire. MARINO MARINI had good early speed off the rail then dueled outside a rival, inched away in midstretch and held on gamely but was caught late. MIDAS EYES went up inside to duel for the lead, fought back on the turn and into the stretch and continued willingly to the end. EYE OF THE TIGER stalked the pace off the rail then between horses leaving the backstretch and on the turn and into the stretch and lacked the needed late response. WATCHEM SMOKEY chased outside a rival then along the inside, came out in upper stretch and split foes at the wire. DOMESTIC DISPUTE settled off the rail then angled in and saved ground, waited behind horses into the stretch, came out in upper stretch and could not offer the necessary late kick. POSSE dropped back outside and settled off the rail, split horses into the turn, was in a bit tight midway on the bend, came between foes into the stretch but also could not summon the needed rally. BLAZONRY unhurried off the rail on the backstretch and turn, came three deep into the stretch and failed to menace. BUDDY GIL close up stalking the pace a bit off the rail, angled in leaving the turn and weakened in the stretch. SPECIAL RATE bobbled a bit at the start, chased outside or off the rail, went between horses on the turn and three deep into the stretch and did not rally. TOCCET well placed stalking the pace wide between horses, dropped back leaving the backstretch, angled in on the turn and weakened. ZAVATA in a good position stalking the pace outside on the backstretch and four wide on the turn, came out into the stretch and had little left.

Owners- 1, Blahut Stables LLC; 2, Rancho San Miguel; 3, Gann Edmund A; 4, Gunther John D; 5, Gann Edmund A; 6, Bienstock Dave and Winner Charles; 7, Heiligbrodt Racing Stable and Vinery Stables; 8, Robertson Sanford R; 9, Desperado Stables Inc McFadden Donnie and Merrill Stables et al; 10, Juddmonte Farms Inc; 11, Borislow Daniel M; 12, Tabor Michael B

Trainers- 1, Machowsky Michael; 2, O'Neill Doug; 3, Frankel Robert J; 4, Hollendorfer Jerry; 5, Frankel Robert J; 6, Gallagher Patrick; 7, Asmussen Steven M; 8, Walsh Kathy; 9, Mullins Jeff; 10, Frankel Robert J; 11, Scanlan John F; 12, Biancone Patrick L

Scratched– Baltic Heights (11Oct03 7SA 1)

$2 Daily Double (1-10) Paid $257.00 ; Daily Double Pool $60,072 .
$1 Pick Three (1/3/5/12-1-10) Paid $679.50 ; Pick Three Pool $105,567 .

NINTH RACE
Calder
DECEMBER 27, 2003

1½ MILES. (Turf) (2.24) LA PREVOYANTE H. Grade II. Purse $200,000 FOR FILLIES AND MARES, THREE YEARS OLD AND UPWARD. By subscription of $200 each which shall accompany the nomination, $2,000 to pass the entry box and an additional $2,000 to start. This race will be limited to 12 Starters, with Also Eligibles. (High Weights Preferred). Supplemental Nominations due at time of entry with a fee of $5,000 to enter and start. Closed Saturday, December 13, 2003 with (19) nominations.

Value of Race: $200,000 Winner $120,000; second $40,000; third $22,000; fourth $12,000; fifth $6,000. Mutuel Pool $486,417.00 Exacta Pool $342,145.00 Trifecta Pool $223,816.00 Superfecta Pool $64,204.00

Last Raced	Horse	M/Eqt.	A.	Wt	PP	¼	½	1	1¼	Str	Fin	Jockey	Odds $1
15Nov03 ^{8}Aqu^{2}	Volga-Ire	L	5	119	7	5^{1}	4^{hd}	$3^{1/2}$	$2^{1/2}$	$1^{1 1/2}$	$1^{2 3/4}$	Migliore R	3.10
6Dec03 ^{5}Hol^{1}	Lady Annaliese-NZ	L	4	116	3	$3^{1 1/2}$	3^{2}	4^{1}	$4^{1/2}$	$3^{1/2}$	$2^{1 1/4}$	Coa E	3.00
6Dec03 ^{9}Crc^{4}	Lost Appeal	L b	5	115	4	11	11	$9^{1/2}$	5^{1}	4^{1}	$3^{3/4}$	Douglas R R	28.90
6Dec03 ^{5}Hol^{2}	Go On Baby	L	5	114	5	$2^{2 1/2}$	$2^{1 1/2}$	$2^{1 1/2}$	1^{1}	$2^{1/2}$	4^{2}	Bridgmohan S	15.00
25Aug03 ^{8}Sar^{1}	Sixty Seconds-NZ	L	5	116	11	9^{2}	$6^{1/2}$	5^{1}	$3^{1/2}$	$5^{1 1/2}$	$5^{1/2}$	Santos J A	5.50
6Dec03 ^{9}Crc^{1}	New Economy	L	5	116	1	7^{hd}	9^{1}	10	$7^{1 1/2}$	6^{2}	$6^{1 1/2}$	Homeister R B Jr	7.80
15Nov03 ^{8}Aqu^{4}	Mariensky	L	4	115	10	6^{1}	7^{hd}	8^{2}	$8^{2 1/2}$	7^{hd}	$7^{3 1/4}$	Blanc B	18.90
7Dec03 ^{6}Crc^{3}	Pillow Talk	L	4	114	2	4^{1}	5^{1}	6^{1}	6^{2}	8^{7}	$8^{9 1/2}$	Alvarado R Jr	77.90
24Oct03 ^{7}Bel^{1}	Shining Jewel	L	3	112	9	8^{hd}	8^{hd}	7^{hd}	9^{3}	9^{4}	9^{6}	Velazquez J R	15.30
24Oct03 ^{2}Crc^{5}	Victory Snit	L f	4	112	8	$1^{1 1/2}$	1^{3}	1^{hd}	10	10	10	Chavez J F	151.10
15Nov03 ^{8}Aqu^{1}	Spice Island	L b	4	118	6	$10^{2 1/2}$	10^{3}	—	—	—	—	Velasquez C H	3.10

OFF AT 3:54 Start Good. Won driving. Course firm.

TIME :23, :48, 1:13, 1:38^{4}, 2:03^{1}, 2:26 (:23.12, :48.00, 1:13.05, 1:38.97, 2:03.23, 2:26.13)

$2 Mutuel Prices:

7 – VOLGA–IRE	8.20	4.60	4.00
3 – LADY ANNALIESE–NZ		4.20	3.20
4 – LOST APPEAL			7.40

$2 EXACTA 7–3 PAID $42.80 $2 TRIFECTA 7–3–4 PAID $482.60
$2 SUPERFECTA 7–3–4–5 PAID $5,207.60

Dk. b or br. m, (Mar), by Caerleon – Verveine, by Lear Fan. Trainer McLaughlin Kiaran P. Bred by Allez France Stables (Ire).

VOLGA (IRE) raced unhurriedly off the hedge, bid in the three path of the final turn, dueled clear midstretch and finished with aggressive handling. LADY ANNALIESE (NZ) rated back inside, steadied approaching the final turn, lacked room through the turn, angled to the hedge entering the stretch and finished well. LOST APPEAL, unhurriedly outside, bid widest on the final turn then finished evenly. GO ON BABY rated of the pace and off the hedge, took the lead inside nearing the final turn, dueled between horses through the upper stretch then weakened the final furlong. SIXTY SECONDS (NZ) rated back toward mid track, bid through the final turn then leveled off in the drive. NEW ECONOMY was in tight on the hedge into the second turn, raced unhurriedly through the backstretch, angled out making a bid on the final turn then finished evenly outside. MARIENSKY, unhurriedly in mid track, lacked room into the final turn and finished empty outside. PILLOW TALK, unhurriedly inside, was steadied on the backstretch, made a mild bid on the final turn then gave way. SHINING JEWEL had her heels clipped into the second turn then never factored after. VICTORY SNIT rated a clear lead early, came off the hedge on the backstretch then faded abruptly into the final turn. SPICE ISLAND clipped the heels of Shining Jewel and fell into the second turn. The stewards reviewed the incident on the second turn and made no changes.

Owners– 1, J Allen; 2, Agri Harvest Inc Blue Vista Inc & R Frankel; 3, Poston Bill and Vicki; 4, Shah Stables; 5, The Leigh Family Stable; 6, R S Evans; 7, Waterville Lake Stable; 8, Backer William M; 9, Dicresce Gary P; 10, Elso George I; 11, Denlea Port Ltd

Trainers– 1, McLaughlin Kiaran P; 2, Frankel Robert J; 3, Edwards Oliver; 4, O'Neill Doug; 5, Clement Christophe; 6, Motion H Graham; 7, Clement Christophe; 8, Tagg Barclay; 9, Bond H James; 10, Thompson Yvette; 11, Pregman John S Jr

$2 Pick Three (5–8–7) Paid $402.80 ; Pick Three Pool $26,765 .

ELEVENTH RACE
Calder
DECEMBER 27, 2003

1½ MILES. (Turf) (2.24) W. L. MCKNIGHT H. Grade II. Purse $200,000 FOR THREE YEAR OLDS AND UPWARD. By subscription of $200 each which shall accompany the nomination, $2,000 to pass the entry box and an additional $2,000 to start. This race will be limited to 12 Starters, with Also Eligibles. (High Weights Preferred). Supplemental Nominations due at time of entry with a fee of $5,000 to enter and start. Closed Saturday, December 13, 2003 with (23) nominations.

Value of Race: $200,000 Winner $120,000; second $40,000; third $22,000; fourth $12,000; fifth $6,000. Mutuel Pool $454,199.00 Exacta Pool $325,702.00 Trifecta Pool $240,160.00 Superfecta Pool $79,184.00

Last Raced	Horse	M/Eqt.	A.	Wt	PP	¼	½	1	1¼	Str	Fin	Jockey	Odds $1
22Nov03 8Aqu1	Balto Star	L	5	121	2	1^{1}	$1^{1½}$	$1^{1½}$	$1^{1½}$	$1^{1½}$	$1^{1½}$	Velazquez J R	2.30
22Nov03 8Hol1	Continuously	L	4	116	8	$8^{3½}$	8^{4}	7^{2}	6^{2}	3^{1}	$2^{½}$	Coa E	3.20
16Nov03 9CD3	Rowans Park	L	3	114	7	6^{2}	6^{2}	3^{hd}	2^{hd}	2^{1}	$3^{2¼}$	Santos J A	5.20
15Nov03 5Crc4	Sir Brian's Sword	L	5	112	10	5^{hd}	5^{hd}	$6^{½}$	$7^{2½}$	$4^{1½}$	$4^{¾}$	Bravo J	32.20
27Nov03 6CD3	Prodigus-Brz	L	4	114	5	$7^{½}$	$7^{½}$	$8^{3½}$	$5^{½}$	6^{hd}	$5^{½}$	Cruz M R	44.80
11Oct03 8Bel1	ThompsonRoug-Ire	L	4	114	3	4^{1}	$4^{1½}$	$4^{½}$	$4^{½}$	5^{hd}	6^{nk}	Velasquez C H	15.10
22Nov03 8Aqu3	Cetewayo	L b	9	115	6	$10^{2½}$	$10^{2½}$	10^{3}	9^{2}	8^{hd}	7^{nk}	Douglas R R	4.00
22Nov03 8Hol4	Runaway Dancer	L	4	114	4	11	11	11	$10^{2½}$	$9^{2½}$	$8^{½}$	Garcia J A	5.90
1Dec03 5Crc1	Father Bryan's Gem	L	4	111	11	$2^{½}$	$2^{1½}$	$2^{1½}$	$3^{1½}$	$7^{1½}$	9^{2}	Castro E	58.10
22Nov03 8Aqu4	Final Prophecy	L	4	115	9	$9^{3½}$	$9^{2½}$	9^{hd}	11	11	10^{1}	Velez J A Jr	66.00
19Oct03 9WO9	Art Variety-Brz	L b	5	115	1	3^{1}	$3^{½}$	5^{1}	8^{hd}	$10^{½}$	11	Blanc B	24.10

OFF AT 4:47 Start Good. Won driving. Course firm.

TIME :24^{1}, :48^{4}, 1:13^{3}, 1:37^{2}, 2:01, 2:24^{4} (:24.36, :48.95, 1:13.60, 1:37.54, 2:01.03, 2:24.87)

$2 Mutuel Prices:			
2 – BALTO STAR	6.60	3.80	3.20
9 – CONTINUOUSLY		3.80	3.00
8 – ROWANS PARK			4.40

$2 EXACTA 2–9 PAID $25.40 $2 TRIFECTA 2–9–8 PAID $117.00
$2 SUPERFECTA 2–9–8–12 PAID $1,501.40

Dk. b or br. g, (Mar), by Glitterman – Miss Livi , by Devil's Bag . Trainer Pletcher Todd A. Bred by Anstu Stables Inc (Ky).

BALTO STAR rated the pace from the inside, was under stout pressure from the top of the stretch and responded well. CONTINUOUSLY rated back outside, bid widest on the final turn then dueled late for place. ROWANS PARK rated back in mid tack, advanced off the rail through the final turn then outfinished in the duel for place. SIR BRIAN'S SWORD, unhurriedly toward the outside, bid saving ground on the final turn, eased out for the drive then leveled off. PRODIGUS (BRZ) showed no speed and passed tiring rivals outside. THOMPSON ROUGE (IRE) rated off the pace toward the outside, gave chase in mid track on the final turn then proved empty angling in. CETEWAYO rated back toward mid track, made a mild bid then finished emptily toward the outside. RUNAWAY DANCER was steadied at the start then outrun. FATHER BRYAN'S GEM rated close in the three path then gave way. FINAL PROPHECY never factored. ART VARIETY (BRZ) rated off the early pace inside, gave chase into the final turn then faded.

Owners– 1, Anstu Stables Inc; 2, Khaled Saud b; 3, Melnyk Eugene and Laura; 4, Jeb Racing Stable Inc; 5, Late Nite Stables LLC; 6, Almaddah Abdullah S; 7, Chandler Dr John A; 8, R L Stable; 9, W Lickle; 10, Howes Dale and Jean; 11, Team Victory

Trainers– 1, Pletcher Todd A; 2, Frankel Robert J; 3, Reinstedler Anthony L; 4, Clement Christophe; 5, McPeek Kenneth G; 6, Mott William I; 7, Dickinson Michael W; 8, Hendricks Dan L; 9, Plesa Edward Jr; 10, Cibelli Jane; 11, McPeek Kenneth G

Scratched– Gran Cesare (ARG) (12Dec03 9Crc1) , Macaw (IRE) (22Nov03 8Aqu2) , In Hand (22Oct03 9Kee3)

TWELFTH RACE
Calder
DECEMBER 27, 2003

1⅛ MILES. (1.50) FRED W. HOOPER H. Grade III. Purse $100,000 FOR THREE YEAR OLDS AND UPWARD. By subscription of $100 each which shall accompany the nomination, $1,000 to pass the entry box and an additional $1,000 to start. Closed Saturday, December 13, 2003 with (13) nominations.

Value of Race: $100,000 Winner $60,000; second $20,000; third $11,000; fourth $6,000; fifth $3,000. Mutuel Pool $332,733.00 Exacta Pool $257,920.00 Trifecta Pool $210,377.00 Superfecta Pool $82,410.00

Last Raced	Horse	M/Eqt.	A.	Wt	PP	St	¼	½	¾	Str	Fin	Jockey	Odds $1
28Nov03 8Crc8	Predawn Raid	L b	4	112	2	1	$1^{1½}$	$1^{1½}$	$1^{1½}$	1^{2}	$1^{4¼}$	Chavez J F	15.40
15Nov03 12Crc1	Best of the Rest	L	8	122	9	9	$7^{1½}$	5^{hd}	5^{hd}	$3^{2½}$	2^{2}	Coa E	2.70
28Nov03 8Lrl1	Deeliteful Guy	L f	4	112	7	6	$4^{½}$	$4^{1½}$	$3^{½}$	2^{1}	$3^{2¼}$	Velazquez J R	12.00
28Nov03 11CD3	Aeneas	L	4	114	1	3	$5^{½}$	6^{1}	$6^{½}$	$4^{1½}$	4^{hd}	Boulanger G	1.10
15Dec03 5Crc2	Dancing Guy	L bf	8	113	3	4	$6^{½}$	$8^{½}$	9	$5^{½}$	$5^{5¼}$	Velez R I	31.30
15Nov03 12Crc3	The Judge Sez Who	L	4	115	4	7	8^{1}	7^{hd}	$7^{½}$	$6^{1½}$	$6^{1¾}$	Velasquez C H	5.10
27Nov03 3Aqu4	Regal Sanction	L	4	114	6	5	2^{1}	3^{hd}	4^{1}	8^{2}	$7^{3½}$	Santos J A	9.40
22Nov03 8Crc1	Demeteor	L	4	112	5	2	$3^{½}$	2^{1}	2^{hd}	$7^{1½}$	$8^{2¼}$	Homeister R B Jr	23.70
27Oct03 7Crc1	Dustys Birthday	L b	4	115	8	8	9	9	$8^{½}$	9	9	Douglas R R	59.80

OFF AT 5:13 Start Good. Won driving. Track fast.

TIME :24, :49^{1}, 1:14^{4}, 1:39^{4}, 1:52^{2} (:24.14, :49.35, 1:14.87, 1:39.92, 1:52.47)

$2 Mutuel Prices:			
2 – PREDAWN RAID	32.80	12.60	8.80
9 – BEST OF THE REST		4.80	3.40
7 – DEELITEFUL GUY			6.40

$2 EXACTA 2–9 PAID $168.80 $2 TRIFECTA 2–9–7 PAID $1,706.20
$2 SUPERFECTA 2–9–7–1 PAID $6,015.80

Gr/ro. g, (Apr), by Sir Cat – Dawn's Flame , by Grey Dawn II . Trainer Stutts Bennie F Jr. Bred by Mt Joy Stables Inc (Ky).

PREDAWN RAID rated the pace off the rail, widened his lead under a drive entering the stretch then finished with moderate hand urging. BEST OF THE REST rated off the pace outside, bid entering the stretch, reached place with a sixteenth to go and finished evenly. DEELITEFUL GUY rated off the pace in mid track, bid in the three path of the final turn then leveled out the last furlong. AENEAS, unhurriedly, bid off the rail through the final turn, was eased out entering the stretch and empty in the drive. DANCING GUY raced unhurriedly in mid track, eased out through the final turn then weakened in the lane. THE JUDGE SEZ WHO raced unhurriedly inside and offered no rally. REGAL SANCTION rated close off the rail then faded saving ground through the final turn. DEMETEOR rated close in the three path then faded on the final turn. DUSTYS BIRTHDAY was outrun.

Owners– 1, Mount Joy Stables Inc; 2, Oxenberg Beatrice; 3, C D and G Stable; 4, Pavlish Patricia; 5, Green Newcomb; 6, Sez Who Racing; 7, Moore Susan and John; 8, Hoffman Kenneth E; 9, Curry Diane and Gentry Lloyd

Trainers– 1, Stutts Bennie F Jr; 2, Plesa Edward Jr; 3, Klesaris Robert P; 4, Wolfson Martin D; 5, Green N; 6, Wolfson Milton W; 7, Jerkens James A; 8, Hoffman Kenneth E; 9, Nazareth John A Sr

---

$2 Daily Double (2–2) Paid $120.40 ; Daily Double Pool $93,298 .
$2 Pick Three (9–2–2) Paid $1,806.00 ; Pick Three Pool $48,716 .
$1 Pick Four (7–9–2–2) Paid $3,415.80 ; Pick Four Pool $238,213 .

Calder Race Course Attendance: 11,361 Mutuel Pool: $1,247,065.00 ITW Mutuel Pool: $550,612.00 ISW Mutuel Pool: $7,366,748.00

SEVENTH RACE
Santa Anita
DECEMBER 27, 2003

7 FURLONGS. (1.20) LA BREA S. Grade I. Purse $250,000 FOR FILLIES, THREE YEARS OLD. (Foals of 2000). By subscription of $200 each to accompany the nomination or by supplementary nomination of $5,000 by time of entry. $2,500 additional to start, with $250,000 guaranteed, of which $150,000 to first, $50,000 to second, $30,000 to third, $15,000 to fourth and $5,000 to fifth. 123 lbs. Non–winners of $100,000 twice in 2003 allowed 2 lbs.; of such a race in 2003 4 lbs.; of $60,000 in 2003 or $35,000 since September 25, 2003, 6 lbs.; of $30,000 at any time, 8 lbs.(Maiden and claiming races not considered). Starters to be named through the entry box by the closing time of entries. A trophy will be presented to the owner of the winner. Closed with 14 nominations.

Value of Race: $250,000 Winner $150,000; second $50,000; third $30,000; fourth $15,000; fifth $5,000. Mutuel Pool $673,907.00 Exacta Pool $389,765.00 Quinella Pool $34,716.00 Trifecta Pool $378,661.00 Superfecta Pool $133,834.00

Last Raced		Horse	M/Eqt.	A.	Wt	PP	St	¼	½	Str	Fin	Jockey	Odds $1
30Nov03	6Hol4	Island Fashion	LB b	3	123	10	2	3¹	2¹½	11½	16	Desormeaux K J	9.40
28Nov03	9Aqu1	Randaroo	LB	3	119	7	3	2hd	1hd	22½	21½	Castillo H Jr	7.00
11Oct03	8SA2	Buffythecenterfold	LB	3	119	3	9	7hd	3½	3hd	3½	Solis A O	8.40
20Nov03	7Hol1	Hope Rises	LB	3	116	2	5	6½	4hd	52½	4½	Flores D R	14.50
30Nov03	6Hol5	Acago	LB b	3	117	1	10	92½	51½	42	53½	Espinoza V	9.60
25Oct03	2SA2	Elloluv	LB	3	121	4	7	8½	91½	71½	61	Nakatani C S	1.20
29Nov03	7GG2	Bartok's Blithe	LB	3	121	9	8	10	10	9½	71	Ramsammy E	94.80
18Apr03	3SA1	Gone Exclusive	LB	3	117	5	4	4hd	8½	6hd	8½	Stevens G L	28.10
25Oct03	1SA1	Stellar	LB	3	119	8	1	1hd	6½	8hd	91½	Smith M E	25.50
24Aug03	9Dmr5	Atlantic Ocean	LB	3	121	6	6	5hd	71	10	10	Valenzuela P A	4.60

OFF AT 3:41 Start Good. Won driving. Track fast.

TIME :22³, :45², 1:09¹, 1:21³ (:22.72, :45.51, 1:09.36, 1:21.79)

	11 – ISLAND FASHION	20.80	10.60	6.40
$2 Mutuel Prices:	8 – RANDAROO		7.40	5.20
	3 – BUFFYTHECENTERFOLD			6.60

$1 EXACTA 11–8 PAID $76.50 $2 QUINELLA 8–11 PAID $103.20
$1 TRIFECTA 11–8–3 PAID $738.90 $1 SUPERFECTA 11–8–3–2 PAID $13,353.20

Gr/ro. f, (Mar), by Petionville – Danzigs Fashion , by A Native Danzig . Trainer Polanco Marcelo. Bred by Everest Stables Inc (Ky).

ISLAND FASHION angled in and dueled three deep on the backstretch and outside a rival into and on the turn, took the lead into the stretch, kicked clear under urging and proved best. RANDAROO between horses early, angled in and dueled inside, fought back on the turn, came a bit off the rail in the stretch and held second. BUFFYTHECENTERFOLD outside a rival early, was taken out and pulled her way up five wide on the backstretch and into the turn, stalked three deep on the turn and into the stretch and held third between foes late. HOPE RISES stalked the pace inside on the backstretch and turn, came out into the stretch and put in a late bid at a minor award three deep on the line. ACAGO off a bit slowly, came off the rail on the backstretch and pulled her way up four wide between foes, angled in and continued between rivals on the turn, was a bit off the rail in the stretch and could not offer the needed late kick. ELLOLUV between horses early, chased a bit off the rail, went up four wide on the turn and three deep into the stretch and lacked the needed rally. BARTOK'S BLITHE allowed to settle off the rail, went five wide into the turn, continued four wide on the bend and was not a threat. GONE EXCLUSIVE had speed off the rail then pulled her way between horses to stalk the pace, was in a bit tight a half mile out then took up sharply into the turn and weakened. STELLAR angled in and dueled between horses on the backstretch, dropped back into the turn and had little left. ATLANTIC OCEAN stalked between horses on the backstretch, steadied in tight early on the turn, dropped back, angled in and weakened thereafter.

Owners– 1, Everest Stables Inc; 2, Allen Joseph; 3, Brian Allen A and Stronach Stables; 4, Jay Em Ess Stable; 5, Wertheimer Farm LLC; 6, Reddam J Paul; 7, 5C Racing Stable LLC; 8, Milch David S; 9, Tabor Michael and Evans Edward P; 10, The Thoroughbred Corporation

Trainers– 1, Polanco Marcelo; 2, McLaughlin Kiaran P; 3, Stute Melvin F; 4, Ellis Ronald W; 5, Mandella Richard E; 6, Dollase Craig; 7, Gutierrez Jorge; 8, Vienna Darrell; 9, Biancone Patrick L; 10, Baffert Bob

Scratched– Princess V. (06Dec03 7GG 1)

$2 Daily Double (1–11) Paid $129.20 ; Daily Double Pool $41,125 .
$1 Pick Three (6–1–11) Paid $448.10 ; Pick Three Pool $116,232 .

EIGHTH RACE
Santa Anita
DECEMBER 28, 2003

1⅛ MILES. (Turf) (1.43⁴) SAN GABRIEL H. Grade II. Purse $150,000 A HANDICAP FOR THREE-YEAR-OLDS AND UPWARD. By subscription of $150 each to accompany the nomination or by supplementary nomination of $3,000 by Sunday, December 21. $1,500 additional to start, with $150,000 guaranteed, of which $90,000 to first, $30,000to second, $18,000 to third, $9,000 to fourth and $3,000 to fifth. Weights Monday, December 22. High weights preferred. Starters to be named through the entry box by the closing time of entries. A trophy will be presented to the owner of the winner. (Railat 15 feet). Closed with 19 Nominations. (Rail at 15 feet).

Value of Race: $150,000 Winner $90,000; second $30,000; third $18,000; fourth $9,000; fifth $3,000. Mutuel Pool $409,386.00 Exacta Pool $226,536.00 Quinella Pool $23,292.00 Trifecta Pool $247,523.00 Superfecta Pool $111,656.00

Last Raced	Horse	M/Eqt. A. Wt	PP	St	¼	½	¾	Str	Fin	Jockey	Odds $1
29Nov03 9Hol1	Redattore-Brz	LB 8 122	9	4	2¹	2¹½	2¹	1¹½	1²	Solis A O	1.40
8Nov03 8SA2	Continental Red	LB 7 116	4	2	8hd	8½	8¹	5¹	2²½	Stevens G L	14.10
29Oct03 5SA1	Denied	LB b 5 116	7	1	1½	1½	1hd	2²½	3hd	Espinoza V	4.00
30Sep03 STC7	French Polo-FR	LB 3 112	5	9	9	9	3½	3hd	4½	Ramsammy E	27.90
7Nov03 7SA1	Trial by Jury	LB b 4 116	2	8	4¹½	4¹	4hd	4¹½	5²	Flores D R	11.00
14Jun03 3Hol5	Blue Steller-Ire	LB 5 116	1	3	7¹½	6¹½	7¹	6¹½	6¹	Nakatani C S	5.80
5Dec03 6Hol6	Maranilla-Ire	LB bf 4 116	3	5	3½	3hd	5¹	7hd	7½	Desormeaux K J	41.80
30Nov03 9Hol7	Sign ofTheWolf-GB	LB 3 115	6	6	5hd	5hd	6½	8¹½	8½	Smith M E	11.40
27Sep03 6BM2	Fateful Dream	LB b 6 115	8	7	6½	7hd	9	9	9	Valenzuela P A	6.00

OFF AT 4:08 Start Good. Won driving. Course firm.
TIME :24, :48, 1:11⁴, 1:35⁴, 1:48 (:24.16, :48.14, 1:11.94, 1:35.89, 1:48.17)

$2 Mutuel Prices:	9 – REDATTORE–BRZ	4.80	3.40	2.60
	4 – CONTINENTAL RED		8.20	4.60
	7 – DENIED			3.60

$1 EXACTA 9–4 PAID $24.60 $2 QUINELLA 4–9 PAID $27.60
$1 TRIFECTA 9–4–7 PAID $96.00 $1 SUPERFECTA 9–4–7–5 PAID $1,747.50

B. h, (Oct), by Roi Normand – Political Intrigue , by Deputy Minister . Trainer Mandella Richard. Bred by Haras Santa Ana do Rio Grande (Brz).

REDATTORE (BRZ) angled in and prompted the pace outside a rival, gained the advantage into the stretch, kicked clear and held gamely under urging. CONTINENTAL RED chased a bit off the rail then inside on the backstretch and second turn, came out in upper stretch and closed willingly for second. DENIED angled in on the early lead, set a pressured pace inside, fought back on the second turn, could not match either of the top pair in the lane but held third. FRENCH POLO (FR) settled outside a rival, launched a bid three deep on the backstretch and into the second turn, continued outside a foe on that bend, was between horses past midstretch and was edged for the show. TRIAL BY JURY close up stalking the pace inside, came off the rail in upper stretch and missed third between foes late. BLUE STELLER (IRE) saved ground then stalked a bit off the rail, split horses into the second turn, came three deep into the stretch and lacked the needed rally. MARANILLA (IRE) close up stalking the pace outside a rival or between horses, weakened in the stretch. SIGN OF THE WOLF (GB) chased between horses then outside on the backstretch, went three deep into and on the second turn and four wide into the stretch and also weakened. FATEFUL DREAM chased outside a rival, dropped back leaving the backstretch and lacked a further response.

Owners– 1, Taunay Luis A; 2, Fitzpatrick Sharon M; 3, Blue Field U S A Inc; 4, Kirkwood Al and Saundra S; 5, Lewis Robert B and Beverly J; 6, Amerman Racing Stables LLC; 7, Reddam J Paul; 8, Vandalsfen Berend; 9, Gann Edmund A

Trainers– 1, Mandella Richard E; 2, Jory Ian P; 3, Mullins Jeff; 4, Lewis Craig A; 5, Baffert Bob; 6, Frankel Robert J; 7, Cecil Ben D; 8, Powell Leonard; 9, Frankel Robert J

$2 Daily Double (1–9) Paid $10.60 ; Daily Double Pool $39,381 .
$1 Pick Three (4–1–9) Paid $36.10 ; Pick Three Pool $75,226 .

ABOUT 6½ FURLONGS. (Turf) (1.11²) MONROVIA H. Grade III. Purse $100,000 A HANDICAP FOR FILLIES AND MARES THREE YEARS OLD AND UPWARD. By subscription of $100 each to accompany the nomination or by supplementary nomination of $2,000 by Monday, December 22. $250 to pass the entry box and $750 additional to start, with $100,000 added, The added money an all fees to be divided 60% to the winner, 20% to second, 12% to third, 6% to fourth and 2% to fifth. Weights Tuesday, December 23. Highweights preferred. Starters to be named through the entry box by the closing time of entries. Atrophy will be presented to the owner of the winner. (Rail at 15 feet.) Closed with 23 Nominations. (Rail at 15 feet.)

FIFTH RACE
Santa Anita
DECEMBER 29, 2003

Value of Race: $109,300 Winner $65,580; second $21,860; third $13,116; fourth $6,558; fifth $2,186. Mutuel Pool $231,406.00 Exacta Pool $143,641.00 Quinella Pool $12,683.00 Trifecta Pool $112,634.00 Superfecta Pool $43,467.00

Last Raced	Horse	M/Eqt. A. Wt	PP	St	¼	½	Str	Fin	Jockey	Odds $1
8Nov03 5SA4	Icantgoforthat	LB b 4 114	6	1	11½	11½	11	1no	Baze T	4.40
5Jly03 7Hol9	Polygreen-FR	LB 4 116	3	3	42	41	2hd	21	Stevens G L	a- 0.50
7Sep03 6Dmr1	Spring Star-FR	LB 4 119	4	6	6	6	51½	32	Solis A O	a- 0.50
8Nov03 5SA6	Roberta's Mango	LB 4 117	2	2	33	2hd	3hd	41	Espinoza V	6.50
14Dec03 8Hol6	Bold Roberta	LB b 5 115	1	4	2½	31	41½	51	Garcia M S	12.50
13Nov03 5Hol2	Reefs Sis-GB	LB 4 115	5	5	51	5hd	6	6	Valenzuela P A	5.30

a–Coupled: Polygreen–Fr and Spring Star–Fr.

OFF AT 2:35 Start Good . Won driving. Course firm.
TIME :22, :44¹, 1:07, 1:13 (:22.03, :44.20, 1:07.10, 1:13.07)

$2 Mutuel Prices:	8 – ICANTGOFORTHAT	10.80	3.00	3.00
	1 – POLYGREEN–FR(a–entry)		2.20	2.10
	1A – SPRING STAR–FR(a–entry)		2.20	2.10

$1 EXACTA 8–1 PAID $11.10 $2 QUINELLA 1–8 PAID $7.80
$1 TRIFECTA 8–1–4 PAID $33.10 $1 SUPERFECTA 8–1–4–2 PAID $73.00

B. f, (Mar), by In Excess–Ire – Texinadress , by Copelan . Trainer Knapp Steve. Bred by Michael E Pegram (Cal).

ICANTGOFORTHAT sped to the early lead off the rail, angled in down the hill, set the pace inside and held on gamely along the fence under urging. POLYGREEN (FR) saved ground stalking the pace, came out in upper stretch, drew alongside the winner past midstretch and continued gamely but could not get by. SPRING STAR (FR) squeezed at the start, angled in and saved ground down the hill, swung out on the dirt and three deep into the stretch and finished well. ROBERTA'S MANGO stalked outside a rival down the hill, also came three deep into the stretch and lacked the needed rally. BOLD ROBERTA angled in and stalked the winner inside on the hill, came out between horses crossing the dirt and into the stretch and weakened in the final furlong. REEFS SIS (GB) chased outside a rival down the hill, came out four wide into the stretch and also weakened. Rail on hill at 7 feet.

Owners– 1, Broberg Andy and Knapp Palmer; 2, Frere and Wertheimer; 3, Frere and Wertheimer; 4, Lucky Ladies Stable LLC; 5, S L U Inc; 6, Vreeland James R

Trainers– 1, Knapp Steve; 2, Mandella Richard E; 3, Mandella Richard E; 4, Canani Julio C; 5, Warren Donald; 6, Walsh Kathy

Scratched– Honest Answer (15Oct03 7SA 1) , Sweetcakesanshakes (08Nov03 5SA 3) , Dedication (FR) (30Nov03 6Hol3) , Dreamers Glory (27Nov03 3Hol4)

$2 Daily Double (8–8) Paid $51.40 ; Daily Double Pool $16,336 .
$1 Pick Three (2/6–8–8) Paid $61.20 ; Pick Three Pool $44,185 .

CANADIAN GRADED STAKES

EIGHTH RACE
Woodbine
APRIL 26, 2003

7 FURLONGS. (1.20^3) 48th Running of THE VIGIL HANDICAP. Grade III. Purse $150,000 For FOUR YEAR OLDS AND UPWARD. By subscription of $150 each which shall accompany the nomination and an additional $1,500 when making entry; with $150,000 added, plus all fees to be divided: 60% to the winner, 20% to second, 11% to third, 6% to fourth and 3% to fifth. Weights Saturday, April 19. Closed Wednesday, April 9, 2003 with 28 nominations. Final entries to be made through the entry box no later than 11:30 a.m. on Wednesday April 23, 2003. Plus up to $8,800 Breeder Awards.

Value of Race: $164,700 Winner $98,820; second $32,940; third $18,117; fourth $9,882; fifth $4,941. Mutuel Pool $134,504.00 Triactor Pool $78,377.00 Exactor Pool $63,263.00

Last Raced	Horse	M/Eqt.	A.	Wt	PP	St	¼	½	Str	Fin	Jockey	Odds $1
22Mar03 ^{8}WO^4	Wake At Noon	Lbf	6	124	3	6	4^2	1½	12½	13¼	Ramsammy E	1.70
14Sep02 ^{8}WO^3	Shaws Creek	L	4	114	1	7	6^1	6^1	42½	2^2	Montpellier C	25.50
30Nov02 ^{8}WO^1	Cheap Talk	Lb	4	120	4	4	5^{hd}	5^1	2½	31¾	Husbands P	4.35
11Apr03 ^{8}WO^3	Forever Grand	Lb	4	115	6	2	1^{hd}	4^1	31½	44¼	Kabel T K	11.15
22Mar03 ^{8}WO^3	Davids Expectation	Lb	4	114	5	1	3^{hd}	3^{hd}	5½	51¼	McKnight J	11.55
22Mar03 ^{8}WO^1	Krz Ruckus	b	6	119	2	5	2^{hd}	2^{hd}	6^2	61¾	Luciani D	4.10
16Nov02 ^{10}Lrl^6	Boston Common	L	4	123	7	3	7	7	7	7	Sutherland C	2.85

OFF AT 4:32 Start Good. Won driving. Track fast.
TIME :22, :44^2, 1:09^4, 1:23^1 (:22.15, :44.44, 1:09.88, 1:23.25)

$2 Mutuel Prices:

3–WAKE AT NOON	5.40	3.40	2.60
1–SHAWS CREEK		13.60	5.30
4–CHEAP TALK			3.40

$2 TRIACTOR 3–1–4 PAID $390.60 $2 EXACTOR 3–1 PAID $102.20

Ch. h, by Cure the Blues–Sermon Time, by Silver Deputy. Trainer Katryan Abraham R. Bred by Schickedanz Bruno (Ont–C).

WAKE AT NOON dueled between KRZ RUCKUS and DAVIDS EXPECTATION while off the rail, gained command early on the turn, drew off through the stretch. SHAWS CREEK bumped at the start, stalked the duel from off the rail, came three wide into the stretch, angled out just past the eighth pole, got up for place five wide late, was vanned off after the race. CHEAP TALK stalked the duel four wide, advanced five wide on the turn, flattened out in the stretch. FOREVER GRAND vied for the early lead, pressed the pace four wide, tired into the stretch. DAVIDS EXPECTATION vied for the early lead, pressed the pace three wide, tired on the turn. KRZ RUCKUS bumped at the start, dueled inside the winner, gave way on the turn. BOSTON COMMON trailed while five wide.

Owners— 1, Schickedanz Bruno; 2, Jam Jar Racing Stable; 3, Lottridge T & Tiller R P; 4, DiGiulio Frank & Tiller R P Jr; 5, Mockingbird Farm Inc; 6, Guidolin R & Partners; 7, Englander Richard A

Trainers—1, Katryan Abraham R; 2, Ross John A; 3, Tiller Robert P; 4, Tiller Robert P; 5, Casse Mark; 6, DePaulo Michael P; 7, Wright Michael Jr

$1 Pick Three (6–8–3) Paid $23.75; Pick Three Pool $10,187.

EIGHTH RACE
Woodbine
MAY 10, 2003

1$\frac{1}{16}$ MILES. (1.40^4) 48th Running of THE ECLIPSE HANDICAP. Grade III. Purse $150,000 FOR FOUR YEAR OLDS AND UPWARD. By subscription of $150 each which shall accompany the nomination and an additional $1,500 when making entry; with $150,000 added, plus all fees to be divided: 60% to the winner, 20% to second, 11% to third, 6% to fourth and 3% to fifth. Weights Saturday, May 3. Final entries to be made through the entry box no later than 11:30 a.m. on Wednesday, May 7. Closed Wednesday, April 23, 2003 with 31 nominations. Plus up to $11,575 Breeder Awards.

Value of Race: $172,650 Winner $103,590; second $34,530; third $18,992; fourth $10,359; fifth $5,179. Mutuel Pool $143,368.00 Triactor Pool $87,194.00 Exactor Pool $71,386.00

Last Raced	Horse	M/Eqt.	A.	Wt	PP	St	¼	½	¾	Str	Fin	Jockey	Odds $1
27Apr03 ^{1}WO^1	Phantom Light	Lb	4	114	4	1	2½	2^1	1½	11½	11½	Landry R C	5.00
26Apr03 ^{9}WO^2	No Comprende	Lb	5	113	5	12	12	12	111½	3^{hd}	22¼	McKnight J	5.10
26Apr03 ^{9}WO^3	Anglian Prince	Lb	4	116	6	3	4^{hd}	4^1	41½	2^3	3^1	Barton J	12.90
26Apr03 ^{9}WO^7	Four Alert	Lb	6	115	8	6	61½	51½	5^{hd}	4^2	4^2	Sutherland C	32.65
26Apr03 ^{9}WO^5	Tails Of The Crypt	Lb	4	115	2	11	11^2	112½	101½	5^1	5¾	Clark D	22.70
13Feb03 ^{9}GP^7	Malmaison	Lb	4	113	12	9	82½	6^{hd}	6^{hd}	6^1	6^2	Somsanith N	25.30
1Dec02 ^{10}WO^1	Attest	L	7	115	11	10	102½	10^1	8½	81½	7^1	McAleney J S	9.40
26Apr03 ^{9}WO^6	Lil Personalitee	L	6	117	7	7	9^2	9½	9½	10½	8¾	Husbands P	16.45
3Mar02 ^{9}FG^6	Kiss A Native	Lb	6	119	10	8	7^{hd}	7^{hd}	71½	9^{hd}	9no	Ramsammy E	5.45
26Apr03 ^{9}WO^1	Tempered Appeal	Lbf	6	116	3	2	1½	1^{hd}	2^1	7½	102¼	Ellis S	8.95
19Apr03 ^{5}Kee^1	Indy Lead	Lb	5	114	1	5	5^{hd}	81½	12	12	111½	Kabel T K	3.10
19Apr03 ^{1}WO^1	Chris's Bad Boy	Lf	6	117	9	4	3^1	3½	3^{hd}	11^2	12	Jones Jono	21.70

OFF AT 4:37 Start Good. Won driving. Track fast.
TIME :23, :46^4, 1:11^4, 1:37, 1:43^3 (:23.15, :46.94, 1:11.98, 1:37.19, 1:43.62)

$2 Mutuel Prices:

4–PHANTOM LIGHT	12.00	7.50	6.10
5–NO COMPRENDE		5.00	4.80
6–ANGLIAN PRINCE			7.30

$2 TRIACTOR 4–5–6 PAID $393.90 $2 EXACTOR 4–5 PAID $67.50

Gr/ro c, by Alphabet Soup–Kirby Meadow, by Meadowlake. Trainer Vella Daniel J. Bred by Adena Springs (Ont–C).

PHANTOM LIGHT pressed the pace outside of TEMPERED APPEAL, gained the lead early on the second turn, turned back a bid from ANGLIAN PRINCE heading into the stretch, drew off in upper stretch and stayed clear of the closing NO COMPRENDE. NO COMPRENDE trailed, came off the rail on the second turn to be seven wide for the drive, rallied late for the place position. ANGLIAN PRINCE stalked the forced pace from off the rail, made a three wide bid on the second turn, held his position in the stretch. FOUR ALERT was four wide on the first turn, stalked the forced pace three wide, made a bid five wide on the second turn, flattened out in the stretch. TAILS OF THE CRYPT raced inside, rallied mildly on the second turn and through the stretch. MALMAISON was four wide throughout. ATTEST raced three wide, rallied five wide on the second turn, checked in upper stretch when squeezed between NO COMPRNDE and MALMAISION. LIL PERSONALITEE raced off the rail and was not a threat. KISS A NATIVE was well placed three wide, dropped back on the second turn. TEMPERED APPEAL set a pressured pace inside the winner, gave way on the second turn. INDY LEAD stalked the forced pace from the inside, was well placed in the backstretch, faded on the second turn. CHRIS'S BAD BOY was four wide on the first turn, pressed the pace three wide outside the winner, gave way into the stretch and faded.

Owners— 1, Stronach Stable; 2, Clarity Stables; 3, Prime Acres Inc; 4, Englander Richard A; 5, Jam Jar Racing Stable; 6, Haras Santa Maria de Araras; 7, Sangara K K; 8, California Stable; 9, Franks John; 10, Schickedanz Bruno; 11, Fipke Charles E; 12, Alpine Stable

Trainers—1, Vella Daniel J; 2, Smith James J; 3, Hardy James M; 4, Wright Michael Jr; 5, Ross John A; 6, Attfield Roger L; 7, Richards Lorne; 8, Cardella John; 9, Bell David R; 10, Katryan Abraham R; 11, Attfield Roger L; 12, Armata Vito

$1 Pick Three (4–6–4) Paid $287.95; Pick Three Pool $8,376.

EIGHTH RACE
Woodbine
MAY 11, 2003

6½ FURLONGS. (1.14^{3}) 29th Running of THE GEORGE C. HENDRIE HANDICAP. Grade III. Purse $150,000 For FILLIES AND MARES, FOUR YEAR OLDS AND UPWARD. By subscription of $150 each which shall accompany the nomination and an additional $1,500 when making entry; with $150,000 added and an additional $50,000 for Canadian Breds, plus all fees to be divided:60% to the winner, 20% to second, 11% to third, 6% to fourth and 3% to fifth. Weights Saturday, May 3. Final entries to be made through the entry box no later than 11:30 a.m. on Thursday, May 8, 2003. Plus $50,000 for Canadian Breds from the Thoroughbred Improvement Program and the Canadian Thoroughbred Horse Society. Closed Wednesday, April 23, 2003 with 23 nominations. Plus up to $11,575 Breeder Awards.

Value of Race: $182,950 Winner $103,770; second $34,590; third $24,525; fourth $13,377; fifth $6,688. Mutuel Pool $139,114.00 Triactor Pool $87,613.00 Exactor Pool $68,807.00

Last Raced	Horse	M/Eqt.	A.	Wt	PP	St	¼	½	Str	Fin	Jockey	Odds $1
27Apr03 ^{8}WO^{1}	El Prado Essence	Lb	6	120	3	10	7^{2}	4^{hd}	1^{1}	1^{4}	Husbands P	3.30
12Apr03 ^{8}WO^{4}	Leading Role	Lf	5	115	4	5	3^{hd}	2^{hd}	2^{2}	$2\frac{1}{2}$	Kabel T K	18.05
12Apr03 ^{8}WO^{1}	Brass In Pocket	L	4	120	6	6	$6\frac{1}{2}$	7^{1}	4^{1}	$31\frac{1}{4}$	Clark D	2.75
27Apr03 ^{8}WO^{2}	Mysterious Affair	Lbf	6	120	8	3	$4\frac{1}{2}$	5^{hd}	$51\frac{1}{2}$	4^{nk}	Landry R C	7.45
11Apr03 ^{4}WO^{1}	Roman Romance	L	5	115	9	4	9^{hd}	$92\frac{1}{2}$	7^{1}	5^{3}	Bahen S R	15.50
20Nov02 ^{6}WO^{1}	Sheila's Prospect	Lb	5	117	1	9	1^{hd}	$31\frac{1}{2}$	3^{1}	6no	McAleney J S	10.05
27Apr03 ^{8}WO^{4}	Mulrainy	Lb	4	118	10	2	5^{hd}	$6\frac{1}{2}$	8^{hd}	$7\frac{1}{2}$	Sutherland C	16.30
11Apr03 ^{4}WO^{3}	Miss Sweep	Lb	5	115	2	8	$2\frac{1}{2}$	1^{hd}	6^{1}	$81\frac{1}{2}$	Todd F Jr	29.40
20Nov02 ^{6}WO^{3}	Lightning Pace	L	5	114	5	7	10^{15}	8^{3}	9^{5}	$98\frac{1}{4}$	Ramsammy E	16.65
5Aug02 ^{8}WO^{3}	Ginger Gold	L	4	119	11	1	8^{hd}	10^{10}	10^{7}	$106\frac{3}{4}$	Dos Ramos R A	3.35
3May03 ^{6}FE^{1}	La Ballerine	Lf	4	115	7	11	11	11	11	11	Lauzon J M	90.50

OFF AT 4:40 Start Good For All But LA BALLERINE Won driving. Track good.
TIME :21^{3}, :43^{4}, 1:08^{4}, 1:15^{3} (:21.65, :43.95, 1:08.98, 1:15.66)

$2 Mutuel Prices:			
5-EL PRADO ESSENCE	8.60	4.10	3.40
6-LEADING ROLE		17.30	10.40
8-BRASS IN POCKET			4.10

$2 TRIACTOR 5-6-8 PAID $481.00 $2 EXACTOR 5-6 PAID $123.80

Ch. m, by El Prado*Ire–Quadrahope, by Quadratic. Trainer Cappuccitti Audre. Bred by Kenneth C Duncan & Neil R Phelps (Ky).

EL PRADO ESSENCE stalked the duel from the inside, came off the rail on the turn to be five wide for the drive, rallied and gained command in mid stretch, drew off under a drive. LEADING ROLE pressed the pace three wide, dueled on the turn, held the place position. BRASS IN POCKET broke outwards slamming into LA BALLERINE, chased four wide, was in tight late on the turn, finished well. MYSTERIOUS AFFAIR chased five wide, gave way into the stretch. ROMAN ROMANCE raced four wide, rallied late three wide. SHEILA'S PROSPECT came through inside to duel with MISS SWEEP, gave way in upper stretch. MULRAINY chased six wide, tired into the stretch. MISS SWEEP dueled outside of SHELIA'S PROSPECT, was between horses on the turn, tired in upper stretch. LIGHTNING PACE steadied leaving the chute, raced off the rail, dropped back in the stretch. GINGER GOLD was five wide and faded on the turn. LA BALLERINE slammed at the break, outrun while three wide.

Owners— 1, Cappuccitti Audre & Gordon; 2, Colne Farm Casselman Gail & Mitchel; 3, DiGiulio Frank D Jr; 4, Hardy James M; 5, Payer Dennis Dean & Michael & DeLuc; 6, Sangara K K; 7, Wings of Erin Farm; 8, Gemini Farms & Kerrio V A; 9, Alpine Stable; 10, Jim Dandy Stable; 11, Lizotte Jeannette

Trainers—1, Cappuccitti Audre; 2, Casselman Gail; 3, Tiller Robert P; 4, Hardy James M; 5, Simms John C; 6, Richards Lorne; 7, O'Keefe Thomas; 8, Biamonte Ralph J; 9, Armata Vito; 10, Attard Sid C; 11, Scheffer Denis

Scratched— Devastating (12Apr03 ^{8}WO^{7}), Spanish Decree (12Apr03 ^{10}WO^{1})

$1 Pick Three (1-3-5) Paid $135.90; Pick Three Pool $10,302.

EIGHTH RACE
Woodbine
MAY 17, 2003

1$\frac{1}{16}$ MILES. (1.40^{4}) 48th Running of THE MARINE. Grade III. Purse $150,000 FOR THREE-YEAR-OLDS. By subscription of $150 each which shall accompany the nomination and an additional $1,500 when making entry; with $150,000 added, plus all fees to be divided: 60% to the winner, 20% to second, 11% to third, 6% to fourth and 3% to fifth. Weight 124 lbs. Non-winners of a sweepstakes of $75,000 three times at a mile or over, 3 lbs. Of a sweepstakes of $75,000 twice at a mile or over, 5 lbs.; Of a sweepstakes of $75,000 once at a mile or over or a sweepstakes of $75,000 twice at any distance, 7 lbs; of a sweepstakes of $75,000 once, 9 lbs. (No Canadian Bred Allowance) Final entries to be made through the entry box no later than 11:30 a.m. on Wednesday, May 14,2003. Closed Wednesday, April 30, 2003 with 32 nominations. Plus up to $11,575 Breeder Awards.

Value of Race: $163,800 Winner $98,280; second $32,760; third $18,018; fourth $9,828; fifth $4,914. Mutuel Pool $180,570.00 Triactor Pool $81,251.00 Exactor Pool $82,872.00

Last Raced	Horse	M/Eqt.	A.	Wt	PP	St	¼	½	¾	Str	Fin	Jockey	Odds $1
19Apr03 ^{8}WO^{1}	Wando	L	3	119	3	2	1^{hd}	$1\frac{1}{2}$	$1\frac{1}{2}$	$12\frac{1}{2}$	$14\frac{1}{2}$	Kabel T K	0.65
19Apr03 ^{8}WO^{3}	El Ruller	Lb	3	117	6	6	$32\frac{1}{2}$	3^{2}	2^{1}	2^{4}	$22\frac{3}{4}$	Sabourin R B	24.65
2Nov02 ^{9}WO^{2}	Arco's Gold	L	3	119	5	3	5^{3}	$52\frac{1}{2}$	$52\frac{1}{2}$	3^{hd}	$33\frac{1}{2}$	Montpellier C	5.00
10May03 ^{1}Hst^{1}	Illusive Force	L	3	119	2	4	2^{1}	2^{hd}	$32\frac{1}{2}$	4^{5}	$44\frac{3}{4}$	Wilson D H	12.35
4Apr03 ^{8}Kee^{5}	Strizzi	L	3	115	4	1	$4\frac{1}{2}$	$43\frac{1}{2}$	4^{2}	5^{2}	$5\frac{3}{4}$	Ramsammy E	11.40
3May03 ^{9}WO^{2}	Quiet Dare	L	3	115	1	5	6	6	6	6	6	Clark D	3.00

OFF AT 4:38 Start Good. Won driving. Track fast.
TIME :22^{4}, :46^{1}, 1:11, 1:36, 1:42^{3} (:22.80, :46.28, 1:11.11, 1:36.14, 1:42.61)

$2 Mutuel Prices:			
3-WANDO	3.30	2.70	2.20
6-EL RULLER		11.40	5.00
5-ARCO'S GOLD			3.10

$2 TRIACTOR 3-6-5 PAID $124.80 $2 EXACTOR 3-6 PAID $25.40

Ch. c, (Feb), by Langfuhr–Kathie's Colleen, by Woodman. Trainer Keogh Michael. Bred by Gustav Schickedanz (Ont-C).

WANDO vied for the early lead with ILLUSIVE FORCE while off the rail, controlled the pace under pressure outside of that one in the backstretch, turned back a bid from EL RULLER on the second turn, drew off in upper stretch. EL RULLER was three wide on the first turn, stalked the forced pace from off the rail, made a bid three wide on the second turn, came up second best. ARCO'S GOLD was three wide on the first turn, raced inside through the backstretch, advanced on the second turn, came off the rail heading into the stretch and continued to rally mildly to gain the show position. ILLUSIVE FORCE vied for the early lead inside of the winner, pressed the pace in the backstretch, gave way on the second turn. STRIZZI was well placed inside, came out three wide on the second turn, and dropped back. QUIET DARE trailed, advanced mildly three wide late in the backstretch, was four wide on the second turn.

Owners— 1, Schickedanz Gustav; 2, Spindler L Silvera Arthur & Moldofs; 3, DiIorio Alex & Steven; 4, Canyon Farms; 5, Stronach Stable; 6, Augustin Stable

Trainers—1, Keogh Michael; 2, Silvera Arthur; 3, Ross John A; 4, VanOverschot Robert; 5, Pierce Malcolm; 6, Benson MacDonald

$1 Pick Three (4-5-3) Paid $28.35; Pick Three Pool $12,372.

EIGHTH RACE
Woodbine
MAY 19, 2003

1¹⁄₁₆ MILES. (1.40⁴) 50th Running of THE SELENE. Grade I. Purse $250,000 For THREE-YEAR-OLD FILLIES. By subscription of $250 each which shall accompany the nomination and an additional $2,500 when making entry. Weight 123 lbs. Non-winners of a sweepstakes of $75,000 twice at a mile or over, 3 lbs.; Of a sweepstakes of $75,000 once at a mile or over, 5 lbs.; Of a sweepstakes of $75,000 at any distance, 7 lbs. (No Canadian Bred Allowance.) Closed Wednesday, April 30, 2003 with 21nominations. Includes $25,000 from the Thoroughbred Improvement Program and the Canadian Thoroughbred Horse Society. Plus up to $17,457 Breeder Awards.

Value of Race: $277,750 Winner $166,650; second $55,550; third $30,553; fourth $16,665; fifth $8,332. Mutuel Pool $190,973.00 Triactor Pool $127,476.00 Exactor Pool $108,378.00

Last Raced	Horse	M/Eqt.	A.Wt	PP	St	¼	½	¾	Str	Fin	Jockey	Odds $1
20Apr03 7WO¹	Too Late Now		3 116	5	3	4¹½	5½	3hd	2hd	1²½	Landry R C	5.80
5Apr03 8WO⁵	Handpainted	L	3 118	6	6	3¹½	2½	2¹½	1hd	2²	Husbands P	9.15
2May03 8WO¹	Winter Garden	L	3 118	4	1	2hd	1½	1hd	3⁴	3¹¼	Sutherland C	3.70
25Apr03 10Kee¹	Seeking The Ring	L	3 116	2	8	5¹	4hd	4²	5¹	4½	Kabel T K	3.60
4May03 8WO²	Mountain Dawn	L	3 116	8	5	8³	6½	5½	4hd	5³½	Clark D	9.45
20Apr03 8WO⁴	Santerra	Lf	3 120	1	2	7hd	8⁵	8¹½	7²	6nk	Montpellier C	44.70
9Apr03 5Kee²	Theology	Lb	3 116	7	9	6hd	7¹	6²½	6¹½	7²¾	Coa E M	1.90
20Apr03 8WO¹	Deputy Cures Blues	Lb	3 116	3	7	9	9	9	8¹	8no	Ramsammy E	25.20
8Mar03 7DeD⁴	Cat's Cat	Lb	3 116	9	4	1hd	3¹	7hd	9	9	Lovato F Jr	26.15

OFF AT 4:35 Start Good For All But SEEKING THE RING, DEPUTY CURES BLUES Won driving. Track fast.
TIME :22⁴, :46³, 1:12, 1:37⁴, 1:44¹ (:22.98, :46.78, 1:12.12, 1:37.92, 1:44.36)

$2 Mutuel Prices:

5-TOO LATE NOW	13.60	9.20	6.00
6-HANDPAINTED		9.20	5.50
4-WINTER GARDEN			4.50

$2 TRIACTOR 5-6-4 PAID $748.90 $2 EXACTOR 5-6 PAID $143.20

B. f, (Mar), by Raj Waki-Half of Everything, by Ten Gold Pots. Trainer Day James E. Bred by James E Day (Ont-C).

TOO LATE NOW steadied heading into the first turn, stalked the forced pace from off the rail, gained command in mid stretch and drew off. HANDPAINTED bumped at the start, vied for the lead three wide on the first turn, pressed the pace outside of WINTER GARDEN in the backstretch, gained a short lead going into the second turn, dueled with WINTER GARDEN from the midway point of the final turn until putting that one away in mid stretch, was over taken by the winner as she gained the place position. WINTER GARDEN vied for the lead from the inside, gained the lead heading into the backstretch, was headed going into the second turn, dueled with the runner up, gave way in mid stretch. SEEKING THE RING bumped and steadied at the start, raced off the rail, advanced four wide on the second turn to reach contention but was unable to stay with the leaders in the stretch. MOUNTAIN DAWN was carried out slightly on the first turn, raced three wide, advanced four wide on the second turn, and could gain no further in the stretch. SANTERRA bumped at the start, was well placed inside, came out three wide on the second turn, and was not a threat. THEOLOGY bumped at the start, steadied and veered out slightly on the first turn, raced off the rail, advanced mildly three wide on the second turn. DEPUTY CURES BLUES had an awkward start, checked heading into the first turn, trailed, passed a tired one three wide. CAT'S CAT vied for the lead while between horses on the first turn, stalked the forced pace from the inside in the backstretch, faded on the second turn.

Owners— 1, Come By Chance Stable; 2, Sikura John & Glen; 3, DiGiulio Frank D Jr; 4, Sam-Son Farms; 5, Ambler M & Partners; 6, Burnett Theodore F; 7, Clifton William L Jr; 8, Chambers Herbert W; 9, Frankel Gerald

Trainers—1, Day James E; 2, Carroll Josie; 3, Tiller Robert P; 4, Frostad Mark; 5, Benson MacDonald; 6, Mattine Michael; 7, Bond Harold James; 8, McCulloch Scott; 9, Stidham Michael

$1 Pick Three (4-9-5) Paid $2,460.40; Pick Three Pool $14,570.

EIGHTH RACE

Woodbine

MAY 24, 2003

1 1/16 MILES. (Turf)(1.39[1]) 69th Running of THE CONNAUGHT CUP. Grade III. Purse $150,000 FOUR YEAR OLDS AND UPWARD. By subscription of $150 each which shall accompany the nomination and an additional $1,500 when making entry; with $150,000 added plus all fees to be divided: 60% to the winner, 20% to second, 11% to third, 6% to fourth and 3% to fifth. Weight 124 lbs. Non-winners of a sweepstakes of $75,000 three times at a mile or over in 2002–2003, 3 lbs.; Of a sweepstakes of $75,000 twice at a mile or over in 2002–2003, 5 lbs.; Of a sweepstakes of $75,000 once at a mile or over in 2002–2003,7 lbs. Final entries to be made through the entry box no later than 11:30 a.m. on Wednesday, May 21, 2003. Plus up to $11,575 Breeder Awards. Closed Wednesday, May 7, 2003 with 37 nominations.

Value of Race: $173,550 Winner $104,130; second $34,710; third $19,091; fourth $10,413; fifth $5,206. Mutuel Pool $135,385.00 Triactor Pool $84,392.00 Exactor Pool $60,227.00

Last Raced	Horse	M/Eqt.	A.Wt	PP	St	1/4	1/2	3/4	Str	Fin	Jockey	Odds $1
13Apr03 7Kee3	Fly Smartly	L b	5 117	10	2	6 1/2	5hd	5 1/2	1hd	1 3/4	Kabel T K	6.30
4May03 10Tam2	Solitary Dancer	L	7 117	3	5	5 1	4 1/2	4 1	2 1	2nk	Husbands P	16.45
16May03 8WO5	Mr. Sulu	L	5 117	9	7	10 1 1/2	10 1	9 2 1/2	6hd	3 1 1/4	Landry R C	11.75
19Apr03 7Kee3	Red Sea-GB	L	7 117	2	11	7 1/2	7 2 1/2	7hd	5 1 1/2	4 3/4	Jones Jono	2.80
17Nov02 9CD7	Stage Classic	L b	5 117	8	4	3 1/2	3hd	3hd	7 3 1/2	5 1	Montpellier C	11.20
10May03 8WO5	Tails Of The Crypt	L b	4 119	4	6	9 1 1/2	9hd	10 1 1/2	9 1 1/2	6hd	Clark D	20.55
10May03 8WO3	Anglian Prince	L b	4 119	5	10	8 2	8 4 1/2	6 2 1/2	8 1/2	7 1 1/4	McAleney J S	14.00
30Nov02 10WO1	Silver Spear	L b	5 117	1	8	2hd	1hd	1hd	4hd	8 1/2	Sabourin R B	4.15
3Nov02 6WO5	Le Cinquieme Essai	L	4 119	6	1	1 1/2	2 1 1/2	2 1 1/2	3hd	9 2 3/4	McKnight J	6.60
16May03 8WO4	Academic	L b	6 117	7	9	11	11	11	10 1/2	10nk	Olguin G L	7.25
24Mar03 9FG7	Gone Fishin	L f	7 117	11	3	4 1/2	6hd	8 1 1/2	11	11	Callaghan S	31.40

OFF AT 4:37 Start Good For All But MR. SULU Won driving. Course soft.

TIME :25, :49⁴, 1:14⁴, 1:40⁴, 1:47³ (:25.13, :49.94, 1:14.98, 1:40.85, 1:47.71)

$2 Mutuel Prices:

11–FLY SMARTLY	14.60	8.80	6.40
3–SOLITARY DANCER		16.10	10.00
10–MR. SULU			8.20

$2 TRIACTOR 11–3–10 PAID $3,350.80 $2 EXACTOR 11–3 PAID $300.00

B. g, by Smart Strike–Spinnakers Flying, by Grey Dawn II. Trainer Frostad Mark. Bred by Sam–Son Farm (Ont–C).

FLY SMARTLY well placed three wide, was between horses on the turn, rallied four wide, bumped with the runner up in the stretch, prevailed. SOLITARY DANCER stalked the duel from off the rail, bumped with the winner in the stretch, gave his best three wide. MR. SULU bobbled at the start, raced three wide, bumped ANGLIAN PRINCE in upper stretch, rallied five wide. RED SEA (GB) well placed inside, waited for running room heading into the stretch, came off the rail in upper stretch and finished well three wide. STAGE CLASSIC pressed the early pace three wide, stalked the duel, finished evenly. TAILS OF THE CRYPT bumped at the start, raced inside, rallied mildly four wide. ANGLIAN PRINCE bumped at the start, was three wide, bumped by MR SULU and checked in upper stretch, gained mildly four wide. SILVER SPEAR came through inside to duel with LE CINQUIEME ESSAI, gave way in mid stretch. LE CINQUIEME ESSAI had a short lead early, dueled outside of SILVER SPEAR, gave way in mid stretch. ACADEMIC trailed while wide, passed a tired one. GONE FISHIN stalked the duel four wide, dropped back in the stretch.

Owners— 1, Sam-Son Farms; 2, Franks John; 3, McMurray A L & Carroll Josie; 4, Werner William Windhaven Farm & Att; 5, Dominion Bloodstock Ball Derek & Ga; 6, Jam Jar Racing Stable; 7, Prime Acres Inc; 8, Stronach Stable; 9, William Scott; 10, Cardella John; 11, Springfield Stable & Dura Racing

Trainers—1, Frostad Mark; 2, Giliforte Layne S; 3, Carroll Josie; 4, Attfield Roger L; 5, Cotey David; 6, Ross John A; 7, Hardy James M; 8, Pierce Malcolm; 9, Nielsen Paul; 10, Cardella John; 11, Doyle Michael J

$1 Pick Three (1–1–11) Paid $7,716.95; Pick Three Pool $10,488.

EIGHTH RACE

Woodbine

JUNE 1, 2003

$1\frac{1}{16}$ MILES. (Turf)(1.39[1]) 48th Running of THE NASSAU. Grade II. Purse $250,000 (plus $50,000 Other Sources) For FILLIES AND MARES, THREE YEAR OLDS AND UPWARD. By subscription of $200 each which shall accompany the nomination and an additional $2, 000 when making entry. Weight: Three year olds 117 lbs.; Older 124 lbs. Non–winners of a sweepstakes of $75,000 three times at a mile or over in 2002–2003, 3 lbs.; Of a sweepstakes of $75,000 twiceat a mile or over in 2002–2003, 5 lbs.; Of a sweepstakes of $75,000 once at a mile or over in 2002 –2003, 7 lbs.; Of $53,400 at a mile or over in 2002–2003, 9 lbs. (No Canadian Br ed Allowance) (Maiden or claiming races not considered). Final entries to be made through the entry box no later than 11:30 a.m. on Thursday, May 29, 2003. Plus $50,000 for Canadian Breds from the Thoroughbred Improvement Program and Canadian Thoroughbred Horse Society. Plus up to $14,612 Breeder Awards. Closed May 14, 2003 with 41 nominations.

Value of Race: $296,700 Winner $166,920; second $65,640; third $36,102; fourth $19,692; fifth $8,346. Mutuel Pool $191,246.00 Triactor Pool $122,769.00 Exactor Pool $88,720.00

Last Raced	Horse	M/Eqt. A.Wt	PP	St	$\frac{1}{4}$	$\frac{1}{2}$	$\frac{3}{4}$	Str	Fin	Jockey	Odds $1
3May03 7CD11	Strait From Texas	L 4 119	6	4	$6\frac{1}{2}$	6^3	$4\frac{1}{2}$	3^4	$1\frac{1}{2}$	Dos Ramos R A	20.75
26Oct02 7AP11	Chopinina	Lb 5 115	1	7	$2\frac{1}{2}$	$2\frac{1}{2}$	1^{hd}	$1\frac{1}{2}$	2^3	Ramsammy E	4.60
3Nov02 4WO1	Byzantine	Lb 7 117	4	9	8^1	8^{hd}	$72\frac{1}{2}$	$5\frac{1}{2}$	$3\frac{1}{2}$	Jones Jono	28.10
11May03 7WO1	One For Rose	L 4 115	9	2	3^4	3^7	2^5	$2\frac{1}{2}$	4^1	Montpellier C	31.25
18May03 7WO3	Five Fishes–FR	L 5 117	3	5	$72\frac{1}{2}$	9	9	$81\frac{1}{2}$	$5\frac{1}{2}$	Husbands P	14.80
9Apr03 9Kee1	Madame Cerito	L 4 115	2	8	9	7^{hd}	$81\frac{1}{2}$	$73\frac{1}{2}$	6^{nk}	Perret C	1.85
18May03 7WO1	Hot Talent	Lb 4 119	5	6	5^{hd}	5^{hd}	5^{hd}	$41\frac{1}{2}$	7^2	Kabel T K	1.75
16May03 7WO3	First Quarter	L 4 119	7	3	$41\frac{1}{2}$	4^{hd}	$61\frac{1}{2}$	6^{hd}	$81\frac{1}{2}$	Landry R C	8.50
11May03 8WO7	Mulrainy	Lb 4 119	8	1	1^1	1^{hd}	$32\frac{1}{2}$	9	9	Sutherland C	27.65

OFF AT 4:38 Start Good For All But ONE FOR ROSE Won driving. Course good.

TIME :23, :46, 1:10, 1:36, 1:424 (:23.17, :46.08, 1:10.09, 1:36.17, 1:42.92)

$2 Mutuel Prices:

7–STRAIT FROM TEXAS	43.50	13.70	10.00
1–CHOPININA		5.60	4.80
5–BYZANTINE			9.50

$2 TRIACTOR 7–1–5 PAID $1,349.10 $2 EXACTOR 7–1 PAID $188.70

Dk. b. or br. f, by Judge T C–Tellum Texan, by Eastern Echo. Trainer Buttigieg Paul M. Bred by Robert H Roberts & Bea Roberts (Ky).

STRAIT FROM TEXAS raced four wide, ranged up in hand heading into the stretch, was asked for run in mid stretch, and rallied to take over late. CHOPININA advanced to press the pace inside of MULRAINY, came off the rail shortly after the eleven sixteenths pole, controlled the pace on the turn under pressure, gave her best inside through the stretch while giving way late. BYZANTINE bumped at the start, raced three wide, and rallied mildly four wide. ONE FOR ROSE broke outwards, stalked the pace three wide, pressed the pace outside of the runner up on the turn, gave way in mid stretch. FIVE FISHES (FR) raced inside, gradually came off the rail on the turn to be six wide for the drive, rallied late. MADAME CERITO raced off the rail, gained mildly five wide in the stretch. HOT TALENT bumped at the start, was three wide while between horses, advanced mildly in mid stretch, was outfinished late. FIRST QUARTER raced inside, was in tight and steadied behind the fading pace setter going into the stretch, came off the rail in upper stretch and was not a threat. MULRAINY had speed to clear early while off the rail, came under pressure after two furlongs, dropped down to the rail when the runner up moved outside of her, gave way on the turn, and faded.

Owners— 1, Michael James A; 2, Knob Hill Stable; 3, Royal Oak Farm; 4, Tucci Stables; 5, Schettine William C; 6, Seitz Fredrick J; 7, Stronach Stable; 8, Come By Chance Stable & Schaedle R; 9, Wings of Erin Farm

Trainers—1, Buttigieg Paul M; 2, Fehr John Alec; 3, Pollock Bruce M; 4, Attard Sid C; 5, Carroll Josie; 6, Ward John T Jr; 7, Pierce Malcolm; 8, Day James E; 9, O'Keefe Thomas

Scratched— Mariensky (31May03 8BEL1)

NINTH RACE

Stampede Pk

JUNE 14, 2003

$1\frac{1}{16}$ MILES. (1.421) 37th Running of THE ALBERTA DERBY. Grade III. Purse $100,000 A Scale weight stakes for three year olds. By subscription of $200 each and a further payment of $1200 to pass the entry box, and an additional $600 to start. Preference will be given to horses with the highest lifetime earnings at entry time as supplied by Equibase. Field limited to twelve starters. Colts and Geldings – 121 lbs. Fillies – 116 lbs. A $10,000 bonus will be paid by the Horse Racing Alberta Breeding Support Program to any Alberta bred winner of this race. Closed Wednesday, June 4, 2003.

Value of Race: $100,000 Winner $63,000; second $20,000; third $10,000; fourth $5,000; fifth $2,000. Mutuel Pool $40,205.00 Exactor Pool $25,974.00

Last Raced	Horse	M/Eqt. A.Wt	PP	St	$\frac{1}{4}$	$\frac{1}{2}$	$\frac{3}{4}$	Str	Fin	Jockey	Odds $1
25May03 7StP1	Taiaslew	L 3 121	5	1	$1\frac{1}{2}$	$1\frac{1}{2}$	1^6	1^6	$17\frac{1}{2}$	Simard R E	0.55
31May03 4Hst1	Gamblin Caper	L 3 121	6	2	2^2	2^1	2^1	$21\frac{1}{2}$	$21\frac{1}{2}$	Wright N	2.45
31May03 2StP1	Rindanica	Lb 3 121	7	4	3^{hd}	3^{hd}	$32\frac{1}{2}$	$33\frac{1}{2}$	$31\frac{3}{4}$	Winters P A	10.95
31May03 2StP2	Beau Brass	3 121	1	7	7	7	5^{hd}	4^{hd}	$41\frac{3}{4}$	Welch Q K	35.00
25May03 7StP2	Shawteesh	3 121	3	5	5^{hd}	5^2	$41\frac{1}{2}$	5^3	$53\frac{1}{2}$	Painter L M	10.30
4Jun03 8StP5	Bet The Breeze	3 121	4	6	6^3	$6\frac{1}{2}$	7	$61\frac{1}{2}$	$65\frac{1}{2}$	Heiler Stephan	46.55
4Jun03 8StP3	Free Pour	b 3 121	2	3	$43\frac{1}{2}$	$41\frac{1}{2}$	6^1	7	7	Wong P	18.65

OFF AT 4:47 Start Good. Won handily. Track fast.

TIME :231, :464, 1:12, 1:371, 1:434 (:23.20, :46.80, 1:12.00, 1:37.20, 1:43.80)

$2 Mutuel Prices:

5–TAIASLEW	3.10	2.20	2.10
6–GAMBLIN CAPER		2.80	2.80
7–RINDANICA			2.40

$2 EXACTOR 5–6 PAID $6.50

Dk. b. or br. c, (Mar), by Slewdledo–Taiayellowribbon, by Sharper One. Trainer Tracy Greg. Bred by Dave Stark (Wash).

TAIASLEW away alertly, set pace, drew clear 1/4 pole, drew off stretch. GAMBLIN CAPER stalked pace, bid backstretch, faded 1/4 pole, held place. RINDANICA close up, evenly, dropped back 1/4 pole, evenly stretch. BEAU BRASS rail, gaining backstretch, flattened out. SHAWTEESH saved ground, no factor. BET THE BREEZE saved ground, evenly, no threat. FREE POUR rail, stalked pace early, dropped back backstretch.

Owners— 1, Tracy Shelli & Ryan Stan; 2, Yu Yan Hua & McNeil Gary; 3, Rick Robertson Engineering Ltd; 4, White Tom; 5, Michaud Denis & Normand Maurice; 6, Champagne Stables Milen Derek & Vik; 7, Lindsay Frank & Red Ron Farms

Trainers—1, Tracy Greg; 2, Jordan Terry; 3, Rycroft Riley; 4, Hedge Rick; 5, Greenwood Dale; 6, Petrowski Joan; 7, Smith Ron K

EIGHTH RACE

Woodbine

JUNE 15, 2003

1⅛ MILES. (Turf)(1.45¹) 96th Running of THE KING EDWARD BREEDERS CUP HANDICAP. Grade II. Purse $300,000 added (includes $100,000 BC – Breeders' Cup). THREE-YEAR-OLDS AND UPWARD. ($100,000 from Breeders' Cup Fund for Cup nominees only). By subscription of $300 each which shall accompany the nomination and an additional $3,000 when making entry; with $200,000 added. Breeders' Cup Fund Monies also correspondingly divided provided a Breeders' Cup nominee has finished in an awarded position. Any Breeders' Cup Fund Monies not awarded will revert back to the fund. Weights Saturday, June 7. This race will not be divided, the starters will be determined at time of entry with preference given to Breeders' Cup nominees only of equal racing quality overweight assignment (respective of sex and weight for age). Plus up to $14,612 Breeder Awards. Closed Wednesday, May 28 with 42 nominations.

Value of Race: $336,600 Winner $203,760; second $67,920; third $37,356; fourth $20,376; fifth $7,188. Mutuel Pool $178,732.00 Triactor Pool $109,250.00 Exactor Pool $81,432.00

Last Raced	Horse	M/Eqt.	A.Wt	PP	St	¼	½	¾	Str	Fin	Jockey	Odds $1
17May03 ¹⁰Pim²	Perfect Soul–IR	Lb	5 119	3	9	8hd	8hd	5½	11½	12½	Landry R C	1.70
27Oct02 ⁶WO¹	Strut The Stage	Lb	5 121	7	3	7²	7½	6½	5¹	2¼	Kabel T K	3.15
17May03 ¹⁰Pim⁴	Del Mar Show	L	6 119	9	1	3¹	3½	3hd	3½	3½	Day P	2.40
11May03 7Bel¹	Tap The Admiral	L	5 116	8	2	2½	1hd	1hd	2½	4½	Husbands P	8.95
29Nov02 8CD⁴	Rhenium–IRE	Lf	6 111	1	8	4hd	4½	4½	4½	5nk	Sutherland C	45.70
24May03 8WO⁹	Le Cinquieme Essai	L	4 112	5	6	9	9	7hd	7½	6¹	McKnight J	32.55
24May03 8WO⁵	Stage Classic	Lb	5 115	2	7	5¹	5hd	9	8hd	7nk	Montpellier C	33.25
24May03 8WO⁴	Red Sea–GB	L	7 113	6	5	6hd	6hd	8hd	9	82½	Callaghan S	15.25
11May03 7Bel⁷	Union Place	L	4 115	4	4	1hd	2¹	2½	6½	9	Dos Ramos R A	14.25

OFF AT 4:38 Start Good For All But PERFECT SOUL (IRE) Won driving. Course good.

TIME :24², :48¹, 1:12⁴, 1:37, 1:49³ (:24.47, :48.38, 1:12.87, 1:37.18, 1:49.60)

$2 Mutuel Prices:

3–PERFECT SOUL–IR	5.40	3.50	2.50
7–STRUT THE STAGE		3.90	2.80
9–DEL MAR SHOW			2.80

$2 TRIACTOR 3–7–9 PAID $61.40 $2 EXACTOR 3–7 PAID $24.40

B. h, by Sadler's Wells–Ball Chairman, by Secretariat. Trainer Attfield Roger L. Bred by Fipke C (Ire).

PERFECT SOUL (IRE) bobbled at the break, was well placed three wide, rallied five wide on the turn, gained command in upper stretch and drew off. STRUT THE STAGE bumped at the start, stalked the forced pace four wide, moved out to the five path in upper stretch, rallied to be second best. DEL MAR SHOW had a short lead early, was close up while three wide, stalked the pace on the turn, gained late for the show position. TAP THE ADMIRAL bumped at the start, gained the lead after half a mile while off the rail, gave way in upper stretch. RHENIUM (IRE) stalked the pace from the inside, came off the rail on the turn, moved back inside for the drive and was not a threat. LE CINQUIEME ESSAI well placed four wide, advanced five wide on the turn, was six wide in the stretch, and gained mildly. STAGE CLASSIC stalked the pace from off the rail, bumped with RED SEA (GB) early on the turn, moved inside on the turn, was off the rail in the lane and did not rally. RED SEA (GB) stalked the pace three wide, bumped with STAGE CLASSIC early on the turn, weakened in the stretch. UNION PLACE led briefly early, pressed the pace inside TAP THE ADMIRAL, gave way into the stretch.

Owners— 1, Fipke Charles E; 2, Sam-Son Farms; 3, Allen E Paulson Living Trust; 4, S Ettinger; 5, Firestone D M; 6, William Scott; 7, Dominion Bloodstock Ball Derek & Ga; 8, Werner William Windhaven Farm & Att; 9, Sorokolit William A Sr

Trainers—1, Attfield Roger L; 2, Frostad Mark; 3, Mott William I; 4, Carroll Del W II; 5, Hopmans C C Jr; 6, Nielsen Paul; 7, Cotey David; 8, Attfield Roger L; 9, Schulhofer Randy

$1 Pick Three (1–5–3) Paid $19.70; Pick Three Pool $10,414.

SIXTH RACE

Woodbine

JUNE 22, 2003

6 FURLONGS. (Turf)(1.07³) 31st Running of THE NEARCTIC STAKES HANDICAP. Grade II. Purse $250,000 For THREE-YEAR-OLDS AND UPWARD. By subscription of $250 each which shall accompany the nomination and an additional $2,500 when making entry; with $250,000 added, plus all fees to be divided: 60% to the winner, 20% to second, 11% to third, 6% to fourth and 3% to fifth. Weights, Saturday, June 14 , 2003. Final entries to be made through the entry box no later than 11:30 a.m. on Thursday, June 19, 2003. Closed Wednesday, June 4, 2003 with 36 nominations.

Value of Race: $286,500 Winner $171,900; second $57,300; third $31,515; fourth $17,190; fifth $8,595. Mutuel Pool $255,420.00 Superfecta Pool $38,640.00 Triactor Pool $159,156.00 Exactor Pool $139,268.00

Last Raced	Horse	M/Eqt.	A.Wt	PP	St	1/4	1/2	Str	Fin	Jockey	Odds $1
4Jun03 4WO1	Soaring Free	L	4 115	11	4	3$\frac{1}{2}$	1$\frac{1}{2}$	12$\frac{1}{2}$	13$\frac{1}{4}$	Kabel T K	2.10
24May03 8WO2	Solitary Dancer	L	7 117	10	11	81	8hd	6hd	2hd	Husbands P	12.50
2May03 7CD5	Nuclear Debate	L	8 121	7	6	6$\frac{1}{2}$	4$\frac{1}{2}$	2hd	3$\frac{1}{2}$	Coa E M	2.45
18Oct02 8WO2	Montezuma's Gold	L	7 114	9	8	9$\frac{1}{2}$	9$\frac{1}{2}$	92	4nk	McAleney J S	18.50
30Nov02 8WO6	Zone Judge	L	5 115	3	1	4hd	5$\frac{2}{1}$	4hd	5hd	Montpellier C	12.15
31May03 7WO1	Chris's Bad Boy	Lf	6 117	5	3	2hd	2$\frac{1}{2}$	3$\frac{1}{2}$	63	Jones Jono	21.35
24May03 8WO11	Gone Fishin	Lf	7 110	1	5	101	10hd	10hd	7nk	Sutherland C	30.75
19May03 6WO7	Relaunch Star	L	5 108	4	2	1hd	3hd	52	8$\frac{3}{4}$	Gulas L L	37.25
11May03 7Bel2	Krieger	Lb	5 116	8	7	72	7$\frac{1}{2}$	8$\frac{1}{2}$	91	Landry R C	4.55
1Jun03 9WO6	Wild Strike	L	5 114	2	10	11	11	11	10hd	Dos Ramos R A	30.85
13Mar03 NAS7	Orchestrated-AU	L	7 114	6	9	5hd	6$\frac{1}{2}$	71	11	Bahen S R	11.05

OFF AT 3:13 Start Good For All But ORCHESTRATED (AUS) Won driving. Course firm.
TIME :21⁴, :44¹, :55⁴, 1:07³ (:21.92, :44.35, :55.84, 1:07.73)

$2 Mutuel Prices:

11–SOARING FREE	6.20	3.90	2.90
10–SOLITARY DANCER		9.80	5.40
7–NUCLEAR DEBATE			3.00

$1 SUPERFECTA 11–10–7–9 PAID $768.30 $2 TRIACTOR 11–10–7 PAID $216.10 $2 EXACTOR 11–10 PAID $61.90

Dk. b. or br. g, by Smart Strike–Dancing With Wings, by Danzig. Trainer Frostad Mark. Bred by Sam–Son Farm (Ont–C).

SOARING FREE had a short lead early, pressed the pace three wide, gained the lead on the turn, gained command in upper stretch, drifted in in mid stretch, drew off under strong encouragement and equaled the course record. SOLITARY DANCER raced four wide, rallied five wide for the place position. NUCLEAR DEBATE stalked the forced pace three wide, made a bid in the stretch, and was outfinished. MONTEZUMA'S GOLD was three wide, came out six wide in upper stretch and rallied late. ZONE JUDGE stalked the pace from the inside, was off the rail into the stretch, angled out in upper stretch to the five path, and was outfinished. CHRIS'S BAD BOY pressed the pace from between horses, gave way in upper stretch. GONE FISHIN was inside, and did not threaten. RELAUNCH STAR set a pressured pace from inside, gave way into the stretch. KRIEGER was three wide, off the rail in the stretch, and not a threat. WILD STRIKE was off the rail, and showed little. ORCHESTRATED (AUS) hit the gate, stalked the forced pace from between horses, was four wide in the stretch and faded.

Owners— 1, Sam–Son Farms; 2, Franks John; 3, Herrick Racing; 4, Stronach Stable; 5, Penny Winston W; 6, Alpine Stable; 7, Springfield Stable & Dura Racing; 8, Castle Peak Farm Ltd; 9, Stronach Stable; 10, Schickedanz Gustav; 11, Darley Stud Management Co Ltd

Trainers—1, Frostad Mark; 2, Giliforte Layne S; 3, Vienna Darrell; 4, Pierce Malcolm; 5, Dwyer David; 6, Armata Vito; 7, Doyle Michael J; 8, Yu Danny; 9, Vella Daniel J; 10, Keogh Michael; 11, McLaughlin Kiaran P

$1 Pick Three (5–8–11) Paid $33.60; Pick Three Pool $17,926.
$1 Win Four (2–5–8–11) Paid $78.20; Win Four Pool $30,492.

EIGHTH RACE
Woodbine
JULY 1, 2003

1¼ MILES. (2.01) 51st Running of THE DOMINION DAY HANDICAP. Grade III. Purse $200,000 added. 3–year–olds. By subscription of $200 each which shall accompany the nomination and an additional $2,000 when making entry. Weights, Saturday, June 21. Final entries to be made through the entry box later than 11:30 a.m. on Saturday, June 28, 2003. Closed Wendesday, June 11 with 20 nominations.

Value of Race: $226,000 Winner $135,600; second $45,200; third $24,860; fourth $13,560; fifth $6,780. Mutuel Pool $151,952.00 Triactor Pool $102,361.00 Exactor Pool $71,177.00

Last Raced	Horse	M/Eqt.	A.Wt	PP	¼	½	¾	1	Str	Fin	Jockey	Odds $1
7Jun03 ^{7}WO^{5}	Phantom Light	Lb	4 115	1	1^{1}	$1^{1\frac{1}{2}}$	1^{1}	$1^{1\frac{1}{2}}$	1^{3}	1^{4}	Kabel T K	6.45
17May03 ^{11}Pim^{2}	Changeintheweather	Lb	4 117	7	7^{2}	7^{1}	$6^{\frac{1}{2}}$	$3^{\frac{1}{2}}$	$3^{1\frac{1}{2}}$	2^{nk}	Prado E S	3.10
13Jun03 ^{2}WO^{1}	Dance To Destiny	Lbf	4 115	3	$3^{\frac{1}{2}}$	$2^{\frac{1}{2}}$	$2^{\frac{1}{2}}$	$2^{2\frac{1}{2}}$	2^{hd}	$3^{1\frac{1}{2}}$	McAleney J S	4.95
7Jun03 ^{7}WO^{1}	No Comprende	Lb	5 117	8	10	10	9^{hd}	6^{2}	4^{4}	$4^{4\frac{1}{4}}$	McKnight J	3.40
7Jun03 ^{7}WO^{3}	Attest	L	7 117	6	9^{5}	$9^{2\frac{1}{2}}$	7^{hd}	$5^{\frac{1}{2}}$	$5^{1\frac{1}{2}}$	$5^{2\frac{3}{4}}$	Baze R A	13.40
18Jun03 ^{3}WO^{1}	Florida Recount	Lb	4 116	4	6^{hd}	6^{1}	5^{hd}	$8^{3\frac{1}{2}}$	7^{2}	$6^{1\frac{1}{2}}$	Husbands P	6.85
7Jun03 ^{7}WO^{4}	Dream Launcher	Lb	5 118	5	5^{hd}	$4^{\frac{1}{2}}$	4^{1}	$4^{1\frac{1}{2}}$	6^{1}	$7^{\frac{1}{2}}$	Dos Ramos R A	25.10
14Jun03 ^{10}CD^{6}	Unbridled Vision	Lb	5 114	2	8^{hd}	8^{hd}	10	$9^{2\frac{1}{2}}$	9^{5}	$8^{2\frac{3}{4}}$	Luzzi M J	6.25
7Jun03 ^{7}WO^{2}	Indy Lead	Lb	5 114	10	4^{1}	5^{hd}	$3^{\frac{1}{2}}$	$7^{\frac{1}{2}}$	$8^{\frac{1}{2}}$	$9^{5\frac{1}{2}}$	Sabourin R B	28.40
7Jun03 ^{7}WO^{8}	Kiss A Native	Lb	6 116	9	2^{hd}	3^{1}	8^{1}	10	10	10	Luciani D	37.70

OFF AT 4:29 Start Good. Won driving. Track fast.
TIME :23^{1}, :46^{2}, 1:11^{2}, 1:36^{1}, 2:01 (:23.21, :46.51, 1:11.47, 1:36.27, 2:01.15)

$2 Mutuel Prices:

1–PHANTOM LIGHT	14.90	7.50	5.00
8–CHANGEINTHEWEATHER		4.70	3.60
3–DANCE TO DESTINY			5.20

$2 TRIACTOR 1–8–3 PAID $338.20 $2 EXACTOR 1–8 PAID $79.50

Gr/ro c, by Alphabet Soup–Kirby Meadow, by Meadowlake. Trainer Vella Daniel J. Bred by Adena Springs (Ont–C).

PHANTOM LIGHT had speed under pressure while three wide the first time through the stretch, cleared on the first turn, raced off the rail through the backstretch, was roused in upper stretch and began to draw off, received two left handed taps of the whip in mid stretch, then was under a strong hand ride to the wire. CHANGEINTHEWEATHER was off the rail while between horses, began to rally early on the second turn, and split horses just before the quarter pole, finished well four wide through the stretch to take the place position. DANCE TO DESTINY bobbled at the start, stalked the pace three wide, came under left handed urging on the second turn, was outfinished for the place position late. NO COMPRENDE trailed while off the rail, rallied three wide, split horses into the stretch, and continued the gain mildly through the stretch from off the rail. ATTEST raced three wide, advanced mildly four wide on the second turn and in the stretch. FLORIDA RECOUNT was well placed off the rail. DREAM LAUNCHER stalked the pace three wide, and was not a threat. UNBRIDLED VISION raced off the rail, and was not a factor. INDY LEAD stalked the pace five wide, weakened on the second turn. KISS A NATIVE advanced early to press the pace five wide the first time through the stretch, stalked the pace four wide on the first turn and early in the backstretch, came under right handed urging midway through the backstretch, and faded.

Owners— 1, Stronach Stable; 2, Pin Oak Stable; 3, Sam-Son Farms; 4, Clarity Stables; 5, Sangara K K; 6, Tucci Stables; 7, Cappuccitti Audre; 8, Lunsford Bruce; 9, Fipke Charles E; 10, Franks John

Trainers—1, Vella Daniel J; 2, Motion H Graham; 3, Frostad Mark; 4, Smith James J; 5, Richards Lorne; 6, Attard Sid C; 7, Cappuccitti Audre; 8, Mott William I; 9, Attfield Roger L; 10, Bell David R

Scratched— Malmaison (15Jun03 ^{6}FE^{4})

$1 Pick Three (6–3–1) Paid $105.60; Pick Three Pool $12,798.

EIGHTH RACE
Hastings
JULY 1, 2003

1⅛ MILES. (1.46^{4}) 43rd Running of THE LIEUTENANNT GOVERNORS' HANDICAP. Grade III. Purse $100,000 (plus up to 13% for BC breds). 3–year–olds and upward. $200 to nominate. $1,000 to enter and $1,000 to pass scratch time. Weights to be announced Sunday, June 22.

Value of Race: $110,582 Winner $66,349; second $22,116; third $12,164; fourth $6,635; fifth $3,318. Mutuel Pool $55,493.00 Triactor Pool $45,638.00 Exactor Pool $26,828.00

Last Raced	Horse	M/Eqt.	A.Wt	PP	St	¼	½	¾	Str	Fin	Jockey	Odds $1
31May03 ^{8}Hst^{3}	Lord Nelson	Lf	6 119	5	6	$3^{\frac{1}{2}}$	$3^{1\frac{1}{2}}$	3^{2}	1^{1}	1^{3}	Fuentes F P	1.05
14Jun03 ^{7}Hst^{1}	Let's Go Rusty	L	6 114	2	7	8	$7^{\frac{1}{2}}$	6^{1}	4^{1}	2^{hd}	Krasner S	3.20
14Jun03 ^{7}Hst^{2}	Commodore Craig	Lbf	4 116	6	2	2^{1}	$2^{\frac{1}{2}}$	2^{1}	2^{2}	$3^{2\frac{1}{4}}$	Loseth C	5.00
14Jun03 ^{7}Hst^{3}	Silver Donn	Lb	4 117	3	3	$4^{\frac{1}{2}}$	$4^{1\frac{1}{2}}$	4^{2}	5^{4}	$4^{\frac{1}{2}}$	Alvarado P V	5.95
15Jun03 ^{9}Hst^{1}	Ekati	Lb	4 112	7	1	1^{1}	$1^{\frac{1}{2}}$	$1^{\frac{1}{2}}$	3^{1}	$5^{6\frac{3}{4}}$	Skelly R V	28.70
1Mar03 ^{10}SA^{10}	Futural	Lb	7 117	1	5	7^{1}	8	7^{2}	6^{5}	6^{6}	Valdez F S	18.35
26Apr03 ^{7}Hst^{5}	Colondelivery		4 112	8	4	$5^{1\frac{1}{2}}$	$6^{1\frac{1}{2}}$	8	$7^{\frac{1}{2}}$	$7^{3\frac{3}{4}}$	Wright N	23.00
14Jun03 ^{7}Hst^{6}	Irish Pleasure	Lb	5 115	4	8	$6^{\frac{1}{2}}$	5^{hd}	$5^{\frac{1}{2}}$	8	8	Stephen A	26.40

OFF AT 4:48 Start Good For All But IRISH PLEASURE Won driving. Track fast.
TIME :23, :47^{4}, 1:12^{2}, 1:37^{1}, 1:50^{2} (:23.04, :47.87, 1:12.53, 1:37.24, 1:50.49)

$2 Mutuel Prices:

5–LORD NELSON	4.10	2.90	2.30
2–LET'S GO RUSTY		3.50	2.70
6–COMMODORE CRAIG			3.40

$2 TRIACTOR 5–2–6 PAID $43.40 $2 EXACTOR 5–2 PAID $13.90

Dk. b. or br. g, by Maudlin–Lady Hamilton, by The Minstrel. Trainer Condilenios Dino. Bred by Mr & Mrs R J Bennett (BC–C).

LORD NELSON away alertly, stalked the leaders from three wide, made a bid and gained command from three wide on the final turn, drew clear driving. LET'S GO RUSTY unhurried early, rallied from between horses turning into the stretch, closed willingly and was up for the place. COMMODORE CRAIG away alertly, pressed the pace from the outside, had the lead between calls at the quarter pole, weakened and gave way. SILVER DONN away alertly and up close, stalked the leaders and went evenly. EKATI hustled along from the outside to gain the lead, set a moderate pace, gave way after three quarters. FUTURAL three wide on the first turn, lost ground, dropped back, showed little. COLONDELIVERY four wide on the first turn, dropped back. IRISH PLEASURE broke slowly, hustled along on the inside, was used up and through after a half.

Owners— 1, Bennett Mr & Mrs R J; 2, Hoggard Les & Leffler Bob; 3, Linwood Stables; 4, J & V Morgan Ventures Ltd; 5, Patzer Mr & Mrs Elmer; 6, Hart Kim N; 7, Raycol Holdings Ltd; 8, Kwan Fred

Trainers—1, Condilenios Dino; 2, Condilenios Dino; 3, Anderson Robert J; 4, Rohman Robert; 5, Barroby Harold J; 6, Bryant Steve; 7, Crawford Ray; 8, Cizik Tony

EIGHTH RACE

Woodbine

JULY 5, 2003

1⅛ MILES. (Turf)(1.45¹) 8th Running of THE DANCE SMARTLY HANDICAP. Grade III. Purse $150,000 FOR FILLIES AND MARES, THREE-YEAR-OLDS AND UPWARD. By subscription of $150 each which shall accompany the nomination and an additional $1,500 when making entry. Weights Saturday, June 28, 2003. Final entries to be made no later than 11:30 a.m. on Wednesday, July 2, 2003. Plus $50,000 for Canadian Breds from the Thoroughbred Improvement Program and Canadian Thoroughbred Horse Society. Closed Wednesday, June 18, 2003 with 35 nominations.

Value of Race: $187,250 Winner $103,050; second $44,350; third $24,393; fourth $10,305; fifth $5,152. Mutuel Pool $141,495.00 Triactor Pool $85,868.00 Exactor Pool $68,558.00

Last Raced	Horse	M/Eqt. A.Wt	PP	St	¼	½	¾	Str	Fin	Jockey	Odds $1
15May03 6Bel3	Madeira Mist-IR	L	4 116	8	4	7²	7½	8½	2½	1no	Husbands P	8.45
1Jun03 8WO8	First Quarter	L	4 114	9	2	6²½	6²½	5¹	4¹	2¹	Somsanith N	30.65
1Jun03 8WO3	Byzantine	Lb	7 117	5	9	10	9¹	9²½	5hd	3½	Jones Jono	16.05
8Sep02 6WO2	Diadella	Lb	6 118	3	10	9hd	10	10	7³	4¹	Clark D	4.75
1Jun03 8WO1	Strait From Texas	L	4 118	7	5	8³½	8¹	7²	1½	5½	Dos Ramos R A	5.35
1Jun03 8WO2	Chopinina	Lb	5 116	1	7	2½	1hd	1½	3hd	6²	Ramsammy E	1.80
7Jun03 8WO2	Ginger Gold	L	4 116	2	6	1hd	3²	3hd	6¹	7⁴½	McAleney J S	9.75
1Jun03 8WO5	Five Fishes-FR	Lb	5 112	6	3	3¹	2½	2hd	8²½	8³¾	Sutherland C	39.80
8Sep02 8Bel5	Cyclorama	Lb	4 116	10	1	4¹	5¹½	4¹	9⁵	9⁸½	Landry R C	4.50
18Jun03 4WO1	Ghazirella	Lf	5 115	4	8	5½	4hd	6hd	10	10	Husbands S P	41.30

OFF AT 4:34 Start Good. Won driving. Course firm.

TIME :22⁴, :45², 1:09², 1:33³, 1:48 (:22.95, :45.49, 1:09.50, 1:33.71, 1:48.05)

$2 Mutuel Prices:

9-MADEIRA MIST-IR	18.90	9.00	6.20
10-FIRST QUARTER		24.10	12.30
6-BYZANTINE			5.60

$2 TRIACTOR 9-10-6 PAID $8,581.00 $2 EXACTOR 9-10 PAID $489.00

B. f, by Grand Lodge-Mountains Of Mist*Ire, by Shirley Heights*GB. Trainer Clement Christophe. Bred by O'Reilly Dr A J & Skymarc Farm (Ire).

MADEIRA MIST (IRE) angled in early to be well placed inside, advanced off the rail into the stretch, moved back to the rail two furlongs out, rallied along the rail through the stretch, gained the lead approaching the sixteenth pole, and won the head bob. FIRST QUARTER was three wide, advanced early on the turn to a stalking position, was in tight in upper stretch, steadied passing the three sixteenths pole, rallied three wide and just missed. BYZANTINE bumped at the start, trailed early while three wide, rallied five wide through the stretch. DIADELLA was well back inside, trailed on the turn, angled out in upper stretch, rallied late eight wide. STRAIT FROM TEXAS raced off the rail, advanced four wide on the turn, rallied five wide in the stretch, led in mid stretch and was outfinished. CHOPININA pressed the pace inside of GINGER GOLD early, gained the lead at the three sixteenths pole, and set fast fractions, gave way off the rail in upper stretch. GINGER GOLD had a short lead early three wide, pressed outside of CHOPINA into the turn, dropped back slightly to stalk in mid turn, made a bid three wide late on the turn, weakened in the stretch. FIVE FISHES (FR) bumped at the start, pressed the pace three wide, faltered into the stretch. CYCLORAMA broke sharply while breaking outwards, stalked the forced pace four wide, made a bid into the stretch, and dropped back. GHAZIRELLA stalked the forced pace from the inside, faded through the stretch.

Owners— 1, Skymarc Farm Inc; 2, Come By Chance Stable; 3, Royal Oak Farm; 4, Stronach Stable; 5, Michael James A; 6, Knob Hill Stable; 7, Jim Dandy Stable; 8, Schettine William C; 9, Clifton William L Jr; 10, Mitchelson William A & Partner

Trainers—1, Clement Christophe; 2, Day James E; 3, Pollock Bruce M; 4, Pierce Malcolm; 5, Buttigieg Paul M; 6, Fehr John Alec; 7, Attard Sid C; 8, Carroll Josie; 9, Bond Harold James; 10, Crean Robert F

Scratched— Hot Talent (1Jun03 8WO7)

$1 Pick Three (8-1-9) Paid $677.65; Pick Three Pool $7,996.

EIGHTH RACE

Woodbine

JULY 12, 2003

1⅛ MILES. (Turf)(1.45¹) 104th Running of THE TORONTO CUP HANDICAP. Grade III. Purse $150,000 For THREE-YEAR-OLDS. By subscription of $150 each which shall accompany the nomination and an additional $1,500 when making entry; with $150,000 added, plus all fees to be divided: 60% to the winner, 20% to second, 1 1% to third, 6% to fourth and 3% to fifth. Weights, Saturday, July 5, 2003. Final entries to be made through the entry box no later than 11:30 a.m. on Wednesday July 9, 2003. Closed Wednesday, June 25, 2003 with 34 nominations.

Value of Race: $164,100 Winner $98,460; second $32,820; third $18,051; fourth $9,846; fifth $4,923. Mutuel Pool $120,748.00 Triactor Pool $66,702.00 Exactor Pool $60,591.00

Last Raced	Horse	M/Eqt. A.Wt	PP	St	¼	½	¾	Str	Fin	Jockey	Odds $1
22Jun03 9WO2	Mobil	L	3 122	2	3	1½	1hd	1hd	1¹	1¹	Kabel T K	0.90
22Jun03 4WO2	Strizzi	L	3 119	5	1	4hd	5²	3¹	3³	2¾	Ramsammy E	4.10
22Jun03 4WO1	Moonshine Hall	L	3 121	4	6	6	6	4¹	2¹	3³¼	Husbands P	1.80
25Jun03 3WO3	Tracy's Tonka Toy	L	3 117	6	2	2¹½	2hd	2hd	4⁴	4²¾	Jones Jono	34.20
8Jun03 4WO1	Pants N Kisses	L	3 116	3	4	5²	4hd	5hd	5⁴	5⁹½	Montpellier C	14.50
22Jun03 9WO12	Illusive Force	L	3 114	1	5	3hd	3¹½	6	6	6	McAleney J S	24.70

OFF AT 4:20 Start Good For All But PANTS N KISSES. Won driving. Course good.

TIME :24², :48¹, 1:12², 1:36², 1:49 (:24.41, :48.20, 1:12.41, 1:36.48, 1:49.15)

$2 Mutuel Prices:

2-MOBIL	3.80	2.50	2.10
5-STRIZZI		4.40	2.60
4-MOONSHINE HALL			2.10

$2 TRIACTOR 2-5-4 PAID $17.40 $2 EXACTOR 2-5 PAID $13.40

B. c, (Jan), by Langfuhr-Kinetigal, by Naskra. Trainer Keogh Michael. Bred by Gustav Schickedanz (Ont-C).

MOBIL set a pressured slow pace from off the rail, came three wide into the stretch, was headed briefly in mid stretch, and prevailed determinedly. STRIZZI was well placed three wide, advanced four wide on the turn to make a bid in the stretch, took the place position late. MOONSHINE HALL trailed while three wide, advanced five wide in the turn, put a head in front briefly in mid stretch, was outfinished for the place position late. TRACY'S TONKA TOY pressed the pace three wide, gave way into the stretch. PANTS N KISSES hit the gate at the start, was well placed off the rail, and showed little. ILLUSIVE FORCE stalked the forced pace from the inside, faded in the stretch.

Owners— 1, Schickedanz Gustav; 2, Stronach Stable; 3, Melnyk Eugene & Laura; 4, Box Arrow Farm; 5, Dominion Bloodstock Ball Derek & Ga; 6, Canyon Farms

Trainers—1, Keogh Michael; 2, Pierce Malcolm; 3, Reinstedler Anthony; 4, Colbourne Gordon C; 5, Cotey David; 6, VanOverschot Robert

---

$1 Pick Three (6-5-2) Paid $52.20; Pick Three Pool $12,758.

EIGHTH RACE
Woodbine
JULY 20, 2003

1⅜ MILES. (Turf)(2.13) 5th Running of THE CHINESE CULTURAL CENTRE. Grade II. Purse $300,000 For THREE-YEAR-OLDS AND UPWARD. By subscription of $300 each which shall accompany the nomination and an additional $3,000 when making entry. Weights: Three-Year-Olds, 118 lbs. Older 124 lbs. Winners of $750,000 at a mile or over since October 1, additional 2 lbs.; Non-winners of $100,000 three times at a mile or over in 2002–2003, 3 lbs.; Of $100,000 twice at a mile or over in 2002–2003, 5 lbs.; Of $100,000 once at a mile or over in 2002–2003, 7 lbs.; Of $75,000 at a mile or over in 2002–2003, 9 lbs. Final entries to be made through the entry box no later than 10:30 a.m. on Thursday, July 17, 2003. Close Wednesday, July 2, 2003 with 23 nominations.

Value of Race: $330,900 Winner $198,540; second $66,180; third $36,399; fourth $19,854; fifth $9,927. Mutuel Pool $198,360.00 Triactor Pool $118,542.00 Exactor Pool $100,091.00

Last Raced	Horse	M/Eqt.	A.Wt	PP	¼	½	¾	1	Str	Fin	Jockey	Odds $1
15Jun03 ^{8}WO^{2}	Strut The Stage	Lb	5 121	4	$4^{1\frac{1}{2}}$	$4^{1\frac{1}{2}}$	$4^{1\frac{1}{2}}$	3^{hd}	$2^{\frac{1}{2}}$	$1^{1\frac{1}{2}}$	Kabel T K	2.05
15Jun03 ^{8}WO^{1}	Perfect Soul-IR	Lb	5 119	3	2^{hd}	3^{2}	3^{2}	$2^{1\frac{1}{2}}$	$1^{\frac{1}{2}}$	$2^{2\frac{3}{4}}$	Landry R C	1.10
21Jun03 ^{5}WO^{3}	Angel On The Wing	L	4 115	7	$1^{1\frac{1}{2}}$	1^{1}	1^{1}	1^{hd}	3^{3}	$3^{\frac{3}{4}}$	Gulas L L	20.40
29Jun03 ^{3}WO^{5}	Portcullis	L	4 119	2	6^{1}	7^{6}	6^{hd}	6^{hd}	4^{hd}	4^{hd}	Callaghan S	14.30
25Jun03 ^{8}Bel^{4}	Deputy Strike	L	5 115	6	5^{hd}	5^{3}	5^{5}	$5^{1\frac{1}{2}}$	5^{hd}	5^{hd}	Somsanith N	5.65
14Jun03 ^{10}CD^{5}	Colonial Colony	L	5 115	5	7^{4}	$6^{\frac{1}{2}}$	$7^{3\frac{1}{2}}$	7^{10}	6^{2}	$6^{4\frac{1}{4}}$	Dos Ramos R A	13.25
29Jun03 ^{3}WO^{2}	Stage Classic	Lb	5 115	1	$3^{2\frac{1}{2}}$	2^{hd}	2^{hd}	$4^{1\frac{1}{2}}$	7^{12}	$7^{15\frac{3}{4}}$	Ramsammy E	17.95
29Jun03 ^{3}WO^{7}	Soldierofpleasure	Lb	4 115	8	8	8	8	8	8	8	McAleney J S	43.05

OFF AT 4:33 Start Good. Won driving. Course firm.
TIME :24^{1}, :49^{1}, 1:13^{2}, 1:37^{1}, 2:13^{4} (:24.25, :49.27, 1:13.45, 1:37.39, 2:13.85)

$2 Mutuel Prices:				
	4–STRUT THE STAGE	6.10	3.00	3.00
	3–PERFECT SOUL–IR		2.50	2.10
	7–ANGEL ON THE WING			6.90

$2 TRIACTOR 4–3–7 PAID $98.20 $2 EXACTOR 4–3 PAID $11.90

Ch. h, by Theatrical*Ire–Ruby Ransom, by Red Ransom. Trainer Frostad Mark. Bred by Jamm Ltd (Ky).

STRUT THE STAGE was well placed three wide, advanced on the second turn to a stalking position, rallied four wide in the stretch, gained command passing the sixteenth pole and drew out. PERFECT SOUL (IRE) stalked the pace three wide, pressed outside of ANGEL ON THE WING on the second turn, gained the lead in upper stretch, but was no match for the winner while clearly second best. ANGEL ON THE WING bumped at the start, set the pace from off the rail, gave way in upper stretch, drifted out, and held his position. PORTCULLIS raced inside, came off the rail on the second turn, was five wide in the stretch, bumped with COLONIAL COLONY through the stretch, and did not threaten. DEPUTY STRIKE bumped at the start, raced off the rail, moved inside on the second turn, and finished evenly in the stretch. COLONIAL COLONY raced off the rail, came six wide in the stretch, bumped with PORTCULLIS through the stretch and had no menace. STAGE CLASSIC stalked the pace from the inside, was off the rail in the stretch, and dropped back. SOLDIEROFPLEASURE was always outrun, and eased.

Owners— 1, Sam-Son Farms; 2, Fipke Charles E; 3, Sam-Son Farms; 4, Sam-Son Farms; 5, West Point Stable; 6, Lakeside Farm; 7, Dominion Bloodstock Ball Derek & Ga; 8, Franks John

Trainers—1, Frostad Mark; 2, Attfield Roger L; 3, Frostad Mark; 4, Frostad Mark; 5, McLaughlin Kiaran P; 6, Bindner Walter M Jr; 7, Cotey David; 8, Bell David R

$1 Pick Three (2–7–4) Paid $171.75; Pick Three Pool $12,083.

EIGHTH RACE
Woodbine
AUGUST 2, 2003

6 FURLONGS. (Turf)(1.07^{3}) 15th Running of THE ROYAL NORTH HANDICAP. Grade III. Purse $150,000 For FILLIES AND MARES, THREE-YEAR-OLDS AND UPWARD. By subscription of $150 each which shall accompany the nomination and an additional $1,500 when making entry. Weights, Saturday, July 26, 2003. Final entries to be made through the entry box no later than 11:30 a.m. on Wednesday, July 30, 2003. $50,000 of this purse has been provided through the Thoroughbred Improvement Program and Canadian Thoroughbred Horse Society. Closed Wednesday, July 16, 2003 with 27 nominations. Plus up to $11,575 Breeder Awards.

Value of Race: $209,050 Winner $131,430; second $43,810; third $18,596; fourth $10,143; fifth $5,071. Mutuel Pool $123,491.00 Triactor Pool $82,257.00 Exactor Pool $66,017.00

Last Raced	Horse	M/Eqt.	A.Wt	PP	St	¼	½	Str	Fin	Jockey	Odds $1
5Jly03 ^{8}WO^{6}	Chopinina	Lb	5 120	7	3	4^{1}	1^{hd}	1^{1}	$1^{2\frac{1}{2}}$	Kabel T K	1.55
30Jun03 ^{8}WO^{1}	Alpha Heat	L	4 117	2	6	$5^{1\frac{1}{2}}$	3^{1}	2^{4}	2^{7}	McAleney J S	2.35
13Jly03 ^{9}WO^{1}	Leading Role	Lf	5 116	4	5	3^{1}	$2^{\frac{1}{2}}$	3^{3}	$3^{\frac{1}{2}}$	Ramsammy E	4.70
22Jun03 ^{9}Cnl^{1}	Twice As Sweet	Lf	5 115	6	2	7	$6^{\frac{1}{2}}$	$4^{\frac{1}{2}}$	$4^{4\frac{1}{4}}$	Verge M E	11.20
5Jly03 ^{9}Cnl^{3}	Formada-AR	L	5 115	5	7	6^{hd}	7	7	$5^{\frac{3}{4}}$	Landry R C	11.80
19Jly03 ^{8}FE^{1}	Mysterious Affair	Lbf	6 121	3	1	2^{hd}	4^{hd}	$6^{2\frac{1}{2}}$	$6^{1\frac{3}{4}}$	Dos Ramos R A	8.75
28Jun03 ^{2}WO^{1}	Mille Feville	L	4 114	1	4	1^{hd}	5^{2}	5^{hd}	7	Callaghan S	11.15

OFF AT 4:21 Start Good. Won driving. Course soft.
TIME :23, :47^{1}, :59^{2}, 1:12 (:23.00, :47.21, :59.41, 1:12.19)

$2 Mutuel Prices:				
	8–CHOPININA	5.10	3.30	2.30
	2–ALPHA HEAT		2.90	2.50
	4–LEADING ROLE			3.00

$2 TRIACTOR 8–2–4 PAID $45.60 $2 EXACTOR 8–2 PAID $14.30

Gr/ro m, by Lear Fan–Lady Aloma, by Cozzene. Trainer Fehr John Alec. Bred by Knob Hill Stable (Ont-C).

CHOPININA was close up while four wide, came five wide into the stretch, gained command in upper stretch, drew off while drifting in under left handed encouragement. ALPHA HEAT stalked the duel from off the rail, advanced three wide into the stretch, split horses in upper stretch to make her bid, came up second best. LEADING ROLE dueled three wide, drifted out slightly into the stretch to be four wide, held her position. TWICE AS SWEET raced three wide, gained mildly four wide in the stretch. FORMADA (ARG) raced off the rail, was five wide in the stretch, and was not a threat. MYSTERIOUS AFFAIR dueled from between horses, weakened in upper stretch. MILLE FEVILLE dueled inside of MYSTERIOUS AFFAIR, gave way into the stretch.

Owners— 1, Knob Hill Stable; 2, Stronach Stable; 3, Colne Farm Casselman Gail & Mitchel; 4, Green Mountain Stables; 5, Behrendt John T; 6, Hardy James M; 7, Haras Santa Maria de Araras

Trainers—1, Fehr John Alec; 2, Baker Reade; 3, Casselman Gail; 4, Motion H Graham; 5, Donk David; 6, Hardy James M; 7, Attfield Roger L

Scratched— Multiple Wins (29Jun03 ^{10}BEL^{4}), Spanish Decree (19Jly03 ^{8}FE^{2}), Marisa Go (13Jly03 ^{9}WO^{7})

$1 Pick Three (4–5–8) Paid $124.15; Pick Three Pool $7,409.

EIGHTH RACE
Assiniboia
AUGUST 4, 2003

1⅛ MILES. (1.47^{3}) MANITOBA DERBY Grade III. Purse $100,000 For 3-year-olds. Weight, Fillies, 121 lbs. Colts & Geldings, 126 lbs. Fees: $200 to nominate – $1,000 to enter– $1,000 to start. Nominations closed Thursday, July 24, 2003 at 10:00 a.m. with 13.

Value of Race: $100,000 Winner $60,000; second $20,000; third $10,000; fourth $5,000; fifth $3,000; sixth $2,000. Mutuel Pool $72,507.00 Quinella Pool $7,221.00 Exactor Pool $27,197.00 Triactor Pool $51,104.00 Superfecta Pool $21,181.00

Last Raced	Horse	M/Eqt.	A.	Wt	PP	St	¼	½	¾	Str	Fin	Jockey	Odds $1
13Jly03 ^{8}Cby^{4}	Hero's Pleasure	L	3	126	9	9	8^{hd}	$8^{\frac12}$	$5^{1\frac12}$	2^{1}	1^{1}	Stevens S A	8.00
13Jly03 ^{7}AsD^{1}	Taiaslew	L	3	126	6	1	$1^{1\frac12}$	1^{1}	1^{2}	1^{5}	$2^{3\frac12}$	Simard R E	1.00
12Jly03 ^{8}WO^{5}	Pants N Kisses	L	3	126	4	6	9^{3}	$9^{2\frac12}$	6^{2}	5^{5}	$3^{1\frac34}$	Montpellier C	2.00
13Jly03 ^{7}AsD^{2}	Fancy Bru	L b	3	126	8	7	$5^{1\frac12}$	$5^{1\frac12}$	$4^{1\frac12}$	3^{hd}	4^{5}	Hightower T W	14.45
13Jly03 ^{7}AsD^{5}	Northern Affair	L f	3	126	1	2	$4^{\frac12}$	3^{2}	2^{1}	$4^{2\frac12}$	$5^{6\frac12}$	Crawford J	38.75
13Jly03 ^{7}AsD^{6}	Wild Ruler		3	126	10	10	10	10	10	$8^{\frac12}$	$6^{4\frac14}$	Evans S P	82.40
13Jly03 ^{6}AP^{1}	Big Glori	L b	3	126	7	8	3^{hd}	$2^{\frac12}$	3^{hd}	$7^{2\frac12}$	$7^{\frac12}$	Bell D C	7.70
19Jly03 ^{7}AsD^{2}	Beetrap		3	126	2	4	$6^{\frac12}$	$7^{2\frac12}$	8^{hd}	$6^{\frac12}$	$8^{3\frac34}$	Leacock J	86.05
13Jly03 ^{10}Sol^{4}	Jubilation	L b	3	126	5	5	$7^{\frac12}$	6^{hd}	7^{1}	9^{3}	$9^{5\frac34}$	Pruitt J	67.65
13Jly03 ^{7}AsD^{3}	Sand Rush	f	3	126	3	3	2^{hd}	$4^{\frac12}$	$9^{\frac12}$	10	10	DesAutels J	63.80

OFF AT 4:43 Start Good . Won driving. Track fast.

TIME :22^{4}, :46^{4}, 1:12^{2}, 1:39^{3}, 1:53^{2} (:22.80, :46.80, 1:12.40, 1:39.60, 1:53.40)

$2 Mutuel Prices:				
	9 – HERO'S PLEASURE	18.00	5.70	3.50
	6 – TAIASLEW		2.60	2.20
	4 – PANTS N KISSES			2.60

$2 QUINELLA 6–9 PAID $13.30 $2 EXACTOR 9–6 PAID $41.10
$2 TRIACTOR 9–6–4 PAID $111.20 $2 SUPERFECTA 9–6–4–8 PAID $497.90

Dk. b or br. c, (Mar), by Sea Hero – Rebeau's Pleasure , by Lord Rebeau . Trainer Oliver Douglas R. Bred by Jean Duke (Ky).

HERO'S PLEASURE rated back and outside early, advanced steadily while off the rail on the final turn, came with a long determined rally outside to get by late. TAIASLEW opened a short clear lead early, increased his margin into the final turn, took a good lead into the stretch, gave way late. PANTS N KISSES, back and inside early, advanced off the rail on the final turn, finished well outside. FANCY BRU stalked widest, advanced outside on the final turn, rallied mildly. NORTHERN AFFAIR, wel placed inside, advanced steadily on the final turn, rallied to passing the eighth pole, hung. WILD RULER trailed to the final turn, advanced outside, passed tired rivals. BIG GLORI, well placed outside, faded passing the three-eighths pole. BEETRAP raced evenly inside. JUBILATION, back and off the rail, did not menace. SAND RUSH, well placed off the rail early, faded after a half mile had been run.

Owners– 1, Duke Jean D; 2, Tracy Shelli and Ryan Stan; 3, Dominion Bloodstock Ball Derek and Galbraith Hugh; 4, Pawluk Ed and Jim and Danelson Gary; 5, K 5 Stables; 6, Kling Guy; 7, Orion Stables; 8, de Marni Caesar and Arlene; 9, G and W Racing Stable; 10, K 5 Stables

Trainers– 1, Oliver Doug; 2, Tracy Greg; 3, Cotey David; 4, Danelson Gary; 5, Corbel Keith; 6, Kling Guy; 7, McCoy James B; 8, De Marni Caesar; 9, Pruitt Lise; 10, Corbel Keith

$2 Pick Three (3–5–9) Paid $147.90 ; Pick Three Pool $3,640 .
$2 Daily Double (5–9) Paid $30.30 ; Daily Double Pool $22,007 .
$2 Pick Six (9–3–5–3–5–9) 5 Correct Paid $208.80 ; Pick Six Pool $1,111 ; Carryover Pool $968.

Attendance: Unavailable Mutuel Pool: $428,727.00

FIFTH RACE
Woodbine
AUGUST 9, 2003

7 FURLONGS. (1.20^{3}) 48th Running of THE DUCHESS. Grade III. Purse $150,000 For THREE-YEAR-OLD FILLIES. By subscription of $150 each which shall accompany the nomination and an additional $1,500 when making entry. Weight, 123 lbs. Winners of a sweepstakes of $75,000 three times in 2003, additional 2 lbs.; Non-winners of a sweepstakes of $75,000 twice in 2003, 3 lbs.; Of a sweepstakes of $75,000 once in 2003, 5 lbs.; Of a sweepstakes of $75,000 in 2002, 7 lbs.; Of $48,540, 9 lbs. (No Canadian Bred Allowance) Plus $50,000 for Canadian Breds from the Thoroughbred Improvement Program and the Canadian Thoroughbred Horse Society. Plus up to $11,575 Breeder Awards Closed Wednesday, July 23, 2003 with 25 nominations.

Value of Race: $177,250 Winner $100,350; second $43,450; third $18,398; fourth $10,035; fifth $5,017. Mutuel Pool $168,084.00 Superfecta Pool $33,045.00 Triactor Pool $97,310.00 Exactor Pool $85,054.00

Last Raced	Horse	M/Eqt.	A.	Wt	PP	St	¼	½	Str	Fin	Jockey	Odds $1
12Jly03 ^{9}EIP^{1}	Finally Here	L	3	117	7	2	$4^{\frac12}$	$3^{\frac12}$	1^{hd}	$1^{\frac12}$	Husbands P	6.60
26Jly03 ^{3}WO^{1}	[D]Winter Garden	L	3	120	2	3	1^{hd}	1^{hd}	2^{1}	$2^{\frac12}$	Sutherland C	1.30
16Jly03 ^{3}WO^{2}	Miss Crissy	Lb	3	118	6	6	$6^{1\frac12}$	$4^{2\frac12}$	3^{2}	$3^{1\frac34}$	Bahen S R	13.85
26Jly03 ^{3}WO^{2}	Smart Angel	L	3	114	8	1	$7^{1\frac12}$	5^{hd}	$5^{2\frac12}$	$4^{3\frac12}$	Kabel T K	4.50
12Jly03 ^{9}Crc^{4}	Littlemiss Sparkle	Lf	3	114	4	4	2^{hd}	$2^{1\frac12}$	4^{hd}	5^{1}	Ramsammy E	3.75
26Jly03 ^{3}WO^{4}	Beautiful Baroness	Lb	3	115	3	7	5^{hd}	$6^{1\frac12}$	$6^{1\frac12}$	6^{nk}	Callaghan S	57.45
1Aug03 ^{8}Mth^{3}	Sanctified	b	3	115	5	8	8	$7^{\frac12}$	7^{15}	$7^{20\frac34}$	Landry R C	25.65
13Jly03 ^{6}WO^{3}	Eclipse Bay	Lbf	3	114	1	5	3^{3}	8	8	8	Hutton G W	6.50

[D]–Winter Garden disqualified and placed 3rd.

OFF AT 3:07 Start Good. Won driving. Track fast.
TIME :22^{1}, :45, 1:10^{2}, 1:24 (:22.24, :45.02, 1:10.44, 1:24.15)

$2 Mutuel Prices:				
	7–FINALLY HERE	15.20	7.00	4.50
	6–MISS CRISSY		10.50	4.90
	2–WINTER GARDEN			2.70

$1 SUPERFECTA 7–6–2–9 PAID $1,227.00 $2 TRIACTOR 7–6–2 PAID $547.80 $2 EXACTOR 7–6 PAID $181.50

Ch. f, (May), by Yarrow Brae–Neolithic, by Deputed Testamony. Trainer Amoss Thomas. Bred by James M Courtney (Md).

FINALLY HERE stalked the forced pace three wide, advanced into the stretch, wore down WINTER GARDEN through the stretch. WINTER GARDEN set a pressured pace from off the rail, drifted in approaching the eighth pole, was very game while inside through the stretch. MISS CRISSY stalked the forced pace from the inside, made a bid in upper stretch, had her path taken away when WINTER GARDEN drifted in approaching the eighth pole, checked, was angled out and finished well three wide. SMART ANGEL raced three wide, rallied mildly four wide in the stretch. LITTLEMISS SPARKLE was a bit rank at the start, pressed the pace three wide, weakened in upper stretch. BEAUTIFUL BARONESS stalked the forced pace from off the rail, and was not a threat. SANCTIFIED trailed, passed a tired one. ECLIPSE BAY pressed the pace inside of WINTER GARDEN, gave way on the turn, and faded. A Stewards' inquiry following the race looking into the stretch run disqualified WINTER GARDEN from second and placed her third for interfering with MISS CRISSY at the eighth pole.

Owners— 1, Pop-A-Top LLC; 2, DiGiulio Frank D Jr; 3, Harlequin Ranches; 4, Werner R Windhaven Allard C & Attfi; 5, Rising Graph Stables; 6, Folino John & Partner; 7, Lewis Lakin; 8, Chiefswood Stable

Trainers— 1, Amoss Thomas; 2, Tiller Robert P; 3, Allain Emile M; 4, Attfield Roger L; 5, Whiting Lynn S; 6, Cardella John; 7, Biancone Patrick L; 8, Coatrieux Eric

Scratched— Power Gem (17Jly03 ^{8}WO^{2})

$1 Pick Three (6–3–7) Paid $937.35; Pick Three Pool $11,408.

EIGHTH RACE
Woodbine
AUGUST 16, 2003

7 FURLONGS. (Turf)(1.20^{1}) 9th Running of THE PLAY THE KING HANDICAP. Grade III. Purse $150,000 For THREE-YEAR-OLDS AND UPWARD. By subscription of $150 each which shall accompany the nomination and an additional $1,500 when making entry; with $150,000 added, plus all fees to be divided: 60% to the winner, 20% to second, 11% to third, 6% to fourth and 3% to fifth. Weights, Saturday, August 9. Closed Wednesday, July 30, 2003 with 40 nominations. Final entries to be made through the entry box no later than 11:30 a.m. on Wednesday, August 13, 2003. Plus up to $11,575 Breeder Awards.

Value of Race: $165,000 Winner $99,000; second $33,000; third $18,150; fourth $9,900; fifth $4,950. Mutuel Pool $152,020.00 Triactor Pool $70,955.00 Exactor Pool $75,296.00

Last Raced	Horse	M/Eqt.	A.Wt	PP	St	¼	½	Str	Fin	Jockey	Odds $1
19Jly03 ^{3}WO^{1}	Soaring Free	L	4 121	6	1	$2^{1\frac{1}{2}}$	1^{hd}	1^{1}	$1^{1\frac{1}{2}}$	Kabel T K	0.85
6Jly03 ^{6}Mth^{1}	Jeb's Wild	Lb	4 114	5	2	1^{1}	$2^{1\frac{1}{2}}$	2^{2}	$2^{1\frac{1}{2}}$	Ramsammy E	16.75
1Aug03 ^{8}WO^{6}	Frank's Selection	Lb	7 113	2	3	5^{hd}	4^{hd}	$3^{1\frac{1}{2}}$	3^{1}	Mailhot P	37.05
26Jly03 ^{5}Dmr^{3}	Golden Arrow	Lb	4 114	1	4	$3^{\frac{1}{2}}$	6	$4^{2\frac{1}{2}}$	$4^{1\frac{1}{2}}$	Blanc B	3.95
19Jly03 ^{3}WO^{2}	Numerous Times	Lf	6 117	3	5	4^{1}	3^{hd}	5^{hd}	5^{nk}	Husbands P	2.95
4Jly03 ^{7}Bel^{1}	Millennium Dragon-GB	L	4 116	4	6	6	$5^{\frac{1}{2}}$	6	6	Landry R C	6.50

OFF AT 4:39 Start Good. Won driving. Course yielding.
TIME :23, :46^{2}, 1:10^{2}, 1:23^{2} (:23.13, :46.51, 1:10.54, 1:23.52)

$2 Mutuel Prices:			
6-SOARING FREE	3.70	2.80	2.40
5-JEB'S WILD		7.70	5.40
2-FRANK'S SELECTION			4.80

$2 TRIACTOR 6-5-2 PAID $266.40 $2 EXACTOR 6-5 PAID $40.60

Dk. b. or br. g, by Smart Strike–Dancing With Wings, by Danzig. Trainer Frostad Mark. Bred by Sam-Son Farm (Ont-C).

SOARING FREE had a short lead early, pressed the pace outside of JEB'S WILD, drew even at the three eighths pole, gained command in upper stretch and held well. JEB'S WILD set a pressured pace inside of the winner, gave way in upper stretch, held the place position. FRANK'S SELECTION was well placed off the rail, advanced between horses on the turn, gained mildly three wide in the stretch. GOLDEN ARROW stalked the forced pace from the inside, and was not a threat. NUMEROUS TIMES stalked the forced pace three wide, was four wide in the stretch, and had no rally. MILLENNIUM DRAGON (GB) stalked the forced pace four wide, came five wide into the stretch, and was not a factor.

Owners— 1, Sam-Son Farms; 2, Croley Thomas L; 3, Elliott-Griem Lynda; 4, Gainsborough Farm LLC; 5, Committee Stable; 6, Darley Stud Management LLC

Trainers—1, Frostad Mark; 2, Hills Timothy A; 3, Griem Robert J; 4, Drysdale Neil; 5, Attard Sid C; 6, McLaughlin Kiaran P

$1 Pick Three (1-2-6) Paid $99.30; Pick Three Pool $9,595.

NINTH RACE
Northlands
AUGUST 23, 2003

1⅜ MILES. (2.15^{4}) 74th Running of THE CANADIAN DERBY. Grade III. Purse $150,000 THREE YEAR OLDS. By subscription of $300 each and a further payment of $1,500 to pass the entry box and an additional $1,200 to pass scratch time. Guaranteed with $94,500 to the winner, $30.000 to second, $15,000 to third, $7,500 to fourth, and $3,000 to fifth. Weights: Fillies, 121 lbs. Colts and geldings, 126 lbs. Closed Wednesday August 13 with 11 nominations. A $10,000 Bonus will be paid by Horse Racing Alberta to the owner of the winning horse if Alberta Bred.

Value of Race: $150,000 Winner $94,500; second $30,000; third $15,000; fourth $7,500; fifth $3,000. Mutuel Pool $91,932.00 Exacta Pool $27,163.00 Triactor Pool $41,260.00

Last Raced	Horse	M/Eqt.	A.Wt	PP	¼	½	¾	1	Str	Fin	Jockey	Odds $1
9Aug03 ^{7}NP^{2}	Raylene	L	3 121	5	5^{hd}	6^{3}	$6^{2\frac{1}{2}}$	6^{4}	2^{2}	1^{1}	Walcott R	5.35
4Aug03 ^{8}AsD^{2}	Taiaslew	L	3 126	2	1^{1}	$1^{\frac{1}{2}}$	$1^{\frac{1}{2}}$	1^{1}	1^{5}	$2^{6\frac{1}{4}}$	Simard R E	2.00
2Aug03 ^{4}NP^{3}	Reb's Drummer	bf	3 126	4	2^{1}	$2^{\frac{1}{2}}$	2^{2}	$2^{1\frac{1}{2}}$	$3^{1\frac{1}{2}}$	$3^{\frac{3}{4}}$	Heiler Stephan	24.05
2Aug03 ^{4}NP^{2}	Rindanica	Lb	3 126	8	4^{2}	$4^{\frac{1}{2}}$	5^{1}	5^{1}	4^{2}	4^{5}	Winters P A	9.65
2Aug03 ^{4}NP^{1}	Beau Brass	L	3 126	1	$7^{1\frac{1}{2}}$	$7^{\frac{1}{2}}$	$7^{\frac{1}{2}}$	$7^{1\frac{1}{2}}$	5^{4}	$5^{4\frac{1}{2}}$	Wilson D H	8.45
1Aug03 ^{4}NP^{1}	Beauzak	Lb	3 126	6	8	8	8	8	7^{3}	6^{1}	Hamel R	24.90
4Aug03 ^{8}AsD^{1}	Hero's Pleasure	L	3 126	7	6^{3}	$5^{1\frac{1}{2}}$	4^{hd}	$4^{\frac{1}{2}}$	$6^{\frac{1}{2}}$	$7^{10\frac{3}{4}}$	Stevens S A	3.05
4Aug03 ^{7}Hst^{2}	Illusive Force	L	3 126	3	$3^{2\frac{1}{2}}$	$3^{\frac{1}{2}}$	$3^{2\frac{1}{2}}$	3^{hd}	8	8	Welch Q K	4.65

OFF AT 4:43 Start Good. Won driving. Track fast.
TIME :23^{2}, :48, 1:13^{2}, 1:40^{4}, 2:07^{3}, 2:21^{3} (:23.40, :48.00, 1:13.40, 1:40.80, 2:07.60, 2:21.60)

$2 Mutuel Prices:			
5-RAYLENE	12.70	5.20	3.50
2-TAIASLEW		4.20	3.20
4-REB'S DRUMMER			7.40

$2 EXACTA 5-2 PAID $47.00 $2 TRIACTOR 5-2-4 PAID $912.50

Dk. b. or br. f, (Mar), by Tabasco Cat–Petite Princess, by Dayjur. Trainer Haynes Rodney. Bred by Kennelot Stables Limited (Ky).

RAYLENE evenly, steady advance, checked 3/8 pole, altered course sharply, rallied, closed fast stretch. TAIASLEW away alertly, set pressured pace, drew clear 1/4 pole, weakened stretch. REB'S DRUMMER pressed pace, outside, flattened out stretch. RINDANICA rail, gaining backstretch, blocked 1/4 pole, evenly stretch. BEAU BRASS slow early, gaining backstretch, evenly stretch. BEAUZAK slow early, evenly, passed tiring rivals. HERO'S PLEASURE evenly, gaining backstretch, flattened out. ILLUSIVE FORCE rail, stalked pace, weakened 3/8 pole, gave way stretch.

Owners— 1, Calmar Stables & Ranch; 2, Tracy Shelli & Ryan Stan; 3, Sycamore Stables; 4, Rick Robertson Engineering Ltd; 5, White Tom; 6, Richard Pilon; 7, Duke Jean D; 8, Canyon Farms

Trainers—1, Haynes Rodney; 2, Tracy Greg; 3, Chabot Rob; 4, Rycroft Riley; 5, Hedge Rick; 6, Simon Stuart; 7, Oliver Douglas R; 8, VanOverschot Robert

EIGHTH RACE
Woodbine
AUGUST 30, 2003

1½ MILES. (Turf)(2.25^{3}) 51st Running of THE NIAGARA BREEDERS' CUP HANDICAP. Grade II. Purse $300,000 (includes $100,000 BC – Breeders' Cup) For THREE-YEAR-OLDS AND UPWARD. (100,000 from the Breeders' Cup Fund for Cup nominees only.) By subscription of $300 each which shall accompany the nomination and an additional $3,000 when making entry. Any Breeders' Cup Fund monies not awarded will revert back to the Fund. Weights Saturday, August 23. This field will be limited to seventeen starters. If more than seventeen entries pass the entry box, the starters will be determined at that time with preference given to Breeders' Cup nominees only of equal racing quality or weight assignment (respective of sex and weight for age). Final entries to be made through the entry box no later than 11:30 a.m. on Wednesday, August 27, 2003. Closed Wednesday, August13, 2003 with 24 nominations. Plus up to $14,612 Breeder Awards.

Value of Race: $337,200 Winner $202,320; second $67,440; third $37,092; fourth $20,232; fifth $10,116. Mutuel Pool $220,892.00 Triactor Pool $140,818.00 Exactor Pool $117,032.00

Last Raced	Horse	M/Eqt.	A.	Wt	PP	¼	½	1	1¼	Str	Fin	Jockey	Odds $1
20Jly03 ^{8}WO^{1}	Strut The Stage	Lb	5	123	5	5^{4}	5^{3}	$6^{1\frac{1}{2}}$	$5^{2\frac{1}{2}}$	1^{hd}	$1^{1\frac{1}{4}}$	Kabel T K	1.15
20Jly03 ^{7}Del^{1}	Revved Up	L	5	118	8	3^{1}	$4^{2\frac{1}{2}}$	4^{1}	1^{1}	2^{1}	$2^{1\frac{1}{2}}$	Husbands P	3.05
26Jly03 ^{9}AP^{2}	Better Talk Now	Lb	4	115	7	$6^{1\frac{1}{2}}$	6^{1}	$5^{\frac{1}{2}}$	4^{hd}	3^{1}	$3^{\frac{3}{4}}$	Douglas R R	5.95
12Aug03 ^{9}Pha^{2}	Bowman Mill	L	5	112	3	$2^{1\frac{1}{2}}$	$1^{\frac{1}{2}}$	2^{1}	$3^{\frac{1}{2}}$	5^{3}	$4^{\frac{1}{2}}$	McKnight J	34.70
10Aug03 ^{6}WO^{1}	Portcullis	L	4	117	4	7^{2}	9^{4}	$8^{1\frac{1}{2}}$	$6^{\frac{1}{2}}$	6^{2}	5^{nk}	Callaghan S	11.00
3Aug03 ^{8}WO^{3}	Mark One	Lb	4	114	1	$1^{\frac{1}{2}}$	2^{2}	1^{hd}	2^{1}	$4^{1\frac{1}{2}}$	$6^{1\frac{1}{2}}$	Landry R C	28.40
16Feb03 ^{10}GP^{10}	Cetewayo	Lb	9	118	2	10	10	10	$9^{\frac{1}{2}}$	$7^{1\frac{1}{2}}$	$7^{1\frac{1}{4}}$	Clark D	10.25
2Aug03 ^{9}Lrl^{4}	Dr. Kashnikow	L	6	118	6	9^{3}	8^{hd}	9^{hd}	10	$8^{2\frac{1}{2}}$	8^{6}	Dos Ramos R A	15.05
5Jly03 ^{8}AP^{3}	Jack's Own Time	L	4	113	10	8^{hd}	7^{3}	7^{4}	$8^{1\frac{1}{2}}$	9^{hd}	$9^{\frac{1}{2}}$	Ramsammy E	21.05
10Aug03 ^{6}WO^{3}	Stage Classic	Lb	5	115	9	4^{3}	$3^{\frac{1}{2}}$	3^{hd}	7^{1}	10	10	Montpellier C	77.25

OFF AT 4:25 Start Good. Won driving. Course firm.

TIME :24^{1}, :49^{2}, 1:13^{3}, 1:38^{1}, 2:02^{3}, 2:27 (:24.38, :49.49, 1:13.66, 1:38.28, 2:02.69, 2:27.13)

$2 Mutuel Prices:

5-STRUT THE STAGE	4.30	2.80	2.30
8-REVVED UP		3.10	2.40
7-BETTER TALK NOW			3.50

$2 TRIACTOR 5-8-7 PAID $45.40 $2 EXACTOR 5-8 PAID $14.00

Ch. h, by Theatrical*Ire-Ruby Ransom, by Red Ransom. Trainer Frostad Mark. Bred by Jamm Ltd (Ky).

STRUT THE STAGE stalked the pace from off the rail, advanced four wide on the final turn, gained command passing the eighth pole and drew out. REVVED UP was close up four wide into the first turn, stalked the pace inside of STAGE CLASSIC, advanced between horses into the stretch to gain the lead, gave way passing the eighth pole and held the place position. BETTER TALK NOW angled in going into the first turn, was well off the rail, advanced inside into the final turn, was in tight, and steadied on the final turn, bumped BOWMAN MILL at the three sixteenths pole, finished well off the rail. BOWMAN MILL pressed the pace outside of MARK ONE, had the lead through the backstretch, drifted out slightly on the final turn, was in tight, bumped and steadied at the three sixteenths pole, did not threaten after that. PORTCULLIS was well placed inside, came off the rail on the final turn, gradually came out five wide in upper stretch, and gained mildly. MARK ONE set a pressured pace inside BOWMAN MILL, pressed that one through the backstretch, regained the lead into the final turn, gave way into the stretch. CETEWAYO trailed three wide, passed tiring rivals. DR. KASHNIKOW was well back while inside, came four wide into the stretch, and had no menace. JACK'S OWN TIME steadied early, raced three to four wide, and showed little. STAGE CLASSIC was close up five wide on the first turn, stalked the pace from off the rail, was three wide in the final turn, dropped back in the stretch.

Owners— 1, Sam-Son Farms; 2, Live Oak Plantation; 3, B Johnson K Barth & C Dwyer; 4, Chandler Dr John A; 5, Sam-Son Farms; 6, Stronach Stable; 7, Chandler Dr John A; 8, Erdenheim Farm; 9, Joan & John Phillips Pam Gartin & R; 10, Dominion Bloodstock Ball Derek & Ga

Trainers—1, Frostad Mark; 2, Clement Christophe; 3, Motion H Graham; 4, Dickinson Michael W; 5, Frostad Mark; 6, Vella Daniel J; 7, Dickinson Michael W; 8, Fisher John R S; 9, Toner James J; 10, Cotey David

EIGHTH RACE
Woodbine
SEPTEMBER 6, 2003

1 MILE. (Turf)(1.32^3) 39th Running of THE NATALMA. Grade III. Purse $150,000 For TWO-YEAR-OLD FILLIES. By subscription of $150 each which shall accompany the nomination and an additional $1,500 when making entry; with $150,000 added and an additional $50,000 for Canadian Breds, plus all fees to be divided: 60% to the winner, 20% to second, 11% to third, 6% to fourth and 3% to fifth. Weight 119 lbs. Winners of a sweepstakes of $75,000 twice, additional 2 lbs.; Non-winners of a sweepstakes of $75,000 once, allowed 3 lbs.; Of a race other than claiming, 5 lbs. (No Canadian Bred Allowance) Final entries to be made through the entry box no later than 11:30 a.m. on Wednesday, September 3, 2003. Plus $50,000 for Canadian Breds from the Thoroughbred Improvement Program and Canadian Thoroughbred Horse Society. Closed with 60 nominations, Wednesday August 20th,2003. Plus up to $11,575 Breeder Awards.

Value of Race: $177,000 Winner $106,200; second $35,400; third $19,470; fourth $10,620; fifth $5,310. Mutuel Pool $171,494.00 Triactor Pool $107,641.00 Exactor Pool $86,024.00

Last Raced	Horse	M/Eqt.	A.	Wt	PP	St	¼	½	¾	Str	Fin	Jockey	Odds $1
17Jly03 ^{4}Bel^1	Pink Champagne	L	2	114	9	8	6^{hd}	6^{hd}	$6^{\frac{1}{2}}$	1^1	1^{hd}	Dos Ramos R A	2.60
19Jly03 Lin^1	Saree-GB	L	2	117	6	10	10	$8^{\frac{1}{2}}$	$7^{1\frac{1}{2}}$	2^{hd}	$2^{2\frac{1}{2}}$	Husbands P	2.35
13Aug03 Sal^2	America America	Lb	2	121	7	3	$5^{1\frac{1}{2}}$	$4^{\frac{1}{2}}$	5^{hd}	$4^{3\frac{1}{2}}$	3^1	Peslier O	6.95
22Aug03 ^{6}WO^2	Do You Love It	L	2	117	1	6	$3^{1\frac{1}{2}}$	3^{hd}	1^{hd}	3^{hd}	$4^{7\frac{3}{4}}$	Jones Jono	17.45
22Aug03 ^{6}WO^4	Coco's My Dream		2	116	10	1	$9^{1\frac{1}{2}}$	7^2	$8^{2\frac{1}{2}}$	6^{hd}	$5^{1\frac{3}{4}}$	Olguin G L	16.10
27Jly03 ^{2}WO^1	Sleek And Powerful	Lb	2	118	2	5	1^{hd}	$1^{\frac{1}{2}}$	2^1	$5^{\frac{1}{2}}$	6^{nk}	Husbands S P	78.95
2Aug03 ^{7}WO^1	Silver Bird	L	2	116	5	7	4^{hd}	$5^{3\frac{1}{2}}$	4^{hd}	$7^{3\frac{1}{2}}$	$7^{1\frac{1}{2}}$	McAleney J S	3.15
3Aug03 ^{4}WO^7	Summerberry	Lb	2	115	3	9	7^{hd}	$9^{\frac{1}{2}}$	10	8^1	8^6	Kabel T K	16.25
22Aug03 ^{6}WO^1	Ralla	L	2	116	8	2	8^{hd}	10	9^2	$9^{1\frac{1}{2}}$	9^7	Callaghan S	19.25
3Aug03 ^{4}WO^3	Molly's Gone	L	2	114	4	4	2^2	$2^{1\frac{1}{2}}$	3^{hd}	10	10	McKnight J	27.00

OFF AT 4:25 Start Good. Won driving. Course firm.
TIME :21^3, :44^1, 1:09^4, 1:36^2 (:21.73, :44.22, 1:09.88, 1:36.53)

$2 Mutuel Prices:

11-PINK CHAMPAGNE	7.20	4.20	3.50
8-SAREE-GB		3.80	3.20
9-AMERICA AMERICA			4.50

$2 TRIACTOR 11-8-9 PAID $127.30 $2 EXACTOR 11-8 PAID $28.40

Dk. b. or br. f, (Mar), by Awesome Again–Turkappeal, by Turkoman. Trainer Kimmel John C. Bred by FarFellow Farms Ltd (Ky).

PINK CHAMPAGNE raced three wide, advanced on the turn while moving inside, came off the rail in upper stretch, gained the lead in mid stretch and was all out to hold off the runner up. SAREE (GB) trailed, advanced off the rail on the turn, lacked room and bumped with AMERICA AMERICA in upper stretch, rallied between horses, and was out gamed by the winner. AMERICA AMERICA stalked the forced pace from off the rail, came three wide into the stretch, was in tight, bumped, and jostled in upper stretch, made a four wide bid through the stretch, lugged in late and was outfinished. DO YOU LOVE IT stalked the forced pace from the inside, came off the rail into the stretch, gained the lead three wide in upper stretch, gave way in mid stretch, was forced in late. COCO'S MY DREAM had a short lead early, raced four wide, came six wide into the stretch, and was not a threat. SLEEK AND POWERFUL set a pressured fast pace from the inside, weakened in upper stretch. SILVER BIRD stalked the forced pace three wide, made a mild bid four wide in upper stretch, and faltered. SUMMERBERRY raced off the rail, moved inside on the turn, was four wide in the stretch, and showed little. RALLA raced three wide, faded in the stretch. MOLLY'S GONE pressed the pace outside of SLEEK AND POWERFUL while three wide, gave way into the stretch, and faded.

Owners— 1, Starview Stable; 2, Mack Earle I; 3, Cameron Express Inc; 4, David & Doris Levitch Bert & Mark B; 5, Henwood Ken; 6, Tropical Stable & O'Callaghan Sarah; 7, Jim McAlpine; 8, Sapara James & Alice; 9, Anderson Farms & Ontario Inc; 10, Franks John

Trainers—1, Kimmel John C; 2, Casse Mark; 3, Mourier Franck; 4, Casse Mark; 5, Attard Sid C; 6, O'Callaghan Daniel M; 7, Baker Reade; 8, Carroll Josie; 9, Frostad Mark; 10, Bell David R

Scratched— Sweetgum, Lotus Land (23Aug03 ^{7}WO^5)

$1 Pick Three (1-7-11) Paid $28.35; Pick Three Pool $8,905.

SIXTH RACE
Woodbine
SEPTEMBER 14, 2003

ABOUT 1⅛ MILES. (Turf)(1.43^3) 49th Running of THE CANADIAN HANDICAP. Grade II. Purse $250,000 For FILLIES AND MARES, THREE-YEAR-OLDS AND UPWARD. By subscription of $250 each which shall accompany the nomination and an additional $2,500 when making entry; with $250,000 added and an additional $50,000 for Canadian Breds, plus all fees to be divided: 60% to the winner, 20% to second, 11% to third, 6% to fourth and 3% to fifth. Weights, Saturday, August 30, 2003. Final entries to be made through the entry box no later than 11:30 a.m. on Thursday, September 11, 2003. Plus $50,000 for Canadian Breds from the Thoroughbred Improvement Program and Canadian Thoroughbred Horse Society. Plus up to $14,612 Breeder Awards. Closed Wednesday, August 20, 2003 with 36 nominations.

Value of Race: $309,000 Winner $197,400; second $55,800; third $30,690; fourth $16,740; fifth $8,370. Mutuel Pool $200,022.00 Superfecta Pool $28,078.00 Triactor Pool $102,165.00 Exactor Pool $95,652.00

Last Raced	Horse	M/Eqt.	A.	Wt	PP	St	¼	½	¾	Str	Fin	Jockey	Odds $1
24Aug03 ^{4}WO^2	Inish Glora	L	5	116	6	3	3^1	$3^{\frac{1}{2}}$	3^1	$1^{1\frac{1}{2}}$	$1^{1\frac{3}{4}}$	Kabel T K	10.05
17Aug03 ^{10}Mth^1	Volga-IR	L	5	118	5	1	4^{hd}	6^1	$5^{\frac{1}{2}}$	$2^{2\frac{1}{2}}$	$2^{1\frac{3}{4}}$	Nakatani C S	1.25
23Aug03 ^{9}WO^2	Diadella	Lb	6	116	2	7	5^{hd}	7^1	8	$5^{\frac{1}{2}}$	$3^{\frac{1}{2}}$	Santos J A	4.40
25Aug03 ^{8}Sar^5	Lady Of The Future	L	5	115	8	2	8	8	7^{hd}	8	4^{nk}	Luzzi M J	17.05
9Jly03 New^7	Hold To Ransom	L	3	112	7	5	7^2	5^{hd}	4^{hd}	$6^{1\frac{1}{2}}$	5no	Ramsammy E	5.75
24Aug03 ^{4}WO^3	Byzantine	Lb	7	117	1	8	6^1	$4^{\frac{1}{2}}$	6^1	7^{hd}	6no	Jones Jono	24.05
24Aug03 ^{4}WO^4	First Quarter	L	4	114	4	4	1^{hd}	2^1	2^{hd}	4^{hd}	$7^{\frac{1}{2}}$	Day P	7.30
23Aug03 ^{9}WO^1	Ginger Gold	L	4	116	3	6	$2^{\frac{1}{2}}$	$1^{\frac{1}{2}}$	1^{hd}	3^{hd}	8	Husbands P	6.60

OFF AT 3:31 Start Good For All But INISH GLORA Won driving. Course firm.
TIME :23^4, :47, 1:44^2 (:23.93, :47.08, 1:44.56)

$2 Mutuel Prices:

6-INISH GLORA	22.10	6.20	3.50
5-VOLGA-IR		3.30	2.80
2-DIADELLA			2.90

$1 SUPERFECTA 6-5-2-8 PAID $821.25 $2 TRIACTOR 6-5-2 PAID $240.20
$2 EXACTOR 6-5 PAID $66.80

B. m, by Regal Classic–Star Guest, by Assert*Ire. Trainer Benson MacDonald. Bred by C G Scott DVM (Ont-C).

INISH GLORA bobbled at the start, was close up while three wide, gained the lead into the stretch, drifted in in mid stretch, and prevailed. VOLGA (IRE) stalked the forced pace three wide, rallied four wide, and was second best. DIADELLA stalked the pace from off the rail, dropped back slightly and moved inside on the turn, came off the rail into the stretch, rallied mildly three wide. LADY OF THE FUTURE was five wide early, trailed, was three wide on the turn, gained mildly four wide in the stretch. HOLD TO RANSOM stalked the forced pace three wide, was four wide on the turn, five wide in the stretch and had no menace. BYZANTINE stalked the forced pace from the inside, came out three wide in mid stretch, and did not rally. FIRST QUARTER had a short lead early, pressed the pace outside of GINGER GOLD, weakened into the stretch. GINGER GOLD pressed the pace inside of FIRST QUARTER early, gained the lead at the ten sixteenths pole, and gave way.

Owners— 1, Costigan Robert J; 2, Allen Joseph; 3, Stronach Stable; 4, Pearson Max H; 5, Gainsborough Farm LLC; 6, Royal Oak Farm; 7, Come By Chance Stable; 8, Jim Dandy Stable

Trainers—1, Benson MacDonald; 2, Clement Christophe; 3, Pierce Malcolm; 4, Greene Thomas M; 5, Dunlop Edward; 6, Pollock Bruce M; 7, Day James E; 8, Attard Sid C

$1 Pick Three (8-4-6) Paid $5,727.95; Pick Three Pool $7,793.

FOURTH RACE
Woodbine
SEPTEMBER 14, 2003

1 MILE. (Turf)(1.32^{3}) 51st Running of THE SUMMER. Grade II. Purse $250,000 For TWO-YEAR-OLDS. By subscription of $250 each which shall accompany the nomination and an additional $2,500 when making entry; with $250,000 added, plus all fees to be divided: 60% to the winner, 20% to second, 11% to third, 6% to fourth and 3% to fifth. Weights 122 lbs. Fillies allowed 3 lbs. (No Canadian Bred Allowance) Final entries to be made through the entry box no later than 11:30 a.m. on Thursday, September 11, 2003. Closed Wednesday, August 20, 2003. with 42 nominations.

Value of Race: $285,500 Winner $171,300; second $57,100; third $31,405; fourth $17,130; fifth $8,565. Mutuel Pool $190,232.00 Triactor Pool $117,625.00 Exactor Pool $104,568.00

Last Raced	Horse	M/Eqt.	A.Wt	PP	St	¼	½	¾	Str	Fin	Jockey	Odds $1
17Aug03 ^{3}WO^{2}	Bachelor Blues	L	2 122	8	1	1^{1}	1^{2}	1^{2}	1^{3}	1^{nk}	Kabel T K	12.75
12Jly03 ^{7}AP^{1}	Victory Light	Lb	2 122	10	2	$5^{\frac{1}{2}}$	5^{1}	5^{1}	3^{1}	2^{5}	Day P	6.50
18Aug03 ^{4}Sar^{1}	[D]Commendation	Lb	2 122	9	3	8^{hd}	$8^{2\frac{1}{2}}$	$2^{\frac{1}{2}}$	$2^{\frac{1}{2}}$	$3^{2\frac{1}{4}}$	Desormeaux K J	8.50
6Sep03 ^{8}WO^{3}	America America	L	2 119	2	10	10	$9^{\frac{1}{2}}$	$6^{1\frac{1}{2}}$	$6^{2\frac{1}{2}}$	4^{2}	Nakatani C S	7.45
31Aug03 ^{7}Mth^{1}	Grand Heritage	L	2 122	1	8	$2^{\frac{1}{2}}$	$3^{\frac{1}{2}}$	$3^{\frac{1}{2}}$	$4^{1\frac{1}{2}}$	5^{hd}	Albarado R J	4.35
23Aug03 ^{4}WO^{1}	Bon Marie	L	2 122	6	7	3^{hd}	2^{hd}	4^{1}	5^{1}	$6^{2\frac{1}{4}}$	Jones Jono	15.45
10Aug03 ^{4}WO^{1}	Dynafire	L	2 122	3	6	$6^{\frac{1}{2}}$	6^{hd}	$7^{\frac{1}{2}}$	$7^{\frac{1}{2}}$	7^{1}	Santos J A	1.40
17Aug03 ^{3}WO^{1}	Spider Canyon	b	2 122	7	4	$4^{\frac{1}{2}}$	$4^{\frac{1}{2}}$	8^{2}	$8^{2\frac{1}{2}}$	$8^{1\frac{1}{4}}$	Dos Ramos R A	22.45
9Aug03 ^{3}WO^{3}	Go Kitty Go	Lb	2 122	5	9	9^{2}	10	$9^{\frac{1}{2}}$	9^{5}	$9^{10\frac{1}{4}}$	Husbands P	20.70
17Aug03 ^{3}WO^{3}	Zakocity	Lb	2 122	4	5	$7^{\frac{1}{2}}$	7^{hd}	10	10	10	McAleney J S	36.10

[D]-Commendation disqualified and placed 10th.

OFF AT 2:24 Start Good For All But AMERICA AMERICA, ZAKOCITY Won driving. Course firm.
TIME :23^{2}, :46^{1}, 1:10^{2}, 1:34^{4} (:23.45, :46.26, 1:10.58, 1:34.95)

$2 Mutuel Prices:				
	8–BACHELOR BLUES	27.50	10.50	6.10
	10–VICTORY LIGHT		8.30	5.40
	2–AMERICA AMERICA			5.20

$2 TRIACTOR 8–10–2 PAID $1,670.40 $2 EXACTOR 8–10 PAID $237.20

Gr/ro c, (Mar), by Smoke Glacken–Wedding Day Blues, by El Prado*Ire. Trainer Carroll Josie. Bred by William Schettine (Ky).

BACHELOR BLUES set a pressured pace from off the rail while under restraint, drew clear at the eleven sixteenths pole, came five wide into the stretch, and lasted. VICTORY LIGHT stalked the pace four wide, came seven wide into the stretch, rallied while drifting in and just missed. COMMENDATION was four wide early, three wide on the turn, angled in midway on the turn, rallied mildly off the rail in the stretch. AMERICA AMERICA broke outwards, trailed while off the rail, was three wide on the turn, gained mildly eight wide in the stretch. GRAND HERITAGE was reluctant to load, pressed the pace inside of the winner, weakened into the stretch. BON MARIE stalked the pace from off the rail, came out six wide in the stretch, and lost ground. DYNAFIRE was well placed inside, and had no menace. SPIDER CANYON stalked the pace three wide, dropped back in the stretch. GO KITTY GO raced three wide, was four wide on the turn and showed little. ZAKOCITY hit the gate at the start, was between horses and steadied in the backstretch, three wide on the turn, checked at the three eighths pole, faded in the stretch. A Stewards' inquiry following the race looking into the turn disqualified COMMENDATION from third and place him tenth for interfering with ZACKOCITY.

Owners— 1, Schettine William C; 2, WinStar Farm LLC; 3, Courtland Farms; 4, Cameron Express Inc; 5, Firestone Mrs Bertram R; 6, HorseN Around Racing Stable & Casse; 7, Allard Cam; 8, Minshall Farms; 9, Tommy Town Thoroughbreds LLC; 10, Franks John

Trainers—1, Carroll Josie; 2, Walden W Elliott; 3, Motion H Graham; 4, Mourier Franck; 5, Mott William I; 6, Casse Mark; 7, Attfield Roger L; 8, Minshall Barbara J; 9, Casse Mark; 10, Bell David R

$1 Pick Three (2–5–8) Paid $171.65; Pick Three Pool $9,523.

NINTH RACE
Woodbine
SEPTEMBER 14, 2003

1 MILE. (Turf)(1.32^3) 7th Running of THE ATTO MILE. Grade I. Purse $1,000,000 For THREE-YEAR-OLDS AND UPWARD. By subscription of $750 each which shall accompany the nomination and an additional $10,000 when making entry. The added money and all fees to be divided: 60% to the winner, 20% to second, 11% to third, 6% to fourth and 3%to fifth. Three-year-olds, 119 lbs.; Older 124 lbs. Non-winners of a Gr. I Race in 2003, allowed 3 lbs.; Of a Gr. II Race in 2003 or a Gr. I Race in 2002, allowed 5 lbs.; Of a Gr. III Race in 2003 or a Gr. II Race in 2002, 7 lbs. (Note: Grades as recognized by the International Cataloguing Standards Committee.) (No Canadian-Bred Allowance) Plus up to $17,457 Breeder Awards. Closed Wednesday, August 13, 2003 with 44 nominations.

Value of Race: $1,000,000 Winner $600,000; second $200,000; third $110,000; fourth $60,000; fifth $30,000. Mutuel Pool $868,483.00 Superfecta Pool $135,008.00 Triactor Pool $489,616.00 Exactor Pool $531,706.00

Last Raced	Horse	M/Eqt.	A.	Wt	PP	St	¼	½	¾	Str	Fin	Jockey	Odds $1
2Aug03 ^{5}Dmr^1	Touch of the Blues-FR	L	6	119	3	8	$9^{3\frac{1}{2}}$	$8^{\frac{1}{2}}$	5^{hd}	$3^{2\frac{1}{2}}$	$1^{\frac{1}{2}}$	Desormeaux K J	5.45
16Aug03 ^{8}WO^1	Soaring Free	L	4	121	11	1	2^{hd}	4^{1}	$2^{\frac{1}{2}}$	$1^{\frac{1}{2}}$	$2^{1\frac{3}{4}}$	Kabel T K	4.40
16Aug03 ^{10}AP^5	Perfect Soul-IR	Lb	5	121	4	11	11	11	11	6^{1}	3^{hd}	Santos J A	3.55
9Aug03 ^{8}WO^1	Wando	L	3	115	5	5	4^{1}	3^{hd}	1^{hd}	$2^{\frac{1}{2}}$	$4^{2\frac{3}{4}}$	Husbands P	3.15
2Aug03 ^{8}WO^1	Chopinina	Lb	5	116	8	3	3^{1}	1^{hd}	$3^{1\frac{1}{2}}$	$4^{\frac{1}{2}}$	$5^{1\frac{1}{4}}$	Dos Ramos R A	26.40
12Jly03 ^{8}WO^3	Moonshine Hall	L	3	112	7	7	$8^{2\frac{1}{2}}$	$9^{1\frac{1}{2}}$	$9^{\frac{1}{2}}$	11	$6^{\frac{3}{4}}$	Day P	17.90
5Jly03 ^{9}CD^2	Freefourinternet	L	5	117	2	10	10^{hd}	$10^{\frac{1}{2}}$	$10^{1\frac{1}{2}}$	7^{1}	7^{1}	Albarado R J	37.75
22Aug03 ^{2}Dmr^1	Sarafan	L	6	121	1	9	$6^{\frac{1}{2}}$	5^{hd}	$6^{1\frac{1}{2}}$	5^{9}	8^{hd}	Nakatani C S	5.95
16Aug03 ^{8}WO^5	Numerous Times	Lf	6	117	6	6	5^{1}	6^{hd}	$8^{1\frac{1}{2}}$	$9^{\frac{1}{2}}$	$9^{\frac{1}{2}}$	Jones Jono	16.75
23Aug03 ^{9}Sar^3	Tap The Admiral	L	5	121	10	4	7^{hd}	7^{2}	7^{hd}	10^{1}	$10^{\frac{1}{2}}$	Luzzi M J	13.20
3Aug03 ^{8}WO^1	Wake At Noon	Lb	6	119	9	2	$1^{1\frac{1}{2}}$	$2^{1\frac{1}{2}}$	$4^{\frac{1}{2}}$	$8^{\frac{1}{2}}$	11	Ramsammy E	45.45

OFF AT 5:14 Start Good. Won driving. Course firm.
TIME :22^4, :45^1, 1:09^1, 1:33^1 (:22.84, :45.38, 1:09.38, 1:33.39)

$2 Mutuel Prices:			
3-TOUCH OF THE BLUES-FR	12.90	6.30	3.90
11-SOARING FREE		6.50	4.40
4-PERFECT SOUL-IR			3.60

$1 SUPERFECTA 3-11-4-5 PAID $468.15 $2 TRIACTOR 3-11-4 PAID $368.70 $2 EXACTOR 3-11 PAID $83.50

B. h, by Cadeaux Genereux*GB-Silabteni, by Nureyev. Trainer Drysdale Neil. Bred by Gainsborough Stud Man. (Fr).

TOUCH OF THE BLUES (FR) raced inside, was three wide into the stretch, came out five wide at the three sixteenths pole, rallied and took over late. SOARING FREE broke sharply to gain a short lead early, stalked the forced pace four wide, gained the lead approaching the eighth pole, drifted out in mid stretch, and gave his best. PERFECT SOUL (IRE) trailed to the three sixteenths pole, rallied late while drifting out to get up for the show position. WANDO stalked the forced pace from off the rail, came through between horses into the stretch, gained the lead briefly in upper stretch, flattened out in mid stretch and was outfinished for the show position. CHOPININA was close up early while off the rail, pressed from along the rail inside of WAKE AT NOON at the seven sixteenths pole, gained the lead at the half pole, gave way in upper stretch. MOONSHINE HALL raced off the rail, was three wide on the turn, came four wide into the stretch, angled out at the three sixteenths pole, and gained mildly eight wide. FREEFOURINTERNET was well back while inside, came four wide into the stretch, advanced mildly seven wide. SARAFAN was reluctant to load, well placed inside, came off the rail in the stretch and was not a threat. NUMEROUS TIMES well placed off the rail while between horses, was three wide on the turn, exchanged bumps with TAP THE ADMIRAL in upper stretch, was four wide in the stretch and had no rally. TAP THE ADMIRAL well placed three wide, was five wide on the turn, bumped with NUMEROUS TIMES in upper stretch, forced out slightly at the three sixteenths pole, and had no menace. WAKE AT NOON gained a clear lead after two furlongs while four wide, was three wide on the turn, lost the lead with half a mile remaining, gave way into the stretch, drifted out at the three sixteenths pole, and faded through the stretch.

Owners— 1, Gainsborough Farm LLC; 2, Sam-Son Farms; 3, Fipke Charles E; 4, Schickedanz Gustav; 5, Knob Hill Stable; 6, Melnyk Eugene & Laura; 7, Equirace Com Stable; 8, Tanaka Gary A; 9, Committee Stable; 10, S Ettinger; 11, Schickedanz Bruno

Trainers—1, Drysdale Neil; 2, Frostad Mark; 3, Attfield Roger L; 4, Keogh Michael; 5, Fehr John Alec; 6, Reinstedler Anthony; 7, Scott Joan; 8, Drysdale Neil; 9, Attard Sid C; 10, Carroll Del W II; 11, Katryan Abraham R

$1 Pick Three (2-8-3) Paid $317.35; Pick Three Pool $17,031.

EIGHTH RACE
Woodbine
SEPTEMBER 20, 2003

1 1/16 MILES. (1.404) 38th Running of THE MAZARINE BREEDERS' CUP. Grade II. Purse $250,000 (includes $75,000 BC – Breeders' Cup) For TWO-YEAR-OLD FILLIES. (Includes $75,000 from Breeders' Cup Fund for nominees only) By subscription of $250 each which shall accompany the nomination and an additional $2,500 when making entry; with $175,000 added, and an additional $75,000 from the Breeders' Cup Fund for Cup nominees only. Weight 120 lbs. Winners of a sweepstakes of $ 75,000 at a mile or over, or a sweepstakes of $75,000 three times at any distance, additional 2 lbs.; Non-winners of a sweepstakes of$75,000 twice at anydistance, allowed 3 lbs.; Of a sweepstakes of $75,000 once, 5 lbs.; Of a race other than claiming, 7 lbs.(No Canadian Bred Allowance) The field will be limited to fourteen starters.

Value of Race: $268,250 Winner $160,950; second $53,650; third $29,508; fourth $16,095; fifth $8,047. Mutuel Pool $146,111.00 Exactor Pool $76,791.00

Last Raced	Horse	M/Eqt.	A.Wt	PP	St	¼	½	¾	Str	Fin	Jockey	Odds $1
29Aug03 5WO1	Dream About	L	2 117	4	2	11½	12	13½	18	18¼	Husbands P	0.55
14Sep03 4WO4	America America	L	2 115	5	3	5	2hd	33	23	28¼	Clark D	5.45
3Aug03 4WO1	Brush With Destiny	L	2 115	3	4	41	5	46	410	31½	Kabel T K	3.75
1Sep03 8WO2	La Grande Mamma	L	2 117	1	1	2½	31½	21	31	410½	McAleney J S	8.10
6Sep03 8WO4	Do You Love It	L	2 117	2	5	34	4hd	5	5	5	Jones Jono	10.00

OFF AT 4:25 Start Good. Won ridden out. Track fast.
TIME :234, :481, 1:123, 1:40, 1:472 (:23.99, :48.29, 1:12.77, 1:40.04, 1:47.54)

$2 Mutuel Prices:

4–DREAM ABOUT	3.10	2.40	2.10
5–AMERICA AMERICA		3.60	2.60
3–BRUSH WITH DESTINY			2.20

$2 EXACTOR 4–5 PAID $8.90

Dk. b. or br. f, (Feb), by Cherokee Run–Social Director, by Deputy Minister. Trainer Carroll Josie. Bred by Windfields Farm Ltd (Ont–C).

DREAM ABOUT gained a clear lead off the rail on the first turn, drew off through the stretch, under minimal encouragement as much the best. AMERICA AMERICA trailed early, advanced between horses in the backstretch, came four wide into the stretch and was second best. BRUSH WITH DESTINY raced three to four wide, and was not a threat. LA GRANDE MAMMA stalked the pace from the inside, dropped back in the stretch. DO YOU LOVE IT stalked the pace three wide, was through early, and faded.

Owners— 1, Arosa Farms; 2, Cameron Express Inc; 3, Sam-Son Farms; 4, Great Plyer; 5, Levitch David & Doris Blieden Bert
Trainers—1, Carroll Josie; 2, Mourier Franck; 3, Frostad Mark; 4, Owens Steve; 5, Casse Mark

---

$1 Pick Three (11–2–4) Paid $41.00; Pick Three Pool $8,369.

NINTH RACE
Hastings
SEPTEMBER 20, 2003

1⅛ MILES. (1.464) 40th Running of THE BRITISH COLUMBIA BREEDERS' CUP OAKS. Grade III. Purse $125,000 (plus $25,000 BC – Breeders' Cup) A Scale Weight Stakes for Three Year Old Fillies. By subscription of $200, $1,250 to enter and $1,250 to pass scratch time. With $125,000 added and an additional $25,000 from the Breeders' Cup Fund for Cup nominees only. All Hastings Entertainment Inc. purse money to be divided 60% to the winner, 20% to second, 11% to third, 6% to fourth, and 3% to fifth. Breeders' Cup Fund monies correspondingly divided providing a Breeders' Cup nominee has finished in an awarded position. Any Breeders' Cup Fund monies not awarded will revert back to the Fund. Preference will be based on lifetime earnings as recorded by The Daily Racing Form at time of entry. In a case where horses have identical earnings, preference will be given to the Breeders' Cup eligible horse. Scale Weight: 121lbs.

Value of Race: $169,612 Winner $104,940; second $33,230; third $16,489; fourth $9,969; fifth $4,984. Mutuel Pool $55,157.00 Superfecta Pool $18,225.00 Triactor Pool $37,513.00 Exactor Pool $24,452.00

Last Raced	Horse	M/Eqt.	A.Wt	PP	St	¼	½	¾	Str	Fin	Jockey	Odds $1
23Aug03 9NP1	Raylene	L	3 121	1	4	42½	43½	3hd	32½	1nk	Walcott R	2.00
1Sep03 4Hst1	Dancewithavixen	Lbf	3 121	6	2	22½	22	1hd	12	24½	Valdez F S	0.65
1Sep03 4Hst4	Payton's Pride	Lb	3 121	7	5	52	51	6hd	52½	3hd	Skelly R V	58.75
1Sep03 4Hst3	Chorus Dancer	Lf	3 121	8	6	64	61½	4½	21	4¾	Loseth C	35.60
31Aug03 8Hst1	Vegas Folly	L	3 121	4	7	7hd	84	7½	4½	52½	May R H	47.85
7Sep03 8Hst3	Class Choice	Lb	3 121	3	8	82	7½	84	61½	6nk	Chaparro C	63.90
23Aug03 9EmD5	La Belle Fleur	Lb	3 121	5	9	9	9	9	71½	73	Fuentes F P	79.30
23Aug03 9EmD3	Brave Miss	Lb	3 121	9	1	3½	3½	52	81½	84¾	Alvarado P V	6.25
7Sep03 8Hst4	Pretty Meadow	Lbf	3 121	2	3	15	12	22	9	9	Wright N	30.90

OFF AT 5:11 Start Good For All But LA BELLE FLEUR Won driving. Track fast.
TIME :223, :463, 1:124, 1:382, 1:52 (:22.76, :46.78, 1:12.80, 1:38.56, 1:52.16)

$2 Mutuel Prices:

1–RAYLENE	6.00	2.60	3.00
6–DANCEWITHAVIXEN		2.30	2.40
7–PAYTON'S PRIDE			7.30

$2 SUPERFECTA 1–6–7–8 PAID $387.00 $2 TRIACTOR 1–6–7 PAID $124.80
$2 EXACTOR 1–6 PAID $9.50

Dk. b. or br. f, (Mar), by Tabasco Cat–Petite Princess, by Dayjur. Trainer Haynes Rodney. Bred by Kennelot Stables Limited (Ky).

RAYLENE away alertly and well placed along the inside, stalked the leaders, rallied on the two path, with a well timed finish was up in the final strides driving. DANCEWITHAVIXEN away alertly, stalked the pace setter, took over the lead on the backstretch, drew clear into the stretch, could not hold off the winner. PAYTON'S PRIDE in the middle of the pack, stalked the pace, put in a mild bid along the inside in the stretch, finished well but was outrun by the top two. CHORUS DANCER never far back, stalked the pace, rallied from three wide leaving the backstretch, weakened in the stretch. VEGAS FOLLY unhurried early, put in a mild bid from four wide on the final turn, was outrun. CLASS CHOICE unhurried early, showed little and failed to menace. LA BELLE FLEUR pinched back at the start, trailed for most of the trip and showed little. BRAVE MISS broke sharply and was well placed, caught three wide on the backstretch, gave way after the half. PRETTY MEADOW broke sharply, assumed command, drew clear, set the pace, gave way on the backstretch.

Owners— 1, Calmar Stables & Ranch; 2, TNT Racing Stable; 3, McLellan Roy E; 4, Linwood Stables; 5, Sangara K K; 6, Lara Racing Stables Ltd; 7, Braithwaite E M & Gorasht I M; 8, Nordahl Leif S; 9, Budget Stable
Trainers—1, Haynes Rodney; 2, Longstaff Tom; 3, Barroby Harold J; 4, Anderson Robert J; 5, Barroby Harold J; 6, Olmos Juan C; 7, Barroby Frank E; 8, Heads Barbara; 9, Armstrong Janet

NINTH RACE
Hastings
SEPTEMBER 21, 2003

1⅛ MILES. (1.46^{4}) 58th Running of THE BRITISH COLUMBIA DERBY. Grade II. Purse $250,000 (plus $30,000 THRIF – British Columbia Bred) A Scale Weight Stakes for Three Year Olds. $250 to nominate. $2,500 to enter and $2,500 to pass scratch time. With $250,000 added, of which 60% goes to the winner, 20% to second, 11% to third, 6% to fourth, and 3% to fifth. Weights: Colts & Geldings 126lbs, Fillies 121 lbs. Preference will be based on lifetime earnings as recorded by The Daily Racing Form at time of entry. Field will be limited to 12 starters.

Value of Race: $326,750 Winner $198,750; second $66,250; third $32,863; fourth $19,925; fifth $8,962. Mutuel Pool $82,281.00 Triactor Pool $51,525.00 Exactor Pool $33,656.00

Last Raced	Horse	M/Eqt.	A.Wt	PP	St	¼	½	¾	Str	Fin	Jockey	Odds $1
1Sep03 ^{9}EmD^{1}	Roscoe Pito	L	3 126	3	2	2^{1}	$2^{1\frac{1}{2}}$	1^{hd}	1^{2}	1^{2}	Alvarado P V	1.40
1Sep03 ^{10}Hst^{2}	Steady Smiler		3 126	8	7	6^{hd}	6^{hd}	$6^{3\frac{1}{2}}$	$5^{1\frac{1}{2}}$	$2^{\frac{1}{2}}$	Valdez F S	7.00
23Aug03 ^{9}NP^{4}	Rindanica	Lb	3 126	1	6	$7^{1\frac{1}{2}}$	4^{hd}	5^{1}	4^{2}	$3^{\frac{1}{2}}$	Winters P A	34.00
23Aug03 ^{9}NP^{2}	Taiaslew	L	3 126	6	1	3^{3}	$3^{2\frac{1}{2}}$	3^{2}	$2^{\frac{1}{2}}$	$4^{2\frac{1}{4}}$	Welch Q K	3.80
29Aug03 ^{4}Dmr^{1}	Royal Place	L	3 126	4	8	8^{2}	8^{2}	7^{1}	$6^{\frac{1}{2}}$	$5^{\frac{1}{2}}$	McAleney J S	a-3.35
22Aug03 ^{8}WO^{2}	Pants N Kisses	L	3 126	2	5	4^{2}	$5^{1\frac{1}{2}}$	4^{hd}	7^{3}	$6^{1\frac{1}{4}}$	Olguin G L	5.70
1Sep03 ^{10}Hst^{8}	Bold Texas	Lb	3 126	5	3	1^{hd}	1^{hd}	2^{4}	3^{hd}	$7^{4\frac{1}{2}}$	Serna F A	39.70
1Sep03 ^{1}Hst^{2}	Prerequisite	Lb	3 126	9	9	9	9	9	8^{1}	8^{nk}	Fuentes F P	52.45
1Sep03 ^{10}Hst^{5}	Johnny Ola	L	3 126	7	4	5^{1}	7^{1}	$8^{\frac{1}{2}}$	9	9	Wilson D H	a-3.35

a–Coupled: Royal Place and Johnny Ola.

OFF AT 5:17 Start Good. Won driving. Track fast.
TIME :23, :47^{1}, 1:11^{3}, 1:37^{3}, 1:51^{2} (:23.00, :47.31, 1:11.70, 1:37.62, 1:51.58)

$2 Mutuel Prices:

4–ROSCOE PITO	4.80	2.90	2.70
7–STEADY SMILER		5.20	4.50
2–RINDANICA			4.80

$2 TRIACTOR 4–7–2 PAID $376.90 $2 EXACTOR 4–7 PAID $30.10

Dk. b. or br. g, (May), by Light of Mine–Perfect Coin, by L'Emigrant. Trainer Snow John. Bred by Robert W Simpson & Robert G Henderson (BC–C).

ROSCOE PITO broke sharply, pressed the pace from the inside while under a hold, gained command on the backstretch, drew clear into the stretch and won driving. STEADY SMILER unhurried early and three wide, rallied from three wide on the final turn and four wide down the stretch, closed well and garnered the place. RINDANICA unhurried early, saved ground, rallied from the inside down the stretch, closed willingly. TAIASLEW broke sharply, well placed on the inside, stalked the leaders, rallied, weakened in the stretch. ROYAL PLACE unhurried early, put in a mild bid on the final turn and was outrun. PANTS N KISSES away alertly and in good position, stalked the pace, was through after three quarters. BOLD TEXAS broke sharply, gained command from the outside, set a pressured pace, gave way on the backstretch. PREREQUISITE trailed for most of the trip and showed little. JOHNNY OLA away alertly and in the middle of the pack, was through early and dropped back.

Owners— 1, Snow John Wildcard Stable Punjab Fo; 2, Maybin Rob; 3, Rick Robertson Engineering Ltd; 4, Tracy Shelli & Ryan Stan; 5, Sangara K K; 6, Dominion Bloodstock Ball Derek & Ga; 7, Swift Financial Services Ltd; 8, Maisey Les; 9, Sangara K K

Trainers—1, Snow John; 2, Maybin Robert; 3, Rycroft Riley; 4, Tracy Greg; 5, Barroby Harold J; 6, Cotey David; 7, Kamps Rick; 8, Brown Jim R; 9, Barroby Harold J

$2 Pick Three (5–1–4) Paid $197.20; Pick Three Pool $4,428.

EIGHTH RACE
Woodbine
SEPTEMBER 28, 2003

1⅜ MILES. (Turf)(2.13) 9th Running of THE SKY CLASSIC HANDICAP. Grade II. Purse $250,000 FOR THREE-YEAR-OLDS AND UPWARD. By subscription of $250 each which shall accompany the nomination and an additional $2,500 when making entry; with $250,000 added, plus all fees to be divided: 60% to the winner, 20% to second, 11% to third, 6% to fourth and 3% to fifth. Weights, Saturday, September 20, 2003. Final entries to be made through the entry box no later than 11:30 a.m. on Thursday, September 25, 2003. Closed Wednesday, September 10, 2003 with 27 nominations.

Value of Race: $271,750 Winner $163,050; second $54,350; third $29,893; fourth $16,305; fifth $8,152. Mutuel Pool $114,499.00 Triactor Pool $60,362.00 Exactor Pool $49,509.00

Last Raced	Horse	M/Eqt.	A.Wt	PP	¼	½	¾	1	Str	Fin	Jockey	Odds $1
30Aug03 ^{8}WO^{4}	Bowman Mill	L	5 113	2	3^{5}	$3^{3\frac{1}{2}}$	$3^{1\frac{1}{2}}$	$2^{\frac{1}{2}}$	$1^{\frac{1}{2}}$	1no	Blanc B	6.90
1Sep03 ^{7}WO^{2}	Lenny the Lender	Lbf	7 110	4	4^{1}	$4^{1\frac{1}{2}}$	5^{hd}	5^{7}	$2^{1\frac{1}{2}}$	2^{4}	Sutherland C	24.50
1Sep03 ^{7}WO^{1}	Mobil	L	3 115	1	1^{1}	1^{hd}	1^{1}	$1^{\frac{1}{2}}$	4^{5}	3^{nk}	Husbands P	2.45
30Aug03 ^{8}WO^{1}	Strut The Stage	Lbf	5 123	3	$5^{3\frac{1}{2}}$	5^{1}	4^{hd}	$3^{1\frac{1}{2}}$	3^{hd}	$4^{10\frac{1}{2}}$	Kabel T K	0.55
6Sep03 ^{9}WO^{1}	Wild Strike	Lbf	5 112	5	6	6	6	4^{hd}	5^{20}	5^{18}	Ramsammy E	13.05
5Sep03 ^{7}WO^{1}	Destiny Red	L	3 106	6	2^{1}	2^{3}	2^{hd}	6	6	6	Pimentel R M	21.45

OFF AT 4:23 Start Good. Won driving. Course soft.
TIME :25^{1}, :50, 1:16^{2}, 1:42^{4}, 2:09^{1}, 2:23 (:25.39, :50.14, 1:16.40, 1:42.88, 2:09.35, 2:23.14)

$2 Mutuel Prices:

2–BOWMAN MILL	15.80	7.70	14.00
4–LENNY THE LENDER		13.30	21.50
1–MOBIL			10.60

$2 TRIACTOR 2–4–1 PAID $712.20 $2 EXACTOR 2–4 PAID $196.70

Ch. h, by Kris S.–Aletta Maria, by Diesis*GB. Trainer Dickinson Michael W. Bred by Dr John A Chandler (Ky).

BOWMAN MILL was close up off the rail, dropped back to stalk the forced pace in the backstretch, advanced into the second turn, steadied mildly at the five eighths pole, was close up outside of MOBIL on the final turn, came three wide into the stretch, gained command in upper stretch, and was all out to prevail while drifting in, bumped with the runner up just past the wire. LENNY THE LENDER bumped at the start, well placed inside, advanced late in the backstretch to reach contention on the final turn, came off the rail in upper stretch, rallied while edging towards the rail through the stretch and just missed, was bumped by the winner just past the wire. MOBIL set a pressured pace from off the rail inside of DESTINY RED, moved inside on the second turn, gave way in upper stretch, came back on late for the show position. STRUT THE STAGE well placed four wide, advanced late in the backstretch and on the second turn, flattened out in the stretch, and was outfinished for the show position. WILD STRIKE bumped at the start, trailed while four wide, advanced on the second turn while angling in to be off the rail, weakened in the stretch. DESTINY RED pressed the pace three wide outside of MOBIL, gave way heading into the second turn, and faded. There was a Stewards' inquiry following the race looking into the final few strides. After reviewing the films the Stewards determined the bumping took place just past the wire, and there was no change to the order of finish.

Owners— 1, Chandler Dr John A; 2, Jukosky Richard H; 3, Schickedanz Gustav; 4, Sam-Son Farms; 5, Schickedanz Gustav; 6, Sam-Son Farms

Trainers—1, Dickinson Michael W; 2, Jukosky Richard H; 3, Keogh Michael; 4, Frostad Mark; 5, Keogh Michael; 6, Frostad Mark

$1 Pick Three (5–3–2) Paid $213.00; Pick Three Pool $10,524.

EIGHTH RACE
Woodbine
OCTOBER 4, 2003

1⅛ MILES. (1.48) 93rd Running of THE DURHAM CUP HANDICAP. Grade III. Purse $150,000 For THREE-YEAR-OLDS AND UPWARD. By subscription of $150 each which shall accompany the nomination and an additional $1,500 when making entry; with $150,000 added, plus all fees to be divided: 60% to the winner, 20% to second, 11% to third, 6%to fourth and 3% to fifth. Weights, Saturday, September 27. Closed Wednesday, September 17, 2003 with 22 nominations. Final entries to be made through the entry box no later than 11:30 a.m. on Wednesday, October 1, 2003. Plus up to $11,575 Breeder Awards.

Value of Race: $163,800 Winner $98,280; second $32,760; third $18,018; fourth $9,828; fifth $4,914. Mutuel Pool $94,958.00 Triactor Pool $51,415.00 Exactor Pool $47,768.00

Last Raced	Horse	M/Eqt.	A.	Wt	PP	St	¼	½	¾	Str	Fin	Jockey	Odds $1
14Sep03 ^{7}WO^{1}	Parose	Lf	9	117	3	6	6	6	6	2½	1^{2}	Jones Jono	3.15
1Sep03 ^{6}WO^{1}	Barbeau Ruckus	Lbf	4	116	1	3	$2^{1½}$	1½	1^{1}	$1^{1½}$	$2^{2¼}$	Luciani D	2.70
14Sep03 ^{9}WO^{11}	Wake At Noon	Lbf	6	121	6	1	1^{hd}	2^{3}	2^{4}	$3^{2½}$	$3^{4½}$	Ramsammy E	1.55
14Sep03 ^{7}WO^{3}	On The Game	Lbf	5	115	4	5	5^{7}	5^{8}	3½	4^{10}	4^{16}	McAleney J S	9.05
5Sep03 ^{3}WO^{1}	Tempered Appeal	Lbf	6	114	2	2	3^{hd}	4^{2}	$5^{1½}$	6	$5^{2¾}$	Sutherland C	11.55
14Sep03 ^{7}WO^{6}	Anglian Prince	Lbf	4	114	5	4	$4^{3½}$	3^{hd}	$4^{2½}$	5½	6	Dos Ramos R A	6.55

OFF AT 4:42 Start Good For All But ANGLIAN PRINCE Won driving. Track fast.
TIME :23^{3}, :47^{1}, 1:11^{1}, 1:38^{4}, 1:53 (:23.77, :47.23, 1:11.37, 1:38.80, 1:53.16)

$2 Mutuel Prices:				
	4–PAROSE	8.30	3.50	2.50
	1–BARBEAU RUCKUS		3.60	2.50
	7–WAKE AT NOON			2.30

$2 TRIACTOR 4–1–7 PAID $68.10 $2 EXACTOR 4–1 PAID $28.50

Ch. g, by Parlay Me–Roses for Classy, by Son of Briartic. Trainer McPherson Alex. Bred by Shewchuk Johnnie P (Alb–C).

PAROSE trailed from off the rail well back of the field, began a long drive four wide on the second turn, gained command passing the sixteenth pole, and drew off. BARBEAU RUCKUS was headstrong early, came through to gain the lead off the rail inside of WAKE AT NOON on the first turn, controlled the pace inside of that one through the backstretch, drew clear into the second turn, gave his best in the stretch. WAKE AT NOON was asked away from the gate, and gained a clear lead three wide the first time through the stretch, pressed the pace outside of the runner up in the backstretch, weakened on the second turn. ON THE GAME was steadied mildly early, well placed off the rail, came out four wide in the backstretch, advanced mildly on the second turn and through the stretch. TEMPERED APPEAL stalked the forced pace from off the rail, dropped back on the second turn. ANGLIAN PRINCE stumbled at the start, stalked the forced pace four wide, faded on the second turn. The jockey of ON THE GAME claimed foul against the rider of WAKE AT NOON for interference away from the gate. After reviewing the films the Stewards disallowed the claim of foul.

Owners— 1, Atto John; 2, Muthulingham Thayalan & Armata S; 3, Schickedanz Bruno; 4, Franks John; 5, Parra Rosendo G; 6, Prime Acres Inc

Trainers—1, McPherson Alex; 2, Armata Ross; 3, Katryan Abraham R; 4, Bell David R; 5, Attard Kevin; 6, Hardy James M

Scratched— Indy Lead (14Sep03 ^{7}WO^{5})

$1 Pick Three (6–5–4) Paid $87.50; Pick Three Pool $6,147.

NINTH RACE
Woodbine
OCTOBER 5, 2003

1$\frac{1}{16}$ MILES. (1.40^{4}) 95th Running of THE GREY BREEDERS' CUP. Grade II. Purse $250,000 (includes $75,000 BC – Breeders' Cup) For TWO-YEAR-OLDS. (Includes $75,000 from Breeders' Cup Fund for Cup nominees only) By subscription of $250 each which shall accompany the nomination and an additional $2,500 when making entry; The host associations added monies and all the fees to be divided: 60% to the winner, 20% to second, 11% to third, 6% to fourth and 3% to fifth. Weight 120 lbs. Winners of a sweepstakes of $75,000 twice at a mile or over, additional 2 lbs.; Non-winners of a sweepstakes of $75,000 once at a mile or over or a sweepstakes of $75,000 three times atany distance, 3 lbs.; Of a sweepstakes of $75,000 twice, 5 lbs.; Of a sweepstakes of $75,000 once, 7 lbs.; Of a race other than maiden or claiming, 9 lbs. (No Canadian Bred Allowance).

Value of Race: $277,250 Winner $166,350; second $55,450; third $30,498; fourth $16,635; fifth $8,317. Mutuel Pool $124,732.00 Triactor Pool $88,269.00 Exactor Pool $59,351.00

Last Raced	Horse	M/Eqt.	A.	Wt	PP	St	¼	½	¾	Str	Fin	Jockey	Odds $1
31Aug03 ^{6}WO^{1}	Smoocher	L	2	113	9	7	9	7^{1}	4½	$1^{2½}$	$1^{2¼}$	McAleney J S	6.35
21Sep03 ^{8}WO^{2}	Organ Grinder	L	2	116	7	4	3^{hd}	4^{hd}	3½	$4^{1½}$	2^{hd}	Husbands S P	14.90
30Aug03 ^{7}WO^{2}	Niigon	Lbf	2	114	1	8	6½	5^{1}	5^{2}	3^{1}	$3^{3¾}$	Dos Ramos R A	6.95
1Sep03 ^{5}WO^{1}	Twisted Wit	L	2	120	2	1	$4^{1½}$	3½	2^{2}	2^{hd}	$4^{3¼}$	Clark D	5.70
21Sep03 ^{8}WO^{3}	Estevan	L	2	114	5	3	1^{1}	1^{hd}	1½	5^{4}	$5^{1¼}$	Montpellier C	9.55
5Sep03 ^{6}WO^{1}	Tobe Suave	b	2	114	3	2	5^{hd}	9	9	6^{4}	$6^{6¾}$	Sutherland C	42.55
30Aug03 ^{7}WO^{1}	Silver Ticket	L	2	111	4	6	$8^{1½}$	$8^{1½}$	7½	7^{3}	7^{7}	Kabel T K	1.50
14Sep03 ^{4}WO^{1}	Bachelor Blues	L	2	117	6	5	7^{hd}	6½	$8^{1½}$	8^{1}	$8^{4¼}$	Husbands P	6.55
21Sep03 ^{8}WO^{5}	San Diego Blowout	Lb	2	115	8	9	2^{hd}	2^{2}	6^{2}	9	9	Ramsammy E	11.20

OFF AT 5:10 Start Good For All But SAN DIEGO BLOWOUT Won driving. Track fast.
TIME :24^{1}, :47^{4}, 1:12^{2}, 1:39^{2}, 1:46^{3} (:24.31, :47.87, 1:12.50, 1:39.54, 1:46.74)

$2 Mutuel Prices:				
	9–SMOOCHER	14.70	9.10	5.40
	7–ORGAN GRINDER		14.60	7.00
	1–NIIGON			5.30

$2 TRIACTOR 9–7–1 PAID $1,095.80 $2 EXACTOR 9–7 PAID $241.40

B. c, (Feb), by Kissin Kris–Alta's Princess, by Screen King. Trainer Bell David R. Bred by John Franks (Fla).

SMOOCHER bumped with SAN DIEGO BLOWOUT heading into the first turn, angled in to race along the rail, rallied to gain command in upper stretch and drifted out, jumped tracks approaching the sixteenth pole while drawing off. ORGAN GRINDER stalked the forced pace three wide, advanced four wide on the second turn, gained late to get up for the place position. NIIGON trailed early, was well placed inside, came out three wide on the second turn, moved back in heading into the stretch, advanced and was outfinished for the place position. TWISTED WIT stalked the forced pace from off the rail, advanced three wide on the second turn to make a bid outside of ESTEVAN, flattened out in the stretch. ESTEVAN had a clear lead on the first turn, was under pressure from SAN DIEGO BLOWOUT in the backstretch while off the rail, gave way into the stretch. TOBE SUAVE swung a little wide into the first turn and bumped with SILVER TICKET, dropped back heading into the backstretch, moved inside on the second turn, passed tiring rivals in the stretch. SILVER TICKET was bumped by TOBE SUAVE and steadied on the first turn, raced three wide, and showed little. BACHELOR BLUES was bumped by SILVER TICKET and steadied on the first turn, raced four wide, and faded. SAN DIEGO BLOWOUT was unprepared for the start and broke slow, was between horses and bumped with the winner into the first turn, advanced on the first turn to press the pace outside of ESTEVAN while three wide, gave way on the second turn, and faded.

Owners— 1, Franks John; 2, S & B Stable; 3, Chiefswood Stable; 4, Davis Rolph A; 5, Sapara James & Alice; 6, Silvera Laurie; 7, Sam-Son Farms; 8, Schettine William C; 9, Kelynack Racing Stable

Trainers—1, Bell David R; 2, Attard Sid C; 3, Coatrieux Eric; 4, Tiller Robert P; 5, Carroll Josie; 6, Silvera Laurie; 7, Frostad Mark; 8, Carroll Josie; 9, Katryan Abraham R

$1 Pick Three (10–1–9) Paid $1,600.00; Pick Three Pool $6,424.

EIGHTH RACE
Hastings
OCTOBER 11, 2003

1⅛ MILES. (1.46^4) BALLERINA BREEDERS' CUP S.. Grade III. Purse $125,000 (includes $25,000 BC – Breeders' Cup) (plus $16,250 THRIF – British Columbia Bred) A Scale Weight Stakes for Three Year Olds and Upward Fillies and Mares. (Includes $25,000 from Breeders' Cup Fund for Cup nominees only). All Hastings Entertainment Inc. purse money to be divided 60% to the winner, 20% to second, 11% to third, 6% to fourth, and 3% to fifth. Breeders' Cup Fund monies correspondingly divided providing a Breeders' Cup nominee has finished in an awarded position. Any Breeders' Cup Fund monies not awarded will revert back to the Fund. Preference will be based on life time earnings as recorded by The Daily Racing Form at time of entry. In a case where horses haveidentical earnings, preference will be given to the Breeders' Cup eligible horse. Scale Weights: 3 year olds 121 lbs, Older 124 lbs.

Value of Race: $172,225 Winner $100,320; second $35,190; third $21,142; fourth $10,557; fifth $5,016. Mutuel Pool $44,385.00 Superfecta Pool $10,672.00 Triactor Pool $25,474.00 Exactor Pool $16,561.00

Last Raced	Horse	M/Eqt.	A.	Wt	PP	St	¼	½	¾	Str	Fin	Jockey	Odds $1
20Sep03 ^{9}Hst^2	Dancewithavixen	Lbf	3	121	9	2	2^{hd}	2^{hd}	1^{hd}	2^2	1^{nk}	Valdez F S	2.20
21Sep03 ^{7}Hst^4	Secondary School	Lf	4	124	1	7	8^5	6^2	6^{hd}	$3^{1\frac{1}{2}}$	$2^{\frac{1}{2}}$	Lacoursiere L J	12.85
21Sep03 ^{7}Hst^1	Shelby Madison	L	4	124	7	1	3^3	3^2	3^1	1^{hd}	3^{nk}	Alvarado P V	2.85
20Sep03 ^{9}Hst^1	Raylene	L	3	121	6	6	5^{hd}	7^{hd}	9	5^{hd}	$4^{2\frac{1}{4}}$	Walcott R	2.30
21Sep03 ^{7}Hst^3	Elana d'Amour		4	124	2	8	7^{hd}	9	8^1	$4^{\frac{1}{2}}$	5^1	May R H	4.95
28Sep03 ^{5}Hst^3	Vaux L'taire	Lf	6	124	5	9	9	$8^{1\frac{1}{2}}$	7^1	6^5	$6^{3\frac{3}{4}}$	Fuentes F P	101.60
21Sep03 ^{7}Hst^7	Catahoula Rose	Lb	5	124	4	4	4^4	$4^{2\frac{1}{2}}$	5^{hd}	7^1	$7^{2\frac{3}{4}}$	Stephen A	81.30
20Sep03 ^{9}Hst^8	Brave Miss	Lb	3	121	3	3	6^1	$5^{1\frac{1}{2}}$	4^{hd}	8^{10}	$8^{17\frac{1}{4}}$	Cuthbertson A	67.40
23Aug03 ^{1}Hst^6	Grace For You	Lbf	4	124	8	5	1^1	1^1	2^1	9	9	Serna F A	21.75

OFF AT 4:40 Start Good. Won driving. Track sloppy.
TIME :22^1, :46, 1:12, 1:38^2, 1:52^2 (:22.30, :46.04, 1:12.10, 1:38.47, 1:52.58)

$2 Mutuel Prices:				
	10–DANCEWITHAVIXEN	6.40	4.10	3.50
	1–SECONDARY SCHOOL		12.70	6.90
	7–SHELBY MADISON			4.00

$2 SUPERFECTA 10–1–7–6 PAID $542.20 $2 TRIACTOR 10–1–7 PAID $214.50 $2 EXACTOR 10–1 PAID $52.80

Dk. b. or br. f, (May), by Vying Victor–Hot Ginger, by Royal Chocolate. Trainer Longstaff Tom. Bred by Cliff Baldwin (BC–C).

DANCEWITHAVIXEN broke sharply, pressed the pace from the outside, gained the lead at the three quarters, headed on the final turn, came again and prevailed driving. SECONDARY SCHOOL unhurried early, gaining, rallied from three wide on the final turn and five wide down the stretch, closed well and just missed. SHELBY MADISON broke sharply, well placed, rallied and gained command from three wide on the final turn, gave way. RAYLENE in the middle of the pack, dropped back, rallied from the inside down the stretch, closed and finished well. ELANA D'AMOUR unhurried early, rallied from four wide on the final turn, weakened in the stretch. VAUX L'TAIRE slow early, put in a mild bid from three wide down the stretch, was outrun. CATAHOULA ROSE away alertly and well placed, three wide on the backstretch, was through after three quarters. BRAVE MISS away alertly and allowed to settle, made a middle move from four wide, gave way. GRACE FOR YOU hustled along from the outside, gained command and the rail, set the pace, gave way after three quarters.

Owners— 1, TNT Racing Stable; 2, Whitham Janis R; 3, Jacobson Roy & Dixie; 4, Calmar Stables & Ranch; 5, Dark Horse Stable; 6, Hart Kim N; 7, Burrows Douglas & William & MacDoug; 8, Nordahl Leif S; 9, Bronco J & Glenvista Stables

Trainers—1, Longstaff Tom; 2, Forster David; 3, Cloutier Jacobson Toni; 4, Haynes Rodney; 5, Apperloo Joe; 6, Bryant Steve; 7, Brown Jim R; 8, Heads Barbara; 9, Jordan Terry

Scratched— Castle Mountain (21Sep03 ^{7}HST^2)

EIGHTH RACE
Hastings
OCTOBER 12, 2003

1⅜ MILES. (2.14^2) PREMIER'S H.. Grade III. Purse $100,000 (plus $13,000 THRIF – British Columbia Bred) A Handicap for Three Year Olds and Upward. $200 to nominate. $1,000 to enter and $1,000 to pass scratch time. With $100,000 added, of which 60% goes to the winner, 20% to second, 11% to third, 6% to fourth, and 3% to fifth.

Value of Race: $127,190 Winner $79,200; second $23,800; third $13,090; fourth $7,140; fifth $3,960. Mutuel Pool $40,261.00 Triactor Pool $28,808.00 Exactor Pool $16,565.00

Last Raced	Horse	M/Eqt.	A.	Wt	PP	¼	½	¾	1	Str	Fin	Jockey	Odds $1
21Sep03 ^{9}Hst^1	Roscoe Pito	L	3	118	6	1^2	1^1	$1^{\frac{1}{2}}$	$1^{\frac{1}{2}}$	$1^{\frac{1}{2}}$	1^{hd}	Alvarado P V	0.95
20Sep03 ^{7}Hst^5	Blowin In The Wind	L	4	118	2	6^1	5^1	5^{hd}	5^1	$3^{\frac{1}{2}}$	$2^{\frac{1}{2}}$	Lacoursiere L J	33.10
20Sep03 ^{7}Hst^1	Futural	Lbf	7	118	1	2^1	$2^{1\frac{1}{2}}$	$2^{1\frac{1}{2}}$	2^2	2^1	$3^{1\frac{3}{4}}$	Valdez F S	6.65
21Sep03 ^{9}Hst^5	Royal Place	L	3	112	5	$4^{\frac{1}{2}}$	4^2	$4^{2\frac{1}{2}}$	$3^{\frac{1}{2}}$	4^4	$4^{5\frac{1}{2}}$	Wright N	8.00
6Sep03 ^{9}NP^3	Let's Go Rusty	L	6	115	4	8	8	7^2	$7^{2\frac{1}{2}}$	$5^{2\frac{1}{2}}$	$5^{4\frac{1}{4}}$	Wilson D H	5.30
28Sep03 ^{1}Hst^1	Ezra	L	4	116	7	$7^{\frac{1}{2}}$	$7^{\frac{1}{2}}$	8	8	6^3	$6^{3\frac{1}{2}}$	May R H	8.20
28Sep03 ^{8}AsD^2	Nugrayontheblock	L	4	115	3	$5^{1\frac{1}{2}}$	6^1	6^2	$6^{\frac{1}{2}}$	7^{hd}	$7^{1\frac{1}{2}}$	Walcott R	31.10
21Sep03 ^{9}Hst^2	Steady Smiler		3	116	8	3^{hd}	3^{hd}	3^{hd}	4^1	8	8	Loseth C	7.90

OFF AT 4:40 Start Good For All But ROYAL PLACE Won driving. Track sloppy.
TIME :24^1, :48^3, 1:14^3, 1:40^1, 2:06, 2:19^4 (:24.37, :48.68, 1:14.78, 1:40.29, 2:06.04, 2:19.86)

$2 Mutuel Prices:				
	6–ROSCOE PITO	3.90	3.10	2.50
	2–BLOWIN IN THE WIND		17.40	6.90
	1–FUTURAL			5.70

$2 TRIACTOR 6–2–1 PAID $237.50 $2 EXACTOR 6–2 PAID $63.10

Dk. b. or br. g, (May), by Light of Mine–Perfect Coin, by L'Emigrant. Trainer Snow John. Bred by Robert W Simpson & Robert G Henderson (BC–C).

ROSCOE PITO broke sharply, assumed command, gained the rail, being well rated led throughout, prevailed driving. BLOWIN IN THE WIND never far back and on the inside, angled out on the backstretch to rally from three wide at the quarter pole, closed gamely and just missed. FUTURAL broke sharply, pressed the pace from the outside, finished well being outfinished. ROYAL PLACE off a step slow, hustled along to be close up from three wide, rallied into the stretch, weakened. LET'S GO RUSTY trailed early, rallied but failed to menace. EZRA slow early and three wide, showed little and was always outrun. NUGRAYONTHEBLOCK unhurried early, showed little and was never a threat. STEADY SMILER away alertly and in good position, stalked the leaders from the inside, was through after a mile.

Owners— 1, Snow John Wildcard Stable Punjab Fo; 2, Forster Stable; 3, Hart Kim N; 4, Sangara K K; 5, Hoggard Les & Leffler Bob; 6, Rakis Michael & Hughes David; 7, Heppner Arnold; 8, Maybin Rob

Trainers—1, Snow John; 2, Forster David; 3, Bryant Steve; 4, Barroby Harold J; 5, Condilenios Dino; 6, Giesbrecht Brian; 7, Anderson Carl; 8, Maybin Robert

SIXTH RACE
Woodbine
OCTOBER 13, 2003

1⅛ MILES. (1.48) ONTARIO DERBY. Grade III. Purse $150,000 For THREE-YEAR-OLDS. By subscription of $150 each which shall accompany the nomination and an additional $1,500 when making entry. Weight: 124 lbs. Non-winners of a sweepstakes of $75,000 three times at a mile or over in 2003, allowed 3 lbs.; Of a sweepstakes of $75,000 twice at a mile or over in 2003, 5 lbs.; Of a sweepstakes of $75,000 once at a mile or over in2003, 7 lbs. (No Canadian Bred Allowance) plus up to $10,045 Breeder Awards. Final entries to be made through the entr y box no later than 11:30 a.m. on Friday, October 10, 2003. Closed Wednesday, September 24, 2003 with 16 nominations.

Value of Race: $159,900 Winner $100,737; second $31,980; third $17,589; fourth $9,594. Mutuel Pool $84,111.00 Exactor Pool $79,699.00

Last Raced	Horse	M/Eqt.	A.	Wt	PP	St	¼	½	¾	Str	Fin	Jockey	Odds $1
28Sep03 8WO3	Mobil	L	3	124	1	3	2¹	1½	1½	12½	16¾	Kabel T K	0.95
21Sep03 5WO4	El Gran Maestro	Lb	3	117	2	2	4hd	2hd	3⁵	3⁸	2no	Ramsammy E	27.30
16Aug03 9WO3	Added Edge	L	3	117	4	5	3½	4²	2hd	21½	3¹⁰	Husbands P	3.10
21Sep03 5WO1	Dance Engagement	L	3	117	5	1	1hd	3¹	4	4	4	Clark D	14.55
21Sep03 7WO1	Arco's Gold	L	3	117	3	4	5	5	—	—	—	Montpellier C	1.80

Arco's Gold:Broke Down;

OFF AT 3:25 Start Good. Won driving. Track fast.
TIME :23³, :47⁴, 1:12, 1:38¹, 1:51⁴ (:23.70, :47.93, 1:12.00, 1:38.31, 1:51.99)

$2 Mutuel Prices:

1-MOBIL	3.90	2.70	—
2-EL GRAN MAESTRO		10.30	—
4-ADDED EDGE		—	—

$2 EXACTOR 1-2 PAID $39.60

B. c, (Jan), by Langfuhr–Kinetigal, by Naskra. Trainer Keogh Michael. Bred by Gustav Schickedanz (Ont–C).

MOBIL pressed the pace from off the rail, gained the lead into the backstretch, turned back bids from EL GRAN MAESTRO and ADDED EDGE on the second turn, came three wide into the stretch, drew off, jumped the tracks left by the starting gate approaching the eighth pole. EL GRAN MAESTRO moved to the inside heading into the first turn, stalked the forced pace, advanced to make a bid on the second turn, took the place position off the rail in the stretch. ADDED EDGE bumped at the start, was close up while four wide on the first turn, stalked in the backstretch, advanced to make a three wide bid on the second turn, came four wide into the stretch, and was outfinished for the place position. DANCE ENGAGEMENT set a pressured pace three wide, pressed the pace outside of the winner, gave way into the second turn and faded. ARCO'S GOLD bumped at the start, stalked the forced pace from off the rail, broke down after half a mile, was pulled up and vanned off. A Stewards inquiry following the race looking into the early part of the backstretch resulted in no change.

Owners— 1, Schickedanz Gustav; 2, Fieldstone Farms; 3, Team Valor Stables & Wilson Robert; 4, Hillsbrook Farms; 5, DiIorio Alex & Steven

Trainers—1, Keogh Michael; 2, Nemett George S; 3, Casse Mark; 4, Ross John A; 5, Ross John A

THIRD RACE
Woodbine
OCTOBER 19, 2003

6 FURLONGS. (1.08) HIGHLANDER H.. Purse $150,000 For THREE-YEAR-OLDS AND UPWARD. By subscription of $150 each which shall accompany the nomination and an additional $1,500 when making entry; with $150,000 added, plus all fees to be divided: 60% to the winner, 20% to second, 11% to third, 6% to fourth and 3% to fifth. Weights, Saturday, October 11,2003. Final entries to be made through the entry box no later than 11:30 a.m. on Thursday, October 16, 2003. Closed Wednesday, October 1, 2003 with 15 nominations. Plus up to $11,575 Breeder Awards.

Value of Race: $161,250 Winner $96,750; second $32,250; third $17,738; fourth $9,675; fifth $4,837. Mutuel Pool $101,365.00 Triactor Pool $34,261.00 Exactor Pool $58,851.00

Last Raced	Horse	M/Eqt.	A.	Wt	PP	St	¼	½	Str	Fin	Jockey	Odds $1
1Sep03 9WO1	Forever Grand	Lb	4	117	4	3	5	5	5	11½	Kabel T K	2.35
27Sep03 5WO1	Sophia's Prince	b	4	116	5	4	4³	4⁴	4½	2nk	Husbands S P	4.20
28Sep03 4WO1	Mulligan The Great	L	4	115	3	1	3⁵	3⁶	2¹	32¼	McAleney J S	1.65
23Aug03 8WO3	Krz Ruckus	L	6	115	2	2	2½	2¹	1hd	45¼	Luciani D	4.50
1Sep03 9WO3	Wild Whiskey	Lb	4	115	1	5	1¹	1hd	3¹	5	Clark D	5.00

OFF AT 1:53 Start Good. Won driving. Track muddy.
TIME :21², :43³, :56², 1:09² (:21.42, :43.75, :56.57, 1:09.53)

$2 Mutuel Prices:

5-FOREVER GRAND	6.70	3.60	2.20
6-SOPHIA'S PRINCE		5.00	2.30
4-MULLIGAN THE GREAT			2.10

$2 TRIACTOR 5-6-4 PAID $47.60 $2 EXACTOR 5-6 PAID $30.30

Dk. b. or br. g, by War Deputy–Braverelle, by Brave Shot*GB. Trainer Tiller Robert P. Bred by Ron Motz & Janet Motz (Ont–C).

FOREVER GRAND trailed to mid stretch, rallied four wide, split horses passing the sixteenth pole, and drew out. SOPHIA'S PRINCE was well placed three wide, finished well five wide, took the place position. MULLIGAN THE GREAT was close up while three wide, gained the lead briefly approaching the sixteenth pole, was outfinished for the place position. KRZ RUCKUS pressed the pace from between horses, dueled with WILD WHISKEY on the turn, gained the lead in upper stretch, gave way in mid stretch. WILD WHISKEY was hustled to set a pressured fast pace inside of KRZ RUCKUS, dueled on the turn with that one, weakened in upper stretch.

Owners— 1, DiGiulio Frank & Tiller R P Jr; 2, Agro Joan C; 3, Simmons Charles E; 4, Guidolin R & Partners; 5, Wellwood Gary & Titchner L

Trainers—1, Tiller Robert P; 2, LeBlanc John P Jr; 3, Hopmans C C Jr; 4, DePaulo Michael P; 5, Ross John A

Scratched— Rare Friends (1Sep03 9WO6)

$1 Pick Three (2-4-5) Paid $88.25; Pick Three Pool $12,135.

FIFTH RACE
Woodbine
OCTOBER 19, 2003

1¼ MILES. (Turf)(2.01) E. P. TAYLOR S.. Grade I. Purse $750,000 For FILLIES AND MARES, THREE-YEAR-OLDS AND UPWARD. By subscription of $750 each which shall accompany the nomination and an additional $7,500 when making entry; the added money and all fees to be divided: 60% to the winner, 20% to second, 11% to third, 6% to fourth and 3% to fifth. Three-Year -Olds, 118 lbs. (53.5 kg); Older, 123 lbs. (55.5 kg) (European Scale) (No Canadian Bred Allowance) Breeder Awards. $50, 000 of this purse has been provided through the Thoroughbred Improvement Program and Canadian Thoroughbred Horse Society. Closed Wednesday, September 17, 2003 with 52 nominations.

Value of Race: $750,000 Winner $450,000; second $150,000; third $82,500; fourth $45,000; fifth $22,500. Mutuel Pool $217,808.00 Superfecta Pool $40,149.00 Triactor Pool $116,165.00 Exactor Pool $107,460.00

Last Raced	Horse	M/Eqt.	A.Wt	PP	¼	½	¾	1	Str	Fin	Jockey	Odds $1
5Oct03 ^{6}Kee^{5}	Volga-IR	L	5 123	10	$8^{\frac{1}{2}}$	7^{1}	7^{1}	5^{hd}	2^{1}	1^{hd}	Migliore R	10.45
20Aug03 Yor^{4}	Tigertail-FR		4 123	7	$6^{1\frac{1}{2}}$	6^{1}	6^{hd}	7^{1}	7^{2}	2no	Blanc B	9.15
2Aug03 Goo^{4}	Hi Dubai-GB	L	3 118	4	3^{hd}	4^{2}	3^{hd}	2^{hd}	1^{hd}	3^{hd}	Dettori Lanfranco	2.95
11Sep03 Lch^{1}	Mer de Corail-IR		4 123	5	10	10	$9^{\frac{1}{2}}$	$8^{\frac{1}{2}}$	$6^{1\frac{1}{2}}$	4^{1}	Spencer J P	9.10
27Sep03 ^{8}Bel^{2}	Walzerkoenigin	L	4 123	9	5^{hd}	5^{1}	5^{1}	6^{hd}	5^{hd}	5^{hd}	Prado E S	2.35
7Sep03 ^{9}Bel^{4}	Baie-FR	L	3 118	2	$4^{1\frac{1}{2}}$	3^{hd}	$4^{1\frac{1}{2}}$	$4^{\frac{1}{2}}$	4^{hd}	$6^{3\frac{1}{4}}$	Smith M E	7.25
14Sep03 ^{6}WO^{1}	Inish Glora	L	5 123	1	1^{hd}	1^{hd}	1^{hd}	$1^{\frac{1}{2}}$	3^{1}	$7^{\frac{3}{4}}$	Kabel T K	7.60
5Oct03 ^{6}Kee^{3}	New Economy	L	5 123	3	7^{hd}	$9^{1\frac{1}{2}}$	10	10	9^{1}	8^{7}	Bridgmohan S X	38.45
7Sep03 ^{8}WO^{1}	Heyahohowdy	Lbf	4 123	8	$2^{1\frac{1}{2}}$	$2^{1\frac{1}{2}}$	$2^{1\frac{1}{2}}$	3^{1}	$8^{1\frac{1}{2}}$	9^{hd}	Ramsammy E	28.40
14Sep03 ^{6}WO^{3}	Diadella	Lb	6 123	6	$9^{1\frac{1}{2}}$	8^{hd}	8^{hd}	$9^{1\frac{1}{2}}$	10	10	Husbands P	12.05

OFF AT 2:56 Start Good. Won driving. Course soft.

TIME :26, $:50^{3}$, $1:15^{2}$, $1:40^{4}$, $2:05^{3}$ (:26.13, :50.78, 1:15.58, 1:40.89, 2:05.68)

$2 Mutuel Prices:				
	10-VOLGA-IR	22.90	10.50	7.00
	7-TIGERTAIL-FR		10.90	5.90
	4-HI DUBAI-GB			3.40

$1 SUPERFECTA 10-7-4-5 PAID $4,462.40 $2 TRIACTOR 10-7-4 PAID $1,543.20 $2 EXACTOR 10-7 PAID $226.10

Dk. b. or br. m, by Caerleon-Verveine, by Lear Fan. Trainer McLaughlin Kiaran P. Bred by Allez France Stables Ltd (Ire).

VOLGA (IRE) bumped at the start with WALZERKOENIGIN, raced three wide, rallied four wide through the stretch, gained the lead in mid stretch and prevailed. TIGERTAIL (FR) was reluctant to load, raced inside, waited for room at the three sixteenths pole, angled out at the eighth pole, rallied late five wide to get up for the place position. HI DUBAI (GB) stalked the forced pace from off the rail outside of BAIE (FR), advanced three wide into the stretch, gained the lead in upper stretch, and missed. MER DE CORAIL (IRE) trailed, bumped with NEW ECONOMY heading into the second turn, was between horses on the second turn, finished well four wide between horses. WALZERKOENIGIN bumped at the start between HEYAHOHOWDY and VOLGA (IRE), raced off the rail, was three wide in the stretch, gained mildly, lacked room late. BAIE (FR) stalked the forced pace inside of HI DUBAI (GB), came off the rail in mid stretch, and was not a threat. INISH GLORA set a pressured pace inside of HEYAHOHOWDY, was headed by that one early on the second turn, gave way in mid stretch. NEW ECONOMY was well placed inside, bumped with MER DE CORAIL (IRE) heading into the second turn, dropped back in the stretch. HEYAHOHOWDY bumped with WALZERKOENIGIN, and was a bit rank at the start, pressed the pace outside of INISH GLORA, gained the lead briefly early on the second turn, weakened in upper stretch. DIADELLA raced three wide, drifted out in the stretch, and faded.

Owners— 1, Allen Joseph; 2, Georges Coude; 3, Godolphin Racing Inc; 4, Magnier Mrs John; 5, Gestuet Schlenderhan; 6, 6 C Stable LLC; 7, Costigan Robert J; 8, Evans Robert S; 9, Kelynack Racing Stable; 10, Stronach Stable

Trainers—1, McLaughlin Kiaran P; 2, Collet Rodolphe; 3, Suroor Saeed Bin; 4, Hammond John; 5, Schiergen Peter; 6, Frostad Mark; 7, Benson MacDonald; 8, Motion H Graham; 9, Katryan Abraham R; 10, Pierce Malcolm

Scratched— Byzantine (14Sep03 ^{6}WO^{6})

$1 Pick Three (5-3-10) Paid $248.25; Pick Three Pool $13,457.

NINTH RACE

Woodbine

OCTOBER 19, 2003

1½ MILES. (Turf)(2.25³) PATTISON CANADIAN INTERNATIONAL S.. Grade I. Purse $***,*** For THREE–YEAR–OLDS AND UPWARD. By subscription of $1,000 each which shall accompany the nomination and an additional $15,000 when making final entry. The added money and all fees to be divided: 60% to the winner, 20% to second, 11% to third,6% to fourhand 3% to fifth. Three–Year–Olds, 119 lbs. (54 kg); Older, 126 lbs. (57 kg) (European Scale) Fillies and Mares 3 lbs. (1.4 kg) allowance. (No Canadian Bred Allowance) Final entries to be made through the entry box no later than 10:30 a.m. on Thursday, October 16, 2003. Supplementary nominations may be made no later than the time of final entry by payment of a non–refundable fee of $60,000 which shall include the entry fee. A trophy will be presented to the winning owner. Plus up to $17,457 Breeder Awards.

Value of Race: $1,500,000 Winner $900,000; second $300,000; third $165,000; fourth $90,000; fifth $45,000.   Mutuel Pool $413,157.00

Superfecta Pool $63,970.00 Triactor Pool $225,481.00 Exactor Pool $214,624.00

Last Raced	Horse	M/Eqt.	A.Wt	PP	¼	½	1	1¼	Str	Fin	Jockey	Odds $1
13Sep03 Dnr³	Phoenix Reach–IR	Lb	3 119	5	1¹	2½	3¹	5½	1hd	1¾	Dwyer Martin	5.40
6Sep03 ⁸Bel⁶	Macaw–IR	Lbf	4 126	3	6½	6¹	6½	6¹	3hd	2hd	Bridgmohan S X	12.25
13Sep03 Dnr¹	Brian Boru–GB	L	3 119	4	10	10	9²	8²½	5½	3¹	Spencer J P	1.25
28Sep03 ⁸WO¹	Bowman Mill	L	5 126	10	4½	4²	2hd	1½	2¹	4⁴	Blanc B	14.45
27Sep03 ⁹Bel⁴	Sabiango–GE	L	5 126	1	3hd	3hd	4hd	4hd	6²½	5¹¾	Pedroza E	6.25
27Sep03 ⁹Bel⁷	Lunar Sovereign	L	4 126	8	5hd	5½	5½	3hd	4¹	6¹½	Migliore R	5.60
16Sep03 ML¹	Gruntled–GB		4 126	2	9½	8¹½	7hd	7¹	7¹	7¹½	Dettori Lanfranco	20.00
21Sep03 ⁷WO³	Shoal Water	L	3 119	9	2¹	1¹	1¹	2½	8²	8²	Kabel T K	18.10
40ct03 ¹⁰Kee¹	Art Variety–BR	Lb	5 126	6	8¹	9¹½	10	10	9¹	9²½	Prado E S	16.40
40ct03 ⁷Kee⁴	Portcullis	L	4 126	7	7½	7hd	8²	9¹½	10	10	Callaghan S	41.20

OFF AT 5:07 Start Good. Won driving. Course yielding.

TIME :25¹, :51², 1:16³, 1:42², 2:08¹, 2:33³ (:25.31, :51.41, 1:16.66, 1:42.51, 2:08.36, 2:33.62)

$2 Mutuel Prices:

5–PHOENIX REACH–IR	12.80	6.00	3.80
3–MACAW–IR		8.40	4.20
4–BRIAN BORU–GB			2.50

$1 SUPERFECTA 5–3–4–10 PAID $1,700.60 $2 TRIACTOR 5–3–4 PAID $353.80 $2 EXACTOR 5–3 PAID $137.50

B. c, (Mar), by Alhaarth*Ire–Carroll's Canyon*Ire, by Hatim. Trainer Balding Andrew. Bred by Kiernan Christine (Ire).

PHOENIX REACH (IRE) was headstrong early, went three wide into the first turn while on the pace, moved to the rail before a quarter of a mile, dropped back to stalk the pace in the backstretch, rallied off the rail through the stretch, gained the lead at the eighth pole and held well. MACAW (IRE) was well placed inside, came off the rail on the final turn, finished well four wide. BRIAN BORU (GB) raced inside, trailed through the backstretch, was three wide on the final turn, rallied seven wide in the stretch. BOWMAN MILL stalked the pace three wide, pressed the pace outside of SHOAL WATER through the backstretch, and on the final turn, gained the lead in upper stretch, gave way at the eighth pole. SABIANGO (GER) stalked the pace from the inside early, came off the rail in the backstretch, advanced three wide on the final turn, flattened out in mid stretch. LUNAR SOVEREIGN was well placed off the rail, advanced four wide on the final turn, made a bid in upper stretch, weakened in mid stretch. GRUNTLED (GB) trailed early, raced off the rail, was three wide on the final turn, and not a factor. SHOAL WATER had a short lead early, pressed the pace outside of the winner early, gained the lead early in the backstretch, controlled the pace under pressure through the backstretch and on the second turn, gave way in upper stretch. ART VARIETY (BRZ) raced three wide, dropped back into the final turn, passed a tiring one in the stretch. PORTCULLIS raced three wide, was four wide on the final turn, faded in the stretch.

Owners— 1, Winterbeck Manor Stud; 2, Melillo George; 3, Magnier Mrs John; 4, Chandler Dr John A; 5, Stiftung Gestuet Faehrhof; 6, Darley Stud Management LLC; 7, Ecurie Chalhoub; 8, Sam-Son Farms; 9, Team Victory; 10, Sam-Son Farms

Trainers—1, Balding Andrew; 2, Tagg Barclay; 3, O'Brien Aidan P; 4, Dickinson Michael W; 5, Wohler Andreas; 6, McLaughlin Kiaran P; 7, Hammond John; 8, Frostad Mark; 9, McPeek Kenneth G; 10, Frostad Mark

Scratched— Ballingarry (31Aug03 ⁸DMR⁴)

$1 Pick Three (7–3–5) Paid $118.40; Pick Three Pool $10,694.

EIGHTH RACE
Woodbine
NOVEMBER 1, 2003

1¼ MILES. (2.01) MAPLE LEAF S.. Grade III. Purse $175,000 For FILLIES AND MARES, THREE-YEAR-OLDS AND UPWARD. By subscription of $175 each which shall accompany the nomination and an additional $1, 750 when making entry. Three-Year-Olds 119 lbs., Older 124 lbs. Winners of a sweepstakes of $75,000 three times at a mile or over in 2003, additional 2 lbs.; Non-winners of a sweepstakes of $75,000 twice at a mile or over in 2003, 3 lbs.; Of a sweepstakes of $75,000 once at a mile or over in 2003, 5 lbs.; Of $53,400 at a mile or over in 2003, 7 lbs. (Maiden or claiming races not considered). Final entries to be made through the entry box no later than 11:30 a.m. on Wednesday, October 29, 2003. Closed Wednesday, October 15, 2003 with 22 nominations. Plus $50,000 for Canadian Breds from the Thoroughbred Improvement Program and Canadian Thoroughbred Horse Society. Plus up to $10,045 Breeder Awards.

Value of Race: $196,250 Winner $117,750; second $39,250; third $21,588; fourth $11,775; fifth $5,887. Mutuel Pool $119,198.00 Triactor Pool $85,299.00 Exactor Pool $54,195.00

Last Raced	Horse	M/Eqt.	A.Wt	PP	¼	½	¾	1	Str	Fin	Jockey	Odds $1
11Oct03 ^{5}WO^{1}	One For Rose	L	4 121	7	1^{1}	1^{1}	1^{1}	1^{2}	$1^{2\frac{1}{2}}$	$1^{6\frac{1}{4}}$	Ramsammy E	0.70
11Oct03 ^{5}WO^{2}	Winning Chance	Lb	4 121	8	$2^{\frac{1}{2}}$	3^{1}	3^{1}	2^{4}	2^{7}	$2^{6\frac{1}{4}}$	Kabel T K	4.50
11Oct03 ^{5}WO^{3}	Clouds Of Gold	L	4 118	4	3^{1}	2^{hd}	$2^{\frac{1}{2}}$	$3^{\frac{1}{2}}$	3^{hd}	$3^{1\frac{1}{2}}$	Jones Jono	12.30
11Oct03 ^{5}WO^{5}	Royal Dalliance	L	6 119	5	$4^{\frac{1}{2}}$	4^{1}	$4^{1\frac{1}{2}}$	5^{3}	4^{2}	$4^{2\frac{1}{4}}$	Clark D	14.35
11Oct03 ^{8}Hst^{4}	Raylene	L	3 119	1	$6^{1\frac{1}{2}}$	$7^{2\frac{1}{2}}$	7^{1}	7^{2}	7^{5}	5^{1}	McAleney J S	4.45
13Oct03 ^{8}WO^{1}	Classic Stamp	L	3 117	2	$5^{\frac{1}{2}}$	$5^{2\frac{1}{2}}$	$5^{1\frac{1}{2}}$	$4^{\frac{1}{2}}$	5^{2}	6^{hd}	Husbands P	12.25
11Oct03 ^{5}WO^{10}	Tuff Chick	Lb	5 117	3	$7^{1\frac{1}{2}}$	$6^{2\frac{1}{2}}$	$6^{3\frac{1}{2}}$	6^{1}	$6^{\frac{1}{2}}$	$7^{11\frac{1}{2}}$	Dos Ramos R A	34.65
4Oct03 ^{7}WO^{5}	Rich Mist	L	6 117	6	8	8	8	8	8	8	Callaghan S	48.35

OFF AT 4:30 Start Good. Won driving. Track fast.
TIME :24^{2}, :49, 1:13^{3}, 1:38, 2:03^{2} (:24.47, :49.19, 1:13.71, 1:38.18, 2:03.50)

$2 Mutuel Prices:				
	9–ONE FOR ROSE	3.40	2.60	2.20
	10–WINNING CHANCE		3.60	2.70
	6–CLOUDS OF GOLD			3.50

$2 TRIACTOR 9–10–6 PAID $44.70 $2 EXACTOR 9–10 PAID $9.70

Dk. b. or br. f, by Tejano Run–Saucyladygaylord, by Lord Gaylord. Trainer Attard Sid C. Bred by Hill 'N' Dale Farms (Ont-C).

ONE FOR ROSE gained a clear lead early while three wide, moved in to be off the rail on the first turn, drew off in the stretch. WINNING CHANCE stalked the pace four wide early, moved to the three path on the first turn, and was second best. CLOUDS OF GOLD stalked the pace from off the rail early, moved inside on the first turn, held the show position. ROYAL DALLIANCE raced off the rail, and was not a threat. RAYLENE was close up inside early, dropped back, came off the rail on the first turn, was three wide in the backstretch, passed tiring rivals five wide in the stretch. CLASSIC STAMP was off the rail early, raced three wide in the backstretch, and had no menace. TUFF CHICK raced three wide, and showed little. RICH MIST trailed.

Owners— 1, Tucci Stables; 2, Stronach Stable; 3, The Valiant Stable & Parsley K; 4, Hughes Dave & Godwin John; 5, Calmar Stables & Ranch; 6, Sorokolit William A Sr; 7, Allard Cam; 8, Springfield Stable & Dura Racing

Trainers—1, Attard Sid C; 2, Vella Daniel J; 3, Parsley Ken B; 4, Iglar-Hughes Joanna; 5, Haynes Rodney; 6, Hopmans C C Jr; 7, Attfield Roger L; 8, Doyle Michael J

Scratched— American Skipper (4Oct03 ^{9}WO^{1}), Byzantine (14Sep03 ^{6}WO^{6})

$1 Pick Three (5–2–9) Paid $42.05; Pick Three Pool $8,237.

EIGHTH RACE
Woodbine
NOVEMBER 8, 2003

$1\frac{1}{16}$ MILES. (1.40^{4}) WOODBINE SLOTS CUP H.. Grade III. Purse $150,000 For THREE-YEAR-OLDS AND UPWARD. By subscription of $150 each which shall accompany the nomination and an additional $1,500 when making entry. Weights, Saturday, November 1, 2003. Final entries to be made through the entry box no later than 11:30 a.m. on Wednesday, November 5, 2003. Plus up to $11,575 Breeder Awards Nominations close Wednesday, October 22, 2003.

Value of Race: $166,650 Winner $99,990; second $33,330; third $18,332; fourth $9,999; fifth $4,999. Mutuel Pool $169,776.00 Triactor Pool $75,304.00 Exactor Pool $73,628.00

Last Raced	Horse	M/Eqt.	A.Wt	PP	St	¼	½	¾	Str	Fin	Jockey	Odds $1
19Oct03 ^{1}WO^{2}	No Comprende	Lb	5 117	6	7	6^{5}	6^{5}	3^{1}	$1^{\frac{1}{2}}$	$1^{1\frac{1}{4}}$	Husbands P	4.10
13Oct03 ^{6}WO^{1}	Mobil	L	3 119	2	2	$2^{1\frac{1}{2}}$	2^{1}	2^{hd}	2^{1}	2^{1}	Dos Ramos R A	3.65
4Oct03 ^{8}WO^{1}	Parose	Lf	9 118	1	4	7	7	6^{2}	4^{hd}	$3^{\frac{1}{2}}$	Kabel T K	2.45
4Oct03 ^{8}WO^{3}	Wake At Noon	Lbf	6 119	4	1	$1^{1\frac{1}{2}}$	1^{1}	$1^{\frac{1}{2}}$	$3^{1\frac{1}{2}}$	4^{1}	Ramsammy E	4.25
4Oct03 ^{8}WO^{2}	Barbeau Ruckus	Lbf	4 116	7	6	3^{hd}	$3^{\frac{1}{2}}$	$4^{1\frac{1}{2}}$	$5^{1\frac{1}{2}}$	$5^{2\frac{1}{2}}$	Montpellier C	6.70
9Oct03 ^{8}Bel^{3}	Free Of Love	Lb	5 118	5	5	4^{hd}	4^{1}	$5^{2\frac{1}{2}}$	6^{5}	$6^{2\frac{1}{4}}$	Landry R C	5.60
19Oct03 ^{8}FE^{1}	Kiss A Native	Lf	6 116	3	3	5^{2}	5^{hd}	7	7	7	Griffith C B	26.50

OFF AT 4:30 Start Good. Won driving. Track fast.
TIME :23^{3}, :47^{1}, 1:11^{1}, 1:37, 1:43^{4} (:23.61, :47.37, 1:11.35, 1:37.16, 1:43.93)

$2 Mutuel Prices:				
	8–NO COMPRENDE	10.20	4.50	2.60
	2–MOBIL		4.90	3.20
	1–PAROSE			2.70

$2 TRIACTOR 8–2–1 PAID $141.60 $2 EXACTOR 8–2 PAID $71.90

Dk. b. or br. g, by Compadre–Sociologie, by Caro*Ire. Trainer Smith James J. Bred by Mr & Mrs Gordon Grayson (Va).

NO COMPRENDE raced three wide, advanced four wide on the second turn, gained the lead in upper stretch, the rider lost the whip approaching the eighth pole, edged away under a strong hand ride. MOBIL stalked the pace three wide, pressed outside of WAKE AT NOON in the backstretch and on the second turn, made a bid between horses into the stretch, gave his best. PAROSE trailed, rallied late four wide. WAKE AT NOON gained a clear lead from off the rail early, was under pressure in the backstretch and on the second turn from the runner up, gave way in upper stretch. BARBEAU RUCKUS went six wide into the first turn, stalked the pace three wide, and was not a threat. FREE OF LOVE went five wide on the first turn, stalked the pace three wide, weakened while inside on the second turn. KISS A NATIVE raced four wide on the first turn, stalked the pace from off the rail, dropped back into the second turn.

Owners— 1, Clarity Stables; 2, Schickedanz Gustav; 3, Atto John; 4, Schickedanz Bruno; 5, Muthulingham Thayalan & Armata S; 6, R Evans & A Aprilante; 7, Franks John

Trainers—1, Smith James J; 2, Keogh Michael; 3, McPherson Alex; 4, Katryan Abraham R; 5, Armata Ross; 6, Violette Richard A Jr; 7, Giliforte Layne S

Scratched— Attest (29Oct03 ^{7}WO^{2}), Florida Recount (8Oct03 ^{7}WO^{1})

$1 Pick Three (8–4–8) Paid $248.20; Pick Three Pool $7,611.

EIGHTH RACE

Woodbine

NOVEMBER 16, 2003

7 FURLONGS. (1.20³) BESSARABIAN H.. Grade III. Purse $150,000 For FILLIES AND MARES, THREE–YEAR–OLDS AND UPWARD. By subscription of $150 each which shall accompany the nomination and an additional $1, 500 when making entry; with $150,000 added and an additional $50,000 for Canadian Breds, plus all fees to be divided: 60% to the winner, 20% to second, 11% to third, 6% to fourth and 3% to fifth. Weights, Saturday, November 8, 2003. Final entries to be made through the entry box no later than 11:30 a.m. on Thursday, November 13, 2003. Plus $50,000 from the Thoroughbred Improvement Program and Canadian Thoroughbred Horse Society for Canadian Breds. plus up to $11,575 Breeder Awards. Closed with 26 nominations Wednesday, October 29, 2003.

Value of Race: $164,400 Winner $98,640; second $32,880; third $18,084; fourth $9,864; fifth $4,932.   Mutuel Pool $96,451.00 Triactor Pool $58,717.00   Exactor Pool $43,627.00

Last Raced	Horse	M/Eqt. A.Wt	PP	St	¼	½	Str	Fin	Jockey	Odds $1
25Oct03 9WO1	Winter Garden	L 3 121	4	3	5¹½	1½	1ʰᵈ	1¹	Clark D	1.10
21Sep03 6WO5	El Prado Essence	Lb 6 120	5	4	6²½	4²	3³½	2¹½	Husbands P	3.90
25Oct03 9WO2	Mille Feville	L 4 115	2	7	3ʰᵈ	3½	2½	3⁵	Callaghan S	9.80
24Oct03 3Kee4	Whiletheiron'shot	L 4 116	6	2	7	7	5¹	4ⁿᵏ	Kabel T K	11.30
25Oct03 9WO5	Acting Deputy	Lf 4 118	3	5	4ʰᵈ	6ʰᵈ	4¹	5²	Jones Jono	17.25
2Nov03 7WO2	Ginger Gold	L 4 117	1	6	2ʰᵈ	5ʰᵈ	6³	6⁷¾	Dos Ramos R A	7.15
25Oct03 9WO3	Sheila's Prospect	L 5 115	7	1	1ʰᵈ	2½	7	7	McAleney J S	4.40

OFF AT 4:27 Start Good. Won driving. Track fast.
TIME :22³, :45⁴, 1:11, 1:24 (:22.78, :45.91, 1:11.07, 1:24.14)

$2 Mutuel Prices:

4–WINTER GARDEN	4.20	2.50	2.40
5–EL PRADO ESSENCE		4.00	3.50
2–MILLE FEVILLE			5.50

$2 TRIACTOR 4–5–2 PAID $68.90 $2 EXACTOR 4–5 PAID $14.60

B. f, (Mar), by Roy–Hillsburgh Rumors, by Bold Ruckus. Trainer Tiller Robert P. Bred by Anomaly Investments LP (Ky).

WINTER GARDEN was close up while three wide, came through to gain the lead at the seven sixteenths pole, drew out late. EL PRADO ESSENCE stalked the forced pace four wide, was three wide on the turn, made a bid into the stretch, and was second best. MILLE FEVILLE was close up early while off the rail, vied into the turn, made a bid inside on the turn and in the stretch, gave way late. WHILETHEIRON'SHOT trailed four wide, passed tiring rivals five wide in the stretch. ACTING DEPUTY close up while three wide early, stalked the forced pace from off the rail, came under left handed urging on the turn, and had no response. GINGER GOLD was close up while inside, vied into the turn, before giving way. SHEILA'S PROSPECT had a short lead early while five wide, pressed outside on the turn, weakened at the quarter pole, and faded.

Owners— 1, DiGiulio Frank D Jr; 2, Cappuccitti Gordon; 3, Haras Santa Maria de Araras; 4, Sam-Son Farms; 5, Alpine Stable; 6, Jim Dandy Stable; 7, Sangara K K

Trainers—1, Tiller Robert P; 2, Mattine Anthony; 3, Attfield Roger L; 4, Frostad Mark; 5, Armata Vito; 6, Attard Sid C; 7, Richards Lorne

$1 Pick Three (5–3–4) Paid $32.40; Pick Three Pool $9,123.

A Huevo
Own: Hopkins Mark S

B. g. 8 (May)
Sire: Cool Joe (Cold Reception)
Dam: Verabald (Baldski)
Br: D Lopez (WV)
Tr: Dickinson Michael W(0 0 0 0 .00) 2003:(152 37 .24)

Life	7	5	0	0	$253,500	113	D.Fst 6 5 0 0 $253,500 113
2003	3	2	0	0	$204,000	113	Wet(317) 1 0 0 0 $0 102
1999	4	3	0	0	$49,500	102	Turf(299) 0 0 0 0 $0 –
	0	0	0	0	$0	–	Dst(0) 0 0 0 0 $0 –

15Nov03-10Lrl fst 6f :214 :442 :5631:084 3↑DeFrncsM-G1 **113** 3 10 1010 85¾ 41¾ 11¾ Dominguez R A L119 f 9.30 95-13 AHuevo1191¾ *ShkeYouDown*123no GtorsNBers115½ Pinched,5wd,hand ride 10
21Sep03-7Del fst 6f :221 :444 :5641:084 3↑OClm 50000N **103** 1 5 43½ 42½ 11 12 Dominguez R A L117 f *1.50 100-06 *A Huevo*1172 *Pop Rocks*1174½ Fleety117hd Mid move,drifted,drvg 6
9Aug03-6Mnr fst 6f :212 :44 :5841:091 3↑HArnltMemH88k **63** 8 10 109½ 1011 77¾ 79¾ Dominguez R A LB109 f *2.10 83-06 Secret Romeo1162¼ Cargi1131 *Tour the Hive*115hd Struggled early 10

Action This Day
Own: Hughes B. W

B. c. 3 (Feb) KEEJUL02 $150,000
Sire: Kris S. (Roberto) $150,000
Dam: Najecam (Trempolino)
Br: Jaime S. Carrion, Trustee (Ky)
Tr: Mandella Richard E(0 0 0 0 .00) 2003:(253 51 .20)

Life	3	2	1	0	$817,200	92	D.Fst 3 2 1 0 $817,200 92
2003	3	2	1	0	$817,200	92	Wet(354) 0 0 0 0 $0 –
2002	0	M	0	0	$0	–	Turf(340) 0 0 0 0 $0 –
	0	0	0	0	$0	–	Dst(0) 0 0 0 0 $0 –

25Oct03-7SA fst 1 1/16 :221 :45 1:0941:433 BesTBCJv-G1 **92** 2 121312 13 106¼ 31½ 12¼ Flores D R LB122 26.80 86-07 ActionThisDay1222¼ MinisterEric1225 ChpelRoyl122no 4 wide, going away 12
28Sep03-1SA fst 1 1/16 :232 :473 1:12 1:453 Md Sp Wt 45k **79** 5 77¾ 712 69½ 52¼ 1no Solis A LB117 *1.00 76-16 *ActionThisDy*117no NtiveApprovl117½ CourgeousAct1174 Bid btwn,gamely 7
5Sep03-2Dmr fst 1 :224 :463 1:1041:37 Md Sp Wt 51k **74** 5 66 66¾ 57½ 46 27 Solis A LB120 4.10 82-10 Coldntight1207 *ActionThisDay*120nk ThtsnOutrge1203 Bit tight 1/16,late 2d 6

Adoration
Own: Amerman Racing Stables LLC

B. m. 5 (Apr) KEESEP00 $40,000
Sire: Honor Grades (Danzig) $15,000
Dam: Sewing Lady (Key to the Mint)
Br: Lucy G. Bassett (Ky)
Tr: Hofmans David E(0 0 0 0 .00) 2003:(113 17 .15)

Life	15	5	2	1	$1,443,856	101	D.Fst 11 4 1 1 $1,362,030 101
2003	5	2	1	1	$1,160,750	101	Wet(343) 0 0 0 0 $0 –
2002	10	3	1	0	$283,106	94	Turf(267) 4 1 1 0 $81,826 93
	0	0	0	0	$0	–	Dst(0) 0 0 0 0 $0 –

7Dec03-8Hol fst 1 1/16 :23 :46 1:0941:41 3↑ⒻBayakoaH-G2 **100** 5 32½ 22 21½ 21 23¼ Valenzuela P A LB121 1.40 96-08 StarParde1123¼ Adortion1214 BreNecessities1193 Bobbled start,2nd best 6
25Oct03-2SA fst 1⅛ :47 1:11 1:3541:49 3↑ⒻBCDistaf-G1 **101** 2 11 11 11½ 12 14½ Valenzuela P A LB123 40.70 89-07 Adoration1234½ Elloluv1192½ Got Koko1233½ Speed,inside,gamely 7
28Sep03-6SA fst 1 1/16 :232 :471 1:1111:424 3↑ⒻLdyScBCH-G2 **99** 3 21½ 2½ 2hd 2½ 43¼ Valenzuela P A LB115 b 25.20 87-16 Got Koko118½ ⒹElloluv1161¾ Azeri1281 Pulld,stdied 1/16,wknd 6
Placed third through disqualification
4Sep03-6Dmr fst 1 :222 :46 1:10 1:352 3↑ⒻⓇPiedraFndH81k **100** 6 21 2½ 2hd 1hd 1no Valenzuela P A LB115 b *1.20e 97-11 Adoration115no RoyllyChosen1151½ *AngelGift*1168 Game,strong hand ride 7
19Jan03-7SA fst 1 1/16 :23 :462 1:1021:421 ⒻElEncino-G2 **99** 3 31½ 3½ 1½ 3½ 44½ Valenzuela P A LB119 9.70 88-17 *GotKoko*1191½ BellBellucci1173 BreNecessities119no 3wd bid,inside,lost 3d 8

Note: Ages on all past performances are as of 2004

Affirmed Success
Own: Fried A Jr

B. g. 10 (Apr)
Sire: Affirmed (Exclusive Native) $30,000
Dam: Towering Success (Irish Tower)
Br: Albert Fried, Jr. (Ky)
Tr: Schosberg Richard E(0 0 0 0 .00) 2003:(187 27 .14)

Life	42	17	10	6	$2,285,315	120	D.Fst	29 11 8 4	$1,255,400	119
2003	4	2	0	1	$114,300	110	Wet(331)	5 3 0 1	$434,475	120
2002	6	2	2	1	$383,120	111	Turf(294)	8 3 2 1	$595,440	109
	0	0	0	0	$0	–	Dst(0)	0 0 0 0	$0	–

12Apr03–9Aqu my	7f		:224	:452	1:091	1:212	3↑ CarterH-G1	83	3 2	1hd	2½	58	514¾	Migliore R	L117	4.60	81–13	Congaree1223½ *Aldebaran*1181¼ Peeping Tom1143¾	Vied outside, tired	5
15Mar03–8Aqu fst	6f	⊡	:214	:441	:561	1:09	3↑ ToboggnH-G3	110	2 5	34½	23	2½	11	Migliore R	L118	*1.75	99–11	AffirmedSuccess1181 PeepingTom117¾ CptinRd115nk	3 wide trip, driving	6
26Feb03–8Aqu fst	6f	⊡	:222	:442	:56	1:074	4↑ Alw 54000N$Y	107	3 3	32½	33	21	31	Migliore R	L118	*.70	104–07	Captain Red111½ Gold I. D.118½ *AffirmedSuccess*1189½	Steadied on rail late	6
10Jan03–8Aqu fst	6f	⊡	:231	:453	:571	1:09	4↑ Alw 54000N$Y	103	2 1	2hd	1hd	11	11	Migliore R	L121	*.90	99–07	AffirmdSuccss1211 LtCrson1146 StormCommndr115½	Vied inside, driving	5

Affluent
Own: Whitham Janis R

Ch. m. 6 (Mar)
Sire: Affirmed (Exclusive Native) $30,000
Dam: Trinity Place (Strawberry Road*Aus)
Br: Janis R. Whitham (Ky)
Tr: McAnally Ronald L(0 0 0 0 .00) 2003:(312 44 .14)

Life	23	8	5	4	$1,497,651	107	D.Fst	16 5 4 3	$806,116	107
2003	4	1	0	1	$184,236	102	Wet(324)	1 0 0 1	$24,000	91
2002	8	2	3	0	$560,615	107	Turf(331)	6 3 1 0	$667,535	103
	0	0	0	0	$0	–	Dst(0)	0 0 0 0	$0	–

13Jly03–4Hol fst	7f	:22	:443	1:083	1:212	3↑ ⒻAGleamH-G2	100	4 3	512	57½	43½	31½	Stevens G L	LB119	1.50	93–15	Cee's Elegance1161½ You121no Affluent1192	3wd into str,missed 2d	5
24May03–8Hol fst	1 1/16	:23	:461	1:10	1:414	3↑ ⒻMladyBCH-G1	90	5 45	43½	32½	55	511	Stevens G L	LB117	4.80	84–05	*Azeri*1253 Enjoy1143 Tropical Blossom1111	3wd bid,weakened	6
5Apr03–8OP fst	1 1/16	:241	:483	1:121	1:43	4↑ ⒻAplBlsmH-G1	96	2 56	55	56	45½	45¼	Solis A	L117	4.20	90–11	*Azeri*123hd Take Charge Lady1183¼ *Mandy's Gold*1162	Evenly off rail	7
25Jan03–8SA fst	7f	:22	:443	1:092	1:22	4↑ ⒻSntMncaH-G1	102	4 2	69¾	75¾	31	1½	Solis A	LB119	2.50	96–07	Affluent119½ Sightseek1151½ Secret of Mecca1103	3wd into lane,gamely	7

Aldebaran
Own: Flaxman Holdings Ltd

B. h. 6 (Feb)
Sire: Mr. Prospector (Raise a Native)
Dam: Chimes of Freedom (Private Account)
Br: Flaxman Holdings Ltd (Ky)
Tr: Frankel Robert J(0 0 0 0 .00) 2003:(411 114 .28)

Life	25	8	12	3	$1,739,186	122	D.Fst	12 5 5 1	$965,006	122
2003	8	5	1	1	$1,110,606	122	Wet(431)	3 1 2 0	$574,400	110
2002	8	1	6	0	$428,800	113	Turf(333)	10 2 5 2	$199,780	105
	0	0	0	0	$0	–	Dst(0)	0 0 0 0	$0	–

25Oct03–5SA fst	6f	:21	:431	:55	1:074	3↑ BCSprint-G1	105	6 12	1312	127	99	65½	Bailey J D	LB126	*2.10	93–05	Cajun Beat1232¼ Bluesthestandard1262 ShakeYouDown126½	Belated rally	13
31Aug03–10Sar fst	7f	:22	:441	1:083	1:211	3↑ ForegoH-G1	122	4 7	79½	57	1½	14¾	Bailey J D	L123 f	*1.60	101–09	Aldebaran1234¾ *Najran*1141¼ Gygistar1196¾	Clear sailing inside	7
4Jly03–8Bel fst	7f	:222	:444	1:093	1:222	3↑ TomFoolH-G2	105	4 6	713	711	2½	12	Bailey J D	L122 f	*.95	88–15	*Aldebaran*1222 Peeping Tom1172½ State City1183¾	Going away on rail	7
14Jun03–10CD fst	1⅛	:464	1:102	1:35	1:472	3↑ SFosterH-G1	101	6 63½	66	63½	56½	39½	Bailey J D	L120	3.20	91–04	*Perfect Drift*115hd *Mineshaft*1239½ *Aldebaran*120½	Improved position	10
26May03–9Bel sly	1	:221	:442	1:083	1:34	3↑ MtropltH-G1	110	6 711	79	51¾	11½	1nk	Bailey J D	L119	4.40	96–14	Aldebaran119nk Saarland1143 *Peeping Tom*1143¾	Ducked out stretch	8
3May03–5CD fst	7f	:222	:45	1:093	1:214	4↑ CDH-G2	111	5 10	1111	97½	32	12½	Bailey J D	L120	*1.30	93–08	*Aldebaran*1202½ Pass Rush117nk Cappuchino115hd	Swung 7w, drew off	12
12Apr03–9Aqu my	7f	:224	:452	1:091	1:212	3↑ CarterH-G1	108	5 1	58¾	56½	35	23½	Bailey J D	L118	2.15	92–13	Congaree1223½ *Aldebaran*1181¼ Peeping Tom1143¾	Game finish on rail	5
2Mar03–7SA fst	7f	:222	:443	1:091	1:212	4↑ SnCrlosH-G1	110	6 2	510	54¾	1hd	15	Valdivia J Jr	LB116	2.40	99–08	Aldebaran1165 Crafty C. T.116½ Grey Memo1163	5wd into lane,clear	6

Allamerican Bertie

Own: Klein Richard, Bertram and Elaine

B. m. 5 (Feb)
Sire: Quiet American (Fappiano) $35,000
Dam: Clever Bertie (Timeless Native)
Br: Bert Klein (Ky)
Tr: Flint Steven B(0 0 0 0 .00) 2003:(116 22 .19)

Life	14	8	1	2	$799,235	105	D.Fst	9	5	0	2	$565,090 105
2003	3	2	0	0	$180,000	105	Wet(373)	3	2	1	0	$196,910 99
2002	11	6	1	2	$619,235	105	Turf(248)	2	1	0	0	$37,235 105
	0	0	0	0	$0	-	Dst(0)	0	0	0	0	$0 -

1Mar03-10GP fst 1⅛ :471 1:102 1:351 1:474 3↑(F)RampartH-G2 104 6 12 11½ 12½ 14½ 17¾ Velazquez J R L122 *.40 103-02 Allamerican Bertie1227¾ *Smok'n Frolic*1186¼ Softly1153¼ Strong hand ride 6

8Feb03-10GP fst 1 1/16 :23 :463 1:111 1:422 3↑(F)SabinH-G3 105 9 1hd 11½ 11½ 13 15¼ Bailey J D L120 *1.10 97-08 *AllmericnBerti*1205¼ SmllPromiss112hd RdoubldMiss1141 Off rail, widened 11

5Jan03-10GP fm 1 1/16 (T) :244 :502 1:151 1:46 +3↑(F)HonyFoxH-G3 85 6 11 11 1hd 4nk 106¼ Day P L116 2.20 59-36 *San Dare*115hd Calista1181½ Laurica114nk Used up 10

Alysweep

Own: Doneson Mark and Dubb, Michael

Ch. r. 4 (Mar) OBSFEB02 $100,000
Sire: End Sweep (Forty Niner) $34,980
Dam: Chronicler (Alysheba)
Br: M. G. G. Holdings (Fla)
Tr: Reynolds Patrick L(0 0 0 0 .00) 2003:(217 38 .18)

Life	11	4	2	1	$289,930	103	D.Fst	7	3	1	1	$224,130 103
2003	8	3	2	0	$263,680	103	Wet(329)	4	1	1	0	$65,800 89
2002	3	1	0	1	$26,250	81	Turf(278)	0	0	0	0	$0 -
	0	0	0	0	$0	-	Dst(0)	0	0	0	0	$0 -

7Jun03-9Bel sly 7f :221 :443 1:084 1:22 RvaRdgBC-G2 84 7 5 54 45 58 612½ Chavez J F L123 f 9.20 78-10 Posse123no MidasEyes1236¼ HloHomewrecker123hd Chased outside, tired 8

24May03-8Bel sly 1⅛ :444 1:084 1:344 1:482 PeterPan-G2 83 4 1hd 1½ 1hd 21 26 Bailey J D L123 f 2.75 82-12 Go Rockin' Robin1176 Alysweep123¾ Supervisor1152 Held on for place 6

3May03-9Aqu fst 1 :223 :45 1:093 1:354 Withers-G3 96 3 52½ 62¾ 51¼ 2½ 2nk Migliore R L123 f 4.90 86-21 Spite the Devil116nk Alysweep1231 Stanislavsky116hd Led between calls 8

5Apr03-8Haw fst 1⅛ :463 1:113 1:382 1:512 IlnosDrb-G2 72 9 31 2½ 1hd 610 723¾ Migliore R L124 fb 3.40 75-19 Ten Most Wanted1144 Fund of Funds1148 Foufa's Warrior118¾ Tired 10

16Mar03-9Aqu fst 170 [•] :234 :473 1:114 1:403 Gotham-G3 103 3 11 11½ 11½ 15½ 14¼ Migliore R L120 fb 9.50 91-15 Alysweep1204¼ *GreyComet*1201½ SpitetheDvil116nk Controlled pace, drive 9

22Feb03-8Aqu sly 6f [•] :224 :46 :58 1:103 BestTurn82k 64 2 7 2½ 32½ 48½ 612 Migliore R L122 b *1.25 79-16 ScondnCommnd1168¾ SprFs1221 Mstbnthfrntrw116½ Chased inside, tired 8

20Jan03-8Aqu fst 6f [•] :221 :46 :582 1:111 FCapossela79k 100 2 4 52½ 41 2hd 11½ Migliore R L116 b 3.45 88-22 Alysweep1161½ PhiladelphiJim1204 *Unswept*11616 Swung wide, drew clear 5

1Jan03-6Aqu sly 6f [•] :233 :473 :594 1:121 Alw 43000N1x 89 1 4 1½ 12½ 18 18¾ Migliore R L120 b *1.15 83-17 *Alysweep*1208¾ Just Vinnie1203½ Devout1151¾ Set pace, driving 6

Amonita (GB)

Own: Haras du Mezeray

Dk. b or b. m. 6 (Feb)
Sire: Anabaa (Danzig) $29,344
Dam: Spectacular Joke (Spectacular Bid)
Br: Ship Commodities International (GB)
Tr: Clement Christophe(0 0 0 0 .00) 2003:(389 75 .19)

Life	15	6	3	0	$318,053	103	D.Fst	0	0	0	0	$0 -
2003	3	1	0	0	$65,665	98	Wet(378)	0	0	0	0	$0 -
2002	3	2	1	0	$83,072	103	Turf(328)	15	6	3	0	$318,053 103
	0	0	0	0	$0	-	Dst(0)	0	0	0	0	$0 -

13Apr03-6Kee fm 1 1/16 (T) :233 :48 1:12 1:414 4↑(F)JenyWily-G3 97 4 33 32 33 21 41½ Samyn J L L116 3.90 90-08 SeaofShowers1161¼ MgicMission116nk SnowDnce116hd 4w bid,empty late 10

2Mar03-10GP fm 1⅛ (T) :493 1:131 1:362 1:474 3↑(F)SwneRvrH-G3 98 5 21 21 21 1hd 12½ Samyn J L L117 5.40 96-02 Amonita1172½ What a Price114no Calista118nk Stdy early, drew clear 9

5Jan03-10GP fm 1 1/16 (T) :244 :502 1:151 1:46 +3↑(F)HonyFoxH-G3 94 4 52¼ 42 31 1hd 62¼ Bailey J D L119 *1.40 63-36 *San Dare*115hd Calista1181½ Laurica114nk Flattened out 10

Apt to Be
Own: Duchossois Richard L

B. g. 7 (Apr)
Sire: Rahy (Blushing Groom*Fr) $80,000
Dam: Lets Do Lunch (Royal Roberto)
Br: Hill N Dale Farm (Ky)
Tr: Block Chris M(0 0 0 0 .00) 2003:(259 50 .19)

Life	25	9	6	4	$350,297	110	D.Fst	16	9	2	1	$288,877	110
2003	5	3	0	0	$110,880	110	Wet(351)	3	0	2	0	$30,400	100
2002	5	2	1	1	$72,040	105	Turf(307)	6	0	2	3	$31,020	95
	0	0	0	0	$0	–	Dst(0)	0	0	0	0	$0	–

26Oct03–9CD	sly	7½f	:224 :452 1:103 1:313	3↑AckAckH-G3	33	6	3	42	55¾	713	733¾	Razo E Jr	L120 b	*2.20	48–26	Cappuchino1172 Pass Rush1161 Twilight Road1162	Not persevered with	7
21Sep03–8AP	fst	7f	:23 :453 1:093 1:222	3↑OClm 100000N	104	5	2	32	31½	1hd	11¾	Razo E Jr	L122 b	*.90	93–13	Apt to Be1221¾ Silver Zipper1181¼ Holy Burrito1164½	Driving	5
29Jun03–8AP	fst	1	:232 :453 1:09 1:342	3↑HanshinH-G3	110	3	21	21½	21	11½	17	Razo E Jr	L117 b	3.90	96–24	*Apt to Be*1177 There's Zealous116hd *San Pedro*116nk	Driving	7
7Jun03–8AP	fst	1	:224 :451 1:092 1:353	3↑DrFager46k	95	5	42½	41½	32	2hd	12¾	Razo E Jr	L120 b	1.70	90–17	*Apt to Be*1202¾ Dulce de Leche118hd Stormy Impact118hd	4 wide, driving	6
17May03–7AP	fst	7f	:223 :451 1:093 1:223	3↑OClm 100000	82	8	3	31½	22	25	66½	Razo E Jr	L120 b	7.20	85–12	Bright Valour120no San Pedro120¾ There's Zealous1182	Tired	10

Ashado
Own: Starlight Stables LLC Saylor, Paul an

Dk. b or b. f. 3 (Feb) KEESEP02 $170,000
Sire: Saint Ballado (Halo) $125,000
Dam: Goulash (Mari's Book)
Br: Aaron U. Jones & Marie D. Jones (Ky)
Tr: Pletcher Todd A(0 0 0 0 .00) 2003:(826 199 .24)

Life	6	4	1	1	$610,800	95	D.Fst	4	2	1	1	$495,000	95
2003	6	4	1	1	$610,800	95	Wet(368)	2	2	0	0	$115,800	93
2002	0	M	0	0	$0	–	Turf(300)	0	0	0	0	$0	–
	0	0	0	0	$0	–	Dst(0)	0	0	0	0	$0	–

29Nov03–7Aqu	fst	1⅛	:47 1:12 1:382 1:524	ⒻDemoisel-G2	84	5	3½	31	1hd	1½	1no	Bailey J D	L117	*.55	72–19	Ashado117no La Reina121½ Dr. Kathy11510	Vied, clear, got nod	7
25Oct03–3SA	fst	1 1/16	:224 :464 1:104 1:423	ⒻBCJuvFil-G1	95	5	32½	31½	41	31½	22½	Velazquez J R	LB119	13.30	88–07	Halfbridled1192½ *Ashado*119nk *Victory U. S. A.*1199¼	Saved ground, rallied	14
4Oct03–6Bel	fst	1 1/16	:231 :471 1:121 1:434	ⒻFrizette-G1	88	3	31½	42	41¾	33	34	Santos J A	L120	2.80	77–26	SocietySlction1201¼ VictoryUSA1202¾ Ashdo1206¾	Stayed on well stretch	8
29Aug03–8Sar	fst	7f	:222 :452 1:103 1:24	ⒻSpinaway-G1	84	2	3	2hd	1hd	1½	11¼	Prado E S	L121	3.10	87–10	Ashado1211¼ *Be Gentle*1218¼ Daydreaming1211¾	Bumped start, gamely	6
23Jly03–9Sar	sly	6f	:22 :452 :582 1:12	ⒻSchylrvl-G2	81	6	5	4¾	2hd	11½	13	Prado E S	L118	*2.55	82–17	*Ashado*1183 Maple Syrple1222½ Hermione's Magic1181	Quick 3 wide move	7
18Jun03–3Bel	sly	5½f	:213 :444 :573 1:042	ⒻMd Sp Wt 43k	93	4	4	1½	1½	12½	17	Velazquez J R	L118	*1.10	91–19	*Ashdo*1187 PleseTkeMeOut1183¾ Menifeeque118nk	When roused, widened	5

Atlantic Ocean
Own: The Thoroughbred Corporation

Dk. b or b. f. 4 (Jan) BARMARD2 $1,900,000
Sire: Stormy Atlantic (Storm Cat) $12,500
Dam: Super Chef (Seattle Slew)
Br: Arthur I. Appleton (Fla)
Tr: Baffert Bob(0 0 0 0 .00) 2003:(674 127 .19)

	Life	17	5	3	2	$678,210	92	D.Fst	10	4	1	1	$366,560	92
	2003	9	2	3	1	$443,430	92	Wet(394)	2	0	0	0	$22,260	64
	2002	8	3	0	1	$234,780	89	Turf(333)	5	1	2	1	$289,390	91
		0	0	0	0			Dst(0)	0	0	0	0	$0	–

Aud
Own: Willmott Stables Inc

Dk. b or b. f. 4 (Feb)
Sire: Wild Again (Icecapade) $50,000
Dam: Gail's Brush (Broad Brush)
Br: Willmott Stable (Ky)
Tr: Reinstedler Anthony L(0 0 0 0 .00) 2003:(190 34 .18)

	Life	11	4	2	0	$228,045	94	D.Fst	2	1	0	0	$26,030	83
	2003	11	4	2	0	$228,045	94	Wet(398)	1	0	0	0	$340	36
	2002	0	M	0	0	$0	–	Turf(301)	8	3	2	0	$201,675	94
		0	0	0	0	$0	–	Dst(0)	0	0	0	0	$0	–

Avanzado (Arg)

Own: Cees Stable LLC

Ch. h. 7 (Sep)
Sire: Luhuk (Forty Niner) $7,500
Dam: Avian Eden (Storm Bird)
Br: La Quebrada (Arg)
Tr: O'Neill Doug(0 0 0 0 .00) 2003:(760 133 .18)

Life	27	10	5	2	$886,188	117	D.Fst	16	6	3	1	$845,179	117
2003	8	2	2	0	$602,645	117	Wet(399)	6	2	1	1	$27,377	90
2002	7	4	0	1	$231,992	111	Turf(316)	5	2	1	0	$13,632	–
	0	0	0	0	$0	–	Dst(0)	0	0	0	0	$0	–

27Nov03–7Hol fst 6f :214 :441 :56 1:084 3↑VOUndrwd-G3 **92** 1 4 1½ 1hd 21 53½ Baze T C **LB**124 f *.70 92–08 WtchmSmoky1121 OurNwRcrut1141½ *HstyKrs*116no Inside duel,weakened 6
5Oct03–7SA fst 6f :212 :432 :5521:08 3↑AnTtlBCH-G1 **107** 4 1 1hd 1½ 11 11½ Baze T C **LB**116 f 8.80 98–06 Avnzdo1161½ CptinSquire117hd Bluesthstndrd1151½ Inside duel,held game 6
6Sep03–4Dmr fst 6f :214 :441 :56 1:074 3↑ⓇPirtsBntyH77k **104** 4 1 2hd 1hd 21½ 25 Baze T C **LB**120 f *1.40 97–09 YnkeeGentlemn1145 *Avnzdo*120hd RushintoAltr1181 Dueled, just held 2nd 8
26Jly03–6Dmr fst 6f :214 :44 :5531:074 3↑BCrsbBCH-G2 **106** 4 5 31½ 42 43 43¾ Baze T C **LB**117 fb 6.00 98–07 BeusTown1191½ CptinSquire117nk Bluesthstndrd1172 Stalked,no late bid 9
5Jly03–8Hol fst 7f :214 :442 1:0821:212 3↑TrBndBCH-G1 **88** 1 5 1hd 1½ 32½ 67½ Baze T C **LB**118 fb *2.40 87–11 JoyFrnco118hd Publcton1161½ ⒹBlsthstndrd1173½ Rail,wkened,stdied 1/8 9
Placed 5th through disqualification
29Mar03♦Nad al Sheba (UAE) ft *6f Str 1:094 3↑Dubai Golden Shaheen-G1 2¾ T Baze 130 – State City130¾ Avanzado1301¾ Captain Squire1301¾ 12
Timeform rating: 115 Stk 2000000 *Soon led,clear 2f out,headed 100y out.My Cousin Matt5th,Abreeze6t*
26Jan03–7SA fst 6f :212 :434 :5521:074 4↑PlsVrdsH-G2 **117** 5 1 1½ 12 12½ 14½ Baze T C **LB**116 fb 6.50 99–10 Avnzdo1164½ MellowFellow117½ Disturbingthpc120nk Speed,dueled,clear 6
1Jan03–7SA fst 5½f :212 :442 :5621:023 4↑ElCnejoH-G3 **97** 6 5 4nk 41¼ 53½ 64 Baze T C **LB**117 3.30 95–09 Kona Gold123nk Radiata115¾ No Armistice116hd 4 wide, weakened 7

Awesome Humor

Own: WinStar Farm LLC

Dk. b or b. f. 4 (Feb) FTKJUL01 $45,000
Sire: Distorted Humor (Forty Niner) $20,000
Dam: Horns Gray (Pass the Tab)
Br: Dr. Naveed Chowhan (Ky)
Tr: Walden W. E(0 0 0 0 .00) 2003:(289 67 .23)

Life	11	6	4	0	$848,950	97	D.Fst	9	4	4	0	$544,810	97
2003	7	2	4	0	$539,835	97	Wet(377)	2	2	0	0	$304,140	96
2002	4	4	0	0	$309,115	95	Turf(240)	0	0	0	0	$0	–
	0	0	0	0	$0	–	Dst(0)	0	0	0	0	$0	–

8Nov03–9CD fst 1 :23 :454 1:11 1:362 3↑ⒻCDDstafH-G2 **97** 4 2½ 23 3nk 11 2½ Melancon L L118 3.60 84–20 *LdStory*114½ AwsomHumor1181¼ BorntoDnc1133¼ Chase,4w,led,outgamed 10
3Oct03–9Hoo my 1$\frac{1}{16}$:23 :463 1:1141:453 ⒻInBCOaks-G3 **96** 4 4¾ 32 1½ 14 1¾ Albarado R J **LB**116 *1.30 81–24 AwsomHmor116¾ ClokfVgnss1143¼ ShtGnFvrt118nk 3wd bid, drifted, held 10
13Sep03–12TP fst 1$\frac{1}{16}$:24 :473 1:12 1:444 3↑ⒻTPBC-G3 **94** 2 42 53¼ 42½ 23 23½ Albarado R J L112 2.10 84–17 SmoknFrolic1223½ *AwesomeHumor*1122½ SoMuchMor1181¾ 5 wide 3/8 pole 9
16Aug03–9Sar fst 1¼ :4821:124 1:3742:05 ⒻAlabama-G1 **92** 6 1½ 2½ 32½ 26 26 Albarado R J L121 15.50 76–14 IslndFshion1216 AwesomeHumor1211 SpoknFur1211¼ Bumped after start 6
19Jly03–8Del fst 1$\frac{1}{16}$:231 :463 1:1121:444 ⒻDelOaks-G3 **83** 1 43½ 32½ 33 24 26½ Albarado R J L115 *1.00 77–17 *IslndFshon*1226½ AwsomHmor1154¼ Ldycho115nk Awkward start,2nd best 9
6Jun03–8AP fst 1⅛ :48 1:12 1:3731:504 3↑ⒻOClm 100000N **93** 1 21½ 21 1hd 11½ 11¼ Douglas R R L114 *.90 89–20 Awesome Humor1141¼ Lakenheath1241½ Spirited Maiden1186½ Driving 6
14May03–8CD fst 6f :213 :442 :56 1:081 3↑ⒻOClm 80000N **76** 3 5 33 44½ 410 414 Day P L108 *.50 83–13 LovTlkn1182¾ *BrownEydButy*1189 AbundntlyBlssd1162¼ Near inside,empty 6

Awesome Time
Own: La Penta Robert V

B. c. 4 (Feb)
Sire: Awesome Again (Deputy Minister) $50,000
Dam: Slew Boyera (Seattle Slew)
Br: F.J.F.M., LLC (Ky)
Tr: Zito Nicholas P(0 0 0 0 .00) 2003:(507 77 .15)

Life	11	3	2	1	$226,210	95	D.Fst	9	2	2	1	$199,810	95
2003	9	2	1	1	$189,610	95	Wet(384)	2	1	0	0	$26,400	91
2002	2	1	1	0	$36,600	80	Turf(226)	0	0	0	0	$0	–
	0	0	0	0	$0	–	Dst(0)	0	0	0	0	$0	–

27Nov03–7Aqu fst 1 :232 :46 1:101 1:344 3↑Alw 52000N3x **57** 2 52¼ 117¼ 1116 1119 1128½ Arroyo N Jr L117 28.75 62–16 Stockholder1214 TheLadysGroom1197 OneTuffFox1231 Brief speed, tired 11
28Sep03–7Bel my 1 ⊗:23 :463 1:111 1:361 3↑Alw 52000N3x **53** 4 1½ 1½ 2hd 55½ 624¼ Prado E S L115 9.60 61–29 Colita115½ Acceptable Venture1142¾ DialaHero1194½ Between rivals, tired 6
23Aug03–10Sar fst 7f :213 :433 1:083 1:22 KngsBshp-G1 **58** 12 3 87¾ 1013 1325 1322¼ Prado E S L121 72.00 75–07 VlidVideo121nk GretNotion117nk *Ghostzpper*1171¾ Wide throughout, tired 13
14Jun03–11Del fst 1 1/16 :223 :46 1:103 1:431 LRichrds-G3 **95** 1 31 31 1hd 1hd 1no Black A S L115 20.30 92–13 AwsomTm115no ChrstnsOutlw115¾ ChroksBoy1224½ Hard drive, prevailed 8
3May03–9Aqu fst 1 :223 :45 1:093 1:354 Withers-G3 **51** 7 42 52¾ 811 815 824 Arroyo N Jr L116 b 26.75 62–21 SpitetheDevil116nk Alysweep1231 Stanislavsky116hd Stumbled start, wide 8
12Apr03–5Aqu my 1⅛ :463 1:104 1:362 1:494 3↑Alw 44000N2L **91** 2 12½ 11½ 12 11 11¼ Arroyo N Jr L116 b 4.30 87–12 AwsomTm1161¼ LookngAround1166½ RnwyRssy116nk Drifted out stretch 7
16Mar03–5Aqu fst 1 ⊡:24 :472 1:113 1:381 Alw 55000N$Y **79** 3 62¼ 68 65½ 63¾ 35 McKee J5 L112 3.80 82–15 AtfirstBlush1171 FundofFunds1174 *AwsomTim*112nk Came wide, mild rally 6
31Jan03–8GP fst 1 1/16 :223 :462 1:12 1:44 Alw 36000N1x **66** 4 66 66½ 73¼ 710 715½ Cruz M R L120 11.00 73–12 TenCentsShine1185¼ SenorSwingr1225¼ RoringFvr1181½ 4 wide, no factor 11
4Jan03–3GP fst 1 1/16 :232 :47 1:113 1:441 Alw 34000N1x **83** 3 2½ 21 2hd 2½ 23½ Chavez J F L122 3.80 84–10 IndyDancer1203½ AwesomeTime122nk HotHnd1202¼ Drifted, up for place 6

Azeri
Own: Allen E. Paulson Living Trust

Ch. m. 6 (May) KEESEP99 $110,000
Sire: Jade Hunter (Mr. Prospector) $10,000
Dam: Zodiac Miss*Aus (Ahonoora*GB)
Br: Allen E. Paulson (Ky)
Tr: De Seroux Laura(0 0 0 0 .00) 2003:(111 14 .13)

Life	16	14	2	0	$3,044,820	111	D.Fst	15	13	2	0	$2,004,820	110
2003	5	4	1	0	$817,080	109	Wet(335)	1	1	0	0	$1,040,000	111
2002	9	8	1	0	$2,181,540	111	Turf(265)	0	0	0	0	$0	–
	0	0	0	0	$0	–	Dst(0)	0	0	0	0	$0	–

28Sep03–6SA fst 1 1/16 :232 :471 1:111 1:424 3↑ⒻLdySclBCH-G2 **101** 5 54½ 53½ 53½ 32 32¼ Smith M E LB128 *.20 88–16 Got Koko118½ D Elloluv1161¾ Azeri1281 3wd into lane,no bid 6
Placed second through disqualification
10Aug03–8Dmr fst 1 1/16 :231 :47 1:11 1:42 3↑ⒻCLHrschH-G2 **100** 1 11 1½ 11½ 12½ 13¼ Smith M E LB127 *.30 95–12 Azeri1273¼ *Got Koko*118hd Tropical Blossom1084½ Bit off rail,handily 5
21Jun03–8Hol fst 1⅛ :471 1:103 1:351 1:482 3↑ⒻVanityH-G1 **109** 6 2½ 1hd 2hd 11 12 Smith M E LB127 *.30 92–14 *Azeri*1272 Sister Girl Blues111½ *Bare Necessities*1184½ Dueled,inched clear 7
24May03–8Hol fst 1 1/16 :23 :461 1:10 1:414 3↑ⒻMladyBCH-G1 **109** 4 2hd 11 12½ 12½ 13 Smith M E LB125 *.20 95–05 *Azeri*1253 Enjoy1143 Tropical Blossom1111 Speed,met bids,clear 6
5Apr03–8OP fst 1 1/16 :241 :483 1:121 1:43 4↑ⒻAplBlsmH-G1 **105** 6 32 42 2½ 21½ 1hd Smith M E L123 *.40 95–11 *Azeri*123hd Take ChargeLady1183¼ *Mandy'sGold*1162 Restrained, 4-w, game 7

Bachelor Blues
Own: Schettine William C

Gr/ro. c. 3 (Mar)
Sire: Smoke Glacken (Two Punch) $15,000
Dam: Wedding Day Blues (El Prado*Ire)
Br: William Schettine (Ky)
Tr: Carroll Josie(0 0 0 0 .00) 2003:(273 47 .17)

Life	8	2	3	0	$265,406	89	D.Fst	3	0	2	0	$39,670	66
2003	8	2	3	0	$265,406	89	Wet(402)	1	0	0	0	$3,636	55
2002	0	M	0	0	$0	–	Turf(265)	4	2	1	0	$222,100	89
	0	0	0	0	$0	–	Dst(0)	0	0	0	0	$0	–

24Oct03–8Kee fm 1 1/16 Ⓣ :231 :472 1:123 1:434 BourbonCo112k **64** 8 11½ 11½ 11½ 67½ 811¼ Albarado R J L122 *2.10 71–21 Commendtion1202¾ Onceroundtwice116½ GrndHritg120nk Pace,4-5w,tired 10
5Oct03–9WO fst 1 1/16 :241 :474 1:122 1:463 GreyBC-G2 **49** 6 73¼ 63¾ 88 816 824¼ Husbands P L117 6.55 49–30 Smoocher1132¼ Organ Grinder116hd Niigon1143¾ Bump steady 4w 9
14Sep03–4WO fm 1 Ⓣ :232 :461 1:102 1:344 Summer-G2 **89** 8 11 12 12 13 1nk Kabel T K L122 12.75 89–06 BchlorBls122nk VctoryLght1225 D *Commndton*1222¼ 2-pth,prevail 5w,lane 10
17Aug03–3WO gd 7f Ⓣ :224 :463 1:12 1:25 Alw 72200N3x **73** 5 3 2hd 1hd 1hd 21½ Landry R C L119 *1.05 75–21 SpiderCanyon1171½ *BchelorBlues*1192½ Zkocity1191 Duel, drifted, bumped 9
26Jly03–4WO fm 6f Ⓣ :222 :46 :581 1:111 Md Sp Wt 60k **72** 7 2 3nk 2hd 12 11 Landry R C L120 *1.75 82–14 BchelorBlues1201 D *BonMrie*1201¾ *SpidrCnyon*1151¾ Chase 2-pth,held well 12
11Jly03–6WO fst 6f :221 :45 :573 1:11 Md Sp Wt 60k **66** 2 5 11½ 11 2hd 21 Landry R C L119 2.25 88–11 Langburg1141 *Bachelor Blues*1192 Third Sacker1154 Gave best 2-path lane 8
14Jun03–8WO fst 5f :214 :45 :574 Victoria137k **54** 3 3 42 57 410 39¼ Landry R C L115 3.30 82–09 D GeminiDrem1152¼ ThirdDy1157 BchlorBlus1151¾ Chse 2-path,steady 3/8 7
Placed second through disqualification
11May03–4WO my 4½f :213 :451 :52 Md Sp Wt 60k **55** 9 8 68 611 44½ Husbands P 119 *1.85 94–12 Stormthebrricd114¾ TruthSrum1192¼ GminiDrm1191½ 4 wide, throughout 9

Badge of Silver
Own: Ramsey Kenneth L. and Sarah K

Dk. b or b. c. 4 (Mar) KEESEP01 $85,000
Sire: Silver Deputy (Deputy Minister) $40,000
Dam: Silveroo (Silver Hawk)
Br: Liberation Farm, Oratis Thoroughbreds & Trackside Farm (Ky)
Tr: Werner Ronny W(0 0 0 0 .00) 2003:(247 55 .22)

Life	4	3	0	0	$161,725	108	D.Fst	4	3	0	0	$161,725	108
2003	3	2	0	0	$130,500	108	Wet(322)	0	0	0	0	$0	–
2002	1	1	0	0	$31,225	–	Turf(290)	0	0	0	0	$0	–
	0	0	0	0	$0	–	Dst(0)	0	0	0	0	$0	–

9Mar03–9FG fst 1 1/16 :232 :463 1:103 1:423 LaDerby-G2 **95** 10 42½ 32 31 21 65¾ Albarado R J L122 *1.20 91–17 *Peace Rules*1222¼ D Kafwain1221 Funny Cide122½ 3w, edge, flattened ot 10
Placed 5th through disqualification
16Feb03–9FG fst 1 1/16 :233 :472 1:12 1:424 RisenStr-G3 **108** 10 21 2hd 1hd 13 110 Albarado R J L116 2.90 96–15 BdgeofSilver11610 LoneStrSky122¾ DfrrsVixn114½ Drew away, ridden out 12
23Jan03–7FG fst 6f :22 :453 :572 1:093 Alw 30000N1x **108** 5 1 1½ 1½ 12½ 17 Albarado R J L119 *.70 92–17 *BadgeofSilver*1197 BrokeAgin1198¼ Givetheboycigr1191½ Clear, ridden out 5

Baileys Edge
Own: Holm Thoroughbred Company

Dk. b or b. g. 7 (May)
Sire: Mister Baileys*GB (Robellino)
Dam: Ocean's Edge (Coastal)
Br: Dr. Brian Davidson & George De Benedicty (Ky)
Tr: Margolis Stephen R(0 0 0 0 .00) 2003:(94 16 .17)

Life	14	7	2	2	$240,623	100	D.Fst	9	3	2	1	$126,040	100
2003	1	1	0	0	$60,000	99	Wet(332)	4	4	0	0	$111,063	99
2002	5	1	2	0	$57,826	93	Turf(303)	1	0	0	1	$3,520	84
	0	0	0	0	$0	–	Dst(0)	0	0	0	0	$0	–

4Jan03–8GP fst 6f :212 :44 :564 1:094 3↑ MrProspH-G3 **99** 4 3 69½ 67½ 21½ 1nk Boulanger G L114 17.80 95–11 Baileys Edge114nk FriendlyFrolic1142¼ OutofFashion1151 Rail trip, all out 6

Ballingarry (Ire)

Own: Port Trust Naify, Marsha and San Gabr

B. c. 5 (Apr)
Sire: Sadler's Wells (Northern Dancer)
Dam: Flamenco Wave (Desert Wine)
Br: Orpendale (Ire)
Tr: De Seroux Laura(0 0 0 0 .00) 2003:(111 14 .13)

Life	16	5	1	4	$1,543,975	111	D.Fst	0 0 0 0		$0	–
2003	5	1	0	1	$194,700	100	Wet(281)	0 0 0 0		$0	–
2002	7	2	1	2	$1,282,645	111	Turf(328)	16 5 1 4		$1,543,975	111
	0	0	0	0	$0	–	Dst(0)	0 0 0 0		$0	–

31Aug03-8Dmr	fm	1⅜	Ⓣ :47^{2} 1:12 1:35^{3} 2:12^{1}	3↑ DelMarH-G2	99	8	9^{9}	9$^{8\frac{1}{2}}$	9$^{8\frac{3}{4}}$	5^{5}	4$^{1\frac{1}{2}}$	Smith M E	LB119	5.70	97-05	IrishWrrior116^{hd} ContinntlRd117½ Contnuously114^{1}	Came out str,late bid	9
9Aug03-9Sar	gd	1½	[T] :49 1:13 2:03^{1} 2:28	3↑ SwrdDncH-G1	76	8	3$^{1\frac{1}{2}}$	4^{2}	11$^{4\frac{1}{2}}$	10^{11}	9$^{17\frac{1}{2}}$	Velazquez J R	L119	4.00	63-20	Whitmore's Conn115 1¼ Macaw114^{nk} Slew Valley114¾	Speed outside, tired	11
5Jly03-8AP	gd	1½	Ⓣ :49^{4} 1:15^{1} 2:04 2:28^{1}	3↑ StrStBCH-G3	100	1	5^{3}	4^{4}	4^{2}	2^{hd}	1½	Douglas R R	L121	*.60	96-04	Ballingarry121½ DrBrendler118$^{2\frac{1}{2}}$ JacksOwnTime112¾	Split horses, driving	9
10May03-7Hol	fm	1½	Ⓣ :49^{1} 1:13^{1} 1:59^{4} 2:25^{1}	3↑ JMurryMemH400k	100	5	6$^{3\frac{1}{2}}$	5$^{4\frac{1}{2}}$	5^{6}	5$^{4\frac{1}{2}}$	3$^{6\frac{1}{2}}$	Valenzuela P A	LB120	7.10	92-12	*Storming Home*122^{2} *Denon*122$^{4\frac{1}{2}}$ *Ballingarry*120^{nk}	Came out str,late 3rd	8
6Apr03-7SA	fm	1⅛	Ⓣ :49^{3} 1:13^{1} 1:36^{1} 1:47^{4}	4↑ ArcadiaH-G2	95	3	5^{5}	5$^{4\frac{1}{2}}$	5$^{4\frac{1}{4}}$	7$^{5\frac{1}{4}}$	7$^{3\frac{1}{4}}$	Desormeaux K J	LB120	*1.60	87-11	Century City114^{nk} *Gondolieri*116^{hd} Sunday Break117½	Off bit slow,no bid	9

Balto Star

Own: Anstu Stables Inc

Dk. b or b. g. 6 (Mar)
Sire: Glitterman (Dewan) $15,000
Dam: Miss Livi (Devil's Bag)
Br: Anstu Stables, Inc. (Ky)
Tr: Pletcher Todd A(0 0 0 0 .00) 2003:(826 199 .24)

Life	33	11	6	2	$1,952,946	113	D.Fst	16 5 4 1		$693,126	113
2003	13	4	2	1	$907,500	111	Wet(391)	4 1 1 0		$322,520	109
2002	6	2	2	0	$192,876	107	Turf(321)	13 5 1 1		$937,300	110
	0	0	0	0	$0	–	Dst(0)	0 0 0 0		$0	–

27Dec03-11Crc	fm	1½	Ⓣ :48^{4} 1:13^{3} 2:01 2:24^{4}	3↑ WLMcKntH-G2	105	2	1$^{1\frac{1}{2}}$	1$^{1\frac{1}{2}}$	1$^{1\frac{1}{2}}$	1$^{1\frac{1}{2}}$	1$^{1\frac{1}{2}}$	Velazquez J R	L121	*2.30	109 -	BaltoStar121 1½ Continuously116½ RowansPark114$^{2\frac{1}{4}}$	Pace,responded well	11
22Nov03-8Aqu	sf	1⅜	Ⓣ :49^{3} 1:15 1:39^{3} 2:18^{4}	3↑ RedSmthH-G2	105	6	1½	1½	1$^{1\frac{1}{2}}$	1^{8}	1$^{3\frac{1}{4}}$	Velazquez J R	L120	4.90	90-10	*Balto Star*120$^{3\frac{1}{4}}$ Macaw118^{nk} Cetewayo116$^{3\frac{1}{2}}$	Drew off when roused	11
25Oct03-8SA	fm	1½	Ⓣ :48^{3} 1:11^{2} 2:00 2:24^{1}	3↑ BCTurf-G1	68	6	1½	1^{hd}	8^{11}	8^{15}	9$^{24\frac{1}{2}}$	Velazquez J R	LB126	24.10	80-04	[DH]High Chaparral126 [DH]Johar126^{hd} *Falbrav*126$^{5\frac{1}{2}}$	Inside trip,gave way	9
27Sep03-9Bel	fm	1½	Ⓣ :50^{1} 1:14^{3} 2:02^{1} 2:27^{2}	3↑ TfClscIv-G1	104	3	1$^{1\frac{1}{2}}$	1½	1$^{1\frac{1}{2}}$	1½	3$^{3\frac{1}{2}}$	Prado E S	L126	6.50e	80-14	Sulamani126$^{2\frac{3}{4}}$ Deeliteful Irving126¾ Balto Star126½	Pace, stayed gamely	7
6Sep03-8Bel	yl	1⅜	Ⓣ :51^{4} 1:17^{1} 1:42 2:17^{4}	3↑ ManOWar-G1	102	7	1^{1}	1^{1}	1^{1}	2^{3}	4$^{4\frac{1}{4}}$	Velazquez J R	L126	4.70e	70-26	LunarSovereign126$^{2\frac{3}{4}}$ SlewVlley126^{nk} Denon126 1¼	Rated pace, weakened	8
9Aug03-9Sar	gd	1½	[T] :49 1:13 2:03^{1} 2:28	3↑ SwrdDncH-G1	74	1	1½	1½	2½	11^{11}	11$^{18\frac{1}{4}}$	Velez J A Jr	L119	5.70	62-20	Whitmore's Conn115 1¼ Macaw114^{nk} Slew Valley114¾	Set pace, gave way	11
5Jly03-10Mth	fm	1⅜	Ⓣ :48^{3} 1:14 1:37^{3} 2:12^{3}	3↑ UntdNtnH-G1	110	1	1^{1}	1^{1}	1^{1}	1^{hd}	1½	Velez J A Jr	L117	37.00	101-03	BaltoStar117½ TheTinMan121^{no} LunrSovereign112^{nk}	Pace,game,held well	7
14Jun03-10Mth	fst	1 1/16	⊗ :22^{4} :45^{1} 1:09^{3} 1:42^{1}	3↑ OcenprtH-G3	98	1	2½	2½	2½	1^{hd}	2$^{1\frac{3}{4}}$	Velez J A Jr	L119 f	2.00	98-06	Runspastum113 1¾ *Balto Star*119^{1} Saint Verre118$^{5\frac{1}{2}}$	Outfinished final 1/16	6
16May03-11Pim	sly	1 3/16	:46^{3} 1:11 1:36^{2} 1:56	4↑ PimSpclH-G1	70	2	1½	1^{hd}	3$^{3\frac{1}{2}}$	9^{22}	9$^{30\frac{3}{4}}$	Velazquez J R	L118	5.70	62-23	Mineshaft121$^{3\frac{3}{4}}$ WesternPride116^{hd} Judge'sCase113 1¾	Rail, dropped back	9
5Apr03-8Aqu	fst	1⅛	:46^{2} 1:10^{2} 1:35 1:48	3↑ ExlsrBCH-G3	104	4	4^{2}	4$^{3\frac{1}{2}}$	3$^{1\frac{1}{2}}$	2^{2}	2½	Castellano J J	L119	2.80	95-16	ClassicEndeavor113½ BltoStr119¾ TempestFugit114¾	Carried out 1/4 pole	5
2Mar03-9FG	fst	1⅛	:47^{4} 1:12^{1} 1:36^{2} 1:48^{4}	4↑ NwOrlnsH-G2	88	3	9$^{5\frac{3}{4}}$	7$^{6\frac{1}{2}}$	7$^{5\frac{3}{4}}$	9^{13}	9^{17}	Martin E M Jr	L120	*3.40	83-17	*Mineshaft*115$^{3\frac{1}{2}}$ Olmodavor117$^{2\frac{1}{2}}$ Strive114 1½	Wide backstretch	11
9Feb03-9FG	fst	1 1/16	:24 :47^{4} 1:12^{4} 1:43^{3}	4↑ WirlwayH-G3	111	4	2^{5}	3^{4}	2^{2}	1^{1}	1$^{2\frac{1}{2}}$	Martin E M Jr	L118	*2.50	92-20	Balto Star118$^{2\frac{1}{2}}$ *Mineshaft*116¾ Bonapaw115$^{3\frac{1}{2}}$	Took over, ridden out	8
4Jan03-10GP	gd	1	Ⓣ :23^{2} :47^{2} 1:12^{1} 1:37^{4}	3↑ AppletnH-G2	76	8	3^{3}	3^{2}	3^{2}	9$^{9\frac{1}{4}}$	8$^{11\frac{1}{2}}$	Velazquez J R	L118	*1.80	65-29	Point Prince115 1¼ Krieger115^{nk} Red Sea114 1¾	Stalked 4 wide	9

Barbara O'Brien

Own: Double S Stable Avanzino, Kenneth and

B. m. 5 (Jan)
Sire: Eltish (Cox's Ridge) $3,500
Dam: Brandy O'Brien (Desert Wine)
Br: Marty Hershe & Galloping Acres Farm (Fla)
Tr: Benson Harry(0 0 0 0 .00) 2003:(98 26 .27)

Life	12	5	4	0	$205,695	104		D.Fst	10	4	3	0	$150,695	104
2003	9	3	4	0	$171,035	104		Wet(387)	2	1	1	0	$55,000	95
2002	3	2	0	0	$34,660	93		Turf(208)	0	0	0	0	$0	–
	0	0	0	0	$0	–		Dst(0)	0	0	0	0	$0	–

13Dec03-10Crc	fst	7f		:22	:444	1:102	1:232	3↑ⒻChSprngH-G3	**104**	7	5	21½	21½	13	15¼	Coa E M	L114	5.60	97-11	Barbara O'Brien1145¼ Holy Bubbette1141 Splasha1143	Kept to task	12
15Nov03-11Crc	fst	1 1/16		:234	:482	1:132	1:462	3↑Ⓕ[S]EHeubckDsH200k	**83**	6	43	21	2hd	41¾	79½	Coa E M	L113f	4.10	70-18	Scpde1131¾ *RedoubledMiss*117½ SecretRequest1121½	Bid far turn, faltered	11
4Oct03-9Crc	fst	6½f		:214	:444	1:103	1:173	3↑ⒻUCanDoItH75k	**96**	8	2	33	33½	22	21½	Cruz M R	L114f	3.70	89-17	*Chispiski*1191½ Barbara O'Brien1143¼ Sea Span1131½	Angled in, 2nd best	9
1Sep03-9Pha	sly	7f		:214	:441	1:091	1:221	3↑ⒻSVanBurenH75k	**95**	11	4	32	32	12	12½	Bravo J	L111f	12.30	96-07	BrbrOBrn1112½ *DrxlMonr*1167½ Smkmfygtm115hd	4 wide move,drew clear	11
16Aug03-7Mth	fst	1		:241	:481	1:131	1:401	3↑ⒻAlw 39000n2x	**76**	2	1hd	1½	11½	12	15	Bravo J	L118f	*1.50	76-21	*BarbrOBrien*1185 YoullBeHppy118½ PisleyPrk108no	Vied inside,drew clear	7
24Jly03-8Mth	fst	5f	⊗	:212	:443		:571	3↑ⒻAlw 39000n2x	**84**	1	5	52¾	34	23½	2½	Bravo J	L118f	*1.00	95-13	DesirblMomnt118½ *BrbrOBrin*1186¼ SflyAtHom1151¼	Steadied 3/8,best late	7
18Jly03-5Mth	fst	6f		:214	:45	:571	1:094	3↑ⒻAlw 39000n2x	**–0**	1	6	627	629	640	686	Bravo J	L118f	*1.10	04-17	FitPrformr1188¼ ElctrickCity1143¼ ClvrBlond1182½	Stumbled badly start	6
25May03-8Mth	gd	5f	⊗	:214	:451		:582	3↑ⒻTJMalley50k	**71**	5	5	54	54	32	2no	Bravo J	L113f	2.90	90-16	PlPrncss115no BrbrOBrn1132¼ Bondnddtrmnd1161¾	Out 1/8,bid,just missd	5
27Apr03-10Crc	fst	6f		:22	:453	:58	1:104	3↑ⒻGoldarama42k	**84**	1	8	53	32½	23	24	Castanon J L	L115f	1.90	86-12	TchulaMiss1154 BarbarOBrien1153½ NotinOrder1151¼	Off slowly, 2nd best	8

Bare Necessities

Own: Iron County Farms Inc

Gr/ro. m. 5 (Mar)
Sire: Silver Deputy (Deputy Minister) $40,000
Dam: Shrewd Vixen (Spectacular Bid)
Br: Iron County Farms Inc. (Ky)
Tr: Dollase Wallace A(0 0 0 0 .00) 2003:(95 24 .25)

Life	17	7	1	4	$733,281	106		D.Fst	14	6	1	4	$548,441	106
2003	8	4	0	3	$431,175	106		Wet(351)	1	1	0	0	$183,840	94
2002	8	3	1	1	$299,706	100		Turf(280)	2	0	0	0	$1,000	77
	0	0	0	0	$0	–		Dst(0)	0	0	0	0	$0	–

7Dec03-8Hol	fst	1 1/16	:23	:46	1:094	1:41	3↑ⒻBayakoaH-G2	**93**	6	54	53¼	53	33½	37¼	Douglas R R	LB119	*.90	92-08	StarParade1123¼ Adoration1214 BareNecessities1193	4wd,3wd,bested rest	6
9Aug03-10ElP	fst	1⅛	:462	1:113	1:372	1:50	3↑ⒻGrdeniaH-G3	**106**	9	68	63¾	62¼	11½	15¼	Douglas R R	L119	*.40	98-08	BreNecessities1195¼ DesrtGold1142¾ SoMuchMor115hd	Split 4w 1/4p,drvg	9
21Jun03-8Hol	fst	1⅛	:471	1:103	1:351	1:482	3↑ⒻVanityH-G1	**105**	5	42½	31	32	33	32½	Solis A	LB118	2.70e	89-14	*Azeri*1272 SisterGirlBlues111½ *BreNecessities*1184½	Stalked 3wd,missed 2nd	7
26Apr03-8Haw	fst	1⅛	:49	1:14	1:393	1:524	3↑ⒻSixtySIH-G3	**102**	2	31½	43	31	1½	12½	Douglas R R	L118	*.60	92-31	BareNecessities1182½ JarmrRin114nk Lkenheth1144¾	Split horses, driving	9
30Mar03-8SA	fst	1 1/16	:222	:454	1:101	1:422	4↑Ⓕ[R]SntaLuciaH82k	**101**	9	43½	52¾	3½	1½	11½	Almeida G F	LB120	2.60	92-16	*Bare Necessities*1201½ Alexine1191¼ Printemps1201½	4wd into lane,led,held	9
9Mar03-4GG	fst	1	:23	:463	1:11	1:354	3↑ⒻSacramntoH64k	**94**	2	55	54¼	41½	12	15	Alvarado F T	LB121	*.40	91-16	*Bare Necessities*1215 Castling1181¼ Lost At Sea1191½	Much the best	7
8Feb03-6SA	fst	1⅛	:463	1:104	1:353	1:482	ⒻLaCanada-G2	**97**	3	32	41¾	41½	42½	45¼	Valdivia J Jr	LB118	15.30	87-11	Got Koko121¾ Sightseek1181½ Bella Bellucci1183	Stalked btwn,weakened	5
19Jan03-7SA	fst	1 1/16	:23	:462	1:102	1:421	ⒻElEncino-G2	**99**	6	44	41½	2½	2½	34½	Valdivia J Jr	LB119	4.10	88-17	*GotKoko*1191½ BellBellucci1173 BreNecessitis119no	4wd bid,btwn,held 3rd	8

Bauhauser (Arg)
Own: Heiligbrodt Racing Stable and Jones J

Gr/ro. m. 6 (Oct)
Sire: Numerous (Mr. Prospector)
Dam: Barbaloot (Relaunch)
Br: Los Cerros de Loma Verde (Arg)
Tr: Asmussen Steven M(0 0 0 0 .00) 2003:(1949 452 .23)

Life	16	9	3	1	$137,535	97	D.Fst	11	7	3	0	$128,906 97
2003	4	2	1	0	$113,750	97	Wet(370)	1	1	0	0	$1,491 –
2002	11	6	2	1	$17,479	–	Turf(296)	4	1	0	1	$7,138 –
	0	0	0	0	$0	–	Dst(0)	0	0	0	0	$0 –

12Oct03–8Kee fst 6f :21² :44² :56³ 1:09³ 3↑ⒻTCA-G3 **89** 1 2 1hd 1hd 2hd 4½ Lanerie C J L124 *1.60 91–08 *SmmrMs*122hd DontContssOt122no BorntoDnc122nk Grudgingly weakened 10
13Sep03–6Bel fst 6f :22 :45 :57¹ 1:10⁴ 3↑ⒻFlrlPrkH-G3 **94** 6 6 3nk 1½ 12½ 1¾ Migliore R L115 5.60 85–18 Bauhauser115¾ ShineAgain120²¼ LiteraryLight113¹¼ 3 wide move, held on 6
7Aug03–8Sar fst 7f :22¹ :45 1:09¹ 1:22¹ 4↑ⒻAlw 56000c **97** 2 4 22½ 2½ 12½ 1¾ Migliore R L118 3.25 96–07 *Buhuser*118¾ SlewsFinlAnswer123²¼ Alchmill123¹½ Dug in gamely, held on 5
2Jly03–8CD fst 6f :22¹ :45⁴ :57³ 1:09³ 3↑ⒻOClm 62500N **92** 2 5 11½ 1½ 1hd 22 Meche L J L118 3.90 88–14 MeteorMircle118² *Buhuser*118½ JnnysProspctor112⁴½ Gamely held second 6

Be Gentle
Own: Van Meter T F II

Dk. b or b. f. 3 (May)
Sire: Tale of the Cat (Storm Cat) $16,139
Dam: Gentlelilstar (Risen Star)
Br: Mrs. Nellie M. Cox & Rose Retreat Farm (Va)
Tr: Lukas D. W(0 0 0 0 .00) 2003:(663 71 .11)

Life	7	4	1	0	$523,078	91	D.Fst	6	4	1	0	$518,578 91
2003	7	4	1	0	$523,078	91	Wet(338)	1	0	0	0	$4,500 52
2002	0	M	0	0	$0	–	Turf(298)	0	0	0	0	$0 –
	0	0	0	0	$0	–	Dst(0)	0	0	0	0	$0 –

29Nov03–10CD fst 1 1/16 :24 :48⁴ 1:13² 1:45⁴ ⒻGoldnRod-G2 **91** 9 11½ 11 1½ 1½ 11 McKee J L122 *2.00 79–24 Be Gentle122¹ Lotta Kim116hd Dynaville116⁵ Rail, driving 11
25Oct03–3SA fst 1 1/16 :22⁴ :46⁴ 1:10⁴ 1:42³ ⒻBCJuvFil-G1 **60** 13 12⁷ 95¾ 117¼ 111⁴ 1122 Velasquez C LB119 37.30 69–07 Halfbridled119²½ *Ashado*119nk *Victory U. S. A.*119⁹¼ Bump start, wide 14
3Oct03–9Kee fst 1 1/16 :23 :47² 1:12¹ 1:45² ⒻAlcibiad-G2 **81** 2 11 1½ 11 13 15½ Velasquez C L118 *1.50 80–23 Be Gentle118⁵½ *GallopingGal*118³½ Deb'sCharm118¹ Control pace,hand urg 7
29Aug03–8Sar fst 7f :22² :45² 1:10³ 1:24 ⒻSpinaway-G1 **81** 3 4 3½ 3½ 2½ 21¼ Velasquez C L121 10.50 86–10 Ashado121¹¼ *Be Gentle*121⁸¼ Daydreaming121¹¾ Vied 3 wide, gamely 6
23Jly03–9Sar sly 6f :22 :45² :58² 1:12 ⒻSchylrvl-G2 **52** 1 7 61¼ 55½ 59 511¾ Velasquez C L122 5.10 70–17 *Ashado*118³ MapleSyrple122²½ HermionesMgic118¹ Steadied backstretch 7
4Jly03–10CD fst 5½f :22 :45¹ :57² 1:03⁴ ⒻDebutant-G3 **83** 4 1 1hd 1½ 11½ 11¼ Velasquez C 117 1.80 93–10 Be Gentle117¹¼ Renaissance Lady117⁴½ *SweetJoJo*117²½ 3w,dueled,driving 8
11May03–3CD fst 5f :22 :45³ :58¹ ⒻMd Sp Wt 34k **79** 7 3 21 2hd 12½ 18½ Velasquez C 118 6.60 94–12 *Be Gentle*118⁸½ Good as Silver118¹ In Rome118⁴¼ Hand urging,going away 10

Beau's Town
Own: Coast To Coast Racing Fund LLC and Hu

Ch. g. 6 (Mar)
Sire: Beau Genius (Bold Ruckus) $7,500
Dam: Frio Town (Kerosene)
Br: Bryant H. Prentice III (Ark)
Tr: Norman Cole(0 0 0 0 .00) 2003:(1086 290 .27)

Life	15	10	3	0	$499,400	116	D.Fst	15	10	3	0	$499,400 116
2003	6	4	1	0	$351,800	116	Wet(320)	0	0	0	0	$0 –
2002	6	4	1	0	$117,600	111	Turf(237)	0	0	0	0	$0 –
	0	0	0	0	$0	–	Dst(0)	0	0	0	0	$0 –

3Oct03–7Kee fst 6f :21⁴ :44³ :56 1:08¹ 3↑PhoenxBC-G3 **78** 4 4 4¾ 53¾ 86¼ 812½ Valenzuela P A L124 f *1.10 85–13 Najran122¹½ EthanMan118² TakeAchnceOnMe118²¾ Stumble,drft in start 8
26Jly03–6Dmr fst 6f :21⁴ :44 :55³ 1:07⁴ 3↑BCrsbBCH-G2 **116** 9 2 2½ 1hd 11½ 11½ Valenzuela P A LB119 5.10 102–07 BeusTown119¹½ CptinSquir117nk Blusthstndrd117² Dueled,led,held game 9
21Jun03–9CD fst 6½f :22⁴ :45⁴ 1:09³ 1:16 3↑AristdsH-G3 **102** 3 2 2hd 2hd 1½ 2hd Theriot H J II L123 *1.60 91–15 Mountain General116hd *Beau's Town*123nk Pass Rush118¾ Dueled,gamely 7
10Apr03–10OP fst 6f :22¹ :45¹ :57 1:09 4↑CtFltSpH-G3 **106** 2 2 22 1hd 11 1½ Theriot H J II L122 *.40 95–14 Beau's Town122½ Honor Me116⁴ Sand Ridge114½ Stalked,fully extended 6
16Mar03–9FG fst 6f :22 :44² :56² 1:08⁴ 3↑PeletriBCH144k **112** 3 4 21 1½ 11½ 12¾ Theriot H J II L118 *1.00 96–13 *BeusTown*118²¾ MountinGenrl121¹¾ Bonpw122¹¾ Luggd out, dropped whp 5
1Feb03–9OP fst 6f :21⁴ :45¹ :57 1:09 4↑KingCotton50k **107** 1 2 11 1hd 11½ 14¼ Lovato A J L116 1.50 95–12 *Beau's Town*116⁴¼ Honor Me118²¼ Padlock114¹ Returned ready 6

Belle of Perintown
Own: Mahler Kenneth and Schloss, Jamie
B. f. 4 (Jan) KEESEP01 $50,000
Sire: Dehere (Deputy Minister) $37,200
Dam: Hot Match (Mr. Prospector)
Br: Bradley Wayne Hughes (Ky)
Tr: Kenneally Eddie(0 0 0 0 .00) 2003:(100 20 .20)

Life 12 3 2 4 $265,465 99 | D.Fst 12 3 2 4 $265,465 99
2003 5 1 0 3 $141,390 99 | Wet(428) 0 0 0 0 $0 -
2002 7 2 2 1 $124,075 92 | Turf(330) 0 0 0 0 $0 -
0 0 0 0 $0 - | Dst(0) 0 0 0 0 $0 -

22Nov03-4CD fst 7f :23 :452 1:0941:223 3↑ⒻOClm 80000N 81 6 1 43 32 21 34½ Deegan J C L116 4.40 84-10 DoblScoop1213¼ ScondrySchool1171¼ BllfPrntwn1162¼ 5w bid,flatten out 6
4Jly03-4CD fst 7f :223 :45 1:0921:221 ⒻAlw 67980NC 80 4 3 46½ 44 22½ 36½ Borel C H L118 1.40 84-10 Molto Vita1204¾ Souris1181¾ Belle of Perintown1185¼ 4-5w,flattened out 4
8Mar03-9FG fst 1 1/16 :241 :48 1:13 1:441 ⒻFGOaks-G2 85 2 32½ 32½ 43 43½ 35¾ Borel C H L121 2.80 83-16 LdyTk1213½ AtlnticOcen1212¼ BellofPrintown121¾ Veered into foe break 6
15Feb03-9FG fst 1 1/16 :232 :464 1:1221:442 ⒻSlvrbltd-G2 99 5 21½ 2½ 2½ 12½ 18¼ Borel C H L122 10.20 88-12 BllfPrntn1228¼ AftrnnDrms1121½ RbrdldDrms117nk Bumped break, easily 8
26Jan03-8FG fst 1 :24 :473 1:1211:383 ⒻTiffnyLass100k 38 5 74¾ 89¼ 813 818 830¼ Borel C H L122 8.40 61-21 *Lady Tak*1222¾ Allspice122hd *My Trusty Cat*1221½ Fractious gate, dull 8

Belleski
Own: Moss Mr. and Mrs. Jerome S
B. m. 5 (Feb) KEESEP00 $150,000
Sire: Polish Numbers (Danzig) $20,000
Dam: Rangoon Belle (Alysheba)
Br: David Garvin, David Camball Garvin, Gabriel Duignan & (Ky)
Tr: Sadler John W(0 0 0 0 .00) 2003:(375 71 .19)

Life 11 5 2 1 $238,019 99 | D.Fst 3 0 1 0 $12,960 76
2003 7 4 1 1 $195,059 99 | Wet(349) 0 0 0 0 $0 -
2002 2 1 1 0 $39,200 80 | Turf(346) 8 5 1 1 $225,059 99
0 0 0 0 $0 - | Dst(0) 0 0 0 0 $0 -

30Nov03-6Hol fm 1 Ⓣ:232 :464 1:1021:342 3↑ⒻMatriarc-G1 71 14 21 21 31 1410 1414½ Espinoza V LB123 40.60 78-17 Heat Haze123nk Musical Chimes120no Dedication123½ 4wd,3wd,weakened 14
11Oct03-8SA fm *6½f Ⓣ:213 :432 1:0621:121 3↑ⒻSKMaddyH-G3 99 8 1 53¾ 53½ 43½ 12 Espinoza V LB117 *1.90 96-06 Belleski1172 Buffythecntrfold1161 Icntgofortht1151 3wd into lane,rallied 10
13Aug03-7Dmr fm 1 1/16 Ⓣ:24 :471 1:1031:403 3↑ⒻⓇOsunitasH79k 98 2 1½ 1½ 11 11 2½ Espinoza V LB117 3.90 97-07 Arabic Song115½ *Belleski*1171 *Spring Star*118no Inside,worn down 7
5Jly03-7Hol fm 1 Ⓣ:233 :472 1:1041:341 3↑ⒻRlHroine-G3 95 5 42 41¼ 62¼ 51¾ 32 Espinoza V LB115 2.30e 91-11 MagicMission115hd LittleTresure1212 Belleski1151½ Waited bit,outkicked 9
29May03-7Hol fm 5½f Ⓣ:214 :44 :56 1:021 4↑ⒻOClm 100000N 94 5 3 46½ 45 32½ 12 Espinoza V LB116 *1.30 93-07 Belleski1162 *Knoll Lake*1181 Icantgoforthat1221½ 3w bid,lugged in,clear 7
23Feb03-3SA fm *6½f Ⓣ:223 :451 1:08 1:134 4↑ⒻOClm 80000N 90 5 2 21 2hd 11 11½ Espinoza V LB120 *.80 88-11 *Belleski*1201½ Nanogram1191 Ile de France118½ Bid,cleared,held 8
19Jan03-2SA fm *6½f Ⓣ:213 :434 1:0621:121 4↑ⒻAlw 52936N1x 93 8 3 32 41¼ 1½ 14 Espinoza V LB120 14.20 96-04 *Belleski*1204 Snowfire1201 Janeian123nk Stalked,bid,clear 11

Belong to Sea
Own: Amling Jeffery, Duncker, C. Steven, Q
B. f. 4 (Apr) OBSFEB02 $115,000
Sire: Belong to Me (Danzig) $22,008
Dam: Windansea (Conquistador Cielo)
Br: Domino Stud of Lexington, LLC (Ky)
Tr: Lewis Lisa L(0 0 0 0 .00) 2003:(99 17 .17)

Life 6 3 0 0 $113,460 88 | D.Fst 2 1 0 0 $60,000 88
2003 6 3 0 0 $113,460 88 | Wet(358) 3 2 0 0 $53,460 85
2002 0 M 0 0 $0 - | Turf(286) 1 0 0 0 $0 -
0 0 0 0 $0 - | Dst(0) 0 0 0 0 $0 -

24Sep03-8Bel yl 1 Ⓣ:231 :464 1:1121:351 ⒻⓇStarine65k - 7 32 42½ 815 - - Migliore R L119 f 13.30 - 16 *BettysWish*1222¼ WhereWeLeftOff115nk *ChngingWorld*1158 Eased stretch 8
1Sep03-5Sar gd 7f :223 :454 1:1111:25 3↑ⒻAlw 51000N3x 73 6 6 12½ 11 3nk 47½ Bridgmohan S X L116 f 2.60 74-21 *Fast Cookie*116hd Actcellent1114¾ Drawing a Blank1192¾ Stutter step start 6
4Jly03-9Bel fst 6f :214 :443 :5641:092 ⒻPrioress-G1 74 8 2 31 2hd 41 69½ Castellano J J L119 f 13.90 82-15 House Party1213¼ Chimichurri119½ Princess V.115½ Chased 3 wide, tired 8
15May03-8Pim fst 6f :23 :454 :58 1:11 ⒻMsPreakn-G3 88 5 2 22½ 2½ 12 1hd Castellano J J L117 f 4.70 90-16 BelongtoS117hd Chimichurri122¾ ForvrPrtnrs1192¼ 3wd bid,dug in,driving 5
30Mar03-3Aqu gd 7f :231 :471 1:1231:253 ⒻAlw 41710N1x 85 4 1 13 12½ 110 115 Castellano J J L122 f *.60 75-27 *Belong to Sea*12215 Blazing Tune1176 Meama1175¼ Drew off, ridden out 4
5Mar03-6Aqu sly 6f ⊡:222 :454 :5831:114 ⒻMd Sp Wt 41k 70 2 7 31 31 1hd 13¼ Castellano J J L120 f 2.20 85-13 *Belong to Sea*1203¼ Pretty Imposing1202 Pattiano1201 Came wide, driving 7

Best of the Rest
Own: Oxenberg Beatrice

Gr/ro. h. 9 (Jun)
Sire: Skip Trial (Bailjumper) $5,000
Dam: Obstinacy (Valid Appeal)
Br: Bea Oxenberg (Fla)
Tr: Plesa E Jr(0 0 0 0 .00) 2003:(437 76 .17)

Life	32	16	8	2	$1,407,796	113		
2003	6	3	2	0	$753,500	107		
2002	9	4	2	0	$308,253	113		
	0	0	0	0	$0	–		
D.Fst	28	13	8	2	$1,300,882	113		
Wet(372)	3	3	0	0	$106,600	107		
Turf(249)	1	0	0	0	$314	53		
Dst(0)	0	0	0	0	$0	–		

27Dec03–12Crc fst 1⅛ :49¹ 1:14⁴ 1:39⁴ 1:52² 3↑FHooperH-G3 **95** 9 74½ 54 53 33 24¼ Coa E M L122 2.70 86– 22 PredwnRid1124¼ BestoftheRst122² DlitfulGuy1122¼ Outside bid,even 2nd 9
15Nov03–12Crc fst 1⅛ :49 1:13¹ 1:39² 1:53¹ 3↑[S]CGRoseClsH200k **98** 1 21½ 2hd 2½ 1hd 11¼ Coa E M L121 *.90 86– 18 BestofthRst1211¼ TourofthCt1171½ ThJudgSzWho115nk All out, prevailed 5
11Oct03–8Crc fst 1¹⁄₁₆ :25 :49⁴ 1:14¹ 1:46¹ 3↑SpdABckH-G3 **97** 6 21½ 21 21 21½ 21 Bailey J D L122 *.80 80– 22 TouroftheCt1161 *BestoftheRest*1221 DncingGuy116³ Stalked, no late gain 8
20Apr03–9GP fst 1¹⁄₁₆ :23³ :46⁴ 1:10⁴ 1:42³ 3↑SkipAwyH-G3 **105** 4 23½ 33 32½ 22 1½ Coa E M L121 *1.50 96– 15 Best of the Rest121½ *Consistency*114½ Roger E1149¾ 3 wide, up late 5
2Mar03–9FG fst 1⅛ :47⁴ 1:12¹ 1:36² 1:48⁴ 4↑NwOrlnsH-G2 **97** 1 32½ 44½ 64¾ 68 611¼ Coa E M L118 5.10 89– 17 *Mineshaft*1153½ Olmodavor1172½ Strive1141½ Between foes, faded 11
25Jan03–7GP fst 1⅛ :45⁴ 1:10² 1:36¹ 1:49² 4↑[R]OclBrdSlCl1000k **107** 7 65 44½ 32 21 1½ Coa E M L122 *3.50 95– 10 Best of the Rest122½ Booklet120hd Grey Memo1221¾ 3 wide, up late 12

Better Talk Now
Own: Bushwood Stables

B. g. 5 (Feb)
Sire: Talkin Man (With Approval) $3,500
Dam: Bendita (Baldski)
Br: Wimborne Farm, Inc. (Ky)
Tr: Motion H. G(0 0 0 0 .00) 2003:(318 55 .17)

Life	17	6	3	2	$337,437	101
2003	7	3	1	2	$240,152	101
2002	9	3	2	0	$97,285	97
	0	0	0	0	$0	–
D.Fst	4	0	2	0	$16,360	90
Wet(314)	0	0	0	0	$0	–
Turf(383)	13	6	1	2	$321,077	101
Dst(0)	0	0	0	0	$0	–

1Nov03–8Aqu gd 1⅛ Ⓣ:50 1:14 1:38¹ 1:50² 3↑KnkrbkrH-G2 **101** 1 6² 55½ 54½ 31½ 1½ Prado E S L116 fb 6.80 88– 12 BttrTlkNow116½ DlMrShw116nk MllnnmDrgn1152¾ Altered course stretch 12
4Oct03–7Kee fm 1½ Ⓣ:50² 1:15⁴ 2:04⁴ 2:29² 3↑SycamrBC-G3 **77** 10 87¼ 11 2½ 74¼ 915 Douglas R R L120 b 9.50 78– 14 Sharbayan1201¾ Cetewayo122½ Deputy Strike1201¼ 5w bid,tired in lane 10
30Aug03–8WO fm 1½ Ⓣ:49² 1:13³ 2:02³ 2:27 3↑NiagrBCH-G2 **99** 7 68½ 52¼ 42½ 31 32¾ Douglas R R L115 b 5.95 92– 12 StruttheStage1231¼ RevvedUp1181½ BetterTlkNow115¾ In tight steadied 10
26Jly03–9AP fm 1¼ Ⓣ:49¹ 1:14 1:38³ 2:02³ 3↑ArlgtnH-G3 **100** 1 99¼ 87¼ 83½ 32½ 2nk Douglas R R L115 9.90 93– 05 HonorinWr120nk BetterTlkNow115¾ MysteryGivr118nk 4 wide 1/4, missed 10
29Jun03–7Del fm 1⅛ Ⓣ:51³ 1:15⁴ 1:39¹ 1:50³ 3↑Eighthrty58k **99** 5 2³ 1hd 1½ 1hd 1nk Dominguez R A L116 2.40 89– 11 BetterTlkNow116nk Pickupspeed1232½ Rochestr116⁶ Bid, pace, prevailed 5
13Feb03–9GP fm *1⅛ Ⓣ:49² 1:13⁴ 1:39⁴ 1:51³ 4↑OClm 100000N **94** 2 4⁸ 4⁹ 3⁴ 21½ 31 Prado E S L122 3.70 82– 23 Mr. Pleasentfar118nk Wertz118¾ *Better Talk Now*122½ Not enough late 9
18Jan03–9GP fm 1 Ⓣ:24¹ :48⁴ 1:13² 1:36² 4↑Alw 38000N3x **94** 5 4³ 42 31½ 41¼ 1nk Prado E S L120 2.50 84– 12 BetterTlkNow120nk GoodBoySm118hd HndsomGorg118½ Up final strides 10

Betty's Wish
Own: Gann Edmund A

Ch. f. 4 (Apr) KEESEP01 $6,000
Sire: Gold Case (Forty Niner) $3,500
Dam: Holy Land Band (Dixieland Band)
Br: Dr. Donald S. Dreyfuss (Fla)
Tr: Frankel Robert J(0 0 0 0 .00) 2003:(411 114 .28)

Life	9	5	2	1	$209,440	97	D.Fst	3	1	1	0	$39,200 94
2003	9	5	2	1	$209,440	97	Wet(395)	3	2	1	0	$46,520 92
2002	0	M	0	0	$0	-	Turf(309)	3	2	0	1	$123,720 97
	0	0	0	0	$0	-	Dst(0)	0	0	0	0	$0 -

20Dec03-9Hol fm 1 1/16 Ⓣ :234 :472 1:11 1:412 3↑Ⓕ DahliaH-G2 94 3 41¾ 42½ 53 52¾ 31½ Nakatani C S LB117 *.90e 87-15 Ktdogwn116no PersonlLegend1151½ BettysWish117½ Waited 1/4,split foes 10
13Oct03-9Bel gd 1⅛ [T] :491 1:144 1:391 1:51 Ⓕ PebblesH-G3 97 7 31½ 31½ 3½ 13½ 13¾ Velazquez J R L116 *.80 75-27 Betty's Wish1163¾ Mystery Itself1121 AndoverLady114½ 3 wide both turns 7
24Sep03-8Bel yl 1 Ⓣ :231 :464 1:112 1:351 Ⓕ[R] Starine65k 95 4 21½ 21 11 11½ 12¼ Velazquez J R L122 2.95 84-16 *BttsWsh*1222¼ WhrWLftOff115nk *ChngngWrld*1158 Drew clear when roused 8
5Sep03-5Bel fst 1 1/16 :224 :462 1:111 1:432 3↑Ⓕ Alw 50000N2X 94 1 3½ 1hd 1½ 14 16 Velazquez J R L120 *.85 83-22 *BettysWish*1206 BuyOutTime1162 SuveQueen1191¼ Vied inside, drew away 6
2Aug03-3Sar my 1⅛ ⊗ :47 1:121 1:38 1:511 3↑Ⓕ Alw 48000N1X 92 4 11 11½ 14½ 112 110½ Bailey J D L115 *1.40 79-21 *BettysWish*115101/2 Alluring11913½ SwtScrmr1151¼ Drew away when roused 7
29Jun03-3Bel fst 1 :223 :454 1:113 1:372 3↑Ⓕ Alw 46000N1X 81 5 41 3½ 2hd 21½ 28 Bailey J D L114 1.25 71-21 *Alchemist*1148 *BettysWish*1143 MoonletMinister12011½ 3 wide, second best 5
4Jun03-8Bel my 1 ⊗ :231 :463 1:111 1:37 3↑Ⓕ Alw 46000N1X 90 1 1½ 1½ 1½ 1½ 2½ Bailey J D L115 *1.60 80-24 Mt. Kobla117½ Betty's Wish1156¾ Moonlet Minister1213 Set pace, gamely 8
10May03-5Bel fst 6f :221 :452 :572 1:102 3↑Ⓕ Alw 45000N2L 68 5 8 61¼ 71¾ 86½ 66¼ Migliore R 117 2.15 81-12 HastLVist114¾ HopeforLove1151¼ ElectrickCity115½ Between rivals, tired 8
Previously trained by Foley Gregory D
22Mar03-2TP gd 6f :224 :463 :59 1:113 Ⓕ Md Sp Wt 18k 81 8 5 1hd 2hd 11 15¾ Lumpkins J L122 *.40 84-17 Betty's Wish1225¾ Ladies Precept1226½ *Our Intention*1229¼ 2 path, driving 9

Bien Nicole
Own: Richter Kristine and John

Ch. m. 6 (Apr)
Sire: Bien Bien (Manila) $4,479
Dam: Dana Nicole (Flying Paster)
Br: The Richter Family Trust (Ky)
Tr: Von Hemel Donnie K(0 0 0 0 .00) 2003:(416 94 .23)

Life	26	12	8	2	$1,074,620	101	D.Fst	4	2	0	0	$147,300 94
2003	10	4	3	0	$690,540	101	Wet(284)	2	1	1	0	$9,750 69
2002	10	6	2	2	$340,610	98	Turf(266)	20	9	7	2	$917,570 101
	0	0	0	0	$0	-	Dst(0)	0	0	0	0	$0 -

22Nov03-9CD fm 1⅛ Ⓣ :491 1:134 1:381 1:502 3↑Ⓕ CardinlH-G3 100 11 1hd 12 11½ 11 2¾ Pettinger D R L120 *2.00 81-24 Riskaverse118¾ Bien Nicole1204 Firth of Lorne1161 Duel early,2ndbest 12
25Oct03-6SA fm 1¼ Ⓣ :463 1:102 1:351 1:59 3↑Ⓕ BCF&MTrf-G1 97 12 15 18 11 52¼ 96¾ Pettinger D R LB123 16.20 91-04 Islington123nk L'Ancresse1182½ Yesterday118no Speed,inside,wkened 12
5Oct03-6Kee fm 1 3/16 Ⓣ :484 1:124 1:38 1:554 3↑Ⓕ WnStGlxy-G2 100 1 16 111 111 16 17¼ Pettinger D R L121 *1.50 92-10 Bien Nicole1217¼ Approach1161¼ New Economy1211¼ Light hand urging 6
16Aug03-8AP gd 1 3/16 Ⓣ :493 1:133 1:38 1:554 3↑Ⓕ BeverlyD-G1 101 3 11½ 12½ 1½ 11½ 21¼ Pettinger D R L123 20.90 94-08 Heat Haze1231¼ *Bien Nicole*123½ Riskaverse1231½ Resisted gamely 7
26Jly03-7AP fm 1 3/16 Ⓣ :473 1:113 1:363 1:55 3↑Ⓕ ModestyH-G3 98 4 1½ 1hd 11 2hd 21 Pettinger D R L119 1.60 98-05 Owsley1201 Bien Nicole1194 Beret1153 Held on gamely 7
28Jun03-10LaD fm *1 Ⓣ :223 :47 1:111 1:342 3↑Ⓕ Honeymoon50k 98 10 21½ 11½ 2hd 12½ 13¼ Doocy T T L120 *.90 102-04 BienNicole1203¼ NaturllyWild1201¼ DuetoWinAgin114no Drove well clear 10
26May03-10LS sf 1 Ⓣ :24 :492 1:154 1:43 3↑Ⓕ WnStDstH-G3 79 9 64¾ 65½ 64½ 78 67¼ Pettinger D R L118 *2.30 50-48 *EagleLake*1162¼ LittleTreasure117¾ *MgicMission*1161½ 4w 1st turn,dull effrt 9
2May03-7LS fst 1 ⊗ :233 :471 1:121 1:382 4↑Ⓕ Alw 42500NC 83 2 45 43½ 32½ 31½ 1½ Pettinger D R L122 *.50 80-23 Bien Nicole122½ *Eagle Lake*119nk Cherylville Slew1225¾ Closed gradually 5
5Apr03-8OP fst 1 1/16 :241 :483 1:121 1:43 4↑Ⓕ AplBlsmH-G1 89 4 43½ 21 43½ 69½ 69¼ Pettinger D R L115 17.30 86-11 *Azeri*123hd TakeChargeLady1183¼ *MndysGold*1162 Mid move 3-w,gave way 7
15Mar03-10OP fst 1 1/16 :241 :482 1:13 1:44 3↑Ⓕ OaklwnBC-G3 94 8 52½ 3½ 2hd 2hd 11¼ Pettinger D R L122 8.00 90-14 Bien Nicole1221¼ Red n'Gold117¾ Mandy's Gold1171 Outside, edged clear 9

Bird Town

Own: Marylou Whitney Stables

B. f. 4 (Apr)
Sire: Cape Town (Seeking the Gold) $7,500
Dam: Dear Birdie (Storm Bird)
Br: Marylou Whitney Stables (Ky)
Tr: Zito Nicholas P(0 0 0 0 .00) 2003:(507 77 .15)

Life	12	4	6	1	$871,251	101	D.Fst	10	3	5	1	$795,656	101
2003	8	3	4	0	$815,976	101	Wet(372)	2	1	1	0	$75,595	98
2002	4	1	2	1	$55,275	80	Turf(302)	0	0	0	0	$0	–
	0	0	0	0	$0	–	Dst(0)	0	0	0	0	$0	–

4Oct03-9Bel	fst	1⅛	:474 1:122 1:363 1:491	3↑ⒻBeldame-G1	100	5	1½	1½	1hd	22½	24½	Gryder A T	L120	11.20	79-26	Sightseek1234½ Bird Town1204¾ Buy the Sport120¾	Pace, second best	7
16Aug03-9Sar	fst	1¼	:482 1:124 1:374 2:05	ⒻAlabama-G1	85	5	33	32	22	57¾	511	Prado E S	L121	1.60	71-14	IslndFshion1216 AwesomeHumor1211 SpoknFur1211¼	Bumped after start	6
26Jly03-9Sar	fst	7f	:223 :451 1:081 1:204	ⒻTest-G1	100	7	1	31	3½	25½	24½	Prado E S	L122	*1.75	98-08	Lady Tak1224½ Bird Town1221½ *House Party*1221¾	3 wide, game finish	7
6Jun03-10Bel	fst	1	:232 :461 1:102 1:351	ⒻAcorn-G1	96	7	2hd	1hd	1½	11	1hd	Prado E S	L121	2.65	90-16	Bird Town121hd *Lady Tak*1211 Final Round1213¼	Game while drifting	7
2May03-10CD	fst	1⅛	:46 1:10 1:353 1:483	ⒻKyOaks-G1	101	5	87	86	74	4nk	13¼	Prado E S	L121	18.20	95-07	*Bird Town*1213¼ Santa Catarina121hd Yell121¾	Stumble start,6w,drv	12
10Apr03-8Kee	my	*7f	:214 :442 1:094 1:264	ⒻBeaumont-G2	98	7	1	2hd	11½	2hd	21¼	Coa E M	L118	3.30	91-15	My Boston Gal1201¼ *Bird Town*1184¾ Midnight Cry1184	Dueled, good try	9
23Feb03-5GP	fst	7f	:214 :444 1:101 1:224	ⒻCharon52k	100	5	3	25	22	17	112½	Coa E M	L120	3.40	94-13	Bird Town12012½ Crafty Brat1181¼ WesterlyBreeze1223¾	Kept to pressure	6
16Jan03-9GP	fst	170	:233 :482 1:132 1:421	ⒻAlw 34000N1x	84	6	11	11	1½	2hd	2nk	Day P	L119	2.80	90-18	*Yell*121nk *Bird Town*1195½ Marnesia Light1172¼	Inside, gamely	7

Birdstone

Own: Marylou Whitney Stables

B. c. 3 (May)
Sire: Grindstone (Unbridled) $5,000
Dam: Dear Birdie (Storm Bird)
Br: Marylou Whitney Stables (Ky)
Tr: Zito Nicholas P(0 0 0 0 .00) 2003:(507 77 .15)

Life	3	2	0	0	$339,000	99	D.Fst	2	1	0	0	$312,000	94
2003	3	2	0	0	$339,000	99	Wet(335)	1	1	0	0	$27,000	99
2002	0	M	0	0	$0	–	Turf(198)	0	0	0	0	$0	–
	0	0	0	0	$0	–	Dst(0)	0	0	0	0	$0	–

4Oct03-7Bel	fst	1 1/16	:234 :481 1:133 1:44	Champagn-G1	94	3	43	31	2½	1hd	12½	Bailey J D	L122	2.25	80-26	Birdstone1222½ ChpelRoyl1226¾ DshbordDrummr1222	3 wide, going away	7
30Aug03-8Sar	fst	7f	:222 :452 1:102 1:232	Hopeful-G1	78	6	1	61¾	51¼	31	46½	Prado E S	L122	2.30	83-11	SilverWgon1224 ChplRoyl1221½ NotoriousRogu1221	Hit gate start, 5 wide	7
2Aug03-4Sar	my	6f	:214 :454 :58 1:101	Md Sp Wt 45k	99	4	5	32½	13	18	112½	Prado E S	L119	3.85	91-12	Birdstone11912½ Bold Love1192½ Hornshope1197¼	When ready, drew off	9

Blazonry

Own: Robertson Sanford R

B. c. 4 (Feb) KEESEP01 $100,000
Sire: Hennessy (Storm Cat) $35,000
Dam: Altair (Alydar)
Br: Sanford R. Robertson (Ky)
Tr: Walsh Kathy(0 0 0 0 .00) 2003:(68 11 .16)

Life	8	2	1	1	$105,454	100	D.Fst	3	1	0	1	$96,720	100
2003	3	1	0	1	$96,720	100	Wet(352)	0	0	0	0	$0	–
2002	5	1	1	0	$8,734	–	Turf(315)	5	1	1	0	$8,734	–
	0	0	0	0	$0	–	Dst(0)	0	0	0	0	$0	–

26Dec03-8SA	fst	7f	:222 :45 1:091 1:223	Malibu-G1	90	3	12	1211	1212	99	87¼	Smith M E	LB117	10.30	86-12	SouthernImage115hd MrinoMrini1151 MidsEyes1193	3wd into lane,no bid	12
26May03-7Hol	fst	7f	:213 :44 1:09 1:22	LBrreraM-G2	99	2	9	95¾	73¾	2hd	12½	Smith M E	LB115	4.70	92-11	Blazonry1152½ Fly to the Wire116½ Jimmy O1151	Off slow,6wd into lane	9
2Apr03-4SA	fst	1	:23 :462 1:103 1:354	Alw 66080N1x	100	2	54	42½	4¾	3½	3nk	Smith M E	LB118	12.50	92-15	McCnnsMojve118hd Sttlspctculr120hd *Blzonry*1182½	Bid 4wd,5wd,willingly	6

Bluesthestandard
Own: Sengara Jeffrey

B. g. 7 (Apr)
Sire: American Standard (In Reality) $1,500
Dam: Bob's Blue (Bob's Dusty)
Br: Terry Brown (Ga)
Tr: West Ted H(0 0 0 0 .00) 2003:(167 39 .23)

Life	27	14	6	3	$807,185	114	
2003	10	4	2	2	$631,975	114	
2002	14	7	4	1	$148,810	99	
	0	0	0	0	$0	-	
D.Fst	27	14	6	3	$807,185	114	
Wet(312)	0	0	0	0	$0	-	
Turf(226)	0	0	0	0	$0	-	
Dst(0)	0	0	0	0	$0	-	

25Oct03–5SA fst 6f :21 :43¹ :55 1:07⁴ 3↑BCSprint-G1 **114** 8 9 10⁶ 74¾ 3² 22¼ Smith M E LB126 13.70 97–05 CjunBet1232¼ Bluesthestndrd1262 ShkeYouDown126½ Split rivals, rallied 13
5Oct03–7SA fst 6f :21² :43² :55² 1:08 3↑AnTtlBCH-G1 **103** 5 3 32½ 4² 3² 31½ Smith M E LB115 7.00 96–06 Avnzdo1161½ CptinSquire117hd Blusthstndrd1151½ 3wd into lane,missd 2d 6
17Aug03–8Dmr fst 7f :22¹ :44 1:08¹ 1:21² 3↑POBrienH-G2 **87** 7 4 1½ 2hd 33½ 78¾ Solis A LB117 *1.50 86–09 Dstrbnthpc1162 RshntAltr1174½ FllMnMdnss119½ Dueled btwn,weakened 10
26Jly03–6Dmr fst 6f :21⁴ :44 :55³ 1:07⁴ 3↑BCrsbBCH-G2 **111** 3 4 52½ 52½ 3³ 31¾ Pedroza M A LB117 9.90 100–07 BeusTown1191½ CptinSquir117nk Blusthstndrd1172 3wd into str,missed 2d 9
5Jly03–8Hol fst 7f :21⁴ :44² 1:08² 1:21² 3↑TrBndBCH-G1 **101** 8 1 41¼ 41½ 2¹ 31½ Pedroza M A LB117 3.90 93–11 JoeyFranco118hd Publiction1161½ [D]Bluesthestndrd1173½ Bid,driftd in 1/8 9
Disqualified and placed 6th
26May03–8LS fst 1 1/16 :22⁴ :46 1:10¹ 1:42 3↑LSParkH-G3 **102** 8 41½ 4³ 2¹ 2² 22¾ •Pedroza M A L120 *1.50 89–08 *PNBrgr*1172¾ [DH]MysvllSlw114 [DH]Blsthstndrd1201½ Pulled early,no match 8
26Apr03–9LS fst 1 :23⁴ :47 1:10⁴ 1:35³ 3↑TexsMile-G3 **108** 9 21½ 22½ 2½ 1² 1⁴ Pedroza M A L120 *1.50 95–16 Bluesthestndrd1204 Bonpw116nk Compendium116½ Drew away,ridden out 9
29Mar03–8SA fst 6½f :21² :44 1:08² 1:14⁴ 4↑PtrGrBCH-G2 **105** 7 5 3² 1hd 1hd 1² Smith M E LB115 f 2.20 99–10 *Bluesthestandard*1152 *JoeyFranco*116½ KonaGold1215½ 3wd bid,cleared,held 7
12Mar03–6SA fst 1 1/16 :23 :46¹ 1:10² 1:43 4↑OClm 100000N **99** 6 2½ 1½ 11½ 1² 1no Almeida G F LB118 f 3.60 89–13 *Blsthstndrd*118no BrngHomThgold1181 BnsPyDy1201 3-4 wd, cleared, held 9
17Feb03–9SA fst 6½f :21⁴ :43⁴ 1:09² 1:15² 4↑OClm 62500N **104** 3 7 1hd 1hd 11½ 1⁴ Krone J A LB119 f 4.10 96–13 *Bluesthestandard*1194 SunsetPlce1182½ Denied119½ Inside,steady handling 9

Bossanova
Own: Rodriguez Lorraine and Rod

Dk. b or b. c. 4 (Apr) OBSFEB02 $220,000
Sire: Pine Bluff (Danzig) $10,000
Dam: Street Tappin (Housebuster)
Br: Kent Wiechert & Katy Wiechert (NY)
Tr: Bond H. J(0 0 0 0 .00) 2003:(196 46 .23)

Life	9	4	1	2	$234,426	109	
2003	7	3	1	1	$204,906	109	
2002	2	1	0	1	$29,520	93	
	0	0	0	0	$0	-	
D.Fst	8	4	0	2	$212,146	109	
Wet(368)	1	0	1	0	$22,280	109	
Turf(292)	0	0	0	0	$0	-	
Dst(0)	0	0	0	0	$0	-	

27Nov03–8Aqu fst 6f :22⁴ :45⁴ :57³ 1:10 3↑FallHwtH-G3 **101** 2 3 1¹ 11½ 12½ 1½ Prado E S L128 b *1.70 90–17 Bossanova128½ Papua132¾ Savoy Special127¾ Pace, clear, held on 6
8Nov03–7Aqu fst 6f :23¹ :46² :58¹ 1:10³ 3↑[S]Alw 45000N2x **97** 3 1 12½ 11½ 1⁶ 12¼ Prado E S L118 b *.20 87–19 *Bossanova*1182¼ Connecting1124 Stars Aligned117¾ A handy score 8
18Oct03–8Bel fst 6f :21³ :44⁴ :57¹ 1:10¹ 3↑[S]HudsonH125k **99** 9 2 12½ 1½ 13½ 41¼ Prado E S L118 b *.70 87–21 One N Three115¾ Impeachthepro117nk No Parole117nk Set strong pace 9
28Jun03–8Bel fst 7f :22³ :45² 1:10 1:22⁴ [S]MikeLee117k **109** 3 1 12½ 14½ 1¹² 113¼ Prado E S L114 b *.70 86–15 Bossnov11413¼ AcceptbleVntur1166¼ LimonFort114½ Widened, hand ride 6
Previously trained by Paasch Christopher S
10May03–9CD sly 6f :21 :43⁴ :56¹ 1:09² MattWinn111k **109** 1 8 1½ 1½ 11½ 2½ Velasquez C L114 b 12.20 90–15 *Posse*120½ *Bossanova*1141¼ *Coach Jimi Lee*1205 Pace,outfinished 9
6Apr03–8Kee fst 7f :21³ :44² 1:09⁴ 1:23 Lafayett-G3 **98** 6 1 1¹ 11½ 3nk 34½ Bailey J D L116 b 12.40 84–16 *Posse*1182¼ Roll Hennessy Roll1182¼ Bossanova1162¼ Pace,tired 6
12Jan03–7SA fst 6f :21¹ :44 :56¹ 1:08³ SnMiguel-G3 **51** 3 4 2¹ 4² 55¼ 5²⁰ Solis A LB115 b 3.70 75–12 Omega Code1211 Only the Best1215 Jimmy O1186 Angled in, gave way 5

Bowman Mill
Own: Chandler Dr. John A

Ch. h. 6 (May)
Sire: Kris S. (Roberto) $150,000
Dam: Aletta Maria (Diesis*GB)
Br: Dr. John A. Chandler (Ky)
Tr: Dickinson Michael W(0 0 0 0 .00) 2003:(152 37 .24)

Life	11	4	4	0	$455,042	105	D.Fst	0	0	0	0	$0 –
2003	5	1	2	0	$327,682	105	Wet(347)	0	0	0	0	$0 –
2002	1	1	0	0	$15,960	91	Turf(359)	11	4	4	0	$455,042 105
	0	0	0	0	$0	–	Dst(0)	0	0	0	0	$0 –

22Nov03–8Hol fm 1½ Ⓣ :513 1:164 2:052 2:29 3↑HolTrfCp-G1 **102** 6 12 12 11½ 1hd 3hd Flores D R LB126 *2.00 80–18 ⒹEpicntr126no Continuously126hd BowmnMill126½ Bumped 1/8,game rail 7
Placed second through disqualification
19Oct03–9WO yl 1½ Ⓣ :512 1:163 2:081 2:333 3↑CanIntnl-G1 **105** 10 42½ 21 1½ 2hd 41¾ Blanc B L126 14.45 60–30 Phoenix Reach119¾ Macaw126hd Brian Boru1191 Press 3w,led, gave way 10
28Sep03–8WO sf 1⅜ Ⓣ :50 1:162 1:424 2:23 3↑SkyClscH-G2 **100** 2 33 31 2½ 1½ 1no Blanc B L113 6.90 50–50 Bowman Mill113no LennytheLender1104 *Mobil*115nk Stalk 2-pth,drifted in 6
30Aug03–8WO fm 1½ Ⓣ :492 1:133 2:023 2:27 3↑NiagrBCH-G2 **98** 3 1½ 2hd 32 53½ 43½ McKnight J L112 34.70 91–12 StruttheStge1231¼ RevvdUp1181½ BttrTlkNow115¾ Press outsde,steadied 10
12Aug03–9Pha gd *1⅛ Ⓣ :494 1:151 1:41 1:533 3↑Alw 22000N3x **92** 7 3½ 32½ 21 12½ 21 Molina V H L117 *.60 89–10 Broadway Johnny1191 Bowman Mill1175 Pegylation117¾ Couldn't last 8

Bowman's Band
Own: Schwartz Martin S

Ch. h. 6 (Mar) KEEAPR00 $260,000
Sire: Dixieland Band (Northern Dancer) $60,000
Dam: Hometown Queen (Pleasant Colony)
Br: John W. Rooker (Ky)
Tr: Jerkens H. A(0 0 0 0 .00) 2003:(359 73 .20)

Life	22	7	8	1	$876,440	112	D.Fst	18	6	7	0	$780,160 109
2003	9	2	3	1	$432,240	112	Wet(400)	3	1	1	0	$89,780 112
2002	9	2	5	0	$333,800	108	Turf(316)	1	0	0	1	$6,500 92
	0	0	0	0	$0	–	Dst(0)	0	0	0	0	$0 –

29Nov03–9Aqu fst 1 :224 :442 1:083 1:341 3↑CigarMiH-G1 **102** 7 62 52½ 55 49½ 49¼ Dominguez R A L118 5.10 85–19 Congaree1245¼ Midas Eyes1153 Toccet1151 Bumped after start 7
25Oct03–5Bel fst 7f :223 :452 1:093 1:22 3↑SportPgH-G3 **106** 2 9 61¾ 61¾ 24½ 22½ Dominguez R A L120 *1.35 87–14 Voodoo1142½ BowmnsBnd120½ HghwyProspctr1143¾ Game finish outside 9
3Oct03–8Med fst 1⅛ :464 1:10 1:341 1:464 3↑MedBC-G2 **109** 4 21½ 21 21 11 11¾ Dominguez R A L119 12.30 98–08 BowmnsBnd1191¾ Dynvr1203 ⒹUnfrgttblMx116nk Close,dueled,clear drv 6
Previously trained by Matz Michael R
26Jly03–9Mth fst 1 :234 :471 1:111 1:354 3↑SalvtrMH-G3 **84** 2 43½ 42 41½ 57 57½ Bravo J L116 *1.00 90–02 Vinemeistr114¾ JrsyGint1172 *HighwyProspctor*113½ Stumbled start,empty 6
12Jly03–6PrM fst 1⅛ :462 1:101 1:353 1:481 3↑CrnhsBCH-G3 **108** 1 66½ 63½ 51¼ 2½ 22 Guidry M LB116 2.70 95–10 *Tenpins*1182 Bowman's Band1165½ Woodmoon1164¾ Quick move, 2nd best 6
7Jun03–7Del sly 1 :24 :463 1:11 1:363 3↑BrandywinH100k **112** 1 2½ 21 1hd 1hd 1nk Dominguez R A L116 3.30 101–13 BowmansBand116nk *PrivteLp*11820 Justifiction1142¼ Sent 3/8, strong ride 5
7May03–8Bel fst 1 :223 :443 1:073 1:321 3↑WschstrH-G3 **93** 5 43 47 37 48½ 69¼ Bailey J D L116 4.40 96–04 Najran1134½ Saarland1143 Justification113½ No response 7
11Apr03–9Kee fm 1 Ⓣ :242 :48 1:122 1:363 4↑Alw 65000c **92** 4 52½ 42½ 41¼ 41¾ 31¼ Dominguez R A L116 2.30 84–13 PerfectDrift117¾ FirstLieutennt116½ BowmnsBnd116nk 5w bid,slight gain 9
1Mar03–4GP fst 170 :234 :464 1:102 1:392 4↑Alw 46000c **98** 6 21½ 31½ 21½ 21 21 Velazquez J R L116 *1.40 103–02 GnrousRosi1161 BowmnsBnd1167 IslndSkippr1201¾ Bid, not good enough 6

Buddy Gil

Own: Desperado Stables Inc., McFadden, Don

B. g. 4 (Feb)
Sire: Eastern Echo (Damascus) $5,000
Dam: Really Rising (For Really)
Br: Billingsley Creek Ranch (Ky)
Tr: Mullins Jeff(0 0 0 0 .00) 2003:(313 94 .30)

Life	11	5	1	1	$729,455	106	D.Fst	7	3	1	1	$508,850	104
2003	6	3	0	0	$668,730	106	Wet(379)	3	1	0	0	$151,875	102
2002	5	2	1	1	$60,725	93	Turf(256)	1	1	0	0	$68,730	106
	0	0	0	0	$0	–	Dst(0)	0	0	0	0	$0	–

26Dec03–8SA	fst	7f	:222 :45 1:091 1:223	Malibu-G1	87	6	6	62¼	42½	55½	98¾	Stevens G L	LB121	3.50	84– 12	SouthernImage115hd MrinoMrini1151 MidsEyes1193	Angled in, weakened	12
3May03–10CD	fst	1¼	:461 1:102 1:353 2:01	KyDerby-G1	100	7	1312	1312	115¾	65	65¾	Stevens G L	L126	7.20	88– 06	*FunnyCide*1261¾ *EmpireMaker*126hd PeaceRules126hd	Bmp start,rail in lane	16
5Apr03–6SA	fst	1⅛	:454 1:10 1:36 1:491	SADerby-G1	104	4	63¼	65	52¾	1½	1hd	Stevens G L	LB122	6.30	88– 14	Buddy Gil122hd Indian Express1222¼ Kafwain1221¼	3wd bid,led,gamely	9
16Mar03–5SA	gd	1 1/16	:224 :462 1:104 1:433	SnFelipe-G2	102	5	51¼	62	53	41	1no	Stevens G L	LB119	9.80	86– 19	*BuddyGil*119no Atswhtmtlknbout116¾ Brncus1161¼	Lckd room,split,surged	10
23Feb03–8SA	fm	*6½f Ⓣ	:214 :432 1:062 1:122	Baldwin-G3	106	8	2	53½	52¾	22½	12	Stevens G L	LB117	26.70	95– 11	*Buddy Gil*1172 *King Robyn*1164 Flirt With Fortune1161	5wd into lane,rallied	11
Previously trained by Jenda Charles J																		
11Jan03–8GG	my	1 1/16	:221 :452 1:103 1:433	GGDerby-G3	76	2	44½	45½	42	43½	74½	Krigger K	LB120	7.70	80– 17	Standard Setter120nk Ozzie Cat1201 Pine for Java120¾	Bid rail, weakened	10

Buffythecenterfold

Own: Brian Allen A. and Stronach Stables

B. f. 4 (Mar) KEESEP01 $40,000
Sire: Capote (Seattle Slew) $30,000
Dam: Augusta Springs (Nijinsky II)
Br: Overbrook Farm (Ky)
Tr: Stute Melvin F(0 0 0 0 .00) 2003:(175 15 .09)

Life	13	5	3	2	$450,975	99	D.Fst	10	5	2	1	$410,575	99
2003	7	2	2	2	$228,815	99	Wet(348)	1	0	0	0	$0	69
2002	6	3	1	0	$222,160	90	Turf(312)	2	0	1	1	$40,400	94
	0	0	0	0	$0	–	Dst(0)	0	0	0	0	$0	–

27Dec03–7SA	fst	7f	:223 :452 1:091 1:213	ⒻLaBrea-G1	92	3	9	72	31½	34	37½	Solis A	LB119	8.40	90– 10	IslndFshion1236 Rndroo1191½ Buffythecenterfold119½	Pulled,5wd to turn	10
11Oct03–8SA	fm	*6½f Ⓣ	:213 :432 1:062 1:121 3↑	ⒻSKMaddyH-G3	94	2	6	41¼	21	21½	22	Solis A	LB116 b	3.70e	94– 06	Belleski1172 Buffythecntrfold1161 Icntgoforthtt1151	Stalked,bid,held 2nd	10
2Aug03–8Dmr	fm	1 Ⓣ	:223 :463 1:102 1:333	ⒻSnClmntH-G2	83	7	2½	2hd	2hd	21	34	Espinoza V	LB118 b	9.10	91– 06	Ktdogwn1162 AtlnticOcen1202 Buffythecentrfold118½	Vied btwn,held 3rd	9
12Jly03–9Crc	fst	6f	:212 :444 :572 1:104	ⒻAzaleaBC-G3	73	6	12	126½	86¼	87¾	611¼	Espinoza V	L121	*1.90	79– 11	EbonyBreeze1184¼ StormFlg1162¾ CrftyBrt1162¾	Jammed back st, 6 wide	13
14Jun03–6Hol	fst	1 1/16	:231 :454 1:092 1:413	ⒻHolBCOak-G2	99	2	32	22½	22	2½	24	Espinoza V	LB113	3.70	92– 04	SantaCtrin1164 Buffythecenterfold1135 PrincessV1146	Bid btwn,2nd best	5
4May03–8Hol	fst	7f	:222 :453 1:093 1:222	ⒻRailbird-G3	88	5	3	32	32	1½	11	Espinoza V	LB123	*.40e	90– 09	Bffythcntrfld1231 HnstAnswr1172 DshfrMny1154½	3wd bid,ducked in 1/16	6
23Mar03–3SA	fst	6½f	:22 :443 1:094 1:162	ⒻSantaPaula79k	91	5	3	4¾	1½	2½	1no	Espinoza V	LB121	2.10	91– 18	*Buffythcntrfold*121no WtchngYou1169½ TvysPln1144½	Battled back bravely	5

Buy the Sport

Own: Georgica Stable Mack, Stephen and Ros

Dk. b or b. f. 4 (Apr) FTFFEB02 $155,000
Sire: Devil's Bag (Halo) $15,000
Dam: Final Accord (D'Accord)
Br: Patricia Calandro (NY)
Tr: Barbara Robert(0 0 0 0 .00) 2003:(201 29 .14)

Life	11	3	0	1	$356,145	95	D.Fst	4	2	0	1	$328,013	95
2003	7	2	0	1	$334,521	95	Wet(341)	0	0	0	0	$0	–
2002	4	1	0	0	$21,624	–	Turf(277)	7	1	0	0	$28,132	–
	0	0	0	0	$0	–	Dst(0)	0	0	0	0	$0	–

25Oct03–2SA fst 1⅛ :47 1:11 1:354 1:49 3↑ Ⓕ BCDistaf-G1 **83** 4 72¾ 74½ 74¼ 78 511 Velazquez J R L119 35.20 78–07 Adoration1234½ Elloluv1192½ Got Koko1233½ Squeezed bit start 7
4Oct03–9Bel fst 1⅛ :474 1:122 1:363 1:491 3↑ Ⓕ Beldame-G1 **92** 1 41½ 42½ 4nk 38½ 39¼ Nakatani C S L120 7.30 75–26 Sightseek1234½ Bird Town1204¾ Buy the Sport120¾ Inside trip, no rally 7
Previously trained by Meehan Brian
6Sep03–7Bel fst 1⅛ :452 1:093 1:344 1:482 Ⓕ GazelleH-G1 **95** 6 2½ 3½ 31½ 35 1½ Day P L113 48.00 88–13 Buy the Sport113½ Lady Tak121no Spoken Fur1218¼ Rallied 4 wide,up late 8
9Jly03♦Newmarket (GB) gd 1 Ⓣ Str 1:38 3↑ Ⓕ Falmouth Stakes-G2 Stk 163000 53 Eddery Pat 118 25.00 Macadamia1271 Waldmark118½ Walzerkoenigin1301½ 8
Timeform rating: 98 *Tracked leader,faded final furlong.Hold To Ransom 7th*
13May03♦York (GB) gd 1 5/16 Ⓣ LH 2:09 Ⓕ Musidora Stakes (1-1/4m,85y)-G3 Stk 99700 56¾ Holland D 120 16.00 Cassis1201 Geminiani1222½ Irtahal1201½ 8
Timeform rating: 91 *Trckd ldrs,bumped over 2f out,one-paced to line.Hold To Ransom6th*
27Apr03♦Capannelle (Ity) gd *1 Ⓣ RH 1:401 Ⓕ Premio Regina Elena(Itln1000G)-G2 Stk 321000 68¼ Holland D 123 5.50 Golden Nepi1234 Vale Mantovani123¾ Kiralik1231 17
Timeform rating: 92 *Led to 2f out,weakened over 1f out*
5Apr03♦Lingfield (GB) ft 1 LH 1:362 Intl Trial Stakes (Listed) (dirt) Hcp 54300 12 Holland D 118 4.00 Buy the Sport1182 Membership1235 *Striking Ambition*1231¼ 6
Timeform rating: 106+ *Led throughout,drew clear 2f out,driving.Al Turf 5th*

Cactus Ridge

Own: Dream Walkin Farms Inc

B. c. 3 (Apr)
Sire: Hennessy (Storm Cat) $35,000
Dam: Double Park*Fr (Lycius)
Br: Dream Walkin' Farms, Inc. (Ky)
Tr: Calhoun W. B(0 0 0 0 .00) 2003:(634 156 .25)

Life	4	4	0	0	$187,850	101	D.Fst	4	4	0	0	$187,850	101
2003	4	4	0	0	$187,850	101	Wet(327)	0	0	0	0	$0	–
2002	0	M	0	0	$0	–	Turf(303)	0	0	0	0	$0	–
	0	0	0	0	$0	–	Dst(0)	0	0	0	0	$0	–

27Sep03–7AP fst 1 :23 :453 1:102 1:352 ArlWaFut-G3 **95** 3 11 11 1½ 12½ 13 Martin E M Jr L122 *.20 91–10 Cactus Ridge1223 Glittergem117nk Texas Deputy119no Bobbled start 6
17Aug03–9EIP fst 7f :214 :443 1:093 1:23 JCEllisJuv98k **94** 4 2 11½ 11 15 16½ Martin E M Jr L122 *1.70 97–11 *CctusRidg*1226½ ProprPrdo1164¼ LightnnNThundr1162 3-4w,drew off,drvg 9
12Jly03–8Cby fst 5½f :22 :45 :564 1:03 CbyJuvnile35k **101** 2 1 12 12 15 115 Walker B J Jr LB120 *.80 102–13 *CctusRdg*12015 WldBckroo1206¼ HymnsofGlory1204¼ Bumped brk, driving 7
7Jun03–6AP fst 4½f :224 :46 :521 Md Sp Wt 26k **71** 4 1 1½ 12 11¾ Meier R 118 3.70 97–13 *CactusRidge*1181¾ *OldKentRoad*1185½ *VictoryLight*1181 Bothered start, bled 10

Cajun Beat

Own: Padua Stable and Iracane John and Jos

Dk. b or b. g. 4 (Mar) KEENOV00 $145,000
Sire: Grand Slam (Gone West) $30,000
Dam: Beckys Shirt (Cure the Blues)
Br: John T. L. Jones Jr. & H. Smoot Fahlgren (Ky)
Tr: Margolis Stephen R(0 0 0 0 .00) 2003:(94 16 .17)

Life	11	5	2	0	$832,300	120	D.Fst	9	5	1	0	$819,500 120
2003	9	4	2	0	$820,000	120	Wet(411)	1	0	0	0	$0 49
2002	2	1	0	0	$12,300	84	Turf(322)	1	0	1	0	$12,800 94
	0	0	0	0	$0	-	Dst(0)	0	0	0	0	$0 -

25Oct03–5SA	fst	6f	:21 :431 :55 1:074	3↑BCSprint-G1	120	11	2	3½	1hd	1½	12¼	Velasquez C	LB123 b	22.80	99–05	CjunBet1232¼ Bluesthestndrd1262 ShkeYouDown126½	4 wide, drifted late	13
13Sep03–13TP	fst	6f	:212 :441 :563 1:092	KyCpSpnt-G3	113	5	3	21	1hd	12½	1¾	Velasquez C	L122 b	7.60	95–17	*Cajun Beat*122¾ *Clock Stopper*1163½ Champali1222½	3 wide, lasted	11
12Jly03–10Crc	fst	6f	:213 :443 :57 1:10	CarryBck-G3	104	3	3	42	41¾	31½	22½	Boulanger G	L117 b	26.90	91–11	*Valid Video*1222½ *Cajun Beat*1171¼ Super Fuse117nk	Steadied early	10
14Jun03–2CD	fm	5f	Ⓣ:213 :434 :56	Alw 52800NC	94	4	1	11	1hd	1hd	2nk	Velasquez C	L120 b	*2.10	98–02	*Skeet*116nk Cajun Beat1206½ *Lx Commander*120hd	Pace,outgamed	6
Previously trained by Gambolati Cam																		
10May03–9CD	sly	6f	:21 :434 :561 1:092	MattWinn111k	49	2	9	33½	58	612	923½	Boulanger G	L120 b	13.00	67–15	*Posse*120½ *Bossanova*1141¼ *Coach Jimi Lee*1205	Weakened after 1/2	9
19Apr03–9GP	fst	7f	:221 :45 1:093 1:223	HllndlBch75k	94	2	5	42	51¾	21½	1nk	Boulanger G	L118 b	1.30	95–09	CajunBeat118nk GetSmarter1188¼ FormalCharde118nk	Stdy bkstr, up late	6
16Mar03–11Tam	fst	1 1/16	:231 :47 1:113 1:443	TampaDby-G3	87	2	22	22½	32	43½	64¾	Boulanger G	L118	10.70	90–06	Region of Merit120¾ Aristocat118nk *Hear No Evil*1231¾	Chased, gave way	8
15Feb03–9GP	fst	7f	:22 :441 1:091 1:223	Hutchesn-G2	6	1	4	42	63½	617	642	Boulanger G	L116	7.60	53–08	LionTmer1186 StrengthWithin116¾ CrftyGuy1223¾	Steadied chute & turn	6
26Jan03–8GP	fst	6f	:214 :442 :563 1:092	Alw 36000N1x	104	8	4	31	31	2hd	11	Bailey J D	L122	3.40	97–11	Cajun Beat1221 *Eugene's Third Son*1209½ Letters118nk	Edged away late	9

Candid Glen

Own: Warren Glen C

Dk. b or b. g. 7 (Apr)
Sire: El Gran Senor (Northern Dancer)
Dam: Candid Moments (Pirate's Bounty)
Br: W. Kenan Rand Jr. (Ky)
Tr: Leggio A Jr(0 0 0 0 .00) 2003:(128 22 .17)

Life	38	10	9	6	$1,210,130	101	D.Fst	1	0	0	1	$2,970 61
2003	8	2	0	0	$543,300	101	Wet(329)	3	1	2	0	$45,400 97
2002	12	2	5	3	$303,240	99	Turf(347)	34	9	7	5	$1,161,760 101
	0	0	0	0	$0	-	Dst(0)	0	0	0	0	$0 -

26Jly03–9AP	fm	1¼	Ⓣ:491 1:14 1:383 2:023	3↑ArlgtnH-G3	85	7	35½	34	51¾	65½	88½	Perrodin E J	L118	19.20	84–05	Honor in War120nk Better Talk Now115¾ Mystery Giver118nk	Tired	10
21Jun03–7LS	fm	1⅛	Ⓣ:47 1:112 1:361 1:483	3↑DllasTfCpH250k	92	8	65	68½	62½	63¾	42¾	Perrodin E J	L118	8.00	99 -	Patrol1181 Slew the Red1141 *Storybook Kid*113¾	Lacked needed rally	10
31May03–8LS	fm	1⅛	Ⓣ:50 1:141 1:38 1:501	4↑Alw 42500NC	88	8	32	51¾	42	52¼	62¼	Perrodin E J	L122	*.50	92–06	StrybkKd116nk SmlnSlw118nk KrsHvngfnn119nk	Roused 1/4,no response	9
23Apr03–8Kee	fm	1½	Ⓣ:512 1:164 2:051 2:291	4↑Elkhorn-G3	98	6	21½	42½	53¾	32½	74	Perrodin E J	L116	13.70	90–09	KmLvsBcky117½ MnFrmWcklw123no WllmsNs1161¼	Tracked 4w,faltered	10
23Mar03–8FG	fm	*1⅛	Ⓣ:482 1:122 1:38 1:51	4↑ExploBdH-G2	101	4	72¾	54½	42½	1hd	1nk	Perrodin E J	L114	84.10	89–11	Candid Glen114nk Rouvres115no Freefourinternet115no	Eased out, driving	11
15Feb03–7Hou	fm	1⅛	Ⓣ:502 1:152 1:41 1:531	3↑ConlyBCTH223k	95	1	42½	52¾	41½	41¼	11½	Perrodin E J	L113	8.80	74–19	*Candid Glen*1131½ Red Mountain113½ Dynameaux114½	Split horses, driving	11
1Feb03–9FG	fm	*1⅛	Ⓣ:502 1:142 1:382 1:502	4↑FGBCH150k	92	7	98¼	910	910	88	84½	Perrodin E J	L115	10.50	88–11	MysteryGiver1173¼ Dynmeux115no Freefourintrnt115hd	Mild rally outside	9
5Jan03–9FG	fm	*1 1/16	Ⓣ:244 :503 1:144 1:451	4↑CERBradlyH75k	94	8	75	75	74¼	65½	42¼	Perrodin E J	L116	8.10	85–13	Royal Spy1161 Dynameaux115nk Freefourinternet1151	Not enough late	11

Candy Ride (Arg)

Own: Craig Sidney H. and Jenny

B. c. 5 (Sep)
Sire: Ride the Rails (Cryptoclearance) $7,500
Dam: Candy Girl*Arg (Candy Stripes)
Br: Abolengo (Arg)
Tr: McAnally Ronald L(0 0 0 0 .00) 2003:(312 44 .14)

Life	6	6	0	0	$749,149	123	D.Fst	3	3	0	0	$636,566 123
2003	3	3	0	0	$724,800	123	Wet(307)	0	0	0	0	$0 -
2002	3	3	0	0	$24,349	-	Turf(250)	3	3	0	0	$112,583 107
	0	0	0	0	$0	-	Dst(0)	0	0	0	0	$0 -

24Aug03–5Dmr	fst	1¼	:464 1:104 1:343 1:59	3↑PacifcCl-G1	123	3	21	2½	2hd	11	13¼	Krone J A	LB124	2.20	104–02	CndyRide1243¼ MedglidOro1247 FleetstrtDncr1242	Bobbled start,gamely	4
4Jly03–7Hol	fm	1⅛	Ⓣ:474 1:11 1:341 1:461	3↑AmericnH-G2	107	5	2½	2hd	2½	2hd	1¾	Stevens G L	LB120	*1.00	98–08	*Candy Ride*120¾ *Special Ring*1182 Irish Warrior1161	Led past 1/16,gamely	5
7Jun03–7Hol	fst	1 1/16	:23 :454 1:093 1:411	4↑OClm 100000N	111	3	1½	2hd	2½	1hd	13	Solis A	LB118	*1.40	98–02	*Candy Ride*1183 Primerica1203 Bonus Pay Day1182½	Dueled,clear,driving	6

Cappuchino

Own: Hollendorfer Litt and Todaro

B. h. 5 (Mar) KEESEP00 $130,000
Sire: Capote (Seattle Slew) $30,000
Dam: Tara Roma (Lyphard)
Br: Emory A. Hamilton (Ky)
Tr: Hollendorfer Jerry(0 0 0 0 .00) 2003:(1216 282 .23)

Life	25	7	2	5	$437,760	105	D.Fst	16	4	1	5	$248,381	105
2003	10	2	0	3	$201,712	105	Wet(377)	5	2	1	0	$158,379	99
2002	10	2	2	0	$154,550	93	Turf(289)	4	1	0	0	$31,000	92
	0	0	0	0	$0	-	Dst(0)	0	0	0	0	$0	-

28Nov03-11CD sly 1⅛ :48¹ 1:13 1:38⁴ 1:52² 3↑ ClarkH-G2 **94** 6 11½ 1½ 1½ 52½ 108¾ Thompson T J L116 fb 59.80 67- 27 ⒹEvening Attire118no Quest1143¼ Aeneas1141¼ Pace,inside,tired 14
15Nov03-8Hoo gd 1 :23¹ :46² 1:11 1:37 3↑ SchaeferMl103k **52** 3 21½ 31 54½ 712 722¾ Court J K LB124 fb 2.60 68- 09 CrftyShw1242¼ CoolNCllctv1194½ FghtngIndns1151 Tracked 2-3wd, tired 7
26Oct03-9CD sly 7½f :22⁴ :45² 1:10³ 1:31³ 3↑ AckAckH-G3 **99** 7 1 2hd 2hd 11 12 Court J K L117 fb 8.00 82- 26 Cappuchino1172 Pass Rush1161 Twilight Road1162 Dueled,4w,driving 7
27Sep03-9TP fst 1 :22⁴ :46¹ 1:11 1:36⁴ 3↑ TPFallCh-G3 **97** 5 52¼ 42 42½ 32½ 33 Court J K L119 fb 7.60 87- 22 Crafty Shaw1172¼ Cat Tracker117¾ *Cappuchino*1192¾ 3 wide, lacked bid 8
23Aug03-8Sac fst 1⅛ :45² 1:10¹ 1:37³ 1:51³ 3↑ GovernorsH60k **83** 1 11½ 11 11 2hd 31½ Gonzalez R M LB120 fb *.50 79- 21 ClssicFool112½ UltriorMotivs1161 Cppuchno1209 Gave ground grudgingly 6
2Aug03-10SR fst 1 1/16 :23² :46³ 1:10³ 1:42 3↑ JTGraceH101k **95** 3 11 11 11 13½ 15 Gonzalez R M LB115 fb 3.50 91- 11 Cappuchino1155 Surprise Halo119¾ Trompolino1162½ Good speed, driving 10
5Jly03-8Hol fst 7f :21⁴ :44² 1:08² 1:21² 3↑ TrBndBCH-G1 **79** 4 2 2hd 2½ 76½ 711½ Garcia M S LB112 fb 39.50 83- 11 JoyFrnco118hd Publicton1161½ ⒹBlusthstndrd1173½ Stdied 1/4,lugged out 9
31May03-8Hol fst 7½f :22² :45 1:08² 1:27 3↑ AckAckH91k **98** 2 4 12½ 12 31½ 55¼ Solis A LB116 fb 10.20 98- 08 *Joey Franco*1181 Kela1173½ Publication116nk Bit off rail,weakened 7
3May03-5CD fst 7f :22² :45 1:09³ 1:21⁴ 4↑ CDH-G2 **105** 6 7 3½ 54 21½ 32¾ Coa E M L115 fb 79.70 90- 08 *Aldebaran*1202½ Pass Rush117nk Cappuchino115hd Steadied rail 1/2 pole 12
22Mar03-4GG fst 6f :21 :42⁴ :54⁴ 1:08 3↑ DanvilleH67k **67** 5 4 34½ 36 59½ 613¾ Warren R J Jr LB116 fb 11.80 83- 11 *PresidioHeights*115nk *ElDordoShootr*1213 TxsChili1152 Chased 3w, gave out 6

Carib Lady (Ire)

Own: Gaillardia Racing LLC

B. f. 5 (Feb)
Sire: Sadler's Wells (Northern Dancer)
Dam: Belle Passe*Ire (Be My Guest)
Br: D. P. O'Brien (Ire)
Tr: Casse Mark E(0 0 0 0 .00) 2003:(465 59 .13)

Life	17	4	3	0	$167,769	97	D.Fst	0	0	0	0	$0	-
2003	8	2	1	0	$124,703	97	Wet(287)	0	0	0	0	$0	-
2002	8	2	2	0	$43,066	-	Turf(352)	17	4	3	0	$167,769	97
	0	0	0	0	$0	-	Dst(0)	0	0	0	0	$0	-

6Dec03-9Crc fm 1⅛ Ⓣ :47² 1:11 1:35 1:46⁴ 3↑ ⒻMyChrmrH-G3 **76** 8 88¼ 1014 1114 1211 89 Blanc B L115 8.80 88 - NewEconomy115½ SomthingVnturd1162½ Ivnvinlot113¾ Failed to menace 12
7Sep03-8WO fm 1½ Ⓣ 2:33⁴ 3↑ ⒻFlaminPage109k **94** 1 1hd 32 31½ 32 2¾ Husbands P L117 *1.60 60- 27 Heyahohowdy117¾ CaribLdy1171 AlphSphire1146½ Close up 3w,took place 7
2Aug03-3WO fm 1 1/16 Ⓣ :24¹ :47⁴ 1:12¹ 1:43³ 3↑ ⒻAlw 89000c **85** 5 55 63¾ 54½ 53¼ 43½ Husbands P L120 2.50 76- 20 Byzantine1182¾ Soundtrack118hd Five Fishes118¾ 3w,turn,4w,lane 7
Previously trained by Pletcher Todd A
12Jly03-9Cnl fm 1⅛ Ⓣ :49 1:12¹ 1:36³ 1:49 3↑ ⒻAlAlngBC-G3 **89** 9 54½ 43 42½ 42½ 42½ Castellano J J L119 11.90 89- 03 DressToThrill117½ LdyLind1171 LdyoftheFutur1171 Willing between foes 9
7Jun03-8Bel sf 1 Ⓣ :24¹ :49¹ 1:16¹ 1:43¹ 3↑ ⒻJsAGmBCH-G3 **68** 4 713 816 812 716 618 Bailey J D L115 8.40 26- 46 Mariensky1162 Riskaverse119hd Wonder Again1196¼ No response 8
17May03-7Pim sf 1 1/16 Ⓣ :24⁴ :51¹ 1:17¹ 1:50³ 3↑ ⒻGalrettH-G3 **97** 3 44½ 52½ 32 2hd 1nk Valenzuela P A L116 6.20 49- 49 CrbLdy116nk AffrmdDncr113¾ LdyofthFutr1142¼ Awaited room 1/4,drvng 7
6Apr03-4Kee fm 1½ Ⓣ :53¹ 1:20¹ 2:10¹ 2:33³ 4↑ ⒻAlw 56225N3X **84** 1 11½ 1½ 1hd 21½ 46¼ Santos J A L118 4.90 66- 20 *Lilac Queen*1235¾ Karsavina116nk Daisyago116nk Slow pace,weakened 8
6Mar03-8GP fm *1½ Ⓣ :51¹ 1:16³ 2:07² 2:31³ 4↑ ⒻAlw 38000N2X **90** 1 33½ 34½ 22 1hd 1½ Santos J A L117 *1.90 91- 11 Carib Lady117½ Flying Marlin1172¼ Miu Miu1175¾ All out, prevailed 8

Carson Hollow
Own: Stronach Stables and Hemlock Hills Fa

B. m. 5 (May)
Sire: Carson City (Mr. Prospector) $35,000
Dam: Lizeality (Hold Your Peace)
Br: Patricia Staskowski Purdy (NY)
Tr: Dutrow R E Jr(0 0 0 0 .00) 2003:(531 132 .25)

Life	10	6	3	0	$500,110	107	D.Fst	8	5	2	0	$434,310	107
2003	3	1	2	0	$164,740	102	Wet(399)	2	1	1	0	$65,800	95
2002	7	5	1	0	$335,370	107	Turf(244)	0	0	0	0	$0	–
	0	0	0	0	$0	–	Dst(0)	0	0	0	0	$0	–

11May03–8Bel fst 6f :214 :442 :562 1:09 3↑ⒻGnunRskH-G2 **94** 4 1½ 1½ 2hd 24 Velazquez J R L122 *.65 90–18 ShineAgin1194 CrsonHollow1221¼ *HrmonyLodg*1166¼ Pace, held place,fog 4
29Mar03–9Aqu fst 7f :22 :442 1:084 1:222 3↑ⒻDistfBCH-G2 **102** 4 3 1½ 1hd 1½ 11¼ Luzzi M J L120 f *.50 91–18 CrsonHollow1201¼ *RgingFever*1181¾ BonefidRson1123½ Determined inside 6
22Feb03–10Lrl sly 7f :224 :452 1:103 1:243 3↑ⒻBFrtcheH-G2 **95** 2 21¾ Desormeaux K J L119 f 1.90 82–14 Xtra Heat1251¾ *Carson Hollow*1191¼ Spelling113hd Fog, gamely inside 7

Castledale (Ire)
Own: Lyons Frank and Knee, Greg

B. c. 3 (Apr)
Sire: Peintre Celebre (Nureyev) $37,206
Dam: Louju (Silver Hawk)
Br: Gigginstown House Stud (Ire)
Tr: Mullins Jeff(0 0 0 0 .00) 2003:(313 94 .30)

Life	8	2	4	1	$109,623	92	D.Fst	0	0	0	0	$0	–
2003	8	2	4	1	$109,623	92	Wet(304*)	0	0	0	0	$0	–
2002	0	M	0	0	$0	–	Turf(358)	8	2	4	1	$109,623	92
	0	0	0	0	$0	–	Dst(0)	0	0	0	0	$0	–

29Nov03–5Hol fm 1 Ⓣ:241 :473 1:112 1:352 Generous-G3 **92** 1 42 43 31½ 11 1no Krone J A LB116 3.70 87–13 Castledale116no Dealer Choice1162 LuckyPulpit1163 3wd bid,led,just held 12
Previously trained by David Wachman
14Sep03♦Curragh (Ire) gf 6f Ⓣ Str 1:114 Blenheim Stakes (Listed) Stk 62200 13½ Hughes R 126 4.50 🄳*Castledale*1263½ Colossus126no Kurlicue1234 5
Timeform rating: 97 *Prssd pace,led hfwy,dueled 2f out,drftd rght,led line.Dqd,plcd 2n*
Disqualified and placed second
6Sep03♦Leopardstwn (Ire) gf 7f Ⓣ LH 1:29 Irish Stallion Farms EBF Hcp Hcp 55500 2hd Kinane M J 127 5.00 Alexander Goldrun124hd Castledale127hd Amourallis1153 11
Timeform rating: 95 *Rated in 7th,3rd 1f out,just missed*
29Aug03♦Tralee (Ire) fm 1 Ⓣ LH 1:394 Irish Stallion Farms EBF Hcp Hcp 55000 2nk Kinane M J 130 4.50 Chestnut Gallinule129nk Castledale1301 Tipper Road1101½ 12
Timeform rating: 95 *5th on rail,led 1-1/2f out,soon clear,caught near line*
13Aug03♦Gowran Park (Ire) fm 7f Ⓣ RH 1:064 Gowran Park Nursery Handicap Hcp 17000 1½ Kinane M J 129 *3.00 Castledale129½ Granted Wish1131½ Broomfield Lad118½ 16
Timeform rating: 85 *Tracked leaders,pressing pace halfway,led over 2f out,handily*
4Aug03♦Naas (Ire) gd 7f Ⓣ LH 1:254 Orpen EBF Maiden Maiden 22800 43 O'Donoghue C3 128 *3.50 Lord Admiral1281 Memorandum1231 *Misty Heights*1231 14
Timeform rating: 81 *Close up,dueled over 3f out,led 2f out,headed 170y out,weakened*
20Jly03♦Tipperary (Ire) hy 7½f Ⓣ LH 1:411 Irish Stallion Farms EBF Mdn Maiden 19300 35½ Manning K J 128 2.75 Magritte1285 Asanine123½ Castledale1283 12
Timeform rating: 83 *Tracked in 5th,2nd over 1f out,lost 2nd late*
10Jly03♦Tipperary (Ire) gf 7f Ⓣ LH 1:382 Irish Stallion Farms EBF Mdn Maiden 18500 21 McDonogh D P 128 9.00 Danticat1281 Castledale128nk Fantasticat1286 7
Timeform rating: 83 *Tracked in 3rd,2nd 1-1/2f out,held by winner*

Caught in the Rain
Own: Heiligbrodt Racing Stable and New Wal

Dk. b or b. f. 5 (Mar)
Sire: Petionville (Seeking the Gold) $6,500
Dam: Jinger Feathers (Fred Astaire)
Br: Casino Royale Farms Inc. (Pa)
Tr: Preciado Guadalupe(0 0 0 0 .00) 2003:(487 73 .15)

Life	17	6	0	3	$316,214	97	D.Fst	5	1	0	2	$34,175	92
2003	9	2	0	1	$120,708	93	Wet(334)	2	1	0	0	$30,000	82
2002	8	4	0	2	$195,506	97	Turf(205)	10	4	0	1	$252,039	97
	0	0	0	0	$0	-	Dst(0)	0	0	0	0	$0	-

20Dec03–8Aqu fst 1¼ ⊡ :51 1:154 1:4112:054 3↑ⒻLadiesH-G3 **81** 4 84 63 41¼ 43½ 54½ Molina V H L113 f *2.90 81–18 Svdbythlight1153 QunsTriomph113hd Rtroctiv1131 4 wide move, flattened 10
28Nov03–9Aqu fst 1 :231 :462 1:1031:362 3↑ⒻTopFlgtH-G2 **92** 111010 97¾ 77½ 69¼ 45½ Molina V H L112 f 50.75 77–29 Randaroo1162 Beauty Halo1153¼ Pocus Hocus116nk Good finish outside 12
8Nov03–9Aqu sf 1 1/16 Ⓣ :25 :51 1:1621:47 3↑ⒻAtheniaH-G3 **93** 6 74½ 75¼ 73 5¾ 1no Migliore R L115 14.80 69–31 Caught intheRain115no Lojo114no ConeyKitty113½ 5 wide move, last jump 8
17Oct03–7Med gd 1 1/16 Ⓣ :244 :493 1:1341:433 3↑ⒻVioletH-G3 **87** 4 71¾ 62¼ 52½ 54½ 55¼ King E L Jr L114 13.60 75–23 Dancal1162 Madeira Mist1161¾ Something Ventured116¾ Had no rally 8
30Aug03–8Pha sly 1 1/16 ⊗ :241 :491 1:1341:451 3↑ⒻⓈMrsPenny50k **82** 6 44 31 11½ 16 110¼ Molina V H L117 f *2.20 86–19 Caught in the Rain11710¼ My PrettyWoman1172½ MagicPeak119½ In hand 6
30Jly03–7Del fm 1 Ⓣ :24 :474 1:1141:351 3↑ⒻAlw 43000N4x **82** 4 45½ 42½ 41¼ 72¾ 62 King E L Jr L117 5.10 95–09 Katzen117no *Madeira Mist*122¾ Niclie112¾ Bid 1/4p, outfinished 8
Previously trained by Asmussen Steven M
2Jly03–9CD fm 1 Ⓣ :234 :47 1:1121:354 3↑ⒻAlw 63825N4x **71** 2 21½ 2½ 34½ 511 516¾ Albarado R J L122 5.30 76–11 *Silent Stream*1228¾ *May Gator*1241¾ Ing Ing1183 Between,tired 8
18May03–9CD gd 1 Ⓣ :24 :48 1:1231:363 3↑ⒻOClm 80000N **79** 6 21 21½ 31½ 23½ 35 Blanc B L117 *.90 84–12 SothrnSrprs1194¼ LoknMghtyFn117¾ CghtnthRn1171¾ Tracked,4w,empty 6
1Mar03–9FG yl *1⅛ Ⓣ :5131:162 1:4211:543 4↑ⒻBayouBCH137k **82** 10 11 1hd 1hd 52½ 87½ Lanerie C J L116 8.10 63–29 Quick Tip116nk HistoireSainte1181¾ SnowDance119nk Set pace, weakened 10

Cee's Elegance
Own: Cees Stable LLC

Gr/ro. m. 7 (Mar)
Sire: Cee's Tizzy (Relaunch) $15,000
Dam: Elegant Beauty (Norcliffe)
Br: Cecilia Straub-Rubens (Cal)
Tr: O'Neill Doug(0 0 0 0 .00) 2003:(760 133 .18)

Life	33	6	7	8	$744,039	103	D.Fst	29	6	6	8	$729,947	103
2003	6	2	1	0	$398,600	103	Wet(395)	2	0	1	0	$11,440	85
2002	8	1	4	0	$148,006	99	Turf(189)	2	0	0	0	$2,652	85
	0	0	0	0	$0	-	Dst(0)	0	0	0	0	$0	-

8Nov03–4SA fst 1 1/16 :232 :471 1:1121:42 3↑ⒻⓈCalCupMatH150k **63** 2 31½ 31½ 32 77¼ 719 Espinoza V LB122 2.70 75–10 RyllyChsn1203½ SmmrWndDncr1151½ BrtksBlth116½ Inside trip,weakened 8
23Aug03–8Dmr fst 6½f :222 :45 1:09 1:152 3↑ⒻRchBrdoH-G3 **90** 1 5 41½ 31½ 43 45 Espinoza V LB119 *2.30 93–10 SecretLiaison1164 LacieGirl1161 *SpringMeadow*117hd Waited bit 1/4,no bid 8
13Jly03–4Hol fst 7f :22 :443 1:0831:212 3↑ⒻAGleamH-G2 **103** 3 2 33½ 21½ 1½ 11½ Espinoza V LB116 9.70 95–15 Cee's Elegance1161½ You121no Affluent1192 Strong hand ride 5
7Jun03–4Hol fst 6f :213 :433 :5611:093 3↑ⒻDstStmrH-G3 **76** 5 3 2hd 3½ 43 66¾ Espinoza V LB120 3.90 85–10 MadmePietr121¾ BerFn1163 JetintoHouston116no Dueled btwn,weakened 6
26Apr03–1Hol fst 7f :22 :441 1:0821:213 4↑ⒻⓈBThoughtfl150k **100** 6 4 31 31 1½ 1¾ Espinoza V LB122 *1.40 94–07 CeesElegnce122¾ JetintoHouston1227½ RelPrnoid1202 3wd bid,ridden out 8
25Jan03–5SA fst 1 1/16 :23 :464 1:1041:432 4↑ⒻⓇVesslsDstf750k **90** 4 11 11 11½ 11 22½ Espinoza V LB120 4.10 84–13 SmoknFrolic1182½ *CeesElegance*120½ SmartLcy118hd Inside, just held 2nd 11

Century City (Ire)
Own: Kitchwa Stables and Nichols Thomas L

B. c. 5 (Feb)
Sire: Danzig (Northern Dancer) $250,000
Dam: Alywow (Alysheba)
Br: Kilcarn Stud (Ire)
Tr: Greely C. B(0 0 0 0 .00) 2003:(126 20 .16)

Life	19	6	2	4	$678,892	103	D.Fst	1 0 0 0 $4,392 98
2003	9	2	0	2	$409,392	103	Wet(393)	0 0 0 0 $0 -
2002	8	3	2	1	$256,533	92	Turf(394)	18 6 2 4 $674,500 103
	0	0	0	0	$0	-	Dst(0)	0 0 0 0 $0 -

25Oct03-4SA	fm	1	Ⓣ:221 :452 1:092 1:334	3↑BCMile-G1	103	7	108¾	116½	107	83½	31	Valdivia J Jr	LB126 b	39.00	92-04	SxPrfctons119¾ TouchofthBlus126nk CntryCty1261¼	Btwn foes,late inside	13
5Oct03-8SA	fm	1	Ⓣ:223 :454 1:091 1:323	3↑OkTrBCMl-G2	103	6	66	67½	75½	74¾	32	Valdivia J Jr	LB119 b	30.50	97-01	Designed for Luck119½ *Sarafan*1191½ Century City119nk	Split foes,late 3rd	8
26May03-8Hol	fm	1	Ⓣ:24 :463 1:091 1:331	3↑ShoeBCM-G1	89	6	43½	44½	67½	811	79¾	Espinoza V	LB124 b	18.70	88-10	Redattore124¾ Special Ring1243 *Touch of the Blues*1242	3 wide, weakened	9
3May03-9CD	fm	1⅛	Ⓣ:474 1:111 1:344 1:463	3↑WRTurfCl-G1	97	7	68¼	65	64	77½	66	Valdivia J Jr	L118 b	7.40	95 -	Honor in War1161¼ Requete116¾ *Patrol*114½	7w lane,empty	8
6Apr03-7SA	fm	1⅛	Ⓣ:493 1:131 1:361 1:474	4↑ArcadiaH-G2	102	5	44½	44½	42¼	42¼	1nk	Valdivia J Jr	LB114 b	19.90	90-11	Century City114nk *Gondolieri*116hd Sunday Break117½	Rallied,up 3wd late	9
23Mar03-8FG	fm	*1⅛	Ⓣ:482 1:122 1:38 1:51	4↑ExploBdH-G2	86	10	2½	2½	21	98½	96¾	Valdivia J Jr	L116	8.90	82-11	CndidGlen114nk Rouvres115no Freefourintrnt115no	Forced pace, stopped	11
1Mar03-8SA	gd	1	Ⓣ:234 :472 1:111 1:344	4↑FKilroeH-G2	102	4	41¼	31½	41¾	42¼	43¼	Stevens G L	LB116 b	22.20	85-16	*Redattore*1201 Good Journey1242 Decarchy118nk	Chased btw,missed 3rd	11
1Feb03-7TuP	fm	1 1/16	Ⓣ:233 :474 1:12 1:422	3↑TuPBCH150k	102	1	31	41½	51¼	2hd	1nk	Pincay L Jr	L117 b	2.70	100 -	Century City117nk Irish Warrior116nk Hataab116¾	Got thru 5wd,up late	9
11Jan03-8SA	fst	1 1/16	:23 :462 1:101 1:421	SnFndoBC-G2	98	7	66	64¼	64	64¼	54¾	Pincay L Jr	LB118 b	6.30	88-07	Pass Rush1163½ Tracemark116½ Tizbud116nk	Wide 7/8,mild bid	8

Champion Lodge (Ire)
Own: Charles Ronald L. and Clear Valley St

B. g. 7 (Feb)
Sire: Sri Pekan (Red Ransom) $6,000
Dam: Legit*Ire (Runnett*GB)
Br: Mrs A. Whitehead (Ire)
Tr: Shulman Sanford(0 0 0 0 .00) 2003:(93 12 .13)

Life	25	6	4	3	$350,119	108	D.Fst	0 0 0 0 $0 -
2003	4	2	0	1	$238,638	108	Wet(321)	0 0 0 0 $0 -
2002	9	2	3	1	$83,616	-	Turf(257)	25 6 4 3 $350,119 108
	0	0	0	0	$0	-	Dst(0)	0 0 0 0 $0 -

20Apr03-9SA	fm	*1¾	Ⓣ1:131 1:383 2:273 2:464	4↑SnJnCpoH-G1	102	2	57	77	32	42½	31¼	Solis A	LB117	*1.20	79-14	Passinetti111½ All the Boys115¾ ChampionLodge117¾	Split foes 1/8,rallied	9
15Mar03-7SA	yl	1½	Ⓣ:501 1:154 2:064 2:332	4↑SanLsRyH-G2	108	2	52	52½	43	2½	16	Solis A	LB116	7.10	59-41	ChmpionLodg1166 SpcilMttr1131 Admnnstrtor1163	Roused 3/8, led,cleard	7
20Feb03-5SA	fm	1¼	Ⓣ:481 1:13 1:37 2:004	4↑ⓇSanMarinoH81k	92	5	610	69	57	54½	52¾	Solis A	LB116	2.80	86-11	Requete114¾ Sumitas117hd T. H. Lear1141	3wd hill,mild bid	6
15Jan03-2SA	fm	1	Ⓣ:244 :481 1:11 1:343	4↑OClm 100000	104	1	32	32	32	31½	1nk	Solis A	LB119	8.30	89-09	ChmpionLodge119nk DukeofGrn1191 CstlGndolfo1172½	Split foes,gamely	5

Chapel Royal
Own: Smith Derrick and Tabor, Michael

Dk. b or b. c. 3 (Mar) OBSFEB03 $1,200,000
Sire: Montbrook (Buckaroo) $20,000
Dam: Cut Class Leanne (Cutlass)
Br: Ocala Stud Farm (Fla)
Tr: Pletcher Todd A(0 0 0 0 .00) 2003:(826 199 .24)

Life	6	3	2	1	$484,755	100	D.Fst	5 2 2 1 $394,755 99
2003	6	3	2	1	$484,755	100	Wet(381)	1 1 0 0 $90,000 100
2002	0	M	0	0	$0	-	Turf(258)	0 0 0 0 $0 -
	0	0	0	0	$0	-	Dst(0)	0 0 0 0 $0 -

25Oct03-7SA	fst	1 1/16	:221 :45 1:094 1:433	BesTBCJv-G1	79	10	3½	2hd	11	11½	37¼	Velazquez J R	LB122	5.70	79-07	ActionThisDy1222¼ MinistrEric1225 ChplRoyl122no	Clear turn, weakened	12
4Oct03-7Bel	fst	1 1/16	:234 :481 1:133 1:44	Champagn-G1	90	7	1hd	1½	1½	2hd	22½	Velazquez J R	L122	*1.55	77-26	Birdstone1222½ ChplRoyl1226¾ DshbordDrummr1222	Set pace, weakened	7
30Aug03-8Sar	fst	7f	:222 :452 1:102 1:232	Hopeful-G1	83	7	5	4¾	3nk	1½	24	Velazquez J R	L122	*.65	86-11	SilverWagon1224 ChpelRoyl1221½ NotoriousRogue1221	4 wide, held place	7
24Jly03-8Sar	sly	6f	:212 :444 :572 1:103	Sanford-G2	100	2	4	41	31½	12	15¾	Velazquez J R	L122	*1.00	89-12	ChplRyl1225¾ BlshngIndn1183½ *FlshngMdws*1181¼	Jumped puddles stretch	7
6Jun03-7Bel	fst	5f	:214 :442 :57	Flash-G3	99	3	2	2hd	1½	11½	15¼	Velazquez J R	L114	*.30	98-12	*Chapel Royal*1145¼ Hasslefree1142¼ Juventus1144¼	When asked, ridden out	4
15May03-2Bel	fst	5f	:22 :451 :58	Md Sp Wt 43k	81	7	7	2hd	2hd	13½	19¼	Velazquez J R	L118	*.65	93-12	*Chapel Royal*1189¼ *Snow Eagle*1183 Golden Diamond118¾	Ducked out start	7

Chiming (Ire)
Own: Castleton Lyons

B. m. 6 (Mar)
Sire: Danehill (Danzig)
Dam: Strutting*Ire (Ela-Mana-Mou*Ire)
Br: Mrs C. A. Waters (Ire)
Tr: Frankel Robert J(0 0 0 0 .00) 2003:(411 114 .28)

Life	23	3	4	4	$137,820	108	D.Fst	0	0	0	0	$0	–
2003	2	1	1	0	$66,000	108	Wet(293)	0	0	0	0	$0	–
2002	9	0	1	2	$23,726	–	Turf(328)	23	3	4	4	$137,820	108
	0	0	0	0	$0	–	Dst(0)	0	0	0	0	$0	–

24May03–7BM fm *1⅛ Ⓣ :481 1:113 1:36 1:452 3↑Ⓕ YrbBnBCH-G3 108 2 43 33 32½ 2½ 13½ Nakatani C S LB116 4.00 104–08 Chiming1163½ Noches De Rosa1193 Lindsay Jean1182¼ Stlkd rail, drvng 7
2May03–7Hol fm 1 Ⓣ :25 :491 1:124 1:353 3↑Ⓕ OClm 80000N 95 6 42½ 42 2hd 1½ 2½ Smith M E LB119 3.30 85–17 *Pertuisane119½ Chiming1193 Runaway Pro1212½* 3wd bid,led,willingly 6

Chopinina
Own: Knob Hill Stable

Gr/ro. m. 6 (May)
Sire: Lear Fan (Roberto) $15,000
Dam: Lady Aloma (Cozzene)
Br: Knob Hill Stable (Ont-C)
Tr: Fehr Alec(0 0 0 0 .00) 2003:(61 9 .15)

Life	16	5	2	1	$613,696	106	D.Fst	0	0	0	0	$0	–
2003	5	1	1	0	$227,070	100	Wet(318)	1	0	0	0	$0	65
2002	4	2	1	0	$292,280	106	Turf(334)	15	5	2	1	$613,696	106
	0	0	0	0	$0	–	Dst(0)	0	0	0	0	$0	–

30Nov03–6Hol fm 1 Ⓣ :232 :464 1:102 1:342 3↑Ⓕ Matriarc-G1 92 5 11 11 11 11 95 Dos Ramos R A LB123 b 38.10 87–17 HeatHaze123nk MusicalChimes120no Dediction123½ Speed,inside,wkened 14
14Sep03–9WO fm 1 Ⓣ :224 :451 1:091 1:331 3↑ AttoMile-G1 95 8 31½ 1hd 3½ 43½ 55 Dos Ramos R A L116 b 26.40 92–06 TouchoftheBlues119½ SoringFree1211¾ *PerfectSoul*121hd Inside, gave way 11
2Aug03–8WO sf 6f Ⓣ :23 :471 :592 1:12 3↑Ⓕ RylNrthH-G3 100 7 3 41¼ 1hd 11 12½ Kabel T K L120 b *1.55 78–22 Chopinina1202½ Alpha Heat1177 Leading Role116½ Close up,4w, drew off 7
5Jly03–8WO fm 1⅛ Ⓣ :452 1:092 1:333 1:48 3↑Ⓕ DncSmrtH-G3 87 1 2hd 1hd 1½ 31 63 Ramsammy E L116 b *1.80 85–15 Madeira Mist116no First Quarter1141 *Byzantine117½* Inside, gave way 10
1Jun03–8WO gd 1 1/16 Ⓣ :23 :46 1:10 1:424 3↑Ⓕ Nassau-G2 93 1 21 2hd 1hd 1½ 2½ Ramsammy E L115 b 4.60 83–19 Strait From Texas119½ Chopinina1153 Byzantine117½ Gave best inside 9

Classic Endeavor
Own: Schwartz Herbert T. and Carol A

Dk. b or b. h. 6 (Mar) OBSMAR00 $40,000
Sire: Silver Buck (Buckpasser) $7,500
Dam: Bold Juana (John Alden)
Br: Diane H. Flowers (Fla)
Tr: Schwartz Scott M(0 0 0 0 .00) 2003:(137 17 .12)

Life	41	11	7	3	$466,355	109	D.Fst	26	7	4	3	$307,465	109
2003	11	5	2	0	$241,595	109	Wet(348)	14	4	3	0	$158,890	100
2002	13	3	2	1	$99,190	101	Turf(208)	1	0	0	0	$0	36
	0	0	0	0	$0	–	Dst(0)	0	0	0	0	$0	–

27Nov03–3Aqu fst 1 :232 :46 1:104 1:362 3↑ Alw 58000c 66 5 2½ 21½ 33 510 518¾ Lopez C C L121 f 6.00 64–16 Abreeze1218 Justification119nk Free of Love119nk Chased outside, tired 6
4Jly03–8Mth fst 1 :233 :471 1:12 1:371 3↑ SkipAway60k 37 4 1hd 11 65½ 614 634¾ Lopez C C L122 f *2.10 56–14 JerseyGint116½ SeofTrnquility1149¾ BewreAvlnch1131 No response,eased 6
7Jun03–7Del sly 1 :24 :463 1:11 1:363 3↑ BrandywinH100k 59 4 31 33½ 56 515 528½ Caraballo J C L118 f 6.30 72–13 Bowman's Band116nk *Private Lap*11820 Justification1142¼ Tired 5
Previously trained by Schwartz Herbert T
25May03–10Mth gd 170 :232 :463 1:103 1:41 3↑ FriskMeNow60k 99 1 11 11 1hd 1hd 11 Lopez C C L119 f *.90 98–07 ClssicEndvor1191 IronChncllor1161½ MyRqust1194¼ Pace,game response 5
Previously trained by Schwartz Scott M
10May03–8Del sly 1 :241 :474 1:123 1:374 3↑ QuickCard59k 100 3 21½ 21 21 21½ 25½ Lopez C C L123 f *1.60 89–19 Private Lap1205½ *Classic Endeavor*1233½ Acrolect1181¼ No match, 2nd best 6
26Apr03–8Aqu sly 1 ⊗ :231 :46 1:094 1:333 3↑ FtMarcyH-G3 83 6 31½ 31½ 45¼ 710 815 Prado E S L118 f *2.25 82–12 SaintVerre1178½ *WindsorCastle*1191 JudgesCase1151¾ Chased 4 wide, tired 8
5Apr03–8Aqu fst 1⅛ :462 1:102 1:35 1:48 3↑ ExlsrBCH-G3 105 1 11½ 12½ 1½ 12 1½ Lopez C C L113 f 3.45 96–16 Classic Endeavor113½ Balto Star119¾ TempestFugit114¾ Set pace, driving 5
16Mar03–7Aqu fst 1⅛ ⊡ :472 1:112 1:363 1:493 3↑ StymieH80k 107 1 2hd 21 1½ 13 2no Chavez Luis L114 f 2.70 89–15 SnkMontn123no *ClsscEndvor*1142½ GrondStorm1174¾ Drifted deep stretch 6
2Feb03–8Aqu fst 1⅛ ⊡ :464 1:111 1:36 1:49 4↑ Alw 56000c 109 1 1hd 23 2½ 15 14 Chavez Luis5 L111 f 2.80 92–23 ClsscEndvor1114 *TmpstFgt*123nk GrondStorm120no When roused, driving 5
12Jan03–5Aqu fst 1¼ ⊡ :483 1:133 1:392 2:04 4↑ Alw 20000s 91 9 2hd 2hd 1hd 1½ 11½ Chavez Luis5 L114 f *.60 95–14 *Classic Endeavor*1141½ *Pay PerWin*1124¾ KenDoll1171¼ Vied outside, driving 9
4Jan03–6Aqu my 170 ⊡ :23 :464 1:10 1:40 4↑ Alw 48000N3x 98 4 21 2½ 1hd 1½ 11 Chavez Luis5 L115 f *1.70 94–13 *ClssicEndevor*1151 *IronChncllor*118½ MistrBlus118no Speed outside, driving 5

Colorful Tour

Own: Irish Acres Farm

Ch. h. 5 (Feb)
Sire: Tour d'Or (Medaille d'Or) $10,000
Dam: For You and Me (For Love and Glory)
Br: Irish Acres Farm (Ill)
Tr: Hickey P. N(0 0 0 0 .00) 2003:(298 37 .12)

Life	21	10	4	1	$495,529	105	D.Fst	14	8	4	0	$335,610	105
2003	9	4	2	0	$209,525	105	Wet(349)	3	2	0	0	$126,600	99
2002	8	3	2	1	$191,345	92	Turf(269)	4	0	0	1	$33,319	85
	0	0	0	0	$0	–	Dst(0)	0	0	0	0	$0	–

12Jly03-6PrM	fst	1⅛	:462 1:101 1:353 1:481	3↑ CrnhsBCH-G3	**87**	4 1hd 1½ 4¾ 57½ 514¼	Quinonez L S	LB115	16.10	83-10	*Tenpins*1182 Bowman's Band1165½ Woodmoon1164¾	Dueled, tired	6
21Jun03-9AP	fm	1 1/16 Ⓣ	:234 :473 1:113 1:42	3↑ [S]CardinalH86k	**83**	10 32½ 31½ 61½ 51¼ 65	Marquez C H Jr	L122	6.60	94-05	Act of War1162 [D]Mystery Giver124hd Scooter Roach117½	Weakened	10
Placed 5th through disqualification													
25May03-8PrM	fst	1 1/16	:23 :461 1:102 1:423	3↑ Precisnist47k	**102**	1 1½ 1hd 2½ 21½ 23	Quinonez L S	LB122	1.30	92-24	PttonsVctory1223 ColorflTor1226¼ *NorthwstHl*1193½	Inside duel, 2nd best	4
19Apr03-8Haw	fst	1⅛	:474 1:122 1:384 1:532	3↑ NtlJCIbH-G3	**47**	7 63 66½ 56½ 717 731½	Bourque C C	L119	2.60	57-29	Fight for Ally116nk Colonial Colony114no Parrott Bay1154¼	Outrun	8
9Apr03-9OP	fst	1 1/16	:233 :473 1:12 1:431	4↑ FfthSesn-G3	**105**	7 43 33½ 33½ 23 21	Quinonez L S	L122	2.90	93-23	PttonsVctory1171 ColorfulTor1223¼ MkorsMrk118¾	Restrained, slow gain	7
16Mar03-9OP	fst	1 1/16	:232 :47 1:114 1:432	4↑ RazrbckH-G3	**98**	3 1½ 1½ 1hd 11½ 1nk	Quinonez L S	L118	1.90	93-12	ColorflTr118nk CrftyShw119hd WndwrdPssg1181	Long, determined drive	7
22Feb03-9OP	my	1 1/16	:233 :474 1:134 1:463	4↑ EssexH-G3	**99**	3 21½ 21½ 52 3nk 11½	Quinonez L S	L116	5.10	77-28	*ColorfulTour*1161½ AsktheLord118no Premdittion1171¾	Patient, full of run	10
1Feb03-5OP	fst	1	:23 :454 1:11 1:374	4↑ OClm 50000N	**92**	3 44½ 34½ 42½ 1hd 11¾	Quinonez L S	L122	*1.60	94-15	*Colorful Tour*1221¾ Forty Nine Deeds116½ Zee Oh Six1191	Angled out 4-w	7
1Jan03-8Haw	fst	1 1/16	:233 :471 1:124 1:461	4↑ ChicagoSix43k	**92**	4 43 31½ 51¾ 2½ 11	Meier R	L120	*1.20	76-23	*Colorful Tour*1201 Saquache1201½ Meadowminer1152	Driving	8

Comic Truth

Own: Jayaraman Kalarikkal K. and Vilasini

Ch. c. 4 (Feb)
Sire: Proudest Romeo (Proud Truth)
Dam: Comic Wish (Lyphard's Ridge)
Br: Dr. K. K. Jayaraman & Dr. Vilasini D. Jayaraman (Fla)
Tr: Daly Patrick J(0 0 0 0 .00) 2003:(72 10 .14)

Life	15	5	2	3	$364,348	111	D.Fst	13	5	2	2	$356,848	111
2003	6	1	0	2	$140,108	111	Wet(316)	2	0	0	1	$7,500	85
2002	9	4	2	1	$224,240	97	Turf(203*)	0	0	0	0	$0	–
	0	0	0	0	$0	–	Dst(0)	0	0	0	0	$0	–

16Nov03-8RP	fst	1⅛	:472 1:112 1:363 1:492	OkDerby-G3	**111**	1 31½ 32 31 15 110	Berry M C	LB115 b	2.50	99-14	ComicTruth11510 Excessiveplesure1242¼ MorningMrry1122½	Light urging	6
4Oct03-9Hoo	fst	1 1/16	:223 :462 1:103 1:432	IndnaDby-G3	**97**	1 87 89½ 87½ 67½ 43½	Bejarano R	LB119 b	30.80	88-29	Excessiveplesure1241 GrndHombre1241¼ Wndo1241¼	4-6wd rally, willingly	8
13Sep03-13TP	fst	6f	:212 :441 :563 1:092	KyCpSpnt-G3	**95**	11 10 1111 911 87¼ 66¾	Bejarano R	L116 b	74.30	88-17	*Cajun Beat*122¾ *Clock Stopper*1163½ Champali1222½	5 wide 3/8 pole	11
Previously trained by Norman Cole													
12Apr03-9OP	fst	1⅛	:452 1:094 1:354 1:481	ArkDerby-G2	**83**	8 75½ 76½ 65 510 613¾	Theriot H J II	L122 b	27.70	85-11	*SirCheroke*1181¾ *EugnsThirdSon*1186½ ChristinsOutlw1181	Lacked late kick	12
22Mar03-10OP	fst	1 1/16	:23 :46 1:111 1:44	Rebel125k	**84**	6 55 45 52 32½ 33¼	Theriot H J II	L117 b	4.50	87-15	Crowned King1151¼ Great Notion1192 Comic Truth1172¼	Traffic 2nd turn	7
1Mar03-10OP	gd	1	:233 :474 1:132 1:384	Southwest75k	**85**	5 46 45 21 24 310¼	Theriot H J II	L119 b	*1.50	79-24	Great Notion1129 Alke1141¼ Comic Truth119¾	Mild bid 3-w, hung	7

Composure
Own: Lewis Robert B. and Beverly J

B. f. 4 (Apr) KEESEP01 $470,000
Sire: Touch Gold (Deputy Minister) $50,000
Dam: Party Cited (Alleged)
Br: Rancho San Peasea S. A. (Ky)
Tr: Baffert Bob(0 0 0 0 .00) 2003:(674 127 .19)

Life	8	4	3	0	$731,300	102	D.Fst	7	4	2	0	$531,300	102
2003	2	2	0	0	$300,000	102	Wet(330)	1	0	1	0	$200,000	101
2002	6	2	3	0	$431,300	101	Turf(259)	0	0	0	0	$0	–
	0	0	0	0	$0	–	Dst(0)	0	0	0	0	$0	–

8Mar03–4SA	fst	1 1/16	:24^{2} :48^{2} 1:11^{4} 1:43^{1}	ⒻSAOaks-G1	**102**	1	4$1\frac{1}{2}$	3½	3½	1hd	1¾	Bailey J D	LB117	*.40	88– 14	Composure117¾ *Elloluv*1174½ Go for Glamour1177½	3wd bid,led,gamely	5
9Feb03–7SA	fst	1	:24^{1} :47^{4} 1:11^{4} 1:36	ⒻLsVrgnes-G1	**96**	5	42	5$1\frac{1}{4}$	3$1\frac{1}{2}$	2$1\frac{1}{2}$	1nk	Bailey J D	LB120	*.80	91– 12	*Composure*120nk Elloluv1223 Watching You1168	Stmbld strt,determined	6

Congaree
Own: Stonerside Stable LLC

Ch. h. 6 (Apr)
Sire: Arazi (Blushing Groom*Fr) $7,336
Dam: Mari's Sheba (Mari's Book)
Br: Stonerside Stable, Ltd. (Ky)
Tr: Baffert Bob(0 0 0 0 .00) 2003:(674 127 .19)

Life	23	12	2	4	$3,241,400	120	D.Fst	18	10	2	3	$2,936,600	120
2003	9	5	2	0	$1,608,000	120	Wet(303)	4	2	0	1	$304,800	116
2002	6	3	0	1	$570,000	120	Turf(297)	1	0	0	0	$0	96
	0	0	0	0	$0	–	Dst(0)	0	0	0	0	$0	–

29Nov03–9Aqu	fst	1	:22^{4} :44^{2} 1:08^{3} 1:34^{1}	3↑CigarMiH-G1	**120**	2	3½	2½	2hd	1$1\frac{1}{2}$	15¼	Bailey J D	L124	*.60	94– 19	Congaree1245¼ Midas Eyes1153 Toccet1151	When roused, drew off	7
25Oct03–9SA	fst	1¼	:46^{1} 1:10^{1} 1:34^{1} 1:59^{4}	3↑BCClasic-G1	**115**	9	2hd	1½	1½	1hd	4$2\frac{1}{2}$	Valenzuela P A	LB126	6.30	103– 07	PlesntlyPerfect1261½ MedglidOro126¾ Dynevr121nk	Broke inward, dueled	10
13Sep03–11TP	fst	1⅛	:48^{1} 1:11^{4} 1:37 1:50^{2}	3↑KyCpClH-G2	**110**	4	1½	11	1hd	1hd	21	Prado E S	L124	*.50	83– 17	*Perfect Drift*1201 Congaree1244 *Crafty Shaw*115½	Bobbled slightly st	5
13Jly03–9Hol	fst	1¼	:45^{3} 1:09^{2} 1:34^{1} 2:00^{2}	3↑HolGldCp-G1	**116**	4	32	1½	1$1\frac{1}{2}$	12½	13	Bailey J D	LB124	*1.20	105– 07	Congaree1243 Harlan's Holiday1242 Kudos1241	Inside bid,clear,held	7
26May03–9Bel	sly	1	:22^{1} :44^{2} 1:08^{3} 1:34	3↑MtropltH-G1	**92**	7	2½	2hd	1hd	42	69¼	Stevens G L	L124	*.80	87– 14	Aldebaran119nk Saarland1143 *Peeping Tom*1143¾	Bobbled start, bumped	8
12Apr03–9Aqu	my	7f	:22^{4} :45^{2} 1:09^{1} 1:21^{2}	3↑CarterH-G1	**116**	2	4	2hd	1½	15	13½	Stevens G L	L122	*.80	96– 13	Congaree1223½ *Aldebaran*1181¼ Peeping Tom1143¾	Vied inside, clear	5
1Mar03–9SA	fst	1¼	:46^{3} 1:11^{1} 1:35^{2} 1:59^{4}	4↑SAH-G1	**116**	5	2½	2hd	1½	1hd	2hd	Bailey J D	LB124	*.60	106– 05	*Milwaukee Brew*119hd *Congaree*1244½ Kudos1171½	Fought back rail,game	6
2Feb03–8SA	fst	1⅛	:46^{2} 1:10^{1} 1:35 1:47^{3}	4↑SnAntnoH-G2	**118**	1	2½	22	2½	12½	12¼	Bailey J D	LB123	*.50	96– 18	Congree1232¼ *MilwukeeBrew*1201 PlesntlyPerfect1175	Led into lane,clear	6
4Jan03–8SA	fst	1 1/16	:23^{4} :47^{3} 1:11^{2} 1:41	4↑SnPsqalH-G2	**115**	5	42	41¼	3nk	1$1\frac{1}{2}$	16	Bailey J D	LB121	*.80	99– 05	*Congaree*1216 Kudos119no Hot Market1161¼	3wd bid,ridden out	9

Continuously
Own: Khaled Saud b

B. h. 5 (Jan)
Sire: Diesis*GB (Sharpen Up*GB) $30,000
Dam: Play On and On (Stop the Music)
Br: Palides Investments N. V. Inc. (Ky)
Tr: Frankel Robert J(0 0 0 0 .00) 2003:(411 114 .28)

Life	13	4	2	1	$307,156	102	
2003	8	3	1	1	$293,200	102	
2002	2	0	0	0	$3,905	-	
	0	0	0	0	$0	-	
D.Fst	0	0	0	0	$0	-	
Wet(266)	0	0	0	0	$0	-	
Turf(314)	13	4	2	1	$307,156	102	
Dst(0)	0	0	0	0	$0	-	

27Dec03-11Crc fm 1½ Ⓣ :484 1:133 2:01 2:244 3↑WLMcKntH-G2 102 8 87½ 75 64 32½ 21½ Coa E M L116 3.20 107 - Balto Star1211½ Continuously116½ Rowans Park1142¼ Outside bid for 2nd 11
22Nov03-8Hol fm 1½ Ⓣ :513 1:164 2:052 2:29 3↑HolTrfCp-G1 102 5 65½ 65½ 64½ 32½ 2no Solis A LB126 6.20 80-18 [D]Epicentr126no Continuously126hd BowmnMill126½ 3wd into lane,gamely 7
Placed first through disqualification
24Oct03-8SA fm 1½ Ⓣ :503 1:154 2:043 2:281 3↑CFBurkeH-G3 91 5 11½ 12 11½ 1½ 84½ Valdivia J Jr LB114 5.90 80-16 RunwyDncer112nk Lbirinto116nk SenorSwingr1141 Inside,clear,weakened 9
28Sep03-3SA fm 1¼ Ⓣ :503 1:152 1:39 2:013 3↑CLHirsch-G1 98 3 22 22 21 32½ 43¼ Valdivia J Jr LB124 12.50 82-13 Storming Home124½ *Johar*1241¼ Irish Warrior1241½ Pulled early,no bid 4
31Aug03-8Dmr fm 1⅜ Ⓣ :472 1:12 1:353 2:121 3↑DelMarH-G2 101 9 77½ 77½ 66 42½ 3½ Valdivia J Jr LB114 11.20 98-05 IrishWrrior116hd ContinntlRd117½ Continuously1141 3wd into lane,rallied 9
28Jly03-1Dmr fm 1⅜ Ⓣ :473 1:121 1:362 2:123 3↑OClm 62500N 95 1 63½ 63 61¾ 12 12 Valdivia J Jr LB121 4.20 97-06 Continuously1212 Gulchie119½ SomthingRushing1212 4wd into lane,clear 8
28Jun03-6Hol fm 1 Ⓣ :232 :464 1:10 1:333 4↑Alw 55000N2x 84 2 88¼ 89¼ 86 87½ 76¼ Valdivia J Jr LB120 9.00 90-13 VanRouge118hd GoldenArrow1181 MrshllRooster1182 Rank early,no rally 10
7Jun03-5Hol fm 1 1/16 Ⓣ :241 :473 1:111 1:411 4↑Alw 51918N1x 88 2 97¾ 96 74¾ 63¾ 1nk •Valdivia J Jr LB118 5.70 90-15 [DH]Continuously118 [DH]GoldenRhy120nk Spinbird1205 Pulled early,rallied 9

Crafty Shaw
Own: Cella Charles J

Ch. h. 6 (Apr) KEESEP99 $130,000
Sire: Crafty Prospector (Mr. Prospector) $25,000
Dam: Her She Shawklit (Air Forbes Won)
Br: Lance K. Robinson (Ky)
Tr: Vestal Peter M(0 0 0 0 .00) 2003:(71 10 .14)

Life	34	13	4	5	$850,440	113
2003	14	4	3	2	$351,185	105
2002	10	4	1	1	$348,445	113
	0	0	0	0	$0	-
D.Fst	21	8	3	3	$614,075	113
Wet(391)	11	5	1	2	$234,835	104
Turf(252)	2	0	0	0	$1,530	93
Dst(0)	0	0	0	0	$0	-

28Nov03-11CD sly 1⅛ :481 1:13 1:384 1:522 3↑ClarkH-G2 91 13 64¼ 63½ 62 129¼ 1110¾ Sellers S J L117 14.50 65-27 [D]Evening Attire118no Quest1143¼ Aeneas1141¼ 5w,tired 14
15Nov03-8Hoo gd 1 :231 :462 1:11 1:37 3↑SchaeferMI103k 94 5 53¾ 42½ 1½ 11½ 12¼ Perret C LB124 *1.40 91-09 CrftyShw1242¼ CoolNCollctiv1194½ FightngIndns1151 3wd bid, mild drive 7
4Nov03-9CD fst 1 1/16 :242 :473 1:114 1:432 3↑Alw 62280c 101 5 2½ 2½ 1½ 1hd 1nk Perret C L123 2.60 91-24 *Crafty Shaw*123nk Pass Rush1175½ American Style117½ Gamely,long drive 8
22Oct03-8Kee fm 1 1/16 Ⓣ :233 :471 1:122 1:421 3↑Alw 58200c 87 9 12 11½ 1hd 54 55 Day P L119 *1.10 85-18 *GreatBloom*1211¼ DrKshnikow1191½ RedMountin1192¼ Moved inside,tired 9
27Sep03-9TP fst 1 :224 :461 1:11 1:364 3↑TPFallCh-G3 103 2 1hd 1½ 11½ 12 12¼ Perret C L117 *.60 90-22 Crafty Shaw1172¼ Cat Tracker117¾ *Cappuchino*1192¾ 3 path, driving 8
13Sep03-11TP fst 1⅛ :481 1:114 1:37 1:502 3↑KyCpClH-G2 104 2 2½ 21 31 34 35 Sellers S J L115 9.50 79-17 *Perfect Drift*1201 Congaree1244 *Crafty Shaw*115½ Inside early, tired 5
25Aug03-7Sar fst 1⅛ :464 1:11 1:36 1:482 4↑Alw 58000c 105 5 16 16 12½ 1½ 21¼ Day P L120 4.20 92-20 EveningAttire1231¼ CraftyShw120no ReglSnction1207¾ Stubbornly inside 6
10Aug03-8Sar sly 1⅛ ⊗ :462 1:111 1:364 1:502 4↑Alw 58000c 102 3 1½ 13 13½ 1hd 2no Day P L118 *1.60 83-22 EventheScore118no CrftyShw1189 FreeofLove1181¼ Game inside, missed 7
14Jun03-10CD fst 1⅛ :464 1:102 1:35 1:472 3↑SFosterH-G1 100 2 1½ 1½ 21½ 34½ 410 Borel C H L113 30.70 91-04 *Perfect Drift*115hd *Mineshaft*1239½ *Aldebaran*120½ Pace,weakened 10
1May03-8CD fst 1 1/16 :234 :471 1:104 1:423 3↑Alw 59540c 98 6 53½ 51¼ 32 22 31¾ Borel C H L119 4.60 93-11 El Gran Papa1171¼ Slider119½ Crafty Shaw1192½ Drift start,empty 5w 6
5Apr03-11OP fst 1⅛ :474 1:12 1:354 1:473 4↑OaklawnH-G2 100 3 33 32 31 57 46¾ Lopez J L114 13.90 95-11 *Medaglia d'Oro*1222¾ Slider112hd *Kudos*1174 Bid, failed to sustain 5
16Mar03-9OP fst 1 1/16 :232 :47 1:114 1:432 4↑RazrbckH-G3 98 2 54½ 53½ 3nk 31½ 2nk Lopez J L119 *1.20 93-12 ColorfulTour118nk CrftyShw119hd WindwrdPssg1181 Bid, drifted slightly 7
22Feb03-9OP my 1 1/16 :233 :474 1:134 1:463 4↑EssexH-G3 93 2 74¾ 65¼ 86 42¼ 43¼ Lopez J L120 *.60 74-28 *ColorfulTour*1161½ AskthLord118no Prmdittion1171¾ Took up early,5-w 1/4 10
8Feb03-10P wf 1 1/16 :233 :471 1:112 1:432 4↑OClm 60000N 93 4 32½ 3½ 1hd 1½ 11¼ Lopez J L122 *.20 93-11 CrftyShw1221¼ DustOntheBottle112½ Nntucketr1193 Tracked 3-w, driving 6

Cuvee

Own: Winchell Thorougbreds LLC and Spendth

Ch. c. 3 (Mar)
Sire: Carson City (Mr. Prospector) $35,000
Dam: Christmas Star (Star de Naskra)
Br: Verne H. Winchell (Ky)
Tr: Asmussen Steven M(0 0 0 0 .00) 2003:(1949 452 .23)

Life	6	4	0	1	$360,704	103	D.Fst	5	3	0	1	$270,704	101
2003	6	4	0	1	$360,704	103	Wet(420)	1	1	0	0	$90,000	103
2002	0	M	0	0	$0	–	Turf(267)	0	0	0	0	$0	–
	0	0	0	0	$0	–	Dst(0)	0	0	0	0	$0	–

25Oct03–7SA	fst	1 1/16	:221	:45	1:094	1:433	BesTBCJv-G1	–0	12	41	4nk	31	1221	1258	Bailey J D	LB122	*1.60	28–	07	ActionThisDy1222¼ MinisterEric1225 ChpelRoyl122no	Stalked, wide, tired	12
14Sep03–7Bel	fst	1	:23	:452	1:10	1:353	Futurity-G1	101	3	2½	2hd	1½	16	18¼	Bailey J D	L120	*1.30	88–	16	Cuvee1208¼ Value Plus1205¼ *El Prado Rob*1207¼	Widened under drive	6
13Aug03–8Sar	sly	6½f	:211	:442	1:091	1:154	SarSpcl-G2	103	7	1	11	11	16	17½	Bailey J D	L122	2.75	96–	03	*Cuvee*1227½ Pomeroy1182¾ Limehouse1224½	Vigorous hand ride	8
6Jly03–10CD	fst	6f	:211	:443	:572	1:103	BshfdMnr-G3	69	1	6	3½	5¾	43	36½	Meche L J	L121	*.50	78–	13	Limehouse1214½ First Money1172 *Cuvee*121no	Bmp start,steady 1/2p	6
26May03–9CD	fst	5½f	:222	:46	:58	1:042	KyBC-G3	93	6	6	3½	1½	1¾	18¼	Meche L J	L117	*.60	90–	17	Cuvee1178¼ First Money1176 Exploit Lad1174	Hop start,hand urging	6
2May03–1CD	fst	4½f	:221	:451		:511	Md Sp Wt 37k	80	3	4	1hd		12½	16¼	Meche L J	L118	2.60	99–	05	*Cuvee*1186¼ Cherniavsky1181½ HeroicMoment1182	Mild hand urging,sharp	6

Cyber Secret

Own: Goldfarb Sanford and Irwin and Team J

B. f. 4 (Mar) EASMAY02 $20,000
Sire: Cyberspace (Forty Niner) $2,500
Dam: Merry Maudie (Maudlin)
Br: Earl Pierport & Teresa Pierport (Fla)
Tr: Dutrow R E Jr(0 0 0 0 .00) 2003:(531 132 .25)

Life	9	5	2	0	$274,707	89	D.Fst	8	5	2	0	$274,707	89
2003	5	3	1	0	$214,107	89	Wet(277)	1	0	0	0	$0	–
2002	4	2	1	0	$60,600	87	Turf(242*)	0	0	0	0	$0	–
	0	0	0	0	$0	–	Dst(0)	0	0	0	0	$0	–

10May03–8Bel	fst	7f		:224	:463	1:11	1:231	[F]NasauCBC-G2	87	2	2	1½	1½	2½	23	Bridgmohan S X	L122	*.65	81–	12	House Party1223 Cyber Secret122½ City Sister1165	Pace, held place	4
18Apr03–8Aqu	fst	1		:231	:451	1:10	1:354	[F]Comely-G3	89	2	11	1½	12½	17	15½	Bridgmohan S X	L122	3.50	86–	13	Cyber Secret1225½ StormFlagFlying1223 Bonay1162¼	Set pace, drew away	5
22Mar03–9Aqu	fst	7f		:22	:444	1:093	1:222	[F]Cicada-G3	88	2	4	2½	2½	15	14½	Bridgmohan S X	L122	4.50	91–	12	*Cyber Secret*1224½ *Roar Emotion*1161¾ Boxer Girl1184	When roused, driving	6
1Mar03–8Aqu	fst	1 1/16	[•]	:242	:483	1:124	1:451	[F]Busher81k	83	5	1½	1hd	2hd	3½	41¾	Samyn J L	L122	2.40	78–	23	ElegntDesigner120hd XtrHert118nk VirginVoyg1181½	Set pace, weakened	7
26Jan03–8Aqu	fst	170	[•]	:234	:472	1:111	1:414	[F]Busanda82k	84	1	13	1½	1½	13½	11	Samyn J L	L116	*1.75	85–	16	CyberSecret1161 XtraHeart1186½ GoldenDamsel118nk	Pace, clear, driving	8

Dancal (Ire)
Own: Aronstam Marlon

B. m. 6 (Mar)
Sire: Mujadil (Storm Bird)
Dam: Majesty's Nurse (Indian King)
Br: Eddie Kavanagh (Ire)
Tr: Pletcher Todd A(0 0 0 0 .00) 2003:(826 199 .24)

Life	22	11	5	1	$263,551	101	D.Fst	5	1	1	0	$68,211 –
2003	9	3	2	0	$223,011	101	Wet(254)	0	0	0	0	$0 –
2002	5	2	2	0	$14,881	–	Turf(242)	17	10	4	1	$195,340 101
	0	0	0	0	$0	–	Dst(0)	0	0	0	0	$0 –

30Nov03–6Hol fm 1 Ⓣ :23² :46⁴ 1:10² 1:34² 3↑ⒻMatriarc-G1 **89** 3 9¼ 9¾ 9⁵¾ 13⁷½ 10⁶½ Castellano J J **LB**123 22.10 86– 17 HeatHaze123nk MusicalChimes120no Dediction123½ 5wd into lane,no rally 14
17Oct03–7Med gd 1 1/16 Ⓣ :24⁴ :49³ 1:13⁴ 1:43³ 3↑ⒻVioletH-G3 **99** 6 1hd 11 1½ 12 12 Castellano J J L116 *1.80 80– 23 Dancl116² MdeirMist1161¾ SomethingVentured116¾ Set pace, drew clear 8
20Sep03–9Bel fm 1 Ⓣ :22² :45² 1:09 1:33 3↑ⒻNblDmslH-G3 **101** 3 56½ 63¾ 63 41¾ 2nk Castellano J J L114 5.10 95– 05 WonderAgin117nk *Dncl*114nk SomethingVnturd1151¾ Game finish outside 11
3Aug03–8Sar yl 1 [T] :23¹ :47² 1:13¹ 1:37¹ 4↑ⒻAlw 58000c **99** 3 57½ 53½ 3nk 11 1no Castellano J J L120 9.70 85– 15 Dancal120no Vespers1183½ Young Star1166¼ 3 wide move, got nod 7
Previously trained by Sateesh Seemar
3Apr03♦Nad al Sheba (UAE) fst *1 LH 1:36 3↑ Jumeirah Intl Classic Handicap Hcp 28600 1116½ McEvoy K 133 - *Al Maali*1263¼ Marhoob133½ *Opportunist*120½ 15
Never a factor.Jalaab (126) 8th,Northern Rock (135) 13th
21Mar03♦Jebel Ali (UAE) ft *1 LH 1:36⁴ 3↑ Jebel Ali Mile (Listed) Stk 95300 1¾ McEvoy K 119 - Dancal119¾ Northern Rock123hd Curule1231 12
Timeform rating: 109 *Mid-pack,rail bid 2f out,led near line.Trademark (123) 8th*
7Mar03♦Jebel Ali (UAE) fst *1 LH 1:37³ 3↑ Insurance Services Mngmnt Hcp Hcp 28600 78¼ Smith W 137 - Saint Malo1121¾ Northern Rock1361½ Takes Tutu115nk 10
Timeform rating: 100 *Tracked leaders,bid 2f out,weakened 1f out.Jalaab (130) 8th*
13Feb03♦Nad al Sheba (UAE) fst *1 LH 1:37¹ 3↑ Burj Nahaar Prep Alw 34000 2nk Smith W 122 - Royal Tryst127nk Dancal1222¼ Calcutta1272¼ 11
Timeform rating: 109 *Tracked leader,led 2-1/2f to 1f out,came again near line*
23Jan03♦Nad al Sheba (UAE) ft *1 LH 1:36⁴ 3↑ Maktoum Challenge-Round 1-G3 Stk 95300 510½ Moore R 123 - Estimraar1281¾ State Shinto128¾ Conflict1281 14
Timeform rating: 90 *Mid-pack on rail,3rd 2-1/2f out,weakened 1f out.Abreeze (128) 6th*

Dancewithavixen
Own: TNT Racing Stable

Dk. b or b. f. 4 (May)
Sire: Vying Victor (Flying Paster) $5,000
Dam: Hot Ginger (Royal Chocolate)
Br: Cliff Baldwin (BC-C)
Tr: Longstaff Tom(0 0 0 0 .00) 2003:(79 18 .23)

Life	17	9	4	2	$387,365	85	D.Fst	16	8	4	2	$287,045 85
2003	11	8	2	0	$335,921	85	Wet(367)	1	1	0	0	$100,320 85
2002	6	1	2	2	$51,444	59	Turf(194)	0	0	0	0	$0 –
	0	0	0	0	$0	–	Dst(0)	0	0	0	0	$0 –

11Oct03–8Hst sly 1⅛ :46 1:12 1:38² 1:52² 3↑ⒻBlrinaBC-G3 **85** 9 21 21 1hd 2hd 1nk Valdez F S L121 fb *2.20 82– 21 Dncwthvxn121nk ScondrySchool124½ ShlbyMdsn124nk Prevailed, driving 9
20Sep03–9Hst fst 1⅛ :46³ 1:12⁴ 1:38² 1:52 ⒻBCBCOaks-G3 **85** 6 25 22 1hd 12 2nk Valdez F S L121 fb *.65 84– 15 Raylene121nk *Dancewithavixen*1214½ *Payton's Pride*121hd Clear, just failed 9
1Sep03–4Hst fst 1 1/16 :22³ :45⁴ 1:11 1:44 Ⓕ[R]FreeVactnH55k **82** 1 22½ 22 1hd 13 17¾ Valdez F S L126 fb *.55 95– 07 Dancewithavixen1267¾ Anabatic110² Chorus Dancer1152¼ Much the best 5
4Aug03–4Hst fst 1 1/16 :23³ :46³ 1:11² 1:45 Ⓕ[R]BCStallH55k **78** 1 1hd 1hd 1hd 13 15¾ Valdez F S L124 fb *.55 90– 09 *Dancewithavixen*1245¾ ChorusDancer1144¼ Dee'sLove119½ Led throughout 6
19Jly03–4Hst fst 1 1/16 :24³ :49 1:13⁴ 1:45 ⒻNanaimoH43k **76** 2 2hd 21 2½ 12 12¼ Valdez F S L123 fb *.40e 90– 15 *Dncewithvixen*1232¼ PytonsPride117⁴ *ClssChoice*1134¼ Pressed, drew clear 5
28Jun03–1Hst fst 1 1/16 :23³ :47¹ 1:12 1:44³ Ⓕ[R]LiberatnH44k **82** 4 1hd 1hd 1hd 12 14½ Valdez F S L120 fb *.45 92– 16 *Dancewithvixen*1204½ ChorusDncer116³ AlwysAnnies112no Led throughout 6
14Jun03–2Hst fst 1 1/16 :23³ :47³ 1:13 1:46¹ ⒻAlw 27931NC **73** 6 2½ 2hd 1hd 15 14¾ Valdez F S L117 fb *.35 84– 13 *Dncewithvixen*1174¾ ClssChoic1171¾ PrhpsMgic1093¾ Drew off, ridden out 6
7Jun03–6Hst fst 6½f :22² :46¹ 1:10² 1:17 ⒻEmrldDwnsH44k **82** 2 1 42 41¼ 21½ 22 Valdez F S L122 fb *.80e 91– 14 Dee's Love118² *Dancewithavixen*1224¼ Aquita117½ 3 wide, second best 10
19May03–8Hst fst 6½f :22¹ :45⁴ 1:11 1:17³ ⒻSupernatlH44k **81** 6 5 53½ 61½ 2½ 13½ Valdez F S L120 fb *1.60 90– 13 Dncewithvixen1203½ *DeesLov*1174¼ SrchinSouth1173¾ Drew off, ridden out 7
3May03–7Hst fst 6½f :22² :45⁴ 1:11⁴ 1:18³ Ⓕ[R]FairLady44k **69** 7 3 63¾ 64¼ 32 12 Valdez F S L119 fb *2.15e 85– 09 *Dancewithavixen*119² Dee's Love117hd Searchin South1173¼ 3 wide, driving 8
Previously trained by Terry Rick
19Apr03–9EmDfst 6f :21² :44¹ :55³ 1:08¹ ⒻUSBank35k **65** 3 9 76 76¾ 47½ 46¾ Valdez F S B117 fb 12.50e 90– 11 BisbeesProspect1164¾ TvysPln1201¼ TopPnny120¾ Swung wide, late gain 9

Dancing Guy
Own: Green Newcomb

Gr/ro. g. 9 (Apr)
Sire: Robyn Dancer (Crafty Prospector) $3,500
Dam: Dancing Myrrh (Gold and Myrrh)
Br: Farnsworth Farms (Fla)
Tr: Green N(0 0 0 0 .00) 2003:(23 4 .17)

Life	84	19	17	17	$880,408	108	D.Fst	62	16	14	13	$782,344	108
2003	10	1	1	2	$103,740	101	Wet(350)	13	1	3	3	$61,584	103
2002	13	1	2	5	$139,153	106	Turf(267)	9	2	0	1	$36,480	95
	0	0	0	0	$0	-	Dst(0)	0	0	0	0	$0	-

27Dec03-12Crc fst 1⅛ :491 1:144 1:394 1:522 3↑FHooperH-G3 **88** 3 64 85¼ 94¾ 57 58½ Velez R I L113 fb 31.30 81- 22 PredwnRid1124¼ BestoftheRest1222 DlitfulGuy1122¼ Mid rack,weakened 9
15Dec03- 5Crc fst 1 ⊗ :241 :474 1:124 1:394 3↑OClm 62500(62.5-57.5)N **90** 6 76¼ 76¼ 65 21½ 2nk Velez R I L117 fb 3.60 82- 22 Marco's Word117nk Dancing Guy1171 LongfordArms1171½ 4 wide, gaining 9
15Nov03-12Crc fst 1⅛ :49 1:131 1:392 1:531 3↑[S]CGRoseClsH200k **93** 2 33½ 33 33½ 43 43 Velez R I L114 fb 9.80 83- 18 BstofthRst1211¼ TorofthCt1171½ ThJdgSzWh115nk 3 wd, no late response 5
11Oct03- 8Crc fst 1 1/16 :25 :494 1:141 1:461 3↑SpdABckH-G3 **96** 1 32 42 32 32 32 Velez R I L116 fb 11.10 79- 22 TouroftheCt1161 *BestoftheRest*1221 DncingGuy1163 Lacked late response 8
27Sep03-10Crc wf 6½f :22 :451 1:103 1:171 3↑[R]PoulainD'r42k **75** 1 1 78¼ 710 810 610¼ Velez R I L117 fb 7.50 83- 15 *Love That Moon*119¾ Showmeitall1153¼ Lawbook110nk No factor 8
26May03-11Crc fst 1 1/16 :234 :473 1:12 1:452 3↑MemDayH-G3 **92** 6 77¼ 67 63½ 42¼ 1nk Velez R I L113 fb 10.00 85- 18 Dancing Guy113nk Shotgun Fire1102¼ *High Ideal*1131¼ Swung out, just up 7
3May03- 7Crc fst 1 :24 :48 1:124 1:383 3↑OClm 62500(62.5-57.5)N **83** 3 55½ 64¾ 43 46½ 49 Ferrer J C L117 fb 3.10 79- 12 High Ideal1174½ Lavender's Lad1173 Sebastian Light1171½ 3 wide, tired 8
Previously trained by Green Newcomb
20Apr03- 9GP fst 1 1/16 :233 :464 1:104 1:423 3↑SkipAwyH-G3 **75** 2 46 48 58½ 512 517 Ferrer J C L114 fb 20.70 79- 15 Best of the Rest121½ *Consistency*114½ Roger E1149¾ No factor 5
21Mar03- 9GP fst 1 1/16 :224 :453 1:093 1:43 4↑OClm 150000N **101** 3 510 510 57 34 32 Santos J A L116 fb 10.40 92- 13 Gander1181½ Wiseman'sFerry116½ DancingGuy1162¾ Angled out, willingly 5
1Mar03- 4GP fst 170 :234 :464 1:102 1:392 4↑Alw 46000c **82** 2 54½ 55 55 46½ 49¾ Santos J A L116 fb 4.90 94- 02 GnrousRosi1161 BowmnsBnd1167 IslndSkippr1201¾ Lacked late response 6

Dashboard Drummer
Own: Double S Stable Preferred Pals Stable

Dk. b or b. g. 3 (Apr)
Sire: Alamocitos (Private Account) $1,000
Dam: Groovin Moment (Magic Moment II*Fr)
Br: Bob Pogue & Paulette Pogue (Okla)
Tr: Iwinski Allen(0 0 0 0 .00) 2003:(598 148 .25)

Life	4	3	0	1	$157,600	85	D.Fst	3	2	0	1	$97,600	85
2003	4	3	0	1	$157,600	85	Wet(318)	1	1	0	0	$60,000	85
2002	0	M	0	0	$0	-	Turf(254)	0	0	0	0	$0	-
	0	0	0	0	$0	-	Dst(0)	0	0	0	0	$0	-

4Oct03- 7Bel fst 1 1/16 :234 :481 1:133 1:44 Champagn-G1 **78** 5 31 41½ 42½ 38 39¼ Espinoza J L L122 15.20 71- 26 Birdstone1222½ ChpelRoyl1226¾ DshbordDrummr1222 Came wide, no rally 7
9Aug03-10Mth sly 6f :211 :434 :563 1:104 Sapling-G3 **85** 1 6 57½ 45½ 34 12½ Ferrer J C L120 4.40 85- 15 DshbordDrmmr1202½ DptyStrm120½ ChrmngJm1202 Drifted out,clear late 7
Previously trained by Pogue William R
27Jun03- 8PrM fst 5f :213 :451 :571 PrGldJuv55k **85** 4 1 31 31 1½ 15 Quinonez L S B116 9.40 95- 14 *DshbordDrummer*1165 WlksLiknAngl1161 Chrnivsky1134 Drew off, driving 6
9May03- 1PrM fst 2f :221 Md Sp Wt 21k **–** 2 2 1½ 1¾ Quinonez L S B117 2.30 - - *Dashboard Drummer*117¾ Irish de Slew117¾ Soriano Cat1174 Driving 6

Della Francesca

Own: Ol Memorial Stable Dell Ridge Farm an

B. h. 5 (Mar)
Sire: Danzig (Northern Dancer) $250,000
Dam: La Affirmed (Affirmed)
Br: Brushwood Stable (Pa)
Tr: O'Callaghan Niall M(0 0 0 0 .00) 2003:(243 25 .10)

Life	17	4	3	2	$314,451	102	D.Fst	0 0 0 0	$0 –
2003	8	2	1	0	$177,360	102	Wet(406)	0 0 0 0	$0 –
2002	6	1	1	1	$106,751	65	Turf(405)	17 4 3 2	$314,451 102
	0	0	0	0	$0	–	Dst(0)	0 0 0 0	$0 –

16Nov03–9CD	yl	1⅛ Ⓣ	:492 1:142 1:391 1:513	3↑RivrCtyH-G3	85	9	4½	5¾	42	7¾	88	Chavez J F	L116 b	5.20	68–26	Hard Buck118½ Warleigh1171 Rowans Park1141	Bmp start,bobbled	10
4Oct03–9Kee	fm	1 Ⓣ	:23 :461 1:114 1:36	3↑ShdwlTfM-G1	90	8	1015	1013	106¼	89¼	77¾	Chavez J F	L126 b	20.50	80–14	PerfectSoul126¾ HonorinWr126½ TouchofthBlus1261¼	Improved position	10
13Sep03–7Bel	fm	1⅛ [T]	:483 1:113 1:352 1:472	3↑BelBCH-G2	102	1	53½	56	54	3½	11½	Chavez J F	L114 b	16.30	93–07	Della Francesca1141½ Rouvres116nk Volponi119½	Came wide, drew clear	7
26Jly03–9AP	fm	1¼ Ⓣ	:491 1:14 1:383 2:023	3↑ArlgtnH-G3	98	2	2½	2hd	2hd	2hd	41¼	Melancon L	L114 b	16.20	92–05	HonorinWar120nk BetterTlkNow115¾ MysteryGiver118nk	Weakened a bit	10
2Jly03–6CD	fm	1 1/16 Ⓣ	:244 :492 1:14 1:434	3↑OClm 62500N	93	4	51¼	2½	2hd	2hd	2nk	Albarado R J	L118 b	1.70	85–11	FostrsLnding118nk DllFrncsc1185¼ PointPrnc118no	Broke in bmp start,4w	6
23Mar03–8FG	fm	*1⅛ Ⓣ	:482 1:122 1:38 1:51	4↑ExploBdH-G2	81	8	1½	1½	11	88	108¾	Melancon L	L113 b	25.70	80–11	Candid Glen114nk Rouvres115no Freefourinternet115no	Pace, emptied out	11
16Feb03–10GP	fm	1⅜ Ⓣ	:481 1:121 1:353 2:113	3↑GPBCH-G1	95	9	42	46½	56	51¾	67¼	Chavez J F	115 b	8.90	91–09	ManFromWicklow1194¾ JustListen113½ Srdukr1141	Lacked late response	10
12Jan03–9GP	fm	*1⅛ Ⓣ	:511 1:151 1:394 1:514	4↑Alw 46000c	97	5	2½	2½	2½	21	1½	Chavez J F	116 b	3.80	82–18	Della Francesca116½ Stokosky116½ First Lieutenant1161	All out, prevailed	7

Delta Princess

Own: Khaled Saud b

Dk. b or b. m. 5 (Feb)
Sire: A.P. Indy (Seattle Slew) $300,000
Dam: Lyphard's Delta (Lyphard)
Br: Palides Investments N. V. Inc (Ky)
Tr: Mott William I(0 0 0 0 .00) 2003:(718 138 .19)

Life	12	6	1	1	$272,683	99	D.Fst	0 0 0 0	$0 –
2003	8	4	0	0	$196,110	99	Wet(419)	1 0 0 1	$12,573 76
2002	3	1	1	1	$51,373	90	Turf(328)	11 6 1 0	$260,110 99
	0	0	0	0	$0	–	Dst(0)	0 0 0 0	$0 –

17Oct03–7Med	gd	1 1/16 Ⓣ	:244 :493 1:134 1:433	3↑ⒻVioletH-G3	89	3	3½	41½	42½	44	44½	Luzzi M J	L115	3.60	75–23	Dncl1162 MdeirMist1161¾ SomethingVentured116¾	Between foes, no rally	8
20Sep03–9Bel	fm	1 Ⓣ	:222 :452 1:09 1:33	3↑ⒻNblDmslH-G3	81	9	36	42	32	812	89¾	Migliore R	L115	7.30	85–05	WonderAgin117nk *Dncl*114nk SomethingVenturd1151¾	Speed 3 wide, tired	11
26Jly03–8Sar	fm	1⅛ Ⓣ	:49 1:13 1:363 1:474	3↑ⒻDianaH-G1	95	4	11	1½	1½	5¾	85¼	Luzzi M J	L116	22.10	85–10	Voodoo Dancer120nk *Heat Haze*1181¾ Pertuisane115¾	Set pace, gave way	8
5Jly03–9Pha	fm	1 1/16 Ⓣ	:23 :464 1:113 1:422	3↑ⒻDrJPennyMH100k	98	6	47	48½	22	12	15	Castillo H Jr	L119	*.40	96–07	Delta Princess1195 Spice Island1143½ Willie's Luv115¾	Drew out	6
7Jun03–8Bel	sf	1 Ⓣ	:241 :491 1:161 1:431	3↑ⒻJsAGmBCH-G3	90	6	48½	47½	4¾	32½	48¼	Luzzi M J	L117	8.10	36–46	Mariensky1162 Riskaverse119hd Wonder Again1196¼	Inside run turn, tired	8
3May03–8Aqu	fm	1 1/16 Ⓣ	:231 :481 1:124 1:421	3↑ⒻBeaugayH-G3	99	6	64½	72½	72¾	2hd	1½	Luzzi M J	L113	7.50	93–05	DeltPrincss113½ WondrAgin118¾ *VoodooDncr*1202¾	Slipped through inside	9
14Mar03–6GP	fm	*1 1/16 Ⓣ	:234 :482 1:131 1:434	+4↑ⒻAlw 40000N3x	94	1	58	512	55	44½	1no	Bailey J D	L121	*1.00	85–14	*DeltPrincess*121no CozyIslnd1171¼ PrimeQun1173¾	Checked chute, just up	8
22Feb03–8GP	fm	1 1/16 Ⓣ	:232 :47 1:111 1:412	+4↑ⒻAlw 38000N2x	93	3	53¼	44	42½	2½	1½	Bailey J D	L117	*.80	88–08	*DeltPrincess*117½ GivendTk1214½ *DvilsGoodGirl*1192¼	Bobbled bkstr, inside	10

Denon
Own: Gann Edmund A. and Flaxman Stable

B. h. 6 (Apr)
Sire: Pleasant Colony (His Majesty)
Dam: Aviance*Ire (Northfields)
Br: Flaxman Holdings, Ltd. (Ky)
Tr: Frankel Robert J(0 0 0 0 .00) 2003:(411 114 .28)

Life 21 6 4 3 $1,739,156 110 | **D.Fst 0 0 0 0 $0 –**
2003 7 1 1 1 $425,000 108 | **Wet(376) 0 0 0 0 $0 –**
2002 7 2 2 0 $917,400 110 | **Turf(285) 21 6 4 3 $1,739,156 110**
0 0 0 0 $0 – | **Dst(0) 0 0 0 0 $0 –**

14Dec03♦Sha Tin (HK) gf *1¼ Ⓣ RH 2:00⁴ 3↑ Hong Kong Cup-G1 Stk 2318400 1113¾ Nakatani C S 126 38.00 Falbrav126² Rakti1261¼ Elegant Fashion122½ 14
Timeform rating: 101 *Rated in 9th,12th 2f out,one-paced to line.Bright Sky 4th*
30Nov03♦Tokyo (Jpn) yl *1½ Ⓣ LH 2:28³ 3↑ Japan Cup-G1 Stk 4404000 812¼ Nakatani C S 126 18.70 Tap Dance City126⁹ That's The Plenty121¾ *Symboli Kris S*126hd 18
Timeform rating: 102+ *Rated in 9th,6th 2-1/2f out,one-paced late.Islington9th,Johar16th*
6Sep03–8Bel yl 1⅜ Ⓣ :51⁴1:17¹ 1:42 2:17⁴ 3↑ManOWar-G1 **105** 8 42½ 42½ 42½ 34 33 Bailey J D L126 *1.40 71–26 Lunar Sovereign1262¾ SlewValley126nk Denon1261¼ 3 wide, outfinished 2d 8
9Aug03–9Sar gd 1½ 🅃 :49 1:13 2:03¹2:28 3↑SwrdDncH-G1 **103** 11 84¼ 62¾ 1½ 1½ 42¼ Bailey J D L122 *2.15 78–20 Whitmore'sConn1151¼ Macaw114nk SlewValley114¾ 4 wide run, weakened 11
5Jly03–10Mth fm 1⅜ Ⓣ :48³1:14 1:37³2:12³ 3↑UntdNtnH-G1 **108** 5 43 42½ 42 41¼ 51 Bailey J D L122 *1.20 100–03 Balto Star117½ The Tin Man121no Lunar Sovereign112nk Close,evenly late 7
7Jun03–10Bel sf 1¼ 🅃 :53⁴1:20³ 1:47²2:14 3↑ManhttnH-G1 **108** 9 75¾ 63½ 3nk 13 1½ Bailey J D L122 *2.15 24–57 Denon122½ Requete1161¼ Dr. Brendler116¹ 4 wide move, held on 10
10May03–7Hol fm 1½ Ⓣ :49¹1:13¹ 1:59⁴2:25¹ 3↑JMurryMemH400k **108** 7 53½ 43½ 42 21 22 Bailey J D LB122 2.40 97–12 *Storming Home*122² *Denon*1224½ *Ballingarry*120nk Inside bid str,2d best 8

Derrianne
Own: Waterville Lake Stable

Gr/ro. f. 4 (Feb) KEESEP01 $75,000
Sire: Cozzene (Caro*Ire) $60,000
Dam: Stormy Gal (Storm Cat)
Br: Warren W. Rosenthal (Ky)
Tr: Clement Christophe(0 0 0 0 .00) 2003:(389 75 .19)

Life 9 3 1 2 $163,655 92 | **D.Fst 0 0 0 0 $0 –**
2003 7 2 1 2 $148,666 92 | **Wet(366) 0 0 0 0 $0 –**
2002 2 1 0 0 $14,989 – | **Turf(353) 9 3 1 2 $163,655 92**
0 0 0 0 $0 – | **Dst(0) 0 0 0 0 $0 –**

18Oct03–9Kee fm 1 1/16 Ⓣ :23² :48¹ 1:13²1:43² ⒻVllyView-G3 **86** 4 87¼ 63 73¼ 33½ 33¾ Blanc B L123 *2.20 80–17 Dyna Da Wyna119¾ Mexican Moonlight116³ Derrianne123½ Broke in air 10
27Sep03–9Pim gd 1 1/16 Ⓣ :23¹ :48¹ 1:13¹1:46² ⒻMWashBC-G3 **92** 3 37½ 35 35 2hd 11¼ Blanc B L122 *1.60 70–30 Derrianne1221¼ Chic Joy115² Twining and Dining115nk Wide, driving 7
Previously trained by Nicolas Clement
2Aug03♦Deauville (Fr) gd *1 Ⓣ RH 1:41³ ⒻPrix de la Calonne (Listed) Hcp 47000 64½ Gillet T 128 *2.50 *State of Art*123² Mabalane123nk Precious Pearl128½ 11
Timeform rating: 101 *In touch in 5th,bumped 1f out,unable to recover.Kiralik 11th*
11Jly03♦Deauville (Fr) yl *7f Ⓣ Str 1:23² ⒻPrix Amandine (Listed) Stk 46300 2no Lemaire C-P 128 8.70 Intercontinental128no Derrianne128¾ Together123nk 12
Timeform rating: 110 *Trailed, wide bid 1f out,just missed.Zinziberine 6th,Valdoura 8th*
1Jun03♦Chantilly (Fr) gd *1 Ⓣ RH 1:35 ⒻPrix de Sandringham-G2 Stk 117000 45½ Lemaire C-P 123 10.40 Maiden Tower1231½ *Acago*123² *Intercontinental*123² 7
Timeform rating: 100 *Tracked in 3rd,4th 3f out,one-paced late*
7May03♦Saint-Cloud (Fr) sf *1 Ⓣ LH 1:46² ⒻPrix d'Angerville (Listed) Stk 46600 11½ Lemaire C-P 123 3.50 Derrianne1231½ Thakeyyah123no Sabkha123¾ 8
Timeform rating: 100 *Rated at rear,rallied to lead 120y out,ridden out*
7Apr03♦Maisons-Laffitte (Fr) gd *7f Ⓣ Str 1:29² ⒻPrix Imprudence (Listed) Stk 43700 31½ Peslier O 126 17.00 Six Perfections1261½ *Campsie Fells*126hd *Derrianne*126½ 7
Timeform rating: 102 *Rated in last,bid 1f out,lost duel for 2nd.Zinziberine 4th*

Designed for Luck
Own: Wilson David W. and Holly F

Ch. g. 7 (Apr)
Sire: Rahy (Blushing Groom*Fr) $80,000
Dam: Fantastic Look (Green Dancer)
Br: Mr. & Mrs. John C. Mabee (Ky)
Tr: Cerin Vladimir(0 0 0 0 .00) 2003:(268 49 .18)

Life	22	9	5	2	$604,320	107	D.Fst	2	1	0	0	$14,400	73
2003	4	3	0	0	$267,735	107	Wet(344)	0	0	0	0	$0	-
2002	3	1	0	1	$75,000	105	Turf(336)	20	8	5	2	$589,920	107
	0	0	0	0	$0	-	Dst(0)	0	0	0	0	$0	-

25Oct03-4SA	fm	1	Ⓣ:22^1	:45^2	1:09^2	1:33^4	3↑BCMile-G1	**94**	2	3^1	2^{hd}	1^{hd}	2^{hd}	7^{4¾}	Valenzuela P A	**LB**126 b	5.30	88-04	SxPrfctons119¾ TochofthBls126^{nk} CntryCty126^{1¼}	Bid btwn,led,weakened	13
5Oct03-8SA	fm	1	Ⓣ:22^3	:45^4	1:09^1	1:32^3	3↑OkTrBCMI-G2	**107**	2	2^2	2^3	2½	1^2	1½	Valenzuela P A	**LB**119 b	3.90	99-01	Designed for Luck119½ *Sarafan*119^{1½} Century City119^{nk}	Bid,cleared,held	8
10Sep03-3Dmr	fm	1	Ⓣ:22^4	:46^3	1:09^4	1:33^1	3↑LiveDreamH76k	**106**	3	3½	3^{1½}	3^{1½}	3^1	1^1	Valenzuela P A	**LB**118 b	2.80	97-08	*Designed forLuck*118^1 GreenLine115^1 Redattore124^1	Tight 6-1/2,waited 1/4	8
18Aug03-7Dmr	fm	1	Ⓣ:22^2	:46	1:09^2	1:33	3↑Alw 70000N$MY	**99**	1	4^{1½}	4^{1¾}	2^1	2^1	2^1	Valenzuela P A	**LB**117 b	3.30	97-05	[D]Denied117^1 *DesignedforLuck*117^{2½} MountinRge117^4	Bumped,stdied late	6

Placed first through disqualification

Dessert
Own: The Thoroughbred Corporation

Dk. b or b. f. 4 (Feb)
Sire: Storm Cat (Storm Bird) $500,000
Dam: Windsharp (Lear Fan)
Br: The Thoroughbred Corporation (Ky)
Tr: Mandella Richard E(0 0 0 0 .00) 2003:(253 51 .20)

Life	8	3	1	1	$259,560	95	D.Fst	0	0	0	0	$0	-
2003	6	3	1	1	$259,560	95	Wet(390)	0	0	0	0	$0	-
2002	2	M	0	0	$0	-	Turf(356)	8	3	1	1	$259,560	95
	0	0	0	0	$0	-	Dst(0)	0	0	0	0	$0	-

9Nov03-8SA	fm	1⅛	Ⓣ:45^4	1:09^3	1:34	1:46	3↑ⒻAvigaition74k	**89**	6	2½	2^{hd}	2½	5^{2¼}	7^7	Nakatani C S	**LB**119	2.90	92-08	Crazy Ensign120½ Garden intheRain116^1 Adalgisa116^{1½}	Dueled, weakened	7
24Aug03-9Dmr	fm	1⅛	Ⓣ:47^2	1:11^4	1:35^1	1:47	ⒻDmrOaks-G1	**95**	4	1^{1½}	1^{1½}	1½	1^1	1^{nk}	Nakatani C S	**LB**122	*2.50e	98-03	Dessert122^{nk} Solar Echo122^1 Personal Legend122^{no}	Rail,clear again,held	8
4Aug03-7Dmr	fm	1⅛	Ⓣ:47^2	1:11^3	1:35^1	1:47^1	3↑ⒻAlw 58000N1x	**93**	5	1½	1½	1^{hd}	1^{2½}	1^{3½}	Nakatani C S	**LB**115	*1.50e	97-04	*Dessert*115^{3½} RunwyLollipop119½ *InfernlMcGoon*121^4	Inside,stdy handling	8
24May03-1Hol	fm	1	Ⓣ:24	:47^3	1:10^4	1:35^1	ⒻOClm 80000N	**87**	5	2^1	2^1	2^1	2^2	2¾	Solis A	**LB**118	*1.00	87-17	Fudge Fatale118¾ *Dessert*118^4 Proven Form118^2	Bit off rail,2nd best	5
23Mar03-2SA	fm	*6½f	Ⓣ:21^4	:43^3	1:07^1	1:13^3	3↑ⒻMd Sp Wt 48k	**81**	2	9	4^{1¼}	3^{1½}	1^{hd}	1¾	Solis A	**LB**116	*.80	89-08	Dessert116¾ *Fudge Fatale*116^1 Bijou Queen116^1	Waited, surged inside	9
20Feb03-1SA	fm	*6½f	Ⓣ:22	:44^2	1:08	1:14^2	ⒻMd Sp Wt 48k	**82**	7	6	5^{2¼}	5^{2½}	4^{2½}	3^1	Solis A	**LB**120	12.10	84-13	Devious Impact120^{no} Quero Quero120^1 *Dessert*120^{3½}	Pulled,tight 5/16	9

Devious Boy (GB)
Own: Vreeland James R

Dk. b or b. g. 4 (Feb)
Sire: Dr Devious*Ire (Ahonoora*GB) $11,003
Dam: Oh Hebe*Ire (Night Shift)
Br: Mrs C. F. van Straubeenzee and A. Gibson Fleming (GB)
Tr: Walsh Kathy(0 0 0 0 .00) 2003:(68 11 .16)

Life 15 5 6 2 $272,912 100 | **D.Fst** 3 0 0 2 $5,900 66
2003 7 2 2 2 $236,480 100 | **Wet(209)** 0 0 0 0 $0 –
2002 8 3 4 0 $36,432 – | **Turf(276)** 12 5 6 0 $267,012 100
0 0 0 0 $0 – | **Dst(0)** 0 0 0 0 $0 –

26Dec03–3SA fst 1 ⊗ :223 :454 1:103 1:36 SirBeufort78k **66** 6 53 64¼ 68 711 721 Valdivia J Jr **LB**122 2.70 70– 13 Buckland Manor1202 Saint Buddy1166 Kewen1181½ Stalked pace, no rally 8
4Oct03–4SA fm 1⅛ Ⓣ :494 1:141 1:371 1:484 OakTrDby-G2 **94** 4 21 22 2½ 1½ 1hd Krone J A **LB**118 *1.10 85– 14 DeviousBoy118hd *SweetReturn*118nk UrbnKing1181½ Held game btwn foes 5
6Sep03–8Dmr fm 1⅛ Ⓣ :472 1:11 1:343 1:462 DmrDerby-G2 **100** 8 31½ 41½ 42 31½ 21¼ Krone J A **LB**122 4.80 100– 05 FirlyRnsom1221¼ *DeviousBoy*122no SweetRturn122½ 3wd into str,game 2nd 9
16Aug03–8Dmr fm 1 1/16 Ⓣ :233 :471 1:103 1:401 LaJollaH-G3 **98** 7 43½ 45 53¾ 33 2½ Krone J A **LB**117 11.90 99– 10 Singletary118½ Devious Boy117½ Senor Swinger120½ Off bit slow,rallied 7
23Jly03–8Dmr fm 1 Ⓣ :23 :47 1:111 1:343 ⓇOceanside84k **93** 2 21½ 21½ 2½ 1½ 1½ Krone J A **LB**116 9.70 90– 11 Devious Boy116½ Fairly Ransom118½ Stanley Park1201 Pulled,bid,led,held 7
Run in divisions Previously trained by Peter Haslam
25Jan03♦Lingfield (GB) fst 1¼ LH 2:084 Bet Direct Conditions St(dirt) 35¾ Enstone L3 122 *1.35 Californian123¾ Arry Dash1275 *Devious Boy*122no 5
Timeform rating: 77 Alw 20000 *Tracked in 3rd,2nd over 2f out,outfinished*
11Jan03♦Lingfield (GB) fst 7f LH 1:26 Littlewoods Bet Direct H(dirt) 31½ Fox D7 126 16.00 Desert Spirit105no Satelcom1081½ Devious Boy126nk 14
Timeform rating: 98 Hcp 33600 *Rated in 6th,outpaced 2f out,gaining late.Agilis (123) 4th*

Dimitrova
Own: Higgins Joseph

B. f. 4 (May)
Sire: Swain*Ire (Nashwan) $25,000
Dam: The Caretaker*Ire (Caerleon)
Br: Muirfield Ventures (Ky)
Tr: Weld Dermot K(0 0 0 0 .00) 2003:(8 3 .38)

Life 9 4 2 1 $1,047,292 103 | **D.Fst** 0 0 0 0 $0 –
2003 7 4 1 1 $1,042,970 103 | **Wet(241)** 0 0 0 0 $0 –
2002 2 M 1 0 $4,322 – | **Turf(362)** 9 4 2 1 $1,047,292 103
0 0 0 0 $0 – | **Dst(0)** 0 0 0 0 $0 –

25Oct03–6SA fm 1¼ Ⓣ :463 1:102 1:351 1:59 3↑ⒻBCF&MTrf-G1 **62** 10 68½ 511 1211 1214 1226¼ Smullen P J **LB**118 11.70 72– 04 Islington123nk L'Ancresse1182½ Yesterday118no 3 wide, gave way 12
27Sep03–8Bel fm 1¼ 🅃 :494 1:144 1:39 2:023 3↑ⒻFlwrBlIv-G1 **103** 5 55 54 52 3nk 11 Bailey J D **L**114 3.70 81– 17 Dimitrova1141 Walzerkoenigin120no HeatHze1231¼ Came wide, clear late 7
7Sep03–9Bel gd 1⅛ 🅃 :464 1:113 1:362 1:482 ⒻGrdCyBCH-G1 **98** 3 44½ 44½ 42½ 11½ 24 Bailey J D **L**122 *.75 84– 17 Indy Five Hundred1134 *Dimitrova*1222¼ CampsieFells1161 Bid, yielded late 8
5Jly03–5Hol fm 1¼ Ⓣ :473 1:114 1:353 1:594 ⒻAmercnOaks750k **94** 10 44½ 43½ 31½ 3nk 12 Flores D R **LB**121 4.60 93– 11 Dimitrova1212 *Sand Springs*121nk Atlantic Ocean121½ 3wd bid,led,gamely 14
25May03♦Curragh (Ire) sf 1 Ⓣ Str 1:404 ⒻIrish 1000 Guineas-G1 3¾ Smullen P J 126 16.00 Yesterday126no Six Perfections126¾ *Dimitrova*1262½ 8
Timeform rating: 114 Stk 470000 *Tracked leader,led 2f to 100y out,gamely.L'Ancresse 4th*
13Apr03♦Leopardstwn (Ire) gd 7f Ⓣ LH 1:28 ⒻLtown 1000 Guineas Trial(Lstd) 1hd Smullen P J 126 *1.75 Dimitrova126hd L'Ancresse1263 Shangri La1232½ 10
Timeform rating: 108+ Stk 53800 *Led throughout,clear over 1-1/2f out,met late challenge,all out*
29Mar03♦Leopardstwn (Ire) gd 1 Ⓣ LH 1:411 ⒻEBF Maiden 11½ Shanahan P 126 *2.50 *Dimitrova*1261½ Sharesha1263 Tus Maith126¾ 15
Timeform rating: 93+ Maiden 21800 *Prompted pace,led 3f out,drew clear 1-1/2f out,handily*

Disturbingthepeace

Own: Milch David S. and Rita and Herrick R

B. g. 6 (Mar)
Sire: Bold Badgett (Damascus) $2,500
Dam: Regal Riot (Sovereign Dancer)
Br: Old English Rancho & Patsy McKuen (Cal)
Tr: Vienna Darrell(0 0 0 0 .00) 2003:(303 51 .17)

Life	22	8	4	4	$662,780	111	D.Fst	19	8	4	2	$634,300	111
2003	6	1	0	2	$142,000	106	Wet(350)	1	0	0	1	$22,000	105
2002	9	6	0	1	$452,640	111	Turf(272)	2	0	0	1	$6,480	82
	0	0	0	0	$0	-	Dst(0)	0	0	0	0	$0	-

17Aug03–8Dmr fst 7f :221 :44 1:081 1:212 3↑ POBrienH-G2 **106** 1 5 4¾ 1hd 12½ 12 Espinoza V LB116 6.20 95–09 Dsturbngthpc1162 RshntoAltr1174½ FllMoonMdnss119½ Inside duel,clear 10
26Jly03–6Dmr fst 6f :214 :44 :553 1:074 3↑ BCrsbBCH-G2 **97** 6 6 73¼ 63 66¼ 67¼ Espinoza V LB118 7.10 95–07 BeausTown1191½ CptinSquire117nk Bluesthestndrd1172 3wd,4wd,no rally 9
10May03–6Hol fst 6f :212 :432 :554 1:082 3↑ LATimesH-G3 **101** 1 5 45 43 42½ 42 Espinoza V LB120 b *1.10e 96–11 HombreRapido1161 Publication1161 Giovnnetti116hd Rail trip,no late bid 8
Previously trained by Vienna Darrell
30Mar03♦Chukyo (Jpn) fm *6f Ⓣ LH 1:08 4↑ Takamatsunomiya Kinen-G1 Stk 1498000 134¾ Take Y 126 10.20 Believe1211 Sunningdale1261¼ Rikiai Taikan126nk 18
Rated in 10th,outfinished.Air Thule 16th,Echo Eddie 17th
Previously trained by Vienna Darrell
22Feb03–9Lrl sly 7f :222 :461 1:093 1:22 3↑ GenGrgeH-G2 **105** 7 21 1hd 3nk 34¼ Fogelsonger R L118 b 3.80 93–14 MyCousinMtt1133 PeepingTom1141¼ Disturbingthepec118nk Dueled 2wd 11
26Jan03–7SA fst 6f :212 :434 :552 1:074 4↑ PlsVrdsH-G2 **104** 1 5 2½ 22 22½ 35 Espinoza V LB120 b 2.40 94–10 Avnzdo1164½ MllowFllow117½ Disturbingthpc120nk Off bit slow,weakened 6

Domestic Dispute

Own: Bienstock Dave and Winner, Charles

Ch. c. 4 (Mar)
Sire: Unbridled's Song (Unbridled) $100,000
Dam: Majestical Moment (Magesterial)
Br: Gary Garber (Ky)
Tr: Gallagher Patrick(0 0 0 0 .00) 2003:(238 24 .10)

Life	14	2	2	2	$289,687	103	D.Fst	11	2	2	2	$275,687	103
2003	8	1	0	1	$155,367	103	Wet(339)	2	0	0	0	$5,000	97
2002	6	1	2	1	$134,320	96	Turf(312)	1	0	0	0	$9,000	90
	0	0	0	0	$0	-	Dst(0)	0	0	0	0	$0	-

26Dec03–8SA fst 7f :222 :45 1:091 1:223 Malibu-G1 **95** 5 11 107¼ 97¼ 87½ 64¾ Solis A LB117 42.40 88–12 Southern Image115hd MarinoMarini1151 MidasEyes1193 Waited into lane 12
4Oct03–4SA fm 1⅛ Ⓣ :494 1:141 1:371 1:484 OakTrDby-G2 **90** 2 11 12 1½ 2½ 41¾ Solis A LB118 8.00 83–14 Devious Boy118hd *Sweet Return*118nk Urban King1181½ Inside,wkened late 5
1Sep03–11Pha sly 1⅛ :463 1:104 1:361 1:49 PaDerby-G3 **78** 9 52¼ 64¼ 85¼ 813 918¼ Nakatani C S L122 8.20 81–16 Grand Hombre1145¼ Gimmeawink1222 Ashmore114nk Chased pace, tired 10
3May03–10CD fst 1¼ :461 1:102 1:353 2:01 KyDerby-G1 **95** 10 74½ 53½ 74½ 75½ 109½ Solis A L126 44.00 85–06 *Funny Cide*1261¾ *Empire Maker*126hd Peace Rules126hd Between,5w,empty 16
Previously trained by Baffert Bob
19Apr03–8Kee fst 1 1/16 :23 :47 1:113 1:452 ClmrLex-G2 **95** 5 64¼ 73¼ 42½ 42 33¼ Bailey J D L116 3.70 77–22 Scrimshw1163 EyeofthTigr116nk DomsticDisput116nk 5w trip,no late gain 7
5Apr03–6SA fst 1⅛ :454 1:10 1:36 1:491 SADerby-G1 **95** 9 41¼ 32 31 32½ 55½ Nakatani C S LB122 10.30 82–14 Buddy Gil122hd IndianExpress1222¼ Kafwain1221¼ Bid 3wd,vied,weakened 9
16Mar03–5SA gd 1 1/16 :224 :462 1:104 1:433 SnFelipe-G2 **97** 6 82¾ 83¾ 42½ 52 53 Bailey J D LB122 *2.00 83–19 *BuddyGil*119no Atswhatimtalknbout116¾ Brncusi1161¼ 4wd 1/4, no late bid 10
18Jan03–7SA fst 1 1/16 :23 :462 1:101 1:421 StCtlina-G2 **103** 8 63½ 63¾ 42½ 2hd 13 Flores D R LB113 2.90 93–15 DomesticDispute1133 OurBobbyV1133½ Scrimshw1154 3wd into lane,clear 8

Dr. Brendler
Own: O'Toole Francis J

B. h. 6 (Apr)
Sire: Distant View (Mr. Prospector) $20,000
Dam: Lady of Vision*Ire (Vision)
Br: Francis J. O'Toole (Md)
Tr: Motion H. G(0 0 0 0 .00) 2003:(318 55 .17)

Life	29	5	3	3	$377,517	104	D.Fst	0	0	0	0	$0 –
2003	8	2	1	1	$259,935	104	Wet(272)	1	0	0	1	$5,390 83
2002	9	2	1	1	$71,916	96	Turf(278)	28	5	3	2	$372,127 104
	0	0	0	0	$0	–	Dst(0)	0	0	0	0	$0 –

9Aug03–9Sar gd 1½ Ⓣ :49 1:13 2:031 2:28 3↑ SwrdDncH-G1 101 3 119¾ 107¾ 73¼ 52¼ 53¼ Guidry M L116 12.40 77–20 WhitmoresConn1151¼ Macaw114nk SlewVlley114¾ 6 wide move, weakened 11
5Jly03–8AP gd 1½ ⓣ :494 1:151 2:04 2:281 3↑ StrStBCH-G3 99 3 75 76¼ 53½ 41¾ 2½ Bourque C C L118 2.70 95–04 Ballingarry121½ DrBrendler1182½ JacksOwnTime112¾ Split horses, missed 9
7Jun03–10Bel sf 1¼ Ⓣ :534 1:203 1:472 2:14 3↑ ManhttnH-G1 104 5 98¾ 84¾ 83 64¼ 31¾ Stevens G L L116 22.30 22–57 Denon122½ Requete1161¼ Dr. Brendler1161 Good finish outside 10
17May03–10Pim sf 1⅛ ⓣ :531 1:183 1:442 1:573 3↑ CitgoDix-G2 99 6 66 65½ 53 1½ 1½ Dominguez R A L117 18.70 52–49 Dr. Brendler117½ *PerfectSoul*1173½ Sardaukar117no Settled,4wd run,drivng 6
5Apr03–4Kee fm 1½ ⓣ :501 1:152 2:054 2:303 4↑ Alw 56713N3X 95 1 54 42 4nk 1hd 1¾ Velazquez J R L116 3.30 87–16 *Dr. Brendler*116¾ SpeedofLight1161½ OnlycookHalfOfit1113¾ 4w, stiff drive 6
21Mar03–8GP fm *1 1/16 ⓣ :241 :492 1:131 1:442 4↑ Alw 40000N3X 93 10 97¼ 98 97¼ 64 42½ Guidry M L118 13.70 79–24 LovethGm1181¾ ThfullCircl122hd HndsomGorg118¾ Slow st, belated rally 10
2Mar03–8GP fm 1⅛ ⓣ :472 1:103 1:351 1:47 4↑ Alw 40000N3X 95 7 75¾ 67 64¾ 73¾ 52¼ Douglas R R L118 8.80 98–02 UnionPlce118no *LovetheGm*1201¾ FinlProphcy122nk 3 wide, mild response 9
18Jan03–9GP fm 1 ⓣ :241 :484 1:132 1:362 4↑ Alw 38000N3X 88 6 64 53 42 64¾ 62½ Douglas R R L118 9.80 81–12 BttrTlkNow120nk GoodBoySm118hd HndsomGrg118½ 4 wide, no response 10

Dream About
Own: Arosa Farms

Dk. b or b. f. 3 (Feb) OBSJUN03 $270,000
Sire: Cherokee Run (Runaway Groom) $20,000
Dam: Social Director (Deputy Minister)
Br: Windfields Farm Ltd (Ont-C)
Tr: Carroll Josie(0 0 0 0 .00) 2003:(273 47 .17)

Life	5	2	1	0	$224,430	85	D.Fst	5	2	1	0	$224,430 85
2003	5	2	1	0	$224,430	85	Wet(414)	0	0	0	0	$0 –
2002	0	M	0	0	$0	–	Turf(253)	0	0	0	0	$0 –
	0	0	0	0	$0	–	Dst(0)	0	0	0	0	$0 –

9Nov03–8WO fst 7f :22 :443 1:10 1:23 ⒻGlorisSong181k 25 1 6 2hd 2hd 715 726¾ Husbands P L119 *1.85 62–09 Silver Bird1164½ Duet1141½ Sweet Problem118hd Duel inside, gave way 7
12Oct03–8WO fst 1 1/16 :234 :471 1:122 1:484 ⒻⓇPrncssEliz250k 43 5 2½ 1½ 1hd 31½ 49¾ Husbands P L119 *.25 52–32 *My Vintage Port*1193¾ *Silver Bird*1195 Oblivious1191 Off rail weakened 6
20Sep03–8WO fst 1 1/16 :234 :481 1:123 1:472 ⒻMazarnBC-G2 85 4 11½ 12 13½ 18 18¼ Husbands P L117 *.55 69–29 DrmAbot1178¼ *AmrcAmrc*1158¼ BrshWthDstny1151½ 2-path,mild hand ride 5
29Aug03–5WO fst 7f :223 :45 1:094 1:233 ⒻMd Sp Wt 60k 82 6 5 1½ 1hd 18 18½ Landry R C L115 *.70 86–19 *Dream About*1158½ Mutual Affair115½ *Finnerty's Frolic*1149 3w, drew off 10
8Aug03–7WO fst 5f :221 :454 :581 ⒻMd Sp Wt 60k 69 2 4 62¾ 23 22½ 22½ Landry R C 115 *1.90 86–13 Ontheqt1152½ *Dream About*1154¼ Finnerty's Frolic114¾ Advance inside 6

Dress To Thrill (Ire)
Own: Moyglare Stud Farm Ltd

B. f. 5 (Feb)
Sire: Danehill (Danzig)
Dam: Trusted Partner (Affirmed)
Br: Moyglare Stud Farm Ltd (Ire)
Tr: Clement Christophe(0 0 0 0 .00) 2003:(389 75 .19)

Life	14	7	1	0	$777,158	105	D.Fst	0	0	0	0	$0 –
2003	5	1	0	0	$187,780	99	Wet(294)	0	0	0	0	$0 –
2002	6	5	0	0	$506,918	105	Turf(341)	14	7	1	0	$777,158 105
	0	0	0	0	$0	–	Dst(0)	0	0	0	0	$0 –

30Nov03–6Hol fm 1 ⓣ :232 :464 1:102 1:342 3↑ ⒻMatriarc-G1 82 10 52½ 51¾ 51¾ 105 129½ Valenzuela P A LB123 15.50 83–17 HeatHze123nk MusiclChimes120no Dediction123½ 4wd bid 2nd turn,wkend 14
27Sep03–8Bel fm 1¼ Ⓣ :494 1:144 1:39 2:023 3↑ ⒻFlwrBlIv-G1 99 3 21½ 21 1½ 1hd 42¼ Nakatani C S L120 10.10 79–17 Dimitrova1141 Wlzerkoenigin120no HetHze1231¼ Gave ground grudgingly 7
16Aug03–8AP gd 1 3/16 ⓣ :493 1:133 1:38 1:554 3↑ ⒻBeverlyD-G1 94 7 63½ 54½ 62 63¾ 64¾ Smullen P J L123 4.40 90–08 Heat Haze1231¼ *Bien Nicole*123½ Riskaverse1231½ 3-4 wide, outrun 7
12Jly03–9Cnl fm 1⅛ ⓣ :49 1:121 1:363 1:49 3↑ ⒻAlAlngBC-G3 95 4 11½ 11½ 11 1½ 1½ Prado E S L117 *.60 92–03 DressToThrill117½ LdyLind1171 LdyofthFutur1171 Unruly gate,drifted1/8 9
26May03–6Hol fm 1⅛ ⓣ :482 1:12 1:351 1:464+3↑ ⒻGamlyBCH-G1 98 5 21½ 21 21 31½ 54 Santos J A LB122 3.30 91–10 Tates Creek1221 Dublino122½ Megahertz118½ Pulled,stalked,wkened 6

Dublino

Own: Geringer Robert, Klein, Michael and N

Dk. b or b. m. 5 (Feb) KEESEP00 $180,000
Sire: Lear Fan (Roberto) $15,000
Dam: Tuscoga (Theatrical*Ire)
Br: Arthur B. Hancock III (Ky)
Tr: De Seroux Laura(0 0 0 0 .00) 2003:(111 14 .13)

Life	10	3	5	0	$570,057	106		
2003	5	1	3	0	$266,067	106		
2002	4	1	2	0	$291,607	97		
	0	0	0	0	$0	–		
D.Fst	0	0	0	0	$0	–		
Wet(316)	0	0	0	0	$0	–		
Turf(343)	10	3	5	0	$570,057	106		
Dst(0)	0	0	0	0	$0	–		

16Aug03-8AP gd 1 3/16 Ⓣ :493 1:133 1:38 1:554	3↑ⒻBeverlyD-G1	95	4	21½	22½	2½	21½	54	Desormeaux K J	L123	2.30	91-08	Heat Haze1231¼ *Bien Nicole*123½ Riskaverse1231½	Challenged, weakened	7		
26Jly03-8Dmr fm 1⅛ Ⓣ :501 1:144 1:373 1:49	3↑ⒻMbe/RnaH-G1	103	2	42½	42½	41½	42	2½	•Desormeaux K J	LB121	3.40	87-08	Megahertz116½ DH *Tates Creek*123 DH Dublino1212	Bid btwn,gamely	5		
28Jun03-8Hol fm 1¼ Ⓣ :502 1:134 1:364 2:004	3↑ⒻBevHilsH-G2	104	1	33½	27	23	11½	2¾	Espinoza V	LB122	*1.00	87-13	*Voodoo Dancer*120¾ Dublino1222½ *Megahertz*1171	Came out,led,caught	5		
26May03-6Hol fm 1⅛ Ⓣ :482 1:12 1:351 1:464+	3↑ⒻGamlyBCH-G1	105	4	53½	43½	53½	41½	21	Desormeaux K J	LB122	*1.50	94-10	Tates Creek1221 Dublino122½ Megahertz118½	4wd into lane,rallied	6		
27Apr03-8Hol fm 1 Ⓣ :23 :462 1:101 1:333	3↑ⒻWilshirH-G3	106	6	63¼	52	32	1½	12½	Desormeaux K J	LB120	2.90e	96-12	Dublino1202½ Southern Oasis1161 Final Destination118½	Bid 3wd,led,clear	9		

During

Own: McIngvale James

Dk. b or b. c. 4 (Feb) KEESEP01 $350,000
Sire: Cherokee Run (Runaway Groom) $20,000
Dam: Blading Saddle (Blade)
Br: Gulf States Racing Stables II (Ky)
Tr: Baffert Bob(0 0 0 0 .00) 2003:(674 127 .19)

Life	13	5	2	1	$514,750	106
2003	13	5	2	1	$514,750	106
2002	0	M	0	0	$0	–
	0	0	0	0	$0	–
D.Fst	9	4	1	1	$427,670	104
Wet(379)	4	1	1	0	$87,080	106
Turf(255)	0	0	0	0	$0	–
Dst(0)	0	0	0	0	$0	–

28Nov03-11CD sly 1⅛ :481 1:13 1:384 1:522	3↑ClarkH-G2	–	9	21½	2½	2½	1318	-	Santos J A	L117 b	5.20	- 27	D Evening Attire118no Quest1143¼ Aeneas1141¼	Gave way, eased late	14
29Oct03-8Aqu my 1⅛ :47 1:112 1:372 1:51	DiscvryH-G3	106	2	21½	2½	2hd	2hd	1no	Santos J A	L120 b	5.20	81-27	During120no UnforgettableMx1141¾ Inmorto1144¼	Gamely inside, prevail	8
13Sep03-8Bel fst 1 :222 :45 1:093 1:361	JeromeH-G2	99	7	3½	3½	1½	11½	1¾	Santos J A	L118 b	6.60	85-19	*During*118¾ Tafaseel1144¾ Pretty Wild1161¼	3 wide move, gamely	9
23Aug03-10Sar fst 7f :213 :433 1:083 1:22	KngsBshp-G1	102	10	2	21½	22½	21½	42¼	Velasquez C	L123 b	31.50	95-07	VlidVideo121nk GretNotion117nk *Ghostzpper*1171¾	Chased 3 wide, weaken	13
3Aug03-9Sar fst 1⅛ :47 1:103 1:35 1:48	JimDandy-G2	92	3	2½	21½	33	612	611	Day P	L121 b	23.60	84-11	Strong Hope121nk Empire Maker1232½ Congrats1151	Speed outside, tired	6
13Jly03-6Hol fst 1⅛ :48 1:113 1:362 1:491	Swaps-G2	96	4	11	11	11	3nk	1hd	Bailey J D	LB115 b	8.20	88-07	During115hd *TenMostWnted*122¾ DH EyeofthTigr118	Inside,headed,gamely	6
14Jun03-7CD fst 1 :22 :44 1:084 1:343	NrthrnDncr111k	99	1	1hd	1hd	41¾	43½	32¾	Velasquez C	L114 b	2.60	91-04	Champali1222 Lone Star Sky120¾ *During*114hd	Gamely held third	8
17May03-9Pim gd 1 1/16 :224 :463 1:114 1:434	SirBarton100k	94	2	2hd	21	1hd	22	23	Day P	L115 b	*1.40	85-12	Best Minister1153 During115½ PenobscotBay11512¾	Duel 2wd 5/16,held wll	5
12Apr03-7Aqu my 7f :214 :443 1:10 1:23	BayShore-G3	65	3	8	3½	53½	710	714¼	Stevens G L	L118 b	*2.00	74-13	HaloHomewrecker1161 DonSix1165¼ Stanislvsky116¾	Chased inside, tired	11
12Mar03-4SA fst 1 :23 :47 1:104 1:36	OClm 80000N	103	3	21	2hd	2hd	1½	1¾	Stevens G L	LB118 b	*.60	91-13	During118¾ Touch the Wire1183½ Special Rate1186	Bid, edged away, held	5
20Feb03-2SA fst 1 1/16 :23 :462 1:101 1:414	Alw 56000N1x	104	5	21	21	2½	1½	2¾	Espinoza V	LB118 b	7.90	94-15	Atswhtmtlknbot118¾ *Drng*1183½ BckIndMnor1202½	Led into lane,2nd best	5
1Feb03-6SA fst 6½f :213 :442 1:092 1:16	Md Sp Wt 48k	94	6	3	2hd	2hd	2½	12	Espinoza V	LB120 b	6.40	93-07	During1202 Grinding It Out1201½ *Popularize*120hd	Dueled btwn,gamely	11
4Jan03-6SA fst 6f :212 :442 :57 1:101	Md Sp Wt 48k	78	6	5	31½	42	42	53½	Bailey J D	LB120	5.00e	83-11	Atswhtmtlknbot120½ *BckIndMnor*120½ MchoImg1201	Angled in, weakened	11

Dyna Da Wyna
Own: WinStar Farm LLC

Gr/ro. f. 4 (May)
Sire: Doc's Leader (Mr. Leader) $5,000
Dam: Dyna Peak (Dynaformer)
Br: Alan M. Klein (Ky)
Tr: Walden W. E(0 0 0 0 .00) 2003:(289 67 .23)

Life	11	5	0	1	$222,277	94	D.Fst	1	0	0	1	$5,760	80
2003	9	5	0	0	$216,517	94	Wet(308)	1	0	0	0	$4,250	74
2002	2	M	0	1	$5,760	80	Turf(356)	9	5	0	0	$212,267	94
	0	0	0	0	$0	–	Dst(0)	0	0	0	0	$0	–

22Nov03–9CD fm	1⅛ Ⓣ :491 1:134 1:381 1:502 3↑	ⒻCardinlH-G3	89	6 2hd 22 31½ 33½ 55¾	Day P	L115 f	6.20	76–24	Riskaverse118¾ Bien Nicole1204 Firth of Lorne1161	4w lane,flatten out	12
18Oct03–9Kee fm	1 1/16 Ⓣ :232 :481 1:132 1:432	ⒻVllyView-G3	94	6 33 31½ 31½ 2½ 1¾	Day P	L119 f	3.50	84–17	Dyna Da Wyna119¾ MexicanMoonlight1163 Derrianne123½	4w,steady drive	10
20Sep03–9LaD fm	1 1/16 Ⓣ :233 :474 1:12 1:431	ⒻDeBrtOaks75k	89	7 21 32½ 32 2½ 1hd	Day P	L118 f	*.90	92–07	*DynaDaWyna*118hd TivsLittleSis120¾ TincnToo1171	Moved inside, just up	9
29Aug03–5Sar fm	1 🅃 :234 :471 1:113 1:352	ⒻClm 100000(100–75)	87	7 2½ 24½ 21 1hd 12¾	Day P	L120 f	*1.85	94–10	*DynDWyn*120¾ Onmorfshn1122½ Cndybdndy115½	Drew clear when roused	10
2Aug03–9EIP my	1 ⊗ :233 :463 1:124 1:392	ⒻAudubonOak75k	74	10 64¾ 74¾ 54¼ 43½ 45½	Blanc B	L117 f	6.60	77–20	Keiai Sakura1191¼ Evil Eye Aly1152 Dress to Impress1192¼	4-5 wide trip	10
14Jun03–8CD fm	1⅛ Ⓣ :471 1:114 1:362 1:483	ⒻRegret-G3	83	11 31 34 32½ 21½ 54	Sellers S J	L116 f	26.70	87–10	SndSprings1183 PersonlLegend116½ Achnshen116hd	Inside,flattened out	12
18May03–7CD gd	1 1/16 Ⓣ :23 :471 1:122 1:433	ⒻAlw 43500N1x	83	3 31½ 44 2hd 21 1nk	Day P	L113 f	*2.10	86–12	Dyna Da Wyna113nk Sweet Trip115nk Radiantly120¾	Bmp start,5w,driving	12
5Apr03–6Kee fm	1⅛ Ⓣ :474 1:124 1:38 1:51	ⒻAlw 56000N1x	74	8 2hd 2½ 42½ 55 53½	McKee J5	L118 f	5.00	78–16	Seattle Tac120¾ Plait1201¼ Angliana Dancer118nk	Drift out start,tired	9
Previously trained by Machowsky Michael											
26Jan03–6SA fm	*6½f Ⓣ :213 :434 1:064 1:124	ⒻMd Sp Wt 48k	83	9 1 11 1hd 11 11	Espinoza V	LB120 f	*1.90	93–05	Dyna Da Wyna1201 Quero Quero1203½ *Bruheria*1201½	Dueled, held game	10

Dynever
Own: Wills Catherine and Karches, Peter

Dk. b or b. c. 4 (Mar)
Sire: Dynaformer (Roberto) $50,000
Dam: Flamboyance (Zilzal)
Br: Catherine Wills (Ky)
Tr: Clement Christophe(0 0 0 0 .00) 2003:(389 75 .19)

Life	9	3	3	1	$1,154,020	116	D.Fst	7	3	3	1	$1,094,020	116
2003	9	3	3	1	$1,154,020	116	Wet(332)	2	0	0	0	$60,000	98
2002	0	M	0	0	$0	–	Turf(328)	0	0	0	0	$0	–
	0	0	0	0	$0	–	Dst(0)	0	0	0	0	$0	–

25Oct03–9SA fst	1¼ :461 1:101 1:341 1:594 3↑	BCClasic-G1	116	6 98¾ 910 67 43½ 32¼	Nakatani C S	LB121	15.20	104–07	Pleasantly Perfect1261½ Medagliad'Oro126¾ Dynever121nk	Pinched break	10
3Oct03–8Med fst	1⅛ :464 1:10 1:341 1:464 3↑	MedBC-G2	106	5 63½ 63 32½ 21 21¾	Nakatani C S	L120	1.80	96–08	BowmnsBnd1191¾ Dynevr1203 🄳UnforgttblMx116nk	Outside,aim,even fin	6
1Sep03–11Pha sly	1⅛ :463 1:104 1:361 1:49	PaDerby-G3	88	7 95¾ 95¼ 62¾ 57 612	Prado E S	L122	*1.50	87–16	GrandHombre1145¼ Gimmeawink1222 Ashmore114nk	Squeezed back start	10
9Aug03–8Mnr fst	1⅛ :472 1:104 1:343 1:461	WVDerby-G3	114	1 53¼ 42½ 21 1hd 2nk	Prado E S	LB117	*1.20	105– -	Soto111nk Dynever1175¼ *Colita*1111½	Abreast foe, out gamed	9
7Jun03–11Bel sly	1½ :483 1:132 2:023 2:281	Belmont-G1	98	5 43 51¾ 46 48 410¼	Prado E S	L126	8.50	81–14	EmpireMker126¾ TenMostWntd1264¼ FunnyCid1265¼	Brushed start, tired	6
10May03–8LS fst	1⅛ :472 1:113 1:373 1:502	LnStrDby-G3	98	4 84¼ 64¼ 63¾ 52½ 11½	Prado E S	L122	*.30	97–16	Dynever1221½ MostFeared1221 CommandersAffir1221½	Blocked 1/4 to 1/8	12
5Apr03–11GP fst	1 1/16 :224 :462 1:113 1:43	Aventura250k	101	3 77¾ 77½ 3½ 2hd 13¼	Prado E S	L122	*.90	94–10	*Dynever*1223¼ Supah Blitz1226½ Massive1221	5 wide, gamely	9
8Mar03–4GP fst	170 :233 :473 1:11 1:401	Md Sp Wt 34k	94	6 21½ 21 1hd 11½ 18¼	Prado E S	L122	*.70	100–04	*Dynever*1228¼ Stone Canyon1221¾ Tempered Steel1222	Rail trip, drew off	9
8Feb03–1GP fst	7f :224 :453 1:102 1:224	Md Sp Wt 34k	87	9 7 85¼ 97¾ 46½ 21¾	Prado E S	122	22.20	92–08	*Nacheezmo*1221¾ *Dynever*1223 Stone Canyon1222	Awkward start, 4 wide	9

Eagle Lake
Own: Turf Express Inc

Dk. b or b. m. 6 (Apr)
Sire: Desert Royalty (Desert Wine) $1,000
Dam: Great Notrariety (Great Above)
Br: Robert Norman & Patricia Norman (Tex)
Tr: Norman Cole(0 0 0 0 .00) 2003:(1086 290 .27)

Life	43	13	10	1	$477,877	103	D.Fst	21	4	6	0	$145,320	98
2003	11	4	3	0	$238,874	98	Wet(321)	8	2	1	0	$62,897	103
2002	11	5	0	1	$111,499	97	Turf(322)	14	7	3	1	$269,660	97
	0	0	0	0	$0	-	Dst(0)	0	0	0	0	$0	-

26Dec03-9FG	fm	*1	Ⓣ :224 :461 1:111 1:36	3↑ⒻFurlSail60k	84	2	12½	12½	11½	2hd	76¼	Melancon G	L117 b	5.60	98-05	Bedanken1191 Flager117hd Due to Win Again1152¾	Set pace, gave way	13
15Nov03-6Hou	fm	1 1/16	Ⓣ :244 :50 1:144 1:46	3↑ⒻⓈSanJacinto50k	86	7	11½	12½	11½	1½	2nk	Melancon G	L123 b	*.20	87-20	BurninMemories118nk EagleLke1231¼ PromDte1154¾	In hand, outfinished	8
4Oct03-7Ret	fm	1	Ⓣ :224 :462 1:101 1:342	3↑ⒻⓈFiestaMile35k	93	2	14	12	12	12½	12½	Melancon G	L122 b	*.40	101 -	EagleLke1222½ LdyMllory1196 MinnepolisBbe1141½	In hand, drew off late	6
13Sep03-8Ret	fst	7f	:22 :443 1:10 1:231	3↑ⒻTxStallion42k	79	4	1	13	15½	21½	210¾	Gondron T D	L122 b	*.80	92-10	Lady Mallory11810¾ *Eagle Lake*1225¼ Hay Allison1185	Fast pace, gave way	6
11Jly03-9LS	fm	1 1/16	Ⓣ :232 :482 1:121 1:432	3↑ⒻAlw 38000NC	85	2	13	1½	1½	2hd	42½	Melancon G	L122 b	*.60	84-16	Janeian1221¼ AcademicAngel122nk *GoldenRhythm*1221	Gave way final 1/16	8
28Jun03-6LS	fst	1	:233 :462 1:102 1:363	3↑ⒻⓈAlBoganMem75k	98	1	11	12	11½	12	13¾	Melancon G	L123 b	*.90	90-14	Eagle Lake1233¾ Coastalota123hd Halo Tyra1188	Drew clear, ridden out	6
26May03-10LS	sf	1	Ⓣ :24 :492 1:154 1:43	3↑ⒻWnStDstH-G3	95	3	12½	14	12	13	12¼	Melancon G	L116 b	8.00	57-48	*EagleLake*1162¼ LittleTresure117¾ *MgicMission*1161½	Responded well, held	9
2May03-7LS	fst	1	⊗ :233 :471 1:121 1:382	4↑ⒻAlw 42500NC	82	4	11	12½	12	11	21½	Melancon G	L119 b	3.20	80-23	BienNicole122½ *EagleLke*119nk CherylvilleSlew1225¾	Clear,overtaken late	5
10Apr03-9LS	fm	1	Ⓣ :244 :484 1:124 1:364	4↑ⒻAlw 37000N1Y	90	6	12½	11½	11½	12	12½	Melancon G	L122 b	2.00	88-15	EagleLake1222½ Strawbailey119¾ DistantValley1161	Well rated,ridden out	7
15Mar03-10P	fst	1 1/16	:223 :461 1:11 1:433	4↑ⒻAlw 36000N2M	67	1	1½	11	11	33½	519	Theriot H J II	L121 b	1.70	73-14	*McKinney*1156 See How She Runs1142¾ Yalta1177½	Bobbled, quick pace	5
15Feb03-9OP	my	1 1/16	:233 :482 1:14 1:481	4↑ⒻPippin50k	84	2	12	11½	11	21½	65	Theriot H J II	L121 b	3.20	64-31	Red n'Gold114½ Reason to Talk118½ McKinney115½	Gave way drive	8

Ebony Breeze
Own: Kinsman Stable

B. f. 4 (Jan)
Sire: Belong to Me (Danzig) $22,008
Dam: Valid Carnauba (Valid Appeal)
Br: Kinsman Farm (Ky)
Tr: Mott William I(0 0 0 0 .00) 2003:(718 138 .19)

Life	13	5	3	3	$403,797	102	D.Fst	9	5	3	1	$381,472	102
2003	8	4	1	2	$365,887	102	Wet(364)	1	0	0	1	$4,950	76
2002	5	1	2	1	$37,910	93	Turf(298)	3	0	0	1	$17,375	86
	0	0	0	0	$0	-	Dst(0)	0	0	0	0	$0	-

10Oct03-9Kee	fst	7f	:214 :441 1:092 1:213	ⒻRavenRun-G3	96	10	8	73¼	54½	21½	22½	Velasquez C	L123	4.80	93-11	Yell1232½ Ebony Breeze1233¾ *Tina Bull*117no	5w bid,2ndbest	12
23Aug03-7Sar	fst	6f	:22 :45 :564 1:093	ⒻVctoryRide76k	92	9	5	62¾	31	31½	31¼	Velasquez C	L122	*3.15	93-07	CountryRomnc116½ ShsZlous114¾ EbonyBrz1222½	Chased 4 wide, gamely	9
12Jly03-9Crc	fst	6f	:212 :444 :572 1:104	ⒻAzaleaBC-G3	102	1	13	41½	21½	2hd	14¼	Velasquez C	L118	9.10	90-11	Ebony Breeze1184¼ Storm Flag1162¾ Crafty Brat1162¾	Off rail, drew clear	13
21May03-7CD	gd	1 1/16	Ⓣ :224 :452 1:101 1:42	ⒻAlw 65300NC	83	2	66½	58½	46½	32½	42¾	Day P	L118	*2.00	91-11	*Sand Springs*1181¾ Keiai Sakura118½ Achnasheen118½	4w lane,empty	7
2May03-5CD	fm	1	Ⓣ :231 :464 1:113 1:351	ⒻEdgewood113k	86	3	23½	27	31½	32½	3½	Guidry M	L120	*1.80	95-03	ForestShdows116nk UnbridledFemme116nk EbonyBrz120½	4-5w,slow gain	6
16Mar03-12Tam	fst	1 1/16	:24 :484 1:133 1:451	ⒻFlaOaks-G3	89	2	1½	2hd	2hd	2hd	1½	Guidry M	L120	*.30	92-06	EbonyBreeze120½ DkotLight122hd CrimsonndRoss1165	Long drive, all out	6
1Feb03-10Tam	fst	7f	:223 :463 1:12 1:25	ⒻGasparilla50k	84	11	9	86	73	1hd	11¾	Judice J C	L122	*.80	88-16	*EbonyBreeze*1221¾ CrimsonandRoses1161¾ Splash1161	Split h,dueled,clear	11
11Jan03-10Tam	fst	6f	:223 :462 :59 1:112	ⒻSandpiper50k	86	5	7	72¼	63¼	11	16¾	Rodriguez P A	L116	3.60	93-14	*EbonyBreeze*1166¾ OzildsNncyL1221 LvndrLss1201	Bid four wide drew off	12

El Dorado Shooter

Own: DeLima Barbara

Ch. h. 7 (Mar)
Sire: Man From Eldorado (Mr. Prospector) $1,500
Dam: Maui Lyphear J.*Jpn (Lypheor*GB)
Br: Clifford DeLima (Cal)
Tr: DeLima Clifford(0 0 0 0 .00) 2003:(178 18 .10)

Life	23	12	5	1	$529,740	116	D.Fst	20	9	5	1	$413,390	104
2003	5	3	2	0	$211,950	102	Wet(323)	3	3	0	0	$116,350	116
2002	6	1	2	0	$81,950	99	Turf(321)	0	0	0	0	$0	–
	0	0	0	0	$0	–	Dst(0)	0	0	0	0	$0	–

7Jun03-3BM	fst	6f	:21^{3}	:43^{2}	:55^{3}	1:08^{3}	3↑ BMBCSprH-G3	**102**	6	1	1^{1}	1^{2}	1^{4}	1$^{4\frac{3}{4}}$	Schvaneveldt C P	**LB**120	2.30	96-12	ElDoradoShooter120$^{4\frac{3}{4}}$ HaloCat118$^{1\frac{1}{4}}$ RadrContct116$^{1\frac{1}{2}}$	Quickest, driving	6
18May03-2BM	fst	6f	:21^{3}	:43^{1}	:55^{1}	1:08^{2}	3↑ SaratogaH73k	**101**	5	3	1^{hd}	1^{3}	1^{6}	1^{6}	Baze R A	**LB**121	*.60	97-14	*ElDoradoShooter*121^{6} RdrContct116^{no} *MyCptin*115$^{1\frac{1}{2}}$	Sluggish start,driving	5
22Mar03-4GG	fst	6f	:21	:42^{4}	:54^{4}	1:08	3↑ DanvilleH67k	**102**	6	1	2^{2}	2^{2}	2^{1}	2^{nk}	Baze R A	**LB**121	*.70	97-11	*PresidioHights*115^{nk} *ElDordoShootr*121^{3} TxsChili115^{2}	Stalked, held off late	6
22Feb03-3GG	fst	6f	:21	:43	:55^{2}	1:09	3↑ Ⓢ KenMadySpH97k	**91**	2	2	1^{hd}	1^{hd}	1$^{\frac{1}{2}}$	1^{hd}	Baze R A	**LB**118	1.80	92-11	ElDordoShootr118^{hd} *Giovnntt*116^{hd} RdrContct116$^{\frac{3}{4}}$	Dueled, dug in gamely	5
19Jan03-3GG	fst	6f	:21^{2}	:43^{2}	:55^{1}	1:07^{3}	4↑ MontclairH67k	**102**	4	1	2^{hd}	1^{hd}	2^{hd}	2^{3}	Krigger K	**LB**120	*1.20	96-13	*HaloCat*118^{3} *ElDoradoShooter*120$^{3\frac{1}{2}}$ RdrContct116^{1}	Dueled,caught,held 2d	5

El Prado Essence

Own: Cappuccitti Ford

Ch. m. 7 (Mar)
Sire: El Prado*Ire (Sadler's Wells) $30,000
Dam: Quadrahope (Quadratic)
Br: Kenneth C. Duncan & Neil R. Phelps (Ky)
Tr: Robillard Joshua(0 0 0 0 .00) 2003:(363 28 .08)

Life	30	10	8	3	$800,246	103	D.Fst	22	7	7	3	$523,632	103
2003	7	2	2	0	$220,108	97	Wet(362)	5	3	1	0	$273,374	97
2002	8	2	3	0	$254,932	93	Turf(268)	3	0	0	0	$3,240	63
	0	0	0	0	$0	–	Dst(0)	0	0	0	0	$0	–

15Dec03-9Mnr	fst	6f	:22^{1}	:46	:59^{2}	1:14^{1}	3↑ Ⓕ Alw 41600NC	**23**	2	5	5^{8}	5^{14}	5^{18}	5$^{26\frac{1}{4}}$	Walker B J Jr	**LB**115 b	*1.00	42-38	FthrMrn116$^{4\frac{1}{2}}$ JstMchl116$^{3\frac{1}{4}}$ AbndntlyBlssd116$^{12\frac{3}{4}}$	Stumbled,trailed,wide	5
Previously trained by Mattine Tony																						
16Nov03-8WO	fst	7f	:22^{3}	:45^{4}	1:11	1:24	3↑ Ⓕ BessarbH-G3	**82**	5	4	6^{2}	4$^{1\frac{1}{2}}$	3$^{\frac{1}{2}}$	2^{1}	Husbands P	**L**120 b	3.90	83-18	WinterGrden121^{1} ElPrdoEssenc120$^{1\frac{1}{4}}$ MillFvill115^{5}	Stlk 4w,bid 3w,2nd bst	7
Previously trained by Cappuccitti Audre																						
21Sep03-6WO	fst	7f	:22^{3}	:46	1:11^{1}	1:24	3↑ Ⓕ Alw 78500N$Y	**82**	6	5	4$^{1\frac{1}{2}}$	3^{1}	4^{2}	5^{5}	Husbands P	**L**120 b	*2.50	79-20	*WintrGrdn*117^{hd} *OnforRos*120$^{1\frac{1}{2}}$ MystriousAffr120$^{3\frac{1}{4}}$	Stalk duel 4w,mild bid	8
31Aug03-8WO	fst	7f	:22^{3}	:45^{2}	1:10^{3}	1:24^{2}	3↑ Ⓕ Seaway173k	**89**	5	4	6$^{2\frac{1}{4}}$	5$^{2\frac{1}{4}}$	3$^{1\frac{1}{2}}$	2$^{1\frac{1}{4}}$	Husbands P	**L**119 b	4.65	81-27	BrssnPockt121$^{1\frac{1}{4}}$ ElPrdEssnc119^{nk} Whlthrnsht115$^{1\frac{1}{4}}$	Stalk duel 2-pth,bid	8
22Jun03-3WO	fst	7f	:22	:44^{3}	1:09^{2}	1:22	3↑ Ⓕ SwtBriarTo108k	**83**	3	6	6$^{4\frac{1}{2}}$	4^{1}	5$^{4\frac{1}{2}}$	5$^{9\frac{1}{2}}$	Husbands P	**L**124 b	1.85	84-09	HrmonyLodge117$^{5\frac{1}{2}}$ *WinterGrden*115^{1} *ActingDputy*117$^{\frac{3}{4}}$	Advance inside, bid	6
11May03-8WO	gd	6½f	:21^{3}	:43^{4}	1:08^{4}	1:15^{3}	4↑ Ⓕ GCHndriH-G3	**97**	3	10	7$^{1\frac{3}{4}}$	4$^{1\frac{3}{4}}$	1^{1}	1^{4}	Husbands P	**L**120 b	3.30	97-09	ElPrdoEssence120^{4} LedingRol115$^{\frac{1}{2}}$ *BrssinPockt*120$^{1\frac{1}{4}}$	Stalk duel rail,rly 5w	11
27Apr03-8WO	fst	6½f	:22^{3}	:45^{3}	1:11	1:17^{3}	4↑ Ⓕ Alw 80900NC	**89**	5	3	4$^{4\frac{1}{4}}$	4^{4}	3^{1}	1$^{1\frac{3}{4}}$	Husbands P	**L**120 fb	3.05	87-18	*ElPrdEssnc*120$^{1\frac{3}{4}}$ MystrsAffr120^{nk} ActngDpty116$^{2\frac{1}{2}}$	Stalk duel 3w,drew out	6

Elloluv

Own: Reddam J. P

B. f. 4 (Feb) KEEAPR02 $120,000
Sire: Gilded Time (Timeless Moment) $15,000
Dam: Currency Quest (Cryptoclearance)
Br: North Wales LLC (Ky)
Tr: Dollase Craig(0 0 0 0 .00) 2003:(142 32 .23)

Life	11	4	3	1	$1,221,475	105	D.Fst	10	3	3	1	$1,196,875 105
2003	8	2	3	0	$978,775	105	Wet(361)	1	1	0	0	$24,600 92
2002	3	2	0	1	$242,700	94	Turf(250)	0	0	0	0	$0 –
	0	0	0	0	$0	–	Dst(0)	0	0	0	0	$0 –

27Dec03-7SA	fst	7f	:223 :452 1:091 1:213	ⒻLaBrea-G1	83	4	7	82	95¾	78¾	612	Nakatani C S	LB121	*1.20	86-10	IslndFshion1236 Rndroo1191½ Buffythecentrfold119½	4wd turn,no late bid	10
25Oct03-2SA	fst	1⅛	:47 1:11 1:354 1:49	3↑ⒻBCDistaf-G1	94	6	31	21	21½	22	24½	Nakatani C S	LB119	8.80	84-07	Adoration1234½ Elloluv1192½ Got Koko1233½	Stalked 3wd,2nd best	7
28Sep03-6SA	fst	1 1/16	:232 :471 1:111 1:424	3↑ⒻLdyScBCH-G2	104	6	33½	32	32	1½	2½	Nakatani C S	LB116	6.30	89-16	Got Koko118½ ⒹElloluv1161¾ Azeri1281	Drifted in, game	6
Disqualified and placed 4th																		
2May03-10CD	fst	1⅛	:46 1:10 1:353 1:483	ⒻKyOaks-G1	94	1	1½	11	1hd	2hd	44	Albarado R J	L121	2.70	91-07	*Bird Town*1213¼ Santa Catarina121hd Yell121¾	Duel,inside,weakened	12
5Apr03-8Kee	fst	1 1/16	:243 :483 1:122 1:432	ⒻAshland-G1	105	5	11	11	1½	12	13¾	Albarado R J	L120	2.10	90-20	Elloluv1203¾ Lady Tak123¾ Holiday Lady1165	Drft in bmp start,drvg	7
8Mar03-4SA	fst	1 1/16	:242 :482 1:114 1:431	ⒻSAOaks-G1	101	4	11	1½	1½	2hd	2¾	Valenzuela P A	LB117	1.60	87-14	Composure117¾ *Elloluv*1174½ Go for Glamour1177½	Fought back rail,game	5
9Feb03-7SA	fst	1	:241 :474 1:114 1:36	ⒻLsVrgnes-G1	96	3	1½	1hd	11½	11½	2nk	Valenzuela P A	LB122	1.30	91-12	*Composure*120nk Elloluv1223 Watching You1168	Drifted in 1/8,caught	6
20Jan03-3SA	fst	7f	:222 :451 1:10 1:23	ⒻSntaYnez-G2	94	5	2	3½	3nk	11	12½	Valenzuela P A	LB121	1.80	91-11	Elloluv1212½ Watching You1168 Himalayan1162	4wd,3wd,pulled clear	5

Empire Maker

Own: Juddmonte Farms Inc

Dk. b or b. c. 4 (Apr)
Sire: Unbridled (Fappiano) $200,000
Dam: Toussaud (El Gran Senor)
Br: Juddmonte Farms, Inc. (Ky)
Tr: Frankel Robert J(0 0 0 0 .00) 2003:(411 114 .28)

Life	8	4	3	1	$1,985,800	111	D.Fst	6	2	3	1	$935,800 110
2003	6	3	3	0	$1,936,200	111	Wet(385)	2	2	0	0	$1,050,000 111
2002	2	1	0	1	$49,600	92	Turf(305)	0	0	0	0	$0 –
	0	0	0	0	$0	–	Dst(0)	0	0	0	0	$0 –

3Aug03-9Sar	fst	1⅛	:47 1:103 1:35 1:48	JimDandy-G2	110	5	56	56½	53½	22	2nk	Bailey J D	L123 b	*.30	95-11	Strong Hope121nk Empire Maker1232½ Congrats1151	Game finish outside	6
7Jun03-11Bel	sly	1½	:483 1:132 2:023 2:281	Belmont-G1	110	1	21	2hd	11	11½	1¾	Bailey J D	L126 b	2.00	91-14	EmpirMkr126¾ TnMostWntd1264¼ FunnyCid1265¼	Stalked 4wide, gamely	6
3May03-10CD	fst	1¼	:461 1:102 1:353 2:01	KyDerby-G1	106	11	85½	84	31½	3½	21¾	Bailey J D	L126 b	*2.50	92-06	*Funny Cide*1261¾ *Empire Maker*126hd Peace Rules126hd	5w bid,2ndbest	16
12Apr03-8Aqu	my	1⅛	:471 1:11 1:354 1:483	WoodMem-G1	111	8	32½	32	31½	1hd	1½	Bailey J D	L123 b	*.55	93-12	Empire Maker123½ *Funny Cide*1237½ Kissin Saint1231	3 wide, drift in late	8
15Mar03-8GP	fst	1⅛	:461 1:103 1:36 1:49	FlaDerby-G1	108	6	42½	31½	21	1½	19¾	Bailey J D	L122 b	2.10	97-10	*Empire Maker*1229¾ Trust N Luck122½ Indy Dancer1222½	Drew off, driving	7
7Feb03-7SA	fst	1⅛	:461 1:102 1:353 1:481	ⓇSham81k	98	5	66½	75½	52¾	32	21	Bailey J D	LB115	*.40	92-11	ManAmongMen1201 *EmpireMaker*1152 Spensive1205½	Split foes,inside bid	7

Eurosilver
Own: Buckram Oak Farm

Dk. b or b. c. 3 (Feb)
Sire: Unbridled's Song (Unbridled) $100,000
Dam: Russian Tango (Nijinsky II)
Br: Buckram Oak Farm (Ky)
Tr: Zito Nicholas P(0 0 0 0 .00) 2003:(507 77 .15)

Life	3	2	1	0	$284,000	98	D.Fst	2	1	1	0	$257,000	98
2003	3	2	1	0	$284,000	98	Wet(323)	1	1	0	0	$27,000	96
2002	0	M	0	0	$0	-	Turf(354)	0	0	0	0	$0	-
	0	0	0	0	$0	-	Dst(0)	0	0	0	0	$0	-

4Oct03-6Kee fst 1 1/16 :224 :462 1:102 1:432 LnsEndFt-G2 **98** 10 6 3½ 7 3¾ 55 1½ 1 4¾ Castellano J J L121 11.90 90-20 Eurosilver121 4¾ Tiger Hunt121no Limehouse1211 Quick move, driving 11
1Sep03-3Sar gd 6½f :221 :46 1:111 1:18 Md Sp Wt 45k **96** 6 3 3 1½ 21 13 15¾ Castellano J J L119 *1.60 85-21 *Eurosilver*119 5¾ ExcitingMtro119 4½ *GrndScor*119 1½ Drew clear under drive 8
8Aug03-4Sar fst 7f :23 :461 1:11 1:234 Md Sp Wt 45k **63** 5 3 1hd 1hd 26 27½ Sellers S J L119 *1.65e 80-10 *Silver Wagon*119 7½ *Eurosilver*119 1¾ Apple Krisp119 1¼ Pace, second best 10

Evolving Tactics (Ire)
Own: Moyglare Stud Farm Ltd

B. c. 4 (Mar)
Sire: Machiavellian (Mr. Prospector)
Dam: Token Gesture*Ire (Alzao)
Br: Moyglare Stud Farm Ltd (Ire)
Tr: Weld Dermot K(0 0 0 0 .00) 2003:(8 3 .38)

Life	7	2	0	2	$181,852	94	D.Fst	0	0	0	0	$0	-
2003	6	2	0	2	$181,852	94	Wet(387)	0	0	0	0	$0	-
2002	1	M	0	0	$0	-	Turf(319)	7	2	0	2	$181,852	94
	0	0	0	0	$0	-	Dst(0)	0	0	0	0	$0	-

16Aug03-11AP gd 1¼ Ⓣ :491 1:14 1:384 2:022 Secretar-G1 **94** 3 6 4½ 10 3¾ 9 4¾ 4 4½ 6 6¾ Smullen P J L121 b 8.10 87-08 Kicken Kris116 3½ Joe Bear1162 Lismore Knight121nk Bid stretch, faltered 11
20Jly03-8AP gd 1 3/16 Ⓣ :51 1:17 1:412 1:59 AmercnDb-G2 **93** 5 2 2½ 22 21 2½ 1nk Smullen P J L117 *1.00 79-16 Evolving Tactics117nk Californian121 2¾ Scottago116 1½ All out, driving 5
19Jun03♦Ascot (GB) gf 1¼ Ⓣ RH 2:062 Hampton Court Stakes (Listed) Stk 83900 3 2¾ Smullen P J 123 5.00 Persian Majesty123nk Foodbroker Founder123 2½ *Evolving Tactics*123½ 11
Timeform rating: 104 *Mid-pack,3rd and bumped 1-1/2f out,stayed on.Great Pyramid 9th*
24May03♦Curragh (Ire) sf 1 Ⓣ Str 1:412 Irish 2000 Guineas-G1 Stk 473000 98 Smullen P J 126 16.00 Indian Haven1261 France126 2½ Tout Seul126½ 16
Timeform rating: 99 *Tracked leaders,weakened 1-1/2f out.Great Pyramid5th,Tomahawk11th*
21Apr03♦Cork (Ire) fm 1 Ⓣ RH 1:391 Newmarket Maiden Maiden 17400 12 Smullen P J 128 1.75 Evolving Tactics1282 Sharesha123 4½ Collectors Item128½ 10
Timeform rating: 96+ *Tracked in 4th,2nd 3f out,led 120y out,drew clear*
6Apr03♦Curragh (Ire) gd 1 Ⓣ Str 1:414 3↑ Newbridge Credit Union Maiden Maiden 17200 3 2¼ Smullen P J 128 4.00 Dalcassian128nk Timawari1432 *Evolving Tactics*128 3½ 27
Timeform rating: 89+ *Tracked in 5th,3rd 1-1/2f out,held by first two*

Excessivepleasure
Own: Leatherman Lee and Ty

Dk. b or b. g. 4 (Apr) BAROCY01 $17,000
Sire: In Excess*Ire (Siberian Express) $25,000
Dam: Pleasing (Falstaff)
Br: Cypress Farms 1991 & Vessels Stallion Farm LLC (Cal)
Tr: O'Neill Doug(0 0 0 0 .00) 2003:(760 133 .18)

Life	11	5	4	0	$921,382	103	D.Fst	11	5	4	0	$921,382	103
2003	9	3	4	0	$821,782	103	Wet(367)	0	0	0	0	$0	-
2002	2	2	0	0	$99,600	93	Turf(373)	0	0	0	0	$0	-
	0	0	0	0	$0	-	Dst(0)	0	0	0	0	$0	-

16Nov03-8RP fst 1⅛ :472 1:112 1:363 1:492 OkDerby-G3 **95** 3 1 1½ 1½ 1½ 25 210 Pettinger D R LB124 b *.90 89-14 ComcTruth11510 Excssvplsr124 2¼ MornngMrry112 2½ Could not keep pace 6
4Oct03-9Hoo fst 1 1/16 :223 :462 1:103 1:432 IndnaDby-G3 **103** 2 11 1½ 1hd 1½ 11 Court J K LB124 b 10.10 92-29 Excessiveplesure1241 GrndHombr124 1¼ Wndo124 1¼ Shook bids, held safe 8
3Aug03-11Mth fst 1⅛ :47 1:104 1:36 1:491 HsklInvH-G1 **79** 7 42 2 1½ 2 1½ 611 718 Court J K L117 b 31.00 77-08 Peace Rules121 1¾ Sky Mesa118 7¼ Funny Cide1231 Stumbled start,faded 7
5Jly03-6PrM fst 1 1/16 :23 :461 1:092 1:404 IowaDerby250k **102** 3 1hd 1 1½ 12 1 2½ 1 2¾ Court J K LB122 b 5.80 104 - Excessivepleasure122 2¾ Saint Liam117 4½ Absent Friend1171 Driving 6
26May03-7Hol fst 7f :213 :44 1:09 1:22 LBrreraM-G2 **74** 8 1 31 5 1¾ 8 6¼ 8 11½ Valenzuela P A LB123 b 4.10 80-11 Blazonry115 2½ Fly to the Wire116½ Jimmy O1151 Steadied 4wd into lane 9
26Apr03-4Hol fst 1⅛ :462 1:104 1:36 1:49 [S]SnowChief250k **86** 3 2hd 21 2½ 2 2½ 27 Valenzuela P A LB124 b *1.40 82-10 ChiefPlanner1167 Excessiveplesure124 2½ TizCoup1172 No match,held 2nd 9
30Mar03-9Sun fst 1 1/16 :22 :441 1:082 1:424 WinStrDrby500k **93** 7 2½ 2½ 2 2½ 1½ 1nk Day P L122 b 3.70 96-08 Excsivplsur122nk Spnsiv122¾ AplchinThundr122 5¼ Breather turn,bid 3wd 8
2Mar03-11Sun fst 1 :22 :45 1:093 1:361 BdrIndDby104k **93** 7 1½ 1hd 1½ 1½ 2nk Jaime R L122 b *.40 97-14 MrDectur122nk *Excessiveplsur*1225 FlrionsFlm115 2¼ Wide 1st turn,led late 8
25Jan03-8GP fst 7f :222 :443 1:091 1:221 [R]OcalStdDsh250k **99** 7 3 1 1½ 1hd 1hd 2½ Valenzuela P A L120 b *.90 96-08 *VlidVideo*120½ Excessiveplesur120 3¼ SuphBlitz120 7¾ Dueled off rail, edged 7

Eye of the Tiger

Own: Gunther John D

B. c. 4 (Apr)
Sire: American Chance (Cure the Blues) $10,000
Dam: Dial a Trick (Phone Trick)
Br: John D. Gunther (Ky)
Tr: Hollendorfer Jerry(0 0 0 0 .00) 2003:(1216 282 .23)

Life	10	3	1	3	$236,329	107	**D.Fst**	10	3	1	3	$236,329 107
2003	8	2	1	2	$214,689	107	**Wet(347)**	0	0	0	0	$0 –
2002	2	1	0	1	$21,640	92	**Turf(233)**	0	0	0	0	$0 –
	0	0	0	0	$0	–	**Dst(0)**	0	0	0	0	$0 –

26Dec03–8SA	fst	7f	:22^{2} :45 1:09^{1} 1:22^{3}	Malibu-G1	**97**	7	8	5$1\frac{3}{4}$	3^{2}	4$4\frac{1}{2}$	44	Pedroza M A	LB117	24.00	89– 12	SouthernImage115^{hd} MrinoMrini115^{1} MidsEyes119^{3}	Stalked btwn,no bid	12
23Aug03–10Sar	fst	7f	:21^{3} :43^{3} 1:08^{3} 1:22	KngsBshp-G1	**99**	11	9	9$8\frac{1}{4}$	7$8\frac{1}{2}$	6$5\frac{1}{4}$	6$3\frac{3}{4}$	Solis A	L121	7.00	93– 07	Valid Video121^{nk} Great Notion117^{nk} *Ghostzapper*117$1\frac{3}{4}$	5 wide trip, tired	13
13Jly03–6Hol	fst	1⅛	:48 1:11^{3} 1:36^{2} 1:49^{1}	Swaps-G2	**95**	5	21	21	21	2^{hd}	$3\frac{3}{4}$	•Solis A	LB118	1.90	87– 07	During115^{hd} *Ten Most Wanted*122$\frac{3}{4}$ DH OuttaHere120	Bid btwn foes,gamely	6
22Jun03–3Hol	fst	1$\frac{1}{16}$	:23^{2} :47 1:10^{4} 1:42^{1}	AffirmdH-G3	**107**	4	3$4\frac{1}{2}$	3$3\frac{1}{2}$	3$1\frac{1}{2}$	1$1\frac{1}{2}$	1$4\frac{1}{2}$	Solis A	LB119	*.90	93– 14	EyofthTigr119$4\frac{1}{2}$ MinistrsWildCt118^{nk} Bullistic115$1\frac{1}{2}$	Rail bid,led 1/4,clear	4
3May03–10CD	fst	1¼	:46^{1} 1:10^{2} 1:35^{3} 2:01	KyDerby-G1	**102**	12	4$2\frac{1}{2}$	43	43	42	5$4\frac{3}{4}$	Coa E M	L126	41.50	89– 06	*FunnyCide*126$1\frac{3}{4}$ *EmpireMker*126^{hd} PeceRuls126^{hd}	Lean in bmp 5/16,empty	16
19Apr03–8Kee	fst	1$\frac{1}{16}$	:23 :47 1:11^{3} 1:45^{2}	ClmrLex-G2	**96**	3	7$4\frac{3}{4}$	5$2\frac{1}{4}$	5$2\frac{1}{2}$	32	23	Albarado R J	L116	7.90	77– 22	Scrimshw116^{3} EyofthTigr116^{nk} DomstcDsput116^{nk}	Sluggish start,bmp,ck	7
22Mar03–6SA	fst	6½f	:21^{1} :43^{2} 1:08^{2} 1:15^{1}	SanPedro80k	**102**	2	3	6$2\frac{1}{4}$	5^{3}	44	$3\frac{3}{4}$	Nakatani C S	LB116	4.40	96– 09	*KingRobyn*116$\frac{1}{2}$ TruckleFeture117^{nk} EyofthTigr116^{2}	Came out 1/8, late bid	6
26Feb03–4GG	fst	6f	:21^{3} :44^{1} :56^{2} 1:08^{3}	OClm 50000N	**95**	4	5	3$2\frac{1}{2}$	3$2\frac{1}{2}$	$1\frac{1}{2}$	1$2\frac{1}{2}$	Baze R A	LB118	*.50	94– 11	EyeoftheTiger118$2\frac{1}{2}$ *Midfternoon*118^{2} WstSrtog118^{2}	Rddn out, impressive	7

Fairly Ransom

Own: Zetcher Arnold

Gr/ro. c. 4 (Jan)
Sire: Red Ransom (Roberto)
Dam: Fairly Grey*Fr (Linamix*Fr)
Br: J. L. Lagardere (Ky)
Tr: McAnally Ronald L(0 0 0 0 .00) 2003:(312 44 .14)

Life	9	4	2	1	$388,529	103	**D.Fst**	0	0	0	0	$0 –
2003	6	2	2	1	$358,819	103	**Wet(300)**	0	0	0	0	$0 –
2002	3	2	0	0	$29,710	–	**Turf(323)**	9	4	2	1	$388,529 103
	0	0	0	0	$0	–	**Dst(0)**	0	0	0	0	$0 –

30Nov03–9Hol	fm	1¼	Ⓣ :51 1:17^{2} 1:41 2:04^{1}	HolDerby-G1	**97**	13	11$7\frac{1}{4}$	12$5\frac{1}{2}$	10$6\frac{1}{2}$	8^{3}	$2\frac{1}{2}$	Solis A	LB122	4.80	70– 17	SweetReturn122$\frac{1}{2}$ FairlyRansom122$\frac{1}{2}$ KickenKris122^{hd}	Pulled,4wd,late bid	13
6Sep03–8Dmr	fm	1⅛	Ⓣ :47^{2} 1:11 1:34^{3} 1:46^{2}	DmrDerby-G2	**103**	4	42	3$1\frac{1}{2}$	3$1\frac{1}{2}$	21	1$1\frac{1}{4}$	Solis A	LB122	4.50	101– 05	FirlyRnsom122$1\frac{1}{4}$ *DeviousBoy*122no SwtRturn122$\frac{1}{2}$	Pulled,bid btwn,gamely	9
16Aug03–8Dmr	fm	1$\frac{1}{16}$	Ⓣ :23^{3} :47^{1} 1:10^{3} 1:40^{1}	LaJollaH-G3	**96**	1	6$6\frac{1}{2}$	68	6$5\frac{3}{4}$	44	4$1\frac{1}{2}$	Solis A	LB117	2.90	98– 10	Singletary118$\frac{1}{2}$ Devious Boy117$\frac{1}{2}$ Senor Swinger120$\frac{1}{2}$	4wd into lane,rallied	7
23Jly03–8Dmr	fm	1	Ⓣ :23 :47 1:11^{1} 1:34^{3}	Ⓡ Oceanside84k	**92**	7	7^{10}	78	7$4\frac{1}{4}$	5$2\frac{1}{2}$	$2\frac{1}{2}$	Solis A	LB118	*1.50	89– 11	Devious Boy116$\frac{1}{2}$ Fairly Ransom118$\frac{1}{2}$ Stanley Park120^{1}	Off slow,late bid	7

Run in divisions Previously trained by Andre Fabre

20Apr03♦Longchamp (Fr) yl *1$\frac{5}{16}$ Ⓣ RH 2:17^{1} Prix Greffulhe-G2 3^{2} Placais O 128 3.10 *Dalakhani*128$\frac{1}{2}$ Jipapibaquigrafo128$1\frac{1}{2}$ Fairly Ransom128^{2} 5
Timeform rating: 108 Stk 103000 *Tracked in 4th,quickened over 1f out,held by first two*

30Mar03♦Longchamp (Fr) gd *1$\frac{5}{16}$ Ⓣ RH 2:12^{1} Prix de Courcelles (Listed) 1^{nk} Soumillon C 123 *.90 Fairly Ransom123^{nk} Well Dressed123^{nk} Risk Seeker123$\frac{1}{2}$ 5
Timeform rating: 102 Stk 44200 *Prompted pace,dueled 150y out,led near line*

False Promises
Own: Maracich David

B. g. 4 (Mar) OBSAPR02 $37,000
Sire: Jules (Forty Niner) $6,000
Dam: Stormy Divorce (Storm Bird)
Br: Arther I. Appleton (Fla)
Tr: Granitz Anthony J(0 0 0 0 .00) 2003:(169 27 .16)

Life	15	4	3	1	$226,340	91	D.Fst	4	0	0	0	$420 65
2003	13	3	3	1	$210,740	91	Wet(364)	2	1	0	0	$15,600 65
2002	2	1	0	0	$15,600	65	Turf(345)	9	3	3	1	$210,320 91
	0	0	0	0	$0	-	Dst(0)	0	0	0	0	$0 -

16Nov03-9CD yl 1⅛ Ⓣ :492 1:142 1:391 1:513	3↑RivrCtyH-G3	85 8 73 77½ 95¼ 108¼ 98¼	Marquez C H Jr	L116	14.50	68-26	Hard Buck118½ Warleigh1171 Rowans Park1141	Bmp start,weakened 10
18Oct03-8Haw fm 1⅛ Ⓣ :472 1:114 1:36 1:482	HawDerby-G3	91 2 93¼ 74½ 63 43½ 11	Marquez C H Jr	L115	7.50	98-06	False Promises1151 Megoman1151 BeauClassic113nk	Split horses, driving 11
20Sep03-9AP fm 1 1/16 Ⓣ :233 :473 1:121 1:431	3↑Alw 30000N2x	89 5 116¾ 1110 116¾ 72½ 11	Marquez C H Jr	L120	*3.30	93-12	*False Promises*1201 El Condor118½ Gottabeachboy118hd	6 wide 1/4, driving 11
28Aug03-7AP fm *1½ Ⓣ :483 1:142 2:063 2:312	3↑Alw 32000N1x	86 8 68 75 42 2½ 11¼	Marquez C H Jr	L116	*2.30	97-16	*False Promises*1161¼ Dynareign1165½ Skiperoo118nk	Driving 11
9Aug03-7AP yl 1 1/16 Ⓣ :223 :461 1:111 1:442	3↑Alw 32000N1x	85 9 69½ 66 62 2hd 2nk	Lovato F Jr	L116	5.40	87-17	Santa'sPlayboy119nk *FalsePromises*1162 ImperialTheatre1192	Just missed 10
12Jly03-8AP yl *1 Ⓣ :244 :482 1:132 1:384	Alw 34000N2x	85 6 43 62 41½ 1hd 2hd	Lovato F Jr	L118	7.60	85-20	Mr Mississippi118hd False Promises1183 Hot Hand118nk	Caught late 7
6Jun03-5AP gd *1 1/16 Ⓣ :25 :501 1:154 1:48	Alw 28000N1x	72 3 2½ 1½ 2½ 2hd 52¼	Marquez C H Jr	L118 b	2.30	71-26	Bannock Burner122hd Tortoni118no Gottabeachboy1181¾	Tired 7
23May03-7AP gd *1 Ⓣ :243 :493 1:16 1:41	Alw 30000N2x	82 2 21½ 22½ 2½ 11 2nk	Lovato F Jr	L118	5.30	74-26	Scottago118nk False Promises1181 Distinguishable1185	Caught late 6
28Apr03-6Haw fm 1 1/16 Ⓣ :224 :463 1:11 1:412	3↑Alw 28000N1x	72 3 11 1½ 21 22½ 33¾	Marquez C H Jr	L115	10.20	93-06	*CharacterWitness*1152 Unlicensed1211¾ FlsePromises1151¾	Lost place late 8
19Apr03-4Haw fst 1 1/16 :25 :494 1:15 1:49	OClm 35000(35-30)N	34 2 75½ 75 78 714 724¼	Marquez C H Jr	L118 b	4.50	38-29	JimmysSber1161¼ Distinguishble1187½ BrinDude1181¾	Trailed throughout 7
17Mar03-6OTC fst 1 1/16 :233 :482 1:13 1:441	ⓇOBSChamp100k	25 1 76½ 66½ 76¼ 821 837	Judice J C	122 b	-	67-05	*TheName'sBond*1223 *CoachJimiLee*1223½ *JustSaytheWord*122½	Showed little 8
Non-wagering event								
1Mar03-10TP my 1 1/16 :224 :463 1:11 1:461	JBttgliaMm100k	47 3 75¾ 77¼ 810 813 824	Morgan M R	114 fb	55.40	57-30	Champali1213¼ Chicken Soup Kid1144¼ Grey Comet1211	Bothered start 9
6Feb03-8TP fst 1 :232 :464 1:12 1:39	Alw 15590N1x	65 5 53½ 35 36 47 58	Butler D P	118 b	6.40	71-27	LxCommndr1152¼ CourtofMxms1153 SlltoSrvv1181¾	Failed to sustain bid 9

Fast Cookie
Own: Stonerside Stable LLC

B. f. 4 (Mar)
Sire: Deputy Minister (Vice Regent) $150,000
Dam: Fleet Lady (Avenue of Flags)
Br: Stonerside Stable (Ky)
Tr: Mott William I(0 0 0 0 .00) 2003:(718 138 .19)

Life	15	5	3	3	$345,910	96	D.Fst	12	3	2	3	$249,713 96
2003	8	4	0	2	$255,787	96	Wet(405)	3	2	1	0	$96,197 89
2002	7	1	3	1	$90,123	88	Turf(304)	0	0	0	0	$0 -
	0	0	0	0	$0	-	Dst(0)	0	0	0	0	$0 -

4Oct03-9Pha fst 1 1/16 :24 :474 1:121 1:454	ⒻCotillnH-G2	96 5 42 31½ 2½ 1½ 13¾	Santagata N	L116 b	2.70	83-17	FastCookie1163¾ Ladyecho1168 Svedbythelight1174¼	Bid 4 wide,drew off 5
1Sep03-5Sar gd 7f :223 :454 1:111 1:25	3↑ⒻAlw 51000N3x	89 4 4 45 53½ 41¼ 1hd	Day P	L116 b	*2.25	82-21	*FastCookie*116hd Actcellent1114¾ DrawingaBlank1192¾	3 wide, final strides 6
31Jly03-8Sar fst 7f :223 :452 1:091 1:223	3↑ⒻAlw 51000N3x	90 6 3 43 46 45 31½	Day P	L115 b	3.40	92-04	Lilah113¾ *Country Romance*119¾ *Fast Cookie*115no	3 wide move, gamely 6
8Jun03-9CD fst 6½f :223 :453 1:10 1:162	3↑ⒻOClm 62500N	75 5 5 41¼ 2hd 43½ 57¾	Velasquez C	114 b	*1.20	81-11	Vicki Vallencourt1185¾ Two Dot Slew1181 ShyDory118¾	Exch bumps start 8
1May03-9CD fst 7f :222 :451 1:093 1:22	ⒻLaTroien-G3	88 5 2 42 3½ 11 32¼	Velasquez C	118 b	8.00	90-07	Final Round1161 Lovely Sage1161¼ Fast Cookie1182	Drift start,brush lane 6
11Apr03-6Kee gd 7f :221 :45 1:104 1:244	ⒻAlw 55718N2x	81 3 3 33 42¾ 31½ 1¾	Velasquez C	120	1.70	80-14	Fast Cookie120¾ MissMaryApples118½ ClassicMoment1113¾	5w,stiff drive 5
14Mar03-7GP fst 7f :22 :442 1:092 1:222	ⒻFrwrdGal-G3	66 2 6 3nk 11 32 611½	Bailey J D	117	*2.80	84-09	Midnight Cry1172¾ *Final Round*117¾ Chimichurri121½	Inside, tired 8
6Feb03-8GP fst 6½f :22 :442 1:101 1:17	ⒻAlw 36000N1x	83 5 7 2½ 2hd 11 14	Bailey J D	117	*.90	91-06	Fast Cookie1174 *Bella Lauren*117nk Scapade1172½	Drew away, driving 10

Feline Story
Own: Robsham Einar P

B. f. 3 (Apr) OBSMAR03 $140,000
Sire: Tale of the Cat (Storm Cat) $16,139
Dam: Shappy (Really Secret)
Br: Eclipse Thoroughbreds Inc. (Ky)
Tr: Hough Stanley M(0 0 0 0 .00) 2003:(289 50 .17)

Life	6	3	1	0	$201,780	87	D.Fst	2	1	0	0	$76,980	87
2003	6	3	1	0	$201,780	87	Wet(318)	4	2	1	0	$124,800	85
2002	0	M	0	0	$0	-	Turf(299)	0	0	0	0	$0	-
	0	0	0	0	$0	-	Dst(0)	0	0	0	0	$0	-

12Oct03-10Bel	sly	6½f	:212 :442 1:102 1:17	ⒻAstarita-G2	80	6	5	5¾	5¼	2hd	2nk	Prado E S	L120	3.25	88-16	SpctclrMoon117nk FlnStory120¼ SmokyGlckn11713	Bumped start, 4 wide	9
14Sep03-6Bel	fst	1	:222 :451 1:103 1:38	ⒻMatron-G1	64	3	41	42¼	51¼	55	47½	Castellano J J	L119	*2.35	68-16	Marylebone119no Lokoya1195¾ Eye Dazzler1191¾	Chased inside, tired	8
30Aug03-10Mth	wf	6f	:214 :452 :574 1:104	ⒻSorority-G3	85	3	6	41¼	1½	13½	15¾	Ferrer J C	L119	*1.40	85-13	FlnStr1195¾ WhrlndChrltt1191¼ StndOnTp1192½	Widened,steady handlng	8
23Jly03-9Sar	sly	6f	:22 :452 :582 1:12	ⒻSchylrvl-G2	65	2	4	3½	43	43	46½	Chavez J F	L122	3.00	75-17	Ashado1183 Maple Syrple1222½ Hermione'sMagic1181	Angled out, no rally	7
29Jun03-9Bel	fst	5½f	:213 :453 :582 1:05	ⒻAstoria108k	87	3	4	1hd	1hd	13	14	Chavez J F	L114	3.00	88-18	FelinStory1144 UnbridldButy1148¾ DixiWltz114hd	Drew clear when roused	6
4Jun03-4Bel	sly	5f	:222 :453 :583	ⒻMd Sp Wt 43k	85	1	2	1hd	11½	17	111½	Chavez J F	L118	4.40	90-18	FelinStory11811½ Dncinndsingin1181 CorinthinStr1188¼	Set pace, hand ride	7

Fight for Ally
Own: Calabrese Frank C

Dk. b or b. g. 7 (Feb)
Sire: Fit to Fight (Chieftain) $5,000
Dam: Colonial Ally (Pleasant Colony)
Br: Justice Farm, Inc. (Ind)
Tr: Catalano Wayne M(0 0 0 0 .00) 2003:(356 106 .30)

Life	30	11	4	6	$536,229	103	D.Fst	23	7	3	6	$352,819	103
2003	5	3	0	0	$198,360	97	Wet(396)	7	4	1	0	$183,410	93
2002	8	2	2	1	$98,760	103	Turf(217)	0	0	0	0	$0	-
	0	0	0	0	$0	-	Dst(0)	0	0	0	0	$0	-

2Aug03-5AP	fst	1	⊗:232 :46 1:094 1:353	3↑Clm 55000(65-55)	86	6	1hd	1hd	2hd	2½	44¼	Razo E Jr	L119 b	*.90	86-17	My Extolled Honor121no Horrible Evening1214 Sunkosi121nk	Weakened	7
10May03-8AP	fst	1⅛	:474 1:122 1:373 1:501	3↑BlckTiAfrH100k	87	2	1hd	1½	2hd	41¼	66½	Bourque C C	L117 b	4.40	85-19	Full Mandate113nk Bonus Pack1162 Woodmoon1163¾	Tired	7
19Apr03-8Haw	fst	1⅛	:474 1:122 1:384 1:532	3↑NtlJClbH-G3	97	2	2½	22	2½	11½	1nk	Razo E Jr	L116 b	7.90	89-29	FghtforAlly116nk ColonlColny114no PrrttBy1154¼	Fully extended-driving	8
5Apr03-6Haw	fst	1 1/16	:24 :47 1:114 1:462	3↑OClm 75000	94	4	31	2½	1hd	11½	11	Bourque C C	L123 b	2.10	75-19	Fight for Ally1231 Fighting Indians1212 Fourth Floor1232¼	Driving	5
15Mar03-8Haw	fst	1 1/16	:242 :481 1:123 1:472	4↑IdesOMarch42k	96	4	33	33	21	2½	1nk	Bourque C C	L118 b	2.30	70-42	Fight for Ally118nk Stormy Impact1183¼ Fighting Indians116nk	Driving	7

Film Maker
Own: Courtlandt Farms

Dk. b or b. f. 4 (Mar)
Sire: Dynaformer (Roberto) $50,000
Dam: Miss Du Bois (Mr. Prospector)
Br: TAC Holdings, Inc. (Ky)
Tr: Motion H. G(0 0 0 0 .00) 2003:(318 55 .17)

Life	10	4	2	3	$459,860	100	D.Fst	1	0	0	1	$2,640	52
2003	9	4	2	2	$457,220	100	Wet(373)	0	0	0	0	$0	-
2002	1	M	0	1	$2,640	52	Turf(345)	9	4	2	2	$457,220	100
	0	0	0	0	$0	-	Dst(0)	0	0	0	0	$0	-

15Nov03-9CD	yl	1 1/16	Ⓣ:233 :474 1:13 1:45	ⒻMrsRvere-G2	81	11	63¾	68½	74¾	97¾	86¼	Velasquez C	L122 b	4.00	73-21	Hoh Buzzard120nk Aud1202 Gamble to Victory116½	5w,weakened lane	12
11Oct03-8Kee	fm	1⅛	Ⓣ:473 1:113 1:354 1:474	ⒻQEIICup-G1	100	9	42	43	44	31½	1no	Prado E S	L121 b	11.60	98-11	FilmMaker121no MaidenTower121¾ CasulLook121¾	Exch bumps late,drvg	10
17Aug03-9Sar	fm	1⅛	Ⓣ:462 1:102 1:36 1:49	ⒻLakPlcdH-G2	91	2	33½	46½	38	22	3¾	Prado E S	L119 b	3.00	83-13	SndSprings121¾ IndyFiveHundred114no FilmMkr1193½	Game finish outside	10
28Jly03-8Sar	fm	1 1/16	Ⓣ:24 :481 1:121 1:414	ⒻLkGeorge-G3	95	4	57	58½	63½	51¼	12½	Prado E S	L115 b	9.00	86-20	Film Maker1152½ Ocean Drive119¾ Gal O Gal122½	Awaited room, found it	11
6Jly03-10Mth	fm	1 1/16	Ⓣ:242 :491 1:13 1:414	+ⒻLitlSilver50k	86	3	44½	53½	53½	63	21	Pimentel J	L112 b	3.70	91-11	Impolite1141 FilmMaker112hd MarcsRinbow1121¼	Late momentum for 2nd	7
8May03-9Pim	gd	1 1/16	Ⓣ:241 :494 1:144 1:463	3↑ⒻAlw 26000N1x	79	2	34	42	42½	11½	13¼	Dominguez R A	L113 b	*.40	69-30	Film Maker1133¼ No Bettor Love1171 Maiden Stone112½	Handily	9
19Apr03-9Kee	gd	1 1/16	Ⓣ:23 :473 1:123 1:433	ⒻAlw 50540N1x	84	1	42	3nk	1hd	11	21¾	Albarado R J	L120 b	*.80	81-13	Snowdrops1201¾ Film Maker1205½ Bayani1201¼	Bmp start,inside bid	9
5Apr03-9Kee	fm	1⅛	Ⓣ:471 1:122 1:38 1:504	ⒻAlw 54320N1x	79	6	42½	44½	42	21	31¼	Albarado R J	L120	2.50	82-16	Achnasheen1181 Pleasant Point118nk Film Maker120no	No final response	8
26Feb03-8GP	fm	*1⅛	Ⓣ:492 1:133 1:391 1:512	ⒻMd Sp Wt 34k	75	10	41	32	32	11½	12¾	Prado E S	L121	3.50	84-14	Film Maker1212¾ Boom Bah Yay121nk Wear1212¼	3 wide, drew clear	10

Final Destination (NZ)

Own: Gann Edmund A

Dk. b or b. m. 6 (Nov)
Sire: O'Reilly*NZ (Last Tycoon*Ire)
Dam: Logical Lady*NZ (Sound Reason)
Br: P. Setchell (NZ)
Tr: Frankel Robert J(0 0 0 0 .00) 2003:(411 114 .28)

Life	12	5	3	2	$224,411	101	D.Fst	0	0	0	0	$0 -
2003	2	1	0	1	$103,320	101	Wet(267)	0	0	0	0	$0 -
2002	2	2	0	0	$40,103	93	Turf(338)	12	5	3	2	$224,411 101
	0	0	0	0	$0	-	Dst(0)	0	0	0	0	$0 -

27Apr03–8Hol fm 1 Ⓣ:23 :462 1:1011:333 3↑ⒻWilshirH-G3 98 3 73¾ 84 86¼ 63½ 33½ Espinoza V LB118 *1.40 92–12 Dublino1202½ SouthernOasis1161 FinlDestintion118½ Tight 7/8,stdied 5/16 9

17Feb03–7SA gd 1 Ⓣ:234 :472 1:1141:354 4↑ⒻBnaVstaH-G2 101 2 34 33 32 2hd 1½ Espinoza V LB115 1.90 83–21 FinlDstintion115½ GrdninthRin1152½ EmbssyBll116hd 3wd into str,led,held 6

Final Round

Own: Humphrey G W Jr

B. f. 4 (Mar)
Sire: Storm Cat (Storm Bird) $500,000
Dam: Profit Column (Private Account)
Br: Dinwiddie Farm Limited Partnership (Ky)
Tr: Arnold G R II(0 0 0 0 .00) 2003:(259 34 .13)

Life	10	3	3	3	$282,536	94	D.Fst	8	2	3	2	$208,016 94
2003	6	1	2	2	$172,416	94	Wet(424)	2	1	0	1	$74,520 77
2002	4	2	1	1	$110,120	77	Turf(344)	0	0	0	0	$0 -
	0	0	0	0	$0	-	Dst(0)	0	0	0	0	$0 -

26Jly03–9Sar fst 7f :223 :451 1:0811:204 ⒻTest-G1 93 4 6 52 63¼ 58 47¾ Day P L120 7.40 95–08 Lady Tak1224½ Bird Town1221½ *House Party*1221¾ Rail trip, no rally 7

28Jun03–9Bel fst 1⅛ :4621:113 1:37 1:502 ⒻMthrGoos-G1 94 1 63¾ 63¾ 61¾ 28 36 Prado E S L121 2.90 72–19 *Spoken Fur*1215¼ Yell121¾ Final Round1218¼ 4 wide move, weakened 6

6Jun03–10Bel fst 1 :232 :461 1:1021:351 ⒻAcorn-G1 94 6 61¼ 41½ 31 31 31 Stevens G L L121 16.40 89–16 Bird Town121hd *Lady Tak*1211 Final Round1213¼ 4 wide move, crowded 7

1May03–9CD fst 7f :222 :451 1:0931:22 ⒻLaTroien-G3 93 2 6 64 52 31 11 Bailey J D L116 *1.20 92–07 Final Round1161 LovelySage1161¼ FastCookie1182 Bmp strt,brsh lane,drv 6

14Mar03–7GP fst 7f :22 :442 1:0921:222 ⒻFrwrdGal-G3 85 7 8 813 812 54½ 22¾ Day P L117 6.10 93–09 Midnight Cry1172¾ *Final Round*117¾ Chimichurri121½ Stumbled badly start 8

5Feb03–8GP fst 170 :23 :47 1:1141:412 ⒻAlw 38000N2X 80 5 32 33 33½ 21½ 22 Day P L117 4.20 92–12 PerfectStory1172 FinalRound1173 NeverFil1173½ Saved ground, 2nd best 6

Finally Here

Own: Pop-A-Top LLC

Ch. f. 4 (May)
Sire: Yarrow Brae (Deputy Minister) $6,000
Dam: Neolithic (Deputed Testamony)
Br: James M. Courtney (Md)
Tr: Amoss Thomas M(0 0 0 0 .00) 2003:(445 118 .27)

Life	8	5	1	1	$189,200	94	D.Fst	8	5	1	1	$189,200 94
2003	8	5	1	1	$189,200	94	Wet(320)	0	0	0	0	$0 -
2002	0	M	0	0	$0	-	Turf(251*)	0	0	0	0	$0 -
	0	0	0	0	$0	-	Dst(0)	0	0	0	0	$0 -

5Nov03–9CD fst 6f :212 :451 :5721:10 ⒻAlw 65800NC – 1 7 76½ - - - Borel C H L120 4.80 - 16 Tina Bull1183¼ Holy Bubbette1201 Put Me In118hd Broke down,fell 7

11Oct03–8Lrl fst 7f :231 :46 1:1011:223 3↑Ⓕ[R]MdMilDstfH95k 94 1 5 41½ 2½ 21 22 Karamanos H A L116 3.60 92–10 Willa On the Move1222 Finally Here116no Bronze Abe1183 Inside bid turn 8

13Sep03–6AP fst 6f :214 :45 :5721:10 ⒻSmartDeb47k 93 4 2 31½ 2hd 11½ 1nk Razo E Jr L121 *1.60 94–12 Finally Here121nk Fabulous Brush1167 Feisty Princess1191½ Gamely 6

9Aug03–5WO fst 7f :221 :45 1:1021:24 ⒻDuchess-G3 84 7 2 43¼ 31½ 1hd 1½ Husbands P L117 6.60 84–16 *Finally Here*117½ [D] *Winter Garden*120½ *Miss Crissy*1181¾ 3w,wore down rival 8

12Jly03–9EIP fst 6f :223 :463 :5911:114 3↑ⒻOClm 40000N 81 9 5 5½ 2hd 1hd 11¾ Borel C H L114 2.70 87–11 *Finally Here*1141¾ *Rubyana*1226¼ Knock Twice1183¾ Lean in bmp 1/8p,drvg 9

Previously trained by Runco Jeff C

14May03–6Pim fst 6f :231 :463 :5911:113 ⒻAlw 26000N1X 84 4 5 65¾ 45¼ 42¾ 13¼ Flores O5 L117 25.00 87–19 *FinllyHer*1173¼ *LovYouMdly*1171½ DncinFlight112hd Off 3way duel,5w,drvng 7

16Apr03–3CT fst 7f :234 :491 1:1511:282 ⒻMd Sp Wt 17k 65 1 2 33 31 1½ 12½ Flores O5 L114 2.10 79–20 *Finally Here*1142½ *Judge's Appeal*1198½ *Regal Jackie*1196 Repulsed rival's bid 10

27Mar03–5CT fst 6½f :242 :483 1:1441:214 ⒻMd Sp Wt 17k 47 6 8 910 67¾ 54¾ 31¼ Flores O5 114 44.60 79–21 Diamond Hunter119nk Judge's Appeal1191 *Finally Here*1142 Finished well 10

First Blush

Own: Cowan Marjorie and Irving M

Ch. c. 4 (May)
Sire: French Deputy (Deputy Minister) $4,372
Dam: Blushing Princess (Crafty Prospector)
Br: Irving Cowan & Marjorie Cowan (Ky)
Tr: Jerkens H. A(0 0 0 0 .00) 2003:(359 73 .20)

Life	18	3	5	5	$210,522	103	D.Fst	14	2	3	4	$123,450 103
2003	13	2	3	4	$153,750	103	Wet(417)	4	1	2	1	$87,072 93
2002	5	1	2	1	$56,772	88	Turf(306)	0	0	0	0	$0 -
	0	0	0	0	$0	-	Dst(0)	0	0	0	0	$0 -

30Dec03-11Crc	fst	6f	:221 :45 :573 1:11	3↑ OClm 40000(40-35)N	84	7 5	41½ 32 32½ 44	Douglas R R	114 b	*.90	85-19	JustSytheWord114nk PttonsChrg1172½ Oswyo1171¼	Mid track,even finish	7
23Nov03-6Aqu	fst	6½f	:223 :45 1:094 1:163	3↑ Alw 51000N3x	93	4 5	55½ 54½ 23½ 2¾	Chavez J F	118 b	*1.60	94-12	Kingmaker121¾ FirstBlush1182 CastleGandolfo119hd	Game finish outside	6
2Nov03-7Aqu	fst	7f	:223 :45 1:092 1:223	3↑ Alw 51000N3x	93	9 2	98½ 86¾ 45 33½	Chavez J F	118 b	*1.95	86-17	New York Hero1182 Don Six1181½ First Blush118nk	Mild rally outside	9
18Oct03-9Lrl	fst	6f	:214 :442 :561 1:084	SonnyHine50k	103	3 6	45½ 32½ 43½ 3¾	Goodwin N	119 b	4.80	94-17	Gators N Bears119¾ Super Fuse117hd First Blush119no	2wd, rallied	8
25Sep03-8Bel	fst	6½f	:223 :451 1:091 1:154	3↑ Alw 51000N3x	99	1 5	21½ 2½ 22 21½	Chavez J F	116 b	2.20	92-21	Bishop Court Hill1181½ First Blush116¾ No Parole1163	Tried winner turn	6
20Aug03-3Sar	fst	6f	:221 :444 :57 1:093	3↑ Alw 51000N3x	93	5 1	31½ 2½ 2hd 2nk	Chavez J F	115 b	3.80	94-06	PinchHitter119nk FirstBlush1151¼ *SunraySpirit*1231½	Speed 3 wide, gamely	5
2Aug03-8Sar	fst	6f	:22 :443 :562 1:083	Amstrdam-G2	92	5 2	53½ 3nk 54¼ 57¾	Chavez J F	123 b	15.00	91-07	Zavata1195¼ Great Notion121½ Trust N Luck123nk	4 wide move, faded	7
10Jly03-5Bel	fst	7f	:214 :442 1:102 1:234	3↑ Alw 49000N3x	92	5 1	32½ 1½ 3½ 31	Rojas R I	117	*1.75	80-19	MidnightChrli117½ TurnBckthTim120½ FrstBlush11712¼	Lost whip stretch	5
16May03-6Bel	fst	6f	:22 :443 :564 1:10	3↑ Alw 47000N2x	93	5 4	4nk 2hd 1hd 11½	Rojas R I	115	*1.00	89-19	First Blush1151½ Mighty Gulch121nk *In High Gear*1216¼	Vied 4 wide, clear	5
3May03-8Del	fst	6f	:221 :452 :58 1:111	FLaBellMem75k	89	5 6	51¾ 51¼ 43 32¾	Rojas R I	122	*2.60	85-16	Gimmeawink1221 Only theBest1191¾ *FirstBlush*1222¾	Willingly, closed gap	6
15Mar03-11GP	fst	7f	:214 :441 1:082 1:21	Swale-G3	71	4 4	61¾ 53 58½ 617¼	Velasquez C	120	10.50	86-05	*Midas Eyes*1169¼ *Posse*1204½ Whywhywhy1222¼	3 wide, no factor	8
15Feb03-9GP	fst	7f	:22 :441 1:091 1:223	Hutchesn-G2	71	2 3	52½ 43 55½ 512¼	Chavez J F	122	7.30	83-08	Lion Tamer1186 Strength Within116¾ Crafty Guy1223¾	Faltered	6
3Jan03-9GP	gd	6f	:213 :444 :572 1:104	SpectBid-G3	93	8 4	42¼ 31 1hd 1½	Chavez J F	116	11.90	90-12	First Blush116½ Crafty Guy120¾ Silver Squire1202	3 wide, steady urging	9

Fiscally Speaking

Own: Whitham Janis R

Ch. g. 5 (Feb)
Sire: Belong to Me (Danzig) $22,008
Dam: Tuesday Evening (Nodouble)
Br: Janis R. Whitham (Ky)
Tr: Nafzger Carl A(0 0 0 0 .00) 2003:(285 31 .11)

Life	14	4	3	2	$187,280	102	D.Fst	4	0	2	1	$16,570 85
2003	8	1	1	1	$94,226	102	Wet(351)	3	2	0	0	$62,484 90
2002	6	3	2	1	$93,054	90	Turf(310)	7	2	1	1	$108,226 102
	0	0	0	0	$0	-	Dst(0)	0	0	0	0	$0 -

20Sep03-6KD	fm	6f	Ⓣ :242 :49 1:122	3↑ KyCpTfDash100k	92	4 6	43½ 52½ 41¼ 42½	Court J K	L117 f	4.80	83-19	Fredericktown115no Abderian1172½ Callthesheriff115no	Angled out,no bid	7
31Aug03-9EIP	sly	5½f	⊗ :221 :451 :571 1:033	3↑ Alw 32900NC	83	4 4	32½ 42¾ 43½ 46¼	Court J K	L118 f	*1.20	92-17	Skeet1152¾ Are You Down1182 Chosen Chief1201½	5-6w trip,empty	4
26May03-6CD	gd	5f	Ⓣ :213 :441 :561	3↑ OClm 80000N	90	2 6	57 47 46½ 34¾	Court J K	L120 f	*1.50	92-03	ChosnChif1164¼ MightyBu116½ FisclySpking120nk	Stumble start,5w lane	7
2May03-7CD	fm	5f	Ⓣ :213 :441 :56	3↑ AgonTfSp-G3	102	11 7	55½ 52¾ 52¾ 1hd	Court J K	L114 f	47.40	98-02	Fiscally Speaking114hd Morluc1221 *Testify*122no	Bobble start,6w,drvg	11
12Apr03-7Kee	fm	5½f	Ⓣ :212 :443 :57 1:031	3↑ Shakrtwn-G3	96	9 4	75¼ 65 64 61¼	Desormeaux K J	L118 f	10.90	91-08	No Jacket Required118nk Testify120hd Abderian120nk	4-5w, no late gain	10
21Mar03-8GP	fm	*1 1/16	Ⓣ :241 :492 1:131 1:442	4↑ Alw 40000N3x	87	7 2½	21½ 21½ 52½ 75¼	Douglas R R	L118 f	7.50	77-24	LovethGm1181¾ ThfullCircl122hd HndsomGorg118¾	Jostled stretch, tired	10
10Feb03-9GP	fm	*1	Ⓣ :233 :474 1:131 1:373	4↑ Alw 40000N3x	93	10 32	31½ 2hd 1hd 2¾	Douglas R R	L118 f	6.80	84-19	FrnchChrmr122¾ FiscllySpking118¾ StrtgcPrtnr1181½	Slim lead, held well	10
5Jan03-9GP	fst	6f	:212 :434 :56 1:082	4↑ OClm 75000N	85	1 4	45 47 46½ 49¼	Douglas R R	L120 f	4.70	93-06	Deer Lake1221¾ *Boston Brat*1206¼ Finder1181¼	No late bid	6

Fly Smartly

Own: Sam-Son Farms

B. g. 6 (Mar)
Sire: Smart Strike (Mr. Prospector) $20,000
Dam: Spinnakers Flying (Grey Dawn II)
Br: Sam-Son Farm (Ont-C)
Tr: Frostad Mark R(0 0 0 0 .00) 2003:(206 44 .21)

Life	20	4	1	5	$261,524	94	D.Fst	3	0	0	0	$3,024	71
2003	4	1	0	2	$114,705	94	Wet(384)	0	0	0	0	$0	–
2002	6	2	0	1	$90,796	87	Turf(301)	17	4	1	5	$258,500	94
	0	0	0	0	$0	–	Dst(0)	0	0	0	0	$0	–

12Oct03-7Kee	fm	1⅛	(T) :472 1:112 1:361 1:482	3↑ Alw 58200c	88	10	51¾	2hd	2hd	21½	53½	Lovato F Jr	L124 b	10.60	91-13	GretchensStar124nk *MysteryGiver*1211¾ BonusPack124½	Forced pace,tired	10
24May03-8WO	sf	1 1/16	(T) :25 :494 1:144 1:473	4↑ ConghtCp-G3	94	10	62½	53¼	52¾	1hd	1¾	Kabel T K	L117 b	6.30	60-40	Fly Smartly117¾ Solitary Dancer117nk Mr.Sulu1171¼	Rallied, 3w, prevailed	11
13Apr03-7Kee	fm	1⅛	(T) :473 1:123 1:364 1:483	4↑ Alw 57200N3x	83	7	2hd	2½	2½	24	37¼	Blanc B	L116 b	10.60	87-08	Perfect Soul1185¼ Illusionary1162 *Fly Smartly*1161½	Pressed,weakened	10
23Mar03-9FG	fm	*1	(T) :242 :491 1:142 1:39	4↑ OClm 75000N	87	5	32½	32½	32½	31½	3¾	Blanc B	L118 b	11.90	88-11	Classic Stag122nk Conserve118½ Fly Smartly118hd	Not enough late	6

For Rubies

Own: Choctaw Racing Stable

B. m. 5 (Feb) EASMAY01 $85,000
Sire: Not For Love (Mr. Prospector) $15,000
Dam: Eliza Donner (Oh Say)
Br: Sharon Maloney (Md)
Tr: Whiting Lynn S(0 0 0 0 .00) 2003:(155 21 .14)

Life	23	8	6	3	$352,743	100	D.Fst	21	6	6	3	$317,143	96
2003	9	3	1	0	$138,873	100	Wet(433)	2	2	0	0	$35,600	100
2002	12	4	4	3	$200,390	96	Turf(318)	0	0	0	0	$0	–
	0	0	0	0	$0	–	Dst(0)	0	0	0	0	$0	–

11Oct03-8Lrl	fst	7f	:231 :46 1:101 1:223	3↑ (F)(R)MdMilDstfH95k	73	6	2	31½	42	510	511¼	Melancon L	L119	12.50	83-10	WillaOntheMove1222 FinllyHere116no BronzeAbe1183	Stalked wide, tired	8
19Sep03-8AP	fst	7f	:222 :442 1:092 1:23	3↑ (F)OClm 100000N	75	8	1	1hd	21	33½	78¼	Melancon L	L122	*1.30	82-17	*Summer Mis*1222 Oglala Sue116½ Sarah Jade1163	Tired	9
6Sep03-9TP	fst	6f	:214 :452 :573 1:102	3↑ (F)WeekndDlt70k	85	3	3	33	2½	2hd	22¾	Melancon L	L122	5.20	87-15	Don't Countess Out1222¾ For Rubies1221 Born toDance1221¼	Inside move	8
10Aug03-9EIP	fst	6f	:223 :453 :573 1:094	3↑ (F)ElpBCH102k	71	3	6	63½	32½	45½	413¼	Perret C	L121	2.80	84-11	VckVllncourt1177¼ MtorMrcl121½ *DontCountssOt*1215½	Broke in air,empty	6
12Jly03-11Crc	fst	6f	:212 :442 :573 1:111	3↑ (F)PrcsRnyH-G2	72	6	7	85½	64½	77	812¼	Perret C	L115	10.40	76-11	Gold Mover118no Vision in Flight1134¼ *Harmony Lodge*116hd	Poor start	8
14Jun03-8AP	fst	7f	:223 :451 1:102 1:241	3↑ (F)ChcgoBCH-G3	95	3	7	21	2hd	1hd	13	Perret C	L116	7.20	84-20	For Rubies1163 Raging Fever1204 *Oglala Sue*1131½	Drew off, driving	8
15May03-7CD	sly	6½f	:223 :452 1:101 1:17	3↑ (F)Alw 50515N$Y	100	6	1	1½	13	13	15½	Melancon L	L120	2.20	86-20	*ForRubies*1205½ MinistersBaby116hd BoldBluff116½	Control pace,hand urg	6
26Apr03-8PrM	fst	6f	:212 :442 1:101	3↑ (F)PrairieRse50k	61	3	4	55½	53¼	56¼	611	Marquez C H Jr	LB120	*1.00	79-15	*Don't CountessOut*113hd PrincessJen114¾ WastedWisdom118nk	No mishap	7
11Apr03-10P	fst	6f	:222 :451 :572 1:094	4↑ (F)Alw 36000N$Y	90	3	2	2hd	11	13½	14¾	Theriot H J II	L118	*1.10	91-13	ForRubies1184¾ DringSmile115¾ GigisSkyflyr1182	Took over,kept to task	5

Forever Grand
Own: DiGiulio Jr., Frank and Tiller, R. P

Dk. b or b. g. 5 (Apr) ONTAUT00 $33,625
Sire: War Deputy (Deputy Minister) $3,500
Dam: Braverelle (Brave Shot*GB)
Br: Ron Motz & Janet Motz (Ont-C)
Tr: Tiller Robert P(0 0 0 0 .00) 2003:(254 73 .29)

Life	22	10	1	4	$781,289	105	D.Fst	17	9	1	4	$673,380 105
2003	10	4	0	3	$385,120	105	Wet(362)	4	1	0	0	$103,855 104
2002	10	5	1	1	$362,761	102	Turf(207)	1	0	0	0	$4,054 81
	0	0	0	0	$0	-	Dst(0)	0	0	0	0	$0 -

29Nov03-8WO gd 6f :212 :43 :55 1:08 3↑KennedyRd137k 92 5 5 57¼ 57½ 68¾ 68½ Kabel T K L124 b 2.15 96-04 ChrissBdBoy1186¾ DvidsExpcttion115¾ MyLuckyStrik118hd 3w, no threat 8
19Oct03-3WO my 6f :212 :433 :562 1:092 3↑HilandrH-G3 104 4 3 59½ 511 52½ 11½ Kabel T K L117 b 2.35 97-06 ForvrGrnd1171½ SophisPrnc116nk MullgnthGrt1152¼ Rally 4w, split horses 5
1Sep03-9WO fst 6f :212 :44 :564 1:094 3↑[R]Kenora130k 105 5 6 613 511 45 11¼ Kabel T K L124 b 4.05 95-19 ForeverGrnd1241¼ MullightheGrt1243 WildWhisky1191¼ Trailed,3w,rally 5w 6
23Aug03-8WO fst 6½f :214 :442 1:101 1:17 3↑[S]Shepperton132k 94 5 7 74½ 74¾ 72¼ 1nk Husbands P L124 b 5.20 90-16 Forever Grand124nk Dillinger118nk Krz Ruckus121hd Trail,rally 6w,in time 7
20Jly03-4WO fst 1$\frac{1}{16}$:234 :473 1:12 1:44 3↑[R]Izvestia106k 87 5 2½ 21 21½ 33½ 37¾ Jones J L120 b 10.55 78-34 WakeAtNoon1241¾ AnglinPrince1206 ForeverGrnd120nk Press 3w, gave way 6
2Jly03-7WO fst 7f :222 :443 1:083 1:22 3↑[S]Overskate137k 82 3 8 53¾ 57½ 57½ 67¾ Kabel T K L122 b 3.35 86-14 MullightheGret122½ SophisPrince1164½ MisterCoop1151½ 3 wide, no threat 10
28May03-7WO fst 1$\frac{1}{16}$:23 :463 1:11 1:45 3↑[S]StdyGrowth128k 79 1 1½ 1½ 2hd 33 36¾ Kabel T K L117 b *.95 74-22 Barbeau Ruckus121½ Geraint1176¼ Forever Grand117¾ Off rail gave way 6
18May03-8WO fst 6f :221 :454 :582 1:104 3↑[S]NwProvdnce127k 91 4 3 47 43 41 12 Kabel T K L117 b 1.70 90-18 ForvrGrnd1172 KrzRuckus119nk MullignthGrt119½ Bobbled start,rally 4w 4
26Apr03-8WO fst 7f :22 :442 1:094 1:231 4↑VigilH-G3 85 6 2 1hd 4¾ 33 47 Kabel T K L115 b 11.15 81-23 WakeAtNoon1243¼ ShawsCreek1142 CheapTlk1201¾ Press 4w,tired stretch 7
11Apr03-8WO fst 6f :214 :443 :572 1:111 4↑JcqCartier134k 88 5 1 55¼ 44 24 33½ Kabel T K L116 b 3.95 84-19 RreFriends1193½ PopRocks115hd ForeverGrnd1163 Bobbled, 3w,outfin 2nd 5

Foufa's Warrior
Own: Bender Sondra D

Ch. g. 4 (May)
Sire: Jade Hunter (Mr. Prospector) $10,000
Dam: Foufa (Storm Bird)
Br: Sondra Bender & Howard M. Bender (Md)
Tr: Murray Lawrence E(0 0 0 0 .00) 2003:(129 22 .17)

Life	12	3	1	3	$331,608	95	D.Fst	5	2	1	1	$144,250 91
2003	10	1	1	3	$257,358	95	Wet(331)	2	0	0	1	$6,600 89
2002	2	2	0	0	$74,250	77	Turf(283)	5	1	0	1	$180,758 95
	0	0	0	0	$0	-	Dst(0)	0	0	0	0	$0 -

22Nov03-8Lrl fst 1⅛ :481 1:12 1:37 1:501 [S]NrthrnDncr75k 73 1 65 56 67 711 810½ Dominguez R A L122 fb *1.00e 80-18 Ironton115no James115nk Conservation122nk Dull effort 8
18Oct03-8Haw fm 1⅛ Ⓣ :472 1:114 1:36 1:482 HawDerby-G3 86 11 51½ 84¾ 104¾ 54 62½ Rose J L122 fb 5.10 96-06 False Promises1151 Megoman1151 Beau Classic113nk Flattened out 11
13Sep03-6Pim sly 1⅛ ⊗ :472 1:121 1:382 1:513 [S]HSFinney60k 82 4 55½ 45½ 32½ 33 33¾ Dominguez R A L122 fb *.50 82-25 Conservtion1153 CheverlyGold115¾ FoufsWrrior12210 Off rail, weakened 5
16Aug03-11AP gd 1¼ Ⓣ :491 1:14 1:384 2:022 Secretar-G1 95 2 75½ 62¼ 116¼ 64¾ 56 Dominguez R A L121 fb 6.90 88-08 Kicken Kris1163½ Joe Bear1162 Lismore Knight121nk Flattened out 11
20Jly03-5Del fm 1⅛ Ⓣ :462 1:094 1:344 1:472 KentBC-G3 95 3 66 610 55 43½ 11¼ Dominguez R A L115 fb 4.40 105 - FoufasWrrior1151¼ Remind115½ LismoreKnight1193¼ Mid m,wore dwn rvls 7
7Jun03-9CD fm 1⅛ Ⓣ :462 1:104 1:354 1:472 JfrsnCup-G3 86 2 34 39 37 63¾ 57¾ Karamanos H A L114 fb 5.60 89-05 Senor Swinger1205½ Remind116no Rapid Proof120½ Came out bmp start 7
17May03-12Pim gd 1$\frac{3}{16}$:47 1:113 1:362 1:553 Preaknes-G1 89 3 98¼ 89½ 76½ 712 716 Dominguez R A L126 fb 22.40 79-12 FunnyCide1269¾ MidwayRoad126¾ Scrimshaw126no Hopped,pinched start 10
2May03-9CD fm 1$\frac{1}{16}$ Ⓣ :231 :464 1:102 1:411 CRAmrTrf-G3 89 8 1013 1011 1012 99½ 33½ Vega H L117 b 11.40 94-03 Senor Swinger1172½ Remind1171 Foufa'sWarrior117½ Broke in air,closing 10
5Apr03-8Haw fst 1⅛ :463 1:113 1:382 1:512 IlnosDrb-G2 91 1 1011 89 711 57½ 312 Vega H L118 fb 33.20 87-19 TenMostWanted1144 FundofFunds1148 FoufasWarrior118¾ Hopped start 10
1Mar03-8Lrl fst 1$\frac{1}{16}$:251 :492 1:142 1:461 [S]DputdTstmy75k 77 3 42 44 45½ 48½ 27¼ Vega H L122 f 3.70 71-30 CheroksBoy1157¼ FoufsWrrior1221¼ BrushAhd115nk Broke in air,mild bid 5

Freefourinternet
Own: Equirace.Com LLC

B. h. 6 (Apr) FTFFEB00 $200,000
Sire: Tabasco Cat (Storm Cat) $17,490
Dam: Dixie Chimes (Dixieland Band)
Br: Edward P. Evans (Ky)
Tr: Scott Joan(0 0 0 0 .00) 2003:(43 9 .21)

Life	25	6	2	6	$522,582	105	D.Fst	2	1	0	0	$22,800 102
2003	11	2	1	5	$418,598	105	Wet(361)	1	0	0	1	$12,708 99
2002	8	2	0	0	$63,256	98	Turf(295)	22	5	2	5	$487,074 105
	0	0	0	0	$0	–	Dst(0)	0	0	0	0	$0 –

14Dec03–9FG fst 1 1/16 ⊗ :233 :47 1:122 1:444 3↑OClm 80000N 102 1 914 913 89 32 11 Albarado R J L119 *1.70 86– 21 Freefourinternet1191 ClassicPar119hd InvestorsDream1192 Along in time 9
25Oct03–4SA fm 1 Ⓣ :221 :452 1:092 1:334 3↑BCMile-G1 98 6 98¾ 106½ 96 94½ 63¼ Espinoza J L LB126 57.10 90– 04 SxPrfctons119¾ TouchofthBls126nk CntryCty1261¼ In tight 1/8,outkicked 13
4Oct03–8Bel fm 1 Ⓣ :24 :471 1:103 1:343 3↑KelsoBCH-G2 105 7 106¾ 109¼ 104 3nk 1no Espinoza J L L113 20.60 87– 15 Freefourinternet113no ProudMn1141 Rouvres1151¼ Bumped start, widest 10
14Sep03–9WO fm 1 Ⓣ :224 :451 1:091 1:331 3↑AttoMile-G1 90 2 1011 107 106¼ 76 77 Albarado R J L117 37.75 90– 06 TouchoftheBlues119½ SoringFree1211¾ *PerfectSoul*121hd Mild advance 7w 11
5Jly03–9CD fm 1 Ⓣ :234 :47 1:103 1:352 3↑FrckrBCH-G2 97 1 812 910 87 63¾ 21¼ Blanc B L114 7.60 94– 12 TptheAdmirl1151¼ Freefourinternet114½ *PckgeStore*1141½ 8w 1/8p,closing 9
7Jun03–5CD fm 1 1/16 Ⓣ :233 :463 1:104 1:413 3↑OClm 80000N 93 1 43 45½ 44 33 32 Blanc B L118 b *1.10 94– 05 BilOuttheKing1181 MjesticThief1221 Frefourintrnt118½ 4-5w,no late gain 6
Previously trained by De Seroux Laura
3May03–8Hol wf 1 1/16 ⊗ :224 :461 1:09 1:401 3↑InglewoodH103k 99 2 48½ 48½ 38 35½ 35 Espinoza V LB116 fb 3.70 98– 03 Gondolieri1163 TrulyJudge1142 Freefourintrnt11612 Some gain,no threat 4
Previously trained by Simon Charles
23Mar03–8FG fm *1⅛ Ⓣ :482 1:122 1:38 1:51 4↑ExploBdH-G2 100 6 62¾ 78 74¼ 41½ 3nk Sellers S J L115 b 61.70 89– 11 Candid Glen114nk Rouvres115no Freefourinternet115no Missed,on rail 11
15Feb03–7Hou fm 1⅛ Ⓣ :502 1:152 1:41 1:531 3↑ConlyBCTH223k 89 4 83¼ 73¾ 72 31 42½ Sellers S J L115 b 4.90 71– 19 *Candid Glen*1131½ Red Mountain113½ Dynameaux114½ In tight, 4w, gaining 11
1Feb03–9FG fm *1⅛ Ⓣ :502 1:142 1:382 1:502 4↑FGBCH150k 95 5 64½ 67¼ 88¼ 65 33¼ Sellers S J L115 b 5.60 89– 11 MysteryGiver1173¼ Dynmeux115no Frefourintrnt115hd Late between foes 9
5Jan03–9FG fm *1 1/16 Ⓣ :244 :503 1:144 1:451 4↑CERBradlyH75k 96 5 54½ 54 53 55 31¼ Sellers S J L115 b 5.80 86– 13 RoyalSpy1161 Dynmeux115nk Freefourinternet1151 Eased out, tried hard 11

Funny Cide
Own: Sackatoga Stable

Ch. g. 4 (Apr) SARAUG01 $22,000
Sire: Distorted Humor (Forty Niner) $20,000
Dam: Belle's Good Cide (Slewacide)
Br: Win Star Farm, LLC (NY)
Tr: Tagg Barclay(0 0 0 0 .00) 2003:(166 16 .10)

Life	11	5	2	2	$2,099,385	114	D.Fst	8	4	1	1	$1,189,385 109
2003	8	2	2	2	$1,963,200	114	Wet(400)	3	1	1	1	$910,000 114
2002	3	3	0	0	$136,185	103	Turf(295)	0	0	0	0	$0 –
	0	0	0	0	$0	–	Dst(0)	0	0	0	0	$0 –

25Oct03–9SA fst 1¼ :461 1:101 1:341 1:594 3↑BCClasic-G1 97 4 52¼ 65¼ 78 1011 914¾ Krone J A LB121 8.70 91– 07 PleasantlyPerfect1261½ MedglidOro126¾ Dynever121nk Drifted wide, tired 10
3Aug03–11Mth fst 1⅛ :47 1:104 1:36 1:491 HsklInvH-G1 94 5 52½ 54½ 55 47½ 39 Santos J A L123 *1.00 86– 08 Peace Rules1211¾ Sky Mesa1187¼ Funny Cide1231 Outside 1/4,mild bid 7
7Jun03–11Bel sly 1½ :483 1:132 2:023 2:281 Belmont-G1 104 4 11 1hd 21 33 35 Santos J A L126 *1.00 86– 14 EmpireMker126¾ TenMostWnted1264¼ FunnyCid1265¼ Set pace 3w, tired 6
17May03–12Pim gd 1 3/16 :47 1:113 1:362 1:553 Preaknes-G1 114 9 32 21 2½ 15 19¾ Santos J A L126 *1.90 95– 12 FunnyCide1269¾ MidwayRod126¾ Scrimshw126no Bmpd brk,ratd 3w,clear 10
3May03–10CD fst 1¼ :461 1:102 1:353 2:01 KyDerby-G1 109 5 32 31½ 2½ 1hd 11¾ Santos J A L126 12.80 94– 06 *Funny Cide*1261¾ *EmpireMaker*126hd PeaceRules126hd Bmp start,stiff drive 16
12Apr03–8Aqu my 1⅛ :471 1:11 1:354 1:483 WoodMem-G1 110 4 21½ 21½ 21 2hd 2½ Santos J A L123 5.20 92– 12 Empire Maker123½ *Funny Cide*1237½ Kissin Saint1231 Bumped after start 8
9Mar03–9FG fst 1 1/16 :232 :463 1:103 1:423 LaDerby-G2 99 2 11 11½ 1½ 43½ 33¼ Santos J A L122 6.10 94– 17 *Peace Rules*1222¼ [D]Kafwain1221 Funny Cide122½ Came again rail 10
Awarded second purse money
18Jan03–10GP fst 1 1/16 :232 :471 1:112 1:43 HolyBull-G3 87 13 72¼ 41½ 44 44 56½ Santos J A L122 5.30 87– 10 Offlee Wild116hd Powerful Touch1163 Bham1182½ Hit gate, wide, tired 13

Gal O Gal

Own: Hugel Max

B. f. 4 (Mar)
Sire: Manlove (Mr. Prospector) $3,000
Dam: Barnard Gal (Harvard Man)
Br: Max Hugel (Fla)
Tr: Blengs Vincent L(0 0 0 0 .00) 2003:(185 26 .14)

Life	17	6	0	3	$196,777	91	D.Fst	2	0	0	0	$1,300	29
2003	11	3	0	3	$156,957	91	Wet(262)	0	0	0	0	$0	-
2002	6	3	0	0	$39,820	80	Turf(293)	15	6	0	3	$195,477	91
	0	0	0	0	$0	-	Dst(0)	0	0	0	0	$0	-

20Dec03-8Crc	fm	7½f	Ⓣ	:224	:454	1:094	1:273	ⒻFAGenter100k	86	4	4	1112	119	75¼	43½	Douglas R R	L121	12.50	97-01	Changing World1182 Campsie Fells121½ Formal Miss1211	Belated rally	12	
27Sep03-9Pim	gd	1 1/16	Ⓣ	:231	:481	1:131	1:462	ⒻMWashBC-G3	84	6	712	710	69	62¾	43½	Jurado E M	L122	2.50	66-30	Derrianne1221¼ ChicJoy1152 TwiningandDining115nk	Wide, passed faders	7	
17Aug03-9Sar	fm	1⅛	Ⓣ	:462	1:102	1:36	1:49	ⒻLakPlcdH-G2	82	6	88¼	812	714	68	54¾	Velazquez J R	L119	6.30	79-13	Sand Springs121¾ *IndyFiveHundred*114no *FilmMaker*1193½	Steadied stretch	10	
28Jly03-8Sar	fm	1 1/16	Ⓣ	:24	:481	1:121	1:414	ⒻLkGeorge-G3	88	9	88½	89¾	53	63¾	33¼	Velazquez J R	L122	9.60	83-20	Film Maker1152½ Ocean Drive119¾ Gal O Gal122½	Steadied backstretch	11	
5Jly03-5Hol	fm	1¼	Ⓣ	:473	1:114	1:353	1:594	ⒻAmercnOaks750k	69	11	55½	53½	54¼	1313	1311½	Decarlo C P	LB121	69.00	82-11	Dimitrova1212 *SandSprings*121nk AtlanticOcen121½	Stalked 3wd,weakened	14	
22Jun03-10Cnl	fm	1 1/16	🅃	:241	:483	1:133	1:444	3↑ ⒻAlw 35000NC	80	6	1016	1113	108¾	66½	55¼	Jurado E M	L114	*2.00	83-15	Lady Linda1191¾ *Morena Park*117nk Media Access1171¾	No threat	11	
15May03-6Bel	fm	1 1/16	Ⓣ	:242	:472	1:111	1:402	3↑ ⒻAlw 50000N3x	91	6	74	82¾	61¾	2½	1½	Velazquez J R	L114	3.70	95-09	Gal O Gal114½ *Young Star*1201½ *Madeira Mist*120½	Bumped start, wide	8	
6Apr03-9GP	fm	1⅛	Ⓣ	:50	1:15	1:384	1:501	ⒻViaBorghes75k	83	2	63½	66	75½	62¾	3¾	Decarlo C P	L122	4.30	83-14	Fencelineneighbor116½ Fortuitous122nk *Gal O Gal*122½	Traffic inside turn	9	
28Feb03-8GP	fm	1⅛	Ⓣ	:482	1:123	1:363	1:483	ⒻGailyGaily74k	82	8	83¾	108¾	104½	64½	33¼	Decarlo C P	L121	3.50	89-11	Devil At the Wire117nk Formal Miss1153 Gal O Gal121nk	5 wide, rallied	11	
1Feb03-10GP	fm	1 1/16	Ⓣ	:242	:49	1:123	1:421	+ ⒻHcmbride-G3	87	1	85¾	87¼	83¾	31	1½	Decarlo C P	L117	3.30	84-06	Gal O Gal117½ Formal Miss1172 *Devil At the Wire*117no	On hedge, prevailed	8	
22Jan03-10GP	fm	*1 1/16	Ⓣ	:234	:49	1:134	1:454	ⒻClm 80000(80-75)	83	1	84½	89¼	64¼	21	13½	Decarlo C P	L121	*1.40	75-24	*Gal O Gal*1213½ Lil Scout1191 Two Sharky Betty117hd	Drew clear, driving	10	

Gators N Bears

Own: Nechamkin II Leo S

B. c. 4 (Feb)
Sire: Stormy Atlantic (Storm Cat) $12,500
Dam: I'll Be Along (Notebook)
Br: Robert W. Camac (NJ)
Tr: Nechamkin L S II(0 0 0 0 .00) 2003:(45 8 .18)

Life	17	7	4	4	$301,840	108	D.Fst	13	6	3	4	$267,020	108
2003	13	5	3	4	$257,270	108	Wet(405)	4	1	1	0	$34,820	92
2002	4	2	1	0	$44,570	91	Turf(305)	0	0	0	0	$0	-
	0	0	0	0	$0	-	Dst(0)	0	0	0	0	$0	-

21Dec03-8Aqu	fst	6f	⊡	:223	:451	:57	1:092	3↑ GravesdH-G3	100	3	4	41	52¼	53½	34	Wilson R	L115 fb	5.30	93-12	ShkeYouDown1242¼ WytotheTop1141¾ GtorsNBrs115¾	Angled out, rallied	7	
15Nov03-10Lrl	fst	6f		:214	:442	:563	1:084	3↑ DeFrncsM-G1	108	4	6	32½	32	31½	31¾	Wilson R	L115 fb	5.40	93-13	AHuevo1191¾ *ShkeYouDown*123no GtorsNBrs115½	Chased,3-4wd bid,game	10	
18Oct03-9Lrl	fst	6f		:214	:442	:561	1:084	SonnyHine50k	105	2	3	22½	1hd	12	1¾	Wilson R	L119 fb	*1.60	95-17	Gators N Bears119¾ Super Fuse117hd First Blush119no	2wd bid 1/4,driving	8	
20Sep03-5Mth	fst	6f		:214	:441	:561	1:084	3↑ ⓈFrndlyLvrH45k	86	4	4	52	35	36	35¼	Lopez C C	L122 fb	*.50	90-15	SomethingSmith1192¼ SecondCollction1153 *GtorsNBrs*1221	Lacked a rally	7	
10Aug03-3Mth	fst	6f		:214	:434	:554	1:082	Rumson48k	107	1	2	2½	32	21	12¼	Lopez C C	L122 fb	*1.30	97-14	GtorsNBrs1222¼ *SomthingSmth*1167¾ RocknOnRdy119½	Inside turn,driving	4	
4Jly03-10Mth	fst	6f		:214	:441	:564	1:094	JerShrBC-G3	106	4	2	2hd	13	14½	1½	Lopez C C	L115 fb	7.30	90-18	*Gators N Bears*115½ Mt. Carson1228¼ Don Six1152¼	Clear turn,steady drve	6	
14Jun03-8Mth	fst	6f		:213	:442	:563	1:091	3↑ ⓈOClm 40000N	91	2	7	11	11½	11	1nk	Lopez C C	L113 fb	*.50	93-12	*GatorsNBears*113nk *Truemericnspirit*1155¾ Vow119½	Game respons,held well	8	
17May03-6Pim	gd	6f		:224	:454	:581	1:104	HrshJacobs100k	92	3	4	44¼	44	2½	22¼	Fogelsonger R	L117 b	5.40	89-10	Mt. Carson1222¼ *GatorsNBears*1172¼ OnlytheBest122nk	Rail bid 1/8, gamely	8	
27Apr03-6Pim	fst	6f		:231	:454	:574	1:102	3↑ OClm 30000(30-25)N	93	3	2	1hd	1hd	12	2½	Vega H	L113 fb	2.60	92-13	Kendrick119½ GtorsNBers1133¾ PrsidntButlr112nk	Pressrd ins,clear,game	4	
12Apr03-7Aqu	my	7f		:214	:443	1:10	1:23	BayShore-G3	-	2	9	1011	1121	-	-	Migliore R	L116 fb	9.50	- 13	Halo Homewrecker1161 DonSix1165¼ Stanislavsky116¾	Lost action, eased	11	
23Mar03-8Lrl	fst	6f		:221	:444	:563	1:09	Horatius50k	100	8	6	42	4nk	1hd	2nk	Vega H	L115 b	*2.10	94-14	Deadline115nk Gators N Bears1153 *Mt. Carson*1221¼	4wd,dueled,hung	8	
8Feb03-9Lrl	fst	1 1/16		:24	:474	1:114	1:43	MiraclWood50k	90	1	1½	12	11½	21	35¼	Vega H	L117 fb	2.40	89-16	Gimmewink1171¼ PenobscotBy1154 GtorsNBrs1172¾	Rail, pace, gave way	7	
17Jan03-7Lrl	fst	6f		:223	:46	:581	1:101	OClm 50000(50-45)N	97	6	2	12	12	12	15¼	Vega H	L117 fb	*.70	88-23	Gators N Bears1175¼ Pud1141¼ Dr. Phil117no	Rail, pace, driving	8	

Ghostzapper

Own: Stronach Stable

B. c. 4 (Apr)
Sire: Awesome Again (Deputy Minister) $50,000
Dam: Baby Zip (Relaunch)
Br: Adena Springs (Ky)
Tr: Frankel Robert J(0 0 0 0 .00) 2003:(411 114 .28)

Life	6	4	0	1	$406,120	116	D.Fst	5	3	0	1	$379,120	116
2003	4	3	0	1	$378,400	116	Wet(399)	1	1	0	0	$27,000	102
2002	2	1	0	0	$27,720	99	Turf(223)	0	0	0	0	$0	–
	0	0	0	0	$0	–	Dst(0)	0	0	0	0	$0	–

27Sep03–7Bel	fst	6½f	:214 :441 1:083 1:143	3↑ Vosburgh-G1	**116**	2	10	1013	79½	3nk	16½	Castellano J J	L123 b	3.10	100–16	Ghostzapper1236½ Aggadan1261¼ Posse1231¾	Quick 4 wide move	10
23Aug03–10Sar	fst	7f	:213 :433 1:083 1:22	KngsBshp-G1	**106**	9	5	1011	811	86	3½	Castellano J J	L117 b	6.30	96–07	ValidVideo121nk GreatNotion117nk *Ghostzpper*1171¾	Finished fast outside	13
26Jly03–7Sar	fst	7f	:222 :443 1:09 1:213	3↑ Alw 49000n2x	**99**	4	5	32½	33	1½	1½	Castellano J J	L119 b	*.60	99–08	Ghostzapper119½ *Clock Stopper*1153½ Bold Truth1201½	3 wide trip, gamely	6
20Jun03–7Bel	my	6f	:22 :443 :564 1:091	3↑ Alw 45000n1x	**102**	3	4	612	57½	44½	13¼	Castellano J J	L114 b	*.95	93–14	*Ghostzapper*1143¼ *As Wicked*1192 Patriot's Song120nk	Rolled home outside	6

Go Rockin' Robin

Own: Schwartz Herbert T. and Carol A

Dk. b or b. c. 4 (Mar)
Sire: Distorted Humor (Forty Niner) $20,000
Dam: Flag Support (Personal Flag)
Br: McMahon Thoroughbreds & Win Star Farm, LLC (NY)
Tr: Schwartz Scott M(0 0 0 0 .00) 2003:(137 17 .12)

Life	20	4	3	6	$309,835	96	D.Fst	17	2	3	6	$162,475	96
2003	11	3	1	2	$233,446	96	Wet(398)	3	2	0	0	$147,360	93
2002	9	1	2	4	$76,389	83	Turf(268)	0	0	0	0	$0	–
	0	0	0	0	$0	–	Dst(0)	0	0	0	0	$0	–

17Dec03–7Aqu	sly	1 1/16 [•]	:23 :463 1:114 1:45	3↑ Alw 48000n3x	**38**	2	43	51¾	68	619	634¾	Luzzi M J	L114 b	4.70	46–27	BostonPark1101¼ BigSidsParty1196¼ CrypticDevil1211½	Failed to respond	6
20Aug03–8Sar	fst	1⅛	:473 1:113 1:362 1:493	[S]Albany168k	**75**	1	32½	42	44½	410	411¾	Velazquez J R	L121 b	5.70	75–11	TrfficChief1212 AcceptbleVentur1193 SpitthDvil1216¾	Steadied first turn	5
26Jly03–8FL	fst	1 1/16	:25 :493 1:141 1:443	[S]NYDerby142k	**79**	5	21	2½	2½	34	37	Gryder A T	L124 b	2.65	91–15	*Traffic Chief*1193 Spite the Devil1244 Go Rockin' Robin1247¾	Weakened	5
6Jly03–10Bel	fst	1 1/16	:231 :453 1:093 1:413	Dwyer-G2	**80**	5	46½	48½	59	618	616¾	Bridgmohan S X	L121 b	15.30	75–11	*Strong Hope*115nk Nacheezmo1153 Sky Mesa1195¼	No response	7
14Jun03–11Del	fst	1 1/16	:223 :46 1:103 1:431	LRichrds-G3	**86**	2	52¾	52¼	54¼	43½	45¼	Luzzi M J	L122 b	*1.50	87–13	AwsomTim115no ChrstnsOutlw115¾ ChroksBoy1224½	Lacked needed rally	8
24May03–8Bel	sly	1⅛	:444 1:084 1:344 1:482	PeterPan-G2	**93**	3	51¾	41½	3nk	11	16	Bridgmohan S X	L117 b	13.00	88–12	GoRockin'Robin1176 Alysweep123¾ Supervisor1152	3 wide move, drew off	6
2May03–7Aqu	fst	1⅛	:471 1:111 1:364 1:494	3↑ Alw 44000n1x	**92**	3	62¾	83½	83¾	1hd	12½	Luzzi M J	L112 b	4.00	87–18	*GoRocknRbn*1122½ IndnCrd1162¾ LkngArnd1213¾	Drew clear when roused	8
19Apr03–10Aqu	fst	1	:223 :444 1:092 1:362	3↑ [S]Alw 46000n2x	**69**	5	62¼	61¾	52¾	59½	79	Luzzi M J	L116 br	*1.00	74–13	JllyRollRomp1213¼ SyCsnLnny1212¾ LkngGrnd118¾	Chased outside, tired	11
28Mar03–8Aqu	fst	1⅛	:481 1:123 1:371 1:494	Alw 50000c	**96**	4	43	51½	41¾	2½	21	Luzzi M J	L113 b	4.50	86–23	KissinSnt1161 GoRocknRobn1135 LookOutEvn1155½	3 wide move, gamely	5
8Feb03–8Aqu	fst	1 1/16 [•]	:24 :48 1:12 1:443	Whirlaway81k	**88**	6	54½	62	53½	43½	33¼	Luzzi M J	L118 b	16.30	80–23	BostonPrk1161 GreyComet1222¼ GoRockinRobin118½	Good finish on rail	6
2Jan03–7Aqu	my	1 [•]	:234 :474 1:131 1:384	[S]Alw 44000n1x	**81**	7	55½	35½	32	2½	1nk	Luzzi M J	L117 b	2.20	84–22	GoRocknRobn117nk PolshJwl1175¾ AwknthDrgn1226	Determined outside	8

Gold Mover
Own: Evans Edward P

Ch. m. 6 (Mar)
Sire: Gold Fever (Forty Niner) $5,000
Dam: Intentional Move (Tentam)
Br: Edward P. Evans (Ky)
Tr: Hennig Mark A(0 0 0 0 .00) 2003:(503 73 .15)

Life	31	13	9	5	$1,523,010	112	D.Fst	28	12	9	4	$1,440,000	112
2003	6	2	2	2	$462,480	107	Wet(301)	3	1	0	1	$83,010	99
2002	9	4	3	0	$503,032	112	Turf(305)	0	0	0	0	$0	-
	0	0	0	0	$0	-	Dst(0)	0	0	0	0	$0	-

24Aug03-9Sar	fst	7f	:223 :45 1:09 1:221	3↑[F]BalrinaH-G1	95	6	3	2½	3½	42	32	Coa E M	L118	8.70e	94-12	*HarmonyLodge*115no ShineAgain1202 GoldMover118hd	Good finish outside	8
12Jly03-11Crc	fst	6f	:212 :442 :573 1:111	3↑[F]PrcsRnyH-G2	103	3	5	2½	21½	2½	1no	Bailey J D	L118	*1.50	88-11	GoldMovr118no VisioninFlight1134¼ *HrmonyLodg*116hd	All out, edged rival	8
8Jun03-8Bel	my	6½f	:224 :454 1:091 1:151	3↑[F]VagrncyH-G2	93	3	2	22	21½	34½	35	Bailey J D	L118	1.45	92-10	Shawklit Mint1151¾ Shine Again1213¼ *Gold Mover*118	Wide, no response	3
3May03-8CD	fst	7f	:222 :452 1:10 1:22	4↑[F]HmnaDstH-G1	97	1	2	41¼	41½	44	24½	Prado E S	L119	3.00	87-08	*Sightseek*1164½ Gold Mover119hd Miss Lodi1142¼	5w bid,all out	8
16Mar03-10GP	fst	6½f	:222 :442 1:09 1:154	3↑[F]HurrcnBrtH100k	107	4	3	1hd	1hd	1½	13½	Prado E S	L117	1.30	97-12	GoldMover1173½ HrmonyLodge1164¼ Belterr1162¾	Vied inside, drew away	5
14Feb03-9GP	fst	7f	:222 :443 1:091 1:221	3↑[F]ShrlJnsH-G3	97	1	2	41¼	42½	33	23	Bailey J D	L117	*.50	94-15	Harmony Lodge1143 *Gold Mover*117½ *NonsuchBay*1172¾	Inside, no late gain	6

Golden Marlin
Own: Estate of Joe Famularo and Glass Will

B. f. 4 (Feb)
Sire: Marlin (Sword Dance*Ire) $8,000
Dam: Golden Reality (Unreal Zeal)
Br: Timothy Thornton (Ky)
Tr: Foley Gregory D(0 0 0 0 .00) 2003:(230 50 .22)

Life	14	5	2	1	$233,065	97	D.Fst	9	4	1	1	$149,920	97
2003	11	4	1	0	$193,970	97	Wet(242)	3	1	1	0	$77,580	91
2002	3	1	1	1	$39,095	87	Turf(224)	2	0	0	0	$5,565	79
	0	0	0	0	$0	-	Dst(0)	0	0	0	0	$0	-

27Nov03-10CD	sly	1⅛	:474 1:123 1:382 1:511	3↑[F]FallCtyH-G2	58	8	42	31½	32½	712	830¼	Perret C	L114	13.10	52-25	Lead Story1166½ Mayo On the Side1146 Cloakof Vagueness1146½	5w,tired	9
9Nov03-4CD	fst	1 1/16	:243 :492 1:142 1:443	3↑[F]Alw 63440c	89	2	1½	1½	3nk	1hd	11	Day P	L117	*.80	85-18	GoldnMrlin1171 MinistrsBby1171½ SwtwtrProms117½	Bmp start,hand urg	6
10Oct03-9Kee	fst	7f	:214 :441 1:092 1:213	[F]RavenRun-G3	71	11	2	83¼	85¾	87¾	714	Bejarano R	L123	15.20	82-11	Yell1232½ Ebony Breeze123¾ *Tina Bull*117no	6-7w trip,no rally	12
14Sep03-9TP	fst	6f	:221 :461 :582 1:103	3↑[F]Alw 30600N$Y	97	5	3	64	2hd	14	19½	Bejarano R	L113	*1.90	89-21	Golden Marlin1139½ Malo116½ Silver Sonnet1163½	Lost footing, 5w	7
4Jly03-6PrM	fst	1 1/16	:224 :454 1:093 1:413	[F]IowaOaks125k	62	6	43	43	58	715	722	Birzer A E	LB121	*1.10	78-11	WildwoodRoyal121¾ GoldenReputashn1122¼ Tulupi1126¾	4 wide first turn	8
14Jun03-8CD	fm	1⅛ [T]	:471 1:114 1:362 1:483	[F]Regret-G3	79	4	42	55½	64	64¼	65¾	Day P	L114	8.40	85-10	SandSprings1183 PersonlLegend116½ Achnsheen116hd	Inside,empty lane	12
17May03-9CD	sly	1 1/16	:234 :48 1:124 1:454	[F]Dogwood-G3	91	7	1½	1½	11½	1hd	11	Sellers S J	L115	3.80	79-24	Golden Marlin1151 Double Scoop1142½ Throne1141½	Repelled bid,driving	7
18Apr03-9Kee	yl	1 [T]	:224 :463 1:12 1:36	[F]Applachian111k	78	4	2½	21	21	34½	48¼	Day P	L116	5.90	80-14	*Ocean Drive*120½ Tangle1176¾ Cheryl's Myth1161	Pressed,weakened	8
22Mar03-8TP	fst	1	:222 :461 1:11 1:372	[F]BourbnttBC147k	95	6	21	2hd	2hd	1hd	11¼	Lumpkins J	L114	*2.80	87-14	[D]GldnMrln1141¼ AdptdDhtr1148¼ UnbrdldFmm1212¾	Drifted in twice str	11
Disqualified and placed second																		
15Feb03-9FG	fst	1 1/16	:232 :464 1:122 1:442	[F]Slvrbltd-G2	77	7	43	32	32	57	612¾	Sellers S J	L119	5.20	75-12	BllofPrntown1228¼ AftrnoonDrms1121½ RbrdldDrms117nk	4-w, 3-w, faded	8
18Jan03-10TP	fst	6½f	:224 :453 1:11 1:18	[F]CinTrophy49k	76	5	6	31	2hd	11	11½	Lumpkins J	L115	*1.00	87-16	GldnMrln1151½ MssMrAppls1191 PmprdPrncss115½	In bit tight,rdden out	8

Got Koko

Own: Headley Aase and Leung, Paul

B. m. 5 (Jan) KEESEP00 $30,000
Sire: Signal Tap (Fappiano) $2,500
Dam: Baby North (Northern Baby)
Br: Eileen H. Hartis (Tex)
Tr: Headley Bruce(0 0 0 0 .00) 2003:(138 29 .21)

Life	14	7	1	3	$930,946	107	D.Fst	11 7 1 2	$922,150 107
2003	6	3	1	1	$688,000	107	Wet(266)	0 0 0 0	$0 –
2002	8	4	0	2	$242,946	98	Turf(264)	3 0 0 1	$8,796 79
	0	0	0	0	$0	–	Dst(0)	0 0 0 0	$0 –

25Oct03–2SA fst 1⅛ :47 1:11 1:35⁴ 1:49 3↑ ⒻBCDistaf-G1 **89** 7 5 1¾ 5 2½ 5 2¾ 4⁵ 3⁷ Solis A LB123 b 4.00 82–07 Adoration123 4½ Elloluv119 2½ Got Koko123 3½ 4wd,3wd,best of rest 7
28Sep03–6SA fst 1 1/16 :23² :47¹ 1:11¹ 1:42⁴ 3↑ ⒻLdySсBCH-G2 **105** 2 6⁷ 6 7½ 6 5½ 4² 1½ Solis A LB118 b 5.00 90–16 Got Koko118½ [D]Elloluv116 1¾ Azeri128¹ 4wd into lane,rallied 6
10Aug03–8Dmr fst 1 1/16 :23¹ :47 1:11 1:42 3↑ ⒻCLHrschH-G2 **94** 2 3 1½ 3 1½ 2 1½ 2 2½ 2 3¼ Solis A LB118 b 4.20 92–12 Azeri127 3¼ *Got Koko*118hd Tropical Blossom108 4½ Bobbled bit start 5
9Mar03–8SA fst 1⅛ :47 1:10³ 1:35³ 1:48¹ 4↑ ⒻSMrgrtaH-G1 **94** 1 3² 4 4½ 4⁷ 4⁴ 4¹⁰ Solis A LB120 b 2.00 83–16 Starrer121² *Sightseek*116³ Bella Bellucci116⁵ Saved ground to lane 5
8Feb03–6SA fst 1⅛ :46³ 1:10⁴ 1:35³ 1:48² ⒻLaCanada-G2 **106** 5 4² 3 1½ 3¹ 3¹ 1¾ Solis A LB121 b 2.10 92–11 Got Koko121¾ Sightseek118 1½ Bella Bellucci118³ 3wd,4wd,determinedly 5
19Jan03–7SA fst 1 1/16 :23 :46² 1:10² 1:42¹ ⒻElEncino-G2 **107** 7 6 5½ 5 1¾ 3½ 1½ 1 1½ Solis A LB119 b 3.20 93–17 *GotKoko*119 1½ BellBellucci117³ BreNcssitis119no 5wd move,led 3wd,game 8

Grand Hombre

Own: Darley Stable

Dk. b or b. g. 4 (Apr)
Sire: Grand Slam (Gone West) $30,000
Dam: Santona*Chi (Winning)
Br: Earl I. Mack (Ky)
Tr: Albertrani Thomas(0 0 0 0 .00) 2003:(41 7 .17)

Life	5	4	1	0	$598,360	108	D.Fst	4 3 1 0	$148,360 104
2003	5	4	1	0	$598,360	108	Wet(392)	1 1 0 0	$450,000 108
2002	0	M	0	0	$0	–	Turf(336)	0 0 0 0	$0 –
	0	0	0	0	$0	–	Dst(0)	0 0 0 0	$0 –

4Oct03–9Hoo fst 1 1/16 :22³ :46² 1:10³ 1:43² IndnaDby-G3 **101** 8 7⁵ 6 4½ 6⁵ 3 3½ 2¹ Prado E S LB124 *1.10 91–29 Excessiveplesure124¹ GrndHombr124 1¼ Wndo124 1¼ 3-4wd rally,closing in 8
Previously trained by Manning Dennis J
1Sep03–11Pha sly 1⅛ :46³ 1:10⁴ 1:36¹ 1:49 PaDerby-G3 **108** 5 6 3¼ 7 4¾ 3² 1¹ 1 5¼ Bravo J L114 5.70 99–16 Grand Hombre114 5¼ Gimmeawink122² Ashmore114nk Drew off, driving 10
25Jly03–8Mth fst 1 1/16 :23¹ :46¹ 1:09⁴ 1:42¹ 3↑ Alw 39000N2x **104** 3 2 1½ 2¹ 2 1½ 1¹ 1 1¾ Cruz C L115 *.50 100–12 *GrandHombre*115 1¾ SirRay115 18¾ MudslideSlim121 1½ Dueled,clear final 1/8 6
29Jun03–8Mth fst 1⁷⁰ :24 :48² 1:13¹ 1:43 3↑ Alw 37000N1x **102** 3 1hd 1hd 1hd 1² 1 2½ Cruz C L114 *.60 88–21 *GrndHombre*114 2½ *Cointreu*115hd PrsonlTouch117 12¼ Pace,steady handling 6
8Mar03–8GP fst 6f :22 :44³ :56⁴ 1:08³ Md Sp Wt 34k **100** 8 3 1hd 1hd 1² 1⁴ Prado E S L121 14.30 101–01 *Grand Hombre*121⁴ *Mazengah*121⁴ *Monty Man*121² Vied, rail, drew away 12

Halfbridled

Own: Wertheimer Farm LLC

Dk. b or b. f. 3 (Feb)
Sire: Unbridled (Fappiano) $200,000
Dam: Half Queen (Deputy Minister)
Br: Wertheimer & Frere (Ky)
Tr: Mandella Richard E(0 0 0 0 .00) 2003:(253 51 .20)

Life	4	4	0	0	$849,400	99	D.Fst	4 4 0 0	$849,400 99
2003	4	4	0	0	$849,400	99	Wet(413)	0 0 0 0	$0 –
2002	0	M	0	0	$0	–	Turf(282)	0 0 0 0	$0 –
	0	0	0	0	$0	–	Dst(0)	0 0 0 0	$0 –

25Oct03–3SA fst 1 1/16 :22⁴ :46⁴ 1:10⁴ 1:42³ ⒻBCJuvFil-G1 **99** 14 7 4½ 5 1¾ 3¹ 1½ 1 2½ Krone J A LB119 *2.30 91–07 Halfbridled119 2½ *Ashado*119nk *Victory U. S. A.*119 9¼ Wide trip, drew off 14
28Sep03–9SA fst 1 1/16 :24 :48 1:12² 1:43³ ⒻOakLeaf-G2 **98** 4 1 1½ 2½ 1¹ 1² 1 4½ Krone J A LB119 *.30 86–16 *Halfbridled*119 4½ Tarlow119½ Hollywood Story119 6½ Inside,clear,gamely 7
30Aug03–8Dmr fst 7f :22⁴ :45¹ 1:09³ 1:22¹ ⒻDmrDeb-G1 **99** 1 4 4² 2hd 1 1½ 1⁵ Krone J A LB116 1.60 91–13 *Hlfbridld*116⁵ HollywoodStory115no VictoryUSA116 1½ Re-bid rail 1/4,clear 6
27Jly03–3Dmr fst 5½f :22 :45¹ :57⁴ 1:04 ⒻMd Sp Wt 49k **87** 1 4 6⁵ 6 4¼ 3¹ 1 4½ Krone J A B118 3.60 95–10 *Halfbridled*118 4½ UppityKitty118² HaleakalSunrise118² 4wd rally,drew off 6

Halo Homewrecker
Own: Evans Edward P

B. c. 4 (Apr)
Sire: Southern Halo (Halo) $21,050
Dam: Marital Spook (Silver Ghost)
Br: Edward P. Evans (Va)
Tr: Hennig Mark A(0 0 0 0 .00) 2003:(503 73 .15)

Life	9	3	0	1	$159,745	97
2003	8	3	0	1	$157,165	97
2002	1	M	0	0	$2,580	54
	0	0	0	0	$0	-

D.Fst	7	2	0	0	$47,745	97
Wet(399)	2	1	0	1	$112,000	97
Turf(301)	0	0	0	0	$0	-
Dst(0)	0	0	0	0	$0	-

9Oct03-6Bel fst	1	:243 :464 1:103 1:36	RCornadoQst65k	79	3	1½	1hd	3nk	53	510	Migliore R	L119 b	10.00	76-12	Newfoundland122¼ Conservation119½ Qais119¼	Vied inside, tired	5
23Aug03-10Sar fst	7f	:213 :433 1:083 1:22	KngsBshp-G1	74	5	7	6¾	6½	1115	1214¾	Migliore R	L121 b	54.50	82-07	Valid Video121nk Great Notion117nk *Ghostzapper*117¾	Inside trip, tired	13
12Jly03-10Crc fst	6f	:213 :443 :57 1:10	CarryBck-G3	86	2	8	7¾	6¾	5½	7¼	Bailey J D	L119	*2.30	85-11	*Valid Video*122½ *Cajun Beat*117¼ Super Fuse117nk	Checked early	10
7Jun03-9Bel sly	7f	:221 :443 1:084 1:22	RvaRdgBC-G2	97	8	1	6½	5½	4½	3¼	Stevens G L	L123	7.40	84-10	Posse123no Midas Eyes123¼ Halo Homewrecker123hd	4 wide run turn	8
3May03-9Aqu fst	1	:223 :45 1:093 1:354	Withers-G3	87	2	2½	3½	41	6¼	6½	Velazquez J R	123	*1.50	81-21	SpitetheDevil116nk Alysweep1231 Stnislvsky116hd	Bumped soundly start	8
12Apr03-7Aqu my	7f	:214 :443 1:10 1:23	BayShore-G3	96	6	4	41	31	21	11	Velazquez J R	116	3.80	88-13	HaloHomewrecker1161 DonSix116¼ Stnislvsky116¾	3 wide move, driving	11
22Mar03-9GP fst	7f	:221 :45 1:092 1:22	Alw 38000N1x	96	5	2	31	21	12	1¾	Bailey J D	122	*.30	98-02	*HloHomewrecker*122¾ Vlenzo118½ SwiftThundr118¼	Drew clear, handily	7
22Feb03-9GP fst	7f	:22 :442 1:084 1:214	Md Sp Wt 34k	97	4	4	1hd	1½	2hd	1nk	Bailey J D	122	6.60	99-07	*Halo Homewrecker*122nk *Erin's Storm*122½ *Buju*122¾	Vied inside, prevailed	10

Happy Trails
Own: Goldfarb Sanford and Team Julep Stabl

Dk. b or b. c. 4 (Mar) EASOCT01 $45,000
Sire: Peaks and Valleys (Mt. Livermore) $10,000
Dam: Part With Pride (Executive Pride*Ire)
Br: Paula E. Parsons (Ky)
Tr: Klesaris Steve B(0 0 0 0 .00) 2003:(347 77 .22)

Life	8	4	1	0	$170,445	91
2003	4	3	0	0	$153,420	91
2002	4	1	1	0	$17,025	69
	0	0	0	0	$0	-

D.Fst	5	2	0	0	$37,185	77
Wet(352)	3	2	1	0	$133,260	91
Turf(228)	0	0	0	0	$0	-
Dst(0)	0	0	0	0	$0	-

14Jun03-7Bel gd	1⅛	⊗:461 1:112 1:364 1:50	HillPrnc-G3	91	4	69	6½	5½	31	1¼	Bridgmohan S X	L120 b	11.10	80-19	Happy Trails120¼ *Traffic Chief*1144 Chilly Rooster114½	Along late outside	6
26May03-10Mth sly	1 1/16	⊗:233 :474 1:124 1:452	JrsyDrby-G3	89	2	5¾	5½	4¾	3nk	1¼	Toribio A R	L114 b	1.90e	84-18	*HappyTrails*114¼ StoneCanyon114¾ AngelicAur115½	Blocked,rallied,clear	6
1May03-6Aqu fst	1	:232 :462 1:103 1:35	Clm 75000(75-65)	76	2	5½	5¼	4½	4½	4½	Bridgmohan S X	L119 b	3.95	84-11	PrsonlTch115¾ TtlCntndr119¼ FghtngRyKlly117½	Bumped start, 3 wide	6
15Mar03-3Aqu fst	1	⊡:243 :482 1:124 1:39	Clm 50000(50-40)	77	1	42	42	4¼	2½	1¼	Bridgmohan S X	L120 b	2.95	83-17	HappyTrails120¼ SubordinatesLad120½ *Krebsie*120¼	Came wide, driving	5

Hard Buck (Brz)
Own: Team Victory II

Dk. b or b. c. 5 (Nov)
Sire: Spend a Buck (Buckaroo)
Dam: Social Secret (Secreto)
Br: Haras Old Friends (Brz)
Tr: McPeek Kenneth G(0 0 0 0 .00) 2003:(400 61 .15)

Life	13	8	2	0	$233,148	103
2003	5	3	1	0	$208,238	103
2002	8	5	1	0	$24,910	-
	0	0	0	0	$0	-

D.Fst	1	0	0	0	$0	-
Wet(323)	0	0	0	0	$0	-
Turf(314)	12	8	2	0	$233,148	103
Dst(0)	0	0	0	0	$0	-

16Nov03-9CD yl	1⅛	Ⓣ:492 1:142 1:391 1:513	3↑ RivrCtyH-G3	103	2	3½	32	3½	21	1½	Blanc B	L118	11.60	76-26	Hard Buck118½ Warleigh1171 Rowans Park1141	Rallied rail, driving	10
20Sep03-9KD fm	1	Ⓣ:263 :48 1:142 1:374	3↑ KyCupMile100k	97	6	23	2½	3½	1hd	1nk	Blanc B	L122	3.30	91-17	*Hard Buck*122nk *Gretchen's Star*1172 Last Stand115½	4w,long drive,gamely	8
1Sep03-10EIP gd	1⅛	Ⓣ:48 1:114 1:36 1:48	3↑ TriStateH57k	98	3	2hd	2hd	1hd	1hd	1½	Bejarano R	L116	1.30	84-22	*Hard Buck*116½ Red Mountain115no Classic Par115	Dueled,driving,clear	3
29Mar03♦Nad al Sheba (UAE) fst	*1¼	LH 2:022	3↑ UAE Derby-G2 Stk 2000000							917½	Murtagh J	128	-		Victory Moon128½ Songlark119¾ Inamorato119¼		14
Timeform rating: 86															*Towards rear,effort 2f out,no threat.Outta Here 4th,Parhelion 10th*		
9Feb03♦Gavea (Brz) fm	*1	Ⓣ LH 1:333	GP Estado do Rio de Janeiro-G1 Stk 24500							25½	Lavor C	123	*.80		Pico Central123½ Hard Buck1231 Naguchi123¾		16

Harlan's Holiday

Own: Starlight Stable LLC

B. h. 5 (Apr) FTKJUL00 $97,000
Sire: Harlan (Storm Cat)
Dam: Christmas in Aiken (Affirmed)
Br: Double D Farm Corp. (Ohio)
Tr: Pletcher Todd A(0 0 0 0 .00) 2003:(826 199 .24)

Life	22	9	6	1	$3,632,664	113	D.Fst	18	8	5	0	$3,175,164	113
2003	6	2	2	0	$1,685,100	113	Wet(362)	4	1	1	1	$457,500	109
2002	10	3	2	1	$1,606,000	109	Turf(308)	0	0	0	0	$0	–
	0	0	0	0	$0	–	Dst(0)	0	0	0	0	$0	–

16Aug03–7Sar fst 1¼ :48 1:114 1:37 2:032 3↑SarBCH-G2 **88** 5 43 53½ 86¾ 810 816¾ Velazquez J R L121 2.55 73–14 Puzzlement1133¼ Volponi1221¾ Iron Deputy1154¼ Bumped start, inside 8
13Jly03–9Hol fst 1¼ :453 1:092 1:341 2:002 3↑HolGldCp-G1 **112** 6 42½ 31½ 21½ 22½ 23 Velazquez J R LB124 3.90 102–07 Congaree1243 Harlan's Holiday1242 Kudos1241 Off rail,2nd best 7
14Jun03–9Bel sly 1⅛ :464 1:10 1:35 1:474 3↑BroklynH-G2 **88** 1 42 41½ 44 513 514½ Velazquez J R L122 *2.00 76–09 Iron Deputy1142½ Volponi1223 Saarland1152½ Off slowly, 4 wide 5
29Mar03♦Nad al Sheba (UAE) ft *1¼ LH 2:002 3↑Dubai World Cup-G1 Stk 6000000 25 Velazquez J R 126 - Moon Ballad1265 Harlan's Holiday1261 *Nayef*126no 11
Trackd ldrs, 2nd str, stayed on well fnl 400m, no chance with wnr
22Feb03–11GP fst 1⅛ :463 1:102 1:353 1:49 3↑DonnH-G1 **113** 11 54¼ 44 31½ 1½ 12½ Velazquez J R L120 *2.20 97–13 HarlnsHolidy1202½ *HerosTribute*1141½ Puzzlement114nk 3 wide, drew clear 11
2Feb03–4GP fst 1$\frac{1}{16}$:23 :462 1:104 1:421 4↑Alw 46000N$MY **111** 2 42½ 43 31 11½ 11¾ Velazquez J R L116 *.70 98–12 *Harlan's Holiday*1161¾ Bonus Pack1163 Mr. John1163 4 wide, fully extended 6

Harmony Lodge

Own: Melnyk Eugene and Laura

Ch. m. 6 (Mar) FTFFEB00 $1,650,000
Sire: Hennessy (Storm Cat) $35,000
Dam: Win Crafty Lady (Crafty Prospector)
Br: Sabine Stables (Ky)
Tr: Pletcher Todd A(0 0 0 0 .00) 2003:(826 199 .24)

Life	18	9	1	4	$675,120	107	D.Fst	14	7	1	4	$611,020	107
2003	8	5	1	2	$516,300	107	Wet(359)	3	2	0	0	$63,600	105
2002	3	1	0	0	$42,600	105	Turf(298)	1	0	0	0	$500	63
	0	0	0	0	$0	–	Dst(0)	0	0	0	0	$0	–

5Oct03–9Bel fst 6½f :233 :464 1:10 1:161 3↑Ⓕ GlntBlmH-G2 **107** 2 1 1hd 1½ 12½ 1½ Migliore R L117 2.05 92–15 HrmonyLodg117½ HousPrty116hd SlwsFinlAnswr1126 Pace, clear, held on 6
24Aug03–9Sar fst 7f :223 :45 1:09 1:221 3↑Ⓕ BalrinaH-G1 **100** 8 1 1½ 1hd 11½ 1no Migliore R L115 12.90 96–12 *HarmonyLodge*115no ShineAgain1202 GoldMover118hd Pace, clear, held on 8
12Jly03–11Crc fst 6f :212 :442 :573 1:111 3↑Ⓕ PrcsRnyH-G2 **92** 2 4 1½ 11½ 1½ 34¼ Coa E M L116 3.30 84–11 GoldMover118no VisioninFlight1134¼ *HrmonyLodge*116hd Inside, gave way 8
22Jun03–3WO fst 7f :22 :443 1:092 1:22 3↑Ⓕ SwtBriarTo108k **104** 1 3 3½ 1½ 13 15½ Coa E M L117 *.90 94–09 HrmonyLodge1175½ *WinterGrdn*1151 *ActingDputy*117¾ Came thru, drew off 6
11May03–8Bel fst 6f :214 :442 :562 1:09 3↑Ⓕ GnunRskH-G2 **90** 1 2½ 2½ 32 35¼ Prado E S L116 7.00 89–18 Shine Again1194 Carson Hollow1221¼ *Harmony Lodge*1166¼ Stubborn, fog 4
16Mar03–10GP fst 6½f :222 :442 1:09 1:154 3↑Ⓕ HurrcnBrtH100k **99** 5 2 2hd 2hd 21½ 23½ Day P L116 *1.10 93–12 Gold Mover1173½ Harmony Lodge1164¼ Belterra1162¾ Vied, weakened 5
14Feb03–9GP fst 7f :222 :443 1:091 1:221 3↑Ⓕ ShrlJnsH-G3 **104** 2 1 2hd 1hd 13 13 Velazquez J R L114 4.70 97–15 Harmony Lodge1143 *Gold Mover*117½ *Nonsuch Bay*1172¾ Inside, drew clear 6
12Jan03–10GP fst 6f :214 :444 :57 1:101 3↑Ⓕ 1stLadyH-G3 **98** 7 5 52¼ 1hd 11 11¾ Velazquez J R L113 6.80 93–13 *HarmonyLodge*1131¾ FlyMeCrazy1141¾ *HuntedLss*1143½ 4 wide, edged away 7

Heat Haze (GB)

Own: Juddmonte Farms Inc

Dk. b or b. f. 5 (Mar)
Sire: Green Desert (Danzig)
Dam: Hasili*Ire (Kahyasi)
Br: Juddmonte Farms (GB)
Tr: Frankel Robert J(0 0 0 0 .00) 2003:(411 114 .28)

Life	14	7	2	2	$1,183,696	105	D.Fst	0	0	0	0	$0	-
2003	7	4	1	1	$1,101,460	105	Wet(330)	0	0	0	0	$0	-
2002	7	3	1	1	$82,236	89	Turf(332)	14	7	2	2	$1,183,696	105
	0	0	0	0	$0	-	Dst(0)	0	0	0	0	$0	-

30Nov03–6Hol	fm	1	Ⓣ :23^2	:46^4	1:10^2	1:34^2	3↑ⒻMatriarc-G1	**103**	11	14^{10}	14^{11}	14^{9}	$9^{3\frac12}$	1^{nk}	Velazquez J R	**LB**123	4.30	92–17	Heat Haze123^{nk} Musical Chimes120^{no} Dedication123$\frac12$	Off slow,rallied,up 14
25Oct03–6SA	fm	1¼	Ⓣ :46^3	1:10^2	1:35^1	1:59	3↑ⒻBCF&MTrf-G1	**104**	3	11^{13}	11^{15}	$10^{6\frac12}$	$6^{3\frac34}$	$4^{2\frac34}$	Bailey J D	**LB**123	7.00	95–04	Islington123^{nk} L'Ancresse118$^{2\frac12}$ Yesterday118^{no}	Shuffled early,rallied 12
27Sep03–8Bel	fm	1¼	[T] :49^4	1:14^4	1:39	2:02^3	3↑ⒻFlwrBlIv-G1	**101**	7	7^{9}	7^{5}	$6^{3\frac12}$	$5^{2\frac14}$	3^{1}	Valdivia J Jr	**L**123	*.85	80–17	Dimitrova114^1 Walzerkoenigin120^{no} Heat Haze123$^{1\frac14}$	Game finish outside 7
16Aug03–8AP	gd	1$\frac{3}{16}$	Ⓣ :49^3	1:13^3	1:38	1:55^4	3↑ⒻBeverlyD-G1	**104**	2	7^{5}	$7^{6\frac12}$	7^{3}	$5^{3\frac12}$	$1^{1\frac14}$	Valdivia J Jr	**L**123	*1.70	95–08	Heat Haze123$^{1\frac14}$ *Bien Nicole*123$\frac12$ Riskaverse123$^{1\frac12}$	4 wide 1/4, driving 7
26Jly03–8Sar	fm	1⅛	Ⓣ :49	1:13	1:36^3	1:47^4	3↑ⒻDianaH-G1	**105**	1	7^{3}	$6^{1\frac34}$	$5^{1\frac12}$	2^{hd}	2^{nk}	Bailey J D	**L**118	*1.45e	90–10	Voodoo Dancer120^{nk} *Heat Haze*118$^{1\frac34}$ Pertuisane115$\frac34$	4 wide move, gamely 8
3May03–7CD	fm	1	Ⓣ :23^2	:46^2	1:10^4	1:33^4	3↑ⒻCtDstTMI-G3	**99**	4	$11^{9\frac12}$	$11^{8\frac14}$	$9^{5\frac12}$	$3^{1\frac12}$	$1^{1\frac12}$	Valdivia J Jr	**L**123	2.40	103 -	Heat Haze123$^{1\frac12}$ Quick Tip123$\frac34$ Sentimental Value121$^{1\frac14}$	8w lane,drvg,clear 11
5Apr03–4SA	fm	*6½f	Ⓣ :22	:44^2	1:07^1	1:13	4↑ⒻLsCngasH-G3	**97**	7	6	$8^{5\frac34}$	$8^{5\frac12}$	4^{4}	1^{3}	Valdivia J Jr	**LB**114	2.80	92–07	*Heat Haze*114^3 Icantgoforthat114^{hd} Paga116^1	5wd into lane,rallied 8

Heckle

Own: Dogwood Stable

Gr/ro. c. 3 (Jan) KEEJUL02 $90,000
Sire: Hennessy (Storm Cat) $35,000
Dam: Bid Me Adieu (Spectacular Bid)
Br: Gaines-Gentry Thoroughbreds & Pacelco S.A. (Ky)
Tr: Pletcher Todd A(0 0 0 0 .00) 2003:(826 199 .24)

Life	4	2	0	0	$103,045	88	D.Fst	2	1	0	0	$71,820	88
2003	4	2	0	0	$103,045	88	Wet(324)	2	1	0	0	$31,225	16
2002	0	M	0	0	$0	-	Turf(322)	0	0	0	0	$0	-
	0	0	0	0	$0	-	Dst(0)	0	0	0	0	$0	-

24Jly03–8Sar	sly	6f	:21^2	:44^4	:57^2	1:10^3	Sanford-G2	**16**	5	6	$3^{\frac12}$	$7^{8\frac14}$	7^{20}	7^{33}	Bailey J D	**L**122	3.30	56–12	ChpelRoyl122$^{5\frac34}$ BlushingIndin118$^{3\frac12}$ *FlushingMedows*118$^{1\frac14}$	Stumbled start 7
28Jun03–7Bel	fst	5½f	:22^1	:45^3	:57^4	1:04^3	Tremont-G3	**88**	6	4	$1^{1\frac12}$	$1^{1\frac12}$	1^{6}	$1^{3\frac14}$	Velazquez J R	**L**114	2.95	90–15	Heckle114$^{3\frac14}$ Adage114^1 Hasslefree114$^{6\frac14}$	Drew away when roused 7
3May03–6CD	fst	5f	:22	:45^2		:57^2	3ChmnyJuv114k	**76**	5	7	3^{1}	$2^{\frac12}$	$3^{1\frac12}$	4^{5}	Bailey J D	**L**118	*.50	93–08	*Limehouse*118$^{1\frac14}$ El Sysco Kid119$^{3\frac12}$ East Bay115^{nk}	Broke awk,bmp gate 7
18Apr03–3Kee	my	4½f	:22	:44^4		:51	Md Sp Wt 48k	–	8	2	$1^{1\frac12}$		1^{3}	$1^{12\frac12}$	Bailey J D	**L**118	*.90	100–12	Heckle118$^{12\frac12}$ SandandSilver118^1 FranticPce118^1	Drew off,mild hand urg 8

Hero's Pleasure

Own: Duke Jean D

Dk. b or b. c. 4 (Mar)
Sire: Sea Hero (Polish Navy) $7,000
Dam: Rebeau's Pleasure (Lord Rebeau)
Br: Jean Duke (Ky)
Tr: Oliver Doug(0 0 0 0 .00) 2003:(274 40 .15)

Life	14	4	2	2	$112,667	85	D.Fst	8	2	0	1	$67,617	73
2003	12	4	2	1	$111,195	85	Wet(332)	3	0	2	1	$13,790	85
2002	2	M	0	1	$1,472	49	Turf(256)	3	2	0	0	$31,260	79
	0	0	0	0	$0	–	Dst(0)	0	0	0	0	$0	–

23Aug03-9NP	fst	1⅜		:48 1:132 1:404 2:213	CanDerby-G3	59	7	52	45	42½	614	718½	Stevens S A	L126	3.05	59-25	Raylene1211 Taiaslew1266¼ Reb's Drummer126¾	Mild bid, faded strtch	8
4Aug03-8AsD	fst	1⅛		:464 1:122 1:393 1:532	MntbDrby-G3	73	9	84¾	88	54½	25	11	Stevens S A	L126	8.00	92-16	HerosPleasure1261 Taislew1263½ PntsNKisses1261¾	Determinedly outside	10
13Jly03-8Cby	fm	*1 1/16	Ⓣ	:242 :484 1:122 1:431	3↑OClm 20000N	74	3	53½	52½	63¼	52½	41½	Stevens S A	LB115 f	*2.30	89-07	Teague118¾ McHenryCo.Kid122¾ MyNameIsFrancis118no	Lacked path 1/8	8
28Jun03-8Cby	wf	1	⊗	:233 :473 1:123 1:392	CbyDerby40k	85	3	76	53	44½	44	23½	Stevens S A	LB122	4.80	82-23	MorningMerry1173½ HerosPlesure122nk GintSlm1174	Steady bid, 2nd best	10
7Jun03-8Cby	my	6f		:222 :453 :581 1:111	StPaul35k	81	6	8	85¾	74¾	64¾	33	Stevens S A	LB122	17.80	85-16	*Quote Me Later*118nk Bohunk1202¾ Hero's Pleasure1223½	Ducked out 3/16	8
1Jun03-6Cby	fm	*1 1/16	Ⓣ	:223 :471 1:12 1:431	3↑Alw 16426N3L	79	5	31	33	1½	11	1½	Stevens S A	LB116	*1.70	91-08	Hero's Pleasure116½ *McHenryCo.Kid*1202¼ *Bassant*1201½	3wd trip, prevailed	8
5Apr03-8TuP	fst	1		:234 :464 1:104 1:364	ChuckNLuck24k	70	4	62¾	52¼	45½	68¾	67	Stevens S A	L122	5.60	82-19	*Unyielding*119nk Icy Tobin118hd Ripley1205½	Mid pack, even effort	8
15Mar03-8TuP	fm	1	Ⓣ	:244 :494 1:14 1:382	TempeH35k	75	8	86¾	84¼	42½	43	1½	Stevens S A	L116	13.20	82-18	HerosPleasure116½ DeputyDoc122½ IcyTobin119no	Long drive 5wd,up late	8
7Mar03-9TuP	fst	6f		:214 :444 :574 1:111	Md Sp Wt 9k	67	7	3	64½	57½	23	1hd	Stevens S A	L121	*2.40	85-19	*Hero's Pleasure*121hd Irony1211½ Uncle Lee1215¾	Bid 3wide, up at wire	10
15Feb03-3TuP	gd	5½f		:222 :454 :58 1:043	Md Sp Wt 9k	57	6	3	42½	55¼	24½	2hd	Martinez S B	L121	6.80	83-18	PlyYourBluff121hd *HerosPlesure*1218½ ElyHsseen121½	Closed fast, gaining	7
1Feb03-8Sun	fst	6f		:221 :45 :573 1:101	Md Sp Wt 17k	–0	1	11	88	1015	1017	1027¾	Ortiz M F Jr	L120	10.20	65-11	PrdhBy1201¾ Hrcmsthmnnw1201½ SmlnTm1206¼	Broke out,bumped,tired	11
12Jan03-8TuP	fst	1		:23 :462 1:111 1:354	Rattlsnake35k	46	3	31½	32	56	716	725	Martinez S B	L118	32.30	69-17	Siberland11910½ Icy Tobin1196¾ Ripley1183¼	Pinched,pressed,empty	7

Hero's Tribute

Own: Oxley John C

Dk. b or b. h. 6 (Mar) KEESEP99 $150,000
Sire: Sea Hero (Polish Navy) $7,000
Dam: Eastern Dawn (Damascus)
Br: Dr. & Mrs. R. Smiser West & Mr. & Mrs. M. Miller (Ky)
Tr: Ward J T Jr(0 0 0 0 .00) 2003:(90 17 .19)

Life	25	8	3	4	$859,550	112	D.Fst	19	5	2	3	$624,790	110
2003	6	2	1	0	$307,660	110	Wet(343)	5	2	1	1	$208,100	112
2002	7	2	1	2	$203,345	110	Turf(274)	1	1	0	0	$26,660	95
	0	0	0	0	$0	–	Dst(0)	0	0	0	0	$0	–

14Nov03-9CD	gd	1	Ⓣ	:243 :484 1:14 1:382	3↑OClm 100000N	95	6	42½	31	41	41	1½	•Day P	L123	4.60	80-22	DH HrosTrbt123 DH GrtBloom123½ InvstorsDrm117½	Moved up rail, all out	8
5Jly03-9Bel	fst	1¼		:483 1:123 1:37 2:012	3↑SuburbnH-G1	88	3	32	42½	66½	715	718¼	Samyn J L	L115	22.90	69-13	*Mineshaft*1212¼ Volponi1214 Dollar Bill1152¼	3 wide trip, empty	8
16May03-11Pim	sly	1 3/16		:463 1:11 1:362 1:56	4↑PimSpclH-G1	74	7	32	32½	43½	818	828¼	Prado E S	L116	3.80	65-23	Mineshft1213¾ WesternPride116hd JudgesCs1131¾	Hard to load,weakened	9
29Mar03-11GP	fst	1¼		:48 1:123 1:38 2:041	3↑GPH-G2	110	4	24	2½	1hd	12½	14	Prado E S	L115	*1.80	87-24	Hero's Tribute1154 Aeneas1151 Puzzlement1141½	Steady urging	8
22Feb03-11GP	fst	1⅛		:463 1:102 1:353 1:49	3↑DonnH-G1	109	2	23	23	2hd	2½	22½	Prado E S	L114	4.10	94-13	HarlnsHolidy1202½ *HerosTribute*1141½ Puzzlement114nk	Hit gate, 2nd best	11
11Jan03-10GP	fst	1 1/16		:231 :463 1:102 1:421	3↑HalHopeH-G3	101	2	41	4¾	41½	41½	44½	Prado E S	L115	*2.00	93-12	Windsor Castle1151½ Saint Verre114nk Najran1142¾	Blocked far turn & str	8

High Chaparral (Ire)
Own: Tabor Michael and Magnier, Mrs. John

B. c. 5 (Mar)
Sire: Sadler's Wells (Northern Dancer)
Dam: Kasora (Darshaan*GB)
Br: S. Coughlan (Ire)
Tr: O'Brien Aidan P(0 0 0 0 .00) 2003:(10 1 .10)

Life	13	10	1	2	$5,331,231	112	
2003	4	3	0	1	$1,717,124	112	
2002	6	5	0	1	$3,436,410	111	
	0	0	0	0	$0	-	
D.Fst	0	0	0	0	$0	-	
Wet(267)	0	0	0	0	$0	-	
Turf(378)	13	10	1	2	$5,331,231	112	
Dst(0)	0	0	0	0	$0	-	

25Oct03–8SA fm 1½ [T] :48³ 1:11² 2:00 2:24¹ 3↑ BCTurf-G1 **112** 3 5² 3¹ 3² 3² 1hd ♦Kinane M J LB126 4.90 105–04 [DH]HighChaparral126 [DH]Johar126hd *Falbrv*126 5½ Came out str,game btwn 9
5Oct03♦Longchamp (Fr) hy *1½ [T] RH 2:32¹ 3↑ Prix de l'Arc de Triomphe-G1 Stk 18720000 3 5¾ Kinane M J 131 2.60 Dalakhani123¾ Mubtaker131⁵ *High Chaparral*131 1½ 13
Timeform rating: 124 *4th on rail,3rd 2f out,no chance with first two.Ange Gabriel 9th*
6Sep03♦Leopardstwn (Ire) gd 1¼ [T] LH 2:03¹ 3↑ Irish Champion Stakes-G1 Stk 1110000 1nk Kinane M J 130 4.00 High Chaparral130nk *Falbrav*130hd *Islington*127 1½ 7
Timeform rating: 128 *Trckd 4th,2nd 2f out,led 1f out,drftd left,held well.Alamshar 4th*
10Aug03♦Curragh (Ire) gd 1¼ [T] RH 2:04⁴ 3↑ Royal Whip Stakes-G2 Stk 147000 1¾ Kinane M J 139 *.90 *High Chaparral*139¾ Imperial Dancer132nk In Time's Eye132² 6
Timeform rating: 128+ *Tracked in 3rd,2nd 1-1/2f out,led 1f out,driving*

Hoh Buzzard (Ire)
Own: Tanaka Gary A

Dk. b or b. f. 4 (Mar)
Sire: Alhaarth*Ire (Unfuwain)
Dam: Indian Express*GB (Indian Ridge*Ire)
Br: R. Hodgins (Ire)
Tr: Cecil Ben D(0 0 0 0 .00) 2003:(77 7 .09)

Life	13	5	1	2	$221,839	95	
2003	10	4	1	2	$214,178	95	
2002	3	1	0	0	$7,661	-	
	0	0	0	0	$0	-	
D.Fst	0	0	0	0	$0	-	
Wet(263)	0	0	0	0	$0	-	
Turf(286)	13	5	1	2	$221,839	95	
Dst(0)	0	0	0	0	$0	-	

20Dec03–9Hol fm 1 1/16 [T] :23⁴ :47² 1:11 1:41² 3↑ [F]DahliaH-G2 **90** 10 1hd 1½ 1½ 11½ 5³ Baze T C LB117 b 8.40 86–15 Ktdogwn116no PersonlLegnd115 1½ BttysWish117½ Dueled,clear,wknd late 10
15Nov03–9CD yl 1 1/16 [T] :23³ :47⁴ 1:13 1:45 [F]MrsRvere-G2 **95** 2 2hd 2hd 1hd 11½ 1nk Fogelsonger R L120 b 7.40 79–21 Hoh Buzzard120nk Aud120² Gamble to Victory116½ Driving,lasted 12
Previously trained by Bell Michael H
13Sep03–8AP yl 1⅛ [T] :48³ 1:12 1:36⁴ 1:49 [F]PuckerUp-G3 **88** 5 3² 31½ 4² 41½ 42¼ Stevens G L L118 b *1.40 92–11 Aud118 1¾ *Hail Hillary*116no Julie's Prize120½ Boxed, no rally 12
24Aug03♦Deauville (Fr) yl *1¼ [T] RH 2:09¹ [F]Prix de la Nonette-G3 Stk 71900 2¾ Mackay J 126 b 9.80 State of Art126¾ Hoh Buzzard126hd Felicity126² 7
Timeform rating: 101 *Led to over 1f out,gave ground grudgingly.Time Ahead 7th*
13Aug03♦Salisbury (GB) gd 1¼ [T] RH 2:07³ 3↑ [F]EBF Upavon Stakes (Listed) Stk 72300 1½ Mackay J 117 b 5.00 Hoh Buzzard117½ Quiet Storm117 1½ Echoes In Eternity119 2¾ 5
Timeform rating: 101 *Led after 1f,met challenge 3f out,held gamely*
30Jly03♦Goodwood (GB) yl 1⅛ [T] RH 1:58² 3↑ [F]Weatherbys Bank Rated Handicap Hcp 26400 1³ Fallon K 127 b *3.50 *Hoh Buzzard*127³ Opera Glass123 1¼ Cuddles119¾ 9
Timeform rating: 99 *Led throughout,drew clear over 1f out,handily*
28Jun03♦Newmarket (GB) gd 1 [T] Str 1:39¹ 3↑ [F]EBF Handicap Hcp 24100 1² Mackay J 121 b 6.00 *Hoh Buzzard*121² Fleet of Light126nk Dame de Noche122 1¾ 8
Timeform rating: 95 *Pressed pace,led after 2-1/2f,ridden out*
5Jun03♦Sandown Park (GB) gd 1 [T] RH 1:41³ IG Index Classified Stakes Alw 13700 3² Fallon K 124 b 7.00 *Leporello*126½ *Desert Opal*127 1½ *Hoh Buzzard*124 2½ 9
Timeform rating: 92 *Dwelt,rank early,soon 3rd,lost place 3f out,lacked room,angld out*
5May03♦Kempton (GB) gd 1⅛ [T] RH 1:53² Kempton.co.uk Handicap Hcp 14100 42¼ Fallon K 132 *2.50 *Chinkara*132½ Fabulous Jet132¹ Bowing133¾ 17
Timeform rating: 83 *Mid-pack,chasing leaders over 3f out,bid 1f out,hung*
21Apr03♦Kempton (GB) gd 1⅛ [T] RH 1:53 Kempton for Weddings Handicap Hcp 13500 31¾ Holland D 129 12.00 Foodbroker Founder133nk Doc Watson131 1½ Hoh Buzzard129¹ 15
Timeform rating: 85 *Tracked leaders,lost place over 3f out,back up for 3rd*

Hollywood Story
Own: Krikorian George

Dk. b or b. f. 3 (Mar) FTKJUL02 $130,000
Sire: Wild Rush (Wild Again) $15,000
Dam: Wife for Life (Dynaformer)
Br: Vinery (Ky)
Tr: Shirreffs John A(0 0 0 0 .00) 2003:(163 33 .20)

Life	5	1	2	1	$356,500	95
2003	5	1	2	1	$356,500	95
2002	0	M	0	0	$0	-
	0	0	0	0	$0	-
D.Fst	5	1	2	1	$356,500	95
Wet(394)	0	0	0	0	$0	-
Turf(337)	0	0	0	0	$0	-
Dst(0)	0	0	0	0	$0	-

21Dec03–9Hol fst 1 1/16 :23 :463 1:1041:424 ⒻHolStrlt-G1 95 4 68 63¼ 33 21 12¾ Valenzuela P A LB120 b 6.30 90– 10 HollywoodStory1202¾ RhyDolly1204½ HosofFrtn1204 3wd,came in,cleared 6
25Oct03–3SA fst 1 1/16 :224 :464 1:1041:423 ⒻBCJuvFil-G1 78 3 53½ 83¼ 72¾ 47½ 412 Valenzuela P A LB119 b 21.20 79– 07 Halfbridled1192½ *Ashado*119nk *Victory U. S. A.*1199¼ Bumped first turn 14
28Sep03–9SA fst 1 1/16 :24 :48 1:1221:433 ⒻOakLeaf-G2 89 6 64½ 63½ 42½ 33½ 35 Valenzuela P A LB119 6.40 81– 16 *Halfbridled*1194½ Tarlow119½ Hollywood Story1196½ Off bit slow,missed 2d 7
30Aug03–8Dmr fst 7f :224 :451 1:0931:221 ⒻDmrDeb-G1 88 5 2 31 41¾ 43 25 Valenzuela P A LB115 8.50 86– 13 *Hlfbrdld*1165 HollywoodStry115no VctryUSA1161½ Angled in 1/4,game 2nd 6
3Aug03–5Dmr fst 6f :222 :452 :5731:101 ⒻMd Sp Wt 49k 67 9 3 41¼ 43½ 34½ 26½ Stevens G L LB118 9.10 83– 14 VctoryUSA1186½ HollywoodStory1182 *DxHgh*1181½ 4wd,angled in,2nd best 9

Hombre Rapido
Own: Granja Vista Del Rio Stable

B. g. 7 (Apr)
Sire: Falstaff (Lyphard) $3,500
Dam: Tengo Prisa (Relaunch)
Br: Granja Vista Del Rio (Ky)
Tr: Sadler John W(0 0 0 0 .00) 2003:(375 71 .19)

Life	20	5	4	5	$313,330	112
2003	3	2	0	0	$160,500	107
2002	5	2	1	1	$75,480	112
	0	0	0	0	$0	-
D.Fst	19	4	4	5	$285,730	112
Wet(362)	1	1	0	0	$27,600	106
Turf(326)	0	0	0	0	$0	-
Dst(0)	0	0	0	0	$0	-

10May03–6Hol fst 6f :212 :432 :5541:082 3↑LATimesH-G3 107 8 1 11 11 11½ 11 Valdivia J Jr LB116 b 6.50 98– 11 HombreRapido1161 Publication1161 Giovnnetti116hd Off rail,held gamely 8
19Mar03–7SA fst 6f :212 :442 :5631:094 4↑Alw 79040c 95 4 2 12 1hd 2½ 43 Valdivia J Jr LB118 b *.60 86– 15 MensExclusive118½ GoldnHr1181½ RidndShin1181 Speed, grew weary late 5
12Jan03–3SA fst 6f :211 :432 :5521:083 4↑OClm 100000N 104 4 1 11 12½ 13 12 Valdivia J Jr LB121 b 1.90 95– 12 HombreRapido1212 RideandShine1211 Komax1193½ Bit off rail,held game 6

Honor in War
Own: 3rd Turn Stables LLC

Ch. h. 5 (Jan) KEESEP00 $140,000
Sire: Lord At War*Arg (General*Fr)
Dam: Catumbella (Diesis*GB)
Br: Mill Ridge Farm Ltd. & W Lazy T., Ltd. (Ky)
Tr: McGee Paul J(0 0 0 0 .00) 2003:(309 46 .15)

Life	17	7	2	3	$732,296	110
2003	9	4	1	1	$616,723	110
2002	5	1	1	1	$48,323	94
	0	0	0	0	$0	-
D.Fst	1	1	0	0	$31,850	68
Wet(335)	1	0	0	1	$3,740	89
Turf(403)	15	6	2	2	$696,706	110
Dst(0)	0	0	0	0	$0	-

4Oct03–9Kee fm 1 Ⓣ:23 :461 1:1141:36 3↑ShdwlTfM-G1 105 7 811 79 41½ 1hd 2¾ Flores D R L126 9.90 87– 14 PrfctSoul126¾ HonorinWr126½ TouchofthBlus1261¼ 5-6w trip,outfinished 10
16Aug03–10AP gd 1¼ Ⓣ:49 1:132 1:3732:021 3↑ArlMilln-G1 101 11 108¼ 108½ 75½ 62½ 93½ Valdivia J Jr L126 13.70 91– 08 ⒹStorming Home126½ *Sulamani*126hd DHKaieteur126 Bid, faltered 13
26Jly03–9AP fm 1¼ Ⓣ:4911:14 1:3832:023 3↑ArlgtnH-G3 100 10 77½ 55½ 1hd 1hd 1nk Flores D R L120 *1.60 93– 05 HonornWr120nk BttrTlkNow115¾ MystryGvr118nk Fully extended-driving 10
7Jun03–10Bel sf 1¼ 🅃:5341:203 1:4722:14 3↑ManhttnH-G1 100 10 22½ 41½ 61½ 54 63½ Flores D R L117 8.90 20– 57 Denon122½ Requete1161¼ Dr. Brendler1161 Close up, no rally 10
3May03–9CD fm 1⅛ Ⓣ:4741:111 1:3441:463 3↑WRTurfCl-G1 110 8 33 42½ 42 11 11¼ Flores D R L116 24.30 101 - Honor in War1161¼ Requete116¾ *Patrol*114½ Hop start,4w,drvg 8
17Apr03–6Kee yl 1⅛ Ⓣ:5131:172 1:4141:532 4↑Alw 63822c 95 1 42½ 41 42 1hd 1½ Desormeaux K J L117 2.10 70– 27 *Honor in War*117½ *Irish Warrior*118¾ Holy Conflict1164¾ Circled 6w,driving 4
3Mar03–9GP fm *1 1/16 Ⓣ:232 :474 1:1121:42 4↑OClm 100000N 97 2 42 43 41¾ 3nk 32½ Douglas R R L122 11.70 91– 12 Sttement1221¾ BsebllChmpion118¾ *HonorinWr*1221 Bumped twice stretch 9
1Feb03–8GP fm 1 Ⓣ:223 :454 1:10 1:334 4↑Alw 40000N3x 100 9 64¾ 52 52¼ 3½ 11¼ Coa E M L118 3.50 97– 06 Honor in War1181¼ Love the Game1203¼ SpruceRun1181 Strong hand ride 10
18Jan03–9GP fm 1 Ⓣ:241 :484 1:1321:362 4↑Alw 38000N3x 89 1 54 63½ 62½ 51¾ 52¼ Day P L118 *2.10 82– 12 BttrTlkNow120nk GoodBySm118hd HndsmGrg118½ Blocked deep stretch 10

House Party

Own: Shields J V Jr

Gr/ro. f. 4 (Apr)
Sire: French Deputy (Deputy Minister) $4,372
Dam: Bill Back (Relaunch)
Br: J. V. Shields Jr. (Fla)
Tr: Jerkens H. A(0 0 0 0 .00) 2003:(359 73 .20)

Life	14	6	3	3	$614,564	108	D.Fst	11	5	2	2	$555,614	108
2003	10	5	1	2	$551,354	108	Wet(418)	3	1	1	1	$58,950	106
2002	4	1	2	1	$63,210	90	Turf(333)	0	0	0	0	$0	–
	0	0	0	0	$0	–	Dst(0)	0	0	0	0	$0	–

5Oct03-9Bel	fst	6½f	:233	:464	1:10	1:161	3↑[F]GlntBlmH-G2	106	6	6	61½	61¾	22½	2½	Santos J A	116	*.75	91-15	HrmonyLodge117½ HousPrty116hd SlwsFinlAnswr1126	3 wide trip, gamely	6
6Sep03-8Del	fst	6f	:214	:442	:563	1:081	3↑[F]EndineH-G3	108	2	7	54¾	43	2hd	11	Santos J A	117	*.80	103-06	House Party1171 VisioninFlight1144½ *MoojiMoo*1152¾	Good energy, closed	8
26Jly03-9Sar	fst	7f	:223	:451	1:081	1:204	[F]Test-G1	97	6	4	62	53¼	37½	36	Santos J A	122	3.60	97-08	Lady Tak1224½ Bird Town1221½ *House Party*1221¾	Mild rally outside	7
4Jly03-9Bel	fst	6f	:214	:443	:564	1:092	[F]Prioress-G1	99	2	6	78¼	64	2½	13¼	Santos J A	121	*2.10	92-15	HouseParty1213¼ Chimichurri119½ PrincessV115½	Swung wide, drew away	8
6Jun03-10Bel	fst	1	:232	:461	1:102	1:351	[F]Acorn-G1	88	5	71½ 51¾	52½	43½	44¼		Santos J A	121	7.10	86-16	Bird Town121hd *Lady Tak*1211 Final Round1213¼	Bobbled start	7
10May03-8Bel	fst	7f	:224	:463	1:11	1:231	[F]NasauCBC-G2	93	4	4	41½	41	1½	13	Santos J A	122	2.25	84-12	HouseParty1223 CyberSecret122½ CitySister1165	Found room, drew clear	4
26Apr03-7Del	sly	6f	:221	:454	:58	1:101	[F]LegalLight75k	106	3	1	21½	2hd	13	18½	Rocco J S Jr	122	*1.70	93-15	*House Party*1228½ Ladyecho122¾ Valley of the Gods1172¼	Bid, ridden out	6
14Mar03-7GP	fst	7f	:22	:442	1:092	1:222	[F]FrwrdGal-G3	82	4	2	64¼	64¼	43½	44	Santos J A	121	2.80	92-09	Midnight Cry1172¾ *Final Round*117¾ Chimichurri121½	Swung out, no rally	8
2Feb03-10GP	fst	6f	:212	:443	:573	1:104	[F]OldHat100k	85	3	5	58	52¾	51¼	11½	Santos J A	115	1.80	90-08	HousePrty1151½ Chimichurri1192 GloriousMiss1191¾	Up late, going away	5
5Jan03-5GP	fst	5f	:214	:444		:571	[F]DameMystrs71k	82	5	7	63¼	51¾	32	32¾	Bailey J D	117	*.80	96-06	FollowMeHome115¾ SomethingSilver1152 *HouseParty*1171¼	Hit gate start	7

Icantgoforthat

Own: Broberg Andy and Knapp, Palmer

B. m. 5 (Mar)
Sire: In Excess*Ire (Siberian Express) $25,000
Dam: Texinadress (Copelan)
Br: Michael E. Pegram (Cal)
Tr: Knapp Steve(0 0 0 0 .00) 2003:(275 32 .12)

Life	25	6	3	5	$392,968	97	D.Fst	17	5	2	2	$261,504	86
2003	12	2	1	4	$210,724	97	Wet(388)	1	0	0	1	$12,864	77
2002	5	2	1	0	$96,604	86	Turf(334)	7	1	1	2	$118,600	97
	0	0	0	0	$0	–	Dst(0)	0	0	0	0	$0	–

29Dec03-5SA	fm	*6½f	[T]	:22	:441	1:07	1:13	3↑[F]MnroviaH-G3	97	6	1	11½	11½	11	1no	Baze T C	LB114 b	4.40	92-08	Icantgoforthat114no Polygreen1161 SpringStr1192	Held on gamely inside	6
8Nov03-5SA	fm	*6½f	[T]	:211	:43	1:06	1:121	3↑[F][S]CalCupDisH150k	88	5	4	31½	31½	61¾	43½	Espinoza V	LB117 b	10.80	92-04	BlindAmbition1152½ BoldRobrt118½ Swtcksnshks118½	4 wide into stretch	12
11Oct03-8SA	fm	*6½f	[T]	:213	:432	1:062	1:121	3↑[F]SKMaddyH-G3	92	3	3	11	11	11½	33	Baze T C	LB115 b	39.00	93-06	Bllski1172 Buffythcntrfold1161 Icntgofortht1151	Speed,angled in,caught	10
19Sep03-10Fpx	fst	6½f		:211	:45	1:101	1:163	3↑[F][S]PioPico50k	75	3	2	2hd	1½	22½	35½	Steiner J J	LB116 b	*2.20	89-09	*BoldRobert*1225 Swetcksnshks114½ Icntgofortht116nk	Dueled,lost 2nd late	8
1Aug03-7Dmr	fm	5f	[T]	:212	:44		:553	3↑[F]DaisycutrH92k	79	5	6	2hd	21	41½	75	Flores D R	LB116 b	17.80	- -	RobrtsMngo117½ SwissLk1161½ GrntMrtyWish115hd	Vied,stalked,wkened	10
19Jly03-8Hol	fm	1	[T]	:233	:472	1:111	1:352	3↑[F][S]Valkyr76k	65	2	11	1hd	1hd	41	712½	Enriquez I D	LB117 b	8.90	74-18	Shalini1232 Sunset Serenade1191½ Calzada Kid1171	Driftd out7/8,rail bid	7
29May03-7Hol	fm	5½f	[T]	:214	:44	:56	1:021	4↑[F]OClm 100000N	85	7	1	2½	21½	22½	33	Valenzuela P A	LB122 b	6.70	90-07	Belleski1162 *Knoll Lake*1181 Icantgoforthat1221½	3wd early,bested rest	7
26Apr03-1Hol	fst	7f		:22	:441	1:082	1:213	4↑[F][S]BThoughtfl150k	77	2	2	1hd	1hd	33½	410¼	Valenzuela P A	LB122 b	9.40	84-07	CeesElegnc122¾ JtintoHouston1227½ RlPrnoid1202	Inside duel,weakened	8
5Apr03-4SA	fm	*6½f	[T]	:22	:442	1:071	1:13	4↑[F]LsCngasH-G3	90	5	2	1½	11½	11½	23	Baze T C	LB114 b	42.30	89-07	*Heat Haze*1143 Icantgoforthat114hd Paga1161	Angled in,just held 2d	8
16Mar03-3SA	gd	6½f	⊗	:212	:442	1:101	1:172	4↑[F][S]IrshOBrien107k	77	5	3	2hd	1hd	22	37	Valenzuela P A	LB121 b	2.80	79-14	JtntoHouston1145 BroknBlrsdn1162 Icntgofortht1214½	Dueled, weakened	6
25Jan03-6GP	fst	6f		:212	:442	:57	1:101	4↑[F][R]PaduaFMSpr250k	52	2	5	2hd	42½	88¾	915¾	Valdivia J Jr	L119 b	13.10	77-08	*Madame Pietra*120nk Shameful119no Chispiski119½	On rail, faded	9
3Jan03-7SA	fst	5½f		:211	:442	:57	1:034	4↑[F][S]Survive107k	84	5	1	1hd	1½	14	13½	Valenzuela P A	LB115 b	9.50	93-11	Icntgofortht1153½ TherssYr1122 KittyOnthTrck117hd	Inside,clear,driving	6

I'madrifter
Own: O'Neill Daniel

Dk. b or b. h. 6 (Mar)
Sire: Slewdledo (Seattle Slew) $2,750
Dam: Exploded's Girl (Exploded)
Br: Paulson Bros Ranch & Roy Dane (Wash)
Tr: Specht Steven(0 0 0 0 .00) 2003:(199 33 .17)

Life	25	7	1	4	$291,212	106	D.Fst	18 4 1 3	$151,212 103
2003	7	2	0	2	$132,287	106	Wet(369)	5 3 0 1	$140,000 106
2002	9	1	1	1	$71,875	106	Turf(302)	2 0 0 0	$0 78
	0	0	0	0	$0	–	Dst(0)	0 0 0 0	$0 –

15Jun03-8EmDfst 1 :231 :454 1:091 1:343 3↑BudEmerldH75k 95 7 11½ 12 12 11 31½ •Gonzalez R M LB119 3.80 91-23 Turbn1181¼ *Alfurune*117nk DH MoonlightMeeting118 Clear pace, flattened 8
26May03-8BM fst 1 1/16 :221 :45 1:094 1:413 3↑SeabsctH-G3 84 1 11 11½ 11½ 23 48¾ Gonzalez R M LB116 4.60 90-05 Reba's Gold1188 Free Corona116no Truly a Judge117¾ Pace off rail, wknd 6
26Apr03-7BM yl 1 Ⓣ:232 :473 1:121 1:371 3↑SnFrnBCH-G2 74 4 11½ 12 1hd 85 813¼ Gonzalez R M LB115 9.00 74-13 Ninebanks117no Nicobar1161 National Anthem1161 Pace off rail, empty 8
29Mar03-7GG fst 1 :22 :443 1:083 1:35 3↑BerkelyH-G3 98 4 11½ 11 12 13½ 12½ Gonzalez R M LB115 10.00 95-11 I'madrifter1152½ Palmeiro1171¼ Skip to the Stone1163 Held driving 6
1Mar03-8GG fst 1 :223 :45 1:09 1:344 3↑SanCarlosH61k 103 4 11½ 12 11½ 2hd 32¼ Gonzalez R M LB116 16.50 94-10 Halo Cat1161¼ Fleetstreet Dancer1161 *I'madrifter*1163 Met bid, weakened 10
30Jan03-7GG fst 1 :22 :443 1:09 1:341 4↑Alw 40300N2M 83 3 13½ 14 12½ 32½ 49¼ Krigger K LB120 *.90e 90-14 Boss Ego1161 Epic Honor1167½ Road Afleet110¾ Gave way inside 7
1Jan03-3GG wf 1 :221 :451 1:09 1:334 4↑LafayetteH83k 106 2 12½ 12 12½ 11½ 11½ Krigger K LB115 *.60e 101-10 I'madrifter1151½ *Halo Cat*1153½ Chinkapin1171 Quickest, driving 9

Indy Five Hundred
Own: Georgica Stable

Ch. f. 4 (Feb) KEESEP01 $210,000
Sire: A.P. Indy (Seattle Slew) $300,000
Dam: Lyphard's Delta (Lyphard)
Br: Palides Investments N. V. Inc (Ky)
Tr: Barbara Robert(0 0 0 0 .00) 2003:(201 29 .14)

Life	10	3	1	1	$239,250	107	D.Fst	4 1 0 1	$32,850 69
2003	7	2	1	0	$206,400	107	Wet(419)	1 0 0 0	$0 31
2002	3	1	0	1	$32,850	69	Turf(328)	5 2 1 0	$206,400 107
	0	0	0	0	$0	–	Dst(0)	0 0 0 0	$0 –

11Oct03-8Kee fm 1⅛ Ⓣ:473 1:113 1:354 1:474 ⒻQEIICup-G1 84 8 52 64½ 66 96½ 107½ Day P L121 *2.00 91-11 Film Maker121no Maiden Tower121¾ Casual Look121¾ 4-5w trip,tired 10
7Sep03-9Bel gd 1⅛ 🅃:464 1:113 1:362 1:482 ⒻGrdCyBCH-G1 107 6 87½ 89 86½ 32 14 Day P L113 7.90 88-17 Indy Five Hundred1134 *Dimitrova*1222¼ Campsie Fells1161 Broke in air 8
17Aug03-9Sar fm 1⅛ Ⓣ:462 1:102 1:36 1:49 ⒻLakPlcdH-G2 91 4 1011 1015 1016 44 2¾ Day P L114 15.70 83-13 SndSprings121¾ *IndyFivHundrd*114no *FilmMkr*1193½ Bumped start, pinched 10
28Jly03-8Sar fm 1 1/16 Ⓣ:24 :481 1:121 1:414 ⒻLkGeorge-G3 85 10 109¾ 1011 98 106 74¾ Day P L115 32.25 81-20 Film Maker1152½ Ocean Drive119¾ Gal O Gal122½ Mild rally outside 11
30May03-8Bel gd 1 ⊗:224 :463 1:123 1:391 3↑ⒻAlw 48000N2X 31 4 2hd 2hd 711 723 731¼ Bridgmohan S X L118 9.50 39-30 LadyLiberty1211¼ GiveandTke1218½ FollowBetsy1214 Bumped after start 7
25Apr03-7Aqu fm 1 1/16 Ⓣ:23 :483 1:14 1:451 ⒻAlw 44000N1X 77 1 1½ 1½ 11½ 12 1½ Bridgmohan S X L118 5.50 78-18 IndyFiveHundrd118½ WintrsQust1222½ MdowBll118½ Pace, dug in, held on 9
26Jan03-8Aqu fst 170 ⊡:234 :472 1:111 1:414 ⒻBusanda82k 51 5 44½ 65¾ 714 719 718¾ Castellano J J L116 5.90 66-16 CyberSecret1161 XtraHeart1186½ GoldenDmsel118nk Speed outside, tired 8

Inish Glora
Own: Costigan Robert J

B. m. 6 (May)
Sire: Regal Classic (Vice Regent) $10,000
Dam: Star Guest (Assert*Ire)
Br: C. G. Scott DVM (Ont-C)
Tr: Benson Macdonald(0 0 0 0 .00) 2003:(120 13 .11)

Life	27	6	7	4	$543,888	98	D.Fst	17 3 6 2	$147,517 88
2003	6	3	1	1	$359,667	98	Wet(330)	0 0 0 0	$0 –
2002	9	1	3	1	$88,329	90	Turf(272)	10 3 1 2	$396,371 98
	0	0	0	0	$0	–	Dst(0)	0 0 0 0	$0 –

19Oct03-5WO sf 1¼ Ⓣ:503 1:152 1:404 2:053 3↑ⒻEPTaylor-G1 88 1 1hd 1hd 1½ 31 74½ Kabel T K L123 7.60 74-30 Volga123hd Tigertail123no Hi Dubai118hd Inside, gave way 10
14Sep03-6WO fm *1⅛ Ⓣ:47 1:442 3↑ⒻCanadinH-G2 98 6 3½ 31½ 3nk 11½ 11¾ Kabel T K L116 10.05 96-06 Inish Glora1161¾ Volga1181¾ Diadella116½ Close up, 3w,prevailed 8
24Aug03-4WO fm 1⅛ Ⓣ:472 1:111 1:342 1:462 3↑ⒻⓇBelleGeste106k 95 2 31 21½ 21 1½ 2nk Kabel T K L119 *.90 96-04 *Heyahohowdy*117nk *Inish Glora*1192½ Byzantine1182¼ Off rail,led,out gamed 6
4Aug03-5WO gd 1 1/16 Ⓣ:233 :464 1:113 1:432 3↑ⒻⓈVictoriana132k 93 4 1hd 2½ 1hd 12½ 12 Kabel T K L115 *1.00 81-27 Inish Glora1152 *Heyahohowdy*1136 *Spanish Decree*115hd 2-pth,held well rail 8
20Jly03-2WO fm 1 1/16 Ⓣ:242 :481 1:112 1:411 3↑ⒻAlw 89000NC 94 1 21 2hd 2hd 11½ 14 Kabel T K L116 3.20 92-06 *InishGlor*1164 StrtFromTxs120no SmllPromss1163¼ Press outside,drew off 5
28Jun03-2WO fst 6½f :23 :453 1:093 1:16 3↑ⒻOClm 80000(80-75)N 88 3 4 31 31 32 3¾ Clark D L120 5.75 94-10 MilleFeville120no NumberOneCt122¾ *InishGlor*1207 Stlk duel 3w,mild gain 5

Ipi Tombe (Zim)

Own: Team Valor Stables Winstar Farm and S

B. m. 6 (Oct)
Sire: Manshood*GB (Mr. Prospector) $700
Dam: Carnet de Danse (Dance in Time)
Br: M. P.J. Moor (Zim)
Tr: Walden W. E(0 0 0 0 .00) 2003:(289 67 .23)

Life	14	12	2	0	$1,529,799	99
2003	4	4	0	0	$1,416,273	99
2002	6	5	1	0	$107,252	-
	0	0	0	0	$0	-

D.Fst	0	0	0	0	$0	-
Wet(381)	0	0	0	0	$0	-
Turf(278*)	14	12	2	0	$1,529,799	99
Dst(0)	0	0	0	0	$0	-

28Jun03–9CD fm 1⅛ Ⓣ :474 1:112 1:351 1:473 3↑ ⒻLcstGrvH-G3 **99** 1 34 32½ 33½ 21½ 1½ Day P L123 *.40 96–08 Ipi Tombe123½ Kiss the Devil116½ Quick Tip1171½ Hesitate strt,hand urg 5
29Mar03♦Nad al Sheba (UAE) gd *1⅛ Ⓣ LH 1:473 3↑ Dubai Duty Free-G1 Stk 2000000 13 Shea K 121 - *Ipi Tombe*1213 Paolini1261 Royal Tryst126½ 12
8th str, headway 400m out, ran on well, led 100m, pushed out
8Mar03♦Nad al Sheba (UAE) gd *1⅛ Ⓣ LH 1:483 3↑ Jebel Hatta-G3 Stk 95300 13¾ Shea K 128 - *Ipi Tombe*1283¾ Sights On Gold126¾ St Expedit126nk 10
Timeform rating: 126 *Rated in 5th,3rd 3f out,angled out,led 2f out,handily.Highdown5th*
6Feb03♦Nad al Sheba (UAE) gd *1 Ⓣ LH 1:37 3↑ Al Fahidi Fort (Listed) Stk 95300 12¼ Shea K 128 - *Ipi Tombe*1282¼ *Royal Tryst*1263¼ Trademark1263½ 10
Timeform rating: 124 *Rated in 6th,led 1-1/2f out,soon clear.Conflict5th,IbnAlHaitham9t*

Irish Warrior

Own: Coleman John, Dasaro, George, Thompso

Ch. h. 6 (Jan) KEESEP99 $90,000
Sire: Irish River*Fr (Riverman) $25,000
Dam: Spiritofpocahontas (Alleged)
Br: Robert B. Berger (Ky)
Tr: Dollase Wallace A(0 0 0 0 .00) 2003:(95 24 .25)

Life	22	6	7	4	$665,000	104
2003	10	2	3	4	$500,300	104
2002	6	2	2	0	$91,400	99
	0	0	0	0	$0	-

D.Fst	0	0	0	0	$0	-
Wet(295)	0	0	0	0	$0	-
Turf(316)	22	6	7	4	$665,000	104
Dst(0)	0	0	0	0	$0	-

29Nov03–9Hol fm 1 1/16 Ⓣ :233 :472 1:111 1:403 3↑ CtationH-G2 **104** 3 68 68 62¾ 2½ 2¾ Flores D R LB117 *1.20 92–13 *Redattore*120¾ Irish Warrior1172½ Mister Acpen116nk 5wd into str,willingly 6
25Oct03–4SA fm 1 Ⓣ :221 :452 1:092 1:334 3↑ BCMile-G1 **100** 1013 13 1310 1310 73¼ 42¼ Solis A LB126 32.90 91–04 SxPrfctons119¾ TouchofthBlus126nk CntryCty1261¼ 6wd into lane,rallied 13
28Sep03–3SA fm 1¼ Ⓣ :503 1:152 1:39 2:013 3↑ CLHirsch-G1 **101** 4 34 35 43½ 43½ 31¾ Krone J A LB124 5.80 83–13 Storming Home124½ *Johar*1241¼ Irish Warrior1241½ Came out str,willing 4
31Aug03–8Dmr fm 1⅜ Ⓣ :472 1:12 1:353 2:121 3↑ DelMarH-G2 **102** 4 56 66 76¼ 31½ 1hd Solis A LB116 3.10 99–05 IrishWrrior116hd ContinntlRd117½ Contnuously1141 4wd into lane,gamely 9
27Jly03–8Dmr fm 1⅛ Ⓣ :472 1:11 1:342 1:454 3↑ EdReadH-G1 **99** 6 53½ 54½ 52¼ 43 35¼ Krone J A LB114 8.30 99–03 Special Ring1175 Decarchy117nk *Irish Warrior*114hd 3-4w, willingly late 6
4Jly03–7Hol fm 1⅛ Ⓣ :474 1:11 1:341 1:461 3↑ AmericnH-G2 **101** 2 43 41¾ 42 32½ 32¾ Solis A LB116 4.40 95–08 *Candy Ride*120¾ *Special Ring*1182 Irish Warrior1161 Stalked btwn,best rest 5
13Jun03–5Hol fm 1 1/16 Ⓣ :24 :471 1:112 1:41 4↑ Alw 65348N1M **100** 1 713 714 79¼ 73¾ 1no Solis A LB116 3.00 91–15 Irish Warrior116no Decarchy1222½ NativeDesert1221 Swung out,rallied,up 8
17Apr03–6Kee yl 1⅛ Ⓣ :513 1:172 1:414 1:532 4↑ Alw 63822c **94** 2 32 2hd 31½ 3½ 2½ Day P L118 *.60 69–27 *Honor in War*117½ *Irish Warrior*118¾ Holy Conflict1164¾ Coming again late 4
21Mar03–7SA fm 1⅛ Ⓣ :481 1:12 1:344 1:463 4↑ OClm 150000N **101** 5 54 53½ 53½ 31½ 31¼ Almeida G F LB118 6.90 95–11 Blue Steller1181 Kappa King118nk Irish Warrior1183½ Off rail, willingly 5
1Feb03–7TuP fm 1 1/16 Ⓣ :233 :474 1:12 1:422 3↑ TuPBCH150k **101** 6 73½ 73¾ 72¾ 4¾ 2nk Almeida G F L116 12.30 100 – Century City117nk Irish Warrior116nk Hataab116¾ 5wide 1/4,bid 6w,closd 9

Iron Deputy

Own: Moore Susan and John

B. h. 5 (Feb) FTKJUL00 $45,000
Sire: Silver Deputy (Deputy Minister) $40,000
Dam: Femme De Fer*Fr (Iron Duke)
Br: Jose Soriano (Ky)
Tr: Jerkens James A(0 0 0 0 .00) 2003:(194 46 .24)

Life	10	5	1	1	$370,900	112	D.Fst	9	4	1	1	$220,900 106
2003	5	2	0	1	$238,620	112	Wet(347)	1	1	0	0	$150,000 112
2002	2	1	0	0	$49,980	90	Turf(260)	0	0	0	0	$0 –
	0	0	0	0	$0	–	Dst(0)	0	0	0	0	$0 –

16Aug03–7Sar	fst	1¼	:48 1:114 1:37 2:032	3↑ SarBCH-G2	106	7	31	32½	31½	31½	35	Santos J A	L115	12.70	85– 14	Puzzlement1133¼ Volponi1221¾ Iron Deputy1154¼	Bumped start, 3 wide	8
19Jly03–9AP	fst	1 3/16	:48 1:104 1:36 1:552	3↑ WashPkH-G2	94	3	11	1½	1hd	42½	411¾	Migliore R	L117	2.20	86– 16	Perfect Drift1205 Aeneas1151¼ Flatter1145½	Gave way stretch	5
14Jun03–9Bel	sly	1⅛	:464 1:10 1:35 1:474	3↑ BroklynH-G2	112	2	1½	1½	11½	12	12½	Migliore R	L114	6.60	91– 09	Iron Deputy1142½ Volponi1223 Saarland1152½	Pace, clear, game	5
4May03–4Aqu	fst	1⅛	:473 1:112 1:36 1:483	4↑ Alw 48000N3x	106	5	3½	2hd	1½	18	111¼	Migliore R	L117	*1.05	93– 15	*IronDeputy*11711¼ PinkyPizwanski1175¼ DilHero123hd	With something left	5
22Mar03–8Aqu	fst	7f	:222 :444 1:09 1:22	4↑ Alw 47000N3x	94	1	7	66	54	4¾	4½	Migliore R	L118	*.85	93– 12	ResontoHil118nk TurnBcktheTim113hd HrlyQuinn123hd	Stutter step start	7

Island Fashion

Own: Everest Stables Inc

Gr/ro. f. 4 (Mar)
Sire: Petionville (Seeking the Gold) $6,500
Dam: Danzigs Fashion (A Native Danzig)
Br: Everest Stables Inc. (Ky)
Tr: Polanco Marcelo(0 0 0 0 .00) 2003:(91 7 .08)

Life	10	4	1	0	$1,112,970	109	D.Fst	9	4	1	0	$1,082,970 109
2003	10	4	1	0	$1,112,970	109	Wet(330)	0	0	0	0	$0 –
2002	0	M	0	0	$0	–	Turf(168)	1	0	0	0	$30,000 101
	0	0	0	0	$0	–	Dst(0)	0	0	0	0	$0 –

27Dec03–7SA	fst	7f	:223 :452 1:091 1:213	Ⓕ LaBrea-G1	109	10	2	3nk	2hd	11½	16	Desormeaux K J	LB123 b	9.40	98– 10	IslndFshion1236 Rndroo1191½ Buffythecntrfold119½	Dueled,clear,driving	10
30Nov03–6Hol	fm	1 Ⓣ	:232 :464 1:102 1:342	3↑ Ⓕ Matriarc-G1	101	8	116¼	117¼	128	83¼	4¾	Puglisi I	LB120 b	87.20	91– 17	Heat Haze123nk MusicalChimes120no Dedication123½	5wd into lane,rallied	14

Previously trained by Tagg Barclay

4Oct03–9Bel	fst	1⅛	:474 1:122 1:363 1:491	3↑ Ⓕ Beldame-G1	85	7	31	32	5½	511	613¼	Velazquez J R	L120 b	13.10	71– 26	Sightseek1234½ Bird Town1204¾ Buy the Sport120¾	Chased 3 wide, tired	7
6Sep03–7Bel	fst	1⅛	:452 1:093 1:344 1:482	Ⓕ GazelleH-G1	80	3	31½	2½	2hd	48	48¾	Velazquez J R	L122 b	3.15	79– 13	Buy the Sport113½ Lady Tak121no Spoken Fur1218¼	Bid between, tired	8
16Aug03–9Sar	fst	1¼	:482 1:124 1:374 2:05	Ⓕ Alabama-G1	101	1	2½	1½	12	16	16	Velazquez J R	L121 b	8.30	82– 14	IslndFshion1216 AwsomHumor1211 SpoknFur1211¼	When roused, driving	6

Previously trained by Canani Nick

19Jly03–8Del	fst	1 1/16	:231 :463 1:112 1:444	Ⓕ DelOaks-G3	94	2	1hd	2hd	11½	14	16½	Puglisi I	L122 b	9.10	84– 17	*IslandFashion*1226½ AwesomeHumor1154¼ Ladyecho115nk	Kept to her task	9
2May03–10CD	fst	1⅛	:46 1:10 1:353 1:483	Ⓕ KyOaks-G1	83	12	43½	52½	63	77¼	710½	Valenzuela P A	L121 b	21.70	84– 07	*Bird Town*1213¼ Santa Catarina121hd Yell121¾	Stalked,5w,weaken	12
29Mar03–9Sun	fst	1	:223 :454 1:101 1:361	Ⓕ WinStarOak256k	91	7	810	77½	42½	22	12	Puglisi I	L122 b	5.00	97– 09	Island Fashion1222 Ela Ela1223 Isit Still Legal1223	Bid 4w,lugged in 1/16	9
5Mar03–4SA	fst	6½f	:214 :444 1:093 1:161	Ⓕ Md Sp Wt 48k	83	3	3	11	11	1½	2no	Stevens G L	LB120 b	2.70	92– 09	RivrbotCsno120no *IslndFshon*1204½ TmHonord120nk	Speed,dueled,gamely	8
1Feb03–8TuP	fst	1 1/16	:232 :471 1:113 1:432	Ⓕ ArizonaOak75k	59	7	43½	44½	23	28	412¾	Flores D R	L121 b	*.80e	78– 10	HrborBlus12111½ Myofficwif1211 ArchLdy121nk	Bid 3wd,weakened betwn	7

Islington (Ire)
Own: Executors Of The Late Lord Weinstock

B. f. 5 (Feb)
Sire: Sadler's Wells (Northern Dancer)
Dam: Hellenic (Darshaan*GB)
Br: Ballymacoll Stud Farm Ltd (Ire)
Tr: Stoute Sir Michael R(0 0 0 0 .00) 2003:(2 1 .50)

Life	15	6	0	4	$1,553,043	109	D.Fst	0	0	0	0	$0	-
2003	6	2	0	2	$955,142	109	Wet(267)	0	0	0	0	$0	-
2002	7	4	0	1	$594,316	105	Turf(378)	15	6	0	4	$1,553,043	109
	0	0	0	0	$0	-	Dst(0)	0	0	0	0	$0	-

30Nov03♦Tokyo (Jpn) yl *1½ Ⓣ LH 2:28³ 3↑ Japan Cup-G1 Stk 4404000 | 913½ Fallon K | 121 18.90 | Tap Dance City126⁹ That's The Plenty121¾ *Symboli Kris S*126hd 18
Timeform rating: 102 — *Tracked in 4th,weakened over 1f out.Denon 8th,Johar 16th*

25Oct03–6SA fm 1¼ Ⓣ :46³ 1:10² 1:35¹ 1:59 3↑ ⒻBCF&MTrf-G1 | **109** 4 5⁸ 6¹¹ 63¼ 2hd 1nk Fallon K | LB123 *2.90 98–04 | Islington123nk L'Ancresse118²½ Yesterday118no Pulled,bid,led,gamely 12

6Sep03♦Leopardstwn (Ire) gd 1¼ Ⓣ LH 2:03¹ 3↑ Irish Champion Stakes-G1 Stk 1110000 | 3nk Fallon K | 127 16.00 | High Chaparral130nk *Falbrav*130hd *Islington*1271½ 7
Timeform rating: 124+ — *Rated at rear,pushed along after 4f,gaining late.Alamshar 4th*

20Aug03♦York (GB) gf 1½ Ⓣ LH 2:27² 3↑ ⒻYorkshire Oaks-G1 Stk 398000 | 1¹ Fallon K | 130 *.70 | Islington130¹ Ocean Silk120³ Summitville1201¾ 8
Timeform rating: 120 — *3rd on rail,led over 2f out,held well.L'Ancresse5th,CasualLook7th*

5Jly03♦Sandown Park (GB) gd 1¼ Ⓣ RH 2:05² 3↑ Eclipse Stakes-G1 Stk 610000 | 62¾ Fallon K | 130 4.50 | Falbrav133¾ Nayef1331¼ Kaieteur133no 15
Timeform rating: 118 — *Mid-pack on rail,3rd 1-1/2f out,faded late.Grandera 8th*

18Jun03♦Ascot (GB) gd 1¼ Ⓣ RH 2:05¹ 4↑ Prince of Wales's Stakes-G1 Stk 587000 | 33½ Fallon K | 123 7.00 | Nayef1262½ *Rakti*126¹ Islington123¹ 10
Timeform rating: 118 — *Trckd ldrs,angld out 1f out,drftd lft,held by first two.Falbrav5t*

Ivanavinalot
Own: Campbell Gilbert G

Dk. b or b. f. 4 (Mar)
Sire: West Acre (Forty Niner) $3,500
Dam: Beaty Sark (Deputy Minister)
Br: Gilbert G. Campbell (Fla)
Tr: O'Connell Kathleen(0 0 0 0 .00) 2003:(511 82 .16)

Life	16	6	2	1	$641,300	96	D.Fst	11	5	2	0	$599,500	96
2003	10	1	2	1	$223,000	95	Wet(396)	2	1	0	0	$30,800	91
2002	6	5	0	0	$418,300	96	Turf(237*)	3	0	0	1	$11,000	89
	0	0	0	0	$0	-	Dst(0)	0	0	0	0	$0	-

31Dec03–10Crc fm 1 1/16 Ⓣ :23¹ :47³ 1:10³ 1:39⁴ 3↑ ⒻAuldLngSyn40k **66** 2 42½ 32½ 5⁵ 10¹⁴ 10¹³ Velazquez J R L114 f 3.40 88–02 AllthHonor112½ BornSomthng1172½ Ccktlsndrms1171¾ 3p,faded final turn 10
20Dec03–8Crc fm 7½f Ⓣ :22⁴ :45⁴ 1:09⁴ 1:27³ ⒻFAGenter100k **67** 12 12 7⁷ 72½ 11¹¹ 1112¼ Scocca D L121 f 10.60 89–01 ChangingWorld118² CampsieFells121½ FormalMiss121¹ Poor start, 4 wide 12
6Dec03–9Crc fm 1⅛ Ⓣ :47² 1:11 1:35 1:46⁴ 3↑ ⒻMyChrmrH-G3 **89** 1 1² 11½ 11½ 1² 3³ Scocca D L113 f 27.10 94 – NwEconomy115½ SomthngVntrd1162½ Ivnvnlot113¾ On hedge, weakened 12
8Nov03–5Crc fst 1 ⊗ :23 :46⁴ 1:12⁴ 1:40³ ⒻSnzleDzle40k **20** 4 42¾ 31½ 53½ 6⁸ 937¼ Boulanger G L121 f *1.90 41–25 Dakota Light121⁶ Bonus Extra1144¼ Firm Reality114½ Stopped, eased late 9
14Jun03–12Crc fst 1 1/16 :24 :47⁴ 1:12² 1:46¹ ⒻOffceQueen100k **71** 7 31½ 3½ 31½ 6⁵ 613¼ Cruz M R L121 f *.50 68–21 Splasha1131¼ CrimsonandRoses1136¼ RunningDebte1211¼ 3 wide, faltered 7
16May03–10Pim sly 1⅛ :47³ 1:12¹ 1:38¹ 1:52¹ ⒻBlkEySsn-G2 **69** 4 21½ 21½ 34½ 4¹¹ 414¾ Prado E S L122 f 2.80 68–23 RoarEmotion122½ Fircroft1198½ *SantaCatarin*1175¾ 3wd,roused 3-1/2,faded 8
5Apr03–8Kee fst 1 1/16 :24³ :48³ 1:12² 1:43² ⒻAshland-G1 **55** 4 6³ 6⁶ 7¹¹ 7²² 728½ Guidry M L123 f 10.70 61–20 Elloluv1203¾ Lady Tak123¾ Holiday Lady116⁵ Off slow,bmp,checked 7
14Mar03–9GP fst 1⅛ :47¹ 1:11⁴ 1:37³ 1:50³ ⒻBonnieMs-G2 **95** 7 21½ 2¹ 2¹ 2½ 11¾ Velazquez J R L122 f *1.00 89–13 Ivanavinalot1221¾ *My Boston Gal*1203¼ Holiday Lady118¹ Edged away late 7
23Feb03–9GP fst 1 1/16 :23 :47¹ 1:12 1:44⁴ ⒻDvonaDal-G2 **86** 3 1² 11½ 1½ 21½ 2⁶ Cruz M R L121 f 1.90 79–19 Yell117⁶ *Ivanavinalot*1215¾ Gold Player115³ Inside, 2nd best 5
25Jan03–3SA fst 7f :22 :44¹ 1:09³ 1:23 ⒻⓇJDeereOaks250k **89** 6 4 21½ 21½ 2¹ 21½ Cruz M R LB120 f *1.40 89–07 AtlnticOcn1201½ Ivnvinlot1202½ HumorousLdy120⁵ Stalked pace,2nd best 11

Joey Franco

Own: Frankel Jerry

Dk. b or b. h. 5 (Feb)
Sire: Avenue of Flags (Seattle Slew) $15,000
Dam: Susan Powter (Native Prospector)
Br: Jerry Frankel (Cal)
Tr: Vienna Darrell(0 0 0 0 .00) 2003:(303 51 .17)

Life	17	8	1	1	$635,091	109	D.Fst	15	8	1	1	$635,091 109
2003	10	4	1	0	$452,361	109	Wet(409)	1	0	0	0	$0 80
2002	6	4	0	0	$164,730	100	Turf(303)	1	0	0	0	$0 87
	0	0	0	0	$0	–	Dst(0)	0	0	0	0	$0 –

4Oct03–5SA	fst	1⅛	:482 1:114 1:36 1:481	3↑ GdwdBCH-G2	97	3	51¾	32	3nk	1hd	44¾	Espinoza V	LB117	4.50	88–13	*PlesntlyPerfect*116½ FleetstrtDncr1131¼ StrCross1103	Bit tight 3/4,3wd bid	8
1Sep03–8Dmr	fst	1	:214 :451 1:092 1:353	3↑ DmrBCH-G2	104	6	42½	4¾	2hd	11½	12	Valenzuela P A	LB116	4.80	96–09	Joey Franco1162 Reba's Gold1161½ Grey Memo117½	Bid 3wd,drftd in,clear	7
3Aug03–8Dmr	fst	1 1/16	:224 :453 1:10 1:423	3↑ SnDiegoH-G2	74	4	3½	41½	31½	45½	816	Valenzuela P A	LB117	*2.40	76–11	TasteofPardise113¾ Gondolieri117nk RebsGold1166½	Tight,stdied 7/8 & 3/4	8
5Jly03–8Hol	fst	7f	:214 :442 1:082 1:212	3↑ TrBndBCH-G1	105	9	3	31	31½	11	1hd	Valenzuela P A	LB118	2.50	95–11	JoyFrnco118hd Publcton1161½ [D]Blusthstndrd1173½	3w,led,driftd out,held	9
31May03–8Hol	fst	7½f	:222 :45 1:082 1:27	3↑ AckAckH91k	109	7	3	53¼	42¼	11½	11	Valenzuela P A	LB118	2.70	103–08	*Joey Franco*1181 Kela1173½ Publication116nk	3wd 3/8,bid,led,held	7
26Apr03–8Hol	fst	7½f	:222 :444 1:092 1:28	4↑ [S]Tiznow150k	102	3	6	41¾	41½	2hd	11	Desormeaux K J	LB122	2.60	98–07	*JoeyFranco*1221 BonusPyDy120½ CommndersFlg1202	3wd into lane,rallied	9
29Mar03–8SA	fst	6½f	:212 :44 1:082 1:144	4↑ PtrGrBCH-G2	100	5	4	43	2hd	2hd	22	Stevens G L	LB116	24.90	97–10	*Bluesthestandard*1152 *JoeyFrnco*116½ KonGold1215½	Rail bid,game,held 2nd	7
Previously trained by Hofmans David																		
1Mar03–3SA	fst	6½f	:213 :441 1:09 1:153	4↑ OClm 100000N	75	3	5	2½	2½	53¼	58¼	Stevens G L	LB118	4.50	87–07	F J's Pace1181¾ Waingarth118½ Mighty David1183	Dueled, weakened	5
12Feb03–7SA	wf	6½f	:212 :434 1:081 1:144	4↑ OClm 100000N	80	2	9	97¼	76	65	66½	Smith M E	LB118	*2.80	92–05	Bold Ranger118½ Waingarth1191½ Ride and Shine1193	Off bit slow,no bid	9
25Jan03–4SA	fst	6f	:211 :432 :552 1:08	4↑ [R]FedExSprnt250k	99	4	8	1010	109	78	57	Smith M E	LB119	19.00	91–07	CaptainSquire1195½ *Men'sExclusive*120½ *FJ'sPace*120½	Off rail,imp position	10

Johar

Own: The Thoroughbred Corporation

B. h. 5 (Feb)
Sire: Gone West (Mr. Prospector) $125,000
Dam: Windsharp (Lear Fan)
Br: The Thoroughbred Corporation (Ky)
Tr: Mandella Richard E(0 0 0 0 .00) 2003:(253 51 .20)

Life	16	6	4	2	$1,494,496	112	D.Fst	2	0	0	0	$920 78
2003	5	2	1	1	$912,281	112	Wet(351)	0	0	0	0	$0 –
2002	11	4	3	1	$582,215	100	Turf(325)	14	6	4	2	$1,493,576 112
	0	0	0	0	$0	–	Dst(0)	0	0	0	0	$0 –

30Nov03♦Tokyo (Jpn)	yl	*1½ Ⓣ LH	2:283	3↑ Japan Cup-G1 Stk 4404000							1638	Solis A	126	15.10		Tap Dance City1269 That's The Plenty121¾ *Symboli Kris S*126hd	*Rated in 8th,weakened 2f out.Denon 8th,Sarafan 17th*	18
25Oct03–8SA	fm	1½ Ⓣ	:483 1:112 2:00 2:241	3↑ BCTurf-G1	112	9	96¼	95¾	75½	44	1hd	♦Solis A	LB126	14.20	105–04	[DH]High Chaparral126 [DH]Johar126hd *Falbrav*1265½	5wd into lane,gamely	9
28Sep03–3SA	fm	1¼ Ⓣ	:503 1:152 1:39 2:013	3↑ CLHirsch-G1	103	1	12	12	11	12	2½	Solis A	LB124	3.00	84–13	Storming Home124½ *Johar*1241¼ Irish Warrior1241½	Inside,worn down late	4
22Aug03–2Dmr	fm	1 1/16 Ⓣ	:261 :504 1:142 1:424	3↑ [R]HFBrubakrH69k	94	1	31½	34	34½	32½	31¼	Solis A	LB123	*1.10	86–10	Sarafan1221 Fateful Dream119nk Johar123	Steadied bit early	3
20Jan03–8SA	fm	1¼ Ⓣ	:463 1:104 1:34 1:574	4↑ SnMarcos-G2	106	6	76	73¾	53½	43	1hd	Solis A	LB120	2.30	104–	Johar120hd *The Tin Man*122no Grammarian122½	Waited 1/4,up 4wd late	7

Just Wonder (GB)
Own: Naify Sugarman and Vistas LLC, et al

B. c. 4 (Mar)
Sire: Hernando*Fr (Niniski) $10,920
Dam: Just Fly (Capote)
Br: Lutz Bongen and Gerd Feldmann (GB)
Tr: De Seroux Laura(0 0 0 0 .00) 2003:(111 14 .13)

Life	8	4	1	0	$207,727	100	D.Fst	1 0 0 0	$0 80
2003	6	3	0	0	$190,330	100	Wet(353)	0 0 0 0	$0 –
2002	2	1	1	0	$17,397	–	Turf(297)	7 4 1 0	$207,727 100
	0	0	0	0	$0	–	Dst(0)	0 0 0 0	$0 –

16Aug03-11AP gd 1¼ Ⓣ :491 1:14 1:384 2:022 Secretar-G1 79 8 107¼ 72¾ 52½ 1014 1014¾ Desormeaux K J L123 *3.10 79-08 Kicken Kris1163½ Joe Bear1162 Lismore Knight121nk Bid, faltered 11
29Jun03-8Hol fm 1⅛ Ⓣ :462 1:10 1:35 1:472 + CinmaBCH-G3 100 7 86¾ 87¼ 84¾ 12 1¾ Desormeaux K J LB117 3.40 92-08 JustWonder117¾ *BisRepetitas*1154 SlewCityCitadel1151 4wd bid,clear,held 8
10May03-8BM fm 1$\frac{1}{16}$ Ⓣ :224 :47 1:112 1:423 AscotH100k 90 2 67½ 65 64¼ 32½ 12 Baze R A LB117 *.90 93-15 *Just Wonder*1172 Rapier Dance116hd Obermeister1122½ Swung 4w, drvng 7
12Apr03-7SA fm 1 Ⓣ :232 :474 1:111 1:343 LaPuente150k 93 6 79½ 77 75¼ 64¼ 52¼ Valdivia J Jr LB114 8.40 87-11 Steelaninch114no Singletary1181 Urban King1171 4 wide into stretch 7
1Mar03-7SA fst 1 :222 :451 1:092 1:354 SnRafael-G2 80 5 42½ 52½ 42½ 64¼ 67½ Desormeaux K J LB116 6.60 84-05 Rojo Toro1151 Spensive1182½ Crowned Dancer1181½ Angled in, no rally 7
31Jan03-4SA fm 1 Ⓣ :232 :472 1:11 1:343 OClm 80000N 87 7 74¼ 74¾ 75 62¾ 1hd Desormeaux K J LB118 *2.30 89-09 JustWonder118hd Macchito120hd SweetReturn118no Swung out,rallied,up 8

Kafwain
Own: The Thoroughbred Corporation

Dk. b or b. c. 4 (Feb) FTFFEB02 $720,000
Sire: Cherokee Run (Runaway Groom) $20,000
Dam: Swazi's Moment (Moment of Hope)
Br: Dr. & Mrs. R. Smiser West (Ky)
Tr: Baffert Bob(0 0 0 0 .00) 2003:(674 127 .19)

Life	11	4	2	2	$715,848	115	D.Fst	11 4 2 2	$715,848 115
2003	3	1	0	1	$180,000	115	Wet(394)	0 0 0 0	$0 –
2002	8	3	2	1	$535,848	102	Turf(253)	0 0 0 0	$0 –
	0	0	0	0	$0	–	Dst(0)	0 0 0 0	$0 –

5Apr03-6SA fst 1⅛ :454 1:10 1:36 1:491 SADerby-G1 100 7 51¼ 43 41¼ 42½ 32¼ Valenzuela P A LB122 b 1.70 86-14 Buddy Gil122hd Indian Express1222¼ Kafwain1221¼ Came out str,best rest 9
9Mar03-9FG fst 1$\frac{1}{16}$:232 :463 1:103 1:423 LaDerby-G2 101 5 53½ 54½ 43 32½ 22¼ Espinoza V L122 b 1.40 95-17 *Peace Rules*1222¼ D Kafwain1221 Funny Cide122½ Not enough late 10
Disqualified from purse money
1Feb03-4SA fst 7f :22 :44 1:08 1:21 SnVicnte-G2 115 5 2 52½ 41½ 12½ 14½ Espinoza V LB123 b *.80 101-07 Kafwain1234½ Sum Trick1201½ *Southern Image*1176 4wd,3wd,ridden out 5

Katdogawn (GB)
Own: Cuchna John R., Jim Ford Inc. and Pea

B. f. 4 (Feb)
Sire: Bahhare (Woodman) $4,341
Dam: Trempkate (Trempolino)
Br: Mrs W. H. Gibson Fleming (GB)
Tr: Cassidy James M(0 0 0 0 .00) 2003:(155 15 .10)

Life	15	5	3	2	$330,645	97	D.Fst	0 0 0 0	$0 –
2003	10	4	3	1	$320,580	97	Wet(283*)	0 0 0 0	$0 –
2002	5	1	0	1	$10,065	–	Turf(281)	15 5 3 2	$330,645 97
	0	0	0	0	$0	–	Dst(0)	0 0 0 0	$0 –

20Dec03-9Hol fm 1$\frac{1}{16}$ Ⓣ :234 :472 1:11 1:412 3↑ⒻDahliaH-G2 97 8 97 85¾ 84¾ 63¾ 1no Smith M E LB116 7.90 89-15 Ktdogwn116no PersonlLegnd1151½ BttysWish117½ Waited into lane,game 10
23Nov03-8Hol fm 1⅛ Ⓣ :491 1:13 1:362 1:49 + ⒻASkirball73k 90 8 84¼ 810 76¾ 44 2½ Krone J A LB120 *2.40 83-16 Fencelineneighbor118½ *Ktdogwn*1202 DesertViw117½ 3wd into lane,rallied 10
24Aug03-9Dmr fm 1⅛ Ⓣ :472 1:114 1:351 1:47 ⒻDmrOaks-G1 82 2 88 88½ 74¾ 77 75¾ Krone J A LB122 2.80e 92-03 Dessert122nk Solar Echo1221 PersonalLegend122no No rally,not urged str 8
2Aug03-8Dmr fm 1 Ⓣ :223 :463 1:102 1:333 ⒻSnClmntH-G2 92 1 52½ 41½ 42 41¼ 12 Krone J A LB116 5.10e 95-06 Ktdogwn1162 AtlntcOcn1202 Bffythcntrfold118½ Swung out,rallied,game 9
6Jly03-8Hol fm 1 Ⓣ :231 :463 1:102 1:341 ⒻFlawlessly112k 92 3 98¼ 97¼ 85½ 64¾ 2¾ Smith M E LB115 8.80 92-12 JustTooToo117¾ *Katdogwn*1151 VlentineDncer119½ Squeezed start,rallied 10
1Jun03-8Hol fm 5½f Ⓣ :22 :442 :562 1:023 ⒻManhttnBch77k 90 5 9 95½ 85¾ 53 12 Smith M E LB116 *1.10e 91-09 Katdogawn1162 SevenGrand1161 MontanaBanana114nk Shuffled,tight 3/8 10
8May03-7Hol fm 5½f Ⓣ :212 :441 :561 1:022 ⒻOClm 80000N 89 3 6 53¼ 43½ 41¾ 11 Smith M E LB120 *1.80 92-08 *Katdogawn*1201 Sharpbill1222 *Fudge Fatale*1202 3wd into lane,rallied 6
13Apr03-3SA fm 1⅛ Ⓣ :473 1:114 1:361 1:474 ⒻProvidncia150k 80 6 2hd 21 21 52½ 64¾ Stevens G L LB116 1.50e 85-10 StrVeg114nk *MkupArtist*1151½ ShpsndShdows1151½ Took up btwn foes 1/8 6
20Mar03-3SA fm 1 Ⓣ :234 :481 1:12 1:353 ⒻAlw 66080n1x 79 7 74½ 63¼ 64 44½ 33½ Smith M E LB116 5.40 80-13 *Just Too Too*1161 Tangle1162½ Katdogawn1162 Off tardily, 3wd rally 7
28Feb03-7SA gd *6½f Ⓣ :214 :442 1:074 1:14 ⒻLaHabra110k 85 7 8 812 87¾ 63½ 2hd Krone J A LB114 18.70e 87-13 Luvah Girl116hd Katdogawn1141 Himalayan1161 Off slow,finished well 8

Keys to the Heart
Own: Nichols Thomas L

Dk. b or b. m. 5 (Feb)
Sire: Wild Again (Icecapade) $50,000
Dam: Gold Shadow (Mr. Prospector)
Br: Thomas L. Nichols (Ky)
Tr: Greely C. B(0 0 0 0 .00) 2003:(126 20 .16)

Life	18	2	2	3	$166,348	97	D.Fst	10	2	1	1	$124,896	97
2003	8	1	1	2	$111,600	97	Wet(405)	1	0	0	0	$7,500	74
2002	5	0	0	0	$14,140	86	Turf(308)	7	0	1	2	$33,952	93
	0	0	0	0	$0	–	Dst(0)	0	0	0	0	$0	–

7Dec03-8Hol	fst	1 1/16		:23 :46 1:094 1:41	3↑Ⓕ BayakoaH-G2	81	3	21½	32	42½	45	514¼	Krone J A	LB113	14.20	85-08	StarPrde1123¼ Adortion1214 BreNecessities1193	Stalked pace, weakened	6
21Jun03-8Hol	fst	1⅛		:471 1:103 1:351 1:482	3↑Ⓕ VanityH-G1	87	4	52½	41½	43½	58½	513	Valdivia J Jr	LB115	49.90	79-14	*Azeri*1272 SisterGirlBlues111½ *BreNecessitis*1184½	Stalked btwn,weakened	7
24May03-8Hol	fst	1 1/16		:23 :461 1:10 1:414	3↑Ⓕ MladyBCH-G1	97	6	56½	55½	44	43	47	Valdivia J Jr	LB115	26.90	88-05	*Azeri*1253 Enjoy1143 Tropical Blossom1111	Angled in,no late bid	6
25Apr03-3Hol	fst	1 1/16		:241 :481 1:12 1:424	3↑Ⓕ HawthrnH-G3	94	3	21	2hd	1hd	12	1½	Valdivia J Jr	LB115	17.50	90-10	KeystotheHert115½ Rhin116hd ⒹSeMeAcbo1123½	Vied,cleared,held game	4
5Apr03-6BM	gd	1 1/16	Ⓣ	:241 :484 1:132 1:443	3↑Ⓕ MissAmrcaH83k	71	3	65½	74¾	65¼	78	810½	Rollins C J	LB116	41.00	73-18	Lindsay Jean118nk *Crazy Ensign*118hd *BushTriumph*116no	Failed to respond	9
1Mar03-1SA	gd	1⅛	Ⓣ	:472 1:112 1:362 1:49	4↑Ⓕ Alw 59360n1x	82	9	22½	24	25	23	36	Pincay L Jr	LB118	5.20	78-16	Trekking1184 SereneinSettle1182 KeystotheHrt118nk	Off rail, just held 3d	9
31Jan03-7SA	fm	1¼	Ⓣ	:48 1:121 1:362 2:00	4↑Ⓕ ReloyH81k	93	3	31½	31½	32	32	31	Pincay L Jr	LB116	12.90	92-09	*NochesDeRos*1151 Snowflke117hd KeystothHrt1162	Pulled,stalkd,missd 2d	7
12Jan03-8SA	fm	1	Ⓣ	:223 :454 1:094 1:331	4↑Ⓕ Alw 56000n1x	89	7	97	89¾	87½	55½	25	Espinoza V	LB119	15.90	91-09	*SouthernOsis*1195 KeystothHrt119hd ChrmSong1172	4wd into lane,late 2nd	10

Kicken Kris
Own: Brushwood Stable

B. c. 4 (Mar) KEESEP01 $400,000
Sire: Kris S. (Roberto) $150,000
Dam: Kicken Grass (Jade Hunter)
Br: Valerie Naify (Ky)
Tr: Matz Michael R(0 0 0 0 .00) 2003:(187 25 .13)

Life	13	4	3	2	$599,600	106	D.Fst	5	0	0	1	$6,400	67
2003	9	4	3	1	$593,540	106	Wet(380)	0	0	0	0	$0	–
2002	4	M	0	1	$6,060	38	Turf(333)	8	4	3	1	$593,200	106
	0	0	0	0	$0	–	Dst(0)	0	0	0	0	$0	–

30Nov03-9Hol	fm	1¼	Ⓣ	:51 1:172 1:41 2:041	HolDerby-G1	96	9	43	2½	2½	41¾	31	Castellano J J	LB122	*3.00	70-17	Sweet Return122½ Fairly Ransom122½ KickenKris122hd	3wd bid,outkicked	13
11Oct03-9Bel	fm	1½	Ⓣ	:501 1:144 2:031 2:274	LawRealH-G3	99	4	22½	2hd	1hd	12½	1¾	Castellano J J	L121	*.55	82-14	KickenKris121¾ RowansPrk115¾ FortuneWriters1134¼	When roused, clear	8
21Sep03-9Bel	fm	1⅛	Ⓣ	:471 1:104 1:342 1:46	JamaicaH-G2	101	6	41	31	3nk	21	22	Castellano J J	L121	3.10	98-12	*Stroll*1212 *Kicken Kris*121no Joe Bear1172½	Wide both turns, game	7
16Aug03-11AP	gd	1¼	Ⓣ	:491 1:14 1:384 2:022	Secretar-G1	106	6	33	31½	3½	11½	13½	Castellano J J	L116	15.00	94-08	Kicken Kris1163½ Joe Bear1162 Lismore Knight121nk	Drew off, driving	11
12Jly03-10Cnl	fm	1¼	Ⓣ	:474 1:114 1:361 2:01	VrgniaDrby500k	93	6	53	53½	42½	24½	21½	Castellano J J	L115	31.10	103-03	Silver Tree1151½ *Kicken Kris*1151¾ King's Drama1152	Swung wide,rallied	8
1Jly03-7Del	fm	1 1/16	Ⓣ	:233 :47 1:104 1:423	Alw 40000n2x	85	2	65	55½	63¾	3½	2no	Castillo O O	L117 b	2.80	93-11	Sigint117no Kicken Kris117½ Hypnotist117nk	Split rivals, missed	7
4Apr03-5GP	fm	*1 1/16	Ⓣ	:24 :501 1:142 1:453	Alw 38000n1x	86	8	73¾	63	21	1½	11¼	Douglas R R	L122 b	3.40	76-21	KcknKrs1221¼ MomboLoco1183 MllnnmGhost1182½	Saved grd, clear late	8
13Mar03-4GP	fm	*1⅛	Ⓣ	:501 1:14 1:393 1:514	Md Sp Wt 34k	81	3	74½	73¾	85¾	65½	1hd	Velasquez C	L122 b	18.90	82-19	*KickenKris*122hd FortuneWriters122nk Sailwy1221¾	Checked chute, just up	10
8Feb03-5GP	fst	1⅛		:472 1:12 1:38 1:51	Md Sp Wt 34k	67	7	31½	21½	53¼	46	59	Boulanger G	L122 b	96.20	78-08	Formal Attire1222¾ Major Decision1221¼ *Trustee Man*1224	Chased, tired	11

Kim Loves Bucky
Own: Glenney John and Kim

B. g. 7 (Mar)
Sire: Green Dancer (Nijinsky II) $15,000
Dam: Moondust Mink (Great Above)
Br: Dr. & Mrs. John Glenney (Ky)
Tr: Glenney John(0 0 0 0 .00) 2003:(86 6 .07)

Life	30	6	2	1	$487,699	105	D.Fst	2	0	0	0	$1,210	65
2003	8	2	0	0	$177,940	105	Wet(305)	0	0	0	0	$0	–
2002	8	1	0	0	$159,657	105	Turf(320)	28	6	2	1	$486,489	105
	0	0	0	0	$0	–	Dst(0)	0	0	0	0	$0	–

4Oct03–7Kee	fm	1½	Ⓣ	:502 1:154 2:044 2:292	3↑SycamrBC-G3	90	8	33½	41¼	1½	2½	67½	Valenzuela P A	L122	13.30	85– 14	Sharbayan1201¾ Cetewayo122½ Deputy Strike1201¼	Tracked,led,weaken	10
20Sep03–14KD	fm	1½	Ⓣ	:501 1:14 2:043 2:311	3↑KyCpTrfH-G3	86	4	811	86¼	82	71½	76¼	Sellers S J	L116	4.60	76– 17	D *Art Variety*111hd Rochester116½ Quest Star116nk	Failed to rally	8
31Aug03–8Dmr	fm	1⅜	Ⓣ	:472 1:12 1:353 2:121	3↑DelMarH-G2	93	7	66	56	44	75½	75¼	Valenzuela P A	LB116	7.00	94– 05	IrishWrrior116hd ContinentlRed117½ Continuously1141	Clipped heels 3/16	9
9Aug03–9Sar	gd	1½	T	:49 1:13 2:031 2:28	3↑SwrdDncH-G1	87	6	2½	2½	63	89¼	711	Sellers S J	L115	20.80	69– 20	Whitmore's Conn1151¼ Macaw114nk Slew Valley114¾	Pressed pace, tired	11
5Jly03–10Mth	fm	1⅜	Ⓣ	:483 1:14 1:373 2:123	3↑UntdNtnH-G1	104	7	53	32	32	62¼	63½	Sellers S J	L115	20.40	98– 03	BaltoStr117½ TheTinMn121no LunrSovereign112nk	5wd,brushed into lane	7
31May03–9CD	fm	1⅜	Ⓣ	:484 1:133 1:373 2:14	3↑LsvillH-G3	104	2	21	2hd	2hd	1hd	1½	Sellers S J	L117	4.20	95– 04	KimLovesBucky117½ Rochstr1171½ DrKshnikow117½	Dueled,gamely,drvg	8
10May03–7Hol	fm	1½	Ⓣ	:491 1:131 1:594 2:251	3↑JMurryMemH400k	96	4	43	76	68	67	58¾	Blanc B	LB115	13.90	90– 12	*Storming Home*1222 *Denon*1224½ *Ballingarry*120nk	Stalked btwn,no bid	8
23Apr03–8Kee	fm	1½	Ⓣ	:512 1:164 2:051 2:291	4↑Elkhorn-G3	105	7	43	32½	31½	21	1½	Desormeaux K J	L117	11.90	94– 09	KmLvsBcky117½ MnFrmWckl123no WllmsNs1161¼	Closed gamely,4w,drv	10

King Robyn
Own: Cornejo Racing Inc

B. g. 4 (Mar)
Sire: Robyn Dancer (Crafty Prospector) $3,500
Dam: Queen's Family (New Prospect)
Br: Farnsworth Farms (Fla)
Tr: Mullins Jeff(0 0 0 0 .00) 2003:(313 94 .30)

Life	19	11	1	1	$493,710	104	D.Fst	11	5	0	1	$167,240	104
2003	11	8	1	0	$436,990	104	Wet(331)	2	1	0	0	$17,600	88
2002	8	3	0	1	$56,720	88	Turf(277)	6	5	1	0	$308,870	103
	0	0	0	0	$0	–	Dst(0)	0	0	0	0	$0	–

28Nov03–9Hol	fm	5½f	Ⓣ	:222 :441 :554 1:02	3↑HolTrExH-G3	102	3	2	1hd	1½	11	1½	Baze T C	LB120	*.90	94– 06	King Robyn120½ Geronimo1161 Golden Arrow1151	Strong hand ride	9
24Oct03–5SA	fm	*6½f	Ⓣ	:214 :434 1:064 1:131	3↑MorvichH-G3	102	3	3	11	11	1½	1hd	Solis A	LB117	*2.60	91– 09	*King Robyn*117hd Medecis116¾ Geronimo115hd	Inside,met bid,gamely	9
12Sep03–11Fpx	fst	6½f		:21 :434 1:084 1:153	Foothill49k	98	7	1	1hd	13½	16	15	Fogelsonger R	LB122	*.60	100– 11	*King Robyn*1225 Hell Cat1141 American Fury122hd	Clear, ridden out	7
20Aug03–7Dmr	fm	5f	Ⓣ	:213 :434 :552	3↑GreenFlshH78k	103	4	2	31½	21½	21½	11	Solis A	LB116	*2.00	- -	*KingRobyn*1161 SwissLke1163 MncingDnnis1171	Came out,wore down foe	7
12Jly03–10Crc	fst	6f		:213 :443 :57 1:10	CarryBck-G3	100	10	1	21	1hd	21	44	Solis A	L117	2.70	90– 11	*Valid Video*1222½ *Cajun Beat*1171¼ Super Fuse117nk	Vied turn, weakened	10
18Jun03–7Hol	fm	5½f	Ⓣ	:221 :442 :553 1:012	Alw 62000NC	100	5	1	2hd	2hd	11½	12½	Solis A	LB118	*.60	97– 06	King Robyn1182½ Royal Robe1181½ Taraval116nk	Dueled,clear,riddn out	5
26May03–7Hol	fst	7f		:213 :44 1:09 1:22	LBrreraM-G2	88	7	2	2hd	1hd	1hd	55	Solis A	LB120	*1.80	87– 11	Blazonry1152½ Fly to the Wire116½ Jimmy O1151	3wd turn,led,wkened	9
23Apr03–7Hol	fm	5½f	Ⓣ	:211 :432 :55 1:011	HHenson82k	99	7	4	33	32½	1hd	13	Solis A	LB121	*.80	98– 02	King Robyn1213 Jimmy O1191½ Slew's Prince1171	3wd into lane,clear	9
22Mar03–6SA	fst	6½f		:211 :432 1:082 1:151	SanPedro80k	104	3	2	1hd	11	12	1½	Solis A	LB116	2.50	97– 09	*KingRobyn*116½ TruckleFeture117nk EyofthTigr1162	Dueled, cleared, held	6
23Feb03–8SA	fm	*6½f	Ⓣ	:214 :432 1:062 1:122	Baldwin-G3	101	4	4	1hd	11	12½	22	Solis A	LB116 b	9.30	93– 11	*Buddy Gil*1172 *KingRobyn*1164 FlirtWithFortune1161	Speed,inside,held 2nd	11
23Jan03–7SA	fst	6½f		:211 :432 1:082 1:152	OClm 80000	88	7	2	2½	1hd	13	1½	Solis A	LB118 b	2.90	96– 10	King Robyn118½ Fly to the Wire1184½ *Martinblestme*118¾	Dueled,clear,held	7

Kiss the Devil

Own: Pollard Carl F

Dk. b or b. m. 6 (Feb) KEESEP99 $150,000
Sire: Kris S. (Roberto) $150,000
Dam: Devil's Nell (Devil's Bag)
Br: Domino Stud Of Lexington (Ky)
Tr: Vance David R(0 0 0 0 .00) 2003:(282 40 .14)

Life	22	6	7	4	$381,629	98	D.Fst	3	0	1	0	$7,340	69
2003	3	1	2	0	$150,626	98	Wet(377)	0	0	0	0	$0	–
2002	8	3	1	2	$112,093	92	Turf(337)	19	6	6	4	$374,289	98
	0	0	0	0	$0	–	Dst(0)	0	0	0	0	$0	–

28Jun03–9CD fm 1⅛ Ⓣ :474 1:112 1:351 1:473 3↑ⒻLcstGrvH-G3 **98** 5 11½ 12 1½ 11½ 2½ Meche L J L116 b 6.60 95–08 Ipi Tombe123½ Kiss the Devil116½ Quick Tip1171½ Pace,no match 5
24May03–9CD fm 1 1/16 Ⓣ :232 :471 1:111 1:413 4↑ⒻETMintJH-G3 **93** 4 2½ 21 2½ 12 1nk Meche L J L115 b 13.80 96–07 KisstheDevil115nk QuickTip1191 CellarsShiraz1201 Pressed,driving,lasted 9
23Apr03–6Kee fm 1 1/16 Ⓣ :233 :472 1:121 1:414 4↑ⒻAlw 59463c **96** 2 11½ 12½ 1½ 11½ 2nk Guidry M L116 b 4.90 92–09 Love n' Kiss S.117nk *Kiss the Devil*1162¾ Decencia1161¼ Could not last 7

Kona Gold

Own: Headley Aase, Molasky, Irwin and Mola

B. g. 10 (Mar)
Sire: Java Gold (Key to the Mint)
Dam: Double Sunrise (Slew o' Gold)
Br: Carlos Perez (Ky)
Tr: Headley Bruce(0 0 0 0 .00) 2003:(138 29 .21)

Life	30	14	7	2	$2,293,384	123	D.Fst	29	14	6	2	$2,261,074	123
2003	4	1	0	1	$95,680	109	Wet(322)	1	0	1	0	$32,310	109
2002	3	1	0	0	$128,340	113	Turf(264)	0	0	0	0	$0	–
	0	0	0	0	$0	–	Dst(0)	0	0	0	0	$0	–

26Jly03–6Dmr fst 6f :214 :44 :553 1:074 3↑BCrsbBCH-G2 **103** 5 7 95¾ 75½ 56 54¾ Solis A LB119 3.50 97–07 BeusTown1191½ CptinSquire117nk Bluesthstndrd1172 No late bid outside 9
29Mar03–8SA fst 6½f :212 :44 1:082 1:144 4↑PtrGrBCH-G2 **99** 6 6 64½ 53¼ 32 32½ Nakatani C S LB121 *1.50 96–10 *Bluesthestandard*1152 *JoeyFrnco*116½ KonGold1215½ 3wd into str,missed 2d 7
26Jan03–7SA fst 6f :212 :434 :552 1:074 4↑PlsVrdsH-G2 **102** 3 4 54½ 33 33 65¾ Solis A LB124 *1.40 93–10 Avnzdo1164½ MellowFllow117½ Disturbingthpc120nk Rail move,no late bid 6
1Jan03–7SA fst 5½f :212 :442 :562 1:023 4↑ElCnejoH-G3 **109** 1 7 74½ 64¾ 41½ 1nk Solis A LB123 *1.30 99–09 Kona Gold123nk Radiata115¾ No Armistice116hd Rail bid,up late,game 7

Kudos

Own: Moss Mr. and Mrs. Jerome S

B. g. 7 (Apr)
Sire: Kris S. (Roberto) $150,000
Dam: Souq (Damascus)
Br: Mr. & Mrs. J. S. Moss (Ky)
Tr: Mandella Richard E(0 0 0 0 .00) 2003:(253 51 .20)

Life	24	7	5	4	$1,238,935	113	D.Fst	10	3	1	4	$1,000,715	113
2003	5	1	1	3	$530,000	109	Wet(367)	0	0	0	0	$0	–
2002	3	2	0	1	$468,735	113	Turf(338)	14	4	4	0	$238,220	102
	0	0	0	0	$0	–	Dst(0)	0	0	0	0	$0	–

13Jly03–9Hol fst 1¼ :453 1:092 1:341 2:002 3↑HolGldCp-G1 **109** 3 615 513 45½ 34½ 35 Solis A LB124 b 2.80 100–07 Congaree1243 Harlan's Holiday1242 Kudos1241 Lagged,rallied for 3rd 7
14Jun03–8Hol fst 1⅛ :463 1:103 1:35 1:474 3↑Calfrnin-G2 **108** 1 67½ 77 76¾ 42¾ 1½ Solis A LB116 b 1.90 95–04 Kudos116½ Piensa Sonando1181½ Reba's Gold1181½ 3wd into lane,rallied 7
5Apr03–11OP fst 1⅛ :474 1:12 1:354 1:473 4↑OaklawnH-G2 **106** 5 57½ 58½ 57 35 32¾ Solis A L117 b 3.70 99–11 *Medaglia d'Oro*1222¾ Slider112hd *Kudos*1174 Getting to runner up 5
1Mar03–9SA fst 1¼ :463 1:111 1:352 1:594 4↑SAH-G1 **109** 4 42½ 43 32 32 34½ Krone J A LB117 b 8.80 101–05 *Milwaukee Brew*119hd *Congaree*1244½ Kudos1171½ Pulled,3wd into lane 6
4Jan03–8SA fst 1 1/16 :234 :473 1:112 1:41 4↑SnPsqalH-G2 **104** 1 31½ 31 52¼ 44 26 Solis A LB119 b 4.30 93–05 *Congaree*1216 Kudos119no Hot Market1161¼ Saved ground to lane 9

La Reina
Own: Hamilton Emory A

Ch. f. 3 (Feb)
Sire: A.P. Indy (Seattle Slew) $300,000
Dam: Queena (Mr. Prospector)
Br: Emory A. Hamilton (Ky)
Tr: McGaughey III Claude R(0 0 0 0 .00) 2003:(259 48 .19)

Life	4	2	2	0	$142,420	90	D.Fst	4 2 2 0	$142,420 90
2003	4	2	2	0	$142,420	90	Wet(440)	0 0 0 0	$0 –
2002	0	M	0	0	$0	–	Turf(332)	0 0 0 0	$0 –
	0	0	0	0	$0	–	Dst(0)	0 0 0 0	$0 –

29Nov03–7Aqu	fst	1⅛	:47 1:12 1:382 1:524	ⒻDemoisel-G2	84	2	2hd	2½	2hd	2½	2no	Velazquez J R	L121	1.90	72–19	Ashado117no La Reina121½ Dr. Kathy11510	Came again on rail	7
4Nov03–8Aqu	fst	1	:232 :463 1:111 1:36	ⒻTempted-G3	90	1	2hd	1hd	2½	1hd	13	Velazquez J R	L115	*1.05	85–15	La Reina1153 Eye Dazzler1155½ Sisti's Pride1152	Going away on rail	8
6Sep03–5Bel	fst	7f	:224 :453 1:104 1:234	ⒻMd Sp Wt 45k	80	4	3	31	22½	21	15	Velazquez J R	L119	*.60	81–16	*La Reina*1195 Storm Minstrel1144¾ Sheer Luck1191¼	Drew away late	8
15Aug03–6Sar	fst	6f	:221 :452 :574 1:104	ⒻMd Sp Wt 45k	81	7	1	53	31	2½	2¾	Velazquez J R	119	2.60	87–11	Home Court119¾ *La Reina*1195¾ *Lady Struck Gold*1191½	Game finish outside	7

Lady Tak
Own: Heiligbrodt Racing Stable

Ch. f. 4 (Apr) KEEAPR02 $75,000
Sire: Mutakddim (Seeking the Gold) $6,500
Dam: Star of My Eye (Lucky North)
Br: John Franks (Fla)
Tr: Asmussen Steven M(0 0 0 0 .00) 2003:(1949 452 .23)

Life	11	6	3	0	$716,270	110	D.Fst	10 5 3 0	$696,430 110
2003	9	4	3	0	$675,350	110	Wet(394)	1 1 0 0	$19,840 94
2002	2	2	0	0	$40,920	103	Turf(334)	0 0 0 0	$0 –
	0	0	0	0	$0	–	Dst(0)	0 0 0 0	$0 –

25Oct03–2SA	fst	1⅛	:47 1:11 1:354 1:49	3↑ ⒻBCDistaf-G1	78	3	41½	41½	31½	33½	713¾	Day P	LB119	10.70	75–07	Adoration1234½ Elloluv1192½ Got Koko1233½	Pulled btwn,weakened	7
6Sep03–7Bel	fst	1⅛	:452 1:093 1:344 1:482	ⒻGazelleH-G1	94	8	42	41½	1hd	13½	2½	Bailey J D	L121	*.95	87–13	Buy the Sport113½ LadyTak121no SpokenFur1218¼	4 wide move, saved 2nd	8
26Jly03–9Sar	fst	7f	:223 :451 1:081 1:204	ⒻTest-G1	110	2	3	2½	2hd	15½	14½	Bailey J D	L122	2.00	103–08	Lady Tak1224½ Bird Town1221½ *House Party*1221¾	Drew off when asked	7
6Jun03–10Bel	fst	1	:232 :461 1:102 1:351	ⒻAcorn-G1	96	2	5¾	61¾	42½	21	2hd	Bailey J D	L121	2.80	90–16	Bird Town121hd *Lady Tak*1211 Final Round1213¼	Game finish outside	7
2May03–10CD	fst	1⅛	:46 1:10 1:353 1:483	ⒻKyOaks-G1	88	7	55	42	2hd	3nk	67¾	Bailey J D	L121	*2.60	87–07	*Bird Town*1213¼ Santa Catarina121hd Yell121¾	Bmp 1st turn,brushed	12
5Apr03–8Kee	fst	1 1/16	:243 :483 1:122 1:432	ⒻAshland-G1	98	2	42	32	32	22	23¾	Lanerie C J	L123 f	*1.30	86–20	Elloluv1203¾ Lady Tak123¾ Holiday Lady1165	3w bid,2ndbest	7
8Mar03–9FG	fst	1 1/16	:241 :48 1:13 1:441	ⒻFGOaks-G2	95	4	43½	43	32½	11	13½	Meche D J	L121	*1.10	89–16	LdyTk1213½ AtlnticOcen1212¼ BellofPrintown121¾	Restrained, ridden out	6
26Jan03–8FG	fst	1	:24 :473 1:121 1:383	ⒻTiffnyLass100k	93	4	21	21	2hd	11½	12¾	Meche D J	L122	*.80	91–21	*Lady Tak*1222¾ Allspice122hd *My Trusty Cat*1221½	Took over, ridden out	8
4Jan03–9FG	fst	6f	:214 :451 :57 1:10	ⒻThelma72k	99	4	1	2½	2hd	13	15	Meche D J	L116	*.20	90–15	*Lady Tak*1165 Allspice1223½ Buffalo Jump1222½	Clear, ridden out	4

Lead Story

Own: Miles A S Jr

Ch. m. 5 (Apr) KEESEP00 $45,000
Sire: Editor's Note (Forty Niner) $5,000
Dam: Gwenjinsky (Seattle Dancer)
Br: Cabotaba Partnership (Ky)
Tr: Nafzger Carl A(0 0 0 0 .00) 2003:(285 31 .11)

Life	29	7	3	4	$606,291	107	D.Fst	16	4	2	3	$328,928	98
2003	11	3	1	1	$449,062	107	Wet(282)	6	2	1	0	$251,689	107
2002	13	3	2	2	$111,749	92	Turf(235)	7	1	0	1	$25,674	79
	0	0	0	0	$0	–	Dst(0)	0	0	0	0	$0	–

27Nov03-10CD	sly	1⅛	:47⁴ 1:12³ 1:38² 1:51¹	3↑ Ⓕ FallCtyH-G2	107	4	7¹⁰	7⁹¼	5⁷	1hd	1⁶½	Borel C H	L116	10.10	82– 25	LedStory1166½ MyoOntheSide1146 ClokofVgueness1146½	Rail trip,driving	9
8Nov03- 9CD	fst	1	:23 :45⁴ 1:11 1:36²	3↑ Ⓕ CDDstafH-G2	98	7	10¹⁰	10¹¹	8⁹¾	3¹½	1½	Borel C H	L114	35.80	85– 20	*LedStory*114½ AwsomHumor1181¼ BorntoDnc1133¼	Angled 5w 1/8p,driving	10
24Oct03- 7Kee	fst	1 1/16	:25 :49³ 1:14¹ 1:46	3↑ Ⓕ Alw 58000c	82	4	6⁴½	6⁴¼	6³¼	4²½	3¹¾	Borel C H	L121	1.80	75– 29	ThereRunsHttie1191½ *Donnree*119nk *LedStory*121no	Bmp start,gaining late	6
20Sep03- 8AP	fm	1 Ⓣ	:24¹ :49 1:13 1:37²	3↑ Ⓕ Flawlessly48k	79	6	10⁶	9⁵¼	8⁵½	6⁴	9⁴	Sibille R	L122	22.90	84– 12	Delmonico Cat118nk You GlitterGirl114½ NaturallyWild118¾	Showed little	11
1Sep03- 8AP	my	1⅛	:48 1:12² 1:37¹ 1:50	3↑ Ⓕ ArlMtrnH-G3	84	3	6¹⁴	6¹³	6¹⁰	5¹⁵	5¹⁴¼	Marquez C H Jr	L116	8.30	79– 12	*Take Charge Lady*12310½ Lakenheath1161¾ To the Queen117nk	Outrun	6
9Aug03-10EIP	fst	1⅛	:46² 1:11³ 1:37² 1:50	3↑ Ⓕ GrdeniaH-G3	93	5	9¹⁸	9¹⁶	8⁶¾	4⁴½	4⁸	Borel C H	L115	7.20	90– 08	BreNecessities1195¼ DesertGold1142¾ SoMuchMor115hd	4w,no late threat	9
12Jly03-10EIP	fst	1	:23² :46⁴ 1:11⁴ 1:37³	3↑ Ⓕ HBPAH97k	98	5	9⁸¼	9⁵½	5³	1hd	1²¼	Borel C H	L114	6.70	92– 21	Lead Story1142¼ ClearDestiny1141¾ *BorntoDance*1156	5w lane,driving,clear	9
26Jun03- 8CD	fst	6½f	:23 :45¹ 1:09² 1:16	3↑ Ⓕ OClm 80000N	94	4	5	6⁷½	6⁸	4⁵	4¹¼	Borel C H	L118	27.30	90– 14	SurfNSnd122nk BetYourFeet124nk *VickiVllencourt*120¾	Bmp, in tight 3/16s	6
26Apr03- 8Haw	fst	1⅛	:49 1:14 1:39³ 1:52⁴	3↑ Ⓕ SixtySlH-G3	71	1	8⁵¾	7⁵¼	7⁵½	7¹⁰	7¹⁹½	Vitek J J	L113	31.70	72– 31	Bare Necessities1182½ Jaramar Rain114nk Lakenheath1144¾	No factor	9
4Apr03- 8GP	fst	1 1/16	:22⁴ :46¹ 1:10⁴ 1:43¹	3↑ Ⓕ BnshBrzH75k	91	4	7¹⁴	7¹⁶	7⁷	5⁴	2⁴¼	Velez J A Jr	L115	32.50	89– 08	NonsuchBy1184¼ LedStory1152¼ *TonightsWgr*113½	Swung 5 wide, 2nd best	9
10Mar03- 8GP	sly	170	:22¹ :46² 1:11⁴ 1:41²	4↑ Ⓕ Alw 46000c	67	5	5⁸	5⁴¾	3²	6⁶½	6¹⁷¾	Prado E S	L119	6.50	76– 15	*Nonsuch Bay*1156¼ Alchemilla1193 Colonial Glitter1153¼	3 wide, faltered	7

Lilac Queen (Ger)

Own: Tanaka Gary A

Dk. b or b. m. 6 (May)
Sire: Law Society (Alleged)
Dam: Lilac Dance*GB (Fabulous Dancer)
Br: Gestut Zoppenbroich (Ger)
Tr: Frankel Robert J(0 0 0 0 .00) 2003:(411 114 .28)

Life	8	5	1	0	$203,777	99	D.Fst	0	0	0	0	$0	–
2003	5	3	0	0	$144,858	99	Wet(305)	0	0	0	0	$0	–
2001	3	2	1	0	$58,919	–	Turf(292)	8	5	1	0	$203,777	99
	0	0	0	0	$0	–	Dst(0)	0	0	0	0	$0	–

4Jly03-10Bel	fm	1¼ Ⓣ	:49¹ 1:13¹ 1:36⁴ 1:59³	3↑ Ⓕ NewYorkH-G2	88	5	6⁴½	6³	6³¼	7⁸¾	8⁷	Bailey J D	L117 f	*.75e	89– 07	Snow Dance1161 Pertuisane115¾ Riskaverse1193¼	Came wide, no rally	8
31May03- 8Bel	sf	1⅜ Ⓣ	:52⁴ 1:20³ 1:47² 2:28	3↑ Ⓕ ShpshdBH-G2	69	6	8⁸	7²¾	3½	3³	5²⁰½	Bailey J D	L119 f	*.70	- -	*Mariensky*1148¼ Owsley1194¾ Silent Crystal1121¾	3 wide move, faltered	8
24Apr03- 8Kee	fm	1½ Ⓣ	:50² 1:15³ 2:05³ 2:29³	4↑ Ⓕ Bewitch-G3	99	7	7³½	6²¼	2hd	1²	1⁴	Bailey J D	L116	*.70	92– 11	LilacQueen1164 BeyondtheWaves116hd SnDre118hd	Rallied 4-5w,hand urg	10
6Apr03- 4Kee	fm	1½ Ⓣ	:53¹ 1:20¹ 2:10¹ 2:33³	4↑ Ⓕ Alw 56225N3x	95	7	4³	3½	3nk	1¹½	1⁵¾	Bailey J D	L123	*.40e	72– 20	*Lilac Queen*1235¾ Karsavina116nk Daisyago116nk	Drew off,hand urging	8
24Jan03- 2SA	fm	1¼ Ⓣ	:46¹ 1:10⁴ 1:35¹ 1:59	4↑ Ⓕ OClm 80000N	91	1	4⁷	4²½	3¹	2¹	1²	Valenzuela P A	LB119	*.40	98– 02	*Lilac Queen*1192 La Vita E Bella119½ Monterey Bay1196½	Led past 1/8,clear	5

Limehouse
Own: Dogwood Stable

Ch. c. 3 (Feb) FTSAUG02 $140,000
Sire: Grand Slam (Gone West) $30,000
Dam: Dixieland Blues (Dixieland Band)
Br: Cheryl A. Curtin (Fla)
Tr: Pletcher Todd A(0 0 0 0 .00) 2003:(826 199 .24)

Life	6	3	0	2	$260,435	92	
2003	6	3	0	2	$260,435	92	
2002	0	M	0	0	$0	-	
	0	0	0	0	$0	-	
D.Fst	5	3	0	1	$243,935	92	
Wet(423)	1	0	0	1	$16,500	79	
Turf(346)	0	0	0	0	$0	-	
Dst(0)	0	0	0	0	$0	-	

4Oct03–6Kee	fst	1 1/16	:224 :462 1:102 1:432	LnsEndFt-G2	90	2	74½	51¾	32	41½	34¾	Albarado R J	L121	13.10	85–20	Eurosilver1214¾ Tiger Hunt121no Limehouse1211	Inside to stretch 11
30Aug03–8Sar	fst	7f	:222 :452 1:102 1:232	Hopeful-G1	74	4	2		3nk	2hd	51¼ 58½	Albarado R J	L122	10.30	81–11	SilverWagon1224 ChpelRoyl1221½ NotoriousRogue1221	Vied 3 wide, tired 7
13Aug03–8Sar	sly	6½f	:211 :442 1:091 1:154	SarSpcl-G2	79	2	6	53½	53¾	39	310¼	Albarado R J	L122	3.00	86–03	*Cuvee*1227½ Pomeroy1182¾ Limehouse1224½	Split rivals, no rally 8
6Jly03–10CD	fst	6f	:211 :443 :572 1:103	BshfdMnr-G3	86	2	5	41½	31½	31	14½	Albarado R J	L121	3.00	85–13	Limehouse1214½ First Money1172 *Cuvee*121no	Bmp start,ck 1/2p,drv 6
3May03–6CD	fst	5f	:22 :452 :572	3ChmnyJuv114k	92	3	3	41½	42½	2½	11¼	Albarado R J	L118	6.60	98–08	*Limehouse*1181¼ El Sysco Kid1193½ East Bay115nk	Tough at gate,rail,drv 7
16Apr03–2Kee	fst	4½f	:22 :453 :52	Md Sp Wt 43k	–	6	3	32		31½	1nk	Albarado R J	L118	4.50	95–17	*Limehouse*118nk Cherniavsky1183½ Cold Trick1185¼	Drift lane,gamely,drv 8

Lindsay Jean
Own: Moss Mr. and Mrs. Jerome S

B. m. 6 (Mar) FTFFEB00 $250,000
Sire: Saint Ballado (Halo) $125,000
Dam: Colony Bay (Pleasant Colony)
Br: Robert Lothenbach (Fla)
Tr: Sherman Art(0 0 0 0 .00) 2003:(501 113 .23)

Life	28	7	9	5	$388,160	98	
2003	7	3	1	2	$182,125	97	
2002	9	1	4	1	$84,995	98	
	0	0	0	0	$0	-	
D.Fst	15	1	6	3	$112,875	92	
Wet(394)	2	1	0	1	$37,000	89	
Turf(286)	11	5	3	1	$238,285	98	
Dst(0)	0	0	0	0	$0	-	

29Nov03–7GG	fst	1 1/16	:224 :462 1:103 1:423	3↑ [F]StarBallH64k	87	4	43	32	41¾	2hd	31¼	Schvaneveldt C P	LB120 f	3.20	89–14	TropicalBlossom116½ BartoksBlithe116¾ LindsayJen1201½	Boxed 2nd turn 8
20Sep03–8BM	fm	1 1/16	[T] :223 :463 1:104 1:45	3↑ [F]HillsboroH60k	88	10	46	45	43¼	1hd	2hd	Schvaneveldt C P	LB120	*1.40	81–18	Ilha Grande113hd Lindsay Jean120¾ Milligram118¾	Bid 4w into lane, led 10
30Aug03–3BM	fm	1	[T] :232 :473 1:122 1:381	3↑ [F]AutmnLvesH63k	89	3	55	55½	54	1hd	1½	Schvaneveldt C P	LB118	*.50	82–20	Lindsay Jean118½ [DH]Pheiffer115 [DH]Marty's Zee1153½	Circled 4w, dug in 5
5Jly03–7Hol	fm	1	[T] :233 :472 1:104 1:341	3↑ [F]RlHroine-G3	88	7	63¼	62¼	41¾	63¼	85½	Schvaneveldt C P	LB119	2.30e	88–11	MgicMission115hd LittleTresure1212 Bellski1151½	Rank early,4wd 2d turn 9
24May03–7BM	fm	*1⅛	[T] :481 1:113 1:36 1:452	3↑ [F]YrbBnBCH-G3	94	7	22	22	21	1½	36½	Schvaneveldt C P	LB118	5.10	97–08	Chiming1163½ Noches De Rosa1193 Lindsay Jean1182¼	Prssd, led, wknd 7
5Apr03–6BM	gd	1 1/16	[T] :241 :484 1:132 1:443	3↑ [F]MissAmrcaH83k	94	5	53	52½	2½	11	1nk	Schvaneveldt C P	LB118	2.30	83–18	LindsyJn118nk *CrzyEnsign*118hd *BushTriumph*116no	Bid 3w, dueled, gamely 9
1Feb03–5GG	yl	1 1/16	[T] :231 :474 1:122 1:441	+4↑ [F]BrwnBssH-G3	97	2	23	22	2hd	12½	11½	Schvaneveldt C P	LB116	6.70	88–14	*Lindsay Jean*1161½ Bush Triumph116no Crazy Ensign1181½	Bid 2w, drvng 9

Lion Heart
Own: Smith Derrick and Tabor, Michael

Ch. c. 3 (Jan) FTFFEB03 $1,400,000
Sire: Tale of the Cat (Storm Cat) $16,139
Dam: Satin Sunrise (Mr. Leader)
Br: Sabine Stable (Ky)
Tr: Biancone Patrick L(0 0 0 0 .00) 2003:(135 26 .19)

Life	3	3	0	0	$310,800	103	
2003	3	3	0	0	$310,800	103	
2002	0	M	0	0	$0	-	
	0	0	0	0	$0	-	
D.Fst	3	3	0	0	$310,800	103	
Wet(335)	0	0	0	0	$0	-	
Turf(322)	0	0	0	0	$0	-	
Dst(0)	0	0	0	0	$0	-	

20Dec03–4Hol	fst	1 1/16	:231 :462 1:103 1:424	HolFut-G1	99	4	12	12½	11	11½	13½	Smith M E	121	*.50	90–11	Lion Heart1213½ St Averil1211 That's an Outrage121½	Bit off rail,riddn out 5
15Nov03–7Hol	fst	7f	:221 :443 1:081 1:203	HolPrevu-G3	103	4	1	11½	1½	11½	16	Smith M E	114	*.50	99–06	*Lion Heart*1146 Cooperation116no Voladero1134	Drifted bit,ridden out 5
24Oct03–6SA	fst	6f	:212 :44 :561 1:091	Md Sp Wt 42k	96	4	6	2½	2hd	1hd	11	Stevens G L	118	2.40	92–13	*LionHeart*1181 Boomzeeboom1183 Preachintthebr1182	Dueled,led,gamely 10

Lion Tamer
Own: Tabor Michael B

Ch. c. 4 (Feb) FTKJUL01 $180,000
Sire: Will's Way (Easy Goer) $7,500
Dam: Tippecanoe Creek (Olympio)
Br: Paul Smith (Ky)
Tr: Pletcher Todd A(0 0 0 0 .00) 2003:(826 199 .24)

Life	6	3	1	0	$171,000	98	
2003	4	2	0	0	$135,400	98	
2002	2	1	1	0	$35,600	89	
	0	0	0	0	$0	–	
D.Fst	5	2	1	0	$144,000	98	
Wet(425)	1	1	0	0	$27,000	89	
Turf(290)	0	0	0	0	$0	–	
Dst(0)	0	0	0	0	$0	–	

12Apr03–9Kee fst 1⅛ :47 1:111 1:374 1:513 BlueGras-G1 **50** 7 65 53½ 42½ 611 633¾ Velasquez C L123 5.70 48–30 Peace Rules123¾½ Brancusi1234½ Offlee Wild12310½ Came out bmp 7/8p 9
22Mar03–10TP fst 1⅛ :463 1:11 1:37 1:503 LanesEnd-G2 **92** 9 83¾ 53 52¾ 42½ 42½ Velazquez J R L121 *.80 80–14 NewYorkHero121nk EugenesThirdSon1212¼ Champli121hd 4 wide 1st turn 9
15Feb03–9GP fst 7f :22 :441 1:091 1:223 Hutchesn-G2 **98** 4 5 2½ 21 1½ 16 Velazquez J R L118 *1.30 95–08 Lion Tamer1186 StrengthWithin116¾ CraftyGuy1223¾ Off slowly, drew off 6
4Jan03–5GP fst 6f :22 :452 :573 1:101 Alw 34000N1x **96** 2 9 74¼ 32 11½ 17½ Velazquez J R L118 *.50 93–11 *LionTamer*1187½ Letters1181 OneEyedWilling118nk Broke slow, ridden out 9

Lismore Knight
Own: Pletcher J. J. and Simon, Barry

B. c. 4 (Jan)
Sire: Woodman (Mr. Prospector) $25,000
Dam: Lismore Lady (Ogygian)
Br: Bon Marche, Wallace (Ky)
Tr: Pletcher Todd A(0 0 0 0 .00) 2003:(826 199 .24)

Life	11	4	1	2	$455,600	96	
2003	6	2	0	2	$208,800	96	
2002	5	2	1	0	$246,800	96	
	0	0	0	0	$0	–	
D.Fst	1	0	0	0	$500	49	
Wet(317)	0	0	0	0	$0	–	
Turf(255)	10	4	1	2	$455,100	96	
Dst(0)	0	0	0	0	$0	–	

18Oct03–8Haw fm 1⅛ Ⓣ :472 1:114 1:36 1:482 HawDerby-G3 **86** 1 41½ 42½ 41½ 33 52¼ Arroyo N Jr L122 *1.50 96–06 False Promises1151 Megoman1151 Beau Classic113nk Inside, no rally 11
21Sep03–9Bel fm 1⅛ 🅃 :471 1:104 1:342 1:46 JamaicaH-G2 **83** 5 3½ 2½ 2hd 54 69¾ Velazquez J R L119 5.10 90–12 *Stroll*1212 *Kicken Kris*121no Joe Bear1172½ Speed 3 wide, tired 7
16Aug03–11AP gd 1¼ Ⓣ :491 1:14 1:384 2:022 Secretar-G1 **96** 1 43 42 42 33½ 35½ Douglas R R L121 4.90 88–08 KickenKris1163½ JoeBear1162 LismoreKnight121nk Inside, no winning bid 11
20Jly03–5Del fm 1⅛ Ⓣ :462 1:094 1:344 1:472 KentBC-G3 **91** 7 44 46 42½ 32½ 31¾ Velazquez J R L119 *1.20 103 – FoufasWrrior1151¼ *Remind*1151½ LismoreKnight1193¼ Posed threat,outfin 7
28Jun03–8AP fm 1 1/16 Ⓣ :241 :484 1:123 1:423 ArlClsc-G2 **93** 2 21½ 42½ 42½ 32½ 1¾ Douglas R R L119 *2.20 96–10 Lismore Knight119¾ Remind116½ Good Day Too1161¼ Angled out, driving 10
17May03–7Bel fm 1 Ⓣ :224 :452 1:092 1:341 3↑ Alw 48000N2x **93** 8 3½ 3½ 2½ 12 11 Velazquez J R L115 *.70 89–11 *Lismore Knight*1151 *Alphabetical*121nk St. Dehere1231 Speed 3 wide, clear 8

Lord Nelson
Own: Bennett Mr. and Mrs. R. J

Dk. b or b. g. 7 (Apr)
Sire: Maudlin (Foolish Pleasure)
Dam: Lady Hamilton (The Minstrel)
Br: Mr. & Mrs. R. J. Bennett (BC-C)
Tr: Condilenios Dino K(0 0 0 0 .00) 2003:(201 39 .19)

Life	24	11	6	3	$455,684	99	
2003	5	2	1	2	$161,023	98	
2002	5	3	1	0	$109,629	99	
	0	0	0	0	$0	–	
D.Fst	19	9	4	2	$363,975	99	
Wet(333)	5	2	2	1	$91,709	95	
Turf(313)	0	0	0	0	$0	–	
Dst(0)	0	0	0	0	$0	–	

24Aug03–8EmDfst 1 :221 :442 1:081 1:33 3↑ LgaMileH-G3 **89** 4 63¾ 74 84¼ 35 38¼ Fuentes F P LB116 f 24.20 93–14 Sky Jack1236¼ Poker Brad1162 Lord Nelson1162¾ Hopped start, wide 10
4Aug03–9Hst fst 1⅛ :471 1:121 1:364 1:494 3↑ ®BCCpClassH72k **95** 5 2½ 2hd 1hd 13 13 Fuentes F P L120 f *.50 95–09 LordNelson1203 VernonInvdr1121¾ JzzyYcht114nk Drew clear, ridden out 6
1Jly03–8Hst fst 1⅛ :474 1:122 1:371 1:502 3↑ LtGovrnH-G3 **98** 5 32 31 31½ 11 13 Fuentes F P L119 f *1.05 92–12 *LordNlson*1193 LtsGoRsty114hd *CommodorCrg*1162¼ Bid 3 wide, drew clear 8
31May03–8Hst fst 6½f :214 :444 1:094 1:163 3↑ HKJockClbH44k **87** 5 6 43 42½ 32 31 Fuentes F P L121 f *.85 94–11 BoldnKeen116nk CommodoreCrig117¾ *LordNlson*121no 3 wide, good effort 8
10May03–8Hst fst 6½f :213 :444 1:10 1:164 3↑ GeorgRoyal41k **91** 3 1 42¼ 41½ 1½ 2no Fuentes F P L122 f *2.90 94–12 Diglett117no Lord Nelson1221 *Bold 'n Keen*1171 Failed to sustain bid 10

Lunar Sovereign
Own: Darley Stud Management LLC

Dk. b or b. h. 5 (Feb) FTKJUL00 $140,000
Sire: Cobra King (Farma Way) $4,000
Dam: January Moon (Apalachee)
Br: Cobra Farm Inc. (Ky)
Tr: McLaughlin Kiaran P(0 0 0 0 .00) 2003:(186 46 .25)

Life	16	5	4	1	$508,452	110	D.Fst	2	0	1	0	$7,883 51
2003	7	2	0	1	$410,000	110	Wet(359)	3	0	2	0	$20,550 99
2002	7	2	3	0	$87,233	105	Turf(300)	11	5	1	1	$480,019 110
	0	0	0	0	$0	–	Dst(0)	0	0	0	0	$0 –

19Oct03–9WO yl 1½ Ⓣ :512 1:163 2:081 2:333 3↑ CanIntnl-G1 **94** 8 54½ 52¼ 31 41¼ 67½ Migliore R L126 5.60 54–30 Phoenix Reach119¾ Macaw126hd Brian Boru1191 Advance 4w,bid, weaken 10
27Sep03–9Bel fm 1½ Ⓣ :501 1:143 2:021 2:272 3↑ TfClscIv-G1 **62** 4 33 31 73¾ 713 726¾ Migliore R L126 3.60 57–14 Sulamani1262¾ Deeliteful Irving126¾ Balto Star126½ Speed 3 wide, tired 7
6Sep03–8Bel yl 1⅜ Ⓣ :514 1:171 1:42 2:174 3↑ ManOWar-G1 **110** 3 54½ 54 54 13 12¾ Migliore R L126 10.00 74–26 Lunar Sovereign1262¾ Slew Valley126nk Denon1261¼ Quick 4 wide move 8
9Aug03–9Sar gd 1½ 🅃 :49 1:13 2:031 2:28 3↑ SwrdDncH-G1 **87** 4 41½ 32 52 75¾ 811¼ Migliore R L114 4.00 69–20 Whitmore'sConn1151¼ Macaw114nk SlewValley114¾ Saved ground, empty 11
5Jly03–10Mth fm 1⅜ Ⓣ :483 1:14 1:373 2:123 3↑ UntdNtnH-G1 **109** 4 64 64 63¼ 31 3½ Migliore R L112 7.60 100–03 BaltoStr117½ TheTinMn121no LunrSovereign112nk Widest bid,closed well 7
21May03–8Bel gd 1⅛ 🅃 :494 1:141 1:384 1:503 3↑ Alw 50000N3X **104** 7 52¼ 61¾ 41½ 11½ 13¾ Bailey J D L119 *1.60 77–23 LunrSovereign1193¾ Epicentr122hd ThfullCircl1194½ 4 wide, strong finish 9
Previously trained by McLaughlin Kiaran P
16Jan03♦Nad al Sheba (UAE) gd *1¼ Ⓣ LH 2:033 3↑ Al Rashidiya Prep Alw 34000 716¼ McGlone A 121 - Nowrass1232¼ Kelly123½ Lightning Arrow1235¼ 10
Tracked leader,weakened 1-1/2f out

M B Sea
Own: Bruder Michael J

Dk. b or b. h. 5 (Mar) KEESEP00 $20,000
Sire: Alphabet Soup (Cozzene) $30,000
Dam: Sea Ditty (Afleet)
Br: Adena Springs (Ky)
Tr: Romans Dale L(0 0 0 0 .00) 2003:(638 113 .18)

Life	29	5	6	4	$359,038	108	D.Fst	19	4	5	2	$300,913 108
2003	12	2	2	1	$197,386	103	Wet(392)	7	1	1	1	$55,245 102
2002	13	3	4	2	$157,512	108	Turf(281)	3	0	0	1	$2,880 73
	0	0	0	0	$0	–	Dst(0)	0	0	0	0	$0 –

28Nov03–11CD sly 1⅛ :481 1:13 1:384 1:522 3↑ ClarkH-G2 **98** 11 97¾ 84½ 93¾ 74½ 76 Perret C L116 b 11.20 70–27 🄳Evening Attire118no Quest1143¼ Aeneas1141¼ Angled 5w,no gain late 14
25Oct03–4Kee fst 1⅛ :501 1:143 1:383 1:501 3↑ Fayette-G3 **103** 7 42 41¼ 31 11 11 Perret C L119 b 34.70 89–11 MBSea1191 Tenpins1212½ DHChngeinthewether119 Exch bmps,4w,driving 7
4Oct03–7Del fst 1 3/16 :491 1:124 1:381 1:58 3↑ KelsoH100k **100** 3 44 43½ 45 5¾ 22½ Black A S L116 b 4.00 92–19 Country Be Gold1152½ *M B Sea*116nk Abreeze1154¾ Up for place 5w 5
13Sep03–11TP fst 1⅛ :481 1:114 1:37 1:502 3↑ KyCpClH-G2 **101** 5 55½ 55½ 54½ 56 56¾ Velasquez C L114 b 33.20 77–17 *Perfect Drift*1201 Congaree1244 *Crafty Shaw*115½ 5 wide 3/8 pole 5
9Aug03–7Mnr fst 1 1/16 :24 :481 1:111 1:41 3↑ WVaGovnrsH102k **99** 2 74½ 76 53 31 21¼ Velasquez C LB114 b 4.20 102 - Be Like Mike1101¼ M B Sea114nk Docent122¾ Bid 4wide for place 7
20Jly03–3EIP fst 1 :241 :472 1:112 1:36 3↑ Alw 42000N$Y **96** 6 64½ 54 42 32 45¼ Butler D P L124 b 3.10 95–11 Trion Georgia1184½ E Z Glory118nk Virtual Zone118½ 5w trip,flatten out 6
20Jun03–8CD fst 1 1/16 :232 :463 1:112 1:424 3↑ OClm 62500N **98** 3 79¾ 67¾ 1hd 12½ 11¾ Velasquez C L118 b 4.60 94–18 M B Sea1181¾ Cat Tracker1182½ Mail Call120hd 5w,stiff drive 9
4Jun03–9CD my 1 1/16 :232 :47 1:122 1:454 3↑ OClm 62500N **88** 1 512 68¾ 64¼ 43 41 Day P L118 b *1.50 78–25 Gold Dollar118½ Freon Flier118½ FortyNineDeeds118hd Ck,lack room 5/16s 6
8May03–9CD fm 1 1/16 Ⓣ :234 :463 1:111 1:413 3↑ OClm 62500N **56** 6 74¼ 810 84¾ 78½ 716¼ Day P L117 b 5.70 80–07 MjesticThief1192 Conserve1174 KingAmongQueens117½ 5-6w trip,no rally 10
9Apr03–6Kee sly 1 1/16 :233 :473 1:113 1:431 4↑ Alw 65000N3X **92** 4 77½ 710 67¾ 44 43½ Day P L118 b 4.40 87–16 *Full Mandate*116no Play It Out118½ Quest1183 Slow start,no late bid 8
9Mar03–10GP fst 1 1/16 :224 :46 1:102 1:421 4↑ OClm 80000N **80** 8 88¾ 88 55 64 58¾ Day P L118 b 2.90 89–07 *Justification*1183 Quest1181¼ Doc Wild1223½ Awkward st, no factor 9
15Feb03–7GP fst 1⅛ :47 1:113 1:373 1:502 4↑ Alw 40000N3X **81** 2 74¾ 75½ 74¼ 45½ 38½ Day P L118 b *1.20 81–13 Changeintheweather1184¾ Aeneas1223¾ M B Sea118no 4 wide, up for 3rd 8

Madame Pietra

Own: C. T. Grether Inc

Dk. b or b. m. 7 (May)
Sire: Roy (Fappiano) $10,000
Dam: Missy White Oak (Baederwood)
Br: Curtis G. Mikkelsen & Patricia J. Horth (Fla)
Tr: Zucker Howard L(0 0 0 0 .00) 2003:(96 5 .05)

Life	17	7	3	2	$437,215	106	D.Fst	15	7	3	1	$431,335 106
2003	3	2	0	0	$201,580	94	Wet(429)	0	0	0	0	$0 –
2002	7	3	3	0	$162,655	98	Turf(313)	2	0	0	1	$5,880 80
	0	0	0	0	$0	–	Dst(0)	0	0	0	0	$0 –

23Aug03–8Dmr fst 6½f :22² :45 1:09 1:15² 3↑Ⓕ RchBrdoH-G3 **84** 4 3 5¹¾ 2¹ 2²½ 6⁷½ Valenzuela P A **LB**122 2.60 90–10 Secret Liaison116⁴ Lacie Girl116¹ *Spring Meadow*117ʰᵈ Btwn 3-1/2,no rally 8
7Jun03–4Hol fst 6f :21³ :43³ :56¹1:09³ 3↑Ⓕ DstStmrH-G3 **94** 2 6 6⁴¼ 5⁴ 3²½ 1¾ Valenzuela P A **LB**121 6.10 92–10 MadmePietr121¾ BerFn116³ JetintoHouston116ⁿᵒ Closed gamely,up late 6
25Jan03–6GP fst 6f :21² :44² :57 1:10¹ 4↑Ⓕ Ⓡ PaduaFMSpr250k **93** 9 3 7⁶½ 6³¼ 4² 1ⁿᵏ Valenzuela P A L120 *1.20 93–08 *Madame Pietra*120ⁿᵏ Shameful119ⁿᵒ Chispiski119½ 4 wide, just up 9

Madeira Mist (Ire)

Own: Skymarc Farm Inc

B. m. 5 (Feb)
Sire: Grand Lodge (Chief's Crown) $27,510
Dam: Mountains of Mist*Ire (Shirley Heights*GB)
Br: Dr. A. J. O'Reilly and Skymarc Farm (Ire)
Tr: Clement Christophe(0 0 0 0 .00) 2003:(389 75 .19)

Life	16	5	4	3	$319,483	96	D.Fst	0	0	0	0	$0 –
2004	1	0	0	1	$11,000	91	Wet(344)	0	0	0	0	$0 –
2003	7	2	3	1	$198,950	96	Turf(296)	16	5	4	3	$319,483 96
	0	0	0	0	$0	–	Dst(0)	0	0	0	0	$0 –

3Jan04–11GP fm 1 1/16 Ⓣ :23⁴ :48¹ 1:12 1:41¹ 3↑Ⓕ HonyFoxH-G3 **91** 1 5²¼ 5⁴ 5³½ 2½ 3¾ Prado E S L117 3.20 90–07 DelmonicoCt116½ ConeyKitty115ⁿᵏ MdirMist117ⁿᵏ Lacked room into lane 10
14Dec03–5Crc fm 1 1/16 Ⓣ :22⁴ :47 1:11 1:41¹ 3↑Ⓕ DsgntdDncr34k **90** 3 5³½ 5³ 6²¼ 5⁶ 2¹¼ Coa E M L122 *1.10 93–06 Young Star117¹¼ Madeira Mist122ⁿᵒ Cat's Glow115¾ Steadied far turn 12
8Nov03–9Aqu sf 1 1/16 Ⓣ :25 :51 1:16²1:47 3↑Ⓕ AtheniaH-G3 **85** 7 3½ 4¹½ 3¹ 7²½ 6³¾ Prado E S L117 2.65 65–31 Caught in the Rain115ⁿᵒ Lojo114ⁿᵒ Coney Kitty113½ 3 wide, no response 8
17Oct03–7Med gd 1 1/16 Ⓣ :24⁴ :49³ 1:13⁴1:43³ 3↑Ⓕ VioletH-G3 **95** 8 4¾ 2¹ 2½ 2² 2² Prado E S L116 3.70 78–23 Dncl116² MdeirMist116¹¾ SomethingVentured116¾ Pressed pace, gamely 8
6Sep03–9Del gd 1 1/16 Ⓣ :23³ :47¹ 1:11⁴1:43⁴ 3↑Ⓕ Ⓡ GRsnbrgrMm75k **96** 7 5³ 5⁶ 4⁴ 3ⁿᵏ 1ⁿᵏ Dominguez R A L116 *.90 87–18 Madeira Mist116ⁿᵏ Media Access114³¾ Katzen118¾ Mid m,lg drive,all out 9
30Jly03–7Del fm 1 Ⓣ :24 :47⁴ 1:11⁴1:35¹ 3↑Ⓕ Alw 43000N4x **87** 7 6⁸ 6⁶ 5²¼ 5¹¼ 2ⁿᵒ Dominguez R A L122 *.90 97–09 Katzen117ⁿᵒ *Madeira Mist*122¾ Niclie112¾ Fin well 7 wide 8
5Jly03–8WO fm 1⅛ Ⓣ :45²1:09² 1:33³1:48 3↑Ⓕ DncSmrtH-G3 **94** 8 7⁵½ 7⁶¾ 8⁴¾ 2½ 1ⁿᵒ Husbands P L116 8.45 88–15 Madeira Mist116ⁿᵒ First Quarter114¹ *Byzantine*117½ Rail rally got nod 10
15May03–6Bel fm 1 1/16 Ⓣ :24² :47² 1:11¹1:40² 3↑Ⓕ Alw 50000N3x **87** 5 6²½ 5¹½ 5¹¾ 5⁴ 3² Prado E S L120 *2.30 93–09 Gal O Gal114½ *Young Star*120¹½ *Madeira Mist*120½ Pinched back start 8

Magic Mission (GB)

Own: Al Maktoum Sheik Maktoum b

B. m. 6 (Jan)
Sire: Machiavellian (Mr. Prospector)
Dam: Dream Ticket (Danzig)
Br: Gainsborough Stud Management Ltd (GB)
Tr: Drysdale Neil D(0 0 0 0 .00) 2003:(182 34 .19)

Life	24	4	6	5	$398,111	103	D.Fst	0	0	0	0	$0 –
2003	8	1	2	1	$190,980	103	Wet(442)	0	0	0	0	$0 –
2002	6	2	1	2	$163,400	101	Turf(371)	24	4	6	5	$398,111 103
	0	0	0	0	$0	–	Dst(0)	0	0	0	0	$0 –

30Nov03–6Hol fm 1 Ⓣ :23² :46⁴ 1:10²1:34² 3↑Ⓕ Matriarc-G1 **97** 12 7⁴ 8³¾ 8⁴¾ 5¹¾ 6²¾ Desormeaux K J **LB**123 b 26.00 89–17 Heat Haze123ⁿᵏ MusicalChimes120ⁿᵒ Dedication123½ 4wd into lane,no bid 14
28Sep03–7SA fm 1¼ Ⓣ :50¹1:14⁴ 1:37⁴2:00³ 3↑Ⓕ YlwRibbn-G1 **103** 4 5⁴ 5⁵ 5³ 5¹¾ 4²¼ Nakatani C S **LB**123 b 3.30e 88–13 TtesCrk123¾ MusiclChims118ⁿᵏ *CrzyEnsign*123¹¼ Saved ground,outkicked 8
7Sep03–6Dmr fm 1 1/16 Ⓣ :24³ :48² 1:11⁴1:40³ 3↑Ⓕ PalmrBCH-G2 **100** 4 5³½ 5³½ 3¹½ 2½ 2ⁿᵏ Nakatani C S **LB**117 b 2.50 98–03 SpringStar116ⁿᵏ MgicMission117ⁿᵒ *GrdenintheRin*114³ 3wd bid,outgamed 5
5Jly03–7Hol fm 1 Ⓣ :23³ :47² 1:10⁴1:34¹ 3↑Ⓕ RlHroine-G3 **100** 8 8⁴¾ 8³¾ 8³¾ 3¹ 1ʰᵈ Nakatani C S **LB**115 b 6.30 93–11 MagicMission115ʰᵈ LittleTresure121² Belleski115¹½ 5wd into str,driftd in 9
26May03–10LS sf 1 Ⓣ :24 :49² 1:15⁴1:43 3↑Ⓕ WnStDstH-G3 **88** 4 7⁸¾ 7¹⁰ 7⁷½ 6⁷½ 3³ Day P L116 b 2.70 54–48 *EagleLake*116²¼ LittleTreasure117¾ *MagicMission*116¹½ Best stride too late 9
13Apr03–6Kee fm 1 1/16 Ⓣ :23³ :48 1:12 1:41⁴ 4↑Ⓕ JenyWily-G3 **98** 1 5⁵½ 6³¼ 5⁴½ 3¹ 2¹¼ Prado E S L116 b 6.50 91–08 Sea of Showers116¹¼ Magic Mission116ⁿᵏ Snow Dance116ʰᵈ Between,3w 10
22Mar03–9SA fm 1⅛ Ⓣ :50¹1:13³ 1:37 1:48¹ 4↑Ⓕ SntaAnaH-G2 **96** 4 4²½ 4² 2¹ 2¹ 4¹¾ Nakatani C S **LB**116 8.50 86–09 NochesDeRos115½ GrdenintheRin116ⁿᵏ *Mghrtz*117¹ 2-3 wd, loomed, game 8
11Jan03–3SA fm 1⅛ Ⓣ :49 1:12⁴ 1:35⁴1:46⁴ 4↑Ⓕ SnGrgnoH-G2 **95** 7 5⁵ 6⁵ 6³ 6⁴¼ 6³¾ Espinoza V **LB**113 3.60 91–12 *Tates Creek*121¾ Megahertz117½ Double Cat114¹½ 4wd into lane,no bid 7

Makeup Artist
Own: Krikorian George

B. f. 4 (May) KEESEP01 $250,000
Sire: Dynaformer (Roberto) $50,000
Dam: Deux Anes*GB (Longleat)
Br: Mike H. Sloan (Ky)
Tr: Shirreffs John A(0 0 0 0 .00) 2003:(163 33 .20)

Life	4	2	2	0	$136,300	90	D.Fst	1	0	1	0	$8,200	75
2003	3	2	1	0	$128,100	90	Wet(282)	0	0	0	0	$0	-
2002	1	M	1	0	$8,200	75	Turf(282)	3	2	1	0	$128,100	90
	0	0	0	0	$0	-	Dst(0)	0	0	0	0	$0	-

17May03–3Hol fm 1 Ⓣ :243 :49 1:131 1:362 ⒻSenorita-G3 **90** 4 64½ 62½ 41¼ 2hd 11½ Espinoza V LB117 *1.00 82– 17 MkpArtst1171½ RttrsRngd117½ ShpsndShdws1171 4wd,3wd,2nd turn,game 7
13Apr03–3SA fm 1⅛ Ⓣ :473 1:114 1:361 1:474 ⒻProvidncia150k **89** 3 43½ 42½ 42 32 2nk Valenzuela P A LB115 2.70 90– 10 StarVega114nk *MkeupArtist*1151½ ShpesndShdows1151½ 3wd bid,drifted in 6
9Jan03–5SA fm 1 Ⓣ :224 :464 1:11 1:344 ⒻMd Sp Wt 50k **86** 3 57½ 53 53 32 12 Espinoza V LB120 *1.90 88– 10 MkeupArtist1202 BrillintMov1201½ GoldnPnny1201½ 3wd into lane,rallied 8

Mambo Slew
Own: Manganaro Frank

Dk. b or b. f. 3 (Apr)
Sire: Kingmambo (Mr. Prospector) $200,000
Dam: Slew Boyera (Seattle Slew)
Br: F.J.F.M., LLC (Ky)
Tr: Biancone Patrick L(0 0 0 0 .00) 2003:(135 26 .19)

Life	3	2	0	0	$88,350	81	D.Fst	1	0	0	0	$1,350	49
2003	3	2	0	0	$88,350	81	Wet(342)	0	0	0	0	$0	-
2002	0	M	0	0	$0	-	Turf(342)	2	2	0	0	$87,000	81
	0	0	0	0	$0	-	Dst(0)	0	0	0	0	$0	-

28Nov03–5Hol fm 1 Ⓣ :232 :47 1:112 1:36 ⒻMiesque-G3 **81** 4 37 25 21 1½ 11½ Smith M E 116 *3.30 84– 23 Mambo Slew1161½ Ticker Tape116½ Winendynme116no Bid btwn,led,held 11
18Oct03–6SA fm 1 Ⓣ :232 :472 1:11 1:352 ⒻMd Sp Wt 45k **78** 2 52½ 52¾ 42 41½ 11 Farina T 117 3.30 85– 09 *MmboSlew*1171 Yingyingying117nk VncdorAmig1171 Came out lane,rallied 8
3Aug03–5Sar fst 6f :214 :451 :573 1:11 ⒻMd Sp Wt 45k **49** 4 9 610 78¼ 610 510¼ Farina T 119 5.90 77– 13 CaughtinaPinch1192½ MainStrem119¾ HighgtePrk1193¾ Greenly, no rally 10

Man From Wicklow
Own: Violette R A Jr

Dk. b or b. g. 7 (Apr)
Sire: Turkoman (Alydar) $3,000
Dam: Star of Wicklow (Fast Play)
Br: J. R. Cavanaugh (Fla)
Tr: Violette R A Jr(0 0 0 0 .00) 2003:(178 28 .16)

Life	28	6	4	5	$609,395	108	D.Fst	2	0	0	0	$1,290	28
2003	3	1	2	0	$190,000	108	Wet(328)	0	0	0	0	$0	-
2002	6	1	1	2	$247,865	105	Turf(263)	26	6	4	5	$608,105	108
	0	0	0	0	$0	-	Dst(0)	0	0	0	0	$0	-

23Apr03–8Kee fm 1½ Ⓣ :512 1:164 2:051 2:291 4↑Elkhorn-G3 **104** 9 54 2½ 2hd 11 2½ Bailey J D L123 b *1.40 93– 09 KmLvsBcky117½ MnFrmWckl123no WllmsNs1161¼ Tracked,led,outgamed 10
22Mar03–10GP fm *1½ Ⓣ :50 1:15 2:041 2:282 3↑PanAmerH-G2 **101** 6 66½ 74¼ 42½ 33 21¾ Bailey J D L122 b *.60 105– 02 Quest Star1131¾ Man From Wicklow1221 Reduit114no Not enough late 9
16Feb03–10GP fm 1⅜ Ⓣ :481 1:121 1:353 2:113 3↑GPBCH-G1 **108** 7 55½ 57 46 3nk 14¾ Bailey J D L119 b *1.60 98– 09 MnFromWicklow1194¾ JustListen113½ Srdukr1141 Angled out, drew away 10

Mandy's Gold
Own: Steeplechase Farm

Ch. m. 6 (Mar) EASMAY00 $87,000
Sire: Gilded Time (Timeless Moment) $15,000
Dam: Manduria (Aloma's Ruler)
Br: Audley Farm Inc. (Va)
Tr: Gorham Michael E(0 0 0 0 .00) 2003:(388 64 .16)

Life	24	11	4	6	$1,081,744	109	D.Fst 20 9 4 5 $853,644 109
2003	6	2	0	3	$243,100	99	Wet(369) 4 2 0 1 $228,100 108
2002	13	5	3	3	$715,404	109	Turf(261) 0 0 0 0 $0 –
	0	0	0	0	$0	–	Dst(0) 0 0 0 0 $0 –

20Jly03-10Del fst 1¼ :49² 1:13⁴ 1:38² 2:02⁴ 3↑Ⓕ DelH-G2 **94** 5 2½ 3½ 5 3¼ 57 5 10¾ Black A S L117 f 12.80 86-09 Wild Spirit117⁶ *Take Charge Lady*120 2¾ *Shiny Sheet*112½ Press off rail,wknd 8
21Jun03-9Bel sly 1 1/16 :22² :45¹ 1:09¹ 1:40⁴ 3↑Ⓕ OPhippsH-G1 **92** 1 48 4 4½ 4 1½ 35 310 Migliore R L118 f 6.80 86-18 *Sightseek*118⁵ TakeChargeLady119⁵ Mandy'sGold118 1¾ Rail run, little left 5
16May03-8Pim sly 1 1/16 :23³ :47³ 1:12³ 1:46¹ 3↑Ⓕ PmBCDsfH-G3 **86** 1 3 1½ 3 1½ 42 32 1nk Bailey J D L117 f *.80 76-23 MndysGold117nk *SmmrColny*121 3¾ StrmyFrlc114 1½ Swung out 1/8, surged 4
5Apr03-8OP fst 1 1/16 :24¹ :48³ 1:12¹ 1:43 4↑Ⓕ AplBlsmH-G1 **99** 7 2 1½ 31 3½ 3 2½ 3 3¼ Douglas R R L116 f 17.30 92-11 *Azeri*123hd TakeChargeLady118 3¼ *MndysGold*116² Promptd pace,fell back 7
15Mar03-10OP fst 1 1/16 :24¹ :48² 1:13 1:44 3↑Ⓕ OaklwnBC-G3 **91** 3 1½ 1½ 3½ 3nk 32 Douglas R R L117 f *.40 88-14 Bien Nicole122 1¼ Red n'Gold117¾ Mandy's Gold117¹ Pace, bad step 7/16 9
24Feb03-4GP fst 6f :22² :45⁴ :57⁴ 1:10¹ 4↑Ⓕ Alw 46000N$Y **98** 3 4 11 11 12 1 2½ Velazquez J R L119 f *.30 93-15 Mandy's Gold119 2½ Lilah105 2½ City Fair115 7½ Off rail, driving 5

Mariensky
Own: Waterville Lake Stable

B. m. 5 (Mar) FTSAUG00 $200,000
Sire: Gulch (Mr. Prospector) $50,000
Dam: Julie La Rousse*Ire (Lomond)
Br: Calumet Farm (Ky)
Tr: Clement Christophe(0 0 0 0 .00) 2003:(389 75 .19)

Life	18	5	2	2	$340,008	108	D.Fst 0 0 0 0 $0 –
2003	7	3	0	0	$255,300	108	Wet(332) 0 0 0 0 $0 –
2002	7	0	1	2	$48,469	95	Turf(278) 18 5 2 2 $340,008 108
	0	0	0	0	$0	–	Dst(0) 0 0 0 0 $0 –

27Dec03-9Crc fm 1½ Ⓣ :48 1:13 2:03¹ 2:26 3↑Ⓕ LaPvyteH-G2 **82** 10 78 8 5¼ 87 77 7 8¾ Blanc B L115 18.90 94 - Volga119 2¾ Lady Annaliese116 1¼ Lost Appeal115¾ Lack room far turn 11
15Nov03-8Aqu yl 1½ Ⓣ :52 1:17² 2:08² 2:32² 3↑Ⓕ LngIlndH-G2 **91** 4 4 2½ 53 4 3½ 4 2½ 4 4½ Castellano J J L116 3.70 79-16 Spice Island117 1¼ *Volga*120 2¾ Banyu Dewi114½ Stayed on well on rail 11
25Aug03-8Sar fm 1⅜ [T] :48⁴ 1:13³ 1:37 2:13⁴ 3↑Ⓕ GlenFlsH-G3 **89** 1 5 5½ 4 6½ 56 6 3¼ 7 4¼ Velazquez J R L119 *2.20 97 - SixtySeconds115hd PrimtimvIntin113nk Altrnt116¾ Saved ground, no rally 9
4Jly03-10Bel fm 1¼ [T] :49¹ 1:13¹ 1:36⁴ 1:59³ 3↑Ⓕ NewYorkH-G2 **90** 6 76 7 4½ 7 4¼ 6 8¼ 6 6¼ Santos J A L117 2.85 90-07 Snow Dance116¹ Pertuisane115¾ Riskaverse119 3¼ Inside, no response 8
7Jun03-8Bel sf 1 Ⓣ :24¹ :49¹ 1:16¹ 1:43¹ 3↑Ⓕ JsAGmBCH-G3 **108** 7 8 13 7 10 3½ 1hd 12 Santos J A L116 3.05 44-46 Mariensky116² Riskaverse119hd Wonder Again119 6¼ 4 wide move, clear 8
31May03-8Bel sf 1⅜ [T] :52⁴ 1:20³ 1:47² 2:28 3↑Ⓕ ShpshdBH-G2 **106** 3 65 6 2¾ 5 2½ 1½ 1 8¼ Velazquez J R L114 13.70 13-87 *Mariensky*114 8¼ Owsley119 4¾ Silent Crystal112 1¾ 3 wide move, drew away 8
4May03-7Aqu fm 1 1/16 Ⓣ :24² :49² 1:13¹ 1:43³ 3↑Ⓕ Alw 46000N2X **89** 2 7 3¼ 6 2½ 84 3nk 12 Prado E S L121 *1.65 86-11 *Mariensky*121² *Pieria*121no D'ohana121no Saved ground, clear 9

Marylebone
Own: Tabor Michael B

Gr/ro. f. 3 (Feb) KEESEP02 $725,000
Sire: Unbridled's Song (Unbridled) $100,000
Dam: Desert Queen (Wavering Monarch)
Br: Runnymede Farm Inc., Catesby W. Clay & Catesby W. Clay (Ky)
Tr: Pletcher Todd A(0 0 0 0 .00) 2003:(826 199 .24)

Life	3	2	0	0	$147,000	78	D.Fst 3 2 0 0 $147,000 78
2003	3	2	0	0	$147,000	78	Wet(330) 0 0 0 0 $0 –
2002	0	M	0	0	$0	–	Turf(314) 0 0 0 0 $0 –
	0	0	0	0	$0	–	Dst(0) 0 0 0 0 $0 –

4Oct03-6Bel fst 1 1/16 :23¹ :47¹ 1:12¹ 1:43⁴ Ⓕ Frizette-G1 **53** 6 6 3½ 8 4¾ 8 8½ 8 21 8 24½ Luzzi M J L120 9.50 56-26 SocietySelection120 1¼ VictoryU.SA120 2¾ Ashado120 6¾ Outrun early, tired 8
14Sep03-6Bel fst 1 :22² :45¹ 1:10³ 1:38 Ⓕ Matron-G1 **78** 5 5 1½ 5 2¼ 4 1¼ 2hd 1no Prado E S L119 7.00 76-16 Marylebone119no Lokoya119 5¾ Eye Dazzler119 1¾ Steadied turn, got nod 8
31Jly03-3Sar fst 5f :21⁴ :45³ :58³ Ⓕ Md Sp Wt 45k **65** 1 2 54 65 46 1nk Velazquez J R L118 *1.40 96-04 *Marylebone*118nk For My Wife118½ Sheer Luck118¹ Greenly, along late 8

Max Forever

Own: Dweck Raymond and Dorothy

Dk. b or b. c. 4 (Feb) OBSFEB02 $200,000
Sire: Montbrook (Buckaroo) $20,000
Dam: Jiffener (Derby Wish)
Br: John Franks (Fla)
Tr: Perkins B W Jr(0 0 0 0 .00) 2003:(190 36 .19)

Life	11	3	3	0	$165,340	99	D.Fst	7	2	2	0	$132,300	99
2003	10	3	2	0	$158,940	99	Wet(358)	4	1	1	0	$33,040	83
2002	1	M	1	0	$6,400	76	Turf(281)	0	0	0	0	$0	-
	0	0	0	0	$0	-	Dst(0)	0	0	0	0	$0	-

1Sep03-11Pha sly	1⅛		:463	1:104	1:361	1:49	PaDerby-G3	**70**	6	1½	1hd	42¼	1015	1023	Ferrer J C	L122	52.60	76- 16	GrndHombre1145¼ Gimmewink1222 Ashmore114nk	Vied for lead,gave way	10	
3Aug03-11Mth fst	1⅛		:47	1:104	1:36	1:491	HsklInvH-G1	**88**	4	74½	75¼	65	57½	512½	Ferrer J C	L115	47.40	82- 08	Peace Rules1211¾ Sky Mesa1187¼ Funny Cide1231	Saved ground, no rally	7	
12Jly03- 9Mth fst	1 1/16		:234	:48	1:113	1:432	LBrnchBC-G3	**99**	3	31½	2½	3nk	2hd	1hd	Ferrer J C	L113	11.50	94- 11	MxForvr113hd ChrstnsOtlw1152¼ ChllyRoostr112hd	Steadied along 1st trn	6	
15Jun03- 9Mth fst	1	⊗	:232	:463	1:112	1:382	Rstoration50k	**81**	8	53	41¾	31½	42¼	42¼	Ferrer J C	L114	7.90	83- 16	Sky Soldier1191 Deadline119nk Poppy's Image1151	Hung wide briefly 1st	8	
25May03- 9Mth gd	1		:233	:464	1:111	1:38	3↑ Alw 37000N1x	**83**	5	1hd	11	1hd	11½	13½	Ferrer J C	L113	*1.20	87- 07	MaxForever1133½ LisasRoylGuy1203½ Runwy1202¾	Vied inside,drew clear	10	
12Apr03-10Aqu my	1		:231	:461	1:111	1:36	Alw 44000N1x	**71**	1	4¾	2hd	22½	210	413¾	Castellano J J	L122 b	4.80	71- 12	Nacheezmo11813 Intelligent Male118¾ Auto City118no	Vied inside, tired	9	
16Mar03- 9Aqu fst	170	⊡	:234	:473	1:114	1:403	Gotham-G3	**78**	7	31	21½	43½	713	713¾	Castellano J J	L116 b	12.80	77- 15	Alysweep1204¼ *Grey Comet*1201½ Spite the Devil116nk	Speed 3 wide, tired	9	
1Mar03- 6Aqu fst	1 1/16	⊡	:231	:464	1:121	1:444	Md Sp Wt 42k	**87**	5	1hd	1½	15	16	16¾	Castellano J J	L120 b	*1.10	82- 23	Max Forever1206¾ *Runaway Russy*1203¼ Touching Gold1202¾	Kept to drive	10	
31Jan03- 6Aqu fst	6f	⊡	:224	:461	:583	1:111	Md Sp Wt 41k	**78**	4	5	45½	46½	34½	21¾	Castellano J J	L121	*.85	86- 12	*New York Hero*1161¾ *Max Forever*121nk Curb1212¼	Good finish outside	9	
5Jan03- 5Aqu gd	6f	⊡	:221	:452	:58	1:103	Md Sp Wt 41k	**78**	5	2	44	53	45	23¼	Castellano J J	L122	*1.65	88- 12	*Colita*1223¼ Max Forever1221¾ *Courting Concorde*1222	Rallied for place	10	

Medaglia d'Oro

Own: Gann Edmund A

Dk. b or b. h. 5 (Apr)
Sire: El Prado*Ire (Sadler's Wells) $30,000
Dam: Cappucino Bay (Bailjumper)
Br: Albert Bell & Joyce Bell (Ky)
Tr: Frankel Robert J(0 0 0 0 .00) 2003:(411 114 .28)

Life	15	7	6	0	$4,254,720	120	D.Fst	14	6	6	0	$3,654,720	120
2003	5	3	2	0	$1,990,000	119	Wet(355)	1	1	0	0	$600,000	113
2002	9	4	3	0	$2,260,600	120	Turf(291)	0	0	0	0	$0	-
	0	0	0	0	$0	-	Dst(0)	0	0	0	0	$0	-

25Oct03- 9SA fst	1¼	:461	1:101	1:341	1:594	3↑ BCClasic-G1	**117**	8	1hd	2½	2½	2hd	21½	Bailey J D	LB126	*2.60	104- 07	PlesntlyPerfect1261½ MedglidOro126¾ Dynever121nk	Bumped brk, gamely	10
24Aug03- 5Dmr fst	1¼	:464	1:104	1:343	1:59	3↑ PacifcCl-G1	**118**	2	11	1½	1hd	21	23¼	Bailey J D	LB124	*.60	101- 02	CndyRide1243¼ MedglidOro1247 FleetstrtDncr1242	Speed,inside,2nd best	4
2Aug03- 9Sar fst	1⅛	:464	1:102	1:344	1:473	3↑ WhitneyH-G1	**114**	5	2½	21½	2hd	1½	11	Bailey J D	L123	*.80	97- 11	Medaglia d'Oro1231 Volponi1201¼ *Evening Attire*118nk	Pace, gamely, clear	7
5Apr03-11OP fst	1⅛	:474	1:12	1:354	1:473	4↑ OaklawnH-G2	**111**	1	11	1½	1½	11½	12¾	Bailey J D	L122	*.10	102- 11	*Medaglia d'Oro*1222¾ Slider112hd *Kudos*1174	Comfortable pace	5
1Feb03- 9SA fst	1⅛	:454	1:094	1:344	1:48	Strub-G2	**119**	6	11	11	13	15	17	Bailey J D	LB123	*.40	94- 16	*Medaglia d'Oro*1237 Olmodavor117½ Tracemark1177	Inside, ridden out	6

Megahertz (GB)
Own: Bello Michael

Ch. f. 5 (May)
Sire: Pivotal*GB (Polar Falcon) $69,316
Dam: Heavenly Ray (Rahy)
Br: Cheveley Park Stud Ltd (GB)
Tr: Frankel Robert J(0 0 0 0 .00) 2003:(411 114 .28)

Life	22	8	3	5	$1,159,094	104	D.Fst	0	0	0	0	$0 -
2003	7	2	1	3	$534,480	104	Wet(320)	0	0	0	0	$0 -
2002	7	5	1	0	$600,180	97	Turf(336)	22	8	3	5	$1,159,094 104
	0	0	0	0	$0	-	Dst(0)	0	0	0	0	$0 -

25Oct03-6SA	fm	1¼	Ⓣ :463 1:102 1:351 1:59	3↑ⒻBCF&MTrf-G1	103	9	1219 1222	118½	104½	53½	Solis A	LB123	16.10	94- 04	Islington123nk L'Ancresse118 2½ Yesterday118no	Best stride late 12
26Jly03-8Dmr	fm	1⅛	Ⓣ :501 1:144 1:373 1:49	3↑ⒻMbe/RnaH-G1	104	3	53	53	52	52½	1½	Solis A	LB116	8.20	88- 08	Megahertz116½ DH Tates Creek123 DH Dublino1212 Swung out,rallied,game 5
28Jun03-8Hol	fm	1¼	Ⓣ :502 1:134 1:364 2:004	3↑ⒻBevHilsH-G2	99	4	55	58½	47	44	33¼	Solis A	LB117	1.90	85- 13	Voodoo Dancer120¾ Dublino122 2½ Megahertz1171	Came out,late for 3rd 5
26May03-6Hol	fm	1⅛	Ⓣ :482 1:12 1:351 1:464+	3↑ⒻGamlyBCH-G1	104	1	69½	66½	65	53½	31½	Solis A	LB118	6.00	93- 10	Tates Creek1221 Dublino122½ Megahertz118½	Swung out,closed game 6
19Apr03-4SA	fm	1¼	Ⓣ :481 1:122 1:361 2:00	4↑ⒻSntBrbrH-G2	102	5	55	54	52½	21	1¾	Solis A	LB117	*1.30	93- 09	Megahertz117¾ Trekking111 1½ Noches De Rosa117hd	Split foes,led,game 5
22Mar03-9SA	fm	1⅛	Ⓣ :501 1:133 1:37 1:481	4↑ⒻSntaAnaH-G2	98	6	74¼	73¼	63	31½	3¾	Solis A	LB117	*1.00	87- 09	Noches De Rosa115½ Garden in the Rain116nk Megahertz1171	Steadied 3/8 8
11Jan03-3SA	fm	1⅛	Ⓣ :49 1:124 1:354 1:464	4↑ⒻSnGrgnoH-G2	101	4	65	55	52½	31½	2¾	Solis A	LB117	3.20	94- 12	Tates Creek121¾ Megahertz117½ Double Cat114 1½	Waited 1/4,rallied 7

Midas Eyes
Own: Gann Edmund A

B. c. 4 (Apr)
Sire: Touch Gold (Deputy Minister) $50,000
Dam: Bayou Plans (Bayou Hebert)
Br: Jacks or Better Farm Inc. (Fla)
Tr: Frankel Robert J(0 0 0 0 .00) 2003:(411 114 .28)

Life	8	3	3	1	$357,928	111	D.Fst	7	3	2	1	$317,928 110
2003	6	2	2	1	$333,788	111	Wet(338)	1	0	1	0	$40,000 111
2002	2	1	1	0	$24,140	84	Turf(204)	0	0	0	0	$0 -
	0	0	0	0	$0	-	Dst(0)	0	0	0	0	$0 -

26Dec03-8SA	fst	7f	:222 :45 1:091 1:223	Malibu-G1	104	1	9	1hd	1½	21	31	Velazquez J R	LB119	*1.10e	92- 12	SouthernImage115hd MrinoMrini1151 MidsEyes1193	Inside duel,best rest 12
29Nov03-9Aqu	fst	1	:224 :442 1:083 1:341	3↑CigarMiH-G1	110	1	2½	1½	1hd	21½	25¼	Velazquez J R	L115	4.70	89- 19	Congaree124 5¼ Midas Eyes1153 Toccet1151	Pace, second best 7
25Oct03-5SA	fst	6f	:21 :431 :55 1:074	3↑BCSprint-G1	96	5	8	41½	62¾	75½	89¼	Velazquez J R	LB123	8.30	90- 05	CjunBet123 2¼ Blusthstndrd1262 ShkYouDown126½	Bumped early, no rally 13
7Jun03-9Bel	sly	7f	:221 :443 1:084 1:22	RvaRdgBC-G2	111	3	3	2½	2½	11½	2no	Bailey J D	L123	*.80	90- 10	Posse123no Midas Eyes123 6¼ HaloHomewrecker123hd	Pressd pce, gamely 8
26Apr03-9CD	fst	1	:224 :46 1:104 1:361	DerbyTrl-G3	105	3	1hd	11½	12½	12½	12½	Bailey J D	L122	*.30	86- 23	MidasEyes122 2½ Champli122 13¼ DesertWrrior118nk	Bmp start,hand urging 6
15Mar03-11GP	fst	7f	:214 :441 1:082 1:21	Swale-G3	110	6	6	2½	1½	16	19¼	Bailey J D	L116	4.30	103- 05	Midas Eyes116 9¼ Posse120 4½ Whywhywhy122 2¼	Stumbled st, drew off 8

Midnight Cry
Own: Barrister Hall Stables LLC

Ch. f. 4 (May) KEEOCT01 $62,000
Sire: Smart Strike (Mr. Prospector) $20,000
Dam: Mythical Dancer (Sovereign Dancer)
Br: Runnymede Farm Inc. & Peter J. Callahan (Ky)
Tr: McPeek Kenneth G(0 0 0 0 .00) 2003:(400 61 .15)

Life	8	3	1	2	$213,152	91	D.Fst	5	3	1	0	$166,152 91
2003	2	1	0	1	$85,000	91	Wet(425)	3	0	0	2	$47,000 89
2002	6	2	1	1	$128,152	87	Turf(308)	0	0	0	0	$0 -
	0	0	0	0	$0	-	Dst(0)	0	0	0	0	$0 -

10Apr03-8Kee	my	*7f	:214 :442 1:094 1:264	ⒻBeaumont-G2	89	9	4	42	41¾	34	36	Prado E S	L118	5.20	86- 15	My Boston Gal120 1¼ Bird Town118 4¾ Midnight Cry1184	Tracked,4w,empty 9
14Mar03-7GP	fst	7f	:22 :442 1:092 1:222	ⒻFrwrdGal-G3	91	1	5	51¾	42	11	12¾	Prado E S	L117	4.60	96- 09	Midnight Cry117 2¾ Final Round117¾ Chimichurri121½	Drew clear, driving 8

Milwaukee Brew

Own: Stronach Stable

B. h. 7 (Jan)
Sire: Wild Again (Icecapade) $50,000
Dam: Ask Anita (Wolf Power*Saf)
Br: Robert Spiegel (Ky)
Tr: Frankel Robert J(0 0 0 0 .00) 2003:(411 114 .28)

Life	24	8	4	5	$2,879,612	118	D.Fst	22	8	3	5	$2,839,612	118
2003	4	2	1	0	$743,000	116	Wet(374)	2	0	1	0	$40,000	103
2002	7	2	0	3	$1,590,000	118	Turf(293)	0	0	0	0	$0	-
	0	0	0	0	$0	-	Dst(0)	0	0	0	0	$0	-

24Aug03-5Dmr fst	1¼	:464 1:104 1:343 1:59	3↑PacifcCl-G1	104	4	44½	31½	45	49	412¼	Prado E S	LB124 b	3.10	92-02	CandyRide1243¼ MedglidOro1247 FleetstreetDncer1242	3wd 3/8,gave way	4
3Aug03-1Mth fst	1 1/16	:241 :473 1:11 1:423	3↑Alw 55000N2M	102	5	61½	62¾	42¼	1½	14¼	Prado E S	L116 b	*.20	98-08	MlwkBrw1164¼ ClNCllctv1161¾ LghtnngStrps119nk	4-w bid,mild hand ride	6
1Mar03-9SA fst	1¼	:463 1:111 1:352 1:594	4↑SAH-G1	116	6	31	3½	2½	2hd	1hd	Prado E S	LB119 b	3.80	106-05	*Milwaukee Brew*119hd *Congaree*1244½ Kudos1171½	Vied 3wd,led past 1/8	6
2Feb03-8SA fst	1⅛	:462 1:101 1:35 1:473	4↑SnAntnoH-G2	114	5	62¼	43½	31	22½	22¼	Prado E S	LB120 b	4.90	94-18	Congree1232¼ *MilwukeeBrew*1201 PlsntlyPrfct1175	4wd into lane,2nd best	6

Mineshaft

Own: Farish William S., Elkins Jr., James

Dk. b or b. h. 5 (May)
Sire: A.P. Indy (Seattle Slew) $300,000
Dam: Prospectors Delite (Mr. Prospector)
Br: W. S. Farish, James Elkins & W. T. Webber Jr. (Ky)
Tr: Howard Neil J(0 0 0 0 .00) 2003:(156 31 .20)

Life	18	10	3	1	$2,283,402	118	D.Fst	10	8	2	0	$1,856,046	117
2003	9	7	2	0	$2,209,686	118	Wet(440)	1	1	0	0	$400,000	118
2002	9	3	1	1	$73,716	104	Turf(332)	7	1	1	1	$27,356	-
	0	0	0	0	$0	-	Dst(0)	0	0	0	0	$0	-

27Sep03-10Bel fst	1¼	:473 1:11 1:344 2:001	3↑JkyClbGC-G1	114	3	32	2½	11½	15	14¼	Albarado R J	L126	*.40	93-09	Mineshaft1264¼ Quest1262¾ Evening Attire1266½	When asked, ridden out	5
6Sep03-9Bel fst	1⅛	:472 1:111 1:342 1:461	3↑Woodward-G1	117	2	43½	42½	32	12½	14¼	Albarado R J	L126	*.30	99-13	*Mineshaft*1264¼ HoldThatTiger1224¾ Puzzlement12611¼	3 wide move, clear	5
5Jly03-9Bel fst	1¼	:483 1:123 1:37 2:012	3↑SuburbnH-G1	115	1	21½	2½	1hd	1½	12¼	Albarado R J	L121	*.75	87-13	*Mineshaft*1212¼ Volponi1214 Dollar Bill1152¼	Cruised when asked	8
14Jun03-10CD fst	1⅛	:464 1:102 1:35 1:472	3↑SFosterH-G1	117	10	52½	53½	11½	11	2hd	Albarado R J	L123	*.70	101-04	*Perfect Drift*115hd *Mineshaft*1239½ *Aldebaran*120½	Bmp start,outgamed	10
16May03-11Pim sly	1 3/16	:463 1:11 1:362 1:56	4↑PimSpclH-G1	118	3	42	42¾	21	11½	13¾	Albarado R J	L121	*1.30	93-23	Mineshaft1213¾ Western Pride116hd Judge's Case1131¾	Driving	9
25Apr03-9Kee fst	1⅛	:474 1:12 1:362 1:482	4↑BenAli-G3	116	1	32½	33	2hd	12½	19	Albarado R J	L120	*.30	98-02	*Mineshaft*1209 AmericanStyle1161¼ Mettron1161¾	Hand urging,much best	4
2Mar03-9FG fst	1⅛	:474 1:121 1:362 1:484	4↑NwOrlnsH-G2	116	6	21½	22½	1hd	11½	13½	Albarado R J	L115	5.00	100-17	*Mineshaft*1153½ Olmodavor1172½ Strive1141½	Took over, driving	11
9Feb03-9FG fst	1 1/16	:24 :474 1:124 1:433	4↑WirlwayH-G3	107	7	57¼	45½	53½	42½	22½	Albarado R J	116	2.70	89-20	Balto Star1182½ *Mineshaft*116¾ Bonapaw1153½	Up for second	8
19Jan03-9FG fst	1 1/16	:241 :472 1:113 1:434	4↑DiplmtWayH75k	103	2	32½	31½	1hd	11	1no	Albarado R J	116	*1.00	91-13	Mineshaft116no Learned1161¼ Discreet Hero1131	Shook free, all out	7

Mister Acpen (Chi)
Own: Noctis Stable Papiano, Neil and Taub,

Dk. b or b. h. 6 (Oct)
Sire: Golden Voyager (Mr. Prospector)
Dam: Gruta Azul (Semenenko)
Br: Haras Matancilla (Chi)
Tr: Mulhall Kristin(0 0 0 0 .00) 2003:(105 15 .14)

Life	21	6	3	1	$317,974	105	D.Fst	0	0	0	0	$0 –
2003	8	2	1	1	$228,200	105	Wet(365*)	1	0	0	0	$0 –
2002	2	1	0	0	$58,920	–	Turf(367)	20	6	3	1	$317,974 105
	0	0	0	0	$0	–	Dst(0)	0	0	0	0	$0 –

14Dec03♦Sha Tin (HK) gf *1 Ⓣ RH 1:341 3↑ Hong Kong Mile-G1 Stk 1803000 — 1011¼ Flores D 126 55.00 Lucky Owners126½ Bowman's Crossing126¾ Lohengrin126¾ — 14
Timeform rating: 96 — *Mid-pack,outpaced turn over 3f out*

29Nov03-9Hol fm 1 1/16 Ⓣ :233 :472 1:111 1:403 3↑ CtationH-G2 **99** 4 22 21½ 2hd 3½ 33¼ Valenzuela P A LB116 b 2.90 90-13 *Redattore*120¾ IrishWrrior117 2½ MisterAcpen116nk Pulled,bid btw,held 3d 6
27Sep03-6BM fm *1⅛ Ⓣ :474 1:122 1:371 1:464 3↑ BMBCH-G3 **105** 6 12½ 12 12 12 11¼ Gonzalez R M LB116 b 4.30 97-16 Mister Acpen116 1¼ Fateful Dream117no Ninebanks1185 Well rated, drvng 10
31Aug03-8Dmr fm 1⅜ Ⓣ :472 1:12 1:353 2:121 3↑ DelMarH-G2 **98** 1 11 11 1hd 21 62¼ Espinoza V LB116 b *2.60 97-05 IrishWrrior116hd ContinntlRd117½ Contnuously1141 Inside trip,weakened 9
27Jly03-8Dmr fm 1⅛ Ⓣ :472 1:11 1:342 1:454 3↑ EdReadH-G1 **99** 2 21 21 31½ 63¼ 55½ Espinoza V LB115 6.50 99-03 Special Ring1175 Decarchy117nk *Irish Warrior*114hd Rail, gamely in lane 6
14Jun03-3Hol fm 1¼ Ⓣ :484 1:132 1:361 2:003 3↑ CWhtghmH-G1 **101** 2 22 2½ 21½ 3½ 2¾ Espinoza V LB115 b 8.40 88-14 Storming Home124¾ Mister Acpen115½ Cagney1141 Pulled,bid btw,willing 6
21May03-7Hol fm 1⅛ Ⓣ :491 1:124 1:36 1:473 +4↑ Alw 62000N$MY **103** 4 13½ 11 11 11½ 12½ Espinoza V LB116 b 7.10 91-16 Mister Acpen116 2½ Gigli116½ *Sarafan*1221 Inside,held on gamely 7
11Apr03-8Kee fm 1 Ⓣ :233 :463 1:112 1:354 4↑ MakrsMrk-G2 **94** 6 99¼ 911 75¾ 67½ 44½ Sellers S J L116 b 29.30 84-13 RoylSpy118 1¼ MsqusApprovl118 1¾ TouchofthBls117 1½ 5w trip,minor gain 9

Mobil
Own: Schickedanz Gustav

B. c. 4 (Jan)
Sire: Langfuhr (Danzig) $20,000
Dam: Kinetigal (Naskra)
Br: Gustav Schickedanz (Ont-C)
Tr: Keogh Michael(0 0 0 0 .00) 2003:(97 17 .18)

Life	15	8	3	1	$1,067,711	98	D.Fst	9	4	3	0	$662,593 98
2003	9	5	2	1	$753,405	98	Wet(340)	1	1	0	0	$47,640 79
2002	6	3	1	0	$314,306	86	Turf(293)	5	3	0	1	$357,478 96
	0	0	0	0	$0	–	Dst(0)	0	0	0	0	$0 –

8Nov03-8WO fst 1 1/16 :233 :471 1:111 1:434 3↑ WoSltCpH-G3 **96** 2 21½ 21 2½ 2½ 21¼ Dos Ramos R A L119 3.65 86-09 No Comprende117 1¼ Mobil1191 Parose118½ Bid btween,gave best 7
13Oct03-6WO fst 1⅛ :474 1:12 1:381 1:514 OntarDby-G3 **96** 1 2hd 1½ 1½ 12½ 16¾ Kabel T K L124 *.95 87-13 Mobil124 6¾ El GranMaestro117no AddedEdge11710 Off rail,jumped tracks 5
28Sep03-8WO sf 1⅜ Ⓣ :50 1:162 1:424 2:23 3↑ SkyClscH-G2 **93** 1 1hd 11 1½ 42 34 Husbands P L115 2.45 46-50 Bowman Mill113no Lenny the Lender1104 *Mobil*115nk Off rail, gave way 6
1Sep03-7WO fm 1⅛ Ⓣ :48 1:12 1:36 1:481 3↑ ⓇHalton131k **96** 6 12½ 11 11 13 13½ Kabel T K L119 *.25 87-13 Mobil119 3½ LennytheLender115 3¾ StedyRuckus117nk Slow pace, drew off 6
9Aug03-8Mnr fst 1⅛ :472 1:104 1:343 1:461 WVDerby-G3 **98** 4 87¾ 78½ 67½ 512 59½ Chavez J F LB117 7.70 95 - Soto111nk Dynever117 5¼ *Colita*111 1½ Stumbled at start 9
12Jly03-8WO gd 1⅛ Ⓣ :481 1:122 1:362 1:49 TrontoCH-G3 **92** 2 1½ 11 1hd 1hd 11 Kabel T K L122 *.90 83-17 Mobil1221 Strizzi119¾ Moonshine Hall121 3¼ Slow pace,gamely 3w 6
22Jun03-9WO fst 1¼ :463 1:114 1:372 2:022 ⓇQueensPlt1000k **98** 6 33½ 32 33 25 29 Kabel T K L126 2.20 93-17 *Wando*1269 *Mobil*126 1½ Rock Again126 2½ Stalk 2-path,2nd best 12
31May03-8WO fst 1⅛ :471 1:12 1:383 1:514 ⓇPlateTrial162k **94** 6 2hd 2hd 1½ 21½ 11½ Kabel T K L126 *.80 87-26 Mobil126 1½ Rock Again1269 Peef1264 Came again off rail 6
3May03-9WO fst 7f :231 :464 1:113 1:241 ⓇQueenston160k **89** 4 1 41½ 31 2hd 11 Kabel T K L119 1.50 83-18 *Mobil*1191 Quiet Dare1173 Awesome Action1152 Stalk 3w,rally 4w 5

Mountain General

Own: Asmussen Keith I

Dk. b or b. g. 6 (Mar)
Sire: Mountain Cat (Storm Cat) $7,500
Dam: Tulira (General Assembly)
Br: Curtis Green (Ky)
Tr: Asmussen Steven M(0 0 0 0 .00) 2003:(1949 452 .23)

Life	26	9	8	2	$539,667	116	D.Fst	23	9	7	2	$496,042	116
2003	6	2	3	0	$212,580	105	Wet(348)	3	0	1	0	$43,625	104
2002	9	4	1	2	$209,347	116	Turf(235)	0	0	0	0	$0	–
	0	0	0	0	$0	–	Dst(0)	0	0	0	0	$0	–

10Aug03–9Sar sly 6f :22 :443 :563 1:09 3↑AGVndbtH-G2 104 1 3 59 57½ 45¾ 25 Day P L118 b 6.70 92–10 *PrivteHorde*1155 MountinGenrl118hd MiksClssic114nk Game finish outside 5
21Jun03–9CD fst 6½f :224 :454 1:093 1:16 3↑AristdsH-G3 102 2 7 76¾ 63½ 62¼ 1hd Lanerie C J L116 b 10.20 91–15 MountainGenerl116hd *BeusTown*123nk PssRush118¾ Steady,bmp 3/16s,rail 7
3May03–5CD fst 7f :222 :45 1:093 1:214 4↑CDH-G2 93 10 5 97¾ 118½ 107½ 108 Meche L J L118 b 13.80 85–08 *Aldebaran*1202½ Pass Rush117nk Cappuchino115hd 8 wide, no threat 12
16Mar03–9FG fst 6f :22 :442 :562 1:084 3↑PeletriBCH144k 105 4 3 45½ 58½ 34 22¾ Lanerie C J L121 b 3.00 93–13 *Beau's Town*1182¾ Mountain General1211¾ Bonapaw1221¾ Finished well 5
23Feb03–9FG fst 6f :221 :454 :573 1:101 4↑TaylrSpclH100k 101 2 4 32½ 42 31½ 1½ Lanerie C J L119 b *.90 89–16 MountinGenerl119½ SpdHuntr115nk DoctorMik115hd Split foes, prevailed 6
12Jan03–9FG fst 6f :212 :444 :57 1:093 4↑ColPowerH75k 101 5 2 67 65½ 51¾ 2¾ Lanerie C J L119 b 2.50 91–15 Cojet115¾ *Mountain General*1193 Kazoo118nk Could not get past 6

Mr. Jester

Own: Biggs Kaaren J

Dk. b or b. c. 3 (Apr) OBSAPR03 $75,000
Sire: Silver Deputy (Deputy Minister) $40,000
Dam: Future Pretense (Fappiano)
Br: G. Watts Humphrey Jr. (Ky)
Tr: Wren Steve(0 0 0 0 .00) 2003:(69 12 .17)

Life	6	4	2	0	$730,800	91	D.Fst	6	4	2	0	$730,800	91
2003	6	4	2	0	$730,800	91	Wet(381)	0	0	0	0	$0	–
2002	0	M	0	0	$0	–	Turf(259)	0	0	0	0	$0	–
	0	0	0	0	$0	–	Dst(0)	0	0	0	0	$0	–

5Dec03–8DeD fst 1 1/16 :23 :454 1:111 1:451 BdGmgDltJk1000k 91 4 52 42½ 21½ 11 1¾ Chapa R L115 14.30 104–05 Mr. Jester115¾ Fire Slam115nk Perfect Moon1151½ Kept to task 10
8Nov03–9DeD fst 1 :23 :47 1:122 1:393 JeanLafitt100k 88 3 52 31½ 21 21½ 22 LeBlanc K P L120 1.20 87–23 Joe Six Pack1152 *Mr. Jester*12025 Vic Mason1161 Best of others 5
13Sep03–10TP fst 1 1/16 :231 :47 1:114 1:463 KyCupJuv-G3 85 6 57½ 56½ 42½ 34 2no Bejarano R L118 20.60 79–17 [D]Pomeroy116no Mr. Jester1181¼ The Cliff's Edge114¾ Drifted 5w 1/4 pole 8
Placed first through disqualification
10Aug03–10LaD fst 5½f :211 :451 :582 1:053 Pioneer50k 68 2 7 66¼ 55¼ 42 1nk Chapa R L116 2.20 88–14 *MrJester*116nk AfternoonChrlie116½ EstbnMigul1171¾ Kicked down leader 7
24Jly03–11LaD fst 5½f :221 :453 :58 1:051 Alw 25000N1x 68 5 1 3nk 3nk 23 21¼ Chapa R L119 *.60 89–18 FullMoonsArisin1191¼ *MrJester*1195¼ GoWestAgin119¾ Vied 3-w, clear 2nd 6
3Jly03–1LaD fst 5f :223 :46 :583 Md Sp Wt 23k 82 5 4 21 2hd 12½ 19¼ Chapa R L118 6.60 91–19 Mr. Jester1189¼ Blackmailer118hd Trifecta1182½ Vied turn, drove clear 7

My Boston Gal

Own: Porter J. Chester, Bloch, Randy and M

B. f. 4 (Feb) KEESEP01 $95,000
Sire: Boston Harbor (Capote) $23,000
Dam: Western League (Forty Niner)
Br: Overbrook Farm (Ky)
Tr: Nafzger Carl A(0 0 0 0 .00) 2003:(285 31 .11)

Life	7	4	1	0	$411,251	101	D.Fst	6	3	1	0	$256,251	95
2003	4	1	1	0	$216,714	101	Wet(335)	1	1	0	0	$155,000	101
2002	3	3	0	0	$194,537	95	Turf(317)	0	0	0	0	$0	–
	0	0	0	0	$0	–	Dst(0)	0	0	0	0	$0	–

2May03–10CD fst 1⅛ :46 1:10 1:353 1:483 ⒻKyOaks-G1 90 2 32½ 31½ 42 63¼ 56½ Day P L121 5.80 88–07 *Bird Town*1213¼ Santa Catarina121hd Yell121¾ 5w late,empty 12
10Apr03–8Kee my *7f :214 :442 1:094 1:264 ⒻBeaumont-G2 101 3 7 52¼ 31½ 1hd 11¼ Day P L120 *2.70 92–15 MyBostonGl1201¼ *BirdTown*1184¾ MidnightCry1184 Rallied between,drvg 9
14Mar03–9GP fst 1⅛ :471 1:114 1:373 1:503 ⒻBonnieMs-G2 92 3 11½ 11 11 1½ 21¾ Day P L120 3.20 87–13 Ivanavinalot1221¾ *My Boston Gal*1203¼ Holiday Lady1181 Inside, 2nd best 7
23Feb03–9GP fst 1 1/16 :23 :471 1:12 1:444 ⒻDvonaDal-G2 60 2 43½ 43 44 48 521 Borel C H L121 *1.50 64–19 Yell1176 *Ivanavinalot*1215¾ Gold Player1153 Saved ground, faded 5

My Cousin Matt
Own: Englander Richard A

Dk. b or b. g. 5 (Jan)
Sire: Matty G (Capote) $7,500
Dam: Conquistamiss (Conquistador Cielo)
Br: Donald Marino (Fla)
Tr: Lake Scott A(0 0 0 0 .00) 2003:(2012 457 .23)

Life	26	7	6	1	$656,579	114	D.Fst	16	4	4	1	$459,979 110
2003	6	1	1	1	$297,500	114	Wet(322)	2	2	0	0	$149,400 114
2002	14	5	2	0	$307,159	110	Turf(244)	8	1	2	0	$47,200 92
	0	0	0	0	$0	–	Dst(0)	0	0	0	0	$0 –

27Sep03–7Bel fst 6½f :214 :441 1:083 1:143 3↑Vosburgh-G1 **91** 9 1 2½ 22½ 5½ 510½ Dunkelberger T L L126 f 26.25 89– 16 Ghostzapper1236½ Aggadan1261¼ Posse1231¾ Pressed pace, tired 10
31Aug03–10Sar fst 7f :22 :441 1:083 1:211 3↑ForegoH-G1 **85** 2 6 43 77½ 69 516¾ Velazquez J R L115 f 7.00 84– 09 Aldebaran1234¾ *Najran*1141¼ Gygistar1196¾ No response 7
12Jly03–12Crc fst 6f :211 :434 :562 1:10 3↑SmlSprtH-G3 **98** 3 5 66 55¾ 36½ 39 Dominguez R A L116 f 3.40 85– 11 ShkYouDown1198¼ *PrvtHord*113¾ MyCosnMtt116½ Angled out, gained 3rd 13
21Jun03–13Suf fst 6f :22 :452 :573 1:102 3↑JBMoslyBCH200k **104** 2 3 2½ 11½ 11 21¾ Dominguez R A LB117 f 2.20 93– 16 PpngTom1151¾ MyCousnMtt1172½ TruDrcton1191¼ Frct in gate, game try 8
29Mar03♦Nad al Sheba (UAE) ft *6f Str 1:094 3↑Dubai Golden Shaheen-G1 54¼ R Dominguez 130 – State City130¾ Avanzado1301¾ Captain Squire1301¾ 12
Timeform rating: 107 Stk 2000000 *Trailed early, 10th halfway, mild late gain. Abreeze 6th*
22Feb03–9Lrl sly 7f :222 :461 1:093 1:22 3↑GenGrgeH-G2 **114** 4 53½ 43½ 1hd 13 Dominguez R A L113 f 4.00 97– 14 MyCousinMtt1133 PepingTom1141¼ Disturbingthpc118nk Strong, driving 11

Mystery Giver
Own: Team Block

B. g. 6 (Apr)
Sire: Dynaformer (Roberto) $50,000
Dam: Ioya (Naskra)
Br: David Block & Patricia Block (Ill)
Tr: Block Chris M(0 0 0 0 .00) 2003:(259 50 .19)

Life	27	9	6	1	$695,510	102	D.Fst	0	0	0	0	$0 –
2003	10	2	2	1	$256,260	102	Wet(339)	1	0	0	0	$1,560 52
2002	9	3	1	0	$302,060	102	Turf(314)	26	9	6	1	$693,950 102
	0	0	0	0	$0	–	Dst(0)	0	0	0	0	$0 –

29Nov03–7CD yl 1 1/16 Ⓣ :243 :49 1:141 1:453 3↑OClm 100000N **84** 9 98¾ 910 74¾ 64½ 64½ Blanc B L123 *1.30 72– 26 MjesticThief117hd BilOuttheKing1193½ PrivtEmblm117½ No late response 10
1Nov03–8Haw fm 1 Ⓣ :234 :471 1:111 1:343 3↑CareyMmH-G3 **98** 1 810 84¾ 84¼ 4nk 1½ Marquez C H Jr L120 *1.90 98– 04 MysteryGiver120½ AlsDearlyBred118¾ MjorRhythm116½ 6 wide 1/4, driving 8
12Oct03–7Kee fm 1⅛ Ⓣ :472 1:112 1:361 1:482 3↑Alw 58200c **95** 8 72½ 86¾ 85¾ 32 2nk Albarado R J L121 *2.20 95– 13 GretchensStr124nk *MysteryGiver*1211¾ BonusPck124½ 5w lane, gaining late 10
20Sep03–9KD fm 1 Ⓣ :263 :48 1:142 1:374 3↑KyCupMile100k **91** 4 813 715 77¼ 74¼ 42¾ ♦Albarado R J L122 *1.80 88– 17 *Hard Buck*122nk *Gretchen's Star*1172 Last Stand115½ 6-7w lane, mild gain 8
17Aug03–8AP gd 1 1/16 Ⓣ :242 :49 1:134 1:432 3↑JohnHenry52k **92** 5 66¼ 64¼ 53 42¼ 2½ Marquez C H Jr L123 *.50 91– 12 ChanChan117½ MysteryGiver123hd RockchlkJyhwk1172 4 wide 1/4, missed 6
26Jly03–9AP fm 1¼ Ⓣ :491 1:14 1:383 2:023 3↑ArlgtnH-G3 **98** 3 89 77 63¼ 44½ 31 Albarado R J L118 6.00 92– 05 Honor in War120nk Better Talk Now115¾ Mystery Giver118nk Belatedly 10
21Jun03–9AP fm 1 1/16 Ⓣ :234 :473 1:113 1:42 3↑ⓈCardinalH86k **90** 9 74¼ 52½ 31 31 22 Douglas R R L124 *.80 97– 05 Act of War1162 ⒹMystery Giver124hd ScooterRoach117½ Came over start 10
Disqualified and placed 9th
23Apr03–8Kee fm 1½ Ⓣ :512 1:164 2:051 2:291 4↑Elkhorn-G3 **99** 3 109¼ 109¼ 75¾ 73¾ 53½ Albarado R J L116 7.90 90– 09 KmLovsBcky117½ MnFrmWcklw123no WllmsNws1161¼ 9w lane, no threat 10
Previously trained by Scherer Richard R
23Mar03–8FG fm *1⅛ Ⓣ :482 1:122 1:38 1:51 4↑ExploBdH-G2 **95** 5 96¼ 1010 95¼ 31 52¾ Albarado R J L116 4.70 86– 11 CndidGlen114nk Rouvres115no Frefourintrnt115no Circled foes, weakened 11
1Feb03–9FG fm *1⅛ Ⓣ :502 1:142 1:382 1:502 4↑FGBCH150k **102** 9 53½ 55¼ 55¼ 41½ 13¼ Albarado R J L117 *1.60 92– 11 MysteryGiver1173¼ Dynmeux115no Frfourintrnt115hd Loomed, ridden out 9

Najran
Own: Buckram Oak Farm

Gr/ro. h. 5 (Feb) KEESEP00 $100,000
Sire: Runaway Groom (Blushing Groom*Fr) $15,000
Dam: Line Command (Capote)
Br: France Weiner & Irv Weiner (Ky)
Tr: Zito Nicholas P(0 0 0 0 .00) 2003:(507 77 .15)

Life	15	7	2	1	$483,448	111	D.Fst	13 6 2 1	$431,321 111
2003	7	2	1	1	$305,700	111	Wet(392)	2 1 0 0	$52,127 103
2002	7	5	1	0	$176,798	106	Turf(280)	0 0 0 0	$0 –
	0	0	0	0	$0	–	Dst(0)	0 0 0 0	$0 –

3Oct03–7Kee	fst	6f	:214 :443 :56 1:081	3↑PhoenxBC-G3	111	7	1	3nk	3nk	2½	1½	Castellano J J	L122	6.00	98–13	Najran1221½ EthanMan1182 TakeAchnceOnMe1182¾	Forced pace,driving	8
31Aug03–10Sar	fst	7f	:22 :441 1:083 1:211	3↑ForegoH-G1	111	7	2	1½	1½	2½	24¾	Castellano J J	L114	12.80	96–09	Aldebaran1234¾ *Najran*1141¼ Gygistar1196¾	Set pressured pace	7
4Jly03–8Bel	fst	7f	:222 :444 1:093 1:222	3↑TomFoolH-G2	87	1	3	33	38½	53½	48¼	Prado E S	L116	3.55	80–15	*Aldebaran*1222 Peeping Tom1172½ State City1183¾	Chased inside, tired	7
26May03–9Bel	sly	1	:221 :442 1:083 1:34	3↑MtropltH-G1	87	3	1½	1hd	2hd	64	712	Prado E S	L116	4.10	84–14	Aldebaran119nk Saarland1143 *Peeping Tom*1143¾	Set pressured back	8
7May03–8Bel	fst	1	:223 :443 1:073 1:321	3↑WschstrH-G3	111	1	12½	13½	15½	18	14½	Prado E S	L113	5.40	105–04	Najran1134½ Saarland1143 Justification113½	Shown whip stretch	7
13Apr03–8Kee	fst	7f	:22 :444 1:092 1:213	3↑CmwlthBC-G2	42	4	6	31	42	717	734¼	Coa E M	L118	3.60	62–13	SmoothJzz1183 CrftyCT1186¼ MultipleChoice1203¾	Unruly gate,hop in air	7
11Jan03–10GP	fst	1 1/16	:231 :463 1:102 1:421	3↑HalHopeH-G3	106	8	51¼	2½	1hd	1½	31¾	Day P	L114	2.60e	96–12	Windsor Castle1151½ Saint Verre114nk Najran1142¾	Slim lead, weakened	8

Native Heir
Own: Gill Michael J

B. g. 6 (Apr) EASSEP99 $20,000
Sire: Makin (Danzig) $2,000
Dam: Mary Had a Lot (Double Zeus)
Br: Spencer F. Young (Va)
Tr: Shuman Mark(0 0 0 0 .00) 2003:(1105 225 .20)

Life	31	15	6	4	$534,436	109	D.Fst	20 7 5 4	$274,313 109
2003	10	4	3	1	$200,280	109	Wet(389)	10 8 1 0	$257,723 105
2002	8	2	1	1	$71,370	95	Turf(252)	1 0 0 0	$2,400 79
	0	0	0	0	$0	–	Dst(0)	0 0 0 0	$0 –

10Oct03–6CT	fst	7f	:224 :462 1:124 1:264	3↑HBPARansnH51k	12	10	7	33½	36	1018	1038	Rosenthal M E	L124 b	2.60	49–20	*DonldsPrid*1171¾ *BostonCommon*1235½ QuitGrtitud1162¾	Nothing left drive	10
1Sep03–10Mth	sly	6f	:211 :44 :563 1:101	3↑Icecapade58k	93	2	1	2hd	11	1½	11	Castellano A Jr	L122 b	2.50	88–10	NtiveHeir1221 TkeAchnceOnMe1174½ HrsZlous1143¼	Drifted,inched clear	4
3Aug03–9Mth	fst	6f	:212 :434 :562 1:093	3↑TeddyDrone75k	95	1	5	12	12	12	2¾	Ferrer J C	L122 b	2.40	90–10	It's a Monster122¾ *Native Heir*1221½ Aggadan122¾	Pace inside,good try	8
Previously trained by Robb John J																			
29Jun03–11Cnl	fst	6f	:22 :443 :563 1:094	3↑[S]WMBailesMm50k	89	3	2	1hd	2hd	21	2¾	Wilson R	L122 b	*.20	95–05	Smashing Beau119¾ Native Heir1222 Fredlea117¾	2wd, dueled, gamely	5
Previously trained by Shuman Mark																			
7Jun03–10Mth	sly	5f	⊗:214 :444 :57	3↑WolfHill50k	100	2	1	1hd	1hd	12	1¾	Rose J	L122 b	*1.10	97–17	Native Heir122¾ *Jeb's Wild*1133 Go Rail Go1134¼	Gamely,drifting out	5
24May03–9Pim	sly	5f	⊗:212 :443 :572	3↑BenCohen58k	103	2	4	27	27	25	11	Wilson R	L119 b	1.50	97–20	*Native Heir*1191 Baby Shark117½ Sassy Hound1176¼	Drifted 8wd,up	5
5Apr03–9GP	fst	7f	:214 :441 1:083 1:213	3↑ArtaxH100k	99	5	1	11	11	34	32¾	Homeister R B Jr	L115 b	2.10e	97–06	Highway Prospector1141¾ Swift Replica1121 *Native Heir*115½	Held well	8
8Mar03–10GP	fst	7f	:221 :442 1:082 1:21	3↑RcSclBCH-G2	94	3	1	1½	11	43	75¾	Velasquez C	L116 b	*.70e	97–01	TouroftheCt116hd BurnngRom1161¼ *HghwyProspctor*114nk	Off rail, faltered	8
9Feb03–10GP	fst	6½f	:212 :432 1:082 1:15	3↑DpMnstrH-G3	109	6	2	11½	12	12½	14½	Velasquez C	L114 b	9.40	101–07	Native Heir1144½ Binthebest1151½ Fire and Glory114¾	Inside, widened	8
22Jan03–9GP	fst	6f	:213 :441 :562 1:091	4↑Alw 46000N$Y	108	8	1	11	12	2hd	2hd	Santos J A	L116 b	8.50	98–12	*HanaHighway*116hd *NativeHeir*1165 DremRun1161¾	Bumped stretch, edged	10

New Economy

Own: Evans Robert S

B. m. 6 (Feb)
Sire: Red Ransom (Roberto)
Dam: Sunyata (Proud Truth)
Br: R. S. Evans (Ky)
Tr: Motion H. G(0 0 0 0 .00) 2003:(318 55 .17)

Life	20	6	3	2	$438,368	96	D.Fst	2	1	0	0	$10,680	71
2003	6	1	0	1	$111,681	96	Wet(322)	0	0	0	0	$0	-
2002	7	3	0	0	$241,200	96	Turf(306)	18	5	3	2	$427,688	96
	0	0	0	0	$0	-	Dst(0)	0	0	0	0	$0	-

27Dec03-9Crc fm	1½	Ⓣ :48 1:13 2:031 2:26	3↑ⒻLaPvyteH-G2	85	1	98¼	107¾	75½	65	67¼	Homeister R B Jr	L116	7.80	96 -	Volga119 2¾ Lady Annaliese116 1¼ Lost Appeal115¾	In tight 2nd turn	11
6Dec03-9Crc fm	1⅛	Ⓣ :472 1:11 1:35 1:464	3↑ⒻMyChrmrH-G3	96	9	75¾	68	69	43	1½	Homeister R B Jr	L115	7.40	97 -	NewEconomy115½ SomethingVentured116 2½ Ivnvinlot113¾	3 wide, up late	12
19Oct03-5WO sf	1¼	Ⓣ :503 1:152 1:404 2:053	3↑ⒻEPTaylor-G1	86	3	96¾	106	105¼	97¼	85¼	Bridgmohan S X	L123	38.45	74- 30	Volga123hd Tigertail123no Hi Dubai118hd	Inside, dropped back	10
5Oct03-6Kee fm	1 3/16	Ⓣ :484 1:124 1:38 1:554	3↑ⒻWnStGlxy-G2	81	6	68½	516	515	511	38½	Douglas R R	L121	28.90	83- 10	Bien Nicole121 7¼ Approach116 1¼ New Economy121 1¼	Improved position	6
24Apr03-8Kee fm	1½	Ⓣ :502 1:153 2:053 2:293	4↑ⒻBewitch-G3	91	3	105¾	95½	85¾	65	54¼	•Albarado R J	L116	8.30	88- 11	LilacQueen1164 BeyondtheWaves116hd SanDre118hd	Between lane,empty	10
8Feb03-8GP fm	1⅜	Ⓣ :481 1:131 1:38 2:133	3↑ⒻVeryOneH-G3	89	7	73¾	73¼	72¾	53¼	76	Homeister R B Jr	L115	8.60	82- 11	SanDre116 2¼ *Tweedside*115½ HiTechHoneycomb113½	Lacked late response	12

New York Hero

Own: Paraneck Stable

Dk. b or b. c. 4 (Mar) EASMAY02 $135,000
Sire: Partner's Hero (Danzig) $5,000
Dam: Nin Two (John Alden)
Br: Dark Hollow Farm & William Beatson (Md)
Tr: Pedersen Jennifer(0 0 0 0 .00) 2003:(320 30 .09)

Life	14	4	3	0	$465,860	101	D.Fst	11	4	3	0	$414,860	101
2003	14	4	3	0	$465,860	101	Wet(371)	2	0	0	0	$45,000	96
2002	0	M	0	0	$0	-	Turf(249)	1	0	0	0	$6,000	88
	0	0	0	0	$0	-	Dst(0)	0	0	0	0	$0	-

20Dec03-11Crc fm	7½f	Ⓣ :224 :453 1:093 1:272	PAxthelm100k	88	1	2	69½	58	57	44½	Santos J A	L119 b	4.10	97- 01	Magic Mecke1171 Hear No Evil122 2¼ SharpImpact122 1¼	Checked far turn	12
29Nov03-9Aqu fst	1	:224 :442 1:083 1:341	3↑CigarMiH-G1	94	3	72½	73½	76	610	613½	Castellano J J	L113 b	30.75	80- 19	Congaree124 5¼ Midas Eyes1153 Toccet1151	Inside, no response	7
2Nov03-7Aqu fst	7f	:223 :45 1:092 1:223	3↑Alw 51000N3x	101	5	7	53	45	24½	12	Castellano J J	L118 b	6.60	90- 17	New York Hero1182 DonSix118 1½ FirstBlush118nk	Stumbled start, gamely	9
19Oct03-8Bel fst	1	:231 :461 1:104 1:36	3↑Alw 52000N3x	98	1	1½	11	11	1hd	1½	Castellano J J	L116 b	15.70	86- 14	D *NewYorkHero*116½ PrivtCity1164 JimThirdsBolro1192	Came out stretch	6
Disqualified and placed second																	
12Sep03-8Bel fst	1 1/16	:232 :462 1:101 1:413	3↑Alw 52000N3x	64	1	31½	32	48½	518	519¼	Prado E S	L116 b	9.80	73- 21	*Newfoundland*120 2¾ Private City116 2¼ Blue Boat123 5¼	Tired after a half	5
14Jun03-11Del fst	1 1/16	:223 :46 1:103 1:431	LRichrds-G3	43	5	2hd	2hd	64¾	815	830	Castillo L A	L122 fb	3.90	62- 13	AwesomTim115no ChristinsOutlw115¾ ChroksBoy122 4½	Vied 2 wide, tired	8
17May03-12Pim gd	1 3/16	:47 1:113 1:362 1:553	Preaknes-G1	94	8	54½	65½	65½	59	612¾	Chavez J F	L126 fb	19.60	82- 12	FunnyCide126 9¾ MidwayRod126¾ Scrimshw126no	Broke out,brushed,wide	10
3May03-9Aqu fst	1	:223 :45 1:093 1:354	Withers-G3	88	1	3½	2hd	3½	52¼	54	Castellano J J	L123 b	3.50	82- 21	SpitetheDevil116nk Alysweep1231 Stnislvsky116hd	Bumped soundly start	8
12Apr03-8Aqu my	1⅛	:471 1:11 1:354 1:483	WoodMem-G1	96	1	11½	11½	11	36	49	Arroyo N Jr	L123 fb	8.90	84- 12	Empire Maker123½ *Funny Cide*123 7½ Kissin Saint1231	Came out start, tired	8
22Mar03-10TP fst	1⅛	:463 1:11 1:37 1:503	LanesEnd-G2	96	6	2½	2½	2hd	1hd	1nk	Arroyo N Jr	L121 b	14.70	83- 14	NewYorkHero121nk EugenesThirdSon121 2¼ Chmpli121hd	Drifted out late	9
27Feb03-8Aqu fst	170	⊡ :23 :464 1:12 1:42	3↑Alw 46000N3L	88	4	3½	22	1½	2½	2½	Castillo L A5	L111 f	*2.65	83- 20	JudgeChris122½ *NewYorkHero*111 2½ FightenBeezi115 3¾	With pace, gamely	8
19Feb03-4Aqu fst	6f	⊡ :224 :454 :58 1:104	Alw 43000N1x	89	7	1	1hd	1hd	1½	11¼	Castillo L A5	L117 f	*1.90	90- 14	NwYorkHro117 1¼ CsnvSlmmr1121 *FfthfHnnssy*117 2½	Between rivals, drive	8
31Jan03-6Aqu fst	6f	⊡ :224 :461 :583 1:111	Md Sp Wt 41k	82	1	4	21½	21½	22	11¾	Castillo L A5	L116 f	4.40	88- 12	*New York Hero*116 1¾ *Max Forever*121nk Curb121 2¼	Drifted out start	9
18Jan03-1Aqu fst	6f	⊡ :224 :462 :582 1:11	Md Sp Wt 41k	79	5	6	68½	57	38	25	Castillo L A5	L116 f	10.70	84- 15	CourtingConcorde1215 *NewYorkHero*116¾ *JohnnyBox*121 3¾	Greenly, 3 wide	8

Ninebanks
Own: Abruzzo Peter

B. g. 6 (Jan)
Sire: Smokester (Never Tabled) $5,000
Dam: Nataka (With Approval)
Br: Trudy McCaffery & John Toffan (Cal)
Tr: Hollendorfer Jerry(0 0 0 0 .00) 2003:(1216 282 .23)

Life	34	10	7	2	$634,693	103	D.Fst	8	2	1	0	$62,570 101
2003	9	3	2	1	$310,400	103	Wet(303)	5	0	1	1	$23,075 90
2002	12	3	3	1	$206,395	99	Turf(356)	21	8	5	1	$549,048 103
	0	0	0	0	$0	–	Dst(0)	0	0	0	0	$0 –

26Oct03–7BM	fm	1 1/16	Ⓣ:24 :48 1:114 1:421	3↑PacificaH68k	**95**	5	3²	5⁴	53½	3⁵	2³	Warren R J Jr	LB120 b	*1.00	92– 12	Vallarta1143 Ninebanks1201 Aly Bubba116no	3w 2nd trn, mild gain 9
27Sep03–6BM	fm	*1⅛	Ⓣ:474 1:122 1:371 1:464	3↑BMBCH-G3	**102**	3	54½	3⁴	42½	2²	31¼	Warren R J Jr	LB118 b	4.10	96– 16	MisterAcpen1161¼ FatefulDream117no Ninebanks1185	Rail trip, no impact 10
1Sep03–8BM	fm	1	Ⓣ:232 :472 1:114 1:372	3↑[S]CalTurfChH100k	**101**	8	32½	32½	3¹	12½	1nk	Warren R J Jr	LB119 b	*1.90	86– 17	Ninebanks119nk Surprise Halo1182½ NativeDesert1171	Bid 3w, led, driving 8
2Aug03–5Dmr	fm	1	Ⓣ:212 :444 1:321	3↑[R]WickerrH76k	**95**	7	3⁷	3¹¹	3⁴	75¾	84¼	Pedroza M A	LB119 b	19.00	98– 06	*TouchoftheBlues*122no Inesperado1211½ Suances1201	Came out lane,no bid 10
4Jly03–7Hol	fm	1⅛	Ⓣ:474 1:11 1:341 1:461	3↑AmericnH-G2	**93**	1	32½	31½	3²	55¼	56¼	Warren R J Jr	LB115 b	14.30	92– 08	*Candy Ride*120¾ *Special Ring*1182 Irish Warrior1161	Shuffled into str,wknd 5
15Jun03–4BM	fm	1 1/16	Ⓣ:241 :483 1:122 1:423	3↑FosterCtyH65k	**99**	2	53¼	32½	3²	4¾	2¾	Warren R J Jr	LB120 b	2.30	92– 14	Handyman Bill116¾ Ninebanks120½ Night Life1172¼	Angled out, rallied 7
26Apr03–7BM	yl	1	Ⓣ:232 :473 1:121 1:371	3↑SnFrnBCH-G2	**103**	3	33½	3³	2hd	1¹	1no	Warren R J Jr	LB117 b	4.60	87– 13	Ninebanks117no Nicobar1161 National Anthem1161	Bid rail, led, gamely 8
16Mar03–3GG	yl	1⅛	Ⓣ:494 1:131 1:373 1:50	3↑GGBrdCpH-G3	**97**	4	2¹	2¹	2½	2hd	1no	Warren R J Jr	LB116 b	2.60	95– 05	*Ninebanks*116no Surprise Halo1166½ Royal Gem1182	Long drive, gamely 4
25Jan03–2SA	fm	1⅛	Ⓣ:464 1:103 1:344 1:462	4↑[R]BarCTBATrf500k	**89**	6	54½	5⁶	3²	41¼	106½	Pedroza M A	LB120 b	17.50	90– 08	Admnnstrtor120no MscsStorm1181 ForbddnAppl1201	Rail trip,outkicked 12

No Comprende
Own: Clarity Stables

Dk. b or b. g. 6 (Apr)
Sire: Compadre (El Gran Senor) $2,500
Dam: Sociologie (Caro*Ire)
Br: Mr. & Mrs. Gordon Grayson (Va)
Tr: Smith James J(0 0 0 0 .00) 2003:(78 10 .13)

Life	28	7	5	4	$580,667	101	D.Fst	18	6	2	3	$448,818 101
2003	10	2	3	1	$298,700	101	Wet(203)	2	0	1	0	$18,942 95
2002	7	1	1	1	$111,307	100	Turf(327)	8	1	2	1	$112,907 100
	0	0	0	0	$0	–	Dst(0)	0	0	0	0	$0 –

8Nov03–8WO	fst	1 1/16	:233 :471 1:111 1:434	3↑WoSltCpH-G3	**98**	6	65¼	63½	3½	1½	11¼	Husbands P	L117 b	4.10	87– 09	No Comprende1171¼ Mobil1191 Parose118½	3w,advnce 4w,edge away 7
19Oct03–1WO	my	1 1/16	:231 :462 1:104 1:433	3↑Alw 86400NC	**95**	1	6¹¹	6¹¹	5⁵	2³	21½	McKnight J	L118 b	*2.05	86– 16	*Open Concert*1181½ *No Comprende*1182½ Attest1183¼	Rally btween,2nd best 6
28Sep03–9Haw	fst	1¼	:493 1:133 1:39 2:033	3↑HawGldCH-G2	**97**	4	53½	54½	4³	4⁴	48¼	Marquez C H Jr	L115 b	49.80	82– 20	Perfect Drift1221¾ Tenpins119½ Aeneas1146	No factor 6
16Aug03–7Sar	fst	1¼	:48 1:114 1:37 2:032	3↑SarBCH-G2	**100**	4	6⁷	76¼	5⁵	55½	49¼	Luzzi M J	L112 b	69.50	81– 14	Puzzlement1133¼ Volponi1221¾ Iron Deputy1154¼	Ducked out stretch 8
1Jly03–8WO	fst	1¼	:462 1:112 1:361 2:01	3↑DomDayH-G3	**99**	8	108¼	94¾	66½	44½	45¾	McKnight J	L117 b	3.40	103– 11	PhntomLight1154 *Chngeinthewethr*117nk DnctoDstiny1151½	3 wide, rallied 10
7Jun03–7WO	fst	1⅛	:473 1:121 1:372 1:501	3↑Alw 89000NC	**101**	6	9¹²	77½	64¼	1²	1⁴	McKnight J	L118 b	4.40	95– 19	No Comprende1184 Indy Lead1181¾ Attest1181	4w, rallied, drew off 9
10May03–8WO	fst	1 1/16	:23 :464 1:114 1:433	4↑EclipseH-G3	**96**	5	12¹²129¾	117¼	34½	21½		McKnight J	L113 b	5.10	86– 20	PhntomLight1141½ *NoComprnd*1132¼ AnglinPrnc1161	Late rally 7w,for 2nd 12
26Apr03–9WO	fst	170	:231 :464 1:113 1:42	4↑Alw 89000NC	**93**	2	7⁹	78¾	65¾	3⁴	24¾	McKnight J	L116 b	2.80	92– 26	TemperdAppl1164¾ NoComprnd1161¾ AnglinPrinc1181¾	Late rally, 4 wide 7
22Mar03–9OP	fst	1 1/16	:234 :474 1:121 1:424	4↑OClm 100000N	**95**	5	5⁴	42½	52¾	3²	32½	Thompson T J	L116 b	12.90	93– 15	Slider1221 Mc Mahon1221½ No Comprende1167¾	Best of rest 7
7Mar03–9OP	fst	1	:24 :473 1:12 1:364	4↑Alw 36000N$Y	**86**	5	96¼	5⁵	4³	4⁵	56½	Castellano A Jr	L115 b	44.50	92– 13	McMhon1154 [D]WtchYorPnns1211 DstOnthBottl112no	Flattened out late 9

No Jacket Required
Own: Webber W T Jr

B. g. 7 (Mar)
Sire: Jolie's Halo (Halo)
Dam: Island Spirit (Shahrastani)
Br: Richard Kaster (Ky)
Tr: Amoss Thomas M(0 0 0 0 .00) 2003:(445 118 .27)

Life	54	7	9	4	$203,049	100	D.Fst	25	2	3	3	$33,485	77
2003	12	4	2	0	$130,454	100	Wet(295)	3	0	0	0	$3,250	49
2002	12	0	3	1	$20,070	84	Turf(240)	26	5	6	1	$166,314	100
	0	0	0	0	$0	–	Dst(0)	0	0	0	0	$0	–

26Dec03–4FG fm *5½f Ⓣ :223 :461 :5741:04 3↑Clm 17500(17.5-15) **74** 1 4 75¼ 76 33 43¼ Albarado R J L119 *.90 93–04 Rapid Raj115nk Roberto's Pride119½ General Express114½ No real threat 9
11Dec03–5FG fm *5½f Ⓣ :222 :46 :5821:043 3↑Clm 25000(25-20) **78** 1 4 44 43½ 23 24 Borel C H L119 *.60 89–07 Grifter1194 NoJacketRequired119½ GrandpaTwo1171 Lacked needed rally 9
20Sep03–6KD fm 6f Ⓣ :242 :49 1:122 3↑KyCpTfDash100k **79** 3 2 75 75½ 73¾ 67½ Blanc B L115 6.60 78–19 Fredericktown115no Abderian1172½ Callthesheriff115no Failed to menace 7
9Aug03–5EIP fm 5½f Ⓣ :212 :441 :5641:021 3↑Alw 37800NC **94** 1 2 45 45 33 2nk Borel C H L122 7.20 91–10 Wudantunoit120nk No Jacket Required1222 *Skeet*1171 Closing late, 6w 8
19Jun03–7CD fm 1 Ⓣ :241 :48 1:1341:381 3↑Alw 25000s **74** 4 62 52¼ 52¼ 62¼ 63¾ Borel C H L118 *.90 77–17 KingofSpeed1181 Nantucketeer120hd GameCalled118nk Inside,empty late 10
26May03–5LS sf 5f Ⓣ :223 :464 1:00 3↑BckAGTfSpH100k **85** 1 6 84½ 85¾ 76¼ 55½ Melancon G L118 14.80 72–22 ThtTt1181 TkAchncOnM1151½ RunwyChoic115hd Saved ground,no threat 9
2May03–7CD fm 5f Ⓣ :213 :441 :56 3↑AgonTfSp-G3 **73** 8 8 914 1017 1013 119 Blanc B L122 10.70 89–02 Fiscally Speaking114hd Morluc1221 *Testify*122no Done early 11
12Apr03–7Kee fm 5½f Ⓣ :212 :443 :57 1:031 3↑Shakrtwn-G3 **100** 7 5 98¼ 108¾ 85¼ 1nk Blanc B L118 12.40 92–08 NoJacketRequired118nk Testify120hd Abderin120nk Bobble early,split,drv 10
20Mar03–9FG fm *5½f Ⓣ :222 :47 :5911:053 4↑OClm c-40000 **93** 2 4 55 55¾ 31 13 Melancon G L122 *1.70 88–15 *No Jacket Required*1223 Brother Love1181¼ McNellis118hd Clearly best 8
Claimed from Englander Richard A. for $40,000, Hansen Scott Trainer 2003(as of 3/20): (41 9 5 2 0.22)
24Feb03–5FG fm *5½f Ⓣ :22 :463 :5831:044 4↑Alw 28000N1X **88** 5 5 54 53½ 43½ 11¼ Melancon G L120 *2.50 92–08 *NoJcketRequired*1201¼ ByouBuster1181¼ FrAwyBell1183½ Ran down leader 8
7Feb03–8FG fst 5½f ⊗ :224 :461 :5831:051 4↑Alw 30000N1X **64** 4 1 42½ 54 56 44¾ Melancon G L122 4.70 85–17 OpenChronicle118hd BullyBully1181¾ TkeAdvntg1183 Lacked serious rally 6
19Jan03–5FG fm *5½f Ⓣ :23 :48 :5931:053 4↑Alw 10000s **85** 6 2 32 31 1hd 12 Melancon G L118 4.60 88–17 No Jacket Required1182 Aldo118¾ Classic Alliance118hd Driving to wire 6

Noches De Rosa (Chi)
Own: Diamond A Racing Corporation

Dk. b or b. m. 6 (Aug)
Sire: Stagecraft*GB (Sadler's Wells)
Dam: Night Girl (Noble Fighter)
Br: Haras Don Alberto (Chi)
Tr: Mandella Richard E(0 0 0 0 .00) 2003:(253 51 .20)

Life	20	6	4	4	$289,473	100	D.Fst	0	0	0	0	$0	–
2003	5	2	1	1	$192,860	100	Wet(340)	0	0	0	0	$0	–
2002	4	0	0	0	$43,889	95	Turf(401)	20	6	4	4	$289,473	100
	0	0	0	0	$0	–	Dst(0)	0	0	0	0	$0	–

24May03–7BM fm *1⅛ Ⓣ :4811:113 1:36 1:452 3↑ⒻYrbBnBCH-G3 **100** 1 75½ 75¼ 74¼ 44½ 23½ Almeida G F LB119 b 3.20 100–08 Chiming1163½ NochesDeRosa1193 LindsayJean1182¼ Caught hold too late 7
19Apr03–4SA fm 1¼ Ⓣ :4811:122 1:3612:00 4↑ⒻSntBrbrH-G2 **97** 1 43½ 42½ 42½ 52½ 32¼ Smith M E LB117 b 4.50 91–09 Megahertz117¾ Trekking1111½ NochesDeRos117hd 3wd 2nd turn,best rest 5
22Mar03–9SA fm 1⅛ Ⓣ :5011:133 1:37 1:481 4↑ⒻSntaAnaH-G2 **100** 7 11½ 11½ 11 11 1½ Smith M E LB115 b 13.00 88–09 NochesDeRos115½ GrdenintheRin116nk *Mghrtz*1171 Deftly rated,held late 8
31Jan03–7SA fm 1¼ Ⓣ :48 1:121 1:3622:00 4↑ⒻReloyH81k **95** 2 21 21 21½ 1½ 11 Krone J A LB115 b 3.80 93–09 *NochesDeRos*1151 Snowflke117hd KeystotheHert1162 Pulled,led,clear,held 7
2Jan03–7SA fm 1 Ⓣ :234 :471 1:11 1:344 4↑ⒻOClm 125000N **89** 3 78½ 56½ 53 43½ 43½ Krone J A LB119 b 5.70 84–12 Nuntll117no *GrdenintheRin*1192½ BushTriumph1211 3wd into str,outkicked 9

Nothing to Lose
Own: Ramsey Kenneth L. and Sarah K

B. c. 4 (Jan)
Sire: Sky Classic (Nijinsky II) $20,000
Dam: Cherlindrea (Clever Trick)
Br: Kenneth L. Ramsey & Sarah K. Ramsey (Ky)
Tr: Lukas D. W(0 0 0 0 .00) 2003:(663 71 .11)

Life	6	4	0	0	$166,010	93	D.Fst	1	0	0	0	$2,650	83
2003	2	2	0	0	$120,000	93	Wet(353)	1	0	0	0	$3,160	72
2002	4	2	0	0	$46,010	89	Turf(331)	4	4	0	0	$160,200	93
	0	0	0	0	$0	–	Dst(0)	0	0	0	0	$0	–

21Feb03–9GP fm 1⅛ Ⓣ :4721:114 1:3611:481 PalmBch-G3 **93** 10 104½ 105 83¼ 63¾ 1½ Bailey J D L122 b *1.60 94–09 Nothing to Lose122½ *White Cat*118½ *Imitation*118¾ Angled out, up late 12
1Jan03–10Crc gd 1⅛ Ⓣ :4831:131 1:3811:502 TrpPkDby-G3 **90** 4 54 62¾ 51¼ 31½ 11¾ Bailey J D L115 b *1.80 79–20 *NothingtoLos*1151¾ MillnnumStorm119hd SuphBltz115¾ Checked first turn 12

Ocean Terrace
Own: Fog City Stable

Ch. c. 4 (Feb) KEESEP01 $700,000
Sire: Saint Ballado (Halo) $125,000
Dam: Crystal River (Black Tie Affair*Ire)
Br: Damara Farm (Ky)
Tr: Hess R B Jr(0 0 0 0 .00) 2003:(215 26 .12)

Life	5	3	0	0	$160,400	101	D.Fst	4	2	0	0	$129,200	93
2003	4	2	0	0	$141,200	101	Wet(371)	1	1	0	0	$31,200	101
2002	1	1	0	0	$19,200	85	Turf(255)	0	0	0	0	$0	–
	0	0	0	0	$0	–	Dst(0)	0	0	0	0	$0	–

Previously trained by Hess R B Jr

19Apr03–8Kee	fst	1$\frac{1}{16}$	:23	:47	1:113	1:452	ClmrLex-G2	–	6	52¼	63¼	716	-	-	Sellers S J	L116	12.50	-	22	Scrimshw1163 EyeoftheTiger116nk DomesticDisput116nk	Gave way,eased	7
5Apr03–6SA	fst	1⅛	:454	1:10	1:36	1:491	SADerby-G1	26	1	1hd	1hd	2hd	922	947½	Desormeaux K J	LB122	6.00	40–	14	Buddy Gil122hd Indian Express1222¼ Kafwain1221¼	Driftd out,tired,eased	9
8Mar03–8GG	fst	1$\frac{1}{16}$	:223	:452	1:092	1:421	ElCamRlD-G3	93	9	31½	2½	21	11	11½	Smith M E	LB115	4.80	92–	12	OcenTerrce1151½ MinistersWildCt117no *TenMostWnted*1151	Bid 2w, drvng	10
16Feb03–3SA	gd	7f	:231	:454	1:094	1:223	Alw 52000N1x	101	3	1	2hd	1hd	1½	11	Desormeaux K J	LB120	*1.60	93–	13	*Ocean Terrace*1201 Fly to the Wire118½ Carthage1204½	Inside duel,gamely	7

Offlee Wild
Own: Azalea Stables LLC

Dk. b or b. c. 4 (Apr) KEESEP01 $325,000
Sire: Wild Again (Icecapade) $50,000
Dam: Alvear (Seattle Slew)
Br: Dorothy A. Matz (Ky)
Tr: Smith Thomas V(0 0 0 0 .00) 2003:(81 7 .09)

Life	10	2	1	2	$188,185	99	D.Fst	10	2	1	2	$188,185	99
2003	7	1	0	2	$152,400	99	Wet(383)	0	0	0	0	$0	–
2002	3	1	1	0	$35,785	90	Turf(301)	0	0	0	0	$0	–
	0	0	0	0	$0	–	Dst(0)	0	0	0	0	$0	–

17Oct03–8Kee	fst	1$\frac{1}{16}$	:231	:463	1:112	1:451	3↑ Alw 54000N2x	89	3	87¾	78½	64¾	11	3nk	Borel C H	L116	*1.20	81–	22	PerfectCut118hd CollateralDamge116hd OffleeWild1164¾	Exch bmps 1/4p	11
4Oct03–9Hoo	fst	1$\frac{1}{16}$	:223	:462	1:103	1:432	IndnaDby-G3	88	5	43	54	53½	78	78¾	Borel C H	LB124	11.20	83–	29	Excessiveplesur1241 GrndHombr1241¼ Wndo1241¼	Inside,stalked,weaken	8
13Sep03–13TP	fst	6f	:212	:441	:563	1:092	KyCpSpnt-G3	89	8	2	76	89¾	109¼	99½	Court J K	L116	6.70	86–	17	*Cajun Beat*122¾ *Clock Stopper*1163½ Champali1222½	Faded	11
3May03–10CD	fst	1¼	:461	1:102	1:353	2:01	KyDerby-G1	92	6	119	95½	64	96½	1211½	Albarado R J	L126	29.90	83–	06	*FunnyCide*1261¾ *EmpireMaker*126hd PeceRules126hd	Bmp repeatedly start	16
12Apr03–9Kee	fst	1⅛	:47	1:111	1:374	1:513	BlueGras-G1	91	3	42½	43	32½	34	38	Day P	L123	5.80	74–	30	Peace Rules1233½ Brancusi1234½ Offlee Wild12310½	Exch bmps 1st turn	9
15Feb03–11GP	fst	1$\frac{1}{16}$	:233	:463	1:104	1:431	FntnOYth-G1	93	8	42¼	54½	52½	46	47½	Guidry M	L120	3.80	85–	13	Trust N Luck1225¼ Supah Blitz1202¼ MidwayCat116hd	4 wide, no response	8
18Jan03–10GP	fst	1$\frac{1}{16}$	:232	:471	1:112	1:43	HolyBull-G3	99	9	31	31	33	2½	1hd	Guidry M	L116	27.40	94–	10	Offlee Wild116hd Powerful Touch1163 Bham1182½	3 wide, prevailed	13

Olmodavor
Own: Wertheimer Farm LLC

B. h. 5 (Apr)
Sire: A.P. Indy (Seattle Slew) $300,000
Dam: Corrazona (El Gran Senor)
Br: Wertheimer et Frere (Ky)
Tr: Mandella Richard E(0 0 0 0 .00) 2003:(253 51 .20)

Life	9	4	3	0	$339,540	110	D.Fst	8	4	3	0	$336,480	110
2003	4	1	2	0	$241,080	110	Wet(396)	0	0	0	0	$0	–
2002	5	3	1	0	$98,460	103	Turf(334)	1	0	0	0	$3,060	88
	0	0	0	0	$0	–	Dst(0)	0	0	0	0	$0	–

6Dec03–8Hol	fst	1⅛	:463	1:103	1:354	1:49	3↑ NtvDivrH-G3	102	2	57½	510	57½	23	1½	Solis A	LB117	*1.20	89–12	Olmodavor117½ Nose TheTrade1151½ Chinkapin1181	Determinedly,up late	5
26Oct03–4SA	fst	6½f	:22	:444	1:09	1:152	3↑ OClm 125000N	101	5	2	46	45½	42¼	51½	Solis A	LB118 b	1.30	95–14	Our New Recruit118¾ Omega Code116½ *Arsen*118hd	4wd into lane,outkickd	5
2Mar03–9FG	fst	1⅛	:474	1:121	1:362	1:484	4↑ NwOrlnsH-G2	110	7	52¾	55	43	21½	23½	Solis A	L117 b	6.80	96–17	*Mineshaft*1153½ Olmodavor1172½ Strive1141½	3-wide early	11
1Feb03–9SA	fst	1⅛	:454	1:094	1:344	1:48	Strub-G2	107	1	55¼	54	45½	36½	27	Solis A	LB117 b	4.30	87–16	*Medaglia d'Oro*1237 Olmodavor117½ Tracemark1177	Late 2nd on rail	6

Omega Code
Own: Team Valor Stables Margaux Farm and W

B. c. 4 (Feb) FTFFEB02 $350,000
Sire: Elusive Quality (Gone West) $30,000
Dam: Tin Oaks (Deputy Minister)
Br: Sally J. Andersen (Fla)
Tr: Ward Wesley A(0 0 0 0 .00) 2003:(508 93 .18)

Life	9	3	3	1	$183,120	103	D.Fst	8	3	3	0	$172,120	103
2003	5	1	2	0	$87,810	103	Wet(331)	1	0	0	1	$11,000	78
2002	4	2	1	1	$95,310	94	Turf(248)	0	0	0	0	$0	–
	0	0	0	0	$0	–	Dst(0)	0	0	0	0	$0	–

27Nov03–7Hol	fst	6f	:214	:441	:56	1:084	3↑ VOUndrwd-G3	84	5	3	3½	31½	43	66½	Valenzuela P A	LB118	7.70	89–08	WtchmSmoky1121 OurNwRcrut1141½ *HstyKrs*116no	3 wide duel, weakened	6
26Oct03–4SA	fst	6½f	:22	:444	1:09	1:152	3↑ OClm 125000N	102	1	4	1½	1½	1hd	2¾	Valenzuela P A	LB116	*1.10	95–14	Our New Recruit118¾ Omega Code116½ *Arsen*118hd	Fought back rail,game	5
28Sep03–4SA	fst	6½f	:211	:433	1:094	1:163	3↑ OClm 100000N	90	2	5	2hd	2hd	11½	22	Valenzuela P A	LB116	*1.70	88–16	Ride and Shine1182 Omega Code1162 C.J.'sHonour1183½	Bobbled bit start	5
20Aug03–3Sar	fst	6f	:221	:444	:57	1:093	3↑ Alw 51000N3X	49	3	2	21½	44½	58¾	517¼	Bailey J D	L115	*1.15	77–06	Pinch Hitter119nk First Blush1151¼ *Sunray Spirit*1231½	Chased inside, tired	5
12Jan03–7SA	fst	6f	:211	:44	:561	1:083	SnMiguel-G3	103	1	3	31	21	1hd	11	Pedroza M A	LB121	1.80	95–12	Omega Code1211 Only the Best1215 Jimmy O1186	Tight5/8,stdy handling	5

One for Rose
Own: Tucci Stables

Dk. b or b. m. 5 (May) ONTSEP00 $10,158
Sire: Tejano Run (Tejano) $5,000
Dam: Saucyladygaylord (Lord Gaylord)
Br: Hill 'N' Dale Farms (Ont-C)
Tr: Attard Sid C(0 0 0 0 .00) 2003:(278 54 .19)

Life	14	8	2	2	$557,411	110	D.Fst	9	6	2	1	$438,334	110
2003	10	6	2	0	$476,377	110	Wet(335)	3	2	0	1	$99,385	93
2002	4	2	0	2	$81,034	78	Turf(267)	2	0	0	0	$19,692	85
	0	0	0	0	$0	–	Dst(0)	0	0	0	0	$0	–

27Nov03–7WO	sly	1 1/16	:23	:463	1:113	1:45	3↑ Ⓕ Alw 86400N$Y	93	3	2hd	1hd	21	22½	1½	Ramsammy E	L122	*.55	81–23	OneforRos122½ WinningChnc1221½ RoylDllinc122hd	Duel 2-pth,cme again	5
1Nov03–8WO	fst	1¼	:49	1:133	1:38	2:032	3↑ Ⓕ MaplLeaf-G3	110	7	11	11	12	12½	16¼	Ramsammy E	L121	*.70	97–19	*OneforRose*1216¼ WinningChnc1216¼ CloudsofGold1181½	Off rail, drew off	8
11Oct03–5WO	fst	1⅛	:48	1:131	1:373	1:502	3↑ Ⓕ Alw 86400NC	103	3	41½	41¾	3nk	13	17¼	Ramsammy E	L118	*1.25	94–10	*OnforRos*1187¼ WnnngChnc1182¼ ClodsofGold1181½	Stlk duel 2pth,drw off	10
21Sep03–6WO	fst	7f	:223	:46	1:111	1:24	3↑ Ⓕ Alw 78500N$Y	93	5	4	61¾	41½	31½	2hd	Ramsammy E	L120	3.10	84–20	*WinterGrdn*117hd *OnforRos*1201½ MystriousAffir1203¼	Stalk duel 3w,waited	8
1Sep03–4WO	fst	1 1/16	:234	:482	1:122	1:434	3↑ Ⓕ Ⓡ Algoma126k	105	2	1½	11	11	13½	19½	Ramsammy E	L113	2.45	87–24	OneforRos1139½ WinningChnc11910¾ SmllPromiss1154½	Off rail, drew off	4
2Aug03–3WO	fm	1 1/16 Ⓣ	:241	:474	1:121	1:433	3↑ Ⓕ Alw 89000C	84	4	2½	1hd	1½	21	64	Montpellier C	L118	4.55	76–20	Byzantine1182¾ Soundtrack118hd Five Fishes118¾	Inside, gave way	7
13Jly03–6WO	fst	7f	:222	:444	1:091	1:221	3↑ Ⓕ Ⓡ Kamar108k	89	5	2	2hd	1hd	2hd	2½	Montpellier C	L118	6.75	92–07	*BrassinPocket*124½ OneforRose1181 EclipseBy1141¾	Duel inside, gave best	7
29Jun03–2WO	fst	1 1/16	:24	:483	1:12	1:44	3↑ Ⓕ OClm 80000(80–75)N	86	6	52¼	4nk	12½	11	12½	Montpellier C	L120	*.40	86–20	One for Rose1202½ Darling Katey1206¾ Rich Mist116½	Stalk 3w, drew off	6
1Jun03–8WO	gd	1 1/16 Ⓣ	:23	:46	1:10	1:424	3↑ Ⓕ Nassau-G2	85	9	31½	3½	2hd	2½	44	Montpellier C	L115	31.25	80–19	Strait From Texas119½ Chopinina1153 Byzantine117½	Press 3w, tired	9
11May03–7WO	my	7f	:22	:44	1:092	1:232	3↑ Ⓕ Alw 67600N2X	79	3	6	31½	31½	1hd	13¼	Ramsammy E	L120	*2.30	87–12	One for Rose1203¼ TouchofGinger1201¼ LadyinTails1204¼	Stalk 3w, rallied	7

Owsley
Own: Hancock A B III

Dk. b or b. m. 6 (Feb)
Sire: Harlan (Storm Cat)
Dam: Insipid (Sham)
Br: Arthur B. Hancock III (Ky)
Tr: Schulhofer Randy(0 0 0 0 .00) 2003:(146 23 .16)

Life	23	8	4	1	$865,705	100	D.Fst	4	1	1	1	$31,510	79
2003	5	1	1	0	$141,744	100	Wet(355)	1	0	1	0	$22,231	72
2002	8	4	0	0	$593,870	100	Turf(293)	18	7	2	0	$811,964	100
	0	0	0	0	$0	–	Dst(0)	0	0	0	0	$0	–

16Aug03–8AP gd 1 3/16 Ⓣ :493 1:133 1:38 1:554 3↑ⒻBeverlyD-G1 **85** 1 4 2½ 4 4½ 4 1½ 7 4¼ 7 8½ Douglas R R L123 7.30 86–08 Heat Haze123 1¼ *Bien Nicole*123½ Riskaverse123 1½ Gave way drive 7
26Jly03–7AP fm 1 3/16 Ⓣ :473 1:113 1:363 1:55 3↑ⒻModestyH-G3 **100** 2 53 5 4¾ 3 2½ 1hd 11 Douglas R R L120 *1.30 99–05 Owsley120 1 Bien Nicole119 4 Beret115 3 3 wide 1/4, driving 7
4Jly03–10Bel fm 1¼ [T] :491 1:131 1:364 1:593 3↑ⒻNewYorkH-G2 **93** 3 33 3 1½ 4 1¾ 5 3¼ 45 Samyn J L L117 11.20 91–07 Snow Dance116 1 Pertuisane115¾ Riskaverse119 3¼ Inside trip, no rally 8
31May03–8Bel sf 1⅜ [T] :524 1:203 1:472 2:28 3↑ⒻShpshdBH-G2 **91** 8 2½ 2½ 2hd 2½ 2 8¼ Prado E S L119 3.80 05–87 *Mariensky*114 8¼ Owsley119 4¾ Silent Crystal112 1¾ With pace, second best 8
3May03–8Aqu fm 1 1/16 Ⓣ :231 :481 1:124 1:421 3↑ⒻBeaugayH-G3 **90** 7 4 2½ 31 3½ 5¾ 44 Castellano J J L118 7.10 89–05 DltPrincss113½ WondrAgin118¾ *VoodooDncr*120 2¾ Speed 3 wide, weakened 9

P Day
Own: Russo Adam

Dk. b or b. g. 9 (May)
Sire: Private Terms (Private Account) $5,000
Dam: Gilded Connection (Gilded Age)
Br: Charles H. Hadry (Md)
Tr: Hadry Charles J(0 0 0 0 .00) 2003:(115 23 .20)

Life	50	16	10	9	$662,218	109	D.Fst	37	15	6	8	$574,332	109
2003	5	3	0	0	$141,000	102	Wet(365)	8	0	4	0	$42,156	98
2002	12	3	4	1	$119,490	109	Turf(270)	5	1	0	1	$45,730	92
	0	0	0	0	$0	–	Dst(0)	0	0	0	0	$0	–

17May03–11Pim gd 1⅛ :481 1:124 1:372 1:50 3↑WDShferH-G3 **97** 4 5 4½ 5 4½ 52 44 4 4½ Fogelsonger R L116 f 3.60 89–12 WindsorCstle117 1¾ Chngeinthewthr113 1¾ TmpstFugit116 1 5wd, no threat 8
19Apr03–9Pim fst 1⅛ :471 1:112 1:362 1:484 3↑BltmrBCH-G3 **102** 3 4 9½ 4 7½ 44 12 1 2¾ Fogelsonger R L118 f 3.30 100–20 PDay118 2¾ Changeinthewether114hd FullBrush115 1 3wd move 1/4,driving 7
15Mar03–8Lrl fst 1⅛ :49 1:122 1:37 1:492 4↑HEJhnsnMmH67k **98** 7 42 4 4½ 43 11 1no Fogelsonger R L117 f 5.10 94–16 *P Day*117no Lyracist116 3¼ My Request114hd 3wd 1st,bid btw,dug in 8
Previously trained by Hadry Charles H
23Feb03–9Lrl gd 1⅛ :481 1:122 1:371 1:494 4↑JCampbellH80k **86** 7 65 67 8 7¼ 8 9¾ 7 9¾ Fogelsonger R L117 f *2.50 82–14 Tempest Fugit117 1 *Quiet Gratitude*113 3¾ Lyracist115 1½ Off rail dull effort 8
11Jan03–8Lrl fst 1⅛ :482 1:122 1:372 1:50 4↑NatvDancer74k **99** 6 34 3 1½ 4 1½ 5 1¼ 1hd Fogelsonger R L115 f 2.80 91–23 PDy115hd FullBrush115hd HyGtoutofmywy115nk Waitd ins,wrkd way btw 7

Parose
Own: Atto John

Ch. g. 10 (Apr)
Sire: Parlay Me (Irish Tower) $1,000
Dam: Roses for Classy (Son of Briartic)
Br: Johnnie P. Shewuck (Alb-C)
Tr: McPherson Alexander F(0 0 0 0 .00) 2003:(173 33 .19)

Life	84	19	20	14	$974,771	101	D.Fst	71	19	18	9	$932,784	101
2003	9	3	1	2	$250,177	101	Wet(354)	11	0	2	5	$39,971	93
2002	9	3	4	1	$283,790	96	Turf(212*)	2	0	0	0	$2,016	87
	0	0	0	0	$0	–	Dst(0)	0	0	0	0	$0	–

30Nov03–9WO fst 1¾ 1:133 1:403 3:001 3↑ValdictryH143k **96** 1 8 4¾ 3 1½ 21 32 3 3½ Kabel T K L118 f 3.25 81–25 Hydrogen113no AffirmedFeeling118 3½ Pros118 2½ Advnce 4w,bid,even out 11
8Nov03–8WO fst 1 1/16 :233 :471 1:111 1:434 3↑WoSltCpH-G3 **94** 1 710 7 8½ 6 5½ 43 3 2¼ Kabel T K L118 f *2.45 85–09 No Comprende117 1¼ Mobil119 1 Parose118½ Late rally, 4 wide 7
4Oct03–8WO fst 1⅛ :471 1:111 1:384 1:53 3↑DurhmCpH-G3 **94** 3 612 613 6 9½ 2 1½ 12 Jones J L117 f 3.15 81–24 Parose117 2 BarbeauRuckus116 2¼ WkeAtNoon121 4½ Trailed, long drive 4w 6
14Sep03–7WO fst 1 1/16 :243 :49 1:133 1:452 3↑Alw 86400nc **99** 2 5 3½ 5 5½ 5 4¾ 4 1½ 11 Kabel T K L118 f 4.95 79–32 *Parose*118 1 Royal Dalliance110nk On the Game118¾ Off rail,late rally 4w 7
25Aug03–7Sar fst 1⅛ :464 1:11 1:36 1:482 4↑Alw 58000c **87** 1 411 413 5 6½ 6 9½ 612 Luzzi M J L120 f 28.50 81–20 EveningAttire123 1¼ CraftyShaw120no RegISnction120 7¾ Inside trip, tired 6
25Jly03–8WO fst 1 1/16 :242 :474 1:121 1:442 3↑OClm 90000(100–90) **101** 3 5 6½ 57 31 1½ 14 Kabel T K L116 f 2.35 84–27 Parose116 4 Open Concert122hd Majestic Thief120 1¼ Rally 4w, drew off 5
1Jly03–9WO fst 1 1/16 :231 :474 1:12 1:422 3↑OClm 75000(80–75) **91** 1 57 4 1½ 1hd 2 1½ 2 3¼ Jones J L118 f 5.50 91–11 Anglian Prince120 3¼ *Parose*118 6 Classic Mike120nk 4w,advance,2nd best 5
9Mar03–10GP fst 1 1/16 :224 :46 1:102 1:421 4↑OClm 80000 **81** 3 9 8¾ 78 6 5½ 54 4 7¾ Guidry M L118 f 18.60 90–07 *Justification*118 3 Quest118 1¼ Doc Wild122 3½ 4 wide, passed tired 9
31Jan03–9GP fst 1 1/16 :232 :463 1:104 1:422 4↑OClm 100000 **80** 8 8 6½ 7 5¾ 77 710 716 Guidry M L120 f 18.90 81–12 Roger E118 1 Strive118 2 Woodmoon120 4½ Outrun 8

Pass Rush

Own: Tabor Michael B

Ch. h. 5 (Apr)
Sire: Crown Ambassador (Storm Cat) $4,000
Dam: Profitable Knight (Knight)
Br: Swifty Farms, Inc. (Ind)
Tr: Byrne Patrick B(0 0 0 0 .00) 2003:(119 25 .21)

Life	23	5	8	2	$506,225	106	
2003	9	1	3	1	$261,865	106	
2002	10	3	4	0	$199,540	104	
	0	0	0	0	$0	–	
D.Fst	16	3	5	2	$382,260	106	
Wet(326)	6	2	3	0	$115,310	98	
Turf(302*)	1	0	0	0	$8,655	86	
Dst(0)	0	0	0	0	$0	–	

15Nov03-8Hoo	gd	1	:231 :462 1:11 1:37	3↑SchaeferMl103k	**76**	1	4 3½	54	65	57	59½	Martinez J R Jr	LB121 b	2.50	81-09	CrftyShw1242¼ ColNCllctv1194½ FghtngIndns1151	Angle 5wd, no late run	7
4Nov03-9CD	fst	1 1/16	:242 :473 1:114 1:432	3↑Alw 62280c	**101**	7	31	31½	2½	2hd	2nk	Day P	L117 b	*1.80	91-24	*CraftyShaw*123nk PassRush1175½ AmericnStyle117½	Long drive,outgamed	8
26Oct03-9CD	sly	7½f	:224 :452 1:103 1:313	3↑AckAckH-G3	**95**	3	2	1hd	1hd	21	22	Day P	L116 b	2.20	80-26	Cappuchino1172 Pass Rush1161 Twilight Road1162	Pace,duel,no match	7
5Jly03-9CD	fm	1	Ⓣ :234 :47 1:103 1:352	3↑FrckrBCH-G2	**86**	6	1½	11½	2hd	31½	56¼	Melancon L	L115 b	5.20	89-12	TptheAdmirl1151¼ Freefourinternet114½ *PckgStor*1141½	Hop start,weaken	9
21Jun03-9CD	fst	6½f	:224 :454 1:093 1:16	3↑AristdsH-G3	**101**	1	4	41¾	41½	32	3nk	Melancon L	L118 b	3.80	91-15	MountainGenerl116hd *BeusTown*123nk PssRush118¾	Lack room,bmp 3/16s	7
26May03-8LS	fst	1 1/16	:224 :46 1:101 1:42	3↑LSParkH-G3	**99**	6	3½	31½	42	33½	54½	Day P	L118 b	1.70	87-08	*PiNBurgr*1172¾ DH MysvllSlw114 DH Blusthstndrd1201½	4w 1st turn,no rally	8
3May03-5CD	fst	7f	:222 :45 1:093 1:214	4↑CDH-G2	**105**	3	3	41½	43½	42½	22½	Farina T	L117 b	10.10	90-08	*Aldebaran*1202½ Pass Rush117nk Cappuchino115hd	Stead 1/2pl, check 1/8	12
1Feb03-9SA	fst	1⅛	:454 1:094 1:344 1:48	Strub-G2	**91**	5	41¼	42	34½	49½	516½	Nakatani C S	LB121 b	6.30	77-16	*Medaglia d'Oro*1237 Olmodavor117½ Tracemark1177	3wd 1st turn,wkened	6
11Jan03-8SA	fst	1 1/16	:23 :462 1:101 1:421	SnFndoBC-G2	**106**	8	32	32	2½	11½	13½	Nakatani C S	LB116 b	3.60	93-07	Pass Rush1163½ Tracemark116½ Tizbud116nk	4wd bid 3/8,clear	8

Passinetti

Own: Tanaka Gary A

B. g. 8 (Mar)
Sire: Slew o' Gold (Seattle Slew) $7,500
Dam: Cloelia (Lyphard)
Br: Katom Ltd & Kilboy Estates (Ky)
Tr: Cecil Ben D(0 0 0 0 .00) 2003:(77 7 .09)

Life	17	3	2	5	$387,983	104	
2003	4	2	0	1	$289,320	104	
1999	12	1	2	4	$95,594	98	
	0	0	0	0	$0	–	
D.Fst	0	0	0	0	$0	–	
Wet(365)	0	0	0	0	$0	–	
Turf(296)	17	3	2	5	$387,983	104	
Dst(0)	0	0	0	0	$0	–	

20Apr03-9SA	fm	*1¾	Ⓣ1:131 1:383 2:273 2:464	4↑SnJnCpoH-G1	**104**	4	45½	45	52¾	32½	1½	Blanc B	LB111	11.10	80-14	Passinetti111½ All the Boys115¾ Champion Lodge117¾	3wd into str,rallied	9
6Apr03-7SA	fm	1⅛	Ⓣ :493 1:131 1:361 1:474	4↑ArcadiaH-G2	**100**	9	33½	33½	32	32	4¾	Baze T C	LB111	16.00	89-11	CenturyCity114nk *Gondolieri*116hd SundyBrek117½	3wd into str,outkicked	9
19Mar03-6SA	fm	1⅛	Ⓣ :444 1:083 1:34 1:463	4↑OClm 40000N	**100**	1	55	55	42	11	13	Desormeaux K J	LB118	3.90	96-14	Pssinetti1183 *PrizedFrind*1181½ GroomOnthRun1201	Bid 3deep,led, cleared	8
16Feb03-5SA	gd	1	Ⓣ :242 :49 1:131 1:374	4↑Alw 56000N1x	**87**	2	74¾	84¾	85¼	76	31½	Krone J A	LB123	9.10	71-23	*Studio Time*117½ Revenescent1191 *Passinetti*123no	Came out,stride late	9

Passing Shot
Own: Shields J V Jr

Dk. b or b. f. 5 (Apr)
Sire: A.P. Indy (Seattle Slew) $300,000
Dam: Aucilla (Relaunch)
Br: J. V. Shields Jr. (Ky)
Tr: Jerkens H. A(0 0 0 0 .00) 2003:(359 73 .20)

Life	19	5	5	3	$448,397	94	D.Fst	14 5 2 3	$417,420 94
2003	10	3	2	2	$362,637	94	Wet(433)	4 0 3 0	$30,977 84
2002	9	2	3	1	$85,760	85	Turf(322)	1 0 0 0	$0 61
	0	0	0	0	$0	-	Dst(0)	0 0 0 0	$0 -

4Oct03- 9Bel fst 1⅛ :47⁴1:12² 1:36³1:49¹ 3↑Ⓕ Beldame-G1 **74** 4 6²½ 6⁴½ 6⁵½ 7¹² 7¹⁹¾ Santos J A L123 18.10 64- 26 Sightseek123⁴½ Bird Town120⁴¾ Buy the Sport120¾ Had no rally 7
13Sep03- 9Bel fst 1 1/16 :23 :45⁴ 1:10 1:41¹ 3↑Ⓕ RuffianH-G1 **94** 4 3² 3¹½ 2hd 3⁷ 3⁸½ Santos J A L115 6.40 85- 19 Wild Spirit121³½ You118⁵ Passing Shot115⁵½ 4 wide move, faded 6
22Aug03- 9Sar fst 1¼ :49³1:14¹ 1:38²2:03¹ 3↑Ⓕ PrsnlEnH-G1 **92** 4 2¹ 2¹ 2hd 2¹ 1no Santos J A L114 11.30 91- 17 Passing Shot114no *Wild Spirit*122⁶¼ Miss Linda114²½ Came again outside 5
30Jly03- 8Sar fst 1⅛ :47¹1:11¹ 1:37¹1:50⁴ 3↑Ⓕ Alw 52000N3x **89** 2 2½ 3² 3²½ 1hd 1¾ Santos J A L124 4.00 81- 19 *PssingShot*124¾ GoldnSont120²½ PocusHocus120½ Wide move, determined 5
11Jly03- 9Bel fst 1 1/16 :23² :46⁴ 1:11⁴1:43⁴ 3↑Ⓕ Alw 48000N2x **87** 5 3½ 3½ 1hd 1²½ 1⁴¼ Santos J A L120 *1.70 81- 24 *PassingShot*120⁴¼ Hanselin114no SuveQueen120³½ Drew clear when roused 6
19Jun03- 8Bel sly 7f :22¹ :44³ 1:09¹1:22² 3↑Ⓕ Alw 47000N2x **84** 2 5 5⁴ 3⁴ 3⁵ 2⁴ Santos J A L120 *1.40e 84- 12 *Danceinthestreets*118⁴ *Passing Shot*120¹ City Sister114³¾ Rallied for place 6
7Jun03- 6Bel sly 1 :22⁴ :45⁴ 1:10³1:37 4↑ⒻⓇ Affirmed65k **67** 3 5⁷½ 5⁶ 5⁷ 5⁹½ 5¹¹¼ Chavez J F L117 5.00 70- 14 Alchemilla119no ShesGottheBet119nk *MistySixes*119²¾ Inside, no response 7
23May03- 8Bel sly 1 :22² :45¹ 1:09³1:36¹ 3↑Ⓕ Alw 48000N2x **83** 6 3¹½ 3¹½ 2hd 2hd 2¹¼ Bravo J L121 *1.50 84- 16 *CherokeeLit*117¹¼ PssingShot121⁷¼ *GloriousJnn*115hd 4 wide move, gamely 6
7May03- 6Bel fst 1 :22⁴ :45 1:09 1:34⁴ 4↑ⒻⓇ YanksMusic60k **75** 6 5³ 5⁵¼ 5³ 5²¼ 4⁴¾ Coa E M L115 2.95 87- 04 MessgeRed115¹½ ShesGottheBt117no SrnitysSmil117³¼ Wide trip, no rally 6
17Apr03- 8Aqu fst 1 :23³ :46¹ 1:10 1:36 4↑Ⓕ Alw 46000N2x **91** 8 6³ 7⁴½ 5⁵ 3²½ 3¹¾ Chavez Luis⁵ L112 *1.90 83- 25 Call an Audible119¹ *Moloko*111¾ Passing Shot112nk Came wide, rallied 8

Patton's Victory
Own: Hwy 1 Racing Stable LLC

Dk. b or b. g. 6 (Feb) KEENOV00 $35,000
Sire: Patton (Lord At War*Arg) $2,500
Dam: Tri Skipping (Skip Trial)
Br: Brereton C. Jones (Ky)
Tr: Roberts Stanley W(0 0 0 0 .00) 2003:(640 90 .14)

Life	31	10	1	4	$270,289	107	D.Fst	25 8 0 3	$243,008 107
2003	13	6	0	2	$223,501	107	Wet(326)	6 2 1 1	$27,281 85
2002	8	2	0	0	$15,302	83	Turf(270)	0 0 0 0	$0 -
	0	0	0	0	$0	-	Dst(0)	0 0 0 0	$0 -

11Dec03- 1Haw fst 1 1/16 :23⁴ :46³ 1:10²1:44¹ 3↑ OClm 100000N **81** 5 1¹ 1½ 1½ 3¹½ 6⁵¾ Meier R L118 b *2.40e 80- 26 Ivan Jay Perry118no Mc Mahon120½ Fighting Indians116¹ Tired 7
15Nov03- 8Hoo gd 1 :23¹ :46² 1:11 1:37 3↑ SchaeferMl103k **80** 7 1¹½ 1¹ 2½ 3³ 4⁷¾ Compton P LB124 b 27.80 83- 09 CrftyShw124²¼ CoolNCollctiv119⁴½ FightingIndns115¹ Off rail, weakened 7
1Nov03- 9Wds fst 1 1/16 :23¹ :47³ 1:11⁴1:43¹ 3↑ WoodIndsH30k **71** 5 1hd 1¹½ 1¹½ 1hd 5⁸ Birzer A E LB125 b *1.80 111 - CnyondOro123² WWRobndHd124³½ MrnngMrry120² Own pace, gave way 10
23Aug03- 9EIP fst 1 :23 :45³ 1:11 1:37¹ 3↑ GovernorsH75k **68** 7 3nk 2¹ 5³½ 6⁸ 5¹⁵¾ Birzer A E L120 b 8.20 78- 06 *Sonic West*110⁴½ Trion Georgia115no Sterling Gold113⁴¼ Bobble start,tired 8
2Aug03- 6PrM fst 1⅛ :48 1:11³ 1:35³1:48 3↑ PrairiMedH75k **101** 5 2¹½ 2¹ 2½ 1hd 2hd Birzer A E LB122 b *1.60 98- 06 ⒹNrthstHll118hd PttnsVctr122⁵ StrmImpct116¹¾ Stalked, bid, outgamed 5
Placed first through disqualification
19Jly03- 9Cby fst 1⅛ :46³1:10³ 1:35³1:49 3↑Ⓡ CCJewel141k **94** 2 1²½ 1² 1³ 2¹½ 3⁵½ Birzer A E LB124 b 2.50 97- 02 Daunting122³¼ FreezeAlert124²¼ *Patton's Victory*124⁴ Pace, rail, weakened 8
12Jly03- 6PrM fst 1⅛ :46²1:10¹ 1:35³1:48¹ 3↑ CrnhsBCH-G3 **91** 3 2hd 2½ 2½ 4⁶½ 4¹²¼ Birzer A E LB116 b 6.90 85- 10 *Tenpins*118² Bowman's Band116⁵½ Woodmoon116⁴¾ Inside duel, tired 6
25May03- 8PrM fst 1 1/16 :23 :46¹ 1:10²1:42³ 3↑ Precisnist47k **107** 4 2½ 2hd 1½ 1¹½ 1³ Birzer A E LB122 b 3.40 95- 24 PttonsVctory122³ ColorflTr122⁶¼ *NrthwstHll*119³½ Stumbled start,driving 4
26Apr03- 9Fon fst 1 1/16 :23 :45³ 1:11²1:43³ 3↑ BslmnGsFnH100k **93** 1 1hd 1hd 3nk 3¹ 3⁵½ Birzer A E LB120 b 2.30 94- 13 DustySpike116¹ CowboyStuff119⁴½ *PttonsVictory*120nk Quick pace, inside 7
9Apr03- 9OP fst 1 1/16 :23³ :47³ 1:12 1:43¹ 4↑ FfthSesn-G3 **107** 4 1¹½ 1²½ 1³ 1³ 1¹ Birzer A E L117 b 12.30 94- 23 PttonsVctory117¹ ColorfulTor122³¼ MkorsMrk118¾ Got slow, enough left 7
16Mar03- 5OP fst 1 1/16 :23² :47² 1:11⁴1:43 4↑ OClm 35000N **101** 6 1² 1¹½ 1² 1³ 1²¾ Birzer A E L115 b *.50e 95- 12 *PattonsVictory*115²¾ AlottNumbers122³ *UnlcedWters*122⁶ Pace, ridden out 7
2Mar03-10OP fst 1 1/16 :23⁴ :48² 1:13²1:45⁴ 4↑ Alw 10000s **99** 2 1¹ 1½ 1² 1⁶ 1¹⁰ Birzer A E L122 b 4.80 81- 21 *PttonsVctory*122¹⁰ Onwngndpryr114³½ SpdDmn114²¾ Pace, rail, ridden out 8
9Feb03- 4OP sly 1 :23² :47² 1:12²1:39⁴ 4↑ Alw 7500s **85** 6 2hd 1hd 1¹½ 1²½ 1¹½ Birzer A E L116 b 9.00 84- 18 *PttonsVictory*116¹½ ForiegnDputy122¹¾ RglDom122²¼ Dueled, clear, lasted 7

Peace Rules

Own: Gann Edmund A

Ch. c. 4 (Apr) OBSMAR02 $35,000
Sire: Jules (Forty Niner) $6,000
Dam: Hold to Fashion (Hold Your Peace)
Br: Newchance Farm (Fla)
Tr: Frankel Robert J(0 0 0 0 .00) 2003:(411 114 .28)

Life	13	6	2	2	$2,059,990	109	D.Fst	6	3	1	2	$1,804,950	109
2003	7	3	1	1	$1,850,000	109	Wet(370)	2	0	0	0	$51,350	98
2002	6	3	1	1	$209,990	102	Turf(306)	5	3	1	0	$203,690	102
	0	0	0	0	$0	–	Dst(0)	0	0	0	0	$0	–

25Oct03–4SA	fm	1	Ⓣ	:221 :452 1:092 1:334	3↑ BCMile-G1	71	1	11	1hd	2hd	125	1315½	Prado E S	LB122	*3.10	77–04	SxPrfctons119¾ TochofthBls126nk CntryCty1261¼	Speed,inside,gave way	13
23Aug03–11Sar	fst	1¼		:461 1:094 1:352 2:02	Travers-G1	105	3	2hd	2½	2hd	2½	24½	Bailey J D	L126	*2.30	92–03	*TenMostWnted*1264½ PeceRuls12610 StrongHop126¾	Vied outside, gamely	6
3Aug03–11Mth	fst	1⅛		:47 1:104 1:36 1:491	HsklInvH-G1	109	1	11½	11½	11½	13	11¾	Prado E S	L121	2.30	95–08	Peace Rules1211¾ Sky Mesa1187¼ Funny Cide1231	Pace off rail,driving	7
17May03–12Pim	gd	1 3/16		:47 1:113 1:362 1:553	Preaknes-G1	98	7	2hd	11	1½	35	410½	Prado E S	L126	2.40	84–12	Funny Cide1269¾ Midway Road126¾ Scrimshaw126no	2wd,brushed,wknd	10
3May03–10CD	fst	1¼		:461 1:102 1:353 2:01	KyDerby-G1	106	4	2½	2hd	1½	2hd	31¾	Prado E S	L126	6.30	92–06	*Funny Cide*1261¾ *Empire Maker*126hd Peace Rules126hd	Pressed,led,gamely	16
12Apr03–9Kee	fst	1⅛		:47 1:111 1:374 1:513	BlueGras-G1	104	2	11½	11½	11	11	13½	Prado E S	L123	*.60	82–30	Peace Rules1233½ Brancusi1234½ Offlee Wild12310½	Rated on pace,driving	9
9Mar03–9FG	fst	1 1/16		:232 :463 1:103 1:423	LaDerby-G2	105	9	21	21½	2½	11	12¼	Prado E S	L122	9.40	97–17	*Peace Rules*1222¼ [D]Kafwain1221 Funny Cide122½	Bid, clear, driving	10

Perfect Drift

Own: Stonecrest Farm

B. g. 5 (Apr)
Sire: Dynaformer (Roberto) $50,000
Dam: Nice Gal (Naskra)
Br: Dr. William A. Reed & Stonecrest Farm (Ky)
Tr: Johnson Murray W(0 0 0 0 .00) 2003:(101 14 .14)

Life	18	9	3	1	$2,221,368	117	D.Fst	13	7	2	1	$2,125,710	117
2003	8	5	0	0	$1,505,388	117	Wet(339)	2	1	1	0	$32,800	95
2002	8	3	2	1	$695,120	107	Turf(314)	3	1	0	0	$62,858	104
	0	0	0	0	$0	–	Dst(0)	0	0	0	0	$0	–

25Oct03–9SA	fst	1¼		:461 1:101 1:341 1:594	3↑ BCClasic-G1	104	7	63¾	55	44	65¼	69¾	Stevens G L	LB126	5.70	96–07	Pleasantly Perfect1261½ Medaglia d'Oro126¾ Dynever121nk	Carried wide	10
28Sep03–9Haw	fst	1¼		:493 1:133 1:39 2:033	3↑ HawGldCH-G2	109	6	21	2½	1hd	1hd	11¾	Day P	L122	*.40	90–20	Perfect Drift1221¾ Tenpins119½ Aeneas1146	Ridden out	6
13Sep03–11TP	fst	1⅛		:481 1:114 1:37 1:502	3↑ KyCpClH-G2	112	3	32½	31½	2hd	2hd	11	Day P	L120	1.40	84–17	*Perfect Drift*1201 Congaree1244 *Crafty Shaw*115½	Mild handling	5
16Aug03–10AP	gd	1¼	Ⓣ	:49 1:132 1:373 2:021	3↑ ArlMilln-G1	101	6	32	32	32	83	83¼	Day P	L126	3.80	92–08	[D]*Storming Home*126½ *Sulamani*126hd [DH]Kaieteur126	Gave way	13
19Jly03–9AP	fst	1 3/16		:48 1:104 1:36 1:552	3↑ WashPkH-G2	112	5	42½	42½	31½	1hd	15	Day P	L120	*.60	98–16	Perfect Drift1205 Aeneas1151¼ Flatter1145½	Ridden out	5
14Jun03–10CD	fst	1⅛		:464 1:102 1:35 1:472	3↑ SFosterH-G1	117	7	41½	42½	52½	21	1hd	Day P	L115	6.80	101–04	*Perfect Drift*115hd *Mineshaft*1239½ *Aldebaran*120½	Bmp start,gamely,5w	10
3May03–9CD	fm	1⅛	Ⓣ	:474 1:111 1:344 1:463	3↑ WRTurfCl-G1	104	5	58	54½	53	34	42½	Desormeaux K J	L123	5.80	98 -	Honor in War1161¼ Requete116¾ *Patrol*114½	5w bid,empty late	8
11Apr03–9Kee	fm	1	Ⓣ	:242 :48 1:122 1:363	4↑ Alw 65000c	95	7	21½	1hd	1hd	11½	1¾	Desormeaux K J	L117	*1.50	85–13	PerfectDrift117¾ FirstLieutnnt116½ BowmnsBnd116nk	Pressed,stiff drive	9

Perfect Moon

Own: Royce S. Jaime Racing Stable Inc

B. g. 3 (Mar) EASOCT02 $4,700
Sire: Malibu Moon (A.P. Indy) $3,000
Dam: Perfectly (Parfaitement)
Br: Mr. & Mrs. Hugh J. O'Donovan (Md)
Tr: O'Neill Doug(0 0 0 0 .00) 2003:(760 133 .18)

Life	10	3	1	3	$353,870	89	
2003	10	3	1	3	$353,870	89	
2002	0	M	0	0	$0	-	
	0	0	0	0	$0	-	
D.Fst	10	3	1	3	$353,870	89	
Wet(373*)	0	0	0	0	$0	-	
Turf(269)	0	0	0	0	$0	-	
Dst(0)	0	0	0	0	$0	-	

5Dec03-8DeD	fst	1 1/16	:23 :454 1:111 1:451	BdGmgDltJk1000k	89	2 41 32½ 31½ 43 31	Espinoza V	L115 b	5.90	103- 05	Mr. Jester115¾ Fire Slam115nk Perfect Moon1151½	Contention, wide gain 10
5Oct03-10SA	fst	1 1/16	:222 :453 1:101 1:411	Norfolk-G2	75	6 63¼ 63 52½ 48¼ 315	Espinoza V	LB120	7.60	83- 08	Ruler's Court12014 Capitano1201 Perfect Moon1203½	Stdied 7/8,4-wide 9
10Sep03-8Dmr	fst	7f	:221 :442 1:092 1:23	DmrFut-G2	77	5 2 52½ 52¾ 42½ 32½	Valenzuela P A	LB122	2.80	84- 09	Siphonizer116½ MinisterEric1162 PerfctMoon122nk	4wd into lane,late 3rd 5
Previously trained by Stute Melvin F												
17Aug03-2Dmr	fst	6½f	:22 :444 1:101 1:164	BestPal-G2	84	9 2 41½ 32½ 31 11¼	Valenzuela P A	LB122	3.70	91- 09	PerfectMoon1221¼ Capitno1181¼ MilitryMndte1181	3wd,bid,led 1/16,clear 10
19Jly03-4Hol	fst	6f	:221 :443 :571 1:101	HolJuvCh-G3	82	2 5 42½ 21½ 21 12½	Valenzuela P A	LB117	3.00	89- 13	*PerfctMoon*1172½ BlirsRorinStr1173 RulrsCourt1173	Driftd in,brushed 1/16 5
21Jun03-4Hol	fst	5½f	:214 :451 :572 1:034	Haggin94k	83	5 4 64¼ 66¼ 54¾ 23	Solis A	LB116	14.70	86- 10	StlkingTiger1143 *PerfectMoon*1167 DvetheDude116½	Split foes 1/8,2d best 7
14May03-3Hol	fst	4½f	:22 :46 :52	Md 40000(40-35)	66	4 1 2hd 11 12	Solis A	LB119	4.00	95- 03	PerfctMoon1192 AnthonyEts1193½ Aryoutlkintom1192	Dueled btwn,clear 10
18Apr03-1SA	fst	2f	:111 :213	Md Sp Wt 47k	–	2 4 31½ 41½	Valenzuela P A	LB118	5.60	95- 13	Speak theLanguage115hd *RealRed*118½ FastSplash1161	Inside, outfinished 8
3Apr03-1SA	fst	2f	:112 :214	Md Sp Wt 48k	–	3 8 33 43½	Atkinson P	LB118	14.10	92- 11	DoublBlvdr1182 PpsPckpockt1151½ AnyQustons118no	Bit slow into stride 10
20Mar03-1SA	fst	2f	:112 :22	Md Sp Wt 48k	–	4 7 93½ 910¾	Desormeaux K J	B118	12.30	84- 11	RollOverRoy1182 TossBothWys1181½ FstSplsh117hd	Bpd brk, checked 1/8 9

Perfect Soul (Ire)

Own: Fipke Charles E

B. h. 6 (Apr)
Sire: Sadler's Wells (Northern Dancer)
Dam: Ball Chairman (Secretariat)
Br: C. Fipke (Ire)
Tr: Attfield Roger L(0 0 0 0 .00) 2003:(330 32 .10)

Life	15	6	3	1	$1,136,215	107	
2003	8	3	2	1	$856,195	107	
2002	7	3	1	0	$280,020	104	
	0	0	0	0	$0	-	
D.Fst	0	0	0	0	$0	-	
Wet(276)	0	0	0	0	$0	-	
Turf(375)	15	6	3	1	$1,136,215	107	
Dst(0)	0	0	0	0	$0	-	

25Oct03-4SA	fm	1	Ⓣ :221 :452 1:092 1:334	3↑ BCMile-G1	92	13 76 63¼ 63 52¾ 96	Santos J A	LB126 b	16.40	87- 04	SxPrfctons119¾ TouchofthBlus126nk CnturyCty1261¼	3 wide, no response 13
4Oct03-9Kee	fm	1	Ⓣ :23 :461 1:114 1:36	3↑ ShdwlTfM-G1	107	3 610 67 72¼ 52¼ 1¾	Prado E S	L126 b	6.50	88- 14	PerfectSoul126¾ HonorinWar126½ TouchoftheBlues1261¼	7w 3/16s,driving 10
14Sep03-9WO	fm	1	Ⓣ :224 :451 1:091 1:331	3↑ AttoMile-G1	101	4 1111 1117½ 117¾ 65 32¼	Santos J A	L121 b	3.55	95- 06	TouchoftheBlues119½ SoringFr1211¾ *PrfctSoul*121hd	Late rally,drifted out 11
16Aug03-10AP	gd	1¼	Ⓣ :49 1:132 1:373 2:021	3↑ ArlMilln-G1	105	5 42½ 53½ 64½ 1hd 5¾	Nakatani C S	L126 b	16.60	94- 08	D *Storming Home*126½ *Sulamani*126hd DH Kaieteur126	Led, gave way 13
20Jly03-8WO	fm	1⅜	Ⓣ :491 1:132 1:371 2:134	3↑ ChneseCC-G2	100	3 31 31 2hd 1½ 21½	Landry R C	L119 b	*1.10	94- 06	*StruttheStge*1211½ PerfectSoul1192¾ AngelOnthWing115¾	3w,led,no match 8
15Jun03-8WO	gd	1⅛	Ⓣ :481 1:124 1:37 1:493	3↑ KngEdBCH-G2	106	3 84¾ 83¾ 52¼ 11½ 12½	Landry R C	L119 b	*1.70	80- 25	PerfectSoul1192½ *StruttheStge*1211¼ DelMrShow119½	3w,rally 5w, drew off 9
17May03-10Pim	sf	1⅛	Ⓣ :531 1:183 1:442 1:573	3↑ CitgoDix-G2	98	4 21 2½ 2½ 2½ 2½	Prado E S	L117 b	1.70	51- 49	Dr. Brendler117½ *PerfectSoul*1173½ Sardaukar117no	Prompted 2wd, gamely 6
13Apr03-7Kee	fm	1⅛	Ⓣ :473 1:123 1:364 1:483	4↑ Alw 57200N3x	99	8 3½ 31½ 32 14 15¼	Prado E S	L118 b	*2.40	94- 08	Perfect Soul1185¼ Illusionary1162 *Fly Smartly*1161½	Tracked,5w,driving 10

Phantom Light

Own: Stronach Stable

Gr/ro. h. 5 (Mar) ONTAUT00 $57,162
Sire: Alphabet Soup (Cozzene) $30,000
Dam: Kirby Meadow (Meadowlake)
Br: Adena Springs (Ont-C)
Tr: Vella Daniel J(0 0 0 0 .00) 2003:(192 42 .22)

Life	10	4	1	0	$355,710	108	D.Fst	10	4	1	0	$355,710	108
2003	6	3	0	0	$299,610	108	Wet(400)	0	0	0	0	$0	–
2002	2	1	0	0	$45,020	78	Turf(281)	0	0	0	0	$0	–
	0	0	0	0	$0	–	Dst(0)	0	0	0	0	$0	–

19Jly03–9AP fst 1 3/16 :48 1:10⁴ 1:36 1:55² 3↑WashPkH-G2 **94** 2 3² 3 2½ 4 2½ 5⁵ 5 11¾ Douglas R R L116 b 11.50 86– 16 Perfect Drift120⁵ Aeneas1151¼ Flatter1145½ Gave way after half 5
1Jly03–8WO fst 1¼ :46² 1:11² 1:36¹ 2:01 3↑DomDayH-G3 **108** 1 1 1½ 1¹ 1 1½ 1³ 1⁴ Kabel T K L115 b 6.45 109– 11 PhntomLight115⁴ Chnginthwthr117nk DnctoDstiny1151½ Off rail, drew off 10
7Jun03–7WO fst 1⅛ :47³ 1:12¹ 1:37² 1:50¹ 3↑Alw 89000NC **87** 4 3⁴ 3 2½ 3 2½ 5 4½ 5 8¾ Landry R C L120 b *1.45 86– 19 No Comprende118⁴ Indy Lead1181¾ Attest118¹ Stalk between 9
10May03–8WO fst 1 1/16 :23 :46⁴ 1:11⁴ 1:43³ 4↑EclipseH-G3 **99** 4 2½ 2hd 1½ 1 1½ 1 1½ Landry R C L114 b 5.00 88– 20 PhntomLight1141½ NoComprende1132¼ AnglinPrince116¹ Off rail drew off 12
27Apr03–1WO fst 1 1/16 :24 :48 1:12⁴ 1:44⁴ 4↑Alw 69900N1X **91** 4 2hd 2¹ 1hd 1 4½ 1⁸ McAleney J S L120 b *.70 82– 22 PhntomLight120⁸ SovereignAttire120no GoldShded1207¾ Off rail, drew off 6
13Apr03–5WO fst 7f :22² :44⁴ 1:10³ 1:24² 4↑Alw 63500N1X **80** 1 10 4³ 3 2½ 4 2½ 4½ McAleney J S L120 b *2.70 82– 15 SouthernChnce120hd AsExpected120hd DncrsGust120nk Stalk duel inside 14

Phoenix Reach (Ire)

Own: Winterbeck Manor Stud

B. c. 4 (Mar)
Sire: Alhaarth*Ire (Unfuwain)
Dam: Carroll's Canyon*Ire (Hatim)
Br: Miss Christine Kiernan (Ire)
Tr: Balding Andrew(0 0 0 0 .00) 2003:(2 1 .50)

Life	5	3	1	1	$1,037,276	108	D.Fst	0	0	0	0	$0	–
2003	4	3	0	1	$1,035,526	108	Wet(280)	0	0	0	0	$0	–
2002	1	M	1	0	$1,750	–	Turf(247)	5	3	1	1	$1,037,276	108
	0	0	0	0	$0	–	Dst(0)	0	0	0	0	$0	–

19Oct03–9WO yl 1½ Ⓣ :51² 1:16³ 2:08¹ 2:33³ 3↑CanIntnl-G1 **108** 5 2¹ 3¹ 5 1¼ 1hd 1¾ Dwyer M L119 b 5.40 62– 30 Phoenix Reach119¾ Macaw126hd Brian Boru119¹ Stalk rail,rally 2-pth 10
13Sep03♦Doncaster (GB) gd 1 13/16 Ⓣ LH 3:04³ St Leger Stakes (1-3/4m,132y)-G1 Stk 641000 3 2¾ Holland D 126 8.00 Brian Boru1261¼ High Accolade1261½ Phoenix Reach126² 12
Timeform rating: 120+ *Tracked leaders,lacked room over 2f out,stayed on*
29Jly03♦Goodwood (GB) gd 1½ Ⓣ RH 2:36² Gordon Stakes-G3 Stk 89300 1no Holland D 122 12.00 Phoenix Reach122no High Accolade127½ Hawk Flyer122½ 10
Timeform rating: 117 *Bumped midpack after 3f,led 2f out,headed 1f out,came again,gamel*
3Jly03♦Newbury (GB) gd 1½ Ⓣ LH 2:35 Stan James Maiden Stakes Maiden 15300 1 1¼ Dwyer M 126 6.50 *Phoenix Reach*1261¼ Arresting126² Fame126¾ 14
Timeform rating: 90+ *Trailed,4th 2f out,no room,bumped 1f out,angld rigth,led 100y out*

Pie N Burger

Own: Kagele Brothers Inc. and Bailey, Jame

Ch. g. 6 (Apr) KEESEP99 $45,000
Sire: Twining (Forty Niner) $10,000
Dam: Abarca (Topsider)
Br: Helen C. Alexander (Ky)
Tr: Norman Cole(0 0 0 0 .00) 2003:(1086 290 .27)

Life	33	11	7	2	$682,933	114	D.Fst	30	11	7	2	$677,918	114
2003	7	5	0	0	$373,800	107	Wet(404)	1	0	0	0	$680	57
2002	10	3	2	0	$147,200	114	Turf(249)	2	0	0	0	$4,335	84
	0	0	0	0	$0	–	Dst(0)	0	0	0	0	$0	–

25Oct03–11SA fst 1 1/16 :22³ :46 1:09⁴ 1:42 3↑SeabscuitH150k **106** 5 2¹ 2½ 2½ 1¹ 1¹ Valenzuela P A LB119 b 7.90 94– 07 Pie N Burger119¹ Chinkapin117¾ Redattore123³ Bid,led 1/4,gamely 11
21Sep03–8LaD yl 1 1/16 Ⓣ :24 :48¹ 1:12² 1:44¹ 3↑LaDH100k **71** 8 2½ 2¹ 2² 8¹³ 9¹⁷ Theriot H J II L123 b 4.40 70– 18 Wrleigh1158¼ OneEyedJoker115½ ChuffeAuRouge118no Chased, gave way 11
16Aug03–8EvD fst 1 :22⁴ :46¹ 1:10⁴ 1:37² 3↑EvdMileH75k **107** 5 2² 2¹ 2hd 1¹ 1 6½ Theriot H J II L121 b *.90 96– 19 PieNBurger1216½ Compendium120nk WlkinthSnow1203¼ Drew out, driving 5
13Jly03–9LS fst 1 :23³ :45⁴ 1:09² 1:35³ 3↑BJohnsnMem60k **107** 2 2¹ 2½ 2hd 1 2½ 1 5½ Theriot H J II L120 b *.60 95– 05 PNBurgr1205½ AgrvtngGnrl1203½ Compndm118½ Drw away,much the best 6
26May03–8LS fst 1 1/16 :22⁴ :46 1:10¹ 1:42 3↑LSParkH-G3 **107** 5 2hd 1hd 1¹ 1² 1 2¾ Theriot H J II L117 b 6.50 92– 08 PNBrgr1172¾ DH MysvllSlw114 DH Blsthstndrd1201½ Edged clear,held well 8
9May03–7LS fst 1 1/16 :23² :46¹ 1:10 1:41³ 4↑Alw 38000N2Y **103** 1 1hd 2hd 1½ 1³ 1³ Theriot H J II L118 b *1.70 94– 18 PieNBurger118³ L.ASpiderLegs119¾ BigNumbers119½ Dueled, kicked clear 6
Previously trained by Machowsky Michael
1Mar03–8GG fst 1 :22³ :45 1:09 1:34⁴ 3↑SanCarlosH61k **86** 10 5 2¾ 5 4½ 4⁴ 7¹⁰ 8 10¾ Puglisi I LB117 b 7.00 85– 10 Halo Cat1161¼ Fleetstreet Dancer116¹ I'madrifter116³ Stlkd wide, empty 10

Pink Champagne
Own: Starview Stable

Dk. b or b. f. 3 (Mar) OBSFEB03 $100,000
Sire: Awesome Again (Deputy Minister) $50,000
Dam: Turkappeal (Turkoman)
Br: FarFellow Farms, Ltd. (Ky)
Tr: Kimmel John C(0 0 0 0 .00) 2003:(317 45 .14)

Life	3	2	0	0	$138,000	77	D.Fst	0 0 0 0	$0 –
2004	1	0	0	0	$6,000	76	Wet(378)	0 0 0 0	$0 –
2003	2	2	0	0	$132,000	77	Turf(195)	3 2 0 0	$138,000 77
	0	0	0	0	$0	–	Dst(0)	0 0 0 0	$0 –

1Jan04–6Crc fm $1\frac{1}{16}$ Ⓣ:24 :48^{4} 1:12^{1}1:42 + ⒻTrpOaks100k **76** 11 7$2\frac{3}{4}$ 5$3\frac{1}{2}$ 5$3\frac{1}{2}$ 42 4$1\frac{3}{4}$ Bravo J L118 4.70 87– 08 Bobbie Use114^{nk} Cold Wynnter116$1\frac{1}{2}$ Last Waltz116^{hd} Bid 3p,finished well 12
6Sep03–8WO fm 1 Ⓣ:21^{3} :44^{1} 1:09^{4}1:36^{2} ⒻNatalma-G3 **75** 9 6$5\frac{1}{4}$ 66 6$1\frac{1}{2}$ 11 1^{hd} Dos Ramos R A L114 2.60 81– 12 PinkChampgne114^{hd} Sree117$2\frac{1}{2}$ AmericAmeric121^{1} Advance inside,all out 10
17Jly03–4Bel fm 6f Ⓣ:22 :45^{1} :57^{3}1:10 ⒻMd Sp Wt 43k **77** 5 12 56 4$3\frac{1}{2}$ 2$\frac{1}{2}$ 12 Prado E S 118 6.50 93– 07 *PinkChmpgne*118^{2} ErnedRun115^{nk} ErthqukRid118$1\frac{1}{2}$ Off slowly, clear late 12

Pioneer Boy
Own: Gill Michael J

B. g. 6 (Mar) KEESEP99 $6,500
Sire: Pioneering (Mr. Prospector) $5,000
Dam: Jovial Wings (Northern Jove)
Br: Ruth C. Brightbill (Tex)
Tr: Robb John J(0 0 0 0 .00) 2003:(430 72 .17)

Life	30	9	3	3	$295,465	107	D.Fst	23 5 3 2	$167,545 107
2003	11	5	2	2	$189,340	107	Wet(383)	6 4 0 1	$127,920 105
2002	8	1	1	1	$19,893	88	Turf(275)	1 0 0 0	$0 49
	0	0	0	0	$0	–	Dst(0)	0 0 0 0	$0 –

9Aug03–8Lrl fst 6f :22 :44^{3} :57 1:09^{3} 3↑DavsFriend50k – 1 3 2^{2} 4^{5} - - Wilson R L124 1.60 - 16 *CrossingPoint*121$\frac{3}{4}$ TkeAchnceOnMe119^{3} DerRun119^{4} Pulled up in distress 6
19Jly03–7Cby fst $6\frac{1}{2}$f :21^{3} :43^{2} 1:08^{2}1:15^{2} 3↑[R]CCRpdTrnst96k **102** 10 2 21 2^{hd} 13 1$2\frac{1}{2}$ Wilson R LB124 2.40 101– 09 Pioneer Boy124$2\frac{1}{2}$ Debonair Joe124$4\frac{1}{4}$ *Bensalem*124^{2} Forged clear, driving 10
22Jun03–9Mth gd 6f :22 :44^{4} :57 1:09^{3} 3↑Longfellow60k **94** 5 1 1$\frac{1}{2}$ 11 11 3$2\frac{1}{4}$ Rose J L119 1.40 89– 17 *It's a Monster*119$1\frac{1}{4}$ Fetch Dinner115^{1} *PioneerBoy*119$3\frac{1}{4}$ Set pace, weakened 5
7Jun03–7Bel sly 6f :21^{2} :44 :56^{1}1:09^{2} 3↑TrNthBCH-G2 **81** 3 2 3^{3} 3^{3} 57 6$10\frac{1}{4}$ Wilson R L115 3.35e 82– 10 *ShkYouDown*118^{nk} HghwyProspctor115$4\frac{1}{2}$ Vodk114$\frac{3}{4}$ Chased outside, tired 6
17May03–4Pim my 6f :23^{3} :46^{1} :57^{4}1:10^{1} 3↑MdBCH-G3 **105** 4 6 1^{hd} 1$2\frac{1}{2}$ 14 1$1\frac{1}{2}$ Rose J L113 *.70e 94– 11 PonrBoy113$1\frac{1}{2}$ SssyHnd113$1\frac{1}{2}$ [DH]TstyCbrngh114 Rushed,pace 2wd,drivng 7
12Apr03–8Pim fst 6f :23^{2} :46 :57^{3}1:09^{3} 3↑FirePlug67k **107** 2 3 1$1\frac{1}{2}$ 11 1$\frac{1}{2}$ 2^{nk} Rose J L117 5.80 97– 14 Love Happy117^{nk} *PioneerBoy*117$4\frac{1}{2}$ SassyHound117^{7} Rail,dueled late,game 5
13Mar03–8Lrl fst 6f :22^{4} :45^{3} :57^{1}1:09^{2} 4↑OClm 30000(30–25)N **102** 5 1 1$1\frac{1}{2}$ 1$1\frac{1}{2}$ 12 1$2\frac{3}{4}$ Rose J L119 2.30 92– 20 PioneerBoy119$2\frac{3}{4}$ Clends117$5\frac{1}{2}$ PresidentButlr112$8\frac{3}{4}$ Pace,3wd 3/16,driving 5
22Feb03–6Lrl sly 6f :23 :45^{4} :57^{2}1:09^{3} 4↑OClm 20000(20–18)N **102** 3 1 1^{hd} 11 1$3\frac{1}{2}$ 1$5\frac{1}{2}$ Rose J L122 *2.30 91– 14 *PionrBoy*122$5\frac{1}{2}$ StndingRoomOnly117$2\frac{1}{2}$ *Tobis*122$2\frac{1}{4}$ 2wd,kicked away,drvng 7
9Feb03–8Lrl fst $5\frac{1}{2}$f :22^{3} :45^{3} :57^{3}1:03^{4} 4↑OClm c-(30–25) **88** 1 2 2^{hd} 1^{hd} 2$\frac{1}{2}$ 3$\frac{3}{4}$ Rose J L119 4.60 92– 15 Kendrick117^{nk} Firstround Ko119$\frac{1}{2}$ *Pioneer Boy*119^{2} Rail, weakened 7
Claimed from Fitzgerald Shelley E. for $30,000, Wilcox Warren Trainer 2003(as of 2/9): (143 17 9 17 0.12)
23Jan03–7Lrl fst 6f :22^{2} :46 :58^{1}1:10^{4} 4↑OClm 20000(20–18)N **85** 1 5 1^{hd} 1$\frac{1}{2}$ 1$1\frac{1}{2}$ 2$\frac{3}{4}$ Rose J L122 3.50 84– 18 Trentino117$\frac{3}{4}$ Pioneer Boy122$\frac{3}{4}$ My Lord117^{3} Rail, grudgingly 14
1Jan03–5Lrl sly 6f :23^{4} :47^{1} :59^{1}1:11^{1} 4↑Alw 26000N1x **89** 4 2 11 2^{hd} 1$3\frac{1}{2}$ 1$3\frac{1}{2}$ Rose J L117 3.60 83– 22 Pioneer Boy117$3\frac{1}{2}$ Fifty East117$\frac{3}{4}$ Govans117$2\frac{1}{4}$ Dueled, driving 7

Pleasantly Perfect
Own: Diamond A Racing Corporation

B. h. 6 (Apr) KEESEP99 $725,000
Sire: Pleasant Colony (His Majesty)
Dam: Regal State (Affirmed)
Br: Clovelly Farms (Ky)
Tr: Mandella Richard E(0 0 0 0 .00) 2003:(253 51 .20)

Life	13	6	2	1	$2,949,880	119	D.Fst	11	6	2	1	$2,947,000	119
2003	4	2	0	1	$2,470,000	119	Wet(376)	0	0	0	0	$0	–
2002	8	4	2	0	$479,880	116	Turf(321)	2	0	0	0	$2,880	76
	0	0	0	0	$0	–	Dst(0)	0	0	0	0	$0	–

25Oct03–9SA fst 1¼ :461 1:101 1:341 1:594 3↑BCClasic-G1 119 2 86¼ 77¼ 55 31½ 11½ Solis A LB126 b 14.20 106–07 PlesntlyPerfect1261½ MedglidOro126¾ Dynever121nk Swung wide, up late 10
4Oct03–5SA fst 1⅛ :482 1:114 1:36 1:481 3↑GdwdBCH-G2 105 2 63¼ 63¼ 41¼ 31½ 1½ Solis A LB116 b *1.40 93–13 *PlesntlyPerfect*116½ FleetstrtDncr1131¼ StrCross1103 Bit tight 3/4,4wd bid 8
1Mar03–9SA fst 1¼ :463 1:111 1:352 1:594 4↑SAH-G1 107 3 63½ 65 53½ 43½ 46 Solis A LB116 b 3.70 100–05 *Milwaukee Brew*119hd *Congaree*1244½ Kudos1171½ No late bid outside 6
2Feb03–8SA fst 1⅛ :462 1:101 1:35 1:473 4↑SnAntnoH-G2 113 6 52 53½ 42 32½ 33¼ Solis A LB117 b 3.10 93–18 Congree1232¼ *MilwukeeBrew*1201 PlesntlyPrfct1175 3wd into str,best rest 6

Pocus Hocus
Own: Moore Susan and John

Gr/ro. m. 6 (Feb)
Sire: Quiet American (Fappiano) $35,000
Dam: Cadabra Abra (Al Hattab)
Br: David Allen (Ky)
Tr: Jerkens James A(0 0 0 0 .00) 2003:(194 46 .24)

Life	23	5	5	3	$287,250	101	D.Fst	18	3	5	3	$230,610	101
2003	11	2	4	3	$176,802	101	Wet(359)	2	2	0	0	$51,600	86
2002	4	2	1	0	$78,978	95	Turf(259)	3	0	0	0	$5,040	74
	0	0	0	0	$0	–	Dst(0)	0	0	0	0	$0	–

28Nov03–9Aqu fst 1 :231 :462 1:103 1:362 3↑ⒻTopFlgtH-G2 92 5 88¾ 87¼ 66 59 35¼ Luzzi M J L116 b 7.30 78–29 Randaroo1162 BeautyHlo1153¼ PocusHocus116nk Bumped, steadied start 12
1Nov03–9Aqu fst 1⅛ :49 1:133 1:38 1:503 3↑ⒻTnbkAlmH-G3 101 4 2½ 2½ 1hd 16 15¼ Santos J A L114 b 12.10 83–19 PocusHocus1145¼ NonsuchBy1151½ MissLnd1181 Drew away when roused 6
11Oct03–7Med fst 1 1/16 :241 :48 1:114 1:431 3↑ⒻLongLook50k 83 1 11 1½ 1½ 1hd 2½ Chavez J F L116 b *1.40 91–13 Drexel Monorail113½ *Pocus Hocus*1161¾ *Artist Johanna*1133¼ Inside, gamely 6
19Sep03–8Bel fst 1 1/16 :233 :472 1:12 1:43 3↑ⒻAlw 52000N3x 92 3 11 11½ 12½ 12½ 12½ Santos J A L119 b 2.50 85–14 PocusHocus1192½ CllnAudible119nk LdyLiberty1194¾ Bobbled start, clear 6
21Aug03–3Sar fst 1⅛ :472 1:112 1:362 1:50 4↑ⒻAlw 56260c 80 3 2½ 1½ 1½ 21½ 24¼ Santos J A L116 b 2.65 81–13 ShesGottheBet1134¼ *PocusHocus*1162½ ForestSecrts120½ Pace, held place 4
30Jly03–8Sar fst 1⅛ :471 1:111 1:371 1:504 3↑ⒻAlw 52000N3x 84 1 1½ 1hd 21½ 36 33¼ Day P L120 b 5.40 78–19 *PassingShot*124¾ GoldenSont1202½ PocusHocus120½ Stayed on well on rail 5
9Jly03–8Bel fst 1 1/16 :224 :46 1:11 1:441 3↑ⒻAlw 50000N3x 67 4 31½ 2½ 1hd 36½ 315½ Santos J A L120 b 2.90 63–21 Arabis1202 Kitty Knight11513½ Pocus Hocus1206½ Stumbled start 5
8Jun03–9Mth fst 1 1/16 :231 :464 1:111 1:432 3↑ⒻMthBeach60k 68 5 54 2½ 11½ 33 613 Lopez C C L113 b 2.50 81–13 TonightsWger1134½ *Anntog*1141½ DncetheSlw1191½ Hesitated slightly brk 9
19Feb03–8Aqu fst 1⅛ ⊡ :481 1:122 1:38 1:51 3↑ⒻRareTreatH77k 79 3 11½ 11 1½ 21½ 26½ Castellano J J L114 b *.75 75–14 EllisMomnt1166½ PocusHocus1142¾ WshfulSplndor1131¾ Pace, held place 4
31Jan03–8Aqu fst 1 1/16 ⊡ :234 :482 1:131 1:441 4↑ⒻⓇVideogenic60k 95 7 11 1½ 11 11 2nk Migliore R L116 b 2.20 85–23 Indy Glory116nk Pocus Hocus1163 Kiss a Miss120hd Set pace, gamely 8
11Jan03–8Aqu fst 1 1/16 ⊡ :221 :454 1:112 1:442 3↑ⒻAfectnyH-G3 59 2 11½ 12 21 413 520½ Migliore R L114 b 3.45 63–16 Zonk1184 Wishful Splendor112nk Kiss a Miss1137¾ Set pace, tired 7

Point Prince
Own: Team Valor Stables LLC and Barber Gar

Dk. b or b. g. 5 (Mar)
Sire: Youmadeyourpoint (Diamond Prospect) $1,000
Dam: Princess of Note (Notebook)
Br: Stanley M. Ersoff (Fla)
Tr: Romans Dale L(0 0 0 0 .00) 2003:(638 113 .18)

Life	12	4	1	2	$148,080	101	D.Fst	2	2	0	0	$21,700	78
2003	5	1	0	1	$94,500	101	Wet(373)	1	0	0	1	$3,400	80
2002	6	2	1	1	$47,580	93	Turf(249)	9	2	1	1	$122,980	101
	0	0	0	0	$0	–	Dst(0)	0	0	0	0	$0	–

25Oct03–3Kee fm 1⅛ Ⓣ :481 1:123 1:38 1:494 3↑Alw 53900N3x 71 3 54½ 52¼ 88¾ 79 610¼ McKee J L119 6.30 78–12 Stydahar119nk Brent's Victory1193¾ Valiant King1193¼ 3-4w,weakened 8
23Aug03–5Sar fm 1 1/16 Ⓣ :231 :462 1:10 1:40 3↑Alw 52000N3x 77 2 47 55¼ 86½ 912 1010¾ Gryder A T L119 40.00 84–03 HesCrafty1233¾ ThefullCircle1192 Epicentre1192 Stumbled start, bumped 12
2Jly03–6CD fm 1 1/16 Ⓣ :244 :492 1:14 1:434 3↑OClm 62500N 82 5 2hd 31 41¾ 32½ 35½ Velasquez C L118 7.90 79–11 FostersLnding118nk DellFrncesc1185¼ PointPrinc118no Dueled,weakened 6
24May03–7CD fm 1⅛ Ⓣ :464 1:103 1:35 1:473 3↑OClm 62500N 38 6 64¼ 68 610 727 726¾ Velasquez C L117 3.30 69–07 *Sharbayan*119no FostersLanding112nk CaptainNichols1192¼ Faded,far turn 7
4Jan03–10GP gd 1 Ⓣ :232 :472 1:121 1:374 3↑AppletnH-G2 101 9 56½ 45 42½ 1hd 11¼ Cruz M R L115 29.30 77–29 Point Prince1151¼ Krieger115nk Red Sea1141¾ Inside move turn 9

Political Attack

Own: Erdenheim Farm

B. g. 5 (Mar)
Sire: Hawk Attack (Silver Hawk) $4,000
Dam: Cope's Light (Copelan)
Br: Brereton C. Jones (Ky)
Tr: Matz Michael R(0 0 0 0 .00) 2003:(187 25 .13)

Life	21	7	1	3	$441,154	103
2003	7	3	0	1	$202,688	103
2002	8	1	1	2	$117,800	96
	0	0	0	0	$0	–

D.Fst	2	1	0	1	$80,000	96
Wet(342)	3	0	0	0	$12,300	91
Turf(268)	16	6	1	2	$348,854	103
Dst(0)	0	0	0	0	$0	–

6Dec03-11Crc	fm	1⅛	Ⓣ :451 1:09 1:34 1:454	3↑ TropTrfH-G3	103	8	44	35½	32	1hd	11½	Douglas R R	L116 b	6.80	102 -	PoliticlAttck116 1½ MillnniumDrgon116no Sforz115nk	Edged away, driving	12
18Oct03-8Del	yl	1 1/16	Ⓣ :231 :474 1:122 1:444	3↑ SussexH100k	99	4	2hd	21	2½	1hd	1¾	Dominguez R A	L117 b	*1.10	82- 18	*Political Attack*117¾ Estio113 3 Stanzaic114 2¼	Bid 3/4, driving	7
13Sep03-7Bel	fm	1⅛	🅃 :483 1:113 1:352 1:472	3↑ BelBCH-G2	93	6	43	44	44	54½	54	Guidry M	L114 b	10.20	89- 07	Della Francesca114 1½ Rouvres116nk Volponi119½	Steadied after start	7
23Aug03-9Sar	fm	1 1/16	Ⓣ :224 :46 1:093 1:391	3↑ 4strdavH-G2	100	9	31½	2hd	2½	32	44¼	Guidry M	L115 b	41.25	95- 03	Trademark118 2 Quest Star116 1¼ Tap the Admiral115 1	Pressed pace, tired	11
11Apr03-8Kee	fm	1	Ⓣ :233 :463 1:112 1:354	4↑ MakrsMrk-G2	81	4	89	810	99¼	912	810½	Guidry M	L116 b	8.90	78- 13	RoylSpy118 1¼ MsqsApprovl118 1¾ TchfthBls117 1½	Stumbled,bmp foe start	9
9Mar03-9GP	fm	1 1/16	Ⓣ :234 :474 1:11 1:402	+ 3↑ CanTurfH-G3	102	4	21	22	2hd	11	1½	Guidry M	L114 b	9.20	93- 10	PoliticlAttck114½ MiesquesApprovl116 1 StrtgicPrtnr114 2	Fully extended	7
24Jan03-9GP	fm	*1	Ⓣ :231 :473 1:123 1:37	4↑ OClm 100000N	96	7	31	3nk	3nk	2hd	31¾	Guidry M	L118 b	6.00	86- 16	Boastful118½ Sardaukar118 1¼ *Political Attack*118¾	3 wide, vied, weakened	10

Posse

Own: Heiligbrodt Racing Stable and Vinery

B. c. 4 (Feb) KEESEP01 $115,000
Sire: Silver Deputy (Deputy Minister) $40,000
Dam: Raska (Rahy)
Br: Robert E. Low & Lawana L Low (Ky)
Tr: Asmussen Steven M(0 0 0 0 .00) 2003:(1949 452 .23)

Life	18	7	2	2	$662,841	111
2003	11	5	1	1	$478,426	111
2002	7	2	1	1	$184,415	86
	0	0	0	0	$0	–

D.Fst	14	3	2	2	$406,548	108
Wet(372)	4	4	0	0	$256,293	111
Turf(290)	0	0	0	0	$0	–
Dst(0)	0	0	0	0	$0	–

26Dec03-8SA	fst	7f	:222 :45 1:091 1:223	Malibu-G1	94	9	3	117¾	107¼	65½	75¼	Lanerie C J	LB119	6.80	88- 12	SouthernImage115hd MarinoMrini115 1 MidsEyes119 3	Bit tight 5/16,no bid	12
27Nov03-9FG	sly	6f	:22 :452 :571 1:092	3↑ ThanksgivH60k	108	1	5	65½	66½	31½	11½	Lanerie C J	L120	*.40	93- 17	Posse120 1½ Aloha Bold117 2½ Price of Honour118 10	Between, big finish	6
25Oct03-5SA	fst	6f	:21 :431 :55 1:074	3↑ BCSprint-G1	107	3	10	116½	96¼	87½	44¾	Day P	LB123	23.50	94- 05	CjunBet123 2¼ Bluesthstndrd126 2 ShkYouDown126½	Steadied 1/2 pl, wide	13
27Sep03-7Bel	fst	6½f	:214 :441 1:083 1:143	3↑ Vosburgh-G1	97	5	4	55½	55	61	37¾	Bailey J D	L123	4.70	92- 16	Ghostzapper123 6½ Aggadan126 1¼ Posse123 1¾	Traffic, alter course	10
23Aug03-10Sar	fst	7f	:213 :433 1:083 1:22	KngsBshp-G1	99	3	10	1214	1113	75½	53½	Lanerie C J	L123	6.90	93- 07	Valid Video121nk Great Notion117nk *Ghostzapper*117 1¾	Rallied thru traffic	13
2Aug03-8Sar	fst	6f	:22 :443 :562 1:083	Amstrdam-G2	96	2	3	75¼	63¼	44	46	Lanerie C J	L123	*1.05	93- 07	Zavata119 5¼ Great Notion121½ Trust N Luck123nk	Came wide, no rally	7
7Jun03-9Bel	sly	7f	:221 :443 1:084 1:22	RvaRdgBC-G2	111	5	6	710	79½	21½	1no	Lanerie C J	L123	3.15	90- 10	Posse123no Midas Eyes123 6¼ Halo Homewrecker123hd	Resolute outside	8
10May03-9CD	sly	6f	:21 :434 :561 1:092	MattWinn111k	110	4	4	65¼	47½	33½	1½	Lanerie C J	L120	*1.20	91- 15	*Posse*120½ *Bossanova*114 1¼ *Coach Jimi Lee*120 5	5w lane,stiff drive	9
6Apr03-8Kee	fst	7f	:213 :442 1:094 1:23	Lafayett-G3	108	2	5	55	44	2hd	12¼	Lanerie C J	L118	*2.00	89- 16	*Posse*118 2¼ Roll Hennessy Roll118 2¼ Bossanova116 2¼	4w,hand urging	6
15Mar03-11GP	fst	7f	:214 :441 1:082 1:21	Swale-G3	89	3	1	51½	43	36½	29¼	Meche D J	L120	3.30	94- 05	*Midas Eyes*116 9¼ *Posse*120 4½ Whywhywhy122 2¼	Angled out, 2nd best	8
10Feb03-7FG	fst	5f	:224 :454 :571	Alw 32000N2x	101	2	2	33½	32	11	16¾	Lanerie C J	L118	*.50	103- 14	Posse118 6¾ Down Play118 4¾ Cashmere Miss115 1	New track record	5

Predawn Raid
Own: Mount Joy Stables Inc

Gr/ro. g. 5 (Apr)
Sire: Sir Cat (Storm Cat) $5,000
Dam: Dawn's Flame (Grey Dawn II)
Br: Mt. Joy Stables Inc (Ky)
Tr: Stutts B F Jr(0 0 0 0 .00) 2003:(44 10 .23)

Life	12	3	2	1	$100,040	102	D.Fst	10	3	2	1	$99,590 102
2003	6	2	1	1	$83,250	102	Wet(373)	0	0	0	0	$0 –
2002	4	1	1	0	$16,790	95	Turf(275)	2	0	0	0	$450 73
	0	0	0	0	$0	–	Dst(0)	0	0	0	0	$0 –

27Dec03-12Crc fst 1⅛ :491 1:144 1:394 1:522 3↑FHooperH-G3 **102** 2 11½ 11½ 11½ 12 14¼ Chavez J F L112 b 15.40 90-22 PredwnRid1124¼ BestoftheRest1222 DlitfulGuy1122¼ Moderate hand ride 9
28Nov03-8Crc fm 1 Ⓣ :224 :454 1:10 1:344 3↑Alw 22000N3L **55** 5 21 2hd 21 78½ 815¾ Coa E M L122 b 5.50 78-11 Schneidr119nk CrtifiblyCrzy1162 TouringEnglnd1193¼ Prompted, faltered 10
3Nov03-8Crc fst 1₁₆ :25 :494 1:141 1:454 3↑OClm 16000(16-14)N **94** 1 11½ 11½ 11 12½ 16½ Coa E M L119 b *1.00 83-24 Predawn Raid1196½ Alegorico1223¾ El Graduado1196½ Strong hand ride 9
6Oct03-2Crc fm 1₁₆ Ⓣ :24 :494 1:132 1:44 3↑OClm 16000(16-14)N **73** 9 53¾ 52½ 41 53¼ 77¼ Cruz M R L119 b 4.10 73-20 Weedle1142¾ Ye of Little Faith1141 Sugarsway1151½ Rank, steadied start 10
3Mar03-8GP fst 1⅛ :47 1:11 1:361 1:494 4↑Alw 36000N1X **78** 9 32½ 32½ 22 23 34 Coa E M L122 b *1.40 89-13 Fiery Sweep1183¼ Runway118¾ Predawn Raid1221¼ Off rail, weakened 9
13Feb03-8GP fst 1₁₆ :231 :464 1:121 1:45 4↑Alw 36000N1X **89** 3 52¼ 41½ 31 21 2nk Coa E M L122 b *2.00 84-22 Monrchoftheglen118nk PredwnRid1221½ Coincide1226¾ Steadied 1st turn 10

Presidentialaffair
Own: Ciresa Edward and Papapandrea, Vincen

B. g. 5 (Apr) EASOCT00 $25,000
Sire: Not For Love (Mr. Prospector) $15,000
Dam: Quite Amazing (Bear Hunt)
Br: Will Run Farm (Pa)
Tr: Ciresa Martin E(0 0 0 0 .00) 2003:(119 22 .18)

Life	13	6	2	1	$210,930	106	D.Fst	11	5	2	1	$186,330 106
2003	9	5	1	1	$188,140	106	Wet(403)	2	1	0	0	$24,600 101
2002	4	1	1	0	$22,790	72	Turf(245)	0	0	0	0	$0 –
	0	0	0	0	$0	–	Dst(0)	0	0	0	0	$0 –

21Dec03-8Aqu fst 6f ⊡ :223 :451 :57 1:092 3↑GravesdH-G3 **86** 2 7 77½ 76¼ 76¾ 79¼ Gryder A T L116 14.00 88-12 ShkeYouDown1242¼ WytotheTop1141¾ GtorsNBrs115¾ Off slowly, outrun 7
11Nov03-8Aqu fst 1⅛ :482 1:12 1:371 1:504 3↑StuyvntH-G3 **106** 4 11½ 1½ 1½ 13½ 1nk Migliore R L115 7.00 82-26 Presidentialaffair115nk *Thunder Blitz*114½ Gander1154 Pace, clear, held on 8
11Oct03-11Lrl fst 1³₁₆ :473 1:12 1:362 1:544 3↑ⓇMdMilClasc190k **105** 9 12 13½ 12 1hd 2no Trujillo E L119 3.20 98-07 Docent123no *Presidentialaffair*1191 Jorgie Stover1192¾ Yielded grudgingly 9
19Sep03-3Mth fst 170 :222 :453 1:092 1:392 3↑OClm 35000(35-30)N **106** 2 12½ 12 12 12 14½ Trujillo E L123 *1.10 106-15 Presidentialffir1234½ GllntSir1187 NtiveTwoStepper11836 Off rail, driving 4
Previously trained by Lynch Cathal
1Sep03-8Mth sly 6f :22 :442 :562 1:084 3↑Alw 39000N2X **101** 7 1 31 11 13 15 Trujillo E L120 2.20 95-10 *Presidentialaffair*1205 Amjad118no HognsSpirit1152¼ Aggressive hand ride 8
6Aug03-8Mth fst 6f :213 :44 :562 1:09 3↑Alw 37000N1X **101** 2 6 42 32 1hd 14½ Trujillo E L118 5.40 94-17 *Presidntilffir*1184½ CourtingConcord1141¼ Lttrs1165½ Duel,drew away 1/16 8
13Jly03-5Mth fst 6f :213 :442 :57 1:10 3↑Alw 37000N1X **82** 8 1 2hd 2hd 2½ 3nk Trujillo E L118 fb 8.10 89-14 Blackberry Springs116hd Cozy Man118nk *Presidentialaffair*1181½ Held well 8
28Jun03-5Mth fst 6f :214 :45 :573 1:111 3↑Clm c-(20-18)N2L **82** 3 6 2hd 12 16 16 Ferrer J C L119 fb 4.80 83-17 Presidentialffir1196 MicMc1171½ MisterRiley1132 Saved ground,clear,drv 10
Claimed from De Saye Michael for $20,000, Ramos Faustino F Trainer 2003(as of 6/28): (168 23 21 18 0.14)
10Jun03-9Pha fst 6f :213 :444 :572 1:11 3↑Alw 21600N1X **66** 1 6 4¾ 52 76½ 84½ Thompson W A L117 fb 5.30 79-18 FthrMrk117nk TwoRisLmt1171 DputyDnnyBoy112nk Well placed,rail,tired 11

Private Chef
Own: Moss Mr. and Mrs. Jerome S

B. g. 4 (Feb) FTKJUL01 $50,000
Sire: Partner's Hero (Danzig) $5,000
Dam: Mississippi Lights (Majestic Light)
Br: Candyland Farm (Md)
Tr: Shirreffs John A(0 0 0 0 .00) 2003:(163 33 .20)

Life	3	2	0	0	$99,633	94	D.Fst	0	0	0	0	$0 –
2003	3	2	0	0	$99,633	94	Wet(335)	1	1	0	0	$19,200 89
2002	0	M	0	0	$0	–	Turf(286)	2	1	0	0	$80,433 94
	0	0	0	0	$0	–	Dst(0)	0	0	0	0	$0 –

29Jun03-8Hol fm 1⅛ Ⓣ :462 1:10 1:35 1:472 + CinmaBCH-G3 **87** 5 63¾ 64¼ 63¼ 64½ 45¾ Espinoza V LB117 b *1.20 86-08 JustWonder117¾ *BisRepetits*1154 SlwCityCitdl1151 Shuffld 5/16,boxed 1/8 8
25May03-8Hol fm 1 Ⓣ :241 :482 1:121 1:352 WilRogrs-G3 **94** 6 66 65¼ 54 33 1¾ Espinoza V LB115 b 6.00 87-13 Private Chef115¾ *Banshee King*1151¼ Singletary1173 3wd 2nd turn,rallied 6
16Feb03-2SA gd 6f :212 :442 :571 1:101 Md Sp Wt 48k **89** 6 7 713 79 73½ 13½ ↓Krone J A LB120 b 10.30 87-13 SpecialRate1203½ *PrivateChef*1203½ *ParkersWyWest*1202 Swung out,surged 7

Private Horde

Own: Tucker Billy R

B. h. 5 (Apr)
Sire: Brunswick (Private Account) $3,000
Dam: Manila Rose (Manila)
Br: Billy Tucker (Ky)
Tr: Cain S. J(0 0 0 0 .00) 2003:(214 45 .21)

Life	24	9	4	0	$487,827	117	D.Fst	14	4	3	0	$249,612	103
2003	9	6	2	0	$411,582	117	Wet(301)	8	5	1	0	$237,430	117
2002	9	1	2	0	$49,905	96	Turf(182)	2	0	0	0	$785	50
	0	0	0	0	$0	–	Dst(0)	0	0	0	0	$0	–

25Oct03-5SA	fst	6f	:21 :431 :55 1:074	3↑BCSprint-G1	90	9	11	127½	139	1213	911¼	Lumpkins J	LB126 fb	29.20	88-05	CjunBet1232¼ Bluesthestndrd1262 ShkYouDown126½	Shuffled back 1/2pl	13
20Sep03-13TP	fst	6½f	:223 :451 1:093 1:16	3↑Marfa75k	103	4	5	31½	2hd	1½	11	Thompson T J	L122 fb	*.60	97-15	Private Horde1221 Deer Lake1183¾ Paging1202½	5 wide move, driving	9
10Aug03-9Sar	sly	6f	:22 :443 :563 1:09	3↑AGVndbtH-G2	117	5	4	32½	32	2hd	15	Lumpkins J	L115 fb	10.00	97-10	*PrivteHorde*1155 MountinGenerl118hd MiksClssic114nk	3 wide move, clear	5
12Jly03-12Crc	fst	6f	:211 :434 :562 1:10	3↑SmlSprtH-G3	100	11	11	98¼	78¼	47½	28¼	Lumpkins J	L113 fb	24.80	86-11	ShkYouDown1198¼ *PrivtHord*113¾ MyCousnMtt116½	4 wide turn, up for 2d	13
21Jun03-8PrM	fst	6f	:22 :443 1:083	3↑IowaSprntH125k	99	1	4	1hd	2hd	11½	2hd	Lumpkins J	LB119 fb	3.10	98-12	Chindi114hd Private Horde119½ Sand Ridge1174½	Dueled, clear, nailed	7
17May03-9Mnr	my	6f	:214 :442 :562 1:09	3↑WtrfrdPrkH76k	100	3	5	41¼	3½	1½	12	Lumpkins J	LB119 fb	*1.10	94-10	PrivtHord1192 *FrnkiRsWnnr*114½ CrossngPont1211¾	Behind duel,bid 3wide	6
3May03-4CD	fst	6f	:204 :442 :563 1:092	3↑Alw 58255N$Y	101	7	4	44½	3½	12½	1nk	•Lumpkins J	L120 fb	3.60	91-08	DH TrionGeorgi116 DH *PrivteHorde*120nk Chindi1165	Swerved in lane,lasted	9
25Jan03-10TP	fst	6½f	:222 :45 1:094 1:162	4↑Forego50k	99	5	5	21	2hd	15	12	Lumpkins J	L117 b	3.80	95-17	*Private Horde*1172 Still Be Smokin'117½ Gallatin Kid115no	Kept to task	9
5Jan03-9TP	my	6f	:222 :453 :573 1:10	4↑Alw 26370N$Y	107	5	3	1hd	1½	12½	15¼	Lumpkins J	L116 b	2.50	92-23	*Private Horde*1165¼ *Are You Down*1163¾ *Storm'n J R*1161	3 path, driving	5

Puerto Banus

Own: Taub Steve, Papiano, Neil and Mulhall

Ch. h. 5 (Feb) FTFFEB01 $345,000
Sire: Supremo (Gone West) $2,500
Dam: Drina (Regal and Royal)
Br: The Thoroughbred Corporation (Ky)
Tr: Mulhall Kristin(0 0 0 0 .00) 2003:(105 15 .14)

Life	14	4	3	1	$241,410	101	D.Fst	9	2	2	1	$106,010	100
2003	8	3	2	0	$183,560	101	Wet(312)	0	0	0	0	$0	–
2002	6	1	1	1	$57,850	91	Turf(251)	5	2	1	0	$135,400	101
	0	0	0	0	$0	–	Dst(0)	0	0	0	0	$0	–

9Aug03-9Sar	gd	1½	T :49 1:13 2:031 2:28	3↑SwrdDncH-G1	101	2	108¼	96¾	83¾	42	63¼	Espinoza V	L115 b	18.20	77-20	Whitmore's Conn1151¼ Macaw114nk Slew Valley114¾	Inside trip, no rally	11
20Jly03-7Hol	fm	1½	Ⓣ :483 1:133 2:03 2:264	3↑SunsetH-G2	101	2	612	53¼	31½	31	1½	Espinoza V	LB113 b	11.90	91-13	Puerto Banus113½ Cagney1161½ Continental Red116½	3wd 3rd turn,rallied	8
22Jun03-8Hol	fm	1¼	Ⓣ :50 1:141 1:372 2:003	4↑Alw 62000N$MY	97	4	33	32	21	21	23½	Espinoza V	LB118 b	2.50	85-13	Asong for Billy1163½ *Puerto Banus*118½ DeltaForm1161½	Altered path in 1/8	6
24May03-6Hol	fm	1¼	Ⓣ :504 1:152 1:39 2:02	4↑OClm 80000N	101	1	55½	41½	31½	31	12	Stevens G L	LB118 b	8.30	82-17	PuertoBnus1182 ChrleyBtes120½ TimberCruisr1183	Came out lane,rallied	9
Previously trained by Baffert Bob																		
18Apr03-8SA	fm	1	Ⓣ :231 :461 1:11 1:343	4↑OClm 80000N	92	3	1011	1016	1010	86¾	63¾	Stevens G L	LB120 b	7.40	85-15	*Denied*1181 Marine118nk Meteor Storm1201½	4wd into str,outkicked	11
2Mar03-5SA	fst	1 1/16	:222 :452 1:101 1:431	4↑Alw 59360N1X	97	7	810	89½	63¼	1½	15	Stevens G L	LB118 b	4.90	88-13	PuertoBanus1185 GeorgeBailey120no CoronClssic1222	4wd 2nd turn,clear	10
9Feb03-4SA	fst	1⅛	:464 1:11 1:354 1:48	4↑Alw 58016N1X	95	6	67½	67	53	43	26	Flores D R	LB117 b	*.90e	88-12	Tough Game1176 *Puerto Banus*1172 Mr. Joe C1232	4wd into lane,2nd best	7
20Jan03-7SA	fst	1	:223 :46 1:103 1:354	4↑Alw 56000N1X	100	10	62¼	62¼	3½	41½	42¾	Nakatani C S	LB117 b	2.00e	89-11	Chinois1191 *Tough Game*117¾ George Bailey1191	5wd,4wd,weakened	10

Puzzlement
Own: Shields J V Jr

B. h. 5 (Jan)
Sire: Pine Bluff (Danzig) $10,000
Dam: Taine (Sir Ivor)
Br: J. V. Shields Jr. (Fla)
Tr: Jerkens H. A(0 0 0 0 .00) 2003:(359 73 .20)

Life	20	5	3	5	$627,590	113	D.Fst	13 3 2 5 $497,740 113
2003	11	2	2	3	$470,450	113	Wet(349)	7 2 1 0 $129,850 108
2002	9	3	1	2	$157,140	100	Turf(302)	0 0 0 0 $0 –
	0	0	0	0	$0	–	Dst(0)	0 0 0 0 $0 –

6Sep03–9Bel fst 1⅛	:472 1:111 1:342 1:461	3↑ Woodward-G1	**102**	1	56½	55	55	36½	39	Chavez J F	L126 b	6.90	90– 13	*Mineshaft*1264¼ Hold That Tiger1224¾ Puzzlement12611¼	Rallied for show	5
16Aug03–7Sar fst 1¼	:48 1:114 1:37 2:032	3↑ SarBCH-G2	**113**	2	89¾	66	42½	1hd	13¼	Chavez J F	L113 b	6.90	90– 14	Puzzlement1133¼ Volponi1221¾ Iron Deputy1154¼	Got through on rail	8
2Aug03–9Sar fst 1⅛	:464 1:102 1:344 1:473	3↑ WhitneyH-G1	**110**	1	712	711	77¼	64	42½	Chavez J F	L112 b	21.70	94– 11	Medaglia d'Oro1231 Volponi1201¼ *Evening Attire*118nk	Good finish outside	7
24Jly03–5Sar sly 1⅛	:474 1:113 1:364 1:494	3↑ Alw 52000N3x	**103**	3	56¾	56¼	43½	3nk	12¼	Chavez J F	L120 b	2.35	86– 15	Puzzlement1202¼ Thunder Blitz120¾ Quest1207¾	Drew clear late	5
5Jly03–9Bel fst 1¼	:483 1:123 1:37 2:012	3↑ SuburbnH-G1	**102**	6	58½	56	44½	49½	48½	Chavez J F	L113 b	33.25	78– 13	*Mineshaft*1212¼ Volponi1214 Dollar Bill1152¼	Inside move, tired	8
12Jun03–5Bel gd 1 1/16	:233 :47 1:10 1:404	4↑ Alw 56260c	**102**	3	44	42	48	210	26	Chavez J F	L116 b	1.95	90– 22	Northern Rock1186 Puzzlement1164¾ Sherpa Guide115nk	Rallied on rail	4
16May03–11Pim sly 1 3/16	:463 1:11 1:362 1:56	4↑ PimSpclH-G1	**108**	1	913	916	910	59	56½	Bailey J D	L114 b	12.50	86– 23	Mineshaft1213¾ Western Pride116hd Judge's Case1131¾	Awaited room 3/8	9
26Apr03–8Aqu sly 1	⊗ :231 :46 1:094 1:333	3↑ FtMarcyH-G3	**90**	2	89	76½	55¾	610	411¼	Arroyo N Jr	L118 b	2.60	86– 12	SaintVerre1178½ *WindsorCastle*1191 Judge'sCase1151¾	5 wide, no response	8
29Mar03–11GP fst 1¼	:48 1:123 1:38 2:041	3↑ GPH-G2	**103**	2	56¾	54¾	3½	35½	35	Velasquez C	L114 b	4.20	82– 24	Hero's Tribute1154 Aeneas1151 Puzzlement1141½	Bid turn, even finish	8
22Feb03–11GP fst 1⅛	:463 1:102 1:353 1:49	3↑ DonnH-G1	**106**	8	1110	1014	109¾	54¼	34	Velasquez C	L114 b	18.80	93– 13	HarlnsHolidy1202½ *HerosTribute*1141½ Puzzlement114nk	Off slowly, rallied	11
25Jan03–10GP fst 1 1/16	:232 :482 1:122 1:434	4↑ Alw 40000N3x	**101**	3	87¼	84½	85¼	64	2hd	Prado E S	L118 b	3.20	90– 10	Blue Burner118hd Puzzlement118¾ Skip a Grade1181	Closed fast, missed	8

Quero Quero
Own: Old Friends Inc

B. f. 4 (Mar) KEESEP01 $55,000
Sire: Royal Academy (Nijinsky II) $20,000
Dam: Big Dreams (Great Above)
Br: John R. Gaines Thoroughbreds & Pacelco S.A. (Ky)
Tr: Lobo Paulo H(0 0 0 0 .00) 2003:(62 7 .11)

Life	6	2	2	1	$192,420	88	D.Fst	1 0 0 1 $11,250 82
2003	6	2	2	1	$192,420	88	Wet(329)	0 0 0 0 $0 –
2002	0	M	0	0	$0	–	Turf(309)	5 2 2 0 $181,170 88
	0	0	0	0	$0	–	Dst(0)	0 0 0 0 $0 –

23Nov03–8Hol fm 1⅛	Ⓣ :491 1:13 1:362 1:49	+ ⒻASkirball73k	**84**	7	106¼	911	98¾	87¾	43	Baze T C	LB123	3.70	81– 16	Fencelineneighbor118½ *Ktdogwn*1202 DesrtViw117½	Saved ground to lane	10
7Jun03–8Hol fm 1⅛	Ⓣ :494 1:14 1:372 1:491	+ ⒻHnymnBCH-G2	**88**	10	42	44	52½	52¼	1nk	Baze T C	LB113	10.30	83– 15	Quero Quero113nk AtlanticOcean1211½ Sharpbill113½	3wd into lane,up late	10
11May03–8Hol fm 1	Ⓣ :24 :482 1:121 1:352	3↑ ⒻMd Sp Wt 46k	**87**	8	32	41½	12	14	12	Valenzuela P A	LB116	*1.10	87– 13	*Quero Quero*1162 *Varnished*1163 Ladoma1162½	Got thru rail 1/4,dvng	10
15Mar03–8GG fst 1 1/16	:214 :443 1:092 1:441	ⒻCalOaks81k	**82**	7	2hd	23½	2hd	1hd	31	Duran F	LB114 b	4.60	81– 11	Amber Hills118nk *Mavoreen*115¾ *Quero Quero*114hd	Off slow, led, wknd	7
20Feb03–1SA fm *6½f	Ⓣ :22 :442 1:08 1:142	ⒻMd Sp Wt 48k	**85**	5	3	4¾	31½	31	2no	Valenzuela P A	LB120 b	*.90	85– 13	DeviousImpact120no QueroQuero1201 *Dessert*1203½	Came out 1/8,willingly	9
26Jan03–6SA fm *6½f	Ⓣ :213 :434 1:064 1:124	ⒻMd Sp Wt 48k	**81**	2	6	44	42	31	21	Valenzuela P A	LB120 b	12.90	92– 05	Dyna Da Wyna1201 QueroQuero1203½ *Bruheria*1201½	Stalked pace,willingly	10

Quest

Own: Hancock III, Arthur B. and Healy, Ger

Ch. h. 5 (Apr)
Sire: Seeking the Gold (Mr. Prospector) $250,000
Dam: Starlore (Spectacular Bid)
Br: Arthur B. Hancock III & Gerald F. Healy (Ky)
Tr: Zito Nicholas P(0 0 0 0 .00) 2003:(507 77 .15)

Life	18	5	4	4	$720,760	108	D.Fst	11	4	3	1	$331,700	108
2003	11	2	4	3	$637,860	108	Wet(370)	6	1	1	3	$389,060	108
2002	7	3	0	1	$82,900	97	Turf(311)	1	0	0	0	$0	88
	0	0	0	0	$0	-	Dst(0)	0	0	0	0	$0	-

28Nov03-11CD sly 1⅛ :48¹ 1:13 1:38⁴ 1:52² 3↑ ClarkH-G2 **108** 8 87¼ 94¾ 72½ 2½ 2no Castellano J J L114 17.40 76–27 [D]Evening Attire118no Quest1143¼ Aeneas1141¼ Bmp,carried out lane 14
Placed first through disqualification
25Oct03-4Kee fst 1⅛ :50¹ 1:14³ 1:38³ 1:50¹ 3↑ Fayette-G3 **97** 1 1½ 1hd 1hd 31 74 Sellers S J L119 2.40 85–11 M BSea1191 Tenpins1212½ [DH]Changeintheweather119 Dueled,inside,tired 7
27Sep03-10Bel fst 1¼ :47³ 1:11 1:34⁴ 2:00¹ 3↑ JkyClbGC-G1 **108** 1 1½ 1½ 21½ 25 24¼ Prado E S L126 22.10 89–09 Mineshaft1264¼ Quest1262¾ Evening Attire1266½ Set pace, gamely 5
27Aug03-8Sar fst 1⅛ :48² 1:12² 1:36³ 1:49¹ 3↑ Alw 52000N3x **106** 6 44½ 33 31 11½ 13½ Prado E S L119 4.20 89–19 Quest1193½ Strive119nk Light Night1194¾ Drew away when roused 7
10Aug03-7Sar sly 1⅛ :50¹ 1:14² 1:38² 1:51² 3↑ Alw 52000N3x **99** 2 31½ 31 32 1hd 2no Prado E S L119 3.45 78–22 Cat Tracker119no *Quest*1195¾ Private City1152 3 wide move, gamely 6
24Jly03-5Sar sly 1⅛ :47⁴ 1:11³ 1:36⁴ 1:49⁴ 3↑ Alw 52000N3x **98** 2 41¼ 42¾ 21½ 2hd 33 Albarado R J L120 4.90 83–15 Puzzlement1202¼ Thunder Blitz120¾ Quest1207¾ Between foes, weakened 5
4Jly03-7Bel fm 1 Ⓣ :23² :46¹ 1:10 1:34 3↑ Alw 50000N3x **88** 6 42 51½ 3½ 54½ 85 Prado E S L120 b 12.90 85–17 MillenniumDrgon120½ ThefullCircle120¾ CelticSky1171½ 3 wide trip, tired 10
6Jun03-8Bel fst 1⅛ :46³ 1:10⁴ 1:36 1:49¹ 3↑ Alw 50000N3x **93** 3 51¾ 61 71¾ 41 31¾ Prado E S L119 b *2.45 82–16 *Almuhathir*119nk *Regal Sanction*1191½ Quest1192½ Good finish outside 9
1May03-6CD fst 1 :22² :44⁴ 1:09² 1:34² 3↑ OClm 62500N **97** 9 55½ 43½ 1hd 1½ 2¾ Stevens G L L117 *1.00 94–11 Unbridled Vision119¾ Quest1171¼ Medal Play1172 7w early,outfinished 9
9Apr03-6Kee sly 1 1/16 :23³ :47³ 1:11³ 1:43¹ 4↑ Alw 65000N3x **97** 3 23 31½ 31½ 31 3½ Coa E M L118 *1.20 90–16 *Full Mandate*116no Play It Out118½ Quest1183 Rail,no late gain 8
9Mar03-10GP fst 1 1/16 :22⁴ :46 1:10² 1:42¹ 4↑ OClm 80000N **90** 2 33 33½ 32 21½ 23 Coa E M L118 3.20 95–07 *Justification*1183 Quest1181¼ Doc Wild1223½ 3 wide, gained 2nd 9

Quest Star

Own: Mansell Stables LLC

Dk. b or b. h. 5 (May) OBSMAR01 $150,000
Sire: Broad Brush (Ack Ack) $100,000
Dam: Tinaca (Manila)
Br: John Messara (Ky)
Tr: Walden W. E(0 0 0 0 .00) 2003:(289 67 .23)

Life	24	5	7	4	$560,035	105	D.Fst	6	1	3	1	$58,260	90
2003	10	3	3	0	$298,380	105	Wet(373)	2	0	0	0	$2,800	97
2002	13	2	4	4	$261,655	95	Turf(321)	16	4	4	3	$498,975	105
	0	0	0	0	$0	-	Dst(0)	0	0	0	0	$0	-

28Nov03-11CD sly 1⅛ :48¹ 1:13 1:38⁴ 1:52² 3↑ ClarkH-G2 **97** 3 53¼ 52½ 82¾ 97½ 97 Melancon L L115 b 41.00 69–27 [D]Evening Attire118no Quest1143¼ Aeneas1141¼ Between,faltered 14
1Nov03-8Aqu gd 1⅛ Ⓣ :50 1:14 1:38¹ 1:50² 3↑ KnkrbkrH-G2 **92** 5 72¼ 88 87¼ 56½ 54¼ Velazquez J R L118 b *1.95 84–12 BttrTlkNow116½ DlMrShw116nk MllnnmDrgn1152¾ Altered course stretch 12
20Sep03-14KD fm 1½ Ⓣ :50¹ 1:14 2:04³ 2:31¹ 3↑ KyCpTrfH-G3 **96** 2 23½ 34½ 1½ 2hd 3½ Albarado R J L116 b *2.50 81–17 [D]*Art Variety*111hd Rochester116½ Quest Star116nk Bmp, checked wire 8
Placed second through disqualification
23Aug03-9Sar fm 1 1/16 Ⓣ :22⁴ :46 1:09³ 1:39¹ 3↑ 4strdavH-G2 **105** 1 1½ 1hd 1½ 2hd 22 Prado E S L116 b 9.20 97–03 Trademark1182 Quest Star1161¼ Tap the Admiral1151 Set pace, gamely 11
12Jly03-10Bel gd 1⅜ Ⓣ :51¹ 1:15¹ 1:39 2:15⁴ 3↑ BwlnGrnH-G2 **104** 2 41¼ 31 31½ 2hd 2½ Velazquez J R L117 b 5.70 83–22 *Whitmore's Conn*116½ Quest Star117nk Macaw116¾ Dug in gamely stretch 9
31May03-9CD fm 1⅜ Ⓣ :48⁴ 1:13³ 1:37³ 2:14 3↑ LsvillH-G3 **97** 7 11 1hd 1hd 2hd 53¾ Melancon L L117 b *2.70 91–04 KimLovesBucky117½ Rochester1171½ DrKshnikow117½ Pace,duel,faltered 8
11May03-9CD gd 1⅛ Ⓣ :49² 1:13¹ 1:38 1:51 3↑ Alw 56240c **97** 4 12 13½ 12½ 13½ 1½ Melancon L L123 b *2.80 79–20 Quest Star123½ Roxinho117½ Chianti117¾ Control pace,driving 8
23Apr03-8Kee fm 1½ Ⓣ :51² 1:16⁴ 2:05¹ 2:29¹ 4↑ Elkhorn-G3 **86** 1 11½ 1½ 1hd 85¾ 810½ Prado E S L118 b 2.40 84–09 KmLovsBcky117½ MnFromWcklow123no WllmsNws1161¼ Pace,weakened 10
22Mar03-10GP fm *1½ Ⓣ :50 1:15 2:04¹ 2:28² 3↑ PanAmerH-G2 **104** 3 11½ 11½ 11 12½ 11¾ Prado E S L113 b 4.90 107–02 Quest Star1131¾ Man From Wicklow1221 Reduit114no On rail, prevailed 9
9Feb03-6GP fm 1⅜ Ⓣ :48¹ 1:12⁴ 1:37 2:13¹ 4↑ Alw 38000N2x **101** 7 22½ 22½ 22 2hd 12¼ Day P L118 b 2.80 90–12 *Quest Star*1182¼ *Reduit*1183¼ Powerful Appeal1182¾ Strong hand ride 10

Raging Fever
Own: Evans Edward P

Dk. b or b. m. 6 (Apr)
Sire: Storm Cat (Storm Bird) $500,000
Dam: Pennant Fever (Seattle Slew)
Br: Edward P. Evans (Ky)
Tr: Hennig Mark A(0 0 0 0 .00) 2003:(503 73 .15)

Life	26	11	7	3	$1,458,198	106	D.Fst	21 9 6 2		$1,213,490	106
2003	7	1	2	1	$176,333	101	Wet(412)	5 2 1 1		$244,708	101
2002	10	4	4	1	$595,160	106	Turf(358)	0 0 0 0		$0	–
	0	0	0	0	$0	–	Dst(0)	0 0 0 0		$0	–

13Sep03–6Bel	fst	6f	:22 :45 :571 1:104	3↑ⒻFlrlPrkH-G3	78	5	5	51¾	53½	57¼	56¼	Bailey J D	L117	5.70	79–18	Bauhauser115¾ Shine Again1202¼ Literary Light1131¼	4 wide, no response	6
18Aug03–5Sar	fst	6f	:221 :451 :571 1:102	4↑ⒻAlw 56000c	86	4	2	31½	31½	32	3½	Gryder A T	L123	*1.35	89–06	Literary Light116hd Lilah109½ Raging Fever123¾	Game finish outside	5
1Aug03–8Sar	sly	6f	:221 :452 :572 1:094	3↑ⒻHnrblMsH-G3	96	1	5	31	32	4¾	53¼	Bailey J D	L118 f	4.70	90–13	WillOnthMov114½ ShinAgin120no SmoknFrolic1171	Chased inside, no bid	6
14Jun03–8AP	fst	7f	:223 :451 1:102 1:241	3↑ⒻChcgoBCH-G3	89	1	3	11	1hd	2hd	23	Gryder A T	L120	*1.00	81–20	For Rubies1163 Raging Fever1204 *Oglala Sue*1131½	Best of others	8
17May03–8Bel	fst	1	:224 :452 1:092 1:342	3↑ⒻShuveeH-G2	69	4	43	41	41¾	613	619½	Gryder A T	L119	3.25	74–17	*Wild Spirit*1153½ Smok'n Frolic1191¼ *You*1204¼	Broke in air, wide	6
19Apr03–9Aqu	fst	1	:233 :47 1:103 1:344	3↑ⒻBdORsBCH-G3	101	5	12	12½	1½	11½	1½	Gryder A T	L119	*.90	91–13	RgingFevr119½ SmoknFrolic1203¼ NonsuchBy1171¾	Game on rail, held on	5
29Mar03–9Aqu	fst	7f	:22 :442 1:084 1:222	3↑ⒻDistfBCH-G2	99	1	5	2½	2hd	2½	21¼	Gryder A T	L118	2.15	90–18	CrsonHollow1201¼ *RgingFever*1181¾ BonefideRson1123½	Tried winner turn	6

Randaroo
Own: Allen Joseph

B. f. 4 (Feb) FTKJUL01 $75,000
Sire: Gold Case (Forty Niner) $3,500
Dam: Validated (Valid Appeal)
Br: Dennis Drazin (Ky)
Tr: McLaughlin Kiaran P(0 0 0 0 .00) 2003:(186 46 .25)

Life	12	6	4	0	$491,680	104	D.Fst	10 5 3 0		$451,680	104
2003	10	4	4	0	$401,500	102	Wet(393)	2 1 1 0		$40,000	94
2002	2	2	0	0	$90,180	104	Turf(302)	0 0 0 0		$0	–
	0	0	0	0	$0	–	Dst(0)	0 0 0 0		$0	–

27Dec03–7SA	fst	7f	:223 :452 1:091 1:213	ⒻLaBrea-G1	96	7	3	2hd	1hd	21½	26	Castillo H Jr	LB119	7.00	92–10	IslndFshion1236 Rndroo1191½ Buffythecentrfold119½	Inside duel,held 2nd	10
28Nov03–9Aqu	fst	1	:231 :462 1:103 1:362	3↑ⒻTopFlgtH-G2	102	10	2½	2½	1hd	1½	12	Castillo H Jr	L116	9.20	83–29	Randaroo1162 Beauty Halo1153¼ Pocus Hocus116nk	Pressed pace, clear	12
25Oct03–4Bel	fst	7f	:222 :453 1:102 1:233	3↑ⒻFrstFltH-G2	93	3	2	1½	1hd	15	1nk	Castillo H Jr	L115	4.60	82–14	*Randaroo*115nk Shine Again1211¼ Zawzooth113½	Pace, clear, held on	8
4Oct03–8Pim	fst	6f	:221 :45 :572 1:102	ⒻSflyKtBC-G3	95	4	3	32	32	22	1¾	Castillo H Jr	L119	9.70	93–19	*Rndroo*119¾ FollowMeHom1172¼ *AwsomChrm*115nk	2wd turn,angld 4w,drvg	8
Previously trained by Dutrow Anthony W																		
23Aug03–6Mth	fst	6f	:214 :451 :58 1:104	ⒻMsWoodford60k	86	1	4	22	11	1hd	21¾	Lopez C C	L121	*1.10e	83–22	Elegant Designer1211¾ *Randaroo*1217¼ Catsuit1151¼	Close,led,duel,yielded	6
2Aug03–10Mth	my	5f	⊗:211 :45 :58	ⒻTrenton50k	83	4	5	67½	65¾	51¾	21¾	Lopez C C	L118	1.50	90–18	FollowMeHome1211¾ Randroo1183½ *NicolesDrem*115½	Shuffled back start	6
4Jly03–9Bel	fst	6f	:214 :443 :564 1:092	ⒻPrioress-G1	88	7	3	21	42	51¼	44¼	Prado E S	L119 f	8.30	88–15	HousePrty1213¼ Chimichurri119½ PrincessV115½	Stumbled start, bumped	8
6Jun03–10Bel	fst	1	:232 :461 1:102 1:351	ⒻAcorn-G1	78	4	1hd	2hd	2½	54	59½	Chavez J F	L121 f	14.50	80–16	Bird Town121hd *Lady Tak*1211 Final Round1213¼	Speed inside, tired	7
13Apr03–8Pim	fst	6f	:231 :462 :583 1:114	ⒻSmartHalo55k	79	1	3	11	1hd	2½	2nk	Pino M G	L122	*.05	86–15	Home Run Hitter115nk Randaroo122nk Bamba1173¼	Urged 2wd,duel,game	5
5Mar03–5Aqu	sly	6f	[•]:22 :45 :57 1:101	ⒻAlw 50000N$Y	94	5	2	2½	1hd	11½	14¾	Pino M G	L122	*.25	93–13	Randaroo1224¾ *Home Run Hitter*114nk Leniently1121	Vied outside, driving	5

Raylene

Own: Calmar Stables and Ranch

Dk. b or b. f. 4 (Mar) KEESEP01 $10,000
Sire: Tabasco Cat (Storm Cat) $17,490
Dam: Petite Princess (Dayjur)
Br: Kennelot Stables Limited (Ky)
Tr: Haynes Rodney(0 0 0 0 .00) 2003:(223 31 .14)

Life	17	10	3	0	$442,202	86		
2003	10	6	2	0	$339,687	86		
2002	7	4	1	0	$102,515	80		
	0	0	0	0	$0	–		
D.Fst	13	7	3	0	$356,045	86		
Wet(329)	4	3	0	0	$86,157	83		
Turf(281)	0	0	0	0	$0	–		
Dst(0)	0	0	0	0	$0	–		

1Nov03–8WO	fst	1¼	:49 1:133 1:38 2:032	3↑ Ⓕ MaplLeaf-G3	**86**	1	78	79	711	714	516¼	McAleney J S	L119	4.45	81– 19	*OnforRos*1216¼ WnnngChnc1216¼ ClodsofGold1181½	Passed tired ones 5w	8
11Oct03–8Hst	sly	1⅛	:46 1:12 1:382 1:522	3↑ Ⓕ BlrinaBC-G3	**83**	6	58	79	94½	54	41	Walcott R	L121	2.30	81– 21	Dncewithvixn121nk ScondrySchool124½ ShlbyMdison124nk	Inside, closed	9
20Sep03–9Hst	fst	1⅛	:463 1:124 1:382 1:52	Ⓕ BCBCOaks-G3	**85**	1	48	44½	32	33	1nk	Walcott R	L121	2.00	84– 15	Raylene121nk *Dancewithavixen*1214½ *Payton's Pride*121hd	Well timed drive	9
23Aug03–9NP	fst	1⅜	:48 1:132 1:404 2:213	CanDerby-G3	**83**	5	63½	66	64	25	11	Walcott R	L121	5.35	78– 25	*Raylene*1211 Taiaslew1266¼ Reb's Drummer126¾	Gaining, chckd, closed	8
9Aug03–7NP	fst	1 1/16	:241 :491 1:142 1:462	Ⓕ Sonoma75k	**84**	2	44	51¼	32½	22	2½	Wilson D H	L124	*.35	82– 22	*A Shaky Start*116½ *Raylene*1247 Lakota Spirit1154½	Steady adv, closed	6
20Jly03–7NP	fst	1	:234 :473 1:13 1:394	Ⓕ NPOaks40k	**83**	3	64¼	610	44	21½	16½	Wilson D H	L122	*.60	85– 27	Raylene1226½ *A Shaky Start*1191 Eradikate1182¼	Steady adv, drew off	7
29Jun03–4NP	fst	6½f	:234 :481 1:132 1:20	Ⓕ ChariotChH40k	**71**	3	4	52¾	43	43	22	Wilson D H	123	*.60	76– 31	A Shaky Start1142 *Raylene*1234 Eradikate1151¼	Rail, closed gap	5
15Jun03–8Stp	fst	1 1/16	:241 :50 1:153 1:46	Ⓕ PennyRdge40k	**58**	3	64½	63¼	62	44¼	1nk	Wilson D H	122	*.25	91– 08	Raylene122nk *Reagally Light*1141½ Eradikate1153¼	Closed fast, up late	7
31May03–4Stp	fst	1	:243 :492 1:142 1:381	Ⓕ LilacH40k	**68**	5	31½	32½	1hd	1½	12½	Wilson D H	122	*.20	91– 14	*Raylene*1222½ *Whataweekend*1167 Jadebquick1172	3 wide, bid, drew clr	5
11May03–7Stp	sl	6f	:233 :482 1:144	Ⓕ MtRoyalH40k	**78**	3	4	45	31½	1½	16¼	Wilson D H	119	*.90e	76– 33	*Raylene*1196¼ Whataweekend1172½ Vying Rose1156	Bid 3 wide, drew clear	5

Read the Footnotes

Own: Klaravich Stables Inc

B. c. 3 (Apr) EASMAY03 $320,000
Sire: Smoke Glacken (Two Punch) $15,000
Dam: Baydon Belle (Al Nasr*Fr)
Br: Lawrence Goichman (NY)
Tr: Violette R A Jr(0 0 0 0 .00) 2003:(178 28 .16)

Life	5	4	0	0	$240,660	105		
2003	5	4	0	0	$240,660	105		
2002	0	M	0	0	$0	–		
	0	0	0	0	$0	–		
D.Fst	5	4	0	0	$240,660	105		
Wet(368)	0	0	0	0	$0	–		
Turf(248)	0	0	0	0	$0	–		
Dst(0)	0	0	0	0	$0	–		

29Nov03–8Aqu	fst	1⅛	:481 1:121 1:373 1:503	Remsen-G2	**105**	9	21	2½	1hd	16	13¾	Bailey J D	L122	*2.00	83– 19	RdthFootnots1223¾ MstrDvd11610¾ *WstVrgn*116¾	When roused, kept busy	11
2Nov03–8Aqu	fst	1	:232 :461 1:102 1:362	Nashua-G3	**92**	1	1½	1½	1hd	12	12¼	Bailey J D	L118	2.90	83– 20	*RedthFootnots*1182¼ Pddington1206½ WhoIsChrisG1163¼	Pace inside, clear	9
4Oct03–7Bel	fst	1 1/16	:234 :481 1:133 1:44	Champagn-G1	**68**	6	2hd	2½	32½	512	615	Santos J A	L122	4.10	65– 26	Birdstone1222½ ChplRoyl1226¾ DshbordDrummr1222	Pressed inside, tired	7
7Sep03–6Bel	fst	7f	:223 :453 1:103 1:232	Alw 47000N1X	**89**	2	4	42	42¼	2½	12½	Bailey J D	116	*.45	83– 20	Read the Footnotes1162½ Adage119nk *Artie Schiller*1194½	Rallied 4 wide	6
17Aug03–2Sar	fst	5f	:22 :451 :572	Ⓢ Md Sp Wt 41k	**93**	4	6	1hd	1½	15½	19¼	Velazquez J R	119	*1.05	102– 08	*RedtheFootnotes*1199¼ RodneyBy1197¼ Sptso119¾	Drew away when roused	8

Reba's Gold

Own: Creston Farms

B. h. 7 (Apr)
Sire: Slew o' Gold (Seattle Slew) $7,500
Dam: Lovely Reba (Herat)
Br: Mereworth Farm (Ky)
Tr: Hendricks Dan L(0 0 0 0 .00) 2003:(176 28 .16)

Life	34	8	7	7	$694,922	115		
2003	5	1	1	2	$183,000	105		
2002	11	3	2	2	$320,642	115		
	0	0	0	0	$0	–		
D.Fst	30	7	7	7	$647,312	115		
Wet(337)	2	1	0	0	$43,710	105		
Turf(289)	2	0	0	0	$3,900	96		
Dst(0)	0	0	0	0	$0	–		

4Oct03–5SA	fst	1⅛	:482 1:114 1:36 1:481	3↑ GdwdBCH-G2	**92**	1	31½	52¼	62¾	64½	67¾	Smith M E	LB115 b	6.80	85– 13	*PlesntlyPrfct*116½ FltstrtDncr1131¼ StrCross1103	Saved ground, weakened	8
1Sep03–8Dmr	fst	1	:214 :451 1:092 1:353	3↑ DmrBCH-G2	**100**	3	53½	52¾	43	33	22	Flores D R	LB116 b	5.20	94– 09	Joey Franco1162 Reba's Gold1161½ Grey Memo117½	3wd into lane,willing	7
3Aug03–8Dmr	fst	1 1/16	:224 :453 1:10 1:423	3↑ SnDiegoH-G2	**100**	1	76	78	64½	23	31	Flores D R	LB116 b	3.00	91– 11	TasteofPardise113¾ Gondolieri117nk RebsGold1166½	5wd into lane,rallied	8
14Jun03–8Hol	fst	1⅛	:463 1:103 1:35 1:474	3↑ Calfrnin-G2	**105**	3	21	21	41	2hd	32	Flores D R	LB118 b	8.30	93– 04	Kudos116½ Piensa Sonando1181½ Reba's Gold1181½	Rail bid,led past 1/8	7
26May03–8BM	fst	1 1/16	:221 :45 1:094 1:413	3↑ SeabsctH-G3	**100**	3	44	45	42	13	18	Rollins C J	LB118 b	*2.00	99– 05	Reba's Gold1188 FreeCorona116no TrulyaJudge117¾	Quick bid 4w, handily	6

Redattore (Brz)

Own: Taunay Luis A

B. h. 9 (Oct)
Sire: Roi Normand (Exclusive Native)
Dam: Political Intrigue (Deputy Minister)
Br: Haras Santa Ana do Rio Grande (Brz)
Tr: Mandella Richard E(0 0 0 0 .00) 2003:(253 51 .20)

Life	32	15	2	6	$1,799,883	111	D.Fst	5 2 0 1		$203,965	108
2003	8	5	0	2	$864,147	111	Wet(357)	4 1 0 1		$9,239	–
2002	5	1	2	1	$309,940	108	Turf(306)	23 12 2 4		$1,586,679	111
	0	0	0	0	$0	–	Dst(0)	0 0 0 0		$0	–

28Dec03–8SA	fm	1⅛	Ⓣ	:48 1:114 1:354 1:48	3↑SnGabrlH-G2	**107**	9	2½	2½	2hd	11½	12	Solis A	LB122	*1.40	89–11	Redattore1222 Continental Red1162½ Denied116hd	Vied,led,clear,gamely	9
29Nov03–9Hol	fm	1 1/16	Ⓣ	:233 :472 1:111 1:403	3↑CtationH-G2	**106**	6	33½	32½	31	1½	1¾	Krone J A	LB120	2.70	93–13	*Redattore*120¾ Irish Warrior1172½ MisterAcpen116nk	Re-bid 3wd,drifted in	6
25Oct03–11SA	fst	1 1/16		:223 :46 1:094 1:42	3↑SeabscuitH150k	**103**	2	42½	32	42	41¼	31¾	Solis A	LB123	6.00	92–07	Pie N Burger1191 Chinkapin117¾ *Redattore*1233	Saved ground to 1/4	11
10Sep03–3Dmr	fm	1	Ⓣ	:224 :463 1:094 1:331	3↑LiveDreamH76k	**102**	8	2½	2½	2½	1hd	32	Solis A	LB124	*.80	95–08	*Designed for Luck*1181 Green Line1151 Redattore1241	Vied,led,outfinished	8
27Jly03–8Dmr	fm	1⅛	Ⓣ	:472 1:11 1:342 1:454	3↑EdReadH-G1	**99**	3	31	31½	21½	22	65½	Solis A	LB121	*1.30	99–03	Special Ring1175 Decarchy117nk *Irish Warrior*114hd	Stalked, bid, tired	6
26May03–8Hol	fm	1	Ⓣ	:24 :463 1:091 1:331	3↑ShoeBCM-G1	**111**	9	22	23½	22	21	1¾	Solis A	LB124	*2.20	98–10	Redttore124¾ SpecilRing1243 *TouchoftheBlues*1242	Bid,led past 1/16,game	9
1Mar03–8SA	gd	1	Ⓣ	:234 :472 1:111 1:344	4↑FKilroeH-G2	**109**	8	1hd	1½	1hd	1hd	11	Solis A	LB120	5.20	88–16	*Redattore*1201 Good Journey1242 Decarchy118nk	Clear past 1/8,game	11
8Feb03–3SA	fm	1	Ⓣ	:242 :482 1:12 1:344	4↑Alw 70000n$my	**109**	6	11½	11	11	13	15½	Pincay L Jr	LB119	*.90	88–14	*Redattore*1195½ Mercenary117½ Kachamandi123no	Inside, ridden out	6

Region of Merit

Own: Kennelot Stables Ltd

Ch. c. 4 (Feb) FTSAUG01 $475,000
Sire: Touch Gold (Deputy Minister) $50,000
Dam: Innocently Astray (Gone West)
Br: Louie J. Roussel III (Ky)
Tr: Clement Christophe(0 0 0 0 .00) 2003:(389 75 .19)

Life	8	4	0	0	$258,336	95	D.Fst	6 4 0 0		$250,200	95
2003	6	3	0	0	$229,986	95	Wet(364)	2 0 0 0		$8,136	82
2002	2	1	0	0	$28,350	81	Turf(254)	0 0 0 0		$0	–
	0	0	0	0	$0	–	Dst(0)	0 0 0 0		$0	–

13Sep03–8Bel	fst	1		:222 :45 1:093 1:361	JeromeH-G2	**52**	5	94¾	95¾	912	918	925¼	Nakatani C S	L118	23.70	60–19	*During*118¾ Tafaseel1144¾ Pretty Wild1161¼	Inside trip, tired	9
14Jun03–7Bel	gd	1⅛	⊗	:461 1:112 1:364 1:50	HillPrnc-G3	**82**	5	41½	32	41½	41½	45¾	Arroyo N Jr	L120	1.90	74–19	Happy Trails1201¼ *Traffic Chief*1144 ChillyRooster114½	Inside, no response	6
12Apr03–9OP	fst	1⅛		:452 1:094 1:354 1:481	ArkDerby-G2	**91**	7	44	34	43	49½	49¼	Coa E M	L122	5.50	90–11	*SirCherokee*1181¾ *EugenesThirdSon*1186½ ChristinesOutlw1181	No late kick	12
16Mar03–11Tam	fst	1 1/16		:231 :47 1:113 1:443	TampaDby-G3	**95**	8	33	33½	22	21	1¾	Coa E M	L120	*1.60	95–06	RegionofMerit120¾ Aristocat118nk *HearNoEvil*1231¾	Stalked,led, prevailed	8
15Feb03–3GP	fst	170		:231 :463 1:114 1:421	Alw 38000n2x	**92**	6	21	2½	1½	14	15	Coa E M	L118	2.10	90–13	*RegionofMerit*1185 SpitetheDvil1184½ ChristmsAwy118½	Drew off, driving	6
11Jan03–6GP	fst	7f		:224 :453 1:102 1:23	Alw 34000n1x	**87**	5	3	21	2hd	21½	11½	Coa E M	L122	3.00	93–06	*Region of Merit*1221½ *Aristocat*1222½ Cheddar1222½	All out, prevailed	8

Riddlesdown (Ire)

Own: Tanaka Gary A

Ch. h. 7 (Apr)
Sire: Common Grounds (Kris*GB) $8,000
Dam: Neat Dish (Stalwart)
Br: John McLoughlin (Ire)
Tr: O'Callaghan Niall M(0 0 0 0 .00) 2003:(243 25 .10)

Life	28	7	4	1	$270,964	104	D.Fst	0 0 0 0		$0	–
2003	3	1	0	0	$66,000	104	Wet(323)	0 0 0 0		$0	–
2002	7	2	0	0	$107,262	99	Turf(272)	28 7 4 1		$270,964	104
	0	0	0	0	$0	–	Dst(0)	0 0 0 0		$0	–

4Oct03–7Kee	fm	1½	Ⓣ	:502 1:154 2:044 2:292	3↑SycamrBC-G3	**41**	3	12½	31	77½	1015	1034¾	Chavez J F	L122	18.10	58–14	Sharbayan1201¾ Cetewayo122½ Deputy Strike1201¼	Gave way readily	10
16Feb03–10GP	fm	1⅜	Ⓣ	:481 1:121 1:353 2:113	3↑GPBCH-G1	**97**	1	11½	11½	11½	1hd	46¼	Velez R I	L115	4.20e	92–09	ManFromWicklow1194¾ JustListen113½ Sardukr1141	On hedge, gave way	10
19Jan03–10GP	fm	1⅜	Ⓣ	:494 1:144 1:39 2:143	3↑MDiarmdH-G3	**104**	4	12	14	13	12½	11½	Velez R I	L113	29.80	83–13	Riddlesdown1131½ Macaw1141¾ Just Listen113nk	Fully extended	12

Riskaverse

Own: Fox Ridge Farm Inc

Dk. b or b. m. 5 (Apr)
Sire: Dynaformer (Roberto) $50,000
Dam: The Bink (Seeking the Gold)
Br: Fox Ridge Farm Inc (Ky)
Tr: Kelly Patrick J(0 0 0 0 .00) 2003:(266 21 .08)

Life	21	7	4	4	$1,000,234	104	D.Fst	2	0	0	2	$59,730	72
2003	8	2	1	2	$336,324	104	Wet(359)	1	1	0	0	$26,400	83
2002	7	2	2	0	$461,160	103	Turf(329)	18	6	4	2	$914,104	104
	0	0	0	0	$0	–	Dst(0)	0	0	0	0	$0	–

22Nov03–9CD	fm	1⅛	Ⓣ :49 1 1:13 4 1:38 1 1:50 2	3↑ⒻCardinlH-G3	102	1	42½	42½	42	21	1¾	Velasquez C	L118	2.70	82–24	Riskaverse118¾ Bien Nicole1204 Firth of Lorne1161	4w lane,stiff drive	12
25Oct03–6SA	fm	1¼	Ⓣ :46 3 1:10 2 1:35 1 1:59	3↑ⒻBCF&MTrf-G1	100	8	46½	39½	32	41¾	65	Velazquez J R	LB123	45.50	93–04	Islington123nk L'Ancresse1182½ Yesterday118no	3 wide,no late bid	12
27Sep03–8Bel	fm	1¼	🅃 :49 4 1:14 4 1:39 2:02 3	3↑ⒻFlwrBlIv-G1	98	1	43½	42½	42	4¾	52½	Velazquez J R	L120	6.60	78–17	Dimitrova1141 Walzerkoenigin120no HeatHze1231¼	Saved ground, no rally	7
16Aug03–8AP	gd	1 3/16	Ⓣ :49 3 1:13 3 1:38 1:55 4	3↑ⒻBeverlyD-G1	100	5	32	33½	31	42	31¾	Day P	L123	7.10	93–08	Heat Haze1231¼ *Bien Nicole*123½ Riskaverse1231½	3wd, no late response	7
26Jly03–8Sar	fm	1⅛	Ⓣ :49 1:13 1:36 3 1:47 4	3↑ⒻDianaH-G1	100	8	31½	3½	31	4¾	42¾	Velazquez J R	L118	9.40	87–10	Voodoo Dancer120nk *Heat Haze*1181¾ Pertuisane115¾	3 wide both turns	8
4Jly03–10Bel	fm	1¼	🅃 :49 1 1:13 1 1:36 4 1:59 3	3↑ⒻNewYorkH-G2	100	7	43½	42	31½	22½	31¾	Velazquez J R	L119	3.60	94–07	Snow Dance1161 Pertuisane115¾ Riskaverse1193¼	Stayed on gamely	8
7Jun03–8Bel	sf	1	Ⓣ :24 1 :49 1 1:16 1 1:43 1	3↑ⒻJsAGmBCH-G3	104	8	59	57¾	2½	2hd	22	Velazquez J R	L119	3.20	42–46	Mariensky1162 Riskaverse119hd Wonder Again1196¼	Led between calls	8
18May03–7Bel	fm	1	Ⓣ :22 4 :46 4 1:09 4 1:33 1	4↑ⒻAlw 58000N4x	97	2	32	21	1hd	2hd	1hd	Velazquez J R	L123	*1.25	94–08	Riskverse123hd LovenKissS1201¼ GoldnCoron118no	Shoulder to shoulder	6

Roar Emotion

Own: Allen Joseph

Dk. b or b. f. 4 (Mar) OBSAPR02 $37,000
Sire: Roar (Forty Niner) $5,000
Dam: Emotional Outburst (Capote)
Br: Brenda Jones (Ky)
Tr: Martin Carlos F(0 0 0 0 .00) 2003:(144 16 .11)

Life	6	3	2	0	$307,260	93	D.Fst	4	2	1	0	$177,660	92
2003	3	1	1	0	$150,660	93	Wet(397)	2	1	1	0	$129,600	93
2002	3	2	1	0	$156,600	92	Turf(313)	0	0	0	0	$0	–
	0	0	0	0	$0	–	Dst(0)	0	0	0	0	$0	–

28Jun03–9Bel	fst	1⅛	:46 2 1:11 3 1:37 1:50 2	ⒻMthrGoos-G1	72	6	1hd	1hd	1hd	511	519½	Santos J A	L121	3.20	58–19	*Spoken Fur*1215¼ Yell121¾ Final Round1218¼	Ducked out start	6
16May03–10Pim	sly	1⅛	:47 3 1:12 1 1:38 1 1:52 1	ⒻBlkEySsn-G2	93	1	11½	11½	1hd	15	1½	Velazquez J R	L122	3.40	83–23	RoarEmotion122½ Fircroft1198½ *SantaCatarin*1175¾	Well rated 2wd,driving	8
22Mar03–9Aqu	fst	7f	:22 :44 4 1:09 3 1:22 2	ⒻCicada-G3	78	1	6	45	42	25	24½	Migliore R	L116	*.80	86–12	*CyberSecret*1224½ *RorEmotion*1161¾ BoxerGirl1184	Came wide, good finish	6

Rochester
Own: Augustin Stable

B. g. 8 (Jun)
Sire: Green Dancer (Nijinsky II) $15,000
Dam: Central City*GB (Midyan)
Br: George Strawbridge Jr. (Pa)
Tr: Sheppard Jonathan E(0 0 0 0 .00) 2003:(460 54 .12)

Life	31	10	6	2	$837,897	109	D.Fst	1	0	0	0	$360	63
2003	8	1	2	1	$164,757	103	Wet(285)	0	0	0	0	$0	-
2002	10	3	3	1	$443,124	109	Turf(295)	30	10	6	2	$837,537	109
	0	0	0	0	$0	-	Dst(0)	0	0	0	0	$0	-

4Oct03-7Kee fm 1½ Ⓣ :502 1:154 2:044 2:292 3↑ SycamrBC-G3 **90** 9 108¾ 1012 109½ 84¼ 77½ Martin E M Jr L122 6.90 85-14 Sharbayan1201¾ Cetewayo122½ Deputy Strike1201¼ 10w lane,no threat 10
20Sep03-14KD fm 1½ Ⓣ :501 1:14 2:043 2:311 3↑ KyCpTrfH-G3 **97** 1 69 76¼ 4¾ 3nk 2hd Martin E M Jr L116 4.90 82-17 D *Art Variety*111hd Rochester116½ Quest Star116nk Bmped late, all out 8
Placed first through disqualification
20Jly03-7Del fm 1½ Ⓣ :493 1:14 2:032 2:262 3↑ CapeHnlpn59k **99** 6 32 31½ 21 22 23½ Decarlo C P L116 1.80 104 - Revved Up1163½ *Rochester*1164¼ Regal Dynasty1161¼ Stalked,bid,2nd best 7
29Jun03-7Del fm 1⅛ Ⓣ :513 1:154 1:391 1:503 3↑ Eightthrty58k **93** 2 47½ 42 41½ 32 32¾ Decarlo C P L116 *.70 86-11 Better Talk Now116nk Pickupspeed1232½ Rochester1166 Bid then evenly 5
31May03-9CD fm 1⅜ Ⓣ :484 1:133 1:373 2:14 3↑ LsvillH-G3 **103** 4 714 712 68¼ 42¼ 2½ Day P L117 5.80 94-04 Kim Loves Bucky117½ Rochester1171½ Dr. Kashnikow117½ Closing 5w late 8
23Apr03-8Kee fm 1½ Ⓣ :512 1:164 2:051 2:291 4↑ Elkhorn-G3 **98** 8 76 64¼ 43½ 53½ 63¾ Guidry M L120 9.00 90-09 KimLovsBucky117½ MnFromWcklow123no WllmsNws1161¼ 5w,empty late 10
16Feb03-10GP fm 1⅜ Ⓣ :481 1:121 1:353 2:113 3↑ GPBCH-G1 **93** 8 78½ 79 78¼ 83¾ 88½ Day P L115 7.80 89-09 Man From Wicklow1194¾ Just Listen113½ Sardaukar1141 No factor 10
19Jan03-10GP fm 1⅜ Ⓣ :494 1:144 1:39 2:143 3↑ MDiarmdH-G3 **97** 9 43½ 35 23 32½ 64 Day P L117 3.00 79-13 Riddlesdown1131½ Macaw1141¾ Just Listen113nk Chased 3 wide, tired 12

Rojo Toro
Own: Earnhardt H J III

Ch. c. 4 (Feb) OBSAPR02 $120,000
Sire: Mountain Cat (Storm Cat) $7,500
Dam: Pinta (Carson City)
Br: Haras El Aguila, S.A. (Fla)
Tr: Baffert Bob(0 0 0 0 .00) 2003:(674 127 .19)

Life	4	3	0	0	$150,674	97	D.Fst	4	3	0	0	$150,674	97
2003	2	1	0	0	$121,614	97	Wet(381)	0	0	0	0	$0	-
2002	2	2	0	0	$29,060	96	Turf(241)	0	0	0	0	$0	-
	0	0	0	0	$0	-	Dst(0)	0	0	0	0	$0	-

Previously trained by Baffert Bob
22Mar03-6SA fst 6½f :211 :432 1:082 1:151 SanPedro80k **97** 6 6 3nk 31½ 22 53 Flores D R **LB**119 b *1.10 94-09 *KingRobyn*116½ TruckleFetur117nk EyofthTigr1162 Forced 3wd, weakened 6
1Mar03-7SA fst 1 :222 :451 1:092 1:354 SnRafael-G2 **94** 6 31 1½ 1hd 11½ 11 Bailey J D **LB**115 b *2.10 92-05 RojoToro1151 Spensive1182½ CrownedDncer1181½ Pulled,dueled,led,held 7

Roscoe Pito

Own: Snow John, Wildcard Stable, Punjab Fo

Dk. b or b. g. 4 (May) BRCOCT01 $2,993
Sire: Light of Mine (Mining) $1,000
Dam: Perfect Coin (L'Emigrant)
Br: Robert W. Simpson & Robert G. Henderson (BC-C)
Tr: Snow John(0 0 0 0 .00) 2003:(50 12 .24)

Life	9	6	1	2	$424,566	93	D.Fst	7	4	1	2	$332,281 93
2003	9	6	1	2	$424,566	93	Wet(345*)	2	2	0	0	$92,285 89
2002	0	M	0	0	$0	–	Turf(215)	0	0	0	0	$0 –
	0	0	0	0	$0	–	Dst(0)	0	0	0	0	$0 –

12Oct03–8Hst sly	1⅜	:483 1:143 1:401 2:194	3↑ PremierH-G3	85	6	11	1½	1½	1½	1hd	Alvarado P V	L118	*.95	85– 19	Roscoe Pito118hd Blowin in the Wind118½ Futural1181¾	Well handled	8
21Sep03–9Hst fst	1⅛	:471 1:113 1:373 1:512	BCDerby-G2	86	3	2hd	2hd	1hd	12	12	Alvarado P V	L126	*1.40	87– 14	*Roscoe Pito*1262 Steady Smiler126½ *Rindanica*126½	Well handled, driving	9
1Sep03–9EmDfst	1⅛	:473 1:112 1:353 1:473	EmDBCDerby105k	85	4	11½	2hd	11	12½	12	Krasner S B	LB122	1.90	89– 13	*RoscoePito*1222 Condotirri1225 KnightsbridgRod1226½	In hand, clear, held	6
4Aug03–7Hst fst	1 1/16	:232 :461 1:104 1:451	Ⓡ BCCupStalH55k	74	3	1½	2hd	11	1½	1nk	Krasner S B	L117	*1.00	89– 09	*Roscoe Pito*117nk Illusive Force1181 *Steady Smiler*1171	Dueled, prevailed	7
20Jly03–4Hst fst	1 1/16	:24 :48 1:122 1:434	JColProvH44k	93	4	1½	11	11½	13	15¼	Krasner S B	L114	1.70	96– 11	*Roscoe Pito*1145¼ General Insanity117¾ Steady Smiler1174	Led throughout	5
28Jun03–7Hst fst	1 1/16	:23 :454 1:103 1:441	BurnabyBCH64k	76	3	21½	2hd	11½	32½	36½	Krasner S B	L113 b	5.55	87– 16	*Stratoplan*1135 Steady Smiler1171½ *RoscoePito*1133¼	Chased, led, gave way	7
31May03–4Hst fst	6½f	:224 :461 1:101 1:164	KlondikeH41k	81	3	3	2½	2hd	22	22½	Krasner S B	L113 b	3.25	91– 11	Gamblin Caper1182½ Roscoe Pito1131 *Bold Texas*1171¼	Pressed, weakened	6
17May03–5Hst gd	6½f	:214 :452 1:104 1:172	Md Sp Wt 21k	89	4	1	11½	11	11	13	Krasner S B	L117 b	3.00	91– 17	Roscoe Pito1173 Kompressor Jack1176¼ Nice Fit1222¾	Led throughout	10
3May03–8Hst fst	6f	:223 :46 :591 1:124	Ⓡ Md Sp Wt 21k	64	3	2	33	43½	31½	33½	Krasner S B	L122 b	20.10	88– 09	Bold Texas1221¾ Kompressor Jack1221¾ *Roscoe Pito*122nk	Stalked, evenly	8

Royal Spy

Own: Jayaraman Kalarikkal K. and Vilasini

B. h. 6 (Apr)
Sire: Peteski (Affirmed) $2,000
Dam: Caro's Beauty (Caro*Ire)
Br: Dr. K. K. Jayaraman & Dr. V. Devi Jayaraman (Fla)
Tr: Amoss Thomas M(0 0 0 0 .00) 2003:(445 118 .27)

Life	21	9	0	3	$584,955	108	D.Fst	4	1	0	0	$17,355 93
2003	3	2	0	0	$169,000	104	Wet(288)	5	1	0	2	$65,600 93
2002	5	2	0	0	$92,860	98	Turf(348)	12	7	0	1	$502,000 108
	0	0	0	0	$0	–	Dst(0)	0	0	0	0	$0 –

11Apr03–8Kee fm	1 Ⓣ	:233 :463 1:112 1:354	4↑ MakrsMrk-G2	104	3	21	1½	11½	12½	11¼	Albarado R J	L118	11.60	89– 13	RoylSpy1181¼ MsqsApprovl1181¾ TochofthBls1171½	Pressed,steady drive	9
1Feb03–9FG fm	*1⅛ Ⓣ	:502 1:142 1:382 1:502	4↑ FGBCH150k	94	4	21	1hd	2hd	3½	63¾	Borel C H	L117	6.20	88– 11	MysteryGiver1173¼ Dynmeux115no Frefourintrnt115hd	Bid, weakened late	9
5Jan03–9FG fm	*1 1/16 Ⓣ	:244 :503 1:144 1:451	4↑ CERBradlyH75k	99	1	21	21	11	11½	11	Albarado R J	L116	5.30	87– 13	Royal Spy1161 Dynameaux115nk Freefourinternet1151	Driving to wire	11

Ruby's Reception

Own: Oasis Racing Stable LLC

Gr/ro. f. 4 (Jan) KEESEP01 $12,000
Sire: Rubiano (Fappiano) $10,000
Dam: Court Reception (A.P. Indy)
Br: Avalon Farm (Ky)
Tr: Jones J. L(0 0 0 0 .00) 2003:(146 33 .23)

Life	14	4	3	2	$356,980	86	D.Fst	7	3	2	1	$247,640 84
2003	7	1	1	1	$147,750	86	Wet(382)	5	1	1	1	$109,340 86
2002	7	3	2	1	$209,230	86	Turf(291)	2	0	0	0	$0 59
	0	0	0	0	$0	–	Dst(0)	0	0	0	0	$0 –

18Oct03–9Kee fm	1 1/16 Ⓣ	:232 :481 1:132 1:432	ⒻVllyView-G3	58	8	2hd	52	98¾	910	916½	Thompson T J	L119 b	21.50	67– 17	DynaDaWyn119¾ MexicnMoonlight1163 Derrinne123½	Weakened,far turn	10
23Aug03–6AP fm	1 1/16 Ⓣ	:233 :481 1:121 1:423	ⒻHatoof53k	59	8	813	811	86¼	713	713½	Thompson T J	L121	5.40	82– 10	Cat's Cat116no Hail Hillary1152 Spiritual Drift1152¼	Outrun	8
2Aug03–9EIP my	1 ⊗	:233 :463 1:124 1:392	ⒻAudubonOak75k	70	7	98¼	95¾	75¼	65½	58	D'Amico A J	L121	2.10	75– 20	Keiai Sakura1191¼ Evil Eye Aly1152 Dress to Impress1192¼	5 wide move	10
4Jly03–6PrM fst	1 1/16	:224 :454 1:093 1:413	ⒻIowaOaks125k	84	3	712	714	612	511	49¾	Thompson T J	LB121	1.70	90– 11	WildwoodRoyl121¾ GoldenRputshn1122¼ Tulupi1126¾	Passed tiring rivals	8
7Jun03–8PrM sly	1	:234 :472 1:112 1:364	ⒻPanthers49k	86	1	36½	46	45	36	33	Thompson T J	LB121	*.40	93– 12	*WldwoodRoyl*1151 MonlghtSnt1142 RbysRcptn1212¾	Angled out, mild rally	5
11Apr03–10OP fst	1 1/16	:224 :454 1:11 1:443	ⒻFantasy-G2	84	2	67	67½	52¼	1½	12¼	Thompson T J	L121	4.70	87– 16	RubysRecption1212¼ HrborBlus1211 GoforGlmour117½	5-w 2nd turn, clear	6
8Mar03–10OP fst	1 1/16	:233 :474 1:123 1:44	ⒻHoneybee75k	82	2	79	75½	53¼	23½	25	Thompson T J	L114	2.90	85– 13	MyTrustyCt1165 *RbysRcpton*1141¼ ExplosvBty1171¼	Back, 5-w 1/4, willing	7

Ruler's Court
Own: Darley Stud Management LLC

Dk. b or b. c. 3 (Apr) OBSFEB03 $400,000
Sire: Doneraile Court (Seattle Slew) $15,000
Dam: Future Guest (Copelan)
Br: Douglas Arnold & Dr. Roy Sadovsky (Ky)
Tr: Harty Eoin G(0 0 0 0 .00) 2003:(110 30 .27)

												Life	4	2	0	1	$197,700	102
												D.Fst	4	2	0	1	$197,700	102
												2003	4	2	0	1	$197,700	102
												Wet(358)	0	0	0	0	$0	–
												2002	0	M	0	0	$0	–
												Turf(270*)	0	0	0	0	$0	–
												Dst(0)	0	0	0	0	$0	–

5Oct03-10SA fst	1 1/16	:222 :453 1:101:411		114	Solis A	LB120 b	4.90	98– 08	Ruler's Court1201 Perfect Moon1203 1/2 5wd 7/8,ridden out	9
17Aug03-2Dmr fst	6 1/2f	:22 :44 1:1011:164	76 8 1 83 54 1/2 42 1/2 43 1/2		Flores D R	LB118	2.10	87– 09	PerfectMoon1211 1/2 Capitano118 1 1/2 MilitryMndte1181 4wd into lane,no bid	10
19Jly03-4Hol fst	6f	:221 :443 :5711:101	68 5 3 31 1/2 31 1/2 32 35 1/2		Flores D R	LB117	*.20	83– 13	PerfectMoon1172 1/2 BlirsRorinStr1173 RulersCourt1173 Stalked 3wd,empty	5
11Jun03-4Hol fst	5f	:211 :443 :572	88 1 3 23 1/2 22 21 12		Flores D R	LB119	*.90	97– 12	RulrsCourt1192 WldWd1192 1/2 WstcostThundr119no Bumped past 1/8,clear	9

Runaway Dancer
Own: R. L. Stable

Gr/ro. g. 5 (Mar)
Sire: Runaway Groom (Blushing Groom*Fr) $15,000
Dam: Salsa Dancer (Dahar)
Br: Reyla Graber (Ky)
Tr: Hendricks Dan L(0 0 0 0 .00) 2003:(176 28 .16)

												Life	15	5	1	1	$204,590	101
												D.Fst	2	1	1	0	$12,870	73
												2003	7	3	0	0	$172,170	101
												Wet(333)	0	0	0	0	$0	–
												2002	8	2	1	1	$32,420	86
												Turf(274)	13	4	0	1	$191,720	101
												Dst(0)	0	0	0	0	$0	–

27Dec03-11Crc fm	1 1/16	① :484 1:133 2:01 2:244	94 4 1116 1113 1010 963 86	3↑ WLMcKntH-G2	Garcia J A	L114	5.90	103	– BaltoStar1211 1/2 Continuously116 1/2 RownsPrk1142 1/4 Steadied start, outrun	11
22Nov03-8Hol fm	1 1/2	① :513 1:164 2:052 2:29	101 7 78 79 1/2 76 53 3/4 43 1/2	3↑ HolTrfCp-G1	Krone J A	LB126	5.10	79– 18 ☐Epicentr126no Continuously126 1/4no BowmmMill126 1/2 5wd into lane,rallied	7
24Oct03-8SA fm	1 1/2	① :503 1:154 2:043 2:281	99 1 97 98 3/4 96 1/2 84 1/2 1nk	3↑ CFBurkeH-G3	Smith M E	LB112	38.10	85– 16 RunawyDncer112nk Lbirinto116nk SenorSwinger1141 Rallied wide,up late	9
27Sep03-6BM fm *11/8	① :4741:122 1:3711:464	90 4 1012 1016 1016 1012 66 1/2	3↑ BMBCH-G3	Rollins C J	LB116	17.80	90– 16 Mister Acpen161 1/4 Fateful Dream117no Ninebanks1185 Closed too late	10
25Aug03-6BM fm 1 1/16	① :4931:13 :5:2500N	94 7 79 77 3/4 74 1/4 42 12	3↑ OClm 6250ON	Smith M E	LB121	9.00	93– 22 Runaway Dancer1212 Gulchie119no Nazirali119nk 4wd into lane,rallied	7
24Jly03-7Dmr fm 1 3/8	① :4931:152 1:4042:162	90 2 52 1/2 63 1/4 41 1/4 32 12	3↑ OClm 4000ON	Smith M E	LB121	10.70	78– 22 Runaway Dancer121 2 Shariya116 1/2 Calster123 1/2 Waited,got thru,clear	10
29Jun03-3Hol fm 1 1/16	① :231 :471 1:1111:404	83 6 86 1/4 87 1/4 77 1/4 63 1/2 55	4↑ Alw 51000N1x	Solis A	LB118	18.50	87– 08 Bayamo1202 Mega Gift1181 Vacamonte118 1/2 Bmpd strt,mild bid	8

Runspastum
Own: Jayeff B Stables

B. h. 7 (Mar)
Sire: Woodman (Mr. Prospector) $25,000
Dam: Erandel (Danzig)
Br: Calumet Farm (Ky)
Tr: Goldberg Alan E(0 0 0 0 .00) 2003:(222 39 .18)

												Life	38	7	6	6	$561,545	105
												D.Fst	25	5	5	3	$374,336	105
												2003	6	1	0	2	$83,779	101
												Wet(366)	5	1	1	1	$125,659	105
												2002	12	1	3	2	$163,262	105
												Turf(327)	8	1	0	2	$61,550	97
												Dst(0)	0	0	0	0	$0	–

4Oct03-8Bel fm	1	① :24 :471 1:1031:343	97 5 84 3/4 73 83 1/4 103 63 3/4	3↑ KelsoBCH-G2	Luzzi M J	L112 b	57.25	83– 15 Freefourinternet113no Proud Man1141 Rouvres1151 1/4 Inside trip, no rally	11
23Aug03-10Mth fst	1 1/8	:48 1:121 1:3721:501	89 9 93 3/4 73 4 3/4 66 1/4 81 2 3/4	3↑ IselnBCH-G3	Ferrer J C	L114 b	25.80	77– 27 Tenpins1191 Aeneas114no Jersey Giant1152 1/4 5wd bid,gave way 1/4	9
19Jly03-9Del fst	1 1/16	:233 :462 1:11 1:441	97 5 711 712 68 45 32 3/4	3↑ RRMCarpH100k	Dominguez R A	L116 b	2.80	84– 17 PrivateLap1181 BagofMischief114 1/4 Runspstum116 3/4 Gamely to close gap	7
14Jun03-10Mth fst	1 1/16	:224 :451 1:0931:421	101 5 69 1/4 58 1/2 44 3 1/2 11 1/2	3↑ OcenprtH-G3	Pimentel J	L113 b	9.20	100– 06 Runspastum113 1 1/2 Balto Star1191 Saint Verre118 3/4 Bid 3wd lane,clr late	6
24May03-10Mth sly	1	⊗ :233 :464 1:1121:373	91 1 46 1/4 44 1/2 43 1/4 34 1/4 31	3↑ RedBankH97k	Pimentel J	L114 fb	6.40	88– 16 Just LeFacts111nk SaintVerre118 3/4 Runspastum114 4 3/4 Finished well outside	4
10May03-8Del sly	1	⊗ :241 :474 1:231:374	87 4 57 53 1/2 54 1/2 55 1/2 512 1/4	3↑ QuickCard59k	Castillo O O	L118 b	8.20	82– 19 Private Lap1205 1/2 Classic Endeavor1233 1/4 Acrolect1181 1/4 Evenly	6

Saint Verre

Own: Allen Joseph

B. h. 6 (Jan) FTFFEB00 $50,000
Sire: Saint Ballado (Halo) $125,000
Dam: Margot Verre (Tom Rolfe)
Br: Georgelina Gonzalez (Fla)
Tr: Jerkens H. A(0 0 0 0 .00) 2003:(359 73 .20)

Life	26	6	4	6	$403,462	112	D.Fst	15 4 1 3	$156,740 106
2003	7	1	2	2	$140,282	112	Wet(371)	6 2 2 1	$194,450 112
2002	8	2	1	1	$148,620	106	Turf(284)	5 0 1 2	$52,272 105
	0	0	0	0	$0	-	Dst(0)	0 0 0 0	$0 -

5Jly03-8Bel	fm	1	Ⓣ:234 :461 1:092 1:324	3↑PokerH-G3	98	7	1½	1½	11	1½	31	Espinoza J L	L112	5.20	95-08	War Zone117½ *Trademark*114½ Saint Verre112 1¼	Set pace, gamely	11
14Jun03-10Mth	fst	1 1/16	⊗:224 :451 1:093 1:421	3↑OcenprtH-G3	96	2	1½	1½	1½	2hd	32¾	Lopez C C	L118	2.60	97-06	Runspastum113 1¾ *Balto Star*1191 Saint Verre118 5½	Pace,dueled,yielded	6
24May03-10Mth	sly	1	⊗:232 :464 1:112 1:373	3↑RedBankH97k	93	3	2hd	2hd	2hd	22	2nk	Espinoza J L	L118	*.20	89-16	JustLeFacts111nk SaintVerre118¾ *Runspstum*114 3¾	Lost ground,came late	4
26Apr03-8Aqu	sly	1	⊗:231 :46 1:094 1:333	3↑FtMarcyH-G3	112	1	1½	11	15	18	18½	Espinoza J L	L117	6.40	97-12	Saint Verre117 8½ *Windsor Castle*1191 Judge'sCase115 1¾	Set pace, drew off	8
5Apr03-8Aqu	fst	1⅛	:462 1:102 1:35 1:48	3↑ExlsrBCH-G3	95	5	21½	22½	2½	54½	55¾	Arroyo N Jr	L114	8.50	90-16	ClassicEndeavor113½ BltoStr119¾ TempestFugit114¾	Drifted out 1/4 pole	5
22Feb03-11GP	fst	1⅛	:463 1:102 1:353 1:49	3↑DonnH-G1	85	5	75¾	78	88¼	1113	1017	Santos J A	L114	14.40	80-13	HrlnsHolidy120 2½ *HerosTribute*114 1½ Puzzlmnt114nk	Rank, steadied 1st trn	11
11Jan03-10GP	fst	1 1/16	:231 :463 1:102 1:421	3↑HalHopeH-G3	106	6	72¾	84	61¾	2½	21½	Santos J A	L114	9.50	96-12	Windsor Castle115 1½ Saint Verre114nk Najran114 2¾	4 wide, outfinished	8

Saintly Look

Own: Carl William A

Dk. b or b. c. 4 (Mar)
Sire: Saint Ballado (Halo) $125,000
Dam: Sensational Eyes (Roman Majesty)
Br: William A. Carl (Ky)
Tr: Stewart Dallas(0 0 0 0 .00) 2003:(308 49 .16)

Life	8	3	2	0	$168,505	106	D.Fst	7 3 2 0	$168,505 106
2003	4	1	1	0	$90,220	106	Wet(357)	1 0 0 0	$0 51
2002	4	2	1	0	$78,285	90	Turf(281)	0 0 0 0	$0 -
	0	0	0	0	$0	-	Dst(0)	0 0 0 0	$0 -

22Nov03-8CD	fst	6½f	:222 :45 1:082 1:143	3↑OClm 62500N	106	3	3	32½	32	32½	2¾	Day P	L115	6.50	97-10	EugnsThirdSon119¾ SntlyLook115 5¼ TotlLmt117 2¾	5w,slowly gaining late	7
22Mar03-10TP	fst	1⅛	:463 1:11 1:37 1:503	LanesEnd-G2	78	1	1½	1½	1hd	54	511¼	Sellers S J	L121	7.20	72-14	NewYorkHero121nk EugenesThirdSon121 2¼ Champali121hd	Tired final 1/8	9
16Feb03-9FG	fst	1 1/16	:233 :472 1:12 1:424	RisenStr-G3	76	1	11	1hd	2hd	35½	518¼	Sellers S J	L122	3.20	78-15	Badge ofSilver11610 LoneStarSky122¾ Defrere'sVixen114½	Headed, faded	12
25Jan03-9FG	fst	1	:233 :464 1:114 1:373	LeComte-G3	95	11	2hd	2hd	2hd	1hd	12¾	Sellers S J	L122	4.30	96-11	Saintly Look122 2¾ *Call Me Lefty*122½ Winning Fans114½	Clearly best	11

San Dare
Own: Mounts David G

B. m. 6 (Apr) KEESEP99 $9,000
Sire: Dare and Go (Alydar) $3,912
Dam: San Empery (Empery)
Br: Sidney Turner (Ky)
Tr: Hiles Rick(0 0 0 0 .00) 2003:(98 13 .13)

Life	44	8	11	9	$484,171	100
2003	10	2	1	2	$190,939	100
2002	14	3	7	2	$225,822	99
	0	0	0	0	$0	–

D.Fst	15	1	5	4	$57,015	85
Wet(253)	5	1	2	0	$56,150	85
Turf(262)	24	6	4	5	$371,006	100
Dst(0)	0	0	0	0	$0	–

22Nov03–9CD fm 1 1/8 Ⓣ :49 1 1:13 4 1:38 1 1:50 2 3↑ ⒻCardinlH-G3 **85** 4 11 7 1/2 11 9 1/4 9 6 1/4 10 7 1/2 8 7 1/2 Martinez W L115 24.70 74– 24 Riskaverse118 3/4 Bien Nicole120 4 Firth of Lorne116 1 6-7w stretch,no rally 12
31Oct03–9CD fm 1 1/16 Ⓣ :24 2 :48 4 1:13 1 1:43 4 3↑ ⒻAlw 64600c **83** 1 5 6 5 5 5 2 4 2 1/2 3 1 3/4 Martinez W L117 4.10 83– 13 Quick Tip117 1 May Gator121 3/4 San Dare117 4 1/4 6w bid,slight gain 6
11Oct03–8Haw fm 1 1/16 Ⓣ :22 4 :46 3 1:09 4 1:39 4 3↑ ⒻIndnMdBCH120k **74** 4 7 12 7 11 7 13 7 8 1/2 7 8 3/4 Silva C H L119 4.20 96 – Janeian118 2 1/4 Delmonico Cat117 1 Delicatessa116 1 1/2 Trailed throughout 7
19Jly03–7Del fm 1 3/8 Ⓣ :49 3 1:14 3 1:39 1 2:15 3↑ ⒻRGDickBCH148k **88** 10 6 6 1/4 7 7 9 4 6 4 1/2 6 3 3/4 Guidry M L117 *1.50 107 – Alternte115 1 1/4 SpiceIsInd114 1/2 LdyoftheFuture115hd Well placed, no rally' 11
28Jun03–9CD fm 1 1/8 Ⓣ :47 4 1:11 2 1:35 1 1:47 3 3↑ ⒻLcstGrvH-G3 **93** 2 5 8 5 6 1/2 5 8 5 6 4 2 1/2 Guidry M L117 11.30 93– 08 Ipi Tombe123 1/2 Kiss the Devil116 1/2 Quick Tip117 1 1/2 5w lane,minor gain 5
24May03–9CD fm 1 1/16 Ⓣ :23 2 :47 1 1:11 1 1:41 3 4↑ ⒻETMintJH-G3 **86** 6 9 7 1/2 8 7 5 6 1/2 4 5 5 3 1/4 Guidry M L119 3.60 93– 07 Kiss the Devil115nk Quick Tip119 1 Cellars Shiraz120 1 Slow start,squeezed 9
24Apr03–8Kee fm 1 1/2 Ⓣ :50 2 1:15 3 2:05 3 2:29 3 4↑ ⒻBewitch-G3 **92** 2 9 5 1/4 10 7 1/2 10 8 1/4 8 5 1/4 3 4 Guidry M L118 3.50 88– 11 LilacQueen116 4 BeyondtheWaves116hd SnDre118hd 10w lane,gaining late 10
23Mar03–8GP sly 1 1/2 ⊗ :48 2 1:14 2:06 1 2:32 1 3↑ ⒻOrchidH-G2 **85** 6 5 8 1/2 5 2 3/4 3 3 1/2 2 4 2 5 1/2 Guidry M L119 2.20 – – Tweedside116 5 1/2 San Dare119 5 HiTechHoneycomb115 4 1/4 Hit gate, 2nd best 7
8Feb03–8GP fm 1 3/8 Ⓣ :48 1 1:13 1 1:38 2:13 3 3↑ ⒻVeryOneH-G3 **100** 11 10 8 1/4 10 6 3/4 12 5 1/2 6 3 1/4 1 2 1/4 Guidry M L116 6.00 88– 11 San Dare116 2 1/4 *Tweedside*115 1/2 Hi Tech Honeycomb113 1/2 5 wide, going away 12
5Jan03–10GP fm 1 1/16 Ⓣ :24 4 :50 2 1:15 1 1:46 +3↑ ⒻHonyFoxH-G3 **99** 7 10 4 1/2 10 7 9 5 3/4 7 2 1hd Guidry M L115 11.60 65– 36 *San Dare*115hd Calista118 1 1/2 Laurica114nk Rallied 5 wide 10

Sand Springs
Own: Willmott Stables Inc

Dk. b or b. f. 4 (May)
Sire: Dynaformer (Roberto) $50,000
Dam: Lovely Martha (Storm Bird)
Br: Willmott Stables, Inc. (Ky)
Tr: Reinstedler Anthony L(0 0 0 0 .00) 2003:(190 34 .18)

Life	12	5	2	1	$519,902	93
2003	7	4	1	0	$451,390	93
2002	5	1	1	1	$68,512	83
	0	0	0	0	$0	–

D.Fst	0	0	0	0	$0	–
Wet(321)	1	0	0	0	$0	–
Turf(330)	11	5	2	1	$519,902	93
Dst(0)	0	0	0	0	$0	–

11Oct03–8Kee fm 1 1/8 Ⓣ :47 3 1:11 3 1:35 4 1:47 4 ⒻQEIICup-G1 **89** 5 6 2 1/4 3 1 1/2 2 2 4 2 9 5 Guidry M L121 10.20 93– 11 FilmMaker121no MaidenTower121 3/4 CsulLook121 3/4 Stumble,bmp foe start 10
7Sep03–9Bel gd 1 1/8 🅃 :46 4 1:11 3 1:36 2 1:48 2 ⒻGrdCyBCH-G1 **80** 2 1 2 1 1 1/2 1 1 7 10 7 12 1/4 Guidry M L120 4.60 76– 17 Indy Five Hundred113 4 *Dimitrova*122 2 1/4 Campsie Fells116 1 Drifted, tired 8
17Aug03–9Sar fm 1 1/8 Ⓣ :46 2 1:10 2 1:36 1:49 ⒻLakPlcdH-G2 **93** 9 1 1 1 6 1 5 1/2 1 2 1 3/4 Guidry M L121 *1.35 84– 13 SndSprings121 3/4 *IndyFivHundrd*114no *FlmMkr*119 3 1/2 Set pace, determinedly 10
5Jly03–5Hol fm 1 1/4 Ⓣ :47 3 1:11 4 1:35 3 1:59 4 ⒻAmercnOaks750k **90** 13 1 1 1/2 1 1 1hd 1hd 2 2 Guidry M LB121 7.20 91– 11 Dimitrova121 2 *SandSprings*121nk AtlanticOcen121 1/2 Fought back,game 2nd 14
14Jun03–8CD fm 1 1/8 Ⓣ :47 1 1:11 4 1:36 2 1:48 3 ⒻRegret-G3 **92** 6 1 1 1 2 1 1 1/2 1 1 1/2 1 3 Guidry M L118 4.90 91– 10 SndSprings118 3 PersonlLegend116 1/2 Achnshn116hd Stumble start,driving 12
21May03–7CD gd 1 1/16 Ⓣ :22 4 :45 2 1:10 1 1:42 ⒻAlw 65300nc **89** 6 1 2 1 3 1 3 1/2 1 2 1/2 1 1 3/4 Guidry M L118 2.60 94– 11 *Sand Springs*118 1 3/4 Keiai Sakura118 1/2 Achnasheen118 1/2 Pace,steady drive 7
26Apr03–10CD fm 1 Ⓣ :23 3 :47 3 1:13 1:37 3 3↑ ⒻAlw 42550n1x **88** 6 1 1/2 2hd 1hd 1 1 1/2 1 7 1/4 Guidry M L114 *2.50 84– 16 *Sand Springs*114 7 1/4 Twilight Glow112 1/2 Constancy114nk Drew off,driving 9

Santa Catarina
Own: Lewis Robert B. and Beverly J

B. f. 4 (Feb) KEESEP01 $950,000
Sire: Unbridled (Fappiano) $200,000
Dam: Purrfectly (Storm Cat)
Br: Dinwiddie Farm (Ky)
Tr: Baffert Bob(0 0 0 0 .00) 2003:(674 127 .19)

Life	10	3	3	2	$645,260	106	
2003	5	2	1	1	$342,680	106	
2002	5	1	2	1	$302,580	95	
	0	0	0	0	$0	-	
D.Fst	7	3	3	0	$458,260	106	
Wet(425)	2	0	0	2	$142,000	85	
Turf(309)	1	0	0	0	$45,000	88	
Dst(0)	0	0	0	0	$0	-	

5Jly03-5Hol	fm	1¼ Ⓣ	:473 1:114 1:353 1:594	ⒻAmercnOaks750k	88	4	21½	21	2hd	2hd	42¾	Stevens G L	LB121	*2.60	90-11	Dimitrova1212 *SandSprings*121nk AtlanticOcen121½	Stalked,bid,outkicked	14
14Jun03-6Hol	fst	1 1/16	:231 :454 1:092 1:413	ⒻHolBCOak-G2	106	1	57½	47½	43½	1½	14	Stevens G L	LB116	*.80	96-04	SantaCatarin1164 Buffythecenterfold1135 PrincessV1146	3wd bid,cleared	5
16May03-10Pim	sly	1⅛	:473 1:121 1:381 1:521	ⒻBlkEySsn-G2	79	6	43	42	2hd	25	39	Stevens G L	L117	*.80	74-23	RoarEmotion122½ Fircroft1198½ *SantaCtrin*1175¾	Rated 4wd,bid,weakened	8
2May03-10CD	fst	1⅛	:46 1:10 1:353 1:483	ⒻKyOaks-G1	96	11	76½	74½	31	1hd	23¼	Stevens G L	L121	5.90	92-07	*Bird Town*1213¼ Santa Catarina121hd Yell121¾	Exch brushes stretch	12
12Mar03-2SA	fst	1	:222 :461 1:104 1:373	ⒻOClm 80000N	87	5	41½	2hd	11	13½	15	Stevens G L	LB118	*.30e	83-13	SntCtrin1185 HonestAnswer1182 *ProvenForm*1182½	Kicked clear, ridn out	6

Savedbythelight
Own: Mack Earle I

Dk. b or b. f. 4 (Mar)
Sire: Saint Ballado (Halo) $125,000
Dam: Wild Royal (Wild Again)
Br: R. C. Durr & George Budig (Ky)
Tr: Violette R A Jr(0 0 0 0 .00) 2003:(178 28 .16)

Life	11	3	2	4	$312,504	94	
2003	7	2	0	4	$229,080	94	
2002	4	1	2	0	$83,424	89	
	0	0	0	0	$0	-	
D.Fst	8	2	1	4	$275,704	94	
Wet(385)	0	0	0	0	$0	-	
Turf(276)	3	1	1	0	$36,800	80	
Dst(0)	0	0	0	0	$0	-	

20Dec03-8Aqu	fst	1¼ ⊡	:51 1:154 1:411 2:054	3↑ⒻLadiesH-G3	88	7	2½	2½	2hd	12½	13	Migliore R	L115 b	4.50	86-18	Svedbythlight1153 QunsTriomph113hd Rtroctiv1131	Pressed pace, driving	10
26Nov03-7Aqu	fst	1⅛	:48 1:121 1:383 1:524	3↑ⒻAlw 50000N2x	78	6	4¾	31½	3½	32½	32½	Chavez J F	L117 b	*1.20	69-28	MissFortunte1172¼ TurquoiseBd121nk *Svdbythlight*117hd	Wide both turns	6
4Oct03-9Pha	fst	1 1/16	:24 :474 1:121 1:454	ⒻCotillnH-G2	76	3	32	53	54½	38½	311¾	Vega H	L117 b	2.90	71-17	Fast Cookie1163¾ Ladyecho1168 Savedbythelight1174¼	Bested rest	5
17Aug03-9Sar	fm	1⅛ Ⓣ	:462 1:102 1:36 1:49	ⒻLakPlcdH-G2	80	1	55	68½	612	57	65¾	Migliore R	L114 b	6.70	78-13	SndSprings121¾ *IndyFiveHundred*114no *FilmMker*1193½	Inside, no response	10
19Jly03-9Bel	fst	1½	:462 1:113 2:033 2:31	ⒻCCAOaks-G1	81	2	616	65¾	46½	410	36	Santos J A	L121 b	6.90	71-17	SpokenFur1213½ Fircroft1212½ Svdbythlight1214¼	3 wide run second turn	7
15Jun03-8Bel	fst	1⅛ ⊗	:462 1:104 1:36 1:49	ⒻSandsPoint114k	94	5	2hd	2hd	2hd	12½	15¾	Migliore R	L115 b	5.60	85-18	Svdbythlight1155¾ VirgnVoyg117hd LttlBonnt1152	Drew away under drive	5
9May03-7Bel	fst	1 1/16	:243 :482 1:122 1:45	3↑ⒻAlw 46000N1x	77	4	21	3½	24½	27	34½	Migliore R	L116 b	*1.30	70-25	*Moonlightndbuty*1124 Alluring122½ *Svdbythlght*1164	Chased outside, no bid	6

Scrimshaw
Own: Lewis Robert B. and Beverly J

Dk. b or b. c. 4 (Apr) KEEAPR02 $550,000
Sire: Gulch (Mr. Prospector) $50,000
Dam: Rogue Girl (Sham)
Br: Stan Stefanski & Ingrid Stefanski (Ky)
Tr: Lukas D. W(0 0 0 0 .00) 2003:(663 71 .11)

Life	10	3	0	2	$408,879	104	
2003	8	1	0	2	$352,479	101	
2002	2	2	0	0	$56,400	104	
	0	0	0	0	$0	-	
D.Fst	8	3	0	1	$308,879	104	
Wet(342)	2	0	0	1	$100,000	98	
Turf(286)	0	0	0	0	$0	-	
Dst(0)	0	0	0	0	$0	-	

23Aug03-10Sar	fst	7f	:213 :433 1:083 1:22	KngsBshp-G1	82	6	6	75¼	911	911	1011¼	Chavez J F	L123 b	20.40	86-07	Valid Video121nk Great Notion117nk *Ghostzapper*1171¾	Brief speed, tired	13
2Aug03-8Sar	fst	6f	:22 :443 :562 1:083	Amstrdam-G2	88	1	5	43	52¾	66¼	69¼	Prado E S	L123 b	5.60	90-07	Zavata1195¼ Great Notion121½ Trust N Luck123nk	Chased inside, tired	7
7Jun03-11Bel	sly	1½	:483 1:132 2:023 2:281	Belmont-G1	74	3	32	31½	59	619	630	Stevens G L	L126 b	11.00	61-14	EmpireMker126¾ TenMostWntd1264¼ FunnyCid1265¼	Drifted 1/4 pl, tired	6
17May03-12Pim	gd	1 3/16	:47 1:113 1:362 1:553	Preaknes-G1	98	2	1hd	32	42½	25	310½	Stevens G L	L126 b	4.90e	84-12	FunnyCide1269¾ MidwayRoad126¾ Scrimshaw126no	Came in, brushed 1/16	10
3May03-10CD	fst	1¼	:461 1:102 1:353 2:01	KyDerby-G1	93	16	64	73¾	84¾	86	1110½	Velasquez C	L126 b	16.50	84-06	*Funny Cide*1261¾ *EmpireMaker*126hd PeaceRules126hd	Drift in bmp start,5w	16
19Apr03-8Kee	fst	1 1/16	:23 :47 1:113 1:452	ClmrLex-G2	101	1	21½	32	32	1½	13	Prado E S	L116 b	6.30	80-22	Scrimshw1163 EyofthTigr116nk DomsticDisput116nk	Bobble,bmp,4w,drvg	7
15Feb03-9GP	fst	7f	:22 :441 1:091 1:223	Hutchesn-G2	75	5	6	31	32	44	410½	Bailey J D	L118 b	2.00	84-08	Lion Tamer1186 Strength Within116¾ Crafty Guy1223¾	Slow start, 3 wide	6
18Jan03-7SA	fst	1 1/16	:23 :462 1:101 1:421	StCtlina-G2	92	6	21	21½	21	32	36½	Solis A	LB115 b	*1.90	86-15	DomsticDsput1133 OurBobbyV1133½ Scrmshw1154	Broke in,3wd,best rest	8

Sea of Showers
Own: Flaxman Stable

B. m. 5 (Apr)
Sire: Seattle Slew (Bold Reasoning) $300,000
Dam: Chimes of Freedom (Private Account)
Br: Flaxman Holdings Ltd (Ky)
Tr: Frankel Robert J(0 0 0 0 .00) 2003:(411 114 .28)

Life	9	4	0	1	$161,449	101	D.Fst	0	0	0	0	$0 -
2003	3	2	0	0	$106,846	101	Wet(387)	0	0	0	0	$0 -
2002	6	2	0	1	$54,603	86	Turf(319)	9	4	0	1	$161,449 101
	0	0	0	0	$0	-	Dst(0)	0	0	0	0	$0 -

23Aug03-8Sar fm $1\frac{1}{16}$ [T] :23^2 :47^1 1:11 1:41 3↑ Ⓕ BlSpaBCH-G3 **80** 2 $7^{7\frac14}$ $8^{5\frac12}$ $8^{5\frac34}$ 9^{10} 9^8 Bailey J D L117 *1.30 91 - Stylish116½ Snow Dance117^1 Cozzy Corner112^{hd} Stutter step stretch 9
13Apr03-6Kee fm $1\frac{1}{16}$ Ⓣ :23^3 :48 1:12 1:41^4 4↑ Ⓕ JenyWily-G3 **101** 2 $8^{8\frac12}$ $9^{5\frac34}$ $9^{5\frac14}$ $6^{2\frac14}$ $1^{1\frac14}$ Bailey J D L116 *2.10 92- 08 SofShowrs116$^{1\frac14}$ MgicMission116^{nk} SnowDnc116^{hd} Under brisk urging,7w 10
17Jan03-7SA fm 1 Ⓣ :23^2 :46^1 1:09^3 1:33^2 4↑ Ⓕ OClm 80000N **97** 10 9^{10} 9^{10} $9^{7\frac34}$ $6^{2\frac14}$ 1^1 Solis A LB119 *1.50 95- 07 *Sea of Showers*119^1 Revenante119$^{1\frac12}$ Nanogram119$^{1\frac12}$ 5wd into lane,rallied 10

Secret Liaison
Own: Desperado Stables Inc

B. m. 6 (Feb) KEESEP99 $75,000
Sire: Housebuster (Mt. Livermore) $7,500
Dam: Pennant Winner (Crafty Prospector)
Br: Needham/ Betz Thoroughbreds, Liberation Farm & Elia (Ky)
Tr: West Ted H(0 0 0 0 .00) 2003:(167 39 .23)

Life	14	7	2	0	$342,719	102	D.Fst	14	7	2	0	$342,719 102
2003	4	2	0	0	$136,719	102	Wet(398)	0	0	0	0	$0 -
2002	4	3	1	0	$137,600	100	Turf(270)	0	0	0	0	$0 -
	0	0	0	0	$0	-	Dst(0)	0	0	0	0	$0 -

23Aug03-8Dmr fst 6½f :22^2 :45 1:09 1:15^2 3↑ Ⓕ RchBrdoH-G3 **102** 8 1 $1^{\frac12}$ 1^1 $1^{2\frac12}$ 1^4 Nakatani C S LB116 3.70 98- 10 Secret Liaison116^4 Lacie Girl116^1 *Spring Meadow*117^{hd} Bit off rail,cleared 8
6Aug03-6Dmr fst 6½f :22^2 :45^1 1:09^2 1:15^4 3↑ Ⓕ OClm 80000N **97** 4 3 $1^{\frac12}$ 1^1 $1^{2\frac12}$ $1^{1\frac12}$ Nakatani C S LB117 *1.60 96- 13 *Secret Liaison*117$^{1\frac12}$ Puxa Saco116$^{2\frac12}$ Wild Tickle117^2 Bit off rail,held game 6
26Mar03-2SA fst 6f :21^1 :44 :56^3 1:10^1 4↑ Ⓕ PineTreeLn78k **79** 5 1 1^{hd} 2^{hd} 1^{hd} $4^{4\frac12}$ Smith M E LB116 2.00 82- 08 Shameful116^1 Wild Tickle116½ Brisquette116^3 Dueled,wkened late 5
22Feb03-8SA fst 6f :21^1 :43^4 :56^2 1:10^1 4↑ Ⓕ LsFlresH-G3 **75** 7 3 3^{nk} 1^{hd} 2^1 $6^{7\frac14}$ Smith M E LB117 3.40 80- 15 Spring Meadow117^{nk} Brisquette116$^{1\frac12}$ Wild Tickle117½ 4wd,3wd,weakened 7

Senor Swinger
Own: Lewis Robert B. and Beverly J

Gr/ro. c. 4 (Apr)
Sire: El Prado*Ire (Sadler's Wells) $30,000
Dam: Smooth Swinger (Kris S.)
Br: Bob Ackerman (Ky)
Tr: Baffert Bob(0 0 0 0 .00) 2003:(674 127 .19)

Life	12	4	0	2	$376,890	103	D.Fst	3	2	0	0	$59,640 93
2003	11	3	0	2	$361,290	103	Wet(396)	2	0	0	0	$22,500 96
2002	1	1	0	0	$15,600	86	Turf(321)	7	2	0	2	$294,750 103
	0	0	0	0	$0	-	Dst(0)	0	0	0	0	$0 -

30Nov03-9Hol fm 1¼ Ⓣ :51 1:17^2 1:41 2:04^1 HolDerby-G1 **92** 12 $9^{6\frac14}$ $10^{5\frac12}$ $12^{8\frac12}$ $12^{5\frac34}$ $12^{3\frac12}$ Bailey J D LB122 4.00 68- 17 Sweet Return122½ Fairly Ransom122½ Kicken Kris122^{hd} Steadied,tight 1/8 13
24Oct03-8SA fm 1½ Ⓣ :50^3 1:15^4 2:04^3 2:28^1 3↑ CFBurkeH-G3 **98** 4 3^2 3^3 $3^{1\frac12}$ $2^{\frac12}$ $3^{\frac12}$ Bailey J D LB114 *3.40 84- 16 RunawayDancer112^{nk} Labirinto116^{nk} SenorSwinger114^1 Bid btwn,led 1/16 9
6Sep03-8Dmr fm 1⅛ Ⓣ :47^2 1:11 1:34^3 1:46^2 DmrDerby-G2 **99** 1 8^5 $7^{5\frac14}$ 6^4 $6^{3\frac12}$ $4^{1\frac34}$ Valdivia J Jr LB122 *1.90 99- 05 FirlyRnsom122$^{1\frac14}$ *DeviousBoy*122no SwetRturn122½ 3wd into str,outkicked 9
16Aug03-8Dmr fm $1\frac{1}{16}$ Ⓣ :23^3 :47^1 1:10^3 1:40^1 LaJollaH-G3 **97** 3 $7^{9\frac12}$ 7^{11} $7^{7\frac34}$ $6^{5\frac34}$ 3^1 Alvarado F T LB120 *1.40 99- 10 Singletary118½ Devious Boy117½ Senor Swinger120½ Split foes,rail rally 7
12Jly03-10Cnl fm 1¼ Ⓣ :47^4 1:11^4 1:36^1 2:01 VrgniaDrby500k **87** 3 $6^{3\frac12}$ $6^{5\frac12}$ 7^5 5^{10} $4^{5\frac14}$ Day P L122 *.20 100- 03 Silver Tree115$^{1\frac12}$ *Kicken Kris*115$^{1\frac34}$ King's Drama115^2 6wd 3/16,by-faders 8
7Jun03-9CD fm 1⅛ Ⓣ :46^2 1:10^4 1:35^4 1:47^2 JfrsnCup-G3 **103** 7 6^9 6^{14} $4^{9\frac12}$ 1^1 $1^{5\frac12}$ Albarado R J L120 *.70 97- 05 Senor Swinger120$^{5\frac12}$ Remind116^{no} Rapid Proof120½ Drew off,hand urg,5w 7
17May03-12Pim gd $1\frac{3}{16}$:47 1:11^3 1:36^2 1:55^3 Preaknes-G1 **94** 10 10^{12} 10^{14} 10^{12} 6^{12} $5^{12\frac12}$ Day P L126 f 4.90e 82- 12 FunnyCide126$^{9\frac34}$ MidwayRoad126$^{\frac34}$ Scrimshw126^{no} Wide belated response 10
2May03-9CD fm $1\frac{1}{16}$ Ⓣ :23^1 :46^4 1:10^2 1:41^1 CRAmrTrf-G3 **97** 3 $7^{4\frac14}$ $7^{6\frac34}$ $8^{7\frac14}$ $5^{3\frac12}$ $1^{2\frac12}$ Day P L117 f 3.10 98- 03 Senor Swinger117$^{2\frac12}$ Remind117^1 Foufa's Warrior117½ 6w lane,stiff drive 10
12Apr03-8Aqu my 1⅛ :47^1 1:11 1:35^4 1:48^3 WoodMem-G1 **96** 5 6^8 6^7 6^7 5^9 $5^{9\frac14}$ Stevens G L L123 17.30 84- 12 Empire Maker123½ *Funny Cide*123$^{7\frac12}$ Kissin Saint123^1 Bumped after start 8
Previously trained by Goldfine Mickey A
15Mar03-8GP fst 1⅛ :46^1 1:10^3 1:36 1:49 FlaDerby-G1 **75** 5 5^5 $5^{4\frac34}$ 4^3 5^9 $5^{20\frac14}$ Prado E S L122 6.70 77- 10 *Empire Maker*122$^{9\frac34}$ Trust N Luck122½ Indy Dancer122$^{2\frac12}$ 4 wide, faltered 7
31Jan03-8GP fst $1\frac{1}{16}$:22^3 :46^2 1:12 1:44 Alw 36000N1x **93** 5 5^4 5^5 3^1 1^1 $1^{5\frac14}$ ♦Prado E S L122 5.50 89- 12 TenCentsShine118$^{5\frac14}$ SnorSwingr122$^{5\frac14}$ RoringFvr118$^{1\frac12}$ 3 wide, just lasted 11

Shake You Down
Own: Cole R L Jr

Ch. g. 6 (Apr)
Sire: Montbrook (Buckaroo) $20,000
Dam: Mauvin Gway (Rajab)
Br: Ocala Stud Farm (Fla)
Tr: Lake Scott A(0 0 0 0 .00) 2003:(2012 457 .23)

Life	36	14	6	4	$998,560	121	D.Fst	28	9	6	4	$800,380 121
2003	13	7	2	2	$829,160	121	Wet(372)	7	5	0	0	$198,180 118
2002	11	3	3	1	$91,640	102	Turf(266)	1	0	0	0	$0 29
	0	0	0	0	$0	-	Dst(0)	0	0	0	0	$0 -

21Dec03–8Aqu fst 6f ⊡ :223 :451 :57 1:092 3↑GravesdH-G3 **110** 4 2 1hd 11 12 12¼ Luzzi M J L124 fb *.90 97–12 ShkYoDown1242¼ WytothTop1141¾ GtorsNBrs115¾ Speed 2 wide, driving 7
15Nov03–10Lrl fst 6f :214 :442 :563 1:084 3↑DeFrncsM-G1 **108** 6 5 21 2hd 1hd 21¾ Luzzi M J L123 fb *.80 93–13 AHuevo1191¾ *ShakeYouDown*123no GatorsNBers115½ Bobbled,2wd,gamely 10
25Oct03–5SA fst 6f :21 :431 :55 1:074 3↑BCSprint-G1 **109** 2 13 2hd 2hd 21½ 34¼ Luzzi M J LB126 fb 3.50 95–05 CjunBet1232¼ Blusthstndrd1262 ShkYouDown126½ Broke slow, rushed up 13
11Sep03–8Bel fst 6f :214 :442 :561 1:083 3↑Alw 56000c **115** 5 3 11 13 16 15¾ Luzzi M J L123 fb *.50 96–12 Shake You Down1235¾ Papua118hd Super Fuse1162¾ Cruised, ridden out 6
10Aug03–9Sar sly 6f :22 :443 :563 1:09 3↑AGVndbtH-G2 **103** 2 1 1hd 1hd 3nk 45¼ Luzzi M J L123 fb *.55 92–10 *PrivteHord*1155 MountinGnrl118hd MiksClssic114nk Vied inside, weakened 5
12Jly03–12Crc fst 6f :211 :434 :562 1:10 3↑SmlSprtH-G3 **121** 13 1 31½ 2hd 14 18¼ Luzzi M J L119 fb *2.80 94–11 ShkeYouDown1198¼ *PrivteHorde*113¾ MyCousinMtt116½ Strong hand ride 13
7Jun03–7Bel sly 6f :212 :44 :561 1:092 3↑TrNthBCH-G2 **108** 6 4 2hd 1½ 12½ 1nk Luzzi M J L118 fb *.85 92–10 *ShkYouDown*118nk HighwyProspctor1154½ Vodk114¾ Duel, dug in, held on 6
10May03–6Bel fst 6f :22 :443 :561 1:082 3↑BoldRlrH-G3 **113** 7 1 11½ 11½ 1½ 11 Luzzi M J L115 fb *1.80 97–12 *ShakeYouDown*1151 HeresZelous1143¼ PeepingTom117¾ Set pace, gamely 7
26Apr03–5Aqu sly 6f :214 :441 :554 1:073 4↑Alw 54000N4X **118** 3 1 11 11½ 15 15¼ Fragoso P7 L112 fb *.80 102–15 *Shake You Down*1125¼ Lethal Weapon1172½ Kazoo1199 Set pce,drew away 5
11Apr03–8Aqu sly 6f :214 :444 :561 1:081 4↑Alw 54000N$Y **118** 3 4 25 1hd 17 17½ Fragoso P7 L111 fb *3.10e 99–19 *ShakeYouDown*1117½ GoldI.D118½ *Heroofthegame*1133¼ Rail run, ridden out 9
12Mar03–6Aqu fst 6f ⊡ :222 :444 :571 1:10 4↑Clm c-(65-55) **92** 3 6 22 21½ 2½ 2nk Delgado A L120 fb 7.00 94–12 Run Kush Run115nk *ShakeYouDown*1202¼ C.L.Rib120¾ Game finish outside 6
Claimed from Hand, Craig E. and Donahue, Timothy O. for $65,000, Feliciano Ben M Jr Trainer 2003(as of 3/12): (50 11 8 9 0.22) Previously trained by Gino Luigi
20Feb03–7Lrl fst 6f :221 :451 :57 1:092 4↑OClm 50000(50-45)N **92** 1 1 12 1½ 33½ 44½ Delgado A L117 fb 12.50 87–18 *LovHppy*122½ *ThDputyIsHom*114½ SssyHond1173½ Sent,pace ins,weakened 8
31Jan03–7Lrl fst 5½f :23 :46 :58 1:04 4↑OClm 50000(50-45)N **86** 7 1 3½ 3nk 31½ 34¼ Delgado A L117 fb 2.00 88–20 *LoveHappy*1192¾ *TakeAchnceOnMe*1171½ ShkeYouDown117¾ Vied,3w, tired 7

Sharbayan (Ire)
Own: Iron County Farms Inc. and Miller Tru

B. g. 6 (Mar)
Sire: Doyoun*Ire (Mill Reef) $5,520
Dam: Sharbata*Ire (Kahyasi)
Br: His Highness the Aga Khan's Studs S.C. (Ire)
Tr: Dollase Wallace A(0 0 0 0 .00) 2003:(95 24 .25)

Life	12	6	2	0	$237,925	104	D.Fst	0	0	0	0	$0 -
2003	5	4	0	0	$162,601	104	Wet(250)	0	0	0	0	$0 -
2002	3	1	0	0	$34,160	96	Turf(315)	12	6	2	0	$237,925 104
	0	0	0	0	$0	-	Dst(0)	0	0	0	0	$0 -

16Nov03–9CD yl 1⅛ Ⓣ :492 1:142 1:391 1:513 3↑RivrCtyH-G3 **96** 1 94¼ 98½ 84¼ 65½ 53¼ Day P L119 b *1.90 73–26 Hard Buck118½ Warleigh1171 Rowans Park1141 9w lane,no real threat 10
4Oct03–7Kee fm 1½ Ⓣ :502 1:154 2:044 2:292 3↑SycamrBC-G3 **104** 2 44 52¼ 31 1½ 11¾ Day P L120 b 2.90 93–14 Sharbayan1201¾ Cetewayo122½ Deputy Strike1201¼ 5w,late hand urging 10
30Aug03–8AP fm *1½ Ⓣ :493 1:152 2:07 2:313 3↑Hcp 45000 **98** 2 318 313 312 33 1¾ Marquez C H Jr L117 b *1.30 96–09 *Sharbayan*117¾ Roxinho1171 Act of War118hd Driving 5
24May03–7CD fm 1⅛ Ⓣ :464 1:103 1:35 1:473 3↑OClm 62500N **97** 3 78¼ 711 712 45½ 1no Day P L119 b *.70 96–07 *Shrbyn*119no FostrsLnding112nk CptinNichols1192¼ Bmp start,force in,drv 7
9Apr03–7Kee gd 1 1/16 Ⓣ :231 :47 1:121 1:44 4↑Alw 51478N2X **96** 3 78 76¾ 54 33½ 1½ Day P L116 b *2.40 81–18 *Shrbyn*116½ SunshineMessngr1162 CmpDvid1161½ Lack room 1/4p,5w,drvg 9

Sharp Impact

Own: Darley Stud Management LLC

Dk. b or b. c. 4 (Mar) FTKJUL01 $425,000
Sire: Siphon*Brz (Itajara) $20,000
Dam: Fast and Early (Carson City)
Br: Brereton C. Jones (Ky)
Tr: McLaughlin Kiaran P(0 0 0 0 .00) 2003:(186 46 .25)

Life	11	4	0	2	$206,568	96	D.Fst	4	2	0	0	$64,800 88
2003	8	2	0	2	$141,768	96	Wet(308)	2	1	0	0	$28,800 82
2002	3	2	0	0	$64,800	88	Turf(258)	5	1	0	2	$112,968 96
	0	0	0	0	$0	–	Dst(0)	0	0	0	0	$0 –

20Dec03-11Crc fm 7½f Ⓣ :224 :453 1:093 1:272 PAxthelm100k **91** 9 7 25 26 34½ 33¼ Douglas R R L122 b 5.20 99- 01 Magic Mecke1171 Hear No Evil1222¼ Sharp Impact1221¼ Not enough late 12
29Oct03- 8Aqu my 1⅛ :47 1:112 1:372 1:51 DiscvryH-G3 – 8 11½ 1½ 53¾ - - Gryder A T L114 b 24.50 - 27 During120no Unforgettable Max1141¾ Inamorato1144¼ Eased stretch 8
21Sep03- 9Bel fm 1⅛ [T] :471 1:104 1:342 1:46 JamaicaH-G2 **72** 7 1½ 1½ 1hd 44 714¾ Migliore R L116 b 10.70 85- 12 *Stroll*1212 *Kicken Kris*121no Joe Bear1172½ Set pace, tired 7
1Sep03-10Sar gd 1 3/16 Ⓣ :48 1:124 1:364 1:552 SaranacH-G3 **94** 3 1½ 11½ 1hd 1½ 32¼ Coa E M L116 b 3.95e 87- 11 ShoalWater1162¼ UrbanKing115hd SharpImpct1161½ Set pace, weakened 6
4Aug03- 8Sar yl 1⅛ [T] :481 1:124 1:371 1:491 HalOFmeH-G2 **77** 1 1hd 1½ 1½ 34½ 711¼ Migliore R L122 b 7.30 81- 08 *Stroll*1174 Urban King1151¼ Saint Stephen115¾ Set pace, tired 11
13Jly03- 9Bel fm 1¼ [T] :501 1:144 1:383 2:023 Lexingtn-G3 **96** 6 11½ 11 12 11 1½ Migliore R L114 b 4.00 81- 20 SharpImpact114½ HiddenTruth1182 UrbnKing114¾ Controlled pace, game 6
8Jun03- 5Bel my 1⅛ ⊗ :46 1:102 1:36 1:494 3↑ Alw 48000N2x **82** 1 1½ 1½ 1½ 11½ 11¼ Migliore R L115 b 3.00 81- 17 *SharpImpct*1151¼ ColonilBy1214½ PoppysImge1154½ Set pace, determined 7
Previously trained by Eoin G Harty
13Feb03♦Nad al Sheba (UAE) fst *1 LH 1:37 3↑ UAE 2000 Guineas (Prestige)-G3 Stk 250000 86¾ O'Donohoe D 117 b - Victory Moon126½ Western Diplomat1171¼ Bourbonnais1191¾ 9
Timeform rating: 94 *Tracked leader,bid 2f out,weakened 1f out.Endemaj 4th,Dublin 7th*

Shawklit Mint

Own: Flatbird Stable

Dk. b or b. f. 5 (Apr)
Sire: Air Forbes Won (Bold Forbes) $2,500
Dam: Shawklit Delight (Pine Bluff)
Br: Treasure Hill Farm, Inc. (NY)
Tr: Reynolds Patrick L(0 0 0 0 .00) 2003:(217 38 .18)

Life	29	10	4	6	$464,654	108	D.Fst	22	5	4	6	$253,999 108
2004	1	0	0	0	$816	–	Wet(346)	7	5	0	0	$210,655 105
2003	11	4	1	0	$232,725	105	Turf(277)	0	0	0	0	$0 –
	0	0	0	0	$0	–	Dst(0)	0	0	0	0	$0 –

13Dec03- 7Aqu fst 6f [•] :233 :47 :584 1:111 3↑ⒻGrlndORssH82k **70** 2 6 63¼ 53 65¼ 66½ Arroyo N Jr L116 3.70 81- 15 Balmy114hd Gazillion1194 Bonefide Reason1121¼ Inside, no rally 9
28Nov03- 9Aqu fst 1 :231 :462 1:103 1:362 3↑ⒻTopFlgtH-G2 **90** 1 31 32 43½ 37½ 56¼ Arroyo N Jr L114 21.50 77- 29 Randaroo1162 Beauty Halo1153¼ Pocus Hocus116nk Bumped after start 12
18Oct03- 6Bel fst 7f :22 :451 1:11 1:241 3↑Ⓕ[S]IroquoisH125k **74** 8 8 99¾ 86¼ 76¼ 56¼ Migliore R L123 6.70 73- 21 PrincessDixie120nk ShesGottheBet1232¾ GrbBg117¾ Bumped start, 5 wide 13
1Aug03- 8Sar sly 6f :221 :452 :572 1:094 3↑ⒻHnrblMsH-G3 **69** 4 1 42½ 64¾ 611 613¾ Migliore R L115 4.80 79- 13 WillOntheMove114½ ShinAgin120no SmoknFrolic1171 Hard ridden, empty 6
12Jly03-11Crc fst 6f :212 :442 :573 1:111 3↑ⒻPrcsRnyH-G2 **77** 5 3 74 87½ 87½ 710½ Velasquez C L116 4.10 78- 11 Gold Mover118no Vision in Flight1134¼ *Harmony Lodge*116hd No factor 8
8Jun03- 8Bel my 6½f :224 :454 1:091 1:151 3↑ⒻVagrncyH-G2 **105** 2 1 12 11½ 12½ 11¾ Migliore R L115 4.30 97- 10 Shawklit Mint1151¾ Shine Again1213¼ *Gold Mover*118 In charge from start 3
22May03- 8Bel sly 6f :222 :444 :564 1:093 4↑ⒻAlw 56000c **85** 1 1 1hd 1hd 1hd 1½ Migliore R L120 *.70 91- 13 *ShwklitMint*120½ BonefideRson1181 *SilkConcord*1162½ Vied, dug in, prevail 5
15Mar03- 7Aqu fst 6f [•] :223 :452 :572 1:102 3↑Ⓕ[S]BroadwayH81k **90** 2 4 3½ 21½ 2½ 11¾ Migliore R L123 *.65 92- 11 *ShwkltMnt*1231¾ Boundnddtrmnd114½ *ShsGotthBt*119nk With pace, driving 7
21Feb03- 8Aqu fst 6f [•] :22 :444 :573 1:103 4↑ⒻAlw 54000N$Y **94** 1 5 36 33 21½ 1½ Migliore R L116 *.65 91- 13 *ShwklitMint*116½ BonefideReson1171 GoldnMd1191¼ Came wide, prevailed 6
1Feb03- 8Aqu fst 6f [•] :231 :463 :59 1:11 3↑ⒻCorrectnH83k **92** 7 3 64¾ 43 3½ 21¼ McKee J L113 *2.15 88- 21 A. P. Andie1121¼ *Shawklit Mint*1134 Golden Made116¾ Game finish outside 9
1Jan03- 9Aqu sly 6f [•] :231 :462 :58 1:10 3↑ⒻInterbrghH81k **69** 2 4 44 46 514 514 Migliore R L115 1.65 80- 17 Wilzada1195 BlindedbyLove114½ BonefideReson1136¼ Wide, no response 7

Shine Again
Own: Bohemia Stable

Dk. b or b. m. 7 (Jan)
Sire: Wild Again (Icecapade) $50,000
Dam: Shiner (Two Punch)
Br: Mrs. Richard C. duPont (Md)
Tr: Jerkens H. A(0 0 0 0 .00) 2003:(359 73 .20)

Life	34	14	10	7	$1,271,840	110	D.Fst	29	13	6	7	$1,078,620 110
2003	7	2	5	0	$275,620	104	Wet(392)	5	1	4	0	$193,220 105
2002	10	4	2	3	$425,500	105	Turf(241)	0	0	0	0	$0 -
	0	0	0	0	$0	-	Dst(0)	0	0	0	0	$0 -

25Oct03-4Bel	fst	7f	:222 :453 1:102 1:233	3↑ⒻFrstFltH-G2	92	1	5	51¼	41¾	25	2nk	Migliore R	L121	*.50	82-14	*Randaroo*115nk Shine Again1211¼ Zawzooth113½	Game finish outside	8
13Sep03-6Bel	fst	6f	:22 :45 :571 1:104	3↑ⒻFlrlPrkH-G3	92	3	4	41¾	43	32½	2¾	Santos J A	L120	*.55	84-18	Bauhauser115¾ Shine Again1202¼ Literary Light1131¼	Game finish outside	6
24Aug03-9Sar	fst	7f	:223 :45 1:09 1:221	3↑ⒻBalrinaH-G1	100	5	5	41½	41½	31½	2no	Santos J A	L120	*2.60	96-12	*HrmonyLodge*115no ShineAgin1202 GoldMover118hd	Steadied backstretch	8
1Aug03-8Sar	sly	6f	:221 :452 :572 1:094	3↑ⒻHnrblMsH-G3	104	5	4	2½	2½	2½	2½	Samyn J L	L120	*1.65	92-13	WillOnthMov114½ ShinAgin120no SmoknFrolic1171	Pressed pace, gamely	6
8Jun03-8Bel	my	6½f	:224 :454 1:091 1:151	3↑ⒻVagrncyH-G2	101	1	3	32½	31½	22½	21¾	Samyn J L	L121	*.70	95-10	Shawklit Mint1151¾ Shine Again1213¼ *Gold Mover*118	Game finish outside	3
11May03-8Bel	fst	6f	:214 :442 :562 1:09	3↑ⒻGnunRskH-G2	104	2		42	41½	1hd	14	Samyn J L	L119	2.10	94-18	ShineAgin1194 CrsonHollow1221¼ *HrmonyLodge*1166¼	Drew away late, fog	4
19Apr03-4Aqu	fst	6f	:22 :444 :57 1:093	4↑ⒻAlw 54000N4x	96	4	4	42½	41¼	2hd	1¾	Samyn J L	L123	*.60	92-15	*ShineAgain*123¾ FreshTracks1162¼ OzildasKaren1162½	Shown whip stretch	5

Shoal Water
Own: Sam-Son Farms

B. g. 4 (Feb)
Sire: Smart Strike (Mr. Prospector) $20,000
Dam: Puffin Island (Pleasant Colony)
Br: Sam-Son Farm (Ont-C)
Tr: Frostad Mark R(0 0 0 0 .00) 2003:(206 44 .21)

Life	10	3	2	2	$412,050	99	D.Fst	5	2	0	1	$146,770 92
2003	7	2	1	2	$325,690	99	Wet(435)	1	0	0	1	$50,000 90
2002	3	1	1	0	$86,360	85	Turf(311)	4	1	2	0	$215,280 99
	0	0	0	0	$0	-	Dst(0)	0	0	0	0	$0 -

19Oct03-9WO	yl	1½	[T] :512 1:163 2:081 2:333	3↑CanIntnl-G1	89	9	11	11	2½	86¼	810½	Kabel T K	L119	18.10	51-30	Phoenix Reach119¾ Macaw126hd Brian Boru1191	Off rail gave way	10
21Sep03-7WO	fst	1 1/16	⊗ :224 :463 1:121 1:462	3↑OClm 80000(80-75)N	87	6	54½	44	41½	42	34	Kabel T K	L117	*.50	70-35	Arco's Gold1153 Pat's Expectation1121 Shoal Water1172	4w, mild rally	7
1Sep03-10Sar	gd	1 3/16	[T] :48 1:124 1:364 1:552	SaranacH-G3	99	6	2½	21½	2hd	2½	12¼	Velazquez J R	L116	*1.15	89-11	ShoalWater1162¼ UrbanKing115hd SharpImpct1161½	Speed outside, clear	6
9Aug03-8WO	fm	1½	[T] :484 1:132 2:032 2:283	[R]Breeders1000k	97	6	33	31	1½	21½	21½	Kabel T K	L126	6.90	85-14	Wando1261½ *ShoalWter*1263¼ ColorfulJudgement1265	Stalk 5w,led,2nd best	8
20Jly03-8FE	my	1 3/16	:462 1:104 1:362 1:554	[R]PrncOWales500k	90	7	2hd	21	21	35	36	Clark D	L126	6.00	95 -	*Wando*1264 Arco's Gold1262 Shoal Water1262	Pressed, gave way	7
22Jun03-9WO	fst	1¼	:463 1:114 1:372 2:022	[R]QueensPlt1000k	92	10	22½	21	21½	36	413	Landry R C	L126	17.15	89-17	*Wando*1269 *Mobil*1261½ Rock Again1262½	Stalk 2-path,bid 3w	12
30May03-7WO	fst	1 1/16	:24 :482 1:13 1:451	Alw 69900N1x	92	5	1hd	1hd	1hd	12	14¼	Kabel T K	L117	2.30	80-25	ShoalWater1174¼ ITestify1171¼ TracysTonkToy1181	Duel 3 wide, drew off	9

Sightseek
Own: Juddmonte Farms Inc

Ch. m. 5 (Feb)
Sire: Distant View (Mr. Prospector) $20,000
Dam: Viviana (Nureyev)
Br: Juddmonte Farms, Inc. (Ky)
Tr: Frankel Robert J(0 0 0 0 .00) 2003:(411 114 .28)

Life	13	8	4	0	$1,433,866	115	D.Fst	11 7 3 0	$1,244,266 115
2003	8	4	3	0	$1,171,888	115	Wet(350)	1 1 0 0	$180,000 110
2002	5	4	1	0	$261,978	100	Turf(333)	1 0 1 0	$9,600 85
	0	0	0	0	$0	–	Dst(0)	0 0 0 0	$0 –

25Oct03–2SA fst 1⅛ :47 1:11 1:354 1:49 3↑ⒻBCDistaf-G1 **84** 5 6²¾ 64 6²¾ 56½ 410½ Bailey J D LB123 *.60 78–07 Adoration1234½ Elloluv1192½ Got Koko1233½ Bit crowded start 7
4Oct03–9Bel fst 1⅛ :474 1:122 1:363 1:491 3↑ⒻBeldame-G1 **107** 2 51½ 53 3nk 12½ 14½ Bailey J D L123 *.30 84–26 Sightseek1234½ Bird Town1204¾ Buy the Sport120¾ When asked, in hand 7
27Jly03–9Sar fst 1⅛ :491 1:132 1:38 1:504 3↑ⒻGoFWandH-G1 **115** 5 31½ 21½ 2½ 18 111½ Bailey J D L121 *.15 81–27 *Sightseek*12111½ *ShesGotthBt*1125 NonsuchBy1134 When ready, ridden out 6
21Jun03–9Bel sly 1 1/16 :222 :451 1:091 1:404 3↑ⒻOPhippsH-G1 **110** 2 2½ 2½ 2hd 11½ 15 Bailey J D L118 *1.05 96–18 *Sightseek*1185 TkeChrgeLdy1195 MndysGold1181¾ Drew clear under drive 5
3May03–8CD fst 7f :222 :452 1:10 1:22 4↑ⒻHmnaDstH-G1 **107** 2 5 51¼ 51½ 11½ 14½ Bailey J D L116 *.80 92–08 *Sightseek*1164½ Gold Mover119hd Miss Lodi1142¼ Split foes,3w,driving 8
9Mar03–8SA fst 1⅛ :47 1:103 1:353 1:481 4↑ⒻSMrgrtaH-G1 **108** 4 11 11 11½ 2hd 22 Valdivia J Jr LB116 2.50 91–16 Starrer1212 *Sightseek*1163 Bella Bellucci1165 Inside, 2nd best 5
8Feb03–6SA fst 1⅛ :463 1:104 1:353 1:482 ⒻLaCanada-G2 **105** 1 1½ 1hd 1hd 1½ 2¾ Valenzuela P A LB118 *.90 91–11 Got Koko121¾ Sightseek1181½ Bella Bellucci1183 Bit off rail,worn down 5
25Jan03–8SA fst 7f :22 :443 1:092 1:22 4↑ⒻSntMncaH-G1 **101** 5 6 41½ 3nk 11 2½ Bailey J D LB115 *.70 95–07 Affluent119½ Sightseek1151½ Secret of Mecca1103 Bid 3wd,led,willingly 7

Silver Wagon
Own: Buckram Oak Farm

Gr/ro. c. 3 (Mar) OBSFEB03 $120,000
Sire: Wagon Limit (Conquistador Cielo) $5,000
Dam: So Ritzy (Darn That Alarm)
Br: Mr. & Mrs. Leverett S. Miller (Fla)
Tr: Ziadie Ralph(0 0 0 0 .00) 2003:(375 44 .12)

Life	4	2	1	1	$162,140	92	D.Fst	4 2 1 1	$162,140 92
2003	4	2	1	1	$162,140	92	Wet(331*)	0 0 0 0	$0 –
2002	0	M	0	0	$0	–	Turf(229*)	0 0 0 0	$0 –
	0	0	0	0	$0	–	Dst(0)	0 0 0 0	$0 –

13Dec03–9Crc fst 1 1/16 :234 :483 1:133 1:453 WhatAPlesr100k **88** 1 21 42½ 53 33 35 Bailey J D L117 *.80 79–25 SecondofJune1155 TwiceasBd111hd SilverWgon1171¾ Steadied first turn 9
30Aug03–8Sar fst 7f :222 :452 1:102 1:232 Hopeful-G1 **92** 5 4 72 61½ 2½ 14 Bailey J D L122 12.50 90–11 SilverWgon1224 ChplRoyl1221½ NotoriousRogu1221 Split rivals, drew off 7
8Aug03–4Sar fst 7f :23 :461 1:11 1:234 Md Sp Wt 45k **79** 4 8 51¼ 51¾ 16 17½ Bailey J D L119 *1.65e 88–10 *Silver Wagon*1197½ *Eurosilver*1191¾ Apple Krisp1191¼ Bumped start, inside 10
28Jun03–10Crc fst 6½f :224 :462 1:123 1:193 Md Sp Wt 28k **67** 4 6 84 65½ 54½ 21¾ Garcia J A L118 6.80 79–12 TwiceasBd1181¾ *SilverWgon*118½ CheethSpeed1181 Angled out, up for 2nd 9

Singletary
Own: Little Red Feather Racing

B. c. 4 (May)   KEE0CT01 $3,200
Sire: Sultry Song (Cox's Ridge) $5,000
Dam:Joiski's Star (Star de Naskra)
Br: Disler Farms Ltd (Ky)
Tr: Chatlos D Jr(0 0 0 0 .00) 2003:(51 8 .16)

											Life	10	3	3	1	$246,822	100	D.Fst	2	0	0	0	$1,120	79
											2003	8	2	2	1	$206,352	99	Wet(348)	0	0	0	0	$0	–
											2002	2	1	1	0	$40,470	100	Turf(270)	8	3	3	1	$245,702	100
																		Dst(0)	0	0	0	0	$0	–

6Sep03–8Dmr fm 1 1/16 ⊕ :472 1:11 1:343 1:462 DmrDerby–G2 98 5 1 1/2 1 1/2 1 11 5 2 1/4 Valenzuela P A LB122 4.30 99–05 FirlyRnsom1221 1/4 DeviousBoy122no SweetReturn1222 1/2 Inside trip,weakened 9
16Aug03–8Dmr fm 1 1/16 ⊕ :233 :471 1:103 1:401 LaJollaH–G3 99 6 1hd 1 1/2 12 1/2 1 1/2 Valenzuela P A LB118 6.80 100–10 Singletary118 1/2 Devious Boy117 1/2 Senor Swinger120 1/2 Angled in,clear,held 7
23Jly03–5Dmr fm 1 1 ⊕ :223 :463 1:10 1:334 ®Oceanside85k 99 3 21 2 1/2 1hd 1hd 21 Valenzuela P A LB120 *.90 93–11 Sweet Return1161 Singletary1201 Requite1164 Pulld bit,led,outkickd 9
Run in divisions
25May03–8Hol fm 1 ⊕ :241 :482 1:121 1:352 WilRogrs–G3 90 1 21 21 21 1/2 22 32 Valenzuela P A LB117 *.40 85–13 PrivateChef115 3/4 BansheeKing151 1/4 Singletary1173 Pulled,stalkd,outkickd 6
12Apr03–7SA fm 1 ⊕ :232 :471 1:111 1:343 LaPuente150k 98 5 44 1/2 43 44 1/2 41 1/4 2no Flores D R LB118 *1.10 89–11 Steelaninch114no Singletary1181 Urban King1171 Bumped btwn 1/8,game 7
14Mar03–7SA fm 1 1/16 ⊕ :233 :464 1:094 1:333 AcademyRd81k 96 8 11 1/2 11 11 12 12 1/2 Flores D R LB116 2.40 94–08 Singletary1162 1/2 Steelaninch1161 Deep Shadow115 1/2 Dictated pace, driving 8
20Feb03–2SA fst 1 1/16 :23 :462 1:011 1:414 Alw 56000N1x 78 4 42 32 1/2 52 57 Pincay L Jr LB118 8.90 80–15 Atswhtmtlknbot118 3/4 Drng1183 1/4 BckindMnor1202 1/2 Pulled,stalkd,gave way 5
18Jan03–7SA fst 1 1/16 :23 :462 1:011 1:421 StCtlina–G2 79 3 52 31 1/2 31 1/2 46 Valenzuela P A LB113 9.70 79–15 DomsticDisput1133 OurBobbyV133 1/2 Scrimshw1154 Tight 7/8,bid,wkened 8

Siphonizer
Own: Hughes B. W

Dk. b or b. c. 3 (Mar) FTKJUL02 $275,000
Sire: Siphon*Brz (Itajara) $20,000
Dam:Thesky'sthelimit (Northern Prospect)
Br: Brereton C. Jones (Ky)
Tr: Mandella Richard E(0 0 0 0 .00) 2003:(253 51 .20)

											Life	5	2	0	0	$197,400	86	D.Fst	5	2	0	0	$197,400	86
											2003	5	2	0	0	$197,400	86	Wet(263)	0	0	0	0	$0	–
											2002	0	M	0	0	$0	–	Turf(252)	0	0	0	0	$0	–
																		Dst(0)	0	0	0	0	$0	–

25Oct03–7SA fst 1 1/16 :221 :45 1:094 1:433 BesTBCJv–G1 52 8 75 3/4 62 1/4 96 1/4 913 1023 Krone J A LB122 22.60 63–07 ActionThisDay1222 1/4 MinisterEric1225 ChpelRoy122no Traffic early, wide 12
50ct03–10SA fst 1 1/16 :222 :453 1:011 1:411 Norfolk–G2 69 4 53 52 1/2 42 1/2 38 418 1/2 Krone J A LB120 3.50 79–08 Ruler's Court1201 Capitano1201 Perfect Moon1203 1/2 3wd 2nd turn,no bid 9
10Sep03–8Dmr fst 7f :221 :442 1:092 1:23 DmrFut–G2 82 1 4 31 2hd 11 1 1/2 Krone J A LB116 5.40 87–09 Siphonizer116 1/2 Minister Eric116 2 Perfect Moon122nk Rail,drifted out,held 5
17Aug03–6Dmr fst 6 1/2f :221 :444 1:011 1:164 BestPal–G2 76 3 7 62 3/4 64 1/2 53 3/4 53 1/2 Krone J A LB118 *1.80 87–09 PerfectMoon1221 1/2 Capitano1121 Military Mndte1181 Stalked,no late bid 10
24Aug03–6Dmr fst 5 1/2f :222 :454 :573 1:034 Md Sp Wt 49k 86 9 1 2 1/2 2hd 11 1 1/2 Flores D R LB120 4.20 96–07 Siphonizer120 3/4 Cooperation1205 1/4 MinisterEric120 1/2 Inched away,held game 10

Sir Cherokee
Own: Domino Stud of Lexington LLC

B. c. 4 (Feb)
Sire: Cherokee Run (Runaway Groom) $20,000
Dam:La Cucina*Ire (Last Tycoon*Ire)
Br: Domino Stud of Lexington, LLC (Ky)
Tr: Tomlinson Michael A(0 0 0 0 .00) 2003:(97 14 .14)

											Life	11	4	3	0	$428,310	106	D.Fst	6	1	2	0	$334,480	106
											2003	5	3	0	0	$365,535	106	Wet(373)	5	3	1	0	$93,330	93
											2002	6	1	3	0	$62,775	90	Turf(248)	0	0	0	0	$0	–
																		Dst(0)	0	0	0	0	$0	–

27Nov03–9CD sly 1 ⊗ :221 :451 1:11 1:374 3+ OClm 62500N 93 6 61 3 711 34 1/2 11 13 Thompson T J L115 *1.40 78–25 Sir Cherokee115 3/4 G P Fleet1211 1/2 Bright Sea1172 4-5w, steady drive 7
12Apr03–9OP fst 1 1/16 ⊗ :452 1:094 1:354 1:481 ArkDerby–G2 106 5 12 16 1217 97 3/4 23 1/2 11 3/4 Thompson T J L118 55.60 91–11 SrChrok118 3/4 EignsThrdSon1186 1/2 ChrstnsOt1w118 1 6-w rally,kicked clear 12
22Mar03–10OP fst 1 1/16 :23 :46 1:111 1:44 Rebel125k 80 5 41 1/2 32 41 53 3/4 45 1/2 Lopez J L114 7.80 84–15 CrowndKing115 1/4 GrtNotion119 2 ComcTruth117 2 1/4 Steadied 1st turn, 4-w 7
1Mar03–10OP gd 1 :233 :474 1:321 1:384 Southwest75k 84 2 710 69 65 3/4 48 411 Lopez J L115 3.40 78–24 Great Notion1129 Alke114 1 1/4 Comic Truth1193 Mild rally 7
8Feb03–9OP wf 1 :224 :464 1:211 1:39 3+ Alw 32000N2L 80 3 67 53 1/2 42 3/4 41 1/4 11 3/4 Lopez J L115 *.80 88–11 SirCherokee115 1 3/4 MavCat115no ProperProspect1233 1/4 Angled out, willing 8

Six Perfections (Fr)
Own: Flaxman Holdings Ltd

Blk. f. 4 (Feb)
Sire: Celtic Swing*GB (Damister) $60,414
Dam: Yogya (Riverman)
Br: Famille Niarchos (Fr)
Tr: Bary Pascal F(0 0 0 0 .00) 2003:(2 1 .50)

Life	10 6 4 0	$1,451,544	105	D.Fst	0 0 0 0	$0 -
2003	6 3 3 0	$1,256,076	105	Wet(245*)	0 0 0 0	$0 -
2002	4 3 1 0	$195,468	-	Turf(302)	10 6 4 0	$1,451,544 105
	0 0 0 0	$0	-	Dst(0)	0 0 0 0	$0 -

25Oct03–4SA fm 1 Ⓣ :221 :452 1:0921:334 3↑BCMile-G1 **105** 12 86¼ 84½ 73½ 42¼ 1¾ Bailey J D B119 5.30 93–04 SixPrfctons119¾ TouchofthBlus126nk CnturyCty1261¼ Balked gate,rallied 13
17Aug03♦Deauville (Fr) yl *1 Ⓣ Str 1:381 3↑ Prix Jacques le Marois-G1 Stk 581000 1nk Thulliez T 121 2.80e *Six Perfections*121nk Domedriver1301 Telegnosis1301 12
Timeform rating: 124+ *Rated 5th,led 1f out,gamely.Special Kaldoun4th,NebraskaTornado6th*
3Aug03♦Deauville (Fr) yl *1 Ⓣ Str 1:372 3↑ ⒻPrix d'Astarte-G2 Stk 113000 2nk Thulliez T 119 *1.20 Bright Sky126nk *Six Perfections*1191½ Marbye119no 12
Timeform rating: 114+ *Tracked in 4th,led over 1f out,headed near line.Acago 4th*
25May03♦Curragh (Ire) sf 1 Ⓣ Str 1:404 ⒻIrish 1000 Guineas-G1 Stk 470000 2no Murtagh J P 126 *.30 Yesterday126no Six Perfections126¾ *Dimitrova*1262½ 8
Timeform rating: 117+ *Towards rear,4th and blocked on rail 2f out,late rush,just failed*
4May03♦Newmarket (GB) gf 1 Ⓣ Str 1:382 Ⓕ1000 Guineas Stakes-G1 Stk 514000 21½ Thulliez T 126 *1.75 *Russian Rhythm*1261½ Six Perfections1261¼ Intercontinental1261½ 19
Timeform rating: 116+ *Towards rear,bumped 2-1/2f out,angled right,finished fast*
7Apr03♦Maisons-Laffitte (Fr) gd *7f Ⓣ Str 1:292 ⒻPrix Imprudence (Listed) Stk 43700 11½ Thulliez T 126 *.60 Six Perfections1261½ *Campsie Fells*126hd *Derrianne*126½ 7
Timeform rating: 106+ *Rank early tracking leaders,bumped 1-1/2f out,led 1f out,handily*

Sixty Seconds (NZ)
Own: The Leigh Family Stable

Dk. b or b. m. 6 (Oct)
Sire: Centaine*Aus (Century*Aus)
Dam: Fifteen Reasons*NZ (Sound Reason)
Br: T E Parae Trust (NZ)
Tr: Clement Christophe(0 0 0 0 .00) 2003:(389 75 .19)

Life	15 6 1 2	$304,229	97	D.Fst	0 0 0 0	$0 -
2003	3 2 0 0	$105,060	97	Wet(320)	0 0 0 0	$0 -
2002	6 3 0 0	$178,625	-	Turf(265)	15 6 1 2	$304,229 97
	0 0 0 0	$0	-	Dst(0)	0 0 0 0	$0 -

27Dec03–9Crc fm 1½ Ⓣ :48 1:13 2:0312:26 3↑ⒻLaPvyteH-G2 **86** 11 67½ 53 31½ 53½ 56¾ Santos J A L116 5.50 96 - Volga1192¾ Lady Annaliese1161¼ Lost Appeal115¾ Mid track,leveled off 11
25Aug03–8Sar fm 1⅜ Ⓣ :4841:133 1:37 2:134 3↑ⒻGlenFlsH-G3 **97** 7 45 56¾ 45½ 2½ 1hd Santos J A L115 3.25 101 - SixtySeconds115hd Primtimvlntin113nk Altrnt116¾ Gamely between rivals 9
11Jly03–8Bel yl 1 Ⓣ :242 :481 1:1221:37 4↑ⒻAlw 52000N4X **96** 6 64½ 63½ 41½ 1½ 13 Bailey J D L119 *1.50 75–25 *Sixty Seconds*1193 Cozzy Corner117no Vespers119nk 4 wide move, clear 7

Sky Jack
Own: Ren–Mar Thoroughbreds

Gr/ro. g. 8 (Apr)
Sire: Jaklin Klugman (Orbit Ruler)
Dam: Sky Captive (Skywalker)
Br: Rene & Margie Lambert (Cal)
Tr: O'Neill Doug(0 0 0 0 .00) 2003:(760 133 .18)

Life	18 10 2 2	$1,115,127	122	D.Fst	14 8 2 2	$1,034,010 122
2003	3 2 0 0	$185,860	115	Wet(335)	0 0 0 0	$0 -
2002	5 2 1 0	$556,900	115	Turf(289)	4 2 0 0	$81,117 98
	0 0 0 0	$0	-	Dst(0)	0 0 0 0	$0 -

24Aug03–8EmDfst 1 :221 :442 1:0811:33 3↑LgaMileH-G3 **105** 3 1hd 2hd 1hd 15 16¼ Baze R A LB123 b *1.50 101–14 Sky Jack1236¼ Poker Brad1162 Lord Nelson1162¾ Vied, clear, widened 10
5Jly03–6Hol fst 1 1/16 :232 :463 1:10 1:41 4↑Alw 76880C **115** 1 1hd 1½ 1½ 11½ 12 Valenzuela P A LB118 b *1.80 99–01 *SkyJck*1182 LegendryWeve1181½ Romnceishope1187 Inside,cleared,game 8
13Jun03–5Hol fm 1 1/16 Ⓣ :24 :471 1:1121:41 4↑Alw 65348N1M **90** 2 1hd 1hd 1hd 1hd 64¾ Valenzuela P A LB122 b 2.90 86–15 IrishWarrior116no Decarchy1222½ NtiveDesert1221 Inside duel,weakened 8

Smokey Glacken
Own: Moore Susan and John

B. f. 3 (Mar) KEESEP02 $150,000
Sire: Forestry (Storm Cat) $50,000
Dam: Majesty's Crown (Magesterial)
Br: Jayeff B Stables (Ky)
Tr: Jerkens James A(0 0 0 0 .00) 2003:(194 46 .24)

Life	4 3 0 1	$140,820	78	D.Fst	3 3 0 0	$124,320	78
2003	4 3 0 1	$140,820	78	Wet(371*)	1 0 0 1	$16,500	78
2002	0 M 0 0	$0	–	Turf(318*)	0 0 0 0	$0	–
	0 0 0 0	$0	–	Dst(0)	0 0 0 0	$0	–

23Nov03–8Aqu fst 6f :213 :45 :572 1:11 ⒻVllyStrm-G3 **77** 1 5 1½ 11½ 15½ 13¾ Santos J A L118 2.50 85–12 Smokey Glacken118¾ Baldomera118½ Stoic1181 Stumbled start, clear 9
12Oct03–10Bel sly 6½f :212 :442 1:102 1:17 ⒻAstarita-G2 **78** 1 7 4¾ 31½ 1hd 31½ Santos J A L117 4.20 86–16 SpctclrMoon117nk FlnStory1201¼ *SmkyGlckn*11713 Wide move, weakened 9
21Sep03–9Mth fst 6f :212 :441 :564 1:101 ⒻForwardGal50k **78** 3 6 1hd 1hd 12 12½ Velez J A Jr L115 *1.10 88–14 SmokeyGlacken1152½ BabaGonzo1214 Amzer1122½ Dueled 2w, drew clear 8
25Aug03–4Sar fst 5½f :213 :453 :581 1:05 ⒻMd Sp Wt 45k **69** 5 6 1½ 12 16 15 Santos J A L119 *1.45 91–15 *Smokey Glacken*1195 *Storm Fleet*1191¾ Mystified119½ Widened when asked 10

Smok'n Frolic
Own: Dogwood Stable

Gr/ro. m. 5 (Apr) OBSFEB01 $85,000
Sire: Smoke Glacken (Two Punch) $15,000
Dam: Cherokyfrolicflash (Green Dancer)
Br: Cherokee Farms Inc. (Fla)
Tr: Pletcher Todd A(0 0 0 0 .00) 2003:(826 199 .24)

Life	25 8 5 1	$1,276,500	104	D.Fst	20 8 5 0	$1,239,764	100
2003	11 3 3 1	$776,856	104	Wet(367)	3 0 0 1	$29,836	104
2002	5 1 0 0	$156,900	97	Turf(272)	2 0 0 0	$6,900	90
	0 0 0 0	$0	–	Dst(0)	0 0 0 0	$0	–

15Nov03–11Crc fst 1 1/16 :234 :482 1:132 1:462 3↑Ⓕ[S]EHeubckDsH200k **91** 11 53½ 31½ 3½ 3nk 54½ Velazquez J R L122 b *.70 75–18 Scpde1131¾ *RedoubledMiss*117½ SecretRequest1121½ 3 wide, bid, weakened 11
4Oct03–9Bel fst 1⅛ :474 1:122 1:363 1:491 3↑ⒻBeldame-G1 **91** 6 2½ 2½ 2hd 49 410 Dominguez R A L123 b 17.00 74–26 Sightseek1234½ Bird Town1204¾ Buy the Sport120¾ Pressed pace, tired 7
13Sep03–12TP fst 1 1/16 :24 :473 1:12 1:444 3↑ⒻTPBC-G3 **100** 8 31½ 1hd 11 13 13½ Prado E S L122 b *1.80 88–17 SmoknFrolic1223½ *AwesomeHumor*1122½ SoMuchMor1181¾ 3 wide, driving 9
24Aug03–9Sar fst 7f :223 :45 1:09 1:221 3↑ⒻBalrinaH-G1 **83** 3 8 72¼ 84¾ 811 87¾ Velazquez J R L117 3.65 88–12 *Harmony Lodge*115no ShineAgain1202 GoldMover118hd Rated, 6 wide, tired 8
1Aug03–8Sar sly 6f :221 :452 :572 1:094 3↑ⒻHnrblMsH-G3 **104** 2 3 54 52¼ 51¼ 3½ Velazquez J R L117 7.80 92–13 WillOnthMov114½ ShinAgin120no SmoknFrolc1171 Gamely between rivals 6
21Jun03–9Bel sly 1 1/16 :222 :451 1:091 1:404 3↑ⒻOPhippsH-G1 **89** 5 33 31 31 49½ 411¾ Velazquez J R L118 5.90 84–18 *Sightseek*1185 TakeChargeLady1195 MndysGold1181¾ Chased 3 wide, tired 5
17May03–8Bel fst 1 :224 :452 1:092 1:342 3↑ⒻShuveeH-G2 **99** 2 22 2½ 2hd 2hd 23½ Velazquez J R L119 3.10 90–17 *Wild Spirit*1153½ Smok'n Frolic1191¼ *You*1204¼ Led between calls 6
19Apr03–9Aqu fst 1 :233 :47 1:103 1:344 3↑ⒻBdORsBCH-G3 **100** 2 22 22½ 2½ 21½ 2½ Velazquez J R L120 2.25 90–13 RgingFever119½ SmoknFrolic1203¼ NonsuchBy1171¾ Game finish outside 5
23Mar03–9Aqu fst 1⅛ :473 1:104 1:354 1:49 3↑ⒻNxtMoveH-G3 **95** 4 1½ 1hd 1½ 13 12¼ Velazquez J R L120 *.90 91–16 Smok'n Frolic1202¼ Ellie's Moment1163¾ Pupil1131 Dictated pace, clear 6
1Mar03–10GP fst 1⅛ :471 1:102 1:351 1:474 3↑ⒻRampartH-G2 **91** 4 22 21½ 22½ 24½ 27¾ Santos J A L118 2.80 95–02 Allamerican Bertie1227¾ *Smok'n Frolic*1186¼ Softly1153¼ Off rail, no match 6
25Jan03–5SA fst 1 1/16 :23 :464 1:104 1:432 4↑Ⓕ[R]VesslsDstf750k **94** 7 84¼ 52½ 43 21 12½ Bailey J D LB118 *1.80 87–13 SmoknFrolic1182½ *CeesElegnce*120½ SmrtLcy118hd Came out str,bid,clear 11

Smoocher
Own: Franks John

B. c. 3 (Feb)
Sire: Kissin Kris (Kris S.) $7,500
Dam: Alta's Princess (Screen King)
Br: John Franks (Fla)
Tr: Bell David R(0 0 0 0 .00) 2003:(298 38 .13)

Life	4	2	1	0	$231,653	90	D.Fst	4	2	1	0	$231,653 90
2003	4	2	1	0	$231,653	90	Wet(324)	0	0	0	0	$0 –
2002	0	M	0	0	$0	–	Turf(235)	0	0	0	0	$0 –
	0	0	0	0	$0	–	Dst(0)	0	0	0	0	$0 –

15Nov03-8WO fst 1 1/16 :224 :463 1:114 1:432 Display135k **86** 2 35 33½ 32½ 28 210 McAleney J S L122 *1.35 79-25 JudthsWldRsh11510 Smoochr12211 *Bgborrowndd*117nk Inside, advance 4w 5
5Oct03-9WO fst 1 1/16 :241 :474 1:122 1:463 GreyBC-G2 **90** 9 95 74¼ 43 12½ 12¼ McAleney J S L113 6.35 73-30 Smoocher1132¼ Organ Grinder116hd Niigon1143¾ Rail rlly,jump tracks 9
31Aug03-6WO fst 7f :224 :462 1:114 1:243 Md Sp Wt 60k **88** 6 4 51¾ 41¼ 2hd 1no McAleney J S L120 *1.50 81-27 *Smoocher*120no Picadilly Bay1154¾ *Campo Lago*1203¾ Duel outsde,got nod 8
9Aug03-3WO fst 6½f :23 :463 1:12 1:182 Md Sp Wt 60k **62** 2 6 63¼ 52¾ 65 54½ McAleney J S L120 10.85 78-16 WintrWhsky1171 WhyNotGold1151½ GoKttyGo120hd Broke in air,5w, turn 6

Smooth Jazz
Own: Tabor Michael B

Dk. b or b. c. 5 (May) KEESEP00 $95,000
Sire: Storm Boot (Storm Cat) $15,000
Dam: Blushing Issue (Blushing John)
Br: San Gabriel Investment & T. F. Van Meter (Ky)
Tr: Pletcher Todd A(0 0 0 0 .00) 2003:(826 199 .24)

Life	11	5	0	1	$321,105	117	D.Fst	9	4	0	1	$290,505 117
2003	2	1	0	0	$175,725	117	Wet(297)	2	1	0	0	$30,600 82
2002	9	4	0	1	$145,380	106	Turf(287)	0	0	0	0	$0 –
	0	0	0	0	$0	–	Dst(0)	0	0	0	0	$0 –

13Apr03-8Kee fst 7f :22 :444 1:092 1:213 3↑ CmwlthBC-G2 **117** 1 1 1½ 11 12 13 Prado E S L118 f 7.00 96-13 Smooth Jazz1183 Crafty C. T.1186¼ MultipleChoice1203¾ Pace,mild urging 7
8Mar03-10GP fst 7f :221 :442 1:082 1:21 3↑ RcSclBCH-G2 **99** 7 2 31 41½ 32½ 53½ Prado E S L114 5.60 99-01 TorofthCt116hd BrnngRom1161¼ *HghwyProspctor*114nk Chased, weakened 8

Smooth Maneuvers
Own: Nick Sanna Stables LLC

Dk. b or b. f. 4 (Apr) KEESEP01 $20,000
Sire: Grindstone (Unbridled) $5,000
Dam: Aerobatics (Caro*Ire)
Br: J D Squires (Ky)
Tr: Pino Michael V(0 0 0 0 .00) 2003:(422 127 .30)

Life	5	4	1	0	$123,900	94	D.Fst	5	4	1	0	$123,900 94
2003	5	4	1	0	$123,900	94	Wet(338)	0	0	0	0	$0 –
2002	0	M	0	0	$0	–	Turf(207)	0	0	0	0	$0 –
	0	0	0	0	$0	–	Dst(0)	0	0	0	0	$0 –

15Nov03-8Lrl fst 1⅛ :493 1:143 1:39 1:512 ⒻAArundel-G3 **88** 1 12 1½ 1hd 12½ 12½ Pino M G L115 f 8.90 84-15 SmthMnvrs1152½ DvtnUnbrdld117nk Alchmst117hd Well rated ins,driving 7
25Oct03-6Del fst 1 :25 :491 1:141 1:39 3↑ ⒻCordially58k **89** 4 11 1hd 1hd 2hd 23¾ Potts C L L116 f 2.10 85-21 Shiny Sheet1183¾ *Smooth Maneuvers*1162 BlueHills1182½ Vied, held on well 5
30Sep03-7Del fst 6f :214 :444 :574 1:102 ⒻAlw 37000n2x **90** 3 5 57½ 55½ 23 11¾ Dominguez R A L122 f *1.00 92-09 SmthMnvrs1221¾ *MrryIndMssy*1171¼ *ItsSpky*1222¾ Quick move, ridden out 6
2Sep03-9Del fst 6f :222 :454 :582 1:11 3↑ ⒻAlw 34000n1x **80** 2 6 52½ 42 21½ 11¾ Dominguez R A L114 f *1.00 89-11 *SmoothMneuvers*1141¾ *Nimmer*1141½ TurquoisBd117¾ Awkward st,ridden o 8
3Aug03-5Del fst 5½f :221 :453 :573 1:034 3↑ ⒻMd c-(25-20) **94** 6 2 12½ 12 14 15½ Alvarado R Jr L118 f 2.90 99-10 *SmthMnvrs*1185½ Cnsstntly11814½ SlsbrySlw1186¾ Unchallenged, ridden o 7
Claimed from Iwin 00 for $25,000, Iwinski Allen Trainer 2003(as of 8/3): (331 77 64 33 0.23)

Snake Mountain

Own: Shelley Jack and Buzas, Paul J., et

Ch. g. 6 (Mar)
Sire: A.P. Indy (Seattle Slew) $300,000
Dam: Coup de Genie (Mr. Prospector)
Br: Flaxman Holdings, Ltd. (Ky)
Tr: Jerkens James A(0 0 0 0 .00) 2003:(194 46 .24)

Life	19 10 0 4	$470,432	107	D.Fst	13 10 0 2 $449,745 107
2003	5 3 0 0	$159,825	107	Wet(440)	2 0 0 0 $18,000 99
2002	10 7 0 2	$307,920	106	Turf(332)	4 0 0 2 $2,687 -
				Dst(0)	0 0 0 0 $0 -

24Oct03-8Bel fst 1¹⁄₁₆ :22 :444 1:102 1:442 3↑ Alw 58000c 94 2 412 416 58¹⁄₂ 21¹⁄₂ 1¹⁄₂ Migliore R L123 1.55 78-29 SnakeMountin123¹ Justifiction1131¹ Cottge1182¹ Game inside, prevailed 5

16May03-41Pim sly 1¹⁄₁₆ :463 1:11 1:362 1:56 4↑ PimSpclH-G1 88 5 64³ 57¹ 67 615 619¹⁄₂ Santos J A L120 10.10 73-23 Mineshift1213³ WesternPride116ʰᵈ JudgesCse1131³ Drifted wide 1/4,tired 9

5Apr03-8Aqu fst 1¹⁄₈ :463 1:102 1:35 1:48 3↑ ExlsrBCH-G3 102 3 54 54²¹⁄₂ 53 44¹⁄₂ 42 Luzzi M J L122 *1.10 94-16 ClassicEndeavor113³ BltoStr119³ TempestFugit1148³ Good finish outside 5

16Mar03-7Aqu fst 1¹⁄₈ ⊡ :472 1:112 1:363 1:493 3↑ StymieH80k 107 2 44 45 43 33 1ⁿᵒ Luzzi M J L123 *.50e 89-15 SnkMontn123ⁿᵒ ClsscEndvor1142¹ GrondStorm1174³ Determinedly outside 6

18Jan03-8Aqu fst 1¹⁄₁₆ ⊡ :233 :474 1:211 1:44 3↑ AquH-G3 104 4 47¹⁄₂ 42 21 17 17¹⁄₂ Luzzi M J L120 *.35e 86-21 SnkMontn1207¹⁄₂ GrondStorm1174¹ CtsAtHom1149 Inside move, hand ride 5

Snow Dance

Own: Oxley John C

Gr/ro. m. 6 (Mar)
Sire: Forest Wildcat (Storm Cat) $60,000
Dam: Northern Pageant (Spectacular Bid)
Br: Aspiration Stable (Ky)
Tr: Ward J T Jr(0 0 0 0 .00) 2003:(90 17 .19)

Life	25 8 5 5	$938,597	104	D.Fst	4 1 1 1 $44,140 81
2003	8 1 1 2	$220,510	104	Wet(346)	0 0 0 0 $0 -
2002	7 1 3 1	$281,687	100	Turf(306)	21 7 4 4 $894,457 104
				Dst(0)	0 0 0 0 $0 -

19Oct03-8Kee fm 1¹⁄₂ ⊕ :5241:181 2:0812:314 3↑ⒻDowager150k 76 3 11¹⁄₂ 11 2¹⁄₂ 32 8¹¹⁄₂ Douglas R R L125 3.80 69-20 SpiceIsland1206¹⁄₂ OceanSilk118³ Peacefally1201¹⁄₂ Broke in air,rush,tire 10

27Sep03-8Bel fm 1¹⁄₄ ⊕ :4941:144 1:39 2:023 3↑ⒻFlwrBllv-G1 92 6 11¹⁄₂ 11 2¹⁄₂ 62³⁄₄ 76¹⁄₄ Migliore R L120 9.00 75-17 Dimitrova114¹ WalzerKoenigin120ⁿᵒ HeatHaze1231¹ Bobbled start, tired 7

23Aug03-8Sar fm 1¹⁄₁₆ ⊕ :233 :471 1:11 1:41 3↑ⒻBISpaBCH-G3 97 6 55¹⁄₂ 54 53¹⁄₂ 41¹⁄₄ 2¹⁄₂ Migliore R L117 5.00 98 - Stylish116¹⁄₄ SnowDance117¹ CozzyCorner112ʰᵈ Broke in air, gamely 9

26Jly03-8Sar fm 1¹⁄₈ ⊕ :49 1:13 1:363 1:474 3↑ⒻDianaH-G1 98 2 86¹⁄₄ 84³⁄₄ 85¹⁄₄ 73¹⁄₂ 73¹⁄₂ Migliore R L117 9.40 87-10 VoodooDancer120ⁿᵏ HeatHaze1181³ Pertuisane1154 Leapt in air start 8

4Jly03-10Bel fm 1¹⁄₄ ⊕ :4911:131 1:3641:593 3↑ⒻNewYorkH-G2 104 4 42²¹⁄₂ 21¹⁄₂ 2ʰᵈ 12¹⁄₂ 11 Migliore R L116 27.00 96-17 SnowDance116¹ Pertuisane1158³ Riskaverse1193¹ Drew clear when roused 8

31May03-8Bel sf 1³⁄₈ ⊕ :5241:203 4:722:28 3↑ⒻSnpshdBH-G2 39 5 75¹ 83¹ 711 624 637 Santos J A L116 5.00 - - Mariensky11484 Owsley11943 SilentCrystal112¹³ Inside,no response 8

13Apr03-6Kee fm 1¹⁄₁₆ ⊕ :233 :48 1:12 1:414 4↑ⒻJenyWily-G3 98 1 10 44¹⁄₂ 53¹⁄₄ 75 42 31¹⁄₄ Santos J A L116 3.90 90-08 SofShowrs1161¹⁄₄ MgicMission116ⁿᵏ SnowDnc116ʰᵈ 4-5w,no final response 10

1Mar03-9FG yl *1¹⁄₈ ⊕ :5131:162 1:4211:543 4↑ⒻBayouBCH137k 95 1 21 43 43 63¹⁄₂ 32 Perret C L119 *1.20 69-29 QuickTip116ⁿᵏ HistoireSainte1181³ SnowDnce119ⁿᵏ Lacked needed finish 10

Soaring Free
Own: Sam–Son Farms

Dk. b or b. g. 5 (Jan)
Sire: Smart Strike (Mr. Prospector) $20,000
Dam: Dancing With Wings (Danzig)
Br: Sam–Son Farm (Ont–C)
Tr: Frostad Mark R(0 0 0 0 .00) 2003:(206 44 .21)

Life	14	7	3	0	$803,682	109	D.Fst	6	3	2	0	$142,520 100
2003	8	5	1	0	$699,200	109	Wet(448)	2	1	0	0	$51,062 109
2002	6	2	2	0	$104,482	94	Turf(355)	6	3	1	0	$610,100 105
	0	0	0	0	$0	–	Dst(0)	0	0	0	0	$0 –

25Oct03–4SA fm 1 Ⓣ :221 :452 1:092 1:334 3↑BCMile-G1 **98** 3 21 3nk 31 1hd 5 3/4 Velazquez J R LB126 22.20 90–04 SxPrfctons119 3/4 TouchofthBls126nk CntryCty126 1 1/4 3wd bid,led,overtaken 13
4Oct03–9Kee fm 1 Ⓣ :23 :461 1:114 1:36 3↑ShdwlTfM-G1 **101** 6 24 1/2 23 1/2 11 2hd 42 1/2 Kabel T K L126 5.20 85–14 PerfectSoul126 3/4 HonorinWr126 1/2 TouchoftheBlues126 1 1/4 Inside,weakened 10
14Sep03–9WO fm 1 Ⓣ :224 :451 1:091 1:331 3↑AttoMile-G1 **105** 11 21 1/2 41 3/4 2hd 1 1/2 2 1/2 Kabel T K L121 4.40 96–06 TouchoftheBlues119 1/2 SoringFree121 1 3/4 *PrfctSoul*121hd Stalk 4w,gave best 11
16Aug03–8WO yl 7f Ⓣ :23 :462 1:102 1:232 3↑PlayKngH-G3 **105** 6 1 21 1hd 11 11 1/2 Kabel T K L121 *.85 85–15 SoringFree121 1 1/2 JebsWild114 1 1/2 FrnksSlction1131 Press outsde,held well 6
19Jly03–3WO fm 7f Ⓣ :223 :444 1:083 1:211 3↑ⓇOntarioJC107k **98** 6 2 2hd 1 1/2 12 1 3/4 Kabel T K L119 *.20 96–04 *Soaring Free*119 3/4 Numerous Times117 3 1/2 MisterCoop117 1/2 Off rail held well 6
22Jun03–6WO fm 6f Ⓣ :214 :441 :554 1:073 3↑NearctcH-G2 **105** 11 4 3nk 1 1/2 12 1/2 13 1/4 Kabel T K L115 *2.10 100 – *SoaringFree*115 3 1/4 SolitaryDncer117hd NuclerDebte121 1/2 Press 3w, drew off 11
4Jun03–4WO sly 6f ⊗ :22 :451 :572 1:094 3↑Alw 80900NC **109** 6 1 33 32 1/2 13 1/2 14 1/4 Kabel T K L118 *2.40 95–13 *SoaringFree*118 4 1/4 ChepTlk1202 *MullgntheGret*120nk Stalk duel 4w,drew off 7
10May03–3WO fst 7f :23 :461 1:111 1:231 3↑Alw 67600N2X **100** 3 1 1 1/2 11 13 1/2 17 3/4 Kabel T K L120 *.65 88–20 *SorngFr*120 7 3/4 TJsLckyMon120 2 3/4 OpnChrncl120 8 1/2 2w,drew off when asked 5

Society Selection
Own: Cowan Marjorie and Irving M

B. f. 3 (Apr)
Sire: Coronado's Quest (Forty Niner) $50,000
Dam: Love That Jazz (Dixieland Band)
Br: Marjorie Cowan & Irving Cowan (Ky)
Tr: Jerkens H. A(0 0 0 0 .00) 2003:(359 73 .20)

Life	3	2	0	0	$327,000	95	D.Fst	3	2	0	0	$327,000 95
2003	3	2	0	0	$327,000	95	Wet(338)	0	0	0	0	$0 –
2002	0	M	0	0	$0	–	Turf(309)	0	0	0	0	$0 –
	0	0	0	0	$0	–	Dst(0)	0	0	0	0	$0 –

25Oct03–3SA fst 1 1/16 :224 :464 1:104 1:423 ⒻBCJuvFil-G1 **67** 6 148 148 1/2 137 1/2 1011 1018 Ganpath R B119 4.10 73–07 Halfbridled119 2 1/2 *Ashado*119nk *Victory U. S. A.*119 9 1/4 Steadied first turn 14
4Oct03–6Bel fst 1 1/16 :231 :471 1:121 1:434 ⒻFrizette-G1 **95** 8 83 3/4 74 1/2 73 1/2 21 1/2 11 1/4 Ganpath R 120 8.20 81–26 SocietySelction120 1 1/4 VictoryUSA120 2 3/4 Ashdo120 6 3/4 Came wide, clear late 8
18Aug03–2Sar fst 5f :22 :453 :58 ⒻMd Sp Wt 45k **78** 7 6 75 63 1/4 4 3/4 13 1/2 Ganpath R 119 17.90 99–06 *SocietySelction*119 3 1/2 ForMyWif119nk Ovrrction119hd Stumbled after start 9

Soto
Own: Galopp LLC

Ch. c. 4 (Feb) KEESEP01 $50,000
Sire: Dehere (Deputy Minister) $37,200
Dam: Subtle Fragrance (Crafty Prospector)
Br: Domino Stud of Lexington, LLC (Ky)
Tr: Dickinson Michael W(0 0 0 0 .00) 2003:(152 37 .24)

Life	6	5	1	0	$666,164	114	D.Fst	6	5	1	0	$666,164 114
2003	3	2	1	0	$473,200	114	Wet(420)	0	0	0	0	$0 –
2002	3	3	0	0	$192,964	94	Turf(293)	0	0	0	0	$0 –
	0	0	0	0	$0	–	Dst(0)	0	0	0	0	$0 –

20Sep03–10LaD fst 1 1/8 :493 1:133 1:374 1:503 SuDyXXIV-G2 **106** 4 41 1/4 32 1/2 2hd 1hd 2 1/2 Dominguez R A L124 f 1.20 87–16 Ten Most Wanted124 1/2 Soto124 5 1/4 Crowned King1241 Stubborn until late 6
9Aug03–8Mnr fst 1 1/8 :472 1:104 1:343 1:461 WVDerby-G3 **114** 3 21 2hd 11 2hd 1nk Dominguez R A LB111 f 2.20 105 – Soto111nk Dynever117 5 1/4 *Colita*111 1 1/2 Hooked ins, battled 9
19Jly03–8Pha fst 6f :22 :45 :564 1:084 3↑Alw 22000N3X **109** 1 4 44 1/2 2hd 11 1/2 13 3/4 Molina V H L112 f *.70 95–15 *Soto*112 3 3/4 Parade of Music117 6 3/4 J. J.'s Joy119 2 1/4 Under wraps 5

Southern Image
Own: Blahut Stables LLC

Dk. b or b. c. 4 (Apr) OBSMAR02 $300,000
Sire: Halo's Image (Halo) $5,000
Dam: Pleasant Dixie (Dixieland Band)
Br: Arthur I. Appleton (Fla)
Tr: Machowsky Michael(0 0 0 0 .00) 2003:(185 28 .15)

Life 4 3 0 1 $231,600 106 | D.Fst 4 3 0 1 $231,600 106
2003 3 2 0 1 $202,800 106 | Wet(332) 0 0 0 0 $0 –
2002 1 1 0 0 $28,800 97 | Turf(227) 0 0 0 0 $0 –
0 0 0 0 $0 – | Dst(0) 0 0 0 0 $0 –

26Dec03–8SA fst 7f :222 :45 1:091 1:223 Malibu-G1 **106** 10 7 31½ 52½ 32½ 1hd Espinoza V LB115 13.70 93–12 Southern Image115hd Marino Marini1151 Midas Eyes1193 4wd,3wd,up late 12
2Aug03–7Dmr fst 1 1/16 :223 :461 1:11 1:424 3↑ Alw 61480n1x **96** 4 64 42 41¼ 13 11 Espinoza V LB115 *1.70 91–09 *SouthernImage*1151 Mr.JoeC1233½ ClassyFella1211½ Off slow,4wd surge 1/4 7
1Feb03–4SA fst 7f :22 :44 1:08 1:21 SnVicnte-G2 **102** 3 5 2½ 3½ 34 36 Nakatani C S LB117 2.50 95–07 Kafwain1234½ Sum Trick1201½ *Southern Image*1176 Off bit slow, 3 wide 5

Speak in Passing
Own: Juddmonte Farms Inc

B. h. 7 (Apr)
Sire: Danzig (Northern Dancer) $250,000
Dam: Diese (Diesis*GB)
Br: Juddmonte Farms (Ky)
Tr: Frankel Robert J(0 0 0 0 .00) 2003:(411 114 .28)

Life 13 5 6 0 $284,778 111 | D.Fst 0 0 0 0 $0 –
2003 1 1 0 0 $82,500 100 | Wet(389) 0 0 0 0 $0 –
2002 1 1 0 0 $34,200 108 | Turf(409) 13 5 6 0 $284,778 111
0 0 0 0 $0 – | Dst(0) 0 0 0 0 $0 –

19Apr03–8SA fm *6½f Ⓣ :213 :432 1:063 1:124 4↑ SnSmeonH-G3 **100** 3 6 54 42 4¾ 1½ Flores D R LB118 2.40 93–10 SpekinPssing118½ Spinelssjllyfish115½ RockyBr1161 4wd into lane,gamely 8

Special Ring
Own: Prestonwood Farm LLC

B. g. 7 (Mar)
Sire: Nureyev (Northern Dancer) $100,000
Dam: Ring Beaune (Bering*GB)
Br: Wertheimer & Frere (Ky)
Tr: Canani Julio C(0 0 0 0 .00) 2003:(165 35 .21)

Life 25 9 4 3 $675,023 111 | D.Fst 0 0 0 0 $0 –
2003 5 1 2 0 $383,000 111 | Wet(343) 0 0 0 0 $0 –
2002 6 4 0 1 $168,975 110 | Turf(355) 25 9 4 3 $675,023 111
0 0 0 0 $0 – | Dst(0) 0 0 0 0 $0 –

25Oct03–4SA fm 1 Ⓣ :221 :452 1:092 1:334 3↑ BCMile-G1 **94** 5 65 73½ 84½ 114½ 85 Flores D R LB126 b 5.10 88–04 SxPrfctons119¾ TouchofthBls126nk CntryCty1261¼ Stdied hard 1/8,no bid 13
5Oct03–8SA fm 1 Ⓣ :223 :454 1:091 1:323 3↑ OkTrBCMl-G2 **102** 5 54½ 55½ 65½ 64¾ 42¼ Flores D R LB121 b *.70 97–01 DesignedforLuck119½ *Srfn*1191½ CenturyCity119nk 4wd into str,missed 3d 8
27Jly03–8Dmr fm 1⅛ Ⓣ :472 1:11 1:342 1:454 3↑ EdReadH-G1 **111** 4 11 11 11½ 12 15 Flores D R LB117 b 3.10 104–03 Special Ring1175 Decarchy117nk *Irish Warrior*114hd Deftly rated, drew off 6
4Jly03–7Hol fm 1⅛ Ⓣ :474 1:11 1:341 1:461 3↑ AmericnH-G2 **105** 3 1½ 1hd 1½ 1hd 2¾ Flores D R LB118 b 2.00 97–08 *Candy Ride*120¾ *Special Ring*1182 Irish Warrior1161 Inside, game effort 5
26May03–8Hol fm 1 Ⓣ :24 :463 1:091 1:331 3↑ ShoeBCM-G1 **109** 8 12 13½ 12 11 2¾ Valdivia J Jr LB124 b 3.20 97–10 Redttore124¾ SpecilRing1243 *TouchoftheBlues*1242 Fought back rail,game 9

Spectacular Moon
Own: Heiligbrodt Racing Stable and Stoners

Dk. b or b. f. 3 (Mar)
Sire: Migrating Moon (Silver Buck) $2,500
Dam: Doctor Danielle (Spectacular Bid)
Br: Nancy Economy (Fla)
Tr: Alecci John V(0 0 0 0 .00) 2003:(146 27 .18)

Life	5	4	0	1	$139,190	81	D.Fst	3	2	0	1	$34,370 69
2003	5	4	0	1	$139,190	81	Wet(305)	2	2	0	0	$104,820 81
2002	0	M	0	0	$0	-	Turf(209)	0	0	0	0	$0 -
	0	0	0	0	$0	-	Dst(0)	0	0	0	0	$0 -

15Nov03–5Lrl fst 1 1/16 :241 :48 1:131 1:443 ⒻSelima100k **64** 5 32 43½ 23½ 38 313¾ Dominguez R A L119 *1.50 72– 15 Richetta1196½ TaittingerRose1197¼ SpectacularMoon119no Dropped back 7
12Oct03–10Bel sly 6½f :212 :442 1:102 1:17 ⒻAstarita-G2 **81** 8 1 812 68¼ 43¼ 1nk Chavez J F L117 28.00 88– 16 SpctclrMoon117nk FlnStory1201¼ *SmkyGlckn*11713 Ducked in start, bump 9
13Sep03–2Pim sly 6f :232 :472 :593 1:122 ⒻOClm 50000(50–45)N **71** 2 1 42¼ 22 11 13¾ Dominguez R A L117 1.40 83– 18 *Spectacular Moon*1173¾ J Star1121½ *Richetta*1222½ 3wd 1/4, ridden out 4
21Aug03–6Lrl fst 6f :223 :454 :583 1:113 ⒻClm c-(40–35) **69** 2 2 2hd 2hd 1hd 14½ Wilson R L117 *1.20 81– 20 *Spectacular Moon*1174½ J Star1174½ *Hop On It*10810¼ Urged,duel ins,drv clr 7
Claimed from Gill Michael J. for $40,000, Robb John J Trainer 2003(as of 8/21): (320 54 56 38 0.17)
2Aug03–4Lrl fst 6f :222 :46 :591 1:123 ⒻMd c-(25–20) **57** 3 6 42½ 21½ 1hd 12¼ Jurado E M L122 3.90 76– 21 *SpectaculrMoon*1222¼ TresLind1227¼ JessiesJoy1222½ Rail bid, drove clear 9
Claimed from Bailey Morris for $25,000, Gaudet Edmond D Trainer 2003(as of 8/2): (183 26 24 27 0.14)

Spice Island
Own: Denlea Park Ltd

Dk. b or b. m. 5 (Mar) KEESEP00 $46,000
Sire: Tabasco Cat (Storm Cat) $17,490
Dam: Crown of Sheba (Alysheba)
Br: Cranford Stud (Ky)
Tr: Pregman J S Jr(0 0 0 0 .00) 2003:(87 11 .13)

Life	21	7	5	2	$392,656	99	D.Fst	7	2	0	1	$38,370 85
2003	13	6	3	1	$361,286	99	Wet(318)	5	1	2	0	$59,346 84
2002	8	1	2	1	$31,370	75	Turf(290)	9	4	3	1	$294,940 99
	0	0	0	0	$0	-	Dst(0)	0	0	0	0	$0 -

27Dec03–9Crc fm 1½ Ⓣ :48 1:13 2:031 2:26 3↑ⒻLaPvyteH-G2 – 6 109¼ - - - - Velasquez C L118 b 3.10 - - Volga1192¾ Lady Annaliese1161¼ Lost Appeal115¾ Clipped heels,fell 11
15Nov03–8Aqu yl 1½ Ⓣ :52 1:172 2:082 2:322 3↑ⒻLngIlndH-G2 **99** 7 53 32 32½ 32 11¼ Carrero V L117 b 7.00 84– 16 Spice Island1171¼ *Volga*1202¾ Banyu Dewi114½ 3 wide move, clear 11
19Oct03–8Kee fm 1½ Ⓣ :524 1:181 2:081 2:314 3↑ⒻDowager150k **97** 7 54 54½ 33 11½ 16¼ Velasquez C L120 b 11.80 81– 20 *Spice Island*1206¼ Ocean Silk118¾ Peacefally1201¼ 4-5w,drew off,driving 10
11Sep03–9Bel fm 1⅛ [T] :49 1:123 1:363 1:482 3↑ⒻAlw 52000N3x **89** 6 52 52 52¼ 5¾ 1½ Prado E S L119 b *3.45 88– 08 *Spice Island*119½ Exchange Bay1152 Vinthea1191½ Traffic, found room 10
6Aug03–8Sar sly 1⅛ ⊗ :484 1:13 1:38 1:511 4↑Ⓕ[R]Waya63k **84** 2 44 46 48 47 46¾ Chavez J F L116 b *1.20 72– 30 May Gator1186½ Kathy K D118hd Suave Queen116nk No response 4
19Jly03–7Del fm 1⅜ Ⓣ :493 1:143 1:391 2:15 3↑ⒻRGDickBCH148k **93** 4 1011 1013 116 96 21¼ Chavez J F L114 b 8.10 110 - Alternate1151¼ Spice Island114½ Lady of the Future115hd Up for place 6w 11
5Jly03–9Pha fm 1 1/16 Ⓣ :23 :464 1:113 1:422 3↑ⒻDrJPennyMH100k **87** 1 57 510 57½ 45½ 25 Carrero V L114 b 6.30 91– 07 Delta Princess1195 Spice Island1143½ Willie's Luv115¾ 2nd best 6
18Jun03–8Bel sly 1¼ ⊗ :481 1:123 1:383 2:051 3↑ⒻAlw 48000N2x **84** 5 49 49 44½ 31 1½ Chavez J F L120 b 2.85 68– 25 Spice Island120½ Miss Hellie1201 Give and Take12016¾ Along late inside 6
3May03–7Haw yl 1 1/16 Ⓣ :241 :49 1:142 1:464 4↑ⒻNicole43k **84** 2 52 52½ 52 2hd 2½ Bourque C C L118 b *1.40 69– 32 Attico118½ *Spice Island*1185¼ I Can Fan Fan118¾ Outfinished 8
17Apr03–9Kee yl 1⅛ Ⓣ :483 1:151 1:402 1:53 4↑ⒻAlw 56788N2x **83** 7 810 910 85¾ 55½ 3¾ Velasquez C L116 b 3.90 71– 27 Jester116no La Belle Simone117¾ Spice Island1161½ Broke in air,closed 5w 9
23Mar03–8GP sly 1½ ⊗ :482 1:14 2:061 2:321 3↑ⒻOrchidH-G2 **74** 3 36½ 32 56 48½ 414¾ Coa E M L113 b 10.80 - - Tweedside1165½ San Dare1195 Hi Tech Honeycomb1154¼ Inside, faltered 7
23Feb03–10GP fst 1 1/16 ⊗ :24 :481 1:124 1:461 4↑ⒻAlw 36000N1x **85** 4 55 56½ 56 35½ 11¼ Chavez J F L117 b 7.00 78– 19 SpiceIslnd1171¼ *VisioninFlight*117½ NnnisSword1173¾ Outside rally, up late 8
8Feb03–11GP fm 1⅛ Ⓣ :483 1:131 1:374 1:491 4↑ⒻClm 50000(50–45) **84** 6 97½ 98½ 95¾ 74½ 1¾ Coa E M L119 b 43.20 89– 11 *Spice Island*119¾ Roses for Ruby119hd Devillious1191¼ Swung out, up late 10

Spite the Devil

Own: Hardwicke Stable

Dk. b or b. g. 4 (Mar)
Sire: Devil His Due (Devil's Bag) $7,500
Dam: Samantha D (Cryptoclearance)
Br: Elisabeth R. Jerkens (NY)
Tr: Jerkens H. A(0 0 0 0 .00) 2003:(359 73 .20)

Life	**21**	**3**	**5**	**5**	**$342,739**	**96**	**D.Fst**	**18 3 5 5**	**$329,179**	**96**
2003	**14**	**1**	**3**	**3**	**$217,924**	**96**	**Wet(344)**	**3 0 0 0**	**$13,560**	**80**
2002	**7**	**2**	**2**	**2**	**$124,815**	**89**	**Turf(238)**	**0 0 0 0**	**$0**	**–**
	0	**0**	**0**	**0**	**$0**	**–**	**Dst(0)**	**0 0 0 0**	**$0**	**–**

26Dec03-7Aqu	fst	1⅛	[•] :482 1:124 1:374 1:503	3↑Alw 46000N2x	**95**	4	21½	31	21	1hd	2½	Cotto P L Jr7	L108 b	5.00	83-16	MkeMyDyJur117½ SpitetheDevil1081¼ Bnnck1214¼	3 wide move, outfinish	9
27Nov03-7Aqu	fst	1	:232 :46 1:101 1:344	3↑Alw 52000N3x	**84**	11	83	73¼	75½	611	514¼	Chavez Luis	L114 b	8.20	77-16	Stockholder1214 TheLdysGroom1197 OnTuffFox1231	5 wide trip, no rally	11
18Oct03-10Bel	fst	1⅛	:463 1:102 1:361 1:492	3↑[S]EmpirClscH250k	**91**	7	86¼	87	79¼	49	45¼	Chavez J F	L114 b	23.10	78-26	WellFancied124½ Gnder1233¼ MrDetermined1121½	Came wide, good finish	9
28Sep03-7Bel	my	1	⊗ :23 :463 1:111 1:361	3↑Alw 52000N3x	**80**	3	610	64	65¾	66	59¾	Velazquez J R	L112 b	4.40	75-29	Colita115½ Acceptable Venture1142¾ DialaHero1194½	Awkward start, wide	6
5Sep03-8Bel	fst	7f	:223 :451 1:092 1:212	3↑[S]GnDMcAthrH109k	**89**	4	8	33	35	36½	39	Chavez J F	L116 b	6.70	84-16	*Well Fancied*1235½ *Gratiaen*1133½ Spite the Devil1161	Bumped start, inside	8
20Aug03-8Sar	fst	1⅛	:473 1:113 1:362 1:493	[S]Albany168k	**86**	3	43	31½	31	34½	35	Chavez J F	121 b	5.50	82-11	TrfficChief1212 AcceptbleVentur1193 SpitthDvil1216¾	Steadied first turn	5
26Jly03-8FL	fst	1 1/16	:25 :493 1:141 1:443	[S]NYDerby142k	**86**	3	32	31	31½	21½	23	Espinoza J L	124 b	5.70	95-15	*TrfficChief*1193 SpitthDvil1244 GoRockinRobin1247¾	4 path 5/16, no match	5
28Jun03-8Bel	fst	7f	:223 :452 1:10 1:224	[S]MikeLee117k	**63**	6	6	67¼	612	621	621	Migliore R	123 b	4.20	65-15	Bossanova11413¼ AcceptbleVenture1166¼ LimoneForte114½	No response	6
24May03-8Bel	sly	1⅛	:441 1:084 1:344 1:482	PeterPan-G2	**78**	6	41¼	51¾	41¾	37	48¾	Castellano J J	121 b	6.90	79-12	Go Rockin' Robin1176 Alysweep123¾ Supervisor1152	Hustled, wide, tired	6
3May03-9Aqu	fst	1	:223 :45 1:093 1:354	Withers-G3	**96**	5	74¾	73¼	62¾	42	1nk	Chavez Luis	116 b	16.90	86-21	SpitetheDevil116nk Alyswep1231 Stnislvsky116hd	Stumbled start, bumped	8
12Apr03-8Aqu	my	1⅛	:471 1:11 1:354 1:483	WoodMem-G1	**71**	2	710	713	714	821	824¼	Luzzi M J	123	57.75	69-12	Empire Maker123½ *Funny Cide*1237½ Kissin Saint1231	Inside trip, tired	8
16Mar03-9Aqu	fst	170	[•] :234 :473 1:114 1:403	Gotham-G3	**93**	5	74	75¼	66	49	35¾	Luzzi M J	116	5.00	85-15	Alysweep1204¼ *Grey Comet*1201½ Spite the Devil116nk	Inside trip, rallied	9
15Feb03-3GP	fst	170	:231 :463 1:114 1:421	Alw 38000N2x	**83**	1	45½	45½	42	24	25	Bailey J D	118	*1.70	85-13	*RegionofMerit*1185 SpitthDvil1184½ ChristmsAwy118½	Drifted str, 2nd best	6
18Jan03-10GP	fst	1 1/16	:232 :471 1:112 1:43	HolyBull-G3	**77**	12	93¾	117½	99	109¼	1012½	Bailey J D	118	14.90	81-10	Offlee Wild116hd PowerfulTouch1163 Bham1182½	Awkward st, no menace	13

Spoken Fur

Own: Amerman Racing Stables LLC

Gr/ro. f. 4 (Mar)
Sire: Notebook (Well Decorated) $15,000
Dam: Siberian Fur (Siberian Express)
Br: George A. Smith & Dr. W. E. Johnston (Fla)
Tr: Frankel Robert J(0 0 0 0 .00) 2003:(411 114 .28)

Life	**12**	**5**	**1**	**4**	**$675,880**	**104**	**D.Fst**	**11 5 1 4**	**$675,880**	**104**
2003	**10**	**5**	**1**	**3**	**$670,630**	**104**	**Wet(382)**	**0 0 0 0**	**$0**	**–**
2002	**2**	**M**	**0**	**1**	**$5,250**	**67**	**Turf(244)**	**1 0 0 0**	**$0**	**89**
	0	**0**	**0**	**0**	**$0**	**–**	**Dst(0)**	**0 0 0 0**	**$0**	**–**

11Oct03-8Kee	fm	1⅛	(T) :473 1:113 1:354 1:474	ⒻQEIICup-G1	**89**	1	72¼	85¼	87	74¾	74¾	Velasquez C	L121	7.80	93-11	Film Maker121no Maiden Tower121¾ Casual Look121¾	Near inside,no rally	10
6Sep03-7Bel	fst	1⅛	:452 1:093 1:344 1:482	ⒻGazelleH-G1	**94**	1	73¼	52	42	23½	3½	Velasquez C	L121	4.30	87-13	Buy theSport113½ LadyTak121no SpokenFur1218¼	Closed btwn, missed 2d	8
16Aug03-9Sar	fst	1¼	:482 1:124 1:374 2:05	ⒻAlabama-G1	**91**	2	45	44½	44½	36	37	Bailey J D	L121	*.85	75-14	Island Fashion1216 Awesome Humor1211 SpokenFur1211¼	No rally on rail	6
19Jly03-9Bel	fst	1½	:462 1:113 2:033 2:31	ⒻCCAOaks-G1	**88**	7	45	2½	12½	18	13½	Bailey J D	L121	*.90	77-17	SpokenFur1213½ Fircroft1212½ Svedbythelight1214¼	Drew off, ridden out	7
28Jun03-9Bel	fst	1⅛	:462 1:113 1:37 1:502	ⒻMthrGoos-G1	**104**	4	41¾	41¾	3nk	18	15¼	Bailey J D	L121	4.50	78-19	*Spoken Fur*1215¼ Yell121¾ Final Round1218¼	Wrapped up late	6
Previously trained by Smith Austin																		
21May03-8CD	fst	1	:231 :464 1:114 1:371	3↑ⒻAlw 39600N2x	**91**	4	84¾	83¾	63¾	32	11¼	Velasquez C	L114	5.50	81-20	*Spoken Fur*1141¼ Gloriosity1172½ First Again117½	Rail,driving,clear	9
30Apr03-8CD	fst	7f	:221 :444 1:10 1:23	ⒻAlw 33460N1x	**86**	8	7	97½	77½	22	1nk	Velasquez C	L121	5.10	87-13	*SpokenFur*121nk MeetMeAtMidnite1173½ *Stellr*1151¼	Bmp start,5w,driving	11
6Apr03-3Kee	fst	7f	:22 :453 1:121 1:244	ⒻMd Sp Wt 43k	**85**	7	3	78	54	12	16¼	Velasquez C	L120	4.10	80-16	*SpoknFur*1206¼ *SkngthRng*1201¼ ContryRomnc12013½	Angled rail lane,drvg	9
9Mar03-4GP	fst	6f	:22 :443 :564 1:09	ⒻMd Sp Wt 34k	**77**	1	6	54	55	33½	36	Guidry M	L121	*1.00	93-07	*Keiai Sakura*1216 Lake West121hd *Spoken Fur*1212¼	Ducked in start	6
2Feb03-5GP	fst	6f	:22 :45 :573 1:103	ⒻMd Sp Wt 34k	**79**	6	1	56½	56½	34	2hd	Guidry M	L121	4.50	91-08	Who Can Tell121hd Spoken Fur1211¼ *Keiai Sakura*1216¼	Full of run, missed	7

Spring Meadow
Own: Fog City Stable

Ch. m. 5 (Apr) OBSAPR01 $200,000
Sire: Meadowlake (Hold Your Peace) $20,000
Dam: Go for It Lady (Mr. Prospector)
Br: John T. L. Jones Jr. & Ashford Stud (Ky)
Tr: Hess R B Jr(0 0 0 0 .00) 2003:(215 26 .12)

Life	23	6	4	5	$496,123	102	D.Fst	21	6	3	5	$479,079	102
2003	10	3	0	3	$204,002	94	Wet(414)	2	0	1	0	$17,044	77
2002	13	3	4	2	$292,121	102	Turf(256)	0	0	0	0	$0	–
	0	0	0	0	$0	–	Dst(0)	0	0	0	0	$0	–

31Dec03–8SA	fst	6½f	:21^{3}	:44^{2}	1:08^{3}	1:14^{4}	3↑ Ⓕ KalooknQnH84k	–	2	6	2hd	2hd	3^{1}	4$5\frac{1}{2}$	Nakatani C S	LB118	4.90	93– 06	D RoyllyChosn119no EmBovry120$5\frac{1}{2}$ SprklingAv113no			Dueled,just lost 3rd	8	
29Nov03–4Hol	fst	6f	:22^{4}	:45^{4}	:57^{2}	1:09^{1}	3↑ Ⓕ OClm 100000N	92	1	2	1hd	1hd	$2\frac{1}{2}$	$3^{4}\frac{1}{4}$	Krone J A	LB123	3.00	90– 15	*Ema Bovary*119nk Bear Fan117^{4} Spring Meadow123^{5}			Off rail lane,wkened	4	
25Oct03–1SA	fst	6f	:21^{3}	:44	:56^{1}	1:09^{3}	3↑ Ⓕ VerySubtlH107k	94	3	3	2hd	1hd	$1\frac{1}{2}$	$4^{1}\frac{1}{4}$	Stevens G L	LB118	4.00	89– 05	Stellar113no Lacie Girl118nk Cee's Valley Girl115^{1}			Inside,wkened late	6	
23Sep03–8Fpx	fst	6½f	:21^{3}	:45^{2}	1:10^{3}	1:17^{1}	3↑ Ⓕ Bangls&Bds49k	83	6	4	$4^{1}\frac{1}{4}$	$1^{2}\frac{1}{2}$	1^{4}	$1^{5}\frac{1}{2}$	Pedroza M A	LB119	*.70	92– 10	SpringMedow119$5\frac{1}{2}$ KissingGirl114^{6} WildTickle118hd			Drew off, ridden out	7	
23Aug03–8Dmr	fst	6½f	:22^{2}	:45	1:09	1:15^{2}	3↑ Ⓕ RchBrdoH-G3	90	3	7	$7^{3}\frac{1}{4}$	$6^{3}\frac{1}{4}$	5^{4}	3^{5}	Krone J A	LB117	8.90	93– 10	Secret Liaison116^{4} LacieGirl116^{1} *SpringMeadow*117hd			Split foes 1/8,late 3d	8	
20Jly03–9Del	fst	6f	:21^{2}	:44^{2}	:57^{3}	1:11	3↑ Ⓕ LightHrtdH100k	83	7	4	$4^{4}\frac{1}{2}$	4^{2}	$2\frac{1}{2}$	3^{1}	Dominguez R A	L117	*1.60	88– 12	LightsOn111^{1} HuntdLss116no SpringMdow117^{5}			Loomed,not good enough	8	
30Jun03–7Del	fst	6f	:21^{3}	:45	:57^{4}	1:10^{2}	3↑ Ⓕ LocalThllr58k	89	4	5	5^{5}	$4^{1}\frac{1}{2}$	$2\frac{1}{2}$	$1\frac{3}{4}$	Dominguez R A	L118	*1.70	92– 08	SpringMeadow118$\frac{3}{4}$ Bruann123$\frac{1}{2}$ DrexelMonoril118$\frac{1}{2}$			Swung4w,edged clear	7	
3May03–8CD	fst	7f	:22^{2}	:45^{2}	1:10	1:22	4↑ Ⓕ HmnaDstH-G1	85	3	6	8^{3}	7^{4}	6^{7}	$5^{9}\frac{3}{4}$	Stevens G L	L117	25.40	82– 08	*Sightseek*116$4\frac{1}{2}$ Gold Mover119hd Miss Lodi114$2\frac{1}{4}$			Bmp start,no threat	8	
9Apr03–8Kee	sly	7f	:21^{4}	:44^{1}	1:10^{1}	1:24^{1}	4↑ Ⓕ Madison132k	36	4	2	4^{3}	4^{5}	$4^{9}\frac{1}{2}$	$4^{24}\frac{1}{4}$	Sellers S J	L116	*1.40	59– 17	A New Twist116$1\frac{1}{2}$ FlaxenFlyer116$9\frac{1}{2}$ ForestSecrets116$13\frac{1}{4}$			4-5w trip, faded	4	
22Feb03–8SA	fst	6f	:21^{1}	:43^{4}	:56^{2}	1:10^{1}	4↑ Ⓕ LsFlresH-G3	94	5	1	$4^{1}\frac{1}{4}$	$4^{1}\frac{3}{4}$	3^{1}	1nk	Nakatani C S	LB117	*2.60	87– 15	SpringMedow117nk Brisquette116$1\frac{1}{2}$ WildTickle117$\frac{1}{2}$			4wd bid,led 1/16,held	7	

Spring Star (Fr)
Own: Frere and Wertheimer

B. f. 5 (May)
Sire: Danehill (Danzig)
Dam: L'Irlandaise (Irish River*Fr)
Br: Wertheimer Et Frere (Fr)
Tr: Mandella Richard E(0 0 0 0 .00) 2003:(253 51 .20)

Life	11	4	1	4	$253,796	101	D.Fst	0	0	0	0	$0	–
2003	5	2	0	3	$182,313	101	Wet(296)	0	0	0	0	$0	–
2002	6	2	1	1	$71,483	90	Turf(330)	11	4	1	4	$253,796	101
	0	0	0	0	$0	–	Dst(0)	0	0	0	0	$0	–

29Dec03–5SA	fm	*6½f	Ⓣ :22	:44^{1}	1:07	1:13	3↑ Ⓕ MnroviaH-G3	94	4	6	6^{8}	$6^{3}\frac{3}{4}$	$5^{2}\frac{3}{4}$	3^{1}	Solis A	LB119	*.50e	91– 08	Icantgoforthtt114no Polygreen116^{1} SpringStr119^{2}	Squeezed strt,3wd lane	6
7Sep03–6Dmr	fm	$1\frac{1}{16}$	Ⓣ :24^{3}	:48^{2}	1:11^{4}	1:40^{3}	3↑ Ⓕ PalmrBCH-G2	101	3	11	$1^{1}\frac{1}{2}$	$1^{1}\frac{1}{2}$	$1\frac{1}{2}$	1nk	Solis A	LB116	*1.50	98– 03	Spring Star116nk Magic Mission117no *Garden in the Rain*114^{3}	Held gamely	5
13Aug03–7Dmr	fm	$1\frac{1}{16}$	Ⓣ :24	:47^{1}	1:10^{3}	1:40^{3}	3↑ Ⓕ Ⓡ OsunitasH79k	96	6	$3\frac{1}{2}$	$2\frac{1}{2}$	2^{1}	$3^{1}\frac{1}{2}$	$3^{1}\frac{1}{2}$	Solis A	LB118	*1.70	96– 07	Arabic Song115$\frac{1}{2}$ *Belleski*117^{1} *Spring Star*118no	Forced out early	7
13Jly03–1Hol	fm	$1\frac{1}{16}$	Ⓣ :23^{3}	:47^{2}	1:11^{1}	1:41^{1}	4↑ Ⓕ Alw 55000N2x	97	2	$2^{1}\frac{1}{2}$	2^{1}	2hd	1^{1}	1^{4}	Solis A	LB118	*.40	90– 14	Spring Star118^{4} Alozaina120$3\frac{1}{2}$ Chautauqua120^{1}	Bid,clear,ridden out	5
21Jun03–3Hol	fm	1	Ⓣ :24^{2}	:48^{1}	1:11^{3}	1:35^{2}	4↑ Ⓕ Alw 55000N2x	90	1	$7^{6}\frac{1}{2}$	7^{9}	$7^{6}\frac{1}{4}$	$7^{4}\frac{1}{4}$	3hd	Solis A	LB118	*.80	87– 18	Mistic Sun118no Reefs Sis118hd *Spring Star*118^{2}	Off slw,pulled,rallied	7

Standard Setter
Own: Equils James W. and Marcia S

Ch. g. 4 (Mar)
Sire: Benchmark (Alydar) $2,000
Dam: When and Where (Siyah Kalem)
Br: Phillip E. Lebherz & Richard William Meister (Cal)
Tr: Carava Jack(0 0 0 0 .00) 2003:(361 61 .17)

Life	12	3	4	1	$112,810	90	D.Fst	9	2	4	0	$52,560	90
2003	6	2	1	0	$72,700	90	Wet(345)	2	1	0	1	$58,300	84
2002	6	1	3	1	$40,110	79	Turf(275*)	1	0	0	0	$1,950	–
	0	0	0	0	$0	–	Dst(0)	0	0	0	0	$0	–

5Dec03–2Hol fst 1 1/16 :24 1 :47 4 1:11 3 1:43 2 Clm c-(16-14) **90** 5 2½ 2 1½ 1 hd 1 1½ 1 2 Valenzuela P A **LB**118 b *1.20 87– 19 Standard Setter118 2 Charmer Baron118 5 Anza118½ 3wd,rail bid,clear 7
Claimed from Vanburger Carl F. for $16,000, Mitchell Mike Trainer 2003(as of 12/5): (244 57 48 45 0.23)
22Nov03–2Hol fst 6f :22 1 :45 4 :58 1:11 Clm c-(12.5-10.5) **80** 2 6 3 1 2½ 1 hd 2 nk Espinoza V **LB**118 b 2.90 85– 15 Sabalucious118 nk *StndrdSetter*118 1 UnusulMist118 12½ Bid,led,caught late 6
Claimed from Lebherz, Philip and Meister, Richard for $12,500, Bonde Jeff Trainer 2003(as of 11/22): (325 58 52 46 0.18)
31Oct03–4SA fst 1 1/16 :22 2 :45 2 1:09 4 1:43 3↑[S]OClm 40000 **53** 3 4 2 4 2 4 4 6 4¾ 7 18½ Desormeaux K J **LB**117 b 9.30 70– 15 Exceeding115 4 Musique Toujours115 4 Sombrio118 2 Pulled,inside,wkened 7
21Sep03–3BM fm 1 1/16 Ⓣ:21 4 :45 1 1:11 1:43 1 HalfMnBayH68k – 5 2½ 2½ 5 6½ 5 21 - Gonzalez R M **LB**118 b 6.90 - 09 BluBloodBoot115 2½ WinningStrips117 nk AtDwn113 3 Bad step, walked off 5
24Aug03–8Sac fst 6f :21 4 :44 3 :57 1:10 1 [S]EMcCabDby52k **36** 6 3 3 1 3 2½ 4 7½ 5 13¼ Gonzalez R M **LB**122 b 1.50 76– 11 I B Bad117 hd *Taraval*122 8 Ichiban Duc117 no 3wide trip, weakened 6
11Jan03–8GG my 1 1/16 :22 1 :45 2 1:10 3 1:43 3 GGDerby-G3 **84** 1 1 2½ 1 2½ 1 1 1½ 1 nk Gonzalez R M **LB**120 b 17.40 85– 17 Standard Setter120 nk Ozzie Cat120 1 Pine for Java120¾ Well rated, drvng 10

Stanley Park
Own: Moss Mr. and Mrs. Jerome S

Ch. c. 4 (Mar) KEESEP01 $240,000
Sire: Swain*Ire (Nashwan) $25,000
Dam: Tricky Bird (Storm Bird)
Br: Fred Seitz (Ky)
Tr: Shirreffs John A(0 0 0 0 .00) 2003:(163 33 .20)

Life	8	3	0	1	$123,316	96	D.Fst	0	0	0	0	$0	–
2003	8	3	0	1	$123,316	96	Wet(276)	0	0	0	0	$0	–
2002	0	M	0	0	$0	–	Turf(351)	8	3	0	1	$123,316	96
	0	0	0	0	$0	–	Dst(0)	0	0	0	0	$0	–

30Nov03–9Hol fm 1¼ Ⓣ:51 1:17 2 1:41 2:04 1 HolDerby-G1 **95** 1 10 7¼ 11 5½ 11 8 10 4½ 8 1¾ Saint-Martin E **LB**122 b 13.10 69– 17 SweetReturn122½ FirlyRnsom122½ KickenKris122 hd Blocked,steadied 1/8 13
1Nov03–8BM fm 1⅛ Ⓣ:48 1:11 1:36 4 1:48 4 BMDerby-G3 **96** 3 7 5¼ 6 7¼ 5 6 2 hd 1 2½ Saint-Martin E **LB**116 b 7.40 100– 09 Stanley Park116 2½ Bis Repetitas118 1¼ Kewen116 1¼ Circled 4w, handily 8
8Oct03–7SA fm 1¼ Ⓣ:47 4 1:12 1:35 2 1:59 1 3↑OClm 80000N **80** 1 7 11 7 11 7 7½ 6 5¾ 6 9¾ Smith M E **LB**115 b 4.70 87– 06 SpecialMatter118¾ Trompolino118 4 RightProof117 2 3wd into lane,no rally 8
16Aug03–8Dmr fm 1 1/16 Ⓣ:23 3 :47 1 1:10 3 1:40 1 LaJollaH-G3 **90** 2 5 4½ 5 6 4 3½ 5 5½ 6 4 Almeida G F **LB**117 b 13.50 96– 10 Singletary118½ Devious Boy117½ Senor Swinger120½ 3wd into lane,no bid 7
23Jly03–8Dmr fm 1 Ⓣ:23 :47 1:11 1 1:34 3 [R]Oceanside84k **91** 5 5 6 3 2½ 3 1½ 3 1½ 3 1 Smith M E **LB**120 b 2.30 89– 11 Devious Boy116½ Fairly Ransom118½ Stanley Park120 1 Split foes,rail bid 7
Run in divisions
2Jly03–7Hol fm 1 Ⓣ:23 3 :47 1 1:10 3 1:34 2 OClm 80000N **92** 4 9 10 9 10 8 5½ 6 2¾ 1 1½ Smith M E **LB**120 b 9.20 92– 11 StnlyPrk120 1½ FlrtWthFortn118 nk CnqrthGlxy120½ Off bit slow,5wd rally 9
26May03–3Hol fm 1 1/16 Ⓣ:24 4 :49 1 1:13 2 1:43 3↑Md Sp Wt 46k **84** 8 9 8¾ 8 5¼ 7 4 2 1½ 1 2 Johnston M T **LB**116 b 16.00 81– 10 *Stanley Park*116 2 Freedom's Key116½ A. P. Slew123 nk 3wd 7/8,rail bid lane 11
19Mar03–8SA fm 1 Ⓣ:22 :46 1:10 3 1:35 4 Md Sp Wt 50k **55** 2 7 10 9 9¾ 9 8½ 8 8¼ 7 13 Espinoza V **LB**120 b 9.50 70– 14 Gassan Royal120 2 *Sci Fi*120 1½ Richard's Boy120 hd Savd ground, no threat 9

Star Parade (Arg)
Own: McClure J. D

Dk. b or b. f. 5 (Oct)
Sire: Parade Marshal (Caro*Ire)
Dam: Clerical Etoile*Arg (The Watcher)
Br: Firmamento (Arg)
Tr: Vienna Darrell(0 0 0 0 .00) 2003:(303 51 .17)

Life	12	4	3	1	$176,112	106	D.Fst	8	4	3	0	$172,825	106
2003	9	3	3	0	$173,396	106	Wet(260)	1	0	0	1	$227	–
2002	3	1	0	1	$2,716	–	Turf(201)	3	0	0	0	$3,060	88
	0	0	0	0	$0	–	Dst(0)	0	0	0	0	$0	–

7Dec03–8Hol fst 1 1/16 :23 :46 1:094 1:41 3↑ⒻBayakoaH-G2 **106** 2 1½ 12 1½ 11 13¼ Espinoza V LB112 12.20 99–08 Star Parade1123¼ Adoration1214 Bare Necessities1193 Bit off rail,cleared 6
13Nov03–5Hol gd 1 1/16 Ⓣ :232 :47 1:11 1:421 3↑ⒻAlw 51000N3x **88** 4 21 21½ 21½ 43½ 45 Flores D R LB121 4.40 80–16 DreamersGlory1191 ReefsSis1211 *LadyAnnliese*1213 Rank,stalked,wkened 5
30Oct03–7SA fst 1 :223 :453 1:10 1:352 3↑ⒻAlw 53000N2x **94** 1 11 12½ 12 11 12 Flores D R LB118 *1.50 94–09 StarParade1182 Sophisticatedbluff1207½ Lyncola1202 Inside, held gamely 6
22Aug03–7Dmr fst 1 :22 :452 1:111 1:373 3↑ⒻOClm 62500N **81** 1 41½ 4¾ 31½ 52¾ 22½ Nakatani C S LB121 *3.40 83–14 BriteSunnyDay1192½ *StarParade*1212 DiamondTiar1192 Steadied 5/16 & 1/4 7
27Jly03–7Dmr fst 1 :223 :461 1:111 1:371 3↑ⒻOClm 40000N **89** 3 11½ 12½ 1½ 1½ 1nk Nakatani C S LB121 14.20 88–09 Star Parade121nk Siphon Honey121½ Lyncola121no Off rail,resisted late 10
Previously trained by Julio Penna
2Apr03♦San Isidro (Arg) fst *7f LH 1:223 ⒻPremio Rain Magic Alw 3500 22 Abregu M 123 6.20 Fairish1232 *Star Parade*1235 Fortina Toss123½ 10
Tracked leader,led 2f to 1f out,second best
12Mar03♦San Isidro (Arg) fst *6f LH 1:121 ⒻPremio Mi Paisano Alw 3300 2¾ Abregu M 123 13.85 Gran Amiga123¾ Star Parade1231½ Miss Dixie1172½ 15
Tracked in 4th,late gain into 2nd
1Mar03♦San Isidro (Arg) gd *6f Ⓣ LH 1:101 ⒻPremio Final Meeting Alw 4400 811¼ Valdivieso J 123 6.60 Free Runner117nk Passion Toss115no La Balada1231½ 9
Chased in 3rd,weakened 2f out
4Jan03♦Hipodromo (Arg) fst *7f LH 1:221 ⒻPremio Romanza Mora Alw 3300 512 Rivero A 123 5.40 *Forty Schoolgirl*1234 Chinese Dress1237 South Korea123¾ 5
Trailed throughout

Starrer
Own: Krikorian George

Dk. b or b. m. 6 (Apr) FTKOCT99 $35,000
Sire: Dynaformer (Roberto) $50,000
Dam: To the Hunt (Relaunch)
Br: Wind Hill Farm (Ky)
Tr: Shirreffs John A(0 0 0 0 .00) 2003:(163 33 .20)

Life	20	6	5	3	$1,043,033	111	D.Fst	18	5	5	3	$811,033	111
2003	2	2	0	0	$300,000	111	Wet(366)	2	1	0	0	$232,000	103
2002	6	1	1	1	$310,000	105	Turf(335)	0	0	0	0	$0	–
	0	0	0	0	$0	–	Dst(0)	0	0	0	0	$0	–

9Mar03–8SA fst 1⅛ :47 1:103 1:353 1:481 4↑ⒻSMrgrtaH-G1 **111** 5 21 21 21½ 1hd 12 Valenzuela P A LB121 b *1.60 93–16 Starrer1212 *Sightseek*1163 Bella Bellucci1165 Stalked,led,clear late 5
16Feb03–6SA gd 1 1/16 :23 :461 1:104 1:423 4↑ⒻSntMriaH-G1 **103** 1 2hd 31½ 1½ 11½ 14½ Valenzuela P A LB119 b *1.10 91–16 *Starrer*1194½ *You*118½ Rhiana1127 Pulled,rail bid,clear 5

Storming Home (GB)

Own: Al Maktoum Sheik Maktoum b

Dk. b or b. h. 6 (Feb)
Sire: Machiavellian (Mr. Prospector)
Dam: Try to Catch Me (Shareef Dancer)
Br: Gainsborough Stud Management Ltd (GB)
Tr: Drysdale Neil D(0 0 0 0 .00) 2003:(182 34 .19)

Life	24	8	4	3	$1,536,704	112	D.Fst	0	0	0	0	$0	–
2003	5	3	0	0	$650,000	112	Wet(345)	0	0	0	0	$0	–
2002	8	2	2	2	$579,080	–	Turf(318)	24	8	4	3	$1,536,704	112
	0	0	0	0	$0	–	Dst(0)	0	0	0	0	$0	–

25Oct03–8SA fm 1½ Ⓣ :483 1:112 2:00 2:241 3↑BCTurf-G1 **96** 5 83¾ 52¼ 42½ 55½ 79 Stevens G L LB126 fb *2.00 96–04 DH High Chaparral126 DH Johar126hd *Falbrav*1265½ 3wd,4wd,no late bid 9
28Sep03–3SA fm 1¼ Ⓣ :503 1:152 1:39 2:013 3↑CLHirsch-G1 **104** 2 45½ 45½ 32½ 22 1½ Stevens G L LB124 fb *.30 85–13 Storming Home124½ *Johar*1241¼ Irish Warrior1241½ 3wd into lane,rallied 4
16Aug03–10AP gd 1¼ Ⓣ :49 1:132 1:373 2:021 3↑ArlMilln-G1 **107** 4 1210 119 42 3nk 1½ Stevens G L L126 b *2.40 95–08 D *Storming Home*126½ *Sulamani*126hd DH Kaieteur126 Duckd out 13
Disqualified and placed 4th
14Jun03–3Hol fm 1¼ Ⓣ :484 1:132 1:361 2:003 3↑CWhtghmH-G1 **103** 5 510 53¾ 53 2hd 1¾ Stevens G L LB124 fb *.30 89–14 Storming Home124¾ Mister Acpen115½ Cagney1141 5wd 1/2,4wd into lane 6
10May03–7Hol fm 1½ Ⓣ :491 1:131 1:594 2:251 3↑JMurryMemH400k **112** 1 74½ 31 3½ 11 12 Stevens G L LB122 b 2.80 99–12 *Storming Home*1222 *Denon*1224½ *Ballingarry*120nk 3wd bid,led,gamely 8

Strait From Texas

Own: Michael James A

Dk. b or b. m. 5 (Apr) FTKOCT00 $12,500
Sire: Judge T C (Judge Smells) $8,500
Dam: Tellum Texan (Eastern Echo)
Br: Robert H. Roberts & Bea Roberts (Ky)
Tr: Buttigieg Paul M(0 0 0 0 .00) 2003:(135 11 .08)

Life	24	7	6	2	$565,630	94	D.Fst	4	0	1	0	$11,697	66
2003	9	3	3	0	$275,936	94	Wet(341)	0	0	0	0	$0	–
2002	9	2	1	2	$185,047	93	Turf(271)	20	7	5	2	$553,933	94
	0	0	0	0	$0	–	Dst(0)	0	0	0	0	$0	–

23Aug03–9WO fm 1 1/16 Ⓣ :24 :472 1:112 1:41 3↑ⒻAlw 89000NC **68** 2 65 75¼ 53 77¾ 710¾ Dos Ramos R A L118 3.60 82–11 Ginger Gold1171¼ Diadella1161 Ghazirella1161½ Rank backstrtch,no rly 8
20Jly03–2WO fm 1 1/16 Ⓣ :242 :481 1:112 1:411 3↑ⒻAlw 89000NC **85** 3 43 31½ 31½ 21½ 24 Dos Ramos R A L120 *.70 88–06 *InishGlora*1164 StraitFromTexs120no SmllPromises1163¼ Stalk rail, bid 3w 5
5Jly03–8WO fm 1⅛ Ⓣ :452 1:092 1:333 1:48 3↑ⒻDncSmrtH-G3 **88** 7 87½ 88¼ 72¾ 1½ 52½ Dos Ramos R A L118 5.35 85–15 Madeira Mist116no First Quarter1141 *Byzantine*117½ Rally 5w,led,outfinish 10
1Jun03–8WO gd 1 1/16 Ⓣ :23 :46 1:10 1:424 3↑ⒻNassau-G2 **94** 6 67 67¾ 47½ 31 1½ Dos Ramos R A L119 20.75 84–19 Strait From Texas119½ Chopinina1153 Byzantine117½ 4w,rallied 9
Previously trained by Maker Michael J
3May03–7CD fm 1 Ⓣ :232 :462 1:104 1:334 3↑ⒻCtDstTMI-G3 **78** 11 44½ 44½ 42½ 116½ 119¾ Day P L123 8.90 93 – Heat Haze1231½ Quick Tip123¾ Sentimental Value1211¼ Stalk,5w,faded 11
Previously trained by Michael James A
16Mar03–10Tam fm 1 1/16 Ⓣ :232 :464 1:11 1:41 4↑ⒻHillsborgh100k **94** 6 1hd 11½ 1½ 11 1½ Castanon J L L118 8.80 93–10 Strait From Texas118½ Dedication1181 Stylish1181 Fast pace, just lasted 11
8Feb03–10Tam fm *1⅛ Ⓣ :49 1:141 1:384 1:504 4↑ⒻEndeavour75k **90** 2 3½ 42 62 42½ 21 Castanon J L L116 4.10 84–21 Wander Mom1221 *Strait From Texas*116½ Kimster116¾ Boxed, split horses 12
23Jan03–9Tam fm *1 1/16 Ⓣ :234 :50 1:152 1:47 4↑ⒻAlw 14300NC **88** 2 85¼ 99½ 68½ 32½ 13½ Castanon J L L118 *1.00 75–29 Strait From Texas1183½ No Deadline118nk Par Golfer1181½ Ridden out 9
13Jan03–8Tam fm *5f Ⓣ :584 4↑ⒻAlw 15800NC **78** 4 10 1010 65¼ 54½ 2½ Henry W T L118 *1.40 – – Take a Look120½ *Strait From Texas*1181¼ Social Top1181 Closed fast 6 wide 10

Stroll

Own: Claiborne Farm

Dk. b or b. c. 4 (Apr)
Sire: Pulpit (A.P. Indy) $60,000
Dam: Maid for Walking*GB (Prince Sabo)
Br: Claiborne Farm (Ky)
Tr: Mott William I(0 0 0 0 .00) 2003:(718 138 .19)

Life	11	6	2	1	$446,547	105	D.Fst	3 0 1 0	$14,867 65
2003	6	5	1	0	$398,800	105	Wet(330)	0 0 0 0	$0 –
2002	5	1	1	1	$47,747	87	Turf(258)	8 6 1 1	$431,680 105
	0	0	0	0	$0	–	Dst(0)	0 0 0 0	$0 –

11Oct03-12Crc fm	1⅛	Ⓣ :474 1:112 1:354 1:481	CrcDerby-G3	97	7	61¾	52	1hd	12½	13¾	Bailey J D	L122	*.20	90– 15	Stroll1223¾ CertifiablyCrazy1152¾ SuperFrolic1192½	Stdy 1st turn, handily	9
21Sep03-9Bel fm	1⅛	T :471 1:104 1:342 1:46	JamaicaH-G2	105	3	2½	41½	41¼	11	12	Bailey J D	L121	*1.40	100– 12	Stroll1212 Kicken Kris121no Joe Bear1172½	Got through on rail	7
4Aug03-8Sar yl	1⅛	T :481 1:124 1:371 1:491	HalOFmeH-G2	102	9	2hd	2½	2½	14½	14	Bailey J D	L117	*2.65	92– 08	Stroll1174 Urban King1151¼ Saint Stephen115¾	Pressed pace, clear	11
5Jly03-8Mth fm	1 1/16	Ⓣ :224 :461 1:10 1:40	+ Lamplghtr50k	99	9	87¾	64¼	52	2hd	12¾	Bailey J D	L115	*.50	101– 03	Stroll1152¾ Purely Classic1134½ Ali's Pride1161	5wd bid,duel,edge away	9
10May03-7Bel fm	1	Ⓣ :233 :47 1:104 1:343	3↑ Alw 46000N1x	97	7	3½	32½	3½	1½	16	Luzzi M J	L116	*1.95	87– 13	Stroll1166 Polympics122nk Wild Maple1221	3 wide move, drew off	12
18Apr03-10Kee yl	1 1/16	Ⓣ :221 :453 1:103 1:431	Alw 56000N1x	86	1	1½	11½	11½	1hd	22	Bailey J D	L120	4.00	83– 14	Hidden Truth1182 Stroll1201¼ Bat Mobile1204½	Pace,no match late	9

Strong Hope

Own: Melnyk Eugene and Laura

B. c. 4 (Feb) FTSAUG01 $1,700,000
Sire: Grand Slam (Gone West) $30,000
Dam: Shining Through (Deputy Minister)
Br: Trackside Farm, G.A. Seelbinder & Liberation Farm (Ky)
Tr: Pletcher Todd A(0 0 0 0 .00) 2003:(826 199 .24)

Life	7	5	0	1	$582,360	110	D.Fst	5 3 0 1	$528,960 110
2003	7	5	0	1	$582,360	110	Wet(423)	2 2 0 0	$53,400 100
2002	0	M	0	0	$0	–	Turf(337)	0 0 0 0	$0 –
	0	0	0	0	$0	–	Dst(0)	0 0 0 0	$0 –

23Aug03-11Sar fst	1¼	:461 1:094 1:352 2:02	Travers-G1	91	2	1hd	1½	3½	36	314½	Velazquez J R	L126	4.40	82– 03	TenMostWanted1264½ PeaceRules12610 StrongHope126¾	Vied inside, tired	6
3Aug03-9Sar fst	1⅛	:47 1:103 1:35 1:48	JimDandy-G2	110	1	1½	11½	1½	12	1nk	Velazquez J R	L121	6.70	95– 11	Strong Hope121nk EmpireMaker1232½ Congrats1151	Pace, dug in, gamely	6
6Jly03-10Bel fst	1 1/16	:231 :453 1:093 1:413	Dwyer-G2	110	3	1½	11	11½	12½	1nk	Velazquez J R	L115	2.50	92– 11	Strong Hope115nk Nacheezmo1153 Sky Mesa1195¼	Took charge early	7
7Jun03-4Bel gd	1	:222 :451 1:092 1:354	3↑ Alw 48000N2x	100	9	1½	11	1½	11	11¾	Velazquez J R	L118	3.75	87– 13	StrongHop1181¾ OurSmmrStorm1214½ Inmorto1151¼	Set pace, drew clear	12
14May03-9Bel fst	1	:231 :462 1:111 1:361	3↑ Alw 46000N1x	97	6	11½	11	11½	12½	1no	Velazquez J R	L117	3.00	85– 22	Strong Hope117no Crimson Hero1147 Mukhtaser1184	Set pace, got nod	10
12Apr03-4Aqu sly	7f	:224 :453 1:093 1:222	3↑ Md Sp Wt 41k	95	2	5	1½	1½	11½	12¼	Velazquez J R	L117	1.75	91– 13	Strong Hope1172¼ Stone Canyon1177¾ Deco's Secret11210	Set pace, driving	7
8Mar03-8GP fst	6f	:22 :443 :564 1:083	Md Sp Wt 34k	74	5	9	31	31	35	410	Velazquez J R	L121	2.20	91– 01	Grand Hombre1214 Mazengah1214 Monty Man1212	3 wide, tired	12

Strut the Stage

Own: Sam–Son Farms

Ch. h. 6 (Mar) KEESEP99 $235,000
Sire: Theatrical*Ire (Nureyev) $75,000
Dam: Ruby Ransom (Red Ransom)
Br: Jamm Ltd. (Ky)
Tr: Frostad Mark R(0 0 0 0 .00) 2003:(206 44 .21)

Life	19	9	2	2	$1,265,923	105	D.Fst	0 0 0 0	$0 –
2003	4	2	1	0	$485,085	104	Wet(320)	0 0 0 0	$0 –
2002	8	3	0	1	$403,542	105	Turf(359)	19 9 2 2	$1,265,923 105
	0	0	0	0	$0	–	Dst(0)	0 0 0 0	$0 –

28Sep03-8WO sf	1⅜	Ⓣ :50 1:162 1:424 2:23	3↑ SkyClscH-G2	92	3	58	42½	31	32	44¼	Kabel T K	L123 fb	*.55	46– 50	BowmnMill113no LennytheLender1104 Mobil115nk	4w,advance,flatten out	6
30Aug03-8WO fm	1½	Ⓣ :492 1:133 2:023 2:27	3↑ NiagrBCH-G2	104	5	55½	62¾	52½	1hd	11¼	Kabel T K	L123 b	*1.15	95– 12	StruttheStge1231¼ RevvedUp1181½ BttrTlkNow115¾	Stalk 2-pth,drew out	10
20Jly03-8WO fm	1⅜	Ⓣ :491 1:132 1:371 2:134	3↑ ChneseCC-G2	103	4	43	43	31½	2½	11½	Kabel T K	L121 b	2.05	96– 06	StruttheStg1211½ PrfctSoul1192¾ AnglOnthWing115¾	3w,rally 4w, drew off	8
15Jun03-8WO gd	1⅛	Ⓣ :481 1:124 1:37 1:493	3↑ KngEdBCH-G2	100	7	72¾	72¼	62¾	55	22½	Kabel T K	L121 b	3.15	77– 25	Perfect Soul1192½ Strut the Stage1211¼ DelMarShow119½	Stalk 4w,rally 5w	9

Stylish

Own: Estate of Ahmed Bin Salman

B. m. 6 (Apr) KEESEP99 $725,000
Sire: Thunder Gulch (Gulch) $65,000
Dam: Miss Lenora (Theatrical*Ire)
Br: Allen E. Paulson (Ky)
Tr: Mott William I(0 0 0 0 .00) 2003:(718 138 .19)

			Life	24	8	6	5	$588,227	99	D.Fst	1	1	0	0	$18,600	64
			2003	6	3	0	1	$270,955	98	Wet(286)	2	0	2	0	$16,800	52
			2002	7	2	2	2	$183,976	99	Turf(306)	21	7	4	5	$552,827	99
										Dst(0)	0	0	0	0	$0	–

20Sep03-9Bel	fm	1	① :222 :46² 1:09 1:33	3↑ⒻNblDmsIH-G3	91	5	10¹⁴	11¹⁰³⁄₄	117	7⁶³⁄₄	55	Castillo H Jr	L118 b	7.00	90 – 05	WonderAgin117ⁿᵏ DncI114ⁿᵏ SomethingVentured115¹³⁄₄	Mild rally outside 11
23Aug03-8Sar	yl	1¹⁄₁₆	⊞ :232 :471 1:11 1:41	3↑ⒻBISpaBCH-G3	98	3	44	43	42	3ⁿᵏ	1¹⁄₂	Velazquez J R	L116 b	8.70	90 –	Stylish116¹⁄₂ Snow Dance1171 Cozzy Corner172ʰᵈ	Dug in gamely, prevail 9
19Jly03-10Mth	sf	1¹⁄₁₆	① :221 :46 1:10²1:41³₊	3↑ⒻEatntwnH-G3	95	7	68	68¹⁄₂	6³¹⁄₄	4ⁿᵏ	1ⁿᵏ	Castillo H Jr	L118 b	*2.00	93 – 07	Stylish118ⁿᵏ SomethingVnturd117¹⁄₂ SwtDimos113ʰᵈ	Long drive,up late yds 9
15Jun03-8Cby	fm	1	① :232 :464 1:03¹:344	3↑ⒻLadyCbyBC98k	91	6	85¹⁄₂	84⁹⁄₄	7³⁄₄	41	13	Blanc B	LB118 b	*1.00	100 –	Stylish1183 Cheryiville Slew120ⁿᵒ Voodoo Lady118³⁄₄	Swung out, drove clear 10
24May03-9CD	fm	1¹⁄₁₆	① :232 :471 1:11¹:41³	4↑ⒻETMintJH-G3	88	5	87	9⁸¹⁄₂	911	7⁶³⁄₄	4²¹⁄₄	Velasquez C	L117 b	5.40	94 – 07	Kiss the Devil115ⁿᵏ Quick Tip1191 Cellars Shiraz1201	In tight start,ck 9
16Mar03-10Tam	fm	1¹⁄₁₆	① :232 :464 1:11 1:41	4↑ⒻHillsborgh100k	91	11	6²¹⁄₄	66	6³¹⁄₂	5⁴¹⁄₂	3¹¹⁄₂	Guidry M	L118 b	6.30	91 – 10	Strait From Texas118¹⁄₂ Dedication1181 Stylish1181	Finished well 4w 11

Sue's Good News

Own: Cresran LLC

Ch. f. 4 (Apr) KEESEP01 $45,000
Sire: Woodman (Mr. Prospector) $25,000
Dam: Montera (Easy Goer)
Br: Carlos Perez (Ky)
Tr: Hobby Steve(0 0 0 0 .00) 2003:(144 30 .21)

			Life	8	5	0	0	$160,800	90	D.Fst	6	5	0	0	$160,800	90
			2003	8	5	0	0	$160,800	90	Wet(345)	1	0	0	0	$0	70
			2002	0	M	0	0	$0	–	Turf(280)	1	0	0	0	$0	86
										Dst(0)	0	0	0	0	$0	–

30ct03-9Hoo	my	1¹⁄₁₆	:23 :46³ 1:11⁴:45³	ⒻInBCOaks-G3	70	2	7⁵³⁄₄	6⁸¹⁄₂	98	6¹²	6¹⁵	Doocy T T	LB121 f	7.60	66 – 24	AwsomHmor116³⁄₄ ClokoFVgnss114²³⁄₄ ShtGnFvrt118ⁿᵏ	Hung 7wd 1/4, tired 10
13Sep03-8AP	yl	1¹⁄₈	:49³1:12 1:36⁴1:49	ⒻPuckerUp-G3	86	4	43	5²¹⁄₂	5³¹⁄₂	74	7³¹⁄₄	Doocy T T	L122 f	6.20	91 – 11	Aud118¹³⁄₄ Hail Hillary116ⁿᵒ Julie's Prize120¹⁄₂	Weakened 12
9Aug03-8AP	fst	1¹⁄₈	:48⁴1:13³ 1:38³1:50²	ⒻSngprPlt-G3	90	4	6³¹⁄₂	63	6³¹⁄₂	3¹⁄₂	1¹¹⁄₄	Doocy T T	L120 f	*2.40	91 – 14	SsGoodNws120¹¹⁄₄ KpngthGold1227 MtMAtMdnt118ⁿᵒ	Angled out, driving 9
19Jly03-8Del	fst	1¹⁄₁₆	:231 :463 1:11²:44⁴	ⒻDelOaks-G3	67	3	5³³⁄₄	56	57¹⁄₂	79²¹⁄₂	6¹⁵³⁄₄	Doocy T T	L117	3.20	68 – 17	Island Fashion1226¹⁄₂ Awesome Humor1154¹⁄₄ Ladyecho115ⁿᵏ	Flattened out 9
19Jun03-8AP	fst	1	:231 :472 1:12¹¹:38¹	3↑ⒻOClm62500N	84	7	2¹⁄₂	21	1ʰᵈ	11	1⁴¹⁄₂	Doocy T T	L116	*.40	77 – 26	Sue's Good News116⁴¹⁄₂ Sassy Bear120ⁿᵏ Playitagain Leo120³⁄₄	Ridden out 8
12Apr03-110P	fst	1	:231 :47 1:12 1:37³	ⒻInstRcgBC70k	87	5	3¹¹⁄₂	42	2¹¹⁄₂	1³¹⁄₂	1⁵¹⁄₂	Doocy T T	L116	*1.30	95 – 11	SuesGoodNws116⁵¹⁄₂ LdyMllory1212¹⁄₄ MkkoHokt116ʰᵈ	Pounced, ridden out 10
23Mar03-100P	fst	6f	:214 :451 :574¹:101	ⒻAlw 31000N1x	88	3	2	5²¹⁄₂	4¹³⁄₂	21	12³⁄₄	Doocy T T	L122	*1.20	89 – 15	SusGoodNws1222³⁄₄ Mschvosly114³ AbondngTrth1141¹⁄₄	Kicked clear, driving 8
2Mar03-10P	fst	6f	:222 :463 :59²¹:122	ⒻMd Sp Wt 30k	81	6	4	4¹¹⁄₂	1¹¹⁄₂	1³¹⁄₂	1⁹³⁄₄	Doocy T T	L116	*1.90	78 – 26	Sue's Good News116⁹³⁄₄ Corrigan123³⁄₄ Miss Legend116³³⁄₄	3-w bid, ridden out 7

Sulamani (Ire)

Own: Godolphin Racing Inc

B. c. 5 (Apr)
Sire: Hernando*Fr (Niniski) $10,920
Dam: Soul Dream (Alleged)
Br: The Niarchos Family (Ire)
Tr: bin Suroor Saeed(0 0 0 0 .00) 2003:(16 2 .12)

Life	12	7	2	0	$3,640,845	110	D.Fst	0	0	0	0	$0	–
2003	6	3	1	0	$2,603,842	110	Wet(318)	0	0	0	0	$0	–
2002	6	4	1	0	$1,037,003	–	Turf(322)	12	7	2	0	$3,640,845	110
	0	0	0	0	$0	–	Dst(0)	0	0	0	0	$0	–

25Oct03–8SA fm 1½ Ⓣ :48^{3} 1:11^{2} 2:00 2:24^{1} 3↑ BCTurf-G1 **101** 4 7¾ 7¼ 6½ 6½ 5¼ Dettori L LB126 3.10 99–04 DH High Chaparral126 DH Johar126^{hd} *Falbrav*126^{5½} Clipped heels 6-1/2 9
27Sep03–9Bel fm 1½ Ⓣ :50^{1} 1:14^{3} 2:02^{1} 2:27^{2} 3↑ TfClscIv-G1 **110** 7 7¼ 7¼ 6¼ 2½ 1¾ Bailey J D L126 *.75 84–14 Sulamani126^{2¾} DeelitefulIrving126¾ BaltoStar126½ Stumbled second turn 7
16Aug03–10AP gd 1¼ Ⓣ :49 1:13^{2} 1:37^{3} 2:02^{1} 3↑ ArlMilln-G1 **106** 1 7¾ 6^{4} 5½ 4¼ 2½ Flores D R L126 2.80 94–08 D *Storming Home*126½ *Sulamani*126^{hd} DH Kaieteur126 Bothered 13
Placed first through disqualification
26Jly03♦Ascot (GB) gd 1½ Ⓣ RH 2:33^{1} 3↑ King George VI & Queen Eliz S-G1 Stk 1218000 2½ Dettori L 133 4.50 Alamshar121^{3½} *Sulamani*133^{2} Kris Kin121½ 12
Timeform rating: 128+ *Towards rear,7th in traffic halfway,2nd 1-1/2f out,veered right*
29Jun03♦Saint-Cloud (Fr) gd *1½ Ⓣ LH 2:30^{4} 3↑ Grand Prix de Saint-Cloud-G1 Stk 403000 5¼ Dettori L 135 *.70e *Ange Gabriel*135^{1½} Polish Summer135^{nk} Millstreet135½ 10
Timeform rating: 117 *Rated in 5th,7th 2-1/2f out,lacked rally.Placed 4th via DQ*
Placed 4th through disqualification
29Mar03♦Nad al Sheba (UAE) gd *1½ Ⓣ LH 2:27^{3} 3↑ Dubai Sheema Classic-G1 Stk 2000000 1¾ Dettori L 123 - Sulamani123¾ *Ange Gabriel*123^{3¼} *Ekraar*123^{1¼} 16
Timeform rating: 127+ *Rated in 15th,long drive to lead 100y out,handily.Highest 7th*

Summer Colony

Own: Evans Edward P

Dk. b or b. m. 6 (Apr)
Sire: Summer Squall (Storm Bird) $50,000
Dam: Probable Colony (Pleasant Colony)
Br: Edward P. Evans (Ky)
Tr: Hennig Mark A(0 0 0 0 .00) 2003:(503 73 .15)

Life	24	10	5	1	$1,448,930	110	D.Fst	18	10	2	1	$1,397,350	110
2003	5	1	1	0	$256,500	93	Wet(358)	4	0	2	0	$40,660	86
2002	8	4	2	1	$992,500	110	Turf(292)	2	0	1	0	$10,920	84
	0	0	0	0	$0	–	Dst(0)	0	0	0	0	$0	–

4Oct03–9Bel fst 1⅛ :47^{4} 1:12^{2} 1:36^{3} 1:49^{1} 3↑ Ⓕ Beldame-G1 **85** 3 7½ 7^{7} 7^{6} 6^{11} 5^{13¼} Fragoso P L123 28.50 71–26 Sightseek123^{4½} Bird Town120^{4¾} Buy the Sport120¾ Inside, no response 7
22Aug03–9Sar fst 1¼ :49^{3} 1:14^{1} 1:38^{2} 2:03^{1} 3↑ Ⓕ PrsnlEnH-G1 **79** 2 5^{4} 5½ 4¼ 4^{4} 4¾ Prado E S L120 6.50 82–17 Passing Shot114^{no} *WildSpirit*122^{6¼} MissLinda114^{2½} Stumbled start, 3 wide 5
20Jly03–10Del fst 1¼ :49^{2} 1:13^{4} 1:38^{2} 2:02^{4} 3↑ Ⓕ DelH-G2 **87** 8 6^{2} 7¾ 6¼ 6^{10} 6^{16} Velazquez J R L122 2.60 81–09 WildSpirit117^{6} *TakeChargeLdy*120^{2¾} *ShinySheet*112½ Moved head, off slow 8
28Jun03–11Mth fst 1⅛ :48^{2} 1:13 1:38^{3} 1:51^{4} 3↑ Ⓕ MPchrBCH-G2 **93** 1 4^{6} 4^{3} 3½ 1½ 1^{3} Stevens G L L120 *.40 82–18 SummrColony120^{3} ShsGotthBt112½ CllnAudbl110½ 3-deep bid, drew clear 4
16May03–8Pim sly 1$\frac{1}{16}$:23^{3} :47^{3} 1:12^{3} 1:46^{1} 3↑ Ⓕ PmBCDsfH-G3 **86** 4 4½ 4½ 3½ 1^{hd} 2^{nk} Velazquez J R L121 1.60 76–23 MndysGold117^{nk} *SmmrColony*121^{3¾} StrmyFrlc114^{1½} Urged,3wd trip,failed 4

Summer Mis
Own: Richard Otto Stables Inc

Dk. b or b. m. 5 (Feb)
Sire: Summer Squall (Storm Bird) $50,000
Dam: Julie Mis (Miswaki)
Br: R. Otto Stables, Inc. (Ill)
Tr: Mitchell Anthony(0 0 0 0 .00) 2003:(67 22 .33)

Life	16	9	1	1	$414,883	96	D.Fst	12 9 0 0	$390,565	96
2003	8	6	0	0	$286,495	96	Wet(333)	1 0 1 0	$18,270	62
2002	4	2	0	1	$90,750	92	Turf(291)	3 0 0 1	$6,048	66
	0	0	0	0	$0	–	Dst(0)	0 0 0 0	$0	–

8Nov03–8Haw	fst	6f	:221 :452 :573 1:102	3↑[F][S]PowerlessH94k	**86**	2 1 1½ 1hd 1½ 12¾	Sterling L J Jr	L127 b	*.80	91– 11	Summer Mis127 2¾ Gracility116no Cashmere Miss116no		Driving	11
12Oct03–8Kee	fst	6f	:212 :442 :563 1:093	3↑[F]TCA-G3	**90**	7 4 3½ 3nk 3nk 1hd	Douglas R R	L122 b	11.90	91– 08	*SmmrMs*122hd DontContssOt122no BorntDnc122nk		Forced pace,3w,driving	10
19Sep03–8AP	fst	7f	:222 :442 1:092 1:23	3↑[F]OClm 100000N	**93**	5 2 2hd 11 13 12	Sterling L J Jr	L122 b	1.90	90– 17	*Summer Mis*1222 Oglala Sue116½ Sarah Jade1163		Ridden out	9
26Jly03–6AP	fst	1	:224 :464 1:092 1:362	3↑[F][S]Hcp 45000	**96**	4 31 1½ 11 12½ 13½	Sterling L J Jr	L124 b	*.80	86– 15	*Summer Mis*124 3½ Gracility116 7½ Ioya Forever116½		Driving	7
21Jun03–5AP	fst	6f	:223 :453 :574 1:103	3↑[F][S]IMurphyH84k	**83**	3 4 31 1½ 11½ 11¼	Sterling L J Jr	L123 b	*1.80	91– 06	*Summer Mis*123 1¼ Seven Brides118¾ Win Won1225		Drifted out stretch	9
14Jun03–8AP	fst	7f	:223 :451 1:102 1:241	3↑[F]ChcgoBCH-G3	**77**	8 1 5 1¼ 32 36 48½	Sterling L J Jr	L115 b	14.50	75– 20	For Rubies1163 Raging Fever1204 *Oglala Sue*113 1½		Weakened	8
25May03–8AP	fst	6f	:223 :46 :582 1:113	3↑[F]OClm 100000N	**85**	2 4 32 3nk 1½ 13	Sterling L J Jr	L118 b	4.30	86– 18	Summer Mis1183 Oglala Sue118hd *Victory At Sea*1181		3 wide, driving	5
3May03–7Haw	yl	1 1/16	[T] :241 :49 1:142 1:464	4↑[F]Nicole43k	**–0**	8 62¼ 62½ 77½ 825 851½	Sterling L J Jr	L115 b	7.50	18– 32	Attico118½ *Spice Island*118 5¼ I Can Fan Fan118¾		Outrun	8

Sweet Return (GB)
Own: Red Oak Stable

Ch. c. 4 (Mar)
Sire: Elmaamul (Diesis*GB) $3,169
Dam: Sweet Revival*GB (Claude Monet)
Br: C. S. Tateson (GB)
Tr: McAnally Ronald L(0 0 0 0 .00) 2003:(312 44 .14)

Life	14	3	3	4	$523,031	101	D.Fst	0 0 0 0	$0	–
2003	9	2	2	2	$500,360	101	Wet(231)	0 0 0 0	$0	–
2002	5	1	1	2	$22,671	–	Turf(246)	14 3 3 4	$523,031	101
	0	0	0	0	$0	–	Dst(0)	0 0 0 0	$0	–

30Nov03–9Hol	fm	1¼	[T] :51 1:172 1:41 2:041	HolDerby-G1	**98**	8 11 1½ 1½ 11½ 1½	Krone J A	LB122	16.70	71– 17	SweetRturn122½ FirlyRnsom122½ KicknKris122hd	Speed,inside,held game	13
4Oct03–4SA	fm	1⅛	[T] :494 1:141 1:371 1:484	OakTrDby-G2	**94**	5 32 44 42 31½ 2hd	Stevens G L	LB118	2.80	85– 14	Devious Boy118hd *SweetReturn*118nk UrbanKing118 1½	Bid,willingly,missed	5
6Sep03–8Dmr	fm	1⅛	[T] :472 1:11 1:343 1:462	DmrDerby-G2	**100**	9 53½ 53½ 53½ 53 31¼	Stevens G L	LB122	20.80	100– 05	Fairly Ransom122 1¼ *DeviousBoy*122no SweetReturn122½	Split foes,late bid	9
16Aug03–8Dmr	fm	1 1/16	[T] :233 :471 1:103 1:401	LaJollaH-G3	**91**	5 31 32 32½ 23 53½	Baze R A	LB117	7.90	96– 10	Singletary118½ Devious Boy117½ Senor Swinger120½	Pulled,stalked,no bid	7
23Jly03–5Dmr	fm	1	[T] :223 :463 1:10 1:334	[R]Oceanside85k	**101**	5 42½ 32 31½ 2hd 11	Nakatani C S	LB116	5.00	94– 11	Sweet Return1161 *Singletary*1201 Requite1164	3wd into lane,game	9
Run in divisions													
2Jly03–7Hol	fm	1	[T] :233 :471 1:103 1:342	OClm 80000N	**87**	2 31½ 32 42 52½ 42¼	Nakatani C S	LB118	4.30	90– 11	StnlyPrk120 1½ FlrtWthFortn118nk CnqrthGlxy120½	Lacked room 1/8-1/16	9
11Jun03–5Hol	fm	1⅛	[T] :474 1:122 1:362 1:49	+ OClm 80000N	**83**	8 54½ 45 54 85¾ 74¼	Solis A	LB118	2.60	80– 21	BnsheeKing118no HelmsDeep120hd Gentlston1201	Pulled,bit crowded 1/8	9
8Mar03–2SA	fm	*6½f	[T] :221 :441 1:064 1:124	OClm 80000N	**88**	5 5 43 42½ 32 21½	Solis A	LB116	*1.10	91– 07	NtionWideNews116 1½ SwtRturn116 1¼ Moujoudh116nk	Btwn dirt,2nd best	6
31Jan03–4SA	fm	1	[T] :232 :472 1:11 1:343	OClm 80000N	**86**	6 87¼ 87¼ 87 73¾ 3nk	Valdivia J Jr	LB118	8.20	89– 09	JustWonder118hd Mcchito120hd SweetReturn118no	Tight start,waited 1/8	8

Taiaslew
Own: Tracy Shelli and Ryan, Stan

Dk. b or b. g. 4 (Mar)
Sire: Slewdledo (Seattle Slew) $2,750
Dam: Taiayellowribbon (Sharper One)
Br: Dave Stark (Wash)
Tr: Tracy Greg(0 0 0 0 .00) 2003:(42 8 .19)

Life 12 8 2 1 $331,241 88 | D.Fst 10 6 2 1 $280,841 88
2003 7 4 2 0 $204,325 86 | Wet(392) 2 2 0 0 $50,400 86
2002 5 4 0 1 $126,916 88 | Turf(302) 0 0 0 0 $0 –
0 0 0 0 $0 – | Dst(0) 0 0 0 0 $0 –

21Sep03–9Hst fst 1⅛ :47¹ 1:11³ 1:37³ 1:51² BCDerby-G2 81 6 3¹ 31½ 3⁴ 2² 4³ Welch Q K L126 3.80 84–14 *Roscoe Pito*126² Steady Smiler126½ *Rindanica*126½ Rallied, weakened 9
23Aug03–9NP fst 1⅜ :48 1:13² 1:40⁴ 2:21³ CanDerby-G3 82 2 1½ 1½ 1¹ 1⁵ 2¹ Simard R E L126 *2.00 77–25 *Raylene*121¹ Taiaslew1266¼ Reb's Drummer126¾ Drew clear, weakened 8
4Aug03–8AsD fst 1⅛ :46⁴ 1:12² 1:39³ 1:53² MntbDrby-G3 71 6 11½ 1¹ 1² 1⁵ 2¹ Simard R E L126 *1.00 91–16 Hero's Pleasure126¹ Taiaslew1263½ Pants N Kisses1261¾ Gave way late 10
13Jly03–7AsD fst 1 1/16 :23² :48¹ 1:13¹ 1:49² DerbyTrial35k 82 5 1¹ 1½ 11½ 1³ 1³ Simard R E L126 *.30 81–25 Taiaslew126³ Fancy Bru1265½ Sand Rush126³ Off rail, drew out 8
14Jun03–9Stp fst 1 1/16 :23¹ :46⁴ 1:12 1:43⁴ AlbrtDby-G3 82 5 11½ 11½ 1½ 1⁶ 17½ Simard R E L121 *.55 102–11 *Taiaslew*1217½ Gamblin Caper1211½ *Rindanica*1211¾ Set pace, drew off 7
25May03–7Stp fst 1 :23¹ :46 1:11³ 1:37³ HfprOMHrtH40k 82 7 2hd 11½ 11½ 1⁵ 18½ Simard R E L123 *.50 94–09 *Taiaslew*1238½ Shawteesh115no *Cool Bender*1152½ Dueled, drew off str 7
11May03–9Stp sl 6f :23¹ :47⁴ 1:14¹ PresidntsH40k 86 6 2 2½ 1½ 1³ 1⁴ Simard R E L120 *.80 79–33 *Taiaslew*120⁴ Judge Ruckus1182½ Shawteesh115⁷ Outside, drew clear 7

Take Charge Lady
Own: Select Stable

B. m. 5 (Feb) FTKJUL00 $175,000
Sire: Dehere (Deputy Minister) $37,200
Dam: Felicita (Rubiano)
Br: William Schettine (Ky)
Tr: McPeek Kenneth G(0 0 0 0 .00) 2003:(400 61 .15)

Life 22 11 7 0 $2,480,377 109 | D.Fst 16 9 5 0 $2,067,311 109
2003 7 2 3 0 $720,026 107 | Wet(399) 6 2 2 0 $413,066 107
2002 10 6 3 0 $1,388,635 109 | Turf(304) 0 0 0 0 $0 –
0 0 0 0 $0 – | Dst(0) 0 0 0 0 $0 –

27Nov03–10CD sly 1⅛ :47⁴ 1:12³ 1:38² 1:51¹ 3↑Ⓕ FallCtyH-G2 76 7 31½ 21½ 2² 35½ 5¹⁹ D'Amico A J L123 *.60 63–25 LedStory1166½ MyoOnthSid114⁶ ClokofVgunss1146½ 4w,bid,far turn,tired 9
25Oct03–2SA fst 1⅛ :47 1:11 1:35⁴ 1:49 3↑Ⓕ BCDistaf-G1 79 1 2¹ 3¹ 41¾ 66½ 613¼ Prado E S LB123 6.80 76–07 Adoration1234½ Elloluv1192½ Got Koko1233½ Saved ground, weakened 7
5Oct03–8Kee fst 1⅛ :47 1:10³ 1:35⁴ 1:49² 3↑Ⓕ Spinster-G1 99 4 3³ 3¹ 2hd 11½ 1hd Prado E S L123 *.50 93–13 Take Charge Lady123hd You123⁴ Miss Linda123¾ 4w,stiff drive,lasted 6
1Sep03–8AP my 1⅛ :48 1:12² 1:37¹ 1:50 3↑Ⓕ ArlMtrnH-G3 107 6 2² 2¹ 1¹ 1⁸ 110½ Sellers S J L123 *.30 93–12 *TkeChrgeLdy*12310½ Lkenheth1161¾ TotheQuen117nk Stalked pace, handily 6
20Jly03–10Del fst 1¼ :49² 1:13⁴ 1:38² 2:02⁴ 3↑Ⓕ DelH-G2 101 3 1½ 1hd 1hd 2² 2⁶ Sellers S J L120 4.30 91–09 Wild Spirit117⁶ *Take Charge Lady*1202¾ *ShinySheet*112½ No match, 2nd best 8
21Jun03–9Bel sly 1 1/16 :22² :45¹ 1:09¹ 1:40⁴ 3↑Ⓕ OPhippsH-G1 101 3 1½ 1½ 1hd 21½ 2⁵ Prado E S L119 1.65 91–18 *Sightseek*118⁵ TakeChargeLady119⁵ Mandy'sGold1181¾ Pace, second best 5
5Apr03–8OP fst 1 1/16 :24¹ :48³ 1:12¹ 1:43 4↑Ⓕ AplBlsmH-G1 105 5 11½ 1¹ 1½ 11½ 2hd Sellers S J L118 3.80 95–11 *Azeri*123hd Take Charge Lady1183¼ *Mandy's Gold*116² Slow early, caught 7

Tap the Admiral
Own: Ettinger Stanley

Ch. h. 6 (Mar) KEESEP99 $32,000
Sire: Pleasant Tap (Pleasant Colony) $25,000
Dam: Polish Buck (Polish Navy)
Br: Highland Farms, Inc. (Ky)
Tr: Carroll D W II(0 0 0 0 .00) 2003:(147 16 .11)

Life 30 6 7 7 $476,686 102 | D.Fst 7 0 1 2 $13,830 78
2003 6 2 0 1 $265,046 102 | Wet(336) 2 0 1 1 $10,710 72
2002 8 2 2 3 $106,860 98 | Turf(263) 21 6 5 4 $452,146 102
0 0 0 0 $0 – | Dst(0) 0 0 0 0 $0 –

14Sep03–9WO fm 1 Ⓣ :22⁴ :45¹ 1:09¹ 1:33¹ 3↑AttoMile-G1 87 10 7⁵ 7³ 74¼ 10⁸ 108¾ Luzzi M J L121 13.20 88–06 Touch of theBlues119½ SoaringFree1211¾ *PerfectSoul*121hd 5w, no menace 11
23Aug03–9Sar fm 1 1/16 Ⓣ :22⁴ :46 1:09³ 1:39¹ 3↑4strdavH-G2 102 4 1063¾ 10⁴ 84¼ 42¼ 33¼ Luzzi M J L115 15.10 96–03 Trademark118² Quest Star1161¼ Tap the Admiral115¹ Broke in air, inside 11
25Jly03–8Sar yl 1⅛ 🅃 :47¹ 1:11² 1:36⁴ 1:49 3↑BBaruchH-G2 96 4 66½ 64½ 6² 4² 46¼ Samyn J L L116 4.50 86–07 *Trademark*1144¾ Rouvres116nk Slew Valley1131½ Wide move, no rally 7
5Jly03–9CD fm 1 Ⓣ :23⁴ :47 1:10³ 1:35² 3↑FrckrBCH-G2 100 4 7⁷ 74½ 62¾ 2¹ 11¼ McKee J L115 7.20 95–12 TptheAdmirl1151¼ Freefourintrnt114½ *PckgStor*1141½ Angled 5-6w,driving 9
15Jun03–8WO gd 1⅛ Ⓣ :48¹ 1:12⁴ 1:37 1:49³ 3↑KngEdBCH-G2 97 8 2hd 1hd 1hd 21½ 44¼ Husbands P L116 8.95 76–25 Perfect Soul1192½ *StruttheStage*1211¼ DelMarShow119½ Off rail, gave way 9
11May03–7Bel fm 1 Ⓣ :23⁴ :46² 1:10 1:34⁴ 4↑Alw 58000c 97 5 2hd 1½ Luzzi M J L117 6.10 86–14 Tap the Admiral117½ Krieger123nk Slew Valley117¾ Determined, fog 8

Tapit
Own: Winchell Thoroughbreds LLC

Gr/ro. c. 3 (Feb) KEESEP02 $625,000
Sire: Pulpit (A.P. Indy) $60,000
Dam: Tap Your Heels (Unbridled)
Br: Oldenburg Farms, LLC (Ky)
Tr: Dickinson Michael W(0 0 0 0 .00) 2003:(152 37 .24)

							Life	2	2	0	0	$79,800	98	D.Fst	2	2	0	0	$79,800	98
							2003	2	2	0	0	$79,800	98	Wet(397)	0	0	0	0	$0	–
							2002	0	M	0	0	$0	–	Turf(273)	0	0	0	0	$0	–
								0	0	0	0			Dst(0)	0	0	0	0	$0	–

15Nov03- 6Lrl fst 1¹⁄₁₆ :24 :46¹ 1:12⁴ 1:43⁴ LrlFut-G3 98 1 4¹¹⁄₂ 4¹¹⁄₂ 4² 1ʰᵈ 1⁴³⁄₄ Dominguez R A L122f *1.00 90– 15 Tapit1224¾ Polish Rifle122½ Ghost Mountain121²¹⁄₂ Hopped,boxed,handily 7
19Oct03- 6Del fst 1 :24⁴ :48² 1:13¹¹ 1:38¹ Md Sp Wt 33k 90 4 2¹¹⁄₂ 2² 12¹⁄₂ 14 17³⁄₄ Caraballo J C L120f 2.30 93– 18 Tapit1207³⁄₄ Fancatstik1204² Mighty Roar1201⁶³⁄₄ Bid 3/8, handily 8

Taste of Paradise
Own: Abrahams Keith and Bloom, Paul

Dk. b or b. h. 5 (Apr)
Sire: Conquistador Cielo (Mr. Prospector) $15,000
Dam: Tastetheteardrops (What Luck)
Br: Abrahams, Snukal & Bloom (Ky)
Tr: Sadler John W(0 0 0 0 .00) 2003:(375 71 .19)

							Life	12	3	2	1	$280,360	102	D.Fst	12	3	2	1	$280,360	102
							2003	7	2	0	0	$222,910	102	Wet(366)	0	0	0	0	$0	–
							2002	4	1	2	1	$57,450	100	Turf(257)	0	0	0	0	$0	–
								0	0	0	0			Dst(0)	0	0	0	0	$0	–

25Oct03-11SA fst 1¹⁄₁₆ :23 :46 1:09⁴ 1:42 3↑ SeabscuitH150k 96 11 53¹⁄₂ 53 53¹⁄₂ 64¹⁄₄ 55¾ Valdivia J Jr LB115 26.10 88– 07 Pie N Burger1191 Chinkapin117¾ Redattore1223 4 wide,no late bid 11
4Oct03- 5SA fst 1¹⁄₈ :48² 1:11⁴ 1:36 1:48¹ 3↑ GdwdBCH-G2 96 4 1¹¹⁄₂ 1¹¹⁄₂ 1ʰᵈ 2ʰᵈ 55¼ Valdivia J Jr LB114 20.00 88– 13 PlesntlyPerfct116½ FltstrtDncr1131½ StrCross1103 Lost whip 1/8,weakened 8
1Sep03- 8Dmr fst 1 :21⁴ :45¹ 1:09²1:35³ 3↑ DmrBCH-G2 96 4 3¹¹⁄₂ 1ʰᵈ 2¹¹⁄₂ 44 Espinoza V LB115 9.60 92– 09 Joey Franco116² Reba's Gold116½ Grey Memo117½ Bid btwn,rail,lost 3rd 7
3Aug03- 8Dmr fst 1¹⁄₁₆ :22⁴ :45³ 1:10 1:42³ 3↑ SnDiegoH-G2 102 8 1¹¹⁄₂ 11 13 1² Espinoza V LB113 37.40 92– 09 TasteofPrdise113¾ Gondolier1117ᴺᴷ RebsGold116⁵¹⁄₂ Angled in,cleared,held 8
12Jly03- 8Hol fst 6f :22 :44² :56⁴1:09¹ 3↑ OClm 62500N 94 5 2 3¹¹⁄₂ 21 22 42¾ Valdivia J Jr LB121 2.50 91– 09 DitchDigger120¾ ToughGm119ⁿᵒ Exprssionist1192 3wd in lane,outkickd 7
7Jun03- 3BM fst 6f :21³ :43³ :55³1:08³ 3↑ BMBCSprH-G3 82 5 2 3³¹⁄₂ 35 47 47¹¹⁄₂ Rollins C J LB116 5.20 88– 12 ElDoradoShooter120⁴¾ HaloCat118¹¼ RdrContcct116¹¹⁄₂ Tracked 3w, empty 6
2May03- 4Hol fst 6f :21² :43¹ :56 1:08² 3↑ OClm 62500N 101 5 4 51¹⁄₄ 51¹⁄₄ 3¹¹⁄₂ 1ʰᵈ Valdivia J Jr LB119 5.30 98– 09 Taste of Paradise119ʰᵈ Sunset Place1193 Fonz's1192¹⁄₂ 3wd,rail bid,gamely 5

Tates Creek
Own: Juddmonte Farms Inc

Ch. m. 6 (Jan)
Sire: Rahy (Blushing Groom*Fr) $80,000
Dam: Viviana (Nureyev)
Br: Juddmonte Farms (Ky)
Tr: Frankel Robert J(0 0 0 0 .00) 2003:(411 114 .28)

							Life	17	11	3	0	$1,471,674	107	D.Fst	1	0	0	0	$840	59
							2003	5	3	1	0	$704,067	107	Wet(378)	0	0	0	0	$0	–
							2002	8	5	2	0	$661,512	105	Turf(361)	16	11	3	0	$1,470,834	107
								0	0	0	0			Dst(0)	0	0	0	0	$0	–

25Oct03- 6SA fm 1¹⁄₄ ⓣ :46³ 1:10² 1:35¹ 1:59 3↑Ⓕ BCF&MTrf-G1 98 1 79 711 95 74¼ 86¹⁄₄ Valenzuela P A LB123 4.70 92– 04 Islington123ⁿᵏ L'Ancresse118¹⁄₂ Yesterday118ⁿᵒ Tight past 1/8,vanned 12
28Sep03- 7SA fm 1¹⁄₄ ⓣ :50¹ 1:14 1:37⁴ 2:00³ 3↑Ⓨ YlwRibbn-G1 107 2 42¹¹⁄₂ 32¹⁄₂ 32 2¹¹⁄₂ 1² Valenzuela P A LB123 *.90 90– 13 TtesCreek123² MusicChims118ⁿᵏ CrzyEnsign1231¾ Blockd,bulled thru 1/8 8
26Jly03- 8Dmr fm 1¹⁄₈ ⓣ :50¹ 1:14 1:37³ 1:49 3↑Ⓕ Mbe/RnaH-G1 103 1 21 2¹¹⁄₂ 2ʰᵈ 11¹⁄₂ 2¹¹⁄₂ Valenzuela P A LB123 *1.10 87– 08 Megahertz116¹⁄₂ TtesCreek123ᴰᴴ Dublino1212 Drifted in 1/8,game 5
26May03- 6Hol fm 1¹⁄₈ ⓣ :48² 1:12 1:35¹ 1:46⁴ 3↑Ⓕ GamlyBCH-G1 107 6 32¹⁄₂ 32 31¹⁄₂ 21 11 Valenzuela P A LB122 3.50 95– 10 Tates Creek1221 Dublino122½ Megahertz118¼ 3w bid,drifted in,game 6
11Jan03- 3SA fm 1¹⁄₈ ⓣ :49 1:12⁴ 1:35⁴ 1:46⁴ 4↑Ⓕ SnGrgnoH-G2 103 3 2¹¹⁄₂ 21 2ʰᵈ 1¹⁄₂ Valenzuela P A LB121 *.90 95– 12 Tates Creek121¾ Megahertz117½ Double Cat114¹¹⁄₂ Bid,led 1/8,held game 7

Ten Most Wanted

Own: Chisholm James, Jarvis, Michael, Redd

Dk. b or b. c. 4 (Feb) FTFFEB02 $145,000
Sire: Deputy Commander (Deputy Minister) $15,000
Dam: Wanted Again (Criminal Type)
Br: Jim H. Plemmons (Ky)
Tr: Dollase Wallace A(0 0 0 0 .00) 2003:(95 24 .25)

Life	11	4	3	1	$1,553,460	112	D.Fst	10	4	2	1	$1,353,460	112
2003	10	4	2	1	$1,544,860	112	Wet(235)	1	0	1	0	$200,000	109
2002	1	M	1	0	$8,600	85	Turf(207)	0	0	0	0	$0	–
	0	0	0	0	$0	–	Dst(0)	0	0	0	0	$0	–

25Oct03–9SA fst 1¼ :461 1:101 1:341 1:594 3↑ BCClasic-G1 **98** 10 74¼ 87¾ 911 911 814¼ Day P LB121 b 4.10 92–07 PleasntlyPerfect1261½ MedglidOro126¾ Dynever121nk Checked first turn 10

20Sep03–10LaD fst 1⅛ :493 1:133 1:374 1:503 SuDyXXIV-G2 **107** 1 31 45 31½ 2hd 1½ Day P L124 b *.50 88–16 Ten Most Wanted124½ Soto1245¼ Crowned King1241 4-w bid, edging away 6

23Aug03–11Sar fst 1¼ :461 1:094 1:352 2:02 Travers-G1 **112** 4 45 42 1hd 1½ 14½ Day P L126 b 2.75 97–03 *TenMostWanted*1264½ PeceRules12610 StrongHope126¾ Bumped first turn 6

13Jly03–6Hol fst 1⅛ :48 1:113 1:362 1:491 Swaps-G2 **96** 1 64½ 63¾ 42 1hd 2hd Day P LB122 *.60e 88–07 During115hd *TenMostWnted*122¾ DHEyeofthTigr118 4wd move,led,outgmd 6

7Jun03–11Bel sly 1½ :483 1:132 2:023 2:281 Belmont-G1 **109** 6 53 41¾ 32 21½ 2¾ Day P L126 f 9.70 90–14 EmpireMker126¾ TenMostWntd1264¼ FunnyCid1265¼ Wide trip, 2nd best 6

3May03–10CD fst 1¼ :461 1:102 1:353 2:01 KyDerby-G1 **98** 15 108½ 107 94¾ 107½ 97¾ Day P L126 6.60 86–06 *FunnyCide*1261¾ *EmpireMker*126hd PeceRules126hd Off slow,bmp,ck,no bid 16

5Apr03–8Haw fst 1⅛ :463 1:113 1:382 1:512 IlnosDrb-G2 **110** 2 76½ 64½ 53½ 21½ 14 Day P L114 *2.30 99–19 TenMostWnted1144 FundofFunds1148 FoufsWrrior118¾ Lacked room 1/4 10

8Mar03–8GG fst 1 1/16 :223 :452 1:092 1:421 ElCamRlD-G3 **90** 2 2½ 31½ 43 42½ 31½ Day P LB115 3.30 90–12 OcenTerrc1151½ MinistrsWildCt117no *TnMostWntd*1151 2w trip, no impact 10

7Feb03–7SA fst 1⅛ :461 1:102 1:353 1:481 RSham81k **86** 2 2½ 2½ 2hd 43½ 48½ Desormeaux K J LB116 b 7.40 84–11 Man AmongMen1201 *EmpireMaker*1152 Spensive1205½ Bumped start,tired 7

5Jan03–7SA fst 1 :222 :461 1:111 1:38 Md Sp Wt 50k **79** 4 54¼ 44½ 21 12½ 18 Desormeaux K J LB120 b *.70 81–15 TenMostWnted1208 SntFeSlew1202 ChestersChoic1202 3wd bid,led,clear 10

Tenpins

Own: Vitello Joseph V

Ch. h. 6 (Mar)
Sire: Smart Strike (Mr. Prospector) $20,000
Dam: Maid's Broom (Deputy Minister)
Br: Joseph Vitello (Mich)
Tr: Winfree Donald R(0 0 0 0 .00) 2003:(80 9 .11)

Life	16	9	2	2	$1,121,449	113	D.Fst	12	7	2	2	$995,310	113
2003	5	2	2	0	$512,760	111	Wet(428)	4	2	0	0	$126,139	110
2002	7	5	0	1	$560,629	113	Turf(303)	0	0	0	0	$0	–
	0	0	0	0	$0	–	Dst(0)	0	0	0	0	$0	–

28Nov03–11CD sly 1⅛ :481 1:13 1:384 1:522 3↑ ClarkH-G2 **91** 12 43 42½ 41 119 1211 Lanerie C J L119 f 3.60 65–27 DEvening Attire118no Quest1143¼ Aeneas1141¼ Broke in air,4w,tired 14

25Oct03–4Kee fst 1⅛ :501 1:143 1:383 1:501 3↑ Fayette-G3 **101** 5 2½ 2hd 2hd 21 21 Albarado R J L121 f *1.10 88–11 MBSea1191 Tenpins1212½ DHChngeinthewether119 Bmp foe 3/16s,2ndbst 7

28Sep03–9Haw fst 1¼ :493 1:133 1:39 2:033 3↑ HawGldCH-G2 **106** 3 11 1½ 2hd 2hd 21¾ Albarado R J L119 f 1.80 88–20 Perfect Drift1221¾ Tenpins119½ Aeneas1146 Gamely, outfinished 6

23Aug03–10Mth fst 1⅛ :48 1:121 1:372 1:501 3↑ IselnBCH-G3 **110** 4 2½ 1hd 1hd 1½ 11 Albarado R J L119 f *1.00 90–27 Tenpins1191 Aeneas114no *Jersey Giant*1152¼ Gamely,edged clear 9

12Jly03–6PrM fst 1⅛ :462 1:101 1:353 1:481 3↑ CrnhsBCH-G3 **111** 5 31½ 3½ 1½ 1½ 12 Albarado R J LB118 *1.30 97–10 *Tenpins*1182 Bowman's Band1165½ Woodmoon1164¾ Drew clear, driving 6

The Cliff's Edge

Own: La Penta Robert V

Dk. b or b. c. 3 (Apr) KEESEP02 $200,000
Sire: Gulch (Mr. Prospector) $50,000
Dam: Zigember (Danzig)
Br: Stoneside Stable (Ky)
Tr: Zito Nicholas P(0 0 0 0 .00) 2003:(507 77 .15)

Life	5	3	1	0	$255,258	101	D.Fst	5	3	1	0	$255,258	101
2003	5	3	1	0	$255,258	101	Wet(401)	0	0	0	0	$0	–
2002	0	M	0	0	$0	–	Turf(336)	0	0	0	0	$0	–
	0	0	0	0	$0	–	Dst(0)	0	0	0	0	$0	–

29Nov03–11CD fst 1 1/16 :241 :482 1:13 1:452 KyJC-G2 **94** 7 84¾ 31½ 1hd 11½ 1¾ Sellers S J L122 *.90 81–24 TheCliffsEdg122¾ GrnProspct1161¾ ProprPrdo1183¾ 4w, took over, lasted 8

2Nov03–9CD fst 1 :222 :45 1:10 1:352 Iroquois-G3 **101** 2 86 53½ 3½ 14 17¾ Sellers S J L117 *2.20 90–14 *TheCliffsEdge*1177¾ KorbynGold121½ GrndScore1171¼ Quick move, driving 9

4Oct03–6Kee fst 1 1/16 :224 :462 1:102 1:432 LnsEndFt-G2 **87** 7 1019 1113 910 75½ 66¼ Sellers S J L121 8.50 84–20 Eurosilver1214¾ Tiger Hunt121no Limehouse1211 Carried in start 11

13Sep03–10TP fst 1 1/16 :231 :47 1:114 1:463 KyCupJuv-G3 **83** 7 79 66½ 3½ 22 31¼ Sellers S J L114 3.50 78–17 DPomeroy116no Mr. Jester1181¼ The Cliff's Edge114¾ In air st, steadied 8

Placed second through disqualification

24Aug03–2Sar fst 6f :222 :454 :581 1:104 Md Sp Wt 45k **82** 1 5 1½ 12 12½ 14 Sellers S J L119 4.10 88–12 ThCliffsEdg1194 ApplKrisp1195¼ HrborthGold1193½ Widened under drive 6

The Tin Man
Own: Todd Aury and Ralph E

Dk. b or b. g. 6 (Feb)
Sire: Affirmed (Exclusive Native) $30,000
Dam: Lizzie Rolfe (Tom Rolfe)
Br: Ralph Todd & Aury Todd (Ky)
Tr: Mandella Richard E(0 0 0 0 .00) 2003:(253 51 .20)

Life	18	7	4	1	$1,074,460	111	D.Fst	0	0	0	0	$0 -
2003	6	1	2	0	$440,840	111	Wet(316)	0	0	0	0	$0 -
2002	9	5	1	1	$598,020	109	Turf(326)	18	7	4	1	$1,074,460 111
	0	0	0	0	$0	-	Dst(0)	0	0	0	0	$0 -

25Oct03–8SA fm 1½ Ⓣ :483 1:112 2:00 2:241 3↑ BCTurf-G1 102 7 2½ 2hd 11 2½ 45½ Smith M E LB126 14.30 99– 04 [DH]High Chaparral126 [DH]Johar126hd *Falbrav*1265½ Vied,led,weakened 9
16Aug03–10AP gd 1¼ Ⓣ :49 1:132 1:373 2:021 3↑ ArlMilln-G1 102 10 21½ 21 2½ 2hd 62½ Smith M E L126 5.90 92– 08 [D]*Storming Home*126½ *Sulamani*126hd [DH]Kaieteur126 Weakened 13
5Jly03–10Mth fm 1⅜ Ⓣ :483 1:14 1:373 2:123 3↑ UntdNtnH-G1 109 2 21 21 21 2hd 2½ Smith M E L121 5.90 100– 03 BaltoStr117½ TheTinMn121no LunrSovereign112nk Held 2nd,needed more 7
10May03–7Hol fm 1½ Ⓣ :491 1:131 1:594 2:251 3↑ JMurryMemH400k 85 3 11½ 11 1½ 43½ 714¾ Smith M E LB123 *1.90 84– 12 *Storming Home*1222 *Denon*1224½ *Ballingarry*120nk Speed,inside,wkened 8
15Feb03–7SA yl 1½ Ⓣ :51 1:153 2:054 2:311 4↑ SLsObspH-G2 111 1 11½ 11½ 12½ 18 19½ Smith M E LB121 *.50 70– 30 TheTinMan1219½ SpecialMatter1131½ Harrisnd116½ Riddn out,in hand late 5
20Jan03–8SA fm 1¼ Ⓣ :463 1:104 1:34 1:574 4↑ SnMarcos-G2 106 3 21 2½ 2½ 2½ 2hd Smith M E LB122 *1.80 104 - Johar120hd *The Tin Man*122no Grammarian122½ Game btwn foes late 7

Thunder Blitz
Own: Stronach Stable

Gr/ro. h. 6 (May)
Sire: Holy Bull (Great Above) $15,000
Dam: Rasant (Assert*Ire)
Br: Adena Springs (Ky)
Tr: Dutrow R E Jr(0 0 0 0 .00) 2003:(531 132 .25)

Life	23	4	6	6	$462,450	110	D.Fst	16	2	5	5	$392,150 110
2003	8	2	3	1	$143,720	110	Wet(359)	4	2	1	0	$64,420 102
2002	3	0	1	1	$14,280	91	Turf(269)	3	0	0	1	$5,880 71
	0	0	0	0	$0	-	Dst(0)	0	0	0	0	$0 -

13Dec03–8Aqu fst 1 3/16 [•] :49 1:132 1:374 1:554 3↑ QeensCoH-G3 110 4 31½ 21 2hd 1½ 11½ Chavez J F L114 4.90 105– 17 ThunderBlitz1141½ EveningAttire123hd SttlFitz1153¼ Stalked, bid, driving 6
11Nov03–8Aqu fst 1⅛ :482 1:12 1:371 1:504 3↑ StuyvntH-G3 106 6 43 31 31 23½ 2nk Prado E S L114 5.10 82– 26 Presidentialaffair115nk *Thunder Blitz*114½ Gander1154 Came again outside 8
Previously trained by Frankel Robert
2Oct03–8Bel fst 1⅛ :463 1:111 1:364 1:492 3↑ Alw 52000N3x 101 1 2½ 1½ 11½ 1hd 21¾ Migliore R L119 2.85 81– 17 Congrats1161¾ Thunder Blitz1191½ *Peekskill*11910¼ Bumped stretch 5
27Aug03–8Sar fst 1⅛ :482 1:122 1:363 1:491 3↑ Alw 52000N3x 91 3 56½ 54½ 42½ 59 59 Bailey J D L119 *1.20 80– 19 Quest1193½ Strive119nk Light Night1194¾ Wide, no response 7
24Jly03–5Sar sly 1⅛ :474 1:113 1:364 1:494 3↑ Alw 52000N3x 99 5 31 2hd 11½ 1hd 22¼ Bailey J D L120 *1.75 84– 15 Puzzlement1202¼ Thunder Blitz120¾ Quest1207¾ Stubbornly on rail 5
6Jly03–4Bel fst 1 1/16 :241 :471 1:111 1:424 4↑ Alw 50000N3x 99 3 2hd 11 1hd 11½ 3hd Bailey J D L118 *.85 86– 11 Regal Sanction118hd Strive118no Thunder Blitz118nk Gamely on rail 5
12Apr03–6Aqu my 1 :233 :46 1:101 1:353 4↑ Alw 46000N2x 102 3 2hd 1hd 12½ 17 16 Bailey J D L117 1.45 87– 12 ThundrBltz1176 *Thbgppl*114hd LghtnngStrps1175¾ When ready, ridden out 5
27Feb03–7SA wf 1 :22 :444 1:091 1:35 4↑ OClm 62500N 81 2 54¾ 53½ 54½ 54½ 58¼ Valdivia J Jr LB119 b 3.00 88– 13 Arsen1171¼ *Primerica*1191 Good Cop Bad Cop1192½ 3wd into lane,no bid 7

Tizdubai
Own: Darley Stud Management LLC

B. f. 3 (Jan) KEENOV01 $950,000
Sire: Cee's Tizzy (Relaunch) $15,000
Dam: Cee's Song (Seattle Song)
Br: Cee's Stable LLC (Cal)
Tr: Harty Eoin G(0 0 0 0 .00) 2003:(110 30 .27)

Life	2	2	0	0	$116,400	79	D.Fst	2	2	0	0	$116,400 79
2003	2	2	0	0	$116,400	79	Wet(412)	0	0	0	0	$0 -
2002	0	M	0	0	$0	-	Turf(218)	0	0	0	0	$0 -
	0	0	0	0	$0	-	Dst(0)	0	0	0	0	$0 -

9Aug03–8Dmr fst 6½f :22 :441 1:101 1:17 ⒻSorrento-G2 79 7 1 22½ 23 21½ 14 Flores D R LB118 2.00 90– 13 Tizdubai1184 Dirty Diana1224½ Solar Fire118½ Bid,led 1/16,clear 8
6Jly03–7Hol fst 5½f :222 :463 :59 1:051 Ⓕ[S]Md Sp Wt 44k 69 7 2 41¼ 51¼ 21½ 11½ Flores D R LB119 *1.00 82– 15 *Tizdubai*1191½ Blowing Bartok1197 Silber1193½ Tight 3/8,blocked 1/4 8

Too Late Now
Own: Come By Chance Stable

B. f. 4 (Mar)
Sire: Raj Waki (Miswaki)
Dam: Half of Everything (Ten Gold Pots)
Br: James E. Day (Ont-C)
Tr: Day James E(0 0 0 0 .00) 2003:(104 14 .13)

Life	7	4	0	1	$566,110	92		
2003	7	4	0	1	$566,110	92		
2002	0	M	0	0	$0	-		
	0	0	0	0	$0	-		
D.Fst	6	4	0	1	$566,110	92		
Wet(302)	0	0	0	0	$0	-		
Turf(226)	1	0	0	0	$0	60		
Dst(0)	0	0	0	0	$0	-		

31Aug03-8WO fst 7f :223 :452 1:103 1:242 3↑ⒻSeaway173k 55 3 8 52¼ 62¾ 812 817½ Landry R C L118 8.20 64-27 BrssnPckt1211¼ ElPrdEssnc119nk Whlthrsht1151¼ Bump brk,stlk,bid,fade 8
24Aug03-8WO fm 1 Ⓣ:22 :442 1:091 1:333 ⒻOntColeenH153k 60 2 42¼ 32 31½ 1010 1014¾ Landry R C L120 5.00 80-04 Shaconage1152¼ HourofJustice1162½ *MyPlLn*1151¼ Stalk duel,bid,weaken 13
1Jly03-8FE fst 1 1/16 :242 :474 1:122 1:441 ⒻⓇBisonCity250k 78 5 4nk 43 42 33 33¾ Landry R C 123 *.85 86-16 DHSeekingthRing114 DHBrttothcor1183¾ TooLtNow123¾ Bid, evened out 6
8Jun03-9WO fst 1⅛ :472 1:124 1:391 1:53 ⒻⓇLbatWoOaks500k 81 5 1hd 11 11 12½ 1nk Landry R C 121 *.65 81-21 TooLateNow121nk *SeekingtheRing*1211½ Snterr121nk 2-pth drew clear,held 10
19May03-8WO fst 1 1/16 :224 :463 1:12 1:441 ⒻSelene-G1 92 5 41¾ 52 31½ 2hd 12½ Landry R C 116 5.80 85-16 *TooLateNow*1162½ Hndpinted1182 WinterGrden1181¼ Stalk forced pace 3w 9
20Apr03-7WO fst 6f :223 :46 :581 1:104 ⒻAlw 63500N1x 87 2 5 41¼ 3½ 2hd 12½ Landry R C 117 *1.70 90-17 *TooLteNow*1172½ GoldlefdMirror1185 LPtitJustic1165¼ Stalk, advanced 4w 8
5Apr03-4WO fst 5f :212 :442 :564 3↑ⒻMd Sp Wt 60k 80 2 5 31½ 2hd 11½ 14½ Landry R C 118 17.95 96-03 *TooLteNow*1184½ Emptythetill118no NwDilignc118¾ Stalk 2w, drew off 3 w 6

Total Impact (Chi)
Own: Al Kabeer Sultan Mohammed Saud and Br

Ch. h. 6 (Aug)
Sire: Stuka (Jade Hunter) $1,500
Dam: Pebbles*Chi (Manos de Piedra)
Br: Haras Don Alberto (Chi)
Tr: De Seroux Laura(0 0 0 0 .00) 2003:(111 14 .13)

Life	11	4	3	0	$598,388	112
2003	6	2	1	0	$163,400	112
2002	3	0	2	0	$414,700	102
	0	0	0	0	$0	-
D.Fst	8	2	3	0	$574,440	112
Wet(339)	2	2	0	0	$20,288	-
Turf(295)	1	0	0	0	$3,660	95
Dst(0)	0	0	0	0	$0	-

6Dec03-8Hol fst 1⅛ :463 1:103 1:354 1:49 3↑NtvDivrH-G3 94 4 32 2hd 2½ 33½ 55 Smith M E LB118 2.60 84-12 Olmodavor117½ NoseTheTrade1151½ Chinkapin1181 Pulled,vied,weakened 5
10May03-8Hol fst 1 1/16 :23 :453 1:092 1:404 3↑MrvnLRyH-G2 110 4 32½ 31 2½ 12 12 Smith M E LB114 *2.30 100-04 TotlImpct1142 FleetstretDncr1144 PinsSonndo1151 Stalked,bid,led,clear 8
5Apr03-10SA fst 1⅛ :462 1:102 1:351 1:482 4↑SnBrdnoH-G3 112 6 41½ 32 31½ 21 2nk Espinoza V LB113 10.60 92-14 WesternPride116nk *TotalImpct*1131 FleetstreetDncer1122½ 3wd bid,missed 8
22Mar03-8SA fst 1 1/16 :23 :461 1:101 1:422 4↑OClm 62500N 100 4 2½ 2hd 1hd 11½ 11 Smith M E LB118 3.80 92-10 Total Impact1181 Tough Game120½ *Denied*1184½ Edged away, held sway 7
6Mar03-3SA fm 1⅛ Ⓣ:462 1:103 1:35 1:47 4↑OClm 80000N 95 3 3½ 3½ 31 32 41 Desormeaux K J LB118 8.40 93-06 *RiverGod*118nk MananMcLir118½ PltinumDuke118nk 3 wide,lost 3rd late 6
25Jan03-1SA fst 7f :22 :441 1:084 1:213 4↑OClm 62500N 90 1 8 813 813 87 58 Desormeaux K J LB119 4.90 90-07 Total Limit1203½ Sunset Place1182 *Arsen*1181 Off bit slow,no threat 8

Touch of the Blues (Fr)
Own: Al Maktoum Sheik Maktoum b

B. h. 7 (Apr)
Sire: Cadeaux Genereux*GB (Young Generation*Ire)
Dam: Silabteni (Nureyev)
Br: Gainesborough Stud Management (Fr)
Tr: Drysdale Neil D(0 0 0 0 .00) 2003:(182 34 .19)

Life	35	8	6	5	$1,655,358	106
2003	6	2	1	3	$1,082,885	106
2002	9	1	2	0	$305,350	104
	0	0	0	0	$0	-
D.Fst	0	0	0	0	$0	-
Wet(309)	0	0	0	0	$0	-
Turf(333)	35	8	6	5	$1,655,358	106
Dst(0)	0	0	0	0	$0	-

25Oct03-4SA fm 1 Ⓣ:221 :452 1:092 1:334 3↑BCMile-G1 103 8 1211 128 118½ 32 2¾ Desormeaux K J LB126 11.90 92-04 SxPrfctons119¾ TouchofthBlus126nk CntryCty1261¼ 4wd into lane,rallied 13
4Oct03-9Kee fm 1 Ⓣ:23 :461 1:114 1:36 3↑ShdwlTfM-G1 104 4 912 911 61¾ 3½ 31¼ Desormeaux K J L126 4.10 87-14 PrfctSoul126¾ HonorinWr126½ TouchofthBlus1261¼ Between,no late gain 10
14Sep03-9WO fm 1 Ⓣ:224 :451 1:091 1:331 3↑AttoMile-G1 106 3 97¾ 85 52½ 31 1½ Desormeaux K J L119 5.45 97-06 Touch of theBlues119½ SoaringFree1211¾ *PerfectSoul*121hd Inside,rally 5w 11
2Aug03-5Dmr fm 1 Ⓣ:212 :444 1:321 3↑ⓇWickerrH76k 105 1 58 612 55 22 1no Desormeaux K J LB122 *2.70 102-06 *TouchoftheBlues*122no Inesperado1211½ Suances1201 Came out 1/8,gamely 10
26May03-8Hol fm 1 Ⓣ:24 :463 1:091 1:331 3↑ShoeBCM-G1 103 4 99¾ 913 89 56½ 33¾ Desormeaux K J LB124 10.10 94-10 Redattore124¾ Special Ring1243 *Touch of the Blues*1242 Bit crowded early 9
11Apr03-8Kee fm 1 Ⓣ:233 :463 1:112 1:354 4↑MakrsMrk-G2 97 9 34½ 46 32½ 33 33 Desormeaux K J L117 3.20 86-13 RoylSpy1181¼ MsqsApprovl1181¾ TochofthBls1171½ Between,no late gain 9

Tour of the Cat
Own: Double G Stables LLC

B. g. 6 (May) OBSAPR00 $18,000
Sire: Tour d'Or (Medaille d'Or) $10,000
Dam: Tune in to the Cat (Tunerup)
Br: C. V. S. Sales Company (Fla)
Tr: Mora Myra(0 0 0 0 .00) 2003:(154 22 .14)

Life	33	10	10	6	$807,261	111	D.Fst	18	7	4	1	$526,876 111
2003	9	3	2	2	$351,070	107	Wet(357)	4	2	1	1	$164,446 102
2002	11	4	3	2	$246,270	111	Turf(289)	11	1	5	4	$115,939 99
	0	0	0	0	$0	-	Dst(0)	0	0	0	0	$0 -

13Dec03-11Crc fst 7f :221 :451 1:102 1:234 3↑KenyNoeJrH100k **93** 10 2 5¹¾ 4²½ 22 3³¼ Cabassa A Jr L119 f 3.60 92- 11 HastyKris116hd WakeAtNoon1163¼ TouroftheCat119hd Rallied three wide 10
15Nov03-12Crc fst 1⅛ :49 1:131 1:392 1:531 3↑[S]CGRoseClsH200k **96** 4 11½ 1hd 1½ 2hd 21¼ Cabassa A Jr L117 f 2.10 85- 18 BstofthRst1211¼ TorofthCt1171½ ThJdgSzWho115nk Off rail, outfinished 5
11Oct03- 8Crc fst 1 1/16 :25 :494 1:141 1:461 3↑SpdABckH-G3 **99** 5 11½ 11 11 11½ 11 Cabassa A Jr L116 f 1.90 81- 22 Tour of the Cat1161 *Best of theRest*1221 DancingGuy1163 Inside, prevailed 8
1Sep03- 5Crc gd 1 ⊗ :24 :472 1:12 1:383 3↑MiaMIBCH-G3 **102** 4 1½ 1½ 1hd 12½ 12½ Cabassa A Jr L115 f 3.30 88- 23 *TouroftheCat*1152½ LastStand113hd LavendersLad114¾ Drew clear, driving 10
12Jly03-12Crc fst 6f :211 :434 :562 1:10 3↑SmlSprtH-G3 **94** 12 2 77 89¼ 710 610¼ Cabassa A Jr L114 f 13.70 84- 11 ShkYouDown1198¼ *PrivtHord*113¾ MyCousinMtt116½ 3 wide, lacked a rally 13
14Jun03- 3Crc fm 5f Ⓣ :221 :45 :564 3↑Linear42k **96** 5 5 64¾ 63¾ 63¼ 31¼ Cabassa A Jr L122 f 4.70 89- 10 SwiftRplc115½ SmsConcord117¾ TourofthCt1222½ Bumped, steadied start 6
5Apr03- 9GP fst 7f :214 :441 1:083 1:213 3↑ArtaxH100k **71** 4 2 42½ 54½ 710 715¼ Cabassa A Jr L118 f 3.10 85- 06 HighwyProspector1141¾ SwiftReplic1121 *NtiveHir*115½ Saved grd, no rally 8
8Mar03-10GP fst 7f :221 :442 1:082 1:21 3↑RcSclBCH-G2 **107** 2 4 42½ 31½ 1½ 1hd Cabassa A Jr L116 f 9.60 103- 01 TorofthCt116hd BrnngRom1161¼ *HghwyPrspctr*114nk Dueled str, prevailed 8
15Feb03-10Tam fm 1 1/16 Ⓣ :233 :481 1:122 1:412 3↑TampaBayBC99k **93** 8 1½ 2hd 2hd 21½ 25 Cabassa A Jr L118 f 6.70 86- 18 BurnngRom1235 *TourofthCt*118no FrstLutnnt116no No match, saved place 12

Trademark (Saf)
Own: Darley Stable

B. g. 8 (Oct)
Sire: Goldmark*Saf (Golden Thatch)
Dam: Popular*Saf (Elliodor*Fr)
Br: D Cohen & Sons (pty) Ltd (Saf)
Tr: McLaughlin Kiaran P(0 0 0 0 .00) 2003:(186 46 .25)

Life	49	11	11	7	$493,747	110	D.Fst	1	0	0	0	$0 -
2003	9	2	1	1	$251,143	110	Wet(280)	0	0	0	0	$0 -
2002	10	1	3	1	$40,014	-	Turf(478)	48	11	11	7	$493,747 110
	0	0	0	0	$0	-	Dst(0)	0	0	0	0	$0 -

4Oct03- 9Kee fm 1 Ⓣ :23 :461 1:114 1:36 3↑ShdwlTfM-G1 **96** 1 48 56 21 63¾ 65 Migliore R L126 *2.50 83- 14 PerfectSoul126¾ HonorinWr126½ TouchoftheBlues1261¼ 4w bid,weakened 10
23Aug03- 9Sar fm 1 1/16 Ⓣ :224 :46 1:093 1:391 3↑4strdavH-G2 **109** 5 41½ 41½ 41½ 1hd 12 Migliore R L118 *2.90 99- 03 Trademark1182 Quest Star1161¼ Tap the Admiral1151 When roused, clear 11
25Jly03- 8Sar yl 1⅛ [T] :471 1:112 1:364 1:49 3↑BBaruchH-G2 **110** 6 43 41 41 1½ 14¾ Migliore R L114 6.60 93- 07 *Trademark*1144¾ Rouvres116nk Slew Valley1131½ Got through inside 7
5Jly03- 8Bel fm 1 Ⓣ :234 :461 1:092 1:324 3↑PokerH-G3 **99** 2 52¼ 41 21 2½ 2½ Coa E M L114 13.80 95- 08 War Zone117½ *Trademark*114½ Saint Verre1121¼ Gamely between foes 11
Previously trained by Sateesh Seemar
10Apr03♦Nad al Sheba (UAE) gd *1 Ⓣ LH 1:401 3↑ Connector Trophy (Amtr Riders) 42¼ al Maktoum R 160 - Walmooh160½ *Nooshman*1601¼ Shaard160½ 12
Timeform rating: 82 Alw 27200 *Tracked in 3rd,lacked rally*
21Mar03♦Jebel Ali (UAE) ft *1 LH 1:364 3↑ Jebel Ali Mile (Listed) 814½ Smith W J 123 - Dancal119¾ Northern Rock123hd Curule1231 12
Timeform rating: 84 Stk 95300 *Tracked leaders,weakened over 2f out.Marhoob 4th,Pacino 6th*
8Mar03♦Nad al Sheba (UAE) gd *1⅛ Ⓣ LH 1:483 3↑ Jebel Hatta-G3 55½ Smith W J 126 - *Ipi Tombe*1283¾ Sights On Gold126¾ St Expedit126nk 10
Timeform rating: 112 Stk 95300 *Trckd ldr,brief bid 2f out,wknd 1f out.Royal Tryst4th,Highdown6th*
6Feb03♦Nad al Sheba (UAE) gd *1 Ⓣ LH 1:37 3↑ Al Fahidi Fort (Listed) 35½ Durcan T E 126 - *Ipi Tombe*1282¼ *Royal Tryst*1263¼ Trademark1263½ 10
Timeform rating: 108 Stk 95300 *Close up,one-paced final furlong.Conflict5th,Millennium Dragon8th*
16Jan03♦Nad al Sheba (UAE) gd *1¼ Ⓣ LH 2:033 3↑ Al Rashidiya Prep 48 Durcan T E 123 - Nowrass1232¼ Kelly123½ Lightning Arrow1235¼ 10
Timeform rating: 91 Alw 34000 *Mid-pack,3rd 2-1/2f out,faded through stretch.West Order 9th*

Trust N Luck
Own: Robsham Einar P

Ch. c. 4 (Apr) OBSMAR02 $200,000
Sire: Montbrook (Buckaroo) $20,000
Dam: Bold Burst (Dahar)
Br: Wiest's-Heather's 2000 (Fla)
Tr: Ziadie Ralph(0 0 0 0 .00) 2003:(375 44 .12)

Life	12	5	3	1	$727,484	110	D.Fst	11	4	3	1	$708,684 110
2003	4	1	1	1	$344,684	106	Wet(320)	1	1	0	0	$18,800 88
2002	8	4	2	0	$382,800	110	Turf(254)	0	0	0	0	$0 -
	0	0	0	0	$0	-	Dst(0)	0	0	0	0	$0 -

2Aug03-8Sar fst 6f :22 :443 :5621:083 Amstrdam-G2 **97** 6 1 1hd 1hd 22½ 35¾ Velasquez C L123 6.50 93-07 Zavata1195¼ Great Notion121½ Trust N Luck123nk Vied outside, weakened 7
19Apr03-8Kee fst 1$\frac{1}{16}$:23 :47 1:1131:452 ClmrLex-G2 **95** 7 11½ 11 11½ 2½ 43½ Velasquez C L123 2.30 76-22 Scrimshw1163 EyofthTigr116nk DomstcDsput116nk Brush gate,weakened 7
15Mar03-8GP fst 1⅛ :4611:103 1:36 1:49 FlaDerby-G1 **92** 1 11 11½ 11 2½ 29¾ Velasquez C L122 *1.00 87-10 *Empire Maker*1229¾ Trust N Luck122½ Indy Dancer1222½ Inside, no match 7
15Feb03-11GP fst 1$\frac{1}{16}$:233 :463 1:1041:431 FntnOYth-G1 **106** 6 12 11½ 11½ 14 15¼ Velasquez C L122 4.90 93-13 Trust N Luck1225¼ Supah Blitz1202¼ Midway Cat116hd Inside, drew away 8

Tweedside
Own: Melnyk Eugene and Laura

B. m. 6 (Apr) KEESEP99 $100,000
Sire: Thunder Gulch (Gulch) $65,000
Dam: Twitchet (Roberto)
Br: Dr. & Mrs. R. S. West & Mr. & Mrs. Mackenzie Miller (Ky)
Tr: Pletcher Todd A(0 0 0 0 .00) 2003:(826 199 .24)

Life	20	7	4	1	$646,791	98	D.Fst	6	1	1	0	$221,030 93
2003	2	1	1	0	$140,000	96	Wet(277)	2	2	0	0	$186,674 91
2002	6	2	0	1	$149,035	98	Turf(306)	12	4	3	1	$239,087 98
	0	0	0	0	$0	-	Dst(0)	0	0	0	0	$0 -

23Mar03-8GP sly 1½ ⊗ :4821:14 2:0612:321 3↑Ⓕ OrchidH-G2 **91** 4 25 22 12½ 14 15½ Douglas R R L116 f *1.20 - - Tweedside1165½ SanDre1195 HiTechHoneycomb1154¼ Drew away, driving 7
8Feb03-8GP fm 1⅜ Ⓣ :4811:131 1:38 2:133 3↑Ⓕ VeryOneH-G3 **96** 9 52¼ 31 1hd 11½ 22¼ Velazquez J R L115 f 4.20 86-11 San Dare1162¼ *Tweedside*115½ Hi TechHoneycomb113½ 3 wide, outfinished 12

Valid Video
Own: Fehsenfeld Mac

Dk. b or b. g. 4 (Mar) OBSOCT00 $29,000
Sire: Valid Wager (Valid Appeal) $10,000
Dam: Miss Video (Star Gallant)
Br: Casey Seaman (Fla)
Tr: Manning Dennis J(0 0 0 0 .00) 2003:(155 21 .14)

Life	10	6	1	0	$565,700	110	D.Fst	7	5	0	0	$524,500 110
2003	7	4	1	0	$474,500	110	Wet(394)	3	1	1	0	$41,200 95
2002	3	2	0	0	$91,200	95	Turf(238)	0	0	0	0	$0 -
	0	0	0	0	$0	-	Dst(0)	0	0	0	0	$0 -

25Oct03-5SA fst 6f :21 :431 :55 1:074 3↑BCSprint-G1 **77** 4 6 83 117 1316 1316¼ Prado E S LB123 8.10 83-05 CajunBeat1232¼ Bluesthestndrd1262 ShkeYouDown126½ Saved grd, tired 13
23Aug03-10Sar fst 7f :213 :433 1:0831:22 KngsBshp-G1 **107** 2 8 42½ 44½ 31½ 1nk Bravo J L121 7.80 97-07 Valid Video121nk Great Notion117nk *Ghostzapper*1171¾ Steadied stretch 13
12Jly03-10Crc fst 6f :213 :443 :57 1:10 CarryBck-G3 **110** 9 2 62¼ 3nk 11 12½ Bravo J L122 8.80 94-11 *Valid Video*1222½ *Cajun Beat*1171¼ Super Fuse117nk 3 wide, edged away 10
24May03-7Mth sly 5f ⊗ :221 :45 :57 GildedTime50k **94** 2 2 32½ 33 23 22¾ Cruz C L122 *.90 94-13 Buzzy's Gold1132¾ *Valid Video*1224 *Rockin On Ready*1192 Inside, 2nd best 5
5Apr03-11GP fst 1$\frac{1}{16}$:224 :462 1:1131:43 Aventura250k **75** 2 31 2½ 2hd 32 614¾ Velasquez C L122 3.10 79-10 *Dynever*1223¼ Supah Blitz1226½ Massive1221 Saved grd, gave way 9
17Mar03-20TC fst 6f :22 :45 :5711:093 [R]OBSSprint50k **92** 2 2 2½ 1½ 1hd 13½ Prado E S L122 - 97 - VlidVideo1223½ SuperFuse1223¾ LughingLuke1223 Repulsed bid, drew off 7
Non-wagering event
25Jan03-8GP fst 7f :222 :443 1:0911:221 [R]OcalStdDsh250k **100** 1 5 31½ 2hd 2hd 1½ Prado E S L120 2.70 97-08 *VlidVideo*120½ Excessiveplesur1203¼ SuphBlitz1207¾ Dueled rail, prevailed 7

Vinemeister

Own: Travin Stables

Dk. b or b. h. 5 (May) OBSAPR01 $52,000
Sire: Williamstown (Seattle Slew) $5,000
Dam: Fairway Jet (Pleasant Colony)
Br: Nestor Camino (Ky)
Tr: Seewald Alan S(0 0 0 0 .00) 2003:(187 31 .17)

Life	23	4	3	2	$222,520	99	D.Fst	18	4	3	1	$212,970	99
2003	8	1	1	1	$75,840	98	Wet(329)	3	0	0	1	$8,850	93
2002	10	1	1	1	$71,780	99	Turf(298)	2	0	0	0	$700	72
	0	0	0	0	$0	-	Dst(0)	0	0	0	0	$0	-

6Dec03-7Crc	fst	6½f	:222 :464 1:114 1:182	3↑ OClm 62500(62.5-57.5)N	90	7	1	21½	1½	2½	2¾	Velez J A Jr	L117	2.80	86- 16	*Boston Fox*114¾ Vinemeister1171½ R. Associate1091	Off rail, gamely	7
1Sep03-3Mth	sly	170	:23 :462 1:11 1:412	3↑ OClm 75000N	93	6	32	21½	2½	41¼	34½	Velez J A Jr	L123	7.40	91- 18	Jarf1191¼ Run to Victory1193¼ Vinemeister1231¼	Outside,tired drive	6
23Aug03-10Mth	fst	1⅛	:48 1:121 1:372 1:501	3↑ IselnBCH-G3	60	1	3½	41¼	85¼	916	930¾	Velez J A Jr	L114	16.20	59- 27	Tenpins1191 Aeneas114no *Jersey Giant*1152¼	Gave way after 5/8	9
26Jly03-9Mth	fst	1	:234 :471 1:111 1:354	3↑ SalvtrMH-G3	98	3	22	21	1hd	12	1¾	Velez J A Jr	L114	14.10	98- 02	Vinemeister114¾ JerseyGint1172 *HighwyProspctor*113½	Stalked,clear,drvg	6
26Jun03-8Mth	fst	6f	:214 :441 :561 1:084	3↑ OClm 40000N	89	1	8	75¾	57	46	44	Velez J A Jr	L118	5.90	91- 15	*Zavata*1141 Rockin On Ready1142¾ SkipaGrade118nk	Steadied briefly start	8
2Mar03-7Aqu	sly	1	⊡ :232 :464 1:121 1:38	4↑ Alw 48000N3x	73	1	32	33	43	57½	511	Bridgmohan S X	L117	5.80	77- 31	Tailfromthecrypt1144 Hero's Glow119nk *Tarek*1173½	No response	5
29Jan03-8Aqu	fst	6f	⊡ :233 :463 :583 1:102	4↑ Alw 47000N3x	85	1	5	52¼	44½	56¼	75¼	Beckner D V	L118	13.30	87- 16	*Papua*1201 Reason to Hail1231 Pop Rocks1181¾	Inside trip, no rally	7
11Jan03-6Aqu	fst	6f	⊡ :213 :443 :564 1:084	4↑ Alw 47000N3x	81	6	2	1hd	2½	43	58¾	Gryder A T	L118	6.80	91- 10	American Century1182 Pop Rocks118½ Alex's Pal1181½	Vied inside, tired	7

Volga (Ire)

Own: Allen Joseph

Dk. b or b. m. 6 (Mar)
Sire: Caerleon (Nijinsky II)
Dam: Verveine (Lear Fan)
Br: Allez France Stables (Ire)
Tr: McLaughlin Kiaran P(0 0 0 0 .00) 2003:(186 46 .25)

Life	19	7	5	2	$1,141,759	105	D.Fst	0	0	0	0	$0	-
2003	6	3	2	0	$730,800	98	Wet(225)	0	0	0	0	$0	-
2002	6	1	1	2	$208,720	105	Turf(337)	19	7	5	2	$1,141,759	105
	0	0	0	0	$0	-	Dst(0)	0	0	0	0	$0	-

27Dec03-9Crc	fm	1½	Ⓣ :48 1:13 2:031 2:26	3↑ ⒻLaPvyteH-G2	98	7	46½	31½	21	11½	12¾	Migliore R	L119	3.10	103 -	Volga1192¾ Lady Annaliese1161¼ Lost Appeal115¾	Aggressive handling	11
15Nov03-8Aqu	yl	1½	Ⓣ :52 1:172 2:082 2:322	3↑ ⒻLngIlndH-G2	97	10	31	21	1hd	11½	21¼	Migliore R	L120	*2.10	83- 16	Spice Island1171¼ *Volga*1202¾ Banyu Dewi114½	With pace, gamely	11
19Oct03-5WO	sf	1¼	Ⓣ :503 1:152 1:404 2:053	3↑ ⒻEPTaylor-G1	96	10	75¾	74¼	52	2hd	1hd	Migliore R	L123	10.45	79- 30	Volga123hd Tigertail123no Hi Dubai118hd	3w,rally 4w, prevailed	10
Previously trained by Clement Christophe																		
5Oct03-6Kee	fm	1 3/16	Ⓣ :484 1:124 1:38 1:554	3↑ ⒻWnStGlxy-G2	76	5	47	312	311	26	510¾	Nakatani C S	L121	2.90	81- 10	Bien Nicole1217¼ Approach1161¼ New Economy1211¼	Tracked,4w,tired	6
14Sep03-6WO	fm	*1⅛	Ⓣ :47 1:442	3↑ ⒻCanadinH-G2	94	5	41½	62½	51¼	21½	21¾	Nakatani C S	L118	*1.25	94- 06	Inish Glora1161¾ Volga1181¾ Diadella116½	Stalk 3w,rally 4w	8
17Aug03-10Mth	gd	1⅛	Ⓣ :474 1:113 1:361 1:481	3↑ ⒻMtchmkrH-G3	97	9	106¾	910	98¾	43	11¾	Bravo J	L116	*2.50	89- 11	Volg1161¾ SomthingVnturd117¾ Cocktlsndrms115no	Well back,out,rallied	10

Voodoo
Own: Moore Susan and John

Ch. g. 6 (Feb)
Sire: Petionville (Seeking the Gold) $6,500
Dam: Slide Show (Slewacide)
Br: Everest Stables Inc. (Ky)
Tr: Jerkens James A(0 0 0 0 .00) 2003:(194 46 .24)

Life	22	7	2	4	$454,356	111	D.Fst	20	7	2	3	$438,344 111
2003	6	2	0	0	$108,942	111	Wet(352)	2	0	0	1	$16,012 89
2002	8	2	1	1	$184,984	109	Turf(215)	0	0	0	0	$0 –
	0	0	0	0	$0	–	Dst(0)	0	0	0	0	$0 –

29Nov03–9Aqu fst 1 :224 :442 1:083 1:341 3↑CigarMiH-G1 **93** 6 5½ 63 6½ 711 714 Santos J A L116 b 12.20 80–19 Congaree1245¼ Midas Eyes1153 Toccet1151 Bumped after start 7
25Oct03–5Bel fst 7f :223 :452 1:093 1:22 3↑SportPgH-G3 **111** 7 4 21 2hd 14½ 12½ Chavez J F L114 b 4.30 90–14 Voodoo1142½ BowmnsBnd120½ HghwyProspctor1143¾ Speed 3 wide, clear 9
27Sep03–7Bel fst 6½f :214 :441 1:083 1:143 3↑Vosburgh-G1 **88** 3 5 1½ 12½ 2hd 611½ Chavez J F L126 b 7.90 88–16 Ghostzapper1236½ Aggadan1261¼ Posse1231¾ Inside, bumped stretch 10
17Aug03–8Sar fst 6f :222 :45 :564 1:093 4↑Alw 56000c **105** 2 6 31 2hd 2hd 1½ Velazquez J R L120 b *2.00 94–08 Voodoo120½ HeresZealous1182¼ HookandLadder1185½ Resolutely outside 7
4Jly03–8Bel fst 7f :222 :444 1:093 1:222 3↑TomFoolH-G2 **86** 6 1 12½ 15½ 1½ 58¾ Velazquez J R L114 b 18.90 79–15 *Aldebaran*1222 Peeping Tom1172½ State City1183¾ Set pace, tired 7
18Jan03–8Aqu fst 1¹⁄₁₆ [•] :232 :474 1:121 1:44 3↑AquH-G3 **62** 1 14½ 11½ 11 412 524½ Migliore R L115 b *.35e 61–21 *SnkeMountin*1207½ GroundStorm1172¼ CtsAtHom1149 Bumped start, tired 5

Voodoo Dancer
Own: Green Hills Farm

B. m. 6 (Apr) KEESEP99 $200,000
Sire: Kingmambo (Mr. Prospector) $200,000
Dam: Zuri (Danzig)
Br: Lazy E Ranch Inc. (Ky)
Tr: Clement Christophe(0 0 0 0 .00) 2003:(389 75 .19)

Life	21	11	4	2	$1,427,952	106	D.Fst	1	0	0	0	$0 35
2003	4	2	0	1	$432,364	106	Wet(369)	0	0	0	0	$0 –
2002	7	3	3	1	$562,638	106	Turf(378)	20	11	4	2	$1,427,952 106
	0	0	0	0	$0	–	Dst(0)	0	0	0	0	$0 –

25Oct03–6SA fm 1¼ (T) :463 1:102 1:351 1:59 3↑(F)BCF&MTrf-G1 **100** 7 910 912 53 94½ 75¼ Nakatani C S LB123 8.90 93–04 Islington123nk L'Ancresse1182½ Yesterday118no Bit tight 6-1/2,5w str 12
26Jly03–8Sar fm 1⅛ (T) :49 1:13 1:363 1:474 3↑(F)DianaH-G1 **106** 3 62½ 72¼ 72¾ 1hd 1nk Nakatani C S L120 2.60 90–10 VoodooDancer120nk *HeatHaze*1181¾ Pertuisane115¾ 5 wide move, resolute 8
28Jun03–8Hol fm 1¼ (T) :502 1:134 1:364 2:004 3↑(F)BevHilsH-G2 **106** 5 44½ 48 34½ 21½ 1¾ Nakatani C S LB120 2.60 88–13 *Voodoo Dancer*120¾ Dublino1222½ *Megahertz*1171 3wd into lane,gamely 5
3May03–8Aqu fm 1¹⁄₁₆ (T) :231 :481 1:124 1:421 3↑(F)BeaugayH-G3 **96** 8 54½ 52 51¼ 4¾ 31¼ Samyn J L L120 *.80 92–05 DeltPrincess113½ WonderAgin118¾ *VoodooDncr*120¾ Game finish outside 9

Wacky Patty
Own: Turf Express Inc., Debruycker and Jac

Dk. b or b. f. 3 (Feb) OBSWIN02 $16,000
Sire: Formal Dinner (Well Decorated) $7,500
Dam: As a Day in June (Fly So Free)
Br: D. W. Frazier MD & Suzanne Sharra Maxwell (Fla)
Tr: Norman Cole(0 0 0 0 .00) 2003:(1086 290 .27)

Life	7	4	0	0	$184,569	86	D.Fst	7	4	0	0	$184,569 86
2003	7	4	0	0	$184,569	86	Wet(348)	0	0	0	0	$0 –
2002	0	M	0	0	$0	–	Turf(239)	0	0	0	0	$0 –
	0	0	0	0	$0	–	Dst(0)	0	0	0	0	$0 –

5Dec03–6DeD fst 1 :223 :463 1:113 1:39 (F)BdGmgDltPr250k **54** 7 21 21 43 68½ 617 Theriot H J II L118 b 4.90 75–05 SltyRomnce1145¼ QuestionblPst1141 TurntoLss1142 Pressed pace, faded 10
7Nov03–9DeD fst 7f :234 :473 1:131 1:264 (F)Chargedup75k **81** 3 3 2½ 11 1hd 1no Theriot H J II L120 b *.80 92–15 Wacky Patty120no Miss Cortina1152½ Cryptos' Best1171 Dueled, got nod 5
28Sep03–8LaD fst 6f :221 :463 :583 1:12 (F)DeltaMiss40k **49** 1 4 12 2hd 37½ 413¾ Melancon G L122 b *.20e 70–21 VinoTinto1186½ GoodisGlor1166¼ Yoursmnours1131 Steadied start,falterd 8

Previously trained by Chapman James K

4Jly03–4Hol fst 6f :22 :443 :571 1:101 (F)Landaluc-G3 **86** 6 1 2hd 2hd 1½ 11 Valdivia J Jr LB119 b *1.90 89–12 WckyPtty1191 ChrishDstiny1165 PltinumPrncss1161 Brushed 3/16,gamely 6
8Jun03–7Hol fst 5½f :213 :444 :572 1:042 (F)Cinderella84k **61** 3 9 85¼ 87½ 68¾ 47½ Valdivia J Jr LB119 b 3.10 78–15 YogsPolrBr1133 SmokBrk1162 OutrgosOystr1162½ Bobbled,crowded start 9
11May03–9Hol fst 5f :22 :453 :581 (F)Nursery81k **74** 1 5 2hd 11 11 12 Nakatani C S LB119 b *1.10 93–12 WackyPatty1192 *YogisPolarBear*114hd *KindLen*1144 Inside,held on gamely 7
30Apr03–8Hol fst 4½f :212 :451 :513 (F)Md Sp Wt 46k **71** 1 1 1½ 11½ 12½ Nakatani C S LB119 b 2.30 97–08 *WckyPtty*1192½ KindLen1191 Shesgotgoldfever1193½ Rail, steady handling 9

Wake At Noon
Own: Schickedanz Bruno

Ch. h. 7 (Apr)
Sire: Cure the Blues (Stop the Music)
Dam: Sermon Time (Silver Deputy)
Br: Bruno Schickedanz (Ont-C)
Tr: Collazo Henry(0 0 0 0 .00) 2003:(477 63 .13)

Life 47 19 6 5 $1,567,492 113 | D.Fst 40 18 6 4 $1,484,407 113
2004 1 0 0 0 $3,000 84 | Wet(362) 4 1 0 1 $83,085 111
2003 10 3 1 1 $303,671 102 | Turf(251) 3 0 0 0 $0 91
0 0 0 0 $0 – | Dst(0) 0 0 0 0 $0 –

3Jan04-10GP fst 6f :221 :444 :5631:09 3↑MrPrpctH-G3 84 5 1 41½ 51¾ 56½ 58 Karamanos H A L116 fb 17.90 89- 10 Cajun Beat1211½ Gygistar118¾ Deer Lake1153 Mid track,faded turn 6
13Dec03-11Crc fst 7f :221 :451 1:1021:234 3↑KenyNoeJrH100k 100 9 3 1hd 11½ 12 2hd Karamanos H A L116 fb 10.00 95- 11 HastyKris116hd WakeAtNoon1163¼ TouroftheCt119hd Yielded grudgingly 10
Previously trained by Katryan Abraham R
8Nov03-8WO fst 1 1/16 :233 :471 1:1111:434 3↑WoSltCpH-G3 93 4 11½ 11 1½ 31½ 42¾ Ramsammy E L119 fb 4.25 84- 09 No Comprende1171¼ Mobil1191 Parose118½ Off rail gave way 7
4Oct03-8WO fst 1⅛ :4711:111 1:3841:53 3↑DurhmCpH-G3 87 6 1hd 2½ 21 32 34¼ Ramsammy E L121 fb *1.55 77- 24 Prose1172 BrbeuRuckus1162¼ WkeAtNoon1214½ Press outsde, weakened 6
14Sep03-9WO fm 1 Ⓣ :224 :451 1:0911:331 3↑AttoMile-G1 86 9 11½ 2hd 42 87 119¼ Ramsammy E L119 b 45.45 88- 06 Touch of the Blues119½ Soaring Free1211¾ *Perfect Soul*121hd 3 wide, faded 11
3Aug03-8WO fst 1 1/16 :23 :462 1:1041:424 3↑SeagramCup136k 102 1 11½ 12 12 1½ 12¾ Ramsammy E L119 b *1.65 92- 18 WkeAtNoon1192¾ AnglinPrince1153¼ MrkOne119hd 2-pth,turned bck rival 6
20Jly03-4WO fst 1 1/16 :234 :473 1:12 1:44 3↑ⓇIzvestia106k 100 4 1½ 11 11½ 1hd 11¾ Ramsammy E L124 b 4.45 86- 34 *WkeAtNoon*1241¾ AnglinPrince1206 *ForvrGrnd*120nk 2-path,turn back rival 6
22Jun03-8WO fst 6½f :214 :441 1:0921:161 3↑Alw 80900N$Y 85 6 1 21 22 23 44¼ Kabel T K L122 fb *1.05 90- 09 WildWhiskey1182¼ CheapTlk1181½ DwnWtcher118½ Chase 3w,outfinished 6
26May03-9Bel sly 1 :221 :442 1:0831:34 3↑MtropltH-G1 41 5 3½ 42 814 826 836¼ Ramsammy E L115 fb 50.75 60- 14 Aldebaran119nk Saarland1143 *Peeping Tom*1143¾ Bumped start, rushed 8
26Apr03-8WO fst 7f :22 :442 1:0941:231 4↑VigilH-G3 100 3 6 4nk 1½ 12½ 13¼ Ramsammy E L124 fb *1.70 88- 23 WakeAtNoon1243¼ ShwsCreek1142 *ChepTlk*1201¾ Duel between, drew off 7
22Mar03-8WO my 5f :212 :441 :571 4↑BriarticH108k 85 4 7 65¼ 65½ 65¾ 42¼ Ramsammy E L124 fb *1.90 92- 11 Krz Ruckus1181 Olympian115¾ Davids Expectation114½ Late rally, 4 wide 8

Wando
Own: Schickedanz Gustav

Ch. c. 4 (Feb)
Sire: Langfuhr (Danzig) $20,000
Dam: Kathie's Colleen (Woodman)
Br: Gustav Schickedanz (Ont-C)
Tr: Keogh Michael(0 0 0 0 .00) 2003:(97 17 .18)

Life 13 8 2 1 $2,379,700 111 | D.Fst 9 6 1 1 $1,161,450 111
2003 8 5 1 1 $2,017,323 111 | Wet(334) 1 1 0 0 $300,000 99
2002 5 3 1 0 $362,377 87 | Turf(296) 3 1 1 0 $918,250 101
0 0 0 0 $0 – | Dst(0) 0 0 0 0 $0 –

4Oct03-9Hoo fst 1 1/16 :223 :462 1:1031:432 IndnaDby-G3 99 6 32½ 3½ 2hd 2½ 32¼ Husbands P LB124 f 2.30 90- 29 Excessiveplesure1241 GrndHombr1241¼ Wndo1241¼ 3wd, bid, aim,faltered 8
14Sep03-9WO fm 1 Ⓣ :224 :451 1:0911:331 3↑AttoMile-G1 101 5 42½ 31½ 1hd 2½ 42¼ Husbands P L115 *3.15 95- 06 TouchoftheBlus119½ SoringFr1211¾ *PrfctSoul*121hd Stalk 2-pth,led,outfin 11
9Aug03-8WO fm 1½ Ⓣ :4841:132 2:0322:283 ⓇBreeders1000k 100 7 21½ 2½ 32 11½ 11½ Husbands P L126 *.50 87- 14 Wando1261½ *ShoalWter*1263¼ ColorfulJudgement1265 Stalk 4w, rallied 3w 8
20Jly03-8FE my 1 3/16 :4621:104 1:3621:554 ⓇPrncOWales500k 99 4 1hd 11 11 14 14 Husbands P L126 *.30 101 - *Wando*1264 Arco's Gold1262 Shoal Water1262 Shook clear, easily 7
22Jun03-9WO fst 1¼ :4631:114 1:3722:022 ⓇQueensPlt1000k 111 4 12½ 11 11½ 15 19 Husbands P L126 *1.40 102- 17 *Wando*1269 *Mobil*1261½ Rock Again1262½ Off rail, drew off 12
17May03-8WO fst 1 1/16 :224 :461 1:11 1:423 Marine-G3 102 3 1hd 1½ 1½ 12½ 14½ Kabel T K L119 *.65 93- 18 *Wando*1194½ *El Ruller*1172¾ Arco's Gold1193½ Off rail, drew off 6
19Apr03-8WO fst 6f :223 :454 :5811:103 Woodstock135k 97 5 3 41¾ 41 2hd 1nk Kabel T K L121 *1.10 91- 14 *Wando*121nk I'm the Tiger1173 El Ruller1192½ Stalk 4w,waited turn 7
30Mar03-8WO fst 6f :22 :452 :5811:11 ⓇAchievmtH161k 93 4 1 31½ 3nk 11½ 2nk Kabel T K L122 *.30 89- 19 MajesticWisdom115nk *Wando*1226¼ BiddysLd1152 Stalk duel 3w,outfnshd 5

War Zone
Own: Juddmonte Farms Inc

B. h. 5 (Jan)
Sire: Danzig (Northern Dancer) $250,000
Dam: Proflare (Mr. Prospector)
Br: Juddmonte Farms, Inc. (Ky)
Tr: Frankel Robert J(0 0 0 0 .00) 2003:(411 114 .28)

Life	15	6	1	1	$259,614	100	D.Fst	0	0	0	0	$0 –
2003	5	2	0	0	$120,436	100	Wet(452)	0	0	0	0	$0 –
2002	4	1	0	0	$47,902	–	Turf(412)	15	6	1	1	$259,614 100
	0	0	0	0	$0	–	Dst(0)	0	0	0	0	$0 –

24Oct03–5SA fm *6½f Ⓣ:214 :434 1:0641:131 3↑MorvichH-G3 98 7 8 89½ 86½ 64½ 51½ Bailey J D LB118 3.50 90–09 *King Robyn*117hd Medecis116¾ Geronimo115hd Came out,rallied btwn 9
23Aug03–9Sar fm 1 1/16 Ⓣ:224 :46 1:0931:391 3↑4strdavH-G2 86 3 95¼ 93¾ 73¾ 109 910¼ Castellano J J L119 3.75 89–03 Trademark1182 Quest Star1161¼ Tap the Admiral1151 No response 11
5Jly03–8Bel fm 1 Ⓣ:234 :461 1:0921:324 3↑PokerH-G3 100 6 85¼ 83¾ 32½ 3½ 1½ Castellano J J L117 *2.45 96–08 War Zone117½ *Trademark*114½ Saint Verre1121¼ Along late outside 11
26May03–8Hol fm 1 Ⓣ:24 :463 1:0911:331 3↑ShoeBCM-G1 95 5 87¾ 79 79 69 57¼ Flores D R LB124 5.20 91–10 Redattore124¾ Special Ring1243 *TouchoftheBlues*1242 Off bit slow,no rally 9
28Mar03–7SA fm *6½f Ⓣ:221 :45 1:0731:131 4↑Alw 65000NC 93 5 5 57 42 2½ 1½ Flores D R LB116 *.80 91–10 War Zone116½ Ecstatic122hd Nuclear Debate1184 Off slow,rail bid,best 5

Watchem Smokey
Own: Gann Edmund A

B. g. 4 (Feb) ARKFEB01 $4,700
Sire: Alphabet Soup (Cozzene) $30,000
Dam: Karon's Dream (Geiger Counter)
Br: Barbara R. Smicklas & John E Smicklas (Okla)
Tr: Frankel Robert J(0 0 0 0 .00) 2003:(411 114 .28)

Life	9	7	0	0	$159,500	107	D.Fst	5	4	0	0	$120,500 107
2003	7	5	0	0	$144,200	107	Wet(396)	3	3	0	0	$35,400 90
2002	2	2	0	0	$15,300	75	Turf(316)	1	0	0	0	$3,600 92
	0	0	0	0	$0	–	Dst(0)	0	0	0	0	$0 –

26Dec03–8SA fst 7f :222 :45 1:0911:223 Malibu-G1 97 2 10 73¼ 63½ 76 54¼ Valenzuela P A LB119 *1.10e 89–12 SouthernImage115hd MrinoMrini1151 MidsEyes1193 Split foes late,no bid 12
27Nov03–7Hol fst 6f :214 :441 :56 1:084 3↑VOUndrwd-G3 101 2 6 44 42½ 31½ 11 Krone J A LB112 3.70 96–08 WtchmSmoky1121 OurNwRcruit1141½ *HstyKrs*116no Came out lane,rallied 6
3Oct03–6SA fm *6½f Ⓣ:221 :44 1:06 1:12 3↑Alw 63600N$Y 92 4 4 31½ 32½ 43½ 44 Solis A LB116 2.40 93–03 ThunderBullet1161 MencingDnnis1201½ NuclrDbt1161½ Stalked rail,no bid 8
Previously trained by Borel Cecil P
5Jly03–10LaD fst 6f :214 :442 :5611:091 Airline50k 107 9 3 32 32½ 1hd 12¾ Simington D E L117 *1.10 98–16 WtchemSmokey1172¾ BookNote117½ *LcLrong*1178¾ Stalked, kicked clear 9
1May03–8LS my 6f :22 :45 :57 1:093 OClm 60000N 90 8 2 31 2hd 11 13¼ Simington D E L120 3.00 92–11 *Watchem Smokey*1203¼ Demopolis120¾ *Slam Bam*1161 Stalked, drew clear 9
22Mar03–8OP fst 6f :214 :452 :5731:10 Alw 31000N1X 89 8 3 31 3nk 1½ 1¾ Quinonez L S L115 *1.10 90–16 *Watchem Smokey*115¾ Either Orr122¾ Kristine's King1153¼ 3-w bid, driving 9
1Mar03–11OP gd 6f :223 :463 :59 1:12 3↑Clm 30000(30-25)N3L 88 2 2 2hd 1hd 12 15¾ Theriot H J II L119 4.00 80–20 *Watchem Smokey*1195¾ ExclusiveSlew1161 *Remaster*124¾ Drew out, driving 9

Western Pride
Own: Chapman Carolyn and McArthur, Theresa

Dk. b or b. h. 6 (May) OBSMAR00 $65,000
Sire: Way West*Fr (Gone West) $2,000
Dam: Strongerthanpride (Proud Birdie)
Br: C. Bowling & C. Thompson (Fla)
Tr: Chapman James K(0 0 0 0 .00) 2003:(126 15 .12)

Life	29	10	4	1	$1,288,569	112	D.Fst	23	8	3	1	$1,024,800 112
2003	6	1	1	0	$214,750	112	Wet(352)	4	2	1	0	$233,769 112
2002	5	1	1	0	$334,640	112	Turf(203)	2	0	0	0	$30,000 100
	0	0	0	0	$0	–	Dst(0)	0	0	0	0	$0 –

27Dec03–10Tam fst 6f :221 :452 :58 1:104 3↑Pelican60k 89 11 4 42½ 43 62½ 43 Rocco J S Jr L117 *2.30 93–14 AbovthWind1171 ScrtRomo1172 WckyforLov122hd Lacked late response 12
3Aug03–8Dmr fst 1 1/16 :224 :453 1:10 1:423 3↑SnDiegoH-G2 76 6 2½ 2½ 76 810 715 Valdivia J Jr LB118 6.10 77–11 TasteofPrdise113¾ Gondolieri117nk RebsGold1166½ 4wd 7/8,vied,gave way 8
13Jly03–9Hol fst 1¼ :4531:092 1:3412:002 3↑HolGldCp-G1 104 5 21 2½ 33 45 58 Valdivia J Jr LB124 13.10 97–07 Congaree1243 Harlan's Holiday1242 Kudos1241 3wd bid 5/8,vied,wkend 7
14Jun03–8Hol fst 1⅛ :4631:103 1:35 1:474 3↑Calfrnin-G2 95 5 11 11 1½ 64¾ 68 Valenzuela P A LB118 *1.20 87–04 Kudos116½ PiensaSonando1181½ RebsGold1181½ Took up btwn 1/4,wkend 7
16May03–11Pim sly 1 3/16 :4631:11 1:3621:56 4↑PimSpclH-G1 112 8 2½ 2hd 11 21½ 23¾ Valenzuela P A L116 3.40 89–23 Mineshft1213¾ WesternPride116hd JudgesCse1131¾ 2wd,clear 3-1/2,faded 9
5Apr03–10SA fst 1⅛ :4621:102 1:3511:482 4↑SnBrdnoH-G3 112 8 2½ 21 2½ 11 1nk Valenzuela P A LB116 4.00 92–14 WestrnPrid116nk *TotlImpct*1131 FltstrtDncr1122½ Led 2nd turn,held game 8

White Cat

Own: Cottrell R H Sr

Ch. c. 4 (Mar) KEESEP01 $30,000
Sire: Mountain Cat (Storm Cat) $7,500
Dam: Our Friend Terry (Cox's Ridge)
Br: Stillmeadow Farm LLC & Dr. Steve Conboy (Ky)
Tr: McPeek Kenneth G(0 0 0 0 .00) 2003:(400 61 .15)

Life	11	3	2	0	$157,778	94	D.Fst	6	2	0	0	$59,428	88
2003	4	1	2	0	$97,000	94	Wet(342)	1	0	0	0	$1,350	60
2002	7	2	0	0	$60,778	88	Turf(235)	4	1	2	0	$97,000	94
	0	0	0	0	$0	–	Dst(0)	0	0	0	0	$0	–

4Apr03–8Kee	fm	1	Ⓣ :224 :46 1:103 1:344	Trnsylvn-G3	**94**	3	43½	45	31½	21½	1hd	Sellers S J	L116 b	3.50	94– 08	White Cat116hd Deep Shadow1181 Christmas Away116nk	4w,stiff drive	9
21Feb03–9GP	fm	1⅛	Ⓣ :472 1:114 1:361 1:481	PalmBch-G3	**92**	5	71½	41¾	3½	1½	2½	Prado E S	L118 b	5.60	93– 09	Nothing to Lose122½ *White Cat*118½ *Imitation*118¾	3 wide, outfinished	12
26Jan03–9GP	fm	1$\frac{1}{16}$	Ⓣ :241 :484 1:123 1:423	+ DaveFeldmn75k	**86**	7	32½	41½	41¾	41¾	2nk	Prado E S	L118 b	6.80	82– 12	Hypnotist116nk White Cat118½ Private Gold118¾	3 wide, just missed	12
1Jan03–10Crc	gd	1⅛	Ⓣ :483 1:131 1:381 1:502	TrpPkDby-G3	**84**	6	86¼	84¾	83¼	72¾	63	Guidry M	L117 b	27.80	76– 20	*NothingtoLos*1151¾ MllnnumStorm119hd SuphBltz115¾	Check 3/8pl, 6 wide	12

Whitmore's Conn

Own: Shanley Michael and Lynn

Dk. b or b. h. 6 (Mar)
Sire: Kris S. (Roberto) $150,000
Dam: Albonita (Deputed Testamony)
Br: Bud Wolf & Joe D'Agostino (NY)
Tr: Schulhofer Randy(0 0 0 0 .00) 2003:(146 23 .16)

Life	28	7	4	5	$740,426	107	D.Fst	5	0	0	2	$23,490	89
2003	6	2	0	1	$404,236	107	Wet(404)	1	1	0	0	$25,200	78
2002	9	3	2	0	$210,100	103	Turf(321)	22	6	4	3	$691,736	107
	0	0	0	0	$0	–	Dst(0)	0	0	0	0	$0	–

6Sep03–8Bel	yl	1⅜	Ⓣ :514 1:171 1:42 2:174	3↑ ManOWar-G1	**97**	4	66	65½	76½	89	77	Day P	L126 b	5.80	67– 26	Lunar Sovereign126 2¾ Slew Valley126nk Denon126 1¼	3 wide turn, no rally	8
9Aug03–9Sar	gd	1½	[T] :49 1:13 2:031 2:28	3↑ SwrdDncH-G1	**107**	5	97¾	118¼	104¼	32	11¼	Samyn J L	L115 b	24.75	80– 20	Whitmore's Conn115 1¼ Macaw114nk Slew Valley114¾	7 wide move, clear	11
12Jly03–10Bel	gd	1⅜	Ⓣ :511 1:151 1:39 2:154	3↑ BwlnGrnH-G2	**105**	1	85¾	75¼	75¾	42¾	1½	Samyn J L	L116 b	11.80	84– 22	*Whitmore's Conn*116½ Quest Star117nk Macaw116¾	Came wide, in time	9
25Jun03–8Bel	gd	1¼	[T] :494 1:142 1:382 2:014	4↑ Alw 58000c	**91**	6	115½	115	108½	712	56¼	Bridgmohan S X	L115 b	6.50	79– 20	State Shinto120½ *Revved Up*118 2½ Dr. Kashnikow120 1¼	Mild rally outside	11
25May03–8Bel	sf	1⅛	[T] :51 1:152 1:401 1:522	3↑ [S]KingstonH113k	**90**	1	54¼	62¼	64¼	37½	35¾	Bridgmohan S X	L122 b	4.00	62– 32	IrishColonil1194 CelticSky118 1¾ WhitmorsConn122 1¾	Inside trip, no rally	9
19Jan03–10GP	fm	1⅜	Ⓣ :494 1:144 1:39 2:143	3↑ MDiarmdH-G3	**91**	1	54	45½	86¾	78½	87	♦Prado E S	L114 b	*2.70	76– 13	Riddlesdown113 1½ Macaw114 1¾ Just Listen113nk	No rally	12

Whoopi Cat

Own: Smith Derrick and Tabor, Michael

Dk. b or b. f. 3 (Feb)
Sire: Tale of the Cat (Storm Cat) $16,139
Dam: Whoopi*NZ (Sky Filou*NZ)
Br: Richard Giacopelli (Ky)
Tr: Biancone Patrick L(0 0 0 0 .00) 2003:(135 26 .19)

Life	2	2	0	0	$115,800	87	D.Fst	0	0	0	0	$0	–
2003	2	2	0	0	$115,800	87	Wet(333)	2	2	0	0	$115,800	87
2002	0	M	0	0	$0	–	Turf(320)	0	0	0	0	$0	–
	0	0	0	0	$0	–	Dst(0)	0	0	0	0	$0	–

11Aug03–8Sar	my	6½f	:211 :443 1:103 1:172	ⒻAdirondk-G2	**83**	5	3	31	2½	2hd	11¼	Prado E S	116	*1.35	88– 11	WhoopiCt116 1¼ UnbridledBeuty116 3¾ EyeDzzler116½	Bobble start, 3 wide	7
11Jly03–3Bel	gd	5f	:22 :451 :572	ⒻMd Sp Wt 43k	**87**	7	5	3½	2½	11	16	Prado E S	118	9.00	96– 17	*Whoopi Cat*1186 Storm Minstrel118¾ For My Wife118¾	3 wide, drew away	7

Wild and Wicked
Own: Randal Mr. and Mrs. R. David

Dk. b or b. c. 4 (Jan)
Sire: Wild Again (Icecapade) $50,000
Dam: Wicked Witchcraft (Good Behaving)
Br: Mr. & Mrs. Robert David Randal (Ky)
Tr: McPeek Kenneth G(0 0 0 0 .00) 2003:(400 61 .15)

Life	5	3	0	0	$358,480	101	D.Fst	4	2	0	0	$331,225	101
2003	5	3	0	0	$358,480	101	Wet(320)	1	1	0	0	$27,255	101
2002	0	M	0	0	$0	–	Turf(257)	0	0	0	0	$0	–
	0	0	0	0	$0	–	Dst(0)	0	0	0	0	$0	–

23Aug03-11Sar fst 1¼ :461 1:094 1:352 2:02 Travers-G1 **90** 5 617 615 69¼ 411 415¼ Sellers S J L126 16.90 82– 03 *TenMostWnted*1264½ PeceRules12610 StrongHope126¾ Inside trip, no rally 6
3Aug03-11Mth fst 1⅛ :47 1:104 1:36 1:491 HsklInvH-G1 **93** 3 21½ 31½ 43 36 410 Sellers S J 118 4.90 85– 08 Peace Rules1211¾ Sky Mesa1187¼ Funny Cide1231 Outside 1/4,wknd drive 7
21Jun03-14Tdn fst 1⅛ :483 1:13 1:373 1:50 OhioDrby-G2 **101** 6 21½ 22½ 2½ 2hd 13¼ Sellers S J 114 *1.10 93– 14 WldndWckd1143¼ Hckndffy1122½ MdwyRd1142¼ Going away,hand ridden 7
25May03-2CD sly 1 1/16 :234 :474 1:124 1:441 Alw 42075N1x **101** 4 11½ 11½ 11½ 13 12¾ Sellers S J 115 *.50 87– 24 *WildndWickd*1152¾ *SintLm*1224¼ StrngthWthn1164½ Control pace,hand urg 6
25Apr03-5Kee fst 7f :224 :453 1:102 1:223 Md Sp Wt 50k **98** 7 1 1hd 1hd 12½ 19½ Sellers S J 120 *1.10 91– 16 *Wild and Wicked*1209½ Grand Scam1206½ *Cointreau*1201¾ Mild hand urging 8

Wild Spirit (Chi)
Own: Sumaya Us Stables

Dk. b or b. f. 5 (Jul)
Sire: Hussonet (Mr. Prospector) $20,000
Dam: Wild Princess (Wild Again)
Br: Haras Sumaya (Chi)
Tr: Frankel Robert J(0 0 0 0 .00) 2003:(411 114 .28)

Life	14	9	4	0	$934,690	110	D.Fst	5	4	1	0	$838,677	110
2003	4	3	1	0	$830,000	110	Wet(480)	9	5	3	0	$96,013	–
2002	10	6	3	0	$104,690	–	Turf(413)	0	0	0	0	$0	–
	0	0	0	0	$0	–	Dst(0)	0	0	0	0	$0	–

13Sep03-9Bel fst 1 1/16 :23 :454 1:10 1:411 3↑Ⓕ RuffianH-G1 **109** 1 54 52 3nk 12 13½ Bailey J D L121 *.55 94– 19 Wild Spirit1213½ You1185 Passing Shot1155½ With something left 6
22Aug03-9Sar fst 1¼ :493 1:141 1:382 2:031 3↑Ⓕ PrsnlEnH-G1 **92** 1 32½ 31½ 31 11 2no Bailey J D L122 *.20 91– 17 Passing Shot114no *Wild Spirit*1226¼ MissLinda1142½ Steadied quarter pole 5
20Jly03-10Del fst 1¼ :492 1:134 1:382 2:024 3↑Ⓕ DelH-G2 **110** 2 41½ 2hd 2hd 12 16 Bailey J D L117 *.80 97– 09 WildSpirit1176 *TakeChargeLdy*1202¾ *ShinySheet*112½ Lost whip, ridden out 8
17May03-8Bel fst 1 :224 :452 1:092 1:342 3↑Ⓕ ShuveeH-G2 **106** 3 32½ 31 31½ 1hd 13½ Castellano J J 115 10.20 94– 17 *Wild Spirit*1153½ Smok'n Frolic1191¼ *You*1204¼ Came wide, drew clear 6

Willa On the Move
Own: Angelos Peter G

Ch. m. 5 (Jan) EASOCT00 $47,000
Sire: Two Punch (Mr. Prospector) $25,000
Dam: Willa Joe*Ire (El Gran Senor)
Br: Robert L. Quinichett (Md)
Tr: Dutrow Anthony W(0 0 0 0 .00) 2003:(297 89 .30)

Life	12	6	3	0	$363,940	106	D.Fst	10	5	2	0	$249,380	106
2003	5	3	0	0	$166,390	106	Wet(370)	2	1	1	0	$114,560	105
2002	7	3	3	0	$197,550	103	Turf(223)	0	0	0	0	$0	–
	0	0	0	0	$0	–	Dst(0)	0	0	0	0	$0	–

28Nov03-9Aqu fst 1 :231 :462 1:103 1:362 3↑Ⓕ TopFlgtH-G2 **78** 9 52 42 33 49 1012½ Prado E S L116 *1.20 70– 29 Randaroo1162 Beauty Halo1153¼ Pocus Hocus116nk 3 wide, no response 12
11Oct03-8Lrl fst 7f :231 :46 1:101 1:223 3↑ⒻⓇ MdMilDstfH95k **98** 4 8 76 54 11 12 Pino M G L122 *.40 94– 10 Willa On the Move1222 FinallyHere116no BronzeAbe1183 Bump brk, 5 wide 8
24Aug03-9Sar fst 7f :223 :45 1:09 1:221 3↑Ⓕ BalrinaH-G1 **95** 2 7 82¾ 53 52¼ 52¼ Albarado R J L116 3.65 94– 12 *HrmonyLodge*115no ShineAgin1202 GoldMover118hd Steadied backstretch 8
1Aug03-8Sar sly 6f :221 :452 :572 1:094 3↑Ⓕ HnrblMsH-G3 **105** 6 6 64½ 42 3½ 1½ Prado E S L114 2.50 93– 13 WillOntheMov114½ ShinAgin120no SmoknFrolic1171 3 wide move, gamely 6
27Jun03-9Bel fst 6f :223 :453 :572 1:093 4↑ⒻⓇ XtraHeat65k **106** 2 4 43½ 4¾ 21 2no Velazquez J R L120 *.80 91– 18 Ⓓ RdhdRiot118no *WillOnthMov*1208¾ FrshTrcks116no Drifted in, out, brush 5
Placed first through disqualification

Windsor Castle

Own: Dogwood Stable

B. h. 6 (Feb) OBSMAR00 $45,000
Sire: Lord Carson (Carson City) $6,000
Dam: Frigidette (It's Freezing)
Br: Windwoods Farm (Ky)
Tr: Alexander Frank A(0 0 0 0 .00) 2003:(147 20 .14)

Life	28	6	7	5	$591,255	110	
2003	7	2	1	1	$165,880	109	
2002	11	1	2	4	$167,275	110	
	0	0	0	0	$0	–	
D.Fst	19	4	4	3	$430,755	110	
Wet(385)	8	2	3	1	$154,780	104	
Turf(285)	1	0	0	1	$5,720	96	
Dst(0)	0	0	0	0	$0	–	

23Jly03-8Sar gd	1⅛	⊗:471 1:113 1:371 1:50	4↑Alw 58000c	94	3	54½	44½	32	45½	39¾	Santos J A	L121	3.90	75-15	EveningAttire1216¾ Onthedeanslist1193 WindsorCstle1211½	3 wide, no rally	6
7Jun03-7Del sly	1	:24 :463 1:11 1:363	3↑BrandywinH100k	70	3	43	45	35	312	422½	Gryder A T	L120	2.70	78-13	Bowman's Band116nk *Private Lap*11820 Justification1142¼	Flattened out	5
17May03-11Pim gd	1⅛	:481 1:124 1:372 1:50	3↑WDShferH-G3	104	7	44	44	42	12½	11¾	Santos J A	L117	4.70	94-12	WndsrCstl1171¾ Chngnththr1131¾ TmpstFgt1161	Stalked,4wd 3/16,drvng	8
26Apr03-8Aqu sly	1	⊗:231 :46 1:094 1:333	3↑FtMarcyH-G3	96	5	42	53	25	28	28½	Coa E M	L119	7.50	88-12	Saint Verre1178½ *Windsor Castle*1191 Judge's Case1151¾	Rallied for place	8
29Mar03-11GP fst	1¼	:48 1:123 1:38 2:041	3↑GPH-G2	87	6	46½	44½	74	812	816	Coa E M	L115	6.60	71-24	Hero's Tribute1154 Aeneas1151 Puzzlement1141½	Gave way turn	8
22Feb03-11GP fst	1⅛	:463 1:102 1:353 1:49	3↑DonnH-G1	104	4	97¼	911	78	66¾	65¾	Coa E M	L116	4.70	91-13	HrlnsHolidy1202½ *HerosTribute*1141½ Puzzlement114nk	Stdy, hit rail 1st trn	11
11Jan03-10GP fst	1 1/16	:231 :463 1:102 1:421	3↑HalHopeH-G3	109	4	83¾	73¾	73¾	52	11½	Coa E M	L115	4.70	98-12	WindsorCastle1151½ SaintVerre114nk Najran1142¾	Swung out, going away	8

Winter Garden

Own: DiGiulio F D Jr

B. f. 4 (Mar) KEEOCT01 $30,000
Sire: Roy (Fappiano) $10,000
Dam: Hillsburgh Rumors (Bold Ruckus)
Br: Anomaly Investments LP (Ky)
Tr: Tiller Robert P(0 0 0 0 .00) 2003:(254 73 .29)

Life	12	8	1	2	$549,328	93	
2003	9	6	1	2	$470,826	93	
2002	3	2	0	0	$78,502	75	
	0	0	0	0	$0	–	
D.Fst	10	7	1	2	$507,186	93	
Wet(436)	2	1	0	0	$42,142	75	
Turf(356)	0	0	0	0	$0	–	
Dst(0)	0	0	0	0	$0	–	

16Nov03-8WO fst	7f	:223 :454 1:11 1:24	3↑ⒻBessarbH-G3	84	4	3	5½	1½	1hd	11	Clark D	L121	*1.10	84-18	WinterGrden1211 ElPrdoEssence1201¼ MilleFeville1155	3w, drew out late	7
25Oct03-9WO fst	6f	:222 :451 :573 1:102	3↑ⒻOntFashnH136k	93	4	2	31	2hd	1hd	11	Clark D	L119	*.75	92-16	*WinterGrden*1191 MilleFeville115½ SheilsProspect115hd	Stalk 3w, held well	6
21Sep03-6WO fst	7f	:223 :46 1:111 1:24	3↑ⒻAlw 78500N$Y	93	8	1	1hd	1hd	1½	1hd	Clark D	L117	2.75	84-20	*WntrGrdn*117hd *OnforRos*1201½ MystrousAffr1203¼	Duel 4w,held on gamely	8
9Aug03-5WO fst	7f	:221 :45 1:102 1:24	ⒻDuchess-G3	83	2	3	1hd	1hd	2hd	2½	Sutherland C	L120	*1.30	83-16	*FinallyHere*117½ Ⓓ*WinterGrden*120½ *MissCrissy*1181¾	Very game inside lane	8
Disqualified and placed third																	
26Jly03-3WO fst	6½f	:222 :451 1:10 1:164	ⒻAlw 80900NC	92	4	1	2½	2hd	11	12	Sutherland C	L119	*.25	91-10	WinterGrden1192 SmrtAngl117½ ExpctdSong1175	Press outside,drew off	6
22Jun03-3WO fst	7f	:22 :443 1:092 1:22	3↑ⒻSwtBriarTo108k	92	2	4	41	51¼	44	25½	Sutherland C	L115	5.15	88-09	HrmonyLodge1175½ *WinterGrdn*1151 *ActingDputy*117¾	3w,bump steady 3/16	6
19May03-8WO fst	1 1/16	:224 :463 1:12 1:441	ⒻSelene-G1	84	4	2hd	1½	1hd	3nk	34½	Sutherland C	L118	3.70	80-16	*Too Late Now*1162½ Handpainted1182 WinterGarden1181¼	Inside, gave way	9
2May03-8WO fst	6f	:22 :451 :572 1:102	3↑ⒻOClm 80000(80-75)N	88	2	5	32½	21	12½	13¼	Sutherland C	L118	*1.00	92-17	WintrGrdn1183¼ TckyAffir1203½ WhistlingMid1205¼	Stalk 2w,drew off 3 w	5
5Apr03-8WO fst	6f	:214 :441 :562 1:09	ⒻStarShoot143k	85	2	2	1hd	1½	1hd	1½	Sutherland C	L116	12.20	99-03	*Winter Garden*116½ *Hour of Justice*1162 Buffalo Jump1182¾	Gamely off rail	6

Wonder Again

Own: Phillips Joan G. and John W

B. m. 5 (Feb)
Sire: Silver Hawk (Roberto) $75,000
Dam: Ameriflora (Danzig)
Br: Phillips Racing Partnership & John Phillips (Ky)
Tr: Toner James J(0 0 0 0 .00) 2003:(102 13 .13)

	Life	14	5	2	2	$499,915	103	D.Fst	1	0	0	0	$0	47
	2003	6	1	1	1	$176,075	103	Wet(302)	1	0	0	1	$4,840	49
	2002	8	4	1	1	$323,840	97	Turf(378)	12	5	2	1	$495,075	103
								Dst(0)	0	0	0	0	$0	-

5Oct03-8Kee fm 1³⁄₁₆ ① .48⁴1:12⁴ 1:38 1:55⁴ 3↑ⒻWnStGlxy-G2	79	4	3⁶	2¹¹	2¹¹	3⁹	4⁹³⁄₄	Prado E S	L121	2.70	82– 10 Bien Nicole121⁷¼ Approach116¹¼ New Economy121¹¼	Empty in drive	6
20Sep03-9Bel fm 1 ① .22² .45² 1:09 1:33 3↑ⒻNblDmslH-G3	102	11	8⁹³⁄₄	8⁶³⁄₄	5²¹⁄₂	3¹¹⁄₂	1ⁿᵏ	Prado E S	L117	6.10	95– 05 WonderAgin117ⁿᵏ Dncl114ⁿᵏ SomethingVnturd115¹³⁄₄	Inside move, gamely	11
23Aug03-8Sar fm 1¹⁄₁₆ ①⊞ .23² .47¹ 1:11 1:41 3↑ⒻBlSpaBCH-G3	87	5	6⁵³⁄₄	6⁴¹⁄₄	6³³⁄₄	8⁴	8⁴³⁄₄	Prado E S	L117	3.20	94– – Stylish116¹⁄₂ Snow Dance117¹ Cozzy Corner112ʰᵈ	Came wide, empty	9
26Jly03-8Sar fm 1¹⁄₈ ① .49 1:13 1:36³ 1:47⁴ 3↑ⒻDianaH-G1	100	5	2¹	2¹⁄₂	2¹⁄₂	3ⁿᵏ	5²³⁄₄	Prado E S	L118	3.85	87– 10 Voodoo Dancer120ⁿᵏ Heat Hazel181⁴³⁄₄ Pertuisane115³⁄₄	Between rivals, tired	8
7Jun03-8Bel sf 1 ① .24¹ .49¹ 1:16¹¹ 1:43¹ 3↑ⒻUsAGmBCH-G3	103	3	6⁹¹⁄₂	6⁹³⁄₄	5¹¹⁄₄	4³	3²	Prado E S	L119	*2.65	42– 46 Mariensky116² Riskaverse119ʰᵈ WonderAgain119⁶¹⁄₄	Traffic inside stretch	8
3May03-8Aqu fm 1¹⁄₁₆ ① .23¹ .48¹ 1:12¹ 1:42¹ 3↑ⒻBeaugayH-G3	98	5	3²	4¹¹⁄₂	4¹	1ʰᵈ	2¹⁄₂	Velazquez J R	L118	2.90	92– 05 DeltPrincess113¹⁄₂ WondrAgin118²³⁄₄ VoodooDncr1202³⁄₄	Game finish between	9

Xtra Heat

Own: Classic Star Stable LLC

B. m. 6 (Mar)
Sire: Dixieland Heat (Dixieland Band) $6,000
Dam: Begin (Hatchet Man)
Br: P. McLean Sr., P. McLean Jr., M. McLean, P. Feringa Jr (Ky)
Tr: Salzman J E Sr(0 0 0 0 .00) 2003:(371 54 .15)

	Life	35	26	5	2	$2,389,635	120	D.Fst	32	24	4	2	$2,163,305	120
	2003	2	2	0	0	$150,000	105	Wet(333)	3	2	1	0	$226,330	108
	2002	11	7	2	1	$965,485	111	Turf(277)	0	0	0	0	$0	-
								Dst(0)	0	0	0	0	$0	-

22Feb03-10Lrl sly 7f .22⁴ .45² 1:10³1:24³ 3↑ⒷBFrtcheH-G2	99	3	1¹¹⁄₂	Wilson R	L125	*1.00	84– 14 Xtra Heat125¹²¼ Carson Hollow119¹¼ Spelling113ʰᵈ	Fog,when rdy 2w,drvng	7
18Jan03-8Lrl fst 6f .23 .46 .57²1:09² 4↑ⒻWhatASummr52k	105	4	1¹	1¹	1²¹⁄₂	1²	1²³⁄₄	Wilson R	L122	*.20	92– 26 Xtra Heat122²³⁄₄ Gazillion119³¼ Bernie's Gold117²	Rail, mild hand ride	6

Yell

Own: Claiborne Farm and Dilschneider Adele

Dk. b or b. f. 4 (Apr)
Sire: A.P. Indy (Seattle Slew) $300,000
Dam: Wild Applause (Northern Dancer)
Br: Claiborne Farm & Mrs. Adele Dilschneider (Ky)
Tr: McGaughey III Claude R(0 0 0 0 .00) 2003:(259 48 .19)

Life	11	4	1	2	$441,077	102	D.Fst	11	4	1	2	$441,077	102
2003	9	3	1	1	$408,527	102	Wet(393)	0	0	0	0	$0	–
2002	2	1	0	1	$32,550	92	Turf(368)	0	0	0	0	$0	–
	0	0	0	0	$0	–	Dst(0)	0	0	0	0	$0	–

8Nov03-9CD	fst	1	:23 :454 1:11 1:362	3↑ⒻCDDstafH-G2	85	8 84¾ 88¼ 76¾ 77¼ 66¾	Day P	L116	*.80	78-20	*LeadStory*114½ AwesomeHumor1181¼ BorntoDnce1133¼	8w lane,no factor	10
10Oct03-9Kee	fst	7f	:214 :441 1:092 1:213	ⒻRavenRun-G3	102	9 9 94¼ 95¾ 31½ 12½	Day P	L123	*1.50	96-11	Yell1232½ Ebony Breeze123¾ *Tina Bull*117no	Rallied 5w,drvg,clear	12
24Aug03-9Sar	fst	7f	:223 :45 1:09 1:221	3↑ⒻBalrinaH-G1	95	1 6 62¼ 64½ 64¼ 42¼	Day P	L113	12.60	94-12	*HrmonyLodge*115no ShineAgin1202 GoldMovr118hd	Altered course stretch	8
19Jly03-9Bel	fst	1½	:462 1:113 2:033 2:31	ⒻCCAOaks-G1	76	3 32½ 1½ 22½ 38½ 410¼	Velazquez J R	L121	1.55	67-17	Spoken Fur1213½ Fircroft1212½ Savedbythelight1214¼	Close up, tired	7
28Jun03-9Bel	fst	1⅛	:462 1:113 1:37 1:502	ⒻMthrGoos-G1	95	3 31½ 31½ 41¼ 38½ 25¼	Velazquez J R	L121	*1.45	73-19	*Spoken Fur*1215¼ Yell121¾ Final Round1218¼	Good finish outside	6
2May03-10CD	fst	1⅛	:46 1:10 1:353 1:483	ⒻKyOaks-G1	95	6 65½ 63½ 52½ 51¾ 33¼	Velazquez J R	L121	6.80	92-07	*Bird Town*1213¼ Santa Catarina121hd Yell121¾	Bmp,ck sharply early	12
5Apr03-8Kee	fst	1 1/16	:243 :483 1:122 1:432	ⒻAshland-G1	88	1 52½ 54 53½ 47 49½	Velazquez J R	L120	2.30	80-20	Elloluv1203¾ Lady Tak123¾ Holiday Lady1165	4w,empty in drive	7
23Feb03-9GP	fst	1 1/16	:23 :471 1:12 1:444	ⒻDvonaDal-G2	96	4 33½ 33 31½ 11½ 16	Velazquez J R	L117	5.20	85-19	Yell1176 *Ivanavinalot*1215¾ Gold Player1153	3 wide, drew off	5
16Jan03-9GP	fst	170	:233 :482 1:132 1:421	ⒻAlw 34000n1x	84	5 31½ 21 2½ 1hd 1nk	Velazquez J R	L121	*.60	90-18	*Yell*121nk *Bird Town*1195½ Marnesia Light1172¼	All out, prevailed	7

You

Own: Gann Edmund A

Dk. b or b. m. 5 (Feb)
Sire: You and I (Kris S.) $6,500
Dam: Our Dani (Homebuilder)
Br: Dolphus C. Morrison (Ky)
Tr: Frankel Robert J(0 0 0 0 .00) 2003:(411 114 .28)

Life	23	9	8	2	$2,101,353	107	D.Fst	19	8	6	1	$1,820,273	107
2003	8	2	4	1	$677,108	103	Wet(381)	4	1	2	1	$281,080	96
2002	9	4	2	1	$883,805	105	Turf(220)	0	0	0	0	$0	–
	0	0	0	0	$0	–	Dst(0)	0	0	0	0	$0	–

5Oct03-8Kee	fst	1⅛	:47 1:103 1:354 1:492	3↑ⒻSpinster-G1	99	2 21½ 2½ 1hd 21½ 2hd	Bailey J D	L123	2.00	93-13	Take Charge Lady123hd You1234 Miss Linda123¾	Drift,bmp start,gamely	6
13Sep03-9Bel	fst	1 1/16	:23 :454 1:10 1:411	3↑ⒻRuffianH-G1	103	3 11½ 11 1hd 22 23½	Coa E M	L118	4.30	90-19	Wild Spirit1213½ You1185 Passing Shot1155½	Pace, second best	6
24Aug03-9Sar	fst	7f	:223 :45 1:09 1:221	3↑ⒻBalrinaH-G1	88	7 4 52 74¾ 79¼ 75½	Castellano J J	L120	3.75	90-12	*HarmonyLodge*115no ShineAgain1202 GoldMover118hd	5 wide, no response	8
13Jly03-4Hol	fst	7f	:22 :443 1:083 1:212	3↑ⒻAGleamH-G2	100	1 4 44 43 33½ 21½	Bailey J D	LB121	*1.20	93-15	Cee's Elegance1161½ You121no Affluent1192	Came out,game for 2nd	5
14Jun03-9CD	fst	1⅛	:48 1:114 1:363 1:49	3↑ⒻFlrDLisH-G2	103	2 21½ 21 2½ 12 13¾	Bailey J D	L119	*.50	93-04	You1193¾ Printemps114nk Nonsuch Bay114hd	4w,stiff drive,clear	6
17May03-8Bel	fst	1	:224 :452 1:092 1:342	3↑ⒻShuveeH-G2	97	1 12 1½ 1hd 3½ 34¾	Bridgmohan S X	L120	*1.45	89-17	*Wild Spirit*1153½ Smok'n Frolic1191¼ *You*1204¼	Set pace, tired	6
2May03-8CD	fst	1 1/16	:231 :454 1:10 1:431	3↑ⒻLouvlBCH-G2	90	2 1½ 2hd 2hd 12½ 17¾	Bailey J D	L118	*.30	92-07	You1187¾ Fly Borboleta1111 Seven FourSeven1139¾	Dueled,drew off,drvg	5
16Feb03-6SA	gd	1 1/16	:23 :461 1:104 1:423	4↑ⒻSntMriaH-G1	95	5 3nk 21 4¾ 21½ 24½	Desormeaux K J	LB118	1.30	86-16	*Starrer*1194½ *You*118½ Rhiana1127	Re-bid 3wd,held 2nd	5

Zavata
Own: Tabor Michael B

B. c. 4 (Feb) FTFFEB02 $575,000
Sire: Phone Trick (Clever Trick) $25,000
Dam: Pert Lady (Cox's Ridge)
Br: Mill Ridge, Jamm Ltd. & Dr. J. Chandler (Ky)
Tr: Biancone Patrick L(0 0 0 0 .00) 2003:(135 26 .19)

Life	13	5	1	1	$346,533	112	D.Fst	12	5	1	1	$344,853	112
2003	7	2	0	0	$120,493	112	Wet(362)	1	0	0	0	$1,680	75
2002	6	3	1	1	$226,040	102	Turf(242)	0	0	0	0	$0	–
	0	0	0	0	$0	–	Dst(0)	0	0	0	0	$0	–

26Dec03–8SA fst 7f :222 :45 1:0911:223 Malibu-G1 **69** 12 2 41¾ 75 1214 1216¾ Desormeaux K J B117 b 16.50 76–12 SouthernImage115hd MrinoMrini1151 MidsEyes1193 Wide trip,weakened 12
25Oct03–5SA fst 6f :21 :431 :55 1:074 3↑BCSprint-G1 **86** 1 5 1hd 41¼ 65½ 1212¾ Stevens G L B123 28.40 86–05 CajunBeat1232¼ Bluesthestndrd1262 ShkeYouDown126½ Dueled rail, tired 13
5Oct03–7SA fst 6f :212 :432 :552 1:08 3↑AnTtlBCH-G1 **97** 3 4 42¾ 32 52¼ 53½ Stevens G L B116 7.30 94–06 Avnzdo1161½ CptinSquire117hd Bluesthstndrd1151½ Stalked inside,no bid 6
23Aug03–10Sar fst 7f :213 :433 1:083 1:22 KngsBshp-G1 **90** 8 4 54½ 55 55¼ 87½ Bailey J D 123 *1.25 89–07 Valid Video121nk Great Notion117nk *Ghostzapper*1171¾ Close up, empty 13
2Aug03–8Sar fst 6f :22 :443 :562 1:083 Amstrdam-G2 **112** 3 4 2hd 2hd 12½ 15¼ Bailey J D 119 3.15 99–07 Zavata1195¼ Great Notion121½ Trust N Luck123nk Vied inside, clear 7
26Jun03–8Mth fst 6f :214 :441 :561 1:084 3↑OClm 40000N **99** 2 4 2hd 2½ 1hd 11 Farina T 114 *.80 95–15 *Zavata*1141 Rockin On Ready1142¾ Skip aGrade118nk Inched clear final 1/8 8
24May03–6Bel sly 6f :212 :432 :55 1:074 3↑Alw 56000c **75** 2 1 1hd 34 411 515½ Farina T L112 3.15 84–11 True Direction1234¼ *Well Fancied*1134½ Vodka1152 Speed inside, tired 5

Zonk
Own: Fox Hill Farms Inc

Ch. m. 6 (Apr) KEESEP99 $85,000
Sire: Farma Way (Marfa)
Dam: In Concert (Riverman)
Br: Vinery & Dale Nelson (Ky)
Tr: Servis John C(0 0 0 0 .00) 2003:(325 62 .19)

Life	21	7	5	1	$559,476	100	D.Fst	17	6	4	1	$499,476	100
2003	3	1	0	0	$77,760	94	Wet(274)	3	1	1	0	$60,000	92
2002	6	2	2	0	$144,516	98	Turf(307)	1	0	0	0	$0	69
	0	0	0	0	$0	–	Dst(0)	0	0	0	0	$0	–

16Jly03–8Bel fst 6f :22 :45 :57 1:093 3↑ⒻMyJuliet65k **52** 5 7 53½ 77¾ 716 718 Elliott S L123 f 7.30 73–15 Zawzooth116¾ Forest Heiress1232¼ Redhead Riot120½ 4 wide trip, tired 7
22Feb03–10Lrl sly 7f :224 :452 1:103 1:243 3↑ⒻBFrtcheH-G2 **92** 5 43 Elliott S L117 f 3.10 81–14 Xtra Heat1251¾ *Carson Hollow*1191¼ Spelling113hd Fog,chased 4w,flattned 7
11Jan03–8Aqu fst 1¹⁄₁₆ ⊡ :221 :454 1:112 1:442 3↑ⒻAfectnyH-G3 **94** 5 410 33½ 11 18 14 Lopez C C L118 *2.00 84–16 Zonk1184 Wishful Splendor112nk Kiss a Miss1137¾ With something left 7

Zosima
Own: Darley Stable

Dk. b or b. f. 3 (May)
Sire: Capote (Seattle Slew) $30,000
Dam: Grafin (Miswaki)
Br: Darley (Ky)
Tr: Harty Eoin G(0 0 0 0 .00) 2003:(110 30 .27)

Life	5	3	1	0	$135,440	89	D.Fst	5	3	1	0	$135,440	89
2003	5	3	1	0	$135,440	89	Wet(364)	0	0	0	0	$0	–
2002	0	M	0	0	$0	–	Turf(278)	0	0	0	0	$0	–
	0	0	0	0	$0	–	Dst(0)	0	0	0	0	$0	–

25Oct03–3SA fst 1¹⁄₁₆ :224 :464 1:104 1:423 ⒻBCJuvFil-G1 **75** 11 43 127½ 94¼ 89¾ 513¾ Day P LB119 24.20 77–07 Halfbridled1192½ *Ashado*119nk *Victory U. S. A.*1199¼ Steadied first turn 14
27Sep03–9AP fst 1 :23 :454 1:101 1:36 ⒻArlWaLas-G3 **89** 5 21 32 32 22 11 Day P L118 2.70 88–10 Zosima1181 Everyday Angel1163½ Cryptos' Best1181 Angled out, driving 10
17Aug03–4AP fst 6f :222 :462 :59 1:12 ⒻAlw 32000N1x **71** 4 2 41 1½ 1½ 12 Bourque C C L117 *.90 84–12 *Zosima*1172 Willow Cove119½ *Stormy Rosa*11710 Drew off, driving 6
27Jly03–6AP fst 5½f :222 :463 :59 1:054 ⒻSilverMadn53k **73** 4 4 42½ 42½ 24 23½ Bourque C C L117 3.20 81–18 *Sweet Jo Jo*1173½ *Zosima*11710 Lady's Room117¾ Second best 8
4Jly03–4AP fst 5f :222 :463 :592 ⒻMd Sp Wt 26k **65** 8 6 51¼ 2hd 11½ 14½ Bourque C C L118 b *.80 89–15 Zosima1184½ Speak Easy118no *Willow Cove*1181½ Ridden out 8

RECORDS OF 2003 LEADERS

OWNERS
TRAINERS
JOCKEYS

(MONEY AND RACES WON)

ANNUAL LEADERS

(MONEY AND RACES WON)

LIFETIME RECORDS
OF LEADING JOCKEYS

Leading Owners in 2003 by Money Won

Owner	St	1st	2d	3d	Purses
Michael J. Gill	2,235	425	339	267	$9,236,530
Stronach Stable	622	126	112	63	7,289,114
Juddmonte Farms, Inc.	122	33	21	12	6,265,030
Edmund A. Gann	83	25	19	8	5,848,681
Richard A. Englander	1,182	227	190	163	5,359,759
Melnyk, Eugene and Laura	455	92	65	60	4,123,765
John Franks	988	143	134	120	4,083,255
Sam-Son Farms	201	44	31	31	3,864,116
The Thoroughbred Corp	227	44	41	26	3,486,782
Gustav Schickedanz	106	29	9	8	*3,361,790
Diamond A Racing Corp	48	10	9	6	3,234,070
Lewis, Robert B. and Beverly J.	312	41	40	46	2,948,528
Stonerside Stable LLC	177	31	21	34	2,841,259
Heiligbrodt Racing Stable	305	64	55	38	2,751,875
Amerman Racing Stables LLC	85	19	14	14	2,610,764
Farish, William S., Elkins Jr., James A. and Webber, Jr., W. Temple	16	9	3	0	2,379,076
Edward P. Evans	222	35	39	32	2,357,266
Moss, Mr. and Mrs. Jerome S.	184	42	29	32	2,344,501
Ramsey, Kenneth L. and Sarah K.	334	81	51	36	2,338,452
Frank Carl Calabrese	457	138	69	55	2,259,392
WinStar Farm LLC	266	56	57	28	2,243,263
Dogwood Stable	287	35	39	33	2,204,564
Sackatoga Stable	21	7	3	4	2,089,125
Augustin Stable	271	45	59	42	2,073,396
Einar Paul Robsham	284	49	45	35	1,984,847
B. Wayne Hughes	143	30	23	23	1,970,099
Everest Stables, Inc.	293	45	37	35	1,946,597
Dale Baird	1,029	132	140	146	1,939,085
Rosendo G. Parra	448	85	76	52	1,917,263
Wertheimer Farm LLC	77	19	12	10	1,888,058
Nelson Bunker Hunt	334	68	51	54	1,876,572
Bruno Schickedanz	610	92	69	93	1,874,011
Turf Express, Inc.	459	113	76	55	1,852,690
Overbrook Farm	344	46	40	39	1,851,634
Paraneck Stable	341	33	43	40	1,799,984
Marylou Whitney Stables	160	20	26	20	1,768,908
Stonecrest Farm	57	13	6	7	1,746,137
Joseph V. Shields, Jr.	72	16	10	13	1,739,508
Robert L. Cole, Jr.	230	57	50	31	1,697,403
Frank D. DiGiulio, Jr.	72	26	13	7	1,620,839
Buckram Oak Farm	210	30	30	36	1,585,724
Sheik Maktoum bin Rashid Al Maktoum	51	9	8	7	1,561,558
Alpine Stable	230	39	27	40	1,550,985
Maggi Moss	449	83	68	60	1,529,749
Joseph Allen	50	10	15	4	1,529,352
Golden Eagle Farm	312	38	50	51	1,527,311
G. Watts Humphrey, Jr.	207	30	30	28	1,487,756
Michael B. Tabor	80	15	14	10	1,487,014
Godolphin Racing, Inc.	39	5	6	9	1,460,204
Gumpster Stable LLC	470	82	81	67	1,458,438
Pin Oak Stable LLC	144	31	24	25	1,414,678
Jay Em Ess Stable	211	35	42	33	1,388,519
J. Paul Reddam	83	10	14	10	1,382,791
Anstu Stables, Inc.	62	15	8	9	1,381,599
Craig, Sidney H. and Jenny	108	20	16	12	1,360,447
Live Oak Plantation	206	39	28	24	1,357,133
John C. Oxley	73	12	8	11	1,338,124
Gary A. Tanaka	135	16	15	15	1,335,756
Hwy 1 Racing Stable LLC	527	90	62	73	1,330,550
Flaxman Holdings, Ltd.	16	7	2	2	1,317,392
Coast To Coast Racing Fund LLC	222	54	35	32	1,303,070
Louis D. O'Brien	708	208	136	112	1,293,698
Wygod, Mr. and Mrs. Martin J.	113	30	20	14	1,262,507
K. K. Sangara	195	35	29	38	1,259,162
Darley Stable	72	11	11	9	1,246,095
Tabor, Michael and Magnier, Mrs. John	15	1	3	3	1,231,920
Flying Zee Stable	366	55	58	46	1,218,238
Tucci Stables	88	22	13	11	1,206,855
Jayeff B Stables	207	39	30	24	1,171,328
Darley Stud Management LLC	105	27	19	8	1,155,158
Wills, Catherine and Karches, Peter	8	3	2	1	1,147,900
Jeffrey Sengara	95	23	19	16	1,139,382
Claiborne Farm	71	19	15	7	1,137,430
Team Valor Stables LLC	101	26	10	16	1,136,999
Padua Stables	201	40	36	31	1,125,698
Michael H. Sherman	453	69	74	65	1,106,447
Earle I. Mack	56	11	6	11	1,096,098
Richter, Kristine and John	111	30	19	15	1,089,326
Daniel J. Chen	660	132	98	75	1,079,683
Allen E. Paulson Living Trust	40	8	9	3	1,075,118
Broman, Mary R. and Chester, Sr.	222	35	26	22	1,069,881
Moore, Susan and John	65	18	15	11	1,067,129
Stan E. Fulton	107	21	14	11	1,058,637
Charles E. Fipke	36	4	10	5	1,044,810
West, Gary L. and Mary E.	138	39	19	20	1,033,453
Leatherman, Lee and Ty	22	3	8	2	1,032,202
Smith, Derrick and Tabor, Michael	17	11	3	2	1,029,355
Sondra D. Bender	130	22	17	13	1,025,859
Come By Chance Stable	62	12	5	4	1,021,037
Jayaraman, Kalarikkal K. and Vilasini D.	137	32	29	18	1,017,692
Tom R. Durant	202	44	41	33	1,009,820
Runnin Horse Farm, Inc.	272	47	45	35	1,003,351
Joseph Higgins	10	3	3	1	1,000,910
James McIngvale	74	13	16	2	999,519
Hobeau Farm	131	23	32	24	995,640
P. T. K. Racing LLC	372	45	65	55	992,810
Kenneth W. Murphy	252	66	43	31	984,520
Minshall Farms	127	16	15	15	983,807
Gainsborough Farm LLC	31	5	6	4	980,722
Chisholm, James, Jarvis, Michael, Reddam, J. Paul, et al	4	2	1	0	980,000
Sumaya Us Stables	14	7	1	2	972,874
Robert D. Bone	178	64	22	23	970,440
Thomas F. Van Meter, II	25	9	4	4	948,620
Willmott Stables, Inc.	82	15	8	12	941,754
Pyrite Stables	412	54	56	57	936,950
Jacks or Better Farm, Inc.	184	31	36	24	921,645
Glen C. Warren	93	16	15	6	916,006
Mac Fehsenfeld	135	15	9	20	911,553
Barry K. Schwartz	117	28	22	16	910,274
Beatrice Oxenberg	38	10	7	7	910,240
George Krikorian	49	6	11	10	907,923
E and G Stables	184	60	33	33	907,269
Patricia A. Generazio	238	27	36	33	905,531
Cees Stable LLC	38	8	5	5	904,592
Winterbeck Manor Stud	1	1	0	0	900,000
Billy Hays	426	76	64	45	890,448
Cowan, Marjorie and Irving M.	81	12	14	18	885,900
Kinsman Stable	119	25	15	15	885,166
Elizabeth Walsh	234	43	41	36	882,143
Luis Alfredo Taunay	12	6	0	2	878,347
Monarch Stables, Inc.	307	53	62	36	868,484
Hollendorfer, Jerry and Todaro, George	227	43	53	35	866,163
Glen Hill Farm	138	31	28	16	863,870
Dominion Bloodstock, Ball, Derek and Galbraith, Hugh	145	14	18	22	858,021
Steven M. Asmussen	223	72	36	29	856,710
Janis R. Whitham	65	15	14	10	850,290
Tracy Farmer	155	23	20	20	841,877

Owner	St	1st	2d	3d	Purses
M. Y. Stables, Inc.	292	61	58	26	840,658
Wilson, David W. and Holly F.	120	22	16	21	837,902
Keith I. Asmussen	115	28	24	16	835,194
William S. Farish	99	16	14	13	814,445
Select Stable	22	3	4	3	806,971
John Atto	116	23	13	14	803,852
John D. Murphy, Sr.	235	34	33	39	801,354
Colebrook Farms	218	22	27	24	796,396
Brushwood Stable	57	12	9	7	795,260
Irish Acres Farm	287	35	38	24	794,854
J. Mack Robinson	221	25	40	33	792,622
Audre Cappuccitti	214	16	26	28	790,867
Peachtree Stable	112	21	18	15	780,694
Klein, Richard, Bertram and Elaine	139	27	25	11	780,634
Shadwell Stable	91	21	14	10	775,108
Cobra Farm, Inc.	103	21	17	14	774,562
Flaxman Stable	9	3	2	0	770,960
Equils, James W. and Marcia S.	185	31	24	31	764,935
Dennis E. Weir	206	51	41	26	763,432
Fox Ridge Farm, Inc.	94	11	7	18	762,815
Knob Hill Stable	65	10	12	3	762,234
Cohen, Philip and Marcia and Klesaris, Steve B.	83	23	15	12	758,561
C D and G Stable	303	41	53	59	758,063
Gilbert G. Campbell	144	24	25	21	756,280
Peter Vegso	145	19	13	20	752,345
Robert V. La Penta	49	12	8	5	742,019
Red Oak Stable	84	9	11	19	741,925
Russell L. Reineman Stable, Inc.	161	30	23	24	732,415
Flatbird Stable	44	11	5	5	729,040
Valene Farms	119	27	19	17	721,655
Michael E. Pegram	115	20	19	11	721,238
Team Block	140	17	22	17	717,960
Claiborne Farm and Dilschneider, Adele B.	30	8	2	4	713,530
Bohemia Stable	68	12	16	6	709,546
Kelynack Racing Stable, Inc.	52	11	6	9	707,709
Arnold Zetcher	52	6	5	4	704,724
DiGiulio, Jr., Frank and Tiller, R. P.	40	11	7	6	704,574
Roddy J. Valente	82	21	12	8	701,504
William C. Schettine	73	10	12	12	698,321
Haras Santa Maria de Araras	131	15	14	24	695,872
Schwartz, Herbert T. and Carol A.	115	12	13	10	694,827
Headley, Aase and Leung, Paul	6	3	1	1	688,000
Gold N. Z. Stable	155	42	33	17	685,589
Courtlandt Farms	66	15	12	7	684,926
Kaaren J. Biggs	3	2	1	0	682,000
Asiel Stable	128	24	16	18	680,628
Francis C. McDonnell	219	38	33	30	676,568
Padua Stable and Iracane, John and Joseph	2	2	0	0	675,600
3rd Turn Stables LLC	25	7	1	4	675,018
Desperado Stables, Inc., McFadden, Donnie and Merrill Stables, et al	4	3	0	0	668,730
Fog City Stable	72	12	7	9	664,204
Acclaimed Racing Stable	148	36	22	15	663,822
Centaur Farms, Inc.	132	18	21	20	658,792
John D. Gunther	73	15	8	14	654,591
Jones, Aaron U. and Marie D.	70	7	13	9	653,906
Michael Bello	21	5	3	7	653,477
Carlo D'Amato	158	13	13	20	648,073
Hardwicke Stable	91	17	19	11	645,703
S J B, Jr. Stable	147	25	18	20	645,494
Lanning, Curt and Lila	196	32	19	32	645,346
Kingfield Farms	62	11	10	9	644,383
Saud bin Khaled	49	12	6	2	642,877
Edward E. Turner	104	32	14	13	641,169
Nico Nierenberg	49	9	5	7	640,825
Jack J. Armstrong	258	53	38	31	639,170
William A. Sorokolit, Sr.	85	10	10	8	638,998
Starlight Stables LLC, Saylor, Paul and Martin, John	7	5	1	1	637,800
Ackerley Brothers Farm	68	14	13	17	633,314
Hancock, III, Arthur B. and Healy, Gerald F.	18	2	3	3	630,630
Iron County Farms, Inc.	102	11	11	25	628,420
West Point Thoroughbreds LLC	67	16	10	9	625,278
Charles, Ronald L. and Clear Valley Stables	84	12	13	14	623,880
William Stiritz	163	34	25	24	620,618
Red Baron's Barn LLC	118	20	20	10	618,577
Fox Hill Farms, Inc.	65	21	9	11	603,228
Martin L. Cherry	65	15	12	13	596,627
S L U, Inc.	109	12	14	16	593,527
New Farm	87	20	5	8	593,438
James R. Lewis, Jr.	120	16	25	19	593,395
Kirkwood, Al and Saundra S.	79	15	14	15	590,102
Mark Yagour, Inc.	530	71	66	66	589,364
Galopp LLC	9	5	2	0	579,000
Martin S. Schwartz	57	7	10	10	578,044
Harris Farms, Inc.	134	22	20	26	576,848
Home Team Stables	196	39	35	30	576,526
Edwin Thomas Broome	109	25	22	17	573,130
John Cardella	85	11	17	11	571,214
James F. Edwards	49	12	6	6	570,248
Klaravich Stables, Inc.	46	9	5	7	565,538
Chisholm, James, Horizon Stable and Jarvis, Michael, et al	5	2	1	1	564,860
Our Sugar Bear Stable	80	17	11	8	557,495
Richard Otto Stables, Inc.	36	16	2	5	557,222
Love 2 Win Stable	69	17	9	15	553,258
Armando Lage	122	32	25	18	552,973
Executors Of The Late Lord Weinstock	1	1	0	0	551,200
Jerry Frankel	27	8	4	2	548,389
Starlight Stable LLC	57	10	13	10	547,782
Noctis Stable, Papiano, Neil and Taub, Steve	28	7	7	2	545,220
Robert E. Meyerhoff	124	24	17	22	544,815
Domino Stud of Lexington LLC	41	6	7	6	544,285
Silverton Hill LLC	134	19	17	14	543,460
Walter Wienkowitz	39	9	9	5	542,742
Molinaro Stable	105	17	15	11	542,078
Orion Stables	332	27	26	25	540,209
A. Stevens Miles, Jr.	26	4	3	5	538,730
Carl R. Moore Management LLC	95	23	15	11	538,078
Nick Sanna Stables LLC	107	37	21	16	533,099
Daniel A. Limongelli	204	34	27	34	531,437
Sandra Rasmussen	157	18	26	18	529,584
Steeplechase Farm	68	12	7	10	528,137
Darrell R. Sapp	220	32	43	38	525,016
Carl F. Pollard	96	11	11	8	524,249
Kupferberg, Saul J. and Max	145	18	30	18	521,265
Joseph V. Vitello	9	2	3	0	517,825
Erdenheim Farm	70	12	6	7	516,737
Star Track Farms	114	19	17	11	516,089
William R. Harris	176	18	18	22	514,995
Kuehne Racing	80	14	9	15	514,833
Michael Barkowski	160	25	25	28	514,352
Arthur I. Appleton	130	21	23	21	509,746
Mohammed bin Rashid Al Maktoum	27	10	5	2	509,744
Tom Boy Stable	74	26	15	8	509,297
Robert J. Amendola	107	25	13	14	508,799

Owner	St	1st	2d	3d	Purses
Robert S. Evans	70	12	8	14	507,762
Zuckerman, Donald S. and Roberta Mary	51	12	7	6	506,680
Cornejo Racing, Inc.	24	12	1	1	506,070
Ren-Mar Thoroughbreds	23	10	2	1	505,060
Sapara, James and Alice	33	9	1	2	504,968
Cuchna, John R., Jim Ford Inc. and Pearson, Daron	43	5	7	7	504,600
Waterville Lake Stable	40	6	6	5	503,980
Taylor Mountain Farm LLC	215	20	22	29	503,733
Robert D. Nash	131	27	22	10	503,596
Coleman, John, Dasaro, George, Thompson, James, et al	11	2	3	4	500,300
Donald R. Dizney	126	20	14	14	498,950
James R. Vreeland	35	7	9	3	494,559
Grant, Mary and Joseph and Kelly, Thomas J.	24	3	4	3	494,120
Doneson, Mark and Dubb, Michael	72	8	14	6	491,761
Robert S. Mitchell Trust	100	26	15	13	490,142
Robert Bakerman	164	19	23	17	488,113
Richard L. Duchossois	110	21	11	11	487,770
Wexler Racing Stables, Inc.	207	24	31	22	486,235
Shanley, Michael and Lynn	19	4	0	5	485,572
Green Hills Farm	11	4	1	2	484,569
Jeffrey L. Nielsen	13	1	0	0	483,888
Theodore F. Burnett	64	7	7	10	483,675
William L. Clifton, Jr.	91	15	12	10	482,902
Finney, Albert and Taylor, Mickey and Karen LLC	60	13	10	12	481,544
Karakorum Farm	161	23	16	19	481,471
Hillsbrook Farms	47	6	8	7	481,340
Puglisi Stables	52	10	10	4	480,543
Scott A. Lake	54	17	6	7	480,530
Astor Racing Stable	60	11	9	5	480,143
J B Stables, Inc.	281	26	28	32	479,072
Charles J. Cella	42	6	7	8	478,415
Steven Dwoskin	154	32	23	27	473,997
J D Farms	114	14	16	18	471,071
Paul P. Pompa, Jr.	90	12	18	17	470,873
Louie J. Roussel, III	100	21	8	16	470,545
Fieldstone Farms	42	6	9	4	469,411
Nikolas DeToro	121	15	10	9	465,952
John V. Alecci Stable, Inc.	118	23	19	8	465,751
Prestonwood Farm LLC	11	3	3	1	462,825
TNT Racing Stable	64	15	12	2	460,812
Joseph S. Parisi	125	22	11	18	460,799
Panic Stable LLC	130	24	15	19	459,271
5C Racing Stable LLC	62	9	9	11	458,384
Ronald L. Shenofsky	121	24	16	24	457,465
Tommy Town T'breds LLC	83	14	12	11	455,555
R. Gary Patrick	431	47	43	50	451,363
Royce Jaime	63	13	9	10	449,133
Janelle D. Grum	69	14	15	6	448,962
Rodriguez, Lorraine and Rod	47	11	4	3	448,947
Todd, Aury and Ralph E.	12	1	4	1	448,590
The Elkstone Group LLC	155	22	15	16	447,662
Jer-Mar Stable LLC	90	22	13	14	447,058
Deckert, Jr., Robert and Deckert, Sr., Robert	137	18	14	23	446,741
George Brunacini	112	18	16	11	446,361
Moyglare Stud Farm, Ltd.	18	5	1	0	445,849
Amherst Stable and Spruce Pond Stable	16	0	5	3	444,566
Timber Creek Farm	257	36	33	34	444,514
Braunsdorf, Robert and Levine, Robert	103	16	12	19	444,470
Chandler, Dr. John A.	31	2	8	5	443,232
Walter Family Trust	119	13	21	14	441,763
Charles W. Everett	174	31	29	26	441,009
Billy R. Tucker	14	8	3	0	440,876
Jack L. Boggs	241	40	39	29	439,927
McKeever Racing Stable LLC	59	10	10	5	437,443
Gaillardia Racing LLC	60	7	7	10	435,800
Springfield Stable and Dura Racing	94	4	13	22	435,302
Georgica Stable	26	5	2	1	435,126
James L. Ingalls	264	23	28	29	433,550
Guerino Antonini	49	18	10	6	432,950
Fishelberg, Leonard and Yolanda	67	14	8	12	432,302
William A. Carl	40	7	9	3	429,454
David J. Lanzman Racing, Inc.	92	13	15	18	428,618
Mercedes Stables LLC	70	11	8	10	427,932
Mark E. Casse	48	10	8	4	427,249
Morris Bailey	113	15	21	17	426,396
Gus Goldsmith	149	19	13	18	426,314
Gerald F. Sleeter	64	14	5	9	423,558
Williams, Mr. and Mrs. Larry D.	106	10	21	16	422,275
Bar None Ranches	183	30	33	34	421,293
Harlequin Ranches	46	6	7	8	421,235
Arosa Farms	37	5	2	6	421,085
Worcester Stable	206	38	32	29	420,923
Sabine Stable	72	14	8	8	420,104
C. R. Trout	87	16	9	12	418,654
Equirace.Com LLC	29	5	1	7	418,495
Daniel M. Ryan	114	23	19	16	417,713
David D. Walters	119	25	18	16	416,584
S. A. Partnership	148	11	21	25	415,831
James B. Tafel	125	7	17	16	415,550
D. J. Stable LLC	139	23	23	19	414,691
Destiny Farm LLC	127	22	15	18	413,659
Lazy Lane Farms, Inc.	96	14	16	15	413,605
Alesia, Bran Jam Stable and Ciaglia	69	9	15	11	411,985
Calmar Stables and Ranch	64	10	9	8	411,142
Florence Gemma Siravo	328	42	48	56	410,384
Kitchwa Stables and Nichols, Thomas L.	9	2	0	2	409,392
Goldmart Farms	94	10	14	13	407,616
International Fair Play, Inc.	3	3	0	0	405,000
Lael Stables	90	10	9	7	404,808
Mansell Stables LLC	18	5	5	0	404,582
Wild Horse Stable	143	32	23	14	402,753
Plan B Stable	71	13	14	5	401,024
Santa Cruz Ranch, Inc.	89	10	6	8	401,012
Stubbs Investment, Inc.	89	9	8	13	400,970
Scarberry, Howard and Penny	160	14	27	27	400,338
Our Canterbury Stables	56	10	6	7	399,819
Rose Family Stable	249	26	30	22	399,265
Warren B. Williamson	52	10	12	6	398,756
Win and Place Stable	61	15	13	12	397,523
Bruno Brothers Farms	32	10	2	2	394,671
Cappuccitti, Audre and Gordon	84	5	8	11	394,020
Lawrence Goichman	42	9	12	4	393,385
Michael L. Reavis	78	26	10	12	393,033
Charles E. Simmons	23	6	2	4	390,790
Prime Time Stable	102	16	20	10	390,444
Loren Gale Cox	233	21	27	39	389,887
Kim Noble Hart	136	23	14	12	388,277
Yasou Stable Trust	151	27	22	19	387,282
Hickory Plains Farm LLC	105	17	12	15	387,034
Dennis A. Drazin	111	17	14	18	386,554
Goldish, Marc D. and Savoy Stable	105	13	25	14	385,112
E. A. Ranches	45	7	10	2	384,737
Joseph P. Morey, Jr. Revocable Trust	60	18	12	6	382,733
Cresran LLC	40	9	6	8	382,334
Bennett, Mr. and Mrs. R. J.	107	14	15	20	381,546
Cynthia Phipps	33	5	4	5	381,110

Owner	St	1st	2d	3d	Purses
Lee Lewis	62	8	11	13	380,817
Clarity Stables	29	5	5	5	380,741
C. T. Grether, Inc.	60	5	6	5	380,182
Humphrey, Jr., G. Watts and					
Louise I.	51	8	6	8	378,845
Wright, Mrs. Frank P.	88	17	16	13	374,773
John D. McKee	227	23	25	18	374,516
Heinz Steinmann	72	9	14	3	374,315
Jpf Investments I LLC	51	8	8	6	373,823
Thomas Vanderhyde	155	19	22	22	372,719
Goldfarb, Sanford, Hoffman,					
Stewart and Flesig, Jonathan	9	5	1	1	372,364
Joseph Clark Faulkner	320	64	57	48	371,410
Classic Star Stable LLC	66	10	7	8	370,290
Jam Jar Racing Stable	31	4	6	3	370,186
La Marca Stable	106	18	12	9	369,464
John Rotella	55	11	7	6	369,457
Columbine Stable	57	7	10	9	369,328
Ben Barnow	97	12	14	19	368,661
Charles F. Burnside	129	26	10	18	367,095
Randal, Mr. and Mrs. R. David	19	3	2	5	366,869
Stone Spire LLC	68	17	11	2	366,822
Rey Wan Racing	149	20	18	24	365,750
John Castro	76	12	11	12	365,296
Vincent S. Scuderi	47	12	10	6	364,717
Robert H. Shepard	112	12	16	15	362,144
Karches, Peter F. and					
Rankowitz, Michael	37	11	3	5	362,124
Diamond Oak Stable	72	26	16	5	361,949
Gene Johnson	80	22	11	17	361,646
Tangarae Farms LLP	119	26	18	19	360,118
Robert J. Costigan	6	3	1	1	359,667
R.M.C. Stable	59	9	3	8	359,400
Maine, J. and Baker, R.	22	5	3	3	359,338
Slick 1 Racing	313	54	44	40	357,951
William T. Stradley	31	6	6	4	356,363
Double G Stables LLC	22	3	3	3	355,560
Snow, John, Wildcard Stable,					
Punjab Foods, Mutti, Raj					
and Gomes, Gus	6	4	1	1	354,082
Ivan Dalos	85	8	9	9	351,673
Larry R. Johnson	102	15	15	16	351,521
Parsley, K. and Pettifer, R.	6	3	2	1	351,051
Kagele Brothers, Inc. and					
Bailey, James A.	5	4	0	0	351,000
Ferro Family Trust and					
Bonde, Jeff	24	9	6	1	350,986
Sez Who Racing	73	11	11	7	350,718
McCaffery, Trudy and					
Toffan, John A.	55	7	7	4	350,352
Tricar Stable, Inc.	140	14	16	33	350,270
Joel A. Kligman	65	18	6	10	350,093
Stuart S. Janney, III	51	7	12	9	349,989
Emory A. Hamilton	26	8	8	3	349,545
Bee Bee Stables, Inc. and					
Tortora, Jacqueline	38	3	11	6	348,430
Albert Fried, Jr.	52	8	6	5	348,294
Cecil N. Peacock	58	8	7	7	346,449
William C. Lickle	57	14	4	7	345,483
Gann, Edmund A. and					
Flaxman Stable	4	1	0	1	345,000
Crown Valley Stable	70	24	16	8	344,370
Plumstead Stables	251	23	18	27	344,219
C R K Stable	51	9	11	7	344,105
Eutrophia Farm	58	17	10	6	344,056
K and K Racing Stable LLC	55	13	7	7	342,909
Michael A. Ward, II	123	16	19	20	341,608
Thorn Stable	41	7	8	3	340,885
J D Racing Stable	182	25	25	31	339,957
Lansdon B. Robbins	36	10	7	3	339,603
David Beard	54	11	8	6	337,969
Seymour Cohn	137	15	26	13	337,343
Steel Your Face Stables	47	11	14	3	336,484
Herbert Washington Chambers	95	5	12	11	336,290
W. Bruce Lunsford	70	13	11	7	335,573
Confetti Farms, Inc.	134	26	19	17	334,833
John H. Peace	79	7	13	17	333,413
Beclawat Stable	47	6	10	7	333,235
Gate2wire Farm and					
Highware Horse Racing	92	10	15	14	332,915
Thorobeam Farm	71	14	6	9	332,528
901 Racing Stables LLC	93	14	23	17	330,989
Donver Stable	76	11	11	16	329,795
Richard Malouf	93	22	16	12	329,780
Noreen Carpenito	88	10	12	22	329,721
River Ridge Ranch	75	21	12	7	328,867
Daniel M. Borislow	89	7	14	20	328,723
Peter J. Callahan	86	16	7	10	328,590
Manfred Roos	113	19	9	13	328,078
Tanourin Stable	55	10	7	7	325,985
Stony Oak Farm LLC	97	18	10	10	325,839
Mark S. Hopkins	10	5	1	2	325,725
Peter Abruzzo	15	4	3	2	325,630
Cassels, James and Zollars, Bob	60	9	5	14	324,716
Lloyd Madison Farms, IV LLC	16	5	4	3	324,432
Lothenbach Stables, Inc.	111	12	11	18	323,132
Barbara DeLima	96	9	16	12	323,109
James A. Michael	68	10	11	5	322,230
Susan Dibari	45	9	4	14	322,036
Larry H. Carlton	95	27	12	11	321,612
Harry J. Aleo	57	13	12	7	321,497
Canyon Farms	50	11	7	8	321,345
Cam Allard	51	8	6	6	320,946
Lloyd DeBruycker	132	18	24	16	320,902
Hidden Lane Farms, Inc.	92	16	12	18	319,267
Forgreen Racing Stable LLC	91	15	14	16	318,172
Emerald Pastures Corp., Inc.	133	18	18	6	317,470
Frank Fletcher Racing					
Operations, Inc.	30	9	5	5	316,800
Frank L. Jones, Jr.	68	10	7	8	316,396
Madeline Auerbach	26	7	1	2	316,346
Mount Joy Stables, Inc.	46	11	9	6	316,154
Rodney C. Faulkner	313	52	47	43	316,128
T. Ray Cannon	89	18	12	7	315,909
Winchell Thoroughbreds LLC	36	6	3	6	315,858
Timothy Cunningham	62	6	11	14	314,754
George Melillo	4	1	1	2	314,330
Denlea Park Ltd.	16	4	3	2	313,846
R.C. Hill Stable	27	5	3	2	313,335
Ten Goal Racing Stable					
and Partner	17	4	1	4	313,213
Stan Stefanski	34	10	5	3	313,164
Coming Home Stables, Inc.	80	15	14	13	312,521
E L R Corp	63	10	4	12	311,773
Tenenbaum Racing Stables	35	9	9	5	310,686
Muthulingham, Thayalan					
and Armata, S.	7	4	2	0	310,585
Three H Racing LLC	112	22	9	11	310,418
The Nonsequitur Stable LLC	73	15	12	14	310,350
Dream Walkin Farms, Inc.	86	8	12	10	309,241
McKee Stables, Inc.	55	7	11	5	308,979
Lakeside Farms LLC	81	10	12	1	307,551
Tradewinds Stable	90	19	18	9	307,460
Chris Powell	382	45	42	35	306,772
Little Red Feather Racing	39	5	6	6	305,872
Barr Three LLC	109	14	12	19	305,861
Ogden Mills Phipps	44	5	9	6	305,380
Dolphus Morrison	55	5	9	5	304,859
Vincent Papandrea	67	10	5	7	304,621
Green Lantern Stables LLC	31	9	2	2	304,230

Owner	Starts	1st	2d	3d	Purses
Tulip Hill Farm	95	18	19	10	303,991
Thomas G. McClay	86	13	14	14	303,936
Gatsas Thoroughbreds LLC	37	10	3	9	303,796
Sanford J. Goldfarb	46	10	6	6	303,534
Joseph F. Graffeo	104	14	14	13	303,360
Freedom Acres, Inc.	40	8	8	6	303,062
Henry E. Pabst	43	5	2	8	302,995
James L. Nicholson	258	26	20	40	302,662
JMJ Racing Stables LLC	76	9	12	8	302,296
Terra Farm	49	5	6	13	302,048
Marablue Farm	128	15	13	11	301,402
Mast Thoroughbreds LLC	63	11	7	7	301,071
Greenoaks Farm	80	15	16	10	301,018
Marta Racing Ventures and Hollendorfer, Jerry	23	7	8	2	300,943
Thompson, G. and Tiller, R.	19	7	2	5	300,831
Patricia B. Blass	68	11	7	13	300,574
William M. Backer	109	14	14	16	300,429
Herrick Racing LLC	74	6	14	9	300,109
Burning Daylight Farms	70	17	12	8	299,231
Joann Davis	133	27	23	19	299,032
Adam Russo	62	13	10	9	298,990
Farfellow Farms, Ltd.	43	9	5	4	298,748
James T. Scatuorchio	34	6	10	5	298,603
Ocean Front Property and Asmussen, Keith	42	11	10	5	297,780
Pleterski, K. and B.	38	6	5	2	296,677
Dapple Stable LLC	46	9	7	8	296,465
Robert Tony Gaito	20	5	4	5	296,434
Johnston, Jr., Mrs. S. K.	85	5	12	15	295,938
Francis J. O'Toole	15	3	2	2	295,885
Whitney J. Zeringue, Jr.	115	14	8	11	295,728
Edwin H. Wachtel	75	9	18	12	295,687
Michael House	28	6	5	1	295,343
Grunwald Racing LLC	50	9	4	9	294,858
Desert Sun Stables	58	13	9	8	294,529
Castle Peak Farm, Ltd.	58	8	5	6	292,755
Candy Stables	83	12	12	6	292,698
Southern Nevada Racing Stables	87	8	12	10	292,522
Michael W. Jester	65	10	10	13	291,770
Charlton Baker	116	27	20	14	291,712
Crown's Way Farm	59	7	15	7	291,653
Leonard Liberto	111	17	15	17	291,611
Hal J. Earnhardt, III	15	4	2	2	291,584
Grenier, Dennis and Norine	58	19	10	7	290,844
Stoneway Farm LLC	74	19	1	7	290,787
Toby Roth	80	14	15	9	290,164
Cherrywood Racing Stables II	70	11	11	3	290,062
Calumet Farm	23	9	1	5	288,431
Stephen A. Richardson	174	27	28	18	288,303
Michael J. Moran	15	4	2	2	286,942
Rancha Fresa, Inc.	106	11	12	17	286,910
Conover Stable	59	10	9	8	286,750
Edward Clouston	169	27	27	25	285,952
Stride Rite Racing Stable, Inc.	61	9	8	10	285,860
Soares, Michael and Suarez, Pablo	25	3	4	9	285,778
Serengeti Stable LLC	7	3	4	0	285,120
Rainbow Stable	139	14	24	26	284,605
Kaster, Nancy R. and Richard S.	63	5	12	6	284,061
Charlotte C. Polin	18	2	4	5	283,593
Richard H. Jukosky	51	6	8	9	282,714
Double S Stable	27	9	3	3	282,020
Theresa McArthur	118	22	21	16	281,946
C. Steven Duncker	48	7	10	7	281,829
Eaton Hall Farm	37	6	7	7	281,814
John C. Sessa	80	13	11	13	281,615
Six Brothers Stable	121	20	11	13	281,367
Ed Few	51	10	11	4	281,071
Sefa's Farm	83	12	16	10	280,902
Frank Huarte	59	7	4	8	280,751
William M. Rickman	135	17	11	15	280,609
Conboy, McClanahan and Wineman, et al	9	5	2	0	280,461
Robison, J. Kirk and Judy	47	10	7	8	279,860
Diamond G Ranch, Inc.	117	25	18	10	279,817
R L Stables LLC	28	6	1	6	279,043
Richard H. Glander	35	11	10	4	278,930
Redbob Farm	117	11	24	20	278,875
Team Victory, II	10	5	0	1	278,844
Patricia Pavlish	28	3	2	2	278,770
Brooks, Joe Dee and Lisa	16	7	7	1	278,339
Michael J. Bruder	39	5	4	3	278,165
R. A. Marcello	27	5	5	5	277,928
Elaine M. Gross	518	45	46	49	277,056
Port Trust, Naify, Marsha and San Gabriel Investments	11	1	3	1	276,765
Seinfeld, Barry and Dodson, Elizabeth K.	39	5	7	5	276,467
Leland P. Cook	103	19	6	14	276,280
Granja Vista Del Rio Stable	31	4	3	7	276,212
John Stahlin	192	21	23	21	276,169
Poston, Bill and Vicki	46	9	7	7	275,589
Cameron Express, Inc.	10	4	2	2	275,579
Rowell Enterprises, Inc.	54	7	6	10	274,770
Jerry Hollendorfer	95	19	16	21	274,574
Circle S Ranch, Inc.	130	20	19	14	274,024
Alec Head	7	1	3	1	274,020
Ted Taylor	90	11	8	9	273,155
Silvera, Laurie and Kilambi, Sriniva	8	3	1	0	272,958
L. T. B., Inc. and Childers, Miles	66	12	9	5	272,947
John T. Behrendt	63	9	8	8	272,304
Jay Manoogian	27	8	4	6	271,293
Confort, John and Weiss, Albert	27	5	4	4	271,068
Frank J. Regalbuto	82	17	13	10	270,411
Astor Stable	124	26	25	20	270,346
Leo S. Nechamkin II	30	6	5	5	270,080

*Includes $500,000 bonus

Snapshot Facts: There were 260 owners whose horses earned $500,000 or more in 2003. There were 93 whose horses earned $1 million or more.

Leading Owners in 2003 by Races Won

Owner	St	1st	2d	3d	Purses
Michael J. Gill	2,235	425	339	267	$9,236,530
Richard A. Englander	1,182	227	190	163	5,359,759
Louis D. O'Brien	708	208	136	112	1,293,698
John Franks	988	143	134	120	4,083,255
Frank Carl Calabrese	457	138	69	55	2,259,392
Dale Baird	1,029	132	140	146	1,939,085
Daniel J. Chen	660	132	98	75	1,079,683
Stronach Stable	622	126	112	63	7,289,114
Turf Express, Inc.	459	113	76	55	1,852,690
Melnyk, Eugene and Laura	455	92	65	60	4,123,765
Bruno Schickedanz	610	92	69	93	1,874,011
Hwy 1 Racing Stable LLC	527	90	62	73	1,330,550
Rosendo G. Parra	448	85	76	52	1,917,263
Maggi Moss	449	83	68	60	1,529,749
Gumpster Stable LLC	470	82	81	67	1,458,438
Ramsey, Kenneth L. and Sarah K.	334	81	51	36	2,338,452
Billy Hays	426	76	64	45	890,448
Steven M. Asmussen	223	72	36	29	856,710
Mark Yagour, Inc.	530	71	66	66	589,364
Michael H. Sherman	453	69	74	65	1,106,447
Nelson Bunker Hunt	334	68	51	54	1,876,572
Kenneth W. Murphy	252	66	43	31	984,520
Heiligbrodt Racing Stable	305	64	55	38	2,751,875
Robert D. Bone	178	64	22	23	970,440
Joseph Clark Faulkner	320	64	57	48	371,410
M. Y. Stables, Inc.	292	61	58	26	840,658
E and G Stables	184	60	33	33	907,269
Robert L. Cole, Jr.	230	57	50	31	1,697,403
WinStar Farm LLC	266	56	57	28	2,243,263
Flying Zee Stable	366	55	58	46	1,218,238
Coast To Coast Racing Fund LLC	222	54	35	32	1,303,070
Pyrite Stables	412	54	56	57	936,950
Slick 1 Racing	313	54	44	40	357,951
Monarch Stables, Inc.	307	53	62	36	868,484
Jack J. Armstrong	258	53	38	31	639,170
Rodney C. Faulkner	313	52	47	43	316,128
Dennis E. Weir	206	51	41	26	763,432
Einar Paul Robsham	284	49	45	35	1,984,847
Runnin Horse Farm, Inc.	272	47	45	35	1,003,351
R. Gary Patrick	431	47	43	50	451,363
Overbrook Farm	344	46	40	39	1,851,634
Augustin Stable	271	45	59	42	2,073,396
Everest Stables, Inc.	293	45	37	35	1,946,597
P. T. K. Racing LLC	372	45	65	55	992,810
Chris Powell	382	45	42	35	306,772
Elaine M. Gross	518	45	46	49	277,056
Sam-Son Farms	201	44	31	31	3,864,116
The Thoroughbred Corp	227	44	41	26	3,486,782
Tom R. Durant	202	44	41	33	1,009,820
Elizabeth Walsh	234	43	41	36	882,143
Hollendorfer, Jerry and Todaro, George	227	43	53	35	866,163
Moss, Mr. and Mrs. Jerome S.	184	42	29	32	2,344,501
Gold N. Z. Stable	155	42	33	17	685,589
Florence Gemma Siravo	328	42	48	56	410,384
Lewis, Robert B. and Beverly J.	312	41	40	46	2,948,528
C D and G Stable	303	41	53	59	758,063
Shelly Radosevich	259	41	45	30	236,261
Padua Stables	201	40	36	31	1,125,698
Jack L. Boggs	241	40	39	29	439,927
Alpine Stable	230	39	27	40	1,550,985
Live Oak Plantation	206	39	28	24	1,357,133
Jayeff B Stables	207	39	30	24	1,171,328
West, Gary L. and Mary E.	138	39	19	20	1,033,453
Home Team Stables	196	39	35	30	576,526
Michael Newell	271	39	39	26	230,974
Golden Eagle Farm	312	38	50	51	1,527,311
Francis C. McDonnell	219	38	33	30	676,568
Worcester Stable	206	38	32	29	420,923
Nick Sanna Stables LLC	107	37	21	16	533,099
Acclaimed Racing Stable	148	36	22	15	663,822
Timber Creek Farm	257	36	33	34	444,514
Edward P. Evans	222	35	39	32	2,357,266
Dogwood Stable	287	35	39	33	2,204,564
Jay Em Ess Stable	211	35	42	33	1,388,519
K. K. Sangara	195	35	29	38	1,259,162
Broman, Mary R. and Chester, Sr.	222	35	26	22	1,069,881
Irish Acres Farm	287	35	38	24	794,854
John D. Murphy, Sr.	235	34	33	39	801,354
William Stiritz	163	34	25	24	620,618
Daniel A. Limongelli	204	34	27	34	531,437
Juddmonte Farms, Inc.	122	33	21	12	6,265,030
Paraneck Stable	341	33	43	40	1,799,984
Stix-N-Stones Stable and Miller, Thomas	135	33	26	16	266,961
Jayaraman, Kalarikkal K. and Vilasini D.	137	32	29	18	1,017,692
Lanning, Curt and Lila	196	32	19	32	645,346
Edward E. Turner	104	32	14	13	641,169
Armando Lage	122	32	25	18	552,973
Darrell R. Sapp	220	32	43	38	525,016
Steven Dwoskin	154	32	23	27	473,997
Wild Horse Stable	143	32	23	14	402,753
Shane M. Spiess	216	32	28	31	229,126
Stonerside Stable LLC	177	31	21	34	2,841,259
Pin Oak Stable LLC	144	31	24	25	1,414,678
Jacks or Better Farm, Inc.	184	31	36	24	921,645
Glen Hill Farm	138	31	28	16	863,870
Equils, James W. and Marcia S.	185	31	24	31	764,935
Charles W. Everett	174	31	29	26	441,009
West Ridge Ranch LLC	137	31	23	15	236,796
B. Wayne Hughes	143	30	23	23	1,970,099
Buckram Oak Farm	210	30	30	36	1,585,724
G. Watts Humphrey, Jr.	207	30	30	28	1,487,756
Wygod, Mr. and Mrs. Martin J.	113	30	20	14	1,262,507
Richter, Kristine and John	111	30	19	15	1,089,326
Russell L. Reineman Stable, Inc.	161	30	23	24	732,415
Bar None Ranches	183	30	33	34	421,293
Stephen M. Zimmerman	161	30	18	23	194,969
Gustav Schickedanz	106	29	9	8	*3,361,790
Buddy Lee Racing Stable	84	29	15	15	163,382
Barry K. Schwartz	117	28	22	16	910,274
Keith I. Asmussen	115	28	24	16	835,194
Gary Owens	110	28	26	11	260,643
My Way Stable	193	28	21	18	129,529
Darley Stud Management LLC	105	27	19	8	1,155,158
Patricia A. Generazio	238	27	36	33	905,531
Klein, Richard, Bertram and Elaine	139	27	25	11	780,634
Valene Farms	119	27	19	17	721,655
Orion Stables	332	27	26	25	540,209
Robert D. Nash	131	27	22	10	503,596
Yasou Stable Trust	151	27	22	19	387,282
Larry H. Carlton	95	27	12	11	321,612
Joann Davis	133	27	23	19	299,032
Charlton Baker	116	27	20	14	291,712
Stephen A. Richardson	174	27	28	18	288,303
Edward Clouston	169	27	27	25	285,952
Frank D. DiGiulio, Jr.	72	26	13	7	1,620,839
Team Valor Stables LLC	101	26	10	16	1,136,999
Tom Boy Stable	74	26	15	8	509,297
Robert S. Mitchell Trust	100	26	15	13	490,142
J B Stables, Inc.	281	26	28	32	479,072
Rose Family Stable	249	26	30	22	399,265
Michael L. Reavis	78	26	10	12	393,033
Charles F. Burnside	129	26	10	18	367,095
Diamond Oak Stable	72	26	16	5	361,949

616 THE AMERICAN RACING MANUAL

Owner	St	1st	2d	3d	Purses
Tangarae Farms LLP	119	26	18	19	360,118
Confetti Farms, Inc.	134	26	19	17	334,833
James L. Nicholson	258	26	20	40	302,662
Astor Stable	124	26	25	20	270,346
Hy-Hopes Farm	117	26	24	10	198,637
Ben Campo	118	26	19	16	183,453
Edmund A. Gann	83	25	19	8	5,848,681
Kinsman Stable	119	25	15	15	885,166
J. Mack Robinson	221	25	40	33	792,622
S J B, Jr. Stable	147	25	18	20	645,494
Edwin Thomas Broome	109	25	22	17	573,130
Michael Barkowski	160	25	25	28	514,352
Robert J. Amendola	107	25	13	14	508,799
David D. Walters	119	25	18	16	416,584
J D Racing Stable	182	25	25	31	339,957
Diamond G Ranch, Inc.	117	25	18	10	279,817
Two S Stable	179	25	22	24	207,773
R-W Racing Stable, Inc.	126	25	23	12	188,918
Chris W. Tuttle	137	25	14	18	160,049
Gilbert G. Campbell	144	24	25	21	756,280
Asiel Stable	128	24	16	18	680,628
Robert E. Meyerhoff	124	24	17	22	544,815
Wexler Racing Stables, Inc.	207	24	31	22	486,235
Panic Stable LLC	130	24	15	19	459,271
Ronald L. Shenofsky	121	24	16	24	457,465
Crown Valley Stable	70	24	16	8	344,370
Michael A. Lecesse	102	24	24	11	176,554
Paul H. Horton	110	24	14	17	147,322
Gary Page	109	24	18	15	118,018
Lowell N. Bunyard	77	24	12	11	35,111
Jeffrey Sengara	95	23	19	16	1,139,382
Hobeau Farm	131	23	32	24	995,640
Tracy Farmer	155	23	20	20	841,877
John Atto	116	23	13	14	803,852
Cohen, Philip and Marcia and Klesaris, Steve B.	83	23	15	12	758,561
Carl R. Moore Mgmnt LLC	95	23	15	11	538,078
Karakorum Farm	161	23	16	19	481,470
John V. Alecci Stable, Inc.	118	23	19	8	465,751
James L. Ingalls	264	23	28	29	433,550
Daniel M. Ryan	114	23	19	16	417,713
D. J. Stable LLC	139	23	23	19	414,691
Kim Noble Hart	136	23	14	12	388,277
John D. McKee	227	23	25	18	374,516
Plumstead Stables	251	23	18	27	344,219
STD Racing Stable	107	23	17	22	239,475
Larry A. Byer	120	23	27	22	237,494
James T. Hines, Jr.	210	23	22	23	227,098
M C P Stables	153	23	21	18	195,965
Paul J. Matties, Jr.	115	23	11	13	145,519
Tucci Stables	88	22	13	11	1,206,855
Sondra D. Bender	130	22	17	13	1,025,859
Wilson, David W. and Holly F.	120	22	16	21	837,902
Colebrook Farms	218	22	27	24	796,396
Harris Farms, Inc.	134	22	20	26	576,848
Joseph S. Parisi	125	22	11	18	460,799
The Elkstone Group LLC	155	22	15	16	447,662
Jer-Mar Stable LLC	90	22	13	14	447,058
Destiny Farm LLC	127	22	15	18	413,659
Gene Johnson	80	22	11	17	361,646
Richard Malouf	93	22	16	12	329,780
Three H Racing LLC	112	22	9	11	310,418
Theresa McArthur	118	22	21	16	281,946
McVey, Rose A. and Ramey, Dan	120	22	19	20	137,430
Varue Wilson	103	22	17	13	35,976
Stan E. Fulton	107	21	14	11	1,058,637
Peachtree Stable	112	21	15	10	780,694
Shadwell Stable	91	21	14	10	775,108
Cobra Farm, Inc.	103	21	17	14	774,562
Roddy J. Valente	82	21	12	8	701,504
Fox Hill Farms, Inc.	65	21	9	11	603,228
Arthur I. Appleton	130	21	23	21	509,746
Richard L. Duchossois	110	21	11	11	487,770
Louie J. Roussel, III	100	21	8	16	470,545
Loren Gale Cox	233	21	27	39	389,887
River Ridge Ranch	75	21	12	7	328,867
John Stahlin	192	21	23	21	276,169
R. Scott Wagner	154	21	25	23	260,556
Doro J. Stable, Inc.	159	21	27	25	238,777
Michael Anthony Ferraro	112	21	19	22	207,434
Scardino USA Stable	167	21	16	22	154,301
Merrit Hudson	78	21	11	13	137,321
Charles Lawson	149	21	24	22	112,825
Fire N Ice Stable	148	21	12	14	105,806
Zimbler, Bettie L. and Gary A.	89	21	20	12	102,387
Marylou Whitney Stables	160	20	26	20	1,768,908
Craig, Sidney H. and Jenny	108	20	16	12	1,360,447
Michael E. Pegram	115	20	19	11	721,238
Red Baron's Barn LLC	118	20	20	10	618,577
New Farm	87	20	5	8	593,438
Taylor Mountain Farm LLC	215	20	22	29	503,733
Donald R. Dizney	126	20	14	14	498,950
Rey Wan Racing	149	20	18	24	365,750
Six Brothers Stable	121	20	11	13	281,367
Circle S Ranch, Inc.	130	20	19	14	274,024
Francis J. Paolangeli	75	20	11	8	204,845
Pecoraro Racing Stable	117	20	9	9	201,074
Eugene E. Weymouth	85	20	6	3	200,141
Red Ron Farms	100	20	13	15	192,063
S. T. C. Racing	125	20	15	14	183,423
Stevark Stable, Inc. and Chronister, S.	105	20	19	21	158,337
Jerry L. Balo	79	20	13	8	149,698
Andrew R. Gordon	153	20	22	16	132,279
Everett Hammond	97	20	17	12	130,157
J. D. Riker	91	20	18	5	114,077
Bobby Hodge	160	20	13	19	111,440
Ray Boucher	131	20	8	18	53,604
Amerman Racing Stables LLC	85	19	14	14	2,610,764
Wertheimer Farm LLC	77	19	12	10	1,888,058
Claiborne Farm	71	19	15	7	1,137,430
Peter Vegso	145	19	13	20	752,345
Silverton Hill LLC	134	19	17	14	543,460
Star Track Farms	114	19	17	11	516,089
Robert Bakerman	164	19	23	17	488,113
Gus Goldsmith	149	19	13	18	426,314
Thomas Vanderhyde	155	19	22	22	372,719
Manfred Roos	113	19	9	13	328,078
Tradewinds Stable	90	19	18	9	307,460
Grenier, Dennis and Norine	58	19	10	7	290,844
Stoneway Farm LLC	74	19	1	7	290,787
Leland P. Cook	103	19	6	14	276,280
Jerry Hollerdorfer	95	19	16	21	274,574
Efrain T. Garcia	165	19	23	20	236,382
Thoroughbred Acadiana LLC	75	19	8	12	234,569
Horky, Theresa and Shelansky, Keith	116	19	13	13	207,594
Anthony J. Distefano, Jr.	98	19	20	16	191,116
Robert M. Gorham	95	19	21	15	173,870
Christy R. Johnson	160	19	19	16	152,359
Hammond, Everett and Cox, Robert L.	91	19	18	13	137,081
Gary Danelson	57	19	11	8	121,556
Mary Ann Thomas	130	19	18	16	98,989
Homer Thoroughbreds	126	19	18	16	50,432
Moore, Susan and John	65	18	15	11	1,067,129
Centaur Farms, Inc.	132	18	21	20	658,792
Sandra Rasmussen	157	18	26	18	529,584
Kupferberg, Saul J. and Max	145	18	30	18	521,265
William R. Harris	176	18	18	22	514,995
Deckert, Jr., Robert and Deckert, Sr., Robert	137	18	14	23	446,741
George Brunacini	112	18	16	11	446,361

Owner	Starts	1st	2d	3d	Purses
Guerino Antonini	49	18	10	6	432,950
Joseph P. Morey, Jr. Revocable Trust	60	18	12	6	382,733
La Marca Stable	106	18	12	9	369,464
Joel A. Kligman	65	18	6	10	350,093
Stony Oak Farm LLC	97	18	10	10	325,839
Lloyd DeBruycker	132	18	24	16	320,902
Emerald Pastures Corp., Inc.	133	18	18	6	317,470
T. Ray Cannon	89	18	12	7	315,909
Tulip Hill Farm	95	18	19	10	303,991
Silver Rod Stables, Inc.	68	18	11	10	254,985
Ryehill Farm	114	18	10	16	250,080
Winning Ways T'breds LLC	95	18	17	15	248,339
Michael Langford	83	18	13	10	247,152
Edith M. Lombardi	62	18	12	8	234,687
Gary Marrone	72	18	4	7	207,421
Stephanie S. Beattie	80	18	18	9	202,412
McCarty Racing	87	18	15	13	196,390
Love-Um LLC	99	18	13	16	192,666
Barbara Rehbein	121	18	14	15	178,220
Michael Watral	82	18	8	13	165,566
Diamond L Stable	121	18	17	26	164,454
Robert D. Lawrence	106	18	14	10	115,142
David W. Geist	94	18	15	11	110,267
Team Block	140	17	22	17	717,960
Hardwicke Stable	91	17	19	11	645,703
Our Sugar Bear Stable	80	17	11	8	557,495
Love 2 Win Stable	69	17	9	15	553,258
Molinaro Stable	105	17	15	11	542,078
Scott A. Lake	54	17	6	7	480,530
Hickory Plains Farm LLC	105	17	12	15	387,034
Dennis A. Drazin	111	17	14	18	386,554
Wright, Mrs. Frank P.	88	17	16	13	374,773
Stone Spire LLC	68	17	11	2	366,822
Eutrophia Farm	58	17	10	6	344,056
Burning Daylight Farms	70	17	12	8	299,231
Leonard Liberto	111	17	15	17	291,611
William M. Rickman	135	17	11	15	280,609
Frank J. Regalbuto	82	17	13	10	270,411
Scuderia Montese Stable	138	17	17	17	250,288
Malvern Stable Inc.	66	17	13	5	247,189
Charles P. Hukill	138	17	23	13	245,224
Sunshine Hill Farm	125	17	18	19	204,132
R Bar S Thoroughbreds LLC	97	17	8	12	192,063
Old Coach Farm	82	17	14	11	190,147
John W. Baird	120	17	13	15	188,974
Touchdown Stable	104	17	16	13	186,412
Gentry Farms	125	17	17	19	185,145
Roger Davis	58	17	8	9	184,084
William J. Smith	61	17	14	10	167,110
Murphy, Timothy and Brown, Dave E.	116	17	14	19	126,678
Stevenson Racing LLC	77	17	12	9	120,029
Jim R. Robinson	53	17	7	7	117,241
Gerald Richards	63	17	12	5	107,191
Jose A. Martinez	95	17	15	12	100,810
Joseph V. Shields, Jr.	72	16	10	13	1,739,508
Gary A. Tanaka	135	16	15	15	1,335,756
Minshall Farms	127	16	15	15	983,807
Glen C. Warren	93	16	15	6	916,006
William S. Farish	99	16	14	13	814,445
Audre Cappuccitti	214	16	26	28	790,867
West Point T'breds LLC	67	16	10	9	625,278
James R. Lewis, Jr.	120	16	25	19	593,395
Richard Otto Stables, Inc.	36	16	2	5	557,222
Braunsdorf, Robert and Levine, Robert	103	16	12	19	444,470
C. R. Trout	87	16	9	12	418,654
Prime Time Stable	102	16	20	10	390,444
Michael A. Ward, II	123	16	19	20	341,608
Peter J. Callahan	86	16	7	10	328,590
Hidden Lane Farms, Inc.	92	16	12	18	319,267

Owner	Starts	1st	2d	3d	Purses
K 5 Stables	97	16	12	14	247,086
Nancy Lee Farms	64	16	8	8	228,170
Mast Thoroughbreds LLC, Bieke, Ron and Gorham, Robert M.	117	16	15	19	221,939
Daniel C. Hurtak	121	16	17	18	217,429
Blackjack Thoroughbreds	77	16	8	9	210,948
Deep Rock Farm	92	16	12	9	196,611
Maxine Rice	81	16	14	12	189,971
Martin Brothers, Inc.	141	16	14	12	188,886
Lee A. Rogalski	97	16	11	12	177,418
JON Stable	150	16	24	19	169,866
Israel Flores	108	16	13	17	168,402
Joseph L. Weir	110	16	14	13	147,694
Three of A Kind Stable	28	16	1	2	137,530
Rizzi Racing Stable	113	16	11	18	130,328
James Centofanti	64	16	10	5	93,548
Raymond V. Feldman	62	16	8	9	84,947
Ross Russell	72	16	10	12	84,477
Redbird Farm	38	16	5	7	35,754
Michael B. Tabor	80	15	14	10	1,487,014
Anstu Stables, Inc.	62	15	8	9	1,381,599
Willmott Stables, Inc.	82	15	8	12	941,754
Mac Fehsenfeld	135	15	9	20	911,553
Janis R. Whitham	65	15	14	10	850,290
Haras Santa Maria de Araras	131	15	14	24	695,872
Courtlandt Farms	66	15	12	7	684,926
John D. Gunther	73	15	8	14	654,591
Martin L. Cherry	65	15	12	13	596,627
Kirkwood, Al and Saundra S.	79	15	14	15	590,102
William L. Clifton, Jr.	91	15	12	10	482,902
Nickolas DeToro	121	15	10	9	465,952
TNT Racing Stable	64	15	12	2	460,812
Morris Bailey	113	15	21	17	426,396
Win and Place Stable	61	15	13	12	397,523
Larry R. Johnson	102	15	15	16	351,521
Seymour Cohn	137	15	26	13	337,343
Forgreen Racing Stable LLC	91	15	14	16	318,172
Coming Home Stables, Inc.	80	15	14	13	312,521
The Nonsequitur Stable LLC	73	15	12	14	310,350
Marablue Farm	128	15	13	11	301,402
Greenoaks Farm	80	15	16	10	301,018
Ralph C. Sessa	71	15	15	12	258,885
Mereworth Farms	201	15	15	19	248,049
Authors Stable LLC	167	15	18	15	242,082
Gerald Silver	64	15	15	7	212,825
Billie Klokstad	91	15	16	10	212,311
Louis Clarizio, III	111	15	10	8	196,090
Timber Creek Farm	55	15	13	6	194,266
Blackacre Farms, Inc.	98	15	25	16	182,795
Driver, Ywachetta H. and James Travis	48	15	7	6	180,165
Sandy Valley Farms	56	15	10	7	167,536
Herb Riecken	158	15	16	24	166,278
Michael G. Weatherly	125	15	21	8	165,971
Darryl B. Jackson	48	15	3	5	162,700
Spooner, Sue and Tim	72	15	15	8	156,259
Volar Corporation	146	15	24	13	153,645
Wanda June Johnson	89	15	12	8	152,750
C. L. Nix	110	15	9	11	151,272
Ramon O. Gonzalez	109	15	17	16	138,945
Tracey J. Wisner	142	15	21	20	136,732
Greg Frye	57	15	6	8	122,049
Jim Bausch	152	15	11	17	114,927
Dan Kjorsvik	69	15	6	15	106,585
Georgie Stuart	80	15	15	9	101,130
Blackjack Stables LLC	181	15	27	25	95,285
Charles David Nielsen	77	15	9	10	95,191
Ronnie Duke	148	15	23	11	93,117
Dunn Bar Ranch	56	15	7	6	88,996
Patricia D. Bellucci	117	15	13	12	81,833
Milton M. Gaede	73	15	11	10	57,097

Owner	Starts	1st	2d	3d	Purses
Jaqueline Smith	51	15	12	6	32,149
Dominion Bloodstock, Ball, Derek and Galbraith, Hugh	145	14	18	22	858,021
Ackerley Brothers Farm	68	14	13	17	633,314
Kuehne Racing	80	14	9	15	514,833
J D Farms	114	14	16	18	471,071
Tommy Town T'breds LLC	83	14	12	11	455,555
Janelle D. Grum	69	14	15	6	448,962
Fishelberg, Leonard and Yolanda	67	14	8	12	432,302
Gerald F. Sleeter	64	14	5	9	423,558
Sabine Stable	72	14	8	8	420,104
Lazy Lane Farms, Inc.	96	14	16	15	413,605
Scarberry, Howard and Penny	160	14	27	27	400,338
Bennett, Mr. and Mrs. R. J.	107	14	15	20	381,546
Tricar Stable, Inc.	140	14	16	33	350,270
William C. Lickle	57	14	4	7	345,483
Thorobeam Farm	71	14	6	9	332,528
901 Racing Stables LLC	93	14	23	17	330,989
Barr Three LLC	109	14	12	19	305,861
Joseph F. Graffeo	104	14	14	13	303,360
William M. Backer	109	14	14	16	300,429
Whitney J. Zeringue, Jr.	115	14	8	11	295,728
Toby Roth	80	14	15	9	290,164
Rainbow Stable	139	14	24	26	284,605
Currie, David and Trish	78	14	14	6	265,064
Hawkins, Arden and Robertson, Glen	39	14	3	5	258,587
Schmidt, Ronald D. and Alice M.	64	14	6	14	256,243
Daniel L. Smucker	130	14	18	16	255,586
Kinross Farm	51	14	9	1	246,620
Kjell H. Qvale	118	14	19	15	238,648
Richard T. Beal	101	14	17	14	235,177
Francisco Parra	138	14	18	25	228,005
Snowden, Diane and Guy B.	67	14	5	5	224,037
Tae Shin	98	14	13	14	212,328
Winfred L. Hess, Jr.	75	14	14	10	210,476
Ron Crockett, Inc.	84	14	19	8	198,811
Anjo Racing, Inc.	149	14	13	23	197,081
Theresa Anderson	77	14	9	8	170,925
JRD Farms, Inc.	92	14	8	14	166,246
James A. Griffin	59	14	8	7	164,913
Terry L. Boyd	62	14	12	4	160,202
L. T. B., Inc.	52	14	6	3	145,682
Doug Clyde	62	14	11	12	132,142
J. Eric Desouza	74	14	13	9	129,798
Keenebridge Farm, Inc.	76	14	4	9	128,182
Agnes J. Perdue	90	14	10	8	124,804
Delphine Miller	61	14	9	9	124,370
Clery Sosa-Barrera	57	14	13	6	107,413
Boyce K. Gooch	121	14	14	19	106,590
Kerwyn Parkening	103	14	14	17	99,889
Donald Murray	72	14	9	12	96,792
Frank F. Clark	67	14	11	17	95,827
Kelly Huval	88	14	15	9	87,159
John E. Cox	87	14	7	13	84,183
Michael L. Barro	53	14	13	6	80,686
Pearl Figueroa	100	14	9	7	77,104
Steven C. Roberts	150	14	14	17	75,168
Amos, William J. and Rowland, Tamela	56	14	11	5	72,186
John P. Petty	69	14	8	10	38,802
Stonecrest Farm	57	13	6	7	1,746,137
James McIngvale	74	13	16	2	999,519
Carlo D'Amato	158	13	13	20	648,073
Finney, Albert and Taylor, Mickey and Karen LLC	60	13	10	12	481,544
Royce Jaime	63	13	9	10	449,133
Walter Family Trust	119	13	21	14	441,763
David J. Lanzman Racing, Inc.	92	13	15	18	428,618
Plan B Stable	71	13	14	5	401,024
Goldish, Marc D. and Savoy Stable	105	13	25	14	385,112
K and K Racing Stable LLC	55	13	7	7	342,909
W. Bruce Lunsford	70	13	11	7	335,573
Harry J. Aleo	57	13	12	7	321,497
Thomas G. McClay	86	13	14	14	303,936
Adam Russo	62	13	10	9	298,990
Desert Sun Stables	58	13	9	8	294,529
John C. Sessa	80	13	11	13	281,615
Brereton C. Jones	69	13	8	10	262,946
Meyerhoff, Harry C. and Thomas O.	57	13	11	7	260,592
Triple AAA Ranch	79	13	12	13	242,723
Germania Farms, Inc.	49	13	11	6	239,775
Tycoon Stable	44	13	7	8	236,237
Richard E. Trebat	104	13	15	11	229,955
Stephen R. Baker	107	13	11	12	227,583
Wags Nags Stable LLC	119	13	18	16	223,733
Two C Stables	86	13	14	10	220,338
Terry Bruner	76	13	14	4	218,680
Amestoy, Pierre Jean and Leslie A.	42	13	5	5	208,881
Eaton, Gretchen M. and Arthur J.	51	13	9	4	207,450
William Bannasch Living Trust	44	13	6	2	206,810
Dennis Ward	92	13	20	20	205,952
Daniel T. Gaffney	100	13	15	2	195,226
Hernandez, Earl and Keith and Duvieilh, John	100	13	15	11	193,441
Rodney D. Moyers	112	13	10	8	187,674
Lori Goodz	44	13	10	6	186,273
Don Eberts	60	13	7	11	186,258
Country Roads	92	13	10	9	176,808
Win More Stable, Inc.	38	13	3	6	175,000
Hogan, Barry and Elizabeth and Meier, Rosemary B.	35	13	5	2	173,883
Warwick Stable	60	13	9	10	168,940
Clifford W. Sise, Jr.	53	13	12	7	167,813
Sheila P. Arnold	92	13	11	14	167,645
Barry R. Ostrager	85	13	9	13	166,465
Eilers, Marilyn and Larry J.	127	13	9	16	163,166
AFM Stables Limited	98	13	18	6	162,733
Charles T. Matses	67	13	9	10	155,677
Jack Waldie	102	13	10	14	155,580
Fatman Stables	30	13	6	4	153,722
Chances Are Racing Stable	91	13	12	7	151,104
Daniel J. Lopez	66	13	11	4	148,043
C. Rutledge Horne	95	13	16	14	144,309
Joel W. Sainer	66	13	11	10	142,715
Lams Racing Stable	32	13	1	2	141,580
Champion Racing Stable, Inc.	106	13	14	14	140,287
C. Les Hogg	69	13	9	20	133,876
Empire Meadows T'bred Park	58	13	3	5	129,240
Cornerstone T'breds LLC	95	13	10	9	127,780
Michael A. Dire	86	13	8	6	115,845
David Lathrop	136	13	21	23	109,798
Bruce D. Anderson	92	13	14	20	101,229
Jim Ates	75	13	8	13	98,852
Hern and LePley Racing	56	13	7	11	95,977
Billingsley Creek Ranch	60	13	4	8	95,339
Gordon C. Severson	122	13	10	12	92,749
Phyllis L. Presswood	67	13	15	10	85,626
Rolling Hills Farm LLC	105	13	19	11	80,624
Elison, Tim W. and Deidre	61	13	14	8	74,694
Margaret Root	69	13	13	3	74,322
British Mist Racing	71	13	15	8	64,988
Miller, Shirley L. and Castellanos, Jaime	81	13	8	11	63,460
Marsue Stable	36	13	5	7	60,291
Peggy Faulkner	48	13	6	6	59,696
Carol J. Kelley	94	13	4	9	46,703
Tawnja Elison	27	13	5	2	45,861

Owner	Starts	1st	2d	3d	Purses
John C. Oxley	73	12	8	11	1,338,124
Come By Chance Stable	62	12	5	4	1,021,037
Cowan, Marjorie and Irving M.	81	12	14	18	885,900
Brushwood Stable	57	12	9	7	795,260
Robert V. La Penta	49	12	8	5	742,019
Bohemia Stable	68	12	16	6	709,546
Schwartz, Herbert T. and Carol A.	115	12	13	10	694,827
Fog City Stable	72	12	7	9	664,204
Saud bin Khaled	49	12	6	2	642,877
Charles, Ronald L. and Clear Valley Stables	84	12	13	14	623,880
S L U, Inc.	109	12	14	16	593,527
James F. Edwards	49	12	6	6	570,248
Steeplechase Farm	68	12	7	10	528,137
Erdenheim Farm	70	12	6	7	516,737
Robert S. Evans	70	12	8	14	507,762
Zuckerman, Donald S. and Roberta Mary	51	12	7	6	506,680
Cornejo Racing, Inc.	24	12	1	1	506,070
Paul P. Pompa, Jr.	90	12	18	17	470,873
Ben Barnow	97	12	14	19	368,661
John Castro	76	12	11	12	365,296
Vincent S. Scuderi	47	12	10	6	364,717
Robert H. Shepard	112	12	16	15	362,144
Lothenbach Stables, Inc.	111	12	11	18	323,132
Candy Stables	83	12	12	6	292,698
Sefa's Farm	83	12	16	10	280,902
L. T. B., Inc. and Childers, Miles	66	12	9	5	272,947
Lynne Ristad-Lidgett	114	12	19	17	268,110
Nicholas B. Alexander	50	12	10	5	262,775
Millsap Stables, Inc.	66	12	10	9	245,889
Lake Forest Stable	43	12	4	7	244,309
Nick Cafarchia	52	12	3	8	239,486
Martha K. Gonzalez	47	12	3	5	230,309
Woodvale Farm	119	12	18	12	227,030
Ernest J. George	157	12	16	26	221,451
A. A. C. Stables	57	12	12	9	220,432
Johnny A. Butler	79	12	8	12	217,245
Lomas, Alma and Roy H.	66	12	4	14	216,790
Kay Hale	75	12	15	11	208,955
Bluestem Farm, Inc.	82	12	12	9	208,514
Girdner, Paul K. and Jones, Reginald C.	58	12	9	3	206,606
Hidden Meadow Farm LLC	54	12	5	12	197,215
Jim Bissett	69	12	13	10	193,804
Barry, Henry and Donald	41	12	4	7	192,930
Charles R. Bosco, Sr.	97	12	7	5	191,689
Tony Schuler	53	12	6	7	191,338
Chumas, Janice and Connie	57	12	12	4	190,271
Pete Sinetos	47	12	6	1	188,090
Broadwall Farm	127	12	21	12	184,371
Hall, William E. and Heather	62	12	8	6	181,140
Childers, Miles, L. T. B., Inc. and Wright, Ed	42	12	6	2	180,805
J. Edwin Shilling	84	12	8	10	175,337
Finish Line Partnership	35	12	4	6	167,891
Diglett Stable	45	12	6	6	165,527
Mary Rohner	87	12	10	12	160,514
Laneve, Nicholas S., Warner, William and Ferraro, M. A.	26	12	3	4	158,916
Harry J. Daut	31	12	5	2	158,484
Anita Racing Stable	100	12	10	16	153,795
Gorsuch, Robert, Kreis, Robert and Makarovich, Jr., Raymond	32	12	8	4	153,790
The Jim Stable	96	12	11	16	150,276
Robert H. Zoellner	76	12	11	12	149,563
Grand Slam Racing Stable	93	12	16	10	148,420
Horned Owl Stables	45	12	2	2	148,127
Martha K. Struthers	94	12	12	12	145,446
Sure Shot Stables	40	12	9	6	144,116
Joseph E. Asbell	81	12	16	14	142,320
Lara Racing Stables, Ltd.	118	12	11	19	141,585
Shotwell Farm	99	12	10	12	138,956
Double D Farm Corp.	136	12	11	16	131,869
R. Legacy Racing, Inc.	34	12	4	7	124,145
John Charles Zimmerman	35	12	9	2	115,099
Dick Cappellucci	33	12	6	4	114,857
Metzen, Thomas F. and Karen	69	12	7	8	111,572
Milltown Road Associates	79	12	10	5	111,183
Dale R. White, Sr.	53	12	7	8	110,224
J. Michael Baird	71	12	10	5	105,774
Robert M. Gorham, Jr.	33	12	2	4	103,294
Distefano, Jr., Anthony and Bourgoyne, Tracey	47	12	14	7	99,236
Oak Tree Stables, Inc. and Cheyenne Stable LLC	37	12	3	6	96,186
Richaleen Turpin	77	12	18	9	94,010
A and R Stables LLC	27	12	1	3	92,406
B H Racing Stables, Inc.	79	12	10	12	88,876
White Lake Farms, Inc.	91	12	12	15	87,634
Richard W. Bibb	47	12	7	4	86,776
Bennie D. Lafever	79	12	11	16	85,202
Heartland Racing Team	84	12	12	15	84,988
Kathy L. Stephens	92	12	11	10	84,701
Johnny Black	72	12	9	6	79,722
East Coast Racing Stables LLC	66	12	15	6	78,940
Thomas J. Terry	38	12	2	2	74,699
Kent Calland	97	12	11	6	73,555
William R. Strange	83	12	11	10	66,857
Melanie Hill	57	12	8	5	66,424
Kathryn Wright	56	12	7	9	64,329
Agustin Murillo	43	12	10	4	60,354
Leavitt Thoroughbreds LLC	60	12	4	7	60,033
Widman, Larry and Hansen, Russell	43	12	6	4	56,700
B. and W. Investors	33	12	5	5	55,796
Tim Disney	95	12	6	8	52,951
Don R. Smith	82	12	5	9	37,267

*Includes $500,000 bonus

Snapshot Facts: There were 37 owners whose horses won 50 or more races in 2003. Seventeen owners won more than 75 races and nine won more than 100.

Annual Leading Owner – Money Won

Year	Owner	Earnings
1902	Green B. Morris	$98,350
1903	William C. Whitney	102,569
1904	H.B. Duryea	200,107
1905	James R. Keene	228,724
1906	James R. Keene	155,519
1907	James R. Keene	397,342
1908	James R. Keene	282,342
1909	Samuel C. Hildreth	159,112
1910	Samuel C. Hildreth	152,645
1911	Samuel C. Hildreth	47,473
1912	John W. Schorr	58,225
1913	Harry Payne Whitney	55,056
1914	John W. Schorr	85,326
1915	L.S. Thompson	104,106
1916	H. Guy Bedwell	71,100
1917	A. King Macomber	68,578
1918	J.K.L. Ross	99,179
1919	J.K.L. Ross	209,303
1920	Harry Payne Whitney	270,675
1921	Rancocas Stable (Harry F. Sinclair)	263,500
1922	Rancocas Stable (Harry F. Sinclair)	239,503
1923	Rancocas Stable (Harry F. Sinclair)	438,849
1924	Harry Payne Whitney	240,193
1925	Glen Riddle Farm Stable (Samuel D. Riddle)	199,143
1926	Harry Payne Whitney	407,139
1927	Harry Payne Whitney	328,769
1928	Edward B. McLean	234,640
1929	Harry Payne Whitney	362,305
1930	C.V. Whitney	385,972
1931	C.V. Whitney	422,923
1932	C.V. Whitney	403,681
1933	C.V. Whitney	241,292
1934	Brookmeade Stable (Mrs. Dodge Soane)	251,138
1935	A.G. Vanderbilt	303,605
1936	Milky Way Farm (Mrs. Ethel V. Mars)	206,450
1937	Mrs. Charles S. Howard	214,559
1938	H. Maxwell Howard	226,495
1939	Belair Stud (William Woodward)	284,250
1940	Charles S. Howard	334,120
1941	Calumet Farm (Warren Wright)	475,091
1942	Greentree Stable (Mrs. Payne Whitney)	414,432
1943	Calumet Farm (Warren Wright)	267,915
1944	Calumet Farm (Warren Wright)	601,660
1945	Maine Chance Farm (Mrs. Elizabeth N. Graham)	589,170
1946	Calumet Farm (Warren Wright)	564,095
1947	Calumet Farm (Warren Wright)	1,402,436
1948	Calumet Farm (Warren Wright)	1,269,710
1949	Calumet Farm (Warren Wright)	1,128,942
1950	Brookmeade Stable (Mrs. Dodge Sloane)	651,399
1951	Greentree Stable (Mrs. C.S. Payne & J.H. Whitney)	637,242
1952	Calumet Farm (Mrs. Gene Markey)	1,283,197
1953	A.G. Vanderbilt	987,306
1954	King Ranch (Robert J. Kleberg Jr.)	837,615
1955	Hasty House Farm (Mr. & Mrs. A.E. Reuben)	832,879
1956	Calumet Farm (Mrs. Gene Markey)	1,057,383
1957	Calumet Farm (Mrs. Gene Markey)	1,150,910
1958	Calumet Farm (Mrs. Gene Markey)	946,262
1959	Cain Hoy Stable (H.F. Guggenheim)	742,081
1960	C.V. Whitney	1,039,091
1961	Calumet Farm (Mrs. Gene Markey)	759,856
1962	Ellsworth Stable (Rex C. Ellsworth)	1,154,454
1963	Ellsworth Stable (Rex C. Ellsworth)	1,096,863
1964	Wheatley Stable (Mrs. Henry C. Phipps)	1,073,572
1965	Marion H. Van Berg	895,246
1966	Wheatley Stable (Mrs. Henry C. Phipps)	1,225,861
1967	Hobeau Farm (J.J. Dreyfus Jr.)	1,120,143
1968	Marion H. Van Berg	1,105,388
1969	Marion H. Van Berg	1,453,679
1970	Marion H. Van Berg	1,347,289
1971	Sigmund Sommer	1,523,508
1972	Sigmund Sommer	1,605,896
1973	Dan R. Lasater	1,498,785
1974	Dan R. Lasater	3,022,960
1975	Dan R. Lasater	2,894,726
1976	Dan R. Lasater	2,894,074
1977	Elmendorf (Max Gluck)	2,309,200
1978	Harbor View Farm	2,097,443
1979	Harbor View Farm	2,701,741
1980	Harbor View Farm	2,207,576
1981	Elmendorf (Max Gluck)	1,928,102
1982	Viola Sommer	2,182,626
1983	John Franks	2,643,251
1984	John Franks	3,070,225
1985	Mr. & Mrs. Eugene V. Klein	5,451,201
1986	John Franks	4,463,375
1987	Mr. & Mrs. Eugene V. Klein	5,746,334
1988	Ogden Phipps	5,858,168
1989	Ogden Phipps	5,438,034
1990	Kinghaven Farms	5,041,280
1991	Sam-Son Farm	6,881,902
1992	Golden Eagle Farm	5,479,484
1993	John Franks	5,682,786
1994	John Franks	4,518,083
1995	Allen Paulson	7,238,800
1996	Overbrook Farm	7,008,802
1997	Allen Paulson	5,259,107
1998	Stronach Stable	7,221,416
1999	Stronach Stable	6,221,147
2000	Stronach Stable	11,198,225
2001	Richard A. Englander	9,783,472
2002	Stronach Stable	8,349,249
2003	Michael J. Gill	9,236,530

Annual Leading Owner – Races Won

Year	Owner	Amount Won	Races Won	Year	Owner	Amount Won	Races Won
1905	E. Corrigan	$41,465	100	1951	William Hal Bishop	232,622	117
1906	B. Schreiber	85,713	120	1952	Marion H. Van Berg	311,560	140
1907	B. Schreiber	68,068	105	1953	W. H. Bishop Stable, Inc.	360,514	153
1908	B. Schreiber	88,329	110	1954	W. H. Bishop Stable, Inc.	334,305	119
1909	B. Schreiber	54,475	143	1955	Marion H. Van Berg	348,580	127
1910	R.F. Carman	64,440	105	1956	T. A. Grissom	335,137	118
1911	W.B. Carson	16,690	74		Mr. and Mrs. Marion H.		
1912	H. Guy Bedwell	47,452	103		Van Berg	315,945	118
1913	H. Guy Bedwell	40,475	80	1957	T. A. Grissom	430,506	139
1914	H. Guy Bedwell	50,465	87	1958	W. H. Bishop Stable, Inc.	670,864	165
1915	H. Guy Bedwell	59,530	123	1959	W. H. Bishop Stable, Inc.	626,149	160
1916	H. Guy Bedwell	71,100	136	1960	Marion H. Van Berg	642,607	221
1917	H. Guy Bedwell	38,790	65	1961	Marion H. Van Berg	556,732	192
1918	R.D. &P.J. Williams	55,831	77	1962	Marion H. Van Berg	597,625	205
1919	K. Spence	40,080	67	1963	Marion H. Van Berg	670,367	201
1920	J.K.L. Ross	250,586	118	1964	Marion H. Van Berg	822,305	258
1921	J.K.L. Ross	167,642	88	1965	Marion H. Van Berg	895,246	270
1922	J.K.L. Ross	169,134	78	1966	Marion H. Van Berg	897,794	277
1923	C.B. Irwin	104,054	147	1967	Marion H. Van Berg	1,001,568	268
1924	H. Guy Bedwell	106,580	86	1968	Marion H. Van Berg	1,105,388	339
1925	G. Frank Croissant	112,081	86	1969	Marion H. Van Berg	1,453,679	393
1926	Harry Payne Whitney	407,139	122	1970	Marion H. Van Berg	1,347,289	391
1927	Seagram Stable			1971	Audley Farm (J. F. Edwards)	1,400,258	370
	(E. F. Seagram)	254,922	95	1972	Audley Farm (J. F. Edwards)	1,175,343	302
	Audley Farm Stable			1973	Audley Farm (J. F. Edwards)	1,162,438	266
	(M. & B. B. Jones)	148,183	95	1974	Dan R. Lasater	3,022,960	494
1928	Audley Farm Stable			1975	Dan R. Lasater	2,894,726	459
	(B. B. Jones)	188,106	83	1976	Dan R. Lasater	2,894,074	404
	Seagram Stable			1977	Dan R. Lasater	1,647,107	263
	(E.F., N. & T. W.Seagram)	173,558	83	1978	Dale Baird	309,685	162
1929	Seagram Stable			1979	Dale Baird	415,045	234
	(E.F., N. & T. W.Seagram)	155,945	88	1980	Dale Baird	409,836	230
1930	C.V. Whitney	385,972	120	1981	Dale Baird	503,021	293
1931	C.V. Whitney	422,923	105	1982	Dale Baird	445,650	259
1932	C.V. Whitney	413,361	119	1983	John Franks	2,643,251	183
1933	C.V. Whitney	241,292	136	1984	John Franks	3,070,225	172
1934	B. B. Stable (Beebe-Byers)	74,295	92	1985	Dale Baird	377,542	202
1935	Mrs. A.M. Creech	103,260	107	1986	John Franks	4,463,115	250
1936	Mrs. Ethel D. Jacobs	137,859	149	1987	John Franks	3,445,736	235
1937	Mrs. Ethel D. Jacobs	115,329	102	1988	John Franks	3,834,908	232
1938	Medway Stable			1989	John Franks	3,852,813	255
	(J. E. Smallman)	78,062	99	1990	Dale Baird	365,639	197
1939	Mrs. Emil Denemark	108,520	88	1991	Dale Baird	424,072	246
1940	Mrs. Emil Denemark	115,207	112	1992	Dale Baird	395,496	222
1941	Mrs. Emil Denemark	123,109	111	1993	Dale Baird	397,194	225
1942	Calumet Farm			1994	Dale Baird	428,314	201
	(Warren Wright)	315,005	72	1995	Dale Baird	614,535	251
1943	Mrs. Ethel D. Jacobs	141,775	81	1996	Dale Baird	923,807	278
1944	C. V. Whitney	172,434	64	1997	Dale Baird	1,129,787	275
1945	Mrs. Lottie Wolf	238,361	127	1998	Dale Baird	1,434,265	264
1946	Willian Helis	458,060	89	1999	Dale Baird	2,122,900	308
1947	Calumet Farm			2000	Dale Baird	2,327,230	241
	(Warren Wright)	1,402,436	100	2001	Richard A. Englander	9,783,472	405
1948	Calumet Farm			2002	Richard A. Englander	7,515,562	278
	(Warren Wright)	1,269,710	92	2003	Michael J. Gill	9,236,530	425
1949	William Hal Bishop	235,901	129				
1950	William Hal Bishop	218,689	127				

Leading Trainers in 2003 by Money Won

Trainer	Starts	1st	2d	3d	Pct.	Purses
Robert J. Frankel	411	114	79	57	0.277	$19,143,289
Todd A. Pletcher	826	199	132	105	0.241	12,356,924
Steven M. Asmussen	1,949	452	352	301	0.232	11,725,782
Richard E. Mandella	253	51	40	38	0.202	9,869,548
Bob Baffert	674	127	119	80	0.188	9,442,281
Scott A. Lake	2,009	454	345	280	0.226	9,152,959
William I. Mott	718	138	101	85	0.192	6,866,320
Doug O'Neill	760	133	119	109	0.175	6,438,799
Jerry Hollendorfer	1,216	282	211	193	0.232	6,260,305
Mark Shuman	1,105	225	177	128	0.204	5,633,150
Christophe Clement	389	75	65	39	0.193	5,558,742
Cole Norman	1,086	290	183	125	0.267	5,496,689
Nicholas P. Zito	507	77	86	59	0.152	5,344,914
H. Allen Jerkens	359	73	82	62	0.203	5,173,434
Richard E. Dutrow, Jr.	531	132	90	85	0.249	4,917,280
Jeff Mullins	313	94	61	35	0.300	4,383,866
Ronald L. McAnally	312	44	38	29	0.141	4,309,058
D. Wayne Lukas	663	71	73	80	0.107	4,179,832
Robert P. Tiller	254	73	41	37	0.287	4,090,391
Allen Iwinski	598	148	117	81	0.248	4,053,035
Dale L. Romans	638	113	98	71	0.177	3,987,852
Mark A. Hennig	503	73	85	74	0.145	3,954,020
Mark R. Frostad	206	44	34	31	0.214	3,918,142
Neil D. Drysdale	182	34	27	37	0.187	3,676,819
Kenneth G. McPeek	400	61	61	57	0.153	3,647,975
Neil J. Howard	156	31	26	18	0.199	3,620,359
Barclay Tagg	166	16	23	24	0.096	3,542,297
W. Elliott Walden	289	67	53	36	0.232	3,509,486
Mark E. Casse	465	59	61	68	0.127	3,466,964
Michael Keogh	97	17	7	8	0.175	3,262,209
Thomas M. Amoss	445	118	84	52	0.265	3,217,121
Wallace A. Dollase	95	24	14	17	0.253	3,168,828
Kiaran P. McLaughlin	186	46	26	20	0.247	3,157,180
W. Bret Calhoun	634	156	120	69	0.246	3,088,177
Roger L. Attfield	330	32	44	50	0.097	2,993,896
Sid C. Attard	278	54	45	26	0.194	2,894,519
H. Graham Motion	318	55	47	53	0.173	2,822,266
Scott H. Fairlie	338	84	55	55	0.249	2,816,357
John W. Sadler	375	71	56	59	0.189	2,782,405
Dale Capuano	778	164	151	95	0.211	2,775,536
Claude R. McGaughey III	259	48	40	36	0.185	2,723,707
Reade Baker	191	48	34	28	0.251	2,687,183
Steve B. Klesaris	347	77	54	55	0.222	2,635,382
Timothy A. Hills	479	81	64	61	0.169	2,617,324
Abraham R. Katryan	301	57	34	48	0.189	2,612,005
Donnie K. Von Hemel	416	94	81	59	0.226	2,576,588

Trainer	Starts	1st	2d	3d	Pct.	Purses
Bernard S. Flint	634	128	81	71	0.202	2,566,975
Edward Plesa, Jr.	437	76	62	60	0.174	2,520,681
Josie Carroll	273	47	39	36	0.172	2,496,163
Anthony W. Dutrow	297	89	65	39	0.300	2,448,827
Daniel J. Vella	192	42	31	13	0.219	2,435,069
Armando Lage	801	141	145	117	0.176	2,407,056
Darrell Vienna	303	51	52	34	0.168	2,393,598
Timothy F. Ritchey	405	79	60	72	0.195	2,388,246
Craig Dollase	142	32	22	20	0.225	2,366,273
David R. Bell	298	38	36	46	0.128	2,358,956
James A. Jerkens	194	46	30	30	0.237	2,303,508
Michael W. Dickinson	152	37	30	19	0.243	2,286,371
Malcolm Pierce	249	34	35	29	0.137	2,259,868
John A. Shirreffs	163	33	18	25	0.203	2,237,892
Gary C. Contessa	528	59	58	64	0.112	2,235,357
Art Sherman	501	113	86	76	0.226	2,129,897
Michael V. Pino	422	127	77	62	0.301	2,111,952
Stanley M. Hough	289	50	55	37	0.173	2,107,589
Wesley A. Ward	508	93	99	79	0.183	2,102,262
Dale Baird	1,072	137	147	150	0.128	2,039,862
Bruce N. Levine	366	66	41	56	0.180	2,038,357
Mike R. Mitchell	262	65	51	48	0.248	2,019,188
John C. Kimmel	317	45	30	46	0.142	2,014,841
Vladimir Cerin	268	49	37	44	0.183	1,997,149
Laura De Seroux	111	14	13	11	0.126	1,965,242
George R. Arnold, II	259	34	47	35	0.131	1,961,444
H. James Bond	196	46	20	16	0.235	1,932,521
Martin D. Wolfson	184	36	39	21	0.196	1,926,533
Wayne M. Catalano	356	106	53	42	0.298	1,917,636
Rafael Becerra	235	48	41	33	0.204	1,897,983
Julio C. Canani	165	35	22	26	0.212	1,896,774
Emanuel Tortora	438	66	64	58	0.151	1,894,152
Carl A. Nafzger	285	31	30	47	0.109	1,868,359
A. Ferris Allen, III	690	98	118	104	0.142	1,861,729
Dallas Stewart	308	49	41	38	0.159	1,855,344
Jonathan E. Sheppard	460	54	63	76	0.117	1,845,326
Michael E. Gorham	388	64	55	60	0.165	1,833,673
Paul J. McGee	309	46	46	41	0.149	1,833,433
Jeff Bonde	358	63	60	49	0.176	1,831,339
Linda Rice	352	51	53	52	0.145	1,818,043
Bruce Headley	138	29	17	26	0.210	1,806,298
Ted H. West	167	39	33	27	0.234	1,802,147
Keith L. Bourgeois	774	144	120	118	0.186	1,783,385
Michael E. Hushion	211	52	36	24	0.246	1,775,506
Gene A. Cilio	353	48	60	44	0.136	1,770,255
Jennifer Pedersen	320	30	41	36	0.094	1,754,294
Anthony L. Reinstedler	190	34	25	17	0.179	1,741,618
Murray W. Johnson	101	14	5	11	0.139	1,732,941

Trainer	Starts	1st	2d	3d	Pct.	Purses
William Spawr	297	65	47	25	0.219	1,715,806
Patrick L. Biancone	135	26	15	21	0.193	1,711,726
Patrick J. Kelly	266	21	31	33	0.079	1,710,927
Vito Armata	242	42	28	41	0.174	1,699,311
Patrick L. Reynolds	217	38	30	32	0.175	1,694,627
Michael R. Matz	187	25	33	19	0.134	1,694,615
John J. Robb	430	72	71	53	0.167	1,686,593
Michael L. Reavis	475	100	73	69	0.211	1,674,666
John C. Servis	325	62	58	43	0.191	1,670,665
Richard A. Violette, Jr.	178	28	19	35	0.157	1,656,468
David E. Hofmans	113	17	10	18	0.150	1,655,369
John Charles Zimmerman	553	132	101	69	0.239	1,654,261
Hugh H. Robertson	412	81	64	55	0.197	1,645,507
William P. White	386	74	41	54	0.192	1,642,373
Clifford W. Sise, Jr.	409	73	63	56	0.179	1,639,135
Jack Carava	361	61	51	57	0.169	1,624,102
Harry F. Thompson, Jr.	1,023	197	162	148	0.193	1,612,005
Robert E. Holthus	312	53	44	51	0.170	1,595,737
Jeff C. Runco	649	118	112	90	0.182	1,585,486
Bruce M. Kravets	1,118	198	159	164	0.177	1,561,062
William E. Morey	401	100	70	68	0.249	1,554,868
John T. Ward, Jr.	90	17	9	13	0.189	1,551,218
Layne S. Giliforte	484	68	94	59	0.141	1,543,790
Ronny W. Werner	247	55	49	33	0.223	1,528,906
Hamilton A. Smith	490	73	64	81	0.149	1,528,726
Barry Abrams	365	38	39	53	0.104	1,526,968
Nick Canani	253	43	40	35	0.170	1,522,828
Aidan P. O'Brien	10	1	2	2	0.100	1,496,800
Albert M. Stall, Jr.	309	53	40	50	0.172	1,495,011
Dennis J. Manning	155	21	10	24	0.136	1,494,773
Stanley W. Roberts	640	90	82	85	0.141	1,489,610
Guadalupe Preciado	487	73	69	80	0.150	1,478,601
Robert P. Klesaris	419	60	69	80	0.143	1,461,391
Kathleen O'Connell	511	82	60	67	0.161	1,451,667
Danny Pish	656	123	95	72	0.188	1,449,831
John A. Ross	142	18	23	25	0.127	1,437,072
C. Cliff Hopmans, Jr.	171	23	23	19	0.135	1,418,810
Dan L. Hendricks	176	28	21	28	0.159	1,413,975
Henry Dominguez	442	108	75	62	0.244	1,413,493
Chris M. Block	259	50	35	31	0.193	1,407,832
Niall M. O'Callaghan	243	25	20	41	0.103	1,406,322
Patrick B. Byrne	119	25	27	14	0.210	1,396,421
Joseph F. Orseno	385	42	64	44	0.109	1,395,614
Ralph Ziadie	375	44	53	55	0.117	1,389,608
Philip G. Johnson	166	20	22	26	0.121	1,376,268
Ronney W. Brown	770	142	93	95	0.184	1,373,599
Gerald S. Bennett	551	103	98	68	0.187	1,350,507
Michael Stidham	292	51	40	43	0.175	1,343,812

Trainer	Starts	1st	2d	3d	Pct.	Purses
John S. McCaslin	366	100	71	51	0.273	1,332,327
Timothy Ritvo	533	71	72	64	0.133	1,329,337
Randy Schulhofer	146	23	16	18	0.158	1,326,465
C. Beau Greely	126	20	13	19	0.159	1,323,774
John E. Salzman, Sr.	371	54	52	67	0.146	1,322,984
Scooter Davis	471	98	72	53	0.208	1,312,698
Benjamin M. Feliciano, Jr.	294	66	46	46	0.225	1,310,170
Michael Machowsky	185	28	33	23	0.151	1,298,638
Ralph Martinez	708	208	136	112	0.294	1,293,698
Patrick Gallagher	238	24	31	32	0.101	1,293,652
Saeed bin Suroor	16	2	4	5	0.125	1,290,330
Rodney Jenkins	263	56	46	33	0.213	1,284,474
Michael J. Doyle	262	17	37	45	0.065	1,278,554
David M. Carroll	132	35	16	15	0.265	1,266,858
Alan E. Goldberg	222	39	33	24	0.176	1,265,895
Frank John Kirby	494	53	64	78	0.107	1,261,312
Eoin G. Harty	110	30	21	9	0.273	1,257,859
Robert Barbara	201	29	16	24	0.144	1,239,853
Catherine Day Phillips	93	18	11	15	0.194	1,234,298
Benjamin W. Perkins, Jr.	190	36	22	19	0.190	1,227,899
John F. Martin	335	103	60	41	0.308	1,222,893
Edward T. Allard	395	71	54	58	0.180	1,218,361
Alexander F. McPherson	173	33	24	19	0.191	1,217,381
Laurie Silvera	147	23	23	15	0.157	1,217,366
Audre Cappuccitti	274	22	32	35	0.080	1,201,140
Jenine Sahadi	155	22	20	16	0.142	1,200,976
Dominic G. Galluscio	239	35	30	33	0.146	1,198,681
Gregory D. Foley	230	50	28	40	0.217	1,196,620
Richard J. Ciardullo, Jr.	406	69	62	42	0.170	1,196,596
Paul G. Aguirre	201	39	34	22	0.194	1,195,370
George Weaver	224	33	30	24	0.147	1,177,404
John Cardella	186	23	30	23	0.124	1,170,397
Hal R. Wiggins	272	37	42	31	0.136	1,163,606
James M. Cassidy	155	15	22	15	0.097	1,158,021
Macdonald Benson	120	13	19	9	0.108	1,156,115
David R. Vance	282	40	30	32	0.142	1,148,462
Bobby C. Barnett	350	45	36	36	0.129	1,143,246
Ralph J. Biamonte	162	42	27	22	0.259	1,142,839
Dick R. Clark	402	77	63	54	0.192	1,142,583
James E. Day	104	14	5	11	0.135	1,139,974
Howard E. Wolfendale	261	73	44	46	0.280	1,130,425
Norman McKnight	247	28	30	26	0.113	1,121,242
Larry Robideaux, Jr.	251	44	39	35	0.175	1,118,345
David Cotey	177	19	23	25	0.107	1,111,582
Dermot K. Weld	8	3	1	0	0.375	1,108,000
Norman R. Pointer	313	51	52	35	0.163	1,104,835
Richard P. Hazelton	253	40	33	40	0.158	1,102,397
Richard E. Schosberg	187	27	27	33	0.144	1,102,228

Trainer	Starts	1st	2d	3d	Pct.	Purses
Kathleen A. Demasi	535	63	62	63	0.118	1,100,301
Henry Collazo	477	63	57	65	0.132	1,099,754
Carla Gaines	159	23	32	20	0.145	1,094,952
Robert B. Hess, Jr.	215	26	25	24	0.121	1,091,267
Stephen R. Margolis	94	16	16	16	0.170	1,089,523
Gary Sciacca	376	18	25	39	0.048	1,077,920
Robert M. Gorham	417	71	63	67	0.170	1,077,422
Andrew Leggio, Jr.	128	22	19	9	0.172	1,075,581
Doris Hebert	409	70	80	70	0.171	1,072,945
Ronald J. Dandy	601	104	96	74	0.173	1,070,833
Thomas M. Agosti	319	66	49	47	0.207	1,068,801
Mark Glatt	235	42	28	20	0.179	1,066,929
Don Von Hemel	294	39	53	46	0.133	1,065,533
Michael P. DePaulo	182	17	23	18	0.093	1,065,288
Patricia Farro	486	69	59	68	0.142	1,063,345
Kristin Mulhall	105	15	20	9	0.143	1,062,473
Thomas F. Tomillo	632	65	61	66	0.103	1,057,825
James Hatchett	264	42	45	32	0.159	1,051,662
Frank LaBoccetta, Jr.	179	43	44	16	0.240	1,050,658
Donald S. Reeder	433	79	69	52	0.182	1,047,158
Chris J. Englehart	575	111	89	82	0.193	1,039,199
J. Eric Kruljac	311	74	52	41	0.238	1,037,384
David G. Donk	270	29	25	48	0.107	1,034,471
Frank A. Alexander	147	20	22	21	0.136	1,033,210
Lawrence E. Murray	129	22	17	13	0.171	1,025,526
Craig Anthony Lewis	209	30	25	26	0.144	1,024,093
Kelly R. Von Hemel	295	51	44	43	0.173	1,013,877
Chris Tuttle	504	65	72	58	0.129	1,009,239

Leading Trainers in 2003 by Races Won

Trainer	Starts	1st	2d	3d	Pct.	Purses
Scott A. Lake	2,009	454	345	280	0.226	$9,152,959
Steven M. Asmussen	1,949	452	352	301	0.232	11,725,782
Cole Norman	1,086	290	183	125	0.267	5,496,689
Jerry Hollendorfer	1,216	282	211	193	0.232	6,260,305
Mark Shuman	1,105	225	177	128	0.204	5,633,150
Ralph Martinez	708	208	136	112	0.294	1,293,698
Todd A. Pletcher	826	199	132	105	0.241	12,356,924
Bruce M. Kravets	1,118	198	159	164	0.177	1,561,062
Harry F. Thompson, Jr.	1,023	197	162	148	0.193	1,612,005
Dale Capuano	778	164	151	95	0.211	2,775,536
W. Bret Calhoun	634	156	120	69	0.246	3,088,177
Allen Iwinski	598	148	117	81	0.248	4,053,035
Keith L. Bourgeois	774	144	120	118	0.186	1,783,385
Ronney W. Brown	770	142	93	95	0.184	1,373,599
Armando Lage	801	141	145	117	0.176	2,407,056
William I. Mott	718	138	101	85	0.192	6,866,320
Dale Baird	1,072	137	147	150	0.128	2,039,862
Doug O'Neill	760	133	119	109	0.175	6,438,799
Rodney C. Faulkner	727	133	113	107	0.183	785,605
Richard E. Dutrow, Jr.	531	132	90	85	0.249	4,917,280
John Charles Zimmerman	553	132	101	69	0.239	1,654,261
Bernard S. Flint	634	128	81	71	0.202	2,566,975
Jose A. Martinez	731	128	109	102	0.175	904,069
Bob Baffert	674	127	119	80	0.188	9,442,281
Michael V. Pino	422	127	77	62	0.301	2,111,952
David C. Anderson	519	125	82	65	0.241	749,333
Danny Pish	656	123	95	72	0.188	1,449,831
Thomas M. Amoss	445	118	84	52	0.265	3,217,121
Jeff C. Runco	649	118	112	90	0.182	1,585,486
Robert J. Frankel	411	114	79	57	0.277	19,143,289
Dale L. Romans	638	113	98	71	0.177	3,987,852
Art Sherman	501	113	86	76	0.226	2,129,897
Chris J. Englehart	575	111	89	82	0.193	1,039,199
Henry Dominguez	442	108	75	62	0.244	1,413,493
Wayne M. Catalano	356	106	53	42	0.298	1,917,636
Ronald J. Dandy	601	104	96	74	0.173	1,070,833
Gerald S. Bennett	551	103	98	68	0.187	1,350,507
John F. Martin	335	103	60	41	0.308	1,222,893
Michael L. Reavis	475	100	73	69	0.211	1,674,666
William E. Morey	401	100	70	68	0.249	1,554,868
John S. McCaslin	366	100	71	51	0.273	1,332,327
A. Ferris Allen, III	690	98	118	104	0.142	1,861,729
Scooter Davis	471	98	72	53	0.208	1,312,698
Michael Anthony Ferraro	408	97	66	53	0.238	874,216
Don J. Mills	339	96	62	45	0.283	828,506
Jeff Mullins	313	94	61	35	0.300	4,383,866
Donnie K. Von Hemel	416	94	81	59	0.226	2,576,588
Wesley A. Ward	508	93	99	79	0.183	2,102,262

Trainer	Starts	1st	2d	3d	Pct.	Purses
Kim Hammond	503	93	79	64	0.185	608,524
Stanley W. Roberts	640	90	82	85	0.141	1,489,610
Anthony W. Dutrow	297	89	65	39	0.300	2,448,827
Gary L. Johnson	658	87	77	78	0.132	835,709
David W. Geist	425	85	56	54	0.200	710,652
Scott H. Fairlie	338	84	55	55	0.249	2,816,357
Kathleen O'Connell	511	82	60	67	0.161	1,451,667
Timothy A. Hills	479	81	64	61	0.169	2,617,324
Hugh H. Robertson	412	81	64	55	0.197	1,645,507
Flint W. Stites	652	81	92	88	0.124	874,855
Timothy F. Ritchey	405	79	60	72	0.195	2,388,246
Donald S. Reeder	433	79	69	52	0.182	1,047,158
Charlton Baker	293	79	47	37	0.270	777,216
Todd M. Beattie	318	78	61	39	0.245	954,343
Nicholas P. Zito	507	77	86	59	0.152	5,344,914
Steve B. Klesaris	347	77	54	55	0.222	2,635,382
Dick R. Clark	402	77	63	54	0.192	1,142,583
Edward Plesa, Jr.	437	76	62	60	0.174	2,520,681
Eddie M. Essenpreis	433	76	65	75	0.176	674,080
Christophe Clement	389	75	65	39	0.193	5,558,742
Jon G. Arnett	407	75	70	59	0.184	776,172
Jeffrey A. Radosevich	469	75	72	56	0.160	731,442
Michael A. Lecesse	378	75	64	58	0.198	660,640
William P. White	386	74	41	54	0.192	1,642,373
J. Eric Kruljac	311	74	52	41	0.238	1,037,384
Dan L. McFarlane	411	74	89	68	0.180	679,479
H. Allen Jerkens	359	73	82	62	0.203	5,173,434
Robert P. Tiller	254	73	41	37	0.287	4,090,391
Mark A. Hennig	503	73	85	74	0.145	3,954,020
Clifford W. Sise, Jr.	409	73	63	56	0.179	1,639,135
Hamilton A. Smith	490	73	64	81	0.149	1,528,726
Guadalupe Preciado	487	73	69	80	0.150	1,478,601
Howard E. Wolfendale	261	73	44	46	0.280	1,130,425
Dale Angelle	380	73	79	49	0.192	950,202
J. Michael Baird	361	73	51	41	0.202	924,841
Joe Woodard	397	73	62	45	0.184	790,108
Michael S. Ferraro	304	73	47	30	0.240	510,423
John J. Robb	430	72	71	53	0.167	1,686,593
Kevin J. Joy	455	72	65	53	0.158	661,822
D. Wayne Lukas	663	71	73	80	0.107	4,179,832
John W. Sadler	375	71	56	59	0.189	2,782,405
Timothy Ritvo	533	71	72	64	0.133	1,329,337
Edward T. Allard	395	71	54	58	0.180	1,218,361
Robert M. Gorham	417	71	63	67	0.170	1,077,422
Ron K. Smith	328	71	61	54	0.217	962,661
Doris Hebert	409	70	80	70	0.171	1,072,945
Richard J. Ciardullo, Jr.	406	69	62	42	0.170	1,196,596
Patricia Farro	486	69	59	68	0.142	1,063,345
Michael W. Nance	375	69	66	34	0.184	939,295

Trainer	Starts	1st	2d	3d	Pct.	Purses
Leroy Hellman	348	69	54	48	0.198	552,731
Layne S. Giliforte	484	68	94	59	0.141	1,543,790
Samuel Breaux	382	68	48	50	0.178	982,876
Barbara I. McBride	328	68	48	36	0.207	437,982
W. Elliott Walden	289	67	53	36	0.232	3,509,486
Bruce N. Levine	366	66	41	56	0.180	2,038,357
Emanuel Tortora	438	66	64	58	0.151	1,894,152
Benjamin M. Feliciano, Jr.	294	66	46	46	0.225	1,310,170
Thomas M. Agosti	319	66	49	47	0.207	1,068,801
Joe S. Offolter	391	66	51	42	0.169	554,371
Jake S. Radosevich	447	66	72	59	0.148	520,967
Mike R. Mitchell	262	65	51	48	0.248	2,019,188
William Spawr	297	65	47	25	0.219	1,715,806
Thomas F. Tomillo	632	65	61	66	0.103	1,057,825
Chris Tuttle	504	65	72	58	0.129	1,009,239
Luis Albert Palacios	339	65	60	50	0.192	893,833
Michael E. Gorham	388	64	55	60	0.165	1,833,673
Michael Lenzini	429	64	53	39	0.149	550,312
Jeff Bonde	358	63	60	49	0.176	1,831,339
Kathleen A. Demasi	535	63	62	63	0.118	1,100,301
Henry Collazo	477	63	57	65	0.132	1,099,754
Randall R. Russell	380	63	46	47	0.166	449,401
John C. Servis	325	62	58	43	0.191	1,670,665
Kenneth G. McPeek	400	61	61	57	0.153	3,647,975
Jack Carava	361	61	51	57	0.169	1,624,102
Timothy Mark Gleason	383	61	41	55	0.159	763,194
Robert P. Klesaris	419	60	69	80	0.143	1,461,391
Steve Manley	379	60	56	50	0.158	491,600
Justin Evans	340	60	53	50	0.177	374,013
Mark E. Casse	465	59	61	68	0.127	3,466,964
Gary C. Contessa	528	59	58	64	0.112	2,235,357
Mark Fusco	298	59	50	41	0.198	890,069
L. Craig Cox	338	58	58	45	0.172	846,969
Randy Allen	394	58	49	59	0.147	835,398
Kevin Lewis	270	58	41	34	0.215	730,996
Abraham R. Katryan	301	57	34	48	0.189	2,612,005
Oscar S. Barrera, Jr.	293	57	45	32	0.195	494,451
Rodney Jenkins	263	56	46	33	0.213	1,284,474
Brian J. Koriner	291	56	51	41	0.192	930,474
Tim McCanna	296	56	46	47	0.189	501,178
Alan Crocker	250	56	32	35	0.224	287,125
H. Graham Motion	318	55	47	53	0.173	2,822,266
Ronny W. Werner	247	55	49	33	0.223	1,528,906
Edward J. Coletti, Jr.	259	55	47	38	0.212	987,350
Gary Danelson	189	55	38	27	0.291	417,424
Bill Brashears	298	55	48	48	0.185	305,084
Sid C. Attard	278	54	45	26	0.194	2,894,519
Jonathan E. Sheppard	460	54	63	76	0.117	1,845,326
John E. Salzman, Sr.	371	54	52	67	0.146	1,322,984

Trainer	Starts	1st	2d	3d	Pct.	Purses
Tommie T. Morgan	368	54	62	45	0.147	807,199
Rodrigo Madrigal, Sr.	246	54	36	23	0.220	794,519
Bart G. Hone	256	54	46	35	0.211	611,980
Robert E. Holthus	312	53	44	51	0.170	1,595,737
Albert M. Stall, Jr.	309	53	40	50	0.172	1,495,011
Frank John Kirby	494	53	64	78	0.107	1,261,312
John W. Baird	383	53	49	40	0.138	844,800
Michael E. Hushion	211	52	36	24	0.246	1,775,506
Angel C. Salinas	335	52	52	39	0.155	898,313
Gary W. Cross	271	52	51	44	0.192	849,264
Phillip T. Aristone	395	52	61	56	0.132	630,553
Michael Newell	471	52	64	53	0.110	571,159
Bernell B. Rhone	301	52	34	35	0.173	517,735
Samuel J. Keyrouze	383	52	44	37	0.136	313,194
Richard E. Mandella	253	51	40	38	0.202	9,869,548
Darrell Vienna	303	51	52	34	0.168	2,393,598
Linda Rice	352	51	53	52	0.145	1,818,043
Michael Stidham	292	51	40	43	0.175	1,343,812
Norman R. Pointer	313	51	52	35	0.163	1,104,835
Kelly R. Von Hemel	295	51	44	43	0.173	1,013,877
Stanley M. Hough	289	50	55	37	0.173	2,107,589
Chris M. Block	259	50	35	31	0.193	1,407,832
Gregory D. Foley	230	50	28	40	0.217	1,196,620
Lloyd C. Mason	274	50	34	36	0.183	801,568

Annual Leading Trainers – Money Won

Year	Trainer	Amount Won	Strts*	No. of Wins	Year	Trainer	Amount Won	Strts*	No. of Wins
1908	J. Rowe	$284,335		50	1957	H. A. Jones	1,150,910		70
1909	S. C. Hildreth	123,942		73	1958	W. Molter	1,116,544		69
1910	S. C. Hildreth	148,010		84	1959	W. Molter	847,290		71
1911	S. C. Hildreth	49,418		67	1960	H. Jacobs	748,349		97
1912	J. F. Schorr	58,110		63	1961	H. A. Jones	759,856		62
1913	J. Rowe	45,936		18	1962	M. A. Tenney	1,099,474		58
1914	R. C. Benson	59,315		45	1963	M. A. Tenney	860,703	192	40
1915	J. Rowe	75,596		19	1964	W. C. Winfrey	1,350,534	287	61
1916	S. C. Hildreth	70,950		39	1965	H. Jacobs	1,331,628	610	91
1917	S. C. Hildreth	61,698		23	1966	E. A. Neloy	2,456,250	282	93
1918	H. G. Bedwell	80,296		53	1967	E. A. Neloy	1,776,089	262	72
1919	H. G. Bedwell	208,728		63	1968	E. A. Neloy	1,233,101	212	52
1920	L. Feustal	186,087		22	1969	Elliott Burch	1,067,936	156	26
1921	S. C. Hildreth	262,768		85	1970	C. Whittingham	1,302,354	551	82
1922	S. C. Hildreth	247,014		74	1971	C. Whittingham	1,737,115	393	77
1923	S. C. Hildreth	392,124		75	1972	C. Whittingham	1,734,020	429	79
1924	S. C. Hildreth	255,608		77	1973	C. Whittingham	1,865,385	423	85
1925	G. R. Thompkins	199,245		30	1974	F. Martin	2,408,419	846	166
1926	S. P. Harlan	205,681		21	1975	C. Whittingham	2,437,244	487	93
1927	W. H. Bringloe	216,563		63	1976	J. Van Berg	2,976,196	2,362	496
1928	J. F. Schorr	258,425		65	1977	L. S. Barrera	2,715,848	781	127
1929	J. Rowe Jr	314,881		25	1978	L. S. Barrera	3,307,164	592	100
1930	J Fitzsimmons	397,355		47	1979	L. S. Barrera	3,608,517	492	98
1931	J. W. Healy	297,300		33	1980	L. S. Barrera	2,969,151	559	99
1932	J. Fitzsimmons	266,650		68	1981	C. Whittingham	3,993,302	376	74
1933	R. A. Smith	135,720		53	1982	C. Whittingham	4,587,457	410	63
1934	R. A. Smith	249,938		43	1983	D. Wayne Lukas	4,267,261	595	78
1935	J. H. Stotler	303,005		87	1984	D. Wayne Lukas	5,835,921	805	131
1936	J. Fitzsimmons	193,415		42	1985	D. Wayne Lukas	11,155,188	1,140	218
1937	R. McGarvey	209,925		46	1986	D. Wayne Lukas	12,345,180	1,510	259
1938	E. H. Sande	226,495		15	1987	D. Wayne Lukas	17,502,110	1,735	343
1939	J. Fitzsimmons	266,205		45	1988	D. Wayne Lukas	17,842,358	1,500	318
1940	T. Smith	269,200		14	1989	D. Wayne Lukas	16,103,998	1,398	305
1941	B. A. Jones	475,318		70	1990	D. Wayne Lukas	14,508,871	1,396	267
1942	J. M. Gaver	406,547		48	1991	D. Wayne Lukas	15,942,223	1,497	289
1943	B. A. Jones	267,915		73	1992	D. Wayne Lukas	9,806,436	1,349	230
1944	B. A. Jones	601,660		60	1993	Robert Frankel	8,883,252	346	79
1945	T. Smith	510,655		52	1994	D. Wayne Lukas	9,250,591	693	147
1946	H. Jacobs	560,077		99	1995	D. Wayne Lukas	12,858,429	840	194
1947	H. A. Jones	1,334,805		85	1996	D. Wayne Lukas	15,967,608	1,007	192
1948	H. A. Jones	1,118,670		81	1997	D. Wayne Lukas	10,355,154	854	175
1949	H. A. Jones	978,587		76	1998	Bob Baffert	16,660,880	721	167
1950	P. M. Burch	637,754		96	1999	Bob Baffert	14,266,707	500	134
1951	J. M. Gaver	616,392		42	2000	Bob Baffert	11,831,605	678	146
1952	B. A. Jones	662,137		29	2001	Robert J. Frankel	14,607,446	390	101
1953	H. Trotsek	1,028,873		54	2002	Robert J. Frankel	17,748,340	480	117
1954	W. Molter	1,107,860		136	2003	Robert J. Frankel	19,143,289	411	114
1955	J. Fitzsimmons	1,270,055		66		*Starts unavailable until 1963			
1956	W. Molter	1,227,402		142					

Annual Leading Trainers – Races Won

Year	Trainer	Amount Won	Strts*	No. of Wins	Year	Trainer	Amount Won	Strts*	No. of Wins
1907	J. Rowe	397,342		70	1954	R. H. McDaniel	834,390		206
1908	A. J. Boyner	170,775		71	1955	F. H. Merrill Jr.	298,794		154
1909	H. G. Bedwell	64,943		122	1956	V. R. Wright	532,344		177
1910	F. Ernest	64,525		105	1957	V. R. Wright	527,271		192
1911	W. B. Carson	16,250		72	1958	F. H. Merrill Jr.	320,827		171
1912	H. G. Bedwell	42,595		84	1959	V. R. Wright	534,319		172
1913	H. G. Bedwell	42,895		87	1960	F. H. Merrill Jr.	344,459		143
1914	H. G. Bedwell	49,430		84	1961	V. R. Wright	442,650		178
1915	H. G. Bedwell	51,015		97	1962	W. H. Bishop	544,261		162
1916	H. G. Bedwell	70,545		123	1963	H. Jacobson	730,418	688	140
1917	H. G. Bedwell	47,585		66	1964	H. Jacobson	801,869	730	169
1918	K. Spence	35,303		58	1965	H. Jacobson	863,721	886	200
1919	K. Spence	67,352		96	1966	L. Cavalaris Jr.	763,201	635	175
1920	K. Spence	94,674		74	1967	E. Hammond	325,905	996	200
	S. A. Clopton	152,312		74	1968	Jack C. Van Berg	776,330	1,152	256
1921	S.C. Hindreth	262,768		85	1969	Jack C. Van Berg	952,207	1,092	239
1922	H. McDaniel	169,134		78	1970	Jack C. Van Berg	974,818	1,312	282
	J. A. Parsons	40,465		78	1971	Dale Baird	290,553	1,130	245
1923	C. B. Irwin	104,054		147	1972	Jack C. Van Berg	1,381,067	1,342	286
1924	J. A. Parsons	42,566		93	1973	Dale Baird	416,592	1,558	305
1925	J. J. Duggan	49,830		70	1974	Jack C. Van Berg	1,567,418	1,712	329
1926	W. Perkins	127,753		82	1975	R. E. Dutrow	1,840,041	1,419	352
1927	S.C. Hindreth	161,569		72	1976	Jack C. Van Berg	2,976,196	2,362	496
1928	J. F. Schorr	258,425		65	1977	K. T. Leatherbury	1,702,112	1,475	322
	J. Reed	63,795		65	1978	K. T. Leatherbury	1,512,048	1,488	304
1929	L. Gentry	65,821		74	1979	Dale Baird	554,333	1,908	316
1930	C. B. Irwin	70,411		92	1980	Dale Baird	542,259	1,964	306
1931	J. C. Mikel	49,770		72	1981	Dale Baird	592,929	1,983	349
1932	G. Alexandra	55,890		76	1982	Dale Baird	477,136	1,763	276
1933	H. Jacobs	76,965		116	1983	Jack C. Van Berg	3,212,318	1,740	258
1934	H. Jacobs	113,055		127	1984	Jack C. Van Berg	4,163,118	1,638	250
1935	H. Jacobs	95,155		114	1985	Dale Baird	453,038	1,670	249
1936	H. Jacobs	155,789		177	1986	Jack C. Van Berg	5,536,478	1,841	266
1937	H. Jacobs	142,474		134	1987	D. Wayne Lukas	17,502,110	1,735	343
1938	H. Jacobs	116,609		109	1988	D. Wayne Lukas	17,842,358	1,500	318
1939	H. Jacobs	100,907		106	1989	D. Wayne Lukas	16,103,998	1,398	305
1940	D. Womeldorff	112,137		108	1990	D. Wayne Lukas	14,508,871	1,396	267
1941	H. Jacobs	165,964		123	1991	Dale Baird	499,475	1,626	296
1942	H. Jacobs	186,371		133	1992	Dale Baird	461,626	1,592	256
1943	H. Jacobs	210,775		128	1993	Dale Baird	475,294	1,673	269
1944	H. Jacobs	306,821		117	1994	Mario Beneito	1,440,880	1,108	247
1945	S. Liepiec	228,361		127	1995	Dale Baird	699,146	1,485	286
1946	W. Molter	329,725		122	1996	Dale Baird	1,077,565	1,520	330
1947	W. Molter	833,970		155	1997	Dale Baird	1,237,322	1,479	300
1948	W. Molter	1,015,547		184	1998	Dale Baird	1,575,592	1,378	290
1949	W. Molter	686,184		129	1999	Dale Baird	2,091,769	1,297	304
	W. H. Bishop	236,131		129	2000	Scott Lake	5,736,002	1,045	337
1950	R. H. McDaniel	441,590		156	2001	Scott Lake	7,817,856	1,566	407
1951	R. H. McDaniel	539,204		164	2002	Steven M. Asmussen	10,246,910	1,810	407
1952	R. H. McDaniel	573,837		168	2003	Scott Lake	9,152,959	2,009	454
1953	R. H. McDaniel	751,957		211					

*Starts unavailable until 1963

Leading North American Trainers – Lifetime Wins

The list below includes the top 50 winning trainers since 1911 and their records through Dec. 31, 2003. It includes wins and earnings from Thoroughbred races in the United States and Canada. Trainer statistics from seasons prior to 1963 include only wins and earnings and exclude trainers which did not saddle at least 10 winners during the year. Statistics prior to 1911 are not available.

Trainer	1st	Purses	Trainer	1st	Purses
Dale Baird	8,883	$27,213,302	Harry F. Thompson, Jr.	2,435	13,760,862
Jack C. Van Berg	6,338	80,185,591	Don Von Hemel	2,417	26,757,198
King T. Leatherbury	6,010	51,786,296	Jonathan E. Sheppard	2,412	46,399,132
Richard P. Hazelton	4,557	35,631,268	Ronald L. McAnally	2,398	110,362,977
D. Wayne Lukas	4,232	234,662,095	Henry P. Mercer	2,365	6,994,981
Frank H. Merrill, Jr.	3,974	16,980,632	Bob E. Arnett	2,349	6,476,765
Jerry Hollendorfer	3,938	69,186,437	Gerald S. Bennett	2,335	16,826,475
Richard E. Dutrow, Sr.	3,665	36,189,085	Philip G. Johnson	2,304	47,152,600
Grover G. Delp	3,604	39,261,182	Scott A. Lake	2,278	36,649,093
Hirsch Jacobs	3,593	15,356,904	Lazaro S. Barrera	2,269	49,932,176
H. Allen Jerkens	3,507	82,930,846	Frank L. Brothers	2,258	42,926,824
Everett Hammond	3,425	7,781,650	Ronald J. Dandy	2,253	17,199,843
William I. Mott	3,168	128,965,926	Dale Capuano	2,236	34,115,431
Frank Martin, Sr.	3,160	44,734,153	Del W. Carroll	2,224	19,059,524
Jere R. Smith, Sr.	3,108	28,865,426	Michael S. Ferraro	2,211	11,901,845
William H. Bishop	3,058	10,337,050	James Fitzsimmons	2,176	12,981,615
Robert J. Frankel	2,993	157,982,076	Edward T. Allard	2,161	24,656,491
David R. Vance	2,875	29,059,604	Steven M. Asmussen	2,160	49,133,413
Bernard S. Flint	2,766	41,042,786	Charles W. Walker	2,141	11,953,492
Jerome C. Meyer	2,741	20,328,532	Ron K. Smith	2,140	13,632,101
Bruce M. Kravets	2,732	16,747,008	Glenn L. Hild	2,135	22,434,004
Mario Beneito	2,695	11,038,092	Robert L. Martin	2,128	16,902,198
Robert E. Holthus	2,546	32,888,029	Martin L. Fallon	2,121	16,088,629
Charles E. Whittingham	2,534	109,215,527	John H. Forbes	2,105	29,225,901
Robert R. Hilton	2,512	6,000,312	Joseph H. Pierce, Jr.	2,091	30,131,159

Leading North American Trainers – Lifetime Earnings

The list below includes the top 50 earning trainers since 1911 and their records through Dec. 31, 2003. It includes records from Thoroughbred races in the United States and Canada. Trainer statistics from seasons prior to 1963 include only wins and earnings and exclude trainers which did not saddle at least 10 winners during the year. Statistics prior to 1911 are not available.

Trainer	Starters	1st	2nd	3rd	Purses
D. Wayne Lukas	23,386	4,232	3,460	2,970	$234,662,095
Robert J. Frankel	14,658	2,993	2,453	2,058	157,982,076
William I. Mott	14,740	3,168	2,434	2,029	128,965,926
Ronald L. McAnally	16,042	2,398	2,202	2,009	110,362,977
Charles E. Whittingham	13,805	2,534	1,868	1,706	109,215,527
Bob Baffert	6,198	1,343	1,010	888	98,770,477
Richard E. Mandella	9,172	1,630	1,442	1,353	95,260,824
H. Allen Jerkens	18,538	3,507	2,527	2,200	82,930,846
Claude R. McGaughey III	5,744	1,363	1,020	885	82,731,027
Jack C. Van Berg	38,375	6,338	5,318	4,672	80,185,591
Jerry Hollendorfer	16,770	3,938	2,810	2,384	69,186,437
Neil D. Drysdale	5,455	1,078	830	804	68,660,648
Roger L. Attfield	7,251	1,387	1,122	983	60,255,218
Nicholas P. Zito	10,464	1,280	1,239	1,194	58,351,537
Flint S. Schulhofer	8,765	1,328	1,208	1,102	54,657,686
Woodford C. Stephens	8,208	1,942	1,173	983	53,014,814
Gary F. Jones	7,900	1,465	1,107	981	52,672,611
King T. Leatherbury	32,965	6,010	4,814	4,225	51,786,296
Melvin F. Stute	14,731	1,897	1,897	1,860	51,644,131
Lazaro S. Barrera	13,201	2,269	1,864	1,729	49,932,176
Todd A. Pletcher	4,558	909	735	561	49,425,030
Steven M. Asmussen	10,691	2,160	1,813	1,517	49,133,413
Philip G. Johnson	13,987	2,304	1,779	1,816	47,152,600
Jonathan E. Sheppard	14,379	2,412	2,168	2,053	46,399,132
Frank Martin, Sr.	17,568	3,160	2,456	2,321	44,734,153
W. Elliott Walden	5,324	968	808	700	43,692,444
Frank L. Brothers	9,798	2,258	1,535	1,208	42,926,824
James E. Day	6,751	1,149	1,000	888	42,535,323
Darrell Vienna	7,014	1,093	979	900	42,455,224
Bernard S. Flint	15,219	2,766	2,234	1,893	41,042,786
Gasper S. Moschera	8,910	1,546	1,355	1,310	40,004,972
Mark A. Hennig	4,567	743	703	597	39,838,654
Grover G. Delp	17,528	3,604	2,774	2,429	39,261,182
Carl A. Nafzger	7,173	937	914	948	39,035,676
George R. Arnold, II	8,099	1,269	1,236	1,065	38,911,353
Harvey L. Vanier	13,846	1,950	1,807	1,717	38,669,750
David E. Hofmans	5,385	852	711	675	38,149,885
John C. Kimmel	4,680	901	769	638	37,983,539
Scott A. Lake	10,001	2,278	1,753	1,415	36,649,093
Richard E. Dutrow, Sr.	18,996	3,665	3,009	2,514	36,189,085
Richard P. Hazelton	24,148	4,557	3,684	3,331	35,631,268
Christophe Clement	3,306	611	549	434	35,616,957
Jerry M. Fanning	12,577	1,533	1,527	1,527	35,592,534
Leroy S. Jolley	6,605	975	889	765	34,373,565
Mike R. Mitchell	8,986	1,860	1,411	1,081	34,363,969
Neil J. Howard	4,426	928	709	608	34,291,988
Dale Capuano	11,315	2,236	1,873	1,543	34,115,431
Thomas M. Amoss	6,209	1,429	1,050	847	34,100,703
Robert E. Holthus	17,761	2,546	2,236	2,127	32,888,029
John W. Sadler	7,339	1,090	1,076	906	32,584,148

Leading Jockeys in 2003 by Money Won

Jockey	Starts	1st	2d	3d	Purses
Jerry D. Bailey	776	206	149	97	$23,354,960
Edgar S. Prado	1,478	259	235	207	18,475,582
Alex O. Solis	1,115	203	170	175	16,304,252
Patrick A. Valenzuela	1,447	287	266	237	15,697,352
John R. Velazquez	1,308	306	193	175	15,425,501
Pat Day	985	215	175	110	13,378,292
Jose A. Santos	1,157	176	183	162	11,472,287
Ramon A. Dominguez	1,627	453	316	252	11,359,767
Todd Kabel	836	160	163	110	11,323,313
Patrick Husbands	882	168	144	117	11,168,817
Robby Albarado	1,123	185	205	180	11,061,314
David Romero Flores	1,039	155	168	122	10,759,008
Cornelio H. Velasquez	1,696	273	249	235	10,577,461
Victor Espinoza	1,325	206	182	203	10,004,495
Javier Castellano	1,235	182	202	177	9,558,978
Richard Migliore	1,027	186	132	133	9,505,289
Corey S. Nakatani	922	124	131	149	8,518,363
Mike E. Smith	939	162	115	99	8,401,045
Eibar Coa	1,275	209	196	176	8,274,472
Julie A. Krone	806	139	103	93	8,202,107
Michael J. Luzzi	1,248	165	157	198	7,772,168
Tyler Baze	1,299	175	178	187	7,518,061
Emile Ramsammy	838	127	104	99	7,203,924
Russell A. Baze	1,359	410	289	192	6,917,825
Shaun Bridgmohan	1,166	154	118	147	6,765,343
Jorge F. Chavez	1,064	154	176	126	6,736,591
James McAleney	734	112	101	95	6,672,531
Shane J. Sellers	971	163	159	124	6,556,788
Rene R. Douglas	1,075	201	170	160	6,482,949
Corey J. Lanerie	1,341	231	225	215	6,187,084
Kent J. Desormeaux	579	78	98	77	6,033,136
John McKee	1,475	212	202	230	6,027,114
Ryan Fogelsonger	1,388	278	234	257	5,903,822
Gary L. Stevens	345	58	62	50	5,829,570
David Clark	662	104	85	70	5,677,197
Jose Valdivia, Jr.	833	82	95	121	5,401,879
Manoel R. Cruz	1,579	262	241	228	5,353,375
Jono C. Jones	646	91	74	101	5,348,472
Mario G. Pino	1,175	247	184	165	5,265,850
Calvin H. Borel	1,220	162	150	136	5,163,800
Joe Bravo	590	128	97	84	4,928,660
Gerard Melancon	1,409	247	205	183	4,927,346
Rafael Bejarano	1,440	260	202	190	4,912,559
Eddie M. Martin, Jr.	1,175	203	179	162	4,846,092
Mark Guidry	868	117	95	109	4,763,739
Constant Montpellier	658	80	96	97	4,678,130
Gary Boulanger	1,254	183	150	181	4,656,376
Charles C. Lopez	995	141	146	148	4,610,902
Jeremy Rose	1,008	154	170	148	4,516,749
Eusebio Razo, Jr.	978	163	148	115	4,410,042
Robert C. Landry	451	53	61	70	4,243,567
Terry J. Thompson	1,171	181	153	161	4,059,292
Roberto Alvarado, Jr.	910	193	154	131	4,026,410
Pablo Fragoso	909	103	120	103	3,987,229
Martin A. Pedroza	946	144	132	126	3,983,182
Jon Kenton Court	1,137	146	151	142	3,965,598
Jamie Theriot	1,105	213	161	121	3,959,033
Eddie Castro	1,256	242	257	174	3,931,877
Ronald J. Warren, Jr.	962	171	150	141	3,823,529
Aaron T. Gryder	756	78	94	94	3,797,879
Horacio Karamanos	1,286	179	176	191	3,740,427
Lonnie Meche	1,026	162	156	131	3,725,447
Christopher A. Emigh	1,117	143	160	160	3,652,638
Deshawn L. Parker	1,497	236	200	183	3,560,616
Stewart Elliott	1,314	249	205	175	3,539,826
Jason P. Lumpkins	958	197	127	129	3,515,564
Anthony S. Black	705	131	127	103	3,466,248
Anthony Mawing	1,453	211	169	192	3,434,041
Carlos H. Marquez, Jr.	841	145	93	113	3,422,747
Abel Castellano, Jr.	1,083	160	157	149	3,374,772
Chad Phillip Schvaneveldt	870	168	142	126	3,345,865
Julian Pimentel	670	107	97	98	3,326,817
Travis L. Dunkelberger	1,105	219	193	131	3,283,544
Roberto M. Gonzalez	855	166	130	104	3,237,018
Curt C. Bourque	867	131	98	122	3,210,402
Rick Wilson	680	127	114	102	3,122,717
Frank T. Alvarado	839	111	124	115	3,074,049
Chance J. Rollins	1,054	168	171	155	3,044,796
Jose C. Ferrer	644	111	90	53	3,041,892
Richard A. Dos Ramos	448	43	61	51	3,040,134
Jose A. Velez, Jr.	588	80	92	86	3,038,413
Luis S. Quinonez	1,018	154	131	133	2,993,293
Kirk Paul LeBlanc	1,030	154	156	126	2,972,269
Steven Ronald Bahen	604	61	56	59	2,915,223
Larry J. Sterling, Jr.	766	130	104	119	2,909,942
Julia Brimo	651	75	96	80	2,906,771
Francisco Duran	1,153	144	165	153	2,883,409
Richard Monterrey	1,164	172	187	143	2,869,556
Luis D. Chavez	612	75	80	84	2,859,212
Manuel Aguilar	1,142	113	167	140	2,846,007
Chad K. Murphy	965	156	132	125	2,794,719
Oliver Castillo	894	103	123	126	2,794,258
Julio A. Garcia	536	105	84	64	2,790,993
Dino Luciani	466	55	54	52	2,784,710
Jose Luis Flores	1,115	205	171	144	2,747,252
Roman Chapa	871	148	129	107	2,745,909
Guy Smith	1,179	181	161	152	2,735,124
Jozbin Z. Santana	923	128	126	121	2,731,042
Rodrigo Madrigal, Jr.	802	119	102	109	2,723,456
Rosemary B. Homeister, Jr.	996	107	127	120	2,717,392
Steven Joseph Bourque	1,026	159	145	165	2,659,284
Chantal Sutherland	471	48	54	60	2,613,807
Luis Garcia	1,270	179	178	165	2,603,914
Martin Ramos Ramirez	928	153	125	109	2,596,851
Slade Callaghan	474	47	42	73	2,592,417
Larry Melancon	521	65	56	58	2,576,557
Jose C. Caraballo	767	107	102	112	2,568,865
Jeremy Beasley	997	201	133	127	2,567,947
Joseph C. Judice	1,221	276	191	155	2,563,372
Brice Blanc	349	41	30	46	2,549,334
Clinton L. Potts	675	116	99	89	2,535,014
James McKnight	292	51	40	45	2,516,379
Oscar Flores	1,044	183	150	127	2,486,401
Carl James Woodley	1,126	203	151	171	2,444,883
Elvis Joseph Perrodin	525	85	66	75	2,432,172
Frank Lovato, Jr.	697	82	94	82	2,400,210
Jean-Luc Samyn	373	36	35	50	2,377,998

Jockey	Starts	1st	2d	3d	Purses	Jockey	Starts	1st	2d	3d	Purses
Gerry Olguin	433	49	44	42	2,362,545	Luis Antonio Gonzalez	933	157	122	108	1,666,350
J. D. Acosta	1,193	152	152	134	2,360,396	Felipe Valdez	647	91	95	94	1,657,853
Willie Martinez	840	82	97	86	2,328,580	Carlos Gonzalez	735	96	88	92	1,651,015
Jesus Lopez Castanon	954	145	126	124	2,320,572	Roberto A. Perez	1,014	95	97	110	1,639,086
Kendrick Carmouche	1,081	147	180	145	2,304,251	Juan Ortega	1,038	101	123	127	1,635,569
Glenn W. Corbett	939	168	155	135	2,285,784	Jeff Johnston	915	123	109	105	1,634,848
Oswald M. Pereira	1,164	155	142	156	2,281,338	Thomas Clifton	961	204	144	110	1,629,820
Dana G. Whitney	903	147	102	124	2,263,859	Mark E. Rosenthal	764	97	84	68	1,628,197
Gary A. Birzer	1,202	142	164	136	2,249,618	Alex Birzer	938	104	125	119	1,624,996
Jake Barton	617	88	100	67	2,228,485	G. F. Almeida	447	40	55	51	1,620,798
Eduardo O. Nunez	944	87	103	141	2,224,296	Christopher Griffith	610	77	89	67	1,617,098
David J. McFadden	870	132	125	97	2,204,176	Julio E. Felix	881	137	104	118	1,615,896
Norberto Arroyo, Jr.	475	48	47	52	2,146,662	Harry Vega	565	100	78	86	1,614,471
Erick D. Rodriguez	1,060	128	155	144	2,132,617	Neil Poznansky	559	87	62	77	1,608,504
Earlie Fires	607	76	77	79	2,130,783	Winston Albert Thompson	860	118	108	106	1,597,691
Jorge Martin Bourdieu	702	123	118	108	2,126,591	William D. Troilo	795	86	89	103	1,594,440
E. T. Baird	697	99	83	86	2,125,954	Dale V. Beckner	522	66	45	53	1,584,120
Joe M. Castro	708	96	102	93	2,118,858	Scott A. Stevens	882	127	126	128	1,575,422
Monte Clifton Berry	1,057	199	175	146	2,114,269	Nicola Wright	518	103	88	63	1,573,058
Donald R. Pettinger	448	71	70	55	2,113,937	James Lopez	565	60	80	55	1,566,172
David G. Lopez	989	123	157	168	2,101,889	Victor Carrero	528	45	52	56	1,565,383
Nick Santagata	1,095	114	130	145	2,078,607	Bobby J. Walker, Jr.	664	96	99	78	1,563,326
Simon P. Husbands	419	38	33	43	2,075,204	Juan Umana	911	96	107	121	1,560,908
Carlos H. Silva	702	84	76	93	2,073,144	Michael Francis Rowland	923	155	152	102	1,554,297
Heberto Castillo, Jr.	537	37	46	40	2,052,260	Christopher P. DeCarlo	459	47	51	56	1,553,865
Rodney A. Prescott	1,564	185	201	186	2,051,659	Kevin Leon Cogburn	969	118	131	152	1,538,569
Kevin Radke	971	186	140	147	2,034,196	David Wilson	769	108	106	123	1,534,562
Ignacio Puglisi	497	46	65	36	2,026,425	Terry A. Stanton	874	126	123	105	1,529,063
John Jacinto	1,163	140	148	129	2,006,702	Perry Wayne Ouzts	1,406	198	187	184	1,523,268
Jose L. Espinoza	536	31	49	46	1,975,306	Timothy T. Doocy	616	67	76	76	1,514,145
Laffit A. Pincay, Jr.	229	49	34	31	1,967,131	Jillian Scharfstein	449	37	54	55	1,512,398
Orlando Mojica	1,365	209	187	165	1,959,350	Zoe Cadman	626	71	71	77	1,508,392
Pedro V. Alvarado	551	124	104	78	1,951,115	Perry Compton	768	155	109	94	1,504,347
Dean P. Butler	1,033	103	102	119	1,948,310	Emilio Flores	1,261	184	159	158	1,487,158
Edwin L. King, Jr.	688	65	87	104	1,946,284	Gary Baze	713	109	106	104	1,473,126
Josiah F. Hampshire, Jr.	833	168	135	89	1,924,804	Alfredo V. Clemente	475	60	45	60	1,461,373
Thomas L. Pompell	1,218	180	161	147	1,907,249	Robert Dean Williams	882	112	113	117	1,457,246
Casey T. Lambert	790	120	106	109	1,898,311	Huber Villa-Gomez	1,012	208	160	138	1,453,253
Francine Villeneuve	563	94	70	78	1,880,371	Leanne M. Painter	677	96	95	108	1,452,572
Felipe F. Martinez	766	59	87	92	1,857,407	Ken S. Tohill	548	93	98	90	1,431,125
Shane Laviolette	853	89	81	109	1,856,532	Luis A. Castillo	472	38	47	54	1,428,241
Joseph Stokes	754	110	130	74	1,830,185	Russell W. Woolsey	789	137	105	109	1,421,536
Na Somsanith	368	42	45	45	1,814,145	Kevin Krigger	629	64	77	92	1,417,232
Jesse M. Campbell	790	83	93	87	1,806,903	Daniel Coa	543	74	60	59	1,399,934
Aurelio Toribio, Jr.	810	104	97	98	1,800,832	Carlos L. Castro	952	96	116	116	1,394,313
Ricardo Jaime	613	117	94	83	1,797,654	Andrew R. Ramgeet	582	76	81	73	1,385,754
Federico Mata	1,378	206	173	168	1,779,351	Perry A. Winters	672	88	96	87	1,375,987
Donald Edward Simington	976	123	143	118	1,773,847	Taylor M. Hole	770	122	115	105	1,358,068
Brian Todd Bochinski	587	80	59	71	1,764,119	Abdiel Toribio	345	37	41	50	1,352,281
Quincy Welch	655	141	131	91	1,761,060	Marlon St. Julien	599	63	72	62	1,347,810
Paul R. Toscano	700	78	68	85	1,753,236	Ken A. Shino	798	95	95	97	1,337,632
Kerwin D. Clark	1,012	155	137	119	1,752,737	Esteban Angel Gomez	1,171	195	166	160	1,333,625
Richard A. Bracho	626	71	81	74	1,699,812	Michael G. Ziegler	937	142	124	121	1,323,996
Matt S. Garcia	462	40	50	58	1,698,728	Isaias D. Enriquez	529	39	47	46	1,307,675
Randall A. Meier	632	74	67	74	1,698,435	Mathew Carroll McGowan	898	95	95	104	1,306,632
Michael C. Baze	633	86	94	94	1,689,908	Seth B. Martinez	667	120	105	86	1,306,289
David Cora	1,265	244	176	172	1,688,801	Mary Elizabeth Doser	805	132	136	112	1,302,322
Tommy Molina	662	71	92	65	1,686,372	Eduardo E. Perez	537	57	68	54	1,294,570
Raymond Brian Sabourin	317	30	41	34	1,685,052	Hector L. Rosario, Jr.	949	161	173	122	1,290,526

Jockey	Starts	1st	2d	3d	Purses	Jockey	Starts	1st	2d	3d	Purses
Vladimir Diaz	1,029	146	150	182	1,288,382	Anthony J. D'Amico	466	51	44	59	1,153,896
Dyn Panell	688	99	106	97	1,278,089	Ricardo A. Valdes	448	60	51	56	1,148,924
Pedro Luis Cotto, Jr.	499	39	54	48	1,274,333	Charles W. Forrest	797	72	89	80	1,138,554
Real E. Simard	634	82	70	77	1,273,095	Stephan Heiler	576	91	80	89	1,137,043
Carlos M. Cruz	355	40	45	46	1,272,164	Adalberto Diaz Lopez	452	56	73	61	1,128,033
Jose R. Martinez, Jr.	517	55	59	55	1,269,915	Miguel Hernandez	1,031	161	177	177	1,122,416
Paul Albert Nicol, Jr.	644	110	94	76	1,259,019	Brian Joseph Hernandez	712	84	95	83	1,113,190
Jesus Sanchez	817	92	72	90	1,256,890	Enrique M. Jurado	406	53	47	45	1,111,905
Joe M. Johnson	554	65	63	60	1,251,770	Hiram G. Rivera	720	97	78	97	1,111,529
Elvis Trujillo	376	46	44	50	1,249,755	Nena Matz	637	116	100	71	1,099,653
Chin C. Yang	990	121	139	129	1,248,572	Omar A. Berrio	419	46	35	48	1,098,777
Joseph Rocco	583	73	66	77	1,244,338	Shannon Uske	227	24	39	25	1,087,016
Cindy Sue Noll	577	67	79	86	1,244,230	Tony Farina	157	22	14	25	1,081,670
Orlando Bocachica	589	94	80	72	1,234,898	Ted D. Gondron	636	93	68	70	1,081,215
Derek C. Bell	563	105	80	72	1,230,614	Jose E. Lopez	611	75	86	88	1,080,804
Victor H. Molina	612	75	72	69	1,223,413	Greta Kuntzweiler	592	51	52	50	1,078,370
Jack M. Lauzon	471	59	55	52	1,222,205	Carlos D. Madeira	502	60	56	65	1,076,508
Jose L. Rivera, Jr.	749	86	80	95	1,222,196	Jason R. Eads	570	67	66	73	1,074,281
Ricardo Feliciano	666	92	100	89	1,212,892	Craig Perret	90	16	13	14	1,061,940
Casey Fusilier	824	98	116	97	1,206,325	Tho Nguyen	598	64	72	72	1,055,902
Daniel J. David	320	70	43	35	1,204,246	Todd Glasser	450	69	65	62	1,047,227
Richard Harvey Hamel	649	82	88	85	1,197,401	Sidney P. LeJeune, Jr.	815	84	91	97	1,040,279
Jeffrey Skerrett	806	108	83	94	1,196,232	Uriel A. Lopez	658	43	74	69	1,040,268
Vernon Bush	693	89	96	74	1,196,008	Michael Duane Pindell	605	66	60	88	1,039,919
Pedro A. Rodriguez	729	112	123	105	1,181,989	John A. Grabowski	553	128	88	85	1,037,942
Carlos Montalvo	596	53	58	64	1,180,555	Mark T. Johnston	440	36	62	44	1,036,783
Mark Phillips	764	107	114	102	1,179,954	Francisco Perez Fuentes	435	59	58	63	1,032,798
Alfredo J. Juarez, Jr.	538	43	59	56	1,179,167	Hector G. Ramos	505	88	62	69	1,024,110
Anibal Prado	906	89	88	109	1,168,620	Brian Dale Peck	363	34	41	33	1,019,526
Martin Escobar	886	113	127	87	1,166,117	Nik G. Goodwin	586	43	69	57	1,002,504
Juan M. Gutierrez	926	194	156	141	1,165,975	*North American earnings only					
John R. Davila, Jr.	720	141	115	89	1,164,666						
Timothy Thornton	417	49	53	47	1,158,983						

Leading Jockeys in 2003 by Races Won

Jockey	Starts	1st	2d	3d	Purses
Ramon A. Dominguez	1,627	453	316	252	$11,359,767
Russell A. Baze	1,359	410	289	192	6,917,825
John R. Velazquez	1,308	306	193	175	15,425,501
Patrick A. Valenzuela	1,447	287	266	237	15,697,352
Ryan Fogelsonger	1,388	278	234	257	5,903,822
Joseph C. Judice	1,221	276	191	155	2,563,372
Cornelio H. Velasquez	1,696	273	249	235	10,577,461
Manoel R. Cruz	1,579	262	241	228	5,353,375
Rafael Bejarano	1,440	260	202	190	4,912,559
Edgar S. Prado	1,478	259	235	207	18,475,582
Stewart Elliott	1,314	249	205	175	3,539,826
Mario G. Pino	1,175	247	184	165	5,265,850
Gerard Melancon	1,409	247	205	183	4,927,346
David Cora	1,265	244	176	172	1,688,801
Eddie Castro	1,256	242	257	174	3,931,877
Deshawn L. Parker	1,497	236	200	183	3,560,616
Corey J. Lanerie	1,341	231	225	215	6,187,084
Travis L. Dunkelberger	1,105	219	193	131	3,283,544
Pat Day	985	215	175	110	13,378,292
Jamie Theriot	1,105	213	161	121	3,959,033
John McKee	1,475	212	202	230	6,027,114
Anthony Mawing	1,453	211	169	192	3,434,041
Eibar Coa	1,275	209	196	176	8,274,472
Orlando Mojica	1,365	209	187	165	1,959,350
Huber Villa-Gomez	1,012	208	160	138	1,453,253
Jerry D. Bailey	776	206	149	97	23,354,960
Victor Espinoza	1,325	206	182	203	10,004,495
Federico Mata	1,378	206	173	168	1,779,351
Jose Luis Flores	1,115	205	171	144	2,747,252
Thomas Clifton	961	204	144	110	1,629,820
Alex O. Solis	1,115	203	170	175	16,304,252
Eddie M. Martin, Jr.	1,175	203	179	162	4,846,092
Carl James Woodley	1,126	203	151	171	2,444,883
Rene R. Douglas	1,075	201	170	160	6,482,949
Jeremy Beasley	997	201	133	127	2,567,947
Monte Clifton Berry	1,057	199	175	146	2,114,269
Perry Wayne Ouzts	1,406	198	187	184	1,523,268
Jason P. Lumpkins	958	197	127	129	3,515,564
Esteban Angel Gomez	1,171	195	166	160	1,333,625
Juan M. Gutierrez	926	194	156	141	1,165,975
Roberto Alvarado, Jr.	910	193	154	131	4,026,410
Richard Migliore	1,027	186	132	133	9,505,289
Kevin Radke	971	186	140	147	2,034,196
Robby Albarado	1,123	185	205	180	11,061,314
Rodney A. Prescott	1,564	185	201	186	2,051,659
Emilio Flores	1,261	184	159	158	1,487,158
Gary Boulanger	1,254	183	150	181	4,656,376
Oscar Flores	1,044	183	150	127	2,486,401
Javier Castellano	1,235	182	202	177	9,558,978
Terry J. Thompson	1,171	181	153	161	4,059,292
Guy Smith	1,179	181	161	152	2,735,124
Thomas L. Pompell	1,218	180	161	147	1,907,249
Horacio Karamanos	1,286	179	176	191	3,740,427
Luis Garcia	1,270	179	178	165	2,603,914
Jose A. Santos	1,157	176	183	162	11,472,287
Tyler Baze	1,299	175	178	187	7,518,061
Richard Monterrey	1,164	172	187	143	2,869,556
Ronald J. Warren, Jr.	962	171	150	141	3,823,529
Patrick Husbands	882	168	144	117	11,168,817
Chad Phillip Schvaneveldt	870	168	142	126	3,345,865
Chance J. Rollins	1,054	168	171	155	3,044,796
Glenn W. Corbett	939	168	155	135	2,285,784
Josiah Francis Hampshire, Jr.	833	168	135	89	1,924,804
Roberto M. Gonzalez	855	166	130	104	3,237,018
Michael J. Luzzi	1,248	165	157	198	7,772,168
Shane J. Sellers	971	163	159	124	6,556,788
Eusebio Razo, Jr.	978	163	148	115	4,410,042
Mike E. Smith	939	162	115	99	8,401,045
Calvin H. Borel	1,220	162	150	136	5,163,800
Lonnie Meche	1,026	162	156	131	3,725,447
Hector L. Rosario, Jr.	949	161	173	122	1,290,526
Miguel Luis Gaeta Hernandez	1,031	161	177	177	1,122,416
Todd Kabel	836	160	163	110	11,323,313
Abel Castellano, Jr.	1,083	160	157	149	3,374,772
Steven Joseph Bourque	1,026	159	145	165	2,659,284
Luis Antonio Gonzalez	933	157	122	108	1,666,350
Chad K. Murphy	965	156	132	125	2,794,719
David Romero Flores	1,039	155	168	122	10,759,008
Oswald M. Pereira	1,164	155	142	156	2,281,338
Kerwin D. Clark	1,012	155	137	119	1,752,737
Michael Francis Rowland	923	155	152	102	1,554,297
Perry Compton	768	155	109	94	1,504,347
Shaun Bridgmohan	1,166	154	118	147	6,765,343
Jorge F. Chavez	1,064	154	176	126	6,736,591
Jeremy Rose	1,008	154	170	148	4,516,749
Luis S. Quinonez	1,018	154	131	133	2,993,293
Kirk Paul LeBlanc	1,030	154	156	126	2,972,269
Martin Ramos Ramirez	928	153	125	109	2,596,851
J. D. Acosta	1,193	152	152	134	2,360,396
Roman Chapa	871	148	129	107	2,745,909
Kendrick Carmouche	1,081	147	180	145	2,304,251
Dana G. Whitney	903	147	102	124	2,263,859
Jon Kenton Court	1,137	146	151	142	3,965,598
Vladimir Diaz	1,029	146	150	182	1,288,382
Carlos H. Marquez, Jr.	841	145	93	113	3,422,747
Jesus Lopez Castanon	954	145	126	124	2,320,572
Martin A. Pedroza	946	144	132	126	3,983,182
Francisco Duran	1,153	144	165	153	2,883,409
Christopher A. Emigh	1,117	143	160	160	3,652,638
Ivan R. Gonzalez	823	143	131	107	980,238
Gary A. Birzer	1,202	142	164	136	2,249,618
Michael G. Ziegler	937	142	124	121	1,323,996
Charles C. Lopez	995	141	146	148	4,610,902
Quincy Welch	655	141	131	91	1,761,060
John R. Davila, Jr.	720	141	115	89	1,164,666
John Jacinto	1,163	140	148	129	2,006,702
Kelly Bridges	788	140	118	115	951,561
Julie A. Krone	806	139	103	93	8,202,107
Marco A. Ccamaque	916	138	111	93	787,850
Julio E. Felix	881	137	104	118	1,615,896
Russell W. Woolsey	789	137	105	109	1,421,536
Jerome Carkeek	831	134	108	116	692,422
David J. McFadden	870	132	125	97	2,204,176
Mary Elizabeth Doser	805	132	136	112	1,302,322
Anthony S. Black	705	131	127	103	3,466,248
Curt C. Bourque	867	131	98	122	3,210,402
Larry J. Sterling, Jr.	766	130	104	119	2,909,942
Carlos Nieto	914	129	126	107	938,243
Armando Martinez	878	129	114	95	631,805
Joe Bravo	590	128	97	84	4,928,660
Jozbin Z. Santana	923	128	126	121	2,731,042
Erick D. Rodriguez	1,060	128	155	144	2,132,617
John A. Grabowski	553	128	88	85	1,037,942
Emile Ramsammy	838	127	104	99	7,203,924
Rick Wilson	680	127	114	102	3,122,717
Scott A. Stevens	882	127	126	128	1,575,422
Terry A. Stanton	874	126	123	105	1,529,063
Corey S. Nakatani	922	124	131	149	8,518,363
Pedro V. Alvarado	551	124	104	78	1,951,115
Jorge Martin Bourdieu	702	123	118	108	2,126,591
David G. Lopez	989	123	157	168	2,101,889
Donald Edward Simington	976	123	143	118	1,773,847
Jeff Johnston	915	123	109	105	1,634,848
Taylor M. Hole	770	122	115	105	1,358,068
Chin C. Yang	990	121	139	129	1,248,572

Jockey	Starts	1st	2d	3d	Purses
Casey T. Lambert	790	120	106	109	1,898,311
Seth B. Martinez	667	120	105	86	1,306,289
Luis A. Belmonte	903	120	130	109	875,121
Rodrigo Madrigal, Jr.	802	119	102	109	2,723,456
Wilson Omar Dieguez	908	119	108	134	987,066
Jose Luis Calo	1,043	119	110	116	687,424
Winston Albert Thompson	860	118	108	106	1,597,691
Kevin Leon Cogburn	969	118	131	152	1,538,569
Alberto R. Higuera	908	118	123	131	849,912
Mark Guidry	868	117	95	109	4,763,739
Ricardo Jaime	613	117	94	83	1,797,654
William P. Otero	808	117	122	100	945,395
Ramsey Zimmerman	633	117	99	80	870,188
Clinton L. Potts	675	116	99	89	2,535,014
Nena Matz	637	116	100	71	1,099,653
Robert Webb	588	115	114	91	385,312
Nick Santagata	1,095	114	130	145	2,078,607
Manuel Aguilar	1,142	113	167	140	2,846,007
Martin Escobar	886	113	127	87	1,166,117
James McAleney	734	112	101	95	6,672,531
Robert Dean Williams	882	112	113	117	1,457,246
Pedro A. Rodriguez	729	112	123	105	1,181,989
Rex A. Stokes, III	718	112	81	77	943,963
Frank T. Alvarado	839	111	124	115	3,074,049
Jose C. Ferrer	644	111	90	53	3,041,892
Joseph Stokes	754	110	130	74	1,830,185
Paul Albert Nicol, Jr.	644	110	94	76	1,259,019
Joel Santiago	842	110	112	89	881,721
Gary Baze	713	109	106	104	1,473,126
David Wilson	769	108	106	123	1,534,562
Jeffrey Skerrett	806	108	83	94	1,196,232
Julian Pimentel	670	107	97	98	3,326,817
Rosemary B. Homeister, Jr.	996	107	127	120	2,717,392
Jose C. Caraballo	767	107	102	112	2,568,865
Mark Phillips	764	107	114	102	1,179,954
Julio A. Garcia	536	105	84	64	2,790,993
Derek C. Bell	563	105	80	72	1,230,614
David Clark	662	104	85	70	5,677,197
Aurelio Toribio, Jr.	810	104	97	98	1,800,832
Alex Birzer	938	104	125	119	1,624,996
Pablo Fragoso	909	103	120	103	3,987,229
Oliver Castillo	894	103	123	126	2,794,258
Dean P. Butler	1,033	103	102	119	1,948,310
Nicola Wright	518	103	88	63	1,573,058
Robert Messina	618	103	82	86	913,588
Juan Ortega	1,038	101	123	127	1,635,569
Harry Vega	565	100	78	86	1,614,471
Travis Wayne Hightower	448	100	66	50	783,767
Jorge A. Guerra	855	100	94	111	577,306
E. T. Baird	697	99	83	86	2,125,954
Dyn Panell	688	99	106	97	1,278,089
Octavio Bernal	860	99	101	116	912,070
Casey Fusilier	824	98	116	97	1,206,325
Mark E. Rosenthal	764	97	84	68	1,628,197
Hiram G. Rivera	720	97	78	97	1,111,529
Joe M. Castro	708	96	102	93	2,118,858
Carlos Gonzalez	735	96	88	92	1,651,015
Bobby J. Walker, Jr.	664	96	99	78	1,563,326
Juan Umana	911	96	107	121	1,560,908
Leanne M. Painter	677	96	95	108	1,452,572
Carlos L. Castro	952	96	116	116	1,394,313
Paul M. Nolan	779	96	94	102	816,496
Roberto A. Perez	1,014	95	97	110	1,639,086
Ken A. Shino	798	95	95	97	1,337,632
Mathew Carroll McGowan	898	95	95	104	1,306,632
Scott T. Saito	591	95	84	96	846,173
Francine Villeneuve	563	94	70	78	1,880,371
Orlando Bocachica	589	94	80	72	1,234,898
Ken S. Tohill	548	93	98	90	1,431,125
Ted D. Gondron	636	93	68	70	1,081,215
Josh M. Romero	991	93	106	106	885,951
Jesus Sanchez	817	92	72	90	1,256,890
Ricardo Feliciano	666	92	100	89	1,212,892
Jono C. Jones	646	91	74	101	5,348,472
Felipe Valdez	647	91	95	94	1,657,853
Stephan Heiler	576	91	80	89	1,137,043
Joe A. Crispin	537	90	98	83	263,458
Shane Laviolette	853	89	81	109	1,856,532
Vernon Bush	693	89	96	74	1,196,008
Anibal Prado	906	89	88	109	1,168,620
Edwin Perez	640	89	82	78	614,853
Jake Barton	617	88	100	67	2,228,485
Perry A. Winters	672	88	96	87	1,375,987
Hector G. Ramos	505	88	62	69	1,024,110
Logan H. Cormier	559	88	74	73	901,083
Eduardo O. Nunez	944	87	103	141	2,224,296
Neil Poznansky	559	87	62	77	1,608,504
Lester Cash Knight	750	87	110	99	929,632
Michael C. Baze	633	86	94	94	1,689,908
William D. Troilo	795	86	89	103	1,594,440
Jose L. Rivera, Jr.	749	86	80	95	1,222,196
Dennis Michael Collins	516	86	77	62	418,348
Elvis Joseph Perrodin	525	85	66	75	2,432,172
Luis Jeronimo Martinez	510	85	72	86	865,781
Mick Ruis	510	85	73	57	727,690
Carlos H. Silva	702	84	76	93	2,073,144
Brian Joseph Hernandez	712	84	95	83	1,113,190
Sidney P. LeJeune, Jr.	815	84	91	97	1,040,279
Sandi Lee Gann	490	84	69	62	640,999
James Christopher Herrell	704	84	86	72	567,724
Jesse M. Campbell	790	83	93	87	1,806,903
Jose Valdivia, Jr.	833	82	95	121	5,401,879
Frank Lovato, Jr.	697	82	94	82	2,400,210
Willie Martinez	840	82	97	86	2,328,580
Real E. Simard	634	82	70	77	1,273,095
Richard Harvey Hamel	649	82	88	85	1,197,401
Lyndon Hannigan	901	82	115	104	683,946
David M. Rivera	667	82	89	83	642,754
Lorenzo Castane Lopez	658	82	86	79	572,035
Frank Albert Gonsalves	533	81	79	67	774,390
Orlando A. Martinez	760	81	113	84	551,312
Vince J. Guerra	698	81	94	94	540,348
Twyla Beckner	397	81	59	65	265,209
Constant Montpellier	658	80	96	97	4,678,130
Jose A. Velez, Jr.	588	80	92	86	3,038,413
Brian Todd Bochinski	587	80	59	71	1,764,119
Leslie Mawing	737	79	102	105	872,808
Manuel Rohena	510	79	80	81	718,753
Luis Ranilla	619	79	91	87	419,760
Kent J. Desormeaux	579	78	98	77	6,033,136
Aaron T. Gryder	756	78	94	94	3,797,829
Paul R. Toscano	700	78	68	85	1,753,236
Baltazar Contreras	347	78	66	45	424,504
Christopher Griffith	610	77	89	96	1,617,098
Colin Skinner	652	77	73	75	613,706
Earlie Fires	607	76	77	79	2,130,783
Andrew R. Ramgeet	582	76	81	73	1,385,754
Luis Espinosa	543	76	59	67	569,019
Julia Brimo	651	75	96	80	2,906,771
Luis D. Chavez	612	75	80	84	2,859,212
Victor H. Molina	612	75	72	69	1,223,413
Jose E. Lopez	611	75	86	88	1,080,804

*North American starts only

Leading Jockeys in 2003 by Stakes Earnings

Jockey	Starts	1st	2d	3d	Purses
Jerry D. Bailey	236	70	49	24	$18,328,237
Edgar S. Prado	236	46	45	29	10,956,804
Alex O. Solis	191	40	28	38	10,032,170
Pat Day	176	33	30	20	6,854,008
John R. Velazquez	210	37	33	31	6,834,040
Patrick A. Valenzuela	193	31	32	30	6,703,750
Robby Albarado	146	29	28	23	6,429,257
Jose A. Santos	182	21	27	35	5,892,636
David Romero Flores	154	20	19	21	5,419,212
Todd Kabel	109	29	20	14	4,635,341
Patrick Husbands	92	20	21	14	4,414,970
Julie A. Krone	110	24	16	12	4,216,717
Richard Migliore	138	28	10	14	3,865,232
Corey S. Nakatani	142	17	18	23	3,844,096
Mike E. Smith	150	23	18	11	3,827,974
Gary L. Stevens	114	15	20	16	3,785,874
Victor Espinoza	162	25	16	24	3,463,215
Cornelio H. Velasquez	153	18	17	23	3,444,474
Ramon A. Dominguez	122	30	27	24	3,410,195
Javier Castellano	122	14	17	25	3,156,922
Kent J. Desormeaux	118	12	21	14	3,060,738
Eibar Coa	126	20	21	20	2,923,482
Jose Valdivia, Jr.	122	13	15	14	2,519,758
Shane J. Sellers	119	15	19	11	2,448,156
Rene R. Douglas	109	20	14	15	2,160,015
Jorge F. Chavez	135	16	15	12	2,094,486
Emile Ramsammy	84	15	13	6	2,064,870
Shaun Bridgmohan	102	12	15	19	2,042,444
Michael J. Luzzi	107	12	8	18	2,040,144
Joe Bravo	80	24	10	11	2,029,800
Tyler Baze	147	6	24	18	1,961,107
Mark Guidry	84	10	7	18	1,658,382
David Clark	61	12	8	4	1,566,457
Gerard Melancon	115	21	15	15	1,518,278
Brice Blanc	57	8	6	7	1,516,997
James McAleney	76	8	10	15	1,465,786
Corey J. Lanerie	101	10	18	16	1,437,536
Robert C. Landry	51	6	5	8	1,425,603
Eddie M. Martin, Jr.	98	17	12	13	1,400,988
Ryan Fogelsonger	93	15	15	21	1,389,595
Terry J. Thompson	74	15	19	9	1,365,687
Gary Boulanger	118	9	18	17	1,336,881
Manoel R. Cruz	117	18	20	14	1,295,663
Calvin H. Borel	98	6	13	6	1,293,865
Jono C. Jones	49	9	3	12	1,242,875
Russell A. Baze	79	17	17	10	1,224,270
Julio A. Garcia	82	14	10	10	1,134,953
Jeremy Rose	86	13	8	20	1,124,121
Jean-Luc Samyn	42	6	7	6	1,082,018
Eusebio Razo, Jr.	69	16	6	5	1,080,841
Elvis Joseph Perrodin	61	7	8	5	1,049,919
Roman Chapa	64	6	8	8	1,044,625
Donald R. Pettinger	47	9	10	5	1,042,533
Jamie Theriot	70	13	7	10	1,034,558
Lonnie Meche	78	12	15	8	1,033,710
Mario G. Pino	81	14	12	18	984,852
Aaron T. Gryder	65	6	11	10	945,951
Jason P. Lumpkins	47	13	8	7	945,075
Jose A. Velez, Jr.	76	6	14	11	924,503
Jon Kenton Court	59	7	5	5	901,809
Martin Dwyer	1	1	0	0	900,000
Michael J. Kinane	4	1	0	0	899,800
Charles C. Lopez	85	13	12	15	886,391
Anthony S. Black	39	10	5	5	882,493
Ignacio Puglisi	50	6	4	3	866,432
Richard Anthony Dos Ramos	51	5	6	4	864,650
Luis S. Quinonez	59	14	11	9	839,600
Jose C. Ferrer	88	15	6	8	838,828
Roberto M. Gonzalez	54	18	1	8	837,622
Kirk Paul LeBlanc	76	15	6	7	781,337
Rafael Bejarano	51	11	4	5	770,304
Rosemary B. Homeister, Jr.	89	10	11	11	768,537
Manuel Aguilar	76	9	7	10	760,870
Constant Montpellier	52	5	5	7	759,087
Frank T. Alvarado	64	7	11	12	749,855
Jeremy Beasley	65	16	12	11	741,950
Julian Pimentel	63	15	10	7	741,044
John McKee	44	5	4	7	739,088
Rick Wilson	63	10	9	7	690,550
Larry Melancon	65	3	7	7	676,960
Felipe Valdez	50	12	7	8	673,346
Curt C. Bourque	64	8	7	14	672,501
Jorge Martin Bourdieu	65	12	12	12	669,586
Ronald J. Warren, Jr.	55	7	11	5	659,900
Oliver Castillo	42	7	6	11	633,913
Carlos H. Marquez, Jr.	53	3	4	10	633,145
Jose L. Espinoza	38	4	5	5	625,082
Martin A. Pedroza	55	8	5	2	594,494
Heberto Castillo, Jr.	38	5	3	3	594,293
Craig Perret	30	5	3	5	584,280
Guy Smith	55	9	13	8	583,090
Pedro V. Alvarado	39	8	4	9	579,499
Ricardo Jaime	61	8	13	11	578,528
Eduardo O. Nunez	62	6	11	3	559,392
Dino Luciani	31	5	3	2	556,033
Kieren Fallon	2	1	0	0	553,985
Sal Gonzalez, Jr.	26	11	2	2	552,606
Ken S. Tohill	45	10	11	4	545,915
Chad Phillip Schvaneveldt	48	7	8	4	543,115
Larry J. Sterling, Jr.	40	7	4	9	542,505
Joseph C. Judice	53	11	8	6	533,721
Abel Castellano, Jr.	57	8	4	6	531,270
Willie Martinez	48	5	10	3	524,405
Anthony Mawing	36	10	5	7	520,875
Norberto Arroyo, Jr.	44	1	3	2	517,114
Rodrigo Madrigal, Jr.	25	6	4	0	496,724
Stewart Elliott	39	8	5	9	494,064
Jesus Lopez Castanon	62	7	6	7	485,805
Jose C. Caraballo	39	7	3	7	479,536
Gary Baze	51	11	8	7	473,509
Scott A. Stevens	85	13	10	19	470,154
Frank Lovato, Jr.	61	6	7	6	460,818
Timothy T. Doocy	47	6	7	5	444,642
Nicola Wright	41	10	9	2	443,363
Carlos Gonzalez	45	8	6	6	440,807
Donnie J. Meche	17	3	2	1	425,500
Real E. Simard	42	10	8	3	423,784
Horacio Karamanos	69	5	8	3	414,158
Glenn W. Corbett	60	10	10	11	413,660
Laffit A. Pincay, Jr.	26	2	3	5	412,149
Steven Joseph Bourque	52	6	8	8	409,632
Slade Callaghan	32	2	3	4	407,052
Casey T. Lambert	54	5	8	11	406,790
Christopher A. Emigh	56	3	9	9	399,018
Jake Barton	25	3	5	3	397,673
Chandra R. Rennie	26	4	0	5	397,100
Jason R. Eads	49	9	5	10	387,923
David Wilson	50	9	7	6	387,583
Chantal Sutherland	36	1	5	4	381,482
Perry A. Winters	35	7	6	10	372,713
Monte Clifton Berry	49	6	7	4	372,618
Seth B. Martinez	58	11	8	7	367,732
Samuel B. Krasner	35	8	4	4	367,440
Brian Dale Peck	30	4	6	3	365,825
Carlos D. Madeira	40	5	5	9	364,811
Chance J. Rollins	43	4	10	4	360,745
Eddie Castro	50	4	7	9	359,757
Tony Farina	20	1	3	2	359,008
Kevin Radke	46	8	3	8	357,193
Abad Cabassa, Jr.	20	3	2	2	356,432
Clinton L. Potts	25	5	4	2	355,473
Carl James Woodley	44	7	4	6	354,360
Tom Foley	31	8	4	1	352,225
Matt S. Garcia	41	2	7	6	350,847
Francisco Duran	44	6	5	8	342,850
Leanne M. Painter	31	8	5	4	340,200
Christopher P. DeCarlo	32	3	4	4	339,465
Jozbin Z. Santana	45	4	4	12	335,280
Julio E. Felix	33	7	8	3	333,585
Ray Ganpath	5	1	1	1	332,000
Simon P. Husbands	24	1	4	3	329,882
William D. Troilo	26	7	2	3	329,594
Dean P. Butler	28	4	5	0	328,906

Jockey	Starts	1st	2d	3d	Purses	Jockey	Starts	1st	2d	3d	Purses
G. F. Almeida	42	2	6	1	326,556	Erick D. Rodriguez	15	3	1	1	179,184
Michael G. Ziegler	62	11	4	6	315,345	Aurelio Toribio, Jr.	41	3	2	4	178,575
Joe M. Castro	38	5	6	2	313,013	Frank Albert Gonsalves	43	6	5	5	177,106
Tommy Molina	24	5	3	2	312,577	Brian Joseph Hernandez	23	3	2	1	176,575
Kerwin D. Clark	57	4	8	5	310,904	Pat Smullen	7	1	0	0	172,000
Federico Mata	41	5	7	6	310,766	Russell W. Woolsey	32	2	4	5	169,757
Alex Birzer	39	5	2	8	307,091	Jose Luis Flores	21	2	4	2	160,195
James McKnight	28	2	2	1	302,995	C. Omar Klinger	22	4	0	2	159,713
Roger I. Velez	42	4	1	5	302,403	Felipe J. Santos	21	2	2	2	158,959
Carlos H. Silva	28	4	4	5	301,699	Randall A. Meier	24	3	1	2	156,112
Juan M. Gutierrez	50	12	6	6	301,246	Richard A. Bracho	28	1	6	4	152,131
Ricardo Feliciano	32	5	6	7	300,122	Miguel Sanchez Fuentes	26	3	2	4	149,532
Terry A. Stanton	41	5	6	1	293,550	Isaias D. Enriquez	27	1	0	6	149,135
Roberto Alvarado, Jr.	36	4	2	2	291,657	Larry J. Lacoursiere	25	2	2	3	146,706
Thomas L. Pompell	35	7	3	1	290,956	Dale V. Beckner	33	1	4	7	146,186
John Jacinto	52	5	5	7	290,862	Lanfranco Dettori	4	0	0	1	146,100
Ben Russell	27	4	7	4	290,677	Anthony J. D'Amico	20	2	2	5	143,576
Bobby J. Walker, Jr.	45	6	3	4	289,388	Martin Ramos Ramirez	20	2	2	2	142,242
Victor Carrero	25	3	3	3	289,340	Enrique M. Jurado	24	2	3	1	141,548
Abdiel Toribio	34	4	3	5	286,299	Dyn Panell	22	4	3	7	141,250
Craig Thornton	6	4	0	0	286,025	Scott T. Saito	35	2	9	7	141,229
Harry Vega	25	2	6	6	284,690	Nena Matz	26	3	2	4	141,112
Nick Santagata	26	4	2	2	283,973	Gary Wilbert Bain	9	1	1	1	140,969
Steven Ronald Bahen	25	1	2	4	277,548	Cyril Murphy	15	3	0	2	140,526
Derek C. Bell	40	8	6	4	276,554	Rodney A. Prescott	41	2	3	8	139,633
Michael Francis Rowland	26	5	4	4	276,327	Leslie Mawing	37	3	5	3	138,820
Rickey Walcott	11	3	1	3	273,997	Richard Monterrey	14	1	4	1	136,851
Kevin Leon Cogburn	42	5	8	7	272,002	Christopher Martin	12	3	3	1	135,368
Esteban Angel Gomez	65	8	10	10	267,146	Elvis Trujillo	18	1	5	1	135,050
Travis L. Dunkelberger	27	3	11	1	264,773	Carlos M. Cruz	22	2	3	2	134,544
Winston Albert Thompson	33	8	4	2	262,125	Mark T. Johnston	24	2	2	3	133,959
Robert Massey	25	5	2	2	261,390	Michael Phillip Iammarino	26	5	3	3	133,140
Kelly Bridges	58	10	8	5	260,939	Vernon Bush	16	5	1	2	132,400
Ricardo A. Valdes	18	5	4	2	258,304	Eric Saint-Martin	7	2	1	0	131,750
Ken A. Shino	39	5	5	9	255,480	Kerry D. Kretzer	16	2	0	1	131,613
Chris Loseth	34	2	8	8	255,394	Gerry Olguin	16	0	3	2	130,440
Hector L. Rosario, Jr.	30	4	5	6	255,036	Wilson Omar Dieguez	39	2	5	6	130,110
Jimmy Ray Coates	31	8	5	1	251,765	Raymond Torres	11	4	1	0	128,168
Donald Edward Simington	42	4	3	6	250,914	Alberto R. Higuera	33	3	4	7	126,391
E. T. Baird	23	5	3	5	249,644	Stephan Heiler	27	2	2	5	125,750
Quincy Welch	44	3	12	3	249,275	David C. Nuesch	19	2	0	2	125,610
Earlie Fires	36	2	6	5	245,714	Eduardo E. Perez	13	1	3	0	124,820
Luis Antonio Gonzalez	24	6	2	2	244,589	Kevin Krigger	14	1	4	0	124,018
James Lopez	28	3	4	1	243,556	Felipe F. Martinez	30	1	3	3	123,809
Perry Compton	42	8	5	4	234,327	Robert W. Johnson	27	2	4	5	123,144
Darryll Holland	1	0	0	1	233,200	Joseph J. Steiner	14	2	1	2	118,113
Michael Dennis Clark	34	5	4	2	230,938	Greta Kuntzweiler	12	2	1	0	117,160
Adan Fuentes	25	3	1	3	229,955	Glen Murphy	13	2	2	3	114,103
Jeff Johnston	31	5	3	3	229,700	Ray Sibille	18	0	1	4	113,974
David Bentley	29	2	5	13	224,231	F. Bruce Miller, Jr.	15	1	8	1	113,484
Richard Harvey Hamel	31	5	3	5	224,200	Omar A. Berrio	18	1	1	2	112,648
Raymond Brian Sabourin	18	1	2	3	223,863	Wade P. Rini	14	2	2	2	111,661
Francine Villeneuve	12	3	0	2	221,689	Tammi Piermarini	30	2	4	4	111,570
Ted D. Gondron	28	4	4	2	221,679	David G. Lopez	21	1	1	4	110,150
Gus M. Brown	16	5	3	0	215,661	Pedro A. Rodriguez	27	3	1	4	110,124
Orlando Mojica	37	5	8	5	211,080	Rohan R. Singh	19	2	8	2	109,490
Jamie Spencer	2	0	0	1	210,000	Danush Sukie	6	2	0	1	108,833
Mary Elizabeth Doser	22	3	6	4	209,995	Larry C. Reynolds	19	3	1	1	108,642
Kendrick Carmouche	24	4	3	4	209,572	Ken Hendricks	14	4	3	2	107,250
Luis Jeronimo Martinez	25	3	4	2	208,799	Nilo Perez	9	2	0	1	106,445
Miguel Luis Gaeta Hernandez	54	8	11	5	202,017	Kelly Michael Murray	22	5	2	2	105,401
Adalberto Diaz Lopez	24	2	1	6	201,920	Shane Laviolette	26	0	3	5	105,398
Edwin L. King, Jr.	45	2	1	6	201,314	Cindy Sue Noll	13	2	1	0	104,942
Josiah Francis Hampshire, Jr.	38	5	9	4	199,895	John A. Grabowski	12	3	1	3	104,898
Paul R. Toscano	46	0	3	7	198,804	Rodney R. Trader	8	2	3	1	104,750
Neil Poznansky	14	3	1	4	197,728	Jerome Carkeek	41	7	8	8	103,425
Luis D. Chavez	10	2	3	0	197,586	Nik G. Goodwin	16	1	3	1	103,350
John R. Davila, Jr.	14	3	5	2	196,416	Omar Camejo	21	2	1	2	103,142
Weldon T. Cloninger, Jr.	25	3	1	4	194,375	Nicholas J. Petro	17	1	2	3	103,120
Chin C. Yang	12	3	2	1	194,170	J. D. Acosta	23	0	5	3	102,749
Joseph Rocco	17	3	2	0	192,767	Tommy Meyers	6	2	1	0	102,700
Francisco Perez Fuentes	29	2	1	3	191,372	Robert V. Skelly	26	0	4	4	102,392
Travis Wayne Hightower	20	8	2	1	185,850	Pablo Fragoso	25	0	2	2	102,341
Na Somsanith	17	2	1	0	185,479	Robert Dean Williams	24	2	2	1	101,319
Andreas Suborics	2	0	1	0	185,000	Sean P. Evans	16	3	1	4	101,066
Gallyn Vick Mitchell	28	4	2	3	184,805	Danny Sorenson	3	2	1	0	101,000
Joe M. Johnson	16	3	1	2	181,801	Julio Molina Pezua	9	1	0	1	100,026

Leading Jockeys in 2003 by Stakes Won

Jockey	Starts	1st	2d	3d	Purses
Jerry D. Bailey	236	70	49	24	$18,328,237
Edgar S. Prado	236	46	45	29	10,956,804
Alex O. Solis	191	40	28	38	10,032,170
John R. Velazquez	210	37	33	31	6,834,040
Pat Day	176	33	30	20	6,854,008
Patrick A. Valenzuela	193	31	32	30	6,703,750
Ramon A. Dominguez	122	30	27	24	3,410,195
Robby Albarado	146	29	28	23	6,429,257
Todd Kabel	109	29	20	14	4,635,341
Richard Migliore	138	28	10	14	3,865,232
Victor Espinoza	162	25	16	24	3,463,215
Julie A. Krone	110	24	16	12	4,216,717
Joe Bravo	80	24	10	11	2,029,800
Mike E. Smith	150	23	18	11	3,827,974
Jose A. Santos	182	21	27	35	5,892,636
Gerard Melancon	115	21	15	15	1,518,278
David Romero Flores	154	20	19	21	5,419,212
Patrick Husbands	92	20	21	14	4,414,970
Eibar Coa	126	20	21	20	2,923,482
Rene R. Douglas	109	20	14	15	2,160,015
Cornelio H. Velasquez	153	18	17	23	3,444,474
Manoel R. Cruz	117	18	20	14	1,295,663
Roberto M. Gonzalez	54	18	1	8	837,622
Corey S. Nakatani	142	17	18	23	3,844,096
Eddie M. Martin, Jr.	98	17	12	13	1,400,988
Russell A. Baze	79	17	17	10	1,224,270
Jorge F. Chavez	135	16	15	12	2,094,486
Eusebio Razo, Jr.	69	16	6	5	1,080,841
Jeremy Beasley	65	16	12	11	741,950
Gary L. Stevens	114	15	20	16	3,785,874
Shane J. Sellers	119	15	19	11	2,448,156
Emile Ramsammy	84	15	13	6	2,064,870
Ryan Fogelsonger	93	15	15	21	1,389,595
Terry J. Thompson	74	15	19	9	1,365,687
Jose C. Ferrer	88	15	6	8	838,828
Kirk Paul LeBlanc	76	15	6	7	781,337
Julian Pimentel	63	15	10	7	741,044
Javier Castellano	122	14	17	25	3,156,922
Julio A. Garcia	82	14	10	10	1,134,953
Mario G. Pino	81	14	12	18	984,852
Luis S. Quinonez	59	14	11	9	839,600
Jose Valdivia, Jr.	122	13	15	14	2,519,758
Jeremy Rose	86	13	8	20	1,124,121
Jamie Theriot	70	13	7	10	1,034,558
Jason P. Lumpkins	47	13	8	7	945,075
Charles C. Lopez	85	13	12	15	886,391
Scott A. Stevens	85	13	10	19	470,154
Twyla Beckner	34	13	4	4	82,151
Kent J. Desormeaux	118	12	21	14	3,060,738
Shaun Bridgmohan	102	12	15	19	2,042,444
Michael J. Luzzi	107	12	8	18	2,040,144
David Clark	61	12	8	4	1,566,457
Lonnie Meche	78	12	15	8	1,033,710
Felipe Valdez	50	12	7	8	673,346
Jorge Martin Bourdieu	65	12	12	12	669,586
Juan M. Gutierrez	50	12	6	6	301,246
Rafael Bejarano	51	11	4	5	770,304
Sal Gonzalez, Jr.	26	11	2	2	552,606
Joseph C. Judice	53	11	8	6	533,721
Gary Baze	51	11	8	7	473,509
Seth B. Martinez	58	11	8	7	367,732
Michael G. Ziegler	62	11	4	6	315,345
Scott Sterr	30	11	2	6	78,851
Mark Guidry	84	10	7	18	1,658,382
Corey J. Lanerie	101	10	18	16	1,437,536
Anthony S. Black	39	10	5	5	882,493
Rosemary B. Homeister, Jr.	89	10	11	11	768,537
Rick Wilson	63	10	9	7	690,550
Ken S. Tohill	45	10	11	4	545,915
Anthony Mawing	36	10	5	7	520,875
Nicola Wright	41	10	9	2	443,363
Real E. Simard	42	10	8	3	423,784
Glenn W. Corbett	60	10	10	11	413,660
Kelly Bridges	58	10	8	5	260,939
Rennie Latchman	25	10	5	1	58,835
Gary Boulanger	118	9	18	17	1,336,881
Jono C. Jones	49	9	3	12	1,242,875
Donald R. Pettinger	47	9	10	5	1,042,533
Manuel Aguilar	76	9	7	10	760,870
Guy Smith	55	9	13	8	583,090
Jason R. Eads	49	9	5	10	387,923
David Wilson	50	9	7	6	387,583
Brice Blanc	57	8	6	7	1,516,997
James McAleney	76	8	10	15	1,465,786
Curt C. Bourque	64	8	7	14	672,501
Martin A. Pedroza	55	8	5	2	594,494
Pedro V. Alvarado	39	8	4	9	579,499
Ricardo Jaime	61	8	13	11	578,528
Abel Castellano, Jr.	57	8	4	6	531,270
Stewart Elliott	39	8	5	9	494,064
Carlos Gonzalez	45	8	6	6	440,807
Samuel B. Krasner	35	8	4	4	367,440
Kevin Radke	46	8	3	8	357,193
Tom Foley	31	8	4	1	352,225
Leanne M. Painter	31	8	5	4	340,200
Derek C. Bell	40	8	6	4	276,554
Esteban Angel Gomez	65	8	10	10	267,146
Winston Albert Thompson	33	8	4	2	262,125
Jimmy Ray Coates	31	8	5	1	251,765
Perry Compton	42	8	5	4	234,327
Miguel Luis Gaeta Hernandez	54	8	11	5	202,017
Travis Wayne Hightower	20	8	2	1	185,850
Elvis Joseph Perrodin	61	7	8	5	1,049,919
Jon Kenton Court	59	7	5	5	901,809
Frank T. Alvarado	64	7	11	12	749,855
Ronald J. Warren, Jr.	55	7	11	5	659,900
Oliver Castillo	42	7	6	11	633,913
Chad Phillip Schvaneveldt	48	7	8	4	543,115
Larry J. Sterling, Jr.	40	7	4	9	542,505
Jesus Lopez Castanon	62	7	6	7	485,805
Jose C. Caraballo	39	7	3	7	479,536
Perry A. Winters	35	7	6	10	372,713
Carl James Woodley	44	7	4	6	354,360
Julio E. Felix	33	7	8	3	333,585
William D. Troilo	26	7	2	3	329,594
Thomas L. Pompell	35	7	3	1	290,956
Jerome Carkeek	41	7	8	8	103,425
Robert Webb	44	7	6	3	84,316
Tim Moccasin	17	7	4	5	43,902
Tyler Baze	147	6	24	18	1,961,107
Robert C. Landry	51	6	5	8	1,425,603
Calvin H. Borel	98	6	13	6	1,293,865
Jean-Luc Samyn	42	6	7	6	1,082,018
Roman Chapa	64	6	8	8	1,044,625
Aaron T. Gryder	65	6	11	10	945,951
Jose A. Velez, Jr.	76	6	14	11	924,503
Ignacio Puglisi	50	6	4	3	866,432
Eduardo O. Nunez	62	6	11	3	559,392
Rodrigo Madrigal, Jr.	25	6	4	0	496,724
Frank Lovato, Jr.	61	6	7	6	460,818
Timothy T. Doocy	47	6	7	5	444,642
Steven Joseph Bourque	52	6	8	8	409,632
Monte Clifton Berry	49	6	7	4	372,618
Francisco Duran	44	6	5	8	342,850
Bobby J. Walker, Jr.	45	6	3	4	289,388
Luis Antonio Gonzalez	24	6	2	2	244,589
Frank Albert Gonsalves	43	6	5	5	177,106
Matt Williams	30	6	2	7	85,024
Jay Conklin	21	6	8	2	47,568
Richard Anthony Dos Ramos	51	5	6	4	864,650
Constant Montpellier	52	5	5	7	759,087
John McKee	44	5	4	7	739,088
Heberto Castillo, Jr.	38	5	3	3	594,293
Craig Perret	30	5	3	5	584,280
Dino Luciani	31	5	3	2	556,033
Willie Martinez	48	5	10	3	524,405
Horacio Karamanos	69	5	8	3	414,158
Casey T. Lambert	54	5	8	11	406,790
Carlos D. Madeira	40	5	5	9	364,811
Clinton L. Potts	25	5	4	2	355,473
Joe M. Castro	38	5	6	2	313,013
Tommy Molina	24	5	3	2	312,577
Federico Mata	41	5	7	6	310,766

Jockey	Starts	1st	2d	3d	Purses	Jockey	Starts	1st	2d	3d	Purses
Alex Birzer	39	5	2	8	307,091	Joe M. Johnson	16	3	1	2	181,801
Ricardo Feliciano	32	5	6	7	300,122	Erick D. Rodriguez	15	3	1	1	179,184
Terry A. Stanton	41	5	6	1	293,550	Aurelio Toribio, Jr.	41	3	2	4	178,575
John Jacinto	52	5	5	7	290,862	Brian Joseph Hernandez	23	3	2	1	176,575
Michael Francis Rowland	26	5	4	4	276,327	Randall A. Meier	24	3	1	2	156,112
Kevin Leon Cogburn	42	5	8	7	272,002	Miguel Sanchez Fuentes	26	3	2	4	149,532
Robert Massey	25	5	2	2	261,390	Nena Matz	26	3	2	4	141,112
Ricardo A. Valdes	18	5	4	2	258,304	Cyril Murphy	15	3	0	2	140,526
Ken A. Shino	39	5	5	9	255,480	Leslie Mawing	37	3	5	3	138,820
E. T. Baird	23	5	3	5	249,644	Christopher Martin	12	3	3	1	135,368
Michael Dennis Clark	34	5	4	2	230,938	Alberto R. Higuera	33	3	4	7	126,391
Jeff Johnston	31	5	3	3	229,700	Pedro A. Rodriguez	27	3	1	4	110,124
Richard Harvey Hamel	31	5	3	5	224,200	Larry C. Reynolds	19	3	1	1	108,642
Gus M. Brown	16	5	3	0	215,661	John A. Grabowski	12	3	1	3	104,898
Orlando Mojica	37	5	8	5	211,080	Sean P. Evans	16	3	1	4	101,066
Josiah Francis Hampshire, Jr.	38	5	9	4	199,895	Huber Villa-Gomez	16	3	2	2	95,250
Michael Phillip Iammarino	26	5	3	3	133,140	Travis Wales	27	3	0	3	91,621
Vernon Bush	16	5	1	2	132,400	Bobby L. Johnson	15	3	0	2	86,785
Kelly Michael Murray	22	5	2	2	105,401	Mark Anthony Villa	17	3	1	1	86,485
Berkley R. Packer	30	5	5	2	66,478	Edwin Molinari	15	3	1	3	82,950
Richard M. Vasquez	14	5	2	1	66,195	Orlando A. Martinez	29	3	7	5	76,938
Daniel Raymond Boag	25	5	6	0	52,592	Daniel Lee Beck	21	3	3	3	62,431
Dennis Michael Collins	25	5	1	1	51,284	Janine Stianson	13	3	3	2	29,109
Terri Landaker	24	5	5	3	39,825	Travis Hamilton	10	3	2	1	17,289
Jose L. Espinoza	38	4	5	5	625,082	Stephen Michael Karr	15	3	2	3	13,961
Chandra R. Rennie	26	4	0	5	397,100	Laffit A. Pincay, Jr.	26	2	3	5	412,149
Brian Dale Peck	30	4	6	3	365,825	Slade Callaghan	32	2	3	4	407,052
Chance J. Rollins	43	4	10	4	360,745	Matt S. Garcia	41	2	7	6	350,847
Eddie Castro	50	4	7	9	359,757	G. F. Almeida	42	2	6	1	326,556
Jozbin Z. Santana	45	4	4	12	335,280	James McKnight	28	2	2	1	302,995
Dean P. Butler	28	4	5	0	328,906	Harry Vega	25	2	6	6	284,690
Kerwin D. Clark	57	4	8	5	310,904	Chris Loseth	34	2	8	8	255,394
Roger I. Velez	42	4	1	5	302,403	Earlie Fires	36	2	6	5	245,714
Carlos H. Silva	28	4	4	5	301,699	David Bentley	29	2	5	13	224,231
Roberto Alvarado, Jr.	36	4	2	2	291,657	Adalberto Diaz Lopez	24	2	1	6	201,920
Ben Russell	27	4	7	4	290,677	Edwin L. King, Jr.	45	2	1	6	201,314
Abdiel Toribio	34	4	3	5	286,299	Luis D. Chavez	10	2	3	0	197,586
Craig Thornton	6	4	0	0	286,025	Francisco Perez Fuentes	29	2	1	3	191,372
Nick Santagata	26	4	2	2	283,973	Na Somsanith	17	2	1	0	185,479
Hector L. Rosario, Jr.	30	4	5	6	255,036	Russell W. Woolsey	32	2	4	5	169,757
Donald Edward Simington	42	4	3	6	250,914	Jose Luis Flores	21	2	4	2	160,195
Ted D. Gondron	28	4	4	2	221,679	Felipe J. Santos	21	2	2	2	158,959
Kendrick Carmouche	24	4	3	4	209,572	Larry J. Lacoursiere	25	2	2	3	146,706
Gallyn Vick Mitchell	28	4	2	3	184,805	Anthony J. D'Amico	20	2	2	5	143,576
C. Omar Klinger	22	4	0	2	159,713	Martin Ramos Ramirez	20	2	2	2	142,242
Dyn Panell	22	4	3	7	141,250	Enrique M. Jurado	24	2	3	1	141,548
Raymond Torres	11	4	1	0	128,168	Scott T. Saito	35	2	9	7	141,229
Ken Hendricks	14	4	3	2	107,250	Rodney A. Prescott	41	2	3	8	139,633
Jason Leacock	19	4	0	2	97,900	Carlos M. Cruz	22	2	3	2	134,544
Gary Kurek	12	4	2	0	90,724	Mark T. Johnston	24	2	2	3	133,959
John B. Woodley	7	4	1	0	85,641	Eric Saint-Martin	7	2	1	0	131,750
Armando Martinez	46	4	10	5	81,946	Kerry D. Kretzer	16	2	0	1	131,613
Lorenzo Castane Lopez	21	4	3	0	75,660	Wilson Omar Dieguez	39	2	5	6	130,110
Anne Von Rosen	10	4	0	0	31,070	Stephan Heiler	27	2	2	5	125,750
Megan Ludlow	14	4	1	4	28,762	David C. Nuesch	19	2	0	2	125,610
Todd J. Nuttall	18	4	2	0	15,237	Robert W. Johnson	27	2	4	5	123,144
Larry Melancon	65	3	7	7	676,960	Joseph J. Steiner	14	2	1	2	118,113
Carlos H. Marquez, Jr.	53	3	4	10	633,145	Greta Kuntzweiler	12	2	1	0	117,160
Donnie J. Meche	17	3	2	1	425,500	Glen Murphy	13	2	2	3	114,103
Christopher A. Emigh	56	3	9	9	399,018	Wade P. Rini	14	2	2	2	111,661
Jake Barton	25	3	5	3	397,673	Tammi Piermarini	30	2	4	4	111,570
Abad Cabassa, Jr.	20	3	2	2	356,432	Rohan R. Singh	19	2	8	2	109,490
Christopher P. DeCarlo	32	3	4	4	339,465	Danush Sukie	6	2	0	1	108,833
Victor Carrero	25	3	3	3	289,340	Nilo Perez	9	2	0	1	106,445
Rickey Walcott	11	3	1	3	273,997	Cindy Sue Noll	13	2	1	1	104,942
Travis L. Dunkelberger	27	3	11	1	264,773	Rodney R. Trader	8	2	3	1	104,750
Quincy Welch	44	3	12	3	249,275	Omar Camejo	21	2	1	2	103,142
James Lopez	28	3	4	1	243,556	Tommy Meyers	6	2	1	0	102,700
Adan Fuentes	25	3	1	3	229,955	Robert Dean Williams	24	2	2	1	101,319
Francine Villeneuve	12	3	0	2	221,689	Danny Sorenson	3	2	1	0	101,000
Mary Elizabeth Doser	22	3	6	4	209,995	David Burton Patton	23	2	3	4	99,734
Luis Jeronimo Martinez	25	3	4	2	208,799	Robert Neal Lester	21	2	4	1	92,140
Neil Poznansky	14	3	1	4	197,728	Taylor M. Hole	25	2	2	5	89,557
John R. Davila, Jr.	14	3	5	2	196,416	Paul M. Nolan	25	2	4	0	88,709
Weldon T. Cloninger, Jr.	25	3	1	4	194,375	Russell Vicchrilli	21	2	6	3	88,496
Chin C. Yang	12	3	2	1	194,170	Matthew Otis McCarron	12	2	0	2	84,000
Joseph Rocco	17	3	2	0	192,767	Jacques DesAutels	20	2	3	2	82,570

Apprentice Jockeys – Money Won in 2003

Jockey	Mts.	1st	2d	3d	Pct.	Purses
Fragoso, Pablo	909	103	120	103	.113	$3,987,229
Castro, Eddie	1,196	234	247	164	.196	3,797,572
Brimo, Julia	651	75	96	80	.115	2,906,771
Monterrey, Richard	1,164	172	187	143	.148	2,869,556
Chavez, Luis D.	500	75	75	69	.150	2,739,336
Fogelsonger, Ryan	679	152	125	137	.224	2,714,321
Garcia, Luis	1,270	179	178	165	.141	2,603,914
McKee, John	591	92	89	85	.156	2,573,148
Flores, Oscar	927	170	127	116	.183	2,188,234
Rodriguez, Erick D.	963	114	147	133	.118	1,875,407
Baze, Michael C.	633	86	94	94	.136	1,689,908
Scharfstein, Jillian	449	37	54	55	.082	1,512,398
Cotto, Jr., Pedro Luis	499	39	54	48	.078	1,274,333
Fusilier, Casey	824	98	116	97	.119	1,206,325
Phillips, Mark	764	107	114	102	.140	1,179,954
Thornton, Timothy	417	49	53	47	.118	1,158,983
Castillo, Luis A.	305	31	41	36	.102	1,151,975
Uske, Shannon	227	24	39	25	.106	1,087,016
Lopez, Jose E.	611	75	86	88	.123	1,080,804
Rivera, Hiram G.	656	92	73	87	.140	1,026,949
Contreras, Cruz	415	46	45	52	.111	881,328
Wright, Nicola	249	50	49	35	.201	824,563
Singh, Sunny	235	25	26	25	.106	789,063
Rivera, Jr., Jose L.	362	42	45	45	.116	764,911
Stortz, Marcia	540	54	55	68	.100	752,048
Boudreau, Daniel	380	42	37	47	.111	746,938
Shepherd, Justin	479	44	41	48	.092	742,363
Ruis, Mick	510	85	73	57	.167	727,690
Duran, Francisco	280	34	31	45	.121	668,736
Perez, Edwin	640	89	82	78	.139	614,853
Bracaloni, Natasha D.	357	29	62	56	.081	572,510
Ramos, Hector G.	284	55	38	31	.194	566,508
Garcia, Alan	209	27	26	32	.129	551,279
Byrne, John	612	40	42	51	.065	441,106
Graham, James	419	20	43	47	.048	434,454
Diego, Iram Vargas	478	45	44	54	.094	430,374
Garcia, Carlos	314	35	32	26	.111	401,399
Beauregard, Shannon	371	46	45	44	.124	382,583
Maldonado-Alicea, E	454	32	30	46	.070	360,496
Morris, Liz	267	22	24	18	.082	353,401
Mendez, Emmanuel	311	25	28	39	.080	350,822
Fuentes, Freddy	263	35	22	34	.133	345,174
Mangold, Kevin	386	21	24	37	.054	344,974
Ramos, Adrian B.	421	30	32	44	.071	337,049
Dorr, Sandi	167	26	22	20	.156	317,834
Carreno, Jorge	271	33	32	29	.122	314,363
Suarez, Gabriel	347	38	39	40	.110	311,783
Quinonez, Belen	361	19	20	33	.053	309,694
McGowan, Mathew C	194	28	20	25	.144	277,760
Lawson, Mark	217	16	21	37	.074	258,477
Santana, Daniel	207	25	20	28	.121	258,091
Nelson, Leroy	213	18	15	20	.085	255,405
Ning, Stan	298	12	25	40	.040	252,197
King, Dallas	381	26	13	25	.068	250,851
DeAlba, Cesar	93	15	9	8	.161	248,780
Romero, Hector R.	195	17	24	18	.087	238,335
Delorme, Larren	241	34	35	36	.141	231,891
Vannozzi, Lauren	232	29	30	27	.125	229,530
Covington, Raina	327	25	23	26	.076	227,689
Thomas, Michael	467	29	37	34	.062	211,597
Perez, Salvador	360	27	24	37	.075	206,730
Diaz, Renzo	195	13	16	20	.067	202,390
Pennington, Frankie	247	28	23	31	.113	195,502
Rohena, Jr., Rafael	231	27	33	19	.117	194,784
Hernandez, Adrian	192	20	17	21	.104	191,594
Rochabrun, John	216	14	15	23	.065	186,140
Mena, Miguel	149	13	11	18	.087	185,655
Fitzpatrick, Ashton	169	12	8	14	.071	176,030
Kenny-Martin, Jocelyne	263	24	30	28	.091	171,131
Abbott, Emma Jane	105	16	15	13	.152	170,058
Hernandez, Jr., Brian J	68	12	16	3	.176	168,249
Zambrana, Eddie Joe	307	24	24	30	.078	167,027
Acosta, J. D.	105	11	12	17	.105	165,592
Teague, Rahede	298	13	20	30	.044	163,397
Bisono, Alex	100	9	10	13	.090	162,048
Cosme, Emanuel	151	15	15	11	.099	155,039
Endres, Jessica	377	27	19	29	.072	148,930
Beckon, Chad	49	3	1	6	.061	138,534
Kinsey, Jill E.	110	11	7	13	.100	133,706
Talman, Katherine G.	320	27	41	44	.084	128,676
Vasquez, Rolando	142	13	13	12	.092	124,807
Whitacre, Brandon	55	7	8	9	.127	109,935
Fraser, Cory	29	4	4	1	.138	106,815
Mello, David	131	8	12	18	.061	105,522
Gomez, Oscar	121	3	2	0	.025	102,743
Olmo, Christian J.	115	6	8	10	.052	101,712
Torres, Jose	202	11	12	19	.054	99,590
Leacock, Jason	93	16	11	9	.172	98,033
Deyan, Carlos	151	8	9	6	.053	91,984
Galvan, Mario A.	162	6	6	11	.037	91,309
Marcial, Alejandro	106	3	10	6	.028	90,428
Torbit, Renee	207	13	21	28	.063	88,128
Terry, Dominic M.	76	6	4	7	.079	86,545
Velez, Pedro J.	208	9	8	18	.043	84,657
Esposito, Anthony C.	158	6	6	9	.038	75,208
Gray, Akili	277	6	10	16	.022	67,646
Crandall, Amanda L.	118	8	11	4	.068	66,912
Hamilton, Quincy	82	7	7	7	.085	64,181
Olivera, Juan Manuel	154	7	14	16	.045	63,732
Velez, Juan J.	110	6	4	6	.055	61,515
Van Hassel, Chip	49	4	4	13	.082	59,522
O'Donnell, Kristin	155	21	15	24	.135	59,520
Raghunath, Raymond	36	2	1	3	.056	57,511
Fuentes, Edwin	105	4	8	7	.038	56,737
Cruz, George Luis	101	7	9	15	.069	56,451
Rojas, Ruben	112	6	14	7	.054	55,597
Schmidt, Jennifer	127	4	12	6	.031	52,447
Offutt, Leigh	77	2	4	7	.026	50,870
Luna, Ramon	78	11	7	5	.141	41,701
Silva, Carlos Ignacio	39	4	2	7	.103	41,413
Von Rosen, Anne	56	3	7	3	.054	37,361
Garcia, Jason	53	1	2	4	.019	36,083
Williams, Justin B.	120	2	3	10	.017	36,077
Han, Amanda	60	4	10	3	.067	34,247
Roche, Jennie	39	4	8	8	.103	33,861
Rice, Jessica	35	2	3	0	.057	29,411
Campbell, Shannon	37	1	0	1	.027	27,468
Nagle, Valerie	38	1	4	2	.026	24,714
Moore, Rory T.	37	2	2	4	.054	22,038
Lake, Anne-Marie	61	2	2	4	.033	21,285
Vazquez, Jeovani	22	2	0	4	.091	21,180
Avila, Juan	59	1	1	4	.017	20,965
Irion, Heather	30	5	2	3	.167	20,236
Shamsie, Clayton P.	31	2	3	3	.065	17,930
Ramos, Ramon	42	1	1	1	.024	17,203
Davila, Jose M.	16	2	2	2	.125	16,386
Talbot, Crista R.	59	1	3	7	.017	15,325

Leading Apprentice Jockeys – Races Won in 2003

Jockey	Mts.	1st	2d	3d	Pct.	Purses
Castro, Eddie	1,196	234	247	164	.196	$3,797,572
Garcia, Luis	1,270	179	178	165	.141	2,603,914
Monterrey, Richard	1,164	172	187	143	.148	2,869,556
Flores, Oscar	927	170	127	116	.183	2,188,234
Fogelsonger, Ryan	679	152	125	137	.224	2,714,321
Rodriguez, Erick D.	963	114	147	133	.118	1,875,407
Phillips, Mark	764	107	114	102	.140	1,179,954
Fragoso, Pablo	909	103	120	103	.113	3,987,229
Fusilier, Casey	824	98	116	97	.119	1,206,325
McKee, John	591	92	89	85	.156	2,573,148
Rivera, Hiram G.	656	92	73	87	.140	1,026,949
Perez, Edwin	640	89	82	78	.139	614,853
Baze, Michael C.	633	86	94	94	.136	1,689,908
Ruis, Mick	510	85	73	57	.167	727,690
Brimo, Julia	651	75	96	80	.115	2,906,771
Chavez, Luis D.	500	75	69		.150	2,739,336
Lopez, Jose E.	611	75	86	88	.123	1,080,804
Ramos, Hector G.	284	55	38	31	.194	566,508
Stortz, Marcia	540	54	55	68	.100	752,048
Wright, Nicola	249	50	49	35	.201	824,563
Thornton, Timothy	417	49	53	47	.118	1,158,983
Contreras, Cruz	415	46	45	52	.111	881,328
Beauregard, Shannon	371	46	45	44	.124	382,583
Diego, Iram Vargas	478	45	44	54	.094	430,374
Shepherd, Justin	479	44	41	48	.092	742,363
Rivera, Jr., Jose L.	362	42	45	45	.116	764,911
Boudreau, Daniel	380	42	37	47	.111	746,938
Byrne, John	612	40	42	51	.065	441,106
Cotto, Jr., Pedro Luis	499	39	54	48	.078	1,274,333
Suarez, Gabriel	347	38	39	40	.110	311,783
Scharfstein, Jillian	449	37	54	55	.082	1,512,398
Garcia, Carlos	314	35	32	26	.111	401,399
Fuentes, Freddy	263	35	22	34	.133	345,174
Duran, Francisco	280	34	31	45	.121	668,736
Delorme, Larren	241	34	35	36	.141	231,891
Carreno, Jorge	271	33	32	29	.122	314,363
Maldonado-Alicea, E	454	32	30	46	.070	360,496
Castillo, Luis A.	305	31	41	36	.102	1,151,975
Ramos, Adrian B.	421	30	32	44	.071	337,049
Bracaloni, Natasha D.	357	29	62	56	.081	572,510
Vannozzi, Lauren	232	29	30	27	.125	229,530
Thomas, Michael	467	29	37	34	.062	211,597
McGowan, Mathew C	194	28	20	25	.144	277,760
Pennington, Frankie	247	28	23	31	.113	195,502
Garcia, Alan	209	27	26	32	.129	551,279
Perez, Salvador	360	27	24	37	.075	206,730
Rohena, Jr., Rafael	231	27	33	19	.117	194,784
Endres, Jessica	377	27	19	29	.072	148,930
Talman, Katherine G.	320	27	41	44	.084	128,676
Dorr, Sandi	167	26	22	20	.156	317,834
King, Dallas	381	26	13	25	.068	250,851
Singh, Sunny	235	25	26	25	.106	789,063
Mendez, Emmanuel	311	25	28	39	.080	350,822
Santana, Daniel	207	25	20	28	.121	258,091
Covington, Raina	327	25	23	26	.076	227,689
Uske, Shannon	227	24	39	25	.106	1,087,016
Kenny-Martin, Jocelyne	263	24	30	28	.091	171,131
Zambrana, Eddie Joe	307	24	24	30	.078	167,027
Morris, Liz	267	22	24	18	.082	353,401
Mangold, Kevin	386	21	24	37	.054	344,974
O'Donnell, Kristin	155	21	15	24	.135	59,520
Graham, James	419	20	43	47	.048	434,494
Hernandez, Adrian	192	20	17	21	.104	191,594
Quinonez, Belen	361	19	20	33	.053	309,694
Nelson, Leroy	213	18	15	20	.085	255,405
Romero, Hector R.	195	17	24	18	.087	238,335
Lawson, Mark	217	16	21	37	.074	258,477
Abbott, Emma Jane	105	16	15	13	.152	170,058
Leacock, Jason	93	16	11	9	.172	98,033
DeAlba, Cesar	93	15	9	8	.161	248,780
Cosme, Emanuel	151	15	15	11	.099	155,039
Rochabrun, John	216	14	15	23	.065	186,140
Diaz, Renzo	195	13	16	20	.067	202,390
Mena, Miguel	149	13	11	18	.087	185,655
Teague, Rahede	298	13	20	30	.044	163,397
Vasquez, Rolando	142	13	13	12	.092	124,807
Torbit, Renee	207	13	21	28	.063	88,128
Ning, Stan	298	12	25	40	.040	252,197
Fitzpatrick, Ashton	169	12	8	14	.071	176,030
Hernandez Jr., Brian J	68	12	16	3	.176	168,249
Acosta, J. D.	105	11	12	17	.105	165,592
Kinsey, Jill E.	110	11	7	13	.100	133,706
Torres, Jose	202	11	12	19	.054	99,590
Luna, Ramon	78	11	7	5	.141	41,701
Bisono, Alex	100	9	10	13	.090	162,048
Velez, Pedro J.	208	9	8	18	.043	84,657
Mello, David	131	8	12	18	.061	105,522
Deyan, Carlos	151	8	9	6	.053	91,984
Crandall, Amanda L.	118	8	11	4	.068	66,912
Whitacre, Brandon	55	7	8	9	.127	109,935
Hamilton, Quincy	82	7	7	7	.085	64,181
Olivera, Juan Manuel	154	7	14	16	.045	63,732
Cruz, George Luis	101	7	9	15	.069	56,451
Olmo, Christian J.	115	6	8	10	.052	101,712
Galvan, Mario A.	162	6	6	11	.037	91,309
Terry, Dominic M.	76	6	4	7	.079	86,545
Esposito, Anthony C.	158	6	6	9	.038	75,208
Gray, Akili	277	6	10	16	.022	67,646
Velez, Juan J.	110	6	4	6	.055	61,515
Rojas, Ruben	112	6	14	7	.054	55,597
Irion, Heather	30	5	2	3	.167	20,236
Fraser, Cory	29	4	4	1	.138	106,815
Van Hassel, Chip	49	4	4	13	.082	59,522
Fuentes, Edwin	105	4	8	7	.038	56,737
Schmidt, Jennifer	127	4	12	6	.031	52,447
Silva, Carlos Ignacio	39	4	2	7	.103	41,413
Han, Amanda	60	4	10	3	.067	34,247
Roche, Jennie	39	4	8	8	.103	33,861
Stinn, Caroline	34	4	9	10	.118	14,439
Rivera, Jr., Jose M.	37	4	1	4	.108	10,880
Beischer, Danielle	30	4	7	5	.133	6,350
Beckon, Chad	49	3	1	6	.061	138,534
Gomez, Oscar	121	3	2	0	.025	102,743
Marcial, Alejandro	106	3	10	6	.028	90,428
Von Rosen, Anne	56	3	7	3	.054	37,361
Itschner, Christine	33	3	2	1	.091	10,027
Raghunath, Raymond	36	2	1	3	.056	57,511
Offutt, Leigh	77	2	4	7	.026	50,870
Williams, Justin B.	120	2	3	10	.017	36,077
Rice, Jessica	35	2	3	0	.057	29,411
Moore, Rory T.	37	2	2	4	.054	22,038
Lake, Anne-Marie	61	2	2	4	.033	21,285
Vazquez, Jeovani	22	2	0	4	.091	21,180
Shamsie, Clayton P.	31	2	3	3	.065	17,930
Davila, Jose M.	16	2	2	2	.125	16,386

Annual Leading Jockeys – Money Won

Jockey	Mts.	1st	2d	3d	Pct.	Purses	Jockey	Mts.	1st	2d	3d	Pct.	Purses
1908 Notter, J.	872	249	178	140	.29	$464,322	1960 Shoemaker, W.	1,227	274	196	158	.22	2,123,961
1909 Dugan, E.	631	143	123	86	.23	166,355	1961 Shoemaker, W.	1,256	304	186	175	.24	2,690,819
1910 Shilling, C. H.	506	172	96	64	.34	176,030	1962 Shoemaker, W.	1,126	311	156	128	.28	2,916,844
1911 Koerner, T.	813	162	133	112	.20	88,308	1963 Shoemaker, W.	1,203	271	193	137	.22	2,526,925
1912 Butwell, J.	684	144	122	110	.21	79,843	1964 Shoemaker, W.	1,056	246	147	133	.23	2,649,553
1913 Buxton, M.	887	146	131	136	.16	82,552	1965 Baeza, B.	1,245	270	200	201	.22	2,582,702
1914 McCahey, J.	824	155	157	130	.19	121,845	1966 Baeza, B.	1,341	298	222	190	.22	2,951,022
1915 Garner, M.	775	151	118	90	.19	96,628	1967 Baeza, B.	1,064	256	184	127	.24	3,088,888
1916 McTaggart, J.	832	150	137	119	.18	155,055	1968 Baeza, B.	1,089	201	184	145	.18	2,835,108
1917 Robinson, F.	731	147	125	108	.20	148,057	1969 Velasquez, J.	1,442	258	230	204	.18	2,542,315
1918 Luke, L.	756	178	123	108	.24	210,864	1970 Pincay, L. Jr.	1,328	269	208	187	.20	2,626,526
1919 Loftus, J.	177	65	36	24	.37	252,707	1971 Pincay, L. Jr.	1,627	380	288	214	.23	3,784,377
1920 Krummer, C.	353	87	79	48	.25	292,376	1972 Pincay, L. Jr.	1,388	289	215	205	.21	3,225,827
1921 Sande, E.	340	112	69	59	.33	263,043	1973 Pincay, L. Jr.	1,444	350	254	209	.24	4,093,492
1922 Johnson, A.	297	43	57	40	.14	345,054	1974 Pincay, L. Jr.	1,278	341	227	180	.27	4,251,060
1923 Sande, E.	430	122	89	79	.28	569,394	1975 Baeza, B.	1,190	196	208	180	.16	3,674,398
1924 Parke, I.	844	205	175	121	.24	290,395	1976 Cordero, A. Jr.	1,534	274	273	235	.18	4,709,500
1925 Fator, L.	315	81	54	44	.26	305,775	1977 Cauthen, S.	2,075	487	345	304	.23	6,151,750
1926 Fator, L.	511	143	90	86	.28	361,435	1978 McHargue, D. G.	1,762	375	294	263	.21	6,188,353
1927 Sande, E.	179	49	33	19	.27	277,877	1979 Pincay, L. Jr.	1,708	420	302	261	.25	8,183,535
1928 McAtee, L.	235	55	43	25	.23	301,295	1980 McCarron, C. J.	1,964	405	318	282	.20	7,661,000
1929 Garner, M.	274	57	39	33	.21	314,975	1981 McCarron, C. J.	1,494	326	251	207	.22	8,397,604
1930 Workman, R.	571	152	88	79	.27	420,438	1982 Cordero, A. Jr.	1,838	397	338	227	.22	9,702,520
1931 Kurtsinger, C.	519	93	82	79	.18	392,095	1983 Cordero, A. Jr.	1,792	362	296	237	.20	10,116,807
1932 Workman, R.	378	87	48	55	.23	385,070	1984 McCarron, C. J.	1,565	356	276	218	.23	12,038,213
1933 Jones, R.	471	63	57	70	.13	226,285	1985 Pincay, L. Jr.	1,409	289	246	183	.21	13,415,049
1934 Wright, W. D.	919	174	154	114	.19	287,185	1986 Santos, J. A.	1,636	329	237	222	.20	11,329,297
1935 Coucci, S.	749	141	125	103	.19	319,760	1987 Santos, J. A.	1,639	305	268	208	.19	12,407,355
1936 Wright, W. D.	670	100	102	73	.15	264,000	1988 Santos, J. A.	1,867	370	287	265	.20	14,877,298
1937 Kurtsinger, C.	765	120	94	106	.16	384,292	1989 Santos, J. A.	1,459	285	238	220	.20	13,847,003
1938 Wall, N.	658	97	94	82	.15	385,161	1990 Stevens, G. L.	1,504	283	245	202	.19	13,881,198
1939 James, B.	904	191	165	105	.21	353,333	1991 McCarron, C. J.	1,440	265	228	206	.18	14,456,073
1940 Arcaro, E.	783	132	143	112	.17	343,661	1992 Desormeaux, K. J.	1,568	361	260	208	.23	14,193,006
1941 Meade, D.	1,164	210	185	158	.18	398,627	1993 Smith, M. E.	1,510	343	235	214	.23	14,008,148
1942 Arcaro, E.	687	123	97	89	.18	481,949	1994 Smith, M.E.	1,483	317	250	196	.21	15,979,820
1943 Longden, J.	871	173	140	121	.20	573,276	1995 Bailey, J.D.	1,265	287	193	144	.23	16,308,230
1944 Atkinson, T.	1,539	287	231	213	.19	899,101	1996 Bailey, J.D.	1,185	297	189	165	.25	17,064,409
1945 Longden, J.	778	180	112	100	.23	981,977	1997 Bailey, J.D.	1,144	272	186	178	.24	15,946,282
1946 Atkinson, T.	1,377	233	213	173	.17	1,036,825	1998 Stevens, G.L.	839	171	141	118	.20	18,884,352
1947 Dodson, D.	646	141	100	75	.22	1,429,949	1999 Bailey, J.D.	972	242	164	135	.25	17,530,905
1948 Arcaro, E.	726	188	108	98	.26	1,686,230	2000 Day, P.	1,219	267	206	186	.22	17,479,838
1949 Brooks, S.	906	209	172	110	.23	1,316,817	2001 Bailey, J. D.	910	226	194	137	.25	18,997,720
1950 Arcaro, E.	888	195	153	144	.22	1,410,160	2002 Bailey, J. D.	832	213	139	118	.26	19,271,814
1951 Shoemaker, W.	1,161	257	197	161	.22	1,329,890	2003 Bailey, J. D.	776	206	149	97	.27	23,354,960
1952 Arcaro, E.	807	188	122	109	.23	1,859,591							
1953 Shoemaker, W.	1,683	485	302	210	.29	1,784,187							
1954 Shoemaker, W.	1,251	380	221	142	.30	1,876,760							
1955 Arcaro, E.	820	158	126	108	.19	1,864,796							
1956 Hartack, W.	1,387	347	252	184	.25	2,343,955							
1957 Hartack, W.	1,238	341	208	178	.28	3,060,501							
1958 Shoemaker, W.	1,133	300	185	137	.26	2,961,693							
1959 Shoemaker, W.	1,285	347	230	159	.27	2,843,133							

Annual Leading Jockeys – Races Won

Year	Jockey	Mts.	1st	2d	3d	Unplc.	Pct.
1895	Perkins, J.	762	192	177	129	264	.25
1896	Scherrer, J.	1,093	271	227	172	423	.24
1897	Martin, H.	803	173	152	116	362	.21
1898	Burns, T.	973	277	213	149	334	.28
1899	Burns, T.	1,064	273	173	266	352	.26
1900	Mitchell, C	874	195	140	139	380	.23
1901	O'Connor, W.	1,047	253	221	192	381	.24
1902	Ranch, J.	1,069	276	205	181	407	.26
1903	Fuller, G. C.	918	229	152	122	415	.25
1904	Hildebrand, E.	1,169	297	230	171	471	.25
1905	Nicol, D.	861	221	143	136	861	.26
1906	Miller, W	1,384	388	300	199	497	.28
1907	Miller, W	1,194	334	226	170	464	.28
1908	Powers, V.	1,260	324	204	185	547	.26
1909	Powers, V.	704	173	121	114	296	.25
1910	Garner, G.	947	200	188	153	406	.20
1911	Koerner, T.	813	162	133	112	406	.20
1912	Hill, P.	967	168	141	129	529	.17
1913	Buxton, M.	887	146	131	136	474	.16
1914	McTaggart, J.	787	157	132	106	392	.20
1915	Garner, M.	775	151	118	90	416	.19
1916	Robinson, F.	791	178	131	124	358	.23
1917	Crump, W.	803	151	140	101	411	.19
1918	Robinson, F.	864	185	140	108	431	.21
1919	Robinson, C.	896	190	145	126	435	.21
1920	Butwell, J.	721	152	129	139	301	.21
1921	Lang, C.	696	135	110	105	346	.19
1922	Fator, M.	859	188	153	116	402	.22
1923	Parke, I.	718	173	105	95	345	.24
1924	Parke, I.	844	205	175	121	343	.24
1925	Mortensen, A.	987	187	145	138	517	.19
1926	Jones, R.	1,172	190	163	152	667	.16
1927	Hardy, L.	1,130	207	192	151	580	.18
1928	Inzelone, J.	1,053	155	152	135	610	.15
1929	Knight, M.	871	149	132	133	547	.17
1930	Riley, H.R.	861	177	145	123	416	.21
1931	Roble, H.	1,174	173	173	155	673	.15
1932	Gilbert, J.	1,050	212	144	160	534	.20
1933	Westrope, J.	1,224	301	235	166	522	.25
1934	Peters, M.	1,045	221	179	147	498	.21
1935	Stevenson, C.	1,099	206	169	146	578	.19
1936	James, B.	1,106	245	196	161	505	.22
1937	Adams, J.	1,265	260	186	177	642	.21
1938	Longden, J.	1,150	236	168	171	575	.21
1939	Meade, D.	1,284	255	221	180	628	.20
1940	Dew, E.	1,377	287	201	180	709	.21
1941	Meade, D.	1,164	210	185	158	611	.18
1942	Adams, J.	1,120	245	185	150	540	.22
1943	Adams, J.	1,069	228	159	171	511	.21
1944	Atkinson, T.	1,539	287	231	213	808	.19
1945	Jessop, J. D.	1,085	290	182	168	445	.27
1946	Atkinson, T.	1,377	233	213	173	758	.17
1947	Longden, J.	1,327	316	250	195	566	.24
1948	Longden, J.	1,197	319	223	161	494	.27
1949	Gilson, G	1,347	270	217	181	679	.20
1950	Culmone, J.	1,676	388	283	218	787	.23
	Shoemaker, W.	1,640	388	266	230	756	.24
1951	Burr, C.	1,319	310	232	192	585	.24
1952	DeSpirito, A.	1,482	390	247	212	633	.26
1953	Shoemaker, W.	1,683	485	302	210	686	.29
1954	Shoemaker, W.	1,251	380	221	142	508	.30
1955	Hartack, W.	1,702	417	298	215	772	.25
1956	Hartack, W.	1,387	347	252	184	604	.25
1957	Hartack, W.	1,238	341	208	178	511	.28
1958	Shoemaker, W.	1,133	300	185	137	511	.26
1959	Shoemaker, W.	1,285	347	230	159	549	.27
1960	Hartack, W.	1,402	307	247	190	658	.22
1961	Sellers, J.	1,394	328	212	227	627	.24
1962	Ferraro, R.	1,755	352	252	226	925	.20
1963	Blum, W.	1,704	360	286	215	843	.21
1964	Blum, W.	1,577	324	274	170	809	.21
1965	Davidson, J.	1,582	319	228	190	845	.20
1966	Gomez, A.	996	318	173	142	363	.32
1967	Velasquez, J.	1,939	438	315	270	916	.23
1968	Cordero Jr., A.	1,662	345	278	219	820	.21
1969	Snyder, L.	1,645	352	290	243	760	.21
1970	Hawley, S.	1,908	452	313	265	878	.24
1971	Pincay Jr., L.	1,627	380	288	214	745	.23
1972	Hawley, S.	1,381	367	269	200	545	.27
1973	Hawley, S.	1,925	515	336	292	782	.27
1974	McCarron, C. J.	2,199	546	392	297	964	.25
1975	McCarron, C. J.	2,194	468	389	305	1,032	.21
1976	Hawley, S.	1,634	413	245	201	778	.25
1977	Cauthen, S.	2,075	487	345	304	939	.23
1978	Delahoussaye, E.	1,666	384	285	238	759	.23
1979	Gall, D.	2,146	479	396	326	945	.22
1980	McCarron, C. J.	1,964	405	318	282	959	.20
1981	Gall, D.	1,917	376	305	297	939	.20
1982	Day, P.	1,870	399	326	255	890	.21
1983	Day, P.	1,725	454	321	251	699	.26
1984	Day, P.	1,694	399	296	259	740	.24
1985	Antley, C. W.	2,335	469	371	288	1,208	.20
1986	Day, P.	1,417	429	246	202	540	.30
1987	Desormeaux, K. J.	2,207	450	370	294	1,093	.20
1988	Desormeaux, K. J.	1,897	474	295	276	852	.25
1989	Desormeaux, K. J.	2,312	598	385	309	1,021	.26
1990	Day, P.	1,421	364	265	222	575	.26
1991	Day, P.	1,405	430	256	213	506	.31
1992	Baze, R. A.	1,691	433	296	237	725	.25
1993	Baze, R. A.	1,579	410	297	225	647	.26
1994	Baze, R. A.	1,587	415	310	266	605	.26
1995	Baze, R. A.	1,537	448	312	233	544	.29
1996	Baze, R. A.	1,465	415	297	201	552	.28
1997	Prado, E. S.	2,046	536	388	307	815	.26
1998	Prado, E. S.	1,969	470	377	285	837	.24
1999	Prado, E. S.	1,902	402	307	276	917	.21
2000	Baze, R.A.	1,513	412	252	239	610	.27
2001	Dominguez, R. A.	1,864	431	368	278	786	.23
2002	Baze, Russell A.	1,508	431	302	219	556	.29
2003	Dominguez, R.A.	1,627	453	316	252	606	.28

All-time Leading Female Jockeys

The leading female jockey of all time is Julie Krone, who returned to riding in November of 2002. The first female jockey to be licensed to ride in North America was Kathy Kusner, a two-time member of the United States Equestrian team who broke her leg at a Madison Square Garden horse show in 1968, before she ever got the chance to ride in a pari-mutuel race.

The first female to actually ride in a race was Diane Crump, who rode Bridle to a sixth place finish at Hialeah Park, February 7, 1969. Two weeks later, Barbara Jo Rubin began a string of historic firsts, by winning aboard Cohesion at Charles Town racetrack in West Virginia and following that by winning with her first two mounts at Aqueduct Racetrack, in New York.

Through the years, many female jockeys have continued to break down the barriers of active, open competition.

Among those who made major contributions to this effort, were Patty Barton, Mary Bacon, Karen Rogers, Mary Russ, Abigal Fuller, Robyn Smith, Andrea Seefeldt, Rosemary Homeister Jr., Diane Nelson, Joyce Jellison, Lisa Kuykendall, Vicky Warhol, Mary Ann Alligood, B.A. Bogichow, Donna Barton, Vicky Aragon-Baze, Patricia Cooksey, Chantal Sutherland, Cindy Noll, and Krone.

Below are the top three female riders of all time in total races and purses won as of Dec. 31, 2003.

LEADING FEMALE JOCKEYS – MONEY WON THROUGH 2003

Name	Starts	Wins	Seconds	Thirds	Earnings
Krone, Julie A	21,408	3,704	3,261	2,912	$90,125,088
Homeister, Rosemary B	12,366	1,660	1,647	1,678	26,484,542
Cooksey, Patricia J	18,244	2,136	2,185	2,119	19,872,992

LEADING FEMALE JOCKEYS – RACES WON THROUGH 2003

Name	Starts	Wins	Seconds	Thirds	Earnings
Krone, Julie A	21,408	3,704	3,261	2,912	$90,125,088
Cooksey, Patricia J	18,244	2,136	2,185	2,119	19,872,992
Aragon-Baze, Vicky	11,235	1,769	1,550	1,402	11,639,868

Leading North American Jockeys – Lifetime Wins

The list below includes the most prolific winning jockeys in racing history and their records through Jan. 11, 2004. It includes any jockey with 1,900 career victories in Thoroughbred races. Verifiable performances in major stakes in Dubai, Europe and Asia also are included. If the jockey retired, the last year of competition is indicated. Among jockeys retiring in 2003 were leader Laffit Pincay Jr. and Eddie Delahoussaye, who announced his retirement in 2003 after having not ridden since an accident in 2002.

Jockeys	Last Rode	Mounts	1st	2d	3d	Win %	Purses
Pincay Laffit A. Jr.	2003	48,486	9,530	7,784	6,650	19.7%	$237,120,625
Shoemaker William	1990	40,350	8,833	6,136	4,987	21.9%	123,375,524
Day Pat		39,353	8,605	6,699	5,561	21.9%	285,282,474
Baze Russell A.		38,936	8,484	6,566	5,542	21.8%	125,124,455
Gall David A.	1999	41,775	7,396	6,525	6,131	17.7%	24,972,821
McCarron Chris J.	2002	34,239	7,141	5,670	4,672	20.9%	263,985,505
Cordero Angel Jr.	1995	38,656	7,057	6,136	5,359	18.3%	164,561,227
Velasquez Jorge	1997	40,852	6,795	6,178	5,755	16.6%	125,544,379
Hawley Sandy	1998	31,455	6,449	4,825	4,159	20.5%	88,681,292
Snyder Larry	1996	35,681	6,388	5,030	3,440	17.9%	47,207,289
Delahoussaye Eddie J.	2002	39,213	6,384	5,676	5,586	16.3%	195,884,940
Gambardella Carl	1994	39,018	6,349	5,953	5,353	16.3%	29,389,041
Fires Earlie		43,643	6,296	5,381	5,200	14.4%	81,486,627
Longden John	1966	32,413	6,032	4,914	4,273	18.6%	24,665,800
Bailey Jerry D.		29,558	5,576	4,339	3,739	18.9%	263,273,711
Pino Mario G.		32,957	5,312	4,837	4,511	16.1%	83,033,994
Vasquez Jacinto	1996	37,337	5,228	4,714	4,510	14.0%	85,754,115
Ardoin Ronald D.		32,335	5,226	4,298	3,793	16.2%	58,908,059
Prado Edgar S.		25,905	4,948	4,212	3,683	19.1%	130,739,792
Wilson Rick		24,586	4,918	4,235	3,451	20.0%	76,789,720
Baez Rodolfo	1999	28,609	4,875	4,291	4,103	17.0%	30,474,225
Arcaro Eddie	1961	24,092	4,779	3,807	3,302	19.8%	30,039,543
Stevens Gary L.		26,863	4,749	4,270	3,856	17.7%	208,664,803
Black Anthony S.		31,094	4,702	4,086	3,985	15.1%	52,593,726
Brumfield Don	1989	33,223	4,573	4,076	3,758	13.8%	43,567,861
Guidry Mark		28,275	4,540	4,044	3,794	16.1%	77,420,715
Ouzts Perry Wayne		35,519	4,495	4,390	4,324	12.7%	25,014,488
Brooks Steve	1975	30,330	4,451	4,219	3,658	14.7%	18,239,817
Maple Eddie	1998	33,974	4,398	4,516	4,335	12.9%	105,338,573
Blum Walter	1975	28,673	4,382	3,913	3,350	15.3%	26,497,189
Perret Craig		26,896	4,377	3,862	3,573	16.3%	111,578,781
Desormeaux Kent J.		21,942	4,372	3,591	3,057	19.9%	166,206,074
Smith Mike E.		25,996	4,334	3,690	3,353	16.7%	161,076,862
Romero Randy P.	1999	26,091	4,294	3,743	3,313	16.5%	75,264,198
Doocy Timothy T.		28,294	4,288	3,764	3,508	15.2%	51,168,967
Lloyd Jeffrey Scott	2000	31,296	4,276	4,318	4,179	13.7%	34,199,413
Hartack William	1975	21,535	4,272	3,370	2,871	19.8%	26,466,758
Sibille Ray		36,816	4,261	4,342	4,364	11.6%	68,802,712
Gomez Avelino	1980	17,028	4,081	2,947	2,405	24.0%	11,777,297
Solis Alex O.		27,199	4,050	3,761	3,840	14.9%	171,701,531
Dittfach Hugo	1989	33,905	4,000	4,092	6,113	11.8%	13,506,052
Rowland Michael F.		26,654	3,992	3,664	3,234	15.0%	28,544,678
Grove Philip	1997	26,901	3,991	3,761	3,580	14.8%	16,511,842
Colton Robert E.	2002	24,932	3,982	3,561	3,395	16.0%	40,779,163
Sellers Shane J.		23,130	3,932	3,418	2,893	17.0%	116,095,779
Borel Calvin H.		25,782	3,881	3,503	2,991	15.1%	68,353,711
Chavez Jorge F.		22,488	3,878	3,197	2,784	17.2%	137,420,033
Migliore Richard		25,959	3,836	3,414	3,252	14.8%	126,491,077
Hulet Leslie	1999	25,286	3,816	3,589	3,293	15.1%	17,847,169
Whited D. E.	1990	28,036	3,795	3,602	3,374	13.5%	25,206,767
Atkinson Ted	1959	23,661	3,795	3,300	2,913	16.0%	17,449,360
Meier Randall A.		29,783	3,777	3,622	3,466	12.7%	51,231,798
Neves Ralph	1964	25,334	3,772	3,547	3,352	14.9%	13,786,239
Moyers Leroy	1992	26,040	3,770	3,529	3,190	14.5%	21,491,585
Baird R. L.	1985	24,822	3,749	3,281	2,912	15.1%	12,592,611

Jockeys	Last Rode	Mounts	1st	2d	3d	Win %	Purses
Santos Jose A.		23,400	3,740	3,342	3,268	16.0%	167,244,583
Krone Julie A.		21,408	3,704	3,261	2,912	17.3%	90,125,088
Santagata Nick		33,050	3,696	3,640	3,721	11.2%	65,528,213
Weiler Dan	1995	27,706	3,694	3,362	3,213	13.3%	12,225,344
Hansen Ron D.	1993	20,430	3,693	3,204	2,839	18.1%	42,635,184
Neff Steve	1995	27,951	3,685	3,384	3,299	13.2%	15,526,196
Williams Robert D.		24,705	3,663	3,229	3,090	14.8%	26,772,449
Gonzalez Roberto M.		26,502	3,618	3,409	3,172	13.7%	47,701,787
Ussery Robert	1974	20,593	3,611	3,941	2,427	17.5%	22,714,074
Loseth Chris		25,573	3,603	3,369	3,074	14.1%	31,513,155
Powell Jim Paul	2001	27,455	3,587	3,400	3,403	13.1%	15,997,565
Toro Fernando	1990	27,496	3,555	3,507	3,484	12.9%	56,299,765
Pierce D.	1985	28,740	3,546	3,655	3,617	12.3%	39,018,422
Bracciale Vincent Jr.	1995	20,291	3,545	3,003	2,712	17.5%	37,817,349
Valenzuela Patrick A.		23,469	3,544	3,535	3,013	15.1%	125,885,595
Passmore William J.	1984	29,409	3,531	3,143	2,994	12.0%	22,992,805
Antley Chris W.	2000	19,723	3,480	2,881	2,494	17.6%	92,261,894
Lively John	1991	26,134	3,468	3,033	3,073	13.3%	32,573,504
Dlugopolski A. R.	2001	25,428	3,453	3,146	2,900	13.6%	10,582,479
Thornburg Buck	1989	27,258	3,433	3,208	3,163	12.6%	22,876,221
Tejeira Jorge E.	2001	21,987	3,419	3,050	2,826	15.6%	28,146,870
Rocco Joseph		25,405	3,401	3,332	3,280	13.4%	47,401,656
Davis Robbie G.	2002	24,260	3,382	3,365	3,108	13.9%	115,732,836
Burton John E.	1999	20,511	3,336	2,816	2,821	16.3%	7,782,602
Hinojosa Herbert	1998	25,160	3,334	3,349	3,246	13.3%	17,962,176
Bravo Joe		18,396	3,332	2,954	2,505	18.1%	73,883,689
Iliescu Arnold	1996	25,972	3,324	3,026	3,139	12.8%	14,840,887
Baze Gary		22,070	3,312	2,910	2,725	15.0%	26,908,646
Whitley Kevin	2001	19,189	3,275	2,580	2,345	17.1%	19,271,837
Adams John	1958	20,159	3,270	2,704	2,635	16.2%	9,743,109
Platts Robin	2000	20,442	3,245	2,835	2,570	15.9%	39,266,629
Stevens Scott A.		23,135	3,213	3,096	3,067	13.9%	21,484,020
Dupuy Larry A.	2000	18,855	3,204	2,780	2,477	17.0%	10,990,706
Rivera Heriberto Jr.	2000	22,110	3,183	3,010	2,825	14.4%	24,110,789
Elliott Stewart		20,740	3,181	2,657	2,506	15.3%	32,881,106
Ferrer Jose C.		21,551	3,180	2,879	2,676	14.8%	48,432,909
Bourque Steven J.		21,664	3,180	2,777	2,579	14.7%	19,885,948
Diaz Juvenal Lopez	2000	20,808	3,164	2,797	2,570	15.2%	41,589,019
Castaneda Marco	1997	27,053	3,163	3,192	3,329	11.7%	53,068,587
Baeza Braulio	1976	17,239	3,140	2,730	2,422	18.2%	36,150,142
Warren Ronald J. Jr.		21,461	3,139	3,079	3,038	14.6%	54,877,543
Krasner Samuel B.		19,631	3,136	2,882	2,527	16.0%	23,485,716
Pettinger Donald R.		19,198	3,133	2,620	2,500	16.3%	39,816,083
Silva Carlos H.		25,602	3,132	3,012	3,026	12.2%	50,860,364
Houghton T. D.		18,203	3,132	2,649	2,323	17.2%	25,471,437
Judice Joseph C.		20,995	3,105	2,873	2,751	14.8%	31,253,001
Bourque Curt C.		20,844	3,103	2,576	2,407	14.9%	36,138,315
Flores Jose Luis		17,876	3,087	2,746	2,306	17.3%	26,052,446
York Ray	2000	25,159	3,082	2,911	2,740	12.3%	14,206,054
Johnston Mark T.		18,731	3,078	2,839	2,630	16.4%	56,627,737
Compton Perry		22,155	3,061	2,832	2,545	13.8%	20,219,826
McCauley W. H.	1998	20,129	3,049	2,892	2,552	15.1%	71,391,327
Davidson Jesse	1988	18,433	3,035	2,440	2,264	16.5%	10,727,089
Morgan Michael R.		21,801	3,034	2,745	2,649	13.9%	25,983,371
Turcotte Ron	1978	20,281	3,032	2,897	2,559	14.9%	28,606,490
McKnight James		21,412	3,021	2,814	2,701	14.1%	35,735,346
Madden Darrel	1974	20,822	3,000	2,607	2,618	14.4%	7,374,831
Lopez Charles C.		20,155	2,996	2,609	2,444	14.9%	51,609,069
D'Amico Anthony J.		21,387	2,996	2,713	2,464	14.0%	35,111,614

Jockeys	Last Rode	Mounts	1st	2d	3d	Win %	Purses
Hampshire J. F. Jr.		17,020	2,995	2,470	2,303	17.6%	25,345,166
Knight Lester Cash		20,705	2,986	3,036	2,998	14.4%	22,269,399
Reynolds Larry C.		19,634	2,975	2,809	2,465	15.2%	36,824,160
Rincon Rudy	1999	23,559	2,975	2,860	2,804	12.6%	9,252,809
Boulanger Gary		19,561	2,974	2,730	2,635	15.2%	53,032,669
Faul Ricky J.		22,814	2,966	2,759	2,727	13.0%	22,444,140
Vargas Jorge L.		19,544	2,945	2,766	2,607	15.1%	22,136,913
Baltazar Chuck	1997	22,618	2,912	2,497	2,405	12.9%	23,902,514
McCarthy Michael J.	2002	17,180	2,907	2,654	2,493	16.9%	44,677,863
Rotz John L.	1973	20,288	2,907	2,495	2,288	14.3%	22,991,932
Court Jon Kenton		23,153	2,883	2,712	2,625	12.5%	48,667,060
Culmone Joe	1972	16,307	2,868	2,496	2,183	17.6%	12,010,447
Woods C. R. Jr.		21,086	2,860	2,601	2,534	13.6%	36,644,771
Salvaggio Mark V.		17,820	2,858	2,657	2,427	16.0%	16,797,405
Nicol Paul Albert Jr.		17,423	2,841	2,563	2,436	16.3%	23,688,055
Velez Jose A. Jr.		20,844	2,838	2,789	2,577	13.6%	54,496,834
Kutz Dean	2002	21,860	2,835	2,682	2,609	13.0%	33,691,225
Miller Donald A. Jr.	1996	18,113	2,830	2,580	2,595	15.6%	37,018,336
Velazquez John R.		17,020	2,823	2,455	2,227	16.6%	119,986,512
Munsell George R.	1999	23,931	2,822	2,762	2,697	11.8%	8,157,106
Albarado Robby		17,750	2,817	2,565	2,351	15.9%	81,174,154
Feliciano Bennie R.	1999	17,566	2,802	2,572	2,370	16.0%	14,063,084
Sellers John	1977	18,636	2,787	2,500	2,371	15.0%	18,359,523
Boulmetis Sam	1966	15,512	2,783	2,308	2,069	17.9%	15,425,953
Mercier Norman	1992	21,275	2,769	2,621	2,524	13.0%	9,004,650
Douglas Rene R.		18,485	2,764	2,713	2,411	15.0%	67,989,894
Barrera Carlos	1997	19,670	2,762	2,510	2,506	14.0%	18,486,045
MacBeth Donald	1986	22,415	2,755	2,822	2,924	12.3%	40,859,309
Dupuy Allen C.		18,309	2,755	2,350	2,150	15.0%	14,135,559
Kabel Todd		15,092	2,752	2,391	2,044	18.2%	72,026,660
Pineda Alvaro	1975	18,007	2,731	2,418	2,165	15.2%	15,327,910
Perrodin Elvis J.		19,070	2,719	2,510	2,432	14.3%	30,858,674
Craig H. A. Jr.	1976	17,454	2,719	2,308	1,984	15.6%	5,138,364
Guerin Eric	1977	20,131	2,712	2,557	2,408	13.5%	17,305,136
Cave Roy	1984	19,937	2,711	2,458	2,469	13.6%	4,305,341
Ecoffey Fred	1984	17,522	2,683	2,471	2,181	15.3%	6,045,127
Vega Harry		15,532	2,677	2,223	2,106	17.2%	30,210,874
Shuk Nick	1981	23,206	2,669	2,586	2,456	11.5%	11,286,518
Hebert Tracy J.	2000	18,249	2,668	2,264	2,072	14.6%	28,491,364
Hinojosa Emede	1990	15,418	2,665	2,188	1,898	17.3%	4,667,134
Trosclair Angelo J.	1998	20,776	2,660	2,470	2,407	12.8%	24,798,012
Grabowski John A.		13,829	2,660	2,211	1,948	19.2%	18,886,563
Fell Jeff	1990	15,165	2,649	2,204	1,954	17.5%	38,742,852
Woodhouse Hedley	1972	21,442	2,642	2,376	2,401	12.3%	14,483,558
Lewis William R. Jr.		18,092	2,642	2,408	2,341	14.6%	7,535,732
Delgado Alberto		21,743	2,637	2,621	2,640	12.1%	34,822,585
Barrow Thomas	1991	21,061	2,627	2,578	2,515	12.5%	12,816,323
Flores David Romero		18,041	2,626	2,460	2,325	14.6%	94,294,972
Gryder Aaron T.		20,352	2,625	2,587	2,652	12.9%	78,056,446
Lapensee Michel		19,466	2,621	2,487	2,341	13.5%	11,637,430
Landing Ray	1983	21,164	2,620	2,692	2,463	12.4%	4,919,246
Lopez Ricardo D.	2002	17,995	2,612	2,668	2,476	14.5%	24,819,034
Manganello Mike	1990	16,773	2,598	2,184	2,042	15.5%	8,946,751
Houghton Rick L.		19,573	2,595	2,585	2,469	13.3%	11,136,223
Nakatani Corey S.		15,420	2,592	2,305	2,160	16.8%	138,022,274
Martin Eddie M. Jr.		19,727	2,591	2,566	2,385	13.1%	42,292,211
Winters Perry A.		16,591	2,591	2,376	2,277	15.6%	17,219,589
Saumell Francisco	1979	18,231	2,591	2,298	2,204	14.2%	3,499,032
Chapman Thomas M.	1996	20,575	2,587	2,554	2,621	12.6%	36,788,641

Jockeys	Last Rode	Mounts	1st	2d	3d	Win %	Purses
Maple Sam	1996	20,211	2,578	2,495	2,366	12.8%	29,091,687
Meza Rafael Q.	2001	19,923	2,573	2,403	2,226	12.9%	48,865,366
Melancon Larry		18,504	2,554	2,435	2,366	13.8%	49,849,424
McHargue D. G.	1988	15,712	2,553	2,154	1,927	16.2%	39,609,526
LeBlanc Kirk Paul		20,137	2,552	2,599	2,464	12.7%	29,036,890
Licata Frank	1999	16,826	2,546	2,302	2,235	15.1%	9,629,846
Valenzuela Ismael	1980	21,203	2,545	2,494	2,346	12.0%	20,122,760
Lambert Jerry	1996	16,564	2,535	2,371	2,249	15.3%	20,933,326
McDowell Michael	1992	19,337	2,517	2,290	2,274	13.0%	16,734,420
Melancon Gerard		18,143	2,516	2,462	2,284	13.9%	29,612,744
St. Leon Gene	1999	18,482	2,514	2,373	2,215	13.6%	24,508,230
Bush Vernon		18,707	2,507	2,389	2,313	13.4%	16,286,011
Diaz Antonio L.	1992	19,081	2,501	2,209	2,056	13.1%	20,525,336
Frazier Ricky		20,554	2,495	2,476	2,406	12.1%	30,316,121
Guillory David	2002	20,649	2,482	2,564	2,429	12.0%	26,706,082
Graell Antonio	2000	18,982	2,481	2,217	2,202	13.1%	22,016,374
Clark David		17,176	2,473	2,272	2,130	14.4%	56,271,962
Bourque Kenneth	1999	19,873	2,467	2,312	2,270	12.4%	20,422,060
Westrope Jack	1958	17,497	2,467	2,406	2,166	14.1%	8,226,677
Coa Eibar		12,734	2,465	1,997	1,638	19.4%	57,626,230
Howard Donald Lee	2001	18,209	2,450	2,219	2,192	13.5%	26,774,427
Samyn Jean-Luc		21,490	2,448	2,500	2,672	11.4%	84,362,390
Johnson Brian G.	2001	16,279	2,445	2,054	2,095	15.0%	16,420,346
Rini Anthony	1975	18,716	2,438	2,429	2,221	13.0%	10,879,825
Molina Victor H.		16,733	2,427	2,216	2,015	14.5%	32,078,834
Duffy Lloyd	1996	21,339	2,419	2,549	2,579	11.3%	24,047,045
Agnello Anthony	1993	15,691	2,414	2,104	1,912	15.4%	10,851,294
Cruguet Jean	1996	20,636	2,407	2,419	2,524	11.7%	51,557,267
Luzzi Michael J.		18,215	2,404	2,182	2,321	13.2%	62,841,967
McCarron Gregg	1995	20,595	2,403	2,316	2,407	11.7%	27,268,536
Walker Bobby J. Jr.		18,044	2,397	2,218	2,051	13.3%	25,640,631
Pedroza Martin A.		20,573	2,396	2,431	2,385	11.6%	59,743,098
Potts Clinton L.		13,844	2,391	1,980	1,823	17.3%	21,593,145
Martinez Luis J.		16,413	2,391	2,095	2,065	14.6%	17,117,254
LaGue Larry	2001	21,287	2,380	2,352	2,440	11.2%	10,210,209
Dunkelberger T. L.		11,296	2,378	1,765	1,553	21.1%	26,203,518
Patterson G.	1990	17,202	2,376	2,214	2,114	13.8%	17,649,667
Ycaza Manuel C.	1970	10,563	2,367	1,749	1,515	22.4%	19,935,226
Attard Larry	1997	19,126	2,366	2,342	2,382	12.4%	34,206,895
Pruitt Jerry		17,667	2,344	2,317	2,201	13.3%	7,179,082
Zook Dana	1997	23,515	2,336	2,690	2,660	9.9%	8,783,561
Guerra Vince J.		18,203	2,326	2,235	2,220	12.8%	11,476,974
Woodley Carl James		17,601	2,323	2,103	2,088	13.2%	16,365,002
Sayler Bernon	2001	26,016	2,302	2,393	2,420	8.8%	11,859,582
Meyers Tommy		13,846	2,301	2,015	1,760	16.6%	12,063,548
Spieth Scott		16,116	2,297	2,171	2,132	14.3%	20,328,039
Sanchez Herson A.	1998	18,313	2,289	2,182	2,117	12.5%	11,048,856
Hendricks Ken		14,334	2,288	1,976	1,893	16.0%	8,492,704
Bartram Brent E.	2002	16,806	2,280	2,211	2,216	13.6%	35,113,773
Solomone Mickey	1990	17,174	2,276	1,846	1,776	13.3%	18,176,887
Martinez Willie		16,570	2,275	2,123	1,887	13.7%	51,269,404
Vigliotti Matthew J.	1996	16,555	2,268	2,216	2,180	13.7%	23,027,131
Campbell Ronald J.	1993	13,874	2,245	1,926	1,706	16.2%	9,403,215
Berry Monte Clifton		16,729	2,231	2,178	2,047	13.3%	20,112,851
Montoya Daryl		19,405	2,228	2,192	2,217	11.5%	22,208,376
Gonsalves Frank A.		17,285	2,217	2,209	2,100	12.8%	13,637,242
Guajardo Alonzo		17,600	2,217	1,997	1,858	12.6%	12,327,742
Aviles Rudy	1997	14,180	2,216	1,970	1,847	15.6%	9,663,913
Avant James E.		12,875	2,215	1,756	1,527	17.2%	10,200,757
McGregor C. H.	2002	13,608	2,214	2,029	2,029	16.3%	12,844,009

Jockeys	Last Rode	Mounts	1st	2d	3d	Win %	Purses
Steinberg Patrick W.	1993	13,884	2,210	1,903	1,681	15.9%	15,698,892
Lopez Adalberto Diaz		14,360	2,207	2,165	1,824	15.4%	28,081,112
Freeman Wayne	2001	17,952	2,188	2,177	2,057	12.2%	4,625,840
Whited Daniel W.	1999	18,343	2,182	2,024	1,928	11.9%	9,062,031
Scocca Dante		18,121	2,164	2,192	2,032	11.9%	13,112,716
Thompson W. A.		15,158	2,163	2,121	2,050	14.3%	17,585,174
Bruin James Edward		22,579	2,162	2,224	2,258	9.6%	25,114,414
Lumpkins Jason P.		10,811	2,153	1,593	1,415	19.9%	24,560,400
Small Stanley	1992	18,088	2,149	2,075	2,118	11.9%	4,453,100
Allen Ronald Dale Jr.	2002	16,734	2,147	2,047	1,963	12.8%	15,647,606
Seymour Don James	1994	11,626	2,141	1,759	1,577	18.4%	31,440,583
Cooksey Patricia J.		18,244	2,136	2,185	2,119	11.7%	19,872,992
Messina Robert		14,041	2,134	1,964	1,808	15.2%	15,253,330
Verge Mario E.		17,208	2,118	2,103	2,064	12.3%	30,976,205
Saumell Larry	1999	17,379	2,098	2,025	1,909	12.1%	24,876,170
Thomas Douglas B.	1997	18,026	2,092	2,103	2,199	11.6%	21,173,003
Markham R. L. Jr.		18,755	2,083	2,062	1,909	11.1%	4,728,642
Moran Michael T.	1995	15,856	2,079	1,968	2,098	13.1%	11,757,349
Troilo William D.		16,722	2,073	1,907	1,942	12.4%	20,207,127
Baker C. J.		17,621	2,063	2,363	2,347	11.7%	12,706,891
Gomez Esteban A.		15,281	2,063	2,008	1,902	13.5%	11,672,076
Edwards James W.	1991	15,202	2,057	1,928	1,898	13.5%	18,456,759
Boland William N.	1969	17,233	2,049	1,895	1,922	11.9%	14,856,095
Vergara Euclides B.	1994	13,449	2,049	1,949	1,843	15.2%	12,501,317
Kaenel Jack Leroy		15,250	2,046	1,831	1,794	13.4%	24,423,893
Gomez Garrett K.	2002	12,886	2,035	1,873	1,686	15.8%	60,312,831
Valovich C. J.	2002	14,351	2,034	1,804	1,661	14.2%	19,655,653
Phelps Billy	1996	16,970	2,026	2,176	1,988	11.9%	8,294,797
Alvarado Pedro V.		11,892	2,025	1,897	1,599	17.0%	13,335,759
Castillo Heberto Jr.		16,198	2,024	1,927	1,952	12.5%	44,120,834
Simonetti Frank	1995	16,593	2,016	2,009	1,956	12.1%	3,696,461
Razo Eusebio Jr.		17,981	2,011	2,267	2,081	11.2%	38,238,312
Romero Shane P.		15,326	2,011	1,703	1,579	13.1%	21,323,763
Hutton Greg W.		15,321	2,004	1,877	1,664	13.1%	27,492,891
Caballero Raul	1995	16,676	2,002	1,927	1,946	12.0%	9,273,564
Ernst Phil	1998	17,430	1,988	2,055	2,026	11.4%	5,195,796
Martinez Orlando A.		15,860	1,986	1,904	1,869	12.5%	12,447,493
Martinez Joe A.		12,560	1,985	1,795	1,692	15.8%	10,628,903
Maese Alex	1998	18,575	1,981	1,992	2,133	10.7%	8,673,676
Best Frank	1999	15,564	1,977	2,012	1,860	12.7%	7,613,461
Shino Ken A.		13,120	1,976	1,748	1,725	15.1%	13,203,362
Rivas Carlos		13,919	1,976	1,724	1,703	14.2%	8,047,742
Lanerie Corey J.		13,936	1,975	1,897	1,806	14.2%	34,033,327
Murphy Glen		15,572	1,968	2,071	1,923	12.6%	19,632,207
Lambert Casey T.		16,350	1,955	1,946	1,855	12.0%	18,003,278
Clark Kerwin D.		16,554	1,954	1,967	1,870	11.8%	25,523,320
Mitchell Gallyn Vick		13,277	1,949	1,802	1,811	14.7%	12,355,583
Grant Howard	1984	10,327	1,944	1,506	1,339	18.8%	12,120,579
Kato Akifumi		18,281	1,939	1,988	2,090	10.6%	5,284,514
Walker Mark K.	2000	13,219	1,935	1,803	1,620	14.6%	12,844,094
Munar Luis H.		11,032	1,933	1,589	1,413	17.5%	12,149,258
Gale Michael Allen		14,973	1,932	2,084	1,965	12.9%	9,797,208
Corbett Glenn W.		13,892	1,924	1,823	1,696	13.8%	18,144,781
Martinez Flavio III	1998	15,512	1,918	1,857	1,768	12.4%	9,715,487
Nelson Eldon	1975	14,415	1,917	1,682	1,535	13.3%	10,084,711
Thompson C. R.	1995	14,832	1,914	1,856	1,834	12.9%	3,590,178
Torres Cesar A.		11,825	1,913	1,649	1,523	16.2%	13,755,491
Saul Dennis	2000	17,819	1,906	2,022	2,294	10.7%	10,385,284
Quinonez Luis S.		13,936	1,905	1,836	1,791	13.7%	22,660,460
Marquez Carlos H. Jr.		14,809	1,902	1,851	1,822	12.8%	35,699,339

World's Leading Jockey – Laffit Pincay Jr.

A legendary career came to an end in 2003 when Laffit Pincay Jr., world's leading jockey with 9,530 winning rides to his credit, retired in the aftermath of an accident at Santa Anita Park.

Pincay, born in Panama on Dec. 29, 1946, started his U.S. riding career in 1966, after winning nearly 450 races in Panama. Within 10 years, he had risen to the height of his profession in North America, leading all jockeys in money won from 1970 through 1974 and earning an Eclipse Award in 1971, 1973 and 1974. His spectacular success warranted election into the Hall of Fame in 1975.

Such success would be sustained. Pincay earned two more Eclipse Awards, in 1979 and 1985, years that again saw him lead all jockeys in earnings.

During his lengthy career, Pincay won the Kentucky Derby in 1984 aboard Swale and rode three consecutive winners of the Belmont, with the Woody Stephens-trained trio of Conquistador Cielo, Caveat and Swale in 1982-1984. He would win seven Breeders' Cup events, including the 1986 Classic aboard Skywalker. Pincay's other Breeders' Cup victories came aboard Bayakoa in the Distaff in 1989 and 1990; with Tasso, Capote and Is It True in the 1985, 1986 and 1988 runnings of the Juvenile, respectively; and Phone Chatter in the 1993 Juvenile Fillies.

The Southern California-based Pincay frequently appeared aboard luminaries such as Affirmed,

Laffit Pincay Jr.

John Henry, Bayakoa, Susan's Girl, Ancient Title and many others.

During his lengthy career, Pincay won over 150 Grade 1 events, including victories in the Arlington Million, Jockey Club Gold Cup, Woodward, Spinster, Metropolitan Handicap, Travers, Florida Derby and Washington D.C. International away from his California home base. He was a dominant force in southern California, winning the Hollywood Gold Cup nine times, the Santa Anita Derby seven times and the Santa Anita Handicap on five occasions.

On Dec. 10, 1999, Pincay surpassed Bill Shoemaker's previous standard of 8,833 winning rides to become racing's all-time leading rider.

Laffit Pincay Jr. Year–by–Year

	Mts	1st	2nd	3rd	Earnings	Year	Mts	1st	2nd	3rd	Earnings
Before 1976, US and Foreign						1988	1,102	198	159	145	8,575,377
	13,677	3,106	2,298	1,942	$28,740,923	1989	1,594	298	224	212	11,361,610
						1990	1,079	150	122	137	6,546,989
						1991	1,433	218	200	173	8,323,411
1976 and Later, US and Foreign						1992	1,283	193	189	128	7,320,773
Year	Mts	1st	2nd	3rd	Earnings	1993	1,214	164	171	167	6,697,141
1976	1,435	386	263	173	$4,377,961	1994	1,211	157	171	172	6,828,999
1977	1,329	295	247	200	4,385,951	1995	1,270	156	187	185	6,181,225
1978	1,428	287	253	205	4,132,993	1996	979	129	122	135	4,160,355
1979	1,707	420	302	260	8,182,260	1997	718	75	94	82	2,520,342
1980	1,419	289	222	222	6,390,355	1998	730	103	101	112	3,917,084
1981	1,511	301	286	229	7,914,392	1999	1,112	170	158	141	6,662,689
1982	1,478	302	240	221	9,076,024	2000	1,090	202	186	136	8,490,360
1983	1,421	299	246	192	8,813,456	2001	1,252	225	180	152	10,049,166
1984	1,407	299	235	192	10,909,948	2002	1,189	205	168	163	9,572,037
1985	1,409	289	246	183	13,315,049	2003	229	49	34	31	1,967,131
1986	1,318	252	208	161	10,168,428	Totals:	48,487	9,530	7,784	6,650	$237,420,625
1987	1,463	313	272	199	11,838,196						

Graded Stakes Events Won By Laffit Pincay Jr.

Year	Stakes Name	Winner
1973	Santa Susana	Belle Marie
1973	Demoiselle	Chris Evert
1973	Golden Rod	Chris Evert
1973	Santa Anita H.	Cougar II
1973	Hollywood Express H.	Crimson Saint
1973	Selima	Dancealot
1973	Stymie H.	Forage
1973	Hollywood Inv H.	Life Cycle
1973	San Miguel	Linda's Chief
1973	Lexington H.	London Company
1973	Manhattan H.	London Company
1973	Santa Anita Derby	Sham
1973	Hollywood Lassie	Special Goddess
1973	Delaware H.	Susan's Girl
1973	Santa Barbara H.	Susan's Girl
1973	Santa Margarita Inv H.	Susan's Girl
1973	Santa Maria H.	Susan's Girl
1973	Susquehanna H.	Susan's Girl
1973	San Marcos H.	Tuqui II
1973	Pasadena	Windy's Daughter
1974	Charles H. Strub	Ancient Title
1974	Los Angeles H.	Ancient Title
1974	Palos Verdes H.	Ancient Title
1974	San Fernando	Ancient Title
1974	Argonaut H.	Battery E.
1974	Baldwin	Battery E.
1974	Santa Maria H.	Convenience
1974	Brighton Beach H.	Crafty Khale
1974	Beldame	Desert Vixen
1974	Matchmaker	Desert Vixen
1974	Hol Juv Champ	Dimaggio
1974	Blue Grass	Judger
1974	Florida Derby	Judger
1974	Adirondack	Laughing Bridge
1974	Sequoia H.	Lt.'s Joy
1974	Hollywood Oaks	Miss Musket
1974	Cygnet	Miss Tokyo
1974	Junior League	Miss Tokyo
1974	Frizette	Molly Ballantine
1974	American H.	Plunk
1974	San Antonio	Prince Dantan
1974	San Carlos H.	Royal Owl
1974	Carleton F. Burke H.	Tallahto
1974	Oak Tree Invitational	Tallahto
1974	Santa Barbara H.	Tallahto
1974	Vanity H.	Tallahto
1974	Whitney	Tri Jet
1974	San Bernardino H.	Wichita Oil
1974	Westchester	Windy Whisper
1975	Californian	Ancient Title
1975	Hol Gold Cup Inv H.	Ancient Title
1975	San Carlos H.	Ancient Title
1975	Los Angeles H.	Big Band
1975	California Derby	Diabolo
1975	Demoiselle	Free Journey
1975	Remsen	Hang Ten
1975	Maskette H.	Let Me Linger
1975	San Luis Obispo H.	Madison Palace
1975	Spinster	Susan's Girl
1976	Santa Anita Derby	An Act
1976	San Luis Rey	Avatar
1976	Beverly Hills H.	Bastonera II
1976	Milady H.	Bastonera II
1976	San Jacinto	Bold Forbes
1976	Thanksgiving Day H.	Classy Surgeon
1976	Del Mar Oaks	Go March
1976	Will Rogers H.	Madera Sun
1976	San Carlos H.	No Bias
1976	Anoakia	Telferner
1976	Del Mar Debutante	Telferner
1976	Volante H.	Today 'n Tomorrow
1976	Del Mar Futurity	Visible
1976	Hollywood Lassie	Wavy Waves
1977	Hol Juv Champ	Affirmed
1977	Century H.	Anne's Pretender
1977	Cinema H.	Bad 'n Big
1977	El Dorado H.	Bad 'n Big
1977	Californian	Crystal Water
1977	Hol Gold Cup H.	Crystal Water
1977	Santa Anita H.	Crystal Water
1977	Honeymoon H.	Joyous Ways
1977	San Fernando	Kirby Lane
1977	Santa Ynez	Wavy Waves
1978	Santa Anita Derby	Affirmed
1978	Thanksgiving Day H.	Always Gallant
1978	American H.	Effervescing
1978	Las Palmas H.	Grenzen
1978	Santa Barbara H.	Kittyluck
1978	Volante H.	Wayside Station
1979	Californian	Affirmed
1979	Charles H. Strub	Affirmed
1979	Hol Gold Cup H.	Affirmed
1979	Jockey Club Gold Cup	Affirmed
1979	Santa Anita H.	Affirmed
1979	Woodward	Affirmed
1979	Jamaica H.	Belle's Gold
1979	Ramona H.	Country Queen
1979	Wilshire H.	Country Queen
1979	Yellow Ribbon	Country Queen
1979	Arcadia H.	Fluorescent Light
1979	San Luis Obispo H.	Fluorescent Light
1979	Demoiselle	Genuine Risk
1979	Santa Maria H.	Grenzen
1979	Santa Monica H.	Grenzen
1979	Ruffian H.	It's in the Air
1979	Native Diver H.	Life's Hope

Year	Stakes Name	Winner	Year	Stakes Name	Winner
1979	Del Mar Derby H.	Relaunch	1982	Oak Leaf	Landaluce
1979	La Jolla Mile	Relaunch	1982	Santa Anita Derby	Muttering
1979	Bel Air H.	Sirlad	1982	Arcadia H.	Perrault
1979	San Bernardino H.	Star Spangled	1982	Hol Gold Cup H.	Perrault
1979	Santa Ynez	Terlingua	1982	San Luis Rey	Perrault
1979	Paterson H.	Valdez	1982	Linda Vista H.	Skillful Joy
1979	Rutgers H.	Valdez	1982	San Marcos H.	Super Moment
1979	Silver Screen H.	Valdez	1982	Hollywood Oaks	Tango Dancer
1979	Swaps	Valdez	1983	Del Mar Debutante	Althea
1980	Los Angeles H.	Beau's Eagle	1983	Del Mar Futurity	Althea
1980	Beverly Hills H.	Country Queen	1983	Hol Juv Champ	Althea
1980	Metropolitan H.	Czaravich	1983	Hollywood Starlet	Althea
1980	Del Mar Derby H.	Exploded	1983	Belmont	Caveat
1980	San Carlos H.	Handsomeness	1983	Longacres Mile H.	Chinook Pass
1980	Frizette	Heavenly Cause	1983	Fountain of Youth	Copelan
1980	Selima	Heavenly Cause	1983	Hollywood Inv H.	Erins Isle
1980	El Encino	It's in the Air	1983	S Juan Capistrano Inv H.	Erins Isle
1980	Vanity H.	It's in the Air	1983	San Luis Rey	Erins Isle
1980	Oak Tree Invitational	John Henry	1983	Del Mar Oaks	Heartlight No. One
1980	Hol Juv Champ	Loma Malad	1983	Hollywood Oaks	Heartlight No. One
1980	Hollywood Lassie	Native Fancy	1983	Ruffian H.	Heartlight No. One
1980	San Gabriel H.	Premiere Ministre	1983	Santa Maria H.	Sangue
1980	Santa Barbara H.	Sisterhood	1983	Super Derby	Sunny's Halo
1980	San Pasqual H.	Valdez	1983	Malibu	Time to Explode
1980	Arl-Wash Futurity	Well Decorated	1984	Delaware H.	Adored
1981	Anoakia	A Kiss for Luck	1984	Milady H.	Adored
1981	Acorn	Heavenly Cause	1984	Santa Susana	Althea
1981	Fantasy	Heavenly Cause	1984	San Gabriel H.	Beldale Lustre
1981	Kentucky Oaks	Heavenly Cause	1984	Santa Ynez	Boo la Boo
1981	Hollywood Inv H.	John Henry	1984	Travers	Carr de Naskra
1981	San Luis Obispo H.	John Henry	1984	San Carlos H.	Danebo
1981	San Luis Rey	John Henry	1984	San Pasqual H.	Danebo
1981	Santa Anita H.	John Henry	1984	Del Mar Debutante	Fiesta Lady
1981	Swaps	Noble Nashua	1984	Matron	Fiesta Lady
1981	Arcadia H.	Premier Ministre	1984	Oak Leaf	Folk Art
1981	Santa Margarita Inv H.	Princess Karenda	1984	AKS Omaha Gold Cup	Gate Dancer
1981	Santa Ana H.	Queen to Conquer	1984	Super Derby	Gate Dancer
1981	Malibu	Raise a Man	1984	Princess	Gene's Lady
1981	El Dorado H.	Seafood	1984	Santa Ynez	Gene's Lady
1981	Bay Meadows H.	Super Moment	1984	Century H.	Interco
1981	Hol Juv Champ	The Captain	1984	S Juan Capistrano Inv H.	Load the Cannons
1982	Gamely H.	Ack's Secret	1984	Rothmans Int	Majesty's Prince
1982	Santa Barbara H.	Ack's Secret	1984	Santa Maria H.	Marisma
1982	Santa Margarita Inv H.	Ack's Secret	1984	Flower Bowl H.	Rossard
1982	Belmont	Conquistador Cielo	1984	Futurity	Spectacular Love
1982	Californian	Erins Isle	1984	Belmont	Swale
1982	Hollywood Inv H.	Exploded	1984	Florida Derby	Swale
1982	San Pasqual H.	Five Star Flight	1984	Kentucky Derby	Swale
1982	Del Mar Derby	Give Me Strength	1984	Eddie Read H.	Ten Below
1982	Malibu	Island Whirl	1984	Silver Screen H.	Tights
1982	Volante H.	Lamerok	1984	Wilshire H.	Triple Tipple
1982	Anoakia	Landaluce	1984	Will Rogers H.	Tsunami Slew
1982	Del Mar Debutante	Landaluce	1985	Hawthorne H.	Adored
1982	Hollywood Lassie	Landaluce	1985	Milady H.	Adored

Year	Stakes Name	Winner	Year	Stakes Name	Winner
1985	Santa Maria H.	Adored	1987	San Fernando	Variety Road
1985	Spinster	Dontstop Themusic	1987	Affirmed H.	W.D. Jacks
1985	Arl-Wash Lassie	Family Style	1987	Mervyn Leroy H.	Zabaleta
1985	Frizette	Family Style	1988	California Derby	All Thee Power
1985	Las Flores H.	Foggy Notion	1988	Rancho Bernardo H.	Clabber Girl
1985	Californian	Greinton	1988	Riva Ridge	Evening Kris
1985	Hol Gold Cup H.	Greinton	1988	Haskell Invitational	Forty Niner
1985	San Bernardino H.	Greinton	1988	La Canada	Hollywood Glitter
1985	San Felipe H.	Image of Greatness	1988	Breeders' Cup Juv	Is It True
1985	Hillsborough H.	Justicara	1988	Malibu	Oraibi
1985	Alibhai H.	Nostalgia's Star	1988	Railbird	Sheesham
1985	Nat Sprint Champ	Pancho Villa	1988	Frizette	Some Romance
1985	Silver Screen H.	Pancho Villa	1988	San Pasqual H.	Super Diamond
1985	Santa Anita Derby	Skywalker	1989	Apple Blossom H.	Bakayoa
1985	Jersey Derby	Spend a Buck	1989	Breeders' Cup Distaff	Bayakoa
1985	Monmouth H.	Spend a Buck	1989	Hawthorne H.	Bayakoa
1985	Dwyer	Stephan's Odyssey	1989	Milady H.	Bayakoa
1985	Jim Dandy	Stephan's Odyssey	1989	Ruffian H.	Bayakoa
1985	Breeders' Cup Juv	Tasso	1989	Santa Margarita Inv H.	Bayakoa
1985	Breeders' Futurity	Tasso	1989	Spinster	Bayakoa
1985	Del Mar Futurity	Tasso	1989	Vanity H.	Bayakoa
1986	Breeders' Cup Juv	Capote	1989	Sorrento	Cheval Volant
1986	Norfolk	Capote	1989	Affirmed H.	Exploding Prospect
1986	Hawthorne H.	Dontstop Themusic	1989	San Vicente	Gum
1986	Santa Anita H.	Greinton	1989	Bay Shore	Houston
1986	San Antonio H.	Hatim	1989	Derby Trial	Houston
1986	Native Diver H.	Hopeful Word	1989	Las Virgenes	Kool Arrival
1986	Princess	Melair	1989	Rancho Bernardo H.	Kool Arrival
1986	San Carlos H.	Phone Trick	1989	Malibu	Music Merci
1986	Breeders' Cup Classic	Skywalker	1989	Will Rogers H.	Notorious Pleasure
1986	Longacres Mile H.	Skywalker	1989	Del Mar Bud BC H.	On the Line
1986	Mervyn Leroy H.	Skywalker	1989	Sierra Madre H.	Oraibi
1986	San Diego H.	Skywalker	1989	Mervyn Leroy H.	Ruhlmann
1986	Bel Air H.	Super Diamond	1989	San Bernardino H.	Ruhlmann
1986	Goodwood H.	Super Diamond	1989	Los Angeles H.	Sam Who
1986	Hol Gold Cup H.	Super Diamond	1989	San Antonio H.	Super Diamond
1987	American H.	Clever Song	1989	San Marcos H.	Trokhos
1987	Jockey Club Gold Cup	Creme Fraiche	1989	Arl-Wash Lassie	Trumpet's Blare
1987	Meadowlands Cup H.	Creme Fraiche	1989	Las Flores H.	Very Subtle
1987	San Gorgonio H.	Frau Altiva	1989	San Gabriel H.	Wretham
1987	Sorrento	Hasty Pasty	1990	Breeders' Cup Distaff	Bayakoa
1987	Washington D. C., Int	Le Glorieux	1990	Chula Vista H.	Bayakoa
1987	Del Mar Futurity	Lost Kitty	1990	Hawthorne H.	Bayakoa
1987	El Camino Real Derby	Masterful Advocate	1990	Milady H.	Bayakoa
1987	San Rafael	Masterful Advocate	1990	Spinster	Bayakoa
1987	San Gabriel H.	Nostalgia's Star	1990	Budweiser Int H.	Fly Till Dawn
1987	Carleton F. Burke H.	Rivlia	1990	Col. F. W. Koester H.	Notorious Pleasure
1987	S Juan Capistrano Inv H.	Rosedale	1990	Silver Screen H.	Stalwart Charger
1987	Eddie Read H.	Sharrood	1990	Hollywood Turf H.	Steinlen
1987	Cinema H.	Something Lucky	1990	Del Mar Derby	Tight Spot
1987	Will Rogers H.	Something Lucky	1991	Rancho Bernardo BC H.	Cascading Gold
1987	Boojum H.	Sun Master	1991	Citation H.	Fly Till Dawn
1987	San Diego H.	Super Diamond	1991	San Marcos H.	Fly Till Dawn
1987	Hollywood Futurity	Tejano	1991	Gamely H.	Miss Josh

Year	Stakes Name	Winner	Year	Stakes Name	Winner
1991	Matchmaker	Miss Josh	1994	Strub	Diazo
1991	River Cities Bud BC	Miss Josh	1994	Matriarch	Exchange
1991	Linda Vista H.	Nice Assay	1994	San Gorgonio H.	Hero's Love
1991	Citation H.	Notorious Pleasure	1994	Del Mar Inv Derby	Ocean Crest
1991	Triple Bend H.	Robyn Dancer	1994	Senorita BC	Rabiadella
1991	Rolling Green H.	Shotiche	1994	Volante H.	Run Softly
1991	Palomar H.	Somethingmerry	1995	Arcadia H.	College Town
1991	American H.	Tight Spot	1995	Orchid H.	Exchange
1991	Arlington Million	Tight Spot	1995	Del Mar Inv H.	Royal Chariot
1991	Eddie Read H.	Tight Spot	1995	Oak Leaf	Tipically Irish
1991	Inglewood H.	Tight Spot	1997	Los Angeles H.	Men's Exclusive
1992	Golden Gate H.	Algenib	1998	Hollywood Futurity	Tactical Cat
1992	San Diego H.	Another Review	1999	Las Flores H.	Enjoy the Moment
1992	Chula Vista H.	Exchange	1999	Hollywood Turf Cup	Lazy Lode
1992	El Encino	Exchange	1999	Beverly Hills H.	Virginie
1992	La Canada	Exchange	2000	Sorrento	Give Praise
1992	Arcadia H.	Fly Till Dawn	2000	Hawthorne Derby	Hymn
1992	San Luis Rey	Fly Till Dawn	2000	Vernon O. Underwood	Men's Exclusive
1992	Laurel Dash	Glen Kate	2000	Native Diver H.	Sky Jack
1992	NYRA Mile H.	Ibero	2000	Hol Juv Champ	Squirtle Squirt
1992	Palos Verdes H.	Individualist	2000	Rancho Bernardo H.	Theresa's Tizzy
1992	Silver Screen H.	Natural Nine	2001	Hollywood Gold Cup	Aptitude
1992	Hollywood Futurity	River Special	2001	Hollywood Prevue	Fonz's
1992	River Cities Bud BC	Sacque	2001	Arcadia H.	Lazy Lode
1992	Lazaro Barrera H.	Star Recruit	2001	Palos Verdes H.	Men's Exclusive
1992	Louisiana Downs H.	Stark South	2001	Vernon O. Underwood	Men's Exclusive
1992	San Francisco Mile H.	Tight Spot	2001	Toyota Blue Grass	Millennium Wind
1993	Swaps	Devoted Brass	2001	Buena Vista H.	Rare Charmer
1993	Malibu	Diazo	2001	Frank E. Kilroe Mile H.	Road to Slew
1993	Pegasus H.	Diazo	2001	Cinema H.	Sligo Bay
1993	Santa Ana H.	Exchange	2001	Bel Air H.	Smile Again
1993	Santa Barbara H.	Exchange	2001	Del Mar H.	Timboroa
1993	Metropolitan H.	Ibero	2002	Monrovia H.	Lil Sister Stich
1993	Breeders' Cup Juv F	Phone Chatter	2002	San Felipe	Medaglia d'Oro
1993	Oak Leaf	Phone Chatter	2002	Native Diver H.	Piensa Sonando
1993	Sorrento	Phone Chatter	2002	Hollywood Gold Cup	Sky Jack
1993	Hollywood Futurity	Valiant Nature	2002	Mervyn LeRoy H.	Sky Jack
1994	San Marcos H.	Bien Bien	2002	Desert Stormer H.	Slewsbox
1994	Lazaro Barrera H.	College Town	2002	Hollywood Turf Cup	Sligo Bay

Russell Baze wins Isaac Murphy Award 9th straight year

Russell Baze continued his monopoly on the Isaac Murphy Award, which is awarded annually to the jockey with the highest win percentage (with a minimum of 500 mounts) during the year. The award, inaugurated in 1995 to honor the legendary black jockey of the 19th century who won 44 percent of his races, has never gone to anyone but Baze. The Isaac Murphy Award is presented by the National Turf Writers Association.

Turning in a particularly strong 2003 season, in which he won 30.2 percent of his starts, Baze was well clear of Ramon Dominguez, with 27.8 percent winning rides.

During 2003, Baze rode 410 winners from 1,359 rides. It was the 11th time in the past 12 years that he has ridden over 400 winners.

Baze concluded 2003 with a lifetime win percent of 21.8. Through Jan. 11, 2004, he had ridden 8,484 winners in his career and is one of only two active jockeys with over 8,000 wins. Pat Day is the other.

Elected to the Hall of Fame at Saratoga in 1999, Baze was the sixth rider in history to reach 7,000 victories in 2000 and in 2002 became the fourth rider to surpass 8,000.

Leading Jockeys of 2003 (by percent wins, with at least 500 rides)	
Jockey	Percent Wins
Russell A. Baze	30.2
Ramon A. Dominguez	27.8
Jerry D. Bailey	26.6
Javier Santiago	25.7
Juan Diaz Rodriguez	24.5
John R. Velazquez	23.4
John A. Grabowski	23.2
Joseph C. Judice	22.6
Pedro V. Alvarado	22.5
Pat Day	21.8

Previous Isaac Murphy Award Statistics

Year	Winner	Percent Wins
1995	Russell Baze	29.1
1996	Russell Baze	28.3
1997	Russell Baze	28.3
1998	Russell Baze	27.6
1999	Russell Baze	28.1
2000	Russell Baze	27.2
2001	Russell Baze	28.1
2002	Russell Baze	28.6
2003	Russell Baze	30.2

Jockeys with 6 or more wins on a single day, 1891–2003

Jockey	Date	Total Wins	Wins	Mts	Track
Antley, C.W.	31-Oct-87	9	4	6	AQU
			5	8	MED
Dunkelberger, Travis L.	30-Mar-00	8	7	8	CT
			1	2	PIM
Shino, Ken A.	2-Apr-00	8	8	10	FON
Umana, Juan	5-Mar-93	8	4	7	GS
			4	8	PHA
Day, P	13-Sep-89	8	8	9	AP
Loseth, C.	9-Apr-84	8	8	10	EP
Williams, R.D.	29-Sep-84	8	8	10	LNN
Gall, D	18-Oct-78	8	8	10	CKA
Tejeira, J.	16-Jun-76	8	3	6	KEY
			5	6	ATL
Jones, H.S.	11-Jun-44	8	8	13	AC
Douglas, Rene R.	24-Jul-03	7	7	9	AP
Pino, Mario G.	7-Jul-02	7	7	10	CNL
Pompell, Thomas L.	19-Jul-02	7	7	9	FP
Karamanos, Horatio	26-Oct-02	7	7	11	LRL
Lanci, Howard L.	30-Jun-01	7	7	9	BF
Moccasin, Tim	25-Aug-01	7	7	7	MD
Valdez, Felipe	23-Dec-01	7	7	9	PM
Compton, Perry	19-Feb-00	7	7	10	FON
Dunkelberger, Travis L.	30-Aug-00	7	7	9	TIM
Houghton, T. D.	19-Jul-98	7	7	9	DET
Rocheleau, Serge R.	16-Aug-98	7	7	9	MD
Andrews, Maureen E.	17-Nov-97	7	7	10	MNR
Bailey, Jerry D.	11-Mar-95	7	7	10	GP
Lovelace, Austin K.	10-Dec-94	7	7	10	HOU
Martinez, Willie	6-Jul-93	7	7	10	ELP
Wash, Jack	22-Jul-93	7	7	9	MD
Baze, Russell A.	16-Apr-92	7	7	9	GG
Baez, Rodolfo	27-Sep-91	7	7	10	RKM
Reynolds, Larry C.	7-Jun-91	7	4	9	CT
			2	3	PIM
			1	1	TRM
Vergara, E.B.	31-Jul-88	7	7	11	DET
Pincay, L. Jr.	14-Mar-87	7	7	8	SA
Fires, E.	25-May-87	7	7	8	AP
Vergara, E.B.	28-Aug-87	7	7	10	DET
Enriquez, H.	26-Jan-86	7	7	11	AC
Gall, D	9-Oct-86	7	7	10	FP
Day, P	20-Jun-84	7	7	8	CD
Frazier, R.L.	27-Oct-84	7	7	11	LAD
Nicol, P.A. Jr.	8-Jun-83	7	7	9	PIM
Fires, E.	16-Aug-83	7	7	8	AP
Wentz, M.	17-Dec-83	7	7	11	TUP
Delgado, A.	16-Aug-82	7	5	6	DEL
			2	2	TIM
Gall, D	26-Sep-81	7	7	11	FP
DePass, R.	15-Mar-80	7	7	7	FD
Gall, D	2-May-80	7	7	9	CKA
Gall, D	6-Jun-79	7	7	9	CKA
Noguez, A.	9-Oct-77	7	7	10	AC
Sorenson, J.	23-Jun-76	7	7	9	ASD
Hawley, S.	10-Oct-74	7	7	9	WO
Pierce, L.	20-May-72	7	7	8	LGA
Hawley, S.	22-May-72	7	7	9	WO
York, R.	14-Jan-70	7	7	10	TUP
Baltazar, C.	15-Dec-69	7	7	8	LRL
Grubb, R.	16-May-67	7	7	8	WO
Moyers, L.	4-Jul-67	7	7	8	SUF
Diaz, J.P.	18-Nov-67	7	7	11	AC
Heath, M.	12-Oct-63	7	7	9	FNO
Heckmann, J.	1-Oct-56	7	7	8	HAW
Turnbull, W.	31-Jul-42	7	7	9	RKM
Sylvester, J.	18-Oct-30	7	7	8	RAV
Compton, Perry	19-Apr-03	6	6	8	FON
Prescott, Rodney A.	03-May-03	6	6	9	IND
Martinez, Armando	29-Aug-03	6	6	9	CLS
Nuttall, Todd J.	21-Sep-03	6	6	7	SJ
Monterrey, Richard	01-Oct-03	6	4	6	CT
			2	5	PIM
Dominguez, Ramon A.	03-Oct-03	6	6	7	MED
Berry, Monte Clifton	24-Oct-03	6	6	9	RP
Pino, Mario G.	25-Oct-03	6	6	9	LRL
Garcia, Luis	20-Nov-03	6	3	6	CT
			3	7	LRL
Gutierrez, Juan M.	01-Dec-03	6	6	9	PM
Lumpkins, Jason P.	21-Apr-02	6	6	8	BM
Carkeek, Jerome	26-Apr-02	6	6	10	FON
Pino, Mario G.	11-May-02	6	6	10	PIM
Bravo, Joe	18-May-02	6	6	8	MTH
Thompson, Terry J.	20-May-02	6	6	9	PRM
Houghton, T. D.	26-May-02	6	6	9	GLD
Clark, Kerwin David	19-Aug-02	6	6	7	EVD
Radke, Kevin	2-Sep-02	6	6	10	EMD
Chapa, Roman	4-Sep-02	6	6	9	RET
Fogelsonger, Ryan	18-Sep-02	6	5	10	PIM
			1	5	CT
Cora, David	18-Oct-02	6	6	8	PEN
Shino, Ken A.	2-Nov-02	6	6	8	WDS
Bourque, Steven Joseph	15-Nov-02	6	6	8	DED
Velasquez, Cornelio H.	24-Nov-02	6	6	10	CRC
Berry, Monte Clifton	30-Sep-01	6	6	9	RP
Dominguez, Ramon A.	13-Dec-01	6	3	6	CT
			3	6	LRL
Dunkelberger, Travis L.	12-Apr-01	6	1	3	CT
			5	7	PIM
Dunkelberger, Travis L.	20-Sep-01	6	1	3	CT
			5	7	
Dunkelberger, Travis L.	27-Jul-01	6	4	7	CT
			2	2	
Lovato, Anthony J.	3-Jul-01	6	6	7	LS
Lumpkins, Jason P.	19-May-01	6	6	9	BM
Messina, Robert	23-Nov-01	6	6	6	FL
Pino, Mario G.	9-Jul-01	6	6	7	CNL
Potts, Clinton L.	8-Feb-01	6	6	8	PEN
Prather, Kris	11-Feb-01	6	6	10	TP
Ramos, Jr., Walter W.	7-Jul-01	6	6	6	MD
Rowland, Michael F.	21-Oct-01	6	1	2	MNR
			5	6	TDN
Thompson, Terry J.	13-Oct-01	6	6	9	HOO
Thompson, Terry J.	20-Oct-01	6	6	9	HOO
Thompson, Terry J.	18-Nov-01	6	6	9	HOO
Thompson, Terry J.	25-Nov-01	6	6	9	HOO
Velazquez, John R.	3-Sep-01	6	6	10	SAR
Wilson, David	8-Jul-01	6	6	8	HST
Avant, James E.	10-Jul-00	6	6	8	EVD
Ayers, Lance K.	18-Jun-00	6	6	9	BOI
Bailey, Jerry D.	11-Mar-00	6	6	9	GP
Bush, Vernon	10-Sep-00	6	6	7	NMP
Castellano, Javier	31-Dec-00	6	6	11	CRC
Compton, Perry	22-Apr-00	6	4	6	FON
			2	4	PRM
Court, Jon Kenton	6-Aug-00	6	6	9	ELP
Dunkelberger, Travis L.	29-Apr-00	6	2	3	CT
			4	9	PIM
Dunkelberger, Travis L.	4-Sep-00	6	6	9	TIM
Dunkelberger, Travis L.	30-Nov-00	6	3	8	CT
			3	5	LRL
Grabowski, John A.	1-Apr-00	6	6	10	FL
Lopez, Lorenzo Castane	21-Oct-00	6	6	8	PM
Nakatani, Corey S.	23-Apr-00	6	6	8	SA
Santos, Felipe J.	25-Sep-00	6	6	9	GLD
Baze, Russell A.	30-Jan-99	6	6	8	BM
Baze, Russell A.	21-Aug-99	6	6	8	BMF
Bielby, James A.	31-May-99	6	6	8	FP
Carkeek, Jerome	26-Jun-99	6	6	9	LNN
Castellano, Javier	9-Dec-99	6	6	8	CRC
Chavez, Jorge F.	13-Feb-99	6	6	10	GP
Day, Pat	13-May-99	6	6	8	CD
Doser, Mary Elizabeth	21-Jun-99	6	6	7	GLD
Gann, Sandi Lee	17-Apr-99	6	6	8	TUP
Gonzalez, Carlos	5-Nov-99	6	6	11	LAD

Jockey	Date	Total Wins	Wins	Mts	Track
Houghton, T. D.	5-Jul-99	6	6	8	GLD
Howarth, Jr., Albert	12-Sep-99	6	6	10	NMP
Morgan, Michael R.	5-Dec-99	6	6	10	HOO
Potts, Clinton L.	1-May-99	6	6	12	CT
Prado, Edgar S.	18-Nov-99	6	4	8	AQU
			2	6	MED
Rollins, Chance J.	22-Dec-99	6	6	10	TUP
Rowland, Michael F.	19-Oct-99	6	6	7	TDN
Rowland, Michael F.	27-Dec-99	6	6	7	MNR
Shino, Ken A.	28-Feb-99	6	6	9	FON
Shino, Ken A.	2-Oct-99	6	1	3	PRM
			5	8	WDS
Whitney, Dana G.	25-Jul-99	6	6	9	MNR
Bridgmohan, Shaun	15-Feb-98	6	6	9	AQU
Clark, David	17-Jul-98	6	6	9	WO
Coa, Eibar	7-Sep-98	6	6	9	CRC
Court, Jon Kenton	12-Sep-98	6	6	10	HOO
Court, Jon Kenton	24-Nov-98	6	6	9	HOO
Dunkelberger, Travis L.	21-Nov-98	6	6	8	CT
Guillory, David	17-Jul-98	6	6	8	LAD
McCarthy, Michael J.	20-May-98	6	6	6	DEL
Melancon, Gerard	8-Aug-98	6	6	9	EVD
Prado, Edgar S.	23-Oct-98	6	6	10	LRL
Reynolds, Larry C.	11-Dec-98	6	5	7	CT
			1	4	LRL
Ardoin, Ronald	17-Jul-97	6	6	7	LS
Baez, Rodolfo	30-May-97	6	6	9	SUF
Bailey, Jerry D.	15-Feb-97	6	6	9	GP
Birzer, Alex	15-Aug-97	6	6	8	CLS
Carkeek, Jerome	26-Oct-97	6	6	10	ATO
Casallas, Eduardo	28-Sep-97	6	6	11	YD
Houghton, T. D.	4-Jul-97	6	6	9	DET
Houghton, T. D.	18-Nov-97	6	6	9	DET
Krasner, Samuel B.	18-Apr-97	6	6	7	HST
McCarthy, Michael J.	2-Nov-97	6	6	9	DEL
Melancon, Kevin Lee	22-Mar-97	6	5	8	DED
			1	1	FG
Prado, Edgar S.	2-Aug-97	6	6	10	LRL
Rowland, Michael F.	20-Oct-97	6	3	5	MNR
			3	5	TDN
Shino, Ken A.	5-Apr-97	6	6	10	FON
Baze, Russell A.	2-May-96	6	6	7	GG
Chavez, Jorge F.	18-Feb-96	6	6	9	AQU
Crispin, Joe A.	6-Jul-96	6	6	9	BOI
Dlugopolski, Anthony R.	29-Apr-96	6	6	7	MNR
Freeman, Wayne	27-Jul-96	6	6	9	GF
Hampshire, Jr., Josiah F.	8-Sep-96	6	6	8	RKM
Houghton, T. D.	26-Jul-96	6	6	9	DET
Houghton, T. D.	27-Oct-96	6	6	11	DET
Ma, Henry C.H.	1-Sep-96	6	6	8	NMP
McCarthy, Michael J.	6-Dec-96	6	3	7	MED
			3	8	PHA
Messina, Robert	4-May-96	6	6	8	FL
Shino, Ken A.	26-May-96	6	6	8	LNN
Avant, James E.	14-Aug-95	6	6	7	EVD
Baez, Rodolfo	19-Aug-95	6	6	9	RKM
Baez, Rodolfo	15-Oct-95	6	6	10	RKM
Day, Pat	20-Feb-95	6	6	8	OP
Delgado, Alberto	30-Aug-95	6	6	9	TIM
Dominguez, Carlos V.	6-Nov-95	6	6	9	FL
Douglas, Rene R.	15-Jul-95	6	6	9	CRC
Houghton, T. D.	28-Apr-95	6	6	9	DET
Hulet, Leslie	21-Nov-95	6	6	10	FL
Jordan, Jimmy	3-Jun-95	6	6	7	ATO
LeBlanc, Kirk Paul	5-Aug-95	6	6	10	EVD
Mitchell, Gallyn Victor	13-Aug-95	6	6	10	YM
Schaefer, Gregory Allen	5-Mar-95	6	6	11	FON
Black, Kenneth	25-Sep-94	6	6	7	MEP
Bravo, Joe	31-Aug-94	6	6	10	MTH
Houghton, T. D.	21-Aug-94	6	6	10	DET
Houghton, T. D.	2-Oct-94	6	6	8	DET
LaGue, Larry	22-Jan-94	6	6	8	BEU
Loseth, Chris	14-Sep-94	6	6	8	HST
Schaefer, Gregory Allen	12-Aug-94	6	6	9	CLS
Schaefer, Gregory Allen	12-Sep-94	6	6	9	CLS
Toscano, Paul R.	29-Jul-94	6	6	9	SR
Vergara, Euclides B.	2-Jun-94	6	6	10	DET
Anderson, Chad W.	16-Apr-93	6	6	9	FON
Bayer, Jason Dwayne	10-Mar-93	6	6	9	YM
Baze, Gary	5-Sep-93	6	6	8	YM
Bergsrud, Scott Alan	11-Jul-93	6	6	8	PLA
Bergsrud, Scott Alan	19-Sep-93	6	6	10	PLA
Black, Kenneth	26-Sep-93	6	6	11	MEP
Borel, Calvin H.	2-May-93	6	6	10	LAD
Day, Pat	11-Mar-93	6	6	8	OP
Doocy, Timothy T.	5-Dec-93	6	6	10	RP
Douglas, Rene R.	8-Dec-93	6	6	7	CRC
Martin, Christopher	6-Sep-93	6	6	10	CT
Umana, Juan	20-Mar-93	6	1	7	GS
			5	9	PHA
Vergara, Euclides B.	15-Jul-93	6	6	10	DET
Winnett, Jr., Buddy G.	6-Nov-93	6	6	9	EP
Ardoin, Ronald	7-Sep-92	6	6	7	LAD
Barnett, Wayne A.	18-Oct-92	6	6	9	CT
Black, Anthony S.	31-Jul-92	6	4	4	ATL
			2	2	PHA
Day, Pat	10-Jun-92	6	6	8	CD
Desormeaux, Kent J.	3-Jul-92	6	6	9	HOL
Doocy, Timothy T.	21-Jun-92	6	6	10	LGA
Flores, David Romero	20-Sep-92	6	6	9	FPX
Flores, David Romero	30-Sep-92	6	6	8	FPX
Green, Brian D.	6-Jun-92	6	6	9	BRD
Guidry, Mark	20-Mar-92	6	6	10	SPT
Guidry, Mark	5-Apr-92	6	6	10	SPT
Guidry, Mark	25-Apr-92	6	6	10	SPT
Jensen, Loren Dale	26-Jun-92	6	6	9	ATO
Pedroza, Martin A.	31-Oct-92	6	6	7	SA
Simard, Real E.	21-Oct-92	6	6	9	STP
Smith, Mike E.	13-Jan-92	6	6	8	AQU
Smith, Mike E.	30-Jan-92	6	6	7	AQU
Whitley, Kevin	21-Aug-92	6	6	8	FL
Aragon, Vicky Ann	24-Nov-91	6	6	7	YM
Borel, Calvin H.	23-Aug-91	6	6	9	LAD
Boulanger, Gary	22-May-91	6	6	9	LGA
Bourque, Curt C.	4-May-91	6	6	8	EVD
Bourque, Curt C.	23-Jun-91	6	6	8	EVD
Day, Pat	30-May-91	6	6	8	CD
Day, Pat	3-Aug-91	6	6	9	AP
Lopez, Adalberto Diaz	16-Mar-91	6	6	8	AC
Lopez, Adalberto Diaz	5-May-91	6	6	10	AC
Lopez, Adalberto Diaz	26-May-91	6	6	10	AC
Romero, Shane P.	10-Feb-91	6	6	10	FG
Romero, Shane P.	24-Feb-91	6	6	8	FG
Rowland, Michael F.	29-Mar-91	6	6	9	TDN
Sellers, Shane J.	6-Sep-91	6	6	9	AP
Sellers, Shane J.	4-Oct-91	6	6	8	AP
Shino, Ken A.	10-Nov-91	6	6	8	CLS
Torres, Hector	12-Aug-91	6	1	4	DMR
			5	9	LA
Winters, Perry A.	15-Aug-91	6	6	7	NP
Elliott, S.	18-Mar-90	6	6	10	RKM
Salvaggio, M.V.	31-Mar-90	6	6	9	PEN
Romero, R.P.	7-Apr-90	6	6	9	KEE
Perret, C.	18-Apr-90	6	6	7	KEE
Hansen, R.D.	21-Apr-90	6	6	9	GG
Elliott, S.	2-May-90	6	6	8	RKM
Jensen, L.D.	23-Jul-90	6	6	9	CLS
Desormeaux, K.J.	17-Feb-89	6	6	8	LRL
Perret, C.	19-Mar-89	6	6	7	HIA
Vega, H.	1-Apr-89	6	6	9	RKM
Fires, E.	19-Jun-89	6	6	6	HAW
Ardoin, R.	4-Jul-89	6	6	8	LAD
Krone, J.	16-Sep-89	6	6	8	MED
Vega, H.	21-Dec-89	6	6	8	RKM

Jockey	Date	Total Wins	Wins	Mts	Track	Jockey	Date	Total Wins	Wins	Mts	Track
Desormeaux, K.J.	26-Apr-88	6	6	8	PIM	Bracciale, V. Jr.	5-Mar-73	6	6	7	BOW
Valenzuela, P.A.	21-Oct-88	6	6	9	SA	Menard, N.	3-Apr-73	6	6	8	JND
Desormeaux, K.J.	12-May-87	6	6	8	PIM	Kirby, C.	30-Sep-73	6	6	8	SAL
Baze, M.B.	28-Jun-87	6	6	7	PLA	Valdez, S.	15-Oct-73	6	6	9	SA
Grove, P.	28-Aug-87	6	6	8	CT	Snyder, L.	27-Oct-73	6	6	8	DET
Steinberg, P.W.	6-Dec-87	6	6	9	TUP	Hawley, S.	26-May-72	6	6	9	WO
Day, P.	17-Feb-87	6	6	7	OP	Snyder, L.	26-May-72	6	6	9	HP
Martinez, L.	7-May-86	6	6	8	DET	Lively, J.	12-Jul-72	6	6	7	AKS
Knight, L.C.	18-Sep-86	6	6	9	DET	Cave, R.	9-Sep-72	6	6	9	PIT
Diaz, J.L.	4-Dec-86	6	6	9	BML	Hinojosa, H.	4-Feb-71	6	6	8	LIB
Romero, R.P.	8-May-85	6	6	8	CD	Hawley, S.	2-May-71	6	6	9	FE
DePass, R.	22-Jun-85	6	6	8	DET	Lively, J.	4-Jun-71	6	6	9	AKS
Romero, R.P.	8-Feb-84	6	6	8	FG	Stewart, R.	16-Jun-71	6	6	8	ASD
Miller, D.A. Jr.	17-Feb-84	6	6	9	BOW	Cox, R.	7-Aug-71	6	6	8	FL
Garcia, J.R.	27-Apr-84	6	6	8	PEN	Tranchina, P.	22-Aug-71	6	6	7	BOI
Edwards, J.W.	28-May-84	6	6	9	DEL	Hawley, S.	1-Sep-71	6	6	9	FE
Antley, C.W.	30-Jul-84	6	6	9	MTH	Platts, R.	8-Sep-71	6	6	9	WO
Snyder, L.	19-Aug-84	6	6	6	LAD	Mitchell, M.	12-Sep-71	6	6	8	PJ
Baze, R.A.	1-Sep-84	6	6	7	BMF	Snyder, L.	25-Oct-71	6	6	7	HP
Santage, J.L.	22-May-83	6	6	8	DET	Shoemaker, W.	24-Jun-70	6	6	7	HOL
Markham, R.L. Jr.	4-Jul-83	6	6	9	WAT	Niblick, D.	7-Aug-70	6	6	9	ELP
Moreno, O.	24-Jul-83	6	6	6	CT	Agnello, A.	27-Aug-70	6	6	9	WAT
Mills, B.L.	28-Aug-83	6	6	8	TDN	Dur'usseau, L.J.	14-Mar-69	6	6	8	TUP
Whitley, K.	20-Jun-82	6	6	8	FL	Snyder, L.	1-Apr-69	6	6	8	OP
Petro, N.	21-Nov-82	6	6	9	SUF	Frey, P.	31-May-69	6	6	9	LGA
Pincay, L. Jr.	4-Mar-81	6	6	8	SA	Perez, A	21-Jun-69	6	6	7	PJ
Platts, R.	3-May-81	6	6	7	WO	Dur'usseau, L.J.	3-Jul-69	6	6	8	AKS
Velasquez, J.	9-Jul-81	6	6	6	BEL	Dur'usseau, L.J.	4-Jul-69	6	6	9	AKS
Delgadillo, C.	5-Sep-81	6	6	8	AC	Dur'usseau, L.J.	5-Jul-69	6	6	9	AKS
Sibille, R.	23-Jun-80	6	6	7	AP	Rosales, R.	6-Sep-69	6	6	9	DMR
Cantagallo, G.J.	28-Jun-80	6	6	8	ATL	Maffeo, C.	20-Sep-69	6	6	8	NAR
Lopez, R.D.	9-Aug-80	6	6	6	HP	Bowcut, D.	20-Sep-69	6	6	8	POC
Seldomridge, A.	19-Aug-80	6	6	9	POC	Turcotte, Rudy	2-Dec-69	6	6	8	AQU
Graell, A.	14-Nov-80	6	6	9	TDN	Cordero, A. Jr.	28-Feb-68	6	6	8	HIA
Hulet, L.	14-Apr-79	6	6	8	FL	Pincay, L. Jr.	27-Apr-68	6	6	9	HOL
Diaz, A.L.	25-Apr-79	6	6	9	GG	Cusimano, G.	16-Jul-68	6	6	9	DEL
Creighton, R.L.	30-Apr-79	6	6	8	EP	Ecoffey, F.	5-Aug-68	6	6	7	LNN
McHargue, D.G.	25-Oct-79	6	6	7	SA	Hinojosa, H.	17-Aug-68	6	6	9	RKM
Perrodin, E.J.	18-Nov-79	6	6	8	FG	Blum, W.	19-Oct-68	6	6	8	GS
Noguez, A.	11-Mar-78	6	6	9	AC	Ecoffey, F.	30-Oct-68	6	6	9	ATO
Mercado, V.V.	1-Apr-78	6	6	8	AC	Vasquez, J.	9-Aug-67	6	6	8	ATL
Orona, W.	11-Jun-78	6	6	8	PJ	Velasquez, J.	30-Aug-67	6	6	7	ATL
Feliciano, B.R.	18-Jun-78	6	6	9	TDN	Madden, D.	9-Sep-67	6	6	8	LD
Pincay, L. Jr.	29-Jul-78	6	6	8	DMR	Whited, D.E.	26-Sep-67	6	6	8	DET
Cauthen, S.	22-Jan-77	6	6	9	AQU	Marquez, C.	20-Jul-66	6	6	7	RD
Cauthen, S.	7-Apr-77	6	6	9	AQU	Fires, E.	6-Sep-66	6	6	7	AP
Gomez, G.J.	12-May-77	6	6	9	CRC	Bowlds, J.P.	11-Mar-65	6	6	8	FG
Edwards, J.W.	24-May-77	6	6	7	ATL	Baze, J.	12-Apr-65	6	6	8	GG
Fann, B.	28-May-77	6	6	9	HAW	Barrera, C.	15-May-65	6	6	8	MEX
Maple, S.	23-Jul-77	6	6	9	AKS	Fires, E.	17-Jun-65	6	6	9	MP
Stahlbaum, G.	5-Aug-77	6	6	6	FE	Frey, P.	3-Sep-65	6	6	9	LGA
Noguez, A.	10-Sep-77	6	6	9	AC	Velasquez, J.	16-Nov-65	6	6	7	GS
Hollingsworth, R.	1-Oct-77	6	6	9	YM	Green, F.	5-Jun-64	6	6	9	WAT
Meaux, C.	2-Oct-77	6	6	6	FP	Rollins, B.	4-Jul-64	6	6	9	CEN
Cauthen, S.	29-Nov-77	6	6	8	AQU	Witmer, R.	10-Oct-64	6	6	7	HAG
Hawley, S.	20-Feb-76	6	6	9	SA	Venezia, M.	7-Dec-64	6	6	9	AQU
Graell, A.	21-Feb-76	6	6	9	TDN	Hinojosa, H.	13-May-63	6	6	9	WAS
Passmore, W.J.	5-Mar-76	6	6	6	BOW	Coy, A.	6-Jul-63	6	6	7	BB
Turcotte, R.	5-Mar-76	6	6	9	AQU	Silva, G.	10-Jul-63	6	6	7	RD
Cordero, A. Jr.	12-Mar-75	6	6	9	AQU	Reynolds, L.	17-Jul-63	6	6	8	MAR
Mucciolo, J.	14-Apr-75	6	6	8	KEY	Whited, D.W.	8-Sep-63	6	6	9	RUI
Wash, J.	20-Jul-75	6	6	9	PJ	Carrozzella, M.	11-Sep-63	6	6	9	LD
Baze, R.	10-Sep-75	6	6	9	LGA	Shoemaker, W.	23-Feb-62	6	6	7	SA
McCarron, G.	6-Jul-74	6	6	8	DEL	Reynolds, L.	3-Aug-62	6	6	9	BLR
Hawley, S.	4-Aug-74	6	6	7	FE	Lucas, W.D.	10-Aug-62	6	6	7	RD
McCarron, C.J.	11-Aug-74	6	6	8	PIM	Davidson, J.	24-Aug-62	6	6	8	SHD
Hawley, S.	11-Aug-74	6	6	9	FE	Davidson, J.	1-Oct-62	6	6	9	SHD
McCarron, C.J.	27-Sep-74	6	6	9	BOW	Blum, W.	19-Jun-61	6	6	8	MTH
McCarron, C.J.	23-Nov-74	6	6	7	LRL	Weiler, D.	12-Aug-61	6	6	8	TDN
McCarron, C.J.	7-Dec-74	6	6	8	PEN	Neves, R.	24-Oct-61	6	6	8	BM
McCarron, C.J.	15-Dec-74	6	6	8	PEN	Barnett, R.L.	7-May-60	6	6	8	SPT
Pincay, L. Jr.	17-Feb-73	6	6	8	SA	Reynolds, L.	1-Oct-60	6	6	9	HAG

Jockey	Date	Total Wins	Wins	Mts	Track	Jockey	Date	Total Wins	Wins	Mts	Track
Grant, H.	16-Mar-59	6	6	8	BOW	Knowles, L.	20-Apr-51	6	6	7	AD
Shoemaker, W.	4-Apr-59	6	6	8	JAM	Craig, H.	2-Jul-51	6	6	8	WAT
Dixon, G.	11-Jun-59	6	6	7	PM	Coppernoll, K.	11-Sep-51	6	6	8	EP
Hunt, G.	19-Jun-59	6	6	9	PM	Shoemaker, W.	13-Oct-50	6	6	8	BM
North't, J.F. Jr.	7-Sep-59	6	6	8	CT	Keene, H.	24-Oct-50	6	6	8	SPT
Coy, A.	25-Apr-58	6	6	7	FE	Keene, H.	4-Nov-50	6	6	9	SPT
Nelson, E.	20-Jun-58	6	6	7	DEL	Culmone, J.	27-Nov-50	6	6	9	BOW
Dittfach, H.	1-Sep-58	6	6	8	CEG	Gomez, A.	22-Jun-49	6	6	8	ASC
Ycaza, M.	7-Apr-57	6	6	9	MEX	Brooks, S.	15-May-48	6	6	8	CD
Ycaza, M.	16-May-57	6	6	8	MEX	Florio, A.	19-Aug-47	6	6	6	MF
Morris, B.	18-Jul-57	6	6	7	MAD	Roy, E.	22-Aug-47	6	6	7	EDM
Bravo, J.	1-Apr-56	6	6	7	MEX	Longden, J.	22-Nov-47	6	6	7	BM
Seller, J.	28-Jul-56	6	6	9	HP	Plesa, E.	3-Oct-46	6	6	7	PLA
Gaudreau, R.	31-Jul-56	6	6	8	CLS	Jessop, J.D.	9-Aug-45	6	6	7	DAD
Hartack, W.	25-Apr-55	6	6	7	LRL	Jessop, J.D.	16-Aug-45	6	6	7	DAD
Shoemaker, W.	16-Aug-55	6	6	7	WAS	Siverwright, J.	21-Jul-44	6	6	7	BRG
Hartack, W.	5-Nov-55	6	6	8	LRL	Atkinson, J.E.	28-Sep-44	6	6	7	GMP
Gomez, A.	21-Mar-54	6	6	7	MEX	McCadden, W.P.	26-Jun-43	6	6	8	FM
Lumm, R.	9-Apr-54	6	6	8	AD	Adams, John	2-Sep-42	6	6	8	TDN
Gomez, A.	11-Apr-54	6	6	7	MEX	Robertson, A.	9-Oct-41	6	6	7	JAM
Harmatz, W.	23-Apr-54	6	6	7	BM	Fonte, C.	23-Sep-39	6	6	7	HAV
Padron, R.	13-Jun-54	6	6	9	HAV	Adams, J.	7-Apr-38	6	6	7	BM
Shoemaker, W.	4-Sep-54	6	6	8	DMR	James, B.	3-May-38	6	6	7	TAN
Meaux, C.	6-Oct-54	6	6	6	CKA	Robertson, A.	19-Feb-33	6	6	7	HAV
Burr, C.	30-Mar-53	6	6	6	GP	Haas, B.	28-Aug-33	6	6	7	TDN
Shoemaker, W.	4-Apr-53	6	6	8	TAN	Adams, A.	11-Sep-30	6	6	6	MAR
Shoemaker, W.	20-Jun-53	6	6	8	HOL	Sande, E.	17-Sep-19	6	6	7	HDG
Knisley, C.	3-Sep-53	6	6	6	HO	Phillips, H.	5-Jul-16	6	6	6	REN
Hartack, W.	6-Oct-53	6	6	8	WAT	Turner, C	9-Apr-12	6	6	7	CHA
Shoemaker, W.	10-Oct-53	6	6	9	GG	Lee, J.	5-Jun-07	6	6	6	CD
DeSpirito, A.	10-Oct-53	6	6	8	RKM	Overton, W.	7-10-1891	6	6	6	OWP
Kaelin, F.	18-Aug-52	6	6	8	WHE						
DeSpirito, A.	20-Aug-52	6	6	8	RKM						
Rossall, R.	26-Oct-52	6	6	8	AC						

Track Abbreviations for Tracks Not Listed Elsewhere

The following are track abbreviations used in the preceding list which are not found on pages 660 and 663. Most of these tracks are closed.

AC	Aqua Caliente	HIA	Hialeah Park
AD	Arizona Downs	HO	Hamilton (Ohio)
AKS	Ak-Sar-Ben	HP	Hazel Park
ASC	Ascot Park	JAM	Jamaica
ATO	Atokad Park	JND	Jefferson Downs
BB	Blue Bonnets	KEY	Keystone
BLR	Bel Air	LD	Lincoln Downs
BML	Balmoral	LGA	Longacres
BOW	Bowie Race Course	LIB	Liberty Bell Park
BRG	Brighouse Park	MAD	Madison Downs
CEG	Victoria Park	MAR	Marlboro
CEN	Centennial Race Track	MEP	MetraPark
CHA	Charleston	MF	Marshfield Fair
CKA	Cahokia Downs	MP	Miles Park
DAD	Dade Park	NAR	Narragansett Park
DET	Detroit Race Course	OWP	Old Washington Park
EDM	Edmonton	PIT	Pitt Park
EP	Exhibition Park	PJ	Park Jefferson
FD	Florida Downs	PLA	Playfair
FM	Fort Miami	POC	Pocono Downs
GMP	Gresham Park	RAV	Ravenna Park
GS	Garden State Park	REN	Reno
HAG	Hagerstown	SHD	Shenandoah Downs
HAV	Oriental Park	SJ	Apache County Fair
HDG	Havre de Grace	TAN	Tanforan
		WAS	Washington Park
		WAT	Waterford Park
		WHE	Wheeling Downs

Top Money-Winning Jockeys and Trainers, by Meet, in 2003

Track	Meet dates		Starts	1st	2d	3d	Win %	Earnings
ALB	9/5 - 9/21	Jockey	Starts	1st	2d	3d	Win %	Earnings
		Ricardo Jaime	53	14	6	10	26	155,062
		Jorge Martin Bourdieu	25	3	7	3	12	67,721
		Casey T. Lambert	28	4	7	4	14	59,848
		Ken S. Tohill	15	3	4	3	20	59,119
		Jimmy Ray Coates	28	3	2	1	11	57,414
ALB	9/5 - 9/21	Trainer	Starts	1st	2d	3d	Win %	Earnings
		Henry Dominguez	38	10	5	6	26	125,748
		Carl M. Dyer	22	3	2	4	14	48,629
		Bart G. Hone	9	2	2	1	22	44,122
		Gary W. Cross	6	2	1	2	33	41,080
		Carl W. Draper	2	2	0	0	100	32,901
ALB	3/14 - 6/8	Jockey	Starts	1st	2d	3d	Win %	Earnings
		Jorge Martin Bourdieu	105	14	25	14	13	228,880
		Adan Fuentes	126	19	20	11	15	191,539
		Ken S. Tohill	70	14	13	11	20	190,802
		Travis Wales	114	22	19	14	19	188,866
		Miguel Sanchez Fuentes	85	13	14	9	15	187,984
ALB	3/14 - 6/8	Trainer	Starts	1st	2d	3d	Win %	Earnings
		Gary W. Cross	66	13	17	7	20	220,595
		Carlos Sedillo	65	15	8	11	23	209,968
		Henry Dominguez	74	22	5	12	30	199,725
		Jon G. Arnett	51	8	12	7	16	87,498
		Ramon O. Gonzalez	77	7	11	11	9	87,378
ANF	7/11 - 7/20	Jockey	Starts	1st	2d	3d	Win %	Earnings
		Megan Ludlow	24	12	3	3	50	23,780
		Jeremy Latham	23	4	3	4	17	12,110
		Juan Padilla	8	4	0	1	50	9,680
		Gary Wade	23	3	7	3	13	9,562
		Stoney D. Whittle	22	0	7	3	0	7,073
ANF	7/11 - 7/20	Trainer	Starts	1st	2d	3d	Win %	Earnings
		Joe Frederick Thomas, Sr.	13	7	2	1	54	13,740
		George Blatchford	5	3	1	0	60	9,840
		Mark Esquibel	13	3	0	4	23	8,724
		Donald G. Black	8	2	2	0	25	5,610
		Zack Ashlock	17	1	7	1	6	5,590
AP	5/9 - 9/27	Jockey	Starts	1st	2d	3d	Win %	Earnings
		Rene R. Douglas	564	132	112	81	23	3,719,651
		Eusebio Razo, Jr.	487	89	75	49	18	2,292,784
		Curt C. Bourque	380	66	49	67	17	1,824,120
		Christopher A. Emigh	471	58	68	68	12	1,696,012
		Carlos H. Marquez, Jr.	390	66	44	61	17	1,595,408
AP	5/9 - 9/27	Trainer	Starts	1st	2d	3d	Win %	Earnings
		Wayne M. Catalano	182	59	22	21	32	985,548
		Gene A. Cilio	169	25	31	13	15	917,358
		Chris M. Block	151	29	21	20	19	835,094
		Steven M. Asmussen	155	19	23	28	12	672,451
		Harvey L. Vanier	191	23	24	28	12	627,216
AQU	10/29 - 12/31	Jockey	Starts	1st	2d	3d	Win %	Earnings
		Richard Migliore	156	30	21	20	19	1,363,170
		Javier Castellano	200	31	28	38	16	1,290,846
		Shaun Bridgmohan	192	32	27	29	17	1,217,289
		John R. Velazquez	116	26	13	16	22	1,195,754
		Michael J. Luzzi	193	26	25	24	13	1,094,471
AQU	10/29 - 12/31	Trainer	Starts	1st	2d	3d	Win %	Earnings
		Todd A. Pletcher	84	22	9	10	26	1,035,791
		Richard E. Dutrow, Jr.	87	30	16	11	34	981,552
		Richard A. Violette, Jr.	30	8	4	5	27	451,894
		James A. Jerkens	36	8	5	10	22	433,930
		Scott A. Lake	58	12	7	7	21	419,681
AQU	3/12 - 5/4	Jockey	Starts	1st	2d	3d	Win %	Earnings
		Michael J. Luzzi	206	39	30	34	19	1,445,329
		Luis D. Chavez	225	33	33	37	15	1,300,300
		Richard Migliore	124	23	17	22	19	1,137,719
		Javier Castellano	182	27	36	25	15	1,133,448
		John R. Velazquez	99	29	20	12	29	1,097,790

			Starts	1st	2d	3d	Win %	Earnings
AQU	3/12 – 5/4	Trainer						
		Richard E. Dutrow, Jr.	80	14	15	17	18	688,480
		H. Allen Jerkens	43	15	9	8	35	658,205
		Robert J. Frankel	4	2	1	0	50	547,600
		Mark A. Hennig	46	12	8	5	26	530,195
		Todd A. Pletcher	39	10	15	2	26	495,824
AQU	1/1 – 3/9	Jockey						
		Javier Castellano	268	44	53	42	16	1,563,281
		Luis D. Chavez	275	42	42	32	15	1,439,036
		Richard Migliore	189	43	31	19	23	1,392,302
		Michael J. Luzzi	238	37	24	40	16	1,276,390
		John McKee	239	35	45	27	15	1,203,139
AQU	1/1 – 3/9	Trainer						
		Richard E. Dutrow, Jr.	65	18	15	11	28	645,112
		Gary C. Contessa	132	15	16	13	11	552,211
		Jennifer Pedersen	92	10	17	17	11	503,592
		Michael E. Hushion	46	15	8	6	33	395,190
		James A. Jerkens	30	10	5	1	33	376,194
ARP	6/6 – 8/25	Jockey						
		Frank Albert Gonsalves	205	46	38	25	22	411,508
		Russell Vicchrilli	138	22	26	8	16	223,785
		Wilson Omar Dieguez	164	24	23	24	15	203,593
		Brian James Theriot	186	21	30	18	11	195,955
		Travis Wales	108	24	14	15	22	178,502
ARP	6/6 – 8/25	Trainer						
		Kenneth Gleason	176	26	30	18	15	319,146
		Jon G. Arnett	116	28	20	21	24	191,522
		Carlos Gonzalez	116	22	12	14	19	180,057
		Gary W. Cross	75	13	11	19	17	149,132
		James E. Jones	75	10	11	9	13	128,356
ASD	5/4 – 9/28	Jockey						
		Travis Wayne Hightower	394	98	63	45	25	757,197
		Juan Crawford	326	55	41	42	17	455,249
		Michael Phillip Iammarino	359	48	32	40	13	410,713
		Jason Leacock	316	47	46	43	15	404,838
		Jacques DesAutels	353	38	55	47	11	393,553
ASD	5/4 – 9/28	Trainer						
		Gary Danelson	189	55	38	27	29	417,424
		Ardell Sayler	223	37	32	28	17	302,053
		Chad Torevell	161	22	20	12	14	200,322
		Clayton Gray	140	22	14	20	16	195,006
		Jack Robertson	105	15	15	14	14	185,294
ATL	4/23 – 5/2	Jockey						
		Victor H. Molina	14	4	1	0	29	50,980
		Kendrick Carmouche	11	3	1	2	27	33,690
		Jody Petty	3	2	0	0	67	30,000
		Edwin L. King, Jr.	8	2	1	1	25	26,710
		Arnaldo Unsihuay	5	3	0	0	60	26,650
ATL	4/23 – 5/2	Trainer						
		Jack Fisher	4	1	2	0	25	24,000
		Kathleen A. Demasi	5	2	1	0	40	23,310
		Edward K. Auwarter	8	1	1	2	13	18,940
		Timothy A. Hills	4	1	1	0	25	16,850
		Richard J. Hendriks	7	1	1	1	14	16,250
ATO	7/19 – 7/20	Jockey						
		Jerome Carkeek	11	3	3	2	27	33,080
		Alejandro T. Granda	11	2	4	1	18	27,355
		Luis Ranilla	12	1	1	3	8	16,657
		Armando Martinez	11	1	1	2	9	16,263
		Yuri Yaranga	12	1	2	0	8	14,893
ATO	7/19 – 7/20	Trainer						
		James R. Compton	2	2	0	0	100	18,000
		David C. Anderson	5	1	1	1	20	12,265
		Herb Riecken	3	1	0	2	33	11,444
		Gene Deroin	4	1	1	0	25	10,205
		Craig Rice	3	1	1	1	33	10,180

BEL	9/5 – 10/26	Jockey	Starts	1st	2d	3d	Win %	Earnings
		Jerry D. Bailey	119	31	14	17	26	3,436,556
		Edgar S. Prado	212	37	38	32	17	2,352,973
		John R. Velazquez	208	44	32	28	21	2,349,989
		Javier Castellano	201	31	35	20	15	1,831,192
		Richard Migliore	177	28	17	17	16	1,672,839

BEL	9/5 – 10/26	Trainer	Starts	1st	2d	3d	Win %	Earnings
		Todd A. Pletcher	96	24	19	17	25	1,598,850
		Robert J. Frankel	20	7	3	5	35	1,372,450
		Neil J. Howard	13	3	2	3	23	975,300
		H. Allen Jerkens	62	8	18	7	13	917,594
		Nicholas P. Zito	42	5	5	4	12	809,655

BEL	5/7 – 7/20	Jockey	Starts	1st	2d	3d	Win %	Earnings
		Jerry D. Bailey	132	29	29	15	22	3,314,185
		John R. Velazquez	267	70	47	37	26	3,250,467
		Edgar S. Prado	301	59	49	41	20	2,979,580
		Jose A. Santos	249	42	42	35	17	2,596,361
		Jorge F. Chavez	283	43	58	34	15	2,055,825

BEL	5/7 – 7/20	Trainer	Starts	1st	2d	3d	Win %	Earnings
		Robert J. Frankel	39	15	8	4	38	2,733,680
		Todd A. Pletcher	133	40	20	17	30	1,649,142
		H. Allen Jerkens	84	19	15	17	23	1,189,577
		Richard E. Dutrow, Jr.	83	22	11	13	27	806,874
		H. James Bond	46	18	7	5	39	799,030

BEU	9/13 – 12/22	Jockey	Starts	1st	2d	3d	Win %	Earnings
		Marco A. Ccamaque	409	83	59	41	20	441,149
		Hector L. Rosario, Jr.	310	49	68	37	16	363,367
		Perry Wayne Ouzts	286	57	38	39	20	329,089
		Jose Luis Calo	315	39	29	25	12	190,265
		Gordon Whitacre	327	29	28	37	9	169,380

BEU	9/13 – 12/22	Trainer	Starts	1st	2d	3d	Win %	Earnings
		Luis Albert Palacios	74	14	17	11	19	195,934
		Bob Jeanotte	38	12	6	6	32	98,288
		Michael W. Nance	18	6	4	2	33	95,125
		Jerry S. Sparks	9	3	2	0	33	89,370
		Timothy E. Hamm	13	3	1	2	23	86,499

BEU	1/10 – 5/3	Jockey	Starts	1st	2d	3d	Win %	Earnings
		Ivan R. Gonzalez	326	78	56	35	24	401,312
		Ramon Luna	308	48	46	42	16	250,508
		Hector L. Rosario, Jr.	168	35	36	22	21	186,898
		Paul M. Nolan	262	33	39	40	13	186,481
		Jose Luis Calo	222	38	32	28	17	180,560

BEU	1/10 – 5/3	Trainer	Starts	1st	2d	3d	Win %	Earnings
		Jake S. Radosevich	147	31	31	16	21	145,243
		Luis Albert Palacios	29	11	3	4	38	96,277
		Geraldine Rodak	107	16	16	11	15	75,457
		David W. Asbury	53	17	9	2	32	70,507
		Rinzy Nocero	90	12	16	11	13	65,012

BM	8/29 – 11/02	Jockey	Starts	1st	2d	3d	Win %	Earnings
		Russell A. Baze	308	96	63	48	31	1,523,970
		Ronald J. Warren, Jr.	226	37	33	33	16	892,388
		Francisco Duran	232	31	39	23	13	633,464
		Jason P. Lumpkins	177	32	20	32	18	611,358
		Joe M. Castro	155	20	26	20	13	559,220

BM	8/29 – 11/02	Trainer	Starts	1st	2d	3d	Win %	Earnings
		Jerry Hollendorfer	219	52	39	34	24	1,007,083
		Armando Lage	182	36	34	24	20	584,085
		Art Sherman	101	25	15	9	25	458,379
		William E. Morey	84	17	18	13	20	371,687
		Brian J. Koriner	66	23	10	10	35	303,263

BM	4/2 – 6/15	Jockey	Starts	1st	2d	3d	Win %	Earnings
		Russell A. Baze	329	97	80	37	29	1,667,034
		Ronald J. Warren, Jr.	242	52	44	32	21	1,111,476
		Roberto M. Gonzalez	221	44	35	32	20	912,922
		Chad Phillip Schvaneveldt	186	32	20	36	17	788,188
		Chance J. Rollins	214	33	40	32	15	727,882

BM	4/2 – 6/15	Trainer	Starts	1st	2d	3d	Win %	Earnings
		Jerry Hollendorfer	240	55	52	32	23	1,311,823
		Armando Lage	156	34	37	24	22	600,913
		Art Sherman	105	23	26	19	22	480,163
		Jeff Bonde	76	16	11	10	21	407,528
		William E. Morey	82	20	20	11	24	318,941

BMF	8/6 – 8/18	Jockey	Starts	1st	2d	3d	Win %	Earnings
		Russell A. Baze	59	18	13	6	31	214,505
		Chad Phillip Schvaneveldt	53	11	16	7	21	199,432
		Francisco Duran	70	11	11	12	16	187,996
		Roberto M. Gonzalez	47	10	10	4	21	145,756
		David G. Lopez	58	9	10	10	16	135,352

BMF	8/6 – 8/18	Trainer	Starts	1st	2d	3d	Win %	Earnings
		Jerry Hollendorfer	37	9	5	6	24	153,850
		Armando Lage	39	7	8	8	18	117,660
		Art Sherman	25	5	4	4	20	78,030
		William E. Morey	22	5	5	3	23	72,206
		Brian J. Koriner	12	4	2	1	33	62,290

BOI	5/3 – 8/10	Jockey	Starts	1st	2d	3d	Win %	Earnings
		Berkley R. Packer	222	51	36	27	23	149,187
		Matt Williams	189	28	21	26	15	126,206
		Robert Webb	220	41	39	37	19	106,942
		Flip John Nollar	257	39	41	38	15	106,737
		Jay Conklin	86	24	20	8	28	79,176

BOI	5/3 – 8/10	Trainer	Starts	1st	2d	3d	Win %	Earnings
		Dru S. Hall	77	23	11	13	30	121,136
		Cindy Rodgers	42	12	6	4	29	53,832
		Steve Duschka	98	20	15	17	20	53,659
		Shawn H. Davis	31	5	7	4	16	46,400
		Tawnja Elison	30	11	8	2	37	45,392

BRD	2/1 – 11/9	Jockey	Starts	1st	2d	3d	Win %	Earnings
		Mike W. Harvell	106	26	19	15	25	53,571
		Fernando Camacho	136	15	25	17	11	47,349
		Jorge L. Fontanez	137	20	13	23	15	46,813
		Wendell John Hilburn	111	14	27	12	13	40,533
		Joel William Allen	125	11	17	13	9	31,909

BRD	2/1 – 11/9	Trainer	Starts	1st	2d	3d	Win %	Earnings
		Britt G. Cranford	44	7	10	7	16	23,314
		Robert L. Roughton	50	10	6	4	20	23,093
		John Hart Garvin	63	9	7	8	14	21,472
		Jim Dale Brooks	57	6	7	8	11	19,788
		Gary L. Anderson	48	8	9	6	17	18,833

BRN	9/6 – 9/7	Jockey	Starts	1st	2d	3d	Win %	Earnings
		Joe A. Crispin	14	3	5	0	21	5,980
		Victor V. Mercado	13	3	2	1	23	5,215
		Melissa Peery	7	3	0	3	43	4,100
		Darlene Braden	9	2	0	1	22	2,768
		Kristin O'Donnell	6	2	0	1	33	2,598

BRN	9/6 – 9/7	Trainer	Starts	1st	2d	3d	Win %	Earnings
		Tammy White	6	2	2	0	33	3,115
		Jaqueline Smith	3	2	1	0	67	2,650
		Don D. Young	5	2	0	1	40	2,410
		Bill Hof	4	2	0	1	50	2,350
		Marion Stitzel	6	0	3	2	0	2,038

CBY	5/16 – 9/1	Jockey	Starts	1st	2d	3d	Win %	Earnings
		Derek C. Bell	324	77	49	38	24	891,747
		Martin Escobar	376	62	60	45	16	659,313
		Seth B. Martinez	273	48	36	37	18	651,621
		Scott A. Stevens	312	38	46	51	12	626,780
		Bobby J. Walker, Jr.	235	40	45	25	17	546,130

CBY	5/16 – 9/1	Trainer	Starts	1st	2d	3d	Win %	Earnings
		Michael E. Biehler	151	27	17	20	18	423,380
		Bernell B. Rhone	169	34	22	19	20	384,951
		David Van Winkle	175	35	22	27	20	383,166
		Hugh H. Robertson	80	22	16	15	28	280,647
		Doug Oliver	130	15	21	15	12	260,749

CD	10/26 – 11/29	Jockey	Starts	1st	2d	3d	Win %	Earnings
		Pat Day	123	41	27	9	33	1,426,891
		Calvin H. Borel	175	28	19	20	16	1,181,573
		Cornelio H. Velasquez	191	26	31	26	14	1,136,997
		John McKee	201	25	22	32	12	1,071,170
		Rafael Bejarano	194	21	23	21	11	752,675
CD	10/26 – 11/29	Trainer	Starts	1st	2d	3d	Win %	Earnings
		Nicholas P. Zito	29	5	2	8	17	688,208
		Carl A. Nafzger	48	7	12	6	15	686,462
		Dale L. Romans	78	20	11	9	26	591,521
		Steven M. Asmussen	77	6	15	15	8	372,129
		Kenneth G. McPeek	44	4	5	8	9	311,602
CD	4/26 – 7/6	Jockey	Starts	1st	2d	3d	Win %	Earnings
		Pat Day	224	51	39	28	23	2,594,611
		Cornelio H. Velasquez	340	63	57	48	19	2,262,086
		Robby Albarado	280	35	47	48	13	1,952,874
		Jerry D. Bailey	31	9	6	2	29	1,333,396
		John McKee	291	42	43	46	14	1,326,335
CD	4/26 – 7/6	Trainer	Starts	1st	2d	3d	Win %	Earnings
		Robert J. Frankel	13	7	4	2	54	1,389,950
		Dale L. Romans	177	39	32	18	22	1,259,400
		Steven M. Asmussen	99	24	13	13	24	821,644
		Barclay Tagg	1	1	0	0	100	800,200
		Thomas M. Amoss	87	20	20	11	23	639,635
CLS	7/24 – 9/14	Jockey	Starts	1st	2d	3d	Win %	Earnings
		Dennis Michael Collins	193	37	34	18	19	157,574
		Armando Martinez	207	41	31	25	20	155,724
		Luis Ranilla	212	38	37	28	18	154,176
		Jerome Carkeek	182	29	26	33	16	126,756
		Yuri Yaranga	200	20	24	30	10	98,080
CLS	7/24 – 9/14	Trainer	Starts	1st	2d	3d	Win %	Earnings
		David C. Anderson	92	17	18	11	18	88,944
		Gene Deroin	41	9	9	5	22	41,730
		Brian M. Roberts	46	8	8	9	17	38,211
		David Grimes	40	10	3	3	25	31,126
		Dale Burns	32	9	6	4	28	30,986
CNL	6/13 – 7/22	Jockey	Starts	1st	2d	3d	Win %	Earnings
		Mario G. Pino	194	38	29	28	20	734,238
		Ryan Fogelsonger	167	42	28	30	25	598,876
		Horacio Karamanos	213	31	29	25	15	562,853
		Edgar S. Prado	6	3	0	0	50	443,844
		Jozbin Z. Santana	161	25	24	13	16	432,957
CNL	6/13 – 7/22	Trainer	Starts	1st	2d	3d	Win %	Earnings
		William I. Mott	2	1	0	0	50	300,000
		Hamilton A. Smith	92	17	12	12	18	229,495
		Jonathan E. Sheppard	70	9	9	14	13	188,790
		Christophe Clement	10	3	3	0	30	162,390
		Michael J. Trombetta	12	7	1	0	58	158,721
CPW	6/15 – 6/22	Jockey	Starts	1st	2d	3d	Win %	Earnings
		Herman Fennell	13	7	2	2	54	5,220
		Frank La Forge	11	1	2	2	9	2,510
		Danielle Beischer	15	1	5	3	7	2,490
		Robert Calva	9	2	1	2	22	2,195
		Chad Warren	9	2	1	1	22	1,730
CPW	6/15 – 6/22	Trainer	Starts	1st	2d	3d	Win %	Earnings
		Dean Martin	11	1	3	2	9	2,200
		Steve Keplin	4	3	1	0	75	1,750
		Joe Thorne	5	3	0	0	60	1,600
		Kevin Keplin	3	1	1	0	33	1,500
		Kelly Kaelberer	7	1	1	0	14	1,425
CRC	10/25/03 – 1/2/04	Jockey	Starts	1st	2d	3d	Win %	Earnings
		Eibar Coa	250	48	43	26	19	1,321,134
		Eddie Castro	447	83	84	63	19	1,299,627
		Manoel R. Cruz	312	50	39	44	16	871,686
		Manuel Aguilar	233	28	23	30	12	556,128
		Rene R. Douglas	109	23	16	14	21	553,395

CRC	10/25/03 – 1/2/04	Trainer	Starts	1st	2d	3d	Win %	Earnings
		Edward Plesa, Jr.	105	21	14	14	20	581,020
		Martin D. Wolfson	38	10	6	2	26	296,373
		Emanuel Tortora	82	14	9	11	17	278,137
		Angel C. Salinas	98	16	14	12	16	270,980
		Todd A. Pletcher	18	3	4	2	17	263,146
CRC	4/25 – 10/24	Jockey	Starts	1st	2d	3d	Win %	Earnings
		Manoel R. Cruz	839	174	156	128	21	3,267,803
		Eddie Castro	817	160	177	113	20	2,671,145
		Gary Boulanger	636	108	92	100	17	2,644,587
		Julio A. Garcia	343	75	52	49	22	1,997,898
		Manuel Aguilar	604	70	108	73	12	1,811,694
CRC	4/25 – 10/24	Trainer	Starts	1st	2d	3d	Win %	Earnings
		William P. White	225	52	25	31	23	1,129,618
		Martin D. Wolfson	103	22	22	13	21	969,910
		Emanuel Tortora	243	35	37	33	14	940,698
		Edward Plesa, Jr.	228	40	35	38	18	906,692
		James Hatchett	157	29	28	20	18	696,392
CT	10/1 – 12/31	Jockey	Starts	1st	2d	3d	Win %	Earnings
		Anthony Mawing	392	64	52	52	16	1,341,901
		Oscar Flores	354	68	58	34	19	1,090,038
		Mark E. Rosenthal	221	46	30	18	21	787,989
		J. D. Acosta	272	40	35	33	15	705,140
		Travis L. Dunkelberger	124	33	20	15	27	509,178
CT	10/1 – 12/31	Trainer	Starts	1st	2d	3d	Win %	Earnings
		Ronney W. Brown	37	7	11	3	19	109,497
		Mark Shuman	28	5	3	2	18	90,625
		Jeff C. Runco	33	5	3	4	15	84,521
		Phil Schoenthal	14	4	1	0	29	62,325
		Dale Capuano	11	4	1	2	36	61,730
CT	7/1 – 9/30	Jockey	Starts	1st	2d	3d	Win %	Earnings
		Anthony Mawing	404	62	43	41	15	887,272
		Travis L. Dunkelberger	217	48	44	24	22	697,188
		Oscar Flores	292	45	48	41	15	643,845
		Luis Garcia	263	46	33	37	17	586,435
		Juan Ortega	310	35	30	36	11	500,393
CT	7/1 – 9/30	Trainer	Starts	1st	2d	3d	Win %	Earnings
		Jeff C. Runco	164	29	27	29	18	410,206
		Ronney W. Brown	203	40	24	30	20	360,268
		Ernest M. Haynes	58	14	6	11	24	191,783
		Bruce M. Kravets	98	16	12	6	16	182,109
		David Walters	68	6	13	4	9	136,429
CT	4/1 – 6/30	Jockey	Starts	1st	2d	3d	Win %	Earnings
		Travis L. Dunkelberger	241	46	51	37	19	595,812
		Anthony Mawing	328	46	38	48	14	579,237
		Luis Garcia	289	36	44	27	12	419,963
		Oscar Flores	209	45	22	26	22	419,300
		Juan Ortega	282	29	26	41	10	368,543
CT	4/1 – 6/30	Trainer	Starts	1st	2d	3d	Win %	Earnings
		Ronney W. Brown	221	35	35	25	16	357,060
		Jeff C. Runco	163	35	26	16	21	349,383
		Bruce M. Kravets	93	14	12	15	15	170,577
		John D. McKee	95	10	15	8	11	150,399
		Amy Albright	27	9	6	2	33	138,390
CT	1/1 – 3/31	Jockey	Starts	1st	2d	3d	Win %	Earnings
		Paul Albert Nicol, Jr.	226	31	27	22	14	433,730
		Mathew Carroll McGowan	292	37	30	41	13	409,685
		Travis L. Dunkelberger	184	33	31	19	18	395,892
		Anthony Mawing	236	31	27	40	13	388,122
		Juan Ortega	214	23	36	27	11	342,449
CT	1/1 – 3/31	Trainer	Starts	1st	2d	3d	Win %	Earnings
		Ronney W. Brown	174	35	22	18	20	316,611
		Jeff C. Runco	140	18	28	26	13	254,571
		Bruce M. Kravets	85	15	12	14	18	168,027
		Dale Capuano	35	14	4	0	40	147,711
		Raimondo Schiano-Dicola	44	10	10	2	23	115,571

			Starts	1st	2d	3d	Win %	Earnings
DED	11/7/02 – 3/23/03	Jockey						
		Steve J. Bourque	534	116	92	71	22	1,836,007
		Guy Smith	547	99	78	69	18	1,616,853
		Carl James Woodley	505	107	79	66	21	1,606,717
		Kerwin D. Clark	429	53	60	51	12	1,026,493
		Jerri Elizabeth Nichols	365	57	53	38	16	721,572
DED	11/7/02 – 3/23/03	Trainer						
		Keith L. Bourgeois	270	55	36	42	20	946,365
		Doris Hebert	241	55	50	38	23	793,679
		Dale Angelle	111	25	21	9	23	482,475
		Steven M. Asmussen	54	21	7	6	39	477,310
		Samuel Breaux	106	24	22	11	23	396,475
DEL	4/26 – 11/9	Jockey						
		Ramon A. Dominguez	836	254	179	120	30	5,847,699
		Roberto Alvarado, Jr.	690	153	125	102	22	3,396,203
		Anthony S. Black	519	96	100	79	18	2,929,379
		Oliver Castillo	633	71	92	94	11	2,110,115
		Jose C. Caraballo	547	83	68	84	15	1,919,531
DEL	4/26 – 11/9	Trainer						
		Scott A. Lake	440	112	86	64	25	2,169,844
		Allen Iwinski	226	76	56	33	34	1,937,168
		Michael V. Pino	270	99	54	37	37	1,526,280
		Timothy F. Ritchey	288	56	45	54	19	1,445,890
		Steve B. Klesaris	141	44	22	20	31	1,299,028
DG	4/12 – 4/20	Jockey						
		Fernando Manuel Gamez	18	8	4	1	44	9,312
		Stephen Michael Karr	18	5	3	2	28	6,649
		Ronald Beverly	17	1	4	6	6	3,557
		Todd J. Nuttall	11	2	2	1	18	3,154
		Anna M. Barrio	16	1	1	2	6	2,174
DG	4/12 – 4/20	Trainer						
		Gene K. Wilson	8	3	4	0	38	3,962
		B. Odell Reidhead	6	3	0	0	50	3,088
		Lowell N. Bunyard	6	1	1	0	17	1,863
		Ricardo Saldana	2	2	0	0	100	1,854
		Jerry Cox	3	1	1	0	33	1,347
DMR	7/23 – 9/10	Jockey						
		Julie A. Krone	253	49	28	33	19	2,985,025
		Patrick A. Valenzuela	294	52	46	46	18	2,673,879
		Alex O. Solis	212	34	31	32	16	2,288,232
		Victor Espinoza	224	34	30	37	15	1,666,734
		Mike E. Smith	176	32	22	14	18	1,544,361
DMR	7/23 – 9/10	Trainer						
		Ronald L. McAnally	66	9	6	9	14	1,394,100
		Bob Baffert	121	23	18	15	19	1,086,834
		Richard E. Mandella	51	12	2	6	24	1,016,612
		Robert J. Frankel	27	5	7	2	19	955,702
		Doug O'Neill	108	13	16	12	12	741,320
DUN	3/15 – 3/23	Jockey						
		Ronald Beverly	15	3	0	3	20	6,402
		Terry Lee Gard	20	4	4	3	20	6,087
		Fernando Manuel Gamez	17	5	2	2	29	5,862
		Todd J. Nuttall	18	3	5	2	17	5,398
		Stephen Michael Karr	22	1	5	5	5	4,285
DUN	3/15 – 3/23	Trainer						
		Michael Megariz, Jr.	2	2	0	0	100	4,676
		Lowell N. Bunyard	8	4	1	2	50	4,305
		Gene K. Wilson	11	2	4	0	18	3,518
		Wiley Aker	10	1	4	1	10	3,272
		Laurie Jones	10	1	3	1	10	2,356
ELK	8/23 – 9/1	Jockey						
		Nathan R. Condie	19	7	3	5	37	13,075
		Matt Williams	16	2	3	3	13	8,735
		Antonio Perez	16	6	2	1	38	8,471
		Travis Hamilton	19	1	6	4	5	6,725
		Todd Thomas	6	2	1	0	33	6,455

ELK	8/23 – 9/1	Trainer	Starts	1st	2d	3d	Win %	Earnings
		Ty J. Garrett	2	1	0	1	50	5,625
		Terrill Gibbs	11	1	4	3	9	5,620
		Blake L. Cragun	6	4	2	0	67	5,535
		Shawn H. Davis	6	1	2	1	17	5,180
		Kyle Dahlke	3	1	0	0	33	4,950
ELP	7/9 – 9/1	Jockey	Starts	1st	2d	3d	Win %	Earnings
		Rafael Bejarano	346	80	52	45	23	1,245,935
		Jon Kenton Court	264	47	46	28	18	795,910
		John McKee	236	32	26	51	14	686,815
		Willie Martinez	164	23	26	18	14	462,940
		Calvin H. Borel	119	19	20	14	16	460,090
ELP	7/9 – 9/1	Trainer	Starts	1st	2d	3d	Win %	Earnings
		Carl A. Nafzger	34	9	2	5	26	235,420
		Robert E. Holthus	45	9	5	11	20	224,200
		Thomas M. Amoss	28	13	4	3	46	210,610
		Dale L. Romans	40	6	4	4	15	179,651
		Merrill R. Scherer	33	12	7	4	36	170,140
EMD	4/19 – 9/22	Jockey	Starts	1st	2d	3d	Win %	Earnings
		Kevin Radke	652	143	101	96	22	1,155,289
		Gary Baze	492	85	78	72	17	928,847
		Juan M. Gutierrez	539	87	79	81	16	813,779
		Gallyn Vick Mitchell	488	70	98	81	14	807,567
		Scott T. Saito	572	90	82	94	16	793,534
EMD	4/19 – 9/22	Trainer	Starts	1st	2d	3d	Win %	Earnings
		Grant T. Forster	118	25	21	25	21	485,472
		Tim McCanna	262	55	45	41	21	465,418
		Bud Klokstad	201	29	31	33	14	384,615
		Frank Lucarelli	243	39	39	36	16	382,433
		Sharon Ross	233	36	40	30	15	360,180
EUR	5/3 – 7/5	Jockey	Starts	1st	2d	3d	Win %	Earnings
		Richard M. Vasquez	37	11	9	9	30	37,717
		Stoney D. Whittle	40	13	4	4	33	21,475
		Dustin W. Williams	48	7	9	9	15	21,461
		Earl Boyd Sutton	29	3	9	5	10	11,575
		Gary L. Worst	37	3	2	7	8	10,717
EUR	5/3 – 7/5	Trainer	Starts	1st	2d	3d	Win %	Earnings
		Joe Frederick Thomas, Sr.	40	12	8	8	30	38,652
		Jose Ibarra	17	6	3	1	35	8,810
		Donald G. Black	15	4	2	2	27	8,802
		Zack Ashlock	28	2	4	5	7	7,968
		Mark Esquibel	20	2	2	5	10	7,743
EVD	4/4 – 9/1	Jockey	Starts	1st	2d	3d	Win %	Earnings
		Carl James Woodley	504	98	71	89	19	680,325
		Rex A. Stokes, III	446	84	61	46	19	492,707
		Guy Smith	261	54	36	34	21	425,715
		Brian Joseph Hernandez	364	55	52	39	15	407,867
		Josh M. Romero	509	56	72	63	11	406,927
EVD	4/4 – 9/1	Trainer	Starts	1st	2d	3d	Win %	Earnings
		Keith L. Bourgeois	282	65	53	46	23	492,856
		Dale Angelle	166	45	34	21	27	316,692
		Donald J. Cormier, Sr.	298	29	36	39	10	243,321
		Samuel Breaux	133	31	14	18	23	223,556
		Doris Hebert	118	20	18	22	17	141,923
FAR	8/22 – 9/14	Jockey	Starts	1st	2d	3d	Win %	Earnings
		Scot A. Schindler	46	18	11	7	39	60,994
		Beth S. Butler	62	17	13	15	27	57,441
		Anne Von Rosen	26	5	5	0	19	37,433
		Megan Ludlow	50	7	6	11	14	29,241
		Donald D. Herber, Jr.	46	3	3	12	7	19,322
FAR	8/22 – 9/14	Trainer	Starts	1st	2d	3d	Win %	Earnings
		John Ness	40	15	6	5	38	39,751
		Ardell Sayler	7	1	2	0	14	17,978
		Ralph Buchholz	2	1	1	0	50	13,833
		Elery H. Scherbenske	3	1	0	0	33	12,624
		Jeff Schindler	17	4	2	3	24	11,723

FE	4/26 – 11/11	Jockey	Starts	1st	2d	3d	Win %	Earnings
		Martin Ramos Ramirez	652	122	98	73	19	2,183,235
		Jake Barton	445	75	84	54	17	1,645,458
		Francine Villeneuve	509	88	64	70	17	1,632,453
		Christopher Griffith	586	77	89	94	13	1,601,778
		Neil Poznansky	515	83	61	70	16	1,517,989
FE	4/26 – 11/11	Trainer	Starts	1st	2d	3d	Win %	Earnings
		Layne S. Giliforte	338	56	65	46	17	1,138,329
		Thomas M. Agosti	211	50	32	29	24	894,141
		Chris Tuttle	322	39	48	36	12	716,630
		Michaela Neubauer	105	30	17	23	29	575,592
		John Simms	183	34	20	29	19	549,531
FER	8/7 – 8/17	Jockey	Starts	1st	2d	3d	Win %	Earnings
		Daniel Raymond Boag	23	8	6	4	35	28,305
		Ramon Guce	22	8	5	6	36	26,997
		Richard A. Sanchez	29	6	6	2	21	25,035
		Robert Boyce	19	3	3	6	16	18,515
		Elliott Demesme	10	2	1	1	20	9,437
FER	8/7 – 8/17	Trainer	Starts	1st	2d	3d	Win %	Earnings
		Dennis Hopkins	16	4	6	2	25	21,985
		Wesley A. Ward	13	5	4	3	38	16,502
		John McDevitt	24	1	3	3	4	10,102
		Santiago C. Rodriguez	6	3	1	0	50	9,701
		David P. Montgomery	1	1	0	0	100	7,575
FG	11/28/02 – 3/31/03	Jockey	Starts	1st	2d	3d	Win %	Earnings
		Robby Albarado	502	102	109	83	20	2,970,129
		Shane J. Sellers	421	88	71	55	21	2,214,320
		Corey J. Lanerie	557	92	97	87	17	2,007,666
		Gerard Melancon	513	86	61	68	17	1,762,727
		Calvin H. Borel	472	57	66	63	12	1,617,595
FG	11/28/02 – 3/31/03	Trainer	Starts	1st	2d	3d	Win %	Earnings
		Steven M. Asmussen	245	63	42	42	26	1,615,182
		Thomas M. Amoss	182	50	38	28	27	1,026,994
		Andrew Leggio, Jr.	70	14	17	6	20	767,766
		Neil J. Howard	41	9	5	5	22	642,560
		Albert M. Stall, Jr.	127	24	18	20	19	543,522
FL	4/18 – 11/29	Jockey	Starts	1st	2d	3d	Win %	Earnings
		John R. Davila, Jr.	703	138	111	88	20	1,140,757
		John A. Grabowski	553	128	88	85	23	1,037,942
		Chin C. Yang	692	91	100	101	13	904,605
		Robert Messina	466	85	67	63	18	704,040
		Manuel Rohena	504	77	80	80	15	687,363
FL	4/18 – 11/29	Trainer	Starts	1st	2d	3d	Win %	Earnings
		Chris J. Englehart	424	95	74	61	22	656,526
		Michael Anthony Ferraro	305	85	55	43	28	630,907
		Charlton Baker	250	72	42	32	29	607,035
		Michael A. Lecesse	350	72	62	54	21	572,001
		Michael S. Ferraro	297	72	47	30	24	496,049
FLG	7/4 – 7/7	Jockey	Starts	1st	2d	3d	Win %	Earnings
		Stephen Michael Karr	16	4	1	1	25	13,620
		Fernando Manuel Gamez	18	3	3	2	17	12,046
		Ronald Beverly	15	3	2	3	20	11,246
		Joseph L. Durigon	15	2	1	1	13	7,858
		Anna M. Barrio	13	1	3	2	8	6,765
FLG	7/4 – 7/7	Trainer	Starts	1st	2d	3d	Win %	Earnings
		George Wern	3	2	0	1	67	5,254
		Lynda R. Tanner	5	1	2	2	20	5,006
		Wiley Aker	5	1	1	1	20	3,991
		Lyndel G. Rutherford	4	1	1	0	25	3,537
		Richard Ramirez	4	1	0	1	25	3,186
FMT	4/10 – 6/7	Jockey	Starts	1st	2d	3d	Win %	Earnings
		Larry D. Payne	45	17	7	10	38	118,982
		G. R. Carter, Jr.	47	12	11	4	26	89,709
		Randy R. Wilson	79	12	16	12	15	89,480
		Curtis Kimes	37	8	9	9	22	54,856
		Tonja A. Arruda	44	6	2	4	14	41,851

FMT	4/10 – 6/7	Trainer	Starts	1st	2d	3d	Win %	Earnings
		Mike R. Teel	28	9	6	5	32	52,785
		Shane Castor	23	7	2	4	30	36,355
		Robert L. Listen	8	3	2	0	38	28,897
		Donnie K. Von Hemel	3	1	2	0	33	28,082
		Greg Frye	8	6	1	1	75	25,620
FNO	10/1 – 10/13	Jockey	Starts	1st	2d	3d	Win %	Earnings
		Macario Rodriguez	49	13	9	9	27	89,404
		Victor Miranda	40	10	4	6	25	60,732
		Ken S. Tohill	30	9	4	5	30	53,107
		Ryan Morris	40	4	6	7	10	40,736
		Berkley R. Packer	29	3	5	4	10	33,102
FNO	10/1 – 10/13	Trainer	Starts	1st	2d	3d	Win %	Earnings
		Rene Amescua	30	10	4	2	33	55,501
		Dennis Hopkins	50	5	10	6	10	52,120
		Michael Lenzini	33	7	2	4	21	46,218
		William Anton	25	4	6	4	16	37,822
		Art Sherman	1	1	0	0	100	27,600
FON	2/8 – 5/4	Jockey	Starts	1st	2d	3d	Win %	Earnings
		Perry Compton	273	91	52	34	33	395,471
		Jerome Carkeek	281	41	34	45	15	212,170
		Armando Martinez	270	30	25	26	11	136,804
		Kelly Michael Murray	164	20	22	16	12	111,450
		Perry S. Whetstone	207	18	27	30	9	104,481
FON	2/8 – 5/4	Trainer	Starts	1st	2d	3d	Win %	Earnings
		David C. Anderson	180	55	32	23	31	303,183
		James R. Compton	62	16	13	10	26	64,317
		Brian M. Roberts	70	12	13	8	17	61,959
		Ricky J. Gustafson	79	10	10	14	13	61,802
		Mark C. Lee	1	1	0	0	100	60,000
FP	4/4 – 10/11	Jockey	Starts	1st	2d	3d	Win %	Earnings
		Joel Santiago	631	101	95	70	16	636,308
		Ramsey Zimmerman	403	79	70	54	20	498,071
		Cynthia M. Medina	312	65	56	52	21	459,489
		Vicente Flores	631	64	71	63	10	411,601
		Michael Allen Gale	359	59	44	60	16	410,194
FP	4/4 – 10/11	Trainer	Starts	1st	2d	3d	Win %	Earnings
		Ralph Martinez	522	140	103	81	27	851,445
		Eddie M. Essenpreis	318	62	55	54	19	443,962
		Leroy Hellman	256	54	44	37	21	346,610
		Steve Manley	212	39	30	31	18	292,813
		Ron L. Brandenburg	210	30	26	30	14	220,829
FPX	9/12 – 9/28	Jockey	Starts	1st	2d	3d	Win %	Earnings
		Martin A. Pedroza	116	31	23	16	27	588,057
		Ryan Fogelsonger	93	22	16	20	24	529,699
		Tyler Baze	104	17	15	20	16	453,375
		Felipe F. Martinez	88	12	15	9	14	317,784
		David C. Nuesch	84	11	11	4	13	284,607
FPX	9/12 – 9/28	Trainer	Starts	1st	2d	3d	Win %	Earnings
		Doug O'Neill	45	10	5	11	22	251,346
		Jeff Mullins	25	8	6	3	32	243,030
		Jack Carava	20	6	4	3	30	128,570
		Donald Warren	9	5	0	1	56	128,300
		Wesley A. Ward	21	10	4	1	48	112,050
GCF	9/27 – 10/5	Jockey	Starts	1st	2d	3d	Win %	Earnings
		Stephen Michael Karr	19	5	3	3	26	6,344
		Fernando Manuel Gamez	18	4	1	2	22	4,863
		Anna M. Barrio	18	3	3	3	17	4,397
		Terry Lee Gard	18	2	4	3	11	4,149
		Charles Lyn McClellan	19	2	2	3	11	3,602
GCF	9/27 – 10/5	Trainer	Starts	1st	2d	3d	Win %	Earnings
		Laurie Jones	9	3	0	1	33	3,071
		Gene K. Wilson	6	2	0	2	33	2,358
		Lyndel G. Rutherford	10	1	2	3	10	2,306
		Lowell N. Bunyard	3	2	0	1	67	2,013
		Richard Ramirez	9	1	1	3	11	1,971

GF	7/4 – 7/27	Jockey	Starts	1st	2d	3d	Win %	Earnings
		Carl Hebert	37	12	4	5	32	20,346
		David P. Stubblefield	38	8	7	7	21	17,014
		Ivan Ortiz, Jr.	32	9	4	4	28	13,866
		Russell David Kingrey	28	5	3	3	18	11,091
		Donald Bruce Hamilton	21	3	3	0	14	9,020
GF	7/4 – 7/27	Trainer	Starts	1st	2d	3d	Win %	Earnings
		Bryan Krone	21	8	4	3	38	12,427
		Mel Berkram	18	8	3	5	44	12,175
		Dale Bagnell	15	3	2	0	20	8,728
		Daniel J. Young	7	2	1	1	29	5,866
		Mark Buckley	13	2	4	2	15	4,865
GG	12/26/02 – 3/30/03	Jockey	Starts	1st	2d	3d	Win %	Earnings
		Russell A. Baze	388	116	82	69	30	2,134,406
		Ronald J. Warren, Jr.	291	58	40	43	20	1,203,783
		Chad Phillip Schvaneveldt	249	56	46	41	22	1,073,811
		Frank T. Alvarado	264	34	52	33	13	864,474
		Francisco Duran	346	42	46	48	12	819,034
GG	12/26/02 – 3/30/03	Trainer	Starts	1st	2d	3d	Win %	Earnings
		Jerry Hollendorfer	296	72	47	60	24	1,662,600
		Armando Lage	196	31	29	27	16	529,825
		Art Sherman	118	27	22	17	23	494,400
		William E. Morey	103	33	10	17	32	412,515
		Jeff Bonde	75	14	17	12	19	405,322
GIL	7/4 – 8/24	Jockey	Starts	1st	2d	3d	Win %	Earnings
		Santos Carrizales	16	3	2	2	19	19,032
		Wayne Womack	5	3	0	1	60	6,848
		Harold Collins	6	1	1	3	17	5,710
		Isaac Chapa	14	1	4	0	7	5,050
		Melody Brooks	10	2	0	1	20	4,920
GIL	7/4 – 8/24	Trainer	Starts	1st	2d	3d	Win %	Earnings
		M. Shawn Finch	10	3	0	1	30	17,084
		Joel Perez	6	1	2	1	17	5,790
		Jimmy L. Ray	5	2	0	1	40	4,890
		Enrique Chavez	3	2	0	1	67	4,180
		Roberto R. Garza	5	1	0	2	20	3,534
GLD	4/26 – 10/28	Jockey	Starts	1st	2d	3d	Win %	Earnings
		Joseph C. Judice	619	151	107	93	24	1,331,643
		Federico Mata	901	160	135	124	18	1,257,574
		Mary Elizabeth Doser	714	114	124	101	16	1,025,032
		Luis Jeronimo Martinez	412	77	61	75	19	732,085
		Felipe J. Santos	618	60	80	86	10	655,900
GLD	4/26 – 10/28	Trainer	Starts	1st	2d	3d	Win %	Earnings
		Gerald S. Bennett	399	82	70	43	21	986,911
		Robert M. Gorham	275	60	46	47	22	783,400
		Randall R. Russell	378	62	46	47	16	433,801
		Richard R. Rettele	303	39	56	38	13	371,825
		Pedro Martinez	203	18	30	27	9	358,332
GP	1/3 – 4/24	Jockey	Starts	1st	2d	3d	Win %	Earnings
		Eibar Coa	501	91	77	65	18	3,139,002
		Edgar S. Prado	403	61	56	64	15	2,484,572
		John R. Velazquez	315	68	42	38	22	2,475,950
		Cornelio H. Velasquez	506	79	84	74	16	2,458,797
		Jerry D. Bailey	159	42	30	23	26	2,222,076
GP	1/3 – 4/24	Trainer	Starts	1st	2d	3d	Win %	Earnings
		Mark Shuman	344	87	58	43	25	1,847,310
		Todd A. Pletcher	118	30	19	10	25	1,561,650
		William I. Mott	148	31	27	17	21	1,028,100
		Edward Plesa, Jr.	84	12	9	6	14	824,250
		Christophe Clement	87	20	10	10	23	732,622
GPR	7/11 – 8/17	Jockey	Starts	1st	2d	3d	Win %	Earnings
		Peter McAleney	52	20	9	12	38	52,125
		Scott Sterr	53	11	13	11	21	34,115
		Terri Landaker	44	12	12	3	27	32,387
		Janine Stianson	39	4	9	2	10	17,156
		Brooke Mellish	49	3	4	16	6	15,039

GPR	7/11 - 8/17	Trainer	Starts	1st	2d	3d	Win %	Earnings
		Jim Meyaard	33	13	8	6	39	36,617
		Stan Marks	24	6	4	6	25	15,971
		Brandt Laczo	18	5	1	3	28	15,603
		Tom Rycroft	34	5	4	11	15	15,140
		Kathy McNally	19	4	3	6	21	11,633

GRP	5/17 - 7/6	Jockey	Starts	1st	2d	3d	Win %	Earnings
		Twyla Beckner	88	26	24	14	30	49,080
		Joe A. Crispin	94	17	24	23	18	38,359
		Melissa Peery	46	11	6	4	24	19,696
		Victor V. Mercado	46	11	6	10	24	19,469
		Monica Barber	40	11	7	6	28	19,230

GRP	5/17 - 7/6	Trainer	Starts	1st	2d	3d	Win %	Earnings
		Jim Keen	34	8	8	11	24	18,979
		Robert Beckner	42	10	9	3	24	17,543
		Gerald E. Robinson	33	6	4	3	18	11,078
		John McDevitt	33	4	6	7	12	11,018
		Vannessa Hunt	18	6	4	2	33	10,343

HAW	9/28/03 - 1/3/04	Jockey	Starts	1st	2d	3d	Win %	Earnings
		Eusebio Razo, Jr.	338	51	50	49	15	1,311,118
		Randall A. Meier	364	56	40	44	15	1,096,828
		Christopher A. Emigh	377	43	56	46	11	1,052,342
		Larry J. Sterling, Jr.	228	37	31	38	16	863,775
		Jesse M. Campbell	366	40	50	42	11	815,543

HAW	9/28/03 - 1/3/04	Trainer	Starts	1st	2d	3d	Win %	Earnings
		Murray W. Johnson	3	2	0	0	67	465,600
		Michael L. Reavis	152	31	21	25	20	448,328
		Wayne M. Catalano	92	22	18	10	24	441,710
		Chris M. Block	69	16	9	4	23	434,120
		Brian Williamson	120	9	16	15	8	387,157

HAW	3/1 - 5/6	Jockey	Starts	1st	2d	3d	Win %	Earnings
		Larry J. Sterling, Jr.	223	56	34	38	25	1,006,870
		Christopher A. Emigh	276	44	39	43	16	929,634
		E. T. Baird	234	41	38	31	18	793,144
		Eusebio Razo, Jr.	156	22	24	18	14	764,055
		Carlos H. Silva	156	23	22	19	15	619,760

HAW	3/1 - 5/6	Trainer	Starts	1st	2d	3d	Win %	Earnings
		Michael L. Reavis	141	45	23	19	32	654,710
		Wallace A. Dollase	2	2	0	0	100	450,000
		Frank John Kirby	137	19	19	27	14	430,990
		Richard P. Hazelton	77	14	11	12	18	429,488
		Thomas F. Tomillo	136	30	13	17	22	362,546

HOL	11/11 - 12/21	Jockey	Starts	1st	2d	3d	Win %	Earnings
		Julie A. Krone	102	23	15	8	23	1,356,893
		Patrick A. Valenzuela	143	27	21	26	19	1,178,196
		Alex O. Solis	99	20	17	18	20	1,055,234
		Mike E. Smith	99	22	17	5	22	988,094
		Tyler Baze	173	23	28	24	13	920,143

HOL	11/11 - 12/21	Trainer	Starts	1st	2d	3d	Win %	Earnings
		Robert J. Frankel	42	12	5	10	29	993,022
		Ronald L. McAnally	27	3	2	3	11	615,720
		Jeff Mullins	38	13	5	7	34	510,360
		Bob Baffert	62	11	13	5	18	507,454
		Doug O'Neill	95	12	19	15	13	434,095

HOL	4/23 - 7/20	Jockey	Starts	1st	2d	3d	Win %	Earnings
		Patrick A. Valenzuela	357	81	54	64	23	3,502,657
		Victor Espinoza	377	69	62	64	18	3,199,393
		Alex O. Solis	256	48	39	43	19	2,700,343
		David Romero Flores	220	41	33	28	19	2,365,212
		Corey S. Nakatani	268	35	50	40	13	1,989,751

HOL	4/23 - 7/20	Trainer	Starts	1st	2d	3d	Win %	Earnings
		Bob Baffert	121	20	20	18	17	1,837,668
		Doug O'Neill	212	37	36	25	17	1,664,452
		Richard E. Mandella	53	9	11	8	17	1,049,824
		Robert J. Frankel	61	14	9	11	23	1,042,833
		Neil D. Drysdale	47	9	9	9	19	970,390

HOO	8/29 – 12/4	Jockey	Starts	1st	2d	3d	Win %	Earnings
		Orlando Mojica	567	100	82	73	18	928,736
		Lester Cash Knight	566	74	83	76	13	722,808
		Rodney A. Prescott	549	78	72	57	14	719,835
		Thomas L. Pompell	465	74	55	55	16	671,444
		Robert Dean Williams	366	48	47	42	13	416,537
HOO	8/29 – 12/4	Trainer	Starts	1st	2d	3d	Win %	Earnings
		Ralph Martinez	164	66	30	25	40	402,938
		Doug O'Neill	1	1	0	0	100	247,080
		R. Gary Patrick	254	23	22	29	9	218,303
		W. Elliott Walden	2	2	0	0	100	190,140
		Kim Hammond	132	23	25	13	17	174,307
HOU	11/1/02 – 3/30/03	Jockey	Starts	1st	2d	3d	Win %	Earnings
		Terry A. Stanton	424	75	63	58	18	798,844
		John Jacinto	478	49	73	56	10	788,789
		Donald Edward Simington	474	75	71	72	16	756,102
		Roman Chapa	357	67	61	38	19	728,582
		Monte Clifton Berry	261	43	40	34	16	446,798
HOU	11/1/02 – 3/30/03	Trainer	Starts	1st	2d	3d	Win %	Earnings
		Steven M. Asmussen	205	57	45	28	28	818,716
		Danny Pish	239	48	29	25	20	528,402
		Tommie T. Morgan	152	29	24	15	19	417,053
		W. Bret Calhoun	141	34	28	16	24	346,512
		Andrew Konkoly	139	27	19	19	19	241,220
HPO	7/10 – 7/13	Jockey	Starts	1st	2d	3d	Win %	Earnings
		Ken A. Shino	12	3	0	3	25	60,443
		Kerry D. Kretzer	1	1	0	0	100	57,600
		Perry Compton	16	1	4	1	6	48,032
		Jerome Carkeek	13	2	0	4	15	44,044
		William Henson	12	1	2	0	8	42,230
HPO	7/10 – 7/13	Trainer	Starts	1st	2d	3d	Win %	Earnings
		Mark C. Lee	1	1	0	0	100	57,600
		David C. Anderson	15	2	1	3	13	48,923
		Boyd Caster	5	1	2	0	20	38,375
		Hugh H. Robertson	2	2	0	0	100	34,080
		Brian M. Roberts	4	2	1	0	50	32,000
HST	4/26 – 11/30	Jockey	Starts	1st	2d	3d	Win %	Earnings
		Pedro V. Alvarado	551	124	104	78	23	1,951,115
		Nicola Wright	511	102	85	63	20	1,524,963
		Felipe Valdez	393	61	63	66	16	1,309,083
		Francisco Perez Fuentes	432	59	58	61	14	993,235
		Chris Loseth	448	59	56	60	13	945,024
HST	4/26 – 11/30	Trainer	Starts	1st	2d	3d	Win %	Earnings
		Dino K. Condilenios	197	38	32	27	19	670,224
		Harold J. Barroby	276	29	47	43	11	602,569
		Robert Van Overschot	179	29	26	31	16	598,468
		Tom Longstaff	78	17	13	3	22	482,425
		John Snow	49	11	5	6	22	430,404
IND	4/11 – 5/26	Jockey	Starts	1st	2d	3d	Win %	Earnings
		Sidney P. LeJeune, Jr.	208	38	30	36	18	410,264
		Orlando Mojica	208	38	31	23	18	392,833
		Rodney A. Prescott	228	27	29	34	12	353,366
		Michael R. Morgan	181	27	27	24	15	330,189
		Luis J. Martinez, Jr.	158	19	22	18	12	224,613
IND	4/11 – 5/26	Trainer	Starts	1st	2d	3d	Win %	Earnings
		R. Gary Patrick	160	25	21	19	16	236,009
		S. Joseph Cain	28	7	6	3	25	100,866
		C. David Norris	24	7	5	2	29	96,967
		Kim Hammond	53	14	9	9	26	92,218
		Raymond E. Stifano	43	4	10	8	9	91,967
KAM	8/10 – 9/7	Jockey	Starts	1st	2d	3d	Win %	Earnings
		Laurina Bugeaud	17	5	7	4	29	17,287
		Ronald Joseph Bilodeau	12	8	3	1	67	14,609
		Caroline Stinn	15	0	3	4	0	4,184
		Lee James	7	2	0	3	29	4,180
		Alan Cuthbertson	2	2	0	0	100	3,420

KAM	8/10 – 9/7	Trainer	Starts	1st	2d	3d	Win %	Earnings
		Murray Cunard	3	1	0	2	33	7,805
		Vicki Anderson	4	2	2	0	50	4,600
		Debbie Spreen	4	1	1	1	25	3,430
		John Rennie Lumsden	3	2	0	1	67	3,220
		Bill Barnes	1	1	0	0	100	3,120
KAM	5/25 – 6/29	Jockey	Starts	1st	2d	3d	Win %	Earnings
		Laurina Bugeaud	18	5	3	3	28	8,740
		Brooke Mellish	14	3	4	3	21	6,220
		Emma Jane Abbott	9	3	2	2	33	5,044
		Ronald Joseph Bilodeau	12	2	3	1	17	4,146
		Amber Dickinson	9	3	0	1	33	4,090
KAM	5/25 – 6/29	Trainer	Starts	1st	2d	3d	Win %	Earnings
		Vicki Anderson	9	3	1	1	33	4,570
		Irene Miller	3	3	0	0	100	3,720
		Murray Cunard	7	2	1	1	29	3,200
		Gail Hochsteiner	3	2	1	0	67	2,840
		Wade Hardie	9	1	0	4	11	2,320
KD	9/13 – 9/23	Jockey	Starts	1st	2d	3d	Win %	Earnings
		Rafael Bejarano	26	4	3	8	15	223,431
		Eddie M. Martin, Jr.	8	1	2	1	13	151,512
		Brice Blanc	23	5	1	2	22	136,320
		Jon Kenton Court	24	2	3	2	8	79,038
		Calvin H. Borel	18	4	1	3	22	74,999
KD	9/13 – 9/23	Trainer	Starts	1st	2d	3d	Win %	Earnings
		Kenneth G. McPeek	11	4	0	2	36	138,170
		Jonathan E. Sheppard	5	1	1	0	20	129,112
		Darrin Miller	3	2	0	0	67	78,940
		John T. Ward, Jr.	3	1	0	0	33	63,680
		W. Elliott Walden	6	0	2	1	0	54,800
KEE	10/3 – 10/25	Jockey	Starts	1st	2d	3d	Win %	Earnings
		Edgar S. Prado	27	6	1	2	22	1,149,109
		Pat Day	87	21	22	8	24	1,098,476
		Cornelio H. Velasquez	93	15	10	10	16	938,891
		Robby Albarado	102	15	17	14	15	893,743
		Corey J. Lanerie	67	9	10	10	13	452,202
KEE	10/3 – 10/25	Trainer	Starts	1st	2d	3d	Win %	Earnings
		Nicholas P. Zito	31	11	6	3	35	767,241
		Kenneth G. McPeek	33	4	5	4	12	621,353
		H. Graham Motion	8	3	0	2	38	482,195
		W. Elliott Walden	22	7	5	2	32	410,820
		D. Wayne Lukas	34	4	3	3	12	398,888
KEE	4/4 – 4/25	Jockey	Starts	1st	2d	3d	Win %	Earnings
		Robby Albarado	95	17	16	12	18	1,309,581
		Edgar S. Prado	42	9	2	7	21	1,174,622
		Pat Day	85	15	21	10	18	1,100,147
		Jerry D. Bailey	51	12	13	11	24	902,423
		Kent J. Desormeaux	61	9	11	4	15	663,282
KEE	4/4 – 4/25	Trainer	Starts	1st	2d	3d	Win %	Earnings
		Robert J. Frankel	8	5	2	0	63	700,299
		D. Wayne Lukas	35	9	5	4	26	597,069
		Todd A. Pletcher	23	5	2	2	22	384,100
		Craig Dollase	4	1	1	1	25	370,533
		Steven M. Asmussen	19	6	2	1	32	361,694
KIN	7/6 – 8/3	Jockey	Starts	1st	2d	3d	Win %	Earnings
		Ronald Joseph Bilodeau	17	5	6	3	29	10,521
		Caroline Stinn	16	4	5	6	25	9,655
		Ty Dangerfield	5	1	2	0	20	4,500
		David Deforest Brown	4	2	0	1	50	3,000
		Brooke Mellish	4	2	0	0	50	2,717
KIN	7/6 – 8/3	Trainer	Starts	1st	2d	3d	Win %	Earnings
		Wade Hardie	15	3	4	2	20	6,706
		Rosa Lee Burbank	4	3	1	0	75	6,550
		Nancy Burbank	7	2	3	1	29	4,890
		Bob Honeyman	3	1	2	0	33	2,795
		John Van Loon	7	1	1	3	14	2,478

KSP	8/15 – 8/24	Jockey	Starts	1st	2d	3d	Win %	Earnings
		Carl Hebert	20	5	4	3	25	9,402
		Joe A. Crispin	18	3	2	3	17	5,181
		Jackie Smith–Hebert	17	3	1	5	18	5,007
		Shannon Wippert	9	2	2	0	22	3,716
		Ronald Joseph Bilodeau	8	3	1	1	38	3,496
KSP	8/15 – 8/24	Trainer	Starts	1st	2d	3d	Win %	Earnings
		Mel Berkram	12	4	2	3	33	7,598
		Janis D. Schoepf	5	2	1	0	40	3,071
		Wilf McDougall	10	2	0	3	20	2,844
		Keith Davis	7	2	2	0	29	2,817
		R. D. Mower	8	1	2	0	13	2,262
LA	12/26/02 – 12/21/03	Jockey	Starts	1st	2d	3d	Win %	Earnings
		Baltazar Contreras	288	78	63	39	27	381,712
		Alex Bautista	156	46	25	32	29	225,243
		Guillermo R. Gutierrez	272	33	44	40	12	215,855
		Gary L. Boag	233	30	31	42	13	189,970
		Juan C. Leyva	181	29	19	30	16	155,478
LA	12/26/02 – 12/21/03	Trainer	Starts	1st	2d	3d	Win %	Earnings
		Jesus Nunez	269	34	34	34	13	202,457
		Charles S. Treece	214	37	27	21	17	201,938
		Barry Holmes	71	15	12	14	21	74,887
		Daniel G. Luna	42	17	7	4	40	72,823
		Erin Lee Anderson	74	13	7	10	18	62,554
LAD	6/27 – 11/9	Jockey	Starts	1st	2d	3d	Win %	Earnings
		Gerard Melancon	517	101	85	64	20	1,538,147
		Kirk Paul LeBlanc	477	98	71	55	21	1,439,776
		Lonnie Meche	391	84	67	53	21	1,280,472
		Jamie Theriot	362	52	50	43	14	833,450
		Timothy T. Doocy	285	38	39	43	13	711,780
LAD	6/27 – 11/9	Trainer	Starts	1st	2d	3d	Win %	Earnings
		Cole Norman	383	95	64	47	25	1,358,598
		Steven M. Asmussen	256	67	48	50	26	1,137,242
		Donnie K. Von Hemel	109	21	21	21	19	419,796
		Larry Robideaux, Jr.	119	21	18	18	18	417,166
		Troy Young	114	19	17	14	17	412,940
LBG	8/30 – 11/2	Jockey	Starts	1st	2d	3d	Win %	Earnings
		Scott Sterr	107	21	18	19	20	114,942
		Terri Landaker	82	25	15	18	30	99,166
		Cliff James Miyashiro	82	11	15	5	13	57,227
		Janine Stianson	60	9	7	9	15	51,967
		Brooke Mellish	94	9	10	13	10	48,703
LBG	8/30 – 11/2	Trainer	Starts	1st	2d	3d	Win %	Earnings
		Stan Marks	35	16	2	4	46	53,423
		Jim Meyaard	50	13	7	3	26	48,243
		Gene Starlin	28	6	6	8	21	40,343
		Robert Gwilliam	36	8	6	5	22	34,668
		Mike Maupin	23	10	4	2	43	27,555
LBG	5/3 – 6/15	Jockey	Starts	1st	2d	3d	Win %	Earnings
		Scott Sterr	59	11	11	6	19	48,288
		Terri Landaker	57	12	9	7	21	42,022
		Peter McAleney	48	6	9	5	13	29,593
		Carl Hebert	46	5	10	6	11	25,256
		Terry R. Roncin	32	7	3	5	22	22,537
LBG	5/3 – 6/15	Trainer	Starts	1st	2d	3d	Win %	Earnings
		Stan Marks	29	8	6	4	28	29,897
		Phil Wiest	16	6	4	2	38	17,886
		Linda Kropius	20	3	4	6	15	14,668
		Mel Berkram	25	3	3	2	12	12,394
		Marlon Draper	20	2	1	2	10	11,827
LNN	5/9 – 7/6	Jockey	Starts	1st	2d	3d	Win %	Earnings
		Jerome Carkeek	258	54	39	30	21	247,062
		Armando Martinez	254	47	42	31	19	225,811
		Dennis Michael Collins	233	35	32	29	15	175,321
		Luis Ranilla	228	28	31	35	12	149,064
		Alejandro T. Granda	216	26	29	28	12	132,768

LNN	5/9 – 7/6	Trainer	Starts	1st	2d	3d	Win %	Earnings
		David C. Anderson	133	40	21	16	30	181,648
		Herb Riecken	71	8	8	9	11	69,024
		Gene Deroin	55	10	12	3	18	42,265
		Paul Linafelter	28	8	5	3	29	37,758
		Steve L. Hall	37	7	4	6	19	36,184
LRL	10/8 – 12/31	Jockey	Starts	1st	2d	3d	Win %	Earnings
		Abel Castellano, Jr.	328	64	40	34	20	1,253,245
		Ramon A. Dominguez	205	48	31	45	23	1,244,080
		Mario G. Pino	259	49	38	37	19	1,125,760
		Erick D. Rodriguez	297	48	44	37	16	828,770
		Jozbin Z. Santana	275	43	37	32	16	798,795
LRL	10/8 – 12/31	Trainer	Starts	1st	2d	3d	Win %	Earnings
		Mark Shuman	123	23	13	10	19	459,050
		Anthony W. Dutrow	55	14	12	8	25	404,090
		Dale Capuano	117	25	20	14	21	391,575
		Hamilton A. Smith	96	15	8	16	16	355,510
		Scott A. Lake	72	17	11	13	24	323,000
LRL	7/24 – 8/22	Jockey	Starts	1st	2d	3d	Win %	Earnings
		Ryan Fogelsonger	158	25	30	26	16	548,685
		Rick Wilson	86	23	13	12	27	424,310
		Horacio Karamanos	108	19	11	24	18	393,145
		Abel Castellano, Jr.	101	20	23	12	20	368,630
		Mario G. Pino	92	19	11	15	21	359,785
LRL	7/24 – 8/22	Trainer	Starts	1st	2d	3d	Win %	Earnings
		John J. Robb	32	10	8	2	31	168,545
		Dale Capuano	55	5	12	7	9	153,465
		Rodney Jenkins	27	6	4	1	22	134,330
		Hamilton A. Smith	45	6	8	8	13	131,015
		Lawrence E. Murray	12	3	1	1	25	128,840
LRL	1/1 – 3/30	Jockey	Starts	1st	2d	3d	Win %	Earnings
		Ryan Fogelsonger	436	93	86	77	21	1,621,800
		Ramon A. Dominguez	282	74	45	49	26	1,373,555
		Mario G. Pino	223	55	41	30	25	1,012,855
		Clinton L. Potts	235	39	30	32	17	752,060
		Jeremy Rose	233	34	38	22	15	740,390
LRL	1/1 – 3/30	Trainer	Starts	1st	2d	3d	Win %	Earnings
		Scott A. Lake	142	29	21	18	20	641,660
		Dale Capuano	141	28	31	19	20	426,315
		John E. Salzman, Sr.	64	15	11	12	23	410,080
		John J. Robb	110	22	11	14	20	399,075
		Anthony W. Dutrow	49	20	10	8	41	373,260
LS	4/3 – 7/13	Jockey	Starts	1st	2d	3d	Win %	Earnings
		Eddie M. Martin, Jr.	391	85	63	47	22	1,826,163
		Corey J. Lanerie	409	86	79	68	21	1,737,111
		Jamie Theriot	333	67	48	39	20	1,330,242
		Gerard Melancon	325	52	49	41	16	1,212,200
		Jeremy Beasley	351	49	34	46	14	885,609
LS	4/3 – 7/13	Trainer	Starts	1st	2d	3d	Win %	Earnings
		Cole Norman	391	98	64	49	25	2,058,162
		Steven M. Asmussen	362	80	67	59	22	1,811,539
		W. Bret Calhoun	160	51	30	16	32	1,031,883
		Donnie K. Von Hemel	86	18	11	10	21	465,060
		Danny Pish	194	24	25	19	12	463,005
MAF	7/18 – 7/20	Jockey	Starts	1st	2d	3d	Win %	Earnings
		Carl Hebert	9	3	0	3	33	3,327
		Jackie Smith–Hebert	9	0	6	1	0	3,008
		Shannon Wippert	2	1	0	0	50	2,968
		Ivan Ortiz, Jr.	6	2	1	0	33	1,904
		David P. Stubblefield	5	1	0	3	20	1,494
MAF	7/18 – 7/20	Trainer	Starts	1st	2d	3d	Win %	Earnings
		Mel Berkram	5	2	1	1	40	3,166
		Janis D. Schoepf	2	1	0	1	50	3,042
		Wilf McDougall	8	1	3	2	13	2,252
		Debbie Smith	3	2	0	0	67	1,776
		Mel Yelvington	3	1	1	0	33	1,055

		Jockey	Starts	1st	2d	3d	Win %	Earnings
MAN	4/5 – 5/11	Jockey	Starts	1st	2d	3d	Win %	Earnings
		Rick L. Knott	42	10	9	4	24	53,174
		Christopher L. Conway	58	8	8	10	14	50,881
		Russell Brown	50	8	6	5	16	34,890
		James Bo White	31	3	6	2	10	33,573
		Casey T. Lambert	3	2	0	0	67	29,376
MAN	4/5 – 5/11	Trainer	Starts	1st	2d	3d	Win %	Earnings
		Earnest Richard	8	3	0	2	38	29,847
		Kevin C. Carden	2	2	0	0	100	29,100
		Laurie Rosenwasser	35	4	6	6	11	22,194
		Andrew Konkoly	1	1	0	0	100	21,000
		Jaime Castellanos	18	4	4	3	22	20,362
MC	5/11 – 5/18	Jockey	Starts	1st	2d	3d	Win %	Earnings
		Jack Cano, Jr.	2	1	0	1	50	2,675
		Russell David Kingrey	1	1	0	0	100	1,800
		Zack Kelsey	3	1	0	0	33	1,740
		Gilbert D. Rivera	3	0	1	0	0	1,130
		Joey Coversup	3	0	1	0	0	710
MC	5/11 – 5/18	Trainer	Starts	1st	2d	3d	Win %	Earnings
		Bryan Krone	2	2	0	0	100	4,200
		Edward Buxbaum	5	1	0	1	20	2,180
		Rod Gibson	1	0	1	0	0	800
		Lisa Sisko	1	0	1	0	0	600
		Earl E. McKinnon	1	0	1	0	0	500
MD	5/23 – 9/6	Jockey	Starts	1st	2d	3d	Win %	Earnings
		Rennie Latchman	166	43	35	24	26	116,249
		Tim Moccasin	161	34	31	21	21	105,080
		Serge R. Rocheleau	179	36	31	29	20	83,275
		Sheldon Chickeness	146	25	15	23	17	66,892
		Andy Scarlett	125	21	17	22	17	55,857
MD	5/23 – 9/6	Trainer	Starts	1st	2d	3d	Win %	Earnings
		Hubert Pilon	52	16	7	10	31	73,790
		Fern Zdunick	47	9	6	14	19	52,252
		Don Bjarnarson	38	16	5	7	42	35,754
		George Gervais	58	15	16	8	26	31,967
		Bob Barr	47	10	8	11	21	25,768
MDA	9/13 – 10/19	Jockey	Starts	1st	2d	3d	Win %	Earnings
		Andy Scarlett	29	6	5	9	21	7,492
		Sheldon Chickeness	32	6	3	8	19	6,982
		Lawrence Durocher	32	5	4	7	16	6,862
		Hector Rabbitskin	27	4	10	2	15	6,455
		Danielle Beischer	19	7	3	1	37	6,259
MDA	9/13 – 10/19	Trainer	Starts	1st	2d	3d	Win %	Earnings
		Mike Tourangeau	42	8	9	5	19	9,913
		Elton Keshane	30	6	5	10	20	7,893
		Pat Hosie	12	5	1	1	42	4,724
		Jim Ross	19	3	4	1	16	4,202
		Lindsey Keshane	20	3	2	3	15	4,099
MED	10/2 – 11/8	Jockey	Starts	1st	2d	3d	Win %	Earnings
		Charles C. Lopez	152	31	31	14	20	613,547
		Jose A. Velez, Jr.	99	19	16	17	19	429,084
		Ramon A. Dominguez	17	6	5	2	35	367,530
		Alan Garcia	138	21	21	21	15	347,904
		Julian Pimentel	87	16	10	17	18	336,618
MED	10/2 – 11/8	Trainer	Starts	1st	2d	3d	Win %	Earnings
		H. Allen Jerkens	2	1	1	0	50	250,000
		Edwin Thomas Broome	39	13	8	7	33	211,840
		Todd A. Pletcher	16	6	4	2	38	198,700
		Teresa M. Pompay	48	9	12	3	19	171,805
		Allen Iwinski	20	6	4	4	30	139,670
MIL	7/1	Jockey	Starts	1st	2d	3d	Win %	Earnings
		Antonio Ramirez	3	1	1	0	33	3,815
		Shannon Wippert	3	1	1	1	33	3,282
		Scott Sterr	3	1	0	0	33	2,117
		Carl Hebert	3	0	1	2	0	2,067
		Randy Cunningham	2	0	0	0	0	323

MIL	7/1	Trainer	Starts	1st	2d	3d	Win %	Earnings
		Ron David	3	1	1	0	33	3,815
		Rita MacDonald	1	1	0	0	100	1,870
		Stan Marks	3	0	1	1	0	1,761
		Jim Depew	1	1	0	0	100	1,760
		Dennis Dorchester	2	0	1	0	0	970
MNR	10/3 – 12/30	Jockey	Starts	1st	2d	3d	Win %	Earnings
		Deshawn L. Parker	438	67	52	55	15	986,593
		Chad K. Murphy	231	47	28	31	20	770,936
		Gary A. Birzer	341	42	46	41	12	686,379
		Andrew R. Ramgeet	214	29	30	23	14	556,864
		Oswald M. Pereira	290	37	34	28	13	544,444
MNR	10/3 – 12/30	Trainer	Starts	1st	2d	3d	Win %	Earnings
		Dale Baird	232	33	26	33	14	466,429
		J. Michael Baird	85	19	10	7	22	296,916
		Scooter Davis	116	23	15	14	20	277,266
		Bernard S. Flint	37	16	4	3	43	236,466
		John W. Baird	93	11	14	12	12	199,607
MNR	7/1 – 9/30	Jockey	Starts	1st	2d	3d	Win %	Earnings
		Deshawn L. Parker	445	86	65	56	19	1,233,112
		Chad K. Murphy	277	42	39	38	15	803,150
		Oswald M. Pereira	364	54	50	44	15	777,731
		Dana G. Whitney	248	49	32	26	20	718,353
		Gary A. Birzer	362	44	50	41	12	682,224
MNR	7/1 – 9/30	Trainer	Starts	1st	2d	3d	Win %	Earnings
		Dale Baird	245	37	41	41	15	629,426
		Michael W. Dickinson	2	1	0	0	50	360,000
		Scooter Davis	134	25	23	16	19	342,010
		J. Michael Baird	90	20	12	16	22	294,278
		Gary L. Johnson	67	19	8	5	28	230,321
MNR	4/1 – 6/30	Jockey	Starts	1st	2d	3d	Win %	Earnings
		Dana G. Whitney	388	73	40	52	19	1,067,073
		Chad K. Murphy	273	44	37	33	16	833,133
		Deshawn L. Parker	368	40	49	47	11	736,868
		Oswald M. Pereira	308	41	42	55	13	643,083
		David J. McFadden	249	34	39	20	14	621,967
MNR	4/1 – 6/30	Trainer	Starts	1st	2d	3d	Win %	Earnings
		Dale Baird	259	28	33	35	11	491,106
		Scooter Davis	130	34	20	12	26	439,891
		Douglas E. Shanyfelt	104	18	7	16	17	246,929
		John W. Baird	119	17	10	6	14	241,998
		Don Roberson	101	15	15	16	15	214,294
MNR	1/11 – 3/31	Jockey	Starts	1st	2d	3d	Win %	Earnings
		David J. McFadden	204	42	27	22	21	614,185
		Deshawn L. Parker	229	42	33	23	18	595,709
		Dana G. Whitney	262	25	30	46	10	476,183
		Chad K. Murphy	184	23	28	23	13	387,500
		Roberto A. Perez	208	25	16	17	12	361,490
MNR	1/11 – 3/31	Trainer	Starts	1st	2d	3d	Win %	Earnings
		Dale Baird	201	18	26	29	9	325,136
		Scooter Davis	91	16	14	11	18	253,531
		Michael C. Pappada	46	15	8	4	33	204,873
		John W. Baird	75	13	11	7	17	194,091
		Don Roberson	80	13	18	8	16	176,263
MOF	5/10 – 5/18	Jockey	Starts	1st	2d	3d	Win %	Earnings
		Robert Boyce	17	4	6	2	24	7,050
		Ronald Beverly	20	3	4	8	15	6,149
		Stephen Michael Karr	17	4	4	2	24	6,133
		Fernando Manuel Gamez	18	3	4	2	17	5,355
		Justin Vanderwoude	17	3	1	0	18	4,819
MOF	5/10 – 5/18	Trainer	Starts	1st	2d	3d	Win %	Earnings
		Lowell N. Bunyard	8	4	2	2	50	5,968
		Scott J. Craigmyle	14	3	5	2	21	5,101
		Gene K. Wilson	11	4	1	0	36	4,862
		Leonard A. Espinoza	4	1	1	1	25	1,636
		Lyndel G. Rutherford	4	1	1	2	25	1,574

MPM	5/3 - 9/28	Jockey	Starts	1st	2d	3d	Win %	Earnings
		Julie Fritz	40	8	9	6	20	30,840
		Mike Simpson	38	6	10	5	16	27,660
		Dale Berryhill	33	6	1	8	18	21,250
		Kelly R. Spanabel	25	7	3	4	28	20,560
		Lee Gates	41	5	4	3	12	19,620
MPM	5/3 - 9/28	Trainer	Starts	1st	2d	3d	Win %	Earnings
		Reid Gross	28	4	7	7	14	20,850
		John R. Grace	26	4	3	1	15	14,160
		Larry O. Smith	20	3	5	2	15	13,750
		Ron Raper	14	4	3	2	29	12,960
		Doug Caraker	17	4	2	4	24	12,560
MTH	5/24 - 9/28	Jockey	Starts	1st	2d	3d	Win %	Earnings
		Joe Bravo	452	110	76	70	24	3,388,310
		Jose A. Velez, Jr.	341	51	62	47	15	2,248,439
		Jose C. Ferrer	377	77	64	27	20	2,200,399
		Julian Pimentel	355	64	49	54	18	1,963,695
		Charles C. Lopez	426	60	65	65	14	1,959,202
MTH	5/24 - 9/28	Trainer	Starts	1st	2d	3d	Win %	Earnings
		Mark Shuman	295	50	58	33	17	1,549,725
		Timothy A. Hills	148	35	20	14	24	945,820
		Todd A. Pletcher	74	10	13	7	14	866,390
		Benjamin W. Perkins, Jr.	94	21	10	10	22	728,995
		Allen Iwinski	94	23	16	11	24	702,210
NMP	8/29 - 9/14	Jockey	Starts	1st	2d	3d	Win %	Earnings
		Edgar Paucar	68	22	10	3	32	55,458
		Willie Belmonte	71	22	6	9	31	46,717
		Albert L. Howarth, Jr.	63	8	10	12	13	25,443
		Ivan Ortiz, Jr.	60	5	12	8	8	23,885
		Howard L. Lanci	49	7	8	9	14	21,310
NMP	8/29 - 9/14	Trainer	Starts	1st	2d	3d	Win %	Earnings
		Samuel J. Keyrouze	47	6	9	4	13	19,810
		Michael Delnegro	23	3	5	5	13	12,635
		Lori L. Lockhart	11	2	0	1	18	12,405
		Carlos R. Figueroa	24	4	1	4	17	10,907
		John J. Jacavone, Jr.	33	2	6	5	6	10,550
NP	6/20 - 10/26	Jockey	Starts	1st	2d	3d	Win %	Earnings
		Quincy Welch	463	97	91	70	21	1,204,553
		Leanne M. Painter	471	68	65	77	14	1,069,507
		Perry A. Winters	410	55	51	51	13	845,972
		David Wilson	415	57	58	64	14	814,660
		Richard Harvey Hamel	366	50	47	57	14	774,879
NP	6/20 - 10/26	Trainer	Starts	1st	2d	3d	Win %	Earnings
		Ron K. Smith	212	46	40	33	22	619,920
		Dale L. Saunders	177	33	28	28	19	498,555
		Don Gilkyson	143	23	13	22	16	420,736
		Ron Grieves	149	25	27	23	17	396,600
		Rodney Haynes	130	16	26	12	12	313,573
OP	1/24 - 4/12	Jockey	Starts	1st	2d	3d	Win %	Earnings
		Terry J. Thompson	353	69	50	55	20	1,686,126
		Jamie Theriot	256	71	45	25	28	1,183,610
		Carlos H. Marquez, Jr.	254	47	32	32	19	893,510
		Jon Kenton Court	244	37	34	41	15	774,306
		Luis S. Quinonez	288	30	27	33	10	667,748
OP	1/24 - 4/12	Trainer	Starts	1st	2d	3d	Win %	Earnings
		Cole Norman	233	71	41	23	30	1,077,040
		Donnie K. Von Hemel	94	19	17	11	20	511,560
		Robert E. Holthus	105	16	15	19	15	452,170
		Stanley W. Roberts	166	22	20	19	13	451,374
		Michael A. Tomlinson	17	6	4	1	35	397,300
OTC	3/17	Jockey	Starts	1st	2d	3d	Win %	Earnings
		Edgar S. Prado	4	3	0	1	75	130,000
		Gary Boulanger	2	1	0	0	50	63,500
		Pat Day	4	0	2	1	0	40,500
		Carlos Gonzalez	2	1	1	0	50	31,000
		Manoel R. Cruz	2	0	1	1	0	25,000

		Trainer	Starts	1st	2d	3d	Win %	Earnings
OTC	3/17	Edward Plesa, Jr.	3	1	0	1	33	73,500
		Frank Gomez	1	1	0	0	100	60,000
		Dennis J. Manning	1	1	0	0	100	30,000
		Kenneth G. McPeek	1	1	0	0	100	30,000
		Teresa M. Pompay	2	1	0	0	50	24,000
PEN	9/11 – 12/30	Jockey	Starts	1st	2d	3d	Win %	Earnings
		David Cora	331	67	42	38	20	419,899
		Emilio Flores	293	54	31	25	18	370,965
		William P. Otero	287	46	36	42	16	360,286
		Thomas Clifton	222	37	37	27	17	313,398
		Vladimir Diaz	271	36	32	51	13	301,554
PEN	9/11 – 12/30	Trainer	Starts	1st	2d	3d	Win %	Earnings
		Harry F. Thompson, Jr.	253	52	38	39	21	326,377
		Jose A. Martinez	238	43	38	30	18	303,761
		Bruce M. Kravets	231	46	32	27	20	269,666
		David W. Geist	132	38	12	14	29	243,587
		John Charles Zimmerman	90	16	18	12	18	185,240
PEN	5/1 – 8/30	Jockey	Starts	1st	2d	3d	Win %	Earnings
		Thomas Clifton	330	76	48	35	23	553,613
		David Cora	418	72	57	60	17	469,007
		Emilio Flores	440	56	57	60	13	448,849
		Vladimir Diaz	347	52	47	53	15	388,963
		William P. Otero	303	43	51	27	14	313,401
PEN	5/1 – 8/30	Trainer	Starts	1st	2d	3d	Win %	Earnings
		Harry F. Thompson, Jr.	276	50	41	42	18	308,150
		Jose A. Martinez	244	42	46	39	17	262,875
		John Charles Zimmerman	111	32	23	11	29	247,810
		Bruce M. Kravets	225	39	30	39	17	242,894
		Todd M. Beattie	90	25	15	7	28	217,216
PEN	1/2 – 4/30	Jockey	Starts	1st	2d	3d	Win %	Earnings
		David Cora	415	94	64	64	23	556,462
		Thomas Clifton	311	73	53	35	23	460,615
		Emilio Flores	405	61	59	62	15	414,817
		Vladimir Diaz	330	50	60	62	15	383,838
		Luis A. Belmonte	288	40	45	39	14	278,798
PEN	1/2 – 4/30	Trainer	Starts	1st	2d	3d	Win %	Earnings
		Harry F. Thompson, Jr.	280	70	46	42	25	423,775
		Bruce M. Kravets	300	55	53	52	18	354,159
		John Charles Zimmerman	122	36	27	21	30	248,930
		Jose A. Martinez	184	35	18	24	19	182,192
		Flint W. Stites	140	20	19	17	14	147,258
PHA	1/1 – 12/30	Jockey	Starts	1st	2d	3d	Win %	Earnings
		Stewart Elliott	1233	235	196	160	19	3,131,613
		Jose Luis Flores	1063	200	159	135	19	2,616,850
		Kendrick Carmouche	986	128	165	136	13	1,908,508
		Nick Santagata	857	98	107	115	11	1,596,041
		Joseph Rocco	568	70	65	75	12	1,176,770
PHA	1/1 – 12/30	Trainer	Starts	1st	2d	3d	Win %	Earnings
		Scott A. Lake	705	170	117	97	24	2,037,176
		John S. McCaslin	279	77	57	40	28	903,843
		John C. Servis	237	46	44	31	19	858,400
		Guadalupe Preciado	328	56	44	54	17	831,965
		Edward T. Allard	222	48	36	30	22	626,386
PIM	9/3 – 10/5	Jockey	Starts	1st	2d	3d	Win %	Earnings
		Horacio Karamanos	138	29	17	16	21	517,315
		Abel Castellano, Jr.	119	15	17	20	13	340,525
		Mario G. Pino	91	18	11	10	20	338,320
		Luis Garcia	123	20	20	16	16	331,395
		Jozbin Z. Santana	102	12	20	15	12	312,035
PIM	9/3 – 10/5	Trainer	Starts	1st	2d	3d	Win %	Earnings
		Dale Capuano	49	18	4	6	37	262,015
		Benjamin M. Feliciano, Jr.	36	7	7	2	19	126,570
		Hamilton A. Smith	49	6	6	8	12	120,405
		John E. Salzman, Sr.	43	7	3	8	16	118,845
		Rodney Jenkins	24	5	6	4	21	114,915

PIM	4/2 – 6/8	Jockey	Starts	1st	2d	3d	Win %	Earnings
		Ryan Fogelsonger	267	62	41	68	23	1,153,891
		Ramon A. Dominguez	150	40	33	20	27	1,099,870
		Mario G. Pino	202	39	36	31	19	846,270
		Rick Wilson	150	40	22	20	27	803,312
		Jose A. Santos	11	2	0	4	18	764,084
PIM	4/2 – 6/8	Trainer	Starts	1st	2d	3d	Win %	Earnings
		Barclay Tagg	1	1	0	0	100	650,000
		Neil J. Howard	2	1	1	0	50	600,000
		Dale Capuano	113	24	25	19	21	535,914
		Mark Shuman	61	16	5	10	26	417,507
		A. Ferris Allen, III	108	21	20	17	19	357,651
PLN	6/25 – 7/6	Jockey	Starts	1st	2d	3d	Win %	Earnings
		Russell A. Baze	65	18	11	10	28	247,921
		Chance J. Rollins	55	9	9	9	16	227,673
		Roberto M. Gonzalez	50	10	7	4	20	198,201
		Francisco Duran	41	11	3	6	27	145,530
		Joe M. Castro	37	8	3	2	22	125,345
PLN	6/25 – 7/6	Trainer	Starts	1st	2d	3d	Win %	Earnings
		Jerry Hollendorfer	44	6	7	8	14	136,802
		Armando Lage	37	5	9	7	14	129,076
		Jeff Bonde	24	6	2	0	25	94,970
		William E. Morey	16	7	2	3	44	90,945
		Art Sherman	27	3	4	5	11	65,535
PM	10/19/02 – 4/27/03	Jockey	Starts	1st	2d	3d	Win %	Earnings
		Juan M. Gutierrez	353	94	76	57	27	307,304
		Robert Webb	268	60	55	39	22	225,593
		Ron W. Keckler	397	52	57	52	13	193,838
		Marijo H. Terleski	363	44	54	47	12	181,501
		Karen Knapp	240	42	32	41	18	149,703
PM	10/19/02 – 4/27/03	Trainer	Starts	1st	2d	3d	Win %	Earnings
		Jim Fergason	234	43	44	31	18	176,778
		Jonathan Nance	192	37	38	41	19	158,314
		Nick Lowe	166	22	32	23	13	112,649
		Margaret Root	75	17	15	10	23	84,921
		Jim Keen	118	29	17	21	25	78,242
PRM	7/4 – 9/13	Jockey	Starts	1st	2d	3d	Win %	Earnings
		Glenn W. Corbett	219	43	31	32	20	664,219
		Alex Birzer	240	37	36	30	15	554,020
		Perry Compton	194	25	27	24	13	474,509
		Ken A. Shino	198	24	29	26	12	402,054
		Robert Dean Williams	162	28	21	19	17	376,928
PRM	7/4 – 9/13	Trainer	Starts	1st	2d	3d	Win %	Earnings
		Dick R. Clark	198	36	24	31	18	511,993
		Kelly R. Von Hemel	95	16	17	15	17	396,841
		David D. McShane	127	22	19	13	17	363,603
		Paul M. Pearson	76	15	11	11	20	344,287
		Timothy Mark Gleason	119	21	11	15	18	252,846
PRM	4/18 – 6/28	Jockey	Starts	1st	2d	3d	Win %	Earnings
		Luis S. Quinonez	304	60	49	37	20	1,092,893
		Terry J. Thompson	352	63	45	51	18	1,034,930
		Cindy Sue Noll	316	43	57	52	14	850,951
		Glenn W. Corbett	299	48	50	41	16	823,936
		John Jacinto	222	34	33	25	15	602,628
PRM	4/18 – 6/28	Trainer	Starts	1st	2d	3d	Win %	Earnings
		Dick R. Clark	204	41	39	23	20	630,590
		David D. McShane	122	22	14	18	18	458,572
		Stanley W. Roberts	153	30	22	26	20	443,320
		Kelly R. Von Hemel	104	23	14	8	22	405,363
		Paul M. Pearson	72	14	13	9	19	397,745
PRV	7/9 – 7/12	Jockey	Starts	1st	2d	3d	Win %	Earnings
		Victor V. Mercado	19	10	2	3	53	15,520
		Kristin O'Donnell	13	4	2	1	31	7,598
		Twyla Beckner	10	2	4	1	20	5,752
		Ty Dangerfield	14	1	4	4	7	4,496
		Joe A. Crispin	11	2	2	1	18	4,278

PRV	7/9 – 7/12	Trainer	Starts	1st	2d	3d	Win %	Earnings
		Scott Nance	7	3	3	0	43	6,080
		Jaqueline Smith	6	3	1	2	50	5,770
		Elbert Applegate	4	2	0	0	50	2,892
		Lyle Magnuson	3	2	0	0	67	2,760
		Marion Stitzel	8	1	1	0	13	2,572
RD	6/22 – 9/1	Jockey	Starts	1st	2d	3d	Win %	Earnings
		Jeff Johnston	181	58	27	15	32	478,937
		Perry Wayne Ouzts	331	43	48	55	13	336,400
		Hector L. Rosario, Jr.	220	33	36	34	15	269,812
		James Christopher Herrell	264	27	44	31	10	196,824
		Orlando Mojica	132	25	21	23	19	171,108
RD	6/22 – 9/1	Trainer	Starts	1st	2d	3d	Win %	Earnings
		W. Elliott Walden	3	1	1	0	33	160,160
		Luis Albert Palacios	65	10	15	13	15	131,403
		Timothy E. Hamm	18	5	4	2	28	130,527
		James E. Morgan	51	7	9	8	14	73,796
		Dennis T. Moore	78	12	9	16	15	71,564
RD	4/12 – 6/21	Jockey	Starts	1st	2d	3d	Win %	Earnings
		Perry Wayne Ouzts	355	67	56	66	19	436,652
		Hector L. Rosario, Jr.	212	37	31	21	17	278,794
		Jorge A. Guerra	250	48	28	33	19	274,411
		Larry Taylor	192	19	26	31	10	156,646
		James Christopher Herrell	154	26	20	14	17	148,161
RD	4/12 – 6/21	Trainer	Starts	1st	2d	3d	Win %	Earnings
		James E. Morgan	42	17	6	5	40	150,037
		Luis Albert Palacios	60	9	15	6	15	121,996
		Dennis T. Moore	59	14	8	9	24	69,835
		Joe Woodard	70	11	12	6	16	69,139
		Richard Estvanko	21	9	2	2	43	49,587
RET	8/1 – 10/19	Jockey	Starts	1st	2d	3d	Win %	Earnings
		Jeremy Beasley	312	70	49	44	22	695,043
		Weldon T. Cloninger, Jr.	279	48	46	43	17	546,615
		Ted D. Gondron	219	35	28	31	16	410,459
		Kerwin D. Clark	237	47	30	32	20	386,629
		Terry A. Stanton	179	36	34	28	20	376,105
RET	8/1 – 10/19	Trainer	Starts	1st	2d	3d	Win %	Earnings
		Steven M. Asmussen	119	37	20	18	31	489,662
		Danny Pish	204	43	33	23	21	356,365
		John G. Locke	122	18	22	16	15	292,460
		Tommie T. Morgan	99	22	14	12	22	235,451
		Cole Norman	12	5	3	2	42	138,001
RIL	1/18 – 3/2	Jockey	Starts	1st	2d	3d	Win %	Earnings
		Fernando Manuel Gamez	65	17	19	7	26	25,031
		Todd J. Nuttall	64	15	8	7	23	21,199
		Stephen Michael Karr	78	10	14	14	13	19,530
		Don Lee French	65	9	7	13	14	15,763
		Terry Lee Gard	44	7	5	6	16	13,957
RIL	1/18 – 3/2	Trainer	Starts	1st	2d	3d	Win %	Earnings
		Eddie Tellez	24	8	3	2	33	9,731
		Leonard A. Espinoza	17	3	4	3	18	6,987
		Jim Crotts	4	2	1	0	50	5,282
		Gene K. Wilson	25	3	3	4	12	4,941
		Krystal Adams	17	3	0	3	18	4,183
RP	8/22 – 11/30	Jockey	Starts	1st	2d	3d	Win %	Earnings
		Monte Clifton Berry	375	100	75	62	27	873,358
		Kevin Leon Cogburn	356	61	61	66	17	616,049
		Nena Matz	356	76	67	42	21	601,860
		Donald R. Pettinger	111	24	19	12	22	276,379
		Tonja A. Arruda	281	42	27	28	15	254,965
RP	8/22 – 11/30	Trainer	Starts	1st	2d	3d	Win %	Earnings
		Donnie K. Von Hemel	95	27	23	12	28	398,975
		Joe S. Offolter	161	41	30	22	25	272,214
		Rick S. Engel	47	14	11	5	30	135,427
		Clinton C. Stuart	80	17	22	16	21	133,910
		Martin Lozano	71	19	22	6	27	126,156

RPD	7/12 – 7/13	Jockey	Starts	1st	2d	3d	Win %	Earnings
		Lawrence Durocher	4	2	1	1	50	1,300
		Frank La Forge	4	1	2	0	25	1,050
		Enoch Quewezance	3	1	0	1	33	700
		Danielle Beischer	4	0	1	1	0	600
		Thomas Strongarm	1	0	0	1	0	150
RPD	7/12 – 7/13	Trainer	Starts	1st	2d	3d	Win %	Earnings
		Elton Keshane	3	2	1	0	67	1,150
		Norbert Beaulieu	5	1	2	1	20	1,100
		Leon Keshane	1	1	0	0	100	450
		Jim Ross	3	0	0	1	0	350
		Herman Eric Mentuck	2	0	1	0	0	250
RUI	5/23 – 9/1	Jockey	Starts	1st	2d	3d	Win %	Earnings
		Ricardo Jaime	194	45	37	25	23	452,020
		Jorge Martin Bourdieu	188	35	24	32	19	423,089
		Michael Dennis Clark	194	22	34	31	11	301,786
		Carlos D. Madeira	139	27	22	26	19	284,394
		Mark Anthony Villa	149	20	12	19	13	204,276
RUI	5/23 – 9/1	Trainer	Starts	1st	2d	3d	Win %	Earnings
		Henry Dominguez	144	38	28	24	26	377,076
		Joel H. Marr	87	20	15	17	23	215,436
		Fred I. Danley	61	8	12	6	13	120,469
		Ralph W. Black, Jr.	89	13	13	9	15	113,592
		Johnnie L. Nall	36	8	7	4	22	108,437
SA	9/28 – 11/9	Jockey	Starts	1st	2d	3d	Win %	Earnings
		Alex O. Solis	143	27	27	18	19	5,392,576
		Patrick A. Valenzuela	166	34	44	29	20	3,259,469
		Jerry D. Bailey	11	1	1	2	9	1,884,186
		Julie A. Krone	163	26	19	16	16	1,716,239
		Victor Espinoza	158	27	19	23	17	1,361,674
SA	9/28 – 11/9	Trainer	Starts	1st	2d	3d	Win %	Earnings
		Richard E. Mandella	38	9	4	3	24	5,315,570
		Robert J. Frankel	45	8	5	3	18	1,610,016
		Aidan P. O'Brien	5	1	1	1	20	1,211,800
		David E. Hofmans	15	4	2	3	27	1,132,920
		Bob Baffert	76	13	12	7	17	849,568
SA	12/26/02 – 4/20/03	Jockey	Starts	1st	2d	3d	Win %	Earnings
		Patrick A. Valenzuela	481	94	100	76	20	4,710,082
		Alex O. Solis	370	69	51	55	19	4,266,552
		David Romero Flores	436	69	70	51	16	3,551,113
		Victor Espinoza	434	51	48	64	12	2,752,306
		Corey S. Nakatani	338	48	42	59	14	2,421,408
SA	12/26/02 – 4/20/03	Trainer	Starts	1st	2d	3d	Win %	Earnings
		Bob Baffert	208	43	40	28	21	3,141,331
		Robert J. Frankel	90	25	18	13	28	2,757,699
		Jeff Mullins	93	30	28	8	32	1,885,242
		Richard E. Mandella	78	16	13	16	21	1,609,181
		Doug O'Neill	144	24	16	23	17	1,132,677
SAC	8/20 – 9/1	Jockey	Starts	1st	2d	3d	Win %	Earnings
		Antonio Lopez Castanon	26	10	4	1	38	78,850
		Chance J. Rollins	22	8	5	2	36	71,080
		Leslie Mawing	37	4	10	6	11	63,370
		Ryan Morris	42	6	6	4	14	60,515
		Berkley R. Packer	36	8	1	4	22	57,695
SAC	8/20 – 9/1	Trainer	Starts	1st	2d	3d	Win %	Earnings
		Michael Lenzini	48	7	8	5	15	72,330
		Dennis Hopkins	31	5	4	5	16	71,180
		Don J. Mills	17	6	7	1	35	65,870
		John F. Martin	9	7	2	0	78	50,425
		Rene Amescua	23	3	8	1	13	38,855
SAF	3/29 – 4/6	Jockey	Starts	1st	2d	3d	Win %	Earnings
		Ronald Beverly	17	5	3	3	29	6,501
		Stephen Michael Karr	17	3	5	3	18	5,344
		Fernando Manuel Gamez	16	2	3	5	13	4,079
		Don Lee French	17	2	0	3	12	3,102
		Justin Vanderwoude	16	2	1	0	13	3,080

SAF	3/29 – 4/6	Trainer	Starts	1st	2d	3d	Win %	Earnings
		Lowell N. Bunyard	5	4	0	1	80	4,129
		Richard Ramirez	9	2	0	2	22	2,482
		Wiley Aker	7	1	2	1	14	1,964
		B. Odell Reidhead	4	1	2	0	25	1,695
		Gene K. Wilson	5	1	1	1	20	1,554
SAR	7/23 – 9/1	Jockey	Starts	1st	2d	3d	Win %	Earnings
		Jerry D. Bailey	156	46	30	17	29	3,488,369
		John R. Velazquez	235	61	29	31	26	3,250,987
		Edgar S. Prado	225	39	34	31	17	2,113,547
		Pat Day	140	22	23	19	16	1,792,906
		Jose A. Santos	126	14	23	22	11	1,324,768
SAR	7/23 – 9/1	Trainer	Starts	1st	2d	3d	Win %	Earnings
		Todd A. Pletcher	125	35	16	20	28	2,061,357
		Robert J. Frankel	33	7	9	6	21	1,638,800
		H. Allen Jerkens	41	7	8	7	17	858,768
		William I. Mott	77	17	9	11	22	824,072
		Barclay Tagg	25	3	5	1	12	667,610
SJ	9/13 – 9/21	Jockey	Starts	1st	2d	3d	Win %	Earnings
		Todd J. Nuttall	15	7	1	3	47	7,431
		Fernando Manuel Gamez	17	5	4	2	29	6,572
		Charles Lyn McClellan	22	3	5	1	14	5,276
		Stephen Michael Karr	21	3	1	7	14	4,697
		Terry Lee Gard	19	1	7	2	5	3,946
SJ	9/13 – 9/21	Trainer	Starts	1st	2d	3d	Win %	Earnings
		Lowell N. Bunyard	10	6	1	1	60	6,103
		Gene K. Wilson	11	4	1	4	36	4,698
		Wiley Aker	14	3	4	2	21	4,628
		Manny A. Figueroa	8	3	2	1	38	3,793
		B. Odell Reidhead	9	1	4	2	11	2,568
SOL	7/9 – 7/20	Jockey	Starts	1st	2d	3d	Win %	Earnings
		Russell A. Baze	38	15	5	7	39	170,410
		Chance J. Rollins	51	11	7	6	22	116,535
		Francisco Duran	46	7	5	5	15	95,445
		David G. Lopez	34	5	7	4	15	93,680
		Roberto M. Gonzalez	27	5	6	2	19	79,615
SOL	7/9 – 7/20	Trainer	Starts	1st	2d	3d	Win %	Earnings
		Jerry Hollendorfer	21	8	2	2	38	113,665
		Armando Lage	22	7	2	4	32	54,265
		Chuck Peery	7	3	0	0	43	51,890
		Gil Matos	14	4	0	0	29	41,360
		William E. Morey	22	1	3	8	5	41,010
SON	4/26 – 5/4	Jockey	Starts	1st	2d	3d	Win %	Earnings
		Todd J. Nuttall	14	6	1	1	43	7,807
		Ronald Beverly	17	3	4	3	18	5,206
		Fernando Manuel Gamez	15	2	2	4	13	3,954
		Stephen Michael Karr	17	2	4	1	12	3,897
		Anna M. Barrio	14	2	2	3	14	3,350
SON	4/26 – 5/4	Trainer	Starts	1st	2d	3d	Win %	Earnings
		Lowell N. Bunyard	6	3	1	1	50	3,540
		Jesus Fernando Ortega, Sr.	2	1	0	1	50	2,489
		Gene K. Wilson	7	2	1	0	29	2,232
		Laurie Jones	8	1	2	2	13	1,959
		Wiley Aker	5	1	2	1	20	1,825
SR	7/23 – 8/4	Jockey	Starts	1st	2d	3d	Win %	Earnings
		Russell A. Baze	64	23	13	10	36	323,160
		Chance J. Rollins	60	14	14	10	23	172,225
		Francisco Duran	48	8	6	1	17	127,954
		Chad Phillip Schvaneveldt	40	8	8	5	20	122,110
		Joe M. Castro	36	5	5	4	14	103,574
SR	7/23 – 8/4	Trainer	Starts	1st	2d	3d	Win %	Earnings
		Jerry Hollendorfer	24	7	4	3	29	161,145
		Armando Lage	32	8	5	5	25	88,960
		Wesley A. Ward	13	4	3	3	31	85,245
		John F. Martin	17	8	6	1	47	72,605
		William E. Morey	10	5	0	1	50	60,315

SRP	9/19 – 11/23	Jockey	Starts	1st	2d	3d	Win %	Earnings
		Casey T. Lambert	137	38	27	11	28	329,254
		Ken S. Tohill	108	23	21	18	21	304,930
		Adan Fuentes	117	11	12	14	9	162,285
		Freddy Fuentes	123	19	14	15	15	161,805
		Brian James Theriot	95	16	17	9	17	157,778
SRP	9/19 – 11/23	Trainer	Starts	1st	2d	3d	Win %	Earnings
		Gary W. Cross	44	13	11	4	30	197,008
		Jon G. Arnett	83	21	13	15	25	163,747
		Fred I. Danley	48	9	11	8	19	126,348
		Carl M. Dyer	30	8	2	9	27	107,100
		Henry Dominguez	33	9	4	3	27	98,140
STK	6/11 – 6/22	Jockey	Starts	1st	2d	3d	Win %	Earnings
		Ken S. Tohill	59	11	8	9	19	115,425
		Ryan Morris	39	9	4	4	23	67,980
		David Burton Patton	17	6	2	0	35	53,630
		Victor G. Navarro	40	4	4	7	10	46,840
		Antonio Lopez Castanon	29	4	8	1	14	44,550
STK	6/11 – 6/22	Trainer	Starts	1st	2d	3d	Win %	Earnings
		William E. Morey	16	5	4	5	31	53,955
		Michael Lenzini	25	4	5	0	16	34,280
		Wesley A. Ward	7	3	0	1	43	29,770
		Gil Matos	13	2	2	4	15	24,960
		Dennis Hopkins	20	1	3	2	5	23,135
STP	4/4 – 6/15	Jockey	Starts	1st	2d	3d	Win %	Earnings
		Real E. Simard	249	38	22	35	15	569,344
		Quincy Welch	190	44	40	21	23	536,582
		David Wilson	250	40	37	38	16	517,082
		Perry A. Winters	261	33	45	35	13	497,152
		Richard Harvey Hamel	246	31	39	27	13	403,672
STP	4/4 – 6/15	Trainer	Starts	1st	2d	3d	Win %	Earnings
		Ron K. Smith	115	25	21	21	22	342,405
		Ron Grieves	104	23	17	9	22	298,401
		Floyd M. Arthur	61	16	9	14	26	199,716
		Robertino Diodoro	99	15	20	16	15	186,721
		Rodney Haynes	90	14	5	14	16	185,354
SUD	4/5 – 5/4	Jockey	Starts	1st	2d	3d	Win %	Earnings
		Ronald Joseph Bilodeau	37	7	6	8	19	13,048
		David Deforest Brown	32	8	5	2	25	10,888
		Jay Conklin	24	6	6	3	25	9,594
		Sean P. Evans	33	4	9	4	12	8,829
		Luis Morgan	44	7	1	5	16	8,716
SUD	4/5 – 5/4	Trainer	Starts	1st	2d	3d	Win %	Earnings
		A. Lynn Homer	27	6	6	3	22	10,130
		Tracy Lebret	25	5	5	3	20	7,804
		Robert L. Lawrence	20	5	2	3	25	7,085
		Jim McDonnell	23	4	2	4	17	5,725
		Thomas E. Hunter	12	3	3	0	25	5,073
SUF	9/15 – 10/27	Jockey	Starts	1st	2d	3d	Win %	Earnings
		Dyn Panell	125	22	23	19	18	285,936
		Winston Albert Thompson	151	23	18	24	15	284,180
		Josiah Francis Hampshire, Jr.	129	24	17	11	19	243,719
		Mark Phillips	98	15	13	9	15	168,609
		Tammi Piermarini	103	8	24	11	8	136,836
SUF	9/15 – 10/27	Trainer	Starts	1st	2d	3d	Win %	Earnings
		Ronald J. Dandy	95	13	17	9	14	143,850
		Kevin J. Joy	75	14	4	10	19	108,544
		John Rigattieri	43	9	6	2	21	92,906
		Frank P. Shannon	44	6	7	7	14	83,770
		Marshall L. Novak	33	5	5	9	15	83,540
SUF	1/1 – 8/27	Jockey	Starts	1st	2d	3d	Win %	Earnings
		Josiah Francis Hampshire, Jr.	626	142	113	73	23	1,568,521
		Winston Albert Thompson	553	90	78	66	16	1,104,863
		Taylor M. Hole	530	81	88	76	15	1,031,814
		Mark Phillips	661	92	101	93	14	1,009,155
		Vernon Bush	505	77	76	63	15	919,557

SUF	1/1 - 8/27	Trainer	Starts	1st	2d	3d	Win %	Earnings
		Ronald J. Dandy	454	79	73	57	17	832,905
		Robert A. Raymond	250	45	30	33	18	433,244
		Kevin J. Joy	273	40	46	32	15	395,703
		John Rigattieri	223	33	34	25	15	378,965
		Karl M. Grusmark	206	28	33	35	14	344,238
SUN	11/19/02 - 4/6/03	Jockey	Starts	1st	2d	3d	Win %	Earnings
		Jorge Martin Bourdieu	353	61	59	60	17	1,232,289
		Ricardo Jaime	335	55	58	38	16	1,213,485
		Casey T. Lambert	262	33	30	44	13	766,935
		Daryl Montoya	264	39	38	27	15	663,638
		Sal Gonzalez, Jr.	128	26	14	10	20	576,032
SUN	11/19/02 - 4/6/03	Trainer	Starts	1st	2d	3d	Win %	Earnings
		Todd W. Fincher	56	23	6	7	41	597,066
		Henry Dominguez	143	31	37	17	22	580,927
		Ramon O. Gonzalez	235	42	29	21	18	561,904
		Steven M. Asmussen	38	16	7	2	42	500,884
		Fred I. Danley	115	9	19	19	8	485,218
TAM	12/14/02 - 5/4/03	Jockey	Starts	1st	2d	3d	Win %	Earnings
		Joseph C. Judice	591	117	80	62	20	1,148,622
		Jesus Lopez Castanon	480	99	66	69	21	1,121,978
		Thomas L. Pompell	504	73	76	53	14	959,538
		Juan Umana	461	71	73	61	15	821,465
		Russell W. Woolsey	410	58	51	59	14	670,911
TAM	12/14/02 - 5/4/03	Trainer	Starts	1st	2d	3d	Win %	Earnings
		Don R. Rice	205	43	42	23	21	619,054
		Richard J. Ciardullo, Jr.	127	28	23	15	22	334,569
		Kathleen O'Connell	138	28	21	13	20	311,384
		Duane Knipe	133	22	19	15	17	264,091
		Lynne M. Scace	150	27	22	13	18	227,048
TDN	3/15 - 12/15	Jockey	Starts	1st	2d	3d	Win %	Earnings
		Huber Villa-Gomez	773	160	131	95	21	1,096,297
		Michael Francis Rowland	739	134	125	80	18	1,071,027
		Luis Antonio Gonzalez	719	130	92	85	18	976,861
		Julio E. Felix	640	104	71	81	16	795,978
		Ricardo Feliciano	513	77	78	72	15	689,768
TDN	3/15 - 12/15	Trainer	Starts	1st	2d	3d	Win %	Earnings
		Rodney C. Faulkner	529	101	82	75	19	593,063
		Rodrigo Madrigal, Sr.	181	43	30	16	24	406,632
		Jerry S. Sparks	186	27	36	32	15	345,942
		Jeffrey A. Radosevich	258	54	41	38	21	336,307
		Miguel A. Feliciano	192	32	32	29	17	331,136
TIL	8/7 - 8/9	Jockey	Starts	1st	2d	3d	Win %	Earnings
		Victor V. Mercado	20	9	2	2	45	12,513
		Melissa Peery	11	5	2	2	45	8,156
		Joe A. Crispin	18	3	6	3	17	6,809
		Ty Dangerfield	12	3	1	4	25	5,188
		Edgar Montehermoso	13	0	4	1	0	2,564
TIL	8/7 - 8/9	Trainer	Starts	1st	2d	3d	Win %	Earnings
		Terry Lee Fergason	6	3	1	1	50	4,134
		Jaqueline Smith	4	2	1	0	50	3,896
		Judi Yearout	7	2	1	3	29	3,538
		Bill Hof	4	2	2	0	50	2,960
		Lee Marll	3	2	0	0	67	2,340
TIM	8/23 - 9/1	Jockey	Starts	1st	2d	3d	Win %	Earnings
		Travis L. Dunkelberger	53	14	9	8	26	153,965
		Mark E. Rosenthal	50	7	8	6	14	144,380
		J. D. Acosta	46	9	8	5	20	108,820
		Luis Garcia	35	7	5	7	20	79,315
		Alberto Delgado	31	4	5	7	13	68,390
TIM	8/23 - 9/1	Trainer	Starts	1st	2d	3d	Win %	Earnings
		Mark Shuman	11	4	1	2	36	78,705
		John J. Robb	18	4	1	2	22	61,360
		Dale Capuano	20	6	7	2	30	46,300
		King T. Leatherbury	19	4	2	2	21	44,250
		Benjamin M. Feliciano, Jr.	7	3	1	2	43	40,005

TP	11/30 – 12/31	Jockey	Starts	1st	2d	3d	Win %	Earnings
		Rafael Bejarano	137	46	26	20	34	512,196
		Jason P. Lumpkins	126	27	19	17	21	354,459
		Rodney A. Prescott	162	17	12	17	10	200,426
		Anthony J. D'Amico	68	12	10	12	18	186,064
		Mark T. Johnston	91	7	12	8	8	166,937
TP	11/30 – 12/31	Trainer	Starts	1st	2d	3d	Win %	Earnings
		Dale L. Romans	29	10	3	5	34	167,985
		Bernard S. Flint	53	10	7	8	19	163,895
		Gregory D. Foley	32	10	4	3	31	116,485
		Paul J. McGee	16	5	3	1	31	74,400
		Randy L. Morse	19	5	6	1	26	65,797
TP	9/3 – 10/2	Jockey	Starts	1st	2d	3d	Win %	Earnings
		Rafael Bejarano	97	27	18	20	28	338,168
		John McKee	144	17	28	21	12	308,656
		Jon Kenton Court	114	21	18	14	18	276,391
		Edgar S. Prado	6	3	1	1	50	267,250
		Pat Day	4	1	1	1	25	251,500
TP	9/3 – 10/2	Trainer	Starts	1st	2d	3d	Win %	Earnings
		Murray W. Johnson	3	1	0	1	33	222,600
		Bob Baffert	8	2	2	0	25	147,865
		Bernard S. Flint	36	9	9	6	25	118,428
		Todd A. Pletcher	1	1	0	0	100	108,500
		Kenneth G. McPeek	14	6	2	0	43	98,617
TP	1/1 – 4/3	Jockey	Starts	1st	2d	3d	Win %	Earnings
		Jason P. Lumpkins	382	112	54	55	29	1,474,278
		Dean P. Butler	331	31	46	45	9	542,537
		Rafael Bejarano	205	41	40	30	20	505,462
		Jeff Johnston	241	26	39	34	11	491,584
		Rodney A. Prescott	292	32	42	29	11	475,566
TP	1/1 – 4/3	Trainer	Starts	1st	2d	3d	Win %	Earnings
		Bernard S. Flint	159	44	21	13	28	660,722
		Gregory D. Foley	49	17	6	11	35	392,824
		Jennifer Pedersen	2	1	0	0	50	307,500
		William Bradley	63	10	8	5	16	183,467
		Dale L. Romans	43	8	8	5	19	173,037
TUP	9/27/02 – 5/18/03	Jockey	Starts	1st	2d	3d	Win %	Earnings
		Seth B. Martinez	779	145	133	99	19	1,218,709
		Esteban Angel Gomez	932	146	126	133	16	1,112,220
		Miguel Luis Gaeta Hernandez	785	106	120	139	14	913,912
		Michael G. Ziegler	629	109	85	68	17	836,723
		Wilson Omar Dieguez	805	103	93	105	13	797,184
TUP	9/27/02 – 5/18/03	Trainer	Starts	1st	2d	3d	Win %	Earnings
		Kevin Lewis	226	51	34	38	23	614,987
		Dan L. McFarlane	298	56	52	56	19	499,890
		Don J. Mills	209	62	31	27	30	391,599
		J. Eric Kruljac	173	43	38	24	25	373,000
		Molly J. Pearson	174	34	27	25	20	314,527
UN	6/6 – 6/8	Jockey	Starts	1st	2d	3d	Win %	Earnings
		Ty Dangerfield	13	6	3	2	46	8,910
		Victor V. Mercado	11	1	5	3	9	4,233
		Johanna Purdome	12	2	1	3	17	4,213
		Melissa Peery	14	1	1	2	7	2,928
		Robert Webb	5	2	0	0	40	2,600
UN	6/6 – 6/8	Trainer	Starts	1st	2d	3d	Win %	Earnings
		Don D. Young	7	2	2	1	29	3,428
		Brian Tschirgi	6	2	1	2	33	3,405
		Silvester Juarez	7	1	1	1	14	2,420
		Marion Stitzel	9	1	0	0	11	2,382
		Wayne L. Bell	5	1	2	1	20	2,160
WDS	9/23 – 11/1	Jockey	Starts	1st	2d	3d	Win %	Earnings
		Ken A. Shino	181	36	26	24	20	248,287
		Alex Birzer	156	21	26	24	13	164,336
		Frank Albert Gonsalves	120	17	13	16	14	139,773
		Russell Vicchrilli	102	13	15	8	13	111,880
		Jason R. Eads	100	14	14	10	14	110,165

WDS	9/23 – 11/1	Trainer	Starts	1st	2d	3d	Win %	Earnings
		Kenneth Gleason	87	17	18	8	20	162,082
		Timothy Mark Gleason	64	16	7	12	25	90,477
		Jeffrey T. Rutland	26	7	2	3	27	62,081
		Ray E. Tracy, Jr.	36	6	7	5	17	61,250
		Joe Frederick Thomas, Sr.	40	8	9	5	20	59,819
WO	3/22 – 11/30	Jockey	Starts	1st	2d	3d	Win %	Earnings
		Todd Kabel	834	160	163	110	19	11,284,853
		Patrick Husbands	793	158	137	107	20	10,537,299
		Emile Ramsammy	795	123	101	98	15	7,104,415
		James McAleney	731	112	101	94	15	6,654,200
		David Clark	657	104	82	69	16	5,591,449
WO	3/22 – 11/30	Trainer	Starts	1st	2d	3d	Win %	Earnings
		Robert P. Tiller	252	71	41	37	28	4,030,391
		Mark E. Casse	409	54	57	59	13	3,307,134
		Mark R. Frostad	135	33	22	18	24	3,251,825
		Sid C. Attard	276	54	45	26	20	2,892,269
		Michael Keogh	92	15	7	7	16	2,878,756
WYO	6/21 – 8/17	Jockey	Starts	1st	2d	3d	Win %	Earnings
		Cody Foster	30	10	6	3	33	14,961
		Travis Hamilton	21	4	7	2	19	11,409
		Casey Greene	11	3	1	3	27	8,473
		Tony F. Guymon	11	4	1	1	36	5,532
		Antonio Perez	23	4	3	3	17	4,315
WYO	6/21 – 8/17	Trainer	Starts	1st	2d	3d	Win %	Earnings
		Mike D. Taylor	26	9	4	4	35	14,430
		Terrill Gibbs	9	2	3	1	22	7,620
		Daren K. Jones	12	1	1	3	8	5,671
		Travis Lusk	5	3	1	0	60	3,885
		Clair Bergeson	5	3	0	1	60	3,820
YAV	5/24 – 9/2	Jockey	Starts	1st	2d	3d	Win %	Earnings
		Miguel Luis Gaeta Hernandez	265	59	58	48	22	269,992
		Esteban Angel Gomez	291	72	51	36	25	269,401
		Kelly Bridges	246	63	37	41	26	240,446
		Orlando A. Martinez	237	30	48	29	13	180,924
		Alberto R. Higuera	261	31	42	40	12	161,151
YAV	5/24 – 9/2	Trainer	Starts	1st	2d	3d	Win %	Earnings
		Bill Brashears	128	34	20	18	27	138,937
		Justin Evans	124	21	22	21	17	112,921
		Dan L. McFarlane	76	24	27	7	32	110,322
		Gary Page	41	13	7	5	32	61,766
		Jerry Atkin	68	20	7	5	29	56,178
YD	8/23 – 9/21	Jockey	Starts	1st	2d	3d	Win %	Earnings
		Joe Holmes, Sr.	41	9	8	10	22	25,376
		Clay Dunbar	53	8	12	11	15	23,134
		David P. Stubblefield	53	10	10	9	19	22,112
		Russell David Kingrey	34	10	3	4	29	17,130
		Dan Karr	38	7	7	4	18	14,139
YD	8/23 – 9/21	Trainer	Starts	1st	2d	3d	Win %	Earnings
		Dale Bagnell	25	4	5	8	16	16,524
		Edward Buxbaum	19	5	5	1	26	9,962
		Doug Johnson	22	2	5	4	9	8,872
		Parke Edwards	19	4	3	4	21	7,872
		Armand Johnson	19	3	5	2	16	7,737
YKT	6/21 – 7/5	Jockey	Starts	1st	2d	3d	Win %	Earnings
		Thomas Strongarm	4	2	0	0	50	4,410
		Lawrence Durocher	12	4	2	1	33	3,994
		Doug A. Jones	8	1	7	0	13	3,436
		Danielle Beischer	8	3	1	1	38	2,950
		Sheldon Chickeness	5	2	2	1	40	2,136
YKT	6/21 – 7/5	Trainer	Starts	1st	2d	3d	Win %	Earnings
		Dan Keshane	8	3	2	1	38	5,860
		Elton Keshane	13	5	2	1	38	4,834
		Irene Britton	14	2	7	1	14	4,424
		Jim Ross	9	2	2	1	22	2,692
		Leon Keshane	6	1	0	3	17	1,346

Top Race–Winning Jockeys and Trainers, by Meet, in 2003

Track	Meet dates		Starts	1st	2d	3d	Win %	Earnings
ALB	9/5 – 9/21	Jockey	Starts	1st	2d	3d	Win %	Earnings
		Ricardo Jaime	53	14	6	10	26	155,062
		Michael Dennis Clark	33	6	3	6	18	49,842
		Ever Romero Olguin	18	6	2	1	33	46,631
		Victor Escobar	33	5	4	4	15	41,702
		Casey T. Lambert	28	4	7	4	14	59,848
ALB	9/5 – 9/21	Trainer	Starts	1st	2d	3d	Win %	Earnings
		Henry Dominguez	38	10	5	6	26	125,748
		Carl M. Dyer	22	3	2	4	14	48,629
		Ralph W. Black, Jr.	16	3	2	1	19	22,567
		Carlos Sedillo	19	3	1	0	16	16,042
		Dick Cappellucci	9	3	0	2	33	30,504
ALB	3/14 – 6/8	Jockey	Starts	1st	2d	3d	Win %	Earnings
		Travis Wales	114	22	19	14	19	188,866
		Adan Fuentes	126	19	20	11	15	191,539
		Robert W. Johnson	106	18	7	19	17	163,328
		Jorge Martin Bourdieu	105	14	25	14	13	228,880
		Ken S. Tohill	70	14	13	11	20	190,802
ALB	3/14 – 6/8	Trainer	Starts	1st	2d	3d	Win %	Earnings
		Henry Dominguez	74	22	5	12	30	199,725
		Carlos Sedillo	65	15	8	11	23	209,968
		Gary W. Cross	66	13	17	7	20	220,595
		Jon G. Arnett	51	8	12	7	16	87,498
		Ramon O. Gonzalez	77	7	11	11	9	87,378
ANF	7/11 – 7/20	Jockey	Starts	1st	2d	3d	Win %	Earnings
		Megan Ludlow	24	12	3	3	50	23,780
		Jeremy Latham	23	4	3	4	17	12,110
		Juan Padilla	8	4	0	1	50	9,680
		Gary Wade	23	3	7	3	13	9,562
		Liz Emerson	14	1	2	3	7	3,190
ANF	7/11 – 7/20	Trainer	Starts	1st	2d	3d	Win %	Earnings
		Joe Frederick Thomas, Sr.	13	7	2	1	54	13,740
		George Blatchford	5	3	1	0	60	9,840
		Mark Esquibel	13	3	0	4	23	8,724
		Donald G. Black	8	2	2	0	25	5,610
		James Sweet	10	2	1	3	20	4,194
AP	5/9 – 9/27	Jockey	Starts	1st	2d	3d	Win %	Earnings
		Rene R. Douglas	564	132	112	81	23	3,719,651
		Eusebio Razo, Jr.	487	89	75	49	18	2,292,784
		Curt C. Bourque	380	66	49	67	17	1,824,120
		Carlos H. Marquez, Jr.	390	66	44	61	17	1,595,408
		Christopher A. Emigh	471	58	68	68	12	1,696,012
AP	5/9 – 9/27	Trainer	Starts	1st	2d	3d	Win %	Earnings
		Wayne M. Catalano	182	59	22	21	32	985,548
		Chris M. Block	151	29	21	20	19	835,094
		Gene A. Cilio	169	25	31	13	15	917,358
		Harvey L. Vanier	191	23	24	28	12	627,216
		Hugh H. Robertson	132	23	23	16	17	620,179
AQU	10/29 – 12/31	Jockey	Starts	1st	2d	3d	Win %	Earnings
		Shaun Bridgmohan	192	32	27	29	17	1,217,289
		Javier Castellano	200	31	28	38	16	1,290,846
		Richard Migliore	156	30	21	20	19	1,363,170
		Michael J. Luzzi	193	26	25	24	13	1,094,471
		John R. Velazquez	116	26	13	16	22	1,195,754
AQU	10/29 – 12/31	Trainer	Starts	1st	2d	3d	Win %	Earnings
		Richard E. Dutrow, Jr.	87	30	16	11	34	981,552
		Todd A. Pletcher	84	22	9	10	26	1,035,791
		Frank LaBoccetta, Jr.	38	14	5	2	37	308,403
		Scott A. Lake	58	12	7	7	21	419,681
		Bruce N. Levine	69	10	9	11	14	325,617
AQU	3/12 – 5/4	Jockey	Starts	1st	2d	3d	Win %	Earnings
		Michael J. Luzzi	206	39	30	34	19	1,445,329
		Luis D. Chavez	225	33	33	37	15	1,300,300
		John R. Velazquez	99	29	20	12	29	1,097,790
		Shaun Bridgmohan	149	29	17	21	19	1,050,896
		Javier Castellano	182	27	36	25	15	1,133,448

AQU	3/12 – 5/4	Trainer	Starts	1st	2d	3d	Win %	Earnings
		H. Allen Jerkens	43	15	9	8	35	658,205
		Richard E. Dutrow, Jr.	80	14	15	17	18	688,480
		Scott A. Lake	54	14	12	6	26	468,335
		Mark A. Hennig	46	12	8	5	26	530,195
		Patrick L. Reynolds	31	11	5	4	35	458,774
AQU	1/1 – 3/9	Jockey	Starts	1st	2d	3d	Win %	Earnings
		Javier Castellano	268	44	53	42	16	1,563,281
		Richard Migliore	189	43	31	19	23	1,392,302
		Luis D. Chavez	275	42	42	32	15	1,439,036
		Michael J. Luzzi	238	37	24	40	16	1,276,390
		John McKee	239	35	45	27	15	1,203,139
AQU	1/1 – 3/9	Trainer	Starts	1st	2d	3d	Win %	Earnings
		Richard E. Dutrow, Jr.	65	18	15	11	28	645,112
		Gary C. Contessa	132	15	16	13	11	552,211
		Michael E. Hushion	46	15	8	6	33	395,190
		Gregory F. Martin	32	12	10	4	38	294,550
		Jennifer Pedersen	92	10	17	17	11	503,592
ARP	6/6 – 8/25	Jockey	Starts	1st	2d	3d	Win %	Earnings
		Frank Albert Gonsalves	205	46	38	25	22	411,508
		Wilson Omar Dieguez	164	24	23	24	15	203,593
		Travis Wales	108	24	14	15	22	178,502
		Russell Vicchrilli	138	22	26	8	16	223,785
		Brian James Theriot	186	21	30	18	11	195,955
ARP	6/6 – 8/25	Trainer	Starts	1st	2d	3d	Win %	Earnings
		Jon G. Arnett	116	28	20	21	24	191,522
		Kenneth Gleason	176	26	30	18	15	319,146
		Carlos Gonzalez	116	22	12	14	19	180,057
		Gary W. Cross	75	13	11	19	17	149,132
		Temple D. Rushton	159	12	16	18	8	89,289
ASD	5/4 – 9/28	Jockey	Starts	1st	2d	3d	Win %	Earnings
		Travis Wayne Hightower	394	98	63	45	25	757,197
		Juan Crawford	326	55	41	42	17	455,249
		Michael Phillip Iammarino	359	48	32	40	13	410,713
		Jason Leacock	316	47	46	43	15	404,838
		Timothy N. Gardiner	348	43	44	42	12	383,444
ASD	5/4 – 9/28	Trainer	Starts	1st	2d	3d	Win %	Earnings
		Gary Danelson	189	55	38	27	29	417,424
		Ardell Sayler	223	37	32	28	17	302,053
		Tom Gardipy, Jr.	148	25	23	24	17	176,391
		Chad Torevell	161	22	20	12	14	200,322
		Clayton Gray	140	22	14	20	16	195,006
ATL	4/23 – 5/2	Jockey	Starts	1st	2d	3d	Win %	Earnings
		Victor H. Molina	14	4	1	0	29	50,980
		Kendrick Carmouche	11	3	1	2	27	33,690
		Arnaldo Unsihuay	5	3	0	0	60	26,650
		Edwin L. King, Jr.	8	2	1	1	25	26,710
		Jody Petty	3	2	0	0	67	30,000
ATL	4/23 – 5/2	Trainer	Starts	1st	2d	3d	Win %	Earnings
		Kathleen A. Demasi	5	2	1	0	40	23,310
		Jack Fisher	4	1	2	0	25	24,000
		Edward K. Auwarter	8	1	1	2	13	18,940
		Richard J. Hendriks	7	1	1	1	14	16,250
		Timothy A. Hills	4	1	1	0	25	16,850
ATO	7/19 – 7/20	Jockey	Starts	1st	2d	3d	Win %	Earnings
		Jerome Carkeek	11	3	3	2	27	33,080
		Alejandro T. Granda	11	2	4	1	18	27,355
		Yuri Yaranga	12	1	2	0	8	14,893
		Luis Ranilla	12	1	1	3	8	16,657
		Armando Martinez	11	1	1	2	9	16,263
ATO	7/19 – 7/20	Trainer	Starts	1st	2d	3d	Win %	Earnings
		James R. Compton	2	2	0	0	100	18,000
		David C. Anderson	5	1	1	1	20	12,265
		Craig Rice	3	1	1	1	33	10,180
		Gene Deroin	4	1	1	0	25	10,205
		Herb Riecken	3	1	0	2	33	11,444

			Starts	1st	2d	3d	Win %	Earnings
BEL	9/5 – 10/26	Jockey						
		John R. Velazquez	208	44	32	28	21	2,349,989
		Edgar S. Prado	212	37	38	32	17	2,352,973
		Javier Castellano	201	31	35	20	15	1,831,192
		Jerry D. Bailey	119	31	14	17	26	3,436,556
		Jorge F. Chavez	182	28	22	27	15	1,330,620
BEL	9/5 – 10/26	Trainer						
		Todd A. Pletcher	96	24	19	17	25	1,598,850
		Richard E. Dutrow, Jr.	53	13	8	7	25	710,302
		Scott A. Lake	52	12	10	10	23	413,730
		William I. Mott	72	11	4	13	15	573,664
		Stanley M. Hough	49	10	8	3	20	441,180
BEL	5/7 – 7/20	Jockey						
		John R. Velazquez	267	70	47	37	26	3,250,467
		Edgar S. Prado	301	59	49	41	20	2,979,580
		Jorge F. Chavez	283	43	58	34	15	2,055,825
		Richard Migliore	211	43	27	29	20	2,004,353
		Jose A. Santos	249	42	42	35	17	2,596,361
BEL	5/7 – 7/20	Trainer						
		Todd A. Pletcher	133	40	20	17	30	1,649,142
		Richard E. Dutrow, Jr.	83	22	11	13	27	806,874
		Kiaran P. McLaughlin	47	20	9	3	43	758,900
		H. Allen Jerkens	84	19	15	17	23	1,189,577
		H. James Bond	46	18	7	5	39	799,030
BEU	9/13 – 12/22	Jockey						
		Marco A. Ccamaque	409	83	59	41	20	441,149
		Perry Wayne Ouzts	286	57	38	39	20	329,089
		Hector L. Rosario, Jr.	310	49	68	37	16	363,367
		Jose Luis Calo	315	39	29	25	12	190,265
		Gordon Whitacre	327	29	28	37	9	169,380
BEU	9/13 – 12/22	Trainer						
		Rodney C. Faulkner	57	19	9	11	33	69,621
		Rinzy Nocero	80	15	9	7	19	56,959
		Luis Albert Palacios	74	14	17	11	19	195,934
		William D. Cowans	41	13	15	1	32	65,828
		Jake S. Radosevich	140	12	21	21	9	80,007
BEU	1/10 – 5/3	Jockey						
		Ivan R. Gonzalez	326	78	56	35	24	401,312
		Ramon Luna	308	48	46	42	16	250,508
		Jose Luis Calo	222	38	32	28	17	180,560
		Hector L. Rosario, Jr.	168	35	36	22	21	186,898
		Paul M. Nolan	262	33	39	40	13	186,481
BEU	1/10 – 5/3	Trainer						
		Jake S. Radosevich	147	31	31	16	21	145,243
		David W. Asbury	53	17	9	2	32	70,507
		Geraldine Rodak	107	16	16	11	15	75,457
		Rinzy Nocero	90	12	16	11	13	65,012
		Luis Albert Palacios	29	11	3	4	38	96,277
BM	8/29 – 11/02	Jockey						
		Russell A. Baze	308	96	63	48	31	1,523,970
		Ronald J. Warren, Jr.	226	37	33	33	16	892,388
		Chance J. Rollins	185	32	27	26	17	542,583
		Jason P. Lumpkins	177	32	20	32	18	611,358
		Francisco Duran	232	31	39	23	13	633,464
BM	8/29 – 11/02	Trainer						
		Jerry Hollendorfer	219	52	39	34	24	1,007,083
		Armando Lage	182	36	34	24	20	584,085
		Art Sherman	101	25	15	9	25	458,379
		Brian J. Koriner	66	23	10	10	35	303,263
		John F. Martin	54	18	7	7	33	213,528
BM	4/2 – 6/15	Jockey						
		Russell A. Baze	329	97	80	37	29	1,667,034
		Ronald J. Warren, Jr.	242	52	44	32	21	1,111,476
		Roberto M. Gonzalez	221	44	35	32	20	912,922
		Chance J. Rollins	214	33	40	32	15	727,882
		Chad Phillip Schvaneveldt	186	32	20	36	17	788,188

BM	4/2 – 6/15	Trainer	Starts	1st	2d	3d	Win %	Earnings
		Jerry Hollendorfer	240	55	52	32	23	1,311,823
		Armando Lage	156	34	37	24	22	600,913
		Art Sherman	105	23	26	19	22	480,163
		William E. Morey	82	20	20	11	24	318,941
		Brent Sumja	71	19	7	4	27	307,398
BMF	8/6 – 8/18	Jockey	Starts	1st	2d	3d	Win %	Earnings
		Russell A. Baze	59	18	13	6	31	214,505
		Chad Phillip Schvaneveldt	53	11	16	7	21	199,432
		Francisco Duran	70	11	11	12	16	187,996
		Roberto M. Gonzalez	47	10	10	4	21	145,756
		David G. Lopez	58	9	10	10	16	135,352
BMF	8/6 – 8/18	Trainer	Starts	1st	2d	3d	Win %	Earnings
		Jerry Hollendorfer	37	9	5	6	24	153,850
		Armando Lage	39	7	8	8	18	117,660
		John F. Martin	15	6	2	0	40	46,885
		William E. Morey	22	5	5	3	23	72,206
		Art Sherman	25	5	4	4	20	78,030
BOI	5/3 – 8/10	Jockey	Starts	1st	2d	3d	Win %	Earnings
		Berkley R. Packer	222	51	36	27	23	149,187
		Robert Webb	220	41	39	37	19	106,942
		Flip John Nollar	257	39	41	38	15	106,737
		Matt Williams	189	28	21	26	15	126,206
		Jay Conklin	86	24	20	8	28	79,176
BOI	5/3 – 8/10	Trainer	Starts	1st	2d	3d	Win %	Earnings
		Dru S. Hall	77	23	11	13	30	121,136
		Steve Duschka	98	20	15	17	20	53,659
		Jason Homer	58	13	10	9	22	33,285
		Kevin Knudsen	72	13	8	9	18	25,955
		Robert L. Lawrence	37	12	9	4	32	33,504
BRD	2/1 – 11/9	Jockey	Starts	1st	2d	3d	Win %	Earnings
		Mike W. Harvell	106	26	19	15	25	53,571
		Jorge L. Fontanez	137	20	13	23	15	46,813
		Fernando Camacho	136	15	25	17	11	47,349
		Wendell John Hilburn	111	14	27	12	13	40,533
		Bobby L. Johnson	46	13	7	8	28	25,747
BRD	2/1 – 11/9	Trainer	Starts	1st	2d	3d	Win %	Earnings
		Don R. Smith	46	12	5	7	26	18,784
		Robert L. Roughton	50	10	6	4	20	23,093
		John Hart Garvin	63	9	7	8	14	21,472
		Gary L. Anderson	48	8	9	6	17	18,833
		Dale Foster	60	8	3	9	13	18,809
BRN	9/6 – 9/7	Jockey	Starts	1st	2d	3d	Win %	Earnings
		Joe A. Crispin	14	3	5	0	21	5,980
		Victor V. Mercado	13	3	2	1	23	5,215
		Melissa Peery	7	3	0	3	43	4,100
		Darlene Braden	9	2	0	1	22	2,768
		Kristin O'Donnell	6	2	0	1	33	2,598
BRN	9/6 – 9/7	Trainer	Starts	1st	2d	3d	Win %	Earnings
		Tammy White	6	2	2	0	33	3,115
		Jaqueline Smith	3	2	1	0	67	2,650
		Don D. Young	5	2	0	1	40	2,410
		Bill Hof	4	2	0	1	50	2,350
		R. Scott Raley	2	1	1	0	50	1,400
CBY	5/16 – 9/1	Jockey	Starts	1st	2d	3d	Win %	Earnings
		Derek C. Bell	324	77	49	38	24	891,747
		Martin Escobar	376	62	60	45	16	659,313
		Seth B. Martinez	273	48	36	37	18	651,621
		Paul M. Nolan	292	44	34	37	15	462,565
		Bobby J. Walker, Jr.	235	40	45	25	17	546,130
CBY	5/16 – 9/1	Trainer	Starts	1st	2d	3d	Win %	Earnings
		David Van Winkle	175	35	22	27	20	383,166
		Bernell B. Rhone	169	34	22	19	20	384,951
		Michael E. Biehler	151	27	17	20	18	423,380
		Jamie Ness	140	26	14	26	19	215,923
		Hugh H. Robertson	80	22	16	15	28	280,647

CD	10/26 – 11/29	Jockey	Starts	1st	2d	3d	Win %	Earnings
		Pat Day	123	41	27	9	33	1,426,891
		Calvin H. Borel	175	28	19	20	16	1,181,573
		Cornelio H. Velasquez	191	26	31	26	14	1,136,997
		John McKee	201	25	22	32	12	1,071,170
		Rafael Bejarano	194	21	23	21	11	752,675
CD	10/26 – 11/29	Trainer	Starts	1st	2d	3d	Win %	Earnings
		Dale L. Romans	78	20	11	9	26	591,521
		Dallas Stewart	35	9	4	3	26	250,936
		Paul J. McGee	46	8	6	5	17	253,035
		Carl A. Nafzger	48	7	12	6	15	686,462
		Thomas M. Amoss	25	7	5	2	28	260,750
CD	4/26 – 7/6	Jockey	Starts	1st	2d	3d	Win %	Earnings
		Cornelio H. Velasquez	340	63	57	48	19	2,262,086
		Pat Day	224	51	39	28	23	2,594,611
		John McKee	291	42	43	46	14	1,326,335
		Robby Albarado	280	35	47	48	13	1,952,874
		Mark Guidry	223	34	26	31	15	1,272,406
CD	4/26 – 7/6	Trainer	Starts	1st	2d	3d	Win %	Earnings
		Dale L. Romans	177	39	32	18	22	1,259,400
		Steven M. Asmussen	99	24	13	13	24	821,644
		Thomas M. Amoss	87	20	20	11	23	639,635
		Bernard S. Flint	112	14	15	7	13	429,945
		D. Wayne Lukas	82	13	10	13	16	584,921
CLS	7/24 – 9/14	Jockey	Starts	1st	2d	3d	Win %	Earnings
		Armando Martinez	207	41	31	25	20	155,724
		Luis Ranilla	212	38	37	28	18	154,176
		Dennis Michael Collins	193	37	34	18	19	157,574
		Jerome Carkeek	182	29	26	33	16	126,756
		Yuri Yaranga	200	20	24	30	10	98,080
CLS	7/24 – 9/14	Trainer	Starts	1st	2d	3d	Win %	Earnings
		David C. Anderson	92	17	18	11	18	88,944
		David Grimes	40	10	3	3	25	31,126
		Gene Deroin	41	9	9	5	22	41,730
		Dale Burns	32	9	6	4	28	30,986
		Paul Linafelter	26	9	3	3	35	27,849
CNL	6/13 – 7/22	Jockey	Starts	1st	2d	3d	Win %	Earnings
		Ryan Fogelsonger	167	42	28	30	25	598,876
		Mario G. Pino	194	38	29	28	20	734,238
		Horacio Karamanos	213	31	29	25	15	562,853
		Jozbin Z. Santana	161	25	24	13	16	432,957
		Enrique M. Jurado	119	15	17	16	13	299,322
CNL	6/13 – 7/22	Trainer	Starts	1st	2d	3d	Win %	Earnings
		Hamilton A. Smith	92	17	12	12	18	229,495
		A. Ferris Allen, III	75	11	10	8	15	151,031
		Jonathan E. Sheppard	70	9	9	14	13	188,790
		W. Robert Bailes	44	9	8	5	20	141,186
		Benjamin M. Feliciano, Jr.	24	7	4	2	29	94,490
CPW	6/15 – 6/22	Jockey	Starts	1st	2d	3d	Win %	Earnings
		Herman Fennell	13	7	2	2	54	5,220
		Robert Calva	9	2	1	2	22	2,195
		Chad Warren	9	2	1	1	22	1,730
		Cameron Campbell	5	2	0	1	40	1,280
		Danielle Beischer	15	1	5	3	7	2,490
CPW	6/15 – 6/22	Trainer	Starts	1st	2d	3d	Win %	Earnings
		Steve Keplin	4	3	1	0	75	1,750
		Joe Thorne	5	3	0	0	60	1,600
		Dwaine Tveit	3	2	1	0	67	1,250
		Dean Martin	11	1	3	2	9	2,200
		Kevin Keplin	3	1	1	0	33	1,500
CRC	10/25/03 – 1/2/04	Jockey	Starts	1st	2d	3d	Win %	Earnings
		Eddie Castro	447	83	84	63	19	1,299,627
		Manoel R. Cruz	312	50	39	44	16	871,686
		Eibar Coa	250	48	43	26	19	1,321,134
		Gary Boulanger	205	32	22	28	16	542,532
		Manuel Aguilar	233	28	23	30	12	556,128

			Starts	1st	2d	3d	Win %	Earnings
CRC	10/25/03 – 1/2/04	Trainer						
		Edward Plesa, Jr.	105	21	14	14	20	581,020
		Timothy Ritvo	115	18	14	15	16	234,570
		Angel C. Salinas	98	16	14	12	16	270,980
		Kathleen O'Connell	99	14	12	17	14	190,960
		Emanuel Tortora	82	14	9	11	17	278,137
CRC	4/25 – 10/24	Jockey						
		Manoel R. Cruz	839	174	156	128	21	3,267,803
		Eddie Castro	817	160	177	113	20	2,671,145
		Gary Boulanger	636	108	92	100	17	2,644,587
		Julio A. Garcia	343	75	52	49	22	1,997,898
		Manuel Aguilar	604	70	108	73	12	1,811,694
CRC	4/25 – 10/24	Trainer						
		William P. White	225	52	25	31	23	1,129,618
		Edward Plesa, Jr.	228	40	35	38	18	906,692
		Henry Collazo	241	38	28	35	16	666,607
		Emanuel Tortora	243	35	37	33	14	940,698
		Angel C. Salinas	206	34	34	23	17	584,588
CT	10/1 – 12/31	Jockey						
		Oscar Flores	354	68	58	34	19	1,090,038
		Anthony Mawing	392	64	52	52	16	1,341,901
		Mark E. Rosenthal	221	46	30	18	21	787,989
		J. D. Acosta	272	40	35	33	15	705,140
		Travis L. Dunkelberger	124	33	20	15	27	509,178
CT	10/1 – 12/31	Trainer						
		Jeff C. Runco	136	31	27	15	23	456,010
		Ronney W. Brown	152	29	11	20	19	324,119
		Mark Shuman	93	21	14	7	23	381,139
		David Walters	64	14	5	4	22	250,101
		Bruce M. Kravets	63	11	7	7	17	143,780
CT	7/1 – 9/30	Jockey						
		Anthony Mawing	404	62	43	41	15	887,272
		Travis L. Dunkelberger	217	48	44	24	22	697,188
		Luis Garcia	263	46	33	37	17	586,435
		Oscar Flores	292	45	48	41	15	643,845
		Juan Ortega	310	35	30	36	11	500,393
CT	7/1 – 9/30	Trainer						
		Ronney W. Brown	203	40	24	30	20	360,268
		Jeff C. Runco	164	29	27	29	18	410,206
		Bruce M. Kravets	98	16	12	6	16	182,109
		Ernest M. Haynes	58	14	6	11	24	191,783
		Henry E. Worcester, III	52	12	11	5	23	114,531
CT	4/1 – 6/30	Jockey						
		Travis L. Dunkelberger	241	46	51	37	19	595,812
		Anthony Mawing	328	46	38	48	14	579,237
		Oscar Flores	209	45	22	26	22	419,300
		Luis Garcia	289	36	44	27	12	419,963
		Juan Ortega	282	29	26	41	10	368,543
CT	4/1 – 6/30	Trainer						
		Ronney W. Brown	221	35	35	25	16	357,060
		Jeff C. Runco	163	35	26	16	21	349,383
		Bruce M. Kravets	93	14	12	15	15	170,577
		John D. McKee	95	10	15	8	11	150,399
		Henry E. Worcester, III	63	10	11	12	16	122,241
CT	1/1 – 3/31	Jockey						
		Mathew Carroll McGowan	292	37	30	41	13	409,685
		Travis L. Dunkelberger	184	33	31	19	18	395,892
		Anthony Mawing	236	31	27	40	13	388,122
		Paul Albert Nicol, Jr.	226	31	27	22	14	433,730
		Charles W. Forrest	136	24	26	12	18	255,157
CT	1/1 – 3/31	Trainer						
		Ronney W. Brown	174	35	22	18	20	316,611
		Jeff C. Runco	140	18	28	26	13	254,571
		Bruce M. Kravets	85	15	12	14	18	168,027
		Dale Capuano	35	14	4	0	40	147,711
		Raimondo Schiano-Dicola	44	10	10	2	23	115,571

DED	11/7/02 – 3/23/03	Jockey	Starts	1st	2d	3d	Win %	Earnings
		Steve J. Bourque	534	116	92	71	22	1,836,007
		Carl James Woodley	505	107	79	66	21	1,606,717
		Guy Smith	547	99	78	69	18	1,616,853
		Jerri Elizabeth Nichols	365	57	53	38	16	721,572
		Kerwin D. Clark	429	53	60	51	12	1,026,493

DED	11/7/02 – 3/23/03	Trainer	Starts	1st	2d	3d	Win %	Earnings
		Doris Hebert	241	55	50	38	23	793,679
		Keith L. Bourgeois	270	55	36	42	20	946,365
		Chad Hassenpflug	130	28	21	20	22	385,970
		Dale Angelle	111	25	21	9	23	482,475
		Samuel Breaux	106	24	22	11	23	396,475

DEL	4/26 – 11/9	Jockey	Starts	1st	2d	3d	Win %	Earnings
		Ramon A. Dominguez	836	254	179	120	30	5,847,699
		Roberto Alvarado, Jr.	690	153	125	102	22	3,396,203
		Anthony S. Black	519	96	100	79	18	2,929,379
		Jose C. Caraballo	547	83	68	84	15	1,919,531
		Rodrigo Madrigal, Jr.	544	81	65	75	15	1,859,752

DEL	4/26 – 11/9	Trainer	Starts	1st	2d	3d	Win %	Earnings
		Scott A. Lake	440	112	86	64	25	2,169,844
		Michael V. Pino	270	99	54	37	37	1,526,280
		Allen Iwinski	226	76	56	33	34	1,937,168
		Timothy F. Ritchey	288	56	45	54	19	1,445,890
		Steve B. Klesaris	141	44	22	20	31	1,299,028

DG	4/12 – 4/20	Jockey	Starts	1st	2d	3d	Win %	Earnings
		Fernando Manuel Gamez	18	8	4	1	44	9,312
		Stephen Michael Karr	18	5	3	2	28	6,649
		Todd J. Nuttall	11	2	2	1	18	3,154
		Ronald Beverly	17	1	4	6	6	3,557
		Anna M. Barrio	16	1	1	2	6	2,174

DG	4/12 – 4/20	Trainer	Starts	1st	2d	3d	Win %	Earnings
		Gene K. Wilson	8	3	4	0	38	3,962
		B. Odell Reidhead	6	3	0	0	50	3,088
		Ricardo Saldana	2	2	0	0	100	1,854
		Lowell N. Bunyard	6	1	1	0	17	1,863
		Jerry Cox	3	1	1	0	33	1,347

DMR	7/23 – 9/10	Jockey	Starts	1st	2d	3d	Win %	Earnings
		Patrick A. Valenzuela	294	52	46	46	18	2,673,879
		Julie A. Krone	253	49	28	33	19	2,985,025
		Alex O. Solis	212	34	31	32	16	2,288,232
		Victor Espinoza	224	34	30	37	15	1,666,734
		Mike E. Smith	176	32	22	14	18	1,544,361

DMR	7/23 – 9/10	Trainer	Starts	1st	2d	3d	Win %	Earnings
		Bob Baffert	121	23	18	15	19	1,086,834
		Jeff Mullins	53	15	8	5	28	560,205
		Doug O'Neill	108	13	16	12	12	741,320
		John W. Sadler	62	13	9	10	21	644,619
		Richard E. Mandella	51	12	2	6	24	1,016,612

DUN	3/15 – 3/23	Jockey	Starts	1st	2d	3d	Win %	Earnings
		Fernando Manuel Gamez	17	5	2	2	29	5,862
		Terry Lee Gard	20	4	4	3	20	6,087
		Todd J. Nuttall	18	3	5	2	17	5,398
		Shannon Wippert	10	3	1	2	30	3,403
		Ronald Beverly	15	3	0	3	20	6,402

DUN	3/15 – 3/23	Trainer	Starts	1st	2d	3d	Win %	Earnings
		Lowell N. Bunyard	8	4	1	2	50	4,305
		Gene K. Wilson	11	2	4	0	18	3,518
		Dale E. Wales	3	2	1	0	67	2,341
		Michael Megariz, Jr.	2	2	0	0	100	4,676
		Wiley Aker	10	1	4	1	10	3,272

ELK	8/23 – 9/1	Jockey	Starts	1st	2d	3d	Win %	Earnings
		Nathan R. Condie	19	7	3	5	37	13,075
		Antonio Perez	16	6	2	1	38	8,471
		Matt Williams	16	2	3	3	13	8,735
		Casey Greene	10	2	3	2	20	4,402
		Todd Thomas	6	2	1	0	33	6,455

			Starts	1st	2d	3d	Win %	Earnings
ELK	8/23 – 9/1	Trainer						
		Blake L. Cragun	6	4	2	0	67	5,535
		Zane G. Alder	7	3	2	1	43	4,190
		Mike Scudder	5	2	2	0	40	2,915
		Tawnja Elison	2	2	0	0	100	2,160
		Glade W. Van Tassell	4	2	0	0	50	2,130
ELP	7/9 – 9/1	Jockey						
		Rafael Bejarano	346	80	52	45	23	1,245,935
		Jon Kenton Court	264	47	46	28	18	795,910
		John McKee	236	32	26	51	14	686,815
		Dean P. Butler	232	26	13	30	11	394,696
		Willie Martinez	164	23	26	18	14	462,940
ELP	7/9 – 9/1	Trainer						
		Kim Hammond	43	15	7	7	35	101,215
		Thomas M. Amoss	28	13	4	3	46	210,610
		Merrill R. Scherer	33	12	7	4	36	170,140
		S. Joseph Cain	37	11	4	4	30	113,935
		Bobby C. Barnett	52	10	5	5	19	152,090
EMD	4/19 – 9/22	Jockey						
		Kevin Radke	652	143	101	96	22	1,155,289
		Scott T. Saito	572	90	82	94	16	793,534
		Juan M. Gutierrez	539	87	79	81	16	813,779
		Gary Baze	492	85	78	72	17	928,847
		Gallyn Vick Mitchell	488	70	98	81	14	807,567
EMD	4/19 – 9/22	Trainer						
		Tim McCanna	262	55	45	41	21	465,418
		Frank Lucarelli	243	39	39	36	16	382,433
		Terry Gillihan	154	37	28	15	24	307,947
		Sharon Ross	233	36	40	30	15	360,180
		Howard Belvoir	225	33	40	32	15	292,159
EUR	5/3 – 7/5	Jockey						
		Stoney D. Whittle	40	13	4	4	33	21,475
		Richard M. Vasquez	37	11	9	9	30	37,717
		Dustin W. Williams	48	7	9	9	15	21,461
		Jeremy Latham	26	4	7	3	15	9,797
		Megan Ludlow	8	4	1	1	50	5,635
EUR	5/3 – 7/5	Trainer						
		Joe Frederick Thomas, Sr.	40	12	8	8	30	38,652
		Jose Ibarra	17	6	3	1	35	8,810
		William E. Clay, Sr.	16	4	3	3	25	7,656
		Donald G. Black	15	4	2	2	27	8,802
		John W. Layton	11	4	2	1	36	7,732
EVD	4/4 – 9/1	Jockey						
		Carl James Woodley	504	98	71	89	19	680,325
		Rex A. Stokes, III	446	84	61	46	19	492,707
		Josh M. Romero	509	56	72	63	11	406,927
		Brian Joseph Hernandez	364	55	52	39	15	407,867
		Guy Smith	261	54	36	34	21	425,715
EVD	4/4 – 9/1	Trainer						
		Keith L. Bourgeois	282	65	53	46	23	492,856
		Dale Angelle	166	45	34	21	27	316,692
		Samuel Breaux	133	31	14	18	23	223,556
		Donald J. Cormier, Sr.	298	29	36	39	10	243,321
		Francis Melancon, Jr.	168	21	22	21	13	133,907
FAR	8/22 – 9/14	Jockey						
		Scot A. Schindler	46	18	11	7	39	60,994
		Beth S. Butler	62	17	13	15	27	57,441
		Megan Ludlow	50	7	6	11	14	29,241
		Orlando O'Farrill	34	5	5	3	15	13,807
		Anne Von Rosen	26	5	5	0	19	37,433
FAR	8/22 – 9/14	Trainer						
		John Ness	40	15	6	5	38	39,751
		Jeff Schindler	17	4	2	3	24	11,723
		Kelly Kaelberer	16	4	1	3	25	10,857
		Peter Davis	10	3	3	3	30	10,455
		Clayton Nagel	6	3	1	1	50	7,670

			Starts	1st	2d	3d	Win %	Earnings
FE	4/26 – 11/11	Jockey						
		Martin Ramos Ramirez	652	122	98	73	19	2,183,235
		Francine Villeneuve	509	88	64	70	17	1,632,453
		Neil Poznansky	515	83	61	70	16	1,517,989
		Christopher Griffith	586	77	89	94	13	1,601,778
		Jake Barton	445	75	84	54	17	1,645,458
FE	4/26 – 11/11	Trainer						
		Layne S. Giliforte	338	56	65	46	17	1,138,329
		Thomas M. Agosti	211	50	32	29	24	894,141
		Chris Tuttle	322	39	48	36	12	716,630
		John Simms	183	34	20	29	19	549,531
		Nicholas Gonzalez	176	33	15	22	19	497,851
FER	8/7 – 8/17	Jockey						
		Daniel Raymond Boag	23	8	6	4	35	28,305
		Ramon Guce	22	8	5	6	36	26,997
		Richard A. Sanchez	29	6	6	2	21	25,035
		Robert Boyce	19	3	3	6	16	18,515
		Elliott Demesme	10	2	1	1	20	9,437
FER	8/7 – 8/17	Trainer						
		Wesley A. Ward	13	5	4	3	38	16,502
		Dennis Hopkins	16	4	6	2	25	21,985
		Scott Tetreault	6	3	1	1	50	6,841
		Santiago C. Rodriguez	6	3	1	0	50	9,701
		F. A. Lowery	7	2	1	0	29	5,795
FG	11/28/02 – 3/31/03	Jockey						
		Robby Albarado	502	102	109	83	20	2,970,129
		Corey J. Lanerie	557	92	97	87	17	2,007,666
		Shane J. Sellers	421	88	71	55	21	2,214,320
		Gerard Melancon	513	86	61	68	17	1,762,727
		Eddie M. Martin, Jr.	523	72	82	74	14	1,570,824
FG	11/28/02 – 3/31/03	Trainer						
		Steven M. Asmussen	245	63	42	42	26	1,615,182
		Thomas M. Amoss	182	50	38	28	27	1,026,994
		W. Bret Calhoun	105	24	19	15	23	487,758
		Albert M. Stall, Jr.	127	24	18	20	19	543,522
		Larry Robideaux, Jr.	79	17	16	12	22	531,253
FL	4/18 – 11/29	Jockey						
		John R. Davila, Jr.	703	138	111	88	20	1,140,757
		John A. Grabowski	553	128	88	85	23	1,037,942
		Chin C. Yang	692	91	100	101	13	904,605
		Robert Messina	466	85	67	63	18	704,040
		David M. Rivera	667	82	89	83	12	642,754
FL	4/18 – 11/29	Trainer						
		Chris J. Englehart	424	95	74	61	22	656,526
		Michael Anthony Ferraro	305	85	55	43	28	630,907
		Michael A. Lecesse	350	72	62	54	21	572,001
		Michael S. Ferraro	297	72	47	30	24	496,049
		Charlton Baker	250	72	42	32	29	607,035
FLG	7/4 – 7/7	Jockey						
		Stephen Michael Karr	16	4	1	1	25	13,620
		Fernando Manuel Gamez	18	3	3	2	17	12,046
		Ronald Beverly	15	3	2	3	20	11,246
		Joseph L. Durigon	15	2	1	1	13	7,858
		Charles Lyn McClellan	14	2	0	0	14	6,345
FLG	7/4 – 7/7	Trainer						
		George Wern	3	2	0	1	67	5,254
		Lynda R. Tanner	5	1	2	2	20	5,006
		Wiley Aker	5	1	1	1	20	3,991
		Lyndel G. Rutherford	4	1	1	0	25	3,537
		Sandra Ehret	2	1	1	0	50	3,093
FMT	4/10 – 6/7	Jockey						
		Larry D. Payne	45	17	7	10	38	118,982
		Randy R. Wilson	79	12	16	12	15	89,480
		G. R. Carter, Jr.	47	12	11	4	26	89,709
		Curtis Kimes	37	8	9	9	22	54,856
		Leroy Allen Sommers, Jr.	51	6	5	5	12	37,351

FMT	4/10 - 6/7	Trainer	Starts	1st	2d	3d	Win %	Earnings
		Mike R. Teel	28	9	6	5	32	52,785
		Shane Castor	23	7	2	4	30	36,355
		Greg Frye	8	6	1	1	75	25,620
		Tara Wilson	5	4	1	0	80	23,015
		Randy Bass	15	3	3	0	20	17,600
FNO	10/1 - 10/13	Jockey	Starts	1st	2d	3d	Win %	Earnings
		Macario Rodriguez	49	13	9	9	27	89,404
		Victor Miranda	40	10	4	6	25	60,732
		Ken S. Tohill	30	9	4	5	30	53,107
		Ryan Morris	40	4	6	7	10	40,736
		Modesto Linares	21	4	3	2	19	26,799
FNO	10/1 - 10/13	Trainer	Starts	1st	2d	3d	Win %	Earnings
		Rene Amescua	30	10	4	2	33	55,501
		Michael Lenzini	33	7	2	4	21	46,218
		Dennis Hopkins	50	5	10	6	10	52,120
		William Anton	25	4	6	4	16	37,822
		Wesley A. Ward	12	4	3	1	33	24,012
FON	2/8 - 5/4	Jockey	Starts	1st	2d	3d	Win %	Earnings
		Perry Compton	273	91	52	34	33	395,471
		Jerome Carkeek	281	41	34	45	15	212,170
		Armando Martinez	270	30	25	26	11	136,804
		Kelly Michael Murray	164	20	22	16	12	111,450
		Perry S. Whetstone	207	18	27	30	9	104,481
FON	2/8 - 5/4	Trainer	Starts	1st	2d	3d	Win %	Earnings
		David C. Anderson	180	55	32	23	31	303,183
		James R. Compton	62	16	13	10	26	64,317
		Milton M. Gaede	52	13	10	5	25	46,324
		Brian M. Roberts	70	12	13	8	17	61,959
		Steve L. Hall	43	11	5	6	26	53,081
FP	4/4 - 10/11	Jockey	Starts	1st	2d	3d	Win %	Earnings
		Joel Santiago	631	101	95	70	16	636,308
		Ramsey Zimmerman	403	79	70	54	20	498,071
		Cynthia M. Medina	312	65	56	52	21	459,489
		Vicente Flores	631	64	71	63	10	411,601
		Danush Sukie	332	61	50	51	18	382,475
FP	4/4 - 10/11	Trainer	Starts	1st	2d	3d	Win %	Earnings
		Ralph Martinez	522	140	103	81	27	851,445
		Eddie M. Essenpreis	318	62	55	54	19	443,962
		Leroy Hellman	256	54	44	37	21	346,610
		Steve Manley	212	39	30	31	18	292,813
		Alan Crocker	176	39	24	22	22	169,575
FPX	9/12 - 9/28	Jockey	Starts	1st	2d	3d	Win %	Earnings
		Martin A. Pedroza	116	31	23	16	27	588,057
		Ryan Fogelsonger	93	22	16	20	24	529,699
		Tyler Baze	104	17	15	20	16	453,375
		Felipe F. Martinez	88	12	15	9	14	317,784
		Omar A. Berrio	66	12	10	9	18	247,826
FPX	9/12 - 9/28	Trainer	Starts	1st	2d	3d	Win %	Earnings
		Doug O'Neill	45	10	5	11	22	251,346
		Wesley A. Ward	21	10	4	1	48	112,050
		Jeff Mullins	25	8	6	3	32	243,030
		Don J. Mills	19	6	5	2	32	68,560
		Jack Carava	20	6	4	3	30	128,570
GCF	9/27 - 10/5	Jockey	Starts	1st	2d	3d	Win %	Earnings
		Stephen Michael Karr	19	5	3	3	26	6,344
		Fernando Manuel Gamez	18	4	1	2	22	4,863
		Anna M. Barrio	18	3	3	3	17	4,397
		Terry Lee Gard	18	2	4	3	11	4,149
		Charles Lyn McClellan	19	2	2	3	11	3,602
GCF	9/27 - 10/5	Trainer	Starts	1st	2d	3d	Win %	Earnings
		Laurie Jones	9	3	0	1	33	3,071
		Gene K. Wilson	6	2	0	2	33	2,358
		Lowell N. Bunyard	3	2	0	1	67	2,013
		Lyndel G. Rutherford	10	1	2	3	10	2,306
		Richard Ramirez	9	1	1	3	11	1,971

GF	7/4 – 7/27	Jockey	Starts	1st	2d	3d	Win %	Earnings
		Carl Hebert	37	12	4	5	32	20,346
		Ivan Ortiz, Jr.	32	9	4	4	28	13,866
		David P. Stubblefield	38	8	7	7	21	17,014
		Russell David Kingrey	28	5	3	3	18	11,091
		Shaunda L. Larsen	27	4	5	4	15	8,525
GF	7/4 – 7/27	Trainer	Starts	1st	2d	3d	Win %	Earnings
		Bryan Krone	21	8	4	3	38	12,427
		Mel Berkram	18	8	3	5	44	12,175
		Dale Bagnell	15	3	2	0	20	8,728
		Mark Buckley	13	2	4	2	15	4,865
		Doug Johnson	12	2	2	2	17	3,871
GG	12/26/02 – 3/30/03	Jockey	Starts	1st	2d	3d	Win %	Earnings
		Russell A. Baze	388	116	82	69	30	2,134,406
		Ronald J. Warren, Jr.	291	58	40	43	20	1,203,783
		Chad Phillip Schvaneveldt	249	56	46	41	22	1,073,811
		Francisco Duran	346	42	46	48	12	819,034
		Roberto M. Gonzalez	174	36	28	17	21	763,379
GG	12/26/02 – 3/30/03	Trainer	Starts	1st	2d	3d	Win %	Earnings
		Jerry Hollendorfer	296	72	47	60	24	1,662,600
		William E. Morey	103	33	10	17	32	412,515
		Armando Lage	196	31	29	27	16	529,825
		Art Sherman	118	27	22	17	23	494,400
		Dean Pederson	42	17	4	5	40	144,243
GIL	7/4 – 8/24	Jockey	Starts	1st	2d	3d	Win %	Earnings
		Santos Carrizales	16	3	2	2	19	19,032
		Wayne Womack	5	3	0	1	60	6,848
		Melody Brooks	10	2	0	1	20	4,920
		George Luis Cruz	3	2	0	0	67	4,560
		Salvador Perez	7	2	0	0	29	3,998
GIL	7/4 – 8/24	Trainer	Starts	1st	2d	3d	Win %	Earnings
		M. Shawn Finch	10	3	0	1	30	17,084
		Jimmy L. Ray	5	2	0	1	40	4,890
		Enrique Chavez	3	2	0	1	67	4,180
		Joel Perez	6	1	2	1	17	5,790
		Harry L. Brasher	4	1	1	0	25	3,038
GLD	4/26 – 10/28	Jockey	Starts	1st	2d	3d	Win %	Earnings
		Federico Mata	901	160	135	124	18	1,257,574
		Joseph C. Judice	619	151	107	93	24	1,331,643
		Mary Elizabeth Doser	714	114	124	101	16	1,025,032
		Luis Jeronimo Martinez	412	77	61	75	19	732,085
		Colin Skinner	642	75	70	75	12	605,786
GLD	4/26 – 10/28	Trainer	Starts	1st	2d	3d	Win %	Earnings
		Gerald S. Bennett	399	82	70	43	21	986,911
		Randall R. Russell	378	62	46	47	16	433,801
		Robert M. Gorham	275	60	46	47	22	783,400
		Barbara I. McBride	191	49	31	20	26	276,781
		Richard R. Rettele	303	39	56	38	13	371,825
GP	1/3 – 4/24	Jockey	Starts	1st	2d	3d	Win %	Earnings
		Eibar Coa	501	91	77	65	18	3,139,002
		Cornelio H. Velasquez	506	79	84	74	16	2,458,797
		John R. Velazquez	315	68	42	38	22	2,475,950
		Mark Guidry	382	66	44	45	17	1,806,830
		Jose A. Santos	391	63	59	48	16	2,172,253
GP	1/3 – 4/24	Trainer	Starts	1st	2d	3d	Win %	Earnings
		Mark Shuman	344	87	58	43	25	1,847,310
		William I. Mott	148	31	27	17	21	1,028,100
		Todd A. Pletcher	118	30	19	10	25	1,561,650
		Allen Iwinski	127	22	22	15	17	460,450
		Daniel C. Hurtak	94	20	15	10	21	235,510
GPR	7/11 – 8/17	Jockey	Starts	1st	2d	3d	Win %	Earnings
		Peter McAleney	52	20	9	12	38	52,125
		Terri Landaker	44	12	12	3	27	32,387
		Scott Sterr	53	11	13	11	21	34,115
		Janine Stianson	39	4	9	2	10	17,156
		Brooke Mellish	49	3	4	16	6	15,039

GPR	7/11 – 8/17	Trainer	Starts	1st	2d	3d	Win %	Earnings
		Jim Meyaard	33	13	8	6	39	36,617
		Stan Marks	24	6	4	6	25	15,971
		Tom Rycroft	34	5	4	11	15	15,140
		Brandt Laczo	18	5	1	3	28	15,603
		Kathy McNally	19	4	3	6	21	11,633

GRP	5/17 – 7/6	Jockey	Starts	1st	2d	3d	Win %	Earnings
		Twyla Beckner	88	26	24	14	30	49,080
		Joe A. Crispin	94	17	24	23	18	38,359
		Monica Barber	40	11	7	6	28	19,230
		Victor V. Mercado	46	11	6	10	24	19,469
		Melissa Peery	46	11	6	4	24	19,696

GRP	5/17 – 7/6	Trainer	Starts	1st	2d	3d	Win %	Earnings
		Robert Beckner	42	10	9	3	24	17,543
		Jim Keen	34	8	8	11	24	18,979
		Gerald E. Robinson	33	6	4	3	18	11,078
		Vannessa Hunt	18	6	4	2	33	10,343
		Sharon Balcom	21	5	3	2	24	9,490

HAW	9/28/03 – 1/3/04	Jockey	Starts	1st	2d	3d	Win %	Earnings
		Randall A. Meier	364	56	40	44	15	1,096,828
		Eusebio Razo, Jr.	338	51	50	49	15	1,311,118
		Christopher A. Emigh	377	43	56	46	11	1,052,342
		Jesse M. Campbell	366	40	50	42	11	815,543
		Larry J. Sterling, Jr.	228	37	31	38	16	863,775

HAW	9/28/03 – 1/3/04	Trainer	Starts	1st	2d	3d	Win %	Earnings
		Michael L. Reavis	152	31	21	25	20	448,328
		Pat Cuccurullo	79	23	15	8	29	244,639
		Wayne M. Catalano	92	22	18	10	24	441,710
		Thomas F. Tomillo	196	19	13	21	10	317,938
		Charles J. Vinci	103	18	13	8	17	288,725

HAW	3/1 – 5/6	Jockey	Starts	1st	2d	3d	Win %	Earnings
		Larry J. Sterling, Jr.	223	56	34	38	25	1,006,870
		Christopher A. Emigh	276	44	39	43	16	929,634
		E. T. Baird	234	41	38	31	18	793,144
		Curt C. Bourque	196	38	19	17	19	594,685
		Zoe Cadman	183	27	27	24	15	529,279

HAW	3/1 – 5/6	Trainer	Starts	1st	2d	3d	Win %	Earnings
		Michael L. Reavis	141	45	23	19	32	654,710
		Thomas F. Tomillo	136	30	13	17	22	362,546
		Frank John Kirby	137	19	19	27	14	430,990
		Wayne M. Catalano	45	15	3	6	33	353,511
		Richard P. Hazelton	77	14	11	12	18	429,488

HOL	11/11 – 12/21	Jockey	Starts	1st	2d	3d	Win %	Earnings
		Patrick A. Valenzuela	143	27	21	26	19	1,178,196
		Victor Espinoza	116	24	20	15	21	746,782
		Tyler Baze	173	23	28	24	13	920,143
		Julie A. Krone	102	23	15	8	23	1,356,893
		Mike E. Smith	99	22	17	5	22	988,094

HOL	11/11 – 12/21	Trainer	Starts	1st	2d	3d	Win %	Earnings
		Jeff Mullins	38	13	5	7	34	510,360
		Doug O'Neill	95	12	19	15	13	434,095
		Robert J. Frankel	42	12	5	10	29	993,022
		Bob Baffert	62	11	13	5	18	507,454
		Craig Dollase	19	8	2	1	42	230,260

HOL	4/23 – 7/20	Jockey	Starts	1st	2d	3d	Win %	Earnings
		Patrick A. Valenzuela	357	81	54	64	23	3,502,657
		Victor Espinoza	377	69	62	64	18	3,199,393
		Alex O. Solis	256	48	39	43	19	2,700,343
		Tyler Baze	325	43	46	47	13	1,911,235
		David Romero Flores	220	41	33	28	19	2,365,212

HOL	4/23 – 7/20	Trainer	Starts	1st	2d	3d	Win %	Earnings
		Doug O'Neill	212	37	36	25	17	1,664,452
		Bob Baffert	121	20	20	18	17	1,837,668
		Mike R. Mitchell	63	20	11	12	32	554,540
		John W. Sadler	90	18	12	17	20	676,188
		William Spawr	65	17	9	6	26	393,412

HOO	8/29 – 12/4	Jockey	Starts	1st	2d	3d	Win %	Earnings
		Orlando Mojica	567	100	82	73	18	928,736
		Rodney A. Prescott	549	78	72	57	14	719,835
		Lester Cash Knight	566	74	83	76	13	722,808
		Thomas L. Pompell	465	74	55	55	16	671,444
		Robert Dean Williams	366	48	47	42	13	416,537

HOO	8/29 – 12/4	Trainer	Starts	1st	2d	3d	Win %	Earnings
		Ralph Martinez	164	66	30	25	40	402,938
		Kim Hammond	132	23	25	13	17	174,307
		R. Gary Patrick	254	23	22	29	9	218,303
		Marvin A. Johnson	113	18	19	15	16	135,465
		Steve Manley	93	16	17	11	17	115,747

HOU	11/1/02 – 3/30/03	Jockey	Starts	1st	2d	3d	Win %	Earnings
		Donald Edward Simington	474	75	71	72	16	756,102
		Terry A. Stanton	424	75	63	58	18	798,844
		Roman Chapa	357	67	61	38	19	728,582
		John Jacinto	478	49	73	56	10	788,789
		Monte Clifton Berry	261	43	40	34	16	446,798

HOU	11/1/02 – 3/30/03	Trainer	Starts	1st	2d	3d	Win %	Earnings
		Steven M. Asmussen	205	57	45	28	28	818,716
		Danny Pish	239	48	29	25	20	528,402
		W. Bret Calhoun	141	34	28	16	24	346,512
		Tommie T. Morgan	152	29	24	15	19	417,053
		Andrew Konkoly	139	27	19	19	19	241,220

HPO	7/10 – 7/13	Jockey	Starts	1st	2d	3d	Win %	Earnings
		Ken A. Shino	12	3	0	3	25	60,443
		Jerome Carkeek	13	2	0	4	15	44,044
		Perry Compton	16	1	4	1	6	48,032
		William Henson	12	1	2	0	8	42,230
		Armando Martinez	14	1	2	0	7	32,840

HPO	7/10 – 7/13	Trainer	Starts	1st	2d	3d	Win %	Earnings
		David C. Anderson	15	2	1	3	13	48,923
		Brian M. Roberts	4	2	1	0	50	32,000
		Hugh H. Robertson	2	2	0	0	100	34,080
		Boyd Caster	5	1	2	0	20	38,375
		Herb Riecken	9	1	1	1	11	29,184

HST	4/26 – 11/30	Jockey	Starts	1st	2d	3d	Win %	Earnings
		Pedro V. Alvarado	551	124	104	78	23	1,951,115
		Nicola Wright	511	102	85	63	20	1,524,963
		Felipe Valdez	393	61	63	66	16	1,309,083
		Francisco Perez Fuentes	432	59	58	61	14	993,235
		Chris Loseth	448	59	56	60	13	945,024

HST	4/26 – 11/30	Trainer	Starts	1st	2d	3d	Win %	Earnings
		Dino K. Condilenios	197	38	32	27	19	670,224
		Harold J. Barroby	276	29	47	43	11	602,569
		Robert Van Overschot	179	29	26	31	16	598,468
		Terry Clyde	140	26	24	20	19	337,444
		Gary E. Demorest	88	26	19	11	30	313,919

IND	4/11 – 5/26	Jockey	Starts	1st	2d	3d	Win %	Earnings
		Orlando Mojica	208	38	31	23	18	392,833
		Sidney P. LeJeune, Jr.	208	38	30	36	18	410,264
		Rodney A. Prescott	228	27	29	34	12	353,366
		Michael R. Morgan	181	27	27	24	15	330,189
		Luis J. Martinez, Jr.	158	19	22	18	12	224,613

IND	4/11 – 5/26	Trainer	Starts	1st	2d	3d	Win %	Earnings
		R. Gary Patrick	160	25	21	19	16	236,009
		Kim Hammond	53	14	9	9	26	92,218
		Ron Powell	55	11	9	8	20	72,152
		Joseph R. Martin	35	9	4	4	26	63,385
		S. Joseph Cain	28	7	6	3	25	100,866

KAM	8/10 – 9/7	Jockey	Starts	1st	2d	3d	Win %	Earnings
		Ronald Joseph Bilodeau	12	8	3	1	67	14,609
		Laurina Bugeaud	17	5	7	4	29	17,287
		Lee James	7	2	0	3	29	4,180
		Alan Cuthbertson	2	2	0	0	100	3,420
		Caroline Stinn	15	0	3	4	0	4,184

KAM	8/10 – 9/7	Trainer	Starts	1st	2d	3d	Win %	Earnings
		Vicki Anderson	4	2	2	0	50	4,600
		Dave Desautel	3	2	1	0	67	3,027
		Gail Hochsteiner	3	2	1	0	67	2,950
		John Rennie Lumsden	3	2	0	1	67	3,220
		Robert Drummond	4	2	0	0	50	2,520

KAM	5/25 – 6/29	Jockey	Starts	1st	2d	3d	Win %	Earnings
		Laurina Bugeaud	18	5	3	3	28	8,740
		Brooke Mellish	14	3	4	3	21	6,220
		Emma Jane Abbott	9	3	2	2	33	5,044
		Amber Dickinson	9	3	0	1	33	4,090
		Ronald Joseph Bilodeau	12	2	3	1	17	4,146

KAM	5/25 – 6/29	Trainer	Starts	1st	2d	3d	Win %	Earnings
		Vicki Anderson	9	3	1	1	33	4,570
		Irene Miller	3	3	0	0	100	3,720
		Murray Cunard	7	2	1	1	29	3,200
		Gail Hochsteiner	3	2	1	0	67	2,840
		Debra Davis	3	1	2	0	33	2,080

KD	9/13 – 9/23	Jockey	Starts	1st	2d	3d	Win %	Earnings
		Brice Blanc	23	5	1	2	22	136,320
		Rafael Bejarano	26	4	3	8	15	223,431
		Calvin H. Borel	18	4	1	3	22	74,999
		Joe M. Johnson	10	3	3	0	30	68,726
		James Graham	20	2	4	0	10	49,221

KD	9/13 – 9/23	Trainer	Starts	1st	2d	3d	Win %	Earnings
		Kenneth G. McPeek	11	4	0	2	36	138,170
		Jeffrey D. Thornbury	6	2	2	0	33	45,400
		Merrill R. Scherer	12	2	1	0	17	33,791
		Darrin Miller	3	2	0	0	67	78,940
		Thomas F. Proctor	4	2	0	0	50	32,400

KEE	10/3 – 10/25	Jockey	Starts	1st	2d	3d	Win %	Earnings
		Pat Day	87	21	22	8	24	1,098,476
		Robby Albarado	102	15	17	14	15	893,743
		Cornelio H. Velasquez	93	15	10	10	16	938,891
		John McKee	101	11	10	14	11	425,692
		Rafael Bejarano	108	9	17	11	8	349,280

KEE	10/3 – 10/25	Trainer	Starts	1st	2d	3d	Win %	Earnings
		Nicholas P. Zito	31	11	6	3	35	767,241
		Steven M. Asmussen	50	7	7	8	14	315,277
		W. Elliott Walden	22	7	5	2	32	410,820
		Kenneth G. McPeek	33	4	5	4	12	621,353
		D. Wayne Lukas	34	4	3	3	12	398,888

KEE	4/4 – 4/25	Jockey	Starts	1st	2d	3d	Win %	Earnings
		Robby Albarado	95	17	16	12	18	1,309,581
		Pat Day	85	15	21	10	18	1,100,147
		Cornelio H. Velasquez	69	13	6	8	19	535,118
		Jerry D. Bailey	51	12	13	11	24	902,423
		Kent J. Desormeaux	61	9	11	4	15	663,282

KEE	4/4 – 4/25	Trainer	Starts	1st	2d	3d	Win %	Earnings
		D. Wayne Lukas	35	9	5	4	26	597,069
		Thomas M. Amoss	13	6	2	2	46	299,614
		Steven M. Asmussen	19	6	2	1	32	361,694
		Kenneth G. McPeek	20	6	0	3	30	262,611
		Dallas Stewart	23	5	3	5	22	224,212

KIN	7/6 – 8/3	Jockey	Starts	1st	2d	3d	Win %	Earnings
		Ronald Joseph Bilodeau	17	5	6	3	29	10,521
		Caroline Stinn	16	4	5	6	25	9,655
		David Deforest Brown	4	2	0	1	50	3,000
		Brooke Mellish	4	2	0	0	50	2,717
		Ty Dangerfield	5	1	0	2	20	4,500

KIN	7/6 – 8/3	Trainer	Starts	1st	2d	3d	Win %	Earnings
		Wade Hardie	15	3	4	2	20	6,706
		Rosa Lee Burbank	4	3	1	0	75	6,550
		Nancy Burbank	7	2	3	1	29	4,890
		Jack E. Lindsey	4	1	2	1	25	2,280
		Bob Honeyman	3	1	2	0	33	2,795

KSP	8/15 – 8/24	Jockey	Starts	1st	2d	3d	Win %	Earnings
		Carl Hebert	20	5	4	3	25	9,402
		Joe A. Crispin	18	3	2	3	17	5,181
		Jackie Smith–Hebert	17	3	1	5	18	5,007
		Ronald Joseph Bilodeau	8	3	1	1	38	3,496
		Shannon Wippert	9	2	2	0	22	3,716

KSP	8/15 – 8/24	Trainer	Starts	1st	2d	3d	Win %	Earnings
		Mel Berkram	12	4	2	3	33	7,598
		Keith Davis	7	2	2	0	29	2,817
		Janis D. Schoepf	5	2	1	0	40	3,071
		Wilf McDougall	10	2	0	3	20	2,844
		Mark Buckley	5	2	0	0	40	2,072

LA	12/26/02 – 12/21/03	Jockey	Starts	1st	2d	3d	Win %	Earnings
		Baltazar Contreras	288	78	63	39	27	381,712
		Alex Bautista	156	46	25	32	29	225,243
		Guillermo R. Gutierrez	272	33	44	40	12	215,855
		Gary L. Boag	233	30	31	42	13	189,970
		Juan C. Leyva	181	29	19	30	16	155,478

LA	12/26/02 – 12/21/03	Trainer	Starts	1st	2d	3d	Win %	Earnings
		Charles S. Treece	214	37	27	21	17	201,938
		Jesus Nunez	269	34	34	34	13	202,457
		Daniel G. Luna	42	17	7	4	40	72,823
		Barry Holmes	71	15	12	14	21	74,887
		Erin Lee Anderson	74	13	7	10	18	62,554

LAD	6/27 – 11/9	Jockey	Starts	1st	2d	3d	Win %	Earnings
		Gerard Melancon	517	101	85	64	20	1,538,147
		Kirk Paul LeBlanc	477	98	71	55	21	1,439,776
		Lonnie Meche	391	84	67	53	21	1,280,472
		Jamie Theriot	362	52	50	43	14	833,450
		John Jacinto	478	52	49	49	11	696,183

LAD	6/27 – 11/9	Trainer	Starts	1st	2d	3d	Win %	Earnings
		Cole Norman	383	95	64	47	25	1,358,598
		Steven M. Asmussen	256	67	48	50	26	1,137,242
		Donnie K. Von Hemel	109	21	21	21	19	419,796
		Larry Robideaux, Jr.	119	21	18	18	18	417,166
		Troy Young	114	19	17	14	17	412,940

LBG	8/30 – 11/2	Jockey	Starts	1st	2d	3d	Win %	Earnings
		Terri Landaker	82	25	15	18	30	99,166
		Scott Sterr	107	21	18	19	20	114,942
		Rennie Latchman	46	12	5	9	26	47,960
		Ron Darryl Blinston	30	12	4	5	40	41,375
		Cliff James Miyashiro	82	11	15	5	13	57,227

LBG	8/30 – 11/2	Trainer	Starts	1st	2d	3d	Win %	Earnings
		Stan Marks	35	16	2	4	46	53,423
		Jim Meyaard	50	13	7	3	26	48,243
		Mike Maupin	23	10	4	2	43	27,555
		Robert Gwilliam	36	8	6	5	22	34,668
		Gene Starlin	28	6	6	8	21	40,343

LBG	5/3 – 6/15	Jockey	Starts	1st	2d	3d	Win %	Earnings
		Terri Landaker	57	12	9	7	21	42,022
		Scott Sterr	59	11	11	6	19	48,288
		Terry R. Roncin	32	7	3	5	22	22,537
		Peter McAleney	48	6	9	5	13	29,593
		Carl Hebert	46	5	10	6	11	25,256

LBG	5/3 – 6/15	Trainer	Starts	1st	2d	3d	Win %	Earnings
		Stan Marks	29	8	6	4	28	29,897
		Phil Wiest	16	6	4	2	38	17,886
		Randy Hedegaard	7	5	0	0	71	10,616
		Linda Kropius	20	3	4	6	15	14,668
		Mel Berkram	25	3	3	2	12	12,394

LNN	5/9 – 7/6	Jockey	Starts	1st	2d	3d	Win %	Earnings
		Jerome Carkeek	258	54	39	30	21	247,062
		Armando Martinez	254	47	42	31	19	225,811
		Dennis Michael Collins	233	35	32	29	15	175,321
		Luis Ranilla	228	28	31	35	12	149,064
		Alejandro T. Granda	216	26	29	28	12	132,768

LNN	5/9 – 7/6	Trainer	Starts	1st	2d	3d	Win %	Earnings
		David C. Anderson	133	40	21	16	30	181,648
		Gene Deroin	55	10	12	3	18	42,265
		Herb Riecken	71	8	8	9	11	69,024
		Paul Linafelter	28	8	5	3	29	37,758
		Ricky J. Gustafson	47	7	13	2	15	34,163
LRL	10/8 – 12/31	Jockey	Starts	1st	2d	3d	Win %	Earnings
		Abel Castellano, Jr.	328	64	40	34	20	1,253,245
		Mario G. Pino	259	49	38	37	19	1,125,760
		Erick D. Rodriguez	297	48	44	37	16	828,770
		Ramon A. Dominguez	205	48	31	45	23	1,244,080
		Jozbin Z. Santana	275	43	37	32	16	798,795
LRL	10/8 – 12/31	Trainer	Starts	1st	2d	3d	Win %	Earnings
		Dale Capuano	117	25	20	14	21	391,575
		Mark Shuman	123	23	13	10	19	459,050
		Scott A. Lake	72	17	11	13	24	323,000
		Hamilton A. Smith	96	15	8	16	16	355,510
		Anthony W. Dutrow	55	14	12	8	25	404,090
LRL	7/24 – 8/22	Jockey	Starts	1st	2d	3d	Win %	Earnings
		Ryan Fogelsonger	158	25	30	26	16	548,685
		Rick Wilson	86	23	13	12	27	424,310
		Abel Castellano, Jr.	101	20	23	12	20	368,630
		Horacio Karamanos	108	19	11	24	18	393,145
		Mario G. Pino	92	19	11	15	21	359,785
LRL	7/24 – 8/22	Trainer	Starts	1st	2d	3d	Win %	Earnings
		John J. Robb	32	10	8	2	31	168,545
		Carlos A. Garcia	21	8	1	4	38	117,325
		Nick Canani	26	6	9	2	23	84,940
		Hamilton A. Smith	45	6	8	8	13	131,015
		Rodney Jenkins	27	6	4	1	22	134,330
LRL	1/1 – 3/30	Jockey	Starts	1st	2d	3d	Win %	Earnings
		Ryan Fogelsonger	436	93	86	77	21	1,621,800
		Ramon A. Dominguez	282	74	45	49	26	1,373,555
		Mario G. Pino	223	55	41	30	25	1,012,855
		Clinton L. Potts	235	39	30	32	17	752,060
		Jeremy Rose	233	34	38	22	15	740,390
LRL	1/1 – 3/30	Trainer	Starts	1st	2d	3d	Win %	Earnings
		Scott A. Lake	142	29	21	18	20	641,660
		Dale Capuano	141	28	31	19	20	426,315
		John J. Robb	110	22	11	14	20	399,075
		Anthony W. Dutrow	49	20	10	8	41	373,260
		Howard E. Wolfendale	62	20	8	14	32	290,005
LS	4/3 – 7/13	Jockey	Starts	1st	2d	3d	Win %	Earnings
		Corey J. Lanerie	409	86	79	68	21	1,737,111
		Eddie M. Martin, Jr.	391	85	63	47	22	1,826,163
		Jamie Theriot	333	67	48	39	20	1,330,242
		Gerard Melancon	325	52	49	41	16	1,212,200
		Jeremy Beasley	351	49	34	46	14	885,609
LS	4/3 – 7/13	Trainer	Starts	1st	2d	3d	Win %	Earnings
		Cole Norman	391	98	64	49	25	2,058,162
		Steven M. Asmussen	362	80	67	59	22	1,811,539
		W. Bret Calhoun	160	51	30	16	32	1,031,883
		Danny Pish	194	24	25	19	12	463,005
		Dallas E. Keen	92	18	12	12	20	284,600
MAF	7/18 – 7/20	Jockey	Starts	1st	2d	3d	Win %	Earnings
		Carl Hebert	9	3	0	3	33	3,327
		Ivan Ortiz, Jr.	6	2	1	0	33	1,904
		Joe Holmes, Sr.	7	1	1	2	14	1,459
		David P. Stubblefield	5	1	0	3	20	1,494
		Shannon Wippert	2	1	0	0	50	2,968
MAF	7/18 – 7/20	Trainer	Starts	1st	2d	3d	Win %	Earnings
		Mel Berkram	5	2	1	1	40	3,166
		Debbie Smith	3	2	0	0	67	1,776
		Wilf McDougall	8	1	3	2	13	2,252
		Mel Yelvington	3	1	1	0	33	1,055
		Janis D. Schoepf	2	1	0	1	50	3,042

MAN	4/5 – 5/11	Jockey	Starts	1st	2d	3d	Win %	Earnings
		Rick L. Knott	42	10	9	4	24	53,174
		Christopher L. Conway	58	8	8	10	14	50,881
		Russell Brown	50	8	6	5	16	34,890
		Charlotte Bronstad	52	6	5	7	12	29,143
		Salvador Perez	43	6	4	6	14	28,605
MAN	4/5 – 5/11	Trainer	Starts	1st	2d	3d	Win %	Earnings
		Robert Fitzpatrick	8	5	1	0	63	14,960
		Laurie Rosenwasser	35	4	6	6	11	22,194
		Jaime Castellanos	18	4	4	3	22	20,362
		Ruth Claflin	18	4	3	0	22	14,207
		Jimmy L. Ray	19	4	2	1	21	16,246
MC	5/11 – 5/18	Jockey	Starts	1st	2d	3d	Win %	Earnings
		Jack Cano, Jr.	2	1	0	1	50	2,675
		Russell David Kingrey	1	1	0	0	100	1,800
		Zack Kelsey	3	1	0	0	33	1,740
		Gilbert D. Rivera	3	0	1	0	0	1,130
		Joey Coversup	3	0	1	0	0	710
MC	5/11 – 5/18	Trainer	Starts	1st	2d	3d	Win %	Earnings
		Bryan Krone	2	2	0	0	100	4,200
		Edward Buxbaum	5	1	0	1	20	2,180
		Rod Gibson	1	0	1	0	0	800
		Lisa Sisko	1	0	1	0	0	600
		Earl E. McKinnon	1	0	1	0	0	500
MD	5/23 – 9/6	Jockey	Starts	1st	2d	3d	Win %	Earnings
		Rennie Latchman	166	43	35	24	26	116,249
		Serge R. Rocheleau	179	36	31	29	20	83,275
		Tim Moccasin	161	34	31	21	21	105,080
		Sheldon Chickeness	146	25	15	23	17	66,892
		Andy Scarlett	125	21	17	22	17	55,857
MD	5/23 – 9/6	Trainer	Starts	1st	2d	3d	Win %	Earnings
		Hubert Pilon	52	16	7	10	31	73,790
		Don Bjarnarson	38	16	5	7	42	35,754
		George Gervais	58	15	16	8	26	31,967
		Bob Barr	47	10	8	11	21	25,768
		Fern Zdunick	47	9	6	14	19	52,252
MDA	9/13 – 10/19	Jockey	Starts	1st	2d	3d	Win %	Earnings
		Danielle Beischer	19	7	3	1	37	6,259
		Andy Scarlett	29	6	5	9	21	7,492
		Sheldon Chickeness	32	6	3	8	19	6,982
		Clint Magera	20	6	2	5	30	5,673
		Cameron Campbell	18	5	5	2	28	5,765
MDA	9/13 – 10/19	Trainer	Starts	1st	2d	3d	Win %	Earnings
		Mike Tourangeau	42	8	9	5	19	9,913
		Elton Keshane	30	6	5	10	20	7,893
		Pat Hosie	12	5	1	1	42	4,724
		Brad Ball	9	4	2	0	44	3,229
		Jim Ross	19	3	4	1	16	4,202
MED	10/2 – 11/8	Jockey	Starts	1st	2d	3d	Win %	Earnings
		Charles C. Lopez	152	31	31	14	20	613,547
		Alan Garcia	138	21	21	21	15	347,904
		Jose A. Velez, Jr.	99	19	16	17	19	429,084
		Julian Pimentel	87	16	10	17	18	336,618
		Richard A. Bracho	122	15	14	14	12	303,070
MED	10/2 – 11/8	Trainer	Starts	1st	2d	3d	Win %	Earnings
		Edwin Thomas Broome	39	13	8	7	33	211,840
		Teresa M. Pompay	48	9	12	3	19	171,805
		Linda Rice	36	9	2	5	25	135,840
		Timothy A. Hills	40	8	3	4	20	130,406
		Patricia Farro	36	8	3	4	22	123,046
MIL	7/1	Jockey	Starts	1st	2d	3d	Win %	Earnings
		Shannon Wippert	3	1	1	1	33	3,282
		Antonio Ramirez	3	1	1	0	33	3,815
		Scott Sterr	3	1	0	0	33	2,117
		Carl Hebert	3	0	1	2	0	2,067
		Randy Cunningham	2	0	0	0	0	323

MIL	7/1	Trainer	Starts	1st	2d	3d	Win %	Earnings
		Ron David	3	1	1	0	33	3,815
		Rita MacDonald	1	1	0	0	100	1,870
		Jim Depew	1	1	0	0	100	1,760
		Stan Marks	3	0	1	1	0	1,761
		Dennis Dorchester	2	0	1	0	0	970
MNR	10/3 – 12/30	Jockey	Starts	1st	2d	3d	Win %	Earnings
		Deshawn L. Parker	438	67	52	55	15	986,593
		Chad K. Murphy	231	47	28	31	20	770,936
		Gary A. Birzer	341	42	46	41	12	686,379
		Oswald M. Pereira	290	37	34	28	13	544,444
		Jeffrey Skerrett	242	31	26	26	13	443,583
MNR	10/3 – 12/30	Trainer	Starts	1st	2d	3d	Win %	Earnings
		Dale Baird	232	33	26	33	14	466,429
		Scooter Davis	116	23	15	14	20	277,266
		J. Michael Baird	85	19	10	7	22	296,916
		Paula S. Capestro	58	18	10	7	31	185,876
		Bernard S. Flint	37	16	4	3	43	236,466
MNR	7/1 – 9/30	Jockey	Starts	1st	2d	3d	Win %	Earnings
		Deshawn L. Parker	445	86	65	56	19	1,233,112
		Oswald M. Pereira	364	54	50	44	15	777,731
		Dana G. Whitney	248	49	32	26	20	718,353
		Gary A. Birzer	362	44	50	41	12	682,224
		Chad K. Murphy	277	42	39	38	15	803,150
MNR	7/1 – 9/30	Trainer	Starts	1st	2d	3d	Win %	Earnings
		Dale Baird	245	37	41	41	15	629,426
		Scooter Davis	134	25	23	16	19	342,010
		J. Michael Baird	90	20	12	16	22	294,278
		Gary L. Johnson	67	19	8	5	28	230,321
		L. Craig Cox	59	15	9	4	25	202,534
MNR	4/1 – 6/30	Jockey	Starts	1st	2d	3d	Win %	Earnings
		Dana G. Whitney	388	73	40	52	19	1,067,073
		Chad K. Murphy	273	44	37	33	16	833,133
		Oswald M. Pereira	308	41	42	55	13	643,083
		Deshawn L. Parker	368	40	49	47	11	736,868
		Gary A. Birzer	305	37	41	28	12	548,364
MNR	4/1 – 6/30	Trainer	Starts	1st	2d	3d	Win %	Earnings
		Scooter Davis	130	34	20	12	26	439,891
		Dale Baird	259	28	33	35	11	491,106
		Douglas E. Shanyfelt	104	18	7	16	17	246,929
		John W. Baird	119	17	10	6	14	241,998
		Don Roberson	101	15	15	16	15	214,294
MNR	1/11 – 3/31	Jockey	Starts	1st	2d	3d	Win %	Earnings
		Deshawn L. Parker	229	42	33	23	18	595,709
		David J. McFadden	204	42	27	22	21	614,185
		Dana G. Whitney	262	25	30	46	10	476,183
		Roberto A. Perez	208	25	16	17	12	361,490
		Joseph Stokes	161	23	30	15	14	341,028
MNR	1/11 – 3/31	Trainer	Starts	1st	2d	3d	Win %	Earnings
		Dale Baird	201	18	26	29	9	325,136
		Scooter Davis	91	16	14	11	18	253,531
		Michael C. Pappada	46	15	8	4	33	204,873
		Don Roberson	80	13	18	8	16	176,263
		John W. Baird	75	13	11	7	17	194,091
MOF	5/10 – 5/18	Jockey	Starts	1st	2d	3d	Win %	Earnings
		Robert Boyce	17	4	6	2	24	7,050
		Stephen Michael Karr	17	4	4	2	24	6,133
		Ronald Beverly	20	3	4	8	15	6,149
		Fernando Manuel Gamez	18	3	4	2	17	5,355
		Justin Vanderwoude	17	3	1	0	18	4,819
MOF	5/10 – 5/18	Trainer	Starts	1st	2d	3d	Win %	Earnings
		Lowell N. Bunyard	8	4	2	2	50	5,968
		Gene K. Wilson	11	4	1	0	36	4,862
		Scott J. Craigmyle	14	3	5	2	21	5,101
		Lyndel G. Rutherford	4	1	1	2	25	1,574
		Leonard A. Espinoza	4	1	1	1	25	1,636

MPM	5/3 – 9/28	Jockey	Starts	1st	2d	3d	Win %	Earnings
		Julie Fritz	40	8	9	6	20	30,840
		Kelly R. Spanabel	25	7	3	4	28	20,560
		Mike Simpson	38	6	10	5	16	27,660
		Dennis P. Berryhill	19	6	4	1	32	16,980
		Dale Berryhill	33	6	1	8	18	21,250
MPM	5/3 – 9/28	Trainer	Starts	1st	2d	3d	Win %	Earnings
		Reid Gross	28	4	7	7	14	20,850
		Ron Raper	14	4	3	2	29	12,960
		John R. Grace	26	4	3	1	15	14,160
		Doug Caraker	17	4	2	4	24	12,560
		George A. Iacovacci	6	4	0	1	67	8,720
MTH	5/24 – 9/28	Jockey	Starts	1st	2d	3d	Win %	Earnings
		Joe Bravo	452	110	76	70	24	3,388,310
		Jose C. Ferrer	377	77	64	27	20	2,200,399
		Julian Pimentel	355	64	49	54	18	1,963,695
		Charles C. Lopez	426	60	65	65	14	1,959,202
		Jose A. Velez, Jr.	341	51	62	47	15	2,248,439
MTH	5/24 – 9/28	Trainer	Starts	1st	2d	3d	Win %	Earnings
		Mark Shuman	295	50	58	33	17	1,549,725
		Timothy A. Hills	148	35	20	14	24	945,820
		Allen Iwinski	94	23	16	11	24	702,210
		Alan S. Seewald	94	21	15	12	22	456,693
		Benjamin W. Perkins, Jr.	94	21	10	10	22	728,995
NMP	8/29 – 9/14	Jockey	Starts	1st	2d	3d	Win %	Earnings
		Edgar Paucar	68	22	10	3	32	55,458
		Willie Belmonte	71	22	6	9	31	46,717
		Albert L. Howarth, Jr.	63	8	10	12	13	25,443
		Howard L. Lanci	49	7	8	9	14	21,310
		Ivan Ortiz, Jr.	60	5	12	8	8	23,885
NMP	8/29 – 9/14	Trainer	Starts	1st	2d	3d	Win %	Earnings
		Samuel J. Keyrouze	47	6	9	4	13	19,810
		Ronald J. Dandy	9	4	2	1	44	8,063
		Carlos R. Figueroa	24	4	1	4	17	10,907
		William E. Hamer, Sr.	16	4	1	2	25	8,720
		Michael Delnegro	23	3	5	5	13	12,635
NP	6/20 – 10/26	Jockey	Starts	1st	2d	3d	Win %	Earnings
		Quincy Welch	463	97	91	70	21	1,204,553
		Leanne M. Painter	471	68	65	77	14	1,069,507
		Stephan Heiler	358	60	53	52	17	761,084
		David Wilson	415	57	58	64	14	814,660
		Perry A. Winters	410	55	51	51	13	845,972
NP	6/20 – 10/26	Trainer	Starts	1st	2d	3d	Win %	Earnings
		Ron K. Smith	212	46	40	33	22	619,920
		Dale L. Saunders	177	33	28	28	19	498,555
		Ron Grieves	149	25	27	23	17	396,600
		Don Gilkyson	143	23	13	22	16	420,736
		Joan Petrowski	215	20	36	26	9	307,887
OP	1/24 – 4/12	Jockey	Starts	1st	2d	3d	Win %	Earnings
		Jamie Theriot	256	71	45	25	28	1,183,610
		Terry J. Thompson	353	69	50	55	20	1,686,126
		Carlos H. Marquez, Jr.	254	47	32	32	19	893,510
		Jon Kenton Court	244	37	34	41	15	774,306
		Luis S. Quinonez	288	30	27	33	10	667,748
OP	1/24 – 4/12	Trainer	Starts	1st	2d	3d	Win %	Earnings
		Cole Norman	233	71	41	23	30	1,077,040
		Stanley W. Roberts	166	22	20	19	13	451,374
		Donnie K. Von Hemel	94	19	17	11	20	511,560
		Robert E. Holthus	105	16	15	19	15	452,170
		David R. Vance	72	16	13	13	22	292,730
OTC	3/17	Jockey	Starts	1st	2d	3d	Win %	Earnings
		Edgar S. Prado	4	3	0	1	75	130,000
		Carlos Gonzalez	2	1	1	0	50	31,000
		Gary Boulanger	2	1	0	0	50	63,500
		Jose Alberto Rivera, II	3	1	0	0	33	24,000
		Pat Day	4	0	2	1	0	40,500

OTC	3/17	Trainer	Starts	1st	2d	3d	Win %	Earnings
		Edward Plesa, Jr.	3	1	0	1	33	73,500
		Frank Gomez	1	1	0	0	100	60,000
		Dennis J. Manning	1	1	0	0	100	30,000
		Kenneth G. McPeek	1	1	0	0	100	30,000
		Teresa M. Pompay	2	1	0	0	50	24,000
PEN	9/11 – 12/30	Jockey	Starts	1st	2d	3d	Win %	Earnings
		David Cora	331	67	42	38	20	419,899
		Emilio Flores	293	54	31	25	18	370,965
		William P. Otero	287	46	36	42	16	360,286
		Luis A. Belmonte	293	42	44	31	14	294,501
		Thomas Clifton	222	37	37	27	17	313,398
PEN	9/11 – 12/30	Trainer	Starts	1st	2d	3d	Win %	Earnings
		Harry F. Thompson, Jr.	253	52	38	39	21	326,377
		Bruce M. Kravets	231	46	32	27	20	269,666
		Jose A. Martinez	238	43	38	30	18	303,761
		David W. Geist	132	38	12	14	29	243,587
		Flint W. Stites	139	22	22	18	16	159,181
PEN	5/1 – 8/30	Jockey	Starts	1st	2d	3d	Win %	Earnings
		Thomas Clifton	330	76	48	35	23	553,613
		David Cora	418	72	57	60	17	469,007
		Emilio Flores	440	56	57	60	13	448,849
		Vladimir Diaz	347	52	47	53	15	388,963
		Edwin Perez	317	49	47	49	15	311,018
PEN	5/1 – 8/30	Trainer	Starts	1st	2d	3d	Win %	Earnings
		Harry F. Thompson, Jr.	276	50	41	42	18	308,150
		Jose A. Martinez	244	42	46	39	17	262,875
		Bruce M. Kravets	225	39	30	39	17	242,894
		John Charles Zimmerman	111	32	23	11	29	247,810
		Todd M. Beattie	90	25	15	7	28	217,216
PEN	1/2 – 4/30	Jockey	Starts	1st	2d	3d	Win %	Earnings
		David Cora	415	94	64	64	23	556,462
		Thomas Clifton	311	73	53	35	23	460,615
		Emilio Flores	405	61	59	62	15	414,817
		Vladimir Diaz	330	50	60	62	15	383,838
		Carlos Nieto	268	41	39	37	15	273,752
PEN	1/2 – 4/30	Trainer	Starts	1st	2d	3d	Win %	Earnings
		Harry F. Thompson, Jr.	280	70	46	42	25	423,775
		Bruce M. Kravets	300	55	53	52	18	354,159
		John Charles Zimmerman	122	36	27	21	30	248,930
		Jose A. Martinez	184	35	18	24	19	182,192
		Flint W. Stites	140	20	19	17	14	147,258
PHA	1/1 – 12/30	Jockey	Starts	1st	2d	3d	Win %	Earnings
		Stewart Elliott	1233	235	196	160	19	3,131,613
		Jose Luis Flores	1063	200	159	135	19	2,616,850
		Kendrick Carmouche	986	128	165	136	13	1,908,508
		Nick Santagata	857	98	107	115	11	1,596,041
		Anibal Prado	871	88	84	101	10	1,127,468
PHA	1/1 – 12/30	Trainer	Starts	1st	2d	3d	Win %	Earnings
		Scott A. Lake	705	170	117	97	24	2,037,176
		John S. McCaslin	279	77	57	40	28	903,843
		Guadalupe Preciado	328	56	44	54	17	831,965
		Donald S. Reeder	306	55	51	36	18	575,613
		Randy Allen	354	50	46	53	14	609,206
PIM	9/3 – 10/5	Jockey	Starts	1st	2d	3d	Win %	Earnings
		Horacio Karamanos	138	29	17	16	21	517,315
		Luis Garcia	123	20	20	16	16	331,395
		Mario G. Pino	91	18	11	10	20	338,320
		Richard Monterrey	71	16	10	9	23	282,565
		Abel Castellano, Jr.	119	15	17	20	13	340,525
PIM	9/3 – 10/5	Trainer	Starts	1st	2d	3d	Win %	Earnings
		Dale Capuano	49	18	4	6	37	262,015
		Benjamin M. Feliciano, Jr.	36	7	7	2	19	126,570
		A. Ferris Allen, III	32	7	4	3	22	75,690
		John E. Salzman, Sr.	43	7	3	8	16	118,845
		Hamilton A. Smith	49	6	6	8	12	120,405

PIM	4/2 – 6/8	Jockey	Starts	1st	2d	3d	Win %	Earnings
		Ryan Fogelsonger	267	62	41	68	23	1,153,891
		Ramon A. Dominguez	150	40	33	20	27	1,099,870
		Rick Wilson	150	40	22	20	27	803,312
		Mario G. Pino	202	39	36	31	19	846,270
		Horacio Karamanos	165	26	29	26	16	576,370
PIM	4/2 – 6/8	Trainer	Starts	1st	2d	3d	Win %	Earnings
		Dale Capuano	113	24	25	19	21	535,914
		A. Ferris Allen, III	108	21	20	17	19	357,651
		Scott A. Lake	81	16	14	12	20	289,435
		Mark Shuman	61	16	5	10	26	417,507
		John J. Robb	88	15	16	10	17	356,845
PLN	6/25 – 7/6	Jockey	Starts	1st	2d	3d	Win %	Earnings
		Russell A. Baze	65	18	11	10	28	247,921
		Francisco Duran	41	11	3	6	27	145,530
		Roberto M. Gonzalez	50	10	7	4	20	198,201
		Chance J. Rollins	55	9	9	9	16	227,673
		Joe M. Castro	37	8	3	2	22	125,345
PLN	6/25 – 7/6	Trainer	Starts	1st	2d	3d	Win %	Earnings
		William E. Morey	16	7	2	3	44	90,945
		Jerry Hollendorfer	44	6	7	8	14	136,802
		Sergio Ledezma	22	6	2	5	27	50,815
		Jeff Bonde	24	6	2	0	25	94,970
		Armando Lage	37	5	9	7	14	129,076
PM	10/19/02 – 4/27/03	Jockey	Starts	1st	2d	3d	Win %	Earnings
		Juan M. Gutierrez	353	94	76	57	27	307,304
		Robert Webb	268	60	55	39	22	225,593
		Ron W. Keckler	397	52	57	52	13	193,838
		Marijo H. Terleski	363	44	54	47	12	181,501
		Karen Knapp	240	42	32	41	18	149,703
PM	10/19/02 – 4/27/03	Trainer	Starts	1st	2d	3d	Win %	Earnings
		Jim Fergason	234	43	44	31	18	176,778
		Jonathan Nance	192	37	38	41	19	158,314
		Jim Keen	118	29	17	21	25	78,242
		Nick Lowe	166	22	32	23	13	112,649
		Norbert E. Norton	85	21	13	18	25	62,973
PRM	7/4 – 9/13	Jockey	Starts	1st	2d	3d	Win %	Earnings
		Glenn W. Corbett	219	43	31	32	20	664,219
		Alex Birzer	240	37	36	30	15	554,020
		Robert Dean Williams	162	28	21	19	17	376,928
		Perry Compton	194	25	27	24	13	474,509
		Ken A. Shino	198	24	29	26	12	402,054
PRM	7/4 – 9/13	Trainer	Starts	1st	2d	3d	Win %	Earnings
		Dick R. Clark	198	36	24	31	18	511,993
		David D. McShane	127	22	19	13	17	363,603
		Timothy Mark Gleason	119	21	11	15	18	252,846
		Kelly R. Von Hemel	95	16	17	15	17	396,841
		Lynn Chleborad	95	15	14	13	16	212,670
PRM	4/18 – 6/28	Jockey	Starts	1st	2d	3d	Win %	Earnings
		Terry J. Thompson	352	63	45	51	18	1,034,930
		Luis S. Quinonez	304	60	49	37	20	1,092,893
		Glenn W. Corbett	299	48	50	41	16	823,936
		Cindy Sue Noll	316	43	57	52	14	850,951
		Joe M. Johnson	257	36	31	27	14	559,970
PRM	4/18 – 6/28	Trainer	Starts	1st	2d	3d	Win %	Earnings
		Dick R. Clark	204	41	39	23	20	630,590
		Stanley W. Roberts	153	30	22	26	20	443,320
		Kelly R. Von Hemel	104	23	14	8	22	405,363
		David D. McShane	122	22	14	18	18	458,572
		Timothy Mark Gleason	126	18	18	17	14	302,750
PRV	7/9 – 7/12	Jockey	Starts	1st	2d	3d	Win %	Earnings
		Victor V. Mercado	19	10	2	3	53	15,520
		Kristin O'Donnell	13	4	2	1	31	7,598
		Twyla Beckner	10	2	4	1	20	5,752
		Joe A. Crispin	11	2	2	1	18	4,278
		Tad Wayne Skaggs	9	2	1	1	22	4,026

PRV	7/9 – 7/12	Trainer	Starts	1st	2d	3d	Win %	Earnings
		Scott Nance	7	3	3	0	43	6,080
		Jaqueline Smith	6	3	1	2	50	5,770
		Elbert Applegate	4	2	0	0	50	2,892
		Lyle Magnuson	3	2	0	0	67	2,760
		Tom Farrell	5	1	1	2	20	2,392

RD	6/22 – 9/1	Jockey	Starts	1st	2d	3d	Win %	Earnings
		Jeff Johnston	181	58	27	15	32	478,937
		Perry Wayne Ouzts	331	43	48	55	13	336,400
		Hector L. Rosario, Jr.	220	33	36	34	15	269,812
		James Christopher Herrell	264	27	44	31	10	196,824
		Orlando Mojica	132	25	21	23	19	171,108

RD	6/22 – 9/1	Trainer	Starts	1st	2d	3d	Win %	Earnings
		Joe Woodard	53	14	9	3	26	65,840
		Jake S. Radosevich	44	14	4	2	32	67,432
		Dennis T. Moore	78	12	9	16	15	71,564
		Luis Albert Palacios	65	10	15	13	15	131,403
		James E. Morgan	51	7	9	8	14	73,796

RD	4/12 – 6/21	Jockey	Starts	1st	2d	3d	Win %	Earnings
		Perry Wayne Ouzts	355	67	56	66	19	436,652
		Jorge A. Guerra	250	48	28	33	19	274,411
		Hector L. Rosario, Jr.	212	37	31	21	17	278,794
		James Christopher Herrell	154	26	20	14	17	148,161
		Orlando Mojica	134	21	17	15	16	124,955

RD	4/12 – 6/21	Trainer	Starts	1st	2d	3d	Win %	Earnings
		James E. Morgan	42	17	6	5	40	150,037
		Dennis T. Moore	59	14	8	9	24	69,835
		Joe Woodard	70	11	12	6	16	69,139
		Luis Albert Palacios	60	9	15	6	15	121,996
		Richard Estvanko	21	9	2	2	43	49,587

RET	8/1 – 10/19	Jockey	Starts	1st	2d	3d	Win %	Earnings
		Jeremy Beasley	312	70	49	44	22	695,043
		Weldon T. Cloninger, Jr.	279	48	46	43	17	546,615
		Kerwin D. Clark	237	47	30	32	20	386,629
		Adrian B. Ramos	298	36	38	37	12	311,008
		Terry A. Stanton	179	36	34	28	20	376,105

RET	8/1 – 10/19	Trainer	Starts	1st	2d	3d	Win %	Earnings
		Danny Pish	204	43	33	23	21	356,365
		Steven M. Asmussen	119	37	20	18	31	489,662
		Tommie T. Morgan	99	22	14	12	22	235,451
		John G. Locke	122	18	22	16	15	292,460
		Jim Bausch	105	13	15	9	12	99,145

RIL	1/18 – 3/2	Jockey	Starts	1st	2d	3d	Win %	Earnings
		Fernando Manuel Gamez	65	17	19	7	26	25,031
		Todd J. Nuttall	64	15	8	7	23	21,199
		Stephen Michael Karr	78	10	14	14	13	19,530
		Don Lee French	65	9	7	13	14	15,763
		Terry Lee Gard	44	7	5	6	16	13,957

RIL	1/18 – 3/2	Trainer	Starts	1st	2d	3d	Win %	Earnings
		Eddie Tellez	24	8	3	2	33	9,731
		Leonard A. Espinoza	17	3	4	3	18	6,987
		Gene K. Wilson	25	3	3	4	12	4,941
		Krystal Adams	17	3	0	3	18	4,183
		Lowell N. Bunyard	7	2	4	0	29	3,190

RP	8/22 – 11/30	Jockey	Starts	1st	2d	3d	Win %	Earnings
		Monte Clifton Berry	375	100	75	62	27	873,358
		Nena Matz	356	76	67	42	21	601,860
		Kevin Leon Cogburn	356	61	61	66	17	616,049
		Tonja A. Arruda	281	42	27	28	15	254,965
		Gregory Allen Schaefer	240	26	35	25	11	253,947

RP	8/22 – 11/30	Trainer	Starts	1st	2d	3d	Win %	Earnings
		Joe S. Offolter	161	41	30	22	25	272,214
		Donnie K. Von Hemel	95	27	23	12	28	398,975
		Martin Lozano	71	19	22	6	27	126,156
		Clinton C. Stuart	80	17	22	16	21	133,910
		Zachary Armstrong	52	17	12	6	33	88,408

RPD	7/12 – 7/13	Jockey	Starts	1st	2d	3d	Win %	Earnings
		Lawrence Durocher	4	2	1	1	50	1,300
		Frank La Forge	4	1	2	0	25	1,050
		Enoch Quewezance	3	1	0	1	33	700
		Danielle Beischer	4	0	1	1	0	600
		Thomas Strongarm	1	0	0	1	0	150
RPD	7/12 – 7/13	Trainer	Starts	1st	2d	3d	Win %	Earnings
		Elton Keshane	3	2	1	0	67	1,150
		Norbert Beaulieu	5	1	2	1	20	1,100
		Leon Keshane	1	1	0	0	100	450
		Herman Eric Mentuck	2	0	1	0	0	250
		Jim Ross	3	0	0	1	0	350
RUI	5/23 – 9/1	Jockey	Starts	1st	2d	3d	Win %	Earnings
		Ricardo Jaime	194	45	37	25	23	452,020
		Jorge Martin Bourdieu	188	35	24	32	19	423,089
		Carlos D. Madeira	139	27	22	26	19	284,394
		Michael Dennis Clark	194	22	34	31	11	301,786
		Mark Anthony Villa	149	20	12	19	13	204,276
RUI	5/23 – 9/1	Trainer	Starts	1st	2d	3d	Win %	Earnings
		Henry Dominguez	144	38	28	24	26	377,076
		Joel H. Marr	87	20	15	17	23	215,436
		Ralph W. Black, Jr.	89	13	13	9	15	113,592
		Clifford C. Lambert, Sr.	69	11	11	8	16	65,983
		Bart G. Hone	46	10	7	10	22	88,571
SA	9/28 – 11/9	Jockey	Starts	1st	2d	3d	Win %	Earnings
		Patrick A. Valenzuela	166	34	44	29	20	3,259,469
		Tyler Baze	163	33	20	29	20	1,154,159
		Alex O. Solis	143	27	27	18	19	5,392,576
		Victor Espinoza	158	27	19	23	17	1,361,674
		Julie A. Krone	163	26	19	16	16	1,716,239
SA	9/28 – 11/9	Trainer	Starts	1st	2d	3d	Win %	Earnings
		Doug O'Neill	80	22	13	10	28	819,057
		Bob Baffert	76	13	12	7	17	849,568
		Rafael Becerra	29	11	4	3	38	325,620
		John W. Sadler	53	10	7	9	19	495,010
		Jeff Mullins	35	9	6	4	26	450,399
SA	12/26/02 – 4/20/03	Jockey	Starts	1st	2d	3d	Win %	Earnings
		Patrick A. Valenzuela	481	94	100	76	20	4,710,082
		David Romero Flores	436	69	70	51	16	3,551,113
		Alex O. Solis	370	69	51	55	19	4,266,552
		Laffit A. Pincay, Jr.	253	52	40	36	21	2,172,713
		Victor Espinoza	434	51	48	64	12	2,752,306
SA	12/26/02 – 4/20/03	Trainer	Starts	1st	2d	3d	Win %	Earnings
		Bob Baffert	208	43	40	28	21	3,141,331
		Jeff Mullins	93	30	28	8	32	1,885,242
		Robert J. Frankel	90	25	18	13	28	2,757,699
		Vladimir Cerin	94	25	9	13	27	679,426
		Doug O'Neill	144	24	16	23	17	1,132,677
SAC	8/20 – 9/1	Jockey	Starts	1st	2d	3d	Win %	Earnings
		Antonio Lopez Castanon	26	10	4	1	38	78,850
		Chance J. Rollins	22	8	5	2	36	71,080
		Berkley R. Packer	36	8	1	4	22	57,695
		Victor Miranda	41	6	7	4	15	56,435
		Ryan Morris	42	6	6	4	14	60,515
SAC	8/20 – 9/1	Trainer	Starts	1st	2d	3d	Win %	Earnings
		Michael Lenzini	48	7	8	5	15	72,330
		John F. Martin	9	7	2	0	78	50,425
		Don J. Mills	17	6	7	1	35	65,870
		Dennis Hopkins	31	5	4	5	16	71,180
		Rene Amescua	23	3	8	1	13	38,855
SAF	3/29 – 4/6	Jockey	Starts	1st	2d	3d	Win %	Earnings
		Ronald Beverly	17	5	3	3	29	6,501
		Stephen Michael Karr	17	3	5	3	18	5,344
		Fernando Manuel Gamez	16	2	3	5	13	4,079
		Justin Vanderwoude	16	2	1	0	13	3,080
		Don Lee French	17	2	0	3	12	3,102

		Trainer	Starts	1st	2d	3d	Win %	Earnings
SAF	3/29 – 4/6	Lowell N. Bunyard	5	4	0	1	80	4,129
		Richard Ramirez	9	2	0	2	22	2,482
		Wiley Aker	7	1	2	1	14	1,964
		B. Odell Reidhead	4	1	2	0	25	1,695
		Gene K. Wilson	5	1	1	1	20	1,554
SAR	7/23 – 9/1	Jockey	Starts	1st	2d	3d	Win %	Earnings
		John R. Velazquez	235	61	29	31	26	3,250,987
		Jerry D. Bailey	156	46	30	17	29	3,488,369
		Edgar S. Prado	225	39	34	31	17	2,113,547
		Pat Day	140	22	23	19	16	1,792,906
		Cornelio H. Velasquez	203	21	19	27	10	1,023,677
SAR	7/23 – 9/1	Trainer	Starts	1st	2d	3d	Win %	Earnings
		Todd A. Pletcher	125	35	16	20	28	2,061,357
		William I. Mott	77	17	9	11	22	824,072
		Nicholas P. Zito	73	10	13	6	14	582,690
		Philip M. Serpe	43	10	6	2	23	326,050
		Mark A. Hennig	56	8	7	9	14	461,048
SJ	9/13 – 9/21	Jockey	Starts	1st	2d	3d	Win %	Earnings
		Todd J. Nuttall	15	7	1	3	47	7,431
		Fernando Manuel Gamez	17	5	4	2	29	6,572
		Charles Lyn McClellan	22	3	5	1	14	5,276
		Stephen Michael Karr	21	3	1	7	14	4,697
		Joseph L. Durigon	13	2	0	3	15	2,650
SJ	9/13 – 9/21	Trainer	Starts	1st	2d	3d	Win %	Earnings
		Lowell N. Bunyard	10	6	1	1	60	6,103
		Gene K. Wilson	11	4	1	4	36	4,698
		Wiley Aker	14	3	4	2	21	4,628
		Manny A. Figueroa	8	3	2	1	38	3,793
		B. Odell Reidhead	9	1	4	2	11	2,568
SOL	7/9 – 7/20	Jockey	Starts	1st	2d	3d	Win %	Earnings
		Russell A. Baze	38	15	5	7	39	170,410
		Chance J. Rollins	51	11	7	6	22	116,535
		Francisco Duran	46	7	5	5	15	95,445
		Chad Phillip Schvaneveldt	21	7	3	3	33	74,077
		David G. Lopez	34	5	7	4	15	93,680
SOL	7/9 – 7/20	Trainer	Starts	1st	2d	3d	Win %	Earnings
		Jerry Hollendorfer	21	8	2	2	38	113,665
		Armando Lage	22	7	2	4	32	54,265
		Gil Matos	14	4	0	0	29	41,360
		John F. Martin	16	3	6	1	19	37,250
		Brian J. Koriner	10	3	4	1	30	37,075
SON	4/26 – 5/4	Jockey	Starts	1st	2d	3d	Win %	Earnings
		Todd J. Nuttall	14	6	1	1	43	7,807
		Ronald Beverly	17	3	4	3	18	5,206
		Stephen Michael Karr	17	2	4	1	12	3,897
		Fernando Manuel Gamez	15	2	2	4	13	3,954
		Anna M. Barrio	14	2	2	3	14	3,350
SON	4/26 – 5/4	Trainer	Starts	1st	2d	3d	Win %	Earnings
		Lowell N. Bunyard	6	3	1	1	50	3,540
		Gene K. Wilson	7	2	1	0	29	2,232
		Laurie Jones	8	1	2	2	13	1,959
		Wiley Aker	5	1	2	1	20	1,825
		Eddie Tellez	5	1	1	0	20	1,531
SR	7/23 – 8/4	Jockey	Starts	1st	2d	3d	Win %	Earnings
		Russell A. Baze	64	23	13	10	36	323,160
		Chance J. Rollins	60	14	14	10	23	172,225
		Chad Phillip Schvaneveldt	40	8	8	5	20	122,110
		Francisco Duran	48	8	6	1	17	127,954
		David G. Lopez	48	8	5	15	17	88,550
SR	7/23 – 8/4	Trainer	Starts	1st	2d	3d	Win %	Earnings
		John F. Martin	17	8	6	1	47	72,605
		Armando Lage	32	8	5	5	25	88,960
		Jerry Hollendorfer	24	7	4	3	29	161,145
		William E. Morey	10	5	0	1	50	60,315
		Wesley A. Ward	13	4	3	3	31	85,245

SRP	9/19 – 11/23	Jockey	Starts	1st	2d	3d	Win %	Earnings
		Casey T. Lambert	137	38	27	11	28	329,254
		Ken S. Tohill	108	23	21	18	21	304,930
		Freddy Fuentes	123	19	14	15	15	161,805
		Brian James Theriot	95	16	17	9	17	157,778
		Perry S. Whetstone	122	15	14	18	12	154,805
SRP	9/19 – 11/23	Trainer	Starts	1st	2d	3d	Win %	Earnings
		Jon G. Arnett	83	21	13	15	25	163,747
		Gary W. Cross	44	13	11	4	30	197,008
		Fred I. Danley	48	9	11	8	19	126,348
		Henry Dominguez	33	9	4	3	27	98,140
		H. Ray Ashford, Jr.	46	8	6	3	17	69,846
STK	6/11 – 6/22	Jockey	Starts	1st	2d	3d	Win %	Earnings
		Ken S. Tohill	59	11	8	9	19	115,425
		Ryan Morris	39	9	4	4	23	67,980
		David Burton Patton	17	6	2	0	35	53,630
		Antonio Lopez Castanon	29	4	8	1	14	44,550
		Victor G. Navarro	40	4	4	7	10	46,840
STK	6/11 – 6/22	Trainer	Starts	1st	2d	3d	Win %	Earnings
		William E. Morey	16	5	4	5	31	53,955
		Michael Lenzini	25	4	5	0	16	34,280
		Lonnie Arterburn	5	3	1	0	60	17,720
		Wesley A. Ward	7	3	0	1	43	29,770
		Gil Matos	13	2	2	4	15	24,960
STP	4/4 – 6/15	Jockey	Starts	1st	2d	3d	Win %	Earnings
		Quincy Welch	190	44	40	21	23	536,582
		David Wilson	250	40	37	38	16	517,082
		Real E. Simard	249	38	22	35	15	569,344
		Perry A. Winters	261	33	45	35	13	497,152
		Richard Harvey Hamel	246	31	39	27	13	403,672
STP	4/4 – 6/15	Trainer	Starts	1st	2d	3d	Win %	Earnings
		Ron K. Smith	115	25	21	21	22	342,405
		Ron Grieves	104	23	17	9	22	298,401
		Joan Petrowski	99	17	8	13	17	176,794
		Floyd M. Arthur	61	16	9	14	26	199,716
		Robertino Diodoro	99	15	20	16	15	186,721
SUD	4/5 – 5/4	Jockey	Starts	1st	2d	3d	Win %	Earnings
		David Deforest Brown	32	8	5	2	25	10,888
		Ronald Joseph Bilodeau	37	7	6	8	19	13,048
		Luis Morgan	44	7	1	5	16	8,716
		Jay Conklin	24	6	6	3	25	9,594
		Kathleen E. Moore	25	5	0	6	20	7,063
SUD	4/5 – 5/4	Trainer	Starts	1st	2d	3d	Win %	Earnings
		A. Lynn Homer	27	6	6	3	22	10,130
		Tracy Lebret	25	5	5	3	20	7,804
		Robert L. Lawrence	20	5	2	3	25	7,085
		Jim McDonnell	23	4	2	4	17	5,725
		Mike DeMatteis	12	4	1	2	33	5,022
SUF	9/15 – 10/27	Jockey	Starts	1st	2d	3d	Win %	Earnings
		Josiah Francis Hampshire, Jr.	129	24	17	11	19	243,719
		Winston Albert Thompson	151	23	18	24	15	284,180
		Dyn Panell	125	22	23	19	18	285,936
		Mark Phillips	98	15	13	9	15	168,609
		Edgar Paucar	109	10	13	10	9	119,319
SUF	9/15 – 10/27	Trainer	Starts	1st	2d	3d	Win %	Earnings
		Kevin J. Joy	75	14	4	10	19	108,544
		Ronald J. Dandy	95	13	17	9	14	143,850
		John Rigattieri	43	9	6	2	21	92,906
		Karl M. Grusmark	51	8	7	7	16	78,074
		Wayne J. Marcoux	39	8	6	5	21	71,860
SUF	1/1 – 8/27	Jockey	Starts	1st	2d	3d	Win %	Earnings
		Josiah Francis Hampshire, Jr.	626	142	113	73	23	1,568,521
		Mark Phillips	661	92	101	93	14	1,009,155
		Winston Albert Thompson	553	90	78	66	16	1,104,863
		Taylor M. Hole	530	81	88	76	15	1,031,814
		Vernon Bush	505	77	76	63	15	919,557

			Starts	1st	2d	3d	Win %	Earnings
SUF	1/1 – 8/27	Trainer						
		Ronald J. Dandy	454	79	73	57	17	832,905
		Robert A. Raymond	250	45	30	33	18	433,244
		Kevin J. Joy	273	40	46	32	15	395,703
		John Rigattieri	223	33	34	25	15	378,965
		Karl M. Grusmark	206	28	33	35	14	344,238
SUN	11/19/02 – 4/6/03	Jockey						
		Jorge Martin Bourdieu	353	61	59	60	17	1,232,289
		Ricardo Jaime	335	55	58	38	16	1,213,485
		Daryl Montoya	264	39	38	27	15	663,638
		Casey T. Lambert	262	33	30	44	13	766,935
		Sal Gonzalez, Jr.	128	26	14	10	20	576,032
SUN	11/19/02 – 4/6/03	Trainer						
		Ramon O. Gonzalez	235	42	29	21	18	561,904
		Henry Dominguez	143	31	37	17	22	580,927
		Todd W. Fincher	56	23	6	7	41	597,066
		Joel H. Marr	119	22	11	10	18	326,642
		Carlos Sedillo	80	16	9	10	20	292,963
TAM	12/14/02 – 5/4/03	Jockey						
		Joseph C. Judice	591	117	80	62	20	1,148,622
		Jesus Lopez Castanon	480	99	66	69	21	1,121,978
		Thomas L. Pompell	504	73	76	53	14	959,538
		Juan Umana	461	71	73	61	15	821,465
		Russell W. Woolsey	410	58	51	59	14	670,911
TAM	12/14/02 – 5/4/03	Trainer						
		Don R. Rice	205	43	42	23	21	619,054
		Richard J. Ciardullo, Jr.	127	28	23	15	22	334,569
		Kathleen O'Connell	138	28	21	13	20	311,384
		Lynne M. Scace	150	27	22	13	18	227,048
		Anthony Pecoraro	79	25	8	4	32	161,647
TDN	3/15 – 12/15	Jockey						
		Huber Villa-Gomez	773	160	131	95	21	1,096,297
		Michael Francis Rowland	739	134	125	80	18	1,071,027
		Luis Antonio Gonzalez	719	130	92	85	18	976,861
		Julio E. Felix	640	104	71	81	16	795,978
		Ricardo Feliciano	513	77	78	72	15	689,768
TDN	3/15 – 12/15	Trainer						
		Rodney C. Faulkner	529	101	82	75	19	593,063
		Jeffrey A. Radosevich	258	54	41	38	21	336,307
		Gary L. Johnson	363	50	42	45	14	322,127
		Rodrigo Madrigal, Sr.	181	43	30	16	24	406,632
		Michael Newell	284	41	43	27	14	243,794
TIL	8/7 – 8/9	Jockey						
		Victor V. Mercado	20	9	2	2	45	12,513
		Melissa Peery	11	5	2	2	45	8,156
		Joe A. Crispin	18	3	6	3	17	6,809
		Ty Dangerfield	12	3	1	4	25	5,188
		Edgar Montehermoso	13	0	4	1	0	2,564
TIL	8/7 – 8/9	Trainer						
		Terry Lee Fergason	6	3	1	1	50	4,134
		Bill Hof	4	2	2	0	50	2,960
		Judi Yearout	7	2	1	3	29	3,538
		Jaqueline Smith	4	2	1	0	50	3,896
		Lee Marll	3	2	0	0	67	2,340
TIM	8/23 – 9/1	Jockey						
		Travis L. Dunkelberger	53	14	9	8	26	153,965
		J. D. Acosta	46	9	8	5	20	108,820
		Mark E. Rosenthal	50	7	8	6	14	144,380
		Luis Garcia	35	7	5	7	20	79,315
		C. Omar Klinger	26	6	5	1	23	66,970
TIM	8/23 – 9/1	Trainer						
		Dale Capuano	20	6	7	2	30	46,300
		King T. Leatherbury	19	4	2	2	21	44,250
		Mark Shuman	11	4	1	2	36	78,705
		John J. Robb	18	4	1	2	22	61,360
		Hamilton A. Smith	7	4	1	1	57	39,165

TP	11/30 – 12/31	Jockey	Starts	1st	2d	3d	Win %	Earnings
		Rafael Bejarano	137	46	26	20	34	512,196
		Jason P. Lumpkins	126	27	19	17	21	354,459
		Rodney A. Prescott	162	17	12	17	10	200,426
		Anthony J. D'Amico	68	12	10	12	18	186,064
		Justin Shepherd	77	11	8	9	14	142,317
TP	11/30 – 12/31	Trainer	Starts	1st	2d	3d	Win %	Earnings
		Bernard S. Flint	53	10	7	8	19	163,895
		Gregory D. Foley	32	10	4	3	31	116,485
		Dale L. Romans	29	10	3	5	34	167,985
		Randy L. Morse	19	5	6	1	26	65,797
		Paul J. McGee	16	5	3	1	31	74,400
TP	9/3 – 10/2	Jockey	Starts	1st	2d	3d	Win %	Earnings
		Rafael Bejarano	97	27	18	20	28	338,168
		Jon Kenton Court	114	21	18	14	18	276,391
		Dean P. Butler	129	18	13	14	14	237,952
		John McKee	144	17	28	21	12	308,656
		William D. Troilo	79	11	7	11	14	128,343
TP	9/3 – 10/2	Trainer	Starts	1st	2d	3d	Win %	Earnings
		Bernard S. Flint	36	9	9	6	25	118,428
		Kenneth G. McPeek	14	6	2	0	43	98,617
		Randy L. Morse	14	6	1	0	43	55,037
		James R. Jackson	14	5	2	1	36	47,710
		Michael J. Maker	13	5	1	0	38	53,913
TP	1/1 – 4/3	Jockey	Starts	1st	2d	3d	Win %	Earnings
		Jason P. Lumpkins	382	112	54	55	29	1,474,278
		Rafael Bejarano	205	41	40	30	20	505,462
		Rodney A. Prescott	292	32	42	29	11	475,566
		Dean P. Butler	331	31	46	45	9	542,537
		Jeff Johnston	241	26	39	34	11	491,584
TP	1/1 – 4/3	Trainer	Starts	1st	2d	3d	Win %	Earnings
		Bernard S. Flint	159	44	21	13	28	660,722
		Gregory D. Foley	49	17	6	11	35	392,824
		Thomas L. Van Berg	47	13	9	6	28	128,113
		Dennis T. Moore	56	11	11	9	20	103,397
		William Bradley	63	10	8	5	16	183,467
TUP	9/27/02 – 5/18/03	Jockey	Starts	1st	2d	3d	Win %	Earnings
		Esteban Angel Gomez	932	146	126	133	16	1,112,220
		Seth B. Martinez	779	145	133	99	19	1,218,709
		Michael G. Ziegler	629	109	85	68	17	836,723
		Miguel Luis Gaeta Hernandez	785	106	120	139	14	913,912
		Leslie Mawing	754	106	88	111	14	777,348
TUP	9/27/02 – 5/18/03	Trainer	Starts	1st	2d	3d	Win %	Earnings
		Don J. Mills	209	62	31	27	30	391,599
		Dan L. McFarlane	298	56	52	56	19	499,890
		Kevin Lewis	226	51	34	38	23	614,987
		Justin Evans	266	47	36	37	18	298,431
		J. Eric Kruljac	173	43	38	24	25	373,000
UN	6/6 – 6/8	Jockey	Starts	1st	2d	3d	Win %	Earnings
		Ty Dangerfield	13	6	3	2	46	8,910
		Johanna Purdome	12	2	1	3	17	4,213
		Robert Webb	5	2	0	0	40	2,600
		Victor V. Mercado	11	1	5	3	9	4,233
		Melissa Peery	14	1	1	2	7	2,928
UN	6/6 – 6/8	Trainer	Starts	1st	2d	3d	Win %	Earnings
		Don D. Young	7	2	2	1	29	3,428
		Brian Tschirgi	6	2	1	2	33	3,405
		Wayne L. Bell	5	1	2	1	20	2,160
		James R. Craig	3	1	2	0	33	1,900
		Silvester Juarez	7	1	1	1	14	2,420
WDS	9/23 – 11/1	Jockey	Starts	1st	2d	3d	Win %	Earnings
		Ken A. Shino	181	36	26	24	20	248,287
		Alex Birzer	156	21	26	24	13	164,336
		Frank Albert Gonsalves	120	17	13	16	14	139,773
		Kelly Michael Murray	113	17	7	6	15	92,267
		Jason R. Eads	100	14	14	10	14	110,165

WDS	9/23 – 11/1	Trainer	Starts	1st	2d	3d	Win %	Earnings
		Kenneth Gleason	87	17	18	8	20	162,082
		Timothy Mark Gleason	64	16	7	12	25	90,477
		Joe Frederick Thomas, Sr.	40	8	9	5	20	59,819
		Temple D. Rushton	66	7	9	9	11	45,388
		Jeffrey T. Rutland	26	7	2	3	27	62,081
WO	3/22 – 11/30	Jockey	Starts	1st	2d	3d	Win %	Earnings
		Todd Kabel	834	160	163	110	19	11,284,853
		Patrick Husbands	793	158	137	107	20	10,537,299
		Emile Ramsammy	795	123	101	98	15	7,104,415
		James McAleney	731	112	101	94	15	6,654,200
		David Clark	657	104	82	69	16	5,591,449
WO	3/22 – 11/30	Trainer	Starts	1st	2d	3d	Win %	Earnings
		Robert P. Tiller	252	71	41	37	28	4,030,391
		Scott H. Fairlie	270	66	45	49	24	2,505,138
		Abraham R. Katryan	298	57	34	48	19	2,611,144
		Mark E. Casse	409	54	57	59	13	3,307,134
		Sid C. Attard	276	54	45	26	20	2,892,269
WYO	6/21 – 8/17	Jockey	Starts	1st	2d	3d	Win %	Earnings
		Cody Foster	30	10	6	3	33	14,961
		Travis Hamilton	21	4	7	2	19	11,409
		Antonio Perez	23	4	3	3	17	4,315
		Tony F. Guymon	11	4	1	1	36	5,532
		Russel Hadley	12	3	2	0	25	2,928
WYO	6/21 – 8/17	Trainer	Starts	1st	2d	3d	Win %	Earnings
		Mike D. Taylor	26	9	4	4	35	14,430
		Justin Clark	6	3	1	1	50	3,260
		Glade W. Van Tassell	9	3	1	1	33	2,238
		Travis Lusk	5	3	1	0	60	3,885
		Clair Bergeson	5	3	0	1	60	3,820
YAV	5/24 – 9/2	Jockey	Starts	1st	2d	3d	Win %	Earnings
		Esteban Angel Gomez	291	72	51	36	25	269,401
		Kelly Bridges	246	63	37	41	26	240,446
		Miguel Luis Gaeta Hernandez	265	59	58	48	22	269,992
		Vince J. Guerra	193	34	29	29	18	152,883
		Alberto R. Higuera	261	31	42	40	12	161,151
YAV	5/24 – 9/2	Trainer	Starts	1st	2d	3d	Win %	Earnings
		Bill Brashears	128	34	20	18	27	138,937
		Dan L. McFarlane	76	24	27	7	32	110,322
		Justin Evans	124	21	22	21	17	112,921
		Jerry Atkin	68	20	7	5	29	56,178
		Gary Page	41	13	7	5	32	61,766
YD	8/23 – 9/21	Jockey	Starts	1st	2d	3d	Win %	Earnings
		David P. Stubblefield	53	10	10	9	19	22,112
		Russell David Kingrey	34	10	3	4	29	17,130
		Joe Holmes, Sr.	41	9	8	10	22	25,376
		Clay Dunbar	53	8	12	11	15	23,134
		Dan Karr	38	7	7	4	18	14,139
YD	8/23 – 9/21	Trainer	Starts	1st	2d	3d	Win %	Earnings
		Edward Buxbaum	19	5	5	1	26	9,962
		Dale Bagnell	25	4	5	8	16	16,524
		Parke Edwards	19	4	3	4	21	7,872
		Armand Johnson	19	3	5	2	16	7,737
		Bryan Krone	21	3	3	3	14	7,043
YKT	6/21 – 7/5	Jockey	Starts	1st	2d	3d	Win %	Earnings
		Lawrence Durocher	12	4	2	1	33	3,994
		Danielle Beischer	8	3	1	1	38	2,950
		Sheldon Chickeness	5	2	2	1	40	2,136
		Thomas Strongarm	4	2	0	0	50	4,410
		Doug A. Jones	8	1	7	0	13	3,436
YKT	6/21 – 7/5	Trainer	Starts	1st	2d	3d	Win %	Earnings
		Elton Keshane	13	5	2	1	38	4,834
		Dan Keshane	8	3	2	1	38	5,860
		Irene Britton	14	2	7	1	14	4,424
		Jim Ross	9	2	2	1	22	2,692
		Lindsey Keshane	2	1	1	0	50	1,122

GENERAL STATISTICS
OF 2003

TREND OF RACING
MUTUEL HANDLE
NUMBER OF RACES AND PURSES
RACES BY STATE OR PROVINCE

Locations of North American

Alb	–	Albuquerque, NM
AP	–	Arlington Park, IL- (Arlington Int'l Race Course)
Aqu	–	Aqueduct, NY
ArP	–	*Arapahoe Park, CO -
AsD	–	*Assiniboia Downs, Man, Canada -
Atl	–	Atlantic City, NJ
Bel	–	Belmont Park, NY
Beu	–	Beulah Park, OH
BM	–	Bay Meadows, CA
Bmf	–	Bay Meadows Fair, CA
Boi	–	*Boise, ID (Les Bois Park)
BRD	–	*Blue Ribbon Downs, OK
Cby	–	Canterbury Park, MN
CD	–	Churchill Downs, KY
Cls	–	*Columbus, NE
Cnl	–	Colonial Downs,VA
Crc	–	Calder Race Course, FL
CT	–	*Charles Town, WV
DeD	–	*Delta Downs, LA
DeP	–	*Desert Park, BC, Canada
Del	–	Delaware Park, DE
Dmr	–	Del Mar, CA
EIP	–	Ellis Park, KY
EmD	–	Emerald Downs, WA
EvD	–	*Evangeline Downs, LA
Fai	–	Fair Hill, MD
FE	–	Fort Erie, Ont, Canada
Fer	–	*Ferndale, CA
FG	–	Fair Grounds, LA
FL	–	Finger Lakes, NY

FMT	–	*Fair Meadows, OK (Tulsa State Fair)
Fno	–	Fresno, CA
Fon	–	*Fonner Park, NE
FP	–	Fairmount Park, IL
Fpx	–	*Fairplex (Pomona), CA
Fs	–	*Flagstaff, AZ
GBF	–	Great Barrington Fair, MA
GF	–	*Great Falls, MT
GG	–	Golden Gate Fields, CA
Gil	–	*Gillespie County Fair, TX
GLD	–	Great Lakes Downs, MI
GP	–	Gulfstream Park, FL (Includes Breeders' Cup)
GrP	–	*Grants Pass, OR
HaP	–	*Harbor Park, WA
Haw	–	Hawthorne, IL
Hia	–	Hialeah Park, FL
Hol	–	Hollywood Park, CA
Hoo	–	Hoosier Park, IN
Hou	–	Sam Houston Race Park, TX
HPO	–	Horsmen's Park, NE
Hst	–	*Hastings Park, BC, Canada (Formerly Exhibition Park)
Ind	–	Indiana Downs, IN
Kam	–	*Kamloops, BC, Canada
KD	–	Kentucky Downs (Formerly Deuling Grounds)
Kee	–	Keeneland, KY
Kin	–	*Kin Park, BC, Canada
LA	–	*Los Alamitos, CA
LaD	–	Louisana Downs, LA
LnN	–	*Lincoln State Fair, NE
Lrl	–	Laurel Park, MD
LS	–	Lone Star Park, TX
MD	–	*Marquis Downs, Sask, Canada
Med	–	Meadowlands, NJ
Mex	–	*Mexico City, Mexico (Hipodromo de las Americas)

Thoroughbred Race Tracks

Man	–	Manor Downs, TX
Mnr	–	Mountaineer Park, WV
MPM	–	*Mt Pleasant Meadows, MI -
Mth	–	Monmouth Park, NJ
Nmp	–	*Northhampton, MA
NP	–	*Northlands Park, Alta, Canada
OP	–	Oaklawn Park, AK
Pen	–	Penn National, PA
Pha	–	Philadelphia Park, PA
Pim	–	Pimlico, MD
Pla	–	*Playfair, WA
Pln	–	Pleasanton, CA
PM	–	Portland Meadows, OR
PrM	–	Prairie Meadows, IA
RD	–	River Downs, OH
Ret	–	Retama Park, TX
Ril	–	*Rillito, AZ
Rkm	–	Rockingham Park,
RP	–	Remington Park, OK
Rui	–	*Ruidoso Downs, NM
SA	–	Santa Anita Park, CA
Sac	–	Sacramento, CA
Sal	–	*Salem, OR (Lone Oak)
Sar	–	Saratoga, NY
SnD	–	*Sunflower Downs, BC, Canada
Sol	–	*Solano (Vallejo) CA
Spt	–	*Sportsman's Park, IL
SR	–	*Santa Rosa, CA
Stk	–	Stockton, CA
StP	–	*Stampede Park, Alta, Canada
SuD	–	*Sun Downs, WA
Suf	–	Suffolk Downs, MA
Sun	–	Sunland Park, NM
Tam	–	Tampa Bay Downs, FL
Tdn	–	Thistledown, OH
Tim	–	*Timonium, MD
TP	–	Turfway Park, KY
TuP	–	Turf Paradise, AZ
Wds	–	Woodlands, KS
WO	–	Woodbine, Ont, Canada
WRD	–	Will Rogers Downs, OK
Wyo	–	*Wyoming Downs, WY
YAV	–	Yavapai Downs, AZ
YD	–	Yellowstone Downs, MT
YM	–	Yakima Meadows, WA

TRENDS IN THOROUGHBRED RACING

General statistics for race meetings that ended in 2003. The statistics on the following pages include race meets scheduled for 2003 and 2004 along with comparisons of total races, purses, numbers of starters, average size of field, and average purse for 2003 by states.

State	Track	Days	Meetings Ending in 2003						Avg. Overnight Purses	Avg Purses .w/Stks	2004 Dates	
			First Day	Last Day	Races	Starters	Favwins	Fwinpct			First Day	Last Day
AR	OP	49	01/24/03	04/12/03	505	4,525	209	41	$164,575	$228,255	01/23/04	04/10/04
AR	**Totals**	**49**			**505**	**4,525**	**209**	**41**				
AZ	DG	4	04/12/03	04/20/03	18	120	6	33	$4,000	$4,500	04/10/04	04/18/04
AZ	DUN	4	03/15/03	03/23/03	23	152	7	30	$5,500	$7,150	03/13/04	03/31/04
AZ	FLG	4	07/04/03	07/07/03	19	144	9	47	$4,750	$4,750	07/02/04	07/05/04
AZ	GCF	4	09/27/03	10/05/03	19	148	5	26	$4,750	$4,750	09/25/04	10/03/04
AZ	MOF	4	05/10/03	05/18/03	20	116	5	25	$4,750	$5,000	05/08/04	05/16/04
AZ	RIL	14	01/18/03	03/02/03	81	592	23	28	$5,500	$5,786	01/17/04	02/29/04
AZ	SAF	4	03/29/03	04/06/03	17	124	3	18	$3,750	$4,250	03/27/04	04/04/04
AZ	SJ	4	09/13/03	09/21/03	23	144	7	30	$5,750	$5,750	09/11/04	09/19/04
AZ	SON	4	04/26/03	05/04/03	17	118	6	35	$3,750	$4,250	04/24/04	05/02/04
AZ	TUP	167	09/27/02	05/18/03	1,515	12,469	536	35	$60,092	$74,476	09/26/03	05/16/04
AZ	YAV	56	05/24/03	09/02/03	373	2,783	161	43	$27,418	$31,000	05/22/04	09/07/04
AZ	**Totals**	**269**			**2,125**	**16,910**	**768**	**36**				
CA	BM	55	04/02/03	06/15/03	467	3,260	164	35	$140,118	$166,118	04/07/04	06/20/04
CA	BM	50	08/29/03	11/02/03	424	2,991	149	35	$134,770	$160,370	09/03/04	11/07/04
CA	BMF	12	08/06/03	08/18/03	104	710	29	28	$121,250	$125,417	08/11/04	08/23/04
CA	DMR	43	07/23/03	09/10/03	372	3,048	126	34	$300,186	$468,093	07/21/04	09/08/04
CA	FER	10	08/07/03	08/17/03	30	173	10	33	$7,520	$12,770	08/12/04	08/22/04

Meetings Ending in 2003

State	Track	Days	First Day	Last Day	Races	Starters	Favwins	Fwinpct	Avg. Overnight Purses	Avg Purses w/Stks	2004 Dates First Day	Last Day
CA	FNO	11	10/01/03	10/13/03	66	510	29	44	$45,055	$49,600	10/06/04	10/17/04
CA	FPX	17	09/12/03	09/28/03	163	1,326	69	42	$161,235	$225,941	09/10/04	09/26/04
CA	GG	104	11/06/02	03/30/03	881	6,590	320	36	$140,971	$162,829	11/05/03	04/04/04
CA	HOL	65	04/23/03	07/20/03	558	4,293	197	35	$264,185	$412,415	04/21/04	07/18/04
CA	HOL	30	11/11/03	12/21/03	258	1,920	98	38	$229,533	$349,367	11/03/04	12/20/04
CA	LA	191	12/26/02	12/21/03	345	2,386	130	38	$10,619	$10,619	12/26/03	12/19/04
CA	PLN	11	06/25/03	07/06/03	94	744	32	34	$114,864	$143,955	06/30/04	07/11/04
CA	SA	85	12/26/02	04/20/03	733	5,936	269	37	$289,082	$452,494	12/26/03	04/18/04
CA	SA	32	09/28/03	11/09/03	278	2,213	104	37	$237,938	$836,063	09/29/04	10/31/04
CA	SAC	11	08/20/03	09/01/03	86	668	38	44	$80,500	$89,667	08/25/04	09/06/04
CA	SOL	10	07/09/03	07/20/03	87	737	32	37	$95,650	$109,650	07/14/04	07/25/04
CA	SR	12	07/23/03	08/04/03	99	789	42	42	$97,000	$118,667	07/28/04	08/09/04
CA	STK	10	06/11/03	06/22/03	73	605	28	38	$77,050	$77,050	06/16/04	06/27/04
CA	**Totals**	**759**			**5,118**	**38,899**	**1,866**	**36**				
CN	ASD	74	05/04/03	09/28/03	585	4,692	204	35	$56,480	$72,520	05/02/04	10/03/04
CN	FE	114	04/26/03	11/11/03	1,117	9,449	353	32	$176,277	$193,499	05/01/04	11/22/04
CN	GPR	18	07/11/03	08/17/03	59	365	28	47	$10,138	$11,217	07/09/04	08/22/04
CN	HST	69	04/26/03	11/30/03	689	5,254	224	33	$113,280	$151,251	04/17/04	11/28/04
CN	KAM	5	05/25/03	06/29/03	19	102	7	37	$7,640	$7,640	05/30/04	07/04/04
CN	KAM	4	08/10/03	09/07/03	17	73	6	35	$8,600	$12,950	08/08/04	09/05/04
CN	KIN	4	07/06/03	08/03/03	19	90	10	53	$9,750	$11,000	07/11/04	08/01/04
CN	LBG	14	05/03/03	06/15/03	68	495	22	32	$21,009	$22,985	05/01/04	07/04/04
CN	LBG	25	08/30/03	11/02/03	131	929	50	38	$21,812	$31,714	09/04/04	10/31/04
CN	MD	30	05/23/03	09/06/03	197	1,257	83	42	$13,873	$18,557	05/28/04	09/18/04
CN	MDA	12	09/13/03	10/19/03	49	297	15	31	$5,342	$5,342	09/11/04	10/17/04

Meetings Ending in 2003

State	Track	Days	First Day	Last Day	Races	Starters	Favwins	Fwinpct	Avg. Overnight Purses	Avg Purses .w/Stks	2004 Dates First Day	Last Day
CN	MIL	1	07/01/03	07/01/03	3	19	1	33	$16,800	$26,500	07/01/04	07/02/04
CN	NP	74	06/20/03	10/26/03	635	4,860	193	30	$87,019	$111,005	06/25/04	10/30/04
CN	RPD	2	07/12/03	07/13/03	4	19	3	75	$2,000	$2,000	07/10/04	07/11/04
CN	STP	39	04/04/03	06/15/03	340	2,529	115	34	$90,584	$104,305	04/02/04	06/20/04
CN	WO	162	03/22/03	11/30/03	1,550	12,718	515	33	$422,566	$553,554	04/17/04	12/12/04
CN	YKT	6	06/21/03	07/05/03	16	85	6	38	$3,133	$4,100	06/19/04	07/03/04
CN	**Totals**	**653**			**5,498**	**43,233**	**1,835**	**33**				
CO	ARP	47	06/06/03	08/25/03	285	2,353	92	32	$42,088	$54,464	06/04/04	08/23/04
CO	**Totals**	**47**			**285**	**2,353**	**92**	**32**				
DE	DEL	141	04/26/03	11/09/03	1,271	9,133	468	37	$193,827	$234,849	04/24/04	10/31/04
DE	**Totals**	**141**			**1,271**	**9,133**	**468**	**37**				
FL	CRC	128	04/25/03	10/24/03	1,325	10,539	497	38	$175,184	$233,309	04/24/04	10/23/04
FL	CRC	53	10/25/03	01/02/04	575	4,871	185	32	$169,689	$228,462	10/24/04	01/02/05
FL	GP	89	01/03/03	04/24/03	897	7,511	302	34	$237,472	$336,685	01/03/04	04/25/04
FL	OTC	1	03/17/03	03/17/03	6	42	0	0	$0	$370,000	03/15/04	03/15/04
FL	TAM	93	12/14/02	05/04/03	983	9,124	292	30	$117,993	$137,203	12/13/03	05/02/04
FL	**Totals**	**364**			**3,786**	**32,087**	**1,276**	**34**				
IA	PRM	52	04/18/03	06/28/03	478	3,715	170	36	$137,871	$156,813	04/16/04	07/04/04
IA	PRM	48	07/04/03	09/13/03	292	2,475	91	31	$70,750	$109,188	07/09/04	09/25/04
IA	**Totals**	**100**			**770**	**6,190**	**261**	**34**				

			Meetings Ending in 2003						Avg. Overnight Purses	Avg Purses .w/Stks	2004 Dates	
State	Track	Days	First Day	Last Day	Races	Starters	Favwins	Fwinpct			First Day	Last Day
ID	BOI	47	05/03/03	08/10/03	293	2,036	105	36	$12,713	$21,676	05/01/04	08/15/04
ID	**Totals**	**47**			**293**	**2,036**	**105**	**36**				
IL	AP	104	05/09/03	09/27/03	969	7,885	364	38	$207,827	$272,923	05/14/04	09/19/04
IL	FP	102	04/04/03	10/11/03	980	7,473	355	36	$54,467	$58,731	03/26/04	09/18/04
IL	HAW	48	03/01/03	05/06/03	447	3,622	144	32	$170,417	$212,917	02/27/04	05/11/04
IL	HAW	69	09/28/03	01/03/04	648	5,860	227	35	$179,920	$215,862	09/24/04	01/02/05
IL	**Totals**	**323**			**3,044**	**24,840**	**1,090**	**36**				
IN	HOO	70	08/29/03	12/04/03	720	6,580	303	42	$90,414	$111,843	09/02/04	11/21/04
IN	IND	30	04/11/03	05/26/03	281	2,474	102	36	$104,650	$113,150	04/16/04	06/20/04
IN	**Totals**	**100**			**1,001**	**9,054**	**405**	**40**				
KS	ANF	6	07/11/03	07/20/03	25	144	14	56	$4,933	$9,933	07/09/04	07/18/04
KS	EUR	21	05/03/03	07/05/03	55	354	18	33	$4,586	$6,164	05/01/04	07/04/04
KS	WDS	30	09/23/03	11/01/03	203	2,018	49	24	$39,818	$49,184	09/21/04	10/30/04
KS	**Totals**	**57**			**283**	**2,516**	**81**	**29**				
KY	CD	52	04/26/03	07/06/03	527	4,687	168	32	$308,488	$432,527	04/24/04	07/05/04
KY	CD	27	10/26/03	11/29/03	275	2,659	94	34	$338,478	$419,959	10/31/04	11/27/04
KY	ELP	41	07/09/03	09/01/03	413	3,761	149	36	$171,610	$197,829	07/07/04	09/06/04
KY	KD	6	09/13/03	09/23/03	36	360	11	31	$109,286	$197,857	09/18/04	09/28/04
KY	KEE	15	04/04/03	04/25/03	138	1,166	50	36	$383,867	$628,867	04/02/04	04/23/04
KY	KEE	17	10/03/03	11/25/03	154	1,488	45	29	$319,706	$584,412	10/08/04	10/30/04
KY	TP	81	12/01/02	04/03/03	793	7,157	251	32	$133,488	$153,918	11/30/03	04/01/04

Meetings Ending in 2003

State	Track	Days	First Day	Last Day	Races	Starters	Favwins	Fwinpct	Avg. Overnight Purses	Avg Purses .w/Stks	2004 Dates First Day	Last Day
KY	TP	22	09/03/03	10/02/03	220	2,021	87	40	$138,473	$187,336	09/08/04	10/07/04
KY	Totals	261			2,556	23,299	855	33				
LA	DED	80	11/07/02	03/23/03	802	7,176	312	39	$147,313	$183,641	10/31/03	03/27/04
LA	EVD	87	04/04/03	09/01/03	870	7,681	298	34	$66,909	$72,811	04/01/04	09/06/04
LA	FG	84	11/28/02	03/31/03	836	6,791	290	35	$177,968	$253,851	11/27/03	03/28/04
LA	LAD	80	06/27/03	11/09/03	906	8,128	316	35	$145,338	$179,838	05/14/04	10/31/04
LA	Totals	331			3,414	29,776	1,216	36				
MA	NMP	9	08/29/03	09/14/03	75	565	31	41	$25,800	$27,300	09/03/04	09/19/04
MA	SUF	122	01/01/03	08/27/03	1,094	9,206	386	35	$97,269	$109,269	05/01/04	11/27/04
MA	SUF	25	09/15/03	10/27/03	205	1,885	72	35	$87,276	$97,076		
MA	Totals	156			1,374	11,656	489	36				
MD	LRL	119	10/08/02	03/30/03	1,059	8,259	396	37	$155,168	$189,688	10/08/03	03/28/04
MD	LRL	22	07/24/03	08/22/03	192	1,517	69	36	$167,409	$188,318	07/22/04	08/27/04
MD	PIM	48	04/02/03	06/08/03	451	3,270	167	37	$171,096	$257,763	03/31/04	06/06/04
MD	PIM	23	09/03/03	10/05/03	203	1,668	73	36	$165,700	$187,100	09/08/04	10/03/04
MD	TIM	8	08/23/03	09/01/03	75	551	31	41	$113,125	$125,625	08/28/04	09/06/04
MD	Totals	220			1,980	15,265	736	37				
MI	GLD	118	04/26/03	10/28/03	1,006	7,766	360	36	$63,840	$78,362	04/25/04	10/30/04
MI	MPM	32	05/03/03	09/28/03	48	314	16	33	$5,909	$5,909	05/01/04	09/26/04
MI	Totals	150			1,054	8,080	376	36				

State	Track	Days	Meetings Ending in 2003						Avg. Overnight Purses	Avg Purses .w/Stks	2004 Dates First Day	Last Day
			First Day	Last Day	Races	Starters	Favwins	Fwinpct				
MN	CBY	63	05/16/03	09/01/03	547	4,628	201	37	$82,429	$110,206	05/14/04	09/06/04
MN	**Totals**	**63**			**547**	**4,628**	**201**	**37**				
MT	GF	8	07/04/03	07/27/03	49	350	16	33	$11,288	$14,138	07/02/04	07/25/04
MT	YD	12	08/23/03	09/21/03	59	388	19	32	$10,040	$11,838	08/21/04	09/19/04
MT	**Totals**	**20**			**108**	**738**	**35**	**32**				
ND	CPW	3	06/15/03	06/22/03	15	85	7	47	$4,333	$5,833	06/12/04	06/27/04
ND	FAR	13	08/22/03	09/14/03	62	375	29	47	$12,500	$20,438	08/06/04	09/06/04
ND	**Totals**	**16**			**77**	**460**	**36**	**47**				
NE	ATO	2	07/19/03	07/20/03	12	115	5	42	$92,500	$92,500	09/18/04	09/19/04
NE	CLS	26	07/24/03	09/14/03	217	1,921	83	38	$32,087	$35,894	07/23/04	09/12/04
NE	FON	35	02/08/03	05/04/03	337	2,973	136	40	$40,711	$51,895	02/14/04	05/08/04
NE	HPO	4	07/10/03	07/13/03	16	152	4	25	$62,500	$122,500	07/15/04	07/18/04
NE	LNN	33	05/09/03	07/06/03	281	2,360	89	32	$39,413	$44,193	05/14/04	07/11/04
NE	**Totals**	**100**			**863**	**7,521**	**317**	**37**				
NJ	ATL	4	04/23/03	05/02/03	26	254	10	38	$106,250	$106,250	05/05/04	05/19/04
NJ	MED	28	10/02/03	11/08/03	266	2,061	100	38	$171,750	$216,357	09/06/04	12/11/04
NJ	MTH	92	05/24/03	09/28/03	896	7,068	307	34	$246,864	$316,647	05/29/04	09/05/04
NJ	**Totals**	**124**			**1,188**	**9,383**	**417**	**35**				
NM	ALB	51	03/14/03	06/08/03	246	2,069	85	35	$42,459	$57,900	04/09/04	07/05/04
NM	ALB	16	09/05/03	09/21/03	73	555	34	47	$25,563	$46,863	09/10/04	09/26/04
NM	RUI	57	05/23/03	09/01/03	292	2,350	95	33	$39,640	$51,482	05/28/04	09/06/04

			Meetings Ending in 2003						Avg. Overnight Purses	Avg Purses .w/Stks	2004 Dates First Day	Last Day
State	Track	Days	First Day	Last Day	Races	Starters	Favwins	Fwinpct				
NM	SRP	40	09/19/03	11/23/03	251	2,048	111	44	$57,300	$70,973	08/02/04	09/07/04
NM	SUN	78	11/19/02	04/06/03	526	4,968	200	38	$110,219	$146,233	09/27/04	11/02/04
											11/25/03	04/11/04
NM	**Totals**	**242**			**1,388**	**11,990**	**525**	**38**				
NV	ELK	4	08/23/03	09/01/03	23	126	8	35	$7,867	$12,442	08/21/04	09/06/04
NV	**Totals**	**4**			**23**	**126**	**8**	**35**				
NY	AQU	63	12/04/02	03/09/03	542	4,507	186	34	$299,580	$334,290	10/29/03	03/07/04
NY	AQU	38	03/12/03	05/04/03	349	2,682	134	38	$309,895	$394,763	03/10/04	05/02/04
NY	AQU	23	10/29/03	11/30/03	211	1,874	74	35	$318,160	$432,960	10/27/04	11/28/04
NY	BEL	55	05/07/03	07/20/03	517	4,039	189	37	$337,455	$510,545	05/05/04	07/25/04
NY	BEL	38	09/05/03	10/26/03	355	3,016	122	34	$332,737	$619,184	09/10/04	10/24/04
NY	FL	154	04/18/03	11/29/03	1,383	10,656	536	39	$70,055	$75,472	04/16/04	11/23/04
NY	SAR	37	07/20/03	09/01/03	346	2,935	138	40	$356,811	$607,216	07/28/04	09/04/04
NY	**Totals**	**408**			**3,703**	**29,709**	**1,379**	**37**				
OH	BEU	70	01/10/03	05/03/03	508	4,114	181	36	$38,364	$40,564	01/10/04	05/01/04
OH	BEU	69	09/13/03	12/21/03	495	4,707	171	35	$38,934	$48,159	09/11/04	12/20/04
OH	RD	122	04/12/03	09/01/03	902	7,839	349	39	$48,299	$55,615	04/09/04	09/06/04
OH	TDN	188	03/15/03	12/16/03	1,348	11,722	485	36	$52,538	$59,080	04/08/04	12/31/04
OH	**Totals**	**449**			**3,253**	**28,382**	**1,186**	**36**				
OK	BRD	66	02/01/03	11/09/03	208	1,728	65	31	$6,663	$7,026	02/21/04	05/01/04
											08/06/04	10/30/04
OK	FMT	33	04/10/03	06/07/03	103	954	46	45	$20,485	$24,185	05/27/04	07/24/04

State	Track	Days	Meetings Ending in 2003 First Day	Last Day	Races	Starters	Favwins	Fwinpct	Avg. Overnight Purses	Avg Purses w/Stks	2004 Dates First Day	Last Day
OK	RP	10	07/25/03	08/17/03	58	576	19	33	$39,513	$39,513	07/30/04	11/28/04
OK	RP	57	08/22/03	11/30/03	503	4,467	190	38	$61,014	$78,909		
OK		**Totals 166**			**872**	**7,725**	**320**	**37**				
OR	BRN	2	09/06/03	09/07/03	14	91	4	29	$14,750	$14,750	09/11/04	09/12/04
OR	GRP	18	05/17/03	07/06/03	120	682	40	33	$13,128	$14,772	05/15/04	07/05/04
OR	PM	81	10/19/02	04/27/03	659	5,186	226	34	$26,317	$30,714	10/18/03	04/24/04
OR	PRV	4	07/09/03	07/12/03	23	151	12	52	$13,875	$13,875	07/07/04	07/10/04
OR	TIL	3	08/07/03	08/09/03	20	115	5	25	$13,367	$14,133	08/12/04	08/14/04
OR	UN	3	06/06/03	06/08/03	14	81	5	36	$9,800	$9,800	06/11/04	06/13/04
OR		**Totals 111**			**850**	**6,306**	**292**	**34**				
PA	PEN	195	01/02/03	12/30/03	1,772	14,452	646	36	$62,409	$63,872	01/02/04	12/30/04
PA	PHA	213	01/01/03	12/30/03	2,065	16,908	693	34	$116,386	$127,915	01/01/04	12/31/04
PA		**408**			**3,837**	**31,360**	**1,339**	**35**				
TX	GIL	8	07/04/03	08/24/03	17	144	5	29	$6,550	$9,238	07/03/04	08/29/04
TX	HOU	80	11/01/02	03/30/03	767	7,147	268	35	$87,864	$201,920	10/23/03	04/10/04
TX	LS	70	04/03/03	07/13/03	681	6,346	263	39	$161,771	$218,736	04/15/04	07/11/04
											10/01/04	10/31/04
TX	MAN	12	04/05/03	05/11/03	73	584	19	26	$27,208	$38,042	02/28/04	04/25/04
TX	RET	48	08/01/03	10/19/03	457	3,953	192	42	$75,271	$97,979	07/22/04	09/25/04
TX		**Totals 218**			**1,995**	**18,174**	**747**	**37**				
VA	CNL	30	06/13/03	07/22/03	293	2,932	87	30	$146,968	$188,903	06/11/04	07/26/04
VA		**Totals 30**			**293**	**2,932**	**87**	**30**				

Meetings Ending in 2003

State	Track	Days	First Day	Last Day	Races	Starters	Favwins	Fwinpct	Avg. Overnight Purses	Avg Purses .w/Stks	2004 Dates First Day	Last Day
WA	EMD	92	04/19/03	09/22/03	830	6,040	282	34	$66,713	$89,484	04/16/04	09/20/04
WA	SUD	10	04/05/03	05/04/03	48	352	19	40	$7,880	$8,245	04/03/04	05/02/04
WA	Totals	102			878	6,392	301	34				
WV	CT	235	01/01/03	12/31/03	2,330	21,307	776	33	$142,062	$149,974	01/01/04	12/26/04
WV	MNR	222	01/11/03	12/30/03	2,190	20,512	663	30	$164,886	$176,309	01/03/04	12/28/04
WV	Totals	457			4,520	41,819	1,439	32				
WY	WYO	18	06/21/03	08/17/03	36	259	15	42	$2,133	$4,343	06/19/04	08/15/04
WY	Totals	18			36	259	15	42				

NOTES: Meet Days are days counted on which at least one official Thoroughbred race occurred; Races are official Thoroughbred Races

Avg. Daily Overnight Purse excl. Stakes is the amount of Daily Overnight Purses excl. Stakes Races divided by Entry Days

Avg. Daily Overnight Purse incl. Stakes is the amount of Daily Overnight Purses incl. Stakes Races divided by Entry Days

PARI-MUTUEL HANDLE

Snapshot Facts: Pari-mutuel handle on Thoroughbred racing in the United States increased .8 % during 2003 (including separate pools first reported in 2000) to more than $15 billion. Combined US and Canadian handle was down .1%. As in all recent years, gains continued to come exclusively from the off-track sector which accounted for almost 87.5% of US handle.

TOTAL NORTH AMERICAN HANDLE 2000-2003

	2000 Total*	2000 % of total	2001 Total*	2001 % of total	2002 Total*	2002 % of total	2003 Total*	2003 % of total
On Track	$2,430	16.2	$2,273	14.8	$2,190	13.81	$2,041	12.99
Off Track	12,612	83.8	13,082	85.2	13,668	86.19	13,672	87.01
TOTAL	15,042		15,355		15,858	(+3.7)	**15,713	(-.1)

UNITED STATES

	2000 Total	2000 * %of total	2001 Total*	2001 %of total	2002 Total*	2002 %of total	2003 Total*	2003 % of total
On Track	$2,270	15.9	$2,112	14.5	$2,029	13.47	$1,902	12.53
Off Track	12,051	84.1	12,487	85.5	13,033	86.53	13,278	87.47
TOTAL	14,321	(+4.4)	14,599	(+1.9)	15,062	(+3.5)	15,180	(+.8)

CANADA

	2000 Total*	2000 %of total	2001 Total*	2001 %of total	2002 Total*	2002 % of total	2003 Total*	2003 % of total
On Track	$150	31.6	$153	28.3	$153	26.98	$139	26.03
Off Track	325	68.4	387	71.7	414	73.02	394	73.78
TOTAL	475		540		567	(+5.0)	534	(-5.8)

PUERTO RICO

	2000 Total	2000 * %of total	2001 Total*	2001 %of total	2002 Total*	2002 %of total	2003 Total*	2003 % of total
On Track	$10	4.1	$8	3.7	$8	3.49	NA	
Off Track	236	95.9	208	96.3	221	96.51	NA	
TOTAL	246		216	(-16.1)	229	(+10.1)	NA	

• All Dollars in Millions. ** 2003 figures include US and Canada only

PARI MUTUEL HANDLE FROM 1988 THROUGH 1999

Year	United States	% change from prior year	Canada	Total
1988	$8,935,978,600	(+7.3%)	$719,365,900	$9,655,344,500
1989	9,285,509,800	(+3.9%)	772,675,600	10,058,185,400
1990	9,385,072,100	(+1.1%)	823,280,300	10,208,352,400
1991	9,393,460,600	(+0.1%)	804,442,500	10,197,903,100
1992	9,638,864,200	(+2.6%)	770,080,900	10,408,945,100
1993	9,600,545,400	(-0.4%)	730,876,000	10,331,421,400
1994	9,897,028,600	(+3.1%)	680,960,500	10,577,989,100
1995	10,428,822,300	(+5.4%)	794,877,000	11,223,699,300
1996	11,627,000,000	(+11.5%)	**642,000,000	12,269,000,000
1997	12,542,000,000	(+7.9)	527,000,000	13,327,000,000
1998	13,115,000,000	(+4.6)	498,000,000	13,805,000,000
1999	13,724,000,000	(+4.7)	439,000,000	14,408,000,000

*-figures in millions of dollars **-includes Breeders' Cup Day

Sources: The Jockey Club; Equibase Company LLC; California Horse Racing Information Management Systems, Association of Racing Commissioners International and El Comandante.

Gross Purses in North America

Following nine consecutive years of growth, gross purses in the United States dipped 1.7 percent in 2003, despite continued gains in pari-mutuel handle. This could indicate a growing shift in wagering toward offshore bookmakers and other non-racing affiliated wagering outlets that contribute little, if anything, back to live racing source markets. Once again, states with the largest percentage increases in available purse money in 2003 were those with tracks featuring expanded gaming options, namely New Mexico (+29.3 percent) and Louisiana (+18.4 percent).

YEAR	US*	(% CHANGE)	CANADA*	PUERTO RICO*	STARTERS	TOTAL*
1990	714.5	(+1.1%)	69.6	12.4	90,938	$796.5
1991	698.7	(-2.2%)	65.2	12.6	88,189	$776.5
1992	709.6	(+1.6%)	68.4	13.6	84,755	$791.6
1993	692.1	(-2.5%)	63.2	14.4	80,238	$769.7
1994	718.4	(+3.8%)	64	14.8	76,539	$797.2
1995	761.6	(+6.0%)	74.7	15.9	73,870	$852.2
1996	792.7	(+4.1%)	**86.3	18	71,982	$897.0
1997	851.5	(+7.4%)	68.7	18.2	70,370	$938.4
1998	904	(+6.2%)	74.3	15.2	70,291	$993.5
1999	962.9	(+6.5%)	87.7	16.1	70,284	$1,066.7
2000	1,030.9	(+7.1%)	114.9	18.8	70,869	$1,164.6
2001	1,067.5	(+3.6%)	131.9	19.5	71,278	$1,218.9
2002	1,074.2	(+0.6%)	149.1	19.1	74,288	$1,242.4
2003	1,055.5	(-1.7%)	150.4	18.7	75,347	$1,224.6

* Dollars in Millions...

** Includes Breeders' Cup Day at Woodbine

Purses include monies not won and returned to state breeder or other funds, but do not include retroactive payments. In Puerto Rico, retroactive payments represent a significant part of total prize money distributed.

Sources: Equibase Company LLC and Racing Sport Administration of Puerto Rico.

Snapshot Facts: For the first time since 1993, U.S. purses decreased from the year before. Even after the slight drop, U.S. purses were nearly 53 percent higher in 2003 than in 1993.

TWO-YEAR-OLD RACING

With two-year-old races representing just 7.7 percent of all races run in North America, two-year-olds today run less frequently and debut later in the calendar year than ever before. The majority of all two-year-old starters do so little more than three times during their brief preparatory season.

Year	2YO Starters	2YO Starts	Avg Sts.	All starters	%all starters	2YO races	All races	%all races	2YO Purses
1988	14,976	59,988	4	90,486	16.6	6,410	78,270	8.2	86,762,000
1989	14,907	57,956	3.9	91,436	16.3	6,280	81,400	7.7	87,680,400
1990	14,685	57,538	3.9	89,716	16.4	6,189	79,971	7.7	90,028,524
1991	14,631	58,305	4	86,937	16.8	6,361	79,303	8	89,021,900
1992	13,561	55,020	4.1	83,404	16.3	6,167	77,712	7.9	89,672,800
1993	12,471	47,562	3.9	78,740	15.9	5,362	72,342	7.4	81,970,300
1994	11,838	45,066	3.8	74,955	15.8	5,275	70,699	7.5	83,261,500
1995	11,415	42,517	3.7	72,399	15.7	4,963	68,245	7.3	91,472,723
1996	10,977	40,757	3.7	70,450	15.6	4,750	64,388	7.4	96,372,058
1997	10,906	39,573	3.6	69,056	15.8	4,701	63,487	7.4	101,129,962
1998	11,056	39,588	3.6	68,697	16.1	4,639	61,293	7.6	106,820,755
1999	10,936	38,603	3.5	68,678	15.9	4,554	60,182	7.6	116,157,359
2000	11,292	39,745	3.5	69,569	16.2	4,743	60,872	7.8	126,795,123
2001	11,519	40,119	3.5	71,278	16.2	4,731	60,738	7.8	128,371,786
2002	11,964	40,827	3.4	72,825	16.4	4,791	59,896	8	131,477,440
2003	11,559	38,360	3.3	73,918	15.6	4,514	59,001	7.7	130,872,472

Above figures include US and Canada only Source: The Jockey Club and Equibase.

SIZE OF FIELD AND STARTS PER HORSE 1950–2003

Average field size remained relatively consistent between 1950 and 1990, at which time began a persistent decline. Over the past several years, the situation has stabilized as a result of increases in the annual registered foal crop. During this time, however, the decline in average starts per runner has quickened, with average starts per runner in 2003 once again the lowest on record.

YEAR	STARTERS	RACES	STARTS	AVG. FIELD	AVG. STARTS PER RUNNER
1950	22,388	26,932	244,343	9.07	10.91
1955	25,924	31,757	287,775	9.06	11.1
1960	29,798	37,661	337,060	8.95	11.31
1965	37,386	47,335	406,646	8.59	10.88
1970	47,778	56,676	488,326	8.62	10.22
1975	58,816	68,210	601,780	8.82	10.23
1980	64,506	68,243	593,849	8.7	9.21
1985	82,548	75,687	683,667	9.03	8.28
1990	89,716	79,971	712,494	8.91	7.94
1991	86,937	79,303	693,614	8.75	7.98
1992	83,404	77,712	669,967	8.62	8.03
1993	78,740	72,342	618,974	8.56	7.86
1994	74,955	70,699	587,404	8.31	7.84
1995	72,399	68,245	559,669	8.2	7.73
1996	70,450	64,388	534,861	8.31	7.59
1997	69,056	63,487	520,880	8.2	7.54
1998	68,697	61,293	500,710	8.17	7.29
1999	68,678	60,182	493,926	8.21	7.19
2000	69,569	60,872	493,682	8.11	7.1
2001	71,278	60,738	496,604	8.18	6.97
2002	72,825	59,896	495,228	8.27	6.80
2003	73,918	59,001	489,503	8.30	6.62

Above figures include US and Canada only. Data provided by Equibase and The Jockey Club

THOROUGHBRED RACING AND BREEDING WORLDWIDE

Today's world of the thoroughbred reaches to the four corners of the Earth, transcending geographical, political and racial boundaries. While the following statistics demonstrate the overall strength of horse racing and breeding in the United States in comparison with other countries, they only hint at the tremendous contribution made by the US to the thoroughbred industries of other countries.

Country	Races	Purses*	Handle*	Mares	Foals	Starts	Starters
Argentina	7,222	31.64	242.82	10,687	6,424	54,938	12,642
Australia	21,125	190.17	7,255.04	26,667	17,953	205,118	31,136
Austria	103	0.53	***	69	41	748	211
Bahrein	152	0.58	▼▼	77	55	1,259	225
Belgium	420	0.85	26.82	172	101	3,322	655
Brazil	5,317	8.32	89.77	4,715	3,429	43,558	6,895
Canada	5,592	149.13	567.17	3,505	2,600	43,718	7,509
Chile	6,369	17.51	137.89	2,288	1,717	66,436	3,524
Cyprus	913	8.65	107.14	739	422	8,588	1,163
Denmark	295	1.80	***	250	175	4,120	590
France	4,366	132.92	6,981.43	8,323	4,272	48,249	7,597
Germany	2,381	28.84	326.71	2,317	1,341	22,727	3,638
Great Britain	4,572	93.46	12,616.50	9,077	5,156	52,998	8,193
Greece	1,339	18.17	352.95	715	456	11,059	1,454
Hong Kong	710	89.30	9,148.81	0	0	9,167	1,258
Hungary	316	1.25	5.94	415	247	2,842	380
India	3,115	10.64	173.05	2,892	1,372	22,406	4,228
Ireland	789	24.73	1,865.05	16,467	10,214	10,647	1,906
Italy	5,242	102.85	***	3,089	2,165	46,627	6,931
Japan	22,274	996.25	30,570.07	11,948	8,670	237,095	28,996
Lebanon	365	0.81	13.82	0	0	3,108	419
Macau	1,116	33.62	339.99	0	0	12,852	1,116
Madagascar	104	0.01	4.89	9	5	***	119
Malaysia	1,177	29.91	1,132.23	57	36	15,006	2,327
Mauritius	232	1.79	48.26	0	0	2,269	405
Mexico	1,321	***	***	488	283	11,182	1,487
Morocco	431	1.78	145.87	234	100	4,942	675
Netherlands	176	0.51	39.47	31	29	1,230	271
New Zealand	2,669	17.48	353.51	9,288	5,060	29,899	5,098
Norway	288	3.60	356.35	110	74	2,799	568
Oman	100	0.31	▼▼	47	22	***	***
Poland	372	1.00	7.89	895	473	2,480	440
Qatar	172	2.20	▼▼	36	13	1,659	296
Russia	1,202	0.07	0.91	1,022	613	6,103	2,192
Saudi Arabia	301	3.08	▼▼	1,319	535	3,429	961
Slovakia	131	0.46	.10	231	131	1,160	392
South Africa	4,166	21.48	***	4,272	2,493	47,056	7,241
South Korea	1,094	55.84	5,895.11	1,388	915	11,918	1,712
Spain	443	3.03	***	200	170	4,293	752
Sweden	702	8.09	1,164.00	495	445	6,885	1,455
Switzerland	158	1.67	76.86	176	49	1,502	304

Thailand	500	3.84	76.99	525	162	3,800	912
Tunisia	400	1.93	18.85	200	140	5,100	500
Turkey	2,763	74.91	646.66	1,528	1,082	31,157	3,095
United Arab Emer.	373	25.15	▼▼	70	55	4,293	1,212
United States	54,304	1,074.25	15,062.13	59,161	32,235	450,063	67,009
Total	167,672	3,275.31	95,851.05	186,194	111,930	1,559,804	230,084

* All totals in millions of US dollars and where applicable they include a conversion from Euro Dollars at 1.00 Euro at US $ 1.047.

Some handle figures in some countries include sums wagered via legal bookmaking firms and some betting handle figures include Harness racing.

*** Not reported. ...▼▼ No wagering.

Snapshot Fact: Among countries reporting purses and the total number of starters, starters in Hong Kong averaged the highest earnings per runner during the season, with over $89 million in purses and 1,258 starters, for an average of almost $71,000 per starter. This figure was twice that of Japan, whose starters averaged just over $34,000.

Statistics provided by The Jockey Club and are based based on 2002 totals made available by the International Statistical Survey of Horse Racing, as compiled by the Societe d' Encouragement and presented at the 37th International Conference of Racing Authorities, Paris, France, Oct. 6, 2003.

TRENDS IN DISTRIBUTION OF RACES BY PURSES AND DISTANCES

Since 1992, in spite of a substantial reduction in the number of races run, the distribution of races for three-year-olds and up has remained relatively stable. Increasing average purse money continues to favor longer distances.

Year	Races 6F, under	Avg. Purses	Races over 6f, under 1M	Avg. Purses	Races 1 Mile– 1 1/4 Mi.	Avg. Purses	Races over 1 1/4 mi.	Avg. Purses
1989	38,304	6,319	11,487	8,400	24,770	12,563	559	41,126
1990	36,398	6,483	11,662	8,587	25,175	12,970	547	40,050
1991	36,370	6,316	11,289	8,665	24,760	13,188	523	40,551
1992	34,971	6,583	11,200	8,799	24,832	13,342	542	39,087
1993	32,031	7,045	10,069	9,272	23,346	13,811	534	36,642
1994	32,422	7,600	9,930	9,539	22,498	14,252	574	34,864
1995	31,482	8,345	9,117	11,060	22,107	16,268	576	37,615
1996	29,266	9,317	8,744	11,920	21,076	18,176	552	41,060
1997	28,738	10,124	8,451	12,580	21,053	18,949	544	41,919
1998	27,798	11,271	8,134	13,934	20,236	20,827	486	48,069
1999	27,137	12,302	8,330	15,535	19,717	22,533	444	60,399
2000	27,904	13,126	8,110	17,651	19,650	24,478	465	61,335
2001	27,767	14,000	8,074	18,290	19,736	25,718	430	62,953
2002	27,135	14,403	8,308	19,391	19,248	26,404	414	64,315
2003	26,959	14,208	8,091	20,113	19,037	26,435	400	65,063

Above figures include US and Canada only. Excludes all two-year-old racing

Source: Equibase Company LLC

Snapshot Facts: During a year which saw a slight decline in total purses, only races at six furlongs and less saw a decrease in average purses.

THE AMERICAN RACING MANUAL

FOAL CROPS BY STATE

UNITED STATES

Kentucky annually leads the list of states producing registered thoroughbred foals, although MRLS significantly curtailed its foal production in 2002. Nevertheless, Kentucky is one of four states among the top 12 foal producers to increase its share of the US foal crop since 1992. The others are Florida, New York and New Mexico, the latter of which supplanted Ohio as the nation's 12th largest producer of registered foals in 2002, a rank it last held in 1974.

State by 2002 Ranking	1992 Reg. Foals	Per Cent US Crop	2001 Reg. Foals	Per Cent US Crop	2002 Reg. Foals	Per Cent US Crop	% Change 1992–02
Kentucky	6,871	19.6	9,824	28.7	8,120	25.8	18.2
Florida	3,574	10.2	4,341	12.7	4,245	13.5	18.8
California	4,170	11.9	3,726	10.9	3,649	11.6	-12.5
Texas	2,256	6.4	1,967	5.7	1,809	5.8	-19.8
New York	1,471	4.2	1,742	5.1	1,747	5.6	18.8
Louisiana	1,600	4.6	1,396	4.1	1,419	4.5	-11.3
Maryland	1,470	4.2	1,118	3.3	962	3.1	-34.6
Oklahoma	1,577	4.5	1,053	3.1	905	2.9	-42.6
Illinois	1,417	4.0	975	2.8	896	2.8	-36.8
Pennsylvania	871	2.5	910	2.7	812	2.6	-6.8
Washington	1,470	4.2	855	2.5	749	2.4	-49.0
New Mexico	550	1.6	547	1.6	642	2.0	16.7
Ohio	911	2.6	632	1.9	591	1.9	-35.1
Indiana	109	0.3	543	1.6	516	1.6	373.4
Iowa	158	0.5	485	1.4	437	1.4	176.6
Virginia	652	1.9	521	1.5	429	1.4	-34.2
New Jersey	517	1.5	335	1.0	370	1.2	-28.4
Michigan	518	1.5	308	0.9	358	1.1	-30.9
West Virginia	472	1.3	363	1.1	345	1.1	-26.9
Arkansas	435	1.2	305	0.9	303	1.0	-30.3
Arizona	379	1.1	342	1.0	293	0.9	-22.7
Oregon	241	0.7	282	0.8	257	0.8	-6.6
Minnesota	398	1.1	211	0.6	250	0.8	-37.2
Colorado	245	0.7	228	0.7	229	0.7	-6.5
Idaho	326	0.9	206	0.6	172	0.5	-47.2
Nebraska	464	1.3	166	0.5	132	0.4	-71.6
Kansas	256	0.7	102	0.3	93	0.3	-63.7
Massachusetts	98	0.3	73	0.2	73	0.2	-25.5
Montana	250	0.7	117	0.3	70	0.2	-72.0
Georgia	144	0.4	57	0.2	65	0.2	-54.9
South Dakota	76	0.2	57	0.2	64	0.2	-15.8
South Carolina	113	0.3	72	0.2	57	0.2	-49.6
Alabama	120	0.3	65	0.2	56	0.2	-53.3
Utah	215	0.6	66	0.2	52	0.2	-75.8
Missouri	156	0.4	43	0.1	47	0.1	-69.9
North Carolina	126	0.4	47	0.1	44	0.1	-65.1
North Dakota	45	0.1	39	0.1	42	0.1	-6.7
Tennessee	84	0.2	46	0.1	39	0.1	-53.6
Mississippi	61	0.2	20	0.1	29	0.1	-52.5
Wyoming	44	0.1	17	0.0	23	0.1	-47.7
Nevada	27	0.1	9	0.0	18	0.1	-33.3
Wisconsin	41	0.1	21	0.1	16	0.1	-61.0
Connecticut	25	0.1	4	0.0	5	0.0	-80.0
New Hampshire	15	0.0	7	0.0	3	0.0	-80.0
Vermont	10	0.0	1	0.0	3	0.0	-70.0
Delaware	3	0.0	0	0.0	2	0.0	-33.3
Maine	2	0.0	3	0.0	1	0.0	-50.0
Hawaii	7	0.0	0	0.0	1	0.0	-85.7
Virgin Islands	1	0.0	3	0.0	1	0.0	0.0
Alaska	2	0.0	0	0.0	0	0.0	-100.0
Rhode Island	7	0.0	0	0.0	0	0.0	-100.0
Total US	35,050		34,270		31,441		-10.3%
Canada	2,777		2,558		2,350		-15.4%
Puerto Rico	610		585		511		-16.2%
Total Crop	38,437		37,413		34,302		-10.8%

Snapshot Facts: The top 11 producers of registered foals in 1974, when New Mexico last ranked in the top dozen, were Kentucky, California, Florida, Maryland, Virginia, Texas, Washington, Louisiana, Oklahoma, Ohio and Illinois.

DISTRIBUTION OF ACTIVE STALLIONS AND MARES BRED

State by 2003 Ranking	Stallions	2001 Mares Bred	Avg. Book	Stallions	2002 Mares Bred	Avg. Book	Stallions	2003 Mares Bred	Avg. Book
Kentucky	449	20,283	45.2	382	19,648	51.4	369	19,829	53.7
California	421	5,733	13.6	399	5,809	14.6	369	5,746	15.6
Texas	437	3,638	8.3	414	3,584	8.7	337	3,039	9.0
Florida	295	7,166	24.3	285	7,148	25.1	240	6,558	27.3
Louisiana	205	2,221	10.8	204	2,268	11.1	196	2,608	13.3
Oklahoma	239	1953	8.2	220	1752	8.0	185	1483	8.0
New York	136	2,272	16.7	154	2,527	16.4	149	2,667	17.9
New Mexico	147	1,210	8.2	155	1,467	9.5	142	1,383	9.7
Pennsylvania	117	976	8.3	107	1,021	9.5	107	982	9.2
Illinois	134	1,279	9.5	120	1,228	10.2	104	1,091	10.5
Indiana	104	814	7.8	111	877	7.9	92	818	8.9
Ohio	114	865	7.6	107	890	8.3	89	573	6.4
Washington	133	1361	10.2	105	1150	11.0	83	1095	13.2
Maryland	109	1,862	17.1	102	1,841	18.0	77	1,615	21.0
West Virginia	58	665	11.5	65	910	14.0	73	966	13.2
Colorado	83	449	5.4	84	473	5.6	71	444	6.3
Michigan	75	566	7.5	69	518	7.5	62	499	8.0
Arkansas	73	569	7.8	75	642	8.6	60	543	9.1
Virginia	91	589	6.5	76	537	7.1	58	422	7.3
Arizona	75	467	6.2	67	540	8.1	54	533	9.9
Oregon	56	452	8.1	42	387	9.2	45	407	9.0
Iowa	68	743	10.9	61	667	10.9	43	593	13.8
Idaho	68	323	4.8	56	297	5.3	42	265	6.3
Nebraska	43	356	8.3	38	336	8.8	38	330	8.7
Montana	51	274	5.4	43	243	5.7	33	172	5.2
New Jersey	50	277	5.5	42	454	10.8	33	316	9.6
Minnesota	32	257	8.0	39	311	8.0	30	323	10.8
Utah	48	212	4.4	33	146	4.4	27	96	3.6
Kansas	31	200	6.5	30	186	6.2	26	168	6.5
South Carolina	25	232	9.3	31	174	5.6	23	145	6.3
Massachusetts	23	110	4.8	29	119	4.1	20	85	4.3
Alabama	22	96	4.4	21	96	4.6	19	112	5.9
Missouri	35	158	4.5	37	164	4.4	18	80	4.4
Georgia	24	103	4.3	31	129	4.2	17	106	6.2
Tennessee	30	91	3.0	29	110	3.8	17	76	4.5
North Carolina	25	73	2.9	24	70	2.9	16	63	3.9
Mississippi	15	74	4.9	15	73	4.9	14	66	4.7
North Dakota	20	123	6.2	12	106	8.8	14	67	4.8
South Dakota	18	167	9.3	16	151	9.4	14	105	7.5
Wisconsin	15	26	1.7	16	38	2.4	12	41	3.4
Wyoming	18	55	3.1	12	36	3.0	11	27	2.5
Nevada	7	30	4.3	6	12	2.0	4	9	2.3
Vermont	3	5	1.7	5	11	2.2	2	2	1.0
Maine	3	3	1.0	2	3	1.5	2	5	2.5
Rhode Island	0	0	0.0	0	0	0.0	2	2	1.0
Alaska	1	1	1.0	1	1	1.0	1	2	2.0
Connecticut	3	7	2.3	0	0	0.0	1	5	5.0
Delaware	0	0	0.0	1	5	5.0	0	0	0.0
Hawaii	1	1	1.0	0	0	0.0	0	0	0.0
New Hampshire	1	5	5.0	1	6	6.0	0	0	0.0
TOTALS	4,231	59,392	14.0	3,974	59,161	14.9	3,441	56,562	16.4

* Initial returns only (as of 02/01/04); ranked by number of stallions. Source: The Jockey Club

Takeout Percentages in North America by State

The following are the pari-mutuel takeout percentages for each state in which legal wagering was conducted in 2003. The breakdown includes the differing percentages for various wagering formats as well as for the type of race meet and/or racing breed involved.

Arizona – 20% on win-place-show, 21% on Daily Double, Quinella and Exacta, 25% on Trifecta, Superfecta, and Pick 3.

Arkansas – 17% on single wagers and 21% on multiple wagers.

California – 15.43 % Win-place-show takeout for Thoroughbred and Quarter Horse meetings; 16% for Harness, Mixed and Fair meetings. Additional takeout on exotic wagering is 4.75% for Thoroughbred, Quarter Horse and Fair meetings; 6.75% for Mixed meetings and 7.75% for Harness meetings.

Colorado – 18.5% on straight wagers, 25% on exotics.

Delaware – For Thoroughbreds, 17% on straight wagers; additional 2% on Daily Doubles and Exactas, plus an additional 8% on other exotic wagers. For Harness, 18% on straight wagers, 20% on multiple wagers on 8-horse field, 25% on multiple wagers with 9 or more horses in the field.

Florida – Individual tracks allowed to determine the level of total takeout.

Idaho – 20% on straight wagers, 20.75% on exotics.

Illinois – 15% on win-place-show, 17.5% on Exacta and Daily Double, 23% on Trifecta, Pick 3, Pick 4 and Superfecta.

Indiana – 18% on straight wagers, 21.5% on exotics.

Iowa – 16% on win-place-show, 19% on on two-horse wagers, 22% on other forms of wagering.

Kansas – 18% on win-place-show, up to 22% on multiple wagers if authorized by racing commission.

Kentucky – For Thoroughbred tracks over $1,200,000 daily average, 16% on straight wagers and 19% on exotics; at tracks under $1,200,000 daily average, 17.5% on straight wagers and 22% on exotics. For Harness, 18% on straight wagers and 25% on exotics. For Quarter Horse, Appaloosa and Arabian, 18% on straight wagers and 25% on exotics.

Louisiana – 17% on win-place-show, 20.5% on two-horse wagers, 25% on three horse wagers.

Maine – 18% on straight wagers, 26% on exotics.

Maryland – At Thoroughbreds tracks, 18% on straight wagers, 21% on two-horse multiples, 25.75% on three-horse multiples, 14% on Pick 4. At the Fair Hill hunt meeting, 22% on all wagers. At Harness tracks over $600,000 daily, 17% on straight wagers, 19% on two-horse multiplesand 25% on three-horse multiples. At Harness tracks under $600,000 daily,18.75% on straight wagers, 20.75% on two-horse wagers and 26.75% on three-horse wagers.

Massachusetts – 19% win-place-show wagers, 26% on exotics, 19% at fairs.

Michigan – 17% on straight wagers, 20.5% on two race multiples and 25% on multiples involving three or more races.

Minnesota – Not to exceed 17% on win-place-show wagering, 23% on exotic wagering.

Montana – 20% on straight wagers and up to 25% on exotics.

Nebraska – Not less than 15% or more than 18% on straight wagers, up to and including 23% on exotic wagers.

New Hampshire – For Thoroughbreds, 19% on win-place-show wagers, 26% on multiple wagers. For Harness, 19% on win-place-show wagers, 25% on multiple wagers.

New Jersey – 17% straight wagers, 19% on two-horse selections, 25% on three or more horse selections regardless of number of races involved, 15% Pick 4.

New Mexico – For Class A tracks, 19% on win-place-show, 21%-25% on exotic wagers. For Class B tracks, 18.75% to 25% on win-place-show, 21% to 30% on exotic wagers.

New York – At NYRA tracks, 14% on straight wagers, 17.5% on Daily Double, Quinella and Exacta, 25% on Trifecta, Pick 3, Pick 4 and Superfecta, 25% on Pick 6 (20% on non-carryover days). For Harness, 18% on straight wagers, 20% on multiple, 25% on exotics and 34% on super exotics. For Quarter Horse, 17% on straight wagers, 19% on multiple, 25% on exotic and 36% on super exotics. Takeout is the same at Off-Track-Betting facilities, but an additional surcharge of 5% is charged by most OTBs on winning straight wagers, and 6% on winning multiples and exotics.

Ohio – 18% on win-place-show wagers, 22% on all other wagers.

Oklahoma – 18% on win-place-show wagers, 20% on multiple-horse wagers and up to three-race wagers, 25% on multiple race wagers involving four or more races.

Oregon – For commercial meets, 18% on win-place-show, 22% on wagers with two or more wagering interests. At fairs and non-profit meets, up to 22%.

Pennsylvania – 17% on regular wagering pools (19% if average daily handle is less than $300,000, 20% on Exactas, Daily Doubles, Quinellas, Pick Threes and 26-35% on Trifectas and Pick Fours.

Texas – 18% on regular wagers, up to 21% on two-horse wagers, up to 25% on wagers involving three or more horses.

Virginia – 18% on straight wagers, 22% on all other wagers.

Washington – 16.1% on win-place-show wagers, 22.1% on all other wagers, (21.1% for non-profit meetings of less than 10 days).

West Virginia – 17.25% on win-place-show wagers, 19% on two-horse wagers, 25% on wagers on three horses or more.

THE AMERICAN RACING MANUAL
North American Racetracks
AQUEDUCT

New York Racing Association Inc.,
Barry K. Schwartz., Chairman and CEO; Peter F. Karches, Vice Chairman; C. Steven Duncker, Vice Chairman; William A Nader, Senior Vice President; Racing Secretary and Handicapper: Michael S. Lakow; Director of Communications: Glen Mathes.

Street Address: 110th Street and Rockaway Blvd.,
Ozone Park, New York 11417
12 miles from Times Square in New York City
Nearest Airport: John F. Kennedy Int l., 1/2 mile from track

Mailing: P.O. Box 90, Jamaica, New York 11417
Phone: (718) 641-4700; Results: 718 976-3333
Fax: (718) 322-3814
Web Site: www.nyra.com

Track Data: Main Course, 1 1/8-mile oval, sandy loam; 100 feet wide, with one-mile chute. Length of stretch, 1,155.6 feet. Winterized, inner dirt course, one mile. Inner turf course, seven furlongs plus 43 feet with 1 1/8-mile diagonal chute. Stable accommodations: **547** horses; Seating capacity: **27,000.** Total capacity: **90,000.** Parking capacity, approximately **16,000** cars.

Opened September **14, 1959,** Aqueduct conducts live racing from the fall through late spring, using the one mile, winterized inner dirt track from December to mid-March. During the **2002-2003** winter meet, daily purses still were pegged at **$334,000,** including stakes. For the 23 day fall **2003** meet purses were almost **$395,000** per day.

TRACK RECORDS

4 1/2 Furs.	About to Burst	2	117	:51.60	Apr. 26, 1984	1-1/4 M.	Damascus	4	130	1:59-1/5	July 20, 1968
5 Furs.	Bazaar	2		:57.00	Jan. 1, 1963	1-5/16 M.	Gold Star Deputy	5	116	2:07.32	Apr. 10, 1999
5 1/2 Furs.	Raise a Native	2	124	1:02.60	July 17, 1963	1-3/8 M.	Demi s Bret	4	116	2:12.31	Oct. 26, 1997
6 Furs.	Captain Red	6	111	107.80	Feb. 26, 2003	1-1/2 M.	Going Abroad	4	116	2:26-1/5	Oct. 12, 1964
6 1/2 Furs.	Coronado s Quest	2	122	1:14-1/5	Oct. 26, 1997	1-5/8 M.	Sharp Gary	4	116	2:40-2/5	Dec. 13, 1975
7 Furs.	Artax	4	114	1:20.04	May 2, 1999	1-3/4 M.	Malmo	5	114	2:53.73	Mar. 30, 1996
1 Mile	Easy Goer	3	123	1:32-2/5	Apr. 8, 1989	1-7/8 M.	Erin Bright	5	118	3:12-4/5	Apr. 18, 1985
1-1/8M.	Riva Ridge	4	130	1:47	Oct. 15, 1973	2 Miles	Kelso	7	124	3:19-1/5	Oct. 31, 1964
1-3/16 M.	Riva Ridge	4	127	1:52-2/5	July 4, 1973	2 -1/4 M.	Paraje	7	113	3:47-4/5	Dec. 15, 1973

Inner Dirt

4 Fur.	Native Moment	2	122	:53.40	Apr. 2, 1979	1-1/4 M.	Transient Trend	3	111	2:01.53	Dec. 21, 1995
4-1/2 Furs.	Call Me Up	2	115	:52.29	Apr. 16, 1998	1-1/2 M.	Piling	5	22	2:29-3/5	Mar. 13, 1983
6 Furs.	Captain Red	6	111	1:07.93	Feb. 26, 2003	1-5/8 M.	Relaxing	4	120	2:42-2/5	Dec. 13, 1980
1 Mile	Tejano Couture	6	116	1:35.79	March 9, 2000	1-3/4 M.	Sophie s Friend	5	113	2:56-3/5	Feb. 10, 1996
1 M 70 Yds	Carry My Colors	4	114	1:38.92	Feb. 5, 2000	2 Miles	Charlie Coast	4	122	3:24-4/5	Feb. 21, 1979
1-1/16 M.	Autoroute	3	115	1:41.06	Dec. 19, 1992	2-1/16 M.	Rollix	4	105	3:38-4/5	Feb. 3, 1983
1-1/8 M.	Conveyor	5	111	1:47.33	Mar. 6, 1993	2-1/8 M.	Peat Moss	6	128	3:40-3/5	Jan. 31, 1981
1-3/16 M.	Victoriously	5	119	1:54-2/5	Jan. 25, 1998	2-1/4 M.	Field Cat	4	110	3:51-4/5	Dec. 31, 1981

Turf Course

1 Mile	Tax Dodge*	4	116	1:34-3/5	Nov. 1, 1985	1 1/4 M.	Fluorescent Light	4	115	2:14-1/5	Nov. 7, 1978
	Possible Mate*	4	116	1:34-3/5	Nov. 1, 1985	1-1/2 M.	Pebbles	4	123	2:27	Nov. 2, 1985
1-1/16 M.	Spindrift	5	118	1:40.88	May 6, 2000	2 M.	Putting Green	4	112	3:30-2/5	Nov. 23, 1984
1-1/8 M.	Slew The Dragon	3	117	1:47	Nov. 3, 1985	* Dead Heat.					

Leading Jockey, inner track, winter, 2003: Javier Castellano, 76 wins; Leading Trainer, inner track, winter, 2003: Gary Contessa, 29 wins
Leading Jockey, spring meet, 2003: John Velazquez, 69 wins.
Leading Trainer, spring meet, 2003: H. Allen Jerkens, 15 wins
Leading Jockey, fall-winter, 2003: John Velazquez, 26 wins; Leading Trainer, fall-winter, 2003: Todd Pletcher, 16 wins.
Record Attendance: 73, 435, May 31, 1965. Record Handle: $8, 171, 520, Nov 2, 1985. (Breeders' Cup Day): $26, 941, 288 November 2, 1985, (Breeders' Cup Day, all sources.)

ARAPAHOE PARK

Racing Associates of Colorado
President: Ty Howard; General Manager: Bruce Seymore; Racing Secretary: William Powers; Public Relations Director: Frank Provenza.

26000 E Quincy Avenue, Aurora, CO 80016
303-690-2400, Fax: 303-690-6730
Free Results 303-227-4726
E-Mail Address: Arapahoe@Wembleyusa.com

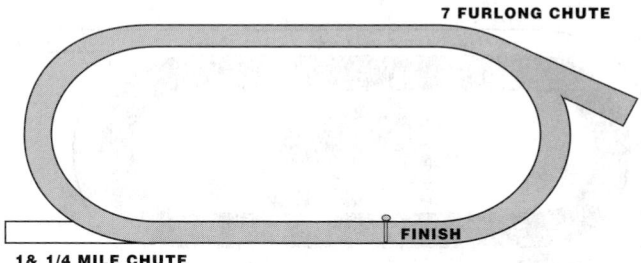

One mile oval, two chutes, seven furlongs and 1-1/4 miles. Distance from last turn to finish 1,029 feet. Seating capacity 2,000. Stable capacity 1,500, Parking for 2,200 cars.

Opened May 24, 1984. Located in Northeastern Colorado, operates the only pari-mutuel racetrack in that state and offered mixed breed racing from June 6 to August 25 in 2003, with total daily purses of over $54,000 per day including stakes funded significantly through Year-round simulcasting.

TRACK RECORDS

Dist.	Horse	Age	Wt	Time	Date	Dist.	Horse	Age	Wt	Time	Date
4 Furs.	Lorenzon	2	118	45.00	June 14, 2003	1 m70yds	Naskra s Advocate	5	118	1:38-1/5	July 23, 1993
4-1/2 Furs	V.G s Catch	2	116	50.40	June 23, 2002	1-1/16 m	I m A Gene	6	122	1:43	July 25, 1992
5 Furls	Nycity	2	118	56.00	July 13, 2002	1-1/8m.	Maysville Slew	6	124	1:49.00	Sept. 1, 2002
5-1/2 Furs	Ribot Line	5	118	1:02.20	June 30, 2002	1-1/4 m	Builder s Boy	6	119	2:05-2/5	June 26, 1992
6 Furs.	Jumbled Pete	5	118	1:08-4/5	Aug. 28, 1993	1-1/2 m	Calgary Classic	6	122	2:33-1/5	July 24, 1993
6-1/2 Furs.	Pray For Booger	3	116	1:18-3/5	Aug. 25, 1995	1-3/4 m	Read My Mind	6	112	3:02	Aug. 9, 1992
7 Furs	Daring Pegasus	5	118	1:21.00	July 4, 2003	2 Miles	Little Reeves	6	116	3:28-2/5	Aug. 27, 1994
1 Mile	Honor Bright	5	116	1:35-1/5	Aug. 7, 1993						

Leading Jockey in 2003: Frank A. Gonsalves, 46 wins.
Leading Trainer in 2003: Jon G. Arnett, 28 wins.

ARLINGTON PARK

Churchill Downs, Inc.

Richard L. Duchossois, Chairman; President: Clifford Goodrich; Vice President of Operations: Ted G. Nicholson; VP Mktg & Sales: Carl Schloessman; William A. Thayer, Senior Vice President of Racing; Frank G. Gabriel, Jr., Executive Vice President of Racing; Dan Leary, Director of Communications: (847) 385-7754.

Street Address: Euclid Avenue & Wilke Road　　　　　P.O. Box 7, Arlington Heights, Illinois 60006-0007
Arlington Heights, Illinois 60006　　　　　　　　　　(847) 385-7500. Fax: (847) 870-6727
Arlington is 26 miles northwest of the Chicago Loop　　　　　　　Press Box: (847) 385-7548
Nearest Airport: O'Hare International, 12 miles from Arlington　　　Web Site: www.arlingtonpark.com
　　　　　　　　　　　　　　　　　　　　　　　　　　e-mail:website @arlingtonpark.com

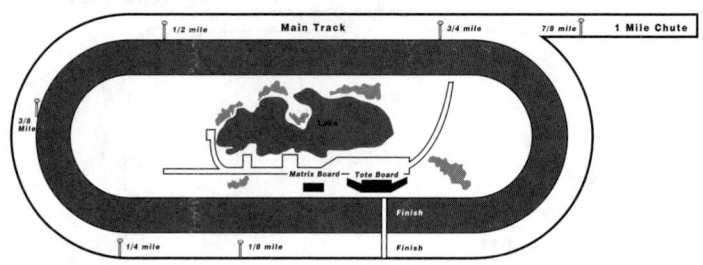

Track Data: 1 1/8-mile oval, sandy loam. One-mile chute. One-mile turf course. five-eighths mile training track. Stalls: 2,140. Seating capacity: 14,000, parking for 8,500 cars.

Originally opened October 13, 1927 and after a crushing fire destroyed the plant in 1985, reopened with a spectacular, ultra modern facility on June 28, 1989, only to close in 1997 after dispute over pari-mutuel takeout percentages with the state government. In 2000, Arlington returned as Arlington International Racecourse, with live racing and more than $290,000 in daily average purses. In 2001, the track changed its name back to 'Arlington Park', complete with a new logo that includes the Twin Spires of Churchill Downs to symbolize the union between the two tracks...The 104-day, 2003 meet ran from May 9 to Sept. 27 and included the prestigious Arlington Million, one of the premier grass races in the world. Daily average purses excluding the rich stakes schedule was in excess of $272,000 per day.

TRACK RECORDS

4-1/2 Furs.	Bold America	2	120	51.64*	June 28, 2002	1-1/16 m.	Mojave	3	109	1:41-2/5*	June 30, 1981
5 Furs.	Zarb s Magic	9	118	57.31*	Sept. 9, 2002	1-1/8 m	Spectacular Bid	4	130	1:46-1/5	July 19, 1980
5-1/2 Furs.	Hey That s Great	5	113	1:02-3/5	June 27, 1992	1-3/16m.	Tenpins	4	116	1:55.07	Sept. 29, 2002
6 Furs.	Taylor s Special	5	118	1:08	Aug. 22, 1986	1-1/4 m.	Private Thoughts	4	117	1:59-2/5	Aug. 20, 1977
6-1/2 Furs.	Pentelicus	6	115	1:14-1/5	July 14, 1990	1-5/16 m.	Rush Home	5	115	2:10	Aug. 7, 1971
7 Furs.	Tumiga	4	120	1:20-2/5	July 13, 1968	1-1/2 m.	El Misterio	5	112	2:28-1/5	Sept. 5, 1960
7-1/2 Furs.	I ll Raise You One	3	112	1:28-4/5	Aug. 3, 1987	1-5/8 m	Fool s Robbery	4	111	2:45-3/5	July 5, 1973
1 Mile	Dr. Fager	4	134	1:32-1/5	Aug. 24, 1968	1-3/4 m	Deaux-Moulins	4	119	2:59-2/5	July 14, 1956
Abt 1-1/16 m.	Ashleigh s Jet	4	120	1:44.10	June 14, 2001	2 Miles.	Swede of Norfolk	6	127	3:26-2/5	Aug. 15, 1970

Turf Course

Abt.5 Furs.	Nicole s Dream	3	120	:56.38	Sep. 18, 2003	Abt 1-1/8 m.	Lotus Pool	4	116	1:47-1/5	Aug. 1, 1991
5 Furs.	Ghost Power	3	117	:56-1/5	Oct. 8, 1993	1-1/8 m.	Mr. Leader	4	116	1:47-2/5	July 4, 1970
Abt. 5-1/2 F.	Loco Kid	4	112	1:01-3/5	May 28, 1969	1-3/16 m.	Reluctant Guest	4	123	1:53-1/5	Sep. 1, 1990
5-1/2 Furs.	Chief Sun Dance	4	115	1:02-3/5	July 6, 1970	Abt.1-1/4 m.	Sir Roberto	5	112	1:57-3/5	June 20, 1990
Abt 1 Mile.	Soaking Smoking	6	113	1:34-4/5	July 24, 1991	1-1/4 m	Awad	5	126	1:58.69	Aug. 27, 1995
1 Mile	Gee Can He Dance	6	113	1:34.50	Sep. 4, 1995	Abt.1-1/2 m.	Noble Savage-Ir	5	112	2:22-1/5	July 20, 1991
Abt.1m70y	Elegant Heir	5	116	1:41-2/5	Aug. 22, 1970	1-1/2m.	Cetewayo	8	118	2:27.50	July 6, 2002
1 M 70 Yds	Pass the Brandy	7	114	1:38-4/5	July 25, 1970	Abt 1-5/8 m	Roman Leader	8	108	2:51	Aug. 19, 1972
Abt 1-1/16 m	Real Attraction	5	115	1:39.60	Aug. 16, 1990						
1-1/16 m.	Zeeruler	4	113	1:41	Sep. 7, 1992						

Leading Jockey in 2003: Rene Douglas, 132 wins
Leading Trainer in 2003: Wayne M. Catalano, 59 wins

Record attendance: 50,568, July 4, 1941. Record handle: $116,059,574 – October 26, 2002 (Breeders' Cup Day). Record handle, non–Breeders' Cup Day: $15,851,625 – August 17, 2002.

ASSINIBOIA DOWNS

Manitoba Jockey Club Inc.
  President: Harvey Warner; General Manager: Sharon Gulyas; Racing Secretary: Ray Miller; Director Media and Corporate Relations: Ernie Nairn.

3975 Portage Avenue, Winnipeg, Manitoba, R3K 2E9
204-885-3330 Fax: 204-831-5348; Free scratch line (204) 889-5137 Free result line (204) 831-0321
E-mail: HYPERLINK mailto:info@assiniboiadowns.com; info@assiniboiadowns.com
Web Site: HYPERLINK http://www.assiniboiadowns.com www.assiniboiadowns.com .

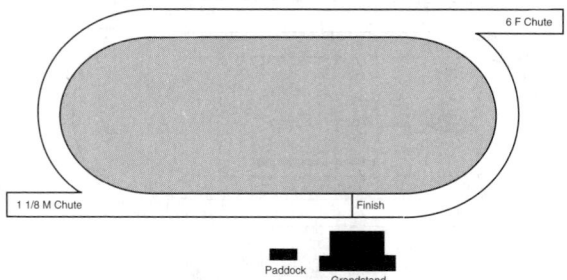

Track: Six and a half furlong oval. Training track four furlongs, with two chutes, six furlongs and 1 1/8 miles. Width of track 80 feet; Distance from last turn to finish 990 feet. Seating capacity 5,000; Stable accommodations 950.
Opened June 10, 1958. . .Operated a 75-day meet in 2003, May 4 to Sept. 28. For the 2004 season, we will have another 75-day meet. Opening day is May 2, 2004, and the meet will conclude on Sunday, Oct. 3, 2004.

TRACK RECORDS

Abt 3 Furs.	Apart	2	120	:29	May 8, 1972	1-1/16 m	Goa	4	118	1:41-3/5	July 23, 1988
4 Furs.	Northern Spike	5	119	:44-2/5	Apr. 23, 1982	1-1/8 m	Overskate	3	126	1:47-3/5	Sep. 9, 1978
4-1/2 Furs.	Astral Moon	9	115	:50-4/5	May 1, 1982	1-1/4 m	Nifty	4	124	2:05	Sep. 20, 1986
5 Furs.	Northern Spike	5	120	:56-2/5	Sep. 5, 1982	1-5/16 m	Scarlet Rich	6	124	2:15-4/5	Oct. 21, 1981
5-1/2 Furs.	Sunny Famous	5	120	1:02-4/5	Sep. 19, 1992	1-3/8 m	Island Fling	6	123	2:16-4/5	Oct. 29, 1977
Abt 6 Furs.	Lone Spruce	7	122	1:12	June 24, 1984	1-1/2 m	Baron Hudec	6	119	2:32	Sep. 9, 1978
6 Furs.	Nephrite	5	122	1:09	Oct. 8, 1989	1-5/8 m	Northern Kip	6	118	2:46-4/5	Oct 30, 1978
Abt 7 Furs.	Proven Reserve	4	121	1:23-3/5	July 9, 1986	1-11/16 m	Hi Executor	8	116	2:56-4/5	Sep. 30, 1984
7 Furs.	Victor s Pride	6	118	1:23-1/5	Aug. 16, 1978	1-3/4 m	Just As Sunny	7	118	3:01-2/5	Oct. 14, 1989
7-1/2 Furs.	Iron Vigors	4	122	1:31	Oct. 9, 1989	2 1/4 Miles	Fremarcton	8	124	3:58-1/5	Aug. 15, 1960
1 mile	Gladiatore II	5	114	1:35-4/5	July 7, 1972						

Leading Jockey in 2003: Travis Hightower, 98 wins.

Leading Trainer in 2003: Gary Danelson, 55 wins

Record attendance: 13,276, August 6, 1979. Record handle $753, 122, July 5, 1981 (16 race–double program.)

ATLANTIC CITY RACE COURSE

Greenwood ACRA, Inc.
   Officers: Harold Handel, Anthony D. Ricci; Racing Secretary: Sal Sinatra; Onsite Management: Maureen Gallagher Bugdon, James A. Miller

Located 14 miles west of Atlantic City
Nearest Airport: Atlantic City International in Pomona,
5 miles from track

4501 Black Horse Pike, Mays Landing, NJ 08330
(609) 641-2190; Fax: (609) 645-8309
Simulcasting: (609) 383-0859

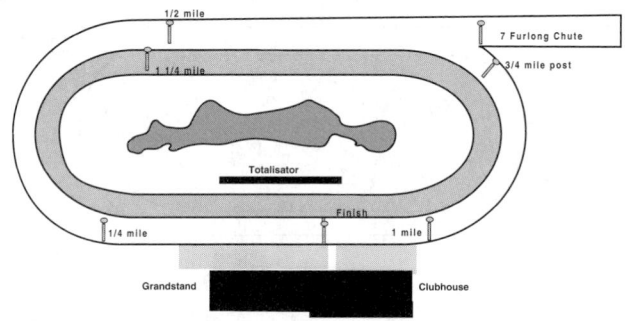

Track data: One and one-eighth mile, oval, with 7/8-mile chute. Distance from last turn to finish line, 947.29 feet; width 100 feet. One mile turf course, width also 100 feet. Both courses lit for night racing One mile and one-eighth oval; sandy loam with seven-furlong chute. Length of homestretch, 947.29 feet. Width of homestretch and backstretch, 100 feet. One mile turf course 100 feet in width. Stable accommodations for 1,602. Seating Capacity 16,000, parking for 4,500. Admission Free.

Opened July 22, 1946 by a virtual "Who's Who" of personalities including Bob Hope and Frank Sinatra. John B. Kelly Sr., Olympic gold medalist and father of the late Princess Grace, was Atlantic City's first president. After more than 50 years of summer racing, AC ran six nights of turf racing in 1999 and 2000, to maintain its simulcast license and was bought by the Greenwood Racing Corp. In 2001 the meet was expanded to 10 dates but in 2002, Atlantic City only was open on May 10, for a one day meet of seven turf races while conducting its nine other racing days at Monmouth Park. After a four-day meet in 2003, featuring purses of just over $100,000, the 2004 meet is set to run May 5 through May 19.

TRACK RECORDS

4-1/2 Furs.	Jo Jo s Sparkle	2	117	:51-2/5	June 22, 1988	1-1/16 M	Prince of Truth	7	121	1:41	June 28, 1975
5 Furs.	Dark Tzarina	5	117	:56-2/5	July 16, 1988	1-1/8 M	World Appeal	3	118	1:46-3/5	July 16, 1983
5-1/2 Furs.	Aeronotic	5	119	1:02-3/5	July 4, 1986	1-3/16 m	Mississippi Mud	4	119	1:54-1/5	Aug. 6, 1977
6 Furs.	Margerine	5	110	1:08-1/5	Aug. 27, 1988	1-1/4 M	Greek Ship	4	119	2:01-4/5	Sep. 29, 1951
6-1/2 Furs.	Zartarian	7	122	1:15-4/5	June 26, 1994	1-3/4 M	Abdallati	6	119	3:06-2/5	Nov. 22, 1973
7 Furs.	Mexican General	4	114	1:20-2/5	July 4, 1977						

Turf Course

Abt 5 Furs.	Bald Smile	7	119	:57-1/5	Aug. 8, 1996	Abt 1-1/8m	Emptor	7	117	1:49-4/5	June 9, 1993
5 Furs.	Chief Whitehair	5	119	:56-2/5	June 28, 1997	1-1/8 m	Marco Bay	4	114	1:46-4/5	June 10, 1994
Abt 5-1/2 F.	Mr. Mink	4	118	1:02-3/5	Sep. 8, 1967	Abt 1-3/16m	Grey Lord II	7	111	1:56-3/5	Sep. 30, 1969
5 1/2 Furs.	Legal Justice	5	119	1:01-4/5	July 12, 1989	1-3/16m	Steinlen	7	124	1:52	July 21, 1990
Abt 1 Mile	Silvino	5	119	1:36-4/5	June 8, 1988	Abt 1-1/2m	Northern Nights	7	115	2:31-4/5	July 10, 1996
1 Mile	Canal	6	120	1:34-1/5	Aug. 19, 1967	1-1/2 M	Advocator	5	115	2:27-1/5	Sep. 21, 1968
Abt 1m40yds	First Grade Reader	5	106	1:40-4/5	June 7, 1991	Abt 1-1/16m	Misty Model	4	115	3:08-3/5	Aug. 19, 1977
1m40yds	Castaneto-Ar	7	115	1:38	June 28, 1991	Abt 2 M	Pier	7	120	3:35-4/5	Sep. 2, 1977
1-1/16m	Road At Sea	3	120	1:41-1/5	Sep. 23, 1967	Abt 2-1/16m	Bangguster	4	117	3:45-4/5	July 6, 1995
	Chiati	6	118	1:41-1/5	July 6, 1979	2-1/16 M	Sticktoitive	8	117	3:42-4/5	Aug. 25, 1993
Abt 1-1/16m	Home Front	5	112	1:43-2/5	June 12, 1976						

Leading Jockey in 2003: Victor H. Molina, 4 wins

Leading Trainer in 2003: Kathleen A. Demasi, 2 wins

Record attendance: 33,404, Sept 7, 1953. Record handle $3,168, 229, August 12,1967

ATOKAD

Horsemen s Atokad Downs
President Robert E. Lee; General Manager, Tom Harris

P.O.Box 518, South Sioux City, Nebraska, 68776
402-494-5722

Track data: Five-eighths-mile oval, with two chutes, 6 1/2 furlongs and 1 1/8 miles. Distance from last turn to finish, 660 feet. Width 68 feet. Stable accommodations: 850; Seating capacity: 3,112.

Opened September 20, 1956. In most years since, Atokad has operated a late summer race meet in the Northwest corner of Nebraska near the South Dakota border. In recent years, Atokad has had short live race meets of one or two days, with two days of racing in 2003. Racing is scheduled for 2004 on Sept. 18 and 19.

TRACK RECORDS

Abt 4 Furs.	Classy Fleet	3	114	:43-4/5	Nov. 19, 1977	1-1/16 m	Great Commander	4	120	1:43-3/5	Nov. 3, 1973
4 Furs.	Shining Sea	6	117	:44-2/5	June 28, 1992	1-/8 m	Reason To Explode	6	114	1:50-1/5	July 13, 1991
5-1/2 Furs.	Slipped in Space	4	115	1:05-1/5	Oct. 24, 1976	1-3/8 m	Barker s Tip	5	111	2:20	Oct. 17, 1964
Abt 6 Furs.	Urgent Valentine	4	121	1:16.40	July 20, 2003	1-7/16	Echo Bar	5	117	2:28	Oct.30, 1968
6 Furs.	Don Rivers	3	122	1:11-2/5	Oct. 28, 1966	Abt.1-7/16 m	Duke of Badgerland	7	115	2:29-3/5	Nov. 6, 1996
6-1/2 Furs.	Spanish Key	7	123	1:16-2/5	Oct. 24, 1970	2 Miles	Navy Grey	5	115	3:30-1/5	Oct. 30, 1962
1 Mile	Quilla Sue	7	120	1:38	Oct. 30, 1973		Middle Road	5	122	3:30-1/5	Nov. 21, 1976
1m 70 yds.	No Mystery	7	117	1:42-1/5	Nov. 5, 1976						

Leading Jockey in 2003: Jerome Carkeek, 3 wins
Leading trainer in 2003: James R. Compton, 2 wins
Record Attendance: 6,200, October18, 1958.Record handle: $483,486, November 9, 1980

BAY MEADOWS
and SAN MATEO COUNTY FAIR

Magna Entertainment
Frank Stronach, Chairman & Director; Bernie Thurman, Vice President and General Manager; Tom Doutrich, Racing Secretary; Richard Lewis, Coordinator of Racing Operations, Tom Ferrall, Publicity Manager.

P.O. Box 5050, San Mateo, California 94402.
Street Address: 2600 South Delaware Street, San Mateo, California 94403.
(650) 574-7223; Fax: (650) 573-4632, Publicity 573-4678.
E-Mail Address: HYPERLINK mailto:webmaster@baymeadows.com; Web Site: www.baymeadows.com.
Nearest Airports: San Francisco International Airport, 7 miles; San Carlos (private), 5 miles.

San Mateo County Fair
2600 South Delaware Street
San Mateo, California 94403
(650) 574-3247

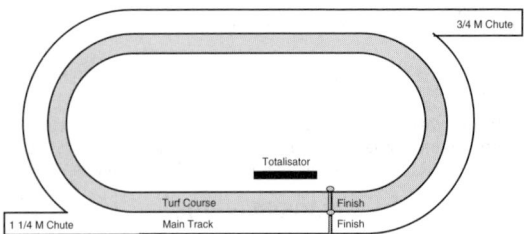

One-mile dirt track with six-furlong and 1 1/4-mile chutes. Length of stretch, 990 feet. Seven-furlong turf course. Stable accommodations, 900 horses. Seating: Grandstand and Infield, 10,000; Club House, 1,500; Turf Club, 1,200. Children's recreational areas in Grandstand and Infield Park. Parking for 5,000 cars.

Opened November 3, 1934. Introduced the totalizator and photo finish camera to United States racing at inaugural meet in 1934. The Bay Meadows Handicap, run since the first Bay Meadows season, is the oldest continuously run stakes in California. Two Thoroughbred meets in 2003 alternating with Golden Gate Fields throughout the major track season in the region. Bay Meadows also plays host annually to the mixed breed, San Mateo County Fair dates (BMf-meet) in August and offers year-round simulcasting. In 2003, purses, including stakes, averaged over $137,000 per day during the two BM meets and about $119,000 during the BMf meet.

TRACK RECORDS

2 Furs.	Royalette	2		21.11	April 12, 2002	1 M 70 Yds	Redress	4	105	1:41-3/5	Dec. 10, 1934
3-1/2 Furs.	Harrogate	2	115	:40-4/5	Mar. 16, 1935	1-1/16 m	Hoedown s Day	5	119	1:38-2/5	Oct. 23, 1983
4 Furs.	Ima Dear	2	112	:46-2/5	Apr. 2, 1935	1-1/8 m	See the King	4	114	1:46-1/5	Oct. 23, 1983
4-1/2 Furs.	Metatron	2	118	:50.59	May 24, 2001	1-3/16 m	Force of Reason	5	117	1:52-4/5	Nov. 5, 1983
5 Furs.	Mr. Doubledown	6	117	:56.44	Mar. 9, 2000	11/4 m	Ask Father	7	112	2:00-2/5	Sep. 28, 1968
5 1/2 Fur.	Rio Oro			1:01.60	Oct. 7, 2001	1-1/2m	Cattle Creek	3	114	2:27-3/5	Dec. 12, 1979
6 Furs.	BlkJackRoad	6	116	1:07-1/5	Oct. 28, 1990	1-5/8 m	Rag King	4	115	2:43-1/5	Dec. 15, 1990
7-1/2 Furs.	Lookabout	3	107	1:30-2/5	Nov. 26, 1936	1-3/4 m	Tornillo	3	108	2:57-3/5	Nov. 21, 1936
1 Mile	Aristocratical	6	113	1:33-3/5	Sep. 10, 1983						

Turf Course

4 1/2 Furs.	Santano	4	123	:50.38	May 17, 2001	1 1/8 M	Ocean Queen	3	110	1:47.80	Oct. 12, 1996
5 Furs	Maria s Mirage	4	116	:56.75	Apr. 20, 2003	Abt. 1 1/8 M	Mula Gula	3	117	1:45.34	Sept. 25, 1999
7 Furs.	First Flyer	4	119	1:24.35	Sept. 25, 1997	1 3/8 M	Peu a Peu	4	115	2:16.39	May 18, 2002
7 1/2 Fur.	Hegemony	4	119	1:28.80	Oct. 12, 1985	Abt. 1 3/8 M	Handsome Weed	4	122	2:17.10	Oct. 24, 1991
1 Mile	Staff Rider	3	118	1:34.68	Aug. 28, 1993	1 1/2 M	Swiss Connection	4	124	2:31.46	Oct. 12,1998
1 1/16 M	Dunant	4	117	1:40.60	Nov. 3, 1985						

Leading Jockey in 2003: Russell Baze, at both BM meets, with 97 and 96 wins, respectively.
Leading Trainer in 2003: Jerry Hollendorfer, at both BM meets, with 55 and 52 wins, respectively.
Leading Jockey BMf in 2003 : Russell Baze, 18 wins.; Leading Trainer BMf in 2003 : Jerry Hollendorfer, 9 wins.
Record attendance:29, 300, April 17, 1948; Record handle: $8,660, 396, Nov 6, 1999

BELMONT PARK

New York Racing Association Inc.
Barry K. Schwartz., Chairman and CEO; Peter F. Karches, Vice Chairman; C. Steven Duncker, Vice Chairman; William A Nader, Senior Vice President; Racing Secretary and Handicapper: Michael S. Lakow; Director of Communications: Glen Mathes.

Street Address: 2150 Hempstead Turnpike
Elmont, New York 11003
Nearest Airports: John F. Kennedy International Airport, six miles south west of track and Laguardia Airport, 12 miles west of track.

P.O. Box 90, Jamaica, New York 11417
Telephone: (718) 641-4700; (516) 488-6000
Fax: (516) 352-0919; Results: 718 976-3333
Email: nyra@nyra.com
Web Site: www.nyra.com

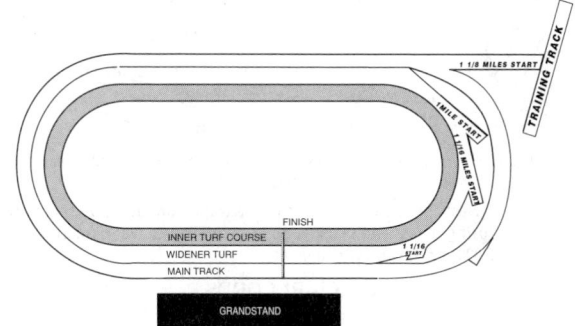

Track Data: 1 1/2-mile oval, sandy surface, length of stretch, 1,097 feet; Widener Turf Course, 1 5/16 miles plus 27 feet with two chutes, one mile and 1 1/16 miles; Inner Turf Course, 1 3/16 miles plus 103 feet, with one chute 1 1/16 miles. Seating 30,000; Capacity: 85–90,000. Parking for 18,500 cars.

Inaugural meet May 4, 1905 and permanent home of the 1 1/2-mile Belmont Stakes, the climax to the world famous Triple Crown series. Also has played host to three of the 20 Breeders' Cup Championships through 2003, including BC VII in 1990, BC XII in 1995, and BC XVIII on Oct. 27, 2001. Purses during the 55-day spring meet in 2003 averaged in excess of $510,000 per day, while purses averaged over $615,000 per day during the 38-day Fall Championship meeting. Belmont's 1 1/2-mile main oval is the largest in North America.

TRACK RECORDS

5 Furs.	Kelly Kip	2	114	:55-3/5	June 21, 1996	1-1/8 m	Secretariat	3	124	1:45-2/5	Sep. 15, 1973
5-1/2Furs.	More Than Ready	2	119	1:02.56	July 4, 1999	1-3/16 m	Rock Hall	4	109	1:56.	May 26, 1986
6 Furs.	Artax	4	120	1:07.66	Oct. 16, 1999	1-1/4 m	In Excess-Ir	4	119	1:58-1/5	July 4, 1991
6-1/2 Furs.	Confide	3	113	1:14.51	Oct. 16, 1997	1-3/8 m	Victoriously	4	118	2:14-3/5	Oct. 16, 1997
7 Furs.	Left Bank	5	121	1:20.17	July 4, 2002	1-1/2 m	Secretariat	3	126	2:24	June 9, 1973
1 Mile	Najran	4	113	1:32.24	May 7, 2003	1 5/8 m	Kelso	3	124	2:40.80	Sept. 28, 1960
1-1/16 m	Rock and Roll	3	112	1:39.51	June 13, 1998						

Widener Turf Course

6 Furs.	Masterclass	4	114	1:07-1/5	May 24, 1992	1-1/4 m	Honey Dear	4	112	2:03-4/5	Oct. 10, 1962
7 Furs.	Official Permission	7	112	1:19.88	July 23, 2000	1-3/8 m	Influent	6	120	2:11	July 13, 1997
1 Mile	Elusive Quality	5	117	1:31.63	July 4, 1998	1-1/2 m	Fantastic Light	5	126	2:24.35	Oct. 27, 2001
1-1/16 m	Fortitude	4	112	1:38.53	Sep. 6, 1997	2 Miles	King s General	5	112	3:20-2/5	July 4, 1983

Inner Turf Course

1-1/16 m	Roman Envoy	4	117	1:39.38	May 23, 1992	1-1/4 m	Paradise Creek	5	124	1:57-3/5	June 11, 1994
1-1/8 m	Subordination	3	113	1:45-3/5	June 15, 1997	1-3/8 m	With Approval	4	118	2:10-1/5	June 17, 1990

Jumps

2 Miles	Warm Spell	4	148	3:36.82	June 4, 1992	2-1/4 m	Popular Gigilo	5	152	4:02-1/5	June 3, 1999
2-1/16 m	Romantic	7	154	4:01-3/5	Sept. 10, 1999	2-1/2 m	Flatterer	5	167	4:40	Sep. 21, 1984

Leading Jockey in 2003 Spring meet: John R. Velazquez, 70 wins.
Leading Trainer in 2003 Spring meet: Todd Pletcher, 40 wins.
Leading Jockey in 2003 Fall meet: John R. Velazquez, 44 wins.
Leading Trainer in 2003 Fall meet: Todd Pletcher, 24 wins.

BEULAH PARK

Heartland Jockey Club Ltd.
President: Charles J. Ruma; General Manager: Michael Weiss; Director of Publicity: Vic Mason;
Racing Secretary: Ed Vomacka   pressbox@beulahpark.com
Street Address: 3664 Grant Avenue   P.O. Box 850, Grove City, Ohio 43123-0850
Grove City, Ohio 43123   (614) 871-9600; Fax: (614) 871-0433
Website: www.beulahpark.com   Racing Office: (614) 871-1938

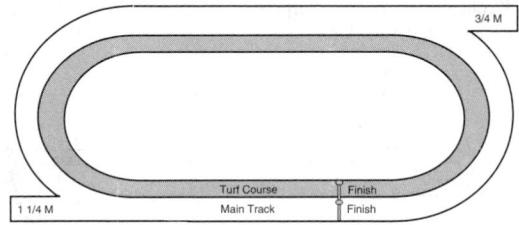

Track Data: One mile oval. Two chutes, six furlongs and 1 1/4 miles. Width of stretch: 80 feet; width of backstretch, 75 feet; distance from last turn to finish line, 1,100 feet. Stable Accommodations: 1,200; Seating capacity 7,200.

Opened April 21, 1923, Beulah Park was Ohio's first racetrack. The track conducts live racing from September to May each year with a fall, winter and spring meet. The track is open seven days a week for full-card simulcasting. Purses per day average approximately $45,000 for the combined meets.

TRACK RECORDS

2 Furs.	Go Chop	2	112	:21-3/5	May 7, 1989	1 3/16 m	World of Magic	4	119	1:55	Sep. 21, 1991
4 Furs.	Float Away	2	117	:46-2/5	May 12, 1938	1 1/4 m	On the Scent	4	122	2:00-1/5	Oct. 19, 1991
4-1/2 Furs.	Last Rebel	8	116	:50.96	April 18, 2003	1 1/2 m	Doctor s Romance	6	117	2:29-2/5	Mar. 26, 1994
5 Furs.	Love Poppa Mucci	5	117	:56-3/5	Feb. 11, 1994	1 5/8 m	Big Beans	4	113	2:46	Oct. 5, 1957
5 1/2 Furs.	Jay's Performer			1:02.78	Mar. 18, 2001	1 3/4 m	Dot Your Eye	4	123	2:57-3/5	Oct. 20, 1971
6 Furs.	Whatta Brave	5	119	1:08 2/5	Oct. 29, 2000	2 Miles	Whipall	4	108	3:27-2/5	Sep. 29, 1951
1 Mile	Appygolucky	6	116	1:35.47	Jan 17, 2003	2 m 70yds	Benomen	5	119	3:29-4/5	Nov. 20, 1993
1 m 70yds.	King s Wailea	5	111	1:40	Nov. 19, 1993	2 1/16 m	She Looks Great	3	122	3:41-2/5	Nov. 28, 1983
1 1/16 m	Din s Dancer	5	122	1:40-4/5	Nov. 3, 1990	2 1/8 m	Second City	4	114	3:48-4/5	Nov. 25, 1984
1 1/8 m	Lord Try On	4	114	1:48-4/5	Sep. 26, 1992	2 1/4 m	Hallay s Pride	6	115	3:48-4/5	May 4, 1991

Turf Course

Abt 6 Furs	Brent s Gail	4	114	1:07	Sep. 1, 1986	Abt.1-3/8 m	Spend Ten	4	113	2:12-4/5	Oct 8, 1988
Abt.1 Mile	Khal Me Sir	7	116	1:38-3/5	Oct. 4, 1992	1 3/8 m	Syncospin	4	115	2:12-3/5	Sep. 25, 1987
1 Mile	Gaelic Cross	7	115	1:35-2/5	Sep. 23, 1987	1 5/8 m	Nigilik	5	121	2:48-1/5	Oct. 24, 1986
Abt 1m 70y	Nail s McNally	4	119	1:40-2/5	Oct. 1, 1988	Abt 2 m	Persian Jig	5	124	3:23-2/5	May 17, 1987
1 m 70yds	Twin To Win	3	108	1:41	Oct. 24, 1986						

Leading Jockey in 2003, Spring meet: Ivan R. Gonzalez, 78 wins.
Leading Trainer in 2003, Spring meet: Jake S. Radosevich, 31 wins
Leading Jockey in 2003, Fall meet: Marco Ccamaque, 83 wins.
Leading Trainer in 2003, Fall meet: Rodney Faulkner, 19 wins
Record attendance: 11,772, May 15, 1954; Record handle: $1,095,950, March 5, 1980; Record handle with simulcasting: $1,478,038, October 5, 2000.

BLUE RIBBON DOWNS

Backstretch, LLC
General Manager: Frank Deal; Assistant General Manager: Blaine Story; Racing Secretary: Shirley Ellis;
Director of Operations and Simulcast Director: Tonya Maxwell; Director of Marketing: Robin Akers.
PO Box 788, Sallisaw, OK 74955-0788   Web Site: www.blueribbondowns.net
Phone: 918-775-7771 Fax: 918-775-5805   E-Mail Address: brd@blueribbondowns.net

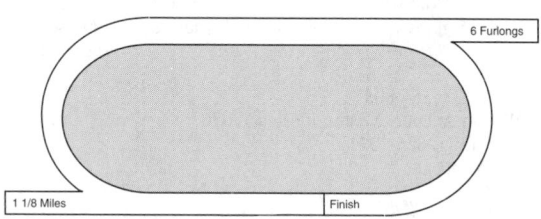

Track Data: Seven-eighth mile plus 30 yards oval, with 6-furlong and 1 1/8-mile chutes. Distance from last turn to finish **845** feet; width **72** feet. Stable accommodations **1,200**. Seating capacity **3,500**.

Opened August 30, 1984. Live mixed breed race meet on weekends. 2004 dates: Feb. 21 to May 1 and Aug. 6 to Oct. 30.

TRACK RECORDS

4 Furs.	Iwontbeback	7	120	:44-3/5	July 3, 1995	1-1/16 m	Just Ask Rudy	6	119	1:43-1/5	Apr. 6, 1996
4-1/2 Furs.	Rebel s Jon	4	118	:50-3/5	June 29, 1996	1-1/8 m	Long On Rowdy	6	120	1:49-3/5	July 17, 1994
5 Furs.	Stites Stride	5	119	:57	Oct. 11, 1987	Abt 1-1/4 m	Indio Jo	6	117	2:09-2/5	Nov. 10, 1985
5-1/2 Furs.	Pro Cat	5	116	1:03.05	March 5, 2000	1-1/4 m	Dare More	6	121	2:03-3/5	Aug. 28, 1994
6 Furs.	Rebel s Jon	3	119	1:08-4/5	July 9, 1995	1-/3/8 m	Say It All	5	121	2:17-1/5	Oct. 1, 1995
7 Furs.	Pretentious Chief	7	118	1:23	Sep. 10, 1995	1-1/2 m	Mr. Sanhedrin	6	119	2:32-3/5	Nov. 14, 1993
7-1/2 Furs.	Karate Kick	6	126	1:29-3/5	Sep. 17, 1994	Abt 1-5/8 m	Chivas Elf	4	120	2:50	Nov. 30, 1986
1 Mile	Staged Attraction	5	122	1:36-1/5	June 10, 1989	1-5/8 m	Askherout	4	118	2:47	Nov. 26, 1989
1-70 yds.	Generain	8	115	1:40.09	Sept. 23, 1994						

Leading Jockey in 2003 (thoroughbred): Mike Harvell, 26 wins
Leading Trainer in 2003 (thoroughbred): Don R. Smith, 12 wins
Record attendance 10,169, August 30, 1984; Record handle $1,152, 006, May 2, 1987.

CALDER RACE COURSE

Calder Race Course, Inc.
Thomas H. Meeker, Chairman and CEO; C. Kenneth Dunn, President; Randall E. Soth, Vice President & General Manager; Racing Secretary: Robert D. Umphrey; Simulcast Director: Diane Stoess; Director of Publicity: Michele Blanco.

Street Address: 21001 NW 27th Avenue
Miami, Florida 33056
Nearest Airports: Ft. Lauderdale-Hollywood Intl.,
8 miles; Miami International, 15 miles

P.O. Box 1808, Miami, Florida 33055-0808
(305) 625-1311 (Dade Co.); (954) 523-4324 (Broward Co.)
Fax: (305) 620-2569; Publicity (305) 624-6284
E-Mail Address: customerservice@calderracecourse.com
Web Site: www.calderracecourse.com

Tropical Park Inc.
P.O. Box 1808, Miami, Florida 33055-0808
Street Address: 21001 NW 27th Avenue, Miami, Florida 33056
Telephone: Office and Track: (305) 625-1311
Officers: C. Kenneth Dunn, President.

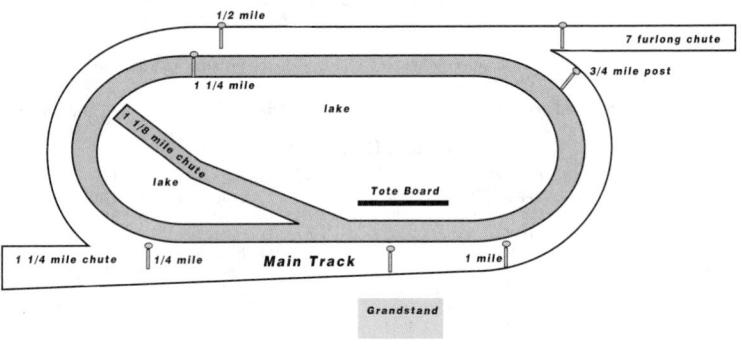

Track Data: One-mile oval. Two chutes: quarter mile, 7 furlongs. Length of stretch: 990 feet. 7-furlong turf course with 1 1/8-mile diagonal chute. Seating for 15,585; Parking for 10,000 cars; Stable Accommodations: 1,850.

Calder Race Course in Miami has grown through its 32 years of existence to become a foundation for the thoroughbred racing industry in south Florida. The track, which opened in 1971 and was acquired by Churchill Downs Incorporated in April of 1999, is located adjacent to Pro Player Stadium, the home of the Miami Dolphins and Florida Marlins. The track annually conducts eight months of live racing, with the Calder meet that runs from late April through late October and the Tropical Park-at-Calder meet that runs from late October to early January. The 2004 Calder stakes schedule features 38 events that carry $5.6 million in purses. Highlights of its racing season include the Festival of the Sun and Summit of Speed.

TRACK RECORDS

2 Furs.	Baby Shark	2		20.81	July 13, 2002		Halo s Image	4	115	1:41-3/5	Oct. 31, 1995
4-1/2 Furs.	Golden Phantom	2	118	51.86	Sept. 16, 2001	1-1/16 m	Castlebrook	4	118	1:42.55	Sept. 15, 2001
5 Furs.	Honest	3	117	57.61	July 1, 1996	1-1/8 m	Jumping Hill	6	117	1:50	Dec. 30, 1978
5-1/2 Furs.	Bernard s Candy	3		1:04.39	Aug. 9, 2002	1-3/16 m	Arctic Honeymoon	4	114	1:59-3/5	Jan. 3, 1987
6 Furs.	Forty One Carats	4	116	1:08.95	Oct. 7, 2000	1-1/4 m	Wicapi	4	114	2:05	June 24, 1996
6-1/2 Furs.	Thrillin Discovery	3	112	1:16.20	Nov. 28, 1998	1-1/2 m	Lead m Home	3	111	2:32-3/5	Dec. 31, 1977
7 Furs.	Constant Escort	4	114	1:21.82	Sep. 28, 1996	1-5/8 miles	Timberlea Tune	5	111	2:50-1/5	Oct. 16, 1971
1 Mile	High Ideal	3	118	1:36.25	Sept. 15, 2001	1-3/4 m	Detective II	7	113	3:03-1/5	Oct. 23, 1971
1 m 70yds	Medieval Mac	3	113	1:41-3/5	July 10, 1993	2 Miles	Detective II	7	130	3:30-1/5	Nov. 11, 1971

Turf Course

5 Furs.	Heckofaralph	5	118	:54-4/5	Aug. 1, 1998	1-1/8 m	The Vid	5	120	1:44-4/5	Nov. 25, 1995
7 Furs.	Carterista	4	119	1:22-1/5	June 19, 1993	1-3/8 m	King s Design	3	113	2:13.18	July 23, 1999
7-1/2 Furs.	Court Lark	6	115	1:26-2/5	July 16, 1994	1-1/2 m	Flag Down	5	116	2:24	Dec. 16, 1995
1 Mile	Mr. Livingston	4	115	1:33.75	Sept. 3, 2001	2 Miles	Skate On Thin Ice	9	117	3:21-4/5	Jan. 2, 1996
1-1/16 m	Spendable	5	117	1:39.33	July 30, 1999						

Leading Jockey in 2003 Calder meet: Manoel Cruz, 174 wins.
Leading Trainer in 2003 Calder meet: William P. White, 52 wins.
Leading Jockey in 2003-2004 Tropical Park meet: Eddie Castro, 83 wins.
Leading Trainer in 2003-2004 Tropical Park meet: Edward Plesa, Jr. 21 wins.

Record attendance: (Calder meet) 23, 103, May 4, 1985 (Derby Day); (Tropical meet) 17,671, January 14, 1978; Record on-track handle: (Calder meet) : $2,954,162 – May 7, 1988 (Derby Day); (Tropical meet) $2,793,767 – January 7, 1989 (Tropical Park Derby Day); Record handle, including simulcasting: (Calder meet) $10,541,440 – July 12, 2003 (Summit of Speed); (Tropical meet) $9,461,604, December 29, 2001 (Grand Slam II Day)

CANTERBURY PARK

Canterbury Park Holding Corp.

Curtis Sampson, Chairman of the Board; Randall Sampson, President, General Manager and CEO; Director of Racing/Racing Secretary: Douglas Schoepf. Media Relations Manager: Joe Anderson.

Nearest Airport: Twin Cities International, 15 minutes east of track.

1100 Canterbury Road, Shakopee, MN 55379
Telephone: (952) 445-7223; (800) 340-6361
Publicity/Press Box (952) 496-6408; Fax: (952) 496-6400
Scratches and results: (952)-233-4818
Web Site: www.canterburypark.com

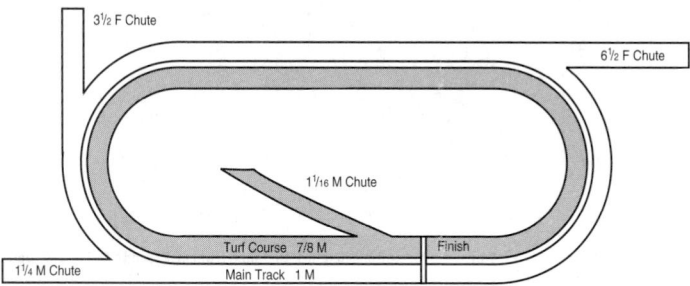

Track Data: One-mile dirt oval, six and one half furlong chute; 7/8-mile turf oval. Stable accommodations, 1,600 horses. Grandstand Capacity, 16,000; Parking for 7,500 cars.

Opened June 26, 1985. After multiple closings into the early 1990's, Canterbury was reopened as Canterbury Park under new management including local horsemen in 1994. In 2004, Canterbury Park will host the sixth renewal of the six-race, $550,000 Claiming Crown, to be held July 17. In addition to its regular May to September race meet, Canterbury purses have doubled to more than $120,000 per day in the years since introducing the first racetrack-based poker facility in the mid-west. At present Canterbury is seeking legislative support for a full fledged casino on the grounds and/or slot machines.

TRACK RECORDS

Abt 3-1/2 F	Bye For Now	3	115	:40	June 30, 1985	1m-70yds	J.P.Jet			1:40.26*	Aug. 3, 2002
3-1/2 Furs.	In Moderation	2	118	:39	May 26, 1997	1-1/16 m	Power Boat	4	112	1:41-4/5	July 30, 1988
4-1/2 Furs.	Gallapiat s Song	2	120	:51-1/5	June 23, 1991	1-1/8 m	Olympio	3	123	1:46-2/5	July 7, 1991
5 Furs.	Feather in My Hat	4	115	:57-1/5	Aug. 25, 1990	1-1/4 m	John Bullit	6	122	2:04-3/5	July 25, 1986
5-1/2 Furs.	Nickel Slot	4	116	1:02-4/5	May 17, 1989	1-1/2 m	Loustros	5	116	2:32-3/5	Aug. 28, 1987
6 Furs.	So Long Seoul	3	114	1:08-3/5	May 6, 1990	1-3/4 m	Luciole	5	118	2:59-4/5	Oct. 12, 1985
6-1/2 Furs.	Don s Irish Melody	5	115	1:14	June 12, 1988	2 Miles	My Tulles Free	4	116	3:25-3/5	Sep. 1, 1986
1 Mile	Minneapple	5	121	1:35-1/5	Sep. 27, 1987						

Turf Course

5 Furs.	Thatsusintheolbean	4	120	:56-2/5	May 23, 1998	Abt 1-1/16 m	Diplomat s Reward	4	116	1:41.34	July 17, 1999
Abt 7-1/2 F	Kiltartan Cross	3	113	1:27-4/5	Aug. 11, 1991	1-1/16 m	Little Bro Lantis	7	118	1:40-1/5	June 17, 1995
7-1/2 Furs.	Honor the Hero	7	122	1:28	June 18, 1995	Abt 1-3/8 m	Le Fabulous Song	4	112	2:14-4/5	Oct. 20, 1991
Abt 1 Mile	Kiltartan Cross	3	112	1:33-2/5	July 10, 1991	1-3/8 m	Treizieme	5	114	2:12-3/5	Aug. 3, 1986
1 Mile	Go Go Jack	4	112	1:33-2/5	June 3, 1995	Abt 1-7/8 m	Mark of Strength	7	118	3:11-2/5	Sep. 12, 1992
Abt 1m 70y	Tainer s Toy	8	109	1:39-1/5	Aug. 10, 1991	1-7/8 m	John Bullit	7	120	3:11-2/5	Sep. 26, 1987
1 m70yds	Numchuek	6	114	1:39-1/5	July 6, 1988						

Leading jockey in 2003: Derek C. Bell, 77 wins.
Leading trainer in 2003: David Van Winkle, 35 wins.
Record attendance: 27,439, April 24, 1987; Record handle: $3,560,228, July 19, 2003

CHARLES TOWN RACES AND SLOTS

PNGI Charles Town Races, LLC
President/COO: Jim Buchanan; Senior VP & Regional Operations Manager: John Finamore; General Manager:
Richard L. Moore; Racing Secretary: Jimmy Hammond; Publicity Director: Jeff Gilleas.
PO Box 551, Charles Town, WV 25414
Phone: 304-725-7001; Fax: 304-725-4384; Free results: 800-795-7001 ext. 384
E-Mail Address: jeff.gilleas@pngaming.com; Web Site: www.charlestownraces.com

Track data: six-furlong oval, with two chutes, 4 1/2 furlongs and 1 5/16 miles. Distance from last turn to finish, 660 feet. Stable accommodations 1,050; seating capacity 6,000.

Charles Town Races opened on Dec. 2, 1933, and was the first northern track to operate during the winter season. Charles Town Races was home to the first black female trainer to be licensed in the United States and featured the first woman jockey to win a pari-mutuel race. Home of the West Virginia Breeders Classics founded by NFL Hall of Fame member, Sam Huff. In 1997, a referendum passed to approve video lottery machines. At present there are 3,500 slots machines. Features a covered parking garage. Charles Town is open year-round for simulcast wagering and slots. Wednesday through Sunday for live night racing, post time is 7:15 pm with Sunday's post at 1 pm. Live racing in 2003 from January to December, split into four seasonal meets totaling 235 racing days, with daily purses of almost $150,000.

TRACK RECORDS

Abt 4 Furs.	Lawrenceville	4	120	:46-2/5	Dec. 30, 1990	1-1/4 m	Belle d Amour	3	112	2:05-3/5	June 28, 1941
4 Furs.	General Stevens	5	112	:45-2/5	July 15, 1978	1-5/16 m	Jim-A-Mike	3	114	2:14	Dec. 3, 1966
4-1/2 Furs.	It s Only Money	4	117	:50.36	July 4, 1999	1-1/2 m	Guasave Breeze	3	118	2:34	June 9, 1972
6-1/2 Furs.	Jet Appeal	5	109	1:17	Jan. 6, 1976	1-9/16 m	Allen Caid	6	115	2:40	Dec. 10, 1941
Abt 7 Furs.	Morgan s Grove	2	117	1:27-3/5	Nov. 5, 1988	1-5/8 m	Cincpac	5	121	2:49-2/5	Nov. 13, 1970
7 Furs.	Ohmylove	5	109	1:24	Jan. 7, 1976	1-13/16 m	Crafty Chris	3	111	3:11-2/5	Nov. 20, 1970
1-1/16 m	My Sister Pearl	5	111	1:43.83	Jan. 4, 2001	1-7/8 m	Gustav II	5	116	3:16-3/5	Nov. 25, 1972
1-1/8 m	Lexington Park	6	126	1:50.20	Sept. 21, 1973						

Leading Jockeys in 2003: Matthew Carroll McGowan, Anthony Mawing and Oscar Flores each won one of four meets; the remaining meet ended in a tie between Travis L. Dunkelberger and Anthony Mawing.

Leading Trainers in 2003: Ronney Brown won two meets and Jeff Runco won one meet; Brown and Runco tied as leaders of the remaining meet.

Record attendance: 21,480 September 17, 1981; Record handle: $2,047,873 May 3, 2003

CHURCHILL DOWNS

Churchill Downs Incorporated.
Thomas H. Meeker, President and CEO; Carl F. Pollard, Chairman; Steve Sexton, President; Karl F.Schmitt Sr. President CD Simulcasting Network; John S. Asher, Vice President Racing Communication; Doug Bredar, Director of Racing, Racing Secretary.

700 Central Avenue   (502) 636-4400; Racing, (502) 636-4470 Louisville, Kentucky 40208-1200
Trackside (simulcasting), (502) 962-2210
Nearest Airport: Louisville International,   Publicity: (502) 636-4460
3 miles from track.   Kentucky Derby Museum: (502) 637-1111
Fax: (502) 636-4430; Publicity (502) 636-4469
Web Site: www.churchilldowns.com

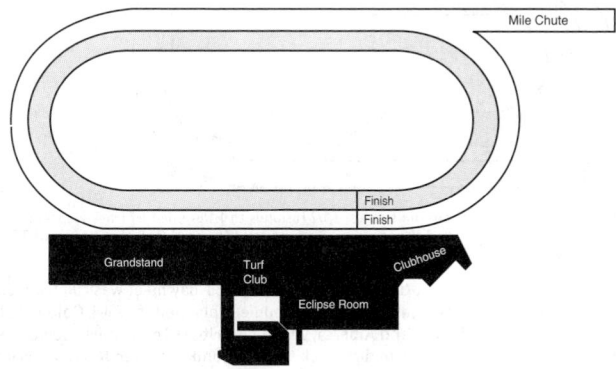

Track Data: One-mile oval, sandy loam with chute for one-mile races. Length of stretch, 1,234 1/2 feet. Matt Winn Turf Course: seven furlongs. Stable capacity, 1,400. Seating for 48,500, capacity 155,000 with infield; Parking for 5,000 cars, with many private lots in surrounding area. NOTE: Derby Day and Oaks seats are sold on an request basis. Derby and Oaks Ticket requests should be directed to Special Events Department, Churchill Downs, 700 Central Avenue, Louisville, Kentucky 40208.
Opened May 17, 1875. The legendary home of the Kentucky Derby and the Kentucky Derby Museum, Churchill Downs is a registered National Historic Landmark. The world-famous Twin Spires were unveiled on Derby Day, May 6, 1895. Churchill also is the oldest North American track with continuous annual racing and daily average purses in 2003 were more than $438,000 during the 52 day spring meet which annually begins with Kentucky Derby week. In 2002, a $121 million Master Plan, more comprehensive than any other construction project in the history of the track, was begun. The first of two phases, 64 luxury suites, was completed in 2003. The second, begun in 2003 and due for completion in 2005, features a long list of improvements and enhancements including more luxury suites; a new Millionaire's Row and Skye Terrace; a new, expanded Turf Club, premium indoor and outdoor box seating; new dining and entertainment areas and much more.

TRACK RECORDS

4 Furs.	Fair Phantom	2	114	:46 3/5*	May 7, 1921	1-1/16 m	Yes Sir	5	110	1:41 3/5	Nov. 25, 1970
4-1/2 Furs.	Chilukki	2	118	:51.00	April 28, 1999	1-1/8 m	Victory Gallop	4	120	1:47.28	June 12, 1999
5 Furs.	Brown Eyed Beauty	4	124	57.12	June 12, 2003	1-3/16 m	Bonnie Andrew	5	110	1:58 3/5	Nov. 14, 1942
5 1/2 Furs.	Cashier's Dream	2	118	1:02.52	July 7, 2001	1-1/4 m	Secretariat	3	126	1:59 2/5	May 5, 1973
6 Furs.	Kona Gold	6	126	1:07.77	Nov. 4, 2000	1-3/8 m	Elliott	6	109	2:20 3/5	Oct. 15, 1906
6 1/2 Furs.	Love At Noon	3	121	1:14.34	May 5, 2001	1 1/2m	A Storm Is Brewing			2:32.02	June 17, 2001
7 Furs.	Alannan	5	116	1:20.50	May 5, 2001	1-5/8 m	Tupolev	5	112	2:49 2/5	July 23, 1983
7 1/2 Furs.	Miss Lodi	4	123	1:28.08	June 1, 2002	1-3/4 m	Caslon Bold	7	114	2:59.64	July 4, 1995
1 Mile	Chilukki	3	116	1:33.57	Nov. 4, 2000	2 Miles	Libertarian	4	113	3:22.26	Nov. 28, 1998
1 m 20yds	Frog Legs	4	107	1:39	May 13, 1913	2-1/16 m	Hi Neighbor	8	117	3:40 4/5	Nov. 11, 1949
1 m 50yds	Hodge	5	120	1:41 4/5	Oct. 4, 1916	2-1/4 m	Raincoat	3	90	3:53	Oct. 7, 1915
1 m 70yds	The Porter	4	110	1:41 3/5	May 30, 1919	3-Miles	Ten Broeck	4	104	5:26 1/2	Sept. 3, 1876
1 m 100yds	The Caxton	4	101	1:49 1/5	May 16, 1902	4-Miles	Sotemia	5	119	7:10 4/5	Oct. 7, 1912

Turf Course

5 Furs.	Are You Down	6	111	55.57	May 14, 2003	1 1/8 m	Lure	4	123	1:46.34	April 30, 1993
1 Mile	Jaggery John	4	113	1:33.78	July 4, 1995	1 3/8 m	Snake Eyes	7	123	2:13.00	May 22, 1997
1 1/16m	Ever With You			1:40.82	Nov. 7, 2001	1 1/2 m	Tikkanen	3	122	2:26.50	Nov 5, 1994

Leading Jockey in 2003 Spring meet: Cornelio H. Velasquez, 63 wins
Leading Trainer in 2003 Spring meet: Dale Romans 39 wins
Leading Jockey in 2003 Fall meet: Pat Day, 41 wins
Leading Trainer in 2003 Fall meet: Dale L. Romans, 20 wins

Spring meet: Record attendance: May 4, 1974 (Derby Day) 163,628. Record handle: May 3, 2003 (Derby Day) $20,583,143 (on-track), $140,379,429 (all sources). Fall meet: Record attendance: November 7, 1998 (Breeders' Cup) 80,452. Record handle: Nov. 4, 2000(Breeders' Cup) $13,579,798.

COLONIAL DOWNS

Colonial Downs Holdings, Inc.
Chief Executive Officer & Board Chairman: Jeff Jacobs; President and CFO: Ian Stewart; General Manager: John E. Mooney (Pres. MD-VA Racing Circuit, Inc.); Racing Secretary: Clayton Beck Public Relations/Marketing Director: Darrell Wood.

10515 Colonial Downs Parkway, New Kent, Virginia 23124
(804) 966-7223 or 1-888-482-8725; Fax: (804) 966-1565. Free results: 1-888-482-8722
Web Site: www.colonialdowns.com.; E-Mail Address: cdwn@richmond.infi.net

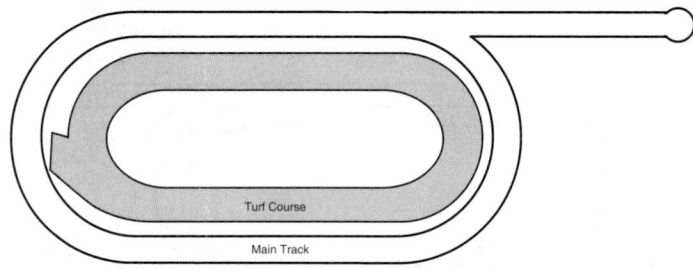

Track Data: 1 1/4 mile dirt track with chute for one-mile races; 7 1/2 furlongs to 1 1/8-mile turf track, depending on rail position, 180 feet wide. Stabling Capacity: 1,050; Seating capacity 6,000 capacity; Parking for 4,000 cars. Operates Virignia OTB facilities in Richmond, Chesapeake, Hampton, and Alberta.

Opened September 1, 1997 as the first pari-mutuel track in Virginia. A 30-day meet was run from June 13 through July 22 in 2003, with a strong accent on turf racing and a similar schedule is planned for 2004. Colonial also operates OTB facilities in Richmond, Chesapeake, Hampton and Alberta, which contribute to the purse structure of almost $189,000 per day. At 1-1/4 miles in circumference, the main dirt track is the second largest in North America. 2004 dates: June 11 to July 26.

TRACK RECORDS

5 Furs.	Timothy Mac	5	122	:55.74	Jul. 1, 2003	1 Mile	Assault John	3	115	1:35.48	Oct. 8, 1997
5-1/2 Furs.	Bid Wild	6	117	1:02.68	Jul. 1, 2003	1-1/16 m	Gold Token	5	115	1:41.09	Sept. 13, 1998
6 Furs.	Capture the Gold	3	119	1:08.55	Oct. 4, 1997	1-1/8 m	Our Toby	3	114	1:48.95	Oct. 4, 1997
6-1/2 Furs.	Cool Ken Jane	5	115	1:16-3/5	Sep. 7, 1997	1-1/4 m	Macgyver	3	114	2:03.54	Sep. 1, 1997
7 Furs.	Sky Watch	4	117	1:20.87	Sep. 1, 1997	1-1/2 m	Lord Mendelson	3	118	2:30.13	Sept. 4, 2000

Turf Course

5 Furs.	Bop	5	117	55.85	June 22, 2002	1-1/8 m	Kerfoot Corner	7	117	1:47.40	Sep. 26, 1998
5 1/2 Fur.	Devereaux	6	115	1:01.93	Sept. 24, 1999	1-3/16 m	Jacksonzac	8	119	1:54.41	Oct. 10, 1998
6 Fur.	Tyaskin	5	122	1:08.11	Sept. 20, 1998	1-1/4 m	Phi Beta Doc	3	117	1:59.97	Oct. 2, 1999
1 Mile	La Reine s Terms	3	115	1:34.24	Sept. 17. 1998	1 1/2 m	Winsox	7	117	2:27.04	Sept. 28, 1998
1 1/16 m	Grass Roots	5	117	1:41.01	Oct. 8, 1999	1 5/8 m	Our Game	4	122	2:44.82'	Sept. 24, 1999

Leading Jockey in 2003: Ryan Fogelsonger, 42 wins
Leading Trainer in 2003: Hamilton A. Smith, 17 wins.

COLUMBUS RACES

Platte County Agricultural Society
Chairman Gary Kruse; GM/Simulcast Director: Gary Bock; Racing Secretary: Dennis Kochevar.

822 15th Street, Columbus, NE 68601
Phone: 402-564-0133 Fax: 402-564-0990
E-Mail: agpark@megavision.com Web Site: www.agpark.com

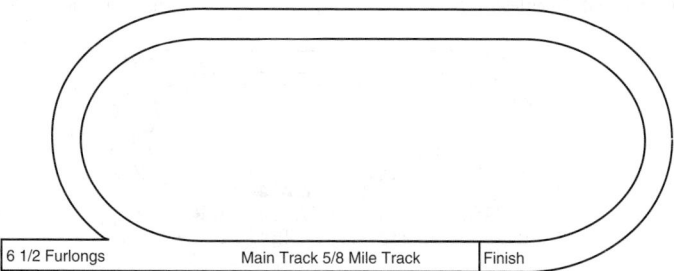

6 1/2 Furlongs   Main Track 5/8 Mile Track   Finish

Track data: five-furlong oval with a 6 1/2-furlong chute Distance from last turn to finish, 720 feet, width of stretch 75 feet. Stable accommodations 900. Seating capacity 4,000.

Opened in the 1940's and usually runs a summer meet of about 25 days with just under $36,000 in daily purses.

TRACK RECORDS

3-1/2 Furs.	Timetoprofit	6	124	39.60	Aug. 24, 2002	1-1/16 m	Foreign Intent	3	114	1:44-2/5	Sep. 21, 1974
5-1/2 Furs.	Foreign Flag	3	114	1:05-1/5	Sep. 30, 1978	1-5/16 m	Too Little Man	4	116	2:19-1/5	Sep. 6, 1969
6 Furs.	Evas Choice	5	117	1:10-2/5	Aug. 27, 1994	1-3/8 m	In Doc s Honor	6	116	2:18-2/5	Sep. 3, 1994
6-1/2 Furs.	Jae Ranch	4	114	1:17	Aug. 12, 1984	1-1/2 m	Skeeter Do	7	117	2:27-4/5	Sep. 12, 1994
1 m 70yds	Ilatan	7	118	1:41-3/5	Sep. 9, 1984	2 Miles	Blazing Don	7	111	3:36-3/5	Sep. 26, 1982

Leading Jockey in 2003: Armando Martinez, 41 wins.
Leading Trainer in 2003: David C. Anderson, 17 wins.
Record attendance, 8,856, September 3, 1973. Record handle $719, 725 September 3, 1984.

DELAWARE PARK

Delaware Racing Association
William M. Rickman Sr., Chairman of the Board; William M. Rickman Jr., President and Chief Executive Officer; William Fasy, Chief Operating Officer; Racing Secretary: Sam Abbey.

777 Delaware Park Blvd.   (302) 994-2521; Free Results: (302) 998-0110
Wilmington, Delaware 19804   Fax: (302) 994-3567; Publicity, (302) 993-2368
Nearest Airport: New Castle County Airport, 4 miles;   Web site: http://www.delawarepark.com
Philadelphia International, 20 miles.   E-mail: programs@delawarepark.com

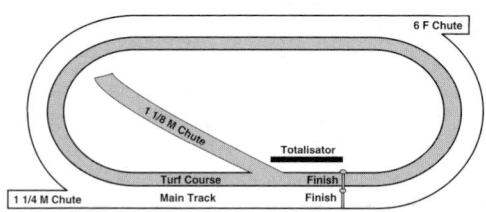

Track Data: One mile sandy loam oval with six-furlong and 1 1/4 mile chutes. Distance from last turn to finish, 995 feet; width 100 feet. Turf course: 7-furlongs. Stable accommodations 1,450. Must be 21 years or older to enter VLT area.

Opened June 26, 1937. Acquired in 1983 by William Rickman, Sr., a Rockville, Md. developer, Delaware Park has enjoyed a major rebirth since video lottery machines were included in the mix on December 29, 1995. In 2003, the 66th season included 141 racing days from April to November with purses in excess of $234,000 including stakes. Highlights included the Delaware Handicap Festival of racing in late July and the prestigious Delaware Handicap. The 2004 live racing season is scheduled for April 24 through Oct. 31. In addition to its two full floors of slot machines, Delaware Park offers full-card, multi-track simulcasting 7 days a week except Christmas and Easter.

TRACK RECORDS

2 Fur.	Glitter River	6	133	:21.60	Sept. 5, 2000	1-1/8 m	Victoria Park	3	122	1:47-2/5	June 18, 1960
4 Furs.	Star Event	2	118	:47	May 5, 1997	1-3/16 m	Gold Star Deputy	5	114	1:56.72	Oct. 31, 1999
4-1/2 Furs.	Erlton	2	118	:51-4/5	May 5, 1998	1-1/4 m	Coup De Fusil	5	114	1:59-4/5	July 25, 1987
5 Furs.	Milky Way Gal	5	116	:56-1/5	July 29, 1989	1-1/2 m	Bam	5	115	2:31	June 26, 1948
5-1/2 Furs.	Dontcloseyoureyes	4	122	1:03	Oct. 14, 1990	1-5/8 m	Flying Retsina Run	5	121	2:46.52	Spet. 4, 2000
6 Furs.	Damitrius	5	115	1:08-1/5	Sep. 2, 1980	1-3/4 m	Cer Vantes	6	118	2:56-2/5	June 27, 1951
1 Mile	Ashlar	4	117	1:35-1/5	June 25, 1960	2 Miles	Dixies Act	5	118	3:29-2/5	Aug. 10, 1975
1 m 70yds	Distinct Vision	3	115	1:39.20	Aug. 25, 2003	2 m 70yds	Wolfe Tone	6	114	3:34	Nov. 7, 1993
1-1/16 m	Lies Of Omission	6	116	1:41-2/5	July 4, 1998	2 1/4 Miles	Sanguine Sword	8	114	3:58-3/5	July 2, 1986

Turf Course

Abt 5 Furs.	Incredible Revenge	4	116	:56	Sep. 4, 1996	1-3/8 m	Cool Prince	5	114	2:12-2/5	July 3, 1965
Abt 1 m	Big Warning	4	122	1:35-2/5	July 22, 1990	Abt 1-1/2 m	Yield	4	116	2:29-4/5	Aug. 26, 1997
1 m	Portsmouth	3	114	1:35	June 17, 1965	1-1/2 m	Revved Up	5	116	2:26.46	July 20, 2003
Abt 1-1/16 m	My Sweet Lord	4	116	1:41-2/5	July 7, 1996	Abt 2 m	Peace Peace Peace	6	141	3:21-4/5	July 18, 1993
1-1/16 m	Charabanc	5	108	1:40-4/5	July 20, 1963	2 Miles	Verdance	4	113	3:24-2/5	Sep. 21, 1986
Abt 1-1/8 m	I m A Lil Devil	5	114	1:48-1/5	July 19, 1992	2-3/8 m	Lively London	5	113	4:09	July 25, 1986
1-1/8 m	Foufa s Warrior	3	115	1:47.44	July 20, 2003	2-7/8 m	Call Louis	4	107	5:08-1/5	Aug. 24, 1986
Abt. 1 3/8M	Go Code			2:17.71	July 10,2001						

Leading jockey in 2003: Ramon A. Dominguez, 254 wins.
Leading trainer in 2003: Scott A. Lake, 112 wins.
Record attendance: 35,473, July 5, 1954. Record handle: $4,837,856 – July 21, 2002

DEL MAR THOROUGHBRED CLUB

Del Mar Thoroughbred Club
President and General Manager, Joe Harper; Executive Vice President, Craig Fravel; Senior VP & CFO, Mike Ernst; Vice President, Marketing, Craig Dado; Vice President, Racing/Racing Secretary, Tom Robbins; Director of Media, Dan Smith.

Street Address: Via De La Valle & Jimmy Durante Blvd.

Nearest Airports: Lindbergh Field, 18 miles south of the track in San Diego. Private planes and helicopters may land at Palomar Airport, 12 miles to the north

P.O. Box 700, Del Mar, California 92014
(858) 755-1141; Fax: (858) 792-1477
Web Site: www.delmarracing.com. E-mail: marys@dmtc.com
Free scratches, results and stretch calls: (858) 793-5544

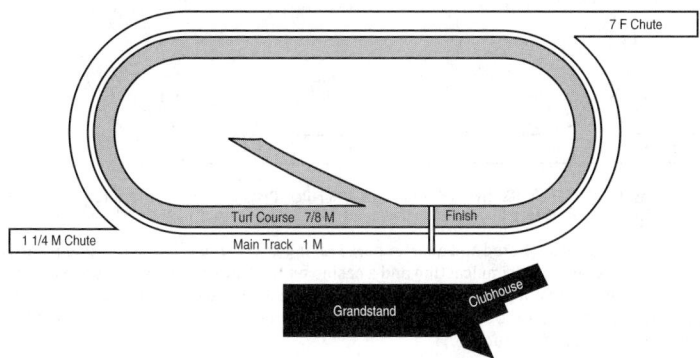

Track Data: One-mile oval with seven-furlong and 1 1/4-mile chutes. Distance from last turn to finish, 919 feet. Jimmy Durante Turf Course, seven-furlong oval, with one-eighth-mile diagonal chute. Stable accommodations: 2,100.
Seating capacity 14,304; Parking for 10,000 cars.

Opened July 3, 1937 with Bing Crosby collecting tickets at the booth. Crosby and several of his Hollywood pals were among Del Mar's original investors. The inaugural meeting also featured the first photo-finish camera (invented by Lorenzo del Riccio, an optical engineer at Paramount Pictures). During the 2003 season, which ran from July 23 through Sept. 10, Del Mar's purses averaged a record $531,055 per day. In 2004, Del Mar's prestigious 43-day meet will run from July 21 to Sept. 8. "Daybreak at Del Mar" - breakfast watching workouts trackside - every weekend 7:30 to 9:30 a.m. First post daily at 2 p.m. with exception of "Four O'Clock Fridays."
Leading Jockey in 2003: Patrick A. Valenzuela, 52 wins.

TRACK RECORDS

5 Furs.	Soldier Girl	3	116	:56-2/5	Aug. 13, 1964	1 1/16 m	Windy Sands	5	122	1:40	Aug. 4, 1962
5-1/2 Furs.	Ack Ack	4	124	1:02-1/5	Sep. 12, 1970	1 1/8 m	Latin Touch	4	109	1:46	Sep. 1, 1979
6 Furs.	King Of Cricket	6	115	1:07-3/5	Aug. 22, 1973	1 3/16 m	Four by Five	7	118	1:56 2/5	Aug. 16, 1954
6-1/2 Furs.	Native Paster	4	117	1:13-3/5	Sep. 4, 1988	Abt 1 1/4m	Ancient Title	7	123	1:55-2/5	Sep. 5, 1977
7 Furs.	Solar Launch	3	122	1:20	Aug. 10, 1990	1 1/4 m	Candy Ride	4	124	1:59.11	Aug. 24, 2003
1 Mile	Precisionist	7	114	1:33-1/5	Aug. 1, 1988	1 1/2 m	Spring Boy	5	116	2:29-2/5	Aug. 16, 1958

Turf Course

5 Furs.	Maria s Mirage	4	119	:55.06	Jul. 28, 2003	1 1/16 m	Allover	4	121	1:39.84	Aug. 27, 2003
71/2 Furs.	Syncopate	6	115	1:27-4/5	Aug. 24, 1981	1 1/8 Miles	Special Ring	6	117	1:45.87	Jul. 27, 2003
1 Mile	Touch of the Blues	6	122	1:32.22	Aug. 2, 2003	1 3/8 Miles	Crazy Ensign	7	121	2:12.07	Aug. 29, 2003

Leading Trainer in 2003: Bob Baffert, 23 wins.
Record Attendance: 44,181, August 10, 1996. Record Handle: $5,657,840 August 15, 1987 (on track). $22,857,782 August 15, 1998 (all sources)

DELTA DOWNS

Delta Downs Racetrack & Casino

Owner: Boyd Gaming Corporation; General Manager: Jack Bernsmeier; Director of Racing and Simulcasting: Chris Warren; Racing Secretary: Trent McIntosh; Public Relations Manager: Cassondra Guilbeau

PO Box 175, Vinton, LA 70668-0175
337-589-7441 Fax: 337-589-2399

Web Site: HYPERLINK http://www.deltadowns.com; www.deltadowns.com;

Track data: six-furlong oval with two chutes, five furlongs and 1 1/16 miles. Distance from last turn to finish line 660 feet. Width of stretch 80 feet; backstretch and turns 70 feet. Stable accommodations 1,320. Seating capacity 3,400; Parking for 3,000 cars.

Opened September 20, 1973. Thoroughbred and quarter horse racing from January to March and from November to late December in 2003 with year round simulcasting and a casino on the track grounds. Purses have increased steadily during the three years of casino operation, with a new high of $183,000 per day registered from November 2002 through March 2003. Dates for 2003-04: Oct. 31 to March 27 and a similar meeting beginning in the fall. A Quarter Horse meet will be run from April 9 to Aug. 15.

TRACK RECORDS

2-1/2 Furs.	Mrs. Deville	2	112	:27	Feb. 19, 1976	1-1/16 m	Norms Promise	4	125	1:43-1/5	Mar. 23, 1975
	Cajun s Two Step	2	115	:27	Feb. 10, 1985	1-1/8 m	Lemon Mousse	4	117	1:56-1/5	Nov. 22, 1992
4 Furs.	Rock Afire	5	119	:46-1/5	Dec. 10 1994	1-3/16 m	Ponderosa Lark	5	114	2:03-3/5	Oct. 31, 1975
4-1/2 Furs.	Raisable Adversary	4	120	:51	Feb. 15, 1992	1-1/4 m	Shy Bull	5	122	2:10-1/5	Nov. 3, 1974
5 Furs.	Britt s Jules	2	117	57.49	Nov. 5, 2003	1-5/16 m	Gentleman Mike	4	115	2:17-3/5	Dec. 1, 1974
6-1/2 Furs.	Chief Okie Dokie	6	118	1:18.76	Feb. 8, 2002	1-3/8 m	Surrogate s Irish	8	118	2:23.52	Mar. 22, 2003
7 Furs.	No Its Not	5	123	1:24.31	Jan. 24, 2003	1-1/2 m	Art Work	6	122	2:41-1/5	Jan. 11, 1974
7-1/2 Furs.	Junior Gent	4	108	1:33-1/5	Mar. 14, 1974	1-9/16 m	Landing Officer	4	122	2:51-4/5	Jan. 15, 1989
1 Mile	Freon Flier	4	118	1:37.52	Mar. 10, 2002	2 Miles	Can Em	5	118	3:43-4/5	Dec. 10, 1988
1 m70yds	Thriller	6	117	1:42-2/5	Sep. 27, 1973						

Record attendance: 10, 824, December 30, 1990; Record handle: $2,477,000, December 5. 2003

Leading Jockey, 2003: Steve J. Bourque, 116 wins.

Leading Trainer, 2003: Doris Hebert and Keith L. Bourgeois, 55 wins (tie).

THE DOWNS AT ALBUQUERQUE

The Downs at Albuquerque, Inc.

President: Paul Blanchard; General Manager: Craig Smith; Director of Administration and Simulcast Coordinator, Beth McKinney; Director of Racing: Don Cook; Racing Secretary: Roddy W. Taylor; Marketing Director: Michael Lazarus.

201 California St. NE, Albq. NM 87108
PO Box 8510, Albuquerque, NM 87198-8510
505-266-5555 Fax: 505-268-1970
E-Mail Address: michaell@abqdowns.com
Web Site: www.abqdowns.com

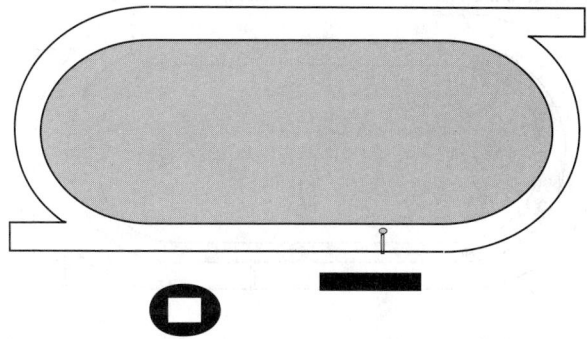

Track data: One-mile oval with 1/4-mile and seven-furlong chutes. Distance from last turn to finish 1,114; width 90 feet. Stable accommodations 1,700.

Opened October of 1938, along old Route 66, as a single-story structure. There are three stories now, all glass enclosed. A casino contributes a percentage of its revenue to the $100,000 daily purse structure. The Downs will run two mixed-breed meets in 2004: Spring, April 9 through July 5; New Mexico State Fair, Sept. 10 through Sept 19 and Sept. 22 through Sept. 26. The Spring meet features The Lineage, a day of racing dedicated to New Mexico-bred horses on a complete card of 10 races, each with a $40,000 purse.

TRACK RECORDS

4 Fur.	Chipper J.	2	118	:45.76	May 6, 2000	1-1/16 m	Ciento	3	120	1:40.60	Sept. 22, 2001
4-1/2 Furs.	Silver Matt	2	115	:51.22	June 17, 2000	1-1/8 m	Moro Grande	8	114	1:48.42	June 8, 2003
5 Furs.	Scout Revolt	3	120	:56.35	Dec. 12, 1998	1-3/16 m	Savage Wind	7	114	2:05-4/5	Oct. 6, 1985
5-1/2 Furs.	Yulla Yulla	5	119	1:01.60	Sept. 23, 2000	1 1/4 m	Luedke	8	119	2:03.69	April 14, 1996
6 Furs.	Huggin the Rail	6	119	1:08.44	Sept. 29, 1996	1-1/2 m	Luedke	6	116	2:33.73	Sept. 25, 1994
6-1/2 Furs.	Ben Told	8	120	1:14.59	May 10, 2002	1 3/4 Miles	Prince De-Or	8	111	2:59.20	Sep. 25, 1966
7 Furs.	Star Smasher			1:21.01*	June 9, 2002	1-13/16 m	Vermejo	6	118	3:05-2/5	Sep. 27, 1970
1 Mile	Curve Ball	6	120	1:35.57	April 27, 2003	2 Miles	Betty Falcon	5	109	3:28-3/5	Oct. 7, 1956
1 m 70yds	Fire Knight	6	112	1:41.60	Sept. 26, 1959						

Leading Jockey, spring meet, 2003: Travis Wales, 22 wins.
Leading Trainer, spring meet, 2003: Henry Dominguez, 22 wins.
Leading Jockey, fall meet, 2003: Ricardo Jaime, 14 wins.
Leading Trainer, fall meet, 2003: Henry Dominguez, 10 wins.
Record attendance: 13,979 September 16, 1990. Record handle: $1,050,700, September 16, 1990, (includes simulcasting.)

ELLIS PARK

Churchill Downs, Inc.

Thomas H. Meeker, Chairman; Steve Sexton, President; Paul D. Kuerzi, General Manager; Racing Secretary and Director of Racing: Doug Bredar; Director of Publicity: Luke Kruytbosch; Marketing Director: Bob Cunningham.

Street Address: 3300 U.S. Highway 41 North   P.O. Box 33, Henderson, Kentucky 42419-0033
Henderson, Kentucky 42420   General Office: (812) 425-1456; Fax (812) 425-0146
Nearest Airport: Evansville, Indiana (8 miles)   Racing Office: (812) 435-8940; Fax: (812) 425-3725

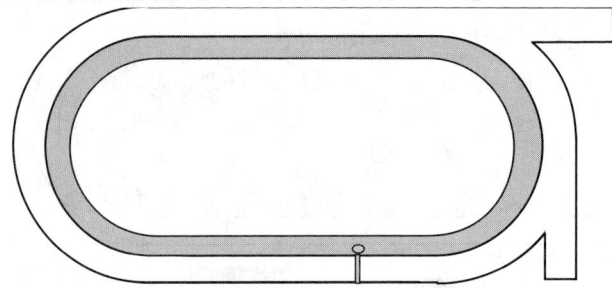

Web site: www.ellisparkracing.com

Track Data: One mile and one-eighth sandy loam oval with seven-furlong and one-mile chutes. Distance from last turn to finish, 1,175 feet; width 100 feet in stetch, 85 feet in backstretch.. One-mile turf course; Stable accommodations for 1,290 stalls; training facilities also available at Kentucky Horse Center in Lexington, (606) 293-1853. Seating for 7,750; Parking for 6,000 cars.

Opened November 8, 1922 and operated by James C. Ellis from 1924 to his death in 1956. Acquired by Churchill Downs in 1998. Several improvements to the facility were made in 2001; in 2003, purses including stakes averaged just under $200,000. For 2004, Ellis Park offers year-round Clubhouse Simulcasting and live racing every day except Tuesday from July 7-Sept. 6, a total of 54 racing d ays.

TRACK RECORDS

5 Furs.	White Image	2	119	:57-3/5	July 9, 1988	1-1/4 m	Won Du Loup	4	115	2:03	Sep. 4, 1988
5-1/2 Furs.	Relentless Seller	3	114	1:03.37	Aug.16, 2002	1-3/8 m	Ramona Jay	4	102	2:23	Aug. 24, 1985
6 Furs.	Stubilem	4	117	1:09	July 1, 1982	1-1/2 m	Unaccountable	5	115	2:29-3/5	July 23, 1988
6-1/2 Furs.	American Chance	5	113	1:15	July 16, 1994	1-5/8 m	Sir Lightning	7	112	2:45-4/5	Aug. 9, 1992
7 Furs.	Sheena Native	4	120	1:21-3/5	July 23, 1988	1-3/4 m	Bondi	3	115	3:00	Aug. 27, 1966
Abt 7-1/2 F	Illbeastar	4	113	1:35-1/5	July 1, 1977	2 Miles	Classic Deal	6	119	3:25-3/5	Aug. 21, 1988
1 Mile	Still Waving	5	118	1:34-3/5	Aug. 13, 1988	2-1/4 m	Bondi	5	115	3:54	Sep. 5, 1966
1-1/8 m	Lt. Lao	4	123	1:47-3/5	Aug. 27, 1988						

Turf Course

5-1/2 Furs.	Bettybird	3	112	1:00.52	Aug. 21, 2002	1-1/4 m	Ye Slew	7	112	1:59-3/5	Aug. 6, 1994
1 Mile	Slewper Imp	5	115	1:32-3/5	July 16, 1995	1-1/2 m	Our Forbes	4	115	2:25-2/5	Aug. 10, 1994
1-1/16 m	Majestic Jove	3	114	1:39-1/5	Aug. 27, 1997	2 Miles	Irish Harbour	6	113	3:20-1/5	Sep. 2, 1996
1-1/8 m	Yaqthan	6	113	1:44-3/5	Sep. 2, 1996						

Leading Jockey in 2003: Rafael Bejarano, 80 wins
Leading Trainer in 2003: Kim Hammond, 15 wins
Record attendance: 15,500 estimated, September 4, 1967.

EMERALD DOWNS

Northwest Racing Associates, LP
President: Ronald D. Crockett; Director of Operations: Bob Fraser ; Director of Racing: Grant Holcomb;
Marketing and Public Relations Director: Susie Sourwine
Street address: 2300 Emerald Downs Dr.Auburn, Wa., 98001
PO Box 617, Auburn, WA 98071-0617 ; 253-288-7000 Fax: 253-288-7010
Web Site: www.emdowns.com

Track data: One-mile oval with two chutes, 1 1/4 miles and 6 1/2 furlongs. Distance from last turn to finish 990 feet.

Opened in 1996 to replace the void left in Seattle area by the termination of racing at Longacres. The 2003 meet featured more than $89,000 in purses, including stakes during a 92-day session from mid–April to mid–September. A similar meet is scheduled for 2004, from April 16 through Sept. 20.

TRACK RECORDS

2 Furs.	Midnight Cruiser	2	112	:21.40	May 4, 2000	1 Mile	Sky Jack	7	123	1:33.00	Aug. 24, 2003
4-1/2 Furs.	I. M. Adevil	2	118	:50-3/5	May 30, 1999	1-1/16 m	Kid Katabatic	5	123	1:39-3/5	July 26, 1998
5 Furs.	Jazzy Mac	5	98	:55.40	Aug. 20, 2000	1-1/8 m	Moonlight Meeting			1:47.00	July 28, 2002
5-1/2 Furs.	Salt Grinder	3	114	1:01.40	Apr. 20, 2002	1-1/4 m	Rapid Stream	7	118	2:01-4/5	Aug. 15, 1998
6 Furs.	Blue Tejano	8	119	1:07.60	June 7, 2002	1-1/2 m	Keen Line	9	120	2:30-3/5	Sep. 6, 1997
6-1/2 Furs.	Bold Ranger			1:13.80*	May 27, 2002	2 Miles	Kavil	5	115	3:26-4/5	Nov. 1, 1996

Leading Jockey in 2003: Kevin Radke, 143 wins.
Leading Trainer in 2003: Tim McCanna, 55 wins.
Record handle: August 22, 1999, $1,217,590; August 22, 1999 $2,731,852, all sources

EVANGELINE DOWNS

Old Evangeline Downs, LLC
GM: David A. Yount.; Racing Secretary: Warren C. Grace. Publicity Director, Sean D. Beirne
PO Box 90270, Lafayette, LA 70506
337-896-7223 Fax: 337-896-5445
E-Mail Address: info@evangelinedowns.com; Web Site: www.evangelinedowns.com

Track data: Seven-furlong oval, with six-furlong and 1 3/16-mile chutes. Distance from last turn to finish 1,020 feet; width 70 feet. Stable accommodations 1,018; Seating capacity 4,800; parking for 3,000 cars.

Opened April 28, 1966 and runs a thoroughbred meet April through Labor Day and a newly added seven-week Quarter Horse meet mid-September to October, with year-round simulcasting and off-track betting sites. Opened Evangeline Downs Racetrack & Casino on Dec. 19, 2003. Racing will move to the new facility in Opelousas, La., in April 2005. Purses for the 2004 season will double from the $63,000 range in 2003 to over $125,000. Evangeline has been the starting point for some of the best jockeys currently in the sport, including recently retired Hall of Famer Eddie Delahoussaye and Randy Romero, a winner of 4,292 races. The great gelding John Henry won his first stakes at Evangeline Downs. On June 3, 2000, the filly Hallowed Dreams won her 14th consecutive race without a defeat, an American record for thoroughbred fillies. The 2004 thoroughbred meet will run 87 days from April 1 to Labor Day, Sept. 6. The 2004 Quarter Horse meet will run 29 days, Sept. 16 to Oct. 31.

TRACK RECORDS

4 Furs.	Rare Trip	2	118	:46.60	May 20, 1977	1 1/16 m	Nin s Pick	3	116	1:43.40	June 19, 1977
4 1/2 Furs.	Bag In Hand		116	51.60	Aug. 28, 2000	1 1/8 Miles	Report to Glory	4	117	1:50.80	Aug. 9, 1993
5 Furs.	Glasspro	7	114	:57.27	Sep. 2, 1995	1 1/4 Miles	Pasquale G.	8	120	2:01.40	July 31, 1977
5 1/2 Furs.	Hunters Halo		119	1:03.80	July 15, 2002	1 7/16 Miles	Paw Paw s Pride		122	2:28.40	July 19, 2002
6 Furs.	Rail	6	121	1:09.20	July 22, 1995	1 1/2 Miles	Just For Charlie	5	117	2:41.40	Sep. 15, 1986
7 1/2 Furs.	Top Silk	4	117	1:31.40	June 2, 1991	1 5/8 Miles	Lucky Man	6	119	2:48.20	Aug. 2, 2002
1 Mile	Winning Connection	4	115	1:36.60	Aug. 19, 2000	1 7/8 Miles	Concho Country	6	122	3:19.40	Aug. 18, 2000
1 M 40 Yds	Mr. D s Prank	7	119	1:43.60	July 11, 1983	2 Miles	Gray Gardner	5	122	3:31.60	Aug. 27, 1990
1 M 70 Yds	State Commander	5	117	1:42.10	Apr. 22, 1991						

Leading Jockey in 2003: Carl James Woodley, 98 wins
Leading Trainer in 2003: Keith L. Bourgeois, 65 wins.

FAIR GROUNDS

Fair Grounds Corp.
Bryan G. Krantz, President and General Manager;
Racing Secretary: Ben Huffman; Director of Marketing/Publicity: Lenny Vangilder

Street Address: 1751 Gentilly Blvd.
New Orleans, Louisiana 70119

P.O. Box 52529, New Orleans, LA 70152
Telephone: (504) 944-5515; Fax: (504) 944-2511
E-mail Address: webmaster@fgno.com
Web Site: http://www.fgno.com

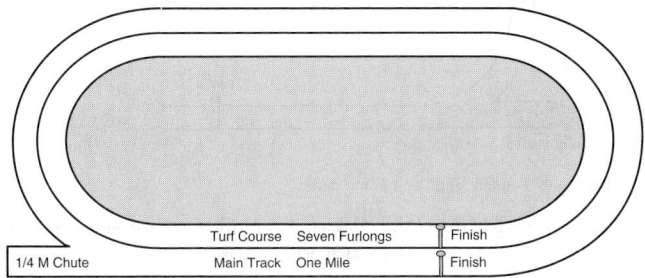

Track Data: One-mile oval, sandy loam. Seven-furlong turf course. One chute, one quarter mile schooling chute. Length of stretch, 1,346 feet. Width of home stretch, 75 feet; backstretch, 70 feet; turns, 75 feet. Stable accommodations, 1,950. Seating capacity 6,500, total capacity 20,000. Parking for 5,000 cars.

Opened April 12, 1872. Suffered a major fire in 1993. After four years of successful meets using tents to replace the burned down grandstand, Fair Grounds opened with a new grandstand in 1997 and has enjoyed some of its most successful meetings in history, averaging more than $260,000 in daily purses each of the last five years. The $600,000 Louisiana Derby is the track's flagship race. Horses to race at Fair Grounds in 2002-2003 included Horse of the Year Mineshaft and Kentucky Derby and Preakness winner Funny Cide. Year-round simulcasting, phone betting and Internet wagering.

TRACK RECORDS

3 Furs.	Henry s Baby	2	112	:33-4/5	Feb. 15, 1971	1-1/16 m	Pie in Your Eye	5	117	1:42.02	Mar. 19, 1994
4-1/2 Furs.	Debs Mini Bars	2	110	:52-1/5	Mar. 8, 1971	1-1/8 m	Phantom On Tour	4	114	1:48.13	Mar. 8, 1998
5 Furs.	Posse	3	118	:57.35	Feb. 10, 2003	1-3/16 m	Half Magic	4	109	1:56-1/5	Mar. 21, 1977
5-1/2 Furs.	Solid Sunny	7	122	1:03-1/5	Mar. 11, 1995	1-1/4 m	Heart	4	116	2:01-4/5	Mar. 16, 1986
	Toby s Success	4	122	1:03.20	Jan. 26. 2004	1-9/16 m	Retintin	7	117	2:42-4/5	Mar. 28, 1970
6 Furs.	Mountain General	4	118	1:08.03	Nov. 28, 2002	1-3/4 m	Aladdin Prince	8	113	3:01-2/5	Apr. 5, 1981
1 Mile	Kitwe	4	112	1:35.94	Mar. 26, 1998	4 Miles	Major Mansir	6	112	8:04.60	Mar. 21, 2003
1 m40yds	Total Rage	4	117	1:38.52	Mar. 23, 1997						

Turf Course

Abt 5 1/2 F	Beware Avalanche		117	1:03.37	Mar. 12, 2000	Abt 1-1/8 m	Rich and Ready	6	117	1:46-4/5	Feb. 21, 1982
Abt 7 1/2 F	Northcote Road		121	1:29.26	Mar. 7, 2000	Abt 1-3/8 m	Present The Colors	5	111	2:17-1/5	Apr. 4, 1982
Abt 1 Mile	Rich and Ready		117	1:35-4/5	Jan. 17, 1982	Abt 1-1/2 m	Palace Panther	5	116	2:32	Apr. 6, 1986
Abt 1-1/16 m	Dixie Poker Ace	7	119	1:42.00	Jan. 8, 1994						

Leading Jockey in 2002-2003 meet: Robby Albarado, 102 wins.

Leading Trainer in 2002-2003 meet: Steven M. Asmussen, 63 wins.

Record attendance: 23, 662, November 27, 1969. Record handle: $9,080,419, March 12, 2000

FAIR MEADOWS

Tulsa State Fairgrounds

P.O. Box 4735 Tulsa, Oklahoma
918-743-7223; Fax (918) 743-8053

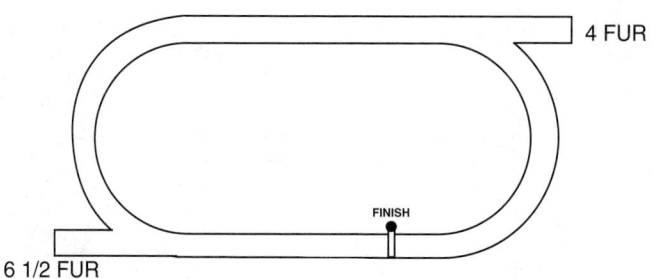

Track data:five-furlong track with 4-furlong and 6 1/2-furlong chutes.

A mixed breed meet scheduled in **2004** from May **27** through July **24**, with daily purses pegged at **$45,000** per day.

TRACK RECORDS

4 Furs.	Only Cash	5	118	:44-2/5	May 30, 1997	1-1/16 m	Stop the Bluffing	5	124	1:45.60	May 29, 2003
5-1/2 Furs.	Double Jack		124	1:03 4/5	Aug. 1, 2001	1-1/8 m	Damascus Slew	4	118	1:51.78	May 30, 1998
6 Furs.	Carsoni	6	122	1:10-4/5	Aug. 3, 1995	1-3/8 m	Second Avie	5	120	2:20	Aug. 5, 1995
6-1/2 Furs.	Tic Tic	4	124	1:16-3/5	July 10, 1998	1-5/8 m	Phantom Cottage	9	118	2:51-4/5	Aug. 1, 1992
1 Mile	Judge North	6	124	1:37	Aug. 5, 1995						

Leading Jockey in 2003: Larry D. Payne, 17 wins.
Leading Trainer in 2003: Mike R. Teel, 9 wins.

FAIRMOUNT PARK

Ogden-Fairmount, Inc.
President, CEO; and General Manager: Brian Zander; Racing Secretary: Robert Pace; Public Relations Director: Jon Sloane; Simulcasting Director: Gregory Graves.

Located on the Illinois side of the
Mississippi River near St. Louis, Missouri

9301 Collinsville Rd., Collinsville, IL 62234
618-345-4300 Fax: 618-344-8218
E-Mail Address: fmtpark@fairmountpark.com
Web Site: www.fairmountpark.com

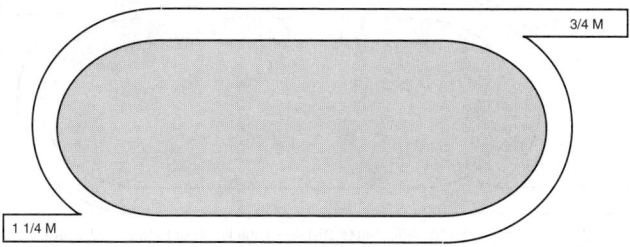

Track data: One-mile oval with 3/4-mile and 1 1/4-mile chutes. Distance from last turn to finish 1,050 feet; width 80 feet stretch and turns, 70 feet in backstretch. Stable accommodations 1,000. Seating capacity 5,500.

Opened September 26, 1925. Former name: Cahokia Downs. The 2003 meet ran 102 dates, from April 4 to October 11, with purses at about $58,000 per day. Dates are scheduled for 2004 from late March through mid-September. Trainer Ralph Martinez, the leading trainer at every Fairmount Park meet since 2000, owns the Fairmount meet record with 157 victories, which he set in 2001. Night racing and extensive simulcasting.

TRACK RECORDS

2 Furs.	Glit	8	122	:20.80	May 3, 2003	1-1/4 m	Leaddrop	4	116	2:03	July 22, 1989
4 Furs.	Aledo	5	120	:45-3/5	June 2, 1994	1-1/2 m	Firth of Tay	5	105	2:33	Sep. 21, 1927
4-1/2 Furs.	Vague Promise	4	122	:51-3/5	May 19, 1978	1-5/8 m	Monthazar	8	120	2:48	Nov. 3, 1973
5 Furs.	Slight in the Rear	2	118	:56-4/5	July 25, 1989	1-3/4 m	Lightin Bill	8	110	3:02-4/5	Oct. 14, 1939
5-1/2 Furs.	Sarof Jr.	4	120	1:03-2/5	June 5, 1980	2 Miles	East Royalty	4	120	3:32-3/5	Dec. 1, 1991
6 Furs.	Ye Country	3	112	1:08-3/5	Nov. 26, 1977	2 m70yds	King Boogie	5	119	3:33-3/5	Sep. 1, 1984
1 Mile	Dusty Appeal	7	116	1:37-2/5	June 20, 1992	2-1/16 m	Tim Trefle	5	113	3:38-4/5	Sep. 10, 1983
1 m 70yds	Dusty Appeal	4	116	1:39-4/5	July 30, 1989	2-1/8 m	Lucrest	5	115	3:46-1/5	Sep. 24, 1983
1-1/16 m	Lt. Lao	5	118	1:40-4/5	July 22, 1989	2-1/4 m	Baye Dawn	5	117	4:00	Oct. 8, 1983
1-1/8 m	Andover Man	3	113	1:47-3/5	Aug. 26, 1989	2-1/2 m	Cat Walk	4	114	4:29	Oct. 22, 1983

Leading Jockey in 2003: Joel Santiago, 101 wins.
Leading Trainer in 2003: Ralph Martinez, 140 wins.
Record attendance: 13,898 September 7, 1953. Record handle: $1,380,880, May 5, 1990

FAIRPLEX PARK

Los Angeles County Fair Association
    VP of Finance and CFO: Michael Seder; Racing Manager: George Bradvica; Racing Secretary: Richard Wheeler; Communications Manager: Wendy Talarico.

PO Box 2250, Pomona, CA 91769
909-623-3111 Fax: 909-865-3602
E-Mail Address: info@fairplex.com
Web Site: www.fairplex.com

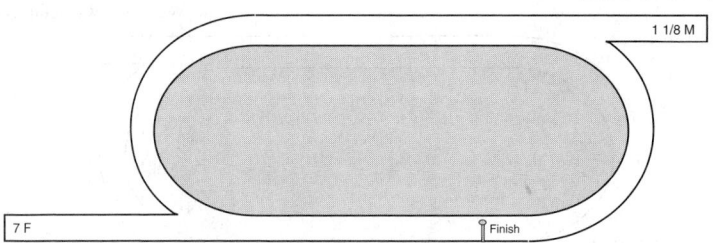

Track data: five-furlong oval with 1/4-mile and 1 1/8-mile chutes. Distance from last turn to finish 757, width 70 feet. Stable accommodations 850. Seating capacity 10,000, parking for 30,000 cars on county fairgrounds.

Opened September 1933. Runs the three week Pomona County Fair meet immediately after Del Mar. In 2003, daily average purses were $225,000 including stakes. Part of the California County Fair system that features numerous short meets throughout the state and has a simulcast pavilion open throughout the year. 2004 dates: Sept. 10 through Sept. 26, with no dark days.

TRACK RECORDS

Abt. 4 Furs.	Quemado	3	120	:44.79	Sep. 25, 2003	1-1/16 m	Monte Parnes-Ar	5	121	1:41-3/5	Sep. 29, 1990
6 Furs.	Drouilly s Boy	4	116	1:09-1/5	Sep. 19, 1989	Abt 1-1/8 m	Dachi s Folly	3	114	1:48-2/5	Sep. 29, 1990
6-1/2 Furs.	Bundle Of Iron	4	116	1:15-1/5	Sep. 23, 1986	1-3/8 m	Mummy s Pleasure	7	120	2:15	Sep. 28, 1986
7 Fur.	Best of Time	4	116	1:22.66	Sep. 16, 2000						

Leading Jockey in 2003: Martin A. Pedroza, 31 wins.
Leading Trainer in 2003: Doug O Neill and Wesley A. Ward, 10 wins (tie).
Record attendance: 28,300 September 25, 1948. Record Handle: $9,455,278 September 19, 1998

FERNDALE

Humboldt County Fair Racing Association

P.O.Box 637
Ferndale, California, 95536
(707)-786-9511

President: Clare Bugeng
Fair Manager: Stuart Titus
Racing Secretary: Ella Robinson

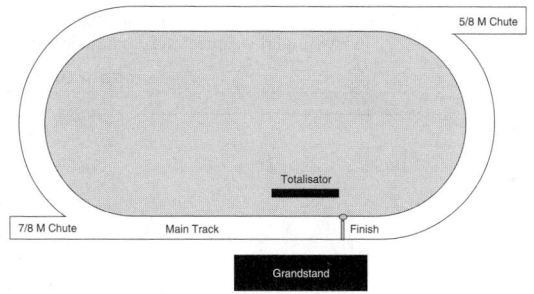

One–half–mile oval with two chutes, five furlongs and 7 furlongs. Distance from last turn to finish 530 feet. Width of track 50 feet.

Opened in the 1950's and has runs an annual short meet during August in a true county fair setting in the redwood forest region of Northern California, near the Oregon border. During 2003, purses averaged about $13,000 per day for 30 total Thoroughbred races on 10 daily cards. 2004 meet: Aug 12 to Aug. 22.

TRACK RECORDS

5 Furs	Fight for Silver	5	118	57.18	Aug. 11, 2002	1-1/8 m	Daytime Bargain	3	120	1:53-1/5	Aug. 22, 1987
6-1/2 Furs.	Rumbita's Lad	5	116	1:19-2/5	Aug. 20, 1992	1-3/8 m	Timnocrea	6	119	2:23	Aug. 20, 1960
7 Furs.	Never Miss T.V.	8	116	1:24-1/5	Aug. 14, 1992	1-5/8 m	Prince Aglo	4	122	2:44-3/5	Aug. 21, 1994
1-1/16 m	Skipper Sam,	6	115	1:43-2/5	Aug. 4, 1969						

Leading Jockey in 2003: Daniel Raymond Boag and Ramon Guce, 8 wins (tie)
Leading Trainer in 2003: Wesley A. Ward, 5 wins.
Record attendance: 7, 142, July 28, 1979. Record handle: $287,548, August 17, 1985

FINGER LAKES

Finger Lakes Racing Association, Inc.

President and General Manager: Christian Riegle; Racing Secretary: James Pambianchi; Publicity and Media: Steve Martin; Director of Simulcasting: Patrick Placito

5857 Rte. 96, Farmington, New York 14425
Mailing address: P.O. Box 25250, Farmington, New York 14425
(585) 924-3232; Fax: Publicity: (585) 924-7275
Free scratch and results line: (585) 935-5252
www.fingerlakesracetrack.com. E-Mail: publicity@fingerlakes.com

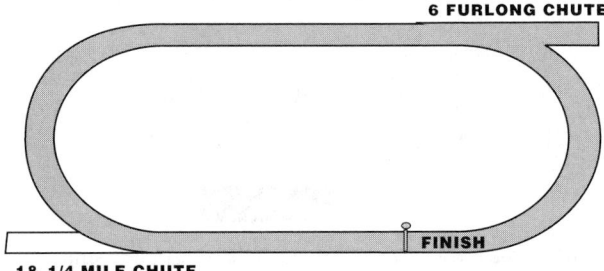

Track Data: One-mile oval; sandy loam. Six-furlong and 1 1/4-mile chutes; length of stretch, 960 feet. Stable accommodations, 1,214. Seating for 6,000; Parking for 4,000 cars.

Opened May 23, 1962 in the picturesque Finger Lakes region and has become the home base for many owners and trainers with New York bred stock. Finger Lakes' daily average purses exceeded $75,000 per day in 2003 for 154 racing days including stakes. A similar meet in 2004 will run from April 16 through November 23.

TRACK RECORDS

2 Furs.	Broadway Blondie	5	116	:21-4/5	Apr. 3, 1998	1-3/4 m	Win Eddie	6	122	3:05-1/5	Aug. 28, 1977
4 Furs.	Valley Cat	9	120	:46-2/5	Apr. 15, 1994	2 Miles	Brier Spirit	8	108	3:47-4/5	Oct. 26, 1980
4-1/2 Furs.	Island Dash	5	120	:51-1/5	Apr. 9, 1996	2 m 40yds	Black Lodge	3	113	3:41	Oct. 5, 1974
5 Furs.	Wonderous Wise	6	115	:57-1/5	Apr. 11, 1989	2 m70yds	Eastern Promise	5	112	3:42-3/5	Oct. 14, 1972
5-1/2 Furs.	Hilary Star	6	111	1:02-4/5	Apr. 16, 1989	2-1/16 m	Tabula	4	110	3:44-3/5	Oct. 13, 1973
6 Furs.	Kelly Kip	4	119	1:08-1/5	June 20, 1998	2-1/8 m	Eastern Promise	5	116	3:5-1/5	Oct. 21, 1972
Abt 7 Furs.	Jerri Prince	7	114	1:26-4/5	Oct. 16, 1976	2-3/16 m	Blazing Cedar	4	113	4:04-1/5	Nov. 10, 1973
1 Mile	Transact	4	119	1:36-1/5	Aug. 29, 1994	2-1/4 m	Amber Dare	3	109	4:11-3/5	Oct. 20, 1973
1 m40yds	Gallant Tiger	4	119	1:40-1/5	June 22, 1975	2-9/16 m	Diamond Platter	7	116	4:50	Oct 12, 1974
1 m70yds	C B Account	4	116	1:40	July 6, 1997	2-5/8 m	Amber Dare	3	115	5:12-2/5	Nov. 17, 1973
1-1/16 m	Fit For Royalty	9	119	1:43	May 19, 1997	2-11/16 m	Polo Prince	3	107	5:14-3/5	Oct. 28, 1972
1-1/8 m	Copper Mount	3	119	1:48-4/5	Aug. 27, 1994	2-3/4 m	Fourth Flight	7	116	5:35-2/5	Nov. 24, 1973
1-3/16 m	North Warning	10	113	1:58-2/5	July 10, 1994	3 m 70yds	Count Mafosta	7	116	5:39-1/5	Oct. 27, 1973
1-1/4 m	Caramba	6	114	2:05-1/5	July 11, 1987	3-1/16 m	Dauntless Pride	4	111	5:45-2/5	Oct. 19, 1974
1-1/2 m	Brave Beast	6	124	2:33-3/5	Sep. 22, 1991	3-1/4 m	Dauntless Pride	4	117	6:15-2/5	Oct. 26, 1974
1-9/16 m	Poor Man s Friend	5	116	2:44	Oct. 16, 1976	4 m 70yds	Gloria Dream	6	113	8:01	Nov. 4, 1972
1-5/8 m	North Warning	10	119	2:46-3/5	Sep. 4, 1994	4-1/16 m	Amber Dare	3	113	8:12-2/5	Nov. 3, 1973
1-11/16 m	Prime Example	6	117	2:58	Nov. 23, 1974	4-1/8 m	Victory Tour	4	115	8:08	Nov. 2, 1974

Leading Jockey in 2003: John R. Davila, Jr, 138 wins.
Leading Trainer in 2003: Chris J. Englehart, 95 wins.

Record attendance: 15, 334, September 3, 1962. Record handle: $765,580, September 24, 1978.

FONNER PARK

Hall County Livestock Improvement Association, Inc.
Francis Gauthier, President; Hugh M. Miner, Jr, Executive Vice President and CEO;
COO: Bruce A. Swihart; Racing Secretary: Doug Schoepf
Street Address: 700 East Stolley Park Road   P.O. Box 490, Grand Island, Nebraska 68802-0490
Grand Island, Nebraska 68801.   (308) 382-4515; Fax: (308) 384-2753
Nearest Airport: Hall County Regional Airport   Email: fonnerpark@aol.com
3 miles north of track, 150 miles from Omaha   Web Site: www.fonnerpark.com

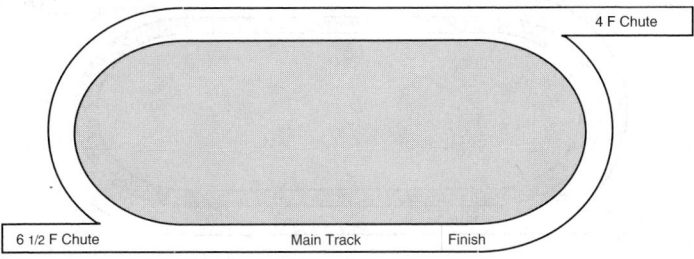

Track Data: five-furlong oval, sandy loam. Distance from last turn to finish line, 700 feet. 6 1/2-furlong and 4-furlong chutes. Width of track 70 feet. Stable accommodations for 1,200. Seating for 5,766; Parking for 5,000 cars.

Opened April 29, 1954. With the demise of Ak-Sar-Ben in the mid-1990's, Fonner Park has run the bulk of Nebraska racing dates. The 2003 season ran from February 8 through May 4 and offered more than $51,000 in daily purses. Fonner Park is the home of the Hall County Fair and many livestock shows. Glass enclosed heated grandstand; extensive simulcasting, 6-7 days per week and the 2004 meet will run Feb. 14 through May 8.

TRACK RECORDS

4 Furs.	Leaping Plum	5	122	:44-1/5	Feb. 17, 1996	1 m 70yds	Shamtastic	6	116	1:40	Apr. 26, 1986
5-1/2 Furs.	Little L. M.	6	115	1:04-2/5	Apr. 12, 1975	1-1/16 m	Sahara King	7	116	1:43	Apr. 27, 1996
6 Furs.	Orphan Kist	5	123	1:10	Apr. 8, 1989	1-1/8 m	Potro	5	117	1:51-2/5	Apr. 25, 1993
6-1/2 Furs.	Majority Of One	5	119	1:17	Mar. 18, 1989	1-3/8 m	Meat Loaf	5	114	2:22-2/5	Apr. 29, 1970
1 Mile	Brian s Star	4	112	1:36-3/5	Apr. 9, 1986						

Leading Jockey in 2003: Perry Compton, 91 wins.

Leading Trainer in 2003: David C. Anderson, 55 wins.

Record Handle: $1,285,011 April 28, 1990. Record Attendance: 10,930 March 17, 1990

FORT ERIE RACETRACK

Eddie Lynn, Vice President of Operations and General Manager; Herb McGirr, Director of Racing; Tom Gostlin, Racing Secretary; Brian Blessing, Public Relations and Television Director.

Street Address: 230 Catherine Street
Fort Erie, Ontario, Canada.

P.O.Box 1130, Fort Erie, Ontario, CA,L2A5N9
905-871-3200;800-295-3770;FAX 905-994-3629,
Web site:www.forterieracing.com;E-mail: femedia@forterieracetrack.com

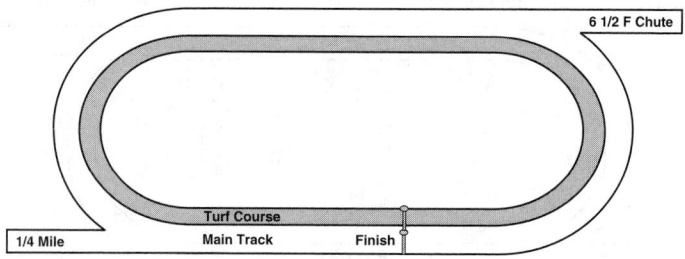

Track Data: One-mile oval with a 6 1/2-furlong and 1 1/4-mile chute. Distance from last turn to finish, about 1,060 feet. Width of stretch 85 feet, backstretch 65 feet; 7-furlong turf course. Stable accommodations for 1,150; seating capacity, 10,700. Parking for 8,500 cars.

Opened June 16, 1897, this beautifully appointed track is home to the Prince of Wales Stakes, second jewel of the Canadian Triple Crown. Fort Erie operated its 106th live race meet in 2003 with 114 racing days from April 26 through November 11. About 1,200 slot machines helped boost purses sharply from $107,000 in 2000 to more than $193,000 in 2003. In 2004, the meet will run from May 1 through Nov. 22, a total of 117 racing days. Located across the Niagara River from Buffalo, N.Y., in close proximity to Niagara Falls...Year-round simulcasting.

TRACK RECORDS

2 Fur.	Leisure Road	5	120	:21.20	Sept. 5, 1998	1-3/16 m	Bruce s Mill	3	126	1:53-4/5	July 31, 1994
4 1/2 Fur.	Island Mission	6	117	:52.02	April 29, 2000	1-1/4 m	Do s Vigil	3	110	2:03-2/5	Aug. 14, 1974
5 Furs.	Dart for Dough	5	114	:56.50	Oct. 6, 2003		French Tambourine	5	115		Aug. 10, 1975
5-1/2 Furs.	Just a Lord	4	113	1:03-3/5	June 15, 1991	1-1/2 m	Itshouldbesoeasy	5	116	2:32.57	Aug. 10, 1999
6 Furs.	Deputy Carson	5	122	1:08.80	Sept. 9, 2001	1-5/8 m	Gay Story	4	112	2:48-3/5	Aug. 27, 1956
6-1/2 Furs.	Muzledick	3	115	1:15-4/5	Aug. 10, 1968	1-3/4 m	Brave Zappa	5	107	2:59	July 9, 1984
1 m 70yds	Myrtle Irene	5	111	1:39-4/5	Aug. 26, 1994	1-13/16 m	Captain Charisma	5	121	3:09-2/5	Aug. 12, 1984
1-1/16 m	Act of Courage	3	119	1:42-1/5	Aug. 7, 1971	1 7/8 m	Frost Prince	7	119	3:22.60	Aug. 20, 1999
	Dimanno	4	118	1:42.20	Sept. 11, 2001	2 m yds	Devils Gold	6	115	3:33	Oct. 6, 1997
1-1/8 m	Lauries Dancer	4	108	1:48	Aug. 23, 1972						

Turf Course

5 Furs.	Oh Mar	6	120	56.99	Sept. 9, 2002	1-1/2 m	Norwick	4	120	2:28	Aug. 21, 1983
Abt 7 Furs.	Native Vigil	5	118	1:22	July 2, 1991	1-3/4 m	Ahead of the Best	4	119	2:56-3/5	Sep. 10, 1991
1 Mile	Fifth and a Jigger	3	115	1:34-1/5	June 10, 1991	Abt 1-7/8 m	Regal Admiral	7	112	3:19-4/5	Aug. 7, 1974
1-1/16 m	Road Of War	4	112	1:40-4/5	June 19, 1994	1-7/8 m	Medlaw	5	123	3:16-1/5	Sep. 30, 1985
1-3/8 m	Lord Vancouver	4	126	2:15	July 30, 1972						

Leading Jockey in 2003: Martin R. Ramirez, 122 wins.
Leading Trainer in 2003: Layne S. Giliforte, 56 wins.
Record Attendance. 17,379 April 8,1961. Record Handle. $1,934,407 Oct 2, 1995.

FRESNO FAIR

Big Fresno Fair
President: Dean Thonesen; CEO: Scott Anderson
Director of Racing: Dan White; Public Relations Director: Susanne Finley

1121 S. Chance Avenue, Fresno, CA 93702
559-650-3247 Fax: 559-650-3226
E-Mail Address: fairpr@fresnofair.com; Web Site: www.fresnofair.com

Track data: One-mile oval with 2-furlong and 6-furlong chutes. Distance from last turn to finish 979 feet. Stable accommodations 900; Seating capacity 6,000, parking for 10,000 cars on county fairgrounds.

Opened September 25, 1935. Runs an 11-day meet in October as part of Northern California Fair circuit and daily average purses were pegged at just under $50,000 during the 2003 meet. The 2004 meet: Oct. 6 to Oct. 17 with year round simulcasting in the pavilion.

TRACK RECORDS

4 Furs	Nellie s Girl	3	127	:44-4/5	Oct. 7, 1978	1 Mile	The Ayes Have It	5	113	1:33-4/5	Nov. 11, 1986
	King Stephen	2	127	:44-4/5	Oct. 7, 1978	1-1/16 m	Dimaggio	4	116	1:39-4/5	Oct. 16, 1976
4-1/2 Furs.	Lovin Laurie	3	118	:51.14	Oct. 8, 2003	1-1/8 m	Minutes Away	3	114	1:46-2/5	Nov. 20, 1985
5 Furs	Big Volume	4	120	:55-2/5	Nov. 15, 1977	1- 1/4 m	Capt. Quicksilver	6	114	1:59-4/5	Oct. 18, 1992
5-1/2 Furs	Knight In Savannah	3	113	1:01-2/5	Nov. 13, 1990	1-1/2 m	El Maduro	5	111	2:30-2/5	Sep. 17, 1980
Abt. 6 Furs	Tia Ping	5	113	1:10-1/5	Oct. 11, 1963	1-11/16 m	Bull Patch	4	111	2:56	Oct. 5, 1954
6 Furs,	Tolemeo	4	122	1:07-2/5	Nov. 12, 1997	2 Miles	Nina s Flag	4	120	3:29-2/5	Oct. 9, 1954

Leading Jockey in 2003: Macario Rodriguez, 13 wins.

Leading Trainer in 2003: Rene Amescua, 10 wins.

Record attendance 15, 596, October 6, 1979.

GILLESPIE COUNTY FAIR

Gillespie Co. Fair & Festivals Association, Inc.
President: James R. Wahrmund; General Manager: Ronnie Esch; Racing Secretary: Scott Sherwood; Public Relations Director: Russell Hartmann

PO Box 526, Fredericksburg, TX 78624
830-997-2359 Fax: 830-997-4923

Began offering pari-mutuel races for quarter horses in the early 1990's. Now runs a quarter horse and/or mixed breed meet during the summer, with 17 Thoroughbred races scheduled in 2003 and a similar schedule in 2004. Extensive simulcasting.

Leading Jockey in 2003: Santos Carrizales and Wayne Womack, 3 wins (tie).

Leading Trainer in 2003: M. Shawn Finch, 3 wins

GOLDEN GATE FIELDS

A Magna Entertainment Facility

Frank Stronach, Chairman and Director; Michael Scalzo, Vice-President and General Manager; Tom Doutrich, Racing Secretary; Richard Lewis, Coordinator of Racing Operations; Tom Ferrall, Publicity Manager.

25 miles Northwest of San Francisco Airport

PO Box 6027, Albany, CA 94706-0027
510-559-7300 Fax: 510-559-7465
Scratch and results line: (510) 559-7419
Web Site: www.goldengatefields.com

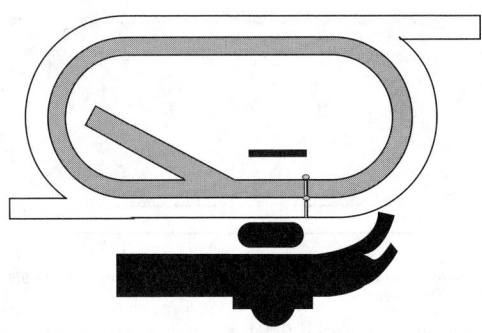

Track data: One-mile oval, with 3/4- and 1 1/4-mile chutes. Distance from last turn to finish **1,000** feet; width of stretch **78** feet, backstretch **75** feet. Turf course: Seven furlongs and **132** feet. Stable accommodations **1,323**; Seating capacity Grandstand, **8,000**; Club House, **5,200**; Turf Club, **1,200**. Parking for **4,723** cars.

Opened February **1, 1941.** Bought by Frank Stronach's Magna Entertainment Inc. in **1999.** The **2002–2003** racing season featured **104** days of racing and was held Nov. **6, 2002,** through March **30, 2003.** Purses averaged about **$137,000.** The track offers year-round simulcasting. Russell Baze was the leading jockey at the **2002–2003** meeting with **176** victories – just two wins shy of the GGF single-season record of **178** he set in **1992.** Baze has won **25** riding titles at GGF. Jerry Hollendorfer saddled a record **114** winners during the **2002–2003** season to earn his **23rd** straight training title at GGF.

TRACK RECORDS

2 Furs.	Extra Kick	2	118	:21.09	Mar. 27, 2003	1-1/16 m	Restless Con	4	118	1:39-2/5	June 24, 1991
4-1/2 Furs.	Victory Found	2	117	:50-1/5	Apr. 30, 1992	1-1/8 m	Simply Majestic	4	114	1:45	Apr. 2, 1988
5 Furs.	Contradiction	4	118	:56.12	Jan. 1, 2003	1-3/16 m	Fleet Bird	4	123	1:52-3/5	Oct. 24, 1953
5-1/2 Furs.	Linear Lights	4	119	1:01.99	Feb. 25, 2004	1-1/4 m	Noor	5	127	1:58-1/5	June 24, 1950
6 Furs.	Smoke Till Dawn	4	117	1:07.45	Dec.17, 2003	1-1/2 m	Bo Donna	5	120	2:29-2/5	June 8, 1979
1 Mile	Caros Love	4	117	1:33	Feb. 13, 1988		Tabular	6	116	2:29-2/5	June 6, 1987

Turf Course

4-1/2 Furs.	Stuttgart	6	119	:49.86	Mar. 29, 2003	1-1/8 m	Blues Traveller	4	112	1:47-3/5	May 14, 1994
5 Furs.	Black Tornado	5	119	:56	May 10, 1975	1-3/8 m	John Henry	9	125	2:13	May 6, 1984
	L Natural	4	114	:56	May 28, 1977	1-1/2 m	Silveyville	6	121	2:27-2/5	June 10, 1984
	Neat Claim	4	113	:56	May 30, 1977		Kings Island	4	116	2:27-2/5	June 9, 1985
	Golden Gordian	4	115	:56	May 27, 1978		Val's Danseur	6	119	2:27-2/5	June 8, 1986
7-1/2 Furs.	Clever Song	4	122	1:28	May 25,1986	1-7/8 m	Paired And Painted	4	114	3:12-1/5	June 28, 1987
1 Mile	Don Alberto	5	114	1:33-2/5	Mar. 22, 1980	2 Miles	Never-Rust	8	114	3:25-3/5	June 26, 1988
1-1/16 m	Announcer	5	115	1:40-2/5	Apr. 16, 1977	Abt 2 3/8 M	Situada	7	115	4:10-4/5	June 25, 1990

Turf Course (from the diagonal, infield chute)

1-1/16 m	Gum	6	116	1:41-1/5	Apr. 11, 1992	2 Miles	Mind Master	5	117	3:29 3/5	Apr. 21, 1990
1-1/8 m	Annoconnor	5	115	1:49-2/5	May 27, 1989						

Leading Jockey in 2002-2003 meet: Russell A. Baze, 176 wins.

Leading Trainer in 2002-2003 meet: Jerry Hollendorfer, 114 wins.

Record attendance 34,967, May 5, 1990. Record handle $8,723,810 May 2, 1998 (includes simulcasts).

GRANTS PASS DOWNS

Southern Oregon Horse Racing Assn.

President: Rod Lowe; Josephine County Fair Manager: Al Westoff.

PO Box 282, Grants Pass, OR 97526
Phone: 541-476-3215

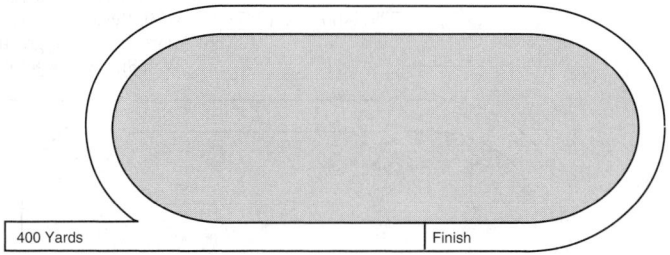

400 Yards   Finish

Track data: One-half-mile oval with a 400-yard chute in the homestretch.

Opened June 21, 1979. Usually runs two and/or three day weekend racing cards from mid-May into July. Simulcasting. 2004 dates: May 15 to July 5.

TRACK RECORDS

4-1/2 Furs.	Nakeen	10	117	:51-4/5	June 4, 1994	6-1/2 Furs.	The Sea King	4	117	1:18-2/5	June 24, 1984
5 Furs.	Dr. Robinson	10	119	:59-1/5	June 20, 1981	1-1/16 m	Handy Man Jeff	7	121	1:45.40	Jul. 6, 2003
5-1/2 Furs.	Tickles Prince	5	119	1:04.14	May 22, 1999	1 3/16 m	Tyonek	4	119	2:01.25	June 19, 1994
Abt 6 Furs.	Lucky May Babe	6	123	1:08-2/5	June 25, 1995	1-5/16 m	A Shot at Fame	6	124	2:14.60	July 4, 2000
6 Furs.	Honest Sea	5	119	1:09-4/5	July 4, 1983	1-3/8 m	Summers Comin	5	122	2:16-2/5	July 4, 1989
Abt 6-1/2 F.	Toll Free	4	122	1:23-3/5	June 30, 1979	1-5/8 m	Moes Cat	5	122	2:52-2/5	July 8, 1990

Leading Jockey, 2003: Twyla Beckner, 26 wins.

Leading Trainer, 2003: Robert Beckner, 10 wins.

Record attendance: 2,540, May 28, 1990. Record handle: $185, 121, July 4, 1987

GREAT FALLS
Montana State Fair Race Meet

Racetrack Management Group, Inc.

President: Erik Ray; General Manager: Edgar O Haire; Racing Secretary: Darrell Ost

PO Box 2810, Great Falls, MT 59403
406-727-8900 Fax: 406-452-8955

Track data: One half mile oval, 5/8- and 7/8-mile chutes. Distance from last turn to finish, 410.1 feet; Width of track 60 feet. Distance from last turn to finish 979 feet. Stable accommodations for 900. Seating capacity 6,000.

Opened in the 1940's as part of the Montana State Fair and has conducted a three week pari-mutuel meet in most years since. Ran eight days from July 4 through July 27 in 2003, with a similar meet scheduled in 2004 starting July 2. . .Extensive simulcasting.

TRACK RECORDS

3 Furs.	My Squeaky Ruler	2	122	:34-2/5	June 8, 1986	Abt. 6-1/2 F.	Charmhersweet	5	122	1:19-4/5	July 30, 1978
Abt. 4 Furs.	Midnight Mackee	4	125	:53-2/5	June 16, 1991	7 Furs.	Diamond Eagle	6	125	1:24.60	Aug. 4, 2000
4-1/2 Furs.	Gay Deil	2	118	:55-2/5	Aug. 7, 1946	1 Mile	Timpanogos	5	128	1:41-3/5	Aug. 9, 1947
5 Furs.	Tiger Sam	4	112	:57-4/5	July 27, 1970	1 m70yds	Proud Barbarian	7	115	1:44.80	July 31, 1986
Abt. 5 Furs.	Happy Vixen	5	110	:56-4/5	Aug. 5, 1946	1-1/16 m	Im Bay	4	122	1:47-4/5	Aug 3, 1986
Abt. 5 1/2	Crown Butte	4	119	1:04.40	June 20, 1999	1-1/8 m	Prince of Queens	4	122	1:52.80	July 26, 1997
6 Furs.	Gallantsia	6	108	1:14-2/5	Aug. 6 1946	Abt. 1-1/8 m	Copper Guard	8	103	1:51	Aug. 10, 1946
6-1/2 Furs.	Lightning Rose	3	114	1:24-1/5	May 28, 1984						

Leading Jockey in 2003: Carl Hebert, 12 wins.

Leading Trainer in 2003: Bryan Krone and Mel Berkram, 8 wins (tie)

Record attendance: 6,597, July 28, 1985. Record handle: $193, 036, August 3, 1985.

GREAT LAKES DOWNS

Magna Entertainment Company
President and General Manager: Chris Dragone; Racing Secretary: Allan Plever; PR/Marketing Director: Mary
Jane Shrauger.

4800 S. Harvey St., Muskegon, MI 49444
(231) 799-2400 Fax: (231) 798-3120; Results via main phone number.
E-Mail Address: glweb@greatlakesdowns.com
Web Site: www.greatlakesdowns.com

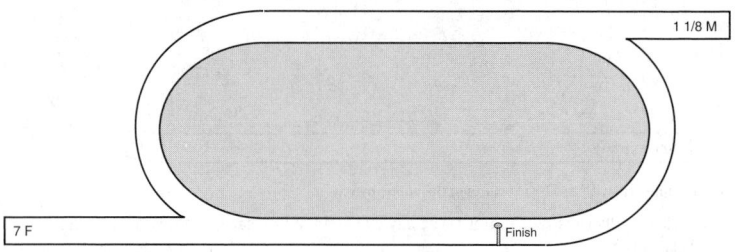

Track data: Five-eighths mile oval, with distance from last turn to finish, **580** feet.

Opened April 23, **1999** and filled the void left by the demise of Detroit Racecourse. The **2004** meet is scheduled to run
from Apr. 25 to Oct. 30...Year-round simulcasting.

TRACK RECORDS

2 Furs.	Roll or Wish	6	110	:23.52	June 22, 1999	7 Furs	Secret Romeo	3	120	1:24.30	Sept. 2, 2001
4 Furs.	Dinner Band	4	114	:45.87	May 15, 2001	1 Mile	Secret Romeo	3	120	1:40.14	Oct. 29, 2001
5 1/2 Furs.	Ambitious Buster	4	115	1:05.37	Sep. 26, 2003	1 m70yds	Secret Romeo	2	122	1:49.20	Nov. 4, 2000
Abt. 5 1/2F.	Double Shift	5	119	1:04.40	June 20, 1999	1-1/16 m	That Monetary	6	115	1:47.28	Aug. 27, 2001
6 Furs.	Native Ruck	4	112	1:11.86	Oct. 11, 2003	1-1/8 m	The Bold Bruiser	4	114	1:54.11	Oct. 28, 2000
6 1/2 Furs.	Native Ruck	3		1:19.43	July 28, 2002						

Leading Jockey in 2003: Federico Mata, 160 wins.
Leading Trainer in 2003: Gerald S. Bennett, 82 wins.

Record attendance 4,427, May 6, 2000. Record handle $966,732, May 15, 2000

GULFSTREAM PARK

Magna Entertainment Corp.

Frank Stronach, Chairman of the Board; Jim McAlpine; President and Chief Executive Officer; Track Chairman: Douglas Donn; Track President and General Manager: Scott Savin; Director of Racing: David Bailey

Nearest Airport: Ft. Lauderdale/Hollywood International   Mailing Address: 901 South Federal Highway Hallandale Beach, Florida 33009

(954) 454-7000; 1-800-771-8873; Fax: (954) 454-7827
Web Site: www.gulfstreampark.com

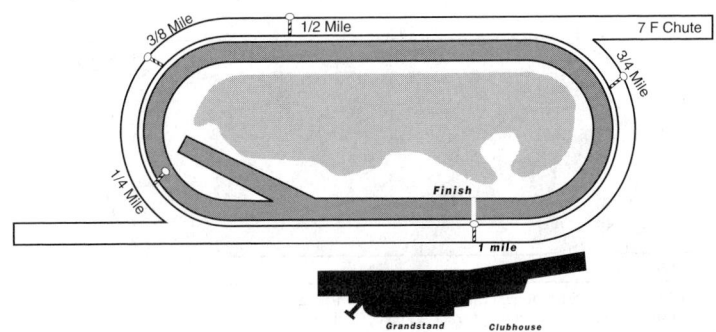

Track Data: One-mile oval, two chutes (three furlongs and seven furlongs); distance from last turn to finish, 952 feet, 2 inches. Stable accommodations for 1,375; Seating capacity: 22,000; Parking for 15,262 cars.

Gulfstream opened Feb. 1, 1939. Gulfstream was purchased by Frank Stronach's Magna Entertainment Corp. in September 1999. Gulfstream hosted the Breeders' Cup three times. Gulfstream's 2004 racing dates are Jan. 3 through April 25. The highlights of the meeting were the $3.6 million Sunshine Millions Day, the $1 million Florida Derby (G1) and the $500,000 Donn Handicap (G1). Gulfstream offered an exceptionally high caliber of thoroughbred competition. The completion of the Palm Meadows Thoroughbred Training Center added 1,440 stalls to augment Gulfstream's stabling facility of 1,375.

TRACK RECORDS

2 1/2 Furs.	Sonnyhero	2	116	:28.05	April 5, 2000	7 Furs.	Elusive Quality	4	119	1:20	Feb. 21, 1997
3 Furs.	El Macho	2	118	:32-1/5	Feb. 26, 1974	1 m70yds	Blacksburg	5	122	1:39	Feb. 6, 1994
4-1/2 Furs.	Iron Rail	2	119	:51-2/5	Apr. 6, 1960	Abt 1-1/8 m	Search the Shadows	3	120	1:48	Mar. 1, 1991
5 Furs.	Boston Brat	6	120	:56.35	Jan. 17, 2003	1-1/16 m	Saxony Warrior	7	107	1:40-1/5	Mar. 6, 1973
5-1/2 Furs.	Boston Brat	6	122	1:02.47	Feb.3, 2003	1-1/8 m	Jumping Hill	7	122	1:46-2/5	Feb. 3, 1979
6 Furs.	Mr. Prospector	3	119	1:07-4/5	Mar. 31, 1973	1-1/4 m	Mat Boy	5	118	1:59	Mar. 24, 1984
	Artax	4	126	1:07.89	Nov. 6, 1999	1-1/2 m	Buffalo Lark	5	120	2:27-3/5	Apr. 12, 1975
6-1/2 Furs.	Federal Hill	3	122	1:15	Mar. 25, 1957	2 Miles	Undue Influence	6	117	3:25-3/5	Mar. 16, 1997
	Alydeed	4		1:15	Mar. 6, 1993						

Turf Course

5 Fur.	Bop	6	124	55.10	Apr. 12, 2003	Abt.1-3/8 m	African Dancer	5	115	2:13-4/5	Mar. 1, 1997
Abt. 5 Furs.	Coyote Willow	4	116	:57.01	May 7, 2000	1-3/8 m	Yagli	6	121	2:10-3/5	Feb. 6, 1999
Abt.1 Mile	Volochine	6	119	1:33-4/5	Feb. 28, 1997	Abt. 1-1/2m	Doctor Disaster	6	117	2:26-1/5	Mar. 5, 1995
1 Mile	Lure	3	122	1:32-4/5	Oct. 31, 1993	1-1/2	Unite s Big Red	5	114	2:23	Mar. 6, 1999
Abt.1-1/16m	Deep Dive	4	122	1:40-2/5	Feb. 21, 1999	Abt 2 Miles	Practitioner	5	121	3:18-1/5	May 6, 1978
1-1/16 m	Federal Trial	5	115	1:39	Feb. 19, 2000	2 Miles	Sabinus	4	115	3:22-2/5	Apr. 17, 1971

Turf Course (infield chute)

Abt.1 Mile	Z. Bengal Tiger	4	116	1:35-3/5	Mar. 8, 1992	Abt 1-1/8 m	Scannapieco	5	117	1:47-1/5	Feb. 24, 1995
1 Mile	Sunny Prince	5	112	1:35-2/5	Mar. 1, 1992	1-1/8 m	Buchman	5	115	1:46-2/5	Mar. 14, 1992
Abt1-1/16m	Weekend Madness	5	113	1:40-1/5	Feb. 12, 1995	Abt 2 Miles	Head Splasher	5	104	3:31-4/5	Mar. 7, 1992
1-1/16 m	Roman Envoy	4	120	1:39-1/5	Nov. 1, 1992						

Leading Jockey in 2003: Eibar Coa, 91 wins.

Leading Trainer in 2003: Mark Shuman, 87 wins.

Record attendance: 51, 342, November 4, 1989, Breeders' Cup Day. Record handle: $100, 336, 230, November 6, 1999 Breeders' Cup Day, all sources, all races

HASTINGS RACECOURSE

Hastings Entertainment Inc.

Jim Ormiston, Chairman; Phil Heard, President and CEO; Debbie Peebles, Director of Racing; Brenda Smith, Director of Marketing , bsmith@hastingsracecourse.com.

Nearest Airport: Vancouver International Airport, 15 miles

Mailing Address: Hastings Racecourse
Vancouver, B.C., Canada V5K 3N8
Race Office: (604) 255-8823; (800) 677-7702; Fax: (604) 251-0428
Free scratch and results line: (604) 254-1631
Web Site: www.hastingsracecourse.com

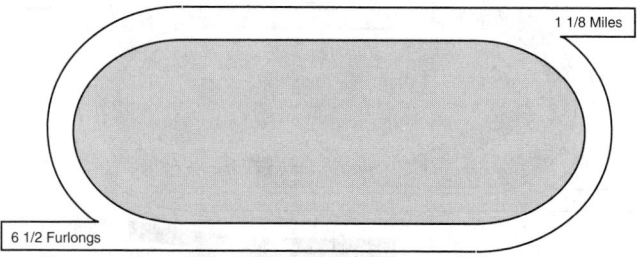

Track Data: Main Course five-furlong, 208-foot oval with 6 1/2 furlongs, 1 1/16- and 1 1/8-mile chutes; four-furlong inner training track; distance from last turn to finish line, 513 feet; width of track, 65 feet. Stable accommodations for 1,000. Seating Capacity 5,600. Parking for 2,500 cars.

Hastings Racecourse will celebrate its 115th anniversary in 2004. On May 1, 2002, Hastings Racecourse was purchased by Woodbine Entertainment Group and became known as Hastings Entertainment Inc doing business as Hastings Racecourse. Hastings Entertainment Inc. (HEI) is a wholly owned subsidiary of Woodbine Entertainment Group (WEG), which also owns and operates Ontario's Woodbine and Mohawk racetracks and the Champions Off-Track wagering teletheatre network. Together, these facilities entertain more than 4.5 million Canadian horse racing customers each season. WEG also developed, owns and operates HorsePlayer Interactive account wagering service and The Racing Network, Canada's only in-home horse racing channel. For 2003, the Hastings meet ran from April 26 through Nov. 30 with purses averaging $151,000 per day including stakes. 2004 dates: April 17 through Nov. 28.

TRACK RECORDS

Abt 3-1/2 F.	Turn to Knight	2	117	:41-1/5	May 27, 1990	1-1/8 M	Artic Son	4	116	1:46-4/5	Aug. 3, 1998
3-1/2 Furs.	Flying Memo	2	116	:39.40	Oct. 26, 2003	1-3/8 M	Irish Bear	3	122	2:14-2/5	Oct. 17, 1987
Abt 6 Furs.	Count The Green	6	123	1:10-4/5	Apr. 17, 1971	1-7/16 M	Who s In Command	5	111	2:23	Aug. 10, 1987
6 Furs.	Great Descretion	4	117	1:10-2/5	May 10, 1969	1-1/2 M	Lucky Son	4	117	2:29	Aug. 25, 1995
6-1/2 Furs.	Torque Converter	6	116	1:15	July 1, 1996	1-11/16 M	Glen Gower	4	114	2:51-1/5	Sep. 9, 1987
1 M 70 Yds	Westbury Road	6	124	1:40-2/5	July 29, 1967	1-3/4 M	Glen Gower	4	119	2:59	Sep. 23, 1987
1-1/16 M	Coral Isle	5	119	1:42-1/5	July 28, 1973	2-1/16 M	Laddie s Prince	4	116	3:30	Oct. 7, 1987
	No Time Flat	3	119	1:42-1/5	Sept. 12, 1987	2-1/8 M	Mr. Chancellor	4	111	3:38-4/5	Oct. 18, 1987
	Timely Stitch	3	118	1:42-1/5	July 6, 1996						

Leading Jockey in 2003: Pedro V. Alvarado, 124 wins.
Leading Trainer in 2003: Dino Condilenios, 38 wins.
Record attendance: 21,156, July 9, 1982. Record handle: $2,612,316 July 9, 1982.

HAWTHORNE RACE COURSE

Hawthorne Race Course, Inc.
General Manager: Thomas F. Carey III.; President: Thomas F. Carey Jr.; Racing Secretary: Gary M. Duch; Director of Media Relations: Jim Miller; Simulcast Director: Lorene Heninger

Mailing Address: 3501 S. Laramie Avenue, Stickney/Cicero, Illinois 60804
(708) 780-3700 and Fax: (708) 780-3677; Press Box: (708) 780-3753
Web Site: www.hawthorneracecourse.com
Nearest Airport: Midway Airport, 2 miles.

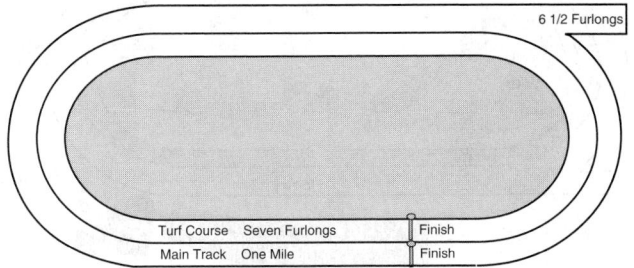

Track Data: Main Course one-mile oval with 6 1/2 furlongs chute; Turf Course, seven furlongs, 184 feet; Distance from last turn to wire 1,320 feet. Stall capacity, (including Sportsman's) 2,400; Seating capacity 18,000; Parking for 7,000 cars.

Opened May 20, 1891. The fifth oldest track in North America, Hawthorne was first owned by Ed Corrigan, who sold to the Carey Family in 1909. Reopened in 1980 after a devastating fire in 1977, and extensively renovated for the 1998 meeting. Took over Sportsman's meet in 2003, running from March 1 to May 6 in the winter and spring and Sept. 28 to Dec. 31 in the fall and winter.

TRACK RECORDS

2 Fur.	Minty Flavors	2	118	:20.88	May 14, 1999	Abt. 1 1/8 m	Crafty Oak	5	114	1:46.69	May 15, 1999
4 1/2 Furs.	Joanies Bella			:51.80	May, 28, 2001	1 3/16 m	Lindy s Lad	5	115	1:59-2/5	Nov. 12, 1980
5 Furs.	De La Concorde	3	119	:57	Nov. 11, 1992		Steal The Account	5	114	1:59 2/5	Aug. 28, 1999
5-1/2 Furs.	Bold Tactics	3	122	1:02-2/5	Oct. 7, 1966	1 1/4 m	Gladwin	4	115	1:58-4/5	Oct. 1, 1970
6 Furs.	Coach Jimi Lee	3	118	1:07.27	Dec. 12, 2003	1 1/2 m	David II	5	113	2:29-3/5	Oct. 1, 1969
6-1/2 Furs.	Dee Lance	3	115	1:14-2/5	July 27, 1988	1 5/8 m	Viale	6	118	2:47.02	Dec. 10, 2000
Abt.6-1/2F.	Sharp Carleen	3	111	1:18-4/5	Sept. 24, 1986	1 3/4 m	America Fore	4	110	3:02-1/5	Oct. 2, 1943
1 m70Yds.	Soldat Bleu	6	116	1:39-1/5	July 27, 1988	2 m70Yds.	Sun N Shine	4	113	3:30-2/5	Oct. 19, 1974
1-/16 m	Sensitive Prince	3	118	1:39-3/5	Sept. 23, 1978	2-1/16 m	Revoque	8	113	3:35-2/5	Oct. 5, 1963
1 1/8 m	Zografos	6	119	1:46-3/5	Oct. 9, 1974	2 1/8 m	Hallandale	3	113	3:41-4/5	Oct. 12, 1963

Turf Course

5 Furs.	Sulemark	5	119	:56	Oct. 25, 1992	Abt.1 1/16m	Galic Boy			1:41.48	May 5, 2001
	Magic Doe	4	119	:56.19	Oct. 28, 1999	1 1/16 m	Janeian	5	118	1:49 4/5	Oct. 11, 2003
Abt. 5 Furs.	Lady Gin	3	114	:56.19	Oct. 22, 2000	1 1/8 m	Rainbows for Life	3	122	1:44-3/5	Oct. 13, 1991
Abt.7 Furs	Point Guard	5	114	1:24-2/5	May 31, 1986	Abt.1 1/8 m	Color by d'Or			1:48.44	May 20, 2001
7 Furs.	Zenobia Empress	5	123	1:22-4/5	July 27, 1986	1 3/16 m	Perth Drummer	7	123	1:57-1/5	July 19, 1986
Abt.7-1/2 F.	Jack s Kingdom	5	119	1:30-3/5	Sept. 1, 1988	Abt.1-1/4 m	Sharp Swinger	5	117	2:08-1/5	Oct. 30, 1987
7-1/2 Furs	Joey Jr.	3	118	1:27-1/5	Nov. 5, 1989	1 1/4 m	Pass The Line	5	117	2:01	Aug. 2, 1986
Abt.1 Mile	Hi Dee Ho Coyote			1:35.62	May 20, 2001	1 3/8 m	Shayzari	6	118	2:15-1/5	Sep. 3, 1988
1 Mile	Niccolo Polo	5	119	1:33-3/5	Sep. 5, 1988	1 1/2 m	Lord Comet	6	117	2:26.87	Oct. 10, 1999
	Sean's Sunshine	5	114	1:36 1/5	Sep. 26, 1999						

Leading Jockey in 2003 Spring meet: Larry Sterling Jr., 56 wins.
Leading Trainer in 2003 Spring meet: Michael L. Reavis, 45 wins.
Leading Jockey in 2003 Fall meet: Randall Meier, 56 wins.
Leading Trainer in 2003 Fall meet: Michael L. Reavis, 31 wins.
Record attendance: 39,033 May 30, 1946 (Lincoln Fields meeting), 37,792, September 6, 1937 (Regular Hawthorne meeting)
Record handle: $11,225,769, October 25, 2003

HOLLYWOOD PARK

Churchill Downs California Company
President: Frederick M. Baedeker; General Manager: Eual G. Wyatt, Jr.; Racing Secretary: Martin Panza;
Public Relations Director: Michael Mooney; Vice President, Marketing: Allen Gutterman.
1050 S. Prairie Ave, Inglewood, CA 90301-0369
310-419-1500 Fax: 310-671-4460 Free Results and Scratches: (310) 242-2150
Web site: www.hollywoodpark.com

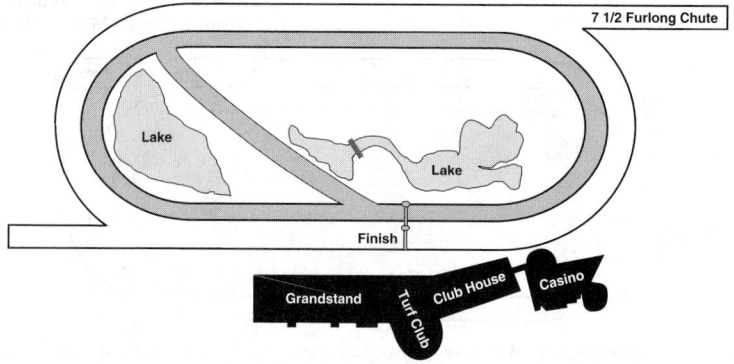

Track data: 1 1/8-mile oval, with one-mile chute. Distance from last turn to finish 1,321 feet. Width of stretch 90 1/2 feet, backstretch 80 1/2 feet. Turf course: One mile and 145 feet, with diagonal straightaway. Stable accommodations for 2,008; Seating capacity 35,000; Parking for 10,000.

Opened June 19, 1938. Was owned and operated by Marje Everett from the 1960's until R.D. Hubbard acquired the track in the early 1990's. Now owned and operated by Churchill Downs, Inc. and has a card casino on the grounds built in the early 1980's. Hollywood has hosted the Breeders' Cup three times, in the inaugural year, 1984, 1987, and 1997. Now hosts two meets each year. The Spring meet in 2003 ran from April 23 through July 20 and offered $412,000 in daily purses, while the 30-day fall meet ran from Nov. 11 through Dec. 21, with $349,000 in purses. The 2004 meets are respectively scheduled for April 21 through July 18 and from Nov. 3 through December 20.

TRACK RECORDS

4-1/2 Furs.	Bridge of Royalty	2	117	:50.59	May 4, 1995	1-1/16 m	Power Forward	4	115	1:40	Dec. 19, 1987
5 Furs.	Magical Mile	2	117	:56-2/5	May 18, 1989	1-1/8 m	Gentlemen	4	121	1:45.35	Dec. 22, 1996
5-1/2 Furs.	Hombre Rapido	5	118	1:01.67	Dec. 20, 2002	1-3/16 m	Dig for It	6	118	1:54.8	May 30, 2001
6 Furs.	Apalachee Ridge	3	114	1:07-2/5	Dec. 12, 1997	1-1/4 m	Greinton	4	120	1:58-2/5	June 23, 1985
6-1/2 Furs.	Lucky Forever	6	118	1:13-1/5	May 20, 1995	1-3/8 m	Golden Ticket	4	116	2:13.42	Dec. 21, 2002
7 Furs.	Mazel Trick	4	115	1:19.97	June 27, 1999	1-5/8 m	Ol Henry	5	115	2:42.50	June 27, 1997
7-1/2 Furs.	Awesome Daze	5	119	1:26-1/5	Nov. 23, 1997	1-3/4 m	Roman Cuzzin	4	113	2:56.77	July 21, 1997
1 Mile	Greinton	4	119	1:32-3/5	June 9, 1985						

Turf Course

5-1/2 Furs.	Pembroke	5	120	1:00-2/5	July 15, 1995	1-1/8 m	Fastness	5	120	1:44-3/5	Nov. 25, 1995
6 Furs.	Answer Do	4	115	1:07	Dec. 15, 1990	1-3/16 m	Kudos	4	123	1:51.80	April 25, 2001
1 Mile	Megan s Interco	5	119	1:32-3/5	May 22, 1994	1-1/4 m	Bien Bien	4	119	1:57-3/5	May 31, 1993
1-1/16 m	Fantastic Fellow	4	118	1:38-3/5	Apr. 26, 1998	1-1/2 m	Talloires	6	116	2:23-2/5	July 21, 1996
Abt 1/8 m	Zoffany	5	116	1:44-4/5	Nov. 16, 1985	Abt 1-3/4 m	Big Warning	4	117	2:50-2/5	Dec. 22, 1990

Leading Jockey in 2003, Spring-summer meet: Patrick A. Valenzuela, 81 wins.
Leading Trainer in 2003, Spring-summer meet: Doug O Neill, 37 wins.
Leading Jockey in 2003, Fall meet: Patrick A. Valenzuela, 27 wins.
Leading Trainer in 2003: fall meet: Jeff Mullins, 13 wins.
Record attendance: 80,340, May 4, 1980. Record handle: $14,352,515, Nov 8, 1987 (Breeders' Cup Day), $73,897,276, November 8, 1997 (Breeders' Cup Day, all sources).

HOOSIER PARK

A Churchill Downs Company
    Chairman: Thomas Meeker (Churchill Downs, president and CEO.); Richard Moore, President, General Manager; Racing Secretary: Warren Groce; Publicity Director: Tammy Knox; Vice President, Marketing, Donna Smith; Vice President, Communications, Thomas Bannon

4500 Dan Patch Circle, Anderson, IN 46013
765-642-7223 Fax: 765-644-0467
Web Site: www.hoosierpark.com

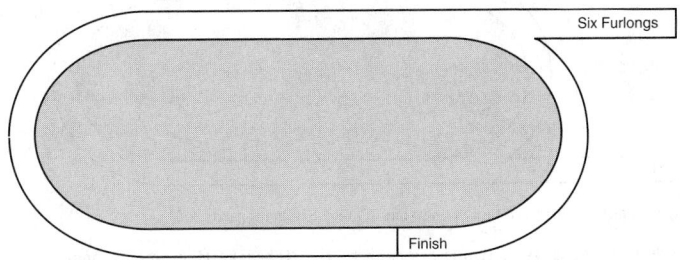

Track data: Seven-eighths mile oval, with a six furlong chute. Distance from last turn to finish 1,255 feet.

Opened Sept. 1, 1994. Runs thoroughbred and harness dates. A controlling interest in the track is owned by Hoosier Park, LP, a subsidiary of Churchill Downs. Annually runs about 70 Thoroughbred dates in the fall and the 2003 meet featured purses worth about $115,000 including stakes. The 2004 dates are Sept. 2 through Nov. 21.

TRACK RECORDS

5-1/2 Furs.	Moro Oro	3	119	1:02-1/5	Sep. 20, 1996	1-1/2 m	Our Forbes	7	119	2:39-1/5	Nov. 7, 1997
6 Furs.	Moro Oro	3	122	1:07-2/5	Nov. 16, 1996	1 5/8 m	Open Space	6	114	2:41.20	Nov. 16, 1996
1 Mile	Vic s Rebel	4	122	1:33-4/5	Oct. 13, 1998	1 7/8 m	Raw New	6	121	3:16.20	Dec. 1, 2000
1-1/16 m	Alydar s Rib	5	120	1:41	Nov. 1, 1996						

Leading Jockey in 2003: Orlando Mojica, 100 wins.
Leading Trainer in 2003: Ralph Martinez, 66 wins.
Record Attendance: 10,827, October 7, 2000. Handle Record $2,207,621, November 14, 2003

HORSEMEN'S PARK

Omaha Exposition and Racing, Inc.
President: Robert E. Lee; Vice President Racing Operations/General Manager: Dick Moore; Racing
Secretary: Greg Hosch

6303 Q Street, Omaha, Nebraska 68117
Telephone: (402) 731-2900; Fax: (402) 731-5122 and (402) 731-5416

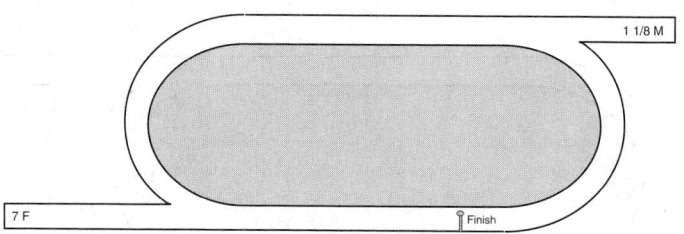

Track Data: 5/8 mile oval. distance from last turn to finish line, 757 feet. Seating capacity, 2800.

Opened July, 1998 with two days of two races each by the Nebraska Horsemen's Benevolent and Protective
Association. While mostly a simulcast facility, a short four-day live meet with purses worth in excess of $120,000 per
day was run in 2003 with a similar meet scheduled for July 15 through July 18 in 2004. Year-round simulcasting of 15–18
tracks per day.

TRACK RECORDS

6 Furs.	Pretty Boy Pete	1:10.20	July 20, 2001	1 Mile	Sure Shot Biscuit		1:35.80	July 22, 2001
6 Furs.	Come a Stridin	1:10.20	July 21, 2001	1 3/8 m	Aly Aly Oxen Free 7	119	2:18.00	July 21, 2002

Leading Jockey in 2003: Ken A. Shino, 3 wins.
Leading Trainer in 2003: David C. Anderson, Brian M. Roberts and Hugh H. Robertson, 2 wins (tie).

INDIANA DOWNS

Oliver Racing, LLC; LHT Capital, LLC
General Manager, Jon Schuster; Director of Racing, Jim Ewart; Thoroughbred Racing Secretary, Butch Cook; Human Resource Manager/Marketing Coordinator, Julie Metz.

4200 N. Michigan Rd.
Shelbyville, IN 46176
(317) 421-0000; Fax, (317) 421-0100
Race Office, (866) 478-7223
www.indianadowns.com

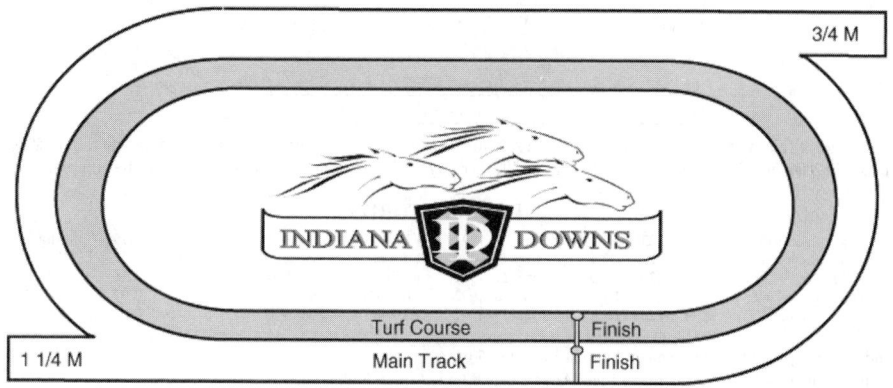

Track Data: One mile dirt track and seven-furlong turf course. Indoor seating 3,000.

TRACK RECORDS

4 1/2 Furs.	Cat Tracks	5	123	:50.75	May 10, 2003	1-70y	K K Avey	3	114	1:41.56	May 7, 2003
5 Furs.	Ship s Silver	6	123	:58.41	Apr. 19, 2003	1-1/16 m	Gonna Gidder	3	110	1:44.20	May 16, 2003
5 1/2 Furs.	Don Golden	8	120	1:03.47	May 8, 2003	1-1/8m	A Secret Scoop	4	117	1:50.62	May 15, 2003
6 Furs.	Lx Commander	3	117	1:09.89	May 26, 2003	1-1/4m	High Chieftain	6	117	2:06.31	May 26, 2003
1 Mile	Kissinleaf	4	117	1:37.76	May 8, 2003						

Opened in December 2002 for harness racing, with first thoroughbred meet commencing on April 11, 2003. In 2003, a meet of 30 days was conducted from April 11 through May 26, featuring purses of over $113,000. Conducts live racing of thoroughbreds, Quarter Horses and standardbreds. Offers year-round full-card simulcasting of thoroughbred and harness racing. An off-site wagering facility is located in Evansville with a second facility in Clarksville due to open in 2004.

Leading Jockey in 2003: Orlando Mojica and Sidney P. LeJeune Jr, 38 wins (tie).
Leading Trainer in 2003: R. Gary Patrick, 25 wins.

KAMLOOPS

479 Chilcotin Road
Kamloops, British Columbia V2H 1G4
(604)828-3590; Fax (606) 828-0836

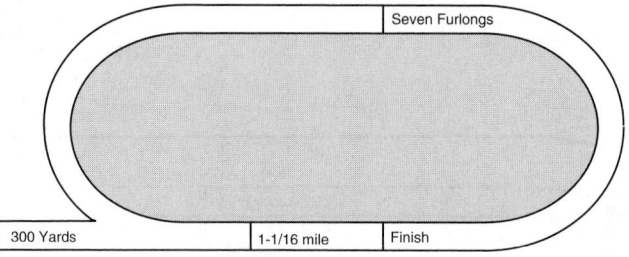

Ran separate four and five day race meetings in 2003 and is scheduled to repeat a similar schedule starting in May and August in 2004. In 2003, purses averaged about $7,500 per day during the spring and $13,000 during the summer.

TRACK RECORDS

3-1/2 furs.	Spooks Classy Lady 2	123	:39-3/5	May 23, 1993	1 Mile	Just Like Light	7	126	1:36.60	Aug. 9, 1998
4 Furs.	Rampaging Alf	2	122	:47	Aug. 8, 1999	1-1/8 m	Winning Edge	6	120	1:51-4/5	Sep. 7, 1992
Abt 4-1/2 F.	War Of Aces	4	126	:48-2/5	June 6, 1992	1-3/16 m	Mondo Key	6	123	1:58	Aug. 29, 1993
6-1/2 Furs.	Gate Hand	7	127	1:17	Aug. 16, 1992	Abt 1-1/4 m	Sidero	6	117	2:07	Aug. 18, 1991
7 Furs.	McBrat	4	123	1:23	Aug. 25, 1991	1-1/4 m	Native Winter	6	126	2:07-1/5	Aug. 29, 1992

Leading Jockey in 2003, Spring meet: Laurina Bugeaud, 5 wins.
Leading Trainer in 2003, Spring meet: Vicki Anderson and Irene Miller, 3 wins (tie)
Leading Jockey in 2003, Summer meet: Ronald Joseph Bilodeau, 8 wins
Leading Trainer in 2003, Summer meet: Many trainers tied with 2 wins.

KEENELAND

Keeneland Association, Incorporated.
Nick Nicholson: President and CEO; W.B. Rogers Beasley, Director of Racing; Ben Huffman, Racing Secretary; Jim Williams, Director of Communications: (859) 288-4220; fax: (859) 288-4254.

Street Address: 4201 Versailles Road
Lexington, Kentucky 40510
Nearest Airport: Blue Grass Field, next to track

P.O. Box 1690, Lexington, Kentucky 40588-1690
(859) 254-3412; (800) 456-3412; Fax: (859) 288-4348
E-mail: keeneland@keeneland.com
Web Site: www.keeneland.com.

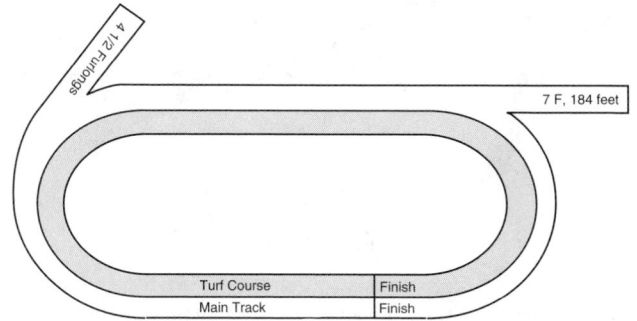

Track Data: Main track, 1 1/16 miles, sandy loam, with 4 1/2- and seven-furlong chutes. Stretch length, 1,174 feet. Turf course, 7 1/2 furlongs. Training Track, five furlongs, sandy loam. Stable accommodations for 1,852. Seating capacity: 8,500; Parking for 10,000 cars.

Opened October 15, 1936, to provide a forum for horses bred in Kentucky and/or bought at the famous Keeneland Yearling sales. Keeneland remains a National Historic Landmark. Its dual live meets – three weeks in April and three more weeks in October – are among the classiest in the sport with purses to match, including numerous Graded stakes and daily average purses nearing $600,000. The Keeneland library, one of the finest Thoroughbred research libraries in the world, is open Monday through Friday with Daily Racing Form archives among the important reference material. Provides announced coverage of workouts on Saturday mornings with trackside breakfast. The 2004 Spring meet is scheduled for Apr. 2 through Apr. 23 and the fall meet from Oct. 8 through Oct. 30. Simulcasting throughout the year.

TRACK RECORDS

4-1/2 Furs.	Quick Swoon	2	121	:51	Apr. 20, 1966	Abt 7 Furs.	Lamb Chop	3	118	1:24-3/5	Oct. 10, 1963
	Royalty Note	2	114	:51	Apr.23, 1968	1-1/16 m	Din s Dancer	5	123	1:40-4/5	Oct. 9, 1990
	Bend The Times	2	117	:51	Apr. 8, 1980	1-1/8 m	Good Command	4	118	1:46-4/5	Oct. 10, 1987
	City Street	2	118	:51.04	Apr. 20, 2001		Grand Jewel	3	120	1:46.87	Oct. 10, 1993
	Heckle	2	118	:51.04	Apr. 18, 2003	1-3/16 m	Arch	3	123	1:53.87	Oct. 11, 1998
6 Furs.	Anjiz	5	114	1:07.78	Oct. 9, 1993	1-1/4 m	Political Fact	4	112	2:02.21	Oct. 15, 1993
6-1/2 Furs.	Number One Sheikh	3	116	1:14.70	Oct. 11, 2000	1-5/8 m	Put-in-Bay	4	113	2:45	Oct. 13, 1967
7 Furs.	Binalong	4	112	1:20.39	Oct. 13, 1993		Mr. Copy Chief	3	118	2:45	Oct. 20, 1971

Turf Course

5-1/2 Furs.	Chris s Thunder	5	123	1:01.72	Oct. 8, 2000	1-3/16 m	Happyanunoit	4	119	1:53.91	Oct. 15, 1999
1 Mile	Altibr	5	126	1:33.72	Oct. 7, 2000	1-1/2 m	Bursting Forth	5	114	2:27.54	Apr. 22, 1999
1-1/16 m	Quiet Resolve	5	116	1:40.30	April 27, 2000	1-5/8 m	Royal Strand	5	117	2:38.68	Oct. 24, 1999
1-1/8 m	Memories of Silver	3	121	1:45.81	Oct. 5, 1996	About distances no longer run over this turf course.					

Leading jockey in 2003 Spring meet: Robby Albarado, 17 wins.
Leading trainer in 2003 Spring meet: D. Wayne Lukas, 9 wins.
Leading jockey in 2003 Fall meet: Pat Day, 21 wins.
Leading trainer in 2003 Fall meet: Nicholas P. Zito, 11 wins.
Record attendance: 29,687, April 15, 2000, 38,501, April 16, 1994 includes intra-state attendance, Record handle: $3,516,621 April 13, 2002,
$17,076,993 April 14, 2001 includes simulcasting.

KENTUCKY DOWNS

Kentucky Downs, LLC.
PO Box 405, Franklin, KY 42134
270-586-7778 Fax: 502-586-8080
Web site:www.turfwaypark.com

General Manager: Ryan Driscoll
Director of Operations: John Goodman II
Racing Secretary: Rick Lee

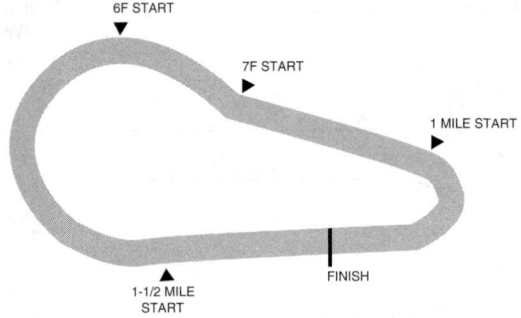

Track data: 1-3/8 miles European turf course in a pear shape that features a sharp first turn and a wide, bulging second turn.

Opened as Dueling Grounds April 22, 1990 and was bought in 1997 by a consortium that included Churchill Downs and Turfway Park. Now managed by Turfway, ran a six-day fall meeting in 2003 with several stakes races, including some steeplechase events over its European style turf course and just under $200,000 in daily purses. A similar meet is scheduled from Sept. 18 to Sept. 28 in 2004. Year-round simulcasting.

TRACK RECORDS

6 Fur.	Morluc	4	116	1:09.66	Sept. 23, 2000	1 Mile	Rob n Gin	4	119	1:35.00	Sept. 19, 1998
7 Fur.	Slew of Deuces	5	116	1:22.77	Sept. 18, 2000	1 1/2 m	Yaqthan	8	115	2:27.60	Sept. 19, 1998

Leading Jockey in 2003: Brice Blanc, 5 wins
Leading Trainer in 2003: Kenneth G. McPeek, 4 wins.

Record attendance: 2,191, May 1999. Record handle: $585,762

KIN PARK

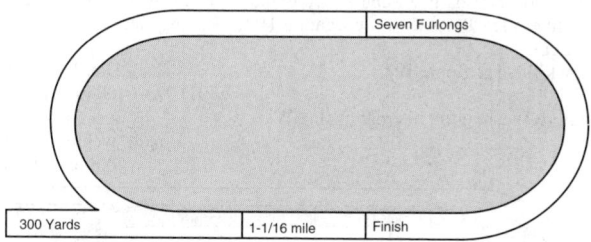

Seven Furlongs

300 Yards   1-1/16 mile   Finish

A 4-day, summer meet in 2003 and a similar meet in 2004.

TRACK RECORDS

Abt 3 Furs.	Mcnoonie	2	122	:34	June 26, 1994	Abt 7 Furs.	Mexican Macho Man	4	126	1:21.00	July 19, 1998
3 Furs.	Rejected Frenchman	3	122	:32-1/5	Aug. 1, 1993	7 Furs.	Gate Hand	6	123	1:22	July 28, 1991
Abt 4 Furs.	Wild Feu	3	118	:44-2/5	May 5, 1996	1 1/16 m	Wicked Advances	7	122	1:45.40	Aug. 7, 1993
5 1/2 Furs.	Tim O Hara	6	123	1:03-1/5	Sep. 20, 1992	Abt 1-1/16m	Gavotte	5	126	1:44.20	July 31, 1999
6 Fur.	Diplomatic Eagle	3	118	1:10.60	July 10, 1994	1 1/8 m	Ninja Warrior	11	120	1:47-2/5	July 16, 1995
Abt 6 Furs.	Detective M	5	126	1:09.60	Aug. 7, 1994	Abt. 1 1/8 m	Conversano	3	134	1:50.80	July 30, 2000
Abt 6-1/2 F.	Little Duke	4	131	1:19.00	July 30, 2000	1-1/4 m	Prospector Bobby	4	123	1:59-1/5	Sep. 29, 1991

Leading Jockey in 2003: Ronald Joseph Bilodeau, 5 wins.
Leading Trainer in 2003: Wade Hardie and Rosa Lee Burbank, 3 wins (tie).

LAUREL PARK

Magna Entertainment Corp.
Frank Stronach, Chairman of the Board; Joseph A. De Francis, President and CEO; Lou Raffetto, COO; Karin
M. De Francis, Executive Vice President; Georganne Hale, Racing Secretary; Mike Gathagan, Director
Broadcast Communications
Street Address: Racetrack Road & Route 198   Box 130, Laurel, Maryland 20725
Laurel, Maryland 20725   (301) 725-0400 or (410) 792-7775 (Baltimore)
Nearest Airport: Baltimore-Washington International (BWI),   Fax: (410) 792-4877
12 miles   E-mail: webmaster@marylandracing.com
       Web Site: www.marylandracing.com

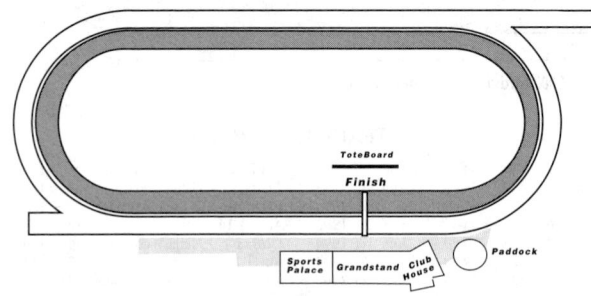

Track Data: 1 1/8-mile loam oval. 7-furlong chute. Length of stretch from last turn to finish line, 1,000 feet. One-mile turf course; Stable
accommodations: 995. Seating capacity: 6,400; Parking for 8,000 cars.

Opened October 2, 1911, Laurel Park has been the sister track of Pimlico Racecourse during the two decades it was
opened and operated by the DeFrancis family. In 2003, Magna Entertainment Corp. purchased a 58 percent stake in
Laurel and a 51 percent stake in Pimlico Race Course, which are both owned and operated by the Maryland Jockey
Club. In 2003, purses including stakes averaged nearly $190,000 at both meets. Dates for 2004 season: Oct. 8, 2003
through March 28, 2004 and July 22 through Aug. 27.

TRACK RECORDS

5 Furs.	Dave s Friend	5	119	:57	Nov. 21, 1980	1-1/16 m	Willard Scott	4	115	1:41-4/5	Nov. 16, 1985
5-1/2 Furs.	Crossing Point	5	117	1:02.45	Nov. 1, 2002	1-1/8 m	Excellent Tipper	4	112	1:47-3/5	July 5, 1992
6 Furs.	Richter Scale	6	123	1:07.95	July 15, 2000	1-3/16 m	Testing	7	121	1:54.51	Oct. 21, 2000
6-1/2 Furs.	Ebonizer	3	115	1:15-2/5	Nov. 23, 1990	1-1/4 m	Ritchie the Coach	5	118	1:59 4/5	Nov. 23, 1996
7 Furs.	Tappiano	5	123	1:21-2/5	Feb. 12, 1989	1-3/4 m	Asserche	6	116	2:58-2/5	Feb. 13, 1994
7-1/2 Furs.	Tidal Surge	4	117	1:29-2/5	Mar. 12, 1994						
1 Mile	Skipper s Friend	4	122	1:34-2/5	Dec. 6, 1980						

Turf Course

5-1/2 Furs.	Oops I Am	5	117	1:02-1/5	June 14, 1994	1-3/16	Gilded Youth	10	117	1:53 3/5	June 27, 1998
6 Furs.	Texas Glitter	4	115	1:08.00	Oct. 28, 2000	1-1/4 m	Dynamic Trick	5	114	1:58.42	Oct. 22, 2000
1 Mile	Portsmouth	3	116	1:34	Oct. 30, 1965	1-1/2 m	Kelso	7	126	2:23-4/5	Nov. 11, 1964
1-1/16 m	Water Moccasin	6	119	1:39-2/5	June 15, 1987	1-3/4 m	Copper Prospect	4	122	2:47-4/5	July 31, 1993
1-1/8 m	La Reine s Terms			1:46.04	Aug. 11, 2002	2 Miles	Summer Ensign	4	118	3:23-3/5	June 15, 1993

Jumps

Abt 2 Miles	Rolling Cart	8	154	4:08	Oct. 9, 1993	Abt 2 Miles	Rolling Cart	8	143	4:14	June 12, 1993
2-1/16 m	Keltie	6	143	4:13-4/5	June 18, 1994						

Leading Jockey in 2003 Winter meet: Ryan Fogelsonger, 93 wins
Leading Trainer in 2003 Winter meet: Scott A. Lake, 29 wins
Leading Jockey in 2003 Summer meet: Ryan Fogelsonger, 25 wins
Leading Trainer in 2003 Summer meet: John J. Robb, 10 wins
Leading Jockey in 2003 Fall meet: Abel Castellano Jr., 64 wins
Leading Trainer in 2003 Fall meet: Dale Capuano, 25 wins

LES BOIS PARK

Les Bois Park, Inc.
General Manager: Duayne Diderickson.

5610 Glenwood Rd., Boise, ID 83714
208-376-7223 Fax: 208-376-7227

Track data: six-furlong oval, with five-furlong and one-mile chutes, the latter also used for two-furlong straightaway races. Distance from last turn to finish 660 feet; width 80 feet.. Stable accommodations 834, Seating capacity 3,300.

Opened May 15, 1970, ran a 46 day meet in 2003, with $21,000 in daily average purses. The 2004 meet is scheduled for May 1 through August 15.

TRACK RECORDS

2 Furs.	Rare n to Syn	4	124	21.40	May 4, 2003	1 Mile	Barsotti	3	122	1:35.60	July 24, 1999
3 Furs.	Big Order	6	117	:33-4/5	May 30, 1970	1-1/8 m	Song Festival	7	122	1:50	June 15, 1991
4 Furs.	We Go Easy	4	123	:45-2/5	June 27, 1976	1-3/16 m	Standup Comedian	8	117	1:58-1/5	June 27, 1987
4-1/2 Furs.	C. K. s Orphan	5	122	:50-3/5	May 25, 1987	1-1/4 m	Talent To Amuse	7	122	2:02	Aug. 11, 1996
5 Furs.	Lord Goodoon	4	122	:55-4/5	May 25, 1987	1-3/8 m	Chikara	4	119	2:17-3/5	Aug. 13, 1988
6 Furs.	Shilne	5	119	1:12-1/5	July 25, 1971	1-1/2	Uncle Maurice	5	122	2:35-3/5	Aug. 12, 1979
6-1/2 Furs.	Stretch the Truth	4	122	1:17	July 12, 1997	1- 3/4 m	Final K.	4	120	2:48-1/5	Sep. 1, 1975
7 Furs.	Pride of Kent	5	122	1:22.60	July 10, 1998	1-7/8 m	Chikara	5	127	2:59-2/5	July 29, 1989
7-1/2 Furs.	Joyous Gard	4	122	1:28.80	June 17, 1998						

Leading Jockey in 2003: Berkley R. Packer, 51 wins
Leading Trainer in 2003: Dru S. Hall, 23 wins

LINCOLN
(Nebraska State Fair Park)

Nebraska State Board of Agriculture
President: Don Virgil; Manager: Patrick Lloyd; Marketing Manager: Christine Rasmussen.

Box 81223, Lincoln, NE 68501-1223
402-474-5371 Fax: 402-473-4114
E-Mail Address: nestatefair@statefair.org; Web Site: www.statefair.org

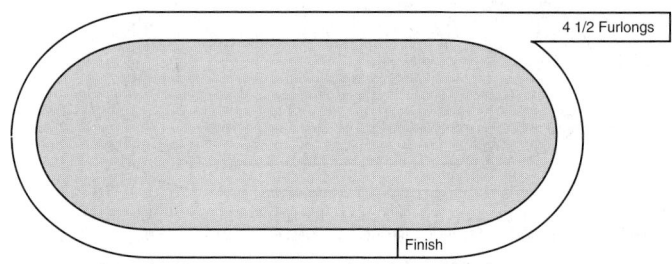

Track data: Five-eighths mile oval, with **4 1/2**-furlong chute. Distance from last turn to finish **480** feet. Stable accommodations **1,200**. Seating capacity **5,800**. Parking for **9,000** cars on the fairgrounds.

Live racing is scheduled in **2004** from May **14** to July **11**; a similar meet in **2003** featured purses of about **$44,000** per day fueled by year round simulcasting.

TRACK RECORDS

4 Furs.	Mr. Mayor	4	120	:46 4/5	Aug. 1, 1975	1-3/16 m	Speedy Rick	6	110	1:54 1/5	Aug. 13, 1977
4-1/2 Furs.	Leaping Plum	4	122	:50	Sep. 17, 1995	1-5/16 m	Famous Event	5	122	2:18 3/5	Oct. 22, 1995
6 Furs.	Genuine Lass	4	120	1:10.20	June 20, 2002	1 3/8 M	Trumpty Dumpty	8	120	2:17.80	June 17, 2001
1 Mile	Sensitive Ghost	8	116	1:36.00	July 14, 2002	1-5/8 m	Hunters Soup	6	120	2:45 4/5	Nov. 5, 1989
1 m70yds	High Dice	6	122	1:39.40	June 24, 2001	2 Miles	Step n Ring	5	116	3:25	July 13, 1996
1-1/16 m	Old n Bold	4	121	1:42 3/5	Aug. 25, 1979	2 3/8 Miles	Naughty Nipper	5	119	4:34 1/5	Nov. 13, 1983
1-1/8 m	Prince Hedstart	6	122	1:49 4/5	Aug. 1, 1982	3 Miles	Hunters Soup	6	121	5:18 3/5	Nov. 19, 1989

Leading Jockey in 2003: Jerome Carkeek, 54 wins.
Leading Trainer in 2003: David C. Anderson, 40 wins.
Record attendance: 10, 107, August 19, 1978.

LONE STAR PARK

Magna Entertainment Corp.
Frank Stronach, Chairman; CEO: Jim McAlpine; Corey S. Johnsen, President; Jeffrey Greco, Vice President and General Manager; Paula Dowell, Vice President of Finance; G.W. Hail, Vice President of Marketing and Sales; Larry Craft, Director of Racing & Racing Secretary, (972) 237-5036; Darren Rogers, Director of Media Relations.

Nearest Airport: Dallas-Fort Worth Int l. Airport, 10 miles .

1000 Lone Star Parkway, Grand Prairie, Texas 75050
(972) 263-7223; Fax: (972) 262-5622; Media: (972) 237-1140
Web Site: www.lonestarpark.com

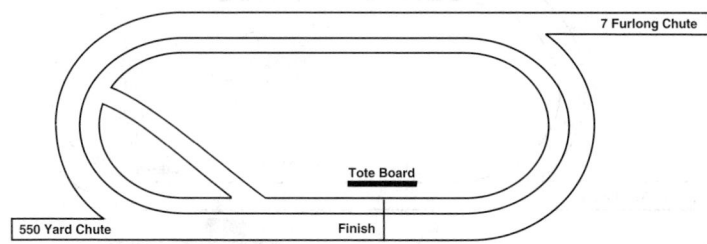

Track Data: One-mile dirt track with a seven-furlong chute. Distance from last turn to finish, 930 feet; width 90 feet. Turf: 7/8-miles with 1 1/8-mile infield chute; width 70 feet. 550-yard Quarter Horse chute. Seating for 12,000; capacity 50,000; Parking for 6,000 cars.

Opened April 1997, Lone Star Park has been the most successful pari-mutuel track in Texas. In 2003, average purses were more than $218,000. The track plays host to the annual NTRA All-Star Jockey Championship. In 2004, Lone Star plays host to the Breeders' Cup. Scheduled dates for 2004: Apr. 15 to July 11 and Oct. 1 through Oct. 31.

TRACK RECORDS

2-1/2 Furs.	Yes He Will	4	124	:26.40	Nov. 7, 1997	1 Mile	Isitingood	6	123	1:34.44	Apr. 20, 1997
4-1/2 Furs.	Rayanegra	2	118	:51.39	May 2, 1997	1-1/16 m	Dixie Dot Com			1:40.53	May 28, 2001
5 Furlongs	Joyful Tune	4	116	:56.25	May 5, 2002	1-1/8 m	Moosekabear	7	115	1:49.69	Apr. 19, 1997
5-1/2 Furs.	That Tat	5	123	1:01.88	Apr. 11, 2003	1-3/16 m	Moosekabear	7	117	1:56.21	May 10, 1997
6 Furs.	Triple Card			1:08.06	May 28, 2001	1-1/4 m	Tali Hai	7	118	2:04.68	June 14, 1997
6-1/2 Furs.	Spiritbound	5	117	1:14.16	May 3, 1997	1-1/2 m	Tali Hai	7	120	2:32.57	July 5, 1997
7 Furs.	Clooney			1:20.98	June, 22,2001	1 3/4 Miles	Sir Moon Dancer	5	114	3:00.46	July 19, 1998

Turf Course

5 Furs.	Icy Morn	5	120	:55-3/5	May 26, 1997	1 Mile	Kiraday	6	116	1:33.56	July 4, 1997
	Caro s Royalty	4	114	:55.60	June 28, 1997	Abt.1 Mile	Royalty Case	3	117	1:34-3/5	July 20, 1997
Abt.5 Furs.	Caro s Royalty	4	122	:56-3/5	July 20, 1997	1-3/8 m	Rugged Bugger	7	114	2:13.53	May 10, 1998
7 1/2 Furs.	Special Moments	5	119	1:28.20	May 24, 1998	1-1/2 m	Final Val	5	114	2:28.20	July 4, 1998
Abt.7-1/2 F.	Sweet Eleanor	4	112	1:28-4/5	July 24, 1997						

Turf Course (out of chute)

Abt.1-1/16m	Seattle Spell	5	115	1:41-4/5	July 19, 1997	1-1/8 m	Toll Paid	7	122	1:46-2/5	June 13, 1997
1-1/16 m	Illusive Ghost	5	115	1:40	July 11, 1997	1-1/8 m	Yaqthan	8	116	1:45.54	May 25, 1998
	Sharpest Image	6	116	1:40.05	May 25, 1998						

Leading Jockey in 2003: Corey J. Lanerie, 86 wins
Leading Trainer in 2003: Cole Norman, 98 wins
Record attendance 33,805, July 3, 2000. Record handle: $3,130, 221, May 1, 1999; $7,218,982, May 1, 1999 (all sources)

LOS ALAMITOS RACE COURSE

Los Alamitos
President: Edward C. Allred; Racing Secretary: Ron Church; Marketing Director: Orlando Gutierrez;
Simulcast Coordinator: Melodie Knuchell

4961 Katella Ave. Los Alamitos, CA 90720
714-820-2800 Fax: 714-236-4534 Free Scratches and Results 714-995-2222
E-Mail Address: larace@losalamitos.com; Web Address: www.losalamitos.com

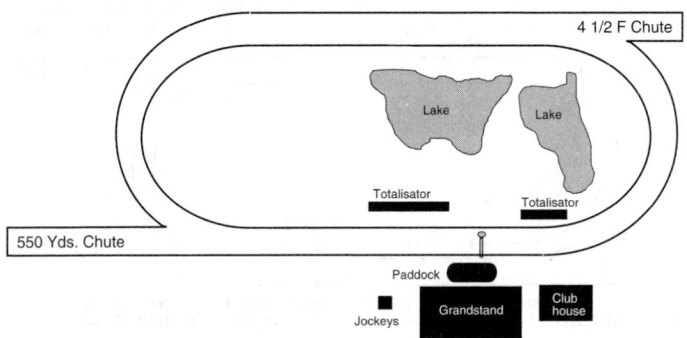

Track data: Five-eighths mile oval, with 4 1/2-furlong and 550-yard straight course. Distance from last turn to finish 558 feet. Width 100 feet in stretch, 90 feet in backstretch and on turns; 6.9 feet banking on turns. Stable accommodations for 1,438. Seating capacity 7,500.

Los Alamitos runs a virtually year-round mixed-breed meet. The 2004 meet is scheduled for Dec. 26, 2003, through Dec. 19, 2004.

THOROUGHBRED TRACK RECORDS

4-1/2 Furs.   Valiant Pete   5   111   :49-1/5   Aug. 11, 1990

Leading Jockey in 2003: Baltazar Contreras, 78 wins
Leading Trainer in 2003: Charles S. Treece, 37 wins
All time single day attendance 19,970 May 6. 1983. All time single day handle $2,127,758 June 30, 1995

LOUISIANA DOWNS

Harrah s Entertainment

Senior Vice President and General Manager: Ted Bogich; Vice President Racing: Ray A. Tromba; Marketing/Publicity Manager-Racing: Jennifer Ray; Racing Secretary: Patrick J. Pope.

Street Address: 8000 East Texas Ave.
Bossier City, Louisiana 71111
Nearest Airport: Shreveport Regional Airport, 12 Miles

P.O. Box 5519, Bossier City, Louisiana 71171-5519
(318) 742-5555; Fax: (318) 741-2615
Web Site: www.ladowns.com
E-Mail: bburgess@harrahs.com

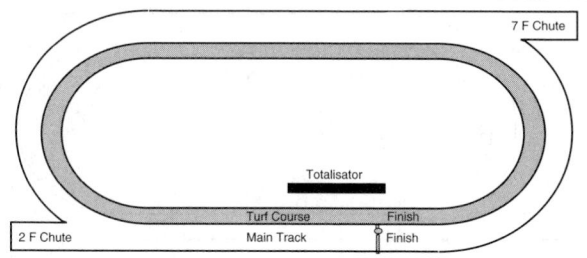

Track Data: One-mile, sandy loam; seven-furlong and 1 1/4-mile chutes; Distance from last turn to finish, **1,010 feet**; Width of stretch and backstretch, **80 feet**; Turf course: 7 furlongs and 50 feet, distance from last turn to finish, **940 feet**, width 70 feet. Stable accommodations for **1,360**. Seating capacity **17,000**; Parking for **4,000** cars.

Opened October, 30, 1974, Louisiana Downs annually runs from mid-May through mid-November. Home of the Super Derby. Slot machines were introduced May 21, 2003, and purses in 2003 averaged almost $180,000 a day. The 2004 meet is scheduled for May 14 through Oct. 31.

TRACK RECORDS

4 Furs.	A Lady For Junius	5	123	:45-2/5	Oct. 9, 1997	1-1/16 m	Nelson	6	113	1:41-2/5	Aug. 15, 1993
4-1/2 Furs.	Sondor	2	119	:51-3/5	May 16, 1984	1-1/8	Mocha Express	5	118	1:48.14	July 24, 1999
5 Furs.	Joyful Tune	4	124	56.90	Sept. 7, 2002	1-3/16	Jungle Pocket	7	118	1:57-2/5	Aug. 15, 1984
5-1/2 Furs.	Fighting K	4	122	1:02-4/5	Sep. 11, 1993	1-1/4 m	Tiznow	3	124	1:59.84	Sept. 30, 2000
6 Furs.	Tangent	4	123	1:08-2/5	Apr. 28, 1984	1-1/2 m	Frankie s Pal	6	110	2:31-4/5	Sep. 3, 1990
	B.J. s Mark			1:08 2/5	July 3, 1999	1-3/4 m	Frankie s Pal	6	113	2:58-4/5	Oct. 14, 1990
6-1/2 Furs.	Prince Of The Mt.	5	117	1:14-4/5	May 23, 1996	2 Miles	Vain Lass	11	110	3:35-1/5	Nov. 16, 1975
7 Furs.	Carrysport	3	116	1:21-3/5	July 4, 1984	2-1/8 m	Woodtie	5	123	3:44-1/5	Oct. 22, 1989
	Contractor			1:21 3/5		2-1/4 m	Eulogize	4	117	3:58-4/5	Nov. 11, 1990
7-1/2 Furs.	Grand Arrival	3	114	1:27	Oct. 25, 1987						
1 m70yds	Country Jim	4	111	1:39-2/5	July 4, 1982						

Turf Course

5 Fur.	Sunshine Classic	5	119	55.79	Aug. 31, 2002	Abt.1 1/8m	Highly Attractive	4	115	1:42	June 17, 1990
Abt.5 Furs.	Mo Dinero			:55 2/5	Sept. 26, 1999	1 1/4 m	Alystorm	4	115	2:05.03	Oct. 1, 1999
Abt.7-1/2 F.	Home In Front	4	112	1:27-2/5	Aug. 22, 1987	Abt.1-1/4 m	Link	6	116	2:04-2/5	Sep. 3, 1994
7-1/2 Furs.	Chuck N Luck	6	113	1:28-2/5	Aug. 5, 1989	Abt.1-3/16m	Symbol Of Pride	5	113	2:16-1/5	July 20, 1986
Abt.1 Mile	Dressy Time	7	114	1:33-2/5	Sep. 1, 1984	1-3/8 m	Semillero	5	116	2:13-1/5	Oct. 12, 1985
1 Mile	Cherokee Circle	4	116	1:34-1/5	July 24, 1983	Abt.1-1/2 m	Comely Dancer	7	117	2:29-3/5	Aug. 12, 1990
Abt.1-1/16m	Inevitable Leader	7	116	1:40	May 26, 1986	Abt.1 13/16	Alamance	6	122	3:05	Sep. 4, 1993
	Vaguely Crafty	6	114	1:40	July 22, 1989	Abt.1 7/8m	Gisela s Dancer	6	128	3:14-2/5	Sep. 18, 1993
1-1/16 m	Clever Song	3	120	1:40-1/5	Aug. 11, 1985	Abt.1 15/16	Woodtie	5	122	3:19	Oct. 8, 1989

Leading Jockey in 2003: Gerard Melancon 101 wins.

Leading Trainer in 2003: Cole Norman, 95 wins

Record attendance: 26,513, May 26, 86. Record handle: $4,371,781, September 27, 1987; $6,773,009, September 20, 2003, all sources.

MARQUIS DOWNS RACECOURSE

Saskatoon Prairieland Exhibition Corp.
Racing Manager: Doug King; Racing Secretary: Rick Fior.

Box 6010, Saskatoon, Sask, CAN S7K 4E4
306-242-6100 Fax: 306-931-7886
E-Mail Address: dking@saskatoonex.com; Web Site: www.saskatoonex.com

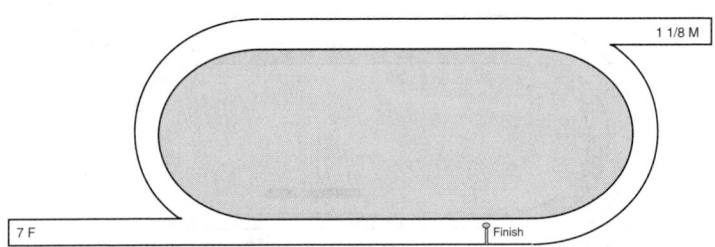

Five-eighths mile oval, 7-furlong and 1 1/8-mile chutes. Distance from last turn to finish **660** feet; width **90** feet. Stable accommodations for **750**. Seating capacity **3,027**.

Opened August **18, 1969** and runs a mixed breed meet on weekends throughout the summer with (with approximately **200** total Thoroughbred races) for a daily average of about **$18,500** per day in purses. 2004 dates: May 28 through Sept. 18.

TRACK RECORDS

3-1/2 Furs.	Kid Dynamo	2	120	:40-2/5	June 20, 1977	1 Mile	Three for You	5	124	1:37-1/5	June 12, 1981
Abt.4 Furs.	Royal Alibi	9	124	:45-1/5	May 20, 1978	1-1/16 m	Little Bo	4		1:42.00	Sept. 1, 1984
4 Furs.	Zizzilin	4	116	:45	May 8, 1981	Abt 1-1/8	Easy Riser	4	119	1:49-2/5	Aug. 25, 1980
5-1/2 Furs.	Mickey s Mark	5	124	1:04-2/5	July 28, 1980	1-1/8 m	Zance	6	124	1:49-3/5	Oct. 10, 1988
6 Furs.	Shotgun Annie	6	119	1:10-2/5	Aug. 7, 1981	1-5/16m	Extrapolate	6	118	2:13	Aug. 29, 1993
Abt.6-1/2 F	Shona Rae	5	120	1:17-4/5	June 11, 1992	1 3/8 m	Secret Cipher	4	127	2:18	Oct. 15, 1983
6-1/2 Furs.	Christmas Country	4	124	1:18-3/5	Aug. 1, 1994	Abt.1-1/2 m	Spring Sunsation	3	115	2:35	Sep. 26, 1993
Abt.7 Furs.	Graceful Klinchit	5	122	1:23-3/5	Aug. 31, 1991	1-5/8 m	Bright Bern	4	115	2:48	July 31, 1976
7 Furs.	T.V. Fling	4		1:24.20	Aug. 28, 1988	1-3/4	Lloyd s Admiral	5	122	3:01-2/5	Oct. 19, 1986

Leading Jockey in 2003: Rennie Latchman, 43 wins.
Leading Trainer in 2003: Hubert Pilon and Don Bjarnarson, 16 wins (tie).

THE MEADOWLANDS

New Jersey Sports & Exposition Authority
President & Chief Executive Officer: James A. DiEleuterio, Jr.; Senior Executive Vice President/Racing: Bruce Garland ; Vice President/Thoroughbred Racing: Robert J. Kulina; Vice President & General Manager Meadowlands: Christopher McErlean; Racing Secretary: Mike Dempsey; Director of Media Relations: Carol Hodes.

Meadowlands Racetrack, 50 Route 120, East Rutherford, New Jersey 07073
(201) 935-8500; (201) 843-2446; Fax:(201) 460-4244
Media/Public Relations, (201) 460-4050. Free scratches & results: (201) 843-2446
E-mail: cmcerlean@njsea.com; Web Site: www.thebigm.com
Nearest Airport: Newark International, 10 miles from track

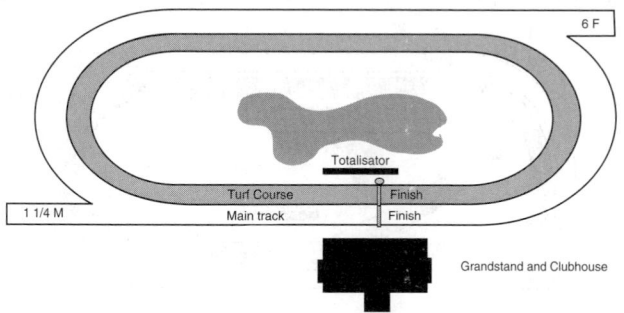

Track Data: One-mile oval, limestone screening and loam with 6-furlong and 1 1/4-mile chutes. Distance from last turn to finish line 990 feet. Width of homestretch , 90 feet; backstretch, 80 feet. Turf course: 7 furlongs. Stable accommodations for 1,760 horses. Seating capacity 6,000; parking for 20,000 cars.

Opened September 6, 1977 with the first night Thoroughbred racing in the metropolitan New York region, which has remained the case into the 21st century. In 2003, The Meadowlands had a 28-day meet that ran from early October into November, featuring purses including stakes of over $215,000 per day. An expanded meet, from Sept. 6 through Dec. 11, is on tap for 2004. Year round simulcasting except Sundays in the fall when NFL Giants play at Giants' Stadium in the Meadowlands Complex.

TRACK RECORDS

5 Furs.	Stu s Choice	3	119	:55-4/5	Sep. 6, 1996	1 1/16 M	Black Forest	4	113	1:40.39	Sept. 26, 1998
5-1/2 Furs.	Red Hot Spot	4	122	1:02.33	Oct. 14, 2003	1-1/8 m	Forty One Carats	3	120	1:45-2/5	Oct. 29, 1999
6 Furs.	Sweet Beast	4	122	1:07-4/5	Nov. 18, 1994	1 3/16 m	Key Lory	5	117	1:53-4/5	Nov. 20, 1999
	Purple Peopleater	8	119	1:07-4/5	Sept. 24, 1999		With Anticipation	5	119	1:53-4/5	Nov. 18, 2000
1 Mile:	On The Tour	4	116	1:34-2/5	Nov. 10, 1999	1-1/4 m	Alysheba	4	127	1:58-4/5	Oct. 14, 1988
1 M 70 Yds	Conveyor	6	122	1:38-2/5	Dec. 9, 1994						

Turf Course

5 Furs.	Special Occasion	6	117	:55.17	Sept. 4, 2000	Abt. 1-70y	Pyrite Search			1:44.01	Oct. 24, 2002
Abt. 5 Furs.	Tangier Sound			:59.05	Nov. 4, 2002	1-1/16 m	Wanderkin	5	118	1:39-2/5	Sep. 30, 1988
1 Mile	Beckon the King	5	113	1:33.88	Oct. 19, 2001	1-3/8 m	Rice	6	126	2:12.00	Sept. 25, 1998
Abt. 1 Mile	Onasilverplatter	4	119	1:38.96	Oct. 23, 2002						
1 m70yds	Cape Playhouse	3	115	1:38	Oct. 25, 1978						

Jumps

Abt.2 Miles	Romeo Lima	4	140	3:43-3/5	Sep. 23, 1980

Leading Jockey in 2003: Charles C. Lopez, 31 wins.
Leading Trainer in 2003: Edwin Thomas Broome, 13 wins.
Record attendance: 44, 462, September 16, 1981. Record handle: $5,025,645 October 14, 1994

MONMOUTH PARK

New Jersey Sports and Exposition Authority
President & Chief Executive Officer: James A. Dieleuterio, Jr.; Senior Executive Vice President/Racing: Bruce Garland; Vice President/Thoroughbred Racing: Robert J. Kulina; Racing Secretary:Mike Dempsey; Director of Media Relations: Bill Knauf.

Monmouth Park, 175 Oceanport Avenue, Oceanport, New Jersey 07757
(732) 222-5100; Fax: (732) 571-8658; Publicity, (732) 571-5539
Free scratches & results: (732) 222-2917
E-mail: mpinfo@njsea.com; Web Site: www.monmouthpark.com
Nearest Airport: Monmouth County Airport, 12 miles from track; Newark International Airport, 40 miles from track; private heliport at Monmouth Park.

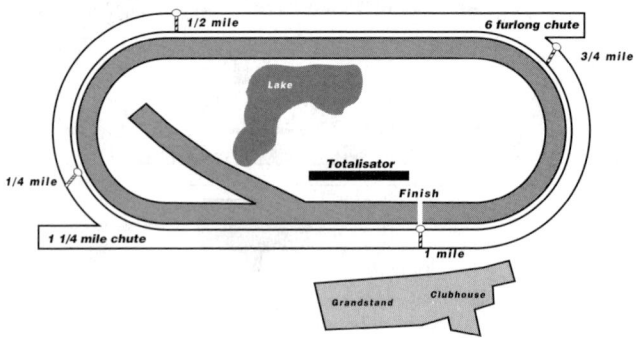

Track Data: One-mile oval, with six-furlong and 1 1/4-mile chutes. Distance from last turn to finish 985 feet; width in stretch 100 feet; backstretch 90 feet. Turf course, 7 furlongs; 90 feet wide, with diagonal chute. Steeplechase racing on turf course. Stable accommodations for 1,550. Seating capacity 18,000. Parking for 14,000.

Opened July 4, 1870 in nearby Long Branch, New Jersey. After being closed for five decades approaching the turn of the century due to state wide anti-gambling legislation, Monmouth was rebuilt in 1946 at its present location in Oceanport, where it has conducted summer racing every year since. In 2003, Monmouth Park had a 92-day meet with purses pegged at more than $315,000 per day, including its rich stakes schedule. The 2004 meet is set for May 29 through Sept. 5.

TRACK RECORDS

5 Furs.	L.B. on Tour	5	120	:56.16	Aug. 21, 1999	1 m70yds	Razzle Dazzle Rey	5	113	1:39-1/5	May 13, 1978
5-1/2 Furs.	American Royale	2	115	1:02-4/5	July 21, 1991	1-1/16 m	Formal Gold	4	121	1:40-1/5	Aug. 23, 1997
6 Furs.	Gilded Time	2	122	1:07-4/5	Aug. 8, 1992	1-1/8 m	Spend A Buck	3	118	1:46-4/5	Aug. 17, 1985
	Delaware Township	4	113	1:07-4/5	Aug. 27, 2000	1-1/4 m	Carry Back	4	124	2:00-2/5	July 14, 1962
1 Mile	Forty Niner	3	114	1:33-4/5	July 16, 1988	1-1/2 m	Chappys Joy	6	112	2:34-1/5	Aug. 5, 1989

Turf Course

5 Furs.	General Express	5	114	:54.60	July 8, 2000	1 1/16 m	Mi Narrow	5	113	1:39.40	July 11, 1999
Abt.5 Furs.	Klassy Briefcase	5	115	:56	June 20, 1990	Abt.1-1/16m	Kali High	7	115	1:41-2/5	June 11, 1993
	Se You In Court	4		:56	June 9, 1993	1-1/16 m	Mi Narrow	5	113	1:39-2/5	July 11, 1999
Abt.1 Mile	Crash Course	3	117	1:34-4/5	June 13, 1999	1-3/8 m	Balto Star	5	117	2:12.78	July 5, 2003
1 Mile	Double Booked	6	122	1:33-1/5	June 2, 1991	1-1/2 m	Agacode	4		2:29-2/5	June 14, 1985
Abt.1-1/16m	Bidding Proud	4	116	1:41-1/5	June 8, 1993	Abt.1-1/8m	Abduct	3	113	1:48-2/5	June 18, 1993
1-1/16 m	Furiously	4	119	1:39-3/5	July 10, 1993	1-1/8 m	Batique			1:46.19	June 6, 2001
Abt.1-7/8 m	Leaping Frog	3	138	3:46	Sep. 29, 1976	Abt.2-1/4m	Ninepins-GB	5	148	4:13-4/5	Sep. 7, 1992
Abt.2 Miles	Summer Colony	5	151	3:33-3/5	June 22, 1988						

Leading Jockey in 2003: Joe Bravo, 110 wins.

Leading Trainer in 2003: Mark Shuman, 50 wins

Record attendance: 47,127, August 5, 2001. Record handle: $11,407,470, August 8, 1999

MOUNTAINEER RACE TRACK & GAMING RESORT
MTR Gaming, Inc.

President & CEO: Edson Arneault; Racing Secretary: Joe Narcavish; Public Relations Director: Tamara Petit. Director of Racing: Rose Mary Williams

PO Box 358, Chester, WV 26034; 304-387-8300 Fax: 304-387-8303
E-Mail Address: info@mtrgaming.com; Web Site: www.mtrgaming.com

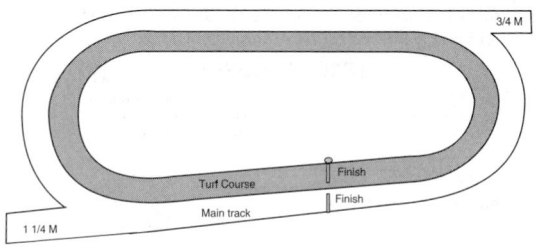

Track data: One-mile oval, with six-furlong and 1 1/4-mile chutes. Distance from last turn to finish 905.31 feet; width, 80 feet. Turf course: 7 furlongs. Stable accommodations for 1,234. Seating capacity 7,400.

Opened as Waterford Park May 19, 1951 when operated by the Charles Town Jockey Club. Renamed Mountaineer Park in 1987 and was a relatively obscure racing venue until slots were legalized in 1993. Live racing five nights a week now is conducted from January to December with extensive simulcasting and 3,220 slot machines on the premises that have boosted purses to more than $176,000 per day. Home of the Grade 3, $600,000 West Virginia Derby, the state's only graded stakes.

TRACK RECORDS

2 Furs.	Promised Cruise	6	120	:21.00	June 23, 1990	1-1/8 M	Soto	3	111	1:46.29	Aug. 9, 2003
4 1/2 Furs.	Baby Shark	5	120	:50.28	Aug. 9, 2003	1 3/16 M	Game Bird	7	115	1:56.66	May 17, 2003
5 Furs.	Mayor Steve	8	115	:55.92	Aug. 31, 2003	Abt.1-1/4 M	Grain	5	119	2:08	May 29, 1974
5 1/2 Furs.	The Dancer	4	121	1:02.24	Dec. 29, 2000	1-1/4 M	Georgie Porgie	4	114	2:03.3	Aug. 6, 1995
6 Furs.	Hustler	6	113	1:07.81	Aug. 11, 2001	1-1/2 M	Pete s Skianno	4	115	2:31.43	June 10, 2000
Abt.1 Mile	Mr. Pantop	4	116	1:36.20	June 26, 1970	1-5/8 M	Prince Swivel	7	119	2:45	Sep. 8, 1973
1 Mile	Find The Mine	5	114	1:33.86	July 4, 2000	1-3/4 M	Chased Again	9	115	2:58.4	July 18, 1959
1 M 40 yds.	Ski Sez	5	115	1:39.4	Mar. 9, 1996	Abt. 2 Miles	Dark Ajax	7	119	3:27.4	June 9, 1973
1 M 70 yds.	Mort	4	121	1:38.81	April 1, 2000	2 Miles	Pleasant Company	4	121	3:30.57	Sep. 1, 2003
1-1/16 M	Be Like Mike	4	110	1:41.15	Aug. 9, 2003	2-1/16 M	Sovereign M.D.	7	121	3:28.40	Dec. 30, 2000

Turf Course

4-1/2 Furs.	Cake N Steak	8	118	:50	Aug. 9, 1993	Abt. 1-1/4 m	King Haigler	5	120	2:09.3	July 4, 1983
Abt. 5 Furs.	Skindles Hotel	6	111	:55.1	July 26, 1960	Abt. 1-5/16 m	Ruff Mack	5	114	2:06	Aug. 25, 1962
5 Furs.	Fina Dur	5	121	:55.52	Sep. 6, 1999	1-3/8 M	Sunset Party	5	113	2:13.23	Sep. 26, 1999
7 Furs.	On to Richmond	4	121	1:21.40	June 16, 2002	Abt. 1-1/2 m	Revenooer	7	116	2:29	July 4, 1959
7-1/2 Furs.	Magical Madness	5	115	1:27.48	May 27, 2002	1-1/2 m	Guild Hall	5	135	2:33.1	June 20, 1969
1 Mile	La Reine s Terms			1:33.49	Sept. 2, 2002	1-3/4 m	Pleasant Company	4	112	2:55.99	Aug. 17, 2003
1 M70yds.	Fast And Friendly	8	121	1:43	Sep. 7, 1964	1-7/8 M	Code s Best	6	121	3:08.23	Sept. 4, 2000
	Poteau	7	120	1:43	July 25, 1982						
Abt.1-1/16 m	Black Eye	4	119	1:40.1	June 28, 1958						

Leading Jockeys in 2003: Deshawn L. Parker, won two of four meets and Dana G. Whitney won one; the remaining meet ended in a tie between Deshawn L. Parker and David J. McFadden.

Leading Trainers in 2003: Dale R. Baird won three of four meets and Scooter Davis won the remaining meet.

Record attendance: 17,934, – August 10, 2002. Record Handle: $2,513,911 – August 9, 2003

MOUNT PLEASANT MEADOWS

Oil Capital Race Ventures
President: Walter Bay; General Manager: Robert Berryhill; Racing Office Manager: Kimberly Devries. General Manager and Racing Office Manager: Robert Berryhill; Mutuels and Simulcast Dir.: Frank Pueschner
PO Box 220, Mt. Pleasant, MI 48858
(989) 773-0012

A mixed breed meet of 32 days spread out between May 3 and Sept. 28 in 2003, with a total of 48 Thoroughbred races and total Thoroughbred purses of $195,000. 2004 dates: May 1 through Sept. 26.

TRACK RECORDS

4 Fur.	Bad Boy Eric			:48.35	Aug. 25, 2001	5 1/2 Fur.	Comedy Routine	7		1:05.40 July 31, 1994
4 1/2 Fur.	Wildcat Express	4	126	:52.35	May 21, 2000	6 Fur.	Tate Express	11	126	1:13.78 Jun. 7, 2003
5 Fur.	My Friend Charlie	8		:59.30	June 29, 1991	1m 70 yds	Halover	7	126	1:51.61 Jul. 6, 2003

Leading Jockey in 2003: Julie Fritz, 8 wins.
Leading Trainer in 2003: Several trainers tied with four wins.

NORTHAMPTON FAIR

Three County Fair Association
Director of Racing: Stanley Stanisewski; Racing Secretary: Jack Bubolz; Racing/PR/Mkg. Director: Sandy Stanisewski.

Hampshire, Franklin & Hampden Agricultural Society
PO Box 305, Northampton, MA 01061-0305
413-584-2237 Fax: 413-648-5214

Track Data: Half-mile oval with banked turns. Distance from last turn to finish 431 feet; width, 50 feet. Stable accommodations for 450. Seating capacity 13,000.

Opened September, 1943 and annually conducts a nine or 10 day late summer meet in the Berkshire region of western Massachussetts. 2004 dates: Sept. 3 through Sept. 19; in 2003, purses averaged approximately $27,000 per day.

TRACK RECORDS

Abt.5 Furs.	Sweetest Music	6	117	:54-4/5 Sept. 2, 1957	Abt.1-1/8 m	Congress Inn	6	119	1:49-1/5 Sept. 10, 1966
Abt.6-1/2 F	Northern Puppy	4	122	1:20-3/5 Sept. 8, 1992	Abt.1-5/8 m	Boss Man Jarett	10	122	2:46.18 Sept. 13, 1999

Leading Jockey in 2003:Edgar Paucar and Willie Belmonte, 22 wins (tie).

Leading Trainer in 2003: Samuel J. Keyrouze, 6 wins.

Record attendance: 30,000 (estimated), September 4, 1972. Record handle to come.

NORTHLANDS PARK

Northlands Park
President: Gordon Wilson; General Manager: Les Butler Racing Secretary: Fred Hilts; Marketing and Communications Manager, Jason Douziech; Communications Coordinator: Jonathan Huntington
PO Box 1480, Edmonton, Alb, CAN T5J 2N5
780-471-7379 Fax: 780-471-7134, Free results line, 780-471-7223
Web Site: www.northlands.com; media relations: jhuntington@northlands.com

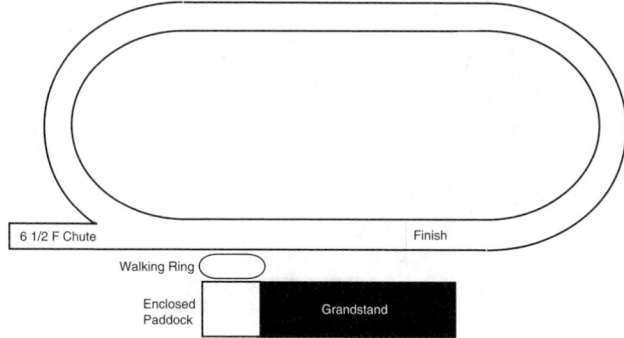

Track data: Five–eighths mile oval with 6 1/2-furlong chute. Distance from last turn to finish 625 feet; width 70 feet. Stable accommodations for 1,100. Seating capacity 9,000.

Opened July 1925 as Edmonton Racetrack, renamed Northlands Park in January 1964. Live racing from mid–June through October, plus extensive simulcasting. In 2003, the 74–day meet averaged purses of $111,000. 2004 dates: June 25 through Oct. 30.

TRACK RECORDS

3-1/2 Furs.	Steel Penny Black	2	115	:38-1/5	June 14, 1984	1-1/16 m	Chilcoton Blaze	4	119	1:42-3/5	Aug. 4, 1984
5-1/2 Furs.	So Long Fellas	5	115	1:04-2/5	Aug. 16, 1975	1-1/4 m	Arctic Laur	7	116	2:09	Aug. 20, 1995
6 Furs.	Lynn s Dream	4	115	1:09.80	July 8, 2000	1-3/8 m	Slyly Gifted	3	126	2:15-4/5	Aug. 30, 1986
6-1/2 Furs.	Timely Ruckus			1:15-2/5	June 26, 1999	1-5/8 m	Dancers Nugget	6	117	2:45.20	Sept. 21, 2001
1 Mile	Bagfull	5	115	1:35-4/5	May 16, 1981						

Leading Jockey in 2003: Quincy Welch, 97 wins.

Leading Trainer in 2003: Ron K. Smith, 46 wins

Record attendance: 15, 922, August 25, 1973; Record handle: $1,652, 940, August 16, 1990.

OAKLAWN PARK

Oaklawn Jockey Club
President: Charles J. Cella; General Manager: R. Eric Jackson; Racing Secretary: Patrick J. Pope; Media Relations Director: Terry Wallace; Director of Simulcast/Mutuels: Bobby Geiger.

Street Address: 2705 Central Avenue
Hot Springs, Arkansas 71901

Mailing Address: P.O. Box 699, Hot Springs, Arkansas 71902
(501) 623-4411 or 1-800-625-5296; Fax: (501) 624-4950
E-mail: winning@oaklawn.com; Web Site: www.oaklawn.com

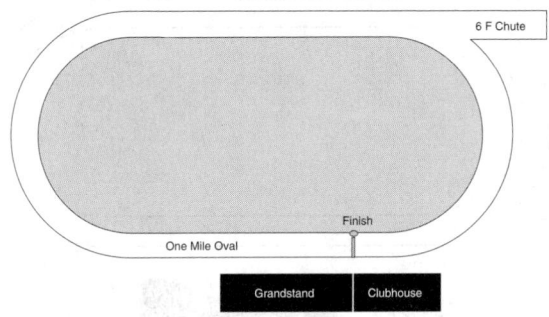

Track Data: One-mile sandy loam oval. Distance from last turn to finish, 1,155 feet; Width, 70 feet on straightaways, 80 feet on turns; Stable accommodations for 1,600. Seating capacity 26,200; Parking for 5,000 cars.

Built in 1904 and opened February 15, 1905, Oaklawn remains the number one tourist attraction in Arkansas. Purses in 2003 exceeded $228,000 per day and $11 million for the meet. The January - April meet annually concludes with the famed Racing Festival of the South, with over $2.6 million in purses for stakes events over a period of one week. Oaklawn offers three major products while it is open 12 months of the year. In addition to the live racing season, the simulcast season runs from May through January. Oaklawn also offers Instant Racing, the innovative pari-mutuel electronic gaming system, which has provided over $1 million in purses since it was introduced in 2000.

TRACK RECORDS

4 Furs.	Crimson Saint	2	119	:44-4/5	Apr. 1, 1971		Hang On Slewpy	4	119	1:40-1/5	Apr. 20, 1991
5-1/2 Furs.	Sis Pleasure Fager	4	115	1:02-3/5	Feb. 15, 1984	1-1/8 m	Snow Chief	4	123	1:46-3/5	Apr. 17, 1987
6 Furs.	Karen s Tom	3	120	1:07-4/5	Apr. 16, 1990	1-3/16 m	Brassy	5	112	1:57-2/5	Mar. 29, 1952
1 Mile	Whitebrush	3	119	1:34-2/5	Mar. 10, 1984	1-1/2 m	Dapper	6	111	2:31-3/5	Mar. 30, 1957
1 m70yds	Win Stat	7	112	1:38-2/5	Mar. 7, 1984	1-3/4 m	Flag Carrier	4	116	2:58	Apr. 18, 1987
1-1/16 m	Heatherten	6	116	1:40-1/5	Apr. 18, 1984						

Leading Jockey in 2003: Jamie Theriot, 71 wins.
Leading Trainer in 2003: Cole Norman, 71 wins
Record attendance: 71,203, April 19, 1986. Record handle: $15,133,537, April 15, 2000

OCALA TRAINING CENTER
TRACK RECORDS

5 Furs.	Hana Highway	5	122	:56.40	Mar. 17, 2003
6 Furs.	Lucky Livi	3		1:09.00	Mar. 20, 2000
1 1/16 m	The Name s Bond	3	122	1:44.20	Mar. 17, 2003

Leading Jockey in 2003: Edgar S. Prado, 3 wins.
Leading Trainer in 2003: No trainer won more than one race.

PENN NATIONAL RACE COURSE

Penn National Gaming Inc.

Peter M. Carlino, Chairman of the Board, President; Richard Orbann, President and CEO; Richard T. Schnaars, Vice-President and General Manager; Director of Publicity: Frederick D. Lipkin.

Street Address: Interstate 81, Exit 80
Grantville, Pennsylvania 17028
Nearest Airport: Harrisburg International,
15 miles from the track

P.O. Box 32, Grantville, Pennsylvania 17028
(717) 469-2211; Fax: (717) 469-2910. 717-469 0921
E-Mail Address: fred.lipkin@pngaming.com
Web Site: www.pnrc.com

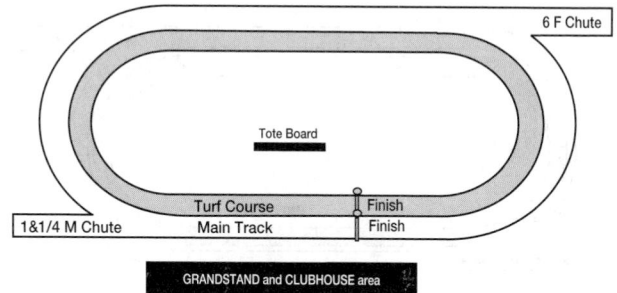

Track Data: One mile, sandy loam with 1/4-mile and 3/4-mile chutes. Distance from last turn to finish, 990 feet. Turf course: 7-furlongs. Stable accommodations, 1,200 horses. Seating capacity: 9,570, Parking for 5,000 cars.

Opened August 30, 1972, Penn National is located 12 1/2 miles Northeast of the Pennsylvania state capital of Harrisburg, Pa. In recent years, including 2003, Penn National has operated approximately 200 days from January to December with purses averaging more than $63,000 per day. But that is only a small part of the picture. In 1982, Penn National Gaming Inc. inaugurated telephone account wagering and soon afterward introduced cable television broadcasts of its races throughout the state. In the early 1990's the parent, public company was formed (Penn National Gaming, Inc.) and began to operate several OTB sites in Pennsylvania while expanding its horizons to own and operate Charles Town racetrack in West Virginia, Pocono Downs in eastern Pennsylvania, and other racing related enterprises and casinos in other states.

TRACK RECORDS

2 Furs.	Five Cousins	3	119	:21.11	Feb. 27, 2003	1 m70yds	Wee Thunder	6	115	1:39-3/5	July 13, 1996
4 Furs.	Gross	2	118	:46-1/5	Apr. 13, 1973	1-1/16 m	A Letter To Harry	4	117	1:41-1/5	Sep. 10, 1978
4-1/2 Furs.	Rita's Best			:50.67	Apr. 27, 2001	1-1/8 m	Collection Agent	4	121	1:49-4/5	Aug. 22, 1987
5 Furs.	On The Phone	4	117	:56-3/5	July 13, 1996	1-3/16 m	Bar Tab	8	114	1:55-2/5	Oct. 14, 1972
5-1/2 Furs.	Cortan	4	113	1:03-1/5	May 29, 1978	1-1/4 m	Adda Nickell	4	122	2:03-3/5	Oct. 30, 1976
	Flaming Emperor				June 26, 1994	1-1/2 m	Holly Holme	5	118	2:31-2/5	Sep. 29, 1973
	Hunter s Ridge				May 1, 1996	1 5/8m	New Episode	8	119	2:48.15	May 18, 2001
6 Furs.	Holiday Music			1:08.89*	May 4, 2002	1-3/4 m	Chasqui	7	119	3:00	June 21, 1980
1 Mile	Vambourine	5	122	1:36-1/5	June 12, 1977	2 Miles	Finny Flyer	6	111	3:28	May 25, 1974
	Agate Bay				Mar 22, 1981						

Turf Course

5 Furs.	Bop	5	121	54.61	Aug. 3, 2002	1-1/16 m	Told	4	123	1:38	Sep. 14, 1980
1 Mile	The Very One	4	110	1:33-1/5	July 15, 1979	1-1/2 m	Coalitioncandidate	5	113	2:27	May 27, 1991
1 m70yds	Aborigine	6	119	1:37-1/5	Aug. 20, 1978						

Leading Jockeys in 2003: David Cora won two of three meets and Thomas Clifton won the remaining meet.
Leading Trainer in 2003: Harry F. Thompson won all three meets.
Record attendance: 15, 442, April 19,1986. Record handle: $2,173,921, December 26, 1998.

PHILADELPHIA PARK

Greenwood Racing

Robert W. Green, Chairman and President; Harold G. Handel, Chief Executive Officer; Director of Phonebet and Player Services: Kimberly Smith; Director of Racing and Racing Secretary: Sal Sinatra; Simulcast Director: Geri Mercer; Director of Public Relations Keith Jones.

Street Address: 3001 Street Road   P.O. Box 1000, Bensalem, Pennsylvania 19020-2096

Bensalem, Pennsylvania 19020   (215) 639-9000; Fax: (215) 639-0337

Nearest Airports: Philadelphia Int l. 16 miles;   Marketing & Publicity: (215) 639-8330

Northeast (private) 3 miles   E-Mail: halhandel@philadelphiapark.com

       Web-Site: www.philadelphiapark.com

Track Data: One mile, sand, clay and loam, with 7-furlong and 1 1/4-mile chutes. Distance from last turn to finish, 974 feet. Width, 80 ft. Turf Course: 7/8 of a mile oval with 1 & 1/8 mile chute. 1,400 stalls. Seating capacity: 8,400; Parking for 5,500:

Opened November 4, 1974, as Keystone Racetrack, changed name in 1984 when acquired by Robert Brennan, owner at the time of newly rebuilt Garden State Park. who was forced out of the racing business in 1990 due to several failed racing related investments. Acquired by present owners Greenwood Racing, a British-based bookmaking operation which has upgraded the facility and stabilized its financial standing. In 2003, Philadelphia Park operated a total of 213 racing days, from January through December, with daily average purses in excess of $127,000 per day including stakes. Like Penn National Gaming, Philadelphia Park operates its own off-track betting parlors in Pennsylvania and telephone wagering accounts.

TRACK RECORDS

2 Furs.	Queen Millie	7	116	:21-1/5	Jan. 30, 1994	1-1/4 m	It s Always Archie	5	116	2:02	Nov. 23, 1974
4 Furs.	Heres A Tip	2	120	:45	June 11, 1982	1-1/2 m	Laugh a Minute	6	117	2:31	Jan. 4, 1992
4-1/2 Furs.	Distinctive Hat	4	114	:51-2/5	May 2, 1994	1-9/16 m	Laugh a Minute	6	122	2:40-4/5	Jan. 18, 1992
5 Furs.	My Favorite Grub	5	119	:56	Sep. 7, 1998	1 5/8 Miles	River Wolf	4	120	2:46-2/5	Oct. 13, 1990
5-1/2 Furs.	Saint Verre	2	118	1:02.65	July 17, 2000	1 3/4 Miles	Johnny s Silencer	3	109	2:57-4/5	Dec. 17, 1988
6 Furs.	Iron Punch	6	114	1:07.89	July 29, 2000	1 13/16 M	Fire North	6	111	3:04-4/5	Mar. 14, 1992
6-1/2 Furs.	Tricky Mister	4	117	1:14-2/5	June 21, 1998	1 7/8 Miles	Haberdasher	5	116	3:13-3/5	Oct. 17, 1987
7 Furs.	Flaming Bridle			1:20.61	Sep. 28, 1999	2 Miles	Perfect To A Tee	4	120	3:25-4/5	Sep. 2, 1996
1 Mile	Regal Count	3	116	1:34-4/5	Dec. 5, 1985	2 1/8 Miles	Heavy Medal Man	5	114	3:39-2/5	Apr. 25, 1992
1 m70yds	Tragedy	4	114	1:38-3/5	Dec. 12, 1995	2 1/4 Miles	Transfer Ticket	4	111	3:56	Dec. 31, 1988
1-1/16m	Cool Spring Park	3	109	1:40-4/5	Nov. 4, 1974	2-1/2 m	Half Chance	5	111	4:24	May 25, 1992
1-1/8 m	Selari Spirit	4	116	1:47	Nov. 30, 1974						
1-3/16 m	Southern Shade	5	113	1:56-2/5	Oct. 20, 1984						

Turf Course

Abt.5 Furs.	Devereux	7	119	:56.67	July 25, 2000	Abt 1-1/8 m	Brenton Reef	7	114	1:50-1/5	Aug. 6, 1989
5 Furs.	Lou s Bucks	4	117	:56	Sept. 20, 1998	1-1/8 m	Whatever For	4	113	1:46-1/5	Sep. 1, 1986
Abt.7-1/2 F.	Mount Bleu	3	109	1:33-3/5	Aug. 27, 1994	1-3/8	Juanca	8	117	2:16-2/5	Sep. 1, 1986
7-1/2 Furs.	Here Comes Scott	4	116	1:30-4/5	Sep. 10, 1994	Abt.1-3/8 m	Quality Affirmed	8	120	2:18.89	July 30, 2002
Abt.1 Mile	King Of Light	4	116	1:40	July 4, 1989	Abt 1-1/2 m	Mort the Sport	4	118	2:31	Aug. 22, 1989
1 Mile	Speak Compelling	3	107	1:39.60	July 24, 2000	1-1/2 m	Lord Zada	7	115	2:28.38	June 10, 2000
Abt.1m70yds	Vin Rouge	5	112	1:41-1/5	July 17, 1994	Abt 2 Miles	Proctor s Image	5	114	3:27-2/5	Oct. 15, 1988
1m70yds	Rolfe s Ruby	6	122	1:39-2/5	June 21, 1986	2 Miles	Chippenham Park	4	113	3:28-4/5	Sep. 1, 1990
Abt.1-1/16m	Mount Bleu	3	108	1:43-1/5	Oct. 4, 1994	Abt. 2-1/16 m	Valay Pass			3:42.54	Oct. 7, 2002
1-1/16 m	Whatever For	4	117	1:40-2/5	June 22, 1986						

Leading Jockey in 2003: Stewart Elliot, 235 wins

Leading Trainer in 2003: Scott A. Lake, 170 wins

Record attendance: 28, 692, May 30, 1983. Record handle: $2,283,057, February 21, 1998

PIMLICO

Magna Entertaiment Corp.

Frank Stronach, Chairman of the Board; Joseph A. De Francis, President and CEO; Lou Raffetto, COO; Karin M. De Francis, Executive Vice President; Georganne Hale, Racing Secretary; Mike Gathagan, Director Broadcast CommunicationsStreet Address: Hayward and Winner Avenues, Maryland Jockey Club, Pimlico Race Course
Baltimore, MD 21215
Nearest Airport, BWIA, 12 miles south on Washington Baltimore Parkway.

Baltimore, Maryland 21215
Telephone: (410) 542-9400; Fax: (410) 466-2521
Media Relations: (410) 466-5622
Free Results and scratches: 410/792-0278 and 301/470-1550
E-mail: webmaster@marylandracing.com Web Site: www.marylandracing.com

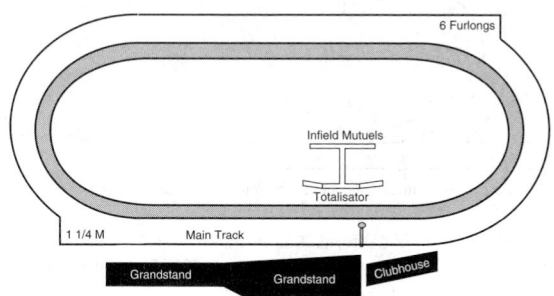

Track Data: One-mile oval with 6-furlong and 1 1/4-mile chutes. Distance from last turn to finish, 1,162 feet, 70 feet wide. Turf course: 7 furlongs. Stable accommodations for 670. Seating capacity: 25,000; total capacity 125,000 with infield on Preakness Day. Parking for 8,000 cars with many private lots in neighborhood. All seats reserved on Preakness Day, mail orders recommended.

Opened October 25, 1870, in Baltimore by the Maryland Jockey Club that was formed in May 1743, in Annapolis, Maryland. The MJC is the nation's oldest sporting organization and Pimlico is the second-oldest track in the United States. Home of the Grade 1 Preakness Stakes, the middle jewel in the Triple Crown, and the Grade 1 Pimlico Special. In 2003, purses during the spring meet averaged just under $260,000. 2004 dates: March 31 through June 6; Sept. 8 through Oct. 3.

TRACK RECORDS

4 1/2 Fur.	Countess Diana	2		:51.50	June 6, 1997	1 m70yds	Sabotage	3	117	1:41-2/5	Dec. 17, 1958
5 Furs.	Crossing Point	6	119	:56	Sep. 14, 2003	1-1/16 m	Deputed Testamony	4	123	1:40-4/5	May 19, 1984
5-1/2 Furs.	Season s Flair	2	119	1:03.40	July 25, 1995	1-1/8 m	Private Terms	4	122	1:47-1/5	May 27, 1989
6 Furs.	Xtra Heat			1:09.07	Aug. 18, 2001	1-3/16 m	Farma Way	4	119	1:52-2/5	May 11, 1991
	Northern Wolf	4	120	1:09.00	Aug. 18,1990	1-1/4 m	Manzotti	5	116	2:01-4/5	Mar. 19, 1988
1 Mile	June Grass	4	110	1:37-3/5	May 2, 1923	1-3/8 m	Narwal	5	120	2:16 2/5	Dec. 15, 1962

Turf Course

5 Fur.	Elberton	4	119	56.00	Sept. 15, 2001	1-1/16m	Air Attack	6	109	1:40-1/5	May 27, 1991
	Splendeed			56.10	May 25, 2002	1-1/8 m	Double Booked	6	118	1:47	May 17, 1991
1 Mile	North East Bound	4	115	1:33.42	May 7, 2000	1-1/2 m	Fort Marcy	6	124	2:27-2/5	May 9, 1970

Jumps

Abt 2 Miles	Age Of Flight	5	146	3:38-2/5	June 18, 1997	Abt 2-1/16m	Mihmaz	6	146	3:51	June 16, 1991

Leading Jockey in Spring meet, 2003: Ryan Fogelsonger, 62 wins.
Leading Trainer, Spring meet, 2003: Dale Capuano, 24 wins
Leading Jockey in Summer-Fall meet, 2003: Horacio Karamanos, 29 wins.
Leading Trainer in Summer-Fall meet, 2003: Dale Capuano, 18 wins
Record attendance: 118,926, May 19, 2001 (Preakness Day). Record handle: $7,357,961 (On track). $71,468,223, May 18, 2002 (all sources)

PLEASANTON

Alameda County Fair Agricultural Association
President: Tim Koopman; General Manager: Rick K. Pickering; Racing Secretary: Greg Brent, PR/Marketing Director: April Chase.

4501 Pleasanton Ave., Pleasanton, CA 94566
925-426-7600 Fax: 925-426-7621
E-Mail Address: jeanne@alamedacountyfair.com; Web Site: www.alamedacountyfair.com

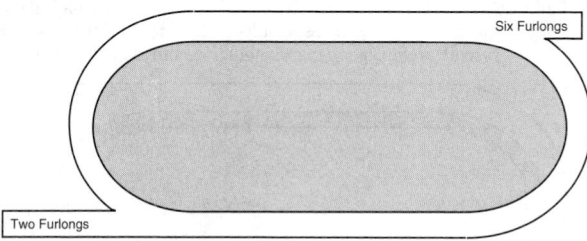

Track data: One-mile oval with two chutes, two furlongs and six furlongs. Distance from last turn to finish, 1085 feet, width 60 feet. Stable accomodations 700; seating capacity 6,808; Parking for 15,000 cars on county fair grounds.

Opened August 10, 1939. Part of the northern California County Fair circuit. Runs a two week mixed breed meet every summer and offered a purse structure in excess of $143,000 per day in 2003. Dates in 2004 are June 30 through July 11.

TRACK RECORDS

4-1/2 Furs.	French Invader	3	115	:51-1/5.	June 27, 1996	6 Furs.	Black Jack Road	8	118	1:08-1/5	July 10, 1993
5 Furs.	Czarina	2	116	:56-3/5.	July 2, 1997	1m-70yds	Call It	4	122	1:38.01	July 5, 2003
5-1/2 Furs.	Boundary Ridge	4	117	1:02	June 29, 1993	1-1/16 m	Aunt Sophie	5	117	1:40.34	July 5, 2003

Leading Jockey in 2003: Russell A. Baze, 18 wins.
Leading Trainer in 2003: William E. Morey, 7 wins.
Record attendance: 21,334–July 4, 1989; Record handle: $3,464,612 July 9, 1989 (includes Quarter Horse racing.)

PORTLAND MEADOWS

The New Portland Meadows, Inc.
President: Arthur L. McFadden; General Manager: Jeffrey L. Grady; Director of Racing & Racing Secretary: Jerry Kohls; Director of Simulcasting: Lynn Stokes.

1001 N. Schmeer Rd., Portland, Oregon 97217
(503) 285-9144; Fax: (503) 286-9763. Free results line: 503-790-2105
E-Mail Address: tnpm@portlandmeadows.com
Web Site: www.portlandmeadows.com

Track data: One-mile oval; with 3/4-mile and 1 1/4-mile chutes. Distance from last turn to finish 990 feet. Seating capacity 6,500.

Opened September 14, 1946, with the first night time racing in America, under direction of William P. Kyne who also built Bay Meadows. Rebuilt in 1971 after a devastating fire, The 'New Portland Meadows, Incorporated' operated the track since from 1991 for 10 years until Magna Entertainment Inc. acquired it in 2001. Live, mixed- breed racing now is the standard with $30,000 in Thoroughbred purses per day for its annual meet from October through April. 2003-04 dates: Oct. 18 to April 24.

TRACK RECORDS

4 Furs.	Wayne S.	2	120	:47	May 22, 1947	1-1/8 m	Hannibal Khal	4	119	1:48-4/5	Dec. 30, 1978
4-1/2 Furs.	Star Expresso	7	122	:51-4/5	Apr. 3, 1999	1-3/16 m	Kitsap Kid	6	121	1:58-2/5	Apr. 27, 1968
5 Furs.	Knight Cover		117	1:09.20	Apr. 26, 1997	1-1/4 m	True Enough	8	122	2:03-1/5	Apr. 9, 1994
5-1/2 Furs.	My Runaway	4	120	1:02-4/5	Jan. 6, 1977	1-1/2 m	Martins Lemon	4	116	2:32	May 13, 1973
6 Furs.	Lethal Grande	4	122	1:09.01	Mar. 30, 2003	1-3/4-m	Moribana	7	124	2:58-3/5	May 27, 1972
1 Mile	Star of Kuwait	7	122	1:36-1/5	May 11, 1975	2 Miles	Martins Lemon	4	120	3:27-3/5	May 20, 1973
1 m70yds	Beau Julian	3	120	1:41-1/5	May 14, 1972						
1-1/16 m	Me Brave	5	120	1:43-1/5	May 5, 1969						

Leading Jockey in 2003: Juan M. Gutierrez, 94 wins.
Leading Trainer in 2003: Jim Fergason, 43 wins.
Attendance record: 12,635, February 6, 1971

PRAIRIE MEADOWS

Prairie Meadows Racetrack and Casino
Robert Farinella, President, CEO, and General Manager; Derron Heldt, Director of Racing; Daniel Doocy, Racing Secretary, Thoroughbred meeting; Mike Jacobsen, Simulcast Coordinator; Mary Lou Coady, Media Communications.

Street Address: 1 Prairie Meadows Drive,
Altoona, Iowa 50009
Nearest Airports: Des Moines International,
(15 miles from track), Ankeny Aviation,
(private charter, 11 miles from track)

P.O. Box 1000, Altoona, Iowa 50009
(515) 967-1000 or (800) 325-9015
Fax: (515) 967-1344; Media, (515) 967-8247
Fax on Demand: 515-967-8576; Results Line: 515-967-8585
E-mail: webmaster@prairiemeadows.com
Web Site: www.prairiemeadows.com

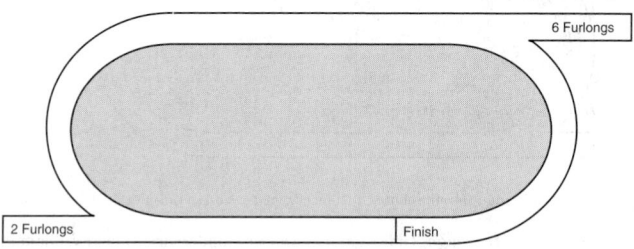

Track Data: One-mile oval, 6-furlong and 1 1/4-mile chutes. Distance from last turn to finish 1,033 feet. Stable accommodations for 1400. Seating Capacity: 7,000; Parking for 3,600 cars.

Opened March 1, 1989, and after suffering financial difficulties in the early 1990s has become one of the most successful tracks in the Midwest, with purses fueled by slots that were legalized in 1995. As usual, there were two meets involving Thoroughbreds in 2003, a 52-day thoroughbred season, beginning April 18, with a daily average purse structure in excess of $156,00 per day, and a mixed-breed session for 48 days from July 4 through Sept. 13, with a total of $11,881,250 in combined thoroughbred purses.

TRACK RECORDS

2 Furs.	Dashboard Drummer	2	117	:22.20	May 9, 2003	1 m70yds	Northwest Hill	5	123	1:39.69	July 4, 2003
4 Furs.	Straight Fever	2	117	:46-1/5	July 16, 1993	1-1/16 m	Excessivepleasure	3	122	1:40.82	July 5, 2003
4-1/2Furs.	Southern Alert	2	118	:51.24	May 7, 2002	1-1/8 m	Beboppin Baby	5	114	1:46-3/5	July 4, 1998
5 Furs.	Dayjob	5	114	:56	May 1, 1999	1-1/4 m	Famous Event	5	119	2:02-3/5	June 23, 1995
5-1/2 Furs.	Leaping Plum	6	122	1:02-2/5	Aug. 5, 1997	1-1/2 m	Famous Event	5	123	2:32	July 9, 1995
6 Furs.	Chindi	4	117	1:08-1/5	July 3, 1998	1-5/8 m	Sir Star	9	118	2:44-3/5	May 12, 1989
1 Mile	Apak	5	117	1:35	Aug. 11, 1998	2 Miles	Gritti Marco	6	114	3:26	July 28, 1995

Leading Jockey in early meet, 2003: Terry J.Thompson, 63 wins
Leading Trainer in early meet, 2003: Dick R. Clark, 41 wins
Leading Jockey in late meet, 2003: Glenn W. Corbett, 43 wins
Leading Trainer in late meet, 2003: Dick R. Clark, 36 wins
Highest Live Handle – On-Track: May 5, 1990 – $488,070 Highest Live Handle – Off-Track: June 2, 1999 – $1,658,931

REMINGTON PARK

Magna Entertrainment Corp.

Chairman: Frank Stronach; President: Corey Johnsen; General Manager: R. D. Logan; Director of Racing and Racing Secretary: Fred Hutton; Director of Media Relations and Marketing: Dale Day.

Nearest Airport: One Remington Place, Oklahoma City, Oklahoma 73111

Will Rogers World Airport, 12 miles   (405) 424-1000; Fax: (405) 425-3297; Press Box (405) 425-3221

Web Site: www.remingtonpark.com

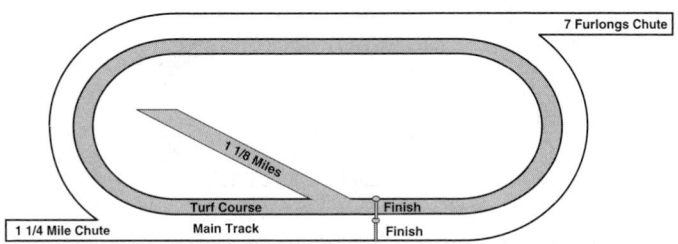

Track Data: One-mile oval, with a seven-furlong and a 1 1/4-mile chute that also is used for straightaway, 2-furlong Quarter Horse races. Distance from last turn to finish 975 feet. Stable accommodations for 1,340. Seating capacity: 8,300; Capacity 24,000. Parking for 6,000 cars.

Opened Sept. 1, 1988, by the DeBartolo corporation and acquired in 1999 by Magna Entertainment., Inc. Conducted 57 thoroughbred dates in 2003, with average daily purses of $71,000, as well as 25 days of mixed-breed racing. In 2004, there are 65 days of racing scheduled from July 30 through Nov. 28, with 28 days of mixed-breed racing scheduled for March 20 through May 31.

TRACK RECORDS

3 Furs.	Raisable Adversary	11	119	:31.20	Aug. 29, 1999	1 M 70 Yds	Marked Tree	3	117	1:39-3/5	Mar. 13, 1993
4 1/2 Fur.	Payday Two	8	117	:52.20	Feb. 26, 2000	1-1-1/16 m	Valid Bonnet	3	123	1:41-1/5	July 26, 1997
5 Furs.	Highland Ice	6	122	:57.20	Dec. 3, 1999	1-1/8 m	Classic Cat	3	124	1:48	Aug. 30, 1998
5-1/2 Furs.	Run Johnny	5	116	1:02	Sep. 6, 1997	1-3/16 m	Wild Rush	3	121	1:53-3/5	Aug. 10, 1997
6 Furs.	Smoke of Ages	5	115	1:08	Sep. 29, 1991	1-1/4 m	Double Platinum	4	117	2:03-2/5	Oct. 10, 1999
6-1/2 Furs.	Kangaroo King	4	119	1:14.40	July 26, 1997	1-3/8 m	Wild and Comfy	5	117	2:17.96	Oct. 18, 2002
7 Furs.	Golden Gear	4	114	1:20-2/5	Mar. 18, 1995	1-1/2 m	Bid the Zeal	4	122	2:31-2/5	Oct. 24, 1998
1 Mile	White Wheels	5	116	1:35-2/5	Aug. 17, 1997	2 Miles	Saavedra	7	114	3:26-4/5	Dec. 10, 1989

Turf Course

5 F (rail in).	Otro Mambo	8		:55.85	Oct. 5, 2001	1-1/16 m	Burbank	4	115	1:39-1/5	Aug. 30, 1997
5 F (rail out)	Dancin in the Park	6		:56.21	Oct. 13, 2000	1-1/8 m	Gauntlett Boy	3	114	1:47-4/5	Nov. 5, 1989
7-1/2 Furs.	Finally Tops	7	116	1:27-3/5	May 1, 1996	1-3/8 m	Vergennes	5	114	2:13.00	Sept. 3, 2000
1 Mile	No More Hard Times	6	118	1:33.80	Sep. 20, 1992	2 Miles	Big Notice	6	119	3:29	Nov. 20, 1993

Leading Jockey in 2003: Monte Clifton Berry, 100 wins.

Leading Trainer in 2003: Joe S. Offolter, 41 wins.

Record attendance: 26,411 February 29,1992. Record handle: $2, 808, 243, February24, 1990

RETAMA PARK

Retama Entertainment Group
Chairman: Joe Straus Jr.; Chief Executive Officer:BryanBrown;General Manager:Robert W.Pollock;Racing Secretary:Larry Craft; Public Relations Director: Doug Vair.

PO Box 47535, San Antonio, TX 78265-7535
210-651-7000 Fax: 210-651-7097
E-Mail: run@retamapark.com; Web Site: www.retamapark.com

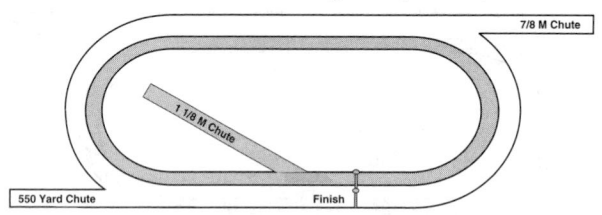

Track data: One-mile oval, with distance from last turn to finish 990 feet. 7 furlong turf course.

Opened April 1995. After financial difficulties that led to bankruptcy protection in 1996, it was acquired by present management in 2001...In 2003, held a 48-day meet from July 22 through Sept. 25 with purses averaging over $97,000 per day.

TRACK RECORDS

Dist.	Horse	Age	Wt.	Time	Date	Dist.	Horse	Age	Wt.	Time	Date
2 1/2 Furs.	Texas Hope	3	107	:28.20	June 28, 1998	7 Furs.	Wild Hawker	5	115	1:22	Apr. 9, 1995
4 1/2 Furs.	Raise a Tab	3	117	:51.06	Aug. 1, 1998	7 Fur.	Bucharest	5	120	1:22.05	May 24, 1995
Abt. 5 Furs.	Mne Glow	4	119	:56.20	Sept. 6, 2002	1 Mile	Paco Loco			1:34.66	
5 Furs.	Play The Jazz	5	115	:57.1	Aug. 23, 1998	1-1/16 m	Chauffe Au Rouge	5	120	1:40.99	Oct. 6, 2001
5 1/2 Furs.	Bailando	5	122	1:02.90	May 13, 1995	1-1/8 m	Fletchers Pride	5	116	1:51.43	Aug. 14, 1998
6 Furs.	Bucharest	5	117	1:08.82	May 10, 1995	1-1/4 m	Call Me Wild	6	120	2:04	Sep. 3, 1995
6 1/2 Furs.	Heavily Armed	5	123	1:15.30	Aug. 30, 1997	1-5/16 m	Opening Remark	7	114	2:13-4/5	Sep. 5, 1996

Turf Course

Dist.	Horse	Age	Wt.	Time	Date	Dist.	Horse	Age	Wt.	Time	Date
5 Furs.	Beach Heat	5	119	:55.69	Aug. 24, 2003	1 1/8 m	Fletcher s Pride	5	116	1:51.43	Aug. 14, 1998
7-1/2 Furs.	Call Me Wild	6	122	1:28.43	Sep. 17, 1995	1 1/4 mi.	Call Me Wild	6	120	2:04.01	Sep. 3, 1995
1 Mile	Eagle Lake	5	122	1:34.54	Oct. 4, 2003	1 5/16 m	Opening Remark	7	114	2:13.99	Sep. 5, 1996
1 1/16 m	Fly Slama Jama	5	115	1:40.79	Oct. 4, 2003	1-3/8 m	Point Click	4	119	2:18.09	Oct. 18, 2003
1-1/8 m	Untraceable	5	115	1:48.13	Aug. 10, 1996	1-13/16 m	Misting Rain	8	115	3:13.22	Sep. 28, 1996

Leading Jockey in 2003: Jeremy Beasely, 70 wins.
Leading Trainer in 2003: Danny Pish, 43 wins.

RILLITO PARK

Pima County Racing Horsemen s Association, Inc.
Public Relations Director, P.A. White .

PO Box 65132, Tucson, AZ 85728-5132
520-293-5011 Fax: 520-293-1287

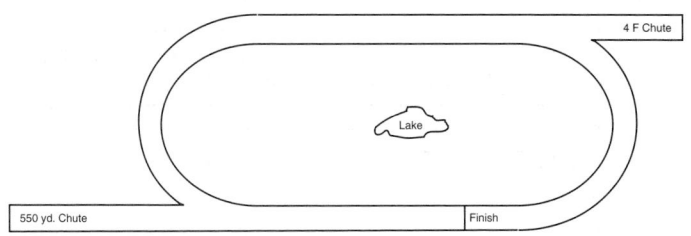

Track data: Five-eighths mile oval with 4 furlong and 6-1/2 furlong chutes. Distance from last turn to finish, 660 feet.

Opened, Nov.1,1953. A mixed breed meet for 14 dates between Jan. 18 and Mar. 2, 2003. A similar schedule is planned for 2004.

TRACK RECORDS

3 Fur.	Alice Be Gay	2	:36.00	March 2, 1974	6 Fur.	Turf s Bounty	5		1:10.20	Nov. 25, 1989
3 1/2 Fur.	Slow Dancing	2	:40.60	Mar. 22, 1981	Abt. 6 Furs.	Loomis Trail	5	124	1:20.00	Feb. 15, 2000
4 Fur.	Blushing God		:44.40	Feb. 3, 2001	6 1/2 Fur.	Club Champ	8		1:15.80	Feb. 18, 1996
5 1/2 Fur.	Cornino Bay		1:04.60	Feb. 4, 2001	7 Fur.	Stalk the Table	5		1:22.60	Jan. 29, 1994

Leading Jockey in 2003: Fernando Manuel Gamez, 17 wins.
Leading Trainer in 2003: Eddie Tellez, 8 wins.

RIVER DOWNS

River Downs Investment Company
President: Dr. J. David Rutherford; Chairman: John C. Hoover; General Manager: Jack Hanessian; Director of Racing and Racing Secretary: Ed Vomacka; Public Relations Director: John Engelhardt.

P.O. Box 30286, Cincinnati, OH 45230
513-232-8000 Fax: 513-232-1412
E-Mail Address: johne@riverdowns.com; Web Site: www.riverdowns.com

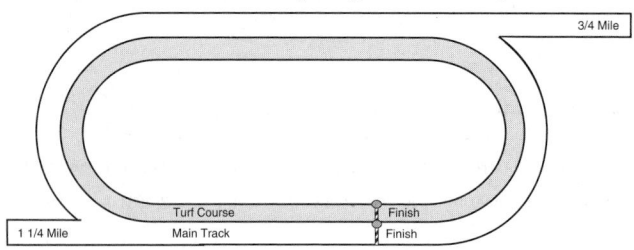

Track data: One–mile oval with six furlongs and 1 1/4–mile chutes. Distance from last turn to finish 1,117 feet, width 80 feet. Turf course: 7–furlongs. Stable accommodations 1,350. Seating capacity 11,000.

Opened July 6, 1925. Operates at least 120 live racing dates each year with 2003 purses at more than $55,000 per day and often offers seven races in tandem with Beulah Park as both tracks swap simulcast signals to complete a statewide 14-race program. The 2004 dates: April 9 through Sept. 6.

TRACK RECORDS

4-1/2 Furs.	Sans Terre	2	119	:52-2/5	May 24, 1971	1-1/8 m	Brown Sugar	3	114	1:49	Sep. 2, 1925
5 Furs.	Banker s Forbes	5	117	:57-3/5	June 7, 1994	1-1/4 m	Crusader	3	126	2:02	July 24, 1926
5-1'/2Furs.	Tazaua	4	120	1:03	Aug. 1, 1964	1-1/2 m	South Dakota	8	116	2:30-3/5	July 1, 1950
6 Furs.	Francine M.	5	124	1:08-3/5	July 4, 1969	1-5/8 m	Sada	8	115	2:45-3/5	Oct. 13, 1934
1 Mile	Alladin Rib	3	119	1:36-1/5	Aug. 8, 1988	1-11/16 m	Distribute	9	109	2:51-3/5	Sep. 7, 1940
1 m 70 yds	South Dakota	3	122	1:40	Aug. 4, 1945	1-3/4 m	Brigler	6	109	2:59-3/5	Oct. 19, 1940
1-1/16 m	Irish Dude	5	126	1:41-4/5	July 5, 1969	1-7/8 m	Shot Bills	7	113	3:26-3/5	Aug. 19, 1979

Turf Course

4-1/2 Furs.	Adena	4	110	:50-4/5	May 26, 1977	1-3/8 m	Hi Rise	4	122	2:15.60	Aug. 15, 2000
5 Furs.	Hobbs	4	122	:56-1/5	Sep. 1, 1991	1-7/16 m	Dina s Pl ymate	11	120	2:25	Aug. 30, 1969
7-1/2 Furs.	Stormy Deep	3	117	1:28-2/5	Aug. 15, 1990	1-1/2 m	Rebel Thunder	4	116	2:28	June 28, 1996
1 Mile	Bad News Blues	3	119	1:34-1/5	July 23, 1994	1-7/8 m	Big Bettor	5	122	3:10-1/5	May 31, 1986
1-1/16 m	Franchise Player	5	112	1:40-3/5	June 12, 1994	2 Miles	Buteo	6	122	3:48-2/5	Sep. 3, 1990

Leading Jockey in 2003 spring meet: Perry Wayne Ouzts, 67 wins.
Leading Trainer in 2003 spring meet: James E. Morgan, 17 wins.
Leading Jockey in 2003 summer meet: Jeff Johnston, 58 wins.
Leading Trainer in 2003 summer meet: Joe Woodard and Jake S. Radosevich, 14 wins (tie).
Record attendance 13,768 May 30, 1956.

ROCKINGHAM PARK

Rockingham Venture, Inc.
President: Joseph E. Carney, Jr.; General Manager: Edward M. Callahan. Director of Publicity: Lynne Snierson.

PO Box 47, Salem, NH 03079
603-898-2311 Fax: 603-898-7163
E-Mail Address: track@rockinghampark.com; Web Site: www.rockinghampark.com

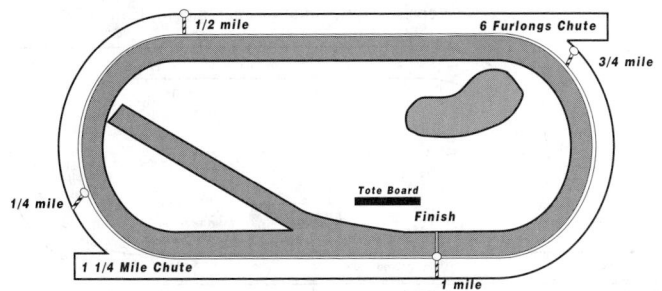

Track data: One-mile oval with 6-furlong and 1 1/4-mile chutes. Distance from last turn to finish 991 feet. Width of stretch 83 feet, backstretch 55 feet. Turf course: 7 furlongs. Stable accommodations: 1,600. Seating capacity: 8,000.

Opened June 28, 1906, rebuilt and reopened on May 26, 1984 after a fire destroyed the grandstand on July 29, 1980. Live racing during the summer of 2002, with purses in excess of $92,000 per day but there was no racing in 2003 and no meeting scheduled for 2004. Year-round simulcasting.

TRACK RECORDS

4 Furs.	Maria s Brown Eyes	2	118	:46-1/5	May 28, 1987	1-1/8 m	Dr. Fager	3	124	1:48-1/5	July 15, 1967
4-1/2 Furs.	Kipper Katz	2	118	:52-2/5	June 25, 1997	1-1/4 m	Dr. Fager	3	120	1:59-4/5	Sep. 2, 1967
5 Furs.	Sneaky Pal	2	118	:56-4/5	July 8, 1974	1-1/2 m	Girder	5	116	2:29-3/5	Oct. 10, 1953
5-1/2 Furs.	Bama Redd	6	122	1:03-4/5	May 21, 1987	2 m 40yds	Zagora	4	114	3:34-2/5	Sep. 2, 1985
6 Furs.	Dandy Blitzen	4	116	1:08-4/5	Aug. 29, 1959	2-1/4 m	Usable	5	114	3:58-2/5	Sep. 4, 1978
1 M 40 Yds	Zafarrancho	5	112	1:38-1/5	June 19, 1987	2-1/2 m	Bert Leo B.	4	115	4:23-3/5	July 5, 1978
1-1/16 m	Herbalist	5	114	1:42	Aug. 19, 1972						

Turf Course

1 Mile	Sword Princess	5	119	1:36.20	June 9, 2002	Abt 1-1/2 m	Padonia	5	122	2:23-1/5	Sep. 8, 1990
Abt1-1/16 m	A Taste For Lace	4	122	1:44-4/5	May 28, 1989	1-3/8 m	Autonomo	6	116	2:20-4/5	June 15, 1991
1-1/16 m	Simply Majestic	5	126	1:42-3/5	June 18, 1989	1-7/8	Hypnotizer	5	116	3:15-3/5	Aug. 19, 1989
	Paris Opera	4	117		July 4, 1990	Abt 2 Miles	Hypnotizer	5	119	3:32	Sep. 23, 1989
Abt 1-1/8 m	Inexplicable	5	114	1:45.04	June 24, 2000						
1-1/8 m	Calista			1:48.62	Aug. 4, 2002						

Jumps

Abt.2 Miles	Dawson	5	155	3:40	July 22, 1989

Leading Jockey in 2002: Josiah F. Hampshire, Jr. 104 wins.

Leading Trainer in 2002: Ronald J. Dandy, 66 wins.

Record attendance 41,509, September 6, 1965. Record handle $2,669,721, September 2, 1968.

RUIDOSO DOWNS RACE TRACK & CASINO

Ruidoso Downs Race Track & Casino
Chairman: R.D. Hubbard; President: Bruce Rimbo; General Manager: Rick Baugh; Racing Secretary: Robert Junk; Director of Marketing and Simulcasting, Neal Mullarky.

1200 Futurity Dr., Ruidoso Downs, NM 88346
505-378-4431 Fax: 505-378-8525
Website: www.ruidownsracing.com; E-mail Address: rdri@zianet.com

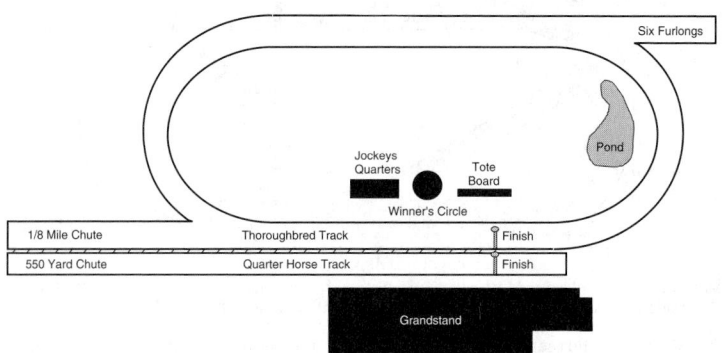

Track data: Seven furlong oval, with 6 furlong and 1-1/8 miles chutes. Distance from last turn to finish 656 feet; width 75 feet. Stable accommodations for 2,000. Seating capacity 7,000, parking for 14,000 cars.

Opened July 1, 1947 and has been the home of the All American Futurity, the richest Quarter Horse race in the world, with a purse worth approximately $2 million. In addition, Ruidoso also conducts about 300 Thoroughbred races during its 50-60 annual racing dates, from late May through Labor Day, when the All American is run.

TRACK RECORDS

4-1/2 Furs.	Bold Approach	2	118	:52.60	June 3, 1988		Strong Arm Robbery				Sept. 1, 2001
5 Furs.	Urlacher	4	119	:56.80	July 13, 2003	1 m-70yds	Brogander	4		1:45.20	Jan. 1, 1954
5-1/2 Furs.	Rocky Gulch	2	120	1:02.00	July 13, 2003	1-1/16 m	Lucky Bluff			1:43.80	Sept. 2, 2001
6 Furs.	Jack Wilson	4	120	1:08.80	Aug. 16, 1992	1-1/8 m	Run John	9	121	1:53.40	July 5, 1996
6 1/2 Fur.	Mr. Tattoo	4		1:17.60	July 4, 1973	1 1/4 mile	Pentelipiano	6	122	2:07.60	Sep. 1, 2003
7 Fur.	Fill Mackis Cup	6		1:24.40	July 15, 1984	1-3/8 m	Start Jumpin	8	122	2:24.20	Aug. 18, 1990
7-1/2 Furs.	Caliban	6	117	1:29.40	July 19, 2003	1-1/2 m	Decidedly Henry C. 6		115	2:37.00	Aug. 19, 1989
1 Mile	Set Records	4	121	1:37.00	July 28, 1995	1-5/8 m	More Than Glory	4	114	2:52.80	Aug. 15, 1992

Leading Jockey in 2003: Ricardo Jaime, 45 wins.
Leading Trainer in 2003: Henry Dominguez, 38 wins.
Record Attendance: 13,526 on September 4, 1999. Record Handle: $1,318,233 on September 4, 1999

SACRAMENTO

California Exposition & State Fair
CEO: Norbert Bartosik, Director of Racing: David Elliott; Racing Secretary: Grant Baker; PR Director: Sally Ash.

1600 Exposition Blvd. Sacramento, CA 95815
916-263-3283 Fax: 916-263-3198
E-Mail Address: delliott@caexpo.com; Web Site: www.bigfun.com

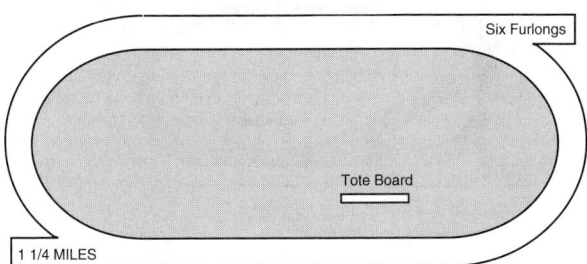

One mile oval, two chutes, six furlongs and 1-1/4 miles. Distance from last turn to finish 990 feet. Width of stretch 80 feet. Seating capacity 6,000; Parking for 12,000 cars on county fair grounds.

Opened September 2, 1935. Annually conducts mixed-breed race meets as part of the California Fair circuit in late August through early September. In 2003, purses were pegged in excess of $89,000 per day for its daily dose of seven-eight Thoroughbred races.

TRACK RECORDS

5 Furs.	Maui Lypheor D	6	116	:554	Sep. 3, 1990	1-1/4 m	Schuss II	7	121	2:01	Sep. 23, 1987
5-1/2 Furs.	Super Donna	4	116	1:01-2/5	Aug. 26, 1990	1-1/2 m	Classy Dame	4	107	2:31-4/5	Sep. 7, 1971
6 Furs.	Passing Game	8	121	1:07-3/5	Sep. 4, 1993		Nordic Chief	8	113	2:31-4/5	Sep. 4, 1979
1 Mile	Makaleha	4	116	1:33-3/5	Aug. 23, 1991	1-3/4 m	Money Buck	5	108	2:56	Aug. 30, 1987
1-1/16 m	Stan s Lad	3	122	1:40-2/5	Aug. 26, 1990						
1-1/18 m	Make Him Famous	4	112	1:46-1/5	Sep . 6, 1982						

Leading Jockey in 2003: Antonio Lopez Castanon, 10 wins.
Leading Trainer in 2003: Michael Lenzini and John F. Martin, 7 wins (tie).
Record attendance 18,722–September 1, 1975. Record handle $1,257, 787, September 7, 1981.

SAM HOUSTON RACE PARK

Sam Houston Race Park, Ltd.

Robert L. Bork, President and General Manager; Ann McGovern, Vice President of Operations; Racing Secretary: Eric Johnston; Director of Communications: Martha Claussen.

7575 North Sam Houston Pkwy. West, Houston, Texas 77064.

(281) 807-8700 or (281) 807-7223; Fax: (281) 807-8777

Press Box, (281) 807-8772.

Web Site: www.shrp.com.

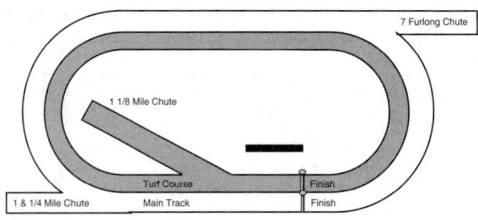

Track Data: One-mile dirt oval; 7/8-mile turf oval. Distance from last turn to finish, **966** feet. Stall accommodations for **1,250**; Seating capacity **14,000**, including simulcast pavilion; Parking for **6,000** cars.

Opened April **29, 1994** as the first Class-1, pari-mutuel track in Texas, home state for fabled King Ranch, but a state that had outlawed pari-mutuel wagering since the Depression. Built and owned by Houston businessman Charles Hurwitz's Maxxam Inc., Sam Houston racetrack suffered through two difficult seasons until Robert Bork was hired as general manager in **1995** and turned the program around with the help of legislative concessions that led to expanded simulcasting revenue and higher purses. In **2002–03**, there were **80** days of racing from late November to the end of March, with average daily purses including stakes of over **$200,000**. **2003–04** dates: Oct. **23** to April **10**.

TRACK RECORDS

4 1/2 Furs.	Angels Lady	2	115	:51.93	May 4, 1997		1 m70yds	Capt Tiff's Beau	5	116	1:40.52	Oct. 24, 1998
5 Fur.	Endofthestorm	4	118	:57.21	Oct. 25, 2003		1-1/16 m	Desert Air	4	124	1:42.74	Feb. 13, 1999
5 1/2 Furs.	Bucharest	6	118	1:02.92	April 13, 1996		1 1/8 m	Lost Soldier	7	120	1:48.75	May 3, 1997
6 Fur.	Bucharest	4	113	1:08.88	April 13, 1996		1 1/4 m	Sauvage Isn't Home	3	114	2:04.75	Dec. 29, 1995
6 1/2 Furs.	Brass Jacks	3	113	1:15.74	May 21, 1994		1-1/2 m	Final Val	5	119	2:32.99	Feb. 20, 1998
7 Furs.	Bucharest	6	118	1:21.29	May 4, 1996		1-3/4 m	Final Val	5	122	3:01.50	Mar. 13, 1998
1 mile	Please Sign In	4	116	1:36.21	Jan. 15, 2001		2 mile	Final Val	5	122	3:31.29	April 3, 1998

Turf Course

5 Fur.	Go Scotty	5	115	:56.93	Mar. 6, 1999		1-1/8 m	Chorwon	6	117	1:47.65	Mar. 6, 1999
1 mile	Mildred s Magic	4	116	1:33.19	Jan. 14, 2000		1-1/2 m	Commander Calhoun	5	116	2:32.56	Oct. 3, 1996
1-1/16 m	Luna Delight	4	116	1:43.24	Dec. 4, 1998							

Leading Jockeys in 2003: Donald Edward Simington and Terry A. Stanton, 75 wins

Leading Trainer in 2003: Steven M. Asmussen, 57 wins

Record attendance: 24,316, July 4, 2003. Record handle: $5,740,955 (Live, Host and Guest) – December 7, 2002; $5,083,955 (Live and Host) – December 7, 2002

SANTA ANITA PARK

A Magna Entertainment Corporation Facility. Los Angeles Turf Club, Incorporated.
Directors: Frank Stronach, Chairman; Vice President/General Manager: Chris McCarron; Director of Racing: Michael J. Harlow; Racing Secretary: Rick Hammerle.
Street Address: 285 W. Huntington Dr.
Arcadia, California 91007

P.O. Box 60014, Arcadia, California 91066-6014
(626) 574-7223; Telex: 675580
Fax: (626) 821-1514; Publicity, (626) 574-6682; Results (626) 446-8501
E-mail: sainfo@santaanita.com; Web Site: www.santaanita.com
Nearest Airports: Hollywood-Burbank, 15 miles. Private planes may land at nearby El Monte Airport.

Oak Tree Racing Association.
Same mailing, street address and Internet site. (626) 574-7223; Fax: (626) 446-9565; Marketing/ Publicity: (626) 574-5074; Executive Vice President: Sherwood Chillingworth; Racing Secretary: Mike Harlow, (626) 574-6472.

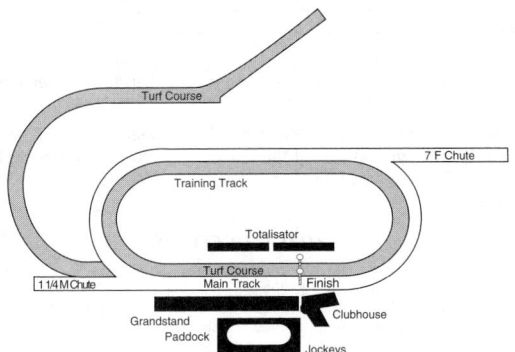

Track Data: One-mile dirt track with seven-furlong and 1 1/4-mile chutes. Distance from last turn to finish, 900 feet; width 85 feet. Turf course: 7 furlongs, plus the downhill chute, 1,408.45 yards from top of the hill to the finish. Stable accommodations for 2,000. Seating Capacity: 19,200. Total capacity with infield 85,000. Parking for 22,000 cars.
Opened December 25, 1934 and built by Charles H. Strub, after races had been conducted without pari-mutuel wagering on virtually the same site north of Los Angeles in the valley of the San Gabriel mountain range where a public one-mile course had been built by E. J. Baldwin in 1907. In more recent times, Santa Anita hosted the Breeders' Cup three times (1986, 1993 and 2003) during the fall dates leased by the Oak Tree Racing Association. During the track's regular winter-spring meet, it is home for the $1 million Santa Anita Handicap, the nation's oldest, continuously run $100,000 race. Santa Anita also features a European style, hillside turf course and was the site for 1984 Olympic Equestrian events...In December 1998, the track was purchased by Frank Stronach's Magna Entertainment, Inc. and Stronach has stated plans to expand the entertainment aspects of the facility. In 2003, Santa Anita had two meets, the 'Oak Tree' meet and regular winter-spring meet that annually begins on Dec. 26. Purses also are among the highest in the nation, pegged at an average of $450,000 per day in the spring and $836,000 at the Oak Tree meet, which included the Breeders' Cup card. Enhancing the Santa Anita experience are public workouts with breakfast served 7:30 to 9:30 AM on racing days at 'Clocker's Corner'; an infield playground with picnic areas for families and Tram Tours of the stable area on weekends.

TRACK RECORDS

2 Furs.	Beautiful Moment	2	118	:21	Apr. 3, 1996	7 Furs.	Spectacular Bid	4	126	1:20	Jan. 5, 1980
4-1/2 Furs.	Willy Float	2	118	:51-2/5	Mar. 23, 1972	1 Mile	Ruhlmann	4	118	1:33-2/5	Mar. 5, 1989
5 Furs.	Zero Henry	2	120	:57-3/5	Oct. 23, 1996	1-1/16 m	Efervescente	5	118	1:39	Jan. 6, 1993
5-1/2 Furs.	Kona Gold	5	119	1:01.74	Jan. 3, 1999	1-1/8 m	Star Spangled	5	117	1:45-4/5	Mar. 24, 1979
6 Furs.	Sunny Blossom	4	115	1:07-1/5	Dec. 30, 1989	1-1/4 m	Spectacular Bid	4	126	1:57-4/5	Feb. 3, 1980
6-1/2 Furs.	Son Of A Pistol	6	114	1:13-3/5	Apr. 4, 1998	1-1/2 m	Queen s Hustler	4	112	2:27-1/5	Feb. 19, 1973

Turf Course

Abt.6-1/2 f	Cayoke	6	117	1:11.45	Jan. 12, 2003		Bequest	5	117	1:57.50	Mar. 31, 1991
1 Mile	Atticus	5	117	1:31-4/5	Mar. 1, 1997	1-1/2 m	Hawkster	3	121	2:22-4/5	Oct. 14, 1989
1-1/16 m	Kostroma-Ir	5	117	1:43-4/5	Oct. 20, 1991	Abt.1-1/2 m	Practicante	6	118	2:26-2/5	Feb. 21, 1972
1-1/4 m	Double Discount	4	116	1:57-2/5	Oct. 9, 1977	Abt.1-3/4 m	Bienamado	5	122	2:42.96	Apr. 14, 2001

Leading Jockey SA 2002-2003 meet: Patrick Valenzuela, 94 wins. Leading Trainer SA 2002-2003 meet: Bob Baffert, 43 wins
Leading Jockey 2003 Oak Tree meet: Patrick Valenzuela, 34 wins. Leading Trainer 2003 Oak Tree meet: Doug O Neill, 22 wins.
Record attendance: 85, 529, March 3, 1985. Record handle: $17,171,465, October 25, 2003 (Breeders' Cup Day); $120,788,128, all sources (Breeders' Cup Day)

SANTA ROSA

Sonoma County Fair and Exposition, Inc.
President: Michael Murphy; General Manager: G. James Moore; Racing Secretary: Gregory Brent, Jr.;
PR Director: Larry Leathers.

PO Box 1536, Santa Rosa, CA 95402
707-545-4200 Fax: 707-573-9342
E-Mail Address: info@sonomacountyfair.com; Web Site: www.sonomacountyfair.com

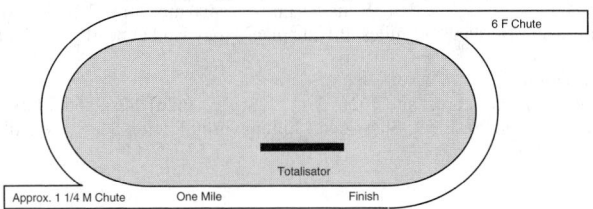

Track data: About one-mile oval (132.6 feet short of one mile), with two chutes, 6 furlongs and 1 1/4 miles, which also is used for two-fur-long straightaway races for Quarter Horses. Distance from last turn to finish 1,145.8 feet, width 80 feet, except for first turn, 60 feet. Stable accommdations 1,022. Seating capacity 8,181. Parking for 12,000 cars on the fairgrounds.

Opened October 8, 1936. Runs a picturesque, two week, mixed-breed meet in the heart of the northern California wine country during late July into early August as part of the Northern California fair circuit. In 2003, purses averaged in excess of $118,000 for the seven Thoroughbred races on the daily 12- and 13-race cards. Year-round simulcasting. 2004 dates: July 28 to August 9.

TRACK RECORDS

4-1/2 Furs.	Westwood Rhythm	5	117	:50.39	July 24, 2003	1 Mile	Magaki	3	115	1:34.40	July 26, 1984
5 Furs.	Valid Redress	5	117	:56.20	Aug. 1, 2003	1-1/16 m	Castle Tweed	4	114	1:39.80	Aug. 2, 1986
5-1/2 Furs	Truely Rude	6	114	1:02.20	Aug. 8, 1982	1-1/8 m	Diplomat Ruler	5	115	1:47.40	July 27, 1985
6 Furs.	Royalty	6	120	1:07.80	Aug. 4, 2000	Abt 1-1/4 m	River Lad	6	113	1:58.00	July 24, 1976

Leading jockey in 2003: Russell A. Baze, 23 wins
Leading Trainer in 2003: John F. Martin and Armando Lage, 8 wins (tie).
Record attendance: 19,208, July 28, 1990. Record handle: $1,056,543, August 8, 1987; $3,967,973, August 7, 1999, all sources.

SARATOGA RACE COURSE

New York Racing Association Inc.
Barry K. Schwartz., Chairman and CEO; Peter F. Karches, Vice Chairman; C. Steven Duncker, Vice Chairman; William A Nader, Senior Vice President; Racing Secretary and Handicapper: Michael S. Lakow; Director of Communications: Glen Mathes.

New York Racing Association Inc.	P.O. Box 564, Saratoga Springs, New York 12866.
P.O. Box 90, Jamaica	Street Address: Union Avenue, Saratoga Springs, New York 12866
New York 11417	(518) 584-6200; or 718-641-4700; Results: 900 443-1111
	E-mail: nyra@nyra.com; Web Site: www.nyra.com

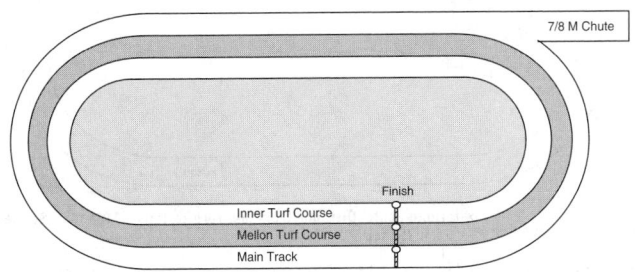

Track data: One and one eighth miles, oval, with a seven furlong chute. Distance from last turn to finish, 1,144. Width of main track **100** feet; Two turf courses: (A: One mile plus **98** feet, and (B: an inner course at 7-furlongs and **304** feet and both turf courses are used for steeplechase racing on a limited basis. Stable accommodations **1,825**; Seating capacity **10,000**, plus **12,000** outside benches; total capacity **65,000**. Parking for **4,000** cars, with many private lots nearby.

Opened August 2, **1864**, Saratoga Race Course is a National Landmark, the oldest track in America and one of the most spectacular and historic venues in the racing world. Located in picturesque Saratoga Springs in the Adirondack Mountains of upstate New York—where the Philadelphia Orchestra and the New York City Ballet are in summer residence–Saratoga Racetrack operates six weeks from late July to Labor Day, with an unmatched graded stakes menu. The 2003 stakes program included 36 stakes worth almost **$9** million and the high quality of racing was supported by average attendance of more than 29,000 fans per day and a total commingled handle of over $550 million. This pushed daily average purses to over **$600,000** per day...In 2004, the Grade 1 Travers for 3-year-olds will be run for the **134th** time on August 28. The dates for the 2004 meet: July 28 through Sept. 4...Please note that most reserved seats for all dates are sold out months in advance via mail.

TRACK RECORDS

Dist.	Horse	Age	Wt	Time	Date		Dist.	Horse	Age	Wt	Time	Date
5 Furs.	Fabulous Force	2	118	:56-3/5	Aug. 18, 1993		1-1/8 m	Left Bank	5	118	1:47.04	Aug. 3, 2002
5-1/2 Furs.	Mayakovsky	2	118	1:03.32	July 25, 2001		1-3/16 m	Winter s Tale	6	117	1:54-3/5	Aug. 21, 1982
6 Furs.	Spanish Riddle	3	113	1:08	Aug. 18, 1972		1-1/4 m	General Assembly	3	126	2:00	Aug. 18, 1979
6-1/2 Furs.	Topsider	5	115	1:14-2/5	Aug. 1, 1979		1-5/8 m	Green Highlander	5	117	2:43-2/5	Aug. 15, 1991
7 Furs.	Darby Creek Road	3	113	1:20-2/5	Aug. 8, 1978		2 Miles	James Boswell	5	116	3:26	Aug. 11, 1983
1 Mile	Key Contender	4	115	1:34-3/5	Aug. 9, 1992							

Turf Course

Dist.	Horse	Age	Wt	Time	Date		Dist.	Horse	Age	Wt	Time	Date
1-1-1/16 m	Fourstardave	6	115	1:38-4/5	July 29, 1991		1-5/8	Tom Swift	5	110	2:37	Aug. 23, 1978
1-1/8 m	Tentam	4	118	1:45-2/5	Aug. 10, 1973		2-1/16 m	Popular Victory	7	120	3:31-2/5	Aug. 23, 1979
1-3/16 m	Phi Beta Doc	3	118	1:51.61	Sept. 1, 1999							

Inner Turf Course

Dist.	Horse	Age	Wt	Time	Date		Dist.	Horse	Age	Wt	Time	Date
1 Mile	Delay of Game	6	122	1:33.67	Sept. 4, 1999		1-3/8 m	Babinda	4	114	2:12	July 26, 1997
1-1/16 m	Roman Envoy	4	119	1:39-4/5	Aug. 3, 1992		1-1/2 m	Awad	7	117	2:23-1/5	Aug. 9, 1997
1-1/8 m	Amarettitorun	5	115	1:46-1/5	July 26, 1997							

Jumps

Dist.	Horse	Age	Wt	Time	Date		Dist.	Horse	Age	Wt	Time	Date
1-5/8 m	Wasted Trip	4	149	2:55-3/5	Aug. 21, 1980		2-1/8 m	Wild Sir	8	148	3:55-3/5	Aug. 15, 1978
1-7/8 m	Coconut Creek	5	141	3:21	Aug. 14, 1980		2-1/4 m	Hokan	5	142	4:12	Aug. 27, 1998
2-1/16 m	Equistar	5	153	3:36.28	Aug. 22, 2002							

Leading jockey in 2003: John R. Velazquez, 61 wins.
Leading trainer in 2003: Todd A. Pletcher, 35 wins.
Record attendance: 77,337, August 17, 2003. Record handle: $9,390,934, August 23, 2003; $39,489,786, August 23, 2003, (all sources, Travers Day)

SOLANO
(Vallejo)

Solano County Fair Association
President: Rebecca Barnes-Lipman; General Manager: Kim Myrman; Racing Secretary: Greg Brent
900 Fairgrounds Drive, Vallejo, CA 94589
Phone: 707-644-4401 Fax: 707-642-7947
E-Mail Address: sricks@scfair.org
Web Address: www.scfair.org

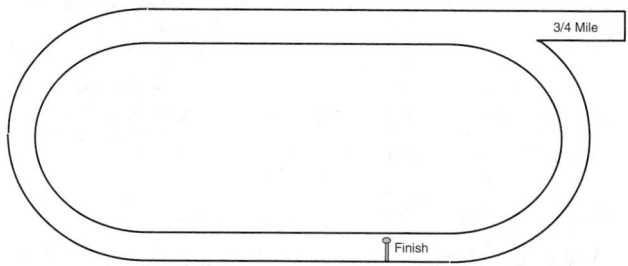

Track data: Seven-eighths mile oval, with six-furlong chute. Distance from last turn to finish, **1,085** feet. Stable accommodations for **1,004**. Seating capacity, **6,500**. Parking for **10,000** cars on the fairgrounds.

Opened June 16, 1951, annually runs a 10 day, mixed-breed summer meet in Vallejo, California on the northeastern corner of the San Francisco Bay as part of the Northern California fair circuit. In 2003, purses were in excess of $109,000 per day for seven-eight Thoroughbred races per day. Year round simulcasting. The dates for the 2004 meet: July 14 through July 25.

TRACK RECORDS

4-1/2 Furs.	Genuine Sparky			51.38	July 20, 2002	1-1/16 m	Hoedown s Day	5	113	1:39-4/5	July 24, 1983
5 Furs.	One Bad Shark	2	118	:56.60	July 14, 2002	1-1/8 m	Baffi s Eagle	7	114	1:48-2/5	July 17, 1984
5-1/2 Furs.	Ridgewood High	5	119	1:02-1/5	July 18, 1982	1-1/4 m	Super Sonet	5	113	2:03-2/5	June 20, 1974
6 Furs.	Salta s Pride	6	116	1:07-4/5	July 13, 1996	1-3/8 m	Rain Storm	6	119	2:15-4/5	June 22, 1973
1 Mile	Kamalii King	6	107	1:34-4/5	July 18, 1982	1-1/2 m	Always King	5	113	2:32-3/5	June 24, 1978

Leading Jockey in 2003: Russell A. Baze, 15 wins.
Leading Trainer in 2003: Jerry Hollendorfer, 8 wins.
Record attendance 18, 127, June 14, 1980.

STAMPEDE PARK

Calgary Exhibition & Stampede
President: Roger Jarvis; General Manager: Steve Edwards; Race Manager: Gail Poole; Racing Secretary: Barry McGrath; Marketing/PR Director: Patti Hunt; Senior Manager, Racing: Keith Marrington.

Box 1060, Calgary, Alberta, CAN T2P 2K8
403-261-0214 Fax: 403-265-7009
E-Mail Address: stpracing@calgarystampede.com; Web Site: www.stampede-park.com

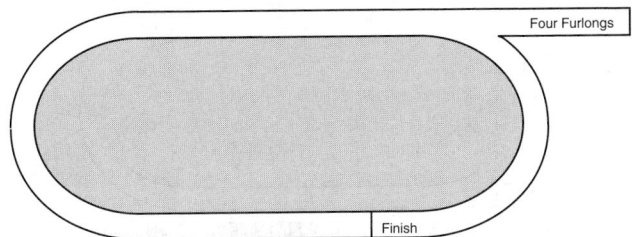

Track data: five-eighths mile oval, with a 4-furlong chute. Distance from last turn to finish, 660 feet; width 70 feet. Stable accommodations for 1,300. Seating capacity 17,800.

Originally opened as Victoria Park in July 1925, renamed Stampede Park in 1973. Current track and grounds rebuilt and reopened June 20, 1974. Runs a 40-50 day spring meet in most years and with a boost from slots, purses reached a new record of $104,000 per day in 2003.

TRACK RECORDS

3-1/2 Furs.	Wild After Dark	2	116	:39-3/5	June 2, 2000	1-1/16 m	Pilotson	7	115	1:42-1/5	Oct. 8, 1988
4 Furs.	Adventuresome Love	7	115	:43-4/5	Apr. 3, 1993	1-1/8 m	Steady Power	3	126	1:47-4/5	Sep. 19, 1987
5-1/2 Furs.	Malawi s Champ	5	108	1:03-4/5	Oct. 29, 1978	1-5/16 m	Postell Man	3	124	2:10-1/5	Oct. 18, 1986
6 Furs.	Classic Rock	3	120	1:09-2/5	Sep. 19, 1981	1-3/8 m	Two Ticky	4	123	2:16-1/5	Oct. 29, 1995
6-1/2 Furs.	Blue Bouncer	3	115	1:19-2/5	June 22, 1974	1-5/8 m	Whiskey Wisker	4	114	2:46-3/5	Oct. 25, 1987
7 Furs.	Edie s Prize	5	115	1:24	June 22, 1974	1-3/4 m	Jubal Tee	4	115	2:59	Nov. 9, 1981
1 Mile	Roll On Briartic	4	123	1:35-4/5	May 21, 1989	2 Miles	Grandin Park	9	118	3:29	Oct. 13, 1979

Leading Jockey in 2003: Quincy Welch, 44 wins.
Leading Trainer in 2003: Ron K. Smith, 25 wins
Record attendance: 6, 167, August 15, 1981.

STOCKTON

San Joaquin County Fair
2nd District Agricultural Association
President: Nanette Martin; CEO, Director of Racing: Forrest White; Racing Secretary: Robert Moreno; Public Relations Director: Lea Isetti.

1658 S. Airport Way, Stockton, CA 95206
Phone: 209-466-5041 Fax: 209-466-5739
Website: www.sanjoaquinfair.com

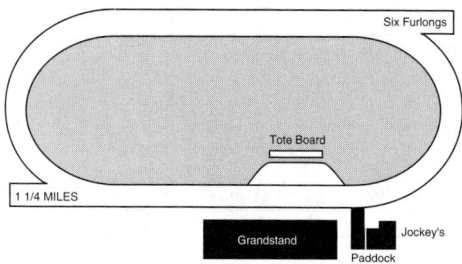

Track data: One-mile oval, with two chutes, 6 furlongs and 1 1/4 miles. Distance from last turn to finish 1,003 feet, width 80 feet. Stable accommodations for 756; Seating capacity 5,660.

Opened in the 1880's, but the first pari-mutuel meet was in August 1934...Runs a 10-day, mixed-breed meet in June as part of the Northern California Fair circuit with year-round simulcasting. Thoroughbred purses were pegged at about $77,000 per day. Dates for 2004: June 16 to June 27.

TRACK RECORDS

5 Furs.	Shining Prince	6	121	:55-4/5	June 26, 1994	1-1/16 m	Athenia Green-En	6	118	1:40-2/5	June 28, 1992
5-1/2 Furs.	Sandy s Era	3	117	1:02-1/5	June 14, 1997	1-1/8 m	Episodic	4	118	1:49-1/5	June 27, 1993
6 Furs.	Lynn s Notebook	4	117	1:07-4/5	June 25, 1995	1-1/4 m	Ali Kato	7	112	2:01-3/5	Aug. 17, 1986
1 Mile	Flying Cuantal	6	117	1:33-2/5	June 15, 1997						

Leading Jockey in 2003: Ken S. Tohill, 11 wins.
Leading Trainer in 2003: William E. Morey, 5 wins.

SUFFOLK DOWNS

Sterling Suffolk Racecourse LLC

Chairperson: Patricia Moseley; Chief Operating Officer: Robert O Malley; Assistant General Manager: Joseph Fatalo; Racing Secretary: Jim Pambianchi.

111 Waldemar Ave., East Boston, MA 02128
Phone: 617-567-3900 Fax: 617-567-7511
Web Site: www.suffolkdowns.com

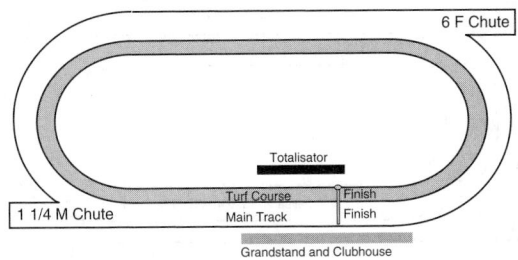

Track data: One-mile oval with six-furlong and 1 1/4-mile chutes. Distance from last turn to finish, **1,030** feet, width in stretch, **90** feet, width in backstretch **70** feet. Turf course: About 7 furlongs. Stable accommodations for **1,300**. Seating capacity **12,000**.

Opened in July 1935...Dates for 2004: 150-day meet, May 1 to Nov. 27. Year-round simulcasting.

TRACK RECORDS

2 Furs.	Adriano s Girl	2	120	:21 4/5	June 4, 1997	1-1/16 m	Talent Show	7	112	1:41 4/5	May 12, 1962
4 Furs.	Crimson Streak	2	120	:45 2/5	Apr. 6, 1970	1-1/8 m	Skip Away	5	130	1:47 1/5	May 30, 1998
4-1/2 Furs.	Lovely Gypsy	2	116	:51 4/5	May 7, 1965	1-3/16 m	Shut Out	3	126	1:55 2/5	July 4, 1942
5 Furs.	Rene Depot	3	124	:57 2/5	June 25, 1972	1-1/4 m	Helioscope	4	126	2:01	May 19, 1955
5-1/2 Furs.	Cocopet	2	113	1:04 3/5	July 17, 1943	1-1/2 m	Connie Rab	6	112	2:30 3/5	May 15, 1954
	Stage Trick	7	115	1:04 3/5	Jan. 14, 2001	1-5/8 m	Count Fire	4	113	2:45 2/5	June 23, 1962
	The Way Holme	3	123	1:04 3/5	Mar. 20, 2002	2 m70yds	On The Square	5	119	3:39 4/5	Apr. 16, 1973
6 Furs.	Canal	5	123	1:08 1/5	May 14, 1966	2-1/16 m	Bold Fencer	6	114	3:35 4/5	Apr. 18, 1983
1 Mile	Back Bay Brave	5	119	1:35 1/5	July 12, 1986	2-1/4 m	Fundy Bay	6	119	3:54 1/5	Dec. 9, 1973
1 m70yds	Half an Hour	7	117	1:40	Jan. 22, 1997						

Turf Course

Abt.5 Furs.	Bishop Ridley	7	118	:57 1/5	July 19, 1987	Abt.1-3/8 m	Gayb k Swan	5	110	2:20 4/5	July 18, 1970
Abt.7 1/2 F.	Times Ahead	6	116	1:32 2/5	Sep. 3, 1988	Abt.1-1/2 m	Akbar Khan	5	120	2:30 3/5	June 17, 1957
Abt.1 Mile	Diablo Reigns	5	119	1:39.35	Sep. 15, 2003	Abt.1-15/16 m	Jamf	9	112	3:11 1/5	July 4, 1975
Abt.1m70yds	Darn Special	6	113	1:42 2/5	May 31, 1997	Abt.2 Miles	Jean-Pierre	5	113	3:19 4/5	June 28, 1969
Abt.1-1/16 m	Landing Court	6	116	1:44 4/5	Oct. 26, 1994						
	Milky Way Guy	5	117	1:44 4/5	July 7, 2003						

Jumps

Abt. 2-1/4 m	Brigade of Guards	5	155	4:24 3/5	June 1, 1997

Leading Jockey in Winter-Spring-Summer meet, 2003: Josiah Francis Hampshire, Jr., 142 wins; Leading Trainer in Winter-Spring-Summer meet, 2003: Ronald J. Dandy, 79 wins
Leading Jockey in Autumn meet, 2003: Josiah Francis Hampshire, Jr., 24 wins; Leading Trainer in Autumn meet, 2003: Kevin Joy, 14 wins
Record attendance: 52,726, August 10, 1935 Record handle: $2,175,836, May 30, 1960. $5,867,414, May 31, 1997, Mass. Cap Day, (includes simulcasting)

SUN DOWNS

Tri-Cities Horse Racing Association

President: Maylon Cowgill; General Manager: Nancy Ann Sorick; Marketing/PR Director: Des Ritari.

PO Box 6662, Kennewick, WA 99336
509-582-5434 Fax: 509-586-9780

Track data: Five-eighths mile oval, with a **6 1/2**-furlong chute. Stable accommodations for **365**. Seating capacity **3,800**.

Opened September 12, 1981 and operated 10 days during in 2003 spread out between April 5 and May 4 A similar meet is scheduled for 2004.
Leading Jockey in 2003: David Deforest Brown, 8 wins.
Leading Trainer in 2003: A. Lynn Homer, 6 wins.

SUNLAND PARK RACETRACK & CASINO

My Way Holdings, LLC
President: Stan Fulton; General Manager: Harold Payne;Racing Secretary: Norm Amundson; Public Relations
Director: Eric Alwan   PO Box 1, Sunland Park, NM 88063
                                                                                        505-874-5200 Fax: 505-589-1518
                                                                        E-Mail Address: sunlandinfo@sunland-park.com.com
                                                                                        Web Site: www.sunland-park.com

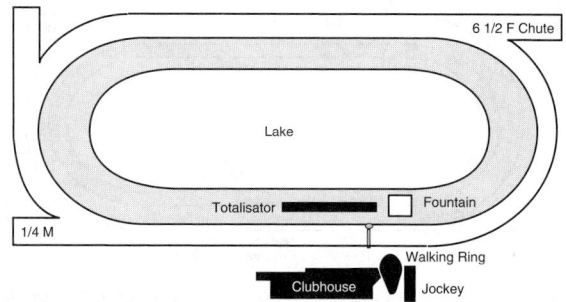

Track data: One-mile oval, with two chutes, 6 1/2 furlongs and 1 1/4 miles, which also is used for straightaway Quarter Horse races. Distance from last turn to finish, 990 feet; width 80 feet. Stable accommodations for 1,600. Seating capacity 5,710.

Opened Sept. 12, 1981 and typically holds a Winter–Spring meet from late November through early April...Bolstered by casino revenue, purses at Sunland were up to nearly $150,000 per day for the 2002–2003 meet. A similar meet is scheduled to run from Nov. 25, 2003, through April 11, 2004.

TRACK RECORDS

2 Furs.	Bekky s Star	2	115	:21-1/5	Feb. 12, 1968	1 Mile	Caliban	6	118	1:35.42	Feb. 16, 2003
3 Furs.	Sara Dier	2	118	:33-3/5	Mar. 31, 1962	1-1/16 m	Winsham Lad	6	120	1:42	Apr. 22, 1962
4 Furs.	Tamran s Jet	2	118	:44-4/5	Mar. 22, 1968	1-1/8 m	Winsham Lad	5	121	1:48-1/5	Jan. 8, 1961
4-1/2 Furs.	Bold Liz	2	118	:50-2/5	Mar. 19, 1972	1-3/16 m	Mickey J.	8	115	1:58-1/5	Nov. 14, 1970
5 Furs.	Draconic s Loom	4	112	:56-2/5	Jan. 13, 1980	1-1/4 m	Curribot	7	124	2:01-2/5	May 6, 1984
5-1/2 Furs.	Treasure Hunt	7	116	1:02.39	Jan. 28, 2003	1-3/8 m	Hot Deck	5	117	2:19-2/5	Jan. 10, 1970
6 Furs.	Pacer	4	120	1:08.36	Jan. 7, 2003	1-1/2 m	Houston Blaze	6	118	2:33-1/5	May 3, 1964
6-1/2 Furs.	Funny Meeting	4	118	1:14.84	Mar. 8, 2003	1-5/8 m	Rush Line	6	120	2:47-3/5	Apr. 6, 1969

Leading Jockey in 2003: Jorge Martin Bourdieu, 61 wins
Leading Trainer in 2003: Ramon O. Gonzalez, 42 wins

SUNRAY PARK & CASINO

Sunray Gaming of New Mexico LLC
    General Manager: Byron Campbell; Director of Racing/Racing Secretary: Hank Demoney; Director of Simulcasting; Toni Wright-Authurs.

39 Road 5568, Farmington, NM 87401
505-566-1200 Fax: 505-326-4292
Web Site: www.sunraygaming.com

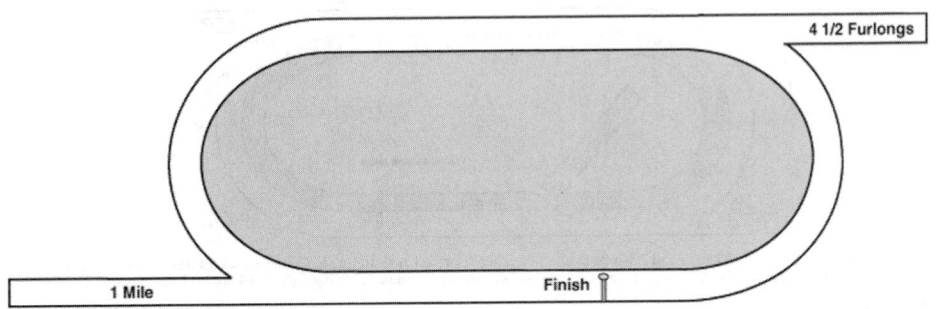

Track data: A six-furlong oval with two chutes, 4 1/2 furlongs and one mile.

Opened in 1984 and located in the northwestern corner of New Mexico, offered mixed breed racing on a limited basis with minimum financial success until closed in 1993. Reopened in 1999 with slot machines to boost purses and currently runs about 40 racing dates from August through November, with Thoroughbred purses over $70,000 per day. 2004 Dates: Aug. 2 through Sept. 7.

TRACK RECORDS

4 Furs.	Absolutely True	3	117	:44.60	Nov. 16, 2003	7 Fur.	Oh Gracie	5	119	1:22.60	Sept. 25, 2000
4 1/2 Furs.	Sky Diver	6	123	:49.80	Oct. 10, 2003	7 1/2 Fur.	Dalt s Kingpin	4	123	1:28.60	Nov. 17, 2003
6 Fur.	Unbridled Set	3	122	1:11.40	Oct. 11, 1999	1 Mile	Ben Told	6	118	1:35.60	Oct. 15, 2000
6-1/2 Fur.	Herecomesthemannow	3	116	1:15.60	Sep. 22, 2003	1 1/8 m	Line Gauge	6	118	1:48.80	Nov. 21, 1999

Leading Jockey in 2003: Casey T. Lambert, 38 wins.
Leading Trainer in 2003: John G. Arnett, 21 wins.

TAMPA BAY DOWNS

Tampa Bay Downs, Inc.

Stella F. Thayer, President and Treasurer; Peter N. Berube, Vice President and General Manager; Director of Racing: Robert Clark; Director of Public Relations: Margo Flynn.

Street Address: 11225 Racetrack Rd., Tampa, Florida 33626   P.O. Box 2007, Oldsmar, Florida 34677
Nearest Airport: Tampa International Airport, 8 miles from track.   (813) 855-4401; Fax: (813) 854-3539
                                               Web Site: www.tampabaydowns.com

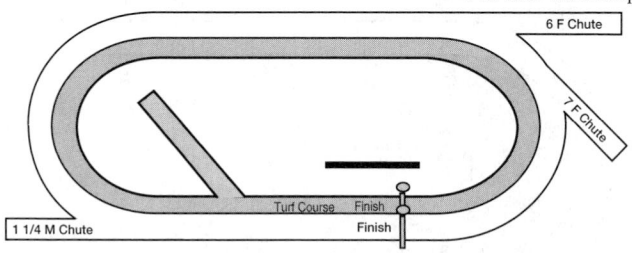

Track Data: One-mile track, 3/8-mile and 7/8-mile chutes; distance from last turn to finish, 976 feet; Turf Course: 7/8-mile with a 1/4-mile chute located inside main track. Stable accommodations for 1,400 horses. Seating Capacity: 6,000; Parking for 5,000 cars.

Originally opened as Tampa Downs on Feb. 18, 1926, the racetrack has amassed a long and colorful history. It was renamed Sunshine Park in 1947 and in 1965, the track was acquired by a group of Tampa sportsmen and renamed Florida Downs. Finally, in 1980, during another change in ownership, the track was renamed again as Tampa Bay Downs. Present ownership assumed the reins just prior to the 1986-1987 season and the facility has been in a state of constant improvement since. In 2003, Tampa Bay Downs launched a state of the art golf practice and wagering facility. The 2004 meet saw the debut of the Silks Card Room, a poker room operating during live racing days from noon to midnight. The 2004 meet also featured a new commingled record handle of over $4.2 million.

TRACK RECORDS

2 Furs.	Silver Dollar Boy	2	120	:21-4/5	Jan. 18, 1980	1-1/16 m	Sunny Prospector	6	119	1:43-2/5	Mar. 29, 1989
3 Furs.	Hot Star	2	117	:33-2/5	Feb. 14, 1980	1-1/8 m	Position Leader	4	122	1:50-3/5	Apr. 9, 1989
4 Furs.	Camp Izard	2	122	:46-4/5	May 1, 1993	1-3/16 m	Warning Flag	8	126	1:59-3/5	Jan. 25, 1986
4-1/2 Furs.	Geronimo J.	2	120	:52-4/5	Mar. 16, 1984	1-1/4 m	Finale Puer	6	119	2:07-2/5	Mar. 7, 1959
5 Furs.	Mr. Buffum			:57.28	Mar. 17, 2002	1-3/8 m	Rugged Zeal	6	120	2:20.68	April 23, 2002
5-1/2 Furs.	That Gift	3	122	1:03.20	Mar. 30, 2000	1-1/2 m	Royal Jacopo	6	118	2:33	Mar. 12, 1955
6 Furs.	Bootlegger s Pet	4	112	1:09	Jan. 26, 1974	1-5/8 m	Most Valiant	11	110	2:48-1/5	Mar. 29, 1997
6 1/2 Furs.	Special Insignia	5	118	1:17.05	Dec. 13, 2003	1-3/4 m	Our Day	4	119	3:00-2/5	Mar. 20, 1957
7 Furs.	Secret Romeo			1:22.62	Jan 22, 2002	2 m	Boss Man Jarett	10	118	3:30.30	April 24, 1999
1 m40yds	Mistum	5	113	1:41-1/5	Mar. 21, 1981						

Turf Course

Abt. 5 Furs.	Ozilda s Nancy Lee	3	112	:57.75	Apr. 21, 2003	1-1/8 m	Lilys Cousin	6	115	1:46.34	May 6, 2000
5 Furs.	Nicole s Dream	3	113	56.00	Mar. 16, 2003	Abt. 1 1/8 m	Cybil	5	115	1:48.48	Jan. 2, 2001
Abt.1 Mile	Mercedes Song	6	116	1:36-4/5	Jan. 12, 1999	Abt. 1-3/8 m	Fun n Gun	6	118	2:24.06	Mar. 30, 2002
1 Mile	Lucky J J	3	115	1:33.79	Feb. 12, 2000	1 3/8 m	Earnest Storm	5	123	2:17.40	Mar. 11, 2003
Abt.1-1/16m	Ben s Quixote	5	116	1:41.23	Dec. 28, 1999	Abt. 1-1/2 m	Top Senor	6	118	2:31.60	Feb. 26, 2002
1-1/16 m	Legs Galore	4	122	1:39-3/5	Feb. 20, 1999						

Leading jockey in 2003: Joseph C. Judice, 117 wins.
Leading Trainer in 2003: Don R. Rice, 43.
Record handle: $4,722,986, all sources.

THISTLEDOWN

Magna Entertainment Corp.
Frank Stronach, Chairman; Jim McAlpine, President & CEO; William D. Murphy, General Manager; William Couch, Director of Racing; Heather McColloch, Director of Communications; Director, Simulcasting: Greg Davis.

Street Address: 21501 Emery Road, North Randall, Ohio, 44128
Nearest Airport: Cleveland Hopkins International, 15 miles

(216) 662-8600; Fax: (216) 662-5339
E-Mail Address: info@thistledown.com
Web Site: www.thistledown.com

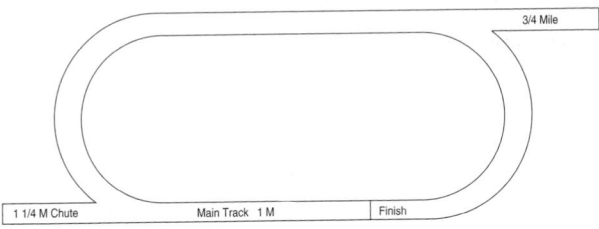

Track Data: One mile oval, six-furlong and 1 1/4 mile chutes; distance from last turn to finish, 978 feet; width 95 feet in the stretch, 75 feet backstretch. Stable accommodations for 1,400. Seating capacity: 6,400; Parking for 6,000 cars.

Opened July 20, 1925, and owned by the DeBartolo Corporation since 1959, Thistledown was acquired in 1999 by Frank Stronach's Magna Entertainment Corp., a spin-off of Magna International, Inc. Annually runs about 185 dates from March to December, plus extensive simulcasting. Note: The CRANWOOD, RANDALL and SUMMIT RACING CLUB race meets were incorporated into Thistledown's regular meet during the DeBartolo years at Thistledown. In 2003, purses were in excess of $59,000 per day. The dates for 2004: April 8 through Dec. 31.

TRACK RECORDS

2 Furs.	Onion Roll	7	111	:20-4/5	Sep. 27, 1993	1 m70yds	Wisdom Seeker	5	122	1:40-4/5	July 22, 1995
4 Furs.	What About Quin	2	118	:45.58	June 5, 2002	1-1/16 m	Entitled to Star	5	112	1:41-1/5	Nov. 25, 1995
4-1/2 Furs.	Onion Roll	6	118	:51-2/5	Nov. 20, 1992	1-1/8 m	Smarten	3	124	1:47-2/5	June 17, 1979
5 Furs.	Jet Bupers	7	118	:57-2/5	June 4, 1978	1-3/16 m	Smoke Screen	5	116	1:55-3/5	July 17, 1954
	Great Allegiance	5	116		May 18, 1997	1-1/4 m	Pert Near	6	117	2:03	Dec. 1, 1979
	Regal Diamond	5	116		Mar. 22, 1997	1-1/2 m	Martha s Wave	6	115	2:31-4/5	June 18, 1955
5-1/2 Furs.	Down Thepike Mike	4	116	1:03-1/5	Aug. 10, 1998	1-5/8 m	Alsang	3	101	2:46	Aug. 8, 1936
6 Furs.	Fancy Threat	5	115	1:08-2/5	Nov. 21, 1987	1-3/4 m	Mala Kee	4	116	2:57-3/5	July 17, 1957
1 Mile	Setting Limits	5	118	1:35-3/5	Nov. 19, 1989	2 Miles	Likely Advice	5	115	3:27	Dec. 15, 1980
1 m40yds	Ifthisbe Britches	5	116	1:38-3/5	Dec. 8, 1989	2 m70yds	Lonely Cloud	8	118	3:41-3/5	May 13, 1990
	North Island	4	119	1:38.60	Dec. 9, 1989	2-1/16 m	Bunker	8	112	3:32-4/5	July 13, 1955

Leading Jockey in 2003: Huber Villa-Gomez, 160 wins.
Leading Trainer in 2003: Rodney C. Faulkner, 101 wins.

TILLAMOOK COUNTY FAIR
Tillamook County Fairgrounds
Fair Board President and racing director, Mel Tupper. General Manager Jerry Underwood.

4603 E Third Street, Tillamook, Oregon.
503-842-2272
Website: wcn.net@tillamookfair
or tillamookfair@wcn.net for any racing information.

Runs a three day mixed-breed during August as part of the Tillamook County Fair with $14,000 in daily Thoroughbred purses. Total purses for the 20 thoroughbred races in 2003 was $42,000.

Leading Jockey in 2003: Victor V. Mercado, 9 wins.
Leading Trainer in 2003: Terry Lee Fergason, 3 wins.

TIMONIUM

Maryland State Fair & Agricultural Society, Inc.
F. Grove Miller, Chairman of the Board; Howard Max Mosner, Jr., President and General Manager; Racing Secretary: Georganne Hale

Street Address: 2200 York Road, Timonium, Maryland 21094

Mailing Address: Maryland State Fair, P.O. Box 188
Timonium, Maryland 21094
Telephone: Office and Track: (410) 252-0200
Free Scratch and Results: 410-792-0278 and/or 301-470-3056
E-Mail Address: msfair@msn.com; Web Site: www.bcpl.lib.md.us/~mdstfair
Nearest Airport: Baltimore-Washington International, 25 miles from track.

Track Data: Five-eighths mile, with 4-furlong and 6 1/2-furlong chutes. Distance from last turn to finish, 700 feet. Stable accommodations, 600. Seating capacity 4,800; Parking for 5,000 cars.

Opened September 1887, Timonium is operated by the Maryland State Fair & Agricultural Society, Inc. The 8-day Fair & Race meeting attracts more than 500,000 fans and concludes on Labor Day. Profits are for the Fair, 4–H Club awards and improvements.

TRACK RECORDS

4 Furs.	Ameri Brilliance	4	121	:43.76	Aug. 23, 2003	1 m70yds	One More Snooze	4	117	1:42	Aug. 31, 1984
Abt.6-1/2F.	Dontcloseyoureyes	5	119	1:15	Aug. 25, 1991	1-1/16 m	Valley Command	4	117	1:42-1/5	Aug. 28, 1990
6-1/2 Furs.	Weather Vane	3	122	1:16-3/5	Sep. 1, 1997	Abt.1-1/16m	Groom s Reckoning	4	117	1:49-1/5	Sep. 2, 1992
1 Mile	Count Off	8	113	1:36-4/5	Aug. 26, 1981	1-1/8 m	Count Disco	4	114	1:49-1/5	July 30, 1983

Leading Jockey in 2003: Travis L. Dunkelberger, 14 wins.
Leading Trainer in 2003: Dale Capuano, 6 wins.
Record Attendance: 17,306, September, 4, 1967. Record handle: $2,452,514, August 29, 1998

TURF PARADISE

Turf Paradise, Inc.
President and General Manager: Randy Fozzard; Racing Secretary: Shawn Swartz; Director of Marketing: Vince Francia

1501 West Bell Road, Phoenix, AZ 85023
602-942-1101 Fax: 602-942-8659
E-Mail Address: webmaster@turfparadise.net; Web Site: www.turfparadise.com

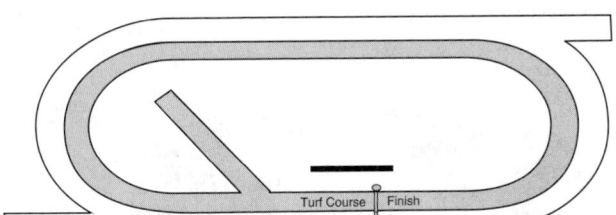

Track data: One-mile oval, with two chutes: 3/8 miles and 6 1/2 furlongs. Distance from last turn to finish, 990 feet. Width 80 feet in stretch, 70 feet in backstretch, 100 feet on turns. Turf course: 7/8 miles, with 1/8 miles infield chute. Stable accommodations for 1,700. Seating capacity 7,284.

Opened January 7, 1956 and after several ownership changes has consistently run an extended Fall–Winter–Spring meet of 160 or more days in recent seasons. During the 167-day session in 2002-2003, purses averaged more than $74,000 per day. Dates in 2004: Sept. 26, 2003 through May 16, 2004.

TRACK RECORDS

2 Furs.	Wandering Boy	6	118	:21-1/5	Dec. 5, 1965	1-1/16 m	Down The Isle	8	117	1:39-1/5	Feb. 11, 1987
3 Furs.	Never Shamed	2	118	:31-3/5	April 1, 1996	1-1/8 m	Our Forbes	6	116	1:47-3/5	Nov. 29, 1996
4-1/2 Furs.	Jazz Hot	2	115	:50.20	April 18, 1995	1-1/4 m	Truly a Pleasure	8	121	2:01-2/5	Mar. 26, 1995
5 Furs.	Zip Pocket	3	122	:55-2/5	April 22, 1967	1-3/8 m	Bloom N Character	4	114	2:15-2/5	Apr. 12, 1980
5-1/2 Furs.	Plenty Zloty	5	118	1:01.10	April 18, 1995	1-5/8 m	Masked Rider	6	119	2:44.40	Feb. 10, 2002
6 Furs.	G Malleah	4	120	1:06-3/5	April 8, 1995	1-3/4 m	Arsenal	7	121	2:55-2/5	Feb. 7, 1971
6-1/2 Furs.	G Malleah	3	116	1:13-4/5	Dec. 3, 1994	2 Miles	Vermejo	5	114	3:24	Apr. 20, 1969
1 Mile	Mr. Pappion	5	118	1:33-1/5	Jan. 30, 1993						

Turf Course

4 1/2 Furs.	Dan s Groovy	7	120	:49.26	Apr. 13, 2003	Abt.1-1/16m	Charging Pete	4	116	1:43-2/5	Apr. 21, 1998
Abt.5 Furs.	J. Zac	5	114	:57-4/5	Feb. 18, 1990	1-1/16 m	Caesour	5	120	1:40-2/5	Feb. 5, 1995
5 Furs.	Amersham			56.29	Feb. 2, 2002	Abt.1-1/8m	Flying Rebel	5	114	1:51	Mar. 28, 1997
Abt.7 Furs.	Faro	4	119	1:25-1/5	Nov. 23, 1986	1-1/8 m	Narghile	5	116	1:48	Feb. 1, 1987
7 Furs.	Bristolville	5	119	1:28.60	Nov. 3, 2001	Abt.1-3/8m	Doctor Trotter	6	121	2:16-4/5	Apr. 18, 1998
Abt.7-1/2F.	Balboa Park	4	119	1:30.40	Dec. 19, 2001	1-3/8 m	Free Corona	5	126	2:15.17	Apr. 27, 2003
7-1/2 Furs.	Briartic Gold	6	119	1:28.18	Apr. 13, 2003	Abt.1-1/2 m	Estonia	7	121	2:34	Apr. 5, 1997
Abt.1 Mile	Oblomov	5	121	1:37-3/5	Apr. 19, 1998	1-1/2 m	Senator McGuire	6	117	2:29-3/5	May 22, 1988
1 Mile	Prose	6	118	1:34.60	Mar. 27, 2001	Abt.1-7/8 m	Amapour	8	115	3:15-1/5	May 18, 1986

Leading Jockey in 2002-3: Esteban Angel Gomez, 146 wins.
Leading Trainer in 2002-3: Don J. Mills, 62 wins
Record attendance: 16,000 estmated, March 18, 1984

TURFWAY PARK

Turfway Park LLC.
President and CEO: Robert N. Elliston; General Manager/Director of Operations: Greg Schmitz;
|Racing Secretary: Richard S. Leigh; Director of Marketing/Communications: Brian Gardner.
Street Address: 7500 Turfway Road,   P.O. Box 8, Florence, Kentucky 41022
Florence, Kentucky 41042   (859) 371-0200, (800) 733-0200; Fax: (859) 647-4730
Nearest Airport: Greater Cincinnati Airport   Media Relations: (859) 647-4842
(2 miles from track)   E-Mail Address: info@turfway.com
                                                                  Web Site: www.turfway.com

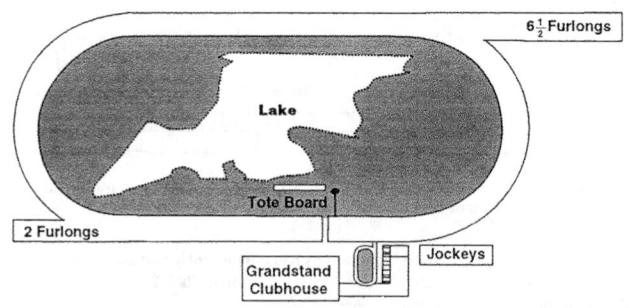

Track Data: One-mile oval with 6 1/2-furlong and 1 1/4-mile chutes. Distance from last turn to finish, 970 feet. Stable accommodations for 1,200. Seating capacity 8,000; Parking for 6,500 cars.

Opened August 27, 1959 and purchased in 1999 by Keeneland Association; Dreamport, Inc., a subsidiary of the GTECH Corporation; and Harrah's Entertainment Inc. Turfway operates three meets each year and is home to the $500,000 Grade 2 Lane's End Stakes, an early prep for the Kentucky Derby, and the Kentucky Cup Day of Champions, five stakes races (four graded) pointing toward the Breeders' Cup. 2004 race dates: Winter/Spring Meet, Jan. 1 through April 1; Fall meet, Sept. 8 through Oct. 7; Holiday Meet, Nov. 28 through Dec. 31. Lane's End Stakes: March 20.
Leading Jockeys, 2003: Rafael Bejarano won two of three meets and Jason P. Lumpkins won the remaining meet.

TRACK RECORDS

2 Furs.	Sizzling Lisa	2	108	:21-3/5	Apr. 2, 1979	1-1/16 m	Anet	3	115	1:40-3/5 Mar. 29, 1997
3 Furs.	Cut Glass	2	11	:34-3/5	Mar. 27, 1976	1-1/8 m	Hansel	3	121	1:46-3/5 Mar. 30, 1991
Abt. 5 Furs.	Blazing Genius	7	129	1:03.20	Aug. 30, 2003	1-1/4 m	Executor	7	117	2:03.82 Dec. 29, 2000
5-1/2 Furs.	Da White Judge	4	119	1:03-2/5	Sep. 29, 1979	1-1/2 m	Canive	4	115	2:31-2/5 Sep. 7, 1963
6 Furs.	Appealing Skier	3	118	1:08-1/5	Sep. 21, 1996	1-5/8 m	Bluegrass Warrior	6	115	2:46-3/5 Feb. 23, 1991
Abt6-1/2 F.	Billy Genn	3	113	1:19-2/5	Sep. 12, 1990	1-11/16 m	Sestos	9	116	2:56-1/5 Jan. 1, 1969
6-1/2 Furs.	Boone s Mill	3	120	1:14-1/5	Dec. 30, 1995	1-3/4 m	Bluegrass Warrior	5	111	2:59 Mar. 10, 1990
1 Mile	Secreto s Hideaway	5	119	1:34	Mar. 5, 1994	2 Miles	Bluegrass Warrior	6	119	3:23-4/5 Mar. 30, 1991

Leading Trainer 2003: Bernard S. Flint won all three meets.
Record Attendance: 22,480, April 25, 2000. Record Handle: $3,223,778, April 2, 1994.

WALLA WALLA RACE TRACK

Walla Walla Fair & Frontier Days
President/Racing Secretary: R. F. Monahan; General Manager: Cory Hewitt.

                                    PO Drawer G , Walla Walla, WA 99362
                                        509-527-3247 Fax: 509-527-3259

WOODBINE

Woodbine Entertainment Group
Jake Howard, Honorary Chairman; David Willmot, Chairman and CEO; James Ormiston, Exec. Vice Pres.;
Steve Lym, Racing Secretary; Glenn Crouter, Vice Pres. of Media and Community Relations.

Street Address: 555 Rexdale Blvd.,
Toronto, Ontario, Canada, M9W 5L2
Nearest Airport: Lester B. Pearson Int l.,
3 kilometers from track

P.O. Box 156, Toronto, Ontario, Canada, M9W 5L2
(416) 675-6110; Fax: (416) 213-2129; Publicity: (416) 213-2122
Web site: www.woodbineentertainment.com;
e-mail: jss@woodbineentertainment.com

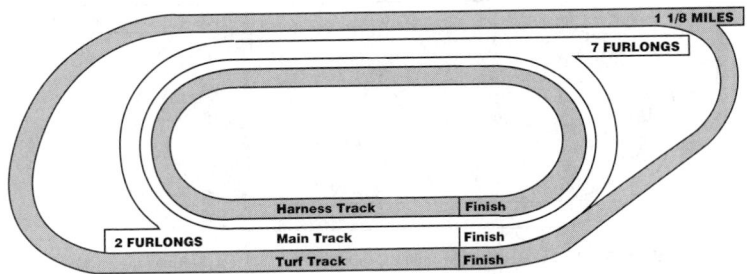

Track Data: One-mile dirt track, with two chutes, 1/4 mile and 7 furlongs. Distance from last turn to finish, 975 feet, width 85 feet in the stretch. Turf course: 1 1/2 miles. Distance from last turn to finish, 1,440 feet, width 100 feet. Also has 7/8-mile Harness track,. Stable accommodations for 1,650. Seating Capacity: 13,500; Parking for 14,700 cars.

The original Woodbine opened in 1874 on the far-eastern outskirts of Toronto, which became Toronto downtown. The name was changed to Old Woodbine in 1956 and Greenwood in 1963. The present facility opened on June 12, 1956. The E.P. Taylor Turf course, unveiled in 1995, is the only 1 1/2-mile grass course in North America and features the longest stretch run in American racing at 1,440 feet. It also rings the one mile dirt track, with a stretch run of 975 feet...In 1996, Woodbine became the first track outside the United States to host the Breeders' Cup and in 2003 with nearly 1,800 slot machines on site, purses for 162 racing dates were more than $550,000, to place Woodbine among the leaders in that category in North America. Dates for 2004: April 17 to Dec. 12.

TRACK RECORDS

3 Furs.	Noble Herod	2	115	:33-3/5	May 5, 1978	1-1/8 m	San Bom Way	6	116	1:47.80	Oct. 12 ,2002
4-1/2 Furs.	Hallmarked	4	118	:50-2/5	Mar. 24, 1996	1-3/16 m	Runnin Roman	3	114	1:55-4/5	Sep. 15, 1974
5 Furs.	Jack and Emma	4	118	:55.95	Apr. 5, 2003	1-1/4 m	Alphabet Soup	5	126	2:01	Oct. 26, 1996
5-1/2 Furs.	Uncle Woger	4	119	1:02.70	Apr. 4, 1999		Set Ablaze	4	109	2:01	July 5, 1996
6 Furs.	Chris s Bad Boy	6	118	1:08.05	Nov. 27, 2003	1-3/8 m	Lovely Sunrise	3	112	2:17	Oct. 26, 1974
6-1/2 Furs.	Fair Juror	4	105	1:14-3/5	Oct. 17, 1961	1-1/2 m	Norcliffe	4	122	2:29-1/5	Oct. 29, 1977
7 Furs.	Oronero	3	114	1:20-3/5	Dec. 6, 1995	1-5/8 m	Eugenia II	4	123	2:43-2/5	Oct. 27, 1956
1 m 70 Yds	Regal Courser	5	115	1:39-3/5	Aug. 8, 1998	1-3/4 m	Major Pots	5	115	2:52.60*	Dec. 8, 1994
1-1/16 m	Kiridashi	4	121	1:40-4/5	Aug. 17, 1996	*-World record					

Turf Course

6 Furs.	Spring Barley		121	1:07.63	Sept. 5, 2001	Abt 1-1/4 m	Desert Waves	5	117	2:02-2/5	June 24, 1995
6-1/2 Furs.	Free Agent on Ice	3	115	1:14.76	June 23, 2000	1-1/4 m	Arbalest	4	115	2:01	June 15, 1995
7 Furs.	Wild Zone	5	120	1:20-1/5	July 30, 1995	Abt 1-3/8 m	Chief Bearhart	3	109	2:16	July 25, 1996
1 Mile	Numerous Times	4	117	1:32.79	Sept. 9, 2001	1-3/8 m	Dawson s Legacy	4	114	2:13.05	Sept. 25, 1999
1-1/16 m	Jet Freighter	4	119	1:39-1/5	June 4, 1995	Abt 1-1/2 m	Mr. Lucky Junction	5	116	2:29-3/5	July 26, 1995
Abt 1-1/8 m	Diadella	4	115	1:43.60	Sept. 9, 2001	1-1/2 m	Raintrap	4	126	2:25-3/5	Oct. 16, 1994
1-1/8 m	Bold Ruritana	5	117	1:45-1/5	June 18, 1995	Abt 1-3/4 m	Moon Bow	6	114	2:46	Sep. 11, 1998

Leading Jockey in 2003: Todd Kabel, 160 wins.
Leading Trainer in 2003: Robert P. Tiller, 71 wins.
Record attendance: 42, 243, October 26, 1996, (Breeders' Cup Day). Record handle: $6, 884, 357 October 26, 1996: $67, 738, 890, October 26, 1996,
(All sources).

THE WOODLANDS

Kansas Racing, LLC
President: William M. Grace; General Manager: Jim Gartland; Racing Secretary: David Keiter; PR/Marketing Director: Connie Loebsack.

9700 Leavenworth Road
Kansas City, KS 66112-0036
913-299-9797 Fax: 913-299-9804
Web Site: www.woodlandskc.com
E-Mail Address: jmelarocca@aol.com;cloebsack@woodlandskc.com

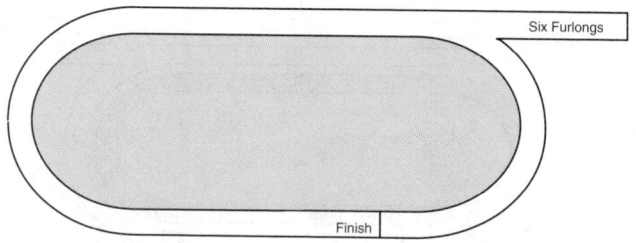

Track data: One-mile oval with 6-furlong chute. Distance from last turn to finish, 1,030 feet. Seating capacity 4,250.

Opened May 24, 1990 for Thoroughbred racing after a year of Greyhound racing which continues to be offered on a separate track in the Woodlands complex. Now runs a one month, mixed-breed meet in the fall with about $50,000 in daily purses. Year-round simulcasting. Dates for 2004: Sept. 21 to Oct. 30.

TRACK RECORDS

4 Furs.	King of Diamonds	5	119	:45.80	Oct. 10, 2001	1-1/16 m	Shatter the Stars	3	114	1:43	July 21, 1991
4-1/2 Furs.	Lanyons Star	2	117	:51-2/5	June 29, 1990	1-1/8 m	Model Age	6	119	1:49-4/5	July 18, 1990
5 Furs.	Tim Dougan	2	118	:57-4/5	June 30, 1991	1-3/16 m	Old Man s Delite	7	124	1:58.00	Oct. 21, 2003
5-1/2 Furs.	Axe Age	6	116	1:03-1/5	Aug. 15, 1993	1-1/4 m	Midway Mail	5	122	2:03-1/5	Sep. 10, 1993
6 Furs.	Great Immunity	4	116	1:08-2/5	June 30, 1991	1-1/2 m	He s a Valentine	4	116	2:33.20	Oct. 14, 1994
1 Mile	French Fritter	4	114	1:36	June 1, 1991	1-3/4 m	Mark of Strength	8	116	3:04-3/5	Sep. 26, 1993
1 m70 Yds	Holly s Wind	4	120	1:40-2/5	June 24, 1990						

Leading Jockey in 2003: Ken A. Shino, 36 wins.
Leading Trainer in 2003: Kenneth Butch Gleason, 17 wins.
Record attendance: 22,015, July 22, 1990

WYOMING DOWNS

Wyoming Horseracing, Inc.
President: Eric Nelson; General Manager and Director of Racing, Dale Parker; Coordinator of Racing Operations, Nina Earll; Director of Operations, Joan Ramos; Controller, Lorie Anderson
Physical Address:
10180 Highway 89 North
Evanston, WY, 82930
(866) 681-7223

Mailing Address:
PO Box 1607, Evanston, WY, 82931
(307) 789-0511; (Fax): (307) 789-9439
E-Mail Address: info@wydowns.com
Web Site: www.wyomingdowns.com

Track data: Seven and one-half furlong oval with two chutes: **6 1/2** furlongs and **550** yards for Quarter Horse and mixed-breed races. Distance from last turn to finish, **1,050** feet. Stable accommodations for **860**. Seating capacity **2,100**.

Opened May 25, 1985, and is scheduled for a summer meet in 2004 from June 19 to Aug. 15. Year-round simulcasting at off-track betting facilities located in Casper, Cheyenne, Evanston and Rock Springs.

TRACK RECORDS

4 Furs	Mister To You	2	122	:46-2/5	Sep. 1, 1991	1 Mile.	Rapt	5	122	1:36	Aug. 9, 1987
4-1/2 Furs.	Truly a Habit	7	124	:51.20	July 22, 2000	1-1/16 m	Running Razor	6	114	1:42-4/5	Sep. 3, 1990
5 Furs.	Briefly Noted	4	122	:56-2/5	Sep. 2, 1990	1-1/8 m	Mud Dancer	9	119	1:49-4/5	Aug. 22,1992
5-1/2Furs.	Beat the Latch	7	124	1:01.80	Aug. 21, 1999	1 1/4 Miles	Prowlin Time	5	122	2:13-1/5	Sep. 2, 1985
6 Furs.	Speed Fancier	4	124	1:08	Aug. 20, 1995	Abt.1 1/4 m	Lurky	6	122	2:03	Aug. 26,1990
7-1/2 Furs.	Become A Lord	6	116	1:29-3/5	July 14, 1990						

Leading jockey in 2003: Cody Foster, 10 wins.
Leading trainer in 2003: Mike D. Taylor, 9 wins.
Record attendance: 9,200 September 2, 1985. Record handle $324, 878, September 2, 1985.

YAVAPAI DOWNS

Yavapai County Fair Association
President: Robert Gray; General Manager: James M. Grundy; Racing Secretary: John Everly
PR/Marketing Director: Gary Spiker; Simulcast Coordinator: Donald Rogers

10401 Highway 89 A
Prescott Valley, AZ 86312-6557
(928) 775-8000 Fax: (928) 445-0408
Web Site: http://www.yavapaidownsatpv.com

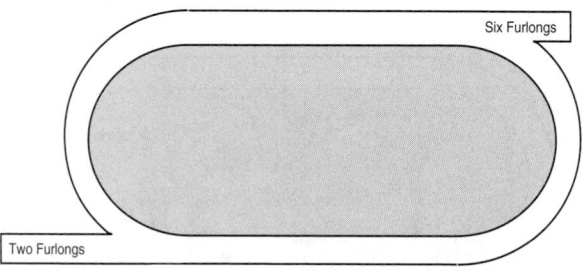

Track data: One-mile oval with 2-furlong and 6-furlong chutes. Distance from last turn to finish 1,020 feet.

Opened May 26, 2001... Located in Prescott Valley, Arizona, 15 miles from the old historic Prescott Downs. The 90-year history of racing in the area continues. The dates for 2004: May 29 though Sept. 2 with thoroughbred purses averaging $40,000 per day.
Leading Jockey in 2003: Estaban Angel Gomez, 72 wins.
Leading Trainer in 2003: Bill Brashears, 34 wins.

TRACK RECORDS

4-1/2 Furs.	Jomax	7	118	:50.40	Aug. 18, 2003	1 Mile	Heightenedinterest			1:35.01	June 3, 2002
5 Furs.	First Snowbound			56.60	June 23, 2002	1-1/16 m	Gusto Forzado			1:42.63	June 24, 2002
5-1/2 Furs.	Hemandan			1:02.36	Aug. 13, 2002	1-1/8 m	Moonray			1:49.40	June 25, 2002
6 Furs.	Miss Pixie			1:08.12	Aug. 24, 2002	1-1/4 m	Cajun Bound	5	126	2:03.20	Aug. 18, 2003

Record attendance: 35,000 – May 26, 2001. Record handle $1,386,000 – June 8, 2002.

YELLOWSTONE DOWNS

Yellowstone Horse Racing Alliance, Inc.
President: Jim Espy; General Manager: Ben Carlson; Racing Secretary: Norm Amundson; Marketing Director: Dan Fuchs

PO Box 1138, Billings, MT 59103
(406) 869-5251

Held 12 days of mixed-breed racing between Aug. 23 and Sept. 21 in 2003, with average daily Thoroughbred purses of almost $12,000. A similar schedule is planned for 2004 to run from Aug. 21 through Sept. 19.
Leading Jockey in 2003: David P. Stubblefield and Russell David Kingrey, 10 wins (tie).
Leading Trainer in 2003: Edward Buxbaum, 5 wins.

Mexico and Puerto Rico

CALIENTE RACETRACK
RACE & SPORTS BOOK
(Agua Caliente,)

MIR Services, Inc.
President: Arturo Alemany; Marketing Manager: Sergio Campos

121 Broadway, # 624, San Diego, CA 92101
Street address: Boulevard Agua Caliente, Tijuana, B.C. Mexico, 22420
619-231-1910; Fax: 619-231-1857
Mexico phone: 011-52-668-62001

Track data: One-mile oval with two chutes, six furlongs and 1 1/4 miles. Distance from last turn to finish line, 990 feet. Width of stretch 90 feet, backstretch 75 feet. Stable accommodations 1,500. Seating capacity 25,000.

Opened Dec. 28, 1929 and is most famous for the 1932 North American race in which the great New Zealand wonder horse Phar Lap ended his career with a victory before his untimely death. Also began the pick six betting format, with the '5-10' (fifth through 10th races) in the 1960's and future book wagering on the Kentucky Derby.

Record attendance, 36,112–May 26, 1963. Record handle $980, 856–March 13, 1977.

JUAREZ RACETRACK

Cesta-Punta Deportes, S.A. De C.V.
President: Carlos Sarabia; General Manager: Steve Sottero; Racing Secretary/SimDir: Jesse Quintana; PR/Marketing Director: Jesse Quintana

240 Thunderbird Dr. Suite C
El Paso, TX 79912
915-587-8304 Fax: 915-587-8382

EL COMMANDANTE
(Puerto Rico)

Hipodromo El Comandante
President: Juan M. Rivera; General Manager: Alejandro Fuentos; Director Public Relations, Press and Marketing: Nidnal Adrover.

El Commandante Management Co LLC
PO Box 1675, Canovanas, PR 00729
787-641-6060 Fax: 787-876-5170
Web Site: comandantepr.com

Track data: One-mile oval, with seven-furlong chute. Width of stretch 85 feet; width of backstretch 75 feet; distance from last turn to finish 900 feet. Stable accommodations for 1,200. Seating capacity 11,000; parking for 4,000 cars.

Opened November 17, 1976. Unsettled racing schedule, pending seasonal weather and other factors. Year-round simulcasting.

Record attendance: 20, 429, December 10, 1978.

RACING ORGANIZATIONS

NATIONAL AND STATE ORGANIZATIONS

INTERNATIONAL ORGANIZATIONS

THE AMERICAN STUD BOOK

Prominent Racing Organizations in North America

NATIONAL THOROUGHBRED RACING ASSOCIATION

NTRA is a tax-exempt membership organization and trade association, formed in 1998 to increase the popularity of Thoroughbred racing and improve economic conditions in the industry. NTRA member contributions, as well as funds from sponsorships and other marketing alliances, are reinvested in programs to grow the horse racing and breeding industries. That reinvestment takes many forms, including marketing, advertising, promotions, television, national consumer research, publicity, economic programs, sponsorship sales and legislative advocacy.

Three years after its founding, NTRA combined operations with Breeders' Cup Limited through a 10-year licensing and operating agreement under which the corporations retained their separate legal identities, Breeders' Cup programs were licensed to the NTRA to manage, and BCL personnel became NTRA employees. The result was one virtual corporation to generate new interest and participation in Thoroughbred racing and its culminating event, the Breeders' Cup World Thoroughbred Championships.

Since its founding, NTRA has developed several subsidiaries, which now include NTRA Productions, NTRA Investments, NTRA Purchasing and NTRA Charities, as well as the NTRA Creative Services program, an in-house marketing agency.

NTRA and Breeders' Cup operate under a single budget, with a combined staff headquartered in Lexington, Ky., and an office of media and sponsorships located in New York City.

2003 NTRA Board of Directors

The 15-member NTRA Board of Directors consists of the NTRA Commissioner and seven representatives each for racetracks and for horsemen, owners and breeders. For a complete listing of NTRA Directors visit the NTRA Web site, NTRA.com, or contact the NTRA at (800) 792-NTRA to request its current Annual Report.

NTRA Commissioner and Chief Executive Officer
Tim Smith

NTRA Commissioner since the organization's inception in 1998, Mr. Smith is the former Deputy Commissioner and Chief Operating Officer of the PGA TOUR.

NTRA Vice Chairman and Breeders' Cup President
D.G. Van Clief, Jr.

Mr. Van Clief assumed the role of NTRA Vice Chairman in January 2001 in addition to that of Breeders' Cup President. He is also a Breeders' Cup representative on the NTRA Board.

NTRA	NTRA
800 Third Avenue	2525 Harrodsburg Road
Suite 901	Fifth Floor
New York, NY 10022	Lexington, KY 40504
Tel (212) 230-9500	Tel (859) 223-5444
Fax (212) 752-3093	Fax (859) 223-3945

Internet: ntra.com
E-mail: ntra@ntra.com

THOROUGHBRED RACING ASSOCIATIONS OF NORTH AMERICA, INC.

Organization of member racetracks and racing associations that was created in 1942, to serve as a unified voice of the Thoroughbred racing industry, to work under a code of Standards and By-Laws. Mission statement: To place maximum emphasis on the integrity of racing and act with other parimutuel industries to promote legislation and provide assistance to member tracks in their relationships with State, Federal or Provincial legislatures. To provide statistical and informational services to all members and to assist in the promotion of racing. To co-sponsor annually, with the National Turf Writers Association and Daily Racing Form, the Eclipse Awards program. To recommend support for organizations and institutions, which engage in equine research, provide formal educational programs designed to produce racetrack management personnel and the protection and promotion of the entire horse industry.

To maintain liaison with other segments of the Thoroughbred industry, and with organizations and associations of other horse breeds. To explore possibilities of group insurance, printing, generic TV commercials, etc. To maintain a register of available part-time personnel such as racing officials, management, publicity, etc.

420 Fair Hill Drive,
Suite 1 Elkton, Maryland 21921-2573
Tel: (410) 392-9200
Fax: (410) 398-1366
E-mail: info@tra-online.com
Web Site: www.tra-online.com

Officers:
Joseph W. Harper, President
Corey S. Johnsen, Vice President
Robert L. Bork, Secretary
William F. Fasy, Treasurer
Christopher N. Scherf, Executive Vice President

Directors:
Don Amos, Magna Entertainment Corp.
Charles W. Bidwill III, National Jockey Club
Robert L. Bork, Sam Houston Race Park
Thomas F. Carey III, Hawthorne Race Course
Charles J. Cella, Oaklawn Park
Sherwood C. Chillingworth, Oak Tree Racing Association
Joseph A. De Francis, Pimlico
Steven Duncker, New York Racing Association
C. Kenneth Dunn, Calder Race Course/Tropical Park
Robert N. Elliston, Turfway Park
Robert A. Farinella, Prairie Meadows Racetrack & Casino
William Gallo, Jr., National Steeplechase Association
Bruce H. Garland, The Meadowlands
Clifford C. Goodrich, Arlington Park
Jeffrey Greco, Lone Star Park
Robert W. Green, Keystone Turf Club
Harold G. Handel, Bensalem Racing Association
Joseph W. Harper, Del Mar Thoroughbred Club
Phil Heard, Hastings Racecourse
Corey S. Johnsen, Magna Entertainment Corp.
Peter Karches, New York Racing Association
Bryan G. Krantz, Fair Grounds
Robert J. Kulina, Monmouth Park
Robert P. Levy, Atlantic City
Jim McAlpine, Santa Anita
Arthur L. McFadden, Portland Meadows
Hugh M. Miner, Jr., Fonner Park
Jerry M. Monahan, Colonial Downs
Richard B. Moore, Horsemen's Park
Howard M. Mosner, Jr., Timonium
Nick Nicholson, Keeneland Association
Richard E. Orbann, Mountainview Racing Association
Louis Raffetto, Laurel Park
William M. Rickman, Jr., Delaware Park

Baird C. Brittingham
Robert S. Gunderson
Lynn Stone

Former Presidents:
1942-1943 John C. Clark
1944-1946 Henry A. Parr III
1947-1948 James E. Dooley
1949-1950 Donald P. Ross
1951-1952 Alfred G. Vanderbilt
1953-1954 John A. Morris
1955-1956 Amory L. Haskell
1957-1958 James D. Stewart
1959-1960 John G. Cella
1961-1962 E. E. Dale Shaffer
1963-1964 Robert P. Strub
1965-1966 Edward P. Taylor
1967-1968 L. L. Haggin III
1969-1970 John D. Schapiro
1971-1973 James E. Brock
1973-1975 Frank M. Basil
1975-1976 Charles J. Cella
1977-1978 Baird C. Brittingham
1979-1980 Robert S. Gunderson
1981-1982 Lynn Stone
1983-1984 Morris J. Alhadeff
1985-1986 James E. Bassett III
1987-1988 Gerard J. McKeon
1989-1990 Robert P. Levy
1991-1992 Thomas H. Meeker
1993-1994 David M. Vance
1995-1996 Clifford C. Goodrich
1997-1998 Harold G. Handel
1999-2000 Stella F. Thayer
2001-2002 Bryan G. Krantz

THOROUGHBRED RACING PROTECTIVE BUREAU
A wholly owned subsidiary of TRA formed in 1946. Bureau of investigation and inter state security for the racing industry.

420 Fair Hill Drive, Suite 2
Elkton, Maryland 21921-2573
Telephone: (410) 398-2261
Fax: (410) 398-1499
E-Mail: trpbinfo@trpb.com
Web Site: http://www.trpb.com

Officers:
Paul W. Berube, President & Treasurer
James P. Gowen, Vice President & Secretary

Board Of Directors:
John E. Mooney - Chairman Colonial Downs
Bryan G. Krantz - Vice Chairman Fair Grounds
Paul W. Berube, TRPB

Robert L. Bork, Sam Houston Race Park
Charles J. Cella, Oaklawn Park
Sherwood C. Chillingworth, Oaktree Racing Association
Richard J. Crofts, Magna Entertainment Corp.
C. Kenneth Dunn, Calder
Christopher McErlean, Meadowlands
Terence J. Meyocks, NTRA
Nick Nicholson, Keeneland Association
Richard T. Schnaars, Penn National
Stella F. Thayer, Tampa Bay Downs

Equibase Company LLC.

Established in 1991 as a general partnership between the Thoroughbred Racing Associations of North America (TRA) and The Jockey Club, Equibase maintains the industry owned, Official database for North American racing. That database is the source material from which Daily Racing Form produces its result charts and comprehensive past performance lines.

821 Corporate Drive
Lexington, Kentucky 40503-2794
Telephone: (859) 224-2860 or (800) 333-2211
Fax: (859) 224-2811
www.equibase.com

Officers:
Chairman, Alan Marzelli
Secretary, Christopher N. Scherf

Management Committee:
Sherwood C. Chillingworth, The Jockey Club
C. Steven Duncker, The Jockey Club
Craig R. Fravel, Del Mar Thoroughbred Club
Alan Marzelli, The Jockey Club
Jim McAlpine, Magna Entertainment Corporation
Terence J. Meyocks, New York Racing Association
Nick Nicholson, Keeneland
Ogden Mills Phipps, The Jockey Club
Steve Sexton, Churchill Downs
Ray Tromba, Louisiana Downs
Michael Weiss, Beulah Park

Executive Staff:
Hank Zeitlin, Executive Vice President and Chief Operating Officer
Chuck Scaravilli, Vice President, Track and Field

Fred Russell-Grantland Rice TRA Sports Writing Scholarship

Begun in 1956, originally named to honor the late Grantland Rice, a Vanderbilt alumnus and one of the best known sports writers of the 20th century. In 1986, the name was changed to also honor Fred Russell, another Vanderbilt alumnus and columnist for the Atlanta Constitution who helped guide the scholarship and its recipients throughout his career. A $500,000 grant was made on behalf of the TRA in 1986 to ensure the future of this valuable stipend. The scholarship, worth $40,000 over 4 years of study, is co-sponsored by Vanderbilt. It is awarded annually to students with special interest and potential in the field of sports writing. The deadline for applying is January 1st each year. High school seniors may obtain a scholarship application form and further information from: Coordinator of Special Scholarships, Undergraduate Admission, Vanderbilt University, 2305 West End Avenue, Nashville, TN 37203-1727; (615) 322-2561.

Among previous winners were nationally prominent sports writers Roy A. Blount, Mill River, Mass, (1959) and 1970 Skip Bayless, Dallas, Tex. The last four winners were:

2000 Mathew James Meenan, McLean, Virginia
2001 Robert Craig Murray III, Brentwood, Tennessee
2002 Byron Patrick Dubow, Alphretta, Georgia
2003 Matthew Collins McDavid, Bethesda, Maryland

THE JOCKEY CLUB

The Jockey Club was originally formed as the Board of Control in 1891 and ratified its first charter as The Jockey Club, February 9, 1894. Through its 110 years, The Jockey Club has served as the official Thoroughbred breed registry for North America and with its family of companies, remains dedicated to the improvement of Thoroughbred breeding and racing. Responsibilities of The Jockey Club consist primarily of maintaining The American Stud Book in a manner that insures integrity of the Thoroughbred in the United States, Canada, and Puerto Rico. In 1996, The Jockey Club began to implement Interactive Registration™, a free service used by approximately 18,000 owners and breeders to fulfill the requirements for registration and naming of Thoroughbreds over the Internet, including submission of digital foal identification photos. The program includes an online 'Names Book' which puts users in direct electronic contact with The Jockey Club's database of names in active use. The Registry also replaced blood-typing with DNA-typing for Thoroughbred parentage verification, beginning with the 2001 foal crop. In addition, The Jockey Club founded Equibase Company in partnership with the Thoroughbred Racing Associations in 1990.

New York Office:
40 East 52nd Street,
New York, New York 10022
(212) 371-5970 Fax (212) 371-6123

Kentucky Office:
821 Corporate Drive
Lexington, Kentucky 40503-2794
(859) 224-2700 Fax (859) 224-2710
Web site: http://www.jockeyclub.com

Officers:
Ogden Mills Phipps, Chairman
William S. Farish, Vice Chairman
James C. Brady, Secretary-Treasurer
Alan Marzelli, President and Chief Operating Officer
Dan Fick, Executive Vice President and Executive Director
James S.J. Liao, Executive Vice President, Finance and Administration

Members:
Josephine E. Abercrombie, * Helen C. Alexander, Joe L. Allbritton, John Ed Anthony, Charles Baker, * John Barr, James E. Bassett III, Rollin W. Baugh, John A. Bell III, Reynolds Bell, Jr., James H. Binger, Gary Biszantz, Edward S. Bonnie, Frank A. Bonsal, Jr., * James C. Brady, Nicholas F. Brady, Larry Bramlage, Michael C. Byrne, Alexander G. Campbell, Jr., Thomas R. Capehart, Charles J. Cella, Mrs. Alice H. Chandler, Helen B. Chenery, Sherwood C. Chillingworth, Robert N. Clay, F. Eugene Dixon, Jr.,

THE JOCKEY CLUB INFORMATION SYSTEMS, INC. (TJCIS)

TJCIS, incorporated in 1989, is a wholly owned subsidiary of The Jockey Club. All profits from TJCIS activities are reinvested in the Thoroughbred industry, funding many industry projects which would otherwise lack financial support.

Operations of the multimedia information and service provider include equineline.com, the Internet-based information network for Thoroughbred and American Quarter Horse industry professionals; catalogue pages for North American Thoroughbreds sold at public auction; and software sales and consulting. Equineline.com features a portfolio service that allows owners and breeders to create a personal profile of their equine interests which can be updated with real-time information. The equineline.com web site also includes a 'trainer program' to help professional horsemen and their assistants streamline or automate the business-related details associated with training horses; and a 'farm program' to help farms organize all of the billing, health care, breeding and foaling records upon which successful operation of their business depends. In addition to its equineline.com services, TJCIS also offers Veterinary Management™ Software to help equine veterinary practices organize all of its health and billing records; and the Horse Farm Management HealthBook™, which enables farm personnel to collect and record reproductive and herd health information in the field through a lightweight Tablet PC.

821 Corporate Drive, Lexington, KY 40503
Toll free (800) 333-1778
(859) 224-2800. . .Fax: (859) 224-2810
http://www.equineline.com
Chairman & CEO: Carl Hamilton

InCompass

As part of a November 2001 corporate restructuring at The Jockey Club family of companies, McKinnie Systems, Inc., the software company that specialized in racing office and horsemen's bookkeeper applications, was re-named InCompass. The re-named entity is a technology solutions company that is centralizing the software applications and systems that serve North American racetracks. Leveraging the power of a centralized database to deliver a wide array of re-engineered solutions, InCompass is helping racetracks achieve operational efficiencies, reduce costs and enhance marketing efforts and business analysis. The roll out of the initial suite of re-engineered products will continue on a track-by-track basis throughout 2004.

821 Corporate Drive, Lexington, KY 40503
(859) 296-3000. . .Fax: (859) 296-3010
http://www.incompass-solutions.com
President: David Haydon
Executive Vice President, Sales and Marketing: David Ruffra

The Jockey Club Technology Services, Inc.
The Jockey Club Technology Services, Inc. (TJCTS) was formed out of the November 2001 corporate restructuring at The Jockey Club family of companies when the business unit that served as the information technology group for The Jockey Club and a technology consultant for the industry at large was spun-off into a wholly-owned subsidiary of The Jockey Club. TJCTS provides infrastructure support services for The Jockey Club family of companies, as well as software design and programming services at the request of other industry organizations.
821 Corporate Drive, Lexington, KY 40503
(859) 224-2700. . .Fax: (859) 224-2777
http://www.tjctechnology.com
President: Robert A. Burch

Grayson-Jockey Club Research Foundation, Inc.
The Grayson Foundation was established in 1940, to raise support for the promotion and funding of equine veterinary research. In 1989, resources were combined with those of The Jockey Club Research Foundation. Over the last two decades, the Foundation has contributed more than $10.2 million toward projects aimed at enhancing the health and safety of horses.
During the year 2003, the Foundation allocated $748,116 for 19 projects at 11 universities continent-wide, confirming its position as the leading private source of equine research funding in the nation. Contributions in support of the Foundation may be addressed to:
The Grayson-Jockey Club Research Foundation
821 Corporate Drive, Lexington, KY 40503
(859) 224-2850. . .Fax: (859) 224-2853
http://www.grayson-jockeyclub.org
President: Edward L. Bowen

The Jockey Club Foundation
Founded in 1943, The Jockey Club Foundation is a charitable trust created to provide relief to needy members of the Thoroughbred industry and their families.

Administered by a Board of Trustees, comprised of members of The Jockey Club, financial aid is extended either through a monthly assistance program or on a one-time lump-sum basis, and includes extensive contributions to other benevolent organizations in the Thoroughbred industry. Since 1985, the Foundation has been able to help thousands of individuals and their families with more than $10.2 million in support. Grants from the Foundation totaled $625,785 in 2003. Contributions in support of the Foundation may be addressed to:
The Jockey Club Foundation
40 East 52nd Street
New York, NY 10022.
(212) 521-5305.Fax: (212) 371-6123
http://www.tjcfoundation.org

Trustees:
C. Steven Duncker
John Hettinger
D.G. Van Clief, Jr.
Treasurer: James S. J. Liao
Executive Director: Nancy Kelly

OTHER RACING ORGANIZATIONS

AMERICAN ASSOCIATION OF EQUINE PRACTITIONERS
Mailing Address: 4075 Iron Works Parkway,
Lexington, KY 40511
Phone: (859) 233-0147 Fax: (859) 233-1968
E-Mail: aaepoffice@aaep.org
President: Dr. Larry Bramlage; Executive Director: David L. Foley

AMERICAN HORSE COUNCIL
Mailing Address: 1616 H. St. NW, 7th floor Washington, D.C. 20006
Phone: (202) 296-4031 Fax: (202) 296-1970
E-Mail: ahc@horsecouncil.org
Chairman: James F. Barton
President: James J. Hickey, Jr.

AMERICAN QUARTER HORSE ASSOCIATION
Mailing Address: P.O. Box 200,
Amarillo, TX 79168
Phone: (806) 376-4811 Fax: (806) 349-6402
E-Mail: racing@aqha.org
Executive Vice President: Bill Brewer
Executive Director of Racing: Gary Carpenter

ASSOCIATION OF RACING COMMISSIONERS INTERNATIONAL, INC.
Mailing Address: 2343 Alexandria Drive, Suite 200,
Lexington, KY 40504-3276
Phone: (859) 224-7070 Fax: (859) 224-7071
E-Mail: ewaters@arci.com
Chairman: Frank Zanzuccki (2004)
Replaces William Jackson
President and CEO: Lonny T. Powell

BREEDERS' CUP LIMITED
Mailing Address: 2525 Harrodsburg Road, Suite 500,
Lexington, KY 40504-3359
Phone: (859) 223-5444 Fax: (859) 223-3945
E-Mail: breederscup@breederscup.com
President: D.G. Van Clief, Jr.
Media Relations Director: James Gluckson, (212) 230-9512

HARNESS TRACKS OF AMERICA
Mailing Address: 4640 East Sunrise, Suite 200,
Tucson, AZ 85718
Phone: (520) 529-2525 Fax: (520) 529-3235
E-Mail: info@harnesstracks.com
President: Christopher McErlean;
Executive Vice President: Stanley F. Bergstein
General Counsel and Secretary: Paul J. Estok

THE JOCKEYS' GUILD, INC.
Mailing Address: P.O. Box 150, Monrovia, CA 91017Phone: 866-GOJOCKS (465-6257) or (626) 305-5605 Fax: (626) 305-5615
President: L. Wayne Gertmenian
Chairman: Tomey Jean Swan
Vice President: Albert Fiss

NATIONAL HORSEMEN'S BENEVOLENT & PROTECTIVE ASSOCIATION
4063 Ironworks Parkway, B2,
Lexington, KY 40511-8905
Email: racing@hbpa.org
Phone: (859) 259-0451
Fax: (859) 259-0452
President: John Roark
Executive Director: Remi Bellocq

NATIONAL RACING COMPACT
Mailing Address: P.O. Box 184
New Kent, VA 23124
Phone: (877) 457-2538
Fax: (804) 966-7422
E-Mail: nrcsupport@racinglicense.com
Chairman: Rick Goodell

NATIONAL TURF WRITERS ASSOCIATION
1244 Meadow Lane
Frankfort, Kentucky, 40601
(502) 875-4864
President: Jennie Rees, 2002 – 2004
Secretary: Dan Liebman
Email:dliebman@bloodhorse.com

NORTH AMERICAN PARI-MUTUEL REGULATORS ASSOCIATION
Mailing Address:
P.O. Box 446, Cheyenne, WY 82003
Phone: (888) 627-7250 Fax: (307) 777-3681
E-Mail: Flamb@state.wy.us
Executive Director: Frank Lamb

RACE TRACK CHAPLAINCY OF AMERICA
Mailing Address: PO Box 91640, Los Angeles, CA 90009
Phone: (310) 419-1640
Fax: (310) 419-1642
Email: etorres@racetrackchaplaincy.org
President: Donald Dean
Executive Director: Dr. Enrique Torres

THOROUGHBRED HORSEMEN'S ASSOCIATIONS, INC.
Mailing Address: 10500 Little Patuxent Pkwy,
Suite 650 Columbia, MD, 21044
Phone: (410) 740-4900 Fax: (410) 740-0800
Email: thassoc@erols.com
Chairman of the Board & CEO: Alan M. Foreman
President: Richard Violette, Jr.

THOROUGHBRED OWNERS & BREEDERS ASSOCIATION
Mailing Address: P.O. Box 4367, Lexington, KY 40544-4367
Phone: (859) 276-2291 Fax: (859) 276-2462
E-mail: toba@toba.org
Chairman of the Board: Gary E. Biszantz
President: Daniel J. Metzger

TRIPLE CROWN PRODUCTIONS LLC
Mailing Address: 700 Central Avenue,
Louisville, KY 40208-1200
Phone: (502) 636 4405 Fax: (502) 638-3894E-Mail: triplecrown@kyderby.com
President: Thomas H. Meeker
Executive Vice-President: Edward P. Seigenfeld

PHONE AND WEB SITES FOR RACING COMMISSIONS IN NORTH AMERICA

ASSOCIATION OF RACING COMMISSIONERS INTERNATIONAL, INC
2343 Alexandria Drive, Suite 200
Lexington, Kentucky, 40504-3276
859/224-7070 Fax: 859/224-7071
Web site: www.arci.com
Contact: Frank Zanzuccki

NORTH AMERICAN PARI-MUTUEL REGULATORS ASSOCIATION
P.O. Box 446
Cheyenne, WY 82003
888/627-7250; Fax 307/777-3681
http://www.napraonline.com
Email: flamb@state.wy.us
Executive Director: Frank Lamb

ALABAMA: BIRMINGHAM RACING COMMISSION
2101 6th Avenue North
Birmingham, 35203
205/328-7223; Fax: 205/328-0632
And:
Macon County Racing Commission
P.O. Box 830724
Tuskegee, 36083
334/727-0121; Fax: 334/727-0182
And:
Mobile County Racing Commission
P.O. Box 1886
Mobile, 36633
251/653-4820; Fax 251/653-4850

ALBERTA RACING CORPORATION
9707 110th Street, Suite 720
Edmonton, Alberta, T5K 2L9, Canada
780/415-5432; Fax: 780/488-5105
http://www.thehorses.com/index_main.html

ARIZONA DEPARTMENT OF RACING
1110 West Washington, Suite 260
Phoenix, 85007
602/364-1700; Fax: 602/364-1703
http://www.raccom.state.az.us/

ARKANSAS STATE RACING COMMISSION
1515 West 7th, Suite 505
P.O. Box 3076
Little Rock, 72203
501/682-1467, Fax: 501/682-5273
http://www. accessarkansas.org/dfa/racing/

BRITISH COLUMBIA RACING COMMISSION
408-4603 Kingsway Avenue
Burnaby, B.C., Canada V5H 4M4
604/660-7400; Fax: 604/660-7414
http://www.pssg.gov.bc.ca/gaming/commercial/tracks.htm

CALIFORNIA HORSE RACING BOARD
1010 Hurley Way, Suite 300
Sacramento, 95825
916/263-6000; Fax: 916/263-6042
http://www.chrb.ca.gov/

CANADIAN PARI-MUTUEL AGENCY
1130 Morrison Drive
Nepean, Ontario K2H 9N6
613/949-0735; Fax: 613/949-0750
http://www.cpma-acpm.gc.ca/cpma_e.html

COLORADO DIVISION OF RACING EVENTS
1881 Pierce Street, Suite 108
Lakewood, 80214
303/205-2990; Fax: 303/205-2950
http://www.revenue.state.co.us/racing_dir/coracing.html

DELAWARE THOROUGHBRED RACING COMMISSION
2320 South DuPont Highway
Dover, 19901
302/698-4500; Fax: 302/697-6287
http://www.state.de.us/deptagri/thoroughbred/index.htm

FLORIDA DIVISION OF PARI-MUTUEL WAGERING
1940 North Monroe Street,
Tallahassee, 32399-1027
850/488-9130, Fax: 850/488-0550
http://www.state.fl.us/dbpr/pmw/index.shtml

IDAHO STATE POLICE RACING COMMISSION
PO Box 700
Meridian, 83680-0700
208/884-7080; Fax: 208/884-7098
http://www.isp.state.id.us/race/index.html

ILLINOIS RACING BOARD
100 West Randolph Street, Suite 11-100
Chicago, 60601
312/814-2600, Fax: 312/814-5062
http://www.state.il.us/agency/irb/

INDIANA HORSE RACING COMMISSION
ISTA Center, Suite 530
150 West Market Street
Indianapolis, 46204
317/233-3119, Fax: 317/233-4470
http://www.in.gov/ihrc/

IOWA RACING AND GAMING COMMISSION
717 East Court Avenue, Suite B
Des Moines, 50309
515/281-7352; Fax: 515/242-6560
http://www3.state.ia.us/irgc/

JAMAICA RACING COMMISSION
P.O. Box 309, Kingston 10, Jamaica
809/926-2718;Fax: 809/926-2207

KANSAS RACING AND GAMING COMMISSION
3400 South West Van Buren
Topeka, 66611-2228
785/296-5800; Fax: 785/296-0900
http://www.accesskansas.org/krc/

KENTUCKY HORSE RACING AUTHORITY
4063 Iron Works Parkway, Building B,
Lexington, 40511
859/246-2040; Fax: 859/246-2039
http://www.state.ky.us/agencies/cppr/krc/

LOUISIANA STATE RACING COMMISSION
320 North Carrollton Avenue, Suite 2-B,
New Orleans, 70119
504/483-4000; Fax: 504/483-4898
http://horseracing.la.gov/

MANITOBA HORSE RACING COMMISSION
Box 46086 RPO Westdale
Winnipeg, Canada R3R 3S3
204/885-7770; Fax: 204/831-0942
http://www.manitobahorsecomm.org/

MARYLAND RACING COMMISSION
500 North Calvert Street, Second Floor, Room 201
Baltimore, 21202-3651
410/230-6330; Fax: 410/333-8308
http://www.dllr.state.md.us/racing/

MASSACHUSETTS STATE RACING COMMISSION
One Ashburton Place, Room 1313
Boston, 02108
617/727-2581; Fax: 617/227-6062
http://www.state.ma.us/src/

MEXICO: NATIONAL RACING COMMISSION OF MEXICO
Apartado Postal 34050, Hipodromo de Las Americas,
Lomas de Sotelo, C.P. 11619, Mexico, D.F.
011-52-5-55 2947933; Fax: 011-52-5-55 2930664

MICHIGAN: THE OFFICE OF RACING COMMISSIONER
37650 Professional Center Drive, Suite 105A,
Livonia, 48154-1100
734/462-2400; Fax: 734/462-2429
http://www.michigan.gov/mda/

MINNESOTA RACING COMMISSION
P.O. Box 630
Shakopee, 55379
952/496-7950, Fax: 952/496-3954
http://www.mnrace.commission.state.ms.us/

MISSOURI GAMING COMMISSION
P.O. Box 1847, 3417 Knipp Drive
Jefferson City, 65102-1847
573/526-4080; Fax: 573/526-1999
http://www.mgc.state.mo.us/horse.html

MONTANA STATE BOARD OF HORSE RACING
301 South Park, Room 68
Helena, 59620
406/444-4287 Fax 406/444-4305
http://www.discoveringmontana.com/liv/
HorseRacing/Index.asp

NEBRASKA STATE RACING COMMISSION
301 Centennial Mall South, 6th floor
Lincoln, 68509
402/471-2577; Fax 402/471-2339
http://horseracing.state.ne.us

NEVADA GAMING COMMISSION AND STATE GAMING CONTROL BOARD
555 E. Washington Ave., Suite 2600
Las Vegas, 89101
702/486-2000; Fax: 702/486-3543
http://gaming.state.nv.us/index.htm

NEW HAMPSHIRE PARI-MUTUEL COMMISSION
244 North Main
Concord, 03301
603/271-2158; 603/271-3381
http://www.state.nh.us/nhpmc/

NEW JERSEY RACING COMMISSION
140 East Front Street, 4th Floor
Trenton, 08625
609/292-0613; Fax: 609/599-1785
http://www.njrconline.com/

NEW MEXICO RACING COMMISSION
300 San Mateo Boulevard N.E. Suite 110
Albuquerque, 87108
505/841-6400; Fax: 505/841-6413

**NEW YORK STATE RACING AND
WAGERING BOARD**
1 Watervliet Avenue Extension, Suite 2
Albany, 12206
Phone: 518/453-8460
http://www.racing.state.ny.us/

NORTH DAKOTA RACING COMMISSION
500 North 9th Street
Bismark, 58501-4509
701/328-4633; Fax 701/328-4280
http://www.ndracingcommission.com/

OHIO STATE RACING COMMISSION
77 South High Street, 18th Floor
Columbus, 43215-6108
614/466-2757; Fax: 614/466-1900
http://www.racing.ohio.gov/

OKLAHOMA HORSE RACING COMMISSION
Shepherd Mall, 2614 Villa Prom
Oklahoma City, 73107
405/943-6472; Fax: 405/943-6474
http://www.ohrc.org/intro.html

ONTARIO RACING COMMISSION
9th Floor, 20 Dundas Street West,
Toronto, Ontario M5G 2C2
416/327-0520; Fax: 416/325-3478

OREGON RACING COMMISSION
800 NE Oregon Street #11, Suite 310
Portland, 97332
503/731-4052; Fax: 503/731-4053
http://www.orednet.org/~orc/

**PENNSYLVANIA STATE HORSE RACING
COMMISSION**
Agriculture Building, Room 304
2301 North Cameron Street
Harrisburg, 17110
717/787-1942; Fax 717/346-1546
http://www.agriculture.state.pa.us/horseracing/
site/default.asp/

**PUERTO RICO RACING SPORT
ADMINISTRATION**
Racing Board-c/o Junta Hipica de Puerto Rico,
Apartado, 30229,
San Juan, 00929-1229
787/768-2005 x 429; Fax: 787/762-5377
And. . .
Office of the Racing Administrator
c/o Administracion del Deporte Hipico
Apartado 29156 65th Infanteria Station,
Rio Piedras 00929-0156
787/768-2005, Fax: 787/762-1105

**RHODE ISLAND DEPT. OF
BUSINESS REGULATION**
Div. of Racing & Athletics
223 Richmond Street
Providence, 02903
401/222-2246; Fax: 401/222-6098
http://www.dbr.state.ri.us/

**SASKATCHEWAN LIQUOR AND GAMING
AUTHORITY**
2500 Victoria Avenue, P.O. Box 5054
Regina, SK S4P 3M3
306/787-4213
http://www.slga.gov.sk.ca/

**SOUTH DAKOTA COMMISSION
OF GAMING**
118 West Capitol Avenue
Pierre, 57501
605/773-6050; Fax: 605/773-6053
http://www.state.sd.us/drr2/reg/gaming/

TEXAS RACING COMMISSION
8505 Cross Park Drive, Suite 110
Austin, 78754
512/833-6699; Fax: 512/833-6907
http://txrc6.txrc.state.tx.us/

**TRINIDAD & TOBAGO
RACING AUTHORITY**
Santa Rosa Park, Churchill Roosevelt Highway,
O'Meara, Arima,
Trinidad, W.I.
809/646-2004; Fax: 809/646-0103

VERMONT RACING COMMISSION
128 Merchants Row
Rutland, 05701
802/786-5050; Fax: 802/786-5051

VIRGINIA RACING COMMISSION
10700 Horsemen's Road, P.O. Box 208
New Kent, 23124
804/966-7400; Fax: 804/966-7418
http://www.vrc.state.va.us/

**WASHINGTON HORSE RACING
COMMISSION**
6326 Martin Way E, Suite 209
Olympia, 98516
360/459-6462; Fax: 360/459-6461
http://www.whrc.wa.gov/

WEST VIRGINIA RACING COMMISSION
106 Dee Drive,
Charleston, 25311
304/558-2150; Fax: 304/558-6319
http://www.wvf.state.wv.us/racing/

**WISCONSIN DEPARTMENT OF
ADMINISTRATION**
Division Of Gaming
2005 West Beltline Highway, Suite 201
P.O. Box 8979
Madison, 53708-8979
608/270-2555; Fax: 608/270-2564
http://www.doa.state.wi.us/gaming/index.asp

WYOMING PARI-MUTUEL COMMISSION
2515 Warren Avenue, Suite 301
Cheyenne, 82002
307/777-5928; Fax: 307/777-3681
http://parimutuel.state.wy.us/

**European and South American Horse Racing
Bureaus:**

International Racing Bureau
Alton House, 117 High Street,
Newmarket, Suffolk, CB8 9WL England
(44) 1 63866 8881

Jockey Club of Buenos Aires
Cerrito 1446
2 Piso-C.P. 1010
Buenos Aires, Republica Argentina

Phone and Internet Directory of Thoroughbred Racing Organizations

North American listings below include phone numbers for the vast majority of active racetracks, county fairs, horsemen's groups, sales companies, breeding and racing organizations, horse rescue and retirement foundations, lobbying groups and select educational institutions with racetrack management programs and/or Veterinary programs.
Foreign listings that follow include the most prominent ruling body of the sport in each country or province and selected racing organizations.

THE UNITED STATES

ALABAMA

Birmingham Racing Commission	Birmingham	(205) 328-7223

ARIZONA

Arizona State Horsemens Association	Phoenix	(602) 390-6806
Arizona Thoroughbred Breeders Association	Phoenix	(602) 942-1310
Apache County Fair	St. Johns	(928) 337-2661
Arizona Department of Racing	Phoenix	(602) 364-1700
Arizona Racing Commission	Phoenix	(602) 364-1700
Cochise County Fair	Douglas	(520) 364-3819
Coconino Fair	Flagstaff	(928) 774-5139
Graham County Fair	Safford	(928) 428-6240
Horsemen's Benevolent & Protective Association	Phoenix	(602) 942-3336
Race Track Industry Program	Tucson	(520) 621-5660
Rillito Park	Tucson	(520) 293-5011
Santa Cruz County Fair	Sonoita	(520) 455-5553
Turf Paradise	Phoenix	(602) 942-1101
Yavapai Downs	Prescott Valley	(928) 775-8000
Yuma County Fair	Yuma	(928) 726-4420

ARKANSAS

Arkansas Horse Council	Jasper	(870) 446-6226
Arkansas State Racing Commission	Little Rock	(501) 682-1467
Arkansas Thoroughbred Breeders' and Horsemen's Assoc	Hot Springs	(501) 624-6328
Horsemen's Benevolent & Protective Association	Hot Springs	(501) 623-7641
Oaklawn Park	Hot Springs	(501) 623-4411

CALIFORNIA

Barretts Equine Sales	Pomona	(909) 629-3099
Bay Meadows	San Mateo	(650) 574-7223
Bay Meadows Fair	San Mateo	(650) 574-3247
California Authority of Racing Fairs	Sacramento	(916) 927-7223
California Assn. of Thoroughbred Racetracks, LLC	Sacramento	(916) 449-6820
California Horse Racing Board	Sacramento	(916) 263-6000
California Thoroughbred Breeders Association	Arcadia	(626) 445-7800
California State Horsemen's Assoc.	Clovis	(559) 325-1055
California Thoroughbred Sales	Arcadia	(626) 445-7753
California Thoroughbred Trainers	Arcadia	(626) 447-2145

Del Mar	Del Mar	(858) 755-1141
Fairplex Park	Pomona	(909) 623-3111
Ferndale/Humboldt	Ferndale	(707) 786-9511
Fresno	Fresno	(559) 650-3247
Golden Gate Fields	Albany	(510) 559-7300
Hollywood Park	Inglewood	(310) 419-1500
Los Alamitos	Los Alamitos	(714) 820-2800
Oak Tree Racing Association	Arcadia	(626) 574-7223
Pleasanton/Alameda	Pleasanton	(925) 426-7600
Sacramento/Cal Expo	Sacramento	(916) 263-3000
Santa Anita Park	Arcadia	(626) 574-7223
Santa Rosa/Sonoma	Santa Rosa	(707) 545-4200
Solano/Vallejo	Vallejo	(707) 551-2000
Stockton/San Joaquin	Stockton	(209) 466-5041
Thoroughbred Owners of California	Arcadia	(626) 574-6620

COLORADO

Arapahoe Park	Aurora	(303) 690-2400
Colorado Horse Council	Denver	(303) 292-4981
Colorado Racing Commission	Lakewood	(303) 205-2990
Horsemen's Benevolent & Protective Association	Aurora	(303) 690-5919
Colorado Thoroughbred Breeders Association	Denver	(303) 294-0260
Colorado Horsemen's Council	Arvada	(303) 279-4546

CONNECTICUT

Connecticut Division of Special Revenue	Newington	(860) 594-0500
Connecticut Horse Council	Durham	(860) 282-0468

DELAWARE

Delaware Thoroughbred Horsemen's Association	Stanton	(302) 994-2521
Delaware Thoroughbred Racing Commission	Dover	(302) 698-4500
Delaware Park	Stanton	(302) 994-2521

FLORIDA

Calder Race Course	Miami	(305) 625-1311
Fasig-Tipton Florida	Lexington, KY	(859) 255-1555
Florida Division of Pari-Mutuel Wagering	Tallahassee	(850) 488-9130
Florida Thoroughbred Breeders & Owners Association	Ocala	(352) 629-2160
Gulfstream Park	Hallandale	(954) 454-7000
Horsemen's Benevolent & Protective Association	Oldsmar	(813) 925-0192
Horsemen's Benevolent & Protective Association	Opa Locka	(305) 625-4591
Ocala Breeders' Sales Co.	Ocala	(352) 237-2154
Sunshine State Horse Council, Inc.	North Fort Meyers	(239) 731-2999
Tampa Bay Downs	Oldsmar	(813) 855-4401

GEORGIA

Georgia Thoroughbred Owners & Breeders Association	Tyrone	(404) 886-6739
Georgia Horse Council	Conyers	(770) 922-3350

IDAHO

Cassia County Fair	Burley	(208) 678-8610
Eastern Idaho State Fair	Blackfoot	(208) 785-2480
Gem County	Emmett	(208) 365-5560
Horsemen's Benevolent & Protective Association	Boise	(208) 376-3991
Idaho Horse Council	Boise	(208) 323-8148
Idaho State Racing Commission	Meridian	(208) 884-7080
Idaho Thoroughbred Breeders Assoc.	Boise	(208) 375-5930
Les Bois Park	Boise	(208) 376-7223
Oneida County Fair	Malad	(208) 766-2247
Pocatello Downs	Pocatello	(208) 238-1721
Rupert Fairgrounds	Rupert	(208) 436-4793
Sandy Downs - Teton Racing	Idaho Falls	(208) 529-0671

ILLINOIS

Arlington Park	Arlington Heights	(847) 385-7500
Fairmount Park	Collinsville	(618) 345-4300
Hawthorne Race Course	Stickney/Cicero	(708) 780-3700
Horsemen's Council of Illinois	Springfield	(217) 585-1600
Illinois Racing Board	Chicago	(312) 814-2600
Illinois Thoroughbred Horsemen's Association	Stickney	(708) 652-2201
Horsemen's Benevolent & Protective Assn. (Chicago)	Barrington	(847) 382-3484
Horsemen's Benevolent & Protective Assn. (Illinois)	Caseyville	(618) 345-7724
Illinois Dept. of Agriculture Horse Racing Programs	Springfield	(217) 782-2172
Illinois Thoroughbred Breeders & Owners Foundation	Caseyville	(618) 344-3427
Illinois Thoroughbred Breeders & Owners Foundation Sales	Caseyville	(618) 344-3427

INDIANA

Hoosier Park	Anderson	(765) 642-7223
Horsemen's Benevolent & Protective Association	Anderson	(866) 663-2001
Indiana Downs	Shelbyville	(317) 421-0000
Indiana Horse Council	Indianapolis	(317) 692-7115
Indiana Horse Racing Commission	Indianapolis	(317) 233-3119
Indiana Thoroughbred Owners and Breeders Association	Carmel	(800) 450-9895

IOWA

Horsemen's Benevolent & Protective Association	Altoona	(515) 967-4804
Iowa Racing & Gaming Commission	Des Moines	(515) 281-7352
Iowa Thoroughbred Breeders and Owners Association	Altoona	(800) 577-1097 and (515) 957-3002
Prairie Meadows	Altoona	(515) 967-1000

KANSAS

Horsemen's Benevolent & Protective Association	Zenda	(620) 243-6641
Kansas Horse Council	Manhattan	(785) 776-0662

Kansas Thoroughbred Association	Fredonia	(620) 378-4772
Kansas Thoroughbred Association/Sales	Edwardsville	(913) 441-0148
Kansas Racing Commission	Topeka	(785) 296-5800
The Woodlands	Kansas City	(913) 299-9797

KENTUCKY

Bluegrass Downs	Paducah	(270) 444-7117
Churchill Downs	Louisville	(502) 636-4400
Ellis Park	Henderson	(812) 425-1456
Fasig-Tipton Company, Inc.	Lexington	(859) 255-1555
Horsemen's Benevolent & Protective Association	Louisville	(502) 363-1077
Keeneland Association, Inc.	Lexington	(859) 254-3412
Kentucky Derby Museum	Louisville	(502) 637-1111
Kentucky Downs	Franklin	(270) 586-7778
Kentucky Horse Council	Lexington	(859) 367-0509
Kentucky Horse Park	Lexington	(859) 233-4303
Kentucky Horse Racing Authority	Lexington	(859) 246-2040
Kentucky Thoroughbred Association	Lexington	(859) 381-1414
Kentucky Thoroughbred Owners & Breeders	Lexington	(859) 259-1643
Lexington Breeders' Sales	Lexington	(859) 269-0695
Stallion Access/Fasig-Tipton	Lexington	(859) 255-1555
Turfway Park Race Course	Florence	(859) 371-0200
University of Louisville Equine Administration Program	Louisville	(502) 852-7617

LOUISIANA

Breeders Sales Co. of Louisiana	New Orleans	(504) 947-4676
Delta Downs	Vinton	(337) 589-7441
Evangeline Downs	Lafayette	(337) 896-7223
Fair Grounds	New Orleans	(504) 944-5515
Fasig-Tipton Louisiana	Lexington, KY	(859) 255-1555
Horsemen's Benevolent & Protective Association	New Orleans	(504) 945-1555
Louisiana Downs	Bossier City	(318) 742-5555
Louisiana State Racing Commission	New Orleans	(504) 483-4000
Louisiana Thoroughbred Breeders Association	New Orleans	(504) 943-7556
Louisiana Thoroughbred Breeders Sales Co.	Carencro	(337) 896-6152

MARYLAND

Fasig-Tipton Midlantic, Inc.	Elkton	(410) 392-5555
Laurel Race Course	Laurel	(410) 792-7775
Maryland Horse Breeders Association	Timonium	(410) 252-2100
Maryland Horse Breeders Foundation	Timonium	(410) 252-2100
Maryland Horse Council, Inc.	Lisbon	(410) 489-7826
Maryland Million, Ltd.	Timonium	(410) 252-2100
Maryland Thoroughbred Horsemen's Association	Baltimore	(410) 265-6842
Maryland Racing Commission	Baltimore	(410) 230-6330
National Steeplechase Association	Elkton	(410) 392-0700
Pimlico Race Course	Baltimore	(410) 542-9400
Timonium	Timonium	(410) 252-0200

MASSACHUSETTS

Horsemen's Benevolent & Protective Assn. (New England)	Revere	(617) 567-3900
Massachusetts State Racing Commission	Boston	(617) 727-2581
Massachusetts Thoroughbred Breeders Association, Inc.	Cambridge	(617) 492-7217
Northampton Fair	Northampton	(413) 584-2237
Suffolk Downs	East Boston	(617) 567-3900

MICHIGAN

Great Lakes Downs	Muskegon	(231) 799-2400
Horsemen's Benevolent & Protective Association	Muskegon	(231) 798-2250
Michigan Horse Council	Lansing	(231) 821-2487
Michigan - Office of the Racing Commissioner	Livonia	(734) 462-2400
Michigan Thoroughbred Owners & Breeders Assn.	Muskegon	(231) 798-7721
Mount Pleasant Meadows	Mt. Pleasant	(989) 773-0012

MINNESOTA

Canterbury Park	Shakopee	(952) 445-7223
Horsemen's Benevolent & Protective Association	Shakopee	(952) 496-6442
Minnesota Horse Council	Coon Rapids	(763) 755-7729
Minnesota Racing Commission	Shakopee	(952) 496-7950
Minnesota Thoroughbred Association	Shakopee	(952) 496-3770
MN. Thoroughbred Association/Sales	Shakopee	(952) 496-3770

MISSISSIPPI

Mississippi Thoroughbred Breeders & Owners Association	Madison	(601) 856-8293

MISSOURI

Missouri Equine Council	Fulton	(800) 313-3327
Missouri Gaming Commission	Jefferson City	(573) 526-4080
Missouri Thoroughbred Owners & Breeders Association	Willard	(417) 742-2624

MONTANA

Great Falls State Fair	Great Falls	(406) 727-8900
Horsemen's Benevolent & Protective Association	Vaughn	(406) 452-2135
Marias Fair	Shelby	(406) 337-3600
Miles City	Miles City	(406) 232-1210
Northwest Montana Fair	Kalispell	(406) 758-5810
State of Montana Board of Horse Racing	Helena	(406) 444-4287
Western Montana Fair	Missoula	(406) 721-3247
Yellowstone Downs	Billings	(406) 869-5251

NEBRASKA

Atokad Downs	South Sioux City	(402) 494-5722
Columbus	Columbus	(402) 564-0133
Fonner Park	Grand Island	(308) 382-4515
Horsemen's Benevolent & Protective Association	Omaha	(402) 731-5300
Horsemen's Park	Omaha	(402) 731-2900

Lincoln	Lincoln	(402) 474-5371
Nebraska State Racing Commission	Lincoln	(402) 471-4155
Neb. Thoroughbred Breeders' Assoc.	Grand Island	(308) 384-4683

NEVADA

Nevada Gaming Commission	Las Vegas	(702) 486-2000

NEW HAMPSHIRE

New Hampshire Pari-Mutuel Comm.	Concord	(603) 271-2158

NEW JERSEY

Atlantic City Racing Association	Atlantic City	(609) 641-2190
Monmouth Park	Oceanport	(732) 222-5100
New Jersey Horse Council	Moorestown	(856) 231-0771
New Jersey Racing Commission	Trenton	(609) 292-0613
New Jersey Thoroughbred Horsemen's Assoc. Inc.	West Long Branch	(732) 263-1022
The Meadowlands	East Rutherford	(201) 935-8500
Thoroughbred Breeders' Association of New Jersey	Long Branch	(732) 870-9718

NEW MEXICO

New Mexico Horse Breeders' Assoc.	Albuquerque	(505) 262-0224
New Mexico Horse Council	Albuquerque	(505) 345-8959
New Mexico Racing Commission	Albuquerque	(505) 841-6400
Ruidoso Downs	Ruidoso Downs	(505) 378-4431
SunRay Park	Farmington	(505) 566-1200
Sunland Park	Sunland Park	(505) 874-5200
The Downs at Albuquerque	Albuquerque	(505) 266-5555

NEW YORK

Aqueduct Race Track	Jamaica	(718) 641-4700
Belmont Park	Elmont	(516) 488-6000
Capital Regional OTB	Schenectady	(518) 370-5151
Catskill Regional OTB	Pomona	(845) 362-0400
Fasig-Tipton Saratoga	Saratoga Springs	(516) 584-4700
Finger Lakes	Farmington	(585) 924-3232
Genesee Valley Breeders Association	Livonia	(716) 924-5285
Horsemen's Benevolent & Protective Assn. (Finger Lakes)	Farmington	(585) 924-3004
Nassau County Regional OTB	Hempstead	(516) 572-2800
New York City Off-Track Betting Corp.	New York	(212) 704-5642
New York State Horse Council	Westport	(518) 962-2316
New York State Racing & Wagering Board	Albany	(518) 453-8460
New York State Thoroughbred Breeding & Dev. Fund Corp.	New York	(212) 465-0660
New York Thoroughbred Breeders	Saratoga	(518) 587-0777
New York Thoroughbred Horsemens Association	Jamaica	(718) 641-4700
Saratoga Race Course	Saratoga Springs	(518) 584-6200
Suffolk Regional OTB	Hauppauge	(631) 853-1000
Western Regional OTB	Batavia	(585)343-1423

NORTH CAROLINA

North Carolina Horse Council	Raleigh	(919) 854-1990
North Carolina Thoroughbred Breeders Assoc.	Raleigh	(800) 957-3490

NORTH DAKOTA

North Dakota Racing Commission	Bismarck	(701) 328-4633

OHIO

Beulah Park	Grove City	(614) 871-9600
Horsemen's Benevolent & Protective Association	Grove City	(614) 875-1269
National Equine Sales	Springfield	(937) 324-5558
Ohio Horseman's Council	Logan	(740) 385-5306
Ohio State Racing Commission	Columbus	(614) 466-2757
Ohio Thoroughbred Breeders & Owners	Cincinnati	(513) 574-0440
River Downs	Cincinnati	(513) 232-8000
Thistledown	North Randall	(216) 662-8600

OKLAHOMA

Blue Ribbon Downs	Sallisaw	(918) 775-7771
Fair Meadows at Tulsa	Tulsa	(918) 743-7223
Heritage Place Sales Company	Oklahoma City	(405) 682-4551
Horsemen's Benevolent & Protective Association	Oklahoma City	(405) 427-8753
Oklahoma Horsemen's Association	Oklahoma City	(405) 843-8333
Oklahoma Horse Racing Commission	Oklahoma City	(405) 943-6472
Oklahoma Thoroughbred Association	Edmond	(405) 330-1006
Remington Park	Oklahoma City	(405) 424-1000

OREGON

Grants Pass Downs	Grants Pass	(541) 476-3215
Oregon Racing Commission	Portland	(503) 731-4052
Horsemen's Benevolent & Protective Association	Portland	(503) 285-4941
Klamath County Fairgrounds	Klamath Falls	(541) 883-3796
Oregon Thoroughbred Breeders' Association	Portland	(503) 285-0658
Portland Meadows	Portland	(503) 285-9144
Tillamook County Fairgrounds	Tillamook	(503) 842-2272

PENNSYLVANIA

Horsemen's Benevolent & Protective Assn (Penn National)	Grantville	(717) 469-2970
Pennsylvania Equine Council	Dallas	(888) 304-0281
Pennsylvania Thoroughbred Horsemen's Association	Bensalem	(215) 638-2012
Penn National	Grantville	(717) 469-2211
Pennsylvania Horse Breeders' Assoc.	Kennett Square	(610) 444-1050
Philadelphia Park	Bensalem	(215) 639-9000
State Horse Racing Commission	Harrisburg	(717) 787-1942

RHODE ISLAND

R.I. Dept. of Business Reg., Div. of Racing & Athletics	Providence	(401) 222-2246

SOUTH CAROLINA

South Carolina Department of Agriculture	Columbia	(803) 734-2210
South Carolina Horsemen's Council	Lexington	(803) 356-4535

SOUTH DAKOTA

South Dakota Commission on Gaming	Pierre	(605) 773-6050

TENNESSEE

Tennessee Department of Agriculture, Marketing Division	Nashville	(615) 837-5103
Tennessee Horse Council	Murfreesboro	(615) 217-3113

TEXAS

Gillespie County Fair	Fredericksburg	(830) 997-2359
Greater Houston Horse Council	Houston	(713) 465-3988
Lone Star Park at Grand Prairie	Grand Prairie	(972) 263-7223
Manor Downs	Austin	(512) 272-5581
Retama Park	Selma	(210) 651-7000
Sam Houston Race Track	Houston	(281) 807-8700
Texas Horsemen's Partnership LLC	Austin	(512) 467-9799
Texas Racing Commission	Austin	(512) 833-6699
Texas Thoroughbred Association	Austin	(512) 458-6133

VERMONT

Vermont Racing Commission	Rutland	(802) 786-5050

VIRGINIA

Colonial Downs	New Kent	(804) 966-7223
Horsemen's Benevolent & Protective Association	Warrenton	(540) 347-0033
Virginia Horse Council	Mineral	(540) 894-0735
Virginia Horse Industry Board	Richmond	(804) 786-5842
Virginia Horsemen's Association	Warrenton	(540) 349-4600
Virginia Racing Commission	New Kent	(804) 966-7400
Virginia Thoroughbred Association	Warrenton	(540) 347-4313

WASHINGTON

Emerald Downs	Auburn	(253) 288-7000
Horsemen's Benevolent & Protective Association	Auburn	(253) 804-6822
Horsemen's Benevolent & Protective Assn. (Inland NW)	Spokane	(509) 536-5123
Sun Downs	Kennewick	(509) 582-5434
Walla Walla Racetrack	Walla Walla	(509) 527-3247
Washington Horse Racing Commission	Olympia	(360) 459-6462
Washington Thoroughbred Breeders Association	Auburn	(253) 288-7878

WEST VIRGINIA

Charles Town Races	Charles Town	(800) 795-7001
Horsemen's Benevolent & Protective Assn. (Charles Town)	Charles Town	(304) 725-1535
Horsemen's Benevolent & Protective Assn. (Mountaineer Pk)	Chester	(304) 387-9772
Mountaineer Park	Chester	(800) 804-0468
West Virginia Racing Commission	Charleston	(304) 558-2150
West Virginia Thoroughbred Breeders Association	Charles Town	(304) 728-6868

WISCONSIN

Wisconsin Gaming Commission	Madison	(608) 270-2555
Wisconsin State Horse Council	Columbus	(920) 623-0393

WYOMING

Wyoming Downs	Evanston	(307) 789-0511
Wyoming Pari-Mutuel Commission	Cheyenne	(307) 777-5928

PUERTO RICO and CANADA

PUERTO RICO

El Comandante	San Juan	(787) 641-6060
Puerto Rico Racing Sport Administration	San Juan	(787) 768-2005
Puerto Rico Thoroughbred		
Breeders Association	San Juan	(787) 876-3944

CANADA

Canadian Thoroughbred Horse Society		
(National Office)	Rexdale, Ont.	(416) 675-3602
The Jockey Club of Canada	Etobicoke, Ont.	(416) 675-7756

ALBERTA

Canadian Thoroughbred Horse Society		
(Alberta Division)	Calgary	(403) 229-3609
Horse Racing Alberta	Edmonton	(780) 415-5432
Northlands Park	Edmonton	(780) 471-7210
Stampede Park	Calgary	(403) 261-0214

BRITISH COLUMBIA

British Columbia Racing Commission	Burnaby	(604) 660-7400
Canadian Thoroughbred Horse Society		
(B.C. Division)	Surrey	(604) 574-0145
Hastings Racecourse	Vancouver	(604) 254-1631
Horsemen's Benevolent		
& Protective Association	Vancouver	(604) 647-2211
Sandown Park	Sidney	(250) 656-1631

MANITOBA

Assiniboia Downs	Winnipeg	(204) 885-3330
Canadian Thoroughbred Horse Society		
(Manitoba Division)	Winnipeg	(204) 832-1702
Horsemen's Benevolent		
& Protective Association (Western)	Winnipeg	(204) 832-4949
Manitoba Horse Racing Commission	Winnipeg	(204) 885-7770

ONTARIO

Canadian Thoroughbred Horse Society		
(Ontario Division)	Rexdale	(416) 675-3602
Fort Erie	Fort Erie	(905) 871-3200
Horsemen's Benevolent		
& Protective Association	Rexdale	(416) 747-5252
Ontario Racing Commission	Toronto	(416) 327-0520
Woodbine	Toronto	(416) 675-7223
Woodbine Entertainment	Rexdale	(416) 675-7223

QUEBEC

Canadian Thoroughbred Horse Society		
(Quebec Division)	Lac Guindon	(450) 475-8648
Quebec Racing Commission	Montreal	(418) 646-1632

SASKATCHEWAN

Canadian Thoroughbred Horse Society (Saskatchewan Div.)	Saskatoon	(306) 329-2422
Marquis Downs	Saskatoon	(306) 242-6100
Saskatchewan Horse Racing Commission	Saskatoon	(306) 933-5997
Saskatchewan Liquor & Gaming Auth.	Regina	(306) 787-4213

AUSTRALIA, EUROPE, ASIA, SOUTH AMERICA and AFRICA

Country	Code	Telephone	Fax
AUSTRALIA			
Australian Jockey Club (Randwick)	(61)	2 9663 8400	2 9663 1679
Australian Stud Book (Randwick)	(61)	2 9663 8411	2 9663 4718
Racing Services Bureau (Flemington)	(61)	3 9258 4700	3 9258 4715
Racing Victoria Ltd (Flemington)	(61)	3 9258 4258	3 9258 4707
BRITAIN			
The Jockey Club (London)	(44)	2 07486 4921	2 07935 8703
Tattersalls (Newmarket)	(44)	1 63866 5931	1 63866 0850
Weatherbys (Wellingborough)	(44)	1 93344 0077	1 93344 0807
GERMANY			
Direktorium Fur Vollblutzucht und Rennen (Cologne)	(49)	221 7498 13	221 7498 68
HONG KONG			
Hong Kong Jockey Club (Happy Valley)	(852)	2966 8111	2966 7000
IRELAND			
Goffs Bloodstock Sales Ltd. (Kill)	(353)	45-886600	45-877119
Horse Racing Ireland (Dublin)	(353)	45-842800	45-842801
Tattersalls (Ireland) Ltd. (Ratoath)	(353)	1 886 4300	1 886 4303
The Turf Club (The Curragh)	(353)	45-445600	45-445601
Weatherbys (Ireland) Ltd. (Naas)	(353)	45-879979	45-879671
ITALY			
U.N.I.R.E.(Rome)	(39)	6 58.33.09.25	6 58.33.09.21
NEW ZEALAND			
New Zealand Racing Conference (Wellington)	(64)	4 385-3988	4 384-5867
SOUTH AFRICA			
Jockey Club of South Africa (Turffontein)	(27)	11 683-9283	11 434-1636
TRINIDAD & TOBAGO RACING AUTHORITY			
Trinidad & Tobago Racing Authority	(868)	646-2004	(868) 646-0103
UNITED ARAB EMIRATES			
The Emirates Racing Association (Dubai)	(971)	4 3313311	4 3313322

FOREIGN RACING WEBSITES

ARGENTINA
www.studbook.com.ar News, stakes results and statistics of Argentine racing. Includes a link to Peruvian racing. In Spanish.
www.monti.com News and results of racing in Argentina. In English.

AUSTRALIA
www.racingvictoria.net.au Official website of the Victoria Racing Club (Flemington).
www.ajc.org.au Official website of the Australian Jockey Club (Randwick).
www.stc.com.au Official website of the Sydney Turf Club (Rosehill).

BRAZIL
www.jcb.br Official website of the Jockey Club Brasileiro. Entries and results of racing in Brazil. In Portuguese.

BRITAIN
www.racingpost.com Racing Post, British racing daily. News, tips, statistics, entries and results for all British and Irish races, plus results of French races on the Parisian circuit, European group races and major stakes races in Asia and North America.
www.sportinglife.com Entries and quick results of British and Irish races, racing news, plus general British and European sports news.

CHILE
www.hipodromo.cl News, entries and results of racing at the Hipodromo Chile, the dirt track in Santiago, Chile. In Spanish.
www.clubhipico.cl News, entries and results of racing at Club Hipico, the turf track in Santiago, Chile. In Spanish.

FRANCE
www.france-galop.com Official website of France-Galop, the French Jockey Club. Nominations, entries and results for all French meetings, plus jockey, trainer and owner stats and descriptions of all French racecourses. In French.
www.paris-turf.com Paris-Turf, French racing daily. News, entries and results for all race in France. Paid subscription necessary for entries and results service. In French.

GERMANY
www.galopp-sport.de Official website of the Direktorium fur Vollblutzucht & Rennen (German Jockey Club). News, entries and results for all races in Germany. In German.
www.horses.de News, entries and results for all German races. In German.

HONG KONG
www.hongkongjockeyclub.com Official website of the Hong Kong Jockey Club. News entries and results of all races in Hong Kong at both Sha Tin and Happy Valley. In English.

IRELAND
www.irish-field.com Irish Field, Irish racing weekly. News, entries and results of all races in Ireland.

ITALY
www.hid.it News, entries and results for all races in Italy. In Italian.
www.trenno.it News, entries and results for all races in Milan (San Siro). In Italian.

JAPAN
www.jair.jrao.ne.jp Official website of the Japan Racing Association and the National Association of Racing. News of Japanese racing. Results of stakes races. Descriptions of all Japanese racecourses. In English.

NEW ZEALAND
www.nzracing.co.nz News, entries and results of racing in New Zealand.

UNITED ARAB EMIRATES
www.emiratesracing.com Official website of the Emirates Racing Association. News, entries and results for all races in the United Arab Emirates. In English.

CORRECTIONS: Please submit information about corrections, deletions or additions to the Phone and Internet directory to arm2004@drf.com.

THE AMERICAN STUD BOOK
Principal Rules and Requirements

RULES FOR REGISTRATION, DNA/BLOODTYPING AND PARENTAGE VERIFICATION

1. ELIGIBILITY FOR FOAL REGISTRATION

A. These rules apply to horses foaled in the United States, Puerto Rico and Canada, provided Rules 11 and 12 apply to horses foaled outside of the United States, Puerto Rico or Canada.

B. Foals must be genetically typed and qualified by parentage verification by a laboratory approved and authorized by The Jockey Club.

C. A foal is eligible for registration provided it is shown to the satisfaction of the Stewards of The Jockey Club that the foal's pedigree authentically traces in all its lines to horses recorded in The American Stud Book or a Foreign Stud Book approved by The Jockey Club and the International Stud Book Committee and if it satisfies all other requirements set forth in these rules. No horse foaled in the United States, Puerto Rico or Canada may be registered unless both its sire and dam have been previously registered in The American Stud Book. The only exception to this rule is a foal imported in utero whose dam is properly registered in The American Stud Book and whose sire was not imported but is properly registered in an approved Foreign Stud Book.

A dead horse is not eligible for registration.

D. To be eligible for registration, a foal must be the result of a stallion's Breeding with a broodmare (which is the physical mounting of a broodmare by a stallion with intromission of the penis and ejaculation of semen into the reproductive tract). As an aid to the Breeding, a portion of the ejaculate produced by the stallion during such mating may immediately be placed in the uterus of the broodmare being bred. A natural gestation must take place in, and delivery must be from, the body of the same broodmare in which the foal was conceived. Without limiting the above, any foal resulting from or produced by the processes of Artificial Insemination, Embryo Transfer or Transplant, Cloning or any other form of genetic manipulation not herein specified, shall not be eligible for registration.

E. If a broodmare is bred to two or more stallions during the same breeding season, The Jockey Club will make every effort to eliminate the incorrect stallion or stallions including:

1. Genetic typing and parentage qualification;

2. Calculation of gestation period; and

3. Applying the principles of two-coat color inheritance, that is, a chestnut sire and a chestnut dam must produce a chestnut or, in some instances, a palomino foal; and a gray/roan foal must have at least one gray/roan parent.

In the case of double qualifying sires, the name of each sire must be recorded as the sire of the foal in the same order that they were bred to the dam. A valid Service Certificate must be supplied with respect to the services of each qualifying sire.

F. A foal is not eligible for registration unless all requirements to register that foal as set forth in Rule 2 are met within one year of the actual foaling date; provided however, under certain limited circumstances, a foal may be eligible for late registration providing the applicant completes all registration requirements, submits the appropriate late registration fee (see Fee Schedule) and The Jockey Club determines that the applicant has sufficiently demonstrated mistake, inadvertence, excusable neglect or other circumstances which justify late registration.

G. A foal is not eligible for registration unless its sire and dam have been genetically typed, as required under Rule 5, provided however, if the sire or dam died prior to being genetically typed, a foal may still be eligible for registration if a notarized statement is submitted by the stallion owner or breeder reporting the death, explaining why the sire or dam was not genetically typed, and requesting that the Stewards of The Jockey Club waive this requirement for the registration of the resulting foal. The deceased sire or dam's Certificate of Foal Registration must also be returned to The Jockey Club (see Rule 16).

If a foal's sire or dam has been blood typed and dies before being DNA typed, it may be necessary to DNA and blood type the foal in order to qualify its parentage.

H. When an application is made to register a foal by an unnamed but registered sire or out of an unnamed but registered dam, the unnamed sire or dam must be named before the registration of the foal can be completed. A fee may be required to claim a name for an unnamed, but registered, sire or dam (see Fee Schedule).

2. REGISTRATION, GENETIC TYPING AND PARENTAGE VERIFICATION OF FOALS

A. A preprinted Live Foal/No Foal Report will be sent to the owner of record of each broodmare listed on a Report of Mares Bred form. If for any reason a breeder does not receive a preprinted Live Foal/No Foal Report by the time the foal is born, the breeder should contact The Jockey Club immediately. The Live Foal/No Foal Report serves a dual purpose; it is used to report the birth of a live foal or to report the status of a broodmare which did not produce a live foal. This report may be submitted through Interactive RegistrationTM at registry.jockeyclub.com.

B. To begin the registration process, each Live Foal Report should be fully completed, signed and returned to The Jockey Club no later than 30 days following the birth of the foal.

If reporting no live foal, submit the No Foal Report within 30 days of the intended birth of the foal. If the mare was not bred submit the No Foal Report in January.

C. A genetic typing kit and a preprinted Registration Application will be sent to the person specified on the Live Foal Report. If the genetic typing kit and preprinted Registration Application are not received within 180 days (6 months) of the foaling date, contact The Jockey Club immediately to request a genetic typing kit.

D. Within 45 days of receipt, the genetic typing kit should be used and the sample sent to the laboratory. The fully completed and signed Registration Application, along with a set of four color photographs of the foal (front, both sides and rear views) clearly showing the color and the markings (or lack of markings) on the head, legs and body, should be submitted to The Jockey Club along with the prescribed fee and a valid service certificate (see Rule 14C). The Registration Application may also be submitted through Interactive RegistrationTM at registry.jockeyclub.com. If either of these requirements are not met, the foal owner may be required to restart the process by obtaining a new genetic typing kit from The Jockey Club and an additional restart fee may be assessed (see Fee Schedule).

E. To correctly identify the foal, a Registration Application must be fully completed and signed each time a genetic sample is submitted.

F. In the case of twins, each twin must be registered separately. The fact that the foal is the product of a twin birth must be reported on the Live Foal Report (see Rule 15). If both twins are alive, the birth of each twin must be reported separately on a Live Foal Report. When submitting the Registration Applications for twins, attach a photocopy of the Service Certificate to the second Registration Application.

G. Upon the completion of all registration requirements within the specified deadlines, and if the foal qualifies as an offspring of its reported sire and dam, a Certificate of Foal Registration will be issued.

If a foal does not qualify as an offspring of its reported sire and/or dam, additional genetic typing may be required. Based on the results of the genetic typing and any other relevant information available, The Jockey Club will make a determination regarding the registration of the foal.

It is the registration applicant's responsibility to resolve doubts regarding parentage.

3. RACING PERMIT

A. The Stewards of The Jockey Club, in their discretion and for good cause, may issue a Racing Permit for any horse which has been genetically typed and parentage analyzed and whose dam qualified, but whose sire did not qualify. The Stewards may consider any other relevant factors in their determination and may require the owner and/or breeder to provide additional information which the Stewards deem necessary. A horse issued a Racing Permit cannot be considered a Thoroughbred for breeding purposes and cannot be entered into The American Stud Book. The term "Racing Permit" must always accompany the name of the horse in any trade journal or racetrack program. Any horse receiving a Racing Permit will never be entitled to receive a Certificate of Foal Registration.

B. To apply for a Racing Permit, the owner must submit a written request to the Stewards.

4. FEES TO REGISTER, GENETIC TYPE AND PARENTAGE VERIFY A FOAL

A. Foal registration fees are assessed according to a Registry Office Fee Schedule. Copies of this Fee Schedule are available from The Jockey Club Registry Office and are periodically included in Registry Office mailings and on The Jockey Club web site.

B. The fee to register a foal as stated in the current Fee Schedule will also cover:

1. Naming, provided a valid attempt to claim a name is received prior to February 1 of the two year old year;

2. The correction of a Certificate of Foal Registration, within six months of the date of issue, if necessary.

3. Subsequent transfers of ownership: and

4. Reissuance of a genetic typing kit for untestable samples.

C. Fees are not refundable, unless a foal dies and the death is reported prior to the issuance of a Certificate of Foal Registration. In this case, a fee will be charged for the genetic typing kit and processing, and upon written request, the remainder of the fee will be refunded (see Fee Schedule).

5. GENETIC TYPING REQUIREMENTS FOR STALLIONS, MARES AND EXPORTED HORSES

A. In addition to genetic typing and parentage verification of all foals as outlined in Rule 2, the following horses must be genetically typed:

1. All stallions and broodmares if not previously genetically typed.

2. All stallions and broodmares for foal crops of 2001 and thereafter must be DNA typed, either from DNA samples extracted from a blood sample already on file with the genetic laboratories or, if none is available, from DNA samples submitted in accordance with this Rule;

3. Foals of 2001 and thereafter that enter the stud for the first time as stallions must be re-DNA typed; and

4. All horses applying for an Export Certificate that have not been previously genetically typed (see Rule 10).

B. To apply for a blood typing kit, complete a Request for a Blood Typing Kit form and submit it to The Jockey Club, along with:

1. A check or money order payable to The Jockey Club for the prescribed fee (see Fee Schedule); and

2. The Certificate of Foal Registration (copies are not acceptable).

DNA typing kits can be obtained from The Jockey Club by request.

C. Within 45 days of receipt, the genetic typing kit should be used and the sample sent to the laboratory. The fully completed Identification form, along with a set of four color photographs of the horse (front, both sides and rear views) clearly showing the color and markings (or lack of markings) on the head, legs and body, must be submitted to The Jockey Club. If either of these requirements are not timely met, the owner may be required to restart the process by obtaining a new genetic typing kit from The Jockey Club, and a restart fee may be assessed (see Fee Schedule).

D. To correctly identify a horse, an Identification form must be fully completed each time a genetic sample is submitted.

E. The Jockey Club shall have the right to require that any horse be genetically typed or re-genetically typed at any time to establish or investigate a horse's identity or pedigree. If at any time The Jockey Club determines that the genetic type of a horse is inconsistent with the genetic type of either or both of its reported parents, The Jockey Club will notify the owner and the Certificate of Foal Registration will be revoked unless the owner provides an explanation satisfactory to the Registrar (or any other person designated by the President of The Jockey Club) within 30 days of notice. In the event that an explanation from the owner is timely received and establishes parentage to the satisfaction of The Jockey Club, a corrected Certificate of Foal Registration may be issued.

F. The Jockey Club will not respond to inquiries, other than pursuant to legal process, Court Order, approved Foreign Stud Book Authorities, recognized State Racing Commissions, Racetrack Authorities or law enforcement agencies with respect to genetic typing information as to specific horses, except upon written request, from a person whose name appears in The Jockey Club records as having an ownership interest in that horse, stating why this information is needed. In these instances, The Jockey Club will state in writing, if requested, whether, based upon information on file, the horse qualifies as an offspring of its reputed parents.

6. NAMING

A. A name may be claimed on the Registration Application, on a Name Claiming Form or through Interactive RegistrationTM at registry.jockeyclub.com. Name selections should be listed in order of preference. Names will be assigned based upon availability and compliance with the naming rules as stated herein. Names may not be claimed or reserved by telephone. When a foreign language name is submitted, an English translation must be furnished to The Jockey Club. An explanation must accompany "coined" or "made-up" names that have no apparent meaning. Horses that were born in the United States, Puerto Rico or Canada and currently reside in another country must be named by The Jockey Club through the Stud Book Authority of their country of residence.

B. If a valid attempt to name a foal is submitted to The Jockey Club by February 1 of the foal's two year old year and such a name is determined not eligible for use, no additional fee is required for a subsequent claim of name for that foal. If a valid attempt to name a foal is not submitted to The Jockey Club by February 1 of the foal's two year old year, a fee is required to claim a name for such a foal (see Fee Schedule).

C. A reserved name must be used within one year from the day it was reserved. Reserved names cannot be used until notification requesting the assignment of the name to a specific horse is received by the Registry Office. If the reserved name is not used within one year from its reservation, it will become available for any horse. A fee is required to reserve a name for a foal (see Fee Schedule).

D. A foal's name may be changed at any time prior to starting in its first race. Ordinarily, no name change will be permitted after a horse has started in its first race or has been used for breeding purposes. However, in the event a name must be changed after a horse has started in its first race, both the old and new names must be used until the horse has raced three times following the name change. The prescribed fee (see Fee Schedule) and the Certificate of Foal Registration must accompany any request to the Registry Office for a change of name.

E. Names of horses over ten years old may be eligible if they are not excluded under Rule 6(F) and have not been used during the preceding five years either in breeding or racing.

Names of geldings and horses that were never used for breeding or racing may be available five years from the date of their death as reported.

F. The following classes of names are not eligible for use:

1. Names consisting of more than 18 letters (spaces and punctuation marks count as letters);

2. Initials such as C.O.D., F.O.B., etc.;

3. Names ending in "filly," "colt," "stud," "mare," "stallion," or any similar horse-related term;

4. Names consisting entirely of numbers. Numbers above thirty may be used if they are spelled out.

5. Names ending with a numerical designation such as "2nd" or "3rd," whether or not such a designation is spelled out;

6. Names of persons unless written permission to use their name is on file with The Jockey Club;

7. Names of "famous" people no longer living unless approval is granted by the Board of Stewards of The Jockey Club;

8. Names of "notorious" people;

9. Names of racetracks or graded stakes races;

10. Recorded names such as assumed names or stable names;

11. Names clearly having commercial significance, such as trade names;

12. Copyrighted material, titles of books, plays, motion pictures, popular songs, etc., unless the applicant furnishes The Jockey Club with proof that the copyright has been abandoned or that such material has not been used within the last five years;

13. Names that are suggestive or have a vulgar or obscene meaning; names considered in poor taste; or names that may be offensive to religious, political or ethnic groups.

14. Names that are currently active either in the stud or on the turf, and names similar in spelling or pronunciation to such names, see 6(E);

15. Permanent names and names similar in spelling or pronunciation to permanent names. The list of criteria to establish a permanent name is as follows:

a. Horses in racing's Hall of Fame;

b. Horses that have been voted Horse of the Year;

c. Horses that have won an Eclipse Award;

d. Horses that have won a Sovereign Award (Canadian Champions);

e. Annual leading sire and broodmare sire by progeny earnings;

f. Cumulative money winners of $2 million or more;

g. Horses that have won the Kentucky Derby, Preakness, Belmont Stakes, The Jockey Club Gold Cup, the Breeders' Cup Classic or the Breeders' Cup Turf; and

h. Horses included in the International List of Protected Names.

G. In addition to the provisions of this Rule 6, the Registrar of The Jockey Club reserves the right of approval on all name claiming requests.

7. TRANSFER AND REPORT OF OWNERSHIP: OWNERSHIP DISPUTES

A. The transfer of ownership for all registered Thoroughbreds may be reported to The Jockey Club by completing a Transfer of Ownership form or through Interactive RegistrationTM at registry.jockey-club.com.

B. The ownership of all Thoroughbred stallions and broodmares must be reported to The Jockey Club each year. For stallions, ownership must be reported by submitting a Report of Mares Bred form (see Rule 14). In the case of a broodmare, ownership must be reported by submitting a Live Foal/No Foal Report (see Rules 2(A), (B), and 15). Based on the ownership reported on the respective forms, The Jockey Club will record any transfer of ownership. If a Thoroughbred stallion or broodmare is sold or otherwise transferred after submitting a Report of Mares Bred Form or Live Foal/No Foal Report, the new ownership must be reported by submitting a Transfer of Ownership Form as in Rule 7(A).

C. If The Jockey Club becomes aware of conflicting information with respect to the ownership of a horse, or other rights in or related to a horse ("Ownership Issues"), The Jockey Club may request additional information and The Jockey Club may defer action related to the horse until the interested parties agree to resolve the Ownership Issues or The Jockey Club may take action based upon Court Order (see Rule 21(F)) or other factors it deems appropriate in its discretion. The Jockey Club shall have no obligation to any party arising out of its decision to defer action or to take action.

In addition, the failure of an owner to submit a valid service certificate pursuant to Rule 2(D) may be considered evidence of an ownership issue to be resolved as set forth above, but in the event action is deferred by The Jockey Club it will process but not issue the Certificate of Foal Registration until a valid service certificate is submitted to The Jockey Club and all other requirements of Rule 2 are satisfied.

D. The Jockey Club will not respond to inquiries, other than pursuant to legal process, Court Order, approved Foreign Stud Book Authorities, recognized State Racing Commissions, Racetrack Authorities or law enforcement agencies with respect to ownership information as to a specific horse, except upon written request, from a person whose name appears in The Jockey Club records as having an ownership interest in that horse.

E. It is advisable that no one complete the purchase of a Thoroughbred until the Certificate of Foal Registration has been transferred by the previous owner. Before completing the sale, the new owner should compare the description on the Certificate of Foal Registration with the actual markings, including cowlicks, found on the horse.

8. CORRECTION OF CERTIFICATE OF FOAL REGISTRATION

A. To obtain a Corrected Certificate of Foal Registration, the following must be submitted to the Registry Office:

1. A check or money order payable to The Jockey Club covering the prescribed fee (see Fee Schedule).

2. A set of four color photographs of the horse (front, both sides, and rear views) clearly showing the color, markings (or lack of markings) on the head, legs and body, and showing any discrepancies, if possible, with the existing Certificate of Foal Registration;

3. A completed and signed Corrected Certificate Form containing the written description of the markings as they now appear on the horse, including the exact location of the head and neck cowlicks; and

4. The Certificate of Foal Registration.

B. Nothing in this rule shall preclude the use of genetic typing information for the purpose of reidenti-fying any horse at any time. If the identity or pedigree of any horse is in question, The Jockey Club may require genetic typing and/or parentage verification to ensure proper identity or pedigree.

9. DUPLICATE CERTIFICATE OF FOAL REGISTRATION

A. If a Certificate of Foal Registration has been lost or destroyed, a Duplicate Certificate of Foal Registration may be issued by the Registry Office upon submission of the following:

1. A check or money order payable to The Jockey Club covering the prescribed fee (see Fee Schedule);

2. A set of four color photographs of the horse (front, both sides, and rear views) clearly showing the color, and the markings (or lack of markings) on the head, legs and body;

3. A completed and signed Duplicate Certificate Form containing the written description of the markings on the horse, including the exact location of the head and neck cowlicks;

4. A notarized statement from the owner or his authorized agent describing the circumstances under which the Certificate of Foal Registration was lost or destroyed;

5. Proof of ownership of that specific horse (for example, a bill of sale or cancelled check including the name or pedigree of the horse, date of sale and the name of the new owner); and

6. Any further evidence and assurances as The Jockey Club may require, such as genetic typing and/or parentage verification.

B. Except as expressly provided in this Rule 9, a Duplicate Certificate of Foal Registration will not be issued as long as the original Certificate of Foal Registration is known to be in existence; provided however, in the event of a sheriff's (or similar) sale or under a non-appealable Court Order, a Duplicate Certificate of Foal Registration will be issued if the Certificate of Foal Registration cannot be obtained from the previous owner only after a good faith effort to recover it is made by the seller and/or the new owner, and in either case, the requirements of Rule 9(A) 1, 2, 3, 5 and 6 must be met and an opinion must be submitted to The Jockey Club from an attorney or an official represen-tative of the court, indicating that the sale (if applicable) was conducted in accordance with the laws of the state and providing such other information as The Jockey Club may request regarding the circumstances and validity of the sale or court order.

C. Once a Duplicate Certificate of Foal Registration is issued, the original Certificate of Foal Registration becomes null and void, and if located, must be returned to the Registry Office.

10. EXPORT REQUIREMENTS

A. When a horse is to be exported to a country outside of the United States, Puerto Rico or Canada, a Certificate of Exportation and passport must be obtained from The Jockey Club within 60 days of exportation. If for any reason the requirements are not completed within 60 days of exportation, the Certificate of Exportation may be obtained only after approval by the Stewards of The Jockey Club and the payment of an additional fee (see Fee Schedule).

B. To obtain a Certificate of Exportation and passport, a horse must be genetically typed, or be in the process of being genetically typed (samples must have arrived at the laboratory in a testable condi-tion) unless the horse was genetically typed previously. If genetic typing is required, a genetic typ-ing kit must be obtained as set forth in Rule 5(B) and the following must be completed and submit-ted to The Jockey Club by the time of the horse's departure:

1. A check or money order payable to The Jockey Club covering the prescribed fee (see Fee Schedule);

2. A set of four color photographs of the horse (front, both sides and rear views) clearly showing the color and the markings (or lack of markings) on the head, legs and body;

3. A completed Export Identification form. The form must be signed by the owner (or owner's authorized agent) and must also indicate the country of destination, name of broker, date of shipment, and ownership of the horse. This form may also be submitted through Interactive RegistrationTM at registry.jockeyclub.com;

4. The Certificate of Foal Registration, 30-Day Racing Permit or Certificate of Foreign Registration;

5. A valid Service Certificate for all mares in foal. If a Service Certificate is not available at the time of shipment, it must be submitted to The Jockey Club as soon as it is received by the owner.

C. The Jockey Club will forward directly to the appropriate Foreign Stud Book Authority the Certificate of Exportation and any other necessary documents as may be reasonably requested by that Stud Book Authority.

D. If a horse is exported to a country whose Stud Book is not approved and then returns to the United States, Puerto Rico or Canada, the owner (or owner's authorized agent) must satisfy all of the requirements of Rule 10(A) and (B), and the horse must be genetically typed and identified within 60 days of its return. No progeny foaled or conceived in a country whose Stud Book is not approved will be eligible for registration in The American Stud Book.

E. Any horse exported without receiving a Certificate of Exportation that returns to the United States, Puerto Rico or Canada must be re-identified, genetically typed, obtain a Certificate of Exportation and pay an additional fee (see Fee Schedule) before The Jockey Club will reissue the Certificate of Foal Registration.

F. Any horse imported into the United States, Puerto Rico or Canada whose sire or dam was not exported properly in accordance with Rule 10 will not receive a Certificate of Foreign Registration until that sire or dam has fulfilled the export requirements.

G. If a horse is imported into the United States, Puerto Rico or Canada and its sire or dam was not exported in accordance with Rule 10, and has since died, The Jockey Club will issue a Certificate of Foreign Registration only upon written application and approval of the Stewards of The Jockey Club to waive the export requirements.

11. IMPORT REQUIREMENTS

A. Horses bred outside of the United States, Puerto Rico or Canada must satisfy the eligibility requirements of Rules 1(C) and 1(D) and must obtain a Certificate of Foreign Registration from The Jockey Club when imported into the United States, Puerto Rico or Canada.

B. To obtain a Certificate of Foreign Registration, the owner or broker must cause the exporting country's registry to submit directly to The Jockey Club within 60 days of arrival of the horse in the United States, Puerto Rico or Canada the following:

1. The Stud Book Certificate or Export Certificate containing the written description and diagrams of the markings on the horse including the exact location of the head and neck cowlicks;

2. A certified copy of the horse's complete racing record. Racing records from the World Hub may also be accepted if available; and

3. A valid Service Certificate if the imported broodmare is in foal.

C. In addition, within 60 days of arrival of the horse in the United States, Puerto Rico or Canada, the owner or broker of the horse must submit the following to The Jockey Club Registry office:

1. A check or money order payable to The Jockey Club covering the prescribed fee (see Fee Schedule);

2. A completed and signed Import Registration Form containing the written description and diagrams of the markings on the horse including the exact location of the head and neck cowlicks. This form may also be submitted through Interactive RegistrationTM at registry.jockeyclub.com.

3. Four color photographs of the horse (front, both sides, and rear views) taken in this country clearly showing the color and the markings (or lack of markings) on the head, legs and body; and

4. The Passport Book, if applicable.

D. If for any reason, the requirements are not completed within 60 days of arrival, the Certificate of Foreign Registration may be obtained only after approval of the Stewards of The Jockey Club and the payment of an additional fee (see Fee Schedule). A horse is not eligible for a Certificate of Foreign Registration unless all requirements, including the appropriate fee (see Fee Schedule), are received by The Jockey Club within one year of the date of arrival in the United States, Puerto Rico or Canada; provided however, the Stewards may, under limited circumstances, grant late registration to a horse that has been in the United States, Puerto Rico, or Canada for more than one year since its arrival provided the following conditions are met:

1. The applicant sets forth in writing to The Jockey Club the reasons the applicant believes he should be relieved from the one year registration requirement; and

2. The Stewards of The Jockey Club determine that the applicant has sufficiently demonstrated mistake, inadvertence, excusable neglect or other circumstances which justify late registration; and

3. The horse had been genetically typed in its country of birth and/or its identity can be established to the satisfaction of the Stewards of The Jockey Club; and

4. The applicant completes all registration requirements, including genetic typing, and submits a late registration fee (see Fee Schedule).

12. 30-DAY FOREIGN RACING PERMIT

A. A 30-Day (Foreign) Racing Permit is a permit issued by the Registry Office of The Jockey Club entitling foreign Thoroughbreds to race in the United States, Puerto Rico or Canada for a period of not longer than 30 days.

B. To obtain a 30-Day (Foreign) Racing Permit, the owner or broker must cause the exporting country's registry to submit directly to The Jockey Club:

1. The Stud Book Certificate or Export Certificate containing the written description of the markings on the horse including the exact location of the head and neck cowlicks, or if neither of these documents are available at that time, a written confirmation of the identity of the horse from the exporting country's Stud Book Authority; and a certified copy of the horse's complete racing record.

C. The owner or broker of the horse must submit the following directly to The Jockey Club Registry Office:

1. A check or money order payable to The Jockey Club covering the prescribed fee (see Fee Schedule);

2. A completed and signed Import Registration Form containing the written description and diagrams of the markings on the horse, including the exact location of the head and neck cowlicks;

3. Four color photographs of the horse (front, both sides and rear views) clearly showing the color and the markings (or lack of markings) on the head, legs and body; and

4. The Passport Book, if applicable.

D. A 30-Day Foreign Racing Permit shall expire upon the expiration date on the permit or earlier if the Thoroughbred leaves the country prior to the expiration date.

E. In the event a Thoroughbred remains in the United States, Puerto Rico or Canada more than 30 days, the owner or authorized agent must apply for a Certificate of Foreign Registration and all import requirements must be satisfied as stated in Rule 11.

13. LEASES AND FOAL-SHARING AGREEMENTS

When a Thoroughbred, through contract or agreement, is leased or entered into foal-sharing, it must be reported to The Jockey Club each year. The lease of a stallion should be reported by checking the lessee box on the Report of Mares Bred form. For a broodmare, a lease or foal-sharing agreement must be reported by checking the lessee or foal-sharing box on the Live Foal Report.

14. STALLION REPORTS (REPORT OF MARES BRED)

A. All stallion owners must report each Thoroughbred broodmare that was bred to their stallion(s) on the Report of Mares Bred form which must be sent to The Jockey Club no later than August 1 of each breeding year. This form may also be submitted through Interactive RegistrationTM at registry.jockeyclub.com. Failure to comply with this deadline will result in delays in the issuance of Service Certificates. Mares bred on Southern Hemisphere time must be reported as soon as possible.

B. A separate Report of Mares Bred form must be completed yearly for each stallion and must be signed by the stallion owner, lessee or authorized agent.

   If the stallion was leased, check the appropriate box provided on the Report of Mares Bred form. If the stallion has died since the last stallion report, a Report of Deaths form should also be submitted.

C. Based on the information on the Report of Mares Bred form submitted by August 1, The Jockey Club will forward to the stallion owner, lessee or authorized agent a preprinted Service Certificate for each broodmare bred, including the name of the stallion, the name of the broodmare, the name of the dam of the broodmare, and the date of the last cover. When the stallion owner, lessee or authorized agent receives the preprinted Service Certificate, it should be examined for accuracy, signed by the stallion owner, lessee or authorized agent and forwarded to the breeder of the foal or submitted to The Jockey Club through Interactive RegistrationTM at registry.jockeyclub.com. The Service Certificate is required to register a foal. Service Certificates will not be issued unless a Report of Mares Bred form is on file at The Jockey Club and until genetic or re-DNA typing of the stallion has been completed (see Rule Five).

D. If the preprinted Service Certificates are lost, duplicate Service Certificates will be issued upon request of the stallion owner, lessee or authorized agent.

15. LIVE FOAL/NO FOAL REPORTS (MARE REPORTS)

A. The breeding status of all Thoroughbred broodmares must be reported yearly to The Jockey Club by submitting a Live Foal/No Foal Report indicating either live foal information or no foal information. This report may also be submitted through Interactive RegistrationTM at registry.jockeyclub.com.

B. In case of a live foal, a fully completed and signed Live Foal Report must be submitted to The Jockey Club within 30 days of the birth of the foal as required in Rule 2.

C. In the case of no foal to be registered, the breeder should submit to The Jockey Club a fully completed and signed No Foal Report within 30 days of the intended birth of the foal. If the mare was not bred submit the No Foal Report in January.

16. DEATH REPORTS

The death of a registered Thoroughbred, or foal for which registration is pending, should be reported to The Jockey Club Registry Office within 30 days of the death by submitting a completed Report of Deaths Form, or through Interactive RegistrationTM at registry.jockeyclub.com and returning the Certificate of Foal Registration, if issued.

17. GELDING REPORTS

If a Colt or Horse has been gelded, the owner or his authorized agent should promptly report that information to The Jockey Club Office by submitting a completed Gelding Report or by furnishing the information through registry.jockeyclub.com. Additionally, The Jockey Club will accept gelding reports from a racetrack recognized by The Jockey Club.

18. SOLD WITHOUT PEDIGREE

A. Any owner who desires a horse no longer to be considered a Thoroughbred for racing or breeding purposes must promptly surrender the Certificate of Foal Registration to The Jockey Club within 60 days of the date of sale with an accompanying notation that the horse was transferred or sold "without pedigree." The notation must be signed by the owner or authorized agent and indicate the date of disposition. In the event the owner or his authorized agent surrenders the Certificate of Foal Registration to The Jockey Club in the above manner more than 60 days after the date of transfer or sale, then the new owner or transferee must also submit a statement that the horse was purchased or received without pedigree.

B. Upon receipt in The Jockey Club Registry Office, the respective Certificate of Foal Registration will be canceled. Once the registration is canceled, the horse cannot be reinstated into the registry, and a Duplicate Certificate of Foal Registration will not be issued.

C. Notations upon a Certificate of Foal Registration which do not clearly indicate transferred or sold without pedigree, including notations such as "not to be raced," shall not result in cancellation of the Certificate of Foal Registration. Such notations could be regarded as defacing the Certificate of Foal Registration and, submission to The Jockey Club of any such defaced Certificate of Foal Registration, may cause a Corrected Certificate of Foal Registration to be issued.

19. DECEPTIVE PRACTICES

A. Any person or entity (collectively "Person") may be denied any or all of the privileges of The American Stud Book in the event:

1. That Person either knowingly misrepresents or aids or abets the misrepresentation of the identity, name, age, appearance, pedigree, genetic type, eligibility for registration or any other information in, or in connection with, any communication to The Jockey Club;

2. That Person steals, counterfeits, forges or alters a certificate or document issued by The Jockey Club or knowingly receives a stolen, counterfeited, forged or altered certificate or document issued by The Jockey Club;

3. That Person intentionally violates any of the Principal Rules and Requirements of The American Stud Book; or

4. There is a final determination by a court (whether civil, criminal or administrative), an official tribunal or an official racing body that such Person: (a) knowingly misrepresented or aided or abetted the misrepresentation of a horse's identity, name, age, appearance, pedigree, genetic type or any other information in connection with either entry in a race or the racing of any horse; (b) knowingly misrepresented or aided or abetted the misrepresentation of a horse's eligibility for registration or any other matter related to The American Stud Book; (c) stole, counterfeited, forged or altered a certificate or document issued by The Jockey Club or knowingly received a stolen, counterfeited, forged or altered certificate or document issued by The Jockey Club; or (d) killed, abandoned, mistreated, neglected or abused, or otherwise committed an act of cruelty to a horse.

B. In the event the Registrar has a reasonable basis upon which to conclude that any of the circumstances identified in subparagraphs (1) through (4) above may apply, the Registrar shall notify such Person in writing (the "Rule 19 Notification"): (i) of the specific subpart(s) of this rule which apply; (ii) of the basis upon which the Registrar believes that the subparts apply; (iii) of the Registrar's proposed action; and (iv) that the Person has the right, within 30 days of the date that Person receives the Rule 19 Notification, either to submit to the Board of Stewards of The Jockey Club ("Stewards") written information to be considered in their determination of the matter or to request a hearing by submitting to the Stewards a written request for a hearing, briefly stating the reasons why that Person asserts that this rule does not apply and/or that the proposed action is not appropriate ("Rule 19 Hearing Request").

C. If a hearing is requested, a non-refundable administrative fee of one thousand dollars ($1,000.00) must be submitted with the Rule 19 Hearing Request.

If no hearing is requested, then all information submitted by the Registrar and the Person shall be considered by the Stewards at their next meeting, at which time the Stewards shall make a final determination as to whether to deny the Person any or all of the privileges of The American Stud Book and the nature and extent of any such denial. The Stewards' determination shall be promptly reduced to writing, stating the decision made and briefly stating the reasons for such decision, and delivered to the Person (and his counsel, if any) and to the Registrar.

If a hearing is requested, then all further proceedings shall be conducted in accordance with the procedures set forth in Rule 20(C).

D. Any Person who receives a Rule 19 Notification may request an expedited determination by submitting a written request to the Stewards with a detailed explanation as to why an expedited determination is warranted.

The authority of the Stewards under this rule and of any Hearing Officer appointed under Rule 20 to hear a matter pursuant to a Rule 19 Hearing Request shall be limited to considering (i) whether a denial of any or all of the privileges of The American Stud Book is warranted under the criteria in this rule and (ii) the nature and extent of any denial of those privileges.

Any determination of the Stewards made pursuant to this Rule 19 shall be final.

20. APPEALS AND HEARINGS

A. Any person or entity ("Person") wishing to object to any action or decision of the Registrar or other officer of The Jockey Club (collectively "Registrar/Officer") (other than Rule 19 Notifications and Rule 19 final determinations) in the application of the Rules to such Person or to such Person's horses(s), may, within 30 days of being advised of such action or decision, submit to the Board of Stewards of The Jockey Club ("Stewards") a written statement ("Statement") including:

1. The specific nature and basis for objecting to the action or decision of the Registrar/Officer;

2. A brief statement of the facts and any documents, affidavits or other written material which that Person believes will be helpful in considering the matter; and

3. If a hearing is desired, a specific request for a hearing.

If a hearing is requested, a non-refundable administrative fee of one thousand dollars ($1,000.00) must be submitted with the Statement.

B. If no hearing is requested, then all information submitted by the Person and the Registrar shall be considered by the Stewards at their next meeting after receipt of the Statement, at which time the Stewards shall make a final determination. That determination shall be promptly reduced to writing, stating the decision made and briefly stating the reasons for such decision, and delivered to the Person (and his counsel, if any) and the Registrar/Officer.

C. If a hearing is requested under either Rule 20(A) or Rule 19 then, within 10 days after receiving the Statement or the Rule 19 Hearing Request, whichever applies, the designee of the Chairman of the Stewards shall provide written notice to the Person of the name, address and telephone number of the individual Steward or independent hearing officer (collectively "Hearing Officer') appointed to hear the matter.

Within 15 days after the date of the appointment of the Hearing Officer, the Hearing Officer shall conduct a telephonic prehearing conference for the purpose of ruling on preliminary matters, clarifying and narrowing the issues, entering into stipulations, scheduling the hearing and considering other issues as may aid in the disposition of the matter. The final hearing shall be scheduled no less than 15 and no more than 30 days after the date of the prehearing conference unless the parties otherwise agree. All hearings shall take place at the offices of The Jockey Club, 821 Corporate Drive, Lexington, Kentucky 40503.

Any Person requesting a hearing may appear personally, if such Person is an individual, or with counsel authorized to act on such Person's behalf and may present witnesses and other evidence. The Registrar/Officer of The Jockey Club may appear with counsel and may testify and present witnesses and other evidence. Any other person having an interest in the subject matter may appear at the hearing if the Hearing Officer determines that such person might materially assist in the determination of the matter.

All testimony at the hearing shall be under oath and stenographically recorded. The Hearing Officer shall not be bound by technical rules of evidence and may receive any evidence which he considers to be reliable and relevant, if not unduly repetitious, including testimony which would be hearsay if presented in a court of law.

The Hearing Officer shall, within 45 days after the close of the hearing, submit written factual findings and recommendations to the Stewards and provide a copy of those findings and recommendations to the Person (and his counsel, if any) and to counsel for the Registrar/Officer. The Stewards shall, no later than the next meeting of the Stewards after the findings and recommendations are made, make a final determination of the matter. The Stewards may accept or reject the findings and/or recommendations in whole or in part. The determination of the Stewards shall then be promptly reduced to writing, stating the decision made and briefly stating the reasons for such decision, and delivered to the Person (and his counsel, if any) and to counsel for the Registrar/Officer.

A Person who has requested a hearing may subsequently waive the right to a hearing by submitting to the Hearing Officer a written statement waiving the right to hearing, in which case, the matter shall proceed under Rule 20(B) or Rule 19, whichever applies, as if no hearing had been requested. Any requests for postponement of a scheduled hearing must be made in writing showing good cause why the postponement should be granted and must actually be received by the Hearing Officer at least 3 business days prior to the scheduled date of the hearing, absent extreme exigent circumstances.

If a Person requests a hearing but fails to appear on the scheduled date, the matter shall proceed under Rule 20(B) or Rule 19, whichever applies, as if no hearing had been requested.

D. Any person submitting a Statement under this rule may request an expedited determination by submitting a written request to the Stewards with a detailed explanation as to why an expedited determination is warranted.

The authority of the Stewards and any Hearing Officer appointed to hear any matter initiated under Rule 20(A) shall be limited to considering whether the Registrar/Officer acted in accordance with the Principal Rules and Requirements of The American Stud Book and any applicable policies of The Jockey Club.

Any determination of the Stewards made pursuant to this Rule 20 shall be final.

21. GENERAL RULES

A. Owners, breeders and authorized agents are responsible for being familiar with the Principal Rules and Requirements of The American Stud Book. Amendments and new rules are available on The Jockey Club web site at jockeyclub.com.

B. Notwithstanding any other provisions in these Rules, it is the responsibility of each applicant to obtain from The Jockey Club all necessary forms and to submit all completed forms and other requirements by the applicable deadlines.

C. Certificates of Foal Registration are issued on the basis of information submitted to The Jockey Club by the applicant and are subject to revocation and cancellation if further information is received by The Jockey Club indicating improper or erroneous issuance. In the event of cancellation or revocation of a Certificate of Foal Registration, that Certificate must be promptly returned to The Jockey Club Registry Office.

D. For the purpose of determining whether a deadline has been met, any document or other material submitted to The Jockey Club shall be deemed to have been submitted to and/or received by The Jockey Club only upon: (1) actual receipt in the appropriate office of The Jockey Club; or (2) if transmitted by United States Mail or other recognized mail carrier, the date such carrier received the material from the sender if that date is noted by the carrier on the outside of the container.

E. Any notices or other material sent by The Jockey Club to any person, including any owner or authorized agent, shall be mailed to the last known address on file with The Jockey Club for the horse which is the subject of the notice or other material regardless of whether the same person has other addresses on file with The Jockey Club for other horses. Change of Address Forms are available from The Jockey Club and may be submitted by the horse owner or authorized agent to notify The Jockey Club of a change of address for mailing notices or other material for any specified horse(s).

F. Notwithstanding any other provisions in these rules, The Jockey Club may require any party(ies) who requests action or inaction from The Jockey Club arising out of or relating to a dispute or controversy with a third party(ies) to settle that dispute in a court of competent jurisdiction and The Jockey Club may defer a decision concerning the matter pending resolution of the dispute as aforesaid. The Jockey Club shall have no obligation to any party arising out of any decision to defer action or to take action under any provision of these Rules.

G. The Jockey Club may decline to process any material received from an owner or breeder not in good standing with The Jockey Club. An owner or breeder will be considered not in good standing if the owner or breeder has any outstanding fees owed to The Jockey Club for any horse including, but not limited to, fees related to registration, genetic typing, naming, imports, exports, duplicates or corrections.

H. Subject to the rules requiring payment of late fees, all fees are due at the time of the submittal of the applicable form or request to The Jockey Club. The Fee Schedule sets forth each submittal to The Jockey Club for which there is a fee and the amount of each fee. In the event any person fails to pay a fee owed to The Jockey Club, then The Jockey Club shall apply any payment subsequently received from that person to the outstanding fees owed by that person to The Jockey Club.

GLOSSARY OF TERMS

The American Stud Book

The American Stud Book is the registry maintained by The Jockey Club for all Thoroughbreds foaled in the United States, Puerto Rico and Canada and for all Thoroughbreds imported into the United States, Puerto Rico and Canada from countries that have a registry recognized by The Jockey Club and the International Stud Book Committee.

Age of a Horse

Foal: A young horse of either sex in its first year of life.

Suckling: A foal of any sex in its first year of life while it is still nursing.

Weanling: A foal of any sex in its first year of life after being separated from its dam.

Yearling: A colt, filly or gelding in its second calendar year of life (Beginning January 1 of the year following its birth).

Two-Year-Old: A colt, filly or gelding in its third calendar year of life (Beginning January 1 of the year following its yearling year).

Breeding Practices Not Approved by The Jockey Club

Artificial Insemination: The process of depositing semen into the reproductive tract of a broodmare in order to get a broodmare in foal (pregnant) without the physical mounting by a stallion.

Cloning: Any method by which the genetic material of an unfertilized egg or an embryo is (i) removed, (ii) replaced by genetic material taken from another organism, (iii) added to with genetic material from another organism, or (iv) otherwise modified by any means in order to produce a live foal.

Embryo Transfer (Transplants): The method whereby a developing embryo or unfertilized egg is removed from its natural dam and implanted into the reproductive tract of either the natural dam or a host dam for a portion of the gestation period in order to produce a live foal.

Breeding Terminology

Bred (Mated): Any filly or mare that has undergone the physical act of breeding (mating).

Bred (Area Foaled): The term "bred" is sometimes used to describe the location where a foal was born, i.e., Kentucky Bred, New York Bred, etc.

Breeder: The breeder of a foal is the owner of the dam at the time of foaling, unless the dam was under a lease or foal-sharing agreement at the time of foaling. In that case, the person(s) specified by the terms of the agreement is (are) the breeder of the foal.

Stallion: A male horse that is used to produce foals.

Sire: A male horse that has produced, or is producing, foals.

Broodmare: A filly or mare that has been bred (mated) and is used to produce foals.

Dam: A female horse that has produced, or is producing, foals.

Maiden: A filly or mare that has never been bred (mated).

In Foal (Pregnant) Broodmare: A filly or mare that was bred (mated), conceived and is currently in foal (pregnant).

Aborted: A term used to describe a broodmare that has been pronounced in foal (pregnant) based on an examination of 42 days or more post breeding (mating) and lost her foal prematurely; or a broodmare from whom an aborted fetus has been observed.

Barren (Not Pregnant): A term used to describe a filly or mare, other than a maiden mare, that was bred (mated) and did not conceive during the last breeding season.

Breeding (Mating): The physical act of a stallion mounting a broodmare with intromission of the penis and ejaculation of semen into the reproductive tract.

Sex

Colt: An entire male horse four-years-old or younger.

Horse: When reference is made to sex, a "horse" is an entire male five-years-old or older.

Ridgling ("rig"): A lay term used to describe either a monorchid or cryptorchid.

Cryptorchid: A male horse of any age that has no testes in his scrotum but was never gelded (the testes are undescended).

Monorchid: A male horse of any age that has only one testicle in his scrotum - the other testicle was either removed or is undescended.

Gelding: A male horse of any age that is unsexed - had both testicles removed.

Filly: A female horse four-years-old or younger.

Mare: A female horse five-years-old or older.

Thoroughbred

A Thoroughbred is a horse which has satisfied the rules and requirements set forth herein and is registered in The American Stud Book or in a Foreign Stud Book recognized by The Jockey Club and the International Stud Book Committee.

United States

The United States includes the 50 states, the District of Columbia, and the insular territories and possessions of the United States of America.

Interactive RegistrationTM

An internet site where breeders, owners and authorized agents can submit registration forms, check registration status and browse the online names book.

Genetic Typing

The process of determining the genetic factors present in a blood or DNA sample.

COLOR GUIDE

The following colors are recognized by The Jockey Club:

Bay: The entire coat of the horse may vary from a yellow-tan to a bright auburn. The mane, tail and lower portion of the legs are always black, unless white markings are present.

Black: The entire coat of the horse is black, including the muzzle, the flanks, the mane, tail and legs, unless white markings are present.

Chestnut: The entire coat of the horse may vary from a red-yellow to a golden-yellow. The mane, tail and legs are usually variations of the coat color, unless white markings are present.

Dark Bay/Brown: The entire coat of the horse will vary from a brown, with areas of tan on the shoulders, head and flanks, to a dark brown, with tan areas seen only in the flanks and/or muzzle. The mane, tail and lower portion of the legs are always black, unless white markings are present.

Gray/Roan: The Jockey Club has combined these colors into one color category. This does not change the individual definitions of the colors for gray and roan and in no way impacts on the two-coat color inheritance principle as stated in Rule 1(E).

Gray: The majority of the coat of the horse is a mixture of black and white hairs. The mane, tail and legs may be either black or gray, unless white markings are present.

Roan: The majority of the coat of the horse is a mixture of red and white hairs or brown and white hairs. The mane, tail and legs may be black, chestnut or roan, unless white markings are present.

Palomino: The entire coat of the horse is golden-yellow, unless white markings are present. The mane and tail are usually flaxen.

White: A rare color not to be confused with the colors gray or roan. The entire coat, including the mane, tail and legs, is white and no other color should be present.

LOCATION OF OFFICES & AVAILABILITY OF FORMS AND INFORMATION

Executive Office:
The Jockey Club
40 East 52nd Street
New York, New York 10022
Telephone: (212) 371-5970
FAX: (212) 371-6123

Registry Office:
The Jockey Club
821 Corporate Drive
Lexington, Kentucky 40503-2794
Telephone: (859) 224-2700
Registration Services: (800) 444-8521
FAX: (859) 224-2710

Canada:
The Jockey Club of Canada
P.O. Box 156
Rexdale, Ontario M9W 5L1
Telephone: (416) 675-7756
FAX: (416) 675-4573
Availability of forms and information only.

All Registry Office forms and current Fee Schedules are available from the Registration Services Department in the Lexington, Kentucky office.

Top Priced North American Yearlings Since 1980

Sale	Horse	Sex	Sire	Dam	Buyer	Sale price
KEE JUL SEL YRLG 85	Seattle Dancer	C	Nijinsky II	My Charmer	BBA (England)	$13,100,000
KEE JUL SEL YRLG 83	Snaafi Dancer	C	Northern Dancer	My Bupers	Aston Upthorpe Stud	10,200,000
KEE JUL SEL YRLG 84	Imperial Falcon	C	Northern Dancer	Ballade	BBA (England)	8,250,000
KEE JUL SEL YRLG 84	Jareer	C	Northern Dancer	Fabuleux Jane	Darley Stud Management	7,100,000
KEE JUL SEL YRLG 85	Laa Etaab	C	Nijinsky II	Crimson Saint	Gainsborough Farm	7,000,000
KEE SEP YRLG 00	Tasmanian Tiger	C	Storm Cat	Hum Along	Demi O'Byrne	6,800,000
KEE JUL SEL YRLG 84	Amjaad	C	Seattle Slew	Desiree	Darley Stud Management	6,500,000
KEE SEP YRLG 01	Van Nistelrooy	C	Storm Cat	Halory	Demi O'Byrne	6,400,000
KEE SEP YRLG 01	Alajwad	C	Storm Cat	La Affirmed	John Ferguson Bloodstock	5,500,000
KEE JUL SEL YRLG 84	Obligato	C	Northern Dancer	Truly Bound	BBA (Ireland)	5,400,000
KEE SEP YRLG 00	King's Consul	C	Kingmambo	Battle Creek Girl	John Ferguson Bloodstock	5,300,000
KEE JUL SEL YRLG 84	Wassl Touch	C	Northern Dancer	Queen Sucree	Darley Stud Management	5,100,000
KEE JUL SEL YRLG 84	Professor Blue	C	Northern Dancer	Mississippi Mud	BBA (England)	4,600,000
FTN YRLG SAR 84	Parlando	C	Northern Dancer	Bubbling	BBA (Ireland)	4,600,000
KEE SEP YRLG 00	Shah Jehan	C	Mr. Prospector	Voodoo Lily	Demi O'Byrne	4,400,000
KEE SEP YRLG 00	Moon's Whisper	F	Storm Cat	East of the Moon	Shadwell Estate Co.	4,400,000
KEE JUL SEL YRLG 82	Empire Glory	C	Nijinsky II	Spearfish	BBA (Ireland)	4,250,000
KEE JUL SEL YRLG 83	Foxboro	C	Northern Dancer	Desert Vixen	BBA (England)	4,250,000
FTN SEL YRLG SAR 00	Distinction	C	Seattle Slew	Omi	David J. Shimmon	4,200,000
KEE JUL SEL YRLG 83	Gallant Archer	C	Nijinsky II	Belle of Dodge Me	Aston Upthorpe Stud	4,100,000
KEE JUL YRLG 01	Warhol	C	Saint Ballado	Charm a Gendarme	Demi O'Byrne	4,000,000
FTN YRLG SAR 84	Elnawaagi	C	Roberto	Gurkhas Band	Darley Stud Management	4,000,000
KEE JUL YRLG 98	Fusaichi Pegasus	C	Mr. Prospector	Angel Fever	Fusao Sekiguchi	4,000,000
KEE SEP YRLG 00	Showlady	F	Theatrical (IRE)	Claxton's Slew	John Ferguson Bloodstock	4,000,000
KEE SEP YRLG 99	Dubai to Dubai	C	Kris S.	Mr. P's Princess	John Ferguson Bloodstock	3,900,000
KEE SEP YRLG 01	Hoyer	C	Mr. Prospector	Destination Mir	John Ferguson Bloodstock	3,800,000
KEE SEP YRLG 03		F	Gone West	Touch of Greatness	John Ferguson	3,800,000
KEE JUL SEL YRLG 84	Alchaasibiyeh	F	Seattle Slew	Fine Prospect	Darley Stud Management	3,750,000
KEE JUL SEL YRLG 87	Warrshan	C	Northern Dancer	Secret Asset	Darley Stud Management	3,700,000
KEE JUL YRLG 01	Virtuosa	F	Seeking the Gold	Escena	Reynolds Bell Jr., agent	3,700,000
KEE SEP YRLG 03		C	Danzig	Queena	Demi O'Byrne	3,600,000
KEE SEP YRLG 00	America's Storm	C	Storm Cat	Lilly Capote	Padua-Gaines-Gentry	3,600,000
KEE JUL YRLG 00	Born Perfect	F	Mr. Prospector	Molly Girl	Padua Stables	3,600,000
KEE JUL YRLG 01	Act of Duty	C	Mr. Prospector	Nuryette	John Ferguson Bloodstock	3,600,000
KEE JUL SEL YRLG 86	Northern State	C	Northern Dancer	South Ocean	Darley Stud Management	3,600,000
KEE JUL SEL YRLG 81	Ballydoyle	C	Northern Dancer	South Ocean	BBA (Ireland)	3,500,000
KEE JUL SEL YRLG 88	Royal Academy	C	Nijinsky II	Crimson Saint	M V O Brien	3,500,000
KEE JAN ALL AGES 98	Inkling	F	Seeking the Gold	Number	Demi O'Byrne	3,400,000
KEE JUL YRLG 00	Sophisticat	F	Storm Cat	Serena's Song	Demi O'Byrne	3,400,000
KEE SEP YRLG 01	Newfoundland	C	Storm Cat	Clear Mandate	Demi O'Byrne	3,300,000
KEE JUL SEL YRLG 81	Shareef Dancer	C	Northern Dancer	Sweet Alliance	Aston Upthorpe Stud	3,300,000
FTN SEL YRLG SAR 01	Habayeb	C	Storm Cat	Gone to Venus	John Ferguson Bloodstock	3,300,000
KEE JUL YRLG 00	Authenticate	C	Gone West	Lakeway	Padua Stables	3,300,000
KEE SEP YRLG 00	Full Mandate	C	A.P. Indy	Clear Mandate	Padua Stables	3,200,000
KEE JUL SEL YRLG 86	Dancing Groom	C	Nijinsky II	Blush With Pride	BBA (Ireland)	3,200,000
KEE JUL YRLG 02	One Cool Cat	C	Storm Cat	Tacha	Demi O'Byrne	3,100,000
FTN YRLG SAR 83	Immortal Dancer	C	Spectacular Bid	Farouche	Aston Upthorpe Stud	3,000,000
KEE JUL YRLG 99	Norway	C	Storm Cat	Weekend Surprise	Demi O'Byrne	3,000,000
FTN SEL YRLG SAR 01	Royal Walk	C	Mr. Prospector	Stone Flower	Bob Baffert, agent	3,000,000
FTN SEL YRLG SAR 01	Russia	C	Kingmambo	Seattle Way	Demi O'Byrne	3,000,000
KEE JUL SEL YRLG 84	Woodman	C	Mr. Prospector	Playmate	BBA (England)	3,000,000
FTN SEL YRLG SAR 99	Ochoco	C	Mr. Prospector	Eaves	Aaron and Marie Jones	3,000,000
KEE JUL YRLG 01	Ustoura	F	Storm Cat	Inca Legacy	John Ferguson Bloodstock	3,000,000
KEE JUL SEL YRLG 81	Fulmar	C	Northern Dancer	Bernie Bird	BBA (England)	2,950,000
KEE JUL SEL YRLG 87	Houston	C	Seattle Slew	Smart Angle	D. Wayne Lukas	2,900,000
KEE JUL SEL YRLG 84	Louisiana Slew	C	Seattle Slew	Wisp O'Will	Jumonville, J. E. Jr.	2,900,000
KEE JUL YRLG 90	A.P. Indy	C	Seattle Slew	Weekend Surprise	BBA (Ireland)	2,900,000

Snapshot Facts: There have been 53 yearlings sold for $3 million or more since 1980. Thirty of them were sold in 1998 or later.

Top Priced North American Yearlings in 2003

Sale	Horse	Sex	Sire	Dam	Buyer	Sale price
KEE SEP YRLG 03		F	Gone West	Touch of Greatness	John Ferguson	$3,800,000
KEE SEP YRLG 03		C	Danzig	Queena	Demi O'Byrne	3,600,000
KEE SEP YRLG 03		C	Unbridled	Serena's Song	Eugene Melnyk	2,800,000
FTN SEL YRLG SAR 03		C	Unbridled	Words of War	Padua Stables	2,700,000
KEE SEP YRLG 03		C	Storm Cat	Bluemamba	Demi O'Byrne	2,600,000
KEE SEP YRLG 03	Unbridled Evil	F	Unbridled	Evil Elaine	Demi O'Byrne	2,400,000
FTN SEL YRLG SAR 03		C	A.P. Indy	Strawberry Reason	Patrick Biancone	1,900,000
KEE SEP YRLG 03		C	A.P. Indy	Adoradancer	Mark Reid Bloodstock	1,850,000
KEE SEP YRLG 03	Saffir	C	Unbridled	Storm Alert	Brushwood Stable	1,800,000
KEE SEP YRLG 03		F	Lemon Drop Kid	Snow Forest	John Ferguson	1,800,000
KEE SEP YRLG 03		C	Storm Cat	Exing (CHI)	Eugene Melnyk	1,750,000
KEE SEP YRLG 03	Kings Ex	C	Kingmambo	Fantastic Ways	John Ferguson	1,700,000
KEE SEP YRLG 03	Ten Centuries	C	Dubai Millennium (Gb)	Fitnah	Palides Investments N.V.	1,600,000
KEE SEP YRLG 03		C	Storm Cat	Seeking Regina	John Ferguson	1,600,000
KEE SEP YRLG 03		F	Gone West	A. P. Assay	John Ferguson	1,600,000
KEE SEP YRLG 03	Saywaan	F	Fusaichi Pegasus	Sharp Cat	Shadwell Estate Co.	1,500,000
KEE SEP YRLG 03		C	Storm Cat	Heeremandi (IRE)	Demi O'Byrne	1,500,000
KEE SEP YRLG 03		C	Old Trieste	Shining Through	Mike Ryan, agent	1,400,000
KEE SEP YRLG 03		F	Saint Ballado	West's Secret	R B and B J Lewis	1,400,000
FTN SEL YRLG SAR 03		C	Unbridled's Song	Silken Cat	John C. Oxley	1,400,000
KEE SEP YRLG 03		F	A.P. Indy	At the Half	Reynolds Bell Jr., agent	1,350,000
KEE SEP YRLG 03		C	Storm Cat	Good Example (FR)	R B and B J Lewis	1,250,000
KEE SEP YRLG 03	King of the Sun	C	Kingmambo	Solar Bound	John Ferguson	1,200,000
KEE SEP YRLG 03		C	Kingmambo	Star Begonia (GB)	John Ferguson	1,200,000
FTN SEL YRLG SAR 03	Seventysevenstreet	C	Storm Cat	Broad Smile	Fleetwood/N.W. Mgmt	1,200,000
KEE SEP YRLG 03		C	Giant's Causeway	Mimi's Golden Girl	My Meadow View Farm	1,150,000
KEE SEP YRLG 03		C	Rahy	Balistroika	John Ferguson	1,100,000
FTN SEL YRLG SAR 03	Harmony Cottage	F	Storm Cat	Jewel Princess	Eugene Melnyk	1,100,000
KEE SEP YRLG 03		F	Unbridled	Banshee Winds	Reynolds Bell Jr., agent	1,100,000
KEE SEP YRLG 03	Ever Elusive	F	Forestry	Shivering Six	Padua Stables	1,000,000
KEE SEP YRLG 03	Tizamazing	F	Cee's Tizzy	Cee's Song	Reynolds Bell Jr., agent	1,000,000
KEE SEP YRLG 03		F	Storm Cat	Successfully	Demi O'Byrne	1,000,000
KEE SEP YRLG 03		C	A.P. Indy	Clear Mandate	Reynolds Bell Jr., agent	975,000
KEE SEP YRLG 03		C	Fusaichi Pegasus	Lakeway	Demi O'Byrne	950,000
KEE SEP YRLG 03	Forest Fighter	C	Forestry	Alyfair	R B and B J Lewis	950,000
KEE SEP YRLG 03		F	A.P. Indy	Better Than Honour	Gayle Van Leer, agent	925,000
KEE SEP YRLG 03		F	A.P. Indy	Red Cat	Frederic Sauque, agent	900,000
FTN SEL YRLG SAR 03	Foxglove	C	Fusaichi Pegasus	Rokeby Rosie	Jeanne G. Vance	900,000
KEE SEP YRLG 03		F	A.P. Indy	Catchascatchcan (Gb)	B. Wayne Hughes	900,000
KEE SEP YRLG 03		F	Unbridled	Rawafed (GB)	B. Wayne Hughes	900,000
KEE SEP YRLG 03		C	Pulpit	Alamosa (GB)	B. Wayne Hughes	900,000
KEE SEP YRLG 03		C	Giant's Causeway	Regina Maria	Demi O'Byrne	875,000
KEE SEP YRLG 03	Sun Sprinkles	F	A.P. Indy	England's Rose	Anthony Stroud Bloodstock	825,000
KEE SEP YRLG 03		F	A.P. Indy	First Night (IRE)	John Ferguson	800,000
KEE SEP YRLG 03		C	Tale of the Cat	Patchiano	Demi O'Byrne	800,000
KEE SEP YRLG 03		F	Thunder Gulch	Save Me the Waltz (Ire)	Demi O'Byrne	800,000
FTK SUM YRLG 03	Chapena	F	Fusaichi Pegasus	La Chaposa (PER)	Fleetwood/N.W. Mgmt	800,000
FTN SEL YRLG SAR 03		C	Unbridled's Song	Stephanie's Road	John Moynihan, agent	800,000
KEE SEP YRLG 03	Princess Omi	F	Unbridled	Omi	John C. Oxley	775,000
FTN SEL YRLG SAR 03		C	Unbridled's Song	La Gueriere	B.T.A. Stable	750,000
KEE SEP YRLG 03	Awesome Buddy	C	Awesome Again	Rosebud (GB)	Fleetwood/N.W. Mgmt	750,000
KEE SEP YRLG 03		C	A.P. Indy	Unbridled Wind	Tracy Farmer	750,000
KEE SEP YRLG 03		C	Cat Thief	Mather Miss	Toyomitsu Hirai	725,000
KEE SEP YRLG 03	Meteor Wells	F	Sadler's Wells	Meteor Stage	R.S. Evans	725,000
KEE SEP YRLG 03		F	Deputy Minister	Go to the Ink	R B and B J Lewis	700,000
KEE SEP YRLG 03		C	Capote	She's a Talent	J.L. Gladwell III	700,000
FTN SEL YRLG SAR 03	Lila's Pegasus	F	Fusaichi Pegasus	Our Dear Ruth	Padua Stables	700,000
FTN SEL YRLG SAR 03		C	Forest Wildcat	Subtle Fragrance	Barry Berkelhammer, agt	675,000
KEE SEP YRLG 03	It's No Joke	C	Distorted Humor	It's Personal	Fleetwood/N.W. Mgmt	675,000
KEE SEP YRLG 03	Unbridled's Folly	F	Unbridled	Carols Folly	Mike Ryan, agent	675,000
KEE SEP YRLG 03	Proud Charm	C	Silver Charm	Proud Run	Fleetwood/N.W. Mgmt	675,000

Snapshot Facts: Six of the 10 most expensive yearling purchases of 2003 were sired by Unbridled or A.P. Indy, neither of which had accounted for a single top 10 high-priced yearling in 2000, 2001 or 2002.

Status of Top Priced North American Yearlings of 2001
(3–Year–Olds of 2003)

Led by $6.4 million purchase Van Nistelrooy, a list of the 26 most expensive yearlings bought at public auction in North America in 2001 is presented below, along with their tabulated race record through 12/31/2003. North American starts are tabulated separately of all foreign starts, as are starts at 2 and 3. If a horse raced more than one season, or both in North America and overseas, a total is given. Stakes winners are indicated in capitalized, bold-face type, while stakes-placed horses are shown in mixed case, bold-face type.

Most successful to date of the top-priced yearlings of 2001 was undefeated Vindication, winner of the 2002 Breeders' Cup Juvenile and Eclipse Award-winning 2-year-old colt or gelding of that year. Other stakes winners, through the conclusion of their 3-year-old season, were Van Nistelrooy, Newfoundland, Tomahawk and Appleby Gardens.

Sale	Horse (Sire – Dam)					Sale Price	Buyer
KEE SEP YRLG 01	**VAN NISTELROOY** (Storm Cat – Halory)					$6,400,000	Demi O'Byrne
	Year	Country	Sts	1st	2d	3rd	Earnings (US Dollars)
	2002	USA/CAN	1	0	0	0	$21,400
	2002	Foreign	5	3	1	1	208,580
	Total		6	3	1	1	229,980
KEE SEP YRLG 01	Alajwad (Storm Cat – La Affirmed)					$5,500,000	John Ferguson Bloodstock
	2003	USA/CAN	4	2	2	0	74,000
	2003	Foreign	2	0	0	1	3,445
	Total		6	2	2	1	77,445
KEE JUL YRLG 01	Warhol (Saint Ballado – Charm a Gendarme)					$4,000,000	Demi O'Byrne
	2002	Foreign	3	0	1	0	6,125
	2003	Foreign	1	1	0	0	12,684
	Total		4	1	1	0	18,809
KEE SEP YRLG 01	Hoyer (Mr. Prospector – Destination Mir)					$3,800,000	John Ferguson Bloodstock
	Unraced						
KEE JUL YRLG 01	Virtuosa (Seeking the Gold – Escena)					$3,700,000	Reynolds Bell Jr., agent
	2003	USA/CAN	3	0	2	0	14,550
KEE JUL YRLG 01	Act of Duty (Mr. Prospector – Nuryette)					$3,600,000	John Ferguson Bloodstock
	2003	Foreign	2	0	1	0	2,954
KEE SEP YRLG 01	**NEWFOUNDLAND** (Storm Cat – Clear Mandate)					$3,300,000	Demi O'Byrne
	2002	Foreign	4	1	0	0	16,550
	2003	USA/CAN	9	4	0	1	137,234
	Total		13	5	0	1	153,784
FTN SEL YRLG SAR 01	Habayeb (Storm Cat – Gone to Venus)					$3,300,000	John Ferguson Bloodstock
	2002	Foreign	2	0	0	1	1,274
	2003	USA/CAN	6	1	0	0	18,550
	Total		8	1	0	1	19,824
FTN SEL YRLG SAR 01	Royal Walk (Mr. Prospector – Stone Flower)					$3,000,000	Bob Baffert, agent
	Unraced						
KEE JUL YRLG 01	Ustoura (Storm Cat – Inca Legacy)					$3,000,000	John Ferguson Bloodstock
	Unraced						
FTN SEL YRLG SAR 01	Russia (Kingmambo – Seattle Way)					$3,000,000	Demi O'Byrne
	2002	Foreign	4	1	1	0	13,192
	2003	USA/CAN	3	0	0	0	740
	Total		7	1	1	0	13,932
KEE JUL YRLG 01	Word of Mouth (Saint Ballado – Katies (IRE))					$2,600,000	The Thoroughbred Corp.
	Unraced						
KEE JUL YRLG 01	**TOMAHAWK** (Seattle Slew – Statuette)					$2,500,000	Demi O'Byrne
	2002	USA/CAN	1	0	0	0	0
	2002	Foreign	4	1	3	0	241,227
	2003	Foreign	5	1	0	0	44,811
	Total		10	2	3	0	219,627

Sale	Name	Price	Buyer
FTN SEL YRLG SAR 01	**Stone Cat** (Storm Cat – Miss Caerleona (FR))	$2,400,000	Live Oak Plantation

Year	Region					Earnings
2002	USA/CAN	1	0	0	0	1,000
2003	USA/CAN	6	2	0	1	102,530
	Total	7	2	0	1	103,530

Sale	Name	Price	Buyer
KEE JUL YRLG 01	British Blue (Storm Cat – Memories of Silver)	$2,400,000	John Ferguson Bloodstock

Year	Region					Earnings
2002	Foreign	2	0	0	0	1,083
2003	USA/CAN	1	0	0	1	4,680
	Total	3	0	0	1	5,763

Sale	Name	Price	Buyer
KEE SEP YRLG 01	Ashraaf (Deputy Minister – Cinnamon Sugar (IRE))	$2,300,000	John Ferguson Bloodstock

Year	Region					Earnings
2002	USA/CAN	4	1	0	0	19,380
2003	USA/CAN	5	1	2	1	53,100
2003	Foreign	2	0	1	1	65,000
	Total	11	2	3	2	137,480

Sale	Name	Price	Buyer
KEE SEP YRLG 01	Triple Act (Theatrical (IRE) – Multiply)	$2,200,000	John Ferguson Bloodstock

Year	Region					Earnings
2003	Foreign	1	0	0	0	0

Sale	Name	Price	Buyer
FTN SEL YRLG SAR 01	**VINDICATION** (Seattle Slew – Strawberry Reason)	$2,150,000	Padua Stables

Year	Region					Earnings
2002	USA/CAN	4	4	0	0	680,950

Sale	Name	Price	Buyer
KEE SEP YRLG 01	Pelican Island (Mr. Prospector – Lady Madonna)	$2,100,000	Eugene Melnyk

Year	Region					Earnings
2003	USA/CAN	5	1	0	0	14,510

Sale	Name	Price	Buyer
FTN SEL YRLG SAR 01	**APPLEBY GARDENS** (A.P. Indy – Larkwhistle)	$2,000,000	Eugene Melnyk

Year	Region					Earnings
2002	USA/CAN	4	1	0	1	174,270
2003	USA/CAN	3	1	0	0	41,940
	Total	7	2	0	1	216,210

Sale	Name	Price	Buyer
KEE JUL YRLG 01	Dubai Lightning (Seeking the Gold – Heraklia)	$2,000,000	John Ferguson Bloodstock

Year	Region					Earnings
2002	Foreign	2	1	1	0	10,022
2003	Foreign	1	0	0	0	0
	Total	3	1	1	0	10,022

Sale	Name	Price	Buyer
KEE JUL YRLG 01	Servaline (Storm Cat – Fitted Crown)	$2,000,000	Brushwood Stable

Year	Region					Earnings
2002	USA/CAN	7	1	0	0	38,580

Sale	Name	Price	Buyer
KEE SEP YRLG 01	Rumansy (Theatrical (IRE) – Tenga)	$2,000,000	Shadwell Estate Co.

Year	Region					Earnings
2003	USA/CAN	7	0	0	1	885

Sale	Name	Price	Buyer
KEE SEP YRLG 01	Hushood (Mr. Prospector – Princess Mitterand)	$1,900,000	Shadwell Estate Co.

Unraced

Sale	Name	Price	Buyer
KEE JUL YRLG 01	Sharp Breeze (Mr. Prospector – Windy Mindy)	$1,900,000	John Ferguson Bloodstock

Year	Region					Earnings
2002	Foreign	1	0	0	0	0
2003	Foreign	6	2	0	2	14,709
	Total	7	2	0	2	14,709

Sale	Name	Price	Buyer
KEE JUL YRLG 01	Unbridled's Comet (Unbridled's Song – Rainbow Promise)	$1,900,000	Buzz Chace, agent

Year	Region					Earnings
2003	USA/CAN	2	0	0	0	1,780

Top Priced Weanlings Sold in North America Since 1980

Sale	Horse	Sex	Sire	Dam	Buyer	Sale Price
*NEWSTEAD FARM FTK 85	Magic of Life	F	Seattle Slew	Larida	BBA (England)	$2,500,000
KEE NOV BRDG 03		C	Storm Cat	Spain	Dromoland Farm	2,400,000
*WARNER JONES KEE 87	Ghashtah	F	Nijinsky II	My Charmer	Shadwell Estates	2,300,000
KEE NOV BRDG 98	King Charlemagne	C	Nureyev	Race the Wild Wind	Demi O'Byrne	1,500,000
KEE NOV BRDG 01	Teeming	F	Storm Cat	Better Than Honour	Josham Farms	1,500,000
KEE NOV BRDG 98	Juniper	C	Danzig	Montage	Demi O'Byrne	1,450,000
KEE NOV BRDG 03	Secret Thyme	F	Storm Cat	Garden Secrets	Brushwood Stable	1,400,000
KEE NOV BRDG 96	Winthrop	C	Storm Cat	Tinnitus	Demi O'Byrne	1,400,000
KEE NOV BRDG 03		F	Storm Cat	Serena's Tune	Dell Ridge Farm	1,400,000
KEE NOV BRDG 99	Restoration	C	Sadler's Wells	Madame Est Sortie (Fr)	M.W. Miller III, agent	1,400,000
KEE NOV BRDG 99	New Trieste	C	A.P. Indy	Lovlier Linda	Paul Shanahan	1,300,000
KEE NOV BRDG 00	She's a Beauty	F	Storm Cat	Now That's Funny	T. Hyde	1,200,000
KEE NOV BRDG 98	Tide Cat	F	Storm Cat	Maytide	505 Farms	1,200,000
KEE NOV BRDG 89	Net Dancer	F	Nureyev	Doubles Partner	E. Hudson	1,200,000
*WARNER JONES KEE 87	Razeen	C	Northern Dancer	Secret Asset	Darley Stud Management	1,175,000
KEE NOV BRDG 00	A. P. Petal	F	A.P. Indy	Golden Petal	B. Wayne Hughes	1,150,000
*NEWSTEAD FARM FTK 85	Worood	F	Vaguely Noble	Farouche	BBA (England)	1,100,000
KEE NOV BRDG 00	Hold That Tiger	C	Storm Cat	Beware of the Cat	Demi O'Byrne	1,100,000
*WARNER JONES KEE 87	Seaside Attraction	F	Seattle Slew	Kamar	Hinton, Monty	1,050,000
KEE NOV BRDG 00	Wildcat Queen	F	Storm Cat	Jetapat	Bradley and Bowden, agents	1,050,000
KEE NOV BRDG 98	Lemon Tart	F	Deputy Minister	Lemon Dove	Brushwood Stable	1,000,000
KEE NOV BRDG 89	Swiss Desert	C	Danzig	Strictly Raised	Gainsborough Farm	1,000,000
KEE NOV BRDG 98	Malibu Karen	F	Seeking the Gold	Regent's Walk	B. Wayne Hughes	1,000,000
KEE NOV BRDG 96	Blissful	F	Mr. Prospector	Angel Fever	J. B. & B. Stables	1,000,000
KEE NOV BRDG 98	Princess Atoosa	F	Gone West	Kooyonga (IRE)	Brushwood Stable	1,000,000
KEE NOV BRDG 00	Baltic Nations	F	Seattle Slew	Baltic Sea	B. Wayne Hughes	975,000
KEE NOV BRDG 00	Perfect Story	F	Tale of the Cat	Turko's Turn	John C. Oxley	975,000
KEE NOV BRDG 89	Khazar	C	Nureyev	Kathleen's Girl	Darley Stud Management	975,000
KEE NOV BRDG 01	Tizdubai	F	Cee's Tizzy	Cee's Song	John Ferguson Bloodstock	950,000
*NEWSTEAD FARM FTK 85	Allen's Alydar	C	Alydar	Kittiwake	Paulson, Allen E.	950,000
KEE NOV BRDG 89	Machikane Aida	F	Alydar	Lady's Secret	Muirfield East	950,000
KEE NOV BRDG 97	Bernstein	C	Storm Cat	La Affirmed	Demi O'Byrne	925,000
KEE NOV BRDG 89	Bevel	C	Mr. Prospector	Bev Bev	Darley Stud Management	900,000
KEE NOV BRDG 99	Costume Party	F	Storm Cat	Now That's Funny	G. Watts Humphrey Jr.	900,000
KEE NOV BRDG 99	Trial by Jury	C	Deputy Minister	Fantastic Ways	R B and B J Lewis	900,000
KEE NOV BRDG 99	Dubai Tiger	C	Storm Cat	Toga Toga Toga	Tim Hyde	900,000
KEE NOV BRDG 99	Lethal Temper	F	Seattle Slew	Shy Princess	LML	875,000
KEE NOV BRDG 98	Lucrative	F	Seeking the Gold	Banker's Lady	John Ferguson Bloodstock	850,000
KEE NOV BRDG 98	Paynes Bay	C	Mr. Prospector	Embellished	Mayfield Equine	825,000
KEE NOV BRDG 03		C	Thunder Gulch	Turko's Turn	Chestnut Valley Farm	800,000
KEE NOV BRDG 02		C	Seattle Slew	Zoe Montana	John Ferguson Bloodstock	800,000
KEE NOV BRDG 89	Fair American	C	Mr. Prospector	Win Nona	Curragh Bloodstock Agency	800,000
KEE NOV BRDG 00	Patriot's Pride	C	A.P. Indy	Windmill Point	Kentucky Properties	800,000
KEE NOV BRDG 99	Sky Legend	F	Deputy Minister	Sky Beauty	Tracy Farmer	800,000
*NEWSTEAD FARM FTK 85	Mrs. Nijinsky	F	Nijinsky II	Mrs. Warren	Delta Thoroughbreds, Inc.	800,000
KEE NOV BRDG 98	Talk Is Money	C	Deputy Minister	Isle Go West	Smithfield Investments	785,000
KEE NOV BRDG 98	Fiddlin Devon	F	Deputy Minister	La Chaposa (PER)	Jane M. Schosberg	775,000
KEE NOV BRDG 99	Wiseman's Ferry	C	Hennessy	Emmaus	Indian Hill Farm	775,000
KEE NOV BRDG 99	Nutcase	F	Forest Wildcat	Raise the Standard	Wertheimer et Frere	775,000
KEE NOV BRDG 99	Sports Hero	C	Mr. Prospector	Alysoft	High Mills Farm	775,000
KEE NOV BRDG 99	Tricky Indy	F	A.P. Indy	Bag of Tricks	B. Wayne Hughes	775,000
KEE NOV BRDG 98	Black Minnaloushe	C	Storm Cat	Coral Dance (FR)	Demi O'Byrne	750,000
KEE NOV BRDG 83	Clef En Or	F	Alydar	Irish Trip	BBA (England)	750,000
KEE NOV BRDG 93	K. G. Beauty	F	Private Account	Maplejinsky	Morio Sakurai	750,000
KEE NOV BRDG 99	Battle Tough	C	Hennessy	Princess Alydar	Chestnut Valley Farm	735,000
KEE NOV BRDG 02		C	Fusaichi Pegasus	Party Cited	John McCormack Bloodstock	725,000
KEE NOV BRDG 99	Nijinsky's Crown	C	Gone West	Nijinsky's Lover	R.A. Adkinson	725,000
KEE NOV BRDG 98	Stellar Slew	F	Seattle Slew	Crown of Love	Karen Taylor, agent	725,000
KEE NOV BRDG 91	Suave Tern	C	Arctic Tern	Suavite	Henri Chalhoub	725,000

* A dispersal sale

Snapshot Facts: There have been 25 Weanlings sold in North America for $1 million or more since 1980. Nine were sired by Storm Cat.

Highest Priced Weanlings Sold at Public Auction in 2003

Only includes Weanlings sold in North America

Sale	Horse	Sex	Sire	Dam	Buyer	Sale Price
KEE NOV BRDG 03		C	Storm Cat	Spain	Dromoland Farm	$2,400,000
KEE NOV BRDG 03		F	Storm Cat	Serena's Tune	Dell Ridge Farm	1,400,000
KEE NOV BRDG 03	Secret Thyme	F	Storm Cat	Garden Secrets	Brushwood Stable	1,400,000
KEE NOV BRDG 03		C	Thunder Gulch	Turko's Turn	Chestnut Valley Farm	800,000
KEE NOV BRDG 03		C	Deputy Minister	Horsafire	Eldon Farm Equine	500,000
KEE NOV BRDG 03		F	Gone West	Poetically	Jon Kelly	500,000
KEE NOV BRDG 03		F	Lemon Drop Kid	Desert Stormette	Lael Stable	460,000
KEE NOV BRDG 03		C	Grand Slam	Sheza Honey	Mike Byrne	400,000
KEE NOV BRDG 03		C	Unbridled's Song	Revonda (IRE)	Shadwell Estate Co.	400,000
KEE NOV BRDG 03		C	Danehill Dancer (Ire)	Glint in Her Eye	Brushwood Stable	375,000
KEE NOV BRDG 03		F	Diesis (GB)	Pent	Blandford Bloodstock	370,000
KEE NOV BRDG 03		C	Point Given	Crafty Queen	Mike Byrne	355,000
KEE NOV BRDG 03		C	Saint Ballado	Alphabulous	Meigs Creek Racing Stable	350,000
KEE NOV BRDG 03		C	Distorted Humor	Gaye's Locket	Bloodstock Services	350,000
KEE NOV BRDG 03		C	Silver Deputy	Ms. Mostly	Heiligbrodt Racing Stable	350,000
KEE NOV BRDG 03		C	High Yield	Here Comes Chelsie	Dromoland & Hartwell farms	335,000
KEE NOV BRDG 03		F	Tiznow	Serena's Sister	Shadwell Estate Co.	300,000
KEE NOV BRDG 03		F	Giant's Causeway	Gouache (ARG)	Hagyard Farm, agent	300,000
KEE NOV BRDG 03		C	Montbrook	Bold Burst	Eaton Sales	300,000
KEE NOV BRDG 03		C	Giant's Causeway	Fountain Lake	BBA Ireland	300,000
KEE NOV BRDG 03		F	Cherokee Run	Jordanesque	Jezebel Farm	290,000
KEE NOV BRDG 03		C	Distorted Humor	Excedius	Brushwood Stable	290,000
KEE NOV BRDG 03		F	Elusive Quality	Indy Flash	Gordon Stollery	290,000
KEE NOV BRDG 03		F	Fantastic Light	Electrostat	Shadwell Estate Co.	280,000
KEE NOV BRDG 03		F	Point Given	Sharp Cat	Chiefswood Stables	275,000
KEE NOV BRDG 03	Lost in the Storm	F	Storm Cat	Lost the Code	Sanford Stable	275,000
KEE NOV BRDG 03		C	Giant's Causeway	Shy Princess	Peter Doyle Bloodstock	260,000
KEE NOV BRDG 03		C	Forestry	Blue Iris (GB)	John Ferguson Bloodstock	250,000
KEE NOV BRDG 03		C	Tale of the Cat	Nurse Dopey	B.N.R. Enterprises	250,000
KEE NOV BRDG 03		C	Ecton Park	Impact Now	Eaton Sales	250,000
KEE NOV BRDG 03		C	War Chant	Montecito	BGH Ranch	250,000
KEE NOV BRDG 03		C	Giant's Causeway	Isle Go West	Eaton Sales	250,000
KEE NOV BRDG 03		F	Pleasant Tap	Fitzy	Edward J. Kelly Jr.	240,000
KEE NOV BRDG 03		F	Grand Slam	Ring Star	Cherokee Equine Int'l	230,000
KEE NOV BRDG 03		F	Thunder Gulch	Bayou Storm	River Downs Stud	230,000
KEE NOV BRDG 03		F	War Chant	West Turn	Pegasus T'bred Training Ctr	230,000
KEE NOV BRDG 03		C	Swain (IRE)	Taanis	R B and B J Lewis	225,000
KEE NOV BRDG 03		C	El Corredor	Inspired Hope	Ferguson Valley Ranch	225,000
KEE NOV BRDG 03		C	Gulch	Classic Reign	Bruce Headley	220,000
KEE NOV BRDG 03		C	Dynaformer	Fashion Delight	George Krikorian	220,000
KEE NOV BRDG 03		C	Honour and Glory	Thirty Six Carat	Jack Smith	210,000
KEE NOV BRDG 03		F	Deputy Minister	Vogueing	K & B Partnership	210,000
KEE NOV BRDG 03		F	Silver Deputy	Gilded Lilly	Fieldcrest Thoroughbreds	210,000
KEE NOV BRDG 03	Em Vee Pea	C	Pulpit	I'll Get There	Jay Em Ess Stable	210,000
KEE NOV BRDG 03		C	El Corredor	Jin Mill	Global Equine	210,000
KEE NOV BRDG 03		F	Aptitude	Colonial Ally	Gage Hill Stables	205,000
KEE NOV BRDG 03		C	Red Ransom	Awwaliya (GB)	Cormac McCormack	205,000
KEE NOV BRDG 03		C	Dynaformer	Earthly Angel	Blandford Bloodstock	200,000
KEE NOV BRDG 03		C	Hennessy	Miss Firefly	Eaton Sales	200,000
KEE NOV BRDG 03		C	Cherokee Run	Subtle Fragrance	EMO Stables	200,000
KEE NOV BRDG 03		C	Carson City	Repeat Royalty	Josham Farms, agent	200,000
KEE NOV BRDG 03		F	Aptitude	Callmeanicepick	D Ingordo Bloodstock Svcs	200,000
KEE NOV BRDG 03		C	Victory Gallop	Sugar Is Gold	Rick Borth	200,000
KEE NOV BRDG 03		C	Rahy	J. D. Flowers	Shadwell Estate Co.	200,000
KEE NOV BRDG 03		C	Hennessy	Lismore Lady	D.E.R. Enterprises	200,000
KEE NOV BRDG 03		F	Point Given	Forever Rainbows	Bluegrass T'bred Svcs, agt	200,000
KEE NOV BRDG 03		C	Hennessy	Lovethespell	Cormac McCormack	200,000
KEE NOV BRDG 03		C	Unbridled's Song	Heat Is On	Durham Co.	200,000

Snapshot Facts: In 2000, 2001, 2002 and 2003, there have been eight weanlings sold for $1 million or more. Seven of them were sired by Storm Cat – the exception being a weanling by A.P. Indy out of Golden Petal sold in 2000.

Average and Median Price Per Yearling

Representing half the dollar volume of the auction sales market, the yearling market is generally accepted as being a true barometer of the health of the Thoroughbred breeding industry. Despite a reduced supply of yearlings due to MRLS, the yearling auction market in 2003 recorded healthy gains in gross sales, average price and median price as demand at the top end of the market returned after a one-year hiatus.

Year	Sale yearlings	Percent change	Yearling sales gross	Percent change	Avg. price	Percent change	Median price	Percent change
1980	7,079	(+11.9)	210,128,000	(+34.1)	29,683	(+19.8)	10,000	(+25.0)
1981	7,949	(+12.3)	279,376,221	(+33.0)	35,146	(+18.4)	11,500	(+15.0)
1982	8,174	(+2.8)	269,376,805	(−3.5)	32,991	(−6.1)	8,116	(−29.4)
1983	8,705	(+6.5)	359,148,103	(+33.2)	41,258	(+25.1)	8,500	(+4.7)
1984	9,268	(+6.5)	383,659,326	(+6.8)	41,396	(+0.3)	6,500	(−23.5)
1985	8,420	(−9.1)	347,842,155	(−9.3)	41,311	(−0.2)	6,800	(+4.6)
1986	8,206	(−2.5)	281,358,236	(−19.1)	34,285	(−17.0)	6,000	(−11.7)
1987	8,845	(+7.8)	313,477,421	(+11.4)	35,441	(+3.3)	6,500	(+8.3)
1988	9,083	(+2.7)	283,845,192	(−9.5)	31,250	(−11.8)	5,500	(−15.0)
1989	8,564	(−5.7)	281,806,185	(−0.7)	32,905	(+5.3)	7,000	(+27.3)
1990	8,760	(+2.3)	257,342,967	(−8.7)	29,377	(−10.7)	7,000	0.0
1991	8,154	(−6.9)	213,905,856	(−16.9)	26,233	(−10.7)	6,028	(−13.9)
1992	7,908	(−3.0)	180,232,617	(−15.7)	22,791	(−13.1)	7,000	(+16.1)
1993	7,413	(+12.0)	188,598,650	(+4.6)	25,442	(+11.6)	8,000	(+14.3)
1994	7,706	(+4.0)	210,336,433	(+11.5)	27,295	(+7.3)	9,162	(+14.5)
1995	7,882	(+2.3)	242,778,829	(+15.4)	30,801	(+12.8)	10,000	(+9.2)
1996	8,025	(+1.8)	277,224,816	(+14.2)	34,539	(+12.1)	9,500	(−5.0)
1997	8,014	(−0.1)	307,607,857	(+11.0)	38,384	(+11.1)	11,500	(+21.1)
1998	8,275	(+3.3)	354,058,332	(+15.1)	42,787	(+11.5)	11,500	0.0
1999	8,738	(+5.6)	440,078,922	(+24.3)	50,364	(+17.7)	12,000	(+4.3)
2000	9,530	(+9.1)	519,443,808	(+18.0)	54,506	(+8.2)	11,500	(−4.2)
2001	9,002	(−5.5)	473,044,553	(−8.9)	52,549	(−3.6)	9,000	(−21.7)
2002	8,941	(−0.7)	390,714,442	(−17.4)	43,699	(−16.8)	11,000	(+22.2)
2003	8,843	(−1.1)	425,251,514	(+8.8)	48,089	(+10.0)	12,000	(+9.1)

Average and Median Price Per Weanling

Year	Sale weanlings	Percent change	Weanling sales gross	Percent change	Avg. price	Percent change	Median price	Percent change
1980	1,480	(+24.9)	21,130,450	(+62.0)	14,277	(+29.7)	N/A	N/A
1981	1,723	(+16.4)	23,944,919	(+13.3)	13,897	(-2.7)	N/A	N/A
1982	1,770	(+2.7)	21,631,160	(-9.7)	12,221	(-12.1)	N/A	N/A
1983	1,656	(-6.4)	24,750,636	(+14.4)	14,946	(+22.3)	N/A	N/A
1984	1,509	(-8.9)	15,609,855	(-36.9)	10,345	(-30.8)	N/A	N/A
1985	1,441	(-4.5)	25,556,965	(+63.7)	17,736	(+71.4)	3,000	N/A
1986	1,432	(-0.6)	22,354,648	(-12.5)	15,611	(-12.0)	3,200	(+6.7)
1987	1,488	(+3.9)	34,660,720	(+55.0)	23,293	(+49.2)	4,200	(+31.3)
1988	1,362	(-8.5)	21,852,247	(-37.0)	16,044	(-31.1)	3,500	(-16.7)
1989	1,475	(+8.3)	35,088,817	(+60.6)	23,789	(+48.3)	5,200	(+48.6)
1990	1,565	(+6.1)	28,406,636	(-19.0)	18,151	(-23.7)	5,500	(+5.8)
1991	1,430	(-8.6)	29,201,455	(+2.8)	20,420	(+12.5)	6,500	(+18.2)
1992	1,505	(+5.2)	23,979,536	(-17.9)	15,933	(-22.0)	6,500	0.0
1993	1,536	(+2.1)	36,244,725	(+51.1)	23,597	(+48.1)	9,000	(+38.5)
1994	1,897	(+23.5)	41,376,763	(+14.2)	21,811	(-7.6)	8,500	(-5.6)
1995	2,000	(+5.4)	52,233,042	(+26.2)	26,111	(+19.7)	11,000	(+29.4)
1996	2,163	(+8.2)	61,083,609	(+16.9)	28,240	(+8.2)	8,500	(-22.7)
1997	2,107	(-2.6)	67,564,249	(+10.6)	32,067	(+13.6)	12,000	(+41.2)
1998	2,282	(+8.3)	89,350,261	(+32.2)	39,154	(+22.1)	12,000	0.0
1999	2,290	(+0.4)	98,109,089	(+9.8)	42,842	(+9.4)	15,000	(+25.0)
2000	2,346	(+2.4)	83,758,024	(-14.6)	35,702	(-16.6)	10,000	(-33.34)
2001	1,933	(-17.6)	52,534,780	(-37.3)	27,178	(-23.9)	7,000	(-30.0)
2002	1,575	(-18.5)	49,061,493	(-6.6)	31,150	(+14.6)	10,000	(+42.9)
2003	1,706	(+8.3)	68,058,938	(+38.7)	39,386	(+26.4)	12,000	(+20.0)

Top Priced 2-Year-Olds Sold in North America Since 1980

Sale	Horse	Sex	Sire	Dam	Buyer	Sale Price
BAR MAR 2YO TRN 03	Diamond Fury	C	Sea of Secrets	Swift Spirit	Charles Fipke	$2,700,000
KEE APR 2YO KY 99	La Salle Street	C	Not For Love	Three Grand	Demi O'Byrne	2,000,000
BAR MAR 2YO TRN 99	Morocco	C	Brocco	Roll Over Baby	The Thoroughbred Corp.	2,000,000
BAR MAR 2YO TRN 00	Gotham City	C	Saint Ballado	What a Reality	David J. Shimmon	2,000,000
FTF FEB SEL 2YO TRN 00	Yonaguska	C	Cherokee Run	Marital Spook	Demi O'Byrne	1,950,000
BAR MAR 2YO TRN 02	Atlantic Ocean	F	Stormy Atlantic	Super Chef	The Thoroughbred Corp.	1,900,000
FTF FEB SEL 2YO TRN 00	Harmony Lodge	F	Hennessy	Win Crafty Lady	Eugene Melnyk	1,650,000
FTF FEB SEL 2YO TRN 03	Lion Heart	C	Tale of the Cat	Satin Sunrise	Demi O'Byrne	1,400,000
BAR MAR 2YO TRN 95	Unbridled's Song	C	Unbridled	Trolley Song	Hiroshi Fujita	1,400,000
*NEWSTEAD FARM FTK 85	Minstress	F	The Minstrel	Fleet Victress	W. S. Farish	1,300,000
FTF FEB SEL 2YO TRN 00	Le Chat	C	Storm Cat	Adorable Micol	John Moynihan, agent	1,250,000
KEE APR 2YO KY 99	Lochlin Slew	F	Seattle Slew	Lochlin	B. Wayne Hughes	1,250,000
OBS SEL 2YO CAL 03	Chapel Royal	C	Montbrook	Cut Class Leanne	Demi O'Byrne	1,200,000
KEE JAN ALL AGES 98	Task	F	Mr. Prospector	Department	Course Investment	1,200,000
BAR MAR 2YO TRN 99	Dance Master	C	Gone West	Nijinsky's Lover	Padua Stables	1,200,000
KEE APR 2YO KY 99	I'm Persuaded	C	Deputy Minister	The Way We Were	Narvick International	1,100,000
FTF FEB SEL 2YO TRN 99	Prather	C	Brocco	Dazzling Dixie	Aaron and Marie Jones	1,100,000
BAR MAR 2YO TRN 97	Scatmandu	C	Storm Cat	Princess Alydar	John C. Kimmel, agent	1,100,000
OBS OPN 2YO 01	Warners	R	Dehere	Sweet Gold	Eugene Melnyk	1,050,000
FTF FEB SEL 2YO TRN 00	Songandaprayer	C	Unbridled's Song	Alizea	Robert and Leslie Hurley	1,000,000
KEE JAN ALL AGES 98	Measure	F	Seeking the Gold	Number	Demi O'Byrne	1,000,000
BAR MAR 2YO TRN 97	Marie J	F	Mr. Prospector	In My Cap	John Ferguson Bloodstock	1,000,000
BAR MAR 2YO TRN 99	Something Else	F	Seeking the Gold	Rythmical	The Thoroughbred Corp.	1,000,000
BAR MAR 2YO TRN 99	Satin Cat	F	Storm Cat	Mended Heart	The Thoroughbred Corp.	1,000,000
BAR MAR 2YO TRN 98	Public Figure	C	Clever Trick	Belle of Killarney	The Thoroughbred Corp.	1,000,000
FTF FEB SEL 2YO TRN 02	Dawson Trail	C	Seeking the Gold	Bounteous (IRE)	Demi O'Byrne	1,000,000
BAR MAR 2YO TRN 03	This Is That	C	El Prado (IRE)	Ask Anita	Tsujimoto and Schettine	1,000,000
FTF FEB SEL 2YO TRN 98	Awesome Cat	C	Storm Cat	Pookette	Chester Broman	1,000,000
FTF FEB SEL 2YO TRN 03	Storm Away	F	Storm Cat	Sun Blush	LeRoy Jolley, agent	1,000,000
FTF FEB SEL 2YO TRN 01	Rosetti	C	Seattle Slew	Chic Shirine	Demi O'Byrne	1,000,000
KEE APR 2YO KY 03	Work	C	Menifee	Pacific City	M & M Racing	950,000
BAR MAR 2YO TRN 99	Barrage	C	Tabasco Cat	Allouette	Robert Waxman	950,000
BAR MAR 2YO TRN 98	Debit Account	F	Mr. Prospector	Awesome Account	Demi O'Byrne	950,000
FTF FEB SEL 2YO TRN 99	Significant	C	Unbridled	Remarkably Easy	R B and B J Lewis	950,000
FTF FEB SEL 2YO TRN 99	Brave Quest	C	Miswaki	Cousin Margaret	John C. Oxley	950,000
FTF FEB SEL 2YO TRN 01	Bella Bellucci	F	French Deputy	Blue Avenue	Demi O'Byrne	925,000
BAR MAR 2YO TRN 96	Native Storm	C	Storm Bird	Aquakiss (FR)	B. Wayne Hughes	900,000
BAR MAR 2YO TRN 97	Clarinova	F	Danzig	Life At the Top (GB)	Demi O'Byrne	900,000
BAR MAR 2YO TRN 97	Malibu Wesley	C	Storm Cat	La Spia	B. Wayne Hughes	900,000
BAR MAR 2YO TRN 95	El Paso Danzig	C	Danzig	Lady in Silver	Hiroshi Fujita	900,000
BAR MAR 2YO TRN 97	Liquid Gold	C	Woodman	Shirley L.	The Thoroughbred Corp.	900,000
FTF FEB SEL 2YO TRN 02	Atswhatimtalknbout	C	A.P. Indy	Lucinda K	B. Wayne Hughes	900,000
FTF FEB SEL 2YO TRN 03	Forest Danger	C	Forestry	Starry Ice	Buzz Chace, agent	900,000
OBS SEL 2YO CAL 01	Max's Buddy	C	Irish River (FR)	Exposed	Buzz Chace, agent	900,000
BAR MAR 2YO TRN 96	Sharp Cat	F	Storm Cat	In Neon	The Thoroughbred Corp.	900,000
BAR MAR 2YO TRN 00	Fun and Sun	C	Southern Halo	Cause I'm Special	Target Bloodstock	900,000
FTF FEB SEL 2YO TRN 99	Chilukki	F	Cherokee Run	Song of Syria	Stonerside Stable	875,000
BAR MAR 2YO TRN 97	Majestic Beauty	F	Danzig	Sister Dot	B. Wayne Hughes	875,000
KEE APR 2YO KY 03	Temescal Ridge	C	Unbridled's Song	Belonging	R B and B J Lewis	875,000
FTF FEB SEL 2YO TRN 96	Speed World	C	Woodman	Gray Tab	Heatherway	875,000
KEE NOV BRDG 99	Saints Cup	C	Saint Ballado	Forever Full	Billy Badgett, agent	850,000
FTF FEB SEL 2YO TRN 03	Fusaichi Donight	C	Kris S.	Key to My Heart	Fusao Sekiguchi	850,000
KEE APR 2YO KY 03	Vencer	C	El Prado (IRE)	La Gueriere	NW Mgmt and Fleetwood	850,000
KEE APR 2YO KY 02	To Teras	C	Unbridled's Song	Whatamiss	Darby Dan Bloodstock	850,000
FTF FEB SEL 2YO TRN 01	Bella Giornata	F	Afternoon Deelites	Lindsali	Katsumi Yoshida	850,000
FTF FEB SEL 2YO TRN 00	Red Carpet	C	Theatrical (IRE)	Rare Bird	Brushwood Stables	825,000
KEE APR 2YO KY 00	Allaroundtheworld	C	Forest Wildcat	Tammy Jean	Demi O'Byrne	825,000
FTF FEB SEL 2YO TRN 99	Ebitda	C	Seattle Slew	French Binnana	Roger King	825,000
BAR MAR 2YO TRN 96	Sapporo Cat	C	Storm Cat	Paris Opera	Hiroshi Fujita	825,000

* A dispersal sale.

Snapshot Facts: There have been 30 2-year-olds sold in North America for $1 million or more since 1980. Among them were future North American graded stakes winners Atlantic Ocean, Chapel Royal, Dance Master, Harmony Lodge, Lion Heart, Scatmandu, Songandaprayer, Unbridled's Song and Yonaguska.

Highest Priced 2–Year–Olds Sold at Public Auction in 2003

Only includes 2–Year–Olds sold in North America

Sale	Horse	Sex	Sire	Dam	Buyer	Sale Price
BAR MAR 2YO TRN 03	Diamond Fury	C	Sea of Secrets	Swift Spirit	Charles Fipke	$2,700,000
FTF FEB SEL 2YO TRN 03	Lion Heart	C	Tale of the Cat	Satin Sunrise	Demi O'Byrne	1,400,000
OBS SEL 2YO CAL 03	Chapel Royal	C	Montbrook	Cut Class Leanne	Demi O'Byrne	1,200,000
FTF FEB SEL 2YO TRN 03	Storm Away	F	Storm Cat	Sun Blush	LeRoy Jolley, agent	1,000,000
BAR MAR 2YO TRN 03	This Is That	C	El Prado (IRE)	Ask Anita	Tsujimoto and Schettine	1,000,000
KEE APR 2YO KY 03	Work	C	Menifee	Pacific City	M & M Racing	950,000
FTF FEB SEL 2YO TRN 03	Forest Danger	C	Forestry	Starry Ice	Buzz Chace, agent	900,000
KEE APR 2YO KY 03	Temescal Ridge	C	Unbridled's Song	Belonging	R B and B J Lewis	875,000
FTF FEB SEL 2YO TRN 03	Fusaichi Donight	C	Kris S.	Key to My Heart	Fusao Sekiguchi	850,000
KEE APR 2YO KY 03	Vencer	C	El Prado (IRE)	La Gueriere	NW Mgmt and Fleetwood	850,000
BAR MAR 2YO TRN 03	Uncle Lee Sam	C	Exploit	Two Punch Lil	J.S. Company	700,000
KEE APR 2YO KY 03	Courageous King	C	Elusive Quality	Pleas Write	Wesley Ward and Roger King	700,000
FTF FEB SEL 2YO TRN 03	Tango Tales	C	Tale of the Cat	Tango's Mambo	John C. Oxley	600,000
KEE APR 2YO KY 03	Snapped Up	C	Forest Wildcat	Starita	J. Paul Reddam	600,000
KEE APR 2YO KY 03	Race for Glory	C	Cape Town	Charming Gal	R B and B J Lewis	600,000
FTF FEB SEL 2YO TRN 03	Indy Snow (GB)	C	A.P. Indy	November Snow	Fleetwood Bloodstock	600,000
FTF FEB SEL 2YO TRN 03	Pro Band	C	Dixieland Band	Dancin Renee	E. Paul Robsham	575,000
FTF FEB SEL 2YO TRN 03	Turnbolt	C	Deputy Minister	Oxford Scholar	B. Wayne Hughes	550,000
KEE APR 2YO KY 03	Estevan	C	Grand Slam	Sandy's Storm	Winsong Farms	525,000
FTF FEB SEL 2YO TRN 03	Victory U. S. A.	F	Victory Gallop	Fordyce	Dr. Tom VanMeter II	525,000
KEE APR 2YO KY 03	Total Command	C	Forestry	Northern Sanction	R B and B J Lewis	500,000
BAR MAR 2YO TRN 03	Fashion Girl	F	Tactical Cat	Ransomed Captive	Overbrook Farm	500,000
KEE APR 2YO KY 03	High Minded	C	Touch Gold	Wild Seven	R B and B J Lewis	500,000
FTF FEB SEL 2YO TRN 03	Street Theatre	C	Theatrical (IRE)	Heart of America	John Ferguson Bloodstock	500,000
KEE APR 2YO KY 03	Elusive Dawn	F	Elusive Quality	Soft Dawn	NW Mgmt and Fleetwood	500,000
FTF FEB SEL 2YO TRN 03	Snow Eagle	C	Wild Again	Music Zone	Michael Gill	485,000
FTF FEB SEL 2YO TRN 03	Sinners N Saints	C	Saint Ballado	Navarra	Int'l Equine Acquisition	475,000
KEE APR 2YO KY 03		C	Machiavellian	Brocatelle (GB)	Fusao Sekiguchi	470,000
KEE APR 2YO KY 03		C	Belong to Me	Battle Creek Girl	B. Wayne Hughes	460,000
FTF FEB SEL 2YO TRN 03	Moss Rose	F	Elusive Quality	Prying (ARG)	R B and B J Lewis	450,000
OBS SEL 2YO CAL 03	Boscobelle	F	Polish Numbers	Biogio's Girl	Eugene Melnyk	450,000
FTF FEB SEL 2YO TRN 03	King Carlos	C	Saint Ballado	Word o' Ransom	Michael Gill	450,000
KEE APR 2YO KY 03	Transept	C	Pulpit	Waviness	John C. Kimmel, agent	425,000
FTF FEB SEL 2YO TRN 03	A. P. Adventure	F	A.P. Indy	Nataliano	R B and B J Lewis	425,000
FTF FEB SEL 2YO TRN 03	Cafe Olympus	C	Grand Slam	Cognac Lady	Ever Union Shokai	425,000
FTF FEB SEL 2YO TRN 03	Greek Sun	C	Danzig	Sunlit Silence	Marathon Farm	425,000
FTF FEB SEL 2YO TRN 03	Wimbledon	C	Wild Rush	Strawberry Clover	M & M Racing	425,000
KEE APR 2YO KY 03	Western Royalty	C	Elusive Quality	Ariadne's Crown	Mike McCarty	420,000
FTF FEB SEL 2YO TRN 03	Orchid Island	F	Broad Brush	Wayward Bound	Guy B. Snowden	400,000
BAR MAR 2YO TRN 03	Danon Victory	C	Victory Gallop	Summer Fantasy	J.S. Company	400,000
OBS SEL 2YO CAL 03	Ruler's Court	F	Doneraile Court	Future Guest	John Ferguson Bloodstock	400,000
BAR MAR 2YO TRN 03	French Flight	F	French Deputy	Heather's Flight	NW Mgmt and Fleetwood	400,000
FTF FEB SEL 2YO TRN 03	Eishin Marukamu	C	Mr. Greeley	Sweetest Gal	Toyomitsu Hirai	400,000
FTF FEB SEL 2YO TRN 03	Princess Sequoia	F	Cherokee Run	Hausman	B. Wayne Hughes	400,000
OBS SPR 2YO 03	Double Lock	F	Double Honor	T. G. for Wanda	William J. Condren	380,000
BAR MAY 2YO HRA 03	Cambira	F	French Deputy	West Forty Two	Headley and Jackson	375,000
FTF FEB SEL 2YO TRN 03	Cherry Bomb	F	Honor Grades	Jealous and Jaded	John Fort	370,000
FTF FEB SEL 2YO TRN 03	Meadow Soprano	F	Meadowlake	Candytuft	B. Wayne Hughes	370,000
KEE APR 2YO KY 03	Island Charm	F	Silver Charm	Tropical Stephanie	Pinebourne Farm	360,000
OBS SEL 2YO CAL 03	Charming Jim	C	Silver Charm	Secret Harbor	Michael Gill	360,000
OBS OPN 2YO 03	Maple Syrple	F	American Chance	Sweet and Lowdown	Team Valor	350,000
KEE APR 2YO KY 03	Big in the Game	C	Touch Gold	Legendary Priness	Int'l Equine Acquisition	350,000
BAR MAY 2YO HRA 03	Evolution	C	Gilded Time	Champaigne Amelia	Alsdorf and La Cresta Farm	335,000
KEE APR 2YO KY 03	Eishin Derinha	C	Exploit	Saratoga Flower	Toyomitsu Hirai	330,000
KEE APR 2YO KY 03	Regina Girl	F	Siphon (BRZ)	Expedicionaria (VEN)	Toyomitsu Hirai	330,000
FTF FEB SEL 2YO TRN 03	Forest Music	F	Unbridled's Song	Defer West	Michael Gill	325,000
OBS OPN 2YO 03	Old Kent Road	C	Two Punch	Gala Goldie	John Ferguson Bloodstock	325,000
FTI SPR 2YO TRN 03	Read the Footnotes	C	Smoke Glacken	Baydon Belle	Klaravich Stables	320,000
KEE APR 2YO KY 03	Tales of Glory	C	Honour and Glory	Dixieland Gal	Demi O'Byrne	320,000
OBS OPN 2YO 03	Salty Romance	F	Salt Lake	Checkerspot	Carl Lizza Jr.	320,000

Snapshot Facts: For the second straight year, the top-priced 2-year-old sold at auction in North America was sired by a stallion represented by his first crop of 2-year-olds.

Top Priced Broodmares Sold at Public Auction Since 1980

Sale	Horse	Age	Sire	Dam	Buyer	Sale Price
KEE NOV BRDG 03	Cash Run	6	Seeking the Gold	Shared Interest	John Magnier	$7,100,000
KEE NOV BRDG 98	Korveya	16	Riverman	Konafa	Reynolds Bell Jr., agent	7,000,000
*NEWSTEAD FARM FTK 85	Miss Oceana	4	Alydar	Kittiwake	Foxfield	7,000,000
KEE NOV BRDG 03	Windsharp	12	Lear Fan	Yes She's Sharp	John Ferguson Bloodstock	6,100,000
FTK SEL FALL MIX 84	Priceless Fame	9	Irish Castle	Comely Nell	Darley Stud Management	6,000,000
KEE NOV BRDG 85	Princess Rooney	5	Verbatim	Parrish Princess	Wichita Equine, Inc.	5,500,000
KEE NOV BRDG 86	Life's Magic	5	Cox's Ridge	Fire Water	E. V. Klein	5,400,000
KEE NOV BRDG 03	Spain	6	Thunder Gulch	Drina	Dromoland Farm	5,300,000
KEE NOV BRDG 83	Producer	7	Nashua	Marion	BBA (England)	5,250,000
KEE JAN ALL AGES 00	Mackie	7	Summer Squall	Glowing Tribute	Britton House Stud	5,000,000
KEE NOV BRDG 00	Jewel Princess	8	Key to the Mint	Jewell Ridge	John Magnier	4,900,000
KEE NOV BRDG 00	Catchascatchcan (Gb)	5	Pursuit of Love	Catawba	Lyons Demesne	4,700,000
KEE NOV BRDG 99	Dance Design (IRE)	6	Sadler's Wells	Elegance in Design (Ire)	Hugo Lascelles, agent	4,700,000
KEE NOV BRDG 00	Myhrr	3	Mr. Prospector	Miesque	Reynolds Bell Jr., agent	4,600,000
KEE NOV BRDG 99	Winglet	11	Alydar	Highest Trump	John Magnier	4,600,000
KEE NOV BRDG 84	It's in the Air	8	Mr. Prospector	A Wind Is Rising	Darley Stud Management	4,600,000
KEE NOV BRDG 83	Two Rings	13	Round Table	Allofthem	Due Process Stable	4,500,000
KEE NOV BRDG 85	Estrapade	5	Vaguely Noble	Klepto	A. E. Paulson	4,500,000
FTK STARS 87	Life's Magic	6	Cox's Ridge	Fire Water	Shadwell Estates	4,400,000
KEE NOV BRDG 00	Magical Allure	5	General Meeting	Rare Lady	Shadwell Estate Co.	4,200,000
KEE NOV BRDG 84	Sangue (IRE)	6	Lyphard	Prodice (FR)	N. B. Hunt	4,100,000
KEE NOV BRDG 84	Love Sign	7	Spanish Riddle	Native Nurse	Arthur I. Appleton	4,100,000
*NEWSTEAD FARM FTK 85	Larida	6	Northern Dancer	Kittiwake	Foxfield	4,000,000
KEE NOV BRDG 02	Bless	3	Mr. Prospector	Angel Fever	ClassicStar	4,000,000
KEE NOV BRDG 00	Blissful	4	Mr. Prospector	Angel Fever	John Magnier	4,000,000
KEE NOV BRDG 01	Twenty Eight Carat	11	Alydar	Voo Doo Dance	Brushwood Stable	4,000,000
KEE NOV BRDG 82	Royal Honoree	9	Round Table	Matriarch	Seth W. Hancock, agent	3,800,000
*NEWSTEAD FARM FTK 85	Kittiwake	17	Sea-Bird	Ole Liz	Mint Tree Stable	3,800,000
KEE NOV BRDG 89	Lady's Secret	7	Secretariat	Great Lady M.	Fares Farm	3,800,000
KEE NOV BRDG 83	Prayers'n Promises	5	Foolish Pleasure	Luiana	Three Chimneys Farm	3,750,000
KEE NOV BRDG 00	Squeak (GB)	6	Selkirk	Santa Linda	John Ferguson Bloodstock	3,700,000
KEE NOV BRDG 85	Barb's Bold	7	Bold Forbes	Goofed	Due Process Stable	3,650,000
KEE NOV BRDG 03	Composure	3	Touch Gold	Party Cited	John Ferguson Bloodstock	3,600,000
KEE JAN ALL AGES 02	Desert Stormer	12	Storm Cat	Breezy Stories	Live Oak Stud	3,600,000
KEE NOV BRDG 01	Phone Chatter	10	Phone Trick	Passing My Way	John Magnier	3,600,000
*GENTRY 86	Crimson Saint	17	Crimson Satan	Bolero Rose	Dorsey, John E.	3,450,000
KEE NOV BRDG 03	Golden Apples (IRE)	5	Pivotal (GB)	Loon (FR)	Shadwell Estate Co.	3,400,000
*ALAN CLORE FTK 88	Triptych	6	Riverman	Trillion	Patrick Biancone	3,400,000
KEE JAN ALL AGES 00	Claxton's Slew	16	Seattle Slew	Nutmeg Native	John Magnier	3,300,000
KEE JAN ALL AGES 99	Escena	6	Strawberry Road (Aus)	Claxton's Slew	Reynolds Bell Jr., agent	3,250,000
KEE NOV BRDG 99	Advancing Star	6	Soviet Star	Fair Advantage	Summer Wind Equine	3,200,000
KEE NOV BRDG 83	Avum	10	Umbrella Fella	Avie	M. H. Goodbody	3,200,000
KEE NOV BRDG 83	Priceless Fame	8	Irish Castle	Comely Nell	Jeffry Morris, agent	3,200,000
KEE NOV BRDG 03	Purrfectly	9	Storm Cat	Perfect Example	Courtlandt Farm	3,150,000
KEE NOV BRDG 03	Sharp Cat	9	Storm Cat	In Neon	John Ferguson Bloodstock	3,100,000
KEE NOV BRDG 00	Caress	9	Storm Cat	La Affirmed	John Ferguson Bloodstock	3,100,000
KEE NOV BRDG 02	Fiji (GB)	8	Rainbow Quest	Island Jamboree	Brushwood Stable	3,100,000
*NEWSTEAD FARM FTK 85	White Star Line	10	Northern Dancer	Fast Line	Darley Stud Management	3,000,000
BAR 505 DISP 00	Manistique	5	Unbridled	Astaire Step	Aaron and Marie Jones	3,000,000
KEE NOV BRDG 01	Dancing Mahmoud	11	Topsider	Execution	Reynolds Bell Jr., agent	3,000,000
KEE NOV BRDG 00	Bright Tiara	11	Chief's Crown	Expressive Dance	John Ferguson Bloodstock	3,000,000
KEE JAN ALL AGES 86	Lucky Lucky Lucky	5	Chieftain	Just One More Time	Shadwell Farm, Inc.	3,000,000
KEE NOV BRDG 83	Solar	7	Halo	Sex Appeal	Due Process Stable	3,000,000
KEE NOV BRDG 03	Arabis	4	Deputy Minister	Aishah	A U and M D Jones	2,900,000
KEE NOV BRDG 03	Habibti	4	Tabasco Cat	Miss Sobriety	Shadwell Estate Co.	2,900,000
KEE NOV BRDG 99	Retrospective	7	Easy Goer	Hay Patcher	John Magnier	2,900,000
KEE NOV BRDG 99	Warm Mood	10	Alydar	Summer Mood	Barronstown Stud	2,850,000
KEE NOV BRDG 99	Sky Beauty	9	Blushing Groom (Fr)	Maplejinsky	John Magnier	2,850,000
KEE JAN ALL AGES 00	Solar Slew	18	Seattle Slew	Gold Sun (ARG)	Lakland	2,800,000
FTK FALL MIX NOV 99	Catinca	4	Storm Cat	Inca Legacy	Brushwood Stables	2,800,000
KEE NOV BRDG 83	Native Nurse	13	Graustark	Indian Nurse	BBA (Ireland)	2,800,000

* A dispersal sale

Snapshot Facts: There have been 26 broodmares sold for $4 million or more since 1980. Four of those $4 million mares were daughters of Mr. Prospector, including full sisters Bless and Blissful.

Top Priced Broodmares Sold at Public Auction in 2003

Only broodmares sold in North America included

Sale	Horse Name	Age	Sire	Dam	Buyer	Sale Price
KEE NOV BRDG 03	Cash Run	6	Seeking the Gold	Shared Interest	John Magnier	$7,100,000
KEE NOV BRDG 03	Windsharp	12	Lear Fan	Yes She's Sharp	John Ferguson Bloodstock	6,100,000
KEE NOV BRDG 03	Spain	6	Thunder Gulch	Drina	Dromoland Farm	5,300,000
KEE NOV BRDG 03	Composure	3	Touch Gold	Party Cited	John Ferguson Bloodstock	3,600,000
KEE NOV BRDG 03	Golden Apples (IRE)	5	Pivotal (GB)	Loon (FR)	Shadwell Estate Co.	3,400,000
KEE NOV BRDG 03	Purrfectly	9	Storm Cat	Perfect Example	Courtlandt Farm	3,150,000
KEE NOV BRDG 03	Sharp Cat	9	Storm Cat	In Neon	John Ferguson Bloodstock	3,100,000
KEE NOV BRDG 03	Arabis	4	Deputy Minister	Aishah	A U and M D Jones	2,900,000
KEE NOV BRDG 03	Habibti	4	Tabasco Cat	Miss Sobriety	Shadwell Estate Co.	2,900,000
KEE NOV BRDG 03	Banshee Winds	13	Known Fact	Quack a Doodledoo	ClassicStar	2,400,000
KEE NOV BRDG 03	Saudi Poetry	6	Storm Cat	Gone to Venus	WinStar Farm, agent	2,200,000
KEE NOV BRDG 03	Poetically	5	Silver Deputy	Primarily	B. Wayne Hughes	2,050,000
KEE NOV BRDG 03	Saganeca	15	Sagace (FR)	Haglette	John Magnier	2,000,000
KEE NOV BRDG 03	Turko's Turn	11	Turkoman	Turbo Launch	ClassicStar	2,000,000
KEE NOV BRDG 03	Alexander Three D (Ire)	4	Pennekamp	Loon (FR)	Castleton Group	1,700,000
KEE NOV BRDG 03	Celtic Melody	5	Mr. Greeley	Ballynaugh	ClassicStar	1,300,000
KEE NOV BRDG 03	Stylelistick	4	Storm Cat	Magnificent Style	ClassicStar	1,300,000
KEE NOV BRDG 03	Descapate	5	Dehere	Scapegoat	WinStar Farm, agent	1,250,000
KEE NOV BRDG 03	Charm	6	Polish Numbers	Banshee Winds	Skara Glen Stables	1,200,000
KEE NOV BRDG 03	Radiant Ring	15	Halo	Gleaming Stone	Jon Kelly	1,100,000
FTK FALL MIX NOV 03	Win Crafty Lady	15	Crafty Prospector	Honeytab	ClassicStar	900,000
KEE NOV BRDG 03	Go Classic	7	Gone West	Seattle Classic	Dell Ridge Farm	900,000
KEE NOV BRDG 03	Magicalmysterykate	5	Woodman	Mysteries	Reynolds Bell Jr., agent	900,000
KEE NOV BRDG 03	Fortuitous	3	Dynaformer	Vermont Connection	Wertheimer et Frere	875,000
KEE NOV BRDG 03	Drina	15	Regal and Royal	Wandering Lace	ClassicStar	850,000
KEE NOV BRDG 03	Amenixa (FR)	9	Linamix (FR)	Amen	Blandford Bloodstock	850,000
KEE NOV BRDG 03	Golden Cat	8	Storm Cat	Eurobird (IRE)	London T'bred Services	800,000
KEE NOV BRDG 03	Regal and Fleet	4	Seattle Slew	Flat Fleet Feet	R.J. Bennett, agent	775,000
KEE NOV BRDG 03	Love At Noon	5	Afternoon Deelites	Lemhi Love	WinStar Farm, agent	750,000
KEE NOV BRDG 03	Hidden Storm	6	Storm Cat	Hidden Garden	Peter Doyle Bloodstock	700,000
KEE NOV BRDG 03	Final Destination (NZ)	5	O'Reilly (NZ)	Logical Lady (NZ)	Fontainebleau Farm	700,000
KEE NOV BRDG 03	French Riviera	4	French Deputy	Actinella	Narvick International	700,000
KEE NOV BRDG 03	Tax Affair	6	Colonial Affair	Pech Di Roma	ClassicStar	675,000
KEE NOV BRDG 03	Erica's Smile	4	Williamstown	Purer Than Pure	Eldon Farm Equine	675,000
KEE NOV BRDG 03	Chimichurri	3	Elusive Quality	Hard Knocker	Black Hawk Stables	675,000
KEE NOV BRDG 03	People's Princess	7	Meadowlake	Cassowary	Summer Wind Farm	650,000
KEE NOV BRDG 03	Polaire (IRE)	7	Polish Patriot	Headrest	London T'bred Services	650,000
KEE NOV BRDG 03	Limelighter	4	Seeking the Gold	Miraloma	John Sikura	650,000
FTK FALL MIX NOV 03	Santa Catalina	15	Cure the Blues	Swept Off Her Feet	Gainesway and Stollery	600,000
KEE NOV BRDG 03	Blue Iris (GB)	10	Petong	Bo' Babbity	John Ferguson Bloodstock	600,000
KEE NOV BRDG 03	Bourbon Belle	8	Storm Boot	Timeless Girl	R.J. Bennett, agent	600,000
KEE NOV BRDG 03	Lucky Rainbow	5	Rainbow Quest	Tinaca	McKeever St. Lawrence	600,000
KEE NOV BRDG 03	Miss Illusion	4	Mr. Prospector	Missy's Mirage	R.J. Bennett, agent	600,000
KEE NOV BRDG 03	Slide Show	12	Slewacide	Screen Landing	Gaines-Gentry T'breds	575,000
KEE NOV BRDG 03	Primaly	8	Alydeed	Primarily	Haruya Yoshida	575,000
KEE NOV BRDG 03	Lamington	4	Danzig	Whirl Series	Barry K. Schwartz	575,000
KEE NOV BRDG 03	September Secret	4	Our Emblem	Andrushka	Greg Knee	575,000
KEE NOV BRDG 03	Westerly Breeze	3	Gone West	On the Brink	Temple Webber Jr.	560,000
KEE NOV BRDG 03	Scapegoat	12	Forty Niner	Old Goat	Gaines-Gentry T'breds	550,000
KEE NOV BRDG 03	Flashy Four	10	Storm Cat	Amy Be Good	Tomoka Hills Farms	550,000
KEE NOV BRDG 03	Call Me Up	7	Miner's Mark	Ring Me Up	Copperhead Stable	550,000
KEE NOV BRDG 03	Erin Moor	5	Holy Bull	Willa Joe (IRE)	Dell Ridge Farm	550,000
KEE NOV BRDG 03	Dake	7	Gulch	Long Silence	Gustav Schickedanz	525,000
KEE NOV BRDG 03	Best Mate	5	Woodman	Ubetshedid	BBA Ireland	525,000
KEE NOV BRDG 03	Zaafira	4	A.P. Indy	Outstandingly	Forging Oaks Farm	525,000

Snapshot Facts: Three broodmares sold for more than $5 million in 2003; prior to this year, only one broodmare – $7 million purchase Korveya in 1998 – had brought more than $5 million since the mid-1980s.

Top-Priced Horses of Racing Age Since 1980

Sale	Horse Name	Sex	Age	Sire	Dam	Buyer	Sale Price
FTK STARS 87	Lady's Secret	F	5	Secretariat	Great Lady M.	Fasig-Tipton, agent	$5,400,000
KEE NOV BRDG 89	Open Mind	F	3	Deputy Minister	Stage Luck	Kazuo Nakamura	4,600,000
KEE NOV BRDG 89	Winning Colors	F	4	Caro (IRE)	All Rainbows	Gainesway Bloodstock Svcs	4,100,000
KEE NOV BRDG 86	Midway Lady	F	3	Alleged	Smooth Bore	BBA (Ireland)	3,300,000
KEE JAN ALL AGES 99	Escena	M	6	Strawberry Road (Aus)	Claxton's Slew	Reynolds Bell Jr., agent	3,250,000
KEE NOV BRDG 84	Hail Bold King	C	3	Bold Bidder	Inca Queen	Due Process Stable	3,200,000
BAR 505 DISP 00	Manistique	M	5	Unbridled	Astaire Step	Aaron and Marie Jones	3,000,000
FTN 2YO TRN HRA 92	Strike the Gold	C	4	Alydar	Majestic Gold	Condren and Cornacchia	2,900,000
BAR MAR 2YO TRN 03	Diamond Fury	C	2	Sea of Secrets	Swift Spirit	Charles Fipke	2,700,000
BAR 505 DISP 00	David Copperfield	C	3	Halo	Bannockburn	Visionary Corp.	2,600,000
DISP WOLFSON FTF 83	Royal Roberto	C	4	Roberto	Princess Roycraft	R.L. Cuchossois	2,200,000
BAR MAR 2YO TRN 00	Gotham City	C	2	Saint Ballado	What a Reality	David J. Shimmon	2,000,000
BAR MAR 2YO TRN 99	Morocco	C	2	Brocco	Roll Over Baby	The Thoroughbred Corp.	2,000,000
KEE APR 2YO KY 99	La Salle Street	C	2	Not For Love	Three Grand	Demi O'Byrne	2,000,000
FTF FEB SEL 2YO TRN 00	Yonaguska	C	2	Cherokee Run	Marital Spook	Demi O'Byrne	1,950,000
BAR MAR 2YO TRN 02	Atlantic Ocean	F	2	Stormy Atlantic	Super Chef	The Thoroughbred Corp.	1,900,000
KEE NOV BRDG 01	Jostle	F	4	Brocco	Moon Drone	Pete Wittmann	1,700,000
FTF FEB SEL 2YO TRN 00	Harmony Lodge	F	2	Hennessy	Win Crafty Lady	Eugene Melnyk	1,650,000
KEE RYEHILL DISP 88	Homebuilder	C	4	Mr. Prospector	Smart Heiress	John Franks	1,600,000
KEE JAN ALL AGES 99	J J'sdream	M	6	Glitterman	Thwack	Robert E. Courtney, agent	1,600,000
FTK STARS 87	Family Style	F	4	State Dinner	Sharp Kitty	Brushwood Stable	1,550,000
FTN HRA SAR 83	Fast Gold	C	4	Mr. Prospector	Flack Attack	J.C. Meyer	1,500,000
KEE NOV BRDG 01	Sequoyah (IRE)	F	3	Sadler's Wells	Brigid	Bill Farish	1,400,000
FTF FEB SEL 2YO TRN 03	Lion Heart	C	2	Tale of the Cat	Satin Sunrise	Demi O'Byrne	1,400,000
BAR MAR 2YO TRN 95	Unbridled's Song	C	2	Unbridled	Trolley Song	Hiroshi Fujita	1,400,000
*NEWSTEAD FARM FTK 85	Minstress	F	2	The Minstrel	Fleet Victress	Farish, W. S.	1,300,000
*ALAN CLORE FTK 88	River Memories	F	4	Riverman	Le Vague a l'Ame	Patrick Biancone	1,300,000
CTS FALL MIX 89	Kool Arrival	F	3	Relaunch	Irish Arrival	Pete Valenti	1,250,000
FTF FEB SEL 2YO TRN 00	Le Chat	C	2	Storm Cat	Adorable Micol	John Moynihan, agent	1,250,000
FTK STARS 87	Pine Tree Lane	F	5	Apalachee	Carealot	Prather, John B.	1,250,000
KEE APR 2YO KY 99	Lochlin Slew	F	2	Seattle Slew	Lochlin	B. Wayne Hughes	1,250,000
FTK STARS 87	North Sider	F	5	Topsider	Back Ack	Mare Haven Farm	1,225,000
FTK SEL FALL MIX 82	Carefully Hidden	F	3	Caro (IRE)	Treasure Chest	King Ranch, Inc.	1,215,000
KEE JAN ALL AGES 98	Task	F	2	Mr. Prospector	Department	Course Investment	1,200,000
OBS SEL 2YO CAL 03	Chapel Royal	C	2	Montbrook	Cut Class Leanne	Demi O'Byrne	1,200,000
BAR MAR 2YO TRN 99	Dance Master	C	2	Gone West	Nijinsky's Lover	Padua Stables	1,200,000
CTS FALL MIX 87	Very Subtle	F	3	Hoist the Silver	Never Scheme	Ben Rochelle	1,200,000
FTK SEL FALL MIX 82	Secrettame	F	4	Secretariat	Tamerett	Mare Haven Farm	1,150,000
KEE NOV BRDG 89	Some Romance	F	3	Fappiano	Zippy Do	Skara Glen Stables	1,150,000
BAR MAR 2YO TRN 97	Scatmandu	C	2	Storm Cat	Princess Alydar	John C. Kimmel, agent	1,100,000
FTK STARS 87	Life At the Top	F	4	Seattle Slew	See You At the Top	Eaton, Lee, agent	1,100,000
FTF FEB SEL 2YO TRN 99	Prather	C	2	Brocco	Dazzling Dixie	Aaron and Marie Jones	1,100,000
KEE APR 2YO KY 99	I'm Persuaded	C	2	Deputy Minister	The Way We Were	Narvick International	1,100,000
KEE NOV BRDG 02	Nasty Storm	F	4	Gulch	A Stark Is Born	Frank Stronach	1,075,000
FTN NOV HRA BEL 83	Luminaire	F	4	Al Hattab	Margaret's Number	Kenneth F. Johnston	1,055,000
OBS OPN 2YO 01	Warners	R	2	Dehere	Sweet Gold	Eugene Melnyk	1,050,000
FTF FEB SEL 2YO TRN 98	Awesome Cat	C	2	Storm Cat	Pookette	Chester Broman	1,000,000
FTN NOV HRA BEL 82	Raise 'n Dance	F	4	Raise a Native	Pink Larkspur	Rutherford, Mike G.	1,000,000
KEE JAN ALL AGES 98	Measure	F	2	Seeking the Gold	Number	Demi O'Byrne	1,000,000
FTF FEB SEL 2YO TRN 03	Storm Away	F	2	Storm Cat	Sun Blush	LeRoy Jolley, agent	1,000,000
BAR MAR 2YO TRN 97	Marie J	F	2	Mr. Prospector	In My Cap	John Ferguson Bloodstock	1,000,000
BAR MAR 2YO TRN 97	Something Else	F	2	Seeking the Gold	Rythmical	The Thoroughbred Corp.	1,000,000
FTF FEB SEL 2YO TRN 02	Dawson Trail	C	2	Seeking the Gold	Bounteous (IRE)	Demi O'Byrne	1,000,000
MAT INT RH 86	Shywing	F	4	Wing Out	Cheyenne Birdsong	Sczesny, E. R.	1,000,000
FTF FEB SEL 2YO TRN 01	Rosetti	C	2	Seattle Slew	Chic Shirine	Demi O'Byrne	1,000,000
FTF FEB SEL 2YO TRN 00	Songandaprayer	C	2	Unbridled's Song	Alizea	Robert and Leslie Hurley	1,000,000
KEE NOV BRDG 89	Is It True	C	3	Raja Baba	Roman Rockette	B. Farmer	1,000,000
BAR MAR 2YO TRN 03	This Is That	C	2	El Prado (IRE)	Ask Anita	Tsujimoto and Schettine	1,000,000
BAR MAR 2YO TRN 99	Satin Cat	F	2	Storm Cat	Mended Heart	The Thoroughbred Corp.	1,000,000
BAR MAR 2YO TRN 98	Public Figure	C	2	Clever Trick	Belle of Killarney	The Thoroughbred Corp.	1,000,000

* A dispersal sale

Snapshot Facts: There have been 60 horses of racing age sold for $1 million or more since 1980. Thirty were 2 year olds.

Top-Priced Horses of Racing Age in 2003

(North American sales only)

Sale	Horse Name	Sex	Age	Sire	Dam	Buyer	Sale Price
BAR MAR 2YO TRN 03	Diamond Fury	C	2	Sea of Secrets	Swift Spirit	Charles Fipke	$2,700,000
FTF FEB SEL 2YO TRN 03	Lion Heart	C	2	Tale of the Cat	Satin Sunrise	Demi O'Byrne	1,400,000
OBS SEL 2YO CAL 03	Chapel Royal	C	2	Montbrook	Cut Class Leanne	Demi O'Byrne	1,200,000
FTF FEB SEL 2YO TRN 03	Storm Away	F	2	Storm Cat	Sun Blush	LeRoy Jolley, agent	1,000,000
BAR MAR 2YO TRN 03	This Is That	C	2	El Prado (IRE)	Ask Anita	Tsujimoto and Schettine	1,000,000
KEE APR 2YO KY 03	Work	C	2	Menifee	Pacific City	M & M Racing	950,000
FTF FEB SEL 2YO TRN 03	Forest Danger	C	2	Forestry	Starry Ice	Buzz Chace, agent	900,000
KEE NOV BRDG 03	Fortuitous	F	3	Dynaformer	Vermont Connection	Wertheimer et Frere	875,000
KEE APR 2YO KY 03	Temescal Ridge	C	2	Unbridled's Song	Belonging	R B and B J Lewis	875,000
KEE APR 2YO KY 03	Vencer	C	2	El Prado (IRE)	La Gueriere	NW Mgmt and Fleetwood	850,000
FTF FEB SEL 2YO TRN 03	Fusaichi Donight	C	2	Kris S.	Key to My Heart	Fusao Sekiguchi	850,000
BAR MAR 2YO TRN 03	Uncle Lee Sam	C	2	Exploit	Two Punch Lil	J.S. Company	700,000
KEE APR 2YO KY 03	Courageous King	C	2	Elusive Quality	Pleas Write	Wesley Ward and Roger King	700,000
KEE NOV BRDG 03	Chimichurri	F	3	Elusive Quality	Hard Knocker	Black Hawk Stables	675,000
KEE APR 2YO KY 03	Snapped Up	C	2	Forest Wildcat	Starita	J. Paul Reddam	600,000
KEE APR 2YO KY 03	Race for Glory	C	2	Cape Town	Charming Gal	R B and B J Lewis	600,000
FTF FEB SEL 2YO TRN 03	Tango Tales	C	2	Tale of the Cat	Tango's Mambo	John C. Oxley	600,000
FTF FEB SEL 2YO TRN 03	Indy Snow (GB)	C	2	A.P. Indy	November Snow	Fleetwood Bloodstock	600,000
FTF FEB SEL 2YO TRN 03	Pro Band	C	2	Dixieland Band	Dancin Renee	E. Paul Robsham	575,000
KEE NOV BRDG 03	Westerly Breeze	F	3	Gone West	On the Brink	Temple Webber Jr.	560,000
FTF FEB SEL 2YO TRN 03	Turnbolt	C	2	Deputy Minister	Oxford Scholar	B. Wayne Hughes	550,000
FTF FEB SEL 2YO TRN 03	Victory U.S.A.	F	2	Victory Gallop	Fordyce	Dr. Tom VanMeter II	525,000
KEE APR 2YO KY 03	Estevan	C	2	Grand Slam	Sandy's Storm	Winsong Farms	525,000
BAR MAR 2YO TRN 03	Fashion Girl	F	2	Tactical Cat	Ransomed Captive	Overbrook Farm	500,000
KEE APR 2YO KY 03	Elusive Dawn	F	2	Elusive Quality	Soft Dawn	NW Mgmt and Fleetwood	500,000
FTF FEB SEL 2YO TRN 03	Street Theatre	C	2	Theatrical (IRE)	Heart of America	John Ferguson Bloodstock	500,000
KEE APR 2YO KY 03	Total Command	C	2	Forestry	Northern Sanction	R B and B J Lewis	500,000
KEE APR 2YO KY 03	High Minded	C	2	Touch Gold	Wild Seven	R B and B J Lewis	500,000
FTF FEB SEL 2YO TRN 03	Snow Eagle	C	2	Wild Again	Music Zone	Michael Gill	485,000
FTF FEB SEL 2YO TRN 03	Sinners N Saints	C	2	Saint Ballado	Navarra	Int'l Equine Acquisition	475,000
KEE APR 2YO KY 03		C	2	Machiavellian	Brocatelle (GB)	Fusao Sekiguchi	470,000
KEE APR 2YO KY 03		C	2	Belong to Me	Battle Creek Girl	B. Wayne Hughes	460,000
FTF FEB SEL 2YO TRN 03	King Carlos	C	2	Saint Ballado	Word o' Ransom	Michael Gill	450,000
OBS SEL 2YO CAL 03	Boscobelle	F	2	Polish Numbers	Biogio's Girl	Eugene Melnyk	450,000
FTF FEB SEL 2YO TRN 03	Moss Rose	F	2	Elusive Quality	Prying (ARG)	R B and B J Lewis	450,000
FTF FEB SEL 2YO TRN 03	Greek Sun	C	2	Danzig	Sunlit Silence	Marathon Farm	425,000
FTF FEB SEL 2YO TRN 03	A. P. Adventure	F	2	A.P. Indy	Nataliano	R B and B J Lewis	425,000
FTF FEB SEL 2YO TRN 03	Cafe Olympus	C	2	Grand Slam	Cognac Lady	Ever Union Shokai	425,000
KEE NOV BRDG 03	Red n'Gold	M	5	Tabasco Cat	Pasampsi	WinStar Farm, agent	425,000
KEE APR 2YO KY 03	Transept	C	2	Pulpit	Waviness	John C. Kimmel, agent	425,000
FTF FEB SEL 2YO TRN 03	Wimbledon	C	2	Wild Rush	Strawberry Clover	M & M Racing	425,000
KEE APR 2YO KY 03	Western Royalty	C	2	Elusive Quality	Ariadne's Crown	Mike McCarty	420,000
BAR MAR 2YO TRN 03	Danon Victory	C	2	Victory Gallop	Summer Fantasy	J.S. Company	400,000
OBS SEL 2YO CAL 03	Ruler's Court	C	2	Doneraile Court	Future Guest	John Ferguson Bloodstock	400,000
FTF FEB SEL 2YO TRN 03	Orchid Island	F	2	Broad Brush	Wayward Bound	Guy B. Snowden	400,000
FTF FEB SEL 2YO TRN 03	Eishin Marukamu	C	2	Mr. Greeley	Sweetest Gal	Toyomitsu Hirai	400,000
FTF FEB SEL 2YO TRN 03	Princess Sequoia	F	2	Cherokee Run	Hausman	B. Wayne Hughes	400,000
BAR MAR 2YO TRN 03	French Flight	F	2	French Deputy	Heather's Flight	NW Mgmt and Fleetwood	400,000
OBS SPR 2YO 03	Double Lock	F	2	Double Honor	T. G. for Wanda	William J. Condren	380,000
BAR MAY 2YO HRA 03	Cambira	F	2	French Deputy	West Forty Two	Headley and Jackson	375,000
FTF FEB SEL 2YO TRN 03	Cherry Bomb	F	2	Honor Grades	Jealous and Jaded	John Fort	370,000
FTF FEB SEL 2YO TRN 03	Meadow Soprano	F	2	Meadowlake	Candytuft	B. Wayne Hughes	370,000
KEE APR 2YO KY 03	Island Charm	C	2	Silver Charm	Tropical Stephanie	Pinebourne Farm	360,000
OBS SEL 2YO CAL 03	Charming Jim	C	2	Silver Charm	Secret Harbor	Mike Gill	360,000
KEE APR 2YO KY 03	Big in the Game	C	2	Touch Gold	Legendary Priness	Int'l Equine Acquisition	350,000
OBS OPN 2YO 03	Maple Syrple	F	2	American Chance	Sweet and Lowdown	Team Valor	350,000
KEE NOV BRDG 03	Colonial Glitter	F	4	Glitterman	Colonial Ally	Dell Ridge Farm	340,000
BAR MAY 2YO HRA 03	Evolution	C	2	Gilded Time	Champaigne Amelia	Alsdorf and La Cresta Farm	335,000
KEE APR 2YO KY 03	Regina Girl	F	2	Siphon (BRZ)	Expedicionaria (Ven)	Toyomitsu Hirai	330,000
KEE APR 2YO KY 03	Eishin Derinha	C	2	Exploit	Saratoga Flower	Toyomitsu Hirai	330,000

Snapshot Facts: Among horses of racing age sold in 2003, the top price of $2.7 million greatly exceeded the best sale of either 2001 or 2002. There were more sold for $1,000,000 or more (five) and $500,000 or more (28) than either of the two preceding years.

Leading Breeders in 2003 by Money Won

Breeder	Starters	Starts	1st	2d	3d	Purses
Adena Springs	.331	1,936	.296	308	238	$11,542,871
Franks John	.464	3,196	.424	393	391	9,529,985
Farnsworth Farms	.423	3,491	.475	449	430	8,114,786
Mockingbird Farm, Inc.	.245	2,323	.309	326	329	7,094,062
Juddmonte Farms	.57	.279	.49	46	33	6,980,540
Jones Brereton C.	.232	1,574	.213	208	234	5,148,902
Mabee John C. Mr. & Mrs.	.244	1,462	.213	192	192	4,795,883
Evans Edward P.	.132	.800	.114	114	110	4,387,687
Sam-Son Farm	.53	.265	.55	44	37	3,743,610
Schickedanz Gustav	.39	.219	.39	21	23	3,608,477
Appleton Arthur I.	.137	.973	.133	122	119	3,419,884
Overbrook Farm	.140	.826	.116	104	99	3,325,554
Stonerside Stable, LLC	.67	.379	.59	34	51	3,290,666
Everest Stables Inc.	.75	.539	.87	80	68	3,090,063
WinStar Farm, LLC	.55	.219	.31	29	23	3,085,433
Campbell Gilbert G.	.141	1,095	.150	138	142	2,771,919
Clovelly Farms	.12	.61	.7	9	11	2,570,591
Ocala Stud Farm	.61	.512	.74	65	75	2,568,240
Paulson Allen E.	.93	.551	.62	63	55	2,543,695
Flaxman Holdings Ltd.	.26	.126	.35	17	19	2,470,075
W. S. Farish, James Elkins & W. T. Webber Jr.	.2	.16	.9	3	0	2,379,076
Harris Farms Inc.	.86	.637	.111	101	103	2,377,896
Albert Bell & Joyce Bell	.4	.30	.14	6	2	2,272,650
The Thoroughbred Corp.	.48	.256	.39	33	42	2,237,059
Kenneth L. Ramsey & Sarah K. Ramsey	.92	.580	.94	78	62	2,209,567
Frazier D. W. Dr.	.128	1,007	.121	135	121	2,200,767
Highland Farms, Inc.	.98	.707	.95	77	96	2,185,081
Wertheimer & Frere	.26	.137	.20	23	14	2,162,036
Wygod Martin J. Mr. & Mrs.	.100	.581	.91	76	61	2,044,044
Newchance Farm	.15	.115	.12	10	10	2,000,495
Shields J. V. Jr.	.29	.195	.35	31	27	1,998,132
Charles Nuckols Jr. & Sons	.103	.758	.96	80	114	1,970,472
Plemmons Jim H.	.38	.217	.32	26	21	1,893,408
J D Farms	.100	.686	.82	79	92	1,866,838
Dr. William A. Reed & Stonecrest Farm	.14	.104	.24	10	11	1,836,189
Mangurian, Jr. Harry T.	.93	.739	.110	88	98	1,804,035
Live Oak Stud	.84	.548	.75	73	52	1,797,955
Schettine William C.	.22	.148	.24	27	17	1,791,995
Minshall Farms	.45	.375	.48	46	51	1,769,319
Sez Who Thoroughbreds	.91	.493	.67	52	62	1,751,559
Claiborne Farm	.44	.260	.40	38	35	1,749,839
Pin Oak Stud, Inc.	.53	.363	.56	62	42	1,740,347
Strawbridge George Jr.	.62	.299	.48	48	42	1,672,981
Farish W. S.	.53	.289	.44	57	32	1,555,748
Robert H. Roberts & Bea Roberts	.71	.657	.86	82	79	1,530,639
Richter Family Trust	.28	.235	.48	41	30	1,525,625
Marylou Whitney Stables	.18	.118	.16	21	15	1,504,246
Prestonwood Farm, LLC	.50	.379	.59	55	50	1,497,731
Jacks or Better Farm Inc.	.45	.306	.51	54	37	1,490,345
John Toffan & Trudy McCaffery	.58	.409	.71	59	43	1,455,845
Moss J. S. Mr. & Mrs.	.26	.178	.30	25	36	1,436,850
Knob Hill Stable	.27	.220	.39	42	22	1,420,790
Bassett Lucy G.	.14	.77	.20	7	9	1,413,520
Toffolon Roger	.53	.481	.75	63	50	1,412,179
Dizney Donald R.	.87	.531	.70	64	66	1,408,951
Hancock Arthur B. III	.70	.448	.58	66	49	1,398,011
Foxfield	.57	.366	.66	58	37	1,389,771
Sondra Bender & Howard M. Bender	.39	.269	.40	31	36	1,364,936
Humphrey G. Watts Jr.	.22	.154	.19	24	29	1,364,432
Marablue Farm	.79	.497	.64	58	60	1,305,906

Breeder	Starters	Starts	1st	2d	3d	Purses
Haras Santa Maria de Araras	46	320	47	39	50	1,296,509
Hermitage Farm LLC	67	441	64	55	55	1,279,779
Nellie M. Cox & Rose Retreat Farm	17	147	23	21	11	1,274,979
Kinsman Farm	53	345	59	42	37	1,272,839
Kinghaven Farms Limited	43	273	37	31	33	1,271,735
Robsham E. Paul	55	455	59	54	45	1,237,198
Stonewall Farm	41	296	56	43	37	1,230,582
North Wales LLC	16	85	7	16	9	1,221,282
Palides Investments N. V. Inc	25	130	26	16	9	1,218,499
Glen Hill Farm	51	350	63	50	42	1,217,316
Hargus Sexton & Sandra Sexton	65	406	46	50	46	1,204,808
Gulf Coast Farms Bloodstock LP	40	240	41	44	33	1,191,691
La Quebrada	38	215	28	25	28	1,182,386
Gainesway Thoroughbreds Ltd.	41	275	52	45	34	1,173,033
Winchell Verne H.	33	234	39	19	32	1,156,384
Wills Catherine	1	9	3	3	1	1,154,020
Meyerhoff Robert E.	49	322	62	41	50	1,153,586
Aaron U. Jones & Marie D. Jones	22	132	21	22	22	1,153,008
Byrne Michael C.	28	190	26	30	18	1,140,860
Anstu Stables Inc	5	23	7	4	1	1,139,957
SLU, Inc.	30	200	30	29	24	1,130,958
Wimborne Farm, Inc.	52	285	38	37	34	1,121,668
The Niarchos Family	2	4	2	0	0	1,113,600
Day James E.	21	121	16	9	13	1,103,086
Irish Acres Farm	60	595	71	67	56	1,097,659
Calumet Farm	54	325	39	31	48	1,091,726
Dreyfuss Donald S. Dr.	64	478	65	72	49	1,091,151
Domino Stud of Lexington, LLC	19	109	13	13	7	1,090,571
Glencrest Farm LLC	57	476	63	50	61	1,089,326
Cherokee Farms, Inc.	11	74	12	10	12	1,088,475
Gainesborough Stud Management	1	6	2	1	3	1,082,885
Double D Farm Corp.	88	650	59	67	83	1,079,337
Sabine Stable	34	241	40	21	29	1,063,026
Hill 'N' Dale Farm	53	334	56	37	33	1,062,199
Adcock J	91	532	66	68	66	1,061,063
Marshall Naify Revocable Trust	47	235	43	39	35	1,050,567
Gainsborough Stud Management Ltd	9	52	8	2	8	1,041,795
Muirfield Ventures	9	62	7	6	5	1,027,766
Carrion, Trustee Jaime S.	10	53	13	9	5	1,027,640
Foxwood Plantation, Inc.	46	377	52	56	35	1,024,924
Seaman Casey	38	231	37	27	25	1,018,629
Gomez Ron E.	62	462	61	67	51	1,014,430
Jayeff B Stables	38	205	36	33	20	1,008,775
Hobeau Farm Ltd.	39	309	32	45	51	998,181
Lussky William	36	279	40	46	37	987,101
Parra Ro	57	355	59	53	36	986,092
Robert Norman & Patricia Norman	35	313	57	52	34	985,061
Swifty Farms Inc.	58	371	52	48	44	984,034
Billingsley Creek Ranch	35	212	49	28	23	976,293
Mt. Brilliant Farm LLC	40	261	39	39	34	975,189
Jones John T. L. Jr.	53	357	50	33	48	943,281
Abolengo	11	65	10	9	8	942,455
Whitham Janis R.	17	106	19	21	14	936,471
Haras Santa Ana do Rio Grande	4	17	8	1	2	935,547
McGinnes Charles Mr. & Mrs.	43	270	33	33	32	932,125
Spiegel Robert	14	94	12	11	19	930,896
Donald & R. Mary Zuckerman, as Tenants by the Entireties	37	187	29	25	14	929,796
Generazio Patricia	39	317	32	50	41	928,266
Glory Days Breeding, Inc.	30	235	54	39	33	924,100
Morrison Dolphus C.	13	88	5	15	7	921,931
C. Fipke	3	18	3	7	2	921,698

Breeder	Starters	Starts	1st	2d	3d	Purses
E & D Enterprises	57	428	54	50	47	916,529
Beclawat Stable	18	114	18	11	16	915,364
Robinson J. Mack	43	316	37	53	43	912,655
Bennett R. J. Mr. & Mrs.	44	383	58	60	54	908,665
duPont Richard C. Mrs.	23	175	23	23	23	905,673
Brylynn Farm, Inc.	56	327	42	44	42	900,451
TAC Holdings, Inc.	26	174	23	25	26	900,354
Miss Christine Kiernan	1	1	1	0	0	900,000
River Ridge Ranch	35	293	52	51	24	895,443
Robinson Lance K.	21	182	29	31	26	893,249
Jerkens Elisabeth R.	21	201	28	36	23	889,005
Schickedanz Bruno	37	329	46	41	40	872,553
Four Horsemen's Ranch	36	247	45	38	32	870,834
Haras Don Alberto	14	116	17	17	17	870,279
Iron County Farms Inc.	33	225	22	21	35	869,775
White Fox Farm	24	174	19	28	30	863,570
Chester Broman & Mary R. Broman	34	201	33	25	23	863,079
Paxson Henry D. Mrs.	38	309	52	38	43	862,208
John T. L. Jones Jr. & H. Smoot Fahlgren	4	28	7	4	2	852,965
Wafare Farm	23	251	29	27	29	848,085
Gardiner Farms Limited	33	235	32	25	28	847,485
Centaur Farms, Inc.	34	230	30	30	35	846,060
Flying Zee Stables	54	396	54	62	54	844,307
Santa Cruz Ranch Inc.	56	391	34	42	43	836,822
Lazy E Ranch Inc	32	187	28	24	20	836,545
Oxenberg Bea	4	35	6	10	5	836,290
Haras Sumaya	2	12	3	1	1	835,180
Hill 'N' Dale Farms	10	71	15	8	8	832,063
George A Smith & Dr. W. E. Johnston	9	72	18	8	10	831,642
CBF Corporation	20	152	31	27	22	829,192
Hunter Barbara	62	415	56	55	63	825,892
Cypress Farms 1991 & Vessels Stallion Farm LLC	1	9	3	4	0	821,782
Robert H Walter Family Trust	44	292	40	41	39	821,120
Meadowbrook Farms, Inc.	46	312	44	33	41	814,924
Colebrook Farms	44	312	34	43	31	808,675
Cobleskill College Found	9	54	13	9	11	799,924
Firmamento	17	111	14	14	19	791,099
Hartis Eileen H.	14	66	10	7	9	784,131
Vanier Harvey L. Mr. & Mrs.	51	403	44	35	43	781,321
Famille Niarchos	2	6	1	0	0	781,200
Rubens Cecilia Straub	13	75	14	6	8	777,210
Ersoff Stanley M.	63	494	51	62	63	770,930
Burning Daylight Farms, Inc.	28	154	31	27	18	765,400
S. Coughlan	1	1	1	0	0	763,200
Dr. & Mrs. R. S. West & Mr. & Mrs. Mackenzie Miller	16	127	15	17	6	760,873
Brunacini George	28	188	26	20	20	758,469
Rooker John W.	12	113	15	20	18	756,406
South River Ranch Inc.	39	313	58	41	34	755,564
Berger Robert B.	16	137	15	16	19	748,017
Triple AAA Ranch	62	395	58	62	61	740,295
Pegram Michael E.	18	102	19	15	14	739,433
Sunrise Stable South	43	345	58	56	56	739,408
Farfellow Farms Ltd.	24	144	22	24	12	738,945
Cobra Farm Inc.	17	112	21	16	10	736,812
Weir Dennis E.	34	270	52	58	41	734,604
McKee Stables Inc	14	80	17	9	13	734,387
Allez France Stables	1	6	3	2	0	730,800
Willmott Stable	16	134	24	20	20	725,960
Rutherford Mike G. Sr.	36	230	33	35	27	720,932
Liberation Farm & Oratis Thoroughbreds	49	247	36	23	29	720,358
Phillips Racing Partnership	33	162	21	28	25	720,096

Breeder	Starters	Starts	1st	2d	3d	Purses
Few Ed	36	238	35	22	20	714,479
Tall Oaks Farm	25	149	18	14	19	714,429
R Bar S Thoroughbreds LLP	51	379	45	41	47	713,672
Watral Michael	40	314	47	42	47	705,607
Audley Farm Inc.	24	151	21	22	24	703,206
G. Watts Humphrey Jr. & Louise I. Humphrey	18	105	23	14	11	703,094
Southern Nevada Racing Stables Inc	41	271	25	36	44	702,556
Goichman Lawrence	18	88	14	15	9	700,284
Curtin Cheryl A.	16	105	19	10	16	698,905
New Farm	17	99	22	6	10	697,240
McDowell Farm	53	385	52	37	43	679,935
Hechavarria Luis de	40	294	32	33	43	679,857
Asiel Stable, L.C.	17	130	25	22	11	672,166
Lazy Lane Stables, Inc.	31	222	35	34	33	666,240
Hettinger John	39	259	28	25	34	655,503
Wind Hill Farm	18	114	21	12	21	649,488
Drazin Dennis	21	147	19	21	19	649,095
Mills Randy	46	352	46	43	34	648,222
McClelland D. G.	16	95	16	12	12	646,840
Hughes B. Wayne	20	97	18	15	16	646,814
Arthur B. Hancock III & Gerald F. Healy	2	19	2	4	3	641,130
Gunther John D.	21	128	21	16	26	638,025
Heiligbrodt Racing Stable	25	184	32	26	22	636,110
Mack Earle Irving	5	25	7	2	3	632,551
Brown Terry	1	10	4	2	2	631,975
Naify Valerie	5	27	6	5	4	631,288
Mereworth Farm	45	337	30	33	36	628,258
Wachtel Edwin	40	336	51	40	45	625,774
Hart Farm, Inc.	45	298	36	37	35	622,323
L. T. Smith Enterprises	41	278	35	35	42	618,810
Mill Ridge Farm Ltd. & W Lazy T. ,Ltd.	1	9	4	1	1	616,723
Brushwood Stable	17	73	16	13	5	613,676
Granja Vista Del Rio	35	198	23	24	29	606,322
Randal Robert David Mr. & Mrs.	22	151	22	17	20	605,001
Summerwind Farm	16	91	22	11	13	604,020
Christiana Stables	25	119	21	17	17	603,305
Nielsen Gerald Mr. & Mrs.	13	94	16	14	7	602,549
Trackside Farm & Liberation Farm & G.A. Seelbinder	2	15	8	2	1	601,340
Cabotaba Partnership	7	46	8	6	6	600,869
Gallagher's Stud	21	171	22	14	13	600,210
Hugel Max	22	176	17	21	23	597,733
Emerald Pastures Corp.	28	213	32	32	22	592,025
Domino Stud, Inc.	16	108	18	15	16	590,278
Malmuth Marvin	23	167	24	24	12	588,642
Robert E Low & Lawana L Low	10	48	8	7	6	588,089
Moyglare Stud Farm, Ltd.	13	94	13	15	5	585,987
J. B. Stables Inc.	48	329	37	32	44	585,129
Hidden Point Farm, Inc.	36	261	37	37	43	581,663
Hurstland Farm	24	184	34	23	19	581,415
Sorokolit William	10	68	11	3	6	577,796
McMakin Nelson	21	167	18	24	19	575,264
Sabiston James T.	17	121	13	19	18	573,953
Baker Reade	9	54	14	7	4	573,938
Chowhan Naveed Dr.	3	17	4	6	1	570,741
Cheveley Park Stud Ltd	5	24	3	1	3	568,687
Casey James W.	44	304	26	25	33	568,458
Justice Farm, Greg Justice & Steve Justice	39	261	25	30	23	565,504
Hubert Pilcher & Docia Pilcher	35	286	32	31	44	563,735
Woodlynn Farm Inc	21	143	23	26	18	562,707
Cohn Seymour	27	190	24	26	22	562,598
Heinlein Herman	39	296	36	32	25	559,037

Breeder	Starters	Starts	1st	2d	3d	Purses
Phipps Ogden Mills	20	121	16	17	14	559,010
Sleeter Carolyn	19	151	27	13	16	558,301
Huckabay Jackie D. MD	22	170	29	23	22	556,450
White Cross Farm	29	247	31	40	30	554,098
Ballymacoll Stud Farm Ltd.	2	2	1	0	0	553,985
Rand, W. Kenan Jr.	5	24	4	1	1	551,825
Gulf States Racing Stables II	6	51	11	7	3	548,702
McKee Ronald E.	15	125	18	22	20	546,218
Greely John J. III	15	109	29	17	11	545,878
Clarkland Farm	32	215	28	29	16	541,713
Dr. K K Jayaraman & Dr. V. Devi Jayaraman	21	152	33	21	23	541,228
Old English Rancho	32	195	24	22	28	535,732
Frankel Jerry	3	24	6	3	1	532,039
Kaster Richard S.	22	154	26	24	18	531,676
Cranford Stud	4	40	13	6	5	531,671
John A Nerud Revocable Trust	21	183	30	26	27	531,306
Novo Oscar	1	6	6	0	0	528,800
Adkins Jerry R.	31	197	28	25	20	528,700
R. C. Durr & George Budig	17	106	19	13	18	528,379
Graham William D.	9	60	8	15	6	528,240
O H Wienges & Son	32	253	44	41	30	527,701
Ryehill Farm	43	303	36	41	26	526,731
Jamm Ltd.	4	31	4	4	4	526,594
Vitello Joseph	4	28	4	4	0	526,239
Frank Digiulio & Frank DiGiulio Jr.	4	21	6	4	2	526,107
Amherst Stable	7	49	3	12	6	525,966
Alexander Helen C.	4	33	9	0	6	525,188
Bakerman Robert	27	204	22	25	24	523,792
Carey John	23	136	21	14	14	522,966
Sapp Darrell R.	31	264	36	51	37	522,431
Shuford Nancy C.	43	294	34	34	41	522,325
Erwin Janet	20	166	26	14	27	522,275
Tommy Town Thoroughbreds, Llc	29	104	15	13	15	521,633
R. Otto Stables, Inc.	3	21	12	1	1	520,990
McFadden Neal	43	300	31	37	44	520,784
Youngman Patricia	16	127	15	32	29	520,210
Vegso Racing Stable	10	59	9	4	6	517,485
Shewchuk Johnnie P.	29	199	29	16	24	517,303
Winsong Farms	14	93	14	14	12	515,985
Kilcarn Stud	4	23	5	2	2	515,712
Timber Creek Farm	44	355	45	44	39	514,238
McDonnell Francis	33	217	41	32	25	513,895
Willmott Stables, Inc.	5	32	7	4	5	509,140
Loch Lea Farm, Inc.	28	183	22	30	21	508,644
Nolan Chris	25	163	25	24	10	507,550
Rosemont Farm Inc.	22	135	19	22	15	506,914
Ralph Todd & Aury Todd	7	50	6	7	8	506,755
Prentice Bryant H. III	16	125	14	10	12	504,788
Byer Larry	46	317	43	62	49	501,923
C. S. Tateson	1	9	2	2	2	500,360
Jan Siegel, Mace Siegel & Samantha Siegel	17	100	13	24	9	499,400
Elliott James R.	29	178	33	20	16	499,137
Dark Hollow Farm & William Beatson	5	29	6	6	2	498,625
Denis and Mrs. Joan Brosnan	2	11	0	4	1	496,500
Hidden Point Farm Inc.	31	190	19	24	25	496,413
Buckram Oak Farm	15	91	12	11	18	495,825
Applebite Farms	27	144	20	20	14	495,317
Tricar Stables Inc	34	254	36	28	40	495,187
Thomas/Lakin	19	66	16	5	9	494,936
Sugar Maple Farm	20	133	16	22	17	494,600
Nor Joanne	16	80	13	9	13	494,470

Breeder	Starters	Starts	1st	2d	3d	Purses
Harris Ross	24	174	32	8	25	494,404
Thomas J. Kelly & Joseph M. Grant	3	24	3	4	3	494,120
Scott C. G. DVM	7	47	6	7	8	486,713
Eaton Hall Farm	19	136	17	16	14	485,668
Carl William A.	23	142	17	16	17	482,662
Evans R. S.	20	120	18	10	15	482,656
Schoenborn Gus Jr.	30	226	22	23	30	482,549
King Betty	22	178	16	23	25	481,710
Hidden Lane Farms Inc.	15	123	17	17	22	481,270
Doyle Mike	4	34	6	5	8	480,001
Lotz Nicholas M	17	160	22	22	22	476,178
Blazing Meadows Farm	28	215	26	26	30	475,103
Farnsworth Farms & Locust Valley Corp.	37	345	36	31	50	473,179
Anomaly Investments LP	1	9	6	1	2	470,826
Cobra Farm	17	116	17	12	15	468,532
Tod Mtn Thoroughbred	36	229	32	31	21	466,155
Roberts Guy C. Mr. & Mrs.	38	307	45	60	37	464,429
Kennelot Stables, Ltd.	8	55	12	7	10	464,417
Chandler John A. Dr.	10	44	5	11	7	464,008
Fuller Peter	34	295	32	45	50	463,464
Candyland Farm	15	74	19	9	6	461,947
Wakefield Farm	29	228	23	30	31	461,593
Purdy Patricia Staskowski	28	183	22	19	25	455,830
McLean Pope	30	177	29	23	17	455,681
Hamilton Emory A.	5	29	7	6	5	453,802
K C Horse Corporation	16	91	20	11	20	453,307
Fox Ridge Farm Inc	7	44	5	3	7	452,865
Stan Stefanski & Ingrid Stefanski	2	11	4	0	2	452,679
Cohen Morry	9	44	7	6	9	451,882
Westwind Farm	21	193	31	21	25	448,780
Spring Farm	27	128	14	11	14	447,595
Jim Robinson & Pam Robinson	22	172	18	25	20	445,640
Kline Alan S.	14	91	13	14	11	445,420
Dinwiddie Farm	6	28	7	2	2	445,249
Humphrey G. Watts	12	87	14	10	10	443,763
Orilla Del Monte	11	72	14	11	9	443,621
Horses of Course Inc.	17	155	22	31	20	441,930
Scott John S.	21	193	29	23	30	437,109
Clover Leaf Farms II, Inc.	20	122	21	17	16	437,053
Elk Manor Farm	18	86	18	5	8	435,666
Cavanaugh J. R.	13	115	13	13	19	435,407
O'Donovan Hugh J. Mr. & Mrs.	7	64	9	10	10	435,403
Aspiration Stable	6	31	6	3	4	434,032
Canyon Farms	24	142	22	21	19	431,561
Ridder Thoroughbred Stable	23	127	16	9	12	431,288
Asmussen Keith I.	24	163	23	24	25	430,503
Sandra's Bent Tree Farm	19	136	19	22	11	430,170
Tackett Paul	19	184	20	24	33	429,728
Harris William	23	162	19	20	15	429,422
Finney & Taylor	1	14	3	4	3	428,733
Everest Stables, Inc.	22	99	18	16	12	428,340
Haras El Palenque & Earl McNeil	21	136	18	15	17	427,778
Bertolino Frank	15	101	16	21	10	427,405
Lovingier Terry C.	26	166	22	20	20	427,310
Tackett Bill	55	317	44	44	27	425,922

Snapshot Facts: There were 293 breeders whose horses earned $500,000 or more in 2003. There were 103 breeders whose horses earned more than $1 million and 30 breeders with $2 million.

Leading Breeders in 2003 by Races Won

Breeder	Starters	Starts	1st	2d	3d	Purses
Farnsworth Farms	423	3,491	475	449	430	$8,114,786
Franks John	464	3,196	424	393	391	9,529,985
Mockingbird Farm, Inc.	245	2,323	309	326	329	7,094,062
Adena Springs	331	1,936	296	308	238	11,542,871
Jones Brereton C.	232	1,574	213	208	234	5,148,902
Mabee John C. Mr. & Mrs.	244	1,462	213	192	192	4,795,883
Campbell Gilbert G.	141	1,095	150	138	142	2,771,919
Appleton Arthur I.	137	973	133	122	119	3,419,884
Frazier D. W. Dr.	128	1,007	121	135	121	2,200,767
Overbrook Farm	140	826	116	104	99	3,325,554
Evans Edward P.	132	800	114	114	110	4,387,687
Harris Farms Inc.	86	637	111	101	103	2,377,896
Mangurian, Jr. Harry T.	93	739	110	88	98	1,804,035
Charles Nuckols Jr. & Sons	103	758	96	80	114	1,970,472
Highland Farms, Inc.	98	707	95	77	96	2,185,081
Kenneth L. Ramsey & Sarah K. Ramsey	92	580	94	78	62	2,209,567
Wygod Martin J. Mr. & Mrs.	100	581	91	76	61	2,044,044
Everest Stables Inc.	75	539	87	80	68	3,090,063
Robert H. Roberts & Bea Roberts	71	657	86	82	79	1,530,639
J D Farms	100	686	82	79	92	1,866,838
Live Oak Stud	84	548	75	73	52	1,797,955
Toffolon Roger	53	481	75	63	50	1,412,179
Ocala Stud Farm	61	512	74	65	75	2,568,240
Irish Acres Farm	60	595	71	67	56	1,097,659
John Toffan & Trudy McCaffery	58	409	71	59	43	1,455,845
Dizney Donald R.	87	531	70	64	66	1,408,951
Sez Who Thoroughbreds	91	493	67	52	62	1,751,559
Adcock J	91	532	66	68	66	1,061,063
Foxfield	57	366	66	58	37	1,389,771
Dreyfuss Donald S. Dr.	64	478	65	72	49	1,091,151
Hermitage Farm LLC	67	441	64	55	55	1,279,779
Marablue Farm	79	497	64	58	60	1,305,906
Glen Hill Farm	51	350	63	50	42	1,217,316
Glencrest Farm LLC	57	476	63	50	61	1,089,326
Meyerhoff Robert E.	49	322	62	41	50	1,153,586
Paulson Allen E.	93	551	62	63	55	2,543,695
Gomez Ron E.	62	462	61	67	51	1,014,430
Double D Farm Corp.	88	650	59	67	83	1,079,337
Kinsman Farm	53	345	59	42	37	1,272,839
Parra Ro	57	355	59	53	36	986,092
Prestonwood Farm, LLC	50	379	59	55	50	1,497,731
Robsham E. Paul	55	455	59	54	45	1,237,198
Stonerside Stable, LLC	67	379	59	34	51	3,290,666
Bennett R. J. Mr. & Mrs.	44	383	58	60	54	908,665
Hancock Arthur B. III	70	448	58	66	49	1,398,011
South River Ranch Inc.	39	313	58	41	34	755,564
Sunrise Stable South	43	345	58	56	56	739,408
Triple AAA Ranch	62	395	58	62	61	740,295
Robert Norman & Patricia Norman	35	313	57	52	34	985,061
Hill 'N' Dale Farm	53	334	56	37	33	1,062,199
Hunter Barbara	62	415	56	55	63	825,892
Pin Oak Stud, Inc.	53	363	56	62	42	1,740,347
Stonewall Farm	41	296	56	43	37	1,230,582
Sam-Son Farm	53	265	55	44	37	3,743,610
E & D Enterprises	57	428	54	50	47	916,529
Flying Zee Stables	54	396	54	62	54	844,307
Glory Days Breeding, Inc.	30	235	54	39	33	924,100
Godolphin Racing Inc.	67	233	54	31	38	281,732
Foxwood Plantation, Inc.	46	377	52	56	35	1,024,924
Gainesway Thoroughbreds Ltd.	41	275	52	45	34	1,173,033
McDowell Farm	53	385	52	37	43	679,935
Paxson Henry D. Mrs.	38	309	52	38	43	862,208

Breeder	Starters	Starts	1st	2d	3d	Purses
River Ridge Ranch	35	293	52	51	24	895,443
Swifty Farms Inc.	58	371	52	48	44	984,034
Weir Dennis E.	34	270	52	58	41	734,604
Ersoff Stanley M.	63	494	51	62	63	770,930
Jacks or Better Farm Inc.	45	306	51	54	37	1,490,345
Wachtel Edwin	40	336	51	40	45	625,774
Jones John T. L. Jr.	53	357	50	33	48	943,281
Billingsley Creek Ranch	35	212	49	28	23	976,293
Hollis Cotton Oil Mill Inc.	52	324	49	27	37	284,393
Juddmonte Farms	57	279	49	46	33	6,980,540
Minshall Farms	45	375	48	46	51	1,769,319
Richter Family Trust	28	235	48	41	30	1,525,625
Strawbridge George Jr.	62	299	48	48	42	1,672,981
Haras Santa Maria de Araras	46	320	47	39	50	1,296,509
Watral Michael	40	314	47	42	47	705,607
Hargus Sexton & Sandra Sexton	65	406	46	50	46	1,204,808
Mills Randy	46	352	46	43	34	648,222
Schickedanz Bruno	37	329	46	41	40	872,553
Four Horsemen's Ranch	36	247	45	38	32	870,834
R Bar S Thoroughbreds LLP	51	379	45	41	47	713,672
Roberts Guy C. Mr. & Mrs.	38	307	45	60	37	464,429
Timber Creek Farm	44	355	45	44	39	514,238
Farish W. S.	53	289	44	57	32	1,555,748
Meadowbrook Farms, Inc.	46	312	44	33	41	814,924
O H Wienges & Son	32	253	44	41	30	527,701
Tackett Bill	55	317	44	44	27	425,922
Vanier Harvey L. Mr. & Mrs.	51	403	44	35	43	781,321
Byer Larry	46	317	43	62	49	501,923
Marshall Naify Revocable Trust	47	235	43	39	35	1,050,567
Brylynn Farm, Inc.	56	327	42	44	42	900,451
Gulf Coast Farms Bloodstock LP	40	240	41	44	33	1,191,691
McDonnell Francis	33	217	41	32	25	513,895
Northwest Farms	40	245	41	29	28	405,218
Town and Country Farms Corp	35	261	41	36	34	342,065
Claiborne Farm	44	260	40	38	35	1,749,839
Hillis Larry O.	31	271	40	37	37	270,418
Lussky William	36	279	40	46	37	987,101
Robert H Walter Family Trust	44	292	40	41	39	821,120
Sabine Stable	34	241	40	21	29	1,063,026
Sondra Bender & Howard M. Bender	39	269	40	31	36	1,364,936
Calumet Farm	54	325	39	31	48	1,091,726
Knob Hill Stable	27	220	39	42	22	1,420,790
Mt. Brilliant Farm LLC	40	261	39	39	34	975,189
Schickedanz Gustav	39	219	39	21	23	3,608,477
The Thoroughbred Corp.	48	256	39	33	42	2,237,059
Winchell Verne H.	33	234	39	19	32	1,156,384
D Stephen Hollis Md	26	258	38	54	33	291,001
Wimborne Farm, Inc.	52	285	38	37	34	1,121,668
Hidden Point Farm, Inc.	36	261	37	37	43	581,663
J. B. Stables Inc.	48	329	37	32	44	585,129
Kinghaven Farms Limited	43	273	37	31	33	1,271,735
Robinson J. Mack	43	316	37	53	43	912,655
Seaman Casey	38	231	37	27	25	1,018,629
Farnsworth Farms & Locust Valley Corp.	37	345	36	31	50	473,179
Hart Farm, Inc.	45	298	36	37	35	622,323
Heinlein Herman	39	296	36	32	25	559,037
Jayeff B Stables	38	205	36	33	20	1,008,775
Liberation Farm & Oratis Thoroughbreds	49	247	36	23	29	720,358
Ryehill Farm	43	303	36	41	26	526,731
Sapp Darrell R.	31	264	36	51	37	522,431
Tricar Stables Inc	34	254	36	28	40	495,187
Fares Farm Inc	47	314	35	45	43	421,436
Few Ed	36	238	35	22	20	714,479
Flaxman Holdings Ltd.	26	126	35	17	19	2,470,075

Breeder	Starters	Starts	1st	2d	3d	Purses
L. T. Smith Enterprises	41	278	35	35	42	618,810
Lazy Lane Stables, Inc.	31	222	35	34	33	666,240
Shields J. V. Jr.	29	195	35	31	27	1,998,132
Colebrook Farms	44	312	34	43	31	808,675
Hurstland Farm	24	184	34	23	19	581,415
Santa Cruz Ranch Inc.	56	391	34	42	43	836,822
Shuford Nancy C.	43	294	34	34	41	522,325
Baker Luann	24	219	33	24	20	351,882
Chester Broman & Mary R. Broman	34	201	33	25	23	863,079
Dr. K K Jayaraman & Dr. V. Devi Jayaraman	21	152	33	21	23	541,228
Elliott James R.	29	178	33	20	16	499,137
Halo Farms	32	241	33	19	33	421,154
James Arnold & Marcia Arnold	42	288	33	34	32	396,435
McGinnes Charles Mr. & Mrs.	43	270	33	33	32	932,125
Rutherford Mike G. Sr.	36	230	33	35	27	720,932
Emerald Pastures Corp.	28	213	32	32	22	592,025
Fuller Peter	34	295	32	45	50	463,464
Gardiner Farms Limited	33	235	32	25	28	847,485
Generazio Patricia	39	317	32	50	41	928,266
Gentry Farms	44	295	32	26	38	328,053
Harris Ross	24	174	32	8	25	494,404
Hechavarria Luis de	40	294	32	33	43	679,857
Heiligbrodt Racing Stable	25	184	32	26	22	636,110
Hobeau Farm Ltd.	39	309	32	45	51	998,181
Hubert Pilcher & Docia Pilcher	35	286	32	31	44	563,735
Plemmons Jim H.	38	217	32	26	21	1,893,408
Tod Mtn Thoroughbred	36	229	32	31	21	466,155
Burning Daylight Farms, Inc.	28	154	31	27	18	765,400
CBF Corporation	20	152	31	27	22	829,192
McFadden Neal	43	300	31	37	44	520,784
Van Andel Peter	17	136	31	14	19	416,039
Westwind Farm	21	193	31	21	25	448,780
White Cross Farm	29	247	31	40	30	554,098
WinStar Farm, LLC	55	219	31	29	23	3,085,433
Centaur Farms, Inc.	34	230	30	30	35	846,060
John A Nerud Revocable Trust	21	183	30	26	27	531,306
Mereworth Farm	45	337	30	33	36	628,258
Moss J. S. Mr. & Mrs.	26	178	30	25	36	1,436,850
SLU, Inc.	30	200	30	29	24	1,130,958
D. & R. M. Zuckerman, as Tenants by the Entireties	37	187	29	25	14	929,796
Golden Richard L.	27	190	29	24	22	405,680
Greely John J. III	15	109	29	17	11	545,878
Huckabay Jackie D. MD	22	170	29	23	22	556,450
McLean Pope	30	177	29	23	17	455,681
Robinson Lance K.	21	182	29	31	26	893,249
Scott John S.	21	193	29	23	30	437,109
Shewchuk Johnnie P.	29	199	29	16	24	517,303
Wafare Farm	23	251	29	27	29	848,085
Adkins Jerry R.	31	197	28	25	20	528,700
Bachman Thomas W.	25	164	28	25	21	387,879
Cashmark Farm	40	240	28	29	27	406,441
Clarkland Farm	32	215	28	29	16	541,713
Granger J. Weldon	28	176	28	21	22	367,782
Hettinger John	39	259	28	25	34	655,503
Hooper Fred W.	35	210	28	23	16	300,713
Jerkens Elisabeth R.	21	201	28	36	23	889,005
La Quebrada	38	215	28	25	28	1,182,386
Lazy E Ranch Inc	32	187	28	24	20	836,545
Richland Ranch & Sue Cook	29	205	28	25	31	408,118
Riecken Herb L.	24	201	28	21	19	209,528
Hines James T. Jr.	39	262	27	26	30	256,853
Karutz W. S. Dr.	23	173	27	20	19	333,135
Our Farm Inc	33	290	27	34	30	355,216
Sleeter Carolyn	19	151	27	13	16	558,301

Breeder	Starters	Starts	1st	2d	3d	Purses
Blazing Meadows Farm	28	215	26	26	30	475,103
Bourke W. John	23	180	26	13	19	337,640
Brunacini George	28	188	26	20	20	758,469
Byrne Michael C.	28	190	26	30	18	1,140,860
Casey James W.	44	304	26	25	33	568,458
Coal Creek Farm	23	153	26	19	22	378,978
Erwin Janet	20	166	26	14	27	522,275
High Mark Farm	18	175	26	25	18	384,981
Kaster Richard S.	22	154	26	24	18	531,676
Larry Millison Inc.	20	175	26	27	19	417,464
Littleton B. L.	26	235	26	33	28	296,710
Palides Investments N. V. Inc	25	130	26	16	9	1,218,499
Stronach Stables	23	177	26	27	28	349,091
Sun Valley Farm	30	170	26	19	21	358,333
Zamora John J.	26	159	26	15	28	293,366
Asiel Stable, L.C.	17	130	25	22	11	672,166
Bluestem Farm Inc.	25	203	25	33	23	353,493
Dinesh Maniar & Getaway Farms	35	180	25	28	21	371,120
Justice Farm, Greg Justice & Steve Justice	39	261	25	30	23	565,504
Nolan Chris	25	163	25	24	10	507,550
Scharbauer Clarence Jr.	21	179	25	22	24	303,754
Southern Nevada Racing Stables Inc	41	271	25	36	44	702,556
Cohn Seymour	27	190	24	26	22	562,598
De La Pomme	19	135	24	15	20	421,545
Dr. William A. Reed & Stonecrest Farm	14	104	24	10	11	1,836,189
Gardner Timothy J. Mrs.	20	141	24	11	23	393,849
Giuffrida Salvatore	20	184	24	17	16	286,192
Malmuth Marvin	23	167	24	24	12	588,642
Old English Rancho	32	195	24	22	28	535,732
Phenix Harold	24	198	24	27	22	194,987
Porter John B.	20	187	24	16	24	359,783
Red Rock Farm	23	186	24	22	35	191,805
Schettine William C.	22	148	24	27	17	1,791,995
Sharp Bayard	13	103	24	12	14	324,740
Sutherland Farm, Inc	40	216	24	25	28	192,200
Tony Bowling & Bobby Dodd	20	147	24	18	20	339,627
Willmott Stable	16	134	24	20	20	725,960
Al Noren & Bunny Noren	26	127	23	20	11	344,725
Allred Edward	14	113	23	19	14	180,322
Asmussen Keith I.	24	163	23	24	25	430,503
Battle Creek Farm	19	112	23	13	13	265,460
Cuprill Charles A. Mr. & Mrs.	23	239	23	30	26	373,434
G. Watts Humphrey Jr. & Louise I. Humphrey	18	105	23	14	11	703,094
Gerrans Al	14	140	23	13	15	264,960
Granja Vista Del Rio	35	198	23	24	29	606,322
Hill 'n' Dale Farm	19	142	23	18	8	302,928
Marty Hershe & Carol Hershe	16	149	23	23	15	335,409
McKathan Farms	21	138	23	12	11	290,922
Nellie M. Cox & Rose Retreat Farm	17	147	23	21	11	1,274,979
Nelson Merv	19	132	23	12	15	202,801
Seeger Roberta	17	172	23	11	12	375,021
Sessa John	24	153	23	17	18	395,152
Shortleaf Stable	25	186	23	21	28	325,477
TAC Holdings, Inc.	26	174	23	25	26	900,354
Wakefield Farm	29	228	23	30	31	461,593
Whiting Ronald J.	13	118	23	17	17	204,456
Woodlynn Farm Inc	21	143	23	26	18	562,707
duPont Richard C. Mrs.	23	175	23	23	23	905,673
Bakerman Robert	27	204	22	25	24	523,792
Brambly Lane Farm	18	121	22	16	18	420,847
Burbach Willard	24	124	22	14	17	368,394
Canyon Farms	24	142	22	21	19	431,561
CresRan LLC	13	111	22	11	9	203,927
Dunn Bar Ranch LLC	17	139	22	15	16	163,086

Breeder	Starters	Starts	1st	2d	3d	Purses
Farfellow Farms Ltd.	24	144	22	24	12	738,945
Gallagher's Stud	21	171	22	14	13	600,210
Horses of Course Inc.	17	155	22	31	20	441,930
Iron County Farms Inc.	33	225	22	21	35	869,775
Loch Lea Farm, Inc.	28	183	22	30	21	508,644
Lotz Nicholas M	17	160	22	22	22	476,178
Lovingier Terry C.	26	166	22	20	20	427,310
Mr. & Mrs. E. M. Dittloff & K. Dittloff	24	193	22	18	23	200,057
Murphy David L.	23	186	22	24	16	198,092
New Farm	17	99	22	6	10	697,240
Newport Farm	15	171	22	21	35	267,984
Noren Al Mr. & Mrs.	20	147	22	21	21	179,358
Oak Crest Farm	18	144	22	18	23	287,628
Purdy Patricia Staskowski	28	183	22	19	25	455,830
Randal Robert David Mr. & Mrs.	22	151	22	17	20	605,001
Red Sunset Farm	19	144	22	17	19	354,427
Schoenborn Gus Jr.	30	226	22	23	30	482,549
Summerwind Farm	16	91	22	11	13	604,020
White Dan W. Dr.	25	177	22	21	14	387,398
Aaron U. Jones & Marie D. Jones	22	132	21	22	22	1,153,008
Allaire Farms	26	153	21	22	19	165,624
Audley Farm Inc.	24	151	21	22	24	703,206
Carey John	23	136	21	14	14	522,966
Carl Cannata & Olivia Cannata	35	211	21	28	27	208,379
Christiana Stables	25	119	21	17	17	603,305
Clover Leaf Farms II, Inc.	20	122	21	17	16	437,053
Cobra Farm Inc.	17	112	21	16	10	736,812
Cypress Farms 1991	20	145	21	21	14	346,934
Gore Terrel Mr. & Mrs.	15	137	21	14	13	408,945
Green Willow Farms	28	166	21	17	15	278,856
Gunther John D.	21	128	21	16	26	638,025
Jonabell Farm Inc.	20	157	21	17	18	328,681
Moseley James B. Mr. & Mrs.	13	121	21	15	15	311,580
Murphy John D.	22	120	21	17	17	365,878
Perez Robert	33	187	21	20	14	339,664
Phillips Racing Partnership	33	162	21	28	25	720,096
Rainbow Stables	22	194	21	37	39	392,157
Thomson Walter J.	22	127	21	17	14	155,105
Wind Hill Farm	18	114	21	12	21	649,488
Winemiller Becky	19	163	21	29	18	289,927
Applebite Farms	27	144	20	20	14	495,317
Bassett Lucy G.	14	77	20	7	9	1,413,520
Bowman Thomas Dr. & Mrs.	17	100	20	14	8	390,244
Darling W. A.	19	110	20	10	13	286,743
Doro J. Stables Ltd.	13	114	20	9	13	185,842
Fennessy Michael	14	121	20	15	9	216,436
Fleming Thoroughbred Farm	23	136	20	23	18	92,367
Fullmer Patricia A.	25	229	20	22	24	242,087
Holtsinger, Inc.	15	81	20	9	10	418,200
Imbesi Joseph	18	146	20	19	12	317,705
Jim Hawkins & Lois Hawkins	11	123	20	15	18	288,003
K C Horse Corporation	16	91	20	11	20	453,307
Kraft Royal B. Sr.	27	196	20	19	22	328,605
Naify Marshall	12	98	20	14	9	299,725
Nordic Thoroughbreds	13	104	20	6	16	249,502
Oxley John	23	129	20	14	18	311,709
Rickman William M.	37	200	20	19	28	265,857
Santen J. D.	21	146	20	24	16	294,389
Saville Donald P.	17	118	20	12	15	335,725
Solomon William J. Dr.	15	131	20	17	14	187,043
Stautberg G. J. Mr. & Mrs.	22	145	20	20	16	397,079
Stearns Daniel C. DVM	28	281	20	19	31	190,796
Tackett Paul	19	184	20	24	33	429,728
Wertheimer & Frere	26	137	20	23	14	2,162,036

Breeder	Starters	Starts	1st	2d	3d	Purses
Baskin Sy	18	135	19	14	13	294,235
Bowling Carl	16	134	19	15	14	389,783
Caldwell Delmar R.	22	135	19	15	10	422,647
Candyland Farm	15	74	19	9	6	461,947
Curtin Cheryl A.	16	105	19	10	16	698,905
Drazin Dennis	21	147	19	21	19	649,095
Gleis Josephine T.	22	160	19	16	20	293,913
Harris William	23	162	19	20	15	429,422
Hidden Point Farm Inc.	31	190	19	24	25	496,413
Humphrey G. Watts Jr.	22	154	19	24	29	1,364,432
Ironwater Farms Joint Venture	29	172	19	26	16	381,209
Landry Harry L.	17	127	19	24	13	388,284
McAllister Norman J.	42	241	19	23	23	345,079
Meeks Mike	17	131	19	20	13	209,064
Moler C. Bruce	22	172	19	21	22	132,445
Ostrager Barry R.	25	149	19	18	21	397,343
Oxley John C.	18	123	19	20	10	399,969
Pabst Frederick L. Mr. & Mrs.	24	117	19	15	10	261,309
Parrish Hill Farm	20	167	19	20	27	343,312
Pegram Michael E.	18	102	19	15	14	739,433
Purdy Clare K.	10	121	19	17	26	114,676
R. C. Durr & George Budig	17	106	19	13	18	528,379
Robert Miller & Delphine Miller	18	139	19	18	20	185,093
Root Jack B. Dr. & Mrs. Jr.	27	190	19	30	18	131,447
Rosemont Farm Inc.	22	135	19	22	15	506,914
Running Luck Ranch Inc	24	160	19	19	19	158,069
Sandra's Bent Tree Farm	19	136	19	22	11	430,170
Spendthrift Farm	11	121	19	17	17	208,456
Vessels Stallion Farm LLC	26	165	19	25	25	208,577
White Fox Farm	24	174	19	28	30	863,570
Whitham Janis R.	17	106	19	21	14	936,471

Snapshot Facts: There were 69 breeders whose horses won 50 races or more in 2003. There were 13 breeders whose horses won 100 races or more.

Annual Leading Breeder – Money Won

Year Breeder	Sts.	1st	2d	3d	Purses
1923 John E. Madden		419	366	323	$623,630
1924 Harry Payne Whitney		272	201	235	482,865
1925 John E. Madden		383	374	376	535,790
1926 Harry Payne Whitney		351	322	308	715,790
1927 Harry Payne Whitney		271	306	234	718,144
1928 Harry Payne Whitney		234	291	269	514,832
1929 Harry Payne Whitney		278	284	234	825,374
1930 Harry Payne Whitney		294	295	281	698,280
1931 Harry Payne Whitney		264	241	244	582,970
1932 Harry Payne Whitney Estate		244	236	217	560,803
1933 Harry Payne Whitney & Cornelius V. Whitney		282	276	320	342,866
1934 Harry Payne Whitney & Cornelius V. Whitney		310	295	287	320,955
1935 Arthur B. Hancock		392	245	252	359,218
1936 Arthur B. Hancock		310	271	265	362,762
1937 Arthur B. Hancock		279	279	223	416,558
1938 Harry Payne Whitney & Cornelius V. Whitney		154	170	169	374,049
1939 Arthur B. Hancock		242	240	261	345,503
1940 Joseph E. Widener		184	161	153	317,961
1941 Calumet Farm (Warren Wright)		124	127	110	528,211
1942 Mrs. Payne Whitney (Greentree Stable)		175	161	163	536,173
1943 Arthur B. Hancock		346	330	315	619,049
1944 Calumet Farm (Warren Wright)		253	227	231	990,612
1945 E. E. Dale Shaffer (Coldstream Stud)		227	147	142	791,477
1946 Meresworth Farm		341	352	344	962,677
1947 Calumet Farm (Warren Wright)		266	207	168	1,807,432
1948 Calumet Farm (Warren Wright)		227	189	160	1,559,850
1949 Calumet Farm (Warren Wright)		270	206	209	1,515,181
1950 Calumet Farm (Warren Wright)		243	219	231	1,090,286
1951 Calumet Farm (Mrs. Gene Markey)		260	180	217	1,198,107
1952 Calumet Farm (Mrs. Gene Markey)		256	217	209	2,060,590
1953 Calumet Farm (Mrs. Gene Markey)		236	168	169	1,573,803
1954 Calumet Farm (Mrs. Gene Markey)		201	145	176	1,139,609
1955 Calumet Farm (Mrs. Gene Markey)		203	175	148	999,737
1956 Calumet Farm (Mrs. Gene Markey)		208	156	163	1,528,727
1957 Calumet Farm (Mrs. Gene Markey)		178	157	124	1,469,473
1958 Claiborne Farm (A. B. Hancock Sr. & A. B. Hancock Jr.)		146	128	133	1,414,355
1959 Claiborne Farm (A. B. Hancock Jr.)		147	144	138	1,322,595
1960 Cornelius V. Whitney		108	106	92	1,193,181
1961 Calumet Farm (Mrs. Gene Markey)		156	120	144	1,078,894
1962 Rex C. Ellsworth		185	181	155	1,678,769
1963 Rex C. Ellsworth	1,468	194	166	150	1,465,069
1964 Bieber-Jacobs Stable (I. Bieber and H. Jacobs)	2,282	271	271	256	1,301,677
1965 Bieber-Jacobs Stable (I. Bieber and H. Jacobs)	2,233	259	278	269	1,994,649
1966 Bieber-Jacobs Stable (I. Bieber and H. Jacobs)	1,785	216	238	217	1,575,027
1967 Bieber-Jacobs Stable (I. Bieber and H. Jacobs)	1,702	183	182	219	1,515,414
1968 Claiborne Farm (A. B. Hancock Jr.)	797	147	116	95	1,493,189
1969 Claiborne Farm (A. B. Hancock Jr.)	728	111	96	98	1,331,485
1970 Harbor View Farm (L. Wolfson)	2,856	366	342	323	1,515,861
1971 Harbor View Farm (L. Wolfson)	3,160	394	348	358	1,739,214
1972 Leslie Combs II	1,693	240	191	203	1,578,851
1973 Elmendorf Farm Max Gluck)	1,604	220	173	175	2,128,080
1974 Edward P.Taylor	2,480	329	326	314	1,926,937
1975 Edward P.Taylor	2,604	344	366	310	2,369,145
1976 Edward P.Taylor	2,718	356	381	313	3,022,181
1977 Edward P.Taylor	2,968	409	417	401	3,414,169
1978 Edward P.Taylor	2,869	442	417	381	3,387,945
1979 Edward P.Taylor	2,671	353	356	360	3,001,108
1980 Edward P.Taylor	2,194	305	270	266	3,111,006
1981 Elmendorf Farm (Max Gluck)	1,179	149	137	145	2,736,029
1982 Elmendorf Farm (Max Gluck)	1,210	143	146	122	3,049,444
1983 Edward P.Taylor	1,813	227	247	206	3,472,128
1984 Claiborne Farm (A. B. Hancock Jr.)	514	87	82	55	5,554,012
1985 Edward P.Taylor	1,691	241	217	189	4,492,453
1986 N. B. Hunt (Bluegrass Farm)	2,481	281	274	284	5,013,667
1987 N. B. Hunt (Bluegrass Farm)	2,855	324	337	298	5,095,050
1988 O. Phipps	249	47	27	32	6,031,305
1989 O. Phipps	166	33	34	17	5,568,537
1990 Tartan Farms	1,081	170	145	113	6,930,043
1991 Sam-Son Farms	648	117	86	78	6,922,993
1992 Mr. & Mrs John C. Mabee	1,805	282	244	217	7,026,627
1993 John Franks	3,967	541	490	471	6,485,545
1994 Allen E. Paulson	1,526	236	187	167	5,776,308
1995 Allen E. Paulson	1,850	283	249	236	10,975,247
1996 Allen E. Paulson	1,986	295	267	230	9,757,559
1997 Allen E. Paulson	1,762	249	229	210	7,728,812
1998 Mr./Mrs. John C. Mabee	1,610	270	219	230	8,225,102
1999 Harry T. Mangurian Jr.	2,779	457	401	369	10,445,981
2000 Harry T. Mangurian Jr.	2,989	455	403	401	10,347,975
2001 Mockingbird Farm, Inc.	2,309	347	311	346	9,155,451
2002 Mockingbird Farm, Inc.	3,279	516	415	456	11,175,975
2003 Adena Springs	1,936	296	308	238	11,542,871

Starts tabulation began in 1963

Annual Leading Breeder – Races Won

Year	Breeder	Races Won	Year	Breeder	Races Won
1918	John E. Madden	213	1961	Edward P. Taylor	265
1919	John E. Madden	311	1962	Edward P. Taylor	263
1920	John E. Madden	313	1963	Edward P. Taylor	300
1921	John E. Madden	424	1964	Edward P. Taylor	305
1922	John E. Madden	366	1965	Edward P. Taylor	290
1923	John E. Madden	419	1966	Edward P. Taylor	310
1924	John E. Madden	318	1967	Edward P. Taylor	288
1925	John E. Madden	383	1968	Edward P. Taylor	280
1926	John E. Madden	368	1969	Edward P. Taylor	302
1927	John E. Madden	362	1970	Harbor View Farm	366
1928	Himyar Stud	331	1971	Harbor View Farm	394
1929	Himyar Stud	335	1972	Harbor View Farm	326
1930	Audley Farm	318	1973	Rex C. Ellsworth	365
1931	Audley Farm	359	1974	Rex C. Ellsworth	415
1932	Himyar Stud	267	1975	Rex C. Ellsworth	402
1933	Harry Payne Whitney & Cornelius V. Whitney	282	1976	Rex C. Ellsworth	361
1934	Harry Payne Whitney & Cornelius V. Whitney	310	1977	Edward P. Taylor	409
			1978	Edward P. Taylor	442
1935	Arthur B. Hancock	292	1979	Edward P. Taylor	353
1936	Arthur B. Hancock	314	1980	Edward P. Taylor	305
1937	Arthur B. Hancock	279	1981	Edward P. Taylor	242
1938	Arthur B. Hancock	300	1982	Edward P. Taylor	233
1939	Willis Sharp Kilmer	269	1983	Edward P. Taylor	227
1940	Arthur B. Hancock	302	1984	Edward P. Taylor	261
1941	Willis Sharp Kilmer	256	1985	Edward P. Taylor	241
1942	Arthur B. Hancock	333	1986	N. B. Hunt (Bluegrass Farm)	281
1943	Arthur B. Hancock	346	1987	N. B. Hunt (Bluegrass Farm)	324
1944	Arthur B. Hancock	322	1988	John Franks	414
1945	Mereworth Farm	307	1989	John Franks	486
1946	Mereworth Farm	350	1990	John Franks	451
1947	Mereworth Farm	358	1991	John Franks	491
1948	Mereworth Farm	330	1992	John Franks	584
1949	Mereworth Farm	347	1993	John Franks	541
1950	Mereworth Farm	313	1994	John Franks	432
1951	Mereworth Farm	299	1995	John Franks	399
1952	Mereworth Farm	270	1996	John Franks	360
1953	Mereworth Farm	246	1997	Farnsworth Farms	360
1954	Calumet Farm	201	1998	Farnsworth Farms	369
1955	Henry H. Knight	223	1999	Harry T. Mangurian Jr.	457
1956	Henry H. Knight	293	2000	Harry T. Mangurian Jr.	455
1957	Henry H. Knight	284	2001	Farnsworth Farms	358
1958	Henry H. Knight	260	2002	Mockingbird Farm, Inc.	516
1959	King Ranch	227	2003	Farnsworth Farms	475
1960	Edward P. Taylor	267			

Breeders of Winners of $1 Million or More in America

Horse	Sex	Born	Sts	1st	2d	3d	Earnings
Abolengo							
Empress Club (ARG)..M		1988	26	16	2	1	1,155,235
Adena Springs							
Perfect Sting	M	1996	21	14	3	0	2,202,042
Macho Uno	H	1998	14	6	1	3	1,851,803
Red Bullet	H	1997	14	6	2	2	1,161,920
Agrovista Hermosa C.A.							
My Own Business (VEN).H		1997	50	37	5	1	1,016,908
Airlie Stud							
Sangue (IRE)	M	1978	30	13	6	3	1,272,086
White Muzzle (GB)	H	1990	17	6	3	2	1,060,443
Mohammed al Maktoum							
Singspiel (IRE)	H	1992	20	9	8	0	5,952,825
Sheikh Mohammed bin Rashid al Maktoum							
Street Cry (IRE)	H	1998	12	5	6	1	5,150,837
Swain (IRE)	H	1992	22	10	4	6	3,797,566
In the Wings (GB)	H	1986	11	7	1	0	1,562,335
Sheikh Mohammed Obaid Al Maktoum							
High-Rise (IRE)	H	1995	13	5	2	2	1,871,726
Alexander & Aykroyd & Groves							
Althea	M	1981	15	8	4	0	1,275,255
Herbert Allen & Ray Stark							
Subordination	H	1994	21	11	3	1	1,221,068
J. Allen							
Slew City Slew	H	1984	42	11	10	6	1,166,296
High Brite	H	1984	45	15	7	9	1,150,519
Allez France Stables							
Steinlen (GB)	H	1983	45	20	10	7	3,297,169
Arcangues	H	1988	19	6	2	2	1,981,423
Volga (IRE)	M	1998	19	7	5	2	1,141,759
E.C. Allred & Crystal Springs Farm & Robert Moore							
Deputy Commander.....H		1994	13	4	3	2	1,906,640
Simoes de Almeida Armenio							
Silic (FR)	H	1995	15	8	2	0	1,422,299
Happy Alter							
Pistols and Roses	H	1989	44	10	4	6	1,680,506
American Livestock Insurance Co & Foxfield							
Helmsman	H	1992	22	6	7	3	1,132,142
Amerigroup Leasing							
Dear Doctor (FR)	H	1987	32	8	7	4	1,742,671
Amherst Stable							
Volponi	H	1998	31	7	12	5	3,187,232
Angmering Park Stud							
Timboroa (GB)	H	1996	25	10	3	3	1,397,228
Anstu Stables Inc							
Balto Star	G	1998	33	11	6	2	1,952,946
Arthur I. Appleton							
Forbidden Apple	H	1995	31	8	6	9	1,680,640
Jolie's Halo	H	1987	20	8	0	2	1,218,120
M. Arbib							
Strategic Choice	H	1991	33	5	5	5	1,126,735
A. Arculli							
River Verdon (IRE)	G	1987	26	16	4	2	1,574,735
Mr & Mrs Roy L. Ash							
Fruits of Love	H	1995	23	5	3	5	1,089,543
Ashford Stud							
Mystic Lady	M	1998	27	10	8	2	1,170,390
Ashford Stud & Worswick							
Indian Skimmer	M	1984	16	10	1	3	1,469,299
R. & M. Aubert							
Volochine (IRE)	H	1991	45	8	12	9	1,205,580
Audley Farm Inc							
Mandy's Gold	M	1998	24	11	4	6	1,081,744
Peggy Augustus & Keswick Stables							
Simply Majestic	H	1984	44	18	4	7	1,667,713
Azienda Agricola Francesca							
Falbrav (IRE)	H	1998	26	13	5	5	5,825,517
John W. Backer							
Dispersal	H	1986	22	12	3	2	1,511,137
Sanford Bacon							
Say Florida Sandy	H	1994	98	33	17	12	2,085,408
Howard J. Baker							
Serena's Song	M	1992	38	18	11	3	3,283,388
Ballylinch Stud Ltd							
River Keen (IRE)	H	1992	42	11	5	5	1,642,385
Ballymacoll Stud Farm Ltd							
Pilsudski (IRE)	H	1992	22	10	6	2	4,080,297
Golan (IRE)	H	1998	11	4	2	1	1,623,376
Fastness (IRE)	H	1990	24	9	6	1	1,581,165
Islington (IRE)	F	1999	15	6	0	4	1,553,043
Mrs Thomas M. Bancroft							
Damascus	H	1964	32	21	7	3	1,176,781
Anna Marie Barnhart							
Skip Away	H	1993	38	18	10	6	9,616,360
Lucy G. Bassett							
Adoration	F	1999	15	5	2	1	1,443,856
Beall & French Jr							
Tejano	H	1985	21	5	6	3	1,428,177
Robert L. Beall							
Dave's Friend	H	1975	76	35	16	8	1,079,915
Jeanne F. Begg							
Victor Cooley	G	1993	39	13	12	3	1,320,475
Belair Stud							
Nashua	H	1952	30	22	4	1	1,288,565
Albert Bell & Joyce Bell							
Medaglia d'Oro	C	1999	15	7	6	0	4,254,720
Richard Bendit							
Ten Keys	H	1984	54	21	8	4	1,209,211
Biddestone Stud							
Mutamam (GB)	H	1995	21	11	2	1	1,388,410
Ela Athena (GB)	M	1996	17	3	7	2	1,125,252
Bieber-Jacobs Stable							
Allez France	M	1970	21	13	3	1	1,262,801
Blue Diamond Ranch							
Snow Chief	H	1983	24	13	3	5	3,383,210
Blue Seas Music Inc							
Soul of the Matter	H	1991	16	7	4	2	2,302,818
Afternoon Deelites	H	1992	12	7	3	0	1,061,193
Bluegrass Farm							
Dahar	H	1981	29	7	6	4	1,207,286
Rivlia	H	1982	41	9	2	8	1,005,041
Peter E. Blum							
Devil His Due	H	1989	41	11	12	3	3,920,405
Richard M. Bonze							
Fourstardave	G	1985	100	21	18	16	1,636,737
Fourstars Allstar	H	1988	59	14	14	9	1,596,760
Bonnie Heath Farm							
Honor Glide	H	1994	38	11	5	2	1,397,187

Horse	Sex	Born	Sts	1st	2d	3d	Earnings		Horse	Sex	Born	Sts	1st	2d	3d	Earnings
Clydene Boots									**John A. Chandler**							
Richter Scale	H	1994	25	12	2	0	1,139,958		Cetewayo	H	1994	36	11	5	4	1,170,258
C. Bowling & C. Thompson									**Cherokee Farms Inc**							
Western Pride	H	1998	29	10	4	1	1,288,569		Smok'n Frolic	F	1999	25	8	5	1	1,276,500
Peter M. Brant									**Cheveley Park Stud Ltd**							
Gulch	H	1984	32	13	8	4	3,095,521		Soviet Line (IRE)	G	1990	48	16	8	6	1,450,130
Thunder Gulch	H	1992	16	9	2	2	2,915,086		Megahertz (GB)	F	1999	22	8	3	5	1,159,094
Track Barron	H	1981	21	12	3	1	1,353,674		**K. Chong, G. Fong & W. Kwok**							
Peter M. Brant & Haras Santa Maria de Araras									Surfers Paradise (NZ)	G	1987	57	17	5	0	1,419,964
Wallenda	H	1990	33	7	5	5	1,205,929		**Christiana Stables**							
Brick Kiln Stud & Lariston Apartments Ltd									Go for Wand	M	1987	13	10	2	0	1,373,338
Labeeb (GB)	H	1992	20	8	3	4	1,464,950		**Cisley Stable & R.P. Levy**							
David Brillembourg									North Sider	M	1982	36	15	7	5	1,126,400
Windsharp	M	1991	29	11	7	3	1,293,075		**Citadel Stud**							
Bronson Stable									Tobougg (IRE)	H	1998	12	3	2	2	1,079,901
Megan's Interco	G	1989	36	16	11	0	1,062,465		**Hal C.B. Clagett**							
Brushwood Stable									Little Bold John	G	1982	105	38	16	14	1,956,406
High Yield	H	1997	14	4	4	3	1,170,196		**Claiborne Farm**							
Buckland Farm									Slew o' Gold	H	1980	21	12	5	1	3,533,534
Sir Beaufort	H	1987	34	10	10	4	1,149,130		Forty Niner	H	1985	19	11	5	0	2,726,000
Martha H. Buckner									Round Table	H	1954	66	43	8	5	1,749,869
Dixie Dot Com	H	1995	23	8	6	1	1,332,775		Swale	H	1981	14	9	2	2	1,583,660
Calbourne Farm									Royal Glint	H	1970	52	21	9	4	1,004,816
Brown Bess	M	1982	36	16	8	6	1,300,920		**Claiborne Farm & The Gamely Corp**							
Mr & Mrs C.D. Callaway III									Lure	H	1989	25	14	8	0	2,515,289
Farma Way	H	1987	23	8	5	1	2,897,175		**A.G. & R.N. Clay & Hermitage Inc**							
Calumet Farm									Gorgeous	M	1986	14	8	4	1	1,171,370
Strike the Gold	H	1988	31	6	8	5	3,457,026		**Albert G. Clay**							
Agnes World	H	1995	20	8	6	1	3,365,680		Albert the Great	H	1997	22	8	6	4	3,012,490
Criminal Type	H	1985	24	10	5	3	2,351,274		**Catesby W. Clay & Runnymede Farm Inc**							
Elmhurst	G	1990	51	8	11	6	1,100,567		Tejano Run	H	1992	21	8	4	6	1,166,842
Citation	H	1945	45	32	10	2	1,085,760		**J.E. Clay**							
Alex G. Campbell Jr									It's the One	H	1978	28	9	7	9	1,038,444
Mr Purple	H	1992	21	6	3	5	1,133,538		**Clear Creek & Highclere Inc**							
Gilbert G. Campbell									Silverbulletday	M	1996	23	15	3	1	3,093,207
Marlin	H	1993	26	9	3	5	2,448,880		**Violet Cleveland & Frank J. Zureick**							
Blazing Sword	G	1994	45	11	7	7	1,184,055		Urbane	M	1992	18	8	4	4	1,018,568
Carl & Olivia Cannata									**William L. Clifton Jr**							
Gourmet Girl	M	1995	33	9	7	10	1,255,373		Rhythm Band	G	1996	18	5	2	2	1,349,066
Cardiff Stud Farm									**Clovelly Farms**							
Letthebighossroll	G	1988	60	18	14	6	1,014,377		Pleasantly Perfect	H	1998	13	6	2	1	2,949,880
Carelaine Farm									Pay the Butler	H	1984	40	5	5	5	1,934,140
Annoconnor	M	1984	29	12	7	5	1,002,420		**James B. Cody**							
Carelaine Farm & Vintage Meadow Farm									Polar Expedition	G	1991	49	20	5	7	1,491,071
Golden Pheasant	H	1986	22	7	4	3	2,453,958		**E.M. Conjuango Jr**							
Carondelet Farm & Vinery									Manila	H	1983	18	12	5	0	2,692,799
Artax	H	1995	25	7	9	3	1,685,840		**J.D. Corcoran**							
Carpinelli & Henwood Brothers									Happyanunoit (NZ)	M	1995	21	9	6	2	1,582,118
Zoffany	H	1980	36	15	10	2	1,225,569		**S. Coughlan**							
James S. Carrion									High Chaparral (IRE)	C	1999	13	10	1	2	5,331,231
Meadow Star	M	1988	20	11	1	2	1,445,740		Ridgewood Pearl (GB)	M	1992	8	6	1	1	1,179,301
Cutlass Reality	H	1982	66	14	12	9	1,405,660		**Courtney & Congleton**							
Recoup the Cash	G	1990	74	23	6	3	1,098,920		Fit to Fight	H	1979	26	14	3	3	1,042,075
Norman E. Casse & Harry Katz									**Mr & Mrs Robert E. Courtney**							
Isitingood	H	1991	24	11	3	4	1,219,430		Dollar Bill	H	1998	22	4	5	5	1,225,546
Ben S. Castleman									**Marjorie Cowan & Irving Cowan**							
Seattle Slew	H	1974	17	14	2	0	1,208,726		Hollywood Wildcat	M	1990	21	12	3	3	1,432,160
Chadds Ford Stable									War Chant	H	1997	7	5	1	0	1,130,600
Keeper Hill	M	1995	21	4	7	5	1,661,281		**E.A. Cox Jr**							
									Ecton Park	H	1996	23	6	4	6	1,503,825

Horse	Sex	Born	Sts	1st	2d	3d	Earnings
Edward I. Cox Jr							
Marquetry	H	1987	36	10	9	4	2,857,886
Joe Crowley and Mr And Mrs A. P. O'Brien							
Rock of Gibraltar (IRE)	C	1999	13	10	2	0	1,888,048
Cuadra T Y T Inc							
Luthier Fever	H	1991	25	6	5	6	1,160,852
Constance DaParma & Flying M Acres							
Flying Pidgeon	H	1981	56	12	9	13	1,154,337
Bud Dardi							
Echo Eddie	G	1997	28	10	7	3	1,044,354
Darley Stud Management							
Annus Mirabilis (FR)	H	1992	30	9	7	6	1,541,938
Noverre	H	1998	21	5	7	4	1,429,344
State City	C	1999	15	6	0	3	1,374,707
Shantou	H	1993	14	6	2	4	1,132,399
D.B. Davidson							
Beau Genius	H	1985	42	19	7	4	1,055,600
W.R. Davis							
Gate Dancer	H	1981	28	7	8	7	2,501,705
Dayton Ltd							
All Along (FR)	M	1979	21	9	4	2	2,125,828
Paul de Moussac							
Subotica (FR)	H	1988	15	6	4	1	1,856,255
Apple Tree (FR)	H	1989	26	7	4	5	1,388,260
Austin Delaney							
Irish Linnet	M	1988	62	19	16	10	1,220,180
Delta Thoroughbreds Inc							
Cardmania	G	1986	76	16	12	20	1,503,780
Julian DeMarco & Mr & Mrs Scott E. Ricker							
North East Bound	G	1996	45	12	7	2	1,357,148
Derry Meeting Farm							
Yankee Affair	H	1982	55	22	14	8	2,282,156
Charles H. Deters							
Down the Aisle	H	1993	21	9	5	5	1,007,988
Dinwiddie Farm							
King Cugat	H	1997	16	7	7	1	1,293,782
Donald R. Dizney							
Wekiva Springs	H	1991	21	10	4	2	1,512,575
DMD Properties & Samara Fm							
Forever Silver	H	1985	47	8	9	9	1,001,974
Double D Farm Corp.							
Harlan's Holiday	C	1999	22	9	6	1	3,632,664
Double J Farm							
Star of Cozzene	H	1988	38	14	8	5	2,308,923
Catherine Dubois							
Starine (FR)	M	1997	33	10	12	1	1,674,491
Due Process Stable							
Open Mind	M	1986	19	12	2	2	1,844,372
Tavner Dunlap Jr							
Mi Selecto	H	1985	40	9	7	9	1,475,762
Mrs Richard C. duPont							
Kelso	G	1957	63	39	12	2	1,977,896
Shine Again	M	1997	34	14	10	7	1,271,840
Pamela duPont & S. Darmstadt							
Go for Gin	H	1991	19	5	7	2	1,380,866
Richard E. Dutrow							
Lite the Fuse	H	1991	21	9	4	6	1,036,882
Echo Valley Horse Farm Inc							
Winning Colors	M	1985	19	8	3	1	1,526,837
James Egan & David Hanley							
Golden Apples (IRE)	M	1998	16	6	6	2	1,672,583
Elcee-H Stable & Breeding Farm Inc							
Island Whirl	H	1978	34	11	6	6	1,144,010
J. Elkins & W.S. Farish & W.T. Webber Jr							
Secret Status	M	1997	19	8	3	4	1,053,705
James Elkins & William S. Farish							
Tomisue's Delight	M	1994	20	7	5	4	1,207,537
Elmendorf Farm							
Flying Continental	H	1986	51	12	15	10	1,815,938
Honor Medal	H	1981	87	19	13	19	1,347,073
Alphabatim	H	1981	22	7	3	5	1,313,175
Top Corsage	M	1983	53	15	7	9	1,110,028
Super Moment	H	1977	47	10	8	5	1,017,940
Antespend	M	1993	24	10	4	2	1,011,954
Mrs C.W. Engelhard							
Exceller	H	1973	33	15	5	6	1,674,587
Robert W. Entenmann							
Victory Speech	H	1993	27	9	2	5	1,289,020
Equigroup Thoroughbreds							
Corporate Report	H	1988	10	3	5	0	1,067,908
Edward P. Evans							
Gold Mover	M	1998	31	13	9	5	1,523,010
Raging Fever	M	1998	26	11	7	3	1,458,198
Summer Colony	M	1998	24	10	5	1	1,448,930
Robert S. Evans							
Sewickley	H	1985	32	11	9	4	1,017,517
Thomas M. Evans							
Pleasant Tap	H	1987	32	9	9	5	2,721,169
Pleasant Variety	H	1984	58	8	10	11	1,123,783
Colonial Waters	M	1985	32	6	12	3	1,112,847
Everest Stables Inc							
Island Fashion	F	2000	10	4	1	0	1,112,970
Famille Niarchos							
Six Perfections (FR)	F	2000	10	6	4	0	1,451,544
Fares Farm Inc							
Da Hoss	G	1992	20	12	5	2	1,931,558
Fares Stables Ltd							
Janet (GB)	M	1997	27	8	4	6	1,027,237
William S. Farish & William S. Kilroy							
Lemon Drop Kid	H	1996	24	10	3	3	3,245,370
A.P. Indy	H	1989	11	8	0	1	2,979,815
Bien Bien	H	1989	26	9	8	1	2,331,875
Summer Squall	H	1987	20	13	4	0	1,844,282
Stephen Got Even	H	1996	11	5	1	1	1,019,200
Farish William S & Parrish Hill Farm							
Charismatic	H	1996	17	5	2	4	2,038,064
William S. Farish Jr							
Burning Roma	H	1998	28	11	4	5	1,324,037
W.S. Farish & E.J. Hudson							
Bet Twice	H	1984	26	10	6	4	3,308,599
W.S. Farish & G.W. Humphrey Jr							
Sacahuista	M	1984	21	6	7	2	1,298,842
W.S. Farish & O.M. Phipps							
Storm Song	M	1994	12	4	1	2	1,020,050
W.S. Farish, James Elkins & W.T. Webber Jr.							
Mineshaft	C	1999	18	10	3	1	2,283,402
Farnsworth Farms							
Beautiful Pleasure	M	1995	25	10	5	2	2,734,078
Mecke	H	1992	40	12	7	9	2,470,550
Jewel Princess	M	1992	29	13	4	7	1,904,060
Frisk Me Now	H	1994	36	12	5	6	1,727,707

Horse	Sex	Born	Sts	1st	2d	3d	Earnings
Fawn Leap Farm Inc							
Editor's Note	H	1993	31	6	4	3	1,601,394
F. Feeney							
April Run (IRE)	M	1978	18	8	2	4	1,182,819
Finney & Taylor							
Peeping Tom	G	1997	41	12	7	7	1,251,016
C. Fipke							
Perfect Soul (IRE)	H	1998	15	6	3	1	1,136,215
Mr & Mrs Bertram R. Firestone							
Paradise Creek	H	1989	25	14	7	1	3,401,416
Theatrical (IRE)	H	1982	22	10	4	2	2,940,036
Chief Honcho	H	1987	34	10	6	3	1,265,719
Myrna Firestone & Mr & Mrs P. O'Dell							
The Very One	M	1975	71	22	12	9	1,104,623
Pamela H. Firman & G. Watts Humphrey							
Creme Fraiche	G	1982	64	17	12	13	4,024,727
Clear Mandate	M	1992	31	10	6	4	1,085,588
Mr & Mrs Weston L. Fitzpatrick							
Continental Red	G	1996	56	7	12	11	1,047,558
Flaxman Holdings Ltd							
Miesque	M	1984	16	12	3	1	2,070,163
Aldebaran	H	1998	25	8	12	3	1,739,186
Denon	H	1998	21	6	4	3	1,739,156
Spinning World	H	1993	14	8	3	1	1,734,477
Good Journey	H	1996	16	7	5	3	1,733,058
Floors Farming & Side Hill Stud							
Brave Act (GB)	H	1994	27	13	6	2	1,546,269
D.G. Foley							
Taylor's Special	H	1981	41	21	7	2	1,065,805
Forest Retreat Farms Inc & Miller							
Roo Art	H	1982	27	10	4	5	1,011,723
D.J. Foster							
Sunny's Halo	H	1980	20	9	3	2	1,247,791
Fountainebleau Farm Inc							
El Senor	H	1984	44	12	7	5	1,769,215
Ski Paradise	M	1990	20	6	8	1	1,470,588
Four Horsemen's Ranch Inc							
Val's Prince	G	1992	52	13	12	5	2,118,785
Fourth Estate Stables & Keswick Stable							
Sabin	H	1980	25	18	0	2	1,098,341
Ahmed M. Foustok							
In Excess (ire)	H	1987	25	11	2	3	1,736,733
Fox Ridge Farm Inc							
Riskaverse	F	1999	21	7	4	4	1,000,234
Francis A. Genter Stable							
Smile	H	1982	27	14	4	3	1,664,027
Tappiano	M	1984	34	17	2	4	1,305,522
Frankfurt Stables							
Temperate Sil	H	1984	19	6	2	1	1,113,775
John Franks							
Sharp Cat	M	1994	22	15	3	0	2,032,575
Royal Anthem	H	1995	12	6	3	1	1,876,876
Kissin Kris	H	1990	35	4	8	5	1,616,936
Halo America	G	1990	40	15	8	2	1,460,992
Littlebitlively	H	1994	33	10	9	5	1,303,343
Kiss a Native	G	1997	30	12	4	2	1,054,817
Silent Eskimo	M	1995	31	9	4	9	1,039,485
Daniel W. Frazier							
Anet	M	1994	19	8	5	0	1,189,873
Carl M. Freeman							
Miss Alleged	M	1987	15	5	4	3	1,757,342
Albert Fried Jr							
Affirmed Success	G	1994	42	17	10	6	2,285,315
Fulmer Farms							
Slew of Damascus	G	1988	48	16	9	8	1,420,350
Gainesway Thoroughbreds Ltd							
Orientate	H	1998	19	10	3	0	1,716,950
Gainsborough Farm Inc							
Fantastic Light	H	1996	25	12	5	3	8,486,957
Hatoof	M	1989	21	9	4	1	1,841,070
Irish Prize	G	1996	28	10	4	2	1,242,364
Gainsborough Stud Management Ltd							
Touch of the Blues (FR)	H	1997	35	8	6	5	1,655,358
Storming Home (GB)	H	1998	24	8	4	3	1,536,704
Sayyedati (GB)	M	1990	22	6	5	3	1,408,616
Galbreath & Phillips Racing Partnership							
Memories of Silver	H	1993	19	9	3	5	1,448,715
Soaring Softly	M	1995	16	9	1	3	1,270,433
John W. Galbreath							
Sunshine Forever	H	1985	23	8	6	3	2,084,800
Mrs John W. Galbreath							
Proud Truth	H	1982	21	10	4	0	2,198,895
Garrison & Hundley							
Fly So Free	H	1988	33	12	5	3	2,330,954
Tom Gentry							
Judge Angelucci	H	1983	22	10	4	2	1,582,535
George G Farm Inc							
Cryptoclearance	H	1984	44	12	10	7	3,376,327
George Waggoner Stables Inc							
Yes It's True	H	1996	22	11	2	3	1,080,700
Gestut Ammerland							
Borgia (GER)	M	1994	22	6	7	2	1,697,771
Gestut Hof Ittlingen							
Lando (GER)	H	1990	24	10	3	1	3,438,727
Mrs W. Gilmour & Mrs W.M. Jason							
Spectacular Bid	H	1976	30	26	2	1	2,781,608
Josephine T. Gleis							
Fly Till Dawn	H	1986	27	10	5	4	1,556,525
Glen Hill Farm							
One Dreamer	M	1988	25	12	6	2	1,266,067
Glen Oak Farm							
Dancing Brave	H	1983	10	8	1	0	1,435,434
Randle L. Glosson							
Vivace	M	1993	40	20	4	6	1,037,671
Golden Chance Farm Inc							
John Henry	G	1975	83	39	15	9	6,591,860
Golden Orb Farm & K. David Schwartz							
Unbridled Elaine	M	1998	11	6	2	1	1,770,740
Glitter Woman	M	1994	23	10	9	3	1,256,805
Sir J. Goldsmith							
Montjeu (IRE)	H	1996	16	11	2	0	3,178,177
Janet Gomez							
Bet On Sunshine	G	1992	47	22	7	10	1,449,882
Frau R. Grunewald							
Kazzia (GER)	F	1999	7	5	0	0	1,094,206
H & Y Bloodstock							
Taiki Blizzard	H	1991	23	6	8	2	5,523,549
Kurofune Mystery	M	1990	21	6	5	4	1,009,342
Cleo & Vivian Hall							
Judy's Red Shoes	M	1983	83	25	13	12	1,085,668

Horse	Sex	Born	Sts	1st	2d	3d	Earnings
Halo Farms							
King Glorious	H	1986	9	8	1	0	1,175,650
Arthur B. Hancock III							
Menifee	H	1996	11	5	4	1	1,732,000
Arthur B. Hancock III & Stonerside Ltd							
Fusaichi Pegasus	H	1997	9	6	2	0	1,994,400
Hancock III & Peters							
Risen Star	H	1985	11	8	2	1	2,029,845
Gato Del Sol	H	1979	39	7	9	7	1,340,107
Haras Abolengo							
Different (ARG)	M	1992	19	9	3	5	1,349,802
Haras Comalal							
Algenib (ARG)	H	1987	21	7	5	2	1,042,299
Haras D'Ecouves							
Jim and Tonic (FR)	G	1994	39	13	13	4	4,975,807
Haras de la Pomme							
Gentlemen (ARG)	H	1992	24	13	4	2	3,608,558
Haras de St. George Ltd							
Al Mamoon	H	1981	32	11	7	3	1,249,906
Haras Don Yayo							
Festin (ARG)	H	1986	24	9	4	4	2,256,295
Haras El Tio							
Carnegie (IRE)	H	1991	13	7	1	1	1,458,787
Haras Figuron							
Lido Palace (CHI)	H	1997	23	11	7	2	2,705,865
Haras General Cruz							
Cougar II	H	1966	50	20	7	17	1,172,625
Haras Karen Sissy							
Trinycarol (VEN)	M	1979	29	18	3	1	2,644,392
Haras Mocito Guapo							
Malek (CHI)	H	1993	23	10	7	2	2,382,623
Haras Principal							
Bayakoa (ARG)	M	1984	39	21	9	0	2,861,701
Haras Rosa del Sur							
Leger Cat (ARG)	H	1986	53	16	5	7	1,211,402
Haras San Ignacio de Loyola							
Ibero (ARG)	H	1987	34	10	7	4	1,345,199
Lazy Lode (ARG)	H	1994	29	8	4	6	1,296,740
Haras Santa Ana do Rio Grande							
Redattore (BRZ)	H	1995	32	15	2	6	1,799,883
Riboletta (BRZ)	M	1995	28	13	3	3	1,555,103
Haras Santa Maria de Araras							
Troyanos (BRZ)	H	1985	13	10	1	1	1,038,083
Haras Santa Olga							
Puerto Madero (CHI)	H	1994	24	11	3	2	1,361,626
Haras Sao Jose da Serra							
Sandpit (BRZ)	H	1989	40	14	11	6	3,812,597
Haras Sao Jose E Expedictus							
Siphon (BRZ)	H	1991	25	12	6	2	3,136,428
Haras Vacacion							
Paseana (ARG)	M	1987	36	19	10	2	3,317,427
Odalea (ARG)	M	1986	21	8	7	2	1,674,812
Harbor View Farm							
Flawlessly	M	1988	28	16	4	3	2,572,536
Affirmed	H	1975	29	22	5	1	2,393,818
Outstandingly	M	1982	28	10	4	3	1,412,206
Zoman	H	1987	24	7	5	3	1,040,372
Mort Hardy							
Mysterious Affair	M	1997	37	12	9	6	1,059,971
Harper & Irish Hill Farm							
Spend a Buck	H	1982	15	10	3	2	4,220,689
W.R. Hawn							
Real Connection	M	1991	72	7	14	7	1,225,018
Mr & Mrs D. Hayden							
Safely Kept	M	1986	31	24	2	3	2,194,206
Highclere Inc & Louie Roussel III							
Star Standard	H	1992	25	7	4	3	1,121,512
Highclere Stud Ltd							
Sheikh Albadou (GB)	H	1988	15	6	4	1	1,229,702
Highview Stud Bloodstock Partnership No 3							
Let's Elope (NZ)	M	1987	26	11	0	5	2,528,902
Hill 'n Dale Farm & Holtsinger Inc & Star Stable							
Touch Gold	H	1994	15	6	3	1	1,679,907
Hill 'N' Dale Farm							
Hawk Wing	C	1999	12	5	5	0	1,610,604
His Highness The Aga Khan's Studs S.C.							
Daylami (IRE)	H	1994	21	11	3	4	4,614,762
Kalanisi (IRE)	H	1996	11	6	4	1	2,148,836
Daliapour (IRE)	H	1996	26	7	3	3	2,123,763
Manndar (IRE)	H	1996	20	4	6	3	1,128,835
Lashkari (GB)	H	1981	13	5	2	2	1,127,658
Timarida (IRE)	M	1992	16	10	2	2	1,116,186
Hobeau Farm Ltd							
Kelly Kip	H	1994	31	15	3	4	1,157,142
Georgia E. Hofmann							
Heritage of Gold	M	1995	28	16	2	4	2,381,762
Louis Quatorze	H	1993	18	7	5	1	2,054,434
Holly Ridge Farms Inc							
Exbourne	H	1986	14	8	5	1	1,000,198
Fred W. Hooper							
Precisionist	H	1981	46	20	10	4	3,485,398
Diplomatic Jet	H	1992	51	9	5	9	1,267,202
Fred W. Hooper Jr							
Susan's Girl	M	1969	63	29	14	11	1,251,668
Al J. Horton							
Silver Goblin	G	1991	26	16	4	3	1,083,895
G. Watts Humphrey Jr & Joe Pierce Jr							
Morluc	H	1996	40	11	9	7	1,045,758
G. Watts Humphrey Jr. & W. S. Farish							
Misil	H	1988	36	14	8	3	1,296,417
G. Humphrey Jr., J. Pierce Jr., A. Gilman & K. Koontz							
Gaily Magnum	G	1993	24	8	2	2	1,218,578
Cyril Humphris							
Halling	H	1991	18	12	1	0	1,332,651
N.B. Hunt & E. Stephenson							
Triptych	M	1982	41	14	5	11	2,318,946
Nelson B. Hunt							
Estrapade	M	1980	30	12	5	5	1,937,142
Lively One	H	1985	36	9	7	5	1,544,100
Dahlia	M	1970	48	15	3	7	1,489,105
Valerie Hunter							
Defensive Play	H	1987	26	6	4	5	1,688,631
International Thoroughbred Breeders Inc							
On the Line	H	1984	37	14	7	2	1,125,810
Irish Acres Farm							
Buck's Boy	G	1993	30	16	5	2	2,750,148
Iron County Farms Inc							
Nuclear Debate	G	1995	52	11	8	10	1,234,054
Jack Syndicate							
Spook Express (SAF)	M	1994	22	11	2	3	1,016,744

Horse	Sex	Born	Sts	1st	2d	3d	Earnings
Jamm Ltd							
Strut the Stage	H	1998	19	9	2	2	1,265,923
Mr & Mrs S.S. Janney Jr							
Private Terms	H	1985	17	12	0	0	1,243,947
Stuart S. Janney III							
Coronado's Quest	H	1995	17	10	2	0	2,046,190
Janus Bloodstock Inc							
Riviera (FR)	H	1994	21	10	4	3	1,018,535
Walter M. Jeffords Jr							
Lonesome Glory	G	1988	44	24	5	6	1,325,868
John R. Gaines Thoroughbreds LLC & De De McGehee							
Imperial Gesture	F	1999	11	6	2	1	1,419,140
Jonabell Farm Inc et al							
Essence of Dubai	C	1999	13	5	1	2	2,001,058
Aaron U. Jones							
Lemhi Gold	H	1978	22	8	3	1	1,131,355
Brereton C. Jones & Warnerton Farm							
Desert Wine	H	1980	25	8	8	3	1,618,043
Brereton C. Jones							
Southjet	H	1983	30	5	7	2	1,040,483
Juddmonte Farms Inc							
Skimming	H	1996	20	8	5	1	2,286,601
Empire Maker	C	2000	8	4	3	1	1,985,800
Aptitude	H	1997	15	5	4	2	1,965,410
Chester House	H	1995	21	6	4	4	1,944,545
Tinners Way	H	1990	27	7	6	4	1,846,546
Banks Hill (GB)	M	1998	15	5	5	3	1,824,008
Beat Hollow (GB)	H	1997	12	7	2	2	1,814,481
Quest for Fame (GB)	H	1987	19	5	4	4	1,790,417
Running Stag	H	1994	40	7	11	2	1,663,227
Tates Creek	M	1998	17	11	3	0	1,471,674
Sightseek	F	1999	13	8	4	0	1,433,866
Ryafan	M	1994	10	7	1	0	1,342,142
Savinio	G	1990	48	11	11	8	1,321,860
Raintrap (GB)	H	1990	28	9	4	2	1,283,707
Wandesta (GB)	M	1991	21	7	3	5	1,255,145
Dushyantor	H	1993	20	5	5	2	1,197,570
Heat Haze (GB)	F	1999	14	7	2	2	1,183,696
Public Purse	H	1994	14	7	1	4	1,103,324
Flute	M	1998	8	4	3	0	1,101,504
Urgent Request (IRE)	H	1990	25	7	4	1	1,035,339
Richard S. Kaster							
Countess Diana	M	1995	14	7	2	0	1,117,185
KCV Stable							
Lottsa Talc	M	1990	65	21	10	12	1,206,248
Mrs Joan Keaney							
Yavana's Pace (IRE)	G	1992	74	16	14	11	1,199,409
H.B. Keck							
Ferdinand	H	1983	29	8	9	6	3,777,978
Mr & Mrs Rodes Kelly							
Formal Gold	H	1993	16	8	4	1	1,533,600
Thomas J. Kelly & Joseph M. Grant							
Evening Attire	G	1998	28	10	6	3	1,952,970
Ken-Mort Stables							
Maxzene	M	1993	23	11	5	0	1,175,259
Kennelot Stables Ltd							
Stephan's Odyssey	H	1982	16	6	4	1	1,255,328
Danzig Connection	H	1983	17	6	5	4	1,002,620
Mrs D.K. Kerr							
King's Swan	H	1980	107	31	19	18	1,924,845
Keswick Stables							
Alwuhush	H	1985	22	5	4	7	1,012,423
Miss Christine Kiernan							
Phoenix Reach (IRE)	C	2000	5	3	1	1	1,037,276
Kilcarn Stud							
Snurge (IRE)	H	1987	30	7	10	5	1,674,441
J. Howard King							
Very Subtle	M	1984	29	12	6	4	1,608,360
Kinghaven Farms Ltd							
With Approval	H	1986	23	13	5	1	2,863,540
Izvestia	H	1987	21	11	2	2	2,702,527
Exchange	M	1988	30	15	7	4	1,287,795
Carotene	M	1983	41	12	8	5	1,287,232
Present Value	H	1984	42	15	5	3	1,153,853
Steady Power	G	1984	70	13	19	9	1,132,197
Kinghaven Farms Ltd & D. Granite							
Cozzene's Prince	G	1987	68	16	10	10	1,270,057
Kinsman Farm							
Dream Supreme	M	1997	16	9	2	2	1,007,680
Kinsman Stud Farm							
Concerto	H	1994	21	10	4	2	1,308,118
Mr & Mrs William Kirkland							
Ancient Title	H	1970	57	24	11	9	1,252,791
Edgar Kitchen							
Track Robbery	M	1976	59	22	12	7	1,098,537
Knob Hill Stables							
Thornfield	G	1994	19	6	1	3	1,206,074
Benburb	G	1989	22	7	2	4	1,159,949
Mr & Mrs R. Koerber							
Sunny Sunrise	G	1987	63	18	12	9	1,367,268
Jean-Luc Lagardere							
Val Royal (FR)	H	1996	12	7	2	0	1,186,687
Rene & Margie Lambert							
Sky Jack	G	1996	18	10	2	2	1,115,127
Landon & Mary A. Sullivan							
Kiri's Clown	G	1989	62	16	6	8	1,005,469
Roger Laubach							
Captain Steve	H	1997	25	9	3	7	6,828,356
Lazy E. Ranch Inc							
Voodoo Dancer	M	1998	21	11	4	2	1,427,952
Lazy F Ranch							
Forego	G	1970	57	34	9	7	1,938,957
Lazy Lane Stables Inc							
Seeking the Pearl	M	1994	21	8	2	3	4,021,716
Gerald W. Leigh							
Barathea (IRE)	H	1990	16	5	4	0	1,189,181
Blanche P. Levy & Murphy Stable							
Housebuster	H	1987	22	15	3	1	1,229,696
Lin-Drake Farm							
Grand Canyon	H	1987	8	4	3	0	1,019,540
Lin-Drake Farm & Pierce & Pierce Inc							
Friendly Lover	H	1988	66	22	13	12	1,247,670
Henry C.B. Lindh							
Grecian Flight	M	1984	40	21	6	3	1,320,215
Little Hill Farm							
Real Quiet	H	1995	20	6	5	6	3,271,802
Marvin Little Jr							
Hansel	H	1988	14	7	2	3	2,936,586
W.P. Little							
Wild Again	H	1980	28	8	7	4	2,204,829

Horse	Sex	Born	Sts	1st	2d	3d	Earnings
Lawrence I Littmann							
Lil E. Tee	H	1989	13	7	4	1	1,437,506
Live Oak Stud							
Sultry Song	H	1988	23	9	3	5	1,616,276
Solar Splendor	G	1987	42	11	3	6	1,386,468
Loblolly Stable							
Pine Bluff	H	1989	13	6	1	3	2,255,884
Prairie Bayou	G	1990	12	7	3	0	1,450,621
Vanlandingham	H	1981	19	10	3	3	1,409,476
De Roche	G	1986	28	5	8	7	1,078,200
Loblolly Stable & A. Hochner Jr							
Lost Mountain	H	1988	36	5	6	8	1,004,939
Mrs E. Longton							
Saumarez (GB)	H	1987	9	5	1	0	1,275,719
Lord Porchester							
Ibn Bey (GB)	H	1984	28	10	3	4	1,626,059
Lowquest Ltd							
Timber Country	H	1992	12	5	1	4	1,560,400
Bruce W. Lunsford							
Golden Missile	H	1995	25	7	7	4	2,194,510
Vision and Verse	H	1996	21	4	3	5	1,030,330
Lyonstown Stud							
Dr Devious (IRE)	H	1989	15	6	4	0	1,484,230
W.G. Lyster III							
Lu Ravi	M	1995	26	11	8	3	1,819,781
W.G. Lyster III & Jayeff 'B' Stables							
Johannesburg	C	1999	10	7	1	0	1,014,585
Mr & Mrs John C. Mabee							
Best Pal	G	1988	47	18	11	4	5,668,245
General Challenge	G	1996	21	9	3	1	2,877,178
Dramatic Gold	G	1991	39	9	13	6	2,567,630
Nostalgia's Star	H	1982	59	9	17	13	2,154,827
Excellent Meeting	M	1996	20	8	5	3	1,402,396
Early Pioneer	G	1995	33	9	9	5	1,156,815
Event of the Year	H	1995	9	5	2	1	1,095,200
Full Moon Madness	G	1995	39	15	6	10	1,015,885
Captain J. Macdonald-Buchanan							
In the Groove (GB)	M	1987	21	7	4	4	1,336,783
Frank E. Mackle Jr							
Waquoit	H	1983	30	19	4	3	2,225,360
Angus M. MacLean							
Twice the Vice	M	1991	23	12	6	1	1,447,064
Preston Madden							
Alysheba	H	1984	26	11	8	2	6,679,242
Mamakos & Stubbin							
Fali Time	H	1981	15	5	4	2	1,033,179
Mandysland Farm							
Unbridled's Song	H	1993	12	5	4	0	1,311,800
Harry T. Mangurian Jr							
Swept Overboard	H	1997	20	8	5	3	1,137,767
Mareinvest-83 Ltd							
Lost Code	H	1984	27	15	5	2	2,085,396
J.D. Marsh							
Majesty's Prince	H	1979	43	12	10	10	2,077,796
Marystead Farm							
Urban Sea	M	1989	23	8	4	3	1,704,553
Talloires	H	1990	28	5	8	3	1,423,949
Robert E. Masterson							
Pleasant Breeze	G	1995	36	10	8	6	1,271,680
Mayland's Stud Co Ltd							
Dernier Empereur	H	1990	30	8	5	4	1,152,425

Horse	Sex	Born	Sts	1st	2d	3d	Earnings
Maylands Stud Farm							
Trempolino	H	1984	11	4	3	3	1,369,233
Richard D. Maynard							
Chief Bearhart	H	1993	26	12	5	3	3,381,557
P. McLean Sr, P. McLean Jr., M. McLean & P. Feringa Jr							
Xtra Heat	M	1998	35	26	5	2	2,389,635
Don McNeill							
Clever Trevor	G	1986	30	15	5	2	1,388,841
Mr Ross	G	1995	44	18	6	10	1,091,046
Meadow Stud Inc							
Secretariat	H	1970	21	16	3	1	1,316,808
Riva Ridge	H	1969	30	17	3	1	1,111,497
Meadowbrook Farm Inc							
Prized	H	1986	17	9	2	3	2,262,555
Ladies Din	G	1995	37	12	6	6	1,966,754
Brocco	H	1991	8	4	2	0	1,003,550
Mellon Paul							
Sea Hero	H	1990	24	6	3	4	2,929,869
Java Gold	H	1984	15	9	3	1	1,908,832
Fort Marcy	G	1964	75	21	18	14	1,109,791
Meon Valley Stud							
Opera House (GB)	H	1988	18	8	4	3	1,397,456
Robert E. Meyerhoff							
Concern	H	1991	30	7	7	11	3,079,350
Broad Brush	H	1983	27	14	5	5	2,656,793
Include	H	1997	20	10	1	4	1,659,560
Valley Crossing	H	1988	48	8	13	8	1,616,490
Lee Miller							
Heatherten	M	1979	53	21	7	4	1,022,699
Mr & Mrs M. Miller & Mr & Mrs R.S. West							
Lite Light	M	1988	26	8	4	4	1,231,596
Mimika Financicia & Warren Hill Stud							
Pebbles (GB)	M	1981	15	8	4	0	1,419,632
Aubrey W. Minshall							
Mt. Sassafras	G	1992	47	8	7	14	1,382,985
Kiridashi	H	1992	44	14	9	8	1,201,981
Bold Ruritana	M	1990	44	14	10	6	1,140,163
Moira & W.S. Tanaka							
Silveyville	H	1978	56	19	11	8	1,282,880
T. J. Monaghan							
Ezzoud (IRE)	H	1989	22	6	5	2	1,171,885
Moor M.P.J.							
Ipi Tombe (ZIM)	M	1998	14	12	2	0	1,529,799
Nancy Penn Morgan							
Skip Trial	H	1982	38	16	7	2	1,837,451
Dolphus C. Morrison							
You	F	1999	23	9	8	2	2,101,353
Mr & Mrs J.S. Moss							
Kudos	G	1997	24	7	5	4	1,238,935
Moyglare Stud Farm Ltd							
Twilight Agenda	H	1986	32	13	5	4	2,174,529
Thomas C. Mueller							
Chorwon	G	1993	44	13	7	8	1,161,795
Muirfield Ventures							
Dimitrova	F	2000	9	4	2	1	1,047,292
Muirfield Ventures & Jayeff B Stables							
Mutafaweq	H	1996	19	7	1	3	1,800,800

Horse	Sex	Born	Sts	1st	2d	3d	Earnings
William F. Murphy							
Silver Ending	H	1987	37	8	1	9	1,073,420
David Nagle							
Petite Ile (IRE)	M	1986	14	6	3	4	1,281,665
Ed Nahem							
Bertrando	H	1989	24	9	6	2	3,185,610
Marshall Naify							
Manistique	M	1995	15	11	1	1	1,311,800
Audrey Narducci							
Squirtle Squirt	H	1998	16	8	4	0	1,112,220
J.A. Nerud							
Clabber Girl	M	1983	39	8	12	6	1,006,261
Newchance Farm							
Peace Rules	C	2000	13	6	2	2	2,059,990
Newgate Stud Co							
Moon Ballad (IRE)	C	1999	14	5	3	1	4,364,791
Newhaven Park Stud Ltd							
Prowl (AUS)	G	1995	22	5	2	2	1,082,344
Newstead Farm							
Miss Oceana	M	1981	19	11	6	1	1,010,385
Niarchos Family The							
Sulamani (IRE)	C	1999	12	7	2	0	3,640,845
S. Niarchos							
Hernando (FR)	H	1990	20	7	4	1	2,081,978
Greinton (GB)	H	1981	22	10	8	0	1,943,605
Dream Well (FR)	H	1995	14	4	4	4	1,439,441
Gerard A. Nielsen							
Capades	M	1986	27	11	9	2	1,051,006
Joanne H. Nor							
Behrens	H	1994	27	9	8	3	4,563,500
North Central Bloodstock							
Tranquility Lake	M	1995	27	11	7	3	1,662,390
North Ridge Farm							
Ruhlmann	H	1985	27	10	3	4	1,824,154
Blushing John	H	1985	19	9	1	2	1,548,081
North Wales LLC							
Elloluv	F	2000	11	4	3	1	1,221,475
Charles Nuckols Jr & Sons							
War Emblem	C	1999	13	7	0	0	3,491,000
Nuckols Brothers							
Fighting Fit	H	1979	49	14	7	8	1,004,174
Gay O'Callaghan							
Earl of Barking (IRE)	H	1990	37	9	3	10	1,230,519
Oak Cliff Thoroughbreds Ltd							
Sunday Silence	H	1986	14	9	5	0	4,968,554
Skywalker	H	1982	20	8	3	3	2,226,750
Ocala Stud Farms Inc							
Bolshoi Boy	G	1983	58	16	7	8	1,039,702
Queen Alexandra	M	1982	46	19	8	5	1,034,144
George L. Onett							
Cherokee Run	H	1990	28	13	5	5	1,531,818
Orpendale							
Ballingarry (IRE)	C	1999	16	5	1	4	1,543,975
Orpendale & John R. Gaines Thoroughbreds							
Caller One	G	1997	20	10	3	2	3,184,500
Orpendale & Michael Tabor							
Giant's Causeway	H	1997	13	9	4	0	3,078,989
C. Ostermann-Richter							
Paolini (GER)	H	1997	23	4	6	4	2,453,469
Overbrook Farm							
Cat Thief	H	1996	30	4	9	8	3,951,012
Boston Harbor	H	1994	8	6	1	0	1,934,605
Surfside	M	1997	15	8	3	2	1,852,987
Mountain Cat	H	1990	11	6	2	0	1,478,901
Grindstone	H	1993	6	3	2	0	1,224,510
Honour and Glory	H	1993	17	6	5	2	1,202,942
Overbrook Farm & David Reynolds							
Tabasco Cat	H	1991	18	8	3	2	2,347,671
The Overbury Stud							
Caitano (GB)	H	1994	44	9	6	7	2,137,459
Ovidstown Bloodstock Ltd							
Kooyonga (IRE)	M	1988	18	9	4	1	1,476,193
OWD Inc.							
A Fleets Dancer	H	1995	45	12	6	8	1,036,649
Bea Oxenberg							
Best of the Rest	H	1995	32	16	8	2	1,407,796
J. Pantos							
Strawberry Road (AUS)	H	1979	50	21	7	9	1,655,678
Mr & Mrs Parrish & D.C. Parrish III							
Life's Magic	M	1981	32	8	11	6	2,255,218
Allen E. Paulson							
Cigar	H	1990	33	19	4	5	9,999,815
Azeri	M	1998	16	14	2	0	3,044,820
Escena	M	1993	29	11	9	3	2,962,639
Fraise	H	1988	34	10	5	6	2,613,105
Geri	H	1992	19	9	4	3	1,707,980
Yagli	H	1993	27	10	6	3	1,702,121
Astra	M	1996	16	11	1	2	1,378,424
Hap	M	1996	20	10	2	2	1,329,210
Ajina	M	1994	17	7	3	2	1,327,915
Eliza	M	1990	12	5	2	2	1,095,316
Payson Stud Inc							
Farda Amiga	F	1999	8	4	1	0	1,282,302
Virginia Kraft Payson							
L'Carriere	G	1991	23	8	4	3	1,726,175
Salem Drive	H	1982	46	13	7	10	1,046,065
John H. Peace							
West by West	H	1989	30	10	3	7	1,038,123
Pedigree Farms Inc							
License Fee	M	1995	43	16	7	6	1,200,416
Pelican Stable							
Holy Bull	H	1991	16	13	0	0	2,481,760
Oscar T. Penn Jr							
Mercedes Won	H	1986	52	12	7	12	1,087,435
Carlos Perez							
Kona Gold	G	1994	30	14	7	2	2,293,384
Stephen D. Peskoff							
Black Tie Affair (IRE)	H	1986	45	18	9	6	3,370,694
Petra Bloodstock Agency Ltd							
Falcon Flight (FR)	H	1996	20	5	2	3	1,428,849
Mr & Mrs J.W. Phillips							
Brian's Time	H	1985	21	5	2	6	1,001,269
Cynthia Phipps							
Versailles Treaty	M	1988	20	9	9	2	1,271,154
Mrs O. Phipps							
My Big Boy	G	1983	50	10	12	10	1,196,102
Ogden Phipps							
Easy Goer	H	1986	20	14	5	1	4,873,770
Seeking the Gold	H	1985	15	8	6	0	2,307,000
Heavenly Prize	M	1991	18	9	6	3	1,825,940
Personal Ensign	M	1984	13	13	0	0	1,679,880
Dancing Spree	H	1985	35	10	6	9	1,470,484
Buckpasser	H	1963	31	25	4	1	1,462,014

Horse	Sex	Born	Sts	1st	2d	3d	Earnings
Personal Flag	H	1983	24	8	4	4	1,258,924
Polish Navy	H	1984	12	7	1	3	1,118,076
Ogden Mills Phipps							
Inside Information	M	1991	17	14	1	2	1,641,806
Rhythm	H	1987	20	6	3	4	1,592,532
My Flag	M	1993	20	6	3	4	1,557,057
Educated Risk	M	1990	23	11	6	4	1,163,717
Dispute	M	1990	19	9	4	4	1,106,907
Pin Oak Stud Inc							
Peaks and Valleys	H	1992	16	9	3	2	1,589,270
Ward C. Pitfield							
Wild Rush	H	1994	16	8	0	3	1,386,302
Jim H. Plemmons							
Precocity	H	1994	33	9	7	5	1,835,798
Ten Most Wanted	C	2000	11	4	3	1	1,553,460
Michael Poland							
King's Theatre (IRE)	H	1991	19	5	3	4	1,154,329
A.F. Polk Jr							
Temperence Hill	H	1977	31	11	4	2	1,567,650
Ronald Popely							
Hever Golf Rose (GB)	M	1991	66	17	11	10	1,020,328
William Powell & Bates Newton							
Drum Taps	H	1986	31	15	5	2	1,140,788
Prestonwood Farm Inc							
Jostle	M	1997	20	8	5	2	1,389,932
J.A. Price							
Carry Back	H	1958	62	21	11	11	1,241,165
W. Kenan Rand Jr							
Candid Glen	G	1997	38	10	9	6	1,210,130
Rathbarry Stud							
Alpride (IRE)	M	1991	26	11	4	4	1,048,270
Raven Brook Farm Inc							
Not Surprising	G	1990	61	23	4	5	1,112,301
H.E. Reed							
Men's Exclusive	G	1993	47	11	16	4	1,447,928
Dr. William A. Reed & Stonecrest Farm							
Perfect Drift	G	1999	18	9	3	1	2,221,368
William O. Reed							
Bonapaw	G	1996	46	18	7	4	1,158,752
Goodbye Halo	M	1985	24	11	5	4	1,706,702
P. Ribes							
Fieldy (IRE)	M	1983	54	19	9	8	1,212,168
The Richter Family Trust							
Bien Nicole	M	1998	26	12	8	2	1,074,620
B.J. Ridder							
Flying Paster	H	1976	27	13	7	2	1,127,460
Ridgeley Farm							
Grey Memo	H	1997	50	8	4	10	1,733,059
B. & T. Roach							
Princess Rooney	M	1980	21	17	2	1	1,343,339
Corbin J. Robertson							
Turkoman	H	1982	22	8	8	3	2,146,924
G. Robins & T.H. Sams							
Tasso	H	1983	23	9	4	4	1,207,884
M.T. Robinson							
Groovy	H	1983	26	12	4	1	1,346,956
Mrs I.M. Roddick							
Rough Habit (NZ)	G	1986	66	28	16	7	2,861,579
Harold Rose							
Hal's Hope	H	1997	33	9	5	3	1,098,422
Rosemont Farm Inc							
River Bay	H	1993	20	8	3	3	1,167,970

Horse	Sex	Born	Sts	1st	2d	3d	Earnings
C. Rosen							
Chief's Crown	H	1982	21	12	3	3	2,191,168
Morton Rosenthal							
Fit for a Queen	M	1986	51	13	14	9	1,226,429
Cecilia Straub Rubens							
Tiznow	H	1997	15	8	4	2	6,427,830
Budroyale	G	1993	52	17	12	2	2,840,810
Angela Rugnetta							
Gander	G	1996	55	14	10	9	1,761,183
Rutledge Farm							
Colonial Affair	H	1990	20	7	4	3	1,635,228
B.L. Ryan							
Royal Heroine (IRE)	M	1980	21	10	4	2	1,229,449
Ryehill Farm							
Awad	H	1990	70	14	10	11	3,270,131
Homebuilder	H	1984	60	11	11	17	1,172,153
Sabine Stables							
Graeme Hall	H	1997	22	7	7	1	1,147,441
R. Sahm							
Super Diamond	H	1980	37	16	5	5	1,469,233
Peter W. Salmen III							
Bourbon Belle	M	1995	40	16	11	5	1,152,223
Sam-Son Farms							
Sky Classic	H	1987	29	15	6	1	3,320,398
Dance Smartly	M	1988	17	12	2	3	3,263,835
Quiet Resolve	G	1995	31	10	6	4	2,346,768
Dancethruthedawn	M	1998	16	7	2	3	1,609,643
Wilderness Song	M	1988	37	15	12	2	1,482,033
Regal Classic	H	1985	27	8	8	3	1,456,584
Desert Waves	G	1990	63	15	9	6	1,241,295
Rainbows for Life	H	1988	36	15	5	3	1,105,926
Regal Intention	H	1985	41	14	7	10	1,083,103
Herman Sarkowsky							
Dixie Union	H	1997	12	7	3	0	1,233,190
Sasse & Sheed							
Perrault (GB)	H	1977	25	9	5	5	1,536,103
Scott C. Savin							
Richman	H	1988	33	14	5	5	1,314,360
SCEA de Maulepaire							
Tuzla (FR)	M	1994	26	12	6	1	1,332,587
SCEA Haras du Mezeray							
Lassigny	H	1991	28	8	2	5	1,318,371
E.A. Scheib							
Fran's Valentine	M	1982	34	13	4	5	1,375,465
William Schettine							
Take Charge Lady	F	1999	22	11	7	0	2,480,377
Bruno Schickedanz							
Wake At Noon	H	1997	46	19	6	5	1,564,492
Gustav Schickedanz							
Wando	C	2000	13	8	2	1	2,379,700
Mobil	C	2000	15	8	3	1	1,067,711
K.C. Schlich							
Sefa's Beauty	M	1979	52	25	7	8	1,171,628
Barry Schwartz							
Peteski	H	1990	11	7	2	1	1,287,866
Herbert T. Schwartz							
Critical Eye	M	1997	38	14	4	3	1,060,984
Selective Seasons							
Family Style	M	1983	35	10	8	7	1,537,118
E.A. Seltzer							
Tank's Prospect	H	1982	14	5	2	2	1,355,645

Horse	Sex	Born	Sts	1st	2d	3d	Earnings
Shadwell Estate Company Limited							
Almutawakel (GB)	H	1995	19	4	4	1	3,643,021
Shadwell Farm Inc							
Dumaani	H	1991	26	7	3	3	1,079,098
Sakhee	H	1997	14	8	3	1	3,253,253
Shady Bend TB							
Sure Shot Biscuit	G	1996	54	23	10	11	1,025,480
Mr & Mrs L.K. Shapiro							
Native Diver	H	1959	81	37	7	12	1,026,500
Shockey & Willow Wood Farm							
Thirty Six Red	H	1987	20	4	3	5	1,094,310
Karen Silva							
Express Tour	H	1998	14	5	1	1	1,767,515
Robert C. Sims							
Hawkster	H	1986	23	6	3	4	1,510,942
J.B. Singer							
Videogenic	M	1982	73	20	9	10	1,154,360
T. Smith							
Frost King	H	1978	55	27	10	3	1,196,954
A.L. Smollin							
Sir Bear	G	1993	71	19	12	14	2,538,422
Hal Snowden Jr & Raymond Simpson							
Two Item Limit	M	1998	28	7	3	5	1,060,585
Hal Snowden Jr.							
Mr Epperson	G	1995	63	19	10	10	1,042,131
Shawnna Sorenson							
Unshaded	G	1997	20	6	3	3	1,318,492
Southeast Associates							
Alphabet Soup	H	1991	24	10	3	6	2,990,270
Spendthrift Farm							
Interco	H	1980	21	10	4	3	1,070,688
Robert Spiegel							
Milwaukee Brew	H	1997	24	8	4	5	2,879,612
R.H. Spreen							
Lady's Secret	M	1982	45	25	9	3	3,021,325
J.D. Squires							
Monarchos	H	1998	10	4	1	3	1,720,830
Stack & Valerio Ltd							
Kostroma (IRE)	M	1986	26	12	2	3	1,200,088
T. Stack							
Corwyn Bay (IRE)	H	1986	15	6	4	0	1,018,749
Stackallan Stud							
Erins Isle (IRE)	H	1978	33	9	9	3	1,233,889
Kathleen D. Standridge							
J J'sdream	M	1993	40	13	11	7	1,022,217
F. & R. Stark							
Cacoethes	H	1986	14	4	3	3	1,169,064
Beverly R. Steinman							
Colstar	M	1996	18	11	2	1	1,053,056
E.L. Stephenson							
Nasr El Arab	H	1985	16	6	2	2	1,198,585
Stetchworth Park Stud Ltd							
User Friendly (GB)	M	1989	16	8	1	2	1,764,938
Stiftung Gestut Fahrhof							
Silvano (GER)	H	1996	18	7	2	2	2,321,024
Stonerside Stable Ltd							
Congaree	H	1998	23	12	2	4	3,241,400
Stratford Place Stud							
Sarafan	G	1997	36	9	9	4	2,390,271
George Strawbridge Jr							
With Anticipation	G	1995	47	15	9	7	2,654,563
Tikkanen	H	1991	17	4	2	3	1,599,335
Music Merci	G	1986	35	12	7	4	1,500,710
Frank H. Stronach							
Awesome Again	H	1994	12	9	0	2	4,374,590
Nite Dreamer	H	1995	37	5	10	6	1,149,788
Basqueian	G	1991	37	13	10	2	1,094,767
Sugar Maple Farm Inc							
Itsallgreektome	G	1987	29	8	10	2	1,994,618
Sky Beauty	M	1990	21	15	2	2	1,336,000
Summa Stable							
Frankly Perfect	H	1985	22	6	6	4	1,272,957
Swettenham Stud							
Missionary Ridge (GB)	H	1987	42	8	5	8	1,864,498
Lit de Justice	H	1990	36	10	8	6	1,397,649
Rodrigo de Triano	H	1989	13	9	0	0	1,354,192
Single Empire (IRE)	H	1994	23	5	5	3	1,110,889
Swettenham Stud and Partners							
Northern Spur (IRE)	H	1991	15	6	4	3	1,614,425
Symboli Bokujo							
Symboli Rudolf (JPN)	H	1981	16	13	1	1	2,764,980
Paul Tackett							
Hopeful Word	H	1981	43	18	12	3	1,073,051
James B. Tafel							
Banshee Breeze	M	1995	18	10	5	2	2,784,798
Tall Oaks Farm							
Victory Gallop	H	1995	17	9	5	1	3,505,895
Tartan Farm Corporation							
Unbridled	H	1987	24	8	6	6	4,489,475
Equalize	H	1982	43	13	9	8	1,455,298
Primal	G	1985	45	17	11	7	1,209,530
Dr. Fager	H	1964	22	18	2	1	1,002,642
Edward P. Taylor							
Glorious Song	M	1976	34	17	9	1	1,004,534
Taylor Made Farm Inc							
Repent	C	1999	10	5	3	1	1,255,660
The Thoroughbred Corporation							
Point Given	H	1998	13	9	3	0	3,968,500
Spain	M	1997	35	9	9	7	3,540,542
Johar	C	1999	16	6	4	2	1,494,496
Third Kirsmith Racing Associates							
Rubiano	H	1987	28	13	6	1	1,252,817
Ralph Todd & Aury Todd							
The Tin Man	G	1998	18	7	4	1	1,074,460
John A. Toffan & Trudy McCaffery							
Free House	H	1994	22	9	5	3	3,178,971
Came Home	C	1999	12	9	0	0	1,835,940
Bienamado	H	1996	16	8	3	0	1,261,089
D Tsui and Orpendale							
Galileo (IRE)	H	1998	8	6	1	0	2,245,373
Mr & Mrs H.L. Vanier							
Western Playboy	H	1986	45	8	7	7	1,128,449
Vintage Meadow Stable							
Classic Cat	H	1995	20	6	3	5	1,221,300
Joseph Vitello							
Tenpins	H	1998	16	9	2	2	1,121,449
Waldemar Farms							
Foolish Pleasure	H	1972	26	16	4	3	1,216,705
Robert H. Walter							
Cavonnier	G	1993	23	8	3	2	1,254,165
Robert H. Walter Family Trust							
Tout Charmant	M	1996	29	9	9	1	1,781,879
Lazy Slusan	M	1995	47	12	7	10	1,150,410

Horse	Sex	Born	Sts	1st	2d	3d	Earnings
Warner L Jones Farm Inc							
Tap to Music	M	1995	21	6	4	4	1,052,526
Marvin L. Warner							
Stalwars	H	1985	79	17	17	8	1,211,556
Fred Watarida							
Native Desert	G	1993	74	21	13	17	1,828,177
James B. Watriss							
Great Communicator	H	1983	56	14	10	7	2,922,615
Georges Wegliszewski							
Celtic Arms (FR)	H	1991	23	5	2	3	1,102,806
R.G. Wehle							
Win	G	1980	44	14	10	3	1,408,980
Irwin Weiner & France Weiner							
Maltese Superb	M	1997	35	4	7	4	1,145,491
Welcome Farm							
Bessarabian	M	1982	37	18	5	4	1,032,640
Wertheimer et Frere							
Kotashaan (FR)	H	1988	22	10	5	2	2,812,114
Dare and Go	H	1991	22	7	7	5	1,608,972
Atticus	H	1992	18	7	3	1	1,205,933
Mr & Mrs R.S. West & Mr & Mrs M. Miller							
Chilukki	M	1997	17	11	3	0	1,201,828
Murray D. West							
Freedom Cry (GB)	H	1991	12	5	5	0	1,089,080
White Fox Farm							
Fleetstreet Dancer	G	1998	23	5	7	2	1,674,806
Janis R. Whitham							
Affluent	M	1998	23	8	5	4	1,497,651
Wickfield Stud Ltd							
Hawksley Hill (IRE)	G	1993	46	14	12	6	1,730,922
Konrad Widmer							
Thunder Rumble	H	1989	19	8	0	1	1,047,552
Edward Wiest							
Captain Bodgit	H	1994	12	7	1	4	1,014,849
Scott S. Willis							
Scott's Scoundrel	H	1992	50	22	4	8	1,270,052
Catherine Wills							
Dynever	C	2000	9	3	3	1	1,154,020
Charles T. Wilson							
Hodges Bay	H	1985	51	7	15	3	1,050,363
Ralph C. Wilson Jr							
Arazi	H	1989	14	9	1	1	1,212,351
Wimborne Farm							
John's Call	G	1991	40	16	11	3	1,571,267
J.D. Wimpfheimer							
Opening Verse	H	1986	30	10	7	2	1,669,357
Bounding Basque	H	1980	40	10	4	6	1,256,258
Win Star Farm LLC							
Funny Cide	G	2000	11	5	2	2	2,099,385
Verne H. Winchell							
Tight Spot	H	1987	21	12	3	1	1,566,100
Olympio	H	1988	17	9	4	0	1,456,315
V.H. Winchell & Katalpa Farm							
Sea Cadet	H	1988	29	10	6	5	1,807,150
Wind Hill Farm							
Starrer	M	1998	20	6	5	3	1,043,033
Windfields Farm							
Flag Down	H	1990	43	11	11	8	1,699,711
Mrs J.A. Winn							
Proper Reality	H	1985	19	10	3	1	1,701,650
Mr & Mrs Robert Witt							
Possibly Perfect	M	1990	18	11	2	4	1,377,634
Wood & Woodhaven Farms							
Pine Tree Lane	M	1982	38	19	4	4	1,150,561
Mr & Mrs M.L. Wood							
Favorite Trick	H	1995	16	12	0	1	1,726,793
Woodcrest							
Del Mar Dennis	G	1990	26	10	1	4	1,023,373
Forty Niner Days	G	1987	45	9	9	3	1,009,625
Woodlynn Farm Inc							
Guided Tour	G	1996	31	12	8	1	1,964,253
More Than Ready	H	1997	17	7	4	1	1,026,229
Mary Lou Wootton							
Silver Charm	H	1994	24	12	7	2	6,944,369
Mrs R.W. Worthington							
Jameela	M	1976	58	27	15	6	1,038,704
John Youngblood & Fletcher Gray							
Left Bank	H	1997	24	14	2	0	1,402,806
Julius H. Zolezzi							
Big Jag	G	1993	30	13	5	3	1,800,329
Donald Zuckerman & R. Mary Zuckerman							
Kalookan Queen	M	1996	25	11	8	4	1,044,474
Edward N. Zurek							
The Wicked North	H	1989	17	8	4	1	1,180,750

This section includes all horses with at least $1 million in career earnings that had at least one start in North America. It includes any foreign earnings and bonus money awarded for racing performance that was reported to *Daily Racing Form*.

Highest Stud Fees in North America for 2003

Stallion	Stud Fee	Stallion	Stud Fee
Storm Cat	$500,000	Carson City	35,000
A.P. Indy	300,000	Cat Thief	35,000
Seeking the Gold	225,000	Hennessy	35,000
Kingmambo	200,000	Maria's Mon	35,000
Fusaichi Pegasus	125,000	Our Emblem	35,000
Giant's Causeway	125,000	Quiet American	35,000
Gone West	125,000	Capote	30,000
Broad Brush	100,000	Diesis	30,000
Deputy Minister	100,000	Dixie Union	30,000
Unbridled's Song	100,000	Elusive Quality	30,000
Rahy	80,000	Grand Slam	30,000
El Prado	75,000	High Yield	30,000
Point Given	75,000	Johannesburg	30,000
Pulpit	75,000	Red Bullet	30,000
Silver Hawk	75,000	Street Cry	30,000
Theatrical	75,000	Tiznow	30,000
Thunder Gulch	65,000	Woodman	30,000
Cozzene	60,000	Aptitude	25,000
Dixieland Band	60,000	Bertrando	25,000
Forest Wildcat	60,000	Crafty Prospector	25,000
War Chant	60,000	Exploit	25,000
Awesome Again	50,000	Golden Missile	25,000
Coronado's Quest	50,000	Monarchos	25,000
Dynaformer	50,000	Old Trieste	25,000
Forestry	50,000	Phone Trick	25,000
Gulch	50,000	Silver Charm	25,000
Lemon Drop Kid	50,000	Swain	25,000
Mr. Greeley	50,000	Tale of the Cat	25,000
Touch Gold	50,000		
Red Ransom	45,000		
Came Home	40,000		
Mt. Livermore	40,000		
Silver Deputy	40,000		

Editor's Note: Some high-profile horses at stud do not have published stud fees and are priced according to individual contracts via private arrangements.

Top North American Sires in 2003 – Money Won

Sire	Perfs	Win Perfs	Starts	1st	2nd	3rd	Unpl	Purses
A.P. Indy	162	86	744	153	116	78	397	$8,827,360
Dynaformer	147	76	907	131	114	129	533	7,788,577
El Prado (IRE)	192	106	1,331	200	175	172	784	7,758,497
Langfuhr	164	94	1,047	175	142	134	596	6,675,994
Saint Ballado	172	83	892	141	148	121	482	5,953,038
Grand Slam	129	71	628	124	93	82	329	5,806,236
Unbridled	121	53	637	93	85	78	381	5,626,637
Silver Deputy	153	86	986	161	123	121	581	5,606,973
Smart Strike	118	68	730	121	106	110	393	5,489,374
Kris S.	98	54	546	90	79	65	312	5,340,284
Carson City	181	103	1,113	191	163	145	614	5,061,522
Distorted Humor	79	50	449	84	67	67	231	4,978,239
Not For Love	157	100	1,177	208	185	153	631	4,969,343
Pleasant Colony	78	42	538	77	71	72	318	4,871,583
Alphabet Soup	137	83	896	132	111	113	540	4,796,799
Wild Again	125	69	851	116	118	128	489	4,744,488
End Sweep	201	135	1,693	253	207	221	1,012	4,712,517
Smoke Glacken	122	75	879	157	132	124	466	4,587,386
In Excess (IRE)	124	63	681	121	88	78	394	4,259,537
Jules	94	56	616	113	71	74	358	4,228,948
Glitterman	147	93	1,084	174	153	123	634	4,156,373
Tabasco Cat	134	85	939	146	137	117	539	4,118,417
Tale of the Cat	134	70	634	98	106	90	340	4,053,160
Gilded Time	134	81	938	146	142	133	517	4,025,053
Cherokee Run	153	79	985	137	147	128	573	3,985,515
Montbrook	112	60	704	107	98	79	420	3,916,782
Unbridled's Song	130	71	649	104	78	84	383	3,825,586
Salt Lake	166	100	1,170	204	194	147	625	3,796,108
Cryptoclearance	223	103	1,653	191	189	203	1,070	3,739,880
Valid Expectations	115	72	896	145	156	118	477	3,728,127
Mr. Greeley	183	93	1,127	154	138	140	695	3,726,374
Dehere	115	63	712	97	129	85	401	3,672,157
Regal Classic	159	83	1,234	145	151	145	793	3,652,402
Dixie Brass	125	73	933	136	139	148	510	3,609,466
Hennessy	141	69	695	112	73	84	426	3,591,219
Holy Bull	147	91	979	159	119	113	588	3,570,267
Crafty Prospector	135	88	949	152	158	123	516	3,567,141
Runaway Groom	171	87	1,116	149	125	142	700	3,550,370
Belong to Me	152	87	959	136	116	133	574	3,537,479
Peaks and Valleys	137	81	1,048	154	161	138	595	3,536,454
Rubiano	139	87	1,117	161	136	159	661	3,525,061
Deputy Commander	88	36	489	54	68	64	303	3,483,253
Deputy Minister	121	54	626	83	91	71	381	3,475,392
Roar	132	73	850	137	112	109	492	3,439,069
Devil His Due	171	102	1,330	186	185	166	793	3,438,838
Notebook	137	76	1,039	143	150	140	606	3,377,149
Allen's Prospect	192	94	1,312	173	144	143	852	3,357,625
Gulch	112	55	739	99	104	99	437	3,320,379
Petionville	93	54	692	104	91	90	407	3,301,287
Capote	120	61	752	98	95	104	455	3,267,146
Quiet American	158	68	936	122	122	131	561	3,248,609
Sadler's Wells	28	9	97	13	11	15	58	3,202,155
Storm Cat	105	43	410	66	53	44	247	3,193,360
Lit de Justice	112	73	836	133	125	92	486	3,188,818
Forest Wildcat	158	80	877	129	89	101	558	3,096,878
Mutakddim	83	54	682	102	94	89	397	3,091,705
Southern Halo	160	73	1,000	120	136	119	625	3,031,599
French Deputy	100	57	574	93	82	75	324	3,025,445
Honor Grades	121	51	746	90	96	85	475	3,010,960
Tour d'Or	118	73	982	158	125	118	581	2,993,015
West by West	171	104	1,399	183	162	179	875	2,975,350
Storm Boot	181	101	1,053	173	128	107	645	2,966,974
Gone West	92	38	448	57	52	55	284	2,955,826

Sire	Perfs	Win Perfs	Starts	1st	2nd	3rd	Unpl	Purses
Mountain Cat	135	74	960	139	140	102	579	2,923,110
Elusive Quality	93	51	466	79	72	48	267	2,915,950
Gold Fever	125	57	744	99	107	119	419	2,906,828
Seeking the Gold	71	36	414	67	56	48	243	2,889,240
Gold Case	107	63	637	106	85	79	367	2,885,508
Marquetry	161	86	1,098	147	141	157	653	2,861,992
Pine Bluff	105	56	723	101	83	109	430	2,840,677
Twining	130	76	1,100	150	145	144	661	2,831,454
Polish Numbers	142	74	805	121	115	102	467	2,826,367
Rahy	92	41	484	67	67	51	299	2,812,767
Two Punch	157	84	929	142	106	139	542	2,808,808
Sea Hero	113	71	911	129	112	125	545	2,767,674
Awesome Again	70	36	368	57	53	56	202	2,759,659
Out of Place	143	80	1,083	145	158	133	647	2,730,120
Sky Classic	133	51	736	74	109	96	457	2,727,998
Roy	97	57	663	107	71	94	391	2,723,175
Broad Brush	100	57	646	104	73	85	384	2,707,093
Woodman	133	65	823	106	68	93	556	2,669,346
Sir Cat	101	66	665	123	110	80	352	2,622,760
Bold Executive	92	49	603	82	78	78	365	2,617,203
Beau Genius	127	69	939	133	139	117	550	2,612,636
Pentelicus	160	92	1,259	172	175	182	730	2,605,459
Mt. Livermore	135	70	881	123	126	93	539	2,603,783
Tactical Advantage	173	87	1,238	138	145	181	774	2,587,942
Honour and Glory	141	73	857	131	119	116	491	2,587,268
Maria's Mon	131	70	760	115	89	107	449	2,586,346
Grindstone	96	57	566	90	76	77	323	2,578,938
Judge T C	156	85	1,266	140	174	136	816	2,575,212
Formal Dinner	148	90	1,307	170	174	150	813	2,570,233
Dixieland Band	129	63	738	98	88	96	456	2,551,284
Wild Rush	86	49	494	91	82	57	264	2,548,056
Distant View	57	27	383	56	50	49	228	2,547,336
Ide	110	72	885	127	109	113	536	2,541,136
With Approval	155	74	1,080	126	127	111	716	2,539,789
You and I	98	60	711	106	105	89	411	2,523,314
Conquistador Cielo	109	52	712	101	85	89	437	2,512,730
Jade Hunter	112	46	703	79	72	62	490	2,507,628
Smokester	139	78	927	145	137	100	545	2,507,258
Boundary	95	59	640	101	105	82	352	2,500,681
Is It True	107	68	809	142	117	103	447	2,484,585
Numerous	145	74	1,058	123	149	135	651	2,478,264
Boston Harbor	105	56	551	92	59	65	335	2,475,884
Defrere	113	62	755	103	104	110	438	2,474,043
Kissin Kris	136	59	893	106	94	103	590	2,458,136
Editor's Note	107	67	844	118	99	106	521	2,424,453
Pulpit	82	42	410	63	57	50	240	2,411,485
Meadowlake	111	64	637	108	75	68	386	2,401,796
Personal Flag	127	64	946	123	114	121	588	2,399,689
Sword Dance (IRE)	144	82	1,095	136	133	142	684	2,398,148
Royal Academy	99	47	499	76	61	57	305	2,364,725
Valid Wager	90	55	707	102	89	99	417	2,350,593
Bertrando	124	56	616	100	75	81	360	2,346,053
Affirmed	62	29	376	50	46	45	235	2,343,824
Indian Charlie	80	43	411	78	59	58	216	2,326,849
Storm Creek	140	63	995	116	109	129	641	2,324,822
Lord Carson	103	64	745	129	89	93	434	2,303,117
Touch Gold	85	33	373	48	51	43	231	2,259,048
High Brite	131	73	983	140	124	130	589	2,250,658
Afternoon Deelites	110	59	797	111	102	110	474	2,245,346
Skip Trial	87	44	601	69	75	77	380	2,241,963
Summer Squall	75	47	531	84	50	69	328	2,226,196
Unaccounted For	96	56	731	105	105	81	440	2,222,355
Souvenir Copy	104	57	529	86	73	72	298	2,212,419
Halo's Image	79	43	615	86	85	95	349	2,195,790

Sire	Perfs	Win Perfs	Starts	1st	2nd	3rd	Unpl	Purses
Robyn Dancer	111	67	932	127	105	102	598	2,193,413
Phone Trick	142	76	956	122	121	139	574	2,178,999
A. P Jet	112	56	721	98	112	84	427	2,177,411
Silver Ghost	119	59	775	104	98	99	474	2,155,020
Flying Continental	136	71	1,044	120	135	131	658	2,151,137
American Chance	101	53	705	97	106	88	414	2,148,378
Cobra King	78	44	551	78	66	68	339	2,133,282
Bold Badgett	67	41	440	63	57	70	250	2,131,846
Vying Victor	103	54	755	108	100	105	442	2,123,434
Private Terms	102	50	695	103	80	87	425	2,052,259
Cape Town	63	36	289	49	29	33	178	2,046,576
Pembroke	120	65	974	134	137	125	578	2,045,784
Cozzene	92	48	551	71	69	84	327	2,041,800
Slew City Slew	121	62	728	112	86	65	465	2,041,332
Tethra	60	35	409	62	60	43	244	2,041,074
Cee's Tizzy	87	47	464	74	62	79	249	2,037,868
Whiskey Wisdom	65	32	378	44	51	46	237	2,035,214
General Meeting	110	50	607	68	85	77	377	2,034,114
Mecke	88	49	676	87	97	88	404	2,033,996
Patton	128	75	1,012	134	104	108	666	2,025,282
Sultry Song	103	51	616	84	71	75	386	2,019,262
Fit to Fight	130	74	1,004	125	138	117	624	2,018,651
Kingmambo	74	35	379	52	48	45	234	2,005,610
Mr. Prospector	41	15	191	27	26	25	113	1,999,854
Distinctive Pro	98	50	753	90	109	120	434	1,988,114
Open Forum	110	56	757	80	98	112	467	1,986,973
Stormy Atlantic	72	33	372	63	45	67	197	1,984,441
Fortunate Prospect	128	69	1,051	138	133	127	653	1,979,103
Captain Bodgit	111	59	681	98	94	85	404	1,970,672
Take Me Out	107	53	709	100	71	88	450	1,958,424
Lost Soldier	102	48	600	76	64	69	391	1,957,014
Cure the Blues	77	42	644	73	75	77	419	1,952,700
Suave Prospect	79	49	655	96	79	94	386	1,928,234
Lear Fan	68	30	409	40	56	55	258	1,925,682
Signal Tap	88	38	624	61	64	61	438	1,923,787
Pioneering	81	54	584	91	87	77	329	1,912,534
Eastern Echo	93	51	664	88	70	82	424	1,885,557
Red Ransom	95	38	453	54	48	60	291	1,883,523
Citidancer	84	52	585	96	85	86	318	1,861,021
Avenue of Flags	91	46	532	89	65	66	312	1,858,685
Lite the Fuse	75	41	506	68	75	80	283	1,855,165
Waquoit	93	47	654	98	102	78	376	1,826,931
Thunder Gulch	87	41	502	56	63	67	316	1,826,050
Formal Gold	79	49	472	77	67	45	283	1,811,473
Friendly Lover	108	61	796	98	112	82	504	1,785,157
Arazi	8	5	67	14	8	8	37	1,778,350
Wekiva Springs	126	64	838	103	112	102	521	1,776,811
Press Card	108	61	803	109	89	113	492	1,766,565
Unreal Zeal	105	68	917	134	98	117	568	1,742,414
War Deputy	56	29	427	55	52	50	270	1,738,196
Devil's Bag	89	45	505	73	57	52	323	1,734,065
Siphon (BRZ)	109	42	502	57	69	72	304	1,726,394
Concorde's Tune	71	45	539	81	68	65	325	1,717,410
Dove Hunt	99	57	739	92	83	74	490	1,709,822
Dance Brightly	93	47	538	71	58	64	345	1,707,304
Seattle Slew	71	28	386	45	48	46	247	1,694,329
Skywalker	86	37	565	73	75	54	363	1,691,212
Wild Zone	111	57	719	93	81	92	453	1,684,562
Double Honor	85	58	586	112	77	62	335	1,651,091
Lord Avie	102	44	612	76	73	79	384	1,648,916
Partner's Hero	64	32	398	55	53	58	232	1,639,645
Danzig	41	20	172	31	20	13	108	1,614,085
Pleasant Tap	104	41	644	67	74	93	410	1,605,609
Alydeed	103	52	757	82	83	127	465	1,591,930

Sire	Perfs	Win Perfs	Starts	1st	2nd	3rd	Unpl	Purses
Candy Stripes	80	46	494	82	72	56	284	1,583,586
Ghazi	104	45	675	81	81	84	429	1,582,746
Lord At War (ARG)	31	17	197	35	29	19	114	1,581,531
Memo (CHI)	74	33	434	65	55	61	253	1,580,689
Tejabo	55	24	474	44	60	62	308	1,572,103
Boone's Mill	117	75	931	128	121	120	562	1,561,681
Louis Quatorze	92	45	496	66	60	57	313	1,560,179
Lost Code	114	53	779	98	110	87	484	1,557,714
Skip Away	95	36	511	51	67	67	326	1,546,413
Unusual Heat	40	22	304	48	39	45	172	1,535,387
Valley Crossing	80	39	574	71	70	74	359	1,535,022
Green Dancer	66	31	445	53	41	49	302	1,515,680
Sandpit (BRZ)	97	56	691	99	82	71	439	1,503,005
Helmsman	70	40	519	75	80	63	301	1,501,782
Prospect Bay	83	51	537	90	93	65	289	1,499,758
Line In The Sand	142	61	1,135	96	127	129	783	1,494,447
Kiridashi	58	26	357	39	33	33	252	1,489,181
Colonial Affair	68	35	460	73	65	56	266	1,488,091
Spinning World	43	26	257	49	34	29	145	1,477,669
Carnivalay	84	45	621	70	78	74	399	1,467,894
Slewdledo	128	66	710	109	87	93	421	1,467,244
Lucky Lionel	61	37	392	55	47	61	229	1,421,516
Swiss Yodeler	54	35	358	55	61	40	202	1,391,389
Sea Salute	62	34	495	77	60	47	311	1,383,584
Mister Baileys (GB)	63	35	449	58	41	53	297	1,380,417
Deerhound	101	45	659	69	92	66	432	1,376,999
Benchmark	49	33	312	58	44	37	173	1,372,242
Rizzi	83	42	566	74	75	69	348	1,369,941
Way West (FR)	76	39	553	65	68	59	361	1,364,935
Dr. Adagio	58	35	489	74	67	60	288	1,362,231
Machiavellian	20	8	89	14	9	12	54	1,358,003
Theatrical (IRE)	66	21	286	29	31	32	194	1,356,134
Swain (IRE)	18	12	76	17	6	11	42	1,352,277
Demaloot Demashoot	85	51	742	97	91	87	467	1,350,968
Chimes Band	61	38	514	64	80	78	292	1,347,541
Tomorrows Cat	74	26	314	39	44	38	193	1,336,519
Cartwright	89	44	631	74	71	84	402	1,324,945
*Hernando (FR)	4	3	11	6	0	0	5	1,324,330
Norquestor	78	41	607	73	78	85	371	1,322,983
Tejano Run	48	25	361	50	54	46	211	1,319,507
Lac Ouimet	88	46	579	79	67	63	370	1,319,247
Miner's Mark	90	47	754	80	106	79	489	1,313,335
Caller I. D.	105	52	709	90	70	100	449	1,312,731
Williamstown	79	40	584	68	70	80	366	1,312,269
Victory Speech	76	41	594	86	63	53	392	1,311,379
Jeblar	93	41	739	83	101	81	474	1,309,151
Birdonthewire	71	35	431	63	62	52	254	1,303,848
Green Desert	8	6	43	10	8	3	22	1,292,972
Clever Trick	105	53	736	89	98	75	474	1,287,634
Mister Jolie	77	50	610	90	91	94	335	1,287,302
Favorite Trick	63	34	434	54	59	70	251	1,285,063
Known Fact	66	34	427	48	58	55	266	1,283,522
Kokand	77	42	553	87	78	72	316	1,280,953
Tricky Creek	91	49	721	85	92	73	471	1,278,733
Coronado's Quest	58	19	225	31	30	28	136	1,278,475
Sea Wall	43	23	318	38	38	41	201	1,273,177
In Case	112	49	695	72	77	81	465	1,267,685
Go for Gin	70	34	484	54	69	63	298	1,266,698
Ascot Knight	60	25	385	41	53	42	249	1,263,576
Evansville Slew	55	39	459	70	66	60	263	1,260,750
Hussonet	12	5	44	8	6	2	28	1,256,344
Concern	70	39	490	71	54	73	292	1,252,978
Marked Tree	103	53	708	101	88	78	441	1,247,920
Regal Remark	93	53	629	98	98	84	349	1,245,995

Sire	Perfs	Win Perfs	Starts	1st	2nd	3rd	Unpl	Purses
Siberian Summer	72	38	466	72	57	52	285	1,235,659
Northern Afleet	43	33	280	63	37	30	150	1,224,867
Cadeaux Genereux (GB)	8	4	54	6	8	10	30	1,224,079
Air Forbes Won	68	35	523	75	80	69	299	1,217,226
Appealing Skier	69	44	463	68	57	59	279	1,216,233
Housebuster	59	33	476	68	64	58	286	1,211,227
Barbeau	39	24	314	53	41	31	189	1,198,796
Will's Way	52	33	357	62	53	47	195	1,189,099
Concerto	47	37	315	56	42	33	184	1,177,356
Miswaki	85	30	485	45	79	53	308	1,174,200
Barkerville	44	24	301	38	22	42	199	1,166,025
Brunswick	55	33	501	70	71	62	298	1,164,443
Gold Legend	66	34	470	65	62	69	274	1,163,390
Prized	89	41	616	59	71	88	398	1,162,925
Hadif	110	62	727	98	95	92	442	1,159,973
Game Plan	90	57	570	95	82	80	313	1,159,721
Foxhound	76	47	644	84	68	81	411	1,142,548
Kipper Kelly	81	42	623	73	83	70	397	1,142,336
Black Tie Affair (IRE)	60	30	511	51	73	64	323	1,134,514
*Alhaarth (IRE)	7	4	16	4	1	3	8	1,133,848
Northern Idol	52	28	352	52	32	45	223	1,130,701
Wayne County (IRE)	66	35	431	60	54	49	268	1,117,955
Katahaula County	66	42	498	64	79	67	288	1,116,897
Arch	47	26	273	39	50	48	136	1,108,938
Strodes Creek	58	39	429	74	63	47	245	1,100,559
Secret Hello	64	36	478	70	74	79	255	1,100,390
Harlan	32	16	238	28	24	34	152	1,100,346
Our Emblem	85	35	488	55	57	51	325	1,099,968
Bag	123	52	703	77	65	85	476	1,093,470
Key Contender	50	33	457	69	61	59	268	1,093,455
Domasca Dan	24	14	169	26	22	11	110	1,093,027
Turkoman	83	41	624	71	90	79	384	1,080,175
Irish River (FR)	38	18	219	26	29	28	136	1,076,709
Caerleon	12	6	53	9	10	5	29	1,066,849
Great Gladiator	34	18	233	31	21	31	150	1,065,698
Free At Last	106	71	820	113	125	115	467	1,049,263
Bien Bien	24	10	151	19	18	15	99	1,045,889
Regal Intention	71	40	473	69	61	66	277	1,045,312
Zarbyev	58	32	443	48	58	51	286	1,044,727
Meadow Monster	39	30	270	53	34	39	144	1,034,173
All Gone	64	35	485	61	63	65	296	1,031,771
Compadre	34	10	210	14	29	20	147	1,030,253
Eltish	42	23	257	47	36	32	142	1,029,213
Future Storm	82	35	589	58	69	57	405	1,025,191
Sefapiano	66	39	464	66	74	63	261	1,024,547
Fast Play	61	28	432	53	47	53	279	1,022,121
Supremo	80	44	674	70	71	66	467	1,020,345
Irish Open	101	53	800	92	91	113	504	1,017,272
Stuka	51	27	388	59	40	43	246	1,015,290
Prospector's Music	64	39	482	70	65	55	292	1,013,777
Prospectors Gamble	86	37	592	60	63	62	407	1,012,744
Explosive Red	93	42	709	72	101	71	465	1,012,346
Ponche	50	25	392	42	66	67	217	1,010,525
Golden Gear	67	35	468	56	58	53	301	1,007,596
Banker's Gold	65	29	368	46	50	54	218	1,007,086
Olympio	77	39	488	60	58	67	303	1,003,763
Alfaari	60	37	436	63	57	72	244	1,000,747

The above list includes only North American earnings
* Foreign based stallion with North American starters
Statistics provided by Equibase

Top North American Sires in 2003 – Races Won

Sire	Perfs	Win Perfs	Starts	1st	2nd	3rd	Unpl	Purses
End Sweep	201	135	1,693	253	207	221	1,012	$4,712,517
Not For Love	157	100	1,177	208	185	153	631	4,969,343
Salt Lake	166	100	1,170	204	194	147	625	3,796,108
El Prado (IRE)	192	106	1,331	200	175	172	784	7,758,497
Carson City	181	103	1,113	191	163	145	614	5,061,522
Cryptoclearance	223	103	1,653	191	189	203	1,070	3,739,880
Devil His Due	171	102	1,330	186	185	166	793	3,438,838
West by West	171	104	1,399	183	162	179	875	2,975,350
Langfuhr	164	94	1,047	175	142	134	596	6,675,994
Glitterman	147	93	1,084	174	153	123	634	4,156,373
Allen's Prospect	192	94	1,312	173	144	143	852	3,357,625
Storm Boot	181	101	1,053	173	128	107	645	2,966,974
Pentelicus	160	92	1,259	172	175	182	730	2,605,459
Formal Dinner	148	90	1,307	170	174	150	813	2,570,233
Silver Deputy	153	86	986	161	123	121	581	5,606,973
Rubiano	139	87	1,117	161	136	159	661	3,525,061
Holy Bull	147	91	979	159	119	113	588	3,570,267
Tour d'Or	118	73	982	158	125	118	581	2,993,015
Smoke Glacken	122	75	879	157	132	124	466	4,587,386
Mr. Greeley	183	93	1,127	154	138	140	695	3,726,374
Peaks and Valleys	137	81	1,048	154	161	138	595	3,536,454
A.P. Indy	162	86	744	153	116	78	397	8,827,360
Crafty Prospector	135	88	949	152	158	123	516	3,567,141
Twining	130	76	1,100	150	145	144	661	2,831,454
Runaway Groom	171	87	1,116	149	125	142	700	3,550,370
Marquetry	161	86	1,098	147	141	157	653	2,861,992
Tabasco Cat	134	85	939	146	137	117	539	4,118,417
Gilded Time	134	81	938	146	142	133	517	4,025,053
Valid Expectations	115	72	896	145	156	118	477	3,728,127
Regal Classic	159	83	1,234	145	151	145	793	3,652,402
Out of Place	143	80	1,083	145	158	133	647	2,730,120
Smokester	139	78	927	145	137	100	545	2,507,258
Notebook	137	76	1,039	143	150	140	606	3,377,149
Two Punch	157	84	929	142	106	139	542	2,808,808
Is It True	107	68	809	142	117	103	447	2,484,585
Saint Ballado	172	83	892	141	148	121	482	5,953,038
Judge T C	156	85	1,266	140	174	136	816	2,575,212
High Brite	131	73	983	140	124	130	589	2,250,658
Mountain Cat	135	74	960	139	140	102	579	2,923,110
Tactical Advantage	173	87	1,238	138	145	181	774	2,587,942
Fortunate Prospect	128	69	1,051	138	133	127	653	1,979,103
Cherokee Run	153	79	985	137	147	128	573	3,985,515
Roar	132	73	850	137	112	109	492	3,439,069
Dixie Brass	125	73	933	136	139	148	510	3,609,466
Belong to Me	152	87	959	136	116	133	574	3,537,479
Sword Dance (IRE)	144	82	1,095	136	133	142	684	2,398,148
Pembroke	120	65	974	134	137	125	578	2,045,784
Patton	128	75	1,012	134	104	108	666	2,025,282
Unreal Zeal	105	68	917	134	98	117	568	1,742,414
Lit de Justice	112	73	836	133	125	92	486	3,188,818

Sire	Perfs	Win Perfs	Starts	1st	2nd	3rd	Unpl	Purses
Beau Genius	127	69	939	133	139	117	550	2,612,636
Alphabet Soup	137	83	896	132	111	113	540	4,796,799
Dynaformer	147	76	907	131	114	129	533	7,788,577
Honour and Glory	141	73	857	131	119	116	491	2,587,268
Forest Wildcat	158	80	877	129	89	101	558	3,096,878
Sea Hero	113	71	911	129	112	125	545	2,767,674
Lord Carson	103	64	745	129	89	93	434	2,303,117
Boone's Mill	117	75	931	128	121	120	562	1,561,681
Ide	110	72	885	127	109	113	536	2,541,136
Robyn Dancer	111	67	932	127	105	102	598	2,193,413
With Approval	155	74	1,080	126	127	111	716	2,539,789
Fit to Fight	130	74	1,004	125	138	117	624	2,018,651
Grand Slam	129	71	628	124	93	82	329	5,806,236
Sir Cat	101	66	665	123	110	80	352	2,622,760
Mt. Livermore	135	70	881	123	126	93	539	2,603,783
Numerous	145	74	1,058	123	149	135	651	2,478,264
Personal Flag	127	64	946	123	114	121	588	2,399,689
Quiet American	158	68	936	122	122	131	561	3,248,609
Phone Trick	142	76	956	122	121	139	574	2,178,999
Smart Strike	118	68	730	121	106	110	393	5,489,374
In Excess (IRE)	124	63	681	121	88	78	394	4,259,537
Polish Numbers	142	74	805	121	115	102	467	2,826,367
Southern Halo	160	73	1,000	120	136	119	625	3,031,599
Flying Continental	136	71	1,044	120	135	131	658	2,151,137
Editor's Note	107	67	844	118	99	106	521	2,424,453
Wild Again	125	69	851	116	118	128	489	4,744,488
Storm Creek	140	63	995	116	109	129	641	2,324,822
Maria's Mon	131	70	760	115	89	107	449	2,586,346
Jules	94	56	616	113	71	74	358	4,228,948
Free At Last	106	71	820	113	125	115	467	1,049,263
Hennessy	141	69	695	112	73	84	426	3,591,219
Slew City Slew	121	62	728	112	86	65	465	2,041,332
Double Honor	85	58	586	112	77	62	335	1,651,091
Afternoon Deelites	110	59	797	111	102	110	474	2,245,346
Press Card	108	61	803	109	89	113	492	1,766,565
Slewdledo	128	66	710	109	87	93	421	1,467,244
Meadowlake	111	64	637	108	75	68	386	2,401,796
Vying Victor	103	54	755	108	100	105	442	2,123,434
Montbrook	112	60	704	107	98	79	420	3,916,782
Roy	97	57	663	107	71	94	391	2,723,175
Gold Case	107	63	637	106	85	79	367	2,885,508
Woodman	133	65	823	106	68	93	556	2,669,346
You and I	98	60	711	106	105	89	411	2,523,314
Kissin Kris	136	59	893	106	94	103	590	2,458,136
Unaccounted For	96	56	731	105	105	81	440	2,222,355
Unbridled's Song	130	71	649	104	78	84	383	3,825,586
Petionville	93	54	692	104	91	90	407	3,301,287
Broad Brush	100	57	646	104	73	85	384	2,707,093
Silver Ghost	119	59	775	104	98	99	474	2,155,020
Defrere	113	62	755	103	104	110	438	2,474,043
Private Terms	102	50	695	103	80	87	425	2,052,259

Top North American Sires in 2003 – Winning Performers

Sire	Perfs	Win Perfs	Starts	1st	2nd	3rd	Unpl	Purses
End Sweep	201	135	1,693	253	207	221	1,012	$4,712,517
El Prado (IRE)	192	106	1,331	200	175	172	784	7,758,497
West by West	171	104	1,399	183	162	179	875	2,975,350
Carson City	181	103	1,113	191	163	145	614	5,061,522
Cryptoclearance	223	103	1,653	191	189	203	1,070	3,739,880
Devil His Due	171	102	1,330	186	185	166	793	3,438,838
Storm Boot	181	101	1,053	173	128	107	645	2,966,974
Not For Love	157	100	1,177	208	185	153	631	4,969,343
Salt Lake	166	100	1,170	204	194	147	625	3,796,108
Langfuhr	164	94	1,047	175	142	134	596	6,675,994
Allen's Prospect	192	94	1,312	173	144	143	852	3,357,625
Glitterman	147	93	1,084	174	153	123	634	4,156,373
Mr. Greeley	183	93	1,127	154	138	140	695	3,726,374
Pentelicus	160	92	1,259	172	175	182	730	2,605,459
Holy Bull	147	91	979	159	119	113	588	3,570,267
Formal Dinner	148	90	1,307	170	174	150	813	2,570,233
Crafty Prospector	135	88	949	152	158	123	516	3,567,141
Runaway Groom	171	87	1,116	149	125	142	700	3,550,370
Belong to Me	152	87	959	136	116	133	574	3,537,479
Rubiano	139	87	1,117	161	136	159	661	3,525,061
Tactical Advantage	173	87	1,238	138	145	181	774	2,587,942
A.P. Indy	162	86	744	153	116	78	397	8,827,360
Silver Deputy	153	86	986	161	123	121	581	5,606,973
Marquetry	161	86	1,098	147	141	157	653	2,861,992
Tabasco Cat	134	85	939	146	137	117	539	4,118,417
Judge T C	156	85	1,266	140	174	136	816	2,575,212
Two Punch	157	84	929	142	106	139	542	2,808,808
Saint Ballado	172	83	892	141	148	121	482	5,953,038
Alphabet Soup	137	83	896	132	111	113	540	4,796,799
Regal Classic	159	83	1,234	145	151	145	793	3,652,402
Sword Dance (IRE)	144	82	1,095	136	133	142	684	2,398,148
Gilded Time	134	81	938	146	142	133	517	4,025,053
Peaks and Valleys	137	81	1,048	154	161	138	595	3,536,454
Forest Wildcat	158	80	877	129	89	101	558	3,096,878
Out of Place	143	80	1,083	145	158	133	647	2,730,120
Cherokee Run	153	79	985	137	147	128	573	3,985,515
Smokester	139	78	927	145	137	100	545	2,507,258
Dynaformer	147	76	907	131	114	129	533	7,788,577
Notebook	137	76	1,039	143	150	140	606	3,377,149
Twining	130	76	1,100	150	145	144	661	2,831,454
Phone Trick	142	76	956	122	121	139	574	2,178,999
Smoke Glacken	122	75	879	157	132	124	466	4,587,386
Patton	128	75	1,012	134	104	108	666	2,025,282
Boone's Mill	117	75	931	128	121	120	562	1,561,681
Mountain Cat	135	74	960	139	140	102	579	2,923,110
Polish Numbers	142	74	805	121	115	102	467	2,826,367
With Approval	155	74	1,080	126	127	111	716	2,539,789
Numerous	145	74	1,058	123	149	135	651	2,478,264
Fit to Fight	130	74	1,004	125	138	117	624	2,018,651
Dixie Brass	125	73	933	136	139	148	510	3,609,466
Roar	132	73	850	137	112	109	492	3,439,069

Sire	Perfs	Win Perfs	Starts	1st	2nd	3rd	Unpl	Purses
Lit de Justice	112	73	836	133	125	92	486	3,188,818
Southern Halo	160	73	1,000	120	136	119	625	3,031,599
Tour d'Or	118	73	982	158	125	118	581	2,993,015
Honour and Glory	141	73	857	131	119	116	491	2,587,268
High Brite	131	73	983	140	124	130	589	2,250,658
Valid Expectations	115	72	896	145	156	118	477	3,728,127
Ide	110	72	885	127	109	113	536	2,541,136
Grand Slam	129	71	628	124	93	82	329	5,806,236
Unbridled's Song	130	71	649	104	78	84	383	3,825,586
Sea Hero	113	71	911	129	112	125	545	2,767,674
Flying Continental	136	71	1,044	120	135	131	658	2,151,137
Free At Last	106	71	820	113	125	115	467	1,049,263
Tale of the Cat	134	70	634	98	106	90	340	4,053,160
Mt. Livermore	135	70	881	123	126	93	539	2,603,783
Maria's Mon	131	70	760	115	89	107	449	2,586,346
Wild Again	125	69	851	116	118	128	489	4,744,488
Hennessy	141	69	695	112	73	84	426	3,591,219
Beau Genius	127	69	939	133	139	117	550	2,612,636
Fortunate Prospect	128	69	1,051	138	133	127	653	1,979,103
Smart Strike	118	68	730	121	106	110	393	5,489,374
Quiet American	158	68	936	122	122	131	561	3,248,609
Is It True	107	68	809	142	117	103	447	2,484,585
Unreal Zeal	105	68	917	134	98	117	568	1,742,414
Editor's Note	107	67	844	118	99	106	521	2,424,453
Robyn Dancer	111	67	932	127	105	102	598	2,193,413
Sir Cat	101	66	665	123	110	80	352	2,622,760
Slewdledo	128	66	710	109	87	93	421	1,467,244
Woodman	133	65	823	106	68	93	556	2,669,346
Pembroke	120	65	974	134	137	125	578	2,045,784
Meadowlake	111	64	637	108	75	68	386	2,401,796
Personal Flag	127	64	946	123	114	121	588	2,399,689
Lord Carson	103	64	745	129	89	93	434	2,303,117
Wekiva Springs	126	64	838	103	112	102	521	1,776,811
In Excess (IRE)	124	63	681	121	88	78	394	4,259,537
Dehere	115	63	712	97	129	85	401	3,672,157
Gold Case	107	63	637	106	85	79	367	2,885,508
Dixieland Band	129	63	738	98	88	96	456	2,551,284
Storm Creek	140	63	995	116	109	129	641	2,324,822
Defrere	113	62	755	103	104	110	438	2,474,043
Slew City Slew	121	62	728	112	86	65	465	2,041,332
Hadif	110	62	727	98	95	92	442	1,159,973
Capote	120	61	752	98	95	104	455	3,267,146
Friendly Lover	108	61	796	98	112	82	504	1,785,157
Press Card	108	61	803	109	89	113	492	1,766,565
Line In The Sand	142	61	1,135	96	127	129	783	1,494,447
Montbrook	112	60	704	107	98	79	420	3,916,782
You and I	98	60	711	106	105	89	411	2,523,314
Boundary	95	59	640	101	105	82	352	2,500,681
Kissin Kris	136	59	893	106	94	103	590	2,458,136
Afternoon Deelites	110	59	797	111	102	110	474	2,245,346
Silver Ghost	119	59	775	104	98	99	474	2,155,020
Captain Bodgit	111	59	681	98	94	85	404	1,970,672

Top 10 Sires and Their Progeny

A.P. Indy, Dk B H (1989)
By Seattle Slew – Weekend Surprise, by Secretariat
162 Performers, 86 winning performers, $8,827,360 total earnings

Progeny	Mare	Age	Sts	1st	2d	3d	Money Won
A Great Team	Pennant Champion	3	6	3	1	1	98,620
A P Credit	Our Dear Sue	3	5	0	1	1	5,470
A. P. Adventure	Nataliano	2	1	1	0	0	27,000
A. P. Amazon	Ampulla	4	5	1	0	0	13,100
A. P. Aspen	Gone for Gusto	4	10	2	3	2	44,700
A. P. Delta	Lyphard's Delta	6	2	0	0	0	420
Abduction	Jurisdictional	5	1	1	0	0	21,600
Addicks	Don't Read My Lips	4	10	1	1	2	50,410
Adrenalin Running	Harda Arda	2	4	0	0	0	2,640
Alchemist	Aldiza	3	6	3	1	1	104,800
Alexi Dancer	Pike Place Dancer	2	3	0	0	0	1,380
Alluring	Educated Risk	4	7	0	4	1	45,140
Almostashar	Destination Mir	5	1	0	0	0	1,020
Anasheed	Flagbird	3	5	1	0	2	39,980
Appleby Gardens	Larkwhistle	3	3	1	0	0	41,940
Arturo	Digit	3	5	1	2	0	46,840
Ashoka	Gallanta (FR)	3	3	1	1	1	43,340
Atswhatimtalknbout	Lucinda K	3	6	2	1	1	209,120
Aztec Pearl	Aurora	4	8	1	1	1	46,860
Big Country	Flanders	3	8	2	1	2	73,260
Brands Hatch	Watch Out	2	2	0	0	0	3,080
Brazen n' Bold	Go for Bold	4	7	2	3	1	22,268
Bridger	Wakonda	9	2	0	1	0	5,460
Brother Indy	Alghuzaylah (IRE)	4	10	0	3	2	3,005
Bubba's Colors	Two Altazano	5	11	0	2	0	21,670
Bushy Park (IRE)	Tis Juliet	5	8	2	1	1	52,000
Catalindy	Catalina Court	2	1	0	0	0	0
Catbaby	Catinca	2	2	0	0	0	0
Chairman A. P.	Morning Dove	5	3	0	0	0	2,660
Charmed Gift	Potridee (ARG)	4	4	1	1	0	58,732
Chic Joy	Chic Corine	3	7	1	2	0	66,600
Chief Pete	Sheepscot	3	10	2	1	2	27,577
Clasp	Hitch	6	7	1	1	1	8,219
Clear Path	Masake	5	3	1	0	0	20,790
Clutch Player	Cambury Angel	5	7	1	0	3	14,167
Compound	Biding Time	2	2	0	0	0	220
Congrats	Praise	3	7	3	0	1	180,388
Connie's Magic	Connie's Gift	7	8	4	2	1	78,750
Crocker Road	Gallanta (FR)	2	1	0	0	0	980
Dahlia Dearest	Miss Dahlia	3	7	0	0	0	1,820
Dancinandsingin	Scoot Yer Boots	2	2	0	1	0	8,600
Dawn Exodus	Grey Parlo	8	9	2	1	2	29,706
Daydreaming	Get Lucky	2	3	1	0	1	79,000
Dealer's Dream	Dream Deal	4	2	0	1	0	2,033
Decision	Gana	5	12	5	2	2	46,471
Delta Princess	Lyphard's Delta	4	8	4	0	0	196,110
Diamond Indy	Adel	2	2	0	0	1	5,400
Endemaj	Miss Union Avenue	3	1	0	0	0	0
Ender's Shadow	Gold Rush Queen	3	7	3	0	1	97,440
Ender's Sister	Gold Rush Queen	2	5	2	2	0	107,900
Extra	Everhope	3	3	0	0	0	0
Fantastic Voyage	Chateaubaby	3	2	0	0	0	0
Fashion Sense	Donna Karan (CHI)	3	8	1	2	1	47,779
Fircroft	Pemaquid	3	7	0	3	0	156,876
Fire Work	Bernique	8	3	0	0	0	152
Fisher Pond	Chipeta Springs	4	6	0	1	2	25,993
Flatter	Praise	4	2	1	0	1	82,845
Flying Passage	Chic Shirine	3	4	1	0	2	37,250
Fragrance	Esther Rose	2	3	1	0	1	25,840
Friends Lake	Antespend	2	3	2	0	0	84,600
Full Mandate	Clear Mandate	4	8	3	1	0	128,263
Game Box	Aucilla	3	2	0	0	0	1,380
Gentle Giant	Retiro Park	6	2	1	0	0	36,600
Glia	Coup de Genie	4	2	0	0	0	0
Gradepoint	Class Kris	2	2	1	0	0	36,285
Handpainted	Daijin	3	2	0	1	0	59,600
Highgate Park	High Heeled Hope	2	6	2	0	1	49,410
Icanseeclearlynow	Ifyoucouldseemenow	4	9	2	3	1	32,980
Idealism	Sovereign Kitty	3	4	1	0	0	20,166
Impetuous Fling	Impetuous Image	3	13	2	1	0	71,914
In Secure	Morelia	3	4	3	0	0	92,040
India Sun	Sultry Sun	2	2	0	0	0	1,350
Indiana Express	Merit Wings	3	6	1	1	0	19,256
Indixie	Dixie Accent	5	9	2	2	1	15,165
Indy	Izana	2	4	0	0	0	7,395
Indy Charmer	Dancing Mirage	2	4	0	1	1	15,640
Indy Dancer	Dance With Grace	3	5	1	0	1	121,900
Indy Five Hundred	Lyphard's Delta	3	7	2	1	0	206,400
Indy Flag	Dixie Flag	3	2	0	0	1	5,980
Indy Glory	Immerse	5	2	1	1	0	45,600
Indy Lead	Court Hostess	5	10	1	2	1	95,163
Indy Snow (GB)	November Snow	2	2	0	0	0	0
Indy Stormy	Stormy Temper	3	2	0	0	0	300
Indy Thunder	Lucky Souvenir	3	1	0	1	0	5,000
Indy Zone	One Dreamer	3	3	0	0	0	60
Indy's Treasure	Treasure Mine	3	5	0	0	0	2,050
Indygo Shiner	Navarra	5	1	0	0	0	420
Kentucky Pride	Voodoo Lily	3	2	0	1	0	10,500
King Augustus	Polish Style	2	3	0	3	0	18,900
King Tutta	Tutta	3	3	0	0	0	125
King's Honor	Great Lady M.	7	2	0	1	1	993
La Reina	Queena	2	4	2	2	0	142,420
Lady Nichola	Macoumba	2	1	0	1	0	9,800
Lethal Litigator	Vinista	2	1	0	0	1	4,320
Lindy Wells	Luna Wells (IRE)	3	2	0	0	1	3,520
Listen Indy	Ecoute	3	5	0	0	1	9,680
Liszy	Silent Account	3	2	0	0	0	680
Liz On Polk Street	Silver Maiden	2	1	1	0	0	15,600
Lovely Rafaela	Campagnarde (ARG)	2	3	1	0	0	36,480
Lunar Perigee	Meteor Colony	3	6	0	0	0	3,750
Mach Speed	Bay Harbor	2	3	1	1	0	44,121
Major Decision	Harbor Springs	3	7	0	5	0	38,460
Mineshaft	Prospectors Delite	4	9	7	2	0	2,209,686
Miss Hellie	Puestera	4	9	3	2	1	97,600
Mithaal	Zakiyya	2	3	0	0	0	4,080
Mon Sang	Trouble Woman	3	3	0	0	0	1,000
Monarchoftheglen	Milliardaire	4	3	1	0	0	21,600
Mrs. Bassett	Ice Cream Cone	2	2	0	0	0	440
Munaadel	Catch Me by Nine	4	3	0	0	0	0
Mymich	Dixie Ghost	3	9	2	2	0	87,574
New Trieste	Lovlier Linda	4	1	0	0	0	1,500
Nor'wester	Pacific Squall	2	1	0	0	0	2,280
Offtheoldblock	Chip	3	5	1	1	0	19,250
Olmodavor	Corrazona	4	4	1	2	0	241,080
Open Flirt	With a Wink	2	2	0	1	0	9,460
Parrott Bay	Agotaras	6	7	0	3	1	63,350
Passing Shot	Aucilla	4	10	3	2	2	362,637
Patriot's Pride	Windmill Point	3	6	1	0	0	10,414
Perfect Cut	Crystal Shard	3	9	3	2	1	111,148
Political Risk	Two Altazano	3	3	2	1	0	57,372
Possibility	Personal Ensign	3	2	1	0	0	28,350
Proxy Statement	Deputation	4	2	0	0	0	1,500
Que Polo	Heartbreak	4	1	0	0	1	1,500
Quick Temper	Halo America	2	2	1	0	1	32,455
Race On Green	Grab the Green	5	3	0	0	0	620
Racey Dreamer	Dahlia's Dreamer	4	4	2	0	0	23,400
Red Wing Evan	Envied	4	6	2	1	1	49,060
Renaissance Lady	Storm Beauty	2	9	1	4	0	111,850
Rock Slide	Prospectors Delite	5	7	2	1	0	169,390
Romantic Comedy	Zagora	3	6	1	0	3	36,190
Rosberg	Bosra Sham	2	2	1	0	0	26,180
Sa Ad	Zakiyya	6	12	5	2	1	73,528
Sandra's Song	Waterside	5	2	0	0	1	4,400
Schwarzenel	Foret Noire	2	7	0	1	0	7,800
Seattle Weekend	Lassie's Lady	2	4	0	0	0	5,455
Seeking the Glory	Seeking Regina	3	3	1	1	0	35,380
Shake Off	Shake the Yoke (GB)	2	2	1	0	0	24,600
Shanghied	Fleet Road	2	3	0	0	0	1,290
Shaniko	Sapphire n' Silk	2	2	0	1	0	11,940
Sharps 'n Flats	Nine Keys	4	2	2	0	0	18,444
Sheer Luck	Vegas Prospector	2	6	2	1	2	79,280
Sign of Love	Fran's Valentine	3	3	0	0	0	1,980
Snake Mountain	Coup de Genie	5	5	3	0	0	159,825
Spin Control	Prospinsky	3	6	3	0	2	79,310
Spring Affair	Powder Bowl	3	2	0	1	0	3,800
Starindy (GB)	Star of Broadway	2	1	0	0	0	840
Suave	Urbane	2	5	1	2	0	41,355
Swing Lord	Dance With Grace	5	8	1	0	3	19,400
Take a Dip	Immerse	9	7	0	0	0	496
Tell J	Prospinsky	4	10	2	1	0	30,200
Tigress Woods	Tigress Woman	4	11	1	0	0	27,298
Tippecanoe	Mousse Glacee (FR)	3	2	0	0	0	700
Trident House	Amizette	3	9	1	1	0	22,100
Twoindytoo	Two Altazano	4	11	1	2	4	19,369
U.S. Indy	Top Secret	3	3	0	0	0	1,580
Under Caution	Coldheartedcat	2	3	1	0	0	18,300
Vintage Champagne	Meadow Star	3	1	0	0	0	0
Walkes Spring	Whiffling	4	5	0	1	0	10,380
War Marshall	U R Unforgetable	2	1	0	1	0	9,000
Winter Glitter	Snow Forest	6	1	0	0	0	130
With Ability	Withallprobability	5	1	0	0	0	0
Yell	Wild Applause	3	9	3	1	1	408,527

Dynaformer, Dk B H (1985)
By Roberto – Andover Way, by His Majesty
147 Performers, 76 winning performers, $7,788,577 total earnings

Progeny	Mare	Age	Sts	1st	2d	3d	Money Won
American Falcon	Standard Equipment	7	1	0	0	0	270
Arremlee	Mama Dearly	6	3	0	0	1	3,271
Baptize	Screening Room	5	1	0	0	0	0
Barney's Mistress	Chief Mistress	5	13	1	2	2	67,169
Bat Mobile	Sherzarcat	3	3	2	0	1	52,400

Progeny	Mare	Age	Sts	1st	2d	3d	Won
Beauty On Duty	K. O. Kathy	3	6	1	0	1	34,420
Bicentennial	Cardonessa	5	1	0	0	0	0
Bigado	Lailee	8	3	0	0	0	0
Bijou Queen	Prebend	3	4	0	1	3	26,000
Blazing Fury	Blazing Kadie	5	4	0	1	0	13,520
Blue Finally	May We	3	8	2	2	1	64,410
Boreas	Blue Grass Baby	7	2	0	0	0	138
Briteliteinthenite	Forbes Sparkler	3	7	1	1	0	30,469
Bulacan	Specificity	7	11	1	1	0	9,018
Calling All Angels	Demon Within	2	5	0	0	3	10,560
Captain Jackson	Wee Miss Bee	3	1	0	0	0	0
Captainofindustry	Regal Mitterand	4	9	1	0	4	37,730
Charge	Wonderlan	3	4	2	0	0	69,113
Chouette Player	Subtle Raise	6	1	0	0	0	59
Corsita	Pareja	3	4	0	2	1	26,740
Crafty Case	Crafty Example	8	8	1	0	1	8,500
Danceyourheartout	Fancy Stockings	3	11	2	0	2	24,130
Dark Prince	Wild Royal	4	1	0	0	0	0
Dark Whisper	Rosalie's Treat	3	5	2	0	0	52,980
Deadly Force	Country Chelsie	8	3	0	0	0	0
Decimate	Ananda	4	6	0	0	0	7,060
Departing Dynamo	All Abord	6	21	4	3	4	32,706
Dinah's Pearls	Diamonds n Pearls	3	7	0	3	0	24,660
Don'tasktheprice	Pretty Pricey	5	17	2	1	2	13,123
Dyna Del	Dance With Del	3	7	2	4	0	62,100
Dyna King	Rekindled	6	18	2	4	4	9,845
Dyna Mae	Refer	4	4	0	0	1	3,250
Dyna Mojo	Our Sun Queen	3	2	0	0	0	368
Dyna My Darlin	Twang	4	1	0	0	0	86
Dyna Penny	Violet Lady	4	12	0	3	2	31,370
Dynability	Fallibility	7	5	2	1	0	44,500
Dynaboy	Oh Boy Valoy	8	7	0	1	1	4,110
Dynafire	Ring of Fire	2	4	1	1	1	54,218
Dynaheart	Maple Heart	3	3	0	0	0	0
Dynalympic	Miswila	2	3	0	0	1	6,165
Dynameaux	Moving Picture	5	5	0	2	1	75,670
Dynameesch	Meesch	6	4	0	0	0	2,070
Dynamia	Shelly River	2	1	0	1	0	4,180
Dynamic Lady	Quick Courtship	4	7	1	0	1	27,440
Dynamic Lisa	Ashley Lindsey	4	6	2	1	0	108,830
Dynamic Performer	Plenty Smart	7	4	0	0	0	0
Dynamic Trick	Pretty Tricky	8	1	0	0	0	150
Dynamism	Charming Ballerina (IRE)	4	3	0	0	0	0
Dynamistic	Sara Six Pack	5	1	0	0	0	0
Dynamite Cocktail	Tutu	3	10	1	1	1	57,030
Dynamite Vic	Dixie Accent	7	8	1	0	2	20,450
Dynamometer	Fly North	3	2	1	0	1	30,140
Dynareign	Sovereign Mistress	3	11	2	2	3	57,855
Dynarhythm	Relic Rhythm	3	4	1	0	1	35,640
Dynaruler	Greek Wedding	3	5	1	0	1	31,940
Dynastyle	Be in Style	3	7	1	1	0	27,640
Dynasure	Noddy's Halo	3	12	3	1	2	62,883
Dynasurf	Hawaiian Bold	8	13	2	1	5	14,154
Dynatron	Such a Nut	8	3	1	0	0	2,488
Dynavolt	Revolution Leader	6	2	0	0	0	0
Dynawave	Warta	4	15	2	3	0	36,470
Dynaway	Lateral	2	5	1	0	1	20,369
Dyno Dancer	Flamboyance	3	9	3	3	1	1,154,020
Echelon	Sue's Last Dance	3	5	0	0	0	2,520
Fair Winds	Galunpe (IRE)	5	8	1	0	0	4,905
Film Critic	Crafty But Sweet	3	8	0	1	1	10,595
Film Maker	Secretariat Lass	4	3	1	0	0	38,558
Forest Lullaby	Miss Du Bois	3	9	4	2	2	457,220
Forever Now	Noontime Jet	3	3	0	1	0	6,280
Formal Affair	Madame Adolphe	3	7	0	2	2	24,060
Fortuitous	Red Ember	5	7	0	0	0	780
Gratz Park	Vermont Connection	3	2	0	1	0	15,000
Great Bloom	Flying Nightengale	2	3	0	2	1	20,600
Greyhame	Lady Skywalker	5	4	2	0	1	62,720
Ground Hero	Motel Swing	4	13	1	2	2	27,705
Gusto Forzado	Moonflute	3	1	0	0	0	2,800
Gym Kid	Pleasure Bought	8	1	0	0	0	184
Harvey Girl	Could Be	2	5	1	0	1	25,200
Heat of the Night	With Gratitude	3	4	1	1	0	33,720
Heptagone	Dark Heat	8	8	0	0	0	270
Intemperate	Seventies	5	11	4	1	2	52,373
Intern	Crazy Canard	3	5	1	0	0	13,360
Island Dynamo	Medicine Woman	7	7	1	2	1	52,338
Jamessonjimmyjames	Burmese	4	8	2	1	3	17,684
Jordyn Macoma	Mollywaki	4	7	0	0	0	967
Komba	Mysterel's Lady	4	2	0	1	1	13,270
Lover Come Back	Grace and Savour	8	18	2	5	3	30,176
Lucky Dynahoosier	Foolish Beauty	3	1	0	0	0	2,880
Makeup Artist	Lucky Lady Dancer	6	13	2	2	2	13,587
Maliziosa	Deux Anes (GB)	3	3	2	1	0	128,100
Martinis Atmidnite	Kuda	4	9	0	1	3	64,005
Maybe Rocco	Oh Sweet Thing	5	5	0	1	3	6,720
McDynamo	Linetta	3	14	2	2	2	32,870
Mezzaluna	Rondonia	6	3	3	0	0	252,025
Milestone Victory	Dolce Amore	4	3	0	0	0	371
	Sovereign Mistress	2	5	1	0	1	36,678
Minimalist	Gdansk's Honour	4	1	0	0	0	380
Miss Kate Rusby	Memories of Madrid	3	2	0	0	0	0
More Ribbons	Royal Setting	4	9	2	1	1	50,496
Mortgage Man	Come Dancing	4	13	2	0	2	68,238
Mt. Kilimanjaro	Explosive Kate	3	4	0	0	0	3,600
Mystery Giver	Ioya	5	10	2	2	1	256,260
Najjm	Azusa	6	9	0	3	2	28,550
Nandina	J'Aime Jeblis	4	9	0	0	0	404
Neutron	Sparkle Colony	2	4	2	0	0	30,268
New Spirits	Canadian Mischief	3	2	0	0	0	360
No Smoochin	No Huggy No Kissy	5	5	0	0	0	720
Not You Me	Icanseeyounow	3	5	0	0	0	897
Notion	Carefree Flyer	7	19	1	6	0	11,911
Nuvem	National Finalist	3	6	1	1	1	42,760
Oakhurst	Blading Saddle	9	9	2	1	0	11,060
Ocean Silk	Mambo Jambo	3	1	0	1	0	30,000
Omit the Dividend	Sovereign Mistress	5	5	0	1	2	12,880
Oyster Cove	Pearl Essence	4	5	1	1	1	28,140
Pacewaster	Haste Ye Back	10	19	1	2	3	6,538
Perfect Drift	Nice Gal	4	8	5	0	0	1,505,388
Piranhurst	Sovereign Mistress	8	6	1	0	1	11,124
Provobay	Del Sovereign	3	4	0	0	1	4,200
Purple Hills	Gray Cashmere	4	9	1	0	2	27,440
Rare Bush	Nutbush One	3	6	1	1	1	27,840
Rasby	Hawaiian Lady	8	13	4	3	3	62,125
Raving	Pelerine	4	3	2	0	0	29,630
Reformer	Evangelical	2	3	0	0	0	3,360
Regal Dynasty	Troubles Trouble	7	1	0	0	1	6,545
Riskaverse	The Bink	4	8	2	1	2	336,324
Sand Springs	Lovely Martha	3	7	4	1	0	451,390
Scorching	Turcomedy	4	9	1	0	3	19,431
Shackelford	Pocketfulof Posies	7	6	1	1	1	5,186
Shapes and Shadows	Isla Mujeres	3	7	0	0	2	58,638
Short Squeeze	Blond Moment	4	14	1	4	0	77,950
Sniper	Sparkle Colony	4	4	0	0	0	4,094
Soul of Wit	Nutbush One	5	1	0	0	0	265
Splendid Form	Splendid Try	6	9	0	1	1	7,450
Starrer	To the Hunt	5	2	2	0	0	300,000
Terraforming	Rose Helen	8	7	0	0	1	814
Thebannerflies	Hoist the Banner	3	1	0	0	0	0
Time to Dyne	Timely (GB)	4	7	1	1	2	20,330
Totally Platinum	Hoist the Banner	2	6	1	2	0	40,900
Transition Time	Sharp Tradition	4	1	0	0	0	0
Turf Surfer	Eloping	6	11	2	1	2	33,530
Unique	Sarajen	3	2	0	0	0	103
Vergennes	Shareefa	8	2	0	0	0	1,560
Vive Le Roi	Cecelia Tudor	5	1	0	0	0	95
Weldlock	Explodent Design	7	14	2	2	3	24,555
Whenthewindblows	Lovelorn Lady	3	5	0	0	1	9,700
Winendynme	Elway Season (IRE)	2	5	2	0	1	66,280
Winged Sumac	Nimble Tread	3	11	1	2	1	23,870

El Prado, Gr H (1989)
By Sadler's Wells – Lady Capulet, by Sir Ivor

192 Performers, 106 winning performers, $7,758,497 total earnings

Progeny	Mare	Age	Sts	1st	2d	3d	Money Won
Academic Ash	College Road	4	7	0	0	1	10,100
Alie's Del Prado	Highland Strike	2	3	0	1	1	7,130
Arch of Triumph	Arches of Gold	3	7	1	1	0	27,280
Are You Home	Mi Louisa	3	8	3	1	1	49,245
Artie Schiller	Hidden Light	2	5	2	1	1	88,275
Avenida Lady	Saturn's Image	4	3	0	0	1	4,785
Babypaws	Hazel Wand	4	2	0	0	0	0
Bermuda Isle	Gone for Gusto	2	1	0	0	0	1,500
Big Gold Martini	Javelin Catcher	6	14	1	1	0	7,285
Blue Guru	Ruffle My Feathers	5	9	3	2	1	103,380
Boca Flyer	Bocamis	4	1	0	0	0	0
Border Blues	Miss the Blues	3	6	1	0	1	26,140
Borrego	Sweet as Honey	2	4	2	0	0	63,300
Bright and Shiny	Sunburst (GB)	2	4	1	0	0	20,030
Bruheria	Miss Witchcraft	3	2	1	0	1	35,760
Calma Prado	Calm Expression	5	13	1	2	2	46,044
Candeias	Bold n Racy	8	13	1	2	2	8,596
Capture D' Oro	Baby Rabbit	3	2	1	0	0	19,560
Catchaser	Do Not Panic	5	8	0	3	0	12,560
Chameleon	Polly's Rumor	3	5	0	1	2	13,040
Checkthisgroove	Flora Spring	3	4	2	0	1	27,300
Chelsea Park	Island Fire	2	1	0	0	1	1,870
Chindi	Rousing	9	7	1	2	2	118,931
Christina Sanchez	Cope's Light	3	2	1	1	0	13,260
Chuckie's in Love	Crusie	3	11	4	3	2	42,638
Clever Crawford	Remda	4	18	4	4	2	88,980
Cloakof Vagueness	Moving Picture	3	10	2	5	2	200,145
Compete	Pete's Heiress	3	3	1	0	1	20,240
Corning	Painted Portrait	4	5	2	0	0	10,380
Costa Nomore	No Cost	8	6	0	0	1	436
Cowpet Bay	Keeling	2	3	1	0	0	3,240
Crimson and Roses	Flower Garden	3	10	2	3	1	109,800

Progeny	Mare	Age	Sts	1st	2d	3d	Won
Crown Pacific	Runaway Royalty	3	2	0	0	1	1,155
Crystal Lyric	Lady Brigand	4	1	0	0	0	0
Destiny's Design	Lady Brigand	3	7	1	0	0	10,085
Donna's Hope	Lil's Crown	2	1	0	0	0	2,100
Dr. Bombay	Valid Design	3	9	1	2	1	13,724
Drawing a Blank	Ivory Princess (IRE)	7	9	2	1	3	72,240
Driftwood Lodge	Luke's Drifter	3	7	3	1	2	63,040
Dwendi	Stately Lady	5	13	4	1	1	40,924
Eagle Bend	Cross of Iron	5	1	0	0	1	640
El Brette	L and n Bride	4	14	3	4	2	59,154
El Caballito	Newborn	4	1	0	0	0	0
El Case	Miss Mauna Lisa	4	11	0	1	0	1,874
El Charro	Peanut Cowgirl	2	6	1	2	0	22,025
El Cielo	Only Above	9	2	1	0	1	36,120
El Cisc	Bazzie	3	11	1	3	2	21,003
El Crusader	Flying Relaunch	4	9	1	2	2	32,042
El Destiny	Proper Destiny	4	4	0	0	1	1,600
El General	Valid Victress	4	9	0	1	2	33,852
El Giuliani	Eileen Dover	4	2	0	0	0	168
El Prado Diamond	Diamonds Again	3	13	2	3	0	22,130
El Prado Essence	Quadrahope	6	7	2	2	0	220,108
El Prado in Action	Gold Action	5	15	1	1	3	28,720
El Prado Light	Light Tina	5	4	0	0	1	2,280
El Prado Rob	Jurisprudence	2	6	2	0	1	93,054
El Prado Star	Mistress (CHI)	3	2	1	0	0	40,116
El Prado's Delight	Robertina	5	1	0	0	0	0
El Prado's Gal	Cazzy B.	2	5	0	0	0	3,750
El Prado's Plata	Diamondsandrubys	3	15	3	1	2	34,030
El Prados Treasure	Racing Treasure	5	11	0	0	0	658
El Providential	Providential Manor	5	5	0	2	0	11,400
El Silverado	Pillow Fight	2	1	0	0	0	1,290
El Swava	Northern Swava	3	1	0	0	0	420
Erin Hall	Wendys Terms	5	7	1	1	0	8,468
Eugapae	Revolution Leader	3	4	1	1	0	10,670
Exaggerate This	Palana	2	2	0	0	0	0
Exceptionally	Swingin Nickel	2	1	0	0	0	1,818
Exclusive Hopper	Eurobid	3	10	2	4	0	43,570
Federal Case	Tough Case	5	8	1	2	0	10,376
Ferene	Rapid Rosa	6	4	0	0	0	105
Fort Prado	Fort Pond	2	2	0	0	1	4,640
Four Oclock Ruby	Red Light Girl	4	10	1	1	1	21,680
Free Agent On Ice	Bubbly On Ice	6	6	0	0	2	9,904
Frisco Belle	Runaway Ashleigh	3	9	3	3	0	126,300
Game Day	Figi Bidders	3	5	0	0	2	9,290
Garden Dance	Clearthedancefloor	4	5	0	1	1	15,810
Gavro	Bunbeg	3	9	1	3	0	84,916
Gun Barrel	Wild Warning	8	5	0	1	0	1,871
Halloween Fun	On Hand	3	3	0	0	1	3,650
High Volt Jolt	Bold Blast	3	3	0	1	0	16,976
Historical Drive	Keep It Legal	3	2	0	0	0	320
Humberto	Sweets for All	7	13	2	3	1	22,155
Iliamna	Well Bred Lass	5	4	0	0	0	255
Image	Shared Reflections	5	13	4	2	2	135,224
Italian Pride	Florenza	7	12	0	1	2	14,426
Julie's Prize	Julie Mis	3	9	4	1	1	202,095
Just Four Austin	All Ability	4	15	4	1	4	58,940
Kitten's Joy	Kitten's First	2	4	2	1	0	80,115
Kristine's King	Santa Cristina	3	14	3	1	3	62,608
La Prada	Amarata	4	11	1	2	0	14,465
La Prado	Crama	4	9	2	3	1	20,620
La Star	A Billion Stars	4	3	0	0	0	70
Lady Drama	Proper Darling	4	11	1	4	3	47,497
Lady Livingston	Vienna Knickers	2	2	0	0	0	390
Little Miss Pamela	Top Tip	3	5	1	1	0	49,490
Longhorn Blues	Explosive Ele	3	6	1	1	0	26,220
Lusty Latin	Scarlet Ann	4	6	0	0	0	6,084
Lyrical Prado	Lyrical Princess	4	9	1	2	2	57,790
Magnolia Park	Her Name in Lights	4	11	1	0	3	21,107
Matter of Pride	Cyclops Sue	5	6	0	0	0	509
Max's Friend	Individual Spirit	5	10	2	2	2	49,970
McKinney	La Milibucks	5	12	2	1	4	89,679
Medaglia d'Oro	Cappucino Bay	4	5	3	2	0	1,990,000
Mexican Moonlight	Nellie Custis	3	16	3	5	1	116,618
Middleworth Bay	Runaway Ashleigh	7	2	0	0	0	680
Mom's Little Guy	Cove Hill Miss	9	9	3	0	0	21,829
Mona Lisa Lady	Artful Player	4	6	2	1	0	20,996
Mr. Livingston	Vienna Knickers	6	10	2	0	2	68,030
Mt. Ouray	Fay Morgan	6	9	1	1	1	11,649
My Amandari	Madame Adolphe	2	3	1	0	0	33,600
My Eugenia	Hawaiian Comic	5	2	0	0	0	4,200
Natural Image	Natural Elegance	3	4	2	0	0	32,400
Northern Darkness	Hot Times Are Here	4	12	0	1	1	4,363
Ohforcraftsakes	Cagey Baby	4	4	0	1	0	11,780
Onella	Perfect Red	3	8	1	0	1	16,290
Our Joy	Landholder	2	2	0	0	0	1,140
P J Prado	Silk Pajamas	3	1	0	0	0	0
Paco El Prado	Accadia Rocket	6	8	0	3	0	12,284
Palatine	Slide by (GB)	3	11	4	2	1	28,975
Phillies Dream	Blossom Time	4	7	3	1	0	26,660
Point of Flight	V Formation	2	2	0	0	1	7,020
Portable Power	Darned Alarming	3	7	0	0	0	1,230

Progeny	Mare	Age	Sts	1st	2d	3d	Won
Power of Elprado	Lovers Power	6	9	2	0	2	21,640
Prada Shoes	April Fifteenth	3	1	0	0	0	0
Prado Lady	Jaded Lady	3	3	1	0	1	14,700
Prado Maximus	Copelan's Charm	3	1	0	0	0	780
Prado Power	Stage Baby	6	14	4	3	2	56,195
Prado Queen	Queen Ellie	4	3	0	0	0	438
Prado Wells	New Season	8	15	2	1	5	25,345
Prado's Lass	Leary Lass	3	8	1	1	0	23,458
Prado's Picture	Losthepicture	3	9	1	0	2	8,839
Pranna	Anna's Halo	3	19	1	3	3	22,305
Precious Prado	Practice	4	15	1	0	3	11,811
Prince Prado	Hardi Lady	3	11	1	5	3	63,895
Princeapecia	Parrish Empress	4	7	1	1	1	12,308
Princess Pelona	Peachtree City	3	4	2	1	0	56,172
Pro Prado	Mama's Pro	2	3	2	0	0	53,784
Proper Prado	Proper Banner	2	9	2	1	3	100,571
Pyrite Lady	Carol Jane	4	13	0	4	6	24,239
Quizzle	Glory's Ghost	3	5	0	2	0	13,200
Raglan Road	J'Aime Jeblis	3	2	0	0	0	0
Rahy Time	From Time to Time	3	6	0	0	0	1,120
Rainbow Smile	Stop the Rain	4	5	0	0	1	7,285
Rainy Parade	September Rain	4	14	5	2	3	89,628
Remagen Bridge	Fine Impression	5	16	0	4	1	12,080
Rhonesquarterswish	Pertinent Wish	8	3	2	0	1	46,420
Richochet	Attach	2	1	0	0	0	2,700
Royalton	Miss Sanmar	4	7	0	0	0	5,520
Ruggles Road	Rivermaid Dancing	3	10	0	1	1	7,435
Run to the Border	Pixies Lass	4	7	2	0	1	26,290
Sabre of Silver	Tough Blade	5	16	2	0	2	95,100
Santa's Elf	Santaclausiscoming	4	2	0	0	0	0
Sayitlikeumeanit	Bounding Boldly	3	1	0	0	0	0
Senor Prado	Forbes Sparkler	6	16	1	0	4	8,693
Senor Swinger	Smooth Smile	3	11	3	0	2	361,290
Sensible	Magari	3	1	0	0	0	340
Seven On Friday	Torch the Track	4	2	0	0	0	0
Seventh Choice	Personal Choice	4	3	0	0	0	4,056
Shaconage	Carita Tostada (CHI)	3	6	2	0	0	113,822
Shamus Shea	Renewable	6	5	0	0	5	21,700
She's Got It	Hanque Bankque	4	13	0	2	1	6,216
Silver Meadow	Cobey's Girl	3	3	1	1	0	21,960
Simmer	Hotunderthecollar	7	8	1	1	1	37,887
Sir Prado	Regally Refined (IRE)	5	11	2	1	1	17,926
Some Buttercup	Try Trading	3	1	0	0	0	0
Soo Much	Smile and Cry	4	3	0	0	0	2,595
Spanish Artist	Summer Sketches	3	14	0	2	1	16,750
Spanish Eyes	Bedford Street	5	14	4	1	2	64,075
Spanish Johnny	It's Windy	4	12	2	2	2	39,954
Spanish Secrets	Secret Vista	2	3	0	0	0	1,595
Superfines Prado	Commercial Diamond	5	14	1	1	2	30,571
Texas Sandman	Retsina Meli	6	4	0	0	0	166
The Gray Spur	Soft Reply	5	15	1	2	0	9,102
The Plains	Jennifer Elaine	3	4	0	0	0	0
The Real Jewel	Arashi Dancer	5	15	5	1	2	52,990
The Sherminator	Humming Sound	3	10	1	0	1	41,695
This Is That	Ask Anita	2	1	0	0	1	5,400
Timo	Elocat's Burglar	2	5	3	2	0	153,515
Tomadache	Too Loud	7	6	0	0	0	0
Tomprado	Crystal Woods	4	10	3	1	1	26,860
Toogie too Shoes	Toogie Too	3	6	1	0	2	21,310
Town Ghost	Tough Case	6	17	0	0	2	3,925
Twilight Parade	Glory's Light	3	4	0	0	0	5,020
Undisputed Terms	Wendys Terms	4	4	0	0	0	80
Whitehorse Pass	Boomtown Beauty	7	2	0	0	0	287
Whytwocayman	Cayman Queen	4	7	0	1	1	5,934
Willing Coalition	Nabla	2	2	0	0	0	2,250
Willy B. Silver	Buck Ridge Green	7	5	2	0	0	6,755
Winspear	Nay Nay Renay	3	11	1	5	1	35,823
Yagudin	Mythical Status	3	8	1	2	1	44,874
Zach Slim and Eddy	Natalie Natalie	2	6	0	0	1	5,130

Langfuhr, B H (1992)
By Danzig – Sweet Briar Too, by Briartic
164 Performers, 94 winning performers, $6,675,994 total earnings

Progeny	Mare	Age	Sts	1st	2d	3d	Money Won
American Falcon	Standard Equipment	6	7	1	1	3	$52,735
Acadian Style	Profound Peace	3	1	1	0	0	4,200
Albarino	Ms. Tenacious	2	4	0	0	0	1,077
Allison's Hope	White Lace	2	2	0	0	0	195
Allocation	Seeking the Circle	4	11	1	1	1	32,305
Amiable Amy	Quiet M. D.	3	4	1	1	0	39,660
Anthonia	Cool Excellence	3	12	3	1	3	120,530
Anyplace Anytime	Stubborn Star	3	9	0	2	4	28,345
Asmokeafterdinner	Best of Friends	3	16	3	0	4	70,827
Baby Star	Little Irish Nut	4	4	0	0	3	2,126
Barnsy	Rose Colored Lady	2	3	1	1	0	36,020
Be Fuhr Real	Imallzealedup	3	11	1	2	0	11,110
Biogio's Dream	Fois Gras	3	3	0	1	0	9,548
Boylan	Irish Shenanigans	3	7	3	1	3	32,225

Progeny	Mare	Age	Sts	1st	2d	3d	Money Won
Brightest Hour	Super Jamie	3	10	0	2	2	12,061
Casino Bound	Casino Babe	3	2	0	0	0	195
Chap Up	Icy Time	4	8	0	2	0	9,898
Constitution	Kentucky Lill	4	10	2	0	1	47,920
Corporate Chalenge	Summer Storm	3	13	2	2	4	36,799
Crafty Dan	Crafty Sarre	2	3	0	0	1	1,639
Creed's Fury	Social Creed	4	7	0	1	2	2,472
Crisp Decision	Dorky	3	1	0	0	0	340
Currahee	A Number One	4	7	1	2	1	8,336
Dancing Baba	Tricky Melody	2	2	0	0	0	3,550
Dawns Early Dancer	A New Dawning	2	5	1	1	0	6,616
Defuhr	Defreeze	2	7	1	3	3	68,535
Diamonds and Fuhr	Cap Diamonds	2	7	0	0	1	1,210
Ding's Thing	Crew Leader	2	4	3	0	0	56,660
Dixie Feline	Southern Cat	4	12	3	0	2	34,250
Dream of Dashing	Dream Mary	3	14	2	1	2	66,710
Engineered	Niner	3	6	2	1	0	39,800
Expresso Love	Donut's Image	4	10	2	1	1	55,439
Far and Near	Close At Hand	4	6	0	1	2	25,806
Fashion Proof	Hollow Gal	3	12	1	2	4	44,858
Fillygris	Silvita	3	1	1	0	0	8,550
Flip	Timeless Girl	3	3	0	1	1	13,060
Formia	Because I'm Gold	4	15	2	0	2	13,931
Fuhr Elise	Perfolia	3	13	1	3	3	22,130
Fuhr Ore	Iron Obsession	3	7	1	3	1	31,280
Fuhr Real	Fundraising	3	4	0	2	0	6,100
Fuhrfy	Redintheface	3	4	0	0	0	268
Fuhrious Fraulein	Golden Image	3	1	0	0	0	530
Fuhrline	D'Auria	4	5	0	1	2	5,200
Fuhrluck	Singular Broad	2	2	0	0	0	0
Fuhrmidable	My Teddies	3	7	0	1	1	5,190
Fuhry	Convertida (ARG)	4	18	2	2	4	28,840
Fuzzy Star	Vivid Impression	4	9	2	4	1	80,650
Ghannam	Katerina Key	4	6	3	0	0	64,120
Givemethejackpot	Jurajackpot	2	5	1	1	1	13,265
Graypast	Back to the Past	2	2	0	0	0	0
Great Commander	Goggles	3	14	5	2	2	70,573
Gulf of Gdansk	Truly a Ransom	2	6	1	2	2	42,000
Heidi's Secret	Secret	3	7	0	2	1	53,580
Hello Gitana	Hello Fanny	2	6	1	2	2	23,440
Herr Apparant	King's Daughter	2	2	0	0	0	600
Hugger	Periphery	3	4	0	1	0	1,966
Hugh's Choice	Late Sailing	4	1	0	1	0	2,000
Idalou	Trendy	4	10	0	1	0	2,122
Idareya	San Empery	2	4	0	0	0	240
Ididarod Trail	Runaway Smoke	4	10	2	2	0	6,970
Il Capriccio	Lost the Code	2	6	0	1	2	18,640
Imperialism	Bodhavista	2	11	3	3	1	74,605
Indiana Knight	Mary Sloan	4	3	0	0	0	540
Inner Drive	Don't Combo	3	4	0	0	0	0
Instead of Red	Redintheface	2	1	0	0	0	0
Jamie's Bad Boy	Good for Her	4	15	1	1	1	11,078
Katie Lang	Cole Code	3	1	0	0	0	1,100
Keeping the Gold	Five Gold Stars	3	6	4	1	0	140,960
Kingmaker	Esscorrie	4	3	2	0	0	47,010
Klubber Lang	Black Tie Lady	3	13	0	2	3	29,200
Lady Lang	Lady Avalon	4	1	0	0	0	1,680
Ladye Langfuhr	Truly a Ransom	3	9	1	2	2	14,840
Lake of Bays	Secret	4	7	0	0	0	4,797
Landana	Gold Issue	3	5	1	0	0	17,346
Landler	Delightful	4	11	7	3	0	95,945
Lang's Glory	Get the Glory	4	1	0	0	0	107
Langburg	Marienburg	2	5	1	1	0	63,357
Langfuhr's Allure	Sultry Allure	3	14	2	0	0	10,257
Langfuhr's Magic	Kyle's Magic	2	5	1	1	1	17,300
Languissa	Lasting Secret	3	7	1	0	0	5,374
Last Answer	Victorious Answer	3	9	2	1	0	108,951
Layn the Smackdown	Radiant Belle	3	14	2	4	1	38,859
Leisa B Ware	Pancho's Secretary	4	1	0	0	0	0
Leniently	Itsoeasy	3	6	1	0	1	33,006
Licenseapproved	Got the License	3	2	1	0	0	5,974
Lily Langfuhr	Punch a Dragon	2	2	0	0	0	420
Lloydtown	Sylvette	3	4	1	0	0	31,336
Long For	Bella Button	3	4	1	0	0	5,083
Lord Burleigh	Palace Lady	4	7	4	0	0	71,524
Lord Langfuhr	Palace Lady	3	5	1	0	1	33,540
Lord Louis	San Empery	3	9	2	4	1	70,500
Love the Princess	Willulovemetomorow	3	12	0	4	2	19,140
Lovely Discovery	Latin Discovery	3	11	1	1	2	7,304
Lovetheprospect	Willulovemetomorow	2	3	0	0	0	870
Lukfata Louis	Molly's Ghost	3	5	1	0	0	18,600
Marilina	Diaspora	4	8	2	0	1	8,636
Mary Langfuhr	Marissiya (GB)	4	4	1	0	0	4,800
Mind of Gold	Flying Honors	4	5	0	1	0	4,220
Miz Lynne Kelly	My Trim	4	12	3	1	1	32,820
Mobil	Kinetigal	3	9	5	2	1	753,405
Mother Molly Boo	Boo Boo Molly	3	5	0	1	0	3,917
Muskatello	Muskrat Suzie	3	2	0	0	0	3,636
My Buddy My Pal	Gunner Bay	2	2	0	0	0	2,700
My Legal Alien	Comedy Court	4	12	1	5	0	74,900
My Man Alex	Senorita Constanza	3	1	0	0	0	0
Narayan	Sunitya	3	17	1	2	2	16,314
Nelsonstreetnancy	Fireinhereyes	3	7	0	0	0	578
Nina's Limelight	Sudden Appearance	2	2	0	0	0	
Nine Carats	Numberonetreasure	2	2	0	0	0	3,636
No Happy Love	Cuthershort	2	6	1	2	1	11,580
Not So Rough R N	Rough M. D.	3	1	0	1	0	7,280
O'Malley	Miss Ireland	4	12	3	2	1	46,530
One and Done	Jamie Joy Deb	3	7	1	2	0	25,970
Pacific Spell	Malibu Magic	4	5	1	1	0	8,970
Paradise Dancer	Ruckus Ridge	3	3	3	0	0	36,900
Parallax	Ticky Tacky	3	5	1	3	0	43,760
Pavlovsk	Money Madam	4	12	2	1	2	62,770
Peef	C. Sharp	3	10	1	2	1	118,472
Prime Agenda	Worthy	3	4	0	0	0	0
Prince of Rhodes	Afirmada	3	6	1	1	0	10,639
Princess Forever	Sassy Ego	4	8	1	1	0	21,139
Push My Buttons	Great Pass	3	3	2	1	0	24,620
Raquette Lake	Fappies Cosy Miss	4	10	3	0	1	19,836
Resplendence	Exellensea	3	6	0	2	2	14,345
Rich Tradition	Homemade Cookie	3	10	2	1	1	10,410
Riel	Renegade Style	4	1	0	0	0	0
Rudi J.	Hilarious Square	4	1	0	0	0	0
Run Rayma Run	Jeanie's Gift	3	7	0	0	0	3,622
Runbeforethewind	Exploding Tower	3	5	1	1	0	10,410
Salty Langfuhn	Over Your Shoulder	2	2	1	0	0	23,526
Saluda	Our Liebling	2	3	0	0	0	3,636
Second Tuesday	Rare Heat	4	9	2	0	2	49,760
Seductive Lady	You'll B Impressed	2	7	2	1	1	36,020
Seven Gold Gems	Seven Gold Stones	4	16	2	1	4	40,500
Shore Breaker	Sunburst (GB)	3	14	2	3	3	42,185
Simbah	Moonsilver	4	1	0	0	0	0
Sir Claude	Queen Randi	3	9	1	0	2	8,246
Sister Star	Little Irish Nut	2	6	1	1	3	39,955
Six Sexy Sisters	Kathie's Colleen	2	2	2	0	0	140,218
Soccer Kylie	Hey How You	2	4	1	0	1	14,990
Spilled Honey	Honey Sipper	4	14	4	5	0	63,610
Strausberg	Classic Imp	3	11	4	0	2	47,528
Summer Stone	Rubies for Alicia	3	12	3	0	2	45,040
Superlang	Super Me	3	14	0	1	3	26,300
Sweet Maria	Marienburg	3	2	1	0	0	18,840
Sweetgum	Wild Linda	2	2	1	0	1	45,288
Talk Show Tony	Golden Vale	2	2	0	0	0	700
Tarfu	Southern Cat	2	1	0	0	0	0
Tasty Lace	A Taste for Lace	4	4	1	1	1	13,130
Theflash	Filet	2	1	0	0	0	145
Tobie Lang	Tobie Ruckus	3	12	1	3	1	40,018
Tony's Birthday	Saratern	2	1	0	0	0	115
Traci's Wild	Wild for Traci	4	9	0	1	1	16,015
Tulla	Princess J V	3	1	0	1	0	2,700
Tullow	Our Colleen	4	4	2	0	0	10,230
Turn On	Dazzlo	2	3	0	0	1	4,070
Wando	Kathie's Colleen	3	8	5	1	1	2,017,323
Weho	Mary Tavy	3	11	1	0	3	25,840
What Fuhr	Jetsetyet	3	6	2	0	1	10,275
White Flame	White Lace	4	5	0	0	0	2,214
Wildforyou	Wild Linda	3	6	0	0	2	25,277
Wildwood Flower	Dial a Trick	2	3	3	0	0	67,100
Winning Note	Never an Angel	3	5	0	0	0	0
Wrzeszcz	Petite d'Accord	2	1	0	0	0	1,275
Z Z's Destiny	Wooden Pudden	3	1	0	0	0	0

Saint Ballado, Dk B H (1989)
By Halo – Ballade, by Herbager

172 Performers, 83 winning performers, $5,953,038 in total earnings

Progeny	Mare	Age	Sts	1st	2d	3d	Money Won
African Skyline	Why Go On Dreaming	4	10	3	3	2	64,870
Appealing Jewel	Chief Appeal	4	1	0	0	0	
Arcola Lane	Star Actress	4	13	3	2	2	38,314
Ashado	Goulash	3	6	4	1	1	610,800
Ashmore	Sapphire Beads	3	11	3	2	4	182,750
Axis	Moscow Tap	4	15	1	4	2	46,990
Bahama John	Rhythm of Life	3	2	1	0	0	28,275
Ballade's Magic	Magic Paintbrush	3	3	0	0	0	4,002
Balladeer	Roman Nile	5	13	2	1	1	20,819
Ballado Breeze	Wild Royal	2	4	1	1	1	27,980
Ballado Chieftan	Flaming Mirage	3	5	1	2	0	58,260
Ballado Hill	Hill Fifty Four	3	5	1	0	0	19,560
Ballado Melody	Oh So Sharp	4	10	1	0	0	13,290
Ballado Star	Dutra Star	6	4	0	0	0	228
Ballado's Baby	Dusty's Mirage	5	14	4	2	2	95,042
Ballado's Devil	Seashore Miss	5	7	3	2	0	56,200
Ballado's Halo	Goulash	4	9	1	3	1	45,500
Ballence	Excellence	3	2	0	1	0	4,590
Bannatyne	Truce in Balance	4	2	0	0	0	214
Base Stealer	Vennila Cream	3	9	0	0	2	6,500
Battle Red	Royal Fit	2	1	0	0	0	0
Bay Head King	Meadow Silk	5	3	2	0	0	24,600
Bella Luce	Holiday Dancer	4	3	0	1	1	12,230

Progeny	Mare	Age	Sts	1st	2d	3d	Money Won
Bellus	Hansel's Beauty	3	3	0	0	0	328
Blossum	Single Flower	4	7	1	1	1	27,670
Braytonville	Mission Park	2	2	0	0	1	5,000
Brilliantly	Girl of Peace	7	1	0	0	0	0
Brother Ballado	Krystle Czaravich	5	1	0	0	0	120
Cajole	Common Threads	3	7	2	2	1	39,360
Cartage Agent	Imaginary Number	2	5	0	5	0	45,400
Classy Date	Date Stone	4	1	0	0	0	960
Comanche Star	Deceit Princess	2	1	0	0	0	2,135
Continuum	Charlies Paradise	3	7	2	0	1	30,960
Cosmah Star	Im a Star Prospect	4	2	1	1	0	37,345
Countess Ballado	Titlebound	3	2	0	0	0	233
Country Romance	Cuddles	3	10	4	2	1	157,230
Coverly	Mended Heart	3	3	0	0	0	2,285
Defy Logic	Clever Monique	3	11	0	4	4	56,470
Devilwithoutacause	Raise the Bridge	4	1	0	0	1	640
Diva Girl	Field Point Road	4	3	0	0	0	2,880
Divine Bird	Migrate	3	2	1	0	0	29,820
Divorce Lawyer Jay	Wishing Mood	3	7	1	1	3	21,980
Dr. Tony	Dr. Velvet	3	4	0	0	0	2,070
Dreamers Point	Dance With Bees	6	15	0	1	3	8,315
Drill Hall	Stephanie's Road	4	10	2	2	1	54,900
Ealing Park	Jeannie the Meanie	4	4	0	0	0	2,340
Eastside Ballad	Eastside Westside	3	5	1	1	2	56,340
Ecclesiastes	River of Stars	3	1	0	0	0	220
Ecumenical	Inca Sun	3	1	0	0	0	0
Exit Laughing	Bolshoi Comedy	3	10	0	0	1	4,024
Father Judge	Surina Star	3	1	0	0	0	0
Feather Boa	Runaway Spy	3	8	2	2	0	67,850
Flawless Diamond	Diamonds n Frills	3	3	2	0	0	55,200
Flinch	Native Expressions	4	1	0	0	0	210
Four Two Won	Mailorder Bride	4	4	1	1	0	10,494
Freska	Franziska (IRE)	2	2	0	0	1	8,820
Fund of Funds	Heather's Flight	3	5	1	2	1	143,170
Gethsemani	Bottle Top	2	7	1	2	3	60,365
Global Hawk	Olay Monique	3	5	1	0	1	16,440
Glorious Grace	Class With Luck	5	10	2	3	0	111,512
Gold Ballad	Christmas Gold	5	9	4	3	0	36,820
Gotta Ballado	Gotta Be Classi	5	9	0	1	1	6,577
Grace Course	Lady Vernalee	4	4	1	1	1	41,880
Gracious Lady	Madam President	3	6	0	0	2	13,890
Handzz Up	Great Escape	3	15	0	6	0	11,302
Hard Quality	Sweetsoutherncross	3	1	0	0	0	0
Harts Gap	Special Test	4	7	0	3	3	35,880
Heros Among Us	Lady Ling (ARG)	2	1	0	0	0	0
Hockey Man	Psalms	4	1	0	1	0	5,460
Hold the Lime	Coming Out Party	4	1	0	0	0	320
Horse Hill	Mt. Cuba	3	3	0	0	0	1,620
How Little We Know	Sophisticatedcielo	3	8	0	0	1	4,230
I'm Just a Peach	I'm a Raisin	6	11	2	2	2	36,701
In Rome	Our Shopping Spree	2	8	2	1	1	88,740
Innovation	Innovate	3	10	0	0	1	7,044
Jangled	Arising	4	22	1	4	2	17,432
Jetset Saint	Jetsetyet	4	10	1	2	0	19,900
Joyful Ballad	Bring Me Joy	3	4	1	1	0	13,370
Judge of Character	Fanny's Frolic	4	2	0	0	0	0
Kathy K D	Stella Cielo	4	3	0	1	0	19,155
King Carlos	Word o' Ransom	2	4	1	2	0	28,710
Kissed Goodbye	Bye Bye Brazil	5	12	2	2	2	26,879
Klassy Katlyn	Chicken Delight	2	6	0	2	0	24,360
Lights On	Chicken Delight	4	9	2	3	0	122,710
Lindsay Jean	Colony Bay	5	7	3	1	2	182,125
Lindt	Harpa	5	11	0	1	2	8,378
Lizzy Cool	Well Supported	3	3	1	1	0	66,120
Lord Ofthe Thunder	Astarte	4	7	2	1	2	99,803
Lottaballado	Truffles Royale	7	8	0	1	1	1,815
Luv Saint Ballado	Sheer Love	4	1	0	0	0	0
Mad Donna	Marchtothemine	3	11	1	1	1	16,300
Mariola	Glad's Legacy	4	7	0	1	1	8,094
Media Saint	Mediation (IRE)	2	3	0	0	1	3,220
Mille Feville	Captivant	4	9	2	3	1	159,329
Minstrel's Melody	Glorious Minstrel	3	8	1	0	3	30,160
Mr. Elway	I'm Italian	6	2	0	0	0	308
Mystics Blue Rose	Sandy Lake	6	3	1	0	0	10,800
National Saint	Ski Nation	7	2	0	0	1	12,000
Northern Ballad	Sloane Street	2	3	0	0	0	3,960
Ocean Terrace	Crystal River	3	4	2	0	0	141,200
Orvald	Snappy Chatter	7	7	1	0	1	9,498
Oyster Bay	Clamorosa	3	2	0	0	1	3,540
Paddington	Painted Portrait	2	5	2	1	0	109,620
Paint Ballado	Donusa	2	3	0	1	0	7,260
Parnell Square	Smart Lady Too	3	6	1	0	0	29,720
Popular	Western Lady	4	7	0	0	3	29,865
Preach It	Arrested Dreams	2	1	0	0	0	0
Primo Primo	Divine Dixie	3	1	0	0	0	0
Princess Legacy	Miswaki's Princess	4	1	0	0	1	1,350
Prospective Saint	A. B. Prospect	2	2	1	0	1	19,080
Rouge Noir	Ardana (IRE)	3	3	1	0	0	6,670
Roused	With Every Wish	2	2	1	0	0	27,455
Royal Duke	Dark Sapphire (IRE)	3	3	0	2	0	6,175
Royal Parade	Deputy Royal	2	2	0	0	1	2,340

Progeny	Mare	Age	Sts	1st	2d	3d	Money Won
Running Saint	Chadra North	2	5	0	1	1	20,724
Sacred Jewel	Rare Ruby	4	3	0	0	0	3,480
Saint Appeal	Nanerpeal	4	4	1	0	0	28,440
Saint Bernadette	Wedding Jitters	4	2	1	0	1	46,284
Saint Brook	Royal Brook	3	2	1	0	0	9,600
Saint Buddy	Heart of America	3	5	1	1	1	51,480
Saint Damien	Wife Begone	5	7	0	1	1	15,410
Saint Greer	Erina	3	1	0	0	0	0
Saint Joseph	Sprucea	6	2	0	0	0	1,620
Saint Liam	Quiet Dance	3	9	3	3	0	141,275
Saint Lorenzo	Twochindordor	3	11	4	2	1	88,880
Saint Marden	The Administrator	4	1	0	0	0	0
Saint Martin	Hope's Ahead	2	3	0	0	0	0
Saint Sabates	Island Splendour	3	10	2	2	1	34,304
Saint Seminole	Smokey Mirage	2	1	0	0	1	6,666
Saint Stephen	Goulash	3	7	1	3	2	72,340
Saint Stormin'	Stormin' In	3	3	0	2	0	3,500
Saint Verre	Margot Verre	5	7	1	2	2	140,282
Saint Waki	Mollywaki	3	12	3	3	3	124,580
Sainted Colony	Probable Colony	3	5	0	1	3	25,480
Saintly Action	Act	4	4	2	0	0	54,540
Saintly Look	Sensational Eyes	3	4	1	1	0	90,220
Saintly Persuasion	Private Persuasion	3	4	2	1	0	70,200
Saintly Slumber	Anesthesiologist	4	1	0	0	0	0
Saints a Plenty	Plenty of Sunshine	3	4	0	1	1	9,500
Saints Cup	Forever Full	6	6	2	0	1	19,540
Saints n' Sinners	Tassie Belle	3	3	0	0	3	14,960
Sainttwok	Day Rate	5	3	0	0	0	4,020
Santa Croce	Broad Dynamite	3	5	1	3	0	54,000
Santa Rosalia	Sugar Is Gold	2	4	0	0	1	7,650
Savedbythelight	Wild Royal	3	7	2	0	4	229,080
Secret of Front	Safe Out Front	6	5	1	1	0	12,470
She Ain't No Saint	Jolie's Valentine	2	1	0	0	0	0
She's a Saint	Dances With Music	4	3	0	2	0	9,040
Sinners N Saints	Navarra	2	1	0	0	0	420
Smiling Eyes	Western Lady	3	1	0	1	0	9,600
So Saintly	Alden's Prissy	5	3	0	0	0	245
Southern Saint	Sharlorraine	5	15	0	2	2	4,895
Special Ballad	Special Mistress	4	3	0	1	0	7,700
Special Saint	Special Token	5	8	1	1	0	8,975
Spirit Run	Jeannie the Meanie	3	3	1	0	0	36,744
Spirited Maiden	Pacific City	4	8	3	0	4	77,247
St Averil	Avie's Fancy	2	2	1	1	0	98,000
Stacie's Ballado	Storm Minister	2	5	1	1	0	14,160
Stanmore Crescent	Majestic Courtesy	3	1	0	0	0	0
Sweet Blessing	Sweet Alabastar	3	10	1	3	1	10,132
Sweet Melody	Interpretive Mood	2	1	0	0	0	0
Sweetheavenlycross	Sweetsoutherncross	4	7	0	0	1	6,940
Taint True	Pretend	3	1	0	0	0	240
Technocat	All Tanked Up	8	1	0	0	0	0
Tequesta	Bodacious Tatas	2	5	1	0	0	33,120
Theo's Saint	Fancy Pan	3	2	0	0	0	220
Timber Cruiser	River of Stars	4	8	2	1	2	91,400
Truckle Feature	Magic Gleam	3	4	0	1	0	26,160
Vagabond Saint	Queens n Vagabonds	2	1	0	0	0	0
Whatasaint	Whatamiss	4	12	4	0	0	70,840
Wild Horses	Waltzing With Deb	4	7	1	2	0	40,980
Windham Flash	Ameritop	3	5	3	0	0	42,190

Grand Slam, Dk B H (1995)
By Gone West – Bright Candles, by El Gran Senor

129 Performers, 71 winning performers, $5,806,236 in total earnings

Progeny	Mare	Age	Sts	1st	2d	3d	Money Won
Aimee	Ammy Hils	3	12	1	1	3	9,490
Alke	Pasampsi	3	4	2	1	0	77,600
All Electric	Electric Shock	2	2	1	0	0	27,815
All the Tricks	Fluffkins	3	7	1	1	1	12,000
Ampsterdam	Peggibonsi	3	1	0	0	0	140
Ann Dear	Cent Nouvelles	3	12	4	1	2	87,975
Bank Onahomerun	Safety Deposit	3	5	0	0	1	3,038
Beebe Lake	Quiet Rumour	3	9	2	4	1	109,380
Before Sunset	Sunset Song	2	1	0	0	0	2,500
Berani	De Puntillas (GB)	3	4	0	1	0	2,611
Big Score	Voluptuous	3	5	1	0	0	24,528
Bocca Al Lupo	Tilt My Halo	3	4	3	1	0	53,910
Bridge Player	Over Your Shoulder	3	4	0	0	0	360
Caesar's Pearl	Prairie Pearl	3	1	0	1	0	9,600
Cajun Beat	Beckys Shirt	3	9	4	2	0	820,000
Call Me Chester	No More Ironing	3	1	0	0	0	50
Canaan Land	Tipsy Girl	3	6	0	2	1	25,640
Candlelight Prince	Widow Women	3	5	0	1	0	16,820
Casanova Slammer	Casanova Storm	3	12	2	4	1	65,710
Charged Up	Sugar Slew	3	10	0	0	1	4,787
Cherish Destiny	Silver Hiawatha	2	4	1	0	1	55,260
Cimmaron Lady	Circus Poster	3	2	0	0	0	0
Clear the Bases	Hay Hanne	2	1	0	0	0	2,700
Cultural Blend	Sovietica (GB)	3	4	0	0	0	0
Cyclotron	Eliot Chacer	3	2	0	1	0	12,740

		Age	Sts	1st	2d	3d	Money
D's Grand Suprise	Dee's Surprise	3	3	0	0	0	1,800
Dance Instructor	Ransom Dance	2	4	0	1	0	6,950
Double Slam	Diversify	3	9	2	1	2	52,635
Doubtless	Leo Larla	3	5	1	3	0	39,440
Ego Sport	Polish Devil	3	1	0	0	0	0
Estevan	Sandy's Storm	2	5	2	0	1	96,405
Everheart	Northern Dynasty	2	2	1	1	0	40,245
Every Trick	Destiny Now	2	1	0	0	0	0
Fire Slam	Miss Firefly	2	3	2	1	0	259,430
First Draw	E. Hagins	3	5	0	0	0	0
Flushing Meadows	Sheepish Grin	2	4	2	0	1	77,100
Fly Me Ali	Psychic Spirit	2	1	0	1	0	3,510
Forward Impact	Sarasota	3	7	1	0	0	11,130
Four Bagger	Call Catherine	3	8	0	3	0	8,580
Four Majors	Mistress S.	3	10	2	2	1	61,040
Four Tens At Once	Ana Belen (CHI)	3	8	1	0	1	4,415
Gainango	Evaluating	2	2	0	1	1	13,950
Giant Slam	Great Lady Mary	3	6	1	0	2	16,428
Glowing Colors	Wheedle	3	7	2	2	2	80,804
Going Going Gone	Skies of Blue	3	3	1	0	1	8,975
Good Lookin'	Our Dear Helen	2	4	0	4	0	15,485
Grand Cap D	Topsa	2	6	1	1	2	24,520
Grand Chance	Gravy Train	3	8	1	1	2	26,960
Grand Flash	Indy Flash	3	4	1	1	2	13,590
Grand Heritage	Minstrel's Lassie	2	6	2	0	2	92,210
Grand Hombre	Santona (CHI)	3	5	4	1	0	598,360
Grand Model	Archimillionnaire	3	6	0	1	1	10,830
Grand Natalie Rose	Foolish Line	3	3	0	0	0	2,760
Grand Player	Ataentsic	3	8	1	2	0	22,970
Grand Prayer	Lyrical Prayer	2	2	0	2	0	18,000
Grand Runner	Larnica	3	9	1	0	2	4,502
Grand Scam	Candid Moments	3	7	0	2	1	21,910
Grand Score	Alaska Queen	2	3	1	0	2	47,545
Grand Slam Jake	Illustre Inconnue	3	11	1	1	1	14,395
Grand Sorcerer	Life's Magic	3	11	1	1	2	9,975
Grand Steal	Steal of the Night	3	10	2	2	2	95,148
Grand Victor	Stephanie's Road	3	3	2	0	0	49,484
Grand Warrior	Heartful Star	2	3	0	0	3	14,610
Grande's Grandslam	Grande Armee	2	3	0	1	0	7,795
Hackleton's Cliff	Leap of the Heart	3	9	4	0	1	72,916
He's No Saint	Fairy Dancer	3	2	1	1	0	36,000
Hit It Here Cafe	Strawberry's Charm	2	2	0	0	0	0
Home Run Hitter	Flying Ten	3	11	4	2	0	111,540
Houndstooth	Shining Through	2	2	0	0	0	0
Hyannis	Coribek	2	1	0	0	0	360
Illustrious Legacy	Dancing On a Slew	3	7	1	0	2	24,330
Imitation	Kovna	3	3	1	0	1	33,800
Impetus	Tornado Cat	3	6	1	1	0	38,930
In the Park	Short Time	2	1	0	0	0	750
Kon Tiki	Far to Fly	3	4	1	1	1	35,860
La Femme Galante	Dahl	3	1	1	0	0	27,320
Limehouse	Dixieland Blues	2	6	3	0	2	260,435
Linda Belinda	Like Liza Can	2	2	0	0	1	7,980
Little Slam	Summertime Val	3	4	0	0	0	365
Little Switz	Operator Seven	2	2	0	1	0	7,160
Long Pond	Light Up New York	2	2	0	1	0	15,756
Lovely Candles	Lovely Reba	3	5	0	0	1	3,165
Lucky Slam	Mi Lucia	2	2	0	1	1	9,050
Luganis	Annoconnor	3	11	3	2	1	66,267
Lukfata Cowboy	Casual Meeting	3	3	0	2	0	11,400
Major Leaguer	Dance Review	3	3	1	0	1	33,360
Mamie Mom	Susana	2	1	0	0	1	1,650
Master David	Nadra (IRE)	2	1	0	1	0	40,000
Middleweight	Dusty Gloves	3	9	2	4	0	99,600
Midnight Rhapsody	Midnight Oil	3	14	1	4	2	56,472
Mizzen Lass	Minstrelsy	2	3	0	0	1	3,715
Mr. Gehrig	Rita's Reatta	3	4	1	0	0	29,120
Nerve Ending	Winter Treasure	2	1	0	0	0	180
Outta the Park	Nijmis	3	2	1	0	0	20,740
Oxford Grad	Chelsea My Love	3	8	1	1	0	4,400
Pacific Island	Pacific Hideaway	2	5	2	1	0	48,050
Parkers Peace	In the Know	2	2	0	0	0	510
Patriotic Duty	Flying Honors	3	4	0	1	0	1,881
Pennant Dreams	Americarr	3	1	0	0	0	1,290
Perfect Present	June Gift	3	7	1	0	0	11,762
Pie Corner	Making Faces	3	8	2	1	0	92,942
Powerful Magic	Faux Pas (IRE)	3	2	0	0	0	700
Prairie Slam	Turk's Flirt	3	6	2	1	1	45,780
Princess Grand	Seattle Princess	3	3	1	0	1	16,600
Queen Maya	Cahooters	3	1	0	0	0	0
Reel Slam	Araadh	3	5	1	1	0	17,220
Regal Slam	Regal Lady Hour	3	5	3	0	2	17,120
Right Out Ro	Top Bonnet	3	9	0	1	3	27,880
Savoy Special	Flashy Four	3	8	3	3	2	122,513
Seatriscuit	Summertime Val	2	5	1	0	1	14,846
Seventh Inning	Artic Strech	3	8	3	0	1	78,315
Silent Picture	Moving Picture	2	1	0	0	0	0
Slam Dancing	Oh How We Danced	2	2	0	0	0	780
Slam Inn	Topacio (URU)	3	7	1	0	0	7,140
Slamma	Chelsea Favourite	3	4	1	0	0	7,140
Slammin' Lil	Luscious Lily	3	10	2	1	0	51,129
Slamminjamminjewel	Jewel Thief	3	4	0	0	1	825
Sliding Home	Flowers and Vines	2	2	0	0	1	6,330
Sophia Ofthe Hills	Out of the Hills	3	2	0	0	0	0
Stellar	Starr County	3	6	2	0	1	95,820
Strong Hope	Shining Through	3	7	5	0	1	582,360
Sweet Jo Jo	Wild Decision	2	7	3	0	2	134,210
T E Jones	Polish Maid	3	2	0	0	0	2,140
Triple Slam	Santona (CHI)	2	2	0	0	0	1,170
Ventura Hotel	Playing Through	3	6	1	0	0	4,284
Victorious Slam	Approve	2	1	0	0	0	137
Wallop	The Ruler's Sister	3	7	2	0	4	28,190
Winning Run	Shardona	2	5	1	0	0	10,075
Zerotosixty	Sawa's Song	3	9	2	2	0	25,936

Unbridled, Dk B H (1987)
By Fappiano – Gana Facil, by Le Fabuleux
129 Performers, 71 winning performers, $5,806,236 in total earnings

Progeny	Mare	Age	Sts	1st	2d	3d	Money Won
Affable	Chinese Empress	3	7	0	1	0	12,608
Affirmative	Tom's a La Mode	4	1	0	0	0	2,880
Alert	Exclusive Bird	4	4	4	0	0	56,400
Alleynedale	In My Cap	5	1	0	0	0	155
Alwaysinbloom	Evening Primrose	4	2	1	0	1	13,490
Any Reason	Valid Carnauba	4	2	1	1	0	30,780
Arcanum	Twin Bet	4	3	0	0	0	141
Backatitagain	Russian Bride	6	13	1	1	0	17,484
Bavarian Girl	Connecting Link	3	3	2	0	0	51,600
Beautiful Treasure	Beautiful Moment	3	11	0	0	0	10,210
Belterra	Cruising Haven	4	1	0	0	1	11,000
Beyond the Limit	Tularosa	3	3	0	0	0	0
Burkhardt	Alylady	9	3	0	0	0	0
Call Me Glory	Bashful Charmer	3	6	2	0	1	29,156
Carefree	Vennila Cream	6	21	3	4	5	33,696
Cavort	Firey Affair	4	4	0	0	0	408
Colihan	Daggett	7	10	0	2	1	6,581
Comic Genius	Squan Song	5	1	0	0	0	0
Consistency	Top Rung	4	7	4	1	0	113,220
Crap Shooter	Bold Mate	4	5	3	1	0	50,560
Crowd	Wild Applause	5	6	1	0	1	15,760
Daring Bid	Whiffling	5	6	1	0	1	10,806
Darling Bride	Darling Danzig	6	2	0	1	1	13,640
Defenman	Young Brodie	7	6	0	2	0	32,998
Devotion Unbridled	Icy Warning	3	8	4	3	1	152,300
Digitech	Jolie Jolie	5	6	1	1	2	13,220
Doctor Hi	Buckeye Search	2	1	0	0	0	525
Dodgeville	Rezagante (ARG)	3	5	0	0	0	2,640
Drewman	Lucky Sign	5	4	2	0	0	66,510
Eddington	Fashion Star	2	1	0	1	0	9,200
Empire Maker	Toussaud	3	6	3	3	0	1,936,000
Famously Free	Jedina	9	20	2	6	6	21,940
Fast Spot	Herbs and Spices	4	6	3	0	0	22,880
Fervid	Facts of Love	3	3	1	0	0	30,580
Firm Believer	Foreign Aid	5	7	1	0	2	17,780
Free Thinking	Danka	2	3	1	0	0	44,889
Frontier Justice (IRE)	Carnation (FR)	4	1	0	0	0	420
Glamorama	Porizkova	3	3	0	0	1	1,300
Grand Appointment	Grand Sophisticate	5	6	2	1	1	94,380
Gross Margin	Forest Fealty	3	5	0	1	1	13,920
Gypsy Jazz	Julie's Jazz	3	6	1	0	0	12,679
Halfbridled	Half Queen	2	4	4	0	0	849,400
Halodyne	Dynamite Blond	4	3	0	0	0	156
Happily Unbridled	Spire	5	5	0	1	0	15,820
Hard Dance	Misty Dancer	3	10	0	1	2	18,700
Hitchin' Post	Polemic	5	8	1	0	2	18,440
Honour Attendant	You'd Be Surprised	5	2	0	0	0	108
Hydration	Good Picker	4	2	2	0	0	37,200
King Bridle	Life's Magic	5	2	0	0	0	92
Kuch	Til Forbid	3	4	0	1	1	14,250
Lady Liberty	Mesabi Maiden	4	9	2	2	1	91,319
Legalize	Legit	3	3	0	1	1	8,200
Liberated	Footy	2	4	0	0	0	2,580
Mellowes	Princesse Timide	5	8	1	0	2	31,750
Mighty Fortress	Whirl Series	3	4	0	0	1	8,960
Molotov	Mary McGlinchy	3	2	0	0	0	340
Moonlight	Cat Appeal	2	2	0	0	0	1,380
Most Admired	Private Seductress	3	1	0	0	1	6,000
Mustanfar	Manwah	2	3	1	0	0	28,980
My Time Now	Darby Trail	2	1	0	0	1	4,270
Navesink River	Sheepscot	2	1	0	0	0	1,350
Nevermore	Teewinot	3	3	0	1	0	10,580
Niigon	Savethelastdance	2	3	0	1	2	50,504
No Armistice	Ataentsic	6	3	0	0	1	14,622
No Stopping	Going Ashore	3	3	0	0	0	680
O'Kelly	Morcote (IRE)	5	15	3	1	4	19,207
Penne Ala Capaese	Daggett	3	7	1	0	2	29,726
Precision Cut	Anything for Love	6	7	1	0	2	8,896
Pupil	Naughty Natisha	4	3	1	1	1	66,080
Rampant Roll	Time to Roll	4	7	1	2	1	11,395
Rayon	Melleray (IRE)	3	7	1	0	2	29,380

Progeny	Mare	Age	Sts	1st	2d	3d	Won
Rebridled	Truly	9	10	2	0	0	42,120
Rebridled Secret	Secret Partner	2	1	0	0	0	0
Reciprocate	Prima Supra	3	10	0	0	2	5,220
Saarland	Versailles Treaty	4	8	2	2	1	263,040
Sansa	Medicine Woman	3	6	0	0	2	13,455
Santa Catarina	Purrfectly	3	5	2	1	1	342,680
Sarie Marais	Aletta Maria	3	3	0	1	0	10,500
Shelby Lane	Buzz My Bell	6	12	1	3	1	37,760
Side	Edge	5	12	2	2	3	14,325
Silent Rapids	Sunset River	4	5	1	1	0	7,760
Sir Bedivere	Bold Windy	4	6	1	0	1	10,170
St. Mary's County	Berth	3	3	0	0	1	850
Stable Secret	Secret Rendezvous	5	3	0	2	0	1,905
Stand and Fight	Dynamite Blond	3	2	0	1	0	3,380
Stonecoldbroke	Star On the Move	5	4	2	0	0	17,871
Strap	Aces	4	6	0	0	0	379
Sunday Dinner	Kat's Chicken	3	4	0	1	0	7,800
Surely a Lady	Surely Georgie's	4	2	0	0	0	2,990
Symphony Sid	Happy Tune	3	4	0	1	1	11,900
Touch Silver	Platinum Lady	7	14	2	7	1	34,740
Tribute to Heroes	Worth Every Penny	7	7	0	2	2	31,390
Twirlaway	Music House	2	6	0	1	0	12,720
Typhoon Alex	Stormagain	3	2	0	0	1	7,940
Unbridled Affair	Northabout	4	8	0	0	1	4,990
Unbridled Ashley	Valid Warning	3	8	1	4	0	29,850
Unbridled Colors	Naskra Colors	3	4	0	0	1	4,620
Unbridled Dignity	Missy's Mirage	5	4	0	0	0	3,750
Unbridled Femme	Grechelle	3	7	1	1	1	80,672
Unbridled Freedom	Debit My Account	3	1	0	0	0	0
Unbridled Fury	Whinheny	6	1	0	0	0	101
Unbridled Gamble	Valid and True	7	10	5	0	0	25,830
Unbridled Lad	Sheba Little (GB)	3	10	0	2	1	12,285
Unbridled Run	Royal Run	3	6	0	0	0	6,025
Unbridled Soul	Red Soul	4	5	0	0	0	1,757
Unbridled Valor	Chartreuse	3	6	1	1	0	26,600
Unbridled Vision	Bunting	5	7	2	1	0	64,495
Unbridled Waters	Waterside	6	1	0	0	0	460
Unbridled's Image	Sugar's Image	3	2	0	0	0	540
Unbridled's Pride	Seewillo	4	2	0	0	0	700
Uncanny	Jah	3	2	1	0	1	13,490
Uncork	Lovat's Lady	3	2	0	0	0	680
Uncoupled	Code Alert	8	12	1	2	0	6,480
Unleash the Law	Li Law	3	7	1	0	0	4,650
Unleash the Power	My Working Gal	3	5	0	0	0	3,880
Unshuttered	Shuttered	2	4	0	1	1	16,360
Unsurpassed	Squan Song	4	4	0	1	0	11,800
Urania	Miss Nance	3	9	1	1	0	41,380
Wagon Train	Gather the Group	4	9	1	2	0	23,786
Wendover	Majestic Legend	5	10	0	2	2	22,760
Windigo	Banshee Winds	2	1	0	0	0	2,500

Silver Deputy, B H (1985)
By Deputy Minister – Silver Valley, by Mr. Prospector
(153 Performers, 86 winning performers, $5,606,973 in total earnings.)

Progeny	Mare	Age	Sts	1st	2d	3d	Money Won
A Beautiful Heart	Oh So Lovely	3	7	0	1	1	4,990
Abby's Magic	Midnight Magic	4	2	0	0	0	244
Acting Deputy	Bastille Opera	4	8	2	0	3	146,155
Air Marshall	Sky Blue Pink	3	7	0	2	3	37,790
Allensky	Sky Ninski	3	6	0	2	0	9,880
Aloha Rosa	Gypsy Monarch	3	11	0	1	2	13,050
Alter Ego	Roan Promise	6	10	2	1	2	58,335
Amsterdam Ave.	Foot Stone	2	4	0	0	1	4,620
Anna Capri	Lyrical Lady	4	17	5	3	2	52,849
Another Day	Karantina	3	8	1	1	1	13,926
Argentum	Berry Berry Good	4	5	1	0	2	22,310
Assumed Risk	Ms. Balding	5	19	1	4	3	30,150
Aurora Guadalupe	Miss Bering	3	10	3	3	1	57,704
Aztec Silver	A Little Bit Tipsy	7	1	0	0	0	54
Badge of Silver	Silveroo	3	3	2	0	0	130,500
Ballroom Deputy	Tango Charlie	2	3	1	0	0	16,345
Bare Necessities	Shrewd Vixen	4	8	4	0	3	431,175
Baroness Silvia	Omnia	2	5	0	0	0	3,180
Bayou Mist	Pecan Bayou	3	7	2	0	0	53,145
Bethestar	Northeros' Lady	4	9	0	1	1	15,680
Blazing Deputy	Renee's Reflection	4	6	0	0	1	4,035
Breakaway	Make Haste	2	6	1	3	0	48,475
Bring Home Thegold	Slewveau	5	3	0	1	0	14,500
Catch Me Deputy	Family Enterprize	4	2	0	0	0	0
Cate's My Angel	Sea Gulch	4	11	1	3	0	17,576
Celtic Park	Cuz's Star	4	13	4	2	1	58,335
Charioteer	New Wave	4	7	1	1	3	45,510
Chasing Stanley	Strong And Steady	4	10	2	0	1	66,287
Cherry Springs	Abrasive	2	3	0	0	0	0
Citizen's Arrest	Ms. Balding	8	7	0	0	0	423
Coco's Minister	Fapany	3	9	3	2	0	46,240
Corruption	Malicious	5	4	0	1	1	9,570
Cosmos Mariner	Antahkarana	2	1	0	0	0	1,350
Crafty Move	Crafty Jam	3	8	1	2	0	46,750
Cryptic Code	Code of Love	4	4	1	1	0	23,510
Darling Deputy	Ada Ruckus	5	3	0	0	0	3,151
Daytime Robbery	Astas Foxy Lady	7	11	4	0	1	81,437
Deputy Country	My Sweet Country	5	6	1	4	1	46,800
Deputy Danny Boy	Chateau Princess	6	18	4	6	3	69,740
Deputy Devil	Crafty Devil	3	1	0	0	0	0
Deputy Diplomat	Political Parfait	5	3	0	0	0	315
Deputy Jack	My Bubbling Belle	3	5	0	0	2	10,985
Deputy's Reward	Anniversary Blues	4	9	0	0	3	13,485
Desert Destiny	Desert Angel	4	2	0	0	0	120
Divisional Champ	Regal Cathy	6	5	0	0	2	2,085
Doubly Brite	Sweet Mama	5	12	3	4	1	63,890
Dundurn	Brushed Halory	2	2	1	0	0	35,280
Enlighting	Light Up New York	3	7	3	1	0	17,750
Fancy Suenancy	Mistariat	5	14	2	3	1	22,140
Five Star Night	Five Star Night	8	1	0	0	0	274
Foramusementonly	Uijongbu	4	10	1	1	3	36,885
Foriegn Deputy	Rosie's Way	6	10	0	2	1	8,079
Fresh Tracks	Take Me Home	4	6	2	2	1	97,231
Full of Luck	Full of Fable	4	4	1	0	1	32,580
Golden Sheriff	Pretty Place	4	11	1	1	0	24,690
Hussar	Aerobic Lady	3	5	1	0	0	12,546
I'm Tryon	Rouquette (GB)	6	8	1	0	0	4,140
Ifyouprefersilver	If Liloy	4	4	1	0	1	99,960
Iron Deputy	Femme De Fer (FR)	4	5	2	0	1	238,620
Isle Arrest You	Isle Deliver	4	1	0	0	0	0
It's About Silver	Zigabout	4	12	1	1	4	65,001
Izamal	Exceedingly (GB)	4	3	0	0	1	620
Joe Six Pack	Dixie Melody	2	4	3	0	0	127,800
Just Missed	Attractive Missile	4	3	0	0	0	600
La Carina	La Bellissima	3	5	0	1	0	5,750
La Tulipe	Tenacite	4	4	0	1	1	6,848
Lingerie	Ligurian	2	4	1	1	0	9,900
Lone Star Deputy	Starlight Way	3	7	2	0	1	78,680
Looseonthegoose	Stalcreek	3	3	0	0	0	0
Lulu Lemon	Chip	2	1	0	0	0	0
Madiera	Andrea Ruckus	4	8	2	0	0	67,980
Mele Kalikimaka	Northeros' Lady	3	4	1	0	0	6,000
Minister Lady	Crafty Devil	4	11	3	1	3	34,539
Mister Cy	Bright and Fancy	7	6	0	2	0	8,468
Montana	Champagne Surprise	6	11	2	1	0	7,675
Morgan Dollar	Classic Ambition	4	1	0	0	0	0
Mr. Jester	Future Pretense	2	6	4	2	0	730,800
Nashinda	Adorned	2	2	2	0	0	148,635
Needham's Point	Miami Vacation	5	13	4	1	2	52,961
Number Juan	Colonial Reef	2	2	0	1	0	12,740
Oak Hill	With Style	3	4	1	0	0	6,350
Oath of Office	Bibical Sense	3	13	5	3	4	84,120
Out of Pocket	By Your Leave	3	3	0	0	2	4,180
Parkers Mill	Seda Fina	2	1	0	0	1	4,100
Perfectly Stunning	Screened	4	6	2	1	0	62,275
Pericles	Orange Sickle	2	3	1	1	0	40,900
Persian Silver	Puzla (IRE)	5	5	0	0	0	184
Petite Diablo	Reet Petite	5	11	1	3	1	33,118
Pierhead	Cotton House Bay	3	4	0	0	2	8,646
Pistareen	Money Tree	5	12	1	2	1	11,056
Polish Police	Walewskaia (IRE)	6	14	3	0	2	20,510
Polished Deputy	All Primed	3	2	0	0	0	900
Posse	Raska	3	11	5	1	1	478,426
Quassapaug	Bacall	4	2	1	0	0	26,720
Rare Deputy	Terra Cotta	4	7	1	0	1	10,190
Sacred Vow	Hausman	3	7	1	1	0	9,620
Saint Julien	Caromist	5	17	2	4	1	19,147
Scrambling	Apelia	2	4	0	0	0	0
Second in Command	Stormeor	3	9	1	2	2	83,090
Secret Deputy	Secretell	12	8	1	0	0	6,172
Senor Sterling	Fraulein Lieber	6	7	0	0	0	2,065
Sexual Harrasment	Smooth and Classy	3	3	0	1	0	6,800
She's Sterling	Miss Turlington	2	1	0	0	0	0
Sheriff's Posse	Starry Val	3	9	2	0	1	40,221
Shingen Deputy	Orlanova	4	2	0	0	0	216
Shrewd Deputy	Shrewd Vixen	2	2	0	0	0	2,978
Silver Artistry	Tank's Fantasy	4	11	2	3	1	13,888
Silver Calling	Glorious Calling	2	2	0	0	0	0
Silver Chadra	Chadra North	7	13	2	1	4	19,240
Silver Clipper	Riverjinsky	4	5	1	1	1	44,620
Silver Debutante	Wladislawa	4	8	3	0	1	28,665
Silver Endeavor	Ole Bow Wower	4	2	0	0	1	698
Silver Jet	Tsar's Treasure	6	18	2	1	2	29,442
Silver Lace	Aroz	3	5	2	1	1	39,964
Silver Mark	Marfietta	3	8	0	0	1	3,600
Silver Midnight	Pococurante	11	5	0	1	1	5,060
Silver Minister	Mint Leaf	2	3	1	2	0	31,890
Silver Mint	Winning Bidder	3	3	0	0	0	1,143
Silver Rolls	Seasonal Splendor	5	12	1	0	2	5,325
Silver Saint	Pandora Queen	7	9	1	1	0	14,591
Silver Set	Petite Duchess	5	9	2	0	0	8,878
Silver Shield	Dactylic	3	1	0	0	0	0
Silver Singer	Singing Heart	3	1	0	0	0	1,980
Silver Sonnet	Dactylic	4	6	1	1	4	35,140

Progeny	Mare	Age	Sts	1st	2d	3d	Won
Silver Sprout	Ligurian	3	5	1	0	1	13,260
Silver Tap	Tops in Taps	4	4	0	1	0	2,640
Silver Ticket	Go First Class	2	3	1	1	0	90,020
Silver Trooper	Franky's Frantic	8	8	1	2	0	7,036
Silverado Ridge	Chardonnay Ridge	5	9	0	1	0	4,058
Silvermin	Min Elreeh	3	14	0	1	1	5,810
Silverton Bay	C. R. B. Beech	4	13	4	3	2	60,350
Silvery	Cope of Flowers	4	1	0	0	0	0
Silvery Pet	K. C. Super Pet	3	6	0	1	0	11,950
Sion Hill	Should Say	3	1	0	0	0	130
Solid Silver Star	Lady in Silver	3	2	2	0	0	36,370
Some Party	Merry Festival	2	1	0	0	0	1,980
Something Silver	Whats Doin	3	3	0	1	0	15,690
Steel Curtain	Taianna	3	2	1	0	0	4,800
Sweet Sammy	Sweet Sondra	3	6	0	1	0	10,930
Sykes Alive	Malicious	6	7	3	2	1	51,534
The Fat Man	Thoughts	3	9	2	0	0	36,770
Third Half	Guiza	3	7	1	3	2	66,220
Three Tee Three	Saratoga Social	3	1	0	0	0	700
Travel Advisory	La Sarcelle	5	2	0	0	0	306
Treasure Beach	Winka	4	3	0	1	0	8,510
Try Again Len	Nickle Lady	3	3	1	0	0	13,237
Two Silver	Moonsilver	5	2	0	0	0	732
Umpqua	Herb's Prospect	5	7	1	0	1	5,077
Veazey	Kalista (GB)	5	12	1	0	0	10,690
Veredus	Slept Thru It	2	5	1	0	1	20,915
Vice Squad	Runaway Babe	5	19	3	0	4	51,267
Whatuc Iswhat Uget	Prime Value	5	16	0	3	1	10,390
Yeowzer	Rebut	6	10	1	0	2	7,670

Smart Strike, B H (1985)
By Mr. Prospector – Classy 'n Smart, by Smarten
118 Performers, 68 winning performers, $5,489,374 in total earnings

Progeny	Mare	Age	Sts	1st	2d	3d	Money Won
A's Anchorman	Ropa Usada	4	17	0	7	2	20,346
Acts Well	Shahra Bay	4	4	0	0	0	180
Added Edge	Sweet Nostalgia	3	4	0	0	3	41,723
Ain't Talkin	Pledge the Fifth	3	7	3	0	0	51,780
American Strike	Americarr	4	8	0	3	1	6,562
Ask Dorothy	Psychic Spirit	4	15	3	0	7	66,270
Asp	Cleopatra's Pearl	3	1	1	0	0	4,260
Aunt Imo	Political Process	4	3	0	0	0	0
Bastione	Hear the Sea	3	1	0	0	0	95
Beached	Pelican Reef	4	6	1	2	0	40,495
Belgrade	Red Star	5	10	1	0	3	8,256
Benny and Bert	Kiara Patricia	3	2	0	0	0	660
Bisbee's Prospect	Bisbee	3	4	2	0	2	39,865
Byback	Eastern Connection	4	6	2	1	1	73,150
Cal's Baby	Silver Dollar Kate	5	9	2	0	2	61,380
Caught Out	Azhaar	5	3	0	0	1	5,500
Chief Black Hawk	Silver Trainor	4	2	0	0	0	0
Classic Mike	Regent n'Flashy	4	8	1	1	2	80,095
Clear Strike	Time for Trumpets	3	3	1	0	0	10,940
Clever Prospector	Clever Actress	4	8	1	2	2	22,230
Dance Star	Dancing Slippers	4	4	1	1	0	21,240
Deputy Strike	Political Process	5	6	0	0	2	36,927
Don't Strike Out	Classy n' Sassy	3	13	4	3	1	22,195
Extreme Strike	Royal Tali	2	2	0	0	0	0
Fine Strike	Perle Fine	2	6	1	1	1	23,332
Fire Strike	Cape Fire	2	4	1	0	0	14,040
Fleetstreet Dancer	Street Ballet	5	9	0	4	2	302,000
Fly Smartly	Spinnakers Flying	5	4	1	0	2	114,705
Free Strike	Free City	2	1	0	0	0	195
Fresh Thunder	Fresh Air	4	11	3	2	1	57,913
Get Smarter	Regal Feeling	3	3	1	1	0	37,800
Good Luck Strikes	Lucky Minister	2	1	0	0	0	0
Gulf of Mexico	Apalachee Princess	2	2	1	0	0	34,400
Hard Edge	Countus In	4	10	3	2	2	175,562
Hellacious Curve	Regency Island	3	10	0	0	2	3,750
Hestosmartforyou	Polish Spirit	5	13	1	2	1	6,345
High Alert	Apalachee Princess	4	7	1	1	3	48,880
High Strike Zone	Danzig Island	3	7	0	5	1	26,460
It's So Simple	Kaylem Ho	5	5	0	0	1	10,920
Jrsoutofcontrol	Chic Chanel	5	5	0	1	1	9,920
Kait Can't Wait	Handmade	3	10	3	0	3	20,165
Kim the Brat	Whow	3	15	2	4	2	31,430
Kristina's Wish	On Kris's Wings	3	8	1	2	2	35,380
Longship	Spinnakers Flying	3	1	0	1	0	4,340
Matched	Call Her	4	13	4	4	3	38,910
McKee's Gallery	Art Gallery	3	11	2	5	1	70,400
Midnight Cry	Mythical Dancer	3	2	1	0	1	85,000
Miss Boomtown	Point of Honor	4	11	0	1	3	22,090
Moonlight Duel	Countus In	2	2	0	0	0	3,882
Mr. J. T. L.	Star Reputation	2	2	0	0	0	3,528
Mr. Technique	Reassert	3	5	1	1	0	81,275
My Lucky Strike	Launch Time	4	12	3	1	5	191,036
Neeshanha	Madame Sunshine	4	1	0	0	0	0
Noble Strike	Green Noble	5	6	1	0	0	24,183

Progeny	Mare	Age	Sts	1st	2d	3d	Won
Parasail	Dancing With Wings	3	5	2	0	0	97,764
Pat the Winner	Karakorum (IRE)	3	6	1	0	2	11,490
Poison Oak Camp	Erina	4	15	0	2	2	5,920
Portcullis	Dancer's Gate	4	6	1	0	0	94,500
Poydras	Debra C.	3	6	1	2	0	50,140
Prospect Won	Strawberry Burrah	4	9	0	0	2	9,835
Prospectors Strike	Zuri	4	7	1	1	1	21,886
Reine des Neiges	Miss Snowflake	4	9	5	0	1	77,160
Roman Peace	Queen of Egypt	4	7	1	2	1	64,584
Run Sarah Run	Breech	3	13	3	2	5	85,460
Sapphire Hill	Dark Sapphire (IRE)	5	9	3	1	1	53,080
Saranac Lake	Lake Champlain (IRE)	4	6	2	0	0	64,292
Say Cousin Lenny	Lolli Lucka Lolli	4	8	0	1	0	13,310
Sea Strike	Sea Regent	5	5	0	0	1	884
Shadow Cast	Daily Special	2	2	1	0	1	30,005
Shadow Steele	Miss Vice	5	13	0	2	0	3,405
Shining Strike	Raj Dancer	4	6	2	0	1	61,140
Shoal Water	Puffin Island	3	7	2	1	2	325,690
Shopping Around	Shes a Calling	4	5	1	1	1	6,030
Slumber Party	Just Us Girls	3	3	0	0	1	4,477
Smart Agenda	Agenda	4	3	0	0	0	0
Smart Ana	Ana Belen (CHI)	4	1	0	0	0	1,050
Smart Angel	Dior's Angel	3	4	0	1	0	26,215
Smart Choice	Ashtabula	4	2	0	0	0	0
Smart Coup	Offshore Account	4	7	1	2	0	45,446
Smart N Classy	Teenage Queen	3	12	2	3	1	82,600
Smart N Sassy	Marsh Cat	4	3	0	0	1	2,963
Smart N Smooth	Wide Country	4	8	4	1	1	66,690
Smart October	October Beauty	4	5	2	2	0	41,400
Smartee	Lil's Lass	3	8	3	0	0	37,980
Snickle Kiss	Sneak a Kiss	3	2	0	0	0	222
Soaring Free	Dancing With Wings	4	8	5	1	0	699,200
Sosella	Mosella	2	1	0	0	0	0
Strategic Strike	Larking	3	14	1	1	2	70,052
Strike and Run	Great Girlfriend	2	2	0	0	0	0
Strike Breaker	Maria Candela (CHI)	3	2	1	0	0	6,000
Strike Em Hard	Crying Out Loud	2	7	2	0	1	78,516
Strike Point	Point of Honor	3	8	1	1	0	17,610
Strike Rate	Harda Arda	3	7	0	1	2	20,885
Strike the Moment	Angry Moment	2	3	0	0	1	2,123
Strikeapromise	Promiseville	4	9	0	0	0	3,293
Strikes No Spares	All Things Nice	4	5	1	1	1	46,760
Striking Audrey	Tomisue's Dancer	2	3	0	1	0	3,780
Striking Flames	Flaming Gold	4	9	0	1	1	4,970
Striking Picture	Sea View Picture	5	5	1	3	1	19,880
Striking Silver	Chic Chanel	3	2	0	0	0	0
Striking T	Rather Be Dancing	2	9	0	1	1	3,640
Strikingly	Torrent	3	12	2	2	1	84,450
Sunnyridge Sam	Know B's	3	6	3	2	0	42,200
Sunup	Streets of Rio	3	7	2	1	0	45,660
Talk About Smart	Charming Sassafras	3	3	0	0	0	5,823
Talk the Walk	Sunset Strip	2	1	0	1	0	4,800
Tenpins	Maid's Broom	5	5	2	2	0	512,760
Three Strikes	Center Box	4	11	2	2	1	26,250
Walls of Jericho	Dancer's Gate	3	1	1	0	0	40,020
Webster's Gold	Devil's Mistress	4	11	1	1	3	52,480
Well Struck	Summer Fantasy	4	1	0	0	0	2,640
Whiletheiron'shot	No More Ironing	4	5	1	0	1	71,625
Whisper Bay	Senita Lane	2	1	0	0	0	0
Wild Strike	Wild Linda	5	7	1	0	0	63,736
Winning Approach	Chateau Rossi	4	8	1	0	2	19,106
Wise Wish	Wish for Candi	3	2	0	0	0	2,046
Wishful Splendor	Kaylem Ho	4	7	1	3	1	61,461
With Assurance	Queen of Egypt	3	2	0	0	0	0

Kris S., Dk B H (1977)
By Roberto – Sharp Queen, by A Special Romance
98 Performers, 54 winning performers, $5,340,284 in total earnings

Progeny	Mare	Age	Sts	1st	2d	3d	Money Won
A Special Romance	So Tenderlee	8	5	0	0	0	523
Action This Day	Najecam	2	3	2	1	0	817,200
Admiralty Inlet	Vashon	2	1	0	0	0	0
Adreamisborn	Erica's Dream	4	7	0	4	0	28,940
Amador	Elevated Love	2	1	0	1	0	6,600
Amorphous	Pirate's Glow	7	4	1	1	0	4,296
Andover Lady	Hard to Copy	3	5	2	1	1	76,533
Ansky	Ms. Teak Wood	6	10	1	0	1	5,718
Avenging Eagle	Poolesta (IRE)	8	10	1	0	0	3,551
Barometric	Fixin to Storm	4	4	2	1	1	73,664
Besttobeabachelor	Prospective Wife	8	14	3	1	1	26,016
Beth's Bo	Beth's Our Choice	7	12	0	2	1	5,585
Big Burner	Secretariat's Fire	4	7	0	0	0	1,935
Black Cove	O My Darling	7	12	3	0	2	12,722
Bold Caleb	Forli's Secret	7	10	0	1	1	4,574
Bowman Mill	Aletta Maria	5	5	1	2	0	327,682
Breathless	Dark Jewel	6	11	0	5	2	12,245
Captain Tripps	Avant's Gold	8	1	0	0	0	0
Chopper Won	Lady Reiko (IRE)	5	3	1	1	0	40,800

Name	Produce	Age	St	1st	2nd	3rd	Earnings
Colonel Gordon	Bought Twice	3	1	0	0	0	0
Count On Kris	Accountess	5	3	0	0	0	235
Crimson	Competitive	2	1	0	0	0	0
Crowned Kris	La Kain	9	3	0	0	0	235
Crystal Cove	Scenic Point	3	5	0	0	1	6,880
Day's Sunset	Kelley's Day	3	8	1	0	1	21,280
Delray Dilemma	Dreamy Mimi	3	3	0	0	1	7,160
Donald David	Tersa	3	6	0	0	0	1,020
Downright	Sheer Risk	4	4	0	0	0	800
Ellie's Moment	Kelley's Day	5	3	1	1	0	84,273
Epicentre	Carya	4	5	1	1	2	82,565
Florik's Baby	Final Say	2	1	0	0	0	140
Flower Forest	Nortena	3	5	2	1	1	65,495
Ford's Creek	Dixie Sass	5	5	1	0	0	11,790
Fortune Writers	Sweet Lexy May	3	7	1	1	2	60,460
Gamble	Bought Twice	4	7	0	0	2	15,625
Gingham and Lace	In the Till	2	3	1	1	0	21,600
High Merit	Snow Cove	4	4	1	0	0	8,540
Iron Prince	Indio Rose	7	7	1	0	0	6,090
Jack's Own Time	Royal Devotion	4	5	2	1	1	88,145
Janis J.	Miswaki Rose	4	9	1	1	1	9,220
Joharra	Colour Chart	3	3	0	2	0	17,800
John's Rockfleet	Win Crafty Lady	7	9	1	1	2	12,122
Kelli Lee	Musical Minister	3	6	1	0	0	30,960
Kernoff	Bottle Top	4	4	1	1	1	32,080
Kicken Kris	Kicken Grass	3	9	4	3	1	593,540
Kingsley Club	All the Crown	3	2	0	0	0	2,040
Kiss the Devil	Devil's Nell	5	3	1	2	0	150,626
Kodiak	Laura's Pistolette	5	9	2	0	1	25,891
Kris Star	Thega	3	6	2	3	0	68,955
Kris's Dancer	Chic Corine	4	9	4	0	1	73,332
Kris'sbest	Cranberry Island	5	12	3	5	0	37,630
Krisana	French Binnana	4	7	1	0	1	16,135
Krisherra	Ausherra	2	2	1	0	0	15,780
Kudos	Souq	6	5	1	1	3	530,000
Ledge	Rim	3	4	0	0	0	520
Leigh Lake	Quick Rhythm	4	3	0	1	0	6,570
Littledancansing	Misspitch	4	5	0	2	1	4,265
Lord of Speed	Halloween Baby	7	11	0	0	1	4,289
Love n' Kiss S.	Key to My Heart	5	8	3	2	0	152,558
Lucky Scarab	Queen of Egypt	5	6	2	2	0	94,560
Mintess	Freshly Minted	4	2	0	0	0	280
Miu Miu	Sunshine Above	4	9	0	2	2	16,416
Mukhtaser	Aurora	3	5	1	0	2	37,280
Music Way	Music Lane	3	4	1	2	1	50,660
My Pal Lana	Palana	3	10	3	2	3	207,224
Natalie's Moment	Rising Moment	5	3	1	0	0	9,034
Natural High	Maple Lake	5	8	2	2	2	19,419
Nature's Power	A Real Native	7	8	2	0	1	16,027
Outcast	Desert Prowler	4	15	0	2	2	5,022
Pack the Tack	Dawn's Black Tie	3	5	0	1	0	9,274
Pat 'n Matt	Royal Linkage	8	2	0	1	0	1,278
Pole to Pole	Annie Arctica	3	2	1	0	0	19,860
Pragmatist	Bello Cielo	4	1	0	0	0	106
Probability	Madame Adolphe	5	4	1	1	0	14,000
Ramona Girl	Suspicions	5	4	1	0	0	19,965
Red Hurricane	Red Rain	3	6	1	0	0	3,363
Regal Dom	Dusty Gloves	7	14	4	1	1	33,058
Risk and Reward	Birr	4	10	4	0	2	57,902
Risotto	Routilante (IRE)	4	6	2	2	1	44,900
Serazzo	La Chaposa (PER)	7	5	2	0	0	22,870
Settle Up	In Conference	3	6	0	2	1	28,860
So Wistfullee	So Tenderlee	7	2	0	0	0	1,622
Status	Aromacor	4	3	1	1	0	41,000
Steady Streak	Langata (IRE)	4	9	0	1	2	26,845
Strategic Partner	Very Special Lite	5	4	0	1	2	25,400
Stunning Image (IRE)	Looking for Gold	3	2	0	0	1	4,130
Super Kris	Irish Shilling	3	4	1	0	0	6,275
Synergistic	J. E.'s Connection	4	6	1	1	0	44,693
Ten Kisses	Tenski	3	4	1	1	1	22,080
Tiger Hunt	Thega	2	4	2	1	0	312,820
Total Gold	Deputy Darlin	6	1	0	0	0	0
Turned On	Falon	3	1	0	0	0	1,700
View At Beaches	Squalling	2	4	0	0	0	3,120
Visual Energy	Sonata Slew	8	1	0	0	0	0
Wagoneer	Prairie Pearl	4	9	0	1	2	8,160
Water Rights	Thirst for Peace	4	2	0	0	0	1,230
Western Cove	Snow Cove	3	12	0	0	3	10,385
Whitmore's Conn	Albonita	5	6	2	0	1	404,236

Annual Leading Sire – Money Won

Year	Sire	Perfs.	Races Won	Amount Won	Year	Sire	Perfs.	Races Won	Amount Won
1914	Broomstick	31	90	99,043	1959	Nasrullah	69	141	1,434,543
1915	Broomstick	47	108	94,387	1960	Nasrullah	64	122	1,419,683
1916	Star Shoot	87	218	138,163	1961	Ambiorix	73	148	936,976
1917	Star Shoot	81	167	131,674	1962	Nasrullah	62	107	1,474,831
1918	Sweep	33	69	139,057	1963	Bold Ruler	26	56	917,531
1919	Star Shoot	55	108	197,233	1964	Bold Ruler	44	88	1,457,156
1920	Fair Play	27	72	269,102	1965	Bold Ruler	51	90	1,091,924
1921	Celt	52	124	206,167	1966	Bold Ruler	51	107	2,306,523
1922	McGee	57	125	222,491	1967	Bold Ruler	63	135	2,249,272
1923	The Finn	16	31	285,759	1968	Bold Ruler	57	99	1,988,427
1924	Fair Play	45	84	296,204	1969	Bold Ruler	59	90	1,357,144
1925	Sweep	65	185	237,564	1970	Hail to Reason	53	82	1,400,839
1926	Man o' War	26	49	408,137	1971	Northern Dancer	44	93	1,288,580
1927	Fair Play	45	84	296,204	1972	Round Table	65	98	1,199,933
1928	High Time	55	109	307,631	1973	Bold Ruler	41	74	1,488,622
1929	Chicle	41	88	289,123	1974	T.V. Lark	98	121	1,242,000
1930	Sir Gallahad III	16	49	422,200	1975	What a Pleasure	90	101	2,011,878
1931	St. Germans	15	47	315,585	1976	What a Pleasure	85	108	1,622,159
1932	Chatterton	47	93	210,040	1977	Dr. Fager	79	124	1,593,079
1933	Sir Gallahad III	49	78	136,428	1978	Exclusive Native	63	106	1,969,867
1934	Sir Gallahad	55	92	180,165	1979	Exclusive Native	71	104	2,872,605
1935	Chance Play	38	88	191,465	1980	Raja Baba	108	149	2,483,352
1936	Sickle	48	128	209,800	1981	Nodouble	92	115	2,800,884
1937	The Porter	45	104	292,262	1982	His Majesty	56	86	2,675,823
1938	Sickle	48	128	209,800	1983	Halo	69	86	2,773,637
1939	Challenger II	42	99	316,281	1984	Seattle Slew	46	49	5,361,259
1940	Sir Gallahad III	63	102	305,610	1985	Buckaroo	49	50	4,145,272
1941	Blenheim II	30	64	378,981	1986	Lyphard	50	49	4,051,985
1942	Equipoise	36	82	437,141	1987	Mr. Prospector	81	104	5,877,385
1943	Bull Dog	75	172	372,706	1988	Mr. Prospector	82	106	8,986,790
1944	Chance Play	71	150	431,100	1989	Halo	93	114	7,520,142
1945	War Admiral	26	59	591,352	1990	Alydar	98	111	6,378,760
1946	Mahmoud	47	101	638,025	1991	Danzig	68	109	6,214,669
1947	Bull Lea	61	128	1,259,718	1992	Danzig	62	83	5,873,773
1948	Bull Lea	63	147	1,334,027	1993	Kris S.	110	142	4,822,888
1949	Bull Lea	73	165	991,842	1994	Broad Brush	92	72	5,403,999
1950	Heliopolis	77	167	852,292	1995	Palace Music	44	22	5,313,060
1951	Count Fleet	64	124	1,160,847	1996	Forty Niner		110	4,820,916
1952	Bull Lea	65	136	1,630,655	1997	Deputy Minister		104	8,519,155
1953	Bull Lea	56	107	1,155,846	1998	Deputy Minister	92	96	8,517,482
1954	Heliopolis	76	148	1,406,638	1999	Storm Cat	104	117	9,657,579
1955	Nasrullah	40	69	1,433,660	2000	Storm Cat	102	99	6,833,882
1956	Nasrullah	50	106	1,462,413	2001	Thunder Gulch	92	82	7,699,918
1957	Princequillo	75	147	1,698,427	2002	El Prado (Ire)	173	154	6,609,533
1958	Princequillo	65	110	1,394,540	2003	A.P. Indy	162	153	8,827,360

Annual Leading Sire – Races Won

Year	Sire	Perfs.	Winning Performers	Races Won
1999	Allen's Prospect	184	105	217
2000	Allen's Prospect	199	125	231
2001	Allen's Prospect	223	132	256
2002	Allen's Prospect	205	129	248
2003	End Swep	201	135	253

Sires of Winners of $1 Million or More in America

Horse	Sex	Born	Sts	1st	2d	3d	Earnings
A.P. Indy							
Mineshaft	C	1999	18	10	3	1	2,283,402
Golden Missile	H	1995	25	7	7	4	2,194,510
Aptitude	H	1997	15	5	4	2	1,965,410
Lu Ravi	M	1995	26	11	8	3	1,819,781
Tomisue's Delight	M	1994	20	7	5	4	1,207,537
Secret Status	M	1997	19	8	3	4	1,053,705
Stephen Got Even	H	1996	11	5	1	1	1,019,200
Acatenango (GER)							
Lando (GER)	H	1990	24	10	3	1	3,438,727
Borgia (GER)	M	1994	22	6	7	2	1,697,771
Accordion							
Yavana's Pace (IRE)	G	1992	74	16	14	11	1,199,409
Ack Ack							
Broad Brush	H	1983	27	14	5	5	2,656,793
Aferd							
Precocity	H	1994	33	9	7	5	1,835,798
Affirmed							
Flawlessly	M	1988	28	16	4	3	2,572,536
Quiet Resolve	G	1995	31	10	6	4	2,346,768
Affirmed Success	G	1994	42	17	10	6	2,285,315
Affluent	M	1998	23	8	5	4	1,497,651
Peteski	H	1990	11	7	2	1	1,287,866
The Tin Man	G	1998	18	7	4	1	1,074,460
Zoman	H	1987	24	7	5	3	1,040,372
Afleet							
Gaily Magnum	G	1993	24	8	2	2	1,218,578
A Fleets Dancer	H	1995	45	12	6	8	1,036,649
Ahmad (ARG)							
Paseana (ARG)	M	1987	36	19	10	2	3,317,427
Ahonoora (GB)							
Dr Devious (IRE)	H	1989	15	6	4	0	1,484,230
Air Forbes Won							
Mercedes Won	H	1986	52	12	7	12	1,087,435
Al Nasr (FR)							
Nasr El Arab	H	1985	16	6	2	2	1,198,585
Alhaarth (IRE)							
Phoenix Reach (IRE)	C	2000	5	3	1	1	1,037,276
Alleged							
Miss Alleged	M	1987	15	5	4	3	1,757,342
Shantou	H	1993	14	6	2	4	1,132,399
Strategic Choice	H	1991	33	5	5	5	1,126,735
Alydar							
Alysheba	H	1984	26	11	8	2	6,679,242
Easy Goer	H	1986	20	14	5	1	4,873,770
Strike the Gold	H	1988	31	6	8	5	3,457,026
Criminal Type	H	1985	24	10	5	3	2,351,274
Turkoman	H	1982	22	8	8	3	2,146,924
Dare and Go	H	1991	22	7	7	5	1,608,972
Althea	M	1981	15	8	4	0	1,275,255
Desert Waves	G	1990	63	15	9	6	1,241,295
Cacoethes	H	1986	14	4	3	3	1,169,064
Miss Oceana	M	1981	19	11	6	1	1,010,385
Clabber Girl	M	1983	39	8	12	6	1,006,261
Alzao							
Alpride (IRE)	M	1991	26	11	4	4	1,048,270
Amerigo							
Fort Marcy	G	1964	75	21	18	14	1,109,791
Apalachee							
Pine Tree Lane	M	1982	38	19	4	4	1,150,561
Arazi							
Congaree	H	1998	23	12	2	4	3,241,400
At the Threshold							
Lil E. Tee	H	1989	13	7	4	1	1,437,506
Avatar							
Honor Medal	H	1981	87	19	13	19	1,347,073
Bahri							
Sakhee	H	1997	14	8	3	1	3,253,253
Bailjumper							
Skip Trial	H	1982	38	16	7	2	1,837,451
Barachois							
Win	H	1980	44	14	10	3	1,408,980
Barathea (IRE)							
Tobougg (IRE)	H	1998	12	3	2	2	1,079,901
Batonnier							
Cavonnier	G	1993	23	8	3	2	1,254,165
Baynoun (IRE)							
Sandpit (BRZ)	H	1989	40	14	11	6	3,812,597
Be My Native							
River Verdon (IRE)	G	1987	26	16	4	2	1,574,735
Believe It							
Al Mamoon	H	1981	32	11	7	3	1,249,906
Best Turn							
High Brite	H	1984	45	15	7	9	1,150,519
Bet Big							
Bet On Sunshine	G	1992	47	22	7	10	1,449,882
Richman	H	1988	33	14	5	5	1,314,360
Bien Bien							
Bienamado	H	1996	16	8	3	0	1,261,089
Bien Nicole	M	1998	26	12	8	2	1,074,620
Big Spruce							
Super Moment	H	1977	47	10	8	5	1,017,940
Bikala							
Apple Tree (FR)	H	1989	26	7	4	5	1,388,260
Black Tie Affair (IRE)							
Evening Attire	G	1998	28	10	6	3	1,952,970
Formal Gold	H	1993	16	8	4	1	1,533,600
License Fee	M	1995	43	16	7	6	1,200,416
Blushing Groom (FR)							
Blushing John	H	1985	19	9	1	2	1,548,081
Sky Beauty	M	1990	21	15	2	2	1,336,000
Arazi	H	1989	14	9	1	1	1,212,351
Bold Bidder							
Spectacular Bid	H	1976	30	26	2	1	2,781,608
Bold Reasoning							
Seattle Slew	H	1974	17	14	2	0	1,208,726
Bold Ruckus							
Kiridashi	H	1992	44	14	9	8	1,201,981
Bold Ruritana	M	1990	44	14	10	6	1,140,163
Beau Genius	H	1985	42	19	7	4	1,055,600
Bold Ruler							
Secretariat	H	1970	21	16	3	1	1,316,808
Bolger							
Sea Cadet	H	1988	29	10	6	5	1,807,150
Bounding Basque							
Basquein	G	1991	37	13	10	2	1,094,767
Broad Brush							
Concern	H	1991	30	7	7	11	3,079,350
Include	H	1997	20	10	1	4	1,659,560
Farda Amiga	F	1999	8	4	1	0	1,282,302

Horse	Sex	Born	Sts	1st	2d	3d	Earnings
Brocco							
Jostle	M	1997	20	8	5	2	1,389,932
Buckaroo							
Spend a Buck	H	1982	15	10	3	2	4,220,689
Lite the Fuse	H	1991	21	9	4	6	1,036,882
Roo Art	H	1982	27	10	4	5	1,011,723
Buckfinder							
Track Barron	H	1981	21	12	3	1	1,353,674
Bucksplasher							
Buck's Boy	G	1993	30	16	5	2	2,750,148
Bull Lea							
Citation	H	1945	45	32	10	2	1,085,760
Busted (GB)							
Erins Isle (IRE)	H	1978	33	9	9	3	1,233,889
Cabrini Green							
Mr. Epperson	G	1995	63	19	10	10	1,042,131
Cadeaux Genereux (GB)							
Touch of the Blues (FR)	H	1997	35	8	6	5	1,655,358
Caerleon							
Missionary Ridge (GB)	H	1987	42	8	5	8	1,864,498
Kostroma (IRE)	M	1986	26	12	2	3	1,200,088
Volga (IRE)	M	1998	19	7	5	2	1,141,759
Corwyn Bay (IRE)	H	1986	15	6	4	0	1,018,749
Candy Stripes							
Different (ARG)	M	1992	19	9	3	5	1,349,802
Capote							
Boston Harbor	H	1994	8	6	1	0	1,934,605
Caro (IRE)							
With Approval	H	1986	23	13	5	1	2,863,540
Golden Pheasant	H	1986	22	7	4	3	2,453,958
Winning Colors	M	1985	19	8	3	1	1,526,837
Tejano	H	1985	21	5	6	3	1,428,177
Carr de Naskra							
L'Carriere	G	1991	23	8	4	3	1,726,175
Carson City							
State City	C	1999	15	6	0	3	1,374,707
Caucasus							
Videogenic	M	1982	73	20	9	10	1,154,360
Caveat							
Awad	H	1990	70	14	10	11	3,270,131
Cee's Tizzy							
Tiznow	H	1997	15	8	4	2	6,427,830
Budroyale	G	1993	52	17	12	2	2,840,810
Gourmet Girl	M	1995	33	9	7	10	1,255,373
Celtic Swing (GB)							
Six Perfections (FR)	F	2000	10	6	4	0	1,451,544
Cherokee Run							
Chilukki	M	1997	17	11	3	0	1,201,828
Chief's Crown							
Chief Bearhart	H	1993	26	12	5	3	3,381,557
Concerto	H	1994	21	10	4	2	1,308,118
Chief Honcho	H	1987	34	10	6	3	1,265,719
Chieftain							
Fit to Fight	H	1979	26	14	3	3	1,042,075
Cinco Grande							
Ibero (ARG)	H	1987	34	10	7	4	1,345,199
Citidancer							
Urbane	M	1992	18	8	4	4	1,018,568
Clever Trick							
Anet	H	1994	19	8	5	0	1,189,873
Kurofune Mystery	M	1990	21	6	5	4	1,009,342
Codex							
Lost Code	H	1984	27	15	5	2	2,085,396
Comic Blush							
Spook Express (SAF)	M	1994	22	11	2	3	1,016,744
Common Grounds							
Earl of Barking (IRE)	H	1990	37	9	3	10	1,230,519
Compliance							
Fourstardave	G	1985	100	21	18	16	1,636,737
Fourstars Allstar	H	1988	59	14	14	9	1,596,760
Comrade in Arms							
Celtic Arms (FR)	H	1991	23	5	2	3	1,102,806
Conquistador Cielo							
Marquetry	H	1987	36	10	9	4	2,857,886
Forty Niner Days	G	1987	45	9	9	3	1,009,625
Consultant's Bid							
Bayakoa (ARG)	M	1984	39	21	9	0	2,861,701
Cool Victor							
Victor Cooley	G	1993	39	13	12	3	1,320,475
Copelan							
Recoup the Cash	G	1990	74	23	6	3	1,098,920
Cormorant							
Gander	G	1996	55	14	10	9	1,761,183
Go for Gin	H	1991	19	5	7	2	1,380,866
Grecian Flight	M	1984	40	21	6	3	1,320,215
Cougar II							
Gato Del Sol	H	1979	39	7	9	7	1,340,107
Cox's Ridge							
Life's Magic	M	1981	32	8	11	6	2,255,218
Sultry Song	H	1988	23	9	3	5	1,616,276
Cardmania	G	1986	76	16	12	20	1,503,780
Vanlandingham	H	1981	19	10	3	3	1,409,476
De Roche	G	1986	28	5	8	7	1,078,200
Lost Mountain	H	1988	36	5	6	8	1,004,939
Cozzene							
Alphabet Soup	H	1991	24	10	3	6	2,990,270
Star of Cozzene	H	1988	38	14	8	5	2,308,923
Running Stag	H	1994	40	7	11	2	1,663,227
Tikkanen	H	1991	17	4	2	3	1,599,335
Rhythm Band	G	1996	18	5	2	2	1,349,066
Cozzene's Prince	G	1987	68	16	10	10	1,270,057
Maxzene	M	1993	23	11	5	0	1,175,259
Chorwon	G	1993	44	13	7	8	1,161,795
Crested Wave							
Surfers Paradise (NZ)	G	1987	57	17	5	0	1,419,964
Crozier							
Precisionist	H	1981	46	20	10	4	3,485,398
Crusader Sword							
Isitingood	H	1991	24	11	3	4	1,219,430
Cryptoclearance							
Victory Gallop	H	1995	17	9	5	1	3,505,895
Volponi	H	1998	31	7	12	5	3,187,232
Crystal Glitters							
Dear Doctor (FR)	H	1987	32	8	7	4	1,742,671
Cure the Blues							
Wake At Noon	H	1997	46	19	6	5	1,564,492
Cutlass							
Cutlass Reality	H	1982	66	14	12	9	1,405,660
Friendly Lover	H	1988	66	22	13	12	1,247,670
D'Accord							
North East Bound	G	1996	45	12	7	2	1,357,148

Horse	Sex	Born	Sts	1st	2d	3d	Earnings
Damascus							
Desert Wine	H	1980	25	8	8	3	1,618,043
Dancing Brave							
White Muzzle (GB)	H	1990	17	6	3	2	1,060,443
Danehill							
Rock of Gibraltar (IRE)	C	1999	13	10	2	0	1,888,048
Banks Hill (GB)	M	1998	15	5	5	3	1,824,008
Danzig							
Agnes World	H	1995	20	8	6	1	3,365,680
Dance Smartly	M	1988	17	12	2	3	3,263,835
Lure	H	1989	25	14	8	0	2,515,289
Pine Bluff	H	1989	13	6	1	3	2,255,884
Chief's Crown	H	1982	21	12	3	3	2,191,168
Versailles Treaty	M	1988	20	9	9	2	1,271,154
Stephan's Odyssey	H	1982	16	6	4	1	1,255,328
War Chant	H	1997	7	5	1	0	1,130,600
Polish Navy	H	1984	12	7	1	3	1,118,076
Dispute	M	1990	19	9	4	4	1,106,907
Dumaani	H	1991	26	7	3	3	1,079,098
Danzig Connection	H	1983	17	6	5	4	1,002,620
Darby Creek Road							
Salem Drive	H	1982	46	13	7	10	1,046,065
Darn That Alarm							
Pistols and Roses	H	1989	44	10	4	6	1,680,506
Darshaan (GB)							
Kotashaan (FR)	H	1988	22	10	5	2	2,812,114
Mutamam (GB)	H	1995	21	11	2	1	1,388,410
Deerhound							
Countess Diana	M	1995	14	7	2	0	1,117,185
Dehere							
Take Charge Lady	F	1999	22	11	7	0	2,480,377
Graeme Hall	H	1997	22	7	7	1	1,147,441
Deputy Commander							
Ten Most Wanted	C	2000	11	4	3	1	1,553,460
Deputy Minister							
Awesome Again	H	1994	12	9	0	2	4,374,590
Deputy Commander	H	1994	13	4	3	2	1,906,640
Open Mind	M	1986	19	12	2	2	1,844,372
Flag Down	H	1990	43	11	11	8	1,699,711
Touch Gold	H	1994	15	6	3	1	1,679,907
Keeper Hill	M	1995	21	4	7	5	1,661,281
Go for Wand	M	1987	13	10	2	0	1,373,338
Victory Speech	H	1993	27	9	2	5	1,289,020
Mr Purple	H	1992	21	6	3	5	1,133,538
Clear Mandate	M	1992	31	10	6	4	1,085,588
Desert Classic							
Native Desert	G	1993	74	21	13	17	1,828,177
Determined King							
Queen Alexandra	M	1982	46	19	8	5	1,034,144
Devil's Due							
Devil His Due	H	1989	41	11	12	3	3,920,405
Devil's Bag							
Twilight Agenda	H	1986	32	13	5	4	2,174,529
Dewan							
It's the One	H	1978	28	9	7	9	1,038,444
Diesis (GB)							
Halling	H	1991	18	12	1	0	1,332,651
Din's Dancer							
Ladies Din	G	1995	37	12	6	6	1,966,754
Distant View							
Sightseek	F	1999	13	8	4	0	1,433,866
Distorted Humor							
Funny Cide	G	2000	11	5	2	2	2,099,385
Dixie Brass							
Dixie Dot Com	H	1995	23	8	6	1	1,332,775
Dixieland Band							
Dixie Union	H	1997	12	7	3	0	1,233,190
Drum Taps	H	1986	31	15	5	2	1,140,788
Del Mar Dennis	G	1990	26	10	1	4	1,023,373
Dixieland Heat							
Xtra Heat	M	1998	35	26	5	2	2,389,635
Djakao							
Perrault (GB)	H	1977	25	9	5	5	1,536,103
Double Bed (FR)							
Jim and Tonic (FR)	G	1994	39	13	13	4	4,975,807
Doyoun (IRE)							
Daylami (IRE)	H	1994	21	11	3	4	4,614,762
Kalanisi (IRE)	H	1996	11	6	4	1	2,148,836
Manndar (IRE)	H	1996	20	4	6	3	1,128,835
Dr. Carter							
Benburb	G	1989	22	7	2	4	1,159,949
Dynaformer							
Perfect Drift	G	1999	18	9	3	1	2,221,368
Dynever	C	2000	9	3	3	1	1,154,020
Critical Eye	M	1997	38	14	4	3	1,060,984
Starrer	M	1998	20	6	5	3	1,043,033
Riskaverse	F	1999	21	7	4	4	1,000,234
Eagle Eyed							
Peeping Tom	G	1997	41	12	7	7	1,251,016
Easy Goer							
My Flag	M	1993	20	6	3	4	1,557,057
Efisio							
Hever Golf Rose (GB)	M	1991	66	17	11	10	1,020,328
El Gran Senor							
Lit de Justice	H	1990	36	10	8	6	1,397,649
Rodrigo de Triano	H	1989	13	9	0	0	1,354,192
Candid Glen	G	1997	38	10	9	6	1,210,130
Helmsman	H	1992	22	6	7	3	1,132,142
El Prado (IRE)							
Medaglia d'Oro	C	1999	15	7	6	0	4,254,720
Nite Dreamer	H	1995	37	5	10	6	1,149,788
Ela-Mana-Mou (IRE)							
Snurge (IRE)	H	1987	30	7	10	5	1,674,441
Emperor Jones							
Janet (GB)	M	1997	27	8	4	6	1,027,237
End Sweep							
Swept Overboard	H	1997	20	8	5	3	1,137,767
Eskimo							
Silent Eskimo	M	1995	31	9	4	9	1,039,485
Eternal Prince							
Val's Prince	G	1992	52	13	12	5	2,118,785
Exclusive Native							
Affirmed	H	1975	29	22	5	1	2,393,818
Outstandingly	M	1982	28	10	4	3	1,412,206
Exclusive Ribot							
Men's Exclusive	G	1993	47	11	16	4	1,447,928
Explodent							
Mi Selecto	H	1985	40	9	7	9	1,475,762
Exchange	M	1988	30	15	7	4	1,287,795
Exbourne	H	1986	14	8	5	1	1,000,198
Ezzoud (IRE)							
Ela Athena (GB)	M	1996	17	3	7	2	1,125,252

Horse	Sex	Born	Sts	1st	2d	3d	Earnings
Fairy King							
Falbrav (IRE)	H	1998	26	13	5	5	5,825,517
Faliraki (IRE)							
Fali Time	H	1981	15	5	4	2	1,033,179
Fappiano							
Unbridled	H	1987	24	8	6	6	4,489,475
Cryptoclearance	H	1984	44	12	10	7	3,376,327
Defensive Play	H	1987	26	6	4	5	1,688,631
Tappiano	M	1984	34	17	2	4	1,305,522
Rubiano	H	1987	28	13	6	1	1,252,817
Tasso	H	1983	23	9	4	4	1,207,884
Grand Canyon	H	1987	8	4	3	0	1,019,540
Far North							
The Wicked North	H	1989	17	8	4	1	1,180,750
Farnesio (ARG)							
Empress Club (ARG)	M	1988	26	16	2	1	1,155,235
First Landing							
Riva Ridge	H	1969	30	17	3	1	1,111,497
Fit to Fight							
Fit for a Queen	M	1986	51	13	14	9	1,226,429
Fly So Free							
Captain Steve	H	1997	25	9	3	7	6,828,356
Flying Continental							
Continental Red	G	1996	56	7	12	11	1,047,558
Flying Paster							
Flying Continental	H	1986	51	12	15	10	1,815,938
Letthebighossroll	G	1988	60	18	14	6	1,014,377
Foolish Pleasure							
Kiri's Clown	H	1989	62	16	6	8	1,005,469
Forceten							
Heatherten	M	1979	53	21	7	4	1,022,699
Forli							
Forego	G	1970	57	34	9	7	1,938,957
Forty Niner							
Coronado's Quest	H	1995	17	10	2	0	2,046,190
Editor's Note	H	1993	31	6	4	3	1,601,394
Ecton Park	H	1996	23	6	4	6	1,503,825
Left Bank	H	1997	24	14	2	0	1,402,806
Friend's Choice							
Dave's Friend	H	1975	76	35	16	8	1,079,915
Full Pocket							
Fighting Fit	H	1979	49	14	7	8	1,004,174
Gallantsky							
Puerto Madero (CHI)	H	1994	24	11	3	2	1,361,626
Geiger Counter							
Nuclear Debate	G	1995	52	11	8	10	1,234,054
General Meeting							
General Challenge	G	1996	21	9	3	1	2,877,178
Excellent Meeting	M	1996	20	8	5	3	1,402,396
Gilded Time							
Elloluv	F	2000	11	4	3	1	1,221,475
Mandy's Gold	M	1998	24	11	4	6	1,081,744
Glitterman							
Balto Star	G	1998	33	11	6	2	1,952,946
Glitter Woman	M	1994	23	10	9	3	1,256,805
J J'sdream	M	1993	40	13	11	7	1,022,217
Go for Gin							
Albert the Great	H	1997	22	8	6	4	3,012,490
Gold Fever							
Gold Mover	M	1998	31	13	9	5	1,523,010
Gold Legend							
Heritage of Gold	M	1995	28	16	2	4	2,381,762
Gone West							
Da Hoss	G	1992	20	12	5	2	1,931,558
Came Home	C	1999	12	9	0	0	1,835,940
Johar	C	1999	16	6	4	2	1,494,496
Lassigny	H	1991	28	8	2	5	1,318,371
West by West	H	1989	30	10	3	7	1,038,123
Graustark							
Proud Truth	H	1982	21	10	4	0	2,198,895
Great Above							
Holy Bull	H	1991	16	13	0	0	2,481,760
Great Nephew (GB)							
Carotene	M	1983	41	12	8	5	1,287,232
Green Dancer							
Greinton (GB)	H	1981	22	10	8	0	1,943,605
Green Desert							
Sheikh Albadou (GB)	H	1988	15	6	4	1	1,229,702
Heat Haze (GB)	F	1999	14	7	2	2	1,183,696
Grey Dawn II							
Bounding Basque	H	1980	40	10	4	6	1,256,258
Gulch							
Thunder Gulch	H	1992	16	9	2	2	2,915,086
Wallenda	H	1990	33	7	5	5	1,205,929
Gummo							
Ancient Title	H	1970	57	24	11	9	1,252,791
Flying Paster	H	1976	27	13	7	2	1,127,460
Habitat							
Steinlen (GB)	H	1983	45	20	10	7	3,297,169
Habitony							
Best Pal	G	1988	47	18	11	4	5,668,245
Richter Scale	H	1994	25	12	2	0	1,139,958
Half a Year							
Full Moon Madness	G	1995	39	15	6	10	1,015,885
Halo							
Sunday Silence	H	1986	14	9	5	0	4,968,554
Goodbye Halo	M	1985	24	11	5	4	1,706,702
Lively One	H	1985	36	9	7	5	1,544,100
Sunny's Halo	H	1980	20	9	3	2	1,247,791
Jolie's Halo	H	1987	20	8	0	2	1,218,120
Present Value	H	1984	42	15	5	3	1,153,853
Glorious Song	M	1976	34	17	9	1	1,004,534
Hansel							
Guided Tour	G	1996	31	12	8	1	1,964,253
Fruits of Love	H	1995	23	5	3	5	1,089,543
Harlan							
Harlan's Holiday	C	1999	22	9	6	1	3,632,664
Menifee	H	1996	11	5	4	1	1,732,000
Hawkin's Special							
Taylor's Special	H	1981	41	21	7	2	1,065,805
Hennessy							
Johannesburg	C	1999	10	7	1	0	1,014,585
Hernando (FR)							
Sulamani (IRE)	C	1999	12	7	2	0	3,640,845
High Estate (IRE)							
High-Rise (IRE)	H	1995	13	5	2	2	1,871,726
His Majesty							
Majesty's Prince	H	1979	43	12	10	10	2,077,796
Tight Spot	H	1987	21	12	3	1	1,566,100
Cetewayo	H	1994	36	11	5	4	1,170,258

Horse	Sex	Born	Sts	1st	2d	3d	Earnings
Hoist the Silver							
Very Subtle	M	1984	29	12	6	4	1,608,360
Hold Your Tricks							
Judy's Red Shoes	M	1983	83	25	13	12	1,085,668
Holy Bull							
Macho Uno	H	1998	14	6	1	3	1,851,803
Honest Pleasure							
Judge Angelucci	H	1983	22	10	4	2	1,582,535
Honor Grades							
Adoration	F	1999	15	5	2	1	1,443,856
Honor Glide	H	1994	38	11	5	2	1,397,187
Horatius							
Safely Kept	M	1986	31	24	2	3	2,194,206
Housebuster							
Morluc	H	1996	40	11	9	5	1,045,758
Icecapade							
Izvestia	H	1987	21	11	2	2	2,702,527
Wild Again	H	1980	28	8	7	4	2,204,829
Ile de Bourbon							
Petite Ile (IRE)	M	1986	14	6	3	4	1,281,665
Imbros							
Native Diver	H	1959	81	37	7	12	1,026,500
In Reality							
Proper Reality	H	1985	19	10	3	1	1,701,650
Smile	H	1982	27	14	4	3	1,664,027
In the Wings (GB)							
Singspiel (IRE)	H	1992	20	9	8	0	5,952,825
Indian Ridge (IRE)							
Ridgewood Pearl (GB)	M	1992	8	6	1	1	1,179,301
Interco							
Megan's Interco	G	1989	36	16	11	0	1,062,465
Intrepid Hero							
Interco	H	1980	21	10	4	3	1,070,688
Irish River (FR)							
Paradise Creek	H	1989	25	14	7	1	3,401,416
Hatoof	M	1989	21	9	4	1	1,841,010
Irish Prize	G	1996	28	10	4	2	1,242,364
River Bay	H	1993	20	8	3	3	1,167,970
Is It True							
Yes It's True	H	1996	22	11	2	3	1,080,700
Itajara							
Siphon (BRZ)	H	1991	25	12	6	2	3,136,428
Jade Hunter							
Azeri	M	1998	16	14	2	0	3,044,820
Yagli	H	1993	27	10	6	3	1,702,121
Jaklin Klugman							
Sky Jack	G	1996	18	10	2	2	1,115,127
Java Gold							
Kona Gold	H	1994	30	14	7	2	2,293,384
John Alden							
Little Bold John	G	1982	105	38	16	14	1,956,406
Jolie's Halo							
Hal's Hope	H	1997	33	9	5	3	1,098,422
Jules							
Peace Rules	C	2000	13	6	2	2	2,059,990
Kalaglow							
Timarida (IRE)	M	1992	16	10	2	2	1,116,186
Keen (GB)							
River Keen (IRE)	H	1992	42	11	5	5	1,642,385
Key to the Kingdom							
Great Communicator	H	1983	56	14	10	7	2,922,615
Key to the Mint							
Java Gold	H	1984	15	9	3	1	1,908,832
Jewel Princess	M	1992	29	13	4	7	1,904,060
Kingmambo							
Lemon Drop Kid	H	1996	24	10	3	3	3,245,370
Voodoo Dancer	M	1998	21	11	4	2	1,427,952
King Cugat	H	1997	16	7	7	1	1,293,782
King's Bishop							
King's Swan	H	1980	107	31	19	18	1,924,845
Kipper Kelly							
Kelly Kip	H	1994	31	15	3	4	1,157,142
Kissin Kris							
Kiss a Native	G	1997	30	12	4	2	1,054,817
Kleven							
Big Jag	G	1993	30	13	5	3	1,800,329
Kodiack							
Polar Expedition	G	1991	49	20	5	7	1,491,071
Kris (GB)							
Single Empire (IRE)	H	1994	23	5	5	3	1,110,889
Riviera (FR)	H	1994	21	10	4	3	1,018,535
Kris S.							
Prized	H	1986	17	9	2	3	2,262,555
Kissin Kris	H	1990	35	4	8	5	1,616,936
Hollywood Wildcat	M	1990	21	12	3	3	1,432,160
Soaring Softly	M	1995	16	9	1	3	1,270,433
Kudos	G	1997	24	7	5	4	1,238,935
Brocco	H	1991	8	4	2	0	1,003,550
Lando (GER)							
Paolini (GER)	H	1997	23	4	6	4	2,453,469
Langfuhr							
Wando	C	2000	13	8	2	1	2,379,700
Imperial Gesture	F	1999	11	6	2	1	1,419,140
Mobil	C	2000	15	8	3	1	1,067,711
Last Tycoon (IRE)							
Ezzoud (IRE)	H	1989	22	6	5	2	1,171,885
Lear Fan							
Sarafan	G	1997	36	9	9	4	2,390,271
Labeeb (GB)	H	1992	20	8	3	4	1,464,950
Ryafan	M	1994	10	7	1	0	1,342,142
Windsharp	M	1991	29	11	7	3	1,293,075
L'Enjoleur							
Scott's Scoundrel	H	1992	50	22	4	8	1,270,052
Little Missouri							
Prairie Bayou	G	1990	12	7	3	0	1,450,621
Lively One							
Littlebitlively	H	1994	33	10	9	5	1,303,343
Lode							
Lazy Lode (ARG)	H	1994	29	8	4	6	1,296,740
Logical							
Leger Cat (ARG)	H	1986	53	16	5	7	1,211,402
Lomitas (GB)							
Silvano (GER)	H	1996	18	7	2	2	2,321,024
Lord At War (ARG)							
John's Call	G	1991	40	16	11	3	1,571,267
Lost Code							
Kalookan Queen	M	1996	25	11	8	4	1,044,474
Louis Quatorze							
Repent	C	1999	10	5	3	1	1,255,660
Lt. Stevens							
Sefa's Beauty	M	1979	52	25	7	8	1,171,628

Horse	Sex	Born	Sts	1st	2d	3d	Earnings
Lyphard							
Manila	H	1983	18	12	5	0	2,692,799
Ski Paradise	M	1990	20	6	8	1	1,470,588
Dancing Brave	H	1983	10	8	1	0	1,435,434
Sangue (IRE)	M	1978	30	13	6	3	1,272,086
Dahar	H	1981	29	7	6	4	1,207,286
Rainbows for Life	H	1988	36	15	5	3	1,105,926
Sabin	M	1980	25	18	0	2	1,098,341
Lypheor (GB)							
Royal Heroine (IRE)	M	1980	21	10	4	2	1,229,449
Machiavellian							
Street Cry (IRE)	H	1998	12	5	6	1	5,150,837
Almutawakel (GB)	H	1995	19	4	4	1	3,643,021
Storming Home (GB)	H	1998	24	8	4	3	1,536,704
Majestic Light							
Simply Majestic	H	1984	44	18	4	7	1,667,713
Solar Splendor	G	1987	42	11	3	6	1,386,468
Lite Light	M	1988	26	8	4	4	1,231,596
Manila							
Bien Bien	H	1989	26	9	8	1	2,331,875
Manshood (GB)							
Ipi Tombe (ZIM)	H	1998	14	12	2	0	1,529,799
Marauding (NZ)							
Prowl (AUS)	G	1995	22	5	2	2	1,082,344
Marfa							
Farma Way	H	1987	23	8	5	1	2,897,175
Maria's Mon							
Monarchos	H	1998	10	4	1	3	1,720,830
Marquetry							
Artax	H	1995	25	7	9	3	1,685,840
Squirtle Squirt	H	1998	16	8	4	0	1,112,220
Mat-Boy (ARG)							
Festin (ARG)	H	1986	24	9	4	4	2,256,295
Maudlin							
Beautiful Pleasure	M	1995	25	10	5	2	2,734,078
Mecke	H	1992	40	12	7	9	2,470,550
Primal	G	1985	45	17	11	7	1,209,530
Meadowlake							
Meadow Star	M	1988	20	11	1	2	1,445,740
Medieval Man							
Not Surprising	G	1990	61	23	4	5	1,112,301
Mehmet							
On the Line	H	1984	37	14	7	2	1,125,810
Memo (CHI)							
Grey Memo	H	1997	50	8	4	10	1,733,059
Mendocino							
Starine (FR)	M	1997	33	10	12	1	1,674,491
Mill Reef							
Ibn Bey (GB)	H	1984	28	10	3	4	1,626,059
Lashkari (GB)	H	1981	13	5	2	2	1,127,658
Miracle Heights							
Sure Shot Biscuit	G	1996	54	23	10	11	1,025,480
Mister Frisky							
Frisk Me Now	H	1994	36	12	5	6	1,727,707
Miswaki							
Black Tie Affair (IRE)	H	1986	45	18	9	6	3,370,694
Urban Sea	M	1989	23	8	4	3	1,704,553
Misil	H	1988	36	14	8	3	1,296,417
Mocito Guapo							
Malek (CHI)	H	1993	23	10	7	2	2,382,623
Mountain Cat							
Classic Cat	H	1995	20	6	3	5	1,221,300

Horse	Sex	Born	Sts	1st	2d	3d	Earnings
Mr. Leader							
Ruhlmann	H	1985	27	10	3	4	1,824,154
Mr. Prospector							
Gulch	H	1984	32	13	8	4	3,095,521
Forty Niner	H	1985	19	11	5	0	2,726,000
Seeking the Gold	H	1985	15	8	6	0	2,307,000
Fusaichi Pegasus	H	1997	9	6	2	0	1,994,400
Chester House	H	1995	21	6	4	4	1,944,545
Aldebaran	H	1998	25	8	12	3	1,739,186
Dancethruthedawn	M	1998	16	7	2	3	1,609,643
Rhythm	H	1987	20	6	3	4	1,592,532
Tank's Prospect	H	1982	14	5	2	2	1,355,645
Homebuilder	H	1984	60	11	11	17	1,172,153
Educated Risk	M	1990	23	11	6	4	1,163,717
Mt. Livermore							
Orientate	H	1998	19	10	3	0	1,716,950
Peaks and Valleys	H	1992	16	9	3	2	1,589,270
Mt. Sassafras	G	1992	47	8	7	14	1,382,985
Housebuster	H	1987	22	15	3	1	1,229,696
Subordination	H	1994	21	11	3	1	1,221,068
Luthier Fever	M	1991	26	6	5	6	1,160,852
Eliza	M	1990	12	5	2	2	1,095,316
Mysterious Vice							
Mysterious Affair	M	1997	37	12	9	6	1,059,971
Naevus							
King Glorious	H	1986	9	8	1	0	1,175,650
Nashwan							
Swain (IRE)	H	1992	22	10	4	6	3,797,566
Wandesta (GB)	M	1991	21	7	3	5	1,255,145
Naskra							
Olympio	H	1988	17	9	4	0	1,456,315
Nasrullah							
Nashua	H	1952	30	22	4	1	1,288,565
Nassipour							
Let's Elope (NZ)	M	1987	26	11	0	5	2,528,902
Night Shift							
In the Groove (GB)	M	1987	21	7	4	4	1,336,783
Nijinsky II							
Ferdinand	H	1983	29	8	9	6	3,777,978
Sky Classic	H	1987	29	15	6	1	3,320,398
Dancing Spree	H	1985	35	10	6	9	1,470,484
Niniski							
Caitano (GB)	H	1994	44	9	6	7	2,137,459
Hernando (FR)	H	1990	20	7	4	1	2,081,978
No Robbery							
Track Robbery	M	1976	59	22	12	7	1,098,537
Norcliffe							
Groovy	H	1983	26	12	4	1	1,346,956
Northern Baby							
Possibly Perfect	M	1990	18	11	2	4	1,377,634
Northern Fling							
Yankee Affair	H	1982	55	22	14	8	2,282,156
Northern Jove							
Equalize	H	1982	43	13	9	8	1,455,298
Northfields							
Fieldy (IRE)	M	1983	54	19	9	8	1,212,168
Northjet (IRE)							
Southjet	H	1983	30	5	7	2	1,040,483

Horse	Sex	Born	Sts	1st	2d	3d	Earnings
Nostalgia							
Nostalgia's Star	H	1982	59	9	17	13	2,154,827
Nureyev							
Theatrical (IRE)	H	1982	22	10	4	2	2,940,036
Skimming	H	1996	20	8	5	1	2,286,601
Miesque	M	1984	16	12	3	1	2,070,163
Spinning World	H	1993	14	8	3	1	1,734,477
Good Journey	H	1996	16	7	5	3	1,733,058
Atticus	H	1992	18	7	3	1	1,205,933
Alwuhush	H	1985	22	5	4	7	1,012,423
Annoconnor	M	1984	29	12	7	5	1,002,420
Oak Dancer (GB)							
Algenib (ARG)	H	1987	21	7	5	2	1,042,299
Ole Bob Bowers							
John Henry	G	1975	83	39	15	9	6,591,860
One for All							
The Very One	M	1975	71	22	12	9	1,104,623
Opening Verse							
Colstar	M	1996	18	11	2	1	1,053,056
Our Emblem							
War Emblem	C	1999	13	7	0	0	3,491,000
Our Hero							
My Big Boy	G	1983	50	10	12	10	1,196,102
Our Native							
Zoffany	H	1980	36	15	10	2	1,225,569
Overskate							
Capades	M	1986	27	11	9	2	1,051,006
Pago Pago							
Island Whirl	H	1978	34	11	6	6	1,144,010
Palace Music							
Cigar	H	1990	33	19	4	5	9,999,815
Pampabird							
Subotica (FR)	H	1988	15	6	4	1	1,856,255
Panoramic (GB)							
Tuzla (FR)	M	1994	26	12	6	1	1,332,587
Partholon (GB)							
Symboli Rudolf (JPN)	H	1981	16	13	1	1	2,764,980
Pass the Glass							
Super Diamond	H	1980	37	16	5	5	1,469,233
Peaks and Valleys							
Dollar Bill	H	1998	22	4	5	5	1,225,546
Pepenador							
Odalea (ARG)	M	1986	21	8	7	2	1,674,812
Perrault (GB)							
Frankly Perfect	H	1985	22	6	6	4	1,272,957
Persian Bold (IRE)							
Brave Act (GB)	H	1994	27	13	6	2	1,546,269
Kooyonga (IRE)	M	1988	18	9	4	1	1,476,193
Falcon Flight (FR)	H	1996	20	5	2	3	1,428,849
Personal Flag							
Say Florida Sandy	H	1994	98	33	17	12	2,085,408
Petionville							
Island Fashion	F	2000	10	4	1	0	1,112,970
Petrone							
Brown Bess	M	1982	36	16	8	6	1,300,920
Silveyville	H	1978	56	19	11	8	1,282,880
Phone Trick							
Caller One	G	1997	20	10	3	2	3,184,500
Favorite Trick	H	1995	16	12	0	1	1,726,793
Pivotal (GB)							
Golden Apples (IRE)	M	1998	16	6	6	2	1,672,583
Megahertz (GB)	F	1999	22	8	3	5	1,159,094
Play Fellow							
Western Playboy	H	1986	45	8	7	7	1,128,449
Pleasant Colony							
Behrens	H	1994	27	9	8	3	4,563,500
Pleasantly Perfect	H	1998	13	6	2	1	2,949,880
Pleasant Tap	H	1987	32	9	9	5	2,721,169
Denon	H	1998	21	6	4	3	1,739,156
Forbidden Apple	H	1995	31	8	6	9	1,680,640
Colonial Affair	H	1990	20	7	4	3	1,635,228
Sir Beaufort	H	1987	34	10	10	4	1,149,130
Pleasant Variety	H	1984	58	8	10	11	1,123,783
Colonial Waters	M	1985	32	6	12	3	1,112,847
Pleasant Tap							
Pleasant Breeze	G	1995	36	10	8	6	1,271,680
Tap to Music	M	1995	21	6	4	4	1,052,526
Polish Navy							
Sea Hero	H	1990	24	6	3	4	2,929,869
Polish Precedent							
Pilsudski (IRE)	H	1992	22	10	6	2	4,080,297
Princequillo							
Round Table	H	1954	66	43	8	5	1,749,869
Private Account							
Personal Ensign	M	1984	13	13	0	0	1,679,880
Inside Information	M	1991	17	14	1	2	1,641,806
Valley Crossing	H	1988	48	8	13	8	1,616,490
Personal Flag	H	1983	24	8	4	4	1,258,924
Private Terms	H	1985	17	12	0	0	1,243,947
Public Purse	H	1994	14	7	1	4	1,103,324
Corporate Report	H	1988	10	3	5	0	1,067,908
Private Terms							
Soul of the Matter	H	1991	16	7	4	2	2,302,818
Afternoon Deelites	H	1992	12	7	3	0	1,061,193
Pulpit							
Essence of Dubai	C	1999	13	5	1	2	2,001,058
Quadrangle							
Susan's Girl	M	1969	63	29	14	11	1,251,668
Quiet American							
Real Quiet	H	1995	20	6	5	6	3,271,802
Rahy							
Fantastic Light	H	1996	25	12	5	3	8,486,957
Serena's Song	M	1992	38	18	11	3	3,283,388
Hawksley Hill (IRE)	G	1993	46	14	12	6	1,730,922
Tranquility Lake	M	1995	27	11	7	3	1,662,390
Tates Creek	M	1998	17	11	3	0	1,471,674
Noverre	H	1998	21	5	7	4	1,429,344
Early Pioneer	G	1995	33	9	9	5	1,156,815
Rainbow Quest							
Quest for Fame (GB)	H	1987	19	5	4	4	1,790,417
Raintrap (GB)	H	1990	28	9	4	2	1,283,707
Saumarez (GB)	H	1987	9	5	1	0	1,275,719
Urgent Request (IRE)	H	1990	25	7	4	1	1,035,339
Raja Baba							
Sacahuista	M	1984	21	6	7	2	1,298,842
Rambunctious							
Jameela	M	1976	58	27	15	6	1,038,704
Red Ransom							
Perfect Sting	H	1996	21	14	3	0	2,202,042
Reflected Glory							
Snow Chief	H	1983	24	13	3	5	3,383,210
Relaunch							
With Anticipation	G	1995	47	15	9	7	2,654,563

Horse	Sex	Born	Sts	1st	2d	3d	Earnings
Skywalker	H	1982	20	8	3	3	2,226,750
Waquoit	H	1983	30	19	4	3	2,225,360
One Dreamer	M	1988	25	12	6	2	1,266,067
Honour and Glory	H	1993	17	6	5	2	1,202,942
Restless Con							
Echo Eddie	G	1997	28	10	7	3	1,044,354
Rich Cream							
Creme Fraiche	G	1982	64	17	12	13	4,024,727
Rich Man's Gold							
Lido Palace (CHI)	H	1997	23	11	7	2	2,705,865
Risen Star							
Star Standard	H	1992	25	7	4	3	1,121,512
Riverman							
Triptych	M	1982	41	14	5	11	2,318,946
Rivlia	H	1982	41	9	2	8	1,005,041
Roberto							
Sunshine Forever	H	1985	23	8	6	3	2,084,800
Brian's Time	H	1985	21	5	2	6	1,001,269
Robin des Bois							
Gentlemen (ARG)	H	1992	24	13	4	2	3,608,558
Roi Normand							
Redattore (BRZ)	H	1995	32	15	2	6	1,799,883
Riboletta (BRZ)	M	1995	28	13	3	3	1,555,103
Roman Diplomat							
Diplomatic Jet	H	1992	51	9	5	9	1,267,202
Roughcast							
Rough Habit (NZ)	G	1986	66	28	16	7	2,861,579
Rough'n Tumble							
Dr. Fager	H	1964	22	18	2	1	1,002,642
Round Table							
Royal Glint	H	1970	52	21	9	4	1,004,816
Rousillon							
Fastness (IRE)	H	1990	24	9	6	1	1,581,165
Royal Academy							
Val Royal (FR)	H	1996	12	7	2	0	1,186,687
Rubiano							
Burning Roma	H	1998	28	11	4	5	1,324,037
Run the Gantlet							
April Run (IRE)	M	1978	18	8	2	4	1,182,819
Runaway Groom							
Cherokee Run	H	1990	28	13	5	5	1,531,818
Wekiva Springs	H	1991	21	10	4	2	1,512,575
Down the Aisle	H	1993	21	9	5	5	1,007,988
Ruritania							
Frost King	H	1978	55	27	10	3	1,196,954
Sabona							
Bonapaw	G	1996	46	18	7	4	1,158,752
Sadler's Wells							
High Chaparral (IRE)	C	1999	13	10	1	2	5,331,231
Montjeu (IRE)	H	1996	16	11	2	0	3,178,177
Galileo (IRE)	H	1998	8	6	1	0	2,245,373
Daliapour (IRE)	H	1996	26	7	3	3	2,123,763
Beat Hollow (GB)	H	1997	12	7	2	2	1,814,481
Northern Spur (IRE)	H	1991	15	6	4	3	1,614,425
In the Wings (GB)	H	1986	11	7	1	0	1,562,335
Islington (IRE)	F	1999	15	6	0	4	1,553,043
Ballingarry (IRE)	C	1999	16	5	1	4	1,543,975
Carnegie (IRE)	H	1991	13	7	1	1	1,458,787
Dream Well (FR)	H	1995	14	4	4	4	1,439,441
Opera House (GB)	H	1988	18	8	4	3	1,397,456
Dushyantor	H	1993	20	5	5	2	1,197,570
Baratea (IRE)	H	1990	16	5	4	0	1,189,181
King's Theatre (IRE)	H	1991	19	5	3	4	1,154,329
Perfect Soul (IRE)	H	1998	15	6	3	1	1,136,215
Sagace (FR)							
Arcangues	H	1988	19	6	2	2	1,981,423
Saggy							
Carry Back	H	1958	62	21	11	11	1,241,165
Saint Ballado							
Captain Bodgit	H	1994	12	7	1	4	1,014,849
Salse							
Timboroa (GB)	H	1996	25	10	3	3	1,397,228
Saros (GB)							
Fran's Valentine	M	1982	34	13	4	5	1,375,465
Sea-Bird							
Allez France	M	1970	21	13	3	1	1,262,801
Seattle Slew							
Taiki Blizzard	H	1991	23	6	8	2	5,523,549
Slew o' Gold	H	1980	21	12	5	1	3,533,534
A.P. Indy	H	1989	11	8	0	1	2,979,815
Surfside	M	1997	15	8	3	2	1,852,987
Swale	H	1981	14	9	2	2	1,583,660
Slew City Slew	H	1984	42	11	10	6	1,166,296
Flute	M	1998	8	4	3	0	1,101,504
Event of the Year	H	1995	9	5	2	1	1,095,200
Seattle Song							
Irish Linnet	M	1988	62	19	16	10	1,220,180
Secretariat							
Lady's Secret	M	1982	45	25	9	3	3,021,325
Risen Star	H	1985	11	8	2	1	2,029,845
Tinners Way	H	1990	27	7	6	4	1,846,546
Seeking the Gold							
Seeking the Pearl	M	1994	21	8	2	3	4,021,716
Heavenly Prize	M	1991	18	9	6	3	1,825,940
Dream Supreme	M	1997	16	9	2	2	1,007,680
Shadeed							
Sayyedati (GB)	M	1990	22	6	5	3	1,408,616
Sharpen Up (GB)							
Pebbles (GB)	M	1981	15	8	4	0	1,419,632
Trempolino	H	1984	11	4	3	3	1,369,233
Shot Gun Scott							
Vivace	M	1993	40	20	4	6	1,037,671
Siberian Express							
In Excess (IRE)	H	1987	25	11	2	3	1,736,733
Sillery							
Silic (FR)	H	1995	15	8	2	0	1,422,299
Silver Buck							
Silver Charm	H	1994	24	12	7	2	6,944,369
Forever Silver	H	1985	47	8	9	9	1,001,974
Silver Deputy							
Silverbulletday	M	1996	23	15	3	1	3,093,207
Silver Ghost							
Silver Goblin	G	1991	26	16	4	3	1,083,895
Silver Hawk							
Mutafaweq	H	1996	19	7	1	3	1,800,800
Hawkster	H	1986	23	6	3	4	1,510,942
Memories of Silver	M	1993	19	9	3	5	1,448,715
Silver Ending	H	1987	37	8	1	9	1,073,420
Singspiel (IRE)							
Moon Ballad (IRE)	C	1999	14	5	3	1	4,364,791
Sir Ivor Again							
Ten Keys	H	1984	54	21	8	4	1,209,211

Horse	Sex	Born	Sts	1st	2d	3d	Earnings
Sir Leon							
Sir Bear	G	1993	71	19	12	14	2,538,422
Skip Trial							
Skip Away	H	1993	38	18	10	6	9,616,360
Best of the Rest	H	1995	32	16	8	2	1,407,796
Sky Classic							
Thornfield	G	1994	19	6	1	3	1,206,074
Skywalker							
Bertrando	H	1989	24	9	6	2	3,185,610
Slew o' Gold							
Dramatic Gold	G	1991	39	9	13	6	2,567,630
Gorgeous	M	1986	14	8	4	1	1,171,370
Thirty Six Red	H	1987	20	4	3	5	1,094,310
Slewacide							
Slew of Damascus	G	1988	48	16	9	8	1,420,350
Clever Trevor	G	1986	30	15	5	2	1,388,841
Mr Ross	G	1995	44	18	6	10	1,091,046
Slewvescent							
Tout Charmant	M	1996	29	9	9	1	1,781,879
Lazy Slusan	M	1995	47	12	7	10	1,150,410
Slip Anchor (GB)							
User Friendly (GB)	M	1989	16	8	1	2	1,764,938
Smart Strike							
Fleetstreet Dancer	G	1998	23	5	7	2	1,674,806
Tenpins	H	1998	16	9	2	2	1,121,449
Smoke Glacken							
Smok'n Frolic	F	1999	25	8	5	1	1,276,500
Smokester							
Free House	H	1994	22	9	5	3	3,178,971
Southern Halo							
More Than Ready	H	1997	17	7	4	1	1,026,229
Sovereign Dancer							
Gate Dancer	H	1981	28	7	8	7	2,501,705
Louis Quatorze	H	1993	18	7	5	1	2,054,434
Itsallgreektome	G	1987	29	8	10	2	1,994,618
Bolshoi Boy	G	1983	58	16	7	8	1,039,702
Soviet Star							
Soviet Line (IRE)	G	1990	48	16	8	6	1,450,130
Volochine (IRE)	H	1991	45	8	12	9	1,205,580
Freedom Cry (GB)	H	1991	12	5	5	0	1,089,080
Spectrum (IRE)							
Golan (IRE)	H	1998	11	4	2	1	1,623,376
Spend a Buck							
Antespend	M	1993	24	10	4	2	1,011,954
Sportin' Life							
Bet Twice	H	1984	26	10	6	4	3,308,599
Stalwart							
Stalwars	H	1985	79	17	17	8	1,211,556
Star de Naskra							
Sewickley	H	1985	32	11	9	4	1,017,517
State Dinner							
Family Style	M	1983	35	10	8	7	1,537,118
Steady Growth							
Steady Power	G	1984	70	13	19	9	1,132,197
Stop the Music							
Temperence Hill	H	1977	31	11	4	2	1,567,650
Music Merci	G	1986	35	12	7	4	1,500,710
Storm Bird							
Summer Squall	H	1987	20	13	4	0	1,844,282
Indian Skimmer	M	1984	16	10	1	3	1,469,299

Horse	Sex	Born	Sts	1st	2d	3d	Earnings
Storm Boot							
Bourbon Belle	M	1995	40	16	11	5	1,152,223
Storm Cat							
Cat Thief	H	1996	30	4	9	8	3,951,012
Giant's Causeway	H	1997	13	9	4	0	3,078,989
Tabasco Cat	H	1991	18	8	3	2	2,347,671
Sharp Cat	M	1994	22	15	3	0	2,032,575
Mountain Cat	H	1990	11	6	2	0	1,478,901
Raging Fever	M	1998	26	11	7	3	1,458,198
High Yield	H	1997	14	4	4	3	1,170,196
Vision and Verse	H	1996	21	4	3	5	1,030,330
Strawberry Road (AUS)							
Escena	M	1993	29	11	9	3	2,962,639
Fraise	H	1988	34	10	5	6	2,613,105
Ajina	M	1994	17	7	3	2	1,327,915
Summer Squall							
Charismatic	H	1996	17	5	2	4	2,038,064
Summer Colony	M	1998	24	10	5	1	1,448,930
Storm Song	M	1994	12	4	1	2	1,020,050
Sunny's Halo							
Dispersal	M	1986	22	12	3	2	1,511,137
Sunny Sunrise	G	1987	63	18	12	9	1,367,268
Swain (IRE)							
Dimitrova	F	2000	9	4	2	1	1,047,292
Swing Till Dawn							
Fly Till Dawn	H	1986	27	10	5	4	1,556,525
Sword Dance (IRE)							
Marlin	H	1993	26	9	3	5	2,448,880
Blazing Sword	G	1994	45	11	7	7	1,184,055
Sword Dancer							
Damascus	H	1964	32	21	7	3	1,176,781
Talc							
Lottsa Talc	M	1990	65	21	10	12	1,206,248
Tale of Two Cities							
Cougar II	H	1966	50	20	7	17	1,172,625
Targowice							
All Along (FR)	M	1979	21	9	4	2	2,125,828
Tejano							
Tejano Run	H	1992	21	8	4	6	1,166,842
Temperence Hill							
Temperate Sil	H	1984	19	6	2	1	1,113,775
The Minstrel							
Opening Verse	H	1986	30	10	7	2	1,669,357
Savinio	G	1990	48	11	11	8	1,321,860
Theatrical (IRE)							
Royal Anthem	H	1995	12	6	3	1	1,876,876
Geri	H	1992	19	9	4	3	1,707,980
Astra	M	1996	16	11	1	2	1,378,424
Hap	H	1996	20	10	2	2	1,329,210
Strut the Stage	H	1998	19	9	2	2	1,265,923
Thunder Gulch							
Point Given	H	1998	13	9	3	0	3,968,500
Spain	M	1997	35	9	9	7	3,540,542
Mystic Lady	M	1998	27	10	8	2	1,170,390
Thunder Puddles							
Thunder Rumble	H	1989	19	8	0	1	1,047,552
Time for a Change							
Fly So Free	H	1988	33	12	5	3	2,330,954
Tom Fool							
Buckpasser	H	1963	31	25	4	1	1,462,014

Horse	Sex	Born	Sts	1st	2d	3d	Earnings
Topsider							
North Sider	M	1982	36	15	7	5	1,126,400
Top Corsage	M	1983	53	15	7	9	1,110,028
Tour d'Or							
Express Tour	H	1998	14	5	1	1	1,767,515
Transworld							
Lonesome Glory	G	1988	44	24	5	6	1,325,868
Trempolino							
Talloires	H	1990	28	5	8	3	1,423,949
Dernier Empereur	H	1990	30	8	5	4	1,152,425
Twining							
Two Item Limit	M	1998	28	7	3	5	1,060,585
Unbridled							
Banshee Breeze	M	1995	18	10	5	2	2,784,798
Empire Maker	C	2000	8	4	3	1	1,985,800
Unshaded	G	1997	20	6	3	3	1,318,492
Manistique	M	1995	15	11	1	1	1,311,800
Unbridled's Song	H	1993	12	5	4	0	1,311,800
Grindstone	H	1993	6	3	2	0	1,224,510
Red Bullet	H	1997	14	6	2	2	1,161,920
Unbridled's Song							
Unbridled Elaine	M	1998	11	6	2	1	1,770,740
Upper Case							
Flying Pidgeon	H	1981	56	12	9	13	1,154,337
Vacilante (ARG)							
Troyanos (BRZ)	H	1985	13	10	1	1	1,038,083
Vaguely Noble							
Estrapade	M	1980	30	12	5	5	1,937,142
Exceller	H	1973	33	15	5	6	1,674,587
Dahlia	M	1970	48	15	3	7	1,489,105
Lemhi Gold	H	1978	22	8	3	1	1,131,355
Val de l'Orne (FR)							
Pay the Butler	H	1984	40	5	5	5	1,934,140
Valdez							
El Senor	H	1984	44	12	7	5	1,769,215
Velvet Cap							
Trinycarol (VEN)	M	1979	29	18	3	1	2,644,392
Verbatim							
Princess Rooney	M	1980	21	17	2	1	1,343,339
Alphabatim	H	1981	22	7	3	5	1,313,175
Hopeful Word	H	1981	43	18	12	3	1,073,051
Vice Regent							
Regal Classic	H	1985	27	8	8	3	1,456,584
Twice the Vice	M	1991	23	12	6	1	1,447,064
Regal Intention	H	1985	41	14	7	10	1,083,103
Bessarabian	M	1982	37	18	5	4	1,032,640
Vigors							
Real Connection	M	1991	72	7	14	7	1,225,018
Hodges Bay	G	1985	51	7	15	3	1,050,363
Voyageur							
My Own Business (VEN)	H	1997	50	37	5	1	1,016,908
Waquoit							
Halo America	M	1990	40	15	8	2	1,460,992
Warning (GB)							
Annus Mirabilis (FR)	H	1992	30	9	7	6	1,541,938
Way West (FR)							
Western Pride	H	1998	29	10	4	1	1,288,569
What a Pleasure							
Foolish Pleasure	H	1972	26	16	4	3	1,216,705
Whiskey Road							
Strawberry Road (AUS)	H	1979	50	21	7	9	1,655,678
Wild Again							
Milwaukee Brew	H	1997	24	8	4	5	2,879,612
Wilderness Song	M	1988	37	15	12	2	1,482,033
Wild Rush	H	1994	16	8	0	3	1,386,302
Shine Again	M	1997	34	14	10	7	1,271,840
Elmhurst	G	1990	51	8	11	6	1,100,567
With Approval							
Maltese Superb	M	1997	35	4	7	4	1,145,491
Woodman							
Hansel	H	1988	14	7	2	3	2,936,586
Hawk Wing	C	1999	12	5	5	0	1,610,604
Timber Country	H	1992	12	5	1	4	1,560,400
Yachtie (AUS)							
Happyanunoit (NZ)	M	1995	21	9	6	2	1,582,118
You and I							
You	F	1999	23	9	8	2	2,101,353
Your Host							
Kelso	G	1957	63	39	12	2	1,977,896
Zinaad (GB)							
Kazzia (GER)	F	1999	7	5	0	0	1,094,206

This section includes all horses with at least $1 million in career earnings that had at least one start in North America. It includes any foreign earnings and bonus money awarded for racing performance that was reported to *Daily Racing Form*.

Top Juvenile Sires in 2003 – Money Won

Sire	Perfs.	Winning Perfs.	Starts	1st	2nd	3rd	Unplaced	Purses
Tale of the Cat	57	24	162	34	26	21	81	$1,918,383
Grand Slam	42	14	115	23	20	22	50	1,369,174
Silver Deputy	23	11	68	17	11	3	37	1,331,908
Saint Ballado	31	11	97	16	19	14	48	1,255,985
Kris S.	9	4	20	6	4	0	10	1,177,260
A.P. Indy	44	18	125	23	22	10	70	1,114,966
Smoke Glacken	29	17	112	29	19	13	51	1,094,563
Unbridled's Song	35	16	100	18	18	12	52	1,071,880
Unbridled	14	3	35	6	4	4	21	1,024,658
Wild Rush	28	11	86	17	19	11	39	997,759
Victory Gallop	40	11	107	14	16	14	63	914,179
Halo's Image	23	9	109	18	11	19	61	892,481
Forest Wildcat	42	23	136	27	19	14	76	837,625
Langfuhr	41	18	147	26	20	22	79	825,193
Valid Expectations	38	17	131	26	18	20	67	814,703
Carson City	28	13	92	19	13	13	47	803,926
Doneraile Court	37	16	154	24	25	18	87	768,687
Tomorrows Cat	45	16	142	20	18	13	91	765,059
El Prado (IRE)	28	11	88	19	8	11	50	761,232
Montbrook	27	8	98	11	12	11	64	732,590
Forestry	19	11	65	18	12	14	21	716,645
Old Trieste	19	8	64	9	14	7	34	692,090
Salt Lake	30	13	90	22	9	13	46	679,760
Boston Harbor	34	18	125	24	12	15	74	667,301
Gold Case	32	11	104	16	17	18	53	664,913
Cherokee Run	35	13	127	17	13	13	84	664,678
Distorted Humor	29	13	76	16	6	12	42	660,199
Grindstone	18	8	58	12	11	4	31	659,176
Malibu Moon	21	12	70	18	10	8	34	652,179
Gold Fever	40	8	121	12	18	14	77	650,260
Lost Soldier	28	11	104	14	12	13	65	640,364
Bold Executive	16	8	69	11	11	12	35	639,798
Hennessy	30	12	83	19	6	2	56	601,014
Double Honor	40	23	172	31	26	21	94	576,513
Silver Charm	30	15	101	16	12	12	61	573,638
Benchmark	15	9	57	17	9	4	27	563,129
Swiss Yodeler	25	14	129	17	24	18	70	558,892
Cape Town	26	9	69	15	9	6	39	554,002
Souvenir Copy	37	15	124	17	16	18	73	550,100
Gulch	10	4	32	7	8	2	15	539,019
Roar	32	15	96	17	17	13	49	538,247
Coronado's Quest	29	5	67	7	5	8	47	536,328
Lit de Justice	21	11	86	14	15	11	46	534,872
Stormin Fever	35	16	124	17	15	19	73	529,054
Stormy Atlantic	38	13	117	18	16	25	58	524,799
Family Calling	33	17	178	24	25	23	106	519,840
Exploit	43	14	145	15	20	19	91	515,992
Mazel Trick	42	13	119	14	9	12	84	514,053
Archers Bay	22	7	66	7	9	12	38	513,021
Quiet American	37	11	122	14	15	15	78	499,637
Tactical Cat	24	10	78	12	14	8	44	491,972
Whiskey Wisdom	11	3	42	5	6	7	24	490,037
Honour and Glory	36	10	101	15	16	18	52	487,049
Storm Boot	47	17	141	24	12	22	83	471,166
Formal Dinner	30	12	152	18	25	18	91	462,161
American Chance	29	11	88	17	13	7	51	457,090

Sire	Perfs.	Winning Perfs.	Starts	1st	2nd	3rd	Unplaced	Purses
Siphon (BRZ)	37	6	106	8	13	19	66	455,534
Skip Away	37	12	138	15	14	18	91	452,071
Kissin Kris	36	7	138	11	16	11	100	449,583
Lord Carson	18	9	78	14	14	7	43	441,296
Seneca Jones	14	8	65	12	13	15	25	435,394
Rizzi	34	12	146	18	15	16	97	434,609
Elusive Quality	36	10	91	11	9	12	59	429,167
Lucky Lionel	28	12	94	14	11	10	59	427,958
Jules	20	10	83	21	5	4	53	424,378
Pulpit	26	10	64	12	8	12	32	423,658
Indian Charlie	21	7	79	11	11	18	39	420,710
Polish Numbers	19	4	60	9	5	9	37	414,140
Belong to Me	24	10	71	11	11	7	42	405,627
Captain Bodgit	25	10	80	14	11	10	45	403,757
Sea of Secrets	24	11	95	17	16	13	49	403,478
Capote	22	6	69	10	6	5	48	399,654
Crafty Prospector	23	12	73	13	18	9	33	394,808
Kiridashi	12	4	33	6	3	4	20	394,382
Glitterman	18	9	69	13	15	11	30	392,611
Sir Cat	27	13	96	16	16	9	55	389,844
Boundary	15	8	46	13	7	5	21	386,078
Bertrando	22	8	61	9	12	12	28	377,898
Menifee	17	7	66	8	15	13	30	373,055
Porto Foricos	3	1	15	3	2	2	8	372,582
Military	16	9	63	13	7	7	36	367,616
Afternoon Deelites	20	9	83	12	17	13	41	366,280
Sword Dance (IRE)	27	11	114	13	14	13	74	365,755
Dance Brightly	36	17	147	19	13	16	99	360,657
Smokester	32	13	102	16	13	10	63	360,416
Peaks and Valleys	17	5	75	7	11	8	49	358,776
Louis Quatorze	29	8	87	11	11	6	59	355,078
Southern Halo	32	7	125	9	22	16	78	354,265
Unreal Zeal	19	9	66	14	6	10	36	352,710
Good and Tough	20	9	80	11	13	10	46	352,341
Katahaula County	17	9	58	14	10	6	28	352,094
Free House	21	7	83	9	7	10	57	349,079
Cryptoclearance	38	10	134	13	14	12	95	346,186
Rodeo	20	8	54	10	10	3	31	343,521
Maria's Mon	33	7	100	7	12	14	67	342,610
Not For Love	17	8	53	9	14	10	20	342,238
Confide	28	7	95	9	11	13	62	341,474
Dixieland Band	21	7	59	11	7	5	36	338,097
Real Quiet	30	8	102	12	9	10	71	329,331
Time Bandit	10	5	46	8	8	14	16	328,928
Accelerator	44	12	160	15	18	15	112	328,541
Appealing Skier	24	16	97	17	15	10	55	327,824
Leestown	30	12	117	15	15	17	70	326,942

Top Juvenile Sires in 2003 – Races Won

Sire	Perfs.	Winning Perfs	Starts	1st	2nd	3rd	Unplaced	Purses
Tale of the Cat	57	24	162	34	26	21	81	$1,918,383
Double Honor	40	23	172	31	26	21	94	576,513
Smoke Glacken	29	17	112	29	19	13	51	1,094,563
Forest Wildcat	42	23	136	27	19	14	76	837,625
Langfuhr	41	18	147	26	20	22	79	825,193
Valid Expectations	38	17	131	26	18	20	67	814,703
Doneraile Court	37	16	154	24	25	18	87	768,687
Boston Harbor	34	18	125	24	12	15	74	667,301
Family Calling	33	17	178	24	25	23	106	519,840
Storm Boot	47	17	141	24	12	22	83	471,166
Grand Slam	42	14	115	23	20	22	50	1,369,174
A.P. Indy	44	18	125	23	22	10	70	1,114,966
Salt Lake	30	13	90	22	9	13	46	679,760
Jules	20	10	83	21	5	4	53	424,378
Tomorrows Cat	45	16	142	20	18	13	91	765,059
Carson City	28	13	92	19	13	13	47	803,926
El Prado (IRE)	28	11	88	19	8	11	50	761,232
Hennessy	30	12	83	19	6	2	56	601,014
Dance Brightly	36	17	147	19	13	16	99	360,657
Fortunate Prospect	23	14	125	19	20	12	74	293,580
Unbridled's Song	35	16	100	18	18	12	52	1,071,880
Halo's Image	23	9	109	18	11	19	61	892,481
Forestry	19	11	65	18	12	14	21	716,645
Malibu Moon	21	12	70	18	10	8	34	652,179
Stormy Atlantic	38	13	117	18	16	25	58	524,799
Formal Dinner	30	12	152	18	25	18	91	462,161
Rizzi	34	12	146	18	15	16	97	434,609
Suave Prospect	24	14	96	18	10	14	54	270,083
Silver Deputy	23	11	68	17	11	3	37	1,331,908
Wild Rush	28	11	86	17	19	11	39	997,759
Cherokee Run	35	13	127	17	13	13	84	664,678
Benchmark	15	9	57	17	9	4	27	563,129
Swiss Yodeler	25	14	129	17	24	18	70	558,892
Souvenir Copy	37	15	124	17	16	18	73	550,100
Roar	32	15	96	17	17	13	49	538,247
Stormin Fever	35	16	124	17	15	19	73	529,054
American Chance	29	11	88	17	13	7	51	457,090
Sea of Secrets	24	11	95	17	16	13	49	403,478
Appealing Skier	24	16	97	17	15	10	55	327,824
Wild Zone	31	12	114	17	16	13	68	313,959
Saint Ballado	31	11	97	16	19	14	48	1,255,985
Gold Case	32	11	104	16	17	18	53	664,913
Distorted Humor	29	13	76	16	6	12	42	660,199
Silver Charm	30	15	101	16	12	12	61	573,638
Sir Cat	27	13	96	16	16	9	55	389,844
Smokester	32	13	102	16	13	10	63	360,416
In Excessive Bull	17	9	56	16	5	9	26	270,906
Slewdledo	23	12	77	16	7	15	39	241,073
Cape Town	26	9	69	15	9	6	39	554,002
Exploit	43	14	145	15	20	19	91	515,992
Honour and Glory	36	10	101	15	16	18	52	487,049
Skip Away	37	12	138	15	14	18	91	452,071
Accelerator	44	12	160	15	18	15	112	328,541
Leestown	30	12	117	15	15	17	70	326,942
Hadif	25	14	121	15	16	11	79	245,166
Slew City Slew	38	14	113	15	12	7	79	231,003
Victory Gallop	40	11	107	14	16	14	63	914,179

Sire	Perfs.	Winning Perfs.	Starts	1st	2nd	3rd	Unplaced	Purses
Lost Soldier	28	11	104	14	12	13	65	640,364
Lit de Justice	21	11	86	14	15	11	46	534,872
Mazel Trick	42	13	119	14	9	12	84	514,053
Quiet American	37	11	122	14	15	15	78	499,637
Lord Carson	18	9	78	14	14	7	43	441,296
Lucky Lionel	28	12	94	14	11	10	59	427,958
Captain Bodgit	25	10	80	14	11	10	45	403,757
Unreal Zeal	19	9	66	14	6	10	36	352,710
Katahaula County	17	9	58	14	10	6	28	352,094
Concerto	19	12	70	14	8	9	39	301,499
Perfect Vision	15	8	71	14	8	6	43	285,247
Kipper Kelly	18	10	82	14	8	13	47	273,202
Wild Event	22	11	96	14	5	9	68	258,723
Cat's Career	19	7	78	14	5	5	54	165,595
Basket Weave	18	12	70	14	9	9	38	107,354
Crafty Prospector	23	12	73	13	18	9	33	394,808
Glitterman	18	9	69	13	15	11	30	392,611
Boundary	15	8	46	13	7	5	21	386,078
Military	16	9	63	13	7	7	36	367,616
Sword Dance (IRE)	27	11	114	13	14	13	74	365,755
Cryptoclearance	38	10	134	13	14	12	95	346,186
Meadowlake	22	9	78	13	6	9	50	311,360
Count the Time	21	10	85	13	10	6	56	289,380
Friendly Lover	21	10	103	13	17	9	64	259,250
Editor's Note	19	10	79	13	8	8	50	252,368
Defrere	26	11	75	13	9	11	42	235,919
Bianconi	26	12	72	13	6	10	43	205,216
Grindstone	18	8	58	12	11	4	31	659,176
Gold Fever	40	8	121	12	18	14	77	650,260
Tactical Cat	24	10	78	12	14	8	44	491,972
Seneca Jones	14	8	65	12	13	15	25	435,394
Pulpit	26	10	64	12	8	12	32	423,658
Afternoon Deelites	20	9	83	12	17	13	41	366,280
Real Quiet	30	8	102	12	9	10	71	329,331
Finest Hour	14	8	51	12	3	9	27	296,527
Honor Grades	22	9	78	12	10	8	48	270,040
Dove Hunt	22	10	105	12	14	11	68	268,667
Crafty Friend	31	10	93	12	10	5	66	240,889
Hazaam	14	9	75	12	9	13	41	226,942
Demidoff	28	10	94	12	7	13	62	206,943
Baquero	20	7	78	12	10	9	47	174,595
Montbrook	27	8	98	11	12	11	64	732,590
Bold Executive	16	8	69	11	11	12	35	639,798
Kissin Kris	36	7	138	11	16	11	100	449,583
Elusive Quality	36	10	91	11	9	12	59	429,167
Indian Charlie	21	7	79	11	11	18	39	420,710
Belong to Me	24	10	71	11	11	7	42	405,627
Louis Quatorze	29	8	87	11	11	6	59	355,078
Good and Tough	20	9	80	11	13	10	46	352,341
Dixieland Band	21	7	59	11	7	5	36	338,097
Pioneering	23	11	93	11	15	10	57	310,661
Mister Jolie	15	5	59	11	10	17	21	256,943
Marquetry	30	8	95	11	10	12	62	243,510
Northern Afleet	14	8	47	11	8	4	24	229,825
Tactical Advantage	25	11	104	11	12	17	64	223,047
Favorite Trick	17	9	65	11	10	9	35	204,539
Devil His Due	20	6	60	11	6	7	36	198,403
Banker's Gold	26	8	91	11	12	10	58	184,374

Top Juvenile Sires in 2003 – Winning Performers

Sire	Perfs.	Winning Perfs	Starts	1st	2nd	3rd	Unplaced	Purses
Tale of the Cat	57	24	162	34	26	21	81	$1,918,383
Forest Wildcat	42	23	136	27	19	14	76	837,625
Double Honor	40	23	172	31	26	21	94	576,513
A.P. Indy	44	18	125	23	22	10	70	1,114,966
Langfuhr	41	18	147	26	20	22	79	825,193
Boston Harbor	34	18	125	24	12	15	74	667,301
Smoke Glacken	29	17	112	29	19	13	51	1,094,563
Valid Expectations	38	17	131	26	18	20	67	814,703
Family Calling	33	17	178	24	25	23	106	519,840
Storm Boot	47	17	141	24	12	22	83	471,166
Dance Brightly	36	17	147	19	13	16	99	360,657
Unbridled's Song	35	16	100	18	18	12	52	1,071,880
Doneraile Court	37	16	154	24	25	18	87	768,687
Tomorrows Cat	45	16	142	20	18	13	91	765,059
Stormin Fever	35	16	124	17	15	19	73	529,054
Appealing Skier	24	16	97	17	15	10	55	327,824
Silver Charm	30	15	101	16	12	12	61	573,638
Souvenir Copy	37	15	124	17	16	18	73	550,100
Roar	32	15	96	17	17	13	49	538,247
Grand Slam	42	14	115	23	20	22	50	1,369,174
Swiss Yodeler	25	14	129	17	24	18	70	558,892
Exploit	43	14	145	15	20	19	91	515,992
Fortunate Prospect	23	14	125	19	20	12	74	293,580
Suave Prospect	24	14	96	18	10	14	54	270,083
Hadif	25	14	121	15	16	11	79	245,166
Slew City Slew	38	14	113	15	12	7	79	231,003
Carson City	28	13	92	19	13	13	47	803,926
Salt Lake	30	13	90	22	9	13	46	679,760
Cherokee Run	35	13	127	17	13	13	84	664,678
Distorted Humor	29	13	76	16	6	12	42	660,199
Stormy Atlantic	38	13	117	18	16	25	58	524,799
Mazel Trick	42	13	119	14	9	12	84	514,053
Sir Cat	27	13	96	16	16	9	55	389,844
Smokester	32	13	102	16	13	10	63	360,416
Malibu Moon	21	12	70	18	10	8	34	652,179
Hennessy	30	12	83	19	6	2	56	601,014
Formal Dinner	30	12	152	18	25	18	91	462,161
Skip Away	37	12	138	15	14	18	91	452,071
Rizzi	34	12	146	18	15	16	97	434,609
Lucky Lionel	28	12	94	14	11	10	59	427,958
Crafty Prospector	23	12	73	13	18	9	33	394,808
Accelerator	44	12	160	15	18	15	112	328,541
Leestown	30	12	117	15	15	17	70	326,942
Wild Zone	31	12	114	17	16	13	68	313,959
Concerto	19	12	70	14	8	9	39	301,499
Slewdledo	23	12	77	16	7	15	39	241,073
Bianconi	26	12	72	13	6	10	43	205,216
Basket Weave	18	12	70	14	9	9	38	107,354
Silver Deputy	23	11	68	17	11	3	37	1,331,908
Saint Ballado	31	11	97	16	19	14	48	1,255,985
Wild Rush	28	11	86	17	19	11	39	997,759
Victory Gallop	40	11	107	14	16	14	63	914,179
El Prado (IRE)	28	11	88	19	8	11	50	761,232
Forestry	19	11	65	18	12	14	21	716,645
Gold Case	32	11	104	16	17	18	53	664,913
Lost Soldier	28	11	104	14	12	13	65	640,364
Lit de Justice	21	11	86	14	15	11	46	534,872
Quiet American	37	11	122	14	15	15	78	499,637

Sire	Perfs.	Winning Perfs.	Starts	1st	2nd	3rd	Unplaced	Purses
American Chance	29	11	88	17	13	7	51	457,090
Sea of Secrets	24	11	95	17	16	13	49	403,478
Sword Dance (IRE)	27	11	114	13	14	13	74	365,755
Pioneering	23	11	93	11	15	10	57	310,661
Wild Event	22	11	96	14	5	9	68	258,723
Defrere	26	11	75	13	9	11	42	235,919
Tactical Advantage	25	11	104	11	12	17	64	223,047
Tactical Cat	24	10	78	12	14	8	44	491,972
Honour and Glory	36	10	101	15	16	18	52	487,049
Elusive Quality	36	10	91	11	9	12	59	429,167
Jules	20	10	83	21	5	4	53	424,378
Pulpit	26	10	64	12	8	12	32	423,658
Belong to Me	24	10	71	11	11	7	42	405,627
Captain Bodgit	25	10	80	14	11	10	45	403,757
Cryptoclearance	38	10	134	13	14	12	95	346,186
Count the Time	21	10	85	13	10	6	56	289,380
Kipper Kelly	18	10	82	14	8	13	47	273,202
Dove Hunt	22	10	105	12	14	11	68	268,667
Friendly Lover	21	10	103	13	17	9	64	259,250
Editor's Note	19	10	79	13	8	8	50	252,368
Distinctive Cat	26	10	91	10	13	19	49	249,993
Crafty Friend	31	10	93	12	10	5	66	240,889
Demidoff	28	10	94	12	7	13	62	206,943
Formal Gold	21	10	62	10	3	7	42	204,449
Halo's Image	23	9	109	18	11	19	61	892,481
Benchmark	15	9	57	17	9	4	27	563,129
Cape Town	26	9	69	15	9	6	39	554,002
Lord Carson	18	9	78	14	14	7	43	441,296
Glitterman	18	9	69	13	15	11	30	392,611
Military	16	9	63	13	7	7	36	367,616
Afternoon Deelites	20	9	83	12	17	13	41	366,280
Unreal Zeal	19	9	66	14	6	10	36	352,710
Good and Tough	20	9	80	11	13	10	46	352,341
Katahaula County	17	9	58	14	10	6	28	352,094
Meadowlake	22	9	78	13	6	9	50	311,360
Lil's Lad	32	9	97	10	14	13	60	301,404
In Excessive Bull	17	9	56	16	5	9	26	270,906
Honor Grades	22	9	78	12	10	8	48	270,040
Lite the Fuse	21	9	75	10	8	17	40	268,648
Hazaam	14	9	75	12	9	13	41	226,942
Favorite Trick	17	9	65	11	10	9	35	204,539
Pentelicus	26	9	114	9	12	15	78	199,188
Line In The Sand	41	9	184	9	21	24	130	196,670
Lil E. Tee	19	9	73	11	8	12	42	181,528

Top 10 Juvenile Sires and Their Progeny

Tale of the Cat, Dk B H (1994)
By Storm Cat – Yarn, by Mr. Prospector
57 Performers, 24 winning performers, $1,918,383 in total earnings

Progeny	Mare	Age	Sts	1st	2d	3d	Money Won
Adage	Firey Affair	2	6	1	3	0	71,575
Ancient Myth	Pleasant Oasis	2	3	0	0	2	5,460
Artemus Sunrise	Eggs Binnedict	2	3	1	1	0	38,495
Be Gentle	Gentlelilstar	2	7	4	1	0	523,078
Belmont Babe	Arizona Star	2	2	0	0	1	4,100
Black Tie Classic	Black Tie M. D.	2	1	0	0	0	0
Blushingkittentale	Blushing Issue	2	8	1	1	1	16,425
Boom a Cat a Boom	Lovely Sebeecha	2	1	0	0	0	780
Brokenhearted Cat	Sheza Valentine	2	1	1	0	0	13,800
Cali Cali	Stem	2	8	0	1	0	2,680
Cat Buster	Big Dreams	2	4	1	0	1	34,330
Cat Sound	Sound It	2	1	0	0	0	0
Cat's Account	Miner's Match	2	4	1	0	0	17,130
Catboat	Northern Fleet	2	3	0	0	1	1,390
Catsgotninelives	Sea Abyss	2	2	0	0	0	0
Chocolate Tale	Shamrock Time	2	2	0	0	0	295
Cielo's Cat	Cielo's Dance	2	2	0	0	1	2,310
Crockett	Shared Magic	2	1	0	0	0	330
Feline Story	Shappy	2	6	3	1	0	201,780
Glamour Cat	Turk Machine	2	1	0	0	0	2,940
Go Kitty Go	Miami Margie	2	5	0	2	2	39,663
Heaven's Cat	Debs Angel	2	1	0	0	1	2,280
Itawtisawaputtytat	Rubies for Alicia	2	2	1	1	0	18,800
Jack of Clubs	Regal Ruby	2	1	0	0	0	1,230
Key to the Cat	Key to Paradise	2	6	1	1	0	24,275
Lil Gary Too	She's Family	2	2	1	0	0	15,600
Lion Heart	Satin Sunrise	2	3	3	0	0	310,800
Lonesomenumberone	Mime (IRE)	2	1	0	0	0	120
Lord of the Cats	Energise	2	5	1	1	1	23,650
Macann's Promise	Bearly Smiling	2	3	0	0	2	7,386
Matching Sox	Silver and Bronze	2	4	0	4	0	47,400
My Turbeau Cat	My Turbulent Beau	2	1	0	0	0	0
One Lucky Storm	Shameem	2	4	1	0	1	11,745
Point Hidden	Rose of Cimarron (FR)	2	1	0	0	0	0
Red Earthquake	Zuppa	2	1	0	0	0	1,800
Relato Del Gato	Sole	2	3	0	0	1	5,400
Remarqable Tale	Marquetry Road	2	1	0	0	0	0
Resplendency	Doppio Espresso	2	3	1	1	0	37,520
Shenanigan Cat	Cool Slate	2	1	0	0	0	330
Speak Easy	Donna Says So	2	2	0	2	0	11,200
Spellbinder	Thorough Fair	2	5	1	0	1	41,260
Stalkerazzi	Haze	2	3	1	1	0	42,045
Story of the Cat	With Brilliance	2	1	0	0	0	0
Sydneyleigh	Noble Dream Maker	2	1	0	0	0	124
Tale of Woe	Robyns Tune	2	2	1	1	0	36,720
Taleofthewampuscat	Gracious Reason	2	1	0	0	0	900
Tango Tales	Tango's Mambo	2	1	0	1	0	8,540
Tencies Cat	Mimi's Brett	2	2	0	0	1	2,970
The Cat's Tail	Safe T Matches	2	8	1	0	1	14,620
Truecat	Bravada	2	1	0	0	0	0
Tune's Tale	Light of the Moon	2	2	0	0	0	2,580
Uppity Kitty	Princess Harriet	2	4	2	1	1	78,780
Whoopi Cat	Whoopi (NZ)	2	2	2	0	0	115,800
Wild Tale	Young and Wild	2	2	1	1	0	27,600
Winitformom	Colonial Feast	2	2	1	0	0	9,000
Winter Tide	Winthrop Arms	2	2	0	0	1	8,232
Zipcody	Rosekris	2	7	2	1	1	33,115
Grand Warrior	Heartful Star	2	3	0	0	3	14,610
Grande's Grandslam	Grande Armee	2	3	0	1	0	7,795
Hit It Here Cafe	Strawberry's Charm	2	2	0	0	0	0
Houndstooth	Shining Through	2	2	0	0	0	0
Hyannis	Coribek	2	1	0	0	0	360
In the Park	Short Time	2	1	0	0	0	750
Limehouse	Dixieland Blues	2	6	3	0	2	260,435
Linda Belinda	Like Liza Can	2	2	0	0	1	7,980
Little Switz	Operator Seven	2	2	0	1	0	7,160
Long Pond	Light Up New York	2	2	0	1	0	15,756
Lucky Slam	Mi Lucia	2	2	0	1	1	9,050
Mamie Mom	Susana	2	1	0	0	1	1,650
Master David	Nadra (IRE)	2	1	0	1	0	40,000
Mizzen Lass	Minstrelsy	2	3	0	0	1	3,715
Nerve Ending	Winter Treasure	2	1	0	0	0	180
Pacific Island	Pacific Hideaway	2	5	2	1	0	48,050
Parkers Peace	In the Know	2	2	0	0	0	510
Seatriscuit	Summertime Val	2	5	1	0	1	14,846
Silent Picture	Moving Picture	2	1	0	0	0	0
Slam Dancing	Oh How We Danced	2	2	0	0	0	780
Sliding Home	Flowers and Vines	2	2	0	0	1	6,330
Sweet Jo Jo	Wild Decision	2	7	3	0	2	134,210
Triple Slam	Santona (CHI)	2	2	0	0	0	1,170
Victorious Slam	Approve	2	1	0	0	0	137
Winning Run	Shardona	2	5	1	0	0	10,075

Silver Deputy, B H (1985)
By Deputy Minister – Silver Valley, by Mr. Prospector
23 Performers, 11 winning performers, $1,331,908 in total earnings

Progeny	Mare	Age	Sts	1st	2d	3d	Money Won
Amsterdam Ave.	Foot Stone	2	4	0	0	1	4,620
Ballroom Deputy	Tango Charlie	2	3	1	0	0	16,345
Baroness Silvia	Omnia	2	5	0	0	0	3,180
Breakaway	Make Haste	2	6	1	3	0	48,475
Cherry Springs	Abrasive	2	3	0	0	0	1,350
Cosmos Mariner	Antahkarana	2	1	0	0	0	
Dundurn	Brushed Halory	2	2	1	0	0	35,280
Joe Six Pack	Dixie Melody	2	4	3	0	0	127,800
Lingerie	Ligurian	2	4	1	1	0	9,900
Lulu Lemon	Chip	2	1	0	0	0	0
Mr. Jester	Future Pretense	2	6	4	2	0	730,800
Nashinda	Adorned	2	2	2	0	0	148,635
Number Juan	Colonial Reef	2	2	0	1	0	12,740
Parkers Mill	Seda Fina	2	1	0	0	1	4,100
Pericles	Orange Sickle	2	3	1	1	0	40,900
Scrambling	Apelia	2	4	0	0	0	0
She's Sterling	Miss Turlington	2	1	0	0	0	0
Shrewd Deputy	Shrewd Vixen	2	2	0	0	0	2,978
Silver Calling	Glorious Calling	2	2	0	0	0	0
Silver Minister	Mint Leaf	2	3	1	2	0	31,890
Silver Ticket	Go First Class	2	3	1	1	0	90,120
Some Party	Merry Festival	2	1	0	0	0	1,980
Veredus	Slept Thru It	2	5	1	0	1	20,915

Saint Ballado, Dk B H (1989)
By Halo – Ballade, by Herbager
31 Performers, 11 winning performers, $1,255,985 in total earnings

Progeny	Mare	Age	Sts	1st	2d	3d	Money Won
Ashado	Goulash	2	6	4	1	1	610,800
Ballado Breeze	Wild Royal	2	4	1	1	1	27,980
Battle Red	Royal Fit	2	1	0	0	0	0
Braytonville	Mission Park	2	2	0	0	1	5,000
Cartage Agent	Imaginary Number	2	5	0	5	0	45,400
Comanche Star	Deceit Princess	2	1	0	0	0	2,135
Freska	Franziska (IRE)	2	2	0	0	1	8,820
Gethsemani	Bottle Top	2	7	1	2	3	60,365
Heros Among Us	Lady Ling (ARG)	2	1	0	0	0	0
In Rome	Our Shopping Spree	2	8	2	1	1	88,740
King Carlos	Word o' Ransom	2	4	1	2	0	28,710
Klassy Katlyn	Chicken Delight	2	6	0	2	0	24,360
Media Saint	Mediation (IRE)	2	3	0	0	1	3,220
Northern Ballad	Sloane Street	2	3	0	0	0	3,960
Paddington	Painted Portrait	2	5	2	1	0	109,620
Paint Ballado	Donusa	2	3	0	1	0	7,260
Preach It	Arrested Dreams	2	1	0	0	0	0
Prospective Saint	A. B. Prospect	2	2	1	0	1	19,080
Roused	With Every Wish	2	2	1	0	0	27,455
Royal Parade	Deputy Royal	2	2	0	0	1	2,340
Running Saint	Chadra Min	2	5	0	1	1	20,724
Saint Martin	Hope's Ahead	2	3	0	0	0	0
Saint Seminole	Smokey Mirage	2	1	0	0	1	6,666
Santa Rosalia	Sugar Is Gold	2	4	0	0	1	7,650

Grand Slam, Dk B H, (1995)
By Gone West – Bright Candles, by El Gran Senor
42 Performers, 14 winning performers, $1,369,174 in total earnings

Progeny	Mare	Age	Sts	1st	2d	3d	Money Won
All Electric	Electric Shock	2	2	1	0	0	27,815
Before Sunset	Sunset Song	2	1	0	0	0	2,500
Cherish Destiny	Silver Hiawatha	2	4	1	2	0	55,260
Clear the Bases	Hay Hanne	2	1	0	0	0	2,700
Dance Instructor	Ransom Dance	2	4	0	1	0	6,950
Estevan	Sandy's Storm	2	5	2	0	1	96,405
Everheart	Northern Dynasty	2	2	1	1	0	40,245
Every Trick	Destiny Now	2	1	0	0	0	0
Fire Slam	Miss Firefly	2	3	2	1	0	259,430
Flushing Meadows	Sheepish Grin	2	4	2	0	1	77,100
Fly Me Ali	Psychic Spirit	2	1	0	1	0	3,510
Gainango	Evaluating	2	2	0	1	1	13,950
Good Lookin'	Our Dear Helen	2	4	0	4	0	15,485
Grand Cap D	Topsa	2	6	1	1	2	24,520
Grand Heritage	Minstrel's Lassie	2	6	2	0	2	92,210
Grand Prayer	Lyrical Prayer	2	2	0	2	0	18,000
Grand Score	Alaska Queen	2	3	1	0	2	47,545

		Age Sts 1st 2d 3d	Won
She Ain't No Saint	Jolie's Valentine	2 1 0 0 0	0
Sinners N Saints	Navarra	2 1 0 0 0	420
St Averil	Avie's Fancy	2 2 1 1 0	98,000
Stacie's Ballado	Storm Minister	2 5 1 1 0	14,160
Sweet Melody	Interpretive Mood	2 1 0 0 0	0
Tequesta	Bodacious Tatas	2 5 1 0 0	33,120
Vagabond Saint	Queens n Vagabonds	2 1 0 0 0	0

Kris S., Dk B H (1977)
By Roberto – Sharp Queen, by Princequillo
9 Performers, 4 winning performers, $1,177,260 in total earnings

Progeny	Mare	Age Sts 1st 2d 3d	Money Won
Action This Day	Najecam	2 3 2 1 0	817,200
Admiralty Inlet	Vashon	2 1 0 0 0	0
Amador	Elevated Love	2 1 0 1 0	6,600
Crimson	Competitive	2 1 0 0 0	0
Florik's Baby	Final Say	2 1 0 0 0	140
Gingham and Lace	In the Till	2 3 1 1 0	21,600
Krisherra	Ausherra	2 2 1 0 0	15,780
Tiger Hunt	Thega	2 4 2 1 0	312,820
View At Beaches	Squalling	2 4 0 0 0	3,120

A.P. Indy, Dk B H (1989)
By Seattle Slew – Weekend Surprise, by Secretariat
44 Performers, 18 winning performers, $1,114,966 in total earnings

Progeny	Mare	Age Sts 1st 2d 3d	Money Won
A. P. Adventure	Nataliano	2 1 1 0 0	27,000
Adrenalin Running	Harda Arda	2 4 0 0 0	2,640
Alexi Dancer	Pike Place Dancer	2 3 0 0 0	1,380
Brands Hatch	Watch Out	2 2 0 0 0	3,080
Catalindy	Catalina Court	2 1 0 0 0	0
Catbaby	Catinca	2 2 0 0 0	0
Compound	Biding Time	2 2 0 0 0	220
Crocker Road	Gallanta (FR)	2 1 0 0 0	980
Dancinandsingin	Scoot Yer Boots	2 2 0 1 0	8,600
Daydreaming	Get Lucky	2 3 1 0 1	79,000
Diamond Indy	Adel	2 2 0 0 1	5,400
Ender's Sister	Gold Rush Queen	2 5 2 2 0	107,900
Fragrance	Esther Rose	2 3 1 0 1	25,840
Friends Lake	Antespend	2 3 2 0 0	84,600
Gradepoint	Class Kris	2 2 1 0 1	36,285
Highgate Park	High Heeled Hope	2 6 2 0 1	49,410
India Sun	Sultry Sun	2 2 0 0 0	1,350
Indy	Izana	2 4 0 0 0	7,395
Indy Charmer	Dancing Mirage	2 4 0 1 1	15,640
Indy Snow (GB)	November Snow	2 2 0 0 0	0
King Augustus	Polish Style	2 3 0 3 0	18,900
La Reina	Queena	2 4 2 2 0	142,420
Lady Nichola	Macoumba	2 1 0 1 0	9,800
Lethal Litigator	Vinista	2 1 0 0 1	4,320
Liz On Polk Street	Silver Maiden	2 1 1 0 0	15,600
Lovely Rafaela	Campagnarde (ARG)	2 3 1 0 0	36,480
Mach Speed	Bay Harbor	2 3 1 1 0	44,121
Mithaal	Zakiyya	2 3 0 0 0	4,080
Mrs. Bassett	Ice Cream Cone	2 2 0 0 0	440
Nor'wester	Pacific Squall	2 1 0 0 0	2,280
Open Flirt	With a Wink	2 2 0 1 0	9,460
Quick Temper	Halo America	2 2 1 0 1	32,455
Renaissance Lady	Storm Beauty	2 9 1 4 0	111,850
Rosberg	Bosra Sham	2 2 1 0 0	26,180
Schwarzwald	Foret Noire	2 7 0 1 0	7,800
Seattle Weekend	Lassie's Lady	2 4 0 0 0	5,455
Shake Off	Shake the Yoke (GB)	2 2 1 0 0	24,600
Shanghied	Fleet Road	2 3 0 0 0	1,290
Shaniko	Sapphire n' Silk	2 2 0 1 0	11,940
Sheer Luck	Vegas Prospector	2 6 2 1 2	79,280
Starindy (GB)	Star of Broadway	2 1 0 0 0	840
Suave	Urbane	2 5 1 2 0	41,355
Under Caution	Coldheartedcat	2 3 1 0 0	18,300
War Marshall	U R Unforgetable	2 1 0 1 0	9,000

Smoke Glacken, Gr/Ro H (1994)
By Two Punch – Majesty's Crown, by Magesterial
29 Performers, 17 winning performers, $1,094,563 in total earnings

Progeny	Mare	Age Sts 1st 2d 3d	Money Won
Bachelor Blues	Wedding Day Blues	2 8 2 3 0	265,406
Black Magic Lady	Feminazi	2 3 1 0 1	15,960
Bold Jubilation	Boldly Victorious	2 5 1 0 1	32,464
Coup de Grace	Ganzania	2 5 0 0 2	8,830
Distressed Debt	Castle Gardens (IRE)	2 4 2 0 0	53,400

		Age Sts 1st 2d 3d	Won
Helen Anna	Illustrious Lady	2 3 0 1 0	7,700
Just Cash	Cash Customer	2 1 0 0 0	100
Kilgowan	Port Roberto	2 2 1 0 1	19,600
King of Mardi Gras	Bourbon Street Gal	2 5 2 0 0	28,915
Lady Glacken	Miss. Greinton	2 3 2 0 0	16,860
Little Smokey	A Whisper Away	2 7 1 1 1	9,161
Mac Daddy	Lona's Love	2 3 0 1 0	5,635
Montsmoke	Montezuma	2 6 1 1 0	9,890
No Communication	Lady Trickery	2 1 1 0 0	15,400
Potomac Chase	Lady Ellen	2 7 2 0 1	33,900
Princess Malice	Beautiful Craft	2 1 0 0 0	1,260
Read the Footnotes	Baydon Belle	2 5 4 0 0	240,660
Roll Your Own	Paris Gem	2 4 0 3 1	18,460
Smoken Smoke	Key to the Sauce	2 1 0 1 0	5,400
Smokey's Jazz	Musical Cure	2 1 0 0 0	750
Smokume	Presume	2 4 3 1 0	118,544
Storm the Beach	Motel Lady	2 2 0 0 0	0
Streak of Smoke	Streak of Malagra	2 6 2 2 0	72,104
Thanks for Smokin	Crystal Stepper	2 6 1 0 1	13,579
Toofastforyou	Too Fast to Catch	2 6 0 2 2	14,420
Two Down Automatic	Lady Doc	2 4 2 1 0	45,000
Watch Me Smoke	Eden Isle	2 1 0 0 0	380
Weatherwise	Weather Vane	2 3 0 0 1	3,125
Willow Cove	I Fell for It	2 5 1 2 1	37,660

Unbridled's Song, Gr/Ro H (1993)
By Unbridled – Trolley Song, by Caro
35 Performers, 16 winning performers, $1,071,880 in total earnings

Progeny	Mare	Age Sts 1st 2d 3d	Money Won
Ambition Unbridled	Retained	2 3 0 2 1	15,100
Annabelle's Song	Ascloseasitgets	2 1 0 1 0	6,600
Cleito	Jungle Woman	2 7 1 0 1	20,650
Code Song	Two Fer Boston	2 2 1 0 0	27,455
Confirmed	Erie Dearie	2 2 0 1 0	10,000
Danesbury	Whatamiss	2 6 1 0 1	32,515
Decibel	Incircle Miss	2 2 1 0 0	28,950
Delivering Speed	Vaguely Regal (IRE)	2 2 1 0 0	27,280
Desnuda	Proper Form	2 4 1 3 0	54,000
Dogleg Left	Bugs Rabbit	2 1 0 0 0	0
Eurosilver	Russian Tango	2 3 2 1 0	284,000
Eyes Wide Open	Haveaheavenlytime	2 4 0 0 0	4,110
Forest Music	Defer West	2 4 1 0 1	23,676
Greygoosegal	Regal Approval	2 2 1 0 0	18,780
Heroic Moment	Call Me Up	2 7 0 0 2	15,670
Hot Jive	Jacuzzi	2 1 0 0 0	0
Illucination	Golden Par	2 5 0 0 3	10,120
In the Weeds	Marfisa	2 2 1 1 0	17,680
Last Song	Queen of Spirit	2 4 1 1 0	38,930
Lloydminster	Born Twice	2 6 0 2 0	16,919
Marylebone	Desert Queen	2 3 2 0 0	147,000
Melissa's Luv Song	Miss Ali King	2 1 0 0 0	50
Naughty Nae	Rockaroller	2 3 0 0 1	7,650
Pure	Nueces Strip	2 4 0 1 0	10,220
Rainbow Rider	Forever Rainbows	2 2 1 1 0	36,000
Rare Gift	Rare Blend	2 1 1 0 0	27,000
Scene Maker	Walk in Time	2 3 0 0 0	2,340
Swaggering	Yamuna	2 1 0 0 1	3,080
Temescal Ridge	Belonging	2 2 0 0 0	0
Tina's Love	Danara	2 1 0 0 1	4,920
Unbridled Beauty	Dreamscape	2 4 1 2 0	88,535
Unchecked Melody	Madam Sandie	2 1 0 0 0	0
Uninhibited Song	Special Mistress	2 1 0 1 0	5,600
Value Plus	Roll Over Baby	2 4 1 1 0	87,000
Whatasassysong	Electrostat	2 1 0 0 0	50

Unbridled, B H (1987)
By Fappiano – Gana Facil, by Le Fabuleux
14 Performers, 3 winning performers, $1,024,658 in total earnings

Progeny	Mare	Age Sts 1st 2d 3d	Money Won
Doctor Hi	Buckeye Search	2 1 0 0 0	525
Eddington	Fashion Star	2 1 0 1 0	9,200
Free Thinking	Danka	2 3 1 0 0	44,889
Halfbridled	Half Queen	2 4 4 0 0	849,400
Liberated	Footy	2 4 0 0 0	2,580
Moonlight	Cat Appeal	2 2 0 0 0	1,380
Mustanfar	Manwah	2 3 1 0 0	28,980
My Time Now	Darby Trail	2 1 0 0 0	4,270
Navesink River	Sheepscot	2 1 0 0 0	1,350
Niigon	Savethelastdance	2 3 0 1 2	50,504
Rebridled Secret	Secret Partner	2 1 0 0 0	0
Twirlaway	Music House	2 6 0 1 0	12,720
Unshuttered	Shuttered	2 4 0 1 1	16,360
Windigo	Banshee Winds	2 1 0 0 0	2,500

Wild Rush, B H (1994)
By Wild Again – Rose Park, by Plugged Nickle
28 Perfomers, 11 winning performers, $997k759 in total earnings

Progeny	Mare	Age	Sts	1st	2d	3d	Money Won
Bank Audit	Mosquera	2	4	0	3	0	21,140
Bank Roll	Sweetly Decorated	2	1	0	0	0	0
Big Bold Rush	Little Bold Lookin	2	1	0	0	0	1,560
Everything Wild	Just Be Lucky	2	1	0	0	0	0
Hawaiin Gold	Chimes Bird	2	1	0	0	0	0
Hollywood Story	Wife for Life	2	5	1	2	1	356,500
J J Wish	Beyond the Sky	2	2	0	0	1	2,530
Judiths Wild Rush	Tie Talk	2	4	3	0	0	141,915
Nice Ice Rush	Nice Mistake	2	1	0	1	0	3,200
Quintons Gold Rush	Hollywood Gold	2	1	0	1	0	7,600
Rush Into Heaven	Glimpse of Heaven	2	7	2	0	0	74,063
Rush Note	Heavenly Note	2	4	1	0	2	12,100
Speedy Rusher	Sincere Dancer	2	4	1	0	1	8,470
Stellar Jayne	To the Hunt	2	5	3	0	0	119,075
Storm Rush	Search for Time	2	2	0	1	0	13,524
Thelittleirishman	French Lake	2	1	0	0	0	0
Tingwithasting	Notable Sword	2	3	1	1	0	36,250
Valid Rush	A Lady With Appeal	2	4	0	1	1	8,060
Vero Missy	Fleet Line Lady	2	3	1	1	0	5,440
Vous	Seattle Moon	2	4	2	1	0	82,400
Wild About Harry	Ashlea's Debut	2	4	1	1	0	11,820
Wild Attraction	Attraction Fatale	2	3	0	0	1	7,117
Wild Bea	Tarquina	2	7	1	2	2	35,855
Wild Ditty	Sea Ditty	2	1	0	0	0	450
Wild Imp	Impulsive Lady	2	1	0	0	0	0
Wildinthepark	Agua Azulita	2	3	0	0	1	2,430
Willow Rush	Reet Petite	2	6	0	2	1	27,680
Wimbledon	Strawberry Clover	2	3	0	2	0	18,580

Annual Leading Juvenile Sire – Money Won

Year	Sire	Winning Perfs.	Races Won	Amount Won	Year	Sire	Winning Perfs.	Races Won	Amount Won
1914	*Ogden	19	56	$339,911	1964	Bold Ruler	11	36	967,814
1915	Broomstick	11	38	178,546	1965	Tom Fool	5	15	592,871
1916	Alambala	5	16	56,289	1966	Bold Ruler	9	24	941,493
1917	Peter Quince	6	18	48,537	1967	Bold Ruler	12	34	1,126,844
1918	Sweep	12	39	97,947	1968	Bold Ruler	11	27	609,243
1919	Fair Play	4	17	90,002	1969	Prince John	5	11	418,183
1920	Peter Pan	7	30	92,965	1970	Hail to Reason	9	16	473,244
1921	Runnymeade	7	23	128,195	1971	First Landing	9	17	551,120
1922	*Allumeur	1	5	94,847	1972	Bold Ruler	6	14	541,990
1923	Black Toney	11	37	115,745	1973	Raise a Native	7	18	311,002
1924	Ultimus	10	31	104,349	1974	What a Pleasure	13	21	387,748
1925	*Sun Briar	1	7	121,630	1975	What a Pleasure	16	25	611,071
1926	*Wrack	12	22	112,504	1976	Raja Baba	13	26	419,872
1927	Luke McLuke	1	6	111,905	1977	In Reality	8	16	432,596
1928	High Time	18	44	229,100	1978	Secretariat	5	12	600,617
1929	Mad Hatter	10	24	77,735	1979	Mr. Prospector	14	26	529,665
1930	Pennant	5	17	182,950	1980	Raja Baba	9	19	807,335
1931	*Dis Donc	13	34	247,916	1981	Hoist The Flag	12	12	680,753
1932	Pompey	11	28	141,025	1982	Olden Times	7	16	948,900
1933	*Royal Minstrel	8	16	102,395	1983	Alydar	4	19	1,136,063
1934	Chance Shot	8	17	94,900	1984	Danzig	10	10	2,146,530
1935	*Sir Gallahad III	13	31	102,670	1985	Fappiano	8	16	1,232,408
1936	Pompey	6	11	87,150	1986	Rajab	4	9	950,335
1937	Pharamound II	22	41	105,875	1987	Mr. Prospector	9	21	1,566,919
1938	John P. Grier	7	20	95,535	1988	Seattle Slew	7	15	911,567
1939	Black Toney	1	6	135,090	1989	Fappiano	9	15	1,416,884
1940	*Bull Dog	14	28	100,676	1990	Habitony	5	11	1,083,588
1941	Good Goods	6	24	118,425	1991	Capote	15	20	1,160,237
1942	*Bull Dog	8	26	221,332	1992	Storm Cat	4	13	1,668,559
1943	*Bull Dog	14	33	178,344	1993	Storm Cat	14	29	1,514,992
1944	Case Ace	10	28	230,525	1994	Seeking The Gold	19	11	1,170,201
1945	*Sickle	7	13	188,150	1995	Storm Cat	28	16	1,252,266
1946	*Mahmoud	18	40	283,983	1996	Capote	31	14	2,694,604
1947	Bull Lea	11	31	420,940	1997	Phone Trick	38	16	1,692,737
1948	War Admiral	6	23	346,260	1998	Storm Cat	24	10	1,408,473
1949	Roman	18	38	227,604	1999	Storm Cat	20	12	1,389,759
1950	War Relic	14	35	272,182	2000	Honour and Glory	22	30	1,439,824
1951	Menow	6	13	247,700	2001	Valid Expectations	27	40	1,393,897
1952	Polynesian	12	28	341,730	2002	Storm Cat	16	11	1,455,651
1953	Roman	15	33	550,966	2003	Tale of the Cat	24	34	1,918,383
1954	*Nasrullah	14	31	625,692					
1955	*Nirgal	12	24	293,800					
1956	*Nasrullah	10	30	422,573					
1957	Jet Jewel	3	8	360,402					
1958	*Turn-To	8	25	463,280					
1959	Determine	6	14	411,765					
1960	*My Babu	9	18	437,240					
1961	Bryan G	9	25	428,810					
1962	*Nasrullah	9	17	574,231					
1963	Bold Ruler	9	17	343,585					

* Denotes Foreign-bred. Note: Prior to 1962, amount won included earnings only from juvenile winning performers.

Top Broodmare Sires in 2003 – Money Won

Broodmare Sire	Perf	Winning Perf	Mares	Starts	1st	2nd	3rd	Unplaced	Purses
Deputy Minister	316	184	176	2,036	311	273	266	1,186	$11,645,931
Mr. Prospector	261	135	167	1,625	250	207	204	964	9,847,587
Relaunch	332	191	186	2,089	347	282	254	1,206	8,067,738
Affirmed	215	122	137	1,515	206	190	185	934	7,440,542
Dixieland Band	298	165	171	2,090	309	263	280	1,238	7,437,808
Valid Appeal	268	167	160	1,975	302	271	254	1,148	7,138,795
Bold Ruckus	221	135	134	1,409	256	198	191	764	6,719,445
Storm Bird	225	118	135	1,440	221	184	205	830	6,654,708
Crafty Prospector	261	146	157	1,742	256	240	218	1,028	6,079,316
Woodman	197	99	114	1,166	170	135	130	731	5,692,256
Danzig	187	96	119	1,125	170	145	131	679	5,662,881
Vice Regent	255	127	148	1,797	226	246	216	1,109	5,514,011
Seattle Slew	224	113	145	1,422	194	173	174	881	5,333,587
Conquistador Cielo	242	136	140	1,638	235	237	187	979	5,297,591
Nureyev	110	55	78	643	100	86	83	374	5,296,035
Pleasant Colony	208	107	119	1,287	193	186	187	721	5,278,602
Green Dancer	205	101	119	1,308	163	161	171	813	5,192,910
Cox's Ridge	268	144	158	1,892	221	244	255	1,172	5,133,980
Halo	286	130	153	1,922	229	255	221	1,217	5,022,274
Private Account	246	119	137	1,580	195	182	208	995	4,991,108
Alleged	170	78	113	1,120	137	144	132	707	4,792,122
Spectacular Bid	204	92	122	1,270	152	176	150	792	4,749,819
Storm Cat	184	90	122	1,074	150	156	140	628	4,739,075
Miswaki	237	117	145	1,443	198	198	187	860	4,729,285
Cure the Blues	209	104	118	1,334	178	173	164	819	4,711,825
Wild Again	225	103	142	1,414	187	169	166	892	4,628,235
Secretariat	230	108	134	1,638	196	217	193	1,032	4,589,893
Clever Trick	277	143	163	1,753	232	224	230	1,067	4,509,542
Naskra	126	53	73	853	112	91	97	553	4,390,031
Fappiano	172	89	110	1,136	169	149	127	691	4,243,864
Saratoga Six	185	108	103	1,218	191	165	178	684	4,148,419
Sovereign Dancer	227	128	127	1,731	236	194	229	1,072	4,141,414
Kris S.	194	97	127	1,157	169	148	149	691	4,114,120
Flying Paster	172	83	102	1,179	148	156	149	726	4,096,306
Hold Your Peace	119	66	70	919	118	120	128	553	4,038,897
Forty Niner	143	84	93	890	149	129	100	512	4,018,963
Mari's Book	83	49	49	554	96	79	74	305	3,981,942
Rahy	147	73	89	909	132	103	112	562	3,976,340
Topsider	160	96	87	1,133	179	157	127	670	3,970,917
Alydar	193	103	119	1,198	171	160	168	699	3,921,744
El Gran Senor	71	35	44	392	59	49	47	237	3,797,049
Devil's Bag	195	85	111	1,167	138	141	148	740	3,722,080
Broad Brush	165	93	98	1,053	162	168	106	617	3,680,598
Nijinsky II	150	75	95	1,079	142	139	132	666	3,654,511
Majestic Light	218	112	129	1,535	205	195	169	966	3,550,633
Mt. Livermore	193	99	109	1,275	161	161	162	791	3,549,320
Afleet	141	76	91	940	136	131	138	535	3,543,800
Lear Fan	115	51	70	695	84	100	72	439	3,541,348
Meadowlake	164	94	97	1,047	148	128	144	627	3,507,431
Capote	153	85	99	982	147	121	125	589	3,449,163
Alysheba	107	54	61	723	103	100	101	419	3,439,854
Mr. Leader	188	97	109	1,329	179	149	174	827	3,338,628
Air Forbes Won	144	79	85	1,100	159	155	141	645	3,326,490
Strawberry Road (AUS)	130	67	81	819	117	116	119	467	3,303,751
Lost Code	171	78	106	987	154	128	119	586	3,243,714
Pirate's Bounty	188	98	130	1,316	171	174	189	782	3,218,600
Key to the Mint	160	77	101	947	106	112	100	629	3,190,715
Smarten	180	80	108	1,149	142	141	159	707	3,165,221
Phone Trick	194	94	134	1,231	159	139	175	758	3,107,706
Dynaformer	102	55	72	680	92	99	84	405	3,087,376
Carson City	110	57	72	650	108	105	103	334	3,065,777
Baldski	138	69	80	985	136	106	119	624	3,027,718
Red Ransom	114	55	77	664	81	85	70	428	3,009,800
Copelan	159	80	93	1,059	138	131	129	661	2,922,240
Cryptoclearance	127	61	86	795	93	104	95	503	2,882,609
Northern Baby	136	62	70	926	110	135	112	569	2,868,547
Stop the Music	191	86	114	1,267	149	147	141	830	2,846,320
Seeking the Gold	106	60	69	624	96	77	96	355	2,842,451
Caveat	148	74	85	995	137	131	118	609	2,829,672
Stalwart	171	89	107	1,060	144	140	127	649	2,815,352
Apalachee	189	89	123	1,246	163	142	159	782	2,809,311
Star de Naskra	174	84	107	1,144	144	153	118	729	2,804,964
Great Above	156	83	96	1,013	128	113	118	654	2,795,155

Broodmare Sire	Perf	Winning Perf	Mares	Starts	1st	2nd	3rd	Unplaced	Purses
Damascus	123	57	76	823	104	114	103	502	2,794,271
His Majesty	170	78	106	1,242	159	156	159	768	2,792,926
Bailjumper	52	26	38	365	54	43	45	223	2,777,488
Wolf Power (SAF)	137	65	82	979	122	123	125	609	2,748,073
Two Punch	118	64	77	778	112	121	96	449	2,744,776
Cozzene	137	67	90	879	114	123	102	540	2,740,716
Slewacide	86	40	47	537	62	59	61	355	2,710,147
Slew o' Gold	136	66	88	943	122	131	110	580	2,701,439
Our Native	176	79	101	1,208	146	144	143	775	2,668,231
Lyphard	120	50	79	763	81	76	92	514	2,654,074
Mining	124	64	84	762	101	123	86	452	2,632,038
Regal Classic	119	61	73	788	114	86	109	479	2,629,869
Cormorant	117	72	76	837	119	103	96	519	2,620,373
Criminal Type	56	31	39	414	59	62	39	254	2,608,774
Explodent	171	91	104	1,172	147	136	139	750	2,606,173
Well Decorated	201	106	117	1,415	150	196	170	899	2,548,383
Tri Jet	128	65	82	897	114	107	101	575	2,509,570
Personal Flag	102	57	60	734	102	96	92	444	2,509,129
Silver Deputy	92	56	66	547	105	77	67	298	2,494,530
Gone West	121	58	76	650	90	92	77	391	2,492,754
Fit to Fight	172	86	107	1,181	136	155	164	726	2,453,370
With Approval	95	46	56	620	69	76	71	404	2,449,686
Spend a Buck	133	71	77	865	122	110	100	533	2,442,034
Theatrical (IRE)	112	57	71	712	93	80	90	449	2,429,597
It's Freezing	149	74	81	1,034	128	135	122	649	2,427,735
Northern Jove	152	81	89	1,071	145	145	128	653	2,413,756
Premiership	168	86	98	1,187	141	134	139	773	2,396,871
Jade Hunter	107	63	73	793	109	90	103	491	2,393,713
Lucky North	81	47	49	627	97	75	74	381	2,379,626
Irish Tower	152	83	97	1,107	132	126	171	678	2,375,550
Distinctive Pro	123	69	77	945	114	131	136	564	2,320,130
Wavering Monarch	129	50	74	762	93	84	92	493	2,311,601
Cutlass	124	66	77	874	102	106	114	552	2,283,405
Time for a Change	156	77	98	973	120	97	115	641	2,282,685
Lord Avie	143	76	97	920	113	131	131	545	2,280,717
Seattle Dancer	94	47	61	577	85	77	78	337	2,267,932
Allen's Prospect	143	75	92	979	139	110	132	598	2,259,101
Ogygian	121	67	79	784	111	106	99	468	2,257,468
Geiger Counter	107	54	69	716	95	65	102	454	2,253,602
Silver Hawk	135	65	84	809	88	104	110	507	2,220,296
Riverman	109	44	71	662	74	71	62	455	2,188,318
Known Fact	119	68	79	752	108	82	100	462	2,174,549
Chief's Crown	104	58	73	702	101	89	79	433	2,164,346
Runaway Groom	174	71	111	1,043	107	111	129	696	2,145,042
Turkoman	107	52	70	749	100	96	116	437	2,130,573
Bates Motel	136	69	75	894	122	133	101	538	2,124,650
Temperence Hill	166	75	104	1,165	133	148	140	744	2,122,033
Talc	116	61	67	784	99	90	85	510	2,098,320
Diesis (GB)	68	38	48	387	54	48	45	240	2,055,049
D'Accord	110	48	63	800	94	92	113	501	2,037,492
Manila	79	36	52	531	66	62	50	353	2,036,399
Trempolino	48	26	32	279	44	28	25	182	2,025,014
Silent Screen	148	79	94	976	136	116	109	615	1,995,460
Risen Star	64	42	42	452	72	60	71	249	1,978,146
Seattle Song	79	39	50	473	68	60	61	284	1,950,381
Irish River (FR)	121	56	75	706	97	75	91	443	1,945,282
Magesterial	96	45	59	624	87	70	73	394	1,942,577
Polish Navy	93	52	49	650	89	92	83	386	1,935,202
Buckaroo	120	67	75	888	115	99	95	579	1,897,332
Sham	90	43	56	570	62	63	74	371	1,891,049
Silver Buck	140	70	89	912	108	107	114	583	1,876,309
Bucksplasher	102	50	58	764	102	80	72	510	1,873,091
Darshaan (GB)	21	9	18	129	16	19	20	74	1,870,150
Lord Gaylord	90	38	55	567	65	78	80	344	1,857,345
Black Tie Affair (IRE)	116	55	83	717	83	104	99	431	1,855,890
Gate Dancer	123	64	69	829	121	75	110	523	1,854,189
Blushing Groom (FR)	93	50	63	530	84	85	58	303	1,852,933
Fortunate Prospect	121	66	78	934	99	124	122	589	1,841,813
Rajab	56	28	31	430	68	61	42	259	1,838,373
L'Enjoleur	123	65	74	1,002	106	135	156	605	1,806,560
In Reality	96	52	62	663	91	98	78	396	1,801,968
Caerleon	37	18	30	181	32	20	19	110	1,790,810
Gulch	95	45	58	652	96	100	76	380	1,764,808
Caro (IRE)	76	39	48	527	76	66	47	338	1,759,155

Horatius	93	43	57	581	91	88	82	320	1,757,005
Slewpy	100	48	68	656	77	84	93	402	1,749,163
Nasty and Bold	110	51	64	780	93	91	97	499	1,746,721
Unreal Zeal	65	37	39	517	75	85	65	292	1,745,010
Northern Dancer	50	28	33	376	50	53	56	217	1,729,543
Pancho Villa	122	71	72	827	116	113	101	497	1,725,715
Notebook	66	42	40	503	83	61	70	289	1,721,995
Green Forest	97	55	59	713	86	89	90	448	1,718,824
Raise a Native	126	54	81	734	92	81	75	486	1,714,533
Sunny's Halo	154	78	97	1,059	120	112	137	690	1,703,708
Big Spruce	98	46	61	674	82	79	75	438	1,695,139
Desert Wine	91	41	60	572	76	70	70	356	1,688,424
The Minstrel	116	45	73	716	78	72	99	467	1,687,394
Dayjur	50	29	33	307	53	38	38	178	1,670,982
Oh Say	106	55	65	722	97	92	77	456	1,670,585
Drone	88	40	60	587	76	85	85	341	1,661,504
Danzig Connection	115	62	66	863	109	92	128	534	1,660,112
Northern Prospect	104	51	69	632	78	81	69	404	1,654,519
Corporate Report	56	34	36	359	58	51	39	211	1,646,496
Skywalker	85	39	53	452	68	59	62	263	1,626,225
Grey Dawn II	132	53	83	921	81	125	114	601	1,615,251
Fast Play	85	56	49	577	91	73	62	351	1,610,263
Tom Rolfe	85	45	55	604	72	84	76	372	1,595,418
Beau Genius	65	36	42	457	69	59	42	287	1,585,037
Kennedy Road	101	52	55	636	104	57	64	411	1,580,680
Deputed Testamony	57	32	36	404	60	56	42	246	1,576,702
Icecapade	111	52	62	763	94	96	104	469	1,576,373
Foolish Pleasure	104	44	70	722	84	80	93	465	1,573,609
Carr de Naskra	93	40	51	558	77	65	72	344	1,572,958
Assert (IRE)	59	31	35	402	51	53	53	245	1,572,239
Zilzal	20	13	15	149	22	23	18	86	1,559,589
Moscow Ballet	105	56	68	656	89	79	97	391	1,555,505
Hagley	89	46	49	602	76	91	87	348	1,552,751
Far Out East	118	53	75	821	84	98	118	521	1,550,824
Eastern Echo	56	33	37	410	60	64	48	238	1,548,558
Blushing John	90	50	61	645	83	84	83	395	1,548,351
General Assembly	89	44	50	590	69	70	69	382	1,538,893
Hatchet Man	91	43	59	613	75	70	66	402	1,533,690
Sir Ivor	106	45	65	645	72	70	66	437	1,532,086
Dahar	56	30	30	429	61	37	52	279	1,528,852
Val de l'Orne (FR)	94	40	51	660	71	67	72	450	1,520,459
Believe It	145	65	100	873	103	106	81	583	1,513,974
Son of Briartic	77	44	49	568	83	76	88	321	1,503,196
Timeless Moment	112	55	71	776	89	106	85	496	1,502,738
John Alden	62	33	34	467	61	49	53	304	1,501,546
Secreto	83	36	48	573	68	78	68	359	1,498,714
Verbatim	87	51	59	684	98	77	79	430	1,492,848
Far North	126	52	83	749	78	79	78	514	1,471,857
Tunerup	69	36	45	445	54	70	47	274	1,462,098
Rare Performer	92	49	63	682	90	78	88	426	1,451,169
Highland Blade	73	43	43	618	77	79	77	385	1,443,930
Rubiano	45	23	32	243	38	39	29	137	1,438,624
Bob's Dusty	51	26	32	421	47	48	48	278	1,436,778
Lord At War (ARG)	91	46	60	484	75	58	51	300	1,430,721
Marshua's Dancer	103	51	71	694	94	98	78	424	1,423,473
Salt Lake	51	33	43	267	58	32	31	146	1,416,697
Silver Ghost	90	42	62	536	66	72	55	343	1,409,454
Waquoit	75	42	45	499	78	65	51	305	1,399,567
Ascot Knight	58	31	37	395	44	50	54	247	1,388,667
Pentelicus	76	38	50	432	59	51	50	272	1,386,333
Vigors	123	49	79	830	83	95	106	546	1,378,503
Shadeed	60	37	34	405	64	42	66	233	1,377,319
Herat	60	32	33	421	65	48	63	245	1,371,436
Falstaff	37	20	24	198	31	32	19	116	1,361,267
Buckfinder	83	47	56	581	87	88	82	324	1,357,908
Raja Baba	103	47	68	740	77	83	84	496	1,354,884
Slew City Slew	59	37	39	454	71	69	54	260	1,346,233
Fire Dancer	98	49	67	870	96	105	84	585	1,329,537
Pass the Tab	41	19	20	281	34	37	39	171	1,326,896
Regal and Royal	66	36	38	457	71	42	61	283	1,326,535
Dr. Carter	61	33	36	448	72	57	43	276	1,326,522
Roberto	95	43	57	624	57	72	75	420	1,317,140
Skip Trial	74	38	48	576	75	75	57	369	1,309,164
Staff Writer	116	63	67	805	119	97	117	472	1,302,322
Knights Choice	123	66	63	829	117	113	103	496	1,281,543
Kahyasi	3	2	3	17	8	3	1	5	1,280,601

Broodmare Sire	Perf	Winning Perf	Mares	Starts	1st	2nd	3rd	Unplaced	Purses
Prospectors Gamble	59	35	38	464	69	66	50	279	1,279,156
At the Threshold	48	27	29	340	48	53	52	187	1,275,756
Blue Ensign	91	49	61	599	82	57	68	392	1,266,151
Imperial Falcon	67	31	42	569	75	66	50	378	1,262,703
Java Gold	80	41	43	479	54	56	67	302	1,258,797
Greinton (GB)	72	40	44	451	71	39	55	286	1,256,828
Great Gladiator	49	28	27	338	51	51	30	206	1,246,414
Bold Forbes	101	58	59	748	110	97	92	449	1,238,896
Tsunami Slew	76	40	49	536	61	61	72	342	1,233,975
Sauce Boat	135	57	82	856	94	108	85	569	1,229,060
On to Glory	83	41	55	632	72	73	76	411	1,218,275
Groovy	81	44	47	547	84	76	52	335	1,212,989
Dr. Blum	88	36	57	498	56	64	64	314	1,210,223
Sunny Clime	82	37	44	573	61	86	85	341	1,209,248
Houston	89	42	62	604	73	72	74	385	1,200,215
Smile	82	35	45	566	56	53	81	376	1,198,224
World Appeal	82	39	45	580	76	82	69	353	1,188,001
Hawaii	82	42	52	547	71	64	60	352	1,181,260
Brave Shot (GB)	40	20	26	336	38	44	40	214	1,180,763
Ack Ack	86	39	54	554	75	68	52	359	1,179,785
A Native Danzig	8	6	6	44	11	5	2	26	1,171,787
Raise a Cup	67	29	42	385	42	60	51	232	1,167,489
Summing	84	44	53	594	80	66	53	395	1,164,527
Proud Birdie	89	42	54	594	65	59	73	397	1,155,174
What Luck	68	31	47	495	64	78	66	287	1,153,254
Track Barron	86	44	49	600	73	76	77	374	1,150,352
Rainbow Quest	24	8	19	119	11	22	14	72	1,148,783
Baederwood	57	28	38	396	50	52	55	239	1,148,400
Bounding Basque	63	34	38	463	59	63	46	295	1,146,790
Homebuilder	33	21	25	252	32	38	34	148	1,139,908
Mehmet	73	41	51	513	72	52	61	328	1,138,364
Housebuster	60	32	44	328	47	46	44	191	1,136,684
Taylor's Falls	70	38	44	528	69	71	64	324	1,129,316
Farma Way	65	39	44	490	61	58	60	311	1,125,838
Marfa	88	41	58	659	78	66	96	419	1,124,350
Native Prospector	57	26	39	343	41	50	40	212	1,122,943
Hooched	66	34	33	541	60	71	76	334	1,120,510
Private Terms	85	39	57	622	71	77	69	405	1,116,558
Bold Executive	30	16	25	166	27	25	22	92	1,112,795
A.P. Indy	40	22	30	191	32	27	23	109	1,108,370
Exuberant	85	36	56	635	63	79	62	431	1,102,242
Hero's Honor	58	34	29	428	65	64	53	246	1,098,225
Unbridled	62	30	45	333	41	35	39	218	1,091,835
Cherokee Fellow	44	24	24	380	50	59	52	219	1,087,852
Briartic	77	30	46	519	50	54	62	353	1,087,829
Strike Gold	96	38	63	575	56	87	84	348	1,086,390
Vanlandingham	68	36	46	436	67	52	36	281	1,086,000
Easy Goer	41	21	26	257	38	38	34	147	1,079,933
Naevus	79	45	52	483	66	69	48	300	1,079,906
Rollicking	71	32	43	463	62	57	65	279	1,072,001
Fred Astaire	74	39	47	484	63	57	57	307	1,071,607
Golden Act	73	41	45	609	65	83	76	385	1,069,316
Medieval Man	77	45	50	562	75	67	56	364	1,049,605
Full Pocket	79	46	51	562	76	68	65	353	1,049,600
Al Nasr (FR)	55	24	35	361	47	33	56	225	1,046,272
Tank's Prospect	65	32	41	434	52	48	55	279	1,032,388
Blade	62	26	42	417	50	46	48	273	1,030,144
Nodouble	92	46	59	668	70	77	88	433	1,028,942
Linkage	76	45	43	590	77	66	73	374	1,024,696
Lyphard's Wish (FR)	114	44	74	779	62	88	76	553	1,024,000
One for All	69	32	35	476	49	68	69	290	1,023,603
Half a Year	48	25	35	264	42	35	35	152	1,018,924
Badger Land	46	28	30	342	56	41	38	207	1,018,256
Lomond	55	28	35	359	41	63	39	216	1,018,230
Time to Explode	70	38	39	496	55	67	62	312	1,017,120
Avatar	79	39	51	554	65	58	58	373	1,015,617
Country Pine	57	41	36	445	76	55	59	255	1,012,650
Darn That Alarm	50	27	35	371	60	49	40	222	1,012,408
Shareef Dancer	14	8	11	89	18	13	13	45	1,009,992
Plugged Nickle	77	36	44	551	50	72	67	362	1,003,393
Stage Door Johnny	75	34	49	492	57	53	60	322	1,003,331

Top Broodmare Sires in 2003 – Races Won

Broodmare Sire	Perf	Winning Perf	Mares	Starts	1st	2nd	3rd	Unplaced	Purses
Relaunch	332	191	186	2,089	347	282	254	1,206	8,067,738
Deputy Minister	316	184	176	2,036	311	273	266	1,186	11,645,931
Dixieland Band	298	165	171	2,090	309	263	280	1,238	7,437,808
Valid Appeal	268	167	160	1,975	302	271	254	1,148	7,138,795
Bold Ruckus	221	135	134	1,409	256	198	191	764	6,719,445
Crafty Prospector	261	146	157	1,742	256	240	218	1,028	6,079,316
Mr. Prospector	261	135	167	1,625	250	207	204	964	9,847,587
Sovereign Dancer	227	128	127	1,731	236	194	229	1,072	4,141,414
Conquistador Cielo	242	136	140	1,638	235	237	187	979	5,297,591
Clever Trick	277	143	163	1,753	232	224	230	1,067	4,509,542
Halo	286	130	153	1,922	229	255	221	1,217	5,022,274
Vice Regent	255	127	148	1,797	226	246	216	1,109	5,514,011
Storm Bird	225	118	135	1,440	221	184	205	830	6,654,708
Cox's Ridge	268	144	158	1,892	221	244	255	1,172	5,133,980
Affirmed	215	122	137	1,515	206	190	185	934	7,440,542
Majestic Light	218	112	129	1,535	205	195	169	966	3,550,633
Miswaki	237	117	145	1,443	198	198	187	860	4,729,285
Secretariat	230	108	134	1,638	196	217	193	1,032	4,589,893
Private Account	246	119	137	1,580	195	182	208	995	4,991,108
Seattle Slew	224	113	145	1,422	194	173	174	881	5,333,587
Pleasant Colony	208	107	119	1,287	193	186	187	721	5,278,602
Saratoga Six	185	108	103	1,218	191	165	178	684	4,148,419
Wild Again	225	103	142	1,414	187	169	166	892	4,628,235
Topsider	160	96	87	1,133	179	157	127	670	3,970,917
Mr. Leader	188	97	109	1,329	179	149	174	827	3,338,628
Cure the Blues	209	104	118	1,334	178	173	164	819	4,711,825
Alydar	193	103	119	1,198	171	160	168	699	3,921,744
Pirate's Bounty	188	98	130	1,316	171	174	189	782	3,218,600
Woodman	197	99	114	1,166	170	135	130	731	5,692,256
Danzig	187	96	119	1,125	170	145	131	679	5,662,881
Fappiano	172	89	110	1,136	169	149	127	691	4,243,864
Kris S.	194	97	127	1,157	169	148	149	691	4,114,120
Green Dancer	205	101	119	1,308	163	161	171	813	5,192,910
Apalachee	189	89	123	1,246	163	142	159	782	2,809,311
Broad Brush	165	93	98	1,053	162	168	106	617	3,680,598
Mt. Livermore	193	99	109	1,275	161	161	162	791	3,549,320
Air Forbes Won	144	79	85	1,100	159	155	141	645	3,326,490
Phone Trick	194	94	134	1,231	159	139	175	758	3,107,706
His Majesty	170	78	106	1,242	159	156	159	768	2,792,926
Lost Code	171	78	106	987	154	128	119	586	3,243,714
Spectacular Bid	204	92	122	1,270	152	176	150	792	4,749,819
Storm Cat	184	90	122	1,074	150	156	140	628	4,739,075
Well Decorated	201	106	117	1,415	150	196	170	899	2,548,383
Forty Niner	143	84	93	890	149	129	100	512	4,018,963
Stop the Music	191	86	114	1,267	149	147	141	830	2,846,320
Flying Paster	172	83	102	1,179	148	156	149	726	4,096,306
Meadowlake	164	94	97	1,047	148	128	144	627	3,507,431
Capote	153	85	99	982	147	121	125	589	3,449,163
Explodent	171	91	104	1,172	147	136	139	750	2,606,173
Our Native	176	79	101	1,208	146	144	143	775	2,668,231
Northern Jove	152	81	89	1,071	145	145	128	653	2,413,756
Stalwart	171	89	107	1,060	144	140	127	649	2,815,352
Star de Naskra	174	84	107	1,144	144	153	118	729	2,804,964
Nijinsky II	150	75	95	1,079	142	139	132	666	3,654,511

Broodmare Sire	Perf	Winning Perf	Mares	Starts	1st	2nd	3rd	Unplaced	Purses
Smarten	180	80	108	1,149	142	141	159	707	3,165,221
Premiership	168	86	98	1,187	141	134	139	773	2,396,871
Allen's Prospect	143	75	92	979	139	110	132	598	2,259,101
Devil's Bag	195	85	111	1,167	138	141	148	740	3,722,080
Copelan	159	80	93	1,059	138	131	129	661	2,922,240
Alleged	170	78	113	1,120	137	144	132	707	4,792,122
Caveat	148	74	85	995	137	131	118	609	2,829,672
Afleet	141	76	91	940	136	131	138	535	3,543,800
Baldski	138	69	80	985	136	106	119	624	3,027,718
Fit to Fight	172	86	107	1,181	136	155	164	726	2,453,370
Silent Screen	148	79	94	976	136	116	109	615	1,995,460
Temperence Hill	166	75	104	1,165	133	148	140	744	2,122,033
Rahy	147	73	89	909	132	103	112	562	3,976,340
Irish Tower	152	83	97	1,107	132	126	171	678	2,375,550
Great Above	156	83	96	1,013	128	113	118	654	2,795,155
It's Freezing	149	74	81	1,034	128	135	122	649	2,427,735
Wolf Power (SAF)	137	65	82	979	122	123	125	609	2,748,073
Slew o' Gold	136	66	88	943	122	131	110	580	2,701,439
Spend a Buck	133	71	77	865	122	110	100	533	2,442,034
Bates Motel	136	69	75	894	122	133	101	538	2,124,650
Gate Dancer	123	64	69	829	121	75	110	523	1,854,189
Time for a Change	156	77	98	973	120	97	115	641	2,282,685
Sunny's Halo	154	78	97	1,059	120	112	137	690	1,703,708
Cormorant	117	72	76	837	119	103	96	519	2,620,373
Staff Writer	116	63	67	805	119	97	117	472	1,302,322
Hold Your Peace	119	66	70	919	118	120	128	553	4,038,897
Strawberry Road (AUS)	130	67	81	819	117	116	119	467	3,303,751
Knights Choice	123	66	63	829	117	113	103	496	1,281,543
Pancho Villa	122	71	72	827	116	113	101	497	1,725,715
Buckaroo	120	67	75	888	115	99	95	579	1,897,332
Cozzene	137	67	90	879	114	123	102	540	2,740,716
Regal Classic	119	61	73	788	114	86	109	479	2,629,869
Tri Jet	128	65	82	897	114	107	101	575	2,509,570
Distinctive Pro	123	69	77	945	114	131	136	564	2,320,130
Lord Avie	143	76	97	920	113	131	131	545	2,280,717
Naskra	126	53	73	853	112	91	97	553	4,390,031
Two Punch	118	64	77	778	112	121	96	449	2,744,776
Ogygian	121	67	79	784	111	106	99	468	2,257,468
Northern Baby	136	62	70	926	110	135	112	569	2,868,547
Bold Forbes	101	58	59	748	110	97	92	449	1,238,896
Jade Hunter	107	63	73	793	109	90	103	491	2,393,713
Danzig Connection	115	62	66	863	109	92	128	534	1,660,112
Carson City	110	57	72	650	108	105	103	334	3,065,777
Known Fact	119	68	79	752	108	82	100	462	2,174,549
Silver Buck	140	70	89	912	108	107	114	583	1,876,309
Runaway Groom	174	71	111	1,043	107	111	129	696	2,145,042
Key to the Mint	160	77	101	947	106	112	100	629	3,190,715
L'Enjoleur	123	65	74	1,002	106	135	156	605	1,806,560
Silver Deputy	92	56	66	547	105	77	67	298	2,494,530
Damascus	123	57	76	823	104	114	103	502	2,794,271
Kennedy Road	101	52	55	636	104	57	64	411	1,580,680
Alysheba	107	54	61	723	103	100	101	419	3,439,854
Believe It	145	65	100	873	103	106	81	583	1,513,974

Top Broodmare Sires in 2003 – Winning Performers

Broodmare Sire	Perf	Winning Perf	Mares	Starts	1st	2nd	3rd	Unplaced	Purses
Relaunch	332	191	186	2,089	347	282	254	1,206	$8,067,738
Deputy Minister	316	184	176	2,036	311	273	266	1,186	11,645,931
Valid Appeal	268	167	160	1,975	302	271	254	1,148	7,138,795
Dixieland Band	298	165	171	2,090	309	263	280	1,238	7,437,808
Crafty Prospector	261	146	157	1,742	256	240	218	1,028	6,079,316
Cox's Ridge	268	144	158	1,892	221	244	255	1,172	5,133,980
Clever Trick	277	143	163	1,753	232	224	230	1,067	4,509,542
Conquistador Cielo	242	136	140	1,638	235	237	187	979	5,297,591
Mr. Prospector	261	135	167	1,625	250	207	204	964	9,847,587
Bold Ruckus	221	135	134	1,409	256	198	191	764	6,719,445
Halo	286	130	153	1,922	229	255	221	1,217	5,022,274
Sovereign Dancer	227	128	127	1,731	236	194	229	1,072	4,141,414
Vice Regent	255	127	148	1,797	226	246	216	1,109	5,514,011
Affirmed	215	122	137	1,515	206	190	185	934	7,440,542
Private Account	246	119	137	1,580	195	182	208	995	4,991,108
Storm Bird	225	118	135	1,440	221	184	205	830	6,654,708
Miswaki	237	117	145	1,443	198	198	187	860	4,729,285
Seattle Slew	224	113	145	1,422	194	173	174	881	5,333,587
Majestic Light	218	112	129	1,535	205	195	169	966	3,550,633
Secretariat	230	108	134	1,638	196	217	193	1,032	4,589,893
Saratoga Six	185	108	103	1,218	191	165	178	684	4,148,419
Pleasant Colony	208	107	119	1,287	193	186	187	721	5,278,602
Well Decorated	201	106	117	1,415	150	196	170	899	2,548,383
Cure the Blues	209	104	118	1,334	178	173	164	819	4,711,825
Wild Again	225	103	142	1,414	187	169	166	892	4,628,235
Alydar	193	103	119	1,198	171	160	168	699	3,921,744
Green Dancer	205	101	119	1,308	163	161	171	813	5,192,910
Woodman	197	99	114	1,166	170	135	130	731	5,692,256
Mt. Livermore	193	99	109	1,275	161	161	162	791	3,549,320
Pirate's Bounty	188	98	130	1,316	171	174	189	782	3,218,600
Kris S.	194	97	127	1,157	169	148	149	691	4,114,120
Mr. Leader	188	97	109	1,329	179	149	174	827	3,338,628
Danzig	187	96	119	1,125	170	145	131	679	5,662,881
Topsider	160	96	87	1,133	179	157	127	670	3,970,917
Meadowlake	164	94	97	1,047	148	128	144	627	3,507,431
Phone Trick	194	94	134	1,231	159	139	175	758	3,107,706
Broad Brush	165	93	98	1,053	162	168	106	617	3,680,598
Spectacular Bid	204	92	122	1,270	152	176	150	792	4,749,819
Explodent	171	91	104	1,172	147	136	139	750	2,606,173
Storm Cat	184	90	122	1,074	150	156	140	628	4,739,075
Fappiano	172	89	110	1,136	169	149	127	691	4,243,864
Stalwart	171	89	107	1,060	144	140	127	649	2,815,352
Apalachee	189	89	123	1,246	163	142	159	782	2,809,311
Stop the Music	191	86	114	1,267	149	147	141	830	2,846,320
Fit to Fight	172	86	107	1,181	136	155	164	726	2,453,370
Premiership	168	86	98	1,187	141	134	139	773	2,396,871
Devil's Bag	195	85	111	1,167	138	141	148	740	3,722,080
Capote	153	85	99	982	147	121	125	589	3,449,163
Forty Niner	143	84	93	890	149	129	100	512	4,018,963
Star de Naskra	174	84	107	1,144	144	153	118	729	2,804,964
Flying Paster	172	83	102	1,179	148	156	149	726	4,096,306
Great Above	156	83	96	1,013	128	113	118	654	2,795,155
Irish Tower	152	83	97	1,107	132	126	171	678	2,375,550
Northern Jove	152	81	89	1,071	145	145	128	653	2,413,756

Broodmare Sire	Perf	Winning Perf	Mares	Starts	1st	2nd	3rd	Unplaced	Purses
Smarten	180	80	108	1,149	142	141	159	707	3,165,221
Copelan	159	80	93	1,059	138	131	129	661	2,922,240
Air Forbes Won	144	79	85	1,100	159	155	141	645	3,326,490
Our Native	176	79	101	1,208	146	144	143	775	2,668,231
Silent Screen	148	79	94	976	136	116	109	615	1,995,460
Alleged	170	78	113	1,120	137	144	132	707	4,792,122
Lost Code	171	78	106	987	154	128	119	586	3,243,714
His Majesty	170	78	106	1,242	159	156	159	768	2,792,926
Sunny's Halo	154	78	97	1,059	120	112	137	690	1,703,708
Key to the Mint	160	77	101	947	106	112	100	629	3,190,715
Time for a Change	156	77	98	973	120	97	115	641	2,282,685
Afleet	141	76	91	940	136	131	138	535	3,543,800
Lord Avie	143	76	97	920	113	131	131	545	2,280,717
Nijinsky II	150	75	95	1,079	142	139	132	666	3,654,511
Allen's Prospect	143	75	92	979	139	110	132	598	2,259,101
Temperence Hill	166	75	104	1,165	133	148	140	744	2,122,033
Caveat	148	74	85	995	137	131	118	609	2,829,672
It's Freezing	149	74	81	1,034	128	135	122	649	2,427,735
Rahy	147	73	89	909	132	103	112	562	3,976,340
Cormorant	117	72	76	837	119	103	96	519	2,620,373
Spend a Buck	133	71	77	865	122	110	100	533	2,442,034
Runaway Groom	174	71	111	1,043	107	111	129	696	2,145,042
Pancho Villa	122	71	72	827	116	113	101	497	1,725,715
Silver Buck	140	70	89	912	108	107	114	583	1,876,309
Baldski	138	69	80	985	136	106	119	624	3,027,718
Distinctive Pro	123	69	77	945	114	131	136	564	2,320,130
Bates Motel	136	69	75	894	122	133	101	538	2,124,650
Known Fact	119	68	79	752	108	82	100	462	2,174,549
Strawberry Road (AUS)	130	67	81	819	117	116	119	467	3,303,751
Cozzene	137	67	90	879	114	123	102	540	2,740,716
Ogygian	121	67	79	784	111	106	99	468	2,257,468
Buckaroo	120	67	75	888	115	99	95	579	1,897,332
Hold Your Peace	119	66	70	919	118	120	128	553	4,038,897
Slew o' Gold	136	66	88	943	122	131	110	580	2,701,439
Cutlass	124	66	77	874	102	106	114	552	2,283,405
Fortunate Prospect	121	66	78	934	99	124	122	589	1,841,813
Knights Choice	123	66	63	829	117	113	103	496	1,281,543
Wolf Power (SAF)	137	65	82	979	122	123	125	609	2,748,073
Tri Jet	128	65	82	897	114	107	101	575	2,509,570
Silver Hawk	135	65	84	809	88	104	110	507	2,220,296
L'Enjoleur	123	65	74	1,002	106	135	156	605	1,806,560
Believe It	145	65	100	873	103	106	81	583	1,513,974
Two Punch	118	64	77	778	112	121	96	449	2,744,776
Mining	124	64	84	762	101	123	86	452	2,632,038
Gate Dancer	123	64	69	829	121	75	110	523	1,854,189
Jade Hunter	107	63	73	793	109	90	103	491	2,393,713
Staff Writer	116	63	67	805	119	97	117	472	1,302,322
Northern Baby	136	62	70	926	110	135	112	569	2,868,547
Danzig Connection	115	62	66	863	109	92	128	534	1,660,112
Cryptoclearance	127	61	86	795	93	104	95	503	2,882,609
Regal Classic	119	61	73	788	114	86	109	479	2,629,869
Talc	116	61	67	784	99	90	85	510	2,098,320

Top 10 Broodmare Sires and Their Progeny

Deputy Minister, Dk B H (1979)
By Vice Regent – Mint Copy, by Bunty's Flight

316 Performers, 184 winning performers, $11,645,931 total earnings

Mare	Progeny (Sire)	Age	Sts	1st	2d	3d	Money Won
Accent On Gold	American Jewel (Rodrigo de Triano)	5	5	0	0	1	2,250
Adorable Minister	Absolutely Joe (Rodeo)	2	2	1	0	0	24,600
Adorable Minister	Gratiaen (Cure the Blues)	6	13	3	1	0	83,090
Adorable Minister	Hope Anew (Personal Flag)	3	7	1	0	0	7,332
Adorable Minister	Slewadora (Seattle Slew)	4	7	1	1	2	9,793
Altar Guild	She Belongs (Belong to Me)	4	5	1	1	0	17,820
Altar Guild	Sky Deputy (Sky Classic)	6	8	1	2	1	43,990
Alya	Vive Bene (Carson City)	3	8	1	1	0	14,220
Am Sensational	Cheeks (Honour and Glory)	5	1	0	0	0	130
Am Sensational	Mystic Storm (Kingmambo)	4	6	1	1	1	26,270
Anthem	Buzzword (Conquistador Cielo)	5	2	0	0	0	1,200
Anthem	Song of Stars (Skywalker)	6	12	0	0	1	1,892
Anthem	Southern Sensation (Southern Halo)	3	2	0	0	0	0
Apex Princess	Kiawah (Rahy)	3	2	0	0	0	435
Approve	Victorious Slam (Grand Slam)	2	1	0	0	0	137
Approve	Xtra Heart (Favorite Trick)	3	6	0	2	1	53,874
Arbitrary Risk	Boogie Woogie Man (Rhythm)	3	14	2	0	2	23,993
Arbitrary Risk	Maladyscat (Sir Cat)	4	16	1	2	6	12,832
Astarte	Dummy (Souvenir Copy)	3	1	1	0	0	6,780
Astarte	Lord Ofthe Thunder (Saint Ballado)	4	7	2	1	2	99,803
Barnie Fife	Neville (Miswaki)	3	14	0	1	2	2,230
Beaty Sark	Ivanavinalot (West Acre)	3	10	1	2	1	223,000
Beaty Sark	Johnnies Wagon (Wheaton)	5	12	2	4	1	20,557
Becomes a Rose	Mrs Miniver (Septieme Ciel)	9	1	0	0	0	0
Border Wish	U Go Hugo (Capote's Prospect)	2	6	1	1	0	4,820
Border Wish	Villa Roja (Pancho Villa)	3	12	1	1	1	9,895
Brief Interlude	Ran for the Dough (Bertrando)	3	6	1	0	0	34,950
Bring Me Joy	Joyful Ballad (Saint Ballado)	3	4	1	1	0	13,370
Butter Cream	Crypto Cream (Cryptoclearance)	4	4	0	0	0	4,230
Calamitous Jen	Country Jeweler (Judge T C)	5	11	0	1	1	6,099
Calamitous Jen	Jo Dinah (Judge T C)	4	17	2	3	2	35,190
Capital Coverup	Chappaquiddick (Cape Town)	3	1	0	0	0	0
Capital Coverup	Gold Scammer (Gold Tribute)	4	2	0	1	0	3,400
Capital Coverup	Thelionshare (Menifee)	2	5	0	0	0	1,061
Captivant	Kir (Relaunch)	6	4	0	0	0	0
Captivant	Mille Feville (Saint Ballado)	4	9	2	3	1	159,329
Captivant	Noisette (Broad Brush)	3	7	3	0	2	95,030
Choral Minister	Honest Grade (Honor Grades)	3	5	1	1	0	8,180
Choral Minister	R McLennen (Roy)	5	3	0	0	1	6,750
Clear Mandate	Full Mandate (A.P. Indy)	4	8	3	1	0	128,263
Clear Mandate	Newfoundland (Storm Cat)	3	9	4	0	1	137,234
Coastal Minister	Maytown (Menifee)	2	4	0	1	0	12,700
Coastal Minister	Minister of Note (Editor's Note)	4	12	1	3	2	16,884
Coastal Minister	Mountain Minister (Mountain Cat)	3	10	1	1	0	12,250
Consolata	Chicka Hermosa (Crusader Sword)	4	10	0	2	2	14,623
Consolata	Monologue (Opening Verse)	6	15	3	2	1	15,184
Continental Divide	Long Division (Private Terms)	3	6	0	0	1	3,210
Continental Divide	Vision of Division (Private Terms)	4	7	2	0	0	11,160
Daijin	Handpainted (A.P. Indy)	3	2	0	1	0	59,600
Daijin	Shadow Hawk (Mr. Prospector)	4	4	1	1	1	30,192
Dave's Deacon	Bruno the Dog (Chief Prospect)	8	10	0	0	1	1,450
Dave's Deacon	Hear Come Peanut (Chief Prospect)	3	7	0	1	0	5,105
Debra C.	Cocoa Mio (Horse Chestnut)	2	5	1	0	0	6,534
Debra C.	Poydras (Smart Strike)	3	6	1	2	0	50,140
Delagating	Candor (Crafty Prospector)	4	2	0	0	0	825
Delagating	Just Ruler (Cox's Ridge)	8	4	0	0	0	1,280
Delagating	Mudslide Slim (Crafty Prospector)	6	8	3	1	1	81,140
Deputation	Embarkation (Coronado's Quest)	2	2	0	0	1	4,750
Deputation	Proxy Statement (A.P. Indy)	4	2	0	0	0	1,500
Deputy Dancer	Best Foot Forward (Bien Bien)	4	10	1	0	5	34,395
Deputy Dancer	Gilded Deputy (Gilded Time)	3	14	1	2	0	6,535
Deputy Darlin	Academy Minister (Royal Academy)	4	1	0	0	1	700
Deputy Darlin	Paint It Black (Mt. Livermore)	3	7	1	1	2	41,010
Deputy Darlin	Total Gold (Kris S.)	6	1	0	0	0	0
Deputy Dear	Bond Arbitrage (Forest Wildcat)	2	4	1	1	1	51,230
Deputy Dear	Near and Dear (Red Ransom)	4	5	1	0	0	27,600
Deputy Double	Deputy Marshall (Cryptoclearance)	5	2	0	0	0	339
Deputy Double	Missing Miss (Unaccounted For)	4	6	3	1	0	145,935
Deputy Double	Twice Removed (Unaccounted For)	2	3	1	0	0	8,380
Deputy Envoy	Recollection (Cherokee Run)	3	9	1	2	1	47,020
Deputy Miss	Another One (Miswaki)	3	2	0	0	0	990
Deputy Miss	Miss Cap (Capote)	4	4	0	1	2	21,680
Deputy Royal	Royal Parade (Saint Ballado)	2	2	0	0	1	2,340
Deputy Snoop	Blues Snoop (Cure the Blues)	6	10	0	1	0	1,598
Deputy Snoop	Polish Snoop (Polish Pro)	5	14	1	1	3	5,395
Deputy Snoop	Snoopy Blues (Cure the Blues)	4	14	1	2	2	30,650
Deputy Snoop	Take Me Out Deputy (Take Me Out)	2	3	1	0	0	5,700
Deputy's Mistress	Crimson Courtier (Montreal Red)	5	7	1	1	1	62,661
Deputy's Mistress	Wild Mistress (Forest Wildcat)	2	8	1	1	0	22,160
Desiray	Romeo Tango (Rubiano)	3	14	2	3	2	34,675
Diva's Debut	Maestro's Debut (Woodman)	6	4	1	1	0	13,415
El Diabla	Hemlock (King of Kings)	3	9	2	0	1	27,089
Electric Brae	Darby Lane (Top Account)	4	9	2	1	2	20,575
Emmy Lou	Luxury Line (Major Impact)	3	10	0	0	2	1,694
Emmy Lou	Major Jonathan (Major Impact)	2	2	0	0	0	1,380
Emmy Lou	Redraw (Repriced)	4	15	1	3	0	39,080
Epistolary	Deputy Lad (Mecke)	3	7	1	1	0	37,817
Epistolary	Galarus (Notebook)	4	9	2	2	1	37,310
Epistolary	Trackofthecat (Forest Wildcat)	5	4	0	1	1	21,420
Fancy Minister	Minister o' War (Silver Buck)	4	4	1	1	0	5,185
Fancy Minister	Nici's Gold (Skip Trial)	2	3	0	0	0	288
Field of Vision	Hidden Image (Cherokee Run)	2	1	0	1	0	4,200
Field of Vision	Holy Vision R. N. (Holy Bull)	3	5	0	1	3	19,300
Fire the Deputy	Brush Up (Broad Brush)	3	5	1	0	0	16,830
Fire the Deputy	Southern Fire (Southern Halo)	2	9	1	1	2	18,540
Fire the Deputy	Ten Alarm Fire (Tabasco Cat)	4	7	2	1	1	35,068
First Minister	Preacher's Passion (Vaudeville)	3	1	0	0	0	420
Fly Butterfly	Fly Borboleta (Pulpit)	4	7	1	3	0	127,946
Fly Butterfly	Flying Pulpit (Pulpit)	3	6	0	2	0	19,620
Flying Minister	Charlie Whiskey (Cryptoclearance)	3	6	1	0	0	27,840
Flying Minister	Lifting Fog (Wild Again)	4	12	2	1	2	27,040
Flying Minister	Planets Aligned (Gold Fever)	2	4	0	0	0	5,520
For The King	King's Cloak (Capote)	7	3	0	1	2	5,880
For The King	Malayeen (Polish Numbers)	3	3	0	0	0	0
Forever Rainbows	Garrison Hill (Cozzene)	4	6	1	2	3	22,780
Forever Rainbows	Rainbow Rider (Unbridled's Song)	2	2	1	1	0	36,000
Foxy Deputy	Krisco Kid (Taj Alriyadh)	5	16	1	0	1	5,965
Foxy Deputy	Taj Shotthe Deputy (Taj Alriyadh)	7	2	0	0	0	290
Frannie Frantic	Crypto Gal (Cryptoclearance)	3	10	1	0	2	16,930
Frannie Frantic	Debi's Sportscar (Gold Tribute)	4	11	2	1	3	61,679
Frannie Frantic	Effrene (Evansville Slew)	5	6	1	0	0	8,550
Frannie Frantic	What a Strike (Strike the Gold)	7	10	3	1	1	36,666
Full Approval	Lisa's Approval (Farma Way)	5	6	1	2	1	23,670
Garfield Holme	Coal Inmy Stocking (Benny the Dip)	3	6	1	1	0	7,213
Gentle Minister	Wine Goddess (Miswaki)	3	2	0	1	1	8,260
Geraldine	Deputy Shaker (Thunder Rumble)	5	2	1	0	0	5,130
Geraldine	Dixie Preacher (Dixie Brass)	3	4	1	1	0	34,030
Good Cents	Count Centavos (Miesque's Son)	5	14	4	3	2	20,790
Good Cents	Fifth of Hennessy (Hennessy)	3	8	1	1	2	56,150
Graceful Minister	Uncontrollable (Wild Again)	2	3	1	1	0	28,560
Grandeur	Another Chapter (Carson City)	3	4	0	0	0	980
Grechelle	Unbridled Femme (Unbridled)	3	7	1	1	1	80,672
Half Queen	Halfbridled (Unbridled)	2	4	4	0	0	849,400
Hanto Yo	High Speed Travel (Bold Ruckus)	6	14	4	1	4	156,307
Hanto Yo	Red Hot Flyer (Slew o' Gold)	7	16	2	0	1	8,976
Hanto Yo	Snake Pit (Kiridashi)	3	4	1	0	0	46,488
Henlopen	Messerschmitt (Sky Classic)	2	2	0	0	0	0
Henlopen	Shining Beacon (Diesis)	3	5	0	2	1	14,000
House of Love	Fly Beside Me (Flying Continental)	5	9	2	1	1	22,389
House of Love	Love Storm (Illinois Storm)	3	10	1	3	3	29,550
House of Love	Not a Dollar Off (Marquetry)	4	8	0	0	2	1,396
I's Right	Eyeofthestorm (Summer Squall)	3	3	1	0	0	15,924
I's Right	Rosie's Sister (Royal Academy)	4	4	0	0	1	4,840
Icanseeyounow	Not You Me (Dynaformer)	3	5	0	0	0	897
Icanseeyounow	You Can't Hide (Alphabet Soup)	2	2	1	0	0	6,145
Illustrated	Piping Hot (Tabasco Cat)	3	1	0	0	0	0
Intriguing	Majority (Unbridled's Song)	3	2	1	1	0	6,276
Kay Bee Bee	Home Tour (Souvenir Copy)	2	5	1	0	1	13,240
Kay Bee Bee	Lest We Forget (Tale of the Cat)	3	1	1	0	0	16,800
Keepin' Peace	Golden Peace (Gold Pack)	4	15	3	2	2	24,552
Knight Minstress	New Opposition (Slew the Surgeon)	2	1	0	0	0	1,302
La Deputay	Don't Dream (Waquoit)	6	7	1	0	1	4,101
La Deputay	Never Delay (Press Card)	4	2	0	0	0	1,165
Lady Allaire	Chanceisalady (American Chance)	6	10	1	0	5	66,272
Lady Allaire	Turbo Bullet (Sky Classic)	5	4	0	0	0	0
Lady Go Faster	Little Wing (Allen's Prospect)	5	3	0	0	0	1,380
Langara	Timely Action (Gilded Time)	4	3	1	0	0	31,140
Lean Queen Cobra	Nacheezmo (Carson City)	3	6	3	1	0	126,600
Lean Queen Cobra	Ripsaw (Red Ransom)	4	15	3	3	0	28,262
Leisurely	Vino Tinto (Boundary)	2	4	2	0	0	37,800
Letthemagicbegin	Reggie's Magic (Confide)	3	5	1	2	0	12,625
Letthemagicbegin	Surprise Punch (Two Punch)	4	3	0	0	0	330
Likely Minister	Top Cappelletti (Capote)	3	9	2	0	2	19,130
Lilac Charm	Ecstatic (Rahy)	4	13	2	5	3	148,400
Lilac's Star	Atticus Star (Atticus)	3	7	2	2	0	69,780
Lilac's Star	Dewars Splash (St. Jovite)	6	12	3	0	2	12,797
Lilac's Star	Joy of Millbrook (Crafty Prospector)	4	6	0	2	0	18,706
Love From the Air	Migwaki (Miswaki)	7	6	3	0	0	15,370
Madam Chairman	Keeping Cool (Carson City)	3	3	0	1	0	3,000
Madame Deputy	Funny Honey (Distorted Humor)	2	3	1	1	0	32,800
Madison's Quest	Request for Parole (Judge T C)	4	12	2	2	1	103,270
Madison's Quest	Star Stretcher (Judge T C)	3	5	0	0	1	1,610
Maid's Broom	It's a Sweep (Jade Hunter)	7	14	2	1	0	7,899
Maid's Broom	Override Battle (Conquistador Cielo)	8	4	0	1	0	5,065
Maid's Broom	Tenpins (Smart Strike)	5	5	2	2	0	512,760
Minister of Music	J. Cash (Present Value)	6	6	0	1	0	3,907
Minister of Music	Jim's Super Bonus (Bonus Money)	2	9	0	0	1	1,294
Minister of Music	Nicco Nicco (Walter Willy)	3	5	0	0	0	0
Minister Wife	Mr. Rubicon (Bertrando)	3	3	0	0	0	3,300
Minister's Flag	Graziella (Honour and Glory)	3	2	1	1	0	18,800
Ministrada	Lone Star Sky (Conquistador Cielo)	3	8	0	2	1	166,760
Miraloma	Limelighter (Seeking the Gold)	3	6	0	2	1	30,985
Miraloma	Traditional (Gone West)	4	16	1	2	2	63,810
Mispillion	Trick Shot Artist (Favorite Trick)	2	3	1	2	0	8,200
Miss Jo	Finest (Conquistador Cielo)	3	2	0	0	0	0

Mare	Progeny (Sire)	Age	Sts	1st	2d	3d	Money Won
Miss Katie C.	C the Minister (Gulch)	3	1	0	0	0	0
Miss Katie C.	Cold Stone Steve (Gulch)	4	8	2	2	1	52,100
Mission Hill	Malone (Affirmed)	4	7	1	0	0	14,850
Morelia	In Secure (A.P. Indy)	3	4	3	0	0	92,040
Mosi Au Tunya	Chanceto Reminisce (American Chance)	7	2	0	0	1	880
Ms. Preacher	B. All Mine (Belong to Me)	4	2	0	0	1	1,380
Ms. Preacher	Be a Smooth Talker (Thunder Gulch)	5	4	1	1	0	32,520
Ms. Strike Zone	Zonaki (Miswaki)	4	3	0	0	0	0
Musical Minister	Kelli Lee (Kris S.)	3	6	1	0	0	30,960
Musical Minister	Minister Eric (Old Trieste)	2	5	1	2	1	387,920
Musical Minister	River God (Bahri)	5	3	2	0	0	79,020
Northern Mynx	Northern Request (Urgent Request)	4	17	1	4	4	12,058
Nuts About You	Princess Itron (Itron)	2	6	0	1	2	5,445
One for Hebe	Litter the Glitter (Glitterman)	3	5	2	0	1	16,485
One for Hebe	Simply Gorgeous (Beau Genius)	5	3	1	0	0	15,000
One for Hebe	Two for Hebe (Farma Way)	8	6	0	2	0	1,000
Open House	Homemaker (Afternoon Deelites)	2	7	2	3	2	85,743
Open Marriage	Affair in the Air (A. P Jet)	5	5	0	2	0	22,360
Open Marriage	Caught Cheatin' (Scarlet Ibis)	4	9	1	0	0	33,150
Particular Style	Diplomat (Black Tie Affair)	8	16	5	2	3	54,345
Pemaquid	Fircroft (A.P. Indy)	3	7	0	3	0	156,876
Picabo Street	Nevada Strip (Carson City)	6	12	3	2	2	64,090
Pixie Rose	Fromheretobrazil (Rubiano)	3	7	0	0	0	477
Pixie Rose	Lively Minister (Lively One)	7	11	2	1	3	63,726
Pixie Rose	With Roses (With Approval)	4	19	1	6	4	15,424
Plenty of Sunshine	Saints a Plenty (Saint Ballado)	3	4	0	1	1	9,500
Political Intrigue	Redattore (BRZ) (Roi Normand)	8	8	5	0	2	864,147
Political Process	Aunt Imo (Smart Strike)	4	3	0	0	0	0
Political Process	Deputy Strike (Smart Strike)	5	6	0	0	2	36,927
Possible Consort	Consort Music (Prospector's Music)	4	12	2	0	3	71,969
Possible Consort	Marina Minister (Rubiano)	3	9	2	0	1	63,006
Prayer Colony	Atlas Peak (Pyramid Peak)	2	3	0	1	0	2,400
Presence Galore	Madame Galore (Fantastic Fellow)	2	1	0	0	0	0
Presence Galore	Road Town (Announce)	3	3	0	0	0	840
Presence Galore	Roberto's Minister (Royal Roberto)	6	14	1	4	4	9,400
Presence Galore	Runaway Victor (Runaway Groom)	7	14	0	2	1	26,238
Pretty Keane	Pretty Pro (Distinctive Pro)	3	4	1	0	0	25,890
Prime Affair	True to Slew (Capote)	3	5	0	0	1	3,119
Primedex	Mystified (Gone West)	2	4	0	0	4	19,800
Primedex	Primerica (Mr. Greeley)	5	7	2	3	2	147,640
Promiscuous Angel	No Curfew (Unaccounted For)	6	17	2	4	1	15,530
Promiscuous Angel	Paper Wings (Editor's Note)	4	8	1	1	0	4,177
Promiscuous Angel	Winewomenandsong (Cape Town)	3	1	0	0	0	760
Proper Form	Desnuda (Unbridled's Song)	2	4	1	3	0	54,000
Psychic Spirit	Ask Dorothy (Smart Strike)	4	15	3	0	7	66,270
Psychic Spirit	Fly Me Ali (Grand Slam)	2	1	0	1	0	3,510
Psychic Spirit	Mystic Beat (Rhythm)	5	5	0	1	1	2,448
Puppet Show	Fear Factory (Gold Case)	3	5	1	0	0	25,398
Queen of Spirit	Last Song (Unbridled's Song)	2	4	1	1	0	38,930
Rebs Odyssey	Rebs Agenda (Twilight Agenda)	2	5	0	2	0	5,600
Rebs Odyssey	Rebs Fortyniner (Marked Tree)	3	4	0	0	0	231
Red Mistress	Alleycat Coat (Caller I. D.)	5	3	0	0	0	1,240
Red Mistress	Drawing Away (River Special)	7	1	0	0	0	0
Red Mistress	Trenchtown (Cape Town)	3	1	0	0	0	1,350
Regina's Vice	Early Snow (Souvenir Copy)	3	12	2	2	3	86,392
Return of Mom	Value Play (Mt. Livermore)	4	10	1	1	3	57,690
Rhythm of Life	Bahama John (Saint Ballado)	3	2	1	0	0	28,275
Rhythm of Life	Sarava (Wild Again)	4	1	0	0	0	0
Rhythm of Life	Wild Rocket (Wild Again)	5	6	0	2	0	5,980
Rightfromthestart	Rosemont Hope (Coronado's Quest)	3	16	1	3	3	30,008
Sabbath Song	Sirona Gold (Gold Case)	3	5	2	0	1	68,683
Sahibah	Quest for Rain (Quest for Fame)	5	5	0	1	1	8,500
Salmon Rush	Hard Delivery (Marquetry)	8	5	1	0	1	29,630
Santa Elena	Buffy Bluegrazz (Rahy)	5	1	0	0	0	0
Santa Elena	Seattle Santa (Seattle Slew)	4	9	1	1	0	15,070
Scottische	Grindstone Deputy (Grindstone)	4	1	0	0	0	0
Scottische	Sweet Scottische (Storm Creek)	3	4	1	1	0	50,334
Second Bloom	La Cicale (D'Hallevant)	5	10	1	0	0	7,314
Second Bloom	Molto Bene (Jules)	4	16	3	2	4	42,702
See Moon	Nault (Woodman)	3	12	2	3	1	69,900
Senta	Double Team (Defensive Play)	8	6	0	1	1	4,225
Seoul	Seoul Wild (Wild Again)	2	1	0	1	0	2,000
Share the Fun	Cape Good Hope (Cape Town)	3	7	3	0	1	68,520
Share the Space	Copy Bien (Bien Bien)	4	2	0	0	0	470
Shaunlee	Banshee Brad (Candy Stripes)	5	14	4	6	2	72,910
Shaunlee	Ruby Brad (Rubiano)	6	8	0	2	2	8,975
Shaunlee	Runaway Twins (Runaway Groom)	4	13	3	1	1	47,675
Shaunlee	Tell Me I'm Pritt (Peaks and Valleys)	3	2	0	1	1	4,090
Sheena	Gold Search (Seeking the Gold)	3	8	0	0	2	4,670
Sherriff's Deputy	Deputy (Hadif)	5	3	0	0	1	3,030
Sherriff's Deputy	Secret Wedge (Excellent Secret)	4	12	1	2	2	20,940
Shining Through	Houndstooth (Grand Slam)	2	2	0	0	0	0
Shining Through	Litigasion (Miesque's Son)	5	8	3	2	0	18,980
Shining Through	Strong Hope (Grand Slam)	3	7	5	0	1	582,360
Sixy Minister	Deputy Carson (Carson City)	7	6	0	0	0	1,565
Social Director	Dream About (Cherokee Run)	2	5	2	1	0	224,430
Special Mistress	Equinox (Unbridled's Song)	5	3	1	0	2	10,710
Special Mistress	Mariatom (Irish Tower)	9	13	0	2	3	11,218
Special Mistress	Special Ballad (Saint Ballado)	4	3	0	1	0	7,700
Special Mistress	Special Way (Runaway Groom)	8	16	5	1	3	42,945
Special Mistress	Twilight Time (Twilight Agenda)	6	12	3	1	4	68,190
Special Mistress	Uninhibited Song (Unbridled's Song)	2	1	0	1	0	5,600
Stanley's Girl	Class Shows (Geri)	4	4	0	0	0	792
Star Deputy	Fourth Daughter (Smoke Glacken)	4	6	1	0	0	14,440
Star Minister	Concerned Minister (Concern)	6	4	1	1	1	22,730
Star Minister	Exploding Star (Exploit)	2	1	0	0	1	1,950
Starlet Minister	Moonlet Minister (Chimes Band)	4	12	2	2	3	75,270
Starlet Minister	More Stars (Mt. Livermore)	7	2	0	0	0	0
Starlet Minister	Unbridled Game (Unbridled's Song)	3	5	1	0	2	28,010
Stately Event	Stately Deputy (Miswaki)	3	4	1	0	0	28,530
Stately Star	Sentimental Value (Diesis)	4	5	0	0	1	19,299
Stolen Beauty	Moonlightandbeauty (Capote)	4	12	3	3	2	129,073
Stolen Beauty	Wholehearted (Carson City)	2	3	0	0	0	2,100
Storm Minister	Stacie's Ballado (Saint Ballado)	2	5	1	1	0	14,160
Story Book	Skip a Page (Skip Trial)	5	10	1	2	3	32,610
Story Book	Story Grinder (Grindstone)	3	3	0	0	1	4,080
Sunset Service	Database (Known Fact)	4	9	3	3	1	106,860
Sunset Service	Service Medal (Our Emblem)	2	3	0	0	0	350
Sunset Service	Vespers (Known Fact)	5	9	1	3	1	65,720
Sweet Carolina	Carolina Ties (Quiet American)	3	4	0	0	0	0
Sweet Carolina	Tricks Are Great (Phone Trick)	4	9	0	1	2	4,407
The Franchise	Joyce Loves Me (Aggressive Chief)	2	1	0	0	0	0
Tin Oaks	Omega Code (Elusive Quality)	3	5	1	2	0	87,810
Tin Oaks	Tempest Fugit (Unaccounted For)	6	4	1	1	2	89,200
Tin Oaks	Wild Success (Forest Wildcat)	4	8	2	1	1	10,710
True Mood	Denimsanddiamonds (Private Terms)	3	12	5	1	1	95,479
True Mood	True Moments (Pioneering)	2	5	1	1	0	18,450
Vandra	Crafty Joanne (Prospect Bay)	5	4	0	0	0	60
Very Popular	Citadella (Slew City Slew)	2	1	0	0	0	320
Very Popular	Seattlespectacular (Seattle Slew)	3	5	1	2	1	61,120
Victory Minister	Demalootphotosh't (Dmal't Dmashoot)	5	8	1	1	1	33,958
Victory Minister	Furious Victory (Furiously)	7	9	2	0	2	3,263
Victory Minister	Grit Victory (Demaloot Demashoot)	4	1	0	0	0	91
Viva Girl	Editiorial (Editor's Note)	3	11	1	1	1	14,600
Vivalita	Big Bad Louie (Loup Sauvage)	2	1	0	0	0	0
Vivalita	Monster Move (Meadow Monster)	3	3	1	1	0	11,560
Waltzing Beauty	Empress Livia (Magic Banner)	5	11	0	1	2	9,066
Waltzing Beauty	Gold Ginny (Gold Legend)	2	3	2	1	0	36,000
Waltzing Beauty	Queen of Wands (Wekiva Springs)	3	4	3	1	0	21,850
Wedding March	Marching (Coronado's Quest)	2	2	0	0	0	1,350
Wedding Photo	Rubyana (Rubiano)	4	10	2	2	1	79,850
Whers the Rainbw	Doppler Radar (Runaway Groom)	4	12	2	2	1	29,320
Whers the Rainbw	Mr. Carpe Diem (Good and Tough)	2	3	0	0	0	100
Wonders to Come	Bookkillrr (Black Tie Affair)	7	4	0	0	0	640
Wonders to Come	Fly for Home (Fly So Free)	6	13	0	0	1	1,880
Wonders to Come	Many Ministers (Numerous)	5	9	4	0	0	20,425
Wonders to Come	Miss Crafty Pal (Crafty Friend)	2	2	1	0	1	21,850
Wonders to Come	Sister Smoke (Smoke Glacken)	4	6	3	0	0	16,225
Xanadu	Twisted (Twining)	5	15	1	1	3	13,548
Xanadu	U. K. Kat (Forest Wildcat)	4	12	1	0	1	8,454
Zonda	This N That (Cryptoclearance)	3	2	1	0	0	11,400

Mr. Prospector, B H (1970)
By Raise a Native – Gold Digger, by Nashua

261 Performers, 135 winning performers, $9,847,587 total earnings

Mare	Progeny (Sire)	Age	Sts	1st	2d	3d	Money Won
A Real Native	Nature's Power (Kris S.)	7	8	2	0	1	16,027
Abrade	Berry Good (Arch)	2	1	0	0	0	360
Abrade	Forty Nine Deeds (Alydeed)	4	13	1	1	2	49,290
Abrade	Wear (Arch)	3	3	0	0	1	5,740
Act	Play Taps (Pleasant Tap)	7	2	0	0	0	450
Act	Saintly Action (Saint Ballado)	4	4	2	0	0	54,540
Addenda	Mr. Slew's Valor (Metfield)	9	13	1	0	0	7,987
Aliata	Ferrazzi (Arazi)	5	14	2	2	3	40,481
Allusion	Alunite (Red Ransom)	5	1	0	0	0	0
Allusion	Rag Time Dancer (Dixieland Band)	2	6	1	1	1	12,220
Alqwani	Fehr (Dumaani)	3	7	1	0	2	42,160
Ambria	Dakini (Nureyev)	3	5	0	0	1	5,110
Ambria	Old Economy (Gentlemen)	2	2	0	0	0	0
Art's Prospector	Countess Gold (Mt. Livermore)	4	3	0	0	0	0
Art's Prospector	Lendy (Theatrical)	7	14	1	1	1	9,346
Autumn Moon	Cycle of Life (Spinning World)	3	4	1	0	0	20,930
Ballerina Princess	Peak Dancer (Mt. Livermore)	6	5	1	0	0	10,335
Bashayer	Mosayter (Storm Cat)	5	4	0	0	0	4,290
Bat Prospector	Cherokee Prospect (Cherokee Run)	6	3	0	0	0	840
Bat Prospector	On Exhibit (Cherokee Run)	3	14	2	6	3	35,450
Be a Prospector	Away (Dixieland Band)	6	1	0	0	0	0
Be a Prospector	Bingo Queen (Hennessy)	3	2	0	0	0	86
Be a Prospector	Rich Find (Exploit)	2	3	1	0	0	16,005
Beau Prospector	Abu Leil (Chief's Crown)	7	11	3	3	1	29,470
Beau Prospector	Cherokee Beau (Cherokee Run)	5	2	0	1	0	6,000
Beau Prospector	Cherokee Maiden (Cherokee Run)	4	13	1	2	5	25,939
Beautiful Gem	Max Jones (Capote)	5	5	0	1	0	9,684
Bejat	Glick (Theatrical)	7	13	4	2	0	111,330
Bernice of Winloc	Quinlan's Lesnjake (Dixieland Band)	6	16	1	1	1	6,620
Blazing Alarmiss	Advance to Go (Reprized)	2	3	0	0	1	1,990
Blue Jean Baby	Blue Jean Racer (Silver Hawk)	7	2	0	0	0	0
Boom and Bust	Brazoom (Belong to Me)	4	1	0	0	0	0
Brenda Lagrange	Bugsy N Tuff (Fly So Free)	5	7	0	2	1	3,516

Brenda Lagrange	Overnight Delivery (Mountain Cat)	4	14	6	1	1	50,768
Brocaro	Caroca (Theatrical)	3	4	0	1	0	12,260
Chic Shirine	Flying Passage (A.P. Indy)	3	4	1	0	2	37,250
Chimes	Bestbandintheland (Dixieland Band)	7	3	0	0	0	68
Colour Chart	Equerry (St. Jovite)	5	2	0	0	0	0
Colour Chart	Joharra (Kris S.)	3	3	0	2	0	17,800
Connie's Prospect	Dos Reyes (Southern Halo)	3	1	0	0	0	0
County Fair	Steaming Home (Salt Lake)	4	6	0	0	1	6,542
Coup de Genie	Glia (A.P. Indy)	4	2	0	0	0	0
Coup de Genie	Loving Kindness (Seattle Slew)	3	1	0	0	0	0
Coup de Genie	Snake Mountain (A.P. Indy)	5	5	3	0	0	159,825
Crystal Shard	Clear Destiny (Deputy Minister)	4	5	2	2	0	113,532
Crystal Shard	Perfect Cut (A.P. Indy)	3	9	3	2	1	111,148
Cuddles	Country Romance (Saint Ballado)	3	10	4	2	1	157,230
Dabble	Afternoon Amour (Afternoon Deelites)	5	20	1	2	1	8,643
Dabble	Blame It On Beau (Beau Genius)	4	5	1	1	1	16,240
Dabble	Tori's Portia (Beau Genius)	3	5	0	0	0	590
Dance With Grace	Dance With Kelly (Devil's Bag)	7	10	0	0	1	593
Dance With Grace	Indy Dancer (A.P. Indy)	3	5	1	0	1	121,900
Dance With Grace	Swing Lord (A.P. Indy)	5	8	1	0	3	19,400
Debt	Tennesee Burbin (Hennessy)	3	7	1	1	0	17,220
Delta Love	Career Day (Cherokee Run)	3	2	0	0	0	340
East Cape	Ottawa Chief (Forestry)	2	4	2	1	1	49,700
Educated Risk	Alluring (A.P. Indy)	4	7	0	4	1	45,140
Elizabeth Bay	Jahaam (Danzig)	7	3	0	0	0	1,040
Envied	Close to Perfect (Stravinsky)	2	7	0	1	3	16,720
Envied	Pantages (Louis Quatorze)	3	8	1	0	0	6,665
Envied	Red Wing Evan (A.P. Indy)	4	6	2	1	1	49,060
Especially	Boston Common (Boston Harbor)	4	8	4	1	0	105,930
Especially	Captain Thunder (Storm Cat)	3	4	3	1	0	79,110
Especially	Special Tactics (Tactical Cat)	2	3	0	0	0	0
Fabulous Prospect	Chum (Fortunate Prospect)	4	10	1	0	1	11,778
Fabulous Prospect	Fabulous Fortune (Fortunate Prospect)	5	19	1	1	3	28,650
Fabulous Prospect	Ghetto (Line In The Sand)	2	9	0	0	1	1,880
Faith's Folly	Maid's Folly (Maria's Mon)	4	16	2	3	2	19,687
Find	Seek (Devil's Bag)	3	6	0	0	0	825
Foolish Gold	Cymbidium (Heaven's Wish)	3	11	0	1	4	10,910
Foolish Gold	Foolish Kiss (Kissin Kris)	5	2	0	1	0	6,435
Foolish Gold	Mr. Foolish (Lively One)	7	2	0	0	0	0
Ganadora	Ganadancer (Moscow Ballet)	4	4	0	2	0	4,750
Garimpeiro	Lasting Pleasure (Theatrical)	4	1	0	0	0	0
Garimpeiro	Tysun (Blushing John)	8	7	0	0	0	1,400
Gay Chiffon	Commander's Flag (Spinning World)	4	8	2	0	4	137,544
Gay Chiffon	Goldman (Dixieland Band)	6	11	3	4	0	23,464
Gay Chiffon	Knight Affair (Black Tie Affair)	8	12	1	0	3	12,966
Get Lucky	Daydreaming (A.P. Indy)	2	3	1	0	1	79,000
Gild	Fungee (Dixieland Band)	2	2	0	0	0	0
Gild	Poker Brad (Go for Gin)	5	11	2	2	2	147,830
Gilded Dancer	Valentine Dancer (In Excess)	3	14	5	3	2	312,846
Glittering Legend	Legendary Run (Runaway Groom)	4	1	0	0	0	0
Go for It Lady	Spring Meadow (Meadowlake)	4	10	3	0	3	204,002
Gold Hearted	Benny the Lip (Benny the Dip)	4	17	3	4	1	24,850
Gold Hearted	Encanto Oro (Charismatic)	2	5	0	1	1	2,925
Gold Hearted	Goldharbor Express (Boston Harbor)	3	4	2	1	0	7,000
Gold Heist	Churchhill (The Prime Minister)	3	1	0	0	0	0
Gold Heist	Prime Jewel (The Prime Minister)	4	12	2	2	1	35,590
Gold Seal	Fixed Image (Halo's Image)	4	24	0	2	2	6,888
Gold Shadow	Day Trade (Dixieland Band)	7	8	1	1	0	13,865
Gold Shadow	Keys to the Heart (Wild Again)	4	8	1	1	2	111,600
Gold Shadow	Shadow of Mine (Belong to Me)	2	6	1	0	0	48,280
Gold Whirl	Whirlacat (Mountain Cat)	7	7	0	0	0	669
Gold Whirl	Whirley (Summer Squall)	6	7	1	0	1	11,975
Golden Attraction	Swift Attraction (Storm Cat)	2	1	0	0	0	675
Golden Petal	Golden Glen (Forestry)	2	5	0	1	1	11,860
Golden Reef	Delightful Reef (Pleasant Colony)	7	13	0	1	2	4,432
Goldminess	Gold Bull (Holy Bull)	5	3	0	0	1	1,000
Grass Skirt	Flaming Dixie (Dixieland Band)	2	3	1	1	0	19,010
Hard to Copy	Andover Lady (Kris S.)	3	5	2	1	1	76,533
Hard to Copy	Zarzuela (Seattle Slew)	4	1	0	0	0	600
Hawkeye's Girl	Houston Hawk (Houston)	11	2	0	0	0	0
Hawkeye's Girl	Low Talker (Phone Trick)	3	7	0	1	2	5,633
Here I Go	Let 'Em Go (Red Ransom)	2	3	0	0	1	4,900
Hollywood Gold	I Testify (Lit de Justice)	3	10	0	1	2	34,291
Hollywood Gold	Quintons Gold Rush (Wild Rush)	2	1	0	1	0	7,600
Hopespringsforevr	Ozzie Cat (Storm Cat)	3	10	0	1	1	32,770
Hot Match	Belle of Perintown (Dehere)	3	5	1	0	3	141,390
Hot Match	Bogangles (Joyeux Danseur)	2	7	2	2	1	74,575
Ikhteyaar	Jovial Joshua (Bahri)	2	4	1	2	0	8,600
Illicit	Double Jeopardy (Horse Chestnut)	2	1	0	0	0	0
Im a Star Prospect	Cosmah Star (Saint Ballado)	4	2	1	1	0	37,345
Im a Star Prospect	Show Biz (Candy Stripes)	5	4	0	0	1	2,000
Im a Star Prospect	Star Raider (Belong to Me)	3	6	1	1	0	13,410
Impetuous Image	Hallucinogin (Go for Gin)	6	6	0	1	0	6,980
Impetuous Image	Impetuous Fling (A.P. Indy)	3	13	2	1	0	71,914
In the Till	Emptythetill (Holy Bull)	3	3	0	2	0	24,240
In the Till	Gingham and Lace (Kris S.)	2	3	1	1	0	21,600
In the Till	Incorrigible (Mt. Livermore)	4	16	2	2	2	24,350
Julia Jane	Magic Trap (Alfaari)	3	11	0	0	2	2,522
Julia Jane	Vancouver Vice (Vice Regent)	8	10	0	2	0	4,490
Kalinka	Claridges (With Approval)	5	6	0	0	0	496
Kalinka	Kamoya (Dayjur)	3	5	1	0	0	4,800
Kettle Ridge	Four Corners (Salt Lake)	4	12	3	2	1	50,373
Key to My Heart	Love n' Kiss S. (Kris S.)	5	8	3	2	0	152,558
Lady Is a Tramp	Privateer (Private Terms)	5	7	3	0	1	15,183
Line	Expressway (Tabasco Cat)	4	8	2	1	0	25,360
Lit'l Rose	Handsome Hunk (Hennessy)	4	1	0	0	0	0
Looking for Gold	Stunning Image (Kris S.)	3	2	0	0	1	4,130
Lost Lode	Dominica (Housebuster)	5	2	0	1	0	9,300
Lost Lode	Silver Diablo (Holy Bull)	3	1	0	0	0	360
Love From Mom	American Liberty (Storm Cat)	3	7	0	1	3	27,340
Macoumba	Lady Nichola (A.P. Indy)	2	1	0	1	0	9,800
Macoumba	Parker's Storm Cat (Storm Cat)	3	3	1	1	0	40,800
Macoumba	Somethingdangerous (Danzig)	5	9	2	0	1	45,700
Margi's Prospect	Orville Forest (Boston Harbor)	3	3	1	0	0	21,940
Margi's Prospect	Prospect's Prize (Prized)	6	2	0	0	0	381
Marie J	Sisti's Pride (Forestry)	2	6	1	1	2	64,427
Mary's Spirit	Tavacat (Tabasco Cat)	3	3	2	0	0	12,600
Meteor Miner	Oro Bandito (Pancho Villa)	9	6	1	1	0	4,020
Meteor Miner	Valiant Leader (Broad Brush)	5	10	1	1	2	8,250
Michelky	Reason Prevails (Ogygian)	12	14	2	0	1	7,901
Minden Rose	Thorn Cat (Storm Cat)	6	1	0	0	0	360
Miner's Game	Looking Afar (Broad Brush)	5	7	1	0	2	28,785
Miner's Game	Polish Gift (Danzig)	3	3	0	0	0	2,640
Miner's Game	Prowling (Storm Cat)	4	4	0	0	0	0
Miss Du Bois	Film Maker (Dynaformer)	3	9	4	2	2	457,220
Mission Pass	Coast Line (Boston Harbor)	2	1	0	0	0	2,700
Mission Pass	Harbor Pass (Boston Harbor)	4	14	4	0	1	51,170
More Flags	Dixiemore (Dixieland Band)	6	27	1	3	5	25,221
More Flags	More Bands (Dixieland Band)	3	8	1	0	3	19,985
More Flags	More Terms (Private Terms)	7	1	0	0	0	0
More Flags	Wildest (Wild Again)	5	14	1	4	1	41,368
Mr. P.'s Girl	Location (Relaunch)	8	6	0	0	1	1,714
Nortena	Aldo (Red Ransom)	6	6	0	1	1	8,650
Nortena	Cherry Tree Hill (Red Ransom)	5	3	1	0	1	12,168
Nortena	Flower Forest (Kris S.)	3	5	2	1	1	65,495
O My Darling	Black Cove (Kris S.)	7	12	3	0	2	12,722
O My Darling	Bullistic Flight (Holy Bull)	4	6	1	0	0	11,490
On Final	Final Attack (Hadif)	3	6	2	0	1	27,283
On Final	Fleet Final (Hadif)	4	17	3	2	5	17,290
On Final	Off the Screen (Hadif)	5	9	1	2	1	9,239
On Final	Radar Trap (Hadif)	7	17	3	4	2	27,124
Onaga	Yarico's Pond (Seattle Slew)	3	4	1	1	1	30,910
Onyx	Classic Onyx (Sky Classic)	5	7	1	3	1	6,426
Onyx	Holmdel (Housebuster)	7	9	4	0	1	21,043
Our Millie	Milliemillie (Compliance)	4	6	0	2	0	6,200
Our Millie	Winlocs Grama Rose (Anjiz)	6	5	0	0	1	6,126
Over All	Vauxhall (Theatrical)	5	1	0	0	0	380
Pedicure	Second Performance (Theatrical)	2	1	0	0	0	2,760
Pedicure	Stagy (Theatrical)	3	5	0	0	2	6,340
Pennant Chmpion	A Great Team (A.P. Indy)	3	6	3	1	1	98,620
Pennant Chmpion	Baseball Champion (Wild Again)	5	3	0	1	0	10,380
Perfect Tune	Violins (Royal Academy)	4	4	0	0	0	50
Praise	Congrats (A.P. Indy)	3	7	3	0	1	180,388
Praise	Flatter (A.P. Indy)	4	2	1	0	1	82,845
Proflare	War Zone (Danzig)	4	5	2	0	0	120,436
Propositioning	American Band (Dixieland Band)	4	5	2	0	0	9,960
Proskona	Calista (Caerleon)	5	2	0	1	1	31,000
Prospect Dalia	Chesapeake Lady (Captain Bodgit)	4	2	0	0	0	0
Prospect Dalia	Lermontov (Alleged)	6	4	1	0	0	23,925
Prospect Digger	Hecandigit (Marlin)	4	6	1	0	1	40,320
Prospective	Charismatic Rob (Charismatic)	2	5	1	0	1	35,050
Prospective	Dixie Drummer (Dixieland Band)	5	10	2	0	3	41,240
Prospective Wife	Besttobeabachelor (Kris S.)	8	14	3	1	1	26,016
Prospective Wife	Ride 'Em Rags (Rahy)	7	13	2	6	4	63,680
Prospective Wife	Tomoka Bound (Boundary)	2	2	0	1	0	5,600
Prospctr's Charm	With Charm (With Approval)	6	4	0	0	1	2,400
Prospector's Fire	Royal Alchemist (Royal Academy)	3	4	0	0	1	1,643
Prospector's First	Pancho Pete (Pancho Villa)	8	12	2	0	1	22,789
Prospectr's Punch	Battle Ghost (Battle Launch)	6	11	0	0	0	749
Prospectr's Queen	High Rank (Gentlemen)	3	10	2	1	0	15,645
Prospectr's Queen	Rahy Rhythm (Rahy)	6	8	1	0	0	14,722
Prospectors Delite	Mineshaft (A.P. Indy)	4	9	7	2	0	2,209,686
Prospectors Delite	Rock Slide (A.P. Indy)	5	7	2	1	0	169,390
Prosperity Found	Our Freya (Skip Away)	3	9	0	2	2	24,185
Prosperity Found	Prospect Green (Green Dancer)	5	7	0	0	2	11,520
Prospinsky	Spin Control (A.P. Indy)	3	6	3	0	2	79,310
Prospinsky	Tell J (A.P. Indy)	4	10	2	1	0	30,200
Pueblo	Cherokee Trail (Seattle Slew)	4	6	0	1	1	6,289
Pueblo	Frontier Trail (Deputy Minister)	6	6	0	0	0	405
Pueblo	Maryneill (Belong to Me)	2	1	0	0	0	720
Queena	La Reina (A.P. Indy)	2	4	2	2	0	142,420
Race Artist	Almost Holy (Holy Bull)	3	10	1	3	0	18,795
Race Artist	Eye of the Artist (Old Trieste)	2	2	0	0	0	180
Race Cam	Frozen Chosin (Deputy Minister)	7	1	0	0	0	0
Rafina	Canberra (Sadler's Wells)	4	2	0	0	0	570
Randi's Queen	Neither One (Fly So Free)	5	1	0	0	0	0
Realm	Devil's Domain (Devil's Bag)	5	6	3	0	0	44,040
Realm	Mauk Hawk (Silver Hawk)	2	1	0	0	0	0
Reckless Star	Lightninginabottle (Lightning Leap)	6	2	0	0	0	237
Ridan Prospector	Polish Account (Polish Numbers)	3	5	1	1	1	24,330
Ridan Prospector	Ridan's Mon (Maria's Mon)	4	6	2	2	0	56,460
Riffle	Double Interest (Red Ransom)	4	1	0	0	0	0

Riffle	San Nicolas (Go for Gin)	5	7	1	0	1	38,795
Rock On Now	Intimate Music (Private Terms)	5	12	3	2	2	40,394
Ryn	Aisle Light (Bertrando)	3	1	0	0	1	4,200
Ryn	I've Decided (Bertrando)	6	9	0	1	1	15,580
Safe Return	Never Left (Seattle Slew)	3	9	2	0	1	42,820
San Angelo	Old Lodge (Lure)	7	8	0	1	1	2,750
Sayedat Alhadh	Musaa Ed (Deputy Minister)	4	11	3	4	1	86,780
Scrape	Sobriquet (Hennessy)	2	1	0	0	0	720
Sealed Bid	Lejos (Charismatic)	2	5	0	1	1	4,874
Sha Tha	State Shinto (Pleasant Colony)	7	5	1	0	0	111,876
Sierra Madre	Hunting Cat (Storm Cat)	8	3	0	0	0	134
Sierra Madre	Sun Cat (Tabasco Cat)	6	12	3	5	0	49,794
Sigh Ho	Ascribe (Lil E. Tee)	2	1	0	0	0	217
Sigh Ho	Restored Again (Lil E. Tee)	5	2	0	0	1	930
Silver Discovery	Discover the Glory (Honour and Glory)	3	11	1	5	1	83,545
Silver Discovery	Father Party (Honour and Glory)	2	2	0	0	2	9,390
Silver Valley	Buzzy's Gold (Touch Gold)	3	9	1	2	2	59,380
Simaat	Makam (Green Desert)	3	10	1	3	0	56,235
Sol de Terre	Lake William (Salt Lake)	7	3	1	1	0	36,000
Sometimsadiamnd	Sky Diamond (Sky Classic)	3	1	0	0	0	0
Special Strike	Beware Avalanche (Mt. Livermore)	7	11	2	1	1	81,120
Special Strike	Hot Sync (Valley Crossing)	4	1	0	0	0	420
Spring Morning	Spring Training (Cherokee Run)	2	4	0	1	1	4,775
Starafar	Malagot (Wild Again)	6	8	1	0	2	5,649
Stutz Goldrush	Sky Chariot (Sky Classic)	7	1	0	0	1	8,734
Sugar Gold	Optimity (Personal Flag)	6	14	0	1	3	3,810
Sweepings	Las Malvinas (Lord At War)	5	2	0	0	0	1,080
Sweetheart	Sweet Band (Dixieland Band)	4	10	2	3	1	88,947
Tacha	Seattle Tac (Seattle Slew)	3	3	1	1	0	43,252
Takreem	Spinning Tales (Spinning World)	4	5	3	0	0	50,190
Tersa	Donald David (Kris S.)	3	6	0	0	0	1,020
Unbeatable Foe	Full Force Gale (Mt. Livermore)	6	8	1	2	2	23,325
Watch Out	Brands Hatch (A.P. Indy)	2	2	0	0	0	3,080
Watch Out	Master O Foxhounds (Deputy Minister)	8	4	1	0	0	7,095
Water Saver	Trinity River (River Special)	6	11	2	2	3	36,450
Wayage	Teresa Ann (Boston Harbor)	4	6	0	1	0	11,400
Wayward Bound	Orchid Island (Broad Brush)	2	1	0	0	0	0
Wayward Bound	Yacht Club (Sea Hero)	3	2	1	0	0	10,030
Whist	Trick Taker (Capote)	4	1	0	0	0	93
Wind Capers	Capable Capers (Native Factor)	4	8	2	2	2	15,811
Winged Prospect	Eclipse Bay (Hennessy)	3	3	1	0	1	48,240
Winloc's Millie	Winloc's Anzio (Katowice)	4	6	1	1	1	13,650
Winloc's Millie	Winlocs Glory Days (Belong to Me)	2	3	0	2	0	17,800
Winze	Gildmore (Gilded Time)	4	11	2	3	2	39,950
Withallprobability	With Ability (A.P. Indy)	5	1	0	0	0	0
Withallprobability	With Probability (Wild Again)	2	1	0	0	0	1,290

Relaunch, Gr H (1976)
By In Reality – Foggy Note, by The Axe II

332 Performers, 191 winning performers, $8,067,738 total earnings

Mare	Progeny (Sire)	Age	Sts	1st	2d	3d	Money Won
A Little Reality	Who You Gonna Call (Ghost Ranch)	2	8	1	0	1	11,240
Advertising	Advantage (CHI) (Repriced)	6	1	0	0	0	100
Aerosilver	Lake Silver (Meadowlake)	5	5	1	0	0	19,708
Aerosilver	Mekko Hokte (Holy Bull)	3	9	1	2	2	41,700
Afto	Line Distribution (Major Impact)	7	7	1	0	1	4,520
Afto	Marci's Doctor (Repriced)	5	2	0	1	0	1,196
All Systems Go	Caller Junction (Caller I. D.)	6	6	1	1	0	4,988
All Systems Go	Florida Recount (Grindstone)	4	7	3	0	0	153,162
All Systems Go	Tinsel Bits (Unbridled's Song)	5	10	2	0	0	37,263
All Systems Go	Union Smoke (Clever Trick)	3	4	2	0	0	12,313
Appian Road	Liberty Creek (Bertrando)	4	11	3	2	0	14,018
Appian Road	Road to Mortlock (Mortlock)	3	4	0	1	0	6,200
Arena Blanca	Boss Nass (Video Ranger)	2	4	0	0	0	4,798
Arena Blanca	Glaringlory (Video Ranger)	4	1	0	0	0	50
Aristocratic Baby	Notoriously Elite (Hubble)	5	3	2	1	0	8,466
Ascloseasitgets	Annabelle's Song (Unbridled's Song)	2	1	0	1	0	6,600
Attractive Missile	Just Missed (Silver Deputy)	4	3	0	0	0	600
Attractive Missile	Rocket Royale (Roy)	3	4	2	1	0	29,100
Aucilla	Game Box (A.P. Indy)	3	2	0	0	0	1,380
Aucilla	Passing Shot (A.P. Indy)	4	10	3	2	2	362,637
Authorized Staff	Dayton's Bluff (Lord At War)	6	9	0	0	1	1,261
Authorized Staff	Slave Driver (Geri)	4	8	1	0	0	6,090
Awesome Launch	Rounce (Hatchet Man)	9	7	0	1	2	2,350
Baby Bar	Paster's Baby (Paster's Caper)	4	7	0	0	1	12,065
Baby Zip	Ghostzapper (Awesome Again)	3	4	3	0	1	378,400
Barbaloot	Bauhauser (Numerous)	5	4	2	1	0	113,750
Beauty Supply	Farma Way Jr. (Farma Way)	3	13	2	1	1	6,766
Before the Wind	Miles for Mickey (Judge T C)	4	11	1	3	0	8,956
Before the Wind	Wind in the Sky (Sky Classic)	5	11	2	2	3	9,560
Big Bold Beauty	Bold Fever (Gold Fever)	5	16	3	0	4	15,166
Big Idea	Goodbye Big Cat (Goodbye Doeny)	3	1	1	0	0	16,920
Big Idea	Whats the Big Idea (Spend a Buck)	6	4	0	0	0	0
Bill Back	Formal Process (Diablo)	4	1	0	0	0	0
Bill Back	House Party (French Deputy)	3	10	5	1	2	551,354
Bonus Buy	Muttface Emily (Jules)	4	2	1	0	0	4,290
Bonus Buy	Muttface Seamus (Foligno)	3	1	0	0	0	636
Brainstorming	Benigni (Fly Till Dawn)	5	6	0	0	0	712
Brand Strategy	Jet Thrust (D'Hallevant)	4	2	0	0	1	638
Breech	Run Sarah Run (Smart Strike)	3	13	3	2	5	85,460
Breech	Unpeteable (Peteski)	6	15	7	3	2	85,709
Bundle of Energy	Reenergize (Repriced)	3	1	0	0	0	80
Cape Fire	Fire Strike (Smart Strike)	2	4	1	0	0	14,040
Cape Fire	Foxy Allure (Foxhound)	3	13	3	2	0	22,560
Cape Fire	Miss Alexis (Dehere)	4	7	2	1	1	63,530
Cardo	C U Around (Torrential)	5	10	0	0	0	2,617
Cardo	Eurhrates (Helmsman)	4	9	3	1	2	12,632
Cardo	Sand Save (Line In The Sand)	2	1	0	0	0	0
Careful Approach	Shaky Town (Peaks and Valleys)	3	7	3	2	0	100,160
Careful Approach	Wild Cure (Cure the Blues)	5	17	0	3	1	22,005
Cash Cow	Dilley Dad Burn It (Formal Dinner)	6	1	0	0	0	0
Cash Cow	Lizard Lick (Way West)	4	6	3	1	0	21,320
Casual Aside	Casual Conflict (Fit to Fight)	9	2	1	0	0	9,150
Casual Aside	Youthful Comment (Lil's Lad)	2	2	0	2	0	12,650
Celestial Bliss	River to Heaven (Irish River)	6	3	0	0	0	150
Cents Off	Pfenning (Cox's Ridge)	5	14	2	2	1	18,479
Cents Off	Tententwotwenty (Phone Trick)	3	5	1	2	0	32,650
Cinco Partes	Five Gold Pieces (Gold Fever)	4	1	0	0	0	180
Cinco Partes	Foggy Song (Sultry Song)	8	2	0	0	0	91
Ciro's Seductress	Glaciers End (Clever Trick)	4	2	0	1	0	8,400
Ciro's Seductress	Sea Squirrel (Private Terms)	5	7	2	0	2	65,560
Classy Women	Polish Pianist (Forty Niner)	7	4	0	1	0	2,087
Cocktail	Cobra Bay (Cobra King)	4	1	0	0	0	0
Cocktail	Sean's Pride (Pentelicus)	3	11	1	1	1	12,240
Colrs Inthe Storm	Princesscassandra (Valid Expectations)	3	7	2	0	0	34,247
Colrs Inthe Storm	Sound of Colors (Valid Expectations)	4	3	0	0	0	682
Constnt Compnion	Constant Thunder (Thunder Gulch)	4	4	2	0	0	37,050
Constnt Compnion	Favorite Companion (Favorite Trick)	3	19	1	2	4	10,347
Controllable	Classic Babe (Regal Classic)	3	1	0	0	0	180
Cross Tab	Got Soup (Alphabet Soup)	2	1	0	0	0	0
Cut 'n Set	Acacian Song (Sultry Song)	7	9	0	0	0	587
Cut Test	Marsh Harbour (Labeeb)	3	14	1	2	2	37,013
Darling Sola	Lasserre (Phone Trick)	5	9	0	2	0	2,597
Darling Sola	Malalco (Meadowlake)	4	9	3	1	0	9,718
Deal Code	Dumaani Deal (Dumaani)	4	4	0	0	0	0
Deal Code	Dumaani Way (Dumaani)	5	1	0	0	0	110
Deep Discount	Final Discount (Repriced)	3	10	3	4	1	104,488
Definition	Let's Dance Nance (Judge T C)	4	12	3	2	2	28,917
Diane's Girl	Code Found (Lost Code)	8	15	1	0	1	4,570
Diane's Girl	Last Intention (End Sweep)	4	10	3	3	0	96,569
Dolce Amore	Mezzaluna (Dynaformer)	4	3	0	0	0	371
Dolce Amore	Noir Et Rouge (Quiet American)	3	4	0	1	0	11,240
Doubl Down Elevn	Artie Takes Two (Artema)	2	4	1	1	1	9,645
Doubl Down Elevn	Onda Ray (On Target)	3	5	1	0	0	26,235
Double Norm	Spy Shark (Spy Signal)	7	6	0	0	0	338
Dream Launch	Wouldn't We All (Woodman)	9	3	1	1	0	6,900
Dream Motel	Dream City (Carson City)	4	11	2	3	2	17,743
Dream Motel	Times Like These (Dixieland Band)	3	2	1	0	0	5,525
Dreamsport	Wildly (Wild Wonder)	2	2	1	0	1	31,950
Due Bill	Launch the Cat (Mountain Cat)	5	1	0	0	0	480
Due Bill	Truly a Legend (Mr. Greeley)	4	9	1	0	0	33,900
Especially Aly	Especially Royal (General Royal)	2	3	1	2	0	8,294
Especially Aly	Freedom Forever (Will's Way)	3	7	1	2	0	9,110
Evening Launch	Cloudy Mist (Twining)	4	8	0	2	0	2,720
Evening Launch	Doctor Price (Flag Down)	3	6	2	1	2	25,050
Existentialist	Governor Hickel (Gulch)	4	6	1	0	0	7,960
Existentialist	Oration (Deputy Minister)	6	7	1	0	1	16,920
Fenimore	Earmark (Personal Flag)	7	5	1	1	1	9,310
Fenimore	Happy Acres (Phone Trick)	6	13	1	1	3	5,347
Fenimore	Joethehorse (Runaway Groom)	2	1	0	0	0	0
Fenimore	Sealed Orders (Cryptoclearance)	8	1	0	0	0	0
Fenimore	With the Works (With Approval)	4	6	0	2	0	11,720
Firma	Firm Reality (Roy)	3	13	3	3	2	60,166
Firma	Relaunch Star (Opening Verse)	5	9	2	0	1	95,024
First Spot	Bull Head (Holy Bull)	3	7	1	0	2	13,610
First Spot	Minerveeni (Afternoon Deelites)	4	3	0	0	0	1,440
First Spot	Spot Check (Cherokee Run)	2	5	1	0	0	17,350
First Spot	Tom the River Rat (Virginia Rapids)	5	5	1	1	0	14,970
First Stage	Stage Clearance (Cryptoclearance)	3	13	2	1	1	9,891
Flycatcher	Ghost Catcher (Ghostly Moves)	3	4	1	0	0	6,164
Flycatcher	Iron Cloud (Little Missouri)	5	19	2	2	4	17,583
Flying Galoshes	Diamond Heirloom (Pembroke)	3	12	2	3	1	48,121
Flying Galoshes	Hello Pepper (Ide)	4	11	0	0	1	2,794
Flying Relaunch	El Crusader (El Prado)	4	9	1	2	2	32,042
Flying Relaunch	Flick Creek (El Mayaguezano)	5	7	1	0	0	7,475
Flying Relaunch	Gold Will (Formal Gold)	2	1	0	0	0	0
Foegal	Enter Twine (Twining)	3	3	0	0	1	1,950
Foegal	Gray Black N White (Quiet American)	2	1	0	0	0	1,500
Foggy Note Mdley	Mr. Piano Man (Rubiano)	2	5	2	0	0	24,410
Foggy Note Mdley	Sour Note (Glitterman)	3	2	0	0	0	160
Fulla Finesse	Artfulnesse (Katowice)	5	3	0	0	1	2,730
Fulla Finesse	Little Gray Storm (Future Storm)	4	10	1	1	2	6,419
Fulla Finesse	S. S. Finesse (Blue Ensign)	7	14	3	2	1	27,990
Fulla Finesse	S. S. Spitfire (Blue Ensign)	6	4	1	0	0	2,820
Gatefold	Isabel's Pride (Binalong)	4	12	1	0	3	10,990
Global Star	Cairne (Gilded Time)	2	4	2	1	0	28,200
Global Star	Smashing Gail (Meadowlake)	3	1	0	0	0	0
Good Response	Competitive Edge (Tactical Advntage)	3	7	1	2	1	15,040
Good Response	Core Idea (Breeders Bonus)	9	17	2	3	4	30,935

Good Response	Fortifier (Major Impact)	6	1	0	0	0	114
Good Response	Restage (Repriced)	4	2	1	1	0	27,720
Gray Cashmere	Astor Street (Pulpit)	3	12	1	5	0	17,345
Gray Cashmere	Purple Hills (Dynaformer)	4	9	1	0	2	27,440
Gray Mood	Look Out Joe (Dehere)	4	2	1	0	0	11,400
Great Escape	Ceely's Classic (Always a Classic)	4	7	0	2	2	17,150
Great Escape	Handzz Up (Saint Ballado)	3	15	0	6	0	11,302
Groomer	Fly Nicky Fly (Fly Till Dawn)	3	3	0	0	0	0
Groomer	Reassess (Prospect Bay)	4	14	7	3	2	48,210
Groomer	Time Lord (Dr. Carter)	9	1	0	0	0	80
Harps and Wings	Battle (Glitterman)	5	8	2	2	1	40,521
Heavenly Launch	Bug in a Bottle (Birdonthewire)	4	13	1	4	2	13,945
Heavenly Launch	Crimson Wave (Ocean Crest)	3	7	0	1	0	4,460
Heavenly Launch	Idle Dreamer (T. H. Fappiano)	2	4	0	0	1	1,560
Heavenly Launch	Sky Hunter (Distant View)	5	6	0	2	0	22,058
Heavenly Times	Grindtime (Grindstone)	3	2	1	1	0	33,600
Heavenly Times	Western Times (Mr. Greeley)	2	5	1	2	0	29,400
Herbs and Spices	Fast Spot (Unbridled)	4	6	3	0	0	22,880
Here for Glory	Owyee (Major Impact)	5	14	2	3	0	10,797
Here for Glory	Tricks of Glory (Favorite Trick)	2	2	2	0	0	32,700
Hidden Valley	Won Arm Bandit (Air Forbes Won)	3	8	1	1	0	9,797
I'll Redo It	Re Book (Montbrook)	5	7	1	2	2	26,800
If At First	Bandana (Academy Award)	6	7	2	2	2	52,791
If At First	Marquet First (Marquetry)	3	13	2	2	1	27,737
If At First	Seven Times (Is It True)	4	9	2	1	2	10,238
Innovate	Innovation (Saint Ballado)	3	10	0	0	1	7,044
Instore	Ravishly (Gold Case)	2	3	1	0	1	24,750
Instore	Souvenier Biz (Souvenir Copy)	3	5	2	2	1	107,996
Investment Spend	Silver Gun (Lit de Justice)	3	2	0	0	0	1,818
Jah	Uncanny (Unbridled)	3	2	1	0	1	13,490
Jo Ann's Gal	Equity Player (Pioneering)	4	1	0	0	0	61
Jo Ann's Gal	Rubiano Star (Rubiano)	3	17	0	1	3	6,809
Judaea	Asserted (Affirmed)	3	5	0	0	1	5,260
Just Rumors	Just Gossip (Affirmed)	4	11	3	1	1	66,540
Kitty Hawk	Kill Devil Hill (Marked Tree)	2	1	0	0	0	174
Kitty Hawk	Paragon John (Marked Tree)	3	15	2	1	3	10,100
La Luminosa	Don't Laugh At Me (Mahogany Hall)	3	7	0	0	1	1,546
La Luminosa	On the Fritz (Mahogany Hall)	5	9	1	4	2	108,711
Lashawn	Miss Hadley (Hadif)	4	3	0	0	0	0
Laun Shaw	Memphis (Hennessy)	5	13	4	1	2	38,980
Laun Shaw	Servant King (Cobra King)	4	11	1	1	1	8,048
Launch At Dawn	Morning Launch (Silver Ghost)	6	1	0	0	0	105
Launch Site	Vigilant Site (Diplomatic Jet)	3	8	3	1	1	30,412
Launch the Clan	Corcovado (Dixieland Band)	6	12	3	1	3	15,808
Launch the Clan	Diamond Dawn (Dehere)	4	9	2	1	1	28,732
Launch the Clan	Morning Riser (In Excess)	3	6	2	0	0	20,550
Launch the Clan	Wynhurst (Mt. Livermore)	7	5	1	0	1	6,075
Launch Time	My Lucky Strike (Smart Strike)	4	12	3	1	5	191,036
Launchable	Compelling Launch (Complling Sound)	6	5	1	0	1	5,138
Launchable	Mingo Springs (Carnivalay)	4	2	0	0	0	0
Launchable	Sarah M. (Carnivalay)	5	5	0	0	0	474
Launching Shot	Angelano (Rubiano)	3	6	0	2	1	3,603
Launching Shot	Dr Noble (Meadowlake)	4	4	1	1	0	11,200
Liberty Mint	Dancewithmewesley (Unfinishd Symph)	4	2	0	0	1	625
Liquid Fill	Lil Charlie Too (Stop the Music)	7	5	0	4	0	28,188
Little Fogger	Foggerinthevalley (Peaks and Valleys)	3	3	0	1	0	7,760
Little Zip	Zip Gun (Oh Say)	3	10	3	1	1	31,145
Little Zip	Zip Zip Boom (Jeblar)	2	6	0	0	0	275
Lollypalooza	Alipalooza (Supremo)	3	15	2	2	4	18,980
Lollypalooza	Ocean Commotion (Ocean Crest)	4	8	2	0	0	8,477
Lollypalooza	Party Case (Gold Case)	2	5	0	0	0	765
Lonely Girl	Four Plus Four (Major Impact)	6	3	0	1	1	20,500
Lonely Girl	Kilkea Castle (Pleasant Colony)	3	5	1	0	0	29,340
Lonely Girl	Power Wing (Sovereign Dancer)	9	14	4	3	1	60,436
Lonely Girl	Solitary (Rahy)	2	5	0	0	0	3,420
Luthier's Launch	Gassan Rock (Cape Town)	2	5	1	1	2	23,660
Luthier's Launch	Launch Stone (Grindstone)	5	8	0	0	2	1,820
Magnolia Springs	She's a Mugs (Doneraile Court)	2	1	0	0	0	66
Main Gain	Prismatic (Bertrando)	4	1	0	0	0	0
Main Gain	Targetry (On Target)	2	1	0	0	0	0
Market News	Bobski (Petionville)	2	3	0	0	0	0
Market News	Dinkers Good News (Yeti)	3	12	1	3	2	16,270
Market News	Dinkers Millennium (Yeti)	4	5	1	1	0	8,094
Marketplace	Package Store (Mister Baileys)	5	4	2	0	2	135,984
Mary Roland	Captain Red (Mr. Greeley)	6	7	2	1	2	86,851
Mary Roland	Roll of the Dice (Green Dancer)	5	4	1	2	1	70,089
Me and Myun	Revolver (Laabity)	4	4	0	0	0	944
Me and Myun	Sweet Cane (Laabity)	3	14	0	1	1	9,939
Me Dooit	Susue Sue (Sky Classic)	7	3	0	0	0	510
Milk Toast	Barrington Lady (Will's Way)	2	7	0	3	0	17,940
Milk Toast	French Toast (Storm Boot)	3	5	1	0	2	10,755
Misty Launch	Leading Lioness (Lion Cavern)	2	6	3	0	1	71,620
Ms. Cuvee Napa	Deb's Charm (Silver Charm)	2	3	1	0	2	71,360
Ms. Cuvee Napa	Harve de Grace (Boston Harbor)	3	2	1	0	0	11,400
Native Connection	Presumption (Acceptable)	2	8	1	0	2	36,498
Naughty Notions	Naughty Mambo (Kingmambo)	5	1	0	0	0	0
O K Three Wire	Ok Monsoon (Maria's Mon)	2	4	0	0	0	0
On the Aisle	Diablo's Aisle (Diablo)	4	11	2	1	1	12,410
One Dreamer	Indy Zone (A.P. Indy)	3	3	0	0	0	60
One Dreamer	W. L.'s Legend (Woodman)	6	3	0	1	1	3,600
One Hot Minute	Doubleback (Gentlemen)	3	6	0	2	0	13,640
Onesta	Eight Chimes (Chimes Band)	5	2	0	0	2	1,900
Onesta	Joan's Gray Beauty (Cat's Career)	3	5	0	2	2	11,780
Paperbck Romnce	Ferriday (Roar)	3	12	2	0	1	13,290
Party On Deck	I Miss You (You and I)	3	9	0	1	2	9,340
Peaceable Mood	Siphonette (Siphon (BRZ))	2	5	0	2	2	28,480
Perfect Launch	Power Launch (Premiership)	2	1	0	0	0	330
Perky Wonder	Any Wonder (Walter Willy)	4	7	1	2	0	5,226
Perky Wonder	Bonus Paid (Bonus Money)	5	4	0	0	0	1,324
Phantom Hill	Wildwood Ghost (Northern Flagship)	6	5	2	1	2	16,221
Photo Please	Jeramiah John (Mercer Mill)	2	2	1	0	0	5,700
Photo Please	The Potters Hand (Bound by Honor)	3	8	1	1	1	6,595
Planet Eros	Bookmylaunch (Notebook)	5	13	0	2	6	19,771
Planet Eros	Jakob Teddy (All Gone)	2	6	0	0	2	2,795
Poker Nell	B's Big Boy (Double Honor)	3	9	1	1	0	3,914
Poker Nell	Mystical Allure (Concern)	4	12	3	1	4	32,258
Prematurely Gray	Decoding the Gray (Cryptoclearance)	7	15	4	2	2	38,695
Prematurely Gray	Queen's Triomphe (Cure the Blues)	4	8	5	1	0	135,865
Proper Destiny	El Destiny (El Prado)	4	4	0	0	1	1,600
Proper Destiny	Fan Destiny (Lear Fan)	3	12	1	1	1	21,895
Proper Reflection	Crafty Reflection (Crafty Prospector)	3	14	0	6	4	29,630
Proper Reflection	Proper Conquest (Conquistadr Cielo)	6	9	3	2	0	39,154
Proper Reflection	Proper Prospector (Crafty Prospectr)	2	8	1	3	1	13,250
Pure Wool	Pure American (Quiet American)	2	3	1	2	0	27,200
Purple Rose	Doc Z Do (Idabel)	7	1	0	0	0	0
Purple Rose	Flamingo Flash (Manzotti)	4	1	0	0	0	0
Purple Rose	Ms Medill (Wallenda)	6	8	0	0	0	275
Quarry Hill	Bartus Christian (Doneraile Court)	2	3	1	0	0	7,906
Quarry Hill	Concrete Block (Sky Classic)	3	5	0	1	0	6,176
Quarry Hill	Mountain Eagle (Sky Classic)	5	12	3	1	3	38,005
Quarry Hill	Stonington (Always a Classic)	4	4	1	2	0	42,690
Quarry Hill	Summit Meeting (Sky Classic)	6	2	0	0	0	0
Rayelle	Erik's the Charm (Silver Charm)	2	2	0	0	1	5,300
Real Orphan	Real Gallant (Feeling Gallant)	5	8	1	0	1	3,004
Realahta	Really Something (Ormsby)	4	10	2	1	2	12,602
Really an Angel	Shining Angel (Dance Brightly)	2	7	1	0	0	14,101
Rearrived	Lila's Dream (The Wicked North)	3	3	0	1	0	2,025
Rebow	Bowkeen (Rakeen)	5	4	1	0	0	17,196
Rebow	Retam (Tamayaz)	3	9	2	1	0	69,460
Rebow	Two Bows (Two Punch)	4	8	0	0	0	280
Reclass	Blind Ambition (Political Ambition)	5	6	3	2	0	206,640
Reclass	Cut Class (Cutlass Reality)	4	8	2	2	1	20,930
Red Star	Belgrade (Smart Strike)	5	10	1	0	3	8,256
Red Star	Caroldean (Dixieland Band)	4	4	0	0	1	5,100
Reilette	Lettet Rumble (Pembroke)	6	8	4	0	1	20,033
Rejoyced	Merry Joyce (Royal Academy)	3	1	0	0	1	3,740
Rejoyced	Pincay (Diesis)	2	2	0	0	1	7,820
Rekindld Romnce	Lady Kabbalah (Lord Carson)	3	5	1	1	1	41,330
Rekindld Romnce	Silvery Crown (Lord Carson)	2	4	0	1	0	6,080
Relasure	Eagles Hill (Boundary)	3	3	1	0	0	29,280
Relasure	Quinton's Gold (Carson City)	6	7	0	1	4	34,840
Relax and Smile	Five to Four (Metfield)	5	15	2	2	0	11,505
Relax and Smile	Justified Attack (Hawk Attack)	4	2	0	0	0	0
Relax and Smile	Miracle Mets (Metfield)	6	3	1	0	1	3,500
Relaxer	Stratify (Stack)	3	4	0	0	0	1,615
Reliant	Whereisspringfield (Pembroke)	6	13	3	3	1	35,315
Remittance	Humor the Rumor (Devil's Cry)	4	7	2	0	0	6,780
Remittance	Olivia's Present (Forty Won)	3	7	0	1	1	2,282
Renewed Delight	Never Take Risk (A. P Jet)	3	5	3	1	0	14,802
Renewed Delight	Vault (Gold Case)	4	2	2	0	0	54,000
Renewed Interest	Legally Gray (Rubiano)	3	4	1	1	0	6,260
Resubmit	Hannaboy (Repriced)	3	12	3	2	2	34,865
Royal Launch	Fred's Passion (Numerous)	4	9	2	1	1	12,897
Royal Launch	Master Sergeant (Play Fellow)	5	2	0	0	0	0
Sally's Spirit	Emma Renee (Defrere)	2	1	1	0	0	8,950
Sally's Spirit	Ice Girl (Devil On Ice)	3	12	3	3	1	36,839
Sally's Spirit	Peanut Parfait (Devil On Ice)	4	1	0	0	0	192
Set to Fly	Historic Speech (Pulpit)	4	5	2	1	0	15,750
Set to Fly	Polish Missile (Polish Numbers)	6	6	0	0	0	477
Set to Fly	Stealth Flier (Quiet American)	2	3	0	0	0	1,800
Shabanu	Shabanu's Jet (A. P Jet)	2	1	0	0	0	0
Shrewd Idea	Cutshin (Forest Wildcat)	3	11	0	1	3	11,264
Si Se Puede	Nino Dorado (Man From Eldorado)	5	10	1	3	1	14,575
Skilaunch	Catlaunch (Noble Cat)	2	5	1	1	0	9,335
Skilaunch	Jet Ski (Wavering Monarch)	8	11	1	4	0	7,591
Skilaunch	Mercer's Launch (Mercer Mill)	4	7	1	1	2	17,395
Skilaunch	Monarchski (Wavering Monarch)	9	4	0	0	0	178
Skilaunch	Scioto Bootski (Storm Boot)	5	6	2	3	0	51,116
So Re So	Bold Banker (Banker's Gold)	3	5	2	0	2	18,860
Social Launch	Relaunch the Fever (Luthier Fever)	3	1	0	0	1	1,128
Solamente Un Vez	Eastern Launch (Eastern Echo)	3	2	0	0	0	300
Space Flower	Blaze of Light (Prospect Bay)	5	2	1	0	0	3,805
Space Flower	Yimmy (Good and Tough)	2	2	1	0	0	12,600
Splendid Launch	Splendid Prospect (Prospect Bay)	3	6	0	0	0	686
Springtique	Kaceysexpelled (Expelled)	2	2	0	0	0	0
Steamy Recipe	Guidebook (Notebook)	3	7	2	1	1	38,440
Stock Price	Super Fund (Jules)	3	9	0	1	1	10,031
Sweet Relaunch	Apache Flyer (Marquetry)	2	6	1	1	1	24,985
Sweet Relaunch	Sweet Country Girl (Roy)	3	3	0	1	0	4,000
Sweet Surprise	Blown Surprise (Valid Expectations)	3	13	4	2	3	56,505
Sweet Surprise	Expect a Surprise (Valid Expctations)	2	3	0	0	1	2,510
Tacomolly	Hezslightlyshady (Fly Till Dawn)	3	16	1	1	2	6,432

Taras Way	Union Station (Railway Cat)	3	6	1	0	1	4,134
Taras Way	Wholesale (Repriced)	2	4	0	0	0	762
Tengo Prisa	Estar de Prisa (Brocco)	5	3	0	1	0	2,938
Tengo Prisa	Estrella Prisa (Star de Naskra)	7	4	1	0	1	6,060
Tengo Prisa	Hombre Rapido (Falstaff)	6	3	2	0	0	160,500
Tengo Prisa	Remonte (Flying Continental)	3	4	1	0	0	14,240
Tengo Prisa	Sombrio (Siberian Summer)	4	9	1	0	2	56,056
That Kind I Want	Kind Lena (Seneca Jones)	2	5	1	2	1	65,330
That Kind I Want	Rado Kid (Half Term)	3	8	1	0	0	6,814
That Kind I Want	Yo Buddy (De Niro)	6	8	0	3	0	2,985
To the Hunt	Starrer (Dynaformer)	5	2	2	0	0	300,000
To the Hunt	Stellar Jayne (Wild Rush)	2	5	3	0	0	119,075
Turbo Launch	Late Charge (Capote)	5	6	0	1	1	6,650
Two Dreamer	Indian Dreamer (Numerous)	3	14	2	2	2	34,985
Two Dreamer	Riviera Kate (Runaway Groom)	5	4	2	0	1	8,350
We Have Lift Off	Kondoa Way (Press Card)	4	8	0	0	3	5,295
Whatevrlolawants	Aloha Lola (Aloha Prospector)	3	10	3	4	1	12,746
Whats Doin	Runnymede Bride (Dehere)	4	1	0	0	0	0
Whats Doin	Something Silver (Silver Deputy)	3	3	0	1	0	15,690
Whats Doin	You're Up (Silver Charm)	2	1	0	0	0	2,180
Wonderwhyme	Account for Me (Unaccounted For)	5	14	3	4	1	77,520
Wonderwhyme	I. M. Awonder (Silver Ghost)	4	6	0	0	0	345

Affirmed, Ch H (1975)

By Exclusive Native – Won't Tell You, by Crafty Admiral

215 Performers, 122 winning performers, $7,440,542 total earnings

Mare	Progeny (Sire)	Age	Sts	1st	2d	3d	Money Won
Abigailthewife	Krieger (Lord At War)	5	5	0	2	1	47,550
Adira	Commander's Gal (Deputy Commndr)	3	6	0	2	1	12,270
Adventre n Speed	Candy Adventure (Candy Stripes)	5	14	1	0	0	24,055
Adventre n Speed	Exzachary (Announce)	2	1	0	0	0	0
Adventre n Speed	Heart Head (Announce)	3	8	0	0	0	110
Affectingly	Mon Sweet's Crypto (Cryptoclearnce)	3	15	1	2	2	6,291
Affection Affrmd	Belgravia (Rainbow Quest)	9	2	1	0	0	4,020
Affirm Foundation	Affirm Strategy (Pentelicus)	3	4	0	0	0	720
Affirm Foundation	Affirming Storm (Storm Creek)	4	7	1	0	1	5,439
Affirm Pass	Mr. Authority (Excellent Secret)	4	14	3	3	1	25,618
Affirm Promise	Alpine Pass (Polish Numbers)	4	4	1	2	1	34,740
Affirmarose	Autumn Accent (Souvenir Copy)	2	1	1	0	0	28,200
Affirmatve Choice	Clair de Lune (Regal Classic)	3	5	0	0	2	19,380
Affirmative Fable	Geri Gold (Geri)	3	3	0	0	0	0
Affirmed Affair	Zydeco Affair (Islefaxyou)	3	10	1	3	0	65,549
Affirmd Ambience	Eli's Dancer (Gate Dancer)	7	7	0	0	0	557
Affirmed Bel	Go Ask Daisy (Mutakddim)	2	4	2	0	1	56,130
Affirmed Class	Amelia E. (Sky Classic)	2	1	0	0	0	0
Affirmed Class	Classy Heroine (Sea Hero)	3	15	3	2	2	32,080
Affirmed Gal	My Lil Cup o' Tee (Lil E. Tee)	8	2	0	0	0	0
Affirmed Style	Kool Daddy D. J. (Tossofthecoin)	3	15	1	1	1	7,555
Affirmed Toor	Explosive Affair (Exploit)	2	2	0	0	1	6,666
Affirming	Cobblers Rock (Cure the Blues)	7	7	2	1	0	77,411
Affirmity	Dad Strikes Gold (Strike the Gold)	7	9	1	0	3	10,561
Affirmity	Gold Not Diamonds (Strike the Gold)	4	10	0	1	1	7,781
Affirmity	Sultry Firm (Sultry Song)	2	1	0	0	0	150
Afirmada	Prince of Rhodes (Langfuhr)	3	6	1	1	0	10,639
Afirmada	Violanda (Southern Halo)	4	6	2	1	0	11,720
Ah Fifi	I Will (Explosive Red)	2	2	0	0	0	270
Ah Fifi	Skip the Country (Skip Trial)	4	3	0	0	0	386
American Storm	Choctaw Lady (Cherokee Run)	3	4	0	0	0	0
An Affirmation	Swirling Sky (Sky Classic)	3	2	0	0	0	0
Annuschka	Go Directlyto Jail (Skip Trial)	2	1	0	0	0	110
Annuschka	My Account (Top Account)	4	15	3	1	1	14,013
Annuschka	Red Sky At Morning (Future Storm)	3	2	0	0	0	150
Art Smart	One Smart Cat (Distinctive Cat)	2	4	1	1	0	22,930
Art Smart	Plus Three (Western Fame)	3	12	1	2	3	64,830
Aunti Hattie	Miccosukee (Cherokee Run)	3	14	2	2	2	17,205
Awareness	Grey Pride (Partner's Hero)	3	6	0	1	1	10,990
Barbed Wire	Classified Secret (Sky Classic)	3	5	0	2	1	34,127
Bernique	Fire Work (A.P. Indy)	8	3	0	0	0	152
Black Marble	My Girl Quigly (Idabel)	8	12	1	3	2	28,318
Blond Moment	Mt. Rainer (Mt. Livermore)	5	7	1	1	1	10,286
Blond Moment	Short Squeeze (Dynaformer)	4	14	1	4	0	77,950
Bobett	Egotist (Storm Creek)	3	8	0	1	1	10,012
Buy the Firm	Complete Package (Boundary)	4	3	0	0	1	2,862
Calling Ann	Calling Ticket (Deposit Ticket)	6	5	1	2	2	7,864
Calling Ann	Risky Cat (Tale of the Cat)	3	8	0	0	1	15,050
Captive Spirit	Spirit Dreamer (Regal Classic)	8	14	1	2	1	17,434
Chanti	Dr. J. Bierwith (Deerhound)	3	11	0	1	1	4,452
Checkerspot	Salty Romance (Salt Lake)	2	3	2	0	1	178,440
Cherry a La Mode	Dillonmyboy (Go for Gin)	6	5	1	1	2	33,380
Christilist	Christy's Spirit (Spirit Voices)	2	4	0	0	0	1,418
Christilist	Lota Spunk (Spunky Rascal)	4	10	2	1	1	8,358
Christmas in Aikn	Brother Bob (Royal Roberto)	6	3	1	0	0	7,055
Christmas in Aikn	Dr. Holiday (Kayrawan)	5	8	1	0	2	8,437
Christmas in Aikn	Harlan's Holiday (Harlan)	4	5	2	1	0	485,100
Christmas in Aikn	Holiday Account (Spirit Voices)	2	4	0	0	0	1,099
Cnfirmation Class	Confirmed Devil (Devil His Due)	6	6	0	0	0	748
Costly Emotion	Tomorrows Peach (Tomorrows Cat)	3	14	7	1	1	69,984
Credendum	Credential (Valid Appeal)	5	2	0	0	0	2,280
Crown and Scptre	Kristys Crown (Caller I. D.)	5	9	0	1	0	1,503
Cuando Quiere	Honey Ryder (Lasting Approval)	2	5	1	1	2	46,080
Dearness	All the Boys (Foreign Survivor)	6	4	2	2	0	151,400
Dearness	Foreverness (Island Whirl)	4	5	1	1	2	56,580
Deb's Honor	Private Retreat (Wild Again)	3	10	4	1	0	49,150
Derrynane	Koorachee (Benny the Dip)	4	2	0	0	1	2,160
Derrynane	R. F. Burton (Diesis)	5	2	0	0	0	700
Destiny's Monarch	Affirmlode (Comstock Lode)	2	10	1	2	1	26,219
Destiny's Monarch	I'm Due (Devil His Due)	4	14	1	3	1	9,374
Devotee	Ohni (Salt Lake)	3	19	0	5	2	15,780
Devotee	Pascagoula (Lil E. Tee)	6	11	1	1	3	4,944
Dice Passer	Elway's Way (Louis Quatorze)	4	2	0	0	0	315
Disclaimed	Call Fiorello (Caller I. D.)	8	12	6	1	1	49,135
Disclaimed	Cinemagic (Exploit)	2	5	1	0	1	9,120
Disclaimed	Devote (Deputy Commander)	3	11	1	2	0	48,811
Disclaimed	E T Phone Laura (Roar)	4	8	3	0	0	39,160
Duck Trap	Trappings (Seeking the Gold)	3	7	0	0	0	4,130
Durability	Hard as Nails (Holy Bull)	3	6	1	2	1	55,620
Encore Amour	Da Birdman (Kissin Kris)	2	5	1	0	0	7,480
Encore Amour	Love Evermore (Dr. Caton)	4	11	4	1	0	20,810
Energica	Positively Wild (Wild Again)	3	9	1	2	2	52,340
Energo	Risk and Return (Subordination)	3	1	0	0	1	4,620
Epicure's Garden	Sun Seasons (Salse)	4	4	0	0	0	3,510
Favorable	Cat Crossing (Railway Cat)	4	13	2	0	2	15,525
Favorable	Say Yes (Spirit Voices)	3	9	1	1	3	9,705
Firm Defiance	Fire the Firm (Lite the Fuse)	4	17	2	5	3	51,118
Firm Defiance	Tempers Rising (Unaccounted For)	3	20	2	4	2	44,230
Firm Inquisition	Firm Affair (Colonial Affair)	5	6	1	0	1	7,440
Firm Inquisition	Firm Kiss (Atticus)	4	1	0	1	0	5,600
Flaming Glen	Flaming Villa (Pancho Villa)	4	4	1	2	0	7,090
Floraffirm	Wild Cowboy (Relaunch a Tune)	5	5	0	2	0	1,990
Go On Dreaming	Inspire (Top Account)	3	3	0	0	0	300
Good Natured	Affirmed Reality (Real Partner)	5	10	2	0	1	19,550
Good Natured	Dustins Mozart (Personal Matter)	3	13	0	1	3	4,037
Good Natured	Reality Affirmed (Real Partner)	2	2	0	0	0	0
Governance	Affirm Cat (Harlan)	4	10	1	1	3	12,155
HerName inLights	Byrneing Passion (Plain Dealing)	5	8	0	2	2	12,767
HerName inLights	Light Up the Board (Nelson)	3	8	2	0	0	27,255
HerName inLights	Magnolia Park (El Prado)	4	11	1	0	3	21,107
I Certainly Am	Chinook Cat (Tabasco Cat)	5	8	2	1	1	23,120
I Certainly Am	King of Siam (Kingmambo)	3	10	2	2	0	37,120
In the Library	Picture Book (Rubiano)	6	11	1	1	2	6,096
It's Binnice	Emphasize (Dare and Go)	5	2	1	0	0	10,800
It's Binnice	Straight (Lil Tyler)	3	4	0	0	0	472
Jelly Roll Frolic	Maximus (Spectaculardynasty)	3	17	3	1	2	18,111
Jiny Pustinya	Bittersweetsymfony (Dispersal)	6	6	0	0	0	696
Jiny Pustinya	Bringhometheloot (Demalt Dmashoot)	4	13	1	3	1	12,069
Just Like Daddy	Firm Command (Deputy Commander)	3	9	1	1	2	27,240
Just Like Daddy	Hunter's Sunrise (Deerhound)	4	1	1	0	0	5,070
Kerplop	Bear Bluff (Pine Bluff)	2	5	0	0	1	4,660
Kerplop	Crack of the Bat (Pentelicus)	4	10	3	2	1	41,390
Kerplop	Pine Breeze (Pine Bluff)	3	2	0	0	1	1,900
Kiss Me Caitland	Hisses N Kisses (Forest Wildcat)	3	6	0	0	0	1,210
La Affirmed	Alajwad (Storm Cat)	3	4	2	2	0	74,000
La Affirmed	Della Francesca (Danzig)	4	8	2	1	0	177,360
La Golodrina	Last Call Lover (At the Threshold)	10	10	2	1	2	7,585
La Golodrina	Proper Man (Harlan)	6	6	0	2	1	11,260
La Riviera	Frenchglen (Forestry)	2	1	0	0	0	0
La Riviera	Golden Embers (Danjur)	3	3	0	1	0	10,000
Ladies Lunch	Guilty Gal (Skip Trial)	7	9	1	1	1	8,530
Ladies Lunch	Soup for Lunch (Alphabet Soup)	3	11	3	3	2	104,042
Lady Affirmed	Campaign Castle (Deputy Minister)	3	1	0	0	0	320
Lady Ping	Keep the Ring (Runaway Groom)	8	9	0	0	0	1,063
Lil's Memory	Hadif Declares (Hadif)	2	5	1	3	0	12,900
Linda K.	Lyles Station (Tinners Way)	4	3	0	0	0	148
LookWho'sDncing	Bojangle's Cat (Tabasco Cat)	2	3	1	0	0	29,255
LookWho'sDncing	Rutledge Dancer (Sky Classic)	4	2	0	1	1	8,760
LookWho'sDncing	Tea Dance (Summer Squall)	3	3	1	0	0	15,940
Market Plaza	Mich's Cure (Cure the Blues)	5	7	0	0	0	2,041
Miss Affirmation	Exfirmed (Excavate)	3	11	0	0	4	13,497
Miss Affirmation	Firmly Done (Goodbye Doeny)	5	7	1	1	2	18,204
Miss Affirmation	Review the List (Bag)	2	1	0	0	0	0
Miss Coast Walk	Pam and Gayla (Russian Courage)	3	3	0	0	0	0
Miss Reserve	Phantom of the Sea (Ocean Crest)	6	14	0	0	1	1,704
Miss Roddey	Salute Y'all (Personal Flag)	4	11	1	0	1	4,080
Mocha Mocha	Cap Jaluca (Arch)	2	2	0	0	0	0
Mockingbrd Valley	Galopin Charger (Devil's Bag)	2	6	1	2	1	11,095
My Friend	Galway Vixen (Foxhound)	4	6	0	0	1	1,100
Nell's Jet	Barkenlor Cat (Mountain Cat)	8	13	1	1	3	4,944
Nell's Jet	Big Show (Islefaxyou)	5	9	0	0	3	10,056
Nell's Jet	Heath's Jet (Defrere)	4	10	3	1	0	52,727
No Hastle	No Hastle Mon (Maria's Mon)	4	12	1	1	2	9,757
No Hastle	Trouble N Beantown (Cape Town)	3	7	1	0	3	9,380
Noble Pursuit	High Purr (Mountain Cat)	4	9	1	2	0	8,740
Northern Sanction	Princess Madmyr (Ocean Crest)	5	3	0	0	0	231
Northern Sanction	Regal Endorsement (Regal Classic)	3	1	0	0	0	0
Northern Sanction	Regal Sanction (Regal Classic)	4	8	2	1	1	92,151
Odbiawinner	Odbeaslewpy (Gray Slewpy)	7	5	1	1	0	3,070
Odbiawinner	Winning Memories (Memo)	3	6	0	0	0	3,823
Our Pesaridan	Aritelli (Leo Castelli)	6	10	2	1	0	15,980
Our Pesaridan	Our Wildcat (Forest Wildcat)	4	8	2	1	2	65,000
Our Pesaridan	Sircatour (Sir Cat)	3	4	3	1	0	80,800

Out of Step	Tender Toes (Storm Boot)	3	11	2	3	1	23,775
Pastel Shade	Spainbird (Bluebird)	5	8	1	0	2	53,220
Prettyasarose	Wheater (Mountain Cat)	4	4	0	0	0	1,165
Prosper	Mahzouz (Charismatic)	2	2	0	0	0	2,760
Ragtime Show	Dreams At Sunset (Sky Classic)	3	3	0	0	0	5,346
Ragtime Show	Winning Shows (Sandpit (BRZ))	4	16	5	3	1	40,342
Regal State	Pleasantly Perfect (Pleasant Colony)	5	4	2	0	1	2,470,000
Reminiscently	Esta A. (Boone's Mill)	6	5	1	0	3	6,500
Reminiscently	Graceful Stepper (Phone Trick)	4	4	1	0	1	6,575
Reminiscently	Runaway Rich (Runaway Groom)	5	4	0	0	0	180
Renewable	Account Renewed (Top Account)	4	13	0	2	2	7,351
Renewable	Shamus Shea (El Prado)	6	5	0	0	5	21,700
Rhapsodies	Greeley's Image (Mr. Greeley)	5	5	0	1	1	2,247
River Crossing	Aspen Falls (Hennessy)	2	4	0	0	0	5,540
Sand Wedge	Affirm Challenge (Lytrump)	6	11	1	2	2	5,752
Sand Wedge	Affirm Trump (Lytrump)	9	3	0	0	0	0
Sand Wedge	High Dice (Lytrump)	8	10	3	2	2	53,522
Sand Wedge	Old Man's Delite (Lytrump)	7	15	6	2	1	27,952
Satin Lilly	Satin Concern (Concern)	3	4	1	0	0	8,661
Satin Lilly	Undercover (Allen's Prospect)	4	4	3	0	1	103,610
Secret Surprise	Mojo Workin (Numerous)	3	5	0	2	2	11,480
Secretsequesterd	Secret Runner (Lord Carson)	3	18	2	4	1	21,392
Serenity Jane	Cash Delivery (Polish Numbers)	3	12	3	1	1	53,300
Serenity Jane	What Me (Concern)	4	13	5	1	0	30,857
Serenity Jane	Whole Lotta Love (Not For Love)	2	5	1	0	0	22,620
She's Something	Got Pizazz (Lion Cavern)	2	5	0	1	1	8,975
Shining Starlet	Starlet Cat (Tale of the Cat)	3	6	1	0	2	7,772
Singing Breeze	Sing Softly (Lord Avie)	4	6	1	0	1	9,038
So Right	Cotton Valley (Pine Bluff)	4	1	0	0	0	0
So Right	Peter the Rock (Devil's Bag)	2	3	1	0	2	24,080
Social Miss	Dr. Guiliani (Honour and Glory)	4	8	2	3	0	72,320
Social Miss	Dylans Destiny (Tomorrows Cat)	2	4	0	1	1	14,350
Social Miss	Social Account (Unaccounted For)	5	15	2	2	2	24,413
Spring Valley	Wes Side Story (Tabasco Cat)	3	10	1	1	1	16,695
Springtim Fantasy	Beaver Cat (Sir Cat)	4	5	1	3	0	29,031
Springtim Fantasy	Devil's Fantasy (Devil His Due)	5	8	0	1	0	2,363
St. Paddy's Pal	Barbarella (Barbeau)	4	2	0	0	0	0
St. Paddy's Pal	Barkerman (Barkerville)	2	2	0	0	0	0
St. Paddy's Pal	Jig o' Scotch (Shotiche)	7	15	0	0	1	8,895
Sunny Sara	Brite Sunny Day (High Brite)	4	9	2	1	2	135,856
Sunny Sara	Sunny Outcome (Cee's Tizzy)	3	4	1	2	1	47,600
Sweet Diva	Red Threat (Red Ransom)	5	5	2	1	1	20,061
Talking Girl	Princess K (King of Kings)	3	5	0	0	0	390
Tanuki	Capn Nathan (Captain Bodgit)	4	6	0	1	0	3,248
Tanuki	Mistda (Runaway Groom)	2	3	1	1	0	33,400
Tanuki	Nora Dooley (Distinctive Pro)	3	11	1	3	3	15,335
Tilted Tiara	Pan de Vida (Islefaxyou)	5	12	1	0	0	8,640
Tilted Tiara	Red Line Seven (Loup Sauvage)	3	10	0	2	2	14,310
To Reminisce	She Did It Her Way (Private Terms)	5	8	1	1	1	16,470
Tri Jackie	Mr. Pistols (Pistols and Roses)	7	9	0	0	0	372
Tri Jackie	Tri M All (Win M All)	4	15	2	3	3	15,717
True Love	San Telmo (Southern Halo)	4	7	1	3	1	57,920
Trusted Partner	Dress To Thrill (Danehill)	4	5	1	0	0	187,780
U R Unforgetable	War Marshall (A.P. Indy)	2	1	0	1	0	9,000
Vicky Dearest	Affirm Rail (Rail)	3	7	1	0	0	3,788
Viva Zapata	Dixie's Secret (Dixieland Band)	5	2	0	1	0	1,500
Whiskey Whisper	Cat's Roar (Tomorrows Cat)	2	5	0	0	1	7,080
Whiskey Whisper	Patriotic Legend (Dehere)	3	11	1	0	2	39,045
Whiskey Whisper	Whispered Call (Phone Trick)	4	4	0	1	0	3,880
Wild Affirmation	Affirmed Manner (Regal Classic)	2	4	0	1	0	4,033
Wild Affirmation	Wild Rice (Regal Classic)	3	14	1	0	1	5,405
Yeside	Executive Air (Grindstone)	4	10	2	2	3	16,744

Dixieland Band, B H (1980)
By Northern Dancer – Mississippi Mud, by Delta Judge

298 Performers, 165 winning performers, $11,645,931 total earnings

Mare	Progeny (Sire)	Age	Sts	1st	2d	3d	Money Won
Abbeville	Bert's Bar (Go for Gin)	3	7	2	0	0	40,043
Adorable Slew	Adorable Julie (Jules)	4	5	0	2	1	6,750
Alexander's Band	Dixieland Creation (Dawn of Creation)	9	9	2	0	1	8,415
Alexander's Band	The Flirt Is On (Moving Shoulder)	2	3	0	0	0	330
All Sweets	Colita (Grindstone)	3	8	4	0	1	184,050
All Sweets	Dixie's Band (Twining)	5	9	1	1	0	18,640
All Sweets	Thunder Boot (Storm Boot)	4	11	5	0	0	86,610
Allison's Pride	Penobscot Bay (Is It True)	3	7	0	2	2	64,949
Allison's Pride	The Pride of Dixie (Editor's Note)	2	2	0	0	0	600
Amore E Baci	Amo Ebaci (Avenue of Flags)	3	15	4	1	5	88,958
Attitude Dancer	Dancer's J B (Conte Di Savoya)	4	1	0	0	0	91
Attitude Dancer	Respository (Mahogany Hall)	5	11	1	0	2	4,246
Attitude Dancer	Stuka's Dancer (Stuka)	7	9	0	1	3	2,430
Attitude Dancer	Tatie Dancer (Unaccounted For)	3	1	0	0	0	195
Ava Singstheblues	Esterhazy (Southern Halo)	6	3	0	0	0	860
Backwater Blues	Backwater Hope (Chilito)	3	10	2	2	1	23,715
Bandique	Emerald Blue (Sultry Song)	3	4	2	0	1	5,760
Bandral	Bandito (Lord Carson)	3	8	1	1	1	15,370
Banjo Lady	Lady of the Press (Press Card)	6	14	4	2	4	38,286
Banjo Lady	Sultry Sound (Demaloot Demashoot)	4	11	3	1	1	39,628
Battl Ofthe Bands	Band of Reflection (Codex's Reflectn)	5	24	1	0	1	5,620
Battl Ofthe Bands	Midnight Explosion (Pyramid Peak)	2	1	0	0	1	2,170
Beal Street Blues	B Gone Blues (Gone West)	3	7	1	1	0	32,340
Beal Street Blues	Koloszar (Pulpit)	2	1	0	0	0	0
Big Band Singer	Secret Rush (Marquetry)	4	9	1	1	1	61,770
Bluegrass Belle	Bluegrass Brass (Fight Over)	8	1	0	0	0	38
Bluegrass Belle	Southern Tee (Lil E. Tee)	7	7	1	2	2	12,578
Bourbon Strt Gal	King of Mardi Gras (Smoke Glacken)	2	5	2	0	0	28,915
Bourbon Strt Gal	Southern Smoke (Smoke Glacken)	3	7	2	3	0	65,796
Box Office Gold	Basic Concern (Concern)	6	3	0	0	1	2,125
Box Office Gold	Golden Concern (Concern)	5	6	1	0	3	18,381
Box Office Gold	New York Gold (Gold Token)	3	13	2	4	0	18,820
Box Office Gold	Tu Z Potts (Gold Case)	4	8	2	0	0	36,432
Bundleofstars	Star's Kandi Kane (Evansville Slew)	2	6	2	0	3	30,270
Bundleofstars	Unome's Star (Unome)	3	4	0	0	0	0
C. C. Overdrive	C. C. Integrity (Mr. Integrity)	6	4	0	0	0	309
C. C. Overdrive	Humoresque (Falstaff)	4	17	0	1	1	3,547
C. C. Overdrive	Summer Special (Siberian Summer)	3	10	0	0	0	3,751
Cacophony	Cat Striker (Tactical Cat)	2	11	1	3	3	90,894
Cajun Colors	Golden Ellen (Gold Fever)	3	9	1	1	2	29,780
Cheerio Charmer	El Galante (Fly So Free)	2	2	1	1	0	19,400
Chordette	Operatic (Gilded Time)	3	5	2	2	1	51,500
Cincinnati Pops	Jacobs Smile (Ops Smile)	3	3	0	1	1	11,900
Cincinnati Pops	Jolie Louise (Mister Jolie)	2	1	0	0	0	75
Cincinnati Pops	Pop n' Tap (Pleasant Tap)	7	10	0	0	0	600
Cincinnati Pops	Twist and Pop (Oliver's Twist)	4	6	1	0	2	17,070
Coastal Wave	Cross the Infield (Mr. Greeley)	4	12	2	1	1	36,777
Coastal Wave	Typical Situation (Distorted Humor)	3	3	0	0	0	450
Courtin' Dixie	Terras Terry (Monetary Gift)	3	8	2	1	1	14,130
Cue Girl	Call Shot (Salt Dome)	6	2	0	0	0	0
Dancin Dixie Miss	Dream Deliverer (Sea Hero)	3	14	2	2	5	68,784
Dancin Dixie Miss	Espresso Oro (Java Gold)	8	11	2	3	0	19,925
Dancin Dixie Miss	Hero's Siren (Sea Hero)	4	6	0	1	1	3,935
Dazzling Dixie	Dazzling Rubies (Rubiano)	4	10	1	3	3	58,182
Desaucered	Go In (Conquistador Cielo)	5	2	1	0	0	8,820
Diamond Star	Starship Diligence (Diligence)	3	10	2	3	1	37,020
Divine Dixie	Primo Primo (Saint Ballado)	3	1	0	0	0	0
Dixie Accent	Dynamite Vic (Dynaformer)	7	8	1	0	2	20,450
Dixie Accent	Indixie (A.P. Indy)	5	9	2	2	1	15,165
Dixie Band	Cielo Girl (Conquistador Cielo)	4	12	5	2	1	180,053
Dixie Belle	Sweetjudyblueeyes (Proud and True)	3	13	3	1	3	19,232
Dixie Blue	Blue Grey (With Approval)	7	8	0	0	1	6,733
Dixie Blue	Mister Blues (Mr. Greeley)	6	2	0	0	1	5,280
Dixie Card	Ian's Thunder (Gulch)	8	3	0	0	0	570
Dixie Chimes	Freefourinternet (Tabasco Cat)	5	11	2	1	5	418,598
Dixie Dame	Dashing in Dixie (Out of Place)	3	3	0	0	0	360
Dixie Dash	Dash Home (Two Punch)	3	7	2	1	0	44,940
Dixie Dash	Gold Sensation (Prized)	6	7	0	0	1	1,120
Dixie Dash	Senor Coqui (Jade Hunter)	4	7	2	1	0	10,300
Dixie de Kay	Lethimrun (Roy)	4	16	2	3	4	36,994
Dixie Derby	Dixie Law (Martial Law)	7	5	1	0	1	37,420
Dixie Distinction	Numerous Lady (Numerous)	3	6	0	0	1	7,727
Dixie Distinction	Wishing Dixie (Lycius)	2	3	0	0	0	1,725
Dixie Doll	Gold Doll (Gold Legend)	4	2	0	0	0	0
Dixie Echo	Greg's Syrah (Cape Town)	3	6	1	0	1	25,015
Dixie Echo	Lead Em Home (Mr. Leader)	7	1	0	0	0	0
Dixie Echo	Monocerus (Lord Carson)	4	3	0	0	0	386
Dixie Echo	Premier Cru (Premiership)	6	2	0	0	0	176
Dixie Favor	Kiralik (Efisio)	3	2	0	0	0	240
Dixie Flag	Indy Flag (A.P. Indy)	3	2	0	0	1	5,980
Dixie Flash	Discipline (Stuka)	6	15	1	1	0	7,470
Dixie Flash	Dixie Stripes (Candy Stripes)	4	6	0	0	0	1,328
Dixie Highway	Miss Allie Gator (Beau Genius)	8	2	0	0	1	2,363
Dixie Highway	Out At Home (Take Me Out)	3	10	2	1	2	63,157
Dixie Highway	Scarlett'sprospect (Native Prospectr)	5	11	1	1	4	5,810
Dixie Holiday	Holiday Runner (Meadowlake)	3	7	1	2	1	50,450
Dixie Honey	Bee My Honey (Southern Halo)	4	7	0	2	2	22,880
Dixie Honey	Old Dixie Home (Home At Last)	3	15	2	4	2	53,400
Dixie Landera	Mr. Carlos (Pine Bluff)	6	2	0	0	0	148
Dixie Lane	Neenamusha (Sandpit (BRZ))	3	6	2	2	0	16,794
Dixie Lass	A Perfectredransom (Red Ransom)	9	7	0	0	1	2,848
Dixie Lite	Bourbon St. Dance (Gold Token)	3	6	1	0	0	5,558
Dixie Lite	Thunder Gold (Strike the Gold)	4	3	0	1	0	4,844
Dixie Luck	Crafty Luck (Crafty Prospector)	4	7	1	0	1	19,290
Dixie Maintenance	Marathon Man (Capote)	3	4	0	0	0	500
Dixie Maintenance	Miss Fairfield (Hennessy)	2	1	0	0	0	0
Dixie Melody	Joe Six Pack (Silver Deputy)	2	4	3	0	0	127,800
Dixie Pirate	Captain Craig (Texas City)	9	17	3	4	4	32,550
Dixie Pirate	Hickory Doc (Two Punch)	3	8	1	2	3	18,900
Dixie Pirate	Prospecting Dixie (Allen's Prospect)	4	8	2	4	1	31,020
Dixie Pirate	Sugar Ray Silver (Two Punch)	5	10	2	0	0	14,394
Dixie Rouge	Albert and Baby (Defrere)	3	1	0	0	0	110
Dixie Rouge	Lilah (Defrere)	6	13	4	5	1	153,520
Dixie Sass	Ford's Creek (Kris S.)	5	5	1	0	0	11,790
Dixie Slippers	Playa Maya (Arch)	3	3	1	1	1	35,980
Dixie Step	Dixie's Irish (Proud Irish)	3	14	0	3	2	12,578
Dixie Step	Proud Yvett (Proud Irish)	4	2	0	0	1	1,350
Dixie Sunrise	Dixie Sunset (Castle Guard)	6	5	1	1	1	6,002
Dixie Sunrise	Dixie Two Thousnd (Private Intrview)	5	3	0	0	0	1,350
Dixieland Bandit	Hamlet (Roaring Camp)	3	6	1	2	1	24,889
Dixieland Belle	Bad Dog (Allen's Prospect)	7	9	0	2	3	8,405
Dixieland Belle	Dixielands Devil (Devil His Due)	5	8	2	2	2	37,180

Dixieland Blues	Comeon Dixie (Mr. Greeley)	3	2	0	0	0	1,350
Dixieland Blues	Limehouse (Grand Slam)	2	6	3	0	2	260,435
Dixieland Dream	Fantasy Valley (Gulch)	5	4	0	1	1	3,128
Dixieland Dream	Seek the Dream (Seeking the Gold)	4	6	1	1	0	4,220
Dixieland Fantasy	Admiration (Marquetry)	4	11	0	3	1	13,980
Dixieland Fantasy	Currituck Springs (Wekiva Springs)	3	8	1	1	3	16,025
Dixieland Fantasy	Dixie High (Anet)	2	5	2	0	1	95,945
Dixieland Gal	Count Dixie (Geiger Counter)	6	4	0	0	1	806
Dixieland Gal	Tales of Glory (Honour and Glory)	2	4	2	0	1	60,750
Dixieland Gold	Dixieland Gulch (Gulch)	3	5	2	1	0	43,500
Dixieland Gold	Yellowstone Lady (Crafty Prospectr)	4	3	0	1	0	12,250
Dixieland Queen	Cheverly Gold (Formal Gold)	3	7	0	2	1	23,060
Dixieland Queen	Oh Please Louise (Allen's Prospect)	4	3	0	0	0	0
Dixieland Queen	She's a Rebel Too (Two Punch)	2	2	1	0	1	17,000
Dixieland Queen	Two Punch Sonny (Two Punch)	7	6	1	1	1	35,880
Dixieland Special	Jazz Music (Jules)	3	7	1	2	0	6,980
Dixieland Special	Special Jule (Jules)	4	7	3	2	0	59,460
Dixieland Special	Special Trial (Skip Trial)	5	7	2	1	2	56,070
Dixieland Stand	Dixieland Girl (Trapp Mountain)	4	2	1	0	0	6,480
Dixity Do Dah	Foxhole (Digging In)	5	11	0	3	2	7,075
Dixity Do Dah	Woodmeister (Holzmeister)	2	11	2	0	1	22,250
Donnan's Holly	Conservation (Tamayaz)	3	11	2	3	1	96,550
Donttellthefluff	Eye Pea Oh (With Approval)	7	6	0	0	3	17,460
Donttellthefluff	Sultry Fluff (Sultry Song)	4	4	1	0	0	52,692
Down South	But (Unaccounted For)	5	1	0	1	0	8,600
Down South	Dean Sperry (Crusader Sword)	3	1	0	0	0	0
Down South	Stowe (A. P Jet)	4	3	0	0	0	754
Dutchess of Dixie	Good Boy Duke (Mr. Integrity)	9	18	1	2	1	5,041
Dutchess of Dixie	Paster's Dutchess (Paster's Caper)	4	6	0	1	1	5,660
Etats Unis	Pollard's Vision (Carson City)	2	6	1	1	2	53,291
Fairytale Ending	Cash Marquet (Marquetry)	3	1	0	0	0	126
Flambeau	Silo (Fortunate Prospect)	3	7	0	1	2	5,910
Fluffkins	All the Tricks (Grand Slam)	3	7	1	1	1	12,000
Fluffkins	Sword of Lords (Crafty Prospector)	2	1	0	0	0	137
For Dixie	Mittens Mambo (Kingmambo)	3	1	0	0	0	195
Force Majeure	Force Ministre (Premier Ministre)	4	3	0	0	0	685
Force Majeure	R Cs Slew (Slewacide)	5	6	1	1	2	13,762
Freddie Frisson	In the Ghetto (Hennessy)	3	8	1	0	2	22,880
Gabrielle P.	Rio Yelcho (Distinctive Pro)	5	11	1	1	1	4,731
Golden Tiy	All Is Gold (Gilded Time)	4	1	0	0	0	330
Goldn Wave Band	Don Lux (Look See)	4	2	0	0	0	1,020
Gunner Lil	Perfect Lil (Perfect)	4	3	0	0	0	0
Gunner Lil	Ragtime Gunner (Cryptoclearance)	5	13	2	1	2	10,300
Hatchet Band	Baltic Maria (Maria's Mon)	3	3	0	0	1	1,975
Hatchet Band	Baltic Marque (Marquetry)	6	20	4	1	6	20,743
Hear the Sea	Absolute Nectar (Carson City)	2	5	2	0	1	50,886
Hear the Sea	Bastione (Smart Strike)	3	1	0	0	0	95
Holy Land Band	Betty's Wish (Gold Case)	3	9	5	2	1	209,440
Holy Land Band	R. Dixie Chick (Pioneering)	5	6	1	0	0	4,925
Hug'm	Smokehouse (Smoke Glacken)	4	1	0	0	1	900
Hum Dixie	Rare Racer (Rare Brick)	4	19	2	3	2	12,339
Hum Dixie	Sans Win (Double Honor)	2	2	1	0	1	14,150
Hum Dixie	Southern Honoree (Double Honor)	3	11	4	0	2	35,895
Ice Classic	Twine Power (Twining)	4	16	4	1	1	19,517
Igotrhythm	Gone Musical (Gone West)	4	3	0	0	0	1,955
Igotrhythm	Gone to War (Gone West)	3	8	1	3	0	53,436
Igotrhythm	Native Rhythm (Woodman)	5	7	2	2	0	73,740
Illusive Note	Captain Greybeard (Runaway Groom)	3	9	1	1	3	13,179
Jazzability	Glitter Baby (Glitterman)	5	14	1	1	2	19,881
Jazzalong	Hamaaly (Unbridled's Song)	3	4	1	0	1	14,460
Jazzalong	Jazzfield (Metfield)	6	11	1	2	0	9,198
Jazzy	B B Blues (Slewacide)	6	18	0	0	0	924
Jazzy	Count Basic (Slewacide)	5	11	2	1	1	16,801
Jazzy	Satchmo (Timeless Native)	9	1	0	0	0	0
Kicker Dancin'	Late to the Dance (With Approval)	4	3	0	0	0	475
Kicker Dancin'	Musashi (Supremo)	6	19	2	3	4	22,630
Kutira	Triptips (Regal Classic)	3	10	2	2	1	10,418
Lady of Tralee	Columbia Gorge (Red Ransom)	8	13	1	0	4	4,409
Lady of Tralee	Mi Camila (Southern Halo)	5	2	0	0	1	563
Lady of Tralee	Velvets and Silks (Southern Halo)	3	11	1	4	2	28,536
Landholder	Our Joy (El Prado)	2	2	0	0	0	1,140
Lizzie Toon	Hot Dancer (Will's Way)	3	5	1	0	0	13,770
Lookaway Dixie	Neera (Runaway Groom)	3	5	1	0	0	4,935
Lookaway Dixie	Swinging Ghost (Silver Ghost)	2	2	0	2	0	16,800
Love That Jazz	Society Selection (Coronado's Quest)	2	3	2	0	0	327,000
Magic in the Music	Pocketful of Magic (Mr. Greeley)	3	2	1	0	0	7,530
Magic in the Music	Tune Lender (Banker's Gold)	2	2	1	0	0	6,540
Magic Music	Cool Runnings (Pleasant Tap)	2	4	0	0	0	480
Mason Dixie	Wood Dixie Dance (Woodman)	2	13	2	2	2	39,150
Masquerade Lady	Freedom Roar (Roar)	4	2	0	0	0	315
Masquerade Lady	Girl Fever (Gold Fever)	3	8	0	0	1	5,200
Masquerade Lady	Up Jump the Devil (Devil His Due)	5	14	5	1	2	27,555
Matika	Rateeki (Patton)	5	10	0	0	1	651
Metalmark	Honorable Mark (Double Honor)	2	9	1	1	3	13,235
Metalmark	Pepesqueez (Judge T C)	4	14	2	1	2	18,555
Miss Blush	Adee (Cherokee Colony)	6	9	0	5	3	12,245
Miss Blush	Strodee (Strodes Creek)	4	6	1	0	0	6,900
Mission Park	Braytonville (Saint Ballado)	2	2	0	0	1	5,000
Mrs. K.	Biddy Biddy (Bet Twice)	9	9	1	1	0	5,118
Mrs. K.	Last Waltz (Ghazi)	2	5	2	2	0	54,155
Mrs. K.	Lethal Agenda (Twilight Agenda)	5	15	0	3	1	5,943
Mrs. K.	Spelling (Alphabet Soup)	4	4	0	1	1	29,560
Musical Delight	Smugglers Basin (Mr. Greeley)	4	8	0	2	0	12,080
Musical Delight	Suprise Me Again (Miner's Mark)	5	7	0	1	2	12,600
Musical Flight	Sapphireontherocks (Go for Gin)	4	5	2	2	0	16,706
Musical Flight	Takenbythesky (Twining)	5	5	3	0	0	31,940
Needlepoint	Sir Rubi (Rubiano)	3	12	2	2	2	16,987
Newhall Road	Bayfront (Prospect Bay)	2	3	1	1	1	16,800
Newhall Road	Elaine's Way (Lord Carson)	3	16	3	4	0	42,162
No Fairytales	Shybynature (Blushing John)	7	8	0	0	0	5,790
No Need to Party	Carouse (Cure the Blues)	4	3	0	0	0	830
No Need to Party	Ms Media (Media Starguest)	6	12	0	1	1	8,166
Nocciolina	Railway (Catrail)	5	22	1	0	4	8,056
Northern Dixie	Impecable Manners (Majesty's Imp)	5	3	0	0	0	154
Northern Dixie	Major Alliance (Crafty Friend)	2	2	0	1	1	3,705
Northern Dixie	Mister Misty (Mister Baileys)	3	13	3	4	0	30,216
O. K. Mom	Perfect Ride (Cherokee Run)	4	11	2	4	1	49,089
One More Flag	Robyn's Pal (Unaccounted For)	2	3	0	1	0	4,590
Pas de Problem	Sweet Problem (Is It True)	2	5	2	1	1	86,852
Play the Scale	Natrona (Lord Avie)	4	8	0	2	1	14,452
Pleasant Dixie	Southern Image (Halo's Image)	3	3	2	0	1	202,800
Pray Lady	Elusive Project (Elusive Quality)	2	2	0	0	0	1,468
Pray Lady	Regal n' Classy (Regal Classic)	5	9	0	1	1	23,188
Pray Lady	Sierra Kitty (Mountain Cat)	3	13	1	0	2	37,764
Preakness Lady	Will Belong (Belong to Me)	4	13	1	2	0	7,997
Quite a Rapper	My Friend Bruce (Dance Brightly)	2	3	1	0	1	22,000
Radioactivity	Champali (Glitterman)	3	10	4	1	3	313,522
Radioactivity	Drexel Monorail (Glitterman)	4	13	2	4	2	142,685
Radioactivity	Shorewalk Drive (Formal Gold)	2	4	1	0	0	17,055
Ragged Glory	Twice Glory (Magloire)	3	4	0	0	0	660
Ragtimely	Siward (Distant View)	5	13	8	2	2	34,768
Ragtimely	Timely Minister (Mane Minister)	6	9	0	2	1	8,744
Ragtimely	Tribe (Cherokee Run)	3	8	3	2	1	79,200
Raise the Band	Matchless Hunter (Jade Hunter)	7	9	0	1	1	5,355
Ramblin Dixie	Dixieland Plan (Game Plan)	4	15	0	2	3	19,582
Ramblin Dixie	My Red Cadillac (Son of Briartic)	8	2	0	0	0	0
Rampart Street	Charmeleon (Smokester)	5	12	2	1	2	8,737
Rampart Street	Street Band (Smokester)	4	8	6	0	0	52,260
Regal Band	Montaraz (Numerous)	3	1	0	0	0	0
Regal Band	My Man Gus (Supremo)	4	7	0	0	1	2,437
Regal Band	Resurgence (Black Tie Affair)	6	5	0	1	0	5,940
Regal Band	Siphonophora (Siphon (BRZ))	2	1	0	0	0	0
Rekindled	Dyna King (Dynaformer)	6	18	2	4	4	9,845
Ritzy Dixie	Fort Donna (Fort Chaffee)	5	1	0	0	0	0
Rockaroller	Naughty Nae (Unbridled's Song)	2	3	0	0	1	7,650
Rockaroller	Nick Bollettieri (Unbridled's Song)	4	10	1	1	1	14,680
Rockaroller	Phone Tech (Favorite Trick)	3	7	0	0	3	2,893
Satchmo's Lady	Red Seattle (Septieme Ciel)	7	7	2	2	1	9,424
Satchmo's Lady	Sssh It'sa Secret (Sea of Secrets)	2	1	0	0	0	0
Satin Promise	Baldwin County (Prized)	5	4	0	1	0	8,280
Satin Promise	Promise of War (Lord At War)	7	8	2	0	1	35,290
Satin Promise	Turtle Beach (Out of Place)	3	2	0	0	0	1,620
Scorched	Burning Marque (Marquetry)	7	8	3	1	0	62,760
Scorched	Genuine Appeal (Affirmed)	5	1	0	0	0	0
Scorched	Pyramid Scheme (Distant View)	3	8	0	2	1	6,185
Sea Jamie Win	Summerfield (Affirmed)	4	6	0	0	0	2,720
Sea Jamie Win	The Herc (Lord Carson)	2	7	3	2	0	118,435
Sheshallhavmusic	No Music (Miner's Mark)	4	12	3	1	0	39,204
Shoe Band	Joseph George (Rubiano)	6	10	3	2	2	4,468
Showemyourclass	Act Classy (Noactor)	2	2	0	0	0	217
Showemyourclass	Actalot (Noactor)	6	13	1	1	1	10,295
Showemyourclass	Actceed (Noactor)	4	4	1	2	1	2,214
Showemyourclass	Josie'slil'actress (Noactor)	3	13	1	0	1	6,975
Simple Dreams	Difficult Times (Honour and Glory)	4	8	0	0	3	2,626
Sing and Swing	Got That Swing (With Approval)	8	12	1	1	0	9,939
Sing and Swing	Quick Start (Hennessy)	2	3	1	0	0	32,365
Smile n Molly	Dont Tell the Kids (Carson City)	6	16	3	0	1	27,456
Smile n Molly	Keep Smilin (Geri)	3	3	0	0	0	3,690
Smile n Molly	Smile N Carson (Carson City)	2	4	1	0	0	9,530
So Jazzy	Brite Future (High Brite)	6	18	2	4	3	19,943
Sorority Jazz	Jazz Flight (Meadow Flight)	4	7	1	0	1	4,093
Southern Sound	Can Rianne (Gulch)	3	4	0	0	0	1,845
Southern Sound	Uncle Walter (Tabasco Cat)	2	4	0	1	0	10,520
Starlight Cove	Frosty Starlight (Sharp Frosty)	6	7	0	0	0	563
Street Corner Jive	Vilma Bankey (Lear Fan)	3	2	0	0	0	0
Sunset Song	Before Sunset (Grand Slam)	2	1	0	0	0	2,500
Sunset Song	Chalmette (Quiet American)	4	3	1	0	0	24,700
Sunset Song	J J Thedotcom Man (Private Terms)	5	18	2	0	2	5,083
Sunshine Again	Sunshine Lake (Meadowlake)	2	2	0	0	0	600
Swingin' Sister	Flaming Fire (Smoke Glacken)	3	9	1	0	1	18,575
Swingin' Sister	Take the A Train (Smoke Glacken)	4	18	2	1	1	23,929
Tajannub	Almungid (Thunder Gulch)	4	15	1	2	1	12,165
That's a Plenty	El Progreso (Latin American)	5	8	2	1	1	24,460
That's a Plenty	Honor Stripes (Candy Stripes)	3	7	0	0	2	7,050
Timeless Tempo	Dekay (Exploit)	2	2	0	0	1	1,555
Tiny's Teardrop	Crypto Child (Cryptoclearance)	6	8	0	3	1	5,047
Tiny's Teardrop	Nut Lovin (Avenue of Flags)	2	1	0	0	0	0
Trust in Dixie	Midnight Miner (Miner's Mark)	7	12	2	4	1	15,540
Twigazuri	Futural (Future Storm)	7	12	2	1	1	62,314
Twigazuri	Justastorm (Storm Creek)	4	4	0	0	1	2,520
Twigazuri	Talara (Hennessy)	3	6	1	0	0	32,640
Unending Love	Exert (Roy)	6	1	0	0	0	220

Unending Love	Mon T. Hauls (Mahogany Hall)	4	6	2	2	1	4,940
Vague Gal	Demidor (Demidoff)	3	1	0	0	0	0
Vague Gal	Miraculousmichel (North Prospect)	5	15	2	4	4	17,481
Wrong Delivery	Heart of Jules (Jules)	2	5	2	0	0	26,260

Valid Appeal, B H (1972)
By In Reality – Desert Trial, by Moslem Chief

268 Performers, 167 winning performers, $7,138,795 total earnings

Mare	Progeny (Sire)	Age	Sts	1st	2d	3d	Money Won
A Lady With Appl	El Condor (Birdonthewire)	4	10	1	5	1	52,700
A Lady With Appl	Lady Gwen (Alphabet Soup)	3	11	1	3	3	58,420
A Lady With Appl	Valid Rush (Wild Rush)	2	4	0	1	1	8,060
Absence of Malice	Soldotna (Unzipped)	6	8	2	0	0	33,240
All You All	Lovey Lovey Lovey (Danzig Cnnction)	9	2	0	0	0	280
Always Asking	Aguara (End Sweep)	3	8	1	2	0	32,470
Alwaysinlove	Hasse (Wayne's Crane)	4	4	2	0	0	14,940
Amavalidhope	Hope for Love (Fortunate Prospect)	3	8	1	2	1	56,860
Amavalidhope	Vesta (Fortunate Prospect)	4	4	0	1	0	13,620
Angel's Appeal	Looks Bold (He's a Looker)	5	12	3	2	2	73,656
Appeal to Me	News to Me (Editor's Note)	3	7	1	1	0	28,612
Appealing Andovr	Grace the Stage (Pembroke)	3	5	2	1	0	15,060
Appealing Andovr	Megan's Appeal (Gold Case)	2	3	1	1	0	110,850
Appealing Blues	Man in Blue (Marquetry)	4	4	0	1	1	2,435
Appealing Bruntte	Diablo's Appealer (Diablo)	4	6	0	0	0	1,090
Appealing Bruntte	Forty Sweeps (End Sweep)	3	9	2	0	2	7,956
Appealing Es	At Ease Diablo (Diablo)	4	9	0	1	1	7,920
Appealing Es	Es Muy Stormy (Storm Creek)	3	10	1	1	3	6,729
Appealing Es	Stars On the Water (Marquetry)	2	2	0	0	0	0
Appealing Gal	Valid Kiss (Kissin Kris)	6	5	0	0	1	858
Appealing Girl	Climbeverymountain (Grindstone)	5	3	0	1	0	2,946
Appealing Gypsy	L S Gypsyannio (Giuseppe)	2	2	0	0	0	411
Appealing Gypsy	Ls Storming Gypsy (Bag)	3	6	1	0	0	6,675
Appealing Inez	Mystery Ship (Storm Creek)	3	8	1	0	2	8,018
Appealing Jeanne	Pull Over Please (Glitterman)	4	7	4	0	1	25,570
Appealing Jeanne	Southern Cure (Cure the Blues)	7	11	4	0	1	32,090
Appealing Jeanne	Wild for Jeanne (Wild Zone)	2	6	2	1	0	29,360
Appealing Kanska	Karroo (Cape Town)	3	3	0	1	0	4,768
Appealing Look	Appealing Song (Concerto)	3	2	1	0	0	5,399
Appealing Look	Special Matter (River Special)	5	9	1	2	1	169,660
Appealing Miss	Dr. Miller (My Prince Charming)	3	7	1	0	1	32,940
Appealing Miss	Like to Keep Busy (Big Sal)	5	7	0	0	0	280
Appealing Miss	Soes Bandit (Buckaroo)	7	9	1	1	1	23,635
Appealing Miss	What's That (My Prince Charming)	2	9	0	1	0	4,920
Appling Miss Cox	Stormy Appeal (Storm Creek)	4	15	1	3	1	11,395
Appealing Sam	Appealing Lauren (Double Cash)	3	4	1	0	1	10,070
Appealing Sam	Appealing Secret (Sea of Secrets)	2	8	4	0	0	69,960
Appealing Sara	Dear to Me (Mister Baileys)	3	3	1	0	0	11,780
Appealing Slew	Appealing Jet (Jessie Jet)	5	12	0	5	2	16,375
Appealing Slew	Spring Jet (Jessie Jet)	6	14	0	0	2	6,520
Appealing Story	Diablo's Fable (Diablo)	5	5	1	1	3	9,990
Appealing Style	Nindawayma (Ascot Knight)	5	11	3	5	0	22,134
Applepeal	Apple Appeal (Sunrise Shower)	3	6	1	1	1	6,235
Applepeal	Chilipin (Sunrise Shower)	5	8	0	2	0	8,202
Applepeal	Peal Out (Sunrise Shower)	4	8	1	0	0	8,021
Applepeal	Valid Sunrise (Sunrise Shower)	6	4	2	0	1	4,956
Bellatre	Pegasus Belle (Groomstick)	4	3	0	1	0	1,813
Belle's Appeal	Harbour Gate (Boston Harbor)	2	1	0	0	1	2,340
Boldly Appealing	Bold Explorer (Open Forum)	2	1	0	0	0	0
Call	Mekena South (Skip Trial)	5	15	2	2	1	34,715
Chelly M.	Hitchcock's Best (Bates Motel)	3	17	6	2	1	41,232
Chelly M.	Monticello (Montbrook)	2	9	1	2	2	13,300
Chelly M.	Skinny Dipper (First and Only)	4	11	2	1	2	22,220
Chief Appeal	Appealing Jewel (Saint Ballado)	4	1	0	0	0	0
Chief Appeal	Cozzene Appeal (Cozzene)	5	13	1	2	3	28,685
Chief Appeal	Rehear (Coronado's Quest)	3	3	0	0	0	0
Chief Appeal	Two Chiefs (Two Punch)	7	4	1	1	1	12,816
Cozily	Cozy (Wallenda)	6	7	1	0	2	40,242
Danielle's Jewel	Dancin Daze (Cure the Blues)	4	5	0	3	2	7,840
Dara's Appeal	Nine's Appealagain (Nines Wild)	5	15	0	0	3	5,356
Dara's Appeal	Wild Romeo (Wild Syn)	3	6	0	0	0	526
Di's Song	Hunting Hillbilly (Dove Hunt)	2	12	1	2	1	28,050
Discover Silver	Sleep Away (Skip Away)	3	16	2	6	2	42,730
Elgin Lady	Sgt. Shelley (Twining)	3	10	1	2	0	8,175
Elgin Lady	Uncle Ack (Housebuster)	4	6	1	1	1	7,647
Elgin Lady	York Hills (Fit to Fight)	5	8	1	1	3	24,584
Enjoy the Silence	Silent Embrace (Twining)	3	8	1	2	0	19,440
Enjoy the Silence	Silver Silence (Rubiano)	5	9	3	2	2	36,660
Expensive Glue	Kalt Cafe (In Excessive Bull)	3	3	1	0	0	7,324
Few Choice Wrds	Commandr Benno (Deputy Commndr)	3	15	2	0	2	23,880
Few Choice Wrds	Miss Jeanne Cat (Tabasco Cat)	4	1	0	0	0	0
Flood Warning	Valid Afleet (Rizzi)	2	4	0	0	0	358
French Appeal	Home James (Whitney Tower)	3	8	0	0	2	2,870
Gee Thanks	If I Were You (Defrere)	4	7	3	0	1	50,788
Gee Thanks	Miss Susan (Defrere)	3	7	1	1	1	5,168
Gee Thanks	Thank You Mom (Holzmeister)	2	5	0	0	1	2,660
Gold Appeal	Appealing Turk (Turkoman)	5	4	0	1	1	840
Heavenly Shadow	Kimberley Regiment (Lost Soldier)	3	5	0	1	0	3,640
Hidden Desire	Cometary (Comet Shine)	4	10	2	0	1	19,405
Hidden Desire	Sheilas Desire (Rodeo)	3	5	1	1	0	15,050
Ice Pop	Camp Valid (Roaring Camp)	4	5	1	2	0	11,315
In Pay	Good Bidness (Crafty Dude)	3	3	0	1	1	2,700
Joyatlast	Rocky Robyn (Robyn Dancer)	8	8	2	0	0	22,710
Key Buy	Sit Rep (Broad Brush)	3	1	0	0	0	500
Kind of Appealing	Shadow Government (Reincarnate)	3	8	0	0	2	2,963
Law N Order	Gambler's Law (Prospectors Gamble)	2	4	0	0	1	1,080
Light Rain	Sexy Appeal (Colonial Affair)	4	8	0	1	1	4,620
Little Sister	Spoiled (Wild Again)	2	3	1	1	0	37,225
Long Lasting	Paso Del Norte (Fierce Fighter)	7	5	0	0	0	674
Mary's Appeal	Scobey (Proud Birdie)	8	11	1	4	0	10,120
Milky Way Gal	Cosmic Snowman (Frosty the Snwmn)	7	11	1	0	0	7,161
Milky Way Gal	Jujuba (Jules)	4	6	0	0	0	676
Milky Way Gal	Milky Way Guy (Skip Trial)	5	9	2	2	0	52,110
Miss Valdance	Miss Dancin Diablo (Diablo)	5	2	0	1	0	1,367
Miss Valdance	Valdancer's Gate (Gate Dancer)	7	8	0	1	1	4,082
Miss Valid Match	Carnival Match (Carnivalay)	5	19	0	2	2	7,503
Miss Valid Match	Halo's Match (Halo's Image)	3	6	1	1	1	10,480
Miss Valid Pache	Valid Pulpit (Pulpit)	3	5	2	0	0	55,845
Miss Valid Storm	Miss Valid Joann (Holy Bull)	2	2	1	1	0	6,715
Moving Appeal	City Appeal (Carson City)	10	4	0	1	0	1,291
Nanerpeal	Saint Appeal (Saint Ballado)	4	4	1	0	0	28,440
Naughty Nora	Don't Ignore Her (Slewdledo)	6	12	6	0	1	33,920
Not My Cp of Tea	Go Not Whoa (Tilt Up)	8	12	1	1	5	22,373
Obstinacy	Best of the Rest (Skip Trial)	8	6	3	2	0	753,500
Oedy's Appeal	Oedy's Riches (Rizzi)	5	10	1	2	3	30,531
Oedy's Appeal	Stormin Oedy (Mystery Storm)	6	11	0	1	4	37,800
Peace Rose	Heart in Hand (Notebook)	6	7	0	0	0	1,575
Perfect Exchange	Cauy (Maria's Mon)	5	12	4	3	0	113,616
Perfect Exchange	Maria's Mirage (Maria's Mon)	4	7	3	1	0	120,323
Perfect Exchange	Perfect Miss (Diligence)	3	11	3	1	3	41,305
Personal Line	Brown Eyed Miss (End Sweep)	3	10	1	4	1	52,836
Personal Line	Erotico (Lost Soldier)	2	2	0	1	0	2,980
Personal Line	Line Sweeper (End Sweep)	4	3	0	2	0	5,200
Personal Line	Personal Sweep (End Sweep)	7	8	2	0	0	10,708
Personal Line	Storm's Lining (Storm Creek)	5	7	2	2	0	10,254
Piney Woods	My Limit (Wagon Limit)	2	3	0	1	0	8,730
Plea	My Alternate (Demons Begone)	4	8	0	0	0	521
Plea	Pazhalsta (Moscow Ballet)	5	10	3	4	3	32,335
Plea	Pleas Deal (Delineator)	3	10	2	2	0	36,240
Proud n' Precious	Matsui (Double Honor)	2	1	1	0	0	11,400
Proud n' Precious	Mooji Moo (Jeblar)	4	10	5	1	1	188,810
Quiet Talk	K. P. Express (Captain Bodgit)	3	6	1	1	2	7,422
Quiet Talk	Whispering Miss (Real Quiet)	2	4	0	0	0	125
Radical Appeal	Dontellannie (Traitor)	3	13	0	0	1	948
Radical Appeal	Knock'em Dead (Knockadoon)	4	7	0	0	1	2,610
Radical Appeal	Lau Mor's Glitter (Glitterman)	2	11	0	3	4	24,890
Radical Appeal	Sunny Stutz (Stutz Blackhawk)	8	8	0	0	1	4,560
Real Jenny	Golden Jenny (Capote)	3	4	1	0	1	17,890
Really Appealing	Note Appeal (Notebook)	2	4	0	1	1	4,495
Really Appealing	Real Forum (Open Forum)	4	5	1	0	0	10,767
Rivkah	Diablo's Rift (Diablo)	5	12	0	1	0	4,700
Say Please	Please Run (Roy)	6	3	1	0	0	6,500
Say Please	Priceless Jet (Mahogany Hall)	3	13	3	1	1	34,720
Sedna	Bag of Tootie's (Bag)	3	3	1	0	0	9,000
Silk Appeal	Concorde's Appeal (Concorde's Tune)	4	11	2	2	0	44,560
Silk Appeal	Silk Concorde (Concorde's Tune)	5	8	2	0	2	74,032
Snubs	Snub the Devil (Devil's Bag)	2	2	0	1	0	4,600
Sober Appeal	Plum Sober (Blumin Affair)	2	3	2	1	0	71,888
Sugar's Image	Unbridled's Image (Unbridled)	3	2	0	0	0	540
Suspicious Appeal	Chief Suspect (Rahy)	8	3	0	0	2	1,000
Sweet Message	Sea of Sweets (Sea of Secrets)	2	4	0	1	0	4,630
Sweet Message	Show Killer (Banker's Gold)	3	5	0	1	1	2,875
Sweet Reality	Starship Garnet (Unzipped)	4	8	1	3	1	13,510
Sweet Reality	Sweets (Unzipped)	3	6	0	1	1	3,225
Tashmo Joe	Appealing Greeley (Mr. Greeley)	4	16	1	1	1	10,265
Tashmo Joe	She's a Sweetheart (Go for Gin)	3	6	1	1	0	33,200
Tashmo Joe	Viasec Son (D'Accord)	6	4	2	0	0	15,492
Temptous	Tempest Run (Alydeed)	3	9	1	3	1	32,223
Tracy V.	American Challenge (You and I)	3	6	1	0	0	15,440
Tracy V.	Norman Vincent (Canyon Creek)	4	1	0	0	0	545
True Melody	Miss Guts (American Chance)	4	11	0	4	3	50,263
True Melody	Princess Nicolette (Torrential)	3	18	1	1	5	35,875
Truly Naughty	One Bad Storm (Siberian Summer)	3	5	0	0	3	10,080
Unchained Appeal	Skip Son (Skip Trial)	2	2	0	0	0	710
Uniquely Appling	Cryptos' Best (Cryptoclearance)	2	12	2	1	3	96,345
Uniquely Appling	Joyous Appeal (Devil His Due)	3	9	3	0	2	40,120
Uniquely Appling	Lazar (Exemplary Leader)	7	15	1	2	2	8,895
Uniquely Appling	Mr. Bo Jo (Devil His Due)	4	16	2	2	2	13,853
United Appeal	Nineandfourfifths (Prospect Bay)	4	1	0	0	0	0
Valid Affect	Intrinsic Worth (Red Ransom)	2	5	1	0	3	31,900
Valid Affect	Obligatory (Belong to Me)	3	7	1	0	0	18,225
Valid Allure	Inclinator (Delineator)	7	8	3	0	1	36,300
Valid Allure	Liberation (Green Dancer)	4	14	4	1	2	51,130
Valid and True	Gold Wings (Our Emblem)	5	8	2	2	1	48,740

Valid and True	True Appeal (Deputy Commander)	3	1	0	0	0	0
Valid and True	Unbridled Gamble (Unbridled)	7	10	5	0	0	25,830
Valid Approval	Fierce Knight (Birdonthewire)	2	3	1	1	0	23,440
Valid Approval	Sand Burner (Touch Gold)	3	9	1	2	0	54,120
Valid Approval	Valid Wire (Birdonthewire)	5	13	2	1	2	28,066
Valid Attraction	Pat's Blast O. (Explosive Red)	5	12	1	0	1	13,441
Valid Blend	Alex's Sister (Storm Creek)	3	2	0	0	0	270
Valid Bonnet	Little Bonnet (Coronado's Quest)	3	9	3	2	2	132,806
Valid Bonnet	Val's Expo (Exploit)	2	1	1	0	0	13,800
Valid Carnauba	Any Reason (Unbridled)	4	2	1	1	0	30,780
Valid Carnauba	Boastful (Cozzene)	5	7	2	2	0	60,220
Valid Carnauba	Ebony Breeze (Belong to Me)	3	8	4	1	2	365,887
Valid Coins	Jewel Creek (Storm Creek)	3	17	1	4	3	12,503
Valid Coins	Rich Coins (Rizzi)	5	17	1	4	4	38,335
Valid Coins	Valid Skip (Skip Trial)	2	8	1	2	0	16,595
Valid Dawn	Rupert Haint (Haint)	3	18	2	1	1	10,903
Valid Dawn	Valid Flight (Meadow Flight)	5	9	3	1	0	58,695
Valid Design	Dr. Bombay (El Prado)	3	9	1	2	1	13,724
Valid Design	Heaven (Septieme Ciel)	6	12	4	1	2	16,030
Valid Doge	Swedish Son (Swedaus)	5	10	0	1	1	4,453
Valid Dream	Fun Maggie (Brogan)	2	4	0	0	0	2,160
Valid Eloquence	Rarest Love (Not For Love)	4	6	1	1	1	13,720
Valid Evidence	Anna's Cat (Storm Creek)	3	4	1	0	1	13,515
Valid Evidence	Coco's My Dream (Silver Ghost)	2	5	0	0	0	12,582
Valid Expression	Rich Expression (Rizzi)	4	9	3	0	1	22,594
Valid Fixation	Fan Appeal (Lear Fan)	4	5	1	0	1	32,320
Valid Fixation	More Influence (Southern Halo)	5	10	2	2	1	27,120
Valid Funding	Itsanewday (Wheaton)	2	4	0	1	0	2,455
Valid Gal	Forever Valid (Sunshine Forever)	8	11	0	1	3	4,225
Valid Gem	Gem of a Girl (Storm Creek)	3	1	0	0	0	0
Valid Gem	Madison's Wish (Eltish)	2	1	0	0	0	2,700
Valid Goddess	Broad Sanctions (Broad Brush)	3	6	1	1	0	7,920
Valid Goddess	Valid (Broad Brush)	4	7	2	1	2	18,255
Valid Joy	Valid Forum (Open Forum)	3	9	0	2	1	5,164
Valid Lassie	Valid Chad (Fuzziano)	3	2	0	0	0	175
Valid Lesson	Actcellent (Noactor)	3	9	2	4	1	105,590
Valid Lesson	Actxpedite (Noactor)	2	1	0	0	0	195
Valid Lesson	Valid Action (Noactor)	4	6	1	1	0	7,705
Valid Linda	Amazon River (River Special)	5	2	0	0	0	0
Valid Looker	Bye Bye Beylen (Fort Chaffee)	4	12	5	1	2	48,932
Valid Looker	Cullen (Repriced)	2	2	0	0	0	2,195
Valid Looker	Jaycejace (You and I)	3	12	1	1	5	21,884
Valid Metaphor	Princess Logan (End Sweep)	3	6	1	0	4	10,421
Valid Miss	Cowboy Cumbia (Kentucky Jazz)	5	7	1	0	1	7,752
Valid Miss	Olympia Prince (Fire Maker)	4	8	3	2	2	17,792
Valid Miss Zenda	Seattle Appeal (Hubble)	7	9	0	0	1	3,886
Valid Ms Cherokee	Waltz King (Leo Castelli)	5	5	0	1	1	14,360
Valid Nany	Bull Leave It (Holy Bull)	5	11	2	0	0	11,468
Valid Nany	Lullaby League (Rubiano)	4	4	1	1	1	28,870
Valid Obsession	Dark Torment (Devil's Bag)	4	3	1	0	0	7,925
Valid Obsession	Endless Obsession (End Sweep)	6	6	1	0	2	9,744
Valid Obsession	Soul Obsession (Diablo)	5	1	0	0	0	0
Valid Pache	Valid Hero (Sea Hero)	3	9	1	0	2	11,210
Valid Peak	Josie's Peak (Regal Search)	3	11	0	1	2	5,319
Valid Polly	Polly Moon (Migrating Moon)	5	14	1	2	4	9,885
Valid Precision	Fred's Notebook (Notebook)	3	2	0	0	0	880
Valid Pride	Case of Pride (Gold Case)	4	15	1	1	1	20,033
Valid Pride	Mc Meese (Notebook)	3	15	2	5	2	17,149
Valid Proclmation	Jeanie Sue (Level Sands)	4	13	2	1	3	51,078
Valid Risk	Risk It (Majesty's Imp)	4	16	2	4	1	9,478
Valid Search	Forum Search (Open Forum)	4	8	1	3	0	63,432
Valid Search	Rich Search (Rizzi)	5	7	4	0	0	45,665
Valid Silk	Valid Pro (Polish Pro)	3	6	1	1	0	35,316
Valid Skater	Cuban Mike (Diablo)	9	17	1	6	2	12,676
Valid Storm	Spankstress (Crafty Prospector)	5	9	1	0	2	5,045
Valid Storm	Storm in Philly (Smoke Glacken)	4	9	3	1	0	56,500
Valid Storm	Sweep in Philly (End Sweep)	3	12	7	1	2	60,310
Valid Story	Appeal to Reality (Real Courage)	6	4	0	0	0	225
Valid Story	Pretty Toni (Bold Anthony)	3	13	1	3	2	13,440
Valid Success	Mr. Meanie (Unzipped)	6	3	0	0	0	382
Valid Success	Outlandishlady (Lucky North)	4	10	0	0	1	2,308
Valid Sylvia	Up the Volume (Stop the Music)	5	7	1	1	1	5,041
Valid Symmetry	Symmetron (Awesome Again)	3	2	1	0	0	36,960
Valid Tenet	Cruzin Free (Free House)	2	6	0	0	1	4,310
Valid Tenet	Rainman's Request (Urgent Request)	4	2	0	0	1	3,960
Valid Trade	The Comissioner (Diplomatic Jet)	2	2	0	0	0	0
Valid Trade	Valid Jet (Diplomatic Jet)	4	11	0	2	0	4,131
Valid Triumph	Big League Lady (End Sweep)	3	3	1	0	0	14,760
Valid Victress	El General (El Prado)	4	9	0	1	2	33,852
Valid Warning	Albert G (Devil's Bag)	4	5	0	1	2	20,100
Valid Warning	Unbridled Ashley (Unbridled)	3	8	1	4	0	29,850
Valid Way	Sweeping Way (End Sweep)	5	14	1	2	2	10,909
Valid Way	Sweeptheway (End Sweep)	3	4	0	0	0	2,860
Valid Way	Valid Again (Awesome Again)	2	2	0	1	1	5,655
Validated	Field of Glory (Meadowlake)	4	8	1	1	1	26,120
Validated	Randaroo (Gold Case)	3	10	4	4	0	401,500
Valley Vixen	Secret Command (West by West)	4	5	1	0	0	6,390
Valnesian	Buffalo Soldier (Tactical Advantage)	3	16	4	2	5	41,250
Velvet Tulip	Cloud Walker (Phone Trick)	3	1	1	0	0	16,800
Velvet Tulip	Ole Rebel (Carson City)	4	6	1	3	0	43,580
Vennila Cream	Base Stealer (Saint Ballado)	3	9	0	0	2	6,500
Vennila Cream	Carefree (Unbridled)	6	21	3	4	5	33,696
Vennila Cream	Kazoo (Tabasco Cat)	5	7	1	1	2	67,590
Very Appealing	Power Appeal (Wolf Power)	6	4	0	1	0	874
Very Appealing	Very Gifted (Gift of Gib)	3	3	2	0	0	15,840
Vivio Appeal	La Chunk (Prospector's Halo)	4	17	5	0	4	66,149
Wellingtns Choice	Double Choice (Double Honor)	3	11	3	3	0	16,376
Wellingtns Choice	Exploit Choice (Exploit)	2	1	0	0	0	0
Wellingtns Choice	Gadir (Sejm)	6	9	0	1	0	3,690
Wrldly Possession	Montezuma's Gold (Red Ransom)	7	5	0	0	0	23,817
Wrldly Possession	Super Case (Gold Case)	3	2	2	0	0	72,240
You'll B Imprssed	Impressive Grades (Honor Grades)	7	3	0	0	1	9,480
You'll B Imprssed	Moon Bird (Meadow Flight)	5	15	1	2	1	22,600
You'll B Imprssed	Seductive Lady (Langfuhr)	2	7	2	1	1	36,020

Bold Ruckus, Dk B H (1976)
By Boldnesian – Raise a Ruckus, by Raise a Native

221 Performers, 135 winning performers, $6,719,445 total earnings

Mare	Progeny (Sire)	Age	Sts	1st	2d	3d	Money Won
Accadia Rocket	Gotta Jiboo (Tactical Advantage)	4	12	2	4	3	33,396
Accadia Rocket	Override (Wolf Power)	5	14	4	1	2	28,778
Accadia Rocket	Paco El Prado (El Prado)	6	8	0	3	0	12,284
Ada Ruckus	Darling Deputy (Silver Deputy)	5	3	0	0	0	3,151
Ada Ruckus	Markada (Miner's Mark)	4	1	0	0	0	1,377
Africo	Roar of Africa (Roar)	2	2	0	0	0	2,100
Air Walker	Air Driver (K. O. Punch)	3	9	2	2	1	34,771
Allegro Dancer	Admired (Deputy Bodman)	3	3	0	0	0	241
Andrea Ruckus	Bold Trader (Forest Wildcat)	2	6	1	2	1	43,169
Andrea Ruckus	Madiera (Silver Deputy)	4	8	2	0	0	67,980
Andrea's Bestgirl	Chris's Counter (Grey Counter)	5	8	1	0	0	8,179
Andrea's Bestgirl	Dames I Have Loved (War Deputy)	6	1	0	0	0	114
Anna's Ruckus	Rubber Neck (Way West)	3	8	1	0	0	4,246
Annie's Ruckus	La Vitesse (Joe Spatts)	7	4	3	0	1	36,480
Antique Ruckus	Cloud City (Miner's Mark)	6	7	0	1	1	9,098
Antique Ruckus	Rare Antique (Always a Classic)	4	10	1	0	1	17,386
Arctiana	Ossabaw (Brunswick)	3	12	2	0	2	12,034
Arctiana	Risen Ruckus (Risen Star)	5	7	0	0	1	1,311
Aromacor	Corenn (Hennessy)	3	5	0	0	0	0
Aromacor	Status (Kris S.)	4	3	1	1	0	41,000
Bald Ruckus	Ruby's Ruby (Mutakddim)	2	4	0	0	1	1,774
Ballybeg	Devil At the Wire (Devil His Due)	3	3	1	1	1	75,520
Bellarose	Super Gal (Tejabo)	4	2	0	0	0	0
Bellarose	Tejabelle (Tejabo)	5	17	3	6	3	35,357
Bodust	Bo's a Ten (Patton)	3	19	2	3	6	27,280
Bodust	Tubby Cat (Personal Flag)	6	3	2	1	0	38,370
Body Works	Body Image (Go for Gin)	4	7	1	2	2	9,218
Body Works	Golden Works (Banker's Gold)	3	1	0	0	0	0
Bolarity	Bolarity's Fuse (Lite the Fuse)	5	9	0	1	3	16,738
Bolarity	Explosive Wish (Explosive Red)	6	5	1	1	1	4,196
Bold Blast	High Volt Jolt (El Prado)	3	3	0	1	0	16,976
Bold Lady	Ring of Gold (Formal Gold)	2	4	1	0	0	5,700
Bold n Racy	Cajun Deputy (French Deputy)	4	10	3	1	1	20,043
Bold n Racy	Candeias (El Prado)	8	13	1	2	2	8,596
Bold Ruritana	Raw Power (Rahy)	3	6	1	0	1	54,708
Bold Threat	Cher Ami (Kitwood)	6	1	0	0	0	0
Bold Threat	Threaten (Mister Baileys)	3	9	0	0	1	3,990
Bold Vevila	Saucy Viv (Dr. Adagio)	3	6	0	0	1	5,482
Boldly	Bravely (Tejabo)	4	8	2	2	2	128,390
Boldly Extravagnt	Promenade Road (Dance Brightly)	3	6	1	2	2	75,703
Bounding Ruckus	Bound to Be Sunny (Sunny's Halo)	2	3	1	0	0	9,114
Bounding Ruckus	Kentucky Ruckus (Alphabet Soup)	4	6	2	0	1	21,065
Broadway Ruckus	Good Knight Story (Ascot Knight)	3	11	0	2	0	18,714
Broadway Ruckus	Hollywood Ending (Eagle Eyed)	5	9	2	2	0	95,578
Bunty's Sister	Lost in the Weeds (Lost Soldier)	4	2	0	0	0	0
Buxton Spice	Spice Rack (Sea Wall)	2	2	1	0	0	22,860
Buxton Spice	Spicy Engagement (Runaway Groom)	4	13	2	0	3	33,388
Calgary Miss	Seasonal Change (A Change for April)	5	5	0	0	0	700
Camomille	Capucine (Dance Brightly)	2	6	1	0	0	29,163
Camomille	Chiado (Meadowlake)	3	2	0	0	0	91
Camomille	Next to Heaven (Dehere)	4	6	1	1	0	8,870
Candid Colours	Orphan Lover (Friendly Lover)	4	11	2	1	3	63,150
Carenage	Goodbye Beautiful (Goodbye Doeny)	2	4	1	0	1	26,091
Carenage	Legs O'Neal (Nelson)	3	7	1	2	0	45,310
Carenage	Silent Ruckus (Silent King)	4	10	3	0	1	15,113
Carenage	Sutter's Ruckus (Sutter's Prospect)	5	12	2	2	2	17,987
Carolina Ruckus	Set to Sparkle (Lite the Fuse)	3	14	2	4	5	59,480
Castlemania	Battlements (Sea Wall)	3	9	4	2	2	265,150
Castlemania	Strike the Harp (Sea Wall)	2	4	1	0	1	46,545
Cause a Ruckus	Levada (Jambalaya Jazz)	2	2	0	0	0	1,077
Cause a Ruckus	Peakaboo Peak (Pyramid Peak)	3	13	2	2	2	86,051
Celmis	Buffalo Jump (Benny the Dip)	3	5	0	1	2	53,253
Celmis	Rheaxthus (Cozzene)	5	8	1	0	2	19,282
Celtic Harp	Celdif (Hadif)	3	3	0	0	1	638
Celtic Harp	Faxamillion (Islefaxyou)	4	8	1	2	1	35,040
Celtic Harp	Harpist (Gold Regent)	2	1	0	0	0	1,085

Certainly Super	Cipriani (Dr. Adagio)	2	1	0	0	0	0
Cheers and Tears	Touchmeifyoucan (Touch Gold)	3	1	0	0	0	0
Chi Sa	Lady Helma (Helmsman)	3	9	4	2	1	82,740
Christy's Ruckus	Conflictingopinion (War Deputy)	6	6	1	2	0	6,572
Christy's Ruckus	Ruff N Ruckus (Supremo)	5	1	0	0	0	0
Coastal Ruckus	A Diligent Ruckus (Diligence)	3	1	0	1	0	3,200
Coastal Ruckus	Red Hot Tequila (Time Bandit)	2	1	1	0	0	9,000
Corinna's Ruckus	Corey's Bluff (Pine Bluff)	5	4	0	1	1	25,863
Courageously	Attitude E. Ree (Character)	3	11	3	3	2	25,600
D'Or Ruckus	Lucky Ride (Sultry Song)	5	3	0	0	0	880
D'Or Ruckus	Oneheckofaruckus (Known Fact)	3	6	1	2	0	19,890
D'Or Ruckus	Taraxacum (Meadowlake)	4	1	1	0	0	9,900
Darley's Ruckus	Sayitain'tso Joe (Dr. Adagio)	3	11	1	2	4	52,734
Delightful	Felica's Ruckus (Barbeau)	3	3	0	0	0	0
Delightful	Landler (Langfuhr)	4	11	7	3	0	95,945
Devoted Angel	Eclipsing (Comet Shine)	2	1	0	0	0	336
Douce Douce	Dillinger (Sea Wall)	4	9	2	3	2	147,817
Douce Douce	Hands On (Friendly Lover)	2	3	2	1	0	41,070
Douce Douce	Piersixer (Sea Wall)	3	10	2	1	3	107,439
Douce Douce	Precision Hunter (Sea Wall)	5	7	0	0	0	332
Duck Legs	Waddle Me This (Consigliere)	3	3	0	0	0	482
Embur Sunshine	Aurora Tiger (Dance Brightly)	3	1	0	0	0	0
Embur Sunshine	Embattle (Phone Trick)	4	13	1	3	3	71,676
Embur Sunshine	Ten Flat (Meadowlake)	5	3	2	1	0	7,040
Fearless Vixen	Moe's Mon (Maria's Mon)	4	5	0	0	1	5,330
Florisa	Big Bloke (Trempolino)	4	2	0	0	0	273
Founder's First	Sweet Share (Danzatore)	3	4	0	0	0	1,500
Francsca's Rckus	Provost Marshall (Brocco)	6	2	0	0	2	2,860
Francsca's Rckus	Urban Space (Barkerville)	3	9	1	1	2	28,911
Full of Sparkle	Easy Design (Polka)	4	2	0	0	0	125
Gal in a Ruckus	Her Own Terms (Storm Cat)	4	2	0	0	0	2,840
Gallant Uproar	Jade's in Uproar (I Can't Believe)	2	2	1	0	0	20,178
Good Pharlap	Dronero (PAN) (Foxtrail)	5	4	0	0	2	2,166
Good Pharlap	Good Company (Quite Special)	6	12	1	0	3	29,461
Good Pharlap	Jolie Good (Mister Jolie)	3	13	2	0	4	25,734
Hillsburgh Rumrs	Winter Garden (Roy)	3	9	6	1	2	470,826
Holly Ruckus	Slewpy Ruckus (Slew of Angels)	3	6	1	1	0	22,512
Holly Ruckus	Slewth Slayer (Slew of Angels)	4	5	0	0	0	2,395
Hurricane Rosy	Legalize It (Lit de Justice)	3	3	0	0	0	0
Inaruckus	Brocco Bob (Brocco)	5	2	1	0	0	7,200
Indiana Jane	Dazzling Jane (Dazzling Falls)	4	9	4	1	2	68,550
Indiana Jane	Dazzling Ruckus (Dazzling Falls)	5	1	0	0	0	105
Josella	Josey Hill (Archers Bay)	2	1	1	0	0	38,820
Josella	Tenantry Road (Tejano Run)	3	8	1	3	1	27,207
Julie's Ruckus	Kiss for Julie (Kissin Kris)	3	12	4	0	1	39,632
Julie's Ruckus	Look Into the Past (Tacticl Advntage)	5	8	1	1	0	16,684
Keen Victory	Jaboo (Tejabo)	7	11	1	2	2	10,031
Keen Victory	Marco's Wish (Red Bishop)	5	1	0	0	0	149
Kennisis Bld Magi	Brass Ruckus (Brass Minister)	4	8	2	3	2	4,720
Lady Summerhill	Alyswell (Alysheba)	8	17	3	5	5	49,430
Lady Summerhill	Gastown (Ghazi)	2	2	0	1	0	12,120
Lady Summerhill	Summerhill Gal (Ghazi)	7	6	1	0	0	24,852
Laetare	Fortunate Buy (Fortunate Prospect)	2	3	1	1	0	18,455
Laetare	Lacy Lady (Jeblar)	4	7	2	0	1	18,575
Laetare	Swift Lad (Line In The Sand)	3	1	0	1	0	2,520
Lahaina Pearl	Back to Work (Signal Tap)	3	10	2	0	0	55,224
Lahaina Pearl	Bensonhurst's Best (Signal Tap)	5	3	0	0	0	795
Lahaina Pearl	Shyla's Diamond (Prosperous)	9	2	0	0	0	788
Last Reagent	Bright Reagent (Dance Brightly)	2	1	0	0	0	0
Last Reagent	Solina (Wild Rush)	3	2	1	1	0	47,040
Last Reagent	Wild Dare (Dare and Go)	5	12	0	2	1	16,053
Lemns Ain't Limes	Limone Forte (Dixie Brass)	3	9	2	3	1	87,870
Little Star Vicky	Starbeau (Barbeau)	5	4	0	0	0	1,315
Louvemeorleavme	Bold Lover (Petionville)	3	7	0	1	3	7,005
Louvemeorleavme	Friendly Departure (Friendly Lover)	4	8	1	2	0	11,140
Lucky Minister	Good Luck Strikes (Smart Strike)	2	1	0	0	0	0
Lucky Minister	Lucky Tec (Technology)	5	10	3	2	1	87,454
Lucky Minister	Meadow Minister (Meadowlake)	3	5	0	2	1	32,289
Lucky Minister	Oh Lucky Me (Belong to Me)	4	4	0	1	1	8,740
Majestic Ruckus	Gold Ruckus (Gold Alert)	5	6	3	2	0	68,000
Majestic Ruckus	Majestic Kris (Kissin Kris)	3	4	0	1	0	10,660
Maragin	Manjrekar (Storm Creek)	2	7	1	0	2	30,961
Miss Blue Bell	Bell's Lass (Tethra)	2	1	0	0	0	3,528
Miss Blue Bell	Mysterious Affair (Mysterious Vice)	6	12	1	3	4	214,926
Miyoshi	Southern Celebrity (Southern Halo)	3	3	0	0	1	4,323
Moonlit	Moonlit Romance (Romanov)	3	6	1	1	1	12,886
My Intended	My Vintage Port (Porto Foricos)	2	6	3	2	1	351,051
My Intended	Swooshel (Barbeau)	5	12	3	3	1	35,764
My Sweet Country	Deputy Country (Silver Deputy)	5	6	1	4	1	46,800
Numbronetreasre	Nine Carats (Langfuhr)	2	2	0	0	0	3,636
Opening Bid	La Grande Mamma (Compadre)	2	4	2	1	0	143,975
Opening Bid	Master Carver (Barbeau)	3	13	2	1	0	32,543
Peek a Boo Rckus	Deputy Ruckus (War Deputy)	3	5	0	0	0	0
Peek a Boo Rckus	Peek a Boo Sara (Great Gladiator)	5	9	1	0	0	44,337
Petite Duchess	Bold Nxs (In Excessive Bull)	2	8	4	1	0	45,586
Petite Duchess	Silver Set (Silver Deputy)	5	9	2	0	0	8,878
Playing Catch Up	Fortune Catcher (Fortunate Prspect)	2	8	1	2	1	24,500
Playing Catch Up	Fourtimesaruler (Formal Dinner)	3	11	1	2	3	22,385
Politely Streaking	Regal Council (Regal Classic)	5	8	1	1	2	6,196
Politely Streaking	Stop Looking (Dr. Adagio)	3	3	0	2	1	47,140
Positivly Stompin	By the Bay (Sea Wall)	3	11	0	0	0	5,139
Positivly Stompin	Spiffee Gal (Sea Wall)	2	1	0	1	0	11,760
Praise the Lady	Devoted Lover (Friendly Lover)	2	6	1	1	0	26,881
Precocious Queen	Tornado Alley (Mr. Greeley)	4	1	0	0	0	204
Princess Revenue	Princess Love (Friendly Lover)	3	6	2	3	1	34,130
Prone to Ruckus	Homecomingprincess (Home At Last)	7	8	1	1	0	12,695
Quick Observation	Midnight Velvet (Game Plan)	2	8	1	5	0	44,900
Quick Observation	Norm's Fire Light (Country Light)	4	4	0	0	2	1,680
Rainbow Mmories	Dr. Mo (Maudlin)	4	12	3	1	2	43,564
Rainbow Mmories	The Wildest Rose (Regal Remark)	7	7	1	1	2	11,235
Rambuckus	Betshe Hath a Way (Gilded Time)	3	1	1	0	0	16,830
Reason to Ruckus	Judge Ruckus (Judge T C)	3	10	1	2	2	25,316
Reason to Ruckus	Reason for Justice (Judge T C)	4	12	2	0	3	28,811
Renee's Reflection	Blazing Deputy (Silver Deputy)	4	6	0	0	1	4,035
Roshenara	Amazonian Brand On (Tethra)	3	3	0	0	0	311
Roshenara	California Kiss (Barbeau)	4	10	4	1	1	42,390
Rosie Ruckus	Raven Power (Known Fact)	4	2	0	0	0	0
Rosie Ruckus	Wild Bid (Wild Zone)	3	2	1	0	0	7,410
Ruck's Beauty	Native Ruck (Native Factor)	5	11	1	4	2	12,384
Ruck's Beauty	Ruck's Rapture (Native Factor)	4	6	0	0	0	402
Ruckin Angel	Ruckus in Court (Doneraile Court)	2	1	1	0	0	24,240
Ruckin Angel	Wings True (Is It True)	4	10	3	1	1	46,423
Ruckitas	Aristas (Sea Wall)	3	3	0	0	0	118
Ruckleberry	Believer's Lucky (I Can't Believe)	4	12	2	2	3	49,990
Ruckleberry	Believer's Ruckus (I Can't Believe)	2	6	0	0	0	3,918
Ruckleberry	Huck Berry (I Can't Believe)	3	5	1	1	0	8,658
Ruckus Pette	Whatta Big Ruckus (Big Wig)	4	9	2	1	2	44,798
Ruckus Ridge	Paradise Dancer (Langfuhr)	3	3	3	0	0	36,900
Ruffled Rose	Rose's Echo (Eastern Echo)	3	11	4	1	1	19,020
Sarannah	Maximum Degree (Jeblar)	4	19	1	2	1	7,245
Sarannah	Nautilus (Jeblar)	5	10	1	2	4	28,208
Sassytoga	Colebrook Creek (Tricky Creek)	7	11	4	2	0	33,482
Seattle Cyrina	Action Attraction (Wild Escapade)	4	11	3	1	1	40,136
Seattle Cyrina	Wild Cyrina (Wild Escapade)	3	15	1	2	2	19,035
Shadow Glen	Lite Ruckus (Matchlite)	4	13	1	0	2	7,798
Sissy Ruckus	Doran (Dr. Schwartzman)	9	5	1	0	0	11,730
Slick Prospector	Sassy and Blue (Dance Brightly)	3	4	1	0	0	11,466
Soft Sparkle	Silvanos (Swamp King)	6	3	0	0	0	366
Soiled Dove	Obliquity (Ascot Knight)	3	4	1	0	0	32,274
South Ocean Lane	Ariel's Melody (Sea Wall)	4	5	0	2	0	38,984
Spritely Strain	Champion Ri (Distorted Humor)	3	5	1	1	1	30,260
Spritely Strain	Tudor Court (Lord Carson)	4	10	4	1	1	89,590
Stanhope Magic	Inspired Magic (Inspired Prospect)	2	4	1	0	0	36,976
Studio Affair	Italian Accent (Bianconi)	2	1	0	0	0	0
Studio Affair	Speak Out (Victory Speech)	3	12	1	0	0	64,819
Summer Ruckus	Excess Summer (In Excess)	3	10	6	2	0	294,261
Sweet and Silent	Not Again Dan (Green Dancer)	2	3	0	0	1	6,666
This Weeks Spcial	Oklahoma Natural (Northern Jay)	2	1	0	0	0	100
This Weeks Spcial	Outrider (Northern Jay)	5	8	1	2	1	3,275
This Weeks Spcial	Raven Riot (Northern Jay)	7	4	0	0	0	265
Tobie Ruckus	Psych (Mazel Trick)	2	1	1	0	0	21,700
Tobie Ruckus	Tobias (Barbeau)	5	4	3	0	1	43,550
Tobie Ruckus	Tobie Lang (Langfuhr)	3	12	1	3	1	40,018
Unique Gal	Unique Devil (Devil His Due)	4	11	1	1	4	34,143
Voile Rouge	Fle'che Rouge (Mr. Greeley)	4	16	3	1	3	40,645
Voile Rouge	Foggia (Unaccounted For)	3	16	6	0	1	41,711
What'salltherckas	Sweet Bay (Archers Bay)	2	1	0	1	0	11,760
Winter Feathers	Goose Feathers (Honour and Glory)	4	1	0	0	0	62
Wolfe Island	Cypress Hill (Tri Line)	3	4	1	1	1	9,950
Yousurearebold	Afterdinnerthunder (Formal Dinner)	2	4	0	0	0	1,437
Yousurearebold	Senorita Sirianni (Strike the Gold)	4	5	0	0	0	1,053
Zadracarta	Carta Gold (Touch Gold)	2	2	0	0	1	3,220
Zadracarta	Major Zee (Dayjur)	10	7	5	0	1	52,052
Zadracarta	Zacharov (Cool Victor)	9	14	5	3	1	47,490
Zandalusia	Zanda's Bonus (Bonus Money)	2	5	0	1	1	13,180

Storm Bird, B H (1978)

By Northern Dancer – South Ocean, by New Providence

225 Performers, 118 winning performers, $6,654,708 total earnings

Mare	Progeny (Sire)	Age	Sts	1st	2d	3d	Money Won
Accounts Squared	Grand Coolee (Souvenir Copy)	3	1	0	0	0	0
Accounts Squared	Welcome Sign (Gulch)	4	7	1	1	0	10,056
Allison's Dance	Seeking Red (Red Ransom)	3	9	1	0	3	9,188
Alydar's Storm	Alyode (Rhodes)	2	3	0	0	0	202
Alydar's Storm	Spunky Storm (Spunky Rascal)	4	8	0	0	0	708
Andrea Gail	Areyoutalkintome (Smokester)	2	3	1	0	2	14,640
Ardor	Circle Z (Wild Gold)	3	14	1	1	3	16,473
Ardor	Sandy Time (Man From Eldorado)	7	6	0	0	0	336
Auction Cat	Livestock Auction (Marlin)	2	6	1	1	2	6,015
Audy's Bird	Reverberation (Roar)	2	4	0	0	0	205
Avian Eden	Avanzado (Luhuk)	6	7	2	1	0	202,645
Balanchine	Gulf News (Woodman)	4	2	0	0	0	0
Bay Colony	Guy Getaway (Meadowlake)	2	2	0	2	0	17,200
Big B's Secretary	Spanish Rioja (Patton)	2	4	1	0	0	3,855
Bird Dance	High Rhode (Rhodes)	5	9	0	1	5	3,919
Bird Dance	Stormy Honor (Bound by Honor)	3	4	0	1	0	1,281
Bird Dance	The Storm Trackerr (Covered Wagon)	4	22	1	5	4	14,342
Bird to the Wire	Tick to the Wire (Supremo)	3	9	0	0	2	2,151

Bluegrass Queen	King Walter (Walter Willy)	3	3	0	0	0	225
Boom Bird	Endeavor (Capote)	5	2	1	0	1	36,925
Boom Bird	Higher Impact (Fly Till Dawn)	8	2	0	0	0	300
Boom Bird	Kakapo (Silver Charm)	2	1	0	0	0	137
Boom Bird	Mauk Eight (Capote)	3	4	2	0	1	48,225
Bruces Blue Lou	All American Blue (Phone Trick)	3	8	2	2	1	70,558
Bruces Blue Lou	Pacing the Cage (Salt Lake)	5	13	3	2	2	53,090
Brutally Honest	Jiffy Lou (Wavering Monarch)	5	11	1	0	0	5,340
Brutally Honest	Then Today Always (Miswaki)	2	2	0	0	1	4,191
Cascateira	Ocnus (Latin American)	5	7	3	0	0	29,040
Castleberry	Glitterberry (Glitterman)	5	8	1	1	1	7,784
Cent Nouvelles	Ann Dear (Grand Slam)	3	12	4	1	2	87,975
Centennial Time	Academy Lass (Royal Academy)	2	5	0	1	0	8,125
Centennial Time	Clay Time (Two Punch)	4	9	3	2	3	15,931
Centennial Time	Finisterre Rock (Miner's Mark)	7	13	1	2	4	22,720
Centennial Time	One Hundred Slews (Seattle Slew)	8	1	0	0	0	0
Centennial Time	Time Goes Fast (Diesis)	3	7	0	1	0	1,877
Chimes Bird	Hawaiin Gold (Wild Rush)	2	1	0	0	0	0
Chimes Bird	Ringading (Gilded Time)	3	2	0	0	1	3,000
Classy Mirage	Golden Prospect (Mr. Prospector)	3	1	0	0	1	6,468
Classy Mirage	Mickey's Mirage (Deputy Minister)	2	2	0	2	0	18,000
Classy Mirage	Mike's Classic (Seeking the Gold)	4	12	5	3	2	183,520
Cruise Ticket	Welcome Aboard (Avenue of Flags)	4	9	3	1	0	37,275
Curlew	Bluebayouman (Boone's Mill)	4	5	1	3	0	6,655
Curlew	Brant Lake (Distinctive Pro)	6	5	0	0	0	423
Curlew	Scotch and Rum (Indian Charlie)	3	2	0	1	0	7,280
Deanna's Special	Corrigan (Pleasant Colony)	4	12	2	2	3	63,880
Dear Birdie	Bird Town (Cape Town)	3	8	3	4	0	815,976
Dear Birdie	Birdstone (Grindstone)	2	3	2	0	0	339,000
Dear Birdie	Brave All the Way (Cryptoclearance)	8	6	0	1	0	2,380
Dear Birdie	Cviano (Rubiano)	6	7	0	0	1	970
Demi Souer	City Sister (Carson City)	3	10	3	2	4	133,330
Demi Souer	Fast Decision (Gulch)	4	4	0	0	2	10,920
Demi Souer	Treasure Seeker (Gold Fever)	2	1	0	0	0	0
Elusive Bird	Classic Bird (Sky Classic)	5	4	0	0	1	5,310
Elusive Bird	Missing Silks (Elusive Quality)	3	5	0	3	0	7,340
Emotional Storm	You and You Alone (You and I)	6	3	1	1	0	7,638
Encorevous	City Fair (Carson City)	5	1	0	0	1	5,980
Encorevous	Lorenzon (Carson City)	2	2	1	0	0	8,820
Endless Storm	Ana's Lady Bird (Lord Carson)	2	4	2	0	1	65,190
Endless Storm	Endless Torrential (Torrential)	5	1	0	0	0	0
Endless Storm	Endofthestorm (Lord Carson)	4	17	3	3	6	32,901
Endless Storm	Macho Image (Clever Trick)	3	7	2	0	1	41,400
Exclusive Bird	Alert (Unbridled)	4	4	4	0	0	56,400
Exclusive Bird	Gone Exclusive (Gone West)	3	3	2	0	0	46,600
Exclusive Bird	Private Ryan (Quiet American)	6	8	0	0	2	9,775
Extraterrestral	Alienated (Gone West)	4	9	3	1	2	81,625
Falconette	Big Head Phil (Stalwars)	4	8	1	1	0	6,889
Falconette	Stormy Wars (Stalwars)	6	7	0	0	2	3,087
Festal	Fax Blitz (Smokester)	4	10	3	1	1	26,220
Fixin to Storm	Barometric (Kris S.)	4	4	2	1	1	73,664
Fixin to Storm	Miffed (Artax)	2	1	0	0	0	1,230
Flaming Gold	Flame Song (Unbridled's Song)	5	11	1	3	0	45,039
Flaming Gold	Striking Flames (Smart Strike)	4	9	0	1	1	4,970
Flamingo's Pride	Expert Design (Event of the Year)	2	2	0	0	1	2,660
Flamingo's Pride	Pride of the Group (General Meeting)	6	15	2	4	4	17,404
Flight to Rome	Fit Zun (BRZ) (Choctaw Ridge)	5	8	0	0	1	4,922
Flying Lauren	Jackdaw (Gulch)	2	1	0	0	1	2,340
Foufa	Certantee (Known Fact)	6	5	1	1	0	57,750
Foufa	Foufa's Warrior (Jade Hunter)	3	10	1	1	3	257,358
Foufa	Full Brush (Broad Brush)	8	11	1	1	1	63,670
Foufa	Maryland Mist (Cozzene)	4	4	0	0	0	3,500
Foufa	Media Access (Devil's Bag)	5	6	0	1	4	42,953
Give a Toast	Juventus (Mazel Trick)	2	2	1	0	1	36,327
Good Taste	A Spire a Dream (Marquetry)	2	2	0	0	0	252
Halcyon Bird	Miss Paranoid (Honor Grades)	2	1	0	0	0	810
Highland Legend	Hanover Hollywood (Gulch)	6	7	0	0	1	7,740
Highland Legend	High Potential (Pleasant Colony)	4	6	0	0	1	6,860
Highland Legend	Personal Legend (Awesome Again)	3	9	2	3	1	183,010
Indian Ocean	Snowball Flannagan (Affirmed)	8	4	1	1	0	29,000
Indian Sunset	Quick Action (Carson City)	2	2	1	0	0	30,030
Karri Valley	Trebizond (Sadler's Wells)	7	8	2	0	1	147,488
Kelpie	Stormin Inthe West (West by West)	3	8	1	0	2	8,613
Knoosh	Anja (Gulch)	3	2	0	0	0	0
Lady for Two	Deep Thunder (Gulch)	4	10	1	1	2	7,266
Lady of Choice	Dr. Walsh (Gulch)	3	3	0	0	0	5,400
Lady of Choice	Multiple Choice (Mt. Livermore)	5	4	0	0	2	39,121
Lady of Mine	Chairman of Vice (Woodman)	3	11	1	0	3	6,530
Louisiana Band	Golden Louisia (Formal Gold)	3	16	1	3	1	17,910
Lovely Martha	Castle Spring (Kingmambo)	4	3	0	0	1	4,420
Lovely Martha	Port Henry (Conquistador Cielo)	5	4	0	1	0	5,570
Lovely Martha	Sand Springs (Dynaformer)	3	7	4	1	0	451,390
Low Pressure	Cedar Summer (Souvenir Copy)	2	8	1	0	2	35,240
Maremaid	Glitter Maid (Glitterman)	3	17	3	3	0	40,860
Maremaid	Tea Is Served (Boston Harbor)	2	4	0	0	0	1,680
Mariscal	Betunome (Unome)	3	1	1	0	0	3,120
Middle Course	Aurora Gold (Mutakddim)	3	10	4	2	1	19,330
Middle Course	Dr. Reed (Affirmed)	8	4	0	0	0	635
Middle Course	General Nancy (Marlin)	4	1	0	0	0	0
Middle Course	Sanskrit (Pancho Villa)	10	5	0	3	1	5,318
Middle Course	Tonyrony (Marquetry)	5	12	3	3	4	42,300
Midway Squall	Itchetucknee (Carson City)	3	5	0	0	0	3,070
Midway Squall	Juniper Springs (Wekiva Springs)	5	2	1	1	0	35,000
Migrate	Divine Bird (Saint Ballado)	3	2	1	0	0	29,820
Miss Madisyn Rse	Christian Gulch (Gulch)	3	10	2	0	2	18,630
Miss Popularity	Paralegal (Skip Trial)	6	6	0	0	1	2,070
Miss Tenenholtz	Extra Check (Chequer)	4	5	0	0	0	14,730
Miss Tenenholtz	Extra Fit (Fit to Fight)	3	12	1	1	1	28,600
Miss Tenenholtz	Margie Golden (Golden Gear)	2	3	1	0	0	15,720
Miss Tenenholtz	Our R. N. (You and I)	5	9	3	2	0	12,372
Namaqua	Goodnight Trail (Gulch)	6	13	0	2	2	17,826
No Ordinary Strm	No Ordinary Stone (Grindstone)	3	3	0	0	2	2,600
Olympic Storm	Olympic Emblem (Our Emblem)	2	1	0	1	0	2,700
Olympic Storm	Storm Gulch (Gulch)	3	3	0	0	0	4,120
Oogie Poogie	Dial for Dollars (Woodman)	7	13	0	0	0	1,516
Oogie Poogie	I'm a Goer (Favorite Trick)	3	11	1	2	3	59,300
Pacific Squall	Nor'wester (A.P. Indy)	2	1	0	0	0	2,280
Pacific Squall	Sea Storm (Gulch)	6	8	0	1	0	3,344
Pacific Squall	Wind Sand n' Stars (Gone West)	3	5	0	0	1	1,912
Pasque Flower	Raging Bird (De Niro)	5	5	0	0	0	620
Pasque Flower	Wolf Running (Wolf Power)	2	1	0	0	0	0
Pasque Flower	Wood Lily (American Chance)	6	20	3	2	5	48,722
Petit Oiseau	Samsville (Barkerville)	3	12	1	1	3	10,145
Petit Oiseau	Stormin' Oiseau (Pioneering)	5	8	1	2	2	7,975
Pocket Beauty	Miss Beauty (Miswaki)	4	2	1	1	0	5,856
Precious Parrot	Birdland (Hazaam)	3	17	2	3	2	31,575
Precious Parrot	Johnny Tornado (Lycius)	2	6	2	1	0	28,612
Queen's Visit	Fiorano (Abaginone)	4	2	0	0	0	0
Rainy Day Woman	Party Boy (Go for Gin)	4	10	0	1	1	3,842
Rajas Secret	Hi School Football (Take Me Out)	5	4	0	0	0	960
Raven Runner	Crafty Runner (Crafty Prospector)	6	15	1	3	1	27,670
Red Rock Lake	Method Actor (De Niro)	3	8	1	0	2	12,745
Red Rock Lake	Waconda Lake (Fantastic Fellow)	2	4	1	0	1	7,950
Red Soul	Paris Sunrise (Cape Town)	3	4	1	2	1	52,220
Red Soul	Unbridled Soul (Unbridled)	4	5	0	0	0	1,757
Rogatien	Buster B Bimbo (Numerous)	6	6	0	1	0	2,488
Rogatien	Gracefully Yours (Prospect Bay)	3	6	0	1	0	2,695
Rogatien	Native Tribe (Our Native)	11	5	0	0	1	1,860
Rogatien	Our Winston (Black Tie Affair)	9	5	0	1	1	1,483
Rosebird	Peekaboo Cat (Crafty Prospector)	2	1	0	0	0	145
Running Redhead	Lethal Instrument (Gulch)	7	5	1	1	0	28,875
Running Redhead	Rouquine (Gulch)	3	3	0	0	1	5,360
Samba Storm	Kinnelon (Our Emblem)	4	9	2	0	0	14,420
Sassy Bird	Chercheuse (Seeking the Gold)	5	3	0	0	1	16,688
Sassy Bird	Osprey (Seeking the Gold)	6	18	2	1	4	10,143
Savannah Storm	Lady in Tails (Black Tie Affair)	6	8	0	2	1	37,064
Savannah's Honor	Star of Savannah (Holy Bull)	3	9	1	0	0	14,805
Secret Harbor	Charming Jim (Silver Charm)	2	7	1	2	1	53,105
Shared Emotion	Golden Authority (Acceptable)	3	8	4	1	1	20,202
Shroud Remark	Bold Glory (Honour and Glory)	5	2	0	0	0	225
Shroud Remark	Quick Draw Makah (Phone Trick)	4	4	0	0	3	4,200
So Bad Your Good	The Voice (Twining)	5	1	0	0	0	0
Sooty Tern	Logan Field (Boston Harbor)	4	1	0	1	0	2,100
Sooty Tern	Lucky Lefty (Boundary)	2	3	1	1	0	36,672
Star Bird	Arbitrage (Banker's Gold)	3	1	0	0	0	150
Star Bird	The Editor's Son (Mr. Greeley)	4	6	1	0	1	11,900
Star Ridge	Five Stars (Bahamian Bounty)	4	1	0	0	0	360
Starfire	Fever Fire (Gold Fever)	2	1	0	0	0	0
Steady Gaze	Prairie View (Honor Grades)	4	7	0	2	2	4,225
Steady Gaze	Raise the Stripes (Pembroke)	3	12	4	1	1	76,890
Storm Alley	Iverson (Rubiano)	4	15	7	2	4	71,280
Storm Alley	Twister Alley (Comstock Lode)	2	3	0	0	1	2,680
Storm Attack	Center (Gulch)	4	6	3	0	0	46,620
Storm Attack	Wild Bill Hiccup (Carson City)	3	19	0	3	0	17,380
Storm Berry	Black Ties Ferrari (Black Tie Affair)	7	10	0	0	2	1,980
Storm Berry	Stormin Tammy (Tamayaz)	4	6	1	0	0	4,746
Storm Bride	Distant Venture (Geiger Counter)	8	13	2	4	3	14,179
Storm in Sight	Andrew the Man (Carson City)	6	8	2	1	0	15,069
Storm o' Fire	Fiery Diablo (Diablo)	5	8	1	3	1	45,190
Storm o' Fire	Fiery Sweep (End Sweep)	4	7	1	0	0	24,160
Storm Riding	Audrey Hep (Crafty Prospector)	3	5	2	2	0	77,374
Storm Struck	Savannah's Gold (Gold Fever)	2	2	0	0	1	1,650
Storm Teal	Gold Storm (Seeking the Gold)	3	5	4	0	0	53,700
Storm's Award	Quick Silver Miss (Silver Ghost)	3	12	2	2	0	24,611
Storm's Award	Stormy Conquest (Cnquistadr Cielo)	4	9	2	0	1	29,280
Storm's Honor	Emeralds (Grindstone)	3	8	1	2	2	7,590
Storm's Honor	Rocaco (Geiger Counter)	6	6	4	0	2	48,000
Stormfeather	Girl Gone Crazy (Roar)	2	1	1	0	0	13,800
Strmin Diamnd A	Jake Skate (Arch)	3	4	0	2	1	18,360
Strmin Diamnd A	Katestormedthebird (Out of Place)	2	1	0	1	0	3,000
Strmin Diamnd A	Rotunda Beauty (Phone Trick)	4	13	2	2	1	10,674
Stormin Jane	Colonial Storm (Colonial Affair)	3	4	0	0	0	0

Stormin' In	Saint Stormin' (Saint Ballado)	3	3	0	2	0	3,500
Storming Lass	Towering Storm (Irish Tower)	9	16	4	3	2	40,575
Stormwilhit	Sir Norman (Brentwood Style)	4	3	1	0	0	1,770
Stormy Bend	Candybedandy (Holy Bull)	3	9	2	1	2	77,260
Stormy Bend	Speedy Ransom (Red Ransom)	4	14	2	1	1	16,350
Stormy Divorce	False Promises (Jules)	3	13	3	3	1	210,740
Stormy Jewel	Stoneringer (West by West)	3	14	1	2	2	6,498
Stormy Lass	Stormy Colebrook (Twining)	5	9	0	0	0	5,840
Stormy Moment	Navesink View (Holy Bull)	4	3	1	0	0	6,000
Stormy Moment	No Approval Needed (Lastng Approvl)	3	1	0	0	0	210
Stormy Moud	American Moud (Quiet American)	2	4	0	0	0	365
Suddenly Sydney	Distorted Humor Jr (Distorted Humr)	3	13	1	1	2	11,135
Suspicious Storm	Raffie's Storm (Raffie's Majesty)	3	10	2	2	2	61,455
Sweet Tease	Bucyrus (Rahy)	2	1	0	0	0	0
Sweet Tease	Raw Speed (Matty G)	4	3	0	0	0	119
Thor Baby	Youmakemethorbaby (Two Punch)	5	1	1	0	0	13,200
Tomisue's Storm	Storm's Roar (Roar)	3	3	1	0	0	4,670
Tricky Bird	Stanley Park (Swain)	3	8	3	0	1	123,316
Umbrella	Parachute (Polish Numbers)	2	1	0	0	0	0
Wajibird	Mel's Marque (Marquetry)	6	14	2	4	3	21,558
Wajibird	No Regular Cat (Cat Doctor)	2	2	0	1	0	1,012
Wajibird	Sedona Run (Boone's Mill)	3	5	0	0	0	588
Wander Storm	Glitter Storm (Glitterman)	3	11	3	2	0	25,730
Wander Storm	Wander Mom (Maria's Mon)	5	3	1	0	0	53,000
Wander Storm	Wander Time (Gilded Time)	2	4	1	0	1	14,250
Water Street	Miss Adams (Quiet American)	2	2	0	0	0	0
Weekend Flight	Dawnie Wonder (Victory Gallop)	2	1	0	0	0	0
Westwood	Stormy Surprise (Mr. Greeley)	4	6	1	0	1	5,668
Windmill Point	Exclamation (Capote)	2	2	0	0	1	7,200
Windmill Point	Patriot's Pride (A.P. Indy)	3	6	1	0	0	10,414
Windmill Point	Sugar Mags (Miswaki)	6	11	3	2	0	33,868
Wings of a Storm	Cryptic Storm (Cryptoclearance)	4	10	0	1	3	3,586
Wings of a Storm	Mistys Dark Angel (Traitor)	3	6	0	0	1	1,128
Youwntmetodowht	Paparazzi (Press Card)	4	13	3	5	4	66,045
Zanzaritaville	Cash Again (Petionville)	3	14	2	1	2	10,430

Crafty Prospector, Ch H (1979)
By Mr. Prospector – Real Crafty Lady, by In Reality

261 Performers, 146 winning performers, $6,079,316 total earnings

Mare	Progeny (Sire)	Age	Sts	1st	2d	3d	Money Won
A Tad Crafty	Crafty Connection (Lake George)	3	4	0	0	0	600
A Tad Crafty	Stubbsville (Truckee)	2	3	0	0	0	0
Above Reproach	Above the Devil (Devil His Due)	2	5	1	0	1	29,330
Above Reproach	Crafty Deed (Alydeed)	6	14	3	2	3	14,991
Above Reproach	Fleur de Sel (Ocean Crest)	5	8	3	1	1	120,409
Above Reproach	Kalki's Pride (Regal Classic)	3	16	1	3	4	48,218
Above Reproach	Regal Reproach (Regal Classic)	4	10	0	2	1	24,634
Ailsa	Regalian (Regal Classic)	4	3	0	0	0	1,152
Amarillo	Mystic Hawk (Joyeux Danseur)	3	8	2	2	2	43,658
Ancora	Amber Run (Hazaam)	4	9	0	0	3	2,980
Ancora	Zam Lady (Hazaam)	3	10	1	0	1	6,963
Annalong	Willy Nilly (Norquestor)	4	10	1	2	1	24,995
Arctic Gold Rush	Gold City Slew (Slew City Slew)	4	6	1	1	0	23,049
Arctic Gold Rush	Symphony of Gold (Chimes Band)	3	9	1	1	2	10,350
Baby Jinx	J's Crafty Cat (Tabasco Cat)	3	3	1	0	0	8,700
Bazzie	Dazzled Bayou (Bayou Blurr)	7	8	1	0	0	3,834
Bazzie	El Cisc (El Prado)	3	11	1	3	2	21,003
Beautiful Craft	Cryptocraft (Cryptoclearance)	3	12	0	3	4	19,055
Beautiful Craft	Princess Malice (Smoke Glacken)	2	1	0	0	0	1,260
Beyond the Sky	Alphabetic (Alphabet Soup)	3	4	2	1	0	33,220
Beyond the Sky	J J Wish (Wild Rush)	2	2	0	0	1	2,530
Blushing Princess	First Blush (French Deputy)	3	13	2	3	4	153,750
Blushing Princess	Mickey's Queenmary (King of Kings)	2	3	0	0	0	95
Bold Brittney	Gentle Brittney (Gentlemen)	2	5	1	0	0	15,000
Brilliant Lew	Here Is Lew (Summer Squall)	2	2	0	0	0	100
Burning Season	Hot Weekend (Summer Squall)	2	7	1	1	3	72,915
Burning Season	Macrorie (Runaway Groom)	3	3	0	0	0	809
C. Windy	C. Garrett (Ogydoug)	3	1	0	0	1	1,155
C. Windy	Lighting Jay (Ogydoug)	4	17	0	1	1	2,915
Cagey Baby	Cagey Codger (Lord Carson)	5	4	2	0	0	7,086
Cagey Baby	Ohforcraftsakes (El Prado)	4	4	0	1	0	11,780
Catchthecat	Catchthegroom (Stravinsky)	2	5	1	1	1	24,670
Chandelle	Beat the Traffic (Stormy Atlantic)	2	6	1	1	0	23,393
Chandelle	Crafty Notebook (Notebook)	3	2	0	0	0	280
Cheap Wine	Ebb n' Flow (Indian Charlie)	3	7	2	2	1	37,090
Cheap Wine	The Blank Vanman (Louis Quatorze)	4	6	3	0	1	45,150
Coffee Springs	Pine for Java (Pine Bluff)	3	14	3	2	1	85,280
Coldncrafty	Danny's Star (Red Screen)	3	7	0	0	0	105
Cool and Smart	Monument Valley (Air Forbes Won)	6	12	4	1	2	46,216
Crafty 'n Sassy	Here 'n' Sassy (Dehere)	3	3	0	0	0	2,080
Crafty 'n Sassy	Miss Crafty (Pyramid Peak)	2	2	0	0	0	0
Crafty 'n Sassy	St. Crafty (St. Jovite)	5	1	0	0	0	0
Crafty Annie	Crafty Deer (Deerhound)	4	9	0	0	0	1,045
Crafty Barbie	Miss Barbie Slew (Ocala Slew)	3	22	1	2	1	9,921
Crafty Belle	Belle of Portugal (Bertrando)	3	5	2	1	1	46,120
Crafty Bride	Crafty Comment (Skip Trial)	7	4	0	0	0	1,636
Crafty Bride	Great Account (Top Account)	3	1	0	0	0	360
Crafty But Sweet	Fair Winds (Dynaformer)	3	8	0	1	1	10,595
Crafty Casa	Crafty Song (Unbridled's Song)	3	7	2	0	1	55,790
Crafty Cassandra	Sugar Lake Lass (Run Softly)	3	11	1	1	0	7,014
Crafty Clementine	Miss Gold Diva (Strike the Gold)	4	6	1	1	2	6,288
Crafty Clementine	So Hot (Fit to Fight)	2	2	1	0	0	6,100
Crafty Country	Mammy (Vaudeville)	2	5	0	0	0	760
Crafty Country	Quick Country (Brunswick)	6	3	0	0	0	132
Crafty Country	Samjack (Cryptoclearance)	3	4	0	1	0	1,170
Crafty Devil	Deputy Devil (Silver Deputy)	3	1	0	0	0	0
Crafty Devil	Minister Lady (Silver Deputy)	4	11	3	1	3	34,539
Crafty Devil	Pensive Mood (Maudlin)	5	5	1	2	1	11,150
Crafty Ember	Crafty Wildcat (Forest Wildcat)	4	11	2	2	1	26,301
Crafty Ember	Pampered Princess (Indian Charlie)	3	7	3	0	3	72,370
Crafty Ember	Storm Craft (Forest Wildcat)	5	7	3	1	0	93,250
Crafty Emerald	Wildcat Dee (Forest Wildcat)	3	2	0	0	0	0
Crafty Example	Crafty Case (Dynaformer)	8	8	1	0	1	8,500
Crafty Gal	Steph's Meadowlake (Meadowlake)	2	2	1	0	0	11,700
Crafty Gypsy	Salt Flat (Salt Lake)	3	2	0	0	0	300
Crafty Jam	Crafty Move (Silver Deputy)	3	8	1	2	0	46,750
Crafty Josie	Crafty Creek (Strodes Creek)	5	9	2	1	0	30,990
Crafty Lady	Pretty Cozzene (Cozzene)	4	9	1	1	4	23,750
Crafty Lady B.	Amanda Rules (Mr. Greeley)	5	3	0	0	0	2,850
Crafty Lady B.	Hadtoomuch (Hadif)	3	17	0	2	1	8,925
Crafty Lass	Beso Del Sol (Whitney Tower)	5	15	1	5	2	42,305
Crafty Lass	Chasmo (Future Storm)	4	11	1	1	2	30,356
Crafty Lass	K. K.'s Kiss (Kipper Kelly)	3	4	0	1	1	6,580
Crafty Magic	Cat's Craft (Mountain Cat)	3	12	3	2	2	36,380
Crafty Marian	Red Booom (Explosive Red)	3	10	2	1	0	26,310
Crafty Marian	Red Wrecker (Explosive Red)	2	3	0	0	0	780
Crafty Melody	Crafty Account (Top Account)	4	7	1	0	0	4,765
Crafty Melody	Picki (Top Account)	3	4	0	0	0	2,130
Crafty Mims	Andrea (Unaccounted For)	2	4	1	1	0	8,380
Crafty Nan	Granite Peak (Mt. Livermore)	5	3	0	0	0	0
Crafty Oak	Harbor Craft (Boston Harbor)	2	3	0	0	0	3,360
Crafty Personality	Guten Tanzen (Green Dancer)	5	2	0	0	0	81
Crafty Personality	Mount Tora Bora (Peaks and Valleys)	3	1	0	0	0	0
Crafty Promise	Calvin's Promise (Polish Numbers)	4	9	1	0	1	6,100
Crafty Promise	Sea of Promises (Sea of Secrets)	2	5	2	3	0	64,250
Crafty Quarry	Barnabus (Sea Salute)	5	5	1	0	0	10,050
Crafty Quarry	Super Skip (Skip Away)	3	3	0	0	1	1,890
Crafty Quarry	Unrelenting Desire (Belong to Me)	6	10	0	1	3	7,105
Crafty Question	Bryce (Gilded Time)	2	2	0	0	0	0
Crafty Question	Crafty Wac (Patton)	3	4	0	1	0	3,551
Crafty Rafk	Nooney Cake (Quick Departure)	6	4	0	1	1	4,680
Crafty Sands	Sandmandu (Scatmandu)	2	3	0	0	0	1,020
Crafty Sarre	Crafty Dan (Langfuhr)	2	3	0	0	1	1,639
Crafty Sarre	Mirush (Alydeed)	3	3	0	0	0	1,890
Crafty Siren	Dolly Dynamite (Lite the Fuse)	3	6	0	2	0	26,988
Crafty Starlet	Tuff Number (American Standard)	10	15	0	0	2	2,773
Crafty Time	Mon Dieux (Montbrook)	2	2	0	0	0	460
Crafty Ville	Concertoville (Concerto)	3	4	0	0	0	1,230
Crafty Ville	Crafty Note (Notebook)	5	3	0	1	0	2,460
Crafty's Star	Pippinella (Personal Flag)	3	4	1	1	1	6,154
Crafty's Wish	Useyourimagination (Quest for Fame)	5	7	2	2	1	33,400
Crama	Formidable Storm (Storm Boot)	2	2	0	1	1	5,580
Crama	La Prado (El Prado)	4	9	2	3	1	20,620
Crama	Stormin Ty (Storm Boot)	3	7	0	0	1	820
D. Lady	Be Concerned (Concern)	3	11	1	1	1	12,047
Dream Queen	Duncan's Gold (Gold Fever)	3	6	1	1	0	5,440
Dream Queen	Sultry Breeze (Sultry Song)	4	1	0	0	0	56
Dylan's Crafty	Ashwood C C (Cryptoclearance)	5	10	5	4	0	184,164
Dylan's Crafty	Dylan's Girl (Well Decorated)	4	5	0	0	0	968
Early Bull	Bull Headed Harry (Northern Afleet)	3	10	1	1	3	23,360
Early Bull	Eric's Toy (Gate Dancer)	7	9	0	0	0	553
El Gato Loco	Takeit Or Leave It (Patton)	3	2	0	0	1	2,820
Emphatic Style	Style Champ (Salt Lake)	4	8	3	2	1	43,410
Emphatic Style	That Phat Cat (Mountain Cat)	3	8	1	0	1	11,000
Emphatic Style	The Madison Man (Sultry Song)	6	13	2	3	2	25,747
Enchanted Acorn	Marlig (Atticus)	2	1	0	0	0	0
Enchanted Acorn	Price of Passion (Romanov)	3	3	0	1	0	3,676
Fair Majesty	Pine Penny (Siberian Pine)	4	4	0	0	0	510
Fair Majesty	Princess Jen (Stutz Blackhawk)	6	11	1	3	0	52,100
Foolish Return	Craft Brewin (Magesterial)	8	10	1	2	0	2,141
Foolish Return	Fit to Keep (Fit to Fight)	3	2	1	0	0	4,520
Foolish Return	She Be Brewin (River Special)	4	3	0	0	0	293
For all Seasons	Jezebella (Wild Again)	4	9	1	0	0	7,300
Forgive Me Please	Michener (Ascot Knight)	7	15	4	4	3	69,526
Forgive Me Please	Mission of Love (Atticus)	3	6	1	1	0	5,128
Foxy Digger	Foxy Guy (Line In The Sand)	3	10	3	2	1	23,615
Freeze the Gold	Year for Gold (Half a Year)	4	1	0	0	0	0
Front Row Center	Heavenly Rose (Helmsman)	4	14	1	2	3	30,905
Gamble for Gold	Grand Gamble (El Gran Senor)	4	3	0	0	0	380

Gamble for Gold	Tactical Gamble (Tactical Cat)	2	3	0	0	0	1,380
Gloria's Pleasure	Bobbinjean (Alphabet Soup)	3	6	1	0	1	20,269
Gloria's Pleasure	Game Set Match (Wild Zone)	4	6	0	0	0	890
Gloria's Pleasure	Kristi's Pleasure (Hadif)	6	15	1	0	4	8,416
Gold Button	Flying Canuck (Alphabet Soup)	3	4	0	0	0	9,396
Golden Chip	Lil's a Real Lady (Peaks and Valleys)	3	5	1	0	2	40,830
Grand Investment	Tall Order (Diamond Sword)	3	3	0	0	0	923
Holly Creek	Will's Journey (Will's Way)	3	2	1	1	0	32,800
Hopeful Prospect	Flashdance Star (Joyeux Danseur)	2	1	0	0	0	0
Hyper Hopper	Shelbi's Star (Brogan)	4	6	0	1	0	1,600
Hypersonic	Brighton Belle (High Brite)	5	7	2	1	0	36,354
Inquisitive Look	Magic Forest (Forestry)	2	1	0	0	0	0
Isla Mujeres	Shapes and Shadows (Dynaformer)	3	7	0	0	2	58,638
Isla Mujeres	Tempestuous Lady (Storm Boot)	2	1	1	0	0	22,800
Islandia Princess	Island Prince (Hunting Hard)	3	2	0	0	0	200
Islandia Princess	Princess Terlingua (Wheaton)	5	12	3	3	1	27,272
Islandia Princess	Sword Princess (Sword Dance)	6	1	0	0	0	143
Jeanne's Fancy	Borders Edge (Tethra)	3	2	0	0	0	214
Jeanne's Fancy	Crocus Rose (Tethra)	2	3	1	0	0	36,350
Key On Me	Crafty Key (Indian Charlie)	3	1	0	0	0	0
Kitcho	Willie B Good (Williamstown)	3	9	0	0	2	1,602
Lady Zip	Salty n' Foxy (Salt Lake)	4	6	3	0	3	58,440
Lalou	Crafty Taylor (Capote)	4	10	1	1	1	21,770
Laughngtothebnk	Aristide the Great (Missionary Ridge)	4	15	3	2	4	21,952
Lead Soprano	Mom's Deer (Deerhound)	4	5	2	0	1	9,930
Lead Soprano	Singing Laur (Sky Classic)	2	6	2	2	0	44,120
Lone Star Angel	Lonely Angel (Dixieland Heat)	3	4	1	1	0	11,300
Looking for a Win	Mandarin Marsh (Sea Hero)	6	4	0	0	1	1,568
Looking for a Win	Tappy (Pleasant Tap)	4	10	1	4	4	75,575
Lunar Gold	Moon Tap (Signal Tap)	3	5	0	0	0	2,200
Meg's Habit	No Bad Habits (Roanoke)	9	8	0	2	3	18,260
Meg's Habit	Schemer (Concern)	2	6	1	2	1	59,770
Meg's Habit	Sea Cloud (Housebuster)	4	9	2	1	2	73,310
Meg's Habit	Smiling Bob (Anjiz)	6	1	0	0	0	115
Merlin's Gold	Hello Judy (Secret Hello)	4	13	1	1	5	11,876
Mischief Seeker	Lookin for Love (Colonial Affair)	6	9	5	1	0	34,465
Miss Digger	Sea Leon (Sir Leon)	5	12	6	2	0	91,030
Miss Golden Circle	Mister Manx (Storm Cat)	3	8	1	0	1	18,270
Miss Gourmet	Fast Dish (Roy)	4	16	5	1	1	22,944
Miss Gourmet	Harry's Rainbow (Sunny's Halo)	5	12	1	1	2	6,694
Miss Moneywise	Wise Money (Mystery Storm)	2	5	1	0	0	15,550
Miss Prospector	Gold Dollar (Seattle Slew)	4	13	1	0	3	53,385
Miss Prospector	Hot Line (Capote)	2	2	0	0	0	650
Miss Tahoe	Colleen's Jackpot (Synastry)	3	16	2	2	1	18,790
Miss Tahoe	Jackpot Party (Synastry)	2	4	1	0	0	6,750
Miss Witchcraft	Bruheria (El Prado)	3	2	1	0	1	35,760
Mr. P's Lady	Further (Manila)	6	1	0	0	0	0
Mr. P's Lady	Wild Tip (Southern Halo)	5	13	4	3	0	37,285
Nay Nay Renay	Ragtime Miss (Rinka Das)	5	8	3	0	1	28,020
Nay Nay Renay	Winspear (El Prado)	3	11	1	5	1	35,823
Nikki B. Mine	Makeup Girl (Vaudeville)	2	5	0	0	0	320
Nikki B. Mine	Newport Nikki (Lit de Justice)	3	2	0	1	0	5,450
No Anxious Mmnts	Danny's Way (Regal Classic)	3	12	2	3	2	16,984
Not So Shy	Sister Breeze (Defrere)	4	10	2	2	2	20,455
Okay Babe	Crafty Babe (Fortunate Prospect)	2	1	0	1	0	3,800
Okay Babe	Ok Kiely (Jeblar)	4	7	1	1	0	4,320
Okay Babe	Our Thomas (Jeblar)	9	3	0	0	0	110
On Line One	Charm Attack (Slew Mood)	4	11	2	1	3	12,934
One Crafty Lady	Samaria (Desert Classic)	6	4	0	0	0	450
One Crafty Lady	Summer Sport (Siberian Summer)	3	7	1	0	0	14,110
Othila	Crafty Conveyor (Conveyor)	6	5	0	2	0	5,358
Othila	Don Hector (Silver Buck)	3	13	2	1	1	26,405
Othila	Notable Craft (Notebook)	7	8	0	3	1	20,240
Pat's Misty Gold	Pat's Cowgirl (Tejano)	5	6	1	2	0	7,690
Pennant Winner	Secret Liaison (Housebuster)	5	4	2	0	0	136,719
Pretty Crafty	Pretty Cagey (Elusive Quality)	3	11	2	4	0	61,720
Pretty Crafty	Pretty Sly (Press Card)	4	13	0	2	4	23,645
Pretty n Crafty	Hadif Time Machine (Hadif)	4	5	2	1	1	23,198
Pretty Quick	Angie A (Signal Tap)	5	10	1	0	0	4,114
Pretty Quick	Dixie Jazz (Dixie Brass)	3	13	1	3	1	9,965
Pretty Quick	Jolie (Crusader Sword)	4	2	0	1	1	13,770
Pretty Quick	Uppatuppa's Charm (Williamstown)	2	6	2	0	0	22,294
Princess Joanne	In the Clear (Cryptoclearance)	4	12	3	1	2	57,425
Princess Joanne	Winning Fans (You and I)	3	6	0	1	1	19,400
Progressive Lady	Bel Air Belle (Runaway Groom)	5	2	1	0	0	13,200
Progressive Lady	Boots Malone (Bates Motel)	7	2	0	0	0	420
Progressive Lady	Lady Bates (Bates Motel)	6	4	0	0	0	215
Progressive Lady	Shesa Strodes Lady (Strodes Creek)	3	10	0	1	1	3,890
Progressive Lady	St Soarbay (Captain Bodgit)	4	12	1	3	0	29,820
Prospectr Diamnd	Ooh Sammy (Odyle)	3	6	0	0	0	530
Prospectr Diamnd	The Grand High Ho (Unaccountd For)	4	16	4	3	2	72,715
Proud n' Crafty	Buck'n and Duck'n (Ocala Slew)	5	12	1	2	1	17,381
Proud n' Crafty	Sune (Maria's Mon)	3	7	0	1	2	9,380
Quick and Kind	Billow (Meadowlake)	5	5	1	0	1	10,257
Quick and Kind	Joyful Kay (Tomorrows Cat)	2	5	1	1	0	7,360
Raining Rainbows	Crystal Vision (Belong to Me)	3	11	1	1	0	21,864
Rapid Rosa	Ferene (El Prado)	6	4	0	0	0	105
Rapid Rosa	Rapid Jett (Groovy Jett)	4	9	0	0	0	0
Ray's Crafty Lady	Really Ladylike (For Really)	3	7	2	1	1	9,147
Real Crafty Belle	Northern Deputy (Deputy Commandr)	2	1	0	0	0	0
Rominna	Crafty Hero (Partner's Hero)	3	14	3	1	2	30,805
Rosey Prospector	Ali's Rose (Ali Gaziba)	5	8	0	2	1	6,240
Sigrun	Drifa (Tabasco Cat)	5	5	0	4	0	23,931
Sigrun	Sira (Capote)	4	10	1	2	3	48,705
Sigrun	Storm Breaking (Storm Cat)	3	2	1	0	1	21,100
Soliloquy Song	Stack Song (Stack)	4	3	0	1	0	2,730
Spend the Money	Invest the Money (Carr de Naskra)	3	2	0	1	0	1,900
Spottd Prospectr	Heybaby (Ocean Crest)	3	3	0	0	0	495
Spottd Prospectr	Mahican (Doneraile Court)	2	6	0	3	0	17,750
Spottd Prospectr	Spotted Flag (Personal Flag)	6	1	0	0	0	0
Streamliner	Premier Liner (Premiership)	5	6	2	1	0	9,385
Streamliner	Silent Olimpian (Olympio)	4	6	1	3	1	21,710
Stringtown Sally	Rufustheroadrunner (Open Forum)	3	7	1	1	2	18,580
Stringtown Sally	Stormy Seas (Storm Creek)	5	9	0	2	1	19,050
Stringtown Sally	Stringtown Wonder (Wild Wonder)	2	5	1	2	1	38,850
Strum the Banjo	Cloud Chief (Cherokee Run)	2	4	1	2	0	11,280
Strum the Banjo	Sheila's Wildcat (Forest Wildcat)	4	6	0	0	1	1,575
Subtle Dancer	Baryshnikov's Song (Sultry Song)	6	5	2	1	0	19,300
Subtle Dancer	Bull's Ear (Hesabull)	2	2	0	0	0	880
Subtle Dancer	Tapper (Lost Code)	5	17	2	4	5	38,716
Subtle Fragrance	Soto (Dehere)	3	3	2	1	0	473,200
Sue's Ruby	Segovia (Cryptoclearance)	3	8	1	0	2	32,680
Svenska Flyer	Canadian Flyer (L'Enjoleur)	6	9	1	0	1	20,920
Svenska Flyer	Dj's Bucky Buster (Fair Skies)	3	9	3	0	2	16,987
Swiss Prospector	Colonel Courtney (Mt. Livermore)	3	11	2	2	1	36,187
Theheartofdixie	Stonewood (Tomorrows Cat)	2	5	1	0	1	13,900
Touch of Joy	Emilin (Scatmandu)	2	1	0	0	0	135
Twist the Knife	Quick Nip (Whiskey Wisdom)	4	6	3	0	1	58,380
Twist the Knife	Shesagamer (Farma Way)	7	2	0	0	0	570
Ultimate Strike	Saturday's Warrior (Red Ransom)	3	2	1	0	0	4,200
Unlimited Prospct	Highlandflowergirl (Haymaker)	4	15	0	3	0	5,500
Up Poplar Creek	Attic (Atticus)	3	7	2	4	0	47,760
Up Poplar Creek	Crafty Cobra (Cobra King)	4	9	1	1	2	9,659
Vegas Prospector	Sheer Luck (A.P. Indy)	2	6	2	1	2	79,280
Win Crafty Lady	Harmony Lodge (Hennessy)	5	8	5	1	2	516,300
Win Crafty Lady	John's Rockfleet (Kris S.)	7	9	1	1	2	12,122
Win Crafty Lady	Mister C's Song (Unbridled's Song)	3	1	1	0	0	25,690
Win Crafty Lady	Win's Fair Lady (Dehere)	4	10	3	2	0	114,185
Winnie D.	Littlebigthing (Unbridled's Song)	4	3	0	1	1	10,500
Winnie D.	Romancer (Mt. Livermore)	5	16	0	2	4	9,390
Yecein	Chatter Fox (Foxhound)	4	14	3	0	3	16,943
Yecein	Hailey B (Beau Genius)	3	14	3	4	3	56,155

Woodman, Ch H (1983)

By Mr. Prospector – Playmate, by Buckpasser

197 Performers, 99 winning performers, $5,692,256 total earnings

Mare	Progeny (Sire)	Age	Sts	1st	2d	3d	Money Won
Acquired Merit	Misconception (Bertrando)	6	8	5	0	1	23,410
Acquired Merit	Silent Thunder (Bertrando)	7	8	2	0	1	18,177
Acquired Merit	Six Penny Lane (Bertrando)	4	3	0	0	0	375
Ajfan	Mutamayyaz (Nureyev)	7	4	1	1	0	35,700
Alibi Pride	Clemency (Lil E. Tee)	5	9	0	2	1	6,987
Alibi Pride	Comprador (Ordway)	3	2	0	1	0	7,700
Alibi Pride	Excuse (With Approval)	4	10	1	2	1	11,686
Arctic Interlude	Arctic Sand (Sandpit (BRZ))	4	13	2	4	1	30,510
Arctic Interlude	Forest Landing (Forest Wildcat)	3	4	3	1	0	84,223
Arctic Interlude	Tabacchi (Horse Chestnut)	2	4	1	2	0	78,400
Arctic Interlude	Wood Kat (Mountain Cat)	7	6	3	2	1	31,420
Artistic Art	Artist's Meeting (General Meeting)	3	8	1	3	0	11,730
Babeinthewoods	Moonstone Bay (Skywalker)	3	3	0	0	0	6,200
Babeinthewoods	Spicoli (Southern Halo)	2	2	0	0	0	0
Birchfrost	Haughty Lady (Tale of the Cat)	3	3	0	1	0	5,210
Bosra Sham	Rosberg (A.P. Indy)	2	2	1	0	0	26,180
Breadcrumb	John Galt (Belong to Me)	4	6	1	1	1	6,174
Broadway Music	Halos for Hibiscus (Southern Halo)	3	13	3	0	1	33,400
Broadway Music	New York Harbor (Boston Harbor)	2	5	2	0	0	69,470
Broadway Music	Santoni (Sea Hero)	7	1	0	0	1	840
Butterwood	Woodmans Smile (Ops Smile)	2	6	1	0	0	7,610
Carelaine	Caesarion (Danehill)	4	1	0	0	0	12,000
Caribbean Sol	Wild Caribe (Wild Zone)	2	6	1	1	1	26,497
Caribbean Sol	Wild Celebration (Wild Zone)	4	1	0	0	1	4,050
Carpenter's Lace	Carpenter's Halo (Sunny's Halo)	7	2	0	0	0	0
Carpenter's Lace	Contested (Prenup)	4	12	2	3	2	39,025
Carpenter's Lace	Organic (Sunny's Halo)	9	18	2	4	5	15,295
Carpenter's Lace	Tap Wood (Pleasant Tap)	3	1	0	0	0	200
Charon Fruits	Dell Place (Royal Academy)	4	8	2	2	1	97,117
Charon Fruits	Nextofkin (Capote)	2	2	0	0	0	0
Crazy Canard	Intemperate (Dynaformer)	3	5	1	0	0	13,360
Crazy Canard	Maxinkuckee (Cryptoclearance)	2	3	0	0	0	0

Crystal Woods	City Diamond (Slew City Slew)	2	2	0	0	0	180
Crystal Woods	Tomprado (El Prado)	4	10	3	1	1	26,860
Crystal Woods	Woodmont (Dumaani)	3	9	1	0	0	5,539
Daad	Daad's Hot (Tabasco Cat)	4	15	3	1	4	33,795
Daad	Kosade (Cozzene)	3	4	1	0	0	24,980
Dinka Raja	Geebeekay (Peintre Celebre)	3	13	2	0	2	15,893
Donusa	Paint Ballado (Saint Ballado)	2	3	0	1	0	7,260
Donusa	Uncle Vic (Spinning World)	4	15	1	2	2	24,918
Elbow	Dr. Kathy (Polish Numbers)	2	6	2	0	3	75,485
Emily Thomas	Port Royal Ciel (Septieme Ciel)	6	3	0	0	1	1,350
Emily Thomas	Sea My Darling (Sea Hero)	3	3	0	0	0	1,514
Energise	Lord of the Cats (Tale of the Cat)	2	5	1	1	1	23,650
Energise	Wekiva Woods (Wekiva Springs)	5	8	1	2	1	10,060
Evening Charmer	Capital Charm (Meadowlake)	2	8	2	0	2	29,420
Evening Charmer	Legendary Prince (Concerto)	3	13	2	4	1	28,790
Fast and Fancy	Fancy M. D. (Glitterman)	4	14	6	0	2	64,780
First Flag	Canadian Alliance (Private Terms)	5	5	0	2	2	14,774
First Flag	Duet (Allied Forces)	2	4	1	2	0	104,845
Flaming Mirage	Ballado Chieftan (Saint Ballado)	3	5	1	2	0	58,260
Floridana	Climay (Ocean Falls)	6	1	0	0	0	0
Flower Garden	Crimson and Roses (El Prado)	3	10	2	3	1	109,800
Flower Garden	Kato's Garden (Katowice)	5	13	0	2	1	7,647
Flower Garden	Petals (Dr. Caton)	2	1	0	0	0	125
Flying Angel	Flight Training (Honour and Glory)	3	11	3	0	0	38,808
Flying Angel	Uncle Arthur (Honour and Glory)	2	1	0	0	0	0
Forest Garden	Deep in the Woods (Southern Halo)	2	1	0	0	0	2,050
Forest Queen	Queens Are Wild (Wild Zone)	2	5	2	0	0	24,754
G I C Verdict	Squaw Valley (Indian Charlie)	3	12	2	0	2	32,540
Gay Gallanta	Gallant (Rainbow Quest)	6	6	1	0	0	27,440
Gliding Lark	A Gentle Man (French Deputy)	3	15	0	1	2	12,820
Gliding Lark	Anne's Girl (Key Contender)	4	2	0	0	0	0
Hawkwood Liz	Mighty Mud Bug (Lord Avie)	6	6	0	1	3	10,735
Hawkwood Liz	Take Me Down (Take Me Out)	3	3	2	0	0	18,240
Hujjab	Hyjab (Rahy)	2	4	1	1	0	29,100
Idle Worker	Idle Storm (Storm Creek)	3	11	1	1	1	5,886
Idle Worker	Wimauma Mama (Dixie Brass)	5	16	3	2	2	28,661
Jolie Bois	Trieste's Honor (Old Trieste)	2	4	0	0	1	8,100
Kathie's Colleen	Six Sexy Sisters (Langfuhr)	2	2	2	0	0	140,218
Kathie's Colleen	Wando (Langfuhr)	3	8	5	1	1	2,017,323
Kindred Soul	Soul of Kindness (American Day)	4	3	0	1	0	8,190
Kurmond	Economy (Furiously)	3	8	1	0	0	5,400
Kurmond	Forthcoming (Furiously)	2	3	1	0	0	7,200
Lady in Waiting	Pick a Winner Max (King of Kings)	3	2	0	0	0	0
Limberlost Star	Did We Win (Patton)	3	11	1	1	2	24,845
Limberlost Star	Spirit Star (Polish Navy)	2	2	0	1	0	1,280
Limberlost Star	Tidal Crest (Ocean Crest)	5	3	0	0	0	0
Limberlost Star	Titanic Star (American Standard)	7	13	1	0	0	3,930
Magic of Sunrise	Award Winning Team (Genrl Meeting)	3	1	0	0	0	0
Maple Heart	Dynaheart (Dynaformer)	3	3	0	0	0	0
Maple Heart	Mauk Me (Keos)	2	5	1	0	0	4,754
Maple Heart	Wild Maple (Wild Again)	4	15	0	2	4	37,000
Markham Fair	Ain't She Quaint (Tabasco Cat)	3	3	0	0	0	320
Markham Fair	Big City (Storm Boot)	4	3	1	0	0	22,640
Mary Sloan	Indiana Knight (Langfuhr)	4	3	0	0	0	540
Mary Sloan	Rush to Defend (Wild Rush)	3	4	0	0	0	1,230
Minkover	Brunswood (Brunswick)	4	8	1	0	1	13,185
Miriah	Railroad Red (Glitterman)	2	1	0	0	1	2,390
Miriah	Red's Honor (Glitterman)	5	7	1	1	0	40,780
Miss Woody	Wonderful Miss (Honor Grades)	3	13	2	2	2	25,829
Mixmatch	Match Up (Afternoon Deelites)	4	1	0	0	1	1,080
Mixmatch	Mixed Truce (Brief Truce)	8	6	1	0	0	5,027
Mixmatch	Three Roses (Southern Halo)	3	4	1	0	1	34,239
Moon Is Up	Seven Moons (Sunday Silence)	3	3	0	1	0	10,960
Mrs. Paddy	Paddy's Dasher (Deputy Commander)	3	7	0	0	0	1,307
Ms. Teak Wood	Ansky (Kris S.)	6	10	0	1	2	5,718
Ms. Teak Wood	Midnightresolution (Capote)	2	5	0	0	1	4,795
My Cherie	Hemisphere (Southern Halo)	2	4	0	0	0	340
My Cherie	Skidoo (Senor Speedy)	4	4	1	0	1	20,100
Novel Encounter	Banned in Boston (Boston Harbor)	3	10	4	2	0	119,870
Novel Encounter	Hydrogen (Pleasant Colony)	4	10	2	3	2	175,764
Nuit Chaud	Nelson Street (Fastness)	5	5	0	0	0	2,908
Parcae	Furious Chad (Furiously)	4	11	0	1	1	10,695
Parcae	Shulana (Shuailaan)	3	3	0	0	1	704
Parker's Cove	Catlike Move (Tabasco Cat)	4	10	0	1	2	25,020
Parker's Cove	Park the Car (Gilded Time)	3	9	2	1	0	48,030
Parker's Cove	Ransom Cove (Red Ransom)	6	1	0	0	0	0
Passionnee	Parfumeur (Anabaa)	3	2	0	0	0	0
Pledge	Bianconi Baby (Bianconi)	2	3	1	1	0	11,203
Pledge	Pledge of Peace (Unaccounted For)	3	6	0	1	2	7,890
Port Plaisance	Best Play (Theatrical)	3	3	0	0	0	1,220
Pressed and Ready	Ready for Glory (Honour and Glory)	3	8	3	0	2	24,462
Pretty Flower	Empire Man (Ride the Rails)	4	5	0	0	0	0
Profound Peace	Acadian Style (Langfuhr)	3	1	1	0	0	4,200
Profound Peace	Patti Peach (Forest Wildcat)	5	6	0	1	0	3,902
Prospctive Prince	Roman N Royal (Royal Academy)	4	1	0	0	0	650
Rawya	Erimos (Desert King)	4	10	2	1	2	44,770
Reed	Reedastraffer (King of Kings)	2	1	0	0	0	0
Roxanne	Master Salty (Salt Lake)	4	14	1	3	1	8,575
Roxanne	The Hanging Judge (Judge T C)	3	3	0	2	0	9,255
S S N Phoenix	Alexandria (Out of Place)	3	17	3	3	7	87,170
Safe Harbor	Private Harbor (Private Terms)	2	2	1	0	0	12,060
Scouting	French Embassy (French Deputy)	2	2	0	0	0	125
Scouting	Rooster's Deputy (French Deputy)	3	4	0	1	0	6,000
Sean's Woodman	Easy Ian (Dixieland Band)	4	5	1	0	0	10,320
Sean's Woodman	Sean's Baby (Thunder Gulch)	2	1	0	0	0	0
She's a Woodman	Sulka (Fast Forward)	5	1	0	0	0	330
Shell Ginger	Clarins (Storm Cat)	2	2	0	1	0	9,200
Shoo Bee Doo	John Dool (Midnight Tiger)	6	5	1	0	0	5,402
Silk Masque	Wildwood Royal (Royal Academy)	3	13	5	1	0	152,150
Silvita	Fillygris (Langfuhr)	3	1	1	0	0	8,550
Silvita	Singleton (Highland Ruckus)	5	1	0	0	0	0
Snow Forest	Winter Glitter (A.P. Indy)	6	1	0	0	0	130
Soft Pine	Sandyland (Silver Hawk)	5	11	2	1	3	18,656
Soft Pine	Twin Pines (Pine Bluff)	6	5	0	0	0	544
Solid Proposal	Snuggle Up (Lord Avie)	5	15	1	1	0	6,773
Splintered Life	Last Place (Fast Play)	2	1	0	0	0	0
Star Mesa	Private Oasis (Private Terms)	5	8	2	2	1	85,525
Star Mesa	Sandina (Capote)	2	4	0	0	0	1,941
Star Mesa	Starlet Approval (With Approval)	3	7	0	0	1	9,539
Star Mesa	With a Star (With Approval)	4	5	0	1	1	8,080
Star Scoop	Cherri Knight (Slew the Knight)	4	14	0	2	2	7,060
Star Scoop	Midnight Summit (Personal Flag)	3	8	0	0	2	10,390
Taylor's Playmate	G. W.'s Squall (Summer Squall)	2	1	0	0	1	3,080
Taylor's Playmate	Warren's Classic (Sky Classic)	3	9	1	3	0	39,287
Tennessee	Don't Be Cruel (Joyeux Danseur)	3	9	1	0	0	15,520
Tennessee	Pansy Garden (Cryptoclearance)	4	9	2	1	1	13,173
Tigress Woman	Ancient Remedy (Wild Again)	3	7	1	1	0	25,042
Tigress Woman	Boston Navigator (Boston Harbor)	2	1	0	0	1	3,300
Tigress Woman	Tigress Woods (A.P. Indy)	4	11	1	0	0	27,298
Tropez	Baby Angel (Gentlemen)	3	6	1	0	0	34,068
Tropez	Dame Sylvieguilhem (Nureyev)	4	3	1	0	0	30,000
True Grit	Kiss Kiss (Pleasant Colony)	4	2	0	2	0	5,600
True Grit	True Charisma (Charismatic)	2	8	0	0	1	3,000
Turf Legend	Legendary Lady (Virginia Rapids)	5	4	0	0	0	4,260
Villa d'Este	Gringo Joe (Botanic)	6	15	4	2	1	35,703
Wildwood Lady	Hero Wood (Sea Hero)	4	6	0	1	1	2,648
Wildwood Lady	Wildwood Skier (Appealing Skier)	2	7	1	1	0	7,490
Willie Wood	Ben's Lady (Atticus)	3	9	1	2	0	4,460
Willie Wood	Camden Pine (Pine Bluff)	5	7	2	1	0	21,625
Willie Wood	Passing Willie (With Approval)	4	4	1	1	1	4,841
Willie Wood	Retention Bonus (French Deputy)	2	5	0	0	0	200
Willow Woodman	Dance Lessons (Foxhound)	4	3	1	1	1	53,140
Willow Woodman	Robyn Regal (Robyn Dancer)	3	1	0	0	0	480
Wood of Binn	Prohibitionist (Capote)	2	2	0	0	0	0
Wood of Binn	Three Wonders (Storm Cat)	6	1	0	0	0	400
Wood Rivr Womn	Agua Fria Express (Just a Tune)	5	3	0	0	0	0
Wood Rivr Womn	Hysteria (Hadif)	7	10	0	1	0	1,056
Wooden Table	Mr. McCabe (Becker)	5	14	1	2	3	32,190
Wooden Table	Real Quiet Heath (Real Quiet)	2	4	0	0	0	1,320
Woodja	Norwoods (Deputy Minister)	3	2	0	0	0	103
Woodja	Saucy Cat (Tabasco Cat)	6	10	1	0	0	19,354
Woodja	Seattle Woodja (Seattle Slew)	5	3	0	0	0	1,786
Woodland Orchid	Cedar Sea (Persian Bold)	4	2	0	0	0	0
Woodman's Girl	Always Ready (Dixieland Band)	4	3	1	1	1	22,280
Woodman's Lady	Ladies Meetings (General Meeting)	3	2	0	0	2	4,800
Woodman's Lady	Papa Sids Girl (Souvenir Copy)	2	2	1	0	1	36,225
Woodman's Pride	Papeete (Lear Fan)	2	6	0	0	1	1,190
Woodmn's Wondr	Fastman (Fastness)	5	2	0	0	0	1,020
Woodmn's Wondr	Out of the Bag (Sir Cat)	4	15	3	2	6	59,850
Woodmiss	French Miss (French Deputy)	5	9	1	2	0	13,820
Woodmiss	French Snob (French Deputy)	3	3	0	0	0	980
Woodsia	Lahooq (Indian Ridge)	4	7	1	1	1	25,235
Woodside Road	Hello Woodson (Secret Hello)	6	8	1	2	1	2,684
Woodside Road	Pasquale (Digression)	7	2	0	0	0	0
Woodsong	Damar Wayne (Moscow Ballet)	4	4	1	0	1	16,380
Woodsong	Winston Chi (Cee's Tizzy)	5	5	0	0	0	6,808
Woodyoubelieveit	Wouldyoutouchgold (Touch Gold)	3	2	0	0	0	795
Woodyousmilfrme	Grave Digger (Red Ransom)	2	4	0	0	0	2,990
Worthy Prospect	Clevertrickyman (Clever Trick)	2	4	0	2	0	5,185
Worthy Prospect	Worthy Adversary (Devil's Bag)	3	6	1	1	0	8,800
Worthy Prospect	Worthy Soldier (Personal Flag)	4	10	3	1	2	41,905
Young and Daring	Daring Skipper (Skip Away)	3	4	0	0	0	909
Zienat	Tree Lover (Dumaani)	2	10	2	3	0	23,020
Zuppa	Red At the Helm (Helmsman)	3	13	3	1	2	33,468
Zuppa	Red Earthquake (Tale of the Cat)	2	1	0	0	0	1,800

Annual Leading Broodmare Sires – Money Won

Year	Sire	Mares	Perfs.	Sts.	1st	2d	3d	Amt. Won	Year	Sire	Mares	Perfs.	Sts.	1st	2d	3d	Amt. Won
1937	Sweep	85	140		271	217	278	$382,744	1971	Double Jay	105	202	2,263	290	319	266	2,051,296
1938	Fair Play	76	129		254	260	230	408,369	1972	Princequillo*	134	238	2,262	297	267	269	2,722,783
1939	Sir Gallahad III*	55	95		168	149	156	480,018	1973	Princequillo*	149	241	2,237	322	246	265	3,071,322
1940	High Time	70	134		247	255	236	335,807	1974	Olympia	103	174	2,058	297	254	235	2,300,121
1941	Sweep	65	115		217	197	236	462,587	1975	Double Jay	131	238	2,651	329	341	358	2,233,642
1942	Chicle*	66	113		205	166	196	533,572	1976	Princequillo*	118	202	2,027	266	250	274	2,778,695
1943	Sir Gallahad III*	110	195		365	334	311	703,301	1977	Double Jay	130	233	2,325	300	321	279	2,696,490
1944	Sir Gallahad III*	129	236		447	432	387	1,024,290	1978	Crafty Admiral	95	172	1,848	260	220	220	2,295,375
1945	Sir Gallahad III*	138	236		362	364	335	1,020,235	1979	Prince John	133	207	1,764	281	226	213	2,895,534
1946	Sir Gallahad III*	153	276		475	470	466	1,529,393	1980	Prince John	132	210	1,875	282	258	223	3,434,042
1947	Sir Gallahad III*	152	273		465	407	432	1,458,309	1981	Double Jay	90	153	1,509	187	193	180	3,471,976
1948	Sir Gallahad III*	156	302		433	462	456	1,468,648	1982	Olden Times	119	185	1,598	256	229	179	3,235,590
1949	Sir Gallahad III*	165	317		537	519	502	1,393,104	1983	Buckpasser	72	114	796	117	111	86	3,482,059
1950	Sir Gallahad III*	178	345		542	568	507	1,376,629	1984	Buckpasser	72	108	794	104	87	117	5,140,500
1951	Sir Gallahad III*	176	341		587	607	578	1,707,823	1985	Speak John	74	122	987	127	96	108	5,189,390
1952	Sir Gallahad III*	173	344		567	575	569	1,656,221	1986	Prince John	140	214	1,825	236	222	217	4,440,027
1953	Bull Dog*	114	234		490	449	429	1,941,345	1987	Hoist the Flag	69	103	664	111	86	73	5,533,406
1954	Bull Dog*	116	243		459	430	379	1,780,267	1988	Graustark	99	157	1,229	182	153	145	7,736,657
1955	Sir Gallahad III*	170	336		591	534	587	1,499,162	1989	Buckpasser	95	150	1,190	181	174	151	9,164,291
1956	Bull Dog*	110	228		420	408	381	1,683,908	1990	Grey Dawn II	146	252	2,161	285	237	264	6,003,127
1957	Mahmoud*	92	171		283	247	260	2,593,782	1991	Diplomat Way	129	216	1,908	232	213	201	5,283,778
1958	Bull Lea	89	172		252	211	227	1,645,812	1992	Secretariat	135	239	1,864	259	215	205	6,665,607
1959	Bull Lea	104	189		335	335	280	1,479,375	1993	Nijinsky II	131	215	1,487	206	179	170	6,363,743
1960	Bull Lea	102	196		352	333	298	1,915,881	1994	Nijinsky II	121	214	1,544	223	211	207	7,059,431
1961	Bull Lea	99	196		364	303	333	1,632,559	1995	Seattle Slew	82	142	941	149	125	104	7,762,384
1962	War Admiral	94	120		348	295	263	1,654,396	1996	Mr. Prospector	162	267	1,922	294	226	269	7,095,747
1963	Count Fleet	114	205	2,287	332	265	232	1,866,809	1997	Mr. Prospector	159	275	1,950	297	256	251	8,788,618
1964	War Admiral	109	212	2,757	351	338	323	2,928,459	1998	Mr. Prospector	175	275	1,897	303	244	255	8,175,483
1965	Roman	118	217	2,572	368	333	309	2,394,944	1999	Mr. Prospector	160	286	1,945	286	262	244	8,869,556
1966	Princequillo*	111	191	2,074	287	268	243	2,007,184	2000	Mr. Prospector	153	292	1,909	270	267	220	8,472,649
1967	Princequillo*	118	215	2,079	323	270	238	2,311,709	2001	Mr. Prospector	179	295	1,764	253	238	215	8,944,180
1968	Princequillo*	131	219	2,179	299	285	264	2,116,648	2002	Deputy Minister	159	270	1,668	241	235	223	8,774,040
1969	Princequillo*	129	215	2,027	275	264	213	2,196,327	2003	Deputy Minister	176	316	2,036	311	273	266	11,645,931
1970	Princequillo*	133	209	2,026	261	243	257	2,454,097		*Foreign-bred							

Top Freshman Sires in 2003 – Money Won

Sire	Perfs.	Winning Perfs.	Starts	1st	2nd	3rd	Unplaced	Purses
Victory Gallop	40	11	107	14	16	14	63	$914,179
Doneraile Court	37	16	154	24	25	18	87	768,687
Forestry	19	11	65	18	12	14	21	716,645
Old Trieste	19	8	64	9	14	7	34	692,090
Malibu Moon	21	12	70	18	10	8	34	652,179
Silver Charm	30	15	101	16	12	12	61	573,638
Stormin Fever	35	16	124	17	15	19	73	529,054
Family Calling	33	17	178	24	25	23	106	519,840
Exploit	43	14	145	15	20	19	91	515,992
Mazel Trick	42	13	119	14	9	12	84	514,053
Archers Bay	22	7	66	7	9	12	38	513,021
Tactical Cat	24	10	78	12	14	8	44	491,972
Sea of Secrets	24	11	95	17	16	13	49	403,478
Menifee	17	7	66	8	15	13	30	373,055
Porto Foricos	3	1	15	7	2	2	8	372,582
Military	16	9	63	13	7	7	36	367,616
Good and Tough	20	9	80	11	13	10	46	352,341
Free House	21	7	83	9	7	10	57	349,079
Real Quiet	30	8	102	12	9	10	71	329,331
Time Bandit	10	5	46	8	8	14	16	328,928
Accelerator	44	12	160	15	18	15	112	328,541
Leestown	30	12	117	15	15	17	70	326,942
Wagon Limit	10	5	40	7	6	8	19	318,950
Stravinsky	20	8	68	9	4	15	40	314,798
Precocity	15	7	60	8	9	9	34	306,966
Lil's Lad	32	9	97	10	14	13	60	301,404
Finest Hour	14	8	51	12	3	9	27	296,527
Wild Event	22	11	96	14	5	9	68	258,723
Crafty Friend	31	10	93	12	10	5	66	240,889
Charismatic	35	5	108	6	7	14	81	228,766
Expelled	18	7	70	9	10	9	42	228,050
Crypto Star	16	6	51	9	6	8	28	222,077
Bianconi	26	12	72	13	6	10	43	205,216
General Royal	18	5	70	8	14	10	38	204,145
Artax	24	3	53	4	7	7	35	203,790
Wild Wonder	21	8	66	9	6	12	39	197,015
Perfect Mandate	5	3	16	4	4	2	6	193,730
Alamocitos	5	3	19	5	1	6	7	184,520
Horse Chestnut (SAF)	15	4	38	4	7	1	26	177,941
Diamond	20	6	55	7	11	4	33	175,555
Holzmeister	17	6	73	8	13	8	44	174,958
Baquero	20	7	78	12	10	9	47	174,595
Scatmandu	25	6	75	7	9	8	51	171,867
Gold Regent	17	7	53	8	9	7	29	165,418
Incurable Optimist	7	3	31	3	3	4	21	153,472
Lucky Roberto	11	2	28	4	1	4	19	146,423
Ciano Cat	17	5	57	10	4	6	37	145,865
Event of the Year	12	3	36	3	11	7	15	144,651
El Amante	17	5	59	8	10	6	35	137,843
Quaker Ridge	13	5	63	5	10	10	38	130,713
Parade Ground	20	4	61	5	4	9	43	124,635
Category Five	7	4	24	7	4	1	12	119,459
Stephanotis	8	4	22	5	7	0	10	116,940
Mud Route	8	3	25	4	0	3	18	102,263
Sahm	14	3	46	4	3	6	33	101,094
Claudius	1	1	6	4	2	0	0	99,816
Comic Strip	17	3	42	4	4	5	29	99,460
Esteem	5	3	16	4	5	1	6	98,864

Sire	Perfs.	Winning Perfs.	Starts	1st	2nd	3rd	Unplaced	Purses
Rubiyat	3	3	11	3	2	3	3	94,560
Chelsey Cat	6	4	35	5	3	8	19	94,140
Safely's Mark	7	4	33	7	1	4	21	92,624
Sand Tunnel	5	5	37	6	9	4	18	86,805
Limit Out	7	4	32	5	6	5	16	84,636
Cloud Cover	9	3	31	5	4	1	21	76,485
Fasliyev	3	1	12	1	3	0	8	74,732
Standing On Edge	7	2	33	2	2	4	25	73,500
King of the Heap	6	2	35	4	3	6	22	73,215
Western Borders	10	3	35	3	4	6	22	72,260
Star of Valor	8	3	33	3	4	7	19	71,907
Act Smart	2	1	7	3	1	0	3	70,358
Halos and Horns	8	2	31	3	7	4	17	69,890
Trail City	7	2	25	2	3	8	12	68,768
Frisk Me Now	11	3	32	3	5	2	22	66,581
Renteria	5	2	22	2	3	2	15	56,805
Emancipator	5	2	14	2	2	3	7	53,815
Bonus Time Cat	3	2	19	4	3	2	10	52,860
Valid Trefaire	3	2	21	3	2	5	11	51,636
Chanate	10	3	27	3	4	4	16	49,873
Crown Attorney	10	1	24	1	1	3	19	49,785
Epic Honor	9	3	30	3	2	4	21	49,112
Sir Fir	6	3	18	3	6	2	7	46,640
Shaheen	6	3	24	4	5	1	14	46,374
Sandia Slew	5	3	14	4	4	1	5	43,876
Minister's Mark	7	3	19	3	2	5	9	43,623
Emerald Creme	4	2	31	3	4	3	21	42,342
My Imperial Slew	2	1	10	1	3	1	5	41,201
Lucayan Prince	4	1	15	2	1	1	11	38,415
American Champ	3	2	16	4	1	2	9	38,180
French Parliament	5	2	21	2	4	4	11	36,760
Reality Road	4	2	21	2	5	2	12	35,986
Let Goodtimes Roll	1	1	2	1	0	0	1	32,100
Classy Prospector	7	1	34	1	3	8	22	31,688
Statesmanship	9	3	41	3	1	5	32	30,122
Rainbow Blues (IRE)	4	1	17	2	2	1	12	30,081
Winthrop	9	3	20	3	4	2	11	28,571
Dr Fong	1	1	3	1	1	1	0	27,400
New Way	7	3	25	3	0	3	19	26,418
Guarani	5		26	0	2	4	20	25,450
Intensity	6	1	11	1	0	0	10	25,230
One Golf Sierra	2	1	9	1	3	1	4	22,600
Canyon Run	2	1	3	1	1	0	1	21,580
Via Lombardia (IRE)	3	1	8	1	1	0	6	21,560
Keos	9	1	35	1	1	4	29	20,402
Cimarron Secret	7	3	17	3	0	0	14	20,026

Top Freshman Sires in 2003 – Races Won

Sire	Perfs.	Winning Perfs.	Starts	1st	2nd	3rd	Unplaced	Purses
Doneraile Court	37	16	154	24	25	18	87	$768,687
Family Calling	33	17	178	24	25	23	106	519,840
Forestry	19	11	65	18	12	14	21	716,645
Malibu Moon	21	12	70	18	10	8	34	652,179
Stormin Fever	35	16	124	17	15	19	73	529,054
Sea of Secrets	24	11	95	17	16	13	49	403,478
Silver Charm	30	15	101	16	12	12	61	573,638
Exploit	43	14	145	15	20	19	91	515,992
Accelerator	44	12	160	15	18	15	112	328,541
Leestown	30	12	117	15	15	17	70	326,942
Victory Gallop	40	11	107	14	16	14	63	914,179
Mazel Trick	42	13	119	14	9	12	84	514,053
Wild Event	22	11	96	14	5	9	68	258,723
Military	16	9	63	13	7	7	36	367,616
Bianconi	26	12	72	13	6	10	43	205,216
Tactical Cat	24	10	78	12	14	8	44	491,972
Real Quiet	30	8	102	12	9	10	71	329,331
Finest Hour	14	8	51	12	3	9	27	296,527
Crafty Friend	31	10	93	12	10	5	66	240,889
Baquero	20	7	78	12	10	9	47	174,595
Good and Tough	20	9	80	11	13	10	46	352,341
Lil's Lad	32	9	97	10	14	13	60	301,404
Ciano Cat	17	7	57	10	4	6	37	145,865
Old Trieste	19	8	64	9	14	7	34	692,090
Free House	21	9	83	9	7	10	57	349,079
Stravinsky	20	8	68	9	4	15	40	314,798
Expelled	18	7	70	9	10	9	42	228,050
Crypto Star	16	6	51	9	6	8	28	222,077
Wild Wonder	21	8	66	9	6	12	39	197,015
Menifee	17	7	66	8	15	13	30	373,055
Time Bandit	10	5	46	8	8	14	16	328,928
Precocity	15	7	60	8	9	9	34	306,966
General Royal	18	5	70	8	14	10	38	204,145
Holzmeister	17	6	73	8	13	8	44	174,958
Gold Regent	17	7	53	8	9	7	29	165,418
El Amante	17	5	59	8	10	6	35	137,843
Archers Bay	22	7	66	7	9	12	38	513,021
Wagon Limit	10	7	40	7	6	8	19	318,950
Diamond	20	6	55	7	11	4	33	175,555
Scatmandu	25	6	75	7	9	8	51	171,867
Category Five	7	4	24	7	4	1	12	119,459
Safely's Mark	7	4	33	7	1	4	21	92,624
Charismatic	35	5	108	6	7	14	81	228,766
Sand Tunnel	5	5	37	6	9	4	18	86,805
Alamocitos	5	3	19	5	1	6	7	184,520
Quaker Ridge	13	5	63	5	10	10	38	130,713
Parade Ground	20	4	61	5	4	9	43	124,635
Stephanotis	8	4	22	5	7	0	10	116,940
Chelsey Cat	6	4	35	5	3	8	19	94,140
Limit Out	7	4	32	5	6	5	16	84,636
Cloud Cover	9	3	31	5	4	1	21	76,485
Bustopher Jones	6	4	12	5	2	1	4	17,320
Artax	24	3	53	4	7	7	35	203,790
Perfect Mandate	5	3	16	4	4	2	6	193,730
Horse Chestnut (SAF)	15	4	38	4	4	1	26	177,941
Lucky Roberto	11	2	28	4	1	4	19	146,423
Mud Route	8	3	25	4	0	3	18	102,263
Sahm	14	3	46	4	3	6	33	101,094

Sire	Perfs.	Winning Perfs.	Starts	1st	2nd	3rd	Unplaced	Purses
Claudius	1	1	6	4	2	0	0	99,816
Comic Strip	17	3	42	4	4	5	29	99,460
Esteem	5	3	16	4	5	1	6	98,864
King of the Heap	6	2	35	4	3	6	22	73,215
Bonus Time Cat	3	2	19	4	3	2	10	52,860
Shaheen	6	3	24	4	5	1	14	46,374
Sandia Slew	5	3	14	4	4	1	5	43,876
American Champ	3	2	16	4	1	2	9	38,180
Porto Foricos	3	1	15	3	2	2	8	372,582
Incurable Optimist	7	3	31	3	3	4	21	153,472
Event of the Year	12	3	36	3	11	7	15	144,651
Rubiyat	3	3	11	3	2	3	3	94,560
Western Borders	10	3	35	3	4	6	22	72,260
Star of Valor	8	3	33	3	4	7	19	71,907
Act Smart	2	1	7	3	1	0	3	70,358
Halos and Horns	8	2	31	3	7	4	17	69,890
Frisk Me Now	11	3	32	3	5	2	22	66,581
Valid Trefaire	3	2	21	3	2	5	11	51,636
Chanate	10	3	27	3	4	4	16	49,873
Epic Honor	9	3	30	3	2	4	21	49,112
Sir Fir	6	3	18	3	6	2	7	46,640
Minister's Mark	7	3	19	3	2	5	9	43,623
Emerald Creme	4	2	31	3	4	3	21	42,342
Statesmanship	9	3	41	3	1	5	32	30,122
Winthrop	9	3	20	3	4	2	11	28,571
New Way	7	3	25	3	0	3	19	26,418
Cimarron Secret	7	3	17	3	0	0	14	20,026
Standing On Edge	7	2	33	2	2	4	25	73,500
Trail City	7	2	25	2	3	8	12	68,768
Renteria	5	2	22	2	3	2	15	56,805
Emancipator	5	2	14	2	2	3	7	53,815
Lucayan Prince	4	1	15	2	1	1	11	38,415
French Parliament	5	2	21	2	4	4	11	36,760
Reality Road	4	2	21	2	5	2	12	35,986
Rainbow Blues (IRE)	4	1	17	2	2	1	12	30,081
Big Sky Chester	1	1	4	2	1	0	1	16,317
Shawklit Player	2	1	6	2	2	1	1	14,142
Fasliyev	3	1	12	1	3	0	8	74,732
Crown Attorney	10	1	24	1	1	3	19	49,785
My Imperial Slew	2	1	10	1	3	1	5	41,201
Let Goodtimes Roll	1	1	2	1	0	0	1	32,100
Classy Prospector	7	1	34	1	3	8	22	31,688
Dr Fong	1	1	3	1	1	1	0	27,400
Intensity	6	1	11	1	0	0	10	25,230
One Golf Sierra	2	1	9	1	3	1	4	22,600
Canyon Run	2	1	3	1	1	0	1	21,580
Via Lombardia (IRE)	3	1	8	1	1	0	6	21,560
Keos	9	1	35	1	1	4	29	20,402
My Favorite Grub	1	1	6	1	0	0	5	18,820
Two Smart	1	1	6	1	0	1	4	17,854
Gold Market	3	1	18	1	2	2	13	17,138
Miswaki Bandit	4	1	13	1	1	1	10	15,620
Banjo	4	1	6	1	3	0	2	14,158
Surachai	2	1	5	1	0	0	4	12,780
Buck Strider	4	1	25	1	0	2	22	12,690
Cat Doctor	5	1	17	1	3	2	11	12,352
Flying With Eagles	5	1	7	1	0	1	5	11,850

Top Freshman Sires in 2003 – Winning Performers

Sire	Perfs.	Winning Perfs.	Starts	1st	2nd	3rd	Unplaced	Purses
Family Calling	33	17	178	24	25	23	106	$519,840
Doneraile Court	37	16	154	24	25	18	87	768,687
Stormin Fever	35	16	124	17	15	19	73	529,054
Silver Charm	30	15	101	16	12	12	61	573,638
Exploit	43	14	145	15	20	19	91	515,992
Mazel Trick	42	13	119	14	9	12	84	514,053
Malibu Moon	21	12	70	18	10	8	34	652,179
Accelerator	44	12	160	15	18	15	112	328,541
Leestown	30	12	117	15	15	17	70	326,942
Bianconi	26	12	72	13	6	10	43	205,216
Victory Gallop	40	11	107	14	16	14	63	914,179
Forestry	19	11	65	18	12	14	21	716,645
Sea of Secrets	24	11	95	17	16	13	49	403,478
Wild Event	22	11	96	14	5	9	68	258,723
Tactical Cat	24	10	78	12	14	8	44	491,972
Crafty Friend	31	10	93	12	10	5	66	240,889
Military	16	9	63	13	7	7	36	367,616
Good and Tough	20	9	80	11	13	10	46	352,341
Lil's Lad	32	9	97	10	14	13	60	301,404
Old Trieste	19	8	64	9	14	7	34	692,090
Real Quiet	30	8	102	12	9	10	71	329,331
Stravinsky	20	8	68	9	4	15	40	314,798
Finest Hour	14	8	51	12	3	9	27	296,527
Wild Wonder	21	8	66	9	6	12	39	197,015
Archers Bay	22	7	66	7	9	12	38	513,021
Menifee	17	7	66	8	15	13	30	373,055
Free House	21	7	83	9	7	10	57	349,079
Precocity	15	7	60	8	9	9	34	306,966
Expelled	18	7	70	9	10	9	42	228,050
Baquero	20	7	78	12	10	9	47	174,595
Gold Regent	17	7	53	8	9	7	29	165,418
Ciano Cat	17	7	57	10	4	6	37	145,865
Crypto Star	16	6	51	9	6	8	28	222,077
Diamond	20	6	55	7	11	4	33	175,555
Holzmeister	17	6	73	8	13	8	44	174,958
Scatmandu	25	6	75	7	9	8	51	171,867
Time Bandit	10	5	46	8	8	14	16	328,928
Wagon Limit	10	5	40	7	6	8	19	318,950
Charismatic	35	5	108	6	7	14	81	228,766
General Royal	18	5	70	8	14	10	38	204,145
El Amante	17	5	59	8	10	6	35	137,843
Quaker Ridge	13	5	63	5	10	10	38	130,713
Sand Tunnel	5	5	37	6	9	4	18	86,805
Horse Chestnut (SAF)	15	4	38	4	7	1	26	177,941
Parade Ground	20	4	61	5	4	9	43	124,635
Category Five	7	4	24	7	4	1	12	119,459
Stephanotis	8	4	22	5	7	0	10	116,940
Chelsey Cat	6	4	35	5	3	8	19	94,140
Safely's Mark	7	4	33	7	1	4	21	92,624
Limit Out	7	4	32	5	6	5	16	84,636
Bustopher Jones	6	4	12	5	2	1	4	17,320
Artax	24	3	53	4	7	7	35	203,790
Perfect Mandate	5	3	16	4	4	2	6	193,730
Alamocitos	5	3	19	5	1	6	7	184,520
Incurable Optimist	7	3	31	3	3	4	21	153,472
Event of the Year	12	3	36	3	11	7	15	144,651
Mud Route	8	3	25	4	0	3	18	102,263
Sahm	14	3	46	4	3	6	33	101,094

Sire	Perfs.	Winning Perfs.	Starts	1st	2nd	3rd	Unplaced	Purses
Comic Strip	17	3	42	4	4	5	29	99,460
Esteem	5	3	16	4	5	1	6	98,864
Rubiyat	3	3	11	3	2	3	3	94,560
Cloud Cover	9	3	31	5	4	1	21	76,485
Western Borders	10	3	35	3	4	6	22	72,260
Star of Valor	8	3	33	3	4	7	19	71,907
Frisk Me Now	11	3	32	3	5	2	22	66,581
Chanate	10	3	27	3	4	4	16	49,873
Epic Honor	9	3	30	3	2	4	21	49,112
Sir Fir	6	3	18	3	6	2	7	46,640
Shaheen	6	3	24	4	5	1	14	46,374
Sandia Slew	5	3	14	4	4	1	5	43,876
Minister's Mark	7	3	19	3	2	5	9	43,623
Statesmanship	9	3	41	3	1	5	32	30,122
Winthrop	9	3	20	3	4	2	11	28,571
New Way	7	3	25	3	0	3	19	26,418
Cimarron Secret	7	3	17	3	0	0	14	20,026
Lucky Roberto	11	2	28	4	1	4	19	146,423
Standing On Edge	7	2	33	2	2	4	25	73,500
King of the Heap	6	2	35	4	3	6	22	73,215
Halos and Horns	8	2	31	3	7	4	17	69,890
Trail City	7	2	25	2	3	8	12	68,768
Renteria	5	2	22	2	3	2	15	56,805
Emancipator	5	2	14	2	2	3	7	53,815
Bonus Time Cat	3	2	19	4	3	2	10	52,860
Valid Trefaire	3	2	21	3	2	5	11	51,636
Emerald Creme	4	2	31	3	4	3	21	42,342
American Champ	3	2	16	4	1	2	9	38,180
French Parliament	5	2	21	2	4	4	11	36,760
Reality Road	4	2	21	2	5	2	12	35,986
Porto Foricos	3	1	15	3	2	2	8	372,582
Claudius	1	1	6	4	2	0	0	99,816
Fasliyev	3	1	12	1	3	0	8	74,732
Act Smart	2	1	7	3	1	0	3	70,358
Crown Attorney	10	1	24	1	1	3	19	49,785
My Imperial Slew	2	1	10	1	3	1	5	41,201
Lucayan Prince	4	1	15	2	1	1	11	38,415
Let Goodtimes Roll	1	1	2	1	0	0	1	32,100
Classy Prospector	7	1	34	1	3	8	22	31,688
Rainbow Blues (IRE)	4	1	17	2	2	1	12	30,081
Dr Fong	1	1	3	1	1	1	0	27,400
Intensity	6	1	11	1	0	0	10	25,230
One Golf Sierra	2	1	9	1	3	1	4	22,600
Canyon Run	2	1	3	1	1	0	1	21,580
Via Lombardia (IRE)	3	1	8	1	1	0	6	21,560
Keos	9	1	35	1	1	4	29	20,402
My Favorite Grub	1	1	6	1	0	0	5	18,820
Two Smart	1	1	6	1	0	1	4	17,854
Gold Market	3	1	18	1	2	2	13	17,138
Big Sky Chester	1	1	4	2	1	0	1	16,317
Miswaki Bandit	4	1	13	1	1	1	10	15,620
Banjo	4	1	6	1	3	0	2	14,158
Shawklit Player	2	1	6	2	2	1	1	14,142
Surachai	2	1	5	1	0	0	4	12,780
Buck Strider	4	1	25	1	0	2	22	12,690
Cat Doctor	5	1	17	1	3	2	11	12,352
Flying With Eagles	5	1	7	1	0	1	5	11,850
Constant Demand	2	1	10	1	0	1	8	11,455

Top 10 Freshman Sires and Their Progeny

Victory Gallop, B H (1995)
By Cryptoclearance – Victorious Lil, by Vice Regent
40 Performers, 11 winning performers, $914,179 in total earnings.

Progeny	Mare	Age	Sts	1st	2d	3d	Money Won
Ace's Cappella	Eliot Chacer	2	5	0	0	1	9,195
Al Sami	Miss Information	2	1	0	0	0	0
Athena Girl	Irish Shilling	2	1	0	0	0	0
C's Victory	Le Famo	2	3	0	0	1	3,750
Comes Unglued	High Fine	2	5	0	0	3	6,979
Dawnie Wonder	Weekend Flight	2	1	0	0	0	0
Denny's Victory	Hopi	2	1	0	1	0	3,600
Gallop to Victory	Flying Red Jet	2	2	0	0	0	1,260
Galloping Gal	Indy Flash	2	5	3	1	0	204,884
Galloping to Tea	Tocar	2	1	0	0	0	0
Gimme a Vee	Torrentina	2	2	0	0	0	0
Hello Victory	Bad Gerty	2	3	0	1	0	2,100
Honest Victor	To Be Honest	2	1	1	0	0	11,700
Hot Chipotle	Cajun Cat	2	5	0	2	1	11,780
J B's Victoria	Urban Distraction	2	1	0	0	1	2,170
Judo	Her Grace	2	3	0	1	0	6,750
Kangaroo Jack	Kris's Intention	2	2	1	0	0	5,340
Morgan's Renegade	Painted Pink	2	2	0	0	0	179
Morine's Victory	Torch	2	3	0	1	0	12,375
No Lo Creo	Believability	2	3	0	0	0	265
Notorious Rogue	Believe It Beloved	2	4	1	0	2	68,730
One More Win	One Final Wish	2	2	0	0	0	300
Red Lifesaver	Brush With Tequila	2	1	0	0	0	980
Roger Wilco	Zama Hummer	2	1	0	0	0	0
Sage's Fifty Six	Queen of Bronze	2	7	1	2	0	51,433
Separato	La Bellissima	2	1	1	0	0	12,000
Shining Victory	Phoenix Sunshine	2	1	0	0	0	0
Shot Gun Terry	Red Will Do	2	7	1	1	0	10,770
Special Topics	Orange Motiff	2	4	0	3	0	8,000
Touch of Victory	Grey Rites	2	2	0	0	0	1,200
Twilight Gallop	Twilight Encounter	2	5	1	0	1	18,525
Victor Watz	Hord	2	1	0	0	0	0
Victorious Kiss	Timeless Kisses	2	1	0	0	0	0
Victory Girl	Usual Lies	2	1	0	0	1	5,880
Victory Light	Very Special Lite	2	4	1	1	1	89,960
Victory Moondance	Take Me Home	2	1	0	0	0	0
Victory U.S.A.	Fordyce	2	6	2	1	2	350,370
Victorytonitehey	Fancy Ruler	2	3	0	0	0	2,500
West Dallas	Blacktie Bid	2	3	1	1	0	11,204
Yougonow	La Feria	2	2	0	0	0	0

Doneraile Court, Dk B H (1996)
By Seattle Slew – Sophisticated Girl, by Stop the Music
37 Performers, 16 winning performers, $768,687 in total earnings

Progeny	Mare	Age	Sts	1st	2d	3d	Money Won
Absolute Rocks	Gravel Queen	2	9	2	1	2	47,817
Aireslew	Leslie's Jet	2	4	0	1	0	8,558
Baldomera	Pleasure Card	2	8	2	3	2	62,530
Bartus Christian	Quarry Hill	2	3	1	0	0	7,906
Basketball Court	Stage Bulletin	2	7	4	1	0	55,090
Boston Bar	San Diego Skyhawk	2	2	0	1	0	3,940
Brightstar High	Elegante Chica	2	5	0	1	0	3,400
C C Forever	Hunt's Corner	2	2	0	0	0	0
Courtcase	Always Red	2	1	0	0	0	0
Courtcase	D Hail Mary	2	7	1	1	1	16,430
Courthouse	Bee the One	2	8	0	1	1	9,710
Cowboy Court	Just Hailly	2	1	0	0	0	145
Delicious Dish	Outlandish	2	4	0	0	0	1,240
Donnas Trial	Effie Bland	2	6	1	0	0	34,236
Emma's Wish	Emma D	2	5	0	1	0	2,960
Horah for Bailey	Horah for the Lady	2	6	2	1	2	58,550
Jazzy Jay	Sanctionize	2	2	1	0	0	36,360
Kesia	Casseattack	2	2	0	0	1	1,400
Late Night Leader	Wantyoutowantme	2	6	2	1	0	42,450
Madrone	Easy to Cope	2	1	1	0	0	15,400
Mahican	Spotted Prospector	2	6	0	3	0	17,750
Muncy	Pyrite Captain	2	6	0	0	1	2,074
Oh Oleg	Jet Ready	2	5	1	1	2	25,056
Patriot's Quest	Cryptic Madam	2	2	0	1	0	5,120
Proud Decision	Pretty n' Proud	2	3	0	0	1	3,235
Pyrite Alena	Blue Sword	2	5	1	1	1	9,125
Robin the Purses	Really Seeking	2	3	0	0	2	3,276
Ruckus in Court	Ruckin Angel	2	1	1	0	0	24,240
Ruler's Court	Future Guest	2	4	2	0	1	197,700
Run Mikey Run	Cadillac Women	2	5	1	0	0	12,400
Shamoiselle	Sissy Sham	2	9	1	3	0	52,978
She's a Mugs	Magnolia Springs	2	1	0	0	0	66
Song of Beauty	Eskimo Song	2	1	0	0	0	90
Sophisticated Babe	Lefty's Dollbaby	2	1	0	0	0	1,010

(continued, Victory Gallop)

Progeny	Mare	Age	Sts	1st	2d	3d	Money Won
Stacy Brew	Balastra	2	1	0	0	0	0
Toledo King	Toledo Queen (IRE)	2	5	0	3	1	6,140
Wannagoto Court	Iron Maiden	2	5	0	0	0	305

Forestry, B H (1996)
By Storm Cat – Shared Interest, by Pleasant Colony
19 Performers, 11 winning performers, $716,645 in total earnings.

Progeny	Mare	Age	Sts	1st	2d	3d	Money Won
Acclimate	Mended Heart	2	7	2	1	2	51,815
Deputy Storm	Deputy Jane West	2	4	2	1	0	78,380
Everyday Angel	Subtle Raise	2	3	1	2	0	55,720
Fall Fashion	Digit	2	3	1	1	1	18,200
Forest Grove	Charm a Gendarme	2	2	0	0	0	350
Forest Kitty	Haleakala (IRE)	2	2	0	0	1	3,500
Forestier	D'Youville Nurse	2	1	1	0	0	27,000
Frenchglen	La Riviera	2	1	0	0	0	0
Golden Glen	Golden Petal	2	5	0	1	1	11,860
Hasslefree	Belle of Abruzzi	2	7	2	2	2	108,869
Imperial Ruler	Alexandrina	2	3	0	0	0	0
Magic Forest	Inquisitive Look	2	1	0	0	0	0
Old Forester	Halo River	2	1	0	0	1	4,730
Ottawa Chief	East Cape	2	4	2	1	1	49,700
Reforest	Tremor	2	2	1	1	0	19,590
Sir Forest	Miss Sib	2	2	0	0	0	0
Sisti's Pride	Marie J	2	6	1	1	2	64,427
Smokey Glacken	Majesty's Crown	2	4	3	0	1	140,820
Stoic	Brink	2	7	2	1	2	81,684

Old Trieste, Ch H (1995)
By A.P. Indy – Lovlier Linda, by Vigors
19 Performers, 8 winning performers, $692,020 in total earnings.

Progeny	Mare	Age	Sts	1st	2d	3d	Money Won
Bellarama	Fee Fi Foe	2	1	0	0	0	2,100
Brave Columbus	Without Feathers	2	5	0	0	0	0
Damariscotta	Ontherightwicket	2	4	0	2	0	3,670
Ellieonthemarch	Marchtothemine	2	3	1	0	1	39,496
Eye of the Artist	Race Artist	2	2	0	0	0	180
Fond	Fontal (ARG)	2	5	2	1	0	59,250
Forgotten Promise	Brush Over	2	3	0	0	0	3,400
Micki Michelle	Madam President	2	3	0	0	1	5,000
Minister Eric	Musical Minister	2	5	1	2	1	387,920
Miss Bergdorf	Storm Key	2	4	0	1	0	11,960
Mr. Trieste	Angel's Tearlet	2	2	1	1	0	35,260
Savage Sue	Early Glow	2	2	0	1	0	2,712
Spencers Storm	Cindy's Guest	2	6	1	0	1	20,320
Steady Course	Steady Cat	2	5	1	3	0	57,405
Striking Cobra	Passerine (ARG)	2	3	1	1	0	17,600
Trieste Cat	Mountain Medley	2	1	0	0	0	0
Trieste's Honor	Jolie Bois	2	4	0	0	1	8,100
Venizia	Future Bright	2	5	1	1	2	28,917
Wild Wadi	Out of Taxes	2	1	0	1	0	8,800

Malibu Moon, B H (1997)
By A.P. Indy – Macoumba, by Mr. Prospector
21 Performers, 12 winning performers, $652,179 in total earnings.

Progeny	Mare	Age	Sts	1st	2d	3d	Money Won
An American Idol	Allyouneedislove	2	2	0	1	0	5,250
Aspen Moon	Aspen Miss	2	2	1	0	0	9,750
Cella Luna	A Sunny Singer	2	2	1	0	0	25,830
Culpeper Moon	Snowrico	2	2	1	1	0	14,460
End of an Era	Gala Runaway	2	3	2	0	1	25,490
Faithtrustpixidust	Irish Tawpie	2	1	0	0	0	0
Fly by Moonlight	Majestic Tempest	2	2	1	0	0	8,658
Foolish Moon	Maile	2	5	0	1	1	6,100
Grant's Moon	Grant a Wish	2	6	2	1	1	60,370
Keet Brown	Perkins Magic	2	1	0	0	0	570
Malibu Al	Georgie Gal	2	2	1	1	0	12,820
Malibu Miss	Mean Nanny Jean	2	3	0	1	0	4,070
Malifino	Silverality	2	1	0	0	0	0
Mascalzone	Private Trail	2	8	1	0	0	13,831
Missacity Luke	Noble's Satin Doll	2	4	2	1	0	41,591
Misty Malibu	Misty Canalu	2	2	0	0	1	1,587
Perfect Moon	Perfectly	2	10	3	1	3	353,870
Point Dume	Tova's Princess	2	6	2	0	1	41,800
Slow and Steady	Salubria	2	2	0	2	0	10,500
Valay Moon	Shang Valay	2	5	1	0	0	14,966
Walking On Water	Crown and Water	2	1	0	0	0	666

Silver Charm, Gr/Ro H (1994)
By Silver Buck – Bonnie's Poker, by Poker
30 Performers, 15 winning performers, $573,638 in total earnings.

Progeny	Mare	Age	Sts	1st	2d	3d	Money Won
Aladdin's Lamp	Desert Dream	2	3	1	0	0	27,885
Aurora's Charm	Color of Love	2	2	0	0	0	145
Charming Jim	Secret Harbor	2	7	1	2	1	53,105
Charming Pat	April Green	2	5	0	0	0	605
Cinema Star	Select Account	2	2	0	0	0	980
Consecrate	How So Oiseau	2	7	1	0	0	88,340
Dancin Kelly Z	Bouche Bee	2	5	1	2	1	19,500
Deb's Charm	Ms. Cuvee Napa	2	3	1	0	2	71,360
Doc Baker's Charm	Who's Sorry Now	2	3	2	0	0	43,200
Erik's the Charm	Rayelle	2	2	0	0	1	5,300
Georgetown Gal	My Big Sis	2	2	0	0	0	3,330
High Silver	Vivace	2	9	1	1	3	34,320
Island Charm	Tropical Stephanie	2	3	0	0	1	7,000
Jacob the Great	Bisbee	2	2	0	0	0	343
Kakapo	Boom Bird	2	1	0	0	0	137
My Little Charm	Returno de Darrow	2	3	0	1	0	5,590
Odds On	Bluffing Girl	2	3	1	1	0	39,200
Platinum Priced	Premium Price	2	7	1	3	0	22,320
Preachinatthebar	Holy Nola	2	4	1	0	1	32,820
Rat Like Cunning	Saratoga Warning	2	1	0	0	0	220
Runaround	Fatal Distraction	2	1	0	0	0	0
Sea of Silver	Liz Cee	2	3	1	0	0	34,420
Silver Indy	Miss Cort'n	2	2	1	0	0	17,580
Silver Lure	Merengue	2	6	1	1	0	20,250
Silver Soul	Guinevere K	2	1	1	0	0	8,100
Silver Warrant	Muffies Muffin	2	2	0	0	0	1,050
Silvercity Lady	Bent Creek City	2	6	1	1	1	32,050
Spellfire	Fume	2	3	0	0	1	1,588
Sunshinenbeer	Pretense d'Or	2	2	0	0	0	720
You're Up	Whats Doin	2	1	0	0	0	2,180

Stormin Fever, Dk B H (1994)
By Storm Cat – Pennant Fever, by Seattle Slew
35 Performers, 16 winning performers, $529,054 in total earnings

Progeny	Mare	Age	Sts	1st	2d	3d	Money Won
After the Tone	Record the Call	2	6	0	2	0	25,080
Certified Fact	White Heron	2	2	0	0	0	285
Charcot	Songs of Praise	2	3	1	0	0	33,515
Darios Fire	Dear Rafaela	2	1	0	0	0	2,500
Demon Fever	Last No Break	2	2	0	0	0	1,275
East Bay	Tee for Three	2	2	1	0	1	42,625
Feb Eleven	Make Your Call	2	7	1	1	2	36,350
Fierce Storm	Never Not Able	2	4	0	1	1	15,370
Franscat	Hopespringsagain	2	3	0	0	2	10,060
Furious Fever	Mama Hawk	2	3	0	0	1	5,800
Jettin Fever	Jerry Bomb	2	4	1	0	0	4,831
Minifever	Minicolony	2	2	0	0	1	3,055
Oz	Expensive Tap	2	1	1	0	0	24,600
Patriotic Fever	Oh Summer	2	7	1	0	1	8,545
Pense	Saturday Feeling	2	3	0	0	0	1,143
Post Op	Cosmetic Lift	2	5	0	0	2	8,510
Quiet Edition	Quiet City	2	2	0	0	1	4,100
Quintara	Traveler's Key	2	2	0	1	0	3,300
Run for Lillie	Miss Spentyouth	2	3	0	0	0	305
Spike the Fever	Miss Bid Flash	2	2	0	2	0	15,000
Storm Country	Flag Country	2	1	0	1	0	4,200
Storm Forward	Be Prepared	2	6	1	0	1	26,490
Stormin Dancer	Muskoka Ice	2	2	1	0	0	6,550
Stormin Greek	Countus Affair	2	5	1	2	0	27,950
Stormin in Style	Be in Style	2	1	0	0	0	0
Stormy Noche	Tokyo Flight	2	1	0	0	0	0
Stormy Siege	Winsome Lassie	2	5	2	0	1	46,050
Sun Stroke	Inca Sun	2	6	0	2	2	7,435
Talladega Sweep	Talladega Sprint	2	1	0	0	0	0
Tango Fever	Tango Red	2	7	1	0	1	12,450
Tarlow	Madam Bear	2	3	1	1	0	79,400
To the Whistle	Clarity	2	6	1	1	1	20,320
War Fever	Gender War	2	3	1	0	0	28,800
Wild Fever	Wild Again Miss	2	7	1	1	0	8,320
Winners Table	Screener	2	6	1	0	1	14,840

Family Calling, B H (1994)
By Mr. Prospector – Sense of Unity, by Northern Dancer
33 Performers, 17 winning performers, $519,840 in total earnings.

Progeny	Mare	Age	Sts	1st	2d	3d	Money Won
April's Prince	Sudden's Image	2	9	2	0	0	30,080
Austin W	Cowgirl Ashlee	2	2	0	1	0	2,660
Byeairmail	Young American	2	10	2	1	0	15,535
Callbright	Bright Cide Up	2	2	0	0	0	509
Callcan	Wish for Candi	2	7	1	0	1	11,280
Callcat	Windcat	2	3	1	1	0	33,400
Callfire	Senorita Foxfire	2	1	0	1	0	4,140
Calling All Forbes	Forbes Favorite	2	7	1	2	2	24,010
Calling Mary Mac	Mary Mac	2	12	1	2	0	8,815
Calling Nicole	Ocala Ace	2	10	0	1	2	7,315
Callnew	Wish I Knew	2	8	1	0	1	13,015
Callone	Starbase Won	2	3	1	1	0	18,040
Callsports	Sports Widow	2	10	1	0	2	8,360
Callter	Fired Heater	2	9	1	1	1	21,035
Callvi	Vigorous Rose	2	2	0	0	0	220
Cashel Calling	Queen of Cashel	2	8	3	1	1	51,460
Cherished Bid	Parting Bid	2	8	2	2	2	90,611
England Calling	Something Cool	2	2	0	0	0	0
Family Book	Bride's Book	2	5	2	0	2	23,820
Family Favorite	Miss Meadowlake	2	6	1	2	0	52,100
Family Money	Illakabucks	2	1	0	0	1	900
Fastnfurious	Raise a Goddess	2	3	0	0	0	1,280
Gamblin	Yuki	2	2	0	2	0	15,000
Katie Jo	Pretty Blue Miss	2	5	0	1	1	3,322
La Dame Amour	Deux Amours	2	2	0	0	0	320
Midwife	Le Nat	2	4	1	0	0	5,865
Mindsweeper	Mariquita's Queen	2	2	1	0	1	19,305
Money Call	Anne's Money Honey	2	8	0	0	2	4,850
Pinecall	Poupine	2	7	0	2	1	4,370
Sky Calling	Sky Crystal	2	2	0	0	0	390
Soon to Be Family	Soontobespectacular	2	3	0	0	0	213
Tyler W	This Ain't Kansas	2	6	0	4	1	8,400
Zipper Zipper De	Zooming Zipper	2	9	2	0	2	39,220

Exploit, Dk B H (1996)
By Storm Cat – My Turbulent Miss, by My Dad George
43 Performers, 14 winning performers, $515,992 in total earnings

Progeny	Mare	Age	Sts	1st	2d	3d	Money Won
Cinemagic	Disclaimed	2	5	1	0	1	9,120
Cohassett Rocks	Prospective Joy	2	3	0	0	0	714
Colonial Reign	Pleasant Reign	2	2	0	0	0	0
Courageous Act	Eastside Westside	2	5	1	1	2	45,160
Currituck Sound	Seattle Angel	2	3	0	0	1	3,060
Dekay	Timeless Tempo	2	2	0	0	1	1,555
Desert Deed	Desert Run	2	2	0	0	0	0
Exist	Sixy Chic	2	6	1	2	0	19,245
Expletive	Alizea	2	1	0	0	0	195
Explicitly	Slabovia	2	2	0	0	2	6,580
Exploding Star	Star Minister	2	1	0	0	1	1,950
Exploit Choice	Wellingtons Choice	2	1	0	0	0	0
Exploit Lad	Breeze Lass	2	11	1	2	2	69,841
Exploit'em	In Excelcis Deo	2	1	0	0	0	0
Exploitation	Prima Supra	2	5	0	0	1	5,880
Exploited	Gold Fashioned	2	6	1	0	1	12,930
Exploited Power	Love Child	2	1	0	0	0	230
Exploited Storm	Sixkissesforsara	2	6	1	1	0	31,885
Exploiting	Sealedwithakriss	2	2	0	0	0	0
Exploitive	So Generous	2	8	0	1	0	6,600
Explosive Affair	Affirmed Toor	2	2	0	0	1	6,666
Gato Bob	Call Me (GB)	2	3	1	0	1	8,946
Heroic Deed	Russian Bride	2	1	0	0	1	1,390
Herrera's Gown	Student Wife	2	7	1	2	0	29,670
Jamocha	How Lovely	2	2	0	0	1	6,020
Juniors Song	Chilly Hostess	2	1	0	0	0	0
Kimmy's Kid	Klassy Kim	2	2	0	0	0	1,540
Lightlively	Doradoradora	2	2	0	0	0	4,080
Maple	Maple Lake	2	1	0	0	0	1,350
Marina de Chavon	T. K. O. Lady	2	5	2	1	0	100,565
Merchandise	I've Been a Gem	2	4	0	1	0	8,100
Moon Feather	Cherokee Miss	2	2	0	0	0	1,350
My Allegiance	Colonial Ally	2	4	0	1	0	16,155
Nicebutnaughty	Affirm the Gold	2	6	1	1	0	10,660
Only Seventeen	Virgin Michael	2	6	1	0	2	6,920
Our Exploit	Reach the Top	2	3	1	1	0	28,350
Private Promise	Private Banking	2	7	0	5	0	21,285
Push Push Push	Pushy	2	3	0	0	0	125
Rich Find	Be a Prospector	2	3	1	0	0	16,005
She's Enough	D'Enough	2	1	0	0	1	1,050
Tank Force	Cahill Connection	2	2	0	0	0	1,920
Val's Expo	Valid Bonnet	2	1	1	0	0	13,800
Worksformoney	Culver City	2	4	0	1	1	15,100

Mazel Trick, Ch H (1995)
By Phone Trick – Mazatleca (Mex), by Ramahorn
42 Performers, 13 winning performers, $14,053 in total earnings

Progeny	Mare	Age	Sts	1st	2d	3d	Money Won
Aron's Matzoballs	Phoenician Miss	2	1	0	0	0	2,460
Artic Dream	Artic Raptor	2	3	0	1	1	11,920

Name							Earnings
Asaja	Miss Salt Lick	2	6	1	0	0	5,360
Austere	Girton Gate	2	1	0	0	0	0
Buffy the Slayer	Lap of Luxury	2	1	0	0	0	0
Byestarterhijudge	Cash Crunch	2	4	0	0	0	1,656
Clever Colleen	Clever Thing	2	7	0	0	0	1,620
Cold Trick	Frigidette	2	1	0	0	1	5,000
Crystal Magic	Lalique	2	1	0	0	0	0
Exclusive Print	Master Print	2	1	0	0	1	2,750
Fast Exercise	Aerobic Exercise	2	9	0	1	1	6,155
Foot Trick	Kelly Amber	2	3	0	0	1	5,495
Happy Day	Joyous Day	2	4	0	0	0	0
Jaglander	Test Shot	2	1	1	0	0	24,600
Juventus	Give a Toast	2	2	1	0	1	36,327
Lasik	Clear Vision	2	4	1	0	1	32,290
Laugh Again	Metropo's Lass	2	1	0	0	0	750
Luckbealadytonight	City Mouse	2	3	1	0	0	21,500
Lucky Guy	Fortunate Vision	2	9	0	3	0	14,360
Major Success	Veil Dance	2	2	1	0	0	25,440
Mazel Pic	Picaresque (GB)	2	2	0	0	1	3,220
Mazel Tov	Flying Honors	2	1	0	0	0	1,250
Mazella	Wonderful	2	7	1	1	2	43,940
Nearctica	Tamarisk	2	1	0	0	0	3,528
No Minimum	Halo Lisa	2	4	0	0	0	3,560
No Time for Games	Pay for the Game	2	1	0	0	0	0
One Trick Pony	Turn and Sparkle	2	2	0	0	0	480
Ontheqt	Confidential	2	4	2	2	0	156,940
Outcashem	Blazed Star	2	1	1	0	0	14,250
Psych	Tobie Ruckus	2	1	1	0	0	21,700
Ridgevalley	Charitable Gift	2	2	0	0	0	3,528
Smart Babe	Lady Be Smart	2	1	0	0	0	690
Society Sam	Society Doon	2	3	1	0	0	21,780
Speedmovesme	Alleged Queen	2	3	0	0	1	635
Sweetsmellofsucces	Remedy	2	2	0	0	0	1,050
Swift Trick	Victorian Village	2	4	1	0	0	16,010
Terror Fabulous	Day After Day	2	1	0	0	0	0
Tiara Gin	Celeste Cielo	2	2	0	0	0	124
Trick Ballet	Policy Issue	2	5	1	0	0	7,200
Tricky Taboo	Strictly Taboo	2	1	0	0	0	725
Tricky Touch	Touch of Honor	2	5	0	1	1	15,760
Vibra	Aggie Gold Rush	2	2	0	0	0	0

Annual Leading Freshman Sire – Money Won

Year	Sire	Winning Perfs.	Races Won	Amount Won	Year	Sire	Winning Perfs.	Races Won	Amount Won
1958	Turn-to	8	25	$463,280	1985	Fappiano	8	16	1,232,408
1959	Determine	6	14	411,765	1986	Sportin' Life	8	12	781,734
1960	Pappa Fourway	3	11	283,073	1987	Crafty Prospector	8	17	349,405
1961	Traffic Judge	10	23	264,354	1988	Secreto	3	5	515,284
1962	Bold Ruler	10	26	170,643	1989	Moscow Ballet	10	15	541,810
1963	Cohoes	8	14	201,397	1990	Meadowlake	3	10	1,025,600
1964	Petare	8	21	543,594	1991	Capote	15	20	1,160,237
1965	Better Bee	9	21	107,140	1992	Silver Deputy	6	13	571,702
1966	Windy Sands	7	11	122,811	1993	Seeking the Gold	8	16	835,792
1967	Never Bend	5	11	216,212	1994	Red Ransom	11	19	666,658
1968	Northern Dancer	8	20	194,960	1995	Farma Way	13	23	819,711
1969	Native Charger	3	6	257,717	1996	Salt Lake	13	20	850,956
1970	Tom Rolfe	5	10	362,279	1997	Gilded Time	12	16	722,072
1971	Buckpasser	5	13	498,566	1998	End Sweep	31	42	935,638
1972	What a Pleasure	11	21	162,147	1999	Cherokee Run	17	26	1,369,126
1973	Drone	9	17	115,012	2000	Honour and Glory	22	30	1,439,824
1974	Dust Commander	6	14	196,742	2001	Valid Expectations	27	40	1,393,897
1975	Al Hattab	11	18	121,146	2002	Distorted Humor	15	27	1,300,602
1976	Raja Baba	13	26	419,872	2003	Victory Gallop	11	14	914,179
1977	Roberto	5	13	237,638					
1978	Mr. Prospector	8	15	308,311					
1979	Tri Jet	6	10	193,282					
1980	Foolish Pleasure	7	15	536,783					
1981	Turn and Count	11	19	283,279					
1982	Seattle Slew	4	11	666,755					
1983	Alydar	4	15	1,136,063					
1984	Danzig	10	22	2,146,530					

Prior to 1962, amount won included earnings only from winning performers.

Prior to 1965, earnings only include money earned in the United States, Canada, Mexico and Puerto Rico.

From 1965 through 1994, earnings only include money earned in the United States, Canada and Mexico.

After 1994, earnings only include the United States and Canada.

World Records

DIST	HORSE	AGE	WT	TRACK	DATE	TIME
2f	Minty Flavors	2	118	Hawthorne	14-May-99	:20.88
2 1/2f	Yes He Will	4	124	Lone Star Park	7-Nov-97	:26.53
3f	Raisable Adversary	11	119	Remington Park	29-Aug-99	:31.20
3 1/2f	Steel Penny Black	2	115	Northlands Park	14-Jun-84	:38.20
4f	Ameri Brilliance	4	121	Timonium	23-Aug-03	:43.76
4 1/2f	Valiant Pete	4	121	Los Alamitos	11-Aug-90	:49.20
5f (T)	General Express	5	114	Monmouth	8-Jul-00	:54.60
5 1/2f (T)	Pembroke	5	120	Hollywood Park	15-Jul-95	1:00.46
6f	G Malleah	4	120	Turf Paradise	8-Apr-95	1:06.60
6 1/2f	Lucky Forever	6	118	Hollywood Park	20-May-95	1:13.24
7f	Rich Cream	5	118	Hollywood Park	28-May-80	1:19.40
	Time To Explode	3	117	Hollywood Park	26-Jun-82	
7 1/2f	Awesome Daze	5	119	Hollywood Park	23-Nov-97	1:26.26
1 mile (T)	Elusive Quality	5	117	Belmont Park	4-Jul-98	1:31.63
1m40 (T)	Castaneto	5	115	Atlantic City	28-Jun-91	1:38.08
1m70 (T)	Aborigine	6	119	Penn National	20-Aug-78	1:37.20
1 1/16m (T)	Told	4	123	Penn National	14-Sep-80	1:38
1 1/8m (T)	Kostroma	5	117	Santa Anita	20-Oct-91	1:43.92
1 3/16m (T)	Toonerville	5	120	Hialeah Park	7-Feb-76	1:51.40
1 1/4m (T)	Double Discount	4	116	Santa Anita	6-Oct-77	1:57.40
1 5/16m (T)	Roberto	3	122	York (England)	15-Aug-72	2:07
1 3/8 (T)	With Approval	4	118	Belmont Park	17-Jun-90	2:10.20
1 7/16m	Who's in Command	5	111	Ellis Park	10-Aug-87	2:23
1 1/2 (T)	Hawkster	3	121	Santa Anita	14-Oct-89	2:22.80
1 9/16	Well Lit	5	120	Sportsman's Park	25-Apr-92	2:35.77
1 5/8m (T)	Tom Swift	5	110	Saratoga	23-Aug-78	2:37
1 11/16m	Glen Gower	4	114	Exhibition Park	9-Sep-87	2:51.20
1 3/4m	Major Pots	5	115	Woodbine	8-Dec-94	2:52.60
1 7/8m (T)	Code's Best	6	121	Mountaineer Racetrack	4-Sep-00	3:08.23
2 m (T)	Petrone	5	124	Hollywood Park	23-Jul-69	3:18
2 1/16m	Midafternoon	4	126	Jamaica	15-Nov-56	3:29.60
2 1/8m	Mr Chancellor	4	111	Exhibition Park	18-Oct-87	3:38.80
2 3/16m	Santiago	5	112	Narragansett	27-Sep-41	3:51.20
2 1/4m	Fenelon	4	119	Belmont Park	4-Oct-41	3:47
2 5/16m	Heiress Marie	3	101	Fairmount Park (Cahokia)	16-Jul-60	4:07.20
2 1/2m	Miss Grillo	6	118	Pimlico	12-Nov-48	4:14.60
3 miles	Farragut	5	113	Agua Caliente, (Mexico)	9-Mar-41	5:15
4 miles	Sotemia	5	119	Churchill Downs	7-Oct-12	7:10.80

Editor's note: All above records are for exact distances and none shorter than 3 1/2 furlongs were set on straight courses. (T) desingates turf. Most times were set in .20 intervals. Exact times in hundredths are noted when available.

North American Dirt Records

DIST	HORSE	AGE	WT	TRACK	DATE	TIME
2f	Onion Roll	7	111	Thistledown	27-Sep-93	:20-4/5
	Nervous Moment	2	120	Sportsman's Park	08-Jun-98	:20-4/5
	Minty Flavors	2	118	Hawthorne	14-May-99	:20-4/5
	Lifeisawhirl	4	122	Calder Race Course	15-Jul-00	:20-4/5
2 1/2f	Nice Choice	7	121	Nuevo Laredo	25-Sep-83	:26-1/5
3f	Raisable Adversary	11	119	Remington Park	29-Aug-99	:31.20
3 1/2f	Steel Penny Black	2	115	Northlands Park	14-Jun-84	:38-1/5
	Spiderwoman	5	122	Douglas	23-Apr-00	:38.20
4f	Ameri Brilliance	4	121	Timonium	23-Aug-03	:43.76
4 1/2f	Valiant Pete	4	121	Los Alamitos	11-Aug-90	:49.20
5f	Chinook Pass	3	113	Longacres	17-Sep-82	:55-1/5
5 1/2f	Plenty Zloty	5	118	Turf Paradise	18-Apr-95	1:01.20
	Silvey's Image	5	116	Turf Paradise	24-Oct-92	1:01 1/5
6f	G Malleah	4	120	Turf Paradise	08-Apr-95	1:06.60
6 1/2f	Lucky Forever	6	118	Hollywood Park	20-May-95	1:13.24
7f	Rich Cream	5	118	Hollywood Park	28-May-80	1:19-2/5
	Time To Explode	3	117	Hollywood Park	26-Jun-82	1:19-2/5
7 1/2f	Awesome Daze	5	119	Hollywood Park	23-Nov-97	1:26.26
1 mile	Dr. Fager	4	134	Arlington	24-Aug-68	1:32 1/5
	Najran	4	113	Belmont Park	07-May-2003	1:32.24
1 1/16m	Hoedown's Day	4	119	Bay Meadows Fair	23-Oct-83	1:38 2/5
1 1/8m	Simply Majestic	4	114	Golden Gate Fields	02-Apr-88	1:45.
1 3/16m	Riva Ridge	4	127	Aqueduct	04-Jul-73	1:52-2/5
	Farma Way	4	119	Pimlico	11-May-91	1:52-2/5
1 1/4m	Spectacular Bid	4	126	Santa Anita Park	03-Feb-80	1:57-4/5
1 5/16m	Gold Star Deputy	5	116	Aqueduct	10-Apr-99	2:07.32

DIST	HORSE	AGE	WT	TRACK	DATE	TIME
1 3/8m	Demi's Bret	4	116	Aqueduct	26-Oct-97	2.12.31
1 7/16m	Who's In Command	5	111	Hastings Park	10-Aug-87	2:23.00
1 1/2m	Secretariat	3	126	Belmont Park	09-Jun-73	2:24.00
1 9/16m	Well Lit	5	120	Sportsman's Park	25-Apr-92	2:35.77
1 5/8m	Swaps	4	130	Hollywood Park	25-Jul-56	2:38.20
1 11/16m	Glen Gower	4	114	Hastings Park	09-Sep-87	2:51-1/5
1 3/4m	Paper Junction	4	123	Lincoln State Fair	10-Nov-85	2:50-2/5
1 13/16m	Fire North	6	111	Philadelphia Park	14-Mar-92	3:04-4/5
1 7/8m	Asserche	6	123	Laurel Park	20-Mar-94	3:11.56
1 15/16m	Chased Again	10	117	Shenandoah Downs	17-Sep-60	3:24-3/5
2 miles	Kelso	7	124	Aqueduct	31-Oct-64	3:19-1/5
2 1/8m	Laddie's Prince	4	116	Hastings Park	07-Oct-87	3:30
2 1/4m	Paraje	7	113	Aqueduct	15-Dec-73	3:47-4/5
2 5/16m	Heiress Marie	3	101	Cahokia Downs	16-Jul-60	4:07-1/5
2 3/8m	Naughty Nipper	5	119	Lincoln State Fair	13-Nov-83	4:34-1/5
2 1/2m	Miss Grillo	6	118	Pimlico	12-Nov-48	4:14-3/5
2 9/16m	Diamond Platter	7	116	Finger Lakes	12-Oct-74	4:50
2 5/8m	Amber Dare	3	115	Finger Lakes	17-Nov-73	5:12-2/5
2 11/16m	Bea Beauty	8	122	Thistledown	08-Sep-73	4:47-4/5
2 3/4m	Fourth Flight	7	116	Finger Lakes	24-Nov-73	5:35-2/5
3 miles	Farragut	5	113	Agua Caliente	09-Mar-41	5:15
3m 40y	Bea Beauty	8	128	Thistledown	22-Sep-73	5:31-4/5
3m 70y	Gloria Dream	6	110	River Downs	09-Aug-72	5:32-1/5
3 1/16m	Dauntless Pride	4	111	Finger Lakes	19-Oct-74	5:45-2/5
3 1/4m	Dauntless Pride	4	117	Finger Lakes	26-Oct-74	6:15-1/5
3 5/8m	Eastern Promise	6	120	Thistledown	06-Oct-73	6:49-3/5
4 miles	Sotemia	5	119	Churchill Downs	07-Oct-22	7:10-4/5
4m 70y	Gloria Dream	6	113	Finger Lakes	04-Nov-72	8:01
4 1/16m	Amber Dare	3	113	Finger Lakes	03-Nov-73	8:12-2/5
4 1/8m	Victory Tour	4	115	Finger Lakes	02-Nov-74	8:08

Editor's Note: Only exact distances are included in this listing, no 'About' distances.

North American Turf Records

DIST	HORSE	AGE	WT	TRACK	DATE	TIME
4f	Fine Tassles	5	122	Rillito	30-Jan-94	:46.-3/5
4 1/2f	Dan's Groovy	7	120	Turf Paradise	13-Apr-03	:49.26
5f	General Express	5	114	Monmouth Park	08-Jul-00	:54.-3/5
	Bop	5	121	Penn National	03-Aug-02	:54.61
5 1/2f	Pembroke	5	120	Hollywood Park	15-Jul-95	1:00.46
6f	Answer Do	4	115	Hollywood Park	15-Dec-90	1:07.00
6 1/2f	Key Twenty Two	6	115	Woodbine	04-Jun-92	1:14-1/5
7f	Officialpermission	6	112	Belmont Park	23-Jul-00	1.19.88
7 1/2ff	Court Lark	6	115	Calder Race Course	16-Jul-94	1:26-2/5
1 mile	Elusive Quality	5	117	Belmont Park	04-Jul-98	1:31.63
1 1/16m	Told	4	123	Penn National	14-Sep-80	1:38.00
1 1/8m	Kostroma	5	117	Santa Anita Park	20-Oct-91	1:43.92
1 3/16m	Toonerville	4	120	Hialeah Park	07-Feb-76	1:51-2/5
1 1/4m	Double Discount	4	116	Santa Anita Park	09-Oct-77	1:57-2/5
1 5/16m	Ruff Mack	5	114	Mountaineer Park	25-Aug-02	2:06
1 3/8m	With Approval	4	118	Belmont Park	17-Jun-90	2:10.20
1 7/16m	Dina's Playmate	11	120	River Downs	30-Aug-69	2:25.00
1 1/2m	Hawkster	3	121	Santa Anita Park	14-Oct-89	2:22-4/5
1 5/8m	Tom Swift	5	110	Saratoga	23-Aug-78	2:37.00
1 3/4m	Pleasant Company	4	112	Mountaineer	17-Aug-03	2:55.99
1 13/16m	Misting Rain	8	115	Retama Park	28-Sep-96	3:13.22
1 7/8m	Code's Best	6	121	Mountaineer Park	04-Sep-00	3:08.23
2 miles	Irish Harbour	6	113	Ellis Park	02-Sep-96	3:20-1/5
2 1/16m	Deux-Moulins	8	124	Arlington	28-Jul-55	3:30-4/5
2 1/4m	Buteo	6	122	River Downs	03-Sep-90	3:48.40
2 3/8m	Lively London	5	113	Delaware Park	25-Jul-86	4:09.00
2 13/16	Augustus Bay	8	142	Camden	16-Nov-74	5:24.00
2 7/8m	Call Louis	4	107	Delaware Park	24-Aug-86	5:08-1/5

Editor's note: All records are exact distances. No 'About' distances included.

Canadian Dirt Records

DIST	HORSE	AGE	WT	TRACK	DATE	TIME
2f	Leisure Road	5	120	Fort Erie	5-Sep-98	:21 1/5
3f	Rejected Frenchman	3	122	Kin Park	1-Aug-93	:32 1/5
3 1/2f	Steel Penny Black	2	115	Northlands Park	14-Jun-84	:38 1/5
4f	Adventuresome Love	8	115	Stampede Park	3-Apr-93	:43 4/5
4 1/2f	Canadian Silver	4	119	Greenwood	22-Mar-92	:50
5f	Jack and Emma	4	118	Woodbine	5-Apr-03	:55.95
5 1/2f	Uncle Woger	4	119	Woodbine	4-Apr-99	1:02 3/5
6f	Great Defender	3	114	Woodbine	27-Nov-99	1:08
6 1/2f	Fair Juror	4	105	Woodbine	17-Oct-61	1:14 3/5
7f	Oronero	3	114	Woodbine	6-Dec-95	1:20 3/5
7 1/2f	Iron Vigors	4	122	Assiniboia Downs	9-Oct-89	1:31
1 mile	Twist The Snow	3	117	Greenwood	2-Dec-89	1:34
1m 1/16	Kiridashi	4	121	Woodbine	17-Aug-96	1:40 4/5
1m 1/8	Artic Son	5	117	Hastings Park	3-Aug-98	1:46 4/5
1m 3/16	Bruce's Mill	3	126	Fort Erie	31-Jul-94	1:53 4/5
1m 1/4	Alphabet Soup	5	126	Woodbine	26-Oct-96	2:01
1m 5/16	Arctic Laur	7	116	Northlands Park	20-Aug-95	2:09
1m 3/8	Irish Bear	3	122	Hastings Park	17-Oct-87	2:14 2/5
1m 7/16	Who's In Command	5	111	Hastings Park	10-Aug-87	2:23
1m 1/2	Lucky Son	4	117	Hastings Park	25-Aug-95	2:29
1m 9/16	Eagle's Game	4	123	Kamloops Ex.	6-Sep-92	2:41
1m 5/8	Eugenia II	4	123	Woodbine	27-Oct-56	2:43 2/5
1m 11/16	Glen Gower	4	114	Hastings Park	9-Sep-87	2:51 1/5
1m 3/4	Major Pots	5	115	Woodbine	8-Dec-94	2:52 3/5
1m 13/16	Captain Charisma	5	121	Fort Erie	12-Aug-84	3:09 2/5
1m 7/8	Flying Commander	3	112	Woodbine	2-Dec-01	3:13 1/5
2 miles	Grandin Park	9	118	Stampede Park	13-Oct-79	3:29
2m 1/16	Laddie's Prince	4	116	Hastings Park	7-Oct-87	3:30
2m 1/4	Fremarcton	8	124	Assiniboia Downs	15-Aug-60	3:58 1/5

Editor's note: Only exact distances included on this list, no 'About' distances. Some records were set on tracks that no longer exist.

Canadian Turf Records

DIST	HORSE	AGE	WT	TRACK	DATE	TIME
5f	Oh Mar	6	120	Fort Erie	9-Sep-02	56:99
6f	Wild Zone	6	119	Woodbine	7-Jul-96	1:07 3/5
6.5f	Key Twenty Two	6	115	Woodbine	4-Jun-92	1:14 1/5
7f	Unduplicated	3	116	Woodbine	23-Jun-91	1:20 1/5
7f	Wild Zone	5	120	Woodbine	30-Jul-95	1:20 1/5
1 mile	Viking King	4	118	Woodbine	20-Jun-91	1:32 3/5
	Numerous Times	4	117	Woodbine	9-Sep-01	1:32.79
1m 1/16	Bravest Shot	6	114	Woodbine	1-Jun-90	1:38 4/5
1m 1/8	Bold Ruritana	5	117	Woodbine	18-Jun-95	1:45 1/5
1m 1/4	Mill Native	9	126	Woodbine	20-Aug-88	2:00
1m 3/8	Dawson's Legacy	4	114	Woodbine	25-Sep-99	2:13
1m 1/2	Raintrap	4	126	Woodbine	16-Oct-94	2:25 3/5
1m 5/8	Dahlia	4	123	Woodbine	27-Oct-74	2:40
1m 3/4	Desperado Dan	4	115	Woodbine	22-Jul-84	2:56 2/5
1m 7/8	Medlaw	5	123	Fort Erie	30-Sep-85	3:16 1/5
2 miles	Sir Axton	4	117	Woodbine	23-Oct-65	3:56 4/5

Editor's note: Only exact distances included, no 'About' distances.

Track	Surf.	Abt.	Distance	Win Time	Date

The Downs at Albuquerque

Track	Surf.	Abt.	Distance	Win Time	Date
ALB	D		5F	:56.68	9/14/03
ALB	D		5 1/2F	1:02.78	5/25/03
ALB	D		6F	1:09.43	4/6/03
ALB	D		6 1/2F	1:15.41	9/9/03
ALB	D		7F	1:21.01	6/8/03
ALB	D		1M	1:35.57	4/27/03
ALB	D		1 1/16M	1:42.85	9/20/03
ALB	D		1 1/8M	1:48.42	6/8/03
ALB	D		1 1/2M	2:35.06	6/8/03
ALB	D		1 13/16M	3:08.50	9/21/03
ALB	NO TURF				

Anthony Fair

Track	Surf.	Abt.	Distance	Win Time	Date
ANF	D		4 1/2F	:56.40	7/20/03
ANF	D		5F	1:01.07	7/12/03
ANF	D	A	5F	1:01.67	7/13/03
ANF	D	A	6 1/2F	1:21.44	7/20/03
ANF	D		7F	1:28.94	7/12/03
ANF	D		1 1/16M	1:52.41	7/19/03
ANF	NO TURF				

Arlington Park

Track	Surf.	Abt.	Distance	Win Time	Date
AP	D		4 1/2F	:52.22	6/7/03
AP	D		5F	:57.87	7/13/03
AP	D		5 1/2F	1:03.70	6/27/03
AP	D		6F	1:08.85	7/11/03
AP	D		6 1/2F	1:15.03	9/5/03
AP	D		7F	1:21.88	8/16/03
AP	D		1M	1:34.40	6/29/03
AP	D		1 1/8M	1:49.73	8/16/03
AP	D		1 3/16M	1:55.49	7/19/03
AP	D		1 1/4M	2:05.59	5/23/03
AP	D		1 1/2M	2:33.43	8/3/03

AP Turf

Track	Surf.	Abt.	Distance	Win Time	Date
AP	T	A	5F	:56.38	9/18/03
AP	T		5F	:56.64	7/19/03
AP	T		1M	1:35.85	6/15/03
AP	T	A	1M	1:35.97	8/10/03
AP	T		1 1/16M	1:42.15	6/21/03
AP	T	A	1 1/16M	1:42.89	9/19/03
AP	T	A	1 1/8M	1:48.31	9/18/03
AP	T		1 1/8M	1:49.16	9/13/03
AP	T		1 3/16M	1:55.06	7/26/03
AP	T		1 1/4M	2:02.29	8/16/03
AP	T		1 1/2M	2:28.30	7/5/03
AP	T	A	1 1/2M	2:29.91	6/27/03

Aqueduct

Track	Surf.	Abt.	Distance	Win Time	Date
AQU	D		4 1/2F	:52.01	4/30/03
AQU	D		6F	1:07.77	4/26/03
AQU	D		6 1/2F	1:16.68	11/23/03
AQU	D		7F	1:21.11	4/25/03
AQU	D		1M	1:33.77	4/26/03
AQU	D		1M 70Y	1:40.11	1/4/03
AQU	D		1 1/16M	1:42.98	1/4/03
AQU	D		1 1/8M	1:48.10	4/5/03
AQU	D		1 3/16M	1:55.90	12/13/03
AQU	D		1 1/4M	2:04.15	1/12/03
AQU	D		1 5/8M	2:45.08	12/27/03

Aqu Turf

Track	Surf.	Abt.	Distance	Win Time	Date
AQU	T		1M	1:35.75	5/2/03
AQU	T		1 1/16M	1:41.42	5/3/03
AQU	T		1 1/8M	1:50.53	11/1/03
AQU	T		1 3/8M	2:18.86	11/22/03
AQU	T		1 1/2M	2:32.58	11/15/03

Arapahoe Park

Track	Surf.	Abt.	Distance	Win Time	Date
ARP	D		4F	:45.00	6/14/03
ARP	D		4 1/2F	:52.60	6/28/03
ARP	D		5F	:56.80	7/8/03
ARP	D		5 1/2F	1:02.60	8/23/03
ARP	D		6F	1:08.80	7/5/03
ARP	D		6F	1:08.80	8/24/03
ARP	D		7F	1:21.00	7/4/03
ARP	D		1M	1:35.60	7/4/03
ARP	D		1 1/16M	1:43.20	6/28/03
ARP	D		1 1/16M	1:43.20	8/23/03
ARP	D		1 1/2M	2:40.00	8/25/03
ARP	NO TURF				

Assiniboia Downs

Track	Surf.	Abt.	Distance	Win Time	Date
ASD	D	A	3F	:29.80	6/28/03
ASD	D		4 1/2F	:54.40	7/18/03
ASD	D		5F	:58.80	5/4/03
ASD	D		5 1/2F	1:04.80	5/24/03
ASD	D		6F	1:10.60	6/15/03
ASD	D		7F	1:27.00	9/7/03
ASD	D		1M	1:39.80	9/20/03
ASD	D		1 1/16M	1:45.40	9/6/03
ASD	D		1 1/8M	1:53.00	8/24/03
ASD	D		1 1/4M	2:11.40	9/12/03
ASD	NO TURF				

Atlantic City Racecourse

Track	Surf.	Abt.	Distance	Win Time	Date
ATL	NO DIRT				
ATL	T		5F	:56.53	4/30/03
ATL	T		5 1/2F	1:02.94	5/2/03
ATL	T		1 1/16M	1:43.54	4/30/03
ATL	T	A	1 1/2M	2:44.80	4/23/03

Atokad

Track	Surf.	Abt.	Distance	Win Time	Date
ATO	D		4F	:45.40	7/20/03
ATO	D		6F	1:13.40	7/20/03
ATO	D	A	6F	1:16.40	7/20/03
ATO	D		1M 70Y	1:45.80	7/20/03
ATO	D		1 1/8M	1:54.60	7/20/03
ATO	NO TURF				

Track	Surf. Abt.	Distance	Win Time	Date

Belmont Park

Track	Surf. Abt.	Distance	Win Time	Date
BEL	D	5F	:56.81	5/23/03
BEL	D	5 1/2F	1:04.21	6/20/03
BEL	D	6F	1:07.86	5/24/03
BEL	D	6 1/2F	1:14.72	9/27/03
BEL	D	7F	1:21.42	9/5/03
BEL	D	1M	1:32.24	5/7/03
BEL	D	1 1/16M	1:40.44	5/7/03
BEL	D	1 1/8M	1:46.21	9/6/03
BEL	D	1 1/4M	2:00.25	9/27/03
BEL	D	1 3/8M	2:16.54	9/19/03
BEL	D	1 1/2M	2:28.26	6/7/03

Bel Turf

Track	Surf. Abt.	Distance	Win Time	Date
BEL	T	6F	1:08.86	10/13/03
BEL	T	7F	1:20.20	9/17/03
BEL	T	1M	1:32.81	7/5/03
BEL	T	1 1/16M	1:39.78	5/7/03
BEL	T	1 1/8M	1:46.02	9/21/03
BEL	T	1 1/4M	1:59.63	7/4/03
BEL	T	1 3/8M	2:13.26	9/21/03
BEL	T	1 1/2M	2:27.51	9/27/03

Beulah Park

Track	Surf. Abt.	Distance	Win Time	Date
BEU	D	4 1/2F	:50.96	4/18/03
BEU	D	5F	:57.40	1/21/03
BEU	D	5 1/2F	1:02.79	2/14/03
BEU	D	6F	1:08.87	12/7/03
BEU	D	1M	1:35.47	1/17/03
BEU	D	1M 70Y	1:40.65	1/12/03
BEU	D	1 1/16M	1:43.43	1/14/03
BEU	D	1 1/8M	1:50.19	2/8/03
BEU	D	1 1/4M	2:03.05	11/23/03
BEU	D	1 1/2M	2:35.83	11/8/03
BEU	D	1 3/4M	3:02.04	11/29/03
BEU	NO TURF			

Bay Meadows

Track	Surf. Abt.	Distance	Win Time	Date
BM	D	2F	:22.34	4/23/03
BM	D	4 1/2F	:50.95	5/1/03
BM	D	5F	:57.04	5/4/03
BM	D	5 1/2F	1:01.75	4/16/03
BM	D	6F	1:07.84	4/19/03
BM	D	1M	1:34.33	9/13/03
BM	D	1 1/16M	1:41.47	4/30/03
BM	D	1 1/8M	1:47.65	4/12/03

BM Turf

Track	Surf. Abt.	Distance	Win Time	Date
BM	T	4 1/2F	:51.12	4/11/03
BM	T	5F	:56.75	4/20/03
BM	T	1M	1:35.47	4/6/03
BM	T	1 1/16M	1:42.30	10/26/03
BM	T A	1 1/8M	1:45.41	5/24/03
BM	T	1 1/8M	1:48.97	11/1/03

Bay Meadows Fair

Track	Surf. Abt.	Distance	Win Time	Date
BMF	D	4 1/2F	:53.47	8/10/03
BMF	D	5F	:58.01	8/9/03
BMF	D	5 1/2F	1:03.74	8/16/03
BMF	D	6F	1:08.87	8/15/03
BMF	D	1M	1:36.06	8/16/03

Bmf Turf

Track	Surf. Abt.	Distance	Win Time	Date
BMF	T	4 1/2F	:51.65	8/16/03
BMF	T	5F	:56.71	8/18/03
BMF	T	1M	1:36.48	8/9/03
BMF	T	1 1/16M	1:42.40	8/17/03

Les Bois Park

Track	Surf. Abt.	Distance	Win Time	Date
BOI	D	2F	:21.40	5/4/03
BOI	D	4 1/2F	:51.20	5/26/03
BOI	D	5F	:57.00	6/28/03
BOI	D	5F	:57.00	7/20/03
BOI	D	5F	:57.00	7/30/03
BOI	D	5F	:57.00	8/9/03
BOI	D	6 1/2F	1:18.40	6/28/03
BOI	D	6 1/2F	1:18.40	7/13/03
BOI	D	6 1/2F	1:18.40	7/16/03
BOI	D	7F	1:23.60	7/5/03
BOI	D	7 1/2F	1:30.20	7/23/03
BOI	D	1M	1:37.20	8/9/03
BOI	D	1M	1:37.20	8/10/03
BOI	NO TURF			

Blue Ribbon Downs

Track	Surf. Abt.	Distance	Win Time	Date
BRD	D	4F	:45.51	6/29/03
BRD	D	4 1/2F	:51.45	5/3/03
BRD	D	5F	:57.90	10/26/03
BRD	D	5 1/2F	1:04.56	3/29/03
BRD	D	6F	1:09.86	3/8/03
BRD	D	7 1/2F	1:30.93	5/3/03
BRD	D	1M	1:37.80	7/19/03
BRD	D	1 1/16M	1:46.45	3/22/03
BRD	D	1 1/8M	1:56.11	8/2/03
BRD	NO TURF			

Harney County Fair

Track	Surf. Abt.	Distance	Win Time	Date
BRN	D	5F	1:00.80	9/7/03
BRN	D	7F	1:28.60	9/6/03
BRN	D	1 1/8M	1:57.40	9/6/03
BRN	NO TURF			

Canterbury Park

Track	Surf. Abt.	Distance	Win Time	Date
CBY	D	3 1/2F	:39.34	6/1/03
CBY	D	5F	:59.32	8/10/03
CBY	D	5 1/2F	1:03.02	7/12/03
CBY	D	6F	1:08.97	7/18/03
CBY	D	6 1/2F	1:15.47	7/19/03

Track	Surf.	Abt.	Distance	Win Time	Date
CBY	D		1M	1:37.61	8/2/03
CBY	D		1M 70Y	1:42.13	9/1/03
CBY	D		1 1/16M	1:44.99	7/19/03
CBY	D		1 1/8M	1:49.17	7/19/03

Cby Turf

Track	Surf.	Abt.	Distance	Win Time	Date
CBY	T		5F	:56.60	7/19/03
CBY	T	A	7 1/2F	1:28.69	7/27/03
CBY	T		7 1/2F	1:29.54	6/14/03
CBY	T		1M	1:34.91	6/15/03
CBY	T	A	1M	1:35.42	7/27/03
CBY	T	A	1 1/16M	1:41.46	7/26/03
CBY	T		1 1/16M	1:41.87	8/2/03
CBY	T		1 3/8M	2:16.02	9/1/03

Churchill Downs

Track	Surf.	Abt.	Distance	Win Time	Date
CD	D		4 1/2F	:51.31	5/2/03
CD	D		5F	:57.12	6/12/03
CD	D		5 1/2F	1:03.70	6/7/03
CD	D		6F	1:08.34	5/14/03
CD	D		6 1/2F	1:14.78	11/22/03
CD	D		7F	1:21.76	6/8/03
CD	D		7 1/2F	1:28.33	6/27/03
CD	D		1M	1:34.13	5/2/03
CD	D		1 1/16M	1:42.29	6/22/03
CD	D		1 1/8M	1:47.55	6/14/03
CD	D		1 1/4M	2:01.19	5/3/03

CD Turf

Track	Surf.	Abt.	Distance	Win Time	Date
CD	T		5F	:55.57	5/14/03
CD	T		1M	1:33.96	5/3/03
CD	T		1 1/16M	1:41.38	5/2/03
CD	T		1 1/8M	1:46.67	5/3/03
CD	T		1 3/8M	2:14.09	5/31/03
CD	T		1 1/2M	2:29.00	6/25/03

Columbus

Track	Surf.	Abt.	Distance	Win Time	Date
CLS	D		3 1/2F	:40.60	8/8/03
CLS	D		6F	1:11.60	9/6/03
CLS	D		6 1/2F	1:19.20	8/30/03
CLS	D		6 1/2F	1:19.20	9/1/03
CLS	D		6 1/2F	1:19.20	9/13/03
CLS	D		1M 70Y	1:44.40	9/14/03
CLS	D		1 1/16M	1:47.80	9/1/03
CLS	D		1 3/8M	2:21.60	8/30/03
CLS	NO TURF				

Colonial Downs

Track	Surf.	Abt.	Distance	Win Time	Date
CNL	D		5F	:55.74	7/1/03
CNL	D		5 1/2F	1:02.68	7/1/03
CNL	D		6F	1:09.06	6/28/03
CNL	D		7F	1:21.97	7/5/03
CNL	D		1M	1:35.65	6/13/03

Track	Surf.	Abt.	Distance	Win Time	Date
CNL	D		1M	1:35.65	7/1/03
CNL	D		1 1/16M	1:42.76	7/20/03
CNL	D		1 1/8M	1:51.59	7/1/03

Cnl Turf

Track	Surf.	Abt.	Distance	Win Time	Date
CNL	T		5F	:57.18	7/4/03
CNL	T		5 1/2F	1:03.52	7/7/03
CNL	T		1M	1:37.34	7/8/03
CNL	T		1 1/16M	1:43.95	7/7/03
CNL	T		1 1/8M	1:49.16	7/12/03
CNL	T		1 3/16M	1:58.37	6/27/03
CNL	T		1 1/4M	2:01.11	7/12/03

Chippewa Downs

Track	Surf.	Abt.	Distance	Win Time	Date
CPW	D		2 1/2F	:32.60	6/22/03
CPW	D		4 1/2F	:56.60	6/22/03
CPW	D		5F	1:02.20	6/21/03
CPW	D		5 1/2F	1:11.00	6/22/03
CPW	D		6 1/2F	1:25.20	6/22/03
CPW	D		1 1/16M	1:56.20	6/22/03

Calder Race Course

Track	Surf.	Abt.	Distance	Win Time	Date
CRC	D		2F	:21.15	7/12/03
CRC	D		4 1/2F	:52.56	6/22/03
CRC	D		5F	:58.47	6/22/03
CRC	D		5 1/2F	1:04.54	7/26/03
CRC	D		6F	1:10.03	7/12/03
CRC	D		6 1/2F	1:17.31	7/26/03
CRC	D		7F	1:23.51	12/13/03
CRC	D		1M	1:38.65	9/1/03
CRC	D		1M 70Y	1:44.85	5/11/03
CRC	D		1 1/16M	1:43.77	7/26/03
CRC	D		1 1/8M	1:52.47	12/27/03
CRC	D		1 1/4M	2:07.55	7/14/03
CRC	D		1 1/2M	2:40.84	6/7/03

Crc Turf

Track	Surf.	Abt.	Distance	Win Time	Date
CRC	T		5F	:55.52	5/20/03
CRC	T		7 1/2F	1:27.41	12/20/03
CRC	T		1M	1:34.64	5/11/03
CRC	T		1 1/16M	1:39.95	12/31/03
CRC	T		1 1/8M	1:45.81	12/6/03
CRC	T		1 1/2M	2:24.87	12/27/03

Charles Town

Track	Surf.	Abt.	Distance	Win Time	Date
CT	D		4F	:46.89	2/9/03
CT	D		4 1/2F	:51.04	11/20/03
CT	D		6 1/2F	1:18.16	1/4/03
CT	D		7F	1:24.47	6/14/03
CT	D		1 1/16M	1:46.17	6/12/03
CT	D		1 1/8M	1:54.81	10/10/03
CT	NO TURF				

Track	Surf. Abt.	Distance	Win Time	Date
Delta Downs				
DED	D	4 1/2F	:52.90	3/22/03
DED	D	5F	:57.49	11/5/03
DED	D	6 1/2F	1:19.01	1/11/03
DED	D	7F	1:24.31	1/24/03
DED	D	7 1/2F	1:35.63	2/20/03
DED	D	1M	1:38.72	11/15/03
DED	D	1 1/16M	1:44.07	11/12/03
DED	D	1 1/8M	1:57.62	1/11/03
DED	D	1 1/4M	2:12.38	2/15/03
DED	D	1 3/8M	2:23.52	3/22/03
DED	NO TURF			
Delaware Park				
DEL	D	2F	:22.72	5/12/03
DEL	D	4 1/2F	:53.47	5/17/03
DEL	D	5F	:57.59	9/6/03
DEL	D	5 1/2F	1:03.48	8/26/03
DEL	D	6F	1:08.35	9/6/03
DEL	D	1M	1:36.08	9/16/03
DEL	D	1M 70Y	1:39.20	8/25/03
DEL	D	1 1/16M	1:42.76	8/31/03
DEL	D	1 1/8M	1:48.89	9/27/03
DEL	D	1 3/16M	1:58.07	10/4/03
DEL	D	1 1/4M	2:02.95	7/20/03
DEL	D	1 1/2M	2:34.71	11/3/03
Del Turf				
DEL	T	1M	1:35.32	7/30/03
DEL	T A	1M	1:38.21	7/5/03
DEL	T	1 1/16M	1:41.72	7/19/03
DEL	T A	1 1/16M	1:44.15	10/11/03
DEL	T	1 1/8M	1:47.44	7/20/03
DEL	T A	1 1/8M	1:50.58	7/26/03
DEL	T	1 3/8M	2:15.04	7/19/03
DEL	T A	1 3/8M	2:17.87	7/27/03
DEL	T	1 1/2M	2:26.46	7/20/03
Cochise County Fair				
DG	D A	3F	:38.60	4/20/03
DG	D	5 1/2F	1:06.00	4/13/03
DG	D	6F	1:13.40	4/13/03
DG	D	7F	1:25.40	4/19/03
DG	NO TURF			
Del Mar				
DMR	D	5 1/2F	1:03.31	7/25/03
DMR	D	6F	1:07.90	9/6/03
DMR	D	6 1/2F	1:15.53	8/23/03
DMR	D	7F	1:21.53	8/17/03
DMR	D	1M	1:35.57	9/5/03
DMR	D	1 1/16M	1:41.84	7/26/03
DMR	D	1 1/8M	1:50.54	8/1/03
DMR	D	1 1/4M	1:59.11	8/24/03
Dmr Park				
DMR	T	5F	:55.06	7/28/03
DMR	T	1M	1:32.22	8/2/03
DMR	T	1 1/16M	1:39.84	8/27/03
DMR	T	1 1/8M	1:45.87	7/27/03
DMR	T	1 3/8M	2:12.07	8/29/03
Greenlee County Fair				
DUN	D	5F	1:01.20	3/15/03
DUN	D	5 1/2F	1:05.60	3/23/03
DUN	D	5 1/2F	1:05.60	3/23/03
DUN	D A	6F	1:11.80	3/15/03
DUN	D	7F	1:27.60	3/15/03
DUN	NO TURF			
Elko				
ELK	D	3 1/2F	:45.07	8/29/03
ELK	D	5 1/2F	1:06.60	8/31/03
ELK	D	5 1/2F	1:06.60	9/1/03
ELK	D	6F	1:14.00	8/29/03
ELK	D	6 1/2F	1:19.80	8/30/03
ELK	D	7F	1:25.20	9/1/03
ELK	D	1M	1:41.00	9/1/03
ELK	NO TURF			
Ellis Park				
ELP	D	5F	:58.70	8/27/03
ELP	D	5 1/2F	1:03.60	8/31/03
ELP	D	6F	1:09.92	8/10/03
ELP	D	6 1/2F	1:16.28	7/26/03
ELP	D	7F	1:22.50	7/17/03
ELP	D	1M	1:36.07	7/20/03
ELP	D	1 1/8M	1:50.09	8/9/03
ELP	D	1 1/2M	2:34.80	8/10/03
ELP	D	2 1/4M	4:01.05	9/1/03
ELP Turf				
ELP	T	5 1/2F	1:01.21	8/15/03
ELP	T	1M	1:33.01	7/20/03
ELP	T	1 1/16M	1:39.48	7/19/03
ELP	T	1 1/8M	1:47.30	8/15/03
ELP	T	1 1/2M	2:26.65	8/27/03
Emerald Downs				
EMD	D	2F	:23.40	4/24/03
EMD	D	4 1/2F	:51.80	5/18/03
EMD	D	4 1/2F	:51.80	7/3/03
EMD	D	4 1/2F	:51.80	8/30/03
EMD	D	5F	:55.40	8/24/03
EMD	D	5 1/2F	1:02.00	4/19/03
EMD	D	6F	1:07.80	4/27/03
EMD	D	6F	1:07.80	8/31/03
EMD	D	6 1/2F	1:14.00	5/18/03
EMD	D	1M	1:33.00	8/24/03

Track	Surf.	Abt.	Distance	Win Time	Date
EMD	D		1 1/16M	1:40.20	7/4/03
EMD	D		1 1/8M	1:46.80	7/27/03
EMD	D		1 1/4M	2:02.00	8/1/03
EMD	D		1 1/2M	2:32.00	8/17/03
EMD	NO TURF				

Eureka

EUR	D		4F	:46.20	6/28/03
EUR	D		6F	1:14.81	6/1/03
EUR	D		7F	1:29.82	6/1/03
EUR	D		1 1/16M	1:54.21	6/21/03
EUR	NO TURF				

Evangeline Downs

EVD	D		4 1/2F	:52.40	5/23/03
EVD	D		5F	:58.40	6/20/03
EVD	D		5 1/2F	1:04.60	5/24/03
EVD	D		6F	1:10.40	6/26/03
EVD	D		7 1/2F	1:32.40	6/5/03
EVD	D		7 1/2F	1:32.40	8/22/03
EVD	D		7 1/2F	1:32.40	8/25/03
EVD	D		1M	1:37.40	8/16/03
EVD	D		1M 70Y	1:44.00	5/2/03
EVD	D		1M 70Y	1:44.00	8/1/03
EVD	D		1M 70Y	1:44.00	8/15/03
EVD	D		1 1/16M	1:44.80	5/3/03
EVD	NO TURF				

North Dakota Horse Park

FAR	D		4F	:51.80	9/1/03
FAR	D		4 1/2F	:56.80	8/24/03
FAR	D		5F	1:01.20	9/7/03
FAR	D		5 1/2F	1:09.20	8/24/03
FAR	D		6F	1:12.40	8/29/03
FAR	D		7F	1:30.20	9/14/03
FAR	D		1M	1:44.00	9/1/03
FAR	D		1M	1:44.00	9/12/03
FAR	NO TURF				

Fort Erie

FE	D		2F	:21.42	6/17/03
FE	D		5F	:56.50	10/6/03
FE	D		6F	1:09.76	6/3/03
FE	D		6 1/2F	1:16.17	11/10/03
FE	D		1M 70Y	1:41.43	6/21/03
FE	D		1 1/16M	1:42.42	9/22/03
FE	D		1 1/8M	1:50.93	8/16/03
FE	D		1 3/16M	1:55.84	7/20/03

FE Turf

FE	T		5F	:57.93	7/1/03
FE	T	A	5F	:58.39	9/8/03
FE	T	A	7F	1:22.35	8/24/03
FE	T		1M	1:38.02	6/24/03
FE	T		1 1/16M	1:43.45	7/20/03
FE	T	A	1 1/16M	1:44.91	7/4/03
FE	T	A	1 3/8M	2:21.93	9/7/03

Ferndale

FER	D		5F	:57.87	8/17/03
FER	D		6 1/2F	1:18.81	8/9/03
FER	D		7F	1:24.56	8/15/03
FER	D		1 1/16M	1:47.09	8/16/03
FER	D		1 5/8M	2:48.34	8/17/03
FER	NO TURF				

Fair Grounds

FG	D		5F	:57.35	2/10/03
FG	D		5 1/2F	1:03.45	3/31/03
FG	D		6F	1:08.83	3/16/03
FG	D		1M	1:36.64	1/25/03
FG	D		1M 40Y	1:40.41	12/11/03
FG	D		1 1/16M	1:42.67	3/9/03
FG	D		1 1/8M	1:48.92	3/2/03

Fair Grounds Turf

FG	T	A	5 1/2F	1:03.46	12/28/03
FG	T	A	7 1/2F	1:33.83	3/31/03
FG	T	A	1M	1:36.19	12/26/03
FG	T	A	1 1/16M	1:44.33	12/27/03
FG	T	A	1 1/8M	1:50.41	2/1/03

Finger Lakes

FL	D		4 1/2F	:52.18	4/25/03
FL	D		5F	:58.52	5/2/03
FL	D		5 1/2F	1:03.37	9/22/03
FL	D		6F	1:09.85	7/4/03
FL	D		1M	1:39.04	8/1/03
FL	D		1M 70Y	1:43.12	10/20/03
FL	D		1 1/16M	1:44.74	7/26/03
FL	D		1 1/8M	1:51.72	9/6/03
FL	D		1 1/4M	2:08.00	9/5/03
FL	NO TURF				

Flagstaff

FLG	D	A	3F	:41.00	7/4/03
FLG	D		5 1/2F	1:09.00	7/4/03
FLG	D		5 1/2F	1:09.00	7/5/03
FLG	D		6F	1:12.80	7/5/03
FLG	D		6 1/2F	1:25.20	7/6/03
FLG	D		7F	1:28.40	7/7/03
FLG	NO TURF				

Fair Meadows

FMT	D		4F	:45.00	4/23/03
FMT	D		5 1/2F	1:05.40	4/27/03
FMT	D		6F	1:11.20	4/12/03

Track	Surf.	Abt.	Distance	Win Time	Date
FMT	D		6 1/2F	1:17.60	5/26/03
FMT	D		1M	1:37.60	5/31/03
FMT	D		1 1/16M	1:45.60	5/29/03
FMT	NO TURF				

Fresno

Track	Surf.	Abt.	Distance	Win Time	Date
FNO	D		4 1/2F	:51.14	10/8/03
FNO	D		5F	:56.81	10/11/03
FNO	D		5 1/2F	1:04.39	10/1/03
FNO	D		6F	1:08.54	10/12/03
FNO	D		1M	1:35.96	10/11/03
FNO	D		1 1/16M	1:43.26	10/4/03
FNO	D		1 1/8M	1:51.14	10/13/03
FNO	NO TURF				

Fonner Park

Track	Surf.	Abt.	Distance	Win Time	Date
FON	D		4F	:46.00	4/17/03
FON	D		6F	1:11.60	3/8/03
FON	D		6 1/2F	1:18.60	4/12/03
FON	D		1M	1:38.20	4/12/03
FON	D		1M 70Y	1:44.40	5/2/03
FON	D		1 1/16M	1:43.60	4/26/03
FON	D		1 1/8M	1:55.40	5/4/03
FON	NO TURF				

Fairmount Park

Track	Surf.	Abt.	Distance	Win Time	Date
FP	D		2F	:20.80	5/3/03
FP	D		4F	:46.80	4/12/03
FP	D		4 1/2F	:52.60	6/4/03
FP	D		5F	:58.20	4/15/03
FP	D		5 1/2F	1:04.80	4/23/03
FP	D		6F	1:10.20	5/9/03
FP	D		1M	1:38.60	6/3/03
FP	D		1M 70Y	1:42.60	8/15/03
FP	D		1 1/16M	1:47.20	9/26/03
FP	D		1 1/8M	1:55.40	8/12/03
FP	D		1 1/4M	2:07.40	8/1/03
FP	NO TURF				

Fairplex Park

Track	Surf.	Abt.	Distance	Win Time	Date
FPX	D	A	4F	:44.79	9/25/03
FPX	D		6F	1:10.04	9/17/03
FPX	D		6 1/2F	1:15.57	9/28/03
FPX	D		7F	1:23.32	9/28/03
FPX	D		1 1/16M	1:43.06	9/13/03
FPX	D	A	1 1/8M	1:48.67	9/28/03
FPX	D		1 3/8M	2:18.63	9/27/03
FPX	NO TURF				

Gila County Fair

Track	Surf.	Abt.	Distance	Win Time	Date
GCF	D		3F	:35.40	10/5/03
GCF	D		5 1/2F	1:06.60	9/27/03
GCF	D		6F	1:13.40	10/4/03
GCF	D		7F	1:28.60	9/28/03
GCF	D		1 1/16M	1:46.40	10/5/03
GCF	NO TURF				

Great Falls

Track	Surf.	Abt.	Distance	Win Time	Date
GF	D		5F	1:00.00	7/4/03
GF	D	A	5F	1:04.00	7/27/03
GF	D		7F	1:27.60	7/27/03
GF	D		1M 70Y	1:49.80	7/27/03
GF	NO TURF				

Golden Gate Fields

Track	Surf.	Abt.	Distance	Win Time	Date
GG	D		2F	:21.09	3/27/03
GG	D		5F	:56.12	1/1/03
GG	D		5 1/2F	1:02.11	11/14/03
GG	D		6F	1:07.45	12/17/03
GG	D		1M	1:33.98	1/1/03
GG	D		1 1/16M	1:41.56	3/15/03
GG	D		1 1/8M	1:49.25	2/6/03
GG	D		1 1/8M	1:49.25	3/5/03
GG	D		1 1/4M	2:02.92	11/9/03

GG Turf

Track	Surf.	Abt.	Distance	Win Time	Date
GG	T		4 1/2F	:49.86	3/29/03
GG	T		1M	1:35.83	3/12/03
GG	T		1 1/16M	1:42.00	2/8/03
GG	T		1 1/8M	1:50.07	3/16/03

Gillespie County Fair

Track	Surf.	Abt.	Distance	Win Time	Date
GIL	D		5 1/2F	1:08.61	7/19/03
GIL	D		6F	1:13.69	7/19/03
GIL	D		7F	1:29.05	8/24/03
GIL	NO TURF				

Great Lakes Downs

Track	Surf.	Abt.	Distance	Win Time	Date
GLD	D		4F	:46.07	9/26/03
GLD	D		5 1/2F	1:05.37	9/26/03
GLD	D		6F	1:11.86	10/11/03
GLD	D		6 1/2F	1:20.01	7/27/03
GLD	D		7F	1:26.43	8/16/03
GLD	D		1M	1:40.99	10/4/03
GLD	D		1 1/16M	1:47.88	9/23/03
GLD	D		1 1/8M	1:54.41	10/11/03
GLD	NO TURF				

Gulfstream Park

Track	Surf.	Abt.	Distance	Win Time	Date
GP	D		3F	:33.34	4/18/03
GP	D		5F	:56.35	1/17/03
GP	D		5 1/2F	1:02.47	2/3/03
GP	D		6F	1:08.56	1/5/03
GP	D		6 1/2F	1:15.17	2/9/03
GP	D		7F	1:20.56	3/22/03
GP	D		1M 70Y	1:39.45	3/1/03
GP	D		1 1/16M	1:42.22	2/2/03

Track	Surf.	Abt.	Distance	Win Time	Date
GP	D		1 1/8M	1:47.92	3/1/03
GP	D		1 1/4M	2:04.24	3/29/03
GP	D		1 1/2M	2:32.36	3/23/03

GP Turf

Track	Surf.	Abt.	Distance	Win Time	Date
GP	T		5F	:55.10	4/12/03
GP	T	A	5F	:56.64	3/26/03
GP	T		1M	1:33.81	2/1/03
GP	T	A	1M	1:34.74	2/1/03
GP	T		1 1/16M	1:40.43	3/9/03
GP	T	A	1 1/16M	1:41.36	4/23/03
GP	T		1 1/8M	1:47.12	3/2/03
GP	T	A	1 1/8M	1:50.05	3/7/03
GP	T		1 3/8M	2:11.62	2/16/03
GP	T	A	1 3/8M	2:16.63	3/5/03
GP	T		1 1/2M	2:26.29	3/1/03
GP	T	A	1 1/2M	2:28.45	3/22/03

Grande Prairie

Track	Surf.	Abt.	Distance	Win Time	Date
GPR	D		4F	:46.40	8/2/03
GPR	D		5 1/2F	1:06.20	8/1/03
GPR	D		6F	1:12.40	8/3/03
GPR	D		6 1/2F	1:19.20	8/16/03
GPR	D		7F	1:25.20	7/27/03
GPR	D		7F	1:25.20	8/15/03
GPR	D		1M	1:40.20	8/10/03
GPR	D		1 1/16M	1:46.40	8/1/03
GPR	D		1 1/8M	1:53.40	8/17/03
GPR	NO TURF				

Grants Pass

Track	Surf.	Abt.	Distance	Win Time	Date
GRP	D		4 1/2F	:52.60	6/21/03
GRP	D		5F	1:00.60	6/15/03
GRP	D		5F	1:00.60	7/4/03
GRP	D		5 1/2F	1:05.20	6/21/03
GRP	D		6 1/2F	1:19.60	6/28/03
GRP	D		6 1/2F	1:19.60	7/4/03
GRP	D		1 1/16M	1:45.40	7/6/03
GRP	NO TURF				

Hawthorne

Track	Surf.	Abt.	Distance	Win Time	Date
HAW	D		6F	1:07.27	12/12/03
HAW	D		6 1/2F	1:15.40	12/12/03
HAW	D		1M 70Y	1:39.73	12/14/03
HAW	D		1 1/16M	1:41.19	12/12/03
HAW	D		1 1/8M	1:51.47	4/5/03
HAW	D		1 1/4M	2:01.28	12/13/03

Haw Turf

Track	Surf.	Abt.	Distance	Win Time	Date
HAW	T		5F	:57.91	11/9/03
HAW	T		1M	1:34.70	11/1/03
HAW	T		1 1/16M	1:39.86	10/11/03
HAW	T		1 1/8M	1:48.02	10/10/03
HAW	T		1 1/2M	2:31.81	10/19/03

Hollywood Park

Track	Surf.	Abt.	Distance	Win Time	Date
HOL	D		4 1/2F	:51.33	5/15/03
HOL	D		5F	:57.40	6/11/03
HOL	D		5 1/2F	1:02.75	5/3/03
HOL	D		6F	1:07.52	11/15/03
HOL	D		6 1/2F	1:14.87	5/16/03
HOL	D		7F	1:20.63	11/15/03
HOL	D		7 1/2F	1:27.13	12/13/03
HOL	D		1 1/16M	1:40.32	5/3/03
HOL	D		1 1/8M	1:47.91	6/14/03
HOL	D		1 1/4M	2:00.48	7/13/03

Hol Turf

Track	Surf.	Abt.	Distance	Win Time	Date
HOL	T		5 1/2F	1:01.35	4/23/03
HOL	T		1M	1:33.37	5/26/03
HOL	T		1 1/16M	1:40.38	7/3/03
HOL	T		1 1/8M	1:46.20	7/4/03
HOL	T		1 3/16M	1:53.62	5/1/03
HOL	T		1 1/4M	1:59.98	7/5/03
HOL	T		1 1/2M	2:25.31	5/10/03

Hoosier Park

Track	Surf.	Abt.	Distance	Win Time	Date
HOO	D		5 1/2F	1:02.92	9/27/03
HOO	D		6F	1:10.19	9/5/03
HOO	D		1M	1:37.18	11/15/03
HOO	D		1 1/16M	1:43.48	10/4/03
HOO	D		1 9/16M	2:41.52	10/24/03
HOO	NO TURF				

Sam Houston Racepark

Track	Surf.	Abt.	Distance	Win Time	Date
HOU	D		5F	:57.21	10/25/03
HOU	D		5 1/2F	1:03.10	3/27/03
HOU	D		6F	1:09.36	11/15/03
HOU	D		6 1/2F	1:17.03	3/1/03
HOU	D		7F	1:22.76	1/4/03
HOU	D		7F	1:22.76	10/29/03
HOU	D		1M	1:36.33	3/8/03
HOU	D		1M 70Y	1:42.27	10/31/03
HOU	D		1 1/16M	1:44.03	2/22/03
HOU	D		1 1/8M	1:49.18	1/18/03

Hou Turf

Track	Surf.	Abt.	Distance	Win Time	Date
HOU	T		5F	:57.49	10/24/03
HOU	T		1M	1:38.29	10/31/03
HOU	T		1 1/16M	1:44.70	11/1/03
HOU	T		1 1/16M	1:44.70	12/6/03
HOU	T		1 1/8M	1:53.21	2/15/03
HOU	T		1 1/2M	2:33.32	3/30/03

Horsemen's Park

Track	Surf.	Abt.	Distance	Win Time	Date
HPO	D		6F	1:11.80	7/11/03
HPO	D		1M	1:37.00	7/12/03
HPO	NO TURF				

Track	Surf.	Abt.	Distance	Win Time	Date
Hastings					
HST	D		3 1/2F	:39.40	10/26/03
HST	D		6F	1:11.88	5/3/03
HST	D		6 1/2F	1:15.83	8/4/03
HST	D		6 1/2F	1:15.83	9/6/03
HST	D		1 1/16M	1:43.50	9/28/03
HST	D		1 1/8M	1:49.58	8/23/03
HST	D		1 3/8M	2:18.46	8/4/03
HST	D	A	1 1/2M	2:30.87	9/6/03
HST	D		1 3/4M	3:02.66	9/27/03
HST	NO TURF				
Indiana Downs					
IND	D		4 1/2F	:50.75	5/10/03
IND	D		5F	:58.41	4/19/03
IND	D		5 1/2F	1:03.47	5/8/03
IND	D		6F	1:09.89	5/26/03
IND	D		1M	1:37.76	5/8/03
IND	D		1M 70Y	1:41.56	5/7/03
IND	D		1 1/16M	1:44.20	5/16/03
IND	D		1 1/8M	1:50.62	5/15/03
IND	D		1 1/4M	2:06.31	5/26/03
IND	NO TURF				
Kamloops					
KAM	D		3 1/2F	:43.20	5/25/03
KAM	D	A	4 1/2F	:49.78	8/17/03
KAM	D		6 1/2F	1:18.80	6/29/03
KAM	D		1M	1:38.51	8/17/03
KAM	NO TURF				
Kentucky Downs					
KD	NO DIRT				
KD	T		6F	1:12.51	9/15/03
KD	T		7F	1:25.88	9/15/03
KD	T		1M	1:37.81	9/20/03
KD	T		1 1/2M	2:31.39	9/20/03
Keeneland					
KEE	D		4 1/2F	:51.04	4/18/03
KEE	D		6F	1:08.32	10/3/03
KEE	D		6 1/2F	1:15.28	10/12/03
KEE	D		7F	1:21.73	4/13/03
KEE	D	A	7F	1:25.33	10/9/03
KEE	D		1 1/16M	1:42.92	10/8/03
KEE	D		1 1/8M	1:48.52	4/25/03
KEE	D		1 3/16M	1:58.96	10/24/03
KEE	D		1 1/4M	2:05.85	10/11/03
Kee Turf					
KEE	T		5 1/2F	1:02.92	10/16/03
KEE	T		1M	1:34.98	4/4/03
KEE	T		1 1/16M	1:41.54	10/8/03
KEE	T		1 1/8M	1:47.82	10/11/03

Track	Surf.	Abt.	Distance	Win Time	Date
KEE	T		1 3/16M	1:55.87	10/5/03
KEE	T		1 1/2M	2:29.39	4/23/03
Kin Park					
KIN	D	A	4F	:44.52	7/13/03
KIN	D	A	6F	1:11.24	7/20/03
KIN	D		6 1/2F	1:19.60	8/3/03
KIN	D	A	6 1/2F	1:19.80	7/6/03
KIN	D	A	7F	1:21.65	7/20/03
KIN	D		1 1/16M	1:46.08	8/3/03
KIN	NO TURF				
Kalispell					
KSP	D		5F	1:03.80	8/16/03
KSP	D		6F	1:11.80	8/24/03
KSP	D		7F	1:27.80	8/17/03
KSP	D		1M 70Y	1:51.00	8/24/03
KSP	NO TURF				
Los Alamitos					
LA	D		4 1/2F	:50.54	12/13/03
LA	NO TURF				
Louisiana Downs					
LAD	D		5F	:58.01	9/12/03
LAD	D		5 1/2F	1:03.62	10/16/03
LAD	D		6F	1:09.01	6/27/03
LAD	D		6 1/2F	1:16.11	7/20/03
LAD	D		7F	1:22.25	11/8/03
LAD	D		1M 70Y	1:41.76	11/1/03
LAD	D		1 1/16M	1:44.17	8/30/03
LAD	D		1 1/8M	1:50.77	9/20/03
LaD Turf					
LAD	T	A	5F	:55.94	8/15/03
LAD	T	A	7 1/2F	1:29.28	8/24/03
LAD	T		7 1/2F	1:29.44	7/5/03
LAD	T	A	1M	1:34.53	6/28/03
LAD	T		1M	1:35.93	8/29/03
LAD	T	A	1 1/16M	1:41.68	8/9/03
LAD	T		1 1/16M	1:41.89	8/16/03
LAD	T	A	1 1/4M	2:05.74	11/1/03
Lethbridge					
LBG	D		3F	:34.20	5/3/03
LBG	D		5F	:58.60	5/17/03
LBG	D		5 1/2F	1:07.20	5/18/03
LBG	D		5 1/2F	1:07.20	10/18/03
LBG	D	A	6F	1:10.20	10/11/03
LBG	D		7F	1:23.20	9/27/03
LBG	D		1 1/16M	1:46.60	10/24/03
LBG	D		1 1/8M	1:53.60	10/11/03
LBG	D		1 3/16M	2:03.60	10/5/03
LBG	NO TURF				

Track	Surf. Abt.	Distance	Win Time	Date

Lincoln State Fair

Track	Surf. Abt.	Distance	Win Time	Date
LNN	D	4F	:49.00	6/6/03
LNN	D	4 1/2F	:50.60	7/3/03
LNN	D	6F	1:11.40	7/3/03
LNN	D	1M	1:39.60	5/22/03
LNN	D	1M 70Y	1:43.00	6/27/03
LNN	D	1 3/8M	2:27.60	6/15/03
LNN	D	2M	3:33.40	7/4/03
LNN	NO TURF			

Laurel Park

Track	Surf. Abt.	Distance	Win Time	Date
LRL	D	5 1/2F	1:03.37	11/1/03
LRL	D	6F	1:08.53	10/8/03
LRL	D	7F	1:22.09	12/18/03
LRL	D	1 1/16M	1:42.74	3/15/03
LRL	D	1 1/8M	1:48.41	7/24/03
LRL	D	1 3/16M	1:54.94	10/11/03

Lrl Turf

Track	Surf. Abt.	Distance	Win Time	Date
LRL	T	5 1/2F	1:03.11	10/12/03
LRL	T	1 1/16M	1:40.85	10/13/03
LRL	T	1 1/8M	1:46.86	10/11/03

Lone Star Park

Track	Surf. Abt.	Distance	Win Time	Date
LS	D	4 1/2F	:51.67	4/12/03
LS	D	5F	:56.47	7/6/03
LS	D	5 1/2F	1:01.88	4/11/03
LS	D	6F	1:08.61	5/14/03
LS	D	6 1/2F	1:15.82	4/10/03
LS	D	7F	1:21.92	7/5/03
LS	D	1M	1:35.67	7/13/03
LS	D	1 1/16M	1:41.77	5/9/03
LS	D	1 1/8M	1:50.43	5/10/03

LS Turf

Track	Surf. Abt.	Distance	Win Time	Date
LS	T	5F	:56.55	6/26/03
LS	T	7 1/2F	1:29.80	6/21/03
LS	T	1M	1:34.03	6/18/03
LS	T	1 1/16M	1:43.02	6/25/03
LS	T	1 1/8M	1:48.75	6/21/03
LS	T	1 3/8M	2:17.95	6/20/03
LS	T	1 1/2M	2:34.49	7/11/03

Marias Fair

Track	Surf. Abt.	Distance	Win Time	Date
MAF	D	5F	1:01.60	7/19/03
MAF	D	5F	1:01.60	7/20/03
MAF	D A	6F	1:12.00	7/19/03
MAF	D	7F	1:27.80	7/19/03
MAF	D	1M 70Y	1:50.00	7/20/03
MAF	NO TURF			

Manor Downs

Track	Surf. Abt.	Distance	Win Time	Date
MAN	D	4 1/2F	:51.97	5/3/03
MAN	D	5F	:57.82	4/6/03
MAN	D	5 1/2F	1:04.60	4/5/03
MAN	D	6F	1:09.68	4/19/03
MAN	D	7 1/2F	1:31.45	4/5/03
MAN	D	1M	1:38.00	5/10/03
MAN	NO TURF			

Miles City

Track	Surf. Abt.	Distance	Win Time	Date
MC	D	5F	1:03.80	5/17/03
MC	D	5 1/2F	1:08.60	5/17/03
MC	D A	6F	1:11.00	5/18/03
MC	NO TURF			

Marquis Downs

Track	Surf. Abt.	Distance	Win Time	Date
MD	D	4F	:46.75	5/30/03
MD	D	6F	1:13.35	6/20/03
MD	D	6F	1:13.35	9/6/03
MD	D	6 1/2F	1:22.25	8/16/03
MD	D A	7F	1:25.42	7/4/03
MD	D	1M	1:39.75	7/18/03
MD	D	1 1/16M	1:47.42	9/6/03
MD	NO TURF			

Melville District Agripar

Track	Surf. Abt.	Distance	Win Time	Date
MDA	D	2F	:22.40	10/12/03
MDA	D A	5F	1:00.20	10/11/03
MDA	D A	7F	1:40.20	9/14/03
MDA	D A	7 1/2F	1:37.40	10/4/03
MDA	D A	1M	1:42.80	10/11/03
MDA	D A	1 1/16M	1:49.20	9/27/03
MDA	NO TURF			

The Meadowlands

Track	Surf. Abt.	Distance	Win Time	Date
MED	D	5F	:56.44	10/29/03
MED	D	5 1/2F	1:02.33	10/14/03
MED	D	6F	1:08.15	10/3/03
MED	D	1M	1:35.70	11/1/03
MED	D	1M 70Y	1:40.52	11/6/03
MED	D	1 1/16M	1:41.97	10/31/03
MED	D	1 1/8M	1:46.84	10/3/03
MED	D	1 1/4M	2:02.78	10/18/03

Med Turf

Track	Surf. Abt.	Distance	Win Time	Date
MED	T	5F	:55.47	10/25/03
MED	T	1M	1:36.37	10/2/03
MED	T	1M 70Y	1:38.71	10/25/03
MED	T	1 1/16M	1:41.52	10/11/03

Millerville

Track	Surf. Abt.	Distance	Win Time	Date
MIL	D	7F	1:28.80	7/1/03
MIL	D	1 1/8M	1:58.00	7/1/03
MIL	NO TURF			

Mountaineer Park

Track	Surf. Abt.	Distance	Win Time	Date
MNR	D	4 1/2F	:50.28	8/9/03
MNR	D	5F	:55.92	8/31/03
MNR	D	5 1/2F	1:02.91	9/2/03
MNR	D	6F	1:08.80	9/7/03
MNR	D	1M	1:35.21	6/17/03
MNR	D	1M 70Y	1:40.81	5/23/03
MNR	D	1 1/16M	1:41.15	8/9/03
MNR	D	1 1/8M	1:46.29	8/9/03
MNR	D	1 3/16M	1:56.66	5/17/03
MNR	D	1 1/4M	2:06.49	5/3/03
MNR	D	1 1/2M	2:35.59	10/19/03
MNR	D	1 5/8M	2:54.36	11/2/03
MNR	D	1 3/4M	3:10.09	11/16/03
MNR	D	2M	3:30.57	9/1/03
MNR	D	2 1/16M	3:44.78	12/29/03

Mnr Turf

Track	Surf. Abt.	Distance	Win Time	Date
MNR	T	4 1/2F	:51.62	7/21/03
MNR	T	5F	:55.87	6/28/03
MNR	T	7F	1:21.44	8/19/03
MNR	T	7 1/2F	1:28.43	8/18/03
MNR	T	1M	1:33.99	8/9/03
MNR	T	1 3/8M	2:15.36	7/15/03
MNR	T	1 3/4M	2:55.99	8/17/03

Mohave County Fair

Track	Surf. Abt.	Distance	Win Time	Date
MOF	D	4F	:45.00	5/11/03
MOF	D	5 1/2F	1:07.60	5/11/03
MOF	D	6F	1:14.20	5/11/03
MOF	D	6 1/2F	1:22.60	5/17/03
MOF	D	7F	1:27.20	5/10/03
MOF	NO TURF			

Mount Pleasant Meadows

Track	Surf. Abt.	Distance	Win Time	Date
MPM	D	4F	:50.05	7/12/03
MPM	D	4 1/2F	:55.04	5/31/03
MPM	D	5F	1:01.55	7/5/03
MPM	D	5 1/2F	1:08.27	7/20/03
MPM	D	6F	1:13.78	6/7/03
MPM	D	1M 70Y	1:51.61	7/6/03
MPM	NO TURF			

Monmouth Park

Track	Surf. Abt.	Distance	Win Time	Date
MTH	D	5F	:56.91	6/13/03
MTH	D	5 1/2F	1:03.24	7/10/03
MTH	D	6F	1:08.17	8/29/03
MTH	D	1M	1:35.89	7/26/03
MTH	D	1M 70Y	1:39.55	9/19/03
MTH	D	1 1/16M	1:41.04	9/13/03
MTH	D	1 1/8M	1:49.32	8/3/03
MTH	D	1 1/4M	2:06.97	8/9/03

Mth Turf

Track	Surf. Abt.	Distance	Win Time	Date
MTH	T	5F	:55.48	8/23/03
MTH	T	1M	1:34.95	7/5/03
MTH	T	1 1/16M	1:39.86	7/13/03
MTH	T	1 1/8M	1:46.39	7/4/03
MTH	T	1 3/8M	2:12.78	7/5/03

Northampton Fair

Track	Surf. Abt.	Distance	Win Time	Date
NMP	D A	5F	:55.40	8/29/03
NMP	D A	6 1/2F	1:21.34	9/6/03
NMP	D A	1 1/16M	1:52.34	9/12/03
NMP	D A	1 5/8M	2:53.76	9/1/03
NMP	NO TURF			

Northlands Park

Track	Surf. Abt.	Distance	Win Time	Date
NP	D	3 1/2F	:40.40	7/30/03
NP	D	3 1/2F	:40.40	8/9/03
NP	D	5 1/2F	1:07.60	7/12/03
NP	D	5 1/2F	1:07.60	7/23/03
NP	D	5 1/2F	1:07.60	7/30/03
NP	D	6F	1:11.80	8/6/03
NP	D	6F	1:11.80	8/17/03
NP	D	6 1/2F	1:17.60	8/4/03
NP	D	1M	1:38.20	10/25/03
NP	D	1 1/16M	1:44.60	10/12/03
NP	D	1 5/16M	2:14.40	8/15/03
NP	D	1 3/8M	2:21.40	9/6/03
NP	D	1 5/8M	2:53.20	9/27/03
NP	NO TURF			

Oaklawn Park

Track	Surf. Abt.	Distance	Win Time	Date
OP	D	5 1/2F	1:03.94	3/9/03
OP	D	6F	1:09.01	4/10/03
OP	D	1M	1:36.88	3/7/03
OP	D	1 1/16M	1:42.95	3/22/03
OP	D	1 1/8M	1:47.66	4/5/03
OP	D	1 3/4M	3:02.79	4/12/03
OP	NO TURF			

Ocala Training Center

Track	Surf. Abt.	Distance	Win Time	Date
OTC	D	5F	:56.40	3/17/03
OTC	D	6F	1:09.60	3/17/03
OTC	D	1 1/16M	1:44.20	3/17/03
OTC	NO TURF			

Penn National Racecourse

Track	Surf. Abt.	Distance	Win Time	Date
PEN	D	2F	:21.11	2/27/03
PEN	D	4 1/2F	:51.29	2/26/03
PEN	D	5F	:57.63	5/14/03
PEN	D	5 1/2F	1:03.45	2/26/03
PEN	D	6F	1:09.45	2/26/03
PEN	D	1M	1:38.18	10/10/03
PEN	D	1M 70Y	1:41.35	2/26/03
PEN	D	1 1/16M	1:45.62	10/11/03
PEN	D	1 1/8M	1:51.22	7/16/03

Track	Surf.	Abt.	Distance	Win Time	Date
PEN	D		1 3/16M	2:00.35	10/18/03
PEN	D		1 1/4M	2:06.32	7/2/03
PEN	D		1 1/2M	2:35.68	11/22/03
PEN	D		1 3/4M	3:04.24	8/13/03

Pen Turf

Track	Surf.	Abt.	Distance	Win Time	Date
PEN	T		5F	:55.82	7/4/03
PEN	T		1M	1:36.24	7/12/03
PEN	T		1M 70Y	1:38.95	7/17/03
PEN	T		1 1/16M	1:41.85	8/29/03
PEN	T		1 1/2M	2:31.08	8/29/03

Philadelphia Park

Track	Surf.	Abt.	Distance	Win Time	Date
PHA	D		4 1/2F	:53.39	6/17/03
PHA	D		5F	:57.17	5/11/03
PHA	D		5 1/2F	1:03.10	1/5/03
PHA	D		6F	1:08.80	7/19/03
PHA	D		6 1/2F	1:15.43	12/16/03
PHA	D		7F	1:21.87	12/13/03
PHA	D		1M	1:38.04	9/1/03
PHA	D		1M 70Y	1:41.10	12/8/03
PHA	D		1 1/16M	1:43.35	1/28/03
PHA	D		1 1/8M	1:49.03	9/1/03
PHA	D		1 1/4M	2:05.68	2/25/03
PHA	D		1 1/2M	2:31.61	6/7/03

Pha Turf

Track	Surf.	Abt.	Distance	Win Time	Date
PHA	T		5F	:56.63	7/19/03
PHA	T	A	5F	:57.39	8/19/03
PHA	T		7 1/2F	1:32.41	7/8/03
PHA	T		1M	1:38.50	7/6/03
PHA	T		1M 70Y	1:41.66	7/20/03
PHA	T	A	1M 70Y	1:43.66	8/3/03
PHA	T		1 1/16M	1:42.48	7/5/03
PHA	T	A	1 1/16M	1:46.15	8/17/03
PHA	T		1 1/8M	1:53.03	7/8/03
PHA	T	A	1 1/8M	1:53.74	8/12/03
PHA	T		1 3/8M	2:22.89	7/14/03
PHA	T		1 1/2M	2:42.45	9/22/03

Pimlico

Track	Surf.	Abt.	Distance	Win Time	Date
PIM	D		4 1/2F	:52.01	5/4/03
PIM	D		5F	:56.46	9/27/03
PIM	D		5 1/2F	1:03.55	9/24/03
PIM	D		6F	1:09.57	9/26/03
PIM	D		1 1/16M	1:42.59	9/11/03
PIM	D		1 1/8M	1:48.94	4/19/03
PIM	D		1 3/16M	1:55.61	5/17/03

Pim Turf

Track	Surf.	Abt.	Distance	Win Time	Date
PIM	T		5F	:56.78	9/11/03
PIM	T		1M	1:36.41	5/3/03
PIM	T		1 1/16M	1:41.99	5/15/03
PIM	T		1 1/8M	1:48.56	9/11/03

Pleasanton

Track	Surf.	Abt.	Distance	Win Time	Date
PLN	D		4 1/2F	:51.35	6/25/03
PLN	D		5F	:56.82	7/4/03
PLN	D		5 1/2F	1:02.28	7/5/03
PLN	D		6F	1:07.86	7/5/03
PLN	D		1M 70Y	1:38.01	7/5/03
PLN	D		1 1/16M	1:40.34	7/5/03
PLN	NO TURF				

Portland Meadows

Track	Surf.	Abt.	Distance	Win Time	Date
PM	D		4 1/2F	:52.60	2/17/03
PM	D		5F	:58.51	4/27/03
PM	D		5 1/2F	1:04.63	3/8/03
PM	D		6F	1:09.06	3/30/03
PM	D		1M	1:36.78	4/27/03
PM	D		1 1/16M	1:45.78	3/22/03
PM	D		1 1/8M	1:52.79	1/26/03
PM	D		1 1/4M	2:07.16	3/16/03
PM	D		1 1/2M	2:34.66	4/6/03
PM	D		2M	3:33.09	4/27/03
PM	NO TURF				

Prairie Meadows

Track	Surf.	Abt.	Distance	Win Time	Date
PRM	D		2F	:22.20	5/9/03
PRM	D		4 1/2F	:51.68	5/18/03
PRM	D		5F	:57.23	6/27/03
PRM	D		5 1/2F	1:03.32	6/16/03
PRM	D		6F	1:08.63	6/21/03
PRM	D		1M	1:36.33	7/28/03
PRM	D		1M 70Y	1:39.69	7/4/03
PRM	D		1 1/16M	1:40.82	7/5/03
PRM	D		1 1/8M	1:48.06	8/2/03
PRM	NO TURF				

Prineville

Track	Surf.	Abt.	Distance	Win Time	Date
PRV	D	A	5F	1:02.60	7/11/03
PRV	D	A	5 1/2F	1:06.40	7/12/03
PRV	D	A	7F	1:30.60	7/12/03
PRV	D	A	1 1/8M	2:02.40	7/12/03
PRV	NO TURF				

River Downs

Track	Surf.	Abt.	Distance	Win Time	Date
RD	D		4 1/2F	:53.00	7/29/03
RD	D		5F	:58.80	5/29/03
RD	D		5F	:58.80	6/13/03
RD	D		5 1/2F	1:05.40	7/21/03
RD	D		6F	1:11.00	5/25/03
RD	D		6F	1:11.00	6/1/03
RD	D		1M	1:38.20	5/10/03
RD	D		1M 70Y	1:42.80	5/10/03
RD	D		1 1/16M	1:44.40	6/22/03
RD	D		1 1/8M	1:54.00	7/26/03
RD	D		1 1/4M	2:09.40	7/8/03
RD	D		1 5/8M	2:55.00	8/4/03
RD	D		1 3/4M	3:09.00	9/1/03

Track	Surf. Abt.	Distance	Win Time	Date
RD Turf				
RD	T	5F	:56.80	7/13/03
RD	T	5F	:56.80	8/1/03
RD	T	7 1/2F	1:29.60	6/28/03
RD	T	7 1/2F	1:29.60	7/26/03
RD	T	1M	1:35.60	8/28/03
RD	T	1 1/16M	1:41.80	8/24/03
RD	T	1 1/2M	2:32.00	7/20/03
Retama Park				
RET	D	4 1/2F	:51.51	8/2/03
RET	D	5F	:57.94	10/10/03
RET	D	5 1/2F	1:04.50	8/3/03
RET	D	6F	1:09.58	8/1/03
RET	D	6 1/2F	1:16.64	10/17/03
RET	D	7F	1:22.83	8/16/03
RET	D	1M	1:37.26	9/20/03
RET	D	1 1/16M	1:44.97	8/8/03
Ret Turf				
RET	T	5F	:55.69	8/24/03
RET	T	7 1/2F	1:28.44	10/18/03
RET	T	1M	1:34.54	10/4/03
RET	T	1 1/16M	1:40.79	10/4/03
RET	T	1 1/8M	1:50.67	9/19/03
RET	T	1 3/8M	2:18.09	10/18/03
Rillito				
RIL	D	4F	:45.20	1/19/03
RIL	D	5 1/2F	1:05.60	1/26/03
RIL	D	6F	1:12.20	1/18/03
RIL	D	6F	1:12.20	1/25/03
RIL	D	6 1/2F	1:20.00	2/1/03
RIL	D	7F	1:25.40	2/8/03
RIL	D	7F	1:25.40	2/9/03
RIL	D	1 1/16M	1:48.80	3/2/03
RIL	NO TURF			
Remington Park				
RP	D	3F	:32.73	8/23/03
RP	D	5F	:57.41	9/11/03
RP	D	5 1/2F	1:03.78	11/28/03
RP	D	6F	1:09.84	10/17/03
RP	D	6 1/2F	1:17.06	11/20/03
RP	D	7F	1:22.83	11/8/03
RP	D	1M	1:38.22	11/30/03
RP	D	1M 70Y	1:42.11	10/24/03
RP	D	1 1/16M	1:44.04	11/29/03
RP	D	1 1/8M	1:49.59	11/16/03
RP	D	1 1/2M	2:32.69	11/21/03
RP Turf				
RP	T	5F	:56.67	8/16/03
RP	T	7 1/2F	1:30.69	8/24/03

Track	Surf. Abt.	Distance	Win Time	Date
RP	T	1M	1:36.75	9/7/03
RP	T	1 1/16M	1:44.13	11/16/03
RP	T	1 1/8M	1:53.57	10/12/03
RP	T	1 3/8M	2:21.66	10/30/03
Rossburn Parkland Downs				
RPD	D	4F	:51.30	7/12/03
RPD	D	6F	1:17.20	7/13/03
RPD	D	1M	1:38.30	7/13/03
RPD	NO TURF			
Ruidoso Downs				
RUI	D	4 1/2F	:53.00	6/21/03
RUI	D	5F	:56.80	7/13/03
RUI	D	5 1/2F	1:02.00	7/13/03
RUI	D	6F	1:09.60	8/2/03
RUI	D	6F	1:09.60	8/3/03
RUI	D	6F	1:09.60	9/1/03
RUI	D	7 1/2F	1:29.40	7/19/03
RUI	D	1M	1:37.40	8/10/03
RUI	D	1 1/16M	1:44.00	9/1/03
RUI	D	1 1/4M	2:07.60	9/1/03
RUI	NO TURF			
Santa Anita Park				
SA	D	2F	:21.33	4/2/03
SA	D	5 1/2F	1:02.63	1/1/03
SA	D	6F	1:07.85	1/26/03
SA	D	6 1/2F	1:14.59	10/24/03
SA	D	7F	1:21.12	2/1/03
SA	D	1M	1:34.96	10/17/03
SA	D	1 1/16M	1:41.04	1/4/03
SA	D	1 1/8M	1:47.60	2/2/03
SA	D	1 1/4M	1:59.80	3/1/03
SA Turf				
SA	T A	6 1/2F	1:11.45	1/16/03
SA	T	1M	1:32.61	10/5/03
SA	T	1 1/8M	1:46.17	11/9/03
SA	T	1 1/4M	1:57.92	1/20/03
SA	T	1 1/2M	2:24.24	10/25/03
SA	T A	1 3/4M	2:46.97	4/20/03
Sacramento				
SAC	D	5F	:57.60	8/31/03
SAC	D	5 1/2F	1:03.39	8/29/03
SAC	D	6F	1:08.16	8/20/03
SAC	D	1M	1:37.00	8/20/03
SAC	D	1 1/16M	1:44.80	8/28/03
SAC	D	1 1/8M	1:51.00	8/28/03
SAC	NO TURF			

Track	Surf. Abt.	Distance	Win Time	Date
Safford				
SAF	D	4F	:45.60	3/30/03
SAF	D	5 1/2F	1:08.20	3/29/03
SAF	D	6F	1:11.60	4/5/03
SAF	D	7F	1:29.20	3/30/03
SAF	D	1M	1:46.20	4/5/03
SAF	NO TURF			
Saratoga				
SAR	D	5F	:57.46	8/13/03
SAR	D	5 1/2F	1:03.82	8/11/03
SAR	D	6F	1:08.64	8/2/03
SAR	D	6 1/2F	1:15.69	8/8/03
SAR	D	7F	1:20.83	7/26/03
SAR	D	1 1/8M	1:47.69	8/2/03
SAR	D	1 3/16M	1:59.61	7/24/03
SAR	D	1 1/4M	2:02.14	8/23/03
Sar Turf				
SAR	T	1M	1:35.03	8/22/03
SAR	T	1 1/16M	1:39.29	8/23/03
SAR	T	1 1/8M	1:47.45	8/25/03
SAR	T	1 3/16M	1:53.16	8/22/03
SAR	T	1 3/8M	2:13.96	8/25/03
SAR	T	1 1/2M	2:28.14	8/9/03
Saint Johns				
SJ	D	4F	:43.80	9/14/03
SJ	D	5 1/2F	1:05.60	9/20/03
SJ	D	6F	1:12.20	9/21/03
SJ	D	7F	1:24.20	9/20/03
SJ	D	1M	1:38.80	9/21/03
SJ	NO TURF			
Solano County Fair				
SOL	D	4 1/2F	:51.62	7/12/03
SOL	D	5F	:57.82	7/9/03
SOL	D	5 1/2F	1:03.03	7/13/03
SOL	D	6F	1:08.95	7/19/03
SOL	D	1M	1:36.42	7/10/03
SOL	D	1 1/16M	1:45.75	7/12/03
SOL	D	1 1/16M	1:45.75	7/20/03
SOL	NO TURF			
Sonoita				
SON	D	5F	1:01.20	4/26/03
SON	D	5F	1:01.20	4/26/03
SON	D	5 1/2F	1:06.20	4/27/03
SON	D	6F	1:12.40	4/26/03
SON	D	7F	1:28.80	4/27/03
SON	NO TURF			
Santa Rosa				
SR	D	4 1/2F	:50.39	7/24/03
SR	D	5F	:56.20	8/1/03
SR	D	5 1/2F	1:02.78	7/26/03
SR	D	6F	1:08.45	7/31/03
SR	D	1M	1:35.04	7/27/03
SR	D	1 1/16M	1:41.96	8/1/03
SR	NO TURF			
Sun Ray Park				
SRP	D	4F	:44.60	11/16/03
SRP	D	4 1/2F	:49.80	10/10/03
SRP	D	6 1/2F	1:15.60	9/22/03
SRP	D	7F	1:22.60	11/23/03
SRP	D	7F	1:22.60	11/23/03
SRP	D	7 1/2F	1:28.60	11/17/03
SRP	D	1M	1:36.00	10/19/03
SRP	D	1M	1:36.00	10/24/03
SRP	D	1 1/8M	1:49.40	11/22/03
SRP	NO TURF			
Stockton				
STK	D	4 1/2F	:51.06	6/21/03
STK	D	5 1/2F	1:03.59	6/11/03
STK	D	6F	1:09.29	6/21/03
STK	D	1M	1:36.51	6/22/03
STK	NO TURF			
Stampede Park				
STP	D	3 1/2F	:39.80	5/30/03
STP	D	4F	:44.80	4/4/03
STP	D	6F	1:10.00	5/21/03
STP	D	1M	1:36.00	5/19/03
STP	D	1 1/16M	1:43.00	6/8/03
STP	NO TURF			
Sun Downs				
SUD	D	4F	:46.40	4/19/03
SUD	D	6F	1:15.00	4/19/03
SUD	D	6 1/2F	1:22.40	5/3/03
SUD	D	7F	1:27.60	5/4/03
SUD	NO TURF			
Suffolk Downs				
SUF	D	5F	:58.66	9/16/03
SUF	D	5 1/2F	1:05.10	6/24/03
SUF	D	6F	1:09.91	4/14/03
SUF	D	1M	1:38.46	2/25/03
SUF	D	1M 70Y	1:41.22	2/1/03
SUF	D	1 1/16M	1:45.33	4/12/03
SUF	D	1 1/8M	2:00.20	10/27/03
Suf Turf				
SUF	T A	5F	:57.88	7/14/03
SUF	T A	1M	1:39.35	9/15/03
SUF	T A	1M 70Y	1:43.14	8/20/03
SUF	T A	1 1/16M	1:44.97	7/7/03

Track	Surf.	Abt.	Distance	Win Time	Date

Sunland Park

SUN	D		4F	:45.88	3/4/03
SUN	D		4 1/2F	:51.45	4/6/03
SUN	D		5F	:56.44	1/26/03
SUN	D		5 1/2F	1:02.39	1/28/03
SUN	D		6F	1:08.36	1/7/03
SUN	D		6 1/2F	1:14.84	3/8/03
SUN	D		1M	1:35.42	2/16/03
SUN	D		1 1/16M	1:42.00	2/8/03
SUN	D		1 1/8M	1:48.60	4/5/03
SUN	D		1 1/4M	2:04.04	4/6/03
SUN	NO TURF				

Tampa Bay Downs

TAM	D		3F	:33.40	4/21/03
TAM	D		5F	:58.08	4/27/03
TAM	D		5 1/2F	1:04.32	3/14/03
TAM	D		6F	1:10.15	3/13/03
TAM	D		6 1/2F	1:17.05	12/13/03
TAM	D		7F	1:23.70	1/13/03
TAM	D		1 1/16M	1:43.94	3/1/03
TAM	D		1 1/8M	1:52.99	3/31/03

Tam Turf

TAM	T		5F	:56.06	3/16/03
TAM	T	A	5F	:57.75	4/21/03
TAM	T		1M	1:36.53	4/12/03
TAM	T	A	1M	1:37.67	2/1/03
TAM	T		1 1/16M	1:40.63	3/16/03
TAM	T	A	1 1/16M	1:42.64	4/14/03
TAM	T	A	1 1/8M	1:48.33	4/6/03
TAM	T		1 3/8M	2:17.40	3/11/03

Thistledown

TDN	D		4F	:45.72	9/8/03
TDN	D		4 1/2F	:53.20	9/22/03
TDN	D		5F	:57.80	12/4/03
TDN	D		5 1/2F	1:03.92	4/16/03
TDN	D		6F	1:08.86	12/4/03
TDN	D		1M	1:37.42	12/8/03
TDN	D		1M 40Y	1:40.82	7/4/03
TDN	D		1M 70Y	1:42.84	6/29/03
TDN	D		1 1/16M	1:43.90	12/3/03
TDN	D		1 1/8M	1:50.08	6/21/03
TDN	D		1 1/4M	2:06.42	7/28/03
TDN	D		1 1/2M	2:36.64	8/18/03
TDN	NO TURF				

Tillamook County Fair

TIL	D	A	5F	1:03.80	8/7/03
TIL	D	A	1 1/16M	2:04.20	8/8/03
TIL	NO TURF				

Timonium

TIM	D		4F	:43.76	8/23/03
TIM	D	A	6 1/2F	1:16.55	8/30/03
TIM	D		6 1/2F	1:19.66	8/28/03
TIM	D		1M	1:39.59	8/23/03
TIM	D		1 1/16M	1:43.93	9/1/03
TIM	NO DIRT				

Turfway Park

TP	D		5F	:57.92	12/4/03
TP	D		5 1/2F	1:03.75	3/23/03
TP	D		6F	1:09.54	9/13/03
TP	D		6 1/2F	1:16.17	9/20/03
TP	D		1M	1:35.39	12/20/03
TP	D		1 1/16M	1:43.29	12/20/03
TP	D		1 1/8M	1:50.43	9/13/03
TP	D		1 1/2M	2:34.26	3/7/03
TP	D		1 3/4M	3:02.64	3/29/03
TP	NO TURF				

Turf Paradise

TUP	D		2F	:22.07	4/4/03
TUP	D		4 1/2F	:50.64	5/2/03
TUP	D		5F	:56.77	9/28/03
TUP	D		5 1/2F	1:01.63	10/20/03
TUP	D		6F	1:08.34	12/28/03
TUP	D		6 1/2F	1:14.67	2/9/03
TUP	D		1M	1:34.39	12/30/03
TUP	D		1 1/16M	1:41.74	2/1/03
TUP	D		1 1/8M	1:51.58	1/24/03
TUP	D		1 1/4M	2:03.65	2/11/03
TUP	D		1 5/8M	2:47.02	3/2/03

TuP Turf

TUP	T		4 1/2F	:49.26	4/13/03
TUP	T		7 1/2F	1:28.18	4/13/03
TUP	T		1M	1:35.51	3/29/03
TUP	T		1 1/16M	1:41.26	4/12/03
TUP	T		1 1/8M	1:49.40	4/14/03
TUP	T		1 3/8M	2:15.17	4/27/03
TUP	T		1 7/8M	3:11.34	5/18/03

Union

UN	D		5F	:59.80	6/8/03
UN	D		5 1/2F	1:04.40	6/6/03
UN	D		6 1/2F	1:24.20	6/7/03
UN	D		1 1/16M	1:49.20	6/8/03
UN	NO TURF				

The Woodlands

WDS	D		4 1/2F	:51.40	9/23/03
WDS	D		5F	:58.80	10/31/03
WDS	D		5 1/2F	1:04.00	10/9/03
WDS	D		5 1/2F	1:04.00	10/30/03

Track	Surf. Abt.	Distance	Win Time	Date
WDS	D	6F	1:10.20	10/25/03
WDS	D	1M	1:40.20	10/3/03
WDS	D	1M 70Y	1:42.40	10/29/03
WDS	D	1 1/16M	1:43.20	11/1/03
WDS	D	1 1/8M	1:51.60	10/25/03
WDS	D	1 3/16M	1:58.00	10/21/03
WDS	D	1 3/4M	3:02.60	11/1/03
WDS	NO TURF			

Woodbine

Track	Surf. Abt.	Distance	Win Time	Date
WO	D	4 1/2F	:51.84	5/17/03
WO	D	5F	:55.95	4/5/03
WO	D	5 1/2F	1:04.03	6/28/03
WO	D	6F	1:08.05	11/29/03
WO	D	6 1/2F	1:15.66	5/11/03
WO	D	7F	1:21.71	7/9/03
WO	D	1M 70Y	1:42.14	4/26/03
WO	D	1 1/16M	1:42.44	7/1/03
WO	D	1 1/8M	1:49.77	6/13/03
WO	D	1 3/16M	1:58.66	11/27/03
WO	D	1 1/4M	2:01.15	7/1/03
WO	D	1 1/2M	2:31.88	11/8/03
WO	D	1 3/4M	3:00.28	11/30/03
WO	D	1 7/8M	3:17.68	11/30/03

WO Turf

Track	Surf. Abt.	Distance	Win Time	Date
WO	T	6F	1:07.73	6/22/03
WO	T	6 1/2F	1:14.88	6/20/03
WO	T	7F	1:21.17	8/1/03
WO	T	1M	1:33.27	6/22/03
WO	T	1 1/16M	1:40.14	6/21/03
WO	T A	1 1/8M	1:44.56	9/14/03
WO	T	1 1/8M	1:46.50	8/24/03
WO	T	1 1/4M	2:03.25	6/29/03
WO	T A	1 1/4M	2:05.60	9/5/03
WO	T	1 3/8M	2:13.85	7/20/03
WO	T	1 1/2M	2:27.13	8/30/03

Wyoming Downs

Track	Surf. Abt.	Distance	Win Time	Date
WYO	D	4 1/2F	:51.91	8/2/03
WYO	D	5F	:57.72	8/10/03
WYO	D	6F	1:09.74	8/3/03
WYO	D	7 1/2F	1:31.57	8/9/03
WYO	D	1M	1:39.17	8/17/03
WYO	NO TURF			

Yavapai Downs

Track	Surf. Abt.	Distance	Win Time	Date
YAV	D	4 1/2F	:50.40	8/18/03
YAV	D	4 1/2F	:50.40	9/2/03
YAV	D	5F	:57.00	8/31/03
YAV	D	5 1/2F	1:02.60	7/15/03
YAV	D	6F	1:08.47	5/24/03
YAV	D	1M	1:36.60	6/8/03
YAV	D	1 1/16M	1:43.80	8/26/03
YAV	D	1 1/8M	1:52.40	8/2/03
YAV	D	1 1/4M	2:03.20	8/26/03
YAV	NO TURF			

Yellowstone Downs

Track	Surf. Abt.	Distance	Win Time	Date
YD	D	5 1/4F	1:02.40	9/20/03
YD	D	7F	1:26.20	9/13/03
YD	D	1M 70Y	1:45.80	9/1/03
YD	NO TURF			

Yorkton Exh Association

Track	Surf. Abt.	Distance	Win Time	Date
YKT	D	5F	1:02.08	6/22/03
YKT	D	6 1/2F	1:22.70	6/22/03
YKT	D	1M	1:46.66	7/4/03
YKT	NO TURF			

Fastest Times During 2003

Dirt

Track	Horse	Age	Wt	Distance	Time	Date	Track	Horse	Age	Wt	Distance	Time	Date
FP	Glit	8	122	2F	:20.80	5/3/03	EMD	Alfurune	5	117	1 1/16M	1:40.20	7/4/03
CPW	Northern Stride	2	136	2 1/2F	:32.60	6/22/03	BEL	Mineshaft	4	126	1 1/8M	1:46.21	9/6/03
RP	Cordell	7	117	3F	:32.73	8/23/03	LRL	Docent	5	123	1 3/16M	1:54.94	10/11/03
CBY	Snowbird	2	118	3 1/2F	:39.34	6/1/03	DMR	Candy Ride (ARG)	4	124	1 1/4M	1:59.11	8/24/03
TIM	Ameri Brilliance	4	121	4F	:43.76	8/23/03	NP	They Call Me Cody	5	119	*1 5/16M	2:14.40	8/15/03
SRP	Sky Diver	6	123	4 1/2F	:49.80	10/10/03	BEL	Patriot's Song	4	119	1 3/8M	2:16.54	9/19/03
EMD	Victor Slew	4	115	5F	:55.40	8/24/03	BEL	Empire Maker	3	126	1 1/2M	2:28.26	6/7/03
YD	Mr. Bo Ally Ray	4	124	5 1/4F	1:02.40	9/20/03	HOO	Go Gavin Go	7	113	*1 9/16M	2:41.52	10/24/03
TUP	One Troy Ounce	5	119	5 1/2F	1:01.63	10/20/03	AQU	Loving (BRZ)	7	114	1 5/8M	2:45.08	12/27/03
HAW	Coach Jimi Lee	3	118	6F	1:07.27	12/12/03	WO	Hydrogen	4	113	1 3/4M	3:00.28	11/30/03
EMD	Turban	4	117	6 1/2F	1:14.00	5/18/03	ALB	Archy	5	115	*1 13/16M	3:08.50	9/21/03
GP	Lord Abounding	4	116	7F	1:20.56	3/22/03	WO	Disappeared	7	112	*1 7/8M	3:17.68	11/30/03
HOL	Excess Summer	3	119	7 1/2F	1:27.13	12/13/03	MNR	Pleasant Company	4	121	2M	3:30.57	9/1/03
BEL	Najran	4	113	1M	1:32.24	5/7/03	MNR	Sir Dorset	8	121	*2 1/16M	3:44.78	12/29/03
FG	Ghannam	4	119	1M 40Y	1:40.41	12/11/03	ELP	Sir Dorset	8	121	*2 1/4M	4:01.05	9/1/03
PLN	Call It	4	122	1M 70Y	1:38.01	7/5/03							

Only one race run at distance

Turf

Track	Horse	Age	Wt	Distance	Time	Date	Track	Horse	Age	Wt	Distance	Time	Date
TUP	Dan's Groovy	7	120	4 1/2F	:49.26	4/13/03	SAR	Trademark (SAF)	7	119	1 1/16M	1:39.29	8/23/03
DMR	Maria's Mirage	4	119	5F	:55.06	7/28/03	CRC	Political Attack	4	116	1 1/8M	1:45.81	12/6/03
ELP	Rubyana	4	120	5 1/2F	1:01.21	8/15/03	SAR	Alajwad	3	118	1 3/16M	1:53.16	8/22/03
WO	Soaring Free	4	115	6F	1:07.73	6/22/03	SA	Johar	4	120	1 1/4M	1:57.92	1/20/03
WO	All Star Lover	4	120	*6 1/2F	1:14.88	6/20/03	GP	Man from Wicklow	6	119	1 3/8M	2:11.62	2/16/03
BEL	MillnnmDragn(GB)	4	116	7F	1:20.20	9/17/03	SA	Johar[1]	4	126	1 1/2M	2:24.24	10/25/03
CRC	Magic Mecke	3	117	7 1/2F	1:27.41	12/20/03	SA	HighChaprral(Ire)[1]	4	126	1 1/2M	2:24.24	10/25/03
DMR	TouchoftheBlus(Fr)	6	122	1M	1:32.22	8/2/03	MNR	Pleasant Company	4	112	*1 3/4M	2:55.99	8/17/03
MED	Royal Affirmed	5	120	1M 70Y	1:38.71	10/25/03	TUP	Pittsburgh Star	6	119	*1 7/8M	3:11.34	5/18/03

Only one race run at distance   [1] *Dead Heat*

Fastest Times at Common Distances
6 Furlongs, Dirt (1991–2003)

Horse	Age	Wt	Track	Date	Time	Horse	Age	Wt	Track	Date	Time
G Malleah	4	120	TUP	4/8/95	1:06.60	Lynn's Notebook	4	117	STK	6/25/95	1:07.80
Honor the Hero	5	113	TUP	2/21/93	1:06.80	Hooten Harry	3	120	TUP	12/21/95	1:07.80
Magical Flyer	4	117	TUP	4/18/95	1:07.00	Left the Latch	5	116	TUP	4/27/96	1:07.80
Ladyteeoff	5	116	TUP	12/19/92	1:07.20	Salta's Pride	6	116	SOL	7/13/96	1:07.80
Last Don B.	7	118	TUP	10/22/94	1:07.20	Tolemeo	4	114	FNO	10/12/97	1:07.80
Da Hoss	2	120	TUP	10/30/94	1:07.20	Handy N Bold	5	117	EMD	4/30/00	1:07.80
Honor the Hero	7	124	TUP	2/25/95	1:07.20	Royalty	6	120	SR	8/4/00	1:07.80
Left the Latch	4	115	TUP	2/28/95	1:07.20	Crowning Meeting	8	117	EMD	4/28/02	1:07.80
Honor the Hero	7	115	TUP	3/19/95	1:07.20	Road Afleet	5	118	EMD	4/27/03	1:07.80
Coach Jimi Lee	3	118	HAW	12/12/03	1:07.27	Just Outrageous	4	119	EMD	8/31/03	1:07.80
Honor the Hero	5	121	TUP	2/7/93	1:07.40	Hay Cody	4	127	MED	9/6/96	1:07.81
Last Don B.	7	121	TUP	1/30/94	1:07.40	Hustler	6	113	MNR	8/11/01	1:07.81
G Malleah	5	123	TUP	2/24/96	1:07.40	Wild Gold	4	114	GG	2/13/94	1:07.83
Moro Oro	3	122	HOO	11/16/96	1:07.40	Purple Peopleater	8	119	MED	9/24/99	1:07.83
Bay Runner	4	114	SR	7/29/00	1:07.40	Gilded Time	2	122	MTH	8/8/92	1:07.84
Ruff Hombre	6	115	SA	2/6/92	1:07.44	Lexicon	4	116	SA	10/17/99	1:07.84
Smoke Till Dawn	4	117	GG	12/17/03	1:07.45	Presidio Heights	5	119	BM	4/19/03	1:07.84
Raving Main E Axe	4	116	RP	2/1/91	1:07.50	Avanzado (ARG)	6	116	SA	1/26/03	1:07.85
Answer Do	5	121	TUP	2/24/91	1:07.50	True Direction	4	123	BEL	5/24/03	1:07.86
Apalachee Ridge	3	114	HOL	12/12/97	1:07.52	Spanish Eyes	5	122	PLN	7/5/03	1:07.86
Tough Game	4	119	HOL	11/15/03	1:07.52	Noble Year	5	117	DMR	8/21/95	1:07.87
Kelly Kip	5	123	AQU	4/10/99	1:07.54	Trickey Trevor	4	119	GG	1/23/03	1:07.87
El Dorado Shooter	4	114	GG	1/20/01	1:07.55	Hall of Gold	3	119	GG	11/17/01	1:07.88
Black Jack Road	8	118	PLN	7/11/92	1:07.57	Artax	4	126	GP	11/6/99	1:07.89
Marshad	4	114	TUP	2/6/92	1:07.60	Iron Punch	6	114	PHA	7/29/00	1:07.89
Night Glider	5	116	TUP	1/31/93	1:07.60	Romanzo	4	118	GG	1/18/01	1:07.89
Passing Game	8	121	SAC	9/4/93	1:07.60	Plum Twist	7	116	RP	2/3/91	1:07.90
Garabee	4	114	TUP	9/23/94	1:07.60	Mr. O. P.	5	115	AC	4/28/91	1:07.90
Plenty Zloty	5	121	TUP	2/12/95	1:07.60	Forest Gazelle	4	117	HOL	4/28/95	1:07.90
Will Meyers	5	121	SAC	8/24/96	1:07.60	Five Star Day	4	119	KEE	10/14/00	1:07.90
Champ's Star	3	118	SAC	8/30/98	1:07.60	Yankee Gentleman	4	114	DMR	9/6/03	1:07.90
Blue Tejano	8	119	EMD	6/7/02	1:07.60	Dat You Miz Blue	4	123	BEL	5/26/01	1:07.92
Kelly Kip	4	117	AQU	4/11/98	1:07.61	Captain Red	6	111	AQU	2/26/03	1:07.93
Halo Cat	5	118	GG	1/19/03	1:07.62	Southern Justice	4	114	SA	1/2/92	1:07.94
Artax	4	120	BEL	10/16/99	1:07.66	Irish Twist	4	119	GG	5/30/93	1:07.94
Mr. Doubledown	6	118	GG	5/13/00	1:07.66	Sweet Beast	4	122	MED	11/18/94	1:07.94
Swept Overboard	4	116	SA	10/6/01	1:07.67	Blue Tejano	6	117	GG	6/16/00	1:07.94
Snow Ridge	4	116	SA	1/27/02	1:07.70	Delaware Township	4	113	MTH	8/27/00	1:07.94
Omega Code	2	117	FNO	10/5/02	1:07.70	Lexicon	6	117	BM	9/8/01	1:07.94
Concept Win	4	115	SA	1/30/94	1:07.71	Con Quixote	5	117	GG	12/18/03	1:07.94
Jetinto Houston	4	119	GG	2/7/03	1:07.71	Crafty Alfel	8	119	AQU	3/30/96	1:07.95
Kona Gold	6	126	CD	11/4/00	1:07.77	Richter Scale	6	123	LRL	7/15/00	1:07.95
Shake You Down	5	112	AQU	4/26/03	1:07.77	Cajun Beat	3	123	SA	10/25/03	1:07.95
Anjiz	5	114	KEE	10/9/93	1:07.78	Beau's Town	5	119	DMR	7/26/03	1:07.96
Drum Sound	5	118	TUP	12/19/92	1:07.80	Tres Paraiso	5	116	BM	9/13/97	1:07.98
Doctor Scott Blurr	5	116	TUP	1/30/93	1:07.80	Amarillo Pride	5	117	GG	1/13/00	1:07.98
Smokin Albert	4	116	TUP	3/13/94	1:07.80	Green Team	4	116	SA	11/8/03	1:07.98
Last Don B.	7	125	TUP	4/9/94	1:07.80	Wild 'n Wet	4	122	GG	6/8/00	1:07.99
Gusto's Marker	6	116	TUP	10/2/94	1:07.80	Presidio Heights	5	117	GG	2/16/03	1:07.99
Bear	3	115	TUP	10/30/94	1:07.80	*Many individual performances at 1:08.00*					
Boomie's Bravo	4	121	TUP	3/28/95	1:07.80						

7 Furlongs, Dirt (1991–2003)

Horse	Age	Wt	Track	Date	Time
Mazel Trick	4	115	HOL	6/27/99	1:19.97
Artax	4	114	AQU	5/2/99	1:20.04
Lit de Justice	5	118	DMR	8/19/95	1:20.06
Elusive Quality	4	119	GP	2/21/97	1:20.17
Left Bank	5	121	BEL	7/4/02	1:20.17
D'Hallevant	4	115	DMR	8/20/94	1:20.25
You and I	3	122	BEL	6/11/94	1:20.33
Binalong	4	112	KEE	10/13/93	1:20.39
Golden Gear	4	114	RP	3/18/95	1:20.40
Early Flyer	3	123	HOL	5/28/01	1:20.42
El Corredor	4	119	DMR	8/12/01	1:20.42
Mamselle Bebette	3	115	SA	12/28/93	1:20.45
Reality Road	4	121	BEL	6/21/96	1:20.48
Another Star	4	122	HOL	4/25/98	1:20.49
Distorted Humor	5	119	KEE	4/11/98	1:20.50
Alannan	5	116	CD	5/5/01	1:20.50
Memo (CHI)	7	120	HOL	7/2/94	1:20.52
A. P. Assay	4	116	HOL	6/28/98	1:20.53
Limit Out	3	115	AQU	4/11/98	1:20.54
Hal's Pal (GB)	4	116	HOL	11/6/97	1:20.55
Lord Abounding	4	116	GP	3/22/03	1:20.56
Oronero	3	114	WO	12/6/95	1:20.60
Toolighttoquit	4	115	RP	10/19/96	1:20.60
Flaming Bridle	4	119	PHA	9/28/99	1:20.61
Crafty Friend	6	116	BEL	7/4/99	1:20.62
Lord Abounding	4	118	GP	2/28/03	1:20.63
Lion Heart	2	114	HOL	11/15/03	1:20.63
Light of Morn	6	118	GP	10/30/92	1:20.64
Light of Morn	6	116	DMR	8/23/92	1:20.65
Shared Interest	4	111	BEL	10/10/92	1:20.65
Star of the Crop	3	118	SA	12/26/92	1:20.67
Siphon (BRZ)	4	117	DMR	7/29/95	1:20.70
Dream Supreme	4	120	CD	5/5/01	1:20.70
Gold Land	4	116	HOL	5/3/95	1:20.71
Left Bank	4	126	BEL	9/22/01	1:20.73
The Exeter Man	5	115	HOL	11/7/97	1:20.76
Brutally Frank	6	114	AQU	3/18/00	1:20.77
Alphabet Soup	5	118	DMR	8/17/96	1:20.79
Missy's Mirage	4	119	AQU	4/18/92	1:20.80
Cat's Cradle	4	118	HOL	5/31/96	1:20.80
Western Winter	4	118	BEL	9/19/96	1:20.80
Flaming West	3	114	HOL	11/22/97	1:20.80
Highland Ice	5	121	RP	9/5/98	1:20.80
Hoist the Baba	6	121	RP	9/18/99	1:20.80
Van Patten	7	118	WO	11/23/00	1:20.80
Son of a Pistol	6	118	HOL	6/28/98	1:20.81
Love That Red	3	122	HOL	5/31/99	1:20.81
Now Listen	6	116	HOL	7/3/93	1:20.83
Lady Tak	3	122	SAR	7/26/03	1:20.83
Gold Land	4	117	HOL	5/29/95	1:20.84
Brulay	3	115	HOL	5/17/98	1:20.84
Tough and Rugged	4	109	GP	1/12/93	1:20.86
Binalong	5	117	GP	1/23/94	1:20.86
Sky Watch	4	117	CNL	9/1/97	1:20.87
Sociallyunencumber	4	117	HOL	11/28/97	1:20.88
Darling My Darling	3	117	KEE	10/11/00	1:20.88
Paster's Caper	4	116	HOL	6/22/95	1:20.89
Wouldn't We All	3	119	AQU	4/12/97	1:20.90
Kelleric	4	118	HOL	7/20/97	1:20.90
Lite the Fuse	5	121	BEL	5/5/96	1:20.92
Birdonthewire	4	119	BEL	7/10/93	1:20.93
Twist Afleet	5	122	BEL	5/4/96	1:20.94
Memo (CHI)	6	118	SA	11/6/93	1:20.95
Migrant Worker	5	116	HOL	5/4/94	1:20.95
Wouldn't We All	5	114	AQU	3/14/99	1:20.95
Powis Castle	3	117	SA	12/26/94	1:20.96
Bold Capital	6	116	HOL	5/10/97	1:20.97
Afternoon Deelites	2	115	HOL	11/13/94	1:20.98
Smoke Glacken	3	123	BEL	6/7/97	1:20.98
Clooney	4	118	LS	6/22/01	1:20.98
Collegian	4	117	BEL	6/23/91	1:20.99
Moscow M D	3	114	DMR	8/15/92	1:21.00
Highland Ice	4	118	RP	8/10/97	1:21.00
Ben Told	3	116	ALB	12/19/97	1:21.00
Forestry	3	124	SAR	8/28/99	1:21.00
Daring Pegasus	5	118	ARP	7/4/03	1:21.00
American Chance	5	119	GP	2/10/94	1:21.01
Score Quick	5	113	HOL	6/29/97	1:21.01
Star Smasher	3	123	ALB	6/9/02	1:21.01
Devil of a Trip	3	118	ALB	6/8/03	1:21.01
Le Casque Gris	4	119	HOL	5/8/98	1:21.02
Finder's Fortune	4	117	HOL	6/18/93	1:21.03
Montbrook	3	122	ATL	6/27/93	1:21.04
Banker's Gold	4	115	BEL	7/5/98	1:21.04
Dat You Miz Blue	4	122	AQU	4/7/01	1:21.06
Midas Eyes	3	116	GP	3/15/03	1:21.06
Silver Charm	3	120	SA	2/8/97	1:21.07
Exotic Wood	6	121	SA	1/24/98	1:21.07
Richter Scale	6	121	KEE	4/16/00	1:21.07
Housebuster	4	126	SAR	8/25/91	1:21.08
Capote Belle	3	115	SAR	7/27/96	1:21.08
Concept Win	5	118	HOL	6/24/95	1:21.09
Disturbingthepeace	4	113	HOL	7/6/02	1:21.09
Robyn Dancer	4	118	HOL	6/29/91	1:21.10
Mystery's Edge	4	115	HOL	7/17/92	1:21.10
Orville N Wilbur's	2	119	HOL	12/11/97	1:21.10
Caller One	3	122	HOL	5/29/00	1:21.10
I'ma Game Master	3	117	HOL	11/18/94	1:21.11
Van Patten	7	122	WO	9/10/00	1:21.11
Ginzano	5	118	AQU	4/25/03	1:21.11
Unbridled	4	122	AP	8/3/91	1:21.12
Private Persuasion	4	116	HOL	6/8/95	1:21.12
Afternoon Deelites	4	124	KEE	4/14/96	1:21.12
Kafwain	3	123	SA	2/1/03	1:21.12
Fly So Free	5	117	BEL	5/6/93	1:21.13
Regal Thunder	5	116	DMR	8/14/99	1:21.13
Mr Ross	7	124	RP	9/2/02	1:21.13
Exotic Wood	3	115	HOL	11/26/95	1:21.14
Boundless Moment	4	119	DMR	7/29/96	1:21.15
Sunshine Man	7	113	HIA	3/22/98	1:21.15
Tour of the Cat	5	116	GP	3/8/03	1:21.15
Strodes Creek	3	116	HOL	12/7/94	1:21.16
Wild Rush	4	117	AQU	5/3/98	1:21.16
Individual Style	2	121	HOL	11/26/93	1:21.17
Diazo	3	120	SA	12/26/93	1:21.17
Sierra Grande	4	122	GP	2/8/97	1:21.17
Ceeband	4	110	HOL	7/1/01	1:21.17

1 Mile, Dirt (1991–2003)

Horse	Age	Wt	Track	Date	Time	Horse	Age	Wt	Track	Date	Time
Najran	4	113	BEL	5/7/03	1:32.24	Wagon Limit	4	114	AQU	4/4/98	1:34.06
Williamstown	3	124	BEL	5/5/93	1:32.79	Flat Fleet Feet	4	121	AQU	4/6/97	1:34.07
Honour and Glory	3	110	BEL	5/27/96	1:32.81	Fusaichi Pegasus	3	124	BEL	9/23/00	1:34.07
Slew of Damascus	5	117	YM	3/28/93	1:33.00	Scan	3	117	BEL	9/2/91	1:34.09
Sky Jack	7	123	EMD	8/24/03	1:33.00	Sir Beaufort	5	115	SA	1/2/92	1:34.09
Langfuhr	5	122	BEL	5/26/97	1:33.11	Hello Chicago	3	115	DMR	8/22/94	1:34.09
Congaree	4	119	AQU	11/30/02	1:33.11	Trebizond	5	117	SA	1/4/91	1:34.10
Mr. Pappion	5	118	TUP	1/30/93	1:33.20	Opinionator	3	114	BEL	6/1/91	1:34.10
Wild Wonder	4	121	EMD	8/23/98	1:33.20	Bowdoin Street	7	115	BEL	10/3/91	1:34.10
Edneator	4	111	EMD	8/20/00	1:33.20	Secreto's Hideaway	5	119	TP	3/5/94	1:34.12
Swept Overboard	5	117	BEL	5/27/02	1:33.34	Topsy Robsy	4	115	BEL	9/19/96	1:34.12
Left Bank	4	120	AQU	11/24/01	1:33.35	Alcaughtup	5	114	AQU	3/29/97	1:34.12
Flying Cuantal	6	117	STK	6/15/97	1:33.40	Forest Landing	3	114	CD	5/2/03	1:34.13
Secret Launch	5	116	EMD	6/16/02	1:33.40	Pinfloron (FR)	3	117	BM	12/10/95	1:34.15
Yankee Victor	4	123	AQU	5/6/00	1:33.45	Activist	3	118	AQU	4/3/97	1:34.15
Wild Rush	4	119	BEL	5/25/98	1:33.50	I'madrifter	3	114	BM	10/8/01	1:34.15
French Deputy	3	113	BEL	9/4/95	1:33.53	Harbor Star	4	118	AQU	3/22/03	1:34.15
Chilukki	3	116	CD	11/4/00	1:33.57	Aldebaran	5	119	BEL	5/26/03	1:34.15
Private Music	5	120	STK	6/22/97	1:33.60	Touch Gold	4	123	CD	6/28/98	1:34.16
Dixie Flag	4	117	AQU	4/18/98	1:33.60	Twilight Agenda	5	122	DMR	9/8/91	1:34.17
Cat's At Home	4	114	AQU	4/7/01	1:33.60	Guided Tour	4	122	CD	7/3/00	1:34.17
Rubiano	4	116	AQU	10/26/91	1:33.68	Affirmed Success	5	118	AQU	11/27/99	1:34.18
Dixie Brass	3	107	BEL	5/25/92	1:33.68	Blade Prospector (BRZ)	6	116	GG	3/31/01	1:34.18
Makaleha	4	116	SAC	8/23/91	1:33.70	Echo of Yesterday	5	115	SA	2/17/94	1:34.19
Dixie Brass	3	126	BEL	5/6/92	1:33.71	Stop and Listen	4	119	AQU	4/15/94	1:34.19
There's Zealous	4	123	AP	8/17/02	1:33.76	Highland Gold	6	116	GG	2/19/01	1:34.19
Saint Verre	5	117	AQU	4/26/03	1:33.77	Furiously	3	113	BEL	9/7/92	1:34.20
Semi Vicious	5	115	TUP	1/19/92	1:33.80	Great Energy	7	118	TUP	1/28/94	1:34.20
Layton Hill	4	115	TUP	2/3/94	1:33.80	Want a Winner	4	117	YM	8/14/94	1:34.20
Secret Past	6	121	TUP	1/22/96	1:33.80	Kemper	7	116	TUP	1/22/95	1:34.20
B. Charlie	4	114	BM	9/15/95	1:33.83	Brumbeau	7	119	TUP	3/28/95	1:34.20
Slewker	4	117	BM	2/10/96	1:33.86	Passiano	4	118	TUP	10/21/95	1:34.20
Find the Mine	5	114	MNR	7/4/00	1:33.86	Snow Blink	5	116	TUP	4/16/96	1:34.20
Colonial Affair	3	110	BEL	5/5/93	1:33.87	Alydar's Rib	5	116	HOO	10/4/96	1:34.20
Jovial (GB)	6	115	SA	1/1/93	1:33.88	It's the Wind	7	117	HOO	10/5/96	1:34.20
Pacific Fleet	5	114	AQU	4/5/97	1:33.88	Bold Zak	7	119	STK	6/11/97	1:34.20
Doneraile Court	3	114	BEL	10/11/99	1:33.88	Kid Katabatic	4	113	EMD	8/17/97	1:34.20
Alexandrina	4	111	WO	6/9/91	1:33.90	You've Got Action	4	117	EMD	6/21/98	1:34.20
Sea Emperor	4	114	BEL	6/20/96	1:33.95	Kid Katabatic	6	122	EMD	6/20/99	1:34.20
Gold Memory	4	117	AP	7/26/97	1:33.95	Doc Art	4	116	TUP	10/26/99	1:34.20
Ibero (ARG)	5	117	AQU	10/24/92	1:33.97	Fleet Pacific	6	120	EMD	8/20/00	1:34.20
Holy Bull	3	112	BEL	5/30/94	1:33.98	Why Change	3	112	BEL	9/15/96	1:34.22
I'madrifter	5	115	GG	1/1/03	1:33.98	Barrage	4	116	AQU	11/15/01	1:34.22
Count the Time	4	119	AP	8/26/93	1:33.99	Crafty Friend	6	115	AQU	4/30/99	1:34.23
Vic's Rebel	4	122	HOO	10/13/98	1:33.99	Code One	5	118	MNR	12/19/00	1:34.23
Bolulight	4	121	LGA	8/23/92	1:34.00	Borodislew	5	119	DMR	7/31/95	1:34.24
Calgary Classic	6	116	TUP	1/28/93	1:34.00	Bold Assert	3	120	SA	3/6/92	1:34.25
Nipsy's Son	6	118	TUP	2/7/94	1:34.00	He's Illustrious	6	122	GG	6/12/93	1:34.25
Classy Mirage	4	117	AQU	4/9/94	1:34.00	Limited War	5	116	BEL	5/27/96	1:34.25
Bell Vigor	5	117	BM	2/24/96	1:34.00	Awful Smart	4	120	CD	6/1/00	1:34.25
Stately Star	4	118	HOO	11/23/96	1:34.00	Inside Information	3	121	BEL	5/8/94	1:34.26
Singing Year	5	120	EMD	6/14/98	1:34.00	How Bout Jose	5	119	BM	5/24/02	1:34.26
Bonapaw	6	121	AP	7/20/02	1:34.00	Boss Ego	7	116	GG	1/30/03	1:34.26
Lykatill Hil	4	118	DMR	9/11/94	1:34.01	West by West	3	112	BEL	10/11/92	1:34.27
Prenup	5	122	BEL	5/12/96	1:34.01	Red Bullet	3	113	AQU	3/19/00	1:34.27
Subordinated Debt	3	126	BEL	5/8/91	1:34.03	Ibero (ARG)	6	119	BEL	5/31/93	1:34.29
Romeo's Royalty	5	117	GG	5/18/94	1:34.04	Wouldn't We All	5	118	AQU	11/27/99	1:34.29
Current Worth	4	120	BM	9/7/97	1:34.04	King of Will	5	119	GG	3/16/91	1:34.30
Sir Bear	5	116	AQU	11/28/98	1:34.05	Ave's Flag	5	123	AQU	4/20/97	1:34.30
You	3	121	BEL	6/7/02	1:34.05	Congaree	5	124	AQU	11/29/03	1:34.30

1 1/16 Miles, Dirt (1991–2003)

Horse	Age	Wt	Track	Date	Time	Horse	Age	Wt	Track	Date	Time
Efervescente (ARG)	5	118	SA	1/6/93	1:39.18	Blare of Trumpets	5	115	BEL	5/7/94	1:40.60
Restless Con	4	118	GG	6/24/91	1:39.50	Sky Beauty	4	125	BEL	5/21/94	1:40.60
Rock and Roll	3	112	BEL	6/13/98	1:39.51	Alki Joe	5	117	STK	6/18/95	1:40.60
Charts	5	114	GG	4/18/92	1:39.58	Funny Tale	5	119	EMD	7/20/97	1:40.60
O. R. Race Rat	4	117	YM	1/15/93	1:39.60	General Royal	5	116	PLN	7/11/99	1:40.60
Kid Katabatic	5	123	EMD	7/26/98	1:39.60	Feverish	5	122	SR	7/30/00	1:40.60
Eagle Mill	4	116	AP	5/31/91	1:39.61	Reds Superstar	4	114	PLN	7/8/01	1:40.60
Gateway to Heaven	3	114	FG	12/29/91	1:39.80	Salt Grinder	3	119	EMD	8/11/02	1:40.60
Richmond Runner	7	119	BEL	7/16/97	1:39.81	Hollywood Wildcat	4	124	SA	10/10/94	1:40.61
Reality Road	6	115	BM	1/31/98	1:39.85	Admiralty	4	122	BEL	9/7/96	1:40.61
Master Waco Willie	5	120	YM	3/1/91	1:39.90	Slew of Damascus	5	116	GG	5/29/93	1:40.62
Fit to Scout	4	118	GG	3/16/91	1:39.90	Worldly Ways (GB)	5	116	GG	6/20/99	1:40.62
Mossflower	4	114	BEL	6/20/98	1:39.90	Admiralty	5	115	BEL	10/18/97	1:40.63
Key Contender	6	117	BEL	6/11/94	1:39.92	Ce Flite	3	112	MED	9/6/96	1:40.64
Grand Circus Park	6	117	DET	7/23/94	1:40.00	It's So Simple	3	116	BEL	7/8/01	1:40.66
New Journey	4	116	HOL	11/27/97	1:40.06	Olanthe	6	117	GG	2/25/95	1:40.67
Jarf	5	115	BEL	6/28/01	1:40.08	Raising Havoc	5	119	GG	5/4/97	1:40.67
Settlers Pub	5	112	TP	2/7/91	1:40.10	Jimmy Z	5	115	GG	11/29/02	1:40.67
Wild Years	4	121	BEL	6/7/02	1:40.11	Mazel Trick	4	117	DMR	8/7/99	1:40.68
Bolulight	4	115	GG	6/29/92	1:40.12	River Keen (IRE)	7	115	HOL	7/10/99	1:40.69
Crafty Friend	4	116	HOL	7/12/97	1:40.12	Colita	3	115	BEL	5/21/03	1:40.69
Hind Most	6	122	PRM	5/14/93	1:40.20	Sea Cadet	3	117	BM	1/19/91	1:40.70
Formal Gold	4	121	MTH	8/23/97	1:40.20	Lee's Tanthem	4	117	STK	6/23/91	1:40.70
Lord Sterling	4	115	SR	8/5/00	1:40.20	Tossofthecoin	5	118	HOL	5/21/95	1:40.70
Alfurune	5	117	EMD	7/4/03	1:40.20	Arrivederci Baby	4	113	GG	11/29/96	1:40.72
Region	5	117	HOL	7/17/94	1:40.21	Anet	3	113	TP	3/29/97	1:40.73
Flying Chevron	3	112	MED	9/22/95	1:40.27	Missy's Mirage	4	116	BEL	5/9/92	1:40.74
Event of the Year	3	115	BM	3/7/98	1:40.27	Afternoon Deelites	2	121	HOL	12/18/94	1:40.74
Basqueing Beauty	2	119	TP	9/15/91	1:40.28	Kingdom Found	7	115	SA	1/12/97	1:40.74
Hang On Slewpy	4	119	OP	4/20/91	1:40.30	Becky's Queen	4	117	FNO	10/11/92	1:40.78
Twilight Agenda	5	116	HOL	7/13/91	1:40.30	Valiant Nature	2	121	HOL	12/19/93	1:40.78
Gondolieri (CHI)	4	116	HOL	5/3/03	1:40.32	Cryptodiplomacy	2	117	BEL	9/9/98	1:40.79
Aunt Sophie	5	117	PLN	7/5/03	1:40.34	Sister Act	4	117	BEL	6/19/99	1:40.79
Riboletta (BRZ)	5	125	BEL	9/16/00	1:40.35	Military Hawk	7	121	SR	8/7/94	1:40.80
E Dubai	3	121	BEL	7/8/01	1:40.38	Kiridashi	4	121	WO	8/17/96	1:40.80
Black Forest	4	113	MED	9/26/98	1:40.39	Stone Canyon	3	117	BEL	5/7/03	1:40.80
A P Valentine	3	112	HIA	3/24/01	1:40.39	Sapor	5	117	BEL	5/8/96	1:40.81
Athenia Green (GB)	6	118	STK	6/28/92	1:40.40	Will's Way	4	114	BEL	5/15/97	1:40.81
Sneakin Jake	7	120	YM	9/19/94	1:40.40	Robb	3	112	BEL	5/27/96	1:40.82
Secret Past	6	115	TUP	1/1/96	1:40.40	Savinio	6	116	DMR	7/27/96	1:40.82
Edneator	4	122	EMD	9/11/00	1:40.44	Take Her to Heart	6	115	BM	9/14/97	1:40.82
Jess C's Whirl	3	118	MED	12/10/93	1:40.44	Musical Gambler	3	111	HOL	12/3/97	1:40.82
Siphon (BRZ)	5	117	HOL	5/4/96	1:40.44	Excessivepleasure	3	122	PRM	7/5/03	1:40.82
Snorter	3	117	BEL	5/7/03	1:40.44	Goldigger's Dream	3	116	HOL	11/21/93	1:40.83
Fleet Lady	3	115	GG	12/21/97	1:40.46	Poor But Honest	5	117	PIM	9/9/95	1:40.83
Model Dancer	5	117	BEL	5/18/92	1:40.47	General Challenge	3	124	HOL	6/26/99	1:40.83
The Exeter Man	4	116	HOL	5/17/96	1:40.47	George Bailey	3	118	HOL	12/20/02	1:40.83
Del Mar Dennis	4	115	HOL	5/15/94	1:40.48	Ayearintime	3	119	GG	12/26/02	1:40.83
Louis Cyphre (IRE)	5	119	GG	4/14/91	1:40.50	Crowning Meeting	6	115	GG	11/24/00	1:40.85
Twilight Agenda	5	114	HOL	6/29/91	1:40.50	Hoovergetthekeys	3	120	GG	3/10/01	1:40.85
Say Dance	5	117	BEL	9/16/93	1:40.52	Northern Rock (JPN)	5	118	BEL	6/12/03	1:40.86
Berkley Fitz	3	117	BEL	5/9/92	1:40.53	Earthrise (IRE)	3	116	HOL	11/16/94	1:40.87
Dixie Dot Com	6	118	LS	5/28/01	1:40.53	Hidden Lake	4	117	BEL	6/28/97	1:40.87
Mr. Bluebird	4	118	BEL	9/17/95	1:40.55	Luftikus	4	114	LS	5/29/00	1:40.87
My Mogul	3	106	BEL	5/5/93	1:40.56	Anet	3	122	LS	4/20/97	1:40.88
Regal Rowdy	5	122	HOL	5/12/94	1:40.58	Total Impact (CHI)	5	114	HOL	5/10/03	1:40.88
Paseana (ARG)	7	123	DMR	8/28/94	1:40.59	Have Fun	5	119	SA	1/29/94	1:40.89
Grand Slam	2	122	BEL	10/18/97	1:40.59	Stuka	4	118	SA	11/3/94	1:40.89
Time to Pass	4	117	LGA	7/4/92	1:40.60	Grajagan (ARG)	4	116	HOL	5/9/98	1:40.89
Ibero (ARG)	6	117	HOL	12/19/93	1:40.60	Sightseek	4	118	BEL	6/21/03	1:40.89

1 1/8 Miles, Dirt (1991–2003)

Horse	Age	Wt	Track	Date	Time
Gentlemen (ARG)	4	121	HOL	12/22/96	1:45.35
Flying Notes	3	122	EMD	9/2/02	1:45.40
Forty One Carats	3	120	MED	10/29/99	1:45.50
Albert the Great	4	120	HIA	3/24/01	1:45.52
Free House	3	122	HOL	7/20/97	1:45.96
Atlanta National	5	116	GP	1/26/91	1:46.00
K. J.'s Appeal	4	112	MED	10/16/98	1:46.06
Steady Reply	3	111	CD	6/28/91	1:46.13
Riboletta (BRZ)	5	123	BEL	10/14/00	1:46.14
Inside Information	4	123	BEL	10/28/95	1:46.15
Lykatill Hil	6	125	SAC	8/24/96	1:46.20
Sharp Cat	4	123	BEL	10/10/98	1:46.20
Formal Gold	4	119	BEL	6/14/97	1:46.21
Mineshaft	4	126	BEL	9/6/03	1:46.21
Soto	3	111	MNR	8/9/03	1:46.29
Lindsay's Hawk	5	111	RKM	5/3/91	1:46.30
Lykatill Hil	5	118	BM	12/9/95	1:46.32
Prepo (CHI)	5	115	BM	9/27/97	1:46.32
In Excess (IRE)	4	126	BEL	9/15/91	1:46.33
Seeking Daylight	4	113	BEL	6/15/02	1:46.35
Running Stag	5	117	BEL	6/12/99	1:46.39
Twice the Vice	6	121	HOL	7/20/97	1:46.41
Doc of the Day	4	119	FNO	10/18/92	1:46.45
Olympio	3	123	CBY	7/7/91	1:46.47
Missouri Ace	6	118	SAC	9/2/91	1:46.50
Hal's Pal (GB)	5	116	BM	9/26/98	1:46.51
Scan	3	119	MED	9/20/91	1:46.53
Old Trieste	4	116	HOL	5/29/99	1:46.55
Volponi	3	114	MED	10/19/01	1:46.55
Lakeway	3	121	BEL	6/12/94	1:46.58
Gator Dancer	4	119	BEL	7/18/97	1:46.58
Strike the Gold	4	116	BEL	6/6/92	1:46.60
Aly's Act	3	119	PLA	10/30/93	1:46.60
Tinners Way	6	116	HOL	6/2/96	1:46.60
Profound Secret	4	114	SAC	8/29/98	1:46.60
Behrens	3	117	MED	9/20/97	1:46.61
Beboppin Baby	5	114	PRM	7/4/98	1:46.62
Twilight Agenda	5	121	MED	10/18/91	1:46.63
Subordination	4	114	BEL	6/13/98	1:46.64
The Wicked North	5	120	HOL	6/5/94	1:46.68
Crafty Oak	5	114	HAW	5/15/99	1:46.69
In Excess (IRE)	4	126	SA	1/19/91	1:46.70
Sell Clause	5	118	GG	3/24/91	1:46.70
Hansel	3	121	TP	3/30/91	1:46.70
Devil His Due	5	120	BEL	6/18/94	1:46.71
Bertrando	5	120	SA	10/15/94	1:46.72
Festin (ARG)	5	116	BEL	6/8/91	1:46.75
Wekiva Springs	5	120	BEL	6/15/96	1:46.78
Jolie's Halo	5	116	MTH	8/8/92	1:46.80
Artic Son	5	117	HST	8/3/98	1:46.80
Pleasantly Perfect	4	115	SA	10/6/02	1:46.80
Poker Brad	5	115	EMD	7/27/03	1:46.80
Sky Jack	4	118	HOL	12/3/00	1:46.81
Saint Ballado	3	120	AP	6/21/92	1:46.82
Bowman's Band	5	119	MED	10/3/03	1:46.84
River Keen (IRE)	7	126	BEL	9/18/99	1:46.85
Grand Jewel	3	126	KEE	10/10/93	1:46.87
Holy Bull	3	121	BEL	9/17/94	1:46.89
J. T.'s Pet	7	115	SA	3/20/91	1:46.90
Latin American	5	116	HOL	4/24/93	1:46.92
Lakeway	3	121	HOL	7/10/94	1:46.93
Tomorrows Cat	3	113	MED	9/25/98	1:46.95
Saratoga Dew	3	119	BEL	10/10/92	1:46.99
Another Review	4	120	DMR	8/8/92	1:47.00
Athenia Green (GB)	7	116	PLN	7/11/93	1:47.00
Bertrando	4	126	BEL	9/18/93	1:47.00
Indian Charlie	3	120	SA	4/4/98	1:47.00
Moonlight Meeting	7	120	EMD	7/28/02	1:47.00
Yanks Music	3	119	BEL	10/6/96	1:47.02
Seattle Fitz (ARG)	4	119	BEL	9/27/03	1:47.02
Missy's Mirage	4	118	BEL	5/31/92	1:47.03
Alphabet Soup	4	117	HOL	12/23/95	1:47.03
Banshee Breeze	3	119	KEE	10/17/98	1:47.04
Left Bank	5	118	SAR	8/3/02	1:47.04
Ibero (ARG)	5	115	SA	2/15/92	1:47.05
Sultry Song	4	126	BEL	9/19/92	1:47.05
Cigar	6	126	BEL	9/14/96	1:47.06
Old Trieste	3	118	HOL	7/19/98	1:47.06
Cigar	5	126	BEL	9/16/95	1:47.07
Anshan (GB)	4	115	SA	3/30/91	1:47.10
Ja Ro De	5	117	LGA	6/30/91	1:47.10
Gander	5	114	MED	9/28/01	1:47.11
Event of the Year	3	121	TP	3/29/98	1:47.12
Imperial Gesture	3	117	BEL	9/7/02	1:47.12
Red Sky's	3	118	GG	5/29/99	1:47.16
Jewel Princess	4	120	HOL	7/21/96	1:47.17
Pleasant Breeze	4	110	MED	10/15/99	1:47.17
Diazo	3	117	MED	9/24/93	1:47.18
Keeper Hill	4	123	KEE	10/16/99	1:47.19
Fleet Renee	3	121	BEL	6/30/01	1:47.19
Dispute	3	120	BEL	9/4/93	1:47.20
Military Hawk	7	116	PLN	7/10/94	1:47.20
Heavenly Prize	3	123	BEL	9/4/94	1:47.20
Majestic Nasr	7	113	SAC	9/5/94	1:47.20
Anchor	5	120	FNO	10/14/95	1:47.20
Flirtacious Girl	3	119	EMD	8/21/99	1:47.20
Western Pride	3	113	MNR	8/11/01	1:47.20
Marquetry	6	120	MED	10/15/93	1:47.21
Silver Charm	4	124	SA	10/17/98	1:47.21
Dispute	3	119	BEL	10/16/93	1:47.22
Cigar	5	120	OP	4/15/95	1:47.22
Balto Star	3	121	TP	3/24/01	1:47.23
Mizzen Mast	4	121	SA	2/2/02	1:47.25
Louis Quatorze	3	124	SAR	8/4/96	1:47.26
Del Mar Dennis	5	117	SA	4/2/95	1:47.27
Silver Charm	4	123	SA	2/7/98	1:47.27
Skip Away	5	130	SUF	5/30/98	1:47.27
Victory Gallop	4	120	CD	6/12/99	1:47.28
Sultry Song	4	115	SAR	8/29/92	1:47.29
Serena's Song	3	124	BEL	9/3/95	1:47.29
Skip Away	3	121	KEE	4/13/96	1:47.29
Variety Road	8	120	BM	1/12/91	1:47.30
Farma Way	4	118	SA	2/17/91	1:47.30
Bargain Doll	4	115	GG	5/4/91	1:47.30
Tossofthecoin	4	117	HOL	6/1/94	1:47.30
Ajina	3	120	HOL	11/8/97	1:47.30
Sweet Misty	4	119	MED	10/16/98	1:47.30
Left Bank	3	119	AQU	10/25/00	1:47.30

1 1/4 Miles, Dirt (1991–2003)

Horse	Age	Wt	Track	Date	Time
In Excess (IRE)	4	119	BEL	7/4/91	1:58.33
Skip Away	4	126	BEL	10/18/97	1:58.89
Pleasant Tap	5	126	BEL	10/10/92	1:58.95
Lemon Drop Kid	4	122	BEL	7/4/00	1:58.97
Best Pal	4	124	SA	3/7/92	1:59.08
Candy Ride (ARG)	4	124	DMR	8/24/03	1:59.11
Skip Away	4	126	HOL	11/8/97	1:59.16
Albert the Great	3	122	BEL	10/14/00	1:59.24
Urgent Request (IRE)	5	116	SA	3/11/95	1:59.25
Gentlemen (ARG)	5	124	HOL	6/29/97	1:59.26
Tinners Way	4	124	DMR	8/13/94	1:59.43
Cigar	5	126	HOL	7/2/95	1:59.46
Marquetry	4	110	HOL	6/29/91	1:59.50
Cat Thief	3	122	GP	11/6/99	1:59.52
Bertrando	4	124	DMR	8/21/93	1:59.55
Cigar	5	126	BEL	10/28/95	1:59.58
Evening Attire	4	126	BEL	9/28/02	1:59.58
Tinners Way	5	124	DMR	8/13/95	1:59.63
Real Quiet	4	124	HOL	6/27/99	1:59.67
Milwaukee Brew	6	119	SA	3/1/03	1:59.80
Tiznow	3	124	LAD	9/30/00	1:59.84
Capt. Quicksilver	6	114	FNO	10/18/92	1:59.85
Dare and Go	5	124	DMR	8/10/96	1:59.85
Best Pal	3	116	DMR	8/10/91	1:59.86
Pleasantly Perfect	5	126	SA	10/25/03	1:59.88
Best Pal	4	124	SA	2/9/92	1:59.95
Richie the Coach	5	118	LRL	11/23/96	1:59.96
Skimming	5	124	DMR	8/19/01	1:59.96
Monarchos	3	126	CD	5/5/01	1:59.97
Dream of Fame (IRE)	6	116	SA	10/29/92	2:00.12
Dare and Go	4	118	SA	2/5/95	2:00.15
Skip Away	5	124	HOL	6/28/98	2:00.16
Best Pal	5	121	HOL	7/3/93	2:00.17
Stuka	4	115	SA	3/5/94	2:00.17
A.P. Indy	3	121	GP	10/31/92	2:00.20
Big Sky Jim	6	115	HOL	5/24/98	2:00.21
On the Scent	4	122	BEU	10/19/91	2:00.22
Sultry Song	4	113	HOL	6/27/92	2:00.23
Siphon (BRZ)	6	120	SA	3/2/97	2:00.23
Mineshaft	4	126	BEL	9/27/03	2:00.25
Free House	4	124	DMR	8/15/98	2:00.29
Farma Way	4	120	SA	3/9/91	2:00.30
Majestic Dinner	4	122	BEU	10/8/01	2:00.32
Pleasant Tap	5	119	BEL	7/18/92	2:00.33
Diazo	4	120	SA	2/6/94	2:00.33
Mecke	3	126	LAD	9/30/95	2:00.34
Albert the Great	4	123	BEL	7/1/01	2:00.39
Ajina	3	121	BEL	7/19/97	2:00.45
Frisk Me Now	4	118	BEL	7/4/98	2:00.45
Scuffleburg	5	113	GP	3/6/94	2:00.46
Congaree	5	124	HOL	7/13/03	2:00.48
Blessedly Bold	7	117	MNR	6/8/91	2:00.50
Siphon (BRZ)	5	117	HOL	6/30/96	2:00.50
Let's Be Curious	4	116	SA	4/24/95	2:00.51
Lite Light	3	121	BEL	7/6/91	2:00.54
Buck's Boy	4	114	HAW	10/11/97	2:00.54
Sir Beaufort	6	119	SA	3/6/93	2:00.55
Gentlemen (ARG)	5	124	DMR	8/9/97	2:00.56
General Challenge	3	117	DMR	8/29/99	2:00.57
Ecton Park	3	126	LAD	10/2/99	2:00.59
Wagon Limit	4	126	BEL	10/10/98	2:00.62
Duckhorn	4	115	LRL	3/18/01	2:00.62
Tiznow	4	126	BEL	10/27/01	2:00.62
Devoted Brass	3	123	HOL	7/24/93	2:00.64
Concerto	4	120	LRL	11/29/98	2:00.65
Free House	5	123	SA	3/6/99	2:00.67
Festin (ARG)	5	126	BEL	10/5/91	2:00.69
Best Pal	3	116	HOL	7/7/91	2:00.70
Skip Away	3	121	BEL	10/5/96	2:00.70
Tiznow	3	122	CD	11/4/00	2:00.75
Slew of Damascus	6	117	HOL	7/2/94	2:00.76
Silver Music	3	119	HOL	7/23/94	2:00.76
Guided Tour	5	116	AP	7/21/01	2:00.76
Siberian Summer	4	118	SA	2/7/93	2:00.78
Arcangues	5	126	SA	11/6/93	2:00.83
It's Just Me	3	117	BEU	10/22/94	2:00.85
Missionary Ridge (GB)	5	124	DMR	8/30/92	2:00.87
Defensive Play	4	122	SA	2/10/91	2:00.90
Deputy Commander	3	126	LAD	9/28/97	2:00.92
E Dubai	4	116	BEL	7/6/02	2:00.95
Free Spirit's Joy	3	126	LAD	9/22/91	2:00.96
Olympio	3	126	AP	8/3/91	2:00.99
Thunder Rumble	3	126	SAR	8/22/92	2:00.99
Yourmissinthepoint	4	113	HAW	11/18/95	2:01.00
Alphabet Soup	5	126	WO	10/26/96	2:01.00
Perfect to a Tee	7	122	LRL	11/27/99	2:01.00
Milwaukee Brew	5	115	SA	3/2/02	2:01.02
Jolie's Halo	4	119	GP	3/23/91	2:01.04
Grindstone	3	126	CD	5/4/96	2:01.06
Behrens	5	121	BEL	7/5/99	2:01.06
Truly a Pleasure	8	115	DMR	8/18/95	2:01.09
Running Stag	5	122	SAR	8/29/99	2:01.11
Irish Swap	5	115	HAW	11/21/92	2:01.12
Fusaichi Pegasus	3	126	CD	5/6/00	2:01.12
War Emblem	3	126	CD	5/4/02	2:01.13
Phantom Light	4	115	WO	7/1/03	2:01.15
Supreme Sound (GB)	5	112	HAW	10/9/99	2:01.19
Funny Cide	3	126	CD	5/3/03	2:01.19
Corporate Report	3	126	SAR	8/17/91	2:01.20
Provins	4	112	SA	3/4/92	2:01.22
Skimming	4	124	DMR	8/26/00	2:01.22
Devil His Due	4	121	BEL	7/4/93	2:01.25
Jean Pierre S	5	119	SA	2/17/94	2:01.27
Thunder Gulch	3	126	CD	5/6/95	2:01.27
Strike Reality	8	116	HAW	12/13/03	2:01.28
Cigar	5	126	BEL	10/7/95	2:01.29
Devil His Due	4	113	GP	3/14/93	2:01.33
Mt. Sassafras	7	113	WO	7/1/99	2:01.38
Volponi	4	126	AP	10/26/02	2:01.39
Truly a Pleasure	8	121	TUP	3/26/95	2:01.40
Firm Dancer	4	115	WO	7/1/97	2:01.40
River Keen (IRE)	7	126	BEL	10/10/99	2:01.40
Early Pioneer	5	124	HOL	7/9/00	2:01.40
Point Given	3	126	SAR	8/25/01	2:01.40
Mignon	4	111	HOL	11/27/97	2:01.42
Came Home	3	117	DMR	8/25/02	2:01.45
General Challenge	4	121	SA	3/4/00	2:01.49
Aptitude	4	126	BEL	10/6/01	2:01.49

1 Mile, Turf (1991–2003)

Horse	Age	Wt	Track	Date	Time
Elusive Quality	5	117	BEL	7/4/98	1:31.63
Atticus	5	117	SA	3/1/97	1:31.89
Isitingood	6	121	SA	2/5/97	1:32.05
Val Royal (FR)	5	126	BEL	10/27/01	1:32.05
Lucky Coin	4	120	BEL	9/20/97	1:32.17
Touch of the Blues (FR)	6	122	DMR	8/2/03	1:32.22
Volponi	4	115	BEL	7/5/02	1:32.24
Urgent Request (IRE)	6	115	SA	10/5/96	1:32.44
Known Ranger (GB)	5	113	BEL	9/9/91	1:32.53
Caress	4	119	BEL	6/11/95	1:32.53
Quake	6	118	SA	9/28/01	1:32.55
Viking King	4	118	WO	6/20/91	1:32.60
Slewper Imp	5	115	ELP	7/16/95	1:32.60
Gilder	6	116	ELP	7/29/97	1:32.60
Suffragette	3	112	ELP	7/24/99	1:32.60
Designed for Luck	6	119	SA	10/5/03	1:32.61
License Fee	6	118	BEL	6/9/01	1:32.62
Megan's Interco	5	119	HOL	5/22/94	1:32.64
Val's Prince	5	114	BEL	6/20/97	1:32.67
Dominant Prospect	4	114	BEL	7/4/94	1:32.69
Antespend	4	117	BEL	5/24/97	1:32.69
Soviet Line (IRE)	7	115	BEL	6/7/97	1:32.72
Special Ring	5	120	DMR	8/2/02	1:32.72
Garbu	4	123	BEL	5/24/98	1:32.73
Fastness (IRE)	6	124	HOL	6/16/96	1:32.74
Pebo's Guy	4	121	BEL	7/15/98	1:32.74
Garbu	6	118	BEL	7/12/00	1:32.75
Spinning World	4	126	HOL	11/8/97	1:32.77
Numerous Times	4	117	WO	9/9/01	1:32.79
Tates Creek	4	119	BEL	9/21/02	1:32.79
Lost Soldier	6	117	WO	7/24/96	1:32.80
Provisions	3	110	ELP	8/24/96	1:32.80
Colcon	4	113	BEL	9/14/97	1:32.80
Oh Nellie	4	116	BEL	10/4/98	1:32.80
Always Sure	3	112	ELP	8/21/99	1:32.80
Rob 'n Gin	5	118	BEL	7/3/99	1:32.81
War Zone	4	117	BEL	7/5/03	1:32.81
Green Fee	6	120	BEL	6/23/02	1:32.83
Elizabeth Bay	4	114	BEL	6/15/94	1:32.85
Debonair Dan	4	114	BEL	5/25/96	1:32.87
In Frank's Honor	5	116	BEL	6/9/01	1:32.87
Valentine Dancer	3	116	SA	10/12/03	1:32.87
Journalism	5	114	HOL	4/25/93	1:32.89
Apache Wings	5	118	SA	3/14/03	1:32.89
Lure	3	122	GP	10/31/92	1:32.90
Memories of Silver	4	120	BEL	6/8/97	1:32.90
Alawal	4	121	BEL	7/17/99	1:32.91
Special Ring	5	117	HOL	7/7/02	1:32.91
Valory	3	114	ELP	8/4/01	1:32.93
Night Patrol	6	119	SA	10/5/02	1:32.93
Silic (FR)	4	124	HOL	6/13/99	1:32.95
Tin Smithen	5	116	ELP	7/25/02	1:32.95
Climate	6	116	SA	3/22/02	1:32.98
Keen Runner	7	121	WO	7/19/95	1:33.00
Yaqthan (IRE)	5	114	ELP	7/23/95	1:33.00
Make'n It Happen	4	118	WO	7/28/95	1:33.00
Make'n It Happen	4	115	WO	8/20/95	1:33.00
Camlan	5	117	WO	5/20/96	1:33.00
American Dynasty	3	112	ELP	8/2/97	1:33.00
Labeeb (GB)	6	121	WO	9/20/98	1:33.00
X Country	5	120	ELP	7/20/03	1:33.01
Fourstardave	8	117	BEL	6/26/93	1:33.02
Dancing Douglas	7	110	BEL	5/31/97	1:33.03
Designed for Luck	6	117	DMR	8/18/03	1:33.04
Tradition Rocks	4	123	DMR	8/10/03	1:33.06
Wonder Again	4	117	BEL	9/20/03	1:33.07
Draw Shot	4	118	BEL	7/4/97	1:33.08
Odalea (ARG)	6	116	HOL	5/9/92	1:33.09
Rutledge Gold	3	117	ELP	8/25/02	1:33.09
Tarquin Joe	4	118	BEL	7/6/97	1:33.10
Scagnelli	4	119	BEL	6/16/99	1:33.11
Joleur	8	114	ELP	9/3/00	1:33.11
Martessa (GER)	4	118	HOL	5/29/92	1:33.13
Jido	3	108	BEL	9/16/94	1:33.14
Unfinished Symph	4	121	HOL	6/10/95	1:33.14
Denied	5	121	DMR	7/30/03	1:33.14
Crystal Hearted (GB)	5	114	DMR	7/30/99	1:33.15
Pride of Summer	6	117	BEL	6/22/94	1:33.16
Golden Dice	5	119	BEL	6/25/00	1:33.17
Package Store	4	121	BEL	9/14/02	1:33.17
Escorpion (CHI)	5	116	HOL	11/29/96	1:33.18
Riviera (FR)	6	117	WO	9/10/00	1:33.18
Eighties	6	120	ELP	8/5/01	1:33.18
Reluctant Guest	5	119	SA	11/3/91	1:33.19
Quiet Resolve	4	117	WO	9/19/99	1:33.19
Alyzig	6	113	SA	1/25/03	1:33.19
Savethelastdance	3	114	WO	6/30/91	1:33.20
I'da Dance	5	115	ELP	7/29/94	1:33.20
Terremoto	4	121	WO	6/16/95	1:33.20
Bonnie Castle	4	111	WO	8/26/95	1:33.20
Slew Valley	3	114	BEL	7/1/00	1:33.20
Exbourne	6	122	SA	4/12/92	1:33.21
Cat's Cradle	5	116	SA	1/31/97	1:33.21
Lucky Coin	4	123	BEL	10/3/97	1:33.21
Val Royal (FR)	5	119	SA	10/7/01	1:33.21
First Titanium	6	119	DMR	8/11/02	1:33.21
Riskaverse	4	123	BEL	5/18/03	1:33.21
Captive Number	3	113	BEL	7/12/96	1:33.22
Special Ring	5	119	SA	2/21/02	1:33.23
Amarettitorun	5	116	BEL	9/26/97	1:33.24
Strategic Mission	5	122	GP	1/17/00	1:33.24
Scott the Great	6	117	BEL	6/27/92	1:33.27
Good Journey	6	121	WO	9/8/02	1:33.27
Moonshine Hall	3	118	WO	6/22/03	1:33.27
Designed for Luck	6	118	DMR	9/10/03	1:33.28
Home of the Free	3	112	BEL	8/30/91	1:33.29
Labeeb (GB)	6	124	HOL	6/14/98	1:33.29
Navesink	3	115	BEL	5/9/01	1:33.29
Madjaristan	5	115	SA	3/9/91	1:33.30
Kanatiyr (IRE)	5	121	SA	3/17/91	1:33.30
Pharisien (FR)	4	113	SA	4/7/91	1:33.30
Island Jamboree	5	121	HOL	5/15/91	1:33.30
Caress	5	117	BEL	6/9/96	1:33.30
Old Alliance	5	116	HOL	5/8/92	1:33.32
Dayflower	4	119	BEL	7/16/94	1:33.32
Fastness (IRE)	5	115	HOL	6/24/95	1:33.32
El Cielo	7	117	SA	1/4/01	1:33.32
High Demand	4	121	DMR	8/22/01	1:33.32
Expresso Bay	6	119	DMR	8/17/03	1:33.32

1 1/8 Miles, Turf (1991–2003)

Horse	Age	Wt	Track	Date	Time	Horse	Age	Wt	Track	Date	Time
Kostroma (IRE)	5	117	SA	10/20/91	1:43.92	Indy Vidual	6	116	SAR	9/2/00	1:46.07
Eton Lad (GB)	4	115	SA	10/10/91	1:44.19	Marlin	3	122	HOL	12/1/96	1:46.08
Yaqthan (IRE)	6	113	ELP	9/2/96	1:44.60	Lure	5	125	SAR	8/12/94	1:46.10
Rainbows for Life	3	122	HAW	10/13/91	1:44.70	Sentimental Moi	7	112	SAR	8/15/97	1:46.11
Fastness (IRE)	5	120	HOL	11/25/95	1:44.78	Stallan	4	115	SAR	8/20/97	1:46.11
Quilma (CHI)	4	116	SA	10/12/91	1:44.87	Forty Niner Days	5	114	HOL	7/2/92	1:46.13
Tight Spot	4	117	HOL	5/8/91	1:44.90	Finder's Choice	7	117	LRL	10/24/92	1:46.13
Illiquidity	4	117	ELP	9/2/00	1:44.91	Flawlessly	4	123	HOL	11/29/92	1:46.14
Classic Fame	5	116	SA	11/8/91	1:44.96	Memories of Silver	5	123	SAR	9/6/98	1:46.14
The Vid	5	120	CRC	11/25/95	1:44.99	Outta My Way Man	5	114	BEL	6/22/97	1:46.15
Toussaud	4	116	HOL	5/30/93	1:45.07	Star Connection	5	117	SAR	8/12/99	1:46.16
Leger Cat (ARG)	7	115	HOL	5/9/93	1:45.19	Hibernian Rhapsody (Ire)	4	114	CRC	11/27/99	1:46.17
Bold Ruritana	5	117	WO	6/18/95	1:45.20	Starine (FR)	4	114	SAR	9/3/01	1:46.17
Majestic Jove	4	117	ELP	8/16/98	1:45.20	Crazy Ensign (ARG)	7	120	SA	11/9/03	1:46.17
Repriced	4	115	HOL	5/22/92	1:45.28	Eternity Range	5	120	HOL	5/20/98	1:46.18
Roxinho (BRZ)	4	114	ELP	9/2/02	1:45.39	Isle de France	4	116	HOL	5/5/99	1:46.18
Military Shot	4	117	SA	4/4/91	1:45.40	Tiffany's Taylor	6	114	SAR	8/24/95	1:46.19
Aboriginal Apex	5	115	ELP	9/7/98	1:45.40	Batique	5	113	MTH	6/16/01	1:46.19
Furiously	4	119	SAR	8/11/93	1:45.46	Durham	3	115	ELP	8/7/94	1:46.20
Stay Sound	5	117	ELP	9/4/00	1:45.51	Texas Town	3	105	ELP	7/19/95	1:46.20
Yaqthan (IRE)	8	116	LS	5/25/98	1:45.54	Slewper Imp	5	110	ELP	9/4/95	1:46.20
Gentlemen (ARG)	4	119	HOL	11/30/96	1:45.55	Duck Trap	3	113	ELP	8/18/96	1:46.20
Hero's Love	5	118	WO	9/19/93	1:45.60	Chief Bearhart	4	119	WO	6/14/97	1:46.20
Mufattish	5	116	HOL	5/21/98	1:45.62	S'No Business	4	113	ELP	7/9/97	1:46.20
Notorious Pleasure	6	117	HOL	6/14/92	1:45.68	Howell's Poet	5	119	ELP	8/31/97	1:46.20
Subordination	3	113	BEL	6/15/97	1:45.69	Colorful Vices	5	118	WO	7/12/98	1:46.20
Sweetest Thing	4	121	WO	7/6/02	1:45.72	Think Red	3	114	WO	6/24/00	1:46.20
Wolf (CHI)	4	121	SA	10/4/91	1:45.73	Candy Ride (ARG)	4	120	HOL	7/4/03	1:46.20
Notorious Pleasure	5	118	HOL	11/30/91	1:45.80	King Chulumbo	4	117	SA	10/2/96	1:46.22
Memories of Silver	3	121	KEE	10/5/96	1:45.81	Amarettitorun	5	115	SAR	7/26/97	1:46.22
Astra	4	117	HOL	6/4/00	1:45.81	Yagli	5	121	SAR	7/31/98	1:46.22
Political Attack	4	116	CRC	12/6/03	1:45.81	Exchange	5	120	SA	3/13/93	1:46.23
Super Quercus (FR)	3	122	HOL	11/28/99	1:45.82	Unite's Big Red	4	114	CRC	7/4/98	1:46.24
Hap	4	115	SAR	7/28/00	1:45.82	Distant Mirage (IRE)	3	114	SAR	8/30/98	1:46.26
Jeune Homme	3	114	HOL	11/28/93	1:45.84	Well Wrapped	4	117	LRL	8/2/91	1:46.27
Fly Till Dawn	5	119	HOL	11/30/91	1:45.86	Medium Cool	3	115	SA	11/6/91	1:46.29
Special Ring	6	117	DMR	7/27/03	1:45.87	Vaguely Hidden	6	118	SA	4/12/91	1:46.30
Sharekann (IRE)	5	116	SA	2/20/97	1:45.90	Sky Classic	4	119	WO	6/16/91	1:46.30
Subordination	4	121	BEL	9/26/98	1:45.90	Happyanunoit (NZ)	4	123	HOL	11/28/99	1:46.30
Slew of Damascus	5	114	BM	10/2/93	1:45.91	Promise of War	5	114	ELP	9/3/01	1:46.30
Ricky's Shadow	6	114	CRC	7/4/98	1:45.93	Signal Tap	4	116	SAR	7/30/95	1:46.32
Heritage of Gold	4	115	SAR	9/5/99	1:45.93	Floriselli	6	115	BEL	7/1/00	1:46.32
Fourstardave	7	122	SAR	8/24/92	1:45.94	Majestic Nasr	4	118	SA	10/30/91	1:46.33
Gravieres (FR)	5	114	BM	10/9/93	1:45.95	New Identity	6	118	MTH	7/10/94	1:46.33
Lazy Lode (ARG)	7	118	SA	3/15/01	1:45.95	Tenski	3	119	SAR	8/26/98	1:46.33
Tangazi	4	119	BEL	6/12/99	1:45.97	Foggy Day (FR)	5	117	SA	12/29/99	1:46.33
Fanatic Boy (ARG)	5	116	SA	2/2/92	1:45.99	Star Performance	7	116	SA	3/23/00	1:46.33
Tight Spot	4	123	HOL	7/4/91	1:46.00	Lure	4	123	CD	4/30/93	1:46.34
Thunder Regent	5	113	WO	6/14/92	1:46.00	Legend of Russia (GB)	4	116	SA	3/12/98	1:46.34
Allijeba	7	121	ELP	8/14/93	1:46.00	Lilys Cousin	6	115	TAM	5/6/00	1:46.34
Kiridashi	4	117	WO	6/16/96	1:46.00	Tiger Trap	3	118	SA	4/6/01	1:46.34
Johar	3	118	SA	10/13/02	1:46.00	Draw Again	5	112	CRC	7/8/00	1:46.35
Madagascar (ARG)	5	123	BEL	6/22/02	1:46.02	Rolled Stocking	5	117	MTH	6/9/01	1:46.35
Stroll	3	121	BEL	9/21/03	1:46.02	Valid Reprized	3	115	CRC	11/29/99	1:46.36
Signal Tap	5	114	HIA	3/31/96	1:46.04	River Flyer	3	115	SA	10/12/94	1:46.39
Tranquility Lake	4	119	HOL	6/6/99	1:46.04	Mr. Light Tres (ARG)	6	114	CRC	7/4/95	1:46.39
La Reine's Terms	7	122	LRL	8/11/02	1:46.04	Rajpoute (FR)	4	116	SA	3/19/98	1:46.39
Fourstars Allstar	4	113	SAR	8/12/92	1:46.06	Dexter Drive	4	118	SA	10/20/99	1:46.39
Kazabaiyn	4	116	SA	3/12/94	1:46.06	Viva Pentelicus	7	116	MTH	7/4/03	1:46.39
Tout Charmant	4	123	HOL	11/26/00	1:46.06						

1 1/4 Miles, Turf (1991–2003)

Horse	Age	Wt	Track	Date	Time	Horse	Age	Wt	Track	Date	Time
Bequest	5	117	SA	3/31/91	1:57.50	Missionary Ridge (GB)	4	117	SA	4/22/91	1:59.50
Konba	5	119	SA	10/14/96	1:57.60	Auntie Mame	4	118	BEL	7/18/98	1:59.50
Hero's Welcome (IRE)	4	112	SA	10/13/91	1:57.70	Superiority	7	118	SA	10/18/03	1:59.51
Bien Bien	4	119	HOL	5/31/93	1:57.75	Sandpit (BRZ)	7	120	HOL	5/27/96	1:59.52
Paradise Creek	5	124	BEL	6/11/94	1:57.79	Spanish Fern	4	123	SA	10/2/99	1:59.52
Johar	4	120	SA	1/20/03	1:57.92	Chenin Blanc	5	124	BEL	5/24/91	1:59.54
Classic Fame	6	120	SA	1/20/92	1:58.02	Lech	3	114	BEL	7/21/91	1:59.55
Who's to Pay	5	117	BEL	9/8/91	1:58.18	Tight Spot	4	126	AP	9/1/91	1:59.55
Chief Bearhart	5	122	BEL	6/6/98	1:58.25	Public Purse	6	119	SA	1/22/00	1:59.58
Boldly Excellent	4	118	SA	10/14/91	1:58.33	Ye Slew	7	112	ELP	8/6/94	1:59.60
Dynamic Trick	5	114	LRL	10/22/00	1:58.42	Manndar (IRE)	4	117	BEL	6/10/00	1:59.61
Dreamer	5	116	SA	2/22/97	1:58.47	Astra	5	121	HOL	6/24/01	1:59.61
Admise (FR)	4	121	SA	10/6/96	1:58.48	All the Boys	6	115	SA	1/8/03	1:59.61
Yagli	6	122	BEL	6/5/99	1:58.48	Kostroma (IRE)	6	121	SA	4/5/92	1:59.63
Jungle Pioneer	5	114	SA	4/6/91	1:58.50	Paradise Creek	5	126	LRL	10/15/94	1:59.63
Astra	6	124	HOL	6/29/02	1:58.56	Lexa (FR)	5	119	SA	12/30/99	1:59.63
Awad	5	121	BEL	6/10/95	1:58.57	England's Legend (FR)	4	115	BEL	7/14/01	1:59.63
Super May	5	117	SA	11/11/91	1:58.58	Snow Dance	5	116	BEL	7/4/03	1:59.63
Janet (GB)	4	123	SA	9/29/01	1:58.64	Polaris Star	6	113	BEL	6/4/94	1:59.67
Fahim (GB)	4	113	LRL	7/4/97	1:58.67	You'd Be Surprised	5	118	BEL	7/10/94	1:59.69
Awad	5	126	AP	8/27/95	1:58.69	Nowrass (GB)	6	116	BEL	7/4/02	1:59.69
Fly Till Dawn	5	120	SA	1/21/91	1:58.70	Golden Apples (IRE)	4	123	SA	10/5/02	1:59.72
Pescagani	4	116	BEL	7/14/94	1:58.71	Is Me	4	116	SA	3/13/94	1:59.73
Sentimental Moi	6	114	BEL	7/7/96	1:58.73	Yashmak	3	114	BEL	10/4/97	1:59.73
Tombstone (ARG)	6	118	SA	10/13/03	1:58.82	Indy Vidual	7	120	BEL	6/27/01	1:59.73
Social Retiree	6	119	LRL	7/11/93	1:58.86	So Sterling	4	117	BEL	6/16/91	1:59.74
Radevore (GB)	7	118	SA	1/13/00	1:58.86	Holy Mountain	3	112	BEL	7/17/94	1:59.74
Hannibal Lad (GB)	7	119	SA	1/16/03	1:58.92	Turkish Tryst	5	121	BEL	7/11/96	1:59.74
Bienamado	4	121	HOL	6/25/00	1:58.93	Vergennes	3	112	BEL	7/16/98	1:59.74
Sharp Performance	3	114	BEL	7/15/01	1:58.93	Academy Award	5	117	BEL	6/7/91	1:59.78
The Tin Man	4	124	SA	10/6/02	1:58.93	Paradise Creek	5	126	AP	8/28/94	1:59.78
Bisbalense (CHI)	5	117	BEL	9/8/94	1:58.95	Earl of Barking (IRE)	5	115	HOL	5/29/95	1:59.78
Big Sky Jim	5	116	SA	4/16/97	1:58.97	Logia (ARG)	6	115	SA	2/15/97	1:59.79
Motto	6	118	SA	10/17/01	1:58.97	Le Famo	5	114	BEL	7/22/91	1:59.81
Quest for Fame (GB)	5	122	HOL	5/25/92	1:58.99	Dowty	5	116	BEL	6/27/97	1:59.81
Star of Cozzene	5	118	BEL	6/6/93	1:58.99	Owsley	4	114	BEL	7/4/02	1:59.81
Aquilegia	4	114	BEL	6/19/93	1:59.05	Royal Mountain Inn	4	110	BEL	7/18/93	1:59.82
Lilac Queen (GER)	5	119	SA	1/24/03	1:59.05	Separated Love	5	113	BEL	10/2/98	1:59.82
Tamhid	5	117	BEL	7/2/98	1:59.06	Arbiter	5	119	HOL	7/11/02	1:59.82
Mash One (CHI)	5	124	SA	10/3/99	1:59.07	Lite Approval	4	119	BEL	7/16/97	1:59.83
Ops Smile	5	116	BEL	6/7/97	1:59.08	Dear Doctor (FR)	5	126	AP	9/6/92	1:59.84
Santovito (IRE)	3	118	SA	10/29/99	1:59.13	Flitch	4	117	LRL	7/4/96	1:59.84
Islington (IRE)	4	123	SA	10/25/03	1:59.13	Donna Viola (GB)	5	120	SA	4/19/97	1:59.85
Grand Flotilla	7	116	HOL	5/30/94	1:59.26	Currency Arbitrage	3	118	BEL	6/28/96	1:59.86
Correntino	6	114	BEL	7/15/95	1:59.30	Indy Vidual	3	116	BEL	9/28/97	1:59.86
Mystic Knight (GB)	5	114	BEL	6/11/98	1:59.31	Storm Trooper	4	118	BEL	6/7/97	1:59.88
Happyanunoit (NZ)	5	121	HOL	7/2/00	1:59.32	Sligo Bay (IRE)	4	118	SA	10/18/02	1:59.88
Free At Last (GB)	5	119	SA	2/29/92	1:59.33	Horatio Luro	4	115	BEL	9/7/91	1:59.89
Auntie Mame	4	121	BEL	10/3/98	1:59.33	Saint Stephen	3	118	BEL	7/6/03	1:59.89
Special Matter	5	118	SA	10/8/03	1:59.33	Got the Votes	4	122	SA	10/13/00	1:59.90
Bienamado	5	124	HOL	6/10/01	1:59.34	Maxzene	4	120	BEL	7/12/97	1:59.91
Super Staff	4	123	SA	11/8/92	1:59.36	Irish Linnet	7	118	BEL	7/9/95	1:59.92
Incessant (IRE)	5	116	HOL	6/6/92	1:59.37	Garden in the Rain (FR)	5	118	SA	10/25/02	1:59.92
Six Zero (FR)	4	116	HOL	5/3/98	1:59.37	Missionary Ridge (GB)	5	119	SA	4/27/92	1:59.93
Foresta	5	121	BEL	6/15/91	1:59.38	Noble Sheba	4	119	BEL	6/17/94	1:59.93
Geri	5	116	BEL	6/14/97	1:59.39	Mufattish	4	121	SA	3/27/97	1:59.96
Barrymore (GB)	5	115	SA	1/19/92	1:59.41	Phi Beta Doc	3	117	CNL	10/2/99	1:59.97
Eternity Range	5	117	SA	4/8/98	1:59.41	Tarsho (IRE)	6	118	HOL	6/7/92	1:59.98
The Seven Seas	5	122	HOL	6/3/01	1:59.42	Dimitrova	3	121	HOL	7/5/03	1:59.98
Senure	5	124	SA	9/30/01	1:59.47						

1 1/2 Miles, Turf (1991–2003)

Horse	Age	Wt	Track	Date	Time
Unite's Big Red	5	114	GP	3/6/99	2:23.15
Awad	7	117	SAR	8/9/97	2:23.20
Buck's Boy	5	115	GP	3/7/98	2:23.43
Talloires	6	116	HOL	7/21/96	2:23.55
Filago	4	126	SA	10/6/91	2:23.62
Whata Brainstorm	4	114	GP	3/11/01	2:23.75
Coretta (IRE)	5	118	GP	3/7/99	2:23.85
Kotashaan (FR)	5	124	SA	3/21/93	2:23.91
Chief Bearhart	4	126	HOL	11/8/97	2:23.92
With Anticipation	7	120	SAR	8/10/02	2:24.06
Fraise	4	126	GP	10/31/92	2:24.08
Rial (ARG)	6	118	SA	2/18/91	2:24.10
Flag Down	5	116	CRC	12/16/95	2:24.11
Deeliteful Irving	4	113	GP	3/23/02	2:24.14
Diplomatic Jet	4	123	CRC	12/21/96	2:24.20
Dernier Empereur	6	118	SA	11/4/96	2:24.24
High Chaparral (IRE)	4	126	SA	10/25/03	2:24.24
Johar	4	126	SA	10/25/03	2:24.24
Navarone	4	126	SA	10/10/92	2:24.29
Fantastic Light	5	126	BEL	10/27/01	2:24.36
Musgrave	4	119	HOL	5/26/99	2:24.37
Out of the Realm	6	113	HIA	3/26/95	2:24.43
Pleasant Variety	7	126	SA	3/24/91	2:24.50
Sky Classic	5	126	BEL	10/3/92	2:24.50
Shanawi (IRE)	5	111	SA	2/17/97	2:24.51
Fraise	6	124	GP	3/13/94	2:24.65
Down the Aisle	4	115	SAR	8/8/97	2:24.67
Daylami (IRE)	5	126	GP	11/6/99	2:24.73
Colonial Play	4	113	GP	3/8/98	2:24.75
Buck's Boy	7	120	GP	3/4/00	2:24.80
Balto Star	5	121	CRC	12/27/03	2:24.87
Bon Point (GB)	6	117	HOL	5/22/96	2:24.93
Mr. Lucky Junction	7	114	SA	2/9/97	2:25.00
Star Standing	4	114	GP	3/24/91	2:25.02
Kotashaan (FR)	5	124	SA	10/10/93	2:25.06
Bienamado	4	122	HOL	7/23/00	2:25.06
Sandpit (BRZ)	5	124	SA	10/9/94	2:25.12
Best of Music	5	115	SAR	8/26/96	2:25.13
Bombard	4	120	HOL	6/15/00	2:25.14
Kotashaan (FR)	5	126	SA	11/6/93	2:25.16
Royal Chariot	5	126	HOL	12/10/95	2:25.18
Innuendo (IRE)	6	116	GP	3/10/01	2:25.24
Bon Point (GB)	6	121	HOL	7/20/96	2:25.28
Persianlux (GB)	4	120	SA	11/3/00	2:25.28
Dr. Kiernan	4	114	BEL	6/13/93	2:25.30
Storming Home (GB)	5	122	HOL	5/10/03	2:25.31
Heavy Rain	6	116	GP	3/12/94	2:25.33
Mashaallah	6	119	HOL	6/25/94	2:25.37
Marlin	4	120	HOL	7/20/97	2:25.39
Our Forbes	4	115	ELP	8/10/94	2:25.40
Trampoli	5	121	GP	3/16/94	2:25.42
Dr. Root	4	109	BEL	7/20/91	2:25.43
Jahafil (GB)	7	117	HOL	7/1/95	2:25.45
Kiri's Clown	6	114	SAR	7/29/95	2:25.45
Sandpit (BRZ)	6	124	HOL	7/22/95	2:25.50
Wall Street Dancer	4	114	GP	3/15/92	2:25.53
Raintrap (GB)	4	126	WO	10/16/94	2:25.60
Lisieux Rose (IRE)	5	114	GP	3/5/00	2:25.64
Exaltado	8	115	GP	3/5/00	2:25.64
Dexter Drive	5	117	HOL	4/30/00	2:25.65
Frenchpark (GB)	4	126	HOL	12/11/94	2:25.66
Spectacular Tide	4	113	HIA	5/1/93	2:25.67
Bien Bien	4	122	HOL	7/25/93	2:25.69
Marvelous Wonder	6	115	SA	4/13/91	2:25.70
Celtic Arms (FR)	5	115	GP	3/9/96	2:25.71
Fairy Garden	5	115	GP	3/31/93	2:25.79
Public Purse	5	119	SA	10/31/99	2:25.83
Lazy Lode (ARG)	5	126	HOL	12/4/99	2:25.85
Fraise	4	113	SAR	8/8/92	2:25.88
Tikkanen	3	121	BEL	10/8/94	2:25.88
Julie Jalouse	4	114	GP	3/24/02	2:25.89
Sahib's Light	5	116	HOL	6/29/91	2:25.90
Parade Ground	3	121	BEL	9/27/98	2:25.94
Tiger Trap	4	118	SA	4/4/02	2:25.96
Bienamado	4	126	HOL	12/2/00	2:25.98
Barow (FR)	8	113	ELP	8/18/96	2:26.00
Dark Moondancer (GB)	5	122	SA	3/18/00	2:26.00
Marco Aurelio	5	117	BEL	5/23/92	2:26.04
Square Cut	6	114	SA	2/20/95	2:26.04
Nazirali (IRE)	5	112	SA	2/16/02	2:26.09
Rigamajig	5	114	CRC	1/5/91	2:26.10
Black Monday (GB)	5	112	HOL	7/21/91	2:26.10
Percutant (GB)	6	120	HOL	6/28/97	2:26.10
Cagney (BRZ)	4	116	SA	10/28/01	2:26.10
Polish Admiral (GB)	5	117	HOL	6/22/96	2:26.13
Volga (IRE)	5	119	CRC	12/27/03	2:26.13
Blueprint (IRE)	6	116	HOL	7/15/01	2:26.16
Full of Wonder	4	115	WO	8/31/02	2:26.18
Charley Bates	4	122	HOL	4/23/03	2:26.19
Special Matter	4	118	SA	10/14/02	2:26.21
Skipping (GB)	5	116	HOL	5/19/02	2:26.23
Wicapi	7	114	CRC	12/18/99	2:26.28
Reduit (GB)	5	118	GP	3/1/03	2:26.29
Splendid Career	5	118	SA	4/14/91	2:26.30
Splendid Career	5	123	HOL	6/16/91	2:26.30
Ringaskiddy	5	115	HOL	4/28/01	2:26.32
Grand Flotilla	7	119	HOL	7/24/94	2:26.35
Listen to Ken	5	118	BEL	9/25/98	2:26.35
Single Dawn	6	115	SA	3/12/93	2:26.38
Interim (GB)	4	116	CRC	12/23/95	2:26.38
Auvergne	6	116	HOL	12/8/96	2:26.38
Viernes (BRZ)	5	114	HOL	11/28/02	2:26.38
Charlie's Dewan	3	126	WO	8/20/95	2:26.40
With Anticipation	6	114	SAR	8/11/01	2:26.41
Shanawi (IRE)	7	122	HOL	7/14/99	2:26.46
Revved Up	5	116	DEL	7/20/03	2:26.46
Fade to Blue	7	116	SA	11/8/03	2:26.46
Glenbarra	6	119	LRL	6/16/96	2:26.47
River Bay	4	126	HOL	12/14/97	2:26.47
Dourbadakan	6	119	HOL	7/10/96	2:26.48
Miss High Blade	6	119	HOL	7/2/94	2:26.49
Tikkanen	3	122	CD	11/5/94	2:26.50
Rougeur	3	112	GP	11/1/92	2:26.51
Musgrave	4	120	HOL	4/24/99	2:26.52
Honor Glide	7	117	WO	9/1/01	2:26.52
Irish Silence	3	110	SAR	7/25/97	2:26.54
Shebane	4	123	HOL	6/22/00	2:26.54
Misty Valley	7	116	HOL	6/25/95	2:26.57

Triple Crown Facts and Figures
TRAINERS WITH MORE THAN ONE WIN IN THE KENTUCKY DERBY

SIX WINNERS:
  Ben A. Jones – Lawrin (1938), Whirlaway (1941), Pensive (1944), Citation (1948),
        Ponder (1949), Hill Gail (1952)

FOUR WINNERS:
  H. J. Thompson – Behave Yourself (1921), Bubbling Over (1926), Burgoo King (1932),
        Brokers Tip (1933)
  D. Wayne Lukas – Winning Colors (1988), Thunder Gulch (1995), Grindstone (1996),
        Charismatic (1999)

THREE WINNERS:
  James Fitzsimmons – Gallant Fox (1930), Omaha (1935), Johnstown (1939)
  Max Hirsch – Bold Venture (1936), Assault (1946), Middleground (1950)
  Bob Baffert – Silver Charm (1997), Real Quiet (1998), War Emblem (2002)

TWO WINNERS:
  Lazaro Barrera – Bold Forbes (1976), Affirmed (1978)
  Henry Forrest – Kauai King (1966), Forward Pass (1968)
  LeRoy Jolley – Foolish Pleasure (1975), Genuine Risk (1980)
  H. A. "Jimmy" Jones – Iron Liege (1957), Tim Tam (1958)
  Lucien Laurin – Riva Ridge (1972), Secretariat (1973)
  Horatio Luro – Decidedly (1962), Northern Dancer (1964)
  Woodford C. "Woody" Stephens – Cannonade (1974), Swale (1984)
  Charles E. "Charlie" Whittingham – Ferdinand(1986), Sunday Silence (1989)
  Nicholas "Nick" Zito – Strike the Gold (1991), Go for Gin (1994)

CONSECUTIVE WINNERS:
  Bob Baffert – Silver Charm (1997), Real Quiet (1998)
  Ben A. Jones – Citation (1948), Ponder (1949)
  H.A. "Jimmy" Jones – Iron Liege (1957), Tim Tam (1958)
  Lucien Lauren – Riva Ridge (1972), Secretariat (1973)
  D. Wayne Lukas – Thunder Gulch (1995), Grindstone (1996)
  Herbert John Thompson – Burgoo King (1932), Brokers Tip (1933)

OLDEST TRAINER OF KENTUCKY DERBY WINNER:
  Charlie Whittingham, 76 – Sunday Silence (1989)

YOUNGEST TRAINER OF KENTUCKY DERBY WINNER:
  James Rowe Sr., 24 – Hindoo (1881)

FATHER-SON WINNING TRAINERS:
  James Rowe Sr. (1881/1915)
  and James Rowe Jr. (1931)

  Ben A. Jones (1938/1941/1944/1948/1949/1952)
  and H. A. "Jimmy" Jones (1957/1958)

WINNER AS JOCKEY AND TRAINER:
  John Longden – Count Fleet (1943); Majestic Prince (1969)

WOMEN TRAINERS:
Mary Hirsch – No Sir (1937, 13th)
Mrs. Albert Roth – Senecas Coin (1949, pulled up)
Mary Keim – Mr. Pak (1965, 6th)
Dianne Carpenter – Biloxi Indian (1984, 12th) and Kingpost (1988, 14th)
Patti Johnson – Fast Account (1985, 4th)
Shelley Riley – Casual Lies (1992, 2nd)
Kathy Walsh – Hanuman Highway (1998, 7th)
Akiko Gothard – K One King (1999, 8th)
Jenine Sahadi – The Deputy (2000, 14th)

JOCKEYS WITH MULTIPLE WINS IN THE KENTUCKY DERBY
FIVE WINNERS:
Eddie Arcaro – Lawrin (1938), Whirlaway (1941), Hoop Jr. (1945), Citation (1948),
          Hill Gail (1952)
Bill Hartack – Iron Liege (1957), Venetian Way (1960), Decidedly (1962),
          Northern Dancer (1964), Majestic Prince (1969)

FOUR WINNERS:
Bill Shoemaker – Swaps (1955), *Tomy Lee (1959), Lucky Debonair (1965),
          Ferdinand (1986)

THREE WINNERS:
Isaac Murphy – Buchanan (1884), Riley (1890), Kingman (1891)
Earl Sande – Zev (1923), Flying Ebony (1925), Gallant Fox (1930)
Angel Cordero, Jr. – Cannonade(1974), Bold Forbes(1976), Spend a Buck (1985)
Gary Stevens – Winning Colors(1988), Thunder Gulch(1995), Silver Charm(1997)

TWO WINNERS:
Willie Sims – Ben Brush (1896), Plaudit (1898)
Jimmy Winkfield – His Eminence (1901), Alan-a-Dale (1902)
Johnny Loftus – George Smith (1916), Sir Barton (1919)
Albert Johnson – Morvich (1922), Bubbling Over (1926)
Linus McAtee – Whiskery (1927), Clyde Van Dusen (1929)
Charles Kurtsinger – Twenty Grand(1931), War Admiral (1937)
Conn McCreary – Pensive (1944), Count Turf (1951)
Ismael Valenzuela – Tim Tam (1958), Forward Pass (1968)
Ron Turcotte – Riva Ridge (1972), Secretariat (1973)
Jacinto Vasquez – Foolish Pleasure(1975), Genuine Risk (1980)
Eddie Delahoussaye – Gato Del Sol(1982), Sunny's Halo (1983)
Chris McCarron – Alysheba (1987), Go for Gin (1994)
Jerry Bailey – Sea Hero (1993), Grindstone (1996)
Chris Antley – Strike the Gold (1991), Charismatic (1999)
Kent Desormeaux – Real Quiet (1998). Fusaichi Pegasus (2000)

TWO IN SUCCESSION:
Isaac Murphy (1890-91), Jimmy Winkfield (1901-02), Ron Turcotte (1972-73), and
Eddie Delahoussaye (1982-83)

MOST MOUNTS:
Bill Shoemaker rode in 26 Kentucky Derbies, his last in 1988
Eddie Arcaro in 21, his last in 1961

AFRICAN-AMERICAN JOCKEYS:
Isaac Murphy (Two wins, as above)
Willie Simms (Two wins, as above,)

Jimmy Winkfield. (Two wins, as above)
Oliver Lewis – Aristides (1875)
William Walker – Baden Baden (1877)
George Lewis – Fonso (1880)
Babe Hurd – Apollo (1882)
Erskine Henderson – Joe Cotton (1885)
Isaac Lewis – Montrose (1887)
Alonzo Clayton – Azra (1892)
James "Soup" Perkins – Halma (1895)

APPRENTICE JOCKEYS with victories in the Kentucky Derby:
Ira Hanford – Bold Venture (1936)
William Boland – Middleground (1950)

WOMEN JOCKEYS with mounts in the Derby:
Diane Crump – Fathom (1970), 15th
Patricia Cooksey – So Vague (1984), 11th
Andrea Seefeldt – Forty Something (1991), 16th
Julie Krone – Ecstatic Ride (1992), 14th; Suave Prospect (1995), 11th

OLDEST WINNING JOCKEY:
Bill Shoemaker, 54 – Ferdinand (1986)

YOUNGEST WINNING JOCKEYS:
Alonzo Clayton, 15 – Azra (1892)
James "Soup" Perkins, 15 – Halma (1895)

KENTUCKY/EPSOM DERBY DOUBLE:
Steve Cauthen is the youngest rider, 18, to complete a sweep of the American Triple Crown, the elusive three-race series that has only been completed by 10 other horses since Sir Barton accomplished the feat for the first time in 1919. Cauthen also is the only rider in history to win both the Kentucky Derby and the historic Epsom Derby, the premier classic race for 3-year-olds in Great Britain.
Cauthen won his Kentucky Derby aboard Affirmed in 1978 and won the Epsom Derby twice-in 1985 aboard Slip Anchor and 1987 aboard Reference Point.

FASTEST CLOCKING:
Secretariat – 1973, 1:59.40

TRIPLE CROWN WINNERS

Through 2003, only the 11 Thoroughbreds listed below had managed to win the Kentucky Derby, Preakness, and Belmont Stakes – the three races that comprise the American Triple Crown for 3-year-old Thoroughbreds.

Year	Horse	Jockey	Trainer
1919	Sir Barton	John Loftus	H.Guy Bedwell
1930	Gallant Fox	Earl Sande	James Fitzsimmons
1935	Omaha	William Saunders	James Fitzsimmons
1937	War Admiral	Charles Kurtsinger	George H. Conway
1941	Whirlaway	Eddie Arcaro	Ben A. Jones
1943	Count Fleet	John Longden	G.D. Cameron
1946	Assault	Warren Mehrtens	Max Hirsch
1948	Citation	Eddie Arcaro	Ben A. Jones
1973	Secretariat	Ron Turcotte	Lucien Laurin
1977	Seattle Slew	Jean Cruguet	William H. Turner Jr.
1978	Affirmed	Steve Cauthen	Lazaro S. Barrera

LEADING PREAKNESS-WINNING TRAINERS

SEVEN WINNERS:
> R.W. Walden – Tom Ochiltree (1875), Duke of Magenta (1878), Harold (1879),
>> Grenada (1880), Saunterer (1881), Vanguard (1882), Refund (1888)

FIVE WINNERS:
> Thomas J. Healey – The Parader (1901), Pillory (1922), Vigil (1923), Display (1926),
>> Dr. Freeland (1929),
> D. Wayne Lukas – Codex (1980), Tank's Prospect (1985), Tabasco Cat (1994),
>> Timber Country (1995), Charismatic (1999)

FOUR WINNERS:
> James Fitzsimmons – Gallant Fox (1930), Omaha (1935), Nashua (1955), Bold Ruler (1957)
> H.A. "Jimmy" Jones – Faultless (1947), Citation (1948), Fabius (1956), Tim Tam (1958)
> Bob Baffert – Silver Charm (1997), Real Quiet (1998), Point Given (2001), War Emblem (2002)

WOMEN TRAINERS:
> Judy Johnson – 1968, Sir Beau, 7th
> Judith Zouck – 1980, Samoyed, 6th
> Nancy Heil – 1990, Fighting Notion, 5th
> Shelley Riley – 1992, Casual Lies, 3rd
> Dean Gaudet – 1992, Speakerphone, 14th
> Penny Lewis – 1993, Hegar, 9th
> Cynthia Reese – 1996, In Contention, 6th
> Jean L. Rofe – 1998, Silver's Prospect, 10th
> Jennifer Pedersen – 2001, Griffinite, 5th
> Nancy Alberts – 2002, Magic Weisner, 2nd
> Jennifer Pedersen – 2003, New York Hero, 6th
> Lisa Lewis – 2003, Kissin Saint, 10th

LEADING PREAKNESS-WINNING JOCKEYS

SIX WINNERS:
> Eddie Arcaro – Whirlaway (1941), Citation (1948), Hill Prince (1950), Bold (1951),
>> Nashua (1955), Bold Ruler (1957)

FIVE WINNERS:
> Pat Day – Tank's Prospect (1985), Summer Squall (1990), Tabasco Cat (1994),
>> Timber Country (1995), Louis Quatorze (1996)

WOMEN RIDERS:
> Patricia Cooksey – 1985, 6th
> Andrea Seefeldt – 1994, 7th

FASTEST CLOCKING:
> Secretariat – 1973, 1:53.40 (DRF timed)
> Tank's Prospect – 1985, 1:53.40
> Louis Quatorze – 1996, 1:53.40

LEADING BELMONT-WINNING TRAINERS

EIGHT WINNERS:
James Rowe – George Kinney (1883), Panique (1884), Commando (1901), Delhi (1904),
        Peter Pan (1907), Colin (1908), Sweep (1910), Prince Eugene (1913)
SEVEN WINNERS:
Samuel Hildreth – Jean Bereaud (1899), Joe Madden (1909), Friar Rock (1916),
        Hourless (1917), Grey Lag (1921), Zev (1923), Mad Play (1924)
SIX WINNERS:
James Fitzsimmons – Gallant Fox (1930), Faireno (1932), Omaha (1935), Granville (1936),
        Johnstown (1939), Nashua (1955)
FIVE WINNERS:
Woody Stephens – Conquistador Cielo (1982), Caveat (1983), Swale (1984),
        Creme Fraiche (1985), Danzig Connection (1986)
FOUR WINNERS:
Max Hirsch – Vito (1928), Assault (1946), Middleground (1950), High Gun (1954)
D. Wayne Lukas – Tabasco Cat (1994), Thunder Gulch (1995), Editor's Note (1996)
        Commendable (2000)
R.W. Walden – Duke of Magenta (1878), Grenada (1880), Saunterer (1881),
        Bowling Brook (1898)

WOMEN TRAINERS:
Sarah Lundy – 1984, Minstrel Star, 11th
Patricia Johnson – 1985, Fast Account, 4th
Dianne Carpenter – 1988, Kingpost, 2nd
Shelley Riley – 1992, Casual Lies, 5th
Cynthia W. Reese – 1996, In Contention, 9th
Nancy Alberts – 2002, Magic Weisner, 4th
Jennifer Leigh-Pedersen – 2002, Artax Too, 11th
Linda Rice – 2003, Supervisor, 5th

LEADING BELMONT-WINNING JOCKEYS

SIX WINNERS:
James McLaughlin – Forester (1882), George Kinney (1883), Panique (1884),
        Inspector B. (1886), Hanover (1887), Sir Dixon (1888)
Eddie Arcaro – Whirlaway (1941), Shut Out (1942), Pavot (1945), Citation (1948)
        One Count (1952), Nashua (1955)

FIVE WINNERS:
Earl Sande – Grey Lag (1921), Zev (1923), Mad Play (1924), Chance Shot (1927)
        Gallant Fox (1930)
Bill Shoemaker – Gallant Man (1957), Sword Dancer (1959), Jaipur (1962), Damascus (1967),
        Avatar (1975)

FIRST WOMAN TO WIN THE BELMONT

In 1993, Julie Krone became the only woman to win a Triple Crown race when she guided Colonial Affair to a 2 1/4-length victory in the Belmont Stakes. Krone is the only woman to have ridden in the Belmont. Her other finishes were a ninth aboard Subordinated Debt in 1991, a sixth on Colony Light in 1992 and a second on Star Standard in 1995. In 1996 she rode South Salem, who was eased.

FASTEST CLOCKING:
Secretariat – 1973, 2:24.00

Breeders' Cup Winners

LEADING BREEDERS' CUP CHAMPIONSHIP OWNERS BY MONEY WON

Name	Starters	1st	2nd	3rd	4th	5th	6th	Earnings
Allen E. Paulson*	32	6	2	7	2	1	1	$7,570,000
Frank Stronach*	21	3	0	2	3	4	2	5,458,000
Godolphin Racing Inc.	31	3	2	3	2	5	2	5,004,200
Michael Tabor/Susan Magnier*	21	3	3	1	1	2	4	4,463,920
Overbrook Farm (W. T. Young)*	27	3	2	4	0	3	0	4,387,000
T'bred Corp./Universal Stb.*	25	3	5	0	2	3	1	4,234,200
D. Wildenstein/Ecurie Wildenstein	20	2	4	1	2	1	2	3,917,000
Ogden Phipps	19	3	5	1	1	0	3	3,611,000
Sheikh Mohammed/Darley Stud	24	2	1	5	4	1	1	3,606,800
Juddmonte Farms (K. Abdullah)	39	1	3	5	5	2	2	3,443,620
Sam-Son Farm	17	2	2	1	2	2	2	2,923,000
Flaxman Holdings Ltd./S. Niarchos	15	5	0	0	1	0	3	2,904,400
Frances A. Genter	8	2	3	1	0	0	0	2,835,000
Eugene V. Klein*	17	4	3	1	0	0	1	2,593,000
Robert B. & Beverly J. Lewis*	13	1	5	1	0	1	0	2,556,800
H.H. Aga Khan	7	2	0	0	2	0	1	2,489,600
M. Cooper & C. Straub-Rubens	1	1	0	0	0	0	0	2,480,400
Edmund A. Gann*	13	0	3	2	2	0	2	2,408,800
Diamond A Racing Corp.	2	1	1	0	0	0	0	2,380,000
Carolyn H. Hine	2	1	0	0	0	0	1	2,288,000
Dorothy & Pamela Scharbauer	3	1	1	1	0	0	0	2,133,000
Amherst Stable & Spruce Pond Stable	2	1	0	0	0	0	0	2,080,000
Cee's Stable	1	1	0	0	0	0	0	2,080,000
Ridder Thoroughbred Stable	1	1	0	0	0	0	0	2,080,000
Ogden Mills Phipps	13	3	1	0	3	0	0	1,858,000
Darby Dan Farm	3	1	1	0	0	0	0	1,800,000
Jeffrey S. Sullivan	3	1	0	1	0	0	0	1,668,000
Augustin Stables	6	1	1	0	0	2	0	1,564,000
La Presle Farm (Wertheimer Bros.)	7	2	0	0	0	0	0	1,560,000
Robert E. Meyerhoff	3	1	0	0	0	0	0	1,560,000
Tsurumaki, Farish, Kilroy, Goodman	1	1	0	0	0	0	0	1,560,000
Buckland Farm	9	1	2	0	0	3	1	1,490,000
Golden Eagle Farm	15	0	3	3	2	3	1	1,443,800
Quarter B Farm	3	1	0	1	1	0	0	1,392,000
Oak Cliff Stable	4	1	0	0	0	0	0	1,350,000
Hancock, Gaillard & Whittingham	1	1	0	0	0	0	0	1,350,000
Mrs. Elizabeth A. Keck	1	1	0	0	0	0	0	1,350,000
Black Chip Stable	1	1	0	0	0	0	0	1,350,000
Marjorie & Irving Cowan	7	2	1	0	0	0	1	1,328,400
Claiborne Farm	4	2	0	0	1	0	0	1,250,000
Roger J. Devenport	1	1	0	0	0	0	0	1,227,200
Peter M. Brant	14	1	0	1	3	2	2	1,198,000
Amerman Racing	2	1	0	1	0	0	0	1,160,000
Madeleine Paulson*	4	1	0	0	1	0	0	1,152,000
Paraneck Stable	2	2	0	0	0	0	0	1,144,000
Michael E. Pegram	6	1	0	1	0	1	1	1,112,400
John Franks	10	1	0	1	1	0	1	1,100,000
Padua Stables*	8	2	0	0	0	0	0	1,076,400

*Does not include earnings in other partnerships

LEADING BREEDERS' CUP CHAMPIONSHIP BREEDERS - MONEY WON

Name	Starters	1st	2nd	3rd	4th	5th	6th	Earnings
Allen E. Paulson	27	6	2	3	2	1	1	$7,734,800
Cecilia Straub-Rubens	3	2	1	0	0	0	0	5,360,400
Overbrook Farm	26	3	4	4	1	2	0	4,843,000
Frank Stronach/Adena Springs	9	3	0	0	1	1	1	4,152,000
Odgen Phipps	17	3	5	1	1	0	3	3,611,000
H. H. Aga Khan	10	3	0	0	2	0	1	3,529,600
Sheikh Mohammed/Darley Stud	20	2	1	4	2	1	0	3,223,600
Juddmonte Farms	39	1	3	5	4	2	1	3,161,320
Flaxman Holdings Ltd./S. Niarchos	22	4	2	1	2	3	3	2,797,200
The Thoroughbred Corp.	6	2	3	0	1	0	1	2,732,400
Oak Cliff Thoroughbreds, Ltd.	3	2	0	0	0	0	0	2,700,000
Sean Coughlan	3	3	0	0	0	0	0	2,541,600
Allez France Stables	10	2	1	0	1	1	0	2,332,800
Anna Marie Barnhart	2	1	0	0	0	0	1	2,288,000
Mr. & Mrs. Bertram Firestone	13	1	4	1	0	0	0	2,240,000
Gainsborough Farm/Stud Mgmt.	16	1	1	1	3	3	0	2,220,240
Preston Madden	3	1	1	1	0	0	0	2,133,000
W.S. Farish & W.S. Kilroy	8	1	1	0	0	2	2	2,085,400
Amherst Stable	2	1	0	0	0	0	0	2,080,000
Clovelly Farms	2	1	0	0	0	0	0	2,080,000
Southeast Associates	1	1	0	0	0	0	0	2,080,000
Sam-Son Farms	14	1	3	1	1	2	0	1,956,000
Ballymacoll Stud Farm Ltd.	6	2	1	1	0	0	1	1,944,800
Swettenham Stud/& Partners	9	1	0	2	0	0	1	1,930,000
Tartan Farms	5	1	0	1	0	0	0	1,710,000
Stephen Peskoff	3	1	0	1	0	0	0	1,668,000
Payson Stud (Virginia K. Payson)	6	1	2	0	0	1	0	1,656,400
George Strawbridge Jr.	8	1	2	0	1	2	1	1,634,000
Georgia E. Hofmann	5	0	2	2	1	0	0	1,608,120
Albert & Joyce Bell	3	0	2	0	0	0	0	1,600,000
Wertheimer et Frere	9	2	0	0	0	0	0	1,560,000
Farnsworth Farms	5	2	0	0	0	0	1	1,560,000
Robert Meyerhoff	3	1	0	0	0	0	0	1,560,000
Mr. & Mrs. John C. Mabee	20	0	3	2	3	3	2	1,555,800
John Franks	11	1	2	1	0	0	0	1,480,000
Mrs. John W. Galbreath	2	1	0	1	0	0	0	1,458,000
Meadowbrook Farms	3	2	0	0	0	0	0	1,420,000
Ogden Mills Phipps	13	2	1	0	3	0	0	1,408,000
Niarchos Family	3	2	0	0	0	1	0	1,400,000
Irish Acres Farm	3	1	0	1	1	0	0	1,392,000
W. Paul Little	2	1	0	0	0	0	0	1,350,000
Howard B. Keck	1	1	0	0	0	0	0	1,350,000
Marjorie & Irving Cowan	7	2	1	0	0	0	1	1,328,400
Kinghaven Farms	10	0	2	1	2	0	1	1,285,000
Jaime S. Carrion	5	2	0	0	0	0	0	1,230,000
Golden Orb Farm (K. D. Schwartz)	1	1	0	0	0	0	0	1,227,200
Thomas Mellon Evans	10	0	3	0	0	3	2	1,215,000
Richard Maynard	3	1	0	0	1	0	0	1,152,000
Claiborne Fm & The Gamely Corp.	7	2	0	1	0	0	0	1,148,000
North Ridge Farm	10	1	1	1	0	1	2	1,109,000

LEADING BREEDERS' CUP CHAMPIONSHIP TRAINERS BY MONEY WON

Name	Starts	1st	2nd	3rd	4th	5th	6th	Purses
D. Wayne Lukas	140	17	20	14	7	11	12	$18,608,400
William I. Mott	40	5	6	4	3	2	2	8,492,560
Robert Frankel	57	2	8	7	9	3	5	7,568,020
Claude R. (Shug) McGaughey III	46	8	8	1	6	3	3	7,253,560
Richard Mandella	26	6	1	0	4	2	1	6,676,960
Andre Fabre	34	3	4	7	1	2	1	6,435,400
Neil Drysdale	30	6	4	2	4	4	4	6,095,840
Bob Baffert	40	3	7	3	6	5	3	5,304,800
Aidan P. O'Brien	25	3	4	3	1	3	4	4,952,720
Jay M. Robbins	6	2	0	0	2	0	0	4,938,400
Charles Whittingham	24	2	2	3	2	2	2	4,298,000
Saeed Bin Suroor	22	2	1	2	1	5	2	4,099,800
David Hofmans	10	2	0	2	1	2	0	3,731,040
Sir Michael Stoute	24	3	1	3	0	1	6	3,724,600
Patrick Byrne	7	3	0	0	0	0	0	3,718,000
Jack Van Berg	14	1	3	3	1	0	2	3,600,000
Ron McAnally	27	4	3	2	2	1	4	3,518,000
Nick Zito	21	1	4	2	1	5	1	3,171,120
Flint Schulhofer	26	2	2	4	1	6	1	2,841,400
Carl Nafzger	15	1	3	1	1	0	1	2,812,840
Wallace Dollase	15	1	4	1	1	1	2	2,484,900
Pascal Bary	7	3	0	0	0	1	1	2,416,400
Hubert (Sonny) Hine	5	1	0	0	0	0	1	2,288,000
Philip (P. G.) Johnson	4	1	0	0	1	0	1	2,170,000
LeRoy Jolley	16	2	1	0	3	2	2	2,145,000
Joseph Orseno	10	2	0	1	1	3	1	2,049,600
John Veitch	5	1	1	1	1	0	0	1,978,000
Jonathan Pease	5	2	1	0	0	0	0	1,812,000
Francois Boutin	19	3	0	2	1	1	2	1,712,000
Mark Frostad	7	1	1	0	1	1	0	1,693,000
Ernie Poulos	3	1	0	1	0	0	0	1,668,000
Richard Small	2	1	0	0	0	0	0	1,560,000
Bruce Headley	11	1	2	3	1	2	0	1,526,640
Jenine Sahadi	7	2	1	1	1	0	1	1,509,600
Jim Day	14	1	2	1	1	1	3	1,455,000
Gary Jones	12	0	2	2	1	1	1	1,439,000
P. Noel Hickey	4	1	0	1	1	0	0	1,392,000
Christopher Speckert	5	1	2	0	0	1	1	1,390,000
Vincent Timphony	1	1	0	0	0	0	0	1,350,000
Michael Whittingham	4	1	0	0	0	0	0	1,350,000
Dallas Stewart	4	1	0	0	0	0	1	1,227,200
Christophe Clement	12	0	2	2	1	1	1	1,209,720
Alex Hassinger Jr.	4	2	0	1	0	0	0	1,196,400
Alain de Royer-Dupre	4	1	0	0	2	0	0	1,180,000
Julio Canani	9	2	0	0	1	0	0	1,172,720
Clive E. Brittain	8	1	0	1	1	0	0	1,152,160
Roger Attfield	11	0	2	1	1	1	1	1,095,000
Craig Dollase	5	1	1	0	2	0	0	1,084,000
Michael Dickinson	6	2	0	0	0	0	1	1,040,000
Laura de Seroux	3	1	0	0	0	0	1	1,040,000
John H. M. Gosden	14	1	0	1	3	1	0	1,036,000
Mel Stute	6	2	0	0	1	1	0	1,020,000

LEADING BREEDERS' CUP CHAMPIONSHIP JOCKEYS – MONEY WON

Name	Starts	1st	2nd	3rd	4th	5th	6th	Purses
Pat Day	112	12	17	11	9	10	9	$22,913,360
Chris McCarron	101	9	12	7	7	7	13	17,669,600
Jerry Bailey	89	14	8	10	6	8	6	17,632,540
Gary Stevens	93	8	15	10	7	8	9	13,441,160
Mike Smith	52	10	6	3	4	6	2	10,505,760
Jose Santos	57	7	2	4	6	8	4	7,948,800
Eddie Delahoussaye	68	7	3	6	9	8	6	7,775,000
Corey Nakatani	48	5	7	7	6	3	3	7,340,280
Alex Solis	47	3	7	4	7	6	5	6,827,660
Laffit Pincay Jr.	61	7	4	9	5	3	6	6,811,000
Patrick Valenzuela	46	7	0	3	7	9	3	6,274,280
Angel Cordero Jr.	48	4	7	7	1	6	8	6,020,000
Lanfranco Dettori	30	3	2	4	5	5	1	5,379,160
Michael Kinane	25	3	3	3	1	1	4	4,590,920
Kent Desormeaux	47	2	3	6	8	1	5	4,545,200
Shane Sellers	29	2	3	4	3	1	0	3,960,600
Pat Eddery	30	2	3	3	1	2	1	3,570,000
Jorge Chavez	40	2	2	1	4	1	6	3,438,640
Jorge Velasquez	18	2	5	1	1	0	1	3,353,000
John Velazquez	39	4	1	4	0	6	2	3,231,600
Craig Perret	31	4	2	1	2	1	4	3,205,000
Bill Shoemaker	14	1	2	2	1	1	2	2,226,000
Edgar Prado	33	0	4	2	2	6	4	2,129,560
Victor Espinoza	17	1	2	0	0	1	1	1,933,200
John Murtagh	5	2	0	0	0	2	0	1,873,800
David Flores	18	2	2	1	0	2	1	1,871,200
Walter Swinburn	19	1	1	1	1	2	4	1,714,000
Randy Romero	17	3	0	1	0	3	2	1,648,000
Yves Saint-Martin	4	2	0	0	1	0	0	1,490,000
Olivier Peslier	13	1	1	1	0	0	0	1,362,800
Julie Krone	17	1	2	1	1	0	2	1,285,000
Kieren Fallon	9	1	1	2	0	1	1	1,254,600
Cash Asmussen	25	1	1	2	1	2	3	1,242,000
Fernando Toro	12	1	0	2	2	0	0	1,162,000
Jacinto Vasquez	12	1	1	1	2	0	1	1,149,000
Walter Guerra	7	2	0	1	1	0	0	1,078,000
Garrett Gomez	8	0	1	1	0	0	0	1,040,000
Eric Legrix	2	1	0	0	0	0	0	1,040,000
Freddie Head	10	2	0	1	0	1	1	1,028,000
Jose Valdivia Jr.	5	1	0	2	0	0	1	902,200
Ray Sibille	1	1	0	0	0	0	0	900,000
Don MacBeth	5	1	0	0	1	1	0	760,000
Richard Quinn	3	0	1	0	0	0	0	675,000
Cornelio Velasquez	4	1	0	0	0	0	0	613,600
Thierry Jarnet	6	0	1	1	1	1	0	592,000
Eddie Maple	14	0	0	0	4	1	2	480,000

LEADING BREEDERS' CUP CHAMPIONSHIP SIRES - MONEY WON

Name	Starters	1st	2nd	3rd	4th	5th	6th	Money Won
Sadler's Wells	36	6	2	4	2	3	3	$6,720,600
Storm Cat	31	3	5	4	2	6	1	6,130,800
Deputy Minister	25	3	1	3	3	2	4	5,370,560
Cee's Tizzy	3	2	1	0	0	0	0	5,360,400
Seattle Slew	26	3	4	3	0	3	2	4,655,400
Alydar	19	1	5	3	0	3	0	4,495,000
Danzig	41	5	4	3	5	0	3	4,321,320
Pleasant Colony	19	2	4	0	1	3	2	4,101,320
Kris S.	13	5	0	1	1	0	1	3,721,900
Cozzene	8	2	1	1	0	0	1	3,468,000
Mr. Prospector	42	3	3	2	5	3	6	3,421,680
Nureyev	22	4	2	2	1	0	3	3,408,400
Fappiano	15	2	2	2	3	3	2	3,386,000
Nijinsky II	12	3	2	2	2	0	1	3,283,000
Sovereign Dancer	11	0	5	3	1	1	0	3,053,000
Relaunch	15	2	1	2	2	2	1	3,004,000
Strawberry Road (Aus)	8	3	0	1	1	0	0	2,832,000
Cox's Ridge	16	3	2	4	0	3	1	2,529,000
Unbridled	9	3	2	1	0	0	0	2,516,400
Cryptoclearance	3	1	0	0	1	0	0	2,366,720
Doyoun (Ire)	3	2	0	0	0	0	0	2,329,600
Gone West	15	3	2	0	1	1	3	2,304,800
Skip Trial	3	1	0	0	0	0	1	2,288,000
Mill Reef	6	1	1	1	2	0	0	2,071,000
Palace Music	2	1	0	1	0	0	0	2,040,000
Thunder Gulch	5	1	2	0	1	0	0	1,969,200
Broad Brush	5	1	1	0	0	0	0	1,960,000
Halo	8	1	0	1	2	0	2	1,888,000
Rahy	15	1	3	0	1	3	0	1,868,480
Miswaki	9	1	0	1	1	1	0	1,758,000
Lyphard	10	1	1	1	1	1	1	1,720,000
Irish River (Fr)	15	0	2	3	2	2	0	1,700,140
El Prado (Ire)	2	0	2	0	0	0	0	1,600,000
Private Account	10	2	0	2	1	1	2	1,600,000
Sagace (Fr)	2	1	0	0	0	0	0	1,560,000
Seeking the Gold	7	2	2	1	0	0	1	1,560,000
Jade Hunter	5	1	1	0	1	0	1	1,552,000
Graustark	2	1	0	1	0	0	0	1,458,000
Bucksplasher	3	1	0	1	1	0	0	1,392,000
Icecapade	4	1	0	0	0	0	1	1,380,000
Sharpen Up (GB)	5	1	1	0	0	1	0	1,370,000
Wild Again	11	1	0	1	1	1	0	1,360,000
Caro (Ire)	6	1	2	2	0	0	0	1,341,000
Mt. Livermore	6	2	0	0	1	0	1	1,336,800
Danehill	7	1	2	1	0	0	0	1,333,200
Phone Trick	11	2	0	1	2	1	0	1,295,600
Alleged	10	1	0	0	1	1	0	1,252,000
Unbridled's Song	2	1	0	0	0	0	0	1,227,200
A.P. Indy	13	1	0	1	1	3	0	1,201,200
Darshaan	5	1	0	0	1	1	0	1,198,800
Chief's Crown	6	1	0	0	1	0	0	1,152,000
Marquetry	2	2	0	0	0	0	0	1,144,000
Exclusive Native	8	1	2	2	0	0	0	1,116,000

STATUS OF PAST BREEEDERS' CUP WINNERS AS OF FEBRUARY, 2004
BREEDERS' CUP CLASSIC

YEAR	WINNER	STATUS
2003	Pleasantly Perfect	Still in Training
2002	Volponi	Stud, Hopewell Farm, Ky.
2001	Tiznow	Stud, WinStar Farm, Ky.
2000	Tiznow	Stud, WinStar Farm, Ky.
1999	Cat Thief	Stud, Overbrook Farm, Ky.
1998	Awesome Again	Stud, Adena Springs Farm, Ky.
1997	Skip Away	Stud, Hopewell Farm, Ky.
1996	Alphabet Soup	Stud, Adena Springs Farm, Ky.
1995	Cigar	Retired, Kentucky Horse Park, Ky.
1994	Concern	Stud, Oklahoma Equine Lameness Ctr., Ok.
1993	Arcangues	Stud, Nakamura Stud, Japan
1992	A.P. Indy	Stud, Lane's End Farm, Ky.
1991	Black Tie Affair (Ire)	Stud, Blue Ridge Farm, Va.
1990	Unbridled	Deceased
1989	Sunday Silence	Deceased
1988	Alysheba	Stud, Janadriya, Saudi Arabia
1987	Ferdinand	Deceased
1986	Skywalker	Deceased
1985	Proud Truth	Stud, Haras Cerro Punta, Panama
1984	Wild Again	Stud, Three Chimneys Farm, Ky.

Breeders' Cup Turf

YEAR	WINNER	STATUS
2003	High Chaparral (Ire)	Stud, Coolmore, Ireland
2003	Johar	Still in Training
2002	High Chaparral (Ire)	Stud, Coolmore, Ireland
2001	Fantastic Light	Stud, Dalham Hall Stud, England
2000	Kalanisi (Ire)	Stud, Gilltown Stud, Ireland
1999	Daylami (Ire)	Stud, Gilltown Stud, Ireland
1998	Buck's Boy	Retired, Quarter B Farm, Il.
1997	Chief Bearhart	Stud, Ibari Stallion Station, Japan
1996	Pilsudski (Ire)	Stud, Shizunai Stallion Station, Japan
1995	Northern Spur (Ire)	Stud, Longfield Farm, Ky.
1994	Tikkanen	Stud, Arrow Stud, Japan
1993	Kotashaan (Fr)	Stud, Ballycurragh Stud, Ireland
1992	Fraise	Retired, Olympic Club Riding School, Japan
1991	Miss Alleged	Broodmare, Haras de Manneville, France
1990	In the Wings (GB)	Stud, Kildangan Stud, Ireland
1989	Prized	Stud, Spendthrift Farm, Ky.
1988	Great Communicator	Deceased
1987	Theatrical (Ire)	Stud, Hill 'N' Dale, Ky.
1986	Manila	Stud, Turkish Jockey Club, Turkey
1985	Pebbles (GB)	Retired, Fukumitsu Farm, Japan
1984	Lashkari (GB)	Deceased

Breeders' Cup Distaff

YEAR	WINNER	STATUS
2003	Adoration	Still in Training
2002	Azeri	Still in Training
2001	Unbridled Elaine	Broodmare, Six-D Farm, Ky.
2000	Spain	Broodmare, Three Chimneys Farm, Ky.
1999	Beautiful Pleasure	Broodmare, John Ward Stables, Ky.
1998	Escena	Broodmare, Diamond A Farm, Ky.
1997	Ajina	Broodmare, Stonerside Farm, Ky.

1996	Jewel Princess	Broodmare, Ashford Stud, Ky.
1995	Inside Information	Broodmare, Claiborne Farm, Ky.
1994	One Dreamer	Broodmare, Glen Hill Farm, Fla.
1993	Hollywood Wildcat	Broodmare, Coolmore, Ireland
1992	Paseana (Arg)	Broodmare, San Ignacio de Loyola, Argentina
1991	Dance Smartly	Broodmare, Sam-Son Farm, Ontario, Canada
1990	Bayakoa (Arg)	Deceased
1989	Bayakoa (Arg)	Deceased
1988	Personal Ensign	Broodmare, Claiborne Farm, Ky.
1987	Sacahuista	Broodmare, Creekview Farm (Ashford), Ky.
1986	Lady's Secret	Deceased
1985	Life's Magic	Broodmare, Trackside Farm, Ky.
1984	Princess Rooney	Broodmare, Gentry Bros. Farm, Ky.

Breeders' Cup Filly & Mare Turf

YEAR	WINNER	STATUS
2003	Islington (Ire)	Broodmare, Ballymacoll Stud, Ireland
2002	Starine (Fr)	Broodmare, Newsells Park Stud, England
2001	Banks Hill (GB)	Broodmare, Juddmonte Farms, Ky.
2000	Perfect Sting	Broodmare, Adena Springs Farm, Ky.
1999	Soaring Softly	Broodmare, Darby Dan Farm, Ky.

Breeders' Cup Juvenile

YEAR	WINNER	STATUS
2003	Action This Day	Still in Training
2002	Vindication	Stud, Hill 'N' Dale, Ky.
2001	Johannesburg	Stud, Ashford Stud, Ky.
2000	Macho Uno	Stud, Adena Springs South, Fla.
1999	Anees	Deceased
1998	Answer Lively	Deceased
1997	Favorite Trick	Stud, Walmac International, Ky.
1996	Boston Harbor	Stud, Shizunai Stallion Station, Japan
1995	Unbridled's Song	Stud, Taylor Made, Ky.
1994	Timber Country	Stud, Lex Stud, Japan
1993	Brocco	Stud, Lex Stud, Japan
1992	Gilded Time	Stud, Vinery, Ky.
1991	Arazi	Stud, Gestut Sohrenhof, Switzerland
1990	Fly So Free	Deceased
1989	Rhythm	Stud, Diamond F Ranch, Ca.
1988	Is It True	Stud, Walmac South, Fla.
1987	Success Express	Stud, Chatswood Stud, Victoria, Australia
1986	Capote	Pensioned, Three Chimneys Farm, Ky.
1985	Tasso	Stud, Janadriya, Saudi Arabia
1984	Chief's Crown	Deceased

Breeders' Cup Juvenile Fillies

YEAR	WINNER	STATUS
2003	Halfbridled	Still in Training
2002	Storm Flag Flying	Still in Training
2001	Tempera	Deceased
2000	Caressing	Broodmare, Hermitage Farm, Ky.
1999	Cash Run	Broodmare, Ashford Stud, Ky.
1998	Silverbulletday	Broodmare, Hill 'N' Dale, Ky.
1997	Countess Diana	Broodmare, WinStar Farm, Ky.
1996	Storm Song	Broodmare, Dalham Hall Stud, England
1995	My Flag	Broodmare, Claiborne Farm, Ky.
1994	Flanders	Broodmare, Overbrook Farm, Ky.

1993	Phone Chatter	Broodmare, Ashford Stud, Ky.
1992	Eliza	Broodmare, Creekview Farm (Ashford), Ky.
1991	Pleasant Stage	Deceased
1990	Meadow Star	Deceased
1989	Go for Wand	Deceased
1988	Open Mind	Deceased
1987	Epitome	Broodmare, Elmwood Farm, Ky.
1986	Brave Raj	Broodmare, Patchen Wilkes Farm, Ky.
1985	Twilight Ridge	Broodmare, Manchester Farm, Ky.
1984	Outstandingly	Deceased

Breeders' Cup Mile

YEAR	WINNER	STATUS
2003	Six Perfections (Fr)	Still in Training
2002	Domedriver (Ire)	Stud, Lanwades Stud, Newmarket, England
2001	Val Royal (Fr)	Stud, Eliza Park Stud, Victoria, Australia
2000	War Chant	Stud, Three Chimneys Farm, Ky.
1999	Silic (Fr)	Stud, Crestwood Farm, Ky.
1998	Da Hoss	Retired, Kentucky Horse Park, Ky.
1997	Spinning World	Stud, Coolmore, Ireland
1996	Da Hoss	Retired, Kentucky Horse Park, Ky.
1995	Ridgewood Pearl (GB)	Broodmare, Mountain View Stud, Ireland
1994	Barathea (Ire)	Stud, Rathbarry Stud, Ireland
1993	Lure	Pensioned, Claiborne Farm, Ky.
1992	Lure	Pensioned, Claiborne Farm, Ky.
1991	Opening Verse	Stud, Egerton Stud, England
1990	Royal Academy	Stud, Ashford Stud, Ky.
1989	Steinlen (GB)	Deceased
1988	Miesque	Broodmare, Oak Tree (Lane's End), Ky.
1987	Miesque	Broodmare, Oak Tree (Lane's End), Ky.
1986	Last Tycoon (Ire)	Stud, Blue Gum Farm, Victoria, Australia
1985	Cozzene	Stud, Gainesway Farm, Ky.
1984	Royal Heroine (Ire)	Broodmare, Longfield Stud, Ireland

Breeders' Cup Sprint

YEAR	WINNER	STATUS
2003	Cajun Beat	Still in Training
2002	Orientate	Stud, Gainesway Farm, Ky.
2001	Squirtle Squirt	Stud, Shizunai Stallion Station, Japan
2000	Kona Gold	Retired, Arcadia, Ca.
1999	Artax	Stud, Taylor Made, Ky.
1998	Reraise	Retired, Virginia
1997	Elmhurst	Retired, Evergreen Farm, Ky.
1996	Lit de Justice	Stud, Magali Farm, Ca.
1995	Desert Stormer	Broodmare, Claiborne Farm, Ky.
1994	Cherokee Run	Stud, Jonabell Farm, Ky.
1993	Cardmania	Retired, Frosty Acres Ranch, Ca.
1992	Thirty Slews	Retired, Privately Owned, Ca.
1991	Sheikh Albadou (GB)	Deceased
1990	Safely Kept	Broodmare, Lakland Farm, Ky.
1989	Dancing Spree	Broodmare, Chisbury Manor Stud, England
1988	Gulch	Stud, Lane's End Farm, Ky.
1987	Very Subtle	Deceased
1986	Smile	Deceased
1985	Precisionist	Privately Owned, Fairfield, Fla.
1984	Eillo	Deceased

TOTAL SIMULCAST WAGERING
North American simulcast outlets

Year	Outlets	Simulcast Total	Year	Outlets	Simulcast Total
1984	19	$8,009,109	1994	748	68,078,006
1985	37	19,741,113	1995	781	56,484,875
1986	53	19,474,381	1996	875	61,813,421
1987	57	21,662,205	1997	921	72,659,391
1988	92	33,713,296	1998	909	77,793,618
1989	149	45,129,419	1999	917	85,419,282
1990	256	46,220,925	2000	1,071	95,018,338
1991	603	55,642,551	2001	1,070	91,057,372
1992	625	66,961,184	2002	1,110	96,173,455
1993	644	67,601,992	2003	n/a	101,780,683

BREEDERS' CUP PICK 7 WAGERING		BREEDERS' CUP PICK 6 WAGERING	
Year	Total	Year	Total
1991	$8,526,985	1997	$3,379,014
1992	5,104,480	1998	6,494,193
1993	5,307,815	1999	5,436,691
1994	4,599,918	2000	5,123,453
1995	3,169,018	2001	4,811,450
1996	3,340,945	2002	4,569,515
		2003	4,489,454

BREEDERS CUP DAY STATISTICS

Race Day	Race Track	Attendance	Wagering*	Weather	Temp
October 25, 2003	Santa Anita, CA	51,648	$107,535,731	Sunny	99
October 26, 2002	Arlington Park, IL	46,118	102,798,989	Cloudy	43
October 27, 2001	Belmont Park, NY.	52,987	98,711,413	Cloudy, windy	50
November 4, 2000	Churchill Downs, KY	76,043	101,283,427	Cloudy	55
November 6, 1999	Gulfstream Park, FL	45,124	96,485,255	Clear	77
November 7, 1998	Churchill Downs, KY	80,452	91,338,477	Clear	54
November 8, 1997	Hollywood Park, CA	51,161	71,639.333	Sunny	74
October 26, 1996	Woodbine, Ontario, Canada	42,243	67,738,890	Sunny	60
October 28, 1995	Belmont Park, NY	37,246	64,075,207	Cloudy	66
November 5, 1994	Churchill Downs, KY	71,671	78,224,530	Clear	75
November 6, 1993	Santa Anita Park, CA	55,130	79,744,742	Sunny	81
October 31, 1992	Gulfstream Park, FL	45,415	76,876,726	Sunny	87
November 2, 1991	Churchill Downs, KY	66,204	67,588,113	Partly Sunny	43
October 27, 1990	Belmont Park, NY	51,236	55,328,195	Sunny	43
November 4, 1989	Gulfstream Park, FL	51,342	55,345,677	Sunny	79
November 5, 1988	Churchill Downs, KY	71,237	42,932,379	Cloudy, Drizzle	50
November 21, 1987	Hollywood Park, CA	57,734	31,864,457	Sunny	73
November 1, 1986	Santa Anita Park, CA	69,155	31,984,490	Sunny	73
November 2, 1985	Aqueduct, NY	42,568	26,941,288	Cloudy	54
November 10, 1984	Hollywood Park, CA	64,254	16,452,179	Sunny	70

* Wagering on Breeders' Cup Championship Races only

HORSES WITH MULTIPLE BREEDERS' CUP CHAMPIONSHIP STARTS

ADJUDICATING
1989 Juvenile 11th
1990 Sprint 4th

AFFIRMED SUCCESS
1998 Sprint 6th
1999 Sprint 12th
2000 Mile, 4th
2001 Mile, 11th

AFLEET
1987 Classic 10th
1988 Sprint 3rd

AIR DISPLAY
1986 Mile 11th
1987 Mile 11th

AL MAMOON
1985 Mile 2nd
1986 Mile 6th

ALBERT THE GREAT
2000 Classic 4th
2001 Classic 3rd

ALDEBARAN
2002 Mile 11th
2003 Sprint 6th

ALICE SPRINGS
1994 Mile 5th
1995 Turf 7th

ALPHABATIM
1984 Turf 5th
1986 Classic 5th

ALY'S ALLEY
1998 Juvenile 2nd
2000 Turf 9th

ALYSHEBA
1986 Juvenile 3rd
1987 Classic 2nd
1988 Classic 1st

APPEALING SKIER
1995 Juvenile 12th
1996 Sprint 10th

ARAZI
1991 Juvenile 1st
1992 Mile 11th

AWAD
1995 Turf 6th
1996 Turf 9th
1997 Turf 9th

BALTO STAR
2001 Mile 4th
2003 Turf 9th

BANKS HILL
2001 F & M Turf 1st
2002 F & M Turf 2nd

BANSHEE BREEZE
1998 Distaff 2nd

1999 Distaff 2nd

BARATHEA
1993 Mile 5th
1994 Mile 1st

BAYAKOA (Arg)
1989 Distaff 1st
1990 Distaff 1st

BEAUTIFUL PLEASURE
1997 Juvenile Fillies 7th
1999 Distaff 1st
2000 Distaff 6th

BEHRENS
1997 Classic 7th
1999 Classic 7th

BERTRANDO
1991 Juvenile 2nd
1993 Classic 2nd
1994 Classic 6th

BEST PAL
1990 Juvenile 6th
1993 Classic 10th
1994 Classic 5th

BET ON SUNSHINE
1997 Sprint 3rd
2000 Sprint 3rd
2001 Sprint, 13th
2002 Classic 5th

BET TWICE
1986 Juvenile 4th
1988 Mile 8th

BIGSTONE
1993 Mile 6th
1994 Mile 8th

BIRDONTHEWIRE
1993 Sprint 11th
1994 Sprint 6th

BLACK TIE AFFAIR (Ire)
1989 Sprint 9th
1990 Sprint 3rd
1991 Classic 1st

BLUSHING JOHN
1988 Mile 10th
1989 Classic 3rd

BOLD ARRANGEMENT (GB)
1986 Classic 7th
1987 Classic 11th

BONAPARTISTE (FR)
1998 Turf 9th
1999 Turf 6th

BORGIA (Ger)
1997 Turf 2nd
1999 F & M Turf 5th

BRAHMS
1999 Juvenile 7th

2001 Mile 6th

BUCK'S BOY
1997 Turf 4th
1998 Turf 1st
1999 Turf 3rd

CAFE LATTE (Ire)
1999 F&M Turf 4th
2000 F&M Turf 9th

CAME HOME
2001 Juvenile 7th
2002 Classic 10th

CAPTAIN STEVE
1999 Juvenile 11th
2000 Classic: 3rd

CARDMANIA
1992 Sprint 12th
1993 Sprint 1st
1994 Sprint 3rd

CAT THIEF
1998 Juvenile 3rd
1999 Classic 1st
2000 Classic 7th

CELTIC ARMS
1994 Turf 10th
1995 Turf 10th

CHARGING FALLS
1984 Sprint 6th
1985 Sprint 9th

CHIEF BEARHART
1996 Turf 11th
1997 Turf 1st
1998 Turf 4th

CHIEF'S CROWN
1984 Juvenile 1st
1985 Classic 4th

CIGAR
1995 Classic 1st
1996 Classic 3rd

CITY ZIP
2000 Juvenile 7th
2001 Mile 9th

CLASSIC CROWN
1987 Juvenile Fillies 6th
1988 Distaff 5th

CLEAR MANDATE
1996 Distaff 6th
1997 Distaff 6th

COLONIAL WATERS
1989 Distaff 8th
1990 Distaff 2nd

CONCERN
1994 Classic 1st
1995 Classic 8th

COZZENE
1984 Mile 3rd
1985 Mile 1st

CRYPTOCLEARANCE
1987 Classic 5th
1988 Classic 5th
1989 Classic 5th

CULTURE VULTURE
1991 Juvenile Fillies 9th
1992 Distaff 10th

DA HOSS
1995 Sprint 13th
1996 Mile 1st
1998 Mile 1st

DANCE SMARTLY
1990 Juvenile Fillies 3rd
1991 Distaff 1st

DANCING SPREE
1989 Sprint 1st
1990 Sprint 6th

DELAWARE TOWNSHIP
2000 Sprint 10th
2001 Sprint 6th

DERNIER EMPEREUR
1993 Turf 12th
1994 Classic 14th

DEVIL HIS DUE
1993 Classic 8th
1994 Classic 11th

DISPERSAL
1989 Sprint 3rd
1990 Classic 12th

DOLLAR BILL
2000 Juvenile 10th
2002 Classic 6th

DOUBLE FEINT
1986 Mile 4th
1987 Mile 12th

DRAMATIC GOLD
1994 Classic 3rd
1996 Classic 9th

DUSHYANTOR
1996 Turf 7th
1998 Turf 3rd

EASY GOER
1988 Juvenile 2nd
1989 Classic 2nd

EDITOR'S NOTE
1995 Juvenile 3rd
1996 Classic 12th

EL SENOR
1988 Turf 6th
1989 Turf 7th
1990 Turf 3rd
1991 Turf 9th

EPITOME
1987 Juvenile Fillies 1st
1988 Distaff 7th

ESCENA
1997 Distaff 3rd
1998 Distaff 1st

EVENING ATTIRE
2002 Classic 4th
2003 Classic 7th

EXCHANGE
1992 Distaff 8th
1994 Distaff 7th

EZZOUD
1993 Classic 7th
1994 Classic 7th

FANTASTIC LIGHT
2000 Turf 5th
2001 Turf 1st

FAVORITE TRICK
1997 Juvenile 1st
1998 Mile 8th

FIGHTING FIT
1984 Sprint 3rd
1985 Sprint 4th

FIVE STAR DAY
2000 Sprint 14th
2001 Sprint 8th

FLAG DOWN
1994 Classic 12th
1997 Turf 3rd

FLAWLESSLY
1990 Juvenile Fillies 7th
1993 Mile 9th

FLY SO FREE
1990 Juvenile 1st
1991 Classic 4th
1993 Sprint 9th

FORBIDDEN APPLE
2000 Mile 7th
2001 Mile 2nd
2002 Mile 4th

FOURSTARS ALLSTAR
1992 Mile 9th
1993 Mile 3rd
1995 Mile 7th

FRAISE
1992 Turf 1st
1993 Turf 4th
1994 Turf 11th

FRAN'S VALENTINE
1984 Juvenile Fillies 10th
1985 Distaff 5th
1986 Distaff 2nd

FRIENDLY LOVER
1995 Sprint 5th

1996 Sprint 11th

FURLOUGH
1998 Sprint 10th
1999 Sprint 10th

GANDER
2000 Classic 9th
2001 Classic 9th

GATE DANCER
1984 Classic 3rd
1985 Classic 2nd

GILDED TIME
1992 Juvenile 1st
1993 Sprint 3rd

GO AND GO (Ire)
1989 Juvenile 8th
1990 Classic dnf

GO FOR WAND
1989 Juvenile Fillies 1st
1990 Distaff dnf

GOLDEN MISSLE
1999 Classic 3rd
2000 Classic 13th

GOODBYE HALO
1988 Distaff 3rd
1989 Distaff 6th

GRAND SLAM
1997 Juvenile dnf
1998 Sprint 2nd

GREAT COMMUNICATOR
1987 Turf 12th
1988 Turf 1st

GROOVY
1985 Juvenile 10th
1986 Sprint 4th
1987 Sprint 2nd

GUIDED TOUR
2000 Classic 12th
2001 Classic 5th

GULCH
1986 Juvenile 5th
1987 Classic 9th
1988 Sprint 1st

HAP
2000 Mile 9th
2001 Turf 5th

HATOOF
1993 Turf 5th
1994 Turf 2nd

HAWKSLEY HILL (Ire)
1998 Mile 2nd
1999 Mile 5th

HEAVENLY PRIZE
1993 Juvenile Fillies 3rd
1994 Distaff 2nd

1995 Distaff 2nd

HELMSMAN
1996 Mile 6th
1997 Mile 10th

HERITAGE OF GOLD
1999 Distaff 3rd
2000 Distaff 3rd

HERNANDO
1993 Turf 10th
1994 Turf 6th
1995 Turf 5th

HIGH BRITE
1987 Sprint 5th
1988 Sprint 12th

HIGH CHAPARRAL (IRE)
2002 Turf 1st
2003 Turf 1st-dh

HOLD THAT TIGER
2002 Juvenile 3rd
2003 Classic 5th

HOLLYWOOD WILDCAT
1993 Distaff 1st
1994 Distaff 6th

HONOR GLIDE
1997 Classic 8th
1999 Turf 8th

HONOUR AND GLORY
1995 Juvenile 4th
1996 Sprint 3rd

IMPERIAL GESTURE
2001 Juv. Fillies 2nd
2002 Distaff 3rd

INTREPIDITY
1993 Turf 13th
1994 Turf 4th

ISLINGTON (IRE)
2002 F & M Turf 3rd
2003 F & M Turf 1st

ITSALLGREEKTOME
1990 Mile 2nd
1991 Turf 2nd

JEWEL PRINCESS
1996 Distaff 1st
1997 Distaff dnf

JOHANN QUATZ
1993 Mile 7th
1994 Mile 2nd

JOLIE'S HALO
1991 Mile 6th
1992 Classic 10th

KEEPER HILL
1998 Distaff 3rd
1999 Distaff 4th

KIRBY'S SONG

1997 Juvenile Fillies 5th
1998 Distaff 8th

KONA GOLD
1998 Sprint 3rd
1999 Sprint 2nd
2000 Sprint 1st
2001 Sprint 7th
2002 Sprint 4th

LADY'S SECRET
1985 Distaff 2nd
1986 Distaff 1st

LASHKARI (GB)
1984 Turf 1st
1985 Turf 4th

LEMON DROP KID
1998 Juvenile 5th
1999 Classic 6th
2000 Classic 5th

LIFE'S MAGIC
1984 Distaff 2nd
1985 Distaff 1st

LIT DE JUSTICE
1995 Sprint 3rd
1996 Sprint 1st

LITE LIGHT
1990 Juvenile Fillies 12th
1992 Classic 6th

LIVELY ONE
1988 Classic 8th
1990 Classic 4th

LURE
1992 Mile 1st
1993 Mile 1st
1994 Mile 9th

MACHO UNO
2000 Juvenile 1st
2001 Classic 4th
2002 Classic 5th

MAGELLAN
1997 Mile 6th
1998 Mile 4th

MAGICAL MAIDEN
1992 Distaff 3rd
1993 Distaff 7th

MARQUETRY
1991 Classic 7th
1992 Classic 11th
1993 Classic 4th

MEADOW STAR
1990 Juvenile Fillies 1st
1992 Distaff 7th

MEAFARA
1992 Sprint 2nd
1993 Sprint 2nd

MEDAGLIA D'ORO
2002 Classic 2nd

2003 Classic 2nd

MI SELECTO
1989 Classic 8th
1990 Classic 9th

MIESQUE
1987 Mile 1st
1988 Mile 1st

MIGHTY FORUM
1995 Mile 9th
1996 Mile 13th

MILESIUS
1988 Turf 5th
1989 Turf 10th

MINISTER'S MELODY
1996 Juvenile Fillies 4th
1997 Distaff 5th

MOGAMBO
1985 Juvenile 6th
1986 Classic 9th

MR. NICKERSON
1989 Sprint 12th
1990 Sprint dnf

MUSIC MERCI
1988 Juvenile 4th
1993 Sprint 6th

MUTAMAM (GB)
2000 Turf 4th
2001 Turf 11th

MY FLAG
1995 Juvenile Fillies 1st
1996 Distaff 4th

NOSTALGIA'S STAR
1986 Classic 4th
1987 Classic 7th

NOVERRE
2000 Juvenile 11th
2001 Mile 7th

OLYMPIC PROSPECT
1988 Sprint 7th
1989 Sprint 4th

ON THE LINE
1987 Sprint 10th
1989 Sprint dnf

OPEN MIND
1988 Juvenile Fillies 1st
1989 Distaff 3rd

OPENING VERSE
1990 Classic 7th
1991 Mile 1st

ORIENTATE
2001 Classic 12th
2002 Sprint 1st

OUTSTANDINGLY

1984 Juvenile Fillies 1st
1986 Distaff 3rd

PALACE MUSIC
1985 Mile 9th
1986 Mile 2nd

PARADISE CREEK
1992 Mile 2nd
1993 Mile 8th
1994 Turf 3rd

PASEANA (Arg)
1992 Distaff 1st
1993 Distaff 2nd

PERFECT DRIFT
2002 Classic 12th
2003 Classic 6th

PERFECT STING
1999 F&M Turf 6th
2000 F&M Turf 1st

PERFECT SOUL (IRE)
2002 Turf 8th
2003 Mile 9th

PERSIAN TIARA (Ire)
1984 Turf 7th
1985 Turf 13th

PINE TREE LANE
1986 Sprint 2nd
1987 Sprint 11th

PLEASANT TAP
1989 Juvenile 6th
1990 Turf 8th
1991 Sprint 2nd
1992 Classic 2nd

PRECISIONIST
1984 Classic 7th
1985 Sprint 1st
1986 Classic 3rd
1988 Sprint 5th

PRIOLO
1990 Mile 3rd
1991 Mile 5th

PRIVATE TREASURE
1990 Juvenile Fillies 2nd
1991 Distaff 11th

QUEST FOR FAME
1991 Turf 3rd
1992 Turf 3rd

QUIET RESOLVE
1999 Mile 14th
2000 Turf 2nd
2001 Turf 10th

RHYTHM
1989 Juvenile 1st
1990 Classic 8th

RICHTER SCALE

1997 Sprint 13th
1998 Sprint 12th

RISKAVERSE
2002 F & M Turf 7th
2003 F & M Turf 6th

ROBYN DANCER
1989 Juvenile 9th
1991 Sprint 3rd

ROYAL ANTHEM
1998 Turf 7th
1999 Turf 2nd

SACAHUISTA
1986 Juvenile Fillies 4th
1987 Distaff 1st

SAFELY KEPT
1989 Sprint 2nd
1990 Sprint 1st

SAVINIO
1995 Mile 5th
1997 Classic 5th

SAYYEDATI (GB)
1993 Sprint 12th
1995 Mile 3rd

SENOR SPEEDY
1990 Sprint 9th
1991 Sprint 4th
1992 Sprint 8th

SERENA'S SONG
1994 Juvenile Fillies 2nd
1995 Distaff 5th
1996 Distaff 2nd

SHARP CAT
1996 Juvenile Fillies 9th
1997 Distaff 2nd

SHEIKH ALBADOU (GB)
1991 Sprint 1st
1992 Sprint 4th

SHOT GUN SCOTT
1989 Juvenile 4th
1990 Mile 11th
SILVERBULLETDAY
1998 Juvenile Fillies 1st
1999 Distaff 6th

SIMPLY MAJESTIC
1988 Mile 3rd
1989 Mile 5th

SKI PARADISE
1993 Mile 2nd
1994 Mile 10th

SKIP AWAY
1997 Classic 1st
1998 Classic 6th

SKY BEAUTY
1993 Distaff 5th

1994 Distaff 9th

SKY CLASSIC
1990 Turf 11th
1991 Turf 4th
1992 Turf 2nd

SKYWALKER
1986 Classic 1st
1987 Classic 12th

SLEW CITY SLEW
1988 Classic 9th
1989 Classic 6th

SMILE
1985 Sprint 2nd
1986 Sprint 1st

STARINE
2001 F & M Turf
2002 F & M Turf

STARRER
2001 Distaff 5th
2002 Distaff 4th

SOLAR SPLENDOR
1992 Turf dnf
1993 Turf 14th

SONIC LADY
1986 Mile 7th
1987 Mile 3rd

SOUL OF THE MATTER
1994 Classic 4th
1995 Classic 4th

SOVIET LINE (Ire)
1995 Mile 6th
1997 Mile 7th

SPAIN
1999 Juv. Fillies 4th
2000 Distaff 1st
2001 Distaff, 2nd

SPINNING WORLD
1996 Mile 2nd
1997 Mile 1st

STEINLEN (GB)
1988 Mile 2nd
1989 Mile 1st
1990 Mile 4th

STRAWBERRY ROAD (Aus)
1984 Turf 4th
1985 Turf 2nd

STRIKE THE GOLD
1991 Classic 5th
1992 Classic 8th

SUCCESSFUL APPEAL
1999 Sprint 5th
2000 Sprint 7th

SULTRY SONG
1991 Mile 14th

1992 Classic 5th

SUNSHINE FOREVER
1988 Turf 2nd
1989 Turf 14th

SUPAH GEM
1992 Juvenile Fillies 4th
1993 Distaff 6th

SURSIDE
1999 Juv. Fillies 3rd
2000 Distaff 2nd

SWAIN (Ire)
1996 Turf 3rd
1998 Classic 3rd

SWEPT OVERBOARD
2001 Sprint 4th
2002 Sprint 8th

SYLVAN EXPRESS (Ire)
1987 Sprint 8th
1988 Sprint 8th

TABASCO CAT
1993 Juvenile 3rd
1994 Classic 2nd

TAIKI BLIZZARD
1996 Classic 13th
1997 Classic 6th

TAKE CHARGE LADY
2001 Juv. Fillies 6th
2002 Distaff 6th
2003 Distaff 6th

TAKE ME OUT
1990 Juvenile 2nd
1991 Sprint 7th

TALLOIRES
1995 Turf 13th
1996 Turf 6th

TAP TO MUSIC
1998 Distaff 5th
1999 Distaff 5th

TAYLOR'S SPECIAL
1986 Sprint 5th
1987 Sprint 6th

THEATRICAL (Ire)
1985 Turf 11th
1986 Turf 2nd

1987 Turf 1st

THIRTY SLEWS
1992 Sprint 1st
1993 Sprint 4th

THE TIN MAN
2002 Turf 4th
2003 Turf 4th

TIZNOW
2000 Classic 1st
2001 Classic 1st

TOCCET
2002 Juvenile 9th
2003 Turf 8th

TOUCH GOLD
1997 Classic 9th
1998 Classic 8th

TOUCH OF THE BLUES (FR)
2002 Mile 10th
2003 Mile 2nd

TRACK BARRON
1984 Classic 4th
1985 Classic 5th

TRACK GAL
1995 Sprint 11th
1997 Sprint 10th

TRANQUILITY LAKE
2000 F&M T 8th
2001 Distaff 9th

TRIPTYCH
1986 Classic 6th
1988 Turf 4th

TSUNAMI SLEW
1984 Mile 5th
1985 Mile 5th

TURKOMAN
1985 Classic 3rd
1986 Classic 2nd

TWILIGHT AGENDA
1991 Classic 2nd
1992 Classic 9th

TWILIGHT RIDGE
1985 Juvenile Fillies 1st
1986 Distaff 6th

TWO ITEM LIMIT
2001 Distaff 3rd

2002 Distaff 7th

UNBRIDLED
1990 Classic 1st
1991 Classic 3rd

VAL DES BOIS
1991 Mile 2nd
1992 Mile 4th

VAL'S PRINCE
1997 Turf 8th
1999 Turf 11th

VERSAILLES TREATY
1991 Distaff 2nd
1992 Distaff 2nd

VERY SUBTLE
1987 Sprint 1st
1988 Sprint 4th

VOLOCHINE
1994 Turf 9th
1996 Mile 8th

VOLPONI
2002 Classic 1st
2003 Classic 10th

WHO'S FOR DINNER
1984 Turf 9th
1985 Turf 9th

WILDERNESS SONG
1990 Juvenile Fillies 8th
1991 Distaff 7th

WITH ANTICIPATION
2001 Turf 7th
2002 Turf 2nd

WINNING COLORS
1988 Distaff 2nd
1989 Distaff 9th

YAGLI
1998 Turf 3rd
1999 Turf 4th

XTRA HEAT
2000 Juvenile Fillies 10th
2001 Sprint 2nd
2002 Sprint 6th

ZAVATA
2002 Juvenile dnf
2003 Sprint 12th

Dams With Multiple Starters in the Breeders' Cup

Baby Grace (Arg)
  King Ruckus (1994 Sprint 12th)
  Repent (2001 Juvenile 2nd)
Barbs Compact
  Green Barb (1989 Turf 8th)
  Tsunami Slew (1984 Mile 5th)
  Tsunami Slew (1985 Mile 5th)
Beaming Bride
  Alwuhush (1990 Turf 4th)
  Simply Majestic (1988 Mile 3rd)
  Simply Majestic (1989 Mile 5th)
Beware of the Cat
  Editor's Note (1995 Juvenile 3rd)
  Editor's Note (1996 Classic 12th)
  Hold That Tiger (2002 Juvenile 3rd)
  Hold That Tiger (2003 Classic 5th)
Blitey
  Dancing Spree (1989 Sprint 1st)
  Dancing Spree (1990 Sprint 6th)
  Furlough (1998 Sprint 10th)
  Furlough (1999 Sprint 10th)
Bold Captive
  Pac Mania (1984 Sprint 9th)
  Skywalker (1986 Classic 1st)
  Skywalker (1987 Classic 12th)
Brocade
  Barathea (Ire) (1993 Mile 5th)
  Barathea (Ire) (1994 Mile 1st)
  Gossamer (GB) (2002 F&M T 5th)
Bunting
  Mot Juste (GB) (2001 F&M T 12th)
  Vision and Verse (1999 Classic 9th)
  Vision and Verse (2000 Classic 8th)
Cadeaux d'Amie
  Hatoof (1993 Turf 5th)
  Hatoof (1994 Turf 2nd)
  Irish Prize (2001 Mile 4th)
Cee's Song
  Budroyale (1999 Classic 2nd)
  Tiznow (2000 Classic 1st)
  Tiznow (2001 Classic 1st)
Cheyenne Birdsong
  Creston (1993 Juvenile 11th)
  Shywing (1986 Distaff 2nd)
Chimes of Freedom
  Aldebaran (2002 Mile 11th)
  Aldebaran (2003 Sprint 6th)
  Good Journey (2002 Mile 3rd)
Clever Miss
  Integra (1988 Distaff 9th)
  Secret Odds (1992 Juvenile 10th)
Coup de Folie
  Coup de Genie (1993 Juv. Fil. 4th)
  Exit to Nowhere (1992 Mile 8th)
Crimson Saint
  Pancho Villa (1985 Sprint 5th)
  Royal Academy (1990 Mile 1st)
Crystal Cup
  First Magnitude (Ire) (1999 Turf 14th)
  Iktamal (1996 Sprint 6th)

Dahlia
  Dahar (1986 Turf 5th)
  Dahlia's Dreamer (1994 Turf 12th)
  Rivlia (1987 Turf 9th)
Dance Number
  Offbeat (1991 Juvenile 4th)
  Rhythm (1989 Juvenile 1st)
  Rhythm (1990 Classic 8th)
Dancing Tribute
  Gold Tribute (1996 Juvenile 6th)
  Souvenir Copy (1997 Juvenile 4th)
Danseur Fabuleux
  Arazi (1991 Juvenile 1st)
  Arazi (1992 Mile 11th)
  Noverre (2000 Juvenile 11th)
  Noverre (2001 Mile 7th)
Desirable
  Dumaani (1996 Mile 12th)
  Shadayid (1991 Mile 7th)
Excellent Lady
  General Challenge (1999 Classic 10th)
  Notable Career (2000 Juv. Fil. 2nd)
Fineza
  Golden Gear (1995 Sprint 9th)
  Keeper Hill (1998 Distaff 3rd)
  Keeper Hill (1999 Distaff 4th)
Flama Ardiente
  Magical Wonder (1986 Mile 8th)
  Mt. Livermore (1985 Sprint 3rd)
Gentle Hands
  Bertrando (1991 Juvenile 2nd)
  Bertrando (1993 Classic 2nd)
  Bertrando (1994 Classic 6th)
  Jade Trade (1987 Juvenile 12th)
Gioconda
  Ciro (2000 Turf 6th)
  Good Command (1987 Classic 6th)
Graceful Gal
  Duluth (1987 Mile 14th)
  Real Courage (1985 Juvenile dnf)
Grecian Banner
  Personal Ensign (1988 Distaff 1st)
  Personal Flag (1988 Classic 6th)
Harbor Springs
  Bay Harbor (1997 Juv. Fil. 14th)
  Boston Harbor (1996 Juvenile 1st)
Hasili (IRE)
  Banks Hill (GB) (2001 F & M Turf 1st)
  Banks Hill (GB) (2002 F & M Turf 2nd)
  Dansili (GB) (2000 Mile 3rd)
  Heat Haze (GB) (2003 F & M Turf 4th)
Hattab Gal
  Exetera (1995 Juvenile 2nd)
  On Target (1994 Juvenile 4th)
Homewrecker
  Honor the Hero (1994 Sprint 7th)
  Prenup (1994 Sprint 13th)
Honor an Offer
  Sardula (1993 Juv. Fil. 2nd)
  Imperial Gesture (2001 Juv. Fil. 2nd)
  Imperial Gesture (2002 Distaff 3rd)

Hope (Ire)
Oasis Dream (GB) (2003 Mile 10th)
Zenda (GB) (2003 F & M Turf 8th)
Hunt's Lark
Dove Hunt (1995 Mile 4th)
Lieutenant's Lark (1986 Mile 9th)
In Neon
Royal Anthem (1998 Turf 7th)
Royal Anthem (1999 Turf 2nd)
Sharp Cat (1996 Juv. Fil. 9th)
Sharp Cat (1997 Distaff 2nd)
Star Recruit (1991 Juvenile 9th)
Island Kitty
Hennessy (1995 Juvenile 2nd)
Shy Tom 1990 Turf 10th)
Iza Valentine
Earl's Valentine (1985 Juv. Fil. 10th)
Fran's Valentine (1984 Juv. Fil. 10th)
Fran's Valentine (1985 Distaff 5th)
Fran's Valentine (1986 Distaff 2nd)
Jealous Appeal
Appealing Skier (1995 Juvenile 12th)
Appealing Skier (1996 Sprint 10th)
Jealous Forum (2001 Juv. Fil. 8th)
Trippi (2000 Sprint 9th)
Kamar
Gorgeous 1989 Distaff 2nd)
Key to the Moon (1985 Sprint 10th)
La Chaposa (Per)
Chaposa Springs (1996 Mile 14th)
You and I (1995 Sprint 10th)
Louisville
Le Belvedere (1987 Mile 9th)
Louis Le Grand (1987 Turf 5th)
Love From Mom
Fight for Love (1992 Juvenile 11th)
Love That Jazz (1996 Juv. Fil. 2nd)
Navajo Princess
Dancing Brave (1986 Turf 4th)
Jolypha (1992 Classic 3rd)
Never Knock
Go For Gin (1994 Classic 8th)
Pleasant Tap (1989 Juvenile 6th)
Pleasant Tap (1990 Turf 8th)
Pleasant Tap (1991 Sprint 2nd)
Pleasant Tap (1992 Classic 2nd)
Nice Assay
A. P. Assay (1998 Sprint 5th)
Came Home (2001 Juvenile 7th)
Came Home (2002 Classic 10th)
No Class
Regal Classic (1987 Juvenile 2nd)
Sky Classic (1990 Turf 11th)
Sky Classic (1991 Turf 4th)
Sky Classic (1992 Turf 2nd)
North of Eden
Forbidden Apple (2000 Mile 7th)
Forbidden Apple (2001 Mile 2nd)
Forbidden Apple (2002 Mile 4th)
Paradise Creek (1992 Mile 2nd)
Paradise Creek (1993 Mile 8th)
Paradise Creek (1994 Turf 3rd)
Wild Event (1997 Mile 9th)

Nuryette
Northern Afleet (1997 Sprint 2nd)
Tap to Music (1998 Distaff 5th)
Tap to Music (1999 Distaff 5th)
Passing Mood
Touch Gold (1997 Classic 9th)
Touch Gold (1998 Classic 8th)
With Approval (1990 Turf 2nd)
Personal Ensign
Miner's Mark (1993 Classic 12th)
My Flag (1995 Juv. Fil. 1st)
My Flag (1996 Distaff 4th)
Our Emblem (1995 Sprint 6th)
Primal Force
Awesome Again (1998 Classic 1st)
Macho Uno (2000 Juvenile 1st)
Macho Uno (2001 Classic 4th)
Macho Uno (2002 Classic 5th)
Primarily
Primaly (1997 Juv. Fil. 3rd)
Whiskey Wisdom (1997 Classic 4th)
Pure Profit
Educated Risk (1992 Juv. Fil. 2nd)
Hidden Reserve 1996 Juv. Fil. 2nd)
Inside Information (1995 Distaff 1st)
Purify
Radu Cool (1997 Distaff 4th)
Chaste (2001 F & M Turf 9th)
Raska
Green Fee (2002 Mile 5th)
Posse (2003 Sprint 4th)
Soul Dream
Dream Well (Fr) (1999 Turf 5th)
Sulamani (Ire) (2003 Turf 5th)
Remote Ruler
Close In (1987 Juv. Fil. 4th)
Mama Mucci (1994 Juv. Fil. 7th)
Repetitious (Ire)
Sarhoob (1988 Turf 8th)
Indian Lodge (Ire) (2000 Mile 13th)
Resolver
Adjudicating (1989 Juvenile 11th)
Adjudicating (1990 Sprint 4th)
Dispute (1993 Distaff 4th)
Rowdy Angel
Demon's Begone (1986 Juvenile 6th)
Pine Bluff (1991 Juvenile 7th)
Safely Home
Partner's Hero (1998 Sprint 8th)
Safely Kept (1989 Sprint 2nd)
Safely Kept (1990 Sprint 1st)
Shared Interest
Cash Run (1999 Juv. Fil. 1st)
Forestry (1999 Sprint 4th)
Sharp Kitty
Family Style (1985 Juv. Fil. 2nd)
Lost Kitty (1987 Juv. Fil. 10th)
Shy Spirit
Izvestia (1990 Classic 6th)
Key Spirit (1991 Sprint 11th)

Six Crowns
  Chief's Crown (1984 Juvenile 1st)
  Chief's Crown (1985 Classic 4th)
  Classic Crown (1987 Juv. Fil. 6th)
  Classic Crown (1988 Distaff 5th)
Slightly Dangerous
  Dushyantor (1996 Turf 7th)
  Dushyantor (1998 Turf 3rd)
  Warning (GB) (1988 Mile 11th)
Stark Winter
  Bien Bien (1993 Turf 2nd)
  Dr. Schwartzman (1985 Mile 4th)
Sultry Sun
  Solar Splendor (1992 Turf dnf)
  Solar Splendor (1993 Turf 14th)
  Sultry Song (1991 Mile 14th)
  Sultry Song (1992 Classic 5th)
Surgery
  Sewickley (1989 Sprint 5th)
  Shared Interest (1992 Distaff 11th)
The Brig
  He's a Saros (1987 Classic 8th)
  Saros Brig (1986 Juv. Fil. 3rd)
Toussaud
  Chester House (1999 Classic 4th)
  Decarchy (2003 Mile 12th)
  Honest Lady (2000 Sprint 2nd)
Tree of Knowledge
  Taiki Blizzard (1996 Classic 13th)
  Taiki Blizzard (1997 Classic 6th)
  Theatrical (Ire) (1985 Turf 11th)
  Theatrical (Ire) (1986 Turf 2nd)
  Theatrical (Ire) (1987 Turf 1st)

Trestle
  Classy Cathy (1986 Distaff 4th)
  Ms. Margi (1987 Distaff 5th)
Turk O Witz
  Mr Purple (1994 Juvenile 8th)
  Queens Court Queen (1991 Juv. Fil. 13th)
Viviana
  Sightseek (2003 Distaff 4th)
  Tates Creek (2003 F & M Turf 8th)
Weekend Surprise
  A.P. Indy (1992 Classic 1st)
  Summer Squall (1991 Classic 9th)
Whakilyric
  Hernando (FR) (1993 Turf 10th)
  Hernando (FR) (1994 Turf 6th)
  Hernando (FR) (1995 Turf 5th)
  Johann Quatz (Fr) (1993 Mile 7th)
  Johann Quatz (Fr) (1994 Mile 2nd)
White Jasmine
  Cinch (1994 Juvenile 7th)
  Til Forbid (1991 Distaff 9th)
Willamae
  Willa on the Move (1988 Distaff 8th)
  Will's Way (1996 Classic 7th)
Zippy Do
  Some Romance (1988 Juv. Fil. 6th)
  Vilzak (1987 Turf 4th)

HORSES

First horse to win two Breeders' Cup races, **Miesque** – 1987 Mile and 1988 Mile

Other two-time Breeders' Cup race winners
Bayakoa – 1989 Distaff and 1990 Distaff
Da Hoss – 1996 Mile and 1998 Mile
High Chaparral – 2002 Turf and 2003 Turf (dh)
Lure – 1992 Mile and 1993 Mile
Tiznow – 2000 Classic and 2001 Classic

First dead-heat for win in a Breeders' Cup race
High Chaparral and Johar, 2003 Turf

Margin of victory
Inside Information holds the mark for the largest margin of victory in any Breeders' Cup race with a 13 1/2-length triumph in the 1995 Distaff at Belmont.

Unbeaten Breeders' Cup winners
Halfbridled, winner of the Juvenile Fillies in 2003, was the ninth horse to remain undefeated after winning a Breeders' Cup race. The others were **Personal Ensign** ('88 Distaff), **Meadow Star** ('90 Juvenile Fillies), **Gilded Time** ('92 Juvenile), **Flanders** ('94 Juvenile Fillies), **Favorite Trick** ('97 Juvenile) and **Johannesburg** ('01 Juvenile), **Storm Flag Flying** ('02 Juvenile Fillies) and **Vindication** ('02 Juvenile).

Multiple Breeders' Cup starts by one horse
Kona Gold became the first horse to start in a Breeders' Cup race five times when he finished fourth in the 2002 Sprint in his fifth consecutive try at the race. Four other horses - **Affirmed Success, El Senor, Pleasant Tap**, and **Precisionist** – have each made four Breeders' Cup appearances.

Performance of Favorites
Through 2003, post-time betting favorites won 53 of 145 Breeders' Cup races, a 37.2 percent rate. There have been 36 odds-on choices with 16 winners.

Medaglia d'Oro, finishing second as the favorite for the second straight year, was the sixth straight favorite that did not win the BC Classic. The 4-year-old colt finished second at odds of $2.60-1...Only five favorites have prevailed in the Classic in 20 years and the most recent was **Skip Away** at odds of $1.80-1 in 1997.

Winning Post Positions through 2003.
Post 1 – 13 Winners
Post 2 – 17 Winners
Post 3 – 13 Winners
Post 4 – 17 Winners
Post 5 – 17 Winners
Post 6 – 12 Winners
Post 7 – 5 Winners
Post 8 – 11 Winners
Post 9 – 8 Winners
Post 10 – 7 Winners
Post 11 – 9 Winners
Post 12 – 10 Winners
Post 13 – 2 Winners
Post 14 – 5 Winners

European performances in the Breeders' Cup
In 2003, 2002 Turf winner **High Chaparral**, who shared victory with North American-based Johar in a dead-heat, became the fifth consecutive winner in the $2 million Turf for European connections. European-based horses have won 11 of 20 runnings in this 1 1/2-mile turf event. The other European

winners were : **Lashkari** (1984), **Pebbles** (1985), **In The Wings** (1990), **Miss Alleged** (1991), **Tikkanen** (1994), **Pilsudski** (1996), **Daylami** (1999), **Kalanisi** (2000) and **Fantastic Light** (2001).

High Chaparral also was the third son of Sadler's Wells to win the Turf. The others were **In The Wings** (1990) and **Northern Spur** (1995).

In 2003, **Six Perfections** gave Europe its ninth victory in the Mile. The other winners: **Last Tycoon** (1986), **Miesque** (1987 and '88), **Royal Academy** (1990), **Barathea** (1994), **Ridgewood Pearl** (1995), **Spinning World** (1997) and **Domedriver** (2002).

TRAINERS

In 2003, **Richard Mandella** became the first trainer to win four Breeders'Cup races in one day, taking the Juvenile Fillies with Halfbridled, the Juvenile with Action This Day, the Turf with Johar (in a dead-heat with High Chaparral) and the Classic with Pleasantly Perfect.

Trainer **D. Wayne Lukas** holds the record for in-the-money finishes in one Breeders' Cup race having swept the 1-2-3 finishing positions in the **1988** Juvenile Fillies with Open Mind, Darby Shuffle, and Lea Lucinda. . .Lukas has won the Juvenile Fillies four times, a record for trainers in a single Breeders' Cup race.

Orientate's victory in the 2002 Sprint also gave Lukas a record 17th Breeders' Cup victory. He also leads all trainers with number of starts and money won. Through 2003, Lukas's record is 140-17-20-14 for total earnings of $18,608,400.

Oldest winning Breeders' Cup trainer
P.G. Johnson, at age 77, became the oldest winning trainer of a Breeders' Cup race when Volponi won the 2002 Classic. Whittingham was 76 years old when Sunday Silence won the 1989 Classic.

Youngest winning Breeders' Cup trainer
Craig Dollase, 27, trained **Reraise**, winner of the 1998 Breeders' Cup Sprint.

First woman to train a Breeders' Cup winner
Jenine Sahadi trained Lit de Justice winner of the 1996 Sprint

JOCKEYS

Win percentage, career BC earnings, wins in consecutive years

Mike Smith, whose best 2003 Breeders' Cup finish was a second-place in the Sprint aboard Bluesthestandard, has won 10 of 52 starts for a winning percentage of 19.2 percent, highest among jockeys with at least five wins.

Pat Day is the only jockey to have appeared in Breeders' Cup races all 20 years. In 2003, Day's record number of Breeders' Cup mounts increased to 112. Day's career BC mounts have earned a BC record, $22,913,360, more than $5 million more than **Chris McCarron**, who retired in July 2002. Bailey is third in career earnings with $17,632,540.

Jerry Bailey, who captured the 2003 Mile aboard Six Perfections, has won a Breeders' Cup race in six consecutive years.

Youngest winning jockey
Walter Guerra, 22, rode Outstandingly, winner of the 1984 Juvenile Fillies.

Oldest winning jockey
Bill Shoemaker, 56, rode Ferdinand, winner of the 1987 Breeders' Cup Classic.

BREEDERS and OWNERS

Breeder **Sean Coughlan** improved his record to a perfect three for three when 2002 Turf winner High Chaparral won the 2003 Turf in a dead-heat. His only other starter, Ridgewood Pearl, won the 1995 Mile.

Breeders' Cup winners that sired Breeders' Cup winners.
A.P. Indy won 1992 Classic; sired Tempera , 2001 Juvenile Fillies.
Capote won 1986 Juvenile; sired Boston Harbor, 1996 Juvenile.
Chief's Crown won 1984 Juvenile; sired Chief Bearhart,1997 Turf.
Cozzene won 1985 Mile; sired Tikkanen,1994 Turf and Alphabet Soup, 1996 Classic.
Royal Academy won 1990 Mile; sired Val Royal, 2001 Mile.
Unbridled won 1990 Classic; sired Unbridled's Song,1995 Juvenile, Anees,1999 Juvenile and Halfbridled, 2003 Juvenile Fillies.
Unbridled's Song won 1995 Juvenile; sired Unbridled Elaine, 2001 Distaff.
Wild Again won 1984 Classic; sired Elmhurst, 1997 Sprint.

Breeders' Cup winners that produced Breeders' Cup winners
Hollywood Wildcat won 1993 Distaff; produced War Chant 2000 Mile.
Personal Ensign won 1988 Distaff; produced My Flag 1995 Juvenile Fillies.
My Flag won 1995 Juvenile Fillies; produced Storm Flag Flying, 2002 Juvenile Fillies.

Dams that produced multiple Breeders' Cup winners
Primal Force produced Awesome Again, winner of 1998 Classic, and Macho Uno, winner of 2000 Juvenile.
Storm Flag Flying completed a third generation Breeders' Cup triple with her victory in the Juvenile Fillies. Her dam, **My Flag,** won the 1995 Juvenile Fillies at Belmont Park. My Flag's dam, **Personal Ensign,** won the 1988 Distaff at Churchill Downs. With her victory, Storm Flag Flying joined Unbridled Elaine as the second horse to complete a third generation Breeders' Cup triple. Unbridled Elaine's sire, Unbridled's Song, won the 1995 Juvenile. Unbridled, the sire of Unbridled's Song, won the 1990 Breeders' Cup Classic.

RECORD PARIMUTUEL WIN PAYOUTS
Lowest winning payout, **Meadow Star**, $2.40, winner of the 1990 Juvenile Fillies.
Highest winning payout, **Arcangues**, $269.20 winner of the 1993 Classic.

2003 BREEDERS CUP WAGERING INFORMATION

Handle
$13,678,118 – On-track handle for Breeders' Cup races
$ 4,489,454 – Total Pick 6 Handle
$639,317 – Head2Head Handle
$555,859 – Official Breeders' Cup Futures' Wagering Pool
$101,780,683 – North American Simulcast Handle

IMPORTANT DATES IN BREEDERS' CUP HISTORY

April 23, 1982, John R. Gaines announces plans for multi-race, multimillion-dollar Breeders' Cup Series at the annual Kentucky Derby Festival 'They're Off' awards luncheon in Louisville, Kentucky.

May 3, 1982, Board of Directors named for Breeders' Cup Limited, the non-profit administrative organization for the Breeders' Cup.

July 27, 1982, Breeders' Cup stakes race program outlined as a one-day, seven-race series with purses totaling $13 million. Series to be known as Racing International's Championship Program.

September 2, 1982, After reviewing proposals from eight different racing associations, Breeders' Cup Track Selection Committee chooses Southern California as locale for inaugural Breeders' Cup Championship in 1984.

February 24, 1983, Hollywood Park in Inglewood, California, selected as site for inaugural Breeders' Cup, November 10, 1984.

April 15, 1983, Nomination of 1,083 stallions, representing more than $10.9 million in fees, announced.

June 8, 1983, $10 million Breeders' Cup Premium Awards Program announced, with allocations slated for 90 racing associations in 22 states and five Canadian provinces.

September 13, 1983, NBC Sports and the Breeders' Cup announce an exclusive, multi-year contract to broadcast all seven Breeders' Cup races live to a worldwide audience in a four-hour television special.

January 2, 1984, The split divisions of the La Prevoyante Handicap at Calder Race Course in Florida become the first races to offer Breeders' Cup Premium Awards.

January 4, 1984, Breeders' Cup Ltd. announces a point system based on first-, second-, and third-place finishes in North American Graded Stakes to be used to determine starters in Breeders' Cup races if any of the races are oversubscribed.

January 17, 1984, The graded stakes panel of the Thoroughbred Owners and Breeders Association announces their unprecedented decision to assign Grade I status to all seven Breeders' Cup races.

February 4, 1984, Ollie Cohen's Eillo, eventual winner of the inaugural Breeders' Cup Sprint, named first Breeders' Cup Horse of the Month.

March 6, 1984, Frank E. Kilroe is named chairman of the five-member Racing Directors / Secretaries Panel, which will select starters for the Breeders' Cup races if fields are oversubscribed.

May 8, 1984, Breeders' Cup Limited announces the official names for the seven Breeders' Cup races, with total purses and nominator awards equaling $10 million, the richest single stakes racing day in racing history.

October 22, 1984, Breeders' Cup unveils its permanent trophy, a 1,850 pound bronze and marble reproduction of the Torrie horse, an ecorche or flayed horse designed by the 16th-century sculptor Giambologna.

October 30, 1984, a total of 77 horses are pre-entered for the seven inaugural Breeders' Cup races.

November 5, 1984, Aqueduct Racetrack in New York is named host track for the 1985 Breeders' Cup, with the races scheduled for November 2, 1985.

November 10, 1984, The inaugural Breeders' Cup is run before 64,254 at Hollywood Park. Chief's Crown wins the first Breeders' Cup race, the Breeders' Cup Juvenile and longshot Wild Again wins the Breeders' Cup Classic in a thrilling, controversial stretch duel with Slew o' Gold and Gate Dancer. After a lengthy inquiry in which NBC television cameras bring the key deliberations and video evidence to the viewing audience in unprecedented detail, the stewards disqualify Gate Dancer from second for interfering with Slew o' Gold in the final furlong.

STATES AND COUNTRIES WHICH PRODUCED
BREEDERS' CUP CHAMPIONSHIP WINNERS

CALIFORNIA (2)
Tiznow (C, 2000, 2001)

FLORIDA (18)
Beautiful Pleasure (D, 1999) Brave Raj (JF, 1986) Brocco (J, 1993) Cherokee Run (S, 1994) Cozzene (M, 1985) Eillo (S, 1984) Gilded Time (J, 1992) Hollywood Wildcat (D, 1993) Jewel Princess (D, 1996) Meadow Star (JF, 1990) One Dreamer (D, 1994) Precisionist (S, 1985) Prized (T, 1989) Skip Away (C, 1997) Smile (S, 1986) Tasso (J, 1985) Twilight Ridge (JF, 1985) Unbridled (C, 1990)

ILLINOIS (1)
Buck's Boy (T, 1998)

KENTUCKY (86)
Action This Day (J, 2003) Adoration (D, 2003) Ajina (D, 1997) Alysheba (C, 1988) Anees (J, 1999) Answer Lively (J, 1998) A.P. Indy (C, 1992) Arazi (J, 1991) Arcangues (C, 1993) Artax (S, 1999) Azeri (D, 2002) Boston Harbor (J, 1996) Cajun Beat (S, 2003) Capote (J, 1986) Cardmania (S, 1993) Caressing (JF, 2000) Cash Run (JF, 1999) Cat Thief (C, 1999) Chief's Crown (J, 1984) Countess Diana (JF, 1997) Da Hoss (M, 1996, 1998) Dancing Spree (S, 1989) Desert Stormer (S, 1995) Eliza (JF, 1992) Elmhurst (S, 1997) Epitome (JF, 1987) Escena (D, 1998), Fantastic Light (T, 2001) Favorite Trick (J, 1997) Ferdinand (C, 1987) Flanders (JF, 1994) Fly So Free (J, 1990) Fraise (T, 1992) Great Communicator (T, 1988) Gulch (S, 1988) Halfbridled (JF, 2003) Inside Information (D, 1995) Is It True (J, 1988) Johannesburg (J, 2001) Johar (T, 2003) Kona Gold (S, 2000) Life's Magic (D, 1985) Lit de Justice (S, 1996) Lure (M, 1992) Lure (M, 1993) Macho Uno (J, 2000) Manila (T, 1986) Miesque (M, 1987) Miesque (M, 1988) Miss Alleged (T, 1991) My Flag (JF, 1995) Opening Verse (M, 1991) Orientate (S, 2002) Outstandingly (JF, 1984) Perfect Sting (FMT, 2000) Personal Ensign (D, 1988) Phone Chatter (JF, 1993) Pleasant Stage (JF, 1991) Pleasantly Perfect (C, 2003) Princess Rooney (D, 1984) Proud Truth (C, 1985) Royal Academy (M, 1990) Rhythm (J, 1989) Sacahuista (D, 1987) Silverbulletday (JF, 1998) Skywalker (C, 1986) Soaring Softly (FMT, 1999) Spain (D, 2000) Squirtle Squirt (S, 2001) Storm Flag Flying (JF, 2002) Storm Song (JF, 1996) Success Express (J, 1987) Sunday Silence (C, 1989) Tempera (JF, 2001) Thirty Slews (S, 1992) Timber Country (J, 1994) Unbridled Elaine (D, 2001) Unbridled's Song (J, 1995) Very Subtle (S, 1987) Vindication (J, 2002) Volponi (C, 2002) War Chant (M, 2000), Wild Again (C, 1984)

MARYLAND (3)

Cigar (C, 1995) Concern (C, 1994) Safely Kept (S, 1990)

NEW JERSEY (1)
Open Mind (JF, 1988)

OKLAHOMA (1)
Lady's Secret (D, 1986)

PENNSYLVANIA (3)
Alphabet Soup (C, 1996) Go for Wand (JF, 1989) Tikkanen (T, 1994)

CANADA (3)
Awesome Again (C, 1998) Chief Bearhart (T, 1997) Dance Smartly (D, 1991)

ARGENTINA (3)
Bayakoa (ARG) (D, 1989) Bayakoa (ARG) (D, 1990) Paseana (ARG) (D, 1992)

FRANCE (5)
Kotashaan (T, 1993) Silic (M, 1999) Six Perfections (M, 2003) Starine (FMT, 2002) Val Royal (M, 2001)

GREAT BRITAIN (7)
Banks Hill (FMT, 2001) In the Wings (T, 1990) Lashkari (T, 1984) Pebbles (T, 1985) Ridgewood Pearl (M, 1995), Sheikh Albadou (S, 1991) Steinlen (M, 1989)

IRELAND (12)
Barathea (M, 1994) Black Tie Affair (C, 1991) Daylami (T, 1999) Domedriver (M, 2002), High Chaparral (T, 2002, 2003) Islington (FMT, 2003) Last Tycoon (M, 1986) Kalanisi (T, 2000) Northern Spur (T, 1995) Pilsudski (T, 1996) Royal Heroine (M, 1984) Theatrical (T, 1987)

(C–Classic; D–Distaff; J–Juvenile; JF–Juvenile Fillies; M–Mile; S–Sprint; T–Turf; FMT–Filly/Mare Turf)

Principles of Handicapping and Betting

By Steve Davidowitz

The art/science of handicapping is one of the most compelling facets of Thoroughbred racing. Through handicapping, players in the grandstand can participate in the racetrack experience as much as the horses, jockeys and trainers. Through use of Daily Racing Form past performances, players may assess the relative merits of each horse in every race and come up with an informed, educated opinion about which horse is likely to be favored by the prevailing conditions, or probable pace scenario.

Below are many of the most prominent terms used in Thoroughbred racing, explained with a slant toward their relevance in handicapping. A betting guide and handicapping primer also is included in this section.

GLOSSARY OF TERMS USED IN THOROUGBRED RACING

Also Eligible - A horse officially entered in a race, but not permitted to start, unless scratches from the eligible horses occur which open up starting spots in the field. As a rule, also eligible horses which make it into the body of the race do not replace scratched horses in post position assignments, but rather assume the first available outside post position. For example, if there are 12 horses in the body of the race and a horse on the also eligible list, a total of 13 horses were officially entered in the race, but only 12 will start.

Should the #1 horse be scratched the day before a race, or in some cases race-day morning, then the first also eligible would get post #12 and all the other horses previously drawn into the field would be moved inside one place to assume their official post positions.

Apprentice - A novice jockey who has not yet ridden for a full year past his or her 35th winner, or some other time frame specified by a given state's racing rules. While jockeys serve their apprenticeship, they are accorded a five-pound weight allowance, or reduction from their respective weight assignments in all races except stakes. (Jockeys who have not yet won 5 races are allowed 10- pound weight allowances in some states, while still other states offer some additional variations of these allowances for their early apprenticeships.)

Backstretch - The straightaway on the far side of the track between the turns. Also, the backstretch is used to describe the area outside the racetrack where the stable area usually is located.

Bandage - Strips of cloth wound around the lower part of a horse's legs for support or protection against injury. As in front leg bandages, noted by the symbol "f" in the Daily Racing Form past performances.

Bearing In -(Or bearing out) A horse deviating from a straight course. May be due to weariness, soreness, or the rider's inability to control the mount.

Beyer Speed Figure (Or "Beyer Fig.") The number provided by Andy Beyer and his associates that measures the actual speed of a given horse in a given race, a "fig" that factors out the relative speed of the track condition. For more on this subject see material pertaining to Beyer Speed Figures on following pages ion this section, or consult Andy Beyer's classic book, "Picking Winners," Houghton Mifflin, 1975.

Bleeder - Horse that bleeds internally, or through the nostrils, during or after a workout or race due to ruptured blood vessels caused by stress. The condition is treated by rest, and/or the pre-race administration of the diuretic Furosemide (Lasix), which veterinarians believe can reduce blood pressure in the lung capillaries.

Blinkers - A hood which limits a horse's vision to prevent him from shying from objects or other horses on either side. Used by trainers to improve a horse's breaking ability from the starting gate and/or his concentration when challenged for the lead.

Breakage - The extra pennies that round mutuel odds down to the next lowest nickel or dime. The breakage left over goes to the track or the state, as per racing rules in that state.

Breezing - Working a horse at a moderate speed; usually without whipping, with less effort than "handily."

Bug - Slang for apprentice allowance or apprentice rider. The term comes from the asterisk that usually accompanies an apprentice rider's name in the overnight entries.

Bullet (or Bullet Work) - The best clocking for a specific distance at a given track on a given day is designated by a bold black dot, or bullet.

Bute (or Butazolidin) - Trade name for phenylbutazone, an ingested analgesic medication that controls or alleviates swelling in the joints. Permitted for use on horses on race day in some racing jurisdictions. Before the era of legalized medication, Dancer's Image was disqualified from a Kentucky Derby victory because a post-race urine test revealed "bute" in his system.

Chalk - The horse favored in a race.

Chalk player- A bettor who wagers on favorites.

Checked - Description of a horse whose momentum is lost for an instant because the horse is cut off or in tight quarters. Also "steadied" and "taken up" are terms to describe similar actions by the rider to avoid varying degrees of interference (from least to most severe: steadied, checked, taken up).

Chute - Extension in the backstretch or homestretch to permit a straightaway run from the start.

CLASS OF RACE. Refers to the overall quality of a specific race. In Thoroughbred racing, horses with similar winning histories are grouped together to foster close competition whenever possible. But the class of race is subject to many variations and subtleties, as the list of race types and their appropriate definitions and eligibility conditions demonstrate.

* **Allowance** - A race in which no horse is eligible to be bought or claimed (see Claiming below). Usually the horses competing in an Allowance race are faster than most horses competing in claiming races, but finite comparisons must be made after examining the conditions of eligibility.

For example, an Allowance race for nonwinners of three races-lifetime, is considerably easier than an Allowance race for non winners of three races in the past six months.

Likewise, horses who have won several high priced claiming races would be formidable contenders in an Allowance race for non winners of two races-lifetime. (See the specific types of races listed below and on succeeding pages for more insight into various class levels and eligibility conditions.)

* **Claiming Race** - (or the rarely used term "selling race") The most common of all races, stipulating a selling price (such as $25,000) for which any horse in the race may be purchased. With purses scaled upward in tandem with claiming prices, lower priced claiming races usually include slower horses than higher priced claiming races.

Typically, here are the rules for interested parties to claim horses out of these claiming races:

Purchase can only be made by a registered owner, or trainer on the track with money on deposit with the horsemen's bookkeeper. Claims must be made in a designated sealed box (the claim box) usually 10 minutes before post time. Purses earned in the race are retained by the owner who entered the horse, but once the gates spring open, the claimed horse becomes the property of the claimant, regardless of what occurs during the running of the race. Also, in many jurisdictions, a claimed horse must be raised in price 25 percent for the next 30 days of racing and can not be moved off the grounds for the duration of the meet, except for stakes engagements.

* **Graded Stakes Race** - (or "Group race" in foreign countries). These are races designated by their respective countries as the most prestigious on the annual racing calendar. In the United States, there are approximately 450 Grade 1, Grade 2, and Grade 3 stakes in America (The lower the number, the higher the Group or Grade ranking.) The Kentucky Derby for instance is a Grade 1 stakes; the Epsom Derby in England is a Group 1 race and the New Hampshire Sweepstakes is a Grade 3.

A "stakes race" also may be a nongraded stakes. Derived from the word "sweepstakes," all stakes races may be run under weight-for-age conditions, allowance conditions, or handicap conditions. Owners typically pay an entry fee to nominate, enter, and run their horses in stakes. These fees are added to the base purse put up by the track.

* **Handicap race** - A race in which the weights are assigned by the racing secretary according to his opinion of the relative merits of the horses nominated to compete. By this method, the best horse is assigned top weight (to be carried by the jockey including his or her own body weight, plus the weight of the saddle and any added lead weights needed to complete the assignment loaded into the saddle pockets). While the best horse is so burdened, the rest of the field is assigned lower weights on the theory that this levels the playing field by respectively improving the chances of the least accomplished horses. By far, the most famous handicap race occurred in 1944, when Brownie (115 pounds), Wait A Bit (118), and Bossuet (127) finished in a triple dead heat in the Carter Handicap at Aqueduct. Weights were assigned by John B. Campbell. Prior to the 1990's, it was commonplace for top handicap horses to carry 126, 128, and even 130 or more pounds. But in recent years, handicap stakes have gone out of favor, as most trainers have many more options to run good horses for big purses and are reluctant to run their star horses under such imposts.

* **Futurity** - Races for 2-year-olds that require advance nomination payments and perhaps sustaining payments too. Such races tend to raise the gross purse substantially over the original base amount. While this form of race is used sparingly in modern Thoroughbred racing, it is the predominant form of stakes racing for 2-year-olds in Quarter Horse racing.

* **Maiden race** - A race exclusively for horses that have never won a race. Once a horse has won a maiden race, it can not race in maiden races and must compete against other winners.

* **Match race** - A special two-horse race, often between highly publicized rivals.

* **Statebred race** - A race carded exclusively for horses bred in the specific state. Usually this type of race may also be carded for statebred maidens, or statebred claiming horses, or fillies, or 3-year-olds, or allowances and/or stakes, etc. Some statebred races also feature incentive bonus awards to encourage local breeders and/or owners to participate in the state breeding program.

Clocker - **(Or official clocker).** One who officially times workouts for publication. Usually employed by the racetrack, or racing association. Other clockers may include privately employed clockers.

Closing odds - Final odds posted on the tote board after all wagering has concluded for a given race interests.

Colors - (Or racing silks) The colors and patterns registered by a given owner's racing stable. Includes the shirt jacket and cap. Among the most famous racing silks in racing history are the devil's-red and blue colors of Calumet Farm, the black and cherry silks of the Phipps stable and the blue and white checked pattern carried by the Meadow Stables, who raced Secretariat.

Colt - Unaltered male horse under five years of age.

Company - **(or company line)** The class of horses in a race and/or the members of the field. The "company line" refers to the 1-2-3 finishers in a given horse's past performance line for a single race.

Coupling - **(Or Coupling, or stable coupling.)** When two or more horses in a race belong to the same owner(s), they are said to be "coupled" and they run as one betting entry, comprising a single betting unit. In other words, a bet on one horse in a stable coupling, or entry, is a bet on both. Regardless of post position, their program numbers would be "1" and "1A", with the horse drawing the post position nearest the rail running as "1" and the outside horse of the two running as "1A." In some races, there may be three or more horses linked together in such a stable coupling in which case the third horse out from the rail would be listed as 1X. There also may be two different stable couplings in the same race. In this case, the second stable coupling would be linked together in the betting as #2 and 2B.

Dam - Mother of a horse.

Dead heat - Two or more horses finishing in a tie at the wire as determined by the photo finish camera and posted by the presiding stewards. A dead heat can occur for any finishing position.

Disqualification (or DQ) - Change in the order of finish by officials for an infraction of the rules. Usually this occurs due to racing interference, as noted by the presiding stewards, or as claimed by a participating jockey and upheld by the stewards after a review of the video tapes. When this occurs, parimutuel payoffs are only made according to the official order of finish. Sometimes, however disqualification may occur long after a race has been declared official, due to drug test violations. In that event, the original parimutuel payoffs are not affected, only the purse awards are changed.

Dogs - Wooden barriers or rubber traffic cones placed a certain distance out from the inner rail during workout hours to prevent horses from churning the footing along the inside path. As in a workout "around the dogs."

Driving - A term used to describe strong urging by the jockey in the stretch.

Dropdown - A horse racing against lower class rivals than his most recent races.

Eased - A horse pulled up before the finish of a race, usually due to injury, sometimes to avoid further mishaps that may have occurred in the race.

Entry - **(see Coupling above.)** Two or more horses with a common interest (same owner and/or trainer) who are coupled as a single betting unit and listed in the program under the same betting numbers as, for example: 1 and 1A; or 2 and 2B.

Equivalent odds - Mutuel price paid for each $1 wagered. As in $4.50 to $1, or 9-2 odds.

Even money - Odds of 1-; profit equals investment in a successful wager.

Exacta (or Perfecta) - See Wagering pools below for explanations of Win, Place, Show, Daily Double, Exacta, Trifecta, Pick Three and Pick Six bets.

Fast track - Footing of the racing surface when it is at its best, relatively dry and evenly manicured.

Field Horse (or Mutuel Field) - Two or more starters running as a single betting unit when there are more entrants than the totalizator board can accommodate. Usually the track handicapper will couple the least-accomplished horses in the field and place them under the last number on the tote board. Such as 12 and 13F being coupled under #12 in a tote board that can only accommodate only 12 betting interests. Or 14F, 15F and 16F, all being coupled under #14, in a tote board that can accommodate 14 different betting interests.

Filly - Female horse under five years of age.

Firm - The condition of a turf course corresponding to FAST on a dirt track.

First Time Starter- A horse making its career debut. As a general rule, precociously bred horses, or horses born of inherently fast parentage tend to win races early in their careers, perhaps at short distances, in their first or second starts.

Foal – Newly born horse, or until weaned. Can be male or female.

Fractional time –(Or fractional splits). The intermediate clockings recorded in a race at the quarter mile split, and/or the half mile split, and/or the three-quarter mile split, etc.

Furlong - One-eighth of a mile; 220 yards; 660 feet. The traditional measuring unit for Thoroughbred races in North America as well as all countries and colonies that were once, or still remain under British domain. (Furlongs are similarly used in other countries, but so too are extensions of 1000 meters.)

Furosemide - (or Lasix) Generic term for a diuretic medication used in the treatment of bleeders. The most common trade name is Lasix or Salix.

Gelding - Castrated male horse of any age. Usually, the procedure is done to settle down high-strung racehorses who are not performing well and have minimal stud value. The most notable geldings in the past 50 years however include five-time Horse of the Year KELSO; three–time Horse of the Year FOREGO, and two-time Horse of the Year, JOHN HENRY, all of whom were gelded before they displayed their best form.

Good track - A drying-out track condition on the dirt or turf course. Often a misnomer, in that a good track can be a tricky, sticky track with tiring qualities depending upon the speed of the drainage system to bring the surface back to normal, or fast. On the turf, a good course definitely has some moisture in it and may play a second or two slower than a firm course.

Handicapper - One who assigns weights for a race, as in the racing secretary, or director of racing. The term also is applied to one who uses past performances to assesses the relative merits of a field in order to make selections. A "public handicapper" is one who publishes or broadcasts his analysis and selections in newsprint, or other media.

Handle - (Or betting handle, wagering handle) The total amount of money wagered into a betting pool. "Total handle" refers to the amount wagered on a complete racing card.

Horse - An ungelded male horse, 5 years or older.

In The Money - A horse finishing first, second, or third.

Inquiry - (Or Stewards' Inquiry) A review of the race ordered by the stewards to check into a possible infraction of the rules. An "objection," or "jockey's objection" is a claim of foul made by a rider in a race, and automatically invokes an inquiry into the race by the presiding stewards.

Juvenile - A 2-year-old horse of either sex.

Key horse- (See Wagering strategies below for explanation and a few examples on how to use Key horses in Exactas and Trifectas.

Key race - A term used to identify unusually strong races, in that it means at least two horses have returned from the given race to win or run second in their next outings. Most effective in evaluating the strength of maiden races and races for lightly raced horses on the turf.

Lasix - (see Furosemide) The diuretic used to reduce exercise-induced pulmonary hemorrhaging (bleeding).

Length - The approximate "length" of a horse from nose to tail, about nine feet. Also, used to describe the approximate distance between horses in a race, such as one length, or five lengths away from the lead. According to racetrack myth, one length equals one fifth of a second and one pound of weight equals one length. However, the value of about five lengths equates to approximately four-fifths of a second at most distances and there is controversial research that suggests that it may take several pounds of added weight to have any influence on horse performance at most distances.

Mare - A female horse, 5 years or older.

Morning Line - The term used to describe the approximate odds quoted in the track program and/or posted on the tote board before the betting begins. The idea behind the morning line is to serve as an estimate of how the closing odds might shape up. Theoretically, the morning line should be comprised of 119-124 percentage points for all the horses in the race. This includes 100 percentage points distributed to all the horses in the race, plus approximately 19-24 percentage points representing the average takeout and breakage removed from the money wagered in the win pool by the track and state combined. The proper Betting Percentage Table for all odds situations appears below, along with a sample morning line for an eight-horse field.

1-10 90 percentage points
1-5 83 percentage points
2-5 71 percentage points
1-2 66 percentage points
3-5 62 percentage points
4-5 55 percentage points
1-1 50 percentage points
6-5 45 percentage points
7-5 42 percentage points
3-2 40 percentage points
8-5 38 percentage points
9-5 35 percentage points
2-1 33 percentage points
5-2 29 percentage points
3-1 25 percentage points
7-2 22 percentage points
4-1 20 percentage points
9-2 18 percentage points
5-1 16 percentage points
6-1 14 percentage points
8-1 11 percentage points
10-1 9 percentage points
12-1 8 percentage points
15-1 6 percentage points
20-1 4.5 percentage points
25-1 4 percentage points
30-1 3+ percentage points
40-1 2.5 percentage points
50-1 2 percentage points
75-1 1.5 percentage points
99-1 1 percentage point.

A sample morning line:
#1 Secretariat. . .2-1 (33   percentage points)
#2 Seattle Slew. . 5-2 (29   percentage points)
#3 Affirmed. . . . 3-1 (25   percentage points)
#5 Kelso. . . . . . 9-2 (18   percentage points)
#6 Cigar. . . . . 15-1 (6   percentage points)
#7 Skip Away. . . 15-1 (6   percentage points)
#8 Alysheba   20-1 (4.5 percentage points)

121.5 Total percentage points

Muddy Track - Deep condition of the racing surface after being soaked by water and after some of that water has worked its way into the track cushion—the top 3-4 inches of soil covering the track base. Not a SLOPPY TRACK, which is a wet track covered by rainfall. Not a WET-FAST track, which is a racing surface that has been rolled, or sealed by track maintenance prior to a rainfall. Both a sloppy track and a wet fast track are relatively glib racing surfaces, while a muddy track is usually slower and stickier. On some muddy tracks, trainers will use MUD CAULKS, which are pronged horse shoes designed to provide better traction on such racing surfaces. Shoe information usually is provided by track announcers, or via the video monitors, or on a shoe board in the paddock.

Mudder - A horse who races well on a wet, or an off track. The ability to run on wet surfaces is considered to be an inherited trait. Knowledge of breeding, or breeding statistics can assist players in their attempts to estimate a good or bad performance of horses that have never raced on wet tracks. For horses with previous wet track racing experience, players should consult the wet-track box score in the horse's past performances for clues, or the Tomlinson ratings for wet track potential, a proprietary numeric rating based on breeding, included in Daily Racing Form past performances.

Among the horses that are considered to be outstanding sires from which wet-track running ability tends to be inherited are:

Beau Genius, Bertrando, Broad Brush, Cee's Tizzy, Cherokee Run, Clever Trick, Cure the Blues, Devil His Due, Dixieland Band, Fit to Fight, Glitterman, Holy Bull, Lord At War, Maria's Mon, Meadowlake, Pine Bluff, Phone Trick, Pleasant Colony, Proud Birdie, Saint Ballado, Smoke Glacken and Wild Again, as well as the following sire-lines that have proven to be prolific wet track sires through more than one generation:

Danzig and his sons, **Polish Numbers** and **Belong to Me.**

Deputy Minister and his sons **French Deputy, Silver Deputy and Dehere.**

Fappiano and his sons **Unbridled, Pentelicus** and **Quiet American.**

Mt.Livermore and his sons **Peaks and Valleys** and **Housebuster.**

Mr. Prospector and many of his sons, including **Crafty Prospector, Kingmambo, Our Emblem, Gulch** and his son **Thunder Gulch; Gone West** and his son **Mr. Greeley; Forty Niner** and his son **Twining; Carson City** and his son **Lord Carson; Conquistador Cielo** and his sons **Norquestor** and **Marquetry,** and **Seeking the Gold** and **Seeking the Gold**'s son **Petionville.**

Roberto and his son **Dynaformer.**

Seattle Slew and his sons **Slew City Slew, Capote,** and **A.P. Indy;** and **A.P. Indy's** son **Pulpit.**

Storm Bird and his sons **Summer Squall** and **Storm Cat** and **Storm Cat's** son **Harlan.**

Nijinsky II and his sons **Sky Classic** and **Royal Academy,** who are also prolific sires of turf runners, another trait that seems to be passed on through bloodlines.

Nasal strip - A strip of adhesive cloth placed across the mid-section of a horse's head which some believe can assist the horse in breathing during competition.

Nose - The narrowest advantage a horse can have at the finish line.

Odds - When a horse is 3-1 to win, it means that you will receive $6 back for every $2 wager, plus your initial wager. Thus a $2 bet at 3-1 pays $3 x 2 + $2 (your original wager) for a total of $8.

Odds-on - Sometimes, horses are bet so heavily that they return less than $2 profit for each $2 wagered. These are "odds-on" choices. For example, a horse that goes off at odds of 1-2 pays $1 for each $2 bet, plus your wager. Thus a $2 bet at 1-2 odds would return $1 profit + the $2 wagered for a total of $3. When the payoff odds figure to be less than $4 ($2 profit for each $2 invested), the horse is said to be "odds-on," or an "odds-on" favorite.

Official - As in the result is declared "official." Also refers to the "official" sign displayed on the tote board when result is confirmed. The term also is used to describe a "racing official", which may include stewards, track owners, and supervisory personnel.

OTB (Off-Track Betting) - An off-site betting facility where players can wager on live racing at an associated racetrack.

Overlay - A horse going to the post at odds seemingly higher than he appears to warrant based on his Past Performances. Occasionally the term is used to describe a higher price than the listed morning line odds. The opposite is an underlay.

Pace - Relative rate of early movement in a race, especially by the leader (setting the pace). The phrase "Pace makes the race" refers to the advantage a front runner may have when the early pace is uncontested, or the advantage stretch running horses may have coming from "off the pace" when there are several horses caught in a "speed duel."

Pace handicapping

Beyond evaluating the overall pace of a given race by comparing running styles, a more scientific oriented approach to pace handicapping involves mathematical comparisons of fractional splits and use of track variants to factor out the speed of the racing surface in these comparisons. Many students of the sport take the discipline even further, by converting the published clockings for various fractional splits into "feet per second" velocity times. This conversion can help to facilitate more precise comparisons between the relative rates of speed for each horse in a given race. Accordingly, if one horse seems to have a distinctly faster velocity rating than the rest of the field, that horse can be expected to control the pace. In addition, many students of pace use velocity ratings to make more accurate comparisons of a horse's potential to make a middle-move, through the middle fractional splits. And of course, they can be used as well to compare each horse's relative finishing punch through the final eighth of a mile, or even through the final 3/16 miles, in races such as 1 1/16 miles where the the final fractional split in past performances is 3/16 miles. For more information on this intriguing subject, I refer you to Tom Brohamer's "Modern Pace Handicapping," published by DRF Press and to my own "Betting Thoroughbreds," 2nd revised edition, published Dutton-Plume.

The chart below spells out feet-per-second calculations for a sample fractional split for every major point of call in any race, as well as the rate of speed in feet per seconds for some sample final clockings at popular racing distances.

EQUIVALANT VELOCITY RATINGS IN FEET PER SECOND
FOR FRACTIONAL CLOCKINGS and POPULAR RACING DISTANCES

1/4 mile in   23.20 -   56.88 ft. per second
1/2 mile in   46.60 -   56.65 ft. per second
5/8 mile in   58.40 -   56.51 ft. per second
3/4 mile in 1:10.40 - 56.25 ft. per second
7/8 mile in 1:23.80 - 55.13 ft. per second
One mile in 1:37.40 - 54.21 ft. per second
1-1/8 miles 1:50.40 - 53.71 ft. per second
1-1/4 miles 2:04.00 - 53.23 ft. per second
1-1/2 miles 2:29.00 - 53.13 ft. per second

ONE MILE CLOCKINGS AND VELOCITY RATINGS IN FEET PER SECOND.

1:34 - 56.17 ft. per second
1:35 - 55.58 ft. per second
1:36 - 55.00 ft. per second
1:37 - 54.43 ft. per second
1:38 - 53.88 ft. per second
1:39 - 53.33 ft. per second

Paddock - Designated area that usually features a saddling enclosure and a walking ring where horses are saddled and paraded before post time.

Parimutuel payoff - The posted amount each bettor will receive for a $2 winning mutuel ticket. The payoff is based on dividing the total money bet, after takeout, by the total of winning bets. For example in a win pool of $200,000 about $40,000 will be removed via the takeout before the balance – $160,000 – is used to calculate possible parimutel payoffs. A winning 3-1 shot for instance, will pay $8 for a $2 bet. This includes $3 in profit for every $1 wagered, plus the return of the original $2 investment. . .Record Parimutel Payoff: The all time record payoff for a $2 win wager is an astonishing $2,922 on Power to Geaux in a race that was simulcast from the Fair Grounds in New Orelans to Ak-Sar-Ben in Nebraska, Dec. 8, 1989. The highest parimutuel payoff for a straight $2 win wager on a race run at the track in which the bet was made, is $1,885.50 on Wishing Ring, at Latonia, Kentucky (now Turfway Park), June 17, 1912.

Post position - The starting gate assignment for a horse in a given race. Usually, post positions are assigned via lottery at entry time. Post position can be an important handicapping factor in races where the starting gate is close to the first turn, or when there is a prevalent running-lane bias at work. (See Track Bias, above.)

Pole - (as in furlong pole, quarter pole, half-mile pole, sixteenth pole). These are markers at measured distances around the track which indicate the exact distance in furlongs from the respective pole to the finish line. The quarter pole for instance is a quarter-mile from the finish, not from the starting gate.

Post parade - Horses going from the paddock to starting gate, past the stands. At most tracks in good weather the post parade begins about 11 minutes before post time and is the first phase of the PRE-RACE WARM-UP. In inclement or very cold weather, the post parade is shortened considerably.

Ridden out - Mild encouragement by rider in the stretch.

Ridgling - A male horse of any age with only one descended testicle.

Scratch - (Early scratch, or late scratch, or vet scratch.) The term for removing a horse, or withdrawing a horse from a race.

EARLY SCRATCHES are made before the program numbers are assigned.

LATE SCRATCHES are made by the trainer, or the track veterinarian after program numbers have been assigned. Some late scratches are permitted when bad weather affects the racing surface, or when a surface-switch from grass-to-dirt is made by the track stewards due to bad weather. Most late scratches require stewards' or veterinary approval.

VET SCRATCHES are made by the track or state vet after they are inspected in the paddock, or perhaps after they have gone to the track for pre race warm-ups. This is a precautionary scratch – to protect an infirm, or sore moving horse. Refunds are usually made whenever a "late scratch" or a "vet scratch" is made, unless specific alternative selections are provided in the rules for a particular wager. For instance, a late scratch in a Pick Six race will automatically switch the wager to the post-time betting favorite.

Shadow Roll - A lambs' wool-covered noseband positioned halfway up a horse's face to keep him from seeing shadows on the ground.

Simulcast - Simultaneous television broadcast of a race(s) to betting facilities away from live track. . . Today, simulcast races with full betting menus are offered in abundance at most tracks in tandem with live racing programs, or during "dark days" when no live racing is scheduled.

Sire - Father of a horse.

Sixteenth - One-sixteenth of a mile; 110 yards; 330 feet.

Sloppy - Track condition when there is visible water on the surface with a firm bottom. (See "Muddy Track" for more on wet tracks.)

Soft - Condition of a turf course that corresponds to muddy on dirt tracks.

Statebred - A horse bred in a particular state and thus eligible to compete in special races restricted to statebreds.

Stewards - Top officials of the race meet responsible for enforcing the rules.

Takeout - The percentage of tax taken from each betting pool at the track and distributed according to state law among the state, horsemen (purses), and racetrack. On average, 17 percent, plus "breakage" is taken out of win, place, and show pools, with a net of 83 percent, less breakage, returned to winning bettors. The takeout also is higher in most states on bets involving two or more horses, or two or more races, such as the Daily Double, Exacta, Trifecta, Pick Three, Superfecta and the Pick Six.

Tomlinson Ratings: A proprietary, numerical rating published in Daily Racing Form's past performances to provide clues to a potential to perform on wet tracks, turf courses, and beginning in 2002 at sprint and route distances. Separate Tomlinson ratings are used for each surface and distance type and they appear in the career boxes of every horse's past performance. These ratings are based on the winning history of specific sires' offspring on wet tracks. For a list of the most potent of these sires, see the sires provided under "Mudders" earlier in this section.

Track bias - A term I coined in the mid-1960's to describe the tendency of some racing surfaces to influence the way a race has been run. When a track bias is noted, the handicapper should downgrade horses that are running against the grain of the bias, and upgrade horses that seem likely to benefit from it. A front-running track bias is a bias favoring horses who take command of the race early in the contest. In such conditions, horses who engage in speed duels are less likely to burn themselves out, while lone front running types will be tough to catch. A stretch running track bias is one in which speed types fail to hold their positions, even when they are given an easy lead and a softer pace scenario.

Some track biases also favor inside running lanes, or outside running lanes, while others are inherently built into the track's geometry by the position of the starting gate relative to the first turn. In such cases, horses forced to go wide around must overcome a severe loss of ground or momentum to be serious win contenders. The value of identifying a genuine track bias can be enormous to astute handicappers in that if it exists, it will provide ample cause to downplay the chances of some contenders including well bet favorites, while giving a chance to longshots that are in position to take advantage of the prevalent bias. Just as important, players who watch races carefully may be able to explain a poor performance through knowledge of an existing track bias, or downgrade a seemingly good effort for the same reason. For more information on this intriguing handicapping principle, I refer you to Andy Beyer's "Picking Winners" and my own "Betting Thoroughbreds," available through DRF Press.

Trainer - The person responsible for conditioning a horse.

Trials - A rarely used racing device designed to determine the qualifiers for finals in a select stakes.

More commonly used in Quarter Horse races in which the qualifying finalists earn starting berths based on the fastest qualifying times, or the order of finish. A trial may sometimes be run without a purse. The term also is used to describe a workout or race that enables a horse to attain fitness.

Trips – A horse is said to have a "good trip" when it was able to avoid traffic problems and/or has benefited from a favorable pace scenario, or was able to secure a ground saving placement around the turn(s) followed by a clear path in the stretch. . .A horse is said to have had a "bad trip" when it encounters poor racing luck, heavy traffic, is forced wide around turns, is weakly ridden, or is forced to deal with an unfavorable pace scenario that taxes its energy, or leaves it vulnerable to less talented horses, or horses that have enjoyed better trips.

Turf course – The infield grass course, a course found at many American tracks. While racing on grass remains the dominant form of racing in Europe – where race meetings are usually very short – in America, where dirt track racing dominates and race meets tend to be scheduled for several weeks or months, turf racing makes up a much smaller percentage of the carded races.

Turf racing - Horses who perform well on dirt are not necessarily able to run as well on grass. Conversely, some horses run much faster and smoother on grass and are therefore known as "grass horses," or "turf horses." Moreover, because the majority of infield turf courses have generally sharper turns than dirt tracks, grass racing itself generally places an accent "trips." (See Trips, above.) In handicapping turf races, the bias of the course is similarly important, as is the amount of moisture in it, as some horses run their best races on firm or relatively hard courses, while others prefer courses with some give to it, as in "yielding" or "good", or "soft" labels tend to suggest.

Interestingly just as the ability to perform well on wet tracks may be an inherited trait, so too may the ability to perform well on grass. Here below is a list of potent "turf sires," all of whom have produced a relatively high percentage of grass horses, including many who show their talent for this type of racing in their very first or second attempt. Also interesting is the fact that some of the sires and sire lines found on the "mudders" list, are among the most potent turf sires, while a few are simply outstanding sires whose offspring perform equally as well on any surface, if not any distance.

Prolific turf sires, include:
Affirmed, Afternoon Deelites, Avenue of Flags French Deputy, Glitterman, Irish River, Lord At War, Maria's Mon, Rahy, Salse, Silver Hawk, Smokester, Theatrical.
Caro and his son **Cozzene**
Gone West and his son **Zafonic. Mr. Prospector** and his son **Kingmambo.**
Roberto and his sons **Red Ransom, Kris S.** and **Dynaformer.**
Seattle Slew and his sons **Septieme Ciel, Capote,** and **A.P. Indy.**
Storm Bird and his son **Storm Cat.**
Nijinsky II and his sons **Royal Academy, Shadeed,** and **Sky Classic. Northern Dancer** and virtually all of his sons and grandsons, including, but not limited to **Lyphard, Nureyev, Sadler's Wells, Dixieland Band, Danzig,** and Danzig's son **Foxhound.**

Beyond those above, most sires based or raced in Europe, where grass racing is predominant, tend to be positive turf sire influences.

WAGERING POOLS (Or types of bets in the pari-mutuel system)
* **Win** - You are a winner if your horse is the official winner of the race. The official winner usually is the horse that finishes first, but no finishing position in any race is official until the presiding stewards have cleared the result for possible infractions and posted the "official" sign on the tote board.
* **Place** - If your horse finishes second or better you will win the bet you have made in the place pool. But because all the holders of place tickets on the horses who finished first and/or second will share in the proceeds, the payoffs in the place pool will often be smaller than the win payoffs. In some instances, however, the payoffs will be quite generous in the place pool. For a comprehensive guide on the nuances of Place and Show Betting, along with some of the higher paying exotic wagers, interested players should consult the Appendix section of "Betting Thoroughbreds," (second revised edition), and "Money Secrets at the Racetrack", by Barry Meadow, as well as other works by other handicapping authors.
* **Show** - If your horse finishes third or better you will win the bet you made in the show pool. But because all the holders of show tickets on the horses who finished first, second and/or third will share

in the proceeds of this pool, your payoffs are generally much smaller than the payoffs for the win pool and place pool.

Note: Because the win, place, and show pools are independently calculated the payoffs in one pool have nothing to do with the payoffs in any of the other two. At the same time, if the player wants to bet one horse to win, place, and show at the same time, you may simplify the bet by telling the mutuel clerk that you wish to wager, for example, "$2 across the board on No. 4." That is the same as asking for separate $2 win, $2 place, and $2 show bets on No. 4.

* **Daily Double** - Type of wager calling for the selection of winners in two specially designated races, usually the first two and last two races. Some tracks also schedule "instant" daily doubles and or "rolling" daily doubles, to set up daily doubles in two consecutive races elsewhere or throughout the racing card. If you bet a "2-6" daily double, No. 2 must win the first race and No. 6 must win the second. To cash this bet, winners of the two races must be included on the same parimutuel ticket.

* **Exacta (or Perfecta)** - A wager calling for a selection of the first and second horses in a race, in their exact order of finish. If you bet a "3-4" exacta, No. 3 must win and No. 4 must finish second.

* **Quinella** - Wager in which first two finishers must be picked on a single parimuutel ticket, but not necessarily in exact order.

* **Pick Three and/or Pick Four** - Essentially, this plays out somewhat like a Daily Double in that the bet can only be won when the horses you play to win each race on a given Pick Three ticket (or Pick Four) actually win the three (or four) designated races.

* **Pick Six** - A form of wagering in which the player must select six straight winners on the same parimutuel ticket. This bet, which is popular in California and a few other locales, offers a "carryover" feature, which comes into play when no one correctly picks six. In such cases, a percentage – usually half – of the wagering pool is not distributed to players with five winners and instead is carried over to the next day's betting pool. This boost to the Pick Six pool thus attracts sizeable additional play.

* **Trifecta (or Triple)** - You must select the first, second, and third horses in a race, in their exact order of finish.

* **Superfecta** - A wager in which the first four finishers in a race must be selected in the exact order of finish on the same parimutuel ticket. Because it is a difficult wager to hit, payoffs often are higher than any other form of wagering except the Pick Six.

Wagering Strategies - Aside from the basic $2 win, place and or show bets, the player has many options to consider in the lay of the game. Below are some of the most popular, most efficient wagering options and strategies.

* **Wheel.** In exacta wagering, this is a bet that hooks up a horse in the win position over the rest of the field. By "wheeling", the player essentially is making a win bet in the Exacta pool because the Key horse must win the race for the bet to succeed. For instance, if you think the No. 5 horse will win, and wish to play it as a key horse in the exacta to take advantage of generous payoff possibilities, you would then "wheel" the No. 5 with every other horse in the race, at a cost of $2 for each of the other Exacta combinations in this particular race.

If there are five other horses in this hypothetical race, "wheeling" your selection with all five will cost $10. As a supplement to this strategy it often makes sense to buy an extra Exacta ticket or two on the combinations you favor the most.

* **Bottom wheel.** In the Exacta pool, the player is betting that the key horse will run second to some other horse in the field. A bottom wheel can be an effective "saver" strategy to a win bet, or the preferred way to play a horse that has a long history of finishing second.

* **Partial Wheel.** A wheel of a key horse over part of the field, as in using the Key Horse on top (or bottom), with some of the members of the field. . . A $2 partial wheel using the key horse with three of the five other horses in the race would cost $6. . .Partial wheels also may involve two key horses in the win position and any number of horses in the place position. For example, a partial wheel of two horses in the win position over the same two horses plus two more horses in the field would layout as follows:
Horse A and Horse B; with A,B,C and D.

Using $2 tickets, this part-wheel would cost $12 for the six different combinations. (Key Horse A over B, C, and D; plus Key Horse B over A, C, D.) . .Wheels, bottom wheels and part wheels can be played in the Trifecta pool in the same way they are played in the Exactas.

For example if you liked Key Horse A in the win position, and also liked B,C,D, in the place position and B,C,D,E,F in the show position, that part wheel would cost $12 for $1 units in the Trifecta.

Yearling - The age of every racehorse in his first year of life, as defined by the full 12 months following the first New Year's Day after he or she was foaled. If a horse were foaled on May 5, 1999, he would be a "yearling" from January 1, 2000, through December 31, 2000.

Yielding - A rain softened turf course in which the footing is between firm and soft. In such conditions, horses with European racing – where courses are often wet – and horses with previous good form on rain softened courses, usually have a decided advantage. The same is true for "soft" turf courses.

TYPES OF RACES AND THEIR SYMBOLS
IN DAILY RACING FORM PAST PERFORMANCES.

Md Sp Wt - Maiden Special Weight race for horses that have never won a race. A race in which all horses are assigned the same, or "special weight."

Md25000 - Maiden claiming race. A claiming, or selling race for non winners, with the listed selling price. (In these examples, a race in which the horse was entered to be claimed for $25,000).

Clm25000 - Claiming race open to all horses, with no restrictions.

fClm25000- Claiming race for fillies with no other eligibility restrictions.

Clm25000 3^ - Claiming race for 3 year olds ands up, with no other eligibility restrictions.

Clm25000N2L - Claiming race for nonwinners of 2 races lifetime.

(Increasing numbers indicate nonwinners of up to 5 races lifetime).

Clm25000N2X - For nonwinners of two races or more, excluding maiden races. May also be for nonwinners of 3X, or 4X, depending on the number after N). At the same time, there also may be additional restrictions described in the eligibility conditions of the race.

Clm25000N1Y - Claiming race for nonwinners of 1 race (or more depending
upon the number after N) in a specific time period, usually six months, or the current calendar year.

Clm25000N1mY - Claiming race for nonwinners of a race at a mile or over in a specific time.
period.

OClm25000 - Optional Claiming race (entered to be claimed).

OClm25000N - Optional Claiming race (entered NOT to be claimed).

Hcp8000s – A nonclaiming race better labeled as a "starter handicap" race. (In this case, the number 8000, indicates the minimum claiming price the horse must have started for during a specific time period to be eligible for this "starter" handicap. Weights assigned by the racing secretary and typically the purse is higher than a race at the corresponding claiming price.)

Alw8000s - A "starter allowance" race, (with the minimum claiming price each horse must have started for in a specific time period). This is a nonclaiming race in which the purse usually is higher than a corresponding claiming price. Weights are assigned according to previous victories.

Alw15000N2L - A nonclaiming, or "Allowance race" for nonwinners of two races lifetime. The figure 15000 refers to the purse value of the allowance race. And in these examples there is a total purse of $15,000 offered.

Alw15000N1X - Allowance race for nonwinners of one race – or more races, depending on number after N – in which victories in maiden, claiming, or starter races do not count against eligibility. In such races, it also is likely that victories in any races for state breds will not count against eligibility.

Alw15000N1Y - Allowance race for nonwinners of 1 (or more, depending on number after N) race(s) in or since a specified time period.

Alw15000N1m - Allowance race for nonwinners of 1 race at a mile or over in a specific time period.

Alw15000N$Y - Allowance race for nonwinners of a specific amount of money in a specified time period.

Alw15000N1T - Allowance race for nonwinners of 1 turf race.

Alw15000N1S - Allowance race for nonwinners of 1 stakes lifetime.

Alw15000NC - Allowance race no eligibility restrictions.

Handicap40k - Overnight handicap (purse was $40,000).

MatchR100k - Match race (purse $100,000).

PrincetonH40k - Ungraded, but named stakes race. (H indicates handicap; 40K = $40,000, purse.)

KyDerby-G1 - Graded stakes race. North American races are graded in order of status, with named stakes graded 1, 2, or 3. (In stakes races, the name, or abbreviation of the name, is shown in the class of race column. If a stakes is graded, the name will be followed by G1, G2, or G3. If ungraded, the name will be followed by the purse value, in thousands. The letter "H" after a name indicates the race was a handicap. The letters "Inv" after a name indicate the race was by invitation only.)

MAJOR ISSUES IN HANDICAPPING

A handicapping primer focusing on some of the most important handicapping issues.

Once a player has a basic understanding of the symbols included in Daily Racing Form past performance profiles, it is most useful to focus upon some key facts and concepts, such as those spelled out below.

SPOTTING THE FIT AND READY TO RUN RACEHORSE:

* **Check the dates of the horse's recent races.** If the horse has been racing regularly it is a sign that he is racing fit. If the horse has not started in 45 days or longer, check the past performances to see how he ran the last time he raced off a similar layoff.

Note: In Daily Racing Form past performances, a layoff of 45 days to one year is indicated by a single solid line (or rule) separating races. A layoff of one year or more is represented by a double rule.

* **Check the WORKOUTS.**

If the horse has been working regularly, he may have achieved fitness in the morning, especially if he shows some "bullet" workouts. Often, horses will improve with racing second and/or third starts back off a layoff.

* **Check for established PATTERNS.**

A winning pattern that replicates, or approaches a pattern being repeated today is an important positive sign.

* **Check for previous performances at TODAY's DISTANCE and today's CLASS LEVEL.**

Horses tend to develop preferences, such as a favorite distance, type of race, particular racing surface, or TRACK CONDITION. Perhaps due to tendencies inherited through breeding, some horses only perform at their best in six furlong "SPRINTS" or even shorter distances, while others may need longer races to be effective, including true "ROUTE RACES" at 1 1/8 miles or longer.

* **Check the CAREER BOX.**

Specific preferences can be gleaned by examining the CAREER BOX which highlights the horse's career record at today's distance as well as his career record at today's racetrack. The turf and wet dirt track records for the horse you are examining also are spelled out in the career box, which also includes Tomlinson ratings for grass racing, wet track, and distance ability as derived from a formula based on the proclivities of the sire to transmit those tendencies.

Generally speaking, Tomlinson ratings above 320 are positive indicators for success on either surface or distance.

* **Note the CLASS OF TODAY's RACE.**

It is very useful to know the class of races the horse has been competing in recently to determine if the horse is a good fit for the race. Has the horse been running well lately against similar company? Is the horse dropping in class in search of a winning level or dropping sharply because he is going off form and/or the trainer is looking to sell him cheaply to avoid feed and possible veterinary bills?

It is also possible that a horse may be in sharp form taking a step up in class and this leads to other intriguing handicapping questions, such as:

Has the horse stepped up too high to a level beyond its capabilities? Is the trainer making a shrewd judgment that this horse is now good enough to compete for higher purses? One means of answering this question is through the comparison of Beyer Speed Figures, which are presented exclusively in Daily Racing Form.

All of the above questions are intuitive, in that they play to the art, not the science of handicapping. But, they also highlight the player's ability to ferret out and use the information in the past-performance profiles to make informed, educated guesses as to trainer intent.

* **Examine Beyer Speed Figures.**

Beyer Figures are numerical representations of every horse's performance in every race. They are computed by noted handicapper Andy Beyer and his team of associates after careful review of the past performances and running times posted every day at recognized American racetracks.

The basic idea behind Beyer Figures is to factor out the inherent, relative speed of the racing surface on the day a given race is run so that only a horse's actual speed is represented by the Beyer Figure. In this system of numbers, 2 1/2 Beyer points are roughly equal to one length in a six-furlong sprint, while 2 Beyer points is roughly equal to one length at one mile. And with the speed of the track factored out, a higher Beyer Figure represents a faster actual performance than a horse earning a lower Beyer Speed Figure.

Two Examples:
1: A track is playing two seconds slower than normal for the day and the winner runs 1:12 flat for six fur-longs. Thus this horse's actual, published Beyer Figure will include an upgrade by two seconds to com-pensate for the slower track.

2: A track is playing one faster than normal for the day and the winning time is 1:09. Thus, this Beyer Figure will include a reduction by one second due to the speed of the track.
If these two races run on different days under different track conditions, the resulting Beyer Speed Figures will be identical to each other.

When using this approach to measure actual speed, Beyer Figures can be regarded as interchangeable from track to track and distance to distance. Keep this in mind when you are trying to answer questions regarding class shifts. Consider for instance the possibility that a horse stepping up in class with recent Beyer Speed Figures in the 90's, actually may be faster than a group of horses dropping out of seeming-ly better races that have been posting Beyer Speed Figures in the 80's.

* Examine the prospective PACE OF THE RACE.
The running lines with FRACTIONAL CALLS and corresponding FRACTIONAL SPLITS provide numerous clues to determine the RUNNING STYLE of the horse.
If the horse is often on, or close to the early lead in the first calls of his races, he can be considered a "SPEED HORSE."
If the horse tends to run near the pace and make his best move approaching the stretch, he may be con-sidered a STALKER – the ideal running style for most races. But should a horse persistently lag early and make his best move in the final furlongs, than he he is a "CLOSER," or even a "DEEP CLOSER" (one with a slow fuse that persistently trails during the early stages).
As a general rule, closers are at a disadvantage in races where there is not likely to be a competitive, or faster than usual pace. Conversely, front runners, or near the pace types, will benefit from a "soft" or moderate pace, one that leaves them with some energy in reserve for the inevitable attack from behind. Thus, it is important to review the running styles of ALL horses in today's race. If there is only one speed horse in a field of closers, he may get away with an easy lead and have plenty in reserve for the stretch run. Conversely, if there are many speed horses in today's race, they may exhaust their reserves in an early speed duel and set the race up for a closer. (See "Pace" in the Glossary of Terms earlier in this section for some additional insights into this school of handicapping.)

* Examine closely the records of trainers and jockeys.
The performance of most horses usually is the direct result of planning by the TRAINER and the han-dling on the track by the JOCKEY. It is an important fact to know that nearly 80 percent of all races are won by the top 20 percent of trainers and jockeys at each track. This fact alone should lead players to a careful evaluation of trainers and jockeys before final decisions are made.
For instance, does the trainer have a good winning percentage, say 15 percent or higher? Is he enjoying banner success at the present race meet? Has he trained this horse to a previous good performance under similar conditions? All this information is contained in the past performances and in the TRAIN-ER's BOX SCORE. Additional information about the trainer, such as his proficiency with first time starters, or first time turf runners, or recently claimed horses can be gleaned over time, by comparing past performance profiles of winning performers trained by the same individual.
The jockey is not necessarily the final link in the handicapping puzzle, but he is the last one to impact

Conformation of the Horse and Nomenclature of Body Parts

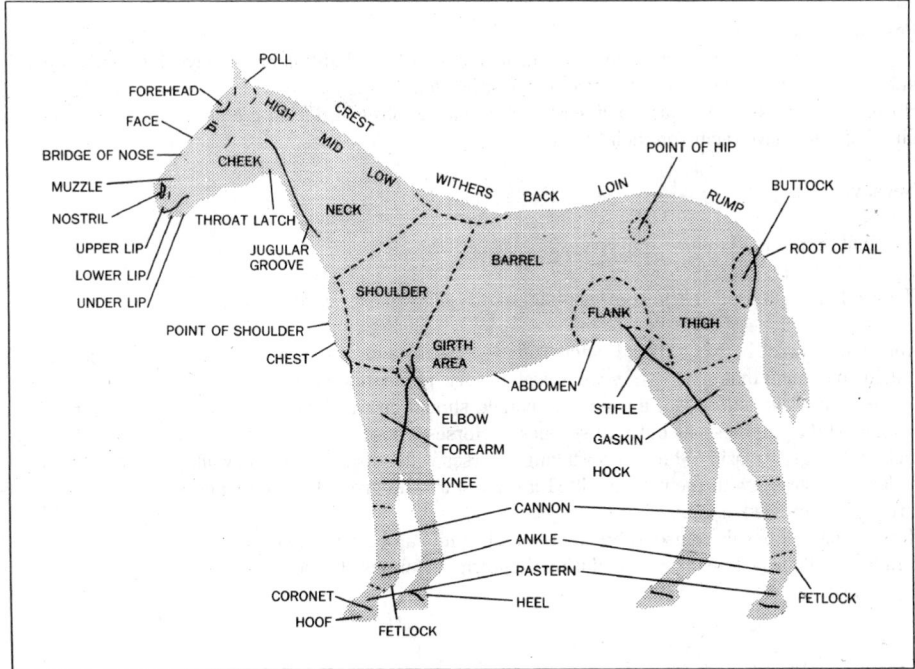

the outcome of the race you are evaluating. Here are some of the major issues handicappers should try to evaluate when assessing the jockey factor. Is today's rider a leading jockey at the meet, or in the national rankings, as posted elsewhere in Daily Racing Form? Has this jockey ridden this horse to a good finish, or prior victory? The JOCKEY's BOX SCORE follows the name of the jockey assigned to ride the respective horse in the past performance profile. Additional statistics about jockeys, such as his record with a given trainer's horses, or his proficiency with turf horses, front runners and betting favorites can be gleaned from result charts and supplemental data provided in Simulcast Weekly, published by Daily Racing Form.

* Put the picture of the race together.

By gaining a feel for each individual horse's current fitness, as well as its best distance and suitability to the racing surface, the handicapper will be able to assess the way a race may be run as well as identify logical contenders and weak threats in the field. Of course, horses are not robots and handicapping is an art, not a science. This leaves ample room for racing luck and human error, including errors made by handicappers. That is why the final link in the handicapping puzzle is the prospective odds being offered on respective contenders in the field. Indeed, the basic betting principle that underlies a winning approach can be summarized by the following few bromides that have stood the test of time.

* Check the physical appearance of the horse.

Horses are athletes who have been purposely trained to run at 35-40 miles per hour for short or long distances. They require months of gallops, workouts and special care and feeding to be fit enough for the task. With or without past performances, it is possible to make good judgments about a horse's relative physical condition through careful observation of its muscle tone, brightness of color, alertness and muscular development.

The illustration of the horse on this page may not provide many insights into how to make such fine line determinations, but it will give you a working language by which you can catalogue observations.

Here are some guidelines from which any player can begin to build a working knowledge of a horse in good or poor condition:

Sprinters, or horses built for distances under one mile, generally have short-cropped bodies and strong hind quarters.

Routers, or horses built for longer distances, have longer, leaner bodies, with broad chests.

Positive Signs:

Fit horses usually have bright shiny coats, coats that reflect sunlight on bright days. Fit horses are alert, but generally not fractious, or unnerved by the surroundings.

Horses that break from a walk to an easy trot into a smooth gait during the post parade are usually in fine shape and have racing on their minds.

Negative Signs

  * Unfit horses tend to have dull coats.

Horses that sweat profusely in cool weather are revealing an excessive nervousness.

Horses that sweat between their hindquarters — "kidney sweat" – also may reveal some nervousness. But, keep in mind that most horses will sweat on very humid, hot days.

Horses who walk "short" during the post parade should be watched during the pre-race warm-up for possible stiff-leggedness, or outright soreness. (Horses whose rear legs do not reach the hoof-prints of their front legs, are said to be "short-walking")Horses with a listless attitude, walking in the post parade under no restraint with their heads tilted lazily toward the ground – even when asked to pick it up – rarely are interested in racing.

Horses that stubbornly refuse to break out of a trot into an easy gallop during the warm-up period post parade should be watched carefully during the warm-up for possible soreness.

* Get fair odds for logical contenders.

Prominent contenders are preferred bets when the odds are generous. Marginal contenders offer little value at low odds. Horses attempting to do something they never have done before – such as a radically new distance, or racing surface – usually are poor bets at short odds. Horses attempting to do something they never have done before, but are bred to handle the situation and are trained by ace trainers with a history of success, are worth strong consideration at generous odds. Horses with multiple losses at the same level and class are poor risks at low odds.

Lightly raced, seemingly fit horses with a probable preference for today's distance and racing surface (as gleaned from their bloodlines, or previous running style, or their respective trainer's known proficiencies) are among the type of horse most likely to improve over previous performances. In other words, this type of horse has the greatest overall potential to outrun relatively moderate or longshot odds.

CLASS and BEYER FIGURES:

Because faster horses run for higher purses, there definitely is a relationship between the Beyer Scale and class levels. Here are some general guidelines that have proven to be true for many years.

The best horses in the country typically earn Beyer Figures from 110 and up.

Good allowance horses or low-grade stakes horses tend to run in the high 90's and low 100's.

A typical $25,000 claiming race usually is run in the low 90s, while $10,000 claiming races tend to earn Beyer Figures in the low to mid-80.

The average winning figure for bottom-level $2,500 claimers at smaller tracks is 57.

Fillies and mares tend to earn Beyer Figures about eight points lower at each class level.

Two-year-olds earn increasingly faster Beyer Figures as they progress through the year, due to obvious maturation and development. The same is true for 3-year-olds as they proceed through their sophomore seasons, into the very early stages of their 4-year-old racing year.

Races restricted to horses bred in a given state tend to earn lower Beyer Figures than "open" races, or races open to all horses.

DAILY RACING FORM's SPEED RATING AND TRACK VARIANTS:
In addition to the Beyer Speed Figures which have been included in Daily Racing Form past performances since 1992, Daily Racing Form also has included its own SPEED RATING and TRACK VARI-
ANT for more than 60 years. The Daily Racing Form Speed Rating provides an alternative means to
gauge a horse's speed in a race. The Speed Rating is a comparison of a horse's final time with the best
time at the distance at that track in the last three years.

HOW DAILY RACING FORM COMPUTES ITS SPEED RATINGS:
The best time at each distance at a given racetrack during the past three years is given a rating of 100.
In any race at that distance at that track, one point will be deducted from 100 for each fifth of a second
by which a given horse fails to equal that time.
Example: In a race where the winner equals the 3 year-best time for a given distance, (100, Speed
Rating), another horse beaten 12 lengths in the same race will get a Speed Rating of 88 (100 minus 12).
As a companion to the Speed Rating, Daily Racing Form's Track Variant takes into consideration all
races run on a particular day under the same conditions of distance and track surface.

HOW DAILY RACING FORM COMPUTES ITS TRACK VARIANTS:
First, the Speed Ratings of all winners in each type of race are added together and an average is computed.
Next, the average is deducted from the par of 100 and the difference is the daily Track Variant.
Example: If the average Speed Rating of winners sprinting on the main track is 86, the Track Variant is
14 (par of 100 minus 86.) Thus, the lower the Track Variant, the faster the track, or perhaps the better
the overall quality of competition that day.

FOREIGN RACES IN DAILY RACING FORM PAST PERFORMANCES LINES.
Daily Racing Form's foreign past performance lines provide exclusive handicapping features not available elsewhere. These features include TIMEFORM RATINGS and refined course conditions needed to
interpret the form of the ever-increasing number of horses being imported from Europe, South
America, New Zealand, Australia, and elsewhere around the world.

Timeform Rating - The race-by-race rating compiled by Britain's most prestigious handicapping
experts at Timeform. Available for races run in Britain, Ireland, and France and some races in Italy,
Germany, and the Pacific Rim. A formula of Timeform rating minus 13 is used to determine an approximate Beyer Speed Figure. (Due to the growing popularity of international racing, Timeform now
includes ratings for America's top horses among its ratings for older horses.)

Track Conditions - Instead of the past practice of labeling a European racing surface "good" to cover
myriad course conditions, Daily Racing Form's foreign track conditions now range from "hard" all the
way down to "heavy."

Course Direction - Foreign courses vary widely in comparison to American tracks, with some races
run on left-handed courses (LH), some on right-handed courses (RH), and some on straight courses
(Str)

Class of Race and Purse - Races are designated as a Stakes (Stk), Handicap (Hcp), Allowance (Alw),
Claiming (Clm), Maiden, Maiden-first time starters (Mdn-FT), or Maiden Claiming, and the total purse
value or claiming price is shown in U.S. dollars.

Race Name and Description - The full race name is given along with its class ranking, as in Group 1,
2, 3, or listed race, an apprentice riders race, or amateur riders race, a ladies race, an auction race, etc.

First Three Finishers - Names are printed in full along with weights and margins, including the margin between third and fourth.

Detailed running line comment - This feature lets you know how the horse was running at every
stage of the race, where he was positioned, trouble if any and how he finished. If the track condition
compromised his chances it would be noted. In addition, if a notable horse or horses in the race finished
out of the first three, the name and finishing position also will be noted.

DRF/NTRA Handicapping Championship–2003–04

By Noel Michaels

LAS VEGAS - Kent Meyer intended to leave Las Vegas early to fly back to Iowa on Saturday night, but his plans quickly changed when the *Daily Racing Form* and the NTRA gave him 100,000 reasons to stick around. Meyer topped a field of 261 of the best horseplayers from around the country to win the fifth annual DRF/NTRA National Handicapping Championship, which concluded on Saturday, Jan. 24 at Bally's - Las Vegas.

Meyer, a 38-year-old landlord from Sioux City, Iowa, won first prize of $100,000 and earned the crown of DRF/NTRA Handicapper of the Year for 2004. Total prize money for the two-day event was a record $240,000.

"I changed my flight to Sunday," Meyer said. "I hadn't counted on winning the thing."

Meyer got out of the gate quickly in the two-day national handicapping finals, hitting a bet on the tournament's first long-odds winner, Jersey Gia, who paid $35 to win and $16.80 to place in Friday's second race at Aqueduct. Meyer then remained in the top three in the standings throughout the tournament thanks to a total of 10 winners in the 30-race contest.

Meyer, who describes himself as an avid horseplayer who is rarely seen not carrying a Racing Form, compiled a contest-winning total of $238.40 based on mythical $2 win-and-place bets on 15 races per day on each day of the two-day contest. The total was good enough to outduel runner-up David Krosunger of Team Monmouth/Meadowlands, who finished a close second with $232.60. Krosunger, a 43-year-old print shop manager from Wallington, Penn., led at the end of day one and at various other times during the contest before settling for the second prize of $40,000.

Eight races each day were mandatory plays and the remaining seven were optional plays on the races from several tracks including Aqueduct, Golden Gate (limited), Gulfstream, Laurel, Oaklawn, Sam Houston (limited), Santa Anita, Turf Paradise, and Turfway (limited). Meyer made only $3.20 in Friday's mandatory plays but crushed his seven optional plays with five winners and $132.40 in total earnings on day one. He then won five more races and $106 on Saturday including Farnum Alley in race five at Gulfstream ($35.20 to win, $10 to place) to cement the victory.

"I usually look at a race and see if I think I can beat the favorite, and you're always looking for prices in tournaments," Meyer said. "My horses weren't finishing second. When my horses were up there they were all winning, and that's probably why I won the tournament."

Meyer was making his second straight National Handicapping Championship appearance after qualifying for the second time at the Bettor Racing OTB in Sioux Falls, South Dakota. He used last year's trip to Las Vegas as an opportunity to elope and ended up finishing 32nd in NHC IV two days later.

After the top two, it was more than $20 back to third-place finisher Randy Franklin, of Scottsdale, Ariz., who finished with $210.70. Franklin, 47, is a former long-time Daily Racing Form handicapper who now works as a money-runner for an Arizona casino. Franklin qualified at Turf Paradise's December tournament and then stuck mainly to playing Turf Paradise in the optional races to compile his tournament total.

The top five was rounded out by Martha Carl of Los Angeles with $201.10 and Brendan Leehy from Omaha, Neb. with $138.40. Carl won $8,000 in prize money. Leehy took home $5,000.

The sixth- through 10th-place finishers all won $2,000 in prize money. They were Brent Shigenaka, Ralph Buston, John Hirsch, Mark Peeples and Larry Kaplan.

Players also competed as members of four-person teams in a separate team contest based on where they qualified. The championship-winning team hailed from Colonial Downs. The quartet of Henry Damgaard, Dave Durkin, Berkley Kern and John Vitale totaled $542.60 and won first prize of $25,000 ($6,250 each). Teams from Horsemen's Park ($499.90) and Arlington ($493.10) finished second and third. The Horsemen's Park team won $10,000 ($2,500 each), while Arlington won $5,000 ($1,250 each).

A media charity contest was also hosted and mirrored the main event. The winners of $10,000 for charity were Team TV, which consisted of Todd Schrupp and Frank Lyons of TVG, and Jeff Medders and Randy Moss of ESPN and was captained by Dave Tuley from the Daily Racing Form.

OFFICIAL NTRA/DRF HANDICAPPING CHAMPIONSHIP STANDINGS

TOP 10 FINISHERS	TEAM	TOURNAMENT BANKROLL	FINAL PRIZE
1st Kent Meyer	Sioux City, Iowa	$238.40	$100,000
2nd David Krosunger	Wallington, Penn.	$232.60	$40,000
3rd Randy Franklin	Scottsdale, Ariz.	$210.70	$15,000
4th Martha Carl	Los Angeles, Calif.	$201.10	$8,000
5th Brendan Leehy	Omaha, Neb.	$183.40	$5,000
6th Brent Shigenaka	Alta Loma, Calif.	$178.20	$2,000
7th Ralph Buston	Auburn, Wash.	$172.60	$2,000
8th John Hirsch	Leesburg, Virginia	$171.40	$2,000
9th Mark Peeples	Rancho Sta. Margarita, Cal.	$167.80	$2,000
10th Larry Kaplan	Northbrook, Ill.	$167.20	$2,000

OFFICIAL 'TEAM' RESULTS

WINNING TEAM	TOTAL	PRIZE
1-Colonial Downs	$542.60	$25,000
2-Horsemen's Park	$499.90	$10,000
3-Arlington Park	$493.10	$5,000

DAY ONE-BONUSES (Awarded for leading first day)

HANDICAPPER	TEAM	TOTAL	PRIZE
1-David Krosunger	Monmouth/Meadowlands	$151.20	$3,000
2-Kent Meyer	Bettor Racing OTB	$132.40	$2,000
3-Martha Carl	Oak Tree at Santa Anita	$123.10	$1,000

DAY TWO-BONUSES (Awarded for leading second day)

HANDICAPPER	TEAM	TOTAL	PRIZE
1-Larry Kaplan	Arlington Park	$146.60	$3,000
2-John Hirsch	Maryland Jockey Club	$138.00	$2,000
3-Ross Gallo	Autotote On The Wire	$135.20	$1,000

DRF/NTRA handicapping champion Kent Meyer (center) with DRF publisher Steven Crist (left) and Keith Chamblin of the NTRA (right).

2003 Qualifiers for the NTRA-DRF National Handicapping Championship
Finals held at Bally's Hotel in Las Vegas, January 2004.

Qualiying Tournaments	Qualifiers			
Feb. 6-8 Reno Hilton	1) Tim Hunt	2) Frank Purkart	3) Joe Kristufek	4) Mike Labriola
Feb. 9-10 Sports Haven	1) Arthur Peters	2) Robert Englander		
Feb. 15-16 Portland Meadows	1) Steve Jackson			
Feb. 28-Mar. 2 Gulfstream Park	1) Kelly Phillips	2) Louis Filoso	3) Dominic Gillotti	4) Brant Allen
Feb. 8-Mar. 15 Tampa Bay Downs	1) Michael Curie	2) Richard Zimmer		
March 15-16 Portland Meadows	1) Bill Marquis			
March 30 Turfway Park	1) Richard Nilsen	2) Sidney Sea		
April 12-13 Portland Meadows	1) Sean Felix			
April 19 Autotote	1) Paul Shurman			
April 18-19 Bally's Moolah	1) Andrew Osborne			
April 19-27 Brisnet	1) Robert Swickard	2) William Stevens	3) Jack Canon	4) Mike Javert
April 6 Laurel	1) Joanne Zielinski	2) Tim O'Leary		
May 2-4 Haw/Nat Jock. Club	1) Rudy Benes	2) Dennis Peterson	3) Don Wright	4) Kay Schriks
Feb.15-May 3 Canterbury	1) John Jaworski			
May 10 Horsemen's Park	1) Wes Watson			
May 31 River Downs	1) Bill Weber 2) Bill O'Neal			
May 31 Bettor Racing OTB	1) H. Mitchell Schuman	2) Tim Stupka	3) Dom Ippolito	4) Kent Meyer
June 14 Delaware Park	1) Shilo Merwitz	2) David Linker		
June 14 Prairie Meadows	1) Mark Brumm	2) Suzanne Nadermann		
June 14-15 Lone Star Park	1) Shelley Hayden	2) Thomas Blosser	3) Dennis Tiernan	4) Marc Gordon
June 20-21 Reno Hilton	1) Larry Hodin	2) Dane Moore	3) Dave Snyder	4) Richard Witt
June 21-22 Belmont Park	1) Joseph Mariconda	2) Patrick Ingram	3) John Russo	4) Mark Fisher
May 7-Jun. 25 Churchill Downs	1) Kyle Bailey	2) Mike Davis		
June 28 Colonial Downs	1) Dave Durkin	2) Berkley Kern Jr.	3) Henry Damgaard	4) John Vitale
July 12 River Downs	1) Jobby Blevins	2) Terri Petty		
July 12-13 Bradley Teletheater	1) John Kopacz	2) Paul Stath		
July 18 Los Alamitos	1) Mark Peeples	2) Paul Truelove	3) John Kayden	4) Anita Papst
July 19 Autotote	1) Dennis Sudul			
July 19 Claiming Crown	1) Jimmy Wells	2) Carolann Zabrouski	3) Henry Collins	4) Douglas Radt
July 25 Ellis Park	1) Rick Strinko			
July 27 Emerald Downs	1) Dave Crabill	2) Claude Davey	3) Michael McNeely	4) Jim Acker
	5) Ralph Buston	6) Nadine Buston	7) Casey Dotson	8) George Strausser
	9) Dave Breuniger	10) Selena Youngman	11) Susan Minshull	12) Joe Pastor
August 1-2 Bally's	1) Brent Shigenaka	2) Bobby Brendler	3) Joe Hinson	
August 2 Keeneland	1) Don Devereaux	2) Jerry Wallace	3) Levi Jasper	4) Jeff Kemper
	5) Bob Ramos			
August 2-3 Sunland Park	1) Mark Senteney	2) Mack McClyment	3) Don Speaks	4) Brian MacClowry
August 8 Ellis Park	1) Robert Schindler			
August 9 Finish Line OTB	1) Howard Dennis	2) Joseph Pepe	3) Chris Savage	
August 9 Suffolk Downs	1) Tony Linares, Jr.	2) Paul Weizer		
August 9-10 Canterbury Park	1) Kim Lettengarver	2) Dave Rasmussen		
August 10 Hawthorne Ill. OTB	1) David Gutfreund	2) Joseph Mudy		
August 22 Ellis Park	1) Travis Culver	2) David Petkovsek		
August 23 Retama Park	1) Calvin Slater	2) Brad Hillman		
August 23-24 Woodbine	1) Phil Werkmeister	2) Stephen Diaz	3) Jack Mahdessian	4) Steve Meyer
August 28-30 Canterbury Park	1) Dan Lynch	2) Paul Navratil	3) John Lynch	4) Wayne Starman
August 21 Cal Expo	1) Andrew Molgilev	2) Robert Bertolucci	3) Theodore Pantages	4) Louis Anagnos
August 30 Monmouth Park	1) Ken Lanyon	2) David Krosunger		
August 30 Horsemen's Park	1) Steve Merrill			

Aug. 20–30 AQHA	1) Mark Bertolucci		
Sept. 6 Twin Spires Club	1) Hy Bueller		
Sept. 6 Prairie Meadows	1) Patrick Lamoreaux	2) James Jarvis	
July 26–Sep. 7 Del Mar on–track	1) Doris Allen	2) John Campana	3) Lindsay Bonifacini
July 26–Sep. 7 Del Mar on–line	1) Michael Eberhard		
Sept. 6–7 Reno Hilton	1) Richard Prozanski	2) Filbea Arnould	3) Mike Mayo 4) Doug Craft
Sept. 6–7 Nat. Orange Show	1) Anthony Sbragia	2) Melissa Sbragia	3) Tom Mulligan 4) Darek Barton
May 5 –Sep. 9 AQHA Dash online	1) Robert L. Beacham		
May 5 –Sep. 9 AQHA Dash ontrack	1) Brett Shelton		
Sept. 13 Twin Spires Club	1) Carlos Chavez		
Sept. 20 Twin Spires Club	1) Mike Wilder		
Sept. 27 Twin Spires Club	1) Nick Compton		
Sept. 27 Retama Park	1) David "Trey" Stiles	2) Earl Wright	
Sept. 27 Arlington Park	1) James Coffey	2) Judith Gonsoulin	3) John Pappalardo 4) Larry Kaplan
Sept. 27 Horsemen's Park	1) Wayne Pearey		
Sept. 13–28 Fairplex	1) Eric Regnolds	2) Dan Trutanich	3) Dennis Decauwer 4) Louis Constan
Oct. 4 Canterbury Park	1) Pete Hill		
Oct. 4 Suffolk Downs	1) Gerard Oberle	2) Wayne Swanstrom	
Oct. 4 Delaware Park	1) John Zielinski, Sr.	2) Joan Houston	
Oct. 4 Sam Houston	1) Jerry Mantooth	2) Steve Lombardo	3) V.R. Daley 4) Tom Elberson
Sep. 27–Oct.11 NTRA/ BC	1) Krzysztof Zawierucha	2) Brady Kosic	3) Doug Smith 4) Gloria Atok
Oct. 11 Horsemen's Park	1) Brendan Leehy		
Oct. 11 Autotote	1) Ross Gallo		
Oct. 12 Hawthorne OTB	1) Bob Wonogas	2) Liz Pold	
Oct. 19 Hastings Racecourse	1) Tom Quan	2) Frasier Rawlinson	3) Owen Hayward 4) Marilla Baird
Nov. 1 Thistledown	1) Jack Wonkovich	2) Shirley Golod	3) Rob Hulsinger 4) David Greene
Nov. 1 Valley Race Park	1) Judy Wagner	2) Bryan Wagner	3) Sally Wang 4) Jay Jones
Nov. 1 Meadowlands	1) Helaine Barash	2) Joseph Scanio	
Nov. 1 AQHA Challenge	1) Stacey L. Wagner		
Sep. 28–Nov. 1 Santa Anita	1) Benny Espinoza	2) Martha Carl	3) Christina Estrada 4) Walter McKee
Aug. 29–Nov. 2 Bay Meadows	1) Cary Martin	2) Ka Man	3) Jennifer Nelson 4) Roger Park
Nov. 15–16 Portland Meadows	1) Kathleen McKee		
Nov. 15–16 Aqueduct	1) Ron Rippey	2) Sal Decarlo	3) William Jackson 4) Darrell Lerner
Oct. 29–Nov. 19 Churchill Downs	1) Robert Breitbeil	2) Raymond Miller	
Nov. 22 Laurel	1) John Hirsch	2) James Koennel	
Nov. 22–23 Remington Park	1) Patti Stevens	2) Jeff Henderson	3) Mike Litowkin 4) Robert Chandler
Nov. 28–30 Hawthorne	1) Robert Gardiner	2) Steven Walker	3) Gloria Slivensky 4) Robert Cochran
Nov. 28–30 Hollywood Park	1) Manuel Rodriguez	2) Jesus Quinoy	3) Gary Goldberg 4) Moshe Shaby
April–Dec. Fair Meadows	1) Kelly Kirby	2) Jack Armstrong	3) Britt Wasson 4) Harry Brook
Dec. 6 Keeneland	1) Daven Turner	2) Jackie Catron	3) Eric Isaacson 4) Bruce Ellison
	5) Gary Templeton	6) Joe Riddell	7) Donna Henry
Dec. 6–7 Fair Grounds	1) Charles Austin	2) William Gonsoulin	3) John Ray 4) James Tunick
	5) Jody Ortego		
Dec. 13 Autotote	1) Steve Wolfson Sr.		
Dec. 13 TVG	1) Fred Hirano	2) Philip Maniatty	3) Juan Lopez 4) Nicholas Grant
Dec. 13 Hoosier Park	1) Ron Kaufmann	2) Bill Downes	3) Mike Elsass 4) Marilyn Broerman
Dec. 13–14 Turf Paradise	1) Charley Witt	2) Lacy Farley	3) Steve Hendricks 4) Howard Hong
	5) Thomas Watrous	6) Howie Falco	7) William Shurman 8) Randy Franklin
Dec. 14 Tampa Bay Downs	1) Gerry Daube	2) Linda Scott	
Dec. 14 Turfway Park	1) Ron Hopkins	2) John Boswell	
Nov. 5–Dec. 21 Golden Gate	1) Zina Smith	2) Kenneth Fregien	3) Sam Edmonds 4) James Wiley
Defending Champion	Steve Wolfson Jr.		

2003 Stakes
and
Graded Stakes
Histories

North American Stakes Run in 2003

Stakes	Date	Race	Trk	Dist/Surf		Winner	Jockey	Gross	Value to winner
AArundelG3	15-Nov-03	8	LRL	1 1/8M	D	Smooth Maneuvers	Pino,Mario	100,000	60,000
AcademyRd	14-Mar-03	7	SA	1M	T	Singletary	Flores,David	103,600	48,660
AccordantH	8-Nov-03	8	MED	6F	D	Mighty Oak	Bridgmohan,Shaun	40,000	24,000
ACFSpeed	30-Mar-03	4	SAF	4F	D	Brooksbobnbucky	Karr,Stephen	2,115	1,184
ACFSpeed	30-Mar-03	6	SAF	4F	D	Jack Dugan	Nuttall,Todd	2,116	1,185
AchievmtH	30-Mar-03	8	WO	6F	D	Majestic Wisdom	Montpellier,Constant	161,100	96,660
AckAckH	31-May-03	8	HOL	7 1/2F	D	Joey Franco	Valenzuela,Patrick	100,325	60,275
AckAckHG3	26-Oct-03	9	CD	7 1/2F	D	Cappuchino	Court,Jon	165,450	102,579
ACKempH	17-Sep-03	8	ALB	7F	D	Hi Teck Man	Coates,Jimmy	32,400	19,440
AcornG1	6-Jun-03	10	BEL	1M	D	Bird Town	Prado,Edgar	250,000	150,000
AdenaTrfSp	30-Aug-03	7	RP	5F	D	Nine Pines	Zambrana,David	36,600	21,000
AdirondkG2	11-Aug-03	8	SAR	6 1/2F	D	Whoopi Cat	Prado,Edgar	150,000	90,000
AfectnyHG3	11-Jan-03	8	AQU	1 1/16M	D	Zonk	Lopez,Charles	109,600	65,760
AffirmdHG3	22-Jun-03	3	HOL	1 1/16M	D	Eye of the Tiger	Solis,Alex	105,200	63,120
Affirmed	7-Jun-03	6	BEL	1M	D	Alchemilla	Velazquez,John	65,900	39,540
Afleet	21-Jun-03	4	WO	6F	D	Battlements	Kabel,Todd	106,000	63,600
AfrcnPrnce	29-Mar-03	7	SUF	6F	D	Jill's Layup	Hole,Taylor	35,000	21,000
Agassiz	23-Aug-03	7	ASD	1M	D	Silver Greek	Gardiner,Timothy	35,000	22,105
AGleamHG2	13-Jul-03	4	HOL	7F	D	Cee's Elegance	Espinoza,Victor	250,000	150,000
AgonTfSpG3	2-May-03	7	CD	5F	T	Fiscally Speaking	Court,Jon	115,300	71,486
AGVndbtHG2	10-Aug-03	9	SAR	6F	D	Private Horde	Lumpkins,Jason	200,000	120,000
Airline	5-Jul-03	10	LAD	6F	D	Watchem Smokey	Simington,Donald	50,000	30,000
AlabamaBel	19-Sep-03	4	LAD	6F	D	Comalagold	Melancon,Gerard	35,000	19,950
AlabamaG1	16-Aug-03	9	SAR	1 1/4M	D	Island Fashion	Velazquez,John	750,000	450,000
AlAlngBCG3	12-Jul-03	9	CNL	1 1/8M	T	Dress To Thrill (IRE)	Prado,Edgar	200,000	120,000
AlamedanH	6-Jul-03	11	PLN	1 1/16M	D	Surprise Halo	Castro,Joe	50,800	27,600
Albany	20-Aug-03	8	SAR	1 1/8M	D	Traffic Chief	Santos,Jose	168,250	100,950
AlbanyH	8-Nov-03	3	GG	6F	D	More Crafty	Radke,Kevin	78,350	33,350
AlbDerby	14-Sep-03	8	ALB	1 1/16M	D	Novel T Dreamer	Coates,Jimmy	32,000	19,200
AlbDerby	7-Jun-03	8	ALB	1 1/16M	D	Fame Ina Minute	Tohill,Ken	43,000	25,800
AlbertaBrd	13-Sep-03	8	LBG	6F	D	Alberta Energy	Sterr,Scott	11,050	6,078
AlbertaBrd	28-Sep-03	9	LBG	7F	D	Guiltybysupiscion	Sterr,Scott	11,050	6,078
AlbertaBrd	13-Sep-03	7	LBG	5F	D	Wintuition	Landaker,Terri	11,050	6,078
AlbertaBrd	13-Sep-03	9	LBG	6F	D	Arctic Horizon	Sterr,Scott	11,200	6,160
AlbertaBrH	20-Sep-03	7	NP	1 1/16M	D	Regal Ability	Hamel,Richard	50,000	31,500
AlbertaOak	20-Sep-03	2	NP	1M	D	A Shaky Start	Painter,Leanne	50,000	31,500
AlBoganMem	28-Jun-03	6	LS	1M	D	Eagle Lake	Melancon,Gerard	75,000	45,000
AlbPremFut	20-Sep-03	6	NP	1M	D	Fly Esteem	Bryan,Desmond	50,000	31,500
AlbrtDbyG3	14-Jun-03	9	STP	1 1/16M	D	Taiaslew	Simard,Real	100,000	63,000
AlcibiadG2	3-Oct-03	9	KEE	1 1/16M	D	Be Gentle	Velasquez,Cornelio	400,000	248,000
ALErwin	15-Aug-03	10	LAD	7F	D	Lac Laronge	Melancon,Gerard	60,000	36,000
AlexMRobbH	28-Dec-03	8	AQU	1 1/16M	D	Salute Him	Migliore,Richard	86,375	51,825
Algoma	1-Sep-03	4	WO	1 1/16M	D	One for Rose	Ramsammy,Emile	126,500	79,695
AllBrandy	6-Sep-03	9	PIM	1 1/8M	T	Cruise Along	Karamanos,Horacio	75,000	45,000
AllianceH	18-Oct-03	10	LAD	1 1/16M	T	Warleigh	Meche,Lonnie	40,000	24,000
AllnEPlsnH	23-Feb-03	7	GP	1M 70Y	D	Cellars Shiraz	Coa,Eibar	75,000	45,000
AllSoldOut	23-Sep-03	2	FP	6F	D	Lady Riss	Woodley,John	36,000	21,600
AlmaNorth	30-Aug-03	9	TIM	1 1/16M	D	Ribbon Cane	Rosenthal,Mark	50,000	30,000
AlmdaCoFMH	5-Jul-03	11	PLN	1 1/16M	D	Aunt Sophie	Gonzalez,Roberto	50,800	27,600
AlwysSilvr	17-Aug-03	10	CRC	6F	D	The Name's Bond	Cruz,Manoel	42,550	27,530
AlyshebaBC	5-Jul-03	9	LS	7F	D	Kool Humor	Martin, Jr.,Eddie	100,000	60,000
AlyssaH	3-May-03	7	BEU	6F	D	So Catty	Gonzalez,Ivan	21,000	9,000
Alywow	31-May-03	4	WO	6 1/2F	T	Hour of Justice	McAleney,James	110,000	66,000
AmadevilH	10-Aug-03	7	CLS	6F	D	Bad Boy Yankee	Collins,Dennis	15,000	9,000
AmbasOLckH	30-Aug-03	6	PHA	7F	D	Run for Joy	Bocachica,Orlando	50,000	30,000
AmercnDbG2	20-Jul-03	8	AP	1 3/16M	T	Evolving Tactics (IRE)	Smullen,Pat	250,000	150,000
AmercnOaks	5-Jul-03	5	HOL	1 1/4M	T	Dimitrova	Flores,David	750,000	450,000
AmericanaH	4-Jul-03	4	CRC	1 1/8M	T	Sea Pleasure	Castanon,Jesus	100,000	60,000
AmericnHG2	4-Jul-03	7	HOL	1 1/8M	T	Candy Ride (ARG)	Stevens,Gary	150,000	90,000
AMFsherDeb	16-Aug-03	9	ELP	7F	D	Sweet Jo Jo	Gonzalez, Jr.,Sal	100,000	45,000
AmliaPbody	4-Oct-03	3	SUF	6F	D	Ask Queenie	Sosa, Jr.,Peter	35,000	21,000

Stakes	Date	Race	Trk	Dist/Surf		Winner	Jockey	Gross	Value to winner
AmrcnBeuty	8-Feb-03	10	OP	6F	D	Emily Ring	Lopez,James	50,000	30,000
AmstrdamG2	2-Aug-03	8	SAR	6F	D	Zavata	Bailey,Jerry	150,000	90,000
AndrsnFwlr	20-Jul-03	9	MTH	5F	T	Only the Best	Cruz,Carlos	50,000	30,000
AnfDerby	18-Jul-03	9	ANF	7F	D	Diggs	Ludlow,Megan	6,400	3,000
AnfTbFut	20-Jul-03	11	ANF	5F	D	Kissin My Friends	Padilla,Juan	11,400	5,500
Angenora	19-Apr-03	13	TDN	6F	D	Alison's Winner	Felix,Julio	40,000	24,000
AngieC	12-Jul-03	9	EMD	6F	D	Melba Jewel	Baze,Gary	38,500	19,058
AngiGo	19-Jul-03	3	BOI	7F	D	Crossfire Trail	Webb,Robert	10,830	6,498
AngiGo	7-Apr-03	9	TUP	1M	D	Deja	Ziegler,Michael	24,514	14,280
AnnArbor	8-Aug-03	7	GLD	1M	D	Cassopolis	Martinez,Luis	45,000	27,000
Anoakia	19-Oct-03	8	SA	6F	D	Wind Flow	Nakatani,Corey	102,825	48,195
AnswerDo	28-Mar-03	7	TUP	6 1/2F	D	Heightenedinterest	Gomez,Esteban	24,920	14,400
AnthonyFrH	20-Jul-03	9	ANF	6 1/2F	D	Sunset Cruise	Latham,Jeremy	5,400	2,400
AnTtlBCHG1	5-Oct-03	7	SA	6F	D	Avanzado (ARG)	Baze,Tyler	210,625	81,375
AOwenDstfH	26-Apr-03	2	TUP	6F	D	Reatta Pass	Martinez,Seth	35,000	21,000
AplBlsmHG1	5-Apr-03	8	OP	1 1/16M	D	Azeri	Smith,Mike	500,000	300,000
Applachian	18-Apr-03	9	KEE	1M	T	Ocean Drive	Bailey,Jerry	111,300	69,006
AppletnHG2	4-Jan-03	10	GP	1M	T	Point Prince	Cruz,Manoel	150,000	90,000
AprisaH	17-Sep-03	10	FPX	6F	D	Thunder Bullet	Pedroza,Martin	50,000	27,500
AquHG3	18-Jan-03	8	AQU	1 1/16M	D	Snake Mountain	Luzzi,Michael	107,400	64,440
Arcadia	20-Jul-03	9	LAD	6F	D	Lac Laronge	Melancon,Gerard	50,000	30,000
ArcadiaHG2	6-Apr-03	7	SA	1 1/8M	T	Century City (IRE)	Valdivia, Jr.,Jose	150,000	90,000
AristdsHG3	21-Jun-03	9	CD	6 1/2F	D	Mountain General	Lanerie,Corey	109,000	67,580
ArizonaOak	1-Feb-03	8	TUP	1 1/16M	D	Harbor Blues	Puglisi,Ignacio	75,000	45,000
ArkDerbyG2	12-Apr-03	9	OP	1 1/8M	D	Sir Cherokee	Thompson,Terry	500,000	300,000
ArlClscG2	28-Jun-03	8	AP	1 1/16M	T	Lismore Knight	Douglas,Rene	175,000	105,000
ArlgtnHG3	26-Jul-03	9	AP	1 1/4M	T	Honor in War	Flores,David	250,000	150,000
ArlMllnG1	16-Aug-03	10	AP	1 1/4M	T	Sulamani (IRE)	Flores,David	1,000,000	600,000
ArlMtrnHG3	1-Sep-03	8	AP	1 1/8M	D	Take Charge Lady	Sellers,Shane	150,000	90,000
ArlSprintH	23-Aug-03	9	AP	6F	D	Out of My Way	Bourque,Curt	100,000	60,000
ArlWaFutG3	27-Sep-03	7	AP	1M	D	Cactus Ridge	Martin, Jr.,Eddie	150,000	90,000
ArlWaLasG3	27-Sep-03	9	AP	1M	D	Zosima	Day,Pat	100,000	60,000
ArpSprintH	15-Jun-03	8	ARP	6F	D	Mr. Tipsy	Dieguez,Wilson	35,000	21,000
ArtaxH	5-Apr-03	9	GP	7F	D	Highway Prospector	Velasquez,Cornelio	100,000	60,000
ArtcQueenH	9-Aug-03	8	FL	6F	D	Ora	Badamo,Joseph	35,000	21,000
AscotGrad	19-Oct-03	8	HST	1 1/16M	D	Joyride	Loseth,Chris	120,650	72,390
AscotH	10-May-03	8	BM	1 1/16M	T	Just Wonder (GB)	Baze,Russell	100,000	55,000
AsDOaks	7-Sep-03	7	ASD	1 1/16M	D	Stolen Sheena	Hightower,Travis	35,000	21,000
AshlandG1	5-Apr-03	8	KEE	1 1/16M	D	Elloluv	Albarado,Robby	551,750	342,085
ASkirball	23-Nov-03	8	HOL	1 1/8M	T	Fencelineneighbor	Valenzuela,Patrick	94,400	45,400
AspenCupH	21-Jun-03	9	RUI	6F	D	Jewels for a Lady	Clark,Michael	31,100	18,660
AspenH	20-Jul-03	8	ARP	6F	D	Debatable	Gonsalves,Frank	35,000	21,000
AspidistrH	23-Aug-03	11	CRC	1M	D	Sara's Success	Castro,Eddie	100,000	60,000
Aspirant	16-Aug-03	8	FL	6F	D	Rb's Glitter	Gryder,Aaron	77,513	46,508
Assault	28-Jun-03	9	LS	1 1/16M	D	Rare Cure	Perrodin,Elvis	100,000	60,000
AstaritaG2	12-Oct-03	10	BEL	6 1/2F	D	Spectacular Moon	Chavez,Jorge	150,000	90,000
Astoria	29-Jun-03	9	BEL	5 1/2F	D	Feline Story	Chavez,Jorge	108,300	64,980
ASwihrtMmH	3-May-03	9	FON	6 1/2F	D	Burning Memories	Compton,Perry	27,500	15,000
ATBASales	18-May-03	9	TUP	5F	D	Bugsy Marrone	Ziegler,Michael	54,954	30,530
ATBASales	18-Oct-03	8	TUP	6F	D	Snowbound Writer	Bridges,Kelly	88,569	30,455
ATBASales	18-Oct-03	7	TUP	6F	D	Bugsy Marrone	Ziegler,Michael	85,142	28,551
ATColeH	20-Sep-03	8	BEL	1 1/8M	D	Quantum Merit	Migliore,Richard	114,700	68,820
AtcTopSFeH	25-Oct-03	7	WDS	6F	D	Jack Black and Ice	Vasquez,Richard	20,000	12,000
AtheniaHG3	8-Nov-03	9	AQU	1 1/16M	T	Caught in the Rain	Migliore,Richard	113,000	67,800
AthertonH	19-Apr-03	3	BM	6F	D	Presidio Heights	Gonzalez,Roberto	78,400	33,400
AttoMileG1	14-Sep-03	9	WO	1M	T	Touch of the Blues (FR)	Desormeaux,Kent	1,000,000	600,000
Auburn	3-May-03	9	EMD	6F	D	Unyielding	Baze,Gary	35,000	19,250
AudubonOak	2-Aug-03	9	ELP	1M	D	Keiai Sakura	McKee,John	75,000	46,250
AuldLngSyn	31-Dec-03	10	CRC	1 1/16M	D	All the Honor	Castro,Eddie	40,650	26,390
AuntieMame	29-Jun-03	10	BEL	1M	T	Something Ventured	Velasquez,John	65,850	39,510
AuRevoir	23-Mar-03	5	DED	5F	D	Mike 'n Doc	Clark,Kerwin	50,000	30,000
AuRevoirH	10-Aug-03	10	BOI	1M	D	Almost Golden	Packer,Berkley	6,700	4,020

Stakes	Date	Race	Trk	Dist/Surf		Winner	Jockey	Gross	Value to winner
AuRevoirH	6-Jul-03	9	GRP	1 1/16M	D	Handy Man Jeff	Mercado,Victor	3,300	1,834
AutmnDzH	1-Sep-03	9	YD	1M 70Y	D	Staged Reality	Kingrey,Russell	3,750	1,875
AutmnLvesH	30-Aug-03	3	BM	1M	T	Lindsay Jean	Schvaneveldt,Chad	78,750	33,750
AutumnCls	8-Nov-03	7	RP	7F	D	Zee Oh Six	Lester,Robert	37,800	22,180
AutumnLve	30-Sep-03	9	MNR	1 1/16M	D	Salzurita (ARG)	Walker, Jr.,Bobby	78,000	46,800
Aventura	5-Apr-03	11	GP	1 1/16M	D	Dynever	Prado,Edgar	250,000	150,000
Avigaition	9-Nov-03	8	SA	1 1/8M	T	Crazy Ensign (ARG)	Solis,Alex	95,150	44,490
Awad	8-Jun-03	8	AP	1M	D	Character Witness	Baird,E.	47,400	28,440
AwatukeExp	4-Oct-03	7	TUP	6F	D	Tulsa	Bridges,Kelly	35,000	21,000
Azalea	15-Mar-03	7	DED	6F	D	Kwik Kash	Cormier,Logan	50,000	30,000
AzaleaBCG3	12-Jul-03	9	CRC	6F	D	Ebony Breeze	Velasquez,Cornelio	300,000	176,000
AZBrdrDrby	26-Apr-03	10	TUP	1 1/16M	D	Moody Slew	Colledge,Cameron	51,903	27,141
AzBrdrFut	29-Nov-03	6	TUP	6F	D	Rockin On	Corbett,Glenn	40,742	21,259
AzBrdrFut	29-Nov-03	7	TUP	6F	D	Steady Breeze	Corbett,Glenn	44,674	23,310
AzCntFrSpd	13-Apr-03	7	DG	5 1/2F	D	Jack Dugan	Nuttall,Todd	2,117	1,185
AzCntFrSpd	13-Apr-03	5	DG	5 1/2F	D	Brooksbobnbucky	Karr,Stephen	2,092	1,171
AZCntSpeed	27-Apr-03	8	SON	5 1/2F	D	Jack Dugan	Nuttall,Todd	2,058	1,153
AzJuvenile	20-Dec-03	7	TUP	6 1/2F	D	Bold Merit	Gomez,Esteban	50,000	30,000
AzStallion	18-May-03	2	TUP	7 1/2F	T	Newark	Martinez,Seth	35,003	19,446
AztecOaks	23-Nov-03	4	SRP	6 1/2F	D	Bounzuz	Hunt,Charleen	69,400	41,640
BabyDoeH	27-Jul-03	9	ARP	7F	D	Cherylville Slew	Quinonez,Luis	35,850	21,510
Bachman	22-Feb-03	8	FON	4F	D	Bevys Affair	Carkeek,Jerome	11,900	7,140
BaldwinG3	23-Feb-03	8	SA	6 1/2F	T	Buddy Gil	Stevens,Gary	114,550	68,730
Ballade	11-Jun-03	7	WO	6F	D	Brass in Pocket	Clark,David	128,875	77,325
BalrinaHG1	24-Aug-03	9	SAR	7F	D	Harmony Lodge	Migliore,Richard	250,000	150,000
Bangls&Bds	23-Sep-03	8	FPX	6 1/2F	D	Spring Meadow	Pedroza,Martin	50,000	27,500
BaraLass	15-Nov-03	2	HOU	7F	D	Sago	Beasley,Jeremy	50,000	30,000
BarCTBATrf	25-Jan-03	2	SA	1 1/8M	T	Adminniestrator	Flores,David	500,000	262,900
BarksdaleH	9-Aug-03	9	LAD	1 1/16M	T	Crook	Jacinto,John	50,000	30,000
BaronaCupH	23-Aug-03	3	DMR	1M	T	Fencelineneighbor	Valdivia, Jr.,Jose	98,850	45,810
BatlrStarH	9-Mar-03	8	FG	6F	D	Itsmybag	Lovato, Jr.,Frank	75,000	45,000
Battlfield	3-Aug-03	10	MTH	1 1/8M	T	Eltawaasul	Martin, Jr.,Eddie	75,000	45,000
Baxter	15-Mar-03	9	FON	6 1/2F	D	Plain Ole John	Carkeek,Jerome	17,250	9,450
Bayakoa	6-Apr-03	10	OP	1 1/16M	D	McKinney	Marquez, Jr.,Carlos	50,000	30,000
BayakoaHG2	7-Dec-03	8	HOL	1 1/16M	D	Star Parade (ARG)	Espinoza,Victor	150,000	90,000
BayouBCH	1-Mar-03	9	FG	1 1/8M	T	Quick Tip	Albarado,Robby	150,000	90,000
BayouCity	25-Jan-03	8	HOU	6F	D	Valid Pulpit	Berry,Monte	35,000	21,000
Bayouland	1-Aug-03	4	LAD	5F	D	Irockdasauce	Carmouche, Jr.,Sylvester	27,500	16,500
BayouState	1-Feb-03	7	DED	7F	D	Oak Hall	LeBlanc,Kirk	75,000	45,000
BayShoreG3	12-Apr-03	7	AQU	7F	D	Halo Homewrecker	Velazquez,John	150,000	90,000
BBaruchHG2	25-Jul-03	8	SAR	1 1/8M	T	Trademark (SAF)	Migliore,Richard	150,000	90,000
BBlckMmDby	17-Aug-03	7	WYO	5 1/2F	D	Cheese Puff	Hamilton,Travis	7,200	4,320
BBRayburn	17-May-03	8	EVD	1M	D	Lota Prince	Tervort,Jason	35,000	21,000
BBrickerH	26-Oct-03	6	BEU	1 1/16M	D	Oh So Easy	Felix,Julio	40,000	24,000
BBrummel	16-Sep-03	8	FPX	6 1/2F	D	P Town John	Alvarado,Frank	50,000	27,500
BCallihanH	31-Aug-03	8	CLS	6 1/2F	D	Flaming Night	Granda,Alejandro	9,175	5,505
BCBCOaksG3	20-Sep-03	9	HST	1 1/8M	D	Raylene	Walcott,Rickey	191,150	104,940
BCClasicG1	25-Oct-03	9	SA	1 1/4M	D	Pleasantly Perfect	Solis,Alex	4,000,000	2,080,000
BCCpClassH	4-Aug-03	9	HST	1 1/8M	D	Lord Nelson	Fuentes,Francisco	72,436	43,462
BCCpDbutnt	4-Aug-03	3	HST	6 1/2F	D	Frozen in Time	Loseth,Chris	58,833	35,300
BCCpDisffH	4-Aug-03	8	HST	1 1/8M	D	Shelby Madison	Alvarado,Pedro	55,590	33,354
BCCpNursry	4-Aug-03	2	HST	6 1/2F	D	Proud Son	Krasner,Samuel	54,680	32,808
BCCpSprntH	4-Aug-03	6	HST	6 1/2F	D	Bold 'n Keen	Wright,Nicola	55,590	33,354
BCCupStalH	4-Aug-03	7	HST	1 1/16M	D	Roscoe Pito	Krasner,Samuel	55,590	33,354
BCDerbyG2	21-Sep-03	9	HST	1 1/8M	D	Roscoe Pito	Alvarado,Pedro	331,250	198,750
BCDistafG1	25-Oct-03	2	SA	1 1/8M	D	Adoration	Valenzuela,Patrick	2,000,000	1,040,000
BCF&MTrfG1	25-Oct-03	6	SA	1 1/4M	T	Islington (IRE)	Fallon,Kieren	1,060,000	551,200
BCJuvFilG1	25-Oct-03	3	SA	1 1/16M	D	Halfbridled	Krone,Julie	1,000,000	520,000
BckAGTfSpH	26-May-03	5	LS	5F	T	That Tat	Martin, Jr.,Eddie	100,000	60,000
BCLottoH	17-Aug-03	7	KAM	1M	D	Slew's Alibi	Bugeaud,Laurina	12,200	7,320
BCJvG1	25-Oct-03	7	SA	1 1/16M	D	Action This Day	Flores,David	1,500,000	780,000
BCMileG1	25-Oct-03	4	SA	1M	T	Six Perfections (FR)	Bailey,Jerry	1,500,000	780,000

Stakes	Date	Race	Trk	Dist/Surf		Winner	Jockey	Gross	Value to winner
BCrsbBCHG2	26-Jul-03	6	DMR	6F	D	Beau's Town	Valenzuela,Patrick	200,000	120,000
BCSprintG1	25-Oct-03	5	SA	6F	D	Cajun Beat	Velasquez,Cornelio	1,180,000	613,600
BCStallH	4-Aug-03	4	HST	1 1/16M	D	Dancewithavixen	Valdez,Felipe	55,720	33,432
BCTurfG1	25-Oct-03	8	SA	1 1/2M	T	High Chaparral (IRE)	Kinane,Michael	2,110,100	763,200
BCTurfG1	25-Oct-03	8	SA	1 1/2M	T	Johar	Solis,Alex	2,110,100	763,200
BCup	11-Oct-03	8	LBG	7F	D	Guiltybysupiscion	Sterr,Scott	11,200	6,160
BCup	18-Oct-03	9	LBG	7F	D	Arctic Horizon	Latchman,Rennie	11,200	6,160
BCup	11-Oct-03	7	LBG	6F	D	Bedford Road	Stianson,Janine	11,050	6,078
BCup	11-Oct-03	5	LBG	5 1/2F	D	Falstaffs's Jewel	Latchman,Rennie	11,200	6,160
BCup	11-Oct-03	9	LBG	1 1/8M	D	Candid Remark	Sterr,Scott	13,200	7,260
BCup	11-Oct-03	6	LBG	6F	D	Feudal Lady	Sterr,Scott	10,900	5,995
BCup	18-Oct-03	6	LBG	5 1/2F	D	Tahoe's Gem	Latchman,Rennie	11,200	6,160
BdGmgDltJk	5-Dec-03	8	DED	1 1/16M	D	Mr. Jester	Chapa,Roman	1,000,000	600,000
BdGmgDltPr	5-Dec-03	6	DED	1M	D	Salty Romance	Smith,Mike	250,000	150,000
BdORsBCHG3	19-Apr-03	9	AQU	1M	D	Raging Fever	Gryder,Aaron	156,600	93,960
BdrIndDby	2-Mar-03	11	SUN	1M	D	Mr. Decatur	Gonzalez, Jr.,Sal	104,100	62,460
Beaufort	20-Sep-03	8	NP	1 1/16M	D	Beau Brass	Wilson,David	50,000	31,500
BeaugayHG3	3-May-03	8	AQU	1 1/16M	T	Delta Princess	Luzzi,Michael	112,400	67,440
BeaumontG2	10-Apr-03	8	KEE	7F	D	My Boston Gal	Day,Pat	250,000	155,000
BeautDay	27-Sep-03	9	DEL	1 1/8M	D	Database	Dominguez,Ramon	59,100	35,460
BelBCHG2	13-Sep-03	7	BEL	1 1/8M	T	Della Francesca	Chavez,Jorge	209,600	125,760
BeldameG1	4-Oct-03	9	BEL	1 1/8M	D	Sightseek	Bailey,Jerry	750,000	450,000
BelleGeste	24-Aug-03	4	WO	1 1/8M	D	Heyahohowdy	Ramsammy,Emile	106,000	63,600
Bellemahne	2-Aug-03	6	WO	1 1/16M	D	Royal Dalliance	Somsanith,Na	108,000	64,800
BelmntDayH	7-Jun-03	6	EUR	7F	D	Won the Derby	Whittle,Stoney	5,550	2,880
BelmontDay	7-Jun-03	11	FMT	6 1/2F	D	Abbi's Choice	Carter, Jr.,G.	30,000	16,500
BelmontG1	7-Jun-03	11	BEL	1 1/2M	D	Empire Maker	Bailey,Jerry	1,000,000	600,000
BelRobrts	21-Sep-03	4	EMD	1 1/16M	D	Infernal McGoon	Gutierrez,Juan	50,000	25,000
BenAliG3	25-Apr-03	9	KEE	1 1/8M	D	Mineshaft	Albarado,Robby	110,300	68,386
Benburb	20-Jul-03	4	FE	1 1/16M	T	Geraint	Husbands,Patrick	68,900	41,340
BenCohen	24-May-03	9	PIM	5F	D	Native Heir	Wilson,Rick	75,000	30,000
BergenCo	24-Oct-03	8	MED	5F	T	College Honor	Santagata,Nick	40,000	24,000
BerkelyHG3	29-Mar-03	7	GG	1M	D	I'madrifter	Gonzalez,Roberto	100,000	55,000
BerniDowdH	19-Jul-03	9	MTH	6F	D	Sheryar Special	Glasser,Todd	50,000	30,000
Bersid	28-Dec-03	3	TUP	1M	T	Fanzoca	Ruis,Mick	21,700	13,020
BessarbHG3	16-Nov-03	8	WO	7F	D	Winter Garden	Clark,David	214,400	98,640
BestPalG2	17-Aug-03	2	DMR	6 1/2F	D	Perfect Moon	Valenzuela,Patrick	150,000	90,000
BestTurn	22-Feb-03	8	AQU	6F	D	Second in Command	Samyn,Jean-Luc	82,800	49,680
BetsyRoss	4-Jul-03	9	MTH	5F	T	Oh Say Vicki	Bravo,Joe	50,000	30,000
BettorInvH	4-Jul-03	8	GRP	6 1/2F	D	Dixie Drifter	Sanchez,Richard	4,975	2,736
BeverlyDG1	16-Aug-03	8	AP	1 3/16M	T	Heat Haze (GB)	Valdivia, Jr.,Jose	700,000	420,000
BevHilsHG2	28-Jun-03	8	HOL	1 1/4M	T	Voodoo Dancer	Nakatani,Corey	200,000	120,000
BewitchG3	24-Apr-03	8	KEE	1 1/2M	T	Lilac Queen (GER)	Bailey,Jerry	112,100	69,503
BFBongard	28-Sep-03	9	BEL	7F	D	Flagshipenterprise	Guidry,Mark	109,500	65,700
BFrtcheHG2	22-Feb-03	10	LRL	7F	D	Xtra Heat	Wilson,Rick	200,000	120,000
BgRedMileH	26-May-03	8	LNN	1M	D	High Dice	Collins,Dennis	15,550	9,330
BGSmithMem	16-Aug-03	8	SUF	1 1/16M	T	Boastful	Hampshire, Jr.,Josiah	35,000	21,000
BHarrison	25-Oct-03	9	HOO	1 1/16M	D	Mr. Mink	Pompell,Thomas	37,300	22,380
BienBien	11-Nov-03	7	HOL	1M	T	Special Rate	Valdivia, Jr.,Jose	93,450	43,470
Bienvenids	26-Sep-03	7	TUP	1M	D	Our Best Man	Stevens,Scott	21,900	13,140
BigJagH	6-Sep-03	3	BM	6F	D	My Captain	Duran,Francisco	78,450	33,450
BigSkyH	27-Jul-03	10	GF	1M 70Y	D	Slick Decision	Stubblefield,David	7,350	3,675
BiminiFlyr	15-Jun-03	5	CRC	1M	D	Win's Fair Lady	Homeister, Jr.,Rosemary	39,225	23,535
Birdcatchr	1-Sep-03	8	NP	6 1/2F	D	Tigger Bay	Painter,Leanne	50,000	31,500
BirdOfPay	30-Aug-03	8	NP	6 1/2F	D	Alta Aire	Walcott,Rickey	50,000	31,500
Birdonwire	11-Oct-03	6	CRC	6F	D	Wynn Dot Comma	Bailey,Jerry	75,000	41,000
BisonCity	1-Jul-03	8	FE	1 1/16M	D	Brattothecore	Barton,Jake	250,000	100,000
BisonCity	1-Jul-03	8	FE	1 1/16M	D	Seeking the Ring	Callaghan,Slade	250,000	100,000
BJohnsnMem	13-Jul-03	9	LS	1M	D	Pie N Burger	Theriot,Jamie	60,000	36,000
BkeyeNatve	10-Aug-03	11	RD	1 1/16M	D	Brother Darcy	Johnston,Jeff	40,000	24,000
BlackGoldH	11-Jan-03	9	FG	7 1/2F	T	Prince Alphie	Sellers,Shane	75,000	45,000
BlackMesa	25-Oct-03	7	RP	7F	D	Bayakoa's Image	Cogburn,Kevin	35,000	20,500

Stakes	Date	Race	Trk	Dist/Surf	Winner	Jockey	Gross	Value to winner
BlackMtnH	8-Mar-03	2	TUP	1 1/16M D	Ceetoit	Sorenson,Danny	35,000	21,000
BlackMtnH	6-Dec-03	8	TUP	1M D	Grimm	Drexler,Hoogie	35,000	21,000
BlackSwan	24-Sep-03	11	FPX	1 1/16M D	Church Editor	Pedroza,Martin	50,000	27,500
BlairsCove	4-Jul-03	8	CBY	1 1/16M D	Bassant	Martinez,Seth	37,250	22,350
BlazingSev	19-Jul-03	6	FE	6F D	Elegant Hunter	Poznansky,Neil	90,000	36,000
BlckTiAfrH	10-May-03	8	AP	1 1/8M D	Full Mandate	Douglas,Rene	100,000	60,000
BldVenturH	19-Jul-03	8	WO	6 1/2F D	Mulligan the Great	McAleney,James	138,500	83,100
BlffsDvdnd	7-Dec-03	9	CRC	5F T	Mooji Moo	Aguilar,Manuel	38,400	25,040
BlkEySsnG2	16-May-03	10	PIM	1 1/8M D	Roar Emotion	Velazquez,John	200,000	120,000
BlomfieldH	19-Oct-03	10	SRP	1M D	Personal Beau	Johnson,Bobby	32,900	19,740
BlrinaBCG3	11-Oct-03	8	HST	1 1/8M D	Dancewithavixen	Valdez,Felipe	192,200	100,320
BlSpaBCHG3	23-Aug-03	8	SAR	1 1/16M T	Stylish	Velazquez,John	213,400	128,040
BltmrBCHG3	19-Apr-03	9	PIM	1 1/8M D	P Day	Fogelsonger,Ryan	125,000	45,000
BlueGrasG1	12-Apr-03	9	KEE	1 1/8M D	Peace Rules	Prado,Edgar	750,000	465,000
BluegrassH	1-Jun-03	8	LNN	6F D	Real Intrusion	Carkeek,Jerome	11,000	6,600
BlueHen	1-Nov-03	8	DEL	1M D	Vogue Girl	Alvarado, Jr.,Roberto	100,000	60,000
BlueMntJuv	14-Nov-03	6	DEL	6F D	Lovely Afternoon	Sterling, Jr.,Larry	53,450	32,070
BlueNorthr	8-Jan-03	7	SA	1M T	Major Idea	Espinoza,Victor	98,800	45,780
BlueRidgeH	14-Jun-03	6	CT	4 1/2F D	Nick's Delight	Jawny,Alvaro	36,750	22,050
BlzngSword	25-Apr-03	5	CRC	7 1/2F T	Mr. Livingston	Cruz,Manoel	42,875	22,725
BlzngSword	25-Apr-03	8	CRC	7 1/2F T	Love the Game	Ferrer,Jose	42,900	27,740
BMBCHG3	27-Sep-03	6	BM	1 1/8M T	Mister Acpen (CHI)	Gonzalez,Roberto	200,000	55,000
BMBCSprHG3	7-Jun-03	3	BM	6F D	El Dorado Shooter	Schvaneveldt,Chad	150,000	82,500
BMDerbyG3	1-Nov-03	8	BM	1 1/8M T	Stanley Park	Saint-Martin,Eric	100,000	55,000
BMJuvenile	19-Oct-03	3	BM	1M D	Market Report	Schvaneveldt,Chad	78,500	43,400
BMLassie	2-Nov-03	3	BM	1M D	Very Vegas	Baze,Russell	78,400	33,400
BMOaks	14-Jun-03	6	BM	1 1/16M T	Amber Hills	Gonzalez,Roberto	83,850	50,100
BnaVstaHG2	17-Feb-03	7	SA	1M T	Final Destination (NZ)	Espinoza,Victor	150,000	90,000
BnnHthTCH	15-Nov-03	5	CRC	1 1/8M T	Stormy Roman	Aguilar,Manuel	150,000	90,000
BnshBrzH	4-Apr-03	8	GP	1 1/16M D	Nonsuch Bay	Coa,Eibar	75,000	45,000
BobBryant	24-May-03	8	PRM	6F D	Coding	Noll,Cindy	57,556	34,534
BobHarding	31-Aug-03	10	MTH	1M T	Spruce Run	Ferrer,Jose	50,000	30,000
BobSlater	13-Apr-03	9	GP	5F D	Petrina Above	Camejo,Omar	75,000	45,000
BoeingH	20-Jul-03	9	EMD	1 1/16M D	Silver Screen Girl	Saito,Scott	40,000	22,000
BoisTbDrby	21-Jun-03	6	BOI	7 1/2F D	Lacenter Flash	Williams,Matt	6,350	3,810
BoldAccntH	8-Feb-03	8	FON	4F D	Burning Memories	Compton,Perry	11,850	6,510
BoldEgoH	4-Jan-03	10	SUN	5 1/2F D	Devious Ways	Quinonez,Luis	54,200	32,520
BoldRlrHG3	10-May-03	6	BEL	6F D	Shake You Down	Luzzi,Michael	108,400	65,040
BoldRuckus	4-Jun-03	3	WO	6F T	Tusayan	Ramsammy,Emile	139,000	83,400
BonnieMsG2	14-Mar-03	9	GP	1 1/8M D	Ivanavinalot	Velazquez,John	200,000	120,000
BooLaBoo	15-Feb-03	8	SA	6F D	Long Term Wish	Solis,Alex	112,500	67,500
BorderCup	20-Jul-03	6	FE	1 1/16M T	Agolo	Husbands,Patrick	65,300	39,180
BossrCityH	26-Jul-03	9	LAD	1 1/16M T	Crowned King	Rennie,Chandra	50,000	30,000
BourbnttBC	22-Mar-03	8	TP	1M D	Adopted Daughter	Butler,Dean	150,000	93,000
BourbonCo	24-Oct-03	8	KEE	1 1/16M T	Commendation	Velasquez,Cornelio	112,800	69,936
Bouwerie	18-May-03	8	BEL	7F D	Golden Damsel	Bailey,Jerry	108,700	65,220
BrandywinH	7-Jun-03	7	DEL	1M D	Bowman's Band	Dominguez,Ramon	100,000	60,000
BraveRaj	20-Sep-03	8	CRC	1M 70Y D	Marina de Chavon	Aguilar,Manuel	100,000	60,000
BrdrsSpcl	28-Jun-03	8	LNN	6F D	Bevys Affair	Beck,Daniel	15,600	9,360
Breeders	9-Aug-03	8	WO	1 1/2M T	Wando	Husbands,Patrick	1,000,000	800,000
BrghsBellH	29-Jun-03	8	HST	1 1/8M D	Shelby Madison	Alvarado,Pedro	44,576	26,746
BriarticH	22-Mar-03	8	WO	5F D	Krz Ruckus	Luciani,Dino	108,000	64,800
Brickyard	19-Oct-03	8	HOO	6F D	If I Were You	Castaneda,Bonnie	39,150	23,490
Bridgeburg	15-Jun-03	6	FE	1 1/16M D	Ocean Front	Ramirez,Martin	90,000	54,000
BrksFields	14-Jun-03	8	CBY	7 1/2F T	Dontbotherknocking	Bell,Derek	40,000	24,000
BrmnghmMdn	14-Jun-03	3	RD	6F D	Bama Royal	Mojica,Orlando	17,500	9,625
BrntsPrncs	24-May-03	12	TDN	6F D	Just Michel	Feliciano,Ricardo	35,000	21,000
BroadwayH	15-Mar-03	7	AQU	6F D	Shawklit Mint	Migliore,Richard	81,600	48,960
BroklynHG2	14-Jun-03	8	BEL	1 1/8M D	Iron Deputy	Migliore,Richard	250,000	150,000
Brookmeade	4-Jul-03	7	CNL	1 1/16M D	Misty Sixes	Pino,Mario	50,000	30,000
BrrettsDeb	20-Sep-03	11	FPX	6 1/2F D	Dixie High	Steiner,Joseph	110,300	60,665
BrrettsJuv	21-Sep-03	11	FPX	6 1/2F D	Don'tsellmeshort	Fogelsonger,Ryan	124,170	68,282

Stakes	Date	Race	Trk	Dist/Surf		Winner	Jockey	Gross	Value to winner
BrthrBrown	19-Oct-03	8	RP	5F	T	Caro's Royalty	Lester,Robert	36,600	21,000
Brumbeau	18-Apr-03	8	TUP	6F	D	Knoll Lake	Bridges,Kelly	23,900	14,340
BrwnBssHG3	1-Feb-03	5	GG	1 1/16M	T	Lindsay Jean	Schvaneveldt,Chad	100,000	55,000
BshfdMnrG3	6-Jul-03	10	CD	6F	D	Limehouse	Albarado,Robby	162,750	100,905
BShinpoch	31-Aug-03	9	EMD	1M	D	Sala de Oro	Russell,Ben	84,000	41,580
BslmnGsFnH	26-Apr-03	9	FON	1 1/16M	D	Dusty Spike	Kretzer,Kerry	110,000	60,000
BstOfOhDst	4-Oct-03	13	BEU	1 1/8M	D	Oh So Easy	Johnston,Jeff	60,000	36,000
BstOfOhEnd	4-Oct-03	14	BEU	1 1/4M	D	Devil Time	Troilo,William	100,000	60,000
BstOfOhSpt	4-Oct-03	12	BEU	6F	D	Scioto Bootski	Rosario, Jr.,Hector	50,000	30,000
BstOhJuvFl	4-Oct-03	10	BEU	1 1/16M	D	Jessica	Woolsey,Russell	60,000	36,000
BstOhJuvnl	4-Oct-03	11	BEU	1 1/16M	D	Floater	Rowland,Michael	60,000	36,000
BThomsMemH	8-Mar-03	11	SUN	6 1/2F	D	Funny Meeting	Lambert,Casey	54,200	32,520
BThoughtfl	26-Apr-03	1	HOL	7F	D	Cee's Elegance	Espinoza,Victor	150,000	90,000
BTuckrmnJr	26-May-03	8	SUF	1 1/16M	D	Freeze Alert	Hampshire, Jr.,Josiah	35,000	21,000
Bucharest	1-Feb-03	8	HOU	6F	D	Mucho Bold	Cogburn,Kevin	35,000	21,000
Buckland	5-Jul-03	9	CNL	5 1/2F	T	All That Glitters	Pino,Mario	60,000	40,000
Buckpasser	10-Oct-03	8	FP	6F	D	Punch Bag	Medina,Cynthia	25,800	15,480
BudChalngr	22-Mar-03	10	TAM	1M	T	Admiral Lance	Rodriguez,Pedro	50,000	30,000
BudEmerldH	15-Jun-03	8	EMD	1M	D	Turban	Mitchell,Gallyn	75,000	41,250
BufaloBayu	1-Nov-03	7	HOU	1 1/16M	T	Skate Away	Gondron,Ted	35,000	21,000
Buffalo	20-Sep-03	7	ASD	1M	D	Coal Smudge	Leacock,Jason	36,000	21,600
BullDog	12-Oct-03	10	FNO	6F	D	My Captain	Duran,Francisco	50,600	27,600
BullPage	27-Jul-03	8	WO	6F	D	Stormthebarricade	Ramsammy,Emile	133,375	80,025
BungalowH	23-Sep-03	9	FP	1M	D	Slick's Lil Sister	Concha,Gilbert	35,800	21,480
BuntyLawls	18-Oct-03	8	WO	1M	T	Tusayan	Ramsammy,Emile	144,750	86,850
BurnabyBCH	28-Jun-03	7	HST	1 1/16M	D	Stratoplan	Wright,Nicola	89,700	38,820
Busanda	26-Jan-03	8	AQU	1M 70Y	D	Cyber Secret	Samyn,Jean-Luc	82,500	49,500
Busher	1-Mar-03	8	AQU	1 1/16M	D	Elegant Designer	Pino,Mario	81,450	48,870
Busls&Bows	18-Sep-03	10	FPX	6 1/2F	D	Wind Flow	Nuesch,David	50,000	27,500
BWineberg	15-Nov-03	8	PM	6F	D	Houston Shuffle	Gutierrez,Juan	18,390	10,115
BwlnGrnHG2	12-Jul-03	10	BEL	1 3/8M	T	Whitmore's Conn	Samyn,Jean-Luc	150,000	90,000
CablsDSolH	11-Oct-03	8	TUP	6F	D	Dan's Groovy	Campbell,Joel	35,000	21,000
Cacapon	21-Jun-03	4	CT	4 1/2F	D	Fancy Buckles	Valdes,Ricardo	36,450	21,870
CactsFlwrH	8-Mar-03	6	TUP	6F	D	Maria's Mirage	Jauregui,Luis	50,000	30,000
CactsWrenH	4-Jan-03	7	TUP	6 1/2F	D	Grimm	Patton,David	38,900	23,340
CactusCupH	1-Mar-03	9	TUP	6 1/2F	D	Top Penny	Gomez,Esteban	35,000	21,000
CaesrsWish	26-Apr-03	8	PIM	1 1/16M	D	Grace Bay	Wilson,Rick	75,000	45,000
Cajun	11-Oct-03	10	LAD	6F	D	Donna's Mailbag	Doocy,Timothy	55,650	33,390
CajunXpres	16-Mar-03	7	DED	5F	D	Believe Im Special	Carmouche, Jr.,Sylvester	50,000	30,000
CalBrdrCh	27-Dec-03	3	SA	7F	D	Silent Sighs	Flores,David	125,000	75,000
CalBrdrCh	26-Dec-03	5	SA	7F	D	Don'tsellmeshort	Solis,Alex	125,000	75,000
Calcasieu	15-Nov-03	7	DED	5F	D	Nitro Chip	LeBlanc,Kirk	50,000	30,000
CalCpClscH	8-Nov-03	9	SA	1 1/8M	D	Tizbud	Espinoza,Victor	250,000	150,000
CalCpMileH	8-Nov-03	8	SA	1M	T	Lennyfromalibu	Fogelsonger,Ryan	175,000	105,000
CalCpStSpH	8-Nov-03	2	SA	6F	D	Coconut Mango	Krone,Julie	50,000	30,000
CalCupDisH	8-Nov-03	5	SA	6 1/2F	T	Blind Ambition	Krone,Julie	150,000	90,000
CalCupDstH	8-Nov-03	3	SA	1 1/4M	D	Moscow Burning	Fogelsonger,Ryan	100,000	60,000
CalCupJuv	8-Nov-03	10	SA	1 1/16M	D	He's the Rage	Espinoza,Victor	125,000	75,000
CalCupJuvF	8-Nov-03	7	SA	1 1/16M	D	House of Fortune	Solis,Alex	125,000	75,000
CalCupMatH	8-Nov-03	4	SA	1 1/16M	D	Royally Chosen	Solis,Alex	150,000	90,000
CalCupSprH	8-Nov-03	6	SA	6F	D	Green Team	Espinoza,Victor	150,000	90,000
CalCupStrH	8-Nov-03	1	SA	1 1/2M	T	Fade to Blue	Espinoza,Victor	50,000	30,000
CalDerby	12-Apr-03	4	BM	1 1/8M	D	Mr. Technique	Gonzalez,Roberto	100,000	55,000
CalderOaks	11-Oct-03	9	CRC	1 1/8M	T	Love Sting	Bain,Gary	200,000	120,000
CalfrninG2	14-Jun-03	8	HOL	1 1/8M	D	Kudos	Solis,Alex	400,000	240,000
CalOaks	15-Mar-03	8	GG	1 1/16M	D	Amber Hills	Baze,Gary	81,150	47,400
CaltechH	30-Mar-03	9	GP	1 1/8M	T	Charge	Coa,Eibar	75,000	45,000
CalTurfChH	1-Sep-03	8	BM	1M	T	Ninebanks	Warren, Jr.,Ronald	100,000	51,700
Camellia	25-Jan-03	8	DED	6 1/2F	D	Prized Amberpro	Woodley,Carl	75,000	45,000
CamRealMIH	27-Apr-03	8	ALB	1M	D	Curve Ball	Coates,Jimmy	42,400	25,440
CanadaDay	1-Jul-03	7	ASD	1M	D	Remiewaterbluz	Crawford,Juan	35,000	21,000
CanadianJu	13-Oct-03	9	NP	1 1/16M	D	Tigger Bay	Painter,Leanne	75,000	47,250

Stakes	Date	Race	Trk	Dist/Surf		Winner	Jockey	Gross	Value to winner
CanadinHG2	14-Sep-03	6	WO	1 1/8M	T	Inish Glora	Kabel,Todd	329,000	197,400
CanDerbyG3	23-Aug-03	9	NP	1 3/8M	D	Raylene	Walcott,Rickey	150,000	94,500
CandyEclar	13-Jul-03	9	MTH	6F	D	Follow Me Home	Pimentel,Julian	50,000	30,000
CanIntnlG1	19-Oct-03	9	WO	1 1/2M	T	Phoenix Reach (IRE)	Dwyer,Martin	1,500,000	900,000
CanTurfHG3	9-Mar-03	9	GP	1 1/16M	T	Political Attack	Guidry,Mark	100,000	60,000
CapeHnlpn	20-Jul-03	7	DEL	1 1/2M	T	Revved Up	Dominguez,Ramon	59,500	35,700
CapitlCtyH	29-Aug-03	2	PEN	1 1/16M	T	Guerdon	Brown,Tracey	30,800	18,480
CaptBoogie	16-Feb-03	8	TUP	1M	D	Free Corona	Ziegler,Michael	23,800	14,280
CaptMyCapt	30-Aug-03	5	PHA	5F	T	Shades of Sunny	Carmouche,Kendrick	50,000	30,000
CaptnCondo	21-Sep-03	8	EMD	6F	D	Millenium Nugget	Gutierrez,Juan	40,000	20,000
CardinalH	21-Jun-03	9	AP	1 1/16M	T	Act of War	Bourque,Curt	86,150	51,690
CardinlHG3	22-Nov-03	9	CD	1 1/8M	T	Riskaverse	Velasquez,Cornelio	175,200	108,624
CareyMmHG3	1-Nov-03	8	HAW	1M	T	Mystery Giver	Marquez, Jr.,Carlos	150,000	90,000
CarmelH	13-Sep-03	7	BM	1 1/16M	T	Cellamare (FR)	Valdivia, Jr.,Jose	78,850	33,850
Carotene	13-Oct-03	8	WO	1 1/8M	T	Classic Stamp	Husbands,Patrick	168,000	100,800
Carousel	29-Mar-03	10	OP	6F	D	Southern Tour	Theriot,Jamie	50,000	30,000
CarryBckG3	12-Jul-03	10	CRC	6F	D	Valid Video	Bravo,Joe	300,000	177,000
CarterHG1	12-Apr-03	9	AQU	7F	D	Congaree	Stevens,Gary	350,000	210,000
CartristaH	10-May-03	8	CRC	1 1/16M	T	Love the Game	Ferrer,Jose	75,000	41,000
CaSprntChH	4-Oct-03	7	BM	6F	D	Trapper	Baze,Russell	100,000	52,800
Cassidy	11-Oct-03	5	CRC	6F	D	Zak's Precocious	Garcia,Julio	75,000	41,000
CasyDrnelH	8-Jun-03	7	ALB	7F	D	Devil of a Trip	Madeira,Carlos	53,300	31,980
Catchrgstr	30-Aug-03	3	CRC	5F	D	Horah for Bailey	Castro,Eddie	54,450	23,670
CatCradleH	14-Dec-03	8	HOL	7 1/2F	D	Valentine Dancer	Espinoza,Victor	105,300	63,180
CavoJuve	3-Aug-03	10	SR	5 1/2F	D	Razen Hazen	Duran,Francisco	53,750	29,850
Cavonnier	1-Oct-03	4	SA	7F	D	Race for Glory	Smith,Mike	80,850	48,510
CBarley	22-Jun-03	4	WO	1M	T	Moonshine Hall	Husbands,Patrick	112,000	67,200
CBStephens	22-Feb-03	7	DED	7F	D	Witt Ante	LeBlanc,Kirk	100,000	60,000
CbyDerby	28-Jun-03	8	CBY	1M	D	Morning Merry	Noll,Cindy	40,000	24,000
CbyJuvnile	12-Jul-03	8	CBY	5 1/2F	D	Cactus Ridge	Walker, Jr.,Bobby	35,000	21,000
CbyLassie	12-Jul-03	7	CBY	5 1/2F	D	Miss Outrageous	Walker, Jr.,Bobby	35,000	21,000
CbyOaks	21-Jun-03	8	CBY	1 1/16M	T	Perfect Moment	Eads,Jason	40,000	24,000
CCAOaksG1	19-Jul-03	9	BEL	1 1/2M	D	Spoken Fur	Bailey,Jerry	500,000	300,000
CCEmerald	19-Jul-03	8	CBY	1 1/16M	T	Image	Krone,Julie	125,000	68,750
CCExpress	19-Jul-03	9	CBY	6F	D	Landler	Fogelsonger,Ryan	50,000	27,500
CCGlsSlipr	19-Jul-03	6	CBY	6 1/2F	D	Mum's Gold	Santagata,Nick	75,000	41,500
CChristian	4-Jul-03	9	BOI	5F	D	Crown Royalty	Hernandez,Miguel	26,100	13,050
CCIrnHorse	19-Jul-03	4	CBY	1 1/16M	D	Ghoastly Prize	Walker, Jr.,Bobby	50,000	27,500
CCJewel	19-Jul-03	9	CBY	1 1/8M	D	Daunting	Krone,Julie	150,000	82,500
CCRpdTrnst	19-Jul-03	7	CBY	6 1/2F	D	Pioneer Boy	Wilson,Rick	100,000	55,000
CDDstafHG2	8-Nov-03	9	CD	1M	D	Lead Story	Borel,Calvin	225,400	139,748
CDHG2	3-May-03	5	CD	7F	D	Aldebaran	Bailey,Jerry	233,800	144,956
CERBradlyH	5-Jan-03	9	FG	1 1/16M	T	Royal Spy	Albarado,Robby	75,000	45,000
CERFH	10-Sep-03	6	DMR	6F	D	Fancee Bargain	Alvarado,Frank	92,300	55,380
CFBurkeHG3	24-Oct-03	8	SA	1 1/2M	T	Runaway Dancer	Smith,Mike	139,250	83,550
CGRoseClsH	15-Nov-03	12	CRC	1 1/8M	D	Best of the Rest	Coa,Eibar	200,000	120,000
Challedon	20-Dec-03	8	LRL	7F	D	Acrolect	Caraballo,Jose	60,000	36,000
ChamisaH	20-Apr-03	8	ALB	7F	D	Take Out the Trash	Bourdieu,Jorge	32,500	19,500
ChampagnG1	4-Oct-03	7	BEL	1 1/16M	D	Birdstone	Bailey,Jerry	500,000	300,000
ChandlerH	8-Nov-03	4	TUP	7 1/2F	T	Frisco Belle	Castro,Joe	35,000	21,000
Chantilly	8-Jun-03	7	ASD	6F	D	Princess Muldoon	DesAutels,Jacques	35,000	21,000
ChapelBell	2-Aug-03	8	LAD	1 1/16M	T	Tiva's Little Sis	Meche,Lonnie	50,000	30,000
Chargedup	7-Nov-03	9	DED	7F	D	Wacky Patty	Theriot,Jamie	75,000	45,000
ChariotChH	29-Jun-03	4	NP	6 1/2F	D	A Shaky Start	Painter,Leanne	40,000	25,200
Charon	23-Feb-03	5	GP	7F	D	Bird Town	Coa,Eibar	52,100	31,260
ChasHHadry	20-Sep-03	9	PIM	1 1/8M	D	Docent	Potts,Clinton	50,000	30,000
ChcgoBCHG3	14-Jun-03	8	AP	7F	D	For Rubies	Perret,Craig	190,750	69,450
ChckredFlg	26-May-03	11	IND	6F	D	Lx Commander	Kuntzweiler,Greta	43,600	26,160
Chenery	19-Jul-03	9	CNL	5 1/2F	D	Urban Warrior	Pino,Mario	50,000	30,000
ChfBearhrt	19-Oct-03	10	WO	1 1/4M	T	Colorful Judgement	Callaghan,Slade	108,000	64,800
ChfNarbona	18-May-03	12	ALB	6F	D	The Eighth Wonder	Coates,Jimmy	35,000	19,250
ChicagIndH	12-Apr-03	9	HAW	6F	D	Classic Appeal	Silva,Carlos	134,392	80,635

Stakes	Date	Race	Trk	Dist/Surf		Winner	Jockey	Gross	Value to winner
ChicagoSix	1-Jan-03	8	HAW	1 1/16M	D	Colorful Tour	Meier,Randall	43,400	26,040
ChinokPass	21-Sep-03	3	EMD	6F	D	Badger K. Eli	Gutierrez,Juan	40,000	20,000
ChneseCCG2	20-Jul-03	8	WO	1 3/8M	T	Strut the Stage	Kabel,Todd	330,900	198,540
Choice	24-Aug-03	10	MTH	1 1/8M	T	Ballonenostrikes	Bravo,Joe	50,000	30,000
ChouCroutH	22-Feb-03	9	FG	1 1/16M	D	Ifyouprefersilver	Lovato, Jr.,Frank	150,000	90,000
Christmas	26-Dec-03	9	MNR	6F	D	Crossing Point	Pino,Mario	77,000	46,200
ChrkeRTfCl	6-Apr-03	11	TAM	1 1/8M	T	Guardianofthegate	Pompell,Thomas	85,250	47,150
CHRussellH	12-Oct-03	3	BM	6F	D	Pheiffer	Warren, Jr.,Ronald	78,500	33,500
ChSprngHG3	13-Dec-03	10	CRC	7F	D	Barbara O'Brien	Coa,Eibar	100,000	60,000
ChuckNLuck	5-Apr-03	8	TUP	1M	D	Unyielding	Lopez,Lorenzo	24,276	14,280
ChuckNLuck	2-Dec-03	8	TUP	7 1/2F	T	Cut of Music	Stevens,Scott	21,700	13,020
CicadaG3	22-Mar-03	9	AQU	7F	D	Cyber Secret	Bridgmohan,Shaun	108,300	64,980
Cigar	16-Aug-03	7	AP	1 1/8M	D	Ask the Lord	Day,Pat	53,600	32,160
CigarMiHG1	29-Nov-03	9	AQU	1M	D	Congaree	Bailey,Jerry	350,000	210,000
CIlesDerby	10-May-03	8	ALB	1M	D	Fame Ina Minute	Summers,Nancy	35,914	21,548
Cimarron	1-Nov-03	7	RP	6 1/2F	D	Aspen Gal	Berry,Monte	36,700	21,850
Cincnatian	6-Jul-03	7	RD	1 1/16M	D	Oh So Easy	Felix,Julio	40,000	24,000
Cinderella	8-Jun-03	7	HOL	5 1/2F	D	Yogi's Polar Bear	Espinoza,Victor	99,825	46,395
CinmaBCHG3	29-Jun-03	8	HOL	1 1/8M	T	Just Wonder (GB)	Desormeaux,Kent	214,550	98,730
CinTrophy	18-Jan-03	10	TP	6 1/2F	D	Golden Marlin	Lumpkins,Jason	50,000	31,300
CitgoDixG2	17-May-03	10	PIM	1 1/8M	T	Dr. Brendler	Dominguez,Ramon	200,000	120,000
CityOVncvr	10-May-03	1	HST	6 1/2F	D	Illusive Force	Wilson,David	44,628	26,777
CJacksnCIH	21-Sep-03	9	ALB	1 13/16M	D	Archy	Fuentes,Freddy	13,450	8,070
CJHindleyH	17-Aug-03	9	FER	1 5/8M	D	Smokeville	Boyce,Robert	13,900	7,575
CLangJrMmH	20-Sep-03	9	RET	1M	D	Compendium	Beasley,Jeremy	35,000	21,000
Clarendon	28-Jun-03	8	WO	5 1/2F	D	Maple Syrple	Husbands,Patrick	166,500	99,900
ClarkCnty	16-Oct-03	8	KEE	5 1/2F	T	On the Fritz	Albarado,Robby	85,425	52,964
ClarkHG2	28-Nov-03	11	CD	1 1/8M	D	Quest	Castellano,Javier	582,000	360,840
CleveKindr	4-Jul-03	10	TDN	5 1/2F	D	Catch My Cat	Fortner,Joddie	40,000	24,000
CleveIndGC	5-Jul-03	11	TDN	1 1/8M	D	Cat Singer	Rosario, Jr.,Hector	100,000	60,000
CLHirschG1	28-Sep-03	3	SA	1 1/4M	T	Storming Home (GB)	Stevens,Gary	250,000	150,000
CLHrschHG2	10-Aug-03	8	DMR	1 1/16M	D	Azeri	Smith,Mike	300,000	180,000
ClmrLexG2	19-Apr-03	8	KEE	1 1/16M	D	Scrimshaw	Prado,Edgar	363,675	225,479
ClsBrdSpcH	30-Aug-03	7	CLS	6 1/2F	D	Sundayblummer	Collins,Dennis	10,350	6,210
ClsDebtant	7-Sep-03	6	CLS	6F	D	Shawklit Premiere	Collins,Dennis	10,300	6,180
ClsFuturty	7-Sep-03	8	CLS	6F	D	Thundering Verzy	Martinez,Armando	10,475	6,285
ClssyNSmrt	19-Nov-03	7	WO	1 1/16M	D	Brass in Pocket	Clark,David	130,750	78,450
ClubHousSp	24-Aug-03	7	CLS	6F	D	Thundering Verzy	Yaranga,Yuri	9,575	5,745
CMcGrgrJrM	26-May-03	6	LS	6F	D	Front Nine	Beasley,Jeremy	50,000	30,000
CmllaUrsoH	9-Nov-03	8	GG	6F	D	Ema Bovary (CHI)	Gonzalez,Roberto	78,700	33,800
CmwlthBCG2	13-Apr-03	8	KEE	7F	D	Smooth Jazz	Prado,Edgar	273,750	169,725
CntLatham	2-Aug-03	4	NP	1 5/16M	D	Beau Brass	Wilson,David	40,000	25,200
CntralIowa	1-Sep-03	6	PRM	1 1/16M	D	Curious Conundrum	Corbett,Glenn	40,000	24,000
CntrlPcCnt	19-Jul-03	8	GPR	6F	D	Disputed Intent	Sterr,Scott	4,072	2,444
CntrStgAnn	1-Jul-03	4	FE	6F	D	Roman Romance	Montpellier,Constant	66,000	39,600
Cocodrie	13-Dec-03	9	DED	6 1/2F	D	Alice From Marigny	Bourque,Steven	40,000	24,000
Colin	13-Jul-03	8	WO	6F	D	San Diego Blowout	Ramsammy,Emile	134,875	84,971
Colleen	3-Aug-03	8	MTH	5 1/2F	D	Fashion Girl	Bravo,Joe	60,000	36,000
Collegian	25-Jan-03	8	SUF	6F	D	Formal Escape	Esposito,Anthony	35,000	21,000
ColmbiaRvr	29-Nov-03	8	PM	6F	D	Runaway Briartic	Beckner,Twyla	10,000	5,500
ColoDerby	3-Aug-03	9	ARP	1 1/16M	D	Cut of Music	Frazier,Don	35,000	21,000
ColPowerH	12-Jan-03	9	FG	6F	D	Cojet	Sellers,Shane	75,000	45,000
ColtsNeck	26-Jul-03	8	MTH	1M	T	Freedom's Honor	Velez, Jr.,Jose	50,000	30,000
Columbia	3-May-03	10	TAM	1 1/8M	T	Guardianofthegate	Pompell,Thomas	50,000	28,500
ComelyG3	18-Apr-03	8	AQU	1M	D	Cyber Secret	Bridgmohan,Shaun	107,900	64,740
Comet	1-Nov-03	6	MED	6F	D	Pleasant Honor	Ortiz,Felix	45,000	27,000
ConghtCpG3	24-May-03	8	WO	1 1/16M	T	Fly Smartly	Kabel,Todd	173,550	104,130
ConlyBCTH	15-Feb-03	7	HOU	1 1/8M	T	Candid Glen	Perrodin,Elvis	223,000	133,800
Conniver	9-Mar-03	8	LRL	7F	D	Gazillion	Dominguez,Ramon	60,000	36,000
Conroe	29-Nov-03	8	HOU	6F	D	Book Note	Clark,Kerwin	35,000	21,000
ContnlMile	31-Aug-03	7	MTH	1M	T	Grand Heritage	Pimentel,Julian	50,000	30,000
Convenence	2-Aug-03	3	CRC	1 1/16M	D	Scapade	Garcia,Julio	50,000	30,000

Stakes	Date	Race	Trk	Dist/Surf		Winner	Jockey	Gross	Value to winner
CoolAir	18-May-03	7	CRC	5F	T	Petrina Above	Camejo,Omar	42,000	27,200
CoolRecept	4-Aug-03	8	FE	1 1/16M	D	Barbeau Ruckus	Luciani,Dino	90,000	54,000
CoorsStr	4-May-03	10	FON	1 1/8M	D	Old Man's Delite	Murray,Kelly	11,775	7,065
CopprTopFt	6-Apr-03	11	SUN	4 1/2F	D	Hecamefromaclaim	Jaime,Ricardo	172,374	86,187
Cordially	25-Oct-03	6	DEL	1M	D	Shiny Sheet	Rose,Jeremy	58,500	35,100
CornadoQst	9-Oct-03	6	BEL	1M	D	Newfoundland	Velazquez,John	65,500	39,300
CoronatnFu	1-Nov-03	10	WO	1 1/8M	D	A Bit O'Gold	Jones,Jono	250,000	150,000
CorrectnH	1-Feb-03	8	AQU	6F	D	A. P. Andie	Chavez,Luis	83,225	49,935
CorteMdera	27-Dec-03	8	GG	1M	D	Swingn' Notes	Schvaneveldt,Chad	78,850	33,650
CotillnHG2	4-Oct-03	9	PHA	1 1/16M	D	Fast Cookie	Santagata,Nick	250,000	150,000
CountFleet	4-Jan-03	8	AQU	1M 70Y	D	Grey Comet	Gryder,Aaron	81,350	48,810
Courtlin	19-Oct-03	7	CRC	5F	T	Petrina Above	Boulanger,Gary	42,850	27,710
Courtship	5-Oct-03	3	BM	6F	D	Uppity Kitty	Lumpkins,Jason	78,700	33,700
CoverGal	1-Oct-03	7	SA	7F	D	House of Fortune	Solis,Alex	80,550	48,330
CoverGirlH	23-Aug-03	1	HST	6 1/2F	D	Elana d'Amour	Krasner,Samuel	44,576	26,746
Cowdin	12-Oct-03	3	BEL	6 1/2F	D	Smokume	Uske,Shannon	78,600	47,354
CoyoteH	15-Feb-03	7	TUP	6F	D	Grimm	Patton,David	50,000	30,000
CPalmerH	9-Aug-03	9	FER	6 1/2F	D	Triviality	Boag,Daniel	8,000	4,225
CptlCtyFut	6-Jul-03	8	LNN	4 1/2F	D	Sheso	Carkeek,Jerome	11,000	6,600
CPWOpenTb	22-Jun-03	6	CPW	1 1/16M	D	River Girl's Boy	La Forge,Frank	2,500	1,250
CpwTbDerby	21-Jun-03	3	CPW	5F	D	Baby Wallys Joy	Fennell,Herman	2,500	1,250
CraftyDrne	12-Oct-03	8	HAW	1M	T	Mc Mahon	Meier,Randall	44,400	26,640
CRAmrTrfG3	2-May-03	9	CD	1 1/16M	D	Senor Swinger	Day,Pat	121,440	75,268
CrankItUp	21-Jun-03	9	MTH	5F	D	Follow Me Home	Pimentel,Julian	50,000	30,000
CrcBCH	26-Apr-03	5	CRC	1 1/16M	D	Stormy Frolic	Santos,Jose	150,000	90,000
CrcDerbyG3	11-Oct-03	12	CRC	1 1/8M	T	Stroll	Bailey,Jerry	200,000	120,000
CrcTurfSpH	12-Jul-03	8	CRC	5F	D	Joe's Son Joey	Bravo,Joe	100,000	60,000
CremDelCrm	14-Nov-03	7	DED	5F	D	Spring Rade	Eads,Jason	50,000	30,000
CremDelCrm	18-Jan-03	8	DED	6 1/2F	D	Scottish Heritage	Rennie,Chandra	50,000	30,000
Criterium	5-Jul-03	8	CRC	5 1/2F	D	Sir Oscar	Garcia,Julio	100,000	60,000
CrnhsBCHG3	12-Jul-03	6	PRM	1 1/8M	D	Tenpins	Albarado,Robby	350,000	210,000
CRodneyH	27-Sep-03	7	DEL	1 1/8M	D	Private Lap	Black,Anthony	200,000	120,000
CrsntCtyDy	18-Jan-03	9	FG	1 1/16M	D	Witt Ante	LeBlanc,Kirk	75,000	45,000
CrystlWtrH	23-Mar-03	7	SA	1M	T	Road to Slew	Flores,David	111,300	66,780
CSalazar	18-May-03	6	ALB	7F	D	Scarzane	Clark,Michael	35,000	19,252
CSHarrisnH	27-Jun-03	7	MD	6F	D	Brite Steel	Moccasin,Tim	5,000	3,000
CstlGuardH	1-Sep-03	5	MTH	1 1/16M	D	Moorish Prince	Baze,Michael	45,000	27,000
CTaliferoM	23-Aug-03	7	RP	6F	D	Where's the Ring	Cogburn,Kevin	36,600	21,000
CtationHG2	29-Nov-03	9	HOL	1 1/16M	T	Redattore (BRZ)	Krone,Julie	400,000	240,000
CTBA	25-Jul-03	7	DMR	5 1/2F	D	Dirty Diana	Smith,Mike	125,000	75,000
CTBABrOaks	4-Aug-03	6	ARP	1 1/16M	D	Tricky Transaction	Gonsalves,Frank	35,000	21,000
CTBADerby	24-Aug-03	11	ARP	1 1/16M	D	This Cat's for You	Wales,Travis	28,000	16,800
CTBAFut	26-Jul-03	9	ARP	5 1/2F	D	C K Jett	Vicchrilli,Russell	35,000	21,000
CTBALassie	17-Aug-03	6	ARP	5 1/2F	D	Ladysgthelooks	Gonsalves,Frank	35,000	21,000
CTBAMarian	22-Sep-03	9	FPX	1 1/16M	D	Amber Hills	Pedroza,Martin	50,000	27,500
CTDashH	4-Jul-03	7	CT	4 1/2F	D	Sea of Green	Perez,Nilo	100,000	65,000
CtDstTMIG3	3-May-03	8	CD	1M	T	Heat Haze (GB)	Valdivia, Jr.,Jose	117,000	72,540
CtFltSpHG3	10-Apr-03	10	OP	6F	D	Beau's Town	Theriot,Jamie	150,000	90,000
CTHSSales	30-Aug-03	8	HST	6 1/2F	D	Proud Son	Krasner,Samuel	66,552	39,931
CTHSSales	30-Aug-03	7	HST	6 1/2F	D	Regal Grace	Villeseche,Anrella	66,396	39,838
CTHSSales	1-Sep-03	4	ASD	6F	D	Coal Smudge	Leacock,Jason	35,000	21,000
CTHSSales	1-Sep-03	7	ASD	6F	D	Sampo's Fool	Hightower,Travis	35,000	21,000
CTT&TOCH	29-Aug-03	7	DMR	1 3/8M	T	Crazy Ensign (ARG)	Solis,Alex	99,025	45,915
CtyBridSop	2-Aug-03	1	MD	1M	D	Stop the Act	Moccasin,Tim	6,500	4,160
CtyEdmtnDH	23-Aug-03	6	NP	1 1/16M	D	Slewability	Winters,Perry	75,000	47,250
CtyOAndrsn	3-Oct-03	7	HOO	5 1/2F	D	Tee's Pearl	Butler,Dean	39,060	23,430
CtyOfRoseH	27-Dec-03	8	PM	1M	D	Chancy Chancy	Beckner,Twyla	10,000	5,500
CtyOfRoses	9-Mar-03	9	PM	6F	D	Wegota Slewzy	Webb,Robert	10,000	5,500
CubKlahrH	22-Jun-03	7	BOI	7F	D	Quiet Syns	Conklin,Jay	5,400	3,240
Cup&Saucer	11-Oct-03	8	WO	1 1/16M	T	Master William	Husbands,Patrick	250,000	150,000
CurribotH	8-Feb-03	11	SUN	1 1/16M	D	Tee Cat	Gonzalez, Jr.,Sal	53,250	31,950
CutIsEnvoy	22-Nov-03	9	CRC	6 1/2F	D	Chispiski	Garcia,Julio	37,650	24,590

Stakes	Date	Race	Trk	Dist/Surf		Winner	Jockey	Gross	Value to winner
CWhtghmHG1	14-Jun-03	3	HOL	1 1/4M	T	Storming Home (GB)	Stevens,Gary	350,000	210,000
CWilsonMH	22-Jun-03	10	GRP	6 1/2F	D	Executive Air	Peery,Melissa	4,475	2,520
CWPardee	26-Apr-03	7	TUP	1M	D	Dead Centre	Schacht,Randy	15,000	9,000
CyclonesH	22-Jun-03	8	PRM	1 1/16M	D	Take Me Up	Quinonez,Luis	70,000	42,000
CyFair	6-Dec-03	8	HOU	7F	D	Souris	Beasley,Jeremy	35,000	21,000
Cypress	11-Jan-03	9	DED	6 1/2F	D	Bet Me Best	Bourque,Steven	50,000	30,000
CzariaH	9-Feb-03	11	SUN	6F	D	Devious Ways	Lambert,Casey	53,650	32,190
D&FSawyrFu	21-Sep-03	6	ALB	6F	D	Queen of Slots	Jaime,Ricardo	61,602	30,801
DadeTurfCl	30-Aug-03	9	ELP	1 1/8M	T	Reason to Talk	Court,Jon	75,000	46,250
DahliaHG2	20-Dec-03	9	HOL	1 1/4M	T	Katdogawn (GB)	Smith,Mike	150,000	90,000
DaHoss	28-Jun-03	9	CNL	1M	D	Tam's Terms	Karamanos,Horacio	50,000	30,000
DaHoss	24-Mar-03	9	TUP	1M	T	Free Corona	Ziegler,Michael	24,260	14,280
DaisycutrH	1-Aug-03	7	DMR	5F	T	Roberta's Mango	Nakatani,Corey	99,025	59,415
DameMystrs	5-Jan-03	5	GP	5F	D	Follow Me Home	Chavez,Jorge	71,400	42,840
DamonRunyn	17-Dec-03	8	AQU	1 1/16M	D	West Virginia	Migliore,Richard	83,675	50,205
DancgCount	1-Jan-03	8	LRL	6F	D	Philadelphia Jim	Dominguez,Ramon	60,000	30,000
DanSueFeat	2-Mar-03	7	RIL	6 1/2F	D	C. R. Cavalier	Gard,Terry	5,257	2,944
DanvilleH	22-Mar-03	4	GG	6F	D	Presidio Heights	Gonzalez,Roberto	78,650	33,650
Danzig	9-May-03	6	PEN	6F	D	Billy Gilman	Diaz,Vladimir	30,600	18,360
Dartsum	7-Jun-03	9	CRC	1M	D	High Ideal	Castanon,Jesus	44,700	23,820
DaveFeldmn	26-Jan-03	9	GP	1 1/16M	T	Hypnotist	Bailey,Jerry	75,000	45,000
DavsFriend	9-Aug-03	8	LRL	6F	D	Crossing Point	Pino,Mario	50,000	30,000
DBernhardt	26-Jul-03	10	ELP	6 1/2F	D	Dubai Sheikh	Lumpkins,Jason	100,000	61,250
DblDelta	6-Jul-03	5	AP	1M	T	Aud	Peck,Brian	47,550	28,530
Dbldogdare	16-Apr-03	8	KEE	1 1/16M	D	Reason to Talk	Day,Pat	108,700	67,394
DblYorFlvr	29-Mar-03	8	HOU	7F	D	Sarastorm	Stanton,Terry	35,000	21,000
DeBartMBCH	1-Sep-03	8	RP	1 1/8M	D	Skate Away	Melancon,Gerard	126,600	75,000
DeBrtOaks	20-Sep-03	8	LAD	1 1/16M	T	Dyna Da Wyna	Day,Pat	75,000	45,000
Debutante	20-Jul-03	8	ASD	5 1/2F	D	Ericka's Lass	Iammarino,Michael	35,000	21,000
DebutantG3	4-Jul-03	10	CD	5 1/2F	D	Be Gentle	Velasquez,Cornelio	110,900	68,758
Decathlon	23-Aug-03	9	MTH	5F	T	Joe's Son Joey	Coa,Eibar	50,000	30,000
DecratnDyH	26-May-03	3	MNR	1M	D	Ashwood C C	Gonzalez,Luis	78,000	46,800
DeFrncsMG1	15-Nov-03	10	LRL	6F	D	A Huevo	Dominguez,Ramon	300,000	180,000
DelHG2	20-Jul-03	10	DEL	1 1/4M	D	Wild Spirit (CHI)	Bailey,Jerry	750,000	450,000
Delicada	19-Jul-03	9	LAD	1 1/16M	D	Blue Guru	Smith,Guy	50,000	30,000
DelMarHG2	31-Aug-03	8	DMR	1 3/8M	T	Irish Warrior	Solis,Alex	250,000	150,000
DelOaksG3	19-Jul-03	8	DEL	1 1/16M	D	Island Fashion	Puglisi,Ignacio	500,000	300,000
DeltaBeau	29-Nov-03	9	DED	5F	D	Britt's Jules	Stokes, III,Rex	40,000	24,000
DeltaBelle	28-Nov-03	9	DED	5F	D	Simply Jolie	Woodley,Carl	40,000	24,000
DeltaLove	7-Jul-03	5	CRC	1 1/16M	T	Dakota Light	Cruz,Manoel	42,325	27,395
DeltaMile	16-Feb-03	7	DED	1M	D	Rhonesquarterswish	Smith,Guy	50,000	30,000
DeltaMiss	28-Sep-03	8	LAD	6F	D	Vino Tinto	LeBlanc,Kirk	40,000	24,000
DemoiselG2	29-Nov-03	7	AQU	1 1/8M	D	Ashado	Bailey,Jerry	200,000	120,000
DepMinistr	15-Oct-03	7	WO	7F	D	Battlements	Kabel,Todd	129,000	77,400
DerbyDayH	3-May-03	8	BRD	6F	D	Carters Boy	Harvell,Mike	9,900	5,940
DerbyDayH	3-May-03	7	EUR	4F	D	D D Dot Comm	Vasquez,Richard	5,550	3,330
DerbyTrial	15-Sep-03	9	FPX	1 1/16M	D	Atouratoura	Martinez,Felipe	50,000	27,500
DerbyTrial	13-Jul-03	7	ASD	1 1/16M	D	Taiaslew	Simard,Real	35,000	21,000
DerbyTrlG3	26-Apr-03	9	CD	1M	D	Midas Eyes	Bailey,Jerry	167,400	103,788
DesertRosH	2-Aug-03	11	RUI	6F	D	Paradise Patty	Bourdieu,Jorge	26,400	15,840
DesertSkyH	29-Mar-03	8	TUP	1M	T	Moonlit Maddie	Higuera,Alberto	36,050	21,000
DevilHonrH	30-Aug-03	9	PHA	7F	D	Roger E	Rocco,Joseph	50,000	30,000
DianaHG1	26-Jul-03	8	SAR	1 1/8M	T	Voodoo Dancer	Nakatani,Corey	500,000	300,000
DianeKem	21-Sep-03	5	EMD	6F	D	Crystal Mt. Stevie	Steiner,Joseph	40,000	20,000
DianeKemH	25-Oct-03	8	PM	6F	D	Icicle Angel	Knapp,Karen	10,000	5,500
Dine	23-Nov-03	10	SRP	6 1/2F	D	Hesa Bad Cat	Zamora,Christopher	70,200	42,120
DiplmtWayH	19-Jan-03	9	FG	1 1/16M	D	Mineshaft	Albarado,Robby	75,000	45,000
DiscvryHG3	29-Oct-03	8	AQU	1 1/16M	D	During	Santos,Jose	111,800	67,080
Display	15-Nov-03	8	WO	1 1/16M	D	Judiths Wild Rush	Luciani,Dino	135,625	81,375
Distaff	1-Sep-03	6	ASD	1M	D	Pete's Surprise	Hendricks,Ken	35,000	21,000
DistfBCHG2	29-Mar-03	9	AQU	7F	D	Carson Hollow	Luzzi,Michael	157,900	94,740
DixieBelle	31-Jan-03	9	OP	6F	D	Explosive Beauty	Theriot,Jamie	50,000	30,000

Stakes	Date	Race	Trk	Dist/Surf		Winner	Jockey	Gross	Value to winner
DixieMiss	23-Aug-03	11	LAD	6F	D	Holy Bubbette	Quinonez,Luis	50,000	30,000
DJuanOnate	18-May-03	5	ALB	6F	D	Hasty Gus	Wales,Travis	35,000	19,250
DLeVineMem	16-Aug-03	9	PHA	7F	D	Highway Prospector	Castellano, Jr.,Abel	75,000	45,000
DLewisMem	1-Aug-03	7	GPR	1 1/16M	D	Gomka	Landaker,Terri	5,540	3,324
DllasTfCpH	21-Jun-03	7	LS	1 1/8M	T	Patrol	Luzzi,Michael	250,000	150,000
DltaCollnH	21-Sep-03	7	HST	1 1/16M	D	Shelby Madison	Alvarado,Pedro	44,160	26,496
DlyCrlngrl	17-May-03	8	GRP	5 1/2F	D	Ancient Traveler	Beckner,Twyla	3,475	1,911
DmrBCHG2	1-Sep-03	8	DMR	1M	D	Joey Franco	Valenzuela,Patrick	250,000	90,000
DmrDebG1	30-Aug-03	8	DMR	7F	D	Halfbridled	Krone,Julie	250,000	150,000
DmrDerbyG2	6-Sep-03	8	DMR	1 1/8M	T	Fairly Ransom	Solis,Alex	300,000	180,000
DmrFutG2	10-Sep-03	8	DMR	7F	D	Siphonizer	Krone,Julie	250,000	150,000
DmrOaksG1	24-Aug-03	9	DMR	1 1/8M	T	Dessert	Nakatani,Corey	300,000	180,000
DncSmrtHG3	5-Jul-03	8	WO	1 1/8M	D	Madeira Mist (IRE)	Husbands,Patrick	221,750	103,050
DogwoodG3	17-May-03	9	CD	1 1/16M	D	Golden Marlin	Sellers,Shane	109,000	67,580
DomDayHG3	1-Jul-03	8	WO	1 1/4M	D	Phantom Light	Kabel,Todd	226,000	135,600
DonaJensen	27-Apr-03	7	PM	1 1/16M	D	Stately's Choice	Webb,Robert	15,000	8,250
DonnaReed	30-Aug-03	5	PRM	1M 70Y	D	Sharky's Review	Quinonez,Luis	79,800	47,880
DonnHG1	22-Feb-03	11	GP	1 1/8M	D	Harlan's Holiday	Velazquez,John	500,000	300,000
Dover	11-Oct-03	7	DEL	1M	D	Capejinsky	Valdes,Ricardo	100,000	60,000
Dowager	19-Oct-03	8	KEE	1 1/2M	T	Spice Island	Velasquez,Cornelio	150,000	93,000
DowdMileH	12-Apr-03	9	FON	1M	D	Tate's Way	Compton,Perry	33,000	19,800
Dowling	9-Aug-03	7	GLD	1M	D	Monetary Star	Faul,Jeffrey	45,000	27,000
DownsAlbH	8-Jun-03	8	ALB	1 1/8M	D	Moro Grande	Tohill,Ken	109,050	65,430
DpMnstrHG3	9-Feb-03	10	GP	6 1/2F	D	Native Heir	Velasquez,Cornelio	100,000	60,000
DputdTstmy	1-Mar-03	8	LRL	1 1/16M	D	Cherokee's Boy	Fogelsonger,Ryan	75,000	45,000
DrDShirley	18-Jan-03	8	RIL	6F	D	Fight for Silver	Barrio,Anna	5,780	3,237
DreamOn	24-Aug-03	9	CRC	1M	D	Spectacular Lisa	Garcia,Julio	44,525	23,715
DrEBenner	20-Sep-03	4	CT	6 1/2F	D	Missacity Luke	Klinger,C.	36,250	23,563
DrFager	7-Jun-03	8	AP	1M	D	Apt to Be	Razo, Jr.,Eusebio	46,800	28,080
DrFschrMmH	5-Oct-03	10	SRP	7F	D	Inox (ARG)	Bourdieu,Jorge	33,400	20,040
DRhudyMem	2-Aug-03	7	DEL	1 1/8M	D	Broad Hopes	Dominguez,Ramon	75,000	45,000
DrJPennyMH	5-Jul-03	9	PHA	1 1/16M	T	Delta Princess	Castillo, Jr.,Heberto	100,000	60,000
DrlyPrcius	15-Feb-03	8	AQU	6F	D	Ladyecho	Castillo,Oliver	81,825	49,095
Drumtop	17-May-03	12	SUF	1 1/16M	T	Ms. Sadira	Vargas,Jorge	35,000	21,000
DsgntdDncr	14-Dec-03	5	CRC	1 1/16M	D	Young Star	Douglas,Rene	39,000	20,400
DstStmrHG3	7-Jun-03	4	HOL	6F	D	Madame Pietra	Valenzuela,Patrick	106,860	64,080
DuchessG3	9-Aug-03	5	WO	7F	D	Finally Here	Husbands,Patrick	217,250	100,350
DuchOfYork	7-Jun-03	7	STP	1 1/16M	D	Sly Lady	Simard,Real	40,000	25,200
DUNHopeful	23-Mar-03	7	DUN	5 1/2F	D	Beautiful Prize	Beverly,Ronald	6,993	3,915
DurhmCpHG3	4-Oct-03	8	WO	1 1/8M	D	Parose	Jones,Jono	163,800	98,280
DVanClief	13-Jul-03	9	CNL	1 1/16M	T	Oxford Tea Party	Torres,Raymond	50,000	30,000
DvonaDalG2	23-Feb-03	9	GP	1 1/16M	D	Yell	Velazquez,John	150,000	90,000
DWilhteMmH	20-Sep-03	5	LAD	1 1/16M	T	Waupaca	Day,Pat	50,000	30,000
DwtPttrsnH	26-Apr-03	9	TUP	1 1/16M	D	All American Chris	Martinez,Seth	35,000	21,000
DwyerG2	6-Jul-03	10	BEL	1 1/16M	D	Strong Hope	Velazquez,John	150,000	90,000
DxPokrAceH	2-Mar-03	7	FG	7 1/2F	T	Mr. Sulu	Albarado,Robby	75,000	45,000
DytnAdwSTf	6-Apr-03	7	TAM	1 1/16M	T	Hear No Evil	Nunez,Eduardo	84,150	46,490
EastView	10-Dec-03	8	AQU	1 1/16M	D	Leedle Dee	Lopez,Charles	81,050	48,630
EatntwnHG3	19-Jul-03	10	MTH	1 1/16M	T	Stylish	Castillo, Jr.,Heberto	100,000	60,000
EBabstMemH	5-Apr-03	12	BEU	6F	D	Devil Time	Rosario, Jr.,Hector	40,000	24,000
EBJohnston	14-Sep-03	11	FPX	1 1/16M	D	Eclipse De Luna (CHI)	Pedroza,Martin	50,000	27,500
EclipseHG3	10-May-03	8	WO	1 1/16M	D	Phantom Light	Landry,Robert	172,650	103,590
Edgewood	2-May-03	5	CD	1M	T	Forest Shadows	Melancon,Larry	113,500	70,370
EdmontnJuv	25-Jul-03	4	NP	6F	D	Excellent Blend	Hamel,Richard	40,000	25,200
EdReadHG1	27-Jul-03	8	DMR	1 1/8M	T	Special Ring	Flores,David	400,000	240,000
EelRiverSp	10-Aug-03	7	FER	5F	D	Truly a Runner	Sanchez,Richard	8,200	4,225
EFinleyH	31-Jul-03	9	SR	6F	D	My Captain	Duran,Francisco	53,550	23,150
EHeubckDsH	15-Nov-03	11	CRC	1 1/16M	D	Scapade	Garcia,Julio	200,000	120,000
Eightthrty	29-Jun-03	7	DEL	1 1/8M	T	Better Talk Now	Dominguez,Ramon	58,700	35,220
Eillo	3-Oct-03	5	MED	6F	D	Outstander	Santana,Jozbin	50,000	30,000
ElanorSear	23-Aug-03	8	SUF	6F	D	African Princess	Bush,Vernon	35,000	21,000
ElCajon	5-Sep-03	7	DMR	1M	D	Excess Summer	Krone,Julie	101,825	61,095

Stakes	Date	Race	Trk	Dist/Surf		Winner	Jockey	Gross	Value to winner
ElCamRIDG3	8-Mar-03	8	GG	1 1/16M	D	Ocean Terrace	Smith,Mike	200,000	110,000
ElCnejoHG3	1-Jan-03	7	SA	5 1/2F	D	Kona Gold	Solis,Alex	108,800	65,280
ElEncinoG2	19-Jan-03	7	SA	1 1/16M	D	Got Koko	Solis,Alex	150,000	90,000
ELGaylrdMm	18-Oct-03	4	RP	1M	T	Notable Okie	Pettinger,Donald	35,000	20,500
Elgin	1-Sep-03	6	WO	1 1/16M	D	Barbeau Ruckus	Luciani,Dino	130,375	82,136
ElkCoTbDby	31-Aug-03	10	ELK	7F	D	Neil's Advice	Williams,Matt	9,450	4,725
ElkCoTbFut	31-Aug-03	6	ELK	5 1/2F	D	Primecat	House,Cody	9,000	4,500
ElkCoTbFut	1-Sep-03	6	ELK	5 1/2F	D	Dismissedhertouch	Thomas,Todd	9,000	4,950
ElkhornG3	23-Apr-03	8	KEE	1 1/2M	T	Kim Loves Bucky	Desormeaux,Kent	150,000	93,000
Elkwood	13-Jul-03	8	MTH	1 1/16M	T	Sir Brian's Sword	Bravo,Joe	50,000	30,000
ELoweStaln	15-Mar-03	6	SUF	6F	D	Stylish Sultan	Thompson,Winston	50,000	30,000
ElPasoTmsH	15-Feb-03	11	SUN	6 1/2F	D	Valid Pulpit	Gonzalez, Jr.,Sal	53,800	32,280
ElpBCH	10-Aug-03	9	ELP	6F	D	Vicki Vallencourt	Bejarano,Rafael	105,050	63,030
ElRasberry	8-Aug-03	11	LAD	7F	D	Letithappencaptain	LeBlanc,Kirk	60,000	24,000
EMcCabDby	24-Aug-03	8	SAC	6F	D	I B Bad	Navarro,Victor	53,000	29,000
EmDBCDerby	1-Sep-03	9	EMD	1 1/8M	D	Roscoe Pito	Krasner,Samuel	125,000	55,000
EmdBCDstfH	24-Aug-03	7	EMD	1M	D	Infernal McGoon	Gutierrez,Juan	100,000	41,250
Emeryville	17-May-03	7	BM	6F	D	Christmas Time	Lopez,Adalberto	78,650	33,650
EmpirClscH	18-Oct-03	10	BEL	1 1/8M	D	Well Fancied	Prado,Edgar	250,000	150,000
EmrldDwnsH	7-Jun-03	6	HST	6 1/2F	D	Dee's Love	Wright,Nicola	44,160	26,496
EmrldExprs	19-Jul-03	9	EMD	6F	D	Sundance Circle	Whitaker,Jennifer	35,000	17,325
EmrldNcklc	13-Sep-03	7	TDN	6F	D	Spring Cat	Villa-Gomez,Huber	35,000	21,000
Endeavour	8-Feb-03	10	TAM	1 1/8M	T	Wander Mom	Cruz,Manoel	75,000	45,000
EndineHG3	6-Sep-03	8	DEL	6F	D	House Party	Santos,Jose	200,000	120,000
EndlsSrprs	16-Mar-03	8	LRL	6F	D	The Deputy Is Home	Dominguez,Ramon	60,000	30,000
EnglndsLgd	22-Oct-03	8	BEL	1M	T	Lojo	Bridgmohan,Shaun	66,050	39,630
EPTaylorG1	19-Oct-03	5	WO	1 1/4M	T	Volga (IRE)	Migliore,Richard	750,000	450,000
EscondidoH	6-Aug-03	7	DMR	1 3/8M	T	Bonus Pack	Desormeaux,Kent	103,675	48,705
EShipmanH	20-Jul-03	8	BEL	1 1/16M	D	Well Fancied	Prado,Edgar	113,100	67,860
EssexHG3	22-Feb-03	9	OP	1 1/16M	D	Colorful Tour	Quinonez,Luis	100,000	60,000
EstrapadeH	15-Aug-03	8	AP	1 1/16M	T	Delicatessa	Razo, Jr.,Eusebio	75,000	45,000
EternlSrch	30-Jul-03	7	WO	1 1/16M	D	Kissed by a Prince	Luciani,Dino	126,625	75,975
ETMintJHG3	24-May-03	9	CD	1 1/16M	T	Kiss the Devil	Meche,Lonnie	168,300	104,346
ETSpringer	6-Sep-03	8	ALB	7F	D	Ciento	Olguin,Ever	37,100	22,260
EurDerby	1-Jun-03	7	EUR	6F	D	Missy Can Do	Vasquez,Richard	13,740	8,244
EurTbrdDb	22-Jun-03	5	EUR	4F	D	Tee Times Two	Vasquez,Richard	14,620	8,773
EvanstnDby	12-Jul-03	6	WYO	6F	D	On the Bill Daily	Greene,Casey	3,800	2,280
EvanstonH	12-Jul-03	11	WYO	4 1/2F	D	Synapse	Hamilton,Travis	3,425	2,055
Evansville	24-Oct-03	10	HOO	1 1/16M	D	Miss Dakota	Butler,Dean	37,250	22,350
EvdMileH	16-Aug-03	8	EVD	1M	D	Pie N Burger	Theriot,Jamie	75,000	45,000
EvdSpntChH	21-Jun-03	8	EVD	6F	D	No Its Not	Hernandez,Brian	35,000	21,000
EvDwnSales	2-Aug-03	9	EVD	5F	D	Streak of Smoke	Weatherly,James	50,000	30,000
ExcellerH	25-Jan-03	9	SA	1M	T	Alyzig	Krone,Julie	102,650	48,090
ExcesEnrgy	12-Nov-03	8	TUP	5 1/2F	D	La Duncan (ARG)	Corbett,Glenn	21,800	13,080
ExlsrBCHG3	5-Apr-03	8	AQU	1 1/8M	D	Classic Endeavor	Lopez,Charles	200,000	90,000
ExploBdHG2	23-Mar-03	8	FG	1 1/8M	T	Candid Glen	Perrodin,Elvis	650,000	390,000
ExpressH	19-Apr-03	8	ALB	5 1/2F	D	Smart Score	Coates,Jimmy	32,100	19,260
FAbadieMem	7-Jun-03	8	EVD	1M	D	Scarlet's Tara	Woodley,Carl	35,000	21,000
FAGenter	20-Dec-03	8	CRC	7 1/2F	T	Changing World	Bravo,Joe	100,000	60,000
FainRdOpen	2-Sep-03	10	YAV	4 1/2F	D	Toast for Mr. Expo	Lopez,Lorenzo	10,000	5,500
Fairfield	19-Jul-03	11	SOL	6F	D	Sharp Miss	Duran,Francisco	54,850	24,050
FairLady	3-May-03	7	HST	6 1/2F	D	Dancewithavixen	Valdez,Felipe	44,368	26,621
FairQueenH	12-Sep-03	8	ALB	6 1/2F	D	Sexy Boots	Tohill,Ken	33,300	19,980
FairwayFun	29-Mar-03	10	TP	1 1/16M	D	Seven Four Seven	Lumpkins,Jason	50,000	31,300
Fall	23-Sep-03	9	MNR	1 1/8M	D	Sonic West	Bejarano,Rafael	76,700	46,020
FallClDisH	20-Sep-03	5	NP	1 1/16M	D	Northern Neechitoo	Welch,Quincy	50,000	31,500
FallCtyHG2	27-Nov-03	10	CD	1 1/8M	D	Lead Story	Borel,Calvin	334,200	207,204
FallHwtHG3	27-Nov-03	8	AQU	6F	D	Bossanova	Prado,Edgar	108,300	64,980
FallsAmssH	11-Jul-03	4	HPO	1M	D	Oglala Sue	Shino,Ken	31,000	17,100
FallSprint	30-Aug-03	7	LBG	5 1/2F	D	Seattle Cue	Landaker,Terri	11,050	6,078
Fanfrelche	26-Oct-03	8	WO	6F	D	Ontheqt	McAleney,James	159,900	95,940
Fantasia	13-Jul-03	10	LAD	6F	D	Letithappencaptain	LeBlanc,Kirk	50,000	30,000

Stakes	Date	Race	Trk	Dist/Surf	Winner	Jockey	Gross	Value to winner
Fantasy	4-Oct-03	8	HST	1 1/16M	D	Comic Opera	Serna,Fernando	63,500	38,100
FantasyG2	11-Apr-03	10	OP	1 1/16M	D	Ruby's Reception	Thompson,Terry	200,000	120,000
FArnsnSire	17-Aug-03	7	ASD	6F	D	Coal Smudge	Leacock,Jason	35,000	21,000
Fashion	5-Jun-03	7	BEL	5F	D	Rodeo Licious	Migliore,Richard	80,000	48,000
FayetteG3	25-Oct-03	4	KEE	1 1/8M	D	M B Sea	Perret,Craig	163,800	101,556
FCapossela	20-Jan-03	8	AQU	6F	D	Alysweep	Migliore,Richard	79,800	47,880
FdrcoTesio	19-Apr-03	8	PIM	1 1/8M	D	Cherokee's Boy	Fogelsonger,Ryan	150,000	90,000
FedExSprnt	25-Jan-03	4	SA	6F	D	Captain Squire	Solis,Alex	250,000	137,500
FedralWayH	11-May-03	9	EMD	6 1/2F	D	Youcan'ttakeme	Baze,Gary	40,000	21,725
FFigueroCl	26-Apr-03	8	SON	6F	D	Fresh Victor	Nuttall,Todd	4,125	2,309
FfthSesnG3	9-Apr-03	9	OP	1 1/16M	D	Patton's Victory	Birzer,Alex	100,000	60,000
FGallMemH	23-Aug-03	8	CT	7F	D	Donald's Pride	Mawing,Anthony	41,750	27,138
FGBCH	1-Feb-03	9	FG	1 1/8M	T	Mystery Giver	Albarado,Robby	150,000	90,000
FGOaksG2	8-Mar-03	9	FG	1 1/16M	D	Lady Tak	Meche,Donnie	350,000	210,000
FGSales	2-Feb-03	8	FG	1M	D	Cypress Cove	Sellers,Shane	80,000	48,000
FHooperHG3	27-Dec-03	12	CRC	1 1/8M	D	Predawn Raid	Chavez,Jorge	100,000	60,000
FiestaMile	4-Oct-03	8	RET	1M	T	Eagle Lake	Melancon,Gerard	35,000	21,000
FillySale	16-Aug-03	2	NP	6 1/2F	D	Classa Red Wine	Welch,Quincy	50,000	30,000
FilMaresH	10-Aug-03	6	BOI	5F	D	Tera Kitty	Taveras,Reino	6,750	4,050
FindH	22-Aug-03	7	LRL	1 1/8M	T	Certantee	Karamanos,Horacio	75,000	45,000
FirecrckrH	4-Jul-03	3	MNR	1M	D	Ashwood C C	Gonzalez,Luis	77,700	46,620
FirePlug	12-Apr-03	8	PIM	6F	D	Love Happy	Dominguez,Ramon	75,000	45,000
FirstLady	23-May-03	9	IND	6F	D	Indy Fire	Coa,Daniel	37,600	22,560
FirstLadyH	14-Jun-03	11	RUI	6F	D	Runawayfun	Villa,Mark	31,400	18,840
FirstLadyHG3	12-Jan-03	10	GP	6F	D	Harmony Lodge	Velazquez,John	100,000	60,000
FKilroeHG2	1-Mar-03	8	SA	1M	T	Redattore (BRZ)	Solis,Alex	400,000	240,000
FLaBellMem	3-May-03	8	DEL	6F	D	Gimmeawink	Potts,Clinton	75,000	45,000
FlaBrDist	17-Mar-03	4	OTC	1 1/16M	D	Kiss Me Twice	Gonzalez,Carlos	35,000	21,000
FlaDerbyG1	15-Mar-03	8	GP	1 1/8M	D	Empire Maker	Bailey,Jerry	1,000,000	600,000
FlagDown	15-Mar-03	12	GP	1 1/8M	D	Woodmoon	Bailey,Jerry	52,700	31,620
FlaminPage	7-Sep-03	8	WO	1 1/2M	T	Heyahohowdy	Sabourin,Raymond	109,000	65,400
FlaOaksG3	16-Mar-03	12	TAM	1 1/16M	D	Ebony Breeze	Guidry,Mark	150,000	90,000
FlashG3	6-Jun-03	7	BEL	5F	D	Chapel Royal	Velazquez,John	106,400	63,955
FlashwayH	27-Apr-03	5	PM	5F	D	Proud Louie	Beckner,Twyla	6,500	3,575
FlaTbChrty	17-Mar-03	8	OTC	5F	D	Hana Highway	Rivera,II,Jose	35,000	21,000
Flawlessly	20-Sep-03	8	AP	1M	T	Delmonico Cat	Douglas,Rene	48,600	29,160
Flawlessly	6-Jul-03	8	HOL	1M	T	Just Too Too	Stevens,Gary	112,300	67,380
FleetTreat	27-Jul-03	6	DMR	7F	D	Tucked Away	Stevens,Gary	100,000	60,000
FLJuvenile	11-Oct-03	8	FL	6F	D	Mr. Fixed Income	Grabowski,John	35,000	21,000
FloorShow	24-May-03	7	DEL	1 1/16M	D	Don Six	Caraballo,Jose	57,900	34,740
FloydDuncn	11-Jan-03	8	SUF	6F	D	Special Jule	Thompson,Winston	35,000	21,000
FlrDLisHG2	14-Jun-03	9	CD	1 1/8M	D	You	Bailey,Jerry	327,900	203,298
FlrlPrkHG3	13-Sep-03	6	BEL	6F	D	Bauhauser (ARG)	Migliore,Richard	108,500	65,100
FlwrBllvG1	27-Sep-03	8	BEL	1 1/4M	T	Dimitrova	Bailey,Jerry	750,000	450,000
FlyingLark	9-Feb-03	8	PM	6F	D	I Won't Apollogize	Jones,Clark	10,000	5,500
FlyngPdgnH	18-Oct-03	5	CRC	1 1/8M	T	French Charmer	DeCarlo,Christopher	100,000	60,000
FMendelMmH	18-Jul-03	6	MD	1M	D	Double Time	Latchman,Rennie	5,000	3,000
FntngoLdy	10-Jul-03	4	HPO	1M	D	Verzene	Shino,Ken	29,800	16,980
FntnOYthG1	15-Feb-03	11	GP	1 1/16M	D	Trust N Luck	Velasquez,Cornelio	200,000	120,000
FolkloreH	31-Aug-03	5	LAD	6 1/2F	D	That Tat	Theriot,Jamie	50,000	30,000
FonPkSpecl	13-Apr-03	9	FON	6F	D	Sundayblummer	Warhol,Vicki	26,100	15,660
FonPkSpecl	5-Apr-03	9	FON	6F	D	Homer's Hero	Carkeek,Jerome	26,275	15,765
FoolExprts	25-Nov-03	7	TUP	6 1/2F	D	Bold Merit	Gomez,Esteban	21,900	13,140
FoolshPlsr	20-Sep-03	10	CRC	1M 70Y	D	Stolen Time	Boulanger,Gary	100,000	60,000
Foothill	12-Sep-03	11	FPX	6 1/2F	D	King Robyn	Fogelsonger,Ryan	50,000	27,500
FordExpres	3-May-03	9	LS	6F	D	That Tat	Martin, Jr.,Eddie	75,000	45,000
Forego	25-Jan-03	10	TP	6 1/2F	D	Private Horde	Lumpkins,Jason	50,000	31,300
ForegoH	6-Sep-03	6	FP	1M 70Y	D	W W Robin de Hood	Woodley,John	25,500	15,300
ForegoHG1	31-Aug-03	10	SAR	7F	D	Aldebaran	Bailey,Jerry	250,000	150,000
Forerunner	17-Apr-03	8	KEE	1 1/8M	T	Californian (GB)	Desormeaux,Kent	111,200	68,944
FortWayne	4-Oct-03	8	HOO	6F	D	Mr. Mink	Pompell,Thomas	39,750	23,850
FortyNinrH	28-Nov-03	7	GG	1 1/16M	D	Star Cross (ARG)	Alvarado,Frank	85,500	51,750

Stakes	Date	Race	Trk	Dist/Surf		Winner	Jockey	Gross	Value to winner
ForwardGal	21-Sep-03	9	MTH	6F	D	Smokey Glacken	Velez, Jr.,Jose	50,000	30,000
ForwrdPass	16-Aug-03	5	AP	7F	D	Coach Jimi Lee	Day,Pat	52,400	31,440
FosterCtyH	15-Jun-03	4	BM	1 1/16M	T	Handyman Bill	Alvarado,Frank	78,000	33,850
FourSeasnH	14-Sep-03	7	BRD	1M	D	Taxauditor	Camacho,Fernando	7,425	4,455
FourstrdavHG2	23-Aug-03	9	SAR	1 1/16M	T	Trademark (SAF)	Migliore,Richard	200,000	120,000
FOXSprtNtH	18-May-03	8	EMD	6 1/2F	D	Turban	Mitchell,Gallyn	35,000	19,250
FoxyJG	19-Jul-03	9	PHA	7F	D	Tri's Passion	Carmouche,Kendrick	55,400	33,240
FranGenter	6-Jul-03	8	CBY	6F	D	Madam Speaker	Bell,Derek	41,325	24,795
FranSlocum	23-Nov-03	8	HOO	1 1/16M	D	Ellens Lucky Star	Mojica,Orlando	38,950	23,370
FrckrBCHG2	5-Jul-03	9	CD	1M	T	Tap the Admiral	McKee,John	288,500	178,870
FrdmOfCity	11-Oct-03	7	NP	1M	D	Waikoloa	Wilson,David	40,000	25,200
FreePress	15-Jun-03	7	ASD	6F	D	Kalfaari	Singh,Rohan	35,000	21,000
FreeSprtsH	22-Jun-03	9	RUI	6F	D	Sky Diver	Bourdieu,Jorge	31,400	18,840
FreeVactnH	1-Sep-03	4	HST	1 1/16M	D	Dancewithavixen	Valdez,Felipe	55,785	33,471
FReidIIIMm	1-Nov-03	4	TUP	5 1/2F	D	Timbers Two	Stevens,Scott	21,800	13,080
Friendship	13-Sep-03	9	LAD	6F	D	Roundabout Jones	Murphy,Glen	71,005	42,603
Friendship	13-Sep-03	11	LAD	6F	D	Hay Lauren	Melancon,Gerard	64,417	38,650
FriskMeNow	25-May-03	10	MTH	1M 70Y	D	Classic Endeavor	Lopez,Charles	60,000	36,000
FrizetteG1	4-Oct-03	6	BEL	1 1/16M	D	Society Selection	Ganpath,Ray	500,000	300,000
FrkFrmFMTf	25-Jan-03	9	GP	1 1/8M	T	Stay Forever	Santos,Jose	350,000	192,500
FrndlyLvrH	20-Sep-03	5	MTH	6F	D	Something Smith	King, Jr.,Edwin	45,000	27,000
FrnsValntn	26-Apr-03	3	HOL	1 1/16M	T	Shalini	Nakatani,Corey	150,000	90,000
FrntRangeH	4-Jul-03	7	ARP	7F	D	Daring Pegasus	Theriot,Brian	35,000	21,000
FrontierH	30-Aug-03	7	GLD	1 1/8M	D	Akatsakat	Molina,Tommy	45,000	27,000
FrostKing	8-Oct-03	6	WO	7F	D	Copper Trail	Villeneuve,Francine	129,250	77,550
FrrBelLeeH	29-Aug-03	7	GLD	1 1/16M	D	Tank Grrrl	Martinez,Luis	45,000	27,000
FrstEpsode	14-Apr-03	5	SUF	1 1/16M	D	Little Time	Thompson,Winston	35,000	21,000
FrstFltHG2	25-Oct-03	4	BEL	7F	D	Randaroo	Castillo, Jr.,Heberto	150,000	90,000
FrwrdGalG3	14-Mar-03	7	GP	7F	D	Midnight Cry	Prado,Edgar	100,000	60,000
FSAffirmed	30-Aug-03	10	CRC	7F	D	Sir Oscar	Garcia,Julio	125,000	75,000
FSawyerH	6-Jul-03	11	RUI	1M	D	Runawayfun	Villa,Mark	26,400	15,840
FSDrFager	9-Aug-03	11	CRC	6F	D	Sir Oscar	Garcia,Julio	75,000	45,000
FSDsrtVixn	9-Aug-03	9	CRC	6F	D	French Village	Penalba,Cecilio	75,000	45,000
FSMyDrGirl	11-Oct-03	10	CRC	1 1/16M	D	Chatter Chatter	Bailey,Jerry	400,000	240,000
FSNReality	11-Oct-03	11	CRC	1 1/16M	D	Sir Oscar	Garcia,Julio	400,000	240,000
FSRmnBrthr	26-Jul-03	1	CRC	1 1/16M	D	Supah Blitz	Castanon,Jesus	50,000	30,000
FSSsnsGirl	30-Aug-03	8	CRC	7F	D	French Village	Boulanger,Gary	125,000	75,000
FtMarcyHG3	26-Apr-03	8	AQU	1M	D	Saint Verre	Espinoza,Jose	117,500	70,500
FurlSail	26-Dec-03	9	FG	1M	T	Bedanken	Pettinger,Donald	60,000	36,000
Fury	4-May-03	8	WO	7F	D	Elusive Thought	McAleney,James	162,750	97,650
FuturityG1	14-Sep-03	7	BEL	1M	D	Cuvee	Bailey,Jerry	200,000	120,000
GailyGaily	28-Feb-03	8	GP	1 1/8M	D	Devil At the Wire	Guidry,Mark	74,200	44,520
GalaLil	22-Mar-03	8	LRL	1 1/8M	D	Undercover	Pino,Mario	75,000	45,000
GallntBobH	4-Oct-03	8	PHA	6F	D	Northern Air	Rocco,Joseph	150,000	90,000
GalntFoxH	27-Dec-03	8	AQU	1 5/8M	D	Loving (BRZ)	Espinoza,Jose	83,925	50,355
GalrettHG3	17-May-03	7	PIM	1 1/16M	T	Carib Lady (IRE)	Valenzuela,Patrick	100,000	60,000
GamlyBCHG1	26-Apr-03	6	HOL	1 1/8M	T	Tates Creek	Valenzuela,Patrick	439,000	263,400
Gardenia	20-Dec-03	9	DED	6 1/2F	D	Kylers Midge	Smith,Guy	40,000	24,000
Gasparilla	1-Feb-03	10	TAM	7F	D	Ebony Breeze	Judice,Joseph	50,000	21,000
GateDancer	9-Aug-03	7	DEL	1 1/8M	D	Changeintheweather	Castillo,Oliver	59,600	35,760
Gaviola	2-Jul-03	8	BEL	1 1/16M	T	Ocean Drive	Bailey,Jerry	65,750	39,450
GazelleHG1	6-Sep-03	7	BEL	1 1/8M	D	Buy the Sport	Day,Pat	250,000	150,000
GCFAAcTxBr	24-Aug-03	6	GIL	7F	D	Bold Reply	Carrizales,Santos	13,600	8,160
GCHndriHG3	11-May-03	8	WO	6 1/2F	D	El Prado Essence	Husbands,Patrick	222,950	103,770
GdwdBCHG2	4-Oct-03	5	SA	1 1/8M	D	Pleasantly Perfect	Solis,Alex	500,000	300,000
GeishaH	7-Dec-03	9	LRL	1 1/16M	D	Cruise Along	Castellano, Jr.,Abel	100,000	60,000
GendelmanH	22-Jun-03	7	RD	1 1/16M	D	Devil Time	Troilo,William	50,000	30,000
GenerousG3	29-Nov-03	5	HOL	1M	T	Castledale (IRE)	Krone,Julie	100,000	60,000
GenGrgeHG2	22-Feb-03	9	LRL	7F	D	My Cousin Matt	Dominguez,Ramon	200,000	120,000
GenPortion	3-Sep-03	6	DMR	6F	D	She's Gottogetaway	Enriquez,Isaias	100,000	60,000
GentillyH	22-Mar-03	9	FG	1M	T	Zarb's Music	Melancon,Gerard	100,000	60,000
GenuinRisk	30-Aug-03	6	FP	1M 70Y	D	Jadester	Medina,Cynthia	25,600	15,360

Stakes	Date	Race	Trk	Dist/Surf		Winner	Jockey	Gross	Value to winner
GenValBrdH	2-Aug-03	8	FL	1 1/16M	D	Noble Adversary	Rohena,Manuel	40,000	24,000
GeorgRoyal	10-May-03	8	HST	6 1/2F	D	Diglett	Alvarado,Pedro	44,160	24,000
GFrncsAscH	19-Jul-03	9	ANF	1 1/16M	D	Was a Zeal	Ludlow,Megan	5,400	3,240
GGBrdCpHG3	16-Mar-03	3	GG	1 1/8M	T	Ninebanks	Warren, Jr.,Ronald	150,000	82,500
GGDerbyG3	11-Jan-03	8	GG	1 1/16M	D	Standard Setter	Gonzalez,Roberto	100,000	55,000
GildedTime	24-May-03	7	MTH	5F	D	Buzzy's Gold	Bravo,Joe	50,000	30,000
GirlPowdrH	18-Oct-03	7	MED	6F	D	Lovely Fiona	Lopez,Charles	40,000	24,000
GKlinchtDH	22-Aug-03	6	MD	1 1/16M	D	Top Stage Dancer	Latchman,Rennie	5,000	3,000
GldnHrshoe	10-Aug-03	8	FE	6 1/2F	D	Spanish Decree	Barton,Jake	90,000	54,000
GldnPhsnt	14-Sep-03	8	AP	1M	T	Al's Dearly Bred	Douglas,Rene	47,700	28,620
GldnPoppyH	18-Oct-03	3	BM	1 1/16M	D	Angel Gift	Baze,Russell	78,500	33,500
GldnStMile	9-Feb-03	8	GG	1M	D	Ministers Wild Cat	Desormeaux,Kent	78,650	33,650
GldnTringl	5-Dec-03	5	DED	6 1/2F	D	Alienated	Gonzalez,Carlos	50,000	30,000
GlendaleH	8-Feb-03	8	TUP	1 1/16M	T	Secret Garden (IRE)	Johnston,Mark	50,000	30,000
GlenFlsHG3	25-Aug-03	8	SAR	1 3/8M	T	Sixty Seconds (NZ)	Santos,Jose	113,100	67,860
GLewisMem	25-Jul-03	13	TDN	1 1/8M	D	Devil Time	Troilo,William	50,000	30,000
Glitterman	21-Jun-03	1	CRC	6F	D	Juggernaut	Cruz,Manoel	42,200	22,320
GlmngChnnl	5-May-03	7	CRC	1 1/16M	T	Sea Pleasure	Velasquez,Cornelio	42,950	27,770
GlntBlmHG2	5-Oct-03	9	BEL	6 1/2F	D	Harmony Lodge	Migliore,Richard	150,000	90,000
GlorisSong	9-Nov-03	8	WO	7F	D	Silver Bird	McAleney,James	186,875	112,125
GlPrincess	19-Dec-03	1	BEU	1M	D	Happy Endings Too	Herrell,James	35,000	21,000
GLStryker	19-Jan-03	8	LRL	7F	D	Cherokee's Boy	Fogelsonger,Ryan	60,000	36,000
GMalleah	7-Dec-03	7	TUP	6F	D	Coded Message	Corbett,Glenn	22,000	13,200
GMaloofFut	21-Sep-03	7	ALB	6F	D	Youareaggravatin'	Jaime,Ricardo	68,480	34,241
GnDMcAthrH	5-Sep-03	8	BEL	7F	D	Well Fancied	Prado,Edgar	109,600	65,760
GnunRskHG2	11-May-03	8	BEL	6F	D	Shine Again	Samyn,Jean-Luc	150,000	90,000
GoddessH	22-Mar-03	9	DED	1M	D	Salty Farma	Meche,Lonnie	100,000	60,000
GoForWand	31-May-03	7	DEL	1 1/16M	D	Hennie's Song	Black,Anthony	100,000	60,000
GoFWandHG1	27-Jul-03	9	SAR	1 1/8M	D	Sightseek	Bailey,Jerry	250,000	150,000
GoingUp	8-Sep-03	8	CRC	7F	D	Honeymooner	Homeister, Jr.,Rosemary	42,250	27,350
Goldarama	27-Apr-03	10	CRC	6F	D	Tchula Miss	Toribio, Jr.,Aurelio	42,225	27,335
GoldBC	28-Sep-03	8	ASD	1 1/8M	D	Sir Pucker	Hightower,Travis	43,750	21,000
GoldCup	15-Nov-03	9	DED	1M	D	Zarb's Luck	Smith,Guy	100,000	60,000
GoldCupH	2-Mar-03	7	DED	1M	D	Prince Slew	Melancon,Gerard	150,000	90,000
GoldenBear	23-Nov-03	7	GG	6F	D	The Herc	Baze,Russell	78,650	33,650
GoldenBoy	7-Jun-03	7	ASD	6F	D	Cool Bender	Blinston,Ron	35,000	21,000
GoldenGull	20-Sep-03	7	CT	4 1/2F	D	Petes Hick Chick	Torres,Raymond	37,100	24,115
Goldfinch	18-Apr-03	8	PRM	6F	D	Elusive Sara	Thompson,Terry	53,000	30,000
GoldnRodG2	29-Nov-03	10	CD	1 1/16M	D	Be Gentle	McKee,John	230,000	142,600
GoldRush	13-Dec-03	7	GG	1M	D	Skipaslew	Saint-Martin,Eric	82,650	48,900
GoldSylviH	17-Jun-03	9	MNR	1M	D	Clear Destiny	Bejarano,Rafael	77,400	46,440
GoodIntent	1-Nov-03	9	CRC	1M	T	Hermans Honor	Nunez,Eduardo	37,875	24,725
GoodIntent	1-Nov-03	5	CRC	1M	T	Gypsy Dot	Homeister, Jr.,Rosemary	37,625	24,575
GothamG3	16-Mar-03	9	AQU	1M 70Y	D	Alysweep	Migliore,Richard	200,000	120,000
GottstnFut	21-Sep-03	9	EMD	1 1/16M	D	Corvallis Dee	Radke,Kevin	100,000	55,000
GovCupFMH	14-Sep-03	11	FAR	7F	D	Red At the Helm	Schindler,Scot	15,700	7,850
GovCupH	31-May-03	8	BOI	7F	D	Quiet Syns	Conklin,Jay	4,751	2,850
GovernorsH	23-Aug-03	8	SAC	1 1/8M	D	Classic Fool	Romero,Hector	60,600	33,100
GovernorsH	23-Aug-03	9	ELP	1M	D	Sonic West	Bejarano,Rafael	75,000	46,250
GovernorsH	3-Aug-03	9	EMD	6 1/2F	D	Handy N Bold	Russell,Ben	50,000	27,500
GovernorsH	19-Jul-03	9	RUI	7 1/2F	D	Caliban	Bourdieu,Jorge	26,100	15,660
GovrnrsCpH	12-Jul-03	4	WYO	1M	D	Pj'salarm	Crane,Dirk	3,525	2,115
GovSpeed	30-Mar-03	8	PM	6F	D	Lethal Grande	Boag,Daniel	10,000	5,500
Gowell	20-Dec-03	10	TP	6F	D	Leading Lioness	Johnston,Mark	50,000	31,300
GPBCHG1	16-Feb-03	10	GP	1 3/8M	T	Man From Wicklow	Bailey,Jerry	200,000	120,000
GPHG2	29-Mar-03	11	GP	1 1/4M	D	Hero's Tribute	Prado,Edgar	300,000	180,000
Graduation	8-Feb-03	8	DED	5F	D	Cleaning House	Bourque,Steven	46,300	23,150
Graduation	30-Jul-03	7	DMR	5 1/2F	D	Don'tsellmeshort	Valenzuela,Patrick	125,000	75,000
Graduation	4-Jul-03	7	ASD	5 1/2F	D	Noble Halo	Iammarino,Michael	35,000	21,428
GrasmickH	22-Feb-03	9	FON	4F	D	Leaping Plum	Wall,Newil	11,525	6,315
GravesdHG3	21-Dec-03	8	AQU	6F	D	Shake You Down	Luzzi,Michael	109,000	65,400
GraysLake	26-May-03	8	PRM	6F	D	Billy Idel	Shino,Ken	59,950	35,970

Stakes	Date	Race	Trk	Dist/Surf		Winner	Jockey	Gross	Value to winner
GrdCyBCHG1	7-Sep-03	9	BEL	1 1/8M	T	Indy Five Hundred	Day,Pat	250,000	150,000
GrdeniaHG3	9-Aug-03	10	ELP	1 1/8M	D	Bare Necessities	Douglas,Rene	200,000	120,000
GreenCarpt	31-May-03	6	RD	1 1/16M	D	Hackendiffy	Rowland,Michael	50,000	30,000
GreenFlshH	20-Aug-03	7	DMR	5F	T	King Robyn	Solis,Alex	98,600	45,660
GreenOaks	23-Feb-03	8	DED	7F	D	Calleybluebayou	Woodley,Carl	100,000	60,000
GrenwodCpH	7-Jun-03	10	PHA	1 1/2M	D	Golden Ticket	DeAlba,Cesar	100,000	60,000
GreyBCG2	5-Oct-03	9	WO	1 1/16M	D	Smoocher	McAleney,James	277,250	166,350
GrIndORssH	13-Dec-03	7	AQU	6F	D	Balmy	Elliott,Stewart	82,950	49,770
GrndCanynH	26-Apr-03	6	TUP	6F	D	Jomax	Gomez,Esteban	35,000	21,000
GroomstckH	16-Aug-03	6	CRC	6 1/2F	D	Built Up	Aguilar,Manuel	75,000	41,000
Groovy	15-Nov-03	9	HOU	7F	D	Roundabout Jones	Beasley,Jeremy	50,000	30,000
GrPrTrfChl	5-Apr-03	9	LS	1M	T	Lone Star Deputy	Martin, Jr.,Eddie	100,000	60,000
GRsnbrgrMm	6-Sep-03	9	DEL	1 1/16M	T	Madeira Mist (IRE)	Dominguez,Ramon	75,000	45,000
GrtMystery	7-Jun-03	6	SUF	6F	D	Glory Be Good	Molinari,Edwin	35,000	21,000
GtwyToGlry	25-Sep-03	11	FPX	1 1/16M	D	Skipaslew	Baze,Tyler	50,000	27,500
GulfCoastH	23-Mar-03	8	DED	1 1/16M	D	No Its Not	Hernandez,Brian	150,000	90,000
GusGrissom	9-Nov-03	9	HOO	1 1/16M	D	Dakota Diamond	Diego,Inosencio	39,150	23,490
GvnrBkyCp	1-Sep-03	9	TDN	1 1/4M	D	Devil Time	Troilo,William	75,000	45,000
GvnrsLdyH	12-Apr-03	5	HAW	6F	D	Seven Brides	Silva,Carlos	131,077	51,705
GWBarker	26-May-03	8	FL	6F	D	Cheap Talk	Grabowski,John	35,000	21,000
GWelchH	6-Jul-03	7	BOI	1M	D	Constantly	Packer,Berkley	7,050	4,230
HAddisonJr	29-Jun-03	8	FE	1 1/16M	D	Barbeau Ruckus	Montpellier,Constant	75,000	45,000
Haggin	21-Jun-03	4	HOL	5 1/2F	D	Stalking Tiger	Almeida,G.	98,550	59,130
HailEmpror	15-Nov-03	7	LRL	1 1/16M	D	Last Intention	Castellano, Jr.,Abel	50,000	30,000
HalfMnBayH	21-Sep-03	3	BM	1 1/16M	T	Blue Blood Boot	Warren, Jr.,Ronald	78,450	33,450
HalHopeHG3	11-Jan-03	10	GP	1 1/16M	D	Windsor Castle	Coa,Eibar	100,000	60,000
HallOFameH	3-Aug-03	7	CLS	6F	D	High Tech Racing	Martinez,Armando	9,200	5,520
HalOFmeHG2	4-Aug-03	8	SAR	1 1/8M	T	Stroll	Bailey,Jerry	150,000	90,000
HalRckDtGm	25-Oct-03	5	LBG	7F	D	The Wildest Rose	Blinston,Ron	11,200	6,160
Halton	1-Sep-03	7	WO	1 1/8M	T	Mobil	Kabel,Todd	131,875	79,125
HanahDustn	12-Feb-03	8	SUF	1M 70Y	D	Ms. Sadira	Bush,Vernon	35,000	21,000
HancockCoH	13-May-03	9	MNR	5F	D	Alison's Winner	Felix,Julio	78,000	46,800
Hansel	22-Mar-03	7	TP	6F	D	Quick Draw	Day,Pat	50,000	24,800
HanshinHG3	29-Jun-03	8	AP	1M	D	Apt to Be	Razo, Jr.,Eusebio	100,000	60,000
HAntnyMemH	2-Aug-03	7	YAV	6F	D	First Snowbound	Martinez,Orlando	15,000	8,250
HArnltMemH	9-Aug-03	6	MNR	6F	D	Secret Romeo	Velasquez,Cornelio	88,000	52,800
HarperCoH	13-Jul-03	13	ANF	5F	D	Grand Strand	Ludlow,Megan	4,900	2,100
HarperCoH	13-Jul-03	9	ANF	5F	D	Sunset Cruise	Latham,Jeremy	4,900	2,100
HarvestH	22-Mar-03	8	ALB	5 1/2F	D	Absolutely True	Summers,Nancy	33,300	19,980
Hatoof	23-Aug-03	6	AP	1 1/16M	T	Cat's Cat	Lovato, Jr.,Frank	53,600	32,160
HawDerbyG3	18-Oct-03	8	HAW	1 1/8M	T	False Promises	Marquez, Jr.,Carlos	250,000	150,000
HawGldCHG2	28-Sep-03	9	HAW	1 1/4M	D	Perfect Drift	Day,Pat	750,000	450,000
HawkeyesH	28-Jun-03	6	PRM	1 1/16M	D	Sharky's Review	Quinonez,Luis	70,000	42,000
HawOaks	15-Nov-03	8	HAW	1 1/16M	D	Beautiful Crazy	Vitek,Justin	100,000	60,000
HawthrnHG3	25-Apr-03	3	HOL	1 1/16M	D	Keys to the Heart	Valdivia, Jr.,Jose	105,400	63,240
HBNoonan	22-Mar-03	15	BEU	6F	D	Southtown Slew	Dasilva,Axel	35,000	22,750
HBPAAlmHvn	20-Jul-03	9	CT	4 1/2F	D	French Republic	Cline,Vincent	41,850	27,203
HBPAChsTnH	10-Oct-03	7	CT	1 1/8M	D	Ribbon Cane	Monterrey,Richard	51,750	33,638
HBPAGovCpH	10-Oct-03	4	CT	4 1/2F	D	Sea of Green	Perez,Nilo	51,300	33,345
HBPAH	12-Jul-03	10	ELP	1M	D	Lead Story	Börel,Calvin	100,000	61,250
HBPAH	7-Jun-03	8	GRP	5 1/2F	D	Tee Tommy Slew	Skaggs,Tad	3,925	2,161
HBPAJeffCo	20-Jul-03	6	CT	1 1/8M	D	Jackyscraftychance	Mawing,Anthony	42,250	27,463
HBPAOpeqon	20-Jul-03	7	CT	4 1/2F	D	Wise Sweep	Jawny,Alvaro	41,600	27,040
HBPARansnH	10-Oct-03	6	CT	7F	D	Donald's Pride	Mawing,Anthony	51,650	33,573
HBPASgbrDy	24-Aug-03	6	KAM	1M	D	Fire Within Fire	Bilodeau,Ronald	5,200	3,120
HBPAWVOaks	20-Jul-03	8	CT	7F	D	Shesanothergrump	Mawing,Anthony	41,800	27,170
HcmbrideG3	1-Feb-03	10	GP	1 1/16M	T	Gal O Gal	DeCarlo,Christopher	100,000	60,000
HCRamsrSrH	12-Oct-03	7	SA	1M	T	Valentine Dancer	Valenzuela,Patrick	113,900	68,340
Heckofrlph	16-Jun-03	4	CRC	5 1/2F	D	Awesome of Course	Cruz,Manoel	41,950	27,170
HEJhnsnMmH	15-Mar-03	8	LRL	1 1/8M	D	P Day	Fogelsonger,Ryan	75,000	45,000
Helena	19-Apr-03	8	SUF	1M	D	Jill's Layup	Hole,Taylor	35,000	21,000
HenryClark	3-May-03	9	PIM	1M	T	Tam's Terms	Karamanos,Horacio	75,000	45,000

Stakes	Date	Race	Trk	Dist/Surf		Winner	Jockey	Gross	Value to winner
HerldGldPH	8-Jun-03	8	STP	1 1/16M	D	They Call Me Cody	Winters,Perry	50,000	31,500
HermosBchH	6-Dec-03	5	HOL	1 1/2M	T	Lady Annaliese (NZ)	Solis,Alex	87,750	40,950
HFBrubakrH	22-Aug-03	2	DMR	1 1/16M	T	Sarafan	Nakatani,Corey	75,675	45,459
HfprOMHrtH	25-May-03	7	STP	1M	D	Taiaslew	Simard,Real	50,000	25,200
HgoodmanSp	28-Jun-03	3	LS	6F	D	Herve	Melancon,Gerard	50,000	30,000
HHenson	23-Apr-03	7	HOL	5 1/2F	T	King Robyn	Solis,Alex	100,200	46,620
HHensonH	5-Apr-03	10	SUN	1M	D	Cielo Girl	Meche,Lonnie	104,350	62,610
HHindmarsh	29-Jun-03	6	FE	1 1/16M	D	Royal Dalliance	Somsanith,Na	75,000	45,000
Highlands	10-Aug-03	10	MTH	1M	D	Uphill Skier	Bravo,Joe	50,000	30,000
HilandHpng	9-Aug-03	8	SUF	1 1/16M	D	Megan's Halo	Bermudez,Jose	35,000	21,000
HilandrHG3	19-Oct-03	3	WO	6F	D	Forever Grand	Kabel,Todd	161,250	96,750
Hildene	18-Oct-03	7	DEL	6F	D	Secret Glow	Black,Anthony	42,000	25,200
HillPrncG3	14-Jun-03	7	BEL	1 1/8M	D	Happy Trails	Bridgmohan,Shaun	113,100	67,860
HillRise	29-Dec-03	1	SA	1M	T	Greek Sun	Solis,Alex	101,250	47,250
Hillsborgh	16-Mar-03	10	TAM	1 1/16M	T	Strait From Texas	Castanon,Jesus	100,000	60,000
HillsboroH	20-Sep-03	8	BM	1 1/16M	T	Ilha Grande	Duran,Francisco	78,950	33,950
Hillsdale	4-Oct-03	7	HOO	5 1/2F	D	Gearbox	Prescott,Rodney	39,300	23,580
Hilltop	10-May-03	9	PIM	1 1/16M	D	City Fire	Rose,Jeremy	75,000	30,000
HJeffrey	24-Aug-03	6	ASD	1 1/8M	D	Northern Affair	Iammarino,Michael	35,000	21,000
HKJockClbH	31-May-03	8	HST	6 1/2F	D	Bold 'n Keen	Wright,Nicola	44,368	26,621
HlieHughsH	2-Mar-03	8	AQU	6F	D	Papua	Migliore,Richard	80,725	48,435
HlIndlBch	19-Apr-03	9	GP	7F	D	Cajun Beat	Boulanger,Gary	75,000	45,000
HmnaDstHG1	3-May-03	8	CD	7F	D	Sightseek	Bailey,Jerry	222,400	137,888
HndPomInvH	28-Sep-03	11	FPX	1 1/8M	D	Chinkapin	Berrio,Omar	100,000	55,000
HnrblMsHG3	1-Aug-03	8	SAR	6F	D	Willa On the Move	Prado,Edgar	107,600	64,560
HnrHrTfExp	26-May-03	8	CBY	5F	T	Flying Supercon	Stevens,Scott	35,000	21,000
HnstPleasr	26-Jul-03	3	AP	5 1/2F	D	Next Bandit	Douglas,Rene	52,800	31,680
HnymnBCHG2	7-Jun-03	8	HOL	1 1/8M	T	Quero Quero	Baze,Tyler	216,950	130,170
HoistHrFlg	31-May-03	8	CBY	6F	D	Don't Countess Out	Thompson,Terry	35,000	21,000
HolBCOakG2	14-Jun-03	6	HOL	1 1/16M	D	Santa Catarina	Stevens,Gary	212,200	127,320
HolDerbyG1	30-Nov-03	9	HOL	1 1/4M	D	Sweet Return (GB)	Krone,Julie	600,000	360,000
HolFutG1	20-Dec-03	8	HOL	1 1/16M	D	Lion Heart	Smith,Mike	382,000	225,600
HolGldCpG1	13-Jul-03	9	HOL	1 1/4M	D	Congaree	Bailey,Jerry	750,000	450,000
HolidayChr	1-Jan-03	9	TP	6F	D	Ultimate Warrior	Peck,Brian	50,000	31,300
HolidayChr	27-Dec-03	10	TP	6F	D	Founding Chairman	D'Amico,Anthony	50,000	31,300
HolidayIng	30-Nov-03	9	TP	6F	D	Halory Leigh	Perret,Craig	50,000	31,300
HolJuvChG3	19-Jul-03	4	HOL	6F	D	Perfect Moon	Valenzuela,Patrick	102,500	61,500
HolPrevuG3	15-Nov-03	7	HOL	7F	D	Lion Heart	Smith,Mike	100,000	60,000
HolStrltG1	21-Dec-03	9	HOL	1 1/16M	D	Hollywood Story	Valenzuela,Patrick	355,500	209,700
HolTrExHG3	28-Nov-03	9	HOL	5 1/2F	T	King Robyn	Baze,Tyler	150,000	90,000
HolTrfCpG1	22-Nov-03	8	HOL	1 1/2M	T	Continuously	Solis,Alex	250,000	150,000
HolWildcat	29-Nov-03	8	CRC	1 1/16M	T	Vous	Bravo,Joe	100,000	60,000
HolyBullG3	18-Jan-03	10	GP	1 1/16M	D	Offlee Wild	Guidry,Mark	100,000	60,000
HolyCapote	14-Sep-03	5	CRC	1 1/16M	T	Lost Appeal	Nunez,Eduardo	43,575	28,145
Honeybee	8-Mar-03	10	OP	1 1/16M	D	My Trusty Cat	Pettinger,Donald	75,000	45,000
HoneyJayH	14-Sep-03	7	BEU	6F	D	Ben's Reflection	Ouzts,Perry	40,000	24,000
Honeymoon	28-Jun-03	10	LAD	1M	T	Bien Nicole	Doocy,Timothy	50,000	30,000
HonkyStar	16-Aug-03	7	DEL	6F	D	Bruanna	Black,Anthony	58,900	35,340
HonyFoxHG3	5-Jan-03	10	GP	1 1/16M	D	San Dare	Guidry,Mark	100,000	60,000
HootersSpt	6-Apr-03	10	TAM	6F	D	Built Up	Coa,Eibar	82,800	45,680
Hoover	20-Jan-03	8	LRL	6F	D	Shake the Dice	Potts,Clinton	60,000	30,000
Hoover	2-Aug-03	5	RD	6F	D	Ding's Thing	Felix,Julio	40,000	24,000
HopefulG1	30-Aug-03	8	SAR	7F	D	Silver Wagon	Bailey,Jerry	200,000	120,000
Horatius	23-Mar-03	8	LRL	6F	D	Deadline	Wilson,Rick	60,000	30,000
Horizon	20-Jul-03	5	RD	1 1/16M	D	Woodburner	Johnston,Jeff	40,000	24,000
HotSprings	23-Mar-03	9	OP	6F	D	Honor Me	Trader,Rodney	50,000	30,000
HouDistafH	11-Jan-03	8	HOU	1 1/16M	D	Reason to Talk	Thompson,Terry	50,000	30,000
HouOaks	15-Mar-03	8	HOU	1M	D	Page Me Later	Jacinto,John	35,000	21,000
HouSprintH	4-Jan-03	8	HOU	7F	D	Term Sheet	Murphy,Glen	50,000	30,000
HouTfSpCp	15-Feb-03	9	HOU	5F	T	Testify	Chapa,Roman	50,000	30,000
HouTxnJuv	15-Nov-03	7	HOU	1 1/16M	D	America America	Chapa,Roman	150,000	90,000
HPBAVernCH	3-Aug-03	6	KIN	1 1/16M	D	Dawns Ben	Dangerfield,Ty	5,250	3,150

Stakes	Date	Race	Trk	Dist/Surf		Winner	Jockey	Gross	Value to winner
HrCmsMyBby	30-Aug-03	6	CRC	5F	D	Wynn Dot Comma	Garcia,Julio	53,875	38,325
HrshJacobs	17-May-03	6	PIM	6F	D	Mt. Carson	Dominguez,Ramon	100,000	60,000
HSFinney	13-Sep-03	6	PIM	1 1/8M	D	Conservation	Jurado,Enrique	60,000	36,000
HsklInvHG1	3-Aug-03	11	MTH	1 1/8M	D	Peace Rules	Prado,Edgar	1,000,000	600,000
HSMitchell	13-Dec-03	7	LRL	6F	D	Excellent Band	Vega,Harry	40,000	24,000
HstaLVstaH	18-May-03	10	TUP	1 7/8M	T	Pittsburgh Star	Higuera,Alberto	50,000	30,000
HstingsPkH	4-May-03	9	EMD	6 1/2F	D	Ema Bovary (CHI)	Gonzalez,Roberto	35,000	19,250
HstLVstaCl	1-Nov-03	10	WDS	1 3/4M	D	Old Man's Delite	Shino,Ken	13,500	6,000
HstSpeedH	6-Sep-03	8	HST	6 1/2F	D	Kalfaari	Evans,Sean	44,472	26,683
HudsonH	18-Oct-03	8	BEL	6F	D	One N Three	Bridgmohan,Shaun	125,000	75,000
HulaChief	1-Mar-03	7	HAW	6F	D	Classic Appeal	Silva,Carlos	43,200	25,920
Huntington	16-Nov-03	8	AQU	6F	D	Excellent Band	Vega,Harry	79,950	47,970
HurrcnBrtH	16-Mar-03	10	GP	6 1/2F	D	Gold Mover	Prado,Edgar	100,000	60,000
HutchesnG2	15-Feb-03	9	GP	7F	D	Lion Tamer	Velazquez,John	150,000	90,000
HvnlyCause	1-Nov-03	8	LRL	7F	D	Richetta	Dominguez,Ramon	60,000	36,000
IaBrdDerby	30-Aug-03	4	PRM	1 1/16M	D	Buzzle Ways	Eads,Jason	74,580	44,748
IaBrdsOaks	30-Aug-03	3	PRM	1M 70Y	D	Soup for Lunch	Birzer,Alex	73,350	44,010
IaDistafBC	11-Jul-03	6	PRM	1 1/16M	D	Missing Miss	Martinez,Willie	127,000	75,000
IaSorority	30-Aug-03	2	PRM	6F	D	Lovethatlegend	Thompson,Terry	72,020	43,212
IaStalInFu	16-Aug-03	6	PRM	6F	D	Okie Style	Williams,Robert	65,208	34,320
Icecapade	1-Sep-03	10	MTH	6F	D	Native Heir	Castellano, Jr.,Abel	60,000	36,000
IdCpClassc	9-Aug-03	7	BOI	1M	D	San Diego Pete	Williams,Matt	35,000	21,000
IdCpDisDby	9-Aug-03	2	BOI	1M	D	Thrill After Dark	Packer,Berkley	33,950	21,000
IdCpDisMat	9-Aug-03	4	BOI	1M	D	Trophy Edition Too	Carreno,Jorge	35,000	21,000
IdCpJuvCh	9-Aug-03	5	BOI	5F	D	Northern Buck	Carreno,Jorge	6,400	3,840
IdCpJuvnl	10-Aug-03	8	BOI	5F	D	Moab	Williams,Matt	46,152	25,384
IdCpSprint	9-Aug-03	9	BOI	5F	D	Jazzing Jack	Averill,Scott	12,078	7,247
IdCupClm	10-Aug-03	3	BOI	7F	D	Ive Been There	Hamilton,Travis	9,464	5,678
IdCupClmng	9-Aug-03	10	BOI	7 1/2F	D	T M T Insider	Talman,Katherine	6,900	4,140
IdCupDerby	10-Aug-03	2	BOI	1M	D	Two Star Story	Condie,Nathan	35,000	21,000
IdesOMarch	15-Mar-03	8	HAW	1 1/16M	D	Fight for Ally	Bourque,Curt	42,800	25,680
IlnosDrby2	5-Apr-03	8	HAW	1 1/8M	D	Ten Most Wanted	Day,Pat	500,000	300,000
IlPrincesH	8-Nov-03	4	HAW	1 1/16M	D	Julie's Prize	Sterling, Jr.,Larry	111,625	51,975
ImSmokin	8-Sep-03	6	DMR	6F	D	Dave the Dude	Solis,Alex	100,000	60,000
IMurphyH	21-Jun-03	5	AP	6F	D	Summer Mis	Sterling, Jr.,Larry	84,550	50,730
Inaugural	24-Jul-03	7	CLS	6F	D	Sundayblummer	Collins,Dennis	9,350	5,610
Inaugural	8-Jun-03	8	ARP	6F	D	River Walk Bob	Wales,Travis	35,000	21,000
Inaugural	13-Dec-03	10	TAM	6F	D	Tricks of Glory	Mata,Federico	60,000	27,000
InauguralH	20-Jun-03	5	MD	6F	D	Double Time	Latchman,Rennie	5,000	3,000
InauguralH	24-May-03	8	YAV	6F	D	Heightenedinterest	Martinez,Orlando	20,000	11,000
InauguralH	3-May-03	8	BOI	6 1/2F	D	Lovers Son	Webb,Robert	6,550	3,930
InauguralH	19-Sep-03	9	SRP	6 1/2F	D	Debatable	Tohill,Ken	32,400	19,440
InauguralH	5-Apr-03	7	EVD	6F	D	Zina Cause	Smith,Guy	35,000	21,000
InauguralH	21-Jun-03	11	WYO	6F	D	Fire Ball John	Foster,Cody	3,725	2,235
InauguralH	18-Oct-03	8	PM	6F	D	Lethal Grande	Boag,Daniel	10,000	5,500
InBCOaksG3	3-Oct-03	9	HOO	1 1/16M	D	Awesome Humor	Albarado,Robby	306,900	184,140
IncdblRvng	7-Sep-03	9	MTH	5F	T	Boozin' Susan	Ferrer,Jose	50,000	30,000
IndepDayH	4-Jul-03	9	EMD	1 1/16M	D	Alfurune	Gutierrez,Juan	40,000	22,000
IndepDayH	4-Jul-03	4	MNR	1M	D	Image of Approval	Stokes,Joseph	77,900	46,740
IndependcH	4-Jul-03	9	LAD	1 1/16M	T	Storybook Kid	Simington,Donald	75,000	45,000
IndnaDbyG3	4-Oct-03	9	HOO	1 1/16M	D	Excessivepleasure	Court,Jon	411,800	247,080
IndnMdBCH	11-Oct-03	8	HAW	1 1/16M	T	Janeian (NZ)	Martin, Jr.,Eddie	150,000	60,000
INewbornMm	21-Jun-03	12	TDN	6F	D	Frankie R's Winner	Sanchez, Jr.,Jose	41,000	21,000
InFuturity	15-Nov-03	9	HOO	6F	D	Edgerrin	Pompell,Thomas	72,650	43,590
IngKnottsH	5-Jul-03	8	ARP	6F	D	Slewannavan	Gonsalves,Frank	35,000	21,000
InglewoodH	3-May-03	8	HOL	1 1/16M	D	Gondolieri (CHI)	Alvarado,Frank	105,900	63,540
INSiresDby	24-May-03	9	IND	6F	D	Storm Tale	McKee,John	38,500	23,100
InStallion	28-Nov-03	8	HOO	6F	D	Down by the Sea	Troilo,William	38,650	23,190
InStallion	29-Nov-03	8	HOO	6F	D	Four Columns	LeJeune, Jr.,Sidney	37,950	22,770
InstRcgBC	12-Apr-03	11	OP	1M	D	Sue's Good News	Doocy,Timothy	75,000	45,000
InterbrghH	1-Jan-03	9	AQU	6F	D	Wilzada	Pino,Mario	81,850	49,110
IowaCradle	30-Aug-03	1	PRM	6F	D	Plum Sober	Thompson,Terry	72,120	43,272

Stakes	Date	Race	Trk	Dist/Surf		Winner	Jockey	Gross	Value to winner
IowaDerby	5-Jul-03	6	PRM	1 1/16M	D	Excessivepleasure	Court,Jon	250,000	150,000
IowaOaks	4-Jul-03	6	PRM	1 1/16M	D	Wildwood Royal	Sukie,Danush	125,000	75,000
IowaSprntH	21-Jun-03	8	PRM	6F	D	Chindi	Doocy,Timothy	125,000	75,000
IowaStalln	26-Jul-03	6	PRM	1M 70Y	D	Perfect Moment	Compton,Perry	75,900	46,200
IowaStFair	23-Aug-03	6	PRM	6F	D	Seven Brides	Murray,Kelly	40,800	24,000
IrishDayH	29-Jun-03	10	EMD	1 1/16M	D	Brave Miss	Russell,Ben	40,000	22,000
IrishSonnt	6-Oct-03	8	DEL	1M	D	From Away	Dominguez,Ramon	58,600	35,160
IroquoisG3	2-Nov-03	9	CD	1M	D	The Cliff's Edge	Sellers,Shane	113,700	70,494
IroquoisH	26-Jul-03	9	PHA	1 1/16M	D	Docent	Elliott,Stewart	53,850	32,310
IroquoisH	18-Oct-03	6	BEL	7F	D	Princess Dixie	Luzzi,Michael	125,000	75,000
IrshOBrien	16-Mar-03	3	SA	6 1/2F	D	Jetinto Houston	Smith,Mike	107,200	64,320
IrvingDstf	12-Apr-03	9	LS	7 1/2F	T	Cherylville Slew	Perrodin,Elvis	75,000	45,000
Isadorable	26-Feb-03	8	SUF	6F	D	Big Miss	Lozano, Jr.,Wilfredo	35,000	21,000
IseInBCHG3	23-Aug-03	10	MTH	1 1/8M	D	Tenpins	Albarado,Robby	200,000	120,000
IslndWhrlH	8-Nov-03	10	LAD	7F	D	Electrode	Gonzalez,Carlos	40,000	24,000
Izvestia	20-Jul-03	4	WO	1 1/16M	D	Wake At Noon	Ramsammy,Emile	106,000	63,600
J&KFletchr	21-Sep-03	6	EMD	1M	D	Getthepartystarted	Radke,Kevin	40,000	20,000
JackHardy	4-Aug-03	7	ASD	1M	D	Jo Me the Money	Bell,Derek	35,000	21,000
JackShoeMe	22-Feb-03	8	RIL	4F	D	Private Creek	Rosales,Arturo	3,694	2,216
JaipurH	26-May-03	8	BEL	7F	D	Garnered	Carrero,Victor	112,100	67,260
JamaicaHG2	21-Sep-03	9	BEL	1 1/8M	T	Stroll	Bailey,Jerry	200,000	120,000
JamedLovly	2-Nov-03	8	WO	7F	D	Willow Bunch	Husbands,Patrick	171,300	102,780
Jameela	1-Feb-03	9	LRL	7F	D	Boxer Girl	Castillo,Oliver	60,000	36,000
JBakerMem	27-Jan-03	3	TUP	6F	D	Deputy Doc	Hernandez,Miguel	23,600	14,160
JBMoslyBCH	21-Jun-03	13	SUF	6F	D	Peeping Tom	Bridgmohan,Shaun	200,000	120,000
JBttgliaMm	1-Mar-03	10	TP	1 1/16M	D	Champali	Lumpkins,Jason	100,000	62,000
JCampbellH	23-Feb-03	9	LRL	1 1/8M	D	Tempest Fugit	Caraballo,Jose	100,000	45,000
JCEllisJuv	17-Aug-03	9	ELP	7F	D	Cactus Ridge	Martin, Jr.,Eddie	100,000	61,250
JColProvH	20-Jul-03	4	HST	1 1/16M	D	Roscoe Pito	Krasner,Samuel	44,576	26,746
JcqCartier	11-Apr-03	8	WO	6F	D	Rare Friends	Husbands,Patrick	134,875	80,925
JDeereOaks	25-Jan-03	3	SA	7F	D	Atlantic Ocean	Flores,David	250,000	137,500
JDiamondFu	14-Sep-03	9	HST	6 1/2F	D	Lord Samarai	Wright,Nicola	106,694	64,016
JDrggrsDeb	13-Dec-03	6	PM	6F	D	Belle Fourche	Saito,Scott	10,000	5,500
JDudlySprH	15-Nov-03	9	CRC	6F	D	Love That Moon	Cruz,Manoel	150,000	90,000
JeanLafitt	8-Nov-03	9	DED	1M	D	Joe Six Pack	Gonzalez,Carlos	100,000	60,000
JEdgarIlFu	20-Dec-03	8	HAW	1 1/16M	D	Sir Fidgity	Sterling, Jr.,Larry	118,575	71,145
JEHStlnStn	17-May-03	7	LS	6 1/2F	D	Coastalota	Perrodin,Elvis	50,000	30,000
JenningsH	7-Jun-03	11	PIM	1 1/8M	D	Pickupspeed	Fogelsonger,Ryan	100,000	60,000
JennyWadeH	1-Aug-03	2	PEN	5F	T	Tangier Sound	Pimentel,Julian	50,000	30,000
JenyWilyG3	13-Apr-03	6	KEE	1 1/16M	T	Sea of Showers	Bailey,Jerry	113,300	70,246
JeromeHG2	13-Sep-03	8	BEL	1M	D	During	Santos,Jose	150,000	90,000
JerseyLily	15-Feb-03	5	HOU	1 1/16M	D	Presumed Innocent	Sellers,Shane	50,000	30,000
JerShrBCG3	4-Jul-03	10	MTH	6F	D	Gators N Bears	Lopez,Charles	100,000	60,000
JersyBrdrH	10-Aug-03	8	MTH	1M	D	Sea of Tranquility	Ferrer,Jose	50,000	30,000
JersyVllge	22-Feb-03	8	HOU	1 1/16M	D	Term Sheet	Beasley,Jeremy	35,000	21,000
JesamineCo	23-Oct-03	8	KEE	1 1/16M	T	Galloping Gal	Blanc,Brice	113,200	70,184
JFLyttleMH	1-Aug-03	10	SR	1 1/16M	D	Allwood	Baze,Russell	53,500	23,100
JfrsnCupG3	7-Jun-03	9	CD	1 1/8M	T	Senor Swinger	Albarado,Robby	220,600	136,772
JGonzalezM	29-Jun-03	11	PLN	5F	D	Lyin Goddess	Gonzalez,Roberto	54,350	23,750
JiffyLube	25-Oct-03	9	HOU	1 1/16M	D	Academic Angel	Beasley,Jeremy	35,000	21,000
JimBowie	23-Aug-03	9	RET	7 1/2F	T	Monsieur Boulanger (GB)	Gondron,Ted	35,000	21,000
JimDandyG2	3-Aug-03	9	SAR	1 1/8M	D	Strong Hope	Velazquez,John	500,000	300,000
JimPowellM	5-Jan-03	6	TUP	6F	D	No Cal Bread	Bridges,Kelly	22,800	13,680
JJReillyH	24-May-03	8	MTH	6F	D	Jersey Giant	Pimentel,Julian	50,000	30,000
JJsDream	28-Jun-03	9	CRC	5 1/2F	D	For All Who Dream	Homeister, Jr.,Rosemary	100,000	60,000
JJShumkerH	1-Aug-03	7	PEN	6F	D	Beau's Surprise	Alvarado, Jr.,Roberto	30,475	18,285
JkBtaBRite	23-Aug-03	9	FL	1 1/16M	D	Moonlightandbeauty	Davila, Jr.,John	40,000	24,000
JkyClbGCG1	27-Sep-03	10	BEL	1 1/4M	D	Mineshaft	Albarado,Robby	1,000,000	600,000
JLeakosSop	1-Aug-03	7	MD	1M	D	She's Nifty	Latchman,Rennie	6,500	3,900
JLongdenH	14-Jun-03	7	HST	1 1/16M	D	Let's Go Rusty	Krasner,Samuel	50,148	30,089
JMcSorley	6-Jul-03	6	MTH	5F	D	Jeb's Wild	Bravo,Joe	50,000	30,000
JMurryMemH	10-May-03	7	HOL	1 1/2M	T	Storming Home (GB)	Stevens,Gary	400,000	240,000

Stakes	Date	Race	Trk	Dist/Surf		Winner	Jockey	Gross	Value to winner
JnLJamisnH	14-Dec-03	10	SUN	6 1/2F	D	Ciento	Gonzalez, Jr.,Sal	133,200	79,920
JoeAGimma	28-Sep-03	8	BEL	7F	D	Capeside Lady	Velazquez,John	108,900	65,340
JOFrrllJvF	15-Nov-03	7	CRC	7F	D	Chatter Chatter	Bailey,Jerry	150,000	90,000
JohnBullit	2-Aug-03	8	CBY	1 1/16M	T	Al's Dearly Bred	Martinez,Seth	40,000	24,000
JohnDMarsh	15-Jun-03	11	CNL	1 1/16M	T	Covering Ground	Castellano, Jr.,Abel	50,000	30,000
JohnHenry	3-Oct-03	7	MED	1 1/16M	T	Tam's Terms	Dominguez,Ramon	50,000	30,000
JohnHenry	17-Aug-03	8	AP	1 1/16M	T	Chan Chan	Emigh,Christopher	52,800	31,680
JohnHenryH	3-May-03	7	EVD	1 1/16M	D	No Its Not	Hernandez,Brian	35,000	21,000
JohnKirby	27-Oct-03	3	SUF	1 1/16M	D	Jill's Layup	Johnson,Richard	35,000	21,000
JohnWayne	17-May-03	8	PRM	6F	D	Take Me Up	Quinonez,Luis	60,000	36,000
JosephneCo	8-Jun-03	7	GRP	5 1/2F	D	Can't Be an Angel	Beckner,Twyla	3,225	1,784
JournalH	21-Jun-03	7	NP	6 1/2F	D	Sixthirtyjoe	Simard,Real	40,000	25,200
JournalStr	25-May-03	8	LNN	6F	D	Homer's Hero	Carkeek,Jerome	11,000	6,600
JPatrickH	19-Jul-03	4	NP	1M	D	Sly Lady	Simard,Real	40,000	25,200
JPriceJuv	15-Nov-03	10	CRC	7F	D	Sir Oscar	Garcia,Julio	150,000	90,000
JrChampion	17-Aug-03	8	MTH	1M	D	Loving Lucy	Ferrer,Jose	50,000	30,000
JRMacomber	2-Aug-03	3	SUF	6F	D	Caramel's Express	Panell,Dyn	35,000	21,000
JRStrausMm	1-Aug-03	9	RET	6F	D	Front Nine	Beasley,Jeremy	35,000	21,000
JrsyDrbyG3	26-May-03	10	MTH	1 1/16M	D	Happy Trails	Toribio,Abdiel	100,000	60,000
JsAGmBCHG3	7-Jun-03	8	BEL	1M	T	Mariensky	Santos,Jose	214,500	128,700
JSnellings	12-Jul-03	8	DEL	1 1/16M	T	Spin Control	Castillo,Oliver	60,300	36,180
JsphBucklw	13-Sep-03	9	MTH	5F	T	Impolite	Ferrer,Jose	50,000	30,000
JstALtKssH	2-Jan-03	11	CRC	5F	T	Flying Birdie	Coa,Eibar	45,285	29,171
JTGraceH	2-Aug-03	10	SR	1 1/16M	D	Cappuchino	Gonzalez,Roberto	101,000	55,100
JudysRdShs	13-Sep-03	5	CRC	1 1/16M	T	Formal Miss	Cruz,Manoel	75,000	41,000
Justakiss	25-Aug-03	7	DEL	1 1/16M	D	Arabis	Dominguez,Ramon	57,900	34,740
JustSmshng	4-Oct-03	8	MED	6F	D	Cupid Season	Lopez,Charles	45,000	27,000
JuvColts	21-Sep-03	8	FE	6F	D	Copper Trail	Villeneuve,Francine	75,000	45,000
Juvenile	7-Sep-03	7	TDN	1 1/16M	D	Floater	Rowland,Michael	75,000	45,000
JuvFillies	20-Sep-03	8	FE	6F	D	Smart Serve	Barton,Jake	75,000	45,000
JWGalbreth	2-Nov-03	6	BEU	1 1/16M	D	Keepyourwitsaboutu	Gonzalez,Luis	50,000	30,000
JWineberg	8-Nov-03	6	PM	6F	D	Americas Pride	Gutierrez,Juan	19,526	10,739
JWPetroMH	21-Jun-03	15	TDN	1 1/16M	D	Golden Tour	Meyers,Tommy	50,000	30,000
JWSifton	14-Sep-03	7	ASD	1 1/8M	D	Fancy Bru	Hightower,Travis	36,000	21,600
Kachina	27-Jul-03	11	RUI	5 1/2F	D	Rama Lassie	Madeira,Carlos	46,635	23,318
KalooknQnH	31-Dec-03	8	SA	6 1/2F	D	Ema Bovary (CHI)	Gonzalez,Roberto	102,400	47,940
Kamar	13-Jul-03	6	WO	7F	D	Brass in Pocket	Clark,David	108,000	64,800
KansasOaks	25-Oct-03	9	WDS	1M 70Y	D	Wildwood Royal	Kurek,Gary	30,000	18,000
KathrynDol	24-Mar-03	4	TUP	5 1/2F	D	Tulsa	Bridges,Kelly	23,930	14,220
Katy	8-Nov-03	8	HOU	7F	D	Appealing Secret	Beasley,Jeremy	35,000	21,000
KBrdkinMem	21-Jun-03	8	SUF	5F	T	Glick	Thompson,Winston	35,000	21,000
KedTrkWstW	20-Jul-03	7	GPR	5 1/2F	D	Bad Toda Bone	McAleney,Peter	3,100	1,860
KelsoBCHG2	4-Oct-03	8	BEL	1M	T	Freefourinternet	Espinoza,Jose	350,000	210,000
KelsoH	4-Oct-03	7	DEL	1 3/16M	D	Country Be Gold	Alvarado, Jr.,Roberto	100,000	60,000
KenMadySpH	22-Feb-03	3	GG	6F	D	El Dorado Shooter	Baze,Russell	100,000	55,000
KennedyRd	29-Nov-03	8	WO	6F	D	Chris's Bad Boy	Jones,Jono	137,375	82,425
Kenora	1-Sep-03	9	WO	6F	D	Forever Grand	Kabel,Todd	130,000	78,000
KentBCG3	20-Jul-03	5	DEL	1 1/8M	T	Foufa's Warrior	Dominguez,Ramon	250,000	150,000
KentH	26-Jul-03	9	EMD	1 1/16M	D	Youcan'ttakeme	Baze,Gary	40,000	21,725
KenyNoeJrH	13-Dec-03	11	CRC	7F	D	Hasty Kris	Douglas,Rene	100,000	60,000
KFlamanMem	5-Jul-03	6	YKT	1M	D	Makewayforbighoss	Strongarm,Thomas	5,800	3,654
Khaled	26-Apr-03	6	HOL	1 1/8M	T	Sea to See	Solis,Alex	150,000	90,000
KindrgrtnH	23-Aug-03	9	PHA	6F	D	Expect the Best	Rocco,Joseph	39,100	23,460
Kingarvie	30-Nov-03	7	WO	1 1/16M	D	Winter Whiskey	Jones,Jono	135,250	81,150
KingCoH	28-Jun-03	9	EMD	1M	D	Strikes No Spares	Radke,Kevin	50,000	27,500
KingCotton	1-Feb-03	9	OP	6F	D	Beau's Town	Lovato,Anthony	50,000	30,000
KingCugat	16-Nov-03	7	AQU	1M	T	Willard Straight	Velazquez,John	60,750	36,450
KingsCourt	27-Jun-03	11	LAD	6F	D	Doctor Mike	Melancon,Gerard	50,000	30,000
KingstonH	25-May-03	8	BEL	1 1/8M	T	Irish Colonial	Castellano,Javier	113,600	68,160
Kingwood	13-Dec-03	9	HOU	1M 70Y	D	Leo's Last Hurrahy	Valdez,Felipe	35,000	21,000
Kissaptmus	22-Mar-03	8	HAW	6F	D	Smoke Chaser	Bourque,Curt	43,600	26,160
KKndrckMmF	26-Oct-03	10	SRP	6 1/2F	D	Speedy Falcon	Escobar,Victor	51,148	24,039

Stakes	Date	Race	Trk	Dist/Surf		Winner	Jockey	Gross	Value to winner
KLAQH	29-Nov-03	10	SUN	5 1/2F	D	This Cat's for You	Tohill,Ken	54,150	32,490
KlondikeH	31-May-03	7	HST	6 1/2F	D	Gamblin Caper	Wright,Nicola	44,576	24,000
KlondikeH	26-Jul-03	8	NP	1 1/16M	D	Kalfaari	Evans,Sean	40,000	25,200
KlsyBrfcse	16-Aug-03	8	MTH	5F	T	Tangier Sound	Pimentel,Julian	50,000	30,000
KmbrltPipe	21-Sep-03	9	KD	6F	T	Freedom Counts	Johnson,Joe	40,000	24,000
KmsCtryDmd	3-Aug-03	11	CRC	6 1/2F	D	Chispiski	Garcia,Julio	42,500	27,500
KngEdBCHG2	15-Jun-03	8	WO	1 1/8M	T	Perfect Soul (IRE)	Landry,Robert	339,600	203,760
KnghtsChc	2-Aug-03	9	EMD	6 1/2F	D	Americas Pride	Radke,Kevin	39,000	19,305
KngsBshpG1	23-Aug-03	10	SAR	7F	D	Valid Video	Bravo,Joe	200,000	120,000
KngsPointH	4-May-03	8	AQU	1 1/8M	D	Lord Ofthe Thunder	Castellano,Javier	81,325	48,795
KnkrbkrHG2	1-Nov-03	8	AQU	1 1/8M	T	Better Talk Now	Prado,Edgar	150,000	90,000
KnsTbDerby	18-Oct-03	9	WDS	1M 70Y	D	Noble Delight	Essman,David	20,000	12,000
KnsTbDerby	18-Oct-03	4	WDS	1M 70Y	D	Morning Merry	Eads,Jason	20,000	12,000
KnsTbrdFut	11-Oct-03	9	WDS	5 1/2F	D	Ama Missprint	Gonsalves,Frank	23,900	14,340
KnsTbrdFut	11-Oct-03	4	WDS	5 1/2F	D	Nick Missed	Vicchrilli,Russell	22,075	13,245
KokopelliH	4-Jan-03	8	TUP	1M	T	Free Corona	Ziegler,Michael	35,000	21,000
KPearsnMmH	19-May-03	8	STP	1M	D	Sly Lady	Simard,Real	40,000	25,200
Kriskimkel	15-Oct-03	4	TUP	1M	D	Playing It Cool	Ziegler,Michael	21,600	12,960
KSPClaimng	24-Aug-03	5	KSP	1M 70Y	D	Neighborhood Bully	Wippert,Shannon	2,900	1,653
KtlOnElJvn	30-Aug-03	8	RET	1M	T	New York Harbor	Stanton,Terry	100,000	60,000
KudzuJuvnl	12-Dec-03	2	FG	5 1/2F	D	Slow Walkin' John	Theriot,Jamie	35,000	19,250
KyAltaH	18-Jul-03	8	NP	1 1/16M	D	Rindanica	Winters,Perry	40,000	25,200
KyBCG3	26-May-03	9	CD	5 1/2F	D	Cuvee	Meche,Lonnie	176,700	109,554
KyCpClHG2	13-Sep-03	11	TP	1 1/8M	D	Perfect Drift	Day,Pat	350,000	221,500
KyCpJuvFil	13-Sep-03	9	TP	1M	D	Class Above	Prado,Edgar	100,000	62,000
KyCpLdsTrf	20-Sep-03	12	KD	1M	T	Apasionata Sonata	Bejarano,Rafael	100,000	62,000
KyCpSpntG3	13-Sep-03	13	TP	6F	D	Cajun Beat	Velasquez,Cornelio	100,000	62,000
KyCpTfDash	20-Sep-03	6	KD	6F	T	Fredericktown	Bejarano,Rafael	100,000	62,000
KyCpTrfHG3	20-Sep-03	14	KD	1 1/2M	T	Rochester	Martin, Jr.,Eddie	200,000	124,000
KyCupJuvG3	13-Sep-03	10	TP	1 1/16M	D	Mr. Jester	Bejarano,Rafael	100,000	62,000
KyCupMile	20-Sep-03	9	KD	1M	D	Hard Buck (BRZ)	Blanc,Brice	100,000	62,000
KyDerbyG1	3-May-03	10	CD	1 1/4M	D	Funny Cide	Santos,Jose	1,100,200	800,200
KyJCG2	29-Nov-03	11	CD	1 1/16M	D	The Cliff's Edge	Sellers,Shane	222,200	137,764
KylasAGem	28-Jun-03	8	SUF	6F	D	Love Not War	Molinari,Edwin	35,000	21,000
KyOaksG1	2-May-03	10	CD	1 1/8M	D	Bird Town	Prado,Edgar	573,800	355,756
Labeeb	2-Nov-03	5	WO	1M 70Y	D	Open Concert	Ramsammy,Emile	114,000	68,400
LaborDayH	1-Sep-03	3	MNR	1M	D	Tour the Hive	Feliciano,Ricardo	76,800	48,384
LaborDayH	1-Sep-03	8	CLS	6 1/2F	D	Doug's Shadow	Ranilla,Luis	9,500	5,700
LaBrdrDrby	11-Oct-03	12	LAD	1 1/16M	D	Spritely Walker	Meche,Lonnie	82,900	49,740
LaBrdrOaks	11-Oct-03	8	LAD	1 1/16M	D	Cute N Noble	Smith,Guy	81,950	49,170
LaBreaG1	27-Dec-03	7	SA	7F	D	Island Fashion	Desormeaux,Kent	250,000	150,000
LaCanadaG2	8-Feb-03	6	SA	1 1/8M	D	Got Koko	Solis,Alex	200,000	120,000
LaClassic	13-Dec-03	9	FG	1 1/8M	D	Spritely Walker	Lanerie,Corey	150,000	90,000
LaConejaH	26-Dec-03	10	SUN	5 1/2F	D	Shemoveslikeaghost	Tohill,Ken	131,600	78,960
LaDerbyG2	9-Mar-03	9	FG	1 1/16M	D	Peace Rules	Prado,Edgar	750,000	450,000
LaDH	21-Sep-03	8	LAD	1 1/16M	T	Warleigh	Meche,Lonnie	100,000	60,000
LadiesHG3	20-Dec-03	8	AQU	1 1/4M	D	Savedbythelight	Migliore,Richard	112,100	67,260
Ladnesian	13-Jul-03	4	HST	6 1/2F	D	Lord Samarai	Alvarado,Pedro	38,913	23,348
LadyAngela	20-Apr-03	8	WO	7F	D	Deputy Cures Blues	Ramsammy,Emile	130,875	78,525
LadyCbyBC	15-Jun-03	8	CBY	1M	T	Stylish	Blanc,Brice	100,000	60,000
LadyFingrs	16-Aug-03	7	FL	6F	D	Mother's Sacrifice	Yang,Chin	79,975	47,985
LadyHalliH	29-Mar-03	6	HAW	1 1/16M	D	Curious Conundrum	Razo, Jr.,Eusebio	100,000	60,000
LadyRazFut	1-Nov-03	4	LAD	6F	D	Chene Rouge	Meche,Lonnie	35,000	21,000
LadySecret	3-Aug-03	3	MTH	1 1/16M	D	Annatoga	Pimentel,Julian	75,000	45,000
LadySecret	9-Nov-03	8	RP	7F	D	Cherylville Slew	Schaefer,Gregory	36,700	21,000
LadySecrtH	24-May-03	8	BOI	7 1/2F	D	Tera Kitty	Taveras,Reino	7,200	4,320
LadySlippr	18-May-03	8	CBY	6F	D	Fancy Injun	Stevens,Scott	37,375	22,425
Lafayette	1-Sep-03	10	EVD	6F	D	Cabildo Bag	Woodley,Carl	50,000	30,000
LafayetteH	1-Jan-03	3	GG	1M	D	I'madrifter	Krigger,Kevin	83,100	49,350
LafayettG3	6-Apr-03	8	KEE	7F	D	Posse	Lanerie,Corey	107,900	66,898
LaFiestaH	14-Mar-03	8	ALB	5 1/2F	D	Princesscassandra	Gonzalez, Jr.,Sal	33,100	19,860

Stakes	Date	Race	Trk	Dist/Surf		Winner	Jockey	Gross	Value to winner
LaFuturity	28-Dec-03	1	FG	6F	D	Brandon's Marfa	Fusilier,Casey	84,965	50,977
LaFuturity	27-Dec-03	8	FG	6F	D	Merry Mary	Lanerie,Corey	84,465	50,679
Laginappe	27-Dec-03	9	DED	1M	D	Our Here Tiz	Hernandez, Jr.,Brian	40,000	24,000
LaHabra	28-Feb-03	7	SA	6 1/2F	T	Luvah Girl (GB)	Smith,Mike	110,800	66,480
LaJollaHG3	16-Aug-03	8	DMR	1 1/16M	T	Singletary	Valenzuela,Patrick	150,000	90,000
LaJuvenile	13-Dec-03	5	FG	6F	D	Walk This Way	Sellers,Shane	100,000	60,000
Lakeway	16-Aug-03	9	RET	7F	D	Lady Mallory	Frazier,Ricky	35,000	21,000
LakPlcdHG2	17-Aug-03	9	SAR	1 1/8M	T	Sand Springs	Guidry,Mark	150,000	90,000
LakvwThFrm	26-Apr-03	7	HOL	7F	D	Five Star Meeting	Flores,David	70,000	42,000
LaLadies	13-Dec-03	8	FG	1 1/16M	D	Cute N Noble	Smith,Guy	100,000	60,000
LaLassie	13-Dec-03	3	FG	6F	D	Rose of Sophia	Gonzalez,Carlos	100,000	60,000
LaLorgnett	27-Sep-03	7	WO	1 1/16M	D	Willow Bunch	Husbands,Patrick	182,375	109,425
Lamplghtr	5-Jul-03	8	MTH	1 1/16M	T	Stroll	Bailey,Jerry	50,000	30,000
LandalucG3	4-Jul-03	4	HOL	6F	D	Wacky Patty	Valdivia, Jr.,Jose	100,300	60,180
LandOEnchH	13-Jul-03	5	RUI	7 1/2F	D	Star Smasher	Bourdieu,Jorge	46,200	27,720
LandOfJazz	15-Aug-03	6	FER	7F	D	Hopso (IRE)	Boag,Daniel	8,310	4,535
LandOfJazz	15-Aug-03	5	FER	7F	D	Lets Pay Cash	Demesme,Elliott	8,310	4,535
LanesEndG2	22-Mar-03	10	TP	1 1/8M	D	New York Hero	Arroyo, Jr.,Norberto	500,000	300,000
Lansing	24-May-03	8	GLD	6F	D	Akatsakat	Judice,Joseph	45,000	27,000
LaPaz	8-Dec-03	8	TUP	6 1/2F	D	Arch Lady	Stevens,Scott	21,800	13,080
LaPrevynte	13-Sep-03	7	WO	1M	T	Miss Crissy	Bahen,Steven	137,125	82,275
LaPuente	12-Apr-03	7	SA	1M	T	Steelaninch (GB)	Espinoza,Victor	150,000	90,000
LaPvyteHG2	27-Dec-03	9	CRC	1 1/2M	T	Volga (IRE)	Migliore,Richard	200,000	120,000
LarkspurH	6-Jun-03	8	GLD	6F	D	Born to Dance	Eads,Jason	45,000	27,000
LasCrucesH	15-Mar-03	11	SUN	1M	D	Dancing Capote	Jaime,Ricardo	79,050	47,430
LaSenoraH	25-Jan-03	10	SUN	6F	D	Inexcessive Play	Fuentes,Adan	132,200	79,320
LaSenorita	30-Aug-03	8	RET	1M	T	Topango	Cloninger, Jr.,Weldon	100,000	60,000
LaSprint	13-Dec-03	6	FG	6F	D	Zarb's Luck	Albarado,Robby	100,000	60,000
Lassie	22-Nov-03	8	PM	6F	D	Quiz the Maid	Martinez,Jaime	10,000	5,500
LassieH	17-Aug-03	1	HST	6 1/2F	D	Overact	Wright,Nicola	39,095	21,000
LaStarterH	13-Dec-03	4	FG	1 1/16M	D	Jacob's Prospect	Lovato, Jr.,Frank	50,000	30,000
LastDance	12-Apr-03	5	SUF	1 1/16M	D	Stylish Sultan	Thompson,Winston	35,000	21,000
LateBloomr	28-Apr-03	7	DEL	6F	D	Skip the Print	Dunkelberger,Travis	58,900	35,340
LATimesHG3	10-May-03	6	HOL	6F	D	Hombre Rapido	Valdivia, Jr.,Jose	200,000	120,000
LaTroienG3	1-May-03	9	CD	7F	D	Final Round	Bailey,Jerry	111,800	69,316
LaTurf	13-Dec-03	7	FG	1 1/16M	D	Silky Zarb	Melancon,Gerard	100,000	60,000
LaurelLane	11-Oct-03	2	LAD	6F	D	Cool Cool Cool	Bourque,Steven	54,300	32,580
LaurieDncr	19-Jul-03	4	FE	1 1/16M	D	Tuff Chick	Dos Ramos,Richard	90,000	36,000
LaVerndrye	14-Jun-03	7	ASD	6F	D	Briara	Hightower,Travis	35,000	21,000
LaVoyageH	23-Mar-03	8	WO	5F	D	Acting Deputy	Kabel,Todd	107,000	64,200
LawRealHG3	11-Oct-03	9	BEL	1 1/2M	T	Kicken Kris	Castellano,Javier	150,000	90,000
LazerShow	26-Sep-03	8	AP	5F	T	Nicole's Dream	Baird,E.	47,400	28,440
LbatWoOaks	8-Jun-03	9	WO	1 1/8M	D	Too Late Now	Landry,Robert	500,000	300,000
LbgHrldMar	27-Sep-03	8	LBG	1 1/16M	D	Gomka	Stianson,Janine	11,220	6,160
LBGOaks	27-Sep-03	7	LBG	6F	D	Flying Lady Cue	Sterr,Scott	10,900	5,995
LBrnchBCG3	12-Jul-03	9	MTH	1 1/16M	D	Max Forever	Ferrer,Jose	100,000	60,000
LBrreraMG2	26-May-03	7	HOL	7F	D	Blazonry	Smith,Mike	150,000	90,000
LBurbankH	27-Jul-03	11	SR	1 1/16M	D	Centerofattention	Castro,Joe	53,900	30,000
LcstGrvHG3	28-Jun-03	9	CD	1 1/8M	T	Ipi Tombe (ZIM)	Day,Pat	164,400	101,928
LdyScBCHG2	28-Sep-03	6	SA	1 1/16M	D	Got Koko	Solis,Alex	300,000	180,000
LdySecretH	1-Sep-03	9	FP	1M 70Y	D	Slick's Lil Sister	Concha,Gilbert	25,700	15,420
LeadrOBand	1-Sep-03	8	DEL	1 1/16M	D	Mile	Castillo,Oliver	59,000	35,400
LeComteG3	25-Jan-03	9	FG	1M	D	Saintly Look	Sellers,Shane	100,000	60,000
LegalLight	26-Apr-03	7	DEL	6F	D	House Party	Rocco, Jr.,Joseph	75,000	45,000
LegJusticH	12-Jul-03	9	PHA	5F	T	Quest of Fate	Molina,Victor	38,300	22,980
Lenta	3-May-03	10	CRC	1 1/16M	T	Formal Miss	Cruz,Manoel	42,850	27,710
LesMackinH	24-Jun-03	5	YAV	1 1/16M	D	Cresco Ruler	Hernandez,Miguel	10,000	5,500
LewsClrkDb	26-Jul-03	8	GF	7F	D	Game Princess	Hebert,Carl	8,000	4,000
LexingtnG3	13-Jul-03	9	BEL	1 1/4M	T	Sharp Impact	Migliore,Richard	150,000	90,000
LgaMileHG3	24-Aug-03	8	EMD	1M	D	Sky Jack	Baze,Russell	250,000	137,500
LghtngJetH	8-Nov-03	7	HAW	6F	D	Bulldog George	Razo, Jr.,Eusebio	111,325	51,795

Stakes	Date	Race	Trk	Dist/Surf		Winner	Jockey	Gross	Value to winner
LiberadaH	1-Jun-03	3	CRC	1M	D	Gentille Alouette	Cruz,Manoel	41,650	26,990
LiberatnH	28-Jun-03	1	HST	1 1/16M	D	Dancewithavixen	Valdez,Felipe	44,576	26,746
Lighthouse	6-Sep-03	9	MTH	1 1/16M	D	Misty Sixes	Bravo,Joe	50,000	30,000
LightHrtdH	20-Jul-03	9	DEL	6F	D	Lights On	Rose,Jeremy	100,000	60,000
LiklyExchg	8-Feb-03	9	TP	1M	D	Seven Four Seven	Lumpkins,Jason	50,000	31,300
LilacH	31-May-03	4	STP	1M	D	Raylene	Wilson,David	50,000	25,200
LilETee	30-Aug-03	7	PHA	1 1/16M	D	Yo	Elliott,Stewart	50,000	30,000
LincolnH	13-Jul-03	2	RUI	6F	D	Lord Imajones	Bourdieu,Jorge	46,600	27,960
LincroftH	28-Jun-03	10	MTH	1M	T	American Freedom	Velez, Jr.,Jose	50,000	30,000
LindsyFrlc	30-Aug-03	14	CRC	1M	D	Pick of the Pack	Homeister, Jr.,Rosemary	52,600	22,560
Lineage	18-May-03	11	ALB	1 1/16M	D	Star Smasher	Fuentes,Miguel	35,000	19,250
LineageClm	18-May-03	1	ALB	6F	D	Choke N Go	Gonzalez, Jr.,Sal	10,000	6,000
Linear	14-Jun-03	3	CRC	5F	T	Swift Replica	Boulanger,Gary	42,000	27,200
LitlSilver	6-Jul-03	10	MTH	1 1/16M	T	Impolite	Ferrer,Jose	50,000	30,000
LittleOnes	23-Aug-03	5	GLD	5 1/2F	D	Heza Mountain Man	Judice,Joseph	45,000	27,000
LiveDreamH	10-Sep-03	3	DMR	1M	T	Designed for Luck	Valenzuela,Patrick	98,725	45,735
LkGeorgeG3	28-Jul-03	8	SAR	1 1/16M	T	Film Maker	Prado,Edgar	114,500	68,700
LKmblDstCh	11-Oct-03	3	SUF	1 1/16M	D	African Princess	Hampshire, Jr.,Josiah	35,000	21,000
LMademosle	16-Aug-03	8	FER	1 1/16M	D	Hot Scramble	Guce,Ramon	10,850	5,950
LMadrinasH	26-Sep-03	11	FPX	1 1/16M	D	Bold Roberta	Nuesch,David	100,000	55,000
LnclnHrtgH	21-Jun-03	7	AP	1 1/16M	D	Kate the Great	Fires,Earlie	84,600	50,760
LndLincoln	12-Apr-03	8	HAW	6F	D	My Beau Mister Joe	Razo, Jr.,Eusebio	140,767	57,780
LngIlndHG2	15-Nov-03	8	AQU	1 1/2M	T	Spice Island	Carrero,Victor	150,000	90,000
LnsEndFtG2	4-Oct-03	6	KEE	1 1/16M	D	Eurosilver	Castellano,Javier	400,000	248,000
LnStrDbyG3	10-May-03	8	LS	1 1/8M	D	Dynever	Prado,Edgar	500,000	277,500
LocalThllr	30-Jun-03	7	DEL	6F	D	Spring Meadow	Dominguez,Ramon	58,900	35,340
LondonLil	30-Nov-03	8	CRC	1 1/16M	T	Where We Left Off (GB)	Coa,Eibar	40,050	21,030
Longfellow	22-Jun-03	9	MTH	6F	D	It's a Monster	Bravo,Joe	60,000	36,000
Longhorn	4-Oct-03	4	RET	6F	D	Front Nine	Beasley,Jeremy	35,000	21,000
LongLook	11-Oct-03	7	MED	1 1/16M	D	Drexel Monorail	Lopez,Charles	50,000	30,000
LouisianaH	2-Jan-03	9	FG	1 1/16M	D	Connected	Melancon,Larry	75,000	45,000
LouvlBCHG2	2-May-03	8	CD	1 1/16M	D	You	Bailey,Jerry	325,500	201,810
Loyalty	16-Aug-03	6	TDN	6F	D	Spring Cat	Villa-Gomez,Huber	35,000	21,000
LRichrdsG3	14-Jun-03	11	DEL	1 1/16M	D	Awesome Time	Black,Anthony	250,000	150,000
LRivloPrCp	9-Aug-03	9	PHA	1M 70Y	D	Gimmeawink	Madrigal, Jr.,Rodrigo	100,000	60,000
LrlFutG3	15-Nov-03	6	LRL	1 1/16M	D	Tapit	Dominguez,Ramon	100,000	60,000
LsCngasHG3	5-Apr-03	4	SA	6 1/2F	T	Heat Haze (GB)	Valdivia, Jr.,Jose	110,000	66,000
LsFlresHG3	22-Feb-03	8	SA	6F	D	Spring Meadow	Nakatani,Corey	135,500	81,300
LSParkHG3	26-May-03	8	LS	1 1/16M	D	Pie N Burger	Theriot,Jamie	300,000	180,000
LstChncDby	30-Dec-03	9	TUP	1 1/16M	T	Vigilant Site	Corbett,Glenn	22,200	13,320
LstCodBrCp	5-Apr-03	9	HAW	6F	D	Coach Jimi Lee	Day,Pat	101,800	61,080
LsvillHG3	31-May-03	9	CD	1 3/8M	T	Kim Loves Bucky	Sellers,Shane	112,000	69,440
LsVrgnesG1	9-Feb-03	7	SA	1M	D	Composure	Bailey,Jerry	200,000	120,000
LtGovrnHG3	1-Jul-03	8	HST	1 1/8M	D	Lord Nelson	Fuentes,Francisco	110,582	66,349
LymanSpChH	28-Jun-03	9	PHA	7F	D	Docent	Elliott,Stewart	54,400	32,640
LyriqueH	1-Sep-03	10	LAD	1 1/16M	T	Tincan Too	Doocy,Timothy	50,000	30,000
MackinacH	20-Sep-03	8	GLD	1 1/16M	D	Monetary Star	Judice,Joseph	45,000	27,000
Mademoisel	22-Mar-03	7	DED	5F	D	Swamp Scare	Meche,Lonnie	50,000	30,000
Madison	9-Apr-03	8	KEE	7F	D	A New Twist	Day,Pat	136,875	84,863
MadmoiselH	8-Aug-03	8	NP	1 1/16M	D	Slewability	Winters,Perry	40,000	25,200
MagaliFms	26-Apr-03	5	HOL	6 1/2F	D	Tucked Away	Stevens,Gary	60,000	36,000
MagicCtyCl	14-Jun-03	7	RD	6F	D	Chief Tudor	Luna,Ramon	35,000	19,250
Magnolia	14-Nov-03	9	DED	7F	D	Prized Amberpro	Woodley,Carl	75,000	45,000
MagnoliaH	1-Mar-03	7	DED	7F	D	Fuse It	Melancon,Gerard	100,000	60,000
MaidOTMist	18-Oct-03	4	BEL	1M	D	Capeside Lady	Velazquez,John	100,000	60,000
MajoretteH	9-Nov-03	10	LAD	7F	D	Distinctive Code	LeBlanc,Kirk	40,000	24,000
MakrsMrkG2	11-Apr-03	8	KEE	1M	T	Royal Spy	Albarado,Robby	200,000	124,000
MalibuG1	26-Dec-03	8	SA	7F	D	Southern Image	Espinoza,Victor	250,000	150,000
Mamzelle	1-May-03	7	CD	5F	T	Full Spectrum	Borel,Calvin	113,500	70,370
ManATBDstf	19-Apr-03	12	MAN	6F	D	Piniante	Simington,Donald	35,000	21,000
Manatee	25-Jan-03	8	TAM	7F	D	Romancin Dixie	Espada,Jose	50,000	28,500

Stakes	Date	Race	Trk	Dist/Surf		Winner	Jockey	Gross	Value to winner
ManDstfCls	10-May-03	10	MAN	1M	D	Blue Guru	Knott,Rick	25,000	15,000
ManhattanH	3-Oct-03	9	WDS	6F	D	Discreetly Irish	Eads,Jason	25,000	15,000
ManhttnBch	1-Jun-03	8	HOL	5 1/2F	T	Katdogawn (GB)	Smith,Mike	99,900	46,440
ManhttnHG1	7-Jun-03	10	BEL	1 1/4M	T	Denon	Bailey,Jerry	400,000	240,000
Manila	25-Sep-03	8	AP	1M	T	Atten Hut	Martin, Jr.,Eddie	46,650	27,990
Manitoba	28-Jun-03	7	ASD	1M	D	Fancy Bru	Hightower,Travis	35,000	21,000
ManOWarG1	6-Sep-03	8	BEL	1 3/8M	T	Lunar Sovereign	Migliore,Richard	500,000	300,000
ManTbrdFut	3-May-03	10	MAN	4 1/2F	D	Marquee	Lambert,Casey	35,000	27,000
MantobaMat	12-Jul-03	7	ASD	1 1/16M	D	Trebbiano	Singh,Rohan	36,000	21,600
MaplLeafG3	1-Nov-03	8	WO	1 1/4M	D	One for Rose	Ramsammy,Emile	246,350	147,810
MarathnSrs	26-Oct-03	6	LBG	1 1/8M	D	Candid Remark	Sterr,Scott	10,900	5,995
Marathon	2-Mar-03	7	TUP	1 5/8M	D	I've Been Crowned	Gann,Sandi	22,700	13,620
MarchMdnsH	23-Mar-03	8	SA	1 1/4M	D	Asong for Billy	Puglisi,Ignacio	85,750	39,750
MardiGrasH	4-Mar-03	9	FG	1M	D	Even the Score	Sellers,Shane	65,000	39,000
Marfa	20-Sep-03	13	TP	6 1/2F	D	Private Horde	Thompson,Terry	75,000	46,950
MargarBCH	2-Aug-03	10	RET	1 1/16M	T	Golden Rhythm	Frazier,Ricky	50,000	30,000
MariahStrm	28-Jun-03	5	AP	1 1/8M	D	Desert Gold	Velasquez,Cornelio	46,650	27,990
Maria'sMon	26-Dec-03	8	AQU	6F	D	Scary Bob	Gryder,Aaron	60,600	36,360
MarineG3	17-May-03	8	WO	1 1/16M	D	Wando	Kabel,Todd	163,800	98,280
MarluelTry	23-Sep-03	7	FP	6F	D	Matthew's Blessing	Lopez,Uriel	36,000	21,600
Marshland	5-Dec-03	7	DED	7F	D	Dusty Spike	Quinonez,Luis	50,000	30,000
Marshua	4-Jan-03	8	LRL	6F	D	Ladyecho	Castillo,Oliver	60,000	30,000
MarshuaRvr	15-Mar-03	9	GP	1M 70Y	D	Dance the Slew	Guidry,Mark	52,700	31,620
MassDerby	13-Oct-03	3	SUF	1 1/16M	D	Mr. Meso	Thompson,Winston	35,000	21,000
MassOaks	27-Sep-03	3	SUF	1 1/16M	D	Amazing Thunder	Panell,Dyn	35,000	21,000
MassTbBrdH	21-Jun-03	6	SUF	1 1/16M	D	Stylish Sultan	Thompson,Winston	75,000	45,000
Matchmaker	15-Jun-03	8	FE	5F	D	Real Doll	Todd, Jr.,Frank	90,000	36,000
MatchmakrH	14-Jun-03	8	LNN	1M	D	Irish Flyer	Anderson,Mark	15,625	9,375
MatriarcG1	30-Nov-03	6	HOL	1M	T	Heat Haze (GB)	Velazquez,John	500,000	300,000
Matron	21-Sep-03	7	ASD	1 1/8M	D	Top Stage Dancer	DesAutels,Jacques	40,000	21,000
MatronG1	14-Sep-03	6	BEL	1M	D	Marylebone	Prado,Edgar	200,000	120,000
MatronH	21-Jun-03	6	MD	6F	D	Tweed	Moccasin,Tim	5,000	3,000
MatronH	30-Aug-03	9	EVD	1M	D	Blue Guru	Smith,Guy	35,000	21,000
MattWinn	10-May-03	8	CD	6F	D	Posse	Lanerie,Corey	111,400	69,068
MaxmGldCpH	18-Jan-03	8	HOU	1 1/8M	D	Valhol	Albarado,Robby	100,000	60,000
MazarnBCG2	20-Sep-03	8	WO	1 1/16M	D	Dream About	Husbands,Patrick	268,250	160,950
Mbe/RnaHG1	26-Jul-03	8	DMR	1 1/8M	T	Megahertz (GB)	Solis,Alex	400,000	240,000
McFaddnMm	2-Mar-03	7	PM	1 1/16M	D	Cee Cruiser	Beckner,Twyla	10,000	5,500
MdBCHG3	17-May-03	4	PIM	6F	D	Pioneer Boy	Rose,Jeremy	200,000	60,000
MddlgrndBC	13-Jul-03	5	LS	6F	D	Korbyn Gold	Beasley,Jeremy	75,000	45,000
MDiarmdHG3	19-Jan-03	10	GP	1 3/8M	T	Riddlesdown (IRE)	Velez,Roger	100,000	60,000
MdJuvChamp	31-Dec-03	8	LRL	1 1/8M	D	Pour It On	Rodriguez,Erick	100,000	60,000
MdJuvChamp	31-Dec-03	6	LRL	1 1/8M	D	White Mountain Boy	Castellano, Jr.,Abel	100,000	60,000
MdMilClasc	11-Oct-03	11	LRL	1 3/16M	D	Docent	Potts,Clinton	200,000	110,000
MdMilDsStH	11-Oct-03	2	LRL	7F	D	Allens Blessing	Carmouche,Kendrick	50,000	27,500
MdMilDstfH	11-Oct-03	8	LRL	7F	D	Willa On the Move	Pino,Mario	100,000	55,000
MdMilLadys	11-Oct-03	7	LRL	1 1/8M	T	Hail Hillary	Castellano, Jr.,Abel	100,000	55,000
MdMilLass	11-Oct-03	4	LRL	7F	D	Richetta	Dominguez,Ramon	100,000	55,000
MdMillOaks	11-Oct-03	6	LRL	1 1/8M	D	River Cruise	Rose,Jeremy	100,000	55,000
MdMillTurf	11-Oct-03	9	LRL	1 1/8M	T	Move Those Chains	Dominguez,Ramon	100,000	55,000
MdMilNrsry	11-Oct-03	5	LRL	7F	D	Polish Rifle	Pino,Mario	100,000	55,000
MdMilSprtH	11-Oct-03	1	LRL	7F	D	My Navy	Dominguez,Ramon	25,000	13,750
MDMilSprtH	11-Oct-03	10	LRL	6F	D	Michael's Pride	Santana,Jozbin	100,000	55,000
MdMilStrtH	11-Oct-03	3	LRL	1 1/8M	D	Irish Colony	Rodriguez,Erick	50,000	27,500
MdmoisellH	19-Jul-03	6	MD	1M	D	Ms. Lady Rose	Scarlett,Andy	5,000	3,000
MdRcngMedH	22-Feb-03	8	LRL	1 1/8M	D	Pupil	Elliott,Stewart	75,000	45,000
Mecke	29-Nov-03	11	CRC	1 1/16M	T	Timo	Coa,Eibar	100,000	60,000
MedBCG2	3-Oct-03	8	MED	1 1/8M	D	Bowman's Band	Dominguez,Ramon	400,000	240,000
MEisenhowr	10-May-03	8	PRM	6F	D	One Fine Shweetie	Thompson,Terry	60,000	36,000
Melair	26-Apr-03	9	HOL	1 1/16M	D	Bartok's Blithe	Espinoza,Victor	200,000	120,000
MemDayH	26-May-03	4	MNR	1M	D	Eagle Time	Magrell,Jane	77,900	46,740

Stakes	Date	Race	Trk	Dist/Surf		Winner	Jockey	Gross	Value to winner
MemDayHG3	26-May-03	11	CRC	1 1/16M	D	Dancing Guy	Velez,Roger	100,000	60,000
MemDaySpdH	26-May-03	7	BOI	4 1/2F	D	Bobbiblue Bayou	Nollar,Flip	7,100	4,260
Memorial	4-Aug-03	6	FE	1 1/16M	D	Sly Butterfly	Poznansky,Neil	90,000	36,000
Merrillvil	11-Oct-03	9	HOO	6F	D	Ellens Lucky Star	Mojica,Orlando	38,800	23,280
MerryTime	7-Jun-03	3	TDN	1 1/16M	D	Lac Ouiloose	Skerrett,Jeffrey	50,000	30,000
MesaH	13-Dec-03	4	TUP	6 1/2F	D	Knoll Lake	Bridges,Kelly	35,000	21,000
MGDCradle	1-Sep-03	12	RD	1 1/16M	D	Tiger Hunt	Melancon,Larry	206,300	120,000
MGoldblatt	16-Mar-03	5	PM	1M	D	Carlyn Road	Terleski,Marijo	10,000	5,500
MHallStrH	18-Oct-03	2	TUP	6 1/2F	D	Credit Call	Campbell,Joel	20,000	12,000
MHarrellMm	13-Sep-03	7	CT	7F	D	Longfield Spud	Reynolds,Larry	35,950	23,368
MiaMIBCHG3	1-Sep-03	5	CRC	1M	D	Tour of the Cat	Cabassa, Jr.,Abad	150,000	90,000
Mia'sHope	6-Jul-03	6	CRC	1 1/16M	T	Hermans Honor	Aguilar,Manuel	42,650	27,590
MiBrdGvCpH	19-Jul-03	8	GLD	1 1/16M	D	Goldinrunner	Rini,Wade	45,000	27,000
MichgnOaks	19-Sep-03	7	GLD	1 1/16M	D	Cantouchis	Doser,Mary	45,000	27,000
MichgnSire	11-Oct-03	8	GLD	1 1/8M	D	Goldinrunner	Martinez,Luis	122,050	73,230
MichgnSire	11-Oct-03	7	GLD	6F	D	Rockem Sockem	Molina,Tommy	121,450	72,870
MichgnSire	11-Oct-03	4	GLD	1 1/16M	D	Clever Moon	Santos,Felipe	124,650	74,790
MichgnSire	11-Oct-03	6	GLD	1 1/8M	D	Sefas Rose	Mata,Federico	123,050	73,830
MichgnSire	11-Oct-03	5	GLD	1 1/16M	D	Monetary Star	Judice,Joseph	121,150	72,690
MichgnSire	11-Oct-03	3	GLD	6F	D	Send 'Em Pakin	Molina,Tommy	124,250	74,550
MichiganFu	28-Oct-03	2	GLD	7F	D	Rockem Sockem	Molina,Tommy	40,137	24,083
MichiganFu	28-Oct-03	1	GLD	7F	D	Heza Mountain Man	Judice,Joseph	40,137	24,083
MichJuvFil	27-Oct-03	2	GLD	7F	D	Cats Copy	Santos,Felipe	40,425	24,255
MichJuvFil	27-Oct-03	1	GLD	7F	D	Gold Ginny	Judice,Joseph	39,675	23,805
MidPeninsl	16-Aug-03	10	BMF	5 1/2F	D	Go Ask Daisy	Castro,Joe	52,100	29,100
MiesqueG3	28-Nov-03	5	HOL	1M	T	Mambo Slew	Smith,Mike	100,000	60,000
MikeLee	28-Jun-03	8	BEL	7F	D	Bossanova	Prado,Edgar	117,000	70,200
MilDerby	1-Jul-03	7	MIL	1 1/8M	D	Sagreeno	Ramirez,Antonio	5,100	2,805
MileHiH	26-Aug-03	5	YAV	1 1/16M	D	Heightenedinterest	Martinez,Orlando	20,000	11,000
MillerLite	14-Jun-03	8	LS	5F	T	Cauy	Martin, Jr.,Eddie	50,000	30,000
MilwakAveH	12-Apr-03	7	HAW	1 1/16M	D	Baker Road	Razo, Jr.,Eusebio	135,667	54,675
Minaret	4-Jan-03	10	TAM	6F	D	Smoke Chaser	Judice,Joseph	50,000	21,000
MinDisClCh	17-Aug-03	3	CBY	1 1/16M	D	She's Scrumpy	Martinez,Seth	39,100	23,460
MinDstfSpr	17-Aug-03	10	CBY	6F	D	Madam Speaker	Bell,Derek	39,250	23,550
MinnClscCh	17-Aug-03	9	CBY	1 1/16M	D	Spoofin	Nolan,Paul	45,400	27,240
MinnDerby	26-Jul-03	9	CBY	1M 70Y	D	Tricky Pick Six	Walker, Jr.,Bobby	52,215	31,329
MinnOaks	26-Jul-03	8	CBY	1M 70Y	D	She's Scrumpy	Martinez,Seth	58,103	34,862
MinSprntCh	17-Aug-03	6	CBY	6F	D	Timberwolf Power	Bell,Derek	39,200	23,520
Minstrel	27-Sep-03	8	LAD	6F	D	Joe Six Pack	Gonzalez,Carlos	40,000	24,000
MiraclWood	8-Feb-03	9	LRL	1 1/16M	D	Gimmeawink	Rose,Jeremy	50,000	30,000
MissAmrcaH	5-Apr-03	6	BM	1 1/16M	T	Lindsay Jean	Schvaneveldt,Chad	83,625	49,875
MissCalif	18-Jan-03	8	GG	6F	D	Denali Cat	Lopez,Adalberto	78,700	43,600
MissGrillo	26-Oct-03	8	BEL	1 1/8M	T	Please Take Me Out	Gryder,Aaron	84,400	50,640
MissMommy	29-Nov-03	5	HAW	6F	D	Bad Kitty	Emigh,Christopher	42,000	25,236
MissOhio	23-Aug-03	9	TDN	6F	D	Baba Gonzo	Gonzalez,Luis	40,000	24,000
MissyGood	11-Jul-03	7	PEN	6F	D	Marquee Kelly	Flores,Jose	30,675	18,405
MisterDiz	26-Jul-03	9	LRL	5 1/2F	T	Ghostly Numbers	Wilson,Rick	50,000	30,000
MisterGus	26-May-03	8	AP	1M	T	Al's Dearly Bred	Douglas,Rene	48,150	28,890
MladyBCHG1	24-May-03	8	HOL	1 1/16M	D	Azeri	Smith,Mike	211,800	127,080
MnHBPAMile	5-Jul-03	8	CBY	1M	T	Passionate Bird	Mawing,Leslie	35,000	21,000
MnHBPASprt	5-Jul-03	7	CBY	6F	D	Silver Zipper	Eads,Jason	35,000	21,000
MNJuvSprnt	27-Jul-03	7	CBY	5 1/2F	D	McKenna Beach	Mawing,Leslie	36,950	22,170
MnrHBPA	14-Oct-03	9	MNR	6F	D	Tour the Hive	Feliciano,Ricardo	77,500	46,500
MnrHPBA	21-Oct-03	9	MNR	6F	D	Cobra Lady	Martinez,Willie	78,400	47,040
MnrMileH	15-Nov-03	9	MNR	1M	D	Sonic West	Bejarano,Rafael	103,175	61,906
MnroviaHG3	29-Dec-03	5	SA	6 1/2F	T	Icantgoforthat	Baze,Tyler	109,300	65,580
MntbDrbyG3	4-Aug-03	8	ASD	1 1/8M	D	Hero's Pleasure	Stevens,Scott	100,000	60,000
MnTurfChmp	17-Aug-03	7	CBY	1M	T	Now Playing	Stevens,Scott	39,500	23,700
Moccasin	16-Nov-03	3	HOL	7F	D	Victory U. S. A.	Krone,Julie	100,000	60,000
MochaExp	11-Apr-03	3	TUP	1M	D	Free Corona	Ziegler,Michael	23,600	14,160
Mockingbrd	24-Apr-03	3	GP	3F	D	Kipper's Night	Trujillo,Elvis	53,000	31,800

Stakes	Date	Race	Trk	Dist/Surf		Winner	Jockey	Gross	Value to winner
ModestyHG3	26-Jul-03	7	AP	1 3/16M	T	Owsley	Douglas,Rene	150,000	90,000
MohawkH	18-Oct-03	9	BEL	1 1/8M	T	Quiet Ruler	Velazquez,John	150,000	90,000
MollyBrwnH	22-Jun-03	8	ARP	6F	D	Waveband	Johnson,Robert	35,000	21,000
MomsCommnd	12-Dec-03	8	AQU	6F	D	Stephan's Angel	Migliore,Richard	60,600	36,360
MoneyPenny	24-Oct-03	6	HAW	1 1/16M	D	Rebridled Dreams	Martin, Jr.,Eddie	43,200	25,920
MontaukH	30-Nov-03	8	AQU	1 1/16M	D	Queen's Triomphe	Espinoza,Jose	82,875	49,725
MontclairH	19-Jan-03	3	GG	6F	D	Halo Cat	Baze,Russell	78,900	33,900
MonzanoClH	8-Jun-03	9	ALB	1 1/2M	D	Cryptotune	Olguin,Ever	13,400	8,040
MoonbeamH	18-Jul-03	7	GLD	1M	D	Sefas Rose	Mata,Federico	45,000	27,000
MorvichHG3	24-Oct-03	5	SA	6 1/2F	T	King Robyn	Solis,Alex	110,800	66,480
MPchrBCHG2	28-Jun-03	11	MTH	1 1/8M	D	Summer Colony	Stevens,Gary	300,000	180,000
MRJnknsMmH	4-May-03	8	STP	6F	D	Sly Lady	Simard,Real	40,000	25,200
MrNikersnH	15-Jun-03	8	PHA	6F	D	Night Caller	Bocachica,Orlando	37,700	22,620
MrProspHG3	4-Jan-03	8	GP	6F	D	Baileys Edge	Boulanger,Gary	100,000	60,000
MrsPenny	30-Aug-03	8	PHA	1 1/16M	D	Caught in the Rain	Molina,Victor	50,000	30,000
MrsRvereG2	15-Nov-03	9	CD	1 1/16M	T	Hoh Buzzard (IRE)	Fogelsonger,Ryan	175,650	108,903
MrvnLRyHG2	10-May-03	8	HOL	1 1/16M	D	Total Impact (CHI)	Smith,Mike	150,000	90,000
Ms	8-Feb-03	8	PM	6F	D	Back Street Gal	Gutierrez,Juan	10,000	5,500
MsCreeker	4-Oct-03	7	HAW	1M	T	Valiant Anna	Montalvo,Carlos	43,800	26,280
MsFuturity	5-Dec-03	1	FG	6F	D	Amanda's Fancy	Riquelme,Jose	23,275	13,461
MsHouston	22-Nov-03	8	HOU	7F	D	Questionable Past	Garner,Cathleen	35,000	21,000
MsIndiana	14-Nov-03	9	HOO	6F	D	Down by the Sea	Troilo,William	74,250	44,550
MsIndyAnna	3-May-03	12	SUF	6F	D	Bruanna	Hampshire, Jr.,Josiah	35,000	21,000
MsKanCityH	27-Sep-03	9	WDS	1 1/16M	D	Market's Best	Vasquez,Richard	30,000	18,000
MsLiberty	25-Oct-03	8	MED	1 1/16M	D	Devotion Unbridled	Pimentel,Julian	45,000	27,000
MsMonypeny	1-Sep-03	6	FE	1 1/16M	D	Soon to Be Single	Villeneuve,Francine	90,000	54,000
MsPreaknG3	15-May-03	8	PIM	6F	D	Belong to Sea	Castellano,Javier	100,000	60,000
MsSoOhio	3-Aug-03	10	RD	1 1/16M	D	Lady Cherie	Felix,Julio	40,000	24,000
MsWoodford	23-Aug-03	6	MTH	6F	D	Elegant Designer	Pino,Mario	60,000	36,000
MTAStalLad	1-Sep-03	7	CBY	6 1/2F	D	Oop's the Red	Escobar,Martin	37,608	22,565
MTAStalLas	1-Sep-03	6	CBY	6 1/2F	D	Lil' Mo' Rhythm	Kimes,Curtis	36,550	21,930
MtchmkrHG3	17-Aug-03	10	MTH	1 1/8M	T	Volga (IRE)	Bravo,Joe	100,000	60,000
MtElbertH	10-Aug-03	8	ARP	1 1/16M	D	Personal Beau	Gonsalves,Frank	22,500	13,500
MthBeach	8-Jun-03	9	MTH	1 1/16M	D	Tonight's Wager	Beckner,Dale	60,000	36,000
MthrGoosG1	28-Jun-03	9	BEL	1 1/8M	D	Spoken Fur	Bailey,Jerry	300,000	180,000
MtRainrBCH	27-Jul-03	7	EMD	1 1/8M	D	Poker Brad	Russell,Ben	100,000	55,000
MtropltHG1	26-May-03	9	BEL	1M	D	Aldebaran	Bailey,Jerry	750,000	450,000
MtRoyalH	11-May-03	7	STP	6F	D	Raylene	Wilson,David	50,000	25,200
MtStHelens	6-Apr-03	5	PM	1M	D	Back Street Gal	Gutierrez,Juan	10,000	5,500
MtVernonH	22-Jun-03	8	BEL	1 1/8M	D	Princess Dixie	Prado,Edgar	114,300	68,580
MTysGilpin	18-Oct-03	3	DEL	6F	D	Tap Day	Bracho,Richard	42,100	25,260
MusgCrkNat	5-Jun-03	10	FMT	6 1/2F	D	Frilly Fun	Payne,Larry	22,900	13,282
Muskoka	1-Sep-03	8	WO	7F	D	My Vintage Port	Jones,Jono	136,375	81,825
MWashBCG3	27-Sep-03	9	PIM	1 1/16M	T	Derrianne	Blanc,Brice	150,000	90,000
MWashngton	17-Feb-03	9	OP	6F	D	Explosive Beauty	Theriot,Jamie	50,000	30,000
MxnPiggott	26-Apr-03	1	TUP	6 1/2F	D	Tulsa	Bridges,Kelly	35,000	21,000
MyCharmer	6-Dec-03	10	TP	1 1/16M	D	Affirmed Dancer	Martinez,Willie	50,000	31,300
MyChrmrHG3	6-Dec-03	9	CRC	1 1/8M	T	New Economy	Homeister, Jr.,Rosemary	100,000	60,000
MyDear	21-Jun-03	8	WO	5F	D	Nashinda	Clark,David	187,125	112,275
MyFairLady	31-May-03	5	SUF	1M 70Y	D	Island Melody	Johnson,Richard	35,000	21,000
MyJuliet	16-Jul-03	8	BEL	6F	D	Zawzooth	Prado,Edgar	65,750	39,450
MyJuliet	26-May-03	8	PHA	6F	D	Astrid	Flores,Jose	100,000	60,000
MysteryJet	12-Mar-03	8	SUF	6F	D	Glory Be Good	Bush,Vernon	35,000	21,000
NanaimoH	19-Jul-03	4	HST	1 1/16M	D	Dancewithavixen	Valdez,Felipe	44,680	26,808
Nandi	26-Jul-03	8	WO	6F	D	La Grande Mamma	Husbands,Patrick	137,375	82,425
NasauCBCG2	10-May-03	8	BEL	7F	D	House Party	Santos,Jose	200,000	120,000
NashuaG3	2-Nov-03	8	AQU	1M	D	Read the Footnotes	Bailey,Jerry	113,100	67,860
NassauG2	1-Jun-03	8	WO	1 1/16M	T	Strait from Texas	Dos Ramos,Richard	328,200	166,920
NatalmaG3	6-Sep-03	8	WO	1M	T	Pink Champagne	Dos Ramos,Richard	227,000	106,200
NATCFut	30-Aug-03	6	DEL	6F	D	Tym Beau	Caraballo,Jose	200,000	120,000
NATCSorFut	30-Aug-03	8	DEL	6F	D	From Away	Dominguez,Ramon	200,000	120,000

Stakes	Date	Race	Trk	Dist/Surf		Winner	Jockey	Gross	Value to winner
NativePetH	11-May-03	8	AP	7F	D	Julie's Prize	Sterling, Jr.,Larry	40,000	24,000
NatvDancer	11-Jan-03	8	LRL	1 1/8M	D	P Day	Fogelsonger,Ryan	75,000	45,000
Navarchus	31-Aug-03	8	CRC	1 1/16M	D	Scottish Bubbly	Aguilar,Manuel	42,750	27,650
NavPrncess	27-Sep-03	9	MTH	1 1/16M	T	Feisty Bull	Lopez,Charles	50,000	30,000
NblDmslHG3	20-Sep-03	9	BEL	1M	T	Wonder Again	Prado,Edgar	150,000	90,000
NcysGltttrH	19-Jul-03	12	CRC	1 1/16M	D	Stormy Frolic	Velez,Roger	75,000	21,000
NDDerby	6-Jul-03	7	ASD	1M	D	Maddies Blues	Hightower,Travis	20,000	10,000
NDFuturity	31-Aug-03	8	ASD	6F	D	Strike an Image	Leacock,Jason	30,000	18,000
NDStallion	2-Aug-03	3	ASD	1 1/16M	D	Suntana	Hendricks,Ken	20,000	10,600
NDStallion	2-Aug-03	6	ASD	6F	D	Sir Augustus	Iammarino,Michael	30,000	15,000
NearctcHG2	22-Jun-03	6	WO	6F	T	Soaring Free	Kabel,Todd	286,500	171,900
NebDerby	4-May-03	9	FON	1M	D	Intervene	Guajardo,Alonzo	27,500	16,500
Needles	6-Sep-03	5	CRC	1 1/16M	D	The Name's Bond	Cruz,Manoel	75,000	41,000
NellieMors	25-Jan-03	8	LRL	1 1/16M	D	Martha's Music	Elliott,Stewart	50,000	30,000
NervosJohn	4-May-03	6	HAW	6F	D	In Secure	Baird,E.	42,400	25,440
NevrMissTV	18-Aug-03	7	YAV	4 1/2F	D	Jomax	Hernandez,Miguel	9,900	5,445
NewBraunfl	11-Oct-03	9	RET	6F	D	Southern Tour	Gondron,Ted	35,000	21,000
NewCastleH	22-Jun-03	7	DEL	1 1/8M	D	Jaramar Rain	Madrigal, Jr.,Rodrigo	100,000	60,000
NewYearEve	30-Dec-03	9	MNR	6F	D	Saratoga Humor	Ramgeet,Andrew	77,300	46,380
NewYorkHG2	4-Jul-03	10	BEL	1 1/4M	T	Snow Dance	Migliore,Richard	250,000	150,000
Niagara	19-Jul-03	8	FL	6F	D	Storm On the Lake	Messina,Robert	35,000	21,000
NiagrBCHG2	30-Aug-03	8	WO	1 1/2M	T	Strut the Stage	Kabel,Todd	337,200	202,320
Nicole	3-May-03	7	HAW	1 1/16M	T	Attico	Douglas,Rene	43,200	25,920
NijskyScrt	25-Jul-03	5	CRC	7 1/2F	T	Mr. Livingston	Cruz,Manoel	44,025	23,415
NJFuturity	7-Nov-03	9	MED	6F	D	War's Prospect	Lopez,Charles	66,032	39,620
NJFuturity	7-Nov-03	7	MED	6F	D	Wild Catseye	King, Jr.,Edwin	65,532	39,320
NMBrdrAscH	6-Oct-03	10	SRP	1M	D	Piute	Fuentes,Adan	67,700	40,620
NMDistaffH	20-Sep-03	9	SRP	6 1/2F	D	Ghost Chatter	Coates,Jimmy	68,200	40,920
NMRcngComH	30-Nov-03	10	SUN	6F	D	Shemoveslikeaghost	Tohill,Ken	132,700	79,620
NMStFairH	21-Sep-03	8	ALB	1 1/8M	D	Personal Beau	Johnson,Bobby	37,550	22,530
NMTbrdDrby	20-Sep-03	8	ALB	1 1/16M	D	Casperino	Jaime,Ricardo	45,427	23,019
NMUnivH	2-Feb-03	10	SUN	1M	D	Ciento	Gonzalez, Jr.,Sal	131,000	78,600
Noel	26-Dec-03	8	DED	1M	D	Boston Fox	Gonzalez,Carlos	40,000	24,000
NoLeHace	18-Oct-03	9	RET	7 1/2F	T	Wishingitwas	Stanton,Terry	35,000	21,000
NorfolkG2	5-Oct-03	10	SA	1 1/16M	D	Ruler's Court	Solis,Alex	250,000	150,000
NorgorDby	9-Aug-03	10	RUI	6F	D	Latenite Trick	Johnson,Robert	32,200	19,320
NormanHall	18-Oct-03	6	SUF	6F	D	Strongestsovereign	Molinari,Edwin	35,000	21,000
Northamptn	6-Sep-03	7	NMP	6 1/2F	D	Mr. Meso	Paucar,Edgar	15,800	9,300
Northernet	17-Aug-03	6	WO	1 1/16M	D	Seeking the Ring	Kabel,Todd	105,000	63,000
NotSurpsng	1-Sep-03	3	CRC	6F	D	Love That Moon	Velasquez,Cornelio	41,950	27,170
NPOaks	20-Jul-03	7	NP	1M	D	Raylene	Wilson,David	40,000	25,200
NRandall	9-Aug-03	10	TDN	6F	D	Ben's Reflection	Cox,Danny	40,000	24,000
NrthnSprBC	12-Apr-03	7	OP	1M	D	Mauk Four	Court,Jon	75,000	45,000
NrthrnDncr	22-Nov-03	8	LRL	1 1/8M	D	Ironton	Petro,Nicholas	75,000	45,000
NrthrnDncr	14-Jun-03	7	CD	1M	D	Champali	Day,Pat	111,100	68,882
NrtMtllcSl	13-Jul-03	7	GPR	6F	D	Wise Dancer	McAleney,Peter	3,600	1,980
NShukMem	23-Jun-03	7	DEL	1 1/16M	D	Gimmeawink	Madrigal, Jr.,Rodrigo	75,000	45,000
NthLitsDeb	17-Aug-03	4	CBY	6F	D	McKenna Beach	Mawing,Leslie	50,250	30,150
NthLitsFut	17-Aug-03	8	CBY	6F	D	Vasant	Ziegler,Michael	52,850	31,710
NtlJClbHG3	19-Apr-03	8	HAW	1 1/8M	D	Fight for Ally	Razo, Jr.,Eusebio	250,000	150,000
NtvDivrHG3	6-Dec-03	8	HOL	1 1/8M	D	Olmodavor	Solis,Alex	100,000	60,000
Nursery	11-May-03	9	HOL	5F	D	Wacky Patty	Nakatani,Corey	99,750	46,350
NvnAlmdCoF	4-Jul-03	11	PLN	5F	D	Lil' Bro Eddie	Rollins,Chance	52,900	29,700
NwOrlnsHG2	2-Mar-03	9	FG	1 1/8M	D	Mineshaft	Albarado,Robby	500,000	300,000
NwProvdnce	18-May-03	8	WO	6F	D	Forever Grand	Kabel,Todd	127,625	80,404
NWstmnstrH	17-Aug-03	2	HST	6 1/2F	D	Lord Samarai	Wright,Nicola	39,004	23,402
NxtMoveHG3	23-Mar-03	9	AQU	1 1/8M	D	Smok'n Frolic	Velazquez,John	108,000	64,800
NYBrdrFut	1-Sep-03	6	FL	6F	D	Mother's Sacrifice	Yang,Chin	155,863	93,518
NYDerby	26-Jul-03	8	FL	1 1/16M	D	Traffic Chief	Davila, Jr.,John	142,200	85,320
NYOaks	1-Sep-03	7	FL	1 1/16M	D	Flag Pin	Bracho,Jorge	60,000	36,000
NYSCrmrnt	9-Nov-03	8	AQU	1M	T	Quantum Merit	Migliore,Richard	100,000	60,000

Stakes	Date	Race	Trk	Dist/Surf		Winner	Jockey	Gross	Value to winner
NYSGrtWtWy	9-Nov-03	7	AQU	6F	D	West Virginia	Bailey,Jerry	125,000	75,000
NYSPfctArc	9-Nov-03	6	AQU	1M	T	Ma Femme	Pezua,Julio	100,000	60,000
NYStl5thAv	9-Nov-03	5	AQU	6F	D	So Sweet a Cat	Velazquez,John	125,000	75,000
NYStlCbCwy	8-Jun-03	6	BEL	1 1/16M	D	Bo Bo's Vice	Chavez,Jorge	250,000	150,000
NYStlnPkAv	27-Apr-03	7	AQU	1M	D	Hanselina	Prado,Edgar	150,000	90,000
NYStlTmSqr	27-Apr-03	8	AQU	1M	D	Grey Comet	Bailey,Jerry	150,000	90,000
NYStStLbty	8-Jun-03	7	BEL	1 1/16M	D	Beautiful America	Santos,Jose	250,000	150,000
Oakhurst	27-Apr-03	10	PM	2M	D	Rattlesnake Ridge	Webb,Robert	10,000	5,500
OaklandH	6-Dec-03	3	GG	6F	D	Boston Common	Schvaneveldt,Chad	78,500	33,500
OaklawnHG2	5-Apr-03	11	OP	1 1/8M	D	Medaglia d'Oro	Bailey,Jerry	500,000	300,000
OakLeafG2	28-Sep-03	9	SA	1 1/16M	D	Halfbridled	Krone,Julie	250,000	150,000
Oakley	22-Jun-03	11	CNL	1 1/16M	T	Little Miss Pamela	Karamanos,Horacio	50,000	30,000
OaklwnBCG3	15-Mar-03	10	OP	1 1/16M	D	Bien Nicole	Pettinger,Donald	200,000	120,000
OakTrDbyG2	4-Oct-03	4	SA	1 1/8M	T	Devious Boy (GB)	Krone,Julie	150,000	90,000
ObeahH	21-Jun-03	7	DEL	1 1/8M	D	Devon Rose	Black,Anthony	100,000	60,000
OBSChamp	17-Mar-03	6	OTC	1 1/16M	D	The Name's Bond	Boulanger,Gary	100,000	60,000
OBSChamp	17-Mar-03	5	OTC	1 1/16M	D	Running Debate	Prado,Edgar	100,000	60,000
OBSSprint	17-Mar-03	2	OTC	6F	D	Valid Video	Prado,Edgar	50,000	30,000
OBSSprint	17-Mar-03	1	OTC	6F	D	Shot Gun Favorite	Prado,Edgar	50,000	30,000
OcalStdDsh	25-Jan-03	8	GP	7F	D	Valid Video	Prado,Edgar	250,000	137,500
Oceanside	23-Jul-03	8	DMR	1M	T	Devious Boy (GB)	Krone,Julie	84,300	50,580
Oceanside	23-Jul-03	5	DMR	1M	T	Sweet Return (GB)	Nakatani,Corey	85,300	51,180
OcenprtHG3	14-Jun-03	10	MTH	1 1/16M	D	Runspastum	Pimentel,Julian	100,000	60,000
OclBrdSlCl	25-Jan-03	7	GP	1 1/8M	D	Best of the Rest	Coa,Eibar	1,000,000	533,500
OcnPlcRsrt	3-Aug-03	7	MTH	1 1/16M	T	In Hand	Pimentel,Julian	75,000	45,000
OffceQueen	14-Jun-03	12	CRC	1 1/16M	D	Splasha	Aguilar,Manuel	100,000	60,000
OgataulH	8-Mar-03	9	FON	6F	D	Tate's Way	Compton,Perry	25,725	15,435
Ogl&CoTfDt	6-Apr-03	9	TAM	1 1/16M	T	Chef's Choice	Pompell,Thomas	84,600	46,760
OhFreshman	16-Nov-03	7	BEU	1M 70Y	D	Dawn's Revenge	Gonzalez,Luis	35,000	21,000
OhioDebH	30-Aug-03	11	TDN	6F	D	Just Michel	Feliciano,Ricardo	40,000	24,000
OhioDrbyG2	21-Jun-03	14	TDN	1 1/8M	D	Wild and Wicked	Sellers,Shane	306,300	180,000
OhioVallyH	27-May-03	9	MNR	6F	D	Timeless Love	Murphy,Chad	77,100	46,260
OkClClassc	27-Sep-03	7	RP	1 1/16M	D	George Taylor	Matz,Nena	75,000	43,530
OkClDistaf	27-Sep-03	3	RP	1M 70Y	D	Bayakoa's Image	Cogburn,Kevin	35,000	20,330
OkClFMTurf	27-Sep-03	1	RP	7 1/2F	T	Slew Ann	LeBlanc,Kirk	35,000	20,330
OkClJuvnl	27-Sep-03	6	RP	6F	D	Okie Style	Pettinger,Donald	35,000	20,330
OkClLassie	27-Sep-03	2	RP	6F	D	Aspen Gal	Berry,Monte	35,000	20,330
OkClSprint	27-Sep-03	5	RP	6F	D	Medium Rare	Berry,Monte	35,000	20,330
OkClTurf	27-Sep-03	4	RP	1M	D	April's Lucky Boy	Pettinger,Donald	35,000	20,330
OkDerbyG3	16-Nov-03	8	RP	1 1/8M	D	Comic Truth	Berry,Monte	160,700	95,400
OklahomaTb	26-May-03	10	FMT	6 1/2F	D	Dance and Dazzle	Payne,Larry	27,300	15,211
OkTrBCMIG2	5-Oct-03	8	SA	1M	T	Designed for Luck	Valenzuela,Patrick	300,000	180,000
OldHat	2-Feb-03	10	GP	6F	D	House Party	Santos,Jose	100,000	60,000
OldIrnsdes	21-Jun-03	12	SUF	1M 70Y	T	Devine Wind	Dominguez,Ramon	35,000	21,000
OldSouthH	4-Oct-03	9	LAD	1 1/16M	D	Due to Win Again	LeBlanc,Kirk	40,000	24,000
Oliver	12-Apr-03	9	IND	6F	D	Santa Fe Strip	Martinez, Jr.,Luis	44,500	26,700
OmahaH	13-Jul-03	4	HPO	1M	D	Dusty Spike	Kretzer,Kerry	110,000	57,600
OntarDbyG3	13-Oct-03	6	WO	1 1/8M	D	Mobil	Kabel,Todd	159,900	100,737
OntarioCo	12-Jul-03	8	FL	6F	D	Strausberg	Grabowski,John	35,000	21,000
OntarioDeb	10-Aug-03	8	WO	6F	D	Slightlymorelikely	Kabel,Todd	136,250	81,750
OntarioJC	19-Jul-03	3	WO	7F	T	Soaring Free	Kabel,Todd	107,000	64,200
OntColeenH	24-Aug-03	8	WO	1M	T	Shaconage	Johnson,Joe	199,375	89,625
OntDamsel	29-Jun-03	8	WO	6 1/2F	T	Dressed for Action	Landry,Robert	166,500	99,900
OntFashnH	25-Oct-03	9	WO	6F	D	Winter Garden	Clark,David	136,125	81,675
OntLassie	23-Nov-03	8	WO	1 1/16M	D	Six Sexy Sisters	Husbands,Patrick	160,950	101,398
OntMatronH	7-Jun-03	8	WO	1 1/16M	D	Winning Chance	Kabel,Todd	189,375	113,625
OnTrustH	13-Dec-03	8	HOL	7 1/2F	D	Excess Summer	Stevens,Gary	107,900	64,740
Open	6-Sep-03	8	LBG	6F	D	Tickle Me Malmo	Smith-Hebert,Jackie	11,200	6,160
Open	31-Aug-03	7	LBG	7F	D	A Knight Mission	Landaker,Terri	11,200	6,160
OpenMind	28-Dec-03	7	AQU	1M 70Y	D	Fond	Carrero,Victor	60,750	36,450
OpenMindH	1-Jun-03	9	MTH	6F	D	Uphill Skier	Bravo,Joe	50,000	30,000

Stakes	Date	Race	Trk	Dist/Surf		Winner	Jockey	Gross	Value to winner
OpenTBDerb	14-Sep-03	10	FAR	1M	D	Maddies Blues	Schindler,Scot	23,016	11,508
OpenTBDerb	1-Sep-03	8	FAR	1M	D	Squirmlikeaworm	Von Rosen,Anne	9,300	4,650
OpenTBInau	14-Sep-03	9	FAR	6F	D	Ski Hero	Butler,Beth	9,100	4,550
OPhippsHG1	21-Jun-03	8	BEL	1 1/16M	D	Sightseek	Bailey,Jerry	300,000	180,000
OrchidHG2	23-Mar-03	8	GP	1 1/2M	D	Tweedside	Douglas,Rene	200,000	120,000
OregonDby	13-Apr-03	8	PM	1 1/8M	D	Glad to Be Here	Boag,Daniel	25,000	13,750
OregonHers	13-Dec-03	7	PM	1M	D	Chancy Chancy	Gutierrez,Juan	10,000	5,500
OregonHis	13-Dec-03	5	PM	1 1/16M	D	Cee Cruiser	Beckner,Twyla	10,000	5,500
OregonOaks	20-Apr-03	8	PM	1 1/16M	D	Back Street Gal	Webb,Robert	15,000	8,250
OrindaH	25-Jan-03	9	GG	6F	D	Lacie Girl	Baze,Russell	78,800	33,800
OrphnKistH	1-Mar-03	9	FON	6F	D	Real Intrusion	Warhol,Vicki	25,825	15,495
OrSprtChmp	13-Dec-03	4	PM	6F	D	Yesss	Beckner,Twyla	10,000	5,500
OsunitasH	13-Aug-03	7	DMR	1 1/16M	T	Arabic Song (IRE)	Nakatani,Corey	102,475	47,985
OSWestFut	13-Dec-03	8	PM	1M	D	Tom Won	Beckner,Twyla	30,295	16,663
OTBASales	1-Nov-03	9	PM	6F	D	Houston Shuffle	Gutierrez,Juan	8,550	4,703
OTBAStalln	4-Jan-03	2	PM	6F	D	Questionable Road	Baze,Gary	10,000	5,500
Overage	2-May-03	8	HAW	1 1/16M	D	Mc Mahon	Fires,Earlie	44,000	26,400
Overnite	7-Jun-03	6	LBG	6F	D	Guiltybysupiscion	Sterr,Scott	11,200	6,160
Overskate	2-Jul-03	7	WO	7F	D	Mulligan the Great	McKnight,James	137,000	82,200
OwnersDayH	6-Sep-03	7	DEL	1 1/8M	D	Country Be Gold	Santos,Jose	75,000	45,000
OzarkHillH	2-Mar-03	7	BRD	4F	D	As de Oro	Goad, Jr.,Kenneth	7,350	4,410
PacifcClG1	24-Aug-03	5	DMR	1 1/4M	D	Candy Ride (ARG)	Krone,Julie	1,000,000	600,000
PacificaH	26-Oct-03	7	BM	1 1/16M	T	Vallarta	Gonzalez,Roberto	78,550	33,550
PaDerbyG3	1-Sep-03	11	PHA	1 1/8M	D	Grand Hombre	Bravo,Joe	750,000	450,000
PaduaFMSpr	25-Jan-03	6	GP	6F	D	Madame Pietra	Valenzuela,Patrick	250,000	137,500
PagoHop	20-Dec-03	9	FG	1M	T	Snowdrops (GB)	Melancon,Gerard	75,000	45,000
PaGovCupH	2-Aug-03	2	PEN	5F	T	Namequest	Klinger,C.	50,000	30,000
PalmBchG3	21-Feb-03	9	GP	1 1/8M	T	Nothing to Lose	Bailey,Jerry	100,000	60,000
PalmrBCHG2	7-Sep-03	6	DMR	1 1/16M	T	Spring Star (FR)	Solis,Alex	200,000	120,000
PaloAltoH	11-Oct-03	8	BM	1M	D	Frisco Belle	Castro,Joe	78,600	33,600
PaloVerdeH	22-Feb-03	4	TUP	6 1/2F	D	Unyielding	Lopez,Lorenzo	35,000	21,000
PanAmerHG2	22-Mar-03	10	GP	1 1/2M	T	Quest Star	Prado,Edgar	200,000	120,000
PanhandleH	3-May-03	9	MNR	5F	D	Crossing Point	Fogelsonger,Ryan	76,500	48,195
Panthers	7-Jun-03	8	PRM	1M	D	Wildwood Royal	Sukie,Danush	50,000	30,000
PanZaretaH	8-Feb-03	9	FG	6F	D	Fuse It	Melancon,Gerard	75,000	45,000
PardisCrek	7-Sep-03	6	AP	1 1/16M	T	Megoman	Perez,Eduardo	46,800	28,080
PardisValH	15-Nov-03	7	TUP	7 1/2F	T	Moody Slew	Dieguez,Wilson	35,000	21,000
ParkIndHer	16-Aug-03	4	MD	1 1/16M	D	She's Nifty	Latchman,Rennie	10,000	6,000
Parnitha	1-Jul-03	6	FE	6F	D	Rare Friends	Landry,Robert	65,000	39,000
Pasco	18-Jan-03	10	TAM	7F	D	Super Fuse	Gonzalez,Carlos	50,000	21,000
PaseanaH	15-Jan-03	7	SA	1 1/16M	D	Printemps (CHI)	Pincay, Jr.,Laffit	102,000	47,700
PassinMood	16-Jul-03	3	WO	7F	T	Cruising Executive	Clark,David	131,000	78,600
Paterson	31-Oct-03	8	MED	1 1/16M	D	Gimmeawink	Potts,Clinton	45,000	27,000
PatrckWood	23-Sep-03	7	GLD	6F	D	Rockem Sockem	Molina,Tommy	45,000	27,000
PaumonokH	25-Jan-03	8	AQU	6F	D	Say Florida Sandy	Luzzi,Michael	80,550	48,330
PAxthelm	20-Dec-03	11	CRC	7 1/2F	T	Magic Mecke	Coa,Eibar	100,000	60,000
PCondelonH	23-Sep-03	6	FP	1M	D	Bulldog George	Razo, Jr.,Eusebio	35,600	21,360
PDShepherd	13-Sep-03	11	FPX	1 1/16M	D	Legendary Weave	Pedroza,Martin	50,000	27,500
PduaSSoCG	6-Apr-03	8	TAM	7F	D	Mychampion	Delgado,Jose	84,500	46,700
PeachofItH	12-Apr-03	4	HAW	1 1/16M	D	Julie's Prize	Sterling, Jr.,Larry	137,092	55,530
PearlNeckl	16-Aug-03	9	LRL	1 1/16M	T	Perfect Blue	Umana,Juan	60,000	36,000
PebblesHG3	13-Oct-03	9	BEL	1 1/8M	D	Betty's Wish	Velazquez,John	110,300	66,180
PeletriBCH	16-Mar-03	8	FG	6F	D	Beau's Town	Theriot,Jamie	150,000	90,000
Pelican	27-Dec-03	10	TAM	6F	D	Above the Wind	Mata,Federico	60,000	27,000
Peninsula	24-Aug-03	8	FE	7F	T	On to Richmond	Ramirez,Martin	90,000	36,000
PennaNurse	22-Nov-03	9	PHA	7F	D	Smarty Jones	Elliott,Stewart	56,100	33,660
PennOaks	1-Sep-03	10	PHA	1M 70Y	D	City Fire	Ferrer,Jose	100,000	60,000
PennyRdge	15-Jun-03	8	STP	1 1/16M	D	Raylene	Wilson,David	40,000	25,200
PepOakFrm	26-Apr-03	10	HOL	6 1/2F	D	Le Mans	Flores,David	60,000	36,000
PeppyAddy	7-Jun-03	9	PHA	7F	D	Yo	Elliott,Stewart	55,000	33,000
PepsBassnt	30-Aug-03	12	RD	6F	D	In Rome	Johnston,Jeff	106,000	60,000

Stakes	Date	Race	Trk	Dist/Surf		Winner	Jockey	Gross	Value to winner
Pepsi	22-Mar-03	9	FON	6F	D	Miss Speed Dial	Murray,Kelly	17,275	10,365
PepsiColaH	18-Jan-03	10	SUN	6F	D	Gulchrunssweet	Fuentes,Adan	132,700	79,620
PepsiColaH	26-May-03	9	EMD	6 1/2F	D	Leather N Lace	Cedeno,Amir	39,000	21,725
Perryville	9-Oct-03	8	KEE	7F	D	Clock Stopper	Albarado,Robby	108,300	67,146
PeterPanG2	24-May-03	8	BEL	1 1/8M	D	Go Rockin' Robin	Bridgmohan,Shaun	200,000	120,000
PhnxGldCpH	8-Mar-03	8	TUP	6F	D	Giovannetti	Sorenson,Danny	100,000	60,000
PhoenixH	25-Oct-03	4	TUP	6F	D	No Turbulence	Stevens,Scott	35,000	21,000
PhoenxBCG3	3-Oct-03	7	KEE	6F	D	Najran	Castellano,Javier	274,000	169,880
PhxLsrTbH	17-Aug-03	11	WYO	1M	D	Gail's Melody	Greene,Casey	7,050	4,230
Piedmont	22-Nov-03	3	GG	6F	D	Wildwood Flower	Radke,Kevin	78,550	33,550
PiedraFndH	4-Sep-03	6	DMR	1M	D	Adoration	Valenzuela,Patrick	98,750	45,750
Pilgrim	19-Oct-03	9	BEL	1 1/8M	T	Timo	Velazquez,John	82,525	49,515
PimSpclHG1	16-May-03	11	PIM	1 3/16M	D	Mineshaft	Albarado,Robby	600,000	400,000
PineTreeLn	26-Mar-03	2	SA	6F	D	Shameful	Flores,David	101,150	47,190
Pinjara	1-Nov-03	8	SA	1M	T	Rush Into Heaven	Puglisi,Ignacio	99,300	46,980
PinonH	23-Mar-03	8	ALB	6 1/2F	D	Spirit de Azure	Fuentes,Miguel	51,800	31,080
Pioneer	10-Aug-03	10	LAD	5 1/2F	D	Mr. Jester	Chapa,Roman	50,000	30,000
PioPico	19-Sep-03	10	FPX	6 1/2F	D	Bold Roberta	Fogelsonger,Ryan	50,000	27,500
Pippin	15-Feb-03	9	OP	1 1/16M	D	Red n'Gold	Thompson,Terry	50,000	30,000
PirtsBntyH	6-Sep-03	4	DMR	6F	D	Yankee Gentleman	Krone,Julie	98,850	45,810
PistolPkrH	9-Aug-03	8	PHA	1 1/16M	D	Mum's Gold	Santagata,Nick	53,600	32,160
PlateTrial	31-May-03	8	WO	1 1/8M	D	Mobil	Kabel,Todd	162,600	97,560
PlayKngHG3	16-Aug-03	8	WO	7F	T	Soaring Free	Kabel,Todd	165,000	99,000
Pleasanton	2-Jul-03	4	PLN	1 1/16M	D	Obermeister	Gonzalez,Roberto	53,500	29,700
PleasntTmp	13-Sep-03	8	KD	1M	T	Powderjay	Troilo,William	40,000	24,000
PlnSenrita	3-Jul-03	9	PLN	1M 70Y	D	Bartok's Blithe	Alvarado,Frank	55,300	30,900
PlsVrdsHG2	26-Jan-03	7	SA	6F	D	Avanzado (ARG)	Baze,Tyler	150,000	90,000
Plymouth	27-Jun-03	7	GLD	7F	D	Cantouchis	Rini,Wade	45,000	27,000
PmBCDsfHG3	16-May-03	8	PIM	1 1/16M	D	Mandy's Gold	Bailey,Jerry	150,000	90,000
PMMileH	27-Apr-03	9	PM	1M	D	Poker Brad	Webb,Robert	35,000	19,250
POBrienHG2	17-Aug-03	8	DMR	7F	D	Disturbingthepeace	Espinoza,Victor	150,000	90,000
Pocahontas	1-Nov-03	9	CD	1M	D	Stellar Jayne	Velasquez,Cornelio	112,300	69,626
PointGiven	28-Sep-03	9	MTH	1 1/16M	D	Rockin On Ready	Clemente,Alfredo	50,000	30,000
PokerHG3	5-Jul-03	8	BEL	1M	T	War Zone	Castellano,Javier	116,200	69,720
Politely	29-Jun-03	9	MTH	1M	T	Southern Fiction	Bravo,Joe	50,000	30,000
Politely	13-Dec-03	8	LRL	7F	D	Worldly Pleasure	Caraballo,Jose	60,000	36,000
PollysJet	5-Jul-03	7	DEL	6F	D	Border Bound	Valdes,Ricardo	59,000	35,400
PomonaDrby	27-Sep-03	11	FPX	1 1/8M	D	Excess Summer	Krone,Julie	100,000	55,000
PoncheH	7-Jun-03	12	CRC	6F	D	Built Up	Aguilar,Manuel	75,000	41,000
PonyExprs	18-May-03	7	ALB	5 1/2F	D	Urlacher	Madeira,Carlos	35,000	19,250
PossblMate	15-May-03	8	BEL	1 1/4M	T	Primetimevalentine	Santos,Jose	60,000	36,000
PostDeb	21-Jun-03	10	MTH	1M 70Y	D	Lake Kinneret	Lopez,Charles	60,000	36,000
PotomacH	12-Apr-03	4	CT	7F	D	Bon Amigo	Garcia,Carlos	36,750	22,050
PoulainD'r	27-Sep-03	10	CRC	6 1/2F	D	Love That Moon	Cruz,Manoel	42,325	27,395
PowerlessH	8-Nov-03	8	HAW	6F	D	Summer Mis	Sterling, Jr.,Larry	118,300	55,980
PraireBayu	13-Dec-03	10	TP	1 1/8M	D	Ask the Lord	Bejarano,Rafael	50,000	31,300
PrairieMle	31-May-03	8	PRM	1M	D	Bodgiteer	Johnson,Joe	50,000	30,000
PrairieRse	26-Apr-03	8	PRM	6F	D	Don't Countess Out	Thompson,Terry	76,500	45,000
PrairiMedH	2-Aug-03	6	PRM	1 1/8M	D	Patton's Victory	Birzer,Alex	50,000	30,000
PrarieExpr	3-May-03	9	PRM	5 1/2F	D	Pie's Lil Brother	Birzer,Alex	43,475	28,085
PrcsFeathr	27-Jul-03	5	CRC	7 1/2F	T	Hermans Honor	Toribio, Jr.,Aurelio	500,000	294,000
PrcsRnyHG2	12-Jul-03	11	CRC	6F	D	Gold Mover	Bailey,Jerry	37,375	22,425
PrcssElain	4-Jul-03	7	CBY	1 1/16M	D	She's Scrumpy	Martinez,Seth	1,000,000	650,000
PreaknesG1	17-May-03	12	PIM	1 3/16M	D	Funny Cide	Santos,Jose	50,000	30,000
Precisnist	25-May-03	8	PRM	1 1/16M	D	Patton's Victory	Birzer,Alex	50,000	30,000
Prelude	30-Aug-03	11	LAD	1 1/16M	D	Kool Humor	Clark,Kerwin	35,000	21,000
Premier	6-Jul-03	9	ARP	7F	D	This Cat's for You	Montoya,Daryl	50,000	30,000
Premiere	3-Apr-03	1	LS	1M	D	Agrivating General	Day,Pat	132,000	79,200
PremierHG3	12-Oct-03	8	HST	1 3/8M	D	Roscoe Pito	Alvarado,Pedro	11,000	6,600
PresCupH	15-Jun-03	8	LNN	6F	D	Buzz Bar	Martinez,Armando	50,000	25,200
PresidntsH	11-May-03	9	STP	6F	D	Taiaslew	Simard,Real		

Stakes	Date	Race	Trk	Dist/Surf	Winner	Jockey	Gross	Value to winner
Preview	22-Mar-03	8	PM	1 1/16M D	Cee Cruiser	Beckner,Twyla	10,000	5,500
PrGldJuv	27-Jun-03	8	PRM	5F D	Dashboard Drummer	Quinonez,Luis	55,000	30,000
PrGldLasse	6-Jul-03	6	PRM	5F D	Berry Berry	Corbett,Glenn	56,750	30,000
Primal	13-Jul-03	8	CRC	1 1/16M D	High Ideal	Castanon,Jesus	41,975	22,185
Primonetta	5-Apr-03	8	PIM	6F D	Balmy	Dominguez,Ramon	75,000	30,000
Princess	11-May-03	8	LNN	6F D	Megans Molly	Ludlow,Megan	11,000	6,000
PrincessH	28-Nov-03	10	SUN	6F D	Homemaker	Gonzalez, Jr.,Sal	55,400	33,240
Princeton	18-Oct-03	8	MED	1 1/16M D	Angelic Aura	Chavez,Jorge	40,000	24,000
PrincsMarg	1-Aug-03	7	NP	6F D	Classa Red Wine	Welch,Quincy	40,000	25,200
PrioressG1	4-Jul-03	9	BEL	6F D	House Party	Santos,Jose	200,000	120,000
PrivatTrms	29-Mar-03	8	LRL	1 1/16M D	Sky Soldier	Madrigal, Jr.,Rodrigo	60,000	36,000
PrknessDay	17-May-03	7	EUR	6F D	Sunset Cruise	Williams,Dustin	5,550	2,880
PrLilySale	30-Aug-03	2	MD	7F D	Royal Rush	Chickeness,Sheldon	27,000	13,500
PrmDebutnt	6-Sep-03	5	PRM	6F D	Aspen Gal	Compton,Perry	40,000	24,000
PrmDerby	13-Sep-03	6	PRM	1 1/16M D	Wiggins	Razo, Jr.,Eusebio	78,000	45,000
PrmFreshmn	6-Sep-03	6	PRM	6F D	Okie Style	Shino,Ken	43,200	24,000
PrmOaks	12-Sep-03	6	PRM	1 1/16M D	Shot Gun Favorite	Thompson,Terry	75,000	45,000
PrmptAngel	16-Nov-03	4	HAW	5F T	Miners Gamble	Emigh,Christopher	43,200	25,920
PrmSprint	9-Aug-03	6	PRM	6F D	Bet On Joe	Corbett,Glenn	50,000	30,000
PrncOWales	20-Jul-03	8	FE	1 3/16M D	Wando	Husbands,Patrick	500,000	300,000
PrncsOPlmH	18-Jan-03	8	TUP	6F D	Knoll Lake	Bridges,Kelly	35,000	21,000
PrncssEliz	12-Oct-03	8	WO	1 1/16M D	My Vintage Port	Jones,Jono	250,000	150,000
PrncssMora	12-Aug-03	3	CRC	5F D	Sea Span	Cruz,Manoel	42,275	27,365
ProOrConH	4-Jan-03	3	SA	1M T	Shalini	Nakatani,Corey	108,400	65,040
ProudPupyH	5-Jul-03	7	FL	6F D	Runaway Tiger	Davila, Jr.,John	35,000	21,000
Providncia	13-Apr-03	3	SA	1 1/8M T	Star Vega (GB)	Smith,Mike	150,000	90,000
PrplViolet	21-Jun-03	4	AP	1M D	Keeping the Gold	Razo, Jr.,Eusebio	86,450	51,870
PrsnlEnHG1	22-Aug-03	9	SAR	1 1/4M D	Passing Shot	Santos,Jose	400,000	240,000
PrspctrGmH	27-Jul-03	7	ARP	1M D	Maysville Slew	Quinonez,Luis	65,200	39,120
PrvateTrms	18-Jan-03	8	SUF	6F D	Pelican Beach	Panell,Dyn	35,000	21,000
PsblyPrfct	4-Jul-03	6	AP	1 1/16M T	Delmonico Cat	Douglas,Rene	45,000	27,834
PtchGround	18-Nov-03	8	TUP	1M T	Grimm	Stevens,Scott	21,800	13,080
PtrGrBCHG2	29-Mar-03	8	SA	6 1/2F D	Bluesthestandard	Smith,Mike	220,000	72,000
PuckerUpG3	13-Sep-03	8	AP	1 1/8M D	Aud	Peck,Brian	175,000	105,000
PunchLine	14-Jun-03	4	CNL	5F T	Bop	Santana,Jozbin	50,000	30,000
PussNBoots	1-Sep-03	8	FE	1 1/16M T	Le Cinquieme Essai	Poznansky,Neil	90,000	54,000
PWrthIlDeb	13-Dec-03	8	HAW	1 1/16M D	Journey Fever	Diego,Iram	111,175	66,705
QeensCoHG3	13-Dec-03	8	AQU	1 3/16M D	Thunder Blitz	Chavez,Jorge	108,300	64,980
QEIICupG1	11-Oct-03	8	KEE	1 1/8M T	Film Maker	Prado,Edgar	500,000	310,000
QnCityOaks	26-Jul-03	9	RD	1 1/8M D	Golden Tour	Meyers,Tommy	100,000	60,000
Queen	22-Mar-03	6	TP	6F D	Belle Artiste	Day,Pat	50,000	31,300
QueenOGrnH	22-Nov-03	8	TUP	1M T	Abbey Bridge	Gomez,Esteban	50,000	30,000
QueensH	12-Jul-03	4	HPO	1M D	Passionate Bird	Granda,Alejandro	33,000	17,700
QueensH	8-Jun-03	7	UN	1 1/16M D	Tender Offer (IRE)	Butterfly,Roger	3,000	1,650
QueensPlt	22-Jun-03	9	WO	1 1/4M D	Wando	Husbands,Patrick	1,000,000	600,000
Queenston	3-May-03	9	WO	7F D	Mobil	Kabel,Todd	160,500	96,300
QuickCard	10-May-03	8	DEL	1M D	Private Lap	Black,Anthony	59,300	35,580
QuicknTree	15-Jun-03	8	HOL	1 1/2M T	Continental Red	Valenzuela,Patrick	102,250	61,350
QuickStepH	10-May-03	8	TDN	6F D	Waist Gunner John	Rowland,Michael	35,000	21,000
RaceArtist	13-Jun-03	8	CRC	5 1/2F D	Crafty Brat	Cruz,Manoel	42,225	27,335
RacnoIngrl	31-Oct-03	9	DED	5F D	Believe Im Special	Faul,Ricky	40,000	24,000
RailbirdG3	4-May-03	8	HOL	7F D	Buffythecenterfold	Espinoza,Victor	107,200	64,320
Rainbow	29-Mar-03	9	OP	6F D	Strodes Commander	Thompson,Terry	58,000	34,800
RainbowCon	19-Jul-03	8	FE	5F T	Mysterious Affair	Dos Ramos,Richard	140,000	84,000
RainbowMis	30-Mar-03	9	OP	6F D	Impetuous Molly	Theriot,Jamie	59,000	35,400
RAllisonFu	27-Dec-03	7	SUN	6 1/2F D	Tin Can Sailor	Madeira,Carlos	173,215	87,926
RalphHayes	30-Aug-03	6	PRM	1 1/16M D	Take Me Up	Quinonez,Luis	82,800	49,680
RampartHG2	1-Mar-03	10	GP	1 1/8M D	Allamerican Bertie	Velazquez,John	200,000	120,000
RareTreatH	19-Feb-03	8	AQU	1 1/8M D	Ellie's Moment	Bridgmohan,Shaun	79,325	47,673
Rattlsnake	12-Jan-03	8	TUP	1M D	Siberland	Corbett,Glenn	35,000	21,000
RavenRunG3	10-Oct-03	9	KEE	7F D	Yell	Day,Pat	174,450	108,159

Stakes	Date	Race	Trk	Dist/Surf		Winner	Jockey	Gross	Value to winner
Ravolia	25-May-03	3	CRC	1M	D	Dakota Light	Castanon,Jesus	42,075	27,245
RazrbckFut	1-Nov-03	10	LAD	6F	D	Gun Town	Trader,Rodney	35,000	21,000
RazrbckHG3	16-Mar-03	9	OP	1 1/16M	D	Colorful Tour	Quinonez,Luis	100,000	60,000
RbtFCareyH	8-Nov-03	9	HAW	1 1/16M	D	Wiggins	Razo, Jr.,Eusebio	119,350	71,610
RCAnderson	5-Jul-03	7	ASD	1M	D	Pete's Surprise	Hendricks,Ken	35,000	21,000
RchBrdoHG3	23-Aug-03	8	DMR	6 1/2F	D	Secret Liaison	Nakatani,Corey	150,000	90,000
RchmdDbyTH	1-Sep-03	10	HST	1 1/16M	D	Mister Mane Man	Lacoursiere,Larry	44,160	17,664
RchmdDbyTH	1-Sep-03	10	HST	1 1/16M	D	Steady Smiler	Valdez,Felipe	44,160	17,664
RchrdKingH	15-Nov-03	3	HOU	1 1/8M	T	Classoffiftyseven	Stanton,Terry	50,000	30,000
RckingChrH	4-Jul-03	9	GRP	6 1/2F	D	Tissington	Beckner,Twyla	2,900	1,632
RckyMtnFut	16-Aug-03	1	WYO	5F	D	Cbknightspretense	Foster,Cody	5,600	3,360
RcSclBCHG2	8-Mar-03	10	GP	7F	D	Tour of the Cat	Cabassa, Jr.,Abad	200,000	120,000
RDBrtloMem	19-Jul-03	16	TDN	1 1/8M	D	Ashwood C C	Gonzalez,Luis	35,000	22,750
RealDelite	31-May-03	7	AP	6F	D	In Secure	Baird,E.	75,000	45,000
RealGdDeal	11-Aug-03	7	DMR	7F	D	Excess Summer	Krone,Julie	100,000	60,000
Rebel	3-Aug-03	9	LAD	5 1/2F	D	Cabildo Bag	Romero,Josh	50,000	30,000
Rebel	22-Mar-03	10	OP	1 1/16M	D	Crowned King	Rennie,Chandra	125,000	75,000
RebsPlicyH	21-Feb-03	7	SA	6 1/2F	T	Grandiser (AUS)	Stevens,Gary	103,600	48,660
RedBankH	24-May-03	10	MTH	1M	D	Just Le Facts	Bravo,Joe	100,000	60,000
RedCmeliaH	30-Mar-03	9	FG	1M	T	Fuse It	Melancon,Gerard	100,000	60,000
RedCross	27-Sep-03	8	MTH	6F	D	Mooji Moo	Toribio,Abdiel	53,000	30,000
RedDiaExpH	20-Sep-03	9	NP	6 1/2F	D	Sixthirtyjoe	Simard,Real	50,000	31,500
RedSmthHG2	22-Nov-03	8	AQU	1 3/8M	T	Balto Star	Velazquez,John	150,000	90,000
RegeyIslnd	19-Jul-03	10	ELP	1 1/16M	T	G P Fleet	Lumpkins,Jason	75,000	30,000
Regret	23-May-03	8	GLD	6F	D	Mercedees Red	Skinner,Colin	45,000	27,000
Regret	3-Aug-03	5	MTH	6F	D	Mooji Moo	Toribio,Abdiel	75,000	45,000
RegretG3	14-Jun-03	8	CD	1 1/8M	T	Sand Springs	Guidry,Mark	231,000	143,220
ReloyH	31-Jan-03	7	SA	1 1/4M	T	Noches De Rosa (CHI)	Krone,Julie	103,600	48,660
RemGreen	16-Nov-03	7	RP	1 1/16M	T	Rockchalk Jayhawk	Cogburn,Kevin	36,700	21,000
RemsenG2	29-Nov-03	8	AQU	1 1/8M	D	Read the Footnotes	Bailey,Jerry	200,000	120,000
RetTurfBCH	9-Aug-03	9	RET	1 1/16M	T	Chauffe Au Rouge	Chapa,Roman	50,000	15,000
Revidere	31-May-03	9	MTH	1M	D	City Fire	Rose,Jeremy	50,000	30,000
RFunkhousr	20-Sep-03	6	CT	7F	D	Fancy Buckles	Valdes,Ricardo	36,400	23,660
RGDickBCH	19-Jul-03	7	DEL	1 3/8M	T	Alternate	Castillo,Oliver	150,000	90,000
RGLevtMemH	9-Aug-03	8	CT	7F	D	Donald's Pride	Mawing,Anthony	36,750	23,888
RGrnSenrFt	13-Jul-03	10	RUI	5 1/2F	D	Rocky Gulch	Clark,Michael	87,386	43,694
RGrnSnrtFt	13-Jul-03	6	RUI	5 1/2F	D	Vipervapor	Bourdieu,Jorge	89,300	44,651
RHedmanMIH	6-Dec-03	10	SUN	1M	D	Rocky Gulch	Bourdieu,Jorge	130,900	78,540
Rhoddndron	14-Jun-03	8	CT	7F	D	Home Run Hitter	Klinger,C.	37,100	22,260
Ribns&LceH	27-Apr-03	9	SUD	6F	D	Chic Crossing	Bilodeau,Ronald	3,650	2,007
Richmond	9-Nov-03	8	HOO	1 1/16M	D	Ellens Lucky Star	Mojica,Orlando	38,300	22,980
RichmondH	16-Feb-03	8	GG	6F	D	Lacie Girl	Baze,Russell	78,550	33,550
RicksMem	6-Sep-03	4	RP	1M	T	Strawbailey	Williams,Robert	36,600	21,000
RillitoMil	2-Mar-03	9	RIL	1 1/16M	D	Dixie Embers	Gard,Terry	3,257	1,824
RiseJim	1-Feb-03	8	SUF	6F	D	Papa Ho Ho	Hampshire, Jr.,Josiah	35,000	21,000
RisenStrG3	16-Feb-03	8	FG	1 1/16M	D	Badge of Silver	Albarado,Robby	150,000	90,000
RiverCitis	6-Sep-03	6	LAD	1 1/16M	T	Academic Angel	Meche,Lonnie	75,000	45,000
RiverMem	2-Nov-03	7	WO	1M 70Y	D	Byzantine	Jones,Jono	114,000	68,400
RivrCtyHG3	16-Nov-03	9	CD	1 1/8M	T	Hard Buck (BRZ)	Blanc,Brice	172,800	107,136
RJSpeers	6-Sep-03	7	ASD	1 1/16M	D	Northern Affair	Iammarino,Michael	35,000	21,000
RKKerlanMH	12-Jul-03	8	HOL	5 1/2F	D	Full Moon Madness	Valdivia, Jr.,Jose	100,800	60,480
RlHroineG3	5-Jul-03	7	HOL	1M	T	Magic Mission (GB)	Nakatani,Corey	112,200	67,320
RoadRunnrH	13-Jul-03	8	RUI	5 1/2F	D	Hasty Gus	Villa,Mark	46,700	28,020
RoamnRachl	12-Jul-03	6	CRC	6 1/2F	D	Outstanding Lady	Chavez,Jorge	52,475	37,485
RocketMan	12-Jul-03	1	CRC	2F	D	Baby Shark	Dunkelberger,Travis	50,000	30,000
Rollicking	8-Nov-03	8	LRL	7F	D	White Mountain Boy	Castellano, Jr.,Abel	60,000	36,000
RollnOnOvr	12-Apr-03	11	BEU	6F	D	Woodburner	Perez,Roberto	35,000	21,000
RomnColonl	5-Jul-03	6	FP	6F	D	Fifteen Rounds	La Sala,Jerry	25,500	15,300
RoundTable	26-Jul-03	5	AP	1 1/8M	D	Wiggins	Razo, Jr.,Eusebio	100,000	60,000
RoyalGlint	31-May-03	11	CRC	1M	D	Patriotic Flame	Homeister, Jr.,Rosemary	50,450	38,270
RoyalNorth	6-Apr-03	11	BEU	6F	D	Heavenly Jet	Gonzalez,Ivan	40,000	24,000

Stakes	Date	Race	Trk	Dist/Surf		Winner	Jockey	Gross	Value to winner
RPMECMile	30-Nov-03	8	RP	1M	D	Depop	Berry,Monte	85,700	51,250
RPOaks	15-Nov-03	4	RP	1M	T	Captain's Daughter	Matz,Nena	41,200	23,700
RRHiltonMm	13-Sep-03	6	CT	7F	D	Cape Power	Mawing,Anthony	36,250	23,563
RRMCarpH	19-Jul-03	9	DEL	1 1/16M	D	Private Lap	Black,Anthony	100,000	60,000
RSanMiguel	26-Apr-03	2	HOL	7F	D	El Nuki	Valenzuela,Patrick	70,000	42,000
Rstoration	15-Jun-03	9	MTH	1M	D	Sky Soldier	Salvaggio,Mark	50,000	30,000
RudyBaez	22-Mar-03	7	SUF	1M	D	Seattle Surprise	Bush,Vernon	35,000	21,000
Ruffian	13-Jul-03	9	ARP	7F	D	Sexy Boots	Tohill,Ken	35,000	21,000
Ruffian	12-Jul-03	8	FP	6F	D	Betty Spaghetti	Flores,Vicente	25,700	15,420
RuffianHG1	13-Sep-03	8	BEL	1 1/16M	D	Wild Spirit (CHI)	Bailey,Jerry	300,000	180,000
RuffKirchH	23-Nov-03	6	BEU	1 1/4M	D	Nate's Rib	Chavez,Casey	40,000	24,000
RuiMileH	10-Aug-03	9	RUI	1M	D	Funny Meeting	Jaime,Ricardo	31,200	18,720
RuiOaks	26-Jul-03	8	RUI	6F	D	Jewels for a Lady	Clark,Michael	26,100	15,660
RuiTbChmpH	1-Sep-03	9	RUI	1 1/16M	D	Caliban	Bourdieu,Jorge	41,800	25,080
RuiTbDerby	31-Aug-03	9	RUI	1 1/16M	D	Novel T Dreamer	Coates,Jimmy	26,600	15,960
RuiTbrdFut	1-Sep-03	7	RUI	6F	D	Hi Teck Man	Jaime,Ricardo	68,731	34,366
RunzaH	19-Apr-03	9	FON	6F	D	Burning Memories	Compton,Perry	17,500	9,600
Rushaway	22-Mar-03	9	TP	1 1/16M	D	Private Gold	Day,Pat	100,000	62,000
Ruthless	5-Jan-03	8	AQU	6F	D	Lizzy Cool	Lopez,Charles	80,425	48,255
RvaRdgBCG2	7-Jun-03	8	BEL	7F	D	Posse	Lanerie,Corey	200,000	120,000
RVnHoozrMm	13-Sep-03	4	CT	7F	D	Shesanothergrump	Mawing,Anthony	35,700	23,205
RylNrthHG3	2-Aug-03	8	WO	6F	T	Chopinina	Kabel,Todd	219,050	131,430
SabinHG3	8-Feb-03	10	GP	1 1/16M	D	Allamerican Bertie	Bailey,Jerry	100,000	60,000
SacramntoH	9-Mar-03	4	GG	1M	D	Bare Necessities	Alvarado,Frank	78,450	33,450
SADerbyG1	5-Apr-03	6	SA	1 1/8M	D	Buddy Gil	Stevens,Gary	750,000	450,000
SafelyKept	16-Aug-03	3	AP	6F	D	Savorthetime	Bourque,Curt	51,550	31,236
SafelyKept	9-Mar-03	4	AQU	6F	D	Saskya	Luzzi,Michael	60,000	36,000
SafelyKptH	4-Jul-03	6	FP	6F	D	Jade's Ace	Woodley,John	25,700	15,420
Saguaro	27-Sep-03	8	TUP	6F	D	Taraval	Stevens,Scott	35,000	21,000
SAHG1	1-Mar-03	9	SA	1 1/4M	D	Milwaukee Brew	Prado,Edgar	1,000,000	600,000
SailOnBy	5-Nov-03	3	TUP	6F	D	Cincinnati Jay	Ziegler,Michael	21,700	13,020
Sale	16-Aug-03	6	NP	6 1/2F	D	Polaris	Heiler,Stephan	50,000	30,000
SalemCo	17-Oct-03	9	MED	1M 70Y	T	Dr. Kathy	Bridgmohan,Shaun	40,000	24,000
SalvtrMHG3	26-Jul-03	9	MTH	1M	D	Vinemeister	Velez, Jr.,Jose	100,000	60,000
SamFDavis	22-Feb-03	10	TAM	1 1/16M	D	White Buck	Velez,Roger	50,000	28,500
SamuelH	20-Dec-03	5	BEU	6F	D	Wedonit	Nolan,Paul	21,000	15,000
SanCarlosH	1-Mar-03	8	GG	1M	D	Halo Cat	Baze,Russell	78,900	33,900
SandiaH	13-Sep-03	8	ALB	5 1/2F	D	Sky Diver	Bourdieu,Jorge	33,000	19,800
Sandpiper	11-Jan-03	10	TAM	6F	D	Ebony Breeze	Rodriguez,Pedro	50,000	21,000
SandsPoint	15-Jun-03	8	BEL	1 1/8M	D	Savedbythelight	Migliore,Richard	114,600	68,760
SanFelipe	20-Dec-03	8	HOU	6F	D	Savorthetime	Bourque,Curt	35,000	21,000
SanfordG2	24-Jul-03	8	SAR	6F	D	Chapel Royal	Velazquez,John	150,000	90,000
SangueH	16-Aug-03	9	LAD	1 1/16M	T	Golden Rhythm	LeBlanc,Kirk	50,000	30,000
SanJacinto	15-Nov-03	6	HOU	1 1/16M	T	Burnin' Memories	Chapa,Roman	50,000	30,000
SanJose	13-Apr-03	8	BM	1 1/16M	D	Mavoreen	Warren, Jr.,Ronald	78,450	33,450
SanLsRyHG2	15-Mar-03	7	SA	1 1/2M	T	Champion Lodge (IRE)	Solis,Alex	250,000	150,000
SanMarinoH	20-Feb-03	5	SA	1 1/4M	T	Requete (GB)	Valdivia, Jr.,Jose	104,400	49,140
SanMateo	28-Sep-03	3	BM	6F	D	Hajji's Honor	Lumpkins,Jason	78,450	33,450
SanPedro	22-Mar-03	6	SA	6 1/2F	D	King Robyn	Solis,Alex	103,200	48,420
SantaPaula	23-Mar-03	3	SA	6 1/2F	D	Buffythecenterfold	Espinoza,Victor	101,925	47,655
SantaTersH	9-Mar-03	11	SUN	6 1/2F	D	Cielo Girl	Gonzalez, Jr.,Sal	53,500	32,100
SantoLalmH	22-Jun-03	10	MTH	1M	D	Willie's Luv	Bravo,Joe	50,000	30,000
SAOaksG1	8-Mar-03	4	SA	1 1/16M	D	Composure	Bailey,Jerry	300,000	180,000
SaplingG3	9-Aug-03	10	MTH	6F	D	Dashboard Drummer	Ferrer,Jose	100,000	60,000
SaranacHG3	1-Sep-03	10	SAR	1 3/16M	T	Shoal Water	Velazquez,John	108,800	65,280
SaratogaH	18-May-03	2	BM	6F	D	El Dorado Shooter	Baze,Russell	78,350	43,250
SarBCHG2	16-Aug-03	7	SAR	1 1/4M	D	Puzzlement	Chavez,Jorge	300,000	180,000
SarLn0tsH	29-Mar-03	9	FG	1M	T	Letithappencaptain	LeBlanc,Kirk	100,000	60,000
SarSpclG2	13-Aug-03	8	SAR	6 1/2F	D	Cuvee	Bailey,Jerry	150,000	90,000
SaskatoonH	28-Jun-03	6	MD	6F	D	Bedford Road	Latchman,Rennie	5,000	3,000
Saylorvlle	28-Jun-03	8	PRM	6F	D	See How She Runs	Pettinger,Donald	102,000	60,000

Stakes	Date	Race	Trk	Dist/Surf		Winner	Jockey	Gross	Value to winner
SBAnthonyH	21-Jun-03	8	FL	6F	D	Miss Royal Ibis	Yang,Chin	35,000	21,000
Scar&GrayH	9-Nov-03	7	BEU	6F	D	Just Michel	Feliciano,Ricardo	40,000	24,000
ScarltCarn	26-May-03	12	TDN	6F	D	Alison's Winner	Sanchez, Jr.,Jose	41,000	27,000
SchaeferMl	15-Nov-03	8	HOO	1M	D	Crafty Shaw	Perret,Craig	103,350	62,010
SchenctdyH	21-Sep-03	8	BEL	6F	D	Travelator	Gryder,Aaron	108,000	64,800
SchprMmBCH	2-Aug-03	9	LRL	1 1/8M	T	French Charmer	DeCarlo,Christopher	150,000	90,000
SchylrvlG2	23-Jul-03	9	SAR	6F	D	Ashado	Prado,Edgar	150,000	90,000
ScklsImage	22-Sep-03	7	GLD	6F	D	Stellar One	Doser,Mary	45,000	27,000
ScndEpsStl	20-Sep-03	5	SUF	6F	D	Stylish Sultan	Thompson,Winston	35,000	21,000
ScttsdaleH	22-Mar-03	8	TUP	1M	T	Friendofthefamily	Stevens,Scott	36,050	21,000
SDiamondFu	14-Sep-03	7	HST	6 1/2F	D	She's a Bombshell	Valdez,Felipe	106,538	63,923
SeabsctHG3	26-May-03	8	BM	1 1/16M	D	Reba's Gold	Rollins,Chance	100,000	55,000
SeabscuitH	25-Oct-03	11	SA	1 1/16M	D	Pie N Burger	Valenzuela,Patrick	150,000	90,000
Seacliff	30-Aug-03	7	CRC	1M	D	Tap Dancer	Nunez,Eduardo	53,525	38,115
SeagramCup	3-Aug-03	8	WO	1 1/16M	D	Wake At Noon	Ramsammy,Emile	136,500	81,900
SeaOErnBCH	15-Jun-03	8	AP	1M	T	Rock Slide	Albarado,Robby	163,650	98,190
SeattleH	27-Apr-03	7	EMD	6F	D	Road Afleet	Baze,Gary	35,000	19,250
Seaway	31-Aug-03	8	WO	7F	D	Brass in Pocket	Clark,David	190,375	114,225
SebsctPrmH	19-Jul-03	7	BOI	5F	D	Guns a Blazen	Williams,Matt	5,600	3,360
SecretarG1	16-Aug-03	11	AP	1 1/4M	T	Kicken Kris	Castellano,Javier	400,000	240,000
Select	30-Aug-03	9	MTH	5F	T	Only the Best	Cruz,Carlos	50,000	30,000
SeleneG1	19-May-03	8	WO	1 1/16M	D	Too Late Now	Landry,Robert	277,750	166,650
Selima	15-Nov-03	5	LRL	1 1/16M	D	Richetta	Wilson,Rick	100,000	60,000
Selma	4-Oct-03	5	RET	5F	T	Jewels for a Lady	Clark,Michael	35,000	21,000
SenApointH	20-Jul-03	8	HST	1 1/16M	D	Jamaari Girl	Wright,Nicola	44,368	26,621
SenoritaG3	17-May-03	8	HOL	1M	T	Makeup Artist	Espinoza,Victor	113,500	68,100
SensatStrH	5-Jan-03	6	SA	6 1/2F	T	Spinelessjellyfish	Krone,Julie	108,300	64,980
SeraStrltH	13-Jul-03	12	RUI	5 1/2F	D	Ghost Chatter	Coates,Jimmy	47,100	28,260
SetlSlwBCH	10-Aug-03	9	EMD	1 1/16M	D	Stratoplan	Wright,Nicola	65,000	22,000
SflyKtBCG3	4-Oct-03	8	PIM	6F	D	Randaroo	Castillo, Jr.,Heberto	150,000	90,000
SFosterHG1	14-Jun-03	10	CD	1 1/8M	D	Perfect Drift	Day,Pat	856,500	531,030
ShadyWell	6-Jul-03	8	WO	5 1/2F	D	Megan's Appeal	Husbands,Simon	164,550	98,730
ShakrtwnG3	12-Apr-03	7	KEE	5 1/2F	T	No Jacket Required	Blanc,Brice	113,700	70,494
Sham	7-Feb-03	7	SA	1 1/8M	D	Man Among Men	Solis,Alex	103,500	48,600
ShckyGreen	15-Jun-03	6	AP	6F	D	Coach Jimi Lee	St. Julien,Marlon	46,800	28,080
ShdwlTfMG1	4-Oct-03	9	KEE	1M	T	Perfect Soul (IRE)	Prado,Edgar	600,000	372,000
ShelbyCnty	2-May-03	8	IND	6F	D	Drop of Rain	Martinez, Jr.,Luis	37,900	22,740
Shenandoah	17-May-03	7	CT	7F	D	Attainable	Pino,Mario	37,250	22,350
Shepperton	23-Aug-03	8	WO	6 1/2F	D	Forever Grand	Husbands,Patrick	132,375	79,425
Shiskabob	11-Oct-03	11	LAD	1 1/16M	T	White Star	LeBlanc,Kirk	82,500	49,500
ShkyGreen	8-Nov-03	7	DEL	1 1/16M	D	Private Lap	Black,Anthony	58,200	34,920
ShkyGreenH	28-Jun-03	8	FP	6F	D	Bulldog George	Gale,Michael	25,600	15,360
ShockerTH	11-Oct-03	7	CRC	1 1/16M	D	Splasha	Aguilar,Manuel	100,000	60,000
ShoeBCMG1	26-May-03	8	HOL	1M	T	Redattore (BRZ)	Solis,Alex	475,000	225,000
ShowtimDeb	8-Nov-03	6	HAW	6F	D	No Beans	McKnight,James	122,275	73,365
ShpshdBHG2	31-May-03	8	BEL	1 3/8M	T	Mariensky	Velazquez,John	150,000	90,000
ShrlJnsHG3	14-Feb-03	9	GP	7F	D	Harmony Lodge	Velazquez,John	100,000	60,000
ShrtgrsHer	16-Aug-03	7	MD	1 1/16M	D	Stop the Act	Moccasin,Tim	10,000	6,000
Shuvee	11-Oct-03	8	FP	6F	D	Lady Riss	Woodley,John	25,800	15,480
ShuveeHG2	17-May-03	8	BEL	1M	D	Wild Spirit (CHI)	Castellano,Javier	200,000	120,000
SilveradoH	6-Apr-03	8	ALB	6F	D	Star Smasher	Fuentes,Miguel	52,300	31,380
SilverMadn	27-Jul-03	6	AP	5 1/2F	D	Sweet Jo Jo	Douglas,Rene	53,200	31,920
SilvrSprBC	12-Jul-03	8	LS	6F	D	Bluegrass Sara	Lanerie,Corey	75,000	45,000
Simcoe	1-Sep-03	5	WO	7F	D	Twisted Wit	Clark,David	139,750	83,850
SirBarton	17-May-03	9	PIM	1 1/16M	D	Best Minister	Prado,Edgar	125,000	60,000
SirBarton	22-Nov-03	8	WO	1 1/16M	D	Time of War	McAleney,James	128,500	77,100
SirBeufort	26-Dec-03	3	SA	1M	D	Buckland Manor	Nakatani,Corey	100,500	46,800
SixtySlHG3	26-Apr-03	8	HAW	1 1/8M	D	Bare Necessities	Douglas,Rene	250,000	150,000
SJuanCComH	22-Nov-03	9	SRP	1 1/8M	D	Moro Grande	Tohill,Ken	51,900	31,140
SJWhitingH	28-Jun-03	11	PLN	6F	D	Texas Chili	Rollins,Chance	50,900	27,600
Skipat	31-May-03	9	PIM	6F	D	Bronze Abe	Rodriguez,Erick	75,000	45,000

Stakes	Date	Race	Trk	Dist/Surf		Winner	Jockey	Gross	Value to winner
SkipAway	4–Jul–03	8	MTH	1M	D	Jersey Giant	Pimentel,Julian	60,000	36,000
SkipAwyHG3	20–Apr–03	9	GP	1 1/16M	D	Best of the Rest	Coa,Eibar	100,000	60,000
SkipTrial	13–Sep–03	3	MTH	1 1/16M	D	Jersey Giant	Pimentel,Julian	59,000	39,000
SKMaddyHG3	11–Oct–03	8	SA	6 1/2F	T	Belleski	Espinoza,Victor	112,000	67,200
Skunktail	13–Jul–03	3	HP0	1M	D	Grayglen	Wall,Newil	31,000	17,100
SkyClscHG2	28–Sep–03	8	WO	1 3/8M	D	Bowman Mill	Blanc,Brice	271,750	163,050
SladyCatIH	20–Sep–03	10	MTH	1M 70Y	D	Vow	Garcia,Matt	45,000	27,000
SleepyHllo	18–Oct–03	5	BEL	1M	D	Friends Lake	Migliore,Richard	100,000	60,000
SlghtNRear	23–Sep–03	8	FP	6F	D	She's Fantastic	Kurek,Gary	35,700	21,420
SliptnFelH	7–Jun–03	9	MNR	1M 70Y	D	Docent	Madrigal, Jr.,Rodrigo	76,700	46,020
SlkStcking	24–Jun–03	7	YAV	5 1/2F	D	Beautiful Prize	Beverly,Ronald	9,700	5,335
SLsObspHG2	15–Feb–03	7	SA	1 1/2M	T	The Tin Man	Smith,Mike	200,000	120,000
SlvrbltdG2	15–Feb–03	9	FG	1 1/16M	D	Belle of Perintown	Borel,Calvin	150,000	90,000
SmartDeb	13–Sep–03	6	AP	6F	D	Finally Here	Razo, Jr.,Eusebio	47,850	28,710
SmartHalo	13–Apr–03	8	PIM	6F	D	Home Run Hitter	Caraballo,Jose	75,000	30,000
SmkGlacken	14–Sep–03	9	MTH	6F	D	Lissau	Ferrer,Jose	50,000	30,000
SmlSprtHG3	12–Jul–03	12	CRC	6F	D	Shake You Down	Luzzi,Michael	500,000	294,000
SmplyMjstc	24–May–03	9	CRC	1 1/16M	D	The Name's Bond	Boulanger,Gary	75,000	41,000
SMrgrtaHG1	9–Mar–03	8	SA	1 1/8M	D	Starrer	Valenzuela,Patrick	300,000	180,000
SmSnsation	13–Mar–03	7	SA	1M	T	Major Idea	Espinoza,Victor	105,850	50,010
SnAntnoHG2	2–Feb–03	8	SA	1 1/8M	D	Congaree	Bailey,Jerry	250,000	150,000
SnBrdnoHG3	5–Apr–03	10	SA	1 1/8M	D	Western Pride	Valenzuela,Patrick	150,000	90,000
SnClmntHG2	2–Aug–03	8	DMR	1M	T	Katdogawn (GB)	Krone,Julie	150,000	90,000
SnCrlosHG1	2–Mar–03	7	SA	7F	D	Aldebaran	Valdivia, Jr.,Jose	200,000	120,000
SnDiegoHG2	3–Aug–03	8	DMR	1 1/16M	D	Taste of Paradise	Espinoza,Victor	250,000	150,000
SnFelipeG2	16–Mar–03	5	SA	1 1/16M	D	Buddy Gil	Stevens,Gary	250,000	150,000
SnFndoBCG2	11–Jan–03	8	SA	1 1/16M	D	Pass Rush	Nakatani,Corey	219,600	131,760
SnFrnBCHG2	26–Apr–03	7	BM	1M	T	Ninebanks	Warren, Jr.,Ronald	200,000	110,000
SnGabrlHG2	28–Dec–03	8	SA	1 1/8M	T	Redattore (BRZ)	Solis,Alex	150,000	90,000
SngprPltG3	9–Aug–03	8	AP	1 1/8M	D	Sue's Good News	Doocy,Timothy	100,000	60,000
SnGrgnoHG2	11–Jan–03	3	SA	1 1/8M	T	Tates Creek	Valenzuela,Patrick	150,000	90,000
SnJnCpoHG1	20–Apr–03	9	SA	1 3/4M	T	Passinetti	Blanc,Brice	400,000	240,000
SnMarcosG2	20–Jan–03	8	SA	1 1/4M	D	Johar	Solis,Alex	150,000	90,000
SnMiguelG3	12–Jan–03	7	SA	6F	D	Omega Code	Pedroza,Martin	107,800	64,680
Sn0Briartc	1–Jun–03	2	EMD	1M	D	Youcan'ttakeme	Baze,Gary	37,000	18,315
SnowChief	26–Apr–03	4	HOL	1 1/8M	D	Chief Planner	Flores,David	250,000	150,000
SnowWhite	20–Dec–03	8	CT	7F	D	Foolishly	Carmouche,Kendrick	72,150	46,898
SnPsqalHG2	4–Jan–03	8	SA	1 1/16M	D	Congaree	Bailey,Jerry	150,000	90,000
SnRafaelG2	1–Mar–03	7	SA	1M	D	Rojo Toro	Bailey,Jerry	200,000	120,000
SnSmeonHG3	19–Apr–03	8	SA	6 1/2F	T	Speak in Passing	Flores,David	137,500	82,500
SntaAnaHG2	22–Mar–03	9	SA	1 1/8M	T	Noches De Rosa (CHI)	Smith,Mike	150,000	90,000
SntaClaraH	3–May–03	8	BM	1M	D	Aunt Sophie	Gonzalez,Roberto	68,550	33,550
SntaLuciaH	30–Mar–03	8	SA	1 1/16M	D	Bare Necessities	Almeida,G.	105,375	49,725
SntaYnezG2	20–Jan–03	3	SA	7F	D	Elloluv	Valenzuela,Patrick	150,000	90,000
SntBrbrHG2	19–Apr–03	4	SA	1 1/4M	T	Megahertz (GB)	Solis,Alex	250,000	150,000
SntMncaHG1	25–Jan–03	8	SA	7F	D	Affluent	Solis,Alex	200,000	120,000
SntMriaHG1	16–Feb–03	6	SA	1 1/16M	D	Starrer	Valenzuela,Patrick	200,000	120,000
SntYsablG3	5–Jan–03	3	SA	1 1/16M	D	Atlantic Ocean	Flores,David	110,900	66,540
SnVicnteG2	1–Feb–03	4	SA	7F	D	Kafwain	Espinoza,Victor	150,000	90,000
SnzleDzle	8–Nov–03	5	CRC	1M	D	Dakota Light	Douglas,Rene	40,325	26,195
SoBelle	25–May–03	8	GRP	5 1/2F	D	Abstract Image	Beckner,Twyla	3,450	1,898
SolCoJuvF	20–Jul–03	10	SOL	5 1/2F	D	Irish Ides	Lopez,David	53,550	30,150
SolnBeachH	1–Sep–03	5	DMR	1M	T	Centerofattention	Desormeaux,Kent	125,000	75,000
SoloHaina	17–May–03	4	CRC	1 1/16M	T	Lost Appeal	Nunez,Eduardo	43,325	27,995
SoMiss0&B	7–Feb–03	2	FG	6F	D	Eastern Memory	Martinez,Willie	35,000	21,000
Somthinryl	21–Jun–03	9	CNL	5 1/2F	T	All That Glitters	Pino,Mario	50,000	30,000
SonnyHine	18–Oct–03	9	LRL	6F	D	Gators N Bears	Wilson,Rick	50,000	30,000
Sonoma	9–Aug–03	7	NP	1 1/16M	D	A Shaky Start	Painter,Leanne	75,000	47,250
SophmrDstf	7–Jun–03	7	BOI	6 1/2F	D	Thrill After Dark	Packer,Berkley	8,580	5,148
Sophomore	7–Jun–03	8	BOI	6 1/2F	D	Ghost to the Post	Conklin,Jay	8,760	5,256
SophSprChm	25–Nov–03	9	MNR	6F	D	Gimmeawink	Lopez,James	78,000	46,800

Stakes	Date	Race	Trk	Dist/Surf		Winner	Jockey	Gross	Value to winner
SororityG3	30-Aug-03	10	MTH	6F	D	Feline Story	Ferrer,Jose	100,000	60,000
SorrentoG2	9-Aug-03	8	DMR	6 1/2F	D	Tizdubai	Flores,David	150,000	90,000
SouthBend	29-Nov-03	9	HOO	1M	D	Edgerrin	Zimmerman,Ramsey	38,100	22,860
SouthOcean	29-Oct-03	4	WO	1 1/16M	D	My Vintage Port	Jones,Jono	133,125	79,875
Southwest	1-Mar-03	10	OP	1M	D	Great Notion	Thompson,Terry	75,000	45,000
SovtPrblmH	23-Mar-03	4	GG	6F	D	Ema Bovary (CHI)	Gonzalez,Roberto	78,500	33,500
SpanglJimH	5-Jul-03	7	NP	1M	D	Kalfaari	Evans,Sean	40,000	25,200
Spartan	28-Jun-03	6	GLD	7F	D	Akatsakat	Judice,Joseph	45,000	27,000
SpdABckHG3	11-Oct-03	8	CRC	1 1/16M	D	Tour of the Cat	Cabassa, Jr.,Abad	100,000	60,000
SpectBidG3	3-Jan-03	9	GP	6F	D	First Blush	Chavez,Jorge	100,000	60,000
SpectclrBd	6-Sep-03	8	AP	7F	D	Korbyn Gold	Lanerie,Corey	46,950	28,170
SpedSeries	18-May-03	6	MOF	6F	D	Revenue	Gamez,Fernando	2,206	1,324
SpeedH	17-May-03	8	LNN	4 1/2F	D	Tonight Rainbow	Jewell,Jerry	11,000	6,000
SpeedToSpr	6-Sep-03	9	NP	1 3/8M	D	Regal Ability	Hamel,Richard	100,000	63,000
SpicyH	23-Aug-03	10	ARP	1 1/16M	D	She's Finding Time	Kutz,Carl	22,500	13,500
SpinawayG1	29-Aug-03	8	SAR	7F	D	Ashado	Prado,Edgar	200,000	120,000
SpinsterG1	5-Oct-03	8	KEE	1 1/8M	D	Take Charge Lady	Prado,Edgar	500,000	310,000
SpiritOTex	15-Nov-03	4	HOU	6F	D	Fitzroyal	Melancon,Gerard	50,000	30,000
SportPgHG3	25-Oct-03	5	BEL	7F	D	Voodoo	Chavez,Jorge	112,700	67,620
Spring	22-Mar-03	8	HOU	7F	D	Faxamillion	Beasley,Jeremy	35,000	21,000
SprngFever	9-Mar-03	9	OP	5 1/2F	D	Brown Eyed Beauty	Court,Jon	50,000	30,000
Sprngfield	21-Jun-03	6	AP	1M	D	Wiggins	Razo, Jr.,Eusebio	86,800	52,080
SprngSprnt	31-May-03	10	LBG	5 1/2F	D	Faiths Hope	Noel,Rory	11,200	6,160
SprntChmpH	21-Jun-03	9	GRP	4 1/2F	D	Natural Wonder	Crispin,Joe	3,450	1,900
SprtSerieH	1-Sep-03	2	RUI	5 1/2F	D	Jenna's Promise	Estrada, Jr.,Salvador	17,100	10,260
SpruceFirH	27-Jul-03	10	MTH	1M	T	Twilights Prayer	Bravo,Joe	50,000	30,000
SptmansPar	9-Mar-03	8	DED	7F	D	Cat Genius	Borel,Calvin	75,000	45,000
SquanSong	27-Dec-03	8	LRL	7F	D	Search for a Cure	Rose,Jeremy	50,000	30,000
SrenasSong	27-Jul-03	9	MTH	1M 70Y	D	City Fire	Ferrer,Jose	60,000	36,000
SRPCasinoH	22-Sep-03	10	SRP	6 1/2F	D	Herecomesthemannow	Johnson,Bobby	32,600	19,560
SskchwnDby	6-Sep-03	6	MD	1 1/16M	D	Beauzak	Hamel,Richard	15,000	9,000
SsktchwnFt	26-Jul-03	2	MD	6F	D	Megan's Way	Evans,Burton	9,025	5,416
SsktchwnFt	26-Jul-03	1	MD	6F	D	Stage Whisper	Moccasin,Tim	8,900	5,340
Stanton	8-Nov-03	5	DEL	6F	D	Little Andrea	Caraballo,Jose	57,900	34,740
StarBallH	29-Nov-03	7	GG	1 1/16M	D	Tropical Blossom	Rollins,Chance	78,800	33,800
StarDNskra	27-Apr-03	8	PIM	6F	D	Love Sam	Jurado,Enrique	60,000	36,000
Stardust	11-Oct-03	6	LAD	6F	D	Nitro Chip	LeBlanc,Kirk	55,700	33,420
Starine	24-Sep-03	8	BEL	1M	T	Betty's Wish	Velazquez,John	65,900	39,540
StarOfTex	15-Nov-03	8	HOU	1 1/16M	D	Record Assembly	Jacinto,John	100,000	40,000
StarOfTex	15-Nov-03	8	HOU	1 1/16M	D	Desert Darby	Beasley,Jeremy	100,000	40,000
StarShoot	5-Apr-03	8	WO	6F	D	Winter Garden	Sutherland,Chantal	185,000	81,000
StarsNStrH	4-Jul-03	8	BOI	7 1/2F	D	I Wood Be a Winner	Packer,Berkley	6,900	4,140
StarterAlw	20-Sep-03	8	LBG	1 1/8M	D	Crown Butte	Stianson,Janine	8,800	4,840
StCtlinaG2	18-Jan-03	7	SA	1 1/16M	D	Domestic Dispute	Flores,David	150,000	90,000
StdyGrowth	28-May-03	8	WO	1 1/16M	D	Barbeau Ruckus	Montpellier,Constant	128,750	77,250
Stefanita	15-Nov-03	9	LRL	7F	D	Gazillion	Prado,Edgar	75,000	45,000
StevensH	14-Sep-03	7	CLS	6 1/2F	D	Intervene	Compton,Perry	15,500	9,300
StFairBrdH	29-Jun-03	8	LNN	1M 70Y	D	High Dice	Beck,Daniel	13,750	8,250
StFairBrdr	13-Jun-03	8	LNN	1M	D	High Tech Racing	Martinez,Armando	15,575	9,345
StFairFut	21-Jun-03	8	LNN	4 1/2F	D	Sheso	Carkeek,Jerome	15,600	9,360
StgDrBttyH	27-Dec-03	10	CRC	1 1/16M	D	Redoubled Miss	Coa,Eibar	100,000	60,000
SthnAccent	12-Jul-03	10	LAD	6F	D	Distinctive Code	Simington,Donald	50,000	30,000
StnHFmSoFl	6-Apr-03	6	TAM	7F	D	Just Bill Me	Homeister, Jr.,Rosemary	84,250	46,550
StNick	20-Dec-03	6	CT	7F	D	Take the Plunge	Martin,Christopher	72,450	47,093
Stonerside	24-May-03	8	LS	7F	D	Miss Bridget Jones	Theriot,Jamie	150,000	90,000
StormCat	5-Oct-03	4	KEE	1M	T	Remind	Bailey,Jerry	84,225	52,220
StPaul	7-Jun-03	8	CBY	6F	D	Quote Me Later	Eads,Jason	35,000	21,000
StPSprChpH	3-May-03	6	STP	6F	D	Fancy As	Hamel,Richard	50,000	25,200
StrAlMrthn	5-Oct-03	7	LBG	1 3/16M	D	Washakie	Mellish,Brooke	8,900	4,895
Stravinsky	19-Apr-03	6	KEE	5 1/2F	T	Repository	Bailey,Jerry	84,375	52,313
StrngRuler	9-Aug-03	9	EMD	6 1/2F	D	Sundance Circle	Whitaker,Jennifer	37,000	18,315

Stakes	Date	Race Trk	Dist/Surf		Winner	Jockey	Gross	Value to winner
StrStBCHG3	5-Jul-03	8 AP	1 1/2M	T	Ballingarry (IRE)	Douglas,Rene	219,500	131,700
StrubG2	1-Feb-03	9 SA	1 1/8M	D	Medaglia d'Oro	Bailey,Jerry	400,000	240,000
SturgnRivr	20-Sep-03	3 NP	1M	D	Bears Little Angel	Winters,Perry	50,000	31,500
StuyvntHG3	11-Nov-03	8 AQU	1 1/8M	D	Presidentialaffair	Migliore,Richard	110,300	66,180
StwbrryMrn	11-May-03	8 HST	6 1/2F	D	Elana d'Amour	Krasner,Samuel	44,368	26,621
StymieH	16-Mar-03	7 AQU	1 1/8M	D	Snake Mountain	Luzzi,Michael	80,975	48,585
SuburbnHG1	5-Jul-03	9 BEL	1 1/4M	D	Mineshaft	Albarado,Robby	500,000	300,000
SuDyXXIVG2	20-Sep-03	10 LAD	1 1/8M	D	Ten Most Wanted	Day,Pat	500,000	300,000
SufDerby	19-Jul-03	8 SUF	1M 70Y	D	Strike 'n Go	Jellison,Jill	35,000	21,000
SufOaks	26-Jul-03	8 SUF	1M 70Y	D	Megan's Halo	Bermudez,Jose	35,000	21,000
SugarBowl	28-Dec-03	9 FG	6F	D	Wildcat Shoes	Albarado,Robby	60,000	36,000
SummerG2	14-Sep-03	4 WO	1M	T	Bachelor Blues	Kabel,Todd	285,500	171,300
SummitSCH	3-May-03	7 TDN	1 1/16M	D	Hackendiffy	Rowland,Michael	50,000	30,000
SummrKing	2-Jun-03	7 DEL	1 1/16M	D	Devon Rose	Rose,Jeremy	58,200	34,920
SumrFinalH	1-Sep-03	4 MNR	1M	D	Salzurita (ARG)	Walker, Jr.,Bobby	78,400	47,040
SunCityH	3-May-03	7 TUP	1M	T	Centerofattention	Drexler,Howie	35,000	21,000
Suncoast	22-Feb-03	6 TAM	1 1/16M	D	Just Bill Me	Homeister, Jr.,Rosemary	50,000	28,500
SunDevil	11-Jan-03	8 TUP	1M	D	Bertrando's Dare	Higuera,Alberto	35,000	21,000
SunflowerH	4-Oct-03	9 WDS	6F	D	Morning Merry	Murray,Kelly	25,000	15,000
SunH	7-Jun-03	8 HST	1 1/16M	D	Secondary School	Lacoursiere,Larry	44,368	24,000
SunlandPkH	5-Apr-03	11 SUN	1 1/8M	D	Night Patrol	Puglisi,Ignacio	105,300	63,180
SunnysHalo	16-Nov-03	6 WO	6 1/2F	D	Night Sky	Kabel,Todd	106,000	63,600
SunnySlope	18-Oct-03	8 SA	6F	D	The Herc	Desormeaux,Kent	104,475	49,185
SunnyvaleH	31-May-03	3 BM	6F	D	Lacie Girl	Baze,Russell	78,000	33,600
SunParkH	28-Dec-03	10 SUN	1 1/16M	D	Ciento	Gonzalez, Jr.,Sal	103,950	62,370
SunPower	8-Nov-03	5 HAW	6F	D	Jaguar Friend	Meier,Randall	115,950	54,720
SunsetGun	12-Jul-03	5 SUF	1 1/16M	T	Sunlit Ridge	Panell,Dyn	35,000	21,000
SunsetHG2	20-Jul-03	7 HOL	1 1/2M	T	Puerto Banus	Espinoza,Victor	150,000	90,000
SunSprtChH	4-Aug-03	7 NP	6 1/2F	D	Sixthirtyjoe	Heiler,Stephan	50,000	31,500
SunYuleDby	13-Dec-03	10 SUN	6 1/2F	D	This Cat's for You	Tohill,Ken	55,550	33,331
SupahJess	12-May-03	7 CRC	6F	D	Crafty Brat	Cruz,Manoel	41,925	27,155
Super	25-Jan-03	10 TAM	7F	D	Above the Wind	Mata,Federico	50,000	21,000
SupernatlH	19-May-03	8 HST	6 1/2F	D	Dancewithavixen	Valdez,Felipe	44,472	26,683
Survive	3-Jan-03	7 SA	5 1/2F	D	Icantgoforthat	Valenzuela,Patrick	107,100	64,260
SusanGrlBC	28-Jun-03	7 DEL	1 1/16M	D	Hennie's Song	Black,Anthony	175,000	105,000
SussexH	18-Oct-03	8 DEL	1 1/16M	T	Political Attack	Dominguez,Ramon	100,000	60,000
SVanBurenH	1-Sep-03	9 PHA	7F	D	Barbara O'Brien	Bravo,Joe	75,000	45,000
SwaleG3	15-Mar-03	11 GP	7F	D	Midas Eyes	Bailey,Jerry	150,000	90,000
SwapsG2	13-Jul-03	6 HOL	1 1/8M	D	During	Bailey,Jerry	400,000	240,000
Sweet&SasH	17-May-03	8 DEL	6F	D	Wish It Were	Toribio,Abdiel	75,000	45,000
Sweetheart	16-Feb-03	9 PM	1 1/16M	D	Stately's Choice	Cedeno,Amir	10,000	5,500
Sweetheart	15-Feb-03	7 DED	7F	D	Meteor Miracle	Santiago,Joel	50,000	30,000
Swift	25-Jan-03	7 TUP	5 1/2F	D	Flying Supercon	Hernandez,Miguel	35,000	21,000
SwneRvrHG3	2-Mar-03	10 GP	1 1/8M	T	Amonita (GB)	Samyn,Jean-Luc	100,000	60,000
SWRandlPlH	23-Aug-03	8 HST	1 1/8M	D	Leloup	Alvarado,Pedro	44,472	26,683
SwrdDncHG1	9-Aug-03	9 SAR	1 1/2M	T	Whitmore's Conn	Samyn,Jean-Luc	500,000	300,000
SwtBriarTo	22-Jun-03	3 WO	7F	D	Harmony Lodge	Coa,Eibar	108,000	64,800
Swynford	21-Sep-03	8 WO	7F	D	Winter Whiskey	Jones,Jono	134,250	80,550
SycamrBCG3	4-Oct-03	7 KEE	1 1/2M	T	Sharbayan (IRE)	Day,Pat	169,200	73,904
TableRun	22-Jun-03	3 EMD	1M	D	Knightsbridge Road	Radke,Kevin	35,000	17,325
TacomaH	13-Jul-03	10 EMD	1 1/16M	D	Condotierri	Mitchell,Gallyn	40,000	21,725
TahDah	13-Jul-03	6 RD	5 1/2F	D	Ding's Thing	Felix,Julio	40,000	24,000
TakinRisks	1-Sep-03	9 TIM	1 1/16M	D	Full Brush	Rosenthal,Mark	50,000	30,000
TampaBayBC	15-Feb-03	10 TAM	1 1/16M	D	Burning Roma	Castanon,Jesus	100,000	60,000
TampaDbyG3	16-Mar-03	11 TAM	1 1/16M	D	Region of Merit	Coa,Eibar	250,000	150,000
TanforanH	8-Feb-03	8 GG	1 1/16M	T	Seinne (CHI)	Warren, Jr.,Ronald	100,000	55,000
TaylorSpec	27-Sep-03	5 AP	5F	T	Skeet	Douglas,Rene	47,550	28,530
TaylrSpclH	23-Feb-03	9 FG	6F	D	Mountain General	Lanerie,Corey	100,000	60,000
TBAutotote	26-Oct-03	9 LBG	1 1/16M	D	Badolstory	Miyashiro,Cliff	13,400	7,370

Stakes	Date	Race	Trk	Dist/Surf		Winner	Jockey	Gross	Value to winner
TbFuturity	14-Sep-03	7	FAR	6F	D	Foxy Scott	Von Rosen,Anne	24,780	12,390
TbFuturity	6-Sep-03	5	FAR	6F	D	Warmnfuzzyfeelin	Von Rosen,Anne	14,500	7,250
TBH	17-Aug-03	7	KSP	7F	D	Dawns Ben	Dangerfield,Ty	2,950	1,711
TBMaiden	17-May-03	6	MC	5 1/2F	D	Ike's Kool Cat	Cano, Jr.,Jack	4,000	2,400
TBMatronH	17-Aug-03	6	KSP	6F	D	Alibi Expert	Hebert,Carl	2,850	1,653
TBMaturity	1-Sep-03	9	FAR	1M	D	Scarlet Lad	Von Rosen,Anne	10,800	5,400
TbMdnDerby	5-Jul-03	8	BOI	6 1/2F	D	Skillful Level	Keckler,Ron	18,005	9,003
TCAG3	12-Oct-03	8	KEE	6F	D	Summer Mis	Douglas,Rene	125,000	77,500
TCNutBrdCl	11-Oct-03	1	CT	4 1/2F	D	Petes Hick Chick	Torres,Raymond	75,000	33,750
TeddyDrone	3-Aug-03	9	MTH	6F	D	It's a Monster	Bravo,Joe	75,000	45,000
TeewrthPlH	18-May-03	9	STP	1M	D	Eternal Secrecy	Painter,Leanne	50,000	25,200
TejanoRun	15-Mar-03	10	TP	1 1/8M	D	Mail Call	Bejarano,Rafael	50,000	31,300
Tejas	4-Oct-03	3	RET	5F	T	Herve	Cloninger, Jr.,Weldon	35,000	21,000
TellikeH	31-May-03	8	EVD	6F	D	High Hopes Irish	Woodley,Carl	35,000	21,000
TempeH	15-Mar-03	8	TUP	1M	T	Hero's Pleasure	Stevens,Scott	35,000	21,000
TemptedG3	4-Nov-03	8	AQU	1M	D	La Reina	Velazquez,John	110,700	66,420
Temptress	22-Aug-03	5	GLD	5 1/2F	D	Zosia's Genius	Judice,Joseph	45,000	27,000
TenaciousH	6-Dec-03	9	FG	1 1/16M	D	G. W.'s Skippie	Lovato, Jr.,Frank	60,000	36,000
TenThouLakes	17-May-03	9	CBY	6F	D	J. P. Jet	Bell,Derek	36,525	21,915
TerreHaute	28-Nov-03	9	HOO	1M	D	Victory Punch	Knight,Lester	38,850	23,310
TerrFair	18-May-03	9	ALB	1 1/16M	D	Casperino	Jaime,Ricardo	35,000	19,250
TestG1	26-Jul-03	8	SAR	7F	D	Lady Tak	Bailey,Jerry	250,000	150,000
Testum	19-Jul-03	1	BOI	7F	D	Dr. Justy	Williams,Matt	9,705	6,006
TexHallFam	4-Oct-03	9	RET	1 1/16M	T	Fly Slama Jama	Cloninger, Jr.,Weldon	100,000	60,000
TexsMileG3	26-Apr-03	9	LS	1M	D	Bluesthestandard	Pedroza,Martin	300,000	170,000
TexsZing	23-Sep-03	10	FP	6F	D	Shandy	Silva,Carlos	36,000	21,600
TexTbBrdrs	19-Jul-03	10	GIL	6F	D	Bold Reply	Carrizales,Santos	7,900	4,740
TfClscIvG1	27-Sep-03	9	BEL	1 1/2M	T	Sulamani (IRE)	Bailey,Jerry	750,000	450,000
TFMoran	24-May-03	5	SUF	1 1/16M	D	Stylish Sultan	Jellison,Jill	35,000	21,000
ThanksgivH	28-Nov-03	6	PM	1M	D	Zip the Bright	Gutierrez,Juan	10,000	5,500
ThanksgivH	27-Nov-03	9	FG	6F	D	Posse	Lanerie,Corey	60,000	36,000
ThbdFut	21-Sep-03	7	YD	5 1/4F	D	Ugotadowhatugotado	Holmes, Sr.,Joe	10,680	5,340
Thelma	4-Jan-03	9	FG	6F	D	Lady Tak	Meche,Donnie	75,000	45,000
TheVeryOne	16-May-03	9	PIM	5F	D	Forest Heiress	Day,Pat	75,000	45,000
ThrbDrb	21-Sep-03	9	YD	7F	D	Nightly Delusions	Holmes, Sr.,Joe	7,150	3,575
ThreeChmnyJuv	3-May-03	6	CD	5F	D	Limehouse	Albarado,Robby	114,000	70,680
ThreeRing	13-Dec-03	12	CRC	1 1/16M	D	Ender's Sister	Velasquez,Cornelio	100,000	60,000
ThreeYOFilSale	5-Sep-03	8	NP	1M	D	A Shaky Start	Painter,Leanne	50,000	30,000
ThrYrOldSl	7-Sep-03	8	NP	1M	D	Double Doc	Painter,Leanne	50,000	30,000
ThtsOurBck	4-May-03	9	CRC	6F	D	Danaher Steve	Homeister, Jr.,Rosemary	41,925	27,155
TicndrogaH	18-Oct-03	7	BEL	1 1/8M	T	Lady Bi Bi	Santos,Jose	150,000	90,000
TiffnyLass	26-Jan-03	8	FG	1M	D	Lady Tak	Meche,Donnie	100,000	60,000
TimbrMusic	13-Jul-03	7	HST	6 1/2F	D	Sungold Skippy	May,Robert	38,913	21,000
Tippett	20-Jul-03	9	CNL	5 1/2F	T	Wage a Penny	Wilson,Rick	50,000	30,000
TipTapH	29-Nov-03	9	RP	1 1/16M	D	Taco Tuesday	Matz,Nena	21,600	11,940
Tiznow	26-Apr-03	8	HOL	7 1/2F	D	Joey Franco	Desormeaux,Kent	150,000	90,000
TJMalley	25-May-03	8	MTH	5F	D	Pali Princess	Velez, Jr.,Jose	50,000	30,000
TllmkDyDby	8-Aug-03	6	TIL	1 1/16M	D	Uncle Whiz	Mercado,Victor	2,300	1,265
TnbkAlmHG3	1-Nov-03	9	AQU	1 1/8M	D	Pocus Hocus	Santos,Jose	107,500	64,500
ToboggnHG3	15-Mar-03	8	AQU	6F	D	Affirmed Success	Migliore,Richard	109,100	65,460
TogaTogaH	8-Jun-03	10	CRC	5 1/2F	D	Storm Flag	Boulanger,Gary	42,850	27,710
TokyoCityH	8-Mar-03	9	SA	1 1/16M	D	Kela	Garcia,Matt	103,150	48,390
TomBane	26-Apr-03	5	TUP	6F	D	Twice the Energy	Martinez,Seth	15,000	9,000
Tomboy	17-May-03	10	RD	1 1/16M	D	Orangeberry	Rosario, Jr.,Hector	50,000	30,000
TomFoolHG2	4-Jul-03	8	BEL	7F	D	Aldebaran	Bailey,Jerry	150,000	90,000
ToMuchCofe	23-Nov-03	9	HOO	1 1/16M	D	Mr. Mink	Pompell,Thomas	38,700	23,220
TondiBudH	29-Mar-03	10	FON	6F	D	Tonight Rainbow	Jewell,Jerry	27,500	15,000
Toon'sH	23-Aug-03	6	MD	1 1/16M	D	Double Time	Latchman,Rennie	5,000	3,000
TopCorsage	19-Jul-03	4	AP	1M	D	Keeping the Gold	Razo, Jr.,Eusebio	52,400	31,440

Stakes	Date	Race	Trk	Dist/Surf		Winner	Jockey	Gross	Value to winner
TopFlgtHG2	28-Nov-03	9	AQU	1M	D	Randaroo	Castillo, Jr.,Heberto	150,000	90,000
TopFlight	5-Sep-03	8	AP	7F	D	I'm a Majek Girl	Lovato, Jr.,Frank	47,700	28,620
TopHat	24-Jun-03	2	YAV	5 1/2F	D	Officer Nasty	Guerra,Vince	9,600	5,280
Topsider	5-Jul-03	8	SUF	6F	D	Dhaffir (CHI)	Piermarini,Tammi	35,000	21,000
TorryPines	7-Sep-03	8	DMR	1M	D	Victory Encounter	Smith,Mike	102,300	47,880
TotahFut	11-Nov-03	10	SRP	6 1/2F	D	Jonnygetachex	Madeira,Carlos	102,352	48,838
ToThePost	31-Jan-03	8	TUP	6F	D	Top Penny	Martinez,Seth	23,700	14,220
Tougaloo	27-Apr-03	7	TDN	6F	D	Ask Linda	Villa-Gomez,Huber	35,000	21,000
TowsleMmH	9-Aug-03	7	TIL	5F	D	Theycallmecolonel	Peery,Melissa	3,800	2,090
TPBCG3	13-Sep-03	12	TP	1 1/16M	D	Smok'n Frolic	Prado,Edgar	175,000	108,500
TPFallChG3	27-Sep-03	9	TP	1M	D	Crafty Shaw	Perret,Craig	100,000	62,000
TPPrevue	4-Jan-03	9	TP	6 1/2F	D	Champali	Lopez,James	50,000	31,300
Trampoli	4-Nov-03	7	AQU	1M	T	Proud Beauty (IRE)	Velazquez,John	61,100	36,660
TraversG1	23-Aug-03	11	SAR	1 1/4M	D	Ten Most Wanted	Day,Pat	1,000,000	600,000
TrBndBCHG1	5-Jul-03	8	HOL	7F	D	Joey Franco	Valenzuela,Patrick	300,000	150,000
TreasurStF	25-Jul-03	5	GF	5F	D	Ugotadowhatugotado	Hamilton,Donald	7,450	3,725
TremontG3	28-Jun-03	7	BEL	5 1/2F	D	Heckle	Velazquez,John	110,200	66,120
Trenton	2-Aug-03	10	MTH	5F	D	Follow Me Home	Pimentel,Julian	50,000	30,000
TrfDstncSt	4-May-03	7	TUP	1 3/8M	T	Icarus in Flight	Martinez,Seth	40,500	24,300
TripleSec	4-Jan-03	9	DED	5F	D	Mighty Merlin	Clark,Kerwin	40,000	24,000
TriStateH	1-Sep-03	10	ELP	1 1/8M	T	Hard Buck (BRZ)	Bejarano,Rafael	75,000	34,500
TriStatFut	25-Oct-03	4	CT	7F	D	Red Velvet Cake	Mawing,Anthony	72,400	47,060
TrlyBoundH	3-Jan-03	9	FG	1 1/16M	D	Lakenheath	Albarado,Robby	75,000	45,000
Trnsylvna3	4-Apr-03	8	KEE	1M	T	White Cat	Sellers,Shane	100,000	62,000
TrNthBCHG2	7-Jun-03	7	BEL	6F	D	Shake You Down	Luzzi,Michael	250,000	90,000
TrontoCHG3	12-Jul-03	8	WO	1 1/8M	T	Mobil	Kabel,Todd	164,100	98,460
TroprSeven	21-Sep-03	7	EMD	1M	D	I'm a Soccer Boy	Mitchell,Gallyn	40,000	20,000
TropTrfHG3	6-Dec-03	11	CRC	1 1/8M	T	Political Attack	Douglas,Rene	100,000	60,000
TrpOaks	1-Jan-03	6	CRC	1 1/16M	T	Sweettrickydancer	Coa,Eibar	100,000	60,000
TrpPkDbyG3	1-Jan-03	10	CRC	1 1/8M	T	Nothing to Lose	Bailey,Jerry	100,000	60,000
TrsRiosJuv	1-Nov-03	10	SRP	6 1/2F	D	Western Ridge	Lambert,Casey	46,377	21,797
TSnchzMmMl	11-May-03	10	MAN	1M	D	Swamp Rat	White,James	35,000	21,000
TTASalesFt	7-Jun-03	10	LS	5F	D	Bluegrass Sara	Meche,Lonnie	138,200	82,920
TTASalesFt	7-Jun-03	8	LS	5F	D	Next Bandit	Martin, Jr.,Eddie	142,930	85,758
TulsaDash	11-Apr-03	10	FMT	4F	D	As de Oro	Goad, Jr.,Kenneth	23,275	12,766
TuPBCH	1-Feb-03	7	TUP	1 1/16M	T	Century City (IRE)	Pincay, Jr.,Laffit	150,000	90,000
TuPDerby	1-Feb-03	6	TUP	1 1/16M	T	Robledo	Flores,David	100,000	60,000
TurfMonstH	31-May-03	9	PHA	5F	T	Testify	Kuntzweiler,Greta	100,000	60,000
TwinLights	16-Aug-03	10	MTH	1 1/16M	D	Feisty Bull	Lopez,Charles	50,000	30,000
Twixt	24-Jul-03	4	LRL	1 1/8M	D	River Cruise	Rose,Jeremy	75,000	45,000
TxHeritage	8-Mar-03	8	HOU	1M	D	Catalissa	Martin, Jr.,Eddie	35,000	21,000
TxStallCon	28-Jun-03	2	LS	5 1/2F	D	Expectacat	Martin, Jr.,Eddie	52,500	31,500
TxStallion	15-Feb-03	3	HOU	1 1/16M	D	Lady Mallory	Valdez,Felipe	75,000	45,000
TxStallion	15-Feb-03	8	HOU	1 1/16M	D	Call Me Lefty	Jacinto,John	75,000	45,000
TxStallion	13-Sep-03	7	RET	7F	D	Fitzroyal	Melancon,Gerard	46,245	27,747
TxStallion	13-Sep-03	8	RET	7F	D	Lady Mallory	Beasley,Jeremy	42,269	25,361
TxStallion	27-Dec-03	9	HOU	1M	D	There Goes Rocket	Perrodin,Elvis	125,000	75,000
TxStallion	27-Dec-03	7	HOU	1M	D	Native Annie	Bourque,Curt	125,000	75,000
TxStallion	28-Jun-03	8	LS	5 1/2F	D	There Goes Rocket	Perrodin,Elvis	122,500	73,500
TxStallion	28-Jun-03	7	LS	5 1/2F	D	Hay Lauren	Martin, Jr.,Eddie	122,500	73,500
TxStallion	4-Oct-03	8	RET	6F	D	Seneca Summer	Gondron,Ted	125,000	75,000
TxStallion	4-Oct-03	6	RET	6F	D	Sago	Beasley,Jeremy	125,000	75,000
Tyro	20-Jul-03	3	MTH	5 1/2F	D	Deputy Storm	Bravo,Joe	50,000	30,000
UCanDoItH	4-Oct-03	9	CRC	6 1/2F	D	Chispiski	Garcia,Julio	75,000	41,000
Unbridled	21-Jun-03	12	CRC	1 1/16M	D	Hear No Evil	Nunez,Eduardo	100,000	60,000
UntdNtnHG1	5-Jul-03	10	MTH	1 3/8M	T	Balto Star	Velez, Jr.,Jose	750,000	450,000
USA	26-May-03	7	LS	1 1/16M	T	Crowned King	Rennie,Chandra	200,000	120,000
USBank	19-Apr-03	9	EMD	6F	D	Bisbee's Prospect	Radke,Kevin	35,000	19,250
VacavilleH	12-Jul-03	10	SOL	6F	D	Lacie Girl	Baze,Russell	50,800	27,600

Stakes	Date	Race	Trk	Dist/Surf		Winner	Jockey	Gross	Value to winner
VagrncyHG2	8-Jun-03	8	BEL	6 1/2F	D	Shawklit Mint	Migliore,Richard	150,000	90,000
Valdale	1-Mar-03	9	TP	1M	D	Unbridled Femme	Peck,Brian	50,000	31,300
ValdictryH	30-Nov-03	9	WO	1 3/4M	D	Hydrogen	Ramsammy,Emile	143,500	86,100
ValidExpec	26-May-03	4	LS	6F	D	See How She Runs	Pettinger,Donald	100,000	60,000
ValidLead	21-Dec-03	8	TUP	6 1/2F	D	Rockin On	Corbett,Glenn	22,100	13,260
ValidLeadr	9-Feb-03	4	TUP	6 1/2F	D	Knoll Lake	Bridges,Kelly	23,700	14,220
ValidLinda	15-Aug-03	9	CRC	6F	D	Secret Request	Castro,Eddie	42,000	27,200
Valkyr	19-Jul-03	8	HOL	1M	T	Shalini	Valenzuela,Patrick	76,875	46,125
Vallejo	15-Feb-03	3	GG	1M	D	Lucky Sabre	Baze,Russell	78,450	33,450
ValorFarm	26-May-03	9	LS	6F	D	Hannah's Royalrock	Day,Pat	50,000	30,000
VAMscrliMH	26-Jul-03	7	DEL	6F	D	Sing Me Back Home	Rose,Jeremy	100,000	60,000
Vandal	17-Aug-03	8	WO	6F	D	Twisted Wit	Clark,David	163,350	98,010
VanityHG1	21-Jun-03	8	HOL	1 1/8M	D	Azeri	Smith,Mike	250,000	150,000
VctoryRide	23-Aug-03	7	SAR	6F	D	Country Romance	Chavez,Jorge	76,200	45,720
VctraLassH	15-Mar-03	9	FG	6F	D	Distinctive Code	Sellers,Shane	100,000	60,000
VDvptRTylr	23-Jul-03	6	BOI	7 1/2F	D	Crystal Cinders	Conklin,Jay	4,300	2,580
VectorComm	11-Jul-03	8	GPR	6F	D	Polish Poppa	Landaker,Terri	3,100	1,860
VeryOneHG3	8-Feb-03	8	GP	1 3/8M	T	San Dare	Guidry,Mark	100,000	60,000
VerySubtlH	25-Oct-03	1	SA	6F	D	Stellar	Farina,Tony	107,200	64,320
VesslsDstf	25-Jan-03	5	SA	1 1/16M	D	Smok'n Frolic	Bailey,Jerry	750,000	411,400
Veterans	26-May-03	9	IND	6F	D	Tee to Green	Mojica,Orlando	37,800	22,680
ViaBorghes	6-Apr-03	9	GP	1 1/8M	T	Fencelineneighbor	Garcia,Julio	75,000	45,000
ViaBrghese	10-Sep-03	8	BEL	1 1/8M	T	Perfect Energy	Castellano,Javier	65,800	39,480
ViceRegent	6-Aug-03	3	WO	1M	T	Tusayan	Ramsammy,Emile	136,500	81,900
Victoria	14-Jun-03	8	WO	5F	D	Third Day	Clark,David	137,750	82,650
Victoria	11-Oct-03	1	LAD	6F	D	Leslie's Love	Melancon,Gerard	53,600	32,160
Victoriana	4-Aug-03	5	WO	1 1/16M	T	Inish Glora	Kabel,Todd	132,875	79,725
VictoriaPk	8-Jun-03	4	WO	1 1/8M	D	Pants N Kisses	Montpellier,Constant	136,875	82,125
VictrQueen	1-Oct-03	7	WO	6F	D	Blonde Executive	Dos Ramos,Richard	130,750	78,450
Videogenic	31-Jan-03	8	AQU	1 1/16M	D	Indy Glory	Bridgmohan,Shaun	60,000	36,000
VigilHG3	26-Apr-03	8	WO	7F	D	Wake At Noon	Ramsammy,Emile	164,700	98,820
Vincennes	3-Oct-03	8	HOO	6F	D	Miss Dakota	Butler,Dean	39,100	23,460
Violet	12-Apr-03	6	HAW	6F	D	Gumbo Love	Cadman,Zoe	133,867	53,595
VioletHG3	17-Oct-03	7	MED	1 1/16M	T	Dancal (IRE)	Castellano,Javier	150,000	90,000
Vivace	22-Jun-03	9	CRC	7F	D	Tchula Miss	Toribio, Jr.,Aurelio	42,500	27,500
VivaciousH	17-Aug-03	12	RD	1 1/16M	D	Oh So Easy	Johnston,Jeff	50,000	30,000
VllyStrmG3	23-Nov-03	8	AQU	6F	D	Smokey Glacken	Santos,Jose	112,200	67,320
VllyViewG3	18-Oct-03	9	KEE	1 1/16M	T	Dyna Da Wyna	Day,Pat	112,900	69,998
VosburghG1	27-Sep-03	7	BEL	6 1/2F	D	Ghostzapper	Castellano,Javier	500,000	300,000
VOUndrwdG3	27-Nov-03	7	HOL	6F	D	Watchem Smokey	Krone,Julie	100,000	60,000
VrgniaDrby	12-Jul-03	10	CNL	1 1/4M	T	Silver Tree	Prado,Edgar	500,000	300,000
VSMyersJr	6-Jul-03	7	CBY	6F	D	One by Design	Bell,Derek	37,585	22,551
Vulcan	28-Mar-03	1	FG	6F	D	Sun Block	Martinez,Willie	35,000	20,650
WafareFarm	19-Apr-03	9	LS	6F	D	Letithappencaptain	LeBlanc,Kirk	50,000	30,000
WaLgslatrH	25-May-03	9	EMD	6 1/2F	D	Ema Bovary (CHI)	Gonzalez,Roberto	35,000	19,250
WalMtchmkr	11-Oct-03	5	LAD	1 1/16M	T	Long Leg Lou	Melancon,Gerard	80,150	48,090
Waquoit	1-Mar-03	7	SUF	1 1/16M	D	Yaeger	Bush,Vernon	35,000	21,000
WashBCOaks	23-Aug-03	9	EMD	1 1/8M	D	Youcan'ttakeme	Baze,Gary	100,000	55,000
WashCupCls	21-Sep-03	10	EMD	1 1/16M	D	Colony Lane	Baze,Gary	50,000	25,000
WashPkHG2	19-Jul-03	9	AP	1 3/16M	D	Perfect Drift	Day,Pat	400,000	240,000
Waya	6-Aug-03	8	SAR	1 1/8M	D	May Gator	Bailey,Jerry	65,750	39,464
Waya	25-Oct-03	9	LRL	1 1/16M	T	Lady of the Future	Rose,Jeremy	75,000	30,000
WaywrdLass	1-Mar-03	10	TAM	1 1/16M	D	Win's Fair Lady	Judice,Joseph	50,000	21,000
WChurchilH	20-Sep-03	7	HST	1 1/8M	D	Futural	Valdez,Felipe	44,576	24,000
WdsDerby	1-Nov-03	8	WDS	1 1/16M	D	Ww Conquistador	Kurek,Gary	30,000	18,000
WDShferHG3	17-May-03	11	PIM	1 1/8M	D	Windsor Castle	Santos,Jose	100,000	60,000
WdsJuv	31-Oct-03	9	WDS	6F	D	Soriano Cat	Murray,Kelly	15,000	9,000
WdswrthMmH	6-Sep-03	8	FL	1 1/8M	D	Right Stop	Woolsey,Russell	35,000	21,000
WEBN	1-Feb-03	9	TP	1M	D	Champali	Lumpkins,Jason	50,000	31,300

Stakes	Date	Race	Trk	Dist/Surf		Winner	Jockey	Gross	Value to winner
WeekndDlt	6-Sep-03	9	TP	6F	D	Don't Countess Out	Thompson,Terry	75,000	46,950
Westerner	15-Aug-03	8	NP	1 5/16M	D	They Call Me Cody	Winters,Perry	40,000	25,200
WesternHer	16-Aug-03	1	MD	6 1/2F	D	Stage Whisper	Moccasin,Tim	10,000	6,000
WestMesaH	19-Sep-03	8	ALB	7F	D	Inox (ARG)	Bourdieu,Jorge	32,000	19,200
WestPointH	8-Aug-03	8	SAR	1 1/8M	T	Finality	Velazquez,John	115,200	69,120
WestrnCanH	1-Jul-03	7	NP	6 1/2F	D	Rindanica	Winters,Perry	40,000	25,200
WFiddleMem	23-Jul-03	8	BOI	7 1/2F	D	Quiet Syns	Conklin,Jay	10,133	6,080
WhatAPlesr	13-Dec-03	9	CRC	1 1/16M	D	Second of June	Velasquez,Cornelio	100,000	60,000
WhatASummr	18-Jan-03	8	LRL	6F	D	Xtra Heat	Wilson,Rick	60,000	30,000
WheatCity	4-Aug-03	6	ASD	1M	D	Deputy Country	Hendricks,Ken	35,000	21,000
Whimsical	12-Apr-03	8	WO	6F	D	Brass in Pocket	Clark,David	190,250	114,150
Whirlaway	8-Feb-03	8	AQU	1 1/16M	D	Boston Park	Bridgmohan,Shaun	81,350	48,810
WhiteOakH	21-Jun-03	8	AP	6F	D	Out of My Way	Bourque,Curt	84,150	50,490
WhitneyHG1	2-Aug-03	8	SAR	1 1/8M	D	Medaglia d'Oro	Bailey,Jerry	750,000	450,000
WhoDrWhoH	12-Jul-03	3	HPO	1M	D	High Dice	Beck,Daniel	30,450	17,070
WhrlgAsh	13-Sep-03	8	DEL	1M	D	Paddington	Madrigal, Jr.,Rodrigo	58,700	35,220
WhtAThreat	16-Nov-03	9	CRC	1 1/16M	T	Magic Mecke	Coa,Eibar	38,000	24,800
WickerrH	2-Aug-03	5	DMR	1M	T	Touch of the Blues (FR)	Desormeaux,Kent	98,975	45,885
WideContry	8-Mar-03	8	LRL	1 1/16M	D	Powers Prospect	Alvarado, Jr.,Roberto	50,000	30,000
Widener	19-Aug-03	8	PHA	1 1/16M	D	Toccet	Chavez,Jorge	35,300	21,180
WildcatH	27-Apr-03	7	TUP	1 3/8M	T	Free Corona	Ziegler,Michael	35,000	21,000
WildNWond	28-Jun-03	8	CT	7F	D	Fancy Buckles	Valdes,Ricardo	36,650	21,990
WildRose	14-Jun-03	8	PRM	1 1/16M	D	Sharky's Review	Quinonez,Luis	62,000	42,000
WildRoseH	28-Jun-03	4	NP	6 1/2F	D	Secret Bullet	Wilson,David	40,000	25,200
Willowbrok	1-Mar-03	8	HOU	5F	T	Sound of Gold	Jacinto,John	35,000	21,000
WilRogrsG3	25-May-03	8	HOL	1M	T	Private Chef	Espinoza,Victor	112,600	67,560
WilshirHG3	27-Apr-03	8	HOL	1M	T	Dublino	Desormeaux,Kent	111,000	66,600
WineCntryH	4-Jul-03	9	FL	6F	D	As Wicked	Rodriguez,Pedro	35,000	21,000
WinningClr	14-Jun-03	8	BOI	7F	D	Heyshe'satrader	Nollar,Flip	11,010	6,606
WinnpegSun	3-Aug-03	7	ASD	1 1/16M	D	Passionate Bird	Hightower,Travis	35,000	21,000
WinshmLadH	11-Jan-03	10	SUN	1M	D	Premeditation	Lambert,Casey	55,550	33,330
WinStarOak	29-Mar-03	9	SUN	1M	D	Island Fashion	Puglisi,Ignacio	256,450	153,870
WinStrDrby	30-Mar-03	9	SUN	1 1/16M	D	Excessivepleasure	Day,Pat	500,000	270,000
Wintrgreen	8-Mar-03	10	TP	1M	D	Seven Four Seven	Lumpkins,Jason	50,000	31,300
WirlwayHG3	9-Feb-03	9	FG	1 1/16M	D	Balto Star	Martin, Jr.,Eddie	125,000	75,000
WishingWel	8-Mar-03	7	DED	7F	D	Souris	Bourque,Steven	75,000	45,000
WishngWell	11-Jan-03	10	TP	6F	D	Honest Deceiver	D'Amico,Anthony	50,000	31,300
WitchesBrw	31-Oct-03	7	MED	5F	T	Tangier Sound	Pimentel,Julian	42,280	24,000
WithersG3	3-May-03	9	AQU	1M	D	Spite the Devil	Chavez,Luis	150,000	90,000
WllmHenHS.	3-May-03	8	IND	6F	D	Indy Energy	Prescott,Rodney	37,800	22,680
WLMcKntHG2	27-Dec-03	11	CRC	1 1/2M	T	Balto Star	Velazquez,John	200,000	120,000
WlmcLSOaks	4-Jul-03	9	LS	1 1/16M	T	Petionville Indeed	Stanton,Terry	100,000	60,000
WLngBrnch	14-Jun-03	9	MTH	6F	D	Slews Final Answer	Pimentel,Julian	60,000	36,000
WmAlmyJr	10-May-03	8	SUF	6F	D	Dhaffir (CHI)	Piermarini,Tammi	35,000	21,000
WmAPurdeyH	20-Sep-03	9	MTH	1M 70Y	D	Powers Prospect	Ferrer,Jose	45,000	27,000
WMBailesMm	29-Jun-03	11	CNL	6F	D	Smashing Beau	Goodwin,Nik	50,000	30,000
WmKyne	26-Jan-03	8	PM	1 1/8M	D	Yesss	Beckner,Twyla	10,000	5,500
WnStDstHG3	26-May-03	10	LS	1M	T	Eagle Lake	Melancon,Gerard	200,000	120,000
WnStGlxyG2	5-Oct-03	6	KEE	1 3/16M	T	Bien Nicole	Pettinger,Donald	500,000	310,000
WntrSlstce	12-Mar-03	7	SA	6 1/2F	T	Repository	Valenzuela,Patrick	102,900	48,240
WodnStar	9-Nov-03	8	HAW	5F	T	Nicole's Dream	Baird,E.	44,000	26,400
WolfHill	7-Jun-03	10	MTH	5F	D	Native Heir	Rose,Jeremy	50,000	30,000
Wolverine	7-Jun-03	8	GLD	6F	D	Deputy Stripe	Doser,Mary	45,000	27,000
WondrDelit	13-Jun-03	6	PEN	6F	D	Tigress Bythetail	Clifton,Thomas	30,700	18,420
WondrWhere	4-Aug-03	8	WO	1 1/4M	T	Alpha Saphire	Ramsammy,Emile	250,000	150,000
WoodchoprH	27-Dec-03	9	FG	1 1/16M	T	Waupaca	Albarado,Robby	75,000	45,000
WoodfordCo	17-Oct-03	9	KEE	5 1/2F	T	Joe's Son Joey	Albarado,Robby	84,525	52,406
Woodlawn	17-May-03	5	PIM	1 1/16M	D	Gang	Mawing,Anthony	125,000	60,000
WoodlndHer	16-Aug-03	3	MD	6 1/2F	D	Allourwishes	Moccasin,Tim	10,000	6,000

Stakes	Date	Race	Trk	Dist/Surf	Winner	Jockey	Gross	Value to winner
WoodIndsH	1-Nov-03	9	WDS	1 1/16M D	Canyon de Oro	Kurek,Gary	30,000	18,000
WoodMemG1	12-Apr-03	8	AQU	1 1/8M D	Empire Maker	Bailey,Jerry	750,000	450,000
WoodsideH	20-Apr-03	8	BM	5F T	Maria's Mirage	Jauregui,Luis	78,850	33,850
Woodstock	19-Apr-03	8	WO	6F D	Wando	Kabel,Todd	135,875	81,525
WoodwardG1	6-Sep-03	9	BEL	1 1/8M D	Mineshaft	Albarado,Robby	500,000	300,000
WorkCrowdH	5-Jan-03	8	GG	1M D	Bob's Lady	Baze,Russell	100,000	55,000
WoSltCpHG3	8-Nov-03	8	WO	1 1/16M D	No Comprende	Husbands,Patrick	166,650	99,990
WPCAOpen	15-Jun-03	7	LBG	7F D	Candid Remark	Sterr,Scott	11,200	6,160
WpgFut	4-Aug-03	5	ASD	6F D	Ghostly Gate	Bell,Derek	40,000	24,490
WProctrMem	18-May-03	8	HOL	5F D	Alpenfest	Espinoza,Victor	99,675	59,805
WRCluerMmH	1-Nov-03	8	TUP	7 1/2F T	Jila (IRE)	Ruis,Mick	35,000	21,000
WrldAppeal	10-Oct-03	8	MED	1M 70Y T	Shining Hawk	Chavez,Jorge	40,000	24,000
WRTurfClG1	3-May-03	9	CD	1 1/8M D	Honor in War	Flores,David	445,300	276,086
WschstrHG3	7-May-03	8	BEL	1M D	Najran	Prado,Edgar	109,700	65,820
WSnappMem	25-May-03	9	BOI	7F D	Quiet Syns	Conklin,Jay	8,800	5,280
WstrnBrdrs	11-May-03	7	CRC	6F D	Awesome of Course	Cruz,Manoel	42,225	27,335
WTBALads	30-Aug-03	9	EMD	1M D	Harvard Avenue	Baze,Gary	38,500	19,058
WthApprovl	16-Aug-03	4	WO	1 1/8M T	Puffer	Kabel,Todd	108,000	64,800
WtrfrdPrkH	17-May-03	9	MNR	6F D	Private Horde	Lumpkins,Jason	76,900	46,140
WVaChrmCpH	9-Aug-03	5	MNR	4 1/2F D	Baby Shark	Dunkelberger,Travis	87,800	52,680
WVaGovnrsH	9-Aug-03	9	MNR	1 1/16M D	Be Like Mike	Chavez,Jorge	102,825	61,697
WVaSpkrCpH	9-Aug-03	4	MNR	1M T	Proud Man	Prado,Edgar	87,800	52,680
WVBrdrClsc	11-Oct-03	7	CT	1 1/8M D	Cape Power	Mawing,Anthony	250,000	112,500
WVCvdaBrCl	11-Oct-03	6	CT	7F D	Sweet Annuity	Cornwell,Richard	150,000	67,500
WVDerbyG3	9-Aug-03	8	MNR	1 1/8M D	Soto	Dominguez,Ramon	600,000	360,000
WVDivTrBCl	11-Oct-03	2	CT	7F D	Ketch a Hello	Richards,Gary	75,000	33,750
WVDs4CsBrC	11-Oct-03	4	CT	4 1/2F D	Earth Power	Reynolds,Larry	75,000	34,425
WVFuturity	15-Nov-03	6	CT	7F D	Petes Hick Chick	Torres,Raymond	39,350	25,578
WVFuturity	15-Nov-03	4	CT	7F D	Take the Plunge	Martin,Christopher	39,350	25,578
WVLotBrCl	11-Oct-03	3	CT	7F D	Longfield Spud	Reynolds,Larry	75,000	33,750
WVMosBrCls	11-Oct-03	8	CT	6 1/2F D	Take the Plunge	Martin,Christopher	75,000	33,750
WVOnJcBrCl	11-Oct-03	5	CT	7F D	Tori's Thunder	Klinger,C.	75,000	33,750
WVPresCupH	9-Aug-03	3	MNR	1M T	Glorious Grace	McKee,John	88,300	52,980
WVSectrStH	9-Aug-03	2	MNR	6F D	Born to Dance	Eads,Jason	88,100	52,860
XtraHeat	27-Jun-03	8	BEL	6F D	Willa On the Move	Velazquez,John	65,550	39,330
YaddoH	15-Aug-03	8	SAR	1 1/8M T	Wake Up Kiss	Prado,Edgar	111,550	66,930
YaddoH	15-Aug-03	5	SAR	1 1/8M T	Dynamic Lisa	Day,Pat	112,550	67,530
YankeAfair	4-Oct-03	7	PHA	1 1/16M T	Oxford Tea Party	Cora,David	57,400	34,440
YankeeAffr	12-Apr-03	9	GP	5F T	Bop	Santana,Jozbin	75,000	45,000
YanksMusic	7-May-03	6	BEL	1M D	Message Red	Castellano,Javier	60,000	36,000
Yaqthan	13-Sep-03	6	KD	1M T	Naraingang (BRZ)	Deegan,Joseph	40,000	24,000
YavapaiH	28-Jun-03	8	YAV	6F D	Augustan	Karr,Stephen	15,000	8,250
YavClsscH	15-Jun-03	8	YAV	6F D	Dance for Gold	Gomez,Esteban	15,000	8,250
YavCoAzBrF	29-Jun-03	8	YAV	5F D	Shesgonnabeastar	Hernandez,Miguel	25,965	13,011
YavDerby	24-Aug-03	7	YAV	1 1/16M D	Beckstein	Lopez,Lorenzo	22,150	12,183
YavDstSrs	26-Aug-03	7	YAV	1 1/4M D	Cajun Bound	Gomez,Esteban	11,475	6,311
YavDwnsFut	1-Sep-03	8	YAV	6F D	River Cha Ching	Bridges,Kelly	27,383	13,900
YavSpntSrs	26-Aug-03	6	YAV	6F D	Fredexpo	Hernandez,Miguel	11,800	6,490
YellowRose	15-Nov-03	5	HOU	6F D	Confiding Winner	Beasley,Jeremy	50,000	30,000
YlwRibbnG1	28-Sep-03	7	SA	1 1/4M T	Tates Creek	Valenzuela,Patrick	500,000	300,000
YnkeeFashn	15-Feb-03	8	SUF	6F D	I'mbackinaction	Lozano, Jr.,Wilfredo	35,000	21,000
YoungMemFt	4-Jul-03	9	EVD	5F D	Ten Times Better	Smith,Guy	93,500	46,750
YrbBnBCHG3	24-May-03	7	BM	1 1/8M T	Chiming (IRE)	Nakatani,Corey	150,000	55,000
Zadracarta	30-Jun-03	8	WO	6F T	Alpha Heat	McAleney,James	107,000	64,200
ZanyTactcs	28-Sep-03	6	HAW	6 1/2F D	Coach Jimi Lee	Day,Pat	42,800	25,680
ZanyTactic	12-Apr-03	8	TUP	6F D	Flying Supercon	Hernandez,Miguel	24,276	14,280
Zydeco	1-Nov-03	9	DED	5F D	Raymond's Dream	Bourque,Steven	40,000	24,000

Histories of Grade 1 Stakes Events

ACORN STAKES, 1 Mile, 3-Year-Old Fillies,
Belmont Park, 2003 Purse: $250,000

Year	Winner	Age	Jockey	Wt.	Second	Wt.	Third	Wt.	Win Value	Time	Beyer
1931	Baba Kenny	3	W. Cannon	121	Lady Legs	113	Romanesque	113	$3,375	1:41.00	
1932	Top Flight	3	R. Workman	121	Parry	114	Unique	114	12,850	1:39.00	
1933	Iseult	3	H. Mills	114	Edelweiss	114	Illusive	114	10,650	1:40.60	
1934	Fleam	3	J. Stout	109	Dusky Princess	112	Lady Reigh	112	8,575	1:38.00	
1935	Good Gamble	3	S. Renick	112	Guiding Star	109	Sorrow	112	7,325	1:39.20	
1936	Blue Sheen	3	J. Stout	112	High Fleet	112	Split Second	121	10,600	1:39.00	
1937	Dawn Play	3	L. Balaski	109	Royal Raiment	112	Drawbridge	115	10,100	1:38.80	
1938	Handcuff	3	C. Kurtsinger	121	Invoke	121	Catalysis	121	10,325	1:40.40	
1939	Hostility	3	L. Haas	121	Wise Lady	121	Red Eye	121	12,100	1:39.80	
1940	Damaged Goods	3	J. Gilbert	121	Fairy Chant	121	War Beauty	121	12,025	1:37.00	
1941	Proud One	3	W. Eads	121	Cis Marion	121	Up the Hill	121	7,275	1:37.60	
1942	Zaca Rosa	3	C. Wahler	121	Vagrancy	121	Bonnet Ann	121	11,300	1:38.20	
1943	Nellie L.	3	W. Eads	121	La Reigh	121	Stefanita	121	10,320	1:38.60	
1944	Twilight Tear	3	C. McCreary	121	Whirlabout	121	Everget	121	10,815	1:37.00	
1945	Gallorette	3	E. Arcaro	121	Monsoon	121	Recce	121	7,930	1:38.00	
1946	Earshot	3	E. Arcaro	121	Bonnie Beryl	121	Rytina	121	9,480	1:37.20	
1947	But Why Not	3	W. Mehrtens	121	Harmonica	121	Alrenie	121	14,300	1:38.00	
1948	Watermill	3	E. Arcaro	121	Alablue	121	Pigreeny	121	12,525	1:37.00	
1949	Nell K.	3	D. Dodson	121	Gaffery	121	Adile	121	13,725	1:38.00	
1950	Siama	3	T. Atkinson	121	Next Move	121	Honey's Gal	121	12,600	1:37.20	
1951	Kiss Me Kate	3	W. Mehrtens	121	Wisteria	121	Jacodema	121	16,750	1:36.40	
1951	Nothirdchance	3	B. Green	121	Gorgeous Reded	121	Vulcania	121	16,550	1:38.00	
1952	Parading Lady	3	J.N. Hardinb'l.	121	Sufie	121	Lily White	121	18,650	1:38.80	
1953	Secret Meeting	3	J. Nichols	121	Wings o' Morn	121	Tritium	121	18,450	1:39.40	
1954	Riverina	3	W. Boland	121			Question Time	121	10,925	1:38.80	
	Happy Mood	3	P. Moreno	121							
1955	High Voltage	3	E. Arcaro	121	Sometime Thing	121	Hen Party	121	22,900	1:38.80	
1956	Beyond	3	C. McCreary	121			Levee	121	12,650	1:37.80	
	Princess Turia	3	H. Moreno	121							
1957	Bayou	3	R. Ussery	121	Teleran	121	Here and There	121	26,000	1:37.00	
1958	Big Effort	3	P. Anderson	121	Polamby	121	Lopar	121	22,952	1:37.40	
1959	Quill	3	R. Ussery	121	Cobul	121	Hope is Eternal	121	38,075	1:37.60	
1960	Irish Jay	3	H. Woodhouse	121	Airmans Guide	121	Sister Antoine	121	38,293	1:35.80	
1961	Bowl of Flowers	3	E. Arcaro	121	Black Darter	121	Seven Thirty	121	37,537	1:37.40	
1962	Cicada	3	W. Shoemaker	121	Tamarona	121	Upswept	121	37,992	1:35.60	
1963	Spicy Living	3	J. Combest	121	Nalee	121	Lamb Chop	121	39,097	1:37.20	
1964	Castle Forbes	3	J.L. Rotz	121	Sceree	121	Face the Facts	121	39,097	1:37.00	
1965	Ground Control	3	D. Pierce	121	Marshua	121	Up Oars	121	38,220	1:37.20	
1966	Marking Time	3	W. Shoemaker	121	Around the Roses	121	Moccasin	121	38,642	1:36.00	
1967	Furl Sail	3	J. Vasquez	121	Quillo Queen	121	Pepperwood	121	44,330	1:35.60	
1968	Dark Mirage	3	M. Ycaza	121	Another Nell	121	Gay Matelda	121	39,065	1:34.80	
1969	Shuvee	3	J. Davidson	121	Hail to Patsy	121	Big Advance	121	38,707	1:35.60	
1970	Royal Signal	3	G. Patterson	121	Cold Comfort	121	Luci Tee.	121	36,969	1:36.20	
1970	Cathy Honey	3	L. Pincay Jr	121	Missile Belle	121	Fast Attack	121	36,969	1:36.00	
1971	Deceit	3	J.L. Rotz	121	Sea Saga	121	Forward Gal	121	38,970	1:36.60	
1972	Susan's Girl	3	V. Tejada	121	Wanda	121	Stacey d'Ette	121	33,720	1:34.60	
1973	Windy's Daughter	3	B. Baeza	121	Poker Night	121	Voler	121	36,541	1:35.40	
1974	Special Team	3	M.A. Rivera	121	Stage Door Betty	121	Raisela	121	33,960	1:35.40	
1974	Chris Evert	3	J. Velasquez	121	Clear Copy	121	Fiesta Libre	121	33,960	1:36.00	
1975	Ruffian	3	J. Vasquez	121	Somethingregal	121	Gallant Trial	121	33,660	1:34.40	
1976	Dearly Precious	3	J. Velasquez	121	Optimistic Gal	121	Tell Me All	121	33,390	1:35.80	
1977	Bring Out the Band	3	D. Brumfield	121	Your Place or Mine	121	Mrs. Warren	121	33,690	1:36.80	
1978	Tempest Queen	3	J. Velasquez	121	Lakeville Miss	121	White Star Line	121	31,920	1:35.40	
1979	Davona Dale	3	J. Velasquez	121	Eloquent	121	Plankton	121	50,130	1:36.00	
1980	Bold 'n Determined	3	E. Delahoussaye.	121	Mitey Lively	121	Sugar and Spice	121	50,400	1:36.80	
1981	Heavenly Cause	3	L. Pincay Jr	121	Dame Mysterieuse	121	Expressive Dance.	121	50,850	1:35.20	
1982	Cupecoy's Joy	3	A. Santiago	121	Nancy Huang	121	Vestris	121	51,750	1:34.20	
1983	Ski Goggle	3	C.J. McCarron	121	Princess Rooney	121	Thirty Flags	121	69,360	1:35.00	
1984	Miss Oceana	3	E. Maple	121	Life's Magic	121	Proud Clarioness	121	135,720	1:35.80	
1985	Mom's Command	3	A. Fuller.	121	Le L'Argent	121	Diplomette	121	113,040	1:35.80	
1986	Lotka	3	J.D. Bailey	121	Dynamic Star	121	Life at the Top	121	113,580	1:35.20	
1987	Grecian Flight	3	C. Perret	121	Fiesta Gal	121	Bound.	121	113,580	1:35.20	
1988	Aptostar	3	R.G. Davis	121	Topicount	121	Avie's Gal	121	109,980	1:34.80	
1989	Open Mind	3	A. Cordero Jr	121	Hot Novel	121	Triple Strike	121	111,960	1:35.40	
1990	Stella Madrid	3	A. Cordero Jr	121	Danzig's Beauty	121	Seaside Attraction.	121	104,580	1:36.00	.95
1991	Meadow Star	3	J.D. Bailey	121	Versailles Treaty	121	Dazzle Me Jolie	121	103,680	1:37.40	.98
1992	Prospectors Delite	3	P. Day.	121	Pleasant Stage	121	Turnback the Alarm	121	113,400	1:35.00	.98
1993	Sky Beauty	3	M.E. Smith	121	Educated Risk	121	In Her Glory.	121	90,000	1:35.40	.103
1994	Inside Information	3	M.E. Smith	121	Cinnamon Sugar	121	Sovereign Kitty	121	90,000	1:34.20	.96

Year	Winner	Age	Jockey	Wt.	Second	Wt.	Third	Wt.	Win Value	Time	Beyer
1995	Cat's Cradle	3	C.W. Antley	121	Country Cat	121	Lucky Lavender Gal	121	90,000	1:37.40	92
1996	Star de Lady Ann	3	M.E. Smith	121	Yanks Music	121	Stop Traffic	121	90,000	1:34.60	96
1997	Sharp Cat	3	G.L. Stevens	121	Dixie Flag	121	Ajina	121	90,000	1:34.40	103
1998	Jersey Girl	3	M.E. Smith	121	Santaria	121	Brave Deed	121	120,000	1:36.32	99
1999	Three Ring	3	J.D. Bailey	121	Better Than Honour	121	Madison's Charm	121	120,000	1:36.16	92
2000	Finder's Fee	3	J. Velazquez	121	C'est L'Amour	121	Roxelana	121	120,000	1:37.38	97
2001	Forest Secrets	3	C.J. McCarron	121	Victory Ride	121	Real Cozzy	121	120,000	1:34.92	93
2002	You	3	J.D. Bailey	121	Willa on the Move	121	Bella Bellucci	121	150,000	1:34.05	97
2003	Bird Town	3	E.S. Prado	121	Lady Tak	121	Final Round	121	150,000	1:35.29	96

Beyer Index: 96.79

ALABAMA STAKES, 1 1/4 Miles, 3-Year-Old Fillies, Saratoga Race Course, 2003 Purse: $750,000

Year	Winner	Age	Jockey	Wt.	Second	Wt.	Third	Wt.	Win Value	Time	Beyer
1872	Woodbine	3	Gradwell	107	Nema	107	Sue Rider	107	2,650	2:06.20	
1873	Minnie W.	3	Ponton	107	Sallie Watson	107	Lizzie Lucas	107	3,050	2:01.60	
1874	Regardless	3	Sparling	107	Countess	107	Madge	107	3,100	2:00.20	
1875	Olitipa	3	Evans	107	Invoice	107	Planet Filly	107	2,800	2:00.20	
1876	Merciless	3	Sparling	107	Patience	107	Athlene	107	2,850	2:00.60	
1877	Susquehanna	3	Hayward	107	Zoo Zoo	107	Oriole	107	3,450	1:57.20	
1878	Belle	3	Hayward	113	Balance All	113	Invermoor	113	2,800	1:59.00	
1879	Ferida	3	Hughes	113	Clarissima	113	Scotilla	113	3,300	2:00.60	
1880	Glidelia	3	W. Donohue	113	Kitty J.	113	Bye and Bye	113	2,600	2:00.00	
1881	Thora	3	W. Donohue	113	Bonnie Lizzie	113	Brambaletta	113	1,450	1:59.20	
1882	Belle of Runnymede	3	Stoval	113	Bonella	113	Olivia	113	3,250	2:08.60	
1883	Miss Woodford	3	J. McLaughlin	113	Bessie	113	Vera	113	3,050	1:57.20	
1884	Tolu	3	Blaylock	113	Mittie B	113	Eulogy	113	3,500	2:01.00	
1885	Ida Hope	3	I. Murphy	113	Elizabeth	113	Banana	113	3,225	1:59.00	
1886	Millie	3	J. McLaughlin	113	Molly McCarthy'sLast	113	Charity	113	3,550	1:59.20	
1887	Grisette	3	West	108	Flageoletta	113	Florimore	113	3,000	2:00.20	
1888	Bella B.	3	J. McLaughlin	115	Los Angeles	113	Prose	108	3,675	1:58.00	
1889	Princess Bowling	3	I. Murphy	114	Cotillion	108	Retrieve	113	2,650	2:03.20	
1890	Sinaloa II	3	Barnes	113	Eminence	110	Daisy F.	113	3,750	1:56.20	
1891	Sallie McClelland	3	Anderson	112	Santa Anna	111			2,075	2:05.60	
1892	Ignite	3	Clayton	112	Engarita	117	Miss Dixie	117	2,475	1:57.20	
1897	Poetess	3	C. Thorpe	114	Sunny Slope	121	Partridge	114	1,425	2:01.20	
1901	Morningside	3	N. Turner	116	Reina	121	Sweet Lavender	110	1,900	1:47.80	
1902	Par Excellence	3	Redfern	116	Lux Casta	116	Josepha	116	3,850	1:47.60	
1903	Stamping Ground	3	Fuller	116	Gravina	116	Astarita	124	4,625	1:56.80	
1904	Beldame	3	O'Neill	124	Dimple	116	Ishlana	116	3,850	1:53.60	
1905	Tradition	3	W. Davis	124	Kiamesha	116	Golden Ten	121	4,850	2:16.40	
1906	Running Water	3	W. Miller	116	Brookdale Nymph	124	Comedienne	121	3,850	1:52.40	
1907	Kennyetto	3	Notter	116	Gold Lady	124	Yankee Girl	124	3,850	1:54.20	
1908	Mayfield	3	C.H. Shilling	106	Anonyma	106	Breckon	110	3,850	2:01.00	

Stamina finished first but was disqualified

Year	Winner	Age	Jockey	Wt.	Second	Wt.	Third	Wt.	Win Value	Time	Beyer
1909	Maskette	3	Scoville	124	Miss Kearney	116	Petticoat	116	3,850	1:59.40	
1910	Ocean Bound	3	C.H. Shilling	124	Cherryola	111	Marigot	111	3,850	1:55.00	
1913	Flying Fairy	3	T. Davies	113	Cadeau	113	Lodona	113	1,455	1:56.20	
1914	Addie M.	3	C. Burlingame	113	Casuarina	117	Early Rose	113	1,740	1:54.40	
1915	Waterblossom	3	E. Martin	126	Lady Rotha	126	Lady Teresa	109	1,160	1:57.60	
1916	Malachite	3	L. Lyke	109	Sprint	109	Jacoba	117	1,720	1:54.60	
1917	Sunbonnet	3	J. Loftus	124	Wistful	124	Fairy Wand	114	3,850	2:07.00	
1918	Eyelid	3	L. Ensor	117	Enfilade	124	Ballymooney	114	6,575	2:04.20	
1919	Vexatious	3	E. Ambrose	114	Milkmaid	124	Polka Dot	124	7,265	2:09.20	
1920	Cleopatra	3	L. McAtee	126	Ethel Gray	114	Edwina	117	7,275	2:07.80	
1921	Prudery	3	L. Fator	124	Bit of White	121	Chat. Thierry	117	7,275	2:04.20	
1922	Nedna	3	F. Keogh	114	Emotion	114	Prudish	124	8,050	2:08.00	
1923	Untidy	3	E. Sande	124	Sally's Alley	121	Sun Quest	114	8,950	2:05.40	
1924	Priscilla Ruley	3	J. Maiben	117	Princess Doreen	126	Sunayr	117	9,925	2:08.80	
1925	Maid at Arms	3	A. Johnson	124	Lightship	114	Sun Tess	114	10,625	2:07.00	
1926	Rapture	3	L. McAtee	124	Black Maria	126	Ruthenia	117	9,275	2:06.00	
1927	Nimba	3	H. Thurber	124	La Palina	114	Recreation	114	12,925	2:06.80	
1928	Nixie	3	D. McAuliffe	121	Valkyr	114	Darkness	114	11,550	2:10.20	
1929	Aquastella	3	P. Walls	121	Lisa	117	White Veil	117	11,775	2:04.80	
1930	Escutcheon	3	L. McAtee	117	Conclave	117	Flying Gal	121	13,875	2:04.20	
1931	Risque	3	E. Steffen	121	Tambour	126	Allez Vite	117	14,200	2:05.60	
1932	Top Flight	3	R. Workman	126	Parry	116	Laughing Queen	121	12,225	2:06.40	
1933	Barn Swallow	3	D. Meade	124	Swivel	121	Edelweiss	126	11,525	2:06.60	
1934	Hindu Queen	3	L Humphries	111	Bazaar	121	Fleam	125	11,050	2:05.00	
1935	Alberta	3	S. Coucci	111	Good Gamble	125	Judy O'Grady	111	7,350	2:05.20	
1936	Floradora	3	D. Brammer	111	High Fleet	125	Valse	111	7,525	2:06.60	
1937	Regal Lily	3	H. Richards	123	Recussion	111	Allowance	111	7,475	2:08.20	
1938	Handcuff	3	J. Westrope	125	Black Wave	114	Anaflame	111	8,275	2:07.40	

Year	Winner	Age	Jockey	Wt.	Second	Wt.	Third	Wt.	Win Value	Time	Beyer
1939	War Plumage	3	M. Peters	124	Bass Wood	111	Hostility	124	10,100	2:05.00	
1940	Calaminia	3	D. Meade	111	Fairy Chant	124	Piquet	122	9,450	2:04.80	
1941	War Hazard	3	C. McCreary	114	Pomayya	114	Dark Discovery	114	8,975	2:04.80	
1942	Vagrancy	3	J. Stout	126	Smiles	126			8,950	2:05.20	
	Bonnet Ann finished first but was disqualified										
1943	Stefanita	3	C. McCreary	117	Askmenow	124	Tack Room	114	11,425	2:04.40	
1944	Vienna	3	J. Stout	114	Twilight Tear	126	Thread o' Gold	117	18,170	2:03.60	
1945	Sicily	3	T. Atkinson	110	Be Faithful	110	Surosa	110	21,015	2:03.40	
1946	Hypnotic	3	E. Guerin	124	Bridal Flower	124	Alma Mater	108	18,250	2:04.20	
1947	But Why Not	3	E. Guerin	126	Cosmic Missile	122	Bee Ann Mac	112	17,975	2:05.00	
1948	Compliance	3	T. Atkinson	112	Alablue	108	Play Tag	108	16,900	2:06.00	
1949	Adile	3	E. Arcaro	112	Plunder	108	Gaffery	120	17,000	2:04.00	
1950	Busanda	3	R. Permane	108	Next Move	126	Antagonism	108	15,850	2:04.40	
1951	Kiss Me Kate	3	E. Arcaro	126	Vulcania	116	Aunt Jinny	122	15,250	2:05.60	
1952	Lily White	3	T. Atkinson	109	Enchanted Eve	114	Gay Grecque	109	17,000	2:05.80	
1953	Sabette	3	J. Higley	114	Grecian Queen	126	Cherry Fizz	109	18,800	2:06.00	
1954	Parlo	3	E. Arcaro	121	Moonsight	111	Open Sesame	111	20,550	2:06.00	
1955	Rico Monte	3	W. Boland	113	Blue Banner	114	Misty Morn	121	20,750	2:05.80	
1956	Tournure	3	E. Guerin	115	Dotted Line	121	Levee	124	18,600	2:05.40	
1957	Here and There	3	E. Nelson	113	Snow White	113	Outer Space	121	20,450	2:06.40	
1958	Tempted	3	R. Ussery	113	Spar Maid	113	Lopar	114	18,712	2:05.80	
1959	High Bid	3	H. Moreno	113	Miss Blue Gem	113	Rich Tradition	117	37,230	2:05.00	
1960	Make Sail	3	M. Ycaza	118	Clear Road	114	Rash Statement	121	38,205	2:04.00	
1961	Primonetta	3	W. Shoemaker	121	Mighty Fair	114	Bowl of Flowers	124	35,555	2:03.20	
1962	Firm Policy	3	J. Sellers	121	Lincoln Center	114	Cicada	124	37,050	2:06.00	
1963	Tona	3	M. Sorrentino	114	Lamb Chop	124	Prodana Neviesta	114	37,310	2:04.20	
1964	Miss Cavandish	3	H. Grant	124	Beautiful Day	114	Castle Forbes	121	36,530	2:03.20	
1965	What a Treat	3	J.L. Rotz	118	Terentia	114	Discipline	118	41,080	2:03.60	
	Discipline finished second but was disqualified and placed third										
1966	Natashka	3	W. Shoemaker	121	Lady Pitt	124	Prides Profile	114	36,790	2:04.20	
	Lady Pitt finished first but was disqualified and placed second										
1967	Gamely	3	W. Shoemaker	118	Treacherous	114	Muse	114	39,130	2:03.20	
1968	Gay Matelda	3	J.L. Rotz	118	Heartland	114	Miss Ribot	118	36,920	2:04.40	
	Heartland finished first but was disqualified and placed second										
1969	Shuvee	3	J. Davidson	124	Pit Bunny	114	Hail to Patsy	118	35,360	2:06.40	
1970	Fanfreluche	3	R. Turcotte	118	Hunnemannia	114	Office Queen	124	38,415	2:03.80	
1971	Lauries Dancer	3	S. Hawley	118	Alma North	118	Forward Gal	121	35,280	2:03.00	
1972	Summer Guest	3	R. Turcotte	121	Light Hearted	118	Betsy Be Good	114	32,640	2:03.40	
1973	Desert Vixen	3	J. Velasquez	119	Bag of Tunes	119	Summer Festival	116	35,620	2:04.20	
1974	Quaze Quilt	3	H. Gustines	121	Chris Evert	121	Fiesta Libre	121	33,660	2:02.60	
1975	Spout	3	J. Cruguet	121	Aunt Jin	121	Funalon	121	49,170	2:04.00	
1976	Optimistic Gal	3	E. Maple	121	Javamine	121	Moontee	121	48,555	2:01.60	
	Dona Maya finished second but was disqualified and placed fourth										
1977	Our Mims	3	J. Velasquez	121	Sensational	121	Cum Laude Laurie	121	66,060	2:03.00	
1978	White Star Line	3	M. Venezia	121	Summer Fling	121	Tempest Queen	121	64,920	2:04.00	
1979	It's in the Air	3	J. Fell	121	Davona Dale	121	Mairzy Doates	121	64,980	2:01.40	
1980	Love Sign	3	R. Hernandez	121	Weber City Miss	121	Sugar and Spice	121	65,880	2:01.00	
1981	Prismatical	3	E. Maple	121	Banner Gala	121	Discorama	121	66,000	2:02.40	
1982	Broom Dance	3	G. McCarron	121	Too Chic	121	Mademoiselle Forli	121	67,680	2:02.20	
1983	Spit Curl	3	J. Cruguet	121	Lady Norcliffe	121	Sabin	121	65,880	2:02.40	
1984	Life's Magic	3	J. Velasquez	121	Lucky Lucky Lucky	121	Class Play	121	86,100	2:02.60	
1985	Mom's Command	3	A. Fuller	121	Fran's Valentine	121	Foxy Deen	121	98,100	2:03.20	
1986	Classy Cathy	3	E. Fires	121	Valley Victory	121	Life at the Top	121	8,400	2:03.20	
1987	Up the Apalachee	3	J. Velasquez	121	Without Feathers	121	Fiesta Gal	121	138,720	2:04.20	
1988	Maplejinsky	3	A. Cordero Jr	121	Make Change	121	Willa on the Move	121	138,240	2:04.00	
1989	Open Mind	3	A. Cordero Jr	121	Dearly Loved	121	Dream Deal	121	136,320	2:01.80	
1990	Go for Wand	3	R.P. Romero	121	Charon	121	Pampered Star	121	139,440	2:04.20	
1991	Versailles Treaty	3	A. Cordero Jr	121	Til Forbid	121	Designated Dancer	121	130,560	2:00.80	111
1992	November Snow	3	C.W. Antley	121	Saratoga Dew	121	Pacific Squall	121	120,000	2:02.40	96
1993	Sky Beauty	3	M.E. Smith	121	Future Pretense	121	Silky Feather	121	120,000	2:02.60	99
1994	Heavenly Prize	3	M.E. Smith	121	Lakeway	121	Sovereign Kitty	121	120,000	2:03.40	98
1995	Pretty Discreet	3	M.E. Smith	121	Friendly Beauty	121	Rogues Walk	121	120,000	2:03.20	111
1996	Yanks Music	3	J.R. Velazquez	121	Escena	121	My Flag	121	120,000	2:02.00	110
1997	Runup the Colors	3	J.D. Bailey	121	Ajina	121	Tomisue's Delight	121	150,000	2:03.00	104
1998	Banshee Breeze	3	J.D. Bailey	121	Lu Ravi	121	Manistique	121	150,000	2:02.20	107
1999	Silverbulletday	3	J.D. Bailey	121	Strolling Belle	121	Gandria	121	150,000	2:03.41	107
2000	Jostle	3	M.E. Smith	121	Secret Status	121	Spain	121	240,000	2:02.71	115
2001	Flute	3	J.D. Bailey	121	Exogenous	121	Two Item Limit	121	450,000	2:04.72	101
2002	Farda Amiga	3	P. Day	121	Allamerican Bertie	121	You	121	450,000	2:01.88	106
2003	Island Fashion	3	J.R. Velazquez	121	Awesome Humor	121	Spoken Fur	121	450,000	2:05.08	101

Beyer Index: 104.71

Distance 1 1/8 miles prior to 1901, in 1904, and from 1906–16; 1 1/16 miles in 1901-02 and on turf in 1903; 1 5/16 miles in 1905

ANCIENT TITLE BREEDERS' CUP HANDICAP, 6 Furlongs,
3-Year-Olds and Up, Santa Anita, 2003 Purse: $156,625

Year	Winner	Age	Jockey	Wt.	Second	Wt.	Third	Wt.	Win Value	Time	Beyer
1985	Temerity Prince	5	W. Ward	120	Debonaire Junior	124	Bid Us	115	37,150	1:09.20	
1986	Groovy	3	J.A. Santos	123	Rosie's K.T.	117	Sun Master	114	49,450	1:08.20	
1987	Zany Tactics	6	J.L. Kaenel	123	On the Line	116	Carload	117	35,500	1:09.00	
1988	Olympic Prospect	4	L. Pincay Jr	123	Sebrof	118	Reconnoitering	114	55,630	1:09.00	
1989	Sam Who	4	L. Pincay Jr	120	Sunny Blossom	116	Don's Irish Melody	114	46,050	1:08.00	
1990	Corwyn Bay	4	E. Delahoussaye	118	Sensational Star	119	Yes I'm Blue	117	61,375	1:08.40	114
1991	Frost Free	6	C.J. McCarron	118	Answer Do	118	Sir Beaufort	113	61,525	1:08.66	104
1992	Gray Slewpy	4	K.J. Desormeaux	118	Trick Me	114	Light of Morn	117	62,950	1:08.48	103
1993	Cardmania	7	E. Delahoussaye	116	Music Merci	117	Bahatur	114	61,975	1:08.04	109
1994	Saratoga Gambler	6	Pedroza MA	113	Uncaged Fury	114	Concept Win	117	62,500	1:08.87	103
1995	Track Gal	4	Stevens GL	116	Siphon	117	Forest Gazelle	116	59,150	1:08.32	105
1996	Lakota Brave	7	E. Delahoussaye	116	Letthebighossroll	119	Paying Dues	118	93,700	1:08.16	106
	Criollito finished third but was disqualified and placed fourth										
1997	Elmhurst	7	C.S. Nakatani	114	Swiss Yodeler	113	Larry the Legend	116	95,000	1:08.82	100
1998	Gold Land	7	K.J. Desormeaux	117	A.P. Assay	116	Swiss Yodeler	114	94,020	1:08.50	105
1999	Lexicon	4	K.J. Desormeaux	116	Kona Gold	120	Regal Thunder	117	125,400	1:07.84	120
2000	Kona Gold	6	A. Solis	124	Regal Thunder	117	Elaborate	116	123,060	1:08.11	117
2001	Swept Overboard	4	E. Delahoussaye	116	Kona Gold	127	I Love Silver	116	124,260	1:07.67	122
2002	Kalookan Queen	6	A. Solis	119	Crafty C.T.	116	Mellow Fellow	117	125,625	1:08.26	109
2003	Avanzado	6	T. Baze	116	Captain Squire	117	Bluesthestandard	115	81,375	1:08.12	107

Beyer Index: 108.86

APPLE BLOSSOM HANDICAP, 1 1/16 Miles, Fillies and Mares, 4-Year-Olds and Up,
Oaklawn Park, 2003 Purse: $500,000

Year	Winner	Age	Jockey	Wt.	Second	Wt.	Third	Wt.	Win Value	Time	Beyer
1973	Levee Night	4	D. Gargan	115	Knightly Belle	120	Royal Pussycat	119	12,000	1:11.00	
1974	Big Dare	4	R. Ussery	116	Gallant Davelle	122	Sixty Sails	114	19,050	1:11.80	
1975	Susan's Girl	6	J. Nichols	124	Truchas	113	Matuta	114	36,720	1:42.40	
1976	Summertime Promise	4	D.G. McHargue	119	Baygo	114	Costly Dream	113	35,760	1:40.60	
1977	Hail Hilarious	4	D. Pierce	121	Kittyluck	112	Summertime Promise	119	82,290	1:41.40	
1978	Northernette	4	D. Brumfield	119	Taisez Vous	124	Cum Laude Laurie	121	74,130	1:42.00	
1979	Miss Baja	4	E. Maple	113	Kit's Double	114	Navajo Princess	121	106,800	1:43.00	
1980	Billy Jane	4	J. Lively	113	Jameela	118	Miss Baja	121	106,290	1:43.60	
1981	Bold 'n Determined	4	E. Delahoussaye	124	La Bonza	111	Karla's Enough	119	131,820	1:44.20	
1982	Track Robbery	6	E. Delahoussaye	124	Andover Way	120	Jameela	123	161,040	1:45.20	
1983	Miss Huntington	6	J. Velasquez	118	Sefa's Beauty	117	Queen of Song	114	172,620	1:44.80	
	Number finished second but was disqualified and placed fourth										
1984	Heatherten	5	S. Maple	116	Try Something New	121	Holiday Dancer	115	167,400	1:40.20	
1985	Sefa's Beauty	6	P. Day	120	Heatherten	127	Life's Magic	123	161,700	1:42.20	
1986	Love Smitten	5	C.J. McCarron	119	Lady's Secret	127	Sefa's Beauty	122	162,180	1:40.40	
1987	North Sider	5	A. Cordero Jr	122	Family Style	120	Queen Alexandra	119	162,300	1:41.20	
1988	By Land By Sea	4	F. Toro	121	Invited Guest	116	Hail a Cab	113	150,000	1:41.20	
1989	Bayakoa	5	L. Pincay Jr	120	Goodbye Halo	125	Invited Guest	116	150,000	1:41.60	
1990	Gorgeous	4	E. Delahoussaye	122	Bayakoa	126	Affirmed Classic	112	210,000	1:40.40	119
1991	Degenerate Gal	6	P. Day	115	Charon	121	Fit to Scout	116	300,000	1:41.20	108
1992	Paseana	5	C.J. McCarron	124	Fit for a Queen	121	Slide out Front	109	300,000	1:42.00	114
1993	Paseana	6	C.J. McCarron	124	Looie Capote	115	Luv Me Luv Me Not	114	300,000	1:41.80	107
1994	Nine Keys	4	M.E. Smith	116	Mamselle Bebette	116	Re Toss	117	300,000	1:42.00	102
1995	Heavenly Prize	4	P. Day	120	Halo America	116	Paseana	122	300,000	1:42.60	104
1996	Twice the Vice	5	C.J. McCarron	117	Halo America	115	Serena's Song	124	300,000	1:41.60	104
1997	Halo America	7	C.H. Borel	117	Jewel Princes	124	Different	121	300,000	1:40.95	113
1998	Escena	5	J.D. Bailey	117	Glitter Woman	119	Toda Una Dama	115	300,000	1:41.64	114
1999	Banshee Breeze	4	J.D. Bailey	122	Sister Act	114	Silent Eskimo	112	300,000	1:42.22	107
2000	Heritage of Gold	5	S.J. Sellers	118	Lu Ravi	114	Bordelaise	113	300,000	1:42.15	110
2001	Gourmet Girl	6	C.H. Borel	113	Lu Ravi	114	Lazy Slusan	116	500,000	1:42.75	110
2002	Azeri	4	M.E. Smith	117	Affluent	118	Miss Linda	118	300,000	1:43.00	105
2003	Azeri	5	M.E. Smith	123	Take Charge Lady	118	Mandy's Gold	116	300,000	1:43.00	105

Beyer Index: 109.36

Distance 6 furlongs 1973-74; 1 mile 70 yards from 1975-79

ARLINGTON MILLION, 1 1/4 Miles (Turf), 3-Year-Olds and Up,
Arlington Park, 2003 Purse: $1,000,000

Year	Winner	Age	Jockey	Wt.	Second	Wt.	Third	Wt.	Win Value	Time	Beyer
1981	John Henry	6	W. Shoemaker	126	The Bart	126	Madam Gay	117	600,000	2:07.60	
1982	Perrault	5	L. Pincay Jr	126	Be My Native	118	Motavato	126	600,000	1:58.80	
1983	Tolomeo	3	P. Eddery	118	John Henry	126	Nijinsky's Secret	126	600,000	2:04.40	
1984	John Henry	9	C.J. McCarron	126	Royal Heroine	122	Gato Del Sol	126	600,000	2:01.40	
1985	Teleprompter	5	T.A. Ives	126	Greinton	126	Flying Pidgeon	126	600,000	2:03.40	
1986	Estrapade	5	F. Toro	122	Divulge	126	Pennine Walk	126	600,000	2:00.80	

Year	Winner	Age	Jockey	Wt.	Second	Wt.	Third	Wt.	Win Value	Time	Beyer
1987	Manila	4	A. Cordero Jr	126	Sharrood	126	Theatrical	126	600,000	2:02.40	
1988	Mill Native	4	C.B. Asmussen	126	Equalize	126	Sunshine Forever	126	600,000	2:00.00	
1989	Steinlen	6	J.A. Santos	126	Lady in Silver	117	Yankee Affair	126	600,000	2:03.60	
1990	Golden Pheasant	4	G.L. Stevens	126	With Approval	126	Steinlen	126	600,000	1:59.60	113
1991	Tight Spot	4	L. Pincay Jr	126	Algenib	122	Kartajana	123	600,000	1:59.40	108
1992	Dear Doctor	5	C.B. Asmussen	126	Sky Classic	126	Golden Pheasant	126	600,000	1:59.80	108
1993	Star of Cozzene	5	J.A. Santos	126	Evanescent	126	Johann Quatz	126	600,000	2:07.40	115
1994	Paradise Creek	5	P. Day	126	Fanmore	126	Muhtarram	126	600,000	1:59.60	111
1995	Awad	5	E. Maple	126	Sandpit	126	The Vid	126	600,000	1:58.60	114
1996	Mecke	4	R.G. Davis	126	Awad	126	Sandpit	126	600,000	2:00.40	111
1997	Marlin	4	G.L. Stevens	126	Sandpit	126	Percutant	126	600,000	2:02.40	107
2000	Chester House	5	J.R. Velazquez	126	Manndar	126	Mula Gula	126	1,200,000	2:01.37	110
2001	Silvano	5	A. Suborics	126	Hap	126	Reddatore	126	600,000	2:02.64	118
2002	Beat Hollow	5	J.D. Bailey	126	Sarafan	126	Forbidden Apple	126	600,000	2:02.94	107
2003	Sulamani	4	D.R. Flores	126	Kaieteur	126			600,000	2:02.29	106
					Paolini	126					

Storming Home finished first but was disqualified and placed fourth

Run at Woodbine in 1988; not run 1998–99

Beyer Index: 110.67

ASHLAND STAKES, 1 1/16 Miles, 3-Year-Old Fillies, Keeneland Race Course, 2003 Purse: $551,750

Year	Winner	Age	Jockey	Wt.	Second	Wt.	Third	Wt.	Win Value	Time	Beyer
1937	Drowsy	3	R. Dotter	110	Ann Jones	110	Sparta	115	2,250	1:45.40	
1940	June Bee	3	K. McCombs	115	Flying Jane	115	Miss Co-Ed	112	2,575	1:13.80	
1941	Valdina Myth	3	B. James	121	Laatokka	112	Blue Lily	115	2,600	1:13.00	
1942	The Swallow	3	E. Arcaro	112	Spiral Pass	115	My Choice	115	2,800	1:17.00	
1943	Valdina Marl	3	F. Zufelt	118	Nippy	115	Askmenow	121	2,550	1:14.20	
1944	Harriet Sue	3	J. Higley	115	Darby Delilah	115	Paddle	109	4,275	1:11.80	
1945	Come and Go	3	C.L. Martin	112	Cross Bayou	112	No Blues	110	3,950	1:13.60	
1946	Sweet Caprice	3	F. Zufelt	115	Bogle	110	Tav	115	4,750	1:12.80	
1947	Cosmic Missile	3	W. Balzaretti	121	Ballarita	115	Happiness	109	9,600	1:12.40	
1948	Bewitch	3	N.L. Pierson	121	Silly Gyp	115	Lea Lark	112	8,250	1:12.00	
1949	Tall Weeds	3	C. McCreary	115	Wistful	115	Warsick	115	9,700	1:11.60	
1950	Wondring	3	H. Manifold	112	Famous Shake	115	Radiant	115	10,250	1:11.00	
1951	Sickle's Image	3	B. Fisk	121	Juliets Nurse	118	How	115	8,750	1:18.00	
1952	Free for Me	3	J.D. Jessop	112	Dalal	109	Fancy Step	115	8,972	1:12.00	
1952	Real Delight	3	E. Arcaro	114	Ave	115	Level Sands	115	8,972	1:11.80	
1953	Cerise Reine	3	D. Dodson	115	Bubbley	118	Sweet Patootie	121	13,997	1:12.20	
1954	Jenjay	3	P.J. Bailey	118	Queen Hopeful	121	Siskey	112	13,100	1:11.00	
1955	Insouciant	3	B. Fisk	112	Courtesy	113	Lea Lane	121	13,360	1:10.80	
1956	Doubledogdare	3	S. Brooks	121	Guard Rail	118	Warning Bell	114	12,027	1:11.40	
1957	Jota Jota	3	P. Anderson	114	Lori-El	115	Nile Lily	114	12,000	1:10.80	
1958	Ramadel	3	W. Hartack	115	Bug Brush	114	Fusilade	112	12,455	1:10.00	
1959	Hidden Talent	3	J. Sellers	115	Narissa	115	Tacking	115	13,072	1:09.80	
1960	Tingle	3	H. Hinjosa	112	Airmans Guide	121	Make Sail	118	16,745	1:10.20	
1961	Goldflower	3	S. Brooks	112	My Portrait	115	Ordie	115	16,640	1:10.60	
1962	Windy Miss	3	R.L. Baird	115	Summer Sea	112	Fortunate Isle	115	17,095	1:11.60	
1963	Sally Ship	3	M. Ycaza	113	Bonnie's Girl	118	Myristyl	115	15,632	1:09.00	
1964	Blue Norther	3	W. Shoemaker	121	Silver Dollar	112	Roman Goddess	115	16,347	1:09.00	
1965	Terentia	3	J. Nichols	112	May's Guide	112	Little Gray Pet	115	15,015	1:10.60	
1965	Bright Bauble	3	K. Knapp	115	Saber Dance	118	Respected	121	14,885	1:10.20	
1966	Justakiss	3	R.J. Campbell	121	Prides Profile	121	Champagne Woman	118	19,532	1:10.00	
1967	Dun-Cee	3	W. Harmatz	115	Furl Sail	118	Woozem	121	19,337	1:09.40	
1968	Miss Swapsco	3	D. Richard	115	Moss	112	Fish Net	118	19,597	1:08.80	
1969	Double Delta	3	C.H. Marquez	115	Nutty Donut	121	Bold Heiress	115	19,565	1:10.00	
1970	Gay Missile	3	R. Broussard	116	Kankakee Miss	115	Three Pigeons	118	20,816	1:10.00	
1971	You All	3	K. Knapp	115	Deceit	121	Silent Beauty	118	20,897	1:11.00	
1972	Barely Even	3	J.L. Rotz	121	Wac	112	La Brisa	115	23,579	1:11.00	

Happens Song finished first but was disqualified and placed eighth

Year	Winner	Age	Jockey	Wt.	Second	Wt.	Third	Wt.	Win Value	Time	Beyer
1973	Raging Whirl	3	W. Sorez	113	Protest	116	A Little Lovin	110	23,611	1:10.80	
1974	Winged Wishes	3	D. Brumfield	116	Cherished Moment	117	Jay Bar Pet	113	29,786	1:28.80	
1974	Maud Muller	3	D. Brumfield	114	Clemanna	113	Irish Sonnet	119	29,834	1:27.00	
1975	Sun and Snow	3	G. Patterson	116	My Juliet	116	Red Cross	114	39,487	1:26.60	
1976	Optimistic Gal	3	B. Baeza	121	Alvarada	116	Confort Zone	113	37,895	1:26.80	
1977	Sound of Summer	3	F. Toro	118	Mrs. Warren	121	Our Mims	118	40,333	1:26.80	
1978	Mucchina	3	J. Amy	113	Grenzen	121	Bold Rendezvous	118	40,527	1:27.20	
1979	Candy Eclair	3	A.S. Black	121	Himalayan	114	Countess North	115	39,618	1:27.00	
1980	Flos Forum	3	R.P. Romero	112	Cerada Ridge	114	Lady Taurian Peace	116	41,210	1:26.40	
1980	Sugar and Spice	3	J. Fell	113	Nice and Sharp	114	Satin Ribera	116	41,210	1:27.20	
1981	Truly Bound	3	W. Shoemaker	121	Wayward Lass	121	Dame Mysterieuse	121	56,778	1:44.00	
1982	Blush With Pride	3	W. Shoemaker	118	Exclusive Love	116	Delicate Ice	113	83,070	1:45.00	
1983	Princess Rooney	3	J. Vasquez	121	Shamivor	114	Decision	116	74,133	1:45.40	

Year	Winner	Age	Jockey	Wt.	Second	Wt.	Third	Wt.	Win Value	Time	Beyer
1984	Enumerating	3	D. Brumfield	114	Miss Oceana	121	Rose of Ashes	113	88,708	1:49.20	
1985	Koluctoo's Jill	3	R.P. Romero	118	Lucy Manette	121	Foxy Deen	121	74,718	1:44.40	
1986	Classy Cathy	3	E. Fires	116	She's a Mystery	116	Patricia J.K.	121	116,513	1:44.00	
1987	Chic Shirine	3	S. Hawley	118	Buryyourbelief	113	Our Little Margie	121	117,683	1:44.60	
1988	Willa on the Move	3	C.J. McCarron	118	On to Royalty	121	Colonial Waters	121	151,125	1:45.80	
1989	Gorgeous	3	E. Delahoussaye	118	Blondeinamotel	115	Some Romance	121	157,430	1:43.20	
1990	Go for Wand	3	R.P. Romero	121	Charon	121	Piper Piper	112	145,665	1:43.60	107
1991	Do It With Style	3	S.J. Sellers	115	Private Treasure	121	Til Forbid	112	182,894	1:43.60	92
1992	Prospectors Delite	3	C. Perret	121	Spinning Round	121	Luv Me Luv Me Not	121	186,063	1:42.60	97
1993	Lunar Spook	3	S.J. Sellers	121	Avie's Shadow	115	Roamin Rachel	115	171,973	1:43.40	95
1994	Inside Information	3	M.E. Smith	121	Bunting	112	Private Status	118	171,197	1:46.80	101
1995	Urbane	3	E. Delahoussaye	115	Conquistadoress	115	Post It	121	207,483	1:43.40	102
1996	My Flag	3	J.D. Bailey	121	Cara Rafaela	121	Mackie	118	335,265	1:42.60	98
1997	Glitter Woman	3	M.E. Smith	121	Anklet	121	Storm Song	121	337,125	1:43.80	104
1998	Well Chosen	3	C.R. Woods Jr.	115	Let	115	Banshee Breeze	120	344,410	1:43.00	96
1999	Silverbulletday	3	J.D. Bailey	123	Marley Vale	115	Gold From the West	115	337,280	1:41.72	108
2000	Rings a Chime	3	S.J. Sellers	116	Zoftig	116	Circle of Life	116	341,155	1:44.43	92
2001	Fleet Renee	3	J.R. Velazquez	116	Golden Ballet	123	Latour	120	357,275	1:43.77	104
2002	Take Charge Lady	3	A. D'Amico	123	Take the Cake	118	Belterra	120	345,805	1:43.29	109
2003	Elloluv	3	R.J. Albarado	120	Lady Tak	123	Holiday Lady	116	342,085	1:43.58	105

Beyer Index: 100.71

Distance 6 furlongs from 1941-73; about seven furlongs from 1974-80; for 3-year-olds and up, fillies and mares, prior to 1940; run at Churchill Downs, 1943-45.

BALLERINA HANDICAP, 7 Furlongs, Fillies and Mares, 3-Year-Olds and Up, Saratoga Race Course, 2003 Purse: $250,000

Year	Winner	Age	Jockey	Wt.	Second	Wt.	Third	Wt.	Win Value	Time	Beyer
1979	Blitey	3	A. Cordero Jr	111	Shukey	116	Bold Rendezvous	116	25,770	1:23.20	
1980	Davona Dale	4	J. Velasquez	119	Misty Gallore	124	It's in the Air	119	33,780	1:22.20	
1981	Love Sign	4	R. Hernandez	119	Jameela	122	Tell a Secret	113	32,400	1:22.60	
1982	Expressive Dance	4	D. MacBeth	122	Tell a Secret	113	Sprouted Rye	113	35,160	1:22.80	
1983	Ambassador of Luck	4	A. Graell	124	Number	119	Broom Dance	122	32,640	1:22.20	
1984	Lass Trump	4	P. Day	122	Adored	122	Sultry Sun	116	51,840	1:21.80	
1985	Lady's Secret	3	D. MacBeth	117	Mrs. Revere	116	Solar Halo	116	67,680	1:22.60	
1986	Gene's Lady	5	R.P. Romero	119	Le Slew	116	Tea Room	110	81,420	1:22.40	
1987	I'm Sweets	4	E. Maple	119	Storm and Sunshine	116	Pine Tree Lane	122	82,260	1:22.60	
1988	Cadillacing	4	A. Cordero Jr	116	Thirty Zip	116	Ready Jet Go	111	69,000	1:21.60	
1989	Proper Evidence	4	C.W. Antley	116	Aptostar	119	Lake Valley	114	73,080	1:23.20	
1990	Feel the Beat	5	J.A. Santos	116	Fantastic Find	116	Proper Evidence	119	71,880	1:22.00	108
1991	Queena	5	M.E. Smith	119	Missy's Mirage	111	Dream Touch	110	72,240	1:22.00	104
1992	Serape	4	C.W. Antley	116	Harbour Club	116	Nannerl	122	71,160	1:21.20	103
1993	Spinning Round	4	J.F. Chavez	119	November Snow	119	Apelia	122	69,120	1:21.40	99
1994	Roamin Rachel	4	P. Day	118	Classy Mirage	123	Twist Afleet	113	65,040	1:21.80	105
1995	Classy Mirage	5	J.A. Krone	119	Inside Information	126	Laura's Pistolette	112	150,000	1:22.40	111
1996	Chaposa Springs	4	S.J. Sellers	120	Capote Belle	117	Broad Smile	114	90,000	1:21.80	107
1997	Pearl City	3	J. Bravo	110	Ashboro	115	Flashy n Smart	112	90,000	1:22.00	107
1998	Stop Traffic	5	S.J. Sellers	118	Runup the Colors	116	U Can Do It	115	120,000	1:22.23	106
1999	Furlough	5	M.E. Smith	114	Bourbon Belle	117	Catinca	121	120,000	1:23.04	103
2000	Dream Supreme	3	P. Day	113	Country Hideaway	117	Bourbon Belle	118	150,000	1:22.97	105
2001	Shine Again	4	J.L. Samyn	113	Country Hideaway	118	Dream Supreme	122	150,000	1:22.33	103
2002	Shine Again	5	J.L. Samyn	116	Raging Fever	121	Mandy's Gold	118	150,000	1:22.26	105
2003	Harmony Lodge	5	R. Migliore	115	Shine Again	120	Gold Mover	118	150,000	1:22.23	100

Beyer Index: 104.71

BELDAME STAKES, 1 1/8 Miles, Fillies and Mares, 3-Year-Olds and Up, Belmont Park, 2003 Purse: $750,000

Year	Winner	Age	Jockey	Wt.	Second	Wt.	Third	Wt.	Win Value	Time	Beyer
1939	Nellie Bly	3	J. Renick	102	Unerring	120	Bala Ormont	115	10,100	1:43.00	
1940	Fairy Chant	3	I. Anderson	119	Dotted Swiss	114	Dolly Val	121	14,050	1:50.80	
1941	Fairy Chant	4	I. Anderson	123	Imperatrice	116	Rosetown	126	14,450	1:51.00	
1942	Barrancosa	7	E. Arcaro	116			Rosetown	126	7,800	1:50.00	
	Vagrancy	3	J. Stout	119							
1943	Mar-Kell	4	B. Thompson	126	Stefanita	116	Vagrancy	122	20,050	1:51.60	
1944	Donitas First	3	T. Atkinson	112	Whirlabout	124	Moon Maiden	114	18,530	1:51.80	
1945	War Date	3	A. Kirkland	119	Letmenow	110	Light of Morn	105	24,100	1:51.00	
1946	Gallorette	4	J. Jessop	126	War Date	113	Kay Gibson	105	39,300	1:51.40	
1946	Bridal Flower	3	A. DeLara	114	Aladear	106	Jupiter Light	108	39,300	1:52.20	
1947	Snow Goose	3	T. Atkinson	106	Gallorette	126	Camargo	112	41,500	1:52.00	
1947	But Why Not	3	E. Arcaro	120	Miss Grillo	126	Elpis	123	42,250	1:51.80	
1948	Conniver	4	D. Dodson	121	Harmonica	114	Gallorette	124	49,700	1:52.40	
1949	Miss Request	4	E. Arcaro	113	Plunder	108	Mother	105	53,600	1:52.80	

Harmonica finished second but was disqualified

Year	Winner	Age	Jockey	Wt.	Second	Wt.	Third	Wt.	Win Value	Time	Beyer
1950	Next Move	3	N. Combest	116	September	108	Wistful	125	47,400	1:50.20	
1951	Thelma Burger	4	W. Shoemaker	110	Bed o' Roses	124	Kiss Me Kate	119	49,300	1:52.00	
1952	Next Move	5	E. Guerin	125	Renew	117	Nilufer	106	43,400	1:51.00	
1952	Real Delight	3	E. Arcaro	126	Marta	117	La Corredora	112	42,400	1:51.00	
1953	Atalanta	5	H.B. Wilson	121	Miss Traffic	106	La Corredora	119	47,600	1:52.20	
1954	Parlo	3	E. Guerin	116	Open Sesame	110	Clear Dawn	114	45,500	1:49.80	
1955	Lalun	3	H. Moreno	116	Clear Dawn	116	Countess Fleet	116	50,800	1:52.00	
1956	Levee	3	R. Broussard	115	Amoret	114	Searching	123	48,100	1:50.00	
1957	Pucker Up	4	W. Shoemaker	125	Plotter	119	Gay Life	104	51,200	1:49.40	
1958	Outer Space	4	W. Harmatz	117	A Glitter	119	Dotted Line	120	44,595	1:49.40	
1959	Tempted	3	E. Nelson	125	Idun	121	High Bid	113	42,905	1:50.20	
1960	Berlo	3	E. Guerin	119	Royal Native	123	Make Sail	119	57,615	1:49.40	
1961	Airmans Guide	4	H. Grant	123	Craftiness	123	Primonetta	118	62,400	1:49.40	
1962	Cicada	3	W. Shoemaker	118	Shirley Jones	123	Firm Policy	118	57,037	1:48.20	
1963	Oil Royalty	5	M. Ycaza	123	Lamb Chop	118	Smart Deb	118	56,972	1:51.00	
1964	Tosmah	3	S. Boulmetis	118	Miss Cavandish	118	Castle Forbes	118	52,552	1:49.60	
1965	What a Treat	3	J.L. Rotz	118	Steeple Jill	123	Straight Deal	118	53,430	1:49.20	
1966	Summer Scandal	4	W. Blum	123	Straight Deal	123	Lady Pitt	118	55,380	1:49.40	
1967	Mac's Sparkler	5	W. Boland	123	Triple Brook	123	Gamely	118	53,235	1:49.80	
1968	Gamely	4	L. Pincay Jr	123	Politely	123	Amerigo Lady	123	53,202	1:49.60	
1969	Gamely	5	L. Pincay Jr	123	Amerigo Lady	123	Shuvee	118	52,877	1:49.20	
1970	Shuvee	4	R. Turcotte	123	Obeah	123	Cold Comfort	118	54,437	1:48.00	
1971	Double Delta	5	K. Knapp	123	Shuvee	123	Cathy Honey	123	49,710	1:48.60	
1972	Susan's Girl	3	L. Pincay Jr	118	Summer Guest	118	Chou Croute	123	67,680	1:48.40	
1973	Desert Vixen	3	L. Pincay Jr	118	Poker Night	118	Susan's Girl	123	65,880	1:46.20	
1974	Desert Vixen	4	L. Pincay Jr	123	Poker Night	123	Tizna	123	68,760	1:46.60	
1975	Susan's Girl	6	B. Baeza	123	Tizna	123	Pass a Glance	123	67,980	1:48.40	
1976	Proud Delta	4	J. Velasquez	123	Revidere	118	Bastonera II	120	64,920	1:46.80	
1977	Cum Laude Laurie	3	A. Cordero Jr	118	What a Summer	123	Charming Story	118	80,025	2:01.80	
1978	Late Bloomer	4	J. Velasquez	123	Pearl Necklace	123	Cum Laude Laurie	123	78,150	2:02.20	
1979	Waya	5	C.B. Asmussen	123	Fourdrinier	118	Kit's Double	123	97,050	2:06.20	
1980	Love Sign	3	R. Hernandez	123	Misty Gallore	123	It's in the Air	123	93,600	2:02.80	
1981	Love Sign	4	W. Shoemaker	123	Glorious Song	123			131,100	2:01.80	
					Jameela	123					
1982	Weber City Miss	5	A. Cordero Jr	123	Mademoiselle Forli	118	Love Sign	123	134,100	2:04.20	
1983	Dance Number	4	A. Cordero Jr	123	Heartlight No. One	118	Mochila	123	133,200	2:00.60	
1984	Life's Magic	3	J. Velasquez	118	Miss Oceana	118	Key Dancer	118	158,280	2:03.20	
1985	Lady's Secret	3	J. Velasquez	118	Isayso	123	Kamikaze Rick	118	160,920	2:03.60	
1986	Lady's Secret	4	P. Day	123	Coup de Fusil	123	Classy Cathy	118	189,600	2:01.60	
1987	Personal Ensign	3	R.P. Romero	118	Coup de Fusil	123	Silent Turn	118	182,100	2:04.40	
1988	Personal Ensign	4	R.P. Romero	123	Classic Crown	118	Sham Say	118	199,440	2:01.20	
1989	Tactile	3	R. Migliore	118	Colonial Waters	123	Rose's Cantina	123	170,100	2:05.20	
1990	Go for Wand	3	R.P. Romero	119	Colonial Waters	123	Buy the Firm	123	167,700	1:45.80	120
1991	Sharp Dance	5	M.E. Smith	123	Versailles Treaty	119	Lady D'Accord	123	150,000	1:48.00	101
1992	Saratoga Dew	3	W.H. McCauley	119	Versailles Treaty	123	Coxwold	123	150,000	1:46.80	108
1993	Dispute	3	J.D. Bailey	119	Shared Interest	123	Vivano	123	150,000	1:47.20	107
1994	Heavenly Prize	3	P. Day	119	Educated Risk	123	Classy Mirage	123	150,000	1:48.80	111
1995	Serena's Song	3	G.L. Stevens	119	Heavenly Prize	123	Lakeway	123	150,000	1:48.60	104
1996	Yanks Music	4	J.R. Velazquez	119	Serena's Song	123	Clear Mandate	123	240,000	1:47.00	111
1997	Hidden Lake	4	R. Migliore	123	Ajina	119	Jewel Princess	123	240,000	1:48.20	105
1998	Sharp Cat	4	C.S. Nakatani	123	Tomisue's Delight	123	Pocho's Dream Girl	123	240,000	1:46.20	119
1999	Beautiful Pleasure	4	J.F. Chavez	123	Silverbulletday	119	Catinca	123	300,000	1:47.74	113
2000	Riboletta	5	C.J. McCarron	123	Beautiful Please	123	Pentatonic	123	450,000	1:46.14	115
2001	Exogenous	3	J.J. Castellano	120	Flute	120	Spain	123	450,000	1:49.20	109
2002	Imperial Gesture	3	J.D. Bailey	120	Mandy's Gold	123	Summer Colony	123	450,000	1:50.63	105
2003	Sightseek	4	J.D. Bailey	123	Bird Town	120	Buy the Sport	120	450,000	1:49.27	107

Distance 1 1/16 miles in 1939; 1 1/4 miles from 1977-89; run at Aqueduct from 1939-56, 1959, 1962-68.

Beyer Index: 109.64

BELMONT STAKES, 1 1/2 Miles, 3-Year-Olds, Belmont Park, 2003 Purse: $1,000,000

Year	Winner	Age	Jockey	Wt.	Second	Wt.	Third	Wt.	Win Value	Time	Beyer
1867	Ruthless	3	J. Gilpatrick	107	De Courcey	110	Rivoli	110	1,850	3:05.00	
1868	General Duke	3	R. Swim	110	Northumberland	110	Fanny Ludlow	107	2,800	3:02.00	
1869	Fenian	3	C. Miller	110	Glenelg	110	Invercauld	107	3,850	3:04.20	
1870	Kingfisher	3	W. Dick	110	Foster	110	Midday	110	3,750	2:59.20	
1871	Harry Basset	3	W. Miller	110	Stockwood	110	By the Sea	107	5,450	2:56.00	
1872	Joe Daniels	3	J. Rowe	110	Meteor	110	Shylock	110	4,500	2:58.20	
1873	Springbok	3	J. Rowe	110	Count d'Orsay	110	Strachino	110	5,200	3:01.60	
1874	Saxon	3	G. Barbee	110	Grinstead	110	Milner	110	4,450	2:42.20	
1875	Calvin	3	R. Swim	110	Aristides	110	Aaron Penn'ton	110	4,200	2:39.20	
1876	Algerine	3	W. Donohue	110	Fiddlesticks	110	Barricade	110	3,700	2:40.20	

Year	Winner	Age	Jockey	Wt.	Second	Wt.	Third	Wt.	Win Value	Time	Beyer
1877	Cloverbrook	3	C. Holloway	110	Loiterer	110	Baden Baden	110	5,200	2:46.00	
1878	Duke of Magenta	3	L. Hughes	118	Bramble	118	Spartan	118	3,850	2:43.20	
1879	Spendthrift	3	S. Evans	118	Monitor	118	Jericho	118	4,250	2:42.60	
1880	Grenada	3	L. Hughes	118	Ferncliffe	118	Turenne	118	2,800	2:47.00	
1881	Saunterer	3	T. Costello	118	Eole	118	Baltic	118	3,000	2:47.00	
1882	Forester	3	J. McLaughlin	118	Babcock	118	Wyoming	115	2,600	2:43.00	
1883	George Kinney	3	J. McLaughlin	118	Trombone	118	Renegade	118	3,070	2:42.20	
1884	Panique	3	J. McLaughlin	118	Himalaya	118			3,150	2:42.00	
1885	Tyrant	3	P. Duffy	118	St. Augustine	118	Tecumseh	118	2,710	2:43.00	
1886	Inspector B.	3	J. McLaughlin	118	The Bard	118	Linden	118	2,720	2:41.00	
1887	Hanover	3	J. McLaughlin	118	Oneko	118			2,900	2:43.20	
1888	Sir Dixon	3	J. McLaughlin	118	Prince Royal	118			3,440	2:40.20	
1889	Eric	3	W. Hayward	118	Diablo	125	Zephyrus	118	4,960	2:47.00	
1890	Burlington	3	S. Barnes	118	Devotee	115	Padishah	113	8,560	2:07.60	
1891	Foxford	3	E. Garrison	118	Montana	117	Laurestan	112	5,070	2:08.60	
1892	Patron	3	W. Hayward	122	Shellbark	122			6,610	2:17.00	
1893	Comanche	3	W. Simms	117	Dr. Rice	122	Rainbow	119	5,310	1:53.20	
1894	Henry of Navarre	3	W. Simms	117	Prig	119	Assignee	115	6,880	1:56.20	
1895	Belmar	3	F. Taral	119	Counter Tenor	126	Nanki Pooh	126	2,700	2:11.20	
1896	Hastings	3	H. Griffin	122	Handspring	125	Hamilton II	110	3,025	2:24.20	
1897	Scottish Chieftain	3	J. Scherrer	115	On Deck	115	Octagon	122	3,550	2:32.20	
1898	Bowling Brook	3	F. Littlefield	122	Previous	122	Hamburg	122	7,810	2:32.00	
1899	Jean Bereaud	3	R.R. Clawson	122	Half Time	119	Glengar	122	9,445	2:23.00	
1900	Ildrim	3	N. Turner	126	Petruchio	126	Missionary	126	14,790	2:21.20	
1901	Commando	3	H. Spencer	126	The Parader	126	All Green	126	11,595	2:21.00	
1902	Masterman	3	J. Bullman	126	Ranald	126	King Hanover	126	13,220	2:22.20	
1903	Africander	3	J. Bullman	126	Whorier	126	Red Knight	126	12,285	2:23.20	
1904	Delhi	3	G. Odom	126	Graziallo	126	Rapid Water	126	11,575	2:06.60	
1905	Tanya	3	E. Hildebrand	121	Blandy	126	Hot Shot	126	17,240	2:08.00	
1906	Burgomaster	3	L. Lyne	126	The Quail	126	Accountant	126	22,700	2:20.00	
1907	Peter Pan	3	G. Mountain	126	Superman	126	Frank Gill	126	22,765	n/a	
1908	Colin	3	J. Notter	126	Fair Play	126	King James	126	22,765	n/a	
1909	Joe Madden	3	E. Dugan	126	Wise Mason	123	Donald McDonald	123	24,550	2:21.60	
1910	Sweep	3	J. Butwell	126	Duke of Ormonde	126			9,700	2:22.00	
1913	Prince Eugene	3	R. Troxler	109	Rock View	128	Flying Fairy	106	2,825	2:18.00	
1914	Luke McLuke	3	M. Buxton	126	Gainer	126	Charlestonian	123	3,025	2:20.00	
1915	The Finn	3	G. Byrne	126	Half Rock	126	Pebbles	126	1,825	2:18.40	
1916	Friar Rock	3	E. Haynes	126	Spur	126	Churchill	126	4,100	2:22.00	
1917	Hourless	3	J. Butwell	126	Skeptic	126	Wonderful	123	5,800	2:17.80	
1918	Johren	3	F. Robinson	126	War Cloud	126	Cum Sah	126	8,950	2:20.40	
1919	Sir Barton	3	J. Loftus	126	Sweep On	126	Natural Bridge	126	11,950	2:17.40	
1920	Man o' War	3	C. Kummer	126	Donnacona	126			7,950	2:14.20	
1921	Grey Lag	3	E. Sande	126	Sporting Blood	126	Leonardo II	126	8,650	2:16.80	
1922	Pillory	3	C.H. Miller	126	Snob II	126	Hea	126	39,200	2:18.80	
1923	Zev	3	E. Sande	126	Chickvale	126	Rialto	126	38,000	2:19.00	
1924	Mad Play	3	E. Sande	126	Mr. Mutt	126	Modest	126	42,880	2:18.80	
1925	American Flag	3	A. Johnson	126	Dangerous	126	Swope	126	38,500	2:16.80	
1926	Crusader	3	A. Johnson	126	Espino	126	Haste	126	48,550	2:32.20	
1927	Chance Shot	3	E. Sande	126	Bois de Rose	126	Flambino	121	60,910	2:32.40	
1928	Vito	3	C. Kummer	126	Genie	126	Diavolo	126	63,430	2:33.20	
1929	Blue Larkspur	3	M. Garner	126	African	126	Jack High	126	59,650	2:32.80	
1930	Gallant Fox	3	E. Sande	126	Whichone	126	Questionnaire	126	66,040	2:31.60	
1931	Twenty Grand	3	C. Kurtsinger	126	Sun Meadow	126	Jamestown	126	58,770	2:29.60	
1932	Faireno	3	T. Malley	126	Osculator	126	Flag Pole	126	55,120	2:32.80	
1933	Hurryoff	3	M. Garner	126	Nimbus	126	Union	126	49,490	2:32.60	
1934	Peace Chance	3	W.D. Wright	126	High Quest	126	Good Goods	126	43,410	2:29.20	
1935	Omaha	3	W. Saunders	126	Firethorn	126	Rosemont	126	35,480	2:30.60	
1936	Granville	3	J. Stout	126	Mr. Bones	126	Hollyrood	126	29,800	2:30.00	
1937	War Admiral	3	C. Kurtsinger	126	Sceneshifter	126	Vamoose	126	38,020	2:28.60	
1938	Pasteurized	3	J. Stout	126	Dauber	126	Cravat	126	34,530	2:29.40	
1939	Johnstown	3	J. Stout	126	Belay	126	Gilded Knight	126	37,020	2:29.60	
1940	Bimelech	3	F.A. Smith	126	Your Chance	126	Andy K.	126	35,030	2:29.60	
1941	Whirlaway	3	E. Arcaro	126	Robert Morris	126	Yankee Chance	126	39,770	2:31.00	
1942	Shut Out	3	E. Arcaro	126	Alsab	126	Lochinvar	126	44,520	2:29.20	
1943	Count Fleet	3	J. Longden	126	Fairy Manhurst	126	Deseronto	126	35,340	2:28.20	
1944	Bounding Home	3	G.L. Smith	126	Pensive	126	Bull Dandy	126	55,000	2:32.20	
1945	Pavot	3	E. Arcaro	126	Wildlife	126	Jeep	126	52,675	2:30.20	
1946	Assault	3	W. Mehrtens	126	Natchez	126	Cable	126	75,400	2:30.80	
1947	Phalanx	3	R. Donoso	126	Tide Rips	126	Tailspin	126	78,900	2:29.40	
1948	Citation	3	E. Arcaro	126	Better Self	126	Escadru	126	77,700	2:28.20	
1949	Capot	3	T. Atkinson	126	Ponder	126	Palestinian	126	60,900	2:30.20	
1950	Middleground	3	W. Boland	126	Lights Up	126	Mr. Trouble	126	61,350	2:28.60	
1951	Counterpoint	3	D. Gorman	126	Battlefield	126	Battle Morn	126	82,000	2:29.00	
1952	One Count	3	E. Arcaro	126	Blue Man	126	Armageddon	126	82,400	2:30.20	

Year	Winner	Age	Jockey	Wt.	Second	Wt.	Third	Wt.	Win Value	Time	Beyer
1953	Native Dancer	3	E. Guerin	126	Jamie K.	126	Royal Bay Gem	126	82,500	2:28.60	
1954	High Gun	3	E. Guerin	126	Fisherman	126	Limelight	126	89,000	2:30.80	
1955	Nashua	3	E. Arcaro	126	Blazing Count	126	Portersville	126	83,700	2:29.00	
1956	Needles	3	D. Erb	126	Career Boy	126	Fabius	126	83,600	2:29.80	
1957	Gallant Man	3	W. Shoemaker	126	Inside Tract	126	Bold Ruler	126	77,300	2:26.60	
1958	Cavan	3	P. Anderson	126	Tim Tam	126	Flamingo	126	73,440	2:30.20	
1959	Sword Dancer	3	W. Shoemaker	126	Bagdad	126	Royal Orbit	126	93,525	2:28.40	
1960	Celtic Ash	3	W. Hartack	126	Venetian Way	126	Disperse	126	96,785	2:29.60	
1961	Sherluck	3	B. Baeza	126	Globemaster	126	Guadalcanal	126	104,900	2:29.20	
1962	Jaipur	3	W. Shoemaker	126	Admiral's Voyage	126	Crimson Satan	126	109,550	2:28.80	
1963	Chateaugay	3	B. Baeza	126	Candy Spots	126	Choker	126	101,700	2:30.20	
1964	Quadrangle	3	M. Ycaza	126	Roman Brother	126	Northern Dancer	126	110,850	2:28.40	
1965	Hail to All	3	J. Sellers	126	Tom Rolfe	126	First Family	126	104,150	2:28.40	
1966	Amberoid	3	W. Boland	126	Buffle	126	Advocator	126	117,700	2:29.60	
1967	Damascus	3	W. Shoemaker	126	Cool Reception	126	Gentleman James	126	104,950	2:28.80	
1968	Stage Door Johnny	3	H. Gustines	126	Forward Pass	126	Call Me Prince	126	117,700	2:27.20	
1969	Arts and Letters	3	B. Baeza	126	Majestic Prince	126	Dike	126	104,050	2:28.80	
1970	High Echelon	3	J.L. Rotz	126	Needles n Pens	126	Naskra	126	115,000	2:34.00	
1971	Pass Catcher	3	W. Blum	126	Jim French	126	Bold Reason	126	97,710	2:30.40	
1972	Riva Ridge	3	R. Turcotte	126	Ruritania	126	Cloudy Dawn	126	93,540	2:28.00	
1973	Secretariat	3	R. Turcotte	126	Twice a Prince	126	My Gallant	126	90,120	2:24.00	
1974	Little Current	3	M.A. Rivera	126	Jolly Johu	126	Cannonade	126	101,970	2:29.20	
1975	Avatar	3	W. Shoemaker	126	Foolish Pleasure	126	Master Derby	126	116,160	2:28.20	
1976	Bold Forbes	3	A. Cordero Jr	126	McKenzie Bridge	126	Great Contractor	126	117,000	2:29.00	
1977	Seattle Slew	3	J. Cruguet	126	Run Dusty Run	126	Sanhedrin	126	109,080	2:29.60	
1978	Affirmed	3	S. Cauthen	126	Alydar	126	Darby Creek Road	126	110,580	2:26.80	
1979	Coastal	3	R. Hernandez	126	Golden Act	126	Spectacular Bid	126	161,400	2:28.60	
1980	Temperence Hill	3	E. Maple	126	Genuine Risk	121	Rockhill Native	126	176,220	2:29.80	
1981	Summing	3	G. Martens	126	Highland Blade	126	Pleasant Colony	126	170,580	2:29.00	
1982	Conquistador Cielo	3	L. Pincay Jr	126	Gato Del Sol	126	Illuminate	126	159,720	2:28.20	
1983	Caveat	3	L. Pincay Jr	126	Slew o' Gold	126	Barberstown	126	215,100	2:27.80	
1984	Swale	3	L. Pincay Jr	126	Pine Circle	126	Morning Bob	126	310,020	2:27.20	
1985	Creme Fraiche	3	E. Maple	126	Stephan's Odyssey	126	Chief's Crown	126	307,740	2:27.00	
1986	Danzig Connection	3	C.J. McCarron	126	Johns Treasure	126	Ferdinand	126	338,640	2:29.80	
1987	Bet Twice	3	C. Perret	126	Cryptoclearance	126	Gulch	126	1,329,160	2:28.20	
1988	Risen Star	3	E. Delahoussaye	126	Kingpost	126	Brian's Time	126	1,303,720	2:26.40	
1989	Easy Goer	3	P. Day	126	Sunday Silence	126	Le Voyageur	126	413,520	2:26.00	
1990	Go and Go	3	M.J. Kinane	126	Thirty Six Red	126	Baron de Vaux	126	411,600	2:27.20	111
1991	Hansel	3	J.D. Bailey	126	Strike the Gold	126	Mane Minister	126	1,417,480	2:28.00	111
1992	A.P. Indy	3	E. Delahoussaye	126	My Memoirs	126	Pine Bluff	126	458,680	2:26.00	111
1993	Colonial Affair	3	J.A. Krone	126	Kissin Kris	126	Wild Gale	126	444,540	2:29.80	104
1994	Tabasco Cat	3	P. Day	126	Go for Gin	126	Strodes Creek	126	392,280	2:26.80	106
1995	Thunder Gulch	3	G.L. Stevens	126	Star Standard	126	Citadeed	126	415,440	2:32.00	101
1996	Editor's Note	3	R.R. Douglas	126	Skip Away	126	My Flag	121	437,880	2:28.80	106
1997	Touch Gold	3	C.J. McCarron	126	Silver Charm	126	Free House	126	432,600	2:28.80	110
1998	Victory Gallop	3	G.L. Stevens	126	Real Quiet	126	Thomas Jo	126	600,000	2:29.16	110
1999	Lemon Drop Kid	3	J.A. Santos	126	Vision and Verse	126	Charismatic	126	600,000	2:27.88	109
2000	Commendable	3	P. Day	126	Aptitude	126	Unshaded	126	600,000	2:31.19	101
2001	Point Given	3	G.L. Stevens	126	A.P. Valentine	126	Monarchos	126	600,000	2:26.56	114
2002	Sarava	3	E. Prado	126	Medaglia d'Oro	126	Sunday Break	126	600,000	2:29.71	105
2003	Empire Maker	3	J.D. Bailey	126	Ten Most Wanted	126	Funny Cide	126	600,000	2:28.26	110

Beyer Index: 107.79

Run at Jerome Park prior to 1890; at Morris Park 189-1904; at Aqueduct 1963-67; no time taken 1906-07. Distance 1 5/8 miles prior to 1874; 1 1/4 miles 1890-92, 1895, 1904-05; 1 1/8 miles 1893-94; 1 3/8 miles 1896-903, 1906-25. Value to winner includes $1 million Triple Crown bonus for Bet Twice in 1987; Risen Star in 1988; and Hansel in 1991.

BEVERLY D. STAKES, 1 3/16 Miles (Turf), Fillies and Mares, 3-Year-Olds and Up, Arlington Park, 2003 Purse: $700,000

Year	Winner	Age	Jockey	Wt.	Second	Wt.	Third	Wt.	Win Value	Time	Beyer
1989	Claire Marine	4	C.J. McCarron	123	Capades	117	Gaily Gaily	123	300,000	2:01.80	
1990	Reluctant Guest	4	R.G. Davis	123	Lady Winner	123	Royal Touch	123	300,000	1:53.20	
1991	Fire the Groom	4	G.L. Stevens	123	Colour Chart	123	Miss Josh	123	300,000	1:53.40	107
1992	Kostroma	6	K.J. Desormeaux	123	Ruby Tiger	123	Dance Smartly	123	300,000	1:54.00	104
1993	Flawlessly	5	C.J. McCarron	123	Via Borghese	123	Let's Elope	123	300,000	1:55.60	103
1994	Hatoof	5	W.R. Swinburn	123	Flawlessly	123	Potridee	123	300,000	1:55.40	104
1995	Possibly Perfect	5	C.S. Nakatani	123	Alice Springs	123	Alpride	123	300,000	1:54.80	105
1996	Timarida	4	J.P. Murtagh	123	Perfect Arc	123	Alpride	123	300,000	1:54.00	109
1997	Memories of Silver	4	J.D. Bailey	123	Maxzene	123	Dance Design	123	300,000	1:54.20	110
2000	Snow Polina	4	J.D. Bailey	123	Happanunoit	123	Country Garden	123	300,000	1:55.87	105
2001	England's Legend	4	C.S. Nakatani	123	The Seven Seas	123	Spook Express	123	300,000	1:55.87	105
2002	Golden Apples	4	P.A. Valenzuela	123	Astra	123	England's Legend	123	420,000	1:56.75	109
2003	Heat Haze	4	J. Valdivia Jr	123	Bien Nicole	123	Riskaverse	123	420,000	1:55.94	104

Beyer Index: 106.18

(TOYOTA) BLUE GRASS STAKES, 1 1/8 Miles, 3-Year-Olds,
Keeneland Race Course, 2003 Purse: $750,000

Year	Winner	Age	Jockey	Wt.	Second	Wt.	Third	Wt.	Win Value	Time Beyer
1911	Governor Gray	3	G. Molesworth	119	Meridian	122	Any Port	122	2,350	1:15.20
1912	Sprite	3	C.H. Schilling	117	Wheelwright	122	Duval	122	1,447	1:51.20
1913	Foundation	3	C. Peak	122	Donerail	122	Gowell	117	906	1:51.20
1914	Bronzewing	3	J.McCabe	117	John Gund	122	Old Ben	119	2,068	1:51.80
1919	Regalo	3	F. Murphy	117	Under Fire	122	Sennings Park	122	3,005	1:51.60
1920	Peace Pennant	3	M. Garner	126	Donnacona	126	Damask	126	3,410	1:51.80
1921	Black Servant	3	N. Barrett	126	Behave Yourself	126	Uncle Velo	126	3,170	1:54.60
1922	Busy American	3	N. Barrett	126	Bet Mosie	126	Startle	121	3,130	1:55.80
1923	Bo McMillan	3	D. Connelly	126	Anna M. Humphrey	121	Aspiration	126	3,120	1:51.80
1924	Altawood	3	L. McDermott	126	Beau Butler	126	Bob Tail	126	3,080	1:51.60
1925	Step Along	3	E. Pool	126	Broadway Jones	126	Bill Strap	126	3,090	1:51.60
1926	Bubbling Over	3	E. Legere	126	Boot to Boot	126	Helen's Babe	121	6,975	1:57.80
1937	Fencing	3	J. Westrope	121	Billionaire	123	Brooklyn	123	4,855	1:49.60
1938	Bull Lea	3	I. Anderson	121	Menow	123	Redbreast	123	5,340	1:54.20
1939	Heather Broom	3	B. James	121	Third Degree	121	Viscount	121	5,575	1:51.00
1940	Bimelech	3	F.A. Smith	123	Roman	123	Bashful Duck	123	10,256	1:51.20
1941	Our Boots	3	C. McCreary	123	Whirlaway	123	Valdina Paul	121	10,042	1:52.40
1942	Shut Out	3	E. Arcaro	123	Bless Me	121	Equinox	121	9,250	1:53.80
1943	Ocean Wave	3	W. Eads	123	Amber Light	123	Crest	121	9,800	1:52.60
1944	Skytracer	3	M. Cafarella	121	Challenge Me	123	Alorter	123	9,500	1:53.40
1945	Darby Dieppe	3	M. Calvert	121	Fighting Step	123	Air Sailor	121	10,450	1:51.60
1946	Lord Boswell	3	E. Arcaro	123	Pellicle	123	In Ernest	121	11,900	1:51.20
1947	Faultless	3	D. Dodson	126	Riskolater	123	John's Pride	126	12,300	1:49.20
1948	Coaltown	3	N.L. Pierson	123	Billings	121	Shy Guy	121	16,050	1:52.60
1949	Halt	3	C. McCreary	121	Johns Joy	126	Wine List	121	16,050	1:52.60
1950	Mr. Trouble	3	D. Dodson	121	Oil Capitol	126	On the Mark	118	20,300	1:50.40
1951	Mameluke	3	R. Adair	121	Phil D.	126	Hall of Fame	121	20,750	1:54.40
1951	Ruhe	3	J.D. Jessop	123	Royal Mustang	121	Counterpoint	121	20,250	1:54.20
	Sonic finished first but was disqualified and placed fourth									
1952	Gushing Oil	3	S. Brooks	123	Cold Command	121	Smoke Screen	121	19,447	1:52.40
1953	Correspondent	3	E. Arcaro	121	Straight Face	126	Money Broker	126	19,967	1:49.00
1954	Goyamo	3	E. Arcaro	123	Hasseyampa	121	Admiral Porter	121	24,290	1:50.60
	Black Metal finished third but was disqualified and placed fourth									
1955	Racing Fool	3	H. Moreno	121	Jean's Joe	123	Munchausen	123	22,112	1:51.80
1956	Toby B.	3	R.L. Baird	121	Career Boy	126	Reaping Right	126	21,235	1:51.00
1957	Round Table	3	R. Neves	126	One-Eyed King	121	Manteau	121	19,600	1:47.40
1958	Plion	3	D. Erb	126	Warren G.	121	Flamingo	117	21,322	1:52.80
1959	Tomy Lee	3	W. Shoemaker	126	Dunce	121	Scotland	123	20,607	1:48.60
1960	Tompion	3	W. Shoemaker	126	Victoria Park	126	Lurullah	121	19,535	1:48.60
1961	Sherluck	3	B. Baeza	121	Flutterby	126	Mr. Consistency	126	22,250	1:48.60
1962	Ridan	3	M. Ycaza	126	Decidedly	121	Roman Line	126	21,580	1:47.60
1963	Chateaugay	3	B. Baeza	121	Get Around	121	Lemon Twist	121	19,695	1:48.00
1964	Northern Dancer	3	W. Hartack	126	Allen Adair	121	Royal Shuck	121	19,207	1:49.80
1965	Lucky Debonair	3	W. Shoemaker	126	Swift Ruler	126	Mr. Pak	121	19,760	1:49.00
1966	Abe's Hope	3	W. Shoemaker	123	Graustark	126	Rehabilitate	123	19,175	1:49.40
1967	Diplomat Way	3	J. Sellers	126	Proud Clarion	121	Gentleman James	126	20,345	1:49.60
1968	Forward Pass	3	I. Valenzuela	126	T.V. Commercial	126	Francie's Hat	121	20,995	1:47.80
1969	Arts and Letters	3	W. Shoemaker	126	Traffic Mark	126	Mr. Coincidence	123	20,182	1:47.80
1970	Dust Commander	3	M. Manganello	126	Corn Off the Cob	126	Naskra	126	21,434	1:51.20
1971	Impetuously	3	E. Guerin	121	Twist the Axe	126	Dynastic	121	22,441	1:49.40
1972	Riva Ridge	3	R. Turcotte	126	Sensitive Music	121	Thurloe Square	121	32,305	1:49.60
1973	My Gallant	3	A. Cordero Jr.	117	Our Native	123	Warbucks	117	37,765	1:49.60
							Impecunious	126		
1974	Judger	3	L. Pincay Jr.	123	Big Latch	117	Gold and Myrrh	114	42,607	1:49.20
1975	Master Derby	3	D.G. McHargue	123	Honey Mark	117	Prince Thou Art	123	39,877	1:49.00
1976	Honest Pleasure	3	B. Baeza	121	Certain Roman	121	Inca Roca	121	73,027	1:49.40
1977	For the Moment	3	A. Cordero Jr.	121	Run Dusty Run	121	Western Wind	121	77,578	1:50.20
1978	Alydar	3	J. Velasquez	121	Raymond Earl	121	Go Forth	121	77,350	1:49.60
1979	Spectacular Bid	3	R.J. Franklin	121	Lot O' Gold	121	Bishop's Choice	121	76,657	1:50.00
1980	Rockhill Native	3	J. Oldham	121	Super Moment	121	Gold Stage	121	84,208	1:50.00
1981	Proud Appeal	3	J. Fell	121	Law Me	121	Golden Derby	121	120,559	1:51.40
1982	Linkage	3	W. Shoemaker	121	Gato Del Sol	121	Wavering Monarch	121	127,774	1:48.00
1983	Play Fellow	3	J. Cruguet	121	Desert Wine	121	Copelan	121	121,924	1:49.40
	Marfa finished second but disqualified and placed fourth									
1984	Taylor's Special	3	P. Day	121	Silent King	121	Charmed Rook	121	133,883	1:52.20
1985	Chief's Crown	3	D. MacBeth	121	Floating Reserve	121	Banner Bob	121	127,740	1:47.60
1986	Bachelor Beau	3	L. Melancon	121	Bolshoi Boy	121	Bold Arrangement	121	171,290	1:51.20
1987	War	3	W.H. McCauley	121	Leo Castelli	121	Alysheba	121	148,135	1:48.40
	Alysheba finished first but was disqualified and placed third									
1988	Granacus	3	J. Vasquez	121	Intensive Command	121	Regal Classic	121	190,856	1:52.20
1989	Western Playboy	3	R.P. Romero	121	Dispersal	121	Tricky Creek	121	185,900	1:51.20

Year	Winner	Age	Jockey	Wt.	Second	Wt.	Third	Wt.	Win Value	Time	Beyer
1990	Summer Squall	3	P. Day	121	Land Rush	121	Unbridled	121	185,006	1:48.60	
1991	Strike the Gold	3	C.W. Antley	121	Fly So Free	121	Nowork All Play	121	260,520	1:48.40	
1992	Pistols and Roses	3	J. Vasquez	121	Conte di Savoya	121	Ecstatic Ride	121	325,000	1:49.00	104
1993	Prairie Bayou	3	M.E. Smith	121	Wallenda	121	Dixieland Heat	121	310,000	1:49.60	96
1994	Holy Bull	3	M.E. Smith	121	Valiant Nature	121	Mahogany Hall	121	310,000	1:50.00	113
1995	Wild Syn	3	R.P. Romero	121	Suave Prospect	121	Tejano Run	121	310,000	1:49.20	109
1996	Skip Away	3	S.J. Sellers	121	Louis Quatorze	121	Editor's Note	121	434,000	1:47.20	113
1997	Pulpit	3	S.J. Sellers	121	Acceptable	121	Stolen Gold	121	434,000	1:49.80	106
1998	Halory Hunter	3	G.L. Stevens	123	Lil's Lad	123	Cape Town	123	465,000	1:47.80	111
1999	Menifee	3	P. Day	123	Cat Thief	123	Vicar	123	465,000	1:48.66	107
2000	High Yield	3	P. Day	123	More Than Ready	123	Wheelaway	123	465,000	1:48.79	106
2001	Millennium Wind	3	L. Pincay Jr.	123	Songandaprayer	123	Dollar Bill	123	465,000	1:48.32	114
2002	Harlan's Holiday	3	E. Prado	123	Booklet	123	Ocean Sound	123	465,000	1:51.51	98
2003	Peace Rules	3	E.S. Prado	123	Brancusi	123	Offlee Wild	123	465,000	1:51.73	104

Beyer Index: **106.75**

Run at old Lexington track prior to 1937; run at Churchill Downs 1943–45

BREEDERS' CUP CLASSIC, 1 1/4 Miles, 3-Year-Olds and Up,
Santa Anita, 2003 Purse: $3,668,000

Year	Winner	Age	Jockey	Wt.	Second	Wt.	Third	Wt.	Win Value	Time	Beyer
1984	Wild Again	4	P. Day	126	Slew o' Gold	126	Gate Dancer	122	1,350,000	2:03.40	

Gate Dancer finished second but was disqualified and placed third

Year	Winner	Age	Jockey	Wt.	Second	Wt.	Third	Wt.	Win Value	Time	Beyer
1985	Proud Truth	3	J. Velasquez	122	Gate Dancer	126	Turkoman	122	1,350,000	2:00.80	
1986	Skywalker	4	L. Pincay Jr	126	Turkoman	126	Precisionist	126	1,350,000	2:00.40	
1987	Ferdinand	4	W. Shoemaker	126	Alysheba	122	Judge Angelucci	126	1,350,000	2:01.40	
1988	Alysheba	4	C.J. McCarron	126	Seeking the Gold	122	Waquoit	126	1,350,000	2:04.80	
1989	Sunday Silence	3	C.J. McCarron	126	Easy Goer	122	Blushing John	126	1,350,000	2:00.20	
1990	Unbridled	3	P. Day	121	Ibn Bey	126	Thirty Six Red	121	1,350,000	2:02.20	116
1991	Black Tie Affair	5	J.D. Bailey	126	Twilight Agenda	126	Unbridled	126	1,560,000	2:02.80	120
1992	A.P. Indy	3	E. Delahoussaye	121	Pleasant Tap	126	Jolypha	118	1,560,000	2:00.20	114
1993	Arcangues	5	J.D. Bailey	126	Bertrando	126	Kissin Kris	122	1,560,000	2:00.80	114
1994	Concern	3	J.D. Bailey	122	Tabasco Cat	122	Dramatic Gold	122	1,560,000	2:02.40	115
1995	Cigar	5	J.D. Bailey	126	L'Carriere	126	Unaccounted For	126	1,560,000	1:59.40	117
1996	Alphabet Soup	5	C.J. McCarron	126	Louis Quatorze	121	Cigar	126	2,080,000	2:01.00	115
1997	Skip Away	4	M.E. Smith	126	Deputy Commander	122	Dowty	126	2,288,000	1:59.00	120

Whiskey Wisdom finished third but was disqualified and placed fourth

Year	Winner	Age	Jockey	Wt.	Second	Wt.	Third	Wt.	Win Value	Time	Beyer
1998	Awesome Again	4	P. Day	126	Silver Charm	126	Swain	126	2,288,000	2:02.16	116
1999	Cat Thief	3	P. Day	122	Budroyale	126	Golden Missile	126	2,080,000	1:59.52	118
2000	Tiznow	3	C.J. McCarron	122	Giant's Causeway	122	Captain Steve	122	2,438,800	2:00.75	116
2001	Tiznow	4	C.J. McCarron	126	Sakhee	126	Albert the Great	126	2,080,000	2:00.62	117
2002	Volponi	4	J.A. Santos	126	Medaglia d'Oro	121	Milwaukee Brew	126	2,080,000	2:01.39	116
2003	Pleasantly Perfect	5	A. Solis	126	Medaglia d'Oro	126	Dynever	121	2,080,000	1:59.88	119

Beyer Index: **116.64**

Run at Hollywood, 1984, 1987, 1997; at Aqueduct, 1985; at Santa Anita, 1986, 1993, 2003; at Churchill Downs, 1988, 1991, 1994, 1998, 2000; at Gulfstream Park, 1989, 1992, 1999; at Belmont Park, 1990, 1995, 2001; at Woodbine, 1996; at Arlington Park, 2002

BREEDERS' CUP DISTAFF, 1 1/8 Miles, Fillies and Mares, 3-Year-Olds and Up,
Santa Anita, 2003 Purse: $1,834,000

Year	Winner	Age	Jockey	Wt.	Second	Wt.	Third	Wt.	Win Value	Time	Beyer
1984	Princess Rooney	4	E. Delahoussaye	123	Life's Magic	119	Adored	123	450,000	2:02.40	
1985	Life's Magic	4	A. Cordero Jr	123	Lady's Secret	119	Dontstop Themusic	123	450,000	2:02.00	
1986	Lady's Secret	4	P. Day	123	Fran's Valentine	123	Outstandingly	123	450,000	2:01.20	
1987	Sacahuista	3	R.P. Romero	119	Clabber Girl	123	Oueee Bebe	119	450,000	2:02.80	
1988	Personal Ensign	4	R.P. Romero	123	Winning Colors	119	Goodbye Halo	119	450,000	1:52.00	
1989	Bayakoa	5	L. Pincay Jr	123	Gorgeous	119	Open Mind	119	450,000	1:47.40	
1990	Bayakoa	6	L. Pincay Jr	123	Colonial Waters	123	Valay Maid	119	450,000	1:49.20	113
1991	Dance Smartly	3	P. Day	120	Versailles Treaty	120	Brought to Mind	123	520,000	1:50.80	107
1992	Paseana	5	C.J. McCarron	123	Versailles Treaty	123	Magical Maiden	119	520,000	1:48.00	105
1993	Hollywood Wildcat	3	E. Delahoussaye	120	Paseana	123	Re Toss	123	520,000	1:48.20	108
1994	One Dreamer	6	G.L. Stevens	123	Heavenly Prize	120	Miss Dominique	123	520,000	1:50.60	105
1995	Inside Information	4	M.E. Smith	123	Heavenly Prize	123	Lakeway	123	520,000	1:46.00	119
1996	Jewel Princess	4	C.S. Nakatani	123	Serena's Song	123	Different	123	520,000	1:48.40	114
1997	Ajina	3	M.E. Smith	120	Sharp Cat	120	Escena	123	520,000	1:47.20	108
1998	Escena	5	G.L. Stevens	123	Banshee Breeze	120	Keeper Hill	120	1,040,000	1:49.89	105
1999	Beautiful Pleasure	4	J.F. Chavez	123	Banshee Breeze	123	Heritage of Gold	123	1,040,000	1:47.56	109
2000	Spain	3	V. Espinoza	120	Surfside	120	Heritage of Gold	123	1,227,200	1:47.66	108
2001	Unbridled Elaine	3	P. Day	120	Spain	123	Two Item Limit	120	1,227,200	1:49.21	102
2002	Azeri	4	M.E. Smith	123	Farda Amiga	119	Imperial Gesture	119	1,040,000	1:48.64	111
2003	Adoration	4	P.A. Valenzuela	123	Elloluv	119	Got Koko	123	1,040,000	1:49.17	101

Beyer Index: **108.21**

Run at Hollywood, 1984, 1987, 1997; at Aqueduct, 1985; at Santa Anita, 1986, 1993, 2003; at Churchill Downs, 1988, 1991, 1994, 1998, 2000; at Gulfstream Park, 1989, 1992, 1999; at Belmont Park, 1990, 1995, 2001; at Woodbine, 1996; at Arlington Park, 2002; Distance 1 1/4 miles prior to 1988

BREEDERS' CUP FILLY AND MARE TURF, 1 1/4 Miles (Turf), Fillies and Mares, 3-Year-Olds and Up, Santa Anita, 2003 Purse: $972,020

Year	Winner	Age	Jockey	Wt.	Second	Wt.	Third	Wt.	Win Value	Time	Beyer
1999	Soaring Softly	4	J.D. Bailey	123	Coretta	123	Zomaradah	123	556,400	2:13.89	105
2000	Perfect Sting	4	J.D. Bailey	123	Tout Charmant	123	Catella	123	629,200	2:13.07	105
2001	Banks Hill	3	O. Peslier	119	Spook Express	123	Spring Oak	119	722,800	2:00.36	112
2002	Starine	5	J.R. Velazquez	123	Banks Hill	123	Islington	118	665,600	2:03.57	109
2003	Islington	4	K. Fallon	123	L'Ancresse	118	Yesterday	118	551,200	1:59.13	109

Beyer Index: **108**

Run at Gulfstream Park, 1999; Churchill Downs, 2000; Belmont Park, 2001; Arlington Park, 2002; Santa Anita, 2003; Distance 1 3/8 miles in 1999 and 2000

(BESSEMER TRUST) BREEDERS' CUP JUVENILE, 1 1/16 Miles, 2-Year-Olds, Santa Anita, 2003 Purse: $1,375,500

Year	Winner	Age	Jockey	Wt.	Second	Wt.	Third	Wt.	Win Value	Time	Beyer
1984	Chief's Crown	2	D. MacBeth	122	Tank's Prospect	122	Spend a Buck	122	450,000	1:36.20	
1985	Tasso	2	L. Pincay Jr	122	Storm Cat	122	Scat Dancer	122	450,000	1:36.20	
1986	Capote	2	L. Pincay Jr	122	Qualify	122	Alysheba	122	450,000	1:43.20	
1987	Success Express	2	J.A. Santos	122	Regal Classic	122	Tejano	122	450,000	1:35.20	
1988	Is It True	2	L. Pincay Jr	122	Easy Goer	122	Tagel	122	450,000	1:46.60	
1989	Rhythm	2	C. Perret	122	Grand Canyon	122	Slavic	122	450,000	1:43.60	
1990	Fly So Free	2	J.A. Santos	122	Take Me Out	122	Lost Mountain	122	450,000	1:43.40	
1991	Arazi	2	P.A. Valenzuela	122	Bertrando	122	Snappy Landing	122	520,000	1:46.40	101
1992	Gilded Time	2	C.J. McCarron	122	It'salilknownfact	122	River Special	122	520,000	1:43.40	87
1993	Brocco	2	G.L. Stevens	122	Blumin Affair	122	Tabasco Cat	122	520,000	1:42.80	97
1994	Timber Country	2	P. Day	122	Eltish	122	Tejano Run	122	520,000	1:44.40	100
1995	Unbridled's Song	2	M.E. Smith	122	Hennessy	122	Editor's Note	122	520,000	1:41.60	103
1996	Boston Harbor	2	J.D. Bailey	122	Acceptable	122	Ordway	122	520,000	1:43.40	99
1997	Favorite Trick	2	P. Day	122	Dawson's Legacy	122	Nationalore	122	520,000	1:44.00	97
1998	Answer Lively	2	J.D. Bailey	122	Aly's Alley	122	Cat Thief	122	520,000	1:42.29	102
1999	Anees	2	G.L. Stevens	122	Chief Seattle	122	High Yield	122	556,400	1:42.05	99
2000	Macho Uno	2	J.D. Bailey	122	Point Given	122	Street Cry	122	520,000	1:42.27	99
2001	Johannesburg	2	M.J. Kinane	122	Repent	122	Siphonic	122	556,400	1:49.61	102
2002	Vindication	2	M.E. Smith	122	Kafwain	122	Hold That Tiger	122	556,400	1:43.62	92
2003	Action This Day	2	D.R. Flores	122	Minister Eric	122	Chapel Royal	122	780,000	1:43.62	

Beyer Index: **98.38**

Run at Hollywood, 1984, 1987, 1997; at Aqueduct, 1985; at Santa Anita, 1986, 1993, 2003; at Churchill Downs, 1988, 1991, 1994, 199, 2000; at Gulfstream Park, 1989, 1992, 1999; at Belmont Park, 1990, 1995, 2001; at Woodbine, 1996; at Arlington Park, 2002; Distance 1 mile in 1984, 1985, and 1987; 1 1/8 miles in 2002

BREEDERS' CUP JUVENILE FILLIES, 1 1/16 Miles, 2-Year-Old Fillies, Santa Anita, 2003 Purse: $917,000

Year	Winner	Age	Jockey	Wt.	Second	Wt.	Third	Wt.	Win Value	Time	Beyer
1984	Outstandingly	2	W.A. Guerra	119	Dusty Heart	119	Fine Spirit	119	450,000	1:37.80	
	Fran's Valentine finished first but was disqualified and placed 10th										
1985	Twilight Ridge	2	J. Velasquez	119	Family Style	119	Steal a Kiss	119	450,000	1:35.80	
1986	Brave Raj	2	P.A. Valenzuela	119	Tappiano	119	Saros Brig	119	450,000	1:43.20	
1987	Epitome	2	P. Day	119	Jeanne Jones	119	Dream Team	119	450,000	1:36.40	
1988	Open Mind	2	R.P. Romero	119	Darby Shuffle	119	Lea Lucinda	119	450,000	1:46.60	
1989	Go for Wand	2	R.P. Romero	119	Sweet Roberta	119	Stella Madrid	119	450,000	1:44.20	
1990	Meadow Star	2	J.A. Santos	119	Private Treasure	119	Dance Smartly	119	450,000	1:44.00	98
1991	Pleasant Stage	2	E. Delahoussaye	119	La Spia	119	Cadillac Women	119	520,000	1:46.40	85
1992	Eliza	2	P.A. Valenzuela	119	Educated Risk	119	Boots 'n Jackie	119	520,000	1:42.80	92
1993	Phone Chatter	2	L. Pincay Jr	119	Sardula	119	Heavenly Prize	119	520,000	1:43.00	95
1994	Flanders	2	P. Day	119	Serena's Song	119	Stormy Blues	119	520,000	1:45.20	92
1995	My Flag	2	J.D. Bailey	119	Cara Rafaela	119	Golden Attraction	119	520,000	1:42.40	95
1996	Storm Song	2	C. Perret	119	Love That Jazz	119	Critical Factor	119	535,600	1:42.00	95
1997	Countess Diana	2	S. Sellers	119	Career Collection	119	Primaly	119	520,000	1:43.68	101
1998	Silverbulletday	2	G.L. Stevens	119	Excellent Meeting	119	Three Ring	119	520,000	1:43.31	93
1999	Cash Run	2	J.D. Bailey	119	Chilukki	119	Surfside	119	582,400	1:42.77	92
2000	Caressing	2	J.R. Velazquez	119	Platinum Tiara	119	She's a Devil Due	119	520,000	1:41.49	107
2001	Tempera	2	D.R. Flores	119	Imperial Gesture	119	Bella Bellucci	119	520,000	1:49.60	102
2002	Storm Flag Flying	2	J.R. Velazquez	119	Composure	119	Santa Catarina	119	520,000	1:42.75	99
2003	Halfbridled	2	J.A. Krone	119	Ashado	119	Victory U.S.A.	119	520,000	1:42.75	

Beyer Index: **95.93**

Run at Hollywood, 1984, 1987, 1997; at Aqueduct, 1985; at Santa Anita, 1986, 1993, 2003; at Churchill Downs, 1988, 1991, 1994, 1998, 2000; at Gulfstream Park, 1989, 1992, 1999; at Belmont Park, 1990, 1995, 2001; at Woodbine, 1996; at Arlington Park, 2002 Distance 1 mile 1984, 1985, and 1987; 1 1/8 miles in 2002

(NETJETS) BREEDERS' CUP MILE, 1 Mile (Turf), 3-Year-Olds and Up,
Santa Anita, 2003 Purse: $1,375,500

Year	Winner	Age	Jockey	Wt.	Second	Wt.	Third	Wt.	Win Value	Time	Beyer
1984	Royal Heroine	4	F. Toro	123	Star Choice	126	Cozzene	126	450,000	1:32.60	
1985	Cozzene	5	W.A. Guerra	126	Al Mamoon	126	Shadeed	123	450,000	1:35.00	
	Palace Music finished second but was disqualified and placed ninth										
1986	Last Tycoon	3	Y. Saint-Martin	123	Palace Music	126	Fred Astaire	123	450,000	1:35.20	
1987	Miesque	3	F. Head	120	Show Dancer	126	Sonic Lady	123	450,000	1:32.80	
1988	Miesque	4	F. Head	123	Steinlen	126	Simply Majestic	126	450,000	1:38.60	
1989	Steinlen	6	J.A. Santos	126	Sabona	126	Most Welcome	126	450,000	1:37.20	
1990	Royal Academy	3	L. Piggott	122	Itsallgreektome	122	Priolo	122	450,000	1:35.20	111
1991	Opening Verse	5	P.A. Valenzuela	126	Val de Bois	126	Star of Cozzene	123	450,000	1:37.40	110
1992	Lure	3	M.E. Smith	126	Paradise Creek	126	Brief Truce	122	520,000	1:32.80	112
1993	Lure	4	M.E. Smith	126	Ski Paradise	120	Fourstars Allstar	126	520,000	1:33.40	112
1994	Barathea	4	L. Dettori	126	Johann Quatz	126	Unfinished Symph	123	520,000	1:34.40	109
1995	Ridgewood Pearl	3	J.P. Murtagh	119	Fastness	126	Sayyedati	123	520,000	1:43.60	114
1996	Da Hoss	4	G.L. Stevens	126	Spinning World	122	Same Old Wish	126	520,000	1:35.80	114
1997	Spinning World	4	C.B. Asmussen	126	Geri	126	Decorated Hero	126	572,000	1:32.60	114
1998	Da Hoss	6	J. Velazquez	126	Hawksley Hil	126	Labeeb	126	520,000	1:35.27	114
1999	Silic	4	C.S. Nakatani	126	Tuzla	123	Docksider	126	520,000	1:34.26	110
2000	War Chant	3	G.L. Stevens	123	North East Bound	126	Dansili	126	608,400	1:34.67	108
2001	Val Royal	5	J. Valdivia Jr.	126	Forbidden Apple	126	Bach	126	592,800	1:32.05	114
2002	Domedriver	4	T. Thulliez	126	Rock of Gibraltar	122	Good Journey	126	556,400	1:36.92	113
2003	Six Perfections	3	J.D. Bailey	119	Touchoftheblues	126	Century City	126	780,000	1:33.86	105

Beyer Index: 111.43

Run at Hollywood, 1984, 1987, 1997; at Aqueduct, 1985; at Santa Anita, 1986,1993, 2003; at Churchill Downs, 1988, 1991, 1994, 1998, 2000; at Gulfstream Park, 1989, 1992, 1999; at Belmont Park, 1990, 1995, 2001; at Woodbine, 1996; at Arlington Park, 2002

BREEDERS' CUP SPRINT, 6 Furlongs, 3-Year-Olds and Up,
Santa Anita, 2003 Purse: $1,082,060

Year	Winner	Age	Jockey	Wt.	Second	Wt.	Third	Wt.	Win Value	Time	Beyer
1984	Eillo	4	C. Perret	126	Commemorate	124	Fighting Fit	126	450,000	1:10.20	
1985	Precisionist	4	C.J. McCarron	126	Smile	124	Mt. Livermore	126	450,000	1:08.40	
1986	Smile	4	J. Vasquez	126	Pine Tree Lane	123	Bedside Promise	126	450,000	1:08.40	
1987	Very Subtle	3	P.A. Valenzuela	121	Groovy	126	Exclusive Enough	124	450,000	1:08.80	
1988	Gulch	4	A. Cordero Jr	126	Play the King	126	Afleet	126	450,000	1:10.40	
1989	Dancing Spree	4	A. Cordero Jr	126	Safely Kept	121	Dispersal	124	450,000	1:09.00	
1990	Safely Kept	4	C. Perret	123	Dayjur	123	Black Tie Affair	126	450,000	1:09.60	116
1991	Sheikh Albadou	3	P. Eddery	124	Pleasant Tap	126	Robyn Dancer	126	520,000	1:09.20	113
1992	Thirty Slews	5	E. Delahoussaye	126	Meafara	120	Rubiano	126	520,000	1:08.20	111
1993	Cardmania	7	E. Delahoussaye	126	Meafara	123	Gilded Time	124	520,000	1:08.60	109
1994	Cherokee Run	4	M.E. Smith	126	Soviet Problem	123	Cardmania	126	520,000	1:09.40	114
1995	Desert Stormer	5	K.J. Desormeaux	123	Mr. Greeley	123	Lit de Justice	126	520,000	1:09.00	107
1996	Lit de Justice	6	C.S. Nakatani	126	Paying Dues	126	Honour and Glory	123	520,000	1:08.60	114
1997	Elmhurst	7	C.S. Nakatani	126	Hesabull	126	Bet on Sunshine	126	613,600	1:08.00	111
1998	Reraise	3	C.S. Nakatani	124	Grand Slam	124	Kona Gold	126	572,000	1:09.07	112
1999	Artax	4	J.F. Chavez	126	Kona Gold	126	Big Jag	126	624,000	1:07.89	124
2000	Kona Gold	6	A. Solis	126	Honest Lady	123	Bet on Sunshine	126	520,000	1:07.77	114
2001	Squirtle Squirt	3	J.D. Bailey	126	Xtra Heat	121	Caller One	126	520,000	1:08.41	119
2002	Orientate	4	J.D. Bailey	126	Thunderello	123	Crafty C. T	126	592,800	1:08.89	114
2003	Cajun Beat	3	C.H. Velasquez	123	Bluesthestandard	126	Shake You Down	126	613,600	1:07.95	120

Beyer Index: 114.14

Run at Hollywood, 1984, 1987, 1997; at Aqueduct, 1985; at Santa Anita, 1986,1993, 2003; at Churchill Downs, 1988, 1991, 1994, 1998, 2000; at Gulfstream Park, 1989, 1992, 1999; at Belmont Park, 1990, 1995, 2001; at Woodbine, 1996; at Arlington Park, 2002

(JOHN DEERE) BREEDERS' CUP TURF, 1 1/2 Miles (Turf), 3-Year-Olds and Up,
Santa Anita, 2003 Purse: $1,944,040

Year	Winner	Age	Jockey	Wt.	Second	Wt.	Third	Wt.	Win Value	Time	Beyer
1984	Lashkari	3	Y. Saint-Martin	122	All Along	123	Raami	122	900,000	2:25.20	
1985	Pebbles	4	P. Eddery	123	Strawberry Road II	126	Mourjane	126	900,000	2:27.00	
1986	Manila	3	J.A. Santos	122	Theatrical	126	Estrapade	123	900,000	2:25.40	
1987	Theatrical	5	P. Day	126	Trempolino	122	Village Star II	126	900,000	2:24.40	
1988	Great Communicator	5	R. Sibille	126	Sunshine Forever	122	Indian Skimmer	123	900,000	2:35.20	
1989	Prized	3	E. Delahoussaye	122	Sierra Roberta	119	Star Lift	126	900,000	2:28.00	
1990	In the Wings	4	G.L. Stevens	126	With Approval	126	El Senor	126	900,000	2:29.60	113
1991	Miss Alleged	4	E. Legrix	123	Itsallgreektome	126	Quest for Fame	126	1,040,000	2:30.80	111
1992	Fraise	4	P.A. Valenzuela	126	Sky Classic	126	Quest for Fame	126	1,040,000	2:24.00	110
1993	Kotashaan	5	K.J. Desormeaux	126	Bien Bien	126	Luazur	126	1,040,000	2:25.00	111
1994	Tikkanen	3	M.E. Smith	122	Hatoof	123	Paradise Creek	126	1,040,000	2:26.40	112
1995	Northern Spur	4	C.J. McCarron	126	Freedom Cry	126	Carnegie	126	1,040,000	2:42.00	114
1996	Pilsudski	4	W.R. Swinburn	126	Singspiel	126	Swain	126	1,040,000	2:30.20	115
1997	Chief Bearhart	4	J.A. Santos	126	Borgia	119	Flag Down	126	1,040,000	2:23.80	110
1998	Buck's Boy	5	S.J. Sellers	126	Yagli	126	Dushyantor	126	1,040,000	2:28.74	111

Year	Winner	Age	Jockey	Wt.	Second	Wt.	Third	Wt.	Win Value	Time	Beyer
1999	Daylami	5	L. Dettori	126	Royal Anthem	126	Buck's Boy	126	1,040,000	2:24.73	118
2000	Kalanisi	4	J.P. Murtagh	126	Quiet Resolve	126	John's Call	126	1,289,600	2:26.96	110
2001	Fantastic Light	5	L. Dettori	126	Milan	126	Timboroa	126	1,112,800	2:24.36	117
2002	High Chaparral	3	M.J. Kinane	121	With Anticipation	126	Falcon Flight	126	1,258,400	2:30.14	111
2003	High Chaparral	4	M.J. Kinane	126			Falbrav	126	763,200	2:24.24	112
	Johar	4	A. Solis	126							

Beyer Index: 112.50

Run at Hollywood, 1984, 1987, 1997; at Aqueduct, 1985; at Santa Anita, 1986, 1993, 2003; at Churchill Downs, 1988, 1991, 1994, 1998, 2000; at Gulfstream Park, 1989, 1992, 1999; at Belmont Park, 1990, 1995, 2001; at Woodbine, 1996; at Arlington Park, 2002

CARTER HANDICAP, 7 Furlongs, 3-Year-Olds and Up, Aqueduct, 2003 Purse: $350,000

Year	Winner	Age	Jockey	Wt.	Second	Wt.	Third	Wt.	Win Value	Time	Beyer
1895	Charade	6	Doggett	100	The Pepper	118	Stephen J.	112	600	2:11.60	
1896	Deerslayer	4	Doggett	100	Charade	105	Lehrman	115	675	1:55.00	
1897	Premier	4	Coylie	114	Storm King	112	Sun Up	116	540	1:49.00	
1898	The Manxman	4	Lewis	114	Don't Care	106	Tabouret	110	1,350	1:29.60	
1899	D. of Middleburg	3	Sullivan	106	Dr. Parker	100	Bannock	118	1,470	1:26.60	
1900	Box	6	Maher	125	Boney Boy	108	The Kentuckian	114	1,560	1:28.00	
1901	Motley	4	Shaw	110	Robert Waddell	99	Pupil	106	1,570	1:28.00	
1902	Ethics	4	H. Cochran	106	Contend	107	Petra	108	1,645	1:28.20	
1903	Ahumada	3	J. Martin	101	Yellow Tail	106	Illyria	85	2,735	1:33.00	
1904	Beldame	3	F. O'Neill	103	Peter Paul	98	Wotan	100	7,710	1:27.00	
1905	Ormonde's Right	4	W. Davis	110	Roseben	113	Little Em.	105	7,140	1:26.80	
1906	Roseben	5	L. Lyne	129	Southern Cross	106	Red Knight	108	7,850	1:26.60	
1907	Glorifier	5	Mountain	119	Roseben	135	Don Diego	108	7,850	1:28.20	
1908	Jack Atkin	4	Musgrave	122	Red River	108	Chapultepec	105	6,850	1:27.80	
1910	Gretna Green	6	G. Burns	105	Alfred Noble	115	Far West	103	1,925	1:27.00	
1914	Roamer	3	M. Buxton	109	Borrow	129	Fl. Fairy	117	1,925	1:24.80	
1915	Phosphor	3	J. Loftus	116	Pomette Bleu	104	Leo. Skolny	105	1,925	1:30.00	
1916	Trial by Jury	4	E. Campbell	121	Ormesdale	105	Sh't Grass	120	1,925	1:25.40	
1917	Old Rosebud	6	A. Schuttinger	130	Bromo	122	The Finn	130	2,825	1:25.80	
1918	Old Koenig	5	G. Byrne	122	Roamer	130	Polymelian	128	2,825	1:23.80	
1919	Naturalist	5	C. Fairbrother	132	Star Master	125	Routledge	104	2,825	1:23.00	
1920	Audacious	4	F. Keogh	117	Constancy	110	Naturalist	124	3,850	1:25.00	
1921	Audacious	5	C. Kummer	126	Sennings Park	113	Idle Dell	96	7,300	1:23.00	
1922	Knobbie	4	L. Fator	120	Careful	115	Bon Homme	109	7,600	1:24.40	
1923	Little Celt	3	C. Turner	116	Knobbie	128	Little Chief	124	7,400	1:25.40	
1924	Sarazen	3	E. Sande	118	Brainstorm	112	Ordinance	115	6,900	1:25.60	
1925	Silver Fox	3	L. Fator	114	Worthmore	128	Candy Kid	106	8,150	1:24.40	
1926	Macaw	3	L. McAtee	123			Extra Dry	99.5	4,750	1:24.60	
	Nedana	4	L. Fator	119							
1927	Happy Argo	4	F. Weiner	119	Black Maria	124	Macaw	124	9,250	1:24.20	
1928	Osmand	4	E. Sande	122	Byrd	110	Happy Argo	129	9,250	1:25.00	
1929	Osmand	5	W. Garner	132	Petee Wrack	123	Distraction	108	8,900	1:26.60	
1930	Flying Heels	3	W. Kelsay	118	Sarazen II	108	Jack High	127	7,650	1:24.40	
1931	Flying Heels	4	C. Kurtsinger	125	Mr. Sponge	116	Hi-jack	130	7,400	1:24.20	
1932	Happy Scot	4	A. Robertson	117	Mr. Sponge	128	Pompeius	111	6,100	1:24.80	
1933	Caterwaul	3	R. Workman	114	Condescend	119	Parry	108	600	1:20.20	
1934	Open Range	3	E. Litzenberger	95	Halcyon	109	Okapi	118	895	1:18.00	
1935	King Saxon	4	C. Rainey	127	Singing Wood	118	Sgt. Byrne	115	6,850	1:23.80	
1936	Clang	4	E. Litzenberger	110	Sation	132	Cycle	112	7,200	1:24.00	
1937	Aneroid	4	C. Rosengarten	123	Deliberator	113	Sgt. Byrne	116	8,875	1:23.60	
1938	Airflame	4	R. Workman	119	Snark	132	Jay Jay	123	7,400	1:23.60	
1939	Fighting Fox	4	J. Stout	119	Can't Wait	112	Rough Time	119	7,600	1:22.80	
1940	He Did	7	G. Woolf	124	Third Degree	124	T.M. Dorsett	113	8,440	1:23.80	
1941	Parasang	4	B. James	114	Harvard Square	120	Omission	117	6,375	1:23.00	
1942	Doublrab	3	B. Thompson	120	Swing and Sway	112	Whirlaway	130	7,250	1:23.00	
1943	Devil Diver	4	G. Woolf	126	Marriage	118	Doublrab	118	7,150	1:24.00	
1944	Bossuet	4	J. Stout	127					3,623	1:23.40	
	Brownie	5	E. Guerin	115							
	Wait a Bit	5	G.L. Smith	118							
1945	Apache	6	J. Stout	130	Wait a Bit	121	First Fiddle	126	7,945	1:24.60	
1946	Flood Town	4	W. Mehrtens	113	King Dorsett	126	Black Swan	112	8,125	1:23.60	
1947	Rippey	4	O. Scurlock	112	Inroc	118	Gallorette	123	19,750	1:23.00	
1948	Gallorette	6	J. Jessop	122	Rippey	132	Skylighter	110	20,550	1:23.40	
1949	Better Self	4	D. Gorman	126	Rippey	123	High Trend	107	20,350	1:25.20	
1950	Guillotine	3	T. Atkinson	109	Noble Impulse	114	Hyphasis	108	16,950	1:23.20	
1951	Arise	4	E. Guerin	122	More Sun	108	Piet	123	16,000	1:23.40	
1952	Northern Star	4	T. Atkinson	115	Crafty Admiral	120	To Market	123	20,250	1:22.00	
1953	Tom Fool	4	T. Atkinson	135	Squared Away	122	Eatontown	113	41,700	1:22.00	
1954	White Skies	5	J. Stout	133	First Aid	115	Royal Vale	126	44,200	1:23.60	
1955	Bobby Brocato	4	R. Broussard	116	Social Outcast	123	Artismo	111	43,000	1:23.40	

Year	Winner	Age	Jockey	Wt.	Second	Wt.	Third	Wt.	Win Value	Time	Beyer
1956	Red Hannigan	5	P.J. Bailey	114	Switch On	119	Artismo	111	40,400	1:23.20	
1957	Portersville	5	T. Atkinson	111	Dedicate	126	Jutland	112	40,800	1:23.00	
1958	Bold Ruler	4	E. Arcaro	135	Tick Tock	113	Gallant Man	128	37,620	1:22.60	
1959	Jimmer	4	J. Ruane	108	Tick Tock	122	Nadir	122	37,490	1:22.60	
1960	Yes You Will	4	L. Adams	122	Mail Order	118	Dunce	119	38,205	1:22.40	
1961	Chief of Chiefs	4	J. Leonard	116	April Skies	127	Natural Bid	111	38,805	1:22.80	
1962	Merry Ruler	4	J. Sellers	119	Hitting Away	119	Rullah Red	113	38,545	1:22.00	
1963	Admiral's Voyage	4	R. Broussard	126	For the Road	117	Saidam	112	37,830	1:22.40	
1964	Ahoy	4	H. Grant	133	Red Gar	112	Gun Bow	126	37,505	1:21.60	
1965	Viking Spirit	5	K. Church	123	Cupid	114	Chieftain	125	35,620	1:21.40	
1966	Davis II	6	C. Stone	116	Time Tested	126	Dapper Dan	113	37,440	1:22.80	
1967	Tumiga	3	B. Feliciano	113	Our Michael	120	Indulto	113	36,790	1:23.80	
1968	In Reality	4	J. Velasquez	124	Tumiga	121	Mr. Washington	119	36,270	1:21.80	
1969	Promise	4	R. Ussery	124	Iron Ruler	121	Royal Exchange	121	37,440	1:22.60	
1970	Tyrant	4	R. Ussery	117	Best Turn	118	Fast Hilarious	126	36,010	1:21.40	
1971	Native Royalty	4	J.L. Rotz	112	Cut the Comedy	112	Shut Eye	116	35,280	1:22.80	

Tyrant finished second but was disqualified and placed last

Year	Winner	Age	Jockey	Wt.	Second	Wt.	Third	Wt.	Win Value	Time	Beyer
1972	Leematt	4	M. Venezia	116	Canonero II	121	Native Royalty	121	34,200	1:22.40	
1973	King's Bishop	4	E. Maple	114	Onion	114	Petrograd	118	35,220	1:20.40	
1974	Forego	4	H. Gustines	129	Mr. Prospector	124	Timeless Moment	113	33,900	1:22.20	
1975	Forego	5	H. Gustines	134	Stop the Music	123	Orders	114	34,860	1:21.60	
1976	Due Diligence	4	J. Amy	111	Honorable Miss	122	Amerrico	122	33,810	1:22.40	
1977	Quiet Little Table	4	E. Maple	119	Gentle King	110	Full Out	117	21,915	1:22.00	
1977	Soy Numero Uno	4	R. Broussard	126	Barrera	119	Gallant Bob	116	31,770	1:22.20	
1978	Pumpkin Moonshine	4	D.A. Bordern	107	Prefontaine	112	Big John Taylor	113	31,920	1:22.20	
1978	Jaipur's Gem	5	J.L. Samyn	115	Vencedor	111	Half High	118	32,070	1:21.60	
1979	Star de Naskra	4	J. Fell	122	Alydar	126	Sensitive Prince	126	48,690	1:21.20	
1980	Czaravich	4	L. Adams	126	Tanthem	122	Nice Catch	120	49,050	1:21.00	
1981	Amber Pass	4	E. Maple	114	Guilty Conscience	111	Dunham's Gift	116	49,410	1:23.00	
1982	Pass the Tab	4	A. Graell	118	Royal Hierarchy	115	Maudlin	114	52,110	1:22.40	
1983	Vittorioso	4	A. Smith	113	Sing Sing	122	Fit to Fight	116	67,800	1:22.80	
1984	Bet Big	4	J.L. Samyn	115	Cannon Shell	109	A Phenomenon	126	73,200	1:21.80	
1985	Mt. Livermore	4	J.D. Bailey	117	Rocky Marriage	122	Carr de Naskra	125	83,340	1:20.80	
1986	Love That Mac	4	E. Maple	117	Ziggy's Boy	118	King's Swan	120	116,460	1:21.60	
1987	Pine Tree Lane	5	R.P. Romero	119	King's Swan	123	Zany Tactics	119	170,400	1:21.20	
1988	Gulch	4	J.A. Santos	124	Afleet	124	Its Acedemic	108	174,300	1:20.40	
1989	On the Line	5	G.L. Stevens	125	True and Blue	114	Dr. Carrington	110	140,880	1:21.40	
1990	Dancing Spree	5	C.W. Antley	123	Dancing Pretense	115	Sewickley	119	137,280	1:22.00	115
1991	Housebuster	4	C. Perret	122	Black Tie Affair	123	Gervazy	116	120,000	1:21.20	119
1992	Rubiano	5	J.A. Santos	118	Kid Russell	112	In Excess	122	140,640	1:21.40	108
1993	Alydeed	4	C. Perret	122	Loach	112	Argyle Lake	113	90,000	1:22.60	111
1994	Virginia Rapids	4	J.L. Samyn	118	Punch Line	114	Cherokee Run	119	90,000	1:21.40	109
1995	Lite the Fuse	4	R.B. Perez	111	Our Emblem	113	You and I	113	90,000	1:21.40	108
1996	Lite the Fuse	5	J.A. Krone	121	Flying Chevron	115	Placid Fund	114	90,000	1:20.80	111
1997	Langfuhr	5	J.F. Chavez	122	Stalwart Member	113	Western Winter	112	90,000	1:22.80	106
1998	Wild Rush	4	K.J. Desormeaux	117	Banker's Gold	114	Western Borders	115	120,000	1:21.16	115
1999	Artax	4	J.F. Chavez	114	Affirmed Success	119	Western Borders	113	120,000	1:20.04	123
2000	Brutally Frank	6	S.X. Bridgmohan	113	Western Expression	113	Affirmed Success	122	120,000	1:21.66	106
2001	Peeping Tom	5	S.X. Bridgmohan	118	Say Florida Sandy	116	Hook And Ladder	118	180,000	1:21.33	113
2002	Affirmed Success	8	R. Migliore	119	Voodoo	113	Burning Roma	117	210,000	1:21.84	111
2003	Congaree	5	G.L. Stevens	122	Aldebaran	118	Peeping Tom	114	210,000	1:21.48	116

Beyer Index: 112.21

Distance 1 1/4 miles 1895; 1 1/8 miles, 1896; 1 1/16 miles, 1897; about 7 furlongs (150 feet short), 1898; 6 1/2 furlongs 1899-1902. Run at old Aqueduct, 1895-1945, 1947-55; at Belmont, 1946, 1956-59, 1968-74, 1996

CHAMPAGNE STAKES, 1 1/16 Miles, 2-Year-Olds,
Belmont Park, 2003 Purse: $500,000

Year	Winner	Age	Jockey	Wt.	Second	Wt.	Third	Wt.	Win Value	Time	Beyer
1867	Sarah B.	2	Washington	97	Lost Cause	97	Boaster	100	1,250	1:45.00	
1868	Cottrill	2	C. Miller	100	Attraction	97			850	1:49.20	
1869	Finesse	2	C. Miller	97	Telegram	100	Cavalier	100	1,200	1:56.00	
1870	Madam Dudley	2	W. Miller	97	Fanchon	97	Barbarian	100	1,350	1:50.20	
1871	Grey Planet	2	Donohue	100	Inverary	104			1,500	1:20.00	
1872	Minnie W.	2	Sparling	97	Delight	97	Survivor	100	1,050	1:19.20	
1873	Grinstead	2	Feakes	100	Dublin	100	Weathercock	100	1,750	1:17.60	
1874	Hyder Ali	2	Donohue	100	James A.	100	Finework	97	1,850	1:20.00	
1875	Virginius	2	W. Clarke	100	Cyclone	97	Tigress	97	2,100	1:19.00	
1876	Bombast	2	Barrett	110	Loiterer	107	Hibernia	107	1,950	1:19.20	
1877	Albert	2	Barbee	110	Maritana	107	Fawn	107	1,900	1:20.60	
1878	Belinda	2	Sparling	107	Boardman	110	Dan Sparling	110	1,275	1:18.00	
1879	Carita	2	Evans	107	Beata	107	Queen's Own	107	2,050	1:18.20	
1880	Lady Rosebery	2	J. McLaughlin	107	Spark	107	Bonnie Lizzie	114	1,175	1:18.20	
1881	Macduff	2	Fisher	110	The Rat	107	Duplex	107	1,150	1:18.20	

Year	Winner	Age	Jockey	Wt.	Second	Wt.	Third	Wt.	Win Value	Time Beyer
1882	Breeze	2	Shauer	108	Cyril	110	Bella	114	1,325	1:20.00
1883	Leo	2	Shauer	110	Pampero	107	Ecuador	110	1,350	1:18.20
1884	Eachus	2	J. McLaughlin	115	St. Augustin	115	Unrest	112	1,225	1:19.20
1885	Dew Drop	2	Olney	122	Inspector B.	115	Lansdowne	115	1,775	1:18.60
1886	Connemarra	2	A. McCarthy Jr	112	Bessie June	112	Belvidere	115	2,100	1:17.00
1887	Cascade	2	Church	102	Fordham	122	Blithesome	119	1,875	1:18.20
1888	Radiant	2	W. Donohue	115	Champagne Charley	115	Stately	119	2,650	1:19.20
1889	June Day	2	Barnes	118	Successor	113	Rosette	105	1,975	1:17.60
1890	Hoodlum	2	Covington	106	Peter	108	Russell	118	2,500	1:46.20
1891	Azra	2	Clayton	108	St. Florian	118	Dagonet	113	3,470	1:30.20
1892	Ramapo	2	Doggett	111	Prince George	115	Runyon	118	3,780	1:28.00
1893	Sir Excess	2	Taral	123	Dobbins	128	Rubicon	106	6,320	1:28.60
1894	Salvation	2	Taral	113	Brandywine	113	Darlen	104	4,880	1:28.20
1895	Ben Brush	2	Simms	120	Prince Lief	110	Merry Prince	110	2,350	1:27.20
1896	The Friar	2	Littlefield	118	Rhodesia	105	Divide	110	3,050	1:28.00
1897	Plaudit	2	R. Williams	125	Lydian	110	San Antonio	112	2,250	1:31.20
1898	Lothario	2	Maher	108	Filigrane	122	Manuel	122	3,250	1:29.60
1899	Kilmarnock	2	Odom	112	Montanic	114	Sadducee	109	3,585	1:27.20
1900	Garry Herrmann	2	Bullman	117	Smile	107	Watercolor	125	2,765	1:27.20
1901	Endurance by Right	2	O'Connor	119	Yankee	122	Caughnawaga	112	4,375	1:28.00
1902	Meltonian	2	Redfern	107	Acefull	122	Grey Friar	119	5,435	1:27.00
1903	Stalwart	2	W. Hicks	112	Pulsus	122	Wotan	112	6,135	1:26.00
1904	Oiseau	2	Odom	122	Tradition	119	Pasadena	122	6,600	1:29.00
1905	Perverse	2	Shaw	119	Whimsical	119	Security	122	6,255	1:23.60
1906	Kentucky Beau	2	W. Miller	119	W.H. Daniel	122	Ballot	122	5,910	1:23.80
1907	Colin	2	W. Miller	122	Stamina	119			5,700	1:23.00
1908	Helmet	2	Notter	122	Selectman	122	Etherial	114	5,625	1:26.00
1909	Fauntleroy	2	McCahey	122	Kingship	112	Candleberry	107	1,060	1:23.60
1914	Paris	2	M. Buxton	110	Charter Maid	116	Sharpshooter	110	1,205	1:22.40
1915	Chicle	2	T. McTaggart	112	Air Man	112	Whimsy	109	1,065	1:24.80
1916	Vivid	2	A. Schuttinger	105	Woodtrap	110			1,455	1:23.40
1917	Lanius	2	F. Robinson	110	Matinee Idol	111	Arrah Go On	105	1,650	1:26.20
1918	War Pennant	2	E. Taplin	106	Terentia	124	Questionnaire	125	2,525	1:25.40
1919	Cleopatra	2	L. McAtee	107	Upset	125	Dr. Clark	104	3,575	1:24.20
1920	Grey Lag	2	L. Ensor	112	Banksia	106	Our Flag	115	4,150	1:24.40
1921	Surf Rider	2	L. Fator	107	Galantman	102	Modo	118	4,400	1:25.40
1922	Nassau	2	C. Fairbrother	112	Miss Smith	109	Coeur de Lion	112	4,650	1:26.40
1923	Sarazen	2	E. Sande	112	Aga Khan	107	Sunspero	119	5,225	1:24.60
1924	Beatrice	2	G. Fields	109	Goldbeater	115	Star Lore	107	6,275	1:26.40
1925	Bubbling Over	2	A. Johnson	122	Espino	112			4,550	1:26.00
1926	Valorous	2	L. McAtee	112	Adios	112	Laddie	116	5,750	1:21.60
1927	Oh Say	2	F. Fields	114	Prate	122	Excalibur	110	6,025	1:22.00
1928	Healy	2	W. Kelsay	115	Chicatie	115	Marine	115	5,825	1:22.60
1929	Whichone	2	L. McAtee	127	Gone Away	115	Boojum	130	6,050	1:21.00
1930	Mate	2	L. Fator	119	Equipoise	132	Sunny Lassie	113	5,525	1:21.80
1931	Sweeping Light	2	F. Coltiletti	116	Pompeius	116	Cambal	116	4,025	1:20.80
1932	Dynastic	2	C. Kurtsinger	119	Kerry Patch	116	De Valera	110	2,170	1:20.80
1933	Hadagal	2	L. Humphries	116	Sgt. Byrne	122	Kawagoe	116	3,520	1:17.40
1934	Balladier	2	W.D. Wright	124	Omaha	117	Plat Eye	126	4,875	1:16.60
1935	Brevity	2	W.D. Wright	113	Snark	113	Granville	113	4,200	1:17.40
1936	Privileged	2	E. Arcaro	122	Dogaway	119	Murph	122	4,225	1:17.00
1937	Menow	2	C. Kurtsinger	113	Bull Lea	116	Fighting Fox	122	4,650	1:17.20
1938	Porter's Mite	2	B. James	119	Impound	116	No Competition	122	5,875	1:14.40
1939	Andy K.	2	J. Longden	124	Calory	113	Strawberry	111	9,675	1:17.00
1940	Monday Lunch	2	E. Arcaro	110	Bold Irishman	113	Swain	122	9,500	1:37.40
1941	Alsab	2	C. Bierman	122	Requested	116	Flaught	110	9,375	1:35.40
1942	Count Fleet	2	J. Longden	116	Blue Swords	119	Attendant	110	10,125	1:34.80
1943	Pukka Gin	2	T. Atkinson	113	Pressure	106	Pensive	110	15,950	1:38.20
1944	Pot o' Luck	2	R. Permane	106	Sir Francis	106	Lady's Reward	110	15,665	1:37.40
1945	Marine Victory	2	D. Padgett	116	Star Pilot	122	Mahout	106	20,550	1:39.20
1946	Donor	2	J. Jessop	116	Phalanx	110	Jet Pilot	119	22,650	1:37.40
1947	Vulcan's Forge	2	A. Kirkland	110	Escadru	113	My Request	119	24,300	1:36.60
1948	Capot	2	T. Atkinson	110	Stone Age	111	Flying Disc	107	23,150	1:37.20
1949	Theory	2	S. Brooks	113	Androcles	110	Sunglow	110	24,050	1:37.00
1950	Uncle Miltie	2	H. Woodhouse	122	Battle Morn	122	Nullify	122	24,050	1:36.60
1951	Armageddon	2	W. Shoemaker	122	Putout	122	Eternal Moon	122	25,600	1:38.20
1952	Laffango	2	N. Shuk	122	Invigorator	122	Country Coz	122	25,700	1:38.00
1953	Fisherman	2	H. Woodhouse	122	Best Years	122	War Piper	122	25,700	1:38.60
1954	Flying Fury	2	H. Moreno	122	Grandpaw	122	Gold Box	122	24,700	1:37.80
1955	Beau Fond	2	E. Arcaro	122	Head Man	122	Ricci Tavi	122	22,700	1:36.40
1957	Jewel's Reward	2	W. Shoemaker	122	Misty Flight	122	Rose Trellis	122	84,225	1:37.60
1958	First Landing	2	E. Arcaro	122	Intentionally	122	Tomy Lee	122	96,870	1:39.40

Tomy Lee finished second but was disqualified and placed third

Year	Winner	Age	Jockey	Wt.	Second	Wt.	Third	Wt.	Win Value	Time	Beyer
1959	Warfare	2	I. Valenzuela	122	Tompion	122	Bally Ache	122	138,195	1:35.20	
1960	Roving Minstrel	2	H. Moreno	122	Garwol	122	Bronzerullah	122	108,035	1:35.60	
1961	Donut King	2	M. Ycaza	122	Jaipur	122	Sir Gaylord	122	146,800	1:36.00	
1962	Never Bend	2	M. Ycaza	122	Master Dennis	122	Outing Class	122	129,675	1:36.60	
1963	Roman Brother	2	J.L. Rotz	122	Traffic	122	Bupers	122	152,150	1:38.00	
1964	Bold Lad	2	B. Baeza	122	Royal Gunner	122	Philately	122	116,825	1:36.40	
1965	Buckpasser	2	B. Baeza	122	Our Michael	122	Advocator	122	163,875	1:36.40	
1966	Successor	2	B. Baeza	122	Dr. Fager	122	Proviso	122	148,325	1:35.00	
1967	Vitriolic	2	B. Baeza	122	Iron Ruler	122	Captain's Gig	122	119,500	1:34.60	
1968	Top Knight	2	M. Ycaza	122	Beau Brummel	122	King Emperor	122	110,450	1:35.20	
1969	Silent Screen	2	J.L. Rotz	122	Brave Emperor	122	Toasted	122	128,150	1:37.20	
1970	Limit to Reason	2	J. Velasquez	122	Arctarus	122	Jim French	122	145,025	1:35.40	

Hoist the Flag finished first but was disqualified last

Year	Winner	Age	Jockey	Wt.	Second	Wt.	Third	Wt.	Win Value	Time	Beyer
1971	Riva Ridge	2	R. Turcotte	122	Chevron Flight	122	Head of the River	122	117,090	1:36.40	
1972	Stop the Music	2	J.L. Rotz	122	Secretariat	122	Step Nicely	122	87,900	1:35.00	

Secretariat finished first but was disqualified and placed second

Year	Winner	Age	Jockey	Wt.	Second	Wt.	Third	Wt.	Win Value	Time	Beyer
1973	Holding Pattern	2	M. Miceli	122	Green Gambados	122	Hosiery	122	55,425	1:36.00	
1973	Protagonist	2	A. Santiago	122	Prince of Reason	122	Cannonade	122	55,425	1:36.00	
1974	Foolish Pleasure	2	J. Vasquez	122	Harvard Man	122	Ramahorn	122	86,850	1:36.00	
1975	Honest Pleasure	2	B. Baeza	122	Dance Spell	122	Whatsyourpleasure	122	89,625	1:36.40	
1976	Seattle Slew	2	J. Cruguet	122	For the Moment	122	Sail to Rome	122	82,350	1:34.40	
1977	Alydar	2	J. Velasquez	122	Affirmed	122	Darby Creek Road	122	80,400	1:36.80	
1978	Spectacular Bid	2	J. Velasquez	122	General Assembly	122	Crest of the Wave	122	80,250	1:34.80	
1979	Joanie's Chief	2	R. Hernandez	122	Rockhill Native	122	Googolplex	122	81,750	1:38.20	
1980	Lord Avie	2	J. Velasquez	122	Noble Nashua	122	Sezyou	122	85,350	1:37.20	
1981	Timely Writer	2	J. Fell	122	Before Dawn	119	New Discovery	122	90,150	1:36.40	
1982	Copelan	2	J.D. Bailey	122	Pappa Riccio	122	El Cubanaso	122	144,000	1:37.80	
1983	Devil's Bag	2	E. Maple	122	Dr. Carter	122	Our Casey's Boy	122	142,200	1:34.20	
1984	For Certain Doc	2	M. Zuniga	122	Mighty Appealing	122	Tank's Prospect	122	171,600	1:49.20	
1985	Mogambo	2	A. Cordero Jr	122	Groovy	122	Mr. Classic	122	194,700	1:37.20	
1986	Polish Navy	2	R.P. Romero	122	Demons Begone	122	Bet Twice	122	199,500	1:35.20	
1987	Forty Niner	2	E. Maple	122	Parlay Me	122	Tejano	122	370,800	1:36.80	
1988	Easy Goer	2	P. Day	122	Is It True	122	Irish Actor	122	334,200	1:34.80	
1989	Adjudicating	2	J. Vasquez	122	Rhythm	122	Senor Pete	122	343,200	1:37.60	
1990	Fly So Free	2	J.A. Santos	122	Happy Jazz Band	122	Subordinated Debt	122	381,600	1:35.60	
1991	Tri to Watch	2	A. Cordero Jr	122	Snappy Landing	122	Pine Bluff	122	300,000	1:36.60	94
1992	Sea Hero	2	J.D. Bailey	122	Secret Odds	122	Press Card	122	300,000	1:34.80	99
1993	Dehere	2	C.J. McCarron	122	Crary	122	Amathos	122	300,000	1:35.80	93
1994	Timber Country	2	P. Day	122	Sierra Diablo	122	On Target	122	300,000	1:44.00	100
1995	Maria's Mon	2	R.G. Davis	122	Diligence	122	Devil's Honor	122	300,000	1:42.20	105
1996	Ordway	2	J.R. Velazquez	122	Traitor	122	Gold Tribute	122	240,000	1:42.00	101
1997	Grand Slam	2	G.L. Stevens	122	Lil's Lad	122	Halory Hunter	122	240,000	1:40.40	102
1998	The Groom Is Red	2	C.S. Nakatani	122	Lemon Drop Kid	122	Weekend Money	122	240,000	1:42.91	93
1999	Greenwood Lake	2	J.L. Samyn	122	Chief Seattle	122	High Yield	122	240,000	1:43.70	91
2000	A P Valentine	2	J.F. Chavez	122	Point Given	122	Yonaguska	122	300,000	1:41.45	98
2001	Officer	2	V. Espinoza	122	Jump Start	122	Heavyweight Champ	122	300,000	1:43.39	102
2002	Toccet	2	J.F. Chavez	122	Icecolbeeratreds	122	Erinsouthernman	122	300,000	1:44.45	97
2003	Birdstone	2	J.D. Bailey	122	Chapel Royal	122	Dashboard Drummer	122	300,000	1:44.50	94

Beyer Index: 97.62

Distance 6 furlongs 1871-89; 7 furlongs, 1891-1904; Widener Course (7 furlongs less 165 feet, 1905-32; 6 1/2 furlongs on Widener Course, 1933-39; 1 1/8 miles, 1984; 1 mile, 1940-83, 1985-93. Run at Jerome Park prior to 1890; at Morris Park 1891-1904; Aqueduct, 1959, 1963-67

CIGAR MILE HANDICAP, 1 Mile, 3-Year-Olds and Up,
Aqueduct, 2003 Purse: $350,000

Year	Winner	Age	Jockey	Wt.	Second	Wt.	Third	Wt.	Win Value	Time	Beyer
1988	Forty Niner	3	W.I. Fox Jr	121	Mawsuff	115	Precisionist	124	340,200	1:34.00	
1989	Dispersal	3	A. Cordero Jr	115	Sewickley	120	Speedratic	117	348,600	1:32.80	
1990	Quiet American	4	C.J. McCarron	116	Dancing Spree	119	Sewickley	124	382,600	1:32.80	124
1991	Rubiano	4	J.A. Santos	116	Sultry Song	111	Diablo	112	300,000	1:33.60	110
1992	Ibero	5	L. Pincay Jr	115	Irish Sweeps	116	Nines Wild	111	300,000	1:32.40	114
1994	Cigar	4	J.D. Bailey	111	Devil His Due	124	Punch Line	112	150,000	1:36.00	115
1995	Flying Chevron	3	R.G. Davis	112	Wekiva Springs	117	Dramatic Gold	120	150,000	1:34.40	112
1996	Gold Fever	3	M.E. Smith	115	Diligence	114	Top Account	117	150,000	1:34.80	108
1997	Devious Course	5	J.F. Chavez	112	Lucayan Prince	114	Basqueian	115	150,000	1:34.80	109
1998	Sir Bear	5	J.D. Bailey	116	Affirmed Success	119	Distorted Humor	116	180,000	1:34.05	111
1999	Affirmed Success	5	J.F. Chavez	118	Adonis	115	Honorifico	113	210,000	1:34.18	109
2000	El Corredor	3	J.D. Bailey	116	Peeping Tom	111	Affirmed Success	120	210,000	1:34.68	112
2001	Left Bank	4	J.R. Velazquez	120	Graeme Hall	118	Red Bullet	118	210,000	1:33.35	118
2002	Congaree	4	J.D. Bailey	119	Aldebaran	116	Crafty C. T.	117	210,000	1:33.11	120
2003	Congaree	5	J.D. Bailey	124	Midas Eyes	115	Toccet	115	210,000	1:34.30	120

Beyer Index: 114

Run as NYRA Mile Handicap prior to 1997

COACHING CLUB AMERICAN OAKS, 1 1/2 Miles, 3-Year-Old Fillies, Belmont Park, 2003 Purse: $500,000

Year	Winner	Age	Jockey	Wt.	Second	Wt.	Third	Wt.	Win Value	Time	Beyer
1917	Wistful	3	W.J. O'Brien	124	Battle	120	The Banshee II.	115	2,300	1:53.60	
1918	Rose d'Or	3	L. Ensor	111	Eyelid	122	Lady Dorothy	115	5,050	2:06.60	
1919	Polka Dot	3	L. Ensor	111	Passing Shower	121	High Born Lady	111	7,790	2:20.20	
1920	Cleopatra	3	L. McAtee	117	La Rablee	111	Oceanna	111	4,075	2:18.80	
1921	Flambette	3	E. Sande	112	Nancy Lee	121	Ten Buttons	124	4,850	2:17.40	
1922	Prudish	3	L. Morris	111	Emotion	111	King's Fancy	111	11,700	2:18.40	
1923	How Fair	3	A. Johnson	112	Gadfly	114	Untidy	121	11,775	2:18.40	
1924	Princess Doreen	3	H. Stutts	121	Relentless	114	Priscilla Ruley	111	12,875	2:19.20	
1925	Florence Nightingale	3	L. McDermott	111	Gamble	113	Extra Dry	113	13,400	2:17.80	
1926	Edith Cavell	3	F. Coltiletti	117	Black Maria	121	Rapture	117	12,100	2:20.60	
1927	Nimba	3	H. Thurber	111	Frilette	117	Flambino	111	15,775	2:19.80	
1928	Bateau	3	E. Sande	121	Darkness	111	Valkyr	111	14,825	2:24.00	
1929	Sweet Verbena	3	J. Maiben	114	Aquastella	118	Golden Anger	114	16,625	2:18.00	
1930	Snowflake	3	L. Schaefer	121	Red Rag	118	Erin	118	19,600	2:18.40	
1931	Tambour	3	F. Coltiletti	121	Scuttle	114	Allez Vite.	114	15,000	2:20.40	
1932	Top Flight	3	R. Workman	121	Argosie	114	Unique	114	15,075	2:20.20	
1933	Edelweiss	3	J. Gilbert	114	Barn Swallow	121	Welcome Gift	114	12,550	2:20.60	
1934	Lady Reigh	3	D. Meade	111	Dusky Princess	111	Hindu Queen	107	9,575	2:18.80	
1935	Black Helen	3	D. Meade	121	Bloodroot	111	Good Gamble	121	7,750	2:18.80	
1936	High Fleet	3	J. Gilbert	111	Split Second	121	Floradora	107	10,575	2:19.60	
1937	Dawn Play	3	L. Balaski	121	Drawbridge	113	Rouge et Noir	107	10,575	2:18.60	
1938	Creole Maid	3	H. Richards	121	Handcuff	121	Gulf Breeze	116	10,425	2:20.80	
1939	War Plumage	3	N. Wall	116	Hostility	121	Wise Lady.	121	11,500	2:16.80	
1940	Damaged Goods	3	J. Gilbert	121	Rosetown	121	Dipsy Doodle.	121	12,550	2:19.00	
1941	Level Best	3	A. Robertson	121	Dark Discovery	121	Nasca	121	10,275	2:17.60	
1942	Vagrancy	3	T. Malley	121	Mackerel	121	Copperette	121	15,425	2:31.60	
1943	Too Timely	3	G. Woolf	121	Askmenow	121	La Reigh	121	13,250	2:35.00	
1944	Twilight Tear	3	C. McCreary	121	Dare Me	121	Plucky Maud.	121	12,495	2:21.00	
1945	Elpis	3	J. Adams	121	Monsoon	121	Segula.	121	15,215	2:18.40	
1946	Hypnotic	3	P. Miller	121	Red Shoes	121	Bonnie Beryl.	121	21,180	2:18.80	
1947	Harmonica	3	J. Adams	121	Cosmic Missile	121	Snow Goose	121	48,200	2:18.20	
1948	Scattered	3	W. Mehrtens	121	Flitabout	121	Challe Anne.	121	43,700	2:18.80	
1949	Wistful	3	S. Brooks	121	Adile	121	Jazz Baby	121	48,700	2:19.60	
1950	Next Move	3	E. Guerin	121	Aegina	121	Busanda.	121	44,500	2:15.80	
1951	How	3	E. Arcaro	121	Kiss Me Kate	121	Jacodema	121	46,800	2:16.80	
1952	Real Delight	3	E. Arcaro	121	Lily White	121	Sufie	121	45,100	2:17.80	
1953	Grecian Queen	3	E. Guerin	121	Sabette	121	Ming Yellow	121	45,500	2:18.60	
1954	Cherokee Rose	3	H. Moreno	121	Open Sesame	121	Riverina	121	43,900	2:19.60	
1955	High Voltage	3	T. Atkinson	121	Lalun	121	Manotick	121	45,800	2:17.60	
1956	Levee	3	H. Woodhouse	121	Princess Turia	121	Lady Swords	121	41,100	2:16.60	
1957	Willamette	3	J. Choquette	121	Bayou	121	Woodlawn	121	48,800	2:16.60	
1958	A Glitter	3	I. Valenzuela	121	Spar Maid	121	Craftiness.	121	45,792	2:20.00	
1959	Resaca	3	M. Ycaza	121	Quill	121	Czarina.	121	58,512	2:02.40	
1960	Berlo	3	E. Guerin	121	Sarcastic	121	Rash Statement	121	55,262	2:04.20	
1961	Bowl of Flowers	3	E. Arcaro	121	Funloving	121	Mighty Fair	121	75,806	2:03.20	
1962	Bramalea	3	R. Ussery	121	Cicada	121	Firm Policy	121	78,081	2:02.60	
1963	Lamb Chop	3	H. Gustines	121	Spicy Living	121	Smart Deb	121	78,244	2:02.80	
1964	Miss Cavandish	3	H. Grant.	121	Castle Forbes	121	Sceree	121	79,544	2:04.00	
1965	Marshua	3	R. Broussard	121	What a Treat	121	Terentia.	121	84,175	2:02.60	
1966	Lady Pitt	3	W. Blum	121	Prides Profile	121	Help on Way	121	77,919	2:05.00	
	Gentle Rain finished second but was disqualified and placed fourth										
1967	Quillo Queen	3	E. Cardone.	121	Muse	121	Pepperwood	121	85,637	2:03.40	
1968	Dark Mirage	3	M. Ycaza	121	Gay Matelda	121	Syrian Sea	121	75,562	2:01.80	
1969	Shuvee	3	J. Davidson	121	Hail to Patsy	121	Secret Verdict	121	77,756	2:03.20	
1970	Missile Belle	3	P. Anderson	121	Cathy Honey	121	Kilts n Kapers.	121	87,019	2:03.80	
1971	Our Cheri Amour	3	J. Kurtz	121	Grafitti	121	Inca Queen.	121	78,975	2:29.80	
1972	Summer Guest	3	R. Turcotte	121	Wanda	121	Susan's Girl.	121	66,360	2:29.40	
1973	Magazine	3	A. Cordero Jr	121	Bag of Tunes	121	Lady Love.	121	70,200	2:27.80	
1974	Chris Evert	3	J. Velasquez	121	Fiesta Libre	121	Maud Muller	121	68,520	2:28.00	
1975	Ruffian	3	J. Vasquez	121	Equal Change	121	Let Me Linger	121	66,720	2:27.80	
1976	Revidere	3	J. Vasquez	121	Optimistic Gal	121	No Duplicate.	121	68,640	2:28.40	
1977	Our Mims	3	J. Velasquez	121	Road Princess	121	Fia.	121	65,880	2:29.40	
1978	Lakeville Miss	3	R. Hernandez	121	Caesar's Wish	121	Tempest Queen.	121	63,540	2:29.40	
1979	Davona Dale	3	J. Velasquez	121	Plankton	121	Croquis	121	79,575	2:30.00	
1980	Bold 'n Determined	3	E. Delahoussaye.	121	Erin's Word	121	Farewell Letter	121	84,000	2:31.80	
1981	Wayward Lass	3	C.B. Asmussen.	121	Real Prize	121	Banner Gala.	121	81,750	2:28.20	
	Real Prize finished first but was disqualified and placed second										
1982	Christmas Past	3	J. Vasquez	121	Cupecoy's Joy	121	Flying Partner	121	84,900	2:28.60	
1983	High Schemes	3	J.L. Samyn	121	Spit Curl	121	Lady Norcliffe	121	107,460	2:30.20	
1984	Class Play	3	J. Cruguet	121	Life's Magic	121	Miss Oceana	121	164,520	2:29.80	
1985	Mom's Command	3	A. Fuller.	121	Bessarabian	121	Foxy Deen	121	142,560	2:32.00	

Year	Winner	Age	Jockey	Wt.	Second	Wt.	Third	Wt.	Win Value	Time	Beyer
1986	Valley Victory	3	R.P. Romero	121	Life at the Top	121	Lotka	121	166,680	2:28.00	
1987	Fiesta Gal	3	A. Cordero Jr	121	Mint Cooler	121	Run Come See	121	172,500	2:31.00	
1988	Goodbye Halo	3	J. Velasquez	121	Aptostar	121	Make Change	121	170,400	2:32.80	
1989	Open Mind	3	A. Cordero Jr	121	Nite of Fun	121	Rose Diamond	121	170,100	2:32.40	
	Nite of Fun finished first but was disqualified and placed second										
1990	Charon	3	C. Perret	121	Crowned	121	Paper Money	121	172,500	2:02.60	103
1991	Lite Light	3	C.S. Nakatani	121	Meadow Star	121	Car Gal	121	150,000	2:00.40	108
1992	Turnback the Alarm	3	C.W. Antley	121	Easy Now	121	Pleasant Stage	121	150,000	2:03.40	92
1993	Sky Beauty	3	M.E. Smith	121	Future Pretense	121	Silky Feather	121	150,000	2:01.40	96
1994	Two Altazano	3	J.A. Santos	121	Plenty of Sugar	121	Sovereign Kitty	121	150,000	2:02.80	97
1995	Golden Bri	3	J.A. Santos	121	Serena's Song	121	Change Fora Dollar	121	150,000	2:03.80	96
1996	My Flag	3	J.D. Bailey	121	Gold n Delicious	121	Weekend in Seattle	121	180,000	2:04.60	102
1997	Ajina	3	M.E. Smith	121	Tomisue's Delight	121	Key Hunter	121	180,000	2:00.40	102
1998	Banshee Breeze	3	J.D. Bailey	121	Keeper Hill	121	Best Friend Stro	121	180,000	2:31.56	102
1999	On a Soapbox	3	J.D. Bailey	121	Dreams Gallore	121	Strolling Belle	121	210,000	2:29.31	98
2000	Jostle	3	M.E. Smith	121	Resort	121	Secret Status	121	210,000	2:29.99	96
2001	Tweedside	3	J.R. Velazquez	121	Exogenous	121	Unbridled Lassie	121	210,000	2:30.70	93
2002	Jilbab	3	M. Luzzi	121	Tarnished Lady	121	Shop Till You Drop	121	210,000	2:31.48	97
2003	Spoken Fur	3	J.D. Bailey	121	Fircroft	121	Savedbythelight	121	300,000	2:31.02	88

Beyer Index: 97.86

Distance 1 1/8 miles in 1917; 1 1/4 miles, 1959–70, 1990–97; 1 3/8 miles 1919–41, 1944–58. Run at Aqueduct 1963–67

FRANK J. DE FRANCIS MEMORIAL DASH, 6 Furlongs, 3-Year-Olds and Up, Laurel, 2003 Purse: $300,000

Year	Winner	Age	Jockey	Wt.	Second	Wt.	Third	Wt.	Win Value	Time	Beyer
1990	Northern Wolf	4	M.J. Luzzi	120	Glitterman	124	Sewickley	126	210,000	1:09.00	111
1991	Housebuster	4	C. Perret	126	Clevor Trevor	123	Safely Kept	121	180,000	1:08.60	118
1992	Superstrike	3	D. Sorenson	112	Parisian Flight	114	King Corrie	117	180,000	1:09.80	110
1993	Montbrook	3	C.J. Ladner III	112	Lion Cavern	117	Flaming Emperor	114	180,000	1:08.60	112
1994	Cherokee Run	4	C. Perret	114	Boom Towner	119	Fu Man Slew	107	180,000	1:08.80	114
1995	Lite the Fuse	4	J.A. Krone	119	Crafty Dude	117	Hot JawsBay	119	180,000	1:08.80	109
1996	Lite the Fuse	5	J.A. Krone	117	Meadow Monster	119	Prospect Bay	114	180,000	1:08.80	117
1997	Smoke Glacken	3	C. Perret	113	Wise Dusty	112	Capote Belle	110	180,000	1:09.40	110
1998	Kelly Kip	4	J.L. Samyn	121	Affirmed Success	114	Partner's Hero	114	180,000	1:08.40	119
1999	Yes It's True	3	J.D. Bailey	114	Good and Tough	123	Storm Punch	114	180,000	1:08.67	106
2000	Richter Scale	6	R. Migliore	123	Just Call Me Carl	119	Falkenburg	114	180,000	1:07.95	111
2001	Delaware Township	5	J.D. Bailey	125	Early Flyer	115	Xtra Heat	117	180,000	1:09.00	116
2002	D'wildcat	4	J.F. Chavez	122	Deer Run	118	Sassy Hound	118	180,000	1:10.81	106
2003	A Huevo	7	R.A. Dominguez	119	Shake You Down	123	Gators n Bears	115	180,000	1:08.90	113

Beyer Index: 112.29

Run at Pimlico in 1990

DEL MAR DEBUTANTE, 7 Furlongs, 2-Year-Old Fillies, Del Mar, 2003 Purse: $250,000

Year	Winner	Age	Jockey	Wt.	Second	Wt.	Third	Wt.	Win Value	Time	Beyer
1951	Tonga	2	G. Glisson	112	Nurse O'War	115	Remolacha	112	15,050	1:12.00	
1952	Lap Full	2	H. Moreno	112	Fortune Teller	112	Smart Barbara	112	23,100	1:10.60	
1953	Lady Cover Up	2	W. Shoemaker	113	Dixie Valor	113	Sweet as Honey	113	20,425	1:11.00	
	Frosty Dawn finished first but but was later found to be ineligible and purse was awarded to Lady Cover Up										
1954	Fair Molly	2	W. Shoemaker	116	Madam Jet	113	Solid Rae	113	21,425	1:10.60	
1955	Miss Todd	2	R. York	119	Snoop	113	Edie's sister	113	20,160	1:10.40	
1956	Blue Vic	2	R. Trejos	113	Darling Adelle	119	Market Basket	113	25,420	1:09.80	
1957	Sally Lee	2	P. Moreno	119	Mrs. E.B.	113	Be My Honey	113	26,950	1:10.40	
1958	Khalita	2	R. York	116	Satina	113	Miss Uppity	116	29,120	1:10.60	
1959	Darling June	2	D. Pierce	113	Fair Maggie	113	Cherokee Miss	113	33,710	1:09.20	
1960	Amri-an	2	A. Maese	113	Chicha	113	Annie Alma	113	27,690	1:09.40	
1961	Spark Plug	2	R. Vasquez	116	Kabema	113	Savaii	113	36,105	1:09.40	
1962	Brown Berry	2	P. Moreno	113	Star Maggie	113	Golden Curra	113	30,550	1:09.40	
1963	Leisurely Kin	2	J. Lambert	113	Loukahl	113	Go Yala	113	35,900	1:09.20	
1964	Admirably	2	R. York	113	Candyean	116	Real Sweet Deal	116	37,465	1:09.80	
							Music Khal	116			
1965	Century	2	W. Hartack	116	Teton Holiday	113	Premise	119	42,175	1:10.00	
1966	Native Honey	2	R. Campas	113	Louisador	113	Supreme Endeavor	113	42,680	1:10.00	
1967	Fast Dish	2	J. Lambert	113	Time to Leave	113	Equimau Pie	113	40,330	1:09.80	
1968	Fourth Round	2	J. Lambert	113	Singing Surf	113	Love You So	113	41,835	1:10.40	
1969	Atomic Wings	2	D. Pierce	113	Minstrel Miss	114	Regal Wine	113	43,025	1:08.60	
1970	Generous Portion	2	D. Tierney	113	June Darling	119	Ulla Britta	113	50,025	1:09.60	
1971	Impressive Style	2	D. Pierce	113	Miss Lady Bug	119	Chargerette	116	47,770	1:09.20	
1972	Windy's Daughter	2	W. Shoemaker	119	King's Edge	113	Rosalie Mae Wynn	116	50,965	1:09.60	
1973	Fleet Peach	2	D. Pierce	116	Fresno Star	113	Divine Grace	113	46,205	1:09.60	
1974	Bubblewin	2	W. Shoemaker	113	Spout	116	Cut Class	114	57,445	1:36.80	
1975	Queen to Be	2	D. McHargue	116	T.V. Terese	113	Awaken	113	57,805	1:36.80	
1976	Telferner	2	L. Pincay Jr.	117	Asterisca	113	Maxine N.	115	65,175	1:37.20	

Year	Winner	Age	Jockey	Wt.	Second	Wt.	Third	Wt.	Win Value	Time	Beyer
1977	Extravagant	2	M. Castaneda	113	Foxy Juliana	115	Honey Jar	113	81,490	1:36.40	
1978	Terlingua	2	D. McHargue	119	Beauty Hour	116	Blowin' Wild	113	79,140	1:36.20	
1979	Table Hands	2	W. Shoemaker	119	Hazel R.	116	Arcades Ambo	117	106,770	1:35.00	
1980	Raja's Delight	2	C.J. McCarron	113	Prestigious Lady	115	Native Fancy	119	110,225	1:37.40	
1981	Skillful Joy	2	C.J. McCarron	113	Marl Lee Ann	115	A Kiss for Luck	117	138,310	1:37.40	
1982	Landaluce	2	L. Pincay Jr.	119	Issues n Answers	116	Granja Reina	113	124,655	1:35.60	
1983	Althea	2	L. Pincay Jr.	119	Diachrony	113	Victorious Joy	113	126,190	1:36.00	
1984	Fiesta Lady	2	L. Pincay Jr.	117	Doon's Baby	119	Trunk	115	93,050	1:38.80	
1984	Full O Wisdom	2	C.J. McCarron	113	Pirate's Glow	115	Wayward Pirate	119	91,050	1:37.40	
1985	Arewehavingfunyet	2	P. Valenzuela	120	Python	117	Wee Lavaliere	117	134,210	1:36.00	
1986	Brave Raj	2	C.A. Black	117	Road to Happiness	113	Soft Copy	115	125,325	1:35.80	
1987	Lost Kitty	2	G.L. Stevens	117	Royal Weekend	113	Hasty Pasty	117	128,850	1:36.00	
1988	Lea Lucinda	2	G.L. Stevens	114	Approved to Fly	114	Beware of the Cat	115	193,850	1:36.40	
	Approved to Fly finished first but was disqualified and placed second										
1989	Rue de Palm	2	R. Baze	115	Dominant Dancer	118	Cheval Volant	118	202,050	1:35.00	
1990	Beyond Perfection	2	A. Solis	114	Lite Light	120	Title Bought	116	191,400	1:34.80	99
1991	La Spia	2	A. Solis	114	Soviet Sojourn	120	Wicked Wit	118	161,000	1:37.00	89
1992	Beal Street Blues	2	G.L. Stevens	115	Fit N Fappy	114	Zoonaqua	120	137,500	1:37.00	84
1993	Sardula	2	E. Delahoussaye	116	Phone Chatter	119	Ballerina Girl	114	137,500	1:21.60	100
1994	Call Now	2	A. Solis	115	How So Oiseau	119	Ski Dancer	116	137,500	1:21.40	97
1995	Batroyale	2	M. Pedroza	119	Proud Dixie	117	General Idea	117	137,500	1:22.40	88
1996	Sharp Cat	2	R.R. Douglas	115	Desert Digger	119	Broad Dynamite	116	150,000	1:23.80	83
1997	Vivid Angel	2	K.J. Desormeaux	115	Griselle	115	Czarina	117	150,000	1:24.20	78
1998	Excellent Meeting	2	K.J. Desormeaux	115	Antahkarana	115	Colorado Song	115	150,000	1:22.20	98
1999	Chilukki	2	D. Flores	121	Spain	115	She's Classy	116	150,000	1:23.54	88
2000	Cindy's Hero	2	G.K. Gomez	114	Notable Career	119	Euro Empire	119	150,000	1:22.61	99
2001	Habibti	2	V. Espinoza	115	Who Loves Aleyna	116	Tempera	119	150,000	1:22.22	99
2002	Miss Houdini	2	G.L. Stevens	116	Santa Catarina	115	Indy Groove	115	150,000	1:23.43	88
2003	Halfbridled	2	J.A. Krone	116	Hollywood Story	115	Victory U.S.A.	116	150,000	1:22.20	99

Beyer Index: 92.07

Distance 6 furlongs 1951–73; 1 mile, 1974–92

DEL MAR OAKS, 1 1/8 Miles (Turf), 3-Year-Old Fillies,
Del Mar, 2003 Purse: $300,000

Year	Winner	Age	Jockey	Wt.	Second	Wt.	Third	Wt.	Win Value	Time	Beyer
1957	Royal Rasher	3	I. Valenzuela	118	Vyg	114	Tourbillonte	114	8,524	1:36.20	
1958	Camloc	3	P. Moreno	114	Gleaming Star	114	Mrs. E.B.	114	8,500	1:36.40	
1959	Pie Queen	3	R. Campas	114	Noorette	114	Khalita	114	8,925	1:36.40	
1960	Linita	3	A. Maese	114	Solid Thought	118	Ypres	114	8,575	1:36.00	
1961	Fun House	3	R. Yanez	112	Amri-An	114	Outfield	114	9,075	1:35.20	
1962	Savall	3	W. Harmatz	116	Table Mate	114	Sunday Slippers	114	9,050	1:35.40	
1963	Hi Rated	3	K. Church	114	Poonetta	114	Curious Clover	114	8,900	1:36.20	
1964	Gin Mah	3	J. Longden	121	Loukahl	121	Spoondee	114	8,925	1:36.80	
1965	Alibarb	3	J. Lambert	114	Miss Rincon	114	Glory's Tryst	114	8,725	1:52.40	
1966	Desert Trial	3	A. Maese	114	Ali's Theme	114	April Dawn	121	7,275	1:51.20	
1966	Mikhaless	3	A. Pineda	114	Windy Kate	114	Fleet Treat	121	7,275	1:51.00	
1967	Forgiving	3	A. Pineda	121	Desert Law	114	My Thel	114	9,725	1:50.80	
1968	Greta	3	R. Campas	114	Baby La	114	Grey Cricket	114	8,725	1:50.60	
1969	Commissary	3	A. Pineda	118	Ynez Queen	115	Serica	114	9,500	1:51.60	
1970	Beja	3	W. Shoemaker	113	Likely Lark	113	Sony Gay	114	9,875	1:49.20	
1970	Thoroly Blue	3	F. Toro	118	Word of Honor	113	Dress Me Up	113	9,875	1:50.20	
1971	Turkish Trousers	3	W. Shoemaker	124	Aladancer	117	Shelf Talker	118	14,750	1:50.00	
1972	House of Cards	3	J. Sellers	115	Pallisima	121	Le Cle	118	18,750	1:50.00	
1973	Sandy Blue	3	D. Pierce	121	Sphere	112	Meileur	118	20,850	1:49.40	
1974	Modus Vivendi	3	D. Pierce	113	Move Abroad	116	Heather Road	115	21,850	1:50.20	
1975	Snap Apple	3	F. Mena	113	Mia Amore	115	Miss Francesca	116	21,450	1:50.00	
1976	Go March	3	L. Pincay Jr	116	Pennygown	113	Franmari	116	25,700	1:49.20	
1977	Taisez Vous	3	D. Pierce	121	Drama Critic	114	Giggling Girl	113	31,550	1:48.80	
1978	Country Queen	3	F. Toro	121	B. Thoughtful	124	Donna Inez	113	33,450	1:49.80	
1979	Our Suiti Pie	3	C.J. McCarron	113	Caline	121	Ancient Art	116	52,300	1:49.80	
1980	Movin' Money	3	P.A. Valenzuela	114	Princess Karenda	122	Tobin's Rose	119	71,000	1:49.40	
1981	French Charmer	3	D.G. McHargue	117	Amber Ever	119	Shimmy	119	82,200	1:49.40	
1982	Castilla	3	R. Sibille	122	Avigaition	119	Skillful Joy	119	81,050	1:50.20	
1983	Heartlight No. One	3	L. Pincay Jr	122	Foggy Moon	115	Fabulous Notion	122	84,100	1:50.20	
1984	Fashionably Late	3	C.J. McCarron	119	Lucky Lucky Lucky	125	Auntie Betty	114	92,400	1:49.40	
1985	Savannah Dancer	3	W. Shoemaker	119	Magnificent Lindy	122	Queen of Bronze	115	94,250	1:48.80	
	Pirate's Glow finished second but was disqualified and fourth										
1986	Hidden Light	3	W. Shoemaker	124	Kraemer	114	Shotgun Wedding	119	92,700	1:47.80	
1987	Lizzy Hare	3	G.L. Stevens	114	Chapel of Dreams	114	Down Again	114	104,300	1:50.40	
1988	No Review	3	R.Q. Meza	115	Do So	124	Jungle Gold	115	96,300	1:49.00	
1989	Stylish Star	3	C.J. McCarron	115	Darby's Daughter	119	General Charge	119	97,500	1:48.60	
1990	Slew of Pearls	3	C.A. Black	117	Adorable Emilie	115	Annual Reunion	117	97,900	1:49.80	
1991	Flawlessly	3	C.J. McCarron	120	Seattle Symphony	120	Fowda	120	96,250	1:49.40	97

Year	Winner	Age	Jockey	Wt.	Second	Wt.	Third	Wt.	Win Value	Time	Beyer
1992	Suivi	3	A. Solis	120	Race the Wild Wind	.120	Alysbelle	120	96,250	1:48.60	94
1993	Hollywood Wildcat	3	E. Delahoussaye	120	Possibly Perfect	120	Miami Sands	120	96,250	1:48.20	102
1994	Twice the Vice	3	G.L. Stevens	120	Malli Star	120	Pharma	120	96,250	1:47.60	100
1995	Bail Out Becky	3	S.J. Sellers	120	Sleep Easy	120	Top Ruhl	120	137,500	1:49.60	97
1996	Antespend	3	C.W. Antley	120	Gastronomical	120	True Flare	120	150,000	1:48.80	100
1997	Famous Digger	3	B. Blanc	120	Golden Arches	121	Seen You Soon	121	150,000	1:49.00	95
1998	Sicy d'Alsace	3	C.S. Nakatani	121	Adel	121	Tranquility Lake	121	150,000	1:48.26	94

Tranquility Lake finished second but was disqualified and placed third

Year	Winner	Age	Jockey	Wt.	Second	Wt.	Third	Wt.	Win Value	Time	Beyer
1999	Tout Charmant	3	D.R. Flores	121	Smooth Player	121	Sweet Ludy	121	150,000	1:48.64	99
2000	No Matter What	3	V. Espinoza	121	Theoretically	121	Premre Creation	121	150,000	1:50.02	94
2001	Golden Apples	3	G.K. Gomez	121	Affluent	121	Reine de Romance	121	180,000	1:47.98	101
2002	Dublino	3	K.J. Desormeaux	121	Megahertz	121	Alozaina	121	180,000	1:47.16	97
2003	Dessert	3	C.S. Nakatani	122	Solar Echo	122	Personal Legend	122	180,000	1:47.04	95

Beyer Index: 97.31

Distance 1 mile, main course, prior to 1965

DIANA HANDICAP, 1 1/8 Miles (Turf), Fillies and Mares, 3-Year-Olds and Up, Saratoga Race Course, 2003 Purse: $500,000

Year	Winner	Age	Jockey	Wt.	Second	Wt.	Third	Wt.	Win Value	Time	Beyer
1939	War Regalia	3	D. Meade	110	Flying Lee	104	Sh'gay Lily	126	2,550	1:52.20	
1940	Piquet	3	E. Arcaro	118	Fairy Chant	118	Rosetown	110	2,425	1:52.00	
1941	Rosetown	4	J. Longden	118	Dorimar	119	Fairy Chant	126	2,650	1:53.40	
1942	Pomayya	4	A. Robertson	124	Key Ring	113	Transient	109	2,450	1:53.00	
1943	Bonnet Ann	4	L. Haas	113	Vagrancy	126	Night Glow	112	4,050	1:50.00	
1944	Whirlabout	3	H. Lindberg	118	Good Morning	120	Vienna	115	8,530	1:50.20	
1945	Surosa	3	A. Snider	110	Legend Bearer	113	Letmenow	109	9,020	1:50.80	
1946	Miss Grillo	4	C. McCreary	124	Jackawake	104	Sicily	119	9,150	1:50.20	
1947	Miss Grillo	5	C. McCreary	126	Humaya	106	Rosa Blanca	114	8,850	1:50.40	
1948	Carolyn A.	4	E. Arcaro	114	Miss Grillo	120	Mother	107	8,025	1:51.80	
1949	Spats	4	T. Atkinson	106	Adile	115	Gaffery	115	7,925	1:52.40	
1950	Ouija	3	W. Bolan	110	Jazz Baby	117	Supersonic	110	8,175	1:51.60	
1951	Vulcania	3	R. Bernhardt	108	Marta	115	Adile	111	7,775	1:52.60	
1952	Busanda	5	T. Atkinson	111	Nilufer	106	Valadium	115	7,675	1:53.40	
1953	Sabette	3	J. Higley	114	Canadiana	115	Dinewisely	105	11,250	1:52.60	
1954	Lavender Hill	5	C. McCreary	121	La Corredora	121	Evening Out	116	16,600	1:52.60	
1955	Misty Morn	3	T. Atkinson	115	Carry the News	110	Oil Painting	118	16,150	1:51.20	
1956	Searching	6	W. Hartack	123	Rico Reto	113	Blue Banner	117	18,950	1:52.00	
1957	Pardala	4	H. Woodhouse	111	Searching	125	Rare Treat	118	19,400	1:53.00	
1958	Searching	6	W. Hartack	123	Endine	116	Rare Treat	112	17,412	1:52.20	
1959	Tempted	4	E. Nelson	122	Polamby	116	Spar Maid	110	36,190	1:50.40	
1960	Tempted	5	E. Nelson	124	Quill	128	Aesthetic	112	24,430	1:51.40	
1961	Craftiness	6	R. Ussery	117	Sarcastic	120	Linda J.A.	107	18,297	1:49.60	
1962	Waltz Song	4	S. Mellon	113	Seven Thirty	124	Honey Dear	111	17,777	1:49.20	
1963	Frimanaha	6	J. Sellers	113	Waltz Song	119	Upswept	112	17,940	1:50.00	
1964	Prodana Neviesta	4	H. Gustines	108	Fool's Play	111	Tona	118	18,492	1:50.60	
1965	Steeple Jill	4	J. Ruane	126	Straight Deal	113	Ho Ho	109	18,752	1:49.60	
1966	Open Fire	5	F. Lovato	117	Reluctant Pearl	108	Mac's Sparkler	113	18,460	1:48.80	
1967	Prides Profile	4	M. Ycaza	114	Straight Deal	127	Malhoa	111	18,655	1:49.60	
1968	Green Glade	4	K. Knapp	110	Gamely	120	Mount Regina	116	18,622	1:49.60	
1969	Gamely	5	E. Belmonte	127	Obeah	118	Amerigo Lady	123	28,925	1:49.60	
1970	Shuvee	4	R. Turcotte	120	Dark Emerald	109	Native Partner	112	31,915	1:49.60	
1971	Shuvee	5	R. Turcotte	128	Double Delta	126	Cathy Honey	116	26,460	1:50.60	
1972	Blessing Angelica	4	E. Belmonte	117	Light Hearted	113	Aladancer	115	16,620	1:49.80	
1973	Cathy Baby	4	J. Velasquez	119	Something Super	113	Worlding	111	13,620	1:46.80	
1973	Lightning Lucy	3	R. Turcotte	116	Flying Fur	114	Summer Guest	122	13,545	1:46.60	
1974	Fairway Flyer	4	J. Velasquez	118	North Broadway	117	Brindabella	117	35,070	1:47.20	
1975	Heloise	4	M. Venezia	113	Victorian Queen	118	Princesse Grey	112	35,250	1:47.40	
1976	Glowing Tribute	3	R. Turcotte	116	Fleet Victress	117	Nijana	111	32,910	1:47.60	
1977	Javamine	4	A. Cordero Jr	114	Pearl Necklace	109	Rich Soil	114	32,640	1:48.40	
1978	Waya	4	A. Cordero Jr	115	Pearl Necklace	125	Fia	110	33,240	1:45.40	
1979	Pearl Necklace	5	J. Fell	124	Island Kiss	114	Terpsichorist	119	35,010	1:48.80	
1980	Just a Game II	4	D. Brumfield	123	The Very One	117	Relaxing	113	35,520	1:49.00	
1981	De La Rose	3	E. Maple	114	Rokeby Rose	115	Euphrosyne	112	36,420	1:50.60	
1982	Hush Dear	4	E. Beitia	109	Larida	114	So Pleasantly	109	34,170	1:47.40	
1982	If Winter Comes	4	E. Beitia	110	Canaille II	112	Noble Damsel	114	34,170	1:47.40	
1983	Geraldine's Store	4	J.L. Samyn	108	Trevita	120	Infinite	111	33,840	1:47.20	
1983	Hush Dear	5	J. Vasquez	123	If Winter Comes	113	First Approach	118	34,080	1:48.40	
1984	Wild Applause	3	W. Guerra	109	Pretty Perfect	109	Spit Curl	112	70,650	1:48.20	
1985	Lake Country	4	J. Fell	117	Possible Mate	118	Key Dancer	120	58,230	1:48.40	
1986	Duty Dance	4	J. Cruguet	118	Dismasted	115	Kapalua Butterfly	112	91,380	1:49.80	
1987	Bailrullah	5	J. Cruguet	111	Perfect Point	114	Videogenic	116	91,860	1:46.20	

Year	Winner	Age	Jockey	Wt.	Second	Wt.	Third	Wt.	Win Value	Time	Beyer
1988	Glowing Honor	3	P. Day	106	Sunny Roberta	111	Graceful Darby	112	73,680	1:49.40	
1989	Glowing Honor	4	J.D. Bailey	115	Wooing	111	Laugh and Be Merry	114	76,200	1:50.20	
1990	Foresta	4	A. Cordero Jr	113	To the Lighthouse	113	Songlines	111	56,790	1:48.40	105
1991	Christiecat	4	J.L. Samyn	117	Virgin Michael	112	Senora Tippy	111	75,360	1:47.60	104
1992	Plenty of Grace	5	W.H. McCauley	114	Ratings	114	Highland Crystal	115	75,960	1:46.60	99
1993	Ratings	5	J.A. Krone	110	Lady Blessington	118	Garendare	113	72,240	1:49.80	95
1994	Via Borghese	5	J.A. Santos	115	Blazing KAdie	110	Coronation Cup	108	83,010	1:52.00	105
1995	Perfect Arc	3	J.R. Velazquez	113	Danish	118	Tiffany's Taylor	113	85,125	1:46.80	108
1996	Electric Society	5	M.E. Smith	117	Powder Bowl	116	Upper Noosh	110	120,000	1:46.40	103
1997	Rumpipumpy	4	J. A. Santos	114	B. A. Valentine	116	Antespend	117	120,000	1:48.40	100
1998	Memories of Silver	5	J.D. Bailey	123	B.A. Valentine	114	Auntie Mame	122	180,000	1:46.00	105
1999	Heritage Of Gold	4	S.J. Sellers	115	Khumba Mela	114	Mossflower	114	180,000	1:45.80	102
2000	Perfect Sting	4	J.D. Bailey	123	License Fee	116	Hello Soso	113	300,000	1:47.01	102
2001	Starine	4	J.R. Velazquez	114	Babae	114	Penny's Gold	120	300,000	1:46.17	111
2002	Tates Creek	4	J.D. Bailey	117	Voodoo Dancer	120	Snow Dance	117	300,000	1:48.00	102
2003	Voodoo Dancer	5	C.S. Nakatani	120	Heat Haze	118	Pertuisane	115	300,000	1:47.98	106

Beyer Index: 103.36

DONN HANDICAP, 1 1/8 Miles, 3-Year-Olds and Up,
Gulfstream Park, 2003 Purse: $500,000

Year	Winner	Age	Jockey	Wt.	Second	Wt.	Third	Wt.	Win Value	Time	Beyer
1959	One-Eyed King	5	J. Sellers	116	Ekaba	117	General Arthur	126	17,925	2:25.80	
1960	One-Eyed King	6	M. Ycaza	121	North Pole II	114	Rafty	115	17,100	2:27.60	
1961	General Arthur	7	L. Gilligan	111	Civic Guard	112	Merry Top II	113	28,395	2:25.80	
1962	Jay Fox	4	L. Gilligan	116	Nasomo	115	Bigfork	112	26,505	2:28.40	
1963	Tutankhamen	5	W. Shoemaker	124	El Loco	112	Parka	117	27,835	2:26.00	
1964	Cedar Key	4	M. Ycaza	122	Parka	119	Suspicious	115	39,750	2:26.00	
1965	Gun Bow	5	W. Blum	127	Temper	108	Lt. Stevens	119	36,650	1:50.00	
1966	Tronado	6	B. Moreira	121	Just About	116	Selari	113	39,550	1:49.20	
1967	Francis U.	4	R.J. Campbell	111	Sky Guy	111	Quinta	117	41,100	1:50.40	
	Quinta finished second but was disqualified and placed third										
1968	Favorable Turn	4	B. Baeza	122	Rixdal	112	Ring Twice	117	45,500	1:48.20	
1969	Funny Fellow	4	B. Baeza	122	Tropic King II	115	Out the Window	114	44,200	1:49.20	
1970	Twogundan	4	E. Fires	112	Beau Brummel	114	Barely Once	113	39,600	1:51.20	
1971	Judgable	4	W. Blum	113	Snow Sporting	119	The Pruner	114	39,120	1:47.00	
1972	Going Straight	4	M. Solomone	116	Mr. Pow Wow	125	Dot Ed's Bluesky	108	37,140	1:48.20	
1973	Triumphant	4	B. Baeza	114	Second Bar	121	Gentle Smoke	113	37,560	1:47.80	
1974	Forego	4	H. Gustines	125	True Knight	123	Proud and Bold	122	39,000	1:48.60	
1975	Proud and Bold	5	G. St. Leon	118	Holding Pattern	121	Arbees Boy	119	35,280	1:48.00	
1976	Foolish Pleasure	4	B. Baeza	129	Packer Captain	114	Home Jerome	112	37,980	1:21.40	
1977	Legion	7	L. Saumell	113	Logical	114	Yamanin	124	37,440	1:48.80	
1978	Man's Man	4	R. Woodhouse	115	Intercontinent	116	Adriatico	110	39,000	1:42.20	
1979	Jumping Hill	7	J. Fell	122	Bob's Dusty	120	Silent Cal	121	60,150	1:46.40	
1980	Lot O' Gold	4	D. Brumfield	119	Addison	111	Going Investor	112	54,600	1:48.80	
1981	Hurry Up Blue	4	C. Lopez	116	Tunerup	126	Joanie's Chief	107	51,345	1:49.00	
1982	Joanie's Chief	5	J.L. Samyn	111	Double Sonic	111	Lord Darnley	113	57,330	1:49.00	
1983	Deputy Minister	4	D. MacBeth	122	Key Count	113	Rivalero	121	60,840	1:48.60	
1984	Play Fellow	4	P. Day	122	Courteous Majesty	111	Jack Slade	114	53,955	1:49.00	
1985	Mo Exception	4	R. Breen	115	Dr. Carter	120	Key to the Moon	122	74,280	1:48.60	
1986	Creme Fraiche	4	E. Maple	122	Skip Trial	122	Minneapple	113	77,280	1:51.20	
1987	Little Bold John	4	M.A. Gonzalez	111	Skip Trial	118	Wise Times	117	96,660	1:48.80	
1988	Jade Hunter	4	J.D. Bailey	112	Cryptoclearance	123	Personal Flag	120	120,000	1:48.80	
1989	Cryptoclearance	5	J.A. Santos	121	Slew City Slew	118	Primal	117	120,000	1:50.20	
1990	Primal	5	E. Fires	120	Ole Atocha	111	Western Playboy	119	120,000	1:50.00	
1991	Jolie's Halo	4	R. Platts	114	Sports View	116	Secret Hello	116	300,000	1:47.40	125
1992	Sea Cadet	4	A. Solis	115	Out of Place	114	Sunny Sunrise	115	300,000	1:48.00	116
1993	Pistols and Roses	4	H. Castillo Jr.	112	Irish Swap	118	Missionary Ridge	118	240,000	1:50.00	101
1994	Pistols and Roses	5	H. Castillo Jr.	114	Eequalsmcsquared	113	Wallenda	118	180,000	1:50.60	110
1995	Cigar	5	J.D. Bailey	115	Primitive Hall	112	Bonus Money	112	180,000	1:49.60	114
1996	Cigar	6	J.D. Bailey	128	Wekiva Springs	117	Heavenly Prize	115	180,000	1:49.00	117
1997	Formal Gold	4	J. Bravo	113	Skip Away	123	Mecke	120	180,000	1:47.40	114
1998	Skip Away	5	J.D. Bailey	126	Unruled	112	Sir Bear	113	180,000	1:50.17	109
1999	Puerto Madero	5	K.J. Desormeaux	120	Behrens	113	Silver Charm	126	300,000	1:48.34	115
2000	Stephen Got Even	4	S.J. Sellers	115	Golden Missile	114	Behrens	121	300,000	1:46.40	120
2001	Captain Steve	4	J.D. Bailey	120	Albert the Great	119	Gander	115	300,000	1:48.95	115
2002	Mongoose	4	E. Prado	114	Kiss a Native	114	Rize	114	300,000	1:49.63	106
	Red Bullet finished second but was disqualified and placed fourth										
2003	Harlan's Holiday	4	J.R. Velazquez	120	Hero's Tribute	114	Puzzlement	114	300,000	1:49.17	113

Beyer Index: 113.46

Distance 1 1/2 miles, turf course, prior to 1965; 1 1/16 miles in 1978; 7 furlongs in 1976

FLORIDA DERBY, 1 1/8 Miles, 3-Year-Olds, Gulfstream Park, 2003 Purse: $1,000,000

Year	Winner	Age	Jockey	Wt.	Second	Wt.	Third	Wt.	Win Value	Time	Beyer
1952	Sky Ship	3	R. Nash	114	Handsome Teddy	117	Sandtop	111	17,550	1:50.80	
1953	Money Broker	3	A. Popara	117	Blaze	111	Jamie K	117	88,000	1:53.80	
							Slim	117			
1954	Correlation	3	W. Shoemaker	119	Goyamo	119	Big Crest	113	100,000	1:55.20	
1955	Nashua	3	E. Arcaro	122	Blue Lem	113	First Cabin	113	100,000	1:53.20	
1956	Needles	3	E. Erb	117	Count Chic	119	Pintor Lea	113	95,200	1:48.60	
1957	Gen. Duke	3	W. Hartack	122	Bold Ruler	122	Iron Liege	118	73,440	1:46.80	
1958	Tim Tam	3	W. Hartack	122	Lincoln Road	118	Grey Monarch	122	77,900	1:49.20	
1959	Easy Spur	3	W. Hartack	122	Sword Dancer	122	Master Palynch	122	75,300	1:47.20	
1960	Bally Ache	3	R. Ussery	122	Venetian Way	122	Victoria Park	122	79,500	1:47.60	
1961	Carry Back	3	J. Sellers	122	Crozier	122	Beau Prince	122	75,100	1:48.80	
1962	Ridan	3	M. Ycaza	122	Cicada	117	Admiral's Voyage	122	85,800	1:50.40	
1963	Candy Spots	3	W. Shoemaker	122	Sky Wonder	122	Cool Prince	122	74,700	1:50.60	
1964	Northern Dancer	3	W. Shoemaker	122	The Scoundrel	122	Dandy K.	122	76,500	1:50.80	
1965	Native Charger	3	J.L. Rotz	122	Hail to All	122	Gallant Lad	122	79,800	1:51.20	
1966	Williamston Kid	3	R.L. Stevenson	122	Bold and Brave	122	Sky Guy	122	83,400	1:50.60	

Abe's Hope finished first but was disqualified and placed fourth

Year	Winner	Age	Jockey	Wt.	Second	Wt.	Third	Wt.	Win Value	Time	Beyer
1967	In Reality	3	E. Fires	122	Biller	122	Reason to Hail	122	99,400	1:50.20	
1968	Forward Pass	3	D. Brumfield	122	Iron Ruler	122	Perfect Tan	118	94,100	1:49.00	
1969	Top Knight	3	M. Ycaza	122	Arts and Letters	122	Al Hattab	122	81,800	1:48.40	
1970	My Dad George	3	R. Broussard	122	Corn off the Cob	122	Cassie Red	122	103,600	1:50.80	
1971	Eastern Fleet	3	E. Maple	118	Executioner	122	Jim French	122	82,680	1:47.40	
1972	Upper Case	3	R. Turcotte	118	Spanish Riddle	122	Gentle Smoke	122	107,760	1:50.00	
1973	Royal and Regal	3	W. Blum	122	Forego	118	Restless Jet	122	78,120	1:47.40	
1974	Judger	3	L. Pincay Jr	118	Cannonade	122	Buck's Bid	118	130,200	1:49.00	
1975	Prince Thou Art	3	B. Baeza	118	Sylvan Place	118	Foolish Pleasure	122	94,440	1:50.40	
1976	Honest Pleasure	3	B. Baeza	122	Great Contractor	122	Proud Birdie	122	94,110	1:47.80	
1977	Coined Silver	3	B. Thornburg	118	Nearly on Time	122	Fort Prevel	122	68,700	1:48.80	
1977	Ruthie's Native	3	C. Perret	122	For the Moment	122	Sir Sir	122	69,900	1:50.20	
1978	Alydar	3	J. Velasquez	122	Believe It	122	Dr. Valeri	122	100,000	1:47.00	
1979	Spectacular Bid	3	R. Franklin	122	Lot o' Gold	122	Fantasy 'n Reality	122	115,000	1:48.80	
1980	Plugged Nickle	3	B. Thornburg	122	Naked Sky	122	Lord Gallant	118	110,000	1:50.20	
1981	Lord Avie	3	C.J. McCarron	122	Akureyri	122	Linnleur	118	147,388	1:50.40	
1982	Timely Writer	3	J. Fell	122	Star Gallant	122	Our Escapade	122	150,000	1:49.60	
1983	Croeso	3	F. Olivares	118	Copelan	122	Law Talk	118	150,000	1:49.80	
1984	Swale	3	L. Pincay Jr	122	Dr. Carter	122	Darn that Alarm	122	180,000	1:47.60	
1985	Proud Truth	3	J. Velasquez	122	Irish Sur	122	Do It Again Dan	122	180,000	1:50.00	
1986	Snow Chief	3	A. Solis	122	Badger Land	122	Mogambo	122	300,000	1:51.80	
1987	Cryptoclearance	3	J.A. Santos	122	No More Flowers	118	Talinum	122	300,000	1:49.60	
1988	Brian's Time	3	R.P. Romero	118	Forty Niner	122	Notebook	122	300,000	1:49.80	
1989	Mercedes Won	3	E. Fires	122	Western Playboy	118	Big Stanley	122	300,000	1:49.60	
1990	Unbridled	3	P. Day	122	Slavic	122	Run Turn	122	300,000	1:52.00	
1991	Fly So Free	3	J.A. Santos	122	Strike the Gold	118	Hansel	122	300,000	1:50.40	
1992	Technology	3	J.D. Bailey	122	Dance Floor	122	Pistols and Roses	122	300,000	1:50.60	101
1993	Bull Inthe Heather	3	W.S. Ramos	122	Storm Tower	122	Wallenda	122	300,000	1:51.20	94
1994	Holy Bull	3	M.E. Smith	122	Ride the Rails	122	Halo's Image	122	300,000	1:47.40	115
1995	Thunder Gulch	3	M.E. Smith	122	Suave Prospect	122	Mecke	122	300,000	1:49.60	101
1996	Unbridled's Song	3	M.E. Smith	122	Editor's Note	122	Skip Away	122	300,000	1:47.80	114
1997	Captain Bodgit	3	A. Solis	122	Pulpit	122	Frisk Me Now	122	300,000	1:50.60	104
1998	Cape Town	3	S.J. Sellers	122	Lil's Lad	122	Halory Hunter	122	450,000	1:49.21	108

Lil's Lad finished first but was disqualified and placed second

Year	Winner	Age	Jockey	Wt.	Second	Wt.	Third	Wt.	Win Value	Time	Beyer
1999	Vicar	3	S.J. Sellers	122	Wondertross	122	Cat Thief	122	450,000	1:50.83	102
2000	Hal's Hope	3	R.I. Velez	122	High Yield	122	Tahkodha Hills	122	450,000	1:51.49	102
2001	Monarchos	3	J.F. Chavez	122	Outofthebox	122	Invisible Ink	122	600,000	1:49.95	105
2002	Harlan's Holiday	3	E. Prado	122	Blue Burner	122	Peekskill	122	600,000	1:48.80	101
2003	Empire Maker	3	J.D. Bailey	122	Trust n Luck	122	Indy Dancer	122	600,000	1:49.05	108

Beyer Index: 104.58

FLOWER BOWL INVITATIONAL STAKES, 1 1/4 Miles (Turf), Fillies and Mares, 3-Year-Olds and Up, Belmont Park, 2003 Purse: $750,000

Year	Winner	Age	Jockey	Wt.	Second	Wt.	Third	Wt.	Win Value	Time	Beyer
1978	Waya	4	A. Cordero Jr	120	Magnificence	108	Leave Me Alone	108	32,490	2:00.60	
1979	Pearl Necklace	5	W. Shoemaker	125	The Very One	112	Terpsichorist	118	68,160	2:02.20	
1980	Just a Game II	4	D. Brumfield	124	Hey Babe	114	Euphrosyne	112	68,640	2:00.80	
1981	Rokeby Rose	4	J. Fell	114	De La Rose	116	Euphrosyne	110	67,200	2:01.60	
1982	Trevita	5	R. Hernandez	117	Hunston	108	Hush Dear	112	71,880	2:01.40	
1983	First Approach	5	J. Velasquez	117	If Winter Comes	113	Mintage	111	68,160	2:00.20	
1984	Rossard	4	L. Pincay Jr	117	Aspen Rose	115	Persian Tiara	116	72,840	2:03.40	
1985	Dawn's Curtsey	3	E. Maple	111	Vers la Caisse	116	Agacerie	117	87,540	2:02.20	
1986	Scoot	3	W. Shoemaker	106			Cope of Flowers	113	65,652	2:00.40	
	Dismasted	4	J.L. Samyn	115							

Year	Winner	Age	Jockey	Wt.	Second	Wt.	Third	Wt.	Win Value	Time	Beyer
1987	Slew's Exceller	5	J.A. Santos	113	Videogenic	118	Fiesta Gal	114	91,020	2:02.20	
1988	Gaily Gaily	5	J.A. Krone	109	Love You by Heart	116	Princely Proof	116	76,800	2:02.80	
1989	River Memories	5	P. Day	112	Capades	116	Miss Unnameable	116	74,880	2:06.80	
1990	Laugh and Be Merry	5	W.H. McCauley	114	Foresta	111	Gaily Gaily	117	78,840	2:00.20	105
1991	Lady Shirl	4	R. Migliore	117	Franc Argument	111	Christiecat	120	120,000	2:02.40	106
1992	Christiecat	5	J.L. Samyn	116	Ratings	114	Plenty of Grace	115	120,000	2:01.00	105
1993	Far Out Beast	6	J.L. Samyn	111	Dahlia's Dreamer	110	Lady Blessington	118	90,000	2:03.80	98
1994	Dahlia's Dreamer	5	J.F. Chavez	112	Alywow	114	Danish	113	120,000	2:05.40	113
1995	Northern Emerald	5	R.B. Perez	113	Danish	116	Duda	113	120,000	2:06.60	105
1996	Chelsey Flower	5	R.G. Davis	115	Powder Bowl	116	Electric Society	118	210,000	2:05.80	108
1997	Yashmak	3	C.S. Nakatani	114	Maxzene	123	Memories of Silver	123	240,000	1:59.60	107
1998	Auntie Mame	4	J.R. Velazquez	121	B.A. Valentine	114	Bahr	118	240,000	1:59.33	104
1999	Soaring Softly	4	J.D. Bailey	118	Coretta	118	Mossflower	115	240,000	2:01.41	103
2000	Colstar	4	J.L. Samyn	116	Snow Polina	121	Pico Teneriffe	115	450,000	2:01.78	105
2001	Lailani	3	J.D. Bailey	118	England's Legend	123	Starine	120	450,000	2:01.88	111
2002	Kazzia	3	J.F. Chavez	118	Turtle Bow	115	Mot Juste	118	450,000	2:05.22	103
2003	Dimitrova	3	J.D. Bailey	114	Walzerkoenigin	120	Heat Haze	123	450,000	2:02.74	103

Beyer Index: 105.43

Run on main track in 1987

FOREGO HANDICAP, 7 Furlongs,
3-Year-Olds and Up, Saratoga Race Course, 2003 Purse: $250,000

Year	Winner	Age	Jockey	Wt.	Second	Wt.	Third	Wt.	Win Value	Time	Beyer
1980	Tanthem	5	J. Velasquez	114	Dr. Patches	114	Hold Your Tricks	116	51,030	1:35.00	
1981	Fappiano	4	A. Cordero	119	Herb Water	108	Guilty Conscience	112	50,220	1:33.80	
1982	Engine One	4	R. Hernandez	112	Rise Jim	121	Pass the Tab	120	33,360	1:21.20	
1983	Maudlin	5	A. Cordero Jr	119	Danebo	115	Singh Tu	115	32,580	1:21.60	
1984	Mugatea	4	R.G. Davis	111	Eskimo	108	I Enclose	111	53,370	1:22.40	
1985	Ziggy's Boy	3	A. Cordero Jr	115	Taylor's Special	124	Knight of Armor	112	66,510	1:21.20	
1986	Groovy	3	J.A. Santos	119	Turkoman	124	Innamorato	110	83,820	1:21.20	
1987	Groovy	4	A. Cordero Jr	132	Purple Mountain	113	Sun Master	118	81,060	1:21.80	
1988	Quick Call	4	P. Day	110	Mawsuff	110	High Brite	122	68,520	1:21.00	
1989	Quick Call	5	P. Day	116	Dancing Spree	117	Sewickley	119	67,920	1:21.80	
1990	Lay Down	6	C.W. Antley	113	Quick Call	120	Traskwood	112	51,840	1:22.80	107
1991	Housebuster	4	C. Perret	126	Senor Speedy	112	Clever Trevor	120	69,480	1:21.00	113
1992	Rubiano	5	J.A. Krone	124	Drummond Lane	115	Diablo	114	70,080	1:22.40	110
1993	Birdonthewire	4	M.E. Smith	117	Harlan	110	Senor Speedy	117	73,080	1:21.80	111
1994	American Chance	5	P. Day	113	Evil Bear	114	Go for Gin	117	66,000	1:22.60	108
1995	Not Surprising	5	R.G. Davis	121	Our Emblem	113	Lite the Fuse	123	64,200	1:21.80	120
1996	Langfuhr	4	J.F. Chavez	110	Top Account	115	Lite the Fuse	121	90,000	1:21.40	109
1997	Score A Birdie	6	W.H. McCauley	113	Victor Cooley	120	Royal Haven	120	120,000	1:22.40	111
1998	Affirmed Success	4	J.F. Chavez	125	Receiver	114	Purple Passion	114	120,000	1:21.80	120
1999	Crafty Friend	6	G.L. Stevens	119	Affirmed Success	119	Sir Bear	119	150,000	1:21.20	115
2000	Shadow Caster	4	J.F. Chavez	113	Intidab	118	Successful Appeal	119	150,000	1:15.00	114
2001	Delaware Township	5	J.D. Bailey	116	Left Bank	115	Alannan	117	150,000	1:15.53	109
2002	Orientate	4	J.D. Bailey	122	Aldebaran	115	Multiple Choice	114	150,000	1:15.68	116
2003	Aldebaran	5	J.D. Bailey	123	Najran	114	Gygistar	119	150,000	1:21.26	122

Beyer Index: 113.21

Distance 6 1/2 furlongs 2000–2002

STEPHEN FOSTER HANDICAP, 1 1/8 Miles,
3-Year-Olds and Up, Churchill Downs, 2003 Purse: $856,500

Year	Winner	Age	Jockey	Wt.	Second	Wt.	Third	Wt.	Win Value	Time	Beyer
1982	Vodika Collins	4	T. Barrow	116	Mythical Ruler	113	Two's a Plenty	115	38,610	1:51.80	
1983	Vodika Collins	5	L. Moyers	118	Mythical Ruler	120	Northern Majesty	114	35,588	1:49.20	
1984	Mythical Ruler	6	J. McKnight	117	Fairly Straight	114	Le Cou Cou	121	34,808	1:49.60	
1985	Vanlandingham	4	P. Day	121	Manantial	112	Sovereign Exchange	113	35,263	1:48.80	
1986	Hopeful Word	5	K.K. Allen	123	Dramatic Desire	114	Ten Gold Pots	122	64,133	1:49.40	
1987	Red Attack	5	J.L. Kaenel	119	Sir Naskra	116	Blue Buckaroo	117	65,254	1:51.20	
1988	Honor Medal	7	L.E. Ortega	123	Outlaws Sham	115	Momsfurrari	109	82,655	1:50.60	
1989	Air Worthy	4	D.J. Soto	115	J.T.'s Pet	115	Present Value	114	73,255	1:49.60	
1990	No Marker	6	A.T. Gryder	115	Western Playboy	117	Lucky Peach	114	72,930	1:49.80	
1991	Black Tie Affair	5	J.L. Diaz	119	Private School	114	Greydar	115	70,915	1:49.80	104
1992	Discover	4	B.E. Bongard	116	Barkerville	113	Classic Seven	113	75,335	1:50.00	111
1993	Root Boy	5	T.G. Turner	113	Discover	114	Flying Continental	117	74,100	1:50.80	99
1994	Recoup the Cash	4	J.L. Diaz	112	Taking Risks	113	Dignitas	113	106,275	1:49.40	108
1995	Recoup the Cash	5	A.T. Gryder	119	Tyus	115	Powerful Punch	113	109,297	1:49.20	105
1996	Tenants Harbor	4	F.C. Torres	112	Pleasant Tango	113	Mt. Sassafras	115	107,933	1:49.80	109
1997	City By Night	4	S.J. Sellers	113	Victor Cooley	115	Semoran	113	101,649	1:50.40	115
1998	Awesome Again	4	P. Day	113	Silver Charm	127	Semoran	115	495,690	1:48.60	118
1999	Victory Gallop	4	J.D. Bailey	120	Nite Dreamer	110	Littlebitlively	115	512,895	1:47.20	116
2000	Golden Missile	5	K.J. Desormeaux	118	Ecton Park	114	Cat Thief	117	502,200	1:49.56	116

Year	Winner	Age	Jockey	Wt.	Second	Wt.	Third	Wt.	Win Value	Time	Beyer
2001	Guided Tour	5	L. Melancon	113	Captain Steve	123	Brahms	114	515,220	1:47.74	116
2002	Street Cry	4	J.D. Bailey	120	Dollar Bill	114	Tenpins	115	516,615	1:47.84	116
2003	Perfect Drift	4	P. Day	115	Mineshaft	123	Aldebaran	120	531,030	1:47.55	117

Beyer Index: 111.69

FOUNTAIN OF YOUTH STAKES, 1 1/16 Miles, 3-Year-Olds, Gulfstream Park, 2003 Purse: $200,000

Year	Winner	Age	Jockey	Wt.	Second	Wt.	Third	Wt.	Win Value	Time	Beyer
1945	Twenty Thirty	2	R. Watson	118	Flag Drill	117	Best Dress	116	3,200	1:45.20	
1947	Atomic Power	3	M. Buxton	116	Skeleton	106	Red Devil	112	6,050	1:40.60	
1947	Tight Squeeze	2	R. Sisto	117	Phar Mon	124	Montayr	115	7,150	1:11.80	
1949	Count-a-Bit	3	J. Robertson	116	Fugitive	113	Top Admiral	114	3,250	1:44.20	
1950	Black George	3	K. Church	110	Theory	123	Erosion	111	3,250	1:23.40	
1951	Alerted	3	W. Cook	114	Pur Sang	118	Blue Speed	115	3,250	1:24.20	
1953	Ram o' War	3	D. Dodson	115	Slim	112	Dr. Stanley	104	12,150	1:42.60	
1953	Tribe	3	B. Green	120	Sickle's Sound	108	Royal Bay Gem	122	12,300	1:43.40	
1954	Sea O Erin	3	J. Adams	112	Remand	112	Bergeruk	104	11,800	1:48.60	
1955	Nance's Lad	3	J. Choquette	117	First Cabin	117	Blue Lem	116	13,550	1:43.60	
1956	Oh Johnny	3	H. Woodhouse	114	Greek Spy	116	Fabius	118	12,765	1:44.20	
1957	Gen. Duke	3	W. Hartack	119	Iron Liege	113	Better Bee	113	11,560	1:44.00	
1958	Tim Tam	3	W. Hartack	122	Grey Monarch	119	Li'l Fella	122	9,725	1:42.80	
1959	Easy Spur	3	W. Hartack	119	Troilus	122	Rare Rice	116	10,275	1:41.80	
1960	Eagle Admiral	3	M. Ycaza	119	Bally Ache	122	Power Dame	116	10,550	1:41.80	
1961	Beau Prince	3	E. Arcaro	113	Crozier	122	Carry Back	122	10,575	1:43.20	
1962	Sharp Count	3	W. Shoemaker	110	Docot Hank K	110	Good Fight	119	10,400	1:43.20	
1963	Cool Prince	3	J. Combest	110	Hot Dust	111	King Toots	119	10,725	1:45.80	
1964	Dandy K	3	M. Solomone	112	Roman Brother	122	Saltville	111	11,075	1:44.80	
1965	Maribeau	3	S. Boulmetis	111	Hail to All	119	Sparkling Johnny	112	11,275	1:44.60	
1966	Kauai King	3	D. Brumfield	113	Amberoid	112	Abe's Hope	116	11,550	1:43.20	
1967	In Reality	3	E. Fires	122	Biller	122	Reason to Hail	119	15,125	1:44.40	
1968	Wise Exchange	3	E. Belmonte	122	Master Bold	119	Subpet	122	14,925	1:43.80	

Forward Pass finished second but was disqualified and placed fourth

Year	Winner	Age	Jockey	Wt.	Second	Wt.	Third	Wt.	Win Value	Time	Beyer
1969	Al Hattab	3	R. Broussard	122	Arts and Letters	119	Ad Majora	122	13,925	1:42.60	
1970	Corn Off the Cob	3	A. Cordero Jr.	113	Naskra	119	Nehoc's Brother	110	24,950	1:44.60	
1971	Authorize	3	J. Vasquez	112	Northfields	113	Glorioso	114	20,160	1:42.40	
1972	Gentle Smoke	3	W. Blum	113	Native Admiral	112	Tarboosh	112	43,020	1:42.00	
1973	Shecky Greene	3	B. Baeza	122	Twice a Prince	117	My Gallant	112	22,950	1:43.80	
1974	Green Gambados	3	C. Baltazar	112	Judger	115	Eric's Champ	112	46,440	1:42.40	
1975	Greek Answer	3	M. Solomone	122	Decipher	115	Gatch	116	22,650	1:42.80	
1976	Sonkisser	3	B. Baeza	117	Proud Birdie	122	Archie Beamish	113	22,770	1:43.80	
1977	Ruthie's Native	3	C. Perret	122	Steve's Friend	112	Fort Prevel	117	26,010	1:42.00	

Fort Prevel finished second but was disqualified and placed third

Year	Winner	Age	Jockey	Wt.	Second	Wt.	Third	Wt.	Win Value	Time	Beyer
1978	Sensitive Prince	3	M. Solomone	114	Believe It	122	Kissing U	113	22,170	1:41.00	
1979	Spectacular Bid	3	R.J. Franklin	122	Lot O' Gold	117	Bishop's Choice	122	35,880	1:41.20	
1980	Naked Sky	3	J.D. Bailey	112	Joanie's Chief	122	Gold Stage	122	29,820	1:43.80	
1981	Akureyri	3	E. Maple	119	Pleasant Colony	122	Lord Avie	122	47,697	1:44.40	
1982	Star Gallant	3	S. Hawley	117	Distinctive Pro	117	Cut Away	113	54,630	1:43.20	
1983	Highland Park	3	D. Brumfield	122	Thalassocrat	117	Chumming	112	45,338	1:44.60	
1983	Copelan	3	L. Pincay Jr.	122	Current Hope	117	Blink	112	44,888	1:43.60	
1984	Darn That Alarm	3	M. Venezia	112	Counterfeit Money	112	Swale	122	73,200	1:43.00	
1985	Proud Truth	3	J. Velasquez	112	Stephan's Odyssey	122	Do It Again Dan	112	106,860	1:43.60	
1986	Ensign Rhythm	3	J. Pezua	112	Jig's Haven	113	Regal Dreamer	117	57,210	1:45.60	
1986	My Prince Charming	3	J.A. Santos	112	Mykawa	117	Papal Power	122	78,060	1:45.00	
1987	Bet Twice	3	C. Perret	122	No More Flowers	112	Gone West	114	100,482	1:43.40	
1988	Forty Niner	3	E. Maple	122	Notebook	122	Buoy	119	98,991	1:43.20	
1989	Dixieland Brass	3	R. Romero	122	Mercedes Won	122	Big Stanley	122	130,000	1:44.60	
1990	Shot Gun Scott	3	D. Penna	122	Smelly	119	Unbridled	117	77,427	1:44.60	99
1991	Fly So Free	3	J.A. Santos	122	Moment of True	117	Subordinated Debt	113	77,737	1:44.20	
1992	Dance Floor	3	C.W. Antley	122	Pistols and Roses	119	Tiger Tiger	112	150,258	1:45.20	98

Careful Gesture finished second but was disqualified and placed fifth

Year	Winner	Age	Jockey	Wt.	Second	Wt.	Third	Wt.	Win Value	Time	Beyer
1993	Duc d' Sligovil	3	J. Krone	112	Bull Inthe Heather	113	Silver of Silver	122	37,698	1:45.00	94
1993	Storm Tower	3	R. Wilson	112	Great Navigator	117	Kissin Kris	117	37,698	1:44.80	96
1994	Dehere	3	C. Perret	119	Go for Gin		Ride the Rails		120,000	1:44.60	99
1995	Thunder Gulch	3	M.E. Smith	119	Suave Prospect	117	Jambalaya Jazz	119	120,000	1:43.20	105
1996	Built for Pleasure	3	G. Boulanger	112	Unbridled's Song	119	Victory Speech	114	120,000	1:43.60	100
1997	Pulpit	3	S.J. Sellers	112	Blazing Sword	117	Captain Bodgit	117	120,000	1:41.80	104
1998	Lil's Lad	3	J.D. Bailey	112	Coronado's Quest	119	Halory Hunter	112	120,000	1:42.60	113
1999	Vicar	3	S.J. Sellers	114	Cat Thief	119	Certain	117	120,000	1:45.64	97
2000	High Yield	3	P. Day	117	Hal's Hope	117	Elite Mercedes	117	120,000	1:42.56	100
2001	Songandaprayer	3	E.S. Prado	117	Outofthebox	114	City Zip	117	120,000	1:43.48	100
2002	Booklet	3	J.F. Chavez	122	Harlan's Holiday	122	Blue Burner	116	120,000	1:44.49	103
2003	Trust n Luck	3	C. Velasquez	122	Supah Blitz	120	Midway Cat	116	120,000	1:43.33	106

Beyer Index: 101

Run twice in 1947. For 2-year-olds in 1945, 1947. Distance 6 furlongs in December 1947; 1 mile 70 yards, March 1947, 1949; 7 furlongs, 1950-51

FRIZETTE STAKES, 1 1/16 Miles, 2-Year-Old Fillies, Belmont Park, 2003 Purse: $500,000

Year	Winner	Age	Jockey	Wt.	Second	Wt.	Third	Wt.	Win Value	Time	Beyer
1945	Bonnie Beryl	2	J. Stout	112	La Liberte	112	Mush Mush	116	8,085	1:11.80	
1946	Bimlette	2	A. DeLara	110	Carolyn A.	122	Pipette	119	14,650	1:12.40	
1947	Slumber Song	2	J. Westrope	113	Grey Flight	112	Watermill	114	14,400	1:12.20	
1948	Our Fleet	2	E. Arcaro	115	Gay Mood	114	Be Sure	114	13,250	1:01.00	
1952	Sweet Patootie	2	T. Atkinson	119	Piedmont Lass	119	Grecian Queen	119	12,050	1:12.40	
1953	Indian Legend	2	T. Atkinson	110	Case Goods	119	Small Favor	115	13,600	1:13.60	
1954	Myrtle's Jet	2	W. Blum	119	Hen Party	119	Sorceress	119	35,000	1:49.20	
1955	Nasrina	2	W. Boland	119	Noors Image	119	Cosmah	119	55,525	1:45.40	
1956	Capelet	2	J. Nichols	119	Light 'n Lovely	119	Romanita	119	58,125	1:45.40	
1957	Idun	2	W. Hartack	119	Lopar	119	Big Fright	119	58,475	1:46.80	
1958	Merry Hill	2	R. Broussard	119	Dance All Night	119	Rich Tradition	119	56,772	1:46.40	
1959	My Dear Girl	2	M.N. Gonzalez	119	Irish Jay	119	Sarcastic	119	59,991	1:40.20	
1960	Bowl of Flowers	2	E. Arcaro	119	Counter Call	119	Good Move	119	69,936	1:35.60	
1961	Cicada	2	W. Shoemaker	119	Firm Policy	119	Jazz Queen	119	83,575	1:36.80	
1962	Pams Ego	2	M. Ycaza	119	Fool;s Play	119	Affectionately	119	73,000	1:38.00	
1963	Tosmah	2	S. Boulmetis	119	Beautiful Day	119	Castle Forbes	119	81,700	1:36.00	
1964	Queen Empress	2	W. Shoemaker	119	Money to Burn	119	Marshua	119	88,875	1:37.40	

Marshua finished second but was disqualified and finished third

Year	Winner	Age	Jockey	Wt.	Second	Wt.	Third	Wt.	Win Value	Time	Beyer
1965	Priceless Gem	2	W. Blum	119	Lady Pitt	119	Swift Lady	119	85,000	1:36.00	
1966	Regal Gleam	2	M. Ycaza	119	Irish County	119	Pepperwood	119	94,675	1:37.40	
1967	Queen of the Stage	2	B. Baeza	119	Gay Matelda	119	Obeah	119	76,975	1:35.40	
1968	Shuvee	2	J. Davidson	119	Gallant Bloom	119	Dihela	119	93,150	1:37.00	
1969	Tudor Queen	2	A. Gomez	119	Cherry Sundae	119	Repoise	119	88,100	1:36.60	
1970	Forward Gal	2	J. Velasquez	119	Isafloridan	119	Make Me Laugh	119	81,525	1:35.60	
1971	Numbered Account	2	B. Baeza	119	Susan's Girl	119	Barely Even	119	68,640	1:37.40	
1972	La Prevoyante	2	J. LeBlanc	121	Cam Axe	121	Fine Tuning	121	72,660	1:36.40	
1973	Bundler	2	J. Vasquez	121	Chris Evert	121	I'm a Pleasure	121	67,140	1:37.00	
1974	Molly Ballantine	2	L. Pincay Jr	121	Copernica	121	Mystery Mood	121	69,360	1:36.80	
1975	Optimistic Gal	2	B. Baeza	121	Artfully	121	Picture Tube	121	67,740	1:36.20	
1976	Sensational	2	J. Velasquez	119	Northern Sea	119	Mrs. Warren	119	64,680	1:37.20	
1977	Lakeville Miss	2	R. Hernandez	119	Misgivings	119	Itsamaza	119	63,780	1:35.40	
1978	Golferette	2	J. Fell	119	It's in the Air	119	Terlingua	119	66,240	1:38.20	
1979	Smart Angle	2	S. Maple	119	Royal Suite	119	Hardship	119	66,000	1:38.00	
1980	Heavenly Cause	2	L. Pincay Jr	119	Sweet Revenge	119	Prayers'n Promises	119	70,920	1:38.80	
1981	Proud Lou	2	D. Beckon	119	Mystical Mood	119	Chilling Thought	119	70,080	1:39.00	
1982	Princess Rooney	2	J. Fell	119	Winning Tack	119	Weekend Surprise	119	68,040	1:36.60	
1983	Miss Oceana	2	E. Maple	119	Life's Magic	119	Lucky Lucky Lucky	119	130,860	1:39.00	
1984	Charleston Rag	2	D. MacBeth	119	Tiltalating	119	Guadery	119	133,200	1:37.20	
1985	Family Style	2	L. Pincay Jr	119	Funistrada	119	Mom's Command	119	161,400	1:36.40	
1986	Personal Ensign	2	R.P. Romero	119	Collins	119	Flying Katuna	119	215,640	1:37.20	
1987	Classic Crown	2	A. Cordero Jr	119	Tap Your Toes	119	Justsayno	119	209,520	1:36.80	
1988	Some Romance	2	L. Pincay Jr	119	Open Mind	119	Ms. Gold Pole	119	176,700	1:38.80	
1989	Stella Madrid	2	A. Cordero Jr	119	Go for Wand	119	Dance Colony	119	171,000	1:35.40	
1990	Meadow Star	2	J.A. Santos	119	Champagne Glow	119	Flawlessly	119	150,000	1:37.20	87
1991	Preach	2	J.A. Krone	119	Vivano	119	Anh Duong	119	150,000	1:36.60	84
1992	Educated Risk	2	J.D. Bailey	119	Standard Equipment	119	Beal Street Blues	119	150,000	1:35.40	94
1993	Heavenly Prize	2	M.E. Smith	119	Facts of Love	119	Footing	119	150,000	1:34.80	102
1994	Flanders	2	P. Day	119	Change Fora Dollar	119	Pretty Discreet	119	150,000	1:42.80	99
1995	Golden Attraction	2	G.L. Stevens	119	My Flag	119	Flat Fleet Feet	119	150,000	1:42.40	96
1996	Storm Song	2	C. Perret	119	Sharp Cat	119	Aldiza	119	240,000	1:42.60	94
1997	Silver Maiden	2	J.D. Bailey	119	Diamond on the Run	119	Brac Drifter	119	240,000	1:42.88	93
1998	Confessional	2	J.D. Bailey	119	Things Change	119	Pico Teneriffe	119	240,000	1:43.18	94
1999	Surfside	2	P. Day	119	Darling My Darling	119	March Magic	119	300,000	1:43.57	81
2000	Raging Fever	2	J.D. Bailey	120	Out of Sync	120	Western Justice	120	300,000	1:43.94	99
2001	You	2	E.S. Prado	120	Cashier's Dream	120	Riskaverse	120	300,000	1:43.94	98
2002	Storm Flag Flying	2	J. Velazquez	120	Santa Catarina	120	Appleby Gardens	120	300,000	1:44.20	95
2003	Society Selection	2	R. Ganpath	120	Victory U.S.A.	120	Ashado	120	300,000	1:43.95	

Beyer Index: 93.54

Distance 5 furlongs, 1948; 6 furlongs, 1945-47, 1952-53; 1 mile, 1959-93. Run at Jamaica Race Course prior to 1959; at Aqueduct, 1960-61, 1963-67.

FUTURITY STAKES, 1 Mile, 2-Year-Olds, Belmont Park, 2003 Purse: $200,000

Year	Winner	Age	Jockey	Wt.	Second	Wt.	Third	Wt.	Win Value	Time	Beyer
1888	Proctor Knott	2	S. Barnes	112	Salvator	108	Galen	115	40,900	1:15.20	
1889	Chaos	2	G. Day	109	St. Carlo	122	Sinaloa II	105	54,500	1:16.80	
1890	Potomac	2	A. Hamilton	115	Masher	108	Strathmeath	124	67,675	1:14.20	
1891	His Highness	2	J. McLaughlin	130	Yorkville Belle	115	Dagonet	108	61,675	1:15.20	

Huron finished second but was disqualified as a starter by Coney Island Jockey Club

Year	Winner	Age	Jockey	Wt.	Second	Wt.	Third	Wt.	Win Value	Time	Beyer
1892	Morello	2	W. Hayward	118	Lady Violet	118	St. Leonards	115	40,450	1:12.20	
1893	Domino	2	F. Taral	130	Galilee	115	Dobbins	130	48,855	1:12.80	

Year	Winner	Age	Jockey	Wt.	Second	Wt.	Third	Wt.	Win Value	Time	Beyer
1894	The Butteflies	2	H. Griffin	112	Brandywine	108	Agitator	110	48,710	1:11.00	
1895	Requittal	2	H. Griffin	115	Silver II	108			53,190	1:11.40	
1896	Ogden	2	F. Turblville	115	Ornament	116	Rodermond	115	43,790	1:10.00	
1897	L'Alouette	2	R. Clawson	115	Uriel	115			34,290	1:11.00	
1898	Martinmas	2	H. Lewis	118	High Degree	113	Mr. Clay	116	36,610	1:12.40	
1899	Chacornac	2	H. Spencer	114	Brigadier	109	Windmere	112	30,630	1:10.40	
1900	Ballyhoo Bey	2	T. Sloan	112	Olympian	112	Tommy Atkins	129	33,580	1:10.00	
1901	Yankee	2	W. O'Connor	119	Lux Casta	109	Barron	112	36,850	1:09.20	
1902	Savable	2	L. Lyne	119	Lord of the Vale	117	Dazzling	116	44,500	1:14.00	
1903	Hamburg Belle	2	G. Fuller	114	Leonidas	123	The Min. Man	122	36,600	1:13.00	
1904	Artful	2	E. Hildebrand	114	Tradition	127	Sysonby	127	40,830	1:11.80	
1905	Ormondale	2	A. Redfern	117	Timber	119	Belmere	117	32,960	1:11.80	
1906	Electioneer	2	W. Shaw	117	Pope Joan	116	De Mund	123	36,880	1:13.60	
1907	Colin	2	W. Miller	125	Bar None	117	Chapultepec	117	26,640	1:11.20	
1908	Maskette	2	J. Notter	118	Sir Martin	127	Helmet	123	26,110	1:11.20	
1909	Sweep	2	J. Butwell	126	Candleberry	117	Grasmere	122	24,100	1:11.80	
1910	Novelty	2	C.H. Shilling	127	Bashti	118	Love Not	114	25,360	1:12.20	
1913	Pennant	2	C. Borel	119	Southern Maid	119	Addie M.	114	15,060	1:15.00	
1914	Trojan	2	C. Burlingame	117	Kaskaskia	120	Harry Junior	122	16,010	1:16.80	
1915	Thunderer	2	J. Notter	122	Bromo	126	Achievement	123	16,590	1:11.80	
1916	Campfire	2	J. McTaggart	125	Rickety	122	Skeptic	122	17,340	1:13.80	
1917	Papp	2	L. Allen	127	Escoba	127	Rosie O'Grady	124	15,600	1:12.00	
1918	Dunboyne	2	A. Schuttinger	127	Sir Barton	117	Purchase	110	23,360	1:12.80	
1919	Man o' War	2	J. Loftus	127	John P. Grier	117	Dominique	122	26,650	1:11.60	
1920	Step Lightly	2	F. Keogh	116	Star Voter	127	Grey Lag	119	35,870	1:12.20	
1921	Bunting	2	F. Coltiletti	117	Galantman	117	D'm of Allah	116	39,700	1:11.40	
1922	Sally's Alley	2	A. Johnson	126	Zev	124	Wilderness	119	47,550	1:11.00	
1923	St. James	2	J. McTaggart	130	Fluvanna	122	Sun Pal.	117	64,810	1:10.40	
1924	Mother Goose	2	L. McAtee	114	Stimulus	122	Single Foot	119	67,730	1:10.80	
1925	Pompey	2	L. Fator	127	Canter	120	Chance Play	119	58,480	1:23.00	
1926	Scapa Flow	2	L. Fator	122	Candy Queen	114	Valorous	122	67,980	1:22.00	
1927	Anita Peabody	2	C. Lang	124	Reigh Count	119	Victorian	119	91,790	1:21.80	
1928	High Strung	2	L. McAtee	122	Roguish Eye	125	Jack High	130	97,990	1:19.00	
1929	Whichone	2	R. Workman	125	Hi-Jack	122	Gallant Fox	122	105,730	1:19.60	
1930	Jamestown	2	L. McAtee	130	Equipoise	130	Mate	122	99,600	1:20.60	
1931	Top Flight	2	R. Workman	127	Mad Pursuit	122	Morfair	122	94,780	1:21.00	
1932	Kerry Patch	2	P. Walls	122	Ladysman	130	Dynastic	122	88,690	1:24.40	
1933	Singing Wood	2	R. Jones	122	Sir Thomas	117	Roustabout	122	81,700	1:21.00	
1934	Chance Sun	2	W.D. Wright	122	Balladier	122	Plat Eye	125	77,510	1:17.60	
1935	Tintagel	2	S. Coucci	122	Hollyrood	122	Jean Bart	122	66,450	1:17.40	
1936	Pompoon	2	H. Richards	127	Privileged	125	Flying Cross	122	55,630	1:16.40	
1937	Menow	2	C. Kurtsinger	119	Tiger	126	Fighting Fox	122	56,800	1:15.20	
1938	Porter's Mite	2	B. James	119	Eight Thirty	122	Third Degree	119	57,045	1:16.80	
1939	Bimelech	2	F.A. Smith	126	Calory	119	Call to Colors	119	57,710	1:16.80	
1940	Our Boots	2	E. Arcaro	119	King Cole	122	Whirlaway	126	65,800	1:15.60	
1941	Some Chance	2	W. Eads	119	Devil Diver	126	Caduceus	119	57,900	1:16.80	
1942	Occupation	2	G. Woolf	126	Askmenow	116	Count Fleet	119	57,890	1:15.20	
1943	Occupy	2	G. Woolf	126	Rodney Stone	122	Platter	114	55,635	1:17.80	
1944	Pavot	2	G. Woolf	126	Alexis	119	Errard	119	53,890	1:15.60	
1945	Star Pilot	2	A. Kirkland	126	Athene	116	Mighty Story	119	52,940	1:17.20	
1946	First Flight	2	E. Arcaro	123	I Will	126	Jet Pilot	122	73,350	1:15.20	
1947	Citation	2	A. Snider	122	Whirling Fox	114	Bewitch	123	78,430	1:15.80	
1948	Blue Peter	2	E. Guerin	126	Myrtle Charm	123	Sport Page	118	88,410	1:14.60	
1949	Guillotine	2	T. Atkinson	122	Theory	122	The Diver	122	87,585	1:15.60	
1950	Battlefield	2	E. Arcaro	122	Big Stretch	122	Rough 'n Tumble	122	81,715	1:15.40	
1951	Tom Fool	2	T. Atkinson	122	Primate	122	Jet's Date	122	86,710	1:17.20	
1952	Native Dancer	2	E. Guerin	122	Tahitian King	122	Dark Star	122	82,845	1:14.40	
1953	Porterhouse	2	W. Boland	122	Artismo	122	Best Years	122	92,875	1:16.00	
1954	Nashua	2	E. Arcaro	122	Summer Tan	122	Royal Coinage	122	88,015	1:15.60	
1955	Nail	2	H. Woodhouse	122	Head Man	122	Polly's Jet.	122	100,425	1:16.80	
1956	Bold Ruler	2	E. Arcaro	122	Greek Game	122	Amarullah	122	91,145	1:15.20	
1957	Jester	2	P.J. Bailey	122	Misty Flight	122	Alhambra	122	81,005	1:16.20	
1958	Intentionally	2	W. Shoemaker	122	First Landing	122	Dunce	122	80,690	1:14.60	
1959	Weatherwise	2	E. Arcaro	122	Udaipur	122	All Hands	122	88,470	1:18.60	
1960	Little Tumbler	2	R. Broussard	122	Globemaster	122	Garwol	122	85,191	1:16.60	
1961	Cyane	2	M. Ycaza	122	Jaipur	122	Sir Gaylord	122	86,650	1:17.20	
1962	Never Bend	2	W. Shoemaker	122	Outing Class	122	Pack Trip	122	94,347	1:17.20	
1963	Bupers	2	A. Gomez	122	Black Mountain	122	Count Bud	122	90,974	1:17.40	
1964	Bold Lad	2	B. Baeza	122	Native Charger	122	Tom Rolfe	122	85,566	1:16.00	
1965	Priceless Gem	2	W. blum	119	Buckpasser	122	Indulto	122	93,827	1:17.20	
1966	Bold Hour	2	J.L. Rotz	122	Successor	122	Pinnacle	122	91,084	1:17.60	
1967	Captain's Gig	2	W. Shoemaker	122	Vitriolic	122	Exclusive Native	122	90,493	1:15.80	
1968	Top Knight	2	M. Ycaza	122	True North	122	Never Confuse	122	88,283	1:16.20	

Year	Winner	Age	Jockey	Wt.	Second	Wt.	Third	Wt.	Win Value	Time	Beyer
1969	High Echelon	2	J.L. Rotz	122	Tepee Rings	122	Irish Castle	122	92,807	1:18.40	
1970	Salem	2	J.L. Rotz	122	Limit to Reason	122	Frozen Delight	122	99,333	1:16.80	
1971	Riva Ridge	2	R. Turcotte	122	Chevron Flight	122	Hold Your Peace	122	87,636	1:16.60	
1972	Secretariat	2	R. Turcotte	122	Stop the Music	122	Swift Courier	122	83,320	1:16.40	
1973	Wedge Shot	2	J. Vasquez	122	Protagonist	122	Judger	122	82,230	1:17.00	

Judger finished second but was disqualified and placed third

Year	Winner	Age	Jockey	Wt.	Second	Wt.	Third	Wt.	Win Value	Time	Beyer
1974	Just the Time	2	M. Castaneda	122	High Steel	122	Valid Appeal	122	66,801	1:16.40	
1975	Soy Numero Uno	2	J. Vasquez	122	Jackknife	122	Beau Talent	122	66,408	1:17.80	
1976	For the Moment	2	E. Maple	122	Banquet Table	122	Western Wind	122	67,353	1:23.20	
1977	Affirmed	2	S. Cauthen	122	Alydar	122	Nasty and Bold	122	63,570	1:21.60	
1978	Crest of the Wave	2	J. Cruguet	122	Strike Your Colors	122			75,660	1:24.00	
					Picturesque	122					

Fuzzbuster finished first but was disqualfied and placed fourth

Year	Winner	Age	Jockey	Wt.	Second	Wt.	Third	Wt.	Win Value	Time	Beyer
1979	Rockhill Native	2	J. Oldham	122	Sportful	122	Gold Stage	122	90,150	1:22.00	
1980	Tap Shoes	2	R. Hernandez	122	Dash o'Pleasure	122	McCracken	122	85,605	1:23.80	
1981	Irish Martini	2	J. Velasquez	122	Herschelwalker	122	Timely Writer	122	103,605	1:24.40	
1982	Copelan	2	J.D. Bailey	122	Satan's Charger	122	Pax in Bello	122	97,110	1:24.20	
1983	Swale	2	E. Maple	122	Shuttle Jet	122	Hail Bold King	122	72,915	1:24.00	
1984	Spectacular Love	2	L. Pincay Jr	122	Chief's Crown	122	Mugzy's Rullah	122	105,900	1:23.20	
1985	Ogygian	2	W.A. Guerra	122	Groovy	122	Mr. Classic	122	81,600	1:22.40	
							Sovereign Don	122			
1986	Gulch	2	A. Cordero Jr	122	Demons Begone	122	Captain Valid	122	82,920	1:22.20	
1987	Forty Niner	2	E. Maple	122	Tsarbaby	122	Crusader Sword	122	80,100	1:22.60	
1988	Trapp Mountain	2	A. Cordero Jr	122	Bio	122	Fast Play	122	74,280	1:23.80	
1989	Senor Pete	2	J.A. Santos	122	Adjudicating	122	Dawn Quixote	122	75,360	1:23.20	
1990	Eastern Echo	2	J.D. Bailey	122	Deposit Ticket	122	Groom's Reckoning	122	69,360	1:22.40	99
1991	Agincourt	2	J.F. Chavez	122	Tri to Watch	122	Pine Bluff	122	72,120	1:23.60	80
1992	Strolling Along	2	C.W. Antley	122	Fight for Love	122	Caponostro	122	69,360	1:23.80	88
1993	Holy Bull	2	M.E. Smith	122	Dehere	122	Prenup	122	69,360	1:23.20	103
1994	Montreal Red	2	J.A. Santos	122	Northern Ensign	122	Wild Escapade	122	66,180	1:36.20	90
1995	Maria's Mon	2	R.G. Davis	122	Louis Quatorze	122	Honour and Glory	122	90,000	1:35.00	101
1996	Traitor	2	J.R. Velazquez	122	Night in Reno	122	Harley Tune	122	90,000	1:35.20	98
1997	Grand Slam	2	G.L. Stevens	122	K.O. Punch	122	Devil's Pride	122	90,000	1:35.60	98
1998	Lemon Drop Kid	2	J.R. Velazquez	122	Yes It's True	122	Medievil Hero	122	90,000	1:37.50	92
1999	Bevo	2	J. Bravo	122	Greenwood Lake	122	More Than Ready	122	90,000	1:36.16	99
2000	Burning Roma	2	R. Wilson	122	City Zip	122	Scorpion	122	120,000	1:37.90	90

City Zip finished first but was disqualified and placed second

Year	Winner	Age	Jockey	Wt.	Second	Wt.	Third	Wt.	Win Value	Time	Beyer
2002	Whywhywhy	2	E.S. Prado	120	Pretty Wild	120	Truckle Feature	120	120,000	1:36.33	102
2003	Cuvee	2	J.D. Bailey	120	Value Plus	120	El Prado Rob	120	120,000	1:35.75	101

Beyer Index: 95.46

Distance 6 furlongs prior to 1892; from 1902–24; 1,263 yards plus 1 foot from 1892–1901; about 7 furlongs, 1925–33; 6 1/2 furlongs, 1934–75; 7 furlongs, 1976–93. Run at Sheepshead Bay prior to 1910; at Saratoga, 1910, 1913–14; at Aqueduct , 1959–60, 1962–67. Run over old straight course prior to 1926; over Widener Straight Course, 1926–58; not run in 2001.

GAMELY BREEDERS' CUP HANDICAP, 1 1/8 Miles (Turf), Fillies and Mares, 3-Year-Olds and Up, Hollywood Park, 2003 Purse: $421,000

Year	Winner	Age	Jockey	Wt.	Second	Wt.	Third	Wt.	Win Value	Time	Beyer
1976	Katonka	4	L. Pincay Jr	121	Fascinating Girl	117	Tizna	126	30,750	1:50.40	
1977	Hail Hilarious	4	D. Pierce	123	Cascapedia	118	Swingtime	119	31,250	1:49.60	
1978	Lucie Manet	5	D.G. McHargue	119	Sensational	120	Glenaris	113	38,975	1:48.20	
1978	Star Ball	6	D.G. McHargue	122	Up to Juliet	114	Teisen Lap	116	38,975	1:48.80	
1979	Sisterhood	4	F. Toro	118	Country Queen	118	Camarado	117	50,450	1:47.80	
1980	Wishing Well	5	F. Toro	119	Country Queen	118	Image of Reality	118	69,600	1:47.80	
1981	Kilijaro	5	M. Castaneda	127	Princess Karenda	121	Wishing Well	122	62,900	1:48.20	
1982	Ack's Secret	6	L. Pincay Jr	122	Miss Huntington	117	Vocalist	114	66,100	1:46.80	
1983	Pride of Rosewood	5	E. Delahoussaye	115	Sangue	123	Mademoiselle Forli	119	64,800	1:48.80	
1984	Sabin	4	E. Maple	125	Triple Tipple	116	Fenny Rough	117	65,400	1:47.40	
1985	Estrapade	5	C.J. McCarron	124	Johnica	115	Possible Mate	116	62,500	1:46.60	
1986	La Koumia	4	R. Sibille	118	Estrapade	123	Tax Dodge	115	92,400	1:45.80	
1987	Northern Aspen	5	G.L. Stevens	119	Reloy	121	Frau Altiva	115	89,800	1:47.60	
1988	Pen Bal Lady	4	E. Delahoussaye	120	Chapel of Dreams	117	Galunpe	120	72,800	1:47.00	
1989	Fitzwilliam Place	5	C. Black	119	Claire Marine	119	Ravinella	121	63,700	1:47.80	
1990	Double Wedge	5	R. Davis	112	Stylish Star	116	Beautiful Melody	115	62,700	1:47.80	103
1991	Miss Josh	5	L. Pincay Jr	118	Island Jamboree	116	Fire the Groom	120	68,000	1:47.40	105
1992	Metamorphose	4	G.L. Stevens	114	Guiza	113	Silvered	116	93,300	1:46.40	100
1993	Toussaud	4	K.J. Desormeaux	116	Gold Fleece	114	Bel's Starlet	116	97,700	1:45.00	106
1994	Hollywood Wildcat	4	E. Delahoussaye	122	Mz. Zill Bear	124	Flawlessly	124	92,900	1:46.40	111
1995	Possibly Perfect	5	K.J. Desormeaux	123	Lady Affirmed	114	Don't Read My Lips	115	92,900	1:46.80	103
1996	Auriette	4	K.J. Desormeaux	118	Flagbird	118	Diplomia	116	128,760	1:46.40	112
1997	Donna Viola	5	G.L. Stevens	121	Real Connection	115	Different	121	120,000	1:47.40	105
1998	Fiji	4	K.J. Desormeaux	123	Kool Kat Katie	119	Squeak	116	158,880	1:47.42	109
1999	Tranquility Lake	4	E. Delahoussaye	119	Midnight Line	117	Green Jewel	117	157,800	1:46.04	112
2000	Astra	4	K.J. Desormeaux	117	Happyanunoit	121	Tout Charmant	119	157,150	1:45.81	107
2001	Happyanunoit	4	B. Blanc	121	Tranquility Lake	124	Beautiful Noise	116	115,710	1:47.34	105

Year	Winner	Age	Jockey	Wt.	Second	Wt.	Third	Wt.	Win Value	Time	Beyer
2002	Astra	6	K.J. Desormeaux	123	Starine	122	Voodoo Dancer	119	...300,000	1:46.93	...105
2003	Tates Creek	5	P.A. Valenzuela ..	122	Dublino	122	Megahertz	118	...263,400	1:46.97	...107

Run on main course 1978

Beyer Index: **106.43**

GARDEN CITY BREEDERS' CUP HANDICAP, 1 1/8 Miles, (Turf), 3-Year-Old Fillies, Belmont Park, 2003 Purse: $244,000

Year	Winner	Age	Jockey	Wt.	Second	Wt.	Third	Wt.	Win Value	Time	Beyer
1979	Danielle B.	3	R. Hernandez	113	Distinct Honor	114	Seascape...........	118	...33,000	1:45.40	
1980	Mitey Lively	3	J. Velasquez	113	Rose of Morn	112	Paintbrush....	112	...33,480	1:36.40	
1981	Banner Gala	3	A. Cordero Jr....	113	Expressive Dance	112	In True Form	118	...33,900	1:35.60	
1982	Nafees	3	J. Velasquez	112	Middle Stage	112	Beau Cougar....	112	...33,120	1:38.40	
1983	Pretty Sensible	3	A. Smith	112	High Schemes	112	Lovin Touch	115	...33,600	1:37.80	
1984	Given	3	M.J. Vigliotti....	118	Maharadoon	112	Recharged	118	...42,960	1:43.40	
1985	Kamikaze Rick	3	A. Cordero Jr....	118	Wising Up	115	Videogenic.	118	...50,490	1:36.00	
1986	Life At the Top	3	C.J. McCarron ...	118	Lotka	118	Funistrada	115	...51,210	1:34.40	
1987	Personal Ensign	3	R.P. Romero	115	One From Heaven ...	118	Key Bid	118	...82,140	1:36.60	
1988	Topicount...........	3	A. Cordero Jr....	115	Toll Fee	112	Fara's Team....	115	...82,260	1:38.00	
1989	Highest Glory	3	J.A. Santos	115	Warfie	118	Tremolos.	113	...70,440	1:37.20	
1990	Aishah	3	J.A. Santos	115	Screen Prospect	115	Vitola	112	...57,690	1:35.40	...103
1991	Dazzle Me Jolie	3	J.A. Santos	115	Grand Girlfriend	112	Wide Country....	124	...72,000	1:35.60	...102
1992	November Snow	3	C.W. Antley	124	Vivano	112	Easy Now	124	...66,480	1:35.80	...100
1993	Sky Beauty	3	M.E. Smith	124	Fadetta	112	For All Seasons	114	...68,400	1:35.60	...100
1994	Jade Flush	3	R.G. Davis	111	Lady Affirmed	117	Saxuality.	117	...67,140	1:46.79	...101
1995	Perfect Arc	3	J.R. Velazquez ...	123	Bail Out Becky	121	Christmas Gift....	118	...101,070	1:42.20	...105
1996	True Flare	3	G.L. Stevens	121	Henlopen	113	Zephyr	124	...128,460	1:42.40	...96
1997	Auntie Mame	3	J.D. Bailey	122	Parade Queen	115	Swearingen....	117	...128,040	1:48.40	...97
1998	Pharatta	3	C.S. Nakatani	120	Tenski	122	Pratella	115	...129,720	1:47.00	...107
1999	Perfect Sting	3	P. Day........	120	Nordican Inch	116	Ronda.	121	...129,900	1:49.41	...101
2000	Gaviola	3	J.D. Bailey	123	Flawly	115	Millie's Quest	116	...150,000	1:48.89	...98
2001	Voodoo Dancer	3	C.S. Nakatani	120	Shooting Party	113	Wander Mom....	116	...150,000	1:47.69	...101
2002	Wonder Again	3	E.S. Prado	119	Riskaverse	119	Pertuisane....	115	...150,000	1:47.33	...96
2003	Indy Five Hundred ...	3	P. Day........	113	Dimitrova	122	Campsie Fells.......	116	...150,000	1:48.44	...107

Beyer Index: **101**

Run on main course prior to 1994. Distance 1 1/16 miles in 1979; 1 mile 70 yards, 1984; 1 mile, 1980–83, 1985–93; 1 1/16 miles on turf, 1994–96; Run as Rare Perfume prior to 1998.

GAZELLE HANDICAP, 1 1/8 Miles, 3-Year-Old Fillies, Belmont Park, 2003 Purse: $250,000

Year	Winner	Age	Jockey	Wt.	Second	Wt.	Third	Wt.	Win Value	Time	Beyer
1887	Firenze	3	Hamilton	113	Flageoletta	103	Mag. Mitchell....	103	1,860	1:56.20	
1888	Winona	3	Martin	108	Blythesome	113	Bella B.............	108	1,775	2:03.00	
1889	Gipsy Queen	3	Fitzpatrick.......	116	Holiday	113	Miss Cody....	113	2,510	2:00.20	
1890	Amazon	3	Hamilton	113	Golden Horn	113	Starlight....	113	3,510	1:58.20	
1891	Ambulance	3	F. Littlefield	117	Reckon	117	Origeuse....	117	3,540	1:59.60	
1892	Yorkville Belle	3	I. Murphy	117	Madrid	117	Ragna....	117	2,840	2:04.00	
1893	Naptha	3	Simms	117	Miss Maude	117	Grace Brown....	117	2,540	1:59.20	
1894	Nahma	3	Littlefield........	117	Jersey Belle	117	Baroness....	117	3,590	2:03.00	
1895	The Butterflies	3	Griffin	117	California	117	Roundelay	117	2,570	1:59.20	
1896	Intermission	3	Taral............	117	Woodvine	117	Bes Browning....	117	2,400	1:58.20	
1897	Casseopia	3	Littlefield........	117	Miss Prim	117	Leonore....	117	2,400	1:59.20	
1898	Geisha	3	T. Sloan........	112	Kitefoot	112	Miss Miriam	112	2,400	1:56.60	
1899	The Rose	3	Maher........	114	Bettie Gray	114	Marmarica....	114	2,400	1:57.20	
1900	Indian Fairy	3	O'Connor	106	Oneck Queen	114	Motley....	106	2,300	1:50.00	
1901	Trigger	3	Odom	106	Janice	114	Morningside....	106	2,300	1:48.20	
1902	Blue Girl	3	T. Burns........	124	Par Excellance	113	Hanover Queen	113	2,300	1:49.40	
1903	Stolen Moments.....	3	Gannon	113	Gloriosa	113	Love Note....	113	3,250	1:49.60	
1904	Beldame	3	F. O'Neill	124	Graceful	121	Little Em....	113	3,590	1:52.60	
1905	Tradition	3	W. Davis	113	Coy Maid	113	Klamesha	113	2,915	1:51.40	
1906	Flip Flap	3	W. Miller......	121	Perverse	124	Meddling Daisy	113	3,390	1:48.00	
1907	Court Dress	3	J. Martin	121	Yankee Girl	121	Estimate	111	4,495	1:47.20	
1908	Stamina	3	E. Dugan	121	Anonyma	111	Laughing Eyes......	111	4,940	1:48.00	
1909	Maskette	3	Scoville........	121	Petticoat	111	Lady Bedford	111	4,045	1:48.00	
1910	Ocean Bound	3	C.H. Shilling	121	Infatuation	106	Ethel D....	106	1,900	1:52.00	
1917	Regret	5	J. Loftus	129	Bayberry Candle	123	Wistful....	105	2,600	1:45.40	
1918	Fairy Wand	4	C. Fairbrother ...	115	Priscilla Mullens	122	Hanovia....	122	2,625	1:45.00	
1919	Milkmaid	3	A. Schuttinger ...	119	Columbine	120	Rose d'Or	107	2,450	1:45.00	
1920	Pen Rose	4	L. Fator	113	Milkmaid	130	Lunetta	113	2,850	1:46.00	
1921	Banksia	3	B. Kennedy	118	Last Straw	109	Chat. Thierry.......	109	3,000	1:47.60	
1922	Lady Baltimore	3	C. Lang	118	Many Smiles	118	Nancy Shanks	110	2,975	1:45.20	
1923	Untidy	3	E. Sande	124	Sun Quest	109	J'line Julian	109	3,100	1:45.80	
1924	Priscilla Ruley	3	J. Maiben	109	Whetstone	109	Sunayr	109	3,225	1:44.40	
	Lady Belle finished third but was disqualified										
1925	Nedana.............	3	L. Fator	118	Primrose	109	Beatrice....	121	2,975	1:44.80	

Year	Winner	Age	Jockey	Wt.	Second	Wt.	Third	Wt.	Win Value	Time	Beyer
1926	Corvette	3	L. Fator	109	Edith Cavell	124	Gavotte	109	2,875	1:44.80	
1927	Flambino	3	D. McAuliffe	110	Frilette	121	Candy May	109	3,325	1:45.00	
1928	Bateau	3	L. McAtee	123	Bradley's Peggy	109	Twitter	121	3,200	1:45.20	
1929	March Hare	3	J.H. Burke	118	Electra	109	Atlantis	121	3,175	1:47.60	
1930	Erin	3	J.H. Burke	118	The Spare	121	Flimsy	118	3,875	1:46.00	
1931	Avenger	3	R. Workman	112	Tambour	121	Lillie D.	105	3,150	1:46.00	
1932	Playfole	3	B. Hanford	111	Argosie	111	Parry	115	2,500	1:45.40	
1936	Gold Seeker	3	W.D. Wright	121	High Fleet	121	Little Miracle	112	3,875	1:44.60	
1937	Regal Lily	3	J. Stout	109	Drawbridge	112	Rosenna	109	5,125	1:44.00	
1938	Invoke	3	J. Stout	109	Creole Maid	121	Bransome	109	4,550	1:45.40	
1939	Red Eye	3	B. James	109	Hostility	121	Ciencia	121	4,400	1:43.20	
1940	Fairy Chant	3	B. James	121	Raise Up	109	Rosetown	112	5,225	1:46.00	
1941	Tangled	3	E. Arcaro	124	Nasca	121	St'nge Device	118	4,825	1:45.80	
1942	Vagrancy	3	J. Stout	121	Smiles	112	Mackerel	112	4,800	1:45.00	
1943	Anthemion	3	J. Longden	121	Stefanita	118	Legend Bearer	112	4,775	1:48.20	
1944	Whirlabout	3	J. Longden	121	Good Thing	112	Leaving	115	8,245	1:43.60	
1945	Ace Card	3	E. Arcaro	121	Bellicose	112	Elpis	124	7,540	1:45.60	
1946	Bridal Flower	3	A. DeLara	111	Hypnotic	121	Bonnie Beryl	116	16,950	1:46.40	
1947	Cosmic Missile	3	H. Pratt	116	Harmonica	121	Mother	116	20,600	1:46.00	
1948	Sweet Dream	3	R. Permane	111	Scattered	121	Compliance	111	19,350	1:45.20	
1949	Nell K.	3	D. Dodson	121	Jazz Baby	111	Adile	111	16,450	1:47.80	
1950	Next Move	3	E. Guerin	121	Bed o' Roses	116	Renew	112	15,250	1:43.60	
1951	Kiss Me Kate	3	W. Mehrtens	121	Boot All	112	Spanish Cream	112	19,450	1:46.00	
1952	Hushaby Baby	3	R. York	113	Aesthete	115	Hadassah	113	19,325	1:45.60	
1953	Grecian Queen	3	E. Guerin	121	Canadiana	121	Sabette	113	20,950	1:45.80	
1954	On Your Own	3	W. Boland	113	Evening Out	113	Fascinator	121	21,000	1:46.60	
1955	Manotick	3	A. Valenzuela	113	Two Stars	113	High Voltage	121	21,400	1:45.60	
1956	Scampering	3	A. Valenzuela	111	Cosmah	116	Dotted Line	124	21,600	1:43.80	
1957	Bayou	3	E. Arcaro	120	Evening Time	118	Pink Velvet	116	21,550	1:43.20	
1958	Idun	3	W. Hartack	124	Munch	122	Tempted	116	18,680	1:43.20	
1959	Sunset Glow	3	W. Shoemaker	108	Royal Native	121	High Bid	118	14,130	1:36.80	
1959	Cee Zee	3	H. Moreno	111	Aesthetic	112	Toluene	115	13,967	1:36.00	
1960	Berlo	3	E. Guerin	122	Sister Antoine	113	Funny Bone	109	14,569	1:35.80	
1960	Sarcastic	3	H. Moreno	115	Twinkle Twinkle	119	Undulation	112	14,569	1:35.40	
1961	Shimmy Dancer	3	M. Ycaza	112	My Portrait	120	Funloving	122	18,752	1:49.00	
1962	Bramalea	3	B. Baeza	122	Cyclopavia	117	Lincoln Center	113	18,687	1:50.00	
1963	Lamb Chop	3	B. Baeza	125	Delhi Maid	119	Smart Deb	123	19,337	1:50.00	
1964	Face the Facts	3	L. Adams	121	Silwall	113	Castle Forbes	121	18,005	1:51.60	
1965	What a Treat	3	J.L. Rotz	123	Terentia	118	Discipline	118	38,675	1:51.40	
1966	Prides Profile	3	M. Ycaza	113	Lady Pitt	124	Swinging Mood	120	36,270	1:52.40	
1967	Sweet Folly	3	H. Gustines	112	Treacherous	116	Swiss Cheese	115	37,415	1:50.20	
1968	Another Nell	3	C. Perret	122	Gay Matelda	123	Pattee Canyon	116	36,400	1:50.80	
1969	Gallant Bloom	3	J.L. Rotz	127	Pit Bunny	116	Shuvee	127	34,970	1:49.00	
1970	Missile Belle	3	P. Anderson	120	Predictable	114	Fanfreluche	122	37,830	1:50.80	
1971	Forward Gal	3	M. Hole	122	Our Cheri Amour	118	Alma North	123	33,720	1:48.60	
1972	Susan's Girl	3	L. Pincay Jr	124	Honestous	112	Light Hearted	121	33,390	1:48.00	
1973	Desert Vixen	3	J. Velasquez	126	Bag of Tunes	117	Poker Night	120	33,780	1:47.40	
1974	Maud Muller	3	A. Cordero Jr	120	Raisela	115	Stage Door Betty	115	33,900	1:46.80	
1975	Land Girl	3	J. Vasquez	114	Hooray Hooray	109	Let Me Linger	119	33,690	1:49.40	
1976	Revidere	3	A. Cordero Jr	124	Pacific Princess	112	Ancient Fables	112	31,950	1:47.80	
1977	Pearl Necklace	3	S. Cauthen	111	Sensational	120	Road Princess	118	31,770	1:48.00	
1978	Tempest Queen	3	J. Velasquez	117	Lulubo	116	Terpsichorist	113	31,710	1:49.80	
1979	Himalayan	3	E. Maple	113	Croquis	113	Fourdrinier	112	32,580	1:48.40	
1980	Love Sign	3	R. Hernandez	121	Sugar and Spice	117	Kelley's Day	112	32,580	1:49.20	
1981	Discorama	3	R. Hernandez	117	Secrettame	114	Tina Tina Too	114	33,300	1:48.20	
1982	Broom Dance	3	G. McCarron	121	Number	113	Mademoiselle Forli	114	33,360	1:47.60	
1983	High Schemes	3	J.L. Samyn	121	Lass Trump	120	Lady Norcliffe	115	66,720	1:48.20	
1984	Miss Oceana	3	E. Maple	121	Sintra	117	Life's Magic	122	66,840	1:47.60	
1985	Kamikaze Rick	3	A. Cordero Jr	113	Overwhelming	112	Fran's Valentine	121	68,880	1:48.60	
1986	Classy Cathy	3	E. Fires	121	Life at the Top	118	Dynamic Star	116	66,480	1:48.40	
1987	Single Blade	3	C.W. Antley	113	Without Feathers	121	Silent Turn	116	80,100	1:48.20	
1988	Classic Crown	3	R.P. Romero	117	Willa on the Move	120	Make Change	118	69,360	1:49.80	
1989	Tactile	3	R. Migliore	114	Dream Deal	117	Fantastic Find	114	67,440	1:48.40	
1990	Highland Talk	3	J.L. Samyn	111	Dance Colony	116	She Can	116	69,960	1:50.80	97
1991	Versailles Treaty	3	A. Cordero Jr	123	Grand Girlfriend	115	Immerse	112	105,840	1:47.40	95
1992	Saratoga Dew	3	W.H. McCauley	120	Vivano	114	Tiney Toast	113	103,140	1:47.60	101
1993	Dispute	3	J.D. Bailey	120	Silky Feather	117	In Her Glory	112	90,000	1:47.20	102
1994	Heavenly Prize	3	M.E. Smith	123	Cinnamon Sugar	118	Sovereign Kitty	118	90,000	1:47.20	106
1995	Serena's Song	3	G.L. Stevens	124	Miss Golden Circle	113	Golden Bri	121	90,000	1:47.20	105
1996	My Flag	3	J.D. Bailey	121	Escena	121	Top Secret	117	120,000	1:48.00	98
1997	Royal Indy	3	P. Day	113	Starry Dreamer	114	Pearl City	117	120,000	1:49.00	96
1998	Tap to Music	3	P. Day	112	Keeper Hill	121	French Braids	115	120,000	1:49.72	96
1999	Silverbulletday	3	J.D. Bailey	124	Queen's Word	113	Awful Smart	115	120,000	1:47.71	100

Year	Winner	Age	Jockey	Wt.	Second	Wt.	Third	Wt.	Win Value	Time	Beyer
2000	Critical Eye	3	M.E. Smith	115	Plenty of Light	116	Resort	116	120,000	1:48.54	104
2001	Exogenous	3	J.J. Castellano	118	Two Item Limit	118	Fleet Renee	122	150,000	1:47.68	110
2002	Imperial Gesture	3	J. Santos	117	Take Charge Lady	121	Bella Bellucci	118	150,000	1:47.12	112
2003	Buy the Sport	3	P. Day	113	Lady Tak	121	Spoken Fur	121	150,000	1:48.57	95

Beyer Index: 101.21

Distance 1 1/16 miles from 1900-58; 1 mile, 1959-60. Run at Gravesend from 1887-1916; at Aqueduct from 1917-55, 1960, 1962-68

GO FOR WAND HANDICAP, 1 1/8 Miles, Fillies and Mares, 3-Year-Olds and Up, Saratoga Race Course, 2003 Purse: $250,000

Year	Winner	Age	Jockey	Wt.	Second	Wt.	Third	Wt.	Win Value	Time	Beyer
1954	Ballerina	4	S. Small	106	Grecian Queen	113	Gay Grecque	112	18,950	1:37.60	
1955	Oil Painting	4	H. Woodhouse	119	Miss Weesie	104	Clear Dawn	116	18,000	1:36.60	
1956	Searching	4	C. McCreary	123	Happy Princess	107	Pucker Up	112	20,100	1:37.00	
1957	Bayou	3	R. Ussery	118	Rare Treat	116	Pink Velvet	113	20,200	1:37.00	
1958	Tempted	3	R. Ussery	113	Alanesian	123	Annie-Lu-San	111	19,070	1:36.40	
1959	Idun	4	E. Guerin	119	Tempted	126	Bornstar	119	18,875	1:36.00	
1960	Tempted	5	E. Nelson	126	Make Sail	118	Craftiness	108	19,200	1:35.60	
1961	teacation	4	R. Broussard	116	Shimmy Dancer	106	Craftiness	120	18,720	1:36.20	
1962	Shirley Jones	6	D. Pierce	122	Linita	122	Waltz Song	115	19,467	1:36.00	
1963	Waltz Song	5	S. Mellon	120	Linita	121	Doll Ina	114	18,882	1:37.20	
1964	Tosmah	3	S. Boulmetis	123	Old Hat	117	Snow Scene II	113	19,630	1:36.60	
1965	Tosmah	4	S. Boulmetis	128	Affectionately	128	Straight Deal	113	18,720	1:35.20	
1966	Summer Scandal	4	W. Blum	123	Straight Deal	119	Treachery	111	18,687	1:37.80	
1967	Politely	4	A. Cordero Jr	115	Triple Brook	117	Lady Pitt	115	18,687	1:35.60	
1968	Amerigo Lady	4	J. Velasquez	120	Serene Queen	114	Green Glade	112	19,077	1:36.40	
1969	Singing Rain	4	B. Baeza	118	Helen Jennings	107	Show Off	110	18,395	1:38.00	
1970	Native Partner	4	A. Cordero Jr	111	Taken Aback	112	Hasty Hitter	107	18,720	1:36.20	
1971	Double Delta	5	K. Knapp	126	Blessing Angelica	107	Lucky Traveler	112	19,830	1:36.20	
1972	Numbered Account	3	A. Cordero Jr	115	Manta	112	Aladancer	114	16,620	1:35.60	
1973	Light Hearted	4	E. Nelson	126	Convenience	121	Krislin	111	17,040	1:34.80	
1974	Ponte Vecchio	4	J. Vasquez	118	Poker Night	116	Twixt	124	35,850	1:34.60	

Desert Vixen finished first but was disqualified from purse money

Year	Winner	Age	Jockey	Wt.	Second	Wt.	Third	Wt.	Win Value	Time	Beyer
1975	Let Me Linger	3	L. Pincay Jr	117	Honorable Miss	121	Susan's Girl	128	34,590	1:35.20	
1976	Artfully	4	P. Day	108	Snooze	108	Land Girl	109	25,920	1:34.00	
1976	Sugar Plum Time	4	J. Imparato	111	Pacific Princess	110	Fleet Victress	115	26,220	1:34.00	
1977	What a Summer	4	J. Vasquez	126	Crab Grass	114	Harvest Girl	111	32,280	1:37.40	
1978	Pearl Necklace	4	R. Hernandez	123	Ida Delia	113	Sensational	117	48,195	1:33.80	
1979	Blitey	3	A. Cordero Jr	112	It's in the Air	122	Pearl Necklace	125	48,015	1:34.80	
1980	Bold n' Determined	3	E. Delahoussaye	122	Genuine Risk	118	Love Sign	120	49,140	1:35.40	
1981	Jameela	5	J. Vasquez	123	Love Sign	123	Island Charm	116	65,280	1:35.00	
1982	Too Chic	4	R. Hernandez	110	Ambassador of Luck	111	Anti Lib	116	67,920	1:34.80	
1983	Ambassador of Luck	4	A. Graell	120	A Kiss for Luck	120	Am Capable	109	67,560	1:36.40	
1984	Miss Oceana	3	E. Maple	120	Paradies	114	Nany	120	70,560	1:35.20	
1985	Lady's Secret	3	J. Velasquez	111	Dowery	117	Mrs. Revere	117	85,020	1:34.80	
1986	Lady's Secret	4	P. Day	125	Steal a Kiss	109	Endear	120	81,060	1:33.40	
1987	North Sider	5	A. Cordero Jr	123	Wisla	116	Funistrada	116	65,500	1:35.00	
1988	Personal Ensign	4	R.P. Romero	123	Winning Colors	118	Sham Say	115	67,080	1:34.20	
1989	Miss Brio	5	J.D. Bailey	116	Proper Evidence	116	Aptostar	123	67,080	1:35.60	
1990	Go for Wand	3	R.P. Romero	114	Feel the Beat	123	Mistaurian	116	68,760	1:35.60	106
1991	Queena	5	A. Cordero Jr	123	Fit to Scout	123	Screen Prospect	116	120,000	1:34.80	104
1992	Easy Now	3	J.D. Bailey	111	Train Robbery	118	Wide Country	116	120,000	1:36.00	95

Nannerl finished second but was disqualified and placed last

Year	Winner	Age	Jockey	Wt.	Second	Wt.	Third	Wt.	Win Value	Time	Beyer
1993	Turnback the Alarm	4	C.W. Antley	123	Nannerl	116	November Snow	116	120,000	1:36.00	96
1994	Sky Beauty	4	M.E. Smith	123	Link River	123	Life Is Delicious	123	90,000	1:49.40	105
1995	Heavenly Prize	4	P. Day	123	Forcing Bid	108	Little Buckles	111	105,000	1:49.80	97
1996	Exotic Wood	4	C. McCarron	115	Shoop	118	Frolic	113	105,000	1:49.40	107
1997	Hidden Lake	4	R. Migliore	123	Flat Fleet Feet	120	Clear Mandate	113	150,000	1:49.60	105
1998	Aldiza	4	M.E. Smith	114	Escena	124	Tomisue's Delight	116	150,000	1:49.88	102
1999	Banshee Breeze	4	J.D. Bailey	124	Beautiful Pleasure	113	Heritage of Gold	117	150,000	1:49.95	109
2000	Heritage of Gold	5	S.J. Sellers	123	Beautiful Pleasure	125	Roza Robata	114	150,000	1:49.84	107
2001	Serra Lake	4	E.S. Prado	113	Pompeii	114	March Magic	114	150,000	1:49.62	102
2002	Dancethruthedawn	4	J.D. Bailey	118	Transcendental	113	Too Scarlet	112	150,000	1:50.21	100
2003	Sightseek	4	J.D. Bailey	121	She's Got the Beat	112	Nonsuch Bay	113	150,000	1:50.92	115

Beyer Index: 103.57

Run as Maskette Stakes prior to 1992. Run at Aqueduct in 1959-60, 1962-68

GULFSTREAM PARK BREEDERS' CUP HANDICAP, 1 3/8 Miles (Turf), 3-Year-Olds and Up, Gulfstream Park, 2003 Purse: $194,000

Year	Winner	Age	Jockey	Wt.	Second	Wt.	Third	Wt.	Win Value	Time	Beyer
1986	Sondrio	5	J.A. Santos	113	Chief Run Run	113	Ends Well	115	74,772	1:40.60	
1987	Bolshoi Boy	4	R. Romero	116	Arctic Honeymoon	114	Little Bold John	115	80,286	1:44.60	

Year	Winner	Age	Jockey	Wt.	Second	Wt.	Third	Wt.	Win Value	Time	Beyer
1988	Salem Drive	6	G. St. Leon	116	Equalize	112	King's River II	113	94,530	1:40.60	
1989	Equalize	3	J.A. Santos	124	Posen	115	Nisswa	111	93,210	1:41.00	
1990	Youmadeyourpoint	4	D. Valiente	112	Blazing Bart	118	Iron Courage	116	94,560	1:39.60	110
1991	Shy Tom	5	C. Perret	115	Dr. Root	112	Runaway Raja	112	94,800	2:14.60	99
1992	Passagere du Soir	5	J.D. Bailey	114	Colchis Island	111	Crystal Moment	116	95,130	2:15.60	99
1993	Stagecraft	6	J.D. Bailey	115	Social Retiree	116	Futurist	116	93,600	2:13.20	106
1994	Strolling Along	4	J.D. Bailey	117	Conveyor	119	Awad	112	93,150	2:05.00	101
1995	Misil	7	J.A. Santos	119	Myrmidon	113	Star of Manila	118	94,200	2:12.40	104
1996	Celtic Arms	5	M.E. Smith	114	Broadway Flyer	117	Flag Down	118	101,880	2:13.80	106
1997	Lassigny	6	J.D. Bailey	116	Flag Down	117	Awad	119	102,840	2:11.20	107
1998	Flag Down	8	J.A. Santos	120	Buck's Boy	115	Copy Editor	116	120,000	2:12.40	109
1999	Yagli	6	J.D. Bailey	121	Wild Event	117	Unite's Big Red	115	120,000	2:10.60	110
2000	Royal Anthem	5	J.D. Bailey	121	Thesaurus	112	Band Is Passing	116	116,400	2:11.34	110
2001	Subtle Power	4	P. Day	113	Whata Brainstorm	114	Stokofsky	114	60,000	2:13.50	103
2002	Cetewayo	8	C. Velasquez	115	Band Is Passing	117	Profit Option	115	120,000	2:17.44	107
2003	Man From Wicklow	6	J.D. Bailey	119	Just Listen	113	Sardaukar	114	120,000	2:11.62	108

Beyer Index: 105.64

Distance 1 1/16 miles 1986–90

HASKELL INVITATIONAL HANDICAP, 1 1/8 Miles, 3-Year-Olds, Monmouth Park, 2003 Purse: $1,000,000

Year	Winner	Age	Jockey	Wt.	Second	Wt.	Third	Wt.	Win Value	Time	Beyer
1968	Balustrade	3	E. Walsh	115	Chompion	113	Funny Fellow	116	50,000	1:50.00	
1969	Al Hattab	3	R. Broussard	126	Dot Ed's Bluesky	111	Hydrologist	115	65,000	1:50.20	
1970	Twice Worthy	3	J. Ruane	117	Roman Scout	113	Dust Commander	122	65,000	1:48.40	
1971	West Coast Scout	3	L. Adams	112	Northfields	114	Alma North	111	65,000	1:48.00	
1972	Freetex	3	M. Hole	117	King's Bishop	115	Cloudy Dawn	117	65,000	1:48.40	
1973	Our Native	3	M.A. Rivera	123	Annihilate 'Em	118	Aljamin	118	65,000	1:48.60	
1974	Holding Pattern	3	M. Miceli	117	Little Current	127	Better Arbitor	119	65,000	1:49.80	
1975	Wajima	3	B. Baeza	118	Intrepid Hero	115	My Friend Gus	116	65,000	1:49.60	
1976	Majestic Light	3	S. Hawley	122	Apassionato	113	Honest Pleasure	126	65,000	1:47.00	
1977	Affiliate	3	M.A. Rivera	117	Don Sebastian	112	Iron Constitution	118	65,000	1:50.60	
1978	Delta Flag	3	D. Nied	112	Dave's Friend	120	Special Honor	118	65,000	1:53.20	
1979	Coastal	3	R. Hernandez	127	Steady Growth	120	Worthy Piper	112	65,000	1:48.80	
1980	Thanks to Tony	3	C. Lopez	111	Superbity	124	Amber Pass	121	90,000	1:49.40	
1981	Five Star Flight	3	C. Perret	119	Lord Avie	126	Ornery Odis	112	120,000	1:48.40	
1982	Wavering Monarch	3	R.P. Romero	117	Aloma's Ruler	126	Lejoli	112	120,000	1:47.80	
1983	Deputed Testamony	3	W.H. McCauley	124	Bet Big	116	Parfaitement	116	120,000	1:49.20	
1984	Big Pistol	3	G. Patterson	119	Birdie's Legend	115	Locust Bayou	115	120,000	1:47.80	
1985	Skip Trial	3	J.L. Samyn	116	Spend a Buck	127	Creme Fraiche	126	180,000	1:48.60	
1986	Wise Times	3	C.P. DeCarlo	114	Personal Flag	114	Danzig Connection	123	180,000	1:48.60	
1987	Bet Twice	3	C. Perret	126	Alysheba	126	Lost Code	124	300,000	1:47.00	
1988	Forty Niner	3	C. Perret	126	Seeking the Gold	125	Primal	117	300,000	1:47.60	
1989	King Glorious	3	C.J. McCarron	123	Music Merci	120	Shy Tom	116	300,000	1:49.80	
1990	Restless Con	3	T.T. Doocy	118	Baron de Vaux	117	Rhythm	121	300,000	1:49.20	
1991	Lost Mountain	3	C. Perret	118	Corporate Report	120	Hansel	126	300,000	1:48.00	107
1992	Technology	3	J.D. Bailey	120	Nines Wild	112	Scudan	113	300,000	1:48.60	108
1993	Kissin Kris	3	J.A. Santos	118	Storm Tower	119	Dry Bean	113	300,000	1:49.40	108
1994	Holy Bull	3	M.E. Smith	126	Meadow Flight	118	Concern	118	300,000	1:48.20	115
1995	Serena's Song	3	G.L. Stevens	124	Pyramid Peak	120	Citadeed	118	300,000	1:48.80	110
1996	Skip Away	3	J.A. Santos	124	Dr. Caton	115	Victory Speech	121	450,000	1:47.60	113
1997	Touch Gold	3	C.J. McCarron	125	Anet	120	Free House	125	850,000	1:47.60	114
1998	Coronado's Quest	3	M.E. Smith	124	Victory Gallop	125	Grand Slam	118	600,000	1:48.60	110
1999	Menifee	3	P. Day	124	Cat Thief	123	Forestry	118	600,000	1:48.06	110
2000	Dixie Union	3	A. Solis	117	Captain Steve	118	Milwaukee Brew	117	600,000	1:50.00	111
2001	Point Given	3	G.L. Stevens	124	Touch Tone	115	Burning Roma	119	900,000	1:49.77	106
2002	War Emblem	3	V. Espinoza	124	Magic Weisner	118	Like a Hero	117	600,000	1:48.21	112
2003	Peace Rules	3	E.S. Prado	121	Sky Mesa	118	Funny Cide	123	600,000	1:49.32	109

Beyer Index: 110.23

Run as Monmouth Inviational Handicap from 1968–80.

CLEMENT L. HIRSCH TURF CHAMPIONSHIP, 1 1/4 Miles (Turf), 3-Year-Olds and Up, Santa Anita, 2003 Purse: $245,000

Year	Winner	Age	Jockey	Wt.	Second	Wt.	Third	Wt.	Win Value	Time	Beyer
1969	Czar Alexander	4	A. Cordero Jr	126	Pink Pigeon	123	Pink Pigeon	126	68,900	2:23.40	
1970	Daryl's Joy	4	J. Sellers	126	Fiddle Isle	126	Cougar II	126	63,600	2:26.20	
1971	Cougar II	5	W. Shoemaker	126	Vegas Vic	121	Manta	123	60,000	2:24.60	
1972	Cougar II	6	W. Shoemaker	126	Queen's Hustler	122	Bicker	122	60,000	2:27.20	
1973	Portentous	3	J. Ramirez	122	Groshawk	122	Kentuckian	126	60,000	2:25.60	
	....		....		....		Kirrary	122			
1974	Tallahto	4	L. Pincay Jr	123	Within Hail	122	Montmartre	126	60,000	2:25.80	

Year	Winner	Age	Jockey	Wt.	Second	Wt.	Third	Wt.	Win Value	Time	Beyer
1975	Top Command	4	W. Shoemaker	126	Top Crowd	126	Buffalo Lark	126	60,000	2:26.00	
1976	King Pellinore	4	W. Shoemaker	126	Royal Derby II	126	L'Heureux	121	60,000	2:31.40	
1977	Crystal Water	4	W. Shoemaker	126	Vigors	126	Ancient Title	126	60,000	2:26.40	
1978	Exceller	5	W. Shoemaker	126	Star of Erin	126	Good Lord	126	90,000	2:24.60	
							As de Copas	126			
1979	Balzac	4	C.J. McCarron	126	Trillion	123	Silver Eagle	126	90,000	2:25.40	
1980	John Henry	5	L. Pincay Jr	126	Balzac	126	Bold Tropic	126	120,000	2:23.40	
1981	John Henry	6	W. Shoemaker	126	Spence Bay	126	The Bart	126	180,000	2:23.40	
1982	John Henry	7	W. Shoemaker	126	Craelius	122	Regalberto	126	180,000	2:24.00	
1983	Zalataia	4	F. Head	123	John Henry	126	Load the Cannons	122	240,000	2:29.20	
1984	Both Ends Burning	4	R.A. Baze	126	Gato Del Sol	126	Raami	121	240,000	2:25.40	
1985	Yashgan	4	C.J. McCarron	126	Both Ends Burning	126	Cariellor	126	240,000	2:27.20	
1986	Estrapade	6	F. Toro	123	Theatrical	126	Uptown Swell	126	240,000	2:26.00	
1987	Allez Milord	4	C.J. McCarron	126	Louis Le Grand	126	Rivlia	126	240,000	2:36.20	
1988	Nasr El Arab	3	G.L. Stevens	121	Great Communicator	126	Circus Prince	126	240,000	2:25.20	
1989	Hawkster	3	R.A. Baze	121	Pay the Butler	126	Saratoga Passage	126	300,000	2:22.80	
1990	Rial	5	R. Meza	126	Eradicate	126	Saratoga Passage	126	300,000	2:23.80	105
1991	Filago	4	P.A. Valenzuela	126	Missionary Ridge	126	Kartajana	123	300,000	2:23.62	109
1992	Navarone	4	P.A. Valenzuela	126	Defensive Play	126	Daros	121	240,000	2:24.29	108
1993	Kotashaan	5	K.J. Desormeaux	124	Luazur	124	Let's Elope	121	180,000	2:25.06	111
1994	Sandpit	5	C.S. Nakatani	124	Grand Flotilla	124	Approach the Bench	124	180,000	2:25.12	112
1995	Northern Spur	4	C.J. McCarron	124	Sandpit	124	Royal Chariot	124	180,000	2:02.37	110
1996	Admise	4	K.J. Desormeaux	121	Khoraz	124	Golden Post	124	180,000	1:58.48	103
	Bon Point (104 Beyer) finished first but was disqualified and placed fifth										
1997	Rainbow Dancer	6	A. Solis	124	Lord Jain	124	Sandpit	124	180,000	2:01.94	108
1998	Military	4	C.S. Nakatani	124	Bonapartiste	124	River Bay	124	180,000	2:02.04	107
	Marlin finished second but was disqualified and placed fourth										
1999	Mash One	5	D.R. Flores	124	Lazy Lode	124	Bonapartiste	124	180,000	1:59.07	108
2000	Mash One	6	D.R. Flores	124	Boatman	124	Asideo	124	180,000	2:00.67	107
2001	Senure	5	A. Solis	124	White Heart	124	Cagney	124	180,000	1:59.47	107
2002	The Tin Man	4	M.E. Smith	124	Sarafan	124	Blue Steller	124	180,000	1:58.93	109
2003	Storming Home	5	G.L. Stevens	124	Johar	124	Irish Warrior	124	150,000	2:01.64	104

Beyer Index: 107.71

Distance 1 1/2 miles prior to 1996; Run as Oak Tree Turf Championship prior to 2000; Run as Oak Tree Invitational 1971-1995; Run as Oak Tree Stakes, 1969-1970

HOLLYWOOD DERBY, 1 1/4 Miles (Turf), 3-Year-Olds, Hollywood Park, 2003 Purse: $600,000

Year	Winner	Age	Jockey	Wt.	Second	Wt.	Third	Wt.	Win Value	Time	Beyer
1938	Specify	3	J. Adams	118	High Strike	118	Fire Marshal	114	11,900	2:04.40	
1939	Shining One	3	J. Westrope	114	Wedding Call	114	Counterpoise	114	18,275	2:03.80	
1940	Big Flash	3	E. Rodriguez	114	Weight Anchor	114	Sweepida	122	18,750	2:03.60	
1941	Staretor	3	G. Woolf	115	Porter's Cap	122	Paperboy	114	19,675	2:03.20	
1945	Busher	3	J. Longden	123	Man o'Glory	112	Quick Reward	121	40,470	1:50.20	
1946	Honeymoon	3	J. Westrope	117	Pere Time	118	Eiffel Tower	118	39,300	2:02.00	
1947	Yankee Valor	3	N. Richardson	118	On Trust	126	Stepfather	118	36,000	2:01.80	
1948	Solidarity	3	J. Longden	119	Drumbeat	122	The Web II	118	33,300	2:02.60	
1949	Pedigree	3	J. Longden	126	Just Why	106	Rhodes Bull	112	42,900	2:03.00	
1950	Valquest	3	J. Westrope	111	Great Circle	126	Sun State	115	17,200	1:49.00	
1951	Grantor	3	W. Shoemaker	110	Australian Ace	111	Gold Note	118	33,600	2:01.80	
1952	A Gleam	3	H. Moreno	118	Arroz	111	Stranglehold	111	36,550	2:01.20	
1953	Rejected	3	R. Neves	110	Fleet Khal	117	Imbros	126	64,500	2:01.40	
1954	Fault Free	3	R. Neves	114	Allied	117	Determine	126	32,850	2:00.80	
1955	Swaps	3	W. Shoemaker	126	Fabulous Vegas	117	Jean's Joe	120	34,700	2:00.60	
1956	Count of Honor	3	E. Arcaro	117	Social Climber	123	Terrang	126	48,950	1:59.40	
1957	Round Table	3	W. Shoemaker	129	Irisher	110	Joe Price	118	69,300	2:00.60	
1958	Strong Bay	3	M. Ycaza	112	The Shoe	122	Hillsdale	118	70,800	2:02.60	
	Hillsdale finished second but was disqualified and placed third										
1959	Bagdad	3	W. Shoemaker	114	Worshiper	111	King O'Turf	110	65,900	1:59.60	
1960	Tempestuous	3	P. Moreno	110	T.V. Lark	122	Blank Check	111	68,700	2:01.40	
1961	Four-and-Twenty	3	J. Longden	126	We're Hoping	110	Bushel-n-Peck	117	77,900	2:00.60	
1962	Drill Site	3	R. Neves	110	Admiral's Voyage	126	Joc Jocoy	122	68,900	2:00.00	
1963	Y Flash	3	E. Burns	123	Get Around	123	Olympiad King	120	79,110	2:00.60	
1964	Real Good Deal	3	J. Longden	123	Close By	123	Performing Art	114	71,000	2:00.80	
1965	Terry's Secret	3	A. Maese	123	Arksoni	123	Easy Lime	114	80,200	2:00.40	
1966	Fleet Host	3	J. Lambert	114	Drin	123	Rehabilitate	114	75,500	2:00.40	
1967	Tumble Wind	3	J. Sellers	117	Duncan Junction	114	Ruken	126	72,900	2:00.20	
1968	Poleax	3	W. Hartack	123	Dewan	123	American Tiger	114	82,000	1:59.80	
1969	Tell	3	D. Pierce	123	Jay Ray	126	Court Road	112	76,600	2:00.00	
1970	Hanalei Bay	3	M. Volzke	114	Corn off the Cob	126	Western Welcome	123	73,200	2:01.20	
1971	Bold Reason	3	L. Pincay Jr	113	Jim French	126	Triple Bend	114	61,200	2:01.00	
1972	Riva Ridge	3	R. Turcotte	129	Bicker	114	Finalista	120	59,900	1:59.60	

Year	Winner	Age	Jockey	Wt.	Second	Wt.	Third	Wt.	Win Value	Time	Beyer
1973	Amen II 3		E. Belmonte 126		Groshawk 126		Kirrary 126	...90,000	2:27.80	
1974	Agitate 3		W. Shoemaker...126		Stardust Mel 126		Top Crowd..........126	...90,000	2:28.20	
1975	Intrepid Hero 3		D. Pierce..........126		Terete 126		Sibirri 126	...90,000	2:29.00	
1976	Crystal Water 3		W. Shoemaker...122		Life's Hope 122		Double Discount....122	...157,750	1:48.40	
1977	Steve's Friend 3		R. Hernandez 122		Affiliate 122		Habitony 122	...140,000	1:47.80	
1978	Affirmed 3		S. Cauthen.......122		Think Snow 122		Radar Ahead 122	...174,750	1:48.20	
1979	Flying Paster 3		D. Pierce..........122		Switch Partners 122		Shamgo 122	...166,750	1:47.60	
1980	Codex 3		E. Delahoussaye .122		Rumbo 122		Cactus Road........122	...195,250	1:47.40	
1981	De La Rose 3		E. Maple 119		High Counsel 122		Lord Trendy 122	...68,700	1:47.60	
1981	Silveyville 3		D. Winick 122		French Sassafras 122		Waterway Drive ...122	...68,700	1:47.60	
1982	Racing is Fun 3		W. Shoemaker...122		Prince Spellbound ..122		Uncle Jeff.........122	...67,150	1:47.20	
1982	Victory Zone 3		E. Delahoussaye .122		The Hague 122		Ask Me.............122	...70,150	1:47.80	
1983	Royal Heroine 3		F. Toro...........119		Interco 122		Pac Mania 122	...87,400	1:48.20	
1983	Ginger Brink 3		F. Toro...........122		Fifth Division 122		Hur Power 122	...86,400	1:49.20	
1984	Procida 3		C.B. Asmussen...122		Executive Pride 122		Reine Mathilde 119	...139,250	1:48.40	
1984	Foscarini 3		D.G. McHargue...122		Roving Minstrel 122		Bean Bag..........122	...140,750	1:47.40	
1985	Charming Duke 3		Y. Saint-Martin..122		Herat 122		La Koumia 119	...171,225	1:46.80	
1985	Slew the Dragon 3		J. Velasquez 122		Savannah Dancer ...119		Catane 122	...168,725	1:46.40	
1986	Thrill Show 3		W. Shoemaker...122		Air Display 122		Bold Arrangement..122	...146,000	1:46.80	
1986	Spellbound 3		R. Sibille 122		Double Feint 122		Bruiser 122	...147,500	1:46.80	
1987	Political Ambition ..3		E. Delahoussaye .122		The Medic 122		Light Sabre 122	...101,600	1:48.20	
1987	Stately Don 3		J. Vasquez 122		Lockton 122		Noble Minstrel.....122	...104,600	1:47.40	
1988	Silver Circus 3		G.L. Stevens 122		Raykour 122		Dr. Death..........122	...110,000	1:48.40	
1989	Live the Dream 3		A. Solis...........122		Charlie Barley 122		River Master........122	...110,000	1:47.00	
1990	Itsallgreektome 3		C.S. Nakatani.....122		Septieme Ciel 122		Anshan 122	...110,000	1:46.60	
1991	Eternity Star........3		E. Delahoussaye .122		Native Boundary ...122		Perfectly Proud ...122	...110,000	1:47.20	...103
1991	Olympio 3		E. Delahoussaye .122		Bistro Garden 122		River Traffic 122	...110,000	1:47.00	...105
1992	Paradise Creek 3		P. Day............122		Bien Bien 122		Kitwood...........122	...220,000	1:47.20	...102
1993	Explosive Red 3		C.S. Nakatani.....122		Jeune Homme 122		Earl of Barking 122	...220,000	1:46.80	...103
1994	River Flyer 3		C.W. Antley......122		Dare and Go 122		Fadeyev 122	...220,000	1:47.40	...107
1995	Labeeb 3		E. Delahoussaye .122		Helmsman 122		Da Hoss 122	...220,000	1:46.40	...108
1996	Marlin 3		J.R. Velazquez ...122		Rainbow Blues 122		Devil's Cup........122	...300,000	1:46.00	...105
1997	Subordination 3		J.D. Bailey 122		Lasting Approval ...122		Blazing Sword 122	...300,000	1:50.00	...105
1998	Vergennes 3		J.R. Velazquez ...122		Dixie Dot Com 122		Lone Bid 122	...300,000	1:49.44	...109
1999	Super Quercus 3		A. Solis...........122		Manndar 122		Fighting Falcon....122	...300,000	1:45.82	...111
2000	Brahms 3		P. Day............122		David Copperfield ..122		Zentsov Street......122	...300,000	1:46.73	...104
	Designed For Luck finished first but was disqualified and placed fifth										
2001	Denon 3		C.J. McCarron ...122		Sligo Bay 122		Aldebaran 122	...300,000	1:49.28	...109
2002	Johar 3		A. Solis...........122		Mananan McLir 122		Royal Gem 122	...300,000	1:48.70	...100
2003	Sweet Return 3		J.A. Krone 122		Fairly Ransom.....122		Kicken Kris 122	...360,000	2:04.27	...98

Beyer Index: **104.93**

Distance 1 1/4 miles 1938–41,1946–49, 1951–72; 1 1/4 miles (turf course), 1973–75. Run on main track 1938–72, 1976–80. Run as Westerner Stakes 1948–58. Run at Santa Anita in 1949.

HOLLYWOOD FUTURITY, 1 1/16 Miles, 2-Year-Olds,
Hollywood Park, 2003 Purse: $376,000

Year	Winner	Age	Jockey	Wt.	Second	Wt.	Third	Wt.	Win Value	Time	Beyer
1981	Stalwart 2		C.J. McCarron ...121		Cassaleria 121		Header Card 118	...365,805	1:47.80	
1982	Roving Boy 2		E. Delahoussaye .121		Desert Wine 121		Fifth Division 121	...418,770	1:41.80	
1983	Fali Time 2		S. Hawley 121		Bold T. Jay 121		Life's Magic 118	...549,485	1:41.60	
1984	Stephan's Odyssey ..2		E. Maple 121		First Norman 121		Right Con 121	...627,000	1:43.40	
1985	Snow Chief 2		A. Solis...........121		Electric Blue 121		Ferdinand.........121	...589,600	1:34.20	
1986	Temperate Sil.......2		W. Shoemaker...121		Alysheba 121		Masterful Advocate 121	...495,000	1:36.20	
1987	Tejano 2		L. Pincay Jr 121		Purdue King 121		Regal Classic......121	...495,000	1:34.60	
1988	King Glorious 2		C.J. McCarron ...121		Music Merci 121		Hawkster 121	...495,000	1:35.60	
1989	Grand Canyon 2		A. Cordero Jr 121		Farma Way 121		Silver Ending 121	...495,000	1:33.00	
1990	Best Pal 2		J.A. Santos.......121		General Meeting ...121		Reign Road 121	...495,000	1:35.40	
1991	A.P. Indy 2		E. Delahoussaye .121		Dance Floor 121		Casual Lies.........121	...329,780	1:42.80	
1992	River Special 2		L. Pincay Jr 121		Stuka 121		Earl of Barking 121	...275,000	1:43.20	...96
1993	Valiant Nature 2		L. Pincay Jr 121		Brocco 121		Flying Sensation...121	...275,000	1:40.60	...106
1994	Afternoon Deelites ..2		K.J. Desormeaux 121		Thunder Gulch 121		A.J. Jett 121	...275,000	1:40.60	...111
1995	Matty G 2		A. Solis...........121		Odyle 121		Ayrton S 121	...275,000	1:41.60	...104
1996	Swiss Yodeler 2		A. Solis...........121		Stolen Gold 121		In Excessive Bull ...121	...348,510	1:42.60	...92
1997	Real Quiet 2		K.J. Desormeaux 121		Artax 121		Nationalore 121	...282,120	1:41.20	...102
1998	Tactical Cat 2		L. Pincay Jr 121		Prime Timber 121		Premier Property..121	...235,800	1:42.63	...93
1999	Captain Steve 2		R.J. Albarado 121		High Yield 121		Cosine.............121	...245,400	1:43.27	...101
2000	Point Given 2		G.L. Stevens 121		Millennium Wind 121		Golden Ticket.......121	...204,300	1:42.21	...101
2001	Siphonic 2		J.D. Bailey 121		The Fonz's 121		Officer 121	...274,050	1:42.09	...103
2002	Toccet 2		J.F. Chavez 121		Domestic Dispute ..121		Coax Kid 121	...243,900	1:41.26	...102
2003	Lion Heart 2		M.E. Smith 121		St Averil 121		That's an Outrage...121	...225,600	1:42.80	...99

Beyer Index: **100.83**

Distance 1 mile 1985–90

HOLLYWOOD GOLD CUP, 1 1/4 Miles, 3-Year-Olds and Up,
Hollywood Park, 2003 Purse: $750,000

Year	Winner	Age	Jockey	Wt.	Second	Wt.	Third	Wt.	Win Value	Time	Beyer
1938	Seabiscuit	5	G. Woolf	133	Specifiy	109	Whichcee	114	37,150	2:03.80	
1939	Kayak II	4	G. Woolf	125	Cravat	126	Specify	118	35,075	2:02.60	
1940	Challedon	4	G. Woolf	133	Specify	117	Can't Wait	115	36,200	2:02.00	
1941	Big Pebble	5	J. Westrope	119	Paperboy	98	Mioland	130	62,475	2:02.60	
1944	Happy Issue	4	H. Woodhouse	119	Bull Reigh	122	Okana	126	60,600	2:01.60	
1945	Challenge Me	4	A. Skoronski	108	Bull Reigh	122	Sirde	111	48,230	2:00.40	
1946	Triplicate	5	B. James	113	Honeymoon	113	Historian	117	79,900	2:00.40	
1947	Cover Up	4	R. Permane	117	Burning Dream	117	Honeymoon	114	73,500	2:00.00	
1948	Shannon II	7	J. Adams	116	On Trust	128	Olhaverry	113	67,600	2:01.60	
1949	Solidarity	4	R. Neves	115	Ace Admiral	115	Pretal	112	100,000	2:01.20	
1950	Noor	5	J. Longden	130	Palestinian	122	Hill Prince	130	100,000	1:59.80	
1951	Citation	6	S. Brooks	120	Bewitch	108	Be Fleet	122	100,000	2:01.00	
1952	Two Lea	6	H. Moreno	113	Cyclotron	100	Sturdy One	108	100,000	2:00.20	
1953	Royal Serenade	5	J. Longden	113	Fleet Bird	122	A Gleam	119	100,000	2:00.80	
1954	Correspondent	4	J. Longden	110	Rejected	126	Trusting	107	100,000	2:00.80	
1955	Rejected	5	G. Glisson	118	Alidon	116	Determine	126	100,000	1:59.60	
1956	Swaps	4	W. Shoemaker	130	Mister Gus	117	Porterhouse	119	102,100	1:58.60	
1957	Round Table	3	W. Shoemaker	109	Porterhouse	119	Find	118	102,100	1:58.60	
1958	Gallant Man	4	W. Shoemaker	130	Eddie Schmidt	110	Seaneen	118	102,100	2:01.60	
1959	Hillsdale	4	T. Barrow	124	Find	112	Terrang	120	102,100	1:59.20	
1960	Dotted Swiss	4	E. Burns	107	Bagdad	122	Eddie Schmidt	112	102,100	1:59.40	
							Prized Host	109			
1961	Prince Blessed	4	J. Longden	114	Grey Eagle	111	Whodunit	113	102,100	1:59.80	
1962	Prove It	5	H. Moreno	125	Windy Sands	111	Cadiz	117	102,100	2:00.00	
1963	Cadiz	7	E. Burns	111	Aldershot	110	Olympiad King	111	102,100	1:59.60	
1964	Colorado King	5	R. York	118	Mustard Plaster	119	Native Diver	117	102,100	2:00.40	
1965	Native Diver	6	J. Lambert	124	Babington	114	Hill Rise	121	102,100	2:00.20	
1966	Native Diver	7	J. Lambert	126	O'Hara	112	Travel Orb	118	102,100	2:00.00	
1967	Native Diver	8	J. Lambert	123	Pretense	131	Biggs	117	102,100	1:58.80	
1968	Princessnesian	4	D. Pierce	117	Racing Room	112	Quicken Tree	119	102,100	1:59.80	
1969	Figonero	4	A. Pineda	115	Nodouble	129	Poleax	118	102,100	1:58.80	
1970	Pleasure Seeker	4	L. Pincay Jr	114	Neurologo	109	T.V. Commercial	112	102,100	1:59.40	
1971	Ack Ack	5	W. Shoemaker	134	Comtal	111	Manta	117	100,000	1:59.80	
1972	Quack	3	D. Pierce	115	Droll Role	119	War Heim	112	100,000	1:58.20	
1973	Kennedy Road	5	W. Shoemaker	120	Quack	127	Cougar II	128	90,000	1:59.40	
1974	Tree of Knowledge	4	W. Shoemaker	115	Ancient Title	125	War Heim	114	90,000	1:59.80	
1975	Ancient Title	5	L. Pincay Jr	125	Big Band	115	E. Tarta	115	90,000	1:59.20	
1976	Pay Tribute	4	M. Castaneda	117	Avatar	123	Riot in Paris	123	150,000	1:58.80	
1977	Crystal Water	4	L. Pincay Jr	129	Cascapedia	116	Caucasus	124	210,000	2:00.00	
1978	Exceller	5	W. Shoemaker	128	Text	118	Vigors	129	192,500	1:59.20	
1979	Affirmed	4	L. Pincay Jr	132	Sirlad	120	Text	119	275,000	1:58.40	
1980	Go West Young Man	5	E. Delahoussaye	116	Balzac	120	Caro Bambino	116	220,000	1:58.80	
1981	Eleven Stitches	4	S. Hawley	122	Caterman	120	Super Moment	117	275,000	2:00.40	
	Caterman finished first but was disqualified and placed second										
1982	Perrault	5	L. Pincay Jr	127	Erins Isle	118	It's the One	125	275,000	1:59.20	
1983	Island Whirl	5	E. Delahoussaye	120	Poley	116	Prince Spellbound	120	275,000	1:59.40	
1984	Desert Wine	4	E. Delahoussaye	122	John Henry	125	Sari's Dreamer	114	275,000	2:00.40	
1985	Greinton	4	L. Pincay Jr	120	Precisionist	125	Kings Island	112	275,000	1:58.40	
1986	Super Diamond	6	L. Pincay Jr	118	Alphabatim	120	Precisionist	127	275,000	2:00.40	
1987	Ferdinand	4	W. Shoemaker	124	Judge Angelucci	118			275,000	2:00.60	
					Tasso	118					
1988	Cutlass Reality	6	G.L. Stevens	116	Alysheba	126	Ferdinand	125	275,000	1:59.40	
1989	Blushing John	4	P. Day	122	Sabona	116	Payant	116	275,000	2:00.40	
1990	Criminal Type	5	J.A. Santos	121	Sunday Silence	126	Opening Verse	119	550,000	1:59.80	121
1991	Marquetry	4	D. Flores	110	Farma Way	122	Itsallgreektome	119	550,000	1:59.40	119
1992	Sultry Song	4	J. Bailey	113	Marquetry	118	Another Review	120	550,000	2:00.20	113
1993	Best Pal	5	C.A. Black	121	Bertrando	118	Major Impact	114	412,500	2:00.00	117
1994	Slew of Damascus	6	G.L. Stevens	117	Fanmore	116	Del Mar Dennis	116	412,500	2:00.60	110
1995	Cigar	5	J.D. Bailey	126	Tinners Way	118	Tossofthecoin	115	550,000	1:59.40	118
1996	Siphon	5	D.R. Flores	117	Geri	118	Helmsman	120	600,000	2:00.40	117
1997	Gentlemen	5	G.L. Stevens	124	Siphon	124	Sandpit	124	600,000	1:59.20	121
1998	Skip Away	5	J.D. Bailey	124	Puerto Madero	124	Gentlemen	124	600,000	2:00.16	117
1999	Real Quiet	4	J.D. Bailey	124	Budroyale	124	Malek	124	600,000	1:59.67	115
2000	Early Pioneer	5	V. Espinoza	124	General Challenge	124	David	124	600,000	2:02.40	112
2001	Aptitude	4	L. Pincay Jr	124	Skimming	124	dq-Futural	124	450,000	2:01.79	107
	Futural (Beyer: 109) finished first but was disqualified and placed third										
2002	Sky Jack	6	L. Pincay Jr	124	Momentum	124	Milwaukee Brew	124	450,000	2:01.73	115
2003	Congaree	5	J.D. Bailey	124	Harlan's Holiday	124	Kudos	124	450,000	2:00.48	116

Beyer Index: 115.57

HOLLYWOOD STARLET, 1 1/16 Miles, 2-Year-Old Fillies,
Hollywood Park, 2003 Purse: $349,500

Year	Winner	Age	Jockey	Wt.	Second	Wt.	Third	Wt.	Win Value	Time	Beyer
1981	Skillful Joy	2	C.J. McCarron	120	Header Card	120	Flying Partner	120	220,900	1:43.20	
1982	Fabulous Notion	2	D. Pierce	120	O'Happy Day	120	Stephanie Bryn	120	271,618	1:42.40	
1983	Althea	2	L. Pincay Jr	120	Life's Magic	120	Spring Loose	120	261,250	1:43.00	
1984	Outstandingly	2	W.A. Guerra	120	Fran's Valentine	120	Wising Up	120	386,403	1:44.00	
1985	I'm Splendid	2	C.J. McCarron	120	Trim Colony	120	Twilight Ridge	120	344,217	1:36.00	
1986	Very Subtle	2	P.A. Valenzuela	120	Sacahuista	120	Infringe	120	267,025	1:37.00	
1987	Goodbye Halo	2	J. Velasquez	120	Variety Baby	120	Jeanne Jones	120	274,505	1:36.20	
1988	Stocks Up	2	A. Solis	120	Fantastic Look	120	One of a Klein	120	292,325	1:35.00	
1989	Cheval Volant	2	A. Solis	120	Annual Reunion	120	Special Happening	120	247,500	1:35.60	
1990	Cuddles	2	G.L. Stevens	120	Lite Light	120	Garden Gal	120	247,500	1:36.20	
1991	Magical Maiden	2	G.L. Stevens	120	Looie Capote	120	Soviet Sojourn	120	138,105	1:42.60	.94
1992	Creaking Board	2	C.S. Nakatani	120	Passing Vice	120	Madame L'Enjoleur	120	139,425	1:43.60	.83
1993	Sardula	2	E. Delahoussaye	120	Princess Mitterand	120	Viz	120	139,095	1:42.20	.98
1994	Serena's Song	2	C.S. Nakatani	120	Urbane	120	Ski Dancer	120	137,500	1:41.80	.103
1995	Cara Rafaela	2	C.S. Nakatani	120	Advancing Star	120	Chile Chatte	120	137,500	1:43.00	.104
1996	Sharp Cat	2	C.S. Nakatani	120	City Band	120	High Heeled Hope	120	165,600	1:44.60	.92
1997	Love Lock	2	K.J. Desormeaux	120	Career Collection	120	Snowberg	120	168,600	1:42.00	.98
1998	Excellent Meeting	2	K.J. Desormeaux	120	Lacquaria	120	Perfect Six	120	240,000	1:42.14	.101
1999	Surfside	2	P. Day	120	She's Classy	120	Abby Girl	120	228,150	1:43.51	.100
2000	I Believe in You	2	A. Solis	120	Jetin Excess	120	Whoopddoo	120	205,050	1:43.57	.90
2001	Habibti	2	V. Espinoza	120	You	120	Tali'sluckybusride	120	214,800	1:43.12	.103
2002	Elloluv	2	P.A. Valenzuela	120	Composure	120	Summer Wind Dancer	120	213,900	1:42.88	.94
2003	Hollywood Story	2	P.A. Valenzuela	120	Rahy Dolly	120	House of Fortune	120	209,700	1:42.87	.95

Beyer Index: **96.54**

Distance 1 mile 1985-90

HOLLYWOOD TURF CUP, 1 1/2 Miles (Turf), 3-Year-Olds and Up,
Hollywood Park, 2003 Purse: $250,000

Year	Winner	Age	Jockey	Wt.	Second	Wt.	Third	Wt.	Win Value	Time	Beyer
1981	Providential II	4	A. Lequeux	126	Queen to Conquer	123	Goldliko	126	325,500	2:26.80	
1982	Prince Spellbound	3	M. Castaneda	122	Majesty's Prince	122	Lithan	126	220,000	2:14.00	
1982	The Hague	3	F. Toro	122	Caterman	126	It's the One	126	220,000	2:13.40	
1983	John Henry	8	C.J. McCarron	126	Zalataia	123	Palikaraki	126	275,000	2:16.60	
1984	Alphabatim	3	C.J. McCarron	122	Raami	122	Both Ends Burning	126	275,000	2:15.80	
							Scruples				
1985	Zoffany	5	E. Delahoussaye	126	Win	126	Vanlandingham	126	275,000	2:28.40	
1986	Alphabatim	5	W. Shoemaker	126	Dahar	126	Theatrical	126	275,000	2:25.80	
1987	Vilzak	4	P. Day	126	Forlitano	126	Political Ambition	122	275,000	2:27.00	
1988	Great Communicator	5	R. Sibille	126	Putting	126	Nasr El Arab	122	275,000	2:34.40	
1989	Frankly Perfect	4	C.J. McCarron	126	Yankee Affair	126	Pleasant Variety	126	275,000	2:26.60	
1990	Itsallgreektome	3	C.S. Nakatani	122	Mashkour	126	Live the Dream	126	275,000	2:24.80	
1991	Miss Alleged	4	C.J. McCarron	123	Itsallgreektome	126	Quest for Fame	126	275,000	2:30.00	.110
1992	Bien Bien	3	C.J. McCarron	122	Fraise	124	Trishyde	119	275,000	2:31.20	.105
	Fraise finished first but was disqualified and placed second										
1993	Fraise	5	C.J. McCarron	126	Know Heights	126	Explosive Red	122	275,000	2:32.20	.111
1994	Frenchpark	4	C.A. Black	126	Dare and Go	122	Regency	126	275,000	2:25.60	.108
1995	Royal Chariot	5	A. Solis	126	Talloires	126	Earl of Barking	126	275,000	2:25.00	.105
1996	Running Flame	4	C.J. McCarron	126	Marlin	126	Talloires	126	300,000	2:28.40	.109
1997	River Bay	4	A. Solis	126	Awad	126	Flag Down	126	300,000	2:26.40	.109
1998	Lazy Lode	4	C.S. Nakatani	126	Yagli	126	Ferrari	126	300,000	2:28.36	.109
1999	Lazy Lode	4	L. Pincay Jr.	126	Public Purse	126	Single Empire	126	240,000	2:25.85	.110
2000	Bienamado	4	C.J. McCarron	126	Northern Quest	126	Lazy Lode	126	240,000	2:25.98	.108
2001	Super Quercus	5	A. Solis	126	Bonapartiste	126	Blazing Fury	126	150,000	2:29.86	.105
2002	Sligo Bay	4	L. Pincay Jr.	126	Grammarian	126	Delta Form	126	150,000	2:27.22	.105
2003	Continuously	4	A. Solis	126	Bowman Mill	126	Epicentre	126	150,000	2:29.01	.102
	Epicentre finished first but was disqualified and placed third										

Beyer Index: **107.38**

Distance 1 3/8 miles 1982-84

HOPEFUL STAKES, 7 Furlongs, 2-Year-Olds,
Saratoga Race Course, 2003 Purse: $200,000

Year	Winner	Age	Jockey	Wt.	Second	Wt.	Third	Wt.	Win Value	Time	Beyer
1903	Delhi	2	C. Gannon	112	Highball	112	Palmbearer	112	22,275	1:13.20	
1904	Tanya	2	E. Hildebrand	127	Rose of Dawn	112	Hot Shot	115	29,790	1:13.40	
1905	Mohawk II	2	A. Redfern	130	Athlete	115	Juggler	112	16,490	1:13.40	
1906	Peter Pan	2	W. Knapp	130	McCarter	122	Jope Joan	112	17,640	1:12.20	
1907	Jim Gaffney	2	D. Nicol	115	Fair Play	125	Bar None	115	17,500	1:15.00	
1908	Helmet	2	J. Notter	115	Perseus	115	Fayette	130	10,990	1:12.20	
1909	Rocky O'Brien	2	V. Powers	122	Sweep	130	Barleythorpe	115	17,160	1:13.20	
1910	Novelty	2	A. Thomas	130	Iron Mask	125	Naushon	125	19,140	1:14.00	
1913	Bringhurst	2	J. Loftus	113	Little Nephew	113	Black Broom	107	4,100	1:12.40	
1914	Regret	2	J. Notter	127	Andrew M.	114	Pebbles	127	9,590	1:16.40	

Year	Winner	Age	Jockey	Wt.	Second	Wt.	Third	Wt.	Win Value	Time	Beyer
1915	Dominant	2	J. Notter	130	Big Smoke	107	Primero	107	9,150	1:13.80	
1916	Campfire	2	J. McTaggart	130	Omar Khayyam	110	Star Master	110	18,850	1:14.60	
1917	Sun Briar	2	W. Knapp	130	Papp	130	Sycamour	115	30,600	1:15.60	
1918	Eternal	2	A. Schuttinger	115	Daydue	115	War Marvel	115	30,150	1:13.60	
1919	Man o' War	2	J. Loftus	130	Cleopatra	112	Constancy	124	24,600	1:13.00	
1920	Leonardo II	2	A. Schuttinger	115	Prudery	127	Oriole	115	33,850	1:12.40	
1921	Morvich	2	A. Johnson	130	Kai-Sang	130	Whiskaway	115	34,900	1:12.60	
1922	Dunlin	2	C. Kummer	115	Goshawk	130	Zev	130	38,950	1:12.40	
1923	Diogenes	2	C. Ponce	115	Bracadale	115	Sunspero	122	46,800	1:12.60	
1924	Master Charlie	2	G. Babin	130	Pas Seul	127	K't'y Cardinal	115	48,700	1:13.00	
1925	Pompey	2	L. Fator	127	Flight of Time	125	Chance Play	122	42,850	1:17.80	
1926	Lord Chaucer	2	F. Coltiletti	115	Termahant	112	Scapa Flow	125	48,850	1:19.80	
1927	Brooms	2	J. Maiben	115	Victorian	115	Nassak	127	55,750	1:20.00	
1928	Jack High	2	G. Ellis	127	Blue Larkspur	130	Chestnut Oak	122	54,100	1:18.40	
1929	Boojum	2	R. Workman	117	Whichone	125	Caruso	127	54,750	1:17.00	
1930	Epithet	2	W. Kelsay	117	Jamestown	130	Novelist	117	56,000	1:17.60	
1931	Tick On	2	P. Walls	117	Sweeping Light	117	Polonaise	122	45,950	1:20.40	
1932	Ladysman	2	R. Jones	130	Sun Archer	122	Happy Gal	127	41,400	1:19.40	
1933	Bazaar	2	D. Meade	119	High Quest	117	Discovery	117	35,550	1:19.00	
1934	Psychic Bid	2	M. Garner	122	Rosemont	117	Esposa	114	38,400	1:19.80	
1935	Red Rain	2	R. Workman	124	Bien Joli	122	Sun Teddy	117	38,400	1:19.80	
1936	Maedic	2	E. Litzenberger	122	Billionaire	119	Tedious	116	32,600	1:20.20	
1937	Sky Larking	2	A. Robertson	119	Bull Lea	116	Fighting Fox	122	31,450	1:20.80	
1938	El Chico	2	N. Wall	126	Ariel Toy	116	Johnstown	116	42,550	1:18.40	
1939	Bimelech	2	F.A. Smith	122	Andy K.	126	Boy Angler	119	33,750	1:18.80	
1940	Whirlaway	2	J. Longden	118	Attention	126	Hy-Cop	116	37,850	1:18.00	
1941	Devil Diver	2	J. Skelly	119	Shut Out	122	Amphitheatre	122	35,950	1:18.60	
1942	Devil's Thumb	2	C. McCreary	122	True Blue	116	Bourmont	116	31,750	1:18.40	
1943	Bee Mac	2	S. Young	119	Boy Knight	122	By Jimminy	122	33,300	1:18.40	
1944	Pavot	2	G. Woolf	126	Esteem	122	Great Power	114	51,775	1:18.80	
1945	Star Pilot	2	A. Kirkland	112	Inroc	112	Revoked	126	55,195	1:16.60	
1946	Blue Border	2	A. DeLara	122	Grand Admiral	126	Johnny Dimick	113	46,450	1:17.00	
	Cosmic Bomb finished second but was disqualified										
1947	Relic	2	J. Adams	114	Whirling Fox	109	My Request	126	48,200	1:17.40	
1948	Blue Peter	2	E. Guerin	126	Sport Page	114	Curandero	114	47,750	1:19.20	
1949	Middleground	2	D. Gorman	114	Navy Chief	118	Mr. Trouble	114	44,050	1:18.40	
1950	Battlefield	2	E. Guerin	122	Battle Morn	122	Big Stretch	122	47,550	1:18.00	
1951	Cousin	2	E. Guerin	122	Tom Fool	122	Hannibal	122	51,700	1:19.20	
1952	Native Dancer	2	E. Guerin	122	Tiger Skin	122	Platan	122	51,450	1:18.80	
1953	Artismo	2	D. Gorman	122	War Piper	122	Turn-to	122	58,900	1:18.00	
1954	Nashua	2	E. Arcaro	122	Summer Tan	122	Pyrenees	122	57,050	1:17.80	
1955	Needles	2	J. Choquette	122	Career Boy	122	Jean Baptiste	122	50,000	1:18.20	
1956	King Hairan	2	E. Arcaro	122	Gannet	122	Cohoes	122	48,400	1:18.40	
1957	Rose Trellis	2	F. Lovato	122	Louis d'Or	122	Jimmer	122	40,075	1:18.40	
1958	First Landing	2	E. Arcaro	122	First Minister	122	That Lucky Day	122	36,700	1:17.80	
1959	Tompion	2	W. Shoemaker	122	Vital Force	122	Bourbon Prince	122	73,434	1:17.40	
1960	Hail to Reason	2	R. Ussery	122	Bronzerullah	122	Chinchilla	122	76,602	1:16.60	
1961	Jaipur	2	E. Arcaro	122	Su Ka Wa	122	Sir Gaylord	122	76,229	1:16.40	
1962	Outing Class	2	D. Pierce	122	Alabama Bound	122	Final Ruling	122	76,407	1:17.00	
1963	Traffic	2	M. Ycaza	122	Amastar	122	Count Bud	122	72,394	1:18.60	
1964	Bold Lad	2	B. Baeza	122	Native Charger	122	Time Tested	122	72,231	1:15.60	
1965	Buckpasser	2	B. Baeza	122	Impressive	122	Indulto	122	71,614	1:16.00	
1966	Bold Hour	2	J.L. Rotz	122	Great Power	122	Top Bid	122	70,005	1:17.20	
1967	What a Pleasure	2	B. Baeza	122	Royal Trace	122	Exclusive Native	122	74,084	1:16.40	
1968	Top Knight	2	M. Ycaza	122	Reviewer	122	Bushido	122	80,145	1:16.00	
1969	Irish Castle	2	B. Baeza	122	Hagley	122	Pontifex	122	73,044	1:17.20	
1970	Proudest Roman	2	J.L. Rotz	122	Pass Catcher	122	Cool Morn	122	85,117	1:18.60	
1971	Rest Your Case	2	J. Vasquez	122	Governor Max	122	Loquacious Dan	122	77,355	1:17.40	
1972	Secretariat	2	R. Turcotte	121	Flight to Glory	121	Stop the Music	121	51,930	1:16.20	
1973	Gusty O'Shay	2	P. Kotenko	121	Take by Storm	121	Prince of Reason	121	50,400	1:16.40	
1974	The Bagel Prince	2	A. Cordero Jr	121	Knightly Sport	121	Cardinal George	121	40,995	1:16.80	
1974	Foolish Pleasure	2	B. Baeza	121	Greek Answer	121	Our Talisman	121	41,445	1:16.00	
1975	Jackknife	2	J. Cruguet	121	Ferrous	121	Whatsyourpleasure	121	41,625	1:16.60	
1975	Eustache	2	J. Nichols	121	Iron Bit	121	Gentle King	121	41,850	1:16.40	
1976	Banquet Table	2	J. Cruguet	122	Turn of Coin	122	P. R. Man.	122	51,345	1:16.20	
1977	Affirmed	2	S. Cauthen	122	Alydar	122	Regal and Royal	122	48,105	1:15.40	
1978	General Assembly	2	D.G. McHargue	122	Exuberant	122	Fuzzbuster	122	48,600	1:16.40	
1979	J.P. Brother	2	J. Imparato	122	Gold Stage	122	Googolplex	122	50,490	1:16.20	
	Rockhill Native finished first but was disqualified and placed sixth										
1980	Tap Shoes	2	R. Hernandez	122	Lord Avie	122	Well Decorated	122	51,750	1:17.00	
1981	Timely Writer	2	R. Danjean	122	Out of Hock	122	Lejoli	122	51,390	1:16.20	
1982	Copelan	2	J.D. Bailey	122	Victorious	122	Aloha Hawaii	122	69,000	1:16.60	
1983	Capitol South	2	J.D. Bailey	122	Don Rickles	122	Swale	122	72,720	1:17.40	

Year	Winner	Age	Jockey	Wt.	Second	Wt.	Third	Wt.	Win Value	Time	Beyer
1984	Chief's Crown	2	D. MacBeth	122	Tiffany Ice	122	Mugzy's Rullah	122	100,440	1:16.00	
1985	Papal Power	2	D. MacBeth	122	Danny's Keys	122	Bullet Blade	122	103,320	1:18.40	
1986	Gulch	2	A. Cordero Jr	122	Persevered	122	Flying Granville	122	126,720	1:16.40	
1987	Crusader Sword	2	R.P. Romero	122	Bill E. Shears	122	Success Express	122	104,850	1:18.60	
1988	Mercedes Won	2	R.G. Davis	122	Fast Play	122	Leading Prospect	122	142,320	1:16.60	
1989	Summer Squall	2	P. Day	122	Sir Richard Lewis	122	Eternal Flight	122	140,000	1:16.80	
1990	Deposit Ticket	2	G.L. Stevens	122	Hansel	122	Link	122	139,680	1:16.20	98
1991	Salt Lake	2	M.E. Smith	122	Slew's Ghost	122	Caller I.D.	122	120,000	1:17.60	
1992	Great Navigator	2	A.T. Gryder	122	Strolling Along	122	England Expects	122	120,000	1:15.60	98
1993	Dehere	2	C.J. McCarron	122	Slew Gin Fizz	122	Whitney Tower	122	120,000	1:15.80	97
1994	Wild Escapade	2	J.F. Chavez	122	Montreal Red	122	Law of the Sea	122	120,000	1:23.20	89
1995	Hennessy	2	G.L. Stevens	122	Louis Quatorze	122	Maria's Mon	122	120,000	1:23.40	100
1996	Smoke Glacken	2	C. Perret	122	Ordway	122	Gunfight	122	120,000	1:23.60	93
1997	Favorite Trick	2	P. Day	122	K.O. Punch	122	Jesse M	122	120,000	1:23.80	91
1998	Lucky Roberto	2	R.G. Davis	122	Tactical Cat	122	Time Bandit	122	120,000	1:23.81	85
1999	High Yield	2	J.D. Bailey	122	Settlement	122	Exciting Story	122	120,000	1:22.85	94
2000	City Zip	2	J.A. Santos	122			Macho Uno	122	80,000	1:24.52	86
	Yonaguska	2	J.D. Bailey	122							
2001	Came Home	2	C.J. McCarron	122	Mayakovsky	122	Thunder Days	122	120,000	1:21.94	108
2002	Sky Mesa	2	E.S. Prado	122	Pretty Wild	122	ZavatA	122	120,000	1:23.08	103
2003	Silver Wagon	2	J.D. Bailey	122	Chapel Royal	122	Notorious Rogue	122	120,000	1:23.47	92

Beyer Index: 94.92

Distance 6 furlongs before 1925; 6 1/2 furlongs, 1925–93. Run over Widener Course, 1943–45

HUMANA DISTAFF HANDICAP, 7 Furlongs,
Fillies and Mares, 4-Year-Olds and Up, Churchill Downs, 2003 Purse: $222,400

Year	Winner	Age	Jockey	Wt.	Second	Wt.	Third	Wt.	Win Value	Time	Beyer
1987	Lazer Show	4	P. Day	120	Weekend Delight		Ten Thousand Stars			1:22.80	
1988	Le L'Argent	6	P. Day	119	Lady Gretchen		Intently			1:22.80	
1989	Sunshine Always	5	P. Day	113	Littlebitapleasure		Lt. Lao			1:24.40	
1990	Medicine Woman	5	P. Day	114	Lost Lode	114	Gallant Ryder	111	36,693	1:23.40	96
1991	Illeria	4	P. Day	112	Nurse Dopey	117	Tipsy Girl	115	37,603	1:23.20	
1992	Ifyoucouldseemenow	4	C. Perret	120	Madam Bear	114	Magal	113	56,599	1:22.22	104
1993	Court Hostess	5	C.J. McCarron	115	Santa Catalina	115	Ifyoucouldseemenow	116	56,550	1:23.18	94
1994	Roamin Rachel	4	M.E. Smith	118	Arches of Gold	121	Glory's Ghost	113	72,345	1:23.83	103
1995	Laura's Pistolette	4	Nakatani CS	114	Morning Meadow	113	Traverse City	114	74,425	1:22.24	97
1996	In Conference	4	M.E. Smith	113	Supah Jess	113	Morris Code	116	72,930	1:23.30	93
1997	Capote Belle	4	J.R. Velazquez	115	Hidden Lake	115	J J'sdream	117	70,060	1:22.38	107
1998	Colonial Minstrel	4	J.R. Velazquez	115	Stop Traffic	114	Meter Maid	114	71,300	1:22.12	105
1999	Zuppardo Ardo	5	S.J. Sellers	114	French Braids	114	Prospector's Song	114	105,183	1:23.40	98
2000	Ruby Surprise	5	J.C. Judice	114	Honest Lady	119	Cassidy	113	102,951	1:21.25	106
2001	Dream Supreme	4	P. Day	120	Le Feminn	115	Nany's Sweep	117	102,300	1:20.70	110
2002	Celtic Melody	4	M. Guidry	114	Gold Mover	115	Hattiesburg	115	141,360	1:22.98	96
	Gold Mover (Beyer: 96) finished first but was disqualified and placed second										
2003	Sightseek	4	J.D. Bailey	116	Gold Mover	119	Miss Lodi	114	137,888	1:22.12	107

Beyer Index: 101.23

JOCKEY CLUB GOLD CUP, 1 1/4 Miles, 3-Year-Olds and Up,
Belmont Park, 2003 Purse: $1,000,000

Year	Winner	Age	Jockey	Wt.	Second	Wt.	Third	Wt.	Win Value	Time	Beyer
1919	Purchase	3	C. Kummer	118					5,350	2:41.60	
1920	Man o' War	3	C. Kummer	118	Damask	118			5,850	2:28.80	
1921	Mad Hatter	5	E. Sande	125	Grey Lad	114	T. Me Not	114	12,100	3:22.40	
1922	Mad Hatter	6	E. Sande	125	Bit of White	122	Pillory	114	12,700	3:22.60	
1923	Homestretch	3	C. Lang	114	Vigil	114	Pettifogger	114	11,300	3:24.20	
1924	My Play	5	A. Schuttinger	125	King Solomon's Seal	125	My Own	125	14,150	3:25.60	
1925	Altawood	4	E. Sande	120	Aga Khan	125	Swope	114	13,050	3:24.60	
1926	Crusader	3	J. Maiben	114	Espino	114	Altawood	125	13,300	3:26.00	
1927	Chance Play	4	E. Sande	125	Display	125	F'er and Ever	125	12,000	3:23.00	
	Brown Bud finished first but was disqualified										
1928	Reigh Count	3	C. Lang	114	Chance Shot	125	Display	125	10,850	3:23.00	
1929	Diavolo	4	J. Maiben	125	Double Pay	125	The Nut	114	10,900	3:24.00	
1930	Gallant Fox	3	E. Sande	118	Yarn	114	Frisius	125	10,300	3:24.40	
1931	Twenty Grand	3	C. Kurtsinger	114	Blenheim	114	Barometer	114	10,400	3:23.40	
1932	Gusto	4	B. Hanford	125	Blenheim	125	Masked Knight	118	9,950	3:25.20	
1933	Dark Secret	4	H. Mills	125	Gusto	125	Equipoise	125	6,400	3:25.20	
1934	Dark Secret	5	C. Kurtsinger	125	Faireno	125	Inlander	125	6,200	3:24.60	
1935	Firethorn	3	E. Arcaro	117	Judy o' Grady	114	Gallant Prince	117	6,550	3:24.20	
1936	Count Arthur	4	J. Stout	124	Memory Book	117	Giant Killer	117	6,750	3:24.40	
1937	Firethorn	5	H. Richards	124	Count Arthur	124	Moonton	117	6,050	3:26.00	
1938	War Admiral	4	W.D. Wright	124	Magic Hour	117	Jolly Tar	117	5,500	3:24.80	
1939	Cravat	4	B. James	124	Isolater	124	Shangay Lily	121	5,550	3:23.00	
1940	Fenelon	3	J. Stout	114	Iron Shot	114	Olympus	125	6,700	3:24.40	

Year	Winner	Age	Jockey	Wt.	Second	Wt.	Third	Wt.	Win Value	Time	Beyer
1941	Market Wise	3	B. James	114	Whirlaway	114	Fenelon	125	7,325	3:20.80	
1942	Whirlaway	4	G. Woolf	124	Alsab	117	Bolingbroke	124	18,350	3:21.60	
1943	Princequillo	3	C. McCreary	117	Fairy Manhurst	117	Bolingbroke	117	18,350	3:21.60	
1944	Bolingbroke	7	R. Permane	125	Strategic	125	Devil Diver	125	17,645	3:27.20	
1945	Pot o' Luck	3	D. Dodson	114	Eurasian	125	Stymie	125	18,335	3:27.40	
1946	Pavot	4	E. Arcaro	124	Stymie	124	Rico Monte	124	18,250	3:22.60	
1947	Phalanx	3	R. Donoso	117	Talon	124	Stymie	124	17,850	3:23.40	
1948	Citation	3	E. Arcaro	117	Phalanx	124	Beauchef.	124	72,700	3:21.60	
1949	Ponder	3	S. Brooks	117	Flying Missel	124	Miss Request	121	36,300	3:22.80	
1950	Hill Prince	3	E. Arcaro	117	Noor	124	Adile	121	36,000	3:23.40	
1951	Counterpoint	3	D. Gorman	117	Hill Prince	124	Kiss Me Kate	114	35,600	3:21.60	
1952	One Count	3	D. Gorman	117	Mark-Ye-Well	117	Crafty Admiral.	124	52,100	3:24.20	
1953	Level Lea	3	W. Boland	117	Alerted	124	Platan	117	55,100	3:27.00	
1954	High Gun	3	E. Arcaro	119	Fisherman	119	Bicarb	124	55,150	3:25.80	
1955	Nashua	3	E. Arcaro	119	Thinking Cap	119	Mark's Puzzle.	119	52,850	3:24.80	
1956	Nashua	4	E. Arcaro	124	Riley	119	Third Brother	119	36,600	3:20.40	
1957	Gallant Man	3	W. Shoemaker	119	Third Brother	124	Reneged	124	53,850	3:23.00	
1958	Inside Tract	4	C. McCreary	124	Dotted Line	121	Civet	124	52,417	3:23.40	
1959	Sword Dancer	3	E. Arcaro	119	Round Table	124	Tudor Era	119	70,790	3:22.20	
1960	Kelso	3	E. Arcaro	119	Don Poggio	124	Bald Eagle	124	70,205	3:19.40	
1961	Kelso	4	E. Arcaro	124	Hillsborough	124	Peace Isle	124	68,770	3:25.80	
1962	Kelso	5	I. Valenzuela	124	Guadalcanal	124	Nickel Boy	124	70,785	3:19.80	
1963	Kelso	6	I. Valenzuela	124	Guadalcanal	124	Garwol	124	70,785	3:22.00	
1964	Kelso	7	I. Valenzuela	124	Roman Brother	119	Quadrangle	119	70,785	3:19.20	
1965	Roman Brother	4	B. Baeza	124	Berenjenal	124	Brave Lad	124	71,500	3:22.60	
1966	Buckpasser	3	B. Baeza	119	Niarkos	124	O'Hara	124	71,825	3:26.20	
1967	Damascus	3	W. Shoemaker	119	Handsome Boy	124	Successor	119	69,290	3:20.20	
1968	Quicken Tree	5	W. Hartack	124	Funny Fellow	119	Chompion	119	71,370	3:22.80	
1969	Arts and Letters	3	B. Baeza	119	Nodouble	124	Harem Lady.	121	69,030	3:22.40	
1970	Shuvee	4	R. Turcotte	121	Loud	119	Hydrologist	124	70,785	3:21.60	
1971	Shuvee	5	J. Velasquez	121	Paraje	124	Loud	124	66,900	3:20.40	
1972	Autobiography	4	A. Cordero Jr	124	Key to the Mint	119	Riva Ridge	119	68,220	3:21.60	
1973	Prove Out	4	J. Velasquez	124	Loud	124	Twice a Prince	119	66,060	3:20.00	
1974	Forego	4	H. Gustines	124	Copte	124	Group Plan.	124	67,140	3:21.20	
1975	Group Plan	5	J. Velasquez	124	Wajima	119	Outdoors	124	95,850	3:23.20	
1976	Great Contractor	3	P. Day	121	Appassopmayp	121	Revidere	118	201,360	2:28.80	
1977	On the Sly	4	G. McCarron	126	Great Contractor	126	Cox's Ridge	121	208,080	2:28.20	
1978	Exceller	5	W. Shoemaker	126	Seattle Slew	126	Great Contractor	126	193,080	2:27.20	
1979	Affirmed	4	L. Pincay Jr	126	Spectacular Bid	121	Coastal	121	225,000	2:27.40	
1980	Temperence Hill	3	E. Maple	121	John Henry	126	Ivory Hunter	126	329,400	2:30.20	
1981	John Henry	6	W. Shoemaker	126	Peat Moss	126	Relaxing	123	340,800	2:28.40	
1982	Lemhi Gold	4	C.J. McCarron	126	Silver Supreme	126	Christmas Past	118	337,800	2:31.20	
1983	Slew o' Gold	3	A. Cordero Jr	121	Highland Blade	126	Bounding Basque.	126	342,000	2:26.20	
1984	Slew o' Gold	4	A. Cordero Jr	126	Hail Bold King	121	Bounding Basque.	126	1,350,400	2:28.80	
1985	Vanlandingham	4	P. Day	126	Gate Dancer	126	Creme Fraiche.	121	516,600	2:27.00	
1986	Creme Fraiche	4	R.P. Romero	126	Turkoman	126	Danzig Connection .	121	510,300	2:28.00	
1987	Creme Fraiche	5	L. Pincay Jr	126	Java Gold	121	Easy n Dirty.	126	650,400	2:30.80	
1988	Waquoit	5	J.A. Santos	126	Personal Flag	126	Easy n Dirty.	126	637,800	2:27.60	
1989	Easy Goer	3	P. Day	121	Cryptoclearance	126	Forever Silver.	126	659,400	2:29.20	
1990	Flying Continental	4	C.A. Black.	126	De Roche	126	Izvestia	121	503,100	2:00.60	117
1991	Festin	5	E. Delahoussaye.	126	Chief Honcho	126	Strike the Gold	121	510,000	2:00.60	114
1992	Pleasant Tap	5	G.L. Stevens	126	Strike the Gold	126	A.P. Indy	121	510,000	1:58.80	117
1993	Miner's Mark	3	C.J. McCarron	121	Colonial Affair	121	Brunswick	126	510,000	2:02.60	106
1994	Colonial Affair	4	J.A. Santos	126	Devil His Due	126	Flag Down	126	450,000	2:02.00	113
1995	Cigar	5	J.D. Bailey	126	Unaccounted For	126	Star Standard.	121	450,000	2:01.20	111
1996	Skip Away	3	S.J. Sellers	121	Cigar	126	Louis Quatorze	121	600,000	2:00.60	115
1997	Skip Away	4	J.D. Bailey	126	Instant Friendship	126	Wagon Limit.	121	600,000	1:58.80	116
1998	Wagon Limit	4	R.G. Davis	126	Gentlemen	126	Skip Away	126	600,000	2:00.62	115
1999	River Keen	7	C.W. Antley	126	Behrens	126	Almutawakel	126	600,000	2:01.40	117
2000	Albert the Great	3	J.F. Chavez	122	Gander	126	Vision and Verse.	126	600,000	1:59.24	119
2001	Aptitude	4	J.D. Bailey	126	Generous Rosi	126	Country Be Gold.	126	600,000	2:01.49	123
2002	Evening Attire	4	S.X. Bridgmohan	126	Lido Palace	126	Harlan's Holiday.	122	600,000	1:59.58	114
2003	Mineshaft	4	R. Albarado	126	Quest	126	Evening Attire	126	600,000	2:00.25	114

Beyer Index: 115.07

Distance 2 miles 1921-75; 1 1/2 miles, 1976-89. Run at Aqueduct 1958-61, 1963-67, 1969-74. Slew o' Gold won a $1 million bonus in 1984 for winning the Woodward, Marlboro Cup, and Jockey Club Gold Cup.

KENTUCKY DERBY, 1 1/4 Miles, 3-Year-Olds,
Churchill Downs, 2003 Purse: $1,100,200

Year	Winner	Age	Jockey	Wt.	Second	Wt.	Third	Wt.	Win Value	Time	Beyer
1875	Aristides	3	O. Lewis	100	Volcano	100	Verdigris	100	2,850	2:37.60	
1876	Vagrant	3	R. Swim	97	Creedmoor	100	Harry Hill	100	2,950	2:38.20	
1877	Baden Baden	3	W. Walker	100	Leonard	100	King William.	100	3,300	2:38.00	
1878	Day Star	3	J. Carter	100	Himyar	100	Leveler	100	4,050	2:37.20	

Year	Winner	Age	Jockey	Wt.	Second	Wt.	Third	Wt.	Win Value	Time	Beyer
1879	Lord Murphy	3	C. Schauer	100	Falsetto	100	Strathmore	100	3,550	2:37.00	
1880	Fonso	3	G. Lewis	105	Kimball	105	Bancroft	105	3,800	2:37.20	
1881	Hindoo	3	J. McLaughlin	105	Lelex	102	Alhambra	105	4,410	2:40.00	
1882	Apollo	3	B. Hurd	102	Runnymede	105	Bengal	105	4,560	2:40.20	
1883	Leonatus	3	W. Donohue	110	Drake Carter	107	Lord Raglan	110	3,760	2:43.00	
1884	Buchanan	3	I. Murphy	110	Loftin	110	Audrain	110	3,990	2:40.20	
1885	Joe Cotton	3	E. Henderson	110	Bersan	110	Ten Booker	110	4,630	2:37.00	
1886	Ben Ali	3	P. Duffy	118	Blue Wing	118	Free Knight	118	4,890	2:36.20	
1887	Montrose	3	I. Lewis	118	Jim Gore	118	Jackobin	118	4,200	2:39.20	
1888	MacBeth II	3	G. Covington	118	Gallifet	118	White	118	4,740	2:38.20	
1889	Spokane	3	T. Kiley	118	Proctor Knott	118	Once Again	118	4,880	2:34.20	
1890	Riley	3	I. Murphy	118	Bill Letcher	118	Robespierre	118	5,460	2:45.00	
1891	Kingman	3	I. Murphy	122	Balgowan	122	High Tariff	122	4,550	2:52.20	
1892	Azra	3	A. Clayton	122	Huron	122	Phil Dwyer	122	4,230	2:41.20	
1893	Lookout	3	E. Kunze	122	Plutus	122	Boundless	122	3,840	2:39.20	
1894	Chant	3	F. Goodale	122	Pearl Song	122	Sigurd	122	4,020	2:41.00	
1895	Halma	3	J. Perkins	122	Basso	122	Laureate	122	2,970	2:37.20	
1896	Ben Brush	3	W. Simms	117	Ben Eder	117	Semper Ego	117	4,850	2:07.60	
1897	Typhoon II	3	F. Garner	117	Ornament	117	Dr. Catlett	117	4,850	2:12.20	
1898	Plaudit	3	W. Simms	117	Lieber Karl	122	Isabey	117	4,850	2:09.00	
1899	Manuel	3	F. Taral	117	Corsini	122	Mazo	117	4,850	2:12.00	
1900	Lieut. Gibson	3	J. Boland	117	Florizar	122	Thrive	122	4,850	2:06.20	
1901	His Eminence	3	J. Winkfield	117	Sannazarro	117	Driscoll	117	4,850	2:07.60	
1902	Alan-A-Dale	3	J. Winkfield	117	Inventor	117	The Rival	117	4,850	2:08.60	
1903	Judge Himes	3	H. Booker	117	Early	117	Bourbon	110	4,850	2:09.00	
1904	Elwood	3	F. Prior	117	Ed Tierney	117	Brancas	117	4,850	2:08.20	
1905	Agile	3	J. Martin	122	Ram's Horn	117	Layson	117	4,850	2:10.60	
1906	Sir Huon	3	R. Troxler	117	Lady Navarre	117	James Reddick	117	4,850	2:08.80	
1907	Pink Star	3	A. Minder	117	Zal	117	Ovelando	117	4,850	2:12.60	
1908	Stone Street	3	A. Pickens	117	Sir Cleges	117	Dunvegan	114	4,850	2:15.20	
1909	Wintergreen	3	V. Powers	117	Miami	117	Dr. Barkley	117	4,850	2:08.20	
1910	Donau	3	F. Herbert	117	Joe Morris	117	Fighting Bob	117	4,850	2:06.40	
1911	Meridian	3	G. Archibald	117	Governor Gray	119	Colston	110	4,850	2:05.00	
1912	Worth	3	C.H. Shilling	117	Duval	117	Flamma	117	4,850	2:09.40	
1913	Donerail	3	R. Goose	117	Ten Point	117	Gowell	112	5,475	2:04.80	
1914	Old Rosebud	3	J. McCabe	114	Hodge	114	Bronzewing	112	9,125	2:03.40	
1915	Regret	3	J. Notter	112	Pebbles	117	Sharpshooter	114	11,450	2:05.40	
1916	George Smith	3	J. Loftus	117	Star Hawk	117	Franklin	117	9,750	2:04.00	
1917	Omar Khayyam	3	C. Borel	117	Ticket	117	Midway	117	16,600	2:04.60	
1918	Exterminator	3	W. Knapp	114	Escoba	117	Viva America	113	14,700	2:10.80	
1919	Sir Barton	3	J. Loftus	112	Billy Kelly	119	Under Fire	122	20,825	2:09.80	
1920	Paul Jones	3	T. Rice	126	Upset	126	On Watch	126	30,375	2:09.00	
1921	Behave Yourself	3	C. Thompson	126	Black Servant	126	Prudery	121	38,450	2:04.20	
1922	Morvich	3	A. Johnson	126	Bet Mosie	126	Joe Finn	126	46,775	2:04.60	
1923	Zev	3	E. Sande	126	Martingale	126	Vigil	126	53,000	2:05.40	
1924	Black Gold	3	J.D. Mooney	126	Chilhowee	126	Beau Butler	126	52,775	2:05.20	
1925	Flying Ebony	3	E. Sande	126	Captain Hal	126	Son of John	126	52,775	2:07.60	
1926	Bubbling Over	3	A. Johnson	126	Bagenbaggage	126	Rock Man	126	50,075	2:03.80	
1927	Whiskery	3	L. McAtee	126	Osmand	126	Jock	126	51,000	2:06.00	
1928	Reigh Count	3	C. Lang	126	Misstep	126	Toro	126	55,375	2:10.60	
1929	Clyde Van Dusen	3	L. McAtee	126	Naishapur	126	Panchio	126	53,950	2:10.80	
1930	Gallant Fox	3	E. Sande	126	Gallant Knight	126	Ned O	126	50,725	2:07.60	
1931	Twenty Grand	3	C. Kurtsinger	126	Sweep All	126	Mate	126	52,350	2:01.80	
1932	Burgoo King	3	E. James	126	Economic	126	Stepenfetchit	126	52,350	2:05.20	
1933	Broker's Tip	3	D. Meade	126	Head Play	126	Charley O	126	48,925	2:06.80	
1934	Cavalcade	3	M. Garner	126	Discovery	126	Agrarian	126	28,175	2:04.00	
1935	Omaha	3	W. Saunders	126	Roman Soldier	126	Whiskolo	126	39,525	2:05.00	
1936	Bold Venture	3	I. Hanford	126	Brevity	126	Indian Broom	126	37,725	2:03.60	
1937	War Admiral	3	C. Kurtsinger	126	Pompoon	126	Reaping Reward	126	52,050	2:03.20	
1938	Lawrin	3	E. Arcaro	126	Dauber	126	Can't Wait	126	47,050	2:04.80	
1939	Johnstown	3	J. Stout	126	Challedon	126	Heather Broom	126	46,350	2:03.40	
1940	Gallahadion	3	C. Bierman	126	Bimelech	126	Dit	126	60,150	2:05.00	
1941	Whirlaway	3	E. Arcaro	126	Staretor	126	Market Wise	126	61,725	2:01.40	
1942	Shut Out	3	W. Wright	126	Alsab	126	Valdina Orphan	126	64,225	2:04.40	
1943	Count Fleet	3	J. Longden	126	Blue Swords	126	Slide Rule	126	60,725	2:04.00	
1944	Pensive	3	C. McCreary	126	Broadcloth	126	Stir Up	126	64,675	2:04.20	
1945	Hoop Jr.	3	E. Arcaro	126	Pot O'Luck	126	Darby Dieppe	126	64,850	2:07.00	
1946	Assault	3	W. Mehrtens	126	Spy Song	126	Hampden	126	96,400	2:06.60	
1947	Jet Pilot	3	E. Guerin	126	Phalanx	126	Faultless	126	92,160	2:06.80	
1948	Citation	3	E. Arcaro	126	Coaltown	126	My Request	126	83,400	2:05.40	
1949	Ponder	3	S. Brooks	126	Capot	126	Palestinian	126	91,600	2:04.20	
1950	Middleground	3	W. Boland	126	Hill Prince	126	Mr. Trouble	126	92,650	2:01.60	
1951	Count Turf	3	C. McCreary	126	Royal Mustang	126	Ruhe	126	98,050	2:02.60	

Year	Winner	Age	Jockey	Wt.	Second	Wt.	Third	Wt.	Win Value	Time	Beyer
1952	Hill Gail	3	E. Arcaro	126	Sub Fleet	126	Blue Man.	126	96,300	2:01.60	
1953	Dark Star	3	H. Moreno	126	Native Dancer	126	Invigorator	126	90,050	2:02.00	
1954	Determine	3	R. York.	126	Hasty Road	126	Hasseyampa	126	102,050	2:03.00	
1955	Swaps	3	W. Shoemaker	126	Nashua	126	Summer Tan	126	108,400	2:01.80	
1956	Needles	3	D. Erb	126	Fabius	126	Come on Red	126	123,450	2:03.40	
1957	Iron Liege	3	W. Hartack	126	Gallant Man	126	Round Table	126	107,950	2:02.20	
1958	Tim Tam	3	I. Valenzuela	126	Lincoln Road	126	Noureddin	126	116,400	2:05.00	
1959	Tomy Lee	3	W. Shoemaker	126	Sword Dancer	126	First Landing	126	119,650	2:02.20	
1960	Venetian Way	3	W. Hartack	126	Bally Ache	126	Victoria Park	126	114,850	2:02.40	
1961	Carry Back	3	J. Sellers	126	Crozier	126	Bass Clef.	126	120,500	2:04.00	
1962	Decidedly	3	W. Hartack	126	Roman Line	126	Ridan.	126	119,650	2:00.40	
1963	Chateaugay	3	B. Baeza	126	Never Bend	126	Candy Spots	126	108,900	2:01.80	
1964	Northern Dancer	3	W. Hartack	126	Hill Rise	126	The Scoundrel	126	114,300	2:00.00	
1965	Lucky Debonair	3	W. Shoemaker	126	Dapper Dan	126	Tom Rolfe	126	112,000	2:01.20	
1966	Kauai King	3	D. Brumfield	126	Advocator	126	Blue Skyer	126	120,500	2:02.00	
1967	Proud Clarion	3	R. Ussery	126	Barbs Delight	126	Damascus	126	119,700	2:00.60	
1968	Forward Pass	3	I. Valenzuela	126	Francie's Hat	126	T.V. Commercial	126	122,600	2:02.20	

Dancer's Image finished first but subsequently was disqualified from the purse money

Year	Winner	Age	Jockey	Wt.	Second	Wt.	Third	Wt.	Win Value	Time	Beyer
1969	Majestic Prince	3	W. Hartack	126	Arts and Letters	126	Dike	126	113,200	2:01.80	
1970	Dust Commander	3	M. Manganello	126	My Dad George	126	High Echelon	126	127,800	2:03.40	
1971	Canonero II	3	G. Avila	126	Jim French	126	Bold Reason	126	145,500	2:03.20	
1972	Riva Ridge	3	R. Turcotte	126	No Le Hace	126	Hold Your Peace.	126	140,300	2:01.80	
1973	Secretariat	3	R. Turcotte	126	Sham	126	Our Native	126	155,050	1:59.40	
1974	Cannonade	3	A. Cordero Jr	126	Hudson County	126	Agitate	126	274,000	2:04.00	
1975	Foolish Pleasure	3	J. Vasquez	126	Avatar	126	Diabolo.	126	209,600	2:02.00	
1976	Bold Forbes	3	A. Cordero Jr	126	Honest Pleasure	126	Elocutionist	126	165,200	2:01.60	
1977	Seattle Slew	3	J. Cruguet	126	Run Dusty Run	126	Sanhedrin	126	214,700	2:02.20	
1978	Affirmed	3	S. Cauthen	126	Alydar	126	Believe It.	126	186,900	2:01.20	
1979	Spectacular Bid	3	R.J. Franklin	126	General Assembly	126	Golden Act.	126	228,650	2:02.40	
1980	Genuine Risk	3	J. Vasquez	121	Rumbo	126	Jaklin Klugman.	126	250,550	2:02.00	
1981	Pleasant Colony	3	J. Velasquez	126	Woodchopper	126	Partez.	126	317,200	2:02.00	
1982	Gato Del Sol	3	E. Delahoussaye	126	Laser Light	126	Reinvested.	126	428,850	2:02.40	
1983	Sunny's Halo	3	E. Delahoussaye.	126	Desert Wine	126	Caveat.	126	426,000	2:02.20	
1984	Swale	3	L. Pincay Jr	126	Coax Me Chad	126	At the Threshold.	126	537,000	2:02.40	
1985	Spend a Buck	3	A. Cordero Jr	126	Stephan's Odyssey	126	Chief's Crown	126	406,800	2:00.20	
1986	Ferdinand	3	W. Shoemaker	126	Bold Arrangement	126	Broad Brush	126	609,400	2:02.80	
1987	Alysheba	3	C.J. McCarron	126	Bet Twice	126	Avie's Copy	126	618,600	2:03.40	
1988	Winning Colors	3	G.L. Stevens	121	Forty Niner	126	Risen Star.	126	611,200	2:02.20	
1989	Sunday Silence	3	P.A. Valenzuela	126	Easy Goer	126	Awe Inspiring.	126	574,200	2:05.00	102
1990	Unbridled	3	C. Perret	126	Summer Squall	126	Pleasant Tap.	126	581,000	2:02.00	
1991	Strike the Gold	3	C.W. Antley	126	Best Pal	126	Mane Minister	126	655,800	2:03.08	
1992	Lil E. Tee	3	P. Day	126	Casual Lies	126	Dance Floor.	126	724,800	2:03.04	107
1993	Sea Hero	3	J.D. Bailey	126	Prairie Bayou	126	Wild Gale	126	735,900	2:02.42	105
1994	Go for Gin	3	C.J. McCarron	126	Strodes Creek	126	Blumin Affair	126	628,800	2:03.72	112
1995	Thunder Gulch	3	G.L. Stevens	126	Tejano Run	126	Timber Country	126	707,400	2:01.27	108
1996	Grindstone	3	J.D. Bailey	126	Cavonnier	126	Prince of Thieves	126	869,800	2:01.06	112
1997	Silver Charm	3	G.L. Stevens	126	Captain Bodgit	126	Free House	126	700,000	2:02.44	115
1998	Real Quiet	3	K.J. Desormeaux	126	Victory Gallop	126	Indian Charlie.	126	738,800	2:02.38	107
1999	Charismatic	3	C.W. Antley	126	Menifee	126	Cat Thief.	126	886,200	2:03.29	108
2000	Fusaichi Pegasus	3	K.J. Desormeaux	126	Aptitude	126	Impeachment.	126	1,038,400	2:01.12	108
2001	Monarchos	3	J.F. Chavez	126	Invisible Ink	126	Congaree	126	812,000	1:59.88	116
2002	War Emblem	3	V. Espinoza	126	Proud Citizen	126	Perfect Drift.	126	1,875,000	2:01.13	114
2003	Funny Cide	3	J.A. Santos	126	Empire Maker	126	Peace Rules.	126	800,200	2:01.19	109

Beyer Index: 109.46

Distance 1 1/2 miles prior to 1896. In 2000, Fusaichi Pegasus earned a $250,000 bonus for winning the Wood Memorial and Kentucky Derby

KENTUCKY OAKS, 1 1/8 Miles, 3-Year-Old Fillies, Churchill Downs, 2003 Purse: $573,800

Year	Winner	Age	Jockey	Wt.	Second	Wt.	Third	Wt.	Win Value	Time	Beyer
1875	Vinaigrette	3	J. Houston	97	Gyptis	97	Elemi	97	1,175	2:39.60	
1876	Necy Hale	3	James	97	Plenty	97	Lady Clipper	97	1,900	2:42.20	
1877	Felicia	3	James	97	Bradamante	97	Aunt Betsy	97	2,550	2:39.00	
1878	Belle of Nelson	3	Booth	97	Buena Vista	97	Fortuna	97	2,650	2:39.00	
1879	Liahtunah	3	Hightower	97	Ada Glenn	97	Buckden Lass.	97	3,350	2:40.20	
1880	Longitude	3	J. McLaughlin	102	Bye and Bye	102	Ersilla	102	3,250	2:41.60	
1881	Lucy May	3	Wolfe	102	Belle of the Highlan	102	Mrs. Chubbs	102	3,000	2:41.00	
1882	Katie Creel	3	Stoval.	102	Pinafore	102	Issie	102	3,240	2:39.00	
1883	Vera	3	Stoval.	102	Orange Blossom	102	Billetta	102	3,220	2:39.60	
1884	Modesty	3	I. Murphy	105	Highflight	105	Bluette	105	3,030	2:48.20	
1885	Lizzie Dwyer	3	Fuller	105	Constellation	105	Exile	105	3,800	2:40.60	
1886	Pure Rye	3	Garrison	113	Red Girl	113	Ada D.	113	4,170	2:41.00	
1887	Florimore	3	Johnston	113	Wary	113	Bannail.	113	3,330	2:40.60	

Year	Winner	Age	Jockey	Wt.	Second	Wt.	Third	Wt.	Win Value	Time	Beyer
1888	Ten Penny	3	A. McCarthy Jr	113	Los Angeles	114	Quindaro Belle	114	3,720	2:42.00	
1889	Jewel Ban	3	Stoval	113	Brandolette	113	Retrieve	113	3,850	2:41.00	
1890	English Lady	3	Hollis	113	Marie K.	113			3,610	2:42.20	
1891	Miss Hawkins	3	Britton	117	Ethel	117	Bonnie Bird	117	3,860	2:18.20	
1892	Miss Dixie	3	Ray	117	Unadilla	117	Greenwich	117	3,470	2:14.20	
1893	Monrovia	3	Reagan	117	Elizabeth L.	117	Joanna	117	2,780	2:16.00	
1894	Selika	3	A. Clayton	117	Charity	117	Shuttle	117	2,600	2:15.00	
1895	Voladora	3	A. Clayton	117	Alabama	117	Kathryn	117	1,830	2:16.60	
1896	Souffe	3	Thorpe	112	Myrtle Harkness	112	La Gascogne	112	2,860	1:54.20	
1897	White Frost	3	T. Burns	112	Rosinante	112	Taluca	112	2,410	1:49.00	
1898	Crocket	3	J. Hill	112	Lennep	112	Alleviate	112	2,860	1:51.20	
1899	Rush	3	J. Hill	112	May Hempstead	117	The L. in Blue	112	2,410	1:52.20	
1900	Etta	3	Overton	112	Scarlet Lily	112	Cleora	112	2,410	1:48.00	
1901	Lady Schorr	3	J. Woods	117	Isobel	112	Edith Q.	112	2,410	1:53.00	
1902	Walnamoinen	3	Coburn	112	Marque	112	Autumn Leaves	112	2,410	1:51.20	
1903	Lemco	3	J. Reiff	112	Mary Lavana	112	The Crisis	112	2,410	1:49.60	
1904	Audience	3	Helgesen	117	Outcome	112	White Plume	112	2,410	1:51.00	
1905	Janeta	3	D. Austin	112	Mum	112	Siss Lee	112	2,410	1:49.60	
1906	King's Daughter	3	E. Robinson	112	Lady Navarre	117	Lady Anne	112	2,410	1:47.80	
1907	Wing Ting	3	J. Lee	112	Altuda	112	Lillie Turner	112	2,410	1:50.20	
1908	Ellen-a-Dale	3	V. Powers	105	Boema	112	Estradia	105	2,410	1:46.60	
1909	Floreal	3	Heidel	112	Pink Wings	105	Cordova	112	2,410	1:49.20	
1910	Samaria	3	Scoville	112	Foxy Mary	112	My Gal	112	1,910	1:50.20	
1911	Bettie Sue	3	T. Rice	112	Ilma	112			1,910	1:48.00	
1912	Flamma	3	Butwell	112	Floral Day	112	Beautiful	105	1,910	1:51.20	
1913	Cream	3	Ganz	112	Floral Park	112	Gowell	117	1,950	1:47.60	
1914	Bronzewing	3	W. Obert	117	Casuarina	112	Brackt'n Belle	112	2,320	1:45.60	
1915	Waterblossom	3	E. Martin	117	One Step	112	Lady Rotha	112	2,530	1:46.60	
1916	Kathleen	3	R. Goose	112	Mandy Hamilton	117	Lady Always	112	2,410	1:47.40	
1917	Sunbonnet	3	J. Loftus	112	Diamond	112	Battle	112	3,035	1:46.80	
1918	Viva America	3	W. Warrington	112	Fern Handley	112	Mistress Polly	112	2,580	1:46.80	
1919	Lillian Shaw	3	T. Murray	117	Milkmaid	117	Dancing Spray	112	4,190	1:45.00	
1920	Lorraine	3	D. Connelly	116	Truly Rural	116	Dresden	116	5,470	1:58.40	
1921	Nancy Lee	3	L. McAtee	116	Prudery	116	Lady Madcap	116	8,980	1:50.40	
1922	Startle	3	D. Connelly	116	Martha Fallon	116	Precious Lula	116	9,920	1:52.60	
1923	Untidy	3	J. Corcoran	116	Sweetheart	116	Gadfly	121	10,060	1:53.00	
1924	Princess Doreen	3	H. Stutts	116	Nellie Morse	121	Befuddle	116	10,160	1:51.80	
1925	Deeming	3	J. McCoy	116	Buckwheat Cake	116	Little Visitor	121	10,280	1:54.00	
1926	Black Maria	3	A. Mortensen	121	Dark Phantom	116	Helen's Babe	116	10,960	1:55.40	
1927	Mary Jane	3	D. Connelly	121	Handy Mandy	111	Fresco	116	10,900	1:53.40	
1928	Easter Stockings	3	W. Crump	116	Pink Lily	116	Reveries' Gal.	121	9,140	1:51.60	
1929	Rose of Sharon	3	W. Crump	121	Lady Broadcast	116	Current	116	10,080	1:51.00	
1930	Alcibiades	3	R. Finnerty	116	Rich Widow	116	Galaday	116	9,760	1:52.60	
1931	Cousin Jo	3	E. James	116	Sunny Lassie	116	Town Limit	116	9,610	1:53.00	
1932	Suntica	3	A. Pascuma	116	I Say	116	Depression	116	4,590	1:52.20	
1933	Barn Swallow	3	D. Meade	116	At Top	116	Bright Bauble	116	4,280	1:51.20	
1934	Fiji	3	G. Elston	116	Far Star	116	Penncote	116	2,230	1:51.60	
1935	Paradisical	3	G. Fowler	116	Mid Victorian	116	Spanish Babe	116	2,310	1:51.20	
1936	Two Bob	3	R. Workman	116	Threadneedle	116	Seventh Heaven	116	4,625	1:52.60	
1937	Mars Shield	3	A. Robertson	121	Shatterproof	116	Alkit	116	4,590	1:53.40	
1938	Flying Lee	3	L. Haas	116	Janice	116	Fantine	116	4,720	1:52.80	
1939	Flying Lill	3	C. Bierman	116	Bala Ormont	116	Rude Awakening	110	4,820	1:51.00	
1940	Inscolassie	3	R.L. Vedder	116	June Bee	116	Shine O'Night	116	4,370	1:54.40	
1941	Valdina Myth	3	G. King	116	Silvestra	116	Mys'y Marvel	116	4,240	1:52.60	
1942	Miss Dogwood	3	J. Adams	116	Questvive	116	Miss Glamour	116	4,810	1:47.00	
	Glide finished first but was disqualified										
1943	Nellie L.	3	W. Eads	116	Valdina Marl	116	Edie Jane	116	4,160	1:48.60	
1944	Canina	3	J. Adams	116	Harriet Sue	121	Paddle	110	4,200	1:48.60	
1945	Come and Go	3	C.L. Martin	121	On-Your-Toes	116	Miss Blindfold	116	3,840	1:49.80	
1946	First Page	3	J.R. Layton	116	Athenia	116	Buzzaround	116	9,175	1:51.40	
1947	Blue Grass	3	J. Longden	116	Cosmic Missile	121	Mother	116	21,680	1:51.60	
1948	Challe Anne	3	W. Garner	116	Reigh Belle	116	Back Talk	116	19,800	1:48.60	
1949	Wistful	3	G. Glisson	116	The Fat Lady	116	Lady Dorimar	116	21,450	1:47.40	
1950	Ari's Mona	3	W. Boland	116	Wondring	121	Diamond Lane	116	21,050	1:43.60	
1951	How	3	E. Arcaro	116	Astro	110	Sickle's Image	121	22,700	1:45.60	
1952	Real Delight	3	E. Arcaro	121	Whirla Lea	116	Big Mo	116	23,100	1:45.40	
1953	Bubbley	3	E. Arcaro	116	Cerise Reine	121	Arab Actress	116	21,750	1:45.60	
1954	Fascinator	3	A. DeSpirito	121	Queen Hopeful	121	Blue Violin	116	22,200	1:45.00	
1955	Lalun	3	H. Moreno	116	Lea Lane	121	Mazza	116	21,350	1:46.00	
1956	Princess Turia	3	W. Hartack	116	Doubledogdare	121	Tournure	116	21,650	1:44.80	
1957	Lori-El	3	L.C. Cook	121	Pillow Talk	121	Dale's Delight	121	29,700	1:44.80	
1958	Bug Brush	3	E. Arcaro	116	Galarullah	116	Hasty Doll	116	26,835	1:44.80	
1959	Wedlock	3	J.L. Rotz	116	Ray's Fairy Gold	116	Aesthetic	110	15,509	1:45.00	

Year	Winner	Age	Jockey	Wt.	Second	Wt.	Third	Wt.	Win Value	Time	Beyer
1959	Hidden Talent	3	M. Ycaza	121	Indian Maid	116	Kathy H.	116	15,509	1:44.40	
1960	Make Sail	3	M. Ycaza	116	Quaze	116	Airmans Guide	116	25,957	1:44.20	
1961	My Portrait	3	B. Baeza	116	Play Time	121	Times Two	116	28,275	1:47.00	
1962	Cicada	3	W. Shoemaker	121	Flaming Page	116	Fortunate Isle	116	27,820	1:44.60	
1963	Sally Ship	3	M. Ycaza	121	Bonnie's Girl	116	Power to Strike	116	29,965	1:44.80	
1964	Blue Norther	3	W. Shoemaker	121	Miss Cavandish	116	Road to Romance	116	31,184	1:44.20	
1965	Amerivan	3	R. Turcotte	116	Gold Digger	116	Terentia	121	31,541	1:44.40	
1966	Native Street	3	D. Brumfield	121	Lady Pitt	121	Naidni Diam.	121	39,357	1:44.80	
1967	Nancy Jr.	3	J. Sellers	121	Gay Sailorette	121	Furl Sail	121	39,620	1:44.40	
1968	Dark Mirage	3	M. Ycaza	121	Miss Ribot	121	Lady Tramp	121	41,437	1:44.60	
1969	Hail to Patsy	3	D. Kassen	121	Double Delta	121	Mrs. Jo Jo	121	38,902	1:44.40	
1970	Lady Vi-E.	3	D.E. Whited	121	Glenary	121	Artists Proof	121	41,437	1:44.80	
1971	Silent Beauty	3	K. Knapp	121	Graffitti	121	At Arms Length	121	42,152	1:44.20	
1972	Susan's Girl	3	V. Tejada	121	Barely Even	121	Fairway Flyer	121	39,894	1:44.20	
1973	Bag of Tunes	3	D. Gargan	121	La Prevoyante	121	Coraggioso	121	43,647	1:44.20	
1974	Quaze Quilt	3	W. Gavidia	121	Special Team	121	Kaye's Commander	121	43,631	1:46.60	
1975	Sun and Snow	3	G. Patterson	121	Funalon	121	Funny Cat.	121	42,315	1:44.60	
1976	Optimistic Gal	3	B. Baeza	121	Comfort Zone	121	Carmelita Gibbs	121	40,186	1:44.60	
1977	Sweet Alliance	3	C.J. McCarron	121	Our Mims	121	Mrs. Warren	121	60,889	1:43.60	
1978	White Star Line	3	E. Maple	121	Grenzen	121	Bold Rendezvous	121	60,498	1:45.20	
1979	Davona Dale	3	J. Velasquez	121	Himalayan	121	Prize Spot.	121	83,590	1:47.20	
1980	Bold 'n Determined	3	E. Delahoussaye	121	Mitey Lively	121	Honest and True	121	83,915	1:44.80	
1981	Heavenly Cause	3	L. Pincay Jr.	121	De la Rose	121	Wayward Lass	121	79,300	1:43.80	
1982	Blush With Pride	3	W. Shoemaker	121	Before Dawn	121	Flying Partner	121	126,133	1:50.20	
1983	Princess Rooney	3	J. Vasquez	121	Bright Crocus	121	Bemissed	121	116,968	1:50.80	
1984	Lucky Lucky Lucky	3	A. Cordero Jr.	121	Miss Oceana	121	My Lucky One	121	112,710	1:51.80	
1985	Fran's Valentine	3	P.A. Valenzuela	121	Foxy Deen	121	Rascal Lass	121	118,365	1:50.00	
1986	Tiffany Lass	3	G.L. Stevens	121	Life at the Top	121	Family Style	121	122,103	1:50.60	
1987	Buryyourbelief	3	J.A. Santos	121	Hometown Queen	121	Super Cook	121	155,415	1:50.40	
1988	Goodbye Halo	3	P. Day	121	Jeanne Jones	121	Willa on the Move	121	156,715	1:50.40	
1989	Open Mind	3	A. Cordero Jr.	121	Imaginary Lady	121	Blondeinamotel	121	150,540	1:50.60	
1990	Seaside Attraction	3	C.J. McCarron	121	Go for Wand	121	Bright Candles	121	156,910	1:52.80	91
1991	Lite Light	3	C.S. Nakatani	121	Withallprobability	121	Til Forbid	121	207,285	1:48.80	106
1992	Luv Me Luv Me Not	3	F.A. Arguello Jr.	121	Pleasant Stage	121	Prospectors Delite.	121	182,455	1:51.40	90
1993	Dispute	3	J.D. Bailey	121	Eliza	121	Quinpool	121	191,230	1:52.40	93
1994	Sardula	3	E. Delahoussaye	121	Lakeway	121	Dianes Halo	121	184,340	1:51.00	99
1995	Gal in a Ruckus	3	W.H. McCauley	121	Urbane	121	Sneaky Quiet	121	235,040	1:50.00	99
1996	Pike Place Dancer	3	C.S. Nakatani	121	Escena	121	Cara Rafaela	121	325,000	1:49.80	101
1997	Blushing K.D.	3	L.J. Meche	121	Tomisue's Delight	121	Storm Song	121	362,514	1:50.20	104
	Sharp Cat finished third but was disqualified and placed eighth										
1998	Keeper Hill	3	D.R. Flores	121	Banshee Breeze	121	Really Polish	121	375,410	1:52.06	100
1999	Silverbulletday	3	G.L. Stevens	121	Dreams Gallore	121	Sweeping Story	121	341,620	1:49.92	107
2000	Secret Status	3	P. Day	121	Rings a Chime	121	Classy Cara	121	378,696	1:50.30	100
2001	Flute	3	J.D. Bailey	121	Real Cozzy	121	Collect Call	121	377,704	1:48.85	98
2002	Farda Amiga	3	C.J. McCarron	121	Take Charge Lady	121	Habibti	121	348,502	1:50.41	108
2003	Bird Town	3	E.S. Prado	121	Santa Catarina	121	Yell	121	355,756	1:48.64	101

Beyer Index: 99.79

Distance 1 1/2 miles from 1875-90; 1 1/4 miles 1891-95; 1 1/16 miles, 1896-1919, 1942-81

KING'S BISHOP STAKES, 7 Furlongs, 3-Year-Olds,
Saratoga Race Course, 2003 Purse: $200,000

Year	Winner	Age	Jockey	Wt.	Second	Wt.	Third	Wt.	Win Value	Time	Beyer
1984	Commemorate	3	F. Lovato Jr.	119	All Fired Up	122	Raja's Shark	115	33,900	1:22.60	
1985	Pancho Villa	3	D. McHargue	122	El Basco	119	Cullendale	115	33,540	1:22.20	
1987	Templar Hill	3	C.J. McCarron	119	Mister S.M.	119	Homebuilder	115	51,660	1:23.00	
1988	King's Nest	3	C.J. McCarron	115	Tejano	117	Parlay Me	115	53,280	1:21.80	
1989	Houston	3	P. Day	119	Fast Play	117	Fierce Fighter	115	51,930	1:22.00	
1990	Housebuster	3	C. Perret	122	Poppiano	115	Sunshine Jimmy	115	54,090	1:21.80	113
1991	Take Me Out	3	M.E Smith	115	Joey the Student	115	To Freedom	119	74,400	1:21.60	
1992	Salt Lake	3	M.E Smith	117	Binalong	115	Agincourt	122	73,440	1:21.40	105
1993	Mi Cielo	3	M.E Smith	115	Williamstown	122	Schossberg	115	74,280	1:21.60	107
1994	Chimes Band	3	J.D. Bailey	117	End Sweep	122	Halo's Image.	117	65,700	1:21.82	110
1995	Top Account	3	P. Day	112	Ft. Stockton	120	Excelerate	113	68,100	1:22.40	107
1996	Honour and Glory	3	J.A. Santos	123	Elusive Quality	112	Distorted Humor	115	64,920	1:21.60	113
1997	Tale of the Cat	3	J.A. Krone	114	Oro de Mexico	116	Trafalger	115	90,000	1:21.60	113
1998	Secret Firm	3	E.S. Prado	121	Mint	121	Scatmandu	116	120,000	1:22.60	107
1999	Forestry	3	C.W. Antley	124	Five Star Day	115	Successful Appeal.	124	120,000	1:21.00	116
2000	More Than Ready	3	P. Day	124	Valiant Halory	114	Millencolin	121	120,000	1:22.49	103
2001	Squirtle Squirt	3	J.D. Bailey	121	Illusioned	119	City Zip	124	120,000	1:21.97	107
2002	Gygistar	3	J.R. Velazquez	124	Boston Common	121	Thunder Days	115	120,000	1:22.85	113
2003	Valid Video	3	J. Bravo	121	Great Notion	117	Ghostzapper	117	120,000	1:22.14	107

Beyer Index: 109.31

LA BREA STAKES, 7 Furlongs, 3-Year-Old Fillies, Santa Anita, 2003 Purse: $250,000

Year	Winner	Age	Jockey	Wt.	Second	Wt.	Third	Wt.	Win Value	Time	Beyer
1974	Niner Power	3	S. Valdez	117	First Majesty	117	Handsome Native	117	20,350	1:43.80	
1975	Bobby Murcer	3	E. Belmonte	120	Bold Clarion	120	Roger's Dandy	117	20,800	1:43.40	
	Run in January										
1975	Featherfoot	3	W. Shoemaker	114	Banyan Road	120	Graham Heagney	114	13,025	1:42.20	
1975	Big Destiny	3	S. Hawley	114	Bending Away	120	Mark's Place	120	13,325	1:42.80	
	Run in December										
1976	Kirby Lane	3	L. Pincay Jr.	117	Tregillick	116	Missing Marbles	116	23,750	1:45.20	
1978	Taisez Vous	3	D. Pierce	121	Ida Delia	114	Sound of Summer	121	26,700	1:22.80	
1979	Great Lady M.	3	L. Pincay Jr.	117	Queen Yasna	114			35,800	1:22.60	
					B. Thoughtful	121					
1980	Terlingua	3	D.G. McHargue	121	Glorious Song	116	Prize Spot	121	31,350	1:20.80	
1981	Dynamite	3	W. Shoemaker	114	Bold 'n Determined	125	Pachena	114	31,750	1:21.40	
1982	Nell's Briquette	3	C.J. McCarron	122	Bannockburn	115	Bee a Scout	117	40,150	1:25.80	
1982	Beautiful Glass	3	C.J. McCarron	114	Skillful Joy	122	Header Card	119	42,450	1:21.00	
1983	Lovlier Linda	3	W. Shoemaker	114	Angel Savage	115	Fabulous Notion	124	40,700	1:22.20	
1985	Mitterand	3	E. Delahoussaye	117	Percipient	119	Lady Trilby	117	39,950	1:21.80	
1985	Savannah Slew	3	W. Shoemaker	119	Lady's Secert	124	Ambra Ridge	117	39,150	1:22.40	
	Run in January and December										
1987	Family Style	3	G.L. Stevens	122	Sari's Heroine	119	Winter Treasure	117	46,700	1:22.60	
1988	Very Subtle	3	P.A. Valenzuela	124	Saros Brig	114	Fold the Flag	117	60,300	1:21.60	
1989	Variety Baby	4	C.A. Black	117	T.V. of Crystal	117	Forewarning	117	49,050	1:21.60	
1990	Akinemod	3	G.L. Stevens	117	Fantastic Look	122	Reluctant Guest	117	62,650	1:21.60	101
1990	Brought to Mind	3	A. Solis	117	A Wild Ride	119	Mama Simba	114	65,000	1:21.60	
1991	D'Or Ruckus	3	C.J. McCarron	115	Good Potential	119	Garden Gal	117	48,800	1:22.05	96
1991	Teresa Mc	3	P.A. Valenzuela	119	Remarkably Easy	119	Suziqcute	119	48,800	1:23.05	87
1992	Arches of Gold	3	E. Delahoussaye	116	Race the Wild Wind	121	Terre Haute	117	64,800	1:21.28	101
1993	Mamselle Bebette	3	C.S. Nakatani	115	Desert Stormer	116	Island Orchid	115	65,900	1:20.45	102
1994	Top Rung	3	G.L. Stevens	115	Klassy Kim	119	Twice the Vice	119	63,700	1:21.84	95
1995	Exotic Wood	3	C.J. McCarron	119	Evil's Pic	119	Jewel Princess	119	80,250	1:21.57	99
1996	Hidden Lake	3	C.J. McCarron	115	Belle's Flag	119	Tiffany Diamond	115	80,900	1:22.00	98
1997	I Ain't Bluffing	3	E. Delahoussaye	119	Minister's Melody	119	Praviana	115	99,540	1:21.23	100
1998	Magical Allure	3	G.L. Stevens	121	Gourmet Girl	117	Tranquility Lake	116	120,000	1:22.06	96
1999	Hookedonthefeelin	3	D.R. Flores	119	Olympic Charmer	119	Kalookan Queen	119	120,000	1:21.84	107
2000	Spain	3	V.L. Espinoza	123	Cover Gal	119	Serenita	115	120,000	1:22.27	96
2001	Affluent	3	E. Delahoussaye	121	Royally Chosen	119	Love At Noon	117	120,000	1:21.29	97
2002	Got Koko	3	A. Solis	117	Spring Meadow	119	Erica's Smile	117	120,000	1:22.57	97
2003	Island Fashion	3	K.J. Desormeaux	123	Randaroo	119	Buffythecenterfold	119	150,000	1:21.79	109

Beyer Index: 98.73

Run at 1 1/16 miles, for 3-year-olds, 1974-76

LAS VIRGENES STAKES, 1 Mile, 3-Year-Old Fillies, Santa Anita, 2003 Purse: $200,000

Year	Winner	Age	Jockey	Wt.	Second	Wt.	Third	Wt.	Win Value	Time	Beyer
1983	Saucy Bobbie	3	L. Pincay Jr	117	A Lucky Sign	121	Little Hailey	113	50,100	1:36.20	
1984	Althea	3	L. Pincay Jr	124	Vagabond Gal	117	My Darling One	114	50,500	1:37.00	
1985	Fran's Valentine	3	P.A. Valenzuela	117	Rascal Lass	121	Wising Up	121	77,150	1:36.40	
1986	Life at the Top	3	R.Q. Meza	114	Twilight Ridge	121	An Empress	117	77,050	1:36.20	
1987	Timely Assertion	3	G.L. Stevens	114	Very Subtle	121	My Turbulent Beau.	114	74,900	1:36.80	
1988	Goodbye Halo	3	J. Velasquez	123	Winning Colors	119	Sadie B. Fast	115	74,750	1:35.80	
1989	Kool Arrival	3	L. Pincay Jr	121	Some Romance	123	Fantastic Look	115	77,200	1:36.20	
1990	Cheval Volant	3	A. Solis	123	Nasers Pride	119	Bright Candles	119	78,150	1:38.00	87
1991	Lite Light	3	C.S. Nakatani	121	Garden Gal	121	Nice Assay	119	93,800	1:35.60	104
1992	Magical Maiden	3	G.L. Stevens	121	Golden Treat	115	Red Bandana	115	96,800	1:36.23	91
1993	Likeable Style	3	G.L. Stevens	117	Incindress	117	Blue Moonlight	119	91,000	1:36.67	92
1994	Lakeway	3	K.J. Desormeaux	117	Fancy 'n Fabulous	114	Princess Mitterand.	116	93,600	1:35.14	103
1995	Serena's Song	3	C.S. Nakatani	122	Cat's Cradle	118	Urbane	116	92,700	1:35.46	108
1996	Antespend	3	C.W. Antley	120	Cara Rafaela	122	Hidden Lake	116	96,900	1:36.45	98
1997	Sharp Cat	3	C.S. Nakatani	122	High Heeled Hope	118	Demon Acquire	116	98,800	1:35.52	101
1998	Keeper Hill	3	D.R. Flores	114	Star of Broadway	116	Occhi Verdi	116	120,000	1:36.94	95
1999	Excellent Meeting	3	K.J. Desormeaux	122	Tout Charmant	116	Weekend Squall	115	120,000	1:35.45	108
2000	Surfside	3	P.Day	121	Spain	115	Rings a Chime	116	117,600	1:37.00	93
2001	Golden Ballet	3	C.J. McCarron	122	Two Item Limit	120	Affluent	116	120,000	1:36.89	97
2002	You	3	J. Bailey	122	Habibti	122	Tali'sluckybusride	120	120,000	1:36.84	93
2003	Composure	3	J.D. Bailey	120	Elloluv	122	Watching You	116	120,000	1:36.13	96

Beyer Index: 97.57

JOHN C. MABEE HANDICAP, 1 1/8 Miles (Turf), Fillies and Mares, 3-Year-Olds and Up, Del Mar, 2003 Purse: $400,000

Year	Winner	Age	Jockey	Wt.	Second	Wt.	Third	Wt.	Win Value	Time	Beyer
1945	Canina	4	J. Westrope	122	Glory Time	113	Frilure	112	3,640	1:37.00	
1959	Boston Again	4	A. Maese	122	Ruwenzori	110	Pie Queen	112	11,150	1:48.40	
1960	Honeys Gem	5	R. Campas	124	Tritoma	115	Jenny Delieu	114	12,750	1:47.60	

Year	Winner	Age	Jockey	Wt.	Second	Wt.	Third	Wt.	Win Value	Time	Beyer
1961	Linita	4	R. Mundorf	121	Wiggle II	119	Amri-An	108	12,900	1:47.80	
	Fun House finished second but was disqualified and placed fourth										
1962	Fun House	4	R. York............	121	Edie Belle	116	Seems a Queen	112	...15,525	1:47.80	
1963	Powder 'n Paint 3		J. Lambert.......	111	Savaii	118	Corolla	115	...16,525	1:48.20	
1964	Jalousie II	5	R. York............	122	Quick Luck	111	Gin Mah............	115	...15,475	1:49.00	
1965	Rullahline	3	K. Church........	112	Hi Rated	113	Poona Queen	115	9,725	1:47.80	
1965	Sea Eagle	3	W. Hartack	116	Lycaste	111	Khai Ireland	116	9,825	1:48.80	
1966	Desert Trial	3	A. Maese........	113	April Dawn	114	Gabriela	106	...10,075	1:48.00	
1966	Fleet Treat	3	R. Menell	114	Maintain	115	Windy Kate	112	...10,175	1:48.20	
1967	Desert Trial	4	A. Maese........	127	Aquilegia	106	Talleeta	113	...17,900	1:48.80	
	....		....		....		Amerigo's Fancy...	119			
1968	Scoop Time.........	4	L. Gilligan......	111	Pombal	114	Sand Creek II	111	...16,075	1:48.20	
1969	Luz del Sol	5	I. Valenzuela....	118	Schatzi Pie	115	Too Angri	110	...11,875	1:48.60	
1969	Greta	4	R. Campas	114	Commissary	115	Scoop Time.........	113	...11,575	1:47.00	
1970	Hi Q.	4	H.K. Wellington	115	Windy Mama	116	Boughs o'Holly	116	...13,600	1:49.80	
1971	Street Dancer	4	F. Toro...........	114	Typecast	116	Manta	130	...15,950	1:48.80	
1972	Street Dancer	5	F. Toro...........	117	Hill Circus	122	Countess Market ...	114	...15,700	1:48.20	
1973	Minstrel Miss	6	D. Pierce........	122	Le Cle	123	Pallisima	118	...19,750	1:49.40	
1974	Tizna	5	W. Shoemaker...	120	Modus Vivendi	118	La Zanzara..........	122	...29,800	1:49.20	
1975	Dulcia	6	W. Shoemaker...	122	Tizna	123	Charger's Star	115	...33,550	1:48.80	
1976	Vagabonda	5	S. Hawley......	115	Stravina	115	Miss Tokyo	116	...34,550	1:51.00	
1977	Dancing Femme	4	D.G. McHargue ..	122	Up to Juliet	113	Swingtime	121	...37,150	1:48.40	
1978	Drama Critic	4	D.G. McHargue ..	120	Country Queen	113	B. Thoughtful.......	115	...47,500	1:49.20	
1979	Country Queen	4	L. Pincay Jr	121	More So	119	Prize Spot..........	116	...69,500	1:48.60	
1980	Queen to Conquer ..	5	W. Shoemaker...	120	A Thousand Stars ..	118	Wishing Well	122	...74,050	1:49.40	
1981	Queen to Conquer ..	6	M. Castaneda....	120	Amber Ever	112	Track Robbery......	113	...84,000	1:48.80	
1982	Honey Fox	4	M. Castaneda....	122	Sangue	123	French Charmer ...	115	...83,900	1:48.80	
1983	Sangue	5	W. Shoemaker...	123	Castilla	121	First Advance.......	115	...80,450	1:48.80	
1984	Flag de Lune	4	F. Olivares	115	Royal Heroine	126	Salt Spring..........	115	...97,200	1:48.40	
1985	Daily Busy	4	W. Shoemaker...	115	Eastland	114	Envie de Rire.......	116	...93,500	1:48.20	
1986	Auspiciante	5	G.L. Stevens	114	Justicara	119	Sauna	119	...81,600	1:48.40	
1987	Short Sleeves	5	E. Delahoussaye.	116	Festivity	117	Auspiciante	120	...97,900	1:50.20	
1988	Annoconnor	4	C.A. Black.......	116	Chapel of Dreams .	118	Short Sleeves	121	...134,000	1:48.40	
1989	Brown Bess	7	J.L Kaenel.......	117	Daring Doone	117	Galunpe	118	...157,750	1:48.80	
1990	Double Wedge	5	R.G. Davis.......	114	Reluctant Guest ...	117	Nikishka	116	...158,000	1:49.00	...107
1991	Campagnarde	4	J.A. Garcia	115	Bequest	118	Somethingmerry ...	118	...196,250	1:49.40	...106
1992	Flawlessly	4	C.J. McCarron ...	123	Re Toss	115	Polemic	116	...187,500	1:50.00	...95
1993	Flawlessly	5	C.J. McCarron ...	125	Heart of Joy	114	Let's Elope..........	118	...186,500	1:48.20	...107
1994	Flawlessly	6	C.J. McCarron ...	124	Hollywood Wildcat .	124	Skimble	116	...181,000	1:48.20	...101
1995	Possibly Perfect ...	5	C.S. Nakatani ...	123	Morgana	115	Yearly Tour	116	...180,600	1:49.80	...104
1996	Matiara	4	C.S. Nakatani ...	118	Alpride	119	Pourquoi Pas	114	...193,500	1:49.20	...103
1997	Escena	4	P. Day............	115	Real Connection ...	115	Different............	121	...180,000	1:49.80	...103
1998	See You Soon	4	C.S. Nakatani ...	114	Sonja's Faith	113	Fiji	125	...180,000	1:47.43	...104
1999	Tuzla	5	D.R. Flores......	121	Happyanunoit	115	Spanish Fern........	115	...240,000	1:47.66	...107
2000	Caffe Latte	4	B.R. Blanc...	117	Tout Charmant	120	Alexine	115	...240,000	1:47.16	...102
2001	Janet	4	D.R. Flores......	116	Tranquility Lake ...	123	Minor Details	112	...240,000	1:48.20	...100
2002	Affluent	4	E. Delahoussaye.	118	Golden Apples	120	Janet	118	...240,000	1:48.37	...103
2003	Megahertz	4	A. Solis...........	116	Dublino	121	....		...240,000	1:49.09	...104
	....		....		Golden Apples	122					
	....		....		Tates Creek	123					

Beyer Index: 103.29

Distance 1 Mile in 1945; Run on main course prior to 1970

MALIBU STAKES, 7 Furlongs, 3-Year-Olds,
Santa Anita, 2003 Purse: $250,000

Year	Winner	Age	Jockey	Wt.	Second	Wt.	Third	Wt.	Win Value	Time	Beyer
1952	Phil D.	4	R. York............	118	Intent	115	Black Douglas	110	...18,500	1:23.00	
1953	A Gleam	4	E. Arcaro	113	Stranglehold	115	Big Noise...........	112	...15,800	1:22.80	
1954	Imbros	4	R. York............	118	Berseem	114	Joe Jones...........	115	...16,600	1:20.60	
1955	Determine	4	R. York............	126	Double Reigh	110	El Drag.............	110	...16,900	1:22.60	
1955	Honeys Alibi	3	B. Boland	120	Hillary	120	Beau Busher	120	...19,050	1:23.00	
	Run in January and December										
1956	Blen Host	3	D. Lewis.......	112	Terrang	124	Count of Honour ...	120	...18,650	1:23.00	
1957	Round Table	3	W. Shoemaker...	130	Seaneen	114	Mystic Eye........	122	...16,550	1:22.00	
1958	Hillsdale	3	T. Barrow	126	Jewel's Reward	126	Swaps Kin	114	...18,800	1:22.40	
1960	Ole Fols	4	W. Boland	122	Bagdad	126	American Comet ...	114	...15,700	1:23.00	
1960	Tompion	3	M. Ycaza........	128	New Policy	124	First Balcony	114	...16,100	1:21.40	
	Run in January and Decembe										
1961	Olden Times	3	W. Shoemaker...	120	Spy Flight	114	Four-and-Twenty ..	128	...16,900	1:22.00	
1962	Native Diver	3	R. Neves	117	Grid Iron Hero	121	Humoso...........	114	...18,050	1:21.60	
1963	More Megaton	3	R. York............	114	Legation	114	Quilta Dude	117	...18,950	1:23.00	
1965	Power of Destiny ...	4	K. Church........	112	Maker's Mark	113	Hill Rise............	122	...19,050	1:22.00	
1966	Terry's Secret	4	A. Maese........	123	Hoist Bar	113	Royal Gunner	117	...18,950	1:23.00	

Year	Winner	Age	Jockey	Wt.	Second	Wt.	Third	Wt.	Win Value	Time	Beyer
1966	Buckpasser	3	B. Baeza	125	Drin	120	Kings Favor	117	18,300	1:22.00	
	Run in January and December										
1968	Damascus	4	W. Shoemaker	126	Rising Market	120	Ruken	123	27,850	1:21.20	
1969	First Mate	4	J. Lambert	117	Skookum	113	Dignitas	117	34,650	1:22.00	
1971	King of Cricket	4	D. Velasquez	113	Hanalei Bay	123	Swift Savage	114	30,450	1:21.20	
1972	Kfar Tov	4	J. Lambert	115	Autobiography	117	Diplomatic Agent	117	28,250	1:21.00	
1972	Wing Out	4	W. Shoemaker	117	Star of Kuwait	113	Tower East	117	29,500	1:21.20	
1973	Bicker	4	G. Brogan	117	Royal Owl	120	Tri Jet	117	39,300	1:21.40	
1974	Ancient Title	4	F. Toro	120	Linda's Chief	126	Dancing Papa	120	34,800	1:22.80	
1975	Lightning Mandate	4	A. Pineda	120	Rocket Review	117	Country's Envoy	120	28,525	1:20.60	
1975	Princely Native	4	B. Baeza	117	First Back	115	Holding Pattern	123	27,775	1:20.80	
1976	Forceten	4	D. Pierce	123	Messenger of Song	120	My Juliet	115	35,450	1:21.00	
1977	Cojak	4	W. Shoemaker	117	Double Discount	117	Little Riva	114	26,050	1:23.00	
1977	Romantic Lead	4	W. Shoemaker	114	Maheras	120	Life's Hope	123	24,800	1:22.40	
1978	J.O. Tobin	4	S. Cauthen	123	Bad 'n Big	120	Eagle Ki	114	35,050	1:23.00	
1979	Little Reb	4	F. Olivares	120	Radar Ahead	123	Affirmed	126	38,200	1:21.00	
1980	Spectacular Bid	4	W. Shoemaker	126	Flying Paster	123	Rosie's Seville	117	47,800	1:20.00	
1981	Doonesbury	4	S. Hawley	117	Roper	114	Unalakleet	114	44,100	1:20.40	
1981	Raise a Man	4	L. Pincay Jr	120	Just Right Mike	114	Aristocratical	117	44,400	1:20.40	
1982	Island Whirl	4	L. Pincay Jr	123	Shanekite	120	It's the One	120	64,000	1:26.00	
1983	Time to Explode	4	L. Pincay Jr	117	Prince Spellbound	123	Wavering Monarch	123	52,550	1:21.00	
1984	Glacial Stream	4	C.J. McCarron	120	Total Departure	120	Hula Blaze	117	43,150	1:22.20	
1984	Pac Mania	4	P.A. Valenzuela	115	Retsina Run	114	Desert Wine	123	43,150	1:22.60	
	Run in two divisions										
1984	Precisionist	3	C.J. McCarron	126	Bunker	117	Milord	115	66,700	1:21.40	
	Run in January and December										
1985	Banner Bob	3	G. Baze	123	Encolure	120	Carload	114	71,600	1:21.00	
1986	Ferdinand	3	W. Shoemaker	123	Snow Chief	126	Don B. Blue	114	72,300	1:21.60	
1987	On the Line	3	A. Cordero Jr	117	Temperate Sil	126	Candi's Gold	123	66,550	1:21.00	
1988	Oraibi	3	L. Pincay Jr	117	Perceive Arrogance	120	Speedratic	114	70,550	1:21.60	
1989	Music Merci	3	L. Pincay Jr	123	Exemplary Leader	117	Doncareer	114	97,300	1:21.60	
1990	Pleasant Tap	3	A. Solis	117	Bedeviled	120	Due to the King	117	67,600	1:21.60	
1991	Olympio	3	E. Delahoussaye	122	Charmonnier	120	Apollo	118	66,850	1:21.28	112
1992	Star of the Crop	3	G.L. Stevens	118	The Wicked North	116	Bertrando	120	67,850	1:20.67	104
1993	Diazo	3	L. Pincay Jr	120	Concept Win	116	Mister Jolie	116	64,700	1:21.00	104
1994	Powis Castle	3	P.A. Valenzuela	117	Ferrara	116	Numerous	118	64,300	1:20.96	113
1995	Afternoon Deelites	3	K.J. Desormeaux	120	Score Quick	120	High Stakes Player	116	100,000	1:21.73	103
1996	King of the Heap	3	K.J. Desormeaux	116	Hesabull	118	Northern Afleet	116	134,300	1:21.84	96
1997	Lord Grillo	3	E. Delahoussaye	119	Silver Charm	123	Swiss Yodeler	115	120,000	1:21.46	109
1998	Run Man Run	3	M.J. Luzzi	115	Artax	119	Event of the Year	121	120,000	1:21.51	105
1999	Love That Red	3	G.K. Gomez	115	Straight Man	118	Cat Thief	123	120,000	1:22.06	102
2000	Dixie Union	3	A. Solis	121	Caller One	119	Wooden Phone	116	120,000	1:21.62	103
2001	Mizzen Mast	3	K.J. Desormeaux	117	Giant Gentleman	115	I Love Silver	117	120,000	1:22.13	105
2002	Debonair Joe	3	J.A. Krone	119	Total Limit	117	American System	117	120,000	1:22.40	94
2003	Southern Image	3	V. Espinoza	115	Marino Marini	115	Midas Eyes	119	150,000	1:22.65	106

Beyer Index: 104.31

MAN O' WAR, 1 3/8 Miles (Turf), 3-Year-Olds and Up, Belmont Park, 2003 Purse: $500,000

Year	Winner	Age	Jockey	Wt.	Second	Wt.	Third	Wt.	Win Value	Time	Beyer
1959	Dotted Line	6	W. Boland	111	Amerigo	121	Prince Willy	112	71,732	2:40.80	
1959	Tudor Era	6	W. Hartack	124	Marlow Road	113	Anisado	111	72,382	2:41.00	
1960	Harmonizing	6	J. Ruane	126	Bald Eagle	126	Sword Dancer	126	70,530	2:33.20	
1961	Wise Ship	4	H. Gustines	108	Harmonizing	119	Geechee Lou	116	65,000	2:50.40	
1962	Beau Purple	5	W. Boland	126	Kelso	126	The Axe II	126	74,620	2:28.60	
1963	The Axe II	5	J.L. Rotz	126	Will I Rule	122	Guadalcanal	126	73,905	2:45.60	
1964	Turbo Jet II	4	H. Grant	126	Gun Bow	126	Knightly Manner	121	72,670	2:42.80	
1965	Hill Rise	4	M. Ycaza	126	Knightly Manner	126	Or et Argent	126	73,255	2:42.60	
1966	Assagai	3	L. Adams	121	Gallip Poll	121	Knightly Manner	126	72,865	2:44.60	
1967	Ruffled Feathers	3	D. Hidalgo	121	Fort Marcy	121	Handsome Boy	126	75,465	2:42.80	
1968	Czar Alexander	3	J. Velasquez	121	Fort Marcy	126	Advocator	126	75,530	2:30.80	
1969	Hawaii	5	J. Velasquez	126	North Flight	126	Fort Marcy	126	73,645	2:27.20	
1970	Fort Marcy	6	J. Velasquez	126	Loud	121	Drumtop	123	75,465	2:33.80	
1971	Run the Gantlet	3	R. Woodhouse	121	Gleaming	121	Practicante	126	67,200	2:33.20	
1972	Typecast	6	A. Cordero Jr	123	Ruritana	121	Droll Role	126	70,380	2:31.80	
1973	Secretariat	3	R. Turcotte	121	Tentam	126	Big Spruce	126	68,160	2:24.80	
1974	Dahlia	4	R. Turcotte	123	Crafty Khale	126	London Company	126	71,700	2:26.60	
1975	Snow Knight	4	J. Velasquez	126	One on the Aisle	121	Drollery	126	68,400	2:29.20	
	One on the Aisle finished first but was disqualified and placed second										
1976	Effervescing	3	A. Cordero Jr	121	Banghi	121	Erwin Boy	126	67,500	2:31.20	
							Rouge Sang				
	Crackle finished third but was disqualified and placed fifth										
1977	Majestic Light	4	S. Hawley	126	Exceller	126	Johnny D.	121	67,860	2:27.60	

Year	Winner	Age	Jockey	Wt.	Second	Wt.	Third	Wt.	Win Value	Time	Beyer
1978	Waya	4	A. Cordero Jr	123	Tiller	126	Mac Diarmida	121	79,725	2:16.20	
1979	Bowl Game	5	J. Velasquez	126	Native Courier	126	Czaravich	121	82,425	2:19.00	
1980	French Colonial	5	J. Vasquez	126	Just a Game II	123	Golden Act	126	84,300	2:15.40	
1981	Galaxy Libra	5	W. Shoemaker	126	Match the Hatch	126	Great Neck	126	99,180	2:14.80	
	Native Courier finished third but was disqualified and placed fourth										
1982	Naskra's Breeze	5	J.L. Samyn	126	Sprink	126	Thunder Puddles	121	103,860	2:13.00	
1983	Majesty's Prince	4	E. Maple	126	Erins Isle	126	L'Emigrant	121	176,700	2:23.60	
1984	Majesty's Prince	5	V. Bracciale Jr	126	Win	126	Cozzene	126	214,200	2:14.60	
1985	Win	5	R. Migliore	126	Bob Back	126	Baillamont	121	183,600	2:15.40	
1986	Dance of Life	3	P. Day	121	Duty Dance	123	Pillaster	121	201,000	2:14.40	
1987	Theatrical	5	P. Day	126	Le Glorieux	121	Midnight Cousins	126	351,000	2:15.40	
1988	Sunshine Forever	3	A. Cordero Jr	120	Pay the Butler	126	My Big Boy	126	357,600	2:14.40	
1989	Yankee Affair	7	J.A. Santos	126	My Big Boy	126	Alwuhush	126	282,240	2:20.80	
1990	Defensive Play	3	P. Eddery	126	Shy Tom	126	Ode	126	284,160	2:17.80	
1991	Solar Splendor	4	W.H. McCauley	126	Dear Doctor	126	Beau Sultan	120	240,000	2:12.00	112
1992	Solar Splendor	5	W.H. McCauley	126	Dear Doctor	126	Spinning	126	240,000	2:12.40	111
1993	Star of Cozzene	5	J.A. Santos	126	Serrant	126	Dr. Kiernan	126	240,000	2:23.00	117
1994	Royal Mountain Inn	5	J.A. Krone	126	Flag Down	126	Fraise	126	240,000	2:11.60	110
1995	Millkom	4	G.L. Stevens	126	Kaldounevees	126	Signal Tap	126	240,000	2:12.80	105
1996	Diplomatic Jet	4	J.F. Chavez	126	Mecke	126	Marlin	126	240,000	2:14.20	111
1997	Influent	6	J.D. Bailey	126	Val's Prince	126	Awad	126	240,000	2:11.60	110
1998	Daylami	4	J.D. Bailey	126	Buck's Boy	126	Indy Vidual	126	240,000	2:13.18	110
1999	Val's Prince	7	J.F. Chavez	126	Single Empire	126	Federal Trial	126	300,000	2:16.69	110
2000	Fantastic Light	4	J.D. Bailey	126	Ela Athena	123	Drama Critic	126	300,000	2:17.44	106
2001	With Anticipation	6	P. Day	126	Silvano	126	Ela Athena	123	300,000	2:25.11	111
2002	With Anticipation	7	P. Day	126	Balto Star	126	Man From Wicklow	126	300,000	2:15.05	108
2003	Lunar Sovereign	4	R. Migliore	126	Slew Valley	126	Denon	126	300,000	2:17.99	110

Beyer Index: 110.08

Distance 1 5/8 miles 1961, 1963–67; 1 1/2 miles, 1959–60, 1962, 1968–77

MANHATTAN HANDICAP, 1 1/4 Miles (Turf), 3-Year-Olds and Up, Belmont Park, 2003 Purse: $400,000

Year	Winner	Age	Jockey	Wt.	Second	Wt.	Third	Wt.	Win Value	Time	Beyer
1896	Belmar	4	T. Sloan	120	Dutch Skater	108	Sir Walter	117	1,450	2:07.20	
1898	Sanders	3	Spencer	107	Swiftmas	112	Irish Reel	124	2,520	1:11.00	
1899	Firearm	4	O'Leary	120	Heliobas	106	Tolulea	102	2,280	1:08.60	
1900	Firearm	5	T. Burns	122	Belle of Lexington	109	Vulcain	112	1,510	1:12.00	
1901	Musette	4	O. Wonderly	100	Redpath	109	King Pepper	98	1,510	1:12.00	
1902	King Pepper	4	Redfern	120	Belle of Lexington	100	Unmasked	120	2,140	1:12.00	
1903	Castalian	3	T. Burns	103	Lux Casta	112	King Pepper	116	2,090	1:09.00	
1904	Broadcloth	4	Crimmins	98	Race King	93	Castalian	105	2,080	1:10.20	
1905	Roseben	4	O'Niell	147	Aeronaut	105	Race King	104	2,120	1:11.60	
1906	Roseben	5	Shaw	147	Suffrage	111	Handzarra	113	2,530	1:12.20	
1907	Baby Wolf	3	E. Dugan	109	Dreamer	112	Jack Atkin	123	2,500	1:12.20	
1908	Delirium	4	Gilbert	104	Half Sovereign	110	Fashion Plate	98	570	1:11.60	
1914	Stromboli	3	C. Turner	122	Comely	107	Frederick L.	115	1,245	1:24.00	
1915	The Finn	3	T. Davis	118	Purdey	108	Montresor	110	1,195	1:26.00	
1916	The Finn	4	A. Schuttinger	130	Short Grass	128	Jacoba	107	1,430	1:39.40	
1917	Stargazer	3	M. Buxton	106	Chiclet	112	Capra	107	1,420	1:39.20	
1918	Naturalist	4	W. Knapp	116	Sunflash II	115	Fairy Wand	104	2,350	1:37.80	
1919	Lucullite	4	L. Fator	118	Star Master	120	Naturalist	137	2,800	1:36.60	
1920	Naturalist	6	C. Kummer	129	Jack Stuart	107	Audacious	117	2,775	1:36.00	
1921	Yellow Hand	4	C.H. Miller	124	Tryster	118	Mad Hatter	132	2,925	1:36.00	
1922	Little Chief	3	L. Fator	115	Thunderclap	130	Brainstorm	103	3,100	1:38.00	
1923	Little Chief	4	E. Sande	119	Untidy	109	Brainstorm	105	3,425	1:35.80	
1924	Sarazen	3	J. Maiben	122	Cherry Pie	108	Mad Play	116	3,500	1:36.40	
1925	Pepp	4	H. Thurber	108	Blind Play	115	Cherry Pie	106	3,575	1:37.40	
1926	Croydon	3	L. McAtee	109	Bumpkin	98	Dr's Parade	115	3,350	1:38.80	
1927	Valorous	4	G. Fields	109	Kiev	109	Osmand	117	3,975	1:37.40	
1928	Victorian	3	L. Fator	118	Princess Tina	109	Penalo	106	3,800	1:37.60	
1929	Ironsides	4	L. McAtee	114	Clean Play	102	Petee-Wrack	128	6,675	1:36.00	
1930	Flying Heels	3	W. Kelsay	114	Petee-Wrack	122	Caruso	104	3,400	1:37.40	
1931	Mr. Sponge	4	M. Garner	121	Jack High	128	Conclave	99	3,325	1:35.80	
1932	Larranga	3	R. Workman	115	Snap Back	103	Mad Frump	111	2,875	1:36.80	
1933	Dark Secret	4	R. Workman	124	Gusto	114	Mr. Khayyam	114	2,560	2:30.00	
1934	Dark Secret	5	C. Kurtsinger	122	Somebody	108	Lady Reigh	106	4,230	2:29.20	
1935	Count Arthur	3	W.D. Wright	117	Judy O'Grady	100	Good Goods	120	4,430	2:30.00	
1936	Action	7	J. Gilbert	122	Count Arthur	112	Ann O'Ruley	103	4,450	2:31.20	
1937	Count Stone	4	F. Kopel	118	Esposa	118	Firethorn	123	4,230	2:30.40	
1938	Isolater	5	J. Stout	108	Regal Lily	108	Seabiscuit	128	4,300	2:31.00	
1939	Sorteado	4	L. Haas	112	Cravat	120	Isolater	118	6,675	2:28.40	
1940	Bolingbroke	3	S. Hebert	95	Mount Vernon II	103	Sickle T.	107	7,725	2:30.00	
1941	Fenelon	4	J. Stout	120	Corydon	110	Welcome Pass	105	8,175	2:29.00	

Year	Winner	Age	Jockey	Wt.	Second	Wt.	Third	Wt.	Win Value	Time	Beyer
1942	Bolingbroke	5	H. Lindberg	115	Whirlaaway	132	King's Abbey	111	8,175	2:27.60	
1943	Bolingbroke	6	S. Brooks	122	The Rhymer	108	King's Abbey	112	7,775	2:30.80	
1944	Devil Diver	5	E. Arcaro	125	Caribou	102	Bolingbroke	126	10,595	2:36.60	
1945	Bankrupt	5	A. Kirkland	116	His Jewel	105	Megogo	117	12,475	2:31.00	
1946	Stymie	5	B. James	126	Pavot	121	Flareback	113	20,050	2:29.40	
							Assault	116			
1947	Rico Monte	5	E. Arcaro	123	Stymie	132	Talon	116	19,250	2:29.80	
1948	Loyal Legion	4	T. Atkinson	123	Donor	113	Tide Rips	110	19,600	2:29.80	
1949	Donor	5	W. Mehrtens	118	My Request	125	Stunts	114	20,400	2:28.00	
1950	One Hitter	4	T. Atkinson	110	Noor	128	Ponder	126	20,800	2:29.20	
1951	County Delight	4	E. Guerin	122	One Hitter	118	Busanda	110	19,550	2:29.60	
1952	Lone Eagle	6	C. Errico	107	Combat Boots	110	One Hitter	117	23,950	2:30.80	
1953	Jampol	4	J. Contreras	110	Alerted	120	Royal Vale	126	23,300	2:30.00	
1954	High Gun	3	E. Arcaro	123	Subahdar	110	Bicarb	116	24,150	2:30.60	
1955	Social Outcast	5	E. Guerin	124	Paper Tiger	111	Icarian	108	22,200	2:30.00	
1956	Flying Fury	4	T. Atkinson	108	Honeys Alibi	117	Paper Tiger	114	37,600	2:30.20	
1957	Reneged	4	R. Ussery	125	Cavort	110	Third Brother	125	37,300	2:29.40	
1958	Warhead	4	E. Arcaro	116	Beau Diable	108	Clem	126	36,515	2:28.60	
1959	Round Table	5	W. Shoemaker	132	Bald Eagle	122	Coloneast	112	37,230	2:42.60	
1960	Don Poggio	4	S. Boulmetis	120	Amber Morn	117	Polylad	118	36,255	2:29.60	
1961	Nickel Boy	6	I. Valenzuela	113	Troubadour II	110	Dress Up	114	36,985	2:10.00	
1962	Tuntankhamen	4	B. Baeza	111	Sensitivo	115	Windy Sands	116	37,765	2:28.40	
1963	Smart	4	E. Nelson	114	Will I Rule	112	Garwol	111	38,220	2:28.00	
1964	Going Abroad	4	R. Broussard	116	Sunrise Flight	117	The Ibex	114	37,635	2:26.20	
1965	Roman Brother	4	B. Baeza	125	Hill Rise	119	Knightly Manner	114	36,790	2:43.20	
1966	Moontrip	5	E. Belmonte	110	O'Hara	116	Niarkos	113	38,545	2:42.40	
1967	Munden Point	5	R. Ussery	126	Dunderhead	113	Moontrip	113	37,180	2:41.60	
1968	Quicken Tree	5	W. Hartack	123	Grace Born	114	Harem Lady	109	37,895	2:28.00	
1969	Harem Lady	5	E. Belmonte	113	Chompion	118	Open Road	112	34,580	2:30.20	
1970	Shelter Bay	4	R. Woodhouse	113	Loud	115	Cougar II	119	40,300	2:14.60	
1971	Happy Way	4	H. Gustines	110	Chompion	116	Elephant Walk	112	27,390	2:16.60	
1971	Big Shot II	6	J. Tejeira	112	Gleaming	116	Red Reality	117	27,990	2:16.40	
1972	Star Envoy	4	J. Velasquez	116	Typecast	122	Exotico	111	28,110	2:13.60	
1972	Ruritania	3	R. Turcotte	111	Droll Role	122	Triangular	110	27,960	2:14.00	
1973	London Company	3	L. Pincay Jr	116	Big Spruce	120	Triangular	110	36,120	2:15.60	
1974	Golden Don	4	J. Cruguet	119	Anono	112	R. Tom Can	114	35,970	2:19.80	
1975	Salt Marsh	5	E. Maple	115	Drollery	109	London Company	118	33,600	2:16.60	
1975	Snow Knight	4	J. Velasquez	123	Shady Character	113	One On the Aisle	114	33,900	2:16.20	
1976	Caucasus	4	F. Toro	120	Trumpeter Swan	113	Kamaraan II	116	33,930	2:14.40	
1977	Gentle King	5	S. Cauthen	111	Double Quill	105	Keep the Promise	112	32,220	2:28.40	
1977	Gallivantor	5	S. Cauthen	112	Gallapiat	112	Togus	112	32,070	2:28.00	
1978	Fabulous Time	4	A. Cordero Jr	112	Bill Brill	109	Tiller	127	48,690	2:01.40	
1979	Fluorescent Light	5	J. Fell	121	Tiller	124	Native Courier	122	51,615	2:04.80	
1980	Morold	5	E. Maple	113	Match the Hatch	111	Foretake	113	53,910	2:00.20	
1981	Match the Hatch	5	J.L. Samyn	114	Mrs. Penny	117	Native Courier	115	52,470	2:03.00	
1982	Sprink	4	J. Miranda	113	Naskra's Breeze	119	Native Courier	116	51,570	2:01.00	
1983	Acaroid	5	A. Cordero Jr	114	Craelius	120	Half Iced	119	72,240	2:00.00	
1984	Win	4	A. Graell	114	Fortnightly	112	Norwick	110	77,520	2:00.60	
1985	Cool	4	J. Vasquez	110	Win	126	Sondrio	107	77,280	2:02.00	
1986	Danger's Hour	4	J.D. Bailey	117	Premier Mister	111	Exclusive Partner	115	87,300	2:02.60	
1987	Silver Voice	4	J.M. Pezua	109	Talakeno	118	Duluth	113	86,220	2:01.40	
1988	Milesius	4	C.W. Antley	112	My Big Boy	114	Maceo	111	71,760	2:04.40	
1989	Milesius	5	R. Migliore	115	Salem Drive	115	My Big Boy	114	73,440	2:00.00	
1990	Phantom Breeze	4	M.E. Smith	113	Green Barb	111	Milesius	116	52,110	2:02.60	
1991	Academy Award	5	A. Madrid Jr	111	Three Coins Up	110	Tarsho	113	111,600	1:59.60	105
1992	Sky Classic	5	P. Day	123	Roman Envoy	111	Leger Cat	116	172,860	2:02.40	107
1993	Star of Cozzene	5	J.A. Santos	118	Lure	124	Solar Splendor	112	90,000	1:58.80	116
1994	Paradise Creek	5	P. Day	124	Solar Splendor	112	River Majesty	113	90,000	1:57.60	117
1995	Awad	5	E. Maple	121	Blues Traveller	119	Kiri's Clown	115	120,000	1:58.40	108
1996	Diplomatic Jet	4	J.F. Chavez	117	Flag Down	119	Kiri's Clown	121	120,000	2:00.00	111
1997	Ops Smile	4	R.G. Davis	116	Flag Down	118	Always a Classic	121	120,000	1:59.00	107
1998	Chief Bearhart	5	J.A. Santos	122	Devonwood	113	Buck's Boy	117	150,000	1:58.25	110
1999	Yagli	6	J.D. Bailey	122	Federal Trial	116	Middlesex Drive	116	180,000	1:58.48	108
2000	Manndar	5	C.S. Nakatani	117	Boatman	113	Spindrift	113	240,000	1:59.61	107
2001	Forbidden Apple	6	C.S. Nakatani	117	King Cugat	120	Tijiyr	115	240,000	2:00.77	110
2002	Beat Hollow	5	A. Solis	118	Forbidden Apple	118	Strut the Stage	117	240,000	2:01.29	110
2003	Denon	5	J.D. Bailey	122	Requete	116	Dr. Brendler	116	240,000	2:14.16	108

Beyer Index: 109.54

Distance 1 1/4 miles in 1896; 6 furlongs over Eclipse Course, 1898–1908; 7 furlongs, 1914–15; 1 mile; 1916–32; 1 1/2 miles, 1933–58, 1960, 1962–64, 1968–69, and 1977, 1 5/16 miles, 1961, 1 5/8 miles, 1959, 1965–67. Run at Morris Park prior to 1905; at Aqueduct, 1959, 1961, 1963–67. Run on main track 1896–1969, 1977, 1979, and 1988

MATRIARCH STAKES, 1 Mile (Turf), Fillies and Mares, 3-Year-Olds and Up, Hollywood Park, 2003 Purse: $500,000

Year	Winner	Age	Jockey	Wt.	Second	Wt.	Third	Wt.	Win Value	Time	Beyer
1981	Kilijaro	.5	L. Pincay Jr	123	Glorious Song	123	Bersid	120	131,600	1:47.00	
1982	Pale Purple	.4	R. Sibille	123	Berry Bush	123	Ticketed	120	104,600	1:48.60	
1982	Castilla	.3	R. Sibille	120	Sangue	123	Star Pastures	123	104,600	1:47.40	
1983	Sangue	.5	W. Shoemaker	123	Castilla	123	Geraldine's Store	123	110,000	1:49.40	
1984	Royal Heroine	.4	F. Toro	123	Reine Mathilde	120	Sabin	123	164,000	1:49.40	
1985	Fact Finder	.6	S. Hawley	123	Tamarinda	123	Possible Mate	123	137,000	1:48.20	
1986	Auspiciante	.5	C.B. Asmussen	123	Aberuschka	123	Reloy	120	110,000	1:48.00	
1987	Asteroid Field	.4	A.T. Gryder	123	Nashmeel	120	Any Song	123	110,000	1:51.00	
1988	Nastique	.4	W. Shoemaker	123	Annoconnor	123	White Mischief II	123	110,000	1:47.00	
1989	Claire Marine	.4	C.J. McCarron	123	General Charge	120	Royal Touch	123	110,000	1:47.40	
1990	Countus In	.5	C.S. Nakatani	123	Taffeta and Tulle	123	Little Brianne	123	110,000	1:46.20	100
1991	Flawlessly	.3	C.J. McCarron	120	Fire the Groom	123	Free at Last	123	110,000	1:46.60	106
1992	Flawlessly	.4	C.J. McCarron	120	Super Staff	123	Kostroma	123	220,000	1:46.00	108
1993	Flawlessly	.5	C.J. McCarron	123	Toussaud	123	Skimble	123	220,000	1:46.60	102
1994	Exchange	.6	L. Pincay Jr	123	Aube Indienne	123	Wandesta	120	220,000	1:49.40	105
1995	Duda	.4	J.D. Bailey	123	Angel in My Heart	120	Wandesta	123	385,000	2:00.20	105
1996	Wandesta	.5	C.S. Nakatani	123	Windsharp	123	Memories of Silver	120	420,000	2:00.00	107
1997	Ryafan	.3	A. Solis	120	Maxzene	123	Yokama	123	420,000	2:05.80	106
1998	Squeak	.3	A.Solis	123	Real Connection	123	Green Jewel	123	420,000	2:05.08	102
1999	Happyanunoit	.4	B. Blanc	123	Tuzla	123	Spanish Fern	123	300,000	1:46.30	107
2000	Tout Charmant	.4	C.J. McCarron	123	Tranquility Lake	123	Happyanunoit	123	300,000	1:46.06	109
2001	Starine	.4	J.R. Velazquez	123	Lethals Lady	120	Golden Apples	120	300,000	1:50.16	101
2002	Dress to Thrill	.3	P.J. Smullen	120	Golden Apples	123	Magic Mission	123	300,000	1:48.31	105
2003	Heat Haze	.4	J.R. Velazquez	123	Musical Chimes	120	Dedication	123	300,000	1:34.43	103

Beyer Index: 104.71

Distance 1 1/4 miles 1995-98; 1 1/8 miles in 1981-1994,1999-2002

MATRON STAKES, 1 Mile, 2-Year-Old Fillies, Belmont Park, 2003 Purse: $200,000

Year	Winner	Age	Jockey	Wt.	Second	Wt.	Third	Wt.	Win Value	Time	Beyer
1892	Sir Francis	.2	Garrison	118	Miss Maude	112	Roche	105	36,770	1:19.00	
1893	Domino	.2	Taral	128	Peacemaker	110	Jack of Spades	121	24,560	1:09.00	
1894	Agitator	.2	Taral	111	Handspun	109	Salvation	111	31,310	1:11.00	
1899	Indian Fairy	.2	J. Slack	111	Redpath	108	Runaway	113	16,697	1:10.20	
1900	Beau Gallant	.2	Bullman	125	Commando	124	The Parader	117	16,297	1:01.20	
1901	Heno	.2	Odom	122	Yankee	129	Whiskey King	125	17,593	1:11.20	
1902	Grey Friar	.2	N. Turner	122	Surbiton	109	Acefull	122	12,180	1:11.20	
1902	Eugenia Burch	.2	Odom	122	Merry Reel	104	Stolen Moments	109	6,790	1:12.20	
1903	The Minute Man	.2	F. O'Neill	117	Hippocrates	111	Collec'r Jessop	112	8,035	1:09.60	
1903	Armenia	.2	W. Hicks	112	For Luck	109	Beldame	123	5,525	1:10.20	
1904	Bedouin	.2	Shaw	114	Glorifier	125	Dandelion	114	12,725	1:09.00	
1904	Sandria	.2	Hildebrand	104	Rose of Dawn	109	Belle Strome	114	13,345	1:08.20	
1905	Burgomaster	.2	L. Lyne	124	Penrhyn	119	Battleaxe	122	10,405	1:12.20	
1905	Perverse	.2	L. Lyne	109	Early and Often	111	Duenna	109	10,485	1:11.20	
1906	Ballot	.2	Radtke	124	Okenite	116	Hickory	112	10,250	1:12.00	
1906	Adoration	.2	W. Miller	116	Fantastic	111	Pope Joan	111	9,030	1:11.80	
1907	Colin	.2	W. Miller	129	Fair Play	122	Royal Tourist	119	9,340	1:12.00	
1907	Stamina	.2	W. Knapp	119	Masquerade	111	Half Sovereign	119	8,940	1:11.80	
1908	Helmet	.2	Notter	124	Joe Madden	122	Practical	112	9,625	1:12.60	
1908	Maskette	.2	Notter	124	Affliction	106		0	5,895	1:20.80	
1909	Radium Star	.2	Creevy	114	Candleberry	112	Rocky O'Brien	129	8,995	1:14.80	
1909	Greenvale	.2	Gilbert	111	Fair Louise	111	Indian Maid	114	8,535	1:15.00	
1910	Naushon	.2	J. Glass	125	Zeus	119	Footprint	122	9,485	1:12.80	
1910	Bashti	.2	C.H. Shilling	117	Love-Not	106	Horizon	106	8,655	1:13.00	
1914	Pebbles	.2	J. Butwell	130	Paris	110	Kilkenny Boy	113	1,130	1:15.00	
1914	Charter Maid	.2	J. McTaggart	111	Coquette	119	Capra	110	1,045	1:14.00	
1923	Tree Top	.2	F. Coltiletti	119	Rosebec	114	Princess Doreen	106	4,150	1:11.60	
1924	Blue Warbler	.2	D. Hurn	122	Swinging	114	Martha Martin	109	10,625	1:13.80	
1925	Taps	.2	A. Johnson	109	Nellie Morse	122	Asinia	114	15,075	1:13.40	
1926	Pantella	.2	L. McAtee	124	Tip Top	119	Bon. Pennant	124	18,275	1:13.40	
1927	Glade	.2	G. Ellis	114	One Hour	122	Bateau	119	21,025	1:12.60	
1928	Dreadnaught	.2	S. O'Donnell	116	Fly Light	109	Bravery	114	21,725	1:12.00	
1929	Dustemall	.2	L. McAtee	124	Murky Cloud	119	Believe Sally	115	25,250	1:11.00	
1930	Baba Kenny	.2	J. Smith	115	Buckup	115	Ladana	122	24,650	1:12.00	
1931	Top Flight	.2	R. Workman	127	Parry	119	Pintail	115	23,750	1:11.60	
1932	Barn Swallow	.2	E. James	115	Iseult	115	Happy Gal	127	20,575	1:11.00	
1933	High Glee	.2	J. Gilbert	115	Bazaar	127	Jabot	115	18,800	1:13.60	
1934	Nellie Flag	.2	E. Arcaro	115	Judy O'Grady	112	Good Gamble	115	20,550	1:10.80	
1935	Beanie M.	.2	D. Meade	119	Victorious Ann	115	Split Second	115	11,900	1:11.80	
1936	Wand	.2	H. Richards	115	Dawn Play	115	Talma Dee	115	12,075	1:11.00	

Year	Winner	Age	Jockey	Wt.	Second	Wt.	Third	Wt.	Win Value	Time	Beyer
1937	Merry Lassie	2	J. Longden	123	Handcuff	115	Creole Maid	115	10,900	1:11.00	
1938	Dinner Date	2	A. Robertson	119	Ciencia	115	Airacuda	115	16,700	1:13.40	
1939	Miss Ferdinand	2	J. Westrope	115	Piquet	115	Thorn Apple	115	14,825	1:12.00	
1940	Misty Isle	2	W.D. Wright	119	Unquote	115	Silvestra	115	15,710	1:10.40	
1941	Petrify	2	R. Donoso	119	Light Lady	119	Ficklebush	110	17,710	1:11.60	
1942	Good Morning	2	H. Lindberg	109	Askmenow	114	Navigating	114	9,525	1:09.20	
1943	Boojiana	2	T. Atkinson	119	Thread o' Gold	119	Bold Anna	114	7,900	1:09.80	
1944	Busher	2	E. Arcaro	119	Twosy	115	Price Level	123	22,530	1:09.40	
1945	Beaugay	2	A. Kirkland	123	Enfilade	119	Athene	115	23,500	1:09.40	
1946	First Flight	2	E. Arcaro	123	Pipette	123	Quarantaine	115	35,535	1:08.60	
1947	Inheritance	2	J. Jessop	123	Vaudeville	115	Ghost Run	123	36,060	1:10.20	
	Bewitch finished first but was disqualified										
1948	Myrtle Charm	2	T. Atkinson	119	Stole	115	Lithe	115	37,805	1:10.60	
1949	Bed o' Roses	2	E. Guerin	119	Fais Do Do	119	Striking	119	40,210	1:11.20	
1950	Atalanta	2	H. Woodhouse	119	Ruddy	119	Sungari	119	38,690	1:12.00	
1951	Rose Jet	2	H. Woodhouse	119	Knot Hole	119	Landmark	119	44,830	1:11.20	
							A Gleam	119			
1952	Is Proud	2	C. McCreary	119	Aerolite	119	Grecian Queen	119	40,960	1:09.00	
1953	Evening Out	2	O. Scurlock	119	Queen Hopeful	119	Clear Dawn	119	41,345	1:10.40	
1954	High Voltage	2	E. Arcaro	119	Blue Banner	119	Lalun	119	49,330	1:10.00	
1955	Doubledogdare	2	E. Arcaro	119	Glamour	119	Beautillion	119	48,620	1:09.80	
1956	Romanita	2	E. Guerin	119	Jet's Charm	119	Lucky Mistake	119	43,020	1:08.60	
1957	Idun	2	W. Hartack	119	Poly Hi	119	Armorial	119	42,900	1:09.60	
1958	Quill	2	P.J. Bailey	119	Rich Tradition	119	Levelix	119	42,610	1:10.00	
1959	Heavenly Body	2	M. Ycaza	119	Irish Jay	119	Rash Statement	119	58,224	1:10.20	
1960	Rose Bower	2	J.L. Rotz	119	Little Tumbler	119	Good Move	119	58,634	1:10.60	
1961	Cicada	2	W. Shoemaker	119	Jazz Queen	119	Pontivy	119	61,028	1:10.60	
1962	Smart Deb	2	R. Ussery	119	Fashion Verdict	119	Affectionately	119	63,889	1:09.80	
1963	Hasty Matelda	2	J. Combest	119	Baraka	119	Beautiful Day	119	63,596	1:12.00	
1964	Candalita	2	R. Ussery	119	Admiring	119	Gold Digger	119	63,680	1:13.00	
1965	Moccasin	2	J. Adams	119	Lyvette	119	Shimmering Gold	119	67,717	1:11.60	
1966	Swiss Cheese	2	J.L. Rotz	119	Great Era	119	Regal Gleam	119	68,659	1:12.80	
1967	Queen of the Stage	2	B. Baeza	119	Gay Matelda	119	Syrian Sea	119	64,733	1:10.00	
1968	Gallant Bloom	2	E. Belmonte	119	Irradiate	119	Queen's Double	119	62,634	1:10.40	
1969	Cold Comfort	2	J. Velasquez	119	Repoise	119	Grab It	119	68,484	1:11.60	
1970	Bonnie and Gay	2	R. Woodhouse	119	Patelin	119	Make Me Laugh	119	68,009	1:11.00	
1971	Numbered Account	2	B. Baeza	119	Stepping High	119	Informative	119	60,306	1:10.40	
1972	La Prevoyante	2	J. LeBlanc	119	Up Above	119	Corraggioso	119	59,874	1:23.60	
1973	Talking Picture	2	R. Turcotte	119	Dancealot	119	Raisela	119	64,050	1:23.20	
1974	Alpine Lass	2	A. Cordero Jr	119	Copernica	119	Spring Is Here	119	52,674	1:23.00	
1975	Optimistic Gal	2	B. Baeza	119	Pacific Princess	119	Prowess	119	51,132	1:23.00	
1976	Mrs. Warren	2	E. Maple	119	Negotiator	119	Resolver	119	51,162	1:24.60	
1977	Lakeville Miss	2	R. Hernandez	119	Stub	119	Akita	119	49,335	1:22.80	
1978	Fall Aspen	2	R.I. Velez	119	Fair Advantage	119	Island Kitty	119	58,980	1:23.80	
1979	Smart Angle	2	S. Maple	119	Royal Suite	119	Nuit D'Amour	119	69,075	1:23.80	
1980	Prayers'n Promises	2	A. Cordero Jr	119	Heavenly Cause	119	Sweet Revenge	119	70,725	1:24.60	
1981	Before Dawn	2	J. Velasquez	119	Arabian Dancer	119	Mystical Mood	119	81,210	1:23.20	
1982	Wings of Jove	2	W.H. McCauley	119	Share the Fantasy	119	Weekend Surprise	119	72,600	1:24.00	
1983	Lucky Lucky Lucky	2	A. Cordero Jr	119	Miss Oceana	119	Buzz My Bell	119	76,590	1:23.60	
1984	Fiesta Lady	2	L. Pincay Jr	119	Tiltalating	119	Contredance	119	47,060	1:24.80	
1985	Musical Lark	2	D. MacBeth	119	Family Style	119	I'm Sweets	119	66,240	1:24.00	
1986	Tappiano	2	J. Cruguet	119	Sea Basque	119	Daytime Princess	119	72,000	1:23.40	
1987	Over All	2	A. Cordero Jr	119	Justsayno	119	Flashy Runner	119	82,140	1:24.80	
1988	Some Romance	2	G.L. Stevens	119	Seattle Meteor	119	Dreamy Mimi	119	68,580	1:24.80	
1989	Stella Madrid	2	A. Cordero Jr	119	Golden Reef	119	Miss Cox's Hat	119	72,720	1:24.40	
1990	Meadow Star	2	J.A. Santos	119	Verbasle	119	Clark Cottage	119	93,240	1:22.80	
1991	Anh Duong	2	A. Cordero Jr	119	Miss Iron Smoke	119	Vivano	119	81,300	1:23.40	.90
1992	Sky Beauty	2	E. Maple	119	Educated Risk	119	Family Enterprize	119	72,480	1:23.20	.92
1993	Strategic Maneuver	2	J.A. Santos	119	Astas Foxy Lady	119	Sovereign Kitty	119	70,680	1:23.80	.96
1994	Flanders	2	P. Day	119	Stormy Blues	119	Pretty Discreet	119	64,740	1:35.00	.101
	Flanders was subsequently disqualified for medication violation										
1995	Golden Attraction	2	G.L. Stevens	119	Cara Rafaela	119	My Flag	119	90,000	1:36.20	.89
1996	Sharp Cat	2	J.D. Bailey	119	Storm Song	119	Fabulously Fast	119	90,000	1:36.00	.90
1997	Beautiful Pleasure	2	J.D. Bailey	119	Diamond on the Run	119	Carrielle	119	90,000	1:35.60	.98
1998	Oh What a Windfall	2	S.J. Sellers	119	Arrested Dreams	119	Marley Vale	119	90,000	1:39.29	.74
1999	Finder's Fee	2	H. Castillo Jr.	119	Darling My Darling	119	Circle of Life	119	90,000	1:36.68	.94
2000	Raging Fever	2	J.D. Bailey	120	Dancinginmydreams	120	Ilusoria	120	120,000	1:38.20	.87
2002	Storm Flag Flying	2	J.R. Velazquez	119	Wild Snitch	119	Fircroft	119	120,000	1:38.52	.93
2003	Marylebone	2	E.S. Prado	119	Lokoya	119	Eye Dazzler	119	120,000	1:38.02	.78

Beyer Index: 90.17

Distance 6 furlongs prior to 1972; 7 furlongs from 1972-93. Run at Morris Park prior to 1905. Run at Pimlico in 1910. Run at Aqueduct 1960, 1962-68. Run over the old straight course 1905-09, 1914, 1923-25. Run on the Widener Course 1926-40, 1942-58. For colts and fillies prior to . 1902. Run in divisions, one for colts and one fillies, 1902-14. Not run in 2001

METROPOLITAN HANDICAP, 1 Mile, 3-Year-Olds and Up,
Belmont Park, 2003 Purse: $750,000

Year	Winner	Age	Jockey	Wt.	Second	Wt.	Third	Wt.	Win Value	Time	Beyer
1891	Tristan	6	Taylor	114	Tenny	129	Clarendon	107	7,300	1:51.20	
1892	Pessara	4	Taral	117	Locohatchee	105	Sleipner	107	12,200	1:54.00	
1893	Charade	4	Doggett	108	His Highness	125	Illume	98	13,740	1:52.20	
1894	Ramapo	4	Taral	117	Roche	105	Henry of Navarre	106	6,145	1:52.20	
1896	Counter Tenor	4	Hamilton	115	St. Maxim	109	Sir Walter	112	3,850	1:53.00	
1897	Voter	3	Lamley	99	The Winner	115	Casseopia	99	3,850	1:40.20	
1898	Bowling Brook	3	P. Clay	102	George Keene	102	Octagon	116	4,280	1:44.00	
1899	Filigrane	3	Clawson	102	Ethelbert	106	Sanders	110	6,750	1:39.60	
1900	Ethelbert	4	Maher	126	Box	121	Imp	127	6,250	1:41.20	
1901	Banastar	6	Odom	123	Contestor	112	All Green	102	6,810	1:42.00	
1902	Arsenal	3	J. Daly	90	Herbert	119	Carbuncle	103	8,920	1:42.00	
1903	Gunfire	4	T. Burns	109	Old England	118	Lux Casta	102	11,080	1:38.60	
1904	Irish Lad	4	Shaw	123	Toboggan	103	Beldame	98	10,880	1:40.00	
1905	Sysonby	3	Shaw	107			Colonial Girl	111	5,655	1:41.60	
	Race King	4	L. Smith	97							
1906	Grapple	4	Garner	97	Okenite	99	Roseben	124	10,850	1:39.00	
1908	Jack Atkin	4	C.H. Shilling	128	Restigouche	98	Don Creole	95	10,650	1:40.80	
1909	King James	4	G. Burns	125	Fayette	108	Juggler	112	3,785	1:40.00	
1910	Fashion Plate	4	M. McGee	105	Prince Imperial	97	Jack Atkin	129	3,800	1:37.80	
1913	Whisk Broom II	6	Notter	126	G.M. Miller	100	Meridian	120	3,500	1:39.00	
1914	Buskin	4	C. Fairbrother	114	Figinny	97	Rock View	127	4,200	1:37.80	
1915	Stromboli	4	C. Turner	118	Sharpshooter	103	Fly Fairy	115	2,325	1:39.80	
1916	The Finn	4	A. Schuttinger	120	Stromboli	122	Spur	100	3,350	1:38.00	
1917	Ormesdale	4	J. McTaggart	111	Spur	117	Borrow	117	3,850	1:39.20	
1918	Trompe La Mort	3	L. McAtee	102	Old Koenig	118	Priscilla Mullens	104	3,865	1:38.40	
1919	Lanius	4	J. Loftus	116	Flags	119	Star Master	116	3,865	1:45.40	
1920	Wildair	3	E. Ambrose	107	Thunderclap	114	On Watch	112	3,865	1:38.80	
1921	Mad Hatter	5	E. Sande	127	Audacious	117	Yellow Hand	110	8,150	1:37.40	
1922	Mad Hatter	6	E. Sande	129	Careful	112	Sennings Park	127	8,550	1:36.60	
1923	Grey Lag	5	E. Sande	133	Dinna Care	107	Exodus	110	7,600	1:38.00	
1924	Laurano	3	H. Thurber	101	Bracadale	110	Rialto	119	9,150	1:38.20	
1925	Sting	4	B. Breuning	114	Shuffle Along	112	Serenader	106	8,625	1:37.00	
1926	Sarazen	5	F. Weiner	129	Senaldo	116	Rock Star	105	9,125	1:38.00	
1927	Black Maria	4	F. Coltiletti	116	Osmand	112	Valorous	108	8,225	1:37.40	
1928	Nimba	4	H. Thurber	114	Chance Shot	118	Scapa Flow	125	8,575	1:40.00	
1929	Petee-Wrack	4	S. O'Donnell	120	Buddy Bauer	117	Bateau	114	8,600	1:40.00	
1930	Jack High	4	L. McAtee	110	Balko	120	Questionnaire	103	8,275	1:35.00	
1931	Questionnaire	4	R. Workman	122	Mokatam	122	Aegis	105	7,575	1:38.60	
1932	Equipoise	4	R. Workman	127	Sun Meadow	118	Mate	128	7,525	1:37.00	
1933	Equipoise	5	R. Workman	128	Okapi	102	Scotch Gold	106	4,725	1:37.40	
1934	Mr. Khayyam	4	R. Jones	119	Sun Archer	106	Ladysman	118	3,480	1:37.00	
	Equipoise finished first but was disqualified										
1935	King Saxon	4	C. Rainey	118	Singing Wood	114	Only One	113	7,225	1:38.20	
1936	Good Harvest	4	S. Renick	107	Whopper	123	Singing Wood	120	6,650	1:36.40	
1937	Snark	4	J. Longden	112	Memory Book	115	Whopper	122	6,675	1:37.80	
1938	Danger Point	4	E. Arcaro	112	Snark	124	Caballero II	122	8,450	1:38.00	
1939	Knickerbocker	3	F.A. Smith	100	Heelfly	116	Jacola	115	7,500	1:37.20	
1940	Third Degree	4	E. Arcaro	123	Can't Wait	109	War Dog	108	10,440	1:35.40	
1941	Eight Thirty	5	H. Richards	132	Bold and Bad	102	Hash	123	10,250	1:37.20	
1942	Attention	4	D. Meade	124	Pictor	120	Market Wise	125	11,300	1:36.40	
1943	Devil Diver	4	G. Woolf	117	Marriage	116	Thumbs Up	117	10,900	1:36.80	
1944	Devil Diver	5	T. Atkinson	134	Alquest	109	Boysy	108	10,080	1:35.80	
1945	Devil Diver	6	T. Atkinson	129	Alex Barth	123	Boy Knight	112	18,280	1:36.40	
1946	Gallorette	4	J.D. Jessop	110	Sirde	124	First Fiddle	126	22,050	1:37.00	
1947	Stymie	6	B. James	124	Brown Mogul	113	Gallorette	116	21,650	1:37.40	
1948	Stymie	7	C. McCreary	126	Colosal	117	Rippey	124	21,200	1:36.80	
1949	Loser Weeper	4	H. Woodhouse	105	Vulcan's Forge	126	But Why Not	119	21,400	1:36.40	
1950	Greek Ship	3	H. Woodhouse	106	Piet	121	Cochise	121	22,450	1:36.00	
1951	Casemate	4	D. Gorman	115	Piet	123	Lights Up	122	26,000	1:35.40	
1952	Mameluke	4	G. Porch	112	Battlefield	125	One Hitter	113	25,200	1:36.40	
1953	Tom Fool	4	T. Atkinson	130	Royal Vale	127	Intent	125	25,800	1:35.80	
1954	Native Dancer	4	E. Guerin	130	Straight Face	117	Jamie K.	110	28,300	1:35.20	
1955	High Gun	4	A. DeSpirito	130	Artismo	115	Joe Jones	119	25,500	1:35.60	
1956	Midafternoon	4	W. Boland	111	Switch On	113	Find	116	37,700	1:35.00	
1957	Traffic Judge	5	E. Arcaro	118	Dedicate	126	Greek Spy	114	44,600	1:36.00	
1958	Gallant Man	4	W. Shoemaker	130	Bold Ruler	135	Clem	114	37,620	1:35.60	
1959	Sword Dancer	3	W. Shoemaker	114	Jimmer	112	Talent Show	115	74,235	1:35.20	
1960	Bald Eagle	5	M. Ycaza	128	First Landing	123	Talent Show	118	73,130	1:33.60	
1961	Kelso	4	E. Arcaro	130	All Hands	117	Sweet William	108	74,100	1:35.60	
1962	Carry Back	4	J.L. Rotz	123	Merry Ruler	120	Rullah Red	111	72,735	1:33.60	
1963	Cyrano	4	R. Ussery	113	George Barton	114	Sunrise County	121	74,815	1:35.00	

Year	Winner	Age	Jockey	Wt.	Second	Wt.	Third	Wt.	Win Value	Time	Beyer
1964	Olden Times	6	H. Moreno	119	Quadrangle	113	Saidam	118	75,010	1:34.40	
1965	Gun Bow	5	W. Blum	130	Chieftain	117	Affectionately	121	72,540	1:34.40	
1966	Bold Lad	4	B. Baeza	132	Hedevar	113	Tio Viejo	115	75,140	1:34.20	
1967	Buckpasser	4	B. Baeza	130	Yonder	108	Impressive	113	70,980	1:34.60	
1968	In Reality	4	J.L. Rotz	124	Advocator	117	Full of Fun	110	70,135	1:35.00	
1969	Arts and Letters	3	J. Cruguet	111	Nodouble	129	Promise	119	75,725	1:34.00	
1970	Nodouble	5	J. Tejeira	126	Reviewer	123	Dewan	122	74,490	1:34.60	
1971	Tunex	5	J. Ruane	113	Protanto	112	Knight in Armor	114	72,960	1:35.80	
1972	Executioner	4	E. Belmonte	119	Bold Reasoning	123	Peace Corps	113	70,290	1:35.40	
1973	Tentam	4	J. Velasquez	116	Key to the Mint	127	King's Bishop	118	68,580	1:35.00	
1974	Arbees Boy	4	E. Maple	112	Forego	134	Timeless Moment	109	67,200	1:34.40	
1975	Gold and Myrrh	4	W. Blum	121	Stop the Music	124	Forego	136	66,840	1:33.60	
1976	Forego	6	H. Gustines	130	Master Derby	126	Lord Rebeau	119	66,660	1:34.80	
1977	Forego	7	W. Shoemaker	133	Co Host	111	Full Out	115	68,640	1:34.80	
1978	Cox's Ridge	4	E. Maple	130	Buckfinder	112	Quiet Little Table	118	66,180	1:34.60	
1979	State Dinner	4	C.J. McCarron	115	Dr. Patches	118	Sorry Lookin	113	64,980	1:34.00	
1980	Czaravich	4	L. Pincay Jr	126	State Dinner	117	Silent Cal	120	83,850	1:35.80	
1981	Fappiano	4	A. Cordero Jr	115	Irish Tower	127	Amber Pass	115	85,650	1:33.80	
1982	Conquistador Cielo	3	E. Maple	111	Silver Buck	111	Star Gallant	111	91,800	1:33.00	
1983	Star Choice	4	J. Velasquez	113	Tough Critic	110	John's Gold	111	145,200	1:33.80	
1984	Fit to Fight	5	J.D. Bailey	124	A Phenomenon	126	Moro	116	209,100	1:34.00	
1985	Forzando II	4	D. MacBeth	118	Mo Exception	113	Track Barron	125	207,600	1:34.40	
1986	Garthorn	4	R.Q. Meza	124	Love That Mac	117	Lady's Secret	120	179,700	1:33.60	
1987	Gulch	3	P. Day	110	King's Swan	121	Broad Brush	128	360,900	1:34.80	
1988	Gulch	4	J.A. Santos	125	Afleet	124	Stacked Pack	110	351,600	1:34.60	
1989	Proper Reality	4	J.D. Bailey	117	Seeking the Gold	126	Dancing Spree	113	353,400	1:34.00	
1990	Criminal Type	5	J.A. Santos	120	Housebuster	113	Easy Goer	127	357,000	1:34.40	117
1991	In Excess	4	P.A. Valenzuela	117	Rubiano	111	Gervaza	114	300,000	1:35.40	117
1992	Dixie Brass	3	J.M. Pezua	107	Pleasant Tap	119	In Excess	121	300,000	1:33.60	111
1993	Ibero	6	L. Pincay Jr	119	Bertrando	121	Alydeed	124	300,000	1:34.20	113
1994	Holy Bull	3	M.E. Smith	112	Cherokee Run	118	Devil His Due	122	300,000	1:33.80	122
1995	You and I	4	J.F. Chavez	112	Lite the Fuse	113	Our Emblem	114	300,000	1:34.60	114
1996	Honour and Glory	3	J.R.Velazquez	110	Lite the Fuse	122			240,000	1:32.80	111
					Afternoon Deelites	123					
1997	Langfuhr	5	J.F. Chavez	122	Western Winter	115	Northern Afleet	117	240,000	1:33.00	112
1998	Wild Rush	4	J.D. Bailey	119	Banker's Gold	115	Accelerator	113	300,000	1:33.50	118
1999	Sir Bear	6	J.R.Velazquez	117	Crafty Friend	114	Liberty Gold	114	300,000	1:34.55	114
2000	Yankee Victor	4	H. Castillo Jr	117	Honest Lady	112	Sir Bear	117	450,000	1:34.64	115
2001	Exciting Story	4	P. Husbands	115	Peeping Tom	119	Alannan	118	450,000	1:37.14	108
2002	Swept Overboard	5	J. Chavez	117	Aldebaran	115	Crafty C.T.	116	450,000	1:33.34	122
2003	Aldebaran	5	J.D. Bailey	119	Saarland	114	Peeping Tom	114	450,000	1:34.15	110

Beyer Index: 114.57

Distance 1 1/8 miles prior to 1897. Run at Morris Park prior to 1905; at Aqueduct from 1960-67, 1969, 1975

MILADY BREEDERS' CUP HANDICAP, 1 1/16 Miles, Fillies and Mares, 3-Year-Olds and Up, Hollywood Park, 2003 Purse: $211,800

Year	Winner	Age	Jockey	Wt.	Second	Wt.	Third	Wt.	Win Value	Time	Beyer
1952	A Gleam	3	P. Moreno	112	Two Lea	117	Spanish Cream	124	16,600	1:21.60	
1953	A Gleam	4	E. LeBlanc	122	Fortune Teller	119	Spanish Cream	115	13,300	1:22.80	
1954	Flitting Past	5	R. Lunn	104	Bubbley	110	Is Proud	115	13,150	1:36.60	
1955	Countess Fleet	4	J. Longden	121	Jet Lady	109	Alibhai Lynn	123	15,050	1:09.20	
1956	Speedy Edie	4	R. Neves	113	Solid Miss	115	Island Queen	110	17,450	1:10.00	
1957	Coverit	4	R. Neves	118	Pucker Up	120	Myrtle	107	12,850	1:09.20	
1958	Born Rich	5	R. York	115	Annie-Lu-San	111	Mateka	115	12,950	1:37.40	
1959	Honeys Gem	4	W. Shoemaker	126	La Plume	111	Penumbra	115	12,950	1:35.40	
1960	Silver Spoon	4	W. Shoemaker	126	Honeys Gem	120	La Plume	110	13,200	1:34.80	
1961	Mountain Glory	5	P. Moreno	113	Tritoma	119	Wiggle II	120	13,800	1:34.60	
1962	Linita	3	J. Longden	120	Bushel-n-Peck	119	Fun House	117	16,250	1:35.20	
1963	Fortunate Isle	4	J. Leonard	111	Savaii	112	Table Mate	122	15,550	1:35.80	
1964	Jalousie II	5	R. York	120	Savaii	117	Star Maggie	115	16,600	1:35.60	
1965	Savaii	6	W. Harmatz	118	Yes Please	113	Curious Clover	121	19,400	1:35.20	
1966	Fleet Treat	3	R. Menell	110	Ormea	114	Hi Hessie	107	20,700	1:36.00	
1967	Desert Trial	4	A. Maese	125	Natashka	123	April Dawn	118	15,700	1:42.40	
1968	Princessnesian	4	L. Pincay Jr	125	Desert Law	114	Courageously	107	18,850	1:42.40	
1969	Desert Law	5	L. Pincay Jr	118	Peggy's World	111	Luz del Sol	112	19,750	1:40.80	
1970	Everything Lovely	5	F. Alvarez	111	Opening Bid	114	Shake a Shadow	114	15,850	1:35.40	
1971	Street Dancer	4	R. Rosales	110			Manta	131	17,250	1:35.80	
	Opening Bid	4	J. Lambert	114							
1972	Typecast	6	V. Tejada	123	Balcony's Babe	114	Convenience	122	26,400	1:34.20	
1973	Minstrel Miss	6	D. Pierce	118	Susan's Girl	128	Pallisima	115	38,000	1:41.80	
1974	Twixt	5	W. Passmore	123	Tallahto	121	La Zanzara	121	33,900	1:41.00	
1975	Modus Vivendi	4	D. Pierce	121	Tizna	124	Mercy Dee	111	32,100	1:42.00	
1976	Bastonera II	5	L. Pincay Jr	117	Swingtime	120	Just a Kick	121	31,600	1:42.00	
1977	Cascadepia	4	S. Hawley	126	Rocky Trip	115	Just a Kick	118	31,250	1:40.80	

Year	Winner	Age	Jockey	Wt.	Second	Wt.	Third	Wt.	Win Value	Time	Beyer
1978	Taisez Vous	4	D. Pierce	127	Drama Critic	118	Sensational	121	32,150	1:41.80	
1979	Innuendo	5	D. Pierce	115	It's in the Air	112	Country Queen	121	32,700	1:41.20	
1980	Image of Reality	4	D.G. McHargue	117	It's in the Air	122	Fondre	113	36,050	1:40.20	
1981	Save Wild Life	4	C.J. McCarron	115	Princess Karenda	120	Swift Bird	115	65,700	1:42.80	
1982	Cat Girl	4	C.J. McCarron	114	Track Robbery	124	Ack's Secret	123	62,500	1:41.60	
1983	Marisma	5	K. Black	118	A Kiss for Luck	113	Sangue	123	63,100	1:42.20	
1984	Adored	4	L. Pincay Jr	119	Princess Rooney	122	Lass Trump	117	63,800	1:41.00	
1985	Adored	5	L. Pincay Jr	125	Lovlier Linda	120	Mitterand	120	73,500	1:33.60	
1986	Dontstop Themusic	6	D.G. McHargue	122	Magnificent Lindy	117	Truffles	110	63,500	1:48.80	
1987	Seldom Seen Sue	4	C.J. McCarron	117	Tiffany Lass	120	Frau Altiva	115	95,000	1:48.20	
1988	By Land By Sea	4	F. Toro	124	Invited Guest	114	Integra	121	89,200	1:43.60	
1989	Bayakoa	5	L. Pincay Jr	124	Flying Julia	113	Carita Tostada	115	91,500	1:42.00	
1990	Bayakoa	6	L. Pincay Jr	127	Fantastic Look	113	Kelly	110	89,700	1:41.20	
1991	Brought to Mind	4	P.A. Valenzuela	118	Luna Elegante	114	Vieille Vigne	117	95,800	1:41.60	
1992	Paseana	5	C.J. McCarron	125	Re Toss	115	Fowda	119	94,200	1:41.40	102
1993	Paseana	6	C.J. McCarron	125	Bold Windy	114	Re Toss	116	94,500	1:41.60	107
1994	Andestine	4	C.J. McCarron	116	Golden Klair	119	Zarani Sidi Anna	116	94,900	1:41.40	105
1995	Pirate's Revenge	4	C.W. Antley	116	Paseana	123	Private Persuasion	116	91,000	1:41.40	106
1996	Twice the Vice	5	C.J. McCarron	120	Jewel Princess	120	Urbane	117	110,100	1:40.80	113
1997	Listening	4	A. Solis	116	Chile Chatte	114	Exotic Wood	118	95,220	1:41.20	101
1998	I Ain't Bluffing	4	C.J. McCarron	120	Fleet Lady	119	Real Connection	112	158,640	1:42.16	102
1999	Gourmet Girl	4	E. Delahoussaye	115	Yolo Lady	115	Victory Stripes	117	112,440	1:40.97	109
2000	Riboletta	5	C.J. McCarron	120	Bordelaise	117	Excellent Meeting	121	121,860	1:42.01	110
2001	Lazy Slusan	6	V. Espinoza	119	Lady Melesi	116	Feverish	118	157,980	1:42.25	103
2002	Azeri	4	M. Smith	122	Affluent	119	Collect Call	115	126,840	1:42.02	109
2003	Azeri	5	M.E. Smith	125	Enjoy	114	Tropical Blossom	111	127,080	1:41.87	109

Beyer Index: 106.33

Distance 7 furlongs in 1952–53; 1 1/8 miles, 1986–87; 6 furlongs, 1955–57; 1 mile, 1954,1958–66, 1970–72, 1985

MOTHER GOOSE STAKES, 1 1/8 Miles, 3-Year-Old Fillies, Belmont Park, 2003 Purse: $300,000

Year	Winner	Age	Jockey	Wt.	Second	Wt.	Third	Wt.	Win Value	Time	Beyer
1957	Outer Space	3	W. Lester	112	Ambulance	112	Gold Finery	112	20,450	1:42.60	
1958	Idun	3	W. Hartack	118	Lopar	112	Lea Moon	113	18,420	1:43.60	
1959	Quill	3	P.J. Bailey	124	Toluene	118	Geechee Lou	112	18,127	1:49.40	
1960	Berlo	3	E. Guerin	114	Chalvedele	111	Make Sail	121	56,794	1:50.60	
1962	Cicada	3	W. Shoemaker	121	Firm Policy	121	Royal Patrice	121	56,014	1:50.00	
1963	Spicy Living	3	J. Combest	121	Smart Deb	121	Lamb Chop	121	59,621	1:50.40	
1964	Sceree	3	L. Adams	121	Face the Facts	121	Just Fancy That	121	58,646	1:50.80	
1965	Cordially	3	B. Baeza	121	What a Treat	121	Up Oars	121	63,180	1:51.60	
1966	Lady Pitt	3	W. Blum	121	Marking Time	121	Prides Profile	121	56,989	1:50.40	
1967	Furl Sail	3	J. Vasquez	121	Quillo Queen	121	Muse	121	63,570	1:49.60	
1968	Dark Mirage	3	M. Ycaza	121	Guest Room	121	Parida	121	55,672	1:49.40	
1969	Shuvee	3	J. Davidson	121	Hail to Patsy	121	Restless Tornado	121	56,599	1:50.20	
1970	Office Queen	3	C.H. Marquez	121	Cathy Honey	121	Missile Belle	121	77,756	1:49.80	
1971	Deceit	3	J.L. Rotz	121	Graffitti	121	Forward Gal	121	53,955	1:50.20	
1972	Wanda	3	J. Velasquez	121	Susan's Girl	121	Summer Guest	121	50,760	1:48.40	
1973	Windy's Daughter	3	E. Belmonte	121	Lady Love	121	North Broadway	121	52,965	1:48.40	
1974	Chris Evert	3	J. Velasquez	121	Maud Muller	121	Quaze Quilt	121	53,775	1:48.60	
1975	Ruffian	3	J. Vasquez	121	Sweet Old Girl	121	Sun and Snow	121	50,220	1:47.80	
1976	Girl in Love	3	J. Cruguet	121	Optimistic Gal	121	Ancient Fables	121	48,510	1:48.80	
1977	Road Princess	3	J. Cruguet	121	Mrs. Warren	121	Cum Laude Laurie	121	51,480	1:48.80	
1978	Caesar's Wish	3	D.R. Wright	121	Lakeville Miss	121	Tempest Queen	121	48,600	1:47.60	
1979	Davona Dale	3	J. Velasquez	121	Eloquent	121	Plankton	121	63,960	1:48.80	
1980	Sugar and Spice	3	J. Fell	121	Bold 'n Determined	121	Erin's Word	121	68,040	1:49.60	
1981	Wayward Lass	3	C.B. Asmussen	121	Heavenly Cause	121	Banner Gala	121	66,720	1:48.80	
1982	Cupecoy's Joy	3	A. Santiago	121	Christmas Past	121	Blush With Pride	121	69,120	1:48.40	
1983	Able Money	3	A. Graell	121	High Schemes	121	Far Flying	121	84,150	1:49.20	
1984	Life's Magic	3	J. Velasquez	121	Miss Oceana	121	Wild Applause	121	127,620	1:48.80	
1985	Mom's Command	3	A. Fuller	121	Le L'Argent	121	Willowy Mood	121	109,800	1:49.60	
1986	Life at the Top	3	J.A. Santos	121	Dynamic Star	121	Family Style	121	132,300	1:49.60	
1987	Fiesta Gal	3	A. Cordero Jr	121	Grecian Flight	121	Chic Shirine	121	150,240	1:50.20	
1988	Goodbye Halo	3	J. Velasquez	121	Make Change	121	Aptostar	121	142,320	1:49.80	
1989	Open Mind	3	A. Cordero Jr	121	Gorgeous	121	Nite of Fun	121	136,320	1:47.40	
1990	Go for Wand	3	R.P. Romero	121	Charon	121	Stella Madrid	121	136,500	1:48.80	104
1991	Meadow Star	3	J.D. Bailey	121	Lite Light	121	Nalees Pin	121	120,000	1:48.80	100
1992	Turnback the Alarm	3	C.W. Antley	121	Easy Now	121	Queen of Triumph	121	120,000	1:48.80	95
1993	Sky Beauty	3	M.E. Smith	121	Dispute	121	Silky Feather	121	120,000	1:49.60	102
1994	Lakeway	3	K.J. Desormeaux	121	Cinnamon Sugar	121	Inside Information	121	120,000	1:46.40	106
1995	Serena's Song	3	G.L. Stevens	121	Golden Bri	121	Forested	121	120,000	1:50.20	101
1996	Yanks Music	3	J.R. Velazquez	121	Escena	121	Cara Rafaela	121	120,000	1:47.80	100
1997	Ajina	3	M.E. Smith	121	Sharp Cat	121	Tomisue's Delight	121	120,000	1:48.40	101
1998	Jersey Girl	3	M.E. Smith	121	Keeper Hill	121	Banshee Breeze	121	120,000	1:47.77	103
1999	Dreams Gallore	3	R.J. Albarado	121	Oh What a Windfall	121	Better Than Honour	121	150,000	1:48.69	101

Year	Winner	Age	Jockey	Wt.	Second	Wt.	Third	Wt.	Win Value	Time	Beyer
2000	Secret Status	3	P. Day	121	Jostle	121	Finder's Fee	121	150,000	1:48.03	102
2001	Fleet Renee	3	J.R. Velazquez	121	Real Cozzy	121	Exogenous	121	150,000	1:47.19	105
2002	Nonsuch Bay	3	J. Bailey	121	Chamrousse	121	Seba	121	150,000	1:49.09	93
2003	Spoken Fur	3	J.D. Bailey	121	Yell	121	Final Round	121	180,000	1:50.41	104

Beyer Index: 101.21

Distance 1 1/16 miles prior to 1959. Run at Aqueduct 1963-67, 1969, 1975.

PACIFIC CLASSIC, 1 1/4 Miles, 3-Year-Olds and Up,
Del Mar, 2003 Purse: $980,000

Year	Winner	Age	Jockey	Wt.	Second	Wt.	Third	Wt.	Win Value	Time	Beyer
1991	Best Pal	3	P.A. Valenzuela	116	Twilight Agenda	124	Unbridled	124	550,000	1:59.80	118
1992	Missionary Ridge	5	K.J. Desormeaux	124	Defensive Play	124	Claret	124	550,000	2:00.80	110
1993	Bertrando	4	G.L. Stevens	124	Missionary Ridge	124	Best Pal	124	550,000	1:59.40	117
1994	Tinners Way	4	E. Delahoussaye	124	Best Pal	124	Dramatic Gold	117	550,000	1:59.40	111
1995	Tinners Way	5	E. Delahoussaye	124	Soul of the Matter	124	Blumin Affair	124	550,000	1:59.60	112
1996	Dare and Go	5	A. Solis	124	Cigar	124	Siphon	124	600,000	1:59.80	116
1997	Gentlemen	5	G.L. Stevens	124	Siphon	124	Crafty Friend	124	600,000	2:00.40	121
1998	Free House	4	C.J. McCarron	124	Gentlemen	124	Pacificbounty	124	600,000	2:00.29	117
1999	General Challenge	3	D.R. Flores	117	River Keen	124	Barter Town	124	600,000	2:00.57	119
2000	Skimming	4	G.K. Gomez	124	Tiznow	117	Ecton Park	124	600,000	2:01.22	117
2001	Skimming	5	G.K. Gomez	124	Dixie Dot Com	124	Dig For It	124	600,000	1:59.96	119
2002	Came Home	3	M.E. Smith	117	Momentum	124	Milwaukee Brew	124	600,000	2:01.45	116
2003	Candy Ride	4	J.A. Krone	124	Medaglia d'Oro	124	Fleetstreet Dancer	124	600,000	1:59.11	123

Beyer Index: 116.62

PERSONAL ENSIGN HANDICAP, 1 1/4 Miles, Fillies and Mares, 3-Year-Olds and Up,
Saratoga Race Course, 2003 Purse: $400,000

Year	Winner	Age	Jockey	Wt.	Second	Wt.	Third	Wt.	Win Value	Time	Beyer
1948	Carolyn A.	4	C. LeBlanc	114	Gallorette	126	Red Shoes	107	19,450	1:46.80	
1949	But Why Not	5	D. Gorman	116	Allie's Pal	111	Conniver	126	19,600	1:44.80	
1950	Red Camelia	4	P. Milligan	110	Roman Candle	113	Nell K.	123	20,250	1:45.40	
1951	Renew	4	B. Green	112	Thelma Burger	109	Next Move	126	23,750	1:50.60	
1952	Next Move	5	E. Guerin	126	Thelma Burger	110	Kiss Me Kate	123	22,900	1:51.20	
1953	Kiss Me Kate	5	D. Gorman	126	Parading Lady	123	La Corredora	123	24,350	1:50.80	
1954	Parlo	3	T. Atkinson	125	Riverina	115	Spinning Top	110	24,700	1:53.40	
1955	Rare Treat	3	R. Mikkonen	112	Searching	118	White Cross	108	24,900	1:50.80	
1956	Blue Banner	4	W. Boland	115	Happy Princess	109	Manotick	119	19,400	1:49.40	
1957	Gay Life	4	J. Ruane	108	Dotted Line	113	Little Pache	111	20,300	1:50.40	
1958	Hoosier Honey	4	J. Ruane	111	Lopar	112	Mlle. Dianne	113	18,290	1:45.40	
1959	Polamby	4	P. Anderson	116	Merry Hill	111	Starlet Miss	112	17,445	1:50.80	
1960	Clear Road	3	R. York	111	Soladesca	118	Big Effort	114	18,160	1:36.40	
1961	Oil Royalty	3	H. Woodhouse	109	Frimanaha	113	Seven Thirty	116	18,525	1:36.60	
1962	Pocosaba	5	W. Boland	114	Lincoln Center	113	Oil Royalty	113	18,265	1:52.00	
1963	Lamb Chop	3	M. Ycaza	126	Waltz Song	123	Dupage Lady	108	18,167	1:49.80	
1964	Steeple Jill	3	J. Ruane	113	Gold Frame	112	Treachery	110	19,305	1:51.80	
1965	Sailor Princess	3	G. Mineau	111	Straight Deal	118	Petticoat	114	35,880	1:52.20	
1966	Straight Deal	4	R. Ussery	118	Mac's Sparkler	113	Belle de Nuit	112	36,595	1:49.60	
1967	Politely	4	B. Baeza	121	Green Glade	114	Princessnesian	111	37,375	1:53.00	
1968	Politely	5	A. Cordero Jr	131	Obeah	112	Serene Queen	114	37,700	1:49.60	
1969	Amerigo Lady	5	J. Velasquez	121	Shuvee	122	Obeah	120	36,790	1:50.00	
1970	Obeah	5	J.L. Rotz	117	Taken Aback	123	Lunation	114	33,960	1:51.20	
1971	Kittiwake	3	H. Gustines	117	Blessing Angelica	112	Sea Saga	118	34,080	1:50.20	
1972	Manta	6	A. Cordero Jr	115	Society Column	110	Kittwake	122	37,660	1:50.00	
1972	Aladancer	4	A. Cordero Jr	114	Summit Joy	108	Sea Saga	111	27,660	1:50.80	
1973	Aglimmer	4	M. Venezia	115	Garland of Roses	111	Cathy Baby	120	36,150	1:49.40	
1974	Lie Low	3	J. Velasquez	116	Aglimmer	116	D. O. Lady	115	27,840	1:49.00	
1974	Twixt	5	W.J. Passmore	121	Garland of Roses	114	Fairway Flyer	124	28,290	1:49.80	
1975	Lie Low	4	J. Velasquez	115	Princesse Grey	114	Carolerno	112	35,910	2:15.20	
1976	Sugar Plum Time	4	A. Cordero Jr	113	Ten Cents a Dance	110	Quacker	111	32,610	1:51.00	
1977	Water Malone	3	J.L. Samyn	121	Northernette	120	Sweet Bernice	113	32,280	1:50.40	
1978	Mrs. Warren	4	J. Velasquez	113	Water Malone	121	One Sum	121	32,190	1:51.40	
1979	Catherine's Bet	4	D. Montoya	113	Water Malone	117	Miss Baja	114	32,340	1:50.20	
1980	Relaxing	4	J. Velasquez	118	Sugar and Spice	115	Plankton	121	33,540	1:49.20	
1981	Tina Tina Too	3	D. MacBeth	114	Explorare	114	Office Wife	113	33,060	1:51.00	
1982	Number	4	E. Maple	114	Sintrillium	112	Norsan	112	32,340	1:51.40	
1983	Chieftain's Command	4	A. Cordero Jr	117	Adept	110	Sintrillium	116	34,440	1:51.60	
1984	Solar Halo	3	R.G. Davis	110	It's Fine	109	Quixotic Lady	115	53,640	1:49.20	
1985	Lady on the Run	3	A. Cordero Jr	109	Verbality	112	Halloween Queen	112	51,210	1:52.00	
1986	Shocker T.	4	G. St. Leon	124	Bharal	115	Natania	115	66,840	1:50.00	
1987	Coup de Fusil	5	A. Cordero Jr	116	Clabber Girl	113	I'm Sweets	118	83,700	1:49.20	
1988	Rose's Cantina	4	J.A. Santos	111	Ms. Eloise	115	Clabber Girl	120	67,080	1:49.80	
1989	Colonial Water	4	A. Cordero Jr	114	Topicount	116	Rose's Cantina	119	67,080	1:50.00	
1990	Personal Business	4	C.W. Antley	111	Buy the Firm	112	Lady Hoolihan	110	70,200	1:51.20	88
1991	Fit to Scout	4	C.W. Antley	114	Train Robbery	112	Her She Shawklit	111	120,000	1:50.20	96

Year	Winner	Age	Jockey	Wt.	Second	Wt.	Third	Wt.	Win Value	Time	Beyer
1992	Quick Mischief	6	C. Perret	113	Versailles Treaty	122	Sahred Interest	111	120,000	1:47.80	106
1993	You'd Be Surprised	4	J.D. Bailey	115	Avian Assembly	111	Gray Cashmere	114	90,000	1:48.40	105
1994	Link River	4	J.A. Krone	114	You'd Be Surprised	120	Dispute	119	120,000	1:50.40	109
1995	Heavenly Prize	4	P. Day	127	Forced Bid	108	Cinnamon Sugar	114	120,000	2:04.00	106
1996	Urbane	4	A. Solis	119	Shoop	114	Frolic	113	180,000	2:03.00	107
1997	Clear Mandate	5	M.E. Smith	115	Shoop	111	Power Play	117	210,000	2:03.60	105
1998	Tomisue's Delight	4	P. Day	115	Tuzla	114	Once Rich Lady	114	240,000	2:04.08	104
1999	Beautiful Pleasure	4	J.F. Chavez	113	Banshee Breeze	124	Keeper Hill	118	240,000	2:02.57	112
2000	Beautiful Pleasure	5	J.F. Chavez	124	Heritage of Gold	124	Pentatonic	113	240,000	2:03.77	103

Back in Shape finished second but was disqualified and placed fourth

Year	Winner	Age	Jockey	Wt.	Second	Wt.	Third	Wt.	Win Value	Time	Beyer
2001	Pompeii		R. Migliore	117	Beautiful Pleasure	117	Irving's Baby	117	240,000	2:04.60	106
2002	Summer Colony	4	J.R. Velazquez	120	Transcendental	114	Dancethruthedawn	120	240,000	2:03.15	107
2003	Passing Shot	4	J.A. Santos	114	Wild Spirit	122	Miss Linda	114	240,000	2:03.33	92

Beyer Index: 103.29

Distance 1 mile, 1960–61; 1 1/16 miles, 1948–51, 1958; 1 1/8 miles, 1952–57, 1959, 1962–74, 1976–94; 1 3/8 miles, 1975. Run as Firenze Handicap prior to 1987; as John A. Morris Handicap, 1987–98

OGDEN PHIPPS HANDICAP, 1 1/16 Miles, Fillies and Mares, 3-Year-Olds and Up,
Belmont Park, 2003 Purse: $300,000

Year	Winner	Age	Jockey	Wt.	Second	Wt.	Third	Wt.	Win Value	Time	Beyer
1961	Disperse	4	W. Boland	111	Don Poggio	125	Air Medal	111	17,712	2:28.40	
1970	Ta Wee	4	J.L. Rotz	132	Process Shot	127	Grey Slacks	111	18,297	1:10.00	
1971	Cold Comfort	4	M. Venezia	118	Process Shot	124	Dorothy Joan	114	19,920	1:11.60	
1972	Summer Guest	3	J. Vasquez	111	Grafitti	115	Judith	110	17,415	1:47.80	
1973	Light Hearted	4	E. Nelson	123	Inca Queen	116	Blessing Angelica	117	32,880	1:48.80	
1974	Poker Night	4	J. Velasquez	114	Krislin	115	Fairway Flyer	117	33,300	1:48.60	
1975	Raisela	4	E. Maple	114	Pass a Glance	114	Sarsar	115	33,510	1:49.20	
1976	Proud Delta	4	J. Velasquez	124	Garden Verse	111	Let Me Linger	114	33,690	1:48.40	
1977	Pacific Princess	4	E. Maple	112	Mississippi Mud	114	Fleet Victress	113	32,700	1:49.20	
1978	Dottie's Doll	5	J. Vasquez	115	One Sum	123	Water Malone	119	32,040	1:47.60	
1979	Pearl Necklace	5	J. Fell	122	Miss Baja	115	Sweet Woodruff	108	31,470	1:48.60	
1980	Misty Gallore	4	D. MacBeth	125	Blitey	115	What'll I Do	110	32,760	1:48.80	
1981	Wistful	4	D. Brumfield	119	Chain Bracelet	119	Love Sign	115	64,200	1:49.80	
1982	Love Sign	5	R. Hernandez	123	Anti Lib	116	Jameela	122	65,280	1:48.00	
1983	Number	4	E. Maple	117	Dance Number	114	Broom Dance	121	65,880	1:48.40	
1984	Heatherten	5	S. Maple	118	Quixotic Lady	118	Thirty Flags	114	92,400	1:49.20	
1985	Heatherten	6	R. Romero	124	Life's Magic	122	Sefa's Beauty	120	84,300	1:48.80	
1986	Endear	4	E. Maple	115	Lady's Secret	128	Ride Sally	124	97,650	1:48.60	
1987	Catatonic	5	D.A. Miller Jr.	116	Ms. Eloise	118	Steal a Kiss	111	137,520	1:50.00	
1988	Personal Ensign	4	R.P. Romero	123	Hometown Queen	109	Clabber Girl	118	131,760	1:47.60	
1989	Rose's Cantina	5	J. Cruguet	117	Make Change	111	Colonial Waters	114	135,120	1:48.60	
1990	Fantastic Find	4	C. Perret	113	Mistaurian	113	Dreamy Mimi	113	139,680	1:50.00	102
1991	A Wild Ride	4	M.E. Smith	120	Fit to Scout	115	Buy the Firm	121	120,000	1:49.00	102
1992	Missy's Mirage	4	E. Maple	118	Harbour Club	110	Versailles Treaty	119	120,000	1:47.00	109
1993	Turnback the Alarm	4	C.W. Antley	119	Deputation	117	You'd Be Surprised	112	90,000	1:48.00	100
1994	Sky Beauty	4	M.E. Smith	128	You'd Be Surprised	118	Schway Baby Sway	109	90,000	1:47.40	107
1995	Heavenly Prize	4	P. Day	122	Little Buckles	111	Sky Beauty	124	90,000	1:43.20	111
1996	Serena's Song	4	J.D. Bailey	125	Shoop	115	Restored Hope	114	120,000	1:41.60	104
1997	Hidden Lake	4	R. Migliore	117	Twice the Vice	121	Jewel Princess	124	150,000	1:40.80	119
1998	Mossflower	4	R.G. Davis	114	Glitter Woman	120	Colonial Minstrel	118	150,000	1:39.90	118
1999	Sister Act	4	P. Day	117	Beautiful Pleasure	117	Catinca	122	150,000	1:40.79	112
2000	Beautiful Pleasure	5	J.F. Chavez	124	Pentatonic	112	Roza Robata	115	150,000	1:41.54	109
2001	Critical Eye	4	M.J. Luzzi	115	Jostle	117	Apple of Kent	117	150,000	1:42.18	104
2002	Raging Fever	4	J.R. Velazquez	120	Transcendental	113	Two Item Limit	117	180,000	1:41.75	102
2003	Sightseek	4	J.D. Bailey	118	Take Charge Lady	119	Mandy's Gold	118	180,000	1:40.89	110

Beyer Index: 107.79

Run as the Hempstead Handicap until 2002. Distance 1 1/2 miles (for both sexes) in 1961; 6 furlongs in 1970–71

PIMLICO SPECIAL HANDICAP, 1 3/16 Miles, 4-Year-Olds and Up,
Pimlico Race Course, 2003 Purse: $600,000

Year	Winner	Age	Jockey	Wt.	Second	Wt.	Third	Wt.	Win Value	Time	Beyer
1937	War Admiral	3	C. Kurtsinger	128	Masked Admiral	100	War Minstrel	109	5,680	1:58.80	
1938	Seabiscuit	5	G. Woolf	120	War Admiral	120			15,000	1:56.60	
1939	Challedon	3	E. Arcaro	120	Kayak II	126	Cravat	126	10,000	1:59.00	
1940	Challedon	4	G. Woolf	126	Can't Wait	126			10,000	2:03.20	
1941	Market Wise	3	W. Eads	120	Haltal	126			10,000	1:58.80	
1942	Whirlaway	4	G. Woolf	126					10,000	2:05.40	
1943	Shut Out	4	E. Arcaro	126	Slide Rule	120	Fairy Manhurst	120	25,000	2:00.20	
1944	Twilight Tear	3	D. Dodson	117	Devil Diver	126	Megogo	126	25,000	1:56.60	
1945	Armed	4	D. Dodson	126	First Fiddle	126	Stymie	126	25,000	1:58.80	
1946	Assault	3	E. Arcaro	120	Stymie	126	Bridal Flower	117	25,000	1:57.00	
1947	Fervent	3	A. Snider	120	Cosmic Bomb	120	Armed	126	25,000	1:58.40	
1948	Citation	3	E. Arcaro	120					10,000	1:59.80	
1949	Capot	3	T. Atkinson	120	Coaltown	126			15,000	1:56.80	

Year	Winner	Age	Jockey	Wt.	Second	Wt.	Third	Wt.	Win Value	Time	Beyer
1950	One Hitter	4	T. Atkinson	126	Chicle II	126	Abstract	126	15,000	1:58.60	
1951	Bryan G.	4	O. Scurlock	126	County Delight	126	Call Over	126	15,000	1:57.40	
1952	General Staff	4	G. Lasswell	126	One Hitter	126			25,000	1:57.40	
1953	Tom Fool	4	T. Atkinson	126	Navy Page	120	Alerted	126	30,000	1:55.80	
1954	Helioscope	3	S. Boulmetis	122	Hasseyampa	122	Fisherman	122	35,000	1:59.00	
1955	Sailor	3	H. Woodhouse	123	Mister Gus	126	Social Outcast	126	40,000	1:57.60	
1956	Summer Tan	4	D. Erb	126	Midafternoon	126	Find	126	35,000	1:56.60	
1957	Promised Land	3	W. Hartack	123	Tick Tock	126	Third Brother	126	35,000	1:57.40	
1958	Vertex	4	S. Boulmetis	126	Sharpsburg	126	Better Bee	126	35,000	2:00.60	
1988	Bet Twice	4	C. Perret	124	Lost Code	126	Cryptoclearance	121	425,000	1:54.20	
1989	Blushing John	4	P. Day	117	Proper Reality	118	Granacus	113	420,000	1:53.20	
1990	Criminal Type	5	J.A. Santos	117	Ruhlmann	124	De Roche	114	600,000	1:53.00	117
1991	Farma Way	4	G.L. Stevens	119	Summer Squall	120	Jolie's Halo	119	450,000	1:52.40	123
1992	Strike the Gold	4	C. Perret	114	Fly So Free	116	Twilight Agenda	122	420,000	1:54.80	111
1993	Devil His Due	4	W.H. McCauley	120	Valley Crossing	112	Pistols and Roses	114	360,000	1:55.40	108
1994	As Indicated	4	R.G. Davis	120	Devil His Due	121	Valley Crossing	113	360,000	1:55.00	115
1995	Cigar	5	J.D. Bailey	122	Devil His Due	121	Concern	121	360,000	1:53.60	114
1996	Star Standard	4	P. Day	111	Key of Luck	120	Geri	118	360,000	1:54.40	111
1997	Gentlemen	5	G.L. Stevens	122	Skip Away	119	Tejano Run	114	360,000	1:53.00	126
1998	Skip Away	5	J.D. Bailey	128	Precocity	115	Hot Brush	113	450,000	1:54.26	118
1999	Real Quiet	4	G.L. Stevens	120	Free House	124	Fred Bear Claw	113	300,000	1:54.31	113
2000	Golden Missile	5	K.J. Desormeaux	116	Pleasant Breeze	113	Lemon Drop Kid	120	450,000	1:54.65	115
2001	Include	4	J.D. Bailey	114	Albert the Great	121	Pleasant Breeze	114	450,000	1:55.61	117
2003	Mineshaft	4	R.J. Albarado	121	Western Pride	116	Judge's Case	113	400,000	1:56.16	118

Beyer Index: 115.85

For 3-year-olds in 1937, 1954; for 4-year-olds and up, 1988–97; Not run 1959–1987, 2002

PREAKNESS STAKES, 1 3/16 Miles, 3-Year-Olds,
Pimlico Race Course, 2003 Purse: $1,000,000

Year	Winner	Age	Jockey	Wt.	Second	Wt.	Third	Wt.	Win Value	Time	Beyer
1873	Survivor	3	G. Barbee	110	John Boulger	110	Artist	110	1,850	2:43.00	
1874	Culpepper	3	W. Donohue	110	King Amadeus	110	Scratch	110	1,900	2:56.20	
1875	Tom Ochiltree	3	L. Hughes	110	Viator	110	Bay Final	110	1,900	2:43.20	
1876	Shirley	3	G. Barbee	110	Rappahannock	110	Algerine	110	1,950	2:44.60	
1877	Cloverbrook	3	C. Holloway	110	Bombast	110	Lucifer	110	1,650	2:45.20	
1878	Duke of Magenta	3	C. Holloway	110	Bayard	110	Albert	110	2,150	2:41.60	
1879	Harold	3	L. Hughes	110	Jericho	110	Rochester	110	2,550	2:40.20	
1880	Grenada	3	L. Hughes	110	Oden	110	Emily F.	110	2,000	2:40.20	
1881	Saunterer	3	W. Costello	110	Compensation	107	Baltic	110	1,950	2:40.20	
1882	Vanguard	3	W. Costello	110	Heck	110	Col. Watson	107	1,250	2:44.20	
1883	Jacobus	3	G. Barbee	110	Parnell	110			1,635	2:42.20	
1884	Knight of Ellerslie	3	S.H. Fisher	110	Welcher	110			1,905	2:39.20	
1885	Tecumseh	3	J. McLaughlin	118	Wickham	118	John C.	118	2,160	2:49.00	
1886	The Bard	3	S.H. Fisher	118	Eurus	118	Elkwood	118	2,050	2:45.00	
1887	Dubine	3	W. Donohue	118	Mahoney	115	Raymond	118	1,675	2:39.20	
1888	Refund	3	F. Littlefield	118	Colt by Ten Broeck	118	Glendale	118	1,185	2:49.00	
1889	Buddhist	3	H. Anderson	118	Japhet	115			1,130	2:17.20	
1890	Montague	5	W. Martin	103	Philosophy	105	Barrister	104	1,215	2:36.60	
1894	Assignee	3	F. Taral	122	Potentate	117	Ed kearney	117	1,830	1:49.20	
1895	Belmar	3	F. Taral	115	April Fool	105	Sue Kittie	110	1,350	1:50.20	
1896	Margrave	3	H. Griffin	115	Hamilton II	107	Intermission	110	1,350	1:51.00	
1897	Paul Kauvar	3	Thorpe	108	Elkins	103	On Deck	108	1,500	1:51.20	
1898	Sly Fox	3	W. Simms	120	The Huguenot	120	Nuto	120	1,500	1:49.60	
1899	Half Time	3	R. Clawson	104	Filigrane	120	Lackland	107	1,580	1:47.00	
1900	Hindus	3	H. Spencer	110	Sarmatian	106	Ten Candies	106	1,900	1:48.40	
1901	The Parader	3	Landry	118	Sadie S.	103	Dr. Barlow	118	1,605	1:47.20	
1902	Old England	3	L. Jackson	115	Maj. Daingerfield	108	Namtor	118	2,240	1:45.80	
1903	Flocarline	3	W. Gannon	113	Mackey Dwyer	108	Rightful	118	1,875	1:44.80	
1904	Bryn Mawr	3	Hildebrand	108	Wotan	108	Dolly Spanker	115	2,355	1:44.20	
1905	Cairngorm	3	W. Davis	114	Kiamesha	104	Coy Maid	109	2,145	1:45.80	
1906	Whimsical	3	W. Miller	108	Content	103	Larable	103	2,355	1:45.00	
1907	Don Enrique	3	G. Mountain	107	Ethon	115	Zambesi	110	2,260	1:45.40	
1908	Royal Tourist	3	E. Dugan	112	Live Wire	108	Robert Cooper	101	2,455	1:46.40	
1909	Effendi	3	W. Doyle	116	Fashion Plate	111	Hill Top	111	2,725	1:39.00	
1910	Layminster	3	Estep	84	Dalhousie	110	Sager	110	2,800	1:40.20	
1911	Watervale	3	E. Dugan	112	Zeus	118	The Nigger	107	2,700	1:51.00	
1912	Col. Holloway	3	C. Turner	107	Bwana Tumbo	120	Tipsand	110	1,450	1:56.60	
1913	Buskin	3	Butwell	117	Kleburne	111	Barnegat	104	1,670	1:53.40	
1914	Holiday	3	A. Schuttinger	108	Brave Cunarder	112	Defendum	106	1,355	1:53.80	
1915	Rhine Maiden	3	D. Hoffman	104	Half Rock	100	Runes	116	1,275	1:58.00	
1916	Damrosch	3	L. McAtee	115	Greenwood	107	Achievement	126	1,380	1:54.80	
1917	Kalitan	3	E. Haynes	117	Al M. Dick	116	Kentucky Boy	116	4,800	1:54.40	
1918	War Cloud	3	J. Loftus	117	Sunny Slope	107	Lanius	110	12,250	1:53.60	
1918	Jack Hare Jr.	3	C. Peak	115	The Porter	107	Kate Bright	105	11,250	1:53.40	

Year	Winner	Age	Jockey	Wt.	Second	Wt.	Third	Wt.	Win Value	Time Beyer
1919	Sir Barton	3	J. Loftus	126	Eternal	126	Sweep On	126	24,500	1:53.00
1920	Man o' War	3	C. Kummer	126	Upset	122	Wildair	114	2,300	1:51.60
1921	Broomspun	3	F. Coltiletti	114	Polly Ann	110	Jeg	114	43,000	1:54.20
1922	Pillory	3	L. Morris	114	Hea	114	June Grass	114	51,003	1:51.60
1923	Vigil	3	B. Marinelli	114	Gen. Thatcher	114	Rialto	114	52,000	1:53.60
1924	Nellie Morse	3	J. Merimee	121	Transmute	126	Mad Play	126	54,000	1:57.20
1925	Coventry	3	C. Kummer	126	Backbone	126	Almadel	126	52,700	1:59.00
1926	Display	3	J. Maiben	126	Blondin	126	Mars	126	53,625	1:59.80
1927	Bostonian	3	A. Abel	126	Sir Harry	126	Whiskery	126	53,100	2:01.60
1928	Victorian	3	R. Workman	126	Toro	126	Solace	126	60,000	2:00.20
1929	Dr. Freeland	3	L. Schaefer	126	Minotaur	126	African	126	52,325	2:01.60
1930	Gallant Fox	3	E. Sande	126	Crack Brigade	126	Snowflake	121	51,925	2:00.60
1931	Mate	3	G. Ellis	126	Twenty Grand	126	Ladder	126	48,225	1:59.00
1932	Burgoo King	3	E. James	126	Tick On	126	Boatswain	126	50,375	1:59.80
1933	Head Play	3	C. Kurtsinger	126	Ladysman	126	Utopia	126	26,850	2:00.40
1934	High Quest	3	R. Jones	126	Cavalcade	126	Discovery	126	25,175	1:58.20
1935	Omaha	3	W. Saunders	126	Firethorn	126	Psychic Bid	126	25,325	1:58.40
1936	Bold Venture	3	G. Woolf	126	Granville	126	Jean Bart	126	27,325	1:59.00
1937	War Admiral	3	C. Kurtsinger	126	Pompoon	126	Flying Scot	126	45,600	1:58.40
1938	Dauber	3	M. Peters	126	Cravat	126	Menow	126	51,875	1:59.80
1939	Challedon	3	G. Seabo	126	Gilded Knight	126	Volitant	126	53,710	1:59.80
1940	Bimelech	3	F.A. Smith	126	Mioland	126	Gallahadion	126	53,230	1:58.60
1941	Whirlaway	3	E. Arcaro	126	King Cole	126	Our Boots	126	49,365	1:58.80
1942	Alsab	3	B. James	126	Requested	126			58,175	1:57.00
					Sun Again	126				
1943	Count Fleet	3	J. Longden	126	Blue Swords	126	Vincentive	126	43,190	1:57.40
1944	Pensive	3	C. McCreary	126	Platter	126	Stir Up	126	60,075	1:59.20
1945	Polynesian	3	W.D. Wright	126	Hoop Jr.	126	Darby Dieppe	126	66,170	1:58.80
1946	Assault	3	W. Mehrtens	126	Lord Boswell	126	Hampden	126	96,620	2:01.40
1947	Faultless	3	D. Dodson	126	On Trust	126	Phalanx	126	98,005	1:59.00
1948	Citation	3	E. Arcaro	126	Vulcan's Forge	126	Bovard	126	91,870	2:02.40
1949	Capot	3	T. Atkinson	126	Palestinian	126	Noble Impulse	126	79,985	1:56.00
1950	Hill Prince	3	E. Arcaro	126	Middleground	126	Dooly	126	56,115	1:59.20
1951	Bold	3	E. Arcaro	126	Counterpoint	126	Alerted	126	83,110	1:56.40
1952	Blue Man	3	C. McCreary	126	Jampol	126	One Count	126	86,135	1:57.40
1953	Native Dancer	3	E. Guerin	126	Jamie K.	126	Royal Bay Gem	126	65,200	1:57.80
1954	Hasty Road	3	J. Adams	126	Correlation	126	Hasseyampa	126	91,600	1:57.40
1955	Nashua	3	E. Arcaro	126	Saratoga	126	Traffic Judge	126	67,550	1:54.60
1956	Fabius	3	W. Hartack	126	Needles	126	No Regrets	126	84,250	1:58.40
1957	Bold Ruler	3	E. Arcaro	126	Iron Liege	126	Inside Tract	126	66,300	1:56.20
1958	Tim Tam	3	I. Valenzuela	126	Lincoln Road	126	Gone Fishin'	126	98,950	1:57.20
1959	Royal Orbit	3	W. Harmatz	126	Sword Dancer	126	Dunce	126	137,800	1:57.00
1960	Bally Ache	3	R. Ussery	126	Victoria Park	126	Celtic Ash	126	122,600	1:57.60
1961	Carry Back	3	J. Sellers	126	Globemaster	126	Crozier	126	126,200	1:57.60
1962	Greek Money	3	J.L. Rotz	126	Ridan	126	Roman Line	126	135,800	1:56.20
1963	Candy Spots	3	W. Shoemaker	126	Chateaugay	126	Never Bend	126	127,500	1:56.20
1964	Northern Dancer	3	W. Hartack	126	The Scoundrel	126	Hill Rise	126	124,200	1:56.80
1965	Tom Rolfe	3	R. Turcotte	126	Dapper Dan	126	Hail to All	126	128,100	1:56.20
1966	Kauai King	3	D. Brumfield	126	Stupendous	126	Amberoid	126	129,000	1:55.40
1967	Damascus	3	W. Shoemaker	126	In Reality	126	Proud Clarion	126	151,500	1:55.20
1968	Forward Pass	3	I. Valenzuela	126	Out of the Way	126	Nodouble	126	142,700	1:56.80
	Dancer's Image finished third but was disqualified									
1969	Majestic Prince	3	W. Hartack	126	Arts and Letters	126	Jay Ray	126	129,500	1:55.60
1970	Personality	3	E. Belmonte	126	My Dad George	126	Silent Screen	126	151,300	1:56.20
1971	Canonero II	3	G. Avila	126	Eastern Fleet	126	Jim French	126	137,400	1:54.00
1972	Bee Bee Bee	3	E. Nelsom	126	No Le Hace	126	Key to the Mint	126	135,300	1:55.60
1973	Secretariat	3	R. Turcotte	126	Sham	126	Our Native	126	129,900	1:55.00
1974	Little Current	3	M.A. Rivera	126	Neapolitan Way	126	Cannonade	126	156,500	1:54.60
1975	Master Derby	3	D.G. McHargue	126	Foolish Pleasure	126	Diabolo	126	158,100	1:56.40
1976	Elocutionist	3	J. Lively	126	Play the Red	126	Bold Forbes	126	129,700	1:55.00
1977	Seattle Slew	3	J. Cruguet	126	Iron Constitution	126	Run Dusty Run	126	138,600	1:54.40
1978	Affirmed	3	S. Cauthen	126	Alydar	126	Believe It	126	136,200	1:54.40
1979	Spectacular Bid	3	R.J. Franklin	126	Golden Act	126	Screen King	126	165,300	1:54.20
1980	Codex	3	A. Cordero Jr	126	Genuine Risk	121	Colonel Moran	126	180,600	1:54.20
1981	Pleasant Colony	3	J. Velasquez	126	Bold Ego	126	Paristo	126	200,800	1:54.60
1982	Aloma's Ruler	3	J.L. Kaenel	126	Linkage	126	Cut Away	126	209,900	1:55.40
1983	Deputed Testamony	3	D.A. Miller Jr.	126	Desert Wine	126	High Honors	126	251,200	1:55.40
1984	Gate Dancer	3	A. Cordero Jr	126	Play On	126	Fight Over	126	243,600	1:53.60
1985	Tank's Prospect	3	P. Day	126	Chief's Crown	126	Eternal Prince	126	423,200	1:53.40
1986	Snow Chief	3	A. Solis	126	Ferdinand	126	Broad Brush	126	411,900	1:54.80
1987	Alysheba	3	C.J. McCarron	126	Bet Twice	126	Cryptoclearance	126	421,100	1:55.80
1988	Risen Star	3	E. Delahoussaye	126	Brian's Time	126	Winning Colors	121	413,700	1:56.20
1989	Sunday Silence	3	P.A. Valenzuela	126	Easy Goer	126	Rock Point	126	438,230	1:53.80

Year	Winner	Age	Jockey	Wt.	Second	Wt.	Third	Wt.	Win Value	Time	Beyer
1990	Summer Squall	3	P. Day	126	Unbridled	126	Mister Frisky	126	445,900	1:53.60	
1991	Hansel	3	J.D. Bailey	126	Corporate Report	126	Mane Minister	126	432,770	1:54.00	117
1992	Pine Bluff	3	C.J. McCarron	126	Alydeed	126	Casual Lies	126	484,120	1:55.60	104
1993	Prairie Bayou	3	M.E. Smith	126	Cherokee Run	126	El Bakan	126	471,835	1:56.60	98
1994	Tabasco Cat	3	P. Day	126	Go for Gin	126	Concern	126	447,720	1:56.40	112
1995	Timber Country	3	P. Day	126	Oliver's Twist	126	Thunder Gulch	126	446,810	1:54.40	106
1996	Louis Quatorze	3	P. Day	126	Skip Away	126	Editor's Note	126	458,120	1:53.40	112
1997	Silver Charm	3	G.L. Stevens	126	Free House	126	Captain Bodgit	126	488,150	1:54.80	118
1998	Real Quiet	3	K.J. Desormeaux	126	Victory Gallop	126	Classic Cat	126	650,000	1:54.75	111
1999	Charismatic	3	C.W. Antley	126	Menifee	126	Badge	126	650,000	1:55.32	107
2000	Red Bullet	3	J.D. Bailey	126	Fusiachi Pegasus	126	Impeachment	126	650,000	1:56.04	109
2001	Point Given	3	G.L. Stevens	126	A P Valentine	126	Congaree	126	650,000	1:55.51	111
2002	War Emblem	3	V. Espinoza	126	Magic Weisner	126	Proud Citizen	126	650,000	1:56.36	109
2003	Funny Cide	3	J.A. Santos	126	Midway Road	126	Scrimshaw	126	650,000	1:55.61	114

Beyer Index: 109.85

Distance 1 1/2 miles prior to 1894; 1 1/4 miles in 1889; 1 1/16 miles from 1894–1900, 1908; 1 mile 70 yards, 1901–07; 1 mile, 1909–10; 1 1/8 miles, 1911–24. For 3-year-olds and up in 1890. Run at Morris Park in 1890; at Gravesend, NY, 1894–1908

PRIORESS, 6 Furlongs,
3-Year-Old Fillies, Belmont Park, 2003 Purse: $200,000

Year	Winner	Age	Jockey	Wt.	Second	Wt.	Third	Wt.	Win Value	Time	Beyer
1948	Itsabet	3	R. Permane	116	Picnic Lunch	116	Alablue	113	17,150	1:13.40	
1949	Nell K.	3	D. Dodson	116	Imacomin	116	Sunny Vale	112	12,100	1:13.40	
1950	Next Move	3	E. Guerin	115	Honey's Gal	116	Miss Degree	112	12,525	1:12.20	
1951	Ruddy	3	T. Atkinson	112	Who Dini	112	Fair Self	112	11,387	1:12.60	
1951	Tilly Rose	3	W. Boland	112	Sweet Talk	115	Miss Meggy	112	11,227	1:11.40	
1952	Landmark	3	D. Gorman	121	Jubling	121	Parading Lady	121	12,250	1:12.20	
1953	Grecian Queen	3	E. Guerin	121	Tritium	121	Flitatious	121	17,300	1:13.40	
1954	Trisong	3	H. Woodhouse	121	Open Sesame	121	Incidentally	121	16,150	1:12.40	
1955	Sometime Thing	3	E. Guerin	121	Minnie Moocher	121	Two Stars	121	17,000	1:12.20	
1956	Royal Lark	3	W. Blum	121	Aiming High	121	Levee	121	16,050	1:12.40	
1957	I Offbeat	3	H. Woodhouse	121	Therapy	121	Mlle. Dianne	121	16,250	1:12.00	
1958	Milady Dares	3	A. Chambers	121	Two Cent Stamp	121	Countess Marcy	121	10,946	1:12.80	
1958	Dixie Miss	3	J. Ruane	121	Locust Time	121	Shy Dancer	121	11,076	1:13.40	
1959	Miss Royal	3	R. Ussery	121	Hope Is Eternal	121	Cobul	121	18,355	1:11.80	
1960	Salt Lake	3	R. Yaka	121	Irish Jay	121	Improve	121	19,362	1:11.80	
1961	Primonetta	3	W. Hartack	121	Apatontheback	121	Mighty Fair	121	15,600	1:10.60	
1962	Some Song	3	J. Sellers	121	Leapfrog	121	Annie O.	121	15,080	1:11.00	
1963	Speedwell	3	W. Shoemaker	121	Fashion Verdict	121	Pams Ego	121	15,405	1:10.60	
1964	Nilene Wonder	3	D. Pierce	121	Enchanting	121	Miss Cavandish	121	18,590	1:12.20	
1965	What a Treat	3	J.L. Rotz	121	Admiring	121	Adorable	121	17,907	1:10.40	
1966	My Boss Lady	3	W. Shoemaker	121	Squeeze	121	Spearfish	121	17,875	1:10.60	
1967	Just Kidding	3	E. Belmonte	121	Great Era	121	Lake Chelan	121	17,907	1:10.40	
1968	Dark Mirage	3	A. Cordero Jr	121	Guest Room	121	Pleasantness	121	18,037	1:10.80	
1969	Ta Wee	3	J.L. Rotz	121	Francis Flower	121	Juliet	121	18,525	1:09.40	
1970	Exclusive Dancer	3	C. Baltazar	121	Restless Life	121	Petunia	121	18,005	1:11.20	
1971	Miss Plumage	3	R. Woodhouse	121	Sea Saga	121	Emperors Desire	121	20,250	1:11.60	
1972	Numbered Account	3	B. Baeza	121	Mindy Malone	121	I Move	121	16,470	1:10.00	
1973	Windy's Daughter	3	B. Baeza	121	Voler	115	Waltz Fan	115	17,355	1:10.20	
1974	Clear Copy	3	D. Montoya	115	Heartful	118	Talking Picture	115	17,745	1:10.20	
1975	Sarsar	3	W. Shoemaker	118	Stulcer	114	Gallant Trial	114	17,070	1:10.80	
1976	Dearly Precious	3	B. Baeza	121	Old Goat	118	Answer	118	22,110	1:09.80	
1977	Ring O'Bells	3	A. Cordero Jr	116	Road Princess	118	Pearl Necklace	116	22,410	1:10.40	
1978	Tempest Queen	3	J. Velasquez	118	Sweet Joyce	112	Silver Ice	115	25,320	1:11.40	
1979	Fall Aspen	3	R.I. Velez	121	Spanish Fake	118	Too Many Sweets	115	25,740	1:11.40	
1980	Lien	3	E. Maple	115	Cybele	112	Nuit D'Amour	115	27,390	1:11.00	
1981	Tina Tina Too	3	C.B. Asmussen	118	Sweet Revenge	121	Ruler's Dancer	112	33,420	1:11.20	
1982	Trove	3	M. Venezia	118	Larida	114	Dearly Too	112	34,380	1:10.00	
1983	Able Money	3	A. Graell	112	Quixotic Lady	118	Captivating Grace	118	34,440	1:11.00	
1984	Proud Clarioness	3	J.L. Samyn	115	Dumdedumdedum	113	Suavite	112	41,400	1:10.40	
1985	Clocks Secret	3	J. Nied Jr	115	Lady's Secret	118	Ride Sally	112	53,010	1:10.00	
1986	Religiosity	3	J.A. Santos	112	Fighter Fox	112	Tromphe de Naskra	114	54,450	1:11.00	
1987	Firey Challenge	3	R. MIgliore	114	Up the Apalachee	118	Monogram	114	69,300	1:10.60	
1988	Fara's Team	3	J.D. Bailey	114	Lake Valley	112	Raging Lady	114	65,700	1:10.20	
1989	Safely Kept	3	A. Cordero Jr	118	Cojinx	114	The Way It's Binn	114	49,770	1:11.60	
1990	Token Dance	3	E. Maple	114	Stella Madrid	121	Charging Fire	114	49,770	1:09.40	
1991	Zama Hummer	3	G.L. Stevens	114	Missy'sirage	114	Devilish Touch	118	74,760	1:09.80	99
1992	American Royale	3	J.A. Santos	118	Debra's Victory	121	Preach	118	68,280	1:09.20	99
1993	Classy Mirage	3	J.A. Krone	114	Missed the Storm	118	Educated Risk	118	67,680	1:08.80	105
1994	Penny's Reshoot	3	J.R. Velazquez	116	Heavenly Prize	121	Beckys Shirt	114	64,500	1:09.00	101
1995	Scotzanna	3	R. Platts	112	Culver City	116	Miss Golden Circle	118	66,840	1:10.60	102
1996	Capote Belle	3	J.R. Velazquez	114	Flat Fleet Feet	118	Miss Maggie	116	67,200	1:08.80	114
1997	Pearl City	3	J.D. Bailey	118	Alyssum	121	Vegas Prospector	121	64,680	1:09.40	100

Year	Winner	Age	Jockey	Wt.	Second	Wt.	Third	Wt.	Win Value	Time	Beyer
1998	Hurricane Bertie	3	P. Day	121	Catinca	114	Foil	114	68,220	1:08.80	99
1999	Sapphire n' Silk	3	P. Day	121	Marley Vale	112	Confessional	118	90,000	1:09.40	94
2000	I'm Brassy	3	J.A. Santos	113	Dat You Miz Blue	114	Lucky Livi	121	90,000	1:09.53	104
2001	Xtra Heat	3	R. Wilson	121	Above Perfection	116	Harmony Lodge	116	120,000	1:08.30	112
2002	Carson Hollow	3	J. Velazquez	114	Spring Meadow	121	Proper Gamble	121	120,000	1:08.79	103
2003	House Party	3	J.A. Santos	121	Chimichurri	119	Princess V.	115	120,000	1:09.45	99

Beyer Index: 102.38

QUEEN ELIZABETH II CHALLENGE CUP INVITATIONAL STAKES, 3-Year-Old Fillies, 1 1/8 Miles (Turf), Keeneland Race Course, 2003 Purse: $500,000

Year	Winner	Age	Jockey	Wt.	Second	Wt.	Third	Wt.	Win Value	Time	Beyer
1984	Sintra	3	K.K. Allen	112	Solar Halo	112	Mr. T's Tune	112	69,644	1:43.40	
1985	Contredance	3	E. Maple	112	Debutante Dancer	116	Folk Art	120	55,608	1:47.00	
1986	Lotka	3	W.A. Guerra	121	Minstress	121	Top Corsage	121	65,000	1:50.00	
1987	Graceful Darby	3	J.D. Bailey	121	Shot Gun Bonnie	121	Sum	121	65,000	1:47.20	
1988	Love You by Heart	3	R.P. Romero	121	Siggebo	121	Glowing Honor	121	65,000	1:44.80	
1989	Coolawin	3	J.A. Velez Jr	121	To the Lighthouse	121	Songlines	121	65,000	1:43.20	
1990	Plenty of Grace	3	J.D. Bailey	121	Christiecat	121	My Girl Jeannie	121	65,000	1:51.40	
1991	La Gueriere	3	B.D. Peck	121	Satin Flower	121	Radiant Ring	121	130,000	1:49.80	101
1992	Captive Miss	3	J.A. Krone	121	Suivi	121	Trampoli	121	124,000	1:48.80	98
1993	Tribulation	3	J.L. Samyn	121	Miami Sands	121	Possibly Perfect	121	124,000	1:53.60	99
1994	Danish	3	J.A. Krone	121	Eternal Reve	121	Avie's Fancy	121	124,000	1:48.80	107
1995	Perfect Arc	3	J.R. Velazquez	121	Auriette	121	Country Cat	121	155,000	1:49.80	106
1996	Memories of Silver	3	R.G. Davis	121	Shake the Yoke	121	Antespend	121	248,000	1:45.80	110
1997	Ryafan	3	A. Solis	121	Auntie Mame	121	Golden Arches	121	248,000	1:46.60	101
1998	Tenski	3	R. Migliore	121	Shires Ende	121	Sierra Virgen	121	248,000	1:48.54	104
1999	Perfect Sting	3	P. Day	121	Tout Charmant	121	Wannabe Grand	121	310,000	1:50.66	103
2000	Collect the Cash	3	S.J. Sellers	121	Blue Moon	121	Theoretically	121	310,000	1:47.94	95
2001	Affluent	3	E. Delahoussaye	121	Golden Apples	121	Snow Dance	121	310,000	1:50.03	99
2002	Riskaverse	3	M. Guidry	121	Zenda	121	Lush Soldier	121	310,000	1:49.84	103
2003	Film Maker	3	E.S. Prado	121	Maiden Tower	121	Casual Look	121	310,000	1:47.82	100

Beyer Index: 102

EDDIE READ HANDICAP, 1 1/8 Miles (Turf), 3-Year-Olds and Up, Del Mar, 2003 Purse: $400,000

Year	Winner	Age	Jockey	Wt.	Second	Wt.	Third	Wt.	Win Value	Time	Beyer
1974	My Old Friend	5	A.L. Diaz	115	Montmartre	116	War Heim	121	22,100	1:49.20	
1975	Blue Times	4	J. Lambert	115	Portentous	112	Confederate Yankee	115	28,200	1:49.20	
1976	Branford Court	6	R. Campas	116	Diode	114	Austin Mittler	115	26,150	1:48.40	
1977	No Turning	4	F. Toro	115	Today 'n Tomorrow	119	Star Ball	111	32,400	1:48.80	
1978	Effervescing	5	L. Pincay Jr	124	Text	123	Bywayofchicago	117	33,050	1:48.60	
1979	Good Lord	8	W. Shoemaker	115	Shagbark	114	True Statement	115	42,450	1:49.20	
1980	Go West Young Man	5	E. Delahoussaye	120	The Bart	118	Bold Tropic	124	64,250	1:47.60	
1981	Wickerr	6	C.J. McCarron	115	Super Moment	117	Mike Fogarty	114	80,750	1:49.80	
1982	Wickerr	7	E. Delahoussaye	119	Spence Bay	122	Perrault	129	95,300	1:48.40	
1983	Prince Spellbound	4	C. Lamance	121	Bel Bolide	117	Ask Me	115	108,000	1:48.80	
1984	Ten Below	5	L. Pincay Jr	117	Silveyville	117	Desert Wine	124	96,200	1:48.20	
1985	Tsunami Slew	4	G.L. Stevens	119	Al Mamoon	118	Both Ends Burning	123	112,300	1:46.80	
1986	Al Mamoon	5	P.A. Valenzuela	121	Zoffany	123	Truce Maker	115	113,400	1:46.60	
1987	Sharrood	4	L. Pincay Jr	120	Santella Mac	115	Skip Out Front	115	133,200	1:48.00	
1988	Deputy Governor	4	E. Delahoussaye	120	Santella Mac	114	Simply Majestic	115	176,500	1:48.80	
1989	Saratoga Passage	4	E. Delahoussaye	116	Skip Out Front	116	Pasakos	116	162,750	1:49.00	
1990	Fly Till Dawn	4	R.Q. Meza	112	Classic Fame	119	Golden Pheasant	122	157,750	1:48.20	
1991	Tight Spot	4	L. Pincay Jr	125	Val des Bois	115	Madjaristan	116	188,500	1:47.20	110
1992	Marquetry	5	D.R. Flores	118	Luthier Enchanteur	116	Leger Cat	115	187,250	1:47.20	112
1993	Kotashaan	5	K.J. Desormeaux	122	Leger Cat	116	Rainbow Corner	114	183,750	1:48.40	109
1994	Approach the Bench	6	C.S. Nakatani	113	Fastness	114	Johann Quatz	116	187,250	1:48.80	104
1995	Fastness	6	G.L. Stevens	115	Romarin	119	Northern Spur	118	182,600	1:48.20	110
1996	Fastness	6	C.S. Nakatani	124	Smooth Runner	114	Gold And Steel	118	193,000	1:47.00	118
1997	Expelled	5	J.A. Garcia	113	El Angelo	119	Marlin	122	180,000	1:48.60	106
1998	Subordination	4	D.R. Flores	117	Bonapartiste	115	Hawksley Hill	120	180,000	1:47.49	107
1999	Joe Who	6	C.W. Antley	116	Ladies Din	119	Bouccaneer	115	240,000	1:48.75	108
2000	Ladies Din	5	K.J. Desormeaux	120	Chester House	114	Gold Nugget	115	240,000	1:48.64	109
2001	Redattore	6	A. Solis	115	Native Desert	116	Super Quercus	115	240,000	1:47.16	106
2002	Sarafan	5	C.S. Nakatani	117	Beat Hollow	122	Redattore	118	240,000	1:46.77	109
3002	Special Ring	6	D.R. Flores	117	Decarchy	117	Irish Warrior	114	240,000	1:45.87	111

Beyer Index: 109.15

RUFFIAN HANDICAP, 1 1/16 Miles, Fillies and Mares, 3-Year-Olds and Up, Belmont Park, 2003 Purse: $300,000

Year	Winner	Age	Jockey	Wt.	Second	Wt.	Third	Wt.	Win Value	Time	Beyer
1976	Revidere	3	J. Vasquez	118	Bastonera II	123	Optimistic Gal	118	79,425	2:01.00	
1977	Cum Laude Laurie	3	A. Cordero Jr	114	Mississippi Mud	123	Cascapedia	128	66,480	1:52.20	
1978	Late Bloomer	4	J. Velasquez	122	Pearl Necklace	124	Tempest Queen	117	64,860	1:47.00	
1979	It's in the Air	3	L. Pincay Jr	122	Blitey	113	Waya	126	79,875	1:47.40	

1980	Genuine Risk	3	J. Vasquez	118	Misty Gallore	124	It's in the Air	118	81,900	1:49.20	
1981	Relaxing	5	A. Cordero Jr	123	Love Sign	120	Jameela	122	97,020	1:47.60	
1982	Christmas Past	3	J. Vasquez	117	Mademoiselle Forli	112	Love Sign	123	100,080	1:48.60	
1983	Heartlight No. One	3	L. Pincay Jr	117	Mochila	113	Try Something New	116	103,140	1:47.20	
1984	Heatherten	5	R.P. Romero	118	Miss Oceana	119	Adored	123	103,320	1:48.20	
1985	Lady's Secret	3	J. Velasquez	116	Isayso	115	Sintrillium	118	128,880	1:47.40	
1986	Lady's Secret	4	P. Day	129	Steal a Kiss	109	Endear	119	165,240	1:46.80	
1987	Coup de Fusil	5	A. Cordero Jr	117	Clabber Girl	112	Sacahuista	114	149,760	1:48.60	
	Sacahuista finished first but was disqualified and placed third										
1988	Sham Say	3	J. Vasquez	113	Classic Crown	115	Make Change	114	146,400	1:48.00	
1989	Bayakoa	5	L. Pincay Jr	125	Colonial Waters	118	Open Mind	120	135,840	1:48.40	
1990	Quick Mischief	4	R.I. Rojas	111	Personal Business	113	Mistaurian	115	144,480	1:42.80	96
1991	Queena	5	A. Cordero Jr	120	Sharp Dance	111	Lady D'Accord	113	120,000	1:41.60	104
1992	Versailles Treaty	4	M.E. Smith	120	Quick Mischief	116	Nannerl	119	120,000	1:41.40	106
1993	Shared Interest	5	R.G. Davis	114	Dispute	115	Turnback the Alarm	123	120,000	1:41.80	107
1994	Sky Beauty	4	M.E. Smith	130	Dispute	117	Educated Risk	114	120,000	1:41.60	106
1995	Inside Information	4	M.E. Smith	125	Unlawful Behavior	110	Incincerate	112	120,000	1:40.80	112
1996	Yanks Music	3	J.R. Velazquez	116	Serena's Song	126	Head East	108	150,000	1:41.80	107
1997	Tomisue's Delight	3	J.D. Bailey	113	Clear Mandate	119	Mil Kilates	114	150,000	1:44.40	95
1998	Sharp Cat	4	C.S. Nakatani	124	Furlough	115	Stop Traffic	119	150,000	1:42.48	112
1999	Catinca	4	R. Migliore	119	Furlough	116	Keeper Hill	118	150,000	1:41.94	102
2000	Riboletta	5	C.J. McCarron	125	Gorumet Girl	114	Country Hideaway	114	150,000	1:40.35	115
2002	Mandy's Gold	4	J.A. Santos	116	You	117	Shine Again	117	180,000	1:42.57	107
2003	Wild Spirit	4	J.D. Bailey	121	You	118	Passing Shot	115	180,000	1:41.23	109

Beyer Index: **106**

Distance 1 1/4 miles in 1976; 1 1/8 miles, 1977–89. Not run in 2001.

SAN CARLOS HANDICAP, 7 Furlongs,
4-Year-Olds and Up, Santa Anita, 2003 Purse: $200,000

Year	Winner	Age	Jockey	Wt.	Second	Wt.	Third	Wt.	Win Value	Time	Beyer
1935	Jabot	4	A. Robertson	109	Riskulus	109	Top Row	103	5,225	1:42.80	
1936	Discovery	5	J. Bejshak	130	Ariel Cross	106	Beefsteak	104	4,025	1:45.40	
1937	Chanceview	5	J. Pollard	110	Indian Broom	116	Boxthorn	117	4,625	1:45.60	
1938	Pompoon	4	J. Gilbert	124	Star Shadow	107	He Did	114	4,600	1:45.00	
1939	Kayak II	4	J. Adams	110	Specify	119	Whichcee	112	10,050	1:42.40	
1940	Specify	5	C. Bierman	115	Lassator	105	Viscounty	109	9,350	1:23.40	
1941	Gen'l Manager	4	R. Neves	110	Viscounty	116	Hysterical	116	10,000	1:24.40	
1946	Sirde	5	J. Gilbert	117	First Fiddle	126	Lou-Bre	109	20,380	1:23.00	
1947	Texas Sandman	6	M. Peterson	114	El Lobo	112	Fighting Frank	121	45,150	1:22.80	
1948	Autocrat	7	A. Skoronski	108	Rippey	115	Prevaricator	114	42,500	1:22.40	
1949	Manyunk	4	E. Guerin	114	Star Reward	120	Miche	116	42,050	1:23.40	
1949	Autocrat	8	J. Nichols	117	Dinner Gong	115	Rippey	124	41,550	1:25.80	
1951	Bolero	5	E. Arcaro	121	Your Host	126	Blue Reading	109	41,300	1:21.00	
1952	To Market	4	E. Arcaro	116	Bryan G.	126	Gold Note	110	17,100	1:24.00	
1953	Blue Reading	6	B. Pearson	121	Ruth Lily	104	Big Noise	112	14,350	1:23.40	
1954	Find	4	E. Guerin	123	Hill Gail	117	Heliowise	116	14,300	1:25.20	
1955	Porterhouse	4	E. Arcaro	115	Imbros	130	Encono	114	14,200	1:22.40	
1956	Porterhouse	5	E. Arcaro	119	Karim	110	Hickory Stick	109	14,650	1:22.80	
1957	Duc de Fer	6	R. Neves	118	Mister Gus	128	Lassabatt	114	13,000	1:23.40	
1958	Seaneen	4	W. Harmatz	114	Porterhouse	126	Ole Fols	120	36,100	1:22.20	
1959	Hillsdale	4	T. Barrow	115	Round Table	132	Micarlo	113	38,750	1:22.20	
1960	Clandestine	4	M. Ycaza	112	Ole Fols	120	Mystic Eye	114	37,000	1:22.20	
1961	First Balcony	4	M. Ycaza	111	T.V. Lark	125	Eddie Schmidt	112	33,300	1:21.80	
1962	Four-and-Twenty	4	J. Longden	124	Ole Fols	117	Finnegan	115	31,300	1:21.80	
1963	Crozier	5	B. Baeza	124	OldenTimes	125	Native Diver	125	38,600	1:21.20	
1964	Admiral's Voyage	5	B. Baeza	124	Cyrano	126	Native Diver	125	36,600	1:22.00	
1965	Native Diver	6	J. Lambert	126	Candy Spots	125	Bonjour	114	36,150	1:21.40	
1966	Cupid	5	R. Ussery	115	Hill Rise	126	Quita Dude	115	38,600	1:22.00	
1967	Native Diver	8	J. Lambert	126	Hoist Bar	115	Pretense	118	39,550	1:22.00	
1968	Suteki	4	W. Blum	113	Postage	106	Quicken Tree	116	34,150	1:22.00	
1969	Rising Market	5	L. Pincay Jr	126	Title Game	115	Tumiga	123	34,350	1:22.60	
1970	Rising Market	6	L. Pincay Jr	121	Tell	125	Fleet Wing	118	24,700	1:21.00	
1971	Ack Ack	5	W. Shoemaker	124	Jungle Savage	120	King of Cricket	119	34,150	1:21.00	
1972	KfarTov	4	J. Lambert	120	Riot	113	Long Position	114	35,450	1:21.40	
1973	Crusading	5	F. Toro	119	Kennedy Road	117	Figonero	118	33,850	1:20.80	
1974	Royal Owl	5	L. Pincay Jr	117	Soft Victory	116	Against the Snow	112	35,600	1:23.40	
1975	Ancient Title	5	L. Pincay Jr	128	Hudson County	116			37,750	1:21.20	
					Bahia Key	117					
1976	No Bias	6	L. Pincay Jr	120	Century's Envoy	126	Bahia Key	120	32,200	1:21.80	
1977	Uniformity	5	F. Toro	115	My Juliet	123	Messenger of Song	121	34,050	1:21.60	
1978	Double Discount	5	F. Mena	117	Impressive Luck	120	Romantic Lead	117	32,650	1:22.00	
1979	O Big Al	4	D.G. McHargue	120	Maheras	122	Bad 'n Big	124	40,800	1:22.00	
1980	Handsomeness	4	L. Pincay Jr	118	Relaunch	121	Beau's Eagle	125	49,100	1:24.00	
1981	Flying Paster	5	J. McCarron	124	To B. or Not	123	Double Discount	115	51,550	1:20.20	

Year	Winner	Age	Jockey	Wt.	Second	Wt.	Third	Wt.	Win Value	Time	Beyer
1982	Solo Guy	4	W. Shoemaker	118	Smokite	116	King Go Go	119	60,700	1:20.80	
1983	Kangroo Court	6	J.J Steiner	118	Dave's Friend	117	Shanekite	118	40,550	1:21.00	
1984	Danebo	5	L. Pincay Jr	117	Pac Mania	118	Poley	119	54,900	1:21.00	
1985	Debonaire Junior	4	C.J. McCarron	125	Tennessee Rite	112	Fifty Six Ina Row	116	64,300	1:21.60	
1986	Phone Trick	4	L. Pincay Jr	125	Temerity Prince	122	My Habitony	117	78,200	1:20.80	
1987	Zany Tactics	6	J.L. Kaenel	118	Bolder Than Bold	116	Epidaurus	115	65,600	1:22.40	
1988	Epidaurus	6	P.A. Valenzuela	117	Super Diamond	125	Lord Ruckus	118	63,500	1:22.00	
1989	Cherokee Colony	4	R.Q. Meza	119	On the Line	126	Happy in Space	116	62,800	1:20.60	
1990	Raise a Stanza	4	R.A. Baze	117	Oraibi	119	Tanker Port	117	64,500	1:21.60	102
1991	Farma Way	4	G.L. Stevens	115	Yes I'm Blue	117	Tanker Port	117	63,500	1:21.40	113
1992	Answer Do	6	G.L. Stevens	120	Individualist	115	Media Plan	116	63,700	1:21.20	107
1993	Sir Beaufort	6	C.J. McCarron	120	Cardmania	117	Excavate	114	62,900	1:22.20	109
1994	Cardmania	8	E. Delahoussaye	122	The Wicked North	117	Portoferraio	115	63,900	1:21.20	106
1995	Softshoe Sure Shot	9	A. Solis	114	Ferrara	115	Subtle Trouble	115	91,600	1:21.40	103
1996	Kingdom Found	6	C.J. McCarron	116	Lakota Brave	114	Lit de Justice	123	98,850	1:22.20	103
1997	Northern Afleet	4	C.J. McCarron	117	Hesabull	117	High Stakes Player	117	97,700	1:21.40	109
1998	Reality Road	6	C.J. McCarron	116	Gold Land	116	Son Of A Pistol	114	100,530	1:21.60	112
1999	Big Jag	6	J. Valdivia Jr.	118	Kona Gold	120	Dramatic Gold	117	90,000	1:21.00	116
2000	Son of a Pistol	8	G.K. Gomez	117	Kona Gold	122	Old Topper	116	96,930	1:22.11	109
2001	Kona Gold	7	A. Solis	125	Blade Prospector	113	Grey Memo	115	90,000	1:21.35	112
2002	Snow Ridge	4	M.E. Smith	118	Alyzig	112	Grey Memo	114	90,000	1:22.02	106
2003	Aldebaran	5	J. Valdivia Jr	116	Crafty C.T.	116	Grey Memo	116	120,000	1:21.53	110

Beyer Index: 108.36

SAN JUAN CAPISTRANO INVITATIONAL HANDICAP, About 1 3/4 Miles (Turf), Santa Anita 4-Year-Olds and Up, 2003 Purse: $400,000

Year	Winner	Age	Jockey	Wt.	Second	Wt.	Third	Wt.	Win Value	Time	Beyer
1935	Head Play	5	C. Kurtsinger	115	Top Row	109	Ladysman	122	9,100	1:51.40	
1936	Whopper	4	W. Saunders	112	Tick On	106	Ariel Cross	103	10,950	1:50.00	
1937	Seabiscuit	4	J. Pollard	120	Grand Manitou	108	Special Agent	116	9,200	1:48.80	
1938	Indian Broom	7	H. Richards	110	Star Shadow	110	Amor Brujo	112	8,700	1:51.40	
1939	Cravat	4	J. Westrope	117	Today	111	Jacola	116	25,200	2:30.40	
1940	Mioland	3	J. Adams	117	Weigh Anchor	115	Sweepida	122	10,250	1:45.20	
1941	Mioland	4	L. Haas	130	Gen'l Manager	107	Best Effort	110	36,840	2:30.80	
1945	Bric-A-Bac	4	C. McCreary	122	Wing and Wing	112	Barrancosa	106	44,310	2:29.20	
1946	Triplicate	5	J.D. Jessop	111	War Valor	109	Old English	110	40,030	2:28.40	
1949	Miss Grillo	7	J. Adams	117	Dinner Gong	118	Rose Beam	109	38,100	2:29.00	
1950	Noor	5	J. Longden	117	Citation	130	Mocopo	107	40,400	2:52.80	
1951	Be Fleet	4	J. Longden	114	Repeluz	116	Mocopo	106	37,800	2:56.00	
1952	Intent	4	E. Guerin	122	Be Fleet	116	Bryan G.	117	33,200	2:55.00	
1953	Intent	5	E. Arcaro	126	Don Rebelde	113	Trusting	121	65,100	2:55.60	
1954	By Zeus	4	R. York	110	Rejected	126	Lucrative	110	73,100	2:26.00	
1955	St. Vincent	4	J. Longden	123	Determine	126	Gigantic	110	69,800	2:46.80	
1956	Bobby Brocato	5	G. Taniguchi	124	Manotick	109	Honeys Alibi	119	68,900	2:49.40	
1957	Corn Husker	4	E. Arcaro	116	Spinney	114	Infantry	111	69,400	2:55.00	
1958	Promised Land	4	I. Valenzuela	121	Tall Chief II	120	Eddie Schmidt	115	70,000	2:52.00	
							Solid Sun.	113			
1959	Royal Living	4	R. Neves	117	Tall Chief II	114	Infantry	112	70,700	2:45.40	
1960	Amerigo	5	W. Hartack	122	King o' Turf	115	Aorangi	109	73,800	2:47.80	
1961	Don't Alibi	5	W. Shoemaker	118	Prince Blessed	116	Notable II	106	68,100	2:48.00	
1962	Olden Times	4	W. Shoemaker	119	Juanro	109	The Axe II	122	73,000	2:53.00	
1963	Pardao	5	I. Valenzuela	119	Juanro	114	Rablero	119	70,660	2:48.20	
1964	Cedar Key	4	M. Ycaza	115	Follow Thru	112	Desert Chief II	113	53,100	2:48.00	
1964	Mr. Consistency	6	K. Church	125	Puyallup	109	Dusky Damion	119	54,100	2:49.00	
1965	George Royal	4	J. Longden	116	Duel	115	Hill Rise	124	75,000	2:46.80	
1966	George Royal	5	J. Longden	118	Plaque	115	Tom Cat.	114	75,000	2:48.80	
1967	Niarkos	7	A. Pineda	120	Biggs	113	Pretense	126	75,000	2:50.20	
1968	Niarkos	8	A. Pineda	121	Jungle Road	115	Rivet	115	75,000	2:47.80	
1969	Petrone	5	J. Sellers	122	Fort Marcy	124	Rivet	115	75,000	2:47.40	
1970	Fiddle Isle	5	W. Shoemaker	125			Fort Marcy	124	50,000	2:46.40	
	Quicken Tree	7	F. Alvarez	124							
1971	Cougar II	5	W. Shoemaker	126	Try Sheep	114	Hill Run	120	75,000	2:46.20	
	Fort Marcy finished second but was disqualified and sixth										
1972	Practicante	6	L. Pincay Jr	118	Cougar II	127	Nor II	120	75,000	2:45.60	
1973	Queen's Hustler	4	R. Rosales	115	Big Spruce	119	Cougar II	127	75,000	2:46.40	
1974	Astray	5	J. Vasquez	126	El Rey	113	Big Spruce	125	75,000	2:45.40	
1975	La Zanzara	5	D. Pierce	114	Astray	125	Stardust Mel	126	75,000	2:52.20	
1976	One on the Aisle	4	S. Hawley	119	Elaborado	113	Top Crowd	121	75,000	2:50.00	
1977	Properantes	4	D.G. McHargue	120	Top Crowd	118	Caucasus	128	85,000	2:47.60	
1978	Exceller	5	W. Shoemaker	126	Noble Dancer	125	Xmas Box	115	120,000	2:51.00	
1979	Tiller	5	A. Cordero Jr	126	Exceller	127	Noble Dancer	128	120,000	2:48.00	
1980	John Henry	5	D.G. McHargue	126	Fiestero	115	The Very One	113	120,000	2:46.80	
1981	Obraztsovy	6	P.A. Valenzuela	121	Exploded	115	Singularity	115	120,000	2:50.40	
1982	Lemhi Gold	4	W. Guerra	121	Exploded	118	Perrault	129	180,000	2:45.60	

Year	Winner	Age	Jockey	Wt.	Second	Wt.	Third	Wt.	Win Value	Time	Beyer
1983	Erins Isle	5	L. Pincay Jr	125	Wolver Heights	118	Victory Zone	115	180,000	2:48.60	
1984	Load the Cannons	4	L. Pincay Jr	119	Jenkins Ferry	114	Norwick	115	180,000	2:48.00	
1985	Prince True	4	C.J. McCarron	124	Estrapade	120	Swoon	117	180,000	2:47.80	
1986	Dahar	5	A. Solis	124	Mountain Bear	115	Jupiter Island	123	220,000	2:47.80	
1987	Rosedale	4	L. Pincay Jr	117	Wylfa	115	Rivlia	115	220,000	2:49.00	
1988	Great Communicator	5	R. Sibille	119	Fiction	116	Carotene	115	220,000	2:51.60	
1989	Nasr El Arab	4	P.A. Valenzuela	123	Pleasant Variety	117	Academic	113	220,000	2:51.40	
1990	Delegant	6	K.J. Desormeaux	115	Valdali	114	Hawkster	123	275,000	2:46.60	108
1991	Mashkour	8	C.J. McCarron	115	River Warden	115	Aksar	116	275,000	2:47.60	104
1992	Fly Till Dawn	6	P.A. Valenzuela	121	Miss Alleged	118	Wall Street Dancer	114	275,000	2:46.53	110
1993	Kotashaan	5	K.J. Desormeaux	121	Bien Bien	119	Fraise	123	220,000	2:45.00	108
1994	Bien Bien	5	C.J. McCarron	122	Grand Flotilla	116	Alex the Great	114	220,000	2:46.69	107
1995	Red Bishop	7	M.E. Smith	119	Special Price	116	Liyoun	112	220,000	2:48.02	107
1996	Raintrap	6	A. Solis	119	Windsharp	116	Awad	120	240,000	2:46.40	107
1997	Marlin	7	E. Delahoussaye	119	Sunshack	118			240,000	2:44.56	107
					African Dancer	114					
1998	Amerique	4	E. Delahoussaye	116	Star Performance	116	Kessem Power	116	240,000	2:47.08	104
1999	Single Empire	5	K.J. Desormeaux	118	Le Paillard	115	Lacayan Indian	113	240,000	2:45.93	105
2000	Sunshine Street	5	J.D. Bailey	115	Single Empire	118	Chelsea Barracks	109	240,000	2:49.06	104
2001	Bienamado	5	C.J. McCarron	122	Persianlux	114	Blueprint	116	240,000	2:42.96	108
2002	Ringaskiddy	6	E. Delahoussaye	116	Staging Post	115	Continental Red	117	240,000	2:44.49	106
2003	Passinetti	7	B. Blanc	111	All the Boys	115	Champion Lodge	117	240,000	2:46.97	104

Beyer Index: 106.36

Distance (main course 1 1/8 miles prior to 1938; 1 1/16 miles in 1940; 1 1/2 miles, 1939, 1941, 1945-49; 1 3/4 miles, 1950-53; (turf course) 1 1/2 miles, 1954. For 3-year-olds in 1940; for 3-year-olds and up in all other years prior to 1968 ..

SANTA ANITA DERBY, 1 1/8 Miles, 3-Year-Olds, Santa Anita, 2003 Purse: $750,000

Year	Winner	Age	Jockey	Wt.	Second	Wt.	Third	Wt.	Win Value	Time	Beyer
1935	Gillie	3	S. Coucci	126	Whiskolo	126	Demonstration	126	19,650	1:44.60	
1936	He Did	3	W.D. Wright	126	Valiant Fox	126	Gold Seeker	121	26,000	1:49.40	
1937	Fairy Hill	3	M. Peters	121	Military	121	Ptolemy	121	45,425	1:45.80	
1938	Stagehand	3	J. Westrope	118	Dauber	118	Sun Egret	118	42,350	1:50.40	
1939	Ciencia	3	C. Bierman	115	Xalapa Clown	120	Impound	120	41,850	1:50.60	
1940	Sweepida	3	R. Neves	120	Royal Crusader	120	Weigh Anchor	120	43,850	1:51.60	
1941	Porter's Cap	3	L. Haas	120	Bull Reigh	120	Copperman	120	44,975	1:54.40	
1945	Bymeabond	3	G. Woolf	119	Busher	121	Best Effort	126	37,250	1:50.00	
1946	Knockdown	3	R. Permane	122	Star Pilot	122	Honeymoon	117	74,680	1:50.60	
1947	On Trust	3	J. Longden	118	W.L. Sickle	118	Tropical Sea	118	81,750	2:03.20	
1948	Salmagundi	3	J. Longden	118	Call Bell	118	Drum Beat	118	79,850	1:51.20	
1949	Old Rockport	3	G. Glisson	118	Olympia	118	Admiral Lea	118	94,700	1:50.20	
1950	Your Host	3	J. Longden	118	Sturdy One	118	Great Circle	118	89,800	1:48.80	
1951	Rough 'n Tumble	3	E. Arcaro	118	Interpretation	118	Aegean	118	81,500	1:50.40	
1952	Hill Gail	3	T. Atkinson	118	Windy City II	118	Arroz	118	92,900	1:50.00	
1953	Chanlea	3	E. Arcaro	118	Merryman	118	Correspondent	118	84,500	1:49.80	
1954	Determine	3	R. York	118	Duke's Lea	118	Travertine	118	84,800	1:48.80	
1955	Swaps	3	J. Longden	118	Jean's Joe	118	Blue Ruler	118	90,400	1:50.00	
1956	Terrang	3	W. Shoemaker	118	Social Climber	118	More Glory	118	111,700	1:51.00	
1957	Sir William	3	H. Moreno	118	Swirling Abbey	118	Round Table	118	9,500	1:54.20	
1958	Silky Sullivan	3	W. Shoemaker	118	Harcall	118	Aliwar	118	83,400	1:49.40	
1959	Silver Spoon	3	R. York	113	Royal Orbit	118	Fightin Indian	118	95,300	1:49.00	
1960	Tompion	3	W. Shoemaker	118	John William	118	Eagle Admiral	118	83,300	1:47.80	
1961	Four-and-Twenty	3	J. Longden	118	Ronnie's Ace	118	Flutterby	118	100,100	1:48.00	
1962	Royal Attack	3	E. Burns	118	Admiral's Voyage	118	Sir Ribot	118	107,100	1:49.60	
1963	Candy Spots	3	W. Shoemaker	118	Sky Gem	118	Round Rock	118	98,300	1:50.20	
1964	Hill Rise	3	D. Pierce	118	Knightly Manner	118	Wil Rad	118	87,400	1:47.40	
1965	Lucky Debonair	3	W. Shoemaker	118	Jacinto	118	Charger's Kin	118	89,300	1:47.00	
1966	Boldnesian	3	W. Blum	118	Saber Mountain	118	Exhibitionist	118	96,900	1:48.40	
1967	Ruken	3	F. Alvarez	118	Tumble Wind	118	Sand Devil	118	94,900	1:49.80	
1968	Alley Fighter	3	L. Pincay Jr	120	Don B.	120	Dewan	120	102,100	1:49.00	
1969	Majestic Prince	3	W. Hartack	120	Mr. Joe F.	120	Lonny's Secret	120	87,200	1:49.20	
1970	Terlago	3	W. Shoemaker	120	George Lewis	120	Aggressively	120	96,400	1:48.40	
1971	Jim French	3	A. Cordero Jr	120	Unconscious	120	Vegas Vic	120	88,400	1:48.20	
1972	Solar Salute	3	L. Pincay Jr	120	Quack	120	Royal Owl	120	88,000	1:47.60	
1973	Sham	3	L. Pincay Jr	120	Linda's Chief	120	Out of the East	120	79,400	1:47.00	
1974	Destroyer	3	I. Valenzuela	120	Aloha Mood	120	Agitate	120	85,200	1:48.80	
1975	Avatar	3	J. Tejeira	120	Rock of Ages	120	Diabolo	120	82,900	1:47.60	
1976	An Act	3	L. Pincay Jr	120	Double Discount	120	Life's Hope	120	97,700	1:48.00	
1977	Habitony	3	W. Shoemaker	120	For the Moment	120	Steve's Friend	120	131,000	1:48.20	
1978	Affirmed	3	L. PIncay Jr	120	Balzac	120	Think Snow	120	127,300	1:48.00	
1979	Flying Paster	3	D. Pierce	120	Beau's Eagle	120	Switch Partners	120	124,900	1:48.00	
1980	Codex	3	P.A. Valenzuela	120	Rumbo	120	Vic's Gold	120	117,200	1:47.60	
1981	Splendid Spruce	3	D.G. McHargue	120	Johnlee n' Harold	120	Hoedown's Day	120	180,600	1:49.00	
1982	Muttering	3	L. Pincay Jr	120	Prince Spellbound	120	Journey at Sea	120	188,300	1:47.60	

Year	Winner	Age	Jockey	Wt.	Second	Wt.	Third	Wt.	Win Value	Time	Beyer
1983	Marfa	3	J. Velasquez	120	My Habitony	120	Naevus	120	198,000	1:49.40	
1984	Mighty Adversary	3	E. Delahoussaye	120	Precisionist	120	Prince True	120	189,700	1:49.00	
1985	Skywalker	3	L. Pincay Jr	122	Fast Account	122	Nostalgia's Star	122	219,500	1:48.40	
1986	Snow Chief	3	A. Solis	122	Icy Groom	122	Ferdinand	122	275,000	1:48.60	
1987	Temperate Sil	3	W. Shoemaker	122	Masterful Advocate	122	Something Lucky	122	278,250	1:49.00	
1988	Winning Colors	3	G.L. Stevens	117	Lively One	122	Mi Preferido	122	275,000	1:47.80	
1989	Sunday Silence	3	P.A. Valenzuela	122	Flying Continental	122	Music Merci	122	275,000	1:47.60	
1990	Mister Frisky	3	G.L. Stevens	122	Video Ranger	122	Warcraft	122	275,000	1:49.00	109
1991	Dinard	3	C.J. McCarron	122	Best Pal	122	Sea Cadet	122	275,000	1:48.00	108
1992	A.P. Indy	3	E. Delahoussaye	122	Bertrando	122	Casual Lies	122	275,000	1:49.25	95
1993	Personal Hope	3	G.L. Stevens	122	Union City	122	Eliza	117	275,000	1:49.03	98
1994	Brocco	3	G.L. Stevens	122	Tabasco Cat	122	Strodes Creek	122	275,000	1:48.33	105
1995	Larry the Legend	3	G.L. Stevens	122	Afternoon Deelites	122	Jumron	122	385,000	1:47.99	106
1996	Cavonnier	3	C.J. McCarron	122	Honour and Glory	122	Corker	122	600,000	1:48.91	104
	Alyrob finished second but was disqualified and placed eighth										
1997	Free House	3	K.J. Desormeaux	122	Silver Charm	122	Hello	122	450,000	1:47.60	110
1998	Indian Charlie	3	G.L. Stevens	122	Real Quiet	122	Artax	122	450,000	1:47.00	111
1999	General Challenge	3	G.L. Stevens	122	Prime Timber	122	Desert Hero	122	450,000	1:48.92	108
2000	The Deputy	3	C.J. McCarron	122	War Chant	122	Captain Steve	122	600,000	1:49.08	109
2001	Point Given	3	G.L. Stevens	122	Crafty C.T.	122	I Love Silver	122	450,000	1:47.77	110
2002	Came Home	3	C. McCarron	122	Easy Grades	122	Lusty Latin	122	450,000	1:50.02	96
2003	Buddy Gil	3	G.L. Stevens	122	Indian Express	122	Kafwain	122	450,000	1:49.36	104

Beyer Index: 105.21

Distance 1 1/16 miles prior to 1938; 1 1/4 miles, 1947

SANTA ANITA HANDICAP, 1 1/4 Miles, 4-Year-Olds and Up,
Santa Anita, 2003 Purse: $1,000,000

Year	Winner	Age	Jockey	Wt.	Second	Wt.	Third	Wt.	Win Value	Time	Beyer
1935	Azucar	7	G. Woolf	117	Ladysman	117	Time Supply	118	108,400	2:02.20	
1936	Top Row	5	W.D. Wright	116	Time Supply	114	Rosemont	116	104,600	2:04.20	
1937	Rosemont	5	H. Richards	124	Seabiscuit	114	Indian Broom	116	90,700	2:02.80	
1938	Stagehand	3	N. Wall	100	Seabiscuit	130	Pompoon	120	91,450	2:01.60	
1939	Kayak II	4	J. Adams	110	Whichcee	112	Main Man	117	91,100	2:01.40	
1940	Seabiscuit	7	J. Pollard	130	Kayak II	129	Whichcee	114	86,650	2:01.80	
1941	Bay View	4	N. Wall	108	Mioland	124	Bolingbroke	106	89,360	2:05.40	
1945	Thumbs Up	6	J. Longden	130	Texas Sandman	116	Gay Dalton	126	82,925	2:01.20	
1946	War Knight	6	J. Adams	115	First Fiddle	126	Snow Boots	112	101,220	2:01.60	
1947	Olhaverry	8	M. Petersen	114	Stitch Again	112	Pere Time	108	98,900	2:01.80	
1948	Talon	6	E. Arcaro	122	On Trust	121	Double Jay	118	102,500	2:03.40	
1949	Vulcan's Forge	4	D. Gorman	119	Dinner Gong	116	Miss Grillo	116	102,000	2:02.80	
1950	Noor	5	J. Longden	114	Citation	132	Two Lea	113	97,900	2:00.80	
1951	Moonrush	5	J. Longden	114	Next Move	116	Sudan	111	97,900	2:02.60	
1952	Miche	7	E. Arcaro	130	Intent	111	Be Fleet	114	104,100	2:01.00	
	Intent finished first but was disqualified and placed second										
1953	Mark-Ye-Well	4	E. Arcaro	130	Trusting	112	First Glance	113	97,900	2:01.20	
1954	Rejected	4	W. Shoemaker	118	Imbros	120	Cyclotron	116	105,900	2:00.60	
1955	Poona II	4	J. Longden	118	Joe Jones	117	Porterhouse	112	103,200	2:03.00	
1956	Bobby Brocato	4	W. Shoemaker	113	Turk's Delight	107	Honeys Alibi	114	97,900	2:04.60	
1957	Corn Husker	4	R. Neves	105	Holandes II	121	Spinney	108	103,600	2:01.80	
1958	Round Table	4	W. Shoemaker	130	Terrang	119	Porterhouse	120	97,900	1:59.80	
1959	Terrang	6	W. Boland	114	Hillsdale	113	Royal Living	111	97,900	2:00.00	
1960	Linmold	4	D. Pierce	110	Fleet Nasrullah	113	Amerigo	120	97,900	2:00.60	
1961	Prove It	4	W. Shoemaker	115	Oink	110	Grey Eagle	108	100,000	2:00.00	
1962	Physician	5	D. Pierce	114	Olden Times	113	Four-and-Twenty	129	100,000	2:02.60	
1963	Crozier	5	B. Baeza	122	Crimson Satan	125			100,000	2:00.80	
					Game	108					
1964	Mr. Consistency	6	K. Church	120	Doc Jocoy	117	Cyrano	125	102,100	2:01.00	
1965	Hill Rise	4	D. Pierce	120	Candy Spots	127	George Royal	114	100,000	2:00.60	
1966	Lucky Debonair	4	W. Shoemaker	124	Cupid	117	Native Diver	126	100,000	2:00.20	
1967	Pretense	4	W. Shoemaker	118	Native Diver	125	O'Hara	113	100,000	2:00.80	
1968	Mr. Right	5	M. Yanez	115	Jungle Road	117	Ala Ram	111	100,000	2:04.60	
1969	Nodouble	4	E. Belmonte	122	Gamely	122	Quicken Tree	126	100,000	2:01.80	
1970	Quicken Tree	7	F. Alvarez	118	Fiddle Isle	119	Field Master	114	100,000	1:59.60	
1971	Ack Ack	5	W. Shoemaker	130	Cougar II	125	The Field	109	100,000	2:03.00	
1972	Triple Bend	4	D. Pierce	119	Cougar II	126	Unconscious	127	105,000	2:00.00	
1973	Cougar II	7	L. Pincay Jr	129	Kennedy Road	119	Cabin	110	105,000	2:00.00	
1974	Prince Dantan	4	R. Turcotte	119	Ancient Title	125	Big Spruce	122	105,000	2:03.60	
1975	Stardust Mel	4	W. Shoemaker	123	Out of the East	112	Okavango	116	105,500	2:06.40	
1976	Royal Glint	6	J. Tejeira	124	Ancient Title	124	Lightning Mandate	120	155,900	2:00.40	
1977	Crystal Water	4	L. Pincay Jr	122	Faliraki	114	King Pellinore	130	173,550	1:59.20	
1978	Vigors	5	D.G. McHargue	127	Mr. Redoy	120	Jumping Hill	115	180,000	2:01.20	
1979	Affirmed	4	L. Pincay Jr	128	Tiller	127	Painted Wagon	115	192,800	1:58.60	
							Exceller	127			
1980	Spectacular Bid	4	W. Shoemaker	130	Flying Paster	123	Beau's Eagle	122	190,000	2:00.60	

Year	Winner	Age	Jockey	Wt.	Second	Wt.	Third	Wt.	Win Value	Time	Beyer
1981	John Henry	6	L. Pincay Jr	128	King Go Go	117	Exploded	115	238,150	1:59.40	
1982	John Henry	7	W. Shoemaker	130	Perrault	126	It's the One	123	318,800	1:59.00	
	Perrault finished first but was disqualified and placed second										
1983	Bates Motel	4	T. Lipham	118	It's the One	123	Wavering Monarch	121	317,350	1:59.60	
1984	Interco	4	P.A. Valenzuela	121	Journey at Sea	117	Gato Del Sol	117	298,650	2:00.60	
1985	Lord at War	5	W. Shoemaker	125	Greinton	120	Gate Dancer	125	275,600	2:00.60	
1986	Greinton	5	L. Pincay Jr	122	Herat	112	Hatim	118	689,500	2:00.00	
1987	Broad Brush	4	A. Cordero Jr	122	Ferdinand	125	Hopeful Word	117	550,000	2:00.60	
1988	Alysheba	4	C.J. McCarron	126	Ferdinand	127	Super Diamond	124	550,000	1:59.80	
1989	Martial Law	4	M. Pedroza	113	Triteamtri	116	Stylish Winner	113	550,000	1:58.80	
1990	Ruhlmann	5	G.L. Stevens	121	Criminal Type	119	Flying Continental	121	550,000	2:01.20	118
1991	Farma Way	4	G.L. Stevens	120	Festin	115	Pleasant Tap	115	550,000	2:00.20	118
1992	Best Pal	4	K.J. Desormeaux	124	Twilight Agenda	124	Defensive Play	115	550,000	1:59.00	123
1993	Sir Beaufort	3	P.A. Valenzuela	119	Star Recruit	117	Major Impact	114	550,000	2:00.55	112
1994	Stuka	4	C.W. Antley	115	Bien Bien	120	Myrakalu	114	550,000	2:00.17	111
	The Wicked North finished first but was disqualified and placed fourth										
1995	Urgent Request	5	G.L. Stevens	116	Best Pal	122	Dare and Go	120	550,000	1:59.25	113
1996	Mr Purple	4	E. Delahoussaye	116	Luthier Fever	114	Just Java	114	600,000	2:02.04	112
1997	Siphon	6	D.R. Flores	120	Sandpit	121	Gentlemen	123	600,000	2:00.23	120
1998	Malek	5	A. Solis	115	Bagshot	113	Don't Blame Rio	117	600,000	2:02.26	108
1999	Free House	5	C.J. McCarron	123	Event of the Year	119	Silver Charm	124	600,000	2:00.67	119
2000	General Challenge	4	C.S. Nakatani	121	Budroyale	122	Puerto Madero	118	600,000	2:01.49	117
2001	Tiznow	4	C.J.McCarron	122	Wooden Phone	117	Tribunal	116	600,000	2:01.55	117
2002	Milwaukee Brew	5	K.J. Desormeaux	115	Western Pride	116	Kudos	116	600,000	2:01.02	116
2003	Milwaukee Brew	6	E.S. Prado	119	Congaree	124	Kudos	117	600,000	1:59.80	116

Beyer Index: 115.71

SANTA ANITA OAKS, 1 1/16 Miles, 3-Year-Old Fillies,
Santa Anita, 2003 Purse: $300,000

Year	Winner	Age	Jockey	Wt.	Second	Wt.	Third	Wt.	Win Value	Time	Beyer
1935	Dunlin Lady	2	W. Saunders	119	Rattlebrain	119	Reelon	118	2,375	0:34.00	
1937	Patty Cake	3	A. Gray	113	Alice G.	113	Coramine	116	3,305	1:12.20	
1938	Minulus	3	C. Corbett	109	First Kiss	111	Midwick	112	4,775	1:11.80	
1939	Sweet Nancy	3	J. Longden	112	Ciencia	112	Morning Breeze	118	10,050	1:25.60	
1940	Augury	3	L. Knapp	121	Less Time	112	Wanna Hygro	112	9,450	1:25.20	
1941	Cute Trick	3	B. James	112	Appeasement	112	Transient	112	9,800	1:23.60	
1945	Busher	3	J. Longden	121	Mist	115	Glory Time	115	18,605	1:23.60	
1946	Enfilade	3	A. Kirkland	117	Honeymoon	121	Lovonsite	111	19,440	1:11.00	
1947	Hubble Bubble	3	B. Layton	113	Maharetta	113	Judy-Rae	117	36,500	1:23.80	
1948	Mrs. Rabbit	3	R. Permane	115	Itsabet	118	Candy Kane	118	41,000	1:24.00	
1949	Gaffery	3	W. Litzenberg	118	June Bride	115	Patmigal	115	45,440	1:24.60	
1950	Special Touch	3	E. Arcaro	115	Talking Point	115	Sea Garden	115	46,000	1:23.80	
1951	Ruth Lily	3	J. Adams	115	Sickle's Image	121	Sweet Talk	115	41,700	1:23.40	
	Sweet Talk finished first but was disqualified and placed third										
1952	Season's Best	3	A. Kolonics	114	Hadassah	108	Your Hostess	117	13,400	1:45.20	
1953	Femme Fatale	3	R. York	111	Schatzi	108	Ramasari	112	13,150	1:45.00	
1954	Quillo Maid	3	J. Phillippi	114	Frosty Dawn	121	Love Factor	119	13,400	1:36.60	
1956	Dupatta	3	R. Trejos	114	Chargers Girl	116	Mrs. Muriel L.	116	11,250	1:24.60	
1957	Market Basket	3	I. Valenzuela	118	Royal Rasher	114	Tourbillonte	116	13,700	1:37.40	
1958	Penumbra	3	W. Boland	112	Well Away	110	Nushie	112	14,100	1:44.80	
1959	Silver Spoon	3	R. York	117	Miss Uppity	117	Bitter Feud	110	13,250	1:41.80	
1960	Darling June	3	D. Pierce	117	Angel Flight	111	Salt Lake	112	13,950	1:44.00	
1961	Fun House	3	G. Taniguchi	111	Oil Royalty	111	Amri-An	117	13,900	1:43.00	
1962	Pixie Erin	3	J. Longden	114	Lincoln Center	112	Dors	112	17,150	1:46.00	
1963	Lamb Chop	3	M. Ycaza	115	Nalee	115	Curious Clover	115	16,150	1:46.40	
1964	Blue Norther	3	W. Shoemaker	115	Face the Facts	115	Roman Goddess	115	26,300	1:41.80	
1965	Desert Love	3	D. Pierce	115	Ardell C.	115	Admiring	115	27,750	1:42.60	
1966	Spearfish	3	D. Pierce	115	Ego Twist	115	Will Hall	115	2,900	1:43.00	
1967	Fish House	3	W. Shoemaker	115	Mira Femme	115			27,800	1:44.20	
					Spinning Around	115					
1968	Allie's Serenade	3	L. Pincay Jr	115	Fish Net	115	Miss Ribot	115	26,550	1:43.20	
1969	Dumpty's Lady	3	W. Shoemaker	115	Hasty Hitter	115	Lover's Quarrel	115	25,900	1:46.00	
1970	Opening Bid	3	D. Pierce	115	Cathy Honey	115	Turn 'n Turn About	115	27,300	1:42.20	
1971	Turkish Trousers	3	W. Shoemaker	115	Generous Portion	115	Sapose Speed	115	31,650	1:42.80	
1972	Susan's Girl	3	V. Teiada	115	Dumpty's Dream	115	Chargerette	115	32,300	1:43.60	
1973	Belle Marie	3	L. Pincay Jr	115	Tallahto	115	Waltz Fan	115	31,800	1:41.80	
1974	Miss Musket	3	W. Shoemaker	115	Out to Lunch	115	Special Team	115	32,800	1:47.00	
1975	Sarsar	3	W. Shoemaker	115	Double You Lou	115	Fascinating Girl	115	33,100	1:42.80	
1976	Girl in Love	3	F. Toro	115	I'm a Charmer	115	Queen to be	115	32,700	1:43.20	
1977	Sound of Summer	3	F. Toro	115	Wavy Waves	115	Lady T.V.	115	33,200	1:42.20	
1978	Grenzen	3	D.G. McHargue	115	Equanimity	115	Mashteen	115	47,800	1:43.80	
1979	Caline	3	W. Shoemaker	115	Terlingua	115	It's in the Air	115	69,000	1:41.60	
1980	Bold 'n Determined	3	E. Delahoussaye	115	Street Ballet	115	Table Hands	115	67,100	1:41.20	
1981	Nell's Briquette	3	W. Shoemaker	115	Bee a Scout	115	Ice Princess	115	82,550	1:42.80	

Year	Winner	Age	Jockey	Wt.	Second	Wt.	Third	Wt.	Win Value	Time	Beyer
1982	Blush With Pride	3	W. Shoemaker	115	Skillful Joy	115	Carry a Tune	115	100,400	1:45.80	
1983	Fabulous Notion	3	D. Pierce	115	Capichi	115	O'Happy Day	115	93,900	1:43.60	
1984	Althea	3	L. Pincay Jr	117	Personable Lady	117	Life's Magic	117	118,500	1:43.60	
1985	Fran's Valentine	3	P.A. Valenzuela	117	Rascal Lass	117	Wising Up	117	122,100	1:42.40	
1986	Hidden Light	3	W. Shoemaker	117	Twilight Ridge	117	An Empress	117	120,200	1:42.40	
1987	Timely Assertion	3	G.L. Stevens	117	Buryyourbelief	117	Very Subtle	117	95,100	1:43.60	
1988	Winning Colors	3	G.L. Stevens	117	Jeanne Jones	117	Goodbye Halo	117	89,900	1:42.00	
1989	Imaginary Lady	3	G.L. Stevens	117	Some Romance	117	Kool Arrival	117	125,400	1:43.40	
1990	Hail Atlantis	3	G.L. Stevens	117	Bright Candles	117	Fit to Scout	117	122,800	1:43.00	97
1991	Lite Light	3	C.S. Nakatani	117	Garden Gal	117	Ifyoucouldseemenow	117	122,100	1:42.40	100
1992	Golden Treat	3	K.J. Desormeaux	117	Magical Maiden	117	Queens Court Queen	117	129,300	1:43.37	90
1993	Eliza	3	P.A. Valenzuela	117	Stalcreek	117	Dance for Vanny	117	129,200	1:42.97	99
1994	Lakeway	3	K.J. Desormeaux	117	Dianes Halo	117	Flying in the Lane	117	122,800	1:41.66	101
1995	Serena's Song	3	C.S. Nakatani	117	Urbane	117	Mari's Sheba	117	121,600	1:42.71	106
1996	Antespend	3	C.W. Antley	117	Cara Rafaela	117	Hidden Lake	117	128,600	1:43.04	99
1997	Sharp Cat	3	C.S. Nakatani	117	Queen of Money	117	Double Park	117	128,800	1:42.22	101
1998	Hedonist	3	K.J. Desormeaux	117	Keeper Hill	117	Nijinsky's Passion	117	150,000	1:44.14	91
1999	Excellent Meeting	3	K.J. Desormeaux	117	Tout Charmant	117	Gleefully	117	150,000	1:43.26	96
2000	Surfside	3	P. Day	117	Kumari Continent	117	Classy Cara	117	180,000	1:44.03	93
2001	Golden Ballet	3	C.J. McCarron	117	Flute	117	Affluent	117	180,000	1:41.83	101
2002	You	3	J.D. Bailey	117	Habibti	117	Ile de France	117	180,000	1:42.70	99
2003	Composure	3	J.D. Bailey	117	Elloluv	117	Go for Glamour	117	180,000	1:43.34	102

Beyer Index: 98.21

Distance 3 furlongs (for 2-year-olds) in 1935; 6 furlongs, 1937-38, 1946; 7 furlongs, 1939-51, 1956; 1 mile in 1954, 1957. Run as Santa Susana Stakes, 1935-51, 1959-85.

SANTA MARGARITA INVITATIONAL HANDICAP, 1 1/8 Miles, Fillies and Mares, 4-Year-Olds and Up, Santa Anita, 2003 Purse: $300,000

Year	Winner	Age	Jockey	Wt.	Second	Wt.	Third	Wt.	Win Value	Time	Beyer
1935	Ted Clark	5	C. Turk	101	Pitter Pat	104	Rock X	104	2,150	1:26.40	
1936	Singing Wood	5	R. Jones	122	Tick On	113	Sound Advice	111	2,130	1:23.00	
1937	Stand Pat	6	W. Saunders	118	Party Spirit	110	Speed to Spare	105	3,145	1:13.00	
1938	Primulus	5	L. Balaski	112	Mars Shield	117	Watersplash	113	4,275	1:49.00	
1939	Flying Lee	4	S. Renick	106	Sweet Nancy	106	Genie Palatine	105	9,500	1:47.20	
1940	Fairy Chant	3	D. Dodson	103	Omelet	110	Sweet Nancy	108	9,000	1:46.80	
1941	Omelet	5	J. Westrope	116	Augury	120	Barrancosa	113	7,100	1:47.20	
1945	Busher	3	J. Longden	126	Whirlabout	123	Canina	117	36,490	1:43.00	
1946	Canina	5	J. Longden	121	Happy Issue	113	Be Faithful	115	39,300	1:43.40	
1947	Monsoon	5	R. Neves	114	Double F.F.	112	Be Faithful	122	3,800	1:43.00	
1948	Miss Doreen	6	J. Longden	116	Elpis	122	Miss Grillo	124	38,400	1:46.00	
1949	Lurline B.	4	W. Litzenberg	108	Danada Gift	112	Alablue	115	38,800	1:53.00	
1950	Two Lea	4	S. Brooks	126	Gaffery	118	But Why Not	116	35,700	1:52.80	
1951	Special Touch	4	W. Shoemaker	114	Bewitch	122	Bed o' Roses	125	36,400	1:48.60	
1952	Bed o' Roses	5	W. Shoemaker	129	Next Move	130	Toto	105	39,550	1:51.40	
1953	Spanish Cream	5	E. Guerin	128	Ruth Lily	112	A Gleam	130	36,800	1:44.80	
1954	Cerise Reine	4	W. Shoemaker	121	Last Wave	112	Wandering Ways	113	38,100	1:47.00	
1955	Blue Butterfly	6	J. Longden	121	Miz Clementine	130	Tessa	112	33,400	1:48.60	
1956	Our Betters	4	E. Arcaro	120	Island Queen	111	Solid Rae	113	34,500	1:49.20	
1957	Our Betters	5	J. Longden	118	Nooran	111	Miss Todd	116	35,600	1:49.00	
1958	Born Rich	5	M. Ycaza	113	Market Basket	123	Nooran	118	34,200	1:50.60	
1959	Bug Brush	4	A. Valenzuela	126	Milly K.	115	Penumbra	110	36,600	1:48.20	
1960	Silver Spoon	4	E. Arcaro	130	Indian Maid	116	Narva	113	34,800	1:48.80	
1961	Sister Antoine	4	W. Harmatz	113	Paris Pike	113	Geechee Lou	118	37,900	1:49.60	
1962	Queen America	6	G. Taniguchi	113	Oil Royalty	117	Tritoma	116	39,600	1:49.40	
1963	Pixie Erin	4	P. Moreno	116	Table Mate	119	Firmannaha	115	36,600	1:54.20	
1964	Curious Clover	4	K. Church	118	Hi Rated	116	Sintesis	119	29,075	1:48.80	
1964	Batteur	4	M. Ycaza	116	Jalousie II	119	Jazz Queen	116	29,075	1:49.00	
1965	Curious Clover	5	K. Church	118	Treachery	117	Petticoat	114	37,850	1:49.60	
1966	Straight Deal	4	W. Shoemaker	121	Pollen	119	Batteur	124	39,300	1:48.60	
1967	Miss Moona	4	L. Pincay Jr	118	Maintain	112	Streamer	114	39,800	1:50.20	
	....	4	....		....		Lost Message	112			
1968	Gamely	4	M. Ycaza	125	Princessnesian	120	Amerigo Lady	123	60,000	1:49.00	
1969	Princessnesian	5	D. Pierce	125	Guest Room	116	Sinking Spring	113	60,000	1:53.00	
1970	Gallant Bloom	4	J.L. Rotz	129	Commissary	117	Tipping Time	117	60,000	1:50.60	
1971	Manta	5	L. Pincay Jr	126	Beja	118	Last of the Line	123	60,000	1:48.80	
1972	Turkish Trousers	4	W. Shoemaker	125	Convenience	118	Typecast	124	60,000	1:47.80	
1973	Susan's Girl	4	L. Pincay Jr	125	Convenience	123	Minstrel Miss	115	60,000	1:47.80	
1974	Tizna	5	F. Toro	117	Penny Flight	113	Tallahto	119	60,000	1:50.80	
1975	Tizna	6	D. Pierce	120	Susan's Girl	123	Gay Style	125	60,000	1:48.60	
1976	Fascinating Girl	4	F. Toro	115	Summertime Promise	114	Charger's Star	114	60,000	1:49.40	
1977	Lucie Manet	4	D.G. McHargue	119	Bastonera II	126	Hope of Glory	114	60,000	1:48.40	
1978	Taisez Vous	4	D. Pierce	125	Sensational	118	Merry Lady III	114	60,000	1:49.00	
1979	Sanedki	5	W. Shoemaker	124	Surera	115	Ida Delia	117	75,000	1:47.80	

Queen Yasna finished second but was disqualified and placed seventh

Year	Winner	Age	Jockey	Wt.	Second	Wt.	Third	Wt.	Win Value	Time	Beyer
1980	Glorious Song	4	C.J. McCarron	120	The Very One	116	Kankam	125	82,500	1:48.40	
1981	Princess Karenda	4	L. Pincay Jr	118	Glorious Song	130	Ack's Secret	122	120,000	1:47.20	
1982	Ack's Secret	6	L. Pincay Jr	118	Track Robbery	123	Past Forgetting	122	150,000	1:47.60	
1983	Marimbula	5	S. Hawley	119	Avigaition	120	Sintrillium	114	150,000	1:48.20	
1984	Adored	4	F. Toro	114	High Haven	118	Weekend Surprise	114	150,000	1:48.60	
1985	Lovlier Linda	5	C.J. McCarron	119	Mitterand	123	Percipient	115	180,000	1:48.00	
1986	Lady's Secret	4	J. Velasquez	125	Johnica	120	Dontstop Themusic	122	180,000	1:47.00	
1987	North Sider	5	A. Cordero Jr	117	Winter Treasure	115	Frau Altiva	117	180,000	1:48.80	
1988	Flying Julia	5	F. Olivares	114	Hollywood Glitter	118	Clabber Girl	118	180,000	1:50.40	
989	Bayakoa	5	L. Pincay Jr	118	Goodbye Halo	125	No Review	117	180,000	1:48.40	
1990	Bayakoa	6	C.J. McCarron	127	Gorgeous	125	Luthier's Launch	113	180,000	1:48.40	110
1991	Little Brianne	6	J.A. Garcia	119	Bayakoa	126	A Wild Ride	119	180,000	1:48.40	110
1992	Paseana	5	C.J. McCarron	122	Laramie Moon	116	Colour Chart	118	180,000	1:47.48	110
1993	Southern Truce	5	C.S. Nakatani	115	Paseana	125	Guiza	114	180,000	1:49.46	100
1994	Paseana	7	C.J. McCarron	123	Kalita Melody	117	Stalcreek	119	180,000	1:49.12	104
1995	Queens Court Queen	6	C.S. Nakatani	120	Paseana	123	Klassy Kim	116	180,000	1:48.81	99
1996	Twice the Vice	5	C.J. McCarron	117	Sleep Easy	115	Jewel Princess	119	180,000	1:49.53	101
1997	Jewel Princess	5	C.S. Nakatani	125	Top Rung	116	Hidden Lake	114	180,000	1:49.30	102
1998	Toda Una Dama	5	G.F. Almeida	114	Exotic Wood	123	Praviana	114	180,000	1:48.87	108
1999	Manistique	4	G.L Stevens	122	Magical Allure	118	India Divina	116	180,000	1:48.31	109
2000	Riboletta	5	C.S. Nakatani	115	Bordelaise	114	Snowberg	114	180,000	1:50.40	98
2001	Lazy Slusan	6	D.R. Flores	116	Spain	122	Critikola	116	180,000	1:48.59	99
2002	Azeri	4	M.E. Smith	115	Spain	118	Printemps	116	180,000	1:49.01	110
2003	Starrer	5	P.A. Valenzuela	121	Sightseek	116	Bella Bellucci	116	180,000	1:48.20	111

Beyer Index: 105.07

Distance 7 furlongs, 1935–36; 6 furlongs, 1937; 1 1/16 miles, 1938–48, 1953–54. For 3-year-olds and up, prior to 1941, 1942–60. Open to both sexes prior to 1938

SANTA MARIA HANDICAP, 1 1/16 Miles, Fillies and Mares, 4-Year-Olds and Up, Santa Anita, 2003 Purse: $200,000

Year	Winner	Age	Jockey	Wt.	Second	Wt.	Third	Wt.	Win Value	Time	Beyer
1934	Wise Daughter	3	J. Westrope	104	Rock X,	104	Wacoche	101	2,180	1:12.40	
1935	Soon Over	4	S. Coucci	109	Sound Advice	112	Beefsteak	110	2,310	1:11.00	
1936	Papenie	3	L. Haas	110	Half Time	118	Grey Count	109	3,575	1:12.80	
1938	Sun Egret	3	A. Shelhamer	114	Short Notice	116	Specify	116	4,900	1:12.00	
1939	Porter's Mite	3	B. James	123	Sweet Patrice	109	Time Alone	120	9,500	1:12.40	
1940	Augury	3	L. Knapp	105	Camp Verde	120	Liberty Franc	111	10,250	1:14.40	
1941	Phar Rong	2	L. Haas	117	Pan Time	117	Fillibeg	114	8,130	:34.40	
1946	Honeymoon	3	T. Atkinson	118	Ariel Belle	115	Going WIth Me	115	17,205	1:37.40	
1947	On Trust	3	R. Neves	117	Stepfather	117	Owners Choice	122	36,800	1:37.40	
1952	Special Touch	5	E. Arcaro	121	Next Move	128	Blue Cloth	108	13,800	1:39.20	
1953	Spanish Cream	5	E. Guerin	124	Mab's Choice	115	Ruth Lily	113	13,200	1:38.20	
1954	Smart Barbara	4	G. Glisson	119	Auntie	116	Cerise Reine	119	15,300	1:25.60	
1955	Blue Butterfly	6	J. Westrope	118	Mab's Choice	115	Alibhai Lynn	122	14,000	1:22.00	
1956	In Reserve	4	J. Longden	120	Manotick	119	Mary Machree	115	15,100	1:23.20	
1957	King's Mistake	7	W. Shoemaker	115	Triple Jay	119	Noors Queen	109	16,900	1:46.00	
1958	Nooran	4	W. Boland	115	Myrtle	111	Ballet Khal	117	17,500	1:42.80	
1959	Two Cent Stamp	4	G. Taniguchi	111	Milly K.	115	Gleaming Star	114	17,400	1:43.60	
1960	Silver Spoon	4	E. Arcaro	127	La Plume	111	Indian Maid	116	17,250	1:42.60	
1961	Tritoma	5	J. Leonard	113	Perizade	109	Swiss Roll	124	18,600	1:43.20	
1962	Rose O'Neill	4	I. Valenzuela	118	Oil Royalty	117	Teacation	118	17,800	1:44.40	
1963	Linita	6	M. Ycaza	121	Pixie Erin	115	Rose O'Neill	121	17,300	1:42.60	
1964	Curious Clover	4	K. Church	113	Jazz Queen	115	Batteur	116	19,050	1:43.20	
1965	Batteur	5	F. Alvarez	119	Affectionately	122	Curious Clover	118	18,650	1:42.80	
1966	Poona Queen	6	M. Ycaza	119	Straight Deal	121	Gallarush	112	20,650	1:42.40	
1967	Natashka	4	W. Shoemaker	123	Miss Moona	118	Streamer	115	20,300	1:42.40	
1968	Gamely	4	M. Ycaza	122	Princessnesian	117	Moog	110	23,400	1:43.80	
1969	Dark Mirage	4	E. Belmonte	126	Desert Law	115	Sinking Spring	112	20,450	1:43.00	
1970	Gallant Bloom	4	J.L. Rotz	126	Commissary	116	Luz Del Sol	114	21,050	1:42.20	
1971	Last of the Line	4	J. Lambert	120	Night Stalker	111	Manta	127	26,850	1:41.60	
1972	Turkish Trousers	4	W. Shoemaker	123	Typecast	126	Street Dancer	123	34,500	1:41.20	
1973	Susan's Girl	4	L. Pincay Jr	125	Convenience	123	Hill Circus	119	32,900	1:42.00	
1974	Convenience	6	L. Pincay Jr	121	Tizna	117	Tallahto	119	34,750	1:42.80	
1975	Gay Style	5	W. Shoemaker	127	Tizna	120	Susan's Girl	124	34,650	1:42.00	
1976	Gay Style	6	D. Pierce	127	Raise Your Skirts	120	Tizna	127	35,100	1:41.40	
1977	Hail Hilarious	4	D. Pierce	122	Swingtime	120	Bastonera II	126	36,050	1:42.00	
1978	Swingtime	6	F. Toro	122	Winter Solstice	124	Granja Sueno	113	37,500	1:41.40	
1979	Grenzen	4	L. Pincay Jr	124	Ida Delia	118	Drama Critic	122	37,650	1:47.20	
1980	Kankam	5	E. Delahoussaye	123	Flaming Leaves	123	Miss Magnetic	117	47,400	1:41.80	
1981	Glorious Song	5	C.J. McCarron	127	Track Robbery	117	Miss Huntington	113	45,450	1:43.20	
1982	Targa	5	F. Olivares	114	Jameela	124	Track Robbery	124	65,100	1:42.00	
1982	Star Pastures	5	W. Shoemaker	119	Sintrillium	116	Viga	112	49,650	1:42.60	
1983	Sangue	5	L. Pincay Jr	124	Cat Girl	115	Happy Bride	116	50,650	1:41.00	

Year	Winner	Age	Jockey	Wt.	Second	Wt.	Third	Wt.	Win Value	Time	Beyer
1984	Marisma	6	L. Pincay Jr	117	Brindy Brindy	114	Sierva	118	69,850	1:44.20	
1984	High Haven	5	R. Sibille	116	Castilla	122	Avigaition	120	50,600	1:42.40	
1985	Adored	5	L. Pincay Jr	124	Dontstop Themusic	121	Lovlier Linda	122	88,800	1:42.40	
1986	Love Smitten	5	C.J. McCarron	120	Johnica	121	North Sider	118	65,600	1:44.60	
1987	Fran's Valentine	5	P.A. Valenzuela	121	North Sider	118	Infinidad	113	91,700	1:42.60	
1988	Mausie	6	G.L. Stevens	114	Miss Alto	118	Novel Sprite	115	63,800	1:43.60	
1989	Miss Brio	5	E. Delahoussaye	119	Bayakoa	118	Annoconnor	122	79,000	1:41.00	
1990	Bayakoa	6	C.J. McCarron	126	Nikishka	117	Carita Tostada	112	90,200	1:43.00	
1991	Little Brianne	6	J. Garcia	117	Luna Elegante	114	Somethingmerry	114	89,700	1:41.60	106
1992	Paseana	5	C.J. McCarron	120	Colour Chart	118	Campagnarde	117	89,100	1:41.94	104
1993	Race the Wild Wind	4	K.J. Desormeaux	117	Paseana	126	Southern Truce	116	90,500	1:41.27	112
1994	Supah Gem	4	C.S. Nakatani	116	Paseana	124	Alysbelle	116	90,700	1:48.83	104
1995	Queens Court Queen	6	C.S. Nakatani	118	Paseana	123	Key Phrase	117	89,300	1:41.61	103
1996	Serena's Song	4	G.L. Stevens	124	Twice the Vice	118	Real Connection	114	95,800	1:42.22	105
1997	Jewel Princess	5	C.S. Nakatani	123	Cat's Cradle	118	Top Rung	117	97,900	1:41.72	114
1998	Exotic Wood	6	C.J. McCarron	121	Toda Una Dama	115	Tuxedo Junction	115	120,000	1:40.95	114
1999	India Divina	5	G.K. Gomez	114	Victory Stripes	115	Belle's Flag	117	120,000	1:42.71	101
2000	Manistique	5	C.S. Nakatani	125	Snowberg	114	Gourmet Girl	115	120,000	1:42.60	105
2001	Lovellon	5	G.L. Stevens	116	Feverish	119	Critikola	115	120,000	1:43.37	99
2002	Favorite Funtime	5	G.L. Stevens	116	Verruma	114	Printemps	116	120,000	1:44.15	101
2003	Starrer	5	P.A. Valenzuela	119	You	118	Rhiana	112	120,000	1:42.75	103

Beyer Index: 105.46

SANTA MONICA HANDICAP, 7 Furlongs, Fillies and Mares, 4-Year-Olds and Up, Santa Anita, 2003 Purse: $200,000

Year	Winner	Age	Jockey	Wt.	Second	Wt.	Third	Wt.	Win Value	Time	Beyer
1957	Mary Machree	6	G. Taniguchi	122	Triple Jay	120	Our Betters	121	13,950	1:22.00	
1958	Market Basket	4	R. York	122	Ballet Khal	117	Cold Hands	109	13,750	1:22.80	
1959	Bug Brush	4	A. Valenzuela	124	Well Away	118	Gleaming Star	114	14,800	1:23.00	
1960	Silver Spoon	4	E. Arcaro	124	Margaretta	121	Indian Maid	120	13,700	1:23.00	
1961	Taboo	4	W. Shoemaker	110	Sue III	117	Paris Pike	113	11,125	1:23.00	
1961	Swiss Roll	4	W. Shoemaker	117	Wiggle II	122	Tritoma	112	10,925	1:22.20	
1962	Perizade	6	R. Campas	115	Queen America	115	Linita	120	14,950	1:22.40	
1963	Table Mate	4	W. Shoemaker	114	Linita	121	My Portrait	118	14,550	1:22.00	
1964	Chop House	4	B. Baeza	116	Sunday Doll	111	Jazz Queen	112	15,650	1:22.80	
1965	Face the Facts	4	M. Ycaza	122	Hi Rated	116	Coliseum Honey	111	12,375	1:22.60	
1965	Chop House	5	I. Valenzuela	120	Affectionately	126	Batteur	118	12,725	1:22.40	
1966	Batteur	6	E. Belmonte	123	Terentia	119	Jalousie II	117	17,450	1:22.40	
1967	Miss Moona	4	L. Pincay Jr	115	Streamer	115	Countess Candy	113	16,650	1:22.40	
1968	Amerigo Lady	4	D. Pierce	118	Amerigo's Fancy	117	Gamely	122	16,450	1:03.00	
1969	Gamely	5	W. Harris	127	Time to Leave	124	Guest Room	115	13,450	1:23.60	
1971	Manta	5	L. Pincay Jr	125	Beja	119	Night Stalker	112	21,900	1:22.20	
1972	Typecast	6	L. Pincay Jr	123	Turkish Trousers	126	Goddess Special	114	29,300	1:21.40	
1973	Chou Croute	5	J.L. Rotz	128	Generous Portion	114	Minstrel Miss	115	27,800	1:23.60	
1974	Tizna	5	F. Toro	116	Susan's Girl	127	Impressive Style	118	28,050	1:24.00	
1975	Sister Fleet	5	F. Toro	115	Susan's Girl	125	Modus Vivendi	123	31,250	1:21.40	
1976	Gay Style	6	D. Pierce	125	Raise Your Skirts	123	Tizna	129	26,650	1:22.00	
1977	Hail Hilarious	4	D. Pierce	119	Bastonera II	125	Modus Vivendi	121	28,150	1:22.60	
1978	Winter Solstice	6	D.G. McHargue	123	Little Happiness	115	Splendid Size	117	27,200	1:21.20	
1979	Grenzen	4	L. Pincay Jr	122	Dottie's Doll	116	Bidding Bold	115	40,600	1:21.60	
1980	Flack Flack	5	W. Shoemaker	117	Shine High	115	Flaming Leaves	123	39,100	1:23.80	
1981	Parsley	5	A. Cordero Jr	116	Ack's Secret	125	Splendid Girl	118	40,050	1:23.40	
1982	Past Forgetting	4	W. Shoemaker	122	Nell's Briquette	118	In True Form	117	49,250	1:20.60	
	Marimbula finished second but was disqualified and placed sixth										
1983	Past Forgetting	5	C.J. McCarron	123	Sierva	119	Bara Lass	115	49,850	1:23.40	
1984	Bara Lass	5	W. Guerra	124	Holiday Dancer	117	Bally Knockan	113	52,250	1:22.00	
1985	Lovlier Linda	5	W. Shoemaker	123	Dontstop Themusic	123	Foggy Nation	119	48,900	1:22.80	
1986	Her Royalty	5	C.J. McCarron	120	North Sider	119	Take My Picture	117	51,300	1:21.60	
1987	Pine Tree Lane	5	A. Cordero Jr	125	Balladry	116	Her Royalty	119	58,140	1:21.80	
1988	Pine Tree Lane	6	G.L. Stevens	121	Fairly Old	115	Le l'Argent	120	73,500	1:23.00	
1989	Miss Brio	5	E. Delahoussaye	117	Valdemosa	116	Josette	115	64,800	1:21.60	
1990	Stormy but Valid	4	G.L. Stevens	119	Survive	118	Hot Novel	117	61,300	1:22.40	108
1991	Devil's Orchid	4	R.A. Baze	116	Stormy but Valid	121	Classic Value	118	90,800	1:21.80	103
	Classic Value finished second but was disqualified and placed third										
1992	Laramie Moon	5	E. Delahoussaye	116	D'Or Ruckus	114	Ifyoucouldseemenow	118	94,700	1:22.66	99
1993	Freedom Cry	5	A. Solis	114	Devil's Orchid	119	Mama Simba	114	91,200	1:21.78	106
1994	Southern Truce	6	G.L. Stevens	116	Arches of Gold	119	Mamselle Bebette	115	93,100	1:21.44	97
1995	Key Phrase	5	C.W. Antley	116	Flying In the Lane	114	Desert Stormer	117	93,100	1:22.82	107
1996	Serena's Song	4	G.L. Stevens	123	Exotic Wood	118	Klassy Kim	116	96,800	1:21.56	108
1997	Toga Toga Toga	5	J.A. Garcia	114	Ski Dancer	117	Grab the Prize	116	96,750	1:23.27	102
1998	Exotic Wood	6	C.J. McCarron	121	Madame Pandit	119	Advancing Star	121	120,000	1:21.07	105
1999	Stop Traffic	6	C.A. Black	120	Belle's Flag	118	Closed Escrow	116	120,000	1:22.17	105
2000	Honest Lady	4	C.S. Nakatani	114	Kalookan Queen	116	Enjoy the Moment	118	132,840	1:21.40	106

Year	Winner	Age	Jockey	Wt.	Second	Wt.	Third	Wt.	Win Value	Time	Beyer
2001	Nany's Sweep	5	K.J. Desormeaux	117	Serenita	115	Surfside	121	120,000	1:22.50	100
2002	Kalookan Queen	6	A. Solis	119	Leading Light	115	Spain	120	120,000	1:22.37	106
2003	Affluent	5	A. Solis	119	Sightseek	115	Secret of Mecca	110	120,000	1:22.17	102

Beyer Index: 103.86

For 3-year-olds and up prior to 1960

SECRETARIAT STAKES, 1 1/4 Miles (Turf), 3-Year-Olds, Arlington Park, 2003 Purse: $400,000

Year	Winner	Age	Jockey	Wt.	Second	Wt.	Third	Wt.	Win Value	Time	Beyer
1974	Glossary	3	A. Santiago	114	Stonewalk	123	Talkative Turn	114	96,400	1:42.80	
1975	Intrepid Hero	3	A. Cordero Jr	123	Gab Bag	117	Larrikin	117	94,000	1:49.80	
1976	Joachim	3	S. Maple	123	Romeo	112	L'Heureux	117	88,400	1:50.80	
1977	Text	3	M. Castaneda	120	Run Dusty Run	126	Flag Officer	123	73,140	1:42.00	
1978	Mac Diarmida	3	J. Cruguet	120	April Axe	120	The Liberal Member	114	99,600	2:29.80	
1979	Golden Act	3	S. Hawley	126	Smarten	120	Flying Dad	120	91,080	2:32.80	
1980	Spruce Needles	3	J.C. Espinoza	123	Proctor	120	The Messenger	123	99,960	2:40.80	
1981	Sing Sing	3	M. Venezia	114	Television Studio	117	Jungle Tough	114	96,240	2:53.60	
1982	Half Iced	3	D. MacBeth	114	Dew Line	114	Continuing	114	90,000	2:31.20	
1983	Fortnightly	3	P. Day	117	Jack Slade	114	Reap	114	102,360	2:32.40	
1984	Vision	3	G. McCarron	114	Mr. Japan	114	Pine Circle	114	117,240	2:38.40	
1985	Derby Wish	3	R.P. Romero	114	Day Shift	114	Duluth	123	146,880	2:01.00	
	Racing Star finished second but was disqualified and placed fourth										
1986	Southjet	3	J.A. Santos	113	Glow	120	Tripoli Shores	115	102,510	2:02.00	
1987	Stately Don	3	J. Vasquez	113	The Medic	120	Zaizoom	120	103,590	2:04.60	
1989	Hawkster	3	P.A. Valenzuela	123	Chenin Blanc	114	Ninety Years Young	114	150,000	2:04.00	
1990	Super Abound	3	R.P. Romero	114	Unbridled	126	Super Fan	117	150,000	2:01.60	
1991	Jackie Wackie	3	P. Day	123	Olympio	126	Sultry Song	114	180,000	2:01.20	100
1992	Ghazi	3	R.G. Davis	114	Paradise Creek	123	Tango Charlie	117	180,000	2:01.00	98
1993	Awad	3	J. Velasquez	120	Explosive Red	123	Brazany	114	240,000	2:08.60	106
1994	Vaudeville	3	G.L. Stevens	123	Dare and Go	114	Jaggery John	120	240,000	2:01.00	100
1995	Hawk Attack	3	P. Day	120	Mecke	117	Petit Poucet	114	240,000	2:00.00	101
1996	Marlin	3	S.J. Sellers	114	Trail City	126	Dancing Fred	114	300,000	2:01.00	106
1997	Honor Glide	3	G.K. Gomez	123	Casey Tibbs	116	Glok	114	240,000	2:02.60	105
2000	Ciro	3	M.J. Kinane	120	King Cugat	123	Guillamou City	117	240,000	2:01.64	108
2001	Startac	3	A. Solis	121	Strut The Stage	123	Sharp Performance	120	240,000	2:04.91	99
2002	Chiselling	3	K.J. Desormeaux	121	Jazz Beat	117	Extra Check	116	240,000	2:04.16	97
2003	Kicken Kris	3	J.J. Castellano	116	Joe Bear	116	Lismore Knight	121	240,000	2:02.53	106

Beyer Index: 102.36

Distance 1 1/16 miles, 1974,1977; 1 1/8 miles, 1975-76, 1 1/2 miles 1978-84. Run on main track in 1977. Run at Hawthorne in 1985. Not run in 1998-99

SHADWELL TURF MILE STAKES, 1 Mile (Turf), 3-Year-Olds and Up, Keeneland Race Course, 2003 Purse: $600,000

Year	Winner	Age	Jockey	Wt.	Second	Wt.	Third	Wt.	Win Value	Time	Beyer
1986	Leprechaun's Wish	4	J.D. Bailey	126	Ingot's Ruler	126	Wop Wop	126	100,848	1:51.80	
1987	Storm on the L'se	4	J.C. Espinoza	126	Uptown Swell	126	Vilzak	126	101,855	1:52.60	
1988	Niccolo Polo	5	D. Brumfield	126	Pollenate	126	Eve's Error	126	101,823	1:53.00	
1989	Steinlen	6	J.A. Santos	116	Crystal Moment	126	Posen	126	122,103	1:52.40	
1990	Itsallgreektome	4	J. Velasquez	126	Opening Verse	126	Super Abound	126	121,973	1:52.20	
1991	Itsallgreektome	4	J. Velasquez	126	Opening Verse	126	Super Abound	126	119,600	1:48.40	109
1992	Lotus Pool	5	C.R. Woods Jr	126	Thunder Regent	126	Chenin Blanc	113	113,646	1:48.20	105
1993	Coaxing Matt	4	E.M. Martin Jr	122	Adam Smith	126	Mr. Light Tres	126	116,420	1:53.00	102
1994	Weekend Madness	4	Sellers SJ	123	Words of War	123	Pennine Ridge	123	116,327	1:38.60	105
1995	Dumaani	4	Krone JA	126	Holy Mountain	126	Mr Purple	123	116,514	1:38.60	99
1996	Dumaani	5	J.A. Krone	126	Desert Waves	126	Dove Hunt	126	133,842	1:35.40	102
1997	Wild Event	4	M. Guidry	126	Trail City	126	Soviet Line	126	134,075	1:34.60	101
1998	Favorite Trick	3	P. Day	123	Soviet Line	126	Wild Event	126	168,795	1:35.00	109
1999	Kirkwall	5	V. Espinoza	126	Delay of Game	126	Ladies Din	126	281,232	1:37.80	103
2000	Altibr	5	R. Migliore	126	Strategic Mission	126	Quiet Resolve	126	279,744	1:33.72	106
2001	Hap	5	J.D. Bailey	126	Where's Taylor	126	Aly's Alley	126	346,270	1:35.98	110
2002	Landseer	3	E.S. Prado	123	Touch of the Blues	126	Beat Hollow	126	372,000	1:35.55	104
2003	Perfect Soul	5	E.S. Prado	126	Honor in War	126	Touch of the Blues	126	372,000	1:36.01	107

Beyer Index: 104.77

SHOEMAKER BREEDERS' CUP MILE, 1 Mile (Turf), 3-Year-Olds and Up, Hollywood Park, 2003 Purse: $415,000

Year	Winner	Age	Jockey	Wt.	Second	Wt.	Third	Wt.	Win Value	Time	Beyer
1938	Air Chute	4	B. James	119	Faithful Maud	107	Speed to Spare	119	2,055	1:11.40	
1939	Don Mike	5	L. Balaski	111	Whichcee	117	Speed to Spare	113	5,325	1:10.80	
1940	Capt. Cal	7	J. Longden	113	Son of War	108	Lassator	117	7,525	1:10.80	
1941	Hysterical	5	E. Rodriguez	123	Exemplify	108	Big Ben	123	8,550	1:11.20	
1944	Civil Code	4	J. Adams	123	Ended	122	Appleknocker	121	7,940	1:12.00	
1945	High Resolve	4	C. Corbett	116	Black Badge	117	stronghold	111	12,472	1:10.80	

Year	Winner	Age	Jockey	Wt.	Second	Wt.	Third	Wt.	Win Value	Time	Beyer
1946	Happy Issue	6	H. Trent	108	Quick Reward	120	Enfilade	116	18,550	1:10.40	
1947	El Lobo	6	W. Bailey	119	Be Sure Now	114	Texas Sandman	117	21,850	1:10.00	
1949	The Shaker	6	J. Adams	110	Star Fiddle	111	Bymeabond	118	19,900	1:10.20	
1950	Star Fiddle	4	H. Trent	108	Your Host	125	Bewitch	114	21,700	1:22.20	
1951	Special Touch	4	W. Shoemaker	122	Manyunk	114	Bullreigh Jr.	110	11,450	1:10.00	
1952	Warcos	3	R. Neves	112	Reighs Bull	119	Mohammedan	114	17,300	1:09.80	
1953	Pet Bully	5	W. Shoemaker	120	Big Noise	111	Blue Trumpeter	110	16,100	1:10.20	
1954	Stranglehold	5	W. Shoemaker	115	Imbros	132	Big Noise	110	15,400	1:09.20	
1955	El Drag	4	J. Longden	112	Berseem	128	Porterhouse	119	15,700	1:09.00	
1956	Cyclotron	8	G. Glisson	112	Porterhouse	118	One Ton Tony	112	16,500	1:09.20	
1957	Find	7	R. York	123	Social Climber	118	Porterhouse	124	15,850	1:09.00	
1958	The Searcher	4	W. Ferguson	107	How Now	115	Sw'ng Abbey	115	13,150	1:09.80	
1959	Fleet Nasrullah	4	I. Valenzuela	116	Terrang	124	Seaneen	118	13,500	1:09.00	
1960	Fleet Nasrullah	5	J. Longden	126	Clandestine	120	Ole Fols	122	12,900	1:08.20	
1961	Revel	5	A. Valenzuela	126	Finnegan	118	Henrijan	117	13,950	1:08.80	
1962	Winonly	5	W. Harmatz	115	Double Lea	117	Prove It	123	14,450	1:08.80	
1963	Winonly	6	I. Valenzuela	121	Kisco Kid	112	Double Lea	115	13,550	1:09.40	
1964	Sledge	5	I. Valenzuela	118	Mustard Plaster	117	Double Lea	117	13,850	1:09.00	
1965	Viking Spirit	5	K. Church	123	Perris	113	Native Diver	127	15,900	1:08.40	
1966	Sledge	7	I. Valenzuela	115	Chiclero	110	Real Good Deal	116	16,200	1:10.20	
1967	Fleet Discovery	4	W. Shoemaker	110	Chiclero	115	Native Diver	131	15,500	1:09.20	
1968	Kissin' George	5	W. Mahorney	126	Rising Market	117	Chiclero	114	15,850	1:08.60	
1969	Indulto	6	D. Pierce	120	Title Game	116	Rising Market	125	16,900	1:08.40	
1970	First Mate	5	J. Lambert	118	Right or Wrong	114	Baffle	124	19,500	1:08.80	
1971	Earl of Milldale	5	J. Lambert	115	King of Cricket	120	Once Over	114	24,750	1:10.40	
1972	Miles Tyson	4	R. Ussery	117	Single Agent	123	Long Position	113	26,900	1:08.00	
1973	Diplomatic Agent	5	R. Rosales	115	Rough Night	111	Selecting	116	20,150	1:09.00	
1974	Beira	5	W. Mahorney	115	Woodland Pines	119	Linda's Chief	124	19,700	1:07.80	
1975	Rise High	5	S. Hawley	116	Selecting	117	Money Lender	115	18,900	1:09.00	

Shirley's Champion finished second but was disqualified and placed fourth

Year	Winner	Age	Jockey	Wt.	Second	Wt.	Third	Wt.	Win Value	Time	Beyer
1976	Sporting Goods	6	F. Toro	115	Century's Envoy	124	Money Lender	115	20,500	1:08.20	
1977	Barrera	5	L. Pincay Jr	119	Beat Inflation	120	Maheras	124	24,650	1:07.40	
1978	J.O. Tobin	4	S. Cauthen	125	Mr. Redoy	121	Miami Sun	115	30,600	1:41.40	
1979	Farnesio	5	W. Shoemaker	119	Harry's Love	114	Star Spangled	120	31,100	1:41.60	
1980	Peregrinator	5	C.J. McCarron	119	Dragon Command	117	Life's Hope	117	31,850	1:41.60	
1984	Massera	4	E. Delahoussaye	115	Sari's Dreamer	112	Barberstown	119	33,350	1:34.20	
1984	Drumalis	6	E. Delahoussaye	119	Bel Bolide	122	Hula Blaze	114	33,950	1:33.80	
1985	Retsina Run	5	E. Delahoussaye	116			Val Danseur	113	26,500	1:33.40	
	Capture Him	4	C.J. McCarron	120							
1985	Native Charmer II	4	S. Hawley	113	Gato Del Sol	120	Both Ends Burning	123	41,000	1:33.60	
1986	Clever Song	4	F. Toro	116	Poly Test	115	Both Ends Burning	124	49,400	1:38.80	
1987	Clever Song	5	F. Toro	119	Al Mamoon	122	Le Belvedere	114	61,900	1:41.20	
1988	Steinlen	4	G.L. Stevens	119	Siyah Kalem	115	Neshad	115	80,200	1:33.20	
1989	Peace	4	W. Shoemaker	115	Steinlen	121	Political Ambition	122	65,700	1:33.00	
1990	Shining Steel	4	C.J. McCarron	114	Super May	117	Brave Capade	111	63,000	1:34.00	103
1991	Exbourne	5	G.L. Stevens	118	Super May	117	Dansil	111	65,300	1:33.40	106
1993	Journalism	5	A. Solis	114	Lomitas	118	Brief Truce	122	63,800	1:32.80	102
1994	Megan's Interco	5	C.A. Black	119	Furiously	116	Rapan Boy	115	63,200	1:32.60	117
1995	Unfinished Symph	4	C.W. Antley	121	Rapan Boy	118	Journalism	117	98,400	1:33.00	111
1996	Fastness	6	C.S. Nakatani	124	Romarin	124	Atticus	124	420,000	1:32.60	111
1997	Pinfloron	5	D. Flores	124	Surachai	124	Helmsman	124	353,400	1:34.40	108
1998	Labeeb	6	K. Desorneaux	124	Fantastic Fellow	124	Hawksley Hill	124	319,200	1:33.20	111
1999	Silic	4	C.S. Nakatani	124	Ladies Din	124	Hawksley Hill	124	280,200	1:32.95	109
2000	Silic	5	K.J. Desormeaux	124	Ladies Din	124	Sharan	124	292,800	1:33.36	109
2001	Irish Prize	5	G.L. Stevens	120	Touch of the Blues	124	Brahms	124	285,000	1:33.68	107
2002	Ladies Din	7	P.A. Valenzuela	124	Redattore	124	Spinelessjellyfish	124	240,000	1:33.39	110
2003	Redattore	8	A. Solis	124	Special Ring	124	Touch of the Blues	124	225,000	1:33.37	111

Beyer Index: **108.85**

Run as Premiere Handicap or Hollywood Premier Handicap prior to 1990. For all ages in 1944. Run at Santa Anita in 1949.
Distance 6 furlongs, 1938–49, 1951–57; 7 furlongs, 1950; 1 1/16 miles, 1978–80, 1986–87. Ron main track prior to 1984

SPINAWAY STAKES, 7 Furlongs, 2-Year-Old Fillies,
Saratoga Race Course, 2003 Purse: $200,000

Year	Winner	Age	Jockey	Wt.	Second	Wt.	Third	Wt.	Win Value	Time	Beyer
1881	Memento	2	Costello	107	Night Cap	107	Tuscaloosa	107	2,100	1:06.00	
1882	Miss Woodford	2	Stoval	103	Tarantella	95	Empress	95	1,800	1:03.00	
1883	Tolu	2	J. McLaughlin	103	Tattoo	100	Economy	95	2,200	1:03.00	
1884	Mission Belle	2	Holloway	103	Radha	95	Floria	107	1,500	1:03.00	
1885	Biggonet	2	Maynard	100	Hattie Carlile	100	Georgie II	95	2,625	1:05.00	
1886	Grisette	2	Miller	103	Lizzie Krepps	103	Agnes	103	2,075	1:03.20	
1887	Los Angeles	2	West	107	Blithesome	103	Cokena	95	2,500	1:02.20	
1888	Gypsy Queen	2	Martin	102	Queen of Trumps	98	Daisy Woodruff	93	2,825	1:03.00	
1889	Daisy F.	2	Richcreek	112	Ruperta	98	Estelle	102	3,750	1:06.20	
1890	Sallie McClelland	2	Allen	117	Helen Rose	107	Ayrshire Lass	104	2,805	1:06.00	

Year	Winner	Age	Jockey	Wt.	Second	Wt.	Third	Wt.	Win Value	Time	Beyer
1891	Promenade	2	Simms	105	Selina D.	98	Salonica	110	2,585	1:03.00	
1901	Rossignol	2	T. Burns	112	Disadvantage	119	Amicitia	119	2,625	1:10.00	
1902	Duster	2	Shaw	122	Astarita	121	Jud. Campbell	122	6,150	1:10.80	
1903	Raglan	2	J. Hicks	119	Little Em	116	Memories	119	10,430	1:12.40	
1904	Tanya	2	Shaw	122	Schulamite	114	Linda Lee	119	10,750	1:07.60	
1905	Edna Jackson	2	F. O'Neill	119	Running Water	119	Curiosity	119	11,750	1:08.80	
1906	Court Dress	2	Radtke	122	Kenyetto	112	Martha	122	7,750	1:07.00	
1907	Julia Powell	2	W. Knapp	112	Half Sovereign	119	Adriana	112	9,170	1:06.80	
1908	Maskette	2	Notter	112	Wedding Bells	112	Lady Hubbard	112	8,250	1:05.80	
1909	Ocean Bound	2	Scoville	115	School Marm	112	Sticker	112	7,750	1:06.60	
1910	Bashti	2	S.H. Shilling	122	Love-not	109	Sweepaway	112	7,820	1:06.80	
1913	Casuarina	2	B. Steele	113	Early Rose	110	Cutaway	116	2,395	1:07.00	
1914	Lady Barbary	2	A. Neylon	122	Kaskaskia	127	Montrosa	104	2,765	1:06.00	
1915	Jacoby	2	M. Garner	107	Lorac	107	Feminist	107	2,425	1:11.00	
1916	Yankee Witch	2	T. Davies	112	Koh-I-Noor	122	Tragedy	122	2,545	1:07.40	
1917	Olive Wood	2	E. Martin	112	Enfilade	119	Rosie O'Grady	124	6,250	1:07.40	
1918	Passing Shower	2	A. Johnson	112	Lady Rosebud	116	Tuscaloosa	112	6,450	1:05.60	
1919	Constancy	2	T. Nolan	109	Wedding Cake	109	Germa	112	5,850	1:05.60	
1920	Prudery	2	E. Ambrose	127	Step Lightly	112	Nancy Lee	127	5,900	1:05.00	
1921	Miss Joy	2	M. Garner	127	Calamity Jane	112	Roulette	112	6,100	1:05.20	
1922	Edict	2	E. Sande	122	Fly by Day	112	Brocade	112	7,425	1:09.00	
1923	Anna Marrone II	2	R. Carter	112	Nellie Morse	124	Tree Top	112	7,675	1:12.60	
1924	Blue Warbler	2	D. Hurn	112	Malbird	109	Lightship	109	7,775	1:12.00	
1925	Cinema	2	E. Barnes	112	Asinia	112	Ruthenia	113	7,425	1:15.40	
1926	Bonnie Pennant	2	J. Maiben	112	Candy May	112	Pandera	127	9,850	1:14.40	
1927	Twitter	2	R. Workman	112	Jollity	112	Bateau	122	9,675	1:12.00	
1928	Atlantis	2	G. Ellis	122	Pennant Lass	111	Bravery	115	10,050	1:15.00	
1929	Goose Egg	2	G. Ellis	122	The Spare	122	Snowflake	115	10,500	1:12.20	
1930	Risque	2	E. Steffen	122	Baba Kenny	115	Panasette	122	10,000	1:16.60	
1931	Top Flight	2	R. Workman	127	Dinner Time	111	Brocado	115	8,400	1:12.60	
1932	Easy Day	2	S. Coucci	111	Crazy Jane	115	Barn Swallow	115	8,425	1:13.40	
1933	Contessa	2	E. Steffen	114	Slapdash	126	Sun Celtic	114	5,850	1:15.00	
1934	Vicaress	2	L. Humphries	116	Clean Out	116	Corinne Dailey	116	4,450	1:12.80	
1935	Forever Yours	2	W.D. Wright	121	Parade Girl	119	Tony's Wife	116	6,725	1:12.80	
1936	Maecloud	2	E. Litzenberger	116	Juliet W.	114	Bad Dreams	110	6,450	1:14.20	
1937	Merry Lassie	2	J. Stout	119	Evening Shadow	114	Jacola	114	7,975	1:12.20	
1938	Dinner Date	2	A. Robertson	113	So Rare	113	Grey Nurse	113	9,450	1:13.00	
1939	Now What	2	R. Workman	122	Piquet	113	Jeanne d'Arc	113	8,350	1:13.20	
1940	Nasca	2	R. Donoso	116	Tangled	116	Level Best	119	8,450	1:12.00	
1941	Mar-Kell	2	W. Eads	113	Equipet	113	Petrify	122	8,125	1:13.60	
1942	Our Page	2	C. McCreary	113	Askmenow	113	Wuskenin	113	8,825	1:12.60	
1943	Bee Mac	2	S. Young	113	Red Wonder	113	Whirlabout	116	8,550	1:12.40	
1944	Price Level	2	J. Gilbert	115	Ace Card	119	Safeguard	111	15,305	1:12.20	
1945	Sopranist	2	T. May	110	Bridal Flower	109	Red Shoes	114	16,670	1:09.20	
1946	Pipette	2	T. May	119	Bright Song	115	Tea Olive	111	16,875	1:11.00	
1947	Bellesoeur	2	T. May	113	Inheritance	111	Grey Flight	113	15,025	1:11.60	
1948	Myrtle Charm	2	A. Skoronski	111	Lady Dorimar	111	Gaffery	115	15,075	1:11.60	
1949	Sunday Evening	2	T. Atkinson	111	Striking	115	Fais Do Do	111	14,100	1:11.40	
1950	Atalanta	2	H. Woodhouse	115	Les Abeilles	108	Wisteria	114	14,950	1:13.00	
1951	Blue Case	2	W. Mehrtens	119	Rose Jet	119	Recess	115	15,575	1:13.20	
1952	Flirtatious	2	D. Gorman	115	Grecian Queen	119	Lot o'Honey	115	15,775	1:13.20	
1953	Evening Out	2	O. Scurlock	123	Alines Pet	111			41,050	1:13.60	
1954	Gandharva	2	N. Shuk	111	My Blue Sky	111	High Voltage	123	44,650	1:12.80	
1955	Register	2	T. Atkinson	114	Doubledogdare	119	Aiming High	119	36,550	1:13.40	
1956	Alanesian	2	W. Boland	119	Jota Jota	119	Magic Forest	119	36,100	1:12.60	
1957	Sequoia	2	R. Ussery	119	Armorial	119	Bridgework	119	32,560	1:12.80	
1958	Rich Tradition	2	W. Boland	119	Recite	119	Quill	119	27,711	1:12.80	
1959	Irish Jay	2	E. Arcaro	119	Warlike	119	Natalma	119	51,235	1:12.20	
	Natalma finished first but was disqualified and placed third										
1960	Good Move	2	E. Guerin	119	Honey Dear	119	Little Tumbler	119	53,672	1:12.40	
1961	Cicada	2	I. Valenzuela	119	Pontivy	119	Jazz Queen	119	52,455	1:12.00	
1962	Affectionately	2	I. Valenzuela	119	Nalee	119	Rare Exchange	119	51,821	1:10.40	
1963	Petite Rouge	2	J. Sellers	119	Hasty Matelda	119	Gailatia	119	53,219	1:12.60	
	Crown Silver finished second but was disqualified and placed last										
1964	Candalita	2	B. Baeza	119	Marshua	119	Queen Empress	119	52,682	1:10.80	
1965	Moccasin	2	L. Adams	119	Swift Lady	119	Forefoot	119	49,627	1:11.00	
1966	Silver True	2	J.L. Rotz	119	Great Era	119	Shirley Heights	119	50,960	1:12.00	
1967	Queen of the Stage	2	B. Baeza	119	Dream Path	119	Gay Matelda	119	52,244	1:10.20	
1968	Queen's Double	2	B. Baeza	119	Show Off	119	Fillypasser	119	52,130	1:11.40	
1969	Meritus	2	M. Ycaza	119	Title	119	Bright Sun	119	51,789	1:10.60	
1970	Forward Gal	2	F. Iannelli	119	Patelin	119	Deceit	119	54,990	1:10.80	
1971	Numbered Account	2	C. Baltazar	119	Rondeau	119	Debby Deb	119	52,770	1:09.80	
1972	La Prevoyante	2	J. LeBlanc	120	Princess Doubleday	120	Behram	120	35,040	1:10.80	

Year	Winner	Age	Jockey	Wt.	Second	Wt.	Third	Wt.	Win Value	Time	Beyer
1973	Talking Picture	2	R. Turcotte	120	Special Team	120	Raisela	120	35,040	1:10.00	
1974	Ruffian	2	V. Bracciale Jr	120	Laughing Bridge	120	Scottish Melody	120	33,060	1:08.60	
1975	Dearly Precious	2	M. Hole	120	Optimistic Gal	120	Quintas Vicki	120	47,880	1:10.60	
1976	Mrs. Warren	2	E. Maple	119	Exerene	119	Sensational	119	33,060	1:10.40	
1977	Sherry Peppers	2	A. Cordero Jr	119	Akita	119	Stub	119	32,340	1:10.80	
1978	Palm Hut	2	R.I. Velez	119	Himalayan	119	Golferette	119	31,770	1:10.60	
1979	Smart Angle	2	S. Maple	119	Jet Rating	119	Marathon Girl	119	48,510	1:10.60	
1980	Prayers 'n Promises	2	A. Cordero Jr	119	Fancy Naskra	119	Companionship	119	50,850	1:11.00	
1981	Before Dawn	2	G. McCarron	119	Betty Money	119	Take Lady Anne	119	52,920	1:09.40	
1982	Share the Fantasy	2	J. Fell	119	Singing Susan	119	Midnight Rapture	119	50,040	1:09.80	
1983	Buzz My Bell	2	J. Velasquez	119	Demetria	119	Bottle Top	119	52,740	1:13.20	
1984	Tiltalating	2	A. Cordero Jr	119	Sociable Duck	119	Contredance	119	85,380	1:11.00	
1985	Family Style	2	D. MacBeth	119	Musical Lark	119	Nervous Baba	119	97,680	1:12.00	
1986	Tappiano	2	J. Cruguet	119	Our Little Margie	119	Daytime Princess	119	130,680	1:11.40	
1987	Over All	2	A. Cordero Jr	119	Bold Lady Anne	119	Flashy Runner	119	101,340	1:11.00	
1988	Seattle Meteor	2	R.P. Romero	119	Love and Affection	119	Moonlight Martini	119	141,120	1:12.60	
1989	Stella Madrid	2	A. Cordero Jr	119	Golden Reef	119	Saratoga Sizzle	119	141,840	1:10.40	
1990	Meadow Star	2	J.A. Santos	119	Garden Gal	119	Good Potential	119	143,040	1:10.20	
1991	Miss Iron Smoke	2	M.A. Pedroza	119	Turnback the Alarm	119	Preach	119	120,000	1:10.60	.84
1992	Family Enterprize	2	P. Day	119	Standard Equipment	119	Sky Beauty	119	120,000	1:09.80	.95

Sky Beauty finished first but was disqualified and placed third
Try in the Sky finished third but was disqualified and placed fourth

Year	Winner	Age	Jockey	Wt.	Second	Wt.	Third	Wt.	Win Value	Time	Beyer
1993	Strategic Maneuver	2	J.A. Santos	119	Astas Foxy Lady	119	Delta Lady	119	120,000	1:10.20	.84
1994	Flanders	2	P. Day	119	Sea Breezer	119	Stormy Blues	119	120,000	1:23.00	.96
1995	Golden Attraction	2	G.L. Stevens	121	Flat Fleet Feet	121	Western Dreamer	121	120,000	1:23.80	.93
1996	Oath	2	S.J. Sellers	121	Pearl City	121	Fabulously Fast	121	120,000	1:23.60	.88
1997	Countess Diana	2	S.J. Sellers	121	Brac Drifter	121	Aunt Anne	121	120,000	1:24.00	.93
1998	Things Change	2	J.A. Santos	121	Extended Applause	121	Miss Jennifer Lynn	121	120,000	1:24.82	.87
1999	Circle of Life	2	J.R. Velazquez	121	Surfside	121	Miss Wineshine	121	120,000	1:23.25	.91
2000	Stormy Pick	2	J. Ferrer	121	Nasty Storm	121	Seeking It All	121	120,000	1:24.33	.82
2001	Cashier's Dream	2	D.J. Meche	121	Smok'n Frolic	121	Magic Storm	121	120,000	1:23.47	.99
2002	Awesome Humor	2	P. Day	121	Forever Partners	121	Midnight Cry	121	120,000	1:24.36	.95
2003	Ashado	2	E.S. Prado	121	Be Gentle	121	Daydreaming	121	120,000	1:24.08	.84

Beyer Index: **90.08**

Distance 5 furlongs prior to 1901; 5 1/2 furlongs, 1901–22; 6 furlongs, 1923–95. Run at Belmont Park, 1943–45. Run on Widener Course, 1945

(OVERBROOK) SPINSTER STAKES, 1 1/8 Miles, Fillies and Mares, 3-Year-Olds and Up, Keeneland Race Course, 2003 Purse: $500,000

Year	Winner	Age	Jockey	Wt.	Second	Wt.	Third	Wt.	Win Value	Time	Beyer
1956	Doubledogdare	3	J. Heckmann	119	Queen Hopeful	123	Lady Swords	119	41,140	1:49.20	
1957	Bornastar	4	K. Church	123	Pucker Up	123	Searching	123	44,480	1:49.20	
1958	Bornastar	5	K. Church	123	Moon Glory	119	Woodlawn	123	43,190	1:49.40	
1959	Royal Native	3	W. Hartack	119	Aesthetic	119	Tacking	119	37,975	1:49.40	
1960	Rash Statement	3	J.L. Rotz	119	Indian Maid	123	Royal Native	123	51,475	1:49.60	
1961	Bowl of Flowers	3	E. Arcaro	119	Primonetta	119	Times Two	119	50,640	1:49.20	
1962	Primonetta	4	W. Shoemaker	123	Royal Patrice	119	Firm Policy	119	44,130	1:48.40	
1963	Lamb Chop	3	M. Ycaza	119	Eleven Keys	119	Laughing Breeze	119	40,635	1:48.40	
1964	Old Hat	5	D. Brumfield	123	Miss Cavandish	119	Time for Bed	119	38,220	1:48.40	
1965	Star Maggie	5	W. Hartack	123	Swoonalong	123	Fairway Fun	119	38,187	1:50.20	
1966	Open Fire	5	B. Baeza	123	Old Hat	123	Summer Scandal	123	38,285	1:50.40	
1967	Straight Deal	5	H. Grant	123	Furl Sail	119	Amerigo Lady	119	39,942	1:49.20	

Amerigo Lady finished second but was disqualified and placed third

Year	Winner	Age	Jockey	Wt.	Second	Wt.	Third	Wt.	Win Value	Time	Beyer
1968	Sale Day	3	E. Guerin	119	Politely	123	Pattee Canyon	119	38,122	1:51.60	
1969	Gallant Bloom	3	J.L. Rotz	119	Miss Ribot	123	Sale Dale	123	37,310	1:48.80	
1970	Taken Aback	4	E. Belmonte	123	Fanfreluche	119	Pattee Canyon	123	40,397	1:51.40	
1971	Chou Croute	3	R. Kotenko	119	Viewpoise	119	Alma North	119	41,015	1:49.00	
1972	Numbered Account	3	L. Pincay Jr	119	Chou Croute	123	Barely Even	119	38,870	1:47.40	
1973	Susan's Girl	4	B. Baeza	123	Light Hearted	119	Coraggioso	119	38,090	1:48.80	
1974	Summer Guest	4	D. Montoya	123	Desert Vixen	119	Coraggioso	123	36,952	1:49.40	
1975	Susan's Girl	6	L. PIncay Jr	123	Flama Ardiente	119	Costly Dream	123	37,830	1:49.80	
1976	Optimistic Gal	3	C. Perret	119	Ivory Wand	119	Rocky Trip	123	53,007	1:51.60	
1977	Cum Laude Laurie	3	A. Cordero Jr	119	Mississippi Mud	123	Ivory Wand	123	54,974	1:48.40	
1978	Tempest Queen	3	J. Velasquez	119	Northernette	123	Likely Exchange	123	72,865	1:49.00	
1979	Safe	3	E. Fires	119	Spark of Life	123	Miss Baja	123	79,852	1:49.20	
1980	Bold 'n Determined	3	E. Delahoussaye	119	Love Sign	119	Likely Exchange	123	114,660	1:49.20	
1981	Glorious Song	5	R. Platts	123	Truly Bound	119	Safe Play	119	106,568	1:49.20	
1982	Track Robbery	6	P.A. Valenzuela	123	Blush With Pride	119	Our Darling	119	110,516	1:47.80	
1983	Try Something New	4	P. Day	123	Dance Number	123	Miss Huntington	123	107,689	1:49.80	
1984	Princess Rooney	4	E. Delahoussaye	123	Lucky Lucky Lucky	119	Heatherten	123	123,840	1:50.40	
1985	Dontstop Themusic	5	L. Pincay Jr	123	Life's Magic	123	Dowery	123	110,419	1:50.40	
1986	Top Corsage	3	S. Hawley	119	Endear	123	Life at the Top	119	142,610	1:48.20	
1987	Sacahuista	3	R.P. Romero	119	Ms. Margi	119	Tall Poppy	123	148,395	1:48.60	
1988	Hail a Cab	5	J. Vasquez	123	Willa On the Move	119	Integra	123	171,600	1:51.00	

Year	Winner	Age	Jockey	Wt.	Second	Wt.	Third	Wt.	Win Value	Time	Beyer
1989	Bayakoa	5	L. Pincay Jr	123	Goodbye Halo	123	Sharp Dance	119	172,413	1:47.80	
1990	Bayakoa	6	L. Pincay Jr	123	Gorgeous	123	Luthier's Launch	123	174,606	1:47.00	113
1991	Wilderness Song	3	P. Day	119	Screen Prospect	123	Til Forbid	119	226,980	1:49.60	103
1992	Fowda	4	P.A. Valenzuela	123	Paseana	123	Meadow Star	123	209,994	1:49.80	106
1993	Paseana	6	C.J. McCarron	123	Gray Cashmere	123	Jacody	119	209,622	1:48.40	102
1994	Dispute	4	P. Day	123	Lets Be Alert	119	Miss Dominique	123	204,414	1:48.80	112
1995	Inside Information	4	M.E. Smith	123	Jade Flush	123	Mariah's Storm	123	198,276	1:50.00	100
1996	Different	4	C.J. McCarron	123	Top Secret	119	Belle of Cozzene	123	336,040	1:49.60	109
1997	Clear Mandate	5	P. Day	123	Feasibility Study	123	Naskra Colors	123	336,350	1:50.40	91
1998	Banshee Breeze	3	R.J. Albarado	119	Runup the Colors	123	Aldiza	123	341,930	1:47.04	115
1999	Keeper Hill	4	K.J. Desormeaux	123	Banshee Breeze	123	A Lady From Dixie	123	344,410	1:47.19	110
2000	Plenty of Light	3	G.K. Gomez	120	Spain	120	Roza Robata	123	336,970	1:48.18	107
2001	Miss Linda	4	R. Migliore	123	Starrer	120	Printemps	123	348,440	1:49.79	109
2002	Take Charge Lady	3	E.S. Prado	120	You	120	Printemps	123	338,520	1:49.90	109
2003	Take Charge Lady	4	E.S. Prado	123	You	123	Miss Linda	123	310,000	1:49.57	99

Beyer Index: **106.07**

For 3-, 4-, and 5-year-olds prior to 1964

SUBURBAN HANDICAP, 1 1/4 Miles,
3-Year-Olds and Up, Belmont Park, 2003 Purse: $500,000

Year	Winner	Age	Jockey	Wt.	Second	Wt.	Third	Wt.	Win Value	Time	Beyer
1884	Gen. Monroe	6	W. Donohue	124	War Eagle	102	J. of Hearts	120	4,945	2:11.60	
1885	Pontiac	4	H. Olney	102	Richmond	110	Rataplan	121	5,855	2:09.20	
1886	Troubadour	4	W. Fitzpatrick	115	Richmond	110	Savanac	100	5,697	2:12.20	
1887	Eurus	4	G. Davis	102	Oriflame	104	Wickham	114	6,065	2:12.00	
1888	Elkwood	5	W. Martin	119	Terra Cotta	122	Firenze	117	6,812	2:07.20	
1889	Raceland	4	E. Garrison	120	Terra Cotta	124	Gorgo	110	6,900	2:09.80	
1890	Salvator	4	I. Murphy	127	Cassius	107	Tenny	126	66,900	2:06.80	
1891	Loantaka	5	M. Bergen	110	Major Domo	108	Cassius	115	9,900	2:07.00	
1892	Montana	4	E. Garrison	115	Major Domo	115	Lamplighter	104	17,750	2:07.40	
1893	Lowlander	5	P. McDermott	105	Terrifier	95	Lamplighter	129	17,750	2:06.60	
1894	Ramopo	4	F. Taral	120	Banquet	119	Sport	114	12,070	2:06.20	
1895	Lazzarone	4	A. Hamilton	115	Sir Walter	126	S'g a Dance	99	4,730	2:07.80	
1896	Henry of Navarre	5	H. Griffin	129	The Commoner	113	Clifford	126	5,850	2:07.00	
1897	Ben Brush	4	W. Simms	123	The Winner	115	Havoc	104	5,850	2:07.20	
1898	Tillo	4	A. Clayton	119	Semper Ego	106	Ogden	109	5,850	2:07.20	
1899	Imp	5	N. Turner	114	Bannockburn	112	Warrenton	114	6,800	2:08.20	
1900	Kinley Mack	4	P. McCue	125	Ethelbert	130	Gulden	100	6,800	2:06.80	
1901	Alcedo	4	H. Spencer	112	Watercure	102	Toddy	100	7,800	2:05.60	
1902	Gold Heels	4	O. Wonderly	124	Pentecost	99	Blues	124	7,800	2:05.20	
1903	Africander	3	G. Fuller	110	Herbert	118	Hunt. Raine	98	16,490	2:10.40	
1904	Hermis	5	A. Redfern	127	The Picket	124	Irish Lad	127	16,800	2:05.00	
1905	Beldame	4	F. O'Neill	123	Proper	109	First Mason	118	16,800	2:05.40	
1906	Go Between	5	W. Shaw	116	Dandelion	107	Colonial Girl	113	16,800	2:05.20	
1907	Nealon	4	W. Dugan	116	Montgomery	104	Beacon Li't	100	16,800	2:06.40	
1908	Ballot	4	J. Notter	127	King James	98	Fair Play	111	19,750	2:03.00	
1909	Fitz Herbert	3	E. Dugan	105	Alfred Noble	104	Fayette	101	3,850	2:03.40	
1910	Olambala	4	G. Archibald	115	Prince Imperial	101	Ballot	129	4,800	2:04.40	
1913	Whisk Broom II	6	J. Notter	139	Lahore	112	Meridian	119	3,000	2:00.00	
1915	Stromboli	4	C. Turner	122	Sam Jackson	100	Sharpshooter	106	3,925	2:05.40	
1916	Friar Rock	3	M. Garner	101	Short Grass	117	Stromboli	123	3,450	2:05.00	
1917	Boots	6	J. Loftus	122	Borrow	115	The Finn	129	4,900	2:05.20	
1918	Johren	3	F. Robinson	110	Hollister	113	Battle	107	5,850	2:06.00	
1919	Corn Tassel	5	L. Ensor	108	Sweep On	108	Boniface	107	5,200	2:02.20	
1920	Paul Jones	3	A. Schuttinger	106	Boniface	115	Exterminator	123	6,350	2:09.60	
1921	Audacious	5	C. Kummer	120	Mad Hatter	130	Sennings Park	110	8,100	2:02.20	
1922	Captain Alcock	5	C. Ponce	108	Flying Cloud	115	Mad Hatter	130	8,200	2:05.40	
1923	Grey Lag	5	E. Sande	135	Snob II	115	Exodus	119	7,800	2:03.00	
1924	Mad Hatter	8	E. Sande	125	Little Celt	114	Aga Khan	102	9,150	2:03.60	
1925	Sting	4	B. Breuning	122	Cherry Pie	108	Mad Play	124	11,300	2:04.20	
1926	Crusader	3	J. Callahan	104	American Flag	124	K. Sol's Seal	107	13,150	2:03.00	
1927	Crusader	4	C. Kummer	127	Black Maria	120	Macaw	120	11,875	2:02.40	
1928	Dolan	4	J. Callahan	105	Chance Shot	120	Scapa Flow	120	13,675	2:06.60	
1929	Bateau	4	E. Ambrose	112	Petee-Wrack	124	Toro	125	14,100	2:03.40	
1930	Petee-Wrack	5	E. Sande	122	Curate	109	Distraction	119	11,850	2:07.40	
1931	Mokatam	4	A. Robertson	123	Questionnaire	128	Her Grace	111	11,200	2:02.40	
1932	White Clover II	6	R. Workman	115	The Nut	110	Sun Meadow	119	11,100	2:03.40	
1933	Equipoise	5	R. Workman	132	Osculator	107	Apprentice	112	7,250	2:02.00	
1934	Ladysman	4	S. Coucci	114	Equipoise	134	War Glory	115	5,750	2:02.60	
1935	Head Play	5	C. Kurtsinger	114	Discovery	123	Only One	110	12,175	2:02.00	
1936	Firethorn	4	H. Richards	116	Granville	108	Whopper	119	12,125	2:04.60	
1937	Aneroid	4	C. Rosengarten	110	Esposa	106	Memory Book	116	10,950	2:01.60	

Year	Winner	Age	Jockey	Wt.	Second	Wt.	Third	Wt.	Win Value	Time	Beyer
1938	Snark	5	J. Longden	120	Pompoon	128	Aneroid	120	17,050	2:01.40	
1939	Cravat	4	J. Westrope	121	Thanksgiving	120	Handcuff	110	17,750	2:02.80	
1940	Eight Thirty	4	H. Richards	127	Can't Wait	109	Third Degree	124	19,850	2:01.60	
1941	Your Chance	4	D. Meade	114	Hash	119	Shot Put	110	25,200	2:02.60	
1942	Market Wise	4	B. James	124	Whirlaway	129	Attention	124	27,800	2:01.80	
1943	Don Bingo	4	J. Renick	104	Attention	121	Lochinvar	105	27,600	2:01.40	
1944	Aletern	5	H. Lindberg	108	Sun Again	128	Alquest	115	39,210	2:01.20	
1945	Devil Diver	6	E. Arcaro	132	Stymie	119	Olympic Zenith	106	34,995	2:04.00	
1946	Armed	5	D. Dodson	130	Reply Paid	110	Stymie	123	43,000	2:02.00	
1947	Assault	4	E. Arcaro	130	Natchez	120	Talon	113	40,100	2:01.80	
1948	Harmonica	4	W. Mehrtens	109	Stymie	128	Colosal	117	39,700	2:03.00	
1949	Vulcan's Forge	4	E. Arcaro	124	But Why Not	117	Flying Missel	108	43,200	2:03.00	
1950	Loser Weeper	5	N. Combest	115	My Request	119	Hill Prince	113	41,400	2:02.00	
1951	Busanda	4	K. Stuart	102	Lone Eagle	110	County Delight	122	42,100	2:02.60	
1952	One Hitter	6	T. Atkinson	112	Crafty Admiral	113	Mameluke	116	41,900	2:02.00	
1953	Tom Fool	4	T. Atkinson	128	Royal Vale	124	Cold Command	114	40,400	2:00.60	
1954	Straight Face	4	T. Atkinson	118	Bassanio	106	Mandingo	106	44,400	2:03.20	
1955	Helioscope	4	S. Boulmetis	128	High Gun	133	Subahdar	119	61,150	2:00.60	
1956	Nashua	4	E. Arcaro	128	Dedicate	111	Subahdar	112	55,900	2:00.80	
1957	Traffic Judge	5	E. Arcaro	124	Lofty Peak	118	Dedicate	126	58,450	2:02.60	
1958	Bold Ruler	4	E. Arcaro	134	Clem	109	Third Brother	110	53,360	2:01.00	
1959	Bald Eagle	4	M. Ycaza	119	Talent Show	125	Plion	119	71,635	2:01.60	
1960	Sword Dancer	4	E. Arcaro	125	First Landing	122	Waltz	115	69,165	2:01.60	
1961	Kelso	4	E. Arcaro	133	Nickel Boy	112	Talent Show	110	72,735	2:02.00	
1962	Beau Purple	5	W. Boland	115	Kelso	132	Garwol	109	68,380	2:00.60	
1963	Kelso	6	I. Valenzuela	133	Saidam	111	Garwol	112	70,525	2:01.80	
1964	Iron Peg	4	M. Ycaza	116	Kelso	131	Olden Times	128	71,500	2:01.80	
1965	Pia Star	4	J. Sellers	117	Smart	119	Tenacle	114	70,720	2:01.00	
1966	Buffle	3	R. Turcotte	110	Pluck	113	Paoluccio	108	72,085	2:02.00	
1967	Buckpasser	4	B. Baeza	133	Ring Twice	111	Yonder	109	71,370	2:02.20	
1968	Dr. Fager	4	B. Baeza	132	Bold Hour	116	Damascus	133	69,615	1:59.60	
1969	Mr. Right	6	A. Cordero Jr	117	Dike	114	Chompion	111	69,550	2:04.80	
1970	Barometer	5	A. Cordero Jr	111	Verbatim	116	Hitchcock	113	71,565	2:01.20	
1971	Twice Worthy	4	J. Ruane	116	Ejemplo	114	Tunex	117	69,240	2:02.20	
1972	Hitchcock	6	C.H. Marquez	113	West Coast Scout	120	Naskra	110	67,980	2:00.00	
1973	Key to the Mint	4	B. Baeza	126	True Knight	118	Cloudy Dawn	113	65,700	2:00.80	
1974	True Knight	5	A. Cordero Jr	127	Plunk	114	Forego	131	68,880	2:01.40	
1975	Forego	5	H. Gustines	134	Arbees Boy	118	Loud	114	66,840	2:27.80	
1976	Foolish Pleasure	4	E. Maple	125	Forego	134	Lord Rebeau	116	65,280	1:55.40	
1977	Quiet Little Table	4	E. Maple	114	Forego	138	Nearly On Time	104	63,840	2:03.00	
1978	Upper Nile	4	J. Velasquez	113	Nearly On Time	109	Great Contractor	114	63,840	2:01.80	
1979	State Dinner	4	J. Velasquez	118	Mister Brea	120	Alydar	127	79,125	2:01.60	
1980	Winter's Tale	4	J. Fell	114	State Dinner	117	Czaravich	127	92,920	2:00.60	
1981	Temperence Hill	4	D. MacBeth	127	Ring of Light	115	Highland Blade	113	100,620	2:02.00	
1982	Silver Buck	4	D. MacBeth	111	It's the One	124	Aloma's Ruler	112	100,620	1:59.60	
1983	Winter's Tale	7	J. Fell	120	Sing Sing	119	Highland Blade	118	168,600	2:01.60	
1984	Fit to Fight	4	J.D. Bailey	126	Canadian Factor	116	Wild Again	116	201,300	2:00.60	
1985	Vanlandingham	4	D. MacBeth	115	Carr de Naskra	120	Dramatic Desire	109	180,600	2:01.00	
1986	Roo Art	4	P. Day	115	Proud Truth	121	Creme Fraiche	121	197,700	2:01.20	
1987	Broad Brush	4	A. Cordero Jr	126	Set Style	112	Bordeaux Bob	112	323,260	2:03.00	
1988	Personal Flag	5	P. Day	117	Waquoit	121	Bet Twice	126	228,060	2:01.40	
1989	Dancing Spree	4	A. Cordero Jr	114	Forever Silver	116	Easy n Dirty	114	258,720	2:02.40	
1990	Easy Goer	4	P. Day	126	De Roche	113	Montubio	113	239,400	2:00.00	119
1991	In Excess	4	G.L. Stevens	119	Chief Honcho	115	Killer Diller	113	300,000	1:58.20	120
1992	Pleasant Tap	5	E. Delahoussaye	119	Strike the Gold	119	Defensive Play	115	300,000	2:00.20	112
1993	Devil His Due	4	W.H. McCauley	121	Pure Rumor	110	West by West	116	180,000	2:01.20	109
1994	Devil His Due	5	M.E. Smith	124	Valley Crossing	113	Federal Funds	110	210,000	2:02.40	110
1995	Key Contender	7	J.D. Bailey	115	Kissin Kris	113	Federal Funds	107	210,000	2:02.20	108
1996	Wekiva Springs	5	M.E. Smith	122	Mahogany Hall	114	L'Carriere	118	300,000	2:02.60	110
1997	Skip Away	4	S.J. Sellers	122	Will's Way	116	Formal Gold	120	210,000	2:02.20	118
1998	Frisk Me Now	4	E.L. King Jr	118	Ordway	110	Sir Bear	117	210,000	2:00.40	112
1999	Behrens	5	J.F. Chavez	121	Catienus	113	Social Charter	113	240,000	2:01.00	110
2000	Lemon Drop Kid	4	E.S. Prado	122	Behrens	122	Lager	113	300,000	1:58.97	117
2001	Albert the Great	4	J.F. Chavez	123	Lido Palace	115	Include	122	300,000	2:00.39	119
2002	E Dubai	4	J.R. Velazquez	116	Lido Palace	119	Macho Uno	119	300,000	2:00.95	114
2003	Mineshaft	4	R.J. Albarado	121	Volponi	121	Dollar Bill	115	300,000	2:01.57	115

Beyer Index: 113.79

SWORD DANCER INVITATIONAL HANDICAP, 1 1/2 Miles (Turf), 3-Year-Olds and Up,
Saratoga Race Course, 2003 Purse: $500,000

Year	Winner	Age	Jockey	Wt.	Second	Wt.	Third	Wt.	Win Value	Time	Beyer
1975	Gallant Bob	3	G. Gallitano	126	Our Hero	113	Due Diligence	113	27,630	1:09.60	
1976	Arabian Law	3	J. Vasquez	112	Full Out	118	Half High	111	26,535	1:10.60	
1977	Effervescing	4	A. Cordero Jr	117	Gentle King	110	Cinteelo	116	33,690	1:39.60	

Year	Winner	Age	Jockey	Wt.	Second	Wt.	Third	Wt.	Win Value	Time	Beyer
1978	True Colors	4	M. Venezia	114	Bill Brill	107	Blue Baron	114	34,020	1:41.00	
1979	Darby Creek Road	5	A. Cordero Jr	119	John Henry	119	Poison Ivory	119	34,320	1:41.60	
1980	Tiller	6	R. Hernandez	126	John Henry	126	Sten	126	96,660	2:25.20	
1981	John Henry	6	W. Shoemaker	126	Passing Zone	126	Peat Moss	126	97,380	2:26.80	
1982	Lemhi Gold	4	C.J. McCarron	126	Erins Isle	126	Field Cat	126	99,000	2:26.00	
1983	Majesty's Prince	4	E. Maple	120	Thunder Puddles	118	Erins Isle	128	141,600	2:34.40	

Hush Dear finished second but was disqualified and placed fourth

Year	Winner	Age	Jockey	Wt.	Second	Wt.	Third	Wt.	Win Value	Time	Beyer
1984	Majesty's Prince	5	E. Maple	124	Nassipour	109	Four Bases	112	176,820	2:31.00	
1985	Tri for Size	4	R.J. Thibeau	110	Talakeno	112	Persian Tiara	113	151,320	2:33.20	
1986	Southern Sultan	4	R.G. Davis	109	Talakeno	114	Tri for Size	111	143,460	2:39.40	
1987	Theatrical	5	P. Day	124	Dance of Life	122	Akabir	114	133,080	2:26.00	

Dance of Life finished first but was disqualified and placed second

Year	Winner	Age	Jockey	Wt.	Second	Wt.	Third	Wt.	Win Value	Time	Beyer
1988	Anka Germania	6	C. Perret	117	Sunshine Forever	114	Carotene	114	141,120	2:32.20	
1989	El Senor	5	W.H. McCauley	118	Nediym	113	My Big Boy	115	139,920	2:27.00	
1990	El Senor	6	A. Cordero Jr	119	With Approval	124	Hodges Bay	114	140,000	2:28.00	
1991	Dr. Root	4	J.L. Samyn	109	Karmani	113	El Senor	116	150,000	2:25.40	102
1992	Fraise	4	J.D. Bailey	113	Wall Street Dancer	116	Montserrat	113	150,000	2:25.80	105
1993	Spectacular Tide	4	J.A. Krone	112	Square Cut	112	Dr. Kiernan	117	120,000	2:30.20	104
1994	Alex the Great	5	P.A. Valenzuela	118	Kiri's Clown	112	L'Hermine	112	150,000	2:28.60	108
1995	Kiri's Clown	6	M.J. Luzzi	114	Awad	121	King's Theatre	113	150,000	2:25.40	109
1996	Broadway Flyer	5	M.E. Smith	118	Kiri's Clown	113	Flag Down	119	150,000	2:32.00	112
1997	Awad	7	P. Day	117	Fahim	110	Val's Prince	112	150,000	2:23.20	108
1998	Cetewayo	4	C.S. Nakatani	115	Val's Prince	113	Dushyantor	119	180,000	2:29.56	107
1999	Honor Glide	5	J.A. Santos	116	Val's Prince	115	Chorwon	114	240,000	2:28.23	109
2000	John's Call	9	J.L. Samyn	114	Aly's Alley	118	Single Empire	119	300,000	2:32.17	112
2001	With Anticipation	6	P. Day	114	King Cugat	120	Slew Valley	114	300,000	2:26.41	109
2002	With Anticipation	7	P. Day	120	Denon	118	Volponi	115	300,000	2:24.06	109
2003	Whitmore's Conn	5	J.L. Samyn	115	Macaw	114	Slew Valley	114	300,000	2:28.14	107

Beyer Index: 107.77

Distance 6 furlongs (main track) for 3-year-olds prior to 1977; 1 1/16 miles, 1977-79. Run at Aqueduct, 1975-76; at Belmont, 1977-91

TEST STAKES, 7 Furlongs, 3-Year-Old Fillies,
Saratoga Race Course, 2003 Purse: $250,000

Year	Winner	Age	Jockey	Wt.	Second	Wt.	Third	Wt.	Win Value	Time	Beyer
1922	Emotion	3	L. McAtee	115	Nedna	115			2,004	2:11.20	
1926	Ruthenia	3	E. Sande	121	Corvette	118	What I'll Do	114	2,900	1:25.60	
1927	Black Curl	3	L. Fator	118	Bonnie Khayyam	111	Fairness	114	3,375	1:26.60	
1928	Nixie	3	D. McAuliffe	121	Lace	114	Tokio	114	2,950	1:25.80	
1929	Dinah Did Upset	3	N. LeBlanc	114	On Her Toes	118	Electa	114	3,450	1:24.20	
1930	Conclave	3	D. Lyons	114	Goose Egg	121	The Beasel	118	3,475	1:24.40	
1931	Buckup	3	M. Garner	118	Ladana	121	Risque	121	3,050	1:25.80	
1932	Suntica	3	M. Garner	128	Parry	118	Unique	118	2,975	1:26.00	
1933	Speed Boat	3	J. Gilbert	106	Barn Swallow	121	White Lies	108	1,820	1:24.20	
1934	Bazaar	3	D. Meade	115	Slapdash	108	Coequal	105	1,820	1:24.60	
1935	Good Gamble	3	S. Renick	122	Mid Victorian	113	Clean Out	110	3,075	1:24.80	
1936	Fair Stein	3	E. Yager	113	Little Miracle	113	Fair Knightness	113	2,750	1:24.80	
1937	Evening Tide	3	C. Kurtsinger	110	That One	112	Sweet Desire	113	3,025	1:26.00	
1938	Black Wave	3	J. Gilbert	113	Anaflame	113			3,175	1:25.80	
					Creole Maid	126					
1939	Redlin	3	D. Meade	114	Red Eye	123	Despondent	114	2,725	1:24.00	
1940	Piquet	3	E. Arcaro	123	Fairy Chant	126	Inkling	114	3,050	1:24.40	
1941	Imperatrice	3	J. Skelly	113	Pomayya	113	Proud One	117	2,850	1:25.20	
1942	Vagrancy	3	J. Stout	123	Taunt	113	Smiles	113	2,575	1:26.00	
1943	Stefanita	3	C. McCreary	117	Best Risk	108	Good Morning	120	4,800	1:25.20	
1944	Whirlabout	3	H. Lindberg	123	Vienna	108	Boiling On	109	6,360	1:24.80	
1945	Safeguard	3	T. Atkinson	111	Monsoon	111	Surosa	106	6,565	1:24.20	
1946	Red Shoes	3	E. Arcaro	123	Upper Level	111	Bridal Flower	121	6,825	1:23.40	
1947	Miss Disco	3	N. Combest	110	Frantie's Bid	112	Ocean Brief	110	7,300	1:24.40	
1948	Alablue	3	E. Guerin	114	Paddleduck	111	Mackinaw	121	7,500	1:25.80	
1949	Lady Dorimar	3	C. McCreary	111	Tall Weeds	116	Gaffery	124	6,975	1:25.20	
1950	Honey's Gal	3	G. Hettinger	111	Faneuil Miss	111	Supersonic	111	6,475	1:24.40	
1951	Vulcania	3	R. Bernhardt	111	Valadium	111	Atalanta	121	6,100	1:26.00	
1952	Gay Grecque	3	R. York	111	Lily White	114	Devilkin	111	5,875	1:26.80	
1953	Canadiana	3	D. Gorman	124	Home-Made	121	Tritium	121	11,700	1:25.60	
1954	Dispute	3	E. Guerin	115	Case Goods	116	Talora	111	13,150	1:25.60	
1955	Blue Banner	3	E. Arcaro	114	Smart Devil	111	Rico Reto	111	12,825	1:24.80	
1956	Glamour	3	S. Cole	121	Medal Play	111	Levee	124	15,750	1:25.80	
1957	Miss Blue Jay	3	T. Atkinson	118	Outer Space	121	Snow White	115	16,600	1:24.40	
1958	Any Morn	3	J. Ruane	115	Dandy Blitzen	115	Armorial	115	16,260	1:25.80	
1959	Shirley Jones	3	P.J. Bailey	115	Mommy Dear	115	Hidden Talent	121	19,785	1:26.00	
1960	Be Cautious	3	R. Ussery	121	Make Sail	121	Clear Road	114	14,617	1:24.00	
1960	Brave Pilot	3	H. Woodhouse	115	Frimanaha	112	Improve	115	14,780	1:23.80	
1962	Polylady	3	B. Baeza	118	Cyclopavia	115	Batter Up	124	11,229	1:23.40	
1962	Firm Policy	3	J. Sellers	121	Look Ma	115	Royal Patrice	115	11,359	1:23.40	

Year	Winner	Age	Jockey	Wt.	Second	Wt.	Third	Wt.	Win Value	Time	Beyer
1963	Bold Consort	3	H. Woodhouse	115	Prodana Neviesta	112	Charspiv	115	11,667	1:25.80	
1963	Barbwolf	3	R. Ussery	115	Lamb Chop	124	No Resisting	121	11,537	1:25.00	
1964	Time for Bed	3	J.L. Rotz	112	Royal Tara	115	Face the Facts	121	20,280	1:23.80	
1965	Discipline	3	W. Blum	118	Terentia	121	Valiant Queen	115	15,454	1:23.60	
1965	Cestrum	3	S. Boulmetis	118	Queen Empress	118	Ground Control	121	15,291	1:23.00	
1966	Belle de Nuit	3	J. Ruane	115	Wake Robin	112	Lady Swaps	112	15,795	1:23.60	
1966	Moccasin	3	B. Baeza	118	Native Street	124	Politely	112	15,632	1:23.40	
1967	Gamely	3	E. Belmonte	121	Wageko	115	Just Kidding	121	15,372	1:21.80	
1967	Treacherous	3	M. Sorrentino	115	Silver True	118	Green Glade	113	15,535	1:23.00	
1968	Heartland	3	J.L. Rotz	115	Twice Cited	115	Teddy's True	115	18,622	1:22.40	
1969	Ta Wee	3	E. Belmonte	124	French Bread	115	Bold Tribute	112	17,940	1:23.60	
1970	Princess Roycraft	3	L. Adams	121	Arachne	115	Meritus	118	14,982	1:22.40	
1970	Hunnemannia	3	E. Belmonte	115	Missile Belle	124	Royal Panic	112	15,307	1:23.60	
1971	Lucky Traveler	3	C. Baltazar	115	Tibb	115	Forward Gal	124	21,300	1:23.80	
1972	Numbered Account	3	J. Vasquez	121	Light Hearted	118	Candid Catherine	121	16,515	1:23.80	
1973	Desert Vixen	3	J. Velasquez	121	Full of Hope	118	Clandenita	118	13,470	1:23.00	
1973	Waltz Fan	3	J. Velasquez	118	Gallant Davelle	116	Tuerta	116	13,545	1:23.60	
1974	Quaze Quilt	3	J. Vasquez	121	Maud Muller	113	Clear Copy	121	20,385	1:22.40	
1974	Maybellene	3	D. Meade Jr	116	Raisela	116	Stage Door Betty	121	20,385	1:23.60	
1975	Hot n Nasty	3	J. Tejeira	122	A Charm	113	Alpine Lass	116	19,665	1:22.00	
	Fleet Victress finished third but was disqualified and placed fourth										
1975	My Juliet	3	J. Vasquez	116	Slip Screen	113	Funalon	113	19,590	1:22.00	
1976	Ivory Wand	3	P. Day	114	Doc Shah's Siren	116	Pacific Princess	114	22,500	1:23.00	
1977	Small Raja	3	M. Solomone	124	Pressing Date	114	Pearl Necklace	116	22,275	1:21.80	
1977	Northern Sea	3	J. Velasquez	121	Northernette	121	Flying Above	114	22,200	1:22.40	
1978	White Star Line	3	J. Fell	121	Silken Delight	114	Zerelda	114	22,095	1:21.40	
1978	Tingle Stone	3	R. Hernandez	114	Mucchina	121	Summer Fling	116	22,020	1:22.00	
1979	Blitey	3	A. Cordero Jr	114	Jameela	118	Spanish Fake	121	25,987	1:22.60	
1979	Clef D'Argent	3	R. Hernandez	114	Alada	114	Syncopating Lady	114	25,988	1:22.20	
1980	Love Sign	3	A. Cordero Jr	116	Weber City Miss	124	Andrea F.	114	33,900	1:22.20	
1981	Cherokee Frolic	3	G. Cohen	121	Maddy's Tune	114	Discorama	114	34,140	1:23.20	
1982	Gold Beauty	3	D. Brumfield	116	Ambassador of Luck	121	Number	114	35,940	1:22.80	
1983	Lass Trump	3	P. Day	114	Medieval Moon	121	Chic Belle	114	34,380	1:22.20	
1984	Sintra	3	K.K. Allen	116	Wild Applause	121	Lucky Lucky Lucky	124	101,040	1:22.60	
1985	Lady's Secret	3	J. Velasquez	121	Mom's Command	124	Majestic Folly	118	99,600	1:21.60	
1986	Storm and Sunshine	3	C. Perret	118	Classy Cathy	121	I'm Sweets	121	103,500	1:22.80	
1987	Very Subtle	3	P.A. Valenzuela	121	Up the Apalachee	121	Silent Turn	121	116,280	1:21.00	
1988	Fara's Team	3	J.D. Bailey	121	Lake Valley	114	Classic Crown	121	109,980	1:22.60	
1989	Safely Kept	3	C. Perret	121	Fantastic Find	114	Cojinx	116	101,520	1:21.40	
1990	Go for Wand	3	R.P. Romero	124	Secret Prospect	118	Token Dance	118	73,440	1:21.00	114
1991	Versailles Treaty	3	A. Cordero Jr	114	Ifyoucouldseemenow	121	Classy Women	116	104,040	1:22.80	101
	Zama Hummer finished third but was disqualified and placed sixth										
1992	November Snow	3	C.W. Antley	116	Meafara	114	Preach	116	105,480	1:21.20	102
1993	Missed the Storm	3	M.E. Smith	114	Miss Indy Anna	114	Educated Risk	114	90,000	1:22.00	98
1994	Twist Afleet	3	J.D. Bailey	114	Penny's Reshoot	118	Heavenly Prize	121	90,000	1:22.00	106
1995	Chaposa Springs	3	J.D. Bailey	120	Miss Golden Circle	114	Daijin	123	90,000	1:21.80	105
1996	Capote Belle	3	J.R. Velazquez	115	Flat Fleet Feet	115	J J'sdream	123	90,000	1:21.00	107
1997	Fabulously Fast	3	J.D. Bailey	114	Aldiza	114	Pearl City	117	90,000	1:21.60	111
1998	Jersey Girl	3	M.E. Smith	123	Brave Deed	114	Catinca	114	120,000	1:23.02	96
1999	Marley Vale	3	J.R. Velazquez	114	Awful Smart	114	Emanating	114	150,000	1:22.77	95
2000	Dream Supreme	3	P. Day	115	Big Bambu	118	Finder's Fee	123	150,000	1:22.66	104
2001	Victory Ride	3	E.S. Prado	116	Xtra Heat	120	Nasty Storm	120	150,000	1:21.72	107
2002	You	3	J.D. Bailey	123	Carson Hollow	123	Spring Meadow	120	150,000	1:22.84	101
2003	Lady Tak	3	J.D. Bailey	122	Bird Town	122	House Party	122	150,000	1:20.83	110

Beyer Index: 104.07

Distance 1 1/4 miles in 1922. Run at Belmont Park 1943-45.

TRAVERS STAKES, 1 1/4 Miles, 3-Year-Olds, Saratoga Race Course, 2003 Purse: $1,000,000

Year	Winner	Age	Jockey	Wt.	Second	Wt.	Third	Wt.	Win Value	Time	Beyer
1864	Kentucky	3	Gillpatrack	100	Tipperary	100	Th'g's N'ck Jr.	100	2,950	3:18.60	
1865	Maiden	3	Sewell	97	Oleata	97	Sarah K.	97	3,400	3:18.20	
1866	Merrill	3	Abe	100	Utrica	97	Bayswater	100	3,500	3:29.00	
1867	Ruthless	3	Gillpatrick	103	R.B. Connolly	100	De Courcey	100	2,850	3:18.20	
1868	The Banshee	3	Smith	97	Boaster	100	Albuera	100	3,150	3:10.60	
1869	Glenelg	3	C. Miller	110	Onyx	110	Invercauld	107	3,000	3:14.00	
1870	Kingfisher	3	C. Miller	110	Telegram	110	Foster	110	4,950	3:15.20	
1871	Harry Bassett	3	W. Miller	110	Nellie Gray	107	Alroy	110	5,600	3:21.60	
1872	Joe Daniels	3	J. Rowe	110	Silent Friend	110	Wade Hampton	110	5,500	3:08.20	
1873	Tom Bowling	3	R. Swim	110	Waverly	110	Merodac	110	5,400	3:09.60	
1874	Attila	3	Barbee	110	Acrobat	110	Steel Eyes	110	5,050	3:09.20	
	Race resulted in a dead heat; Attila won the run-off in 3:08.75										
1875	D'Artagnan	3	Barbee	110	Milner	110	Aristides	110	4,850	3:06.20	
1876	Sultana	3	Hayward	107	Barricade	110	Fredericktown	110	3,700	3:15.20	

Year	Winner	Age	Jockey	Wt.	Second	Wt.	Third	Wt.	Win Value	Time	Beyer
1877	Baden Baden	3	Sayers	110	Bradamante	107	St. James	110	4,550	3:12.20	
1878	Duke of Magenta	3	Hughes	118	Bramble	118	Spartan	118	4,250	3:08.00	
1879	Falsetto	3	I. Murphy	118	Spendthrift	118	Harold	118	4,950	3:09.20	
1880	Grenada	3	Hughes	118	Open	118	Turfman	118	3,750	3:12.20	
1881	Hindoo	3	J. McLaughlin	118	Catoctin	118	Getaway	118	2,950	3:07.20	
1882	Carley B.	3	Quantrell	115	Tom Plunkett	118	Mandamus	118	3,450	3:28.60	
1883	Barnes	3	J. McLaughlin	118	Tennyson	118			3,400	3:18.00	
1884	Rataplan	3	Fitzpatrick	118	Blast	118	Tecoma	118	4,150	3:07.20	
1885	Bersan	3	Spellman	118	Irish Pat	118	Boot Black	118	4,025	3:08.20	
1886	Inspector B.	3	J. McLaughlin	118	Elkwood	118	Silver Cloud	118	3,825	3:10.20	
1887	Carey	3	Baylock	118	Oarsman	118	Pendennis	118	3,825	3:17.60	
1888	Sir Dixon	3	J. McLaughlin	118	Los Angeles	113	Falcon	118	4,625	3:07.60	
1889	Long Dance	3	Barnes	118	Flood Tide	118			3,700	3:08.60	
1890	Sir John	3	Bergan	118	Frontenac	118	Burlington	118	4,925	2:39.00	
1891	Vallera	3	R. Williams	122	Hoodlum	122	Silver King	115	2,900	2:49.00	
1892	Azra	3	Clayton	122	Ronald	122			2,750	2:43.60	
1893	Stowaway	3	McDermott	107	Mirage	110	Walnut	107	2,450	2:10.60	
1894	Henry of Navarre	3	Taral	125	Joe Ripley	110	Rey el Santa Anita	125	2,350	2:10.20	
1895	Liza	3	Griffin	104	Rey del Caredes	109	Maurice	111	1,125	1:55.20	
1897	Rensselaer	3	Taral	126	Tragedian	114	Don de Oro	131	1,425	2:12.00	
1901	Blues	3	Shaw	126	Dublin	111	The Parader	129	6,750	1:58.60	
1902	Hermist	3	Rice	111	Gold Cure	116	Cunard	111	6,750	1:54.80	
1903	Ada Nay	3	F. O'Neill	106	Reliable	126	Gimcrack	111	8,150	1:57.00	
1904	Broomstick	3	T. Burns	129	Bobadil	116	Auditor	111	5,850	2:06.80	
1905	Dandelion	3	Shaw	111	Merry Lark	126	Glenecho	126	8,350	2:08.00	
1906	Gallavant	3	W. Miller	111	Mohawk II	111	Reidmore	111	5,800	2:08.20	
1907	Frank Gill	3	Notter	129	Golf Ball	116	Cork Hill	111	5,800	2:07.00	
1908	Dorante	3	J. Lee	116	King James	111	Beaucoup	111	5,800	2:09.60	
1909	Hilarious	3	Scoville	129	Practical	108	Fayette	121	5,800	2:06.00	
1910	Dalmatian	3	C.H. Shilling	111	Barleythorpe	111	Hampton Court	111	4,825	2:10.00	
1913	Rock View	3	T. McTaggart	129	Prince Eugene	126	Barnegat	115	2,725	2:06.60	
1914	Roamer	3	J. Butwell	123	Surprising	126	Gainer	121	3,000	2:04.00	
1915	Lady Rotha	3	M. Garner	106	Saratoga	124	Iron Duke	111	2,150	2:11.40	
	Trial by Jury finished first but was disqualified										
1916	Spur	3	J. Loftus	129	Star Hawk	116	Franklin	111	3,125	2:05.00	
1917	Omar Khayyam	3	J. Butwell	129	Rickety	123	Ticket	120	5,350	2:08.80	
1918	Sun Briar	3	W. Knapp	120	Johren	126	War Cloud	126	7,700	2:03.20	
1919	Hannibal	3	L. Ensor	120	War Pennant	120	Thunderclap	115	9,835	2:02.80	
1920	Man o' War	3	A. Schuttinger	129	Upset	123	John P. Grier	115	9,275	2:01.80	
1921	Sporting Blood	3	L. Lyke	123	Prudery	121			10,275	2:05.80	
1922	Little Chief	3	L. Fator	120	Kai-Sang	120	Sweep By	123	11,325	2:13.40	
1923	Wilderness	3	B. Marinelli	120	Flagstaff	120	Rialto	110	13,550	2:04.00	
1924	Sun Flag	3	F. Keogh	115	Aga Khan	115	Mr. Mutt	120	14,675	2:04.40	
1925	Dangerous	3	C. Kummer	115	Swope	120	Silver Fox	129	13,425	2:10.80	
1926	Mars	3	F. Coltiletti	123	Pompey	123	Display	123	15,050	2:04.60	
1927	Brown Bud	3	L. Fator	120	Nimba	121	Valorous	120	29,925	2:05.40	
1928	Petee-Wrack	3	S. O'Donnell	117	Victorian	126	Sun Edwin	123	30,550	2:08.00	
1929	Beacon Hill	3	A. Robertson	117	Marine	123	The Nut	117	31,825	2:04.20	
1930	Jim Dandy	3	F.J. Baker	120	Gallant Fox	126	Whichone	126	27,050	2:08.00	
1931	Twenty Grand	3	L. McAtee	126	St. Brideaux	120	Sun Meadow	120	33,000	2:04.60	
1932	War Hero	3	J. Gilbert	115	Monday	115	Sunmelus	115	23,150	2:05.80	
1933	Inlander	3	R. Jones	126	Golden Way	115	Keep Out	115	21,050	2:08.00	
1934	Observant	3	L. Humphries	112	Collateral	117	Roustabout	117	14,650	2:05.60	
1935	Gold Foam	3	S. Coucci	112	St. Bernard	115	Count Arthur	112	14,675	2:04.60	
1936	Granville	3	J. Stout	127	Sun Teddy	122	Count Morse	122	14,700	2:05.80	
1937	Burning Star	3	W.D. Wright	117	Up and Doing	112	Matey	120	14,550	2:04.80	
1938	Thanksgiving	3	E. Arcaro	117	Jolly Tar	112	Fighting Fox	124	14,400	2:03.60	
1939	Eight Thirty	3	H. Richards	117	Sun Lover	122	Sir Marlboro	122	16,575	2:06.60	
1940	Fenelon	3	J. Stout	122	Your Chance	122	Asp	112	17,425	2:04.40	
1941	Whirlaway	3	A. Robertson	130	Fairymant	112	Lord Kitch'er	112	16,900	2:05.80	
1942	Shut Out	3	E. Arcaro	130	Trierarch	112	Star Beacon	113	17,825	2:04.40	
1943	Eurasian	3	S. Brooks	112	Fairy Manhurst	112	Famous Victory	112	19,850	2:03.80	
1944	By Jimminy	3	E. Arcaro	126	Free Lance	112	Bounding Home	126	25,015	2:03.40	
1945	Adonis	3	C. McCreary	110	Burning Dream	110	Sir Francis	116	28,680	2:02.80	
1946	Natchez	3	T. Atkinson	124	Mahout	122	School Tie	112	24,750	2:08.00	
1947	Young Peter	3	T. May	124	Phalanx	128	Colonel O'F	122	19,375	2:06.20	
1948	Ace Admiral	3	T. Atkinson	108	Better Self	124	Alairne	108	19,650	2:05.00	
1949	Arise	3	C. Errico	108	Daiquiri	108	Sun Bahram	122	16,600	2:06.20	
1950	Lights Up	3	G. Hettinger	110	Bed o' Roses	126	Passenson	110	16,350	2:03.00	
1951	Battlefield	3	E. Arcaro	123	Yildiz	126	Big Stretch	114	15,000	2:06.20	
1952	One Count	3	E. Guerin	126	Armageddon	123	Tom Fool	114	16,450	2:07.40	
1953	Native Dancer	3	E. Guerin	126	Dictar	120	Guardian II.	114	18,850	2:05.60	
1954	Fisherman	3	H. Woodhouse	120	Lychnus	114	Chevation	120	19,500	2:06.00	

Year	Winner	Age	Jockey	Wt.	Second	Wt.	Third	Wt.	Win Value	Time	Beyer
1955	Thinking Cap	3	J.P. Bailey	120	Traffic Judge	124	Grandpaw	124	19,150	2:06.40	
1956	Oh Johnny	3	H. Woodhouse	116	Tick Tock	112	Bill's Sky Boy	112	33,200	2:06.20	
1957	Gallant Man	3	W. Shoemaker	126	Bureaucracy	116	Field of Honor	112	29,500	2:04.00	
1958	Piano Jim	3	R. Ussery	112	Grey Monarch	112	Warhead	113	29,920	2:05.80	
1959	Sword Dancer	3	M. Ycaza	126	Middle Brother	112	Nimmer	120	51,962	2:04.20	
1960	Tompion	3	W. Hartack	126	Count Amber	115	Don Rickles	114	53,165	2:03.40	
1961	Beau Prince	3	S. Brooks	126	Guadalcanal	114	Ambiopoise	126	54,210	2:03.00	
1962	Jaipur	3	W. Shoemaker	126	Ridan	126	Military Plume	114	53,722	2:01.60	
1963	Crewman	3	E. Guerin	120	Hot Dust	114	Chateaugay	126	52,910	2:02.40	
1964	Quadrangle	3	M. Ycaza	126	Knightly Manner	120	Hill Rise	123	52,032	2:04.40	
1965	Hail to All	3	J. Sellers	123	Pass the Word	114	Cornish Prince	114	56,777	2:02.20	
1966	Buckpasser	3	B. Baeza	126	Amberoid	123	Buffle	120	53,690	2:01.60	
1967	Damascus	3	W. Shoemaker	126	Reason to Hail	120	Tumiga	117	52,065	2:01.60	
1968	Chompion	3	J. Cruguet	114	Forward Pass	126	Funny Fellow	114	55,802	2:04.80	
1969	Arts and Letters	3	B. Baeza	126	Dike	120	Distray	114	69,290	2:01.60	
1970	Loud	3	J. Vasquez	114	Judgable	117	Plymouth	114	73,385	2:01.00	
1971	Bold Reason	3	L. Pincay Jr	120	West Coast Scout	120	Good Counsel	114	66,420	2:02.40	
1972	Key to the Mint	3	B. Baeza	117	Tentam	114	True Knight	114	66,600	2:01.20	
1973	Annihilate 'Em	3	R. Turcotte	120	Stop the Music	122	See the Jaguar	120	68,280	2:01.60	
1974	Holding Pattern	3	M. Miceli	121	Little Current	126	Chris Evert	121	69,660	2:05.20	
1975	Wajima	3	B. Baeza	126	Media	126	Prince Thou Art	126	65,220	2:02.00	
1976	Honest Pleasure	3	C. Perret	126	Romeo	126	Dance Spell	126	65,040	2:00.20	
1977	Jatski	3	S. Maple	126	Run Dusty Run	126	Silver Series	126	68,160	2:01.60	

Run Dusty Run finished first but was disqualified and placed second

Year	Winner	Age	Jockey	Wt.	Second	Wt.	Third	Wt.	Win Value	Time	Beyer
1978	Alydar	3	J. Velasquez	126	Affirmed	126	Nasty and Bold	126	62,880	2:02.00	

Affirmed finished first but was disqualified and placed second

Year	Winner	Age	Jockey	Wt.	Second	Wt.	Third	Wt.	Win Value	Time	Beyer
1979	General Assembly	3	J. Vasquez	126	Smarten	126	Private Account	126	80,850	2:00.00	
1980	Temperence Hill	3	E. Maple	126	First Albert	126	Amber Pass	126	100,980	2:02.80	
1981	Willow Hour	3	E. Maple	126	Pleasant Colony	126	Lord Avie	126	135,600	2:03.80	
1982	Runaway Groom	3	J. fell	126	Aloma's Ruler	126	Conquistador Cielo	126	132,900	2:02.60	
1983	Play Fellow	3	P. Day	126	Slew o' Gold	126	Hyperborean	126	135,000	2:01.00	
1984	Carr de Naskra	3	L. Pincay Jr	126	Pine Circle	126	Morning Bob	126	211,500	2:02.60	
1985	Chief's Crown	3	A. Cordero Jr	126	Turkoman	126	Skip Trial	126	202,800	2:01.20	
1986	Wise Times	3	J.D. Bailey	126	Danzig Connection	126	Personal Flag	126	203,700	2:03.40	

Broad Brush finished second but was disqualified and placed fourth

Year	Winner	Age	Jockey	Wt.	Second	Wt.	Third	Wt.	Win Value	Time	Beyer
1987	Java Gold	3	P. Day	126	Cryptoclearance	126	Polish Navy	126	673,800	2:02.00	
1988	Forty Niner	3	C.J. McCarron	126	Seeking the Gold	126	Brian's Time	126	653,100	2:01.40	
1989	Easy Goer	3	P. Day	126	Clevor Trevor	126	Shy Tom	126	653,100	2:00.80	
1990	Rhythm	3	C. Perret	126	Shot Gun Scott	126	Sir Richard Lewis	126	707,100	2:02.60	104
1991	Corporate Report	3	C.J. McCarron	126	Hansel	126	Fly So Free	126	600,000	2:01.20	109
1992	Thunder Rumble	3	W.H. McCauley	126	Devil His Due	126	Dance Floor	126	600,000	2:00.80	109
1993	Sea Hero	3	J.D. Bailey	126	Kissin Kris	126	Miner's Mark	126	600,000	2:01.80	109
1994	Holy Bull	3	M.E. Smith	126	Concern	126	Tabasco Cat	126	450,000	2:02.00	115
1995	Thunder Gulch	3	G.L. Stevens	126	Pyramid Peak	126	Malthus	126	450,000	2:03.60	110
1996	Will's Way	3	J.F. Chavez	126	Louis Quatorze	126	Skip Away	126	450,000	2:02.40	114
1997	Deputy Commander	3	C.J. McCarron	126	Behrens	126	Awesome Again	126	450,000	2:04.00	110
1998	Coronado's Quest	3	M.E. Smith	126	Victory Gallop	126	Raffie's Majesty	126	450,000	2:03.40	107
1999	Lemon Drop Kid	3	J.A. Santos	126	Vision and Verse	126	Menifee	126	600,000	2:02.19	110
2000	Unshaded	3	S.J. Sellers	126	Albert the Great	126	Commendable	126	600,000	2:02.59	109
2001	Point Given	3	G.L. Stevens	126	E Dubai	126	Dollar Bill	126	600,000	2:01.40	117
2002	Medaglia d'Oro	3	J.D. Bailey	126	Repent	126	Nothing Flat	126	600,000	2:02.53	113
2003	Ten Most Wanted	3	P. Day	126	Peace Rules	126	Strong Hope	126	600,000	2:02.14	112

Beyer Index: 110.57

Distance 1 3/4 miles prior to 1890; 1 1/2 miles 1890–92; 1 1/8 miles, 1895, 1901–03. Run at Belmont Park, 1943–45

TRIPLE BEND BREEDERS' CUP INVITATIONAL HANDICAP, 7 Furlongs,
3-Year-Olds and Up, Hollywood Park, 2003 Purse: $300,000

Year	Winner	Age	Jockey	Wt.	Second	Wt.	Third	Wt.	Win Value	Time	Beyer
1979	White Rammer	5	W. Shoemaker	120	Arachnoid	124	Bad 'n Big	122	24,650	1:21.20	
1980	Rich Cream	5	W. Shoemaker	118	I'm Smokin	115	Dragon C'mmand	116	32,250	1:19.40	
1981	Summer Time Guy	5	C.J. McCarron	118	Back'n Time	118	Life's Hope	115	37,400	1:20.20	
1982	Never Tabled	5	C.J. McCarron	112	Shanekite	117	Pompeii Court	116	31,750	1:21.00	
1983	Regal Falcon	5	E. Delahoussaye	117	Island Whirl	123	Kang'roo Court	118	30,700	1:23.40	
1984	Debonair Junior	3	C.J. McCarron	114	Croeso	116	Night Mover	120	37,980	1:21.20	
1985	Fifty Six Ina Row	4	L. Pincay Jr	117	Premiership	115	French Legion'aire	117	38,500	1:20.80	
1986	Sabona	4	C.J. McCarron	114	Innamorato	113	Michadilla	115	47,150	1:21.00	
1987	Bedside Promise	5	R.Q. Meza	124	Zabaleta	118	Bolder Than Bold	118	46,500	1:21.00	
1988	Perfec Travel	6	C.A. Black	115	Rec'nntring	115	Dons Irish M'lody	115	49,600	1:22.20	
1989	Sensational Star	5	R.Q. Meza	114	Oraibi	120	Hot Operator	113	49,700	1:21.40	
1990	Prospectors Gamble	5	J.A. Garcia	114	Raise a Stanza	117	Hot Operator	113	64,200	1:21.40	107
1991	Robyn Dancer	4	L. Pincay Jr	118	Bruho	117	Black Jack Road	118	62,700	1:21.00	
1992	Slew the Surgeon	4	M.G. Linares	111	Softshoe Sure Shot	114	Record Boom	114	64,600	1:21.40	100

Year	Winner	Age	Jockey	Wt.	Second	Wt.	Third	Wt.	Win Value	Time	Beyer
1993	Now Listen	6	K.J. Desormeaux	116	Cardmania	116	Star of the Crop	120	66,400	1:20.80	110
1994	Memo	7	P. Atkinson	120	Minjinsky	115	Slerp	119	62,400	1:20.40	113
1995	Concept Win	5	Valenzuela PA	118	Gold Land	116	Lucky Forever	119	63,100	1:21.00	102
1996	Letthebighossroll	8	C.J. McCarron	116	Score Quick	113	Comininalittlehot	116	125,460	1:21.40	105
1997	Score Quick	5	G.F. Almeida	113	Elmhurst	115	First Intent	116	100,980	1:21.00	104
1998	Son Of A Pistol	6	A. Solis	118	The Exeter Man	114	Benchmark	118	120,000	1:20.80	110
1999	Mazel Trick	4	C.J. McCarron	115	Christmas Boy	111	Regal Thunder	115	180,000	1:19.80	118
2000	Elaborate	5	V. Espinoza	114	Cliquot	116	Lexicon	117	180,000	1:21.19	111
2001	Ceeband	4	M.S. Garcia	110	Squirtle Squirt	114	Elaborate	118	180,000	1:21.17	112
2002	Disturbingthepeace	4	V. Espinoza	113	D'wildcat	115	Mellow Fellow	120	180,000	1:21.09	111
2003	Joey Franco	4	P.A. Valenzuela	118	Publication	116	Primerica	113	180,000	1:21.56	105

Bluesthestandard finished third but was disqualified and placed sixth

Beyer Index: 108.31

TURF CLASSIC INVITATIONAL, 1 1/2 Miles (Turf), 3-Year-Olds and Up, Belmont Park, 2003 Purse: $750,000

Year	Winner	Age	Jockey	Wt.	Second	Wt.	Third	Wt.	Win Value	Time	Beyer
1977	Johnny D.	3	S. Cauthen	122	Majestic Light	126	Crow	126	130,000	2:33.20	
1978	Waya	4	A. Cordero Jr	123	Tiller	126	Trillion	123	130,000	2:26.80	
1979	Bowl Game	5	J. Velasquez	126	Trillion	123	Native Courier	126	150,000	2:28.20	
1980	Anifa	4	A. Gibert	123	Golden Act	126	John Henry	126	180,000	2:39.60	
1981	April Run	3	P. Paquet	118	Galaxy Libra	126	The Very One	123	180,000	2:31.20	
1982	April Run	4	C.B. Asmussen	123	Naskra's Breeze	126	Bottled Water	126	286,080	2:29.80	
1983	All Along	4	W.R. Swinburn	123	Thunder Puddles	126	Erins Isle	126	351,420	2:34.00	
1984	John Henry	9	C.J. McCarron	126	Win	126	Majesty's Prince	126	375,150	2:25.20	
1985	Noble Fighter	3	A. Lequeux	119	Win	126	Strawberry Road II	126	431,100	2:25.40	
1986	Manila	3	J.A. Santos	119	Damister	126	Danger's Hour	126	428,150	2:27.80	
1987	Theatrical	5	P. Day	126	River Memories	116	Talakeno	126	360,000	2:29.20	
1988	Sunshine Forever	3	A. Cordero Jr	121	My Big Boy	126	Most Welcome	126	360,000	2:33.80	
1989	Yankee Affair	7	J.A. Santos	126	El Senor	126	My Big Boy	126	392,550	2:27.20	
1990	Cacoethes	4	R. Cochrane	126	Alwuhush	126	With Approval	126	360,000	2:25.00	111
1991	Solar Splendor	4	W.H. McCauley	126	Dear Doctor	126	Fortune's Wheel	121	300,000	2:27.80	112

Spinning finished third but was disqualified and placed fourth

Year	Winner	Age	Jockey	Wt.	Second	Wt.	Third	Wt.	Win Value	Time	Beyer
1992	Sky Classic	5	P. Day	126	Fraise	126	Solar Splendor	126	300,000	2:24.40	110
1993	Apple Tree	4	M.E. Smith	126	Solar Splendor	126	George Augustus	126	300,000	2:28.20	111
1994	Tikkanen	3	C.B. Asmussen	121	Vaudeville	121	Yenda	118	300,000	2:25.80	113
1995	Turk Passer	5	J.R. Velazquez	126	Hernando	126	Celtic Arms	126	300,000	2:36.60	109
1996	Diplomatic Jet	4	J.F. Chavez	126	Awad	126	Marlin	121	300,000	2:27.40	111
1997	Val's Prince	5	M.E. Smith	126	Flag Down	126	Ops Smile	126	300,000	2:28.80	109
1998	Buck's Boy	5	S.J. Sellers	126	Cetewayo	126	Lazy Lode	126	300,000	2:33.25	111
1999	Val's Prince	7	J.F. Chavez	126	Dream Well	126	Fahris	126	360,000	2:28.63	108
2000	John's Call	9	J.L. Samyn	126	Craigsteel	126	Ela Athena	123	450,000	2:28.58	109
2001	Timboroa	5	E.S. Prado	126	King Cugat	126	Cetewayo	126	450,000	2:29.43	109
2002	Denon	4	E.S. Prado	126	Blazing Fury	126	Delta Form	126	450,000	2:28.47	108
2003	Sulamani	4	J.D. Bailey	126	Deeliteful Irving	126	Balto Star	126	450,000	2:27.51	110

Beyer Index: 110.07

Run at Aqueduct 1975 and 1976, and 1981 – 1983

UNITED NATIONS HANDICAP, 1 3/8 Miles (Turf), 3-Year-Olds and Up, Monmouth Park, 2003 Purse: $750,000

Year	Winner	Age	Jockey	Wt.	Second	Wt.	Third	Wt.	Win Value	Time	Beyer
1953	Iceberg II	5	J. Contreras	120	Brush Burn	118	Royal Governor	118	43,050	1:55.80	
1954	Closed Door	4	W. Hartack	117	Royal Vale	120	Kaster	114	50,000	1:57.00	
1955	Blue Choir	4	W. Hartack	126	Chevation	117	Klairon	111	73,600	2:00.00	
1956	Career Boy	3	S. Boulmetis	116	Find	117	Mister Gus	119	65,000	1:56.20	
1957	Round Table	3	W. Shoemaker	118	Tudor Era	112	Find	122	65,000	1:56.20	
1958	Clem	4	W. Shoemaker	113	Round Table	130	Combustion II	115	65,000	1:54.60	
1959	Round Table	5	W. Shoemaker	136	Noureddin	117	Li'l Fella	120	65,000	1:55.20	
1960	T.V. Lark	3	J. Sellers	120	Sword Dancer	127	Bally Ache	122	65,000	1:57.00	
1961	Oink	4	L. Gilligan	119	Tompion	117	Art Market	116	65,000	1:56.00	
1962	Mongo	3	C. Burr	117	T.V. Lark	123	Wise Ship	123	65,000	1:56.60	
1963	Mongo	4	W. Chambers	124	Never Bend	118	Carry Back	127	75,000	1:55.20	
1964	Western Warrior	5	H. Gustines	114	Parka	121	Turbo Jet II	116	75,000	1:57.80	
1965	Parka	7	W. Blum	119	Hill Rise	118	Chieftain	122	75,000	1:57.80	
1966	Assagai	3	L. Adams	118	Ginger Fizz	114	Toulore	118	65,000	1:58.60	
1967	Flit-to	4	H. Woodhouse	110	Assagai	122	Fort Marcy	117	65,000	1:54.00	

Munden Point finished third but was disqualified and placed fourth

Year	Winner	Age	Jockey	Wt.	Second	Wt.	Third	Wt.	Win Value	Time	Beyer
1968	Dr. Fager	4	B. Baeza	134	Advocator	112	Fort Marcy	118	65,000	1:55.20	
1969	Hawaii	4	J. Velasquez	124	North Flight	117	Fort Marcy	130	75,000	2:00.60	
1970	Fort Marcy	6	J. Velasquez	125	Fiddle Isle	127	Mr. Leader	119	75,000	1:56.00	
1971	Run the Gantlet	3	R. Woodhouse	117	Twice Worthy	118	Chompion	116	65,000	2:02.00	
1972	Acclimatization	4	R. Woodhouse	117	Dubasoff	117	Red Reality	119	65,000	1:54.00	
1973	Tentam	4	J. Velasquez	123	Star Envoy	116	Return to Reality	113	75,000	1:54.60	
1974	Halo	5	J. Velasquez	118	London Company	123	Scantling	115	65,000	1:56.80	

Year	Winner	Age	Jockey	Wt.	Second	Wt.	Third	Wt.	Win Value	Time	Beyer
1975	Royal Glint	5	J. Tejeira	120	Stonewalk	120	R. Tom Can	116	65,000	1:57.00	
1976	Intrepid Hero	4	S. Hawley	125	Improviser	116	Break Up the Game	120	65,000	1:53.40	
1977	Bemo	7	D. Brumfield	116	Quick Card	124	Alias Smith	112	65,000	1:54.00	
1978	Noble Dancer II	6	S. Cauthen	127	Upper Nile	118	Dan Horn	117	81,250	1:56.40	
1979	Noble Dancer II	7	J. Vasquez	125	Dom Alaric	120	Overskate	128	75,000	1:56.60	
1980	Lyphard's Wish	4	A. Cordero Jr	118	Match the Hatch	115	Scythian Gold	111	82,500	1:53.80	
1981	Key to Content	4	G. Martens	121	Ben Fab	123	Match the Hatch	115	82,500	1:52.80	
1982	Naskra's Breeze	5	J.L. Samyn	117	Acaroid	115	Don Roberto	116	90,000	1:53.40	
1983	Acaroid	5	A. Cordero Jr	113	Trevita	116	Majesty's Prince	120	106,200	1:54.00	
1984	Hero's Honor	4	J.D. Bailey	123	Cozzene	114	Who's For Dinner	110	106,200	1:54.00	
1985	Ends Well	4	M.R. Morgan	114	Who's For Dinner	116	Cool	111	107,820	1:54.60	
1986	Manila	3	J.A. Santos	114	Uptown Swell	116	Lieutenant's Lark	112	104,040	1:52.60	
1987	Manila	4	J. Vasquez	124	Racing Star	115	Air Display	110	90,000	1:58.80	
1988	Equalize	6	J.A. Santos	116	Wanderkin	115	Bet Twice	124	120,000	1:52.60	
1989	Yankee Affair	7	P. Day	121	Salem Drive	117	Simply Majestic	119	120,000	1:53.20	
1990	Steinlen	7	J.A. Santos	124	Capades	112	Alwuhush	121	300,000	1:52.00	113
1991	Exbourne	5	C.J. McCarron	122	Forty Niner Days	116	Goofalik	114	300,000	1:52.60	109
1992	Sky Classic	5	P. Day	123	Chenin Blanc	115	Lotus Pool	114	300,000	1:52.20	106
1993	Star of Cozzene	5	J.A. Santos	120	Lure	123	Finder's Choice	114	300,000	1:53.20	117
1994	Lure	5	M.E. Smith	123	Fourstars Allstar	117	Star of Cozzene	121	300,000	1:52.60	107
1995	Sandpit	6	C.S. Nakatani	122	Celtic Arms	118	Alice Springs	115	300,000	1:57.20	107
1996	Sandpit	7	C.S. Nakatani	122	Diplomatic Jet	117	Northern Spur	122	300,000	1:55.60	111
1997	Influent	6	J.L. Samyn	117	Geri	113	Flag Down	118	240,000	1:53.60	111
1999	Yagli	6	J.D. Bailey	124	Supreme Sound	113	Amerique	115	150,000	2:16.02	103
2000	Down the Aisle	7	R.G. Davis	114	Aly's Alley	111	Honor Glide	116	210,000	2:13.63	102
2001	Senure	5	R.G. Davis	116	With Anticipation	113	Gritty Sandie	112	300,000	2:13.56	106
	With Anticipation (Beyer: 106) finished first but was disqualified and placed second										
2002	With Anticipation	7	P. Day	119	Denon	118	Sarafan	117	300,000	2:12.81	110
2003	Balto Star	5	J.A. Velez Jr	117	The Tin Man	121	Lunar Sovereign	121	450,000	2:12.78	110

Beyer Index: **108.62**

Run at Atlantic City through 1997; Run as Caesars International 1991-97

VANITY INVITATIONAL HANDICAP, 1 1/8 Miles, Fillies and Mares, 3-Year-Olds and Up, Hollywood Park, 2003 Purse: $250,000

Year	Winner	Age	Jockey	Wt.	Second	Wt.	Third	Wt.	Win Value	Time	Beyer
1940	Etoila II	6	N. Pariso	112	Flying Wild	122	Augury	114	7,275	1:37.20	
1941	Painted Veil	3	J. Westrope	113	Cute Trick	114	African Queen	109	7,350	1:43.40	
1944	Happy Issue	4	H. Woodhouse	122	Paula's Lulu	112	Regimental	116	17,150	1:44.00	
1945	Busher	3	J. Longden	126	Canina	114	Paula's Lulu	113	17,455	1:43.80	
1946	Be Faithful	4	J. Westrope	119	Lasting Peace	107	Double F.F.	112	17,850	1:42.00	
1947	Honeymoon	4	J. Westrope	119	Good Excuse	112	Nepotism	108	18,350	1:42.00	
1948	Hemet Squaw	4	R. Neves	114	Iron Maiden	108	Canina	112	16,350	1:43.60	
1949	Silver Drift	4	N. Brennan	105	Honeymoon	124	Good Excuse	112	19,300	1:43.60	
1950	Next Move	3	E. Guerin	128	Bewitch	124	Wistful	125	18,250	1:49.40	
1951	Bewitch	6	S. Brooks	125	Fleet Rings	106	Great Dream	108	16,950	1:42.80	
1952	Two Lea	6	H. Moreno	122	Wistful	112	Jennie Lee	117	15,900	1:43.40	
1953	Fleet Khal	3	J. Burton	114	A Gleam	126	Spanish Cream	125	15,500	1:42.40	
1954	Bubbley	4	R. York	116	Is Proud	118	Lap Full	107	15,350	1:49.60	
1955	Countess Fleet	4	J. Longden	126	Quillo Maid	107	Frosty Dawn	112	15,100	1:47.60	
1956	Mary Machree	5	B. Pulido	113	Our Betters	120	Solid Miss	119	22,200	1:48.60	
1957	Annie-Lu-San	4	W. Skuse	108	Miss Todd	115	Beautillion	122	23,400	1:48.80	
1958	Annie-Lu-San	5	W. Skuse	112	Ballet Khal	114	Summer Story	115	22,700	1:50.00	
1959	Zev's Joy	4	W. Shoemaker	115	Honeys Gem	129	Sybil Brand	109	21,550	1:48.20	
1959	Tender Size	3	W. Shoemaker	106	La Plume	112	Cellyar	112	21,050	1:48.00	
1960	Silver Spoon	4	J. Longden	130	Tritoma	107	Honeys Gem	118	22,950	1:49.00	
1961	Perizade	5	A. Maese	112	Mountain Glory	121	Solid Thought	113	26,900	1:48.60	
1962	Linita	5	J. Longden	126	Fun House	116	Kissing Belle	109	33,150	1:48.40	
1963	Table Mate	4	W. Shoemaker	120	Pixie Erin	118	Dingle Bay	108	33,150	1:48.40	
1964	Star Maggie	4	W. Shoemaker	115	Curious Clover	121	Jalousie II	123	34,700	1:48.40	
1965	Jalousie II	6	J. Longden	115	Yes Please	115	Savaii	121	31,550	1:48.40	
1966	Khal Ireland	6	S. Trevino	110	Ormea	114	Pollen	115	33,400	1:49.20	
1967	Desert Love	4	J. Lambert	114	Natashka	122	Ali's Theme	106	35,100	1:48.80	
1968	Gamely	4	W. Harris	131	Princessnesian	128	Desert Law	115	47,150	1:47.60	
1969	Desert Law	5	L. Pincay Jr	119	Gamely	128	Amerigo Lady	125	47,600	1:48.20	
1970	Commissary	4	W. Harris	118	Pattee Canyon	124	Tipping Time	120	46,500	1:47.60	
1971	Hi Q.	4	F. Toro	113	Manta	129	Swoon's Flower	116	57,000	1:48.80	
1972	Convenience	4	J. Lambert	121	Typecast	126	Street Dancer	115	55,900	1:47.40	
1973	Convenience	5	J.L. Rotz	121	Minstrel Miss	121	Susan's Girl	127	64,500	1:47.80	
1974	Tallahto	4	L. Pincay Jr	126	La Zanzara	120	Dogtooth Violet	118	66,500	1:47.00	
1975	Dulcia	6	W. Shoemaker	118	Susan's Girl	123	La Zanzara	120	67,500	1:47.40	
1976	Miss Toshiba	4	F. Toro	120	Bastonera II	120	Bold Baby	115	67,200	1:48.00	
1977	Cascapedia	4	S. Hawley	129	Bastonera II	122	Swingtime	117	65,500	1:47.60	
1978	Afifa	4	W. Shoemaker	113	Drama Critic	117	Dottie's Doll	117	77,050	1:46.40	
1979	It's in the Air	3	W. Shoemaker	113	Country Queen	121	Innuendo	116	77,950	1:47.40	

Year	Winner	Age	Jockey	Wt.	Second	Wt.	Third	Wt.	Win Value	Time	Beyer
1980	It's in the Air	4	L. Pincay Jr	120	Conveniently	111	Image of Reality	119	94,600	1:47.00	
1981	Track Robbery	5	P.A. Valenzuela	120	Princess Karenda	118	Save Wild Life	117	110,000	1:47.00	
1982	Sangue	4	W. Shoemaker	120	Track Robbery	123	Cat Girl	117	110,000	1:48.00	
1983	A Kiss for Luck	4	C.J. McCarron	114	Try Something New	118	Sangue	122	110,000	1:49.20	
1984	Princess Rooney	4	E. Delahoussaye	120	Adored	120	Salt Spring	113	150,500	1:46.20	
1985	Dontstop Themusic	5	A. Cordero Jr	118	Salt Spring	114	Estrapade	119	110,000	1:47.80	
1986	Magnificent Lindy	4	C.J. McCarron	116	Dontstop TheMusic	124	Outstandingly	118	137,000	2:02.00	
1987	Infinidad	5	C. Black	113	North Sider	121	Clabber Girl	115	110,000	2:00.60	
1988	Annoconnor	4	C. Black	114	Pen Bal Lady	119	Abloom II	113	110,000	1:49.20	
1989	Bayakoa	5	L. Pincay Jr	125	Flying Julia	112	Goodbye Halo	122	110,000	1:47.20	
1990	Gorgeous	4	E. Delahoussaye	124	Fantastic Look	112	Kelly	110	110,000	1:48.20	111
1991	Brought to Mind	4	P.A. Valenzuela	120	Fit to Scout	115	Luna Elegante	114	110,000	1:48.40	94
1992	Paseana	5	C.J. McCarron	127	Fowda	118	Re Toss	115	165,000	1:48.00	98
1993	Re Toss	6	E. Delahoussaye	115	Paseana	126	Guiza	114	165,000	1:47.80	104
1994	Potridee	4	A. Solis	114	Exchange	118	Golden Klair	119	165,000	1:48.00	103
1995	Private Persuasion	4	G.L. Stevens	114	Top Rung	116	Wandesta	119	165,000	1:48.20	108
1996	Jewel Princess	4	C.S. Nakatani	120	Serena's Song	125	Top Rung	116	150,000	1:47.00	116
1997	Twice the Vice	6	K.J. Desormeaux	114	Real Connection	114	Jewel Princess	123	240,000	1:46.40	110
1998	Escena	5	J.D. Bailey	124	Housa Dancer	115	Different	119	210,000	1:48.13	114
1999	Manistique	4	C.J. McCarron	122	Yolo Lady	115	Bella Chiarra	116	240,000	1:48.06	103
2000	Riboletta	5	C.J. McCarron	123	Speaking of Time	108	Excellent Meeting	120	180,000	1:48.54	111
2001	Gourmet Girl	6	G.L. Stevens	119	Lazy Slusan	122	Setareh	114	150,000	1:49.21	100
2002	Azeri	4	M. Smith	125	Affluent	119	Starrer	117	150,000	1:48.88	107
							Collect Call	115			
2003	Azeri	5	M.E. Smith	127	Sister Girl Blues	111	Bare Necessities	118	150,000	1:48.48	109

Beyer Index: 106.29

Distance 1 mile in 1940, 1 1/16 miles, 1941-53, 1 1.4 miles, 1986-87. Run at Santa Anita in 1949

VOSBURGH, 6 1/2 Furlongs, 3-Year-Olds and Up,
Belmont Park, 2003 Purse: $500,000

Year	Winner	Age	Jockey	Wt.	Second	Wt.	Third	Wt.	Win Value	Time	Beyer
1940	Joe Schenck	5	R.L. Vedder	115	Nitro	108	T.M. Dorsett	120	4,400	1:23.20	
1941	Joe Schenck	6	W. Eads	109	The Chief	114	Roman	132	4,500	1:24.20	
1942	Parasang	5	D. Meade	112	Devil Diver	124	Rosetown	112	6,375	1:23.00	
1943	Wait a Bit	4	C. Givens	115	Sun Again	117	Adulator	110	6,600	1:23.00	
1944	Cassis	5	T. Atkinson	121			Ariel Lad	116	4,792	1:23.40	
	Paperboy	6	W. Mehrtens	115							
1945	Buzfuz	3	T. Luther	120	First Fiddle	130	Coincidence	112	7,765	1:23.20	
1946	Coincidence	4	T. Atkinson	118	Alexis	109	Polynesian	130	13,950	1:23.80	
1947	With Pleasure	4	J. Westrope	132	Bridal Flower	114	Rabies	105	19,900	1:23.40	
1948	Colosal	5	O. Scurlock	118	Spy Song	129	First Flight	124	22,300	1:23.80	
1949	Loser Weeper	4	E. Guerin	116	Lithe	105	Colosal	118	12,750	1:23.00	
1950	Tea-Maker	7	J. Robertson	118	More Sun	106	Piet	124	13,150	1:23.00	
1951	War King	4	C. McCreary	108	Bryan G.	122	General Staff	112	13,125	1:23.20	
	Miche finished first but was disqualified										
1952	Parading Lady	3	J.N. Hard'b'k	105	Tea-Maker	123	Cyclotron	110	16,150	1:23.80	
1953	Indian Land	4	T. Atkinson	111	Navy Page	115	Cold Command	118	17,200	1:23.60	
1954	Joe Jones	4	C. McCreary	116	Pet Bully	134	Hyphasis	111	17,800	1:23.80	
1955	Nance's Lad	3	H. Woodhouse	112	Red Hannigan	119	Bunny's Babe	110	16,650	1:24.00	
1956	Summer Tan	4	E. Guerin	124	Joe Jones	121	Le Beau Prince	121	17,200	1:23.60	
1957	Bold Ruler	3	E. Arcaro	130	TIck Tock	117	St. Amour II	114	16,000	1:21.40	
1958	Tick Tock	5	W. Shoemaker	115	Mister Jive	122	Nashville	116	15,187	1:23.00	
1959	Rick City	3	R.L. Stevenson	115	The Irishman	117	Nahodah	115	18,550	1:22.80	
1960	Mail Order	4	E. Nelson	110	Wiggle II	112	Four Lane	121	19,330	1:22.60	
1961	Gyro	4	B. Baeza	118	Rose Net	111	Humane Leader	110	14,950	1:23.20	
1962	Commend	4	T. Bove	109	Misty Day	119	Surfer	114	15,762	1:22.20	
1963	Ornamento	3	B. Baeza	111	Uppercut	112	Merry Ruler	120	15,275	1:23.80	
1964	Affectionately	4	H. Grant	120	Red Gar	113	Bonjour	114	18,622	1:22.00	
1965	R. Thomas	4	L. Adams	117	Choker	112	Pia Star	126	39,325	1:23.00	
1966	Gallant Romeo	5	K. Knapp	123	Davis II	122	Flag Raiser	121	37,505	1:22.80	
1967	Dr. Fager	3	B. Baeza	128	Jim J.	115	R. Thomas	122	37,310	1:21.60	
1968	Dr. Fager	4	B. Baeza	139	Kissin' George	127	Jim J.	125	37,050	1:20.20	
1969	Ta Wee	3	J.L. Rotz	123	Plucky Lucky	116			38,220	1:21.60	
					Rising Market	120					
1970	Best Turn	4	L. Adams	115	True North	115	Ocean Bar	113	38,545	1:21.40	
1971	Duck Dance	4	J. Ruane	122	Summer Air	120	Coup Landing	118	36,660	1:21.20	
1972	Triple Bend	4	L. Pincay Jr	116	Tunex	112	Favorecidian	117	35,310	1:22.00	
1973	Aljamin	3	A. Cordero Jr	118	Highbinder	115	Timeless Moment	112	33,660	1:21.20	
1974	Forego	4	H. Gustines	131	Stop the Music	118	Prince Dantan	119	35,550	1:21.40	
1975	No Bias	5	A. Santiago	116	Step Nicely	126	Lonetree	117	34,590	1:22.80	
1976	My Juliet	4	A.S. Black	120	It's Freezing	113	Bold Forbes	126	31,980	1:21.80	
	Bold Forbes finished second but was disqualified and placed third										
1977	Affiliate	3	C. Perret	114	Broadway Forli	118	Great Above	112	49,905	1:21.00	
1978	Dr. Patches	4	A. Cordero Jr	117	What a Summer	124	Sorry Lookin	109	48,960	1:21.00	

Year	Winner	Age	Jockey	Wt.	Second	Wt.	Third	Wt.	Win Value	Time	Beyer
1979	General Assembly	3	J. Vasquez	123	Dr. Patches	126	Syncopate	126	48,195	1:21.00	
1980	Plugged Nickle	3	C.B. Asmussen	123	Dave's Friend	126		0	67,440	1:21.40	
1981	Guilty Conscience	5	C.B. Asmussen	126	Rise Jim	126	Well Decorated	123	67,921	1:22.00	
1982	Engine One	4	R. Hernandez	126	Gold Beauty	120	Maudlin	126	65,760	1:23.80	

Mike Mitchell finished second but was disqualified and placed fourth

Year	Winner	Age	Jockey	Wt.	Second	Wt.	Third	Wt.	Win Value	Time	Beyer
1983	A Phenomenon	3	A. Cordero Jr	123	Fit to Fight	126	Deputy Minister	126	69,000	1:21.00	
1984	Track Barron	3	A. Cordero Jr	123	Timeless Native	126	Raja's Shark	123	109,800	1:22.00	
1985	Another Reef	3	N. Santagata	124	Pancho Villa	124	Whoop Up	126	102,420	1:21.80	
1986	King's Swan	6	J.A. Santos	126	Love That Mac	126	Cutlass Reality	126	141,840	1:21.80	
1987	Groovy	4	A. Cordero Jr	126	Moment of Hope	126	Sun Master	126	139,680	1:22.60	
1988	Mining	4	R.P. Romero	126	Gulch	126	High Brite	126	133,920	1:22.40	
1989	Sewickley	4	R.P. Romero	126	Once Wild	126	Mr. Nickerson	123	135,120	1:23.00	
1990	Sewickley	5	A. Cordero Jr	126	Sunshine Jimmy	122	Glitterman	126	142,080	1:21.00	118
1991	Housebuster	4	C. Perret	126	Senator to Be	126	Sunshine Jimmy	126	120,000	1:21.80	115
1992	Rubiano	5	J.A. Krone	126	Sheikh Albadou	126	Salt Lake	123	120,000	1:22.80	113
1993	Birdonthewire	4	M.E. Smith	126	Take Me Out	126	Lion Cavern	126	120,000	1:22.20	114
1994	Harlan	5	J.D. Bailey	126	American Chance	126	Cherokee Run	126	120,000	1:21.80	107
1995	Not Surprising	5	R.G. Davis	126	You and I	126	Our Emblem	126	120,000	1:22.40	106
1996	Langfuhr	4	J.F. Chavez	126	Honour and Glory	122	Lite the Fuse	126	120,000	1:21.20	113
1997	Victory Cooley	4	J.F. Chavez	126	Score a Bride	126	Tale of the Cat	122	120,000	1:22.00	113
1998	Affirmed Success	4	J.F. Chavez	126	Stormin Fever	126	Tale of the Cat	126	150,000	1:21.99	119
1999	Artax	5	J.F. Chavez	126	Stormin Fever	126	Mountain Top	126	150,000	1:21.65	111
2000	Trippi	3	J.D. Bailey	123	More Than Ready	123	One Way Love	126	180,000	1:21.66	111
2001	Left Bank	4	J.R. Velazquez	126	Squirtle Squirt	123	Big E E	126	180,000	1:20.73	118
2002	Bonapaw	6	G. Melancon	126	Aldebaran	126	Voodoo	126	180,000	1:22.34	112
2003	Ghostzapper	3	J. Castellano	123	Aggadan	126	Posse	123	300,000	1:14.72	116

Beyer Index: 113.29

For all ages prior to 1958. Run at Aqueduct in 1959, 1961-74, 1976-77, 1979-83, 1985-86. Distance 7 furlongs prior to 2003

WHITNEY HANDICAP, 1 1/8 Miles, 3-Year-Olds and Up, Saratoga Race Course, 2003 Purse: $750,000

Year	Winner	Age	Jockey	Wt.	Second	Wt.	Third	Wt.	Win Value	Time	Beyer
1928	Black Maria	5	L. Fator	121	Chance Shot	126	Whiskery	126	6,500	2:06.00	
1929	Bateau	4	E. Ambrose	121	Comstockery	117	Display	126	5,850	2:09.40	
1930	Whichone	3	R. Workman	117	Marine	121	Vanity	116	7,100	2:04.00	
1931	St. Brideaux	3	L. McAtee	117	Curate	116	Blenheim	107	6,900	2:05.00	
1932	Equipoise	4	R. Workman	126	Gusto	117	Rocky News	116	5,450	2:05.60	
1933	Caesars Ghost	3	D. Belizzi	107	Sun Archer	107	Golden Way	102	2,425	2:10.80	
1934	Discovery	3	D. Meade	105	Fleam	107	Time Clock	112	2,475	2:07.80	
1935	Discovery	4	J. Bejshak	126	Esposa	100	Good Goods	114	3,125	2:04.60	
1936	Discovery	5	J. Bejshak	126	Esposa	121	Rust	106	3,250	2:06.80	
1937	Esposa	5	N. Wall	121	Matey	117	Count Arthur	126	3,000	2:05.20	
1938	War Admiral	4	W.D. Wright	126	Esposa	121	Fighting Fox	117	2,725	2:03.80	
1939	Eight Thirty	3	H. Richards	117	Shangay Lily	121	Handcuff	121	2,750	2:06.20	
1940	Challedon	4	G. Woolf	126	Isolater	126	Dusky Fox	117	2,700	2:03.20	
1941	Fenelon	4	J. Stout	120	Big Pebble	130	Welcome Pass	107	5,000	2:06.40	
1942	Swing and Sway	4	D. Meade	117	Corydon	117	Haltal	117	4,975	2:05.40	
1943	Bolingbroke	6	H. Lindberg	117	Princequillo	103	Water Pearl	103	7,900	2:02.00	
1944	Devil Diver	6	E. Arcaro	117	Princequillo	117	Bolingbroke	117	11,495	2:02.00	
1945	Trymenow	3	H. Lindberg	103	Pavot	117	Stymie	126	12,135	2:02.20	
1946	Stymie	5	B. James	120	Mahout	103	Trymenow	112	19,350	2:07.40	
1947	Rico Monte	5	R. Donoso	113	Gallorette	112	Stymie	126	18,550	2:02.60	
1948	Gallorette	6	A. Kirkland	115	Loyal Legion	112	Natchez	114	15,450	2:05.20	
1949	Round View	6	S. Perez	110	Donor	116	My Request	126	15,400	2:03.20	
1950	Piet	5	N. Combest	116	Sun Bahram	116	Adile	115	16,200	2:06.60	
1951	One Hitter	5	T. Atkinson	120	Cochise	126	Lone Eagle	114	15,300	2:05.00	
1952	Counterpoint	4	D. Gorman	123	Mandingo	114	One Hitter	126	15,800	2:05.60	
1953	Tom Fool	4	T. Atkinson	126	Combat Boots	114			18,250	2:05.40	
1954	Social Outcast	4	E. Guerin	115	Fisherman	121	Domquil	108	40,300	2:04.40	
1955	First Aid	5	H. Woodhouse	113	Diving Board	113	Chevation	120	18,100	1:51.60	
1956	Dedicate	4	W. Boland	116	Summer Tan	120	Paper Tiger	112	31,500	1:49.80	
1957	Kingmaker	4	R. Ussery	115	Riley	112	Tick Tock	111	31,440	1:52.80	
1958	Cohoes	4	J. Ruane	114	Admiral Vee	126	Inside Tract	112	29,205	1:51.60	
1959	Plion	4	M. Ycaza	114	Amerigo	112	Village Idiot	112	37,165	1:53.00	
1960	Warhead	5	W. Sorrentino	111	Talent Show	123	Manassa Mauler	121	37,750	1:51.00	
1961	Kelso	4	E. Arcaro	130	Our Hope	111	Rienzi	114	36,400	1:48.00	

Our Hope finished first but was disqualified and placed second

Year	Winner	Age	Jockey	Wt.	Second	Wt.	Third	Wt.	Win Value	Time	Beyer
1962	Carry Back	4	J. Sellers	130	Crozier	111	Garwol	110	37,310	1:50.00	
1963	Kelso	6	I. Valenzuela	130	Saidam	111	Sunrise County	117	36,270	1:50.40	
1964	Gun Bow	4	W. Blum	130	Mongo	130	Delta Judge	111	35,295	1:49.20	
1965	Kelso	8	I. Valenzuela	130	Malicious	114	Pia Star	127	35,360	1:49.80	
1966	Staunchness	4	E. Cardone	109	Prolijo	113	Malicious	122	36,140	1:50.20	
1967	Stupendous	4	E. Belmonte	114	Ring Twice	114	Straight Deal	116	36,530	1:48.20	
1968	Dr. Fager	4	B. Baeza	132	Spoon Bait	114	Fort Drum	114	34,775	1:48.80	

Year	Winner	Age	Jockey	Wt.	Second	Wt.	Third	Wt.	Win Value	Time	Beyer
1969	Verbatim	4	P. Anderson	121	Tropic King II	114	Dewan	117	35,945	1:50.00	
1970	Judgable	3	R. Woodhouse	112	Hydrologist	119	Dewan	121	39,260	1:48.40	
1971	Protanto	4	J. Velasquez	117	Peace Corps	114	Shuvee	116	36,300	1:49.40	
1972	Key to the Mint	3	B. Baeza	113	Tunex	117	Loud	117	34,350	1:49.20	
1973	Onion	4	J. Vasquez	119	Secretariat	119	Rule by Reason	119	32,310	1:49.20	
1974	Tri Jet	5	L. Pincay Jr	123	Infuriator	120	Stop the Music	120	33,390	1:47.00	
1975	Ancient Title	5	S. Hawley	128	Group Plan	115	Arbees Boy	118	50,085	1:48.20	
1976	Dancing Gun	4	R.I. Velez	108	American History	109	Erwin Boy	116	17,902	1:50.00	
1977	Nearly On Time	3	S. Cauthen	103	American History	112	Dancing Gun	112	49,545	1:49.40	
1978	Alydar	3	J. Velasquez	123	Buckaroo	112	Father Hogan	114	49,545	1:47.40	
1979	Star de Naskra	4	J. Fell	120	Cox's Ridge	117	The Liberal Member	120	65,040	1:47.60	
1980	State Dinner	5	R. Hernandez	120	Dr. Patches	114	Czaravich	123	99,540	1:48.20	
1981	Fio Rito	6	L. Hulet	113	Winter's Tale	121	Ring of Light	114	105,300	1:48.00	
1982	Silver Buck	4	D. MacBeth	115	Winter's Tale	119	Tap Shoes	113	99,000	1:47.80	
1983	Island Whirl	5	E. Delahoussaye	123	Bold Style	114	Sunny's Halo	116	103,860	1:48.40	
1984	Slew o' Gold	4	A. Cordero Jr	126	Track Barron	117	Thumbsucker	115	165,744	1:48.60	
1985	Track Barron	4	A. Cordero Jr	124	Carr de Naskra	120	Vanlandingham	124	160,680	1:47.60	
1986	Lady's Secret	4	P. Day	119	Ends Well	116	Fuzzy	112	202,500	1:49.80	
1987	Java Gold	3	P. Day	113	Gulch	117	Broad Brush	127	173,100	1:48.40	
1988	Personal Ensign	4	R.P. Romero	117	Gulch	124	King's Swan	123	162,300	1:47.80	
1989	Easy Goer	3	P. Day	119	Forever Silver	122	Cryptoclearance	122	172,500	1:47.40	
1990	Criminal Type	5	G.L. Stevens	126	Dancing Spree	121	Mi Selecto	117	140,640	1:48.60	115
1991	In Excess	4	G.L. Stevens	121	Chief Honcho	115	Killer Diller	112	150,000	1:48.00	116
1992	Sultry Song	4	J.D. Bailey	115	Out of Place	115	Chief Honcho	116	150,000	1:47.20	112
1993	Brunswick	4	M.E. Smith	112	West by West	115	Devil His Due	122	150,000	1:47.40	115
1994	Colonial Affair	4	J.A. Santos	117	Devil His Due	125	West by West	113	210,000	1:48.60	111
1995	Unaccounted For	4	P. Day	114	L'Carriere	111	Silver Fox	112	210,000	1:49.20	111
1996	Mahogany Hall	5	J.A. Santos	113	Serena's Song	116	Peaks and Valleys	121	210,000	1:48.60	110
1997	Will's Way	5	J.D. Bailey	117	Formal Gold	120	Skip Away	125	210,000	1:48.20	126
1998	Awesome Again	4	P. Day	117	Tale of the Cat	114	Crypto Star	116	240,000	1:49.71	110
1999	Victory Gallop	4	J.D. Bailey	123	Behrens	123	Catienus	113	360,000	1:48.66	116
2000	Lemon Drop Kid	4	E.S. Prado	123	Cat Thief	117	Behrens	122	680,000	1:48.30	118
2001	Lido Palace	4	J.D. Bailey	115	Albert The Great	124	Gander	113	540,000	1:47.94	114
2002	Left Bank	5	J.R. Velazquez	118	Street Cry	123	Lido Palace	119	450,000	1:47.04	121
2003	Medaglia d'Oro	4	J.D. Bailey	123	Volponi	120	Evening Attire	118	450,000	1:47.69	114

Beyer Index: 114.93

Closed to geldings prior to 1971. Distance 1 1/4 miles prior to 1955. For 4-year-olds and up from 1957-59. Run at Belmont, 1961-62. Lemon Drop Kid earned a $230,000 bonus in 2000. Lido Palace earned a $90,000 bonus in 2001

CHARLES WHITTINGHAM HANDICAP, 1 1/4 Miles (Turf), 3-Year-Olds and Up, Hollywood Park, 2003 Purse: $350,000

Year	Winner	Age	Jockey	Wt.	Second	Wt.	Third	Wt.	Win Value	Time	Beyer
1969	Fort Marcy	5	M. Ycaza	124	Poleax	117	Court Fool	115	55,000	2:27.20	
1970	Fiddle Isle	5	W. Shoemaker	128	Fort Marcy	126	Governors Party	112	55,000	2:25.60	
1972	Typecast	6	J. Lambert	117	Violonor	110	Cougar II	129	68,750	2:25.80	
1973	Life Cycle	5	L. Pincay Jr	115	Wing Out	118	Cougar II	130	75,000	2:25.60	
1974	Court Ruling	4	W. Mahorney	117	Outdoors	113	London Company	123	75,000	2:27.60	
1975	Barclay Joy	5	A.L. Diaz	113	Captain Cee Jay	117	Chief Hawk Ear	119	75,000	2:27.00	
1976	Dahlia	6	W. Shoemaker	117	Caucasus	119	Pass the Glass	121	120,000	2:26.80	
1977	Vigors	4	J. Lambert	117	Causasus	126	Anne's Pretender	122	120,000	2:26.80	
1978	Exceller	5	W. Shoemaker	127	Bowl Game	123	Noble Dancer II	126	110,000	2:25.80	
1979	Johnny's Image	5	S. Hawley	123	Star Spangled	122	Dom Alaric	119	137,500	2:25.20	
1980	John Henry	5	D.G. McHargue	128	Balzac	120	Go West Young Man	117	137,500	2:25.40	
1981	John Henry	6	L. Pincay Jr	130	Caterman	122	Galaxy Libra	118	110,000	2:27.80	
1982	Exploded	5	L. Pincay Jr	117	Lemhi Gold	123	The Bart	125	165,000	2:25.20	
1983	Erins Isle	5	L. Pincay Jr	127	Exploded	115	Prince Spellbound	120	165,000	2:25.80	
1984	John Henry	9	C.J. McCarron	126	Galant Vert	116	Load the Cannons	120	165,000	2:25.00	
1985	Both Ends Burning	5	E. Delahoussaye	121	Dahar	123	Swoon	114	165,000	2:25.60	
1986	Flying Pidgeon	5	S. Soto	120	Dahar	126	Both Ends Burning	122	165,000	2:27.00	
1987	Rivlia	5	C.J. McCarron	117	Great Communicator	112	Schiller	116	165,000	2:24.20	
1988	Political Ambition	4	E. Delahoussaye	119	Baba Karam	116	Great Communicator	120	165,000	1:58.60	
							Skip Out Front	115			
1989	Great Communicator	6	R. Sibille	123	Nasr El Arab	124	Equalize	124	275,000	1:59.40	
1990	Steinlen	7	L. Pincay Jr	124	Hawkster	122	Santangelo	110	275,000	2:03.00	109
1991	Exbourne	5	G.L. Stevens	119	Itsallgreektome	123	Prized	123	275,000	2:00.00	108
1992	Quest for Fame	5	G.L. Stevens	122	Classic Fame	120	River Traffic	114	275,000	1:58.80	105
1993	Bien Bien	4	C.J. McCarron	119	Best Pal	122	Leger Cat	116	275,000	1:57.60	108
1994	Grand Flotilla	7	G.L. Stevens	116	Bien Bien	124	Blues Traveller	114	275,000	1:59.20	110
1995	Earl of Barking	5	G.F. Almeida	115	Sandpit	122	Savinio	117	275,000	1:59.60	110
1996	Sandpit	7	C.S. Nakatani	120	Northern Spur	123	Awad	119	300,000	1:59.40	112
1997	Rainbow Dancer	6	A. Solis	116	Sunshack	118	Marlin	120	240,000	2:00.00	106
1998	Storm Trooper	5	K.J. Desormeaux	117	River Bay	121	Prize Giving	116	240,000	2:03.05	104
1999	River Bay	6	A. Solis	119	Majorien	117	Alvo Certo	115	240,000	2:00.66	105
2000	White Heart	5	K.J. Desormeaux	117	Self Feeder	116	Deploy Venture	112	180,000	2:00.83	103

Year	Winner	Age	Jockey	Wt.	Second	Wt.	Third	Wt.	Win Value	Time	Beyer
2001	Bienamado	5	C.J. McCarron	124	Senure	117	Timboroa	116	210,000	1:59.34	111
2002	Denon	4	G. Gomez	116	Night Patrol	114	Skipping	117	210,000	2:01.47	108
2003	Storming Home	5	G.L. Stevens	124	Mister Acpen	115	Cagney	114	210,000	2:00.66	103

Beyer Index: 107.29

Distance 1 1/2 miles 1969–87. Run as Hollywood Turf Handicap prior to 1999

WOOD MEMORIAL, 1 1/8 Miles,
3-Year-Olds, Aqueduct, 2003 Purse: $750,000

Year	Winner	Age	Jockey	Wt.	Second	Wt.	Third	Wt.	Win Value	Time	Beyer
1925	Backbone	3	I. Parke	110	Voltaic	117	Swope	120	7,600	1:43.60	
1926	Pompey	3	B. Breuning	120	Navigator	120	Espino	110	8,700	1:42.00	
1927	Saxon	3	G. Ellis	117	Black Panther	110	Bostonian	110	9,050	1:43.60	
1928	Distraction	3	D. McAuliffe	120	Genie	111	Doctor Wilson	123	11,300	1:46.00	
1929	Essare	3	M. Garner	110	Annapolis	110	Upset Lad	123	11,000	1:44.00	
1930	Gallant Fox	3	E. Sande	120	Crack Brigade	120	Desert Light	120	10,150	1:43.60	
1931	Twenty Grand	3	C. Kurtsinger	120	Clock Tower	110	Camper	110	10,200	1:42.60	
1932	Universe	3	L. McAtee	120	Economic	120	Curacao	114	10,400	1:43.00	
1933	Mr. Khayyam	3	P. Walls	122	De Valera	117	Head Play	126	3,760	1:42.60	
1934	High Quest	3	D. Bellizzi	120	Speedmore	112	Spy Hill	112	3,990	1:43.80	
1935	Today	3	R. Workman	112	Plat Eye	122	Omaha	112	11,350	1:42.80	
1936	Teufel	3	E. Litzenberger	112	Granville	117	Delphinium	117	10,775	1:43.20	
1937	Melodist	3	J. Longden	120	Sir Damian	120	Jewell Dorsett	115	19,150	1:42.80	
1938	Fighting Fox	3	J. Stout	120	Can't Wait	120	Opera Hat	120	17,450	1:43.00	
1939	Johnstown	3	J. Stout	120	Voitant	120	Impound	120	17,675	1:42.00	
1940	Dit	3	L. Haas	120	Red Dock	120	Devil's Crag	120	19,225	1:45.80	
1941	Market Wise	3	D. Meade	120	Curious Coin	120	King Cole	120	16,650	1:45.60	
1942	Requested	3	W.D. Wright	120	Bleu d'Or	120	Apache	120	22,900	1:45.20	
1943	Count Fleet	3	J. Longden	126	Blue Swords	126	Twoses	126	20,150	1:43.00	
1944	Stir Up	3	E. Arcaro	126	Stymie	126	Autocrat	126	19,625	1:44.20	
1944	Lucky Draw	3	J. Longden	126	Broad Grin	126	Hoodoo	126	20,115	1:46.20	
1945	Jeep	3	A. Kirkland	126	Gallorette	121	Dockstader	126	18,945	1:45.80	
1945	Hoop Jr.	3	E. Arcaro	126	Alexis	126	Sir Francis	126	18,945	1:45.00	
1946	Assault	3	W. Mehrtens	126	Hampden	126	Marine Victory	126	22,600	1:46.60	
1947	Phalanx	3	E. Arcaro	126	Carolyn A.	121	Owners Choice	126	31,325	1:43.60	
1947	I Will	3	E. Arcaro	126	Stepfather	126	Cornish Knight	126	31,625	1:45.00	
1948	My Request	3	D. Dodson	126	Mount Marcy	126	Better Self	126	34,600	1:46.20	
1949	Olympia	3	E. Arcaro	126	Palestinian	126	Capot	126	31,850	1:45.00	
1950	Hill Prince	3	E. Arcaro	126	Middleground	126	Ferd	126	34,500	1:43.60	
1951	Repetoire	3	P. McLean	126	Battle Morn	126	Intent	126	35,250	1:44.40	
1952	Master Fiddle	3	D. Gorman	126	Tom Fool	126	Pintor	126	45,200	1:52.40	
1953	Native Dancer	3	E. Guerin	126	Tahitian King	126	Invigorator	126	87,000	1:50.60	
1954	Correlation	3	W. Shoemaker	126	Fisherman	126	High Gun	126	86,000	1:50.00	
1955	Nashua	3	T. Atkinson	126	Summer Tan	126	Simmy	126	75,100	1:50.60	
1956	Head Man	3	E. Arcaro	126	Golf Ace	126	Oh Johnny	126	42,400	1:50.20	
1957	Bold Ruler	3	E. Arcaro	126	Gallant Man	126	Promised Land	126	40,800	1:48.80	
1958	Jewel's Reward	3	E. Arcaro	126	Noureddin	126	Martins Rullah	126	37,575	1:50.20	
1959	Manassa Mauler	3	R. Broussard	126	First Landing	126	Our Dad	126	55,915	1:49.60	
1960	Francis S.	3	W. Shoemaker	126	Never Give In	126	John William	126	60,465	1:50.20	
1961	Globemaster	3	J.L. Rotz	126	Carry Back	126	Ambiopoise	126	56,062	1:50.20	
1962	Admiral's Voyage	3	B. Baeza	126	Sunrise County	126	Donut King	126	59,702	1:49.80	
1963	No Robbery	3	J.L. Rotz	126	Bonjour	126	Top Gallant	126	59,020	1:49.20	
1964	Quadrangle	3	W. Hartack	126	Mr. Brick	126	Roman Brother	126	58,012	1:49.20	
1965	Flag Raiser	3	R. Ussery	126	Hail to All	126	Bold Lad	126	60,222	1:50.20	
1966	Amberoid	3	W. BOland	126	Advocator	126	Buffle	126	74,425	1:49.60	
1967	Damascus	3	W. Shoemaker	126	Gala Performance	126	Dawn Glory	126	73,060	1:49.60	
1968	Dancer's Image	3	R. Ussery	126	Iron Ruler	126	Verbatim	126	73,775	1:49.00	
1969	Dike	3	J. Velasquez	126	Al Hattab	126	Reviewer	126	72,085	1:49.60	
1970	Personality	3	E. Belmonte	126	Silent Screen	126	Delaware Chief	126	76,570	1:49.40	
1971	Good Behaving	3	C. Baltazar	126	Eastern Fleet	126	Executioner	126	67,320	1:49.80	
1972	Upper Case	3	R. Turcotte	126	True Knight	126	Head of the River	126	71,040	1:49.00	
1973	Angle Light	3	J. Vasquez	126	Sham	126	Secretariat	126	68,940	1:49.80	
1974	Flip Sal	3	A. Cordero Jr	126	Triple Crown	126	Sharp Gary	126	69,360	1:51.40	
1974	Rube the Great	3	M.A. Rivera	126	Friendly Bee	126	Hudson County	126	69,660	1:49.60	
1975	Foolish Pleasure	3	J. Vasquez	126	Bombay Duck	126	Media	126	72,840	1:48.80	
1976	Bold Forbes	3	A. Cordero Jr	126	On the Sly	126	Sonkisser	126	67,560	1:47.40	
1977	Seattle Slew	3	J. Cruguet	126	Sanhedrin	126	Catalan	126	66,180	1:49.60	
1978	Believe It	3	E. Maple	126	Darby Creek Road	126	Track Reward	126	65,940	1:49.80	
1979	Instrument Landing	3	A. Cordero Jr	126	Screen King	126	Czaravich	126	85,650	1:49.20	
1980	Plugged Nickle	3	B. Thornburg	126	Colonel Moran	126	Genuine Risk	121	87,300	1:50.80	
1981	Pleasant Colony	3	J. Fell	126	Highland Blade	126	Cure the Blues	126	98,280	1:49.60	
1982	Air Forbes Won	3	A. Cordero Jr.	126	Shimatoree	126	Laser Light	126	105,120	1:51.00	

Year	Winner	Age	Jockey	Wt.	Second	Wt.	Third	Wt.	Win Value	Time	Beyer
1983	Bounding Basque	3	G. McCarron	126	Country Pine	126	Aztec Red	126	100,980	1:51.40	
1983	Slew o' Gold	3	E. Maple	126	Parfaitement	126	High Honors	126	101,700	1:51.00	
1984	Leroy S.	3	J. Cruguet	126	Raja's Shark	126	Bear Hunt	126	207,000	1:51.40	
1985	Eternal Prince	3	R. Migliore	126	Proud Truth	126	Rhoman Rule	126	204,900	1:48.80	
1986	Broad Brush	3	V. Bracciale Jr	126	Mogambo	126	Groovy	126	178,500	1:50.60	
1987	Gulch	3	J.A. Santos	126	Gone West	126	Shawklit Won	126	354,300	1:49.00	
1988	Private Terms	3	C.W. Antley	126	Seeking the Gold	126	Cherokee Colony	126	359,400	1:47.20	
1989	Easy Goer	3	P. Day	126	Rock Point	126	Triple Buck	126	340,800	1:50.60	
1990	Thirty Six Red	3	M.E. Smith	126	Burnt Hills	126	Champagneforashley	126	362,400	1:50.40	103
1991	Cahill Road	3	C. Perret	126	Lost Mountain	126	Happy Jazz Band	126	300,000	1:48.40	109
1992	Devil His Due	3	M.E. Smith	126	West by West	126	Rokeby	126	300,000	1:49.20	99
1993	Storm Tower	3	R. Wilson	126	Tossofthecoin	126	Marked Tree	126	300,000	1:48.40	99
1994	Irgun	3	G.L. Stevens	123	Go for Gin	123	Shiprock	123	300,000	1:49.00	109
1995	Talkin Man	3	S.J. Sellers	123	Knockadoon	123	Is Sveikatas	123	300,000	1:49.20	106
1996	Unbridled's Song	3	M.E. Smith	123	In Contention	123	Romano Gucci	123	300,000	1:49.80	103
1997	Captain Bodgit	3	A. Solis	123	Accelerator	123	Smokin Mel	123	300,000	1:48.20	105
1998	Coronado's Quest	3	R.G. Davis	123	Dice Dancer	123	Parade Ground	123	300,000	1:47.40	116
1999	Adonis	3	J.F. Chavez	123	Best of Luck	123	Cliquot	123	360,000	1:47.30	103
2000	Fusaichi Pegasus	3	K.J. Desormeaux	123	Red Bullet	123	Aptitude	123	450,000	1:47.92	111
2001	Congaree	3	V. Espinoza	123	Monarchos	123	Richly Blended	123	450,000	1:47.96	108
2002	Buddha	3	P. Day	123	Medaglia d'Oro	123	Sunday Break	123	450,000	1:48.61	105
2003	Empire Maker	3	J.D. Bailey	123	Funny Cide	123	Kissin Saint	123	450,000	1:48.70	111

Beyer Index: 106.21

WOODFORD RESERVE TURF CLASSIC, 1 1/8 Miles (Turf), 3-Year-Olds and Up, Churchill Downs, 2003 Purse: $445,300

Year	Winner	Age	Jockey	Wt.	Second	Wt.	Third	Wt.	Win Value	Time	Beyer
1987	Manila	4	J. Vasquez	120	Vilzak	112	Lieutenant's Lark	120	110,045	1:48.80	
1988	Yankee Affair	6	P. Day	118	Yucca	112	First Patriot	112	121,225	1:50.00	
1989	Equalize	7	J.A. Santos	118	Yankee Affair	116	Gallant Mel	114	114,140	1:51.40	
1990	Ten Keys	6	K.J. Desormeaux	120	Yankee Affair	120	Stellar Rival	113	110,435	1:50.80	105
1991	Opening Verse	5	C.J. McCarron	116	Itsallgreektome	123	Pedro the Cool	112	125,060	1:47.20	106
1992	Cudas	4	P.A. Valenzuela	117	Sky Classic	123	Fourstars Allstar	118	124,703	1:46.40	105
1993	Lure	4	M.E. Smith	123	Star of Cozzene	118	Cleone	116	181,050	1:46.20	112
1994	Paradise Creek	5	P. Day	118	Lure	123	Yukon Robbery	116	152,067	1:48.20	107
1995	Romarin	5	C.S. Nakatani	118	Blues Traveller	120	Hasten to Add	120	169,585	1:46.80	107
1996	Mecke	4	P. Day	123	Petit Poucet	116	Winged Victory	116	154,960	1:49.40	106
1997	Always a Classic	4	J.D. Bailey	120	Labeeb	118	Down the Aisle	114	145,328	1:49.40	106
1998	Joyeux Danseur	5	R.J. Albarado	123	Lasting Approval	120	Hawksley Hill	120	174,282	1:48.14	111
1999	Wild Event	6	S.J. Sellers	120	Garbu	116	Hawksley Hill	120	206,646	1:47.25	109
2000	Manndar	4	C.S. Nakatani	114	Falcon Flight	118	Yagli	120	217,310	1:47.91	103
2001	White Heart	6	G.L. Stevens	116	King Cugat	120	Brahms	123	216,938	1:48.75	108
2002	Beat Hollow	5	A. Solis	115	With Anticipation	123	Hap	123	280,550	1:47.35	108
2003	Honor in War	4	D.R. Flores	116	Requete	116	Patrol	114	276,086	1:46.67	110

Beyer Index: 107.36

For 4-year-olds and up prior to 1992. Run as Early Times Turf Classic prior to 2000

WOODWARD, 1 1/8 Miles, 3-Year-Olds and Up, Belmont Park, 2003 Purse: $500,000

Year	Winner	Age	Jockey	Wt.	Second	Wt.	Third	Wt.	Win Value	Time	Beyer
1954	Pet Bully	6	W. Hartack	126	Joe Jones	111	Impasse	113	43,700	1:35.60	
1955	Traffic Judge	3	E. Arcaro	118	Paper Tiger	107	Dedicate	110	40,000	1:48.20	
1956	Mister Gus	5	W. Hartack	126	Nashua	126	Jet Action	126	52,950	2:03.00	
1957	Dedicate	4	W. Hartack	126	Gallant Man	120	Bold Ruler	120	70,500	2:01.00	
1958	Clem	4	W. Shoemaker	126	Nadir	120	Reneged	126	71,080	2:01.00	
1959	Sword Dancer	3	E. Arcaro	120	Hillsdale	126	Round Table	126	70,170	2:04.40	
1960	Sword Dancer	4	E. Arcaro	126	Dotted Swiss	126	Bald Eagle	126	71,730	2:01.20	
1961	Kelso	4	E. Arcaro	126	Divine Comedy	126	Carry Back	120	71,240	2:00.00	
1962	Kelso	5	I. Valenzuela	126	Jaipur	120	Guadalcanal	126	74,880	2:03.20	
1963	Kelso	6	I. Valenzuela	126	Never Bend	120	Crimson Satan	126	70,720	2:00.80	
1964	Gun Bow	4	W. Blum	126	Kelso	126	Quadrangle	121	70,330	2:02.40	
1965	Roman Brother	4	B. Baeza	126	Royal Gunner	121	Malicious	126	71,240	2:01.80	
1966	Buckpasser	3	B. Baeza	121	Royal Gunner	126	Buffle	121	73,190	2:02.80	
1967	Damascus	3	W. Shoemaker	120	Buckpasser	126	Dr. Fager	120	70,070	2:00.60	
1968	Mr. Right	5	H. Gustines	126	Damascus	126	Grace Born	126	69,420	2:03.00	
1969	Arts and Letters	3	B. Baeza	120	Nodouble	126	Verbatim	126	68,900	2:01.00	
1970	Personality	3	E. Belmonte	121	Hydrologist	126			71,435	2:01.80	
					Twogundan	126					
1971	West Coast Scout	3	J.L. Rotz	121	Tinajero	121	Cougar II	126	67,860	2:00.60	

Cougar II finished first but was disqualified and placed third

Year	Winner	Age	Jockey	Wt.	Second	Wt.	Third	Wt.	Win Value	Time	Beyer
1972	Key to the Mint	3	B. Baeza	119	Autobiography	126	Summer Guest	116	69,300	2:28.40	

Summer Guest finished second but was disqualified and placed third

Year	Winner	Age	Jockey	Wt.	Second	Wt.	Third	Wt.	Win Value	Time	Beyer
1973	Prove Out	4	J. Velasquez	126	Secretariat	119	Cougar II	126	64,920	2:25.80	
1974	Forego	4	H. Gustines	126	Arbees Boy	126	Group Plan	126	69,240	2:27.60	
1975	Forego	5	H. Gustines	126	Wajima	119	Group Plan	126	64,920	2:27.20	
1976	Forego	6	W. Shoemaker	135	Dance Spell	115	Stumping	108	103,920	1:45.80	
							Honest Pleasure	121			
1977	Forego	7	W. Shoemaker	133	Silver Series	114	Great Contractor	115	105,000	1:48.00	
1978	Seattle Slew	4	A. Cordero Jr	126	Exceller	126	It's Freezing	126	97,800	2:00.00	
1979	Affirmed	4	L. Pincay Jr	126	Coastal	120	Czaravich	120	114,600	2:01.60	
1980	Spectacular Bid	4	W. Shoemaker	126					73,300	2:02.40	
	Walkover										
1981	Pleasant Colony	3	A. Cordero Jr	123	Amber Pass	126	Herb Water	116	137,400	1:47.20	
1982	Island Whirl	4	A. Cordero Jr	123	Silver Buck	126	Silver Supreme	126	136,500	1:46.80	
1983	Slew o' Gold	3	A. Cordero Jr	118	Bates Motel	123	Sing Sing	117	138,900	1:46.60	
1984	Slew o' Gold	4	A. Cordero Jr	126	Shifty Sheik	116	Bet Big	116	175,200	1:47.80	
1985	Track Barron	4	A. Cordero Jr	123	Vanlandingham	123	Chief's Crown	121	200,400	1:46.60	
1986	Precisionist	5	C.J. McCarron	126	Lady's Secret	121	Personal Flag	110	199,200	1:46.00	
1987	Polish Navy	3	R.P. Romero	116	Gulch	118	Creme Fraiche	119	357,000	1:47.00	
1988	Alysheba	4	C.J. McCarron	126	Forty Niner	119	Waquoit	122	498,600	1:59.40	
1989	Easy Goer	3	P. Day	122	Its Acedemic	109	Forever Silver	119	485,400	2:01.00	
1990	Dispersal	4	C.W. Antley	123	Quiet American	117	Rhythm	120	354,000	1:45.80	118
1991	In Excess	4	G.L. Stevens	126	Farma Way	126	Festin	120	300,000	1:46.20	116
1992	Sultry Song	4	J.D. Bailey	126	Pleasant Tap	126	Out of Place	126	300,000	1:47.00	115
1993	Bertrando	4	G.L. Stevens	126	Devil His Due	126	Valley Crossing	126	425,000	1:47.00	125
1994	Holy Bull	3	M.E. Smith	121	Devil His Due	126	Colonial Affair	126	300,000	1:46.80	116
1995	Cigar	5	J.D. Bailey	126	Star Standard	121	Golden Larch	126	300,000	1:47.00	111
1996	Cigar	6	J.D. Bailey	126	L'Carriere	126	Golden Larch	126	300,000	1:47.00	116
1997	Formal Gold	4	K.J. Desormeaux	126	Skip Away	126	Will's Way	126	300,000	1:47.40	125
1998	Skip Away	5	J.D. Bailey	126	Gentlemen	126	Running Stag	126	300,000	1:47.80	119
1999	River Keen	7	C.W. Antley	126	Almutawakel	126	Stephen Got Even	121	300,000	1:46.85	117
2000	Lemon Drop Kid	4	E.S. Prado	126	Behrens	126	Gander	126	300,000	1:50.53	105
2001	Lido Palace	4	J.D. Bailey	126	Albert The Great	126	Tiznow	126	300,000	1:47.42	113
2002	Lido Palace	5	J.F. Chavez	126	Gander	126	Express Tour	126	300,000	1:47.75	105
2003	Mineshaft	4	R.J. Albarado	126	Hold That Tiger	122	Puzzlement	126	300,000	1:46.21	117

Beyer Index: 115.57

Distance 1 mile in 1954; 1 1/4 miles, 1956–71, 1978–80, 1988–89; 1 1/2 miles, 1972–75. Run at Aqueduct 1959–60, 1962–67

YELLOW RIBBON STAKES, 1 1/4 Miles (Turf), Fillies and Mares, 3-Year-Olds and Up, Santa Anita, 2003 Purse: $500,000

Year	Winner	Age	Jockey	Wt.	Second	Wt.	Third	Wt.	Win Value	Time	Beyer
1977	Star Ball	5	H. Grant	123	Swingtime	123	Theia	123	60,000	2:02.60	
1978	Amazer	3	W. Shoemaker	119	Drama Critic	123	Surera	123	90,000	1:59.20	
1979	Country Queen	4	L. Pincay Jr	123	Prize Spot	119	Giggling Girl	123	90,000	2:00.20	
1980	Kilijaro	4	A. Lequeux	123	Ack's Secret	123	Queen to Conquer	123	120,000	1:59.20	
1981	Queen to Conquer	5	M. Castaneda	123	Star Pastures	119	Ack's Secret	123	180,000	1:58.60	
1982	Castilla	3	R. Sibille	119	Avigaition	123	Sangue	123	180,000	1:58.60	
	Avigation finished first but was disqualified and placed second										
1983	Sangue	5	W. Shoemaker	123	L'Attrayante	119	Infinite	119	240,000	2:02.20	
1984	Sabin	4	E. Maple	123	Grise Mine	118	Estrapade	123	240,000	2:00.00	
1985	Estrapade	4	W. Shoemaker	123	Alydar's Best	118	La Koumia	123	240,000	2:00.40	
1986	Bonne Ile	5	F. Toro	123	Top Corsage	118	Carotene	118	240,000	2:01.40	
1987	Carotene	4	J.A. Santos	123	Nashmeel	119	Khariyda	119	240,000	2:03.80	
1988	Delighter	3	C.J. McCarron	119	Nastique	123	No Review	119	240,000	2:02.40	
1989	Brown Bess	7	J.L. Kaenel	123	Darby's Daughter	119	Colorado Dancer	119	240,000	1:57.60	
1990	Plenty of Grace	3	W.H. McCauley	119	Petite Ile	123	Royal Touch	123	240,000	1:58.40	
1991	Kostroma	5	K.J. Desormeaux	123	Flawlessly	119	Fire the Groom	123	240,000	2:01.01	106
1992	Super Staff	4	K.J. Desormeaux	123	Flawlessly	123	Campagnarde	123	240,000	1:59.36	106
1993	Possibly Perfect	3	C.S. Nakatani	118	Tribulation	118	Miatuschka	122	240,000	2:02.91	101
1994	Aube Indienne	4	K.J. Desormeaux	122	Fondly Remembered	122	Zoonaqua	122	240,000	2:02.32	102
1995	Alpride	4	C.J. McCarron	122	Angel in My Heart	118	Bold Ruritana	122	360,000	2:01.68	105
1996	Donna Viola	4	G.L. Stevens	122	Real Connection	122	Dixie Pearl	122	360,000	2:00.62	105
1997	Ryafan	3	A. Solis	118	Fanjica	122	Memories of Silver	123	300,000	2:03.69	105
1998	Fiji	4	K.J. Desormeaux	122	Sonja's Faith	122	Pomona	122	300,000	2:05.23	108
	See You Soon finished second but was disqualified and placed fourth										
1999	Spanish Fern	4	C.J. McCarron	123	Caffe Latte	118	Shabby Chic	118	300,000	1:59.52	104
2000	Tranquility Lake	5	E. Delahoussaye	123	Spanish Fern	123	Polaire	123	300,000	2:02.98	100
2001	Janet	4	D.R. Flores	123	Tranquility Lake	123	Al Desima	123	300,000	1:58.64	104
2002	Golden Apples	4	P.A. Valenzuela	123	Voodoo Dancer	123	Banks Hill	123	300,000	1:59.72	108
2003	Tates Creek	5	P.A. Valenzuela	123	Musical Chimes	118	Crazy Ensign	123	300,000	2:00.77	107

Beyer Index: 104.69

Histories of Grade 2 Stakes Events

A GLEAM INVITATIONAL HANDICAP, 7 Furlongs,
Fillies and Mares, 3-Year-Olds and Up, Hollywood Park, 2003, Purse: $250,000

Year	Winner	Age	Jockey	Wt.	Second	Wt.	Third	Wt.	Win Value	Time	Beyer
1979	Delice	4	E. Delahoussaye	116	Great Lady M.	117	Sateen	111	25,100	1:08.80	
1980	Great Lady M.	5	P.A. Valenzuela	115	Double Deceit	114	Splendid Girl	122	30,550	1:08.40	
1981	She Can't Miss	4	P.A. Valenzuela	117	Cherokee Frolic	114	Shine High	122	32,050	1:09.00	
1982	Happy Bride	4	W.A. Guerra	113	Lucky Lady Ellen	117	Jones Time Machine	112	30,700	1:08.40	
1983	Matching	4	R. Sibille	121	Sierva	117	Bara Lass	117	31,800	1:22.40	
1984	Lass Trump	4	C.J. McCarron	116	Pleasure Cay	116	Angel Savage	112	39,400	1:21.20	
1985	Dontstop the Music	5	L. Pincay Jr	121	Lovlier Linda	122	Mimi Baker	110	36,500	1:21.20	
1986	Outstandingly	4	G.L. Stevens	120	Eloquack	110	Shywing	120	46,100	1:21.80	
1987	Le L'Argent	5	G.D. McHargue	118	Sari's Heroine	117	Rare Starlet	115	48,650	1:23.00	
1988	Integra	4	G.L. Stevens	118	Behind the Scenes	116	Carol's Wonder	117	46,100	1:23.00	
1989	Daloma	5	C.J. McCarron	115	Survive	116	Winning Colors	123	47,900	1:21.60	
1990	Stormy but Valid	4	G.L. Stevens	120	Hot Novel	121	Tis Juliet	117	61,300	1:21.20	103
1991	Survive	7	R.A. Baze	119	Stormy but Valid	121	Brought to Mind	117	62,400	1:22.00	95
1992	Forest Fealty	5	M.A. Pedroza	116	Brought to Mind	120	Devil's Orchid	120	64,800	1:22.00	99
1993	Bold Windy	4	G.L. Stevens	115	La Spia	115	Bountiful Native	122	65,700	1:21.60	98
1994	Golden Klair	4	C.J. McCarron	117	Cargo	117	Minidar	117	60,400	1:22.00	100
1995	Angi Go	5	G.L. Stevens	117	Desert Stormer	118	Dancing Mirage	115	62,700	1:21.40	100
1996	Igotrhythm	4	E. Delahoussaye	116	Klassy Kim	116	Cat's Cradle	118	63,840	1:21.40	102
1997	Toga Toga Toga	5	G.L. Stevens	119	Our Summer Bid	115	Radu Cool	116	65,040	1:22.60	100
1998	A.P. Assay	4	E. Delahoussaye	116	Exotic Wood	124	Closed Escrow	114	150,000	1:20.40	115
1999	Enjoy the Moment	4	D.R. Flores	117	Snowberg	115	Woodman's Dancer	117	120,000	1:21.20	100
2000	Honest Lady	4	K.J. Desormeaux	121	Seth's Choice	115	Hookedonthefeelin	116	120,000	1:21.47	107
2001	Go Go	4	E. Delahoussaye	124	Kitty On the Track	115	Nany's Sweep	117	120,000	1:22.19	100
2002	Irguns Angel	4	E. Delahoussaye	116	Secret Liaison	116	Kalookan Queen	122	120,000	1:22.50	100
2003	Cee's Elegance	6	V. Espinoza	116	You	121	Affluent	119	150,000	1:21.47	103

Beyer Index: 101.57

ADIRONDACK, 6 1/2 Furlongs, 2-Year-Old Fillies
Saratoga Race Course, 2003 Purse: $150,000

Year	Winner	Age	Jockey	Wt.	Second	Wt.	Third	Wt.	Win Value	Time	Beyer
1901	Smart Set	2	O'Connor	114	Saturday	112	Leonid	108	4,325	1:16.60	
1902	Molly Brant	2	Odom	109	Wild Thyme	104	Sir Voorhees	112	6,375	1:13.20	
1903	Sweet Gretchen	2	Fuller	102	Leonidas	115	Gold Saint	112	3,025	1:15.80	
1904	Broadcloth	2	T. Burns	113	Pasadena	112	Blue Coat	98	3,850	1:15.20	
1905	Tangle	2	O'Neill	110	Juggler	111	Ravena	106	3,850	1:13.40	
1906	Salvidere	2	Sewell	128	Don Enrique	110	Aletheuo	108	3,850	1:14.80	
1907	Beaucoup	2	E. Dugan	110	Falcada	104	Fultonville	104	3,850	1:14.00	
1908	Sea Cliff	2	Notter	114	Statesman	114	Con'ght Ranger	109	505	1:15.20	
1909	Scarpia	2	C. Grand	102	Chickasaw	116	Joe Morris	115	1,925	1:13.00	
1910	Zeus	2	Butwell	110	Round the World	120	Iron Mask	124	4,500	1:11.60	
1913	Little Nephew	2	Killingsworth	125	Black Broom	116	Spearhead	106	1,925	1:15.00	
1914	Lady Barbary	2	H. Sunter	114	Trial by Jury	117	Luke	119	2,175	1:14.20	
1915	Friar Rock	2	E. Dugan	116	Achievement	110	Kilmer	102	1,925	1:17.80	
1916	Ultimatum	2	R. Troxler	116	Woodtrap	105	Tragedy	108	2,675	1:14.80	
1917	Happy Go Lucky	2	F. Robinson	109	Matinee Idol	111	Jack Hare Jr.	125	3,750	1:13.60	
1918	Routledge	2	E. Ambrose	111	Daydue	108	Hannibal	125	3,925	1:12.00	
1919	Grayssian	2	T. Nolan	111	Kinnoul	122	Sammy	115	3,925	1:12.80	
1920	Exodus	2	E. Ambrose	125	Jeg	114	Quecreek	110	3,925	1:11.80	
1921	Oil Man	2	E. Haynes	119	Modo	115	Sir Hugh	125	3,925	1:11.80	
1922	Cartoonist	2	C. Kummer	116	Bud Lerner	125	Cherry Pie	122	3,925	1:12.00	
1923	Elvina	2	J. Callahan	112	Sunspero	113	Big Blaze	117	4,350	1:12.00	
	Befuddle finished third but was disqualified										
1924	Cloudland	2	C. Lang	115	Buttin In	110	Pas Seul	118	4,075	1:15.00	
1925	Blockhead	2	A. Johnson	112	Navigator	124	Mar. Militaire	118	3,925	1:13.60	
1926	Friedjof Nansen	2	H. Richards	107	Laddie	116	Easy Money	104	4,525	1:14.60	
1927	One Hour	2	L. Fator	110	Excalibur	110	Glade	108	4,275	1:12.20	
1928	The Worker	2	E. Barnes	107	Sun Worship	116	Hypolux	114	4,225	1:15.40	
1929	War Saint	2	L. McAtee	118	Gold Brook	106	Raccoon	114	5,200	1:12.00	
1930	Ladana	2	L. Fator	120	Chicsu	115	Sovietta	123	4,400	1:12.00	
1931	Brocado	2	M. Garner	120	Mea	114	Pintail	116	3,825	1:14.00	
1932	Speed Boat	2	J. Gilbert	114	Barn Swallow	116	Enactment	112	3,075	1:12.00	
1933	Sun Celtic	2	D. Bellizzi	111	Some Pomp	110	Contessa	109	2,200	1:16.00	
1934	Bird Flower	2	D. Meade	116	Corinne Dailey	111	Pretty Night	114	2,175	1:15.00	
1935	Beanie M.	2	D. Meade	112	Tony's Wife	116	Parade Girl	121	2,300	1:13.80	
1936	Juliet W.	2	D. Brammer	119	Maecloud	123	Swiftply	119	2,550	1:13.00	
1937	Creole Maid	2	H. Richards	120	Miyako	114	Polyata	112	2,275	1:13.20	
1938	Matterhorn	2	J. Longden	105	Grey Nurse	116	Easy Does It	112	4,250	1:15.00	

Year	Winner	Age	Jockey	Wt.	Second	Wt.	Third	Wt.	Win Value	Time	Beyer
1939	Rosetown	2	H. Richards	112	Miss Ferdinand	117	Piquet	119	4,800	1:13.60	
1940	Tangled	2	E. Arcaro	121	Dark Discovery	114	Nasca	122	3,675	1:12.00	
1941	Romping Home	2	J. Longden	116	Equipet	120	Horn	114	4,500	1:13.60	
1942	La Reigh	2	J. Longden	123	Navigating	119	Wuskenin	110	3,775	1:12.40	
1943	Fire Sticky	2	H. Lindberg	108	Mrs. Ames	124	Threat o' Gold	116	5,225	1:10.80	
1944	Busher	2	E. Arcaro	123	War Date	114	Leslie Grey	116	7,530	1:11.60	
1945	Rytina	2	C. McCreary	112	Red Shoes	121	Phantasy	111	7,090	1:11.00	
1953	Riant	2	T. Atkinson	111	Case Goods	119	Fascinator	114	8,525	1:05.40	
1954	Hidden Ship	2	J. Nichols	112	Sorceress	119	Bless Pat	114	8,425	1:05.80	
1955	Dark Charger	2	A. DeSpirito	119	Levee	115	First Asking	111	8,875	1:04.40	
1962	Fashion Verdict	2	H. Woodhouse	114	Fast Luck	114	First Nominee	114	15,957	1:12.00	
1963	Petite Rouge	2	J. Sellers	114	Magna Mater	114	Always Modest	114	16,055	1:13.00	
1964	Candalita	2	B. Baeza	114	Queen Empress	123	Marshua	123	15,697	1:10.80	
1965	Lady Dulcinea	2	M. Carrozzella	114	Lovely Gypsy	120	Prides Profile	123	16,542	1:11.60	
1966	Tainted Lady	2	E. Belmonte	115	Intriguing	115	Silver True	115	16,900	1:12.60	
1967	Wildwook	2	H. Gustines	115	Morgaise	123	Syrian Sea	123	16,965	1:11.60	
1968	Process Shot	2	C. Baltazar	123	Fillypasser	115	Big Advance	123	16,575	1:10.60	
1969	Meritus	2	M. Ycaza	115	Cherry Sundae	114	I'm Gorgeous	114	20,085	1:12.60	
1970	Dutiful	2	L. Pincay Jr	114	Forward Gal	122	Patelin	122	19,402	1:10.80	
1971	Debby Deb	2	E. Belmonte	114	Fance Partner	114	Numbered Account	122	20,820	1:10.20	
1972	Faithful Girl	2	C.H. Marquez	120	Behram	120	Bel Sheba	120	16,965	1:11.80	
1973	Talking Picture	2	B. Baeza	120	In Hot Pursuit	120	Bedknob	120	17,625	1:11.00	
1974	Laughing Bridge	2	L. Pincay Jr	120	Stulcer	120	Some Swinger	120	16,950	1:10.80	
1975	Optimistic Gal	2	B. Baeza	120	Glory Glory	120	Against All Fl'gs	120	22,515	1:11.20	
1976	Harvest Girl	2	J. Cruguet	114	Bonnie Empress	114	Drama Critic	119	22,545	1:11.20	
1977	L'Alezane	2	R. Turcotte	121	Sunny Bay	121	Misgivings	114	22,335	1:10.60	
1978	Whisper Fleet	2	J. Cruguet	119	Island Kitty	114	Golferette	114	22,410	1:10.00	
1979	Smart Angle	2	S. Maple	119	Lucky My Way	114	Andrea F.	114	26,835	1:11.00	
1980	Sweet Revenge	2	J. Velasquez	114	Companionship	114	Honey's Appeal	114	34,080	1:10.40	
1981	Thrilld n Delightd	2	J. Velasquez	114	Apalachee Honey	119	Trove	116	35,160	1:10.80	
1982	Jelly Bean Holiday	2	J. Fell	116	Midnight Rapture	114	Flying Lassie	114	34,920	1:10.80	
1983	Buzz My Bell	2	J. Velasquez	114	Upturning	116	Mrs. Flagler	116	33,720	1:12.40	
1984	Contredance	2	E. Maple	114	Outstandingly	114	Oriental	114	53,100	1:10.40	
1985	Nervous Baba	2	J. Velasquez	114	Family Style	114	Steal a Kiss	114	54,450	1:09.60	
1986	Sacahuista	2	C.J. McCarron	119	Collins	114	Release the Lyd	116	53,280	1:11.00	
1987	Over All	2	A. Cordero Jr	121	Flashy Runner	114	Careless Flirt	114	64,890	1:10.60	
1988	Pat Copelan	2	P. Day	114	Channel Three	116	Premier Playmate	116	66,780	1:10.80	
1989	Dance Colony	2	J.A. Santos	116	In Full Cry	114	Saratoga Sizzle	114	52,200	1:11.80	
1990	Really Quick	2	A. Cordero Jr	114	Devilish Touch	119	Ferber's Follies	119	54,270	1:11.44	79
1991	American Royale	2	A.T. Gryder	119	Bless Our Home	114	Turnbackthe Alarm	119	71,640	1:10.60	
1992	Sky Beauty	2	E. Maple	116	Missed the Storm	114	Distinct Habit	121	70,560	1:10.00	96
1993	Astas Foxy Lady	2	R.P. Romero	119	Footing	114	Casa Eire	119	68,520	1:10.00	89
1994	Seeking Regina	2	J.D. Bailey	114	Changing Ways	119	Phone Bird	114	66,600	1:18.40	72
1995	Flat Fleet Feet	2	M.E. Smith	113	Steady Cat	112	Western Dreamer	120	65,760	1:16.60	95
1996	Storm Song	2	P. Day	113	Last Two States	113	(DH) Larkwhistle	116	84,075	1:17.60	76
1997	Salty Perfume	2	S.J. Sellers	114	Brac Drifter	114	Joustabout	114	90,000	1:17.80	93
1998	Things Change	2	J.A. Santos	114	Extended Applause	117	Brittons Hill	114	90,000	1:18.00	84
1999	Regally Appealing	2	E.S. Prado	114	Miss Wineshine	122	Trump My Heart	114	90,000	1:16.80	92
2000	Raging Fever	2	J.D. Bailey	122	Two Item Limit	117	Secret Lover	117	90,000	1:17.47	101
2001	You	2	E.S. Prado	115	Cashier's Dream	122	Magic Storm	115	90,000	1:15.16	107
2002	Awesome Humor	2	P. Day	122	Stellar	116	Holiday Runner	122	90,000	1:17.75	89
2003	Whoopi Cat	2	E.S. Prado	116	Unbridled Beauty	116	Eye Dazzler	116	90,000	1:17.51	83

Beyer Index: 88.92

Run at 5 1/2 furlongs 1953-55; 6 furlongs 1901-52, 1956-93

(DARLEY) ALCIBIADES, 1 1/16 Miles, 2-Year-Old Fillies, Keeneland Race Course, 2003 Purse: $400,000

Year	Winner	Age	Jockey	Wt.	Second	Wt.	Third	Wt.	Win Value	Time	Beyer
1952	Sweet Patootie	2	S. Armstrong	119	Good Call	119	Aerolite	119	17,617	1:23.60	
1953	Oil Painting	2	A. Popara	119	Pegeen	119	Queen Hopeful	119	19,390	1:24.40	
1954	Myrtle's Jet	2	W. Blum	119	Lea Lane	119	Gandharva	119	22,718	1:23.00	
1955	Doubledogdare	2	S. Brooks	119	Ament	119	Supple	119	23,039	1:24.20	
1956	Leallah	2	S. Boulmetis	119	Bluebility	119	Nantua	119	25,525	1:27.00	
1957	Moon Glory	2	J. Heckmann	119	My Carrie	119	Carrie Louise	119	26,273	1:27.20	
1958	Fiji	2	J. Nichols	119	Tacking	119	Lindaway	119	28,941	1:28.00	
1959	Rash Statement	2	J.L. Rotz	119	Patty's Song	119	Monarchy	119	21,579	1:25.60	
1960	Little Tumbler	2	R. Broussard	119	Times Two	119	Bright Silver	119	20,685	1:26.60	
1961	Journalette	2	W. Carstens	119	Dulaturee	119	Swoon's Princess	119	21,352	1:27.20	
1962	Abrogate	2	R.L. Baird	119	Sally Ship	119	Village Beauty	119	22,324	1:27.20	
1963	Secret Veil	2	W.D. Lucas	119	Kahgahgee	119	Shama	119	22,054	1:27.40	
1964	Fairway Fun	2	J. Leonard	119	Terentia	119	Kalispell	119	22,324	1:26.40	
1965	Moccasin	2	L. Adams	119	Chalina	119	Hurry Star	119	23,390	1:25.80	
1966	Teacher's Art	2	L. Pincay Jr	119	Thong	119	T.V's Princess	119	31,967	1:28.40	

Year	Winner	Age	Jockey	Wt.	Second	Wt.	Third	Wt.	Win Value	Time	Beyer
1967	Lady Tramp	2	I. Valenzuela	119	Sweet Tooth	119	Walk My Lady	119	31,814	1:28.00	
1968	Lil's Bag	2	D. Brumfield	119	Show Off	119	Foolish Miss	119	35,864	1:28.40	
1969	Belle Noire	2	H. Arroyo	119	Song Sparrow	119	Cloudland	119	36,237	1:27.20	
1970	Patelin	2	L. Pincay Jr	119	Bonnie and Gay	119	Secret Retreat	119	34,118	1:27.00	
1971	Mrs. Cornwallis	2	G. Mora	119	La Brisa	119	Stepping High	119	32,068	1:28.40	
1972	Coraggioso	2	D. Brumfield	119	Bag of Tunes	119	Vaguely Familiar	119	34,284	1:27.00	
1973	City Girl	2	E. Fires	119	Fairway Fable	119	Quick Cure	119	44,925	1:27.80	
1974	Hope of Glory	2	J. Nichols	119	Funny Cat	119	Snow Doll	119	54,197	1:27.20	
1975	Optimistic Gal	2	D.G. McHargue	119	Old Goat	119	Answer	119	79,592	1:28.00	
1976	Sans Supplement	2	W. Gavidia	119	Avilion	119	Resolver	119	89,732	1:27.60	
1977	L'Alezane	2	R. Turcotte	119	Robalea	119	No No-Nos	119	80,990	1:27.20	
1978	Angel Island	2	E. Delahoussaye	119	Terlingua	119	Too Many Sweets	119	89,619	1:26.40	
1979	Salud	2	J.C. Espinosa	119	Diorama	119	Sweetest Roman	119	93,503	1:28.20	
1980	Sweet Revenge	2	J. Velasquez	119	Expressive Dance	119	Masters Dream	119	99,190	1:28.00	
1981	Apalachee Honey	2	W. Shoemaker	118	Chilling Thought	118	Casual	118	102,034	1:45.20	
1982	Jelly Bean Hollida	2	D. Brumfield	118	Quarrel Over	118	Issues n' Answers	118	97,825	1:45.80	
1983	Lucky Lucky Lucky	2	J. Vasquez	118	Flippers	118	Geevilla	118	119,675	1:47.00	
1984	Foxy Deen	2	D. Montoya	118	Weekend Delight	118	Dusty Heart	118	117,224	1:45.60	
1985	Silent Account	2	K.K. Allen	118	Steal a Kiss	118	Python	118	132,321	1:46.20	
1986	Zero Minus	2	S. Hawley	118	Bound	118	Desirous	118	125,567	1:45.20	
1987	Terra Incognita	2	D.E. Foster	118	Epitome	118	Pearlie Gold	118	102,996	1:44.60	
1988	Wonders Delight	2	G.L. Stevens	118	Affirmed Classic	118	Seattle Meteor	118	130,000	1:46.40	
1989	Special Happening	2	J.A. Santos	118	Talltalelady	118	Fashion Delight	118	141,375	1:44.60	
1990	Private Treasure	2	J.D. Bailey	118	Through Flight	118	Southern Bar Girl	118	173,420	1:43.80	
1991	Spinning Round	2	J.M. Johnson	118	Queens Court Queen	118	Midnight Society	118	122,200	1:47.20	82
1992	Eliza	2	P.A. Valenzuela	118	Avie's Shadow	118	True Affair	118	122,200	1:43.20	99
1993	Stellar Cat	2	S.J. Sellers	118	Slew Kitty Slew	118	Beau Blush	118	122,200	1:44.60	77
1994	Post It	2	S. Maple	118	Morris Code	118	Cat Appeal	118	66,650	1:46.20	84
1995	Cara Rafaela	2	P. Day	118	Birr	118	Gold Sunrise	118	139,252	1:44.40	90
1996	Southern Playgirl	2	R.P. Romero	118	Screamer*	118	Private Pursuit	118	168,330	1:46.80	85
1997	Countess Diana	2	S.J. Sellers	118	Lily O' Gold	118	Beautiful Pleasure	118	266,600	1:45.20	85
1998	Silverbulletday	2	G.L. Stevens	118	Extended Applause	118	Grand Deed	118	281,976	1:42.40	97
1999	Scratch Pad	2	W.Martinez	118	Rare Beauty	118	Cash Run	118	274,288	1:44.00	82
2000	She's a Devil Due	2	M. Guidry	118	Nasty Storm	118	Cash Deal	118	270,320	1:44.86	83
2001	Take Charge Lady	2	A.J. D'Amico	118	Never Out	118	Cunning Play	118	280,736	1:46.23	93
2002	Westerly Breeze	2	R.J. Albarado	118	Ruby's Reception	118	Final Round	118	276,024	1:46.90	89
2003	Be Gentle	2	C.H. Velasquez	118	Galloping Gal	118	Deb's Charm	118	248,000	1:45.51	81

Beyer Index: 86.69

Run at about 7 furlongs prior to 1982

AMERICAN DERBY, 1 3/16 Miles (Turf),
3-Year-Olds, Arlington Park, 2003 Purse: $250,000

Year	Winner	Age	Jockey	Wt.	Second	Wt.	Third	Wt.	Win Value	Time	Beyer
1884	Modesty	3	I. Murphy	117	Kosciusko	117	Bob Cook	115	10,700	2:42.75	
1885	Volante	3	I. Murphy	123	Favor	123	Troubadour	123	9,570	2:49.50	
1886	Silver Cloud	3	I. Murphy	121	Blu Wing	121	Sir Joseph	118	8,160	2:37.25	
1887	C.H. Todd	3	Hamilton	118	Miss Ford	113	Wary	116	13,690	2:36.50	
1888	Emperor of Norfolk	3	I. Murphy	123	Falcon	121	Los Angeles	116	14,340	2:40.50	
1889	Spokane	3	T. Kiley	121	Sorrento	118	Retrieve	116	15,400	2:41.25	
1890	Uncle Bob	3	T. Kiley	116	Santiago	118	Ben Kingsbury	109	15,260	2:55.75	
1891	Strathmeath	3	Covington	112	Poet Scout	115	Kingman	129	18,610	2:49.25	
1892	Carlsbad	3	R. Williams	122	Zaldivar	122	Cicero	115	16,930	3:04.25	
1893	Boundless	3	E. Garrison	122	St. Leonards	122	Clifford	122	49,500	2:36.00	
1894	Rey el Santa Anita	3	E. Van Kuren	122	Senator Grady	122	Despot	122	19,750	2:36.00	
1898	Pink Coat	3	W. Martin	127	Warrenton	122	Isabey	122	9,225	2:42.60	
1900	Sidney Lucas	3	J. Bullman	122	James	122	Lieut. Gibson	129	9,425	2:40.20	
1901	Robert Waddell	3	J. Bullman	119	Terminus	127	The Parader	122	19,275	2:33.80	
1902	Wyeth	3	L. Lyne	122	Lucien Appleby	122	Aladdin	122	19,875	2:40.20	
1903	The Picket	3	Helgesen	115	Claude	127	Bernays	122	27,025	2:33.00	
1904	Highball	3	G.C. Fuller	122	Woodson	122	Rapid Water	122	26,325	2:33.00	
1916	Dodge	3	F. Murphy	126	Faux-Col	126	Franklin	122	6,850	2:04.60	
1926	Boot to Boot	3	A. Johnson	121	Display	126	Black Maria	116	89,000	2:30.20	
1927	Hydromel	3	L. McDermott	116	Handy Mandy	111	Buddy Bauer	121	22,750	2:29.00	
1928	Toro	3	E. Ambrose	126	Misstep	126	Solace	126	21,925	2:05.80	
1929	Windy City	3	L. McDermott	118	Naishapur	126	African	118	47,550	2:10.00	
1930	Reveille Boy	3	W. Frank	118	Gallant Knight	121	Zenofol	114	51,300	2:04.80	
1931	Mate	3	G. Ellis	126	Pittsburgher	118	Joey Bibb	118	48,675	2:04.20	
1932	Gusto	3	S. Coucci	118	Osculator	118	Prince Hotspur	118	48,200	2:10.60	
1933	Mr Khayyam	3	P. Walls	121	Head Play	126	Fair Rochester	118	23,410	2:04.20	
1934	Cavalcade	3	M. Garner	126	Discovery	118	Singing Wood	121	23,310	2:04.00	
1935	Black Helen	3	D. Meade	118	Count Arthur	118	Tearout	121	25,025	2:10.40	

Year	Winner	Age	Jockey	Wt.	Second	Wt.	Third	Wt.	Win Value	Time	Beyer
1937	Dawn Play	3	L. Balaski	116	Burning Star	118	Dellor	118	25,400	2:05.00	
1940	Mioland	3	J. Adams	123	Sirocco	126	Weigh Anchor	118	44,900	2:05.80	
1941	Whirlaway	3	A. Robertson	126	Bushwhacker	121	Delray	118	44,975	2:04.00	
1942	Alsab	3	G. Woolf	126	With Regards	121	Anticlimax	121	60,850	2:06.60	
1943	Askmenow	3	G. Woolf	115	Bold Captain	117	Famous Victory	117	56,150	2:07.00	
1944	By Jimminy	3	G. Woolf	122	Old Kentuck	118	Nelson Dunstan	118	61,650	2:03.00	
1945	Fighting Step	3	G. South	118	War Jeep	118	Pot o' Luck	122	68,950	2:02.80	
1946	Eternal Reward	3	R. Campbell	118	Pellicle	118	The Dude	122	83,450	2:02.60	
1947	Fervent	3	D. Dodson	118	Cosmic Bomb	118	Phalanx	126	70,950	2:00.60	
1948	Citation	3	E. Arcaro	126	Free America	118	Volcanic	118	66,450	2:01.60	
1949	Ponder	3	S. Brooks	126	Ky. Colonel	118	Johns Joy	118	66,150	2:00.40	
1950	Hill Prince	3	E. Arcaro	126	All Blue	114	Your Host	126	60,050	2:01.20	
1951	Hall of Fame	3	T. Atkinson	122	Abbe Sting	114	Bernwood	118	61,200	2:01.20	
1952	Mark-Ye-Well	3	E. Arcaro	120	Sub Fleet	114	Marcador	117	103,325	1:49.60	
1953	Native Dancer	3	E. Arcaro	128	Landlocked	120	Precious Stone	114	66,500	1:48.40	
1954	Errard King	3	S. Boulmetis	124	High Gun	124	Hasty Road	124	68,900	1:49.80	
1955	Swaps	3	W. Shoemaker	126	Traffic Judge	119	Parador	113	89,600	1:54.60	
1956	Swoon's Son	3	E. Arcaro	122	The Warrior	116	Toby B.	116	102,600	1:59.20	
1957	Round Table	3	W. Shoemaker	126	Iron Liege	126	Ekaba	120	100,350	1:55.00	
1958	Nadir	3	M. Ycaza	120	Victory Morn	123	Talent Show	120	114,600	1:51.60	
1959	Dunce	3	L.C. Cook	126	Demobilize	120	Little Tytus	120	93,700	1:49.60	
1960	T.V. Lark	3	J. Sellers	123	New Policy	120	Heroshogala	111	70,500	1:47.20	
1961	Beau Prince	3	S. Brooks	112	Editorialist	113	Flutterby	114	71,400	1:51.60	
1962	Black Sheep	3	J. Longden	117	Ridan	123	Jam-Tootin	115	71,250	2:01.60	
1963	Candy Spots	3	W. Shoemaker	126	B. Major	123	Crowdus	114	65,833	2:02.40	
1964	Roman Brother	3	F. Alvarez	122	Lt. Stevens	116	Close By	120	89,300	2:01.40	
1965	Tom Rolfe	3	W. Shoemaker	126	Royal Gunner	112	Mr. Pak	112	83,100	2:00.60	
1966	Buckpasser	3	B. Baeza	128	Jolly Jet	116	Advocator	116	84,100	1:47.00	
1967	Damascus	3	W. Shoemaker	126	In Reality	120	Favorable Turn	112	75,000	1:46.80	
1968	Forward Pass	3	I. Valenzuela	123	Nodouble	116	Poleax	120	70,600	1:48.80	
1969	Fast Hilarious	3	L. Pincay Jr	114	Night Invader	119	Dike	126	55,000	1:48.20	
1970	The Pruner	3	B. Baeza	117	Robin's Bug	114	Coaltown Cat	114	65,300	1:47.80	
1971	Bold Reason	3	L. Pincay Jr	124	Mr. Pow Wow	122	Northfields	119	81,950	1:52.60	
1972	Dubasoff	3	J. Vasquez	123	King's Bishop	122	Tri Jet	116	72,800	1:50.80	
1973	Bemo	3	W.J. Passmore	117	Golden Don	115	Buffalo Lark	109	69,400	1:49.60	
1974	Determined King	3	D. Montoya	112	Orders	114	Sr. Diplomat	111	92,000	1:47.80	
1975	Honey Mark	3	G. Patterson	116	High Steel	112	Go to the Bank	111	93,400	1:44.40	
1976	Fifth Marine	3	R. Turcotte	121	Majestic Light	121	Play the Red	121	93,400	1:49.20	
1977	Silver Series	3	L. Snyder	126	Run Dusty Run	126	Brach's Hilarious	112	68,880	2:02.40	
1978	Nast y and Bold	3	J.L. Samyn	114	Star de Naskra	114	Beau Sham	114	68,100	2:03.40	
1979	Smarten	3	S. Maple	126	Super Hit	114	Weather Tamer	114	63,600	2:05.20	
1980	Hurry Up Blue	3	S. Gallitano	114	Tizon	114	Spruce Needles	123	83,400	2:04.40	
1981	Pocket Zipper	3	H.R. Sibille	120	Fairway Phantom	123	Double Sonic	123	84,000	2:03.80	
1982	Wolfie's Rascal	3	R.A. Hernandez	123	Dew Line	114	Northern Majesty	120	65,100	2:05.60	
1983	Play Fellow	3	P. Day	123	Le Cou Cou	114	Brother	114	65,100	2:04.40	
1984	At the Threshold	3	P. Day	126			Par Flite	114	46,800	2:04.00	
	High Alexander	3	G. Gallitano	120							
1985	Creme Fraiche	3	E. Maple	123	Red Attack	114	Smile	123	96,000	2:01.60	
1987	Fortunate Moment	3	E. Fires	118	Fast Forward	118	Gem Master	118	100,350	2:03.80	
1989	Awe Inspiring	3	C. Perret	126	Dispersal	123	Caesar	114	124,500	2:02.40	
1990	Real Cash	3	P.A. Valenzuela	123	Home at Last	123	Adjudicating	117	180,000	2:02.00	112
1991	Olympio	3	E. Delahoussaye	126	Discover	114	Jackie Wackie	123	180,000	2:00.80	112
1992	The Name's Jimmy	3	P. Day	120	Standiford	114	May I Inquire	114	180,000	1:59.40	101
1993	Explosive Red	3	S.J. Sellers	120	Earl of Barking	120	Newton's Law	114	180,000	1:59.80	103
1994	Overbury	3	S.J. Sellers	115			Star Campaigner	114	120,000	1:55.20	101
	Vaudeville	3	A.D. Lopez	114							
1995	Gold and Steel	3	A.T. Gryder	114	Torrential	120	Unanimous Vote	120	180,000	1:55.00	100
1996	Jaunatxo	3	J.L. Diaz	114	Trail City	120	Marlin	114	180,000	1:55.80	104
	Trail City finished first but was disqualified and placed second										
1997	Honor Glide	3	G.K. Gomez	120	Worldly Ways	120	Daylight Savings	114	120,000	1:55.80	103
2000	Pine Dace	3	E Ahern	114	Hymn	114	Del Mar Show	114	120,000	1:55.46	96
2001	Fan Club's Mister	3	R. Meier	121	Monsieur Cat	116	Royal Spy	123	150,000	2:03.27	97
2002	Mananan McLir	3	R.R. Douglas	116	Jazz Beat	117	Extra Check	116	135,000	1:57.11	95
2003	Evolving Tactics	3	P.J. Smullen	117	Californian	121	Scottago	116	150,000	1:59.04	93

Beyer Index: 101.42

AMERICAN HANDICAP, 1 1/8 Miles (Turf),
3-Year-Olds and Up, Hollywood Park, 2003 Purse: $150,000

Year	Winner	Age	Jockey	Wt.	Second	Wt.	Third	Wt.	Win Value	Time	Beyer
1938	Ligaroti	6	N. Richardson	122	Whichcee	122	Frexo	111	6,650	1:50.00	
1939	Kayak II	4	G. Woolf	120	Gosum	107	Olimpo	107	9,800	1:49.80	
1940	Viscounty	4	N. Pariso	115	Hysterical	117	Specify	122	10,700	1:49.00	

Year	Winner	Age	Jockey	Wt.	Second	Wt.	Third	Wt.	Win Value	Time	Beyer
1941	Mioland	4	L. Haas	126	Woof Woof	114	Big Pebble	117	15,750	1:49.40	
1944	Paperboy	6	G. Woolf	122	Happy Issue	118	Lou–Bre	112	17,350	1:49.60	
1945	Bull Reigh	7	H. Trent	114	Paperboy	119	Sirde	112	2,600	1:43.40	
1946	Quick Reward	4	A. Skoronski	120	Olhaverry	111	Autocrat	108	39,750	1:43.20	
1947	Burning Dream	5	J. Londen	112	Cover Up	114	Texas Sandman	115	34,300	1:48.20	
1948	Stepfather	4	G. Pederson	111	Autocrat	112	On Trust	130	32,400	1:50.40	
1949	Double Jay	5	C. Bierman	119	Solidarity	117	Dinner Gong	122	33,250	1:48.60	
1950	Noor	5	J. Longden	132	Dharan	100	Frankly	107	32,500	2:00.20	
1951	Citation	6	S. Brooks	123	Bewitch	106	Sturdy One	112	33,050	1:48.40	
1952	Admiral Drake	5	G. Glisson	113	Sturdy One	115	Intent	127	32,800	1:48.20	
1953	Royal Serenade	5	J. Longden	123	A Gleam	118	Fleet Bird	122	33,350	1:48.60	
1954	Rejected	4	W. Shoemaker	123	High Scud	116	Imbros	126	32,100	1:48.00	
1955	Alidon	4	J. Longden	116	Mister Gus	114	Rejected	118	30,700	1:46.60	
1956	Swaps	4	W. Shoemaker	130	Mister Gus	111	Bobby Brocato	115	57,700	1:46.80	
1957	Find	7	R. Neves	121	Hoop Band	110	Festin	111	32,500	1:48.00	
1958	How Now	5	W. Harmatz	122	Seaneen	116	Eddie Schmidt	120	31,150	1:48.40	
1959	Hillsdale	4	T. Barrow	130	Find	109	Ying and Yang	108	30,600	1:47.20	
1960	Prize Host	5	W. Harmatz	109	Twentyone Guns	108	Bagdad	126	31,150	1:47.60	
1961	Prince Blessed	4	J. Longden	114	Dress Up	112	Sea Orbit	122	33,350	1:47.60	
1962	Prove It	5	H. Moreno	124	Windy Sands	113	Harpie	110	32,850	1:47.60	
1963	Dr. Kacy	4	W. Shoemaker	114	Admiral's Voyage	123	Mr. Consistency	116	34,550	1:48.20	
							Your Alibhai	110			
1964	Colorado King	5	R. York	119	Mustard Plaster	120	Viking Spirit	111	32,700	1:46.40	
1965	Native Diver	6	J. Lamber	125	Tronado	118	Hill Rise	122	31,250	1:47.20	
1966	Travel Orb	4	W. Harmatz	118	Native Diver	128	Real Good Deal	112	34,250	1:47.80	
1967	Pretense	4	J. Sellers	131	Native Diver	123	Biggs	117	32,200	1:47.00	
1968	Pink Pigeon	4	W. Harris	118	Saintex	112	Racing Room	117	34,300	1:47.80	
1969	Figonero	4	L. Pincay Jr	118	Baffle	115	Rivet	113	33,250	1:48.00	
1969	Poleax	4	D. Pierce	120	Bargain Day	114	Revolution	112	31,750	1:48.40	
1970	Fiddle Isle	5	W. Shoemaker	130	Baffle	125	Pinjara	122	31,750	1:47.60	
1971	Ack Ack	5	W. Shoemaker	130	Divide and Rule	121	Figonero	119	45,900	1:47.20	
1972	Buzkashi	5	W. Shoemaker	111	Single Agent	119	Wustenchef	117	49,600	1:48.60	
1973	Kentuckian	4	R. Campas	114	Life Cycle	121	Wing Out	118	50,400	1:48.00	
1974	Plunk	4	L. Pincay Jr	117	Scantling	115	Mr. Cockatoo	114	51,900	1:48.20	
1975	Pass the Glass	4	F. Toro	115	Big Band	116	Against the Snow	114	53,800	1:48.20	
1975	Montmartre	5	F. Toro	115	Top Crowd	115	Ancient Title	128	51,800	1:49.60	
1976	King Pellinore	4	W. Shoemaker	121	Riot in Paris	123	Caucasus	120	59,200	1:48.00	
1977	Hunza Dancer	5	J. Cruguet	120	Anne's Pretender	121	Legendaire	115	68,900	1:47.20	
1978	Effervescing	5	L. Pincay Jr	119	Diagramatic	123	April Axe	113	65,500	1:47.20	
1979	Smoggy	5	D.G. McHargue	119	Dom Alaric	120	Inkerman	119	65,500	1:47.40	
1980	Bold Tropic	5	W. Shoemaker	122	Inkerman	115	Borzoi	117	65,700	1:46.40	
1981	Bold Tropic	6	W. Shoemaker	126	The Bart	117	Don Roberto	112	98,100	1:46.80	
1982	Spence Bay	7	F. Toro	122	The Bart	124	Peter Jones	113	100,300	1:47.20	
1983	John Henry	8	C.J. McCarron	127	Prince Florimund	120	Tonzarun	114	87,100	1:48.40	
1984	Bel Bolide	6	T. Lipham	121	Silveyville	118	Vin St. Bernet	118	123,600	1:46.80	
1985	Tsunami Slew	4	G.L. Stevens	117	Al Mamoon	117	Dahar	123	122,300	1:46.20	
1986	Al Mamoon	5	P.A. Valenzuela	119	Truce Maker	111	Will Dancer	114	107,000	1:09.20	
1987	Clever Song	5	L. Pincay Jr	114	Skip Out Front	114	Barberry	115	127,800	1:45.60	
1988	Skip Out Front	6	C.J. McCarron	115	Steinlen	121	World Court	113	120,800	1:46.40	
1989	Mister Wonderful	6	F. Toro	115	Steinlen	121	Pranke	117	183,600	1:47.20	
1990	Classic Fame	4	E. Delahoussaye	117	Steinlen	125	Pleasant Variety	116	126,800	1:47.80	
1991	Tight Spot	4	L. Pincay Jr	123	Exbourne	122	Super May	118	129,400	1:46.00	.111
1992	Man From Eldorado	4	K.J. Desormeaux	114	Bold Russian	116	Golden Pheasant	123	122,000	1:47.00	.104
1993	Toussaud	4	K.J. Desormeaux	114	Man From Eldorado	116	Journalism	117	126,000	1:46.80	.104
1994	Blues Traveller	4	C.W. Antley	115	Gothland	119	Johann Quatz	116	128,000	1:46.40	.106
1995	Silver Wizard	5	G.L. Stevens	118	Romarin	120	Savinio	118	91,900	1:46.00	.108
1996	Labeeb	4	E. Delahoussaye	119	Gold And Steel	118	Earl OF Barking	116	66,120	1:45.60	.108
1997	El Angelo	5	A. Solis	118	Naninja	114	Wavy Run	117	96,360	1:46.80	.100
1998	Magellan	5	G.L. Stevens	116	Bonapartiste	116	Sharekann	112	90,000	1:47.00	.106
1999	Takarian	4	G.K. Gomez	114	Montemiro	112	Special Quest	115	90,000	1:47.20	.101
2000	Dark Moondancer	5	C.J. McCarron	122	Sardaukar	113	Sunshine Street	119	90,000	1:46.74	.106
2001	Takarian	6	G.K. Gomez	114	Fighting Falcon	114	Fateful Dream	116	90,000	1:48.19	.101
2002	The Tin Man	4	M.E. Smith	115	Devine Wind	115	Kappa King	116	90,000	1:46.82	.105
2003	Candy Ride	4	G.L. Stevens	120	Special Ring	118	Irish Warrior	116	90,000	1:46.20	.107

Beyer Index: 105.15

AMSTERDAM, 6 Furlongs,
3-Year-Olds, Saratoga Race Course, 2003 Purse: $150,000

Year	Winner	Age	Jockey	Wt.	Second	Wt.	Third	Wt.	Win Value	Time	Beyer
1995	Kings Fiction	3	P. Day	112	Lord Carson	115	Ft. Stockton	115	32,250	1:09.60	.104
1996	Distorted Humor	3	P. Day	115	Gold Fever	121	Stu's Choice	115	32,820	1:09.00	.105

Year	Winner	Age	Jockey	Wt.	Second	Wt.	Third	Wt.	Win Value	Time	Beyer
1997	Oro de Mexico	3	C.W. Antley	117	Trafalger	122	Kelly Kip	122	49,275	1:10.80	103
1998	Mint	3	Coa E. M.	119			Southern Bostonion	119	33,060	1:10.20	104
	Secret Firm	3	Prado E. S.	117					33,060		
1999	Successful Appeal	3	Prado E. S.	122	Lion Hearted	114	Silver Season	119	50,340	1:10.20	102
2000	Personal First	3	P. Day	120	Disco Rico	123	Trippi	123	66,000	1:09.33	106
2001	City Zip	3	J.F. Chavez	123	Speightstown	118	Smile My Lord	118	81,420	1:11.03	100
2002	Listen Here	3	P. Day	121	Boston Common	123	Bold Truth	115	90,000	1:09.58	98
2003	Zavata	3	J.D. Bailey	119	Great Notion	121	Trust n Luck	123	90,000	1:08.64	112

Beyer Index: 103.78

Formerly run as the Screen King

APPLETON HANDICAP, 1 Mile (Turf),
3-Year-Olds and Up, Gulfstream Park, 2003 Purse: $150,000

Year	Winner	Age	Jockey	Wt.	Second	Wt.	Third	Wt.	Win Value	Time	Beyer
1952	Alerted	4	O. Scurlock	116	Why Not Now	116	Going Away	110	7,575	1:43.00	
1953	Battlefield	5	A. Schmidt	122	Golden Gloves	108	Mandingo	106	11,150	1:48.80	
1954	Dr. Stanley	4	H. Woodhouse	112	Count Cain	114	Wise Margin	109	11,500	1:50.00	
1955	Fly Wheel	5	H. Woodhouse	116	Immense	112	Sampan	110	11,250	1:49.20	
1956	Mielleux	4	W. Blum	109	Two Fisted	113	Fabulist	112	11,150	1:49.40	
1957	Bardstown	5	W. Hartack	130	First Served	114	Piecesofeight	110	10,535	1:59.40	
1958	Better Bee	4	S. Boulmetis	112	Go Lightly	103	Oh Johnny	122	9,250	1:47.80	
1959	Better Bee	5	J. Choquette	117	Amerigo	117	Bill's Sky B'y	109	10,475	1:47.40	
1960	Oligarchy	6	J. Sellers	112	Stratmat	115	Tudor Era	123	9,700	1:47.80	
1961	Tudor Way	5	W. Hartack	119	Nickel Boy	117	Derrick	117	10,350	1:48.40	
1962	Beau Purple	5	R. Ussery	114	Trans-Way	113	Garwol	110	10,500	1:48.80	
1963	Key Issue	4	H. Woodhouse	108	Sunrise Flight	119	Jay Fox	115	10,550	1:50.40	
1964	Frankie's nod	4	W. Blum	113	Romancero II	113	Garwol	116	10,150	1:49.80	
1965	Ampose	4	K. Knapp	115	Old Hat	122	Editorialist	115	9,600	1:23.80	
1966	Pollux	5	R. Broussard	120	Country Friend	114	Br'yn Bridge	116	9,675	1:22.60	
1967	Canal	6	W. Boland	114	Tom Poker	112	Chinatowner	113	11,975	1:35.20	
1968	Rego	5	E. Fires	108	Quite an Accent	113	Pistacho II	110	12,100	1:36.00	
1969	Quite an Accent	6	B. Thornburg	113	John Jacob	112	Arundel	110	13,575	1:38.60	
1969	Go Marching	4	M. Ycaza	119	Sea Castle	113	Hespero	112	13,575	1:37.80	
1970	Prevailing	4	C. Baltazar	112	Zarco	112	Great Cohoes	120	26,600	1:37.00	
1971	Rocky Mount	4	J. Vasquez	112	Rouge Chanteur	110	Tudor Rew'rd	113	17,490	1:35.80	
1971	Broker's Tip II	6	M. Hole	113	Lonesome River	111	Barking Steeple	113	17,490	1:36.00	
1972	No No Billy	5	D. MacBeth	114	Droll Role	112	De'ri the Greek	111	16,560	1:23.20	
1972	Mr. Pow Wow	4	J. Vasquez	123	G. Lafayette	109	Speedy Zephyr	119	16,410	1:22.80	
1973	Life Cycle	4	F. Ianelli	112	Roundhouse	108	Hope Eternal	112	16,290	1:35.20	
1973	Windtex	4	J.L. Rotz	113	Getajetholme	112	Pri'e of Tr'h	114	16,140	1:35.00	
1974	Right On	5	E. Maple	112	Rey Maya	112	Rapid Sage	114	21,930	1:37.80	
1975	Duke Tom	5	P.I. Grimm	113	Dartsum	116	Return to Real'ty	110	17,460	1:36.20	
1975	Beau Bugle	5	M. Hole	116	The Grok	114	Mr. Door	115	16,860	1:36.20	
1976	Step Forward	4	M. Solomone	114	Faithful Diplomat	111	Pass'n'te Pete	111	20,775	1:34.00	
1976	Improviser	4	J. Cruguet	113	Odd Man	112	Peppy Addy	113	21,195	1:35.60	
1977	Gay Jitterbug	4	L. Saumell	110	What a Threat	110	Riverside Sam	109	16,185	1:36.40	
1977	Cinteelo	4	B. Thornburg	115	Commanding Lead	110	El Guindo	111	16,335	1:36.20	
1978	Qui Native	4	D. MacBeth	117	All Friends	115	Tablao	114	19,350	1:36.40	
1978	Do Lishus	4	J.D. Bailey	110	Haverty	113	Le'd'r of the B'd	113	19,500	1:37.20	
1979	Fleet Gar	4	J. Fell	114	Romeo	118	Vic's Magic	121	19,005	1:36.40	
1979	Regal and Royal	4	J. Fell	120	North Course	114	Bob's Dusty	121	19,155	1:37.00	
1980	Morning Frolic	5	A. Cordero Jr	117	Match the Hatch	111	Nar	113	19,365	1:35.40	
1980	Pipe Dreamer	5	J. Cruguet	113	Houdini	119	Once Over Lightly	114	18,915	1:34.40	
1981	North Course	6	B. Thornburg	115	Proctor	120	Royal Centurion	113	23,292	1:34.80	
1981	Drum's Captain	6	A. Gibert	114	Foretake	116	Poverty Boy	114	23,082	1:35.00	
1982	Gleaming Channel	4	C. Perret	114	Double Cadet	111	Victorian Double	112	18,375	1:36.00	
1982	King of Mardi Gr's	6	A. Smith Jr	113	Some One Frisky	114	Explosive Bid	115	18,225	1:36.40	
1983	Northrop	4	J. Velasquez	116	Forkali	114	North Course	113	26,754	1:22.00	
1984	Super Sunrise	5	C. Perret	118	Smart and Sharp	110	Guston	115	23,628	1:34.40	
1984	Great Substance	6	G. St. Leon	113	Dr. Schwartzman	109	Rising Raja	113	23,418	1:35.00	
1985	Smart and Sharp	6	M.L. Russ	117	Amerilad	112	Dr. Schwartzman	117	31,740	1:34.60	
1985	Star Choice	6	J. McKnight	118	Late Act	121	Solidified	114	31,440	1:34.40	
1986	Cool	5	J. Vasquez	116	Dr. Schwartzman	120	Rising Raja	113	39,690	1:39.60	
1987	Regal Flier	6	J. Vasquez	113	Wollaston	112	Hi Ideal	113	27,375	1:35.60	
1987	Racing Star	5	S.B. Soto	111	Trubulare	111	Onyxly	116	27,975	1:35.60	
1988	Yankee Affair	6	R.P. Romer	116	Performing Pappy	114	King's River II	114	60,000	1:35.00	
1989	Fabulous Indian	4	E.O. Nunez	109	Equalize	125	Simply Majestic	121	60,000	1:35.00	
1990	Highland Springs	6	C. Perret	118	Prince Randi	115	Wanderkin	116	60,000	1:35.20	107
1991	Jolie's Halo	4	R. Platts	114	Rowdy Regal	112	Shot Gun Scott	118	60,000	1:40.40	
1992	Royal Ninja	6	J.D. Bailey	112	Archies Laughter	114	Native Boundary	116	60,000	1:42.40	98
1993	Cigar Toss	6	B.G. Moore	112	Bidding Proud	117	Archies Laughter	114	60,000	1:43.40	100
1994	Paradise Creek	5	M.E. Smith	121	Fourstars Allstar	117	Elite Jeblar	111	60,000	1:40.80	106

Year	Winner	Age	Jockey	Wt.	Second	Wt.	Third	Wt.	Win Value	Time	Beyer
1995	Dusty Screen	7	W.H.McCauley	.116	The Vid	114	Dove Hunt	114	60,000	1:42.60	106
1996	The Vid	6	W.H. McCauley	.122	Dove Hunt	120	Montreal Red	114	60,000	1:41.60	111
1997	Montjoy	5	M.E. Smith	116	Mighty Forum	114	Elite Jeblar	114	60,000	1:39.80	106
1998	Sir Cat	5	J. D. Bailley	119	Wild Event	114	Kingcanrunallday	116	60,000	1:42.60	111
1999	Behaviour	7	S.J. Sellers	113	Notoriety	112	Legs Galore	113	60,000	1:45.77	100
2000	Band Is Passing	4	E.M. Coa	115	Hibernian Rhapsody	115	Shamrock City	114	60,000	1:40.11	104
2001	Associate	6	J.F. Chavez	114	Band Is Passing	119	El Mirasol	115	60,000	1:33.69	100
2002	Pisces	5	R.I. Velez	113	North East Bound	117	Capsized	114	90,000	1:39.41	102
2003	Point Prince	4	M.R. Cruz	115	Krieger	115	Red Sea	114	90,000	1:37.84	101

Beyer Index: 104

Run on main track in 1999. Run at one mile in 2001.

ARCADIA HANDICAP, 1 1/8 Miles (Turf),
4-Year-Olds and Up, Santa Anita, 2003 Purse: $150,000

Year	Winner	Age	Jockey	Wt.	Second	Wt.	Third	Wt.	Win Value	Time	Beyer
1988	Steinlen	5	G.L. Stevens	117	Political Ambition	120	Neshad	117	88,760	1:34.80	
1989	Political Ambition	5	E. Delahoussaye	121	Patchy Groundfog	118	Steinlen	122	62,600	1:35.60	
1990	Steinlen	7	J.A. Santos	125	Bruho	117	Wonder Dancer	111	63,200	1:33.40	105
1991	Pharisien	4	C.S. Nakatani	117	Exbourne	118	Tartas	112	102,500	1:33.20	105
1992	Exbourne	6	G.L. Stevens	122	Repriced	113	Madjaristan	115	95,000	1:33.20	106
1993	Val des Bois	7	P.A. Valenzuela	118	Star of Cozzene	122	C. Sam Maggio	113	77,750	1:35.00	108
1994	Norwich	7	P.A. Valenzuela	117	Megan's Interco	119	Gothland	118	75,850	1:34.00	109
1995	Savinio	5	C.J. McCarron	116	River Flyer	121	Romarin	120	91,800	1:34.60	108
1996	Tychonic	6	G.L. Stevens	118	Debutant Trick	117	Savinio	117	80,300	1:35.80	108
1997	Labeeb	5	E. Delahoussaye	120	Talloires	118	Pinfloron	115	80,100	1:35.80	106
1998	Hawksley Hill	5	G.L. Stevens	117	Precious Ring	114	Kirkwall	117	100,410	1:49.80	106
1999	Commitisize	4	D.R. Flores	117	Majorien	117	Ladies Din	119	90,000	1:48.20	104
2000	Falcon Flight	4	B. Blanc	114	Bonapartiste	118	Otavalo	114	97,950	1:47.88	102
2001	Lazy Lode	7	L. Pincay Jr.	121	Night Patrol	116	Wake the Tiger	114	90,000	1:49.74	111
2002	Seinne	5	C.J. McCarron	115	Irish Prize	122	Kerrygold	116	90,000	1:47.16	104
2003	Century City	4	J. Valdivia Jr	114	Gondolieri	116	Sunday Break	117	90,000	1:47.84	102

Beyer Index: 106

ARKANSAS DERBY, 1 1/8 Miles,
3-Year-Olds, Oaklawn Park, 2003 Purse: $500,000

Year	Winner	Age	Jockey	Wt.	Second	Wt.	Third	Wt.	Win Value	Time	Beyer
1936	Holl Image	3	H.W. Fischer	117	Understand	117	My Auntie	121	4,110	1:53.40	
1937	Eastport	3	R. Hightshoe	117	Zor	117	Sir Midas	117	4,030	1:50.80	
1938	Tiger	3	A. Robertson	125	Silver Sarah	112	Gov. Chandler	117	4,060	1:50.80	
1939	Ariel Toy	3	L. Hardy	117	Radio Gold	117	Torch Stick	112	3,850	1:52.40	
1940	Super Chief	3	J. Richard	117	Colorado Ore	112	The Fop	117	3,810	1:52.20	
1941	He Rolls	3	P. Mills	117	Oakmont	117	Quizzle	117	3,870	1:52.60	
1942	With Regards	3	J. Longden	120	Cerebus	117	Columbus Day	117	4,080	1:50.00	
1943	Seven Hearts	3	J. Adams	120	Ocean Wave	123	Dove Pie	117	7,170	1:52.20	
1944	Challenge Me	3	A. Skoronski	120	Shut Up	117	Bell-Buzzer	117	7,450	1:50.20	
1946	Bob Murphy	3	W. Eads	117	Cid Play	117	Ariel Ace	120	7,460	1:51.80	
1947	Fleetridge	3	A. Craig	117	Sun Beau Go	117	Mel Van Orman	115	7,550	1:51.40	
1948	Fertile Lands	3	P. Glidewell	117	Lucky Codine	117	Beaukiss	112	7,225	1:51.00	
1949	Cacomo	3	B. Fisk	123	Lyle's First	117	Polly Lass	115	7,100	1:54.60	
1950	Big Ike	3	H. Keene	126	Smoke Screen	117	Virtue	112	7,150	1:52.00	
1951	Ruhe	3	J.D. Jessop	120	Enforcer	120	Good Question	120	7,125	1:51.00	
1952	Gushing Oil	3	A. Popara	120	Lextown	123	Our Challenge	120	7,425	1:49.20	
1953	Curragh King	3	J. Adams	111	Supreme's Bub	111	Wismo	108	7,500	1:49.60	
1954	Timely Tip	3	H. Craig	123	Winning Count	117	Super Devil	120	7,650	1:49.80	
1955	Trim Destiny	3	L.C. Cook	113	Styrunner	117	Shannon Comet	114	7,475	1:49.60	
1956	Johns Chic	3	J.L. Rotz	117	Come on Red	117	Mr. Bob W.	114	7,275	1:51.20	
1957	Kentucky Roman	3	J. Delahoussaye	117	Cosmic Force	114	Lori-El	114	9,200	1:49.60	
1958	Count deBlanc	3	J. Sellers	110	Benedicto	116	Little Hunk	105	14,685	1:53.80	
1959	Al Davelle	3	R. Baldwin	110	Sputnik	116	Am Away	116	14,880	1:48.80	
1960	Spring Broker	3	E. Curry	116	Por Prophet	113	El Zag	122	11,499	1:54.40	
1960	Persian Gold	3	J. Combest	110	Tony Graff	122	Deemster	119	11,628	1:53.00	
1961	Light Talk	3	R. Nono	116	Loyal Son	110	Bass Clef	122	18,639	1:50.20	
1962	Areopolis	3	R.L. Baird	110	Prince Dale	116	Eidolon	119	18,655	1:49.60	
1963	Cosmic Tip	3	R. Mundorf	110	Lemon Twist	116	Snow Fort	113	18,460	1:50.40	
1964	Prince Davelle	3	C. Burr	110	Royal Shuck	110	Goff's Gay	110	19,305	1:51.40	
1965	Swift Ruler	3	L. Spraker	122	Flash Climber	110	Mark-Ye-Royal	113	34,110	1:52.20	
1966	Better Sea	3	J. Sellers	122	Eladio	113	Taipan	116	35,640	1:49.20	
1967	Monitor	3	J. Nichols	116	Ask the Fare	122	Barbs Delight	116	35,520	1:48.60	
1968	Nodouble	3	W. McKeever	116	Te Vega	119	Etony	119	35,220	1:50.00	
1969	Traffic Mark	3	P.I. Grimm	122	King of the Castle	122	Sheik of Bagdad	116	36,600	1:50.60	
1970	Herbalist	3	J. Nichols	116	Don't Stop Me	111	Admiral's Shield	122	35,010	1:50.20	

Year	Winner	Age	Jockey	Wt.	Second	Wt.	Third	Wt.	Win Value	Time	Beyer
1971	Twist the Axe	3	G. Patterson	120	Barbizon Streak	123	Bixa	115	38,010	1:49.20	
1972	No Le Hace	3	P. Rubbicco	126	Hassi's Image	120	Great Bear Lake	120	78,660	1:48.80	
1973	Impecunious	3	J. Velasquez	126	Vodika	123	Warbucks	123	74,130	1:49.60	
1974	J.R.'s Pet	3	D.G. McHargue	123	Silver Florin	120	Nick's Folly	120	86,910	1:50.60	
1975	Promised City	3	D.E. Whited	126	Bold Chapeau	117	My Friend Gus	120	82,140	1:51.80	
1976	Elocutionist	3	J. Lively	126	New Collection	117	Klen Klitso	120	81,480	1:49.20	
1977	Clev Er Tell	3	R. Broussard	126	Kodiack	117	Best Person	117	80,520	1:50.60	
1978	Esops Foibles	3	C.J. McCarron	126	Chief of Dixieland	117	Special Honor	120	82,470	1:52.20	
1979	Golden Act	3	S. Hawley	126	Smarten	120	Strike the Main	125	107,280	1:50.00	
1980	Temperence Hill	3	D. Haire	123	Bold 'n Rulling	117	Sun Catcher	120	107,160	1:50.60	
1981	Bold Ego	3	J.L. Lively	123	Top Avenger	120	Woodchopper	123	137,160	1:50.40	
1982	Hostage	3	J. Fell	117	El Baba	126	Bold Style	123	170,580	1:51.60	
1983	Sunny's Halo	3	E. Delahoussaye	126	Caveat	120	Exile King	117	176,340	1:49.40	
1984	Althea	3	P.A. Valenzuela	121	Pine Circle	118	Gate Dancer	118	360,150	1:46.80	
1985	Tank's Prospect	3	G. Stevens	123	Encolure	126	Irish Fighter	115	349,650	1:48.40	
1986	Rampage	3	P. Day	118	Wheatly Hall	115	Family Style	121	300,000	1:48.20	
1987	Demon's Begone	3	P. Day	123	Lookinforthebigone	118	You're No Bargain	115	300,000	1:47.60	
1988	Proper Reality	3	J.D. Bailey	118	Primal	115	Sea Trek	123	300,000	1:48.40	
1989	Dansil	3	L. Snyder	121	Clevor Trevor	126	Advocate Training	115	240,000	1:49.20	
1990	Silver Ending	3	G.L. Stevens	122	Real Cash	122	Power Lunch	118	300,000	1:48.00	
1991	Olympio	3	E. Delahoussaye	122	Corporate Report	118	Richman	122	300,000	1:47.60	
1992	Pine Bluff	3	J.D. Bailey	122	Lil E. Tee	122	Desert Force	122	300,000	1:49.40	.107
1993	Rockamundo	3	C.H. Borel	118	Kissin Kris	122	Foxtrail	122	300,000	1:48.00	.103
1994	Concern	3	G.K. Gomez	118	Blumin Affair	118	Silver Goblin	122	300,000	1:48.00	.109
1995	Dazzling Falls	3	G.K. Gomez	122	Flitch	118	On Target	122	300,000	1:50.60	.95
1996	Zarb's Magic	3	R. Ardoin	122	Grindstone	122	Halo Sunshine	122	300,000	1:49.20	.100
1997	Crypto Star	2	P. Day	122	Phantom On Tour	122	Pacificbounty	122	300,000	1:49.20	.108
1998	Victory Gallop	3	A. Solis	122	Hanuman Highway	118	Favorite Trick	122	300,000	1:49.80	.101
1999	Certain	3	K.J. Desormeaux	122	Torrid Sand	118	Ecton Park	122	300,000	1:49.20	.94
	Valhol (101 Beyer) finished first but was subsequently disqualified										
2000	Graeme Hall	3	R.J. Albarado	118	Snuck In	122	Impeachment	118	300,000	1:49.08	.104
2001	Balto Star	3	M. Guidry	122	Jamaican Rum	122	Son of Rocket	122	300,000	1:49.04	.109
2002	Private Emblem	3	D.J. Meche	122	Wild Horses	118	Windward Passage	122	300,000	1:50.20	.100
							Bay Monster	118			
2003	Sir Cherokee	3	T.J. Thompson	118	Eugene's Third Son	118	Christine's Outlaw	118	300,000	1:48.39	.106

Beyer Index: 103

ARLINGTON CLASSIC, 1 1/16 Miles (Turf)
3-Year-Olds, Arlington Park, 2003 Purse: $175,000

Year	Winner	Age	Jockey	Wt.	Second	Wt.	Third	Wt.	Win Value	Time	Beyer
1929	Blue Larkspur	3	M. Garner	126	Live Oak	119	Clyde Van Dusen	126	59,900	2:14.40	
1930	Gallant Fox	3	E. Sande	126	Gallant Knight	123	Ned O.	121	64,750	2:03.80	
1931	Mate	3	A. Robertson	126	Spanish Play	123	Twenty Grand	126	73,650	2:02.40	
1932	Gusto	3	S. Coucci	126	Stepenfetchit	121	Evergold	121	76,600	2:03.60	
1933	Inlander	3	R. Jones	118	Golden Way	118	War Glory	121	32,755	2:12.00	
1934	Cavalcade	3	M. Garner	126	Discovery	121	Hadagal	121	30,325	2:02.80	
1935	Omaha	3	W.D. Wright	126	St. Bernard	121	Bloodroot	113	28,975	2:01.40	
1936	Granville	3	J. Stout	126	Mr. Bones	121	Hollywood	123	28,400	2:03.20	
1937	Flying Scot	3	J. Gilbert	123	Eagle Pass	118	Burning Star	118	27,375	2:05.80	
1938	Nedayr	3	W.D. Wright	121	Bull Lea	121	Cravat	123	27,500	2:06.20	
1939	Challedon	3	H. Richards	126	Sun Lover	121	Johnstown	128	35,600	2:02.00	
1940	Sirocco	3	G. Woolf	121	Gallahadion	126	Bimelech	126	37,935	2:03.00	
1941	Attention	3	C. Bierman	121	Whirlaway	126	Bushwhacker	121	42,450	2:02.80	
1942	Shut Out	3	E. Arcaro	126	Valdina Orphan	126	With Regards	118	69,700	2:01.40	
1943	Slide Rule	3	F. Zufelt	120	Bourmont	117	Chop Chop	123	53,450	2:04.60	
1944	Twilight Tear	3	L. Haas	114	Old Kentuck	119	Pensive	126	62,050	2:03.60	
1945	Pot o' Luck	3	D. Dodson	119	Air Sailor	119	Fighting Step	119	67,150	2:05.80	
1946	The Dude	3	M. Duhon	119	Sgt. Spence	119	Mighty Story	122	76,950	2:02.60	
1947	But Why Not	3	W. Mehrtens	117	Fervent	122	Cosmic Bomb	118	71,500	2:01.80	
1948	Papa Redbird	3	R.L. Baird	122	Shy Gyu	119	Loujac	119	66,600	2:03.00	
1949	Ponder	3	S. Brooks	126	Admiral Lea	119	Palestinian	126	65,450	2:03.20	
1950	Greek Song	3	O. Scurlock	120	Bed o' Roses	110	Your Host	126	58,950	2:01.80	
1951	Hall of Fame	3	T. Atkinson	120	Battlefield	123	Ruhe	120	62,975	2:03.20	
1952	Mark-Ye-Well	3	E. Arcaro	122	Armageddon	120	Sub Fleet	112	105,375	1:39.20	
1953	Native Dancer	3	E. Guerin	126	Sir Mango	120	Van Crosby	120	97,725	1:38.00	
1954	Errard King	3	S. Boulmetis	120	Helioscope	120	High Gun	123	104,475	1:35.00	
1955	Nashua	3	E. Arcaro	126	Traffic Judge	120	Impromptu	120	91,675	1:35.20	
1956	Swoon's Son	3	D. Erb	120	Ben A. Jones	117	Doubledogdare	112	102,000	1:36.80	
1957	Clem	3	C. McCreary	117	Iron Liege	123	Manteau	117	105,950	1:36.60	
1958	A Dragon Killer	3	J. Combest	117	Talent Show	117	Nadir	120	101,100	1:36.40	
1959	Dunce	3	L.C. Cook	117	On-and-On	117	Intentionally	123	78,700	1:35.00	

Year	Winner	Age	Jockey	Wt.	Second	Wt.	Third	Wt.	Win Value	Time	Beyer
1960	T.V. Lark	3	J. Sellers	120	John William	123	Venetian Way	123	85,500	1:36.20	
1961	Globemaster	3	J.L. Rotz	119	Editorialist	113	Crozier	114	72,900	1:35.40	
1962	Ridan	3	A. Gomez	123	Mighty Fennec	114	Admiral's Voyage	123	64,750	1:38.00	
1963	Candy Spots	3	W. Shoemaker	126	Admiral Vic	114	B. Major	123	88,833	1:35.80	
1964	Tosmah	3	S. Boulmetis	115	Lt. Stevens	118	Close By	120	69,000	1:36.20	
1965	Tom Rolfe	3	W. Shoemaker	124	Royal Gunner	118	Sum Up	118	62,500	1:34.80	
1966	Buckpasser	3	B. Baeza	125	Creme Dela Creme	123	He Jr.	116	63,000	1:32.60	
1967	Dr. Fager	3	B. Baeza	120	Lightning Orphan	116	Diplomat Way	118	61,000	1:36.00	
1968	Exclusive Native	3	I. Valenzuela	113	Iron Ruler	116	Good Investment	116	63,000	1:36.00	
1969	Ack Ack	3	B. Baeza	120	King of the Castle	120	Fast Hilarious	120	66,800	1:34.40	
1970	Corn off the Cob	3	E. Belmonte	117	Tenacious Jr.	114	George Lewis	120	64,500	1:36.00	
1971	Son Ange	3	C. Baltazar	114	Mr. Pow Wow	117	Staunch Avenger	117	68,400	1:36.00	
1972	King's Bishop	3	E. Maple	114	Brick Door	117	Gun Tune	114	67,000	1:35.00	
1973	Linda's Chief	3	B. Baeza	123	Blue Chip Dan	114	Golden Don	114	72,200	1:44.60	
1977	Private Thoughts	4	R. Perez	117	Pay Tribute	118	Dragset	114	90,000	1:59.40	
1978	Alydar	3	J. Fell	126	Chief of Dixieland	114	Gordie H.	114	63,000	2:00.40	
1979	Steady Growth	3	B. Swatuk	123	Private Account	114	Third and Lex	114	65,400	2:00.60	
1980	Spruce Needles	3	M.R. Morgan	114	I'ma Hell Raiser	114	Stone Manor	126	81,000	1:49.20	
1981	Fairway Phantom	3	J. Lively	114	Golden Derby	114	Television Studio	117	84,000	1:53.40	
1982	Wolfie's Rascal	3	A. Cordero Jr	114	Drop Your Drawers	114	Dew Line	114	72,600	1:49.00	
1983	Play Fellow	3	P. Day	123	Bet Big	114	Passing Base	114	65,400	1:49.00	
1984	At the Threshold	3	P. Day	126	Par Flite	114	Dugan Knight	114	71,400	1:50.20	
1985	Smile	3	J. Vasquez	117	Red Attack	114	Clever Allemont	123	114,000	1:51.20	
1986	Sumptious	3	R.P. Romero	115	Glow	120	Cheapskate	123	96,720	1:49.40	
1987	Lost Code	3	G. St. Leon	123	Gem Master	120	Avies Copy	120	99,090	1:49.60	
1989	Clever Trevor	3	D.R. Pettinger	126	Bio	114	Western Playboy	123	124,500	1:49.40	
1990	Sound of Cannons	3	P. Day	114	Adjudicating	117	Home at Last	123	150,000	1:47.40	101
1991	Whadjathink	3	J. Velasquez	120	Freezing Dock	114	Character	120	180,000	1:49.00	108
1992	Saint Ballado	3	J.A. Krone	120	Desert Force	114	Star Recruit	117	180,000	1:46.80	104
1993	Boundlessly	3	P. Day	120	Hegar	114	Williamstown	123	78,000	1:49.80	97
1994	Eagle Eyed	3	C.S. Nakatani	120	Mr. Angel	120	Star Campaigner	114	180,000	1:48.40	102
1995	Hawk Attack	3	P. Day	114	Via Lombardia	120	Bryntirion	114	120,000	1:48.00	102
1996	Trail City	3	P. Day	114	More Royal	120	Winter Quarters	114	120,000	1:48.60	104
1997	Honor Glide	3	G.K. Gomez	114	Brave Act	120	Daylight Savings	114	75,000	1:47.40	103
2000	King Cugat	3	R.J. Albarado	123	Boyum	114	El Ballezano	114	90,000	1:48.16	106
2001	Baptize	3	M.Guidry	121	Indygo Shiner	121	Cherokee Kim	116	120,000	1:48.80	99
2002	Mr. Mellon	3	R.R. Douglas	121	Doc Holiday	121	Seainsky	116	105,000	1:41.95	94
2003	Lismore Knight	3	R.R. Douglas	119	Remind	116	Good Day Too	116	105,000	1:42.73	93

Beyer Index: 101.08

ASTARITA, 6 1/2 Furlongs,
2-Year-Old Fillies, Belmont Park, 2003 Purse: $150,000

Year	Winner	Age	Jockey	Wt.	Second	Wt.	Third	Wt.	Win Value	Time	Beyer
1946	Keynote	2	H. Woodhouse	116	Quarantaine	114	Kai Kai	111	10,325	1:11.20	
1947	Bellsoeur	2	T. May	119	Grey Flight	116	Dusty Legs	111	9,650	1:12.60	
1948	Nell K.	2	D. Dodson	114	Tassel	110	Flying Ship	116	10,275	1:14.60	
1949	Blue Kay	2	T. Atkinson	113	High Frequency	124	Sweetlucybell	115	9,375	1:14.00	
1950	Jacodema	2	R. Permane	113	Self Assurance	116	Ruddy	116	8,950	1:12.00	
1951	Place Card	2	A. Kirkland	111	Landmark	110	Rose Jet	119	9,575	1:12.60	
1952	Grecian Queen	2	E. Guerin	119	Piedmont Lass	116	Flirtatious	122	8,925	1:13.60	
1953	Make a Play	2	B. Green	113	When in Rome	115	Riant	122	8,450	1:13.20	
1954	Two Stars	2	N. Shuk	119	High Voltage	125	My Blue Sky	110	12,800	1:12.80	
1955	Cosmah	2	K. Korte	116	Noors Image	110	Levee	113	12,200	1:11.40	
1956	Alanesian	2	W. Boland	122	Jet's Charm	112	Miss Blue Jay	110	11,450	1:10.00	
1957	Polamby	2	P. Anderson	116	Merry Lark	112	Lopar	114	18,550	1:25.80	
1961	Cicada	2	W. Shoemaker	122	Firm Policy	116	Jazz Queen	112	19,630	1:24.40	
1962	Main Swap	2	B. Baeza	112	Pams Ego	119	Fool's Play	116	19,272	1:23.00	
1963	Petite Rouge	2	J. Sellers	122	Castle Forbes	122	Little Red Belle	112	14,349	1:23.60	
1963	Tosmah	2	S. Boulmetis	119	Beautiful Day	119	Teo Pepi	116	14,511	1:23.00	
1964	I Deceive	2	F. Alvarez	119	Queen Empress	122	Admiring	122	19,955	1:26.60	
1965	Swift Lady	2	H. Gustines	116	Forefoot	114	Lady Diplomat	116	15,697	1:23.60	
1965	Prides Profile	2	D. Pierce	119			Destro	116	10,157	1:23.00	
	Lady Pitt	2	R. Turcotte	116							
1966	Irish County	2	B. Baeza	116	Pepperwood	116	Green Glade	116	19,370	1:24.40	
1967	Syrian Sea	2	R. Ussery	119	Good Game	116	Dawn of Tomorrow	112	19,175	1:22.60	
1968	Show Off	2	E. Belmonte	122	Shoo Fly	122	Roundamene	116	14,804	1:25.00	
1968	Dihela	2	R. Turcotte	112	Imbibe	112	Shuvee	112	14,966	1:24.20	
1969	Cherry Sundae	2	J.L. Rotz	116	Corte Madera	116	Royal Picnic	112	19,890	1:24.80	
1970	Deceit	2	R. Turcotte	122	Make Me Laugh	113	Bonnie and Gay	119	19,402	1:23.80	
1971	Barely Even	2	T. Barrow	119	Miss Gunflint	116	Bridget o' Brick	112	21,120	1:23.40	
1972	Princess Doubleday	2	B. Baeza	114	Tuerta	116	Cherry Jay	114	13,965	1:17.20	

Year	Winner	Age	Jockey	Wt.	Second	Wt.	Third	Wt.	Win Value	Time	Beyer
1972	Waltz Fan	2	J. Mallano	117	Behram	114	Fine Tuning	114	14,040	1:17.80	
1973	Raisela	2	R. Turcotte	113	Nancy G	113	Quick Cure	115	17,610	1:16.80	
1974	Stulcer	2	A. Cordero Jr	113	Copernica	113	But Exclusive	116	17,040	1:16.40	
1975	Picture Tube	2	E. Maple	113	La Tamborera	115	Dottie's Doll	113	23,340	1:18.40	
1976	Sensational	2	A. Cordero Jr	112	Tickle My Toes	112	Spy Flag	112	22,185	1:17.40	
1977	Lakeville Miss	2	R. Hernandez	112	Sherry Peppers	116	Tempermental P't	112	21,990	1:17.80	
1978	Fall Aspen	2	R.I. Velez	112	Whisper Fleet	112	Island Kitty	112	25,755	1:17.00	
1979	Royal Suite	2	J. Fell	114	Andrea F.	112	Smart Angle	116	25,815	1:17.20	
1980	Sweet Revenge	2	J. Velasquez	116	Expressive Dance	113	Hagley's Point	112	33,360	1:17.20	
1981	Before Dawn	2	J. Velasquez	119	Betty Money	112	Take Lady Anne	112	33,540	1:16.60	
1982	Wings of Jove	2	W.H. McCauley	112	On the Bench	112	Bammer	112	32,220	1:16.80	
1983	Tina's Ten	2	R. Migliore	112	Masked Barb	112	Upturning	112	34,740	1:19.20	
1984	Mom's Command	2	A. Fuller	116	Self Image	116	Winters' Love	112	54,900	1:17.80	
1985	Guadery	2	A. Cordero Jr	112	Musical Lark	112	I'm Sweets	112	64,800	1:17.00	
1986	Cagey Exuberance	2	J. Nied Jr	116	Sea Basque	113	Maxi Ruler	116	51,300	1:18.20	
1987	Flashy Runner	2	J. Vasquez	112	Tap Your Toes	112	Galway Song	112	70,560	1:16.60	
1988	Channel Three	2	C. Barrera	116	Pat Copelan	119	Mistaurian	112	83,460	1:17.00	
1989	Dance Colony	2	J.A. Santos	119	Charging Fire	114	Trumpet's Blare	114	68,640	1:17.80	
1990	Devilish Touch	2	C. Perret	116	Makin Faces	112	Missy's Mirage	112	71,760	1:18.00	
1991	Easy Now	2	M.E. Smith	112	Stolen Beauty	112	Celeste Cielo	112	69,240	1:22.80	93
1992	Missed the Storm	2	M.E. Smith	119	Dispute	119	Statuette	119	67,920	1:24.80	92
1993	Shapely Scrapper	2	J. Bravo	119	Brighter Course	119	Fashion Maven	119	67,560	1:24.00	77
1994	Miss Golden Circle	2	J.A. Krone	119	Golden Bri	119	Mistress S.	119	64,740	1:23.60	86
1995	Top Secret	2	M.E. Smith	119	Plum Country	119	Mesabi Maiden	119	69,480	1:36.60	84
1996	Broad Dynamite	2	D.W. Cordova	119	Glitter Woman	119	Biding Time	119	63,960	1:24.00	81
1997	Ninth Inning	2	R.G. Davis	119	Salty Perfume	119	Madame Fireplace	119	64,680	1:17.40	83
1998	Paved in Gold	2	J.F. Chavez	119	Blushing Deed	119	Paula's Girl	119	63,780	1:18.80	81
1999	Silentlea	2	R.G. Davis	119	Valerie's Dream	119	Lucky Livi	119	67,620	1:17.40	74
2000	Xtra Heat	2	M.T. Johnston	117	Gold Mover	119	Major Wager	117	66,060	1:16.71	85
2001	Bella Bellucci	2	G.L. Stevens	117	Forest Heiress	120	Speed to Burn	117	63,955	1:16.67	97
2002	Humorous Lady	2	J.D. Bailey	117	Fast Cookie	117	Chimichurri	117	90,000	1:17.76	83
2003	Spectacular Moon	2	J.F. Chavez	117	Feline Story	120	Smokey Glacken	117	90,000	1:17.16	81

Beyer Index: **84.38**

BARBARA FRITCHIE HANDICAP, 7 Furlongs,
Fillies and Mares, 3-Year-Olds and Up, Laurel Park, 2003 Purse: $200,000

Year	Winner	Age	Jockey	Wt.	Second	Wt.	Third	Wt.	Win Value	Time	Beyer
1952	Singing Beauty	3	N. Shuk	110	My Nell	102	Chalalette	103	14,875	1:51.60	
1953	Sunshine Nell	5	H. Woodhouse	122	La Corredora	123	Sunny Dale	119	15,075	1:46.20	
1954	Sotto Voce	3	W. Blum	111	Mlle. Loretta	117	Canadiana	118	11,750	1:44.80	
1955	Guayana	4	W. Blum	114	Another World	116	Cerise Reine	124	18,900	1:24.40	
1956	Sometime Thing	4	E. Guerin	124	Searching	122	Myrtle's Jet	124	19,050	1:22.80	
1957	Solar System	6	J. Lynch	113	Scansion	112	Cool Stream	117	18,950	1:12.00	
1958	Movitave	3	N. Shuk	112	Gay Warbler	116	Derry	114	18,117	1:13.60	
1959	Tinkalero	4	A. Sherman	121	Mlle. Dianne	113	H'sier Honey	118	17,982	1:10.80	
1961	Sun Glint	4	J. Sellers	116	Cherry Flip	106	Miss Orestes	120	17,712	1:40.20	
1962	Call Card	5	J. Culmone	114	Sun Glint	121	Basking	108	14,235	1:25.60	
1963	All Brandy	4	S. Boulmetis	117	Coppahaunk	123	Think Piece	115	17,387	1:10.80	
1964	Pams Ego	4	R. Ferraro	121	Vitamin Shot	114	Srta. Monica	113	21,612	1:24.40	
1965	Basking	7	O. Cutshaw	113	Redpoll	116	County Maid	124	22,360	1:25.00	
1966	Tosmah	5	S. Boulmetis	121	Queen Empress	123	Privileged	111	38,935	1:23.40	
1967	Holly-O	4	F. Lovato	117	Moccasin	120	Lady Diplomat	111	38,935	1:21.80	
1968	Too Bald	4	M. Ycaza	118	Straight Deal	122	Treacherous	121	37,895	1:21.80	
1969	Too Bald	5	M. Ycaza	129	Miss Spin	117	Double Ripple	107	37,115	1:23.80	
1970	Process Shot	4	L. Adams	123	Serica	111	Kushka	113	38,740	1:23.60	
1971	Cold Comfort	4	M. Venezia	114	Take Warning	110	Double Delta	117	38,415	1:23.60	
1973	First Bloom	5	A. Gomez	117	Pas de Nom	116	Winged Affair	111	38,025	1:23.40	
1974	Twixt	5	W.J. Passmore	124	Groton Miss	112	In the Mat's	109	38,350	1:24.40	
1975	Twixt	6	W.J. Passmore	126	Crackerfax	109	Donetta	112	38,350	1:25.40	
1976	Donetta	5	J.W. Moseley	119	Pinch Pie	117	Heydairya	108	37,765	1:24.60	
1977	Mt. Airy Queen	4	D.R. Wright	114	Avum	109	Forty Nine Sunsets	118	36,270	1:23.80	
1978	Bold Brat	5	J.W. Moseley	115	Spot Two	116	Satin Dancer	114	37,375	1:23.40	
1979	Skipat	5	J.W. Edwards	125	Pearl Necklace	122	The Very One	113	53,755	1:22.40	
1980	Misty Gallore	4	D. MacBeth	121	Gladiolus	122	Silver Ice	116	55,770	1:23.60	
1981	Skipat	7	C.B. Asmussen	124	Whispy's Lass	114	Secret Emotion	113	72,865	1:23.00	
1982	Lady Dean	4	D.A. Miller Jr	119	Sweet Revenge	114	Sinister Queen	114	46,768	1:24.20	
1982	The Wheel Turns	4	G. McCarron	121	Island Charm	122	Up the Flagpole	119	46,118	1:23.60	
1983	Stellarette	5	A. Delgado	114	Hoist Emy's Flag	116	Cheap Seats	122	74,100	1:24.40	
1984	Pleasure Cay	4	D.A. Miller Jr	114	Kattegat's Pride	117	Amanti	117	56,325	1:22.80	
1984	Bara Lass	5	D.A. Miller Jr	125	Owned by All	109	Willamae	113	55,025	1:24.00	
1985	Dumdedumdedum	3	D.A. Miller Jr	115	Kattegat's Pride	117	Amanti	117	87,993	1:25.00	

Year	Winner	Age	Jockey	Wt.	Second	Wt.	Third	Wt.	Win Value	Time	Beyer
1985	Flip's Pleasure	5	J.L. Samyn	115	Applause	120	Gene's Lady	109	71,793	1:24.00	
1986	Willowy Mood	4	B. Thornbug	115	Aerturas	116	Alabama Nana	119	73,840	1:25.40	
1987	Spring Beauty	4	J.A. Santos	115	Notches Trace	110	Pine Tree Lane	126	88,770	1:25.40	
1988	Psyched		K.J. Desormeaux	113	Spring Beauty	116	Kerygma	115	81,250	1:22.60	
1989	Tappiano	5	K.J. Desormeaux	123	Very Subtle	124	Tops in Taps	114	120,000	1:21.40	
1990	Amy Be Good	4	M.E. Smith	112	Channel Three	111	Banbury Fair	110	120,000	1:23.40	95
1991	Fappaburst	4	A. Cordero Jr	114	Devil's Orchid	118	Diva's Debut	116	120,000	1:23.20	104
1992	Wood So	4	M.G. Pino	113	Wide Country	120	W't for the Lady	111	120,000	1:24.40	97
1993	Moon Mist	4	T.G. Turner	112	Ritchie Trail	113	Femma	114	120,000	1:23.40	107
1994	Mixed Appeal	6	A.C. Salazar	111	Known as Nancy	111	Winka	115	120,000	1:23.20	94
1995	Smart 'n Noble	4	M.G. Pino	117	Dust Bucket	114	Gooni Goo Hoo	110	120,000	1:24.00	96
1996	Lottsa Talc	6	F.T. Alvarado	117	Up an Eighth	114	Evil's Pic	116	120,000	1:22.60	97
1997	Miss Golden Circle	5	R. Migliore	118	Lottsa Talc	119	Whaleneck	113	120,000	1:23.00	98
1998	J J'sdream	5	L.C. Reynolds	115	Palette Knife	113	Stylish Encore	114	150,000	1:24.20	102
1999	Passeggiata	5	M.G. Pino	113	Catinca	121	Nothing Special	108	150,000	1:23.40	97
2000	Tap to Music	5	J. Bravo	115	Her She Kisses	114	Di's Time	114	120,000	1:24.75	95
2001	Prized Stamp	4	T.L. Dunkelberger	113	Superduper Miss	114	Tax Affair	113	120,000	1:23.74	94
2002	Xtra Heat	4	H. Vega	128	Prized Stamp	114	Kimbralata	114	120,000	1:22.70	101
2003	Xtra Heat	5	R. Wilson	125	Carson Hollow	119	Spelling	113	120,000	1:24.76	99

Beyer Index: 98.29

LAZARO BARRERA MEMORIAL,
7 Furlongs, 3-Year-Olds, Hollywood Park, 2003 Purse:$150,000

Year	Winner	Age	Jockey	Wt.	Second	Wt.	Third	Wt.	Win Value	Time	Beyer
1953	Perfection	3	W. Shoemaker	118	Laska	112	Speedy Wave	115	10,375	1:23.20	
1954	Milla's Abbey	3	W. Shoemaker	112	Blessed Gal		Hassle		9,475	1:10.80	
1995	Flying Standby	3	C.W. Antley	115	Desert Pirate	119	Boundless Moment	118	40,200	1:09.00	101
1996	Future Quest	3	K.J. Desormeaux	122	Slews Royal Son	119	Tiger Talk	120	35,100	1:15.00	101
1998	Reraise	3	E. Delahoussaye	116	Souvenir Copy	122	Full Moon Madness	117	39,930	1:08.40	115
1999	Love That Red	3	G. Gomez	122	Apremont	118	O'Rey Fantasma	118	56,910	1:20.80	108
2000	Caller One	3	C.S. Nakatani	122	Dixie Union	122	Swept Overboard	122	60,960	1:21.00	116
2001	Early Flyer	3	C.J. McCarron	123	Squirtle Squirt	123	Top Hit	118	65,160	1:20.42	110
2002	Captain Squire	3	C.J. Rollins	123	Fonz's	123	Kamsack	117	90,000	1:21.95	100
2003	Blazonry	3	M.E. Smith	115	Fly to the Wire	116	Jimmy O	115	90,000	1:22.19	99

Beyer Index: 106.25

Run as the Playa Del Ray prior to 1999. Run at 6 furlongs, 1954, 1995, 1998; at 6 1/2 furlongs 1996

BERNARD BARUCH HANDICAP, 1 1/8 Miles (Turf),
3-Year-Olds and Up, Saratoga Race Course, 2003 Purse: $150,000

Year	Winner	Age	Jockey	Wt.	Second	Wt.	Third	Wt.	Win Value	Time	Beyer
1959	Middle Brother	3	R. Ussery	113	Bagdad	123	Nimmer	114	18,322	1:49.00	
1960	Tompion	3	M. Ycaza	123	Don Rickles	114	Careless John	116	18,127	1:50.00	
1961	Shield Bearer	6	M. Ycaza	117	Art Market	111	Gawain	110	18,980	1:47.00	
1962	Hitting Away	4	H. Woodhouse	122	Wise Ship	126	Niksar	111	18,752	1:42.20	
1963	Endymion	4	M. Sorrentino	111	Marlin Bay	111	David K.	113	18,980	1:45.80	
1964	Western Warrior	5	R. Ussery	119	Quick Pitch	117	Endymion	109	19,987	1:42.40	
1965	Quick Pitch	5	J. Combest	111	Flag	114	Circus	113	19,337	1:42.60	
1966	Assagai	3	L. Adams	115	Ginger Fizz	114	Northern D'm'n	113	19,727	1:40.00	
1967	Flit-to	4	H. Woodhouse	113	Spoon Bait	113	Flag	115	15,275	1:40.40	
1967	Fort Marcy	3	R. Turcotte	117	Assagai	126	Paoluccio	112	14,950	1:40.40	
1968	Go Marching	3	L. Adams	117	Jollify	109	Ski Lift	109	15,031	1:42.40	
1968	More Scents	4	A. Cordero Jr	126	Grace Born	111	Flit-to	117	14,544	1:42.60	
1969	Larceny Kid	3	L. Pincay Jr	112	Ludham	113	Baitman	110	15,307	1:41.00	
1969	Hawaii	5	M. Ycaza	122	Rhinelander II	113	Mara Lark	113	15,145	1:42.00	
1970	Big Shot II	5	A. Cordero Jr	111	Shelter Bay	111	Pleas'nt H'b'r	112	15,600	1:39.40	
1970	Bailar	5	A. Cordero Jr	112	Chompion	111	Naskra	110	15,762	1:39.80	
1971	Red Reality	5	J. Velasquez	117	Shelter Bay	120	Close Attention	112	21,180	1:42.20	
1972	Scrimsaw	4	R. Woodhouse	109	Maraschino II	111	New Alibhai	115	14,280	1:46.40	
1972	Chrisaway	4	R. Howard	110	North Flight	117	Apollo Nine	112	1,435	1:46.20	
1973	Tentam	4	J. Velasquez	118	Scrims'aw	111	Astray	114	14,265	1:45.40	
1973	Red Reality	7	J. Velasquez	120	Tri Jet	121	Ruritana	113	14,190	1:46.60	
1974	Golden Don	4	V. Bracciale Jr	113	Halo	119	Scantling	117	23,580	1:46.00	
1975	Salt Marsh	5	E. Maple	116			Drollery	112	18,060	1:49.80	
	Ward McAllister	4	D. Montoya	110							
1976	Intrepid Hero	4	E. Maple	123	Modred	118	Erwin Boy	126	22,530	1:50.40	
1977	Majestic Light	4	S. Hawley	126	Alias Smith	112	Clout	114	23,175	1:46.20	
1978	Dominion	6	J.L. Samyn	115	Bill Brill	111	Upper Nile	119	24,480	1:49.00	
1979	Overskate	4	R. Platts	128	Timbo	108	Native Courier	115	35,610	1:51.80	
1980	Premier Ministre	4	R.I. Encinas	116	Great Neck	112	Tiller	126	35,700	2:13.60	
1981	Native Courier	6	E. Maple	114	Manguin	105	Proctor	118	33,450	1:47.40	

Year	Winner	Age	Jockey	Wt.	Second	Wt.	Third	Wt.	Win Value	Time	Beyer
1981	Great Neck	5	A. Cordero Jr	119	War of Words	111	Match the Hatch	114	33,690	1:47.60	
1982	Pair of Deuces	4	R. Hernandez	115	Native Courier	117	McCann	112	36,300	1:47.80	
1983	Tantalizing	4	J.D. Bailey	115	Ten Below	115	Acaroid	115	34,140	1:48.80	
1983	Fray Star	5	O. Vergara	114	Fortnightly	113	Who's for Dinner	109	34,380	1:48.40	
1984	Win	4	A. Graell	112	Intensify	113	Cozzene	114	57,510	1:47.40	
1985	Win	5	R. Migliore	124	Cozzene	120	Sitzmark	112	59,400	1:47.00	
1986	Exclusive Partner	4	J. Velasquez	112	I'm a Banker	111	Creme Fraiche	117	82,200	1:50.80	
1987	Talakeno	7	A. Cordero Jr	115	Manila	127	Duluth	114	85,380	1:47.40	
1988	My Big Boy	5	R.P. Romero	113	Steinlen	120	Wanderkin	115	72,600	1:46.80	
1989	Steinlen	6	J.A. Santos	121	Soviet Lad	111	Brian's Time	112	73,920	1:51.00	
1990	Who's to Pay	4	J.L. Samyn	110	Steinlen	126	River of Sin	115	52,920	1:48.40	
1991	Double Booked	6	A. Madrid Jr	122	Who's to Pay	118	Solar Splendor	113	71,400	1:49.00	.101
1992	Fourstars Allstar	4	M.E. Smith	113	Lotus Pool	113	Maxigroom	114	70,680	1:46.00	.105
1993	Furiously	4	J.D. Bailey	119	Star of Cozzene	123	Royal Mountain Inn	114	70,320	1:45.40	.108
1994	Lure	5	M.E. Smith	125	Paradise Creek	126	Fourstardave	114	64,920	1:46.00	.112
1995	Fourstars Allstar	7	J.A. Santos	120	Turk Passer	114	Compadre	112	66,240	1:47.60	.107
1996	Volochine	5	P. Day	113	Green Means Go	116	Compadre	108	68,700	1:47.40	.105
1997	Sentimental Moi	7	C. P. Decarlo	112	Jambalaya Jazz	115	Boyce	120	66,480	1:46.00	.105
1998	Yagli	5	J.D. Bailey	121	Tamhid	113	Jambalaya Jazz	115	85,380	1:46.20	.105
1999	Middlesex Drive	4	S.J. Sellers	117	Tanghazi	114	Comic Strip	116	90,000	1:46.40	.104
2000	Hap	4	J.D. Bailey	115	Inexplicable	115	Draw Shot	114	90,000	1:45.82	.104
2001	Hap	5	J.D. Bailey	121	Royal Strand	115	Dr. Kashnikow	114	90,000	1:47.06	.107
2002	Del Mar Show	5	J.D. Bailey	120	Volponi	116	Forbidden Apple	121	90,000	1:48.51	.110
2003	Trademark	7	R. Migliore	114	Rouvres	116	Slew Valley	113	90,000	1:49.06	.110

Beyer Index; 106.38

BAYAKOA HANDICAP, 1 1/16 Miles,
Fillies and Mares, 3-Year-Olds and Up, Hollywood Park, 2003 Purse: $150,000

Year	Winner	Age	Jockey	Wt.	Second	Wt.	Third	Wt.	Win Value	Time	Beyer
1993	Golden Klair	3	CJ. McCarron	115	Pacific Squall	118	Cargo	116	63,500	1:41.20	.101
1994	Thirst for Peace	5	A. Solis	115	Glass Ceiling	117	Dancing Mirage	119	63,500	1:42.20	.101
1995	Pirate's Revenge	4	C.W. Antley	119	Urbane	120	Ashtabula	116	61,900	1:41.80	.101
1996	Listening	3	C.J. McCarron	120	Cat's Cradle	120	Belle's Flag	117	64,920	1:42.60	.102
1997	Sharp Cat	3	A. Solis	121	WALKOVER				60,000	1:42.60	
1998	Manistique	3	G.L. Stevens	119	India Divina	114	Numero Uno	115	60,000	1:42.40	.108
1999	Manistique	4	C.S. Nakatani	124	Snowberg	115	Riboletta	116	90,000	1:43.00	.105
2000	Feverish	5	E. Delahoussaye	119	Gourmet Girl	118	Lazy Slusan	117	90,000	1:42.26	.104
2001	Starrer	3	J.D. Bailey	118	Queenie Belle	118	Tropical Lady	115	90,000	1:42.52	.99
2002	Starrer	4	P.A. Valenzuela	118	Cee's Elegance	113	Angel gift	115	90,000	1:41.74	.105
2003	Star Parade	4	V. Espinoza	112	Adoration	121	Bare Necessities	119	90,000	1:41.02	.106

Beyer Index: 103.2

(STONERSIDE) BEAUMONT STAKES, About 7 Furlongs,
3-Year-Old Fillies, Keeneland Race Course, 2003 Purse: $250,000

Year	Winner	Age	Jockey	Wt.	Second	Wt.	Third	Wt.	Win Value	Time	Beyer
1990	Go for Wand	3	R.P. Romero	122	Trumpet's Blare	119	Seaside Attraction	119	53,983	1:26.40	.104
1991	Ifyoucouldseemenow	3	M.A. Pedroza	122	Versailles Treaty	114	Ever a Lady	114	54,275	1:27.00	
1992	Fluttery Danseur	3	S.J. Sellers	122	Miss Iron Smoke	119	Spinning Round	122	53,918	1:27.40	.89
1993	Roamin Rachel	3	C.W. Antley	122	Added Asset	114	Fit to Lead	122	69,998	1:26.40	.98
1994	Her Temper	3	P. Day	112	Lotta Dancing	113	Term Limits	121	67,456	1:28.40	.84
1995	Dixieland Gold	3	D. Penna	118	Niner's Home	113	Conquistadoress	118	69,874	1:27.40	.94
1996	Golden Gale	3	M.E. Smith	115	Birr	115	Bright Time	115	84,398	1:26.00	.96
1997	Screamer	3	R.J. Albarado	112			Move	121	57,041	1:28.00	.91
	Make Haste	3	P. Day	112							
1998	Star of Broadway	3	P. Day	119	Santaria	119	Bourbon Belle	119	91,140	1:26.60	.99
1999	Swingin On Ice	3	R.J. Albarado	115	Secret Hills	115	Appealing Phylly	123	83,917	1:25.30	.95
2000	Sahara Gold	3	J.D. Bailey	123	Swept Away	118	Darling My Darling	116	84,847	1:26.58	.97
2001	Xtra Heat	3	R. Wilson	120	Mountain Bird	116	Raging Fever	123	155,000	1:27.86	.89
2002	Proper Gamble	3	J.J. Castellano	118	Respectful	116	Vicki Vallencourt	118	155,000	1:28.79	.89
2003	My Boston Gal	3	P. Day	120	Bird Town	118	Midnight Cry	118	155,000	1:26.87	.101

Beyer Index: 94.31

BELMONT BREEDERS' CUP HANDICAP, 1 1/8 Miles (Turf),
3-Year-Olds and Up, Belmont Park, 2003 Purse: $209,600

Year	Winner	Age	Jockey	Wt.	Second	Wt.	Third	Wt.	Win Value	Time	Beyer
1986	Danger's Hour	4	J.D. Bailey	116	Salem Drive	116	Silver Voice	112	95,280	1:40.80	
1987	Talakeno	7	A. Cordero Jr	117	Lightning Leap	110	Glaros	111	93,090	1:49.40	
1988	Steinlen	5	P. Day	120	Iron Courage	113	Barood	110	93,540	1:43.40	

Year	Winner	Age	Jockey	Wt.	Second	Wt.	Third	Wt.	Win Value	Time	Beyer
1989	Highland Springs	5	K.J. Desormeaux	117	Maceo	113	Slew City Slew	118	93,180	1:39.20	
1990	Who's to Pay	4	J.D. Bailey	113	Jalaajel	115	Caltech	120	93,570	1:46.00	
1991	Solar Splendor	4	W.H. McCauley	113	Who's to Pay	118	Jalaajel	114	93,210	1:41.00	106
1992	Roman Envoy	4	C. Perret	113	Lotus Pool	114	Daarik	114	34,800	1:41.40	106
1993	Fourstars Allstar	5	J.A. Santos	116	Lech	115	Cleone	113	92,880	1:39.80	109
1994	A in Sociology	4	Samyn JL	116	Fourstars Allstar	119	Home of the Free	114	34,290	1:40.00	104
1995	Dove Hunt	4	P. Day	121	Fly Cry	116	Unfinished Symph	122	92,970	1:40.00	107
1996	Gentleman Beau	4	J.A. Santos	114	Kiri's Clown	114	Volochine	116	127,140	1:41.00	105
1997	Fortitude	4	R.G. Davis	112	Green Means Go	113	Boyce	118	126,600	1:38.40	104
1998	Subordination	4	D.R. Flores	121	Yagli	122	Bomfim	114	127,020	1:45.80	111
1999	With the Flow	4	J.A. Santos	114	Comic Strip	118	Wised Up	112	127,620	1:49.20	104
2000	Forbidden Apple	5	J.A. Santos	114	Val's Prince	118	Altibr	115	126,000	1:51.73	107
2002	Startac	4	J.D. Bailey	116	Volponi	117	Dr. Kashnikow	115	125,160	1:46.60	105
2003	Della Francesca	4	J.F. Chavez	114	Rouvres	116	Volponi	119	125,760	1:47.48	102

Beyer Index: 105.83

Not run in 2001

BEST PAL, 2-Year-Olds,
6 1/2 Furlongs, Del Mar, 2003 Purse: $150,000

Year	Winner	Age	Jockey	Wt.	Second	Wt.	Third	Wt.	Win Value	Time	Beyer
1972	Brave Dance	2	F. Toro	120	Groshawk	115	River Lad	118	12,625	1:29.80	
1973	Battery E.	2	W. Harris	115	Jenny's Boy	120	Ma'hen McTavish	115	12,750	1:30.60	
1974	Diabolo	2	W. Shoemaker	120	Trond Sang	114	Neat Claim	114	13,050	1:35.60	
1975	Crazy Channon	2	D. Pierce	115	Classy Surgeon	114	Lexington Laugh	117	15,500	1:37.20	
1976	Visible	2	L. Pincay Jr	117	Habitony	114	Replant	115	16,200	1:35.80	
1977	Spanish Way	2	L. Pincay Jr	117	Tampoy	114	Misrepresentation	114	16,700	1:36.00	
1978	Flying Paster	2	D. Pierce	117	Roman Oblisk	117	Runaway Hit	114	19,500	1:35.60	
1979	Doonesbury	2	S. Hawley	113	Executive Counsel	115	Defiance	115	19,300	1:35.40	
1980	Bold and Gold	2	D.C. Hall	113	Splendid Spruce	115	Sir Dancer	113	22,550	1:37.40	
1981	The Captain	2	L. Pincay Jr	117	Distant Heart	115	Gato del Sol	115	26,400	1:36.60	
1982	Roving Boy	2	E. Delahoussaye	115	Encourager	115	Full Choke	117	30,650	1:35.40	
1983	Party Leader	2	R. Sibille	116	Juliet's Pride	115	Gumboy	115	31,550	1:37.20	
1984	Saratoga Six	2	A. Cordero Jr	120	Private Jungle	117	Indigenous	115	31,650	1:36.80	
1985	Swear	2	E. Delahoussaye	116	Bright Tom	116	Smokey Orbit	114	32,750	1:36.60	
1986	Temperate Sil	2	W. Shoemaker	117	Polar Jet	117	Gold on Green	115	32,250	1:23.00	
1987	Purdue King	2	C.J. McCarron	121	Accomplish Ridge	117	Mixed Pleasure	119	38,500	1:23.20	
1988	Rob an Plunder	2	C.J. McCarron	119	Mountain Ghost	117	Pokarito	117	47,750	1:23.00	
1989	A Sir Dancer	2	E. Delahoussaye	117	Drag Race	115	Patches	113	47,550	1:23.00	
1990	Best Pal	2	P.A. Valenzuela	119	Xray	117	Sunshine Machine	117	46,575	1:22.20	
1991	Scherando	2	F. Mena	121	Star Recruit	117	Prince Wild	119	47,620	1:22.40	92
1992	Devil Diamond	2	K.J. Desormeaux	117	Wheeler Oil	119	Crafty	117	45,900	1:22.60	86
1993	Creston	3	C.A. Black	117	Troyalty	121	Flying Sensation	115	45,900	1:16.20	89
1994	Timber Country	2	Solis A	117	Desert Mirage	115	Supremo	117	46,575	1:16.60	79
1995	Cobra King	2	Baze RA	117	Northern Afleet	117	Desert Native	117	60,350	1:15.80	93
1996	Swiss Yodeler	2	A. Solis	121	Golden Bronze	117	Deeds Not Words	117	65,550	1:16.00	97
1997	Old Topper	2	A. Solis	117	King of the Wild	117	Souvenir Copy	117	68,825	1:16.40	92
1998	Worldly Manner	2	G.L. Stevens	117	Domination	117	Waki American	115	65,580	1:16.60	96
1999	Dixie Union	2	A. Solis	121	Exchange Rate	117	Captain Steve	117	90,000	1:16.40	97
2000	Flame Thrower	2	C.S. Nakatani	117	Trailthefox	121	Legendary Weave	117	90,000	1:16.51	96
2001	Officer	2	V. Espinoza	121	Metatron	117	Essence of Dubai	117	90,000	1:15.08	106
2002	Kafwain	2	V. Espinoza	117	Chief Planner	117	Outta Here	117	90,000	1:17.00	93
2003	Perfect Moon	2	P.A. Valenzuela	122	Capitano	118	Military Mandate	118	90,000	1:16.90	84

Beyer Index: 92.31

BEVERLY HILLS HANDICAP, 1 1/4 Miles (Turf Course), Fillies and Mares,
3-Year-Olds and Up, Hollywood Park, 2003 Purse: $200,000

Year	Winner	Age	Jockey	Wt.	Second	Wt.	Third	Wt.	Win Value	Time	Beyer
1938	Brown Jade	4	N. Richardson	115	Rolling Ball	107	Pala Chief	104	4,725	1:45.80	
1939	Bubbling Boy	3	J. Robertson	118	Smoky Snyder	112	Maysette	108	2,110	1:40.20	
1968	Pink Pigeon	4	W. Harris	127	Desert Law	118	Pombal	114	19,700	2:15.20	
1969	Miss Ribot	4	D. Pierce	116	Courageously	111	Princess Endeavour	109	16,850	2:16.40	
1970	Pattee Canyon	5	W. Shoemaker	124	Blow Up II	117	Summer Sorrow	108	32,950	2:13.00	
1971	Manta	4	L. Pincay Jr	127	Typecast	116	Hail the Grey	107	39,400	2:12.20	
1972	Hill Circus	4	W. Shoemaker	115	Manta	116	Typecast	127	37,600	2:13.20	
1973	Le Cle	4	W. Shoemaker	119	Pallisima	115	Convenience	124	49,900	2:14.80	
1974	La Zanzara	4	D. Pierce	120	Mon Miel	114	Dogtooth Violet	116	38,000	2:14.20	
1975	La Zanzara	5	D. Pierce	122	Dulcia	123	Mercy Dee	110	46,500	2:14.80	
1976	Bastonera II	5	L. Pincay Jr	121	Miss Toshiba	124	Miss Tokyo	115	38,800	1:50.20	
1977	Swingtime	5	F. Toro	120	Fortunate Betty	115	Bastonera II	126	25,200	1:48.40	
1978	Swingtime	6	F. Toro	119	Grande Brisa	115	Drama Critic	118	48,000	1:48.40	
1979	Giggling Girl	5	C.J. McCarron	117	Country Queen	123	More So	116	50,100	1:47.60	

Year	Winner	Age	Jockey	Wt.	Second	Wt.	Third	Wt.	Win Value	Time	Beyer
1980	Country Queen	5	L. Pincay Jr	122	Wishing Well	122	The Very One	117	50,550	1:47.40	
1981	Track Robbery	5	P.A. Valenzuela	120	Princess Karenda	121	Save Wild Life	115	61,800	1:46.80	
1982	Sangue	4	W. Shoemaker	119	Ack's Secret	123	Miss Huntington	117	64,300	1:47.40	
1983	Absentia	4	F. Toro	115	Latrone	110	Triple Tipple	118	68,500	1:49.00	
1984	Royal Heroine	4	F. Toro	123	Adored	121	Comedy Act	118	93,200	1:47.20	
1985	Johnica	4	G.L. Stevens	115	Estrapade	125	L'Attrayante	118	61,900	1:48.20	
1986	Estrapade	6	F. Toro	122	Treizieme	115	Sauna	117	63,800	1:59.00	
1987	Auspiciante	6	P.A. Valenzuela	117	Reloy	120	Festivity	114	64,600	1:47.20	
1988	Fitzwilliam Place	4	A. Gryder	119	Ladanum	114	Chapel of Dreams	117	98,200	1:47.20	
1989	Claire Marine	4	C.J. McCarron	120	Fitzwilliam Place	121	No Review	116	93,100	1:47.20	
1990	Beautiful Melody	4	K.J. Desormeaux	115			Stylish Star	116	82,300	1:47.00	99
	Reluctant Guest	4	R.G. Davis	116							
1991	Alcando	5	J. Garcia	113	Fire the Groom	120	Countus In	117	130,200	1:46.40	106
1992	Flawlessly	4	C.J. McCarron	122	Kostroma	124	Alcando	113	184,000	1:47.00	103
1993	Flawlessly	5	C.J. McCarron	123	Jolypha	121	Party Cited	117	180,200	1:47.00	108
1994	Corrazona	4	G.L. Stevens	119	Hollywood Wildcat	124	Flawlessly	124	188,400	1:47.40	102
1995	Alpride	4	C.J. McCarron	115	Possibly Perfect	124	Wandesta	119	185,000	1:46.60	108
1996	Different	4	C.J. McCarron	117	Bail Out Becky	118	Flagbird	118	163,800	2:00.60	105
1997	Windsharp	6	C.S. Nakatani	122	Different	121	Donna Viola	122	180,000	2:00.60	108
1998	Squeak	4	G.L. Stevens	115	Sixy Saint	115	Freeport Flight	114	180,000	2:01.56	102
1999	Virginie	5	L. Pincay Jr	118	Tranquility Lake	122	Keeper Hill	118	150,000	2:00.21	108
2000	Happyanunoit	5	B. Blanc	121	Sweet Life	115	Polaire	116	150,000	1:59.32	107
2001	Astra	5	K.J. Desormeaux	121	Happyanunoit	122	Kalypso Katie	116	120,000	1:59.61	107
2002	Astra	6	K.J. Desormeaux	124	Peu a Peu	116	Crazy Ensign	117	150,000	1:58.56	107
2003	Voodoo Dancer	5	C.S. Nakatani	120	Dublino	122	Megahertz	117	120,000	2:00.80	106

Beyer Index: 105.43

Distance 1 1/16 miles for California foals in 1938; 1 mile for California-foaled 3-year-olds (both sexes) in 1939; 1 3/8 miles 1968-75; 1 1/4 miles in 1986. Run on main course in 1938 and 1939

BLACK-EYED SUSAN, 1 1/8 Miles,
3-Year-old Fillies, Pimlico, 2003 Purse: $200,0000

Year	Winner	Age	Jockey	Wt.	Second	Wt.	Third	Wt.	Win Value	Time	Beyer
1952	Real Delight	3	E. Arcaro	121	Dinewisely	121	Parading Lady	121	16,500	1:51.80	
1953	Spinning Top	3	C. Burr	121	Milspals	121	Wings o' Morn	121	17,750	1:47.20	
1954	Queen Hopeful	3	J. Adams	121	Gweny G.	121	Walla	121	16,550	1:45.80	
1955	High Voltage	3	E. Arcaro	121	Bless Pat	121	Hen Party	121	1,100	1:46.20	
1956	Princess Turia	3	W. Hartack	121	Beyond	121	Hadareward	121	15,500	1:45.60	
1957	Pillow Talk	3	W. Hartack	121	Jota Jota	121	Woodlawn	121	17,350	1:45.00	
1958	Daumay	3	C. Rogers	121	Movitave	121	Stay Smoochie	121	16,100	1:46.60	
1959	Toulene	3	K. Korte	121	Corvina	121	San Ju Lee	121	15,090	1:48.80	
1960	Airmans Guide	3	W. Harmatz	121	Chalvedele	121	Warlike	121	14,862	1:46.20	
1961	Funloving	3	R, Ussery	121	My Portrait	121	First Sitting	121	15,665	1:45.80	
1962	Batter Up	3	L. Adams	121	Narola	121	Spooky Creature	121	16,347	1:45.80	
1963	Nalee	3	W. Chambers	121	Medici	121	Batteur	121	15,975	1:46.80	
1964	Bold Queen	3	T. Lee	121	Sceree	121	Sabemar	121	15,600	1:47.00	
1965	Sue Baru	3	R. Witmer	121	Wendy's Crown	121	Cavans Rose	121	15,584	1:48.40	
1966	Holly-O	3	J. Culmone	121	Chalina	121	Justakiss	121	18,980	1:44.80	
1967	Farest Nan	3	O. Rosado	111	Back in Paris	111	Devotedly	111	18,882	1:44.00	
1968	Singing Rain	3	G. Patterson	111	Syrian Sea	121	Copper Canyon	111	22,360	1:44.20	
1969	Process Shot	3	C. Baltazar	121	Loyal Ruler	113	Around the Horn	111	22,880	1:44.00	
1970	Office Queen	3	C.H. Marquez	118	Princess Roycraft	116	Artists Proof	116	22,522	1:43.80	
1971	At Arms Length	3	R. Barnes	116	Movette	116	Sew to Bed	114	23,367	1:43.20	
1972	Summer Guest	3	R. Turcotte	114	Twixt	113	Barely Even	121	23,140	1:44.00	
1973	Fish Wife	3	D. Gargan	111	Guided Missile	112	Out Cold	116	2,265	1:44.00	
1974	Blowing Rock	3	A. Agnello	111	Heydairya	111	Shantung Silk	116	22,425	1:43.00	
1975	My Juliet	3	A. Hill	116	Gala Lil	114	Funalon	121	37,635	1:44.00	
1976	What a Summer	3	C.J. McCarron	111	Dearly Precious	121	Artfully	114	37,895	1:42.40	
1977	Small Raja	3	A. Cordero Jr	114	Northern Sea	121	Enthused	116	54,503	1:42.80	
1978	Caesar's Wish	3	D. Wright	121	Jevalin	116	Miss Baja	121	55,120	1:44.20	
1979	Davona Dale	3	J. Velasquez	121	Phoebe's Donkey	118	Plankton	121	72,670	1:42.60	
1980	Weber City Miss	3	V. Bracciale Jr	118	Bishop's Ring	111	Champagne Star	114	74,620	1:44.40	
1981	Dame Mysterieuse	3	E. Maple	121	Wayward Lass	121	Real Prize	121	72,800	1:44.20	
1982	Delicate Ice	3	D. Brumfield	114	Trove	121	Milingo	121	74,945	1:44.60	
1983	Batna	3	L.D. Ruch	121	Lovin Touch	116	Weekend Surprise	121	75,400	1:42.40	
1984	Lucky Lucky Lucky	3	A. Cordero Jr	121	Sintra	116	Duo Disco	121	100,060	1:41.20	
1985	Koluctoo's Jill	3	C.J. McCarron	121	Denver Express	116	A Joyful Spray	116	74,295	1:43.00	
1986	Family Style	3	C.J. McCarron	121	Steel Maiden	121	Firgie's Jule	121	100,385	1:44.60	
1987	Grecian Flight	3	C. Perret	121	Bal du Bois	121	Arctic Cloud	121	101,750	1:44.20	
1988	Costly Shoes	3	P. Day	121	Thirty Eight Go Go	121	Lost Kitty	121	97,915	1:44.80	
1989	Imaginary Lady	3	G. Stevens	122	Some Romance	122	Moonlight Martini	117	150,000	1:48.20	
1990	Charon	3	C. Perret	122	Valay Maid	122	Bright Candles	122	150,000	1:48.40	95

Year	Winner	Age	Jockey	Wt.	Second	Wt.	Third	Wt.	Win Value	Time	Beyer
1991	Wide Country	3	S.N. Chavez	122	John's Decision	117	Nalees Pin	117	150,000	1:51.20	97
1992	Miss Legality	3	C.J. McCarron	122	Known Feminist	114	Diamond Duo	114	150,000	1:51.00	94
1993	Aztec Hill	3	M.E. Smith	122	Traverse City	114	Jacody	117	120,000	1:49.60	103
1994	Calipha	3	R. Wilson	114	Bunting	114	Golden Braids	114	120,000	1:51.00	95
1995	Serena's Song	3	G.L. Stevens	122	Conquistadoress	115	Rare Opportunity	115	120,000	1:48.40	113
1996	Mesabi Maiden	3	M. E. Smith	115	Cara Rafaela	122	Ginny Lynn	122	120,000	1:51.00	93
1997	Salt It	3	C.H. Marquez Jr.	117	Buckeye Search	122	Holiday Ball	115	120,000	1:50.40	97
1998	Added Gold	3	J.R. Velazquez	115	Tappin' Ginger	115	Hansel's Girl	117	120,000	1:49.60	95
1999	Silverbulletday	3	G.L. Stevens	122	Dreams Gallore	117	Vee Vee Star	115	120,000	1:47.80	109
2000	Jostle	3	K.J. Desormeaux	122	March Magic	122	Impending Bear	117	120,000	1:52.56	93
2001	Two Item Limit	3	R. Migliore	122	Indy Glory	117	Tap Dance	122	120,000	1:50.84	96
2002	Chamrousse	3	J.D. Bailey	115	Shop Till You Drop	117	Autumn Creek	115	120,000	1:51.61	92
2003	Roar Emotion	3	J.R. Velazquez	122	Fircroft	119	Santa Catarina	117	120,000	1:52.33	93

Beyer Index: 97.5

BONNIE MISS, 1 1/8 Miles,
3-Year-Old Fillies, Gulfstream Park, 2003 Purse: $200,000

Year	Winner	Age	Jockey	Wt.	Second	Wt.	Third	Wt.	Win Value	Time	Beyer
1971	Able Jan	5	R. Breen	113	Director	113	Field Avenue	113	10,035	1:45.20	
1972	Candid Catherine	3	J. Vasquez	117	Barely Even	117	Mrs. Cornwallis	114	21,150	1:23.20	
1973	Fun Palace	4	E. Fires	111	Hasty Jude	119	Viewpoise	113	14,145	1:44.40	
1974	City Girl	3	E. Maple	112	Maud Muller	112	Double Bend	112	21,540	1:22.60	
1975	Cheers Marion	4	M. Castaneda	113	Hinterland	116	Sum'r Sprite	114	10,207	1:42.20	
1975	Diomedia	4	M. Castaneda	116	Gems and Roses	122	Exclusive Lady	113	10,207	1:42.00	
1976	Get Swinging	5	A. Ramos	111	Twenty Six Girl	112	North of B'st'n	114	17,400	1:45.80	
1977	Herecomesthebride	3	L. Saumell	114	Grand Luxe	112	Rich Soil	112	20,970	1:21.80	
1978	Jevalin	3	M. Solomone	114	Raise a Companion	110	Sharp Belle	114	18,600	1:23.80	
1979	Davona Dale	3	J. Velasquez	122	Candy Eclair	122	Prove Me Special	114	17,546	1:21.00	
1980	Lien	3	E. Maple	112	Wistful	115	Champagne Ginny	114	18,510	1:22.00	
1981	Dame Mysterieuse	3	J.L. Samyn	118	Banner Gala	113	Heavenly Cause	121	52,335	1:44.40	
1982	Christmas Past	3	J. Vasquez	121	Norsan	113	Our Darling	112	34,830	1:44.20	
1983	Unaccompanied	3	R. Woodhouse	116	Bright Crocus	114	Dewl Reason	112	58,320	1:45.40	
1984	Miss Oceana	3	E. Maple	121	Enumerating	114	Katrinka	112	70,605	1:42.40	
1985	Lucy Manette	3	C. Perret	121	Outstandingly	121	Micki Bracken	121	72,240	1:44.80	
1986	Patricia J.K.	3	J.A. Santos	121	Noranc	121	Family Style	121	135,570	1:45.20	
1987	Mar Mar	3	W.A. Guerra	121	Super Cook	121	Without Feathers	118	90,000	1:44.60	
1988	On to Royalty	3	C. Perret	121	Tomorrow's Child	121	Make Change	112	120,000	1:45.60	
1989	Open Mind	3	A. Cordero Jr	121	Seattle Meteor	121	Surging	114	120,000	1:43.80	
1990	Charon	3	E. Fires	121	Trumpet's Blare	121	De La Devil	121	120,000	1:44.60	
1991	Withallprobability	3	C. Perret	117	Fancy Ribbons	117	Outlasting	114	120,000	1:43.20	
1992	Spectacular Sue	3	W.S. Ramos	114	Spinning Round	117	Tricky Cinderella	112	120,000	1:44.00	92
1993	Dispute	3	J.D. Bailey	114	Sky Beauty	114	Lunar Spook	117	120,000	1:43.60	95
1994	Inside Information	3	M.E. Smith	114	Cinnamon Sugar	113	Jade Flush	114	120,000	1:42.80	93
1995	Mia's Hope	3	K.L. Chapman	117	Minister Wife	119	Incredible Blues	117	120,000	1:44.80	91
1996	My Flag	3	J.D. Bailey	117	Escena	114	La Rosa	117	120,000	1:45.60	100
1997	Glitter Woman	3	M.E. Smith	117	Southern Playgirl	119	Dixie Flag	114	120,000	1:43.20	103
1998	Banshee Breeze	3	R.P. Romero	114	Santaria	114	Cotton House Bay	114	120,000	1:46.40	89
1999	Three Ring	3	J.R. Velazquez	122	Olympic Charmer	117	Marley Vale	117	120,000	1:43.60	105
2000	Cash Run	3	J.D. Bailey	119	Deed I Do	114	Bejoyfulandrejoyce	114	120,000	1:44.11	96
2001	Tap Dance	3	J.D. Bailey	122	Halo Reailty	117	Unbridled Lassie	122	120,000	1:52.05	87
2002	Chamrousse	3	J.D. Bailey	115	Shop Till You Drop	117	Autumn Creek	115	120,000	1:51.61	92
2003	Ivanavinalot	3	J.R. Velazquez	122	My Boston Gal	120	Holiday Lady	118	120,000	1:50.72	95

Beyer Index: 94.83

BOWLING GREEN HANDICAP, 1 3/8 Miles (Turf),
3-Year-Olds and Up, Belmont Park, 2003 Purse: $150,000

Year	Winner	Age	Jockey	Wt.	Second	Wt.	Third	Wt.	Win Value	Time	Beyer
1958	Rafty	6	E. Guerin	124	One-Eyed King	116	Master Boing	122	18,810	2:17.20	
1959	Bell Hop	4	R. Ussery	116	King Grail	109	Pop Corn	120	18,810	2:14.60	
1960	Amber Morn	4	P. Anderson	113	Dunce	123	North Pole II	117	38,010	2:29.20	
1961	Dead Center	4	J. Yother	107	Wolfram	130	Leix	107	25,772	2:29.80	
1962	Royal Record	4	H. Woodhouse	110	Wise Ship	126	S'shine Cake	110	18,752	2:33.20	
1963	Pollingford	4	W. Harmatz	111	Tutankhamen	127	Hunter's Rock	107	18,070	2:45.40	
1964	Cedar Key	4	M. Ycaza	130	Irish Dandy	110	Chicoco	110	18,752	2:41.80	
1965	Or et Argent	4	W. Blum	113	Hot Dust	119	Pr'ce o'Pilsen	112	38,675	2:40.60	
1966	Moontrip	5	L. Adams	112	Flag	113	Knightly Manner	116	38,610	2:38.80	
1967	Poker	4	W. Boland	112	Assagai	127	Buckpasser	135	36,010	2:41.40	
1968	High Hat	4	E. Belmonte	128	Irish Rebellion	125	Ruffled Feathers	119	36,465	2:29.80	
1969	Czar Alexander	4	J. Velasquez	126	Ruffled Feathers	113	Jean-Pierre	115	38,610	2:27.40	
1970	Fort Marcy	6	J. Velasquez	127	Drumtop	120	Hitchcock	118	37,310	2:26.60	
1971	Drumtop	5	C. Baltazar	124	Fort Marcy	128	Practicante	115	34,080	2:25.40	

Year	Winner	Age	Jockey	Wt.	Second	Wt.	Third	Wt.	Win Value	Time	Beyer
1972	Run the Gantlet	4	R. Woodhouse	121	king Klig	112	Onandaga	114	33,600	2:27.80	
1973	Summer Guest	4	J. Vasquez	119	Red Reality	124	Astray	113	34,200	2:29.20	
1974	Take Off	5	R. Turcotte	120	Garland of Roses	109	Astray	126	34,260	2:26.40	
1975	Barcas	4	M. Castaneda	113	Drollery	113	Telefonico	124	33,240	2:32.20	
1976	Erwin Boy	5	R. Turcotte	120	Drollery	111	Trumpeter Swan	111	34,740	2:26.00	
1977	Hunza Dancer	5	J. Cruguet	117	Improviser	122	Noble Dancer II	117	68,580	1:58.80	
1978	Tiller	4	J. Fell	117	Proud Arion	111	Bowl Game	124	70,260	2:12.40	
1979	Overskate	4	R. Platts	117	Waya	125	Bowl Game	123	84,525	2:11.40	
1980	Sten	5	J. Fell	117	John Henry	128	Lyphard's Wish	120	86,550	2:13.20	
1981	Great Neck	5	A. Cordero Jr	114	Key to Content	119	Match the Hatch	115	84,450	2:12.00	
1982	Open Call	4	J. Velasquez	124	Johnny Dance	114	Baltimore Canyon	116	89,850	2:24.80	
1983	Tantalizing	4	J. Vasquez	113	Sprink	113	Majesty's Prince	122	105,120	2:14.80	
1984	Hero's Honor	4	J.D. Bailey	120	Nassipour	110	Super Sunrise	123	144,120	2:14.00	
1985	Sharannpour	5	A. Cordero Jr	114	Flying Pigeon	116	Equalize	116	156,300	2:18.20	
1986	Uptown Swell	4	E. Maple	114	Palace Panther	116	Equalize	116	147,690	2:14.80	
1987	Theatrical	5	P. Day	123	Akabir	116	Dance of Life	121	144,960	2:14.00	
1988	Coeur de Lion	4	C. Perret	117	Pay the Butler	112	Milesius	115	151,680	2:13.40	
1989	El Senor	5	W.H. McCauley	117	Coeur de Lion	121	Pay the Butler	116	144,960	2:18.60	
1990	With Approval	4	C. Perret	118	Chenin Blanc	113	El Senor	121	113,280	2:10.20	108
1991	Three Coins Up	3	J.D. Bailey	111	Phantom Breeze	117	Beyond the Lake	115	120,000	2:10.80	105
1992	Wall Street Dancer	4	P. Day	114	Fraise	113	Libor	109	120,000	2:12.80	101
1993	Dr. Kiernan	4	C. Antley	114	Spectacular Tide	111	Lomitas	117	90,000	2:17.60	106
1994	Turk Passer	4	J.R. Velazquez	110	Sea Hero	117	Fraise	124	90,000	2:13.20	109
1995	Sentimental Moi	5	R.B. Perez	111	Awad	121	Proceeded	108	90,000	2:15.40	107
1996	Flag Down	6	J.A. Santos	118	Broadway Flyer	118	Diplomatic Jet	119	90,000	2:13.20	106
1997	Influent	6	J.L.Samyn	120	Flag Down	118	Notoriety	108	90,000	2:11.00	107
1998	Cetewayo	4	J.R. Velazquez	112	Officious	113	Chief Bearhart	124	90,000	2:13.40	106
1999	Honor Glide	5	J.A. Santos	114	Parade Ground	118	Fahris*	114	90,000	2:11.00	105
	Federal Trial finished third but was disqualified and placed fourth										
2000	Elhayq	5	S.X. Bridgmohan	113	Yankee Dollar	110	Carpenter's Halo	115	90,000	2:13.81	106
2001	King Cugat	4	J.D. Bailey	119	Slew Valley	112	Man From Wicklow	112	90,000	2:10.62	114
2002	Whitmore's Conn	4	S.X. Bridgmohan	112	Staging Post	115	Moon Solitaire	116	90,000	2:13.43	102
2003	Whitmore's Conn	5	J.L. Samyn	116	Quest Star	117	Macaw	116	90,000	2:15.92	105

Beyer Index: 106.21

(LANE'S END) BREEDERS' FUTURITY, 1 1/16 Miles, 2-Year-Olds, Keeneland, 2003 Purse: $400,000

Year	Winner	Age	Jockey	Wt.	Second	Wt.	Third	Wt.	Win Value	Time	Beyer
1910	Housemaid	2	P. Powers	115	Golden Egg	115	Little Oasis	115	2,543	:48.60	
1911	The Manager	2	T. Koerner	115	Bachelor Girl	115	Wheelwright	115	4,848	:48.00	
1912	Helios	2	Molesworth	115	Forward	121	Chris Star	118	4,154	:54.00	
1913	Imperator	2	B. Steele	115	John Gund	118	B. Brother	115	5,803	1:00.60	
1914	Luke	2	W.W. Taylor	118	Chaimers	118	Ed Crump	118	3,800	1:00.60	
1915	Kinney	2	J. Loftus	118	Jacoba	115	Bellita	115	4,259	1:00.80	
1916	Harry Kelly	2	G. Garner	118	Westy Hogan	118	Yeymila	115	3,614	:58.80	
1917	Escoba	2	W. Knapp	123	Atalanta	115	Gipsy Queen	115	7,246	1:10.60	
1918	Colonel Livingston	2	W. Lilley	120	Col. Taylor	118	Ginger	118	5,574	1:09.60	
1919	Blazes	2	C. Robinson	123	Peace Pennant	118	Lorraine	115	6,018	1:09.60	
1920	Believe Idle Hour	2	E. Pool	120	Star Voter	123	Sir T. Kean	118	6,393	1:09.20	
1921	Gentilly	2	H.J. Burke	122	Sayno	114	Jahn Finn	127	12,827	1:11.60	
1922	Donges	2	E. Fator	127	Easter Bells	122	Sweetheart	110	15,018	1:09.80	
1923	Worthmore	2	W. Kelsay	122	Sayno	114	Black Gold	122	16,201	1:11.40	
1924	Candy Kid	2	I. Parke	122	Almadel	122	Annihilator	122	15,984	1:12.20	
1925	Flight of Time	2	J. Malben	127	Bubbling Over	127	Helen's Babe	119	16,527	1:08.80	
1926	Wood Lore	2	J.H. Burke	122	Candy Queen	119	Creek Indian	122	17,899	1:11.00	
1927	Wacker Drive	2	J. Heupel	122	Happy Time	127	Blackwood	122	18,070	1:13.00	
1928	Current	2	E. Pool	124	Windy City	122	Clyde Van Dusen	122	21,231	1:08.80	
1929	Gallant Knight	2	C. McCrossen	122	Busy	122	Galaday	119	19,229	1:12.60	
1930	Mate	2	M. Garner	122	Pennate	122	Blind Bowboy	122	16,975	1:09.20	
1931	The Bull	2	R. Workman	122	Air Pilot	122	Kakapo	119	17,325	1:09.80	
1932	Technique	2	T. Elston	119	The Darb	122	Caterwaul	127	15,099	1:10.40	
1933	Mata Hari	2	H. Schutte	124	Giggling	119	Discovery	122	15,064	1:09.60	
1938	Johnstown	2	J. Stout	119	Allegro	117	Lightspur	117	9,335	1:11.40	
1939	Roman Flag	2	L. Haas	119	Dit	117	Star Chance	117	10,866	1:10.60	
1940	Whirlaway	2	J. Longden	122	Blue Pair	119	Our Boots	122	7,835	1:11.20	
1941	Devil Diver	2	M. McCreary	122	Miss Dogwood	114	Dogpatch	117	7,884	1:11.80	
1942	Occupation	2	L. Haas	124	Amber Light	117	Dove Pie	117	11,140	1:14.00	
1943	Durazna	2	J. Higley	116	Occupy	122	Mr. Rabbit	117	9,886	1:11.60	
1944	Air Sailor	2	L. Haas	119	Bymeabond	117	Be Fearless	117	11,244	1:12.20	
1945	Pellicle	2	S. Brooks	117	Mr. Chairman	117	Warf	117	12,676	1:12.80	
1946	Education	2	S. Brooks	122	John's Pride	117	Turf	117	16,338	1:11.60	

Year	Winner	Age	Jockey	Wt.	Second	Wt.	Third	Wt.	Win Value	Time	Beyer
1947	Shy Guy	2	S. Brooks	117	Carrara Marble	117	Pennon	117	20,855	1:11.80	
1948	Olympia	2	W. Garner	122	Johns Joy	122	Fleeting Star	117	27,120	1:11.60	
1949	Oil Capitol	2	K. Church	122	French Admiral	117	Roman Bath	122	28,517	1:12.20	
1950	Big Stretch	2	T. Atkinson	117	Royal Mustang	117	Streaking	117	27,674	1:23.60	
1951	Alladier	2	C. Bierman	117	Ed's Pride	119	Smoke Screen	114	27,052	1:23.80	
1952	Straight Face	2	B. Green	117	Jimminy Baxter	117	Spy Defense	119	27,052	1:23.80	
1953	Hasty Road	2	J. Adams	122	Revolt	119	Homestake	119	32,127	1:23.20	
1954	Brother Tex	2	P. Anderson	122	Traffic Judge	122	Irish Brush	122	37,883	1:24.40	
1955	Jovial Jove	2	D. Dodson	122	Swoon's Son	122	Pester	122	33,606	1:23.60	
1956	Round Table	2	S. Brooks	122	Missile	122	Tranquil	122	38,949	1:26.80	
1957	Fulcrum	2	J. Delahoussaye	122	Can Trust	122	Nunya	122	37,214	1:26.40	
1958	Namon	2	J. Combest	122	Pilot	122	Derrick	122	38,722	1:26.60	
1959	Toby's Brother	2	J.L. Rotz	122	All Hands	122	Malaysia	122	35,527	1:27.20	
1960	He's a Pistol	2	L. Hansman	122	Zebadiah	122	Busher's Beauty	122	33,619	1:27.00	
1961	Roman Line	2	W.M. Cook	122	Times Roman	122	Crafty Actor	122	36,754	1:26.60	
1962	Ornamento	2	J. Lynch	122	Copy Chief	122	No Reprieve	122	35,457	1:26.40	
1963	Duel	2	W.D. Lucas	122	Ishkoodah	122	Bleacherite	122	35,399	1:26.20	
1964	Umbrella Fella	2	J. Nazareth	122	Seafes	122	Florida State	122	35,461	1:26.60	
1965	Tinsley	2	J. Nichols	122	Francis U.	122	Woodford	122	37,554	1:28.40	
1966	Gentleman James	2	J. Nichols	122	Monitor	122	Yorkville	122	39,978	1:28.00	
1967	T.V. Commercial	2	M. Ycaza	122	Family Fun	122	Tampa Trouble	122	39,988	1:26.80	
1968	Dike	2	E. Fires	122	Mr. Leader	122	The Heir	122	40,955	1:26.80	
1969	Hard Work	2	D. Brumfield	122	Toasted	122	Lanyon	122	39,055	1:25.60	
1970	Man of the Moment	2	D. Brumfield	122	Whisk	122	Raja Baba	122	41,574	1:28.80	
1971	Windjammer	2	L. Pincay Jr	122	Central Paris	122	Brilliant Native	122	39,948	1:27.20	
1972	Annihilate 'Em	2	D. Brumfield	122	Rocket Pocket	122	Crimson Falcon	122	38,886	1:27.00	
1973	Provante	2	M. Manganello	122	Training Table	122	Wage Raise	122	48,327	1:27.20	
1974	Packer Captain	2	D. Brumfield	122	Master Derby	122	Ruggles Ferry	122	53,277	1:25.80	
1975	Harbor Springs	2	E. Maple	122	Best Bee	122	Scrutiny	122	82,046	1:27.00	
1976	Run Dusty Run	2	D.G. McHargue	122	Banquet Table	122	Get the Axe	122	84,695	1:27.40	
1977	Gonquin	2	F. Olivares	122	Sunny Songster	122	Jaycean	122	83,866	1:28.00	
1978	Strike Your Colors	2	E. Delahoussaye	122	Lot o' Gold	122	Uncle Fudge	122	92,284	1:26.20	
1979	Gold Stage	2	D. Brumfield	121	Degenerate Jon	121	Tonka Wakhen	121	81,608	1:26.80	
1980	Fairway Phantom	2	J. Lively	121	Total Pleasure	121	Quick Ice	121	94,575	1:28.80	
1981	D'Accord	2	D.G. McHargue	121	Lets Dont Fight	121	Shooting Duck	121	94,575	1:44.40	
1982	Highland Park	2	J.L. Lively	121	Caveat	121	Bright Baron	121	97,825	1:43.60	
1983	Swale	2	E. Maple	121	Spender	121	Back Bay Barrister	121	108,631	1:44.00	
1984	Crater Fire	2	D. Montoya	121	Nickel Back	121	Cullendale	121	110,474	1:45.80	
1985	Tasso	2	L. Pincay Jr	121	Regal Dreamer	121	Thundering Force	121	122,424	1:46.00	
1986	Orono	2	S. Hawley	121	Alysheba	121	Pledge Card	121	116,711	1:45.20	
1987	Forty Niner	2	E. Maple	121	Hey Pat	121	Sea Trek	121	104,868	1:43.80	
1988	Fast Play	2	A. Cordero Jr	121	Lorenzoni	121	Bio	121	129,350	1:45.20	
1989	Slavic	2	J.A. Santos	121	Top Snob	121	Harry	121	159,770	1:44.60	
1990	Sir Bordeaux	2	W.S. Ramos	121	Wall Street Dancer	121	Fire in Ice	121	145,925	1:44.40	.82
1991	Dance Floor	2	C.R. Woods Jr	121	Star Recruit	121	Count the Time	121	122,200	1:44.20	.100
1992	Mountain Cat	2	P. Day	121	Living Vicariously	121	Boundlessly	121	122,200	1:45.40	.86
1993	Polar Expedition	2	C.C. Bourque	121	Goodbye Doeny	121	Solly's Honor	121	122,200	1:42.20	.96
1994	Tejano Run	2	J.D. Bailey	121	Cinch	121	Gold Miner	121	71,548	1:44.60	.89
1995	Honour and Glory	2	P. Day	121	City by Night	121	Blushing Jim	121	139,252	1:43.20	.101
1996	Boston Harbor	2	J.D. Bailey	121	Blazing Sword	121	Haint	121	168,005	1:45.20	.93
1997	Favorite Trick	2	P. Day	121	Time Limit	121	Laydown	121	265,112	1:43.20	.100
1998	Cat Thief	2	P. Day	121	Answer Lively	121	Yes It's True	121	272,552	1:44.00	.97
1999	Captain Steve	2	G.K. Gomez	121	Graeme Hall	121	Millencolin	121	274,040	1:42.40	.95
2000	Arabian Light	2	S.J. Sellers	121	Dollar Bill	121	Holiday Thunder	121	279,744	1:43.18	.94
2001	Siphonic	2	C.J. McCarron	121	Harlan's Holiday	121	Metatron	121	281,728	1:43.79	.97
2002	Sky Mesa	2	E.S. Prado	121	Lone Star Sky	121	Truckle Feature	121	269,576	1:46.78	.93
2003	Eurosilver	2	J. Castellano	121	Tiger Hunt	121	Limehouse	121	248,000	1:43.42	.98

Beyer Index: **94.36**

BROOKLYN HANDICAP, 1 1/8 Miles,
3-Year-Olds and Up, Belmont Park, 2003 Purse: $250,000

Year	Winner	Age	Jockey	Wt.	Second	Wt.	Third	Wt.	Win Value	Time	Beyer
1887	Dry Monopole	4	A. McCarthy	106	Blue Wing	112	Hidalgo	115	5,850	2:07.00	
1888	The Bard	5	W. Hayward	125	Hanover	125	Exile	114	6,925	2:13.00	
1889	Exile	7	A. Hamilton	116	Prince Royal	120	Terra Cotta	125	6,900	2:07.50	
1890	Castaway II	4	W. Bunn	100	Badge	114	Eric	110	6,900	2:10.00	
1891	Tenny	5	Barnes	128	Prince Royal	117	Tea Tray	116	14,800	2:10.00	
1892	Judge Morrow	5	A. Covington	116	Pessarra	115	Russell	114	17,750	2:08.75	
1893	Diablo	7	F. Taral	112	Lamplighter	125	Leonawell	110	17,750	2:09.00	
1894	Dr. Rice	4	F. Taral	112	Henry of Navarre	100	Sir Walter	120	17,750	2:07.25	
1895	Hornpipe	4	A. Hamilton	105	Lazzarone	114	Sir Walter	124	7,750	2:11.25	

Year	Winner	Age	Jockey	Wt.	Second	Wt.	Third	Wt.	Win Value	Time Beyer
1896	Sir Walter	6	F. Taral	113	Clifford	125	St. Maxim	108	7,750	2:08.50
1897	Howard Mann	4	H. Martin	106	Lake Shore	106	Volley	95	7,750	2:09.75
1898	Ornament	4	T. Sloan	127	Ben Holladay	121	Sly Fox	92	7,800	2:10.00
1899	Banastar	4	D. Maher	110	Lanky Bob	105	Filigrane	98	7,800	2:06.25
1900	Kinley Mack	4	P. McCue	122	Raffaello	113	Herbert	99	7,800	2:10.00
1901	Conroy	3	W. O'Connor	103	Herbert	99	Standing	113	7,800	2:09.00
1902	Reina	4	W. O'Connor	104	Advance Guard	117	Pentecost	100	7,800	2:07.00
1903	Irish Lad	3	F. O'Neill	103	Gunfire	111	Heno	113	14,950	2:05.40
1904	The Picket	4	E. Helgesen	119	Irish Lad	125	Proper	110	15,800	2:06.60
1905	Delhi	4	T. Burns	124	Ostrich	96	Graziallo	109	15,800	2:06.20
1906	Tokalon	5	W. Bedell	108	Dandelion	107	The Picket	120	15,800	2:05.60
1907	Superman	3	W. Miller	99	Beacon Light	100	Nealon	114	15,800	2:09.00
1908	Celt	3	J. Notter	106	Fair Play	99	Mas Robert	95	19,750	2:04.20
1909	King James	4	E. Dugan	126	Restigouche	114	Celt	127	3,850	2:04.00
1910	Fitz Herbert	4	E. Dugan	130	Olambala	116	Pr. Imperial	97	4,800	2:05.60
1913	Whisk Broom II	6	J. Notter	130	G.M. Miller	106	Sam Jackson	108	3,125	2:03.40
1914	Buckhorn	5	J. McCahey	113	Ruskin	119	Rock View	128	3,350	2:08.00
1915	Tartar	5	J. McTaggart	103	Roamer	125	Borrow	128	3,850	1:50.60
1916	Friar Rock	3	E. Haynes	108	Pennant	123	Slumber II	111	3,850	1:50.00
1917	Borrow	9	W. Knapp	117	Regret	122	Old Rosebud	120	4,850	1:49.40
1918	Cudgel	4	L. Lyke	129	Roamer	120	Geo. Smith	122	4,850	1:50.20
1919	Eternal	3	A. Schuttinger	105	Purchase	117	Questionnaire	100	4,850	1:49.00
1920	Cirrus	4	L. Esnor	108	Boniface	122	Mad Hatter	115	5,850	1:50.00
1921	Grey Lag	3	L. Fator	112	John P. Grier	124	Exterminator	129	7,600	1:49.80
1922	Exterminator	7	A. Johnson	135	Grey Lag	126	Polly Ann	103	7,600	1:50.00
1923	Little Chief	4	E. Sande	114	Bunting	126	Knobbie	112	7,600	1:50.00
1924	Hephaistos	5	J. Maiben	106	Susini	102	Enchantment	111	7,600	1:50.80
1925	Mad Play	4	L. Fator	123	Sting	127	Catalan	107	7,600	1:50.00
1926	Single Foot	4	C. Turner	123	Peanuts	111	Dangerous	108	11,950	1:50.40
1927	Peanuts	5	H. Thurber	112	Chance Play	121	Display	112	13,150	1:48.80
1928	Black Panther	4	J. Maiben	105	Victorian	112	Diavolo	106	13,750	1:51.20
1929	Light Carbine	6	G. Rose	97	Diavolo	120	Sun Beau	124	14,300	1:50.60
1930	Sortie	5	P. Walls	111	Jack High	122	Curate	107	10,800	1:49.80
1931	Questionnaire	4	R. Workman	127	St. Brideaux	104	S. Grant	106	13,900	1:49.00
1932	Blenheim	4	H. Mills	109	Pari-Mutuel	97	Mate	124	9,800	1:51.00
1933	Dark Secret	4	H. Mills	115	Kerry Patch	112	Apprentice	109	3,380	1:51.20
1934	Discovery	3	J. Bejshak	113	Dark Secret	126	Fleam	108	2,925	1:49.80
1935	Dicovery	4	J. Bejshak	123	King Saxon	127	Omaha	114	10,200	1:48.20
1936	Discovery	5	L. Fallon	136	Good Gamble	110	Roman Soldier	126	10,575	1:50.00
1937	Seabiscuit	4	J. Pollard	122	Aneroid	122	Memory Book	114	18,025	1:50.20
1938	The Chief	3	J. Longden	105	Stagehand	110	Unfailing	106	18,450	1:48.40
1939	Cravat	4	B. James	126	Our Ketcham	101	The Chief	112	18,250	1:48.20
1940	Isolater	7	J. Stout	119	Can't Wait	111	Eight Thirty	130	16,900	2:03.00
1941	Fenelon	4	J. Stout	119	Dit	110	Your Chance	121	19,250	2:03.60
1942	Whirlaway	4	G. Woolf	128	Swing and Sway	110	Attention	122	23,650	2:02.60
1943	Devil Diver	4	S. Brooks	123	Market Wise	128	Don Bingo	113	23,200	2:03.40
1944	Four Freedoms	4	E. Arcaro	116	Wait a Bit	116	First Fiddle	126	3,720	2:02.80
1945	Stymie	4	R. Permane	116	Devil Diver	132	Olympic Zenith	110	37,120	2:02.20
1946	Gallorette	4	J. Jessop	128	Stymie	128	Burning Dream	110	41,100	2:05.00
1947	Assault	4	E. Arcaro	133	Stymie	124	Larky Day	110	38,100	2:03.60
1948	Conniver	4	T. Atkinson	114	Gallorette	119	Stymie	130	39,300	2:05.80
1949	Assault	6	D. Gorman	129	Vulcan's Forge	129	Flying Missel	117	40,600	2:02.80
1950	My Request	5	T. Atkinson	119	Double Brandy	115	Hypocrite II	103	41,000	2:03.00
1951	Palestinian	5	S. Boulmetis	121	Sheilas Reward	117	County Delight	124	39,000	2:03.40
1952	Crafty Admiral	4	E. Guerin	116	County Delight	122	To Market	119	41,700	2:01.80
1953	Tom Fool	4	T. Atkinson	136	Golden Gloves	110	High Scud	109	37,900	2:04.40
1954	Invigorator	4	E. Arcaro	114	Find	122	Cold Command	116	40,500	2:03.00
1955	High Gun	4	E. Arcaro	132	Paper Tiger	107	Straight Face	116	37,900	2:03.40
1956	Dedicate	4	E. Arcaro	124	Midafternoon	116	Find	119	37,600	1:55.80
1957	Portersville	5	E. Nelson	116	Admiral Vee	120	Tick Tock	118	37,700	1:55.20
1958	Cohoes	4	J. Ruane	110	Third Brother	110	Inside Tract	106	36,450	1:55.60
1959	Babu	5	C. McCreary	112	Sword Dancer	124	Amerigo	117	72,545	1:56.40
1960	On-and-On	4	I. Valenzuela	118	Greek Star	110	Waltz	112	70,010	2:03.00
1961	Kelso	4	E. Arcaro	136	Divine Comedy	118	Yorky	122	73,320	2:01.60
1962	Beau Purple	5	W. Boland	116	Garwol	106	Polylad	114	71,240	2:00.00
1963	Cyrano	4	R. Ussery	113	Sunrise County	116	Lanvin	108	72,800	2:01.60
1964	Gun Bow	4	W. Blum	122	Olden Times	122	Sunrise Flight	113	71,500	1:59.60
1965	Pia Star	4	J. Sellers	121	Roman Brother	121	Kelso	132	69,680	2:00.60
1966	Buckpasser	3	B. Baeza	120	Buffle	113	Pluck	113	69,615	2:01.80
1967	Handsome Boy	4	E. Belmonte	116	Buckpasser	136	Mr. Right	113	69,355	2:00.20
1968	Damascus	4	M. Ycaza	130	Dr. Fager	135	Mr. Right	114	71,110	1:59.20
1969	Nodouble	4	E. Belmonte	116	Verbatim	120	Dike	114	70,850	2:00.40
1970	Dewan	5	L. Pincay Jr	118	Pleasure Seeker	117	Hydrologist	114	69,810	2:02.80
1971	Never Bow	5	R. Ussery	126	Protanto	111	Royal Harmony	111	69,060	2:03.60

Year	Winner	Age	Jockey	Wt.	Second	Wt.	Third	Wt.	Win Value	Time	Beyer
1972	Key to the Mint	3	B. Baeza	112	Autobiography	122	West Coast Scout	114	70,860	1:54.80	
1973	Riva Ridge	4	R. Turcotte	127	True Knight	117	Tentam	119	67,200	1:52.60	
1974	Forego	4	H. Gustines	129	Billy Come Lately	114	Arbees Boy	116	66,600	1:54.80	
1975	Forego	5	H. Gustines	132	Monetary Principle	109	Stop the Music	121	66,780	1:59.80	
1976	Forego	6	H. Gustines	134	Lord Rebeau	114	Foolish Pleasure	126	67,860	2:01.20	
1977	Great Contractor	4	A. Cordero Jr	112	Forego	137	American History	112	66,600	2:26.20	
1978	Nasty and Bold	3	J.L. Samyn	112	Father Hogan	116	Great Contractor	122	63,900	2:26.00	
1979	The Liberal Member	4	R.I. Encinas	114	Bowl Game	119	State Dinner	123	99,000	2:28.80	
1980	Winter's Tale	4	J. Fell	120	State Dinner	121	Ring of Light	114	130,200	2:28.60	
1981	Hechizado	5	R. Hernandez	116	The Liberal Member	113	Peat Moss	111	138,300	2:26.00	
1982	Silver Supreme	5	J. Vasquez	117	Princelet	112	Baltimore Canyon	113	131,700	2:29.40	
1983	Highland Blade	5	J. Vasquez	117	Sing Sing	118	Silver Supreme	113	172,800	2:31.00	
1984	Fit to Fight	5	J.D. Bailey	129	Vision	111	Dew Line	116	201,600	2:27.40	
1985	Bounding Basque	5	A. Graell	111	Life's Magic	114	Pine Circle	115	207,300	2:26.40	
1986	Little Missouri	4	J.L. Samyn	109	Roo Art	118	Creme Fraiche	118	195,900	2:26.40	
1987	Waquoit	4	C.J. McCarron	123	Bordeaux Bob	112	Full Courage	108	249,480	2:28.40	
1988	Waquoit	5	J.A. Santos	121	Personal Flag	120	Creme Fraiche	118	229,740	2:28.80	
1989	Forever Silver	4	J. Vasquez	116	Drapeau Tricolore	112	Jack of Clubs	112	238,560	2:28.60	
1990	Montubio	5	J. Vasquez	113	Mi Selecto	114	De Roche	113	241,920	2:28.60	
1991	Timely Warning	6	M.J. Luzzi	112	Chief Honcho	121	De Roche	115	210,000	2:14.00	107
1992	Chief Honcho	5	R.P. Romero	117	Valley Crossing	113	Lost Mountain	114	210,000	2:16.80	109
1993	Living Vicariously	3	R.G. Davis	111	Michelle Can Pass	116	Jacksonport	111	150,000	2:17.80	107
1994	Devil His Due	5	M.E. Smith	120	Wallenda	118	Sea Hero	119	150,000	1:46.60	116
1995	You and I	4	J.F. Chavez	115	Key Contender	112	Slick Horn	113	150,000	1:49.00	114
1996	Wekiva Springs	5	M.E. Smith	120	Mahogany Hall	114	Admiralty	111	180,000	1:46.60	107
1997	Formal Gold	4	J.D. Bailey	119	Stephanotis	116	Circle of Light	111	180,000	1:46.20	113
1998	Subordination	4	E.M. Coa	114	Sir Bear	118	Mr. Sinatra	114	180,000	1:46.60	109
1999	Running Stag	5	S.J. Sellers	115	Deputy Diamond	113	Sir Bear	119	210,000	1:46.20	118
2000	Lemon Drop Kid	4	E.S. Prado	120	Lager	114	Down the Aisle	112	150,000	1:49.93	115
2001	Albert The Great	4	J.F. Chavez	122	Perfect Cat	115	Top Official	113	150,000	1:47.41	114
2002	Seeking Daylight	4	E.S. Prado	113	Country Be Gold	113	Griffinite	114	150,000	1:47.84	112
2003	Iron Deputy	4	R. Migliore	114	Volponi	122	Saarland	115	150,000	1:47.84	112

Beyer Index: 111.54

BUENA VISTA HANDICAP, 1 Mile (Turf),
Fillies and Mares, 4-Year-Olds and Up, Santa Anita, 2003 Purse: $150,000

Year	Winner	Age	Jockey	Wt.	Second	Wt.	Third	Wt.	Win Value	Time	Beyer
1988	Davie's Lamb	4	F. Toro	117	Sly Charmer	114	Pen Bal Lady	119	63,050	1:39.00	
1989	Annoconnor	5	C.A. Black	121	Daring Doone	112	Daloma	116	65,800	1:36.40	
1990	Saros Brig	6	P.A. Valenzuela	116	Royal Touch	123	Nikishka	118	68,100	1:34.20	104
1991	Taffeta and Tulle	5	C.J. McCarron	120	Bequest	117	Somethingmerry	114	67,200	1:34.20	101
1992	Gold Fleece	4	A. Solis	114	Elegance	115	Danzante	114	52,100	1:33.40	106
1992	Appealing Missy	5	C.J. McCarron	117	Exchange	120	Re Toss	117	52,100	1:34.20	100
1993	Marble Maiden	4	K.J. Desormeaux	118	Suivi	117	Party Cited	116	65,000	1:36.20	102
1994	Lady Blessington	6	E. Delahoussaye	119	Skimble	118	Hero's Love	121	66,300	1:34.80	103
1995	Lyin to the Moon	6	K.J. Desormeaux	116	Jacodra's Devil	115	Exchange	122	61,700	1:36.60	99
1996	Matiara	4	G.L. Stevens	119	Real Connection	114	Dirca	116	81,800	1:35.60	105
1997	Media Nox	4	C.S. Nakatani	115	Traces Of Gold	115	Grafin	116	85,250	1:33.40	102
1998	Dance Parade	4	K.J. Desormeaux	116	Shake The Yoke	116	Donna Viola	121	101,520	1:36.80	104
1999	Tuzla	4	C.S. Nakatani	120	Supercilious	117	Green Jewel	116	90,000	1:35.60	102
2000	Lexa	6	B. Blanc	115	Here's to You	114	Sierra Virgen	114	97,290	1:36.17	99
2001	Rare Charmer	6	L. Pincay Jr.	117	Elegant Ridge	117	Uncharted Haven	116	90,000	1:36.67	97
2002	Blue Moon	5	B. Blanc	113	Queen of Wilshire	116	Old Money	118	90,000	1:35.57	97
2003	Final Destination	5	V. Espinoza	115	Garden in the Rain	115	Embassy Belle	116	90,000	1:35.99	101

Beyer Index: 101.47

CALIFORNIAN, 1 1/8 Miles,
3-Year-Olds and Up, Hollywood Park, 2003 Purse: $400,000

Year	Winner	Age	Jockey	Wt.	Second	Wt.	Third	Wt.	Win Value	Time	Beyer
1954	Imbros	4	J. Longden	118	Determine	115	High Scud	114	75,300	1:41.00	
1955	Swaps	3	D. Erb	115	Determine	126	Mister Gus	117	63,700	1:40.40	
1956	Porterhouse	4	I. Valenzuela	118	Swaps	127	Mister Gus	118	63,700	1:40.80	
1957	Social Climber	4	W. Shoemaker	119	Round Table	105	Find	119	71,800	1:40.40	
1958	Seaneen	4	J. Longden	109	Round Table	130	Terrang	115	63,300	1:41.00	
1959	Hillsdale	4	T. Barrow	123	Amerigo	107	Ying and Yang	109	67,900	1:40.80	
1960	Fleet Nasrullah	5	J. Longden	119	Eddie Schmidt	113	Bagdad	123	66,300	1:40.60	
1961	First Balcony	4	E. Burns	115	Prove It	127	Sea Orbit	115	67,700	1:40.40	
1962	Cadiz	6	W. Harmatz	111	Prove It	123	Olden Times	123	71,200	1:41.60	
1963	Winonly	6	J. Leonard	115	Mr. Consistency	111	Harpie	115	77,300	1:41.80	
1964	Mustard Plaster	5	J. Leonard	111	Mr. Consistency	123	Colorado King	123	70,500	1:41.60	

Year	Winner	Age	Jockey	Wt.	Second	Wt.	Third	Wt.	Win Value	Time	Beyer
1965	Viking Spirit	5	K. Church	115	Quadrangle	123	Tronado	114	67,900	1:40.80	
1966	Travel Orb	4	W. Harmatz	112	Make Money	112	Sledge	112	75,100	1:41.80	
1967	Biggs	7	W. Harmatz	112	Make Money	112	Pretense	130	74,200	1:41.60	
1968	Dr. Fager	4	B. Baeza	130	Gamely	116	Rising Market	121	74,600	1:40.80	
1969	Nodouble	4	E. Belmonte	127	Rising Market	121	London Jet	112	70,400	1:40.40	
1970	Baffle	5	J. Lambert	113	Figonero	124	Nodouble	130	62,800	1:40.20	
1971	Cougar II	5	W. Shoemaker	124	Master Hand	112	Fleet Surprise	118	81,100	1:41.20	
1972	Cougar II	6	W. Shoemaker	127	Kennedy Road	119	Miles Tyson	118	76,400	1:39.20	
1973	Quack	4	D. Pierce	126	Royal Owl	125	Tri Jet	118	65,300	1:41.40	
1974	Quack	5	D. Pierce	126	Ancient Title	126	Woodland Pines	120	70,900	1:40.20	
1975	Ancient Title	5	L. Pincay Jr	126	Big Band	117	Century's Envoy	117	73,100	1:40.20	
1976	Ancient Title	6	S. Hawley	127	Pay Tribute	117	Austin Mittler	116	65,300	1:41.20	
1977	Crystal Water	4	L. Pincay Jr	128	Mark's Place	121	Ancient Title	123	65,300	1:41.00	
1978	J.O. Tobin	4	S. Cauthen	126	Replant	120	Cox's Ridge	127	124,550	1:41.00	
1979	Affirmed	4	L. Pincay Jr	130	Syncopate	114	Harry's Love	117	159,900	1:41.20	
1980	Spectacular Bid	4	W. Shoemaker	130	Paint King	115	Caro Bambino	118	184,450	1:45.80	
1981	Eleven Stitches	4	S. Hawley	122	Temperence Hill	130	Kilijaro	123	207,600	1:48.40	
1982	Erins Isle	4	L. Pincay Jr	117	It's the One	128	Major Sport	118	200,200	1:48.00	
1983	The Wonder	5	W. Shoemaker	119	Prince Spellbound	122	Poley	117	192,000	1:48.40	
1984	Desert Wine	4	E. Delahoussaye	121	Interco	126	Sari's Dreamer	116	193,600	1:47.60	
1985	Greinton	4	L. Pincay Jr	119	Precisionist	126	Lord at War	126	179,600	1:32.60	
1986	Precisionist	5	C.J. McCarron	126	Super Diamond	117	Skywalker	121	188,400	1:33.60	
1987	Judge Angelucci	4	G. Baze	118	Iron Eyes	115	Snow Chief	126	193,200	1:48.20	
1988	Cutlass Reality	6	C.J. McCarron	115	Gulch	126	Judge Angelucci	126	180,200	1:47.60	
1989	Sabona	7	C.J. McCarron	115	Blushing John	124	Lively One	118	185,800	1:46.80	
1990	Sunday Silence	4	P.A. Valenzuela	126	Stylish Winner	115	Charlatan III	111	168,400	1:48.00	113
1991	Roanoke	4	E. Delahoussaye	116	Anshan	118	Marquetry	113	175,600	1:48.20	109
1992	Another Review	4	K.J. Desormeaux	119	Defensive Play	120	Ibero	119	119,400	1:48.00	105
1993	Latin American	5	G.L. Stevens	116	Missionary Ridge	116	Memo	118	220,000	1:46.80	111
1994	The Wicked North	5	K.J. Desormeaux	120	Kingdom Found	116	Slew of Damascus	116	165,000	1:46.60	116
1995	Concern	4	M.E. Smith	122	Tossofthecoin	118	Tinners Way	116	160,900	1:47.60	108
1996	Tinners Way	6	E. Delahoussaye	116	Helmsman	122	Mr Purple	122	151,980	1:46.60	113
1997	River Keen	5	K.J. Desormeaux	117	Hesabull	118	Benchmark	118	150,000	1:47.20	112
1998	Mud Route	4	C.J. McCarron	116	Deputy Commander	122	Worldly Ways	117	150,000	1:48.00	109
1999	Old Trieste	4	C.J. McCarron	116	Budroyale	120	Puerto Madero	122	180,000	1:46.40	118
2000	Big Ten	5	A. Solis	116	Early Pioneer	118	Mojave Moon	116	150,000	1:49.22	104
2001	Skimming	5	G.K. Gomez	116	Futural	120	Aptitude	116	300,000	1:48.12	111
2002	Milwaukee Brew	5	K.J. Desormeaux	122	Bosque Redondo	118	Momentum	118	300,000	1:48.06	114
2003	Kudos	6	A. Solis	116	Piensa Sonando	118	Reba's Gold	118	240,000	1:47.91	108

Beyer Index: 110.79

CHURCHILL DOWNS DISTAFF HANDICAP, 1 Mile,
Fillies and Mares, 3-Year-Olds and Up, Churchill Downs, 2003 Purse: $225,400

Year	Winner	Age	Jockey	Wt.	Second	Wt.	Third	Wt.	Win Value	Time	Beyer
1986	Lazer Show	3	C.R. Woods Jr	120	Balladry	116	Mrs. Revere	120	102,473	1:22.60	
1987	Bound	3	E. Maple	113	Miss Bid	115	Intently	114	103,253	1:37.00	
1988	Darien Miss	3	P.A. Johnson	116	Sheena Native	117	Coastal Connection	112	102,928	1:36.80	
1989	Classic Value	3	P. Day	114	Coastal Connection	115	Rose's Record	117	102,960	1:35.40	
1990	Oh My Jessica Pie	3	M.A. Gonzalez	114	Seaside Attraction	115	Sweet Nostalgia	111	102,993	1:36.80	94
1991	Fit for a Queen	5	R.D. Lopez	121	Wilderness Song	118	Summer Matinee	113	100,555	1:38.60	101
1992	Wilderness Song	4	C. Perret	120	Miss Jealski	110	Dance Colony	113	102,440	1:36.20	101
1993	Miss Indy Anna	3	P. Day	111	One Dreamer	115	Deputation	119	141,635	1:37.60	108
1994	Educated Risk	4	P. Day	118	Pennyhill Park	117	Alcovy	116	138,125	1:35.60	114
1995	Lakeway	4	K.J. Desormeaux	122	Alcovy	113	Laura's Pistolette	115	137,280	1:35.80	110
1997	Feasibility Study	5	R.J. Albarado	120	J J'sdream	113	Mama's Pro	115	146,196	1:37.60	100
1996	Fast Catch	4	W. Martinez	109	Serena's Song	125	Bedroom Blues	112	139,624	1:36.20	103
1998	Dream Scheme	5	C.H. Borel	113	Sister Act	111	Beautiful Pleasure	111	138,624	1:34.40	116
1999	Let	4	C.H. Borel	113	Roza Robata	114	Dif A Dot	115	138,880	1:34.40	109
2000	Chilukki	3	G.L. Stevens	116	Reciclada	113	Rose of Zollern	114	154,008	1:33.57	108
2001	Nasty Storm	3	P. Day	115	Forest Secrets	113	Trip	117	137,764	1:35.30	101
2002	Softly	4	J.K. Court	114	Bare Necessities	115	Victory Ride	118	138,632	1:35.07	96
2003	Lead Story	4	C.H. Borel	114	Awesome Humor	118	Born to Dance	113	139,748	1:36.55	98

Beyer Index: 104.21

Run at 7 furlongs in 1986

CHURCHILL DOWNS HANDICAP, 7 Furlongs,
4-Year-Olds and Up, Churchill Downs, 2003 Purse: $233,800

Year	Winner	Age	Jockey	Wt.	Second	Wt.	Third	Wt.	Win Value	Time	Beyer
1911	Carlton G.	4	Taplin	107	Messenger Boy	92	Star Charter	107	1,990	1:51.80	
1912	Any Port	6	Byrne	103	Mary Davis	105	Star O'Ryan	100	1,580	1:51.60	

Year	Winner	Age	Jockey	Wt.	Second	Wt.	Third	Wt.	Win Value	Time	Beyer
1913	Rudolfo	4	Loftus	115	Yankee Notions	106	Gowell	103	700	1:51.80	
1938	Arabs Arrow	4	W.L. Johnson	112	Knee Deep	104	Bacon	116	2,145	1:26.80	
1939	Kings Blue	4	C. Kurtsinger	109	Arabs Arrow	119	Janice	106	1,382	1:24.80	
1940	Arabs Arrow	6	C. Bierman	119	Mucho Gusto	110	Bucking	107	2,285	1:39.80	
1941	My Bill	3	C. McCreary	100	Potranco	116	Betty's B'by	109	2,185	1:36.60	
1942	Royal Crusader	5	A. Craig	111	Aonbarr	115	Moscow II	105	2,270	1:37.60	
1943	Best Seller	5	J. Longden	118	Wishbone	115	Three Clovers	102	2,200	1:38.40	
1944	Traffic Court	6		111	Amber Light	114	Ale'tern	117	4,120	1:36.80	
1945	Equifox	8	A. Bodiou	122	Sigma Kappa	100	Mina J.	100	4,000	1:40.00	
1946	Bull Play	4	R. Campbell	111	Letmenow	110	Sigma Kappa	112	8,175	1:42.40	
1947	Dark Jungle	4	S. Brooks	113	Jack S.L.	114	Joe's Choice	108	8,725	1:25.20	
1948	George Gains	5	A.J. Fernandez	116	Joe's Choice	111	Eternal Reward	115	8,500	1:25.20	
1949	Free America	4	S. Brooks	120	Armed	118	Phar Mon	108	7,750	1:25.00	
1950	Fleeting Star	4	S. Brooks	117	Ol' Skipper	117	Sun Herod	119	8,550	1:24.00	
1951	Johns Joy	5	W.M. Cook	118	Roman Bath	118	Mr. Trouble	115	8,400	1:22.80	
1952	Here's Hoping	5	S. Brooks	113	Futuramatic	107	Air Mail	107	8,100	1:11.00	
1953	Roaming	4	J. Contreras	114	Pomace	110	Pet Bully	120	8,050	1:10.60	
1954	Sunny Dale	6	P.J. Bailey	114	Mon-Pharo	118	Gala Fete	116	8,850	1:11.00	
1955	Torch of War	5	J. Adams	113	Tuosix	115	Vagabond King	115	8,025	1:11.20	
1956	Scrutinized	6	W.M. Cook	110	Styrunner	112	Happy Go L'cky	109	8,700	1:25.40	
1957	Swoon's Son	4	D. Erb	128	Sea O Erin	119	Invalidate	113	8,375	1:24.60	
1958	Shan Pac	4	J. Heckmann	115	Ezgo	120	Dogoon	122	7,447	1:22.00	
1959	Cuvier Boy	4	S. Brooks	113	Greek Chief	116	Yemen	115	7,431	1:22.40	
1960	Little Fitz	5	A.W. Peake	115	Better Bee	118	Aesthetic	110	7,399	1:22.40	
1961	Cactus Tom	4	L. Hansman	118	Eight Again	119	Matthias	115	7,540	1:22.40	
1962	Editorialist	4	W. Shoemaker	125	Weatherton	115	Playgoer	112	7,507	1:22.60	
1963	Editorialist	5	M. Ycaza	128	Bass Clef	111	Times Roman	119	7,394	1:22.40	
1964	Olden Times	6	W. Shoemaker	124	Piper's Son	113	Lemon Twist	115	7,475	1:21.40	
1965	Little Lu	4	M. Manganello	110	Big Brigade	114	Clem Pac	124	9,100	1:22.40	
1966	Bay Phantom	4	R.J. Campbell	125	Big Brigade	117	Mr. Pak	110	10,627	1:22.00	
1967	Bay Phantom	5	E. Fires	117	Cabildo	122	Slade	112	11,424	1:22.00	
1968	Cabildo	5	J. Combest	122	Tartan Man	114	Gay Flight	115	10,904	1:23.20	
1969	Judge Kilday	4	D.E. Whited	115	Barbs Delight	122	Gr'd Premiere	115	11,180	1:23.60	
1970	True North	4	M. Manganello	113	Advance Party	113	Sh'k of Bagdad	114	11,050	1:22.60	
1971	No No Billy	4	D. MacBeth	111	Great Mystery	119	Rio Bravo	117	15,340	1:23.20	
1972	List	4	J. Nichols	118	Staunch Avenger	116	Tribal Line	117	15,762	1:23.20	
1973	Code of Honor	5	E. Fires	115	Knight Counter	122	Hook It Up	115	15,096	1:23.00	
1974	Barbizon Streak	6	R. Wilson	115	Grocery List	117	Jim's Alibhi	114	15,015	1:25.40	
1975	Navajo	5	J. Nichols	123	Silver Hope	116	Silver Badge	110	14,804	1:24.40	
1976	Yamanin	4	G. Patterson	115	It's Freezing	120	Easter Island	115	14,495	1:23.80	
1977	It's Freezing	5	E. Delahoussaye	120	Buddy Larosa	112	Silver Hope	119	14,528	1:23.40	
1978	To the Quick	4	J. Amy	116	It's Freezing	117	Prince Majestic	121	14,511	1:25.00	
1979	Trimlea	5	J. Velasquez	113	Dr. Riddick	119	Cabrini King	118	19,240	1:24.60	
1980	Dr. Riddick	6	D. Brumfield	114	Cregan's Cap	112	Silent Dignity	119	17,615	1:23.20	
1981	Dreadnought	4	J.C. Espinoza	112	Tiger Lure	113	Turbulence	119	19,874	1:23.60	
1982	Top Avenger	4	R.P. Romero	114	It's a Rerun	110	Shot n' Missed	117	21,662	1:23.00	
1982	Bayou Black	6	R. Ardoin	119	Vodika Collins	118	Prince Crimson	116	23,433	1:22.80	
1983	Shot n' Missed	6	L. Moyers	118	Vodika Collins	112	Gall'nt Gentleman	115	21,239	1:23.60	
1984	Habitonia	4	P. Day	118	Roman Jamboree	114	Euathlos	113	20,914	1:23.00	
1985	Rapid Gray	6	P. Day	120	Roxbury Park	114	Steel Robbing	115	24,391	1:24.00	
1985	Bayou Hebert	4	J. McKnight	111	Harry 'n Bill	117	Never Company	117	24,196	1:23.40	
1986	Sovereign's Ace	4	P. Rubbicco	117	Artichoke	120	Clever Wake	116	21,957	1:22.60	
1987	Sovereign's Ace	5	L. Pincay Jr	117	Sun Master	123	Savings	114	21,236	1:22.00	
1988	Conquer	4	G.L. Stevens	117	Homebuilder	121	Carborundum	115	36,823	1:23.20	
1989	Dancing Spree	4	P. Day	116	Carborundum	117	Broadway Chief	115	38,253	1:24.00	
1990	Beau Genius	5	R.D. Lopez	119	Traskwood	113	Learn by Heart	115	37,830	1:23.20	99
1991	Thirty Six Red	4	J.D. Bailey	117	Private School	113	Bratt's Choice	115	37,635	1:22.00	111
1992	Pleasant Tap	5	E. Delahoussaye	120	Take Me Out	120	Cantrell Road	113	55,526	1:22.20	104
1993	Callide Valley	5	G.L. Stevens	114	Furiously	117	Ojai	110	56,063	1:22.00	106
1994	Honor the Hero	6	Gomez GK	116	Memo	121	Saratoga Gambler	116	71,370	1:23.00	113
1995	Goldseeker Bud	4	Martinez W	109	Level Sands	112	Go for Gin	115	75,205	1:21.60	104
1996	Criollito	5	C.J. McCarron	114	Forty Won	115	Powis Castle	114	74,620	1:22.00	107
1997	Diligence	4	M.E. Smith	114	Victor Cooley	115	Criollito	115	70,432	1:22.20	107
1998	Distorted Humor	5	G.L. Stevens	119	Gold Land	116	El Amante	113	103,509	1:21.00	117
1999	Rock and Roll	5	P. Day	112	Liberty Gold	114	Run Johnny	113	103,137	1:22.80	105
2000	Straight Man	4	J.F. Chavez	112	Mula Gula	114	Patience Game	114	104,904	1:21.53	103
2001	Alannan	4	E.S. Prado	116	Bonapaw	116	Exchange Rate	113	111,321	1:20.50	113
2002	D'wildcat	4	K.J. Desormeaux	115	Snow Ridge	119	Binthebest	113	106,299	1:22.37	102
	Snow Ridge finished first but was disqualified and placed second										
2003	Aldebaran	5	J.D. Bailey	120	Pass Rush	117	Cappuchino	115	144,956	1:21.80	111

Beyer Index: 107.29

Run as Winnercom Handicap in 2000

CITATION HANDICAP, 1 1/16 Miles (Turf),
3-Year-Olds and Up, Hollywood Park, 2003 Purse: $400,000

Year	Winner	Age	Jockey	Wt.	Second	Wt.	Third	Wt.	Win Value	Time	Beyer
1977	Painted Wagon	4	C. Baltazar	117	Legendaire	114	Pay Tribute	118	48,500	1:42.00	
1978	Effevescing	5	L. Pincay Jr	120	Dr. Patches	116	Text	122	62,700	1:40.20	
1979	Text	5	W. Shoemaker	122	Farnesio	117	Bad 'n Big	119	63,600	1:40.40	
1980	Caro Bambino	5	P.A. Valenzuela	118	Life's Hope	116	Island Sultan	114	36,950	1:33.20	
1981	Tahitian King	5	W. Shoemaker	120	King Go Go	115	Cajun Prince	113	136,000	1:48.80	
1982	Caterman	6	C.J. McCarron	121	Cajun Prince	118	Island Whirl	123	45,700	1:41.00	
1983	Beldale Lustre	4	C.J. McCarron	113	The Hague	115	Sir Pele	114	53,000	1:49.40	
1983	Pewter Grey	4	R. Sibille	115	Belmont Bay	119	Lucence	115	53,500	1:49.60	
1984	Lord at War	4	W. Shoemaker	117	Executive Pride	116	Prairie Breaker	116	68,300	1:50.60	
1985	Zoffany	5	E. Delahoussaye	116	Lord at War	125	Foscarini	115	69,100	1:44.80	
1986	Al Mamoon	5	G.L. Stevens	122	Silveyville	118	Will Dancer	115	123,700	1:48.00	
1987	Forlitano	6	P.A. Valenzuela	120	Conquering Hero	115	Ifrad	115	71,500	1:47.40	
1988	Forlitano	7	P.A. Valenzuela	118	Precisionist	121	Skip out Front	117	69,200	1:46.60	
1989	Fair Judgment	5	E. Delahoussaye	117	Quiet Boy	113	Skip out Front	117	63,300	1:50.00	
1990	Colway Rally	6	C.A. Black	114	Exclusive Partner	117	The Medic	116	62,300	1:47.80	...97
1991	Notorious Pleasure	5	L. Pincay Jr	118	Somethingdifferent	114	Classic Fame	118	102,600	1:45.80	.107
1991	Fly Till Dawn	5	L. Pincay Jr	119	Best Pal	119	Wolf	119	102,600	1:45.80	.107
1992	Leger Cat	6	C.S. Nakatani	114	Trishyde	111	Luthier Enchanteur	117	137,500	1:46.40	.103
1993	Jeune Homme	3	T. Jarnet	114	Paradise Creek	120	Johann Quatz	120	137,500	1:45.80	.110
1994	Southern Wish	5	C.S. Nakatani	115	Square Cut	114	Jeune Homme	118	137,500	2:00.20	.108
1995	Fastness	5	G.L. Stevens	120	Earl of Barking	116	Silver Wizard	117	165,000	1:44.60	.112
1996	Gentlemen	4	G.L. Stevens	119	Smooth Runner	115	Via Lombardia	116	180,000	1:45.40	.108
1997	Geri	5	J.D. Bailey	121	Mufattish	116	Martiniquais	116	180,000	1:48.20	.106
1998	Military	4	G.K. Gomez	118	Mr. Lightfoot	117	Worldly Ways	114	180,000	1:50.40	.107
1999	Brave Act	5	A. Solis	119	Native Desert	116	Bouccaneer	119	300,000	1:39.60	.109
2000	Charge d'Affaires	5	J.A. Santos	116	Ladies Din	122	Native Desert	116	300,000	1:40.30	.103
2001	Good Journey	5	C.J. McCarron	115	Decarchy	117	Irish Prize	122	300,000	1:44.30	.105
2002	Good Journey	6	P. Day	123	Seinneq	115	White Heart	115	300,000	1:41.45	.106
2003	Redattore	8	J.A. Krone	120	Irish Warrior	117	Mister Acpen	116	240,000	1:40.74	.106

Beyer Index: 106.27

CLARK HANDICAP, 1 1/8 Miles,
3-Year-Olds and Up, Churchill Downs, 2003 Purse: $582,000

Year	Winner	Age	Jockey	Wt.	Second	Wt.	Third	Wt.	Win Value	Time	Beyer
1875	Voltigeur	3	McGrath	110	Calvin	100	Millionaire	100	1,425	3:50.75	
1876	Credmoor	3	W. Williams	100	Vagrant	97	Henry Owings	100	2,150	3:34.75	
1877	McWhirter	3	Miller	100	Vera Cruz	97	Hyena	97	2,000	3:30.50	
1878	Leveller	3	Swim	100	Day Star	100			2,150	3:37.00	
					Solicitor	100					
1879	Falsetto	3	I. Murphy	100	Bucktie	100	Trinidad	100	2,100	3:40.50	
1880	Kinkead	3	J. McLaughlin	105	Aurora's Baby	105	Bye and Bye	102	2,350	3:37.75	
1881	Hindoo	3	J. McLaughlin	105	Alfambra	105	Bootjack	105	3,500	2:10.25	
1882	Runnymede	3	J. McLaughlin	105	Babcock	105	Apollo	102	3,180	2:15.50	
1883	Ascender	3	Stoval	102	Cardinal McCloskey	102	Markland	103	3,270	2:18.00	
1884	Buchanan	3	I. Murphy	110	Loftin	110	Audrain	110	3,230	2:12.00	
1885	Bersan	3	I. Murphy	110	Troubadour	110	Joe Cotton	110	3,420	2:09.25	
1886	Blue Wing	3	Garrison	118	Free Knight	118	Endurer	118	4,190	2:10.00	
1887	Jim Gore	3	L. Jones	118	Libretto	118	Ban Cloche	118	3,630	2:11.25	
1888	Gallifet	3	A. McCarthy	118	White	118	Long Roll	118	3,510	2:15.25	
1889	Spokane	3	Kiley	118	Proctor Knott	118	Once Again	118	3,510	2:12.50	
1890	Riley	3	I. Murphy	118	Robespierre	118	Bill Letcher	118	4,140	2:16.25	
1891	High Tariff	3	Overton	122	Dickerson	122	Milt Young	118	3,370	2:12.00	
1892	Azra	3	A. Clayton	122	Phil Dwyer	122			3,340	2:20.00	
1893	Boundless	3	Kunze	122	Buck McCann	122	Decapod	122	2,300	2:12.00	
1894	Chant	3	W. Martin	122	Pearl Song	122	Buckrene	122	2,730	2:19.50	
1895	Halma	3	Perkins	122	Curator	122			1,720	2:15.50	
1896	Ben Eder	3	Simms	117	Semper Ego	117	Parson	109	3,350	1:56.50	
1897	Ornament	3	A. Clayton	117	Dr. Catlett	117	Panmure	117	3,350	1:55.00	
1898	Plaudit	3	R. Williams	127	Lieber Karl	122			3,350	1:56.50	
1899	Corsini	3	N. Turner	122	Hapsburg	117	His Lordship	110	3,350	2:01.75	
1900	Lieutenant Gibson	3	Boland	127	Flaunt	117	Dieudonne	107	3,350	1:54.00	
1901	His Eminence	3	Winkfield	127	The Puritan	117	Driscoll	110	3,350	1:55.00	
1902	Death	7	Slack	116	Jim Clark	101	L. Strathm're	108	1,900	1:47.00	
1903	Lover's Labor	6	Scully	100	Harry New	111	Airlight	92	2,150	1:48.00	
1904	Colonial Girl	5	Lyne	109	Monsieur Beaucaire	116	Reservation	116	2,170	1:48.75	
1905	Batts	4	Nicol	104	Early Boy	98	Brancas	109	2,070	1:53.75	
1906	Hyperion II	3	W. McIntyre	103	Envoy	104	Kercheval	108	2,100	1:49.00	
1907	The Minks	4	Nicol	110	Brancas	110	Harry Scott	102	1,820	1:50.80	
1908	Polly Prim	3	V. Powers	117	The Minks	107	Pinkola	105	1,670	1:58.80	

Year	Winner	Age	Jockey	Wt.	Second	Wt.	Third	Wt.	Win Value	Time	Beyer
1909	Miami	3	M. McGee	103	Arcite	112	Huck	105	1,820	1:45.20	
1910	King's Daughter	7	T. Koerner	124	T.M. Green	109	Crystal Maid	114	1,600	1:45.60	
1911	Star Charter	3	J. Wilson	105	Countless	132	Joe Morris	108	1,620	1:45.20	
1912	Adams Express	4	C.H. Shilling	122	Mary Davis	100	Cherryola	106	1,900	1:47.80	
1913	Buckhorn	4	Goose	122	Flora Fina	106	Any Port	102	2,080	1:48.20	
1914	Belloc	3	A. Mott	95	Cream	108	Old Ben	92	2,510	1:45.00	
1915	Hodge	4	C. Borel	108	Short Grass	124	B's Choice	112	2,380	1:44.60	
1916	Hodge	5	C. Hunt	120	Ed Crump	120	Dr. Carmen	107	2,520	1:45.40	
1917	Old Rosebud	6	D. Connelly	117	Roamer	128	Embroidery	106	2,230	1:45.20	
1918	Beaverkill	4	O. Willis	104	Fruit Cake	110	Midway	119	2,380	1:48.20	
1919	Midway	5	H. Thurber	117	Beaverkill	109	Hodge	109	436	1:46.60	
1920	Boniface	5	E. Sande	121	Ginger	108	King Gorin	121	10,360	1:45.80	
1921	Ginger	5	T. Murray	112	Upset	122	Dan. Spray	97	9,495	1:45.00	
1922	Exterminator	7	B. Kennedy	133	Lady Madcap	111	Rouleau	107	11,375	1:50.00	
1923	Audacious	7	B. Kennedy	120	Anna M. Humphrey	99	Bon Homme	108	11,200	1:54.60	
1924	Chilhowee	3	B. Harvey	100	Chacolet	124	Hopeless	111	11,200	1:54.40	
1925	Spic and Span	4	G. Fields	103	Son of John	103	Little Celt	117	12,000	1:47.60	
1926	San Utar	5	M. Garner	114	Moonraker	107	Roycrofter	104	13,750	1:45.40	
1927	Helen's Babe	4	W. Lilley	113	Old Slip	114	Percentage	108	12,325	1:46.00	
1928	Jock	4	E. Ambrose	122	Cartago	106	Flat Iron	124	10,925	1:45.00	
1929	Martie Flynn	4	C. Meyer	113	Easter Stockings	111	Cartago	111	10,975	1:46.60	
1930	Stars and Bars	4	L. Jones	108	Easter Stockings	113	Pigeon Hole	106	10,900	1:47.40	
1931	Bargello	5	K. Russell	110	Royal Julian	105	Playtime	109	10,325	1:44.80	
1932	Pittsburgher	4	C. Corbett	112	Spanish Play	115	Canfli	106	4,310	1:50.20	
1933	Osculator	4	S. Coucci	112	The Nut	109	Waylayer	111	4,840	1:45.40	
1934	Esseff	4	L. Humphries	115	Barn Swallow	112	Tick On	114	2,170	1:44.00	
1935	Beaver Dam	3	R. Montgomery	102	Blackbirder	109	Bring Back	108	2,270	1:47.40	
1936	Corinto	4	C. Kurtsinger	114	Ariel Cross	116	Coldstream	109	4,510	1:44.80	
1937	Count Morse	4	I. Anderson	119	Sir Jim James	110	G'nt Killer	112	9,200	1:45.20	
1938	Main Man	4	W.F. Ward	124	Teddy Haslam	109	Old Nassau	112	4,530	1:46.80	
1939	Arabs Arrow	5	C. Bierman	116	Torchy	116	Sortie Star	110	2,130	1:45.80	
1940	Up the Creek	4	G. Wallace	110	Arabs Arrow	120	Shot Put	108	2,175	1:46.00	
1941	Haltal	4	C. McCreary	115	Viscounty	115	Gallahadion	120	2,110	1:44.80	
1942	Whirlaway	4	W. Eads	127	Aonbarr	115	Fairmond	110	2,150	1:44.80	
1943	Anticlimax	4	C. Bierman	112	Corydon	110	Shot Put	108	2,175	1:46.00	
1944	Alquest	4	J. Adams	116	Anticlimax	114	Parasang	108	4,050	1:45.20	
1945	Sentiment Sake	4	F. Wirth	102	Old Kentuck	110	Black Pepper	107	3,910	1:47.20	
1946	Hail Victory	4	D. Dodson	118	Top Reward	111	Bull Play	110	7,775	1:47.80	
1947	Jack S.L.	7	S. Brooks	116	Pellicle	118	Letmenow	110	7,825	1:49.60	
1948	Star Reward	4	S. Brooks	117	Jack S.L.	111	Sun Herod	109	8,175	1:46.60	
1949	Shy Guy	4	C. McCreary	123	Free America	115	Armed	120	7,350	1:45.20	
1950	Mount Marcy	5	S. Brooks	121	Ol' Skipper	114	Dart By	114	8,125	1:44.60	
1951	Wistful	4	D. Dodson	116	Shy Guy	113	Johns Joy	120	7,975	1:44.00	
1952	Seaward	7	K. Church	113	Gay Hunter	102	Hedgewood	110	7,825	1:44.40	
1953	Chombro	6	L.C. Cook	105	Whither	110	Royal Mustang	116	10,887	1:45.60	
1953	Second Avenue	6	C. Bierman	114	Eljay	110	Ad'ms Off Ox	120	10,987	1:45.60	
1954	Bay Bloom	5	J. King	111	Gala Fete	116	Second Avenue	112	11,925	1:44.00	
1955	Happy Go Lucky	6	L.C. Cook	111	Smoke Screen	112	Hasseyampa	121	11,650	1:51.60	
1956	Swoon's Son	3	D. Erb	128	Bernburgoo	111	Mister Black	113	21,925	1:50.60	
1957	Ezgo	3	J. Delahoussaye	114	Aurecolt	111	Styrunner	114	17,957	1:50.80	
1958	My Night Out		E.J. Knapp	116	Shan Pac	116	Praised	108	18,169	1:50.00	
1959	Las Olas	4	F.A. Smith	111	Dru Away	119	Beauguerre	110	17,811	1:48.40	
1960	Counterate	3	J.L. Rotz	114	Little Fitz	118	Cuvier Relic	112	17,925	1:49.00	
1961	Aeroflint	3	E. Curry	116	Neewollah	111	Rev-Up	108	18,785	1:48.40	
1962	Crimson Satan	3	H. Hinojosa	121	Tumble Turbie	116	Bass Clef	117	18,070	1:50.00	
1963	Copy Chief	3	D. Brumfield	117	Lemon Twist	115	Brenner Pass	112	17,842	1:49.20	
1964	Lemon Twist	4	B. Phelps	119	Copy Chief	119	City Line	123	17,842	1:50.60	
1965	Big Brigade	4	J. Nichols	118	Special Prince	110	King of Kentucky	112	18,622	1:50.80	
1966	Flick II	4	H. Pilar	112	Carpenter's Rule	118	King of Kentucky	115	18,574	1:49.60	
1967	Random Shot	4	B. Phelps	114	Maris	116	Backbiter	114	18,639	1:50.80	
1968	Bold Favorite	3	R. Nono	113	Ask the Fare	117	Monitor	116	18,330	1:49.20	
1969	Bold Favorite	4	D. Richard	120	Frederick Street	115	Dorileo	116	18,460	1:50.40	
1970	Watch Fob	5	D. Gargan	114	Spud	113	Dust Commander	118	17,859	1:51.20	
1971	Sado	4	D. Brumfield	116	French Corners	111	New Round	113	18,850	1:53.60	
1972	Fairway Flyer	3	D.E. Whited	114	Code of Honor	116	Dartsum	113	18,444	1:53.80	
1973	Golden Don	3	M. Manganello	122	Amber Prey	115	Rastaferian	118	22,392	1:52.80	
1974	Mr. Door	3	W. Gavidia	114	Fairway Flyer	116	Cut the Talk	115	17,989	1:52.20	
1975	Warbucks	5	L. Melancon	124	Silver Badge	118	Shoo Dear	111	17,761	1:54.40	
1976	Yamanin	4	G. Patterson	120	Warbucks	115	Play Boy	113	21,661	1:54.40	
1977	Bob's Dusty	3	R. Depass	118	Packer Captain	116	Almost Grown	113	21,889	1:49.80	
1978	Bob's Dusty	4	R. Depass	116	Kodiack	114	Raymond Earl	117	34,629	1:50.20	
1979	Lot o' Gold	3	J.C. Espinoza	123	Poverty Boy	114	Capital Idea	114	38,383	1:50.80	
1980	Sun Catcher	3	D. Brumfield	117	Belle's Ruler	116	Withholding	116	35,636	1:53.40	

Year	Winner	Age	Jockey	Wt.	Second	Wt.	Third	Wt.	Win Value	Time	Beyer
1981	Withholding	4	L. Melancon	121	Recusant	111	Hard Up	115	37,213	1:52.00	
1982	Hechizado	6	R.P. Romero	117	Withholding	116	Pleasing Times	115	36,823	1:52.40	
1983	Jack Slade	3	J. McKnight	117	Northern Majesty	122	Cad	118	36,823	1:52.40	
1984	Eminency	6	P. Day	121	Jack Slade	122	Bayou Hebert	114	36,400	1:49.00	
1985	Hopeful Word	4	P. Day	118	Dramatic Desire	113	Big Bobcat	111	49,510	1:51.00	
1986	Come Summer	4	P.A. Johnson	112	Taylor's Special	126	Sumptious	120	47,363	1:49.80	
1987	Intrusion	5	L. Melancon	114	Savings	116	Mister C.	116	47,655	1:51.40	
1988	Balthazar B.	5	K.J. Desormeaux	112	Clever Secret	115	Slew City Slew	123	80,835	1:51.20	
1989	No Marker	5	D.W. Cox	113	Set a Record	114	Stop the Stage	111	75,205	1:51.20	
1990	Secret Hello	3	P. Day	115	Din's Dancer	119	De Roche	121	72,410	1:50.60	
1991	Out of Place	4	W.H. McCauley	119	Echelon's Ice Man	110	British Banker	111	74,230	1:52.20	94
1992	Zeeruler	4	G.K. Gomez	113	Flying Continental	118	Echelon's Ice Man	109	76,050	1:50.00	109
1993	Mi Cielo	3	M.E. Smith	117	Take Me Out	115	Forry Cow How	115	150,540	1:51.40	105
1994	Sir Vixen	6	Kutz D	112	Danville	113	Prize Fight	115	142,480	1:51.20	104
1995	Judge TC	4	Johnson JM	115	Tyus	113	Alphabet Soup	117	153,140	1:49.80	105
1996	Isitingood	5	D.R. Flores	120	Savinio	119	Coup d'Argent	110	174,220	1:48.80	114
1997	Concerto	3	J.D. Bailey	113	Terremoto	114	Rod and Staff	107	284,704	1:49.60	106
1998	Silver Charm	4	G.L. Stevens	124	Littlebitlively	113	Wild Rush	117	275,776	1:49.00	113
1999	Littlebitlively	5	C.H. Borel	118	Pleasant Breeze	112	Nite Dreamer	114	284,456	1:50.80	105
2000	Surfside	3	P. Day	113	Guided Tour	114	Maysville Slew	113	276,272	1:48.75	116
2001	Ubiquity	4	C. Perret	113	Include	120	Mr Ross	114	280,240	1:48.26	106
2002	Lido Palace	5	J.F. Chavez	121	Crafty Shaw	115	Hero's Tribute	114	283,464	1:49.13	112
2003	Quest	4	J. Castellano	114	Evening Attire	118	Aeneas	114	360,840	1:52.42	108

Evening Attire finished first but was disqualified and placed second

Beyer Index: 107.46

COMMONWEALTH BREEDERS' CUP, 7 Furlongs,
3-Year-Olds and Up, Keeneland Race Course, 2003 Purse: $273,750

Year	Winner	Age	Jockey	Wt.	Second	Wt.	Third	Wt.	Win Value	Time	Beyer
1987	Exclusive Enough	3	M.E. Smith	111	Lazer Show	120	High Brite	120	101,010	1:08.40	
1988	Calestoga	6	D. Brumfield	120	You're No Bargain	117	Carload	120	101,628	1:09.40	
1989	Sewickley	4	R.P. Romero	115	Irish Open	118	Dancing Spree	115	36,368	1:22.40	
1990	Black Tie Affair	4	M. Guidry	121	Shaker Knit	115	Momsfurrari	118	120,608	1:22.00	
1991	Black Tie Affair	5	J.L. Diaz	124	Housebuster	124	Exemplary Leader	115	118,625	1:21.80	106
1992	Pleasant Tap	5	E. Delahoussaye	116	To Freedom	115	Run on the Bank	118	118,138	1:22.40	105
1993	Alydeed	4	C. Perret	115	Binalong	118	Senor Speedy	115	113,057	1:21.40	109
1994	Memo	7	P. Atkinson	118	American Chance	115	British Banker	115	149,900	1:22.20	116
1995	Golden Gear	4	C. Perret	118	Turkomatic	112	Lit de Justice	121	130,758	1:22.00	105
1996	Afternoon Deelites	4	K.J. Desormeaux	124	Western Winter	113	Our Emblem	115	131,068	1:21.00	104
1997	Victor Cooley	5	E.M. Martin Jr.	114	Western Winter	112	Appealing Skier	121	129,332	1:22.60	107
1998	Distorted Humor	5	G.L. Stevens	119	El Amante	114	Partner's Hero	121	130,820	1:20.40	116
1999	Good and Tough	4	S.J. Sellers	115	Purple Passion	115	Crucible	115	127,906	1:22.00	107
2000	Richter Scale	6	R. Migliore	121	Son's Corona	117	Deep Gold	117	128,836	1:21.07	114
2001	Alannan	5	E.S. Prado	118	Valiant Halory	118	Liberty Gold	118	170,965	1:22.39	100
2002	Orientate	4	P. Day	120	Aldebaran	118	Twilight Road	118	168,997	1:21.54	109
2003	Smooth Jazz	4	E.S. Prado	118	Crafty C.T.	118	Multiple Choice	120	169,725	1:21.73	117

Beyer Index: 108.85

COTILLION HANDICAP, 1 1/16 Miles,
3-Year-Old Fillies. Philadelphia Park, 2003 Purse: $250,000

Year	Winner	Age	Jockey	Wt.	Second	Wt.	Third	Wt.	Win Value	Time	Beyer
1969	Shuvee	3	J. Davidson	124	Class Is Out	113	Secret Verdict	114	33,120	1:43.20	
1970	Office Queen	3	J.L. Rotz	123	Ellen Girl	117	Fast Attack	116	34,500	1:44.00	
1971	Alma North	3	F. Lovato	116	Forward Gal	123	Miss Pat R.	110	33,480	1:43.60	
1972	Susan's Girl	3	V. Tejada	125	Groton miss	119	Honestous	115	35,970	1:44.20	
1973	Lilac Hill	3	D. MacBeth	113	Ladies Agreement	114	Suzi Sunshine	114	34,590	1:43.60	
1974	Honky Star	3	D.G. McHargue	121	Special Team	118	Kudara	121	32,910	1:44.00	
1975	My Juliet	3	D. Brumfield	116	Hot n Nasty	116	Gala Lil	118	20,160	1:43.60	
1976	Revidere	3	J. Vasquez	118	Critical Miss	116	Hay Patcher	116	20,190	1:44.00	
1977	Suede Shoe	3	A.S. Black	116	Raise Old Glory	113	Bafflin Lil	116	27,930	1:42.60	
1978	Queen Lib	3	D. MacBeth	121	Silken Delight	116	Sharp Belle	116	28,620	1:43.20	
1979	Alada	3	J. Fell	116	Too Many Sweets	116	Heavenly Ade	118	33,090	1:43.80	
1980	Sugar and Spice	3	G. Martens	116	Pepi Valley	118	Nijit	116	34,800	1:45.00	
1981	Truly Bound	3	R.J. Franklin	121	Pukka Princess	118	Debonair Dancer	118	33,810	1:42.80	
1982	Lady Eleanor	3	C. Perret	122	Smart Heiress	122	Glass House	117	34,800	1:45.00	
1983	Quixotic Lady	3	G. McCarron	122	Lady Hawthorn	117	Springtime Sharon	117	33,180	1:42.80	
1984	Squan Song	3	R.Z. Hernandez	122	Given	122	You're Too Special	113	60,945	1:42.80	
1984	Dowery	3	V. Bracciale Jr	122	Duo Disco	122	Hot Milk	117	60,945	1:42.80	
1985	Koluctoo's Jill	3	W.H. McCauley	119	Overwhelming	115	Tabayour	118	65,520	1:42.80	
1986	Toes Knows	3	D.R. Wright	119	Life at the Top	121	I'm Sweets	119	65,880	1:42.80	
1987	Silent Turn	3	R.P. Romero	118	Sacahuista	119	Single Blade	117	65,280	1:42.80	

Year	Winner	Age	Jockey	Wt.	Second	Wt.	Third	Wt.	Win Value	Time	Beyer
1988	Aquaba	3	J. Cruguet	115	Ice Tech	113	Mother of Eight	114	79,320	1:44.40	
1989	Sharp Dance	3	K. Castaneda	115	Misty Ivor	113	Tactile	117	81,900	1:45.80	
1990	Valay Maid	3	L. Saumell	119	Toffeefee	115	Trumpet's Blare	116	81,600	1:43.80	109
1992	Star Minister	3	A.J. Seefeldt	117	Diamond Duo	121	Squirm	116	80,760	1:44.00	95
1993	Jacody	3	T.G. Turner	118	Aztec Hill	121	Cearas Dancer	109	95,520	1:43.20	104
1994	Sovereign Kitty	3	W.H. McCauley	118	Cinnamon Sugar	120	Cavada	116	97,440	1:43.40	95
1995	Clear Mandate	3	J.C. Ferrer	113	Blue Sky Princess	114	Country Cat	118	164,550	1:42.80	98
1996	Double Dee's	3	F. Leon	111	Ginny Lynn	121	Princess Eloise	113	90,000	1:44.60	90
1997	Snit	3	R.E. Colton	114	Proud Run	116	Salt It	117	90,000	1:43.80	101
1998	Lu Ravi	3	W. Martinez	121	Sister Act	115	Let	117	90,000	1:43.40	100
1999	Skipping Around	3	M.J. McCarthy	114	Strolling Belle	120	Waltz	114	120,000	1:43.40	95
2000	Jostle	3	M.E. Smith	124	Gold For My Gal	112	Prized Stamp	114	120,000	1:42.54	106
2001	Mystic Lady	3	E.M. Coa	121	Zonk	117	Celtic Melody	115	150,000	1:43.86	103
2002	Smok'n Frolic	3	J.A. Velez Jr.	118	Pupil	114	Jilbab	120	150,000	1:44.27	96
2003	Fast Cookie	3	N. Santagata	116	Ladyecho	116	Savedbythelight	117	150,000	1:45.83	96

Beyer Index: 99.08

BING CROSBY BREEDERS' CUP HANDICAP, 6 Furlongs, 3-Year-Olds and Up, Del Mar, 2003 Purse: $191,000

Year	Winner	Age	Jockey	Wt.	Second	Wt.	Third	Wt.	Win Value	Time	Beyer
1946	War Allies	4	R. Neves	119			Pride of Hy'ro	122	3,250	1:11.40	
	Indian Watch	6	M. Peterson	105							
1947	Be Fearless	5	L. Balaski	121	Barbastel	111	War Valor	108	4,700	1:10.80	
1948	Prevaricator	5	J. Bravo	122	Tape Buster	115	Capt. Flagg	114	6,600	1:11.20	
1949	Cover Up	6	M. Volzke	114	Roman In	115	Barsard	116	6,800	1:10.00	
1950	Imperium	4	W. Shoemaker	122	Akimbo	105	Brave Fox	115	4,500	1:09.80	
1951	Blue Reading	4	B. Pearson	118	Kit Carson	121	Mrs. Fuddy	108	4,450	1:10.40	
1952	Gustaf	9	W. Marsh	107	Blue Reading	123	Trusting	110	4,425	1:10.00	
1953	Ode	6	R. York	111	Big Noise	112	Stranglehold	120	6,200	1:10.20	
1954	Alibhai Lynn	4	J. Phillippi	111	Karim	115	Stranglehold	122	7,100	1:09.60	
1955	One Ton Tony	5	P. Moreno	115	Karim	119	Bobby Brocato	121	6,800	1:09.20	
1956	Colonel Mack	4	R. Neves	122	Poona II	123	Moolah Bux	107	8,700	1:08.80	
1957	How Now	4	R. York	122	Jeddar Ruler	115	Noredski	118	8,725	1:09.20	
1958	How Now	5	W. Harmatz	128	Swirling Abbey	120	Little Moon	110	8,300	1:09.40	
1959	Ole Fols	3	I. Valenzuela	122	Coup de Vent	109	Silky Sullivan	122	8,775	1:08.80	
1960	High Performance	5	R. Campas	110	Little Moon	113	Aliwar	124	8,825	1:09.00	
1961	Ann's Knight	5	R. Mundorf	114	Revel	127	W'nsome Winner	115	8,650	1:08.60	
1962	Sea Orbit	6	R. York	118	Ann's Knight	118	Mr. Wag	114	7,375	1:08.60	
1962	Crazy Kid	4	A. Valenzuela	118	Cadiz	122	Henrijan	118	7,375	1:07.80	
1963	Sledge	4	M. Yanez	117	Testum	119	Gallant Host	114	8,475	1:08.60	
1964	Soldier Girl	3	J. Longden	116	More Megaton	116			8,525	1:09.40	
1964					Rich Mel	118					
1965	Viking Spirit	5	K. Church	128	Perris	115	Nearco Blue	110	8,500	1:08.60	
1966	Chiclero	4	D. Pierce	119	Traveling Dust	112	Aurelius II	115	8,775	1:08.80	
1967	Kissin' George	4	W. Mahorney	122	Wolfgang	110	Royal Step	114	10,375	1:08.60	
1968	Pretense	4	D. Pierce	122	Kissin' George	125	Dizzy Babe	114	8,500	1:07.80	
1969	Kissin' George	6	W. Mahorney	127	Time to Leave	121	Canterbury Road	119	10,450	1:07.80	
1970	Bargain Day	5	R. Rosales	113	Pinjara	125	Imaginative	117	9,025	1:27.60	
1971	Haveago	4	J. Sellers	115	Long Position	119	Fl't Surprise	123	9,075	1:08.20	
1972	Dominant Star	4	F. Alvarez	112	Restless Runner	114	Crimson Saint	118	9,100	1:08.00	
1973	Pataha Prince	8	W. Shoemaker	114	King of Cricket	114	Rough Night	120	13,700	1:08.00	
1974	Rise High	4	J. Tejeira	113	Tragic Isle	121	Against the Snow	115	13,250	1:09.00	
1975	Messenger of Song	3	J. Lambert	119	Stake Driver	114	Century's Envoy	122	12,450	1:08.80	
1976	Cherry River	6	L. Pincay Jr	120	Sawtooth	111	Fast Spot	115	15,900	1:09.40	
1977	Cherry River	7	L. Pincay Jr	120	Leinster House	111	Mark's Place	124	15,800	1:08.40	
1978	Bad 'n Big	4	W. Shoemaker	124	Amadevil	121	Decoded	115	19,400	1:07.80	
1979	Syncopate	4	S. Hawley	116	White Rammer	122	Fleet Twist	116	22,750	1:08.40	
1980	Reb's Golden Ale	5	S. Hawley	117	Bolger	114	Bad 'n Big	118	24,400	1:08.80	
1981	Syncopate	6	E. Delahoussaye	122	Reb's Golden Ale	119	To B. or Not	122	31,100	1:08.60	
1982	Pencil Point	4	P.A. Valenzuela	114	Terresto's Singer	114	Shanekite	115	32,650	1:09.00	
1983	Chinook Pass	4	L. Pincay Jr	125	Vagabond Song	116	Haughty but Nice	115	32,000	1:08.60	
1984	Night Mover	4	L.E. Ortega	120	Premiership	119	Pac Mania	115	31,800	1:08.60	
1985	My Favorite Mom't	4	E. Delahoussaye	116	Rosie's K.T.	116	Fifty Six Ina Row	119	33,350	1:09.80	
1986	American Legion	6	E. Delahoussaye	119	Bold Brawley	113	Ondarty	112	38,000	1:08.20	
1987	Zany Tactics	6	J.L. Kaenel	120	Bolder Than Bold	118	My Favorite Mom't	115	38,600	1:09.00	
1988	Olympic Prospect	4	A. Solis	121	Faro	118	Sebrof	119	59,410	1:08.80	
1989	On the Line	5	G.L. Stevens	124	Speedratic	117	Cresting Water	115	63,800	1:08.00	
1990	Sensational Star	6	R.Q. Meza	113	Frost Free	116	Timeless Answer	116	60,150	1:08.00	110
1991	Bruho	5	C.S. Nakatani	116	Thirty Slews	115	Due to the King	116	62,900	1:08.20	112
1992	Thirty Slews	5	E. Delahoussaye	116	Slerp	115	Anjiz	114	64,900	1:08.20	106
1993	The Wicked North	4	C.A. Black	116	Thirty Slews	121	Black Jack Road	115	61,200	1:08.40	112

Year	Winner	Age	Jockey	Wt.	Second	Wt.	Third	Wt.	Win Value	Time	Beyer
1994	King's Blade	3	Nakatani CS	112	Memo	121	Gundaghia	118	62,400	1:08.60	107
1995	Gold Land	4	Delahoussaye E	116	Lucky Forever	118	G Malleah	116	89,300	1:08.00	112
1996	Lit de Justice	6	C.S. Nakatani	121	Concept Win	116	Gold Land	116	126,750	1:08.00	113
1997	First Intent	8	R.R. Douglas	115	Boundless Moment	118	High Stakes Player	120	102,000	1:08.80	110
1998	Son of a Pistol	6	A. Solis	120	Gold Land	117	Boundless Moment	116	97,200	1:08.00	118
1999	Christmas Boy	6	C.S. Nakatani	114	Son of a Pistol	123	Expressionist	116	96,360	1:08.00	117
2000	Kona Gold	6	A. Solis	123	Love That Red	118	Lexicon	117	124,200	1:08.50	118
2001	Kona Gold	7	A. Solis	126	Caller One	124	Swept Overboard	115	120,000	1:08.22	119
2002	Disturbingthepeace	4	V. Espinoza	116	Freespool	115	Mellow Fellow	118	90,000	1:09.21	110
2003	Beau's Town	5	P.A. Valenzuela	119	Captain Squire	117	Bluesthestandard	117	120,000	1:07.96	116

Beyer Index: 112.86

DAHLIA HANDICAP, 1 1/16 Miles (Turf),
Fillies and Mares, 3-Year-Olds and Up, Hollywood Park, 2003 Purse: $150,000

Year	Winner	Age	Jockey	Wt.	Second	Wt.	Third	Wt.	Win Value	Time	Beyer
1982	Sangue	4	L. Pincay Jr	122	Star Pastures	118	Pat's Joy	115	31,900	1:41.40	
1982	Milingo	3	T. Lipham	124	Pink Safir	113	Berry Bush	117	33,400	1:42.60	
1983	Geraldine's Store	4	J.L. Samyn	118	Northerly Glow	111	Satin Ribera	115	32,500	1:42.40	
1983	First Advance	4	T. Lipham	114	Absentia	116	Bersid	112	33,500	1:42.00	
1984	Lina Cavalieri	4	E. Delahoussaye	117	Pampas	115	Salt Spring	117	53,050	1:44.20	
1985	Capricorn Belle	4	C.J. McCarron	118	Justicara	118	Solva	115	66,200	1:41.60	
1986	Aberuschka	4	P.A. Valenzuela	122	An Empress	117	Reloy	118	80,740	1:41.60	
1987	Invited Guest	3	W. Shoemaker	114	Secuencia	115	Smooch	117	71,950	1:43.40	
1987	Top Corsage	4	J.A. Santos	118	Any Song	116	Aberuschka	120	48,700	1:43.20	
1988	Balbonella	4	F. Toro	117	Goodbye Halo	120	Pen Bal Lady	117	75,100	1:42.80	
1989	Stylish Star	3	C.J. McCarron	116	Ariosa	113	Sugar Plum Gal	114	51,600	1:40.40	
1989	Saros Brig	5	G.L. Stevens	114	Nikishka	120	Beat	115	49,600	1:40.40	
1990	Petalia	5	K.J. Desormeaux	113	Bequest	117	Island Jamboree	113	48,900	1:41.40	96
1990	Little Brianne	5	J.A. Garcia	119	Stylish Star	119	Girl of France	115	50,900	1:40.60	105
1991	Re Toss	4	C.S. Nakatani	115	Elegance	115	Gaelic Bird	114	70,400	1:40.60	102
1992	Kostroma	6	G.L. Stevens	124	Vijaya	114	Guiza	116	66,500	1:41.40	102
1993	Kalita Melody	5	C.A. Black	115	Vinista	116	Gumpher	116	64,500	1:44.60	99
1994	Skimble	5	E. Delahoussaye	118	Queens Court Queen	118	Shir Dar	115	66,000	1:42.20	100
1995	Didina	3	E. Delahoussaye	115	Dirca	114	Rapunzel Runz	116	68,300	1:45.20	107
1996	Sixieme Sens	4	C.S. Nakatani	115	Grafin	116	Admise	121	66,600	1:42.20	103
1997	Golden Arches	3	C.J. McCarron	117	Sonja's Faith	113	Traces Of Gold	116	60,000	1:41.00	100
1998	Tuzla	4	C.S. Nakatani	119	Sonja's Faith	118	Curitiba	115	60,000	1:41.60	102
1999	Lady At Peace	3	G.K. Gomez	113	Cyrillic	117	Country Garden	115	90,000	1:41.40	98
2000	Follow The Money	4	V. Espinoza	115	Smooth Player	120	Beautiful Noise	117	90,000	1:40.71	98
2001	Verruma	5	G.K. Gomez	115	Vencera	115	Heads Will Roll	117	90,000	1:43.24	99
2002	Tout Charmant	6	A. Solis	119			Honestly Darling	114	60,000	1:44.45	99
	Surya	4	P.A. Valenzuela	118							
2003	Katdogawn	3	M.E. Smith	116	Personal Legend	115	Betty's Wish	117	90,000	1:41.52	97

Beyer Index: 100.47

DAVONA DALE, 1 1/16 Miles,
3-Year-Old Fillies, Gulfstream Park, 2003 Purse: $150,000

Year	Winner	Age	Jockey	Wt.	Second	Wt.	Third	Wt.	Win Value	Time	Beyer
1988	Charming Tigress	5	P. Day	115	Polar Wind		No Doublet		21,069	1:24.60	
1988	Cadillacing	4	R.P. Romero	122	Easter Mary		Saucey Missy		21,429	1:23.00	
1989	Waggley	6	J.L. Samyn	122	Plate Queen		Ataentsic		20,640	1:22.60	
1990	Big Pride	3	E. Fires	112	Crowned		Sonic Gray		21,000	1:26.00	91
1991	Fancy Ribbons	3	C. Perret	118	Hula Pride		Designated Dancer		45,420	1:42.00	92
1992	Miss Legality	3	J.A. Krone	116	November Snow	114	Spectacular Sue	114	30,000	1:42.00	96
1993	Lunar Spook	3	M. Guidry	118	Boots 'n Jackie	121	In Her Glory	118	30,000	1:42.00	99
1994	Cut the Charm	3	J.D. Bailey	116	She Rides Tonite	114	Delightful Bet	113	60,000	1:41.40	82
1995	Mia's Hope	3	Chapman KL	114	Minister Wife	121	Culver City	112	60,000	1:43.20	90
1996	Plum Country	3	P. Day	118	My Flag	118	La Rosa	118	60,000	1:42.00	98
	Rare Blend finished second but was disqualified and placed sixth										
1997	Glitter Woman	3	M.E. Smith	114	City Band	121	Southern Playgirl	121	60,000	1:39.20	108
1998	Diamond On the Run	3	P. Day	112	Uanme	114	Dixie Melody	113	60,000	1:42.60	92
1999	Three Ring	3	J.R. Velazquez	118	Golden Temper	113	Gold From The West	116	60,000	1:41.40	106
2000	Cash Run	3	J.D. Bailey	118	Regally Appealing	116	Secret Status	114	60,000	1:40.37	105
2001	Latour	3	J.R. Velazquez	112	Gold Mover	116	Courageous Maiden	113	60,000	1:45.51	83
2002	Ms Brookski	3	R.B. Homeister	121	Colonial Glitter	117	French Satin	115	60,000	1:45.14	89
2003	Yell	3	J.R. Velazquez	117	Ivanavinalot	121	Gold Player	115	90,000	1:44.96	96

Beyer Index: 94.79

Run at 7 furlongs 1988-1990

DEL MAR BREEDERS' CUP HANDICAP, 1 Mile,
3-Year-Olds and Up, Del Mar, 2003 Purse: $178,000

Year	Winner	Age	Jockey	Wt.	Second	Wt.	Third	Wt.	Win Value	Time	Beyer
1987	God Command	4	C.J. McCarron	114	Stop the Fighting	116	Candi's Gold	113	86,250	1:34.80	
1988	Precisionist	7	C.J. McCarron	125	Lively One	114	He's a Saros	116	85,150	1:34.60	
1989	On the Line	5	L. Pincay Jr	124	Good Taste	117	Lively One	125	115,400	1:33.40	
1990	Stalwart Charger	3	R.M. Gonzalez	115	Flying Continental	120	Ruhlmann	123	116,300	1:34.60	
1991	Twilight Agenda	5	K.J. Desormeaux	122	Opening Verse	117	Robyn Dancer	117	116,950	1:34.00	
1992	Reign Road	4	D.R. Flores	114	Sir Beaufort	116	Charmonnier	115	122,000	1:35.20	
1993	Region	4	C.S. Nakatani	115	Lottery Winner	115	L'Express	115	122,100	1:34.80	
1994	Lykatill Hil	4	E. Delahoussaye	118	D'hallevant	117	Stuka	116	62,200	1:34.00	..110
1995	Alphabet Soup	4	C.J. McCarron	115	Lykatill Hil	117	Luthier Fever	115	117,150	1:34.20	..110
1996	Dramatic Gold	5	K.J. Desormeaux	118	Alphabet Soup	120	Savinio	118	125,650	1:34.60	..110
1997	Benchmark	6	E. Delahoussaye	117	Crafty Friend	118	Northern Afleet	120	126,700	1:35.40	..107
1998	Old Trieste	3	C.J. McCarron	116	Grajagan	111	Stalwart Tsu	116	123,172	1:35.20	..104
1999	Hollycombe	5	G.L. Stevens	116	Flying With Eagles	115	Old Trieste	122	126,060	1:35.40	..106
2000	El Corredor	3	V. Espinoza	111	Cliquot	117	Literal Prowler	112	158,160	1:35.05	..110
2001	El Corredor	4	V. Espinoza	121	Figlio Mio	113	Performing Magic	116	150,000	1:35.24	..114
2002	Congaree	4	M. Smith	119	Kela	117	Reba's Gold	116	150,000	1:36.24	..105
2003	Joey Franco	4	P.A. Valenzuela	116	Reba's Gold	116	Grey Memo	117	90,000	1:35.70	..104

Beyer Index: 107.90

DEL MAR DERBY, 1 1/8 Miles (Turf),
3-Year-Olds, Del Mar, 2003 Purse: $300,000

Year	Winner	Age	Jockey	Wt.	Second	Wt.	Third	Wt.	Win Value	Time	Beyer
1948	Frankly	3	G. Pederson	124	Barsard	118	Smoke Tree	118	11,875	1:42.80	
1949	Bolero	3	J. Westrope	124	Elbutte	118	Dharan	108	12,225	1:42.00	
1950	Great Circle	3	R. Neves	123	Mrs. Fuddy	109	Blue Reading	126	9,400	1:48.40	
1951	Grantor	3	W. Shoemaker	124	Mucho Hosso	116	Oats	122	8,900	1:48.60	
1952	Southarlington	3	R. Summers	108	Blue Trumpeter	109	Arroz	122	9,750	1:48.80	
1953	Apple Valley	3	B. Pearson	109	Smart Barbara	113	Chanlea	122	9,050	1:49.40	
1954	Musselshell	3	W. Shoemaker	115	Spring Count	110	Tussle Patch	110	9,650	1:48.80	
1955	Hi Pardner	3	W. Harmatz	108	Golden Land	119	Count Jac	117	15,500	1:49.00	
1956	Bounty Bay	3	J.R. Adams	113	Lucky G.I.	114	Proselyte	114	17,125	1:48.00	
1957	Mystic Eye	3	W. Skuse	120	Judgar Ruler	115	Seaneen	120	16,275	1:48.20	
1958	The Shoe	3	A. Maese	122	Cowboy Book	110	Sir Ruler	122	15,125	1:48.60	
1959	Mr. Eiffel	3	G. Taniguchi	111	King Ara	122	King o' Turf	112	15,425	1:47.60	
1960	Nagea	3	A. Maese	122	Have Tux	111	Djeddah Pat	109	15,575	1:47.60	
1961	Speak John	3	P. Moreno	121	Shelbyville	122	Aldershot	111	15,425	1:48.00	
1962	Bayou Bourg	3	P. Moreno	114	Sunday Slippers	112	Savail	117	16,475	1:48.20	
1963	Big Raff	3	R. Campas	115	Nevada Battler	118	Real Luck	119	12,425	1:48.00	
1963	Olympiad King	3	J. Longden	126	More Megaton	111	Mary Mel	104	12,425	1:47.80	
1964	Pop's Harmony	3	G. Taniguchi	111	Pelegrin	117	Maker's Mark	112	15,675	1:48.60	
1965	Hasty Trip	3	B. Jennings	113	Terry's Secret	126	Nasharco	119	16,825	1:47.60	
1966	Drin	3	D. Pierce	122	Fleet Host	119	Desert Trial	116	15,325	1:47.40	
1967	Charlie Boots	3	A. Pineda	116	Gentlemans Game	112	Kahl Kabee	120	17,750	1:47.40	
1968	Prince Hemp	3	J. Lambert	114			Fiddle Isle	120	10,087	1:46.60	
	Glory Hallelujah	3	R. Caballero	110							
1969	Commissary	3		116	Commissary	116	Neutral	116	16,500	1:47.40	
1970	War Heim	3	F. Toro	113	Mickey McGuire	113	Freeway Kid	113	13,500	1:49.20	
1970	Mayhedo	3	J. Lambert	114	Sir Wiggle	113	Woodie Can	113	13,750	1:49.20	
1971	Regal Case	3	H. Grant	117	Great Career	113	High and Mighty	114	20,450	1:49.00	
1972	Bicker	3	G. Brogan	113	Oh Hello	113	Queen's Hustler	113	23,750	1:49.00	
1973	Right Honorable	3	J. Lambert	115	Groshawk	119	Dancing Papa	113	28,650	1:10.80	
1974	Lightning Mandate	3	A. Pineda	116	Within Hail	113	Prince Petrone	113	27,900	1:50.00	
1975	Larrikin	3	D. Pierce	116	Messenger of Song	116	Wood Carver	115	28,900	1:48.80	
1976	Montespan	3	D.G. McHargue	115	Dr. Krohn	117	Today 'n Tomorrow	118	26,550	1:48.40	
1977	Text	3	D.G.McHargue	122	Pay the Toll	119	Hill Fox	115	32,750	1:49.40	
1978	Misrepresentation	3	D. Pierce	119	Singular	119	Wayside Station	115	33,450	1:49.60	
1979	Relaunch	3	L. Pincay Jr	121	Kamalii Reiung	112	Pole Position	120	51,450	1:48.80	
1980	Exploded	3	L. Pincay Jr	117	Aristocratical	120	Son of a Dodo	118	70,300	1:49.60	
1981	Juan Barrera	3	F. Toro	115	Buen Chico	114	Rock Softly	115	83,950	1:49.00	
1982	Give Me Strength	3	L. Pincay Jr	123	Water Bank	117	Take the Floor	117	88,350	1:49.00	
1983	Tanks Brigade	3	R.Q. Meza	117	Ansuan	115	Evening M'Lord	117	85,350	1:49.00	
1984	Tsunami Slew	3	E. Delahoussaye	119	Prince True	119	Majestic Shore	115	99,650	1:48.00	
1985	First Norman	3	G.L. Stevens	117	Pretensor	116	Catane	112	82,300	1:48.00	
1986	Vernon Castle	3	G.L. Stevens	117	Prince Bobby B.	119	Mazaad	119	95,500	1:48.40	
1987	Deputy Governor	3	E. Delahoussaye	119	Stately Don	120	The Medic	118	98,700	1:48.40	
1988	Silver Circus	3	R.A. Baze	118	Perfecting	118	Roberto's Dancer	116	127,900	1:49.00	
1989	Hawkster	3	P.A. Valenzuela	121	River Master	119	Lode	116	130,500	1:48.00	
1990	Itsallgreektome	3	L. Pincay Jr	122	Predacessor	122	Pro for Sure	122	165,000	1:49.60	
1991	Eternity Star	3	F.J. Alvarado	122	Stark South	122	June's Reward	122	165,000	1:49.20	..100

Year	Winner	Age	Jockey	Wt.	Second	Wt.	Third	Wt.	Win Value	Time	Beyer
1992	Daros	3	E. Delahoussaye	122	Smiling and Dancin	.122	Major Impact	122	.165,000	1:48.80	...98
1993	Guide	3	K.J. Desormeaux	122	Future Storm	122	The Real Vaslav ...	122	.165,000	1:49.60	...93
1994	Ocean Crest	3	L. Pincay Jr	122	Unfinished Symph	.122	Powis Castle	122	.165,000	1:48.60	.100
1995	Da Hoss	3	R.R. Douglas	...122	Lake George	.122	Tabor	122	.165,000	1:48.00	.103
1996	Rainbow Blues	3	C.S. Nakatani	...122	The Barking Shark	.122	Mateo	122	.180,000	1:50.00	...99
1997	Anet	3	G.L. Stevens	...121	Brave Act	121	Worldly Ways	121	.180,000	1:48.40	.108
1998	Ladies Din	3	K.J. Desormeaux	121	Expressionist	121	Scooter Brown	121	.180,000	1:48.40	.108
1999	Val Royal	3	C.S. Nakatani	...121	Fighting Falcon	121	In Frank's Honor ...	121	.180,000	1:48.40	.102
2000	Walkslikeaduck	3	E. Delahoussaye	121	Purely Cozzene	121	New Story	118	.180,000	1:46.66	.107
2001	Romanceishope	3	C.J. McCarron	..121	Indygo Shiner	121	Blue Steller	121	.180,000	1:47.93	...96
2002	Inesperado	3	C.S. Nakatani	...121	Johar	121	Rock Opera	121	.180,000	1:47.49	.102
2003	Fairly Ransom	3	A. Solis	122	Devious Boy	122	Sweet Return	122	.180,000	1:46.45	.103

Beyer Index: 101.46

DEL MAR FUTURITY, 7 Furlongs,
2-Year-Olds, Del Mar, 2003 Purse: $250,000

Year	Winner	Age	Jockey	Wt.	Second	Wt.	Third	Wt.	Win Value	Time	Beyer
1948	Star Fiddle	2	H. Trent	122	Buddy Hunter	110	Tom's Pride	114	...6,825	1:11.80	
1949	Your Host	2	F. Chojnacki	115	Blue Rings	112	Sturdy One	118	...31,725	1:10.40	
1950	Patch	2	J. Longden	118	Gay Cavalier	118	Gold Capitol	112	..23,700	1:10.60	
1951	Big Noise	2	R. Neves	115	Challtack	115	Arroz	115	..26,000	1:10.40	
1952	Hour Regards	2	E. LeBlanc	115	Chanlea	118	Decorated	118	..32,200	1:09.80	
1953	Double Speed	2	J. Phillippi	116	James Session	119	For Example	116	..29,475	1:10.40	
1954	Blue Ruler	2	W. Shoemaker	..119	Colonel Mack	119	Riparlus	116	..25,350	1:09.80	
1955	Blen Host	2	R. York	116	Gilding Wings	116	Fortuneway	116	..40,440	1:10.60	
1956	Swirling Abbey	2	D. Lewis	116	Mr. Sam S	119	Prince Khaled	116	..34,990	1:08.80	
1957	Old Pueblo	2	E. Arcaro	119	Disdainful	116	Strong Bay	116	..40,570	1:09.00	
1958	Tomy Lee	2	W. Shoemaker	..122	Royal Orbit	116	Bagdad	116	..50,980	1:09.20	
1959	Azure's Orphan	2	E. Burns	116	Salatom	116	Warfare	119	..50,720	1:09.60	
1960	Short Jacket	2	R. Neves	116	Mr. America	116	Nashua Blue	116	..46,760	1:09.00	
1961	Weldy	2	R. York	116	Snappy King	116	Donut King	116	..62,390	1:09.20	
1962	Slipped Disc	2	R. Yaka	116	Beekeeper	116	Y Flash	119	..56,115	1:09.80	
1963	Perris	2	A. Maese	116	Oldie	116	Harry H.	116	..60,200	1:09.40	
1964	Terry's Secret	2	A. Maese	116	Azure Te	116	Ky. Front	116	..64,945	1:10.20	
1965	Coursing	2	K. Church	116	Couple o'Quid	116	Ri Tux	116	..60,060	1:08.80	
1966	Ruken	2	F. Alvarez	116	Sand Devil	116	Wolfgang	116	..66,285	1:09.40	
1967	Baffle	2	W. Blum	116	Broad Shadows	116	Poleax	116	..67,050	1:09.60	
1968	Fleet Allied	2	J. Lambert	116	Fleet Kirsch	119	Pellinore	116	..57,130	1:08.20	
1969	George Lewis	2	W. Hartack	116	Swarming Bee	116	Atomic Wings	116	..63,270	1:08.20	
1970	June Darling	2	W. Mahorney ...	119	Kfar Tov	119	Bold Joey	116	..64,895	1:08.80	
1971	MacArthur Park	2	W. Shoemaker	..119	Dorreno	116	Normandy Grey ...	116	..41,975	1:29.00	
1971	D,B. Carm	2	F. Toro	119	Master Ribot	116	Royal Connections	.116	..41,975	1:29.00	
1972	Groshawk	2	W. Shoemaker	..116	Lucky Mike	119	Bottle Brush	116	..67,135	1:28.60	
1973	Such a Rush	2	W. Shoemaker	..116	Fast Pappa	116	The Gay Greek	116	..65,740	1:29.80	
1974	Diabolo	2	W. Shoemaker	..116	George Navonod ...	119	Dimaggio	122	..67,120	1:35.40	
1975	Telly's Pop	2	F. Mena	117	Lexington Laugh ...	114	Body Bend	114	..66,275	1:36.00	
1976	Visible	2	L. Pincay Jr	117	Habitony	114	Washoe County ...	115	..74,535	1:35.60	
1977	Go West Young Man	.2	F. Olivares	114	Tampoy	114	Spanish Way	117	..85,845	1:35.60	
1978	Flying Paster	2	D. Pierce	117	Priority	117	Roman Oblisk	117	.100,400	1:34.80	
1979	The Carpenter	2	C.J. McCarron	..114	Doonesbury	117	Executive Counsel	.114	..98,710	1:35.20	
1980	Bold and Gold	2	D.C. Hall	117	Looks Like Rain ...	114	Sir Dancer	117	.129,630	1:36.20	
1981	Gato Del Sol	2	E. Delahoussaye	114	The Captain	120	Ring Proud	115	.160,720	1:37.40	
1982	Roving Boy	2	E. Delahoussaye	117	Desert Wine	120	Balboa Native	114	.159,945	1:38.80	
1983	Althea	2	L. Pincay Jr	117	Juliet's Pride	115	Gumboy	114	.147,865	1:34.80	
1984	Saratoga Six	2	A. Cordero Jr ...	120	Indigenous	114	Lomax	117	.173,440	1:36.00	
1985	Tasso	2	L. Pincay Jr	114	Arewehavingfunyet	.117	Snow Chief	117	.155,760	1:37.00	
1986	Qualify	2	G.L. Stevens	114	Sacahuista	117	Brevito	116	.158,535	1:35.60	
1987	Lost Kitty	2	L. Pincay Jr	117	Bold Second	118	Purdue King	118	.174,800	1:36.20	
1988	Music Merci	2	C.J. McCarron	..114	Bruho	114	Texian	117	.229,300	1:35.40	
1989	Drag Race	2	F. Olivares	114	Rue de Palm	114	Single Dawn	114	.241,600	1:35.40	
1990	Best Pal	2	P.A. Valenzuela	120	Pillaring	116	Got to Fly	117	.231,600	1:35.40	
1991	Bertrando	2	A. Solis	114	Zurich	114	Star Recruit	115	.188,500	1:36.40	...84
1992	River Special	2	C.J. McCarron	..115	Sudden Hush	120	Seattle Street	114	.137,500	1:36.60	...88
1993	Winning Pact	2	C.S. Nakatani	...115	Ramblin Guy	119	Ferrara	115	.137,500	1:22.00	...93
1994	On Target	2	A. Solis	115	Supremo	115	Timber Country ...	119	.137,500	1:22.20	...90
1995	Future Quest	2	K.J. Desormeaux	115	Othello	115	Cavonnier	117	.137,500	1:21.80	...94
1996	Silver Charm	2	D.R. Flores	116	Gold Tribute	115	Swiss Yodeler	121	.150,000	1:22.80	...97
1997	Souvenir Copy	2	C.J. McCarron	..115	Old Topper	119	Commitisize	115	.150,000	1:23.00	...91
1998	Worldly Manner	2	K.J. Desormeaux	119	Daring General	119	Waki American	114	.150,000	1:23.00	...95
1999	Forest Camp	2	D.R. Flores	116	Dixie Union	121	Captain Steve	115	.150,000	1:21.60	.106

Year	Winner	Age	Jockey	Wt.	Second	Wt.	Third	Wt.	Win Value	Time	Beyer
2000	Flame Thrower	2	J.D. Bailey	119	Street Cry	116	Arabian Light	119	150,000	1:22.00	103
2001	Officer	2	V. Espinoza	121	Kamsack	115	Metatron	116	150,000	1:22.33	99
2002	Icecoldbeeratreds	2	D. Flores	119	Kafwain	119	Chief Planner	115	150,000	1:22.94	94
2003	Siphonizer	2	J.A. Krone	116	Minister Eric	116	Perfect Moon	122	150,000	1:23.10	82

Beyer Index: **93.54**

DEL MAR HANDICAP, 1 3/8 Miles (Turf), 3-Year-Olds and Up, Del Mar, 2003 Purse: $250,000

Year	Winner	Age	Jockey	Wt.	Second	Wt.	Third	Wt.	Win Value	Time	Beyer
1937	Sallys Booster	5	T. Sena	114	Sir Ridgway	107	The Fighter	120	4,225	1:44.80	
1938	Ligaroti	6	W. Moran	128	Capt. Cal	115	Sweepalot	115	3,925	1:43.80	
1939	Wedding Call	3	W.F. Ward	108	Pageboy	107	First Kiss	107	3,975	1:44.00	
1940	Big Flash	3	E. Rodriguez	113	Royal Crusader	107	Woof Woof	110	3,750	1:43.00	
1941	Royal Crusader	4	L. Balaski	113	Wedding Call	112	Lassator	108	6,250	1:43.60	
1945	Texas Sandman	4	M. Peterson	126	Dogpatch	117	Wedding Call	112	10,385	1:43.20	
1946	Olhaverry	7	M. Peterson	116	Adrogue	106	Canina	119	12,100	1:43.20	
1947	Iron Maiden	6	W. Parnell	112	Be Fearless	120	Sierra Fox	115	9,950	1:43.60	
1948	Frankly	3	J. Westrope	112	Hemet Squaw	115			18,350	1:42.40	
					Prevaricator	129					
1949	Top's Boy	5	R. Neves	120	Honeymoon	117	Prevaricator	120	6,450	1:48.80	
1950	Frankly	5	W. Shoemaker	120	Top's Boy	112	Mercenary	112	9,650	1:48.60	
1951	Blue Reading	4	B. Pearson	124	Sturdy One	116	Alderman	117	9,200	1:48.40	
1952	Grantor	4	J. Longden	113	Stormy Cloud	108	Moonrush	117	15,450	1:47.40	
1953	Goose Khal	4	W. Shoemaker	119	Fleet Bird	124	Bernwood	108	14,750	1:48.60	
1954	Stranglehold	5	W. Shoemaker	126	Fleet Khal	109	Blue Tr'peter	108	14,800	1:48.40	
1955	Arrogate	4	J. Longden	116	Bobby Brocato	114	Trigonometry	118	14,800	1:47.40	
1956	Arrogate	5	J. Longden	118	Honeys Alibi	121	Brisk 'n Br't	110	18,050	1:47.00	
1957	How Now	4	R. York	118	Pirnie	109	Windsor Serial	118	18,300	1:47.60	
1958	Noredski	5	D. Pierce	111	Solid Son	112	How Now	126	17,400	1:47.60	
1959	Twentyone Guns	4	G. Taniguchi	118	Mr. Snack	113	Find	122	17,800	1:47.20	
1960	How Now	7	E. Burns	122	Honeys Gem	117	Ying and Yang	113	17,100	1:46.60	
1961	Scotland	5	M. Volzke	112	Nagea	120	Grey Eagle	116	18,000	1:46.80	
1962	Crazy Kid	4	A. Maese	120	Sea Orbit	122	Songman	110	17,950	1:47.60	
1963	Mr. Consistency	5	K. Church	116	Rapido	116	Mr. Wag	113	18,650	1:47.00	
1964	Viking Spirit	4	K. Church	123	Hold Me	119	M're M'g't'n	116	18,700	1:48.00	
1965	Terry's Secret	3	A. Maese	120	Aurelius II	118	Perris	113	18,500	1:47.00	
1966	Old Mose	4	D. Pierce	123	Biggs	115	My Captain	107	18,550	1:47.20	
1967	Native Diver	8	J. Lambert	130	Sharp Decline	109	Quicken Tree	117	23,650	1:46.60	
1968	Quicken Tree	5	W. Hartack	120	Fiddle Isle	113	Rivet	116	17,450	1:46.40	
1969	Figonero	4	A. Pineda	124	Triple Tux	112	Balsamo II	116	27,250	1:46.20	
1970	Daryl's Joy	4	J. Sellers	123	Cougar II	120	Contratodos	110	33,450	2:15.40	
1971	Pinjara	6	W. Shoemaker	121	Makor	110	Great Career	110	51,950	2:15.60	
1972	Hill Circus	4	F. Toro	117	War Heim	116	Wing Out	121	40,000	2:16.00	
1972	Chrisaway	4	R. Howard	112	Marlivam	116	Tetrack	113	40,500	2:16.20	
1973	Red Reality	7	B. Baeza	122	Wing Out	119	Life Cycle	124	60,000	2:17.00	
1974	Redtop III	5	F. Toro	115	My Old Friend	115	Nantwice	111	60,000	2:16.00	
1975	Cruiser II	6	F. Olivares	117	Top Crowd	115	Against the Snow	117	60,000	2:14.40	
1976	Riot in Paris	5	Wl. Shoemaker	122	Avatar	122	Good Report	115	60,000	1:57.40	
1977	Ancient Title	7	D.G. McHargue	123	Painted Wagon	118	Cascapedia	117	60,000	1:55.40	
1978	Palton	5	H.E. Moreno	114	Farnesio	119	Vic's Magic	119	60,000	1:57.40	
1979	Ardiente	4	C.J. McCarron	118	Quick Turnover	122	Sudanes	111	75,000	1:56.80	
1980	G'w'sty'ngman	5	E. Delahoussaye	123	Relaunch	118	Balzac	121	75,000	1:58.20	
1981	Wickerr	6	C.J. McCarron	118	Tahitian King	121	Galaxy Libra	121	82,500	1:57.40	
1982	Muttering	3	W. Shoemaker	117	Regalberto	119	Exploded	121	82,500	1:57.00	
1983	Bel Bolide	5	W. Shoemaker	117	Gato del Sol	123	Egg Toss	117	82,500	1:58.20	
1984	Precisionist	3	C.J. McCarron	117	Pair by Deuces	116	Super Diamond	117	137,000	1:56.80	
1985	Barberstown	5	F. Toro	117	My Habitony	118	First Norman	114	137,000	1:58.00	
1986	Raipillan	4	R.A. Baze	114	Schiller	113	Shulich	113	165,000	2:14.40	
1987	Swink	4	W. Shoemaker	120	Santella Mac	116	Skip Out Front	115	165,000	2:13.80	
1988	Sword Dance	4	C.J. McCarron	114	Great Communicator	120	Baba Karam	115	165,000	2:15.80	
1989	Payant	5	R.G. Davis	118	Saratoga Passage	118	No Review	112	165,000	2:15.20	
1990	Live the Dream	4	A. Solis	118	Mehmetori	107	Soft Machine	113	165,000	2:13.00	104
1991	My Style	4	K.J. Desormeaux	115	Forty Niner Days	118	Super May	117	165,000	2:13.40	109
1992	Navarone	4	P.A. Valenzuela	117	Qathif	117	Stark South	117	137,500	2:15.00	107
1993	Luazur	4	P. Day	116	Kotashaan	123	Myrakalu	114	137,500	2:15.00	108
1994	Navarone	6	P.A. Valenzuela	117	Approach the Bench	116	Sir Mark Sykes	116	137,500	2:14.20	105
1995	Royal Chariot	5	L. Pincay Jr	117	River Rhythm	117	Party Season	116	137,500	2:13.60	104
1996	Dernier Empereur	6	P.A. Valenzuela	116	Talloires	119	Party Season	117	150,000	2:13.80	107
1997	Rainbow Dancer	6	A. Solis	118	Dowty	119	Lord Jain	114	150,000	2:14.00	106
1998	Bonapartiste	4	C.J. McCarron	115	River Bay	123	Military	116	150,000	2:14.00	106
1999	Sayarshan	5	B. Blanc	115	Dancing Place	116	Ladies Din	120	150,000	2:14.20	104

Year	Winner	Age	Jockey	Wt.	Second	Wt.	Third	Wt.	Win Value	Time	Beyer
2000	Northern Quest	5	C.J. McCarron	116	Perssonet	114	Alvo Certo	115	150,000	2:12.65	103
	Alvo Certo finished second but was disqualified and placed third										
2001	Timboroa	5	L. Pincay Jr.	118	C.J. McCarron	116	Super Quercus	117	150,000	2:12.59	105
2002	Delta Form	6	G. Almeida	115	The Tin Man	117	Blue Stellar	117	150,000	2:12.15	106
2003	Irish Warrior	5	A. Solis	116	Continental Red	117	Continuously	114	150,000	2:12.28	102

Beyer Index: 105.43

DELAWARE HANDICAP, 1 1/4 Miles,
Fillies and Mares, 3-Year-Olds and Up, Delaware Park, 2003 Purse: $750,000

Year	Winner	Age	Jockey	Wt.	Second	Wt.	Third	Wt.	Win Value	Time	Beyer
1937	Rosenna	3	M. Peters	108	Fair Knightess	118	Esposa	123	8,125	1:43.80	
1938	Marica	5	R. Dotter	125	Savage Beauty	109	Esposa	120	8,300	1:45.60	
1939	Shangay Lily	7	R. Donoso	113	Bunny Baby	108	Lady Maryland	118	9,175	1:46.00	
1940	Tedbriar	3	J. Lynch	109	War Beauty	106	Orcades	107	9,625	1:45.20	
1941	Dotted Swiss	4	M. Peters	114	Bala Ormont	116	Fairy Chant	126	8,550	1:49.00	
1942	Monida	5	A. DeLara	112	Rosetown	119	War Hazard	123	8,850	1:45.60	
1944	Everget	3	A. Kirkland	113	Donitas First	110	Anthemion	119	8,975	1:44.80	
1945	Plucky Maud	4	R. Permane	115	Legend Bearer	125	Rampart	111	12,450	1:42.60	
1946	Bridal Flower	3	A. DeLara	111	Surosa	114	Mahmoudess	114	20,200	1:43.80	
1947	Elpis	5	L. Hansman	108	Rampart	111	Bridal Flower	125	22,200	1:46.60	
1948	Miss Grillo	6	I. Hanford	119	Elpis	119	Rampart	117	20,850	1:49.00	
1949	Allie's Pal	4	R.J. Martin	114	Paddleduck	119	Dobodura	110	19,950	1:46.40	
1950	Adile	4	J. Gilbert	119	The Mater	107	Jazz Baby	109	21,650	1:44.60	
1951	Busanda	4	E. Guerin	126	Leading Home	109	How	115	42,600	2:04.60	
1952	Kiss Me Kate	4	R. Nash	126	Renew	123	My Celeste	113	43,250	2:02.60	
1953	Grecian Queen	3	T. Atkinson	114	Devilkin	120	My Celeste	117	84,600	2:02.80	
1954	Gainsboro Girl	4	A. Catalano	113	Sunshine Nell	126	Lavender Hill	111	101,800	2:02.60	
1955	Parlo	4	E. Guerin	128	Open Sesame	114	Clear Dawn	119	99,900	2:02.40	
1956	Flower Bowl	4	L. Batchellor	112	Manotick	122	Open Sesame	113	104,875	2:03.00	
1957	Princess Turia	4	W. Hartack	119	Pucker Up	117	Little Pache	115	110,875	2:05.00	
1958	Endine	4	E. Nelson	111	Dotted Line	116	Woodlawn	108	106,875	2:03.00	
1959	Endine	5	P.J. Bailey	117	Polamby	114	Tempted	119	98,312	2:03.60	
1960	Quill	4	R. Ussery	125	Royal Native	129	Geechee Lou	110	94,750	2:02.40	
1961	Airmans Guide	4	H. Grant	121	Royal Native	120	Tritoma	118	104,687	2:02.40	
1962	Seven Thirty	4	L. Adams	120	Cicada	114	Bramalea	115	92,375	2:02.60	
1963	Waltz Song	5	S. Mellon	116	Cicada	128	Table Mate	123	112,062	2:04.00	
1964	Old Hat	5	B. Thornburg	113	Miss Cavandish	115	Waltz Song	116	79,254	2:04.00	
1965	Steeple Jill	4	J. Ruane	123	Ho Ho	109	Miss Cavandish	123	80,122	2:02.80	
1966	Open Fire	5	F. Lovato	110	Treachery	110	Discipline	119	79,930	2:00.40	
1967	Straight Deal	5	R. Ussery	125	Malhoa	112	Miss Spin	114	76,879	2:02.20	
1968	Politely	4	A. Cordero Jr	126	Plucky Pan	117	Treacherous	113	76,476	2:02.80	
1969	Obeah	4	J.L. Rotz	113	Double Ripple	111	Pattee Canyon	115	74,168	2:04.20	
1970	Obeah	5	L. Moyers	114	What a Dream	116	Helen J'nnings	114	8,215	2:02.60	
1971	Blessing Angelica	3	J. Vasquez	111	Deceit	115	Cathy Honey	114	80,860	2:03.40	
1972	Blessing Angelica	4	F. Belmonte	114	Grafitti	113	Numbered Account	115	74,100	2:00.60	
1973	Susan's Girl	4	L. Pincay Jr	127	Summer Guest	122	Light Hearted	125	71,305	2:00.60	
1974	Krislin	5	A. Cordero Jr	115	Twixt	124	Summer Guest	114	74,555	2:01.60	
1975	Susan's Girl	6	R. Broussard	125	Pass a Glance	116	Raisela	117	70,915	2:01.80	
1976	Optimistic Gal	3	E. Maple	119	T.V. Vixen	116	Vodka Time	115	65,040	2:01.00	
1977	Our Mims	3	J. Velasquez	117	Mississippi Mud	124	Dottie's Doll	118	70,785	2:01.00	
1978	Late Bloomer	4	J. Velasquez	119	Dottie's Doll	117	Cum Laude Laurie	119	73,938	2:02.20	
1979	Likely Exchange	5	M.S. Sellers	112	Sans Critique	111	Plain and Simple	110	73,938	2:03.40	
1980	Heavenly Ade	4	J.D. Bailey	112	Croquis	112	Blitey	113	93,893	2:00.00	
1981	Relaxing	5	A. Cordero Jr	119	Wistful	121	Lady of Promise	111	75,075	2:01.00	
1982	Jameela	6	J.L. Kaenel	121	Zvetlana	111	Love Sign	125	74,523	2:02.60	
1983	May Day Eighty	4	J. Vasquez	115	Try Something New	116	Broom Dance	119	66,720	2:03.20	
1984	Adored	4	L. Pincay Jr	120	Mademoiselle Forli	114	Weekend Surprise	112	94,680	2:03.20	
1985	Basie	4	J. Cruguet	110	Heatherten	126	Life's Magic	122	93,360	2:02.00	
1986	Shocker T.	4	G. St. Leon	122	Endear	122	Leecoo	112	69,120	2:02.60	
1987	Coup de Fusil	5	A. Cordero Jr	114	Steal a Kiss	113	Catatonic	118	68,760	1:59.80	
1988	Nastique	4	E. Maple	116	Ms. Eloise	117	Lawyer Talk	112	67,410	2:07.60	
1989	Nastique	5	E. Maple	120	Colonial Waters	117	Thirty Eight Go Go	118	64,890	2:01.20	
1990	Seattle Dawn	4	R.E. Colton	115	Warfie	112	Thirty Eight Go Go	115	68,160	2:03.00	
1991	Crowned	4	R. Wilson	117	Naskra's Lady	114	Tia Juanita	113	69,420	2:04.00	94
1992	Brilliant Brass	5	E.S. Prado	117	Train Robbery	111	Risen Colony	113	93,780	2:03.00	101
1993	Green Darlin	4	M.J. Luzzi	113	Girl on a Mission	116	Starry Val	112	96,300	2:03.60	96
1994	With a Wink	4	Migliore R	114	Passing Vice	115	Alphabulous	111	95,130	2:03.20	100
1995	Night Fax	4	Carle JD	108	Cavada	113	It's Personal	114	95,070	2:02.80	96
1996	Urbane	4	A. Solis	117	Alcovy	117	Shoop	115	180,000	2:01.80	114
1997	Power Play	5	L.C. Reynolds	114	Gold n Delicious	115	Effectiveness	113	210,000	2:03.40	106
1998	Amarillo	4	J.A Krone	110	Tuxedo Junction	115	Timely Broad	110	300,000	2:04.20	96

Year	Winner	Age	Jockey	Wt.	Second	Wt.	Third	Wt.	Win Value	Time	Beyer
1999	Tap to Music	4	P. Day	116	Keeper Hill	120	Unbridled Hope	114	300,000	2:02.15	107
2000	Lu Ravi	5	P. Day	117	Tap to Music	116	Silverbulletday	119	360,000	2:02.21	107
2001	Irving's Baby	4	R.A. Dominguez	113	Under the Rug	115	Lazy Slusan	121	360,000	2:05.21	98
2002	Summer Colony	5	J.R. Velazquez	118	Your Out	113	Two Item Limit	115	360,000	2:04.52	101
2003	Wild Spirit	4	J.D. Bailey	117	Take Charge Lady	120	Shiny Sheet	112	450,000	2:02.95	110

Run as New Castle Handicap prior to 1955; run at 1 1/16 miles prior to 1951; run at Saratoga 1983 to 1985

Beyer Index: 102

DEMOISELLE, 1 1/8 Miles,
2-Year-Old Fillies, Aqueduct, 2003 Purse: $200,000

Year	Winner	Age	Jockey	Wt.	Second	Wt.	Third	Wt.	Win Value	Time Beyer
1908	Melisande	2	Notter	124	Cotytto	105	Arondack	110	2,720	1:06.40
1910	Round the World	2	Herbert	122	Horizon	122	Leah	105	1,150	1:08.60
1914	Couette	2	M. Buxton	119	Comely	126	Brig's Sister	122	1,165	1:07.00
1915	Celandria	2	M. Buxton	122	Malachite	110	Miss Puzzle	112	1,515	1:07.00
1916	Tragedy	2	T. Davis	122	Marie Odile	110	Q. o' th' Water	110	1,925	1:07.00
1917	Wawbeck	2	M. Buxton	113	Rosie O'Grady	125	Quietude	113	2,325	1:09.00
1918	Lady Rosebud	2	J. Collins	109	Kiss Again	113	Luke's Pet	109	2,325	1:07.60
1919	Panoply	2	W. Knapp	125	Indiscretion	109	Luke's Pet	114	2,325	1:09.20
1920	Nancy Lee	2	L. Lyke	112	Pantalette	109	Maiden's Ballet	110	3,170	1:07.80
1921	My Reverie	2	C. Kummer	119	Penitent	109	Nancy F.	116	3,720	1:07.60
1922	Cresta	2	L. Penman	119	Suweep	119	Twaddle	109	3,710	1:07.60
1923	Fluvanna	2	G. Babin	116	Cave Woman	109	Parasol	113	3,715	1:06.40
1924	Maud Muller	2	L. McAtee	125	Swinging	113	Extra Dry	107	3,765	1:06.60
1925	Ethereal	2	F. Coltiletti	109	Hayai	114	Adria	109	3,765	1:07.00
1926	Pandera	2	L. McAtee	126	Recreation	109	Glen Sprite	109	3,765	1:06.00
1927	Fair Mist	2	J. Craigmile	105	Giggleorum	110	One Hour	122	3,765	1:07.00
1928	Toki	2	L. McAtee	109	Ma Mie	105	Ritzy	109	4,425	1:07.60
1929	The Beasel	2	W. Kelsay	109	Murky Cloud	122	Greyola	109	4,575	1:07.00
1930	Straying	2	L. McAtee	108	Ladana	122	Double Time	110	4,375	1:06.60
1931	Straightlace	2	E. Barnes	109	Morden	109	Morush	109	4,175	1:08.40
1932	Disdainful	2	A. Robertson	127	Teaberry	107	Clare Lee	107	2,325	1:07.00
1936	Broad Ripple	2	J. Gilbert	113	Drawbridge	113	Sophia Tucker	119	3,585	1:10.60
1937	Inhale	2	J. Gilbert	122	Miyako	113	Black Wave	113	3,635	1:11.20
1938	Donita M.	2	W.D. Wright	122	Lady Nicotine	113	Sweet Patrice	122	3,425	1:11.40
1939	Now What	2	R. Workman	119	Piquet	113	Ponemah	113	3,275	1:09.00
1940	Level Best	2	B. James	115	Strange Device	122	Tangled	119	6,425	1:09.20
1941	Pig Tails	2	J. Skelly	107	War Melody	115	Jane Blenheim	112	5,625	1:10.20
1942	Optimism	2	J. Longden	111	Bras	111	Demolition	111	5,100	1:09.40
1943	Thread o' Gold	2	J. Stout	111	Boojiana	111	Vietta	106	5,450	1:13.80
1944	Drumuir	2	R. Permane	115	Safeguard	113	Flyweight	119	9,885	1:13.00
1945	War Kilt	2	A. Kirkland	115	Phantasy	106	Upper Level	112	8,230	1:12.40
1946	Carolyn A.	2	E. Arcaro	115	Pipette	119	With Honor	115	33,550	1:12.60
1947	Ghost Run	2	R. Donoso	114	Bellesoeur	114	Shimmer	114	33,100	1:13.60
1948	Lithe	2	W. Garner	116	Lady Dorimar	119	Stole	119	47,025	1:48.20
1949	Bed o' Roses	2	E. Guerin	116	Next Move	119	Rare Perfume	116	38,800	1:45.80
1950	Aunt Jinny	2	N. Wall	116	Vulcania	119	Rose Fern	119	30,700	1:45.80
1951	Rose Jet	2	H. Woodhouse	116	Papoose	119	No Store	119	32,600	1:46.20
1952	Grecian Queen	2	E. Guerin	119	Ballerina	119	Tritium	114	33,325	1:46.60
1953	O'Alison	2	J. Nichols	119	Parlo	119	Case Goods	119	50,775	1:46.40
1958	Khalita	2	E. Arcaro	122	Rich Tradition	122	Sybil Brand	116	15,512	1:25.60
1959	Irish Jay	2	E. Arcaro	122	Rash Statement	113	Space Happy	113	22,595	1:23.60
1963	Windsor Lady	2	W. Hartack	116	Lovejoy	114	Hem and Haw	112	18,720	1:37.40
1964	Discipline	2	I. Valenzuela	113	Lay Aft	115	Cordially	112	18,525	1:39.20
1965	Indian Sunlite	2	W. Boland	114	Lady Pitt	116	Prides Profile	116	19,500	1:38.20
1966	Woozem	2	K. Knapp	119	On the Carpet	113	Amherst	112	18,785	1:35.60
1967	Allie's Serenade	2	J.L. Rotz	113	A. Pleasant Sort	112	Wish Well	112	18,167	1:40.40
1968	Queen's Double	2	B. Baeza	119	Dauntless Dora	112	Mizzle	114	18,250	1:39.20
1969	Native Fern	2	J. Ruane	114	Luci Tee	116	Grab It	114	18,655	1:38.80
1970	Inca Queen	2	A. Cordero Jr	112	Deceit	122	Emperors Desire	114	19,532	1:36.40
1971	Dresden Doll	2	G. St.. Leon	114	Susan's Girl	119	Brenda Beauty	122	21,600	1:35.80
1972	Protest	2	A. Santiago	114	Flightoletti	116	Rose Chapeau	115	18,405	1:37.60
1973	Chris Evert	2	L. Pincay	121	Amberalero	116	Khaled's Kaper	116	17,370	1:36.40
1974	Land Girl	2	J. Vasquez	116	Alpine Lass	121	Funalon	118	35,940	1:36.20
1975	Free Journey	2	L. Pincay Jr	117	Artfully	112	Dottie's Doll	114	51,210	1:50.20
1976	Bring out the Band	2	D. Brumfield	116	Our Mims	113	Road Princess	112	49,500	1:50.80
1977	Caesar's Wish	2	D.R. Wright	116	Lakeville Miss	121	Island Kiss	114	47,565	1:50.60
1978	Plankton	2	R. Hernandez	112	Distinct Honor	113	Belladora	112	48,465	1:50.00
1979	Genuine Risk	2	L. Pincay Jr	116	Smart Angle	121	Spruce Pine	112	49,185	1:51.20
1980	Rainbow Connection	2	A. Cordero Jr	119	De la Rose	116	Tina Tina Too	116	48,870	1:50.80
1981	Snow Plow	2	A. Cordero Jr	121	Larida	113	Vain Gold	121	49,680	1:52.00

Year	Winner	Age	Jockey	Wt.	Second	Wt.	Third	Wt.	Win Value	Time	Beyer
1982	Only Queens	2	M.A. Rivera	116	Good Spruce	113	National Banner	113	49,680	1:52.00	
1983	Qualique	2	M. Venezia	112	Lucky Lucku Lucky	121	Buzz My Bell	121	65,160	1:51.20	
1984	Diplomette	2	R. Hernandez	112	Golden Silence	114	Koluctoo's Jill	113	72,360	1:54.60	
1985	I'm Sweets	2	E. Maple	121	Family Style	121	Steal a Kiss	112	98,280	1:50.20	
1986	Tappiano	2	J. Cruguet	121	Soaring Princess	112	Graceful Darby	112	131,940	1:53.20	
1987	Goodbye Halo	2	A. Cordero Jr	113	Tap Your Toes	112	Galway Song	119	142,080	1:53.00	
1988	Open Mind	2	A. Cordero Jr	121	Darby's Daughter	119	Gild	121	147,120	1:52.00	
1989	Rootentootenwooten	2	J.D. Bailey	112	Bookkeeper	113	Why Go on Dreaming	113	109,440	1:51.60	
1990	Debutant's Halo	2	C. Perret	116	Private Treasure	121	Slept Thru It	113	69,960	1:53.80	.85
1991	Stolen Beauty	2	C.W. Antley	113	Turnback the Alarm	116	Easy Now	116	120,000	1:52.00	.92
1992	Fortunate Faith	2	A. Madrid Jr	112	True Affair	116	Our Tomboy	112	120,000	1:53.40	.80
1993	Strategic Maneuver	2	J.D. Bailey	116	Sovereign Kitty	112	Bunting	112	120,000	1:53.60	.86
1994	Minister Wife	2	J.D. Bailey	121	Miss Golden Circle	118	Special Broad	121	120,000	1:53.40	.93
1995	La Rosa	2	J.A. Krone	114	Quiet Dance	114	Escena	112	120,000	1:50.80	.89
1996	Ajina	2	P. Day	121	Hidden Reserve	114	Biding Time	114	120,000	1:53.60	.83
1997	Clark Street	2	M.E. Smith	121	Soft Senorita	114	Mercy Me	121	120,000	1:53.80	.74
1998	Better Than Honour*	2	R. Migliore	113	Waltz On By	115	Oh What a Windfall	121	120,000	1:52.60	.68
	Tutorial finished first but was disqualified and placed fifth										
1999	Jostle	2	S. Elliott	121	March Magic	112	Shawnee Country	121	120,000	1:51.40	.82
2000	Two Item Limit	2	R. Migliore	122	Sweep Dreams	116	Kingsland	116	120,000	1:52.25	.88
2001	Smok'n Frolic	2	J.R. Velazquez	121	Lady Shari	121	Proxy Statement	117	120,000	1:50.57	.94
2002	Roar Emotion	2	J.R. Velazquez	115	Savedbydaylight	115	Feisty Step	115	120,000	1:51.43	.92
2003	Ashado	2	J.D. Bailey	117	La Reina	121	Dr. Kathy	115	120,000	1:52.88	.84

Beyer Index: 85

DISTAFF BREEDERS' CUP HANDICAP, 7 Furlongs, Fillies and Mares, 3-Year-Olds and Up, Aqueduct, 2003 Purse: $152,400

Year	Winner	Age	Jockey	Wt.	Second	Wt.	Third	Wt.	Win Value	Time	Beyer
1954	Mab's Choice	5	A. Valenzuela	109	Sunshine Nell	126	Brazen Brat	125	21,000	1:24.40	
1955	Oil Painting	4	H. Woodhouse	115	Good Child	113	Canadiana	121	20,300	1:24.00	
1956	Blue Banner	4	E. Arcaro	115	Peignoir	108	Myrtle's Jet	123	15,000	1:23.80	
1957	Searching	5	C. McCreary	124	Fanciful Miss	112	Plotter	110	16,700	1:24.40	
1958	Happy Princess	6	H. Woodhouse	116	Outer Space	117	Searching	123	15,675	1:24.00	
1959	Happy Princess	7	H. Woodhouse	114	Mlle. Dianne	115	Idun	125	18,290	1:24.20	
1960	Mommy Dear	4	M. Ycaza	125	Tinkalero	119	Craftiness	115	17,607	1:23.00	
1961	Teacation	4	R. Broussard	117	Sister Antoine	119	Make Sail	117	14,722	1:23.60	
1962	Rose O'Neill	4	I. Valenzuela	118	Seven Thirty	121	Mighty Fair	116	15,015	1:23.80	
1963	Cicada	4	W. Shoemaker	125	Pocosaba	119	Royal Patrice	120	14,527	1:21.60	
1964	Charspiv	4	R. Ussery	117	Look Ma	109	Suiti	112	13,926	1:24.00	
1964	Smart Deb	4	W. Hartack	125	Pams Ego	121	D'c'l C'n'ge	110	13,764	1:25.20	
1965	Affectionately	5	W. Blum	128	Treachery	115	Petticoat	113	18,102	1:24.00	
1966	Sailor Princess	4	G. Mineau	111	Queen Empress	123	Petticoat	112	18,102	1:22.40	
1967	Cologne	4	B. Baeza	113	Lady Diplomat	114	Miss Moona	122	18,070	1:24.20	
1968	Just Kidding	4	J. Velasquez	113	Shirley Heights	111	Serene Queen	107	18,395	1:23.20	
1969	Heartland	4	J.L. Rotz	121	Amerigo Lady	123	C'ms F'ry G'd	113	18,200	1:22.40	
1970	Process Shot	4	C. Baltazar	120	Ta Wee	134	Dedicated to Sue	115	18,037	1:22.80	
1971	Double Delta	5	B. Baeza	116	Cold Comfort	114	I'm for Mama	115	19,980	1:22.80	
1972	Royal Signal	5	C. Baltazar	121	Red Shoes	118	Aladancer	117	16,545	1:24.20	
1973	Ferly	5	R. Turcotte	113	Wakefield Miss	115	Twixt	112	16,920	1:24.00	
1974	Krislin	5	V. Bracciale Jr	113	Batacuda	116	Ladies Agreement	112	16,770	1:22.00	
1975	Something Super	5	J. Cruguet	115	Shy Dawn	121	Second Coming	108	16,995	1:22.20	
1976	Shy Dawn	5	A. Cordero Jr	118	Land Girl	114	Ladies Agreement	114	22,590	1:24.20	
1977	What a Summer	4	E. Maple	118	Secret Lanvin	112	Shy Dawn	120	21,975	1:11.60	
1978	Vandy Sue	4	A.M. Rodriguez	112	Sea Drone	108	Dalton Road	118	22,185	1:12.00	
1979	Skipat	5	J.W. Edwards	122	Sweet Joyce	106	Unpossible	107	32,520	1:10.40	
1980	Misty Gallore	4	D. MacBeth	124	Lady Lonsdale	114	Spanish Fake	112	33,240	1:24.60	
1981	Lady Oakley	4	J. Fell	114	It's in the Air	120	Lovin' Lass	110	33,900	1:25.40	
1982	Lady Dean	4	D.A. Miller Jr	120	Westport Native	114	Raise 'n Dance	107	33,000	1:23.80	
1983	Jones Time Machine	4	A. Cordero Jr	112	Fancy Naskra	113	Adept	111	32,880	1:23.20	
1984	Am Capable	4	A. Cordero Jr	125	Sweet Missus	104	Fissure	107	52,290	1:11.00	
1985	Give Me a Hint	5	W.A. Ward	109	Nany	121	Descent	106	55,080	1:25.20	
1986	Ride Sally	4	W.A. Guerra	118	Willowy Mood	116	Clocks Secret	122	54,540	1:21.60	
1987	Pine Tree Lane	5	A. Cordero Jr	125	Spring Beauty	117	Gene's Lady	117	52,650	1:22.40	
1988	Cadillacing	4	R.P. Romero	112	Cagey Exuberance	118	Bishop's Delight	111	50,670	1:22.60	
1989	Avie's Gal	4	N. Santagata	112	Haiati	112	Topicount	117	51,660	1:24.00	
1990	Channel Three	4	J.F. Chavez	111	Divine Answer	113	Hedgeabout	112	54,090	1:23.20	
1991	Devil's Orchid	4	R. Baze	117	Your Hope	112	Fappaburst	114	64,080	1:21.00	.115
1992	Nannerl	5	M.E. Smith	112	Missy's Mirage	119	Withallprobability	117	68,880	1:24.60	.101
1994	Classy Mirage	4	R.G. Davis	114	Jill Miner	114	Air Port Won	109	66,480	1:11.20	.100
1995	Recognizable	4	M.E. Smith	120	Beckys Shirt	113	Kurofune Mystery	116	66,540	1:22.80	.102
1996	Lottsa Talc	6	F.T. Alvarado	120	Traverse City	120	Dust Bucket	116	75,820	1:24.00	.100
1997	Miss Golden Circle	5	R. Migliore	120	Inquisitive Look	110	Punkin Pie	109	65,400	1:24.40	.96

Year	Winner	Age	Jockey	Wt.	Second	Wt.	Third	Wt.	Win Value	Time	Beyer
1998	Parlay	4	R. Migliore	114	Lucky Marty	113	Green Light	114	67,260	1:24.00	89
1999	Furlough	5	H. Castillo Jr	115	Catinca	121	Tomorrows Sunshine	113	112,260	1:23.20	104
2000	Honest Lady	4	B. Blanc	117	Her She Kisses	115	Tap to Music	118	111,300	1:22.10	103
2001	Dream Supreme	4	A.T. Gryder	119	Folly Dollar	113	Country Hideaway	118	108,960	1:23.66	96
2002	Raging Fever	4	J.R. Velazquez	120	Prized Stamp	114	La Galerie	115	94,680	1:21.78	105
2003	Carson Hollow	4	M.J. Luzzi	120	Raging Fever	118	Bonafide Reason	112	94,740	1:22.42	102

Beyer Index: 101.08

(CITGO) DIXIE, 1 1/8 Miles (Turf),
3-Year-Olds and Up, Pimlico Race Course, 2003 Purse: $200,000

Year	Winner	Age	Jockey	Wt.	Second	Wt.	Third	Wt.	Win Value	Time Beyer
1870	Preakness	3	Hayward	110	Ecliptic	107	Foster	110	6,400	3:47.50
1871	Harry Bassett		Rowe	110					6,500	
1872	Hubbard	3	McCabe	110	Joe Daniels	110	True Blue	110	13,200	3:36.50
1873	Tom Bowling	3	Swim	110	Merodac	110	Lizzie Lucas	107	4,000	3:58.00
1874	Vandalite	3	Houston	107	Madge	107	Brigand	110	13,200	3:35.50
1875	Tom Ochiltree	3	Evans	110	Viator	107	Joe Cerns	110	4,350	3:42.50
1876	Vigil	3	Spillman	110	Parole	107	Heretog	110	4,300	3:41.50
1877	King Faro	3	Walker	110	Major Barker	110	Susquehanna	107	4,450	3:55.00
1878	Duke of Magenta	3	Hughes	110	Bonnie Wood	107	Spartan	110	4,200	3:41.00
1879	Monitor	3	Hughes	107	Lord Murphy	110	Harold	110	4,850	3:34.75
1880	Grenada	3	Hughes	110	Oden	110	Ferncliffe	110	4,200	3:38.00
1881	Crickmore	3	Hughes	107	Eole	110	Barrett	110	3,550	3:37.00
1882	Monarch	3	Schauer	110	Hilarity	110	Blenheim	107	3,500	3:44.00
1883	George Kinney	3	J. McLaughlin	110	Trafalgar	110	Gonfalon	110	3,600	3:56.00
1884	Loftin	3		113	Blast	110	Thackeray	110	3,595	3:37.75
1885	East Lynne	3	W. Donahue	115	Richmond	118	Longview	118	3,595	3:49.75
1886	The Bard	3	W. Hayward	118	Blue Wing	118	Wheatley	115	3,290	3:33.00
1887	Hanover	3	J. McLaughlin	123	Glenmound	118			4,560	3:51.75
1902	Adelaide Prince	3	W.L. Powers	113	Potheen	116	Flintlock	113	1,530	3:06.60
1903	Colonsay	3	W.C. Daly	114					1,750	3:41.40
1904	The Southerner	3	M. Corbett	116	Ostrich	123	Andrew Mack	116	3,310	3:06.60
1924	Chacolet	6	M. Garner	116	Martingale	120	Rev. Agent	100	24,840	1:59.20
1925	Sarazen	4	E. Sande	130	Spot Cash	115	Joy Smoke	104	25,950	2:02.00
1926	Sarazen	5	F. Weiner	128	Sun Pal	105	G. Th'tcher	118	24,550	2:00.80
1927	Mars	4	F. Coltiletti	124	Display	120	Edisto	113	26,375	1:59.40
1928	Mike Hall	4	H. Richards	110	Scapa Flow	120	Sir Harry	112	24,975	1:59.00
1929	Diavolo	4	J. Maiben	112	Victorian	122	Display	124	27,600	2:00.00
1930	Sandy Ford	4	F. Catrone	106	Inception	114	Sir Harry	112	26,025	1:59.20
1931	Paul Bunyan	5	E. Gianelloni	110	Frisius	112	William T.	110	15,425	2:01.20
1932	Gallant Knight	5	H. Schutte	121	Sun Meadow	118	Aegis	112	14,550	1:58.00
1933	Stepenfetchit	4	E. Steffen	112	Keep Out	101	Tred Avon	117	5,100	2:01.80
1934	Equipoise	6	R. Workman	130	Chatmoss	110	Fla'g Mamie	102	4,190	2:01.80
1935	Only One	4	R. Merritt	108	Head Play	120	Howard	113	4,520	2:01.80
1936	Dark Hope	7	R. Jones	113	Good Goods	115	Gallant Mc	109	9,500	1:58.00
1937	Calumet Dick	5	J. Wagner	108	Finance	118	Aneroid	109	9,450	1:58.40
1938	Pompoon	4	G. Woolf	118	Busy K.	110	M'ked G'eral	107	20,950	1:56.80
1939	Sir Damion	5	D. Meade	113	Tatterdemalion	111	Jacola	117	22,025	1:58.60
1940	Honey Cloud	6	H. Mora	113	Filisteo	112	Aethelwold	107	18,250	1:58.60
1941	Haltal	4	C. McCreary	110	Mioland	129	Dit	110	19,850	1:58.40
1942	Whirlaway	4	E. Arcaro	128	Attention	124	Mioland	126	19,275	1:57.00
1943	Riverland	5	S. Brooks	123	Attention	123	Anticlimax	113	17,775	1:56.40
1944	Sun Again	5	F.A. Smith	120	Rounders	117	Alquest	106	25,700	1:58.20
1945	Rounders	6	F. Remerscheid	118	He Rolls	116	Gay Bit	108	25,400	1:56.80
1946	Armed	5	D. Dodson	130	Stymie	124	Trymenow	117	25,700	1:58.40
1947	Assault	4	E. Arcaro	129	Rico Monte	120	Talon	115	24,700	1:57.80
1948	Fervent	4	N.L. Pierson	121	Stymie	127	Incline	107	21,950	2:01.60
1949	Chains	4	J.D. Jessop	109	Contest	110	Pilaster	120	21,150	1:56.60
1950	Loser Weeper	5	N. Combest	108	Double Brandy	110	Going Away	106	18,450	1:56.20
1951	County Delight	4	J. Nichols	114	On the Mark	107	Why Not Now	116	18,650	1:58.80
1952	Alerted	4	R. Sisto	112	Auditing	111	Hull Down	104	20,400	1:58.00
1953	Royal Vale	5	J. Westrope	120	Cold Command	115	Crafty Admiral	126	18,800	1:51.80
1954	Straight Face	4	B. Green	115	Golden Gloves	113	Capeador	116	19,550	1:51.00
1955	St. Vincent	4	B. James	126	Kaster	120	Maharajah	113	20,250	2:15.40
1956	Chevation	5	C. Rogers	117	Akbar Khan	111	Maharahah	110	21,000	2:17.40
1957	Akbar Khan	5	E. Nelson	113	Jabneh	120	Blue Choir	116	19,675	2:16.20
1958	Pop Corn	4	J. Ruane	110	Master Boing	122	Adare II	110	19,650	2:21.60
1959	One-Eyed King	5	M. Ycaza	120	Oligarchy	116	Mystic II	110	18,712	2:15.40
1960	Shield Bearer	5	N. Shuk	114	Harmonizing	126	Mystic II	114	19,070	2:32.40
1961	Hunter's Rock	3	F. Lovato	111	Shield Bearer	120	Art Market	113	19,857	2:36.20
1962	Wise Ship	5	H. Gustines	123	Sunshine Cake	108	El Bandito	118	41,437	2:42.40

Year	Winner	Age	Jockey	Wt.	Second	Wt.	Third	Wt.	Win Value	Time	Beyer
1963	Cedar Key	3	T. Lee	110	Mr. Steu	112	Parka	119	40,885	2:32.20	
1964	Will I Rule	4	R. Turcotte	118	Turbo Jet II	132	Your Alibhai	109	40,852	2:40.00	
1965	Or et Argent	4	W. Blum	116	Kentucky Jug	112	Desert Love	109	22,847	2:30.20	
1965	Flag	5	T. Lee	114	Ribot's Fling	109	Lancastrian	111	22,945	2:29.00	
1966	Knightly Manners	5	T. Lee	112	Marchio	110	Paoluccio	112	37,830	2:30.80	
1967	War Censor	4	E. Fires	125	Deck Hand	114	Needle Him	111	38,740	2:36.60	
1968	High Hat	4	R. Broussard	116	Irish Rebellion	117	Royal Mal'bar	112	36,270	2:29.80	
1969	Czar Alexander	4	W. Hartack	122	Taneb	117	Jean-Pierre	115	37,895	2:30.80	
1970	Fort Marcy	6	J. Velasquez	124	War Censor	112	Jungle Cove	114	37,375	2:27.40	
1971	Chompion	6	M. Hole	119	Tudor Reward	114	North Flight	116	36,920	2:34.20	
1972	Onandaga	6	J. Kurtz	110	Star Envoy	116	New Alibhai	112	38,350	2:30.00	
1973	Laplander	6	V. Bracciale Jr	111	Chrisaway	112	Wustenchef	112	38,675	2:30.40	
1974	London Company	3	A. Cordero Jr	122	Scrimshaw	110	Mister Diz	110	38,025	2:28.80	
1975	Bemo	5	C.J. McCarron	114	Outdoors	115	Drollery	114	39,325	2:33.40	
1976	Barcas	5	V. Bracciale Jr	112	One on the Aisle	122	Neapolitan Way	108	37,375	2:29.60	
1977	Improviser	5	M. Rivera	120	Grey Beret	114	Oilfield	118	56,875	2:29.40	
1978	Fluorescent Light	4	V. Bracciale Jr	114	That's a Nice	115	Improviser	118	37,343	2:33.20	
1978	Bowl Game	4	J. Velasquez	120	Oilfield	110	Trumpeter Swan	110	37,993	2:33.40	
1979	The Very One	4	C. Cooke	108	That's a Nice	116	Fluorescent Light	124	72,995	2:28.60	
1980	Marquee Universal	4	H. Pilar	118	The Very One	113	Match the Hatch	115	77,155	2:29.60	
1981	El Barril	5	J. Vasquez	116	Buckpoint	119	Birthday List	108	73,255	2:29.80	
1982	Robsphere	5	J. Velasquez	120	Present the Colors	113	Rich and Ready	115	76,960	2:30.20	
1983	Khatango	4	V. Bracciale Jr	114	London Times	108	Super Sunrise	114	75,075	2:28.60	
1984	Persian Tiara	4	R.L. Shelton	109	Crazy Moon	112	Canadian Factor	118	88,675	2:41.00	
1985	Nassipour	5	V. Bracciale Jr	115	Persian Tiara	113	C'mpters Choce	116	72,800	2:27.80	
1986	Uptown Swell	4	W. Guerra	117	Southern Sultan	112	Castelets	117	92,445	2:27.40	
1987	Akabir	6	C. Perret	115	Little Bold John	117	Vilzak	113	74,360	2:28.60	
1988	Kadial	5	G. Stevens	112	Top Guest	118	Milesius	120	71,045	2:45.00	
1989	Coeur de Lion	5	J. Cruguet	121	Dance Card Filled	115	Dynaformer	118	90,000	2:38.40	
1990	Two Moccasins	4	R.P. Romero	114	My Big Boy	115	Marksmanship	113	90,000	2:35.80	73
1991	Double Booked	6	P. Day	118	Chas' Whim	116	Opening Verse	118	90,000	1:47.00	107
1992	Sky Classic	5	P. Day	122	Fourstars Allstar	116	Social Retiree	112	90,000	1:47.80	105
1993	Lure	5	M.E. Smith	124	Star of Cozzene	119	Binary Light	115	90,000	1:47.60	109
1994	Paradise Creek	5	P. Day	124	Lure	124	Astudillo	115	90,000	1:48.40	102
1995	The Vid	5	J.D. Bailey	119	Pennine Ridge	117	Blues Traveller	115	90,000	1:52.20	111
1996	Gold And Steel	4	A. Solis	121	Same Old Wish	115	Comstock Lode	115	120,000	1:52.80	105
1997	Ops Smile	5	E.S. Prado	115	Brave Note	115	Sharp Appeal	121	120,000	1:48.20	103
1998	Yagli	5	J.D. Bailey	121	Sky Colony	115	Blazing Sword	115	120,000	1:51.00	105
1999	Middlesex Drive	4	P. Day	115	Sky Colony	115	Divide and Conquer	115	120,000	1:48.60	97
2000	Quiet Resolve	5	R.J. Albarado	117	Haami	117	Holditholditholdit	117	120,000	1:50.42	103
2001	Hap	4	J.D. Bailey	119	Make No Mistake	119	Cynics Beware	119	120,000	1:48.56	101
2002	Strut the Stage	4	R.J. Albarado	117	Del Mar Show	119	Slew the Red	117	120,000	1:51.70	104
2003	Dr. Brendler	5	R.A. Dominguez	117	Perfect Soul	117	Sardaukar	117	120,000	1:57.78	99

Beyer Index: 101.71

DWYER, 1 1/16 Miles,
3-Year-Olds, Belmont Park, 2003 Purse: $150,000

Year	Winner	Age	Jockey	Wt.	Second	Wt.	Third	Wt.	Win Value	Time	Beyer
1918	War Cloud	3	M. Buxton	126	Jack Hare Jr.	124	Johren	127	4,850	1:50.20	
1919	Purchase	3	W. Knapp	118	Sir Barton	127	Crystal Ford	109	4,850	1:52.60	
1920	Man o' War	3	C. Kummer	126	John P. Grier	108			4,850	1:49.20	
1921	Grey Lag	3	E. Sande	123	Sporting Blood	112	Copper Demon	108	7,100	1:49.00	
1922	Ray Jay	3	C. Ponce	117	Letterman	108	Oceanic	108	7,150	1:52.60	
1923	Dunlin	3	C. Lang	123	Moonraker	108	Picketer	112	7,150	1:51.20	
1924	Ladkin	3	J. Maiben	123	Mad Play	123	Aga Khan	108	7,750	1:49.80	
1925	American Flag	3	A. Johnson	126	Dangerous	112	Silver Fox	123	8,900	2:10.60	
1926	Crusader	3	E. Sande	123	Chance Play	120	Espino	108	15,000	2:29.60	
1927	Kentucky II	3	J. Maiben	108	Chance Shot	126	Bois de Rose	108	18,500	2:31.80	
1928	Genie	3	W. Kelsay	110	Sun Beau	110	Ironsides	117	19,600	2:31.60	
1929	Grey Coat	3	S. O'Donnell	117	Blue Larkspur	124	Flag Day	110	19,450	2:34.00	
1930	Gallant Fox	3	E. Sande	126	Xenofol	110	Limbus	110	11,500	2:32.40	
1931	Twenty Grand	3	C. Kurtsinger	126	Blenheim	112	Barometer	110	11,500	2:34.40	
1932	Faireno	3	T. Malley	124	Gusto	122	Sansarica	111	12,200	2:31.40	
1933	War Glory	3	J. Gilbert	118	Jovius	116	Kerry Patch	121	4,250	2:31.80	
1934	Rose Cross	3	S. Coucci	116	Growler	116	Singing Wood	121	4,090	2:32.00	
1935	Omaha	3	W.D. Wright	126	Good Gamble	114	Cheshire	116	92,000	1:49.20	
1936	Mr. Bones	3	J. Gilbert	119	Pullman	116	Memory Book	119	8,500	1:49.80	
1937	Strabo	3	S. Renick	116	Rudie	119	Sceneshifter	116	10,750	1:51.40	
1938	The Chief	3	G. Woolf	119	Mythical King	119	Stagehand	126	8,900	1:48.40	
1939	Johnstown	3	J. Stout	126	Sun Lover	116	Challedon	126	9,250	1:48.40	
1940	Your Chance	3	W.D. Wright	116	Gen'l Manager	116	Andy K.	122	9,650	2:03.80	
1941	Whirlaway	3	E. Arcaro	126	Market Wise	122	Robert Morris	119	8,075	2:04.40	

Year	Winner	Age	Jockey	Wt.	Second	Wt.	Third	Wt.	Win Value	Time	Beyer
1942	Valdina Orphan	3	C. Bierman	116	Shut Out	126	Lochinvar	119	21,150	2:01.40	
1943	Vincentive	3	J. Gilbert	111	Famous Victory	110	Princequillo	110	19,600	2:05.00	
1944	By Jimminy	3	T. Atkinson	114	Stir Up	120	Lucky Draw	120	39,170	2:03.40	
1945	Wildlife	3	T. Atkinson	116	Gallorette	116	Esteem	116	38,835	2:05.20	
1946	Assault	3	W. Mehrtens	126	Windfields	116	Lord Boswell	121	40,700	2:06.80	
1947	Phalanx	3	R. Donoso	126	But Why Not	111	Brabancon	116	40,800	2:05.80	
1948	My Request	3	T. Atkinson	121	Better Self	121	Loser Weeper	111	39,200	2:02.00	
1949	Shackleton	3	R. Bernhardt	111	One Hitter	111	Going Away	121	39,200	2:07.80	
1950	Greek Song	3	O. Scurlock	116	Hill Prince	111	LIghts Up	116	27,400	2:03.00	
1951	Battlefield	3	E. Arcaro	121	Alerted	111	Hull Down	111	39,800	2:04.40	
1952	Blue Boy	3	C. McCreary	126	Hitex	114	Golden Gloves	118	39,300	2:01.80	
1953	Native Dancer	3	E. Guerin	126	Guardian II	114	By Zeus	114	38,100	2:05.20	
1954	High Gun	3	E. Guerin	126	Palm Tree	114	Paper Tiger	114	39,300	2:05.00	
1955	Nashua	3	E. Arcaro	126	Saratoga	122	Mainlander	114	37,200	2:03.80	
1956	Riley	3	T. Atkinson	121	Oh Johnny	123	Bill's Sky Boy	114	30,400	1:57.40	
1957	Bureaucracy	3	W. Boland	114	Little Hermit	107	Tenacious	113	30,500	1:55.40	
1958	Victory Morn	3	E. Guerin	115	Nasco	119	Day Court	112	20,270	1:58.80	
1959	Waltz	3	S. Boulmetis	121	MIddle Brother	113	Hoist Away	110	52,515	1:54.80	
1960	Francis S.	3	P.J. Bailey	119	Irish Lancer	121	Weatherwise	117	34,565	2:03.00	
1961	Hitting Away	3	H. Woodhouse	119	Baldpate	110	Beau Prince	121	54,340	2:03.80	
1962	Cyane	3	E. Nelson	116	Flying Johnnie	111	Noble Jay	119	54,957	2:01.60	
1963	Outing Class	3	R. Ussery	122	Tenacle	108	Chateaugay	129	55,250	2:01.60	
1964	Quadrangle	3	M. Ycaza	126	Malicious	120	Roman Brother	124	53,170	2:01.40	
1965	Staunchness	3	R. Ussery	114	Duc de Great	113	Hail to All	127	53,397	2:01.80	
1966	Mr. Right	3	E. Cardone	110	Exhibitionist	115	Buffle	123	53,527	2:02.80	
1967	Damascus	3	W. Shoemaker	128	Favorable Turn	112	Blasting Charge	116	54,177	2:03.00	
1968	Stage Door Johnny	3	H. Gustines	129	Out of the Way	123	Chompion	110	53,235	2:01.60	
1969	Gleaming Light	3	L. Adams	112	Jay Ray	119	Distray	112	52,747	2:04.00	
1970	Judgable	3	R. Woodhouse	108	Aggressively	112	Needles n Pens	117	54,892	2:02.60	
1971	Jim French	3	A. Cordero Jr	125	Farewell Party	113	Epic Journey	111	49,020	2:01.60	
1972	Cloudy Dawn	3	W. Hartack	118	Ruritana	112	Halo	112	51,525	2:03.20	
1973	Stop the Music	3	H. Gustines	120	Arbees Boy	115	Duc de Fl'n'gan	111	50,625	2:02.60	
1974	Hatchet Man	3	R. Turcotte	114	Rube the Great	124	Kin Run	112	51,120	2:01.20	
1975	Valid Appeal	3	J.S. Long	111	Wajima	118	Hunka Papa	116	50,400	1:48.40	
1976	Quiet Little Table	3	E. Maple	111	Sir Lister	116	Dance Spell	117	50,895	1:49.00	
1977	Bailjumper	3	A. Cordero Jr	116	Lynn Davis	112	Iron Constitution	121	48,870	1:47.60	
1978	Junction	3	J. Fell	120	Buckaroo	127	Darby Creek Road	121	47,025	1:48.80	
1979	Coastal	3	R. Hernandez	126	Private Account	114	Quiet Crossing	119	63,840	1:47.00	
1980	Amber Pass	3	D. MacBeth	114	Temperence Hill	129	Comptroller	119	67,440	1:49.00	
1981	Noble Nashua	3	C.B. Asmussen	119	Tap Shoes	126	Silver Express	114	68,160	1:49.20	
1982	Conquistador Cielo	3	E. Maple	126	John's Gold	114	Reinvested	119	67,560	1:46.80	
1983	Au Point	3	J.D. Bailey	114	Potentiate	114	Intention	114	68,640	1:48.20	
1984	Track Barron	3	J. Cruguet	119	Darn That Alarm	123	Slew the Coup	114	99,600	1:47.80	
1985	Stephan's Odyssey	3	L. PIncay Jr	123	Cutlass Reality	114	Important Business	126	88,500	1:49.20	
1986	Ogygian	3	W.A. Guerra	119	Johns Treasure	114	Personal Flag	114	112,680	1:48.40	
1987	Gone West	3	E. Maple	123	Pledge Card	114	Polish Navy	123	138,240	1:48.40	
1988	Seeking the Gold	3	P. Day	123	Evening Kris	119	Gay Rights	123	137,040	1:48.00	
1989	Roi Danzig	3	E. Maple	114	Contested Colors	114	Rampart Road	114	133,680	1:49.20	
1990	Profit Key	3	J.A. Santos	123	Rhythm	123	Graf	114	102,960	1:47.40	
1991	Lost Mountain	3	C. Perret	123	Smooth Performance	114	Fly So Free	126	120,000	1:49.20	.102
1992	Agincourt	3	J.F. Chavez	119	Three Peat	119	Windundermywings	114	120,000	1:47.80	.106
1993	Cherokee Run	3	P. Day	123	Miner's Mark	123	Silver of Silver	123	120,000	1:47.60	.102
1994	Holy Bull	3	M.E. Smith	124	Twining	122	Bay Street Star	119	90,000	1:41.00	.119
1995	Hoolie	3	R.G. Davis	117	Reality Road	112	Western Larla	119	90,000	1:42.60	.100
1996	Victory Speech	3	J.D. Bailey	117	Gold Fever	119	Robb	117	99,000	1:41.40	.109
1997	Behrens	3	J.D. Bailey	117	Glitman	114	Banker's Gold	122	90,000	1:42.20	.104
1998	Coronado's Quest	3	M.E. Smith	124	Ian's Thunder	112	Scatmandu	122	90,000	1:42.40	.101
1999	Forestry	3	J.D. Bailey	119	Doneraile Court	119	Successful Appeal	122	90,000	1:41.00	.104
2000	Albert The Great	3	R. Migliore	115	More Than Ready	119	Red Bullet	123	90,000	1:42.62	.108
2001	E Dubai	3	J.D. Bailey	121	Windsor Castle	119	Hero's Tribute	121	90,000	1:40.38	.105
2002	Gygistar	3	J.R. Velazquez	121	Nothing Flat	117	American Style	115	90,000	1:42.59	.97
2003	Strong Hope	3	J.R. Velazquez	115	Nacheezmo	115	Sky Mesa	119	90,000	1:41.76	.110

Beyer Index: 105.15

EL ENCINO, 1 1/16 Miles,
4-Year-Old Fillies, Santa Anita, 2003 Purse: $150,000

Year	Winner	Age	Jockey	Wt.	Second	Wt.	Third	Wt.	Win Value	Time	Beyer
1968	Hill Shine	4	A. Pineda	119	Aurelius II	117	Khalborough	115	14,650	1:42.60	
1969	Gene's Dancer	4	E. Fires	114	Royal Comedian	122	Injunction	119	15,200	1:43.40	
1971	Efa	5	D. Pierce	114	Crimson Hills	115	M'nt'na W'ds	115	16,900	1:41.80	
1972	Thorn	4	J. Sellers	115	Wildcat Hills	115	Efa	117	19,550	1:42.00	

Year	Winner	Age	Jockey	Wt.	Second	Wt.	Third	Wt.	Win Value	Time	Beyer
1973	Class A	5	D. Tierney	122	Sitka D.	119	Cabin	119	18,950	1:44.60	
1974	Wild World	5	W. Shoemaker	118	Class A	115	Proper Escort	112	18,150	1:49.80	
1975	Triggairo	6	D. Pierce	119	Benson	116	Lanquinet	119	19,700	1:49.40	
1976	Fascinating Girl	4	S. Hawley	115	Bold Baby	115	Just a Kick	121	18,850	1:42.40	
1977	Woodsome	4	M. Sellers	115	Lucie Manet	115	Granja Sueno	115	27,450	1:42.20	
1978	Taisez Vous	4	D. Pierce	121	Little Happiness	116	Table the Rumor	121	30,200	1:41.80	
1979	B. Thoughtful	4	D. Pierce	121	Queen Yasma	116	Petron's Love	114	38,200	1:41.40	
1980	It's in the Air	4	L. Pincay Jr	124	Prize Spot	121	Glorious Song	116	38,750	1:41.20	
1981	Princess Karenda	4	E. Delahoussaye	122	Swift Bird	117	Lisawan	114	49,650	1:42.00	
1982	Edge	4	C.B. Asmussen	114	Safe Play	119	Northern Fable	117	68,000	1:41.20	
1983	Beautiful Glass	4	C.J. McCarron	119	Header Card	119	Skillful Joy	122	50,550	1:41.20	
1984	Lovlier Linda	4	W. Shoemaker	117	Weekend Surprise	117	Angel Savage	114	51,250	1:42.00	
1985	Mitterand	4	E. Delahoussaye	119	Percipient	117	Allusion	117	61,600	1:42.00	
1986	Lady's Secret	4	C.J. McCarron	124	Shywing	119	Sharp Ascent	119	65,850	1:41.80	
1987	Seldom Seen Sue	4	W. Shoemaker	114	Miraculous	117	Top Corsage	122	61,850	1:43.00	
1988	By Land By Sea	4	F. Toro	115	Very Subtle	122	Annoconnor	114	64,300	1:41.60	
1989	Goodbye Halo	4	P. Day	124	T.V. of Crystal	117	Savannah's Honor	114	60,200	1:41.80	
1990	Akinemod	4	G.L. Stevens	119	Luthier's Launch	117	Kelly	116	62,900	1:41.20	.119
1991	A Wild Ride	4	C.J. McCarron	122	Highland Tide	114	Somethingmerry	117	63,500	1:42.40	.103
1992	Exchange	4	L. Pincay Jr	117	Grand Girlfriend	115	Damewood	115	67,000	1:43.20	.99
1993	Pacific Squall	4	C.J. McCarron	119	Avian Assembly	117	Magical Maiden	119	63,900	1:45.60	.96
1994	Supah Gem	4	C.S. Nakatani	117	Sensational Eyes	117	Stalcreek	119	64,500	1:41.20	.100
1995	Klassy Kim	4	K.J. Desormeaux	117	Twice the Vice	119	Crissy Aya	119	61,400	1:42.40	.102
1996	Jewel Princess	4	A. Solis	117	Sleep Easy	119	Urbane	119	78,800	1:41.80	.104
1997	Belle's Flag	4	C.S. Nakatani	117	Housa Dancer	115	Listening	119	82,650	1:41.60	.103
1998	Fleet Lady*	4	G.K. Gomez	117	Minister's Melody	117	I Ain't Bluffing	119	96,840	1:43.00	.104

I Ain't Bluffing finished first but was disqualified and placed third …

Year	Winner	Age	Jockey	Wt.	Second	Wt.	Third	Wt.	Win Value	Time	Beyer
1999	Manistique	4	G.L. Stevens	119	Gourmet Girl	117	Magical Allure	119	90,000	1:43.20	.95
2000	Olympic Charmer	4	C.J. McCarron	119	Her She Kisses	115	Smooth Player	117	97,470	1:42.71	.99
2001	Chilukki	4	G.L. Stevens	119	Spain	122	Queenie Belle	119	90,000	1:42.55	.96
2002	Affluent	4	E. Delahoussaye	119	Royally Chosen	117	Sea Reel	115	90,000	1:42.60	.98
2003	Got Koko	4	A. Solis	119	Bella Bellucci	117	Bare Necessities	119	90,000	1:42.25	.107

Beyer Index: 101.79

EXPLOSIVE BID HANDICAP, About 1 1/8 Miles (Turf), 4-Year-Olds and Up, Fair Grounds, 2003 Purse: $650,000

Year	Winner	Age	Jockey	Wt.	Second	Wt.	Third	Wt.	Win Value	Time	Beyer
1992	Slick Groom		K. Leblanc	112	Little Bro Lantis	113	Brownsboro	117	31,590	1:52.60	.90
1993	Coaxing Matt		E. Martin Jr.	114	Dixie Poker Ace	120	Spending Record	115	47,010	1:50.80	.97
1994	Pride of Summer		R. King Jr.		Alpine Choice	114	Empire Pool	116	76,425	1:49.40	.97
1994	Snake Eyes		B. Bartram	115	Yukon Robbery	115	Cozzene's Prince	122	76,305	1:49.40	.97
							Dipotamos	111			
1995	Earl Of Barking		G.Almeida	115	Kazabaiyn	114	Coaxing Matt	113	93,375	1:52.00	.103
1996	Kazabaiyn	6	K.Desormeaux	113	Party Season	116	Coaxing Matt	112	93,195	1:51.51	.102
1997	Always A Classic	4	Martin E. M. Jr.	114	Rainbow Blues	120	Snake Eyes	118	131,970	1:54.80	.107
1998	Joyeux Danseur	5	Albarado R. J.	121	Martiniquais	118	Hollie's Chief	113	223,980	1:49.20	.112
1999	Lord Smith	4	Gomez G. K.	117	Hawksley Hill	122	Chorwon	116	398,160	1:51.20	.106
2000	Brave Act	6	C.B. Asmussen	121	Where's Taylot	113	Chester House	114	360,000	1:48.98	.107
2001	Tijiyr	5	R.J. Albarado	110	Northcote Road	115	King Cugat	121	360,000	1:50.72	.108
2002	Sarafan	5	C.S. Nakatani	116	Beat Hollow	115	Even the Score	116	420,000	1:48.88	.105
2003	Candid Glen	6	E.J. Perrodin	114	Rouvres	115	Freefourinternet	115	390,000	1:51.15	.101

Beyer Index: 102.46

FAIR GROUNDS OAKS, 1 1/16 Miles, 3-Year-Old Fillies, Fair Grounds, 2003 Purse: $350,000

Year	Winner	Age	Jockey	Wt.	Second	Wt.	Third	Wt.	Win Value	Time	Beyer
1966	Help on Way	3	L. Gilligan	115	Dutch Maid	115	Ge Ma	115	9,350	1:52.60	
1967	Furl Sail	3	J.R. Lopez	121	Nancy Jr.	118	Filly Folly	115	10,550	1:45.20	
1968	Trapeze	3	J. Nichols	115	Sale Day	115	Le Bijou	115	11,325	1:46.20	
1969	Royal Fillet	3	L. Moyers	121	Around the Horn	115	Scat Kat	115	9,850	1:46.60	
1970	Kay Emy	3	M. Heath	118	Lady Vi-E.	113	Ellen Girl	113	12,075	1:47.60	
1971	Rosemone Bow	3	K. Knapp	121	Cruline	112	Olney's Pet	112	10,925	1:43.40	
1972	My Charmer	3	L. Melancon	112	Color Me Blue	112	Bugle Bow	115	14,350	1:46.00	
1973	Knitted Gloves	3	J.C. Espinoza	118	Fussy Girl	121	Westward	118	14,825	1:46.00	
1974	Bold Rosie	3	P. Rubbicco	118	Trade Me Later	112	Kaye's Co'mander	118	20,625	1:46.60	
1975	Lucky Leslie	3	D. Brumfield	118	Regal Rumor	121	Decanter	118	19,650	1:46.60	
1976	Bronze Point	3	H. Arroyo	118	Little Broadway	118	Confort Zone	118	20,075	1:44.40	
1977	Table the Rumor	3	W. Shoemaker	112	La Doree	112	Ivory Castle	118	57,800	1:52.40	
1978	Shadycroft Lady	3	R. Martinez Jr	109	Miss Baja	117	B'lle of D'ge Me	114	25,738	1:52.60	
1978	La Doree	4	B. Fann	107	Royal Graustark	114	B'rn the M'n'y	107	25,738	1:52.40	
1980	Honest and True	3	A. Guajardo	118	Smart Angle	121	Lady Taurian Peace	118	33,875	1:44.40	
1981	Truly Bound	3	W. Shoemaker	121	Lou's Dance	118	Sunwontshine	112	61,400	1:44.80	

Year	Winner	Age	Jockey	Wt.	Second	Wt.	Third	Wt.	Win Value	Time	Beyer
1982	Before Dawn	3	J. Velasquez	121	Girlie	121	Linda North	118	66,400	1:45.40	
1983	Bright Crocus	3	S. Hawley	121	Miss Molly	118	Shamivor	115	66,100	1:45.80	
1984	My Darling One	3	C.J. McCarron	112	Texas Cowgirl Nite	118	Rays Joy	112	101,400	1:44.60	
1985	Marshua's Echelon	3	R.J. Franklin	121	Golden Silence	113	Little Biddy Comet	118	113,400	1:44.80	
1986	Tiffany Lass	3	R.L. Frazier	121	Patricia J.K.	121	Turn and Dance	112	97,400	1:45.00	
1987	Up the Apalachee	3	M.R. Torres	121	Cathy Quick	118	Out of the Bid	121	60,000	1:45.40	
1988	Quite a Gem	3	E.J. Perrodin	115	False Glitter	118	Sable Decor	118	59,580	1:46.40	
1989	Mistaurian	3	D. Valiente	113	Affirmed Classic	121	Exquisite Mistress	118	57,900	1:44.80	
1990	Pampered Star	3	S.P. Romero	112	Windansea	118	Gayla's Pleasure	115	59,520	1:44.60	
1991	Rare Pick	3	P.A. Johnson	112	Nalees Pin	121	Lady Blockbuster	118	65,640	1:46.40	.93
1992	Prospectors Delite	3	P. Day	118	Glitzi Bj	118	Desert Radiance	118	63,990	1:44.20	.92
1993	Silky Feather	3	E.J. Perrodin	113	She's a Little Shy	121	Sum Runner	121	64,080	1:43.80	.87
1994	Two Altazano	3	Leblanc KP	112	Tricky Code	121	Minority Dater	112	93,840	1:42.40	.101
1995	Brushing Gloom	3	Brown JE	112	Kuda	118	Legendary Princess	121	90,000	1:45.00	.84
1996	Bright Time	3	L.F. Diaz	112	Mackie	121	Proper Dance	114	90,000	1:45.80	.82
1997	Blushing K.D.	3	L. Meche	121	Tomisue's Delight	121	Cozy Blues	112	105,000	1:42.20	.102
1998	Lu Ravi	3	W. Martinez	112	Well Chosen	112	Silent Eskimo	112	180,000	1:43.60	.89
1999	Silverbulletday	3	G.L. Stevens	121	Runaway Venus	112	Brushed Halory	114	210,000	1:44.80	.101
2000	Shawnee Country	3	D.J. Meche	121	Eden Lodge	121	Zoftig	121	210,000	1:44.81	.92
2001	Real Cozzy	3	E. Martin Jr.	121	Mystic Lady	121	She's a Devil Due	121	210,000	1:44.58	.86
2002	Take Charge Lady	3	A.J. D'Amico	121	Lake Lady	121	Chamrousse	121	210,000	1:43.30	.107
2003	Lady Tak	3	D.J. Meche	121	Atlantic Ocean	121	Belle of Perintown	121	210,000	1:44.36	.95

Beyer Index: 93.15

FALLS CITY HANDICAP, 1 1/8 Miles,
Fillies and Mares, 3-Year-Olds and Up, Churchill Downs, 2003 Purse: $334,200

Year	Winner	Age	Jockey	Wt.	Second	Wt.	Third	Wt.	Win Value	Time	Beyer
1875	Camargo	3	R. Swim	100	Ascension	100			1,125	1:43.25	
1876	Red Coat	3	Hughes	100	Patriot	100	Leamington	100	975	1:46.00	
1877	Flying Locust	3	B. Walker	100	Commodore Parrisot	100	Kinlock	100	625	1:45.00	
1882	Freeland	3	C. Taylor	104	Katie Creel	104	Anglia	104	800	2:42.50	
1883	Washburn	4	H. Blaylock	114	Silvio	114	McGlinty	97	625	2:49.25	
1884	Chance	3	J. Stoval	109	Hiflight	109	Ascender	118	900	1:55.00	
1892	Wadsworth	3	T. Britton	113	Kindora	97			1,450	1:47.00	
1910	Melisande	4	T. Koerner	121	Jack Atkin	136	Ocean Bound	122	1,440	1:12.00	
1911	High Private	5	G. Taplin	108	Princess Calaway	100	Cherryola	105	1,210	1:51.60	
1912	Buckhorn	3	W. Andress	114	High Private	122	Countless	110	1,180	1:13.20	
1913	Wilhite	4	Borel	109	The Widow Moon	103	K'eburne	110	2,010	1:13.80	
1914	Leochares	4	R. Goose	116	Helen Barbee	116	Governor Hughes	114	1,750	1:13.00	
1915	Prince Hermis	5	E. Pool	108	Vogue	107	Pan Zareta	125	2,060	1:13.20	
1916	Kathleen	3	D. Connelly	117	Bringhurst	117	Vogue	112	2,170	1:13.00	
1917	Vogue	5	J. Callahan	113	Bradley's Choice	108	Pan Zareta	131	1,970	1:13.00	
1918	Last Coin	6	L. Gentry	111	Sedan	111	Ocean Sweep	104	1,885	1:13.00	
1919	King Gorin	6	L. Lyke	118	Jack Hare, Jr.	132	Midway	118	4,485	1:48.00	
1920	Woodtrap	6	D. Connelly	113	Sands of Pleasure	105	Sterling	108	5,080	1:56.60	
1921	Bit of White	3	L. Lyke	110	Rangoon	118	Ginger	108	5,420	1:51.20	
1922	Chatterton	3	B. Kennedy	104	Rockminster	108	Rouleau	109	4,860	1:51.00	
1923	Guest of Honor	3	M. Garner	108	Audacious	122	Cherry Tree	111	5,060	1:53.00	
1924	Princess Doreen	3	H. Stutts	113	Hopeless	107	Just David	102	5,280	1:51.60	
1925	Deeming	3	L. Steinhart	106	Sir Peter	114	Balboa	108	50,000	1:55.00	
1926	Rothermel	4	W. Garner	109	Rhin'ock	112	Longworth	100	4,780	1:55.80	
1927	Rhin'ock	4	C. Hunt	108	Percentage	106	Hydromel	114	4,820	1:52.60	
1941	Misty Isle	3	A. Bodiou	116	Meggy	113	Blue Delight	113	1,975	1:37.60	
1942	Pig Tails	3	O. Scurlock	108	Meggy	108	Montsin	107	2,025	1:40.60	
1943	Burgoo Maid	3	W. Morrissey	114	Flying Easy	112	Fiddler's Bit	104	2,035	1:37.40	
1944	Traffic Court	6	W. Garner	118	Bold Style	109	S'ttm't Sake	107	3,980	1:39.40	
1945	Jack's Jill	3	A. LoTurco	115	Sigma Kappa	118	Annie's Reply	108	4,220	1:39.20	
1946	Miss Balladier	4	H. Wallace	107	Jack's Jill	119	First Gun	113	7,700	1:39.60	
1947	Say Blue	3	S. Brooks	113	Jack's Jill	112	Be Faithful	110	7,950	1:39.60	
1948	Jack's Jill	4	F.A. Smith	118	Miss Mommy	113	Speedy Lee	117	7,975	1:38.40	
1949	Brownian	5	A.D. Rivera	116	Blue Helen	113	Blue Note	105	6,250	1:38.80	
1950	Our Request	4	T. Barrow	111	Miss Highbrow	116	Here's Hoping	120	5,775	1:39.40	
1951	Dickie Sue	3	H. Craig	104	Our Request	115	Lyceum	113	5,800	1:37.40	
1952	Peu-a-Peu	3	P.A. Ward	108	Gray Challenge	110	Our Request	114	6,125	1:38.40	
1953	Gala Fete	4	A. Kirkland	117	Cajole	107	Belle Rebelle	106	8,350	1:36.60	
1954	Gala Fete	5	A. Kirkland	120	Close Play	106	Vixen Fixit	115	8,250	1:39.00	
1955	Oil Pollution	4	D. Dodson	121	Pegeen	112	Jenjay	111	8,525	1:41.20	
1956	Doubledogdare	3	S. Brooks	121	Queen Hopeful	122	Lycka	117	15,175	1:37.00	
1957	Leallah	3	D. Erb	114	Beautillion	118	Lady LaRue	111	14,319	1:36.20	
1958	Bornastar	5	K. Church	122	Little Pache	113	Woodlawn	111	14,416	1:37.20	
1959	Indian Maid	3	J.L. Rotz	122	Lindaway	109	Ruling Beauty	114	14,465	1:35.40	
1960	Indian Maid	4	J. Sellers	124	Gerts Image	113	Chance G'ge	110	14,172	1:37.20	

Year Winner	Age	Jockey	Wt.	Second	Wt.	Third	Wt.	Win Value	Time	Beyer
1961 Indian Maid	5	C. Meaux	120	My Sister Kate	112	Times Two	115	15,145	1:38.00	
1962 Primonetta	4	R.L. Baird	126	Old Hat	113	Fortunate Isle	110	14,739	1:35.60	
1963 Alecee	4	V. Cruz	115	Abrogate	116	Mon Petite	109	15,421	1:36.40	
1964 Old Hat	5	D. Brumfield	128	De Cathy	113	Abrogate	117	18,850	1:35.60	
1965 De Cathy	4	E. Eades	113	Abrogate	117	Really Trying	112	18,216	1:36.00	
1966 Old Hat	7	K. Church	116	Naidni Diam	110	Mac's Sparkler	117	18,184	1:35.00	
1967 Amerigo Lady	3	P. Anderson	116	Gusher	113	Likely Swap	113	18,866	1:36.00	
1968 T.V's Princess	4	E. Fires	111	Frederick Street	112	Pattee Canyon	117	14,649	1:35.80	
1968 Sale Day	3	E. Guerin	119	I've Arrived	112	Drover's Dr'm	107	14,649	1:36.80	
1969 Dedicated to Sue	3	M. Manganello	113	Frederick Street	120	Kelly Keim	111	14,682	1:35.60	
1969 Yes Sir	3	D. Brumfield	115	T.V's Princess	118	Cast Ahead	111	14,682	1:36.00	
1970 Mistong	3	J. Soto	110	Double Delta	123	Yes Sir	111	18,882	1:39.80	
1971 Strider	4	M. Manganello	114	Shee Clachan	115	Golden Circlet	114	18,306	1:37.20	
1971 Magnabid	3	D. Brumfield	113	Hard and Fast	113	Deceit	125	18,143	1:36.00	
1972 Fairway Flyer	3	D.E. Whited	117	Brenda Beauty	116	Turning Bold	112	14,909	1:38.40	
1972 Barely Even	3	R. Broussard	128	Silent Beauty	118	Secret Retr't	116	14,747	1:37.80	
1973 Delta Empress	3	E. Fires	111	Pig Party	113	Fine Tuning	115	15,348	1:37.40	
1973 Fairway Flyer	3	D.E. Whited	115	Nalee's Folly	118	Knitted Gloves	113	15,186	1:37.20	
1974 Susan's Girl	5	W. Gavidia	126	Crystal Stone	114	Enc't Native	112	18,184	1:37.40	
1975 Flama Ardiente	3	B. Fann	119	Costly Dream	120	Go on Dreaming	116	18,622	1:38.20	
1976 Hope of Glory	4	D. Brumfield	118	Hail to El	116	Flama Ardiente	117	21,937	1:48.20	
1977 Time for Pleasure	3	T. Barrow	115	Dear Irish	114	Famed Princess	115	2,084	1:46.20	
1978 Navajo Princess	4	C. Perret	123	Love to Tell	118	Likely Exchange	120	36,043	1:45.40	
1979 Holy Mount	3	M.R. Morgan	112	Impetuous Gal	118	Cup of Honey	115	39,163	1:47.60	
1980 Sweet Audrey	3	C.R. Woods Jr	113	Likely Exchange	123	Impetuous Gal	122	36,156	1:48.20	
1981 Safe Play	3	S.A. Spencer	123	Sweetest Chant	118	Friendly Frolic	112	37,993	1:46.20	
1982 Mezimica	4	D.E. Foster	112	Charge My Account	111	Shade Miss	112	39,910	1:51.40	
1982 What Glitter	4	D. Brumfield	114	Sprite Flight	114	Betty Money	118	36,823	1:52.80	
1983 Narrate	3	M.S. Sellers	117	Queen of Song	116	Promising Native	116	36,335	1:51.60	
1984 Pretty Perfect	4	G. Gallitano	121	Electric Fanny	116	Queen of Song	122	37,115	1:50.80	
1985 Donut's Pride	3	L. Melancon	112	Playful Queen	114	My Inheritance	111	35,743	1:53.20	
1985 Electric Fanny	4	J.C. Espinoza	115	Mrs. Revere	121	Chattahoochee	113	25,780	1:52.60	
1986 Queen Alexandra	4	D. Brumfield	124	Kapalua Butterfly	113	Gerrie Singer	116	49,248	1:51.40	
1987 Royal Cielo	3	K.K. Allen	114	Firgie's Jule	115	Fantasy Lover	113	47,330	1:53.00	
1988 Top Corsage	5	D. Brumfield	121	Epitome	116	Lawyer Talk	111	76,895	1:51.80	
1989 Degenerate Gal	4	L. Melancon	116	Luthier's Launch	113	Blackened	112	72,410	1:52.60	
1990 Screen Prospect	3	P. Day	114	Sleek Feet	110	Degenerate Gal	119	75,920	1:51.40	100
1991 Screen Prospect	4	S.J. Sellers	117	Fit for a Queen	124	Bungalow	112	73,580	1:51.20	105
1992 Bungalow	5	P. Day	118	Wilderness Song	123	Auto Dial	115	70,915	1:52.03	91
1993 Gray Cashmere	4	P. Day	120	Avie's Shadow	110	Princess Polonia	112	142,090	1:51.96	98
1994 Alcovy	4	S.E.Miller	114	Pennyhill Park	115	Hey Hazel	114	141,440	1:51.16	101
1995 Mariah's Storm	4	R.N. Lester	120	Alcovy	112	Heavenliness	112	143,390	1:51.37	106
1996 Halo America	6	C.H. Borel	118	Bedroom Blues	115	Debit My Account	113	171,120	1:49.08	107
1997 Feasibility Study	5	M.E. Smith	122	Omi	114	Naskra Colors	112	170,345	1:50.65	101
1998 Tomisue's Delight	4	S.J. Sellers	121	Top Secret	115	Silent Eskimo	113	171,740	1:51.05	99
1999 Silent Eskimo	4	C.H. Borel	117	Let	116	Pleasant Temper	115	171,585	1:48.85	106
2000 Bordelaise	5	P. Day	117	Spain	122	On a Soapbox	116	168,020	1:50.01	108
2001 Forest Secrets	3	C. Perret	113	Printemps	117	Unbridled Elaine	121	169,570	1:49.49	102
2002 Allamerican Bertie	3	P. Day	117	Take Charge Lady	122	Softly	116	167,400	1:49.60	102
2003 Lead Story	4	C.H. Borel	116	Mayo on the Side	114	Cloakof Vagueness	114	207,204	1:51.23	107

Beyer Index: 102.36

FANTASY, 1 1/16 Miles,
3-Year-Old Fillies, Oaklawn Park, 2003 Purse: $200,000

Year Winner	Age	Jockey	Wt.	Second	Wt.	Third	Wt.	Win Value	Time Beyer
1973 Knitted Gloves	3	J.C. Espinosa	121	Fussy Girl	121	Westward	118	96,960	1:42.60
1974 Miss Musket	3	W. Shoemaker	121	Out to Lunch	115	Fairway Fable	118	79,740	1:44.80
1975 Hoso	3	M. Solomone	121	Luxury	114	Dancers Countess	118	70,830	1:46.00
1976 T.V. Vixen	3	B. Walt	121	Answer	121	All Rainbows	112	73,170	1:43.40
1977 Our Mims	3	D. Brumfield	112	Sweet Alliance	118	Meteor Dancer	110	83,970	1:45.00
1978 Equanimity	3	H.E. Moreno	110	Ba Ba Bee	115	Miss Baja	121	77,850	1:44.60
1979 Davona Dale	3	J. Velasquez	121	Caline	121	Very Special Lady	110	101,610	1:44.40
1980 Bold 'n Determined	3	E. Delahoussaye	121	Satin Ribera	115	Honest and True	118	101,940	1:45.20
1981 Heavenly Cause	3	L. Pincay Jr	121	Nell's Briquette	121	Wayward Lass	121	133,890	1:43.80
1982 Flying Partner	3	R. Sibille	118	Skillful Joy	121	Before Dawn	121	163,020	1:47.00
1983 Brindy Brindy	3	K. Jones	115	Fifth Question	115	Choose a Partner	112	169,080	1:44.60
1984 My Darling One	3	C.J. McCarron	121	Althea	121	Personable Lady	118	160,440	1:41.20
1985 Rascal Lass	3	R. Sibille	118	Denver Express	113	Little Biddy Comet	114	169,620	1:43.20
1986 Tiffany Lass	3	G.L. Stevens	121	Lotka	116	Turn and Dance	112	164,640	1:42.00
1987 Very Subtle	3	C.J. McCarron	121	Up the Apalachee	121	Hometown Queen	116	16,270	1:42.40
1988 Jeanne Jones	3	W. Shoemaker	118	Fara's Team	112	Costly Shoes	114	150,000	1:42.20
1989 Fantastic Look	3	C.J. McCarron	113	Imaginary Lady	121	Affirmed Classic	114	150,000	1:43.20

Year	Winner	Age	Jockey	Wt.	Second	Wt.	Third	Wt.	Win Value	Time	Beyer
1990	Silvered	3	D.L. Howard	112	Lonely Girl	114	Fit to Scout	118	150,000	1:44.20	
1991	Lite Light	3	C.S. Nakatani	121	Withallprobability	121	Nalees Pin	121	150,000	1:41.80	100
1992	Race the Wild Wind	3	C.J. McCarron	117	Golden Treat	121	Now Dance	117	150,000	1:43.60	100
1993	Aztec Hill	3	M.E. Smith	121	Adorydar	117	Stalcreek	117	150,000	1:44.20	94
1994	Two Altazano	3	K.P. Leblanc	121	Slide Show	121	Flying in the Lane	121	150,000	1:43.60	91
1995	Cat's Cradle	3	C.W. Antley	121	Forever Cherokee	117	Humble Eight	121	150,000	1:44.20	89
1996	Escena	3	P. Day	117	Antespend	121	Ski Trail	121	150,000	1:43.80	93
1997	Blushing K.D.	3	L.J. Meche	121	Valid Bonnet	121	Ajina	121	150,000	1:42.60	110
1998	Silent Eskimo	3	C.V. Gonzalez	117	Misty Hour	121	Came Unwound	121	150,000	1:43.80	97
1999	Excellent Meeting	3	K.J. Desormeaux	121	The Happy Hopper	121	Dreams Gallore	121	150,000	1:42.60	106
2000	Classy Cara	3	I.L. Puglisi	121	Eden Lodge	117	Gold For My Gal	117	120,000	1:43.95	93
2001	Mystic Lady	3	E.M. Coa	121	Collect Call	121	Mysia Jo	117	120,000	1:43.32	98
2002	See How She Runs	3	D.R. Pettinger	117	:Lake Lady	121	Chamrousse	117	120,000	1:43.80	98
2003	Ruby's Reception	3	T.J. Thompson	121	Harbor Blues	121	Go for Glamour	117	120,000	1:44.61	84

Beyer Index: 96.39

FIRECRACKER BREEDERS' CUP HANDICAP, 1 Mile (Turf),
3-Year-Olds and Up, Churchill Downs, 2003 Purse: $288,500

Year	Winner	Age	Jockey	Wt.	Second	Wt.	Third	Wt.	Win Value	Time	Beyer
1993	Cleone	4	C. Perret	115	Magesterial Cheer	113	Harlan	110	74,815	1:35.80	102
1994	First and Only	7	T.J. Hebert	118	Weekend Madness	111	Avid Affection	112	73,580	1:35.20	100
1995	Jaggery John	4	D. Kutz	113	Rare Reason	115	Fly Cry	119	74,360	1:33.60	103
1996	Rare Reason	5	P. Johnson	115	Artema	114	Wavy Run	116	131,950	1:33.80	106
1997	Soviet Line	7	P. Day	114	Volochine	115	Same Old Wish	113	126,077	1:37.60	107
1998	Claire's Honor	4	A.J. D'Amico	109	Soviet Line	115	Optic Nerve	113	177,630	1:35.80	103
1999	Joe Who	6	R.J. Albarado	113	Middlesex Drive	116	Wild Event	121	132,680	1:36.78	107
2000	Conserve	4	S.J. Sellers	116	Riviera	115	King Slayer	115	177,940	1:35.12	102
2001	Irish Prize	5	G.L. Stevens	122	Aly's Alley	117	Where's Taylor	114	175,770	1:34.68	107
2002	Good Journey	6	P.Day	118	Morluc	114	Even the Score	114	181,350	1:34.83	107
	Where's Taylor finished second but was disqualified and placed third										
2003	Tap the Admiral	5	J. McKee	115	Freefourinternet	114	Package Store	114	178,870	1:35.48	100

Beyer Index: 104

FIRST FLIGHT HANDICAP, 7 Furlongs,
Fillies and Mares, 3-Year-Olds and Up, Belmont, 2003 Purse: $150,000

Year	Winner	Age	Jockey	Wt.	Second	Wt.	Third	Wt.	Win Value	Time	Beyer
1978	What a Summer	5	J. Fell	126	Flying Above	120	Mrs. Warren	113	25,410	1:22.20	
1979	Gladiolus	5	L. Pincay Jr	120	Imarebel	117	Plankton	114	25,740	1:22.40	
1980	Samarta Dancer	4	C.B. Asmussen	112	Jedina	115	Damask Fan	112	33,780	1:25.60	
1981	Island Charm	4	R. Migliore	120	Tax Holiday	116	Chain Bracelet	123	33,720	1:23.60	
1982	Number	3	E. Maple	112	Lady Dean	123	Privacy	118	34,500	1:22.80	
1983	Pert	4	F. Lovato Jr	112	Pretty Sensible	112	Quixotic Lady	121	34,620	1:25.20	
1984	Shortley	4	M.G. Pino	114	Quixotic Lady	116	Rarely Layte	108	42,060	1:22.60	
1985	Alabama Nana	4	J. Velasquez	121	Gene's Lady	115	Paradies	119	50,040	1:22.20	
1986	Chaldea	6	J.L. Samyn	115	Le Slew	114	Gene's Lady	120	53,100	1:22.40	
1987	Al's Helen	4	J. Velasquez	121	Girl Powder	117	Willowy Mood	118	54,180	1:21.80	
1988	Cagey Exuberance	4	J. Imparato	119	Nasty Affair	114	Intently	111	55,350	1:24.40	
1989	Grecian Flight	5	C. Perret	122	Feel the Beat	121	Dance Teacher	112	51,480	1:22.00	
1990	Queena	4	J.D. Bailey	113	Quick Mischief	115	A Penny Is a Penny	122	51,480	1:22.40	106
1991	Missy's Mirage	3	E. Maple	113	Makin Faces	112	Withallprobability	114	74,160	1:21.80	105
1992	Shared Interest	4	J.D. Bailey	111	Missy's Mirage	121	Nannerl	119	120,000	1:20.60	111
1993	Raise the Heck	5	R.I. Velez	114	Regal Victress	113	Shared Interest	121	69,000	1:23.40	106
1994	Twist Afleet	3	J.D. Bailey	117	Ann Dear	117	Incinerate	113	66,000	1:23.00	98
1995	Twist Afleet	4	G.L. Stevens	121	Igotrhythm	109	Lottsa Talc	116	66,780	1:22.80	101
1996	Thunder Achiever	3	R.G. Davis	112	Miss Golden Circle	117	Call Account	110	81,864	1:21.60	105
1997	Dixie Flag	3	M.J. Luzzi	113	Silent City	113	Aldiza	116	64,800	1:22.80	99
1998	Catinca	3	R. Migliore	116	Glitter Woman	121	Blue Begonia	115	82,260	1:22.00	105
1999	Country Hideaway	3	H. Castillo Jr	114	Harpia	117	Anklet	114	90,000	1:23.00	99
2000	Country Hideaway	4	J.L. Espinoza	117	Go To The Ink	115	Cat Cay	114	90,000	1:22.60	101
2001	Shine Again	4	J.L. Samyn	116	Dream Supreme	121	Kalookan Queen	119	90,000	1:23.21	110
2002	Shine Again	5	J.L. Samyn	117	Redhead Riot	112	Raging Fever	119	90,000	1:23.75	102
2003	Randaroo	3	H. Castillo Jr	115	Shine Again	121	Zawzooth	113	90,000	1:23.65	93

Beyer Index: 102.93

FLEUR DE LIS HANDICAP, 1 1/8 Miles,
Fillies and Mares, 3-Year-Olds and Up, Churchill Downs, 2003 Purse: $327,900

Year	Winner	Age	Jockey	Wt.	Second	Wt.	Third	Wt.	Win Value	Time	Beyer
1975	Bundler	4	J. Nichols	120	Jay Bar Pet	112	Tappahannock	116	14,511	1:39.40	
1976	Pago Hop	4	H. Arroyo	116	Flama Ardiente	122	Prec'us Proof	113	14,056	1:38.40	

Year	Winner	Age	Jockey	Wt.	Second	Wt.	Third	Wt.	Win Value	Time	Beyer
1977	Go on Dreaming	5	P. Nicolo	115	B.J. King	114	Kittyluck	117	14,381	1:43.80	
1978	Likely Exchange	4	J. McKnight	113	Time for Pleasure	123	Bold Rendezvous	114	13,894	1:45.40	
1979	Table the Rumor	5	D.E. Whited	118	Likely Exchange	123	Pretty Delight	116	22,864	1:45.20	
1980	Likely Exchange	6	J.S. Sellers	121	Salzburg	116	Smooth Bore	115	23,026	1:45.00	
1981	Forever Cordial	4	D. Haire	114	Salud	114	Passolyn	118	23,205	1:45.40	
1982	Classic Ambition	4	W. Gavidia	112	Beyond Reproof	113	Mean Martha	117	36,855	1:44.80	
1983	Try Something New	4	P. Day	121	Naskra Magic	116	Header Card	117	35,328	1:51.60	
1984	Heatherten	5	S. Maple	124	Satiety	110	Hotsy Totsy	112	35,233	1:51.40	
1985	Straight Edition	5	C.R. Woods Jr	113	Dusty Gloves	110	Del Dun Gee	110	36,108	1:50.80	
1986	Queen Alexandra	4	D. Brumfield	117	Tide	111	Zn'bia Express	119	66,083	1:49.20	
1987	Infinidad	5	M. Solomone	118	Marianna's Girl	117	Queen Alexandra	126	64,815	1:50.60	
1988	Lt. Lao	4	D. Brumfield	116	Lawyer Talk	111	She's a Mystery	111	72,215	1:49.60	
1989	Stoneleigh's Hope	4	J.C. Deegan	112	Way It Should Be	111	Lt. Lao	116	71,435	1:52.60	
1990	A Penny Is a Penny	5	A.T. Gryder	120	Stoneleigh's Hope	115	Lady Hoolihan	112	70,980	1:51.20	91
1991	Maskra's Lady	4	J.M. Johnson	111	Fit for a Queen	116	Under Oath	113	73,515	1:50.40	99
1992	Bungalow	5	F. Torres	114	Til Forbid	113	Beth Believes	112	74,815	1:50.87	94
1993	Quilma	6	R.P. Romero	117	Fappies Cosy Miss	111	Hitch	112	71,240	1:50.80	99
1994	Trishyde	5	C.J. McCarron	117	Eskimo's Angel	115	Ma Guerre	109	107,347	1:51.34	95
1995	Fit to Lead	5	Sellers SJ	117	Pennyhill Park	118	Low Key Affair	112	107,055	1:51.59	102
1996	Serena's Song	4	G.L. Stevens	124	Halo America	117	Alcovy	117	109,493	1:50.30	105
1997	Gold 'n Delicious	4	C.H. Borel	113	Effectiveness	111	Everhope	111	104,718	1:52.87	99
1998	Escena	5	S.J. Sellers	123	One Rich Lady	113	Tomisue's Delight	118	199,020	1:50.19	113
1999	Banshee Breeze	4	R.J. Albarado	124	Silent Eskimo	114	Meadow Vista	109	197,718	1:50.02	110
2000	Heritage of Gold	5	S.J. Sellers	121	Silvebulletday	119	Roza Robata	115	201,252	1:48.26	116
2001	Saudi Poetry	4	V. Espinoza	114	Secret Status	119	Asher	112	206,460	1:49.27	101
2002	Spain	5	J.F. Chavez	121	With Ability	117	Dancethruthedawn	119	204,228	1:49.64	100
2003	You	4	J.D. Bailey	119	Printemps	114	Nonsuch Bay	114	203,298	1:49.12	103

Beyer Index: 101.93

FOREST HILLS HANDICAP, 6 Furlongs,
3-Year-Olds and Up, Belmont Park, 2002 Purse: $250,000

Year	Winner	Age	Jockey	Wt.	Second	Wt.	Third	Wt.	Win Value	Time	Beyer
1975	Relent	4	J. Vasquez	113	Lonetree	118	Cumulo Nimbus	117	27,015	1:09.60	
1976	Soy Numero Uno	3	P. Day	118	It's Freezing	112	Queen City Lad	112	23,295	1:08.60	
1977	Broadway Forli	3	P. Day	115	Full Out	119	It's Freezing	113	22,875	1:09.60	
1978	Big John Taylor	4	J. Vasquez	115	Amadevil	119	Super Pleasure	110	25,365	1:08.80	
1979	Syncopate	4	L. Pincay Jr	118	King's Fashion	119	Tilt Up	116	32,370	1:10.20	
1980	Double Zeus	5	J. Fell	120	Candy Eclair	124	King's Fashion	123	34,260	1:10.60	
1981	Guilty Conscience	5	C.B. Asmussen	115	Imperial Dilemma	112	Maudlin	115	33,480	1:09.20	
1982	Engine One	4	R. Hernandez	115	Maudlin	115	Pass the Tab	118	33,420	1:09.40	
1983	Chas Conerly	3	J. Miranda	118	Gold Beauty	123	Shimatoree	120	33,120	1:10.60	
1984	Tarantara	5	R. Migliore	111	Muskoka Wyck	115	Cannon Shell	117	42,300	1:09.20	
1985	Mt. Livermore	4	J. Velasquez	120	Zany Tactics	114	For Halo	117	54,180	1:09.00	
1986	King's Swan	6	R. Migliore	114	Raja's Shark	119	Boltin Holme	111	50,670	1:08.60	
1987	Sun Master	6	L. Pincay Jr	117	Banker's Jet	115	Play the King	122	51,210	1:09.20	
1988	Claramount	4	C.W. Antley	113	Quick Call	112	High Brite	121	68,400	1:10.60	
1989	Mr. Nickerson	3	C. Perret	114	Sewickley	117	Final Luck	113	67,800	1:11.00	
1990	Carson City	3	J.D. Bailey	116	Mr. Nickerson	121	Once Wild	118	68,400	1:08.00	112
1991	Senor Speedy	4	J.F. Chavez	117	Diablo	114	For Really	113	71,280	1:09.40	108
1992	Belong to Me	3	M.E. Smith	112	Diablo	117	Fast Turn	108	71,280	1:10.00	109
1993	Boom Towner	5	F. Lovato Jr	113	Take Me Out	123	Thelastcrusade	115	69,360	1:09.00	112
1994	Meritocrat	3	M.E. Smith	113	Birdonthewire	117	Lite the Fuse	110	83,025	1:09.00	115
1995	Friendly Lover	7	R. Wilson	118	Lite the Fuse	120	Mining Burrah	114	86,100	1:10.00	108
1996	Lord Carson	4	S.J. Sellers	116	Honour and Glory	119	Splendid Sprinter	110	105,000	1:08.60	114
1997	Kelly Kip	3	J.L. Samyn	111	Crafty Friend	117	Royal Haven	119	120,000	1:08.80	111
1998	Punch Line	8	J.F. Chavez	118	King Roller	114	Johnny Legit	115	120,000	1:09.60	107
1999	Artax	4	J.F. Chavez	120	Good and Tough	118	Intidab	116	150,000	1:07.60	123
2000	Delaware Township	4	P. Day	114	Bevo	114	Valiant Halory	113	150,000	1:08.56	110
2001	Delaware Township	5	E.M. Coa	118	Hook And Ladder	114	Yonaguska	113	150,000	1:09.49	115
2002	Avanzado	5	T.C. Baze	116	Dash for Daylight	115	Esteemed Friend	113	150,000	1:11.00	106

Not run in 2003

Beyer Index: 111.53

FOURSTARDAVE HANDICAP, 1 1/16 Miles (Turf),
3-Year-Olds and Up, Saratoga Race Course, 2003 Purse: $200,000

Year	Winner	Age	Jockey	Wt.	Second	Wt.	Third	Wt.	Win Value	Time	Beyer
1988	Sans the Shadow	4	A. Cordero Jr	115	My Big Boy	117	Real Courage	115	56,340	1:40.00	
1989	Steinlen	6	A. Cordero Jr	122	Expensive Decision	117	Sparkling Wit	110	53,955	1:41.00	
1989	Highland Springs	5	E.S. Prado	122	Fourstardave	122	Soviet Lad	115	53,955	1:41.60	

Year	Winner	Age	Jockey	Wt.	Second	Wt.	Third	Wt.	Win Value	Time	Beyer
1990	Fourstardave	5	M.E. Smith	115	Foreign Survivor	119	Wanderkin	119	57,150	1:41.20	
1991	Fourstardave	6	M.E. Smith	115	Who's to Pay	122	Kate's Valentine	117	71,640	1:38.80	
1992	Now Listen	5	J.R. Velazquez	119	Crackedbell	119	Cold Hoist	115	71,640	1:36.60	98
1993	Lure	4	M.E. Smith	122	Fourstardave	122	Scott the Great	115	71,640	1:40.80	108
1994	A in Sociology	4	Samyn JL	115	Namaqualand	113	Fourstars Allstar	120	68,340	1:41.20	107
1995	Pride of Summer	7	Maple E	115	Fourstars Allstar	120	Jaggery John	120	69,240	1:40.80	109
1996	Da Hoss	4	J.R. Velazquez	113	Green Means Go	113	Rare Reason	118	71,100	1:40.40	109
1997	Soviet Line	7	P. Day	118	Val's Prince	114	Outta My Way Man	118	67,500	1:39.80	106
1998	Wild Event	5	M. Guidry	116	Bomfim	114	Rob 'n Gin	119	68,940	1:39.20	108
1999	Comic Strip	4	P. Day	115	Divide and Conquer	114	Bomfim	113	90,000	1:41.76	108
2000	Hap	4	J.D. Bailey	118	Altibr	115	Weatherbird	112	120,000	1:40.24	104
2001	Dr. Kashnikow	4	J.R. Velazquez	113	Tubrok	113	Aly's Alley	117	120,000	1:39.30	104
2002	Capsized	6	J.A. Santos	115	Pure Prize	119	Pyrus	113	120,000	1:50.90	108
2003	Trademark	7	R. Migliore	118	Quest Star	116	Tap the Admiral	115	120,000	1:39.29	109

Beyer Index: 106.5

Run on main track, 2002

GALLANT BLOOM HANDICAP, 6 1/2 Furlongs,
Fillies and Mares, 3-Year-Olds and Up, Belmont Park 2003 Purse: $150,000

Year	Winner	Age	Jockey	Wt.	Second	Wt.	Third	Wt.	Win Value	Time	Beyer
1994	Vivano	6	W.H. McCauley	116	Ann Dear	118	Strategic Reward	113	48,255	1:19.80	97
1995	Classy Mirage		J.Bailey	123	Dust Bucket	114	Fantastic Woman	110	48,375	1:17.20	97
1996	Miss Golden Circle	5	R.Migliore	115	J J'sdream	119	Nappelon	117	50,040	1:16.20	97
1997	Top Secret	4	Velazquez J. R.	120	Aldiza	116	Dixie Flag	114	49,260	1:16.00	99
1998	Catinca	3	Migliore R.	114	Dixie Flag	117	Crab Grass	114	50,595	1:15.60	101
1999	Positive Gal	3	Bailey J. D.	116	Flamingo Way	114	Torch	113	65,820	1:16.80	96
2000	Dream Supreme	3	P. Day	118	Finder's Fee	116	Tropical Punch	114	64,380	1:15.86	103
2001	Finder's Fee	4	J.R. Velazquez	113	Cedar Knolls	114	Gold Mover	115	79,928	1:17.60	93
2002	Nasty Storm	4	J.A. Santos	114	Raging Fever	120	Shine Again	118	90,000	1:17.89	100
2003	Harmony Lodge	5	R. Migliore	117	House Party	116	Slews Final Answer	112	90,000	1:16.20	107

Beyer Index: 99

GENERAL GEORGE HANDICAP, 7 Furlongs,
3-Year-Olds and Up, Laurel Park 2003 Purse: $200,000

Year	Winner	Age	Jockey	Wt.	Second	Wt.	Third	Wt.	Win Value	Time	Beyer
1973	Ecole Etage	3	G. Cusimano	113	Bid Red L	113	S'ect Perf'nce	110	18,265	1:44.60	
1974	Sharp Gary	3	C. Barrera	122	Jolly Johu	119	Ground Breaker	110	19,045	1:46.60	
1975	Pendulum Sam	3	L. Gino	110	King of Fools	113	Broadway Reviewer	110	18,005	1:48.20	
1976	Princely Game	3	A. Agnello	119	On the Sly	110	Troll By	116	17,940	1:44.60	
1977	Do the Bump	3	C.J. McCarron	122	John U to Berry	115	Steel Bandit	113	17,778	1:47.20	
1978	Ten Ten	3	W.J. Passmore	122	Game Prince	113	Gala Forecast	113	18,200	1:45.80	
1980	Galaxy Road	3	G. McCarron	122	Leader of the Pack	113	Ashanti Gold	110	36,660	1:24.60	
1981	Classic Go Go	3	W.J. Passmore	122	Thirty Eight Paces	122	Aztec Crown	115	37,115	1:23.20	
1984	Judge McGuire	3	C.H. Mendoza	122	American Artist	110	S.S. Hot Sauce	122	55,543	1:46.60	
1985	Roo Art	3	D.A. Miller Jr	122	Joyfull John	112	I Am the Game	119	55,380	1:37.60	
1986	Broad Brush	3	V. Bracciale Jr	122	Fast Step	113	Swallow	116	54,373	1:44.20	
1986	Lil Tyler	3	M.T. Hunter	122	Fobby Forbes	116	Fork Union Cadet	110	53,723	1:45.60	
1987	Templar Hill	3	G.W. Hutton	116	Hay Halo	122	Win Dusty Win	114	74,620	1:44.00	
1988	Private Terms	3	K.J. Desormeaux	116	Dynaformer	122	Delightful Doctor	122	74,328	1:38.80	
1989	Little Bold John	7	D.A. Miller Jr	122	Oraibi	119	Finder's Choice	117	120,000	1:22.80	
1990	King's Nest	5	M.T. Hunter	119	Wind Splitter	117	Notation	119	120,000	1:22.00	109
1991	Star Touch	5	M.J. Luzzi	118	Profit Key	118	Fire Plug	118	120,000	1:22.80	
1992	Senor Speedy	5	J.F. Chavez	126	Sunny Sunrise	123	Formal Dinner	123	120,000	1:21.80	108
1993	Majesty's Turn	4	A. Delgado	118	Senor Speedy	118	Ameri Valay	123	120,000	1:22.60	105
1994	Blushing Julian	4	R.E. Colton	118	Chief Desire	123	Who Wouldn't	118	120,000	1:22.80	111
1995	Who Wouldn't	4	J. Rocco	119	Storm Tower	116	Powis Castle	118	120,000	1:22.00	110
1996	Meadow Monster	5	R. Wilson	120	Splendid Sprinter	113	Cat Be Nimble	114	120,000	1:22.00	118
1997	Why Change	4	M. Guidry	113	Appealing Skier	118	Le Grand Pos	111	120,000	1:22.40	108
1998	Royal Haven	6	R. Migliore	122	Purple Passion	116	Wire Me Collect	117	150,000	1:23.00	111
1999	Esteemed Friend	5	M.J. Luzzi	116	Star of Valor	114	Purple Passion	117	150,000	1:22.40	106
2000	Affirmed Success	6	J.F. Chavez	121	Young At Heart	114	Badge	117	120,000	1:22.02	114
2001	Peeping Tom	4	S.X. Bridgmohan	114	Delaware Township	120	Disco Rico	117	120,000	1:22.00	113
2002	Wrangler	4	A.T. Gryder	115	Rusty Spur	111	Affirmed Success	121	120,000	1:22.53	107
2003	My Cousin Matt	4	R.A. Dominguez	113	Peeping Tom	114	Disturbingthepeace	118	120,000	1:22.12	1"

Beyer Index·

GENUINE RISK HANDICAP, 6 Furlongs,
Fillies and Mares, 3-Year-Olds and Up, Belmont Park, 2003 Purse: $145,500

Year	Winner	Age	Jockey	Wt.	Second	Wt.	Third	Wt.	Win Value	Time	Beyer
1984	On the Bench	4	J. Cruguet	115	Nany	117	Grateful Friend	119	33,060	1:09.60	
1985	Alabama Nana	4	J. Velasquez	117	Hare Brain	119	Two Ours	119	49,260	1:10.60	
1986	Clocks Secret	4	W. Shoemaker	122	Le Slew	119	Liz Taylor	109	48,900	1:10.00	
1987	Pine Tree Lane	5	A. Cordero Jr	122	Silent Account	117	Royal Tali	117	47,970	1:10.20	
1988	Tappiano	4	J. Vasquez	122	Cagey Exuberance	122	Hedgeabout	117	50,040	1:09.00	
1989	Safely Kept	3	A. Cordero Jr	114	Aptostar	122	Cagey Exuberance	122	49,410	1:09.40	
1990	Safely Kept	4	C. Perret	122	Diva's Debut	117	Levitation	117	49,140	1:10.20	
1991	Safely Kept	5	C. Perret	122	Missy's Mirage	109	Token Dance	117	68,400	1:10.00	.104
1992	Parisian Flight	4	J.A. Santos	117	Serape	117	Devil's Orchid	119	70,680	1:09.00	.105
1993	Apelia	4	L. Attard	119	Santa Catalina	117	Reach for Clever	117	69,600	1:10.00	.103
1994	Apelia	5	L. Attard	119	Spinning Round	119	Ann Dear	114	64,680	1:09.00	.106
1995	Classy Mirage	5	J.A. Krone	122	Through the Door	111	Lottsa Talc	117	64,080	1:11.20	.93
1996	Exotic Wood	4	M.E. Smith	119	Lottsa Talc	118	Miss Golden Circle	113	65,100	1:08.40	.111
1997	Miss Golden Circle	5	R. Migliore	120	Start At Once	111	Nappelon	110	65,040	1:09.40	.102
1998	J J'sdream	5	L.C. Reynolds	118	Tate	112	Capote Belle	118	83,310	1:10.20	.93
1999	Foil	4	J.L. Samyn	114	Harpia	118	Gold Princess	115	90,000	1:10.43	.101
2000	Imperfect World	4	R.G. Davis	113	Gold Princess	113	Tropical Punch	115	90,000	1:10.00	.99
2001	Katz Me If You Can	4	J. Bravo	113	Lucky Livi	114	Shine Again	115	90,000	1:09.55	.100
2002	Xtra Heat	4	H. Vega	126	Shine Again	117	La Galerie	114	90,000	1:10.24	.108
2003	Shine Again	6	J.L. Samyn	119	Carson Hollow	122	Harmony Lodge	116	90,000	1:09.19	.104

Beyer Index: 102.23

GOLDEN ROD, 1 1/16 Miles,
2-Year-Olds Fillies, Churchill Downs, 2003 Purse: $230,000

Year	Winner	Age	Jockey	Wt.	Second	Wt.	Third	Wt.	Win Value	Time	Beyer
1910	Helen Barbee	2	Nolan	93	Helene	96	The Hague	102	1,050	1:13.80	
1911	Kaiser	2	Skirvin	98	Island Queen	104	Azylade	102	1,270	1:12.80	
1912	Gowell	2	Loftus	107	Nobby	105	Donerail	103	1,470	1:13.40	
1913	Edith W.	2	J. McCabe	102	Brig's Brother	108	Old Ben	107	1,480	1:12.40	
1914	Vogue	2	J. Metcalf	102	Grecian	98	Aunt Josie	101	1,290	1:13.80	
1915	Milestone	2	A. Mott	104	Checks	103	Pockichoo	105	1,260	1:16.00	
1916	Fan G.	2	M. Buxton	106	Milbrey	98	Opportunity	100	1,400	1:14.80	
1917	Fern Handley	2	O. Willis	100	Sweet Alyssum	100	Hamilton A.	107	1,040	1:15.00	
1918	Legal	2	J. Howard	103	Madge F.	104	Sam Reh	113	1,395	1:14.20	
1919	Busy Signal	2	L. Lyke	110	Prince Pal	112	Orlova	100	5,705	1:40.00	
1920	Rangoon	2	L. Lyke	116	White Star	105	Sir Thos. Kean	106	6,120	1:26.60	
1921	Jeanne Bowdre	2	F. Weiner	105	Rockminister	117	John Finn	117	5,980	1:24.40	
1922	Great Luck	2	E. Pool	109	Alice Blue Gown	105	Donges	119	5,960	1:25.60	
1923	Glide	2	W. Fronk	110	Lord Martin	104	Chilhowee	113	6,480	1:25.00	
1924	Captain Hal	2	J. Heupel	127	King Nadi	110	Blue Ridge	113	5,880	1:26.00	
1925	Rhinock	2	E. Scobie	118	My Colonel	109	Great Sport	103	6,440	1:28.60	
1926	Rolled Stocking	2	W. Crump	111	Ethel Dear	112	Lovely Mannersr	112	6,020	1:25.80	
1927	Easter Stockings	2	R. Russell	107	Mickey D.	110	General Grant	110	5,800	1:27.00	
1962	Sequent	2	F. Callico	114	Golden Sage	113	Power to Strike	114	11,375	1:25.20	
1963	Ivalinda	2	R. Gallimore	114	Cadabra	111	Grecian Princess	114	7,678	1:24.40	
1963	Royal Bund	2	D. Brumfield	119	Valeene	116	Intentorpoise	108	7,776	1:24.40	
1964	Wild Song	2	K. Church	114	Wild Note	114	May's Guide	115	7,654	1:23.80	
1964	Torrid Miss	2	R. Gallimore	114	Kalispell	114	Gallizzie	119	7,654	1:24.20	
1965	Chalina	2	L. Kunitake	113	Trade Mark	112	Holiday Wish	115	25,990	1:25.40	
1966	Woozem	2	K. Knapp	113	Scottish Heath	110	Thong	116	27,979	1:23.40	
1967	Shenow	2	L. Pincay Jr	119	Moss	113	Lady Tramp	116	40,703	1:23.80	
1968	Spring Sunshine	2	D. Brumfield	116	Double Delta	113	Pink Stocking	113	40,310	1:24.00	
1969	Goddess Special	2	H. Viera	116	Mito Sal	116	Native Tumbler	116	36,166	1:27.00	
1970	Levee Night	2	E. Snell	113	Secret Retreat	116	Magnabid	113	43,186	1:23.60	
1971	Barely Even	2	T. Barrow	119	Apple Jackie	113	La Brisa	116	32,194	1:25.80	
1972	Cam Axe	2	E. Fires	113	Bold Memory	113	Patsy's Girl	113	36,569	1:24.00	
1973	Chris Evert	2	L. Pincay Jr	116	Bundler	119	Kiss Me Darlin	116	38,200	1:25.20	
1974	Mirthful Flirt	2	W.J. Passmore	113	Sun and Snow	113	Yale Coed	116	38,597	1:26.60	
1975	Old Goat	2	M. Hole	119	Co'fort Zone	113	Silent Bidder	114	37,940	1:24.80	
1976	Bring out the Band	2	D. Brumfield	114	Shady Lou	116	Ciao	113	38,688	1:25.20	
1977	Bold Rendezvous	2	P. Nicolo	113	Rainy Princess	116	Silver Spook	113	46,449	1:27.00	
1978	Angel Island	2	E. Delahoussaye	119	Safe	113	Too Many Sweets	119	36,325	1:24.20	
1979	Remote Ruler	2	S. Maple	116	Forever Cordial	116	Peachblow	116	43,095	1:25.00	
1980	Mamzelle	2	M.S. Sellers	116	Switch Point	116	Brent's Star	119	83,236	1:46.20	
1981	Betty Money	2	D. Brumfield	119	Hoist Emy's Flag	116	Subdeb	119	91,669	1:45.80	
1982	Weekend Surprise	2	P. Day	119	National Banner	116	Quarrel Over	116	77,701	1:47.00	
1983	Flippers	2	P. Day	119	Robin's Rob	116	Mallorca	116	86,158	1:47.60	
1984	Kamikaze Rick	2	R. Migliore	118	Boldly Dared	114	Gallant Libby	118	101,156	1:47.80	
1985	Slippin n' Slyding	2	C.R. Woods	116	Turn and Dance	110	Bonded Miss	113	95,693	1:46.20	

Year	Winner	Age	Jockey	Wt.	Second	Wt.	Third	Wt.	Win Value	Time	Beyer
1986	Stargrass	2	K.K. Allen	118	Zero Minus	121	Laserette	113	.98,358	1:46.60	
1987	Darien Miss	2	P.A. Johnson	118	Tap Your Toes	118	Most Likely	118	.83,814	1:48.20	
1988	Born Famous	2	E. Fires	120	Coax Chelsie	120	Darby Shuffle	120	.97,500	1:48.20	
1989	De la Devil	2	J.A. Krone	117	Crowned	120	Flew by Em	117	.97,500	1:44.60	
1990	Fancy Ribbons	2	J.E. Bruin	114	Nice Assay	115	Til Forbid	113	.97,500	1:45.40	..88
1991	Vivid Imagination	2	J.M. Johnson	115	Met Her Dream	113	Pennant Fever	113	.97,500	1:46.20	..85
1992	Boots 'n Jackie	2	M.A. Lee	120	Mollie Creek	115	Dance Account	113	.97,500	1:47.20	..79
1993	At the Half	2	P. Day	122	Spiritofpocahontas	115	Mystic Union	111	.97,500	1:46.60	..88
1994	Lilly Capote	2	D.M. Barton	113	Morris Code	113	Cat Appeal	119	.97,500	1:46.60	..88
1995	Gold Sunrise	2	Martinez W	113	Birr	119	Solana	113	.111,150	1:45.40	..82
1996	City Band	2	S.J. Sellers	122	Glitter Woman	113	Water Street	122	.139,996	1:46.80	..95
1997	Love Lock	2	R.J. Albarado	119	Barefoot Dyana	119	Grechelle	111	.139,996	1:44.40	..90
1998	Silverbulletday	2	G.L. Stevens	122	Here I Go	113	Lefty's Dollbaby	113	.134,202	1:43.80	..104
1999	Humble Clerk	2	J.K Court	119	Cash Run	122	Secret Status	111	.138,880	1:45.26	..84
2000	Miss Pickums	2	J.J. Vitek	122	Nasty Storm	112	My White Corvette	119	.138,384	1:48.84	..81
2001	Belterra	2	J.K. Court	117	Take Charge Lady	122	Lotta Rhythm	122	.133,424	1:43.82	..88
2002	My Boston Gal	2	C.H. Borel	117	Holiday Lady	115	My Trusty Cat	115	.136,152	1:45.00	..91
2003	Be Gentle	2	J. McKee	122	Lotta Kim	116	Dynaville	116	.142,600	1:45.91	..91

Beyer Index: 88.14

GOODWOOD BREEDERS' CUP HANDICAP, 1 1/8 Miles, 3-Year-Olds and Up, Santa Anita, 2003 Purse: $482,000

Year	Winner	Age	Jockey	Wt.	Second	Wt.	Third	Wt.	Win Value	Time	Beyer
1982	Cajun Prince	5	W.A. Guerra	115	Caterman	122	Rock Softly	116	46,350	1:40.20	
1983	Pettrax	5	K. Black	117	Konewah	115	Stancharry	117	..46,650	1:42.60	
1984	Lord at War	4	W. Shoemaker	117	Video Kid	118	Menswear	117	..60,150	1:42.00	
1985	Lord at War	4	W. Shoemaker	125	Matafao	106	Last Command	115	..62,800	1:50.20	
1986	Super Diamond	6	L. Pincay Jr	122	Epidaurus	115	Prince Don B.	115	..65,500	1:41.20	
1987	Ferdinand	4	W. Shoemaker	127	Candi's Gold	117	Skywalker	123	..102,500	1:50.80	
1988	Cutlass Reality	6	G.L. Stevens	124	Lively One	116	Stylish Winner	113	.130,400	1:47.20	
1989	Present Value	5	E. Delahoussaye	119	Rahy	121	Happy Toss	116	.128,800	1:47.20	
1990	Lively One	5	A. Solis	120	Miserden	112	Festin	116	.126,800	1:48.00	..105
1991	The Prime Minister	4	C.J. McCarron	115	Marquetry	119	Pleasant Tap	117	.152,300	1:47.80	..108
1992	Reign Road	4	K.J. Desormeaux	116	Sir Beaufort	116	Marquetry	120	.125,200	1:48.20	..109
1993	Lottery Winner	4	K.J. Desormeaux	114	Region	116	Pleaant Tango	115	.127,200	1:47.00	..105
1994	Bertrando	5	G.L. Stevens	120	Dramatic Gold	115	Tossofthecoin	115	.124,400	1:46.60	..113
1995	Soul of the Matter	4	K.J. Desormeaux	121	Tinners Way	121	Alphabet Soup	116	.144,450	1:47.40	..106
1996	Savinio	6	C.S. Nakatani	117	Dare And Go	122	Alphabet Soup	120	.189,300	1:47.80	..110
	Alphabet Soup finished first but was disqualified and placed third										
1997	Benchmark	6	E. Delahoussaye	118	Score Quick	114	Hesabull	117	.158,700	1:47.60	..108
1998	Silver Charm	4	G.L. Stevens	124	Free House	124	Score Quick	115	.262,800	1:47.20	..111
1999	Budroyale	6	G.K. Gomez	119	General Challenge	120	Old Trieste	120	.300,000	1:48.20	..118
2000	Tiznow	3	C.J. McCarron	116	Captain Steve	117	Euchre	115	.300,000	1:47.38	..119
2001	Freedom Crest	5	K.J. Desormeaux	116	Skimming	123	Tiznow	124	.300,000	1:48.86	..108
2002	Pleasantly Perfect	4	A. Solis	115	Momentum	119	Reba's Gold	116	.300,000	1:46.80	..116
2003	Pleasantly Perfect	5	A. Solis	116	Fleetstreet Dancer	113	Star Cross	110	.300,000	1:48.37	..105

Beyer Index: 110..07

GULFSTREAM PARK HANDICAP, 1 1/4 Miles, 3-Year-Olds and Up, Gulfstream Park, 2003 Purse: $300,000

Year	Winner	Age	Jockey	Wt.	Second	Wt.	Third	Wt.	Win Value	Time	Beyer
1946	Do-Reigh-Mi	5	B. Strange	112	Reply Paid	120	Cat Bridge	108	..11,000	2:07.60	
1947	Armed	6	D. Dodson	129	Pot o' Luck	117	Concordian	116	..23,000	2:01.40	
1948	Rampart	6	M. Basile	108	Armed	130	Incline	110	..20,050	2:02.00	
1949	Coaltown	4	O. Scurlock	128	Three Rings	118	Armed	116	..13,000	1:59.80	
1950	Chicle II	5	H. Woodhouse	125	Count-A-Bit	114	Gangway	106	..9,750	2:03.00	
1951	Ennobled	5	J. Stout	113	Mount Marcy	120	Lambent	112	..9,500	2:01.60	
1952	Crafty Admiral	4	C. Errico	114	Alerted	114	Why Not Now	113	..19,850	2:01.00	
1953	Crafty Admiral	5	K. Church	128	Battlefield	125	Dulat	114	..37,400	2:00.80	
1954	Wise Margin	4	K. Stuart	106	Ruhe	114	Intencion	103	..43,500	2:02.80	
1955	Mister Black	6	J. Adams	113	Wise Margin	116	Maharajah	112	..42,100	2:01.80	
1956	Sailor	4	W. Hartack	119	Mielleux	110	Find	116	..83,300	2:00.60	
1957	Bardstown	5	W. Hartack	130	Fabius	123	Needles	126	..76,400	2:00.40	
1958	Round Table	4	W. Shoemaker	130	Meeting	111	Oligarchy	111	..69,800	1:59.80	
1959	Vertex	5	S. Boulmetis	125	Amerigo	114	Air Pilot	110	..80,700	2:01.60	
1960	Bald Eagle	5	M. Ycaza	126	Amerigo	123	On-and-On	121	..71,400	2:01.20	
1961	Tudor Way	5	W. Hartack	124	Derrick	112	Don Poggio	122	..74,000	2:01.60	
1962	Jay Fox	4	L. Gilligan	112	Yorky	121	Carry Back	126	..72,800	2:01.60	
	Yorky finished first but was disqualified and placed second										
1963	Kelso	6	I. Valenzuela	130	Sensitivo	112	Jay Fox	113	..70,500	2:03.20	
1964	Gun Bow	4	W. Shoemaker	125	Garwol	113	Admiral Vic	124	..76,600	2:01.80	
	Admiral Vic finished second but was disqualified and placed third										

Year	Winner	Age	Jockey	Wt.	Second	Wt.	Third	Wt.	Win Value	Time	Beyer
1965	Ampose	4	K. Knapp	112	Tronado	112	Gun Bow	130	71,900	2:04.40	
1966	First Family	4	E. Fires	112	Selari	113	Tie Viejo	113	74,200	2:03.00	
1967	Pretense	4	J. Sellers	126	Amberoid	116	Quinta	117	97,600	2:01.80	
1968	Gentleman James	4	R. Grubb	110	Sacramento	110	Sette Bello	114	86,000	2:02.20	
	Rixdal finished second but was disqualified and placed sixth										
1969	Court Recess	4	M. Miceli	108	Nodouble	125	Tropic King II	116	86,400	2:01.40	
1970	Snow Sporting	4	A. Pineda	118	Twogundian	115	Al Hattab	114	83,600	2:04.00	
1971	Fast Hilarious	5	C. Perret	116	The Pruner	113	Snow Sporting	119	77,040	1:59.40	
1972	Executioner	4	C. Barrera	122	Urgent Message	110	Panicum Repens	110	80,880	2:04.00	
1973	West Coast Scout	5	L. Adams	116	Super Sail	110	Freetex	113	80,880	2:01.00	
1974	Forego	4	H. Gustines	127	True Knight	123	Golden Don	118	72,360	1:59.80	
1975	Gold and Myrhh	4	W. Blum	114	Proud and Bold	120	Buffalo Lark	117	74,520	2:01.80	
1976	Hail the Pirates	6	B. Baeza	116	Legion	113	Packer Captain	113	73,560	2:01.80	
1977	Strike Me Lucky	5	J.D. Bailey	109	Legion	115	Yamanin	122	88,200	2:00.80	
1978	Bowl Game	4	J. Velasquez	112	True Statement	108	Silver Series	126	100,000	2:00.60	
1979	Sensitive Prince	4	J. Vasquez	120	Jumping Hill	126	Silent Cal	119	100,000	1:59.20	
1980	Private Account	4	J. Fell	119	Lot o' Gold	120	Silent Cal	118	100,000	2:01.40	
1981	Hurry Up Blue	4	C. Lopez	119	Yosi Boy	111	Imperial Dilemma	113	114,888	2:03.20	
1982	Lord Darnley	4	M.L. Russ	113	Joanie's Chief	113	Double Sonic	111	91,200	2:01.80	
1983	Christmas Past	4	J. Velasquez	117	Crafty Prospector	115	Rivalero	120	111,630	2:02.60	
1984	Mat Boy	5	J. Valdivieso	118	Lord Darnley	109	Courteous Majesty	114	87,700	1:59.00	
1985	Dr. Carter	4	J. Velasquez	119	Key to the Moon	120	Pine Circle	116	171,480	2:02.00	
1986	Skip Trial	4	R.P. Romero	121	Proud Truth	125	Important Business	113	180,000	2:03.20	
1987	Skip Trial	5	R.P. Romero	118	Creme Fraiche	120	Snow Chief	124	150,000	2:02.80	
1988	Jade Hunter	4	J.D. Bailey	113	Cryptoclearance	122	Creme Fraiche	122	180,000	2:01.60	
1989	Slew City Slew	5	A. Cordero Jr	117	Bold Midway	113	Cryptoclearance	123	180,000	2:03.20	
1990	Mi Selecto	5	J.D. Bailey	114	Tour d'Or	118	Lay Down	113	180,000	2:03.60	109
1991	Jolie's Halo	4	R. Platts	119	Primal	117	Chief Honcho	118	180,000	2:01.00	117
1992	Sea Cadet	4	A. Solis	119	Strike the Gold	115	Sunny Sunrise	114	180,000	2:01.60	120
1993	Devil His Due	4	W.H. McCauley	114	Offbeat	112	Pistols and Roses	114	300,000	2:01.20	114
1994	Scuffleburg	5	C. Perret	113	Migrating Moon	114	Wallenda	117	300,000	2:00.40	109
1995	Cigar	5	J.D. Bailey	118	Pride of Burkaan	114	Mahogany Hall	113	300,000	2:02.80	116
1996	Wekiva Springs	5	J.D. Bailey	117	Star Standard	112	Powerful Punch	113	300,000	2:03.00	110
1997	Mt. Sassafras	5	J.D. Bailey	113	Skip Away	122	Tejano Run	114	300,000	2:02.20	118
1998	Skip Away	5	J.D. Bailey	127	Unruled	112	Behrens	114	300,000	2:03.21	114
1999	Behrens	5	J.F. Chavez	114	Archers Bay	114	Sir Bear	118	210,000	2:01.91	111
2000	Behrens	6	J.F. Chavez	120	Adonis	115	With Anticipation	113	210,000	2:01.79	111
2001	Sir Bear	8	E. Coa	116	Pleasant Breeze	115	Broken Vow	114	120,000	2:02.96	110
2002	Hal's Hope	5	R. Velez	113	Mongoose	115	Sir Bear	117	180,000	2:02.91	109
2003	Hero's Tribute	5	E.S. Prado	115	Aeneas	115	Puzzlement	114	180,000	2:04.24	110

Beyer Index: 112.71

For 4–year–olds and up in 1946

HAWTHORNE GOLD CUP HANDICAP, 1 1/4 Miles, 3-Year-Olds and Up, Hawthorne, 2003 Purse: $750,000

Year	Winner	Age	Jockey	Wt.	Second	Wt.	Third	Wt.	Win Value	Time	Beyer
1928	Display	5	J. Maiben	126	Mike Hall	126	Crusader	126	20,200	2:03.00	
1929	Sun Beau	4	F. Coltiletti	126	Misstep	126	Diavolo	126	21,900	2:01.60	
1930	Sun Beau	5	F. Coltiletti	126	Pigeon Hole	126	Alcibiades	117	23,800	2:04.60	
1931	Sun Beau	6	J. Maiben	126	Mate	120	Plucky Play	126	20,700	2:05.00	
1932	Plucky Play	5	G. Woolf	126	Faireno	117	Mate	126	21,450	2:04.20	
1933	Equipoise	5	R. Workman	126	Fal'ant Sir	126	Mr. Khayyam	117	17,250	2:02.80	
1935	Discovery	4	J. Bejshak	126	Top Dog	120	Spanish Babe	117	11,125	2:04.40	
1937	Sahri II	4	F.A. Smith	110	Infantry	116	Dellor	114	11,125	2:04.40	
1938	Espo'se	6	N. Wall	120	Cardinalis	110	Mucho Gusto	118	10,825	2:13.80	
1939	Challedon	3	H. Richards	120	Gridiron	106	Chief On'w'y	108	10,900	2:03.20	
1946	Jack's Jill	4	J. Higley	111	Spy Song	114	Eternal Reward	118	19,450	2:03.00	
1947	Be Faithful	5	W. Garner	116	Letmenow	103	Stud Poker	100	38,500	2:03.20	
1948	Billings	3	M. Peterson	122	Sun Herod	124	Scotch Secret	103	39,700	2:06.00	
1949	Volcanic	4	A.D. Rivera	125	Sun Herod	115	Vulcan's Forge	126	38,100	2:02.80	
1950	Dr. Ole Nelson	4	G. Porch	110	Curandero	112	Volcanic	125	19,750	2:01.40	
1951	Seaward	6	A. Gomez	113	Picador	105	Ruhe	110	27,250	2:04.20	
1952	To Market	4	W. Boland	123	Dr. Ole Nelson	111	Abbe Sting	107	39,800	2:01.40	
1953	Sub Fleet	4	S. Brooks	115	Smoke Screen	114	Indian Hemp	109	67,350	2:00.60	
1954	Rejected	4	E. Guerin	123	Mister Black	114	Hasseyampa	109	61,550	2:11.60	
1955	Hasseyampa	4	B. Fisk	111	Mister Black	117	Sea o Erin	118	55,200	2:04.80	
1956	Dedicate	4	W. Boland	120	Summer Tan	119	Find	119	80,750	2:02.40	
1957	Round Table	3	W. Harmatz	121	Swoon's Son	128	Find	119	75,950	2:00.20	
1958	Round Table	4	W. Shoemaker	126	Swoon's Son	123	Ekaba	113	73,250	1:59.80	
1959	Day Court	4	H. Moreno	113	Easy Spur	115	Tudor Era	116	71,300	1:59.20	
1960	Kelso	3	E. Arcaro	117	Heroshogala	119	On-and-On	122	88,900	2:02.00	
1961	T.V. Lark	4	J. Longden	113	Heroshogala	109	Run for Nurse	119	78,250	2:02.60	

Year	Winner	Age	Jockey	Wt.	Second	Wt.	Third	Wt.	Win Value	Time	Beyer
1962	Beau Purple	5	W. Boland	123	Bass Clef	117	Sensitivo	118	82,250	2:04.20	
1963	Admiral's Vic	3	M. Solomone	122	Donut King	115	Piper's Son	110	78,500	2:03.80	
1964	Going Abroad	4	R. Broussard	120	Intercepted	118	Olden Times	123	71,100	2:01.60	
1965	Moss Vale	4	R. Baldwin	116	Lemon Twist	113	Peter P'kin	112	79,600	2:07.80	
1966	Bold Bidder	4	P. Anderson	121	Tronado	118	Come On II	113	75,200	2:02.60	
1967	Dr. Fager	3	B. Baeza	123	Whisper Jet	114	Pointmenow	108	72,360	2:01.20	
1968	Nodouble	3	M. Heath	117	Cabildo	120	Irish Dude	112	83,680	1:59.20	
1969	Nodouble	4	E. Belmonte	125	Vif	111	Verbatim	124	74,280	1:59.80	
1970	Gladwin	4	R. Turcotte	115	Red Reality	117	Etony	114	81,320	1:58.80	
1971	Twice Worthy	4	L. Pincay Jr	119	Royal Harmony	115	Wing Out	105	73,880	1:59.40	
1972	Droll Role	4	E. Maple	113	Good Counsel	118	Hitchcock	117	69,780	2:00.40	
1973	Tri Jet	4	B. Baeza	117	Golden Don	113	Cloudy Dawn	114	75,720	2:01.40	
1974	Group Plan	4	J. Velasquez	115	Buffalo Lark	117	Billy Come Lately	119	66,120	1:58.80	
1975	Royal Glint	5	J. Tejeira	124	Buffalo Lark	123	Group Plan	126	74,480	2:02.20	
1976	Almost Grown	4	M. Morgan	110	Teddy's Courage	113	Romeo	113	86,720	2:01.60	
1977	On the Sly	4	G. McCarron	121	Milwaukee Avenue	114	Romeo	111	75,072	2:01.60	
1979	Young Bob	4	R.L Turcotte	114	All the More	113	Architect	121	62,310	1:51.00	
1980	Tunerup	4	J. Vasquez	125	Pole Position	120	The Trader Man	112	82,590	2:00.60	
1981	Spruce Bouquet	4	K. Clark	119	Lord Gallant	114	Bill Monroe	119	101,760	2:04.20	
1982	Recusant	4	R.J. Hirdes Jr	122	Harham's Sizzler	116	Irish Heart	115	98,760	2:01.80	
1983	Water Bank	4	C. Lamance	114	Cad	116	Gallant Gentlem'n	111	130,050	2:01.40	
1984	Proof	4	E. Delahoussaye	118	Jack Slade	119	Bounding Basque	117	160,170	2:01.20	
1985	Garthorn	5	R. Meza	116	Magic North	115	Leroy S.	114	158,220	2:01.80	
1986	Ends Well	5	R.P. Romero	121	Harham's Sizzler	115	Inevitable Leader	113	182,340	2:00.60	
1987	Nostalgia's Star	5	F. Toro	117	Savings	114	Minneapple	117	277,440	2:02.00	
1988	Cryptoclearance	5	J.A. Santos	117	Cutlass Reality	124	Nostalgia's Star	113	303,690	2:00.20	
1989	Cryptoclearance	5	J.A. Santos	122	Proper Reality	120	Classic Account	112	305,730	2:00.40	
1990	Black Tie Affair	4	J.L. Diaz	116	Mi Selecto	115	Silver Tower	112	307,800	2:03.40	116
1991	Sunny Sunrise	4	C.W. Antley	114	Sports View	116	Discover	114	309,840	2:04.00	111
1992	Irish Swap	5	B.E. Poyadou	115	Sea Cadet	121	Evanescent	112	240,000	2:01.80	115
1993	Evanescent	6	A.T. Gryder	115	Marquetry	123	Valley Crossing	117	240,000	2:02.00	109
1994	Recoup the Cash	4	J.L. Diaz	117	Run Softly	114	Kissin Kris	118	240,000	2:01.80	109
1995	Yourmissinthepoint	4	M. Guidry	113	Basqueian	114	Sky Carr	112	150,000	2:01.00	108
1996	Come On Flip	5	C.A. Emigh	113	Michael's Star	114	Mt. Sassafras	120	180,000	2:03.40	107
1997	Buck's Boy	4	M. Guidry	114	Cairo Express	115	Beboppin Baby	115	180,000	2:00.40	108
1998	Awesome Again	4	P. Day	123	Unruled	114	Muchacho Fino	114	240,000	2:02.60	104
1999	Supreme Sound	5	R. Meier	112	Golden Missile	115	Beboppin Baby	113	300,000	2:01.19	105
2000	Dust on the Bottle	5	T.T. Doocy	114	Guided Tour	114	Maysville Slew	113	300,000	2:03.00	107
2001	Duckhorn	4	R. Meier	112	Lido Palace	114	Guided Tour	116	300,000	2:01.61	116
2002	Hail the Chief	5	J.F. Chavez	114	Dollar Bill	114	Parade Leader	115	300,000	2:02.80	113
2003	Perfect Drift	4	P. Day	122	Tenpins	119	Aeneas	114	450,000	2:03.63	109

Beyer Index: 109.79

CLEMENT L. HIRSCH HANDICAP, 1 1/16 Miles,
Fillies and Mares, 3-Year-Olds and Up, Del Mar, 2003 Purse: $300,000

Year	Winner	Age	Jockey	Wt.	Second	Wt.	Third	Wt.	Win Value	Time	Beyer
1967	Daystar II	5	W. Hartack	118	Nevada Marga	121	Maintain	119	9,050	1:35.20	
1973	Grotonian	4	W. Shoemaker	117	Expediter	115	China Silk	114	12,600	1:50.60	
1974	Bahia Key	4	A. Pineda	120	Trotteur	117	Soft Victory	122	13,650	1:34.20	
1975	Bahia Key	5	W. Harris	119	Fair Test	119	Top Command	117	12,750	1:34.00	
1976	Uniformity	4	R. Campas	115	White Fir	118	Royal Derby II	119	16,900	1:28.20	
1977	Notably Different	4	C. Baltazar	113	Key Account	114	Pikehall	109	13,375	1:29.40	
1977	Authorization	5	D.G. McHargue	113	Cherry River	117	Mister Dan	114	13,175	1:29.20	
1978	Nantequos	5	D.G. McHargue	120	Lunar Probe	118	Crew of Ocala	114	20,250	1:29.40	
							Around We Go	117			
1979	He's Dewan	4	D.G. McHargue	119	Caro Bambino	119	No No	115	23,950	1:29.00	
1980	Wayside Station	5	P.A. Valenzuela	113	Concussion	117	Mike Fogarty	115	19,775	1:28.80	
1980	Galaxy Libra	4	W. Shoemaker	118	Wickerr	117	T. Be or Not	116	19,375	1:29.00	
1981	Save Wild Life	4	C.J. McCarron	118	Princess Karenda	120	Track Robbery	125	47,650	1:41.60	
1982	Matching	4	R. Sibille	116	Miss Huntington	116	Cat Girl	117	45,850	1:40.00	
1983	Sangue	5	W. Shoemaker	121	Avigation	122	Skillful Joy	117	46,600	1:42.20	
1984	Princess Rooney	4	P.A. Valenzuela	123	Flag de Lune	115	Moment to Buy	116	60,100	1:40.40	
1985	Dontstop the Music	5	D.G. McHargue	122	Golden Screen	112	Lovlier Linda	119	45,650	1:41.80	
1986	Fran's Valentine	4	W. Shoemaker	119	Cenyak's Star	116	Dontstop the Music	123	59,500	1:41.40	
1987	Infinidad	5	C.A. Black	118	Margaret Booth	117	Le L'Argent	117	63,540	1:41.40	
1988	Clabber Girl	5	C.J. McCarron	120	Annoconnor	118	Integra	119	75,100	1:41.60	
1989	Goodbye Halo	4	C.A. Black	120	Flying Julia	112	Kool Arrival	115	77,450	1:41.80	
1990	Bayakoa	6	L. Pincay Jr	127	Fantastic Look	113	Formidable Lady	112	88,500	1:40.60	100
1991	Vieille Vigne	4	M.A. Pedroza	116	Formidable Lady	113	Lite Light	121	120,300	1:42.60	99
1992	Exchange	4	L. Pincay Jr	120	Fowda	120	Brought to Mind	119	122,100	1:42.00	109
1993	Magical Maiden	4	G.L. Stevens	120	Vieille Vigne	111	Party Cited	117	123,600	1:42.60	92

Year	Winner	Age	Jockey	Wt.	Second	Wt.	Third	Wt.	Win Value	Time	Beyer
1994	Paseana	7	C.J. McCarron	123	Exchange	120	Magical Maiden	118	117,100	1:40.40	108
1995	Borodislew	5	C.J. McCarron	118	Lakeway	121	Golden Klair	118	178,100	1:41.80	98
1996	Different	4	C.J. McCarron	120	Top Rung	116	Borodislew	117	189,200	1:42.40	99
1997	Radu Cool	5	C.J. McCarron	117	Supercilious	113	Swoon River	110	180,000	1:42.60	102
1998	Sharp Cat	4	C.S. Nakatani	124	Supercilious	115	Numero Uno	116	180,000	1:42.00	101
1999	A Lady From Dixie	4	C.W. Antley	116	Manistique	124	Yolo Lady	116	180,000	1:43.40	98
2000	Riboletta	5	C.J. McCarron	125	Bordelaise	115	Gourmet Girl	115	180,000	1:42.06	107
2001	Tranquility Lake	6	E. Delahoussaye	120	Gourmet Girl	122	Nany's Sweep	116	180,000	1:41.78	104
2002	Azeri	4	M.E. Smith	126	Angel Gift	114	Se Me Acabo	114	180,000	1:42.66	105
2003	Azeri	5	M.E. Smith	127	Got Koko	118	Tropical Blossom	108	180,000	1:42.12	100

Beyer Index: 101.57

Run as Chula Vista prior to 2000

HOLLYWOOD BREEDERS' CUP OAKS, 1 1/16 Miles,
3-Year-Old Fillies, Hollywood Park, 2003 Purse: $206,200

Year	Winner	Age	Jockey	Wt.	Second	Wt.	Third	Wt.	Win Value	Time	Beyer
1946	Honyemoon	3	J. Westrope	126	Aptos Honey	112	Good Excuse	106	16,500	1:38.20	
1947	U Time	3	L. Balaski	118	Cold Roll	109	Hemet Squaw	115	18,750	1:23.40	
1948	Flying Rhythm	3	J.W. Martin	110	Belle Jolie	116	Boswell Lady	120	19,050	1:39.60	
1949	June Bride	3	J. Longden	112	Just Why	112	Cosmopolite	113	18,750	1:37.40	
1950	Mrs. Fuddy	3	W. Shoemaker	109	Sea Garden	113	Foxie Green	109	11,750	1:37.20	
1951	Ruth Lily	3	R. Neves	121	Mrs. Traffic	112	Royal Mink	109	15,350	1:44.20	
1952	A Gleam	3	H. Moreno	118	Princess Lygia	118	Tonga	115	16,650	1:42.60	
1953	Fleet Khal	3	J. Burton	117	Smart Barbara	110	Perfection	109	15,000	1:42.80	
1954	Miz Clementine	3	I. Valenzuela	124	Frosty Dawn	115	Free Country	112	14,600	1:50.00	
1955	Baby Alice	3	R. York	112	Auntie Bell	112	Week-End	112	15,050	1:49.20	
1956	Candy Dish	3	W. Shoemaker	112	Triple Jay	121	Tumbling	112	15,800	1:49.60	
1957	Market Basket	3	R. York	121	Pamper Me	115	Molly Maid	109	16,550	1:49.60	
1958	Midnight Date	3	L. Leon	112	Sally Lee	112	Nushie	115	16,050	1:51.00	
1959	Sybil Brand	3	W. Boland	112	Tender Size	112	Ruwenzori	115	15,650	1:49.80	
1960	Paris Pike	3	I. Valenzuela	113	Nathleen	112	Linita	115	16,800	1:48.60	
1961	Rose O'Neill	3	I. Valenzuela	112	Bushel-n-Peck	121	Oil Royalty	118	15,300	1:48.60	
1962	Dingle Bay	3	J. Longden	113	Wish n Wait	112	Table Mate	112	33,650	1:49.80	
1963	Delhi Maid	3	W. Shoemaker	118	Hi Rated	112	Curious Clover	113	34,850	1:49.20	
1964	Loukahl	3	E. Burns	115	Fran La Femme	121	Duchess Khaled	121	34,150	1:49.60	
1965	Straight Deal	3	J. Sellers	112	Sea Eagle	112	Gala Host	118	33,650	1:49.80	
1966	Spearfish	3	D. Pierce	121	Windy Kate	112	Ali's Theme	112	35,950	1:50.20	
1967	Amerigo Lady	3	A.R. Valenzuela	112	Gamely	121	Princessnesian	113	33,300	1:49.20	
1968	Hooplah	3	A. Pineda	112	Morgaise	115	Too Angri	113	32,750	1:48.60	
1969	Tipping Time	3	D. Pierce	121	Commissary	118	Ynez Queen	114	32,100	1:47.40	
1970	Last of the Line	3	J. Lambert	114	Beja	121	Loved	112	32,650	1:48.00	
1971	Turkish Trousers	3	W. Shoemaker	124	Convenience	115	Balcony's Babe	115	37,650	1:47.80	
1972	Pallisima	3	W. Shoemaker	112	Bert's Tryst	112	Susan's Girl	124	37,350	1:48.60	
1973	Sandy Blue	3	D. Pierce	121	Cellist	121	Jungle Princess	112	50,550	1:48.00	
1974	Miss Musket	3	L. Pincay Jr	124	Lucky Spell	121	Modus Vivendi	121	49,550	1:47.80	
1975	Nicosia	3	W. Shoemaker	121	Snap Apple	112	Mia Amore	112	49,400	1:48.40	
1976	Answer	3	D.G. McHargue	121	Franmari	116	I Going	115	49,200	1:48.40	
1977	Glenaris	3	W. Shoemaker	116	One Sum	116	Taisez Vous	121	68,100	1:48.80	
1978	B. Thoughtful	3	D. Pierce	121	Country Queen	121	Grenzen	121	65,400	1:47.60	
1979	Prize Spot	3	S. Hawley	121	It's in the Air	121	Variety Queen	124	63,300	1:48.20	
1980	Princess Karenda	3	D. Pierce	121	Secretarial Queen	121	Disconiz	121	67,400	1:48.20	
1981	Past Forgetting	3	C.J. McCarron	121	Balletomane	121	Glitter Hitter	121	64,100	1:50.00	
1982	Tango Dancer	3	L. Pincay Jr	121	Faneuil Lass	121	Royal Donna	121	66,100	1:49.00	
1983	Heartlight No. One	3	L. Pincay Jr	121	Preceptress	121	Ready for Luck	121	63,900	1:49.80	
1984	Moment to Buy	3	T.M. Chapman	121	Mitterand	121	Lucky Lucky Lucky	121	97,150	1:49.20	
1985	Fran's Valentine	3	C.J. McCarron	121	Magnificent Lindy	121	Deal Price	121	120,300	1:47.40	
1986	Hidden Light	3	W. Shoemaker	121	An Empress	121	Family Style	121	116,600	1:47.80	
1987	Perchance to Dream	3	R. Sibille	121	Sacahuista	121	Pen Bal Lady	121	93,200	1:48.60	
1988	Pattern Step	3	C.J. McCarron	121	Super Avie	121	Comedy Court	121	94,700	1:48.60	
1989	Gorgeous	3	E. Delahoussaye	121	Kelly	121	Lea Lucinda	121	92,700	1:47.80	
1990	Patches	3	G.L. Stevens	121	Jefforee	121	Pampered Star	121	96,100	1:49.60	102
1991	Fowda	3	E. Delahoussaye	121	Grand Girlfriend	121	Masake	121	94,400	1:49.60	91
1992	Pacific Squall	3	K.J. Desormeaux	121	Race the Wild Wind	121	Alysbelle	121	127,200	1:48.00	109
1993	Hollywood Wildcat	3	E. Delahoussaye	121	Fit to Lead	121	Adorydar	121	130,400	1:48.40	107
1994	Lakeway	3	K.J. Desormeaux	121	Sardula	121	Fancy 'n Fabulous	121	120,000	1:46.80	117
1995	Sleep Easy	3	C.S. Nakatani	121	Predicted Glory	121	Bello Cielo	121	122,400	1:50.20	91
1996	Listening	3	C.J. McCarron	121	Antespend	121	Ocean View	121	110,640	1:48.60	102
1997	Sharp Cat	3	A. Solis	121	Freeport Flight	121	Really Happy	121	120,000	1:49.60	98
1998	Manistique	3	G.L. Stevens	115	Sweet and Ready	119	Yolo Lady	116	120,000	1:48.40	110

Year	Winner	Age	Jockey	Wt.	Second	Wt.	Third	Wt.	Win Value	Time	Beyer
1999	Smooth Player	3	E. Delahoussaye	117	Excellent Meeting	121	Nany's Sweep	116	90,000	1:48.00	102
2000	Kumari Continent	3	K.J. Desormeaux	117	Queenie Belle	119	Saudi Poetry	115	90,000	1:49.13	91
2001	Affluent	3	E. Delahoussaye	116	Collect Call	115	Secret of Mecca	116	90,000	1:49.20	97
2002	Adoration	3	G.K. Gomez	115	Sister Girl Blues	114	Saint Bernadette	115	160,080	1:43.73	94
2003	Santa Catarina	3	G.L. Stevens	116	Buffythecenterfold	113	Princess V.	114	127,320	1:41.62	106

Beyer Index: 101.21

HONEYMOON BREEDERS' CUP HANDICAP, 1 1/8 Miles (Turf),
3-Year-Old Fillies, Hollywood Park, 2003 Purse: $215,950

Year	Winner	Age	Jockey	Wt.	Second	Wt.	Third	Wt.	Win Value	Time	Beyer
1956	Triple Jay	3	A. Maese	115	Shes Quick	115	Candy Dish	112	13,500	1:36.40	
1957	Great Pride	3	W. Shoemaker	109	Tourbillonte	109	Inquisitive	110	12,450	1:36.60	
1957	Fanciful Miss	3	J. Longden	109	Royal Rasher	112	Pamper Me	118	12,450	1:36.00	
1958	Foreverett	3	J. Longden	113	Well Away	115	Midnight Date	112	13,600	1:37.60	
1959	Cellyar	3	A. Maese	112	Sybil Brand	112	Just Chargit	112	15,150	1:36.60	
1960	Solid Thought	3	D. Pierce	118	Paris Pike	113	Cherokee Miss	112	13,640	1:36.20	
1961	Bushel-n-Peck	3	W. Shoemaker	112	Rose O'Neill	112	Oil Royalty	118	12,800	1:34.80	
1962	Refanute	3	R. Campas	112	Savaii	112	Sweet Cee Cee	112	16,900	1:36.60	
1963	Molly O'Malley	3	R. York	112	Delhi Maid	118	Hi Rated	112	16,800	1:37.40	
1964	Gim Mah	3	E. Burns	112	Fran La Femme	121	Lil's Nite Out	112	15,500	1:37.20	
1965	Rullahline	3	D. Gorman	112	Bubble Bath	113	Madoo	112	18,825	1:35.80	
1965	Mine Lovely	3	I. Valenzuela	118	Istria	112	Queen Hostess	112	19,325	1:35.40	
1966	April Dawn	3	D. Hall	112	Miss Breakage	112	Fleet Treat	121	20,300	1:36.40	
1967	Spinning Around	3	M. Valenzuela	112	Amerigo Lady	114	Native Honey	118	16,550	1:36.60	
1968	Miss Ribot	3	J. Sellers	118	Time to Leave	121	Saipan	113	15,950	1:42.20	
1969	Marjorie's Theme	3	J. Lambert	114	Commissary	121	Dumpty's Lady	121	16,800	1:41.60	
1970	Street Dancer	3	R. Rosales	112	Opening Bid	121	Hail the Grey	114	16,550	1:34.60	
1971	Turkish Trousers	3	W. Shoemaker	121	Convenience	115	Mia Mood	114	19,850	1:42.40	
1972	Le Cle	3	L. Pincay Jr	115	Pallisima	112	Cautious Bidder	118	20,200	1:42.40	
1973	Meilleur	3	D. Pierce	118	Sphere	118	Goddess Roman	116	20,350	1:42.40	
1974	Bedknob	3	A. Pineda	115	Bold Tullah	118	Bold Ballet	116	20,750	1:42.20	
1975	Katonka	3	L. Pincay Jr	123	Nicosia	125	Just a Kick	118	33,150	1:42.40	
1976	Cascapedia	3	W. Shoemaker	121	Go March	117	Dream of Spring	118	26,750	1:42.20	
1977	Joyous Ways	3	L. Pincay Jr	116	Penny Pueblo	113	Glenaris	119	26,150	1:43.00	
1978	Country Queen	3	M. Castaneda	114	Collect Call	116	Equanimity	121	33,700	1:43.20	
1979	Variety Queen	3	M. Castaneda	114	Prize Spot	117	Whydidju	121	32,550	1:41.60	
1980	Lady Roberta	3	S. Hawley	116	Finance Charge	112	Street Ballet	123	60,050	1:41.80	
1981	Amber Ever	3	C.J. McCarron	114	Verbalize	117	Bee a Scout	115	50,950	1:41.60	
1982	Castilla	3	R. Sibille	116	Tango Dancer	117	Skillful Joy	121	61,400	1:40.60	
1983	Stagedoor C'nt'n	3	C.J. McCarron	118	Saucy Bobbie	117	Hot n Pearly	115	65,200	1:42.00	
1984	Vagabond Gal	3	E. Delahoussaye	115	Heartlight	119	Allusion	115	65,100	1:41.40	
1985	Sharp Ascent	3	E. Delahoussaye	115	Rose Cream	117	Akamini	119	79,400	1:41.40	
1986	An Empress	3	P.A. Valenzuela	115	Top Corsage	118	Miraculous	118	66,900	1:41.80	
1987	Pen Bal Lady	3	E. Delahoussaye	119	Some Sensation	117	Davie's Lamb	115	80,300	1:41.20	
1988	Do So	3	A. Solis	118	Pattern Step	119	Jeanne Jones	120	75,400	1:41.80	
1989	Hot Option	3	E. Delahoussaye	116	Formidable Lady	118	Black Stockings	113	62,600	1:40.20	
1990	Materco	3	E. Delahoussaye	117	Annual Reunion	119	Slew of Pearls	117	65,800	1:41.40	90
1991	Masake	3	M.A. Pedroza	115	Haunting	114	Now Showing	116	60,400	1:42.00	96
1992	Pacific Squall	3	K.J. Desormeaux	115	Miss Turkana	119	Morriston Belle	118	67,100	1:41.00	90
1993	Likeable Style	3	E. Delahoussaye	122	Adorydor	114	Vinista	113	61,200	1:46.20	95
1994	Work the Crowd	3	McCarron CJ	114	Malli Star	117	Fancy 'n Fabulous	118	64,700	1:39.60	103
1995	Auriette	3	Delahoussaye E	117	Artica	119	Top Shape	118	62,100	1:41.60	94
1996	Antespend	3	C.W. Antley	122	Clamorosa	116	Najecam	113	82,410	1:47.40	100
1997	Famous Digger	3	B. Blanc	116	Freeport Flight	115	Kentucky Kaper	117	65,460	1:47.60	94
1998	Country Garden	3	K.J. Desormeaux	120	Janine Rose	113	Chenille	114	64,080	1:48.60	92
1999	Sweet Ludy	3	G.L. Stevens	116	Tout Charmant	118	Aviate	118	65,160	1:48.05	99
2000	Classy Cara	3	I.L. Puglisi	122	Kumari Continent	119	Minor Details	117	90,000	1:48.05	91
2001	Innit	3	C. McCarron	117	Live Your Dreams	115	Beefeater Baby	115	120,000	2:01.28	93
2002	Megahertz	3	P.A. Valenzuela	120	Arabic Song	117	High Society	116	97,830	1:51.97	91
2003	Quero Quero	3	T.C. Baze	113	Atlantic Ocean	121	Sharpbill	113	130,170	1:49.34	88

Beyer Index: 94

HUTCHESON, 7 Furlongs,
3-Year-Olds, Gulfstream Park, 2003 Purse: $150,000

Year	Winner	Age	Jockey	Wt.	Second	Wt.	Third	Wt.	Win Value	Time	Beyer
1954	Buttevant	3	K. Church	113	Jilted Gob	108	Brachs Admiral	111	4,875	1:10.80	
1955	Nance's LAd	3	J. Choquette	113	First Cabin	111	Rouge Falcon	113	9,400	1:16.40	
1956	Decathlon	3	G.R. Martin	122	Busher Fantasy	122	Getthere Jack	122	8,000	1:16.00	
1957	Jet Colonel	3	R. Ussery	119	Barbizon	122	We Trust	144	8,000	1:16.00	
1958	Yemen	3	R. Ussery	114	Belleau Chief	114	Lincoln Road	112	7,425	1:15.80	
1959	Easy Spur	3	L. Batchellor	122	Pointer	114	Octopus	122	7,750	1:16.00	

Year	Winner	Age	Jockey	Wt.	Second	Wt.	Third	Wt.	Win Value	Time	Beyer
1960	Will Ye	3	S. Boulmetis	112	Vox Pop	114	Run for Nurse	118	7,825	1:16.20	
1961	Nashua Blue	3	R. Ussery	116	Beau Prince	116	Intensive	122	7,750	1:23.00	
1962	Eidolon	3	L. Adams	112	Sharp Count	115	Two Block Fox	116	8,425	1:24.80	
1963	Sky Wonder	3	R. Ussery	122	Bold Commander	112	Nashver	114	8,375	1:23.40	
1964	Ky Pioneer	3	L. Adams	114	Kentucky Jug	114	Buz On	113	10,900	1:24.00	
1965	Gallant Lad	3	B. Baeza	114	Prime Minister	112	Good Trouble	116	10,700	1:23.80	
1966	Bold and Brave	3	K. Knapp	112	Kauai King	114	All Love	116	11,625	1:22.80	
1967	Glengary	3	J. Giovanni	110	Sir Winzalot	114	Sun Seeker	110	15,025	1:23.20	
1968	Pappa Steve	3	R. Ussery	119	Addy Boy	114	Intentdamless	112	15,175	1:22.80	
1969	Al Hattab	3	R. Broussard	122	I Found Gold	112	Sail Ahoy	112	15,000	1:22.60	
1970	Cassie Red	3	W. Blum	112	Ring for Nurse	122	Native Royalty	113	22,950	1:22.60	
1971	Landing More	3	R. Woodhouse	119	Son Ange	114	Raja Baba	119	20,910	1:21.80	
1972	Spanish Riddle	3	F.Iannelli	114	Gentle Smoke	114	Delta Oil	114	29,820	1:22.80	
1973	Shecky Greene	3	B. Baeza	122	Forego	116	Leo's Pisces	112	17,170	1:20.80	
1974	Frankie Adams	3	R. Turcotte	114	Judger	110			31,845	1:22.40	
					Training Table	113					
1975	Greek Answer	3	M. Castaneda	122	Fashion Sale	113	Rich Sun	122	20,370	1:21.60	
1976	Sonkisser	3	B. Baeza	116	Gay Jitterbug	116	Star of the Sea	122	19,350	1:21.00	
1977	Silver Series	3	L. Snyder	112	Medieval Man	114	One in a Million	114	20,610	1:22.80	
1978	Sensitive Prince	3	M. Solomone	114	Kissing U.	114	Pipe Major	114	19,890	1:20.80	
1979	Spectacular Bid	3	R.J. Franklin	122	Lot o' Gold	114	Northern Prospect	114	17,766	1:21.40	
1980	Plugged Nickle	3	B. Thornburg	122	Execution's Reason	122	One Son	114	17,640	1:22.60	
1981	Lord Avie	3	C.J. McCarron	122	Spirited Boy	114	Linnleur	114	34,080	1:23.40	
1982	Distinctive Pro	3	J. Velasquez	117	Center Cut	114	Real Twister	114	34,650	1:22.40	
1983	Current Hope	3	A. Solis	114	Highland Park	122	Country Pine	112	39,330	1:22.80	
1984	Swale	3	E. Maple	122	For Halo	114	Darn That Alarm	112	38,790	1:22.20	
1985	Banner Bob	3	K.K. Allen	114	Creme Fraiche	114	Do It Again Dan	114	45,720	1:21.60	
1986	Papal Power	3	D. MacBeth	122	Raja's Revenge	122	Mr. Classic	112	55,440	1:23.80	
1987	Well Selected	3	J. Vasquez	113	Gone West	114	Faster Than Sound	119	53,376	1:23.00	
1988	Perfect Spy	3	J.L. Samyn	114	Forty Niner	122	Notebook	122	52,335	1:23.00	
1989	Dixieland Brass	3	R.P. Romero	114	Western Playboy	112	Tricky Creek	112	58,320	1:22.80	
1990	Housebuster	3	R.P. Romero	119	Yonder	122	Stalker	114	56,787	1:24.40	
1991	Fly So Free	3	J.A. Santos	122	To Freedom	119	Sunny and Pleasant	114	55,527	1:23.20	
1992	My Luck Runs North	3	R.D. Lopez	117	Sneaky Solicitor	117	Frosted Spy	117	55,008	1:24.80	.86
1993	Hidden Trick	3	R.P. Romero	114	Great Navigator	119	Forever Whirl	119	54,108	1:23.60	.91
1994	Holy Bull	3	M.E. Smith	122	Patton	113	You and I	119	45,000	1:21.20	.108
1995	Valid Wager	3	M.A. Pedroza	119	Mr. Greeley	117	Don Juan A	114	45,000	1:23.40	.97
1996	Appealing Skier	3	R. Wilson	119	Unbridled's Song	119	Gold Fever	117	45,000	1:24.60	.104
1997	Frisk Me Now	3	E. L. King Jr.	112	Confide	117	Crown Ambassador	117	60,000	1:22.40	.96
1998	Time Limit	3	J.D. Bailey	119	Coronado's Quest	122	Zippy Zeal	114	60,000	1:22.40	.107
1999	Bet Me Best	3	J.D. Bailey	122	Texas Glitter	119	Cat Thief	119	90,000	1:22.20	
2000	More Than Ready	3	J.R. Velazquez	122			American Bullet	113	60,000	1:21.76	.102
	Summer Note	3	S.J. Sellers	113							
2001	Yonaguska	3	J.D. Bailey	119	City Zip	122	Sparkling Sabre	112	90,000	1:22.63	.95
2002	Showmeitall	3	J.F. Chavez	118	Monthir	116	Royal Lad	116	90,000	1:26.07	.96
2003	Lion Tamer	3	J.R. Velazquez	118	Strength Within	116	Crafty Guy	122	90,000	1:22.60	.98

Beyer Index: 98.42

ILLINOIS DERBY, 1 1/8 Miles,
3-Year-Olds, Hawthorne, 2003 Purse: $500,000

Year	Winner	Age	Jockey	Wt.	Second	Wt.	Third	Wt.	Win Value	Time	Beyer
1923	In Memoriam	3	N. Barrett	118	General Thatcher	118	Prince K.	115	9,250	2:04.20	
1933	Sweeprush	3	W. Moran	115	Fair Rochester	115	Col. Hatfield	118	3,455	2:00.00	
1934	Mata Hari	3	L. Humphries	117	New Deal	119	Plight	122	8,230	1:49.20	
1935	Sun Portland	3	C. Kurtsinger	114	Roman Soldier	122	Tearout	116	7,570	1:50.00	
1936	Rushaway	3	J. Longden	120	Count Morse	114	Reelon	113	9,660	1:50.80	
1937	Case Ace	3	A. Robertson	126	Grey Count	120	Heelfly	120	9,590	1:51.80	
1938	Gov. Chandler	3	W. Garner	118	Xavier	116	Dolly Val	113	9,560	1:58.00	
1963	Lemon Twist	3	S. LeJeune	119	Finklehoffe	114	Cosmic Tip	124	18,167	1:52.60	
1964	Nushka	3	R. Lawless	114	Climax II	114	Goff's Gay	122	26,211	1:53.60	
1965	Terra Hi	3	L. Spraker	119	Aria	109	Bust Him In	116	20,804	1:51.60	
1965	Turn to Reason	3	T. Powell	116	Asdum	116	Travel Agent	113	20,735	1:52.00	
1966	Michigan Avenue	3	M. Ycaza	119	Abe's Hope	124	B. Golden	121	29,466	1:51.40	
1967	Royal Malabar	3	C. Stone	119	Pointmenow	121	Gentleman James	126	37,922	1:51.20	
1968	Bold Favorite	3	R. Nono	114	Three Carrswold	116	Jet's KIngdom	114	43,629	1:50.20	
1969	King of the Castle	3	B. Baeza	126	Rush Date	119	Happy Intellectual	116	43,697	1:51.40	
1972	Fame and Power	3	A. Rini	119	Gun Tune	119	Beau Julian	126	43,986	1:49.40	
1973	Big Whippendeal	3	L. Adams	119	What Will Be	121	Golden Don	126	43,491	1:50.20	
1974	Sharp Gary	3	G. Gallitano	124	Sr. Diplomat	114	Sports Editor	119	63,060	1:50.00	
1975	Colonel Power	3	P. Rubbicco	124	Ruggles Ferry	124	Methdioxya	124	63,360	1:50.20	
1976	Life's Hope	3	S. Hawley	124	Wardlaw	124	New Collection	116	77,295	1:51.40	

Year	Winner	Age	Jockey	Wt.	Second	Wt.	Third	Wt.	Win Value	Time	Beyer
1977	Flag Officer	3	L. Ahrens	124	Time Call	116	Cisk	116	62,955	1:52.20	
1978	Batonnier	3	R.J. Hirdes Jr	124	Raymond Earl	121	Silver Nitrate	124	62,280	1:51.60	
1979	Smarten	3	S. Maple	124	Clever Trick	124	Julie's Dancer	116	91,710	1:49.40	
1980	Ray's Word	3	R. DePass	124	Mighty Return	114	Stutz Blackhawk	121	92,970	1:52.00	
1981	Paristo	3	D.C. Ashcroft	126	Pass the Tab	126	Bitterrook	114	93,300	1:49.60	
1982	Star Gallant	3	R. Sibille	126	Drop Your Drawers	122	Soy Emperor	119	126,420	1:52.60	
1983	Gen'l Practitioner	3	J.A. Santiago	126	Passing Base	114	Aztec Red	124	127,200	1:50.40	
1984	Delta Trace	3	K.K. Allen	124	Wind Flyer	122	Birdie's Legend	124	127,530	1:51.80	
1985	Important Business	3	J.L. Diaz	116	Nostalgia's Star	122	Another Reef	124	192,786	1:51.60	
1986	Bolshoi Boy	3	R. Migliore	118	Speedy Shannon	118	Blue Buckaroo	116	189,432	1:52.20	
1987	Lost Code	3	G. St. Leon	124	Blanco	119	Valid Prospect	112	188,130	1:49.60	
1988	Proper Reality	3	J.D. Bailey	124	Jim's Orbit	122	Classic Account	112	321,000	1:50.20	
1989	Music Merci	3	G.L. Stevens	124	Notation	119	Endow	124	310,150	1:50.20	
1990	Dotsero	3	A.T. Gryder	117	Sound of Cannons	112	Hofre	112	190,290	1:50.60	
1991	Richman	3	J.D. Bailey	124	Doc of the Day	119	Nowork All Play	114	319,200	1:49.20	109
1992	Dignitas	3	J.D. Bailey	117	American Chance	112	Straight to Bed	114	320,100	1:49.00	104
1993	Antrim Rd.	3	A.T. Gryder	114	Seattle Morn	114	Secret Negotiator	114	300,000	1:48.60	93
1994	Rustic Light	3	E. Fires	117	Amathos	103	Seminole Wind	113	300,000	1:51.80	98
1995	Peaks and Valleys	3	J.A. Krone	124	Da Hoss	117	Western Echo	117	300,000	1:48.80	108
1996	Natural Selection	3	R P Romero	114	El Amante	124	Irish Conquest	114	300,000	1:48.60	108
1997	Wild Rush	3	K.J. Desormeaux	117	Anet	124	Saratoga Sunrise	119	300,000	1:47.40	114
1998	Yarrow Brae	3	W. Martinez	114	One Bold Stroke*	117	Orville N Wilbur's	124	300,000	1:51.20	107
1999	Vision and Verse	3	H. Castillo Jr	114	Prime Timber	117	Pineaff	122	300,000	1:48.40	103
2000	Performing Magic	3	S.J. Sellers	119	Country Only	117	Country Coast	114	300,000	1:50.86	101
2001	Distilled	3	M.E. Smith	114	Saint Damien	119	Dream Run	114	300,000	1:51.37	94
2002	War Emblem	3	L.J. Sterling Jr.	114	Repent	124	Fonz's	117	300,000	1:49.92	112
2003	Ten Most Wanted	3	P. Day	114	Fund of Funds	114	Foufa's Warrior	118	300,000	1:51.47	110

Beyer Index: **104.69**

JAMAICA HANDICAP, 1 1/8 Miles (Turf), 3-Year-Olds, Belmont Park, 2003 Purse: $200,000

Year	Winner	Age	Jockey	Wt.	Second	Wt.	Third	Wt.	Win Value	Time	Beyer
1975	Funalon	3	V. Bracciale Jr	113	Busy Saxon	114	Precious Elaine	113	34,140	1:35.80	
1976	Dance Spell	3	R. Hernandez	119	Cojak	119	Quiet Little Table	114	33,330	1:34.00	
1977	Affiliate	3	A. Cordero Jr	124	Buckfinder	113	Proud Arion	115	33,660	1:35.20	
1978	Regal and Royal	3	J. Fell	116	Squire Ambler	111	Roman Reasoning	112	32,460	1:35.00	
1979	Belle's Gold	3	L. Pincay Jr	118	Lean Lad	108	Gallant Best	113	33,180	1:33.60	
1980	Far Out East	3	C.B. Asmussen	113	Dunham's Gift	112	Settlement Day	111	35,100	1:34.00	
1981	Pass the Tab	3	J. Velasquez	113	Spirited Boy	117	Counter Espionage	112	33,300	1:35.20	
1982	John's Gold	3	A. Cordero Jr	113	Lord Lister	111	Estoril	114	33,180	1:37.00	
1983	Bounding Basque	3	G. McCarron	115	A Phenomenon	120	Bet Big	115	51,480	1:34.00	
1984	Raja's Shark	3	R. Migliore	112	Is Your Pleasure	116	Leroy S.	117	52,560	1:36.60	
1985	Don's Choice	3	D. MacBeth	114	I Enrich	110	Easton	109	53,010	1:36.00	
1986	Waquoit	3	R. Migliore	111	Mogambo	119	Moment of Hope	111	53,280	1:34.20	
1987	Stacked Pack	3	R.P. Romero	110	Gulch	123	Homebuilder	112	67,770	1:34.80	
1988	Ruhlmann	3	G.L. Stevens	113	Teddy Drone	112	Din's Dancer	112	84,540	1:35.40	
1989	Domasca Dan	3	S. Hawley	116	Garemma	114	Is It True	120	70,920	1:35.40	
1990	Confidential Talk	3	J.F. Chavez	111	Rubiano	112	Sunshine Jimmy	114	52,470	1:35.60	106
1991	Sultry Song	3	C.W. Antley	113	Honest Ensign	110	Take Me Out	116	70,320	1:34.40	108
1992	West by West	3	J.L. Samyn	112	Offbeat	111	Portroe	111	70,320	1:34.20	103
1993	Mi Cielo	3	M.E. Smith	116	Prospector's Flag	113	Cherokee Run	120	70,440	1:35.20	106
1994	Pennine Ridge	3	J.R. Velazquez	118	Holy Mountain	116	I'm Very Irish	113	66,540	1:35.00	101
1996	Allied Forces	3	R. Migliore	119	Cliptomania	116	Lite Approval	114	86,325	1:40.80	111
1997	Subordination	3	J.F. Chavez	120	Premier Krischief	113	Skybound	121	90,000	1:49.00	98
1998	Vergennes	3	J.R. Velazquez	115	Tanghazi	114	Middlesex Drive	114	90,000	1:50.40	104
1999	Monarch's Maze	3	J. Bravo	117	Killer Joe	112	Monkey Puzzle	118	90,000	1:51.60	98
2000	King Cugat	3	J.D. Bailey	123	Mandarin Marsh	114	Parade Leader	115	120,000	1:49.63	95
2001	Navesink	3	E.S. Prado	118	Strategic Partner	118	Baptize	123	120,000	1:51.53	105
2002	Finality	3	J.R. Velazquez	116	Union Place	115	Chiseling	121	120,000	1:46.66	104
2003	Stroll	3	J.D. Bailey	121	Kicken Kris	121	Joe Bear	117	120,000	1:46.02	105

Beyer Index: **103.38**

JEROME HANDICAP, 1 Mile, 3-Year-Olds, Belmont Park, 2003 Purse: $150,000

Year	Winner	Age	Jockey	Wt.	Second	Wt.	Third	Wt.	Win Value	Time	Beyer
1866	Watson	3	Abe	110	Ulrica	107	Local	110	2,850	1:48.75	
1867	Metairie	3	Hennessey	110	Fanny Cheatham	107	Morrissey	110	2,100	1:49.50	
1868	Bayonet	3	C. Miller	110	Australia	107	Fanny Ludlow	107	2,900	1:45.25	
1869	Glenelg	3	C. Miller	110	Inverness	107	Onyx	110	3,300	1:48.50	
1870	Kingfisher	3	Burns	110	Haric	110	Midday	107	3,950	1:49.00	

Year	Winner	Age	Jockey	Wt.	Second	Wt.	Third	Wt.	Win Value	Time Beyer
1871	Harry Bassettt	3	J. Rowe	110	Monarchist	110	Alroy	110	5,450	3:54.75
1872	Joe Daniels	3	J. Rowe	110	Mate	110	Meteor	110	4,450	3:49.25
1873	Tom Bowling	3	Swim	110	Springbok	110	Fellowcraft	110	4,950	0:00.00
1874	Acrobat	3	Sparling	110	Madge	107	Bannerette	107	4,150	2:37.75
1875	Aristides	3	Swim	110	Calvin	110	Joe Cerns	110	3,900	3:43.00
1876	Charley Howard	3	W. Lakeland	110	Sunburst	110	Red Coat	110	3,550	3:47.75
1877	Basil	3	Evans	110	Susquehana	107	Bombast	110	4,400	3:43.00
1878	Duke of Magenta	3	Hughes	118	Spartan	118	Albert	118	3,450	3:11.50
1879	Monitor	3	Hughes	118	Spendthrift	118	Report	118	4,100	3:12.00
1880	Grenada	3	Hughes	118	Ferncliff	118	Oden	118	3,200	3:12.75
1881	Barrett	3	Feakes	118	Priam	118			2,800	3:13.00
1882	Carley B.	3	J. McLaughlin	115	Elkhorn Lass	115	Duplex	115	2,900	3:21.50
1883	George Kinney	3	Fitzpatrick	125	Euclid	115	Clonmel	118	3,220	3:19.00
1884	Water Lily	3	Feakes	115	Bull's Head	118	Thackeray	121	3,920	3:16.00
1885	Longview	3	Fitzpatrick	118	Tecumseh	118	Saltpetre	118	2,580	3:20.00
1886	The Bard	3	W. Hayward	125	Elkwood	121	Mollie McCarty's L	115	2,900	0:00.00
1887	Firenze	3	Garrison	122	Hanover	125			2,403	3:09.75
1888	Prince Royal	3	Garrison	128	Tea Tray	115	Larchmont	118	3,870	3:10.25
1889	Longstreet	3	I. Murphy	121	Philosophy	104			3,990	3:11.00
1890	Tournament	3	Hayward	125	Banquet	118	Masterlode	104	6,100	2:16.00
1891	Picknicker	3	Clayton	125	Hoodlum	115	Rey del Rey	129	6,250	2:22.75
1892	Tammany	3	Garrison	129	Yorkville Belle	122	Azra	129	18,415	2:36.25
1893	Young Arion	3	J. Lamley	93	Don Alonzo	130	Roche	110	3,190	2:08.75
1894	Rubicon	3	Midgely	122	Declare	107	Harrington	110	5,260	2:09.75
1895	Counter Tenor	3	Simms	121	Brandywine	105	Maurice	98	1,412	1:54.00
1896	Souffle	3	J. Hill	112	The Winner	120	Rondo	108	1,950	2:09.25
1897	Rensselaer	3	Howitt	116	Don d'Oro	115	Tillo	124	1,900	2:07.00
1898	Handball	3	N. Turner	110	Whistling Con	104	Sailor King	106	2,185	2:06.00
1899	King Barleycorn	3	Odom	114	Maid of Harlem	100	Sir Hubert	95	2,155	2:09.00
1900	Alcedo	3	McCue	110	Gonfalon	106	McMeekin	121	2,030	2:07.00
1901	Blues	3	Shaw	126	Baron Pepper	107	Hernando	111	1,995	2:05.75
1902	Hermis	3	Rice	126	Hunter Raine	100	Oom Paul	110	2,240	2:06.20
1903	Eugenia Burch	3	Fuller	116	Grey Friar	111			1,950	2:15.00
1904	Ostrich	3	Crimmius	93	The Southerner	102	Outcome	106	2,325	2:13.00
1905	Bedouin	3	Shaw	111	St. Bellane	102	Von Tromp	112	2,415	2:10.60
1906	Ironsides	3	Radtke	107	Good Luck	114	Running Water	122	2,770	2:10.60
1907	Perseverance	3	R. McDaniel	102	McCarter	114	Gretna Green	105	3,275	2:13.80
1908	Fair Play	3	Gilbert	125	Master Robert	106	Gowan	95	2,940	2:10.40
1909	Fitz Herbert	3	E. Dugan	130	Olambala	120	Mary Davis	99	1,060	2:11.00
1914	Stromboli	3	C. Turner	117	Gainer	109	Figinny	108	1,060	2:36.60
1915	Trial by Jury	3	T. McTaggart	127	The Finn	126	Hauberk	105	1,100	1:38.40
1916	Spur	3	J. Loftus	130	Crimper	120	Air Man	105	2,350	1:39.00
1917	Bally	3	L. Lyke	107	Straight Forward	114	Liberty Loan	126	2,175	1:38.00
1918	Sunny Slope	3	J. Callahan	120	Motor Cop	123	Lady Gertrude	108	1,925	1:38.40
1919	Thunderclap	3	L. Fator	117	Over There	115	Tetley	95	2,575	1:39.40
1920	Busy Signal	3	C. Kummer	115	Pilgrim	96	On Watch	120	2,625	1:37.60
1921	Tryster	3	F. Coltiletti	124	Knobbie	118	Frigate	102	2,375	1:38.20
1922	Kai-Sang	3	L. Fator	133	Athelstan	100	Brainstorm	114	2,850	1:37.00
1923	Cherry Pie	3	F. Coltiletti	113	Prince of Umbria	106	Flagstaff	120	2,975	1:35.40
1924	Priscilla Ruley	3	J. Maiben	111	Mad Play	122	Initiate	107	3,400	1:37.80
1925	Primrose	3	J. Maiben	106	Maid at Arms	114	Bright Steel	104	2,975	1:38.60
1926	Croyden	3	L. McAtee	120	Edith Cavell	114	Bumpkin	109	3,275	1:38.00
1927	Osmand	3	E. Sande	122	Jock	115	Candy Hog	100	3,250	1:38.00
1928	Sun Edwin	3	L. McAtee	118	Royal Stranger	122	Sublevado	105	3,600	1:36.80
1929	Soul of Honor	3	G. Fields	106	Chicatie	108	Comstockery	110	3,525	1:36.20
1930	Mr. Sponge	3	M. Garner	117	Caruso	106	Questionnaire	126	3,200	1:37.40
1931	Ironclad	3	L. Pinchon	102	Mountain Elk	111	Halcyon	109	3,050	1:37.00
1932	Larranaga	3	R. Workman	117	Dark Secret	115	Sweeping Light	110	2,725	1:37.60
1933	Golden Way	3	M. Garner	114	Sun Archer	114	Caesars Ghost	116	1,535	1:38.60
1934	Kievex	3	W.D. Wright	115	Roustabout	111	Somebody	110	4,090	1:37.00
1935	Good Harvest	3	S. Renick	107	Whopper	114	Psychic Bid	116	5,410	1:36.20
1936	Goldeneye	3	I. Hanford	105	Maeriel	110	Tatterdemalion	107	5,290	1:36.60
1937	Pasha	3	L. Balaski	117	Regal Lily	119	Rudie	122	4,920	1:38.20
1938	Cravat	3	A. Robertson	115	Can't Wait	116	The Chief	119	5,050	1:36.40
1939	Easy Mon	3	L. Haas	110	Third Degree	120	Golden Voyage	116	7,225	1:35.80
1940	Roman	3	W.D. Wright	121	Weigh Anchor	112	Tola Rose	116	6,425	1:37.20
1941	Stimady	3	P. Roberts	110	Misty Isle	118	Minnelusa	110	6,825	1:37.20
1942	King's Abbey	3	C. Bierman	112	Bless Me	122	Devil Diver	126	6,325	1:36.40
1943	Slide Rule	3	J. Westrope	122	Eurasian	119	Famous Victory	115	7,075	1:37.40
1944	Occupy	3	G. Grohs	110	Bounding Home	120	Free Lance	112	8,050	1:37.20
1945	Buzfuz	3	T. Luther	115	Greek Warrior	114	Pavot	125	13,010	1:37.20
1946	Mahout	3	E. Arcaro	114	Rippey	117	Athenia	112	14,000	1:37.00
							Kitchen Police	108		

Year	Winner	Age	Jockey	Wt.	Second	Wt.	Third	Wt.	Win Value	Time	Beyer
1947	Donor	3	J.D. Jessop	115	Cosmic Bomb	126	Cornish Knight	113	21,550	1:37.40	
1948	Coaltown	3	N.L. Pierson	126	Mount Marcy	115	Free America	126	21,450	1:36.00	
1949	Capot	3	T. Atkinson	126	Arise	116	Double Brandy	109	17,400	1:36.80	
1950	Hill Prince	3	E. Arcaro	129	Greek Ship	122	Navy Chief	108	17,150	1:35.80	
1951	Alerted	3	O. Scurlock	115	Mandingo	102	Hall of Fame	128	17,650	1:36.20	
1952	Tom Fool	3	T. Atkinson	120	Marcador	111	Mark-Ye-Well	130	17,100	1:37.00	
1953	Navy Page	3	N. Shuk	114	Scent	106	Landlocked	125	18,800	1:37.00	
							First Aid	118			
1954	Martyr	3	S. Small	110	Fisherman	126	Full Flight	118	18,000	1:35.80	
1955	Traffic Judge	3	E. Arcaro	126	Star Rover	121	Impromptu	118	21,750	1:35.20	
1956	Reneged	3	A. Valenzuela	117	Tick Tock	121	Countermand	115	21,550	1:35.40	
1957	Bold Ruler	3	E. Arcaro	130	Bureaucracy	113	Winged Mercury	106	19,950	1:35.00	
1958	Warhead	3	E. Arcaro	118	Piano Jim	121	Jester	118	19,362	1:37.20	
1959	Intentionally	3	M. Ycaza	126	Atoll	120	Seven Corners	110	35,995	1:35.40	
1960	Kelso	3	E. Arcaro	121	Careless John	116	Four Lane	119	37,945	1:34.80	
1961	Carry Back	3	J. Sellers	128	Garwol	111	Beau Prince	126	37,505	1:36.00	
1962	Black Beard	3	B. Baeza	114	Fauve	109	Dedimoud	116	38,285	1:34.60	
1963	Chateugay	3	B. Baeza	128	Accordant	117	Outing Class	123	37,245	1:36.00	
1964	Irvkup	3	J.L. Rotz	113	Lt. Stevens	114	Quadrangle	109	36,140	1:35.00	
1965	Bold Bidder	3	E. Nelson	110	Cornish Prince	123	Slystitch	114	38,870	1:36.00	
1966	Bold and Brave	3	B. Baeza	115	Understanding	107	Our Michael	116	37,765	1:38.00	
1967	High Tribute	3	L. Pincay Jr	113	In Reality	126	Jim J.	116	37,440	1:34.80	
1968	Iron Ruler	3	J. Velasquez	120	Captain's Gig	122	Dewan	119	38,220	1:35.20	
1969	Mr. Leader	3	J. Velasquez	113	Oil Power	110	Hydrologist	111	37,635	1:36.00	
1970	Great Mystery	3	P.I. Grimm	117	Knight of the Road	112	Estimator Dave	107	37,895	1:34.80	
1971	Tinajero	3	E. Belmonte	116	Twin Time	117	Sic Em Judge	117	34,200	1:35.80	
1972	True Knight	3	A. Cordero Jr	114	Tentam	116	Great Bear Lake	109	35,100	1:36.60	
1973	Step Nicely	3	A. Cordero Jr	118	Forego	124	Linda's Chief	126	34,800	1:34.00	
1974	Stonewalk	3	A. Cordero Jr	126	Best of It	117	Heir to the Line	113	34,470	1:34.00	
1975	Guards Up	3	C. Lopez	114	Valid Appeal	119	Great Above	114	33,720	1:34.20	
1976	Dance Spell	3	R. Hernandez	117	Soy Numero Uno	117	Clean Bill	112	66,600	1:35.00	
1977	Broadway Forli	3	P. Day	111	To the Quick	112	Affiliate	120	66,360	1:36.20	
1978	Sensitive Prince	3	J. Vasquez	118	Darby Creek Road	122	Sorry Lookin	112	62,940	1:36.00	
1979	Czaravich	3	J. Cruguet	122	Valdez	122	Gallant Best	112	65,580	1:35.20	
1980	Jaklin Klugman	3	C.J. McCarron	122	Fappiano	114	Plugged Nickle	124	67,320	1:34.20	
1981	Noble Nashua	3	C.B. Asmussen	120	Maudlin	112	Sing Sing	109	69,000	1:33.20	
1982	Fit to Fight	3	J.D. Bailey	112	John's Gold	115	Lord Lister	107	101,880	1:35.40	
1983	A Phenomenon	3	A. Cordero Jr	116	Desert Wine	124	Copelan	118	104,940	1:35.00	
1984	Is Your Pleasure	3	D. MacBeth	114	Track Barron	124	Concorde Bound	115	109,080	1:35.20	
1985	Creme Fraiche	3	E. Maple	124	Pancho Villa	119	El Basco	114	109,260	1:34.60	
1986	Ogygian	3	W.A. Guerra	126	Mogambo	119	Moment of Hope	111	127,620	1:34.00	
1987	Afleet	3	G. Stahlbaum	115	Stacked Pack	109	Templar Hill	117	107,640	1:33.80	
1988	Evening Kris	3	J.D. Bailey	119	Parlay Me	113	Din's Dancer	113	176,400	1:37.80	
1989	De Roche	3	D. Carr	108	Fast Play	116	I'm Influential	111	134,880	1:34.40	
1990	Housebuster	3	C. Perret	126	Citidancer	114	D'Parrot	112	102,060	1:34.00	.118
1991	Scan	3	J.A. Santos	117	Excellent Tipper	113	King Mutesa	113	120,000	1:34.00	.112
1992	Furiously	3	J.D. Bailey	113	Colony Light	111	Dixie Brass	122	120,000	1:34.20	.107
1993	Schossberg	3	J.D. Bailey	118	Williamstown	118	Mi Cielo	116	120,000	1:35.40	.104
1994	Prenup	3	J.D. Bailey	113	Ulises	112	End Sweep	118	120,000	1:34.40	.108
1995	French Deputy	3	G.L Stevens	113	Mr. Greeley	117	Top Account	115	120,000	1:33.40	.119
1996	Why Change	3	C.C. Lopez	112	Distorted Humor	115	Diligence	117	90,000	1:34.20	.108
1997	Richter Scale	3	S.J. Sellers	118	Trafalger	117	Smokin Mel	115	90,000	1:35.80	.111
1998	Limit Out	3	J.L. Samyn	117	Grand Slam	120	Scatmandu	115	90,000	1:36.20	.105
1999	Doneraile Court	3	C.W. Antley	117	Vicar	120	Badger Gold	115	150,000	1:35.60	.100
2000	Fusaichi Pegasus	3	K.J. Desormeaux	124	El Corredor	117	Albert The Great	120	90,000	1:34.07	.115
2001	Express Tour	3	J.R. Velazquez	117	Illusioned	117	Burning Roma	120	90,000	1:34.57	.104
2002	Boston Common	3	J.F. Chavez	118	Vinemeister	115	No Parole	115	90,000	1:36.12	.107
2003	During	3	J.A. Santos	118	Tafaseel	114	Pretty Wild	116	90,000	1:36.32	.199

Beyer Index: 108.36

JIM DANDY, 1 1/8 Miles,
3-Year-Olds, Saratoga Race Course, 2003 Purse: $500,000

Year	Winner	Age	Jockey	Wt.	Second	Wt.	Third	Wt.	Win Value	Time	Beyer
1964	Malicious	3	J.L. Rotz	119	Quadrangle	126	Knightly Manner	117	18,265	1:35.60	
1965	Cornish Prince	3	R. Turcotte	114	Pass the Word	114	Beaupy	114	18,655	1:35.60	
1966	Indulto	3	J.L. Rotz	119	Imam	114	Federalist Boy	114	18,427	1:37.00	
1967	Gala Performances	3	E. Belmonte	114	Great Power	119	Tumiga	119	19,565	1:36.20	
1968	Captain's Gig	3	M. Ycaza	119	Dewan	117	Pamir	114	18,817	1:35.80	
1969	Arts and Letters	3	B. Baeza	126	Gleaming Light	119	Mr. Mag	114	18,102	1:36.20	
1970	Personality	3	L. Pincay Jr	126	Loud	114	Plymouth	114	19,532	1:35.80	
1971	Brazen Brother	3	M. Hole	114	Marshua's Dancer	114	Silver Mallet	114	20,820	1:22.80	
1972	Tentam	3	J. Velasquez	114	True Knight	115	Halo	114	17,430	1:49.60	

Year	Winner	Age	Jockey	Wt.	Second	Wt.	Third	Wt.	Win Value	Time	Beyer
1973	Cheriepe	3	E. Belmonte	117	Arbees Boy	120	Bemo	123	17,310	1:50.20	
1974	Sea Songster	3	A. Cordero Jr	114	Hatchet Man	120	Bobby Murcer	114	22,860	1:50.60	
1975	Forceten	3	D. Pierce	126			Northerly	114	25,725	1:48.40	
1976	Father Hogan	3	M. Venezia	114	Dance Spell	121	El Portugues	114	22,410	1:48.80	
1977	Music of Time	3	M. Venezia	114	Sanhedrin	114	Super Joy	114	22,830	1:50.40	
1978	Affirmed	3	S. Cauthen	128	Sensitive Prince	119	Addison	114	22,155	1:47.80	
1979	Private Account	3	J. Fell	114	Instrument Landing	126	Pianist	114	25,500	1:48.40	
1980	Plugged Nickle	3	J. Fell	128	Current Legend	121	Herb Water	114	34,140	1:49.40	
1981	Willow Hour	3	E. Maple	117	Lemhi Gold	117	Silver Supreme	114	34,200	1:49.20	
1982	Conquistador Cielo	3	E. Maple	126	Lejoli	114	No Home Run	114	32,700	1:48.60	
1983	A Phenomenon	3	A. Cordero Jr	114	Timeless Native	126	Head of the House	114	33,900	1:49.40	
1984	Carr de Naskra	3	E. Maple	114	Slew the Coup	114	Raja's Shark	114	75,720	1:47.40	
1985	Stephan's Odyssey	3	L. Pincay Jr	123	Don's Choice	114	Government Corner	121	73,080	1:48.80	
1986	Lac Ouimet	3	E. Maple	114	Moment of Hope	114	Wayar	114	69,360	1:48.00	
1987	Polish Navy	3	P. Day	117	Pledge Card	117	Cryptoclearance	126	106,740	1:48.40	
1988	Brian's Time	3	A. Cordero Jr	126	Evening Kris	121	Din's Dancer	114	109,980	1:48.20	
1989	Is It True	3	J.A. Santos	121	Fast Play	114	Roi Danzig	126	99,180	1:48.40	
1990	Chief Honcho	3	M.E. Smith	114	Senator to Be	114	Paradise Found	114	67,680	1:51.60	
1991	Fly So Free	3	J.A. Santos	126	Upon My Soul	114	Strike the Gold	128	107,820	1:48.80	106
1992	Thunder Rumble	3	W.H. McCauley	117	Dixie Brass	126	Devil His Due	126	108,000	1:47.40	110
1993	Miner's Mark	3	C.J. McCarron	117	Virginia Rapids	121	Colonial Affair	126	90,000	1:49.00	105
1994	Unaccounted For	3	J.A. Santos	114	Tabasco Cat	103	Ulises	114	80,820	1:49.60	108
1995	Composer	3	J.D. Bailey	112	Malthus	112	Pat n Jac	112	82,575	1:51.00	106
1996	Louis Quatorze	3	P. Day	124	Will's Way	114	Secreto de Estado	114	90,000	1:47.20	119
1997	Awesome Again	3	M.E. Smith	116	Glitman	114	Affirmed Success	114	150,000	1:51.00	107
1998	Favorite Trick	3	P. Day	119	Deputy Diamond	114	Raffie's Majesty	114	150,000	1:50.00	103
1999	Ecton Park	3	A. Solis	116	Lemon Drop Kid	124	Badger Gold	114	180,000	1:49.40	112
2000	Graeme Hall	3	J.D. Bailey	120	Curule	114	Unshaded	120	240,000	1:48.95	106
2001	Scorpion	3	J.D. Bailey	114	Free Of Love	114	Congaree	123	360,000	1:48.90	105
2002	Medaglia d'Oro	3	J.D. Bailey	121	Gold Dollar	115	Essence of Dubai	115	300,000	1:47.82	120

Quest finished second but was disqualified and placed eighth

| 2003 | Strong Hope | 3 | J.R. Velazquez | 121 | Empire Maker | 123 | Congrats | 115 | 300,000 | 1:48.10 | 110 |

Beyer Index: 109

KELSO BREEDERS' CUP HANDICAP, 1 Mile (Turf),
3-Year-Olds and Up, Belmont Park, 2003 Purse: $347,000

Year	Winner	Age	Jockey	Wt.	Second	Wt.	Third	Wt.	Win Value	Time	Beyer
1980	Peat Moss	5	F. Lovato Jr	108	Ivory Hunter	114	Ring of Light	117	68,160	3:24.60	
1981	Peat Moss	6	F. Lovato Jr	126	Field Cat	114	Birthday List	114	66,240	3:20.80	
1982	Worthy Too	4	J.L. Samyn	109	Nice Pirate	112	J'd'sa T'k'r	113	69,840	3:24.40	
1984	Who's for Dinner	5	W.A. Guerra	115	Pin Puller	112	Norwick	109	71,100	2:01.20	
1985	Mourjane	5	R. Migliore	117	Cool	116	Palace Panther	116	70,560	2:02.00	
1986	I'm a Banker	4	A. Graell	111	Duluth	113	Premier Mister	113	54,720	2:03.20	
1987	I'm a Banker	5	A. Graell	107	Tertiary Zone	113	Island Sun	112	76,920	2:10.80	
1988	Sans the Shadow	4	C.W. Antley	116	Posen	117	Tinchens Prince	114	72,240	1:42.00	
1989	I Rejoice	6	J.D. Bailey	114	Quick Call	113	Wanderkin	118	75,360	1:36.40	
1990	Expensive Decision	4	J.L. Samyn	114	Who's to Pay	115	Great Commot'n	113	57,420	1:32.40	112
1991	Star of Cozzene	4	J.A. Santos	113	Known Ranger	113	Fourstardave	117	69,720	1:33.20	106
1992	Roman Envoy	4	C. Perret	117	Lure	111	Val des Bois	118	120,000	1:36.20	108
1993	Lure	4	M.E. Smith	125	Paradise Creek	120	Daarik	112	120,000	1:35.80	111
1994	Nijinsky's Gold	5	Santos JA	114	Lure	128	A in Sociology	117	120,000	1:34.00	110
1995	Mighty Forum	4	Delahoussaye E	115	Fastness	119	Dowty	112	120,000	1:39.40	105
1996	Same Old Wish	6	S.J. Sellers	113	Da Hoss	120	Volochine	116	105,000	1:34.60	106
1997	Lucky Coin	4	R.G. Davis	119	Hawksley Hill	115	Colcon	112	120,000	1:33.60	112
1998	Dixie Bayou	4	J.F. Chavez	112	Sahm	115	Let Goodtimes Roll	112	120,000	1:36.20	103
1999	Middlesex Drive	4	S.J. Sellers	117	Divide and Conquer	114	Wised Up	113	150,000	1:35.40	110
2000	Forbidden Apple	5	J.L. Samyn	116	Affirmed Success	120	Johnny Dollar	113	150,000	1:34.39	109
2001	Forbidden Apple	6	J.A. Santos	118	Sarafan	114	City Zip	112	150,000	1:36.77	104
2002	Green Fee	6	J.R. Velazquez	113	Forbidden Apple	121	Moon Solitaire	117	210,000	1:33.83	110
2003	Freefourinternet	5	J.L. Espinoza	113	Proud Man	114	Rouvres	115	210,000	1:34.73	105

Beyer Index: 107.93

KENTUCKY CUP CLASSIC HANDICAP, 1 1/8 Miles,
3-Year-Olds and Up, Turfway Park, 2003 Purse: $350,000

Year	Winner	Age	Jockey	Wt.	Second	Wt.	Third	Wt.	Win Value	Time	Beyer
1994	Tabasco Cat	3	P. Day	120	Mighty Avanti	115	Best Pal	115	260,000	1:50.20	103
1995	Thunder Gulch	3	G.L. Stevens	121	Judge TC	112	Bound by Honor	113	260,000	1:49.40	108
1996	Atticus	4	C.S. Nakatani	115	Judge TC	116	Isitingood	114	325,000	1:47.40	109
1997	Semoran	4	K.J. Desormeaux	116	Distorted Humor	116	Coup d'Argent	114	217,000	1:48.00	107
1998	Silver Charm	4	G.L. Stevens	123			Acceptable	117	207,250	1:47.40	123
	Wild Rush	4	P. Day	117							

Year	Winner	Age	Jockey	Wt.	Second	Wt.	Third	Wt.	Win Value	Time	Beyer
1999	Da Devil	4	C.H. Borel	112	Social Charter	115	Cat Thief	117	.314,500	1:50.40	.108
2000	Captain Steve	3	S.J. Sellers	115	Golden Missile	121	Early Pioneer	120	.314,500	1:49.95	.116
2001	Guided Tour	5	L. Melancon	118	Balto Star	114	A Fleets Dancer	115	.254,000	1:47.90	.113
2002	Pure Prize	4	M.E. Smith	115	Dollar Bill	117	Hero's Tribute	113	.254,000	1:51.24	.108
2003	Perfect Drift	4	P. Day	120	Congaree	124	Crafty Shaw	115	.221,500	1:50.43	.112

Beyer Index: 110.7

KENTUCKY JOCKEY CLUB, 1 1/16 Miles,
2-Year-Olds, Churchill Downs, 2003 Purse: $222,200

Year	Winner	Age	Jockey	Wt.	Second	Wt.	Third	Wt.	Win Value	Time	Beyer
1920	Tryster	2	F. Coltiletti	122	Grey Lag	122	Behave Yourself	122	.23,695	1:38.40	
1921	Startle	2	D. Connell	119	Rocket	122	John Finn	122	.22,175	1:38.60	
1922	Enchantment	2	L. McAtee	122	Picketer	122	Dongos	122	.25,315	1:38.80	
1923	Wise Counsellor	2	M. Garner	122	Mad Play	122	Chilhowee	122	.26,990	1:37.40	
1924	Master Charlie	2	C. Kummer	122	Pas Seul	122	Kentucky Cardinal	122	.26,010	1:38.20	
1925	Canter	2	C. Turner	122	Flight of Time	122	Rhinock	122	.23,315	1:41.00	
1926	Valorous	2	L. McAtee	122	Bostonian	122	Candy Queen	119	.26,785	1:43.60	
1927	Reigh Count	2	C. Lang	122	Vito	122	Algernon	122	.28,480	1:40.00	
1928	Clyde Van Dusen	2	C. McCrossen	122	Current	119	Windy CIty	122	.32,800	1:38.80	
1929	Desert Light	2	P. Walls	119	Alcibiades	119	Gallant Knight	122	.26,865	1:39.00	
1930	Twenty Grand	2	C. Kurtsinger	122	Equipoise	122	Knight's Call	122	.25,030	1:36.00	
1931	Kakapo	2	E. Pool	119	Pompeius	122	Air Pilot	122	.24,040	1:43.80	
1932	The Darb	2	A. Robertson	122	Caesar's Ghost	122	Dynastic	122	.19,945	1:46.80	
1933	Mata Hari	2	H. Schutte	119	Discovery	122	Collateral	122	.16,230	1:39.80	
1934	Nellie Flag	2	E. Arcaro	119	Good Flavor	122	Myrtlewood	119	.9,820	1:37.60	
1935	Grand Slam	2	W. Hanka	122	Hollyrood	122	Boston Pal	122	.9,835	1:39.60	
1936	Reaping Reward	2	A. Robertson	122	Privileged	122	Dellor	122	.10,140	1:40.00	
1937	Mountain Ridge	2	A. Robertson	122	King's Heir	122	Dah He	122	.8,510	1:38.60	
1938	T.M. Dorsett	2	L. Haas	122	Steel Heels	122	Lightspur	122	.8,450	1:38.60	
1946	Double Jay	2	J. Gilbert	122	Education	122	Patmiboy	116	.22,690	1:37.00	
1947	Bold Gallant	2	F.A. Smith	116	Shy Guy	119	Papa Redbird	116	.21,180	1:38.80	
1948	Johns Joy	2	J. Combest	119	Fleeting Star	116	Our Request	113	.23,545	1:37.00	
1949	Roman Bath	2	D. Scurlock	116	Bolingover	116	Sunglow	116	.21,340	1:38.20	
1950	Pur Sang	2	T. Barrow	116	Bernwood	116	Mameluke	116	.21,995	1:36.60	
1951	Sub Fleet	2	J. Adams	116	Alladier	122	Smoke Screen	113	.38,740	1:40.00	
1952	Straight Face	5	B. Green	122	Spy Defense	116	Berseem	116	.36,545	1:37.40	
1953	Hasty Road	2	J. Adams	122	Goyamo	116	Pinetum	113	.36,185	1:36.00	
1954	Prince Noor	2	J. Adams	113	Fleet Path	116	Parador	116	.36,300	1:38.60	
1955	Royal Sting	2	J. Heckmann	116	Jovial Jove	122	Roman Fan	116	.40,635	1:37.60	
1956	Federal Hill	2	W. Carstens	119	Tranquil	116	Jet Colonel	116	.40,685	1:37.40	
1957	Hill Country	2	L.C. Cook	116	Can Trust	116	Page Seven	113	.34,235	1:38.00	
1958	Winsome Winner	2	S. Brooks	116	Pilot	119	John Bruce	116	.32,020	1:36.40	
1959	Oil Wick	2	R. Dever	116	All Hands	116	Run for Nurse	116	.30,314	1:39.40	
1960	Crimson Fury	2	W. Carstens	117	Safe Swap	116	Wooden Nickel	116	.26,574	1:38.00	
1961	Su Ka Wa	2	H. Clark	119	Times Roman	116	Sharp Count	116	.29,341	1:36.80	
1962	Sky Gem	2	B. Baeza	119	Copy Chief	116	Telethon	116	.34,343	1:37.40	
1963	Journalist	2	K. Church	116	Duel	122	Bleacherite	116	.32,074	1:36.40	
1964	Umbrella Fella	2	J. Nazareth	122	Florida State	116	Black Dad	122	.32,909	1:36.60	
1965	War Censor	2	R. York	116	Tinsley	122	Old Bag	122	.32,909	1:37.60	
1966	Lightning Orphan	2	R. Broussard	119	Gentleman James	116	Monitor	116	.33,790	1:37.60	
1967	Mr. Brogann	2	D. Richard	116	Gin-Rob	122	T.V. Commercial	122	.36,832	1:35.00	
1968	Traffic Mark	2	C.H. Marquez	119	Indian Emerald	119	Hawaiian Ruler	116	.39,705	1:38.20	
1969	Evasive Action	2	J. Tejeira	116	Hard Work	122	Admiral's Shield	116	.35,444	1:33.80	
1970	Line City	2	D. Brumfield	116	Granbid	118	Dothan	116	.40,908	1:36.80	
1971	Windjammer	2	L. Pincay Jr	122	Billy Rogell	116	Thurloe Square	116	.35,685	1:36.80	
1972	Puntilla	2	B. Baeza	116	Golden Don	116	Annihilate 'Em	122	.37,895	1:35.60	
1973	Cannonade	2	P. Anderson	119	Satan's Hills	116	Don't Be Late Jim	116	.49,510	1:36.80	
1974	Circle Home	2	M. Hole	116	Master Derby	122	Ruggles Ferry	116	.36,748	1:36.00	
1975	Play Boy	2	D. Brumfield	116	Khyber King	119	Please Find John	116	.30,491	1:36.80	
1975	Pastry	2	B.R. Feliciano	116	Bold Laddie	119	Bid to Fame	116	.30,329	1:36.80	
1976	Run Dusty Run	2	D.G. McHargue	122	Get the Axe	116	Silver Series	116	.34,830	1:37.20	
1977	Going Investor	2	R. Depass	119	Jaycean	119	Silver Nitrate	119	.36,121	1:38.20	
1978	Lot o' Gold	2	R. Depass	119	Arctic Action	116	Uncle Fudge	119	.37,645	1:37.80	
1979	King Neptune	2	D. Brumfield	116	Royal Sporan	119	Silver Shears	116	.37,001	1:37.80	
1980	Television Studio	2	D. Brumfield	116	Linnleur	116	Bear Creek Dam	116	.73,226	1:47.00	
1981	El Baba	2	R.P. Romero	119	Crown the King	116	Talent Town	119	.85,888	1:45.20	
1982	Highland Park	2	D. Brumfield	122	Coax Me Matt	116	Caveat	122	.75,859	1:47.00	
1983	Biloxi Indian	2	G. Patterson	119	Country Manor	119	Taylor's Special	119	.71,721	1:46.20	
1984	Fuzzy	2	D. Brumfield	114	Banner Bob	119	Nordic Scandal	113	.106,902	1:45.00	
1985	Mustin Lake	2	P. Day	116	Bachelor Beau	116	Regal Dreamer	122	.87,432	1:46.80	
1986	Mt. Pleasant	2	K.K. Allen	116	Mondulick	113	Funny Tunes	113	.93,561	1:46.40	

Year	Winner	Age	Jockey	Wt.	Second	Wt.	Third	Wt.	Win Value	Time	Beyer
1987	Notebook	2	J.A. Santos	122	Buoy	122	Hey Pat	119	74,701	1:47.40	
1988	Tricky Creek	2	L. Melancon	118	Western Playboy	116	Revive	118	106,083	1:45.40	
1989	Grand Canyon	2	A. Cordero Jr	121	Insurrection	121	Dusty's Command	118	95,550	1:44.60	
1990	Richman	2	P. Day	121	Discover	116	Honor Grades	116	107,718	1:45.40	
1991	Dance Floor	2	C.W. Antley	121	Waki Warrior	116	Choctaw Ridge	116	104,891	1:45.20	.93
1992	Wild Gale	2	S.J. Sellers	116	Mi Cielo	116	Shoal Creek	121	105,918	1:45.60	.87
1993	War Deputy	2	G.K. Gomez	112	Tarzans Blade	122	Rustic Light	119	97,500	1:46.60	.90
1994	Jambalaya Jazz	2	Maple S	113	You're the One	112	Peaks and Valleys	119	97,500	1:46.40	.90
1995	Ide	2	Perret C	122	Editor's Note	119	El Amante	113	106,373	1:44.20	.94
1996	Concerto	2	C.H. Marquez Jr.	119	Celtic Warrior	113	Carmen's Baby	122	142,104	1:46.80	.95
1997	Cape Town	2	W. Martinez	113	Time Limit	119	Real Quiet	116	142,228	1:43.80	.96
1998	Exploit	2	C.J. McCarron	122	Vicar	113	Grits n' Hard Toast	113	140,740	1:44.00	.101
1999	Captain Steve	2	R.J. Albarado	122	Mighty	122	Personal First	119	143,840	1:43.00	.105
2000	Dollar Bill	2	C.H. Borel	113	Holiday Thunder	113	Gift Of The Eagle	113	136,656	1:47.18	.96
2001	Repent	2	A.J. D'Amico	122	Request for Parole	117	High Star	115	134,540	1:44.42	.92
2002	Soto	2	L. Melancon	117	Ten Cents a Shine	115	Most Feared	122	143,344	1:44.67	.94
2003	The Cliff's Edge	2	S.J. Sellers	122	Gran Prospect	116	Proper Prado	118	137,764	1:45.50	.94

Beyer Index: 94.38

FRANK E. KILROE MILE HANDICAP, 1 Mile,
4-Year-Olds and Up, Santa Anita, 2003 Purse: $400,000

Year	Winner	Age	Jockey	Wt.	Second	Wt.	Third	Wt.	Win Value	Time	Beyer
1960	American Comet	4	T. Barrow	118	Porter	110	Aorangi	112	16,650	2:04.40	
1961	Wolfram	5	J.L. Rotz	122	Balsarroch Boy	111	Geechee Lou	121	17,600	2:01.00	
1962	Art Market	4	I. Valenzuela	120	Oink	124	Grey Eagle	116	17,600	2:01.00	
1963	The Axe II	5	P. Moreno	122	Rableno	120	Hy-Nat	116	18,600	2:04.20	
1964	Mr. Consistency	6	K. Church	124	Marlin Bay	118	Cedar Key	118	18,100	1:58.60	
1965	Cedar Key	5	W. Shoemaker	122	Dusky Damion	114	Brambles	116	18,800	2:00.80	
1966	Tudor Fame	4	J. Lambert	113	Plaque	112	Aurelius II	115	18,200	2:02.80	
1967	Fleet Host	4	A. Pineda	116	The Dancer	108			18,050	1:59.80	
					Biggs	113					
1968	Nashua Pilot	4	J. Sellers	114	Tumble Wind	120	Mr. Right	118	21,250	2:00.00	
1969	Rivet	5	M. Volzke	118	Palestin	116	Easy Mark	115	21,850	2:03.20	
1970	Royal Dynasty	4	L. Pincay Jr	114	Quicken Tree	120	High Tribute	111	19,300	2:06.80	
1971	Daryl's Joy	5	J. Sellers	126	Magic Hope II	115	Obelisco	113	26,000	1:59.60	
1972	Buzkashi	5	W. Shoemaker	117	Mayhedo	115	Perpetual	114	22,350	2:00.80	
1972	Knight in Armor	5	D. Pierce	120	Big Shot II	125	Golden Eagle II	119	21,950	2:01.80	
1973	River Buoy	8	D. Pierce	117	Wing Out	116	Mazus	121	20,875	2:02.80	
1973	Kobuk King	7	J. Lambert	116	Triggairo	114	Presidual	116	20,475	2:02.80	
1974	Court Ruling	4	B. Baeza	114	Scantling	116	Barrydown	116	32,800	2:01.40	
1975	Ga Hai	4	J. Vasquez	114	Indefatigable	115	Gold Standard	111	32,800	2:07.00	
1976	Ga Hai	5	F. Olivares	115	Riot in Paris	120	Copper Mel	117	34,050	2:00.40	
1977	Caucasus	5	F. Toro	124	Exact Duplicate	115			33,900	2:00.00	
					Victorian Prince	116					
1978	Exceller	5	W. Shoemaker	126	Soldier's Lark	113	Tacitus	115	31,750	2:01.20	
1979	Fluorescent Light	5	L. Pincay Jr	121	Waya	123	As de Copas	118	39,650	2:03.60	
1980	Henschel	6	W. Shoemaker	114	Silver Eagle	120	Balzac	122	40,900	1:58.80	
1981	Premier Ministre	5	L. Pincay Jr	117	Galaxy Libra	119	Bold Tropic	126	38,350	2:02.60	
1982	Perrault	5	L. Pincay Jr	124	Silveyville	117	Le Duc de Bar	111	47,700	2:04.60	
1983	Manantial	5	K. Black	115	Bohemian Grove	115	Western	120	46,500	2:03.40	
1984	Sir Pele	5	R.Q. Meza	114	Lucence	117	Ginger Brink	117	49,850	2:01.20	
1985	Fatih	5	W. Shoemaker	117	Tsunami Slew	119	Swoon	113	64,300	1:59.60	
1986	Strawberry Road II	7	G.L. Stevens	125	Hail Bold King	116	Schiller	115	75,800	2:03.40	
1987	Thrill Show	4	W. Shoemaker	121	Skywalker	123	Aventino	115	92,150	1:35.00	
1988	Mohamed Abdu	4	E. Delahoussaye	118	The Medic	118	The Scout	118	95,300	1:37.00	
1989	Bello Horizonte	6	E. Delahoussaye	116	Sarhoob	120	Patchy Groundfog	117	64,700	1:36.20	
1990	Prized	4	E. Delahoussaye	124	Happy Toss	115	On the Menu	112	67,000	1:34.40	.107
1991	Madjaristan	5	E. Delahoussaye	114	Trebizond	116	Major Moment	111	105,400	1:33.20	
1992	Fly Till Dawn	6	L. Pincay Jr	120	Itsallgreektome	123	Qathif	115	100,200	1:34.60	.110
1993	Leger Cat	7	C.S. Nakatani	114	Luthier Enchanteur	116	The Name's Jimmy	115	70,800	1:34.00	.107
1994	Megan's Interco	5	C.A. Black	118	Tinners Way	115	Ibero	118	64,400	1:33.80	.108
1995	College Town	4	L. Pincay Jr	117	Romarin	120	Finder's Fortune	114	63,800	1:40.60	.99
1996	Tychonic	6	G.L. Stevens	116	Debutant Trick	117	Silver Wizard	117	99,400	1:35.40	.108
1997	Atticus	5	C.S. Nakatani	117	Pinfloron	115	Rainbow Blues	121	97,400	1:31.80	.115
1998	Hawksley Hill	5	P. Day	115	Via Lombardia	117	A Magicman	120	101,190	1:34.80	.106
1999	Lord Smith	4	G.K. Gomez	116	Hawksley Hill	122	Ladies Din	120	90,000	1:34.40	.111
2000	Commitisize	5	V. Espinoza	112	Chullo	117	Sultry Substitute	114	120,000	1:36.61	.106
2001	Road to Slew	6	L. Pincay Jr.	117	Val Royal	118	Hawksley Hill	118	240,000	1:35.96	.106
							Exchange Rate	115			
2002	Decarchy	5	K.J. Desormeaux	119	Sarafan	116	Designed For Luck	117	180,000	1:34.04	.104
2003	Redattore	8	A. Solis	120	Good Journey	124	Decarchy	118	240,000	1:34.94	.109

Beyer Index: 107.38

Run as Arcadia Handicap through 2000; run on main track, 1975, 1976, 1978, 1983, 1995, and 2000; run at 1 1/4 miles prior to 1987.

KNICKERBOCKER HANDICAP, 1 1/8 Miles (Turf),
3-Year-Olds and Up, Aqueduct, 2003 Purse: $150,000

Year	Winner	Age	Jockey	Wt.	Second	Wt.	Third	Wt.	Win Value	Time	Beyer
1960	Quiz Star	4	W. Shoemaker	119	Catapult	108	Leix	109	18,712	2:49.40	
1961	T.V. Lark	4	J. Longden	119	Nasomo	113	Wise Ship	120	19,077	2:40.00	
1962	The Axe II	4	W. Shoemaker	120	Mongo	120	Irish Dandy	112	19,532	2:13.20	
1963	Parka	5	W. Shoemaker	110	Cedar Key	112	Thygold	110	14,105	1:55.20	
1963	Hellenic Hero	5	H. Woodhouse	109	Lucky Turn	111	Mr. Consistency	113	14,105	1:54.00	
1964	Third Martini	5	M. Ycaza	115	Grand Applause	108	Will I Rule	116	19,305	1:56.20	
1965	Circus	4	M. Sorrentino	112	Purser	110	C'ry F'ord II	116	18,655	1:55.80	
1966	Rego	3	H. Woodhouse	112	Paoluccio	118	Gallup Poll	112	19,597	1:59.60	
1967	Flag	7	S. Hernandez	112	Niarkos	115	Ruffled Feathers	120	14,771	1:58.00	
1967	Dunderhead	4	E. Cardone	111	Kentucky Kin	113	Jean-Pierre	114	14,934	1:58.20	
1968	Flit-to	5	M. Ycaza	117	Sea Castle	116	Goodwood II	111	19,337	1:56.00	
1969	Vent du Nord	4	R.L. Turcotte	116	Nez Perce	113	B'u of the w't	109	15,031	1:57.60	
1969	Zarco	3	R. Turcotte	112	Red Reality	116	Eagle's Sw'p	112	15,031	1:56.40	
1970	Mongo's Pride	3	C.H. Marquez	115	Barking Steeple	106	Asp'sia III	112	19,110	2:44.00	
1971	Fresh Alibhai	3	J. Ruane	109	Specious	110	Triangular	108	20,970	2:57.40	
1972	Triangular	5	J.L. Rotz	119	Dendron	112	Up II	108	16,665	2:57.20	
1973	Asray	4	C. Baltazar	112	Triangular	114	Yvetot	112	34,710	2:39.80	
1974	Shady Character	3	A. Cordero Jr	115	John Drew	111	Crafty Khale	126	33,690	2:41.40	
1975	Shady Character	4	A. Cordero Jr	113	Blue Times	115	Yvetot	113	33,900	2:16.20	
1976	Javamine	3	J. Velasquez	111	Recupere	112	Banghi	118	26,400	2:20.60	
1976	Oilfield	3	S. Hawley	112	Royal Mission	111	Trumpeter Swan	112	26,100	2:22.60	
1977	Dance D'Espoir	5	J. Cruguet	112	Java Rajah	106	Diagramatic	112	26,010	2:05.00	
1977	Keep the Promise	5	J. Cruguet	110	Soldier's Lark	110	Star Spangled	114	26,460	2:04.40	
1978	Fluorescent Light	4	J. Cruguet	115	Banquet Table	109	Scythian Gold	110	34,560	2:14.20	
1979	French Colonial	4	J. Vasquez	114	T.V. Series	113	Golden Reserve	112	35,880	2:21.40	
1980	Foretake	4	J. Ruane	112	El Barril	113	Ministrel	109	33,450	2:22.20	
1980	Lobsang II	4	M. Venezia	111	Match the Hatch	115	King Crimson	111	33,450	2:23.60	
1981	Euphrosyne	5	R. Migliore	110	Our Captain Willie	115	Naskra's Breeze	115	33,300	2:18.40	
1981	Ghazwan	4	C. Hernandez	110	Wicked Will	108	Hunston	107	33,540	2:20.60	
1982	Half Iced	3	D. MacBeth	114	No Neck	109	Erin's Tiger	113	33,330	2:18.20	
1982	If Winter Comes	4	M. Venezia	108	Ten Below	113	Forkali	112	33,330	2:19.60	
1983	Four Bases	4	R.J. Thibeau	105	Moon Spirit	114	Ask Me	117	34,230	2:17.80	
1983	Piling	5	E. Maple	114	Chem	116	Charging Through	110	34,470	2:19.00	
1984	He's Vivacious	4	R.G. Davis	109	Nassipour	109	Lucky Scott	107	46,440	2:26.00	
1985	Putting Green	5	E. Maple	112	Domynsky	105	Capricorn Son	109	54,405	2:23.80	
1985	Rocanadour II	6	J. Cruguet	112	Sondrio	115	He's Vivacious	111	54,405	2:23.80	
1986	Duluth	4	J. Cruguet	113	Dance of Life	122	Broadway Tommy	109	55,710	2:20.80	
1987	Laser Lane	4	J.A. Santos	113	Yankee Affair	116	Wanderkin	112	73,260	1:51.60	
1988	Jimmy's Bronco	4	J. Cruguet	112	Coeur de Lion	118	Gai Minois	113	58,590	1:54.80	
1989	Trans Banner	4	J.L. Samyn	112	Soviet Lad	112	Impersonator	114	58,770	1:53.60	
1990	Who's to Pay	4	J.D. Bailey	115	Yankee Affair	120	Gr'n L'ne Express	121	57,240	1:49.20	106
1991	Home of the Free	3	J.R. Velazquez	109	Turkey Point	114	Fourstars Allstar	113	56,070	1:48.60	101
1992	Binary Light	3	J. Cruguet	111	Share the Glory	110	Turkey Point	113	56,160	1:52.60	94
1993	River Majesty	4	M.E. Smith	115	Daarik	114	Home of the Free	118	52,920	1:54.40	98
1994	Kiri's Clown	5	Luzzi MJ	114	River Majesty	117	Red Earth	111	52,335	1:49.20	105
1995	Diplomatic Jet	3	M.E. Smith	113	Flag Down	114	Easy Miner	109	87,870	2:04.80	107
1996	Mr. Bluebird	5	M.E. Smith	113	Devil's Cup	107	Ops Smile	116	69,660	1:49.20	105
1997	Sir Cat	4	M.E. Smith	116	Tahmid	116	Outta My Way Man	115	69,060	1:50.00	96
1998	Sahm	4	J.R. Velazquez	116	Glok	113	Let Goodtimes Roll	112	67,440	1:48.60	104
1999	Charge d'Affaires	4	J.A. Santos	114	Comic Strip	119	Nat's Big Party	113	66,480	1:49.00	100
2000	Charge d'Affaires	5	J.A. Santos	115	Devine Wind	116	Understood	111	90,000	1:49.01	103
2001	Sumitas	5	E.S. Prado	115	Manndar	116	Crash Course	115	90,000	2:02.55	103
2002	Dawn of the Condor	5	J.F. Chavez	114	Serial Bride	114	Polish Miner	114	90,000	1:52.54	98
2003	Better Talk Now	4	E.S. Prado	116	Del Mar Show	116	Millennium Dragon	115	90,000	1:50.53	101

Beyer Index: 101.5

LA CANADA, 1 1/8 Miles,
4-Year-Old Fillies, Santa Anita, 2003 Purse: $200,000

Year	Winner	Age	Jockey	Wt.	Second	Wt.	Third	Wt.	Win Value	Time	Beyer
1975	Chris Evert	4	J. Velasquez	128	Mercy Dee	116	Lucky Spell	119	35,400	1:41.60	
1976	Raise Your Skirts	4	W. Shoemaker	119	Fascinating Girl	117	Our First Delight	117	50,150	1:48.40	
1977	Lucie Manet	4	W. Shoemaker	115	Hail Hilarious	121	Up to Juliet	116	68,300	1:48.20	
1978	Taisez Vous	4	D. Pierce	120	Drama Critic	116	Table the Rumor	117	65,000	1:49.80	
1979	B. Thoughtful	4	D. Pierce	117	Petron's Love	117	Island Kiss	115	69,900	1:48.80	
1980	Glorious Song	4	C.J. McCarron	118	Prize Spot	119	It's in the Air	125	80,350	1:47.60	
1981	Summer Siren	4	M. Castaneda	117	Miss Huntington	116	Tobin's Rose	118	86,250	1:48.60	
1982	Safe Play	4	D. Brumfield	119	Rainbow Connection	116	Native Plunder	117	100,800	1:47.60	
1983	Avigaition	4	E. Delahoussaye	117	Elusive	115	Etoile du Matin	116	101,900	1:49.80	
1984	Sweet Diane	4	R. Sibille	120	Weekend Surprise	115	Lovlier Linda	120	117,200	1:49.20	

Year	Winner	Age	Jockey	Wt.	Second	Wt.	Third	Wt.	Win Value	Time	Beyer
1985	Mitterand	4	E. Delahoussaye	121	Percipient	117	Life's Magic	126	90,700	1:48.80	
1986	Lady's Secret	4	C.J. McCarron	126	Shywing	119	North Sider	118	120,200	1:49.80	
1987	Family Style	4	G.L. Stevens	122	Winter Treasure	117	Sari's Heroine	121	94,800	1:49.60	
1988	Hollywood Glitter	4	L. Pincay Jr	117	By Land By Sea	119	Very Subtle	126	94,200	1:49.20	
1989	Goodbye Halo	4	P. Day	126	Seattle Smooth	117	Savannah's Honor	115	125,300	1:54.40	
1990	Gorgeous	4	E. Delahoussaye	125	Luthier's Launch	117	Kelly	116	122,000	1:50.00	105
1991	Fit to Scout	4	J.A. Garcia	120	Vieille Vigne	116	A Wild Ride	121	126,700	1:48.40	
1992	Exchange	4	L. Pincay Jr	119	Winglet	117	Damewood	116	128,250	1:49.80	95
1993	Alysbelle	4	E. Delahoussaye	116	Pacific Squall	119	Interactive	117	130,850	1:48.80	100
1994	Stalcreek	4	G.L. Stevens	119	Alyshena	115	Hollywood Wildcat	122	120,000	1:48.80	96
1995	Dianes Halo	4	C.S. Nakatani	115	Twice the Vice	119	Klassy Kim	119	123,000	1:49.20	93
1996	Jewel Princess	4	A. Solis	119	Dixie Pearl	116	Privity	117	129,900	1:49.40	98
1997	Belle's Flag	4	C.S. Nakatani	119	Chile Chatte	115	Housa Dancer	115	133,200	1:48.20	105
1998	Fleet Lady	4	G.K. Gomez	119	Minister's Melody	117	I Ain't Bluffing	117	120,000	1:48.40	103
1999	Manistique	4	G.L. Stevens	119	Magical Allure	119	Gourmet Girl	117	120,000	1:48.80	107
2000	Scholars Studio	4	C.S. Nakatani	116	Smooth Player	117	The Seven Seas	116	120,000	1:49.14	104
2001	Spain	4	V. Espinoza	122	Chilukki	119	Letter Of Intent	116	120,000	1:49.74	92
2002	Summer Colony	4	G.L. Stevens	119	Azeri	115	Ask Me No Secrets	115	120,000	1:49.26	105
2003	Got Koko	4	A. Solis	121	Sightseek	118	Bella Bellucci	118	120,000	1:48.41	106

Beyer Index: 100.69

LA PREVOYANTE HANDICAP, 1 1/2 Miles (Turf),
Fillies and Mares, 3-Year-Olds and Up, Calder Race Course, 2003 Purse: $200,000

Year	Winner	Age	Jockey	Wt.	Second	Wt.	Third	Wt.	Win Value	Time	Beyer
1976	Forty Nine Sunsets	3	C. Marquez	116	Cycylya Zee	121	Satan's Cheer	116	27,510	1:46.00	
1976	Redundancy	5	A. Haldar	117	Katonka	125	Yes Dear Maggy	121	26,040	1:41.60	
1978	Len's Determined	4	A. Smith Jr	114	Regal Gal	120	Carolina Moon	114	38,400	1:48.40	
1979	Unreality	5	J.D. Bailey	119	Excitable	117	Sans Arc	117	37,200	1:48.20	
1980	Impetuous Gal	5	E. Fires	113	Tangerine Doll	118	Highland Gypsy	116	23,775	1:52.20	
1980	Jolie Dutch	4	B. Thornburg	116	Reina del Rulo	116	Behave Taurian	108	23,925	1:54.60	
1981	Mairzy Doates	5	O.B. Aviles	121	Champagne Ginny	118	Knightly Noble	110	41,670	1:47.20	
1981	Deuces Over Seven	4	G. Gallitano	114	Little Bounty	121	Quick as Lightning	119	40,950	1:48.00	
1982	Judgable Gypsy	4	J. O'Driscoll	114	Castle Royale	110	Imayrrahtoo	110	42,165	1:50.20	
1982	Just a Game II	6	A. Cordero Jr	123	Sweetest Chant	115	Irish Joy	114	41,655	1:50.40	
1983	London Lil	4	A. Smith Jr	117	Betty Money	116	Dana Calqui	114	54,680	1:47.40	
1983	Fact Finder	4	A. Cordero Jr	115	Sunny Sparkler	122	Seaholme	112	54,380	1:48.00	
1983	Canaille II	5	A. Cordero Jr	118	Castle Royale	115	Genuine Diamond	113	54,380	1:46.60	
1984	Bolt From the Blue	4	J.L. Samyn	113	Bezique	112	Gabfest	110	51,960	2:33.40	
1984	Sabin	4	E. Maple	120	Grunip	113	Pat's Joy	118	52,260	2:32.80	
1985	Persian Tiara	4	J. Terry	120	Dictina	117	Silver in Flight	115	85,335	2:28.80	
1985	Sabin	5	D. Brumfield	126	Key Dancer	118	Burst of Colors	117	72,285	2:27.40	
1986	Powder Break	5	J.A. Santos	116	Shocker T.	119	Devalois	118	120,000	2:30.40	
1987	Lotka	4	E. Maple	121	Bonne Ile	116	After Party	112	120,000	2:36.00	
1988	Singular Bequest	5	E. Fires	115	Autumn Glitter	114	Green Oasis	114	120,000	2:25.20	
1989	Judy's Red Shoes	6	D. Valiente	120	Gaily Gaily	111	Beauty Cream	118	90,000	2:26.40	
1990	Yestday's Kisses	4	W.H. McCauley	113	Black Tulip	115	Coolawin	116	60,000	2:30.80	98
1991	Rigamajig	4	J.F. Chavez	114	Roseate Tern	117	Ahead	112	60,000	2:26.00	
1992	Sardaniya	4	J. Cruguet	113	Flaming Torch	112	Expensiveness	111	90,000	2:29.60	99
1993	Lemhi Go	5	M.A. Gonzalez	112	Indian Chris	112	Silvered	118	60,000	2:37.40	90
1994	Trampoli	4	M.E. Smith	120	Putthepowdertoit	115	Adoryphar	112	90,000	2:28.00	103
1994	Abigailthewife	5	J.A. Santos	114	Trampoli	118	Market Booster	118	90,000	2:28.80	102
1995	Interim	4	C.S. Nakatani	116	Northern Emerald	116	Caromana	114	90,000	2:26.20	100
1996	Ampulla	5	S.J. Sellers	122	Miss Caerleona	115	eclectic Society	117	90,000	2:27.40	104
1997	Last Approach	6	J.A. Krone	110	Flying Concert	118	Grey Way	110	90,000	2:39.00	88
1998	Coretta	4	J.A. Santos	117	Starry Dreamer	114	(DH) Tedarshana	113	90,000	2:26.60	101
1999	Coretta	5	J.A. Santos	120	Idle Rich	116	St. Bernadette	114	90,000	2:27.20	97
2000	Prospectress	4	J.D. Bailey	114	Innuendo	114	Orange Sunset	114	90,000	2:26.97	99
2001	Krisada	5	P. Day	115	Sweetest Thing	115	Great Fever	113	90,000	2:26.63	99
2002	New Economy	4	R.B. Homeister Jr.	113	Jennasietta	112	Tweedside	114	120,000	2:28.55	96
2003	Volga	5	R. Migliore	119	Lady Annaliese	116	Lost Appeal	115	120,000	2:26.13	98

Beyer Index: 98.14

LADY'S SECRET BREEDERS' CUP HANDICAP, 1 1/16 Miles,
Fillies and Mares, 3-Year-Olds and Up, Santa Anita, 2003 Purse: $300,000

Year	Winner	Age	Jockey	Wt.	Second	Wt.	Third	Wt.	Win Value	Time	Beyer
1993	Hollywood Wildcat	3	E. Delahoussaye	117	Re Toss	117	Wedding Ring	113	61,700	1:41.00	106
1995	Borodislew	5	G.L. Stevens	120	Top Rung	116	Golden Klair	117	74,000	1:41.60	109
1996	Top Rung	5	E. Fires	116	Jewel Princess	122	Sleep Easy	116	109,450	1:41.80	107
1997	Sharp Cat	3	A. Solis	117	Twice The Vice	122	Minister's Melody	115	109,400	1:41.40	111
1998	Magical Allure	3	D.R. Flores	116	Victory Stripes	114	Housa Dancer	117	110,280	1:42.40	103
1999	Manistique	4	C.S. Nakatani	123	Cookin Vickie	111	Kalosca	114	125,100	1:42.20	103

Year	Winner	Age	Jockey	Wt.	Second	Wt.	Third	Wt.	Win Value	Time	Beyer
2000	Smooth Player	4	E. Delahoussaye	116	Speaking of Time	109	Bordelaise	116	126,360	1:42.27	99
2001	Queenie Belle	4	B. Blanc	116	Letter of Intent	116	Nany's Sweep	116	126,240	1:43.64	96
2002	Azeri	4	M.E. Smith	127	Starrer	115	Mystic Lady	116	130,500	1:41.10	102
2003	Got Koko	4	A. Solis	118	Azeri	128	Adoration	115	180,000	1:42.92	105

Elloluv finished second but was disqualified and placed fourth

Beyer Index: **104.1**

LAKE PLACID HANDICAP, 1 1/8 Miles (Turf),
3-Year-Old Fillies, Saratoga Race Course, 2003 Purse: $150,000

Year	Winner	Age	Jockey	Wt.	Second	Wt.	Third	Wt.	Win Value	Time	Beyer
1986	An Empress	3	J.A. Santos	121	Fama	114	Spring Innocence	114	52,200	1:42.00	
1987	Graceful Darby	3	J.D. Bailey	116	Spectacular Bev	114	Token Gift	114	50,760	1:41.40	
1988	Betty Lobelia	3	J.A. Santos	116	Curlew	114	Tunita	114	66,780	1:41.60	
1988	Love You by Heart	3	R.P. Romero	114	Another Paddock	116	Flashy Runner	114	66,780	1:41.80	
1989	Capades	3	A. Cordero Jr	121	To the Lighthouse	116	Vanities	114	55,620	1:41.00	
1990	Jefforee	3	J.A. Santos	114	Toffeefee	114	Colonial Runner	114	60,030	1:49.00	99
1991	Jinski's World	3	J.A. Santos	121	Belleofbasinstreet	114	Verbasle	114	59,760	1:41.00	91
1991	Grab the Green	3	A. Cordero Jr	114	Shareefa	121	Irish Linnet	114	59,280	1:40.20	98
1992	Shannkara	3	M.E. Smith	114	Tiney Toast	116	Favored Lady	114	73,380	1:41.80	90
1992	Heed	3	M.E. Smith	114	Captive Miss	114	Mystic Hawk	114	72,420	1:40.80	91
1993	Amal Hayati	3	J.D. Bailey	121	Eloquent Silver	114	Irving's Girl	114	56,940	1:40.80	95
1993	Statuette	3	M.E. Smith	114	Icy Warning	114	Dispute	118	55,980	1:41.40	88
1994	Coronation Cup	3	J.D. Bailey	114	Stretch Drive	114	Golden Tajniak	118	65,760	1:43.80	102
1994	Alywow	3	M.E. Smith	121	Irish Forever	121	Knocknock	114	66,660	1:43.80	102
1995	Class Kris	3	P. Day	112	In a Daydream	112	Shocking Pleasure	113	67,380	1:40.80	102
1995	Bail Out Becky	3	Sellers SJ	115	Fashion Star	112	Grand Charmer	120	67,680	1:41.80	96
1996	Memories of Silver	3	J.D. Bailey	115	Unify	113	Henlopen	112	68,640	1:47.80	106
1997	Witchful Thinkin	3	S.J. Sellers	123	Miss Huff n' Puff	114	Majestic Sunlight	114	90,000	1:47.60	96
1998	Tenski	3	R. Migliore	119	Naskra's de Light	117	Caveat Competor	118	90,000	1:46.20	102
1999	Badouizm	3	R.G. Davis	113	Confessional	115	Emanating	115	90,000	1:46.40	93
2000	Gaviola	3	J.D. Bailey	122	Good Game	117	Millie's Quest	117	90,000	1:48.04	96
2001	Snow Dance	3	R. Migliore	116	Wander Mom	116	Mystic Lady	117	90,000	1:47.42	95
2002	Wonder Again	3	E.S. Prado	114	Riskaverse	120	Miss Marcia	114	90,000	1:49.24	97
2003	Sand Springs	3	M. Guidry	121	Indy Five Hundred	114	Film Maker	119	90,000	1:49.03	93

Beyer Index: **96.47**

Run as Nijana prior to 1998

LANE'S END, 1 1/8 Miles,
3-Year-Olds, Turfway Park, 2003 Purse: $500,000

Year	Winner	Age	Jockey	Wt.	Second	Wt.	Third	Wt.	Win Value	Time	Beyer
1972	Big Dot	3	J. Murchison	109	Tiz Tiz Lou	111	G'sF'rwr'd Thr'st	114	7,125	1:38.80	
1973	Jacks Chevron	3	B. Phelps	117	Trip Stop	116	Mr. Champ	116	9,785	1:42.00	
1973	Bootlegger's Pet	3	M. Solomone	116	Out Ahead	117	Babington's Image	113	9,720	1:41.00	
1974	King of Rome	3	K. Wirth	112	Consigliori	112	Aroyoport	116	12,204	1:44.60	
1974	Aglorite	3	J. Beech Jr	119	Joint Agreement	114	Robard	112	12,236	1:45.40	
1975	Naughty Jake	3	G. Vasquez	119	Promenade Left	114	Jim Dan Bob	112	15,840	1:40.00	
1975	Ambassador's Image	3	E. Snell	122	Clarence Henry	116	Upper Need	116	15,870	1:38.40	
1976	Inca Rosa	3	W. Nemeti	122	Here Comes Jo	116	Brentwood Prince	116	18,780	1:37.40	
1977	Smiley's Dream	3	W. DeStefano	114	Lighten the Load	111	Vestry's Best	111	12,788	1:39.40	
1977	Bob's Dusty	3	J.C. Espinoza	122	A Letter to Harry	116	John Washington	116	12,818	1:38.80	
1978	Five Star General	3	J.C. Espinoza	113	As in Elbow	113	Doc's Rock	119	12,900	1:37.80	
1978	Raymond Earl	3	J.C. Espinoza	113	Washington County	119	Shake Rattle'n Fly	113	12,960	1:38.80	
1979	Lot o' Gold	3	D. Brumfield	122	Julie's Dancer	113	Will Henry	113	29,030	1:37.60	
1980	Major Run	3	M.S. Sellers	119	Ray's Word	122	Misty Bell	113	18,740	1:37.60	
1980	Spruce Needles	3	J.C. Espinoza	119	Avenger M.	122	Summer Advocate	113	18,441	1:36.20	
1981	Mythical Ruler	3	K.B. Wirth	114	Classic Go Go	122	Iron Gem	115	36,460	1:38.00	
1982	Good n' Dusty	3	M.T. Moran	120	Fast Gold	120	Cupecoy's Joy	115	125,450	1:44.60	
1983	Marfa	3	J. Velasquez	120	Noble Home	120	Hail to Rome	120	151,515	1:42.40	
1984	At the Threshold	3	P. Day	121	Bold Southerner	121	The Wedding Guest	121	195,000	1:42.80	
1985	Banner Bob	3	K.K. Allen	121	Image of Greatness	121	Roo Art	121	227,500	1:42.00	
1986	Broad Brush	3	V. Bracciale Jr	121	Miracle Wood	121	Bachelor Beau	121	210,000	1:44.20	
1987	J.T.'s Pet	3	P. Day	121	Faster Than Sound	121	Homebuilder	121	300,000	1:42.80	
1988	Kingpost	3	E.J. Sipus	121	Stalwars	121	Brian's Time	121	300,000	1:50.80	
1989	Western Playboy	3	P. Day	121	Feather Ridge	121	Mercedes Won	121	300,000	1:49.00	
1990	Summer Squall	3	P. Day	121	Bright Again	121	Yonder	121	300,000	1:49.40	
1991	Hansel	3	J.D. Bailey	121	Ruchman	121	Wilder Than Ever	121	300,000	1:46.60	105
1992	Lil E. Tee	3	P. Day	121	Vying Victor	121	Treekster	121	300,000	1:53.40	95
1993	Prairie Bayou	3	C.J. McCarron	121	Proudest Romeo	121	Miner's Mark	121	360,000	1:50.80	98
1994	Polar Expedition	3	C.C. Bourque	121	Powis Castle	121	Chimes Band	121	360,000	1:49.00	103
1995	Serena's Song	3	C.S. Nakatani	116	Tejano Run	121	Mecke	121	360,000	1:49.60	114
1996	Roar	3	M.E. Smith	121	Ensign Ray	121	Victory Speech	121	360,000	1:49.60	95

Year	Winner	Age	Jockey	Wt.	Second	Wt.	Third	Wt.	Win Value	Time	Beyer
1997	Concerto	3	C.H. Marquez Jr.	121	Jack Flash	121	Shammy Davis	121	360,000	1:48.20	102
1998	Event of the Year	3	R.A. Baze	121	Yarrow Brae	121	Truluck	121	360,000	1:47.00	114
1999	Stephen Got Even	3	S.J. Sellers	121	K One King	121	Epic Honor	121	450,000	1:49.00	104
2000	Globalize	3	F.C. Torres	121	Elite Mercedes	121	Rollin With Nolan	121	360,000	1:49.16	97
2001	Balto Star	3	M. Guidry	121	Halo's Stride	121	Mongoose	121	360,000	1:47.23	112
2002	Perfect Drift	3	E. Delahoussaye	121	Azillion	121	Request for Parole	121	300,000	1:48.83	102
2003	New York Hero	3	N. Arroyo Jr	121	Eugene's Third Son	121	Champali	121	300,000	1:50.68	96

Beyer Index: 102.85

LAS PALMAS HANDICAP, 1 1/8 Miles (Turf), Fillies and Mares, 3-Year-Olds and Up, Santa Anita, 2002 Purse: $200,000

Year	Winner	Age	Jockey	Wt.	Second	Wt.	Third	Wt.	Win Value	Time	Beyer
1969	Manta	3	R. Rosales	116	Commisary	119	Miss Ribot	122	26,850	1:41.80	
1970	Manta	4	R. Rosales	125	Beja	119	Thoroly Blue	115	19,350	1:46.60	
1971	Typecast	5	W. Shoemaker	126	Hail the Grey	116	Aladancer	119	19,150	1:49.80	
1972	Resoutely	5	J. Lambert	115	Pallisima	123	Cruz de Roble	117	24,550	1:47.80	
1973	Minstrel Miss	6	D. Pierce	123	Cruz de Roble	113	Veiled Desire	111	27,100	1:47.80	
1974	Lucky Spell	3	J. Tejeira	117	Bold Ballet	117	Fresh Pepper	112	26,750	1:47.40	
1975	Charger's Star	5	W. Shoemaker	116	Tizna	126	Hinterland	116	26,000	1:47.20	
1976	Vagabonda	5	O. Vergara	118	Bastonera II	122	Accra II	115	34,500	1:48.60	
1977	Swingtime	5	F. Toro	119	Theia	113	Summertime Promise	118	25,650	1:47.20	
1978	Grenzen	3	L. Pincay Jr	119	Country Queen	119	Drama Critic	123	39,400	1:48.40	
1979	High Pheasant	4	F. Olivares	114	Prize Spot	119	Axe Me Dear	114	39,700	1:54.00	
1980	Ack's Secret	4	P.A. Valenzuela	114	A Thousand Stars	119	Princess Toby	117	40,400	1:46.00	
1981	Ack's Secret	5	D.G. McHargue	119	Queen to Conquer	123	Berry Bush	118	50,500	1:47.00	
1982	Berry Bush	5	M. Castaneda	115	Satin Ribera	115	Northern Fable	115	70,400	1:47.40	
1983	Castilla	4	C.J. McCarron	121	Night Fire	113	Berry Bush	117	64,300	1:49.20	
1984	Fenny Rough	4	K. Black	117	Comedy Act	117	Pride of Rosewood	115	78,800	1:47.40	
1985	Estrapade	5	W. Shoemaker	124	L'Attrayante	118	Johnica	118	69,100	1:47.20	
1986	Outstandingly	4	G.L. Stevens	118	Shywing	118	Justicara	118	63,400	1:47.60	
1987	Autumn Glitter	4	P. Day	116	Galunpe	119	Festivity	117	91,800	1:50.40	
1988	Annoconnor	4	C.A. Black	120	No Review	114	Goodbye Halo	120	97,800	1:47.00	
1989	Nikishka	4	E. Delahoussaye	116	No Review	117	Agirlfromars	111	96,800	1:46.60	
1990	Little Brianne	5	J.A. Garcia	115	Double Wedge	117	Reluctant Guest	121	93,200	1:46.80	103
1991	Kostroma	5	K.J. Desormeaux	117	Kikala	113	Campagnarde	118	80,750	1:43.80	105
1992	Super Staff	4	K.J. Desormeaux	116	Flawlessly	124	Re Toss	115	77,750	1:46.80	106
1993	Miatuschka	5	C.A. Black	114	Skimble	115	Potridee	115	62,600	1:47.80	99
1994	Aube Indienne	4	K.J. Desormeaux	115	Queens Court Queen	115	Skimble	116	61,300	1:49.60	101
1995	Onceinabluemamoon	4	B. Blanc	116	Yearly Tour	117	Don't Read My Lips	117	76,400	1:50.20	103
1996	Wandesta	5	C.S. Nakatani	120	Real Connection	113	Alpride	120	79,700	1:46.60	106
1997	Real Connection	6	G.F. Almeida	115	Toda Una Dama	114	Luna Wells	119	75,000	1:47.60	104
1998	Sonja's Faith	4	E. Ramsammy	115	See You Soon	116	Idealistic Cause	113	90,000	1:48.80	104
1999	Sapphire Ring	4	G.L. Stevens	118	Cyrillic	117	Country Garden	113	150,000	1:48.20	100
2000	Smooth Player	4	E. Delahoussaye	115	Beautiful Noise	115	Happyanunoit	121	150,000	1:46.99	97
2001	Golden Apples	3	G.K. Gomez	115	Dancingonice	113	Janet	120	150,000	1:46.61	105
2002	Tates Creek	4	J.D. Bailey	120	Voodoo Dancer	121	Magic Mission	113	120,000	1:47.69	102

Beyer Index: 102.69

Not run in 2003.

MERVYN LeROY HANDICAP, 1 1/16 Miles, 3-Year-Olds and Up, Hollywood Park, 2003 Purse: $150,000

Year	Winner	Age	Jockey	Wt.	Second	Wt.	Third	Wt.	Win Value	Time	Beyer
1980	Spectacular Bid	4	W. Shoemaker	132	Peregrinator	119	Beau's Eagle	121	120,400	1:40.40	
1981	Eleven Stitches	4	S. Hawley	115	Glorious Song	121	Summertime Guy	114	97,100	1:36.40	
1982	Mehmet	4	S. Hawley	116	A Run	112	Major Sport	114	63,100	1:34.60	
1983	Fighting Fit	4	W. Shoemaker	115	Island Whirl	122	Kang'roo Court	116	63,600	1:35.80	
1984	Sari's Dreamer	5	R.Q. Meza	112	Fighting Fit	120	Ancestral	115	95,000	1:34.20	
1985	Precisionist	4	C.J. McCarron	126	Greinton	121	My Habitony	115	118,700	1:32.80	
1986	Skywalker	4	L. Pincay Jr	117	Sabona	113	Al Mamoon	120	123,600	1:34.80	
1987	Zabaleta	4	L. Pincay Jr	117	Nostalgia's Star	116	Sabona	114	127,000	1:34.80	
1988	Judge Angelucci	5	E. Delahoussaye	123	Simply Majestic	118	Mark Chip	117	129,600	1:40.80	
1989	Ruhlmann	4	L. Pincay Jr	121	Sabona	114	Perfec Travel	115	122,800	1:40.20	
1990	Super May	4	R.G. Davis	116	Charlatan III	110	Lively One	122	121,600	1:40.80	
1991	Louis Cyphre	5	J.A. Santos	114	Warcraft	115	Anshan	116	110,600	1:40.80	110
1992	Another Review	4	K.J. Desormeaux	116	Sir Beaufort	116	Marquetry	119	86,300	1:41.20	110
1993	Marquetry	6	K.J. Desormeaux	117	Potrillon	117	Lottery Winner	115	92,800	1:49.00	110
1994	Del Mar Dennis	4	S. Gonzales Jr	115	Tinners Way	114	Hill Pass	115	93,300	1:40.40	108
1995	Tossofthecoin	5	C.S. Nakatani	118	Ferrara	114	Polar Route	116	64,600	1:40.60	107
1996	Siphon	5	D.R. Flores	117	Del Mar Dennis	119	Dramatic Gold	117	61,500	1:40.60	116
1997	Hesabull	4	G. F. Alameida	116	Region	112	Kingdom Found	116	63,720	1:41.20	108

Year	Winner	Age	Jockey	Wt.	Second	Wt.	Third	Wt.	Win Value	Time	Beyer
1998	Wild Wonder	4	E. Delahoussaye	116	Budroyale	116	Flick	117	64,320	1:40.80	113
1999	Budroyale	6	G.K. Gomez	118	Moore's Flat	107	Wild Wonder	120	90,000	1:42.00	111
2000	Out of Mind	5	E. Delahoussaye	116	Early Pioneer	116	Skimming	111	90,000	1:41.82	112
2001	Futural	5	C.J. McCarron	117	Skimming	119	Moonlight Charger	114	90,000	1:42.02	108
2002	Sky Jack	6	L. Pincay Jr.	117	Bosque Redondo	117	Devine Wind	114	90,000	1:41.36	115
2003	Total Impact	5	M.E. Smith	114	Fleetstreet Dancer	114	Piensa Sonando	115	90,000	1:40.88	110

Beyer Index: 110.62

(COOLMORE) LEXINGTON, 1 1/16 Miles,
3-Year-Olds, Keeneland Race Course, 2003 Purse: $363,675

Year	Winner	Age	Jockey	Wt.	Second	Wt.	Third	Wt.	Win Value	Time	Beyer
1984	He Is a Great Deal	3	J.C. Espinoza	111	Swale	123	Timely Advocate	112	34,450	1:45.40	
1985	Stephan's Odyssey	3	L. Pincay Jr	118	Tajawa	112	Northern Bid	112	34,775	1:42.60	
1986	Wise Times	3	K.K. Allen	112	Country Light	115	Momentus	118	71,793	1:44.80	
1987	Risen Star	3	J. Vasquez	118	Forty Niner	121	Stalwars	118	68,673	1:46.00	
1989	Notation	3	P. Day	115	Bionic Prospect	114	Charlie Barley	118	71,663	1:44.40	
1990	Home at Last	3	J.D. Bailey	118	Pleasant Tap	115	Thirty Slews	116	73,385	1:43.40	104
1991	Hansel	3	J.D. Bailey	121	Shotgun Harry J.	115	Speedy Cure	118	86,743	1:42.60	105
1992	My Luck Runs North	3	R.D. Lopez	115	Lure	118	Agincourt	115	89,083	1:44.00	100
1993	Grand Jewel	3	J.D. Bailey	118	El Bakan	113	Truth of It All	118	87,219	1:43.60	91
1994	Southern Rhythm	3	G.K. Gomez	118	Soul of the Matter	118	Ulises	113	85,095	1:45.60	104
1995	Star Standard	3	P. Day	115	Royal Mitch	118	Guadalcanal	115	99,882	1:45.00	97
1996	City By Night	3	S.J. Sellers	113	Prince of Thieves	118	Roar	118	123,473	1:42.20	99
1997	Touch Gold	3	G.L. Stevens	115	Smoke Glacken	118	Deeds Not Words	112	116,963	1:43.20	106
1998	Classic Cat	3	R.J. Albarado	114	Voyamerican	114	Grand Slam	123	228,300	1:42.80	108
1999	Charismatic	3	J.D. Bailey	115	Yankee Victor	115	Finder's Fee	115	234,794	1:41.00	108
2000	Unshaded	3	S.J. Sellers	116	Globalize	120	Harlan Traveler	116	221,588	1:43.72	99
2001	Keats	3	L. Melancon	116	Griffinite	116	Bay Eagle	116	230,315	1:43.54	110
2002	Proud Citizen	3	M.E. Smith	116	Crimson Hero	116	Easyfromthegitgo	116	226,083	1:44.58	95
2003	Scrimshaw	3	E.S. Prado	116	Eye of the Tiger	116	Domestic Dispute	116	225,479	1:45.47	101

Beyer Index: 101.93

LONG ISLAND HANDICAP, 1 1/2 Miles (Turf),
Fillies and Mares, 3-Year-Olds and Up, Aqueduct, 2003 Purse: $150,000

Year	Winner	Age	Jockey	Wt.	Second	Wt.	Third	Wt.	Win Value	Time	Beyer
1956	Third Brother	3	I. Valenzuela	120	Beau Diable	114	Thinking Cap	123	19,300	2:44.00	
1957	Promethean	3	J. Ruane	106	Cavort	117	Beam Rider	114	20,200	2:44.00	
1958	Beau Diable	5	H. Woodhouse	124	Casual Friend	117	Whatit'dyou	122	18,192	2:43.00	
1959	Tudor Era	6	W. Hartack	126	Sailor's Guide	124	Anisado	114	14,227	1:54.00	
1959	One-Eyed King	5	W. Shoemaker	121	Tharp	120	Find	116	14,227	1:54.40	
1960	El Espectador	5	B. Baeza	117	General Arthur	120	Quiz Star	118	19,135	2:16.60	
1961	Wise Ship	4	H. Gustines	115	Wolfram	126	Eurasia	115	18,525	1:58.80	
1962	The Axe II	4	W. Shoemaker	117	T.V. Lark	124	Shield Bearer	118	14,609	2:15.60	
1962	Irish Dandy	4	J. Ruane	109	Royal Record	117	Djezzar	110	13,959	2:15.80	
1963	David K.	4	W. Shoemaker	113	The Axe II	126	Never Bend	120	19,142	1:54.80	
1964	Parka	6	W. Blum	123	Cedar Key	126	Will I Rule	112	18,492	1:54.60	
1965	Parka	7	W. Blum	125	Or et Argent	116	Polar Sea	120	19,207	1:54.60	
1966	Paoluccio	4	H. Gustines	115	Gallup Poll	110	Mostar	107	14,982	1:58.60	
1966	Rego	3	H. Woodhouse	109	Pluck	113	Dunderhead	104	15,145	1:59.20	
1967	Munden Point	5	R. Ussery	117	Royal Comedian	109	Isokeha	112	15,177	1:54.80	
1967	Assagai	4	B. Baeza	126	Fast Count	109	Kentucky Kin	113	15,177	1:54.80	
1968	Ruth's Rullah	3	A. Cordero Jr	112	Ruffled Feathers	118	Czar Alexander	115	15,242	2:14.80	
1968	Flit-to	5	M. Ycaza	115	Tobin Bronze	118	Advocator	120	15,080	2:15.20	
1969	The University	4	A. Cordero Jr	113	Vent du Nord	113	North Flight	118	14,917	2:17.20	
1969	Red Reality	3	J. Velasquez	113	Rhinelander II	113	Tradesman	112	15,080	2:16.80	
1970	Larceny Kid	4	C. Baltazar	112	Bailer	119	Mongolia	114	14,901	2:02.00	
1970	Mongo's Pride	3	C.H. Marquez	113	Shelter Bay	122	Pl't Harbour	116	14,739	2:01.20	
1971	Rudo Bird	3	J. Velasquez	109	Red Reality	116	Bark'g St'ple	107	21,210	2:03.20	
1972	Primsie	3	L. Pincay Jr	114	Candid Catherine	114	Roba Bella	123	14,040	1:37.80	
1972	Twixt	5	R. Woodhouse	112	Table Flirt	116	Bold Place	114	13,965	1:39.20	
1973	Tuerta	3	J. Vasquez	116	North of Venus	117	Spring in the Air	118	17,850	1:43.80	
1974	D.O. Lady	3	M.A. Rivera	115	Speak Action	113	Gulls Cry	116	28,080	1:43.20	
1974	Lie Low	3	J. Velasquez	114	Victorian Queen	120	Markimoff	115	28,080	1:42.00	
1975	Slip Screen	3	G. Intellisano	115	Fleet Victress	115	Jabot	115	33,930	1:42.80	
1976	Javamine	3	J. Velasquez	113	Nijana	115	Fun Forever	112	33,270	1:41.60	
1977	Pearl Necklace	3	R. Hernandez	123	Javamine	121	Leave Me Alone	113	32,430	1:43.80	
1978	Terpsichorist	3	A. Cordero Jr	116	Leave Me Alone	109	Proud Event	113	48,555	2:34.00	
1979	Flitalong	3	R.I. Encinas	107	Terpsichorist	122	Catherine's Bet	114	52,245	2:31.40	
1980	The Very One	5	J. Velasquez	120	Relaxing	113	Proud Barbara	113	68,400	2:35.20	
1981	Euphrosyne	5	R. Migliore	110	Mairzy Doates	120	Noble Damsel	112	70,440	2:33.00	

Year	Winner	Age	Jockey	Wt.	Second	Wt.	Third	Wt.	Win Value	Time	Beyer
1982	Hush Dear	4	E. Beitia	111	Canaille II	112	Mintage	111	71,160	2:31.40	
1983	Hush Dear	5	J.L. Samyn	125	Mintage	111	If Winter Comes	113	70,920	2:34.60	
1984	Heron Cove	4	J. Cruguet	114	Key Dancer	115	Secret Sharer	110	109,650	2:32.80	
1985	Faburola	4	E. Legrix	114	Halloween Queen	107	Easy to Copy	114	105,675	2:29.40	
1985	Videogenic	3	J. Cruguet	116	Duty Dance	114	Mariella	110	92,175	2:29.20	
1986	Dismasted	4	J.L. Samyn	120	Dawn's Curtsey	113	Devalois	114	115,560	2:30.40	
1987	Stardusk	3	J. Cruguet	109	Spruce Fir	121	Videogenic	118	115,740	2:30.40	
1988	Dancing All Night	4	J.J. Vasquez	108	Casey	113	Gaily Gaily	111	112,320	2:34.20	
1989	Warfie	3	W.H. McCauley	111	River Memories	113	Noble Links	111	72,480	2:14.40	
1990	Rigamajig	4	J.F. Chavez	110	Narwala	115	Roberto's Hope	112	72,120	2:29.60	
1990	Peinture Bleue	3	J.A. Santos	115	Franc Argument	113	Roseate Tern	119	72,600	2:29.80	108
1991	Shaima	3	L.F. Dettori	115	Highland Penny	116	Franc Argument	111	73,560	2:31.40	101
1992	Villandry	4	M.E. Smith	115	Ratings	116	Gina Romantica	113	71,160	2:29.00	101
1993	Trampoli	4	M.E. Smith	119	Bright Generation	114	Northern Emerald	108	68,760	2:31.40	105
1994	Market Booster	5	M.J. Lukas	115	Tiffany's Taylor	114	Lady Affirmed	113	87,495	2:31.80	103
1995	Yenda	4	C.S. Nakatani	114	Windsharp	111	Market Booster	118	86,440	2:37.00	110
1996	Ampulla	5	S.J. Sellers	121	Wandering Star	118	Beyrouth	113	87,270	2:30.60	108
1997	Sweetzie	5	J.F. Chavez	115	Sweet Smoke	114	Scenic Point	120	90,000	2:16.60	85
1998	Coretta	4	J.A. Santos	114	Starry Dreamer	115	Dixie Ghost	114	60,000	2:29.60	105
1998	Yokama	5	J.D. Bailey	120	Moments of Magic	113	Bristol Channel	114	60,000	2:31.00	96
1999	Midnight Line	4	J.D. Bailey	120	Win For Us	116	Horatia	112	90,000	2:29.60	95
2000	Moonlady	3	C.P. DeCarlo	114	Playact	114	La Ville Rouge	118	90,000	2:17.94	96
2001	Queue	4	J.L. Espinoza	115	Sweetest Thing	115	Lady Dora	114	90,000	2:29.36	97
2002	Uriah	3	N. Arroyo Jr.	112	Sunstone	114	Mot Juste	119	90,000	2:42.48	100
2003	Spice Island	4	V. Carrero	117	Volga	120	Banyu Dewi	114	90,000	2:32.58	99

Beyer Index: 100.6

Run on main track in 1997, 2000 at 1 3/8 Miles

LOUISIANA DERBY, 1 1/16 Miles,
3-Year-Olds, Fair Grounds, 2003 Purse: $750,000

Year	Winner	Age	Jockey	Wt.	Second	Wt.	Third	Wt.	Win Value	Time	Beyer
1920	Damask	3	E. Ambrose	118	Bullet Proof	118	Bred Man	118	4,975	1:51.80	
1923	Amole	3	J.D. Mooney	118	Calcutta	122	Setting Sun	118	9,180	1:57.80	
1924	Black Gold	3	J.D. Mooney	126	Brilliant Cast	117	Rinkey	112	14,750	1:57.60	
1925	Quatrain	3	H. Stutts	126	Benedict Vow	114	Brave Bob	114	17,350	1:56.00	
1926	Baggenbaggage	3	E. Blind	116	Boot to Boot	112	Navigator	122	9,800	1:51.20	
1927	Boo	3	G. Johnson	114	Fred Jr.	122	Fly Hawk	122	14,250	1:51.80	
1928	Jack Higgins	3	C.E. Allen	118	Beauregard	118	Time Maker	118	15,450	1:52.00	
1929	Calf Roper	3	F. Coltiletti	117	Panchio	114	McGonigle	117	15,825	1:56.00	
1930	Michigan Boy	3	J. Shelton	117	Bad News Bob	117	Brother Rank	117	9,225	2:00.20	
1931	Spanish Play	3	C. Landolt	120	Prince d'Amour	120	Anne Arundel	107	7,475	1:51.20	
1932	Lucky Tom	3	A. Pascuma	120	Open Hearth	116	Prince Hotspur	116	9,375	1:53.60	
1933	Col. Hatfield	3	C. Meyer	116	Spicson	113	Gyro	113	4,750	1:56.40	
1934	Hickory Lad	3	J. Westrope	113	Cursor	113	Morning Cry	105	2,870	1:53.40	
1935	McCarthy	3	P. Keester	117	Dark Woman	106	Bulstrode	111	2,150	1:54.00	
1936	Rushaway	3	J. Longden	116	Lolschen	111	Professor Paul	119	3,900	1:50.80	
1937	Grey Count	3	C. Corbett	116	Dead Calm	114	Trina	114	7,730	1:50.80	
1938	Wise Fox	3	J. Longden	114	Bunny Baby	111	Sir Raleigh	116	9,510	1:51.20	
1939	Day Off	3	E. Arcaro	114	Alms	111	Patrol Scout	116	9,510	1:52.60	
1943	Amber Light	3	J. Longden	117	Ocean Wave	126	Pops Pick	116	10,750	1:52.60	
1944	Olympic Zenith	3	N. Jemas	117	Gay Bit	120	Weyanoke	120	11,525	1:54.00	
1946	Pellicle	3	A. LoTurco	117	Earshot	115	Kendor	120	11,675	1:52.80	
1947	Carolyn A.	3	R. Nash	118	Lady's Ace	108	Jobstown	117	15,700	1:57.80	
1948	Bovard	3	W. Saunders	111	Shy Guy	123	Riverlane	114	11,500	1:51.60	
1949	Rookwood	3	J. Delahoussaye	111	Petey Cotter	114	Great Shuffle	111	11,600	1:51.20	
1950	Greek Ship	3	C. Errico	123	Sunglow	111	Yogi	111	12,900	1:51.00	
1951	Whirling Bat	3	P. Anderson	111	Bulverde	111	Running Seas	111	15,900	1:53.40	
1952	Gushing Oil	3	A. Popara	111	Happy Go Lucky	111	Hiram Jr.	111	16,400	1:51.20	
1953	Matagorda	3	P.J. Bailey	111	Money Broker	111	Spy Defense	111	31,875	1:51.80	
1954	Gigantic	3	R. McLaughlin	111	Bobby Brocato	117	Red Hannigan	111	36,325	1:53.20	
1955	Roman Patrol	3	D. Dodson	123	Speed Rouser	111	Portersville	111	34,175	1:49.80	
1956	Reaping Right	3	R.L. Baird	111	Mr. Bob W.	111	Frosty Mr.	112	35,525	1:51.00	
1957	Federal Hill	3	W. Carstens	123	Shan Pac	114	Federal Judge	112	33,275	1:49.60	
1958	Royal Union	3	J. Heckmann	114	Noureddin	111	Ebony Pearl	111	34,850	1:52.00	
1959	Master Palynch	3	R. Broussard	115	Sputnik	114	Festival King	114	35,600	1:49.40	
1960	Tony Graff	3	W. Chambers	111	Yorktown	111	Lurullah	111	35,975	1:52.00	
1961	Bass Clef	3	R. Baldwin	111	Loyal Son	111	King of Kentucky	112	37,700	1:50.20	
1962	Admiral's Voyage	3	R. Broussard	121	Roman Line	125	Green Hornet	119	38,150	1:52.60	
1963	City Line	3	R.L. Baird	119	Lemon Twist	119	All Fool's Day	117	31,750	1:50.20	
1964	Grecian Princess	3	K. Broussard	116	Whit's Pride	117	I Owe	117	33,300	1:50.80	
1965	Dapper Delegate	3	J. Heckmann	121	Doctor Brocato	112	Flash Climber	115	33,900	1:50.20	
1966	Blue Skyer	3	R. Broussard	116	Stupendous	115	Williamston Kid	123	36,000	1:50.60	
1967	Ask the Fare	3	D. Holmes	115	Diplomat Way	126	Grand Premiere	120	36,550	1:50.00	
1968	Kentucky Sherry	3	J. Combest	118	Problem Solver	113	Port Digger	120	37,500	1:50.20	

Year	Winner	Age	Jockey	Wt.	Second	Wt.	Third	Wt.	Win Value	Time	Beyer
1969	King of the Castle	3	C.H. Marquez	115	Jay Ray	120	Walking Stick	113	35,700	1:52.40	
1970	Jim's Alibi	3	R. Baldwin	115	Elva's King	115	Herbalist	115	38,850	1:55.60	
1971	Northfields	3	W. Blum	118	List	115	Will Hays	115	38,550	1:50.20	
1972	No Le Hace	3	P. Rubbicco	120	Feloniously	117	Fame and Power	115	36,400	1:52.80	
1973	Leo's Pisces	3	R. Breen	115	Navajo	120	Angle Light	118	50,000	1:51.60	
1974	Sellout	3	M. Castaneda	118	Buck's Bid	115	Beau Groton	120	55,800	1:51.20	
1975	Master Derby	3	D.G. McHargue	123	Colonel Power	120	Honey Mark	118	61,000	1:49.60	
1976	Johnny Appleseed	3	M. Castaneda	118	Glassy Dip	113	Gay Jitterbug	118	61,000	1:49.80	
1977	Clev Er Tell	3	R. Broussard	120	Run Dusty Run	123	A Letter to Harry	115	61,000	1:48.80	
1978	Esops Foibles	3	C.J. McCarron	118	Quadratic	123	Battonier	120	79,750	1:50.80	
1979	Golden Act	3	S. Hawley	123	Rivalero	115	Incredible Ease	120	100,750	1:51.20	
1980	Prince Valiant	3	M.A. Gonzalez	115	Native Uproar	118	Brent's Trans Am	123	97,150	1:50.40	
1981	Woodchopper	3	J. Velasquez	113	A Run	123	Beau Rit	126	125,800	1:50.80	
1982	El Baba	3	D. Brumfield	123	Linkage	120	Spoonful of Honey	113	112,000	1:50.60	
1983	Balboa Native	3	J. Velasquez	118	Found Pearl Harbor	113	Slewpy	123	112,000	1:50.60	
1984	Taylor's Special	3	S. Maple	118	Silent King	123	Fight Over	123	112,000	1:49.60	
1985	Violado	3	J. Vasquez	115	Creme Fraiche	120	Irish Fighter	113	112,000	1:50.20	
1986	Country Light	3	P. Day	123	Bolshoi Boy	118	Lightning Touch	118	112,000	1:50.40	
1987	J.T.'s Pet	3	P. Day	115	Authentic Hero	118	Plumcake	115	70,260	1:51.00	
1988	Risen Star	3	S.P. Romero	120	Word Pirate	118	Pastourelles	118	98,520	1:43.20	
1989	Dispersal	3	J.A. Santos	118	Majesty's Imp	118	Dansil	123	100,560	1:43.80	
1990	Heaven Again	3	C.S. Nakatani	113	Big E.Z.	113	Very Formal	113	100,440	1:43.80	96
1991	Richman	3	P. Day	122	Near the Limit	114	Far Out Wadleigh	122	120,000	1:44.40	99
1992	Line in the Sand	3	P. Day	117	Hill Pass	117	Colony Light	112	120,000	1:43.40	93
1993	Dixieland Heat	3	R.P. Romero	117	Offshore Pirate	117	Tossofthecoin	115	180,000	1:44.80	93
1994	Kandaly	3	Perret C	118	Game Coin	118	Argolid	118	195,750	1:42.80	97
1995	Petionville	3	C.W. Antley	122	In Character	118	Moonlight Dancer	122	210,000	1:42.80	96
1996	Grindstone	3	J.D. Bailey	118	Zarb's Magic	122	Commander's Palace	118	222,000	1:42.60	102
1997	Crypto Star	3	P. Day	118	Stop Watch	118	Smoke Glacken	122	240,000	1:42.60	98
1998	Comic Strip	3	S.J. Sellers	122	Nite Dreamer	122	Captain Maestri	122	300,000	1:43.20	94
1999	Kimberlite Pipe	3	R.J. Albarado	122	Answer Lively	122	Ecton Park	122	384,000	1:43.29	105
2000	Mighty	3	S.J. Sellers	122	More Than Ready	122	Captain Steve	122	450,000	1:43.29	103
2001	Fifty Stars	3	D. Meche	122	Millennium Wind	122	Hero's Tribute	120	450,000	1:44.78	94
2002	Repent	3	J.D. Bailey	122	Easyfromthegitgo	122	It'sallinthechase	120	450,000	1:43.86	95
2003	Peace Rules	3	E.S. Prado	122	Kafwain	122	Funny Cide	122	450,000	1:42.67	105

Beyer Index: 97.86

LOUISVILLE BREEDERS' CUP HANDICAP, 1 1/16 Miles,
Fillies and Mares, 3-Year-Olds and Up, Churchill Downs, 2003 Purse: $325,500

Year	Winner	Age	Jockey	Wt.	Second	Wt.	Third	Wt.	Win Value	Time	Beyer
1986	Hopeful Word	5	P. Day	119	Little Missouri	116	Czar Nijinsky	121	99,808	1:49.40	
1987	Queen Alexandra	5	D. Brumfield	117	Infinidad	116	I'm Sweets	116	100,295	1:42.80	
1988	By Land by Sea	4	F. Toro	124	Bound	115	Bestofbothworlds	113	100,198	1:43.20	
1989	Darien Miss	4	P.A. Johnson	115	Savannah's Honor	119	Miss Barbour	109	100,750	1:46.00	
1990	Connie's Gift	4	P. Day	111	Affirmed Classic	115	Barbarika	115	100,425	1:45.80	94
1991	Fit for a Queen	5	J.D. Bailey	113	Crowned	115	Topsa	109	101,530	1:43.00	101
1992	Fowda	4	P.A. Valenzuela	117	Dance Colony	114	Fit for a Queen	120	100,750	1:44.00	97
1993	Quilma	6	J.A. Santos	113	Looie Capote	118	Hitch	113	37,570	1:44.60	103
1994	One Dreamer	6	G.L. Stevens	115	Kalita Melody	117	Added Asset	114	136,630	1:43.60	106
1995	Fit to Lead	5	K.J. Desormeaux	116	Jade Flush	115	Teewinot	109	138,125	1:43.40	99
1996	Jewel Princess	4	C.J. McCarron	122	Serena's Song	123	Naskra Colors	113	143,000	1:42.40	108
1997	Halo America	7	C.H. Borel	120	Escena	116	Rare Blend	116	138,012	1:42.60	110
1998	Escena	5	J.D. Bailey	119	One Rich Lady	113	Three Fanfares	109	178,405	1:44.80	104
1999	Silent Eskimo	4	C.H. Borel	113	Lu Ravi	118	Leo's Gypsy Dancer	112	169,415	1:43.80	102
2000	Heritage of Gold	5	S.J. Sellers	119	Roza Robata	112	Bella Chiarra	116	170,655	1:42.99	106
2001	Saudi Poetry	4	V. Espinoza	112	Royal Fair	113	Dreams Gallore	114	172,980	1:42.53	96
2002	Spain	5	J.D. Bailey	118	Mystic Lady	118	De Bertie	115	207,204	1:43.93	102
2003	You	4	J.D. Bailey	118	Fly Borboleta	111	Seven Four Seven	113	201,810	1:43.21	90

Beyer Index: 101.29

MAKER'S MARK MILE, 1 Mile (Turf),
4-Year-Olds and Up, Keeneland Race Course, 2003 Purse: $200,000

Year	Winner	Age	Jockey	Wt.	Second	Wt.	Third	Wt.	Win Value	Time	Beyer
1997	Influent	6	J.L. Samyn	116	Chief Bearhart	114	Foolish Pole	113	69,936	1:34.40	105
1998	Lasting Approval	4	R.J. Albarado	122	Soviet Line	113	Same Old Wish	122	70,060	1:35.40	105
1999	Soviet Line	9	J.R. Velazquez	115	Trail City	115	Rob 'n Gin	120	68,696	1:35.37	101
2000	Conserve	4	S.J. Sellers	116	Marquette	120	Inkatha	116	105,927	1:35.08	102
2001	North East Bound	5	J.A. Velez Jr.	120	Brahms	123	Strategic Mission	116	140,492	1:34.44	108
2002	Touchoftheblues	5	K.J. Desormeaux	116	Pisces	123	Boastful	116	124,000	1:35.02	102
2003	Royal Spy	5	R.J. Albarado	118	Miesque's Approval	118	Touch of the Blues	117	124,000	1:35.82	104

Beyer Index: 103.86

MASSACHUSETTS HANDICAP, 1 1/8 Miles,
3-Year-Olds and Up, Suffolk Downs, 2002 Purse: $500,000

Year	Winner	Age	Jockey	Wt.	Second	Wt.	Third	Wt.	Win Value	Time	Beyer
1935	Top Row	4	G. Woolf	116	Whopper	108	Discovery	138	18,750	1:49.40	
1936	Time Supply	5	R. Workman	121	Gov. Sholtz	100	Stand Pat	119	23,500	1:49.80	
1937	Seabiscuit	4	J. Pollard	130	Caballero II	108	Fair K'htess	108	51,780	1:49.00	
1938	Menow	3	N. Wall	107	Busy K.	107	War Minstrel	106	40,550	1:52.60	
1939	Fighting Fox	4	J. Stout	113	Pompoon	120	Burning Star	110	49,250	1:52.00	
1940	Eight Thirty	4	H. Richards	126	Hash	115	Challedon	130	46,550	1:49.00	
1941	War Relic	3	T. Atkinson	102	Foxbrough	122	Royal Man	106	48,350	1:48.60	
1942	Whirlaway	4	G. Woolf	130	Rounders	108	Attention	122	43,850	1:48.20	
1943	Market Wise	5	V. Nodarse	126	Salto	103	Don Bingo	114	39,650	1:52.00	
1944	First Fiddle	6	J. Longden	124	Alex Barth	114	Alquest	115	41,850	1:49.00	
1945	First Fiddle	6	J. Longden	121	Dinner Party	108	Megogo	106	42,750	1:49.40	
1946	Pavot	4	A. Kirkland	120	Dinner Party	113	Gallorette	119	41,150	1:49.80	
1947	Stymie	6	C. McCreary	128	Elpis	111	Blue Yonder	111	47,250	1:50.00	
1948	Beauchef	5	R. Denoso	115	Harmonica	110	Double Jay	123	47,750	2:02.60	
1949	First Nighter	4	J. Renick	104	Going Away	103	Michigan III	117	39,200	2:04.60	
1950	Cochise	4	E. Arcaro	120	My Request	119	Loser Weeper	118	21,400	2:01.80	
1951	One Hitter	5	T. Atkinson	113	Lights Up	121	Outland	101	22,000	2:02.20	
1952	To Market	4	W. Boland	110	Tio Ciro	105	One Hitter	116	32,600	2:01.40	
1953	Royal Vale	5	J. Westrope	125	Larry Ellis	113	Count Turf	107	43,300	2:02.20	
1954	Wise Margin	4	K. Stuart	111	Find	121	Royal Vale	126	43,100	2:01.60	
1955	Helioscope	4	S. Boulmetis	126	Social Outcast	126	Wise Margin	114	36,000	2:01.00	
1956	Midafternoon	4	W. Boland	110	Find	118	Miellux	109	38,200	2:04.00	
1957	Greek Spy	4	E. Guerin	118	Illusionist	109	Tick Tock	123	39,100	2:03.20	
1958	Promised Land	4	P. Anderson	119	One-Eyed King	111	Clem	114	36,255	2:01.80	
1959	Air Pilot	5	J. Leonard	116	Day Court	115	Bald Eagle	112	53,880	2:02.40	
1960	Talent Show	5	R. Broussard	117	Polylad	116	Battle Neck	107	35,865	2:03.60	
1961	Polylad	5	E. Arcaro	112	Our Hope	114	Nickel Boy	113	37,505	2:01.80	
1962	Air Pilot	8	L. Moyers	105	Polylad	116	Ambiopoise	118	37,115	2:01.40	
1963	Crimson Satan	4	H. Hinojosa	124	Admiral's Voyage	125	Sunrise County	120	38,545	2:01.20	
1964	Smart	5	E. Nelson	115	Sunrise County	114	Steel Viking	106	35,880	2:03.20	
1965	Smart	6	E. Nelson	117	Gun Bow	131	Tenacle	117	36,205	2:01.60	
1966	Fast Count	3	M. Venezia	108	Pluck	113	Baitman	113	53,430	2:01.20	
1967	Good Knight	5	K. Korte	113	Understanding	114	Heronslea	112	40,154	2:02.40	
1968	Out of the Way	3	J.L. Rotz	112	Big Rock Candy	114	King's Place	114	39,682	2:02.80	
1969	Beau Marker	4	L. Moyers	109	Spring Double	122	Chompion	113	36,741	2:04.60	
1970	Semillant	5	J. Cruguet	111	Drumtop	119	Jungle Cove	115	54,730	2:37.20	
1971	Chompion	6	J. Velasquez	116	The Pruner	113	Close Attention	108	54,421	2:34.40	
1972	Droll Role	4	E. Maple	115	Hitchcock	115	Native Royalty	114	75,920	1:49.20	
1973	Riva Ridge	4	R. Turcotte	125	Crafty Khale	112	Loud	113	36,432	1:48.20	
1974	Billy Come Lately	4	D. MacBeth	109	Forage	114	North Sea	111	45,000	1:48.60	
1975	Stonewalk	4	R. Turcotte	117	Group Plan	118	Mongongo	115	60,000	1:48.60	
1976	Dancing Champ	4	C.J. McCarron	118	Rushing Man	114	El Pitirre	117	60,000	1:49.20	
1977	Blue Times	6	A. Cordero Jr.	113	Pension Plan	109	Nearly On Time	106	42,930	1:49.40	
1977	Swinging Hal	4	S.R. Pagano	110	El Pitirre	113	Gentle King	108	43,410	1:49.20	
1978	Big John Taylor	4	J. Vasquez	112	Giboulee	114	Buckfinder	114	67,200	1:48.60	
1979	Island Sultan	4	J. Ruane	110	Western Front	113	Quiet Jay	116	70,140	1:48.60	
1980	Ring of Light	5	F. Lovato Jr.	121	Crow's Nest	114	Niteange	110	68,400	1:50.40	
1981	Soldier Boy	5	R. Danjean	111	Niteange	108	Driving Home	114	72,000	1:49.40	
1982	Silver Supreme	4	E. Beitia.	111	Reef Searcher	117	Frost King	127	100,740	1:48.80	
1983	Let Burn	4	J.C. Penney	115	Space Mountain	110	Bemedalled	112	98,220	1:48.80	
1984	Dixieland Band	4	D.J. Murphy	115	Ward Off Trouble	113	Vigumand	107	126,300	1:52.00	
1985	Bounding Basque	5	A. Graell	110	Dr. Carter	122	Hail Bold King	120	124,560	1:47.60	
1986	Skip Trial	4	J.L. Samyn	123	Creme Fraiche	121	El Basco	118	128,040	1:49.80	
1987	Waquoit	4	C.J. McCarron	117	Broad Brush	126	Tour d'Or	114	124,560	1:49.00	
1988	Lost Code	4	C. Perret	127	Waquoit	122	Afleet	123	154,108	1:50.20	
1989	Private Terms	4	K.J. Desormeaux	119	Granacus	113	Simply Majestic	120	180,000	1:49.40	
1995	Cigar	5	J.D. Bailey	124	Poor But Honest	107	Double Calvados	113	450,000	1:48.60	.117
1996	Cigar	6	J.D. Bailey	130	Personal Merit	111	Prolanizer	110	300,000	1:49.60	.112
1997	Skip Away	4	S.J. Sellers	119	Formal Gold	114	Will's Way	114	500,000	1:47.80	.122
1998	Skip Away	5	J.D. Bailey	130	Puerto Madero	116	K.J.'s Appeal	113	500,000	1:47.20	.121
1999	Behrens	5	J.F. Chavez	118	Running Stag	113	Real Quiet	121	400,000	1:49.00	.117
2000	Running Stag	6	J.R. Velazquez	116	Out Of Mind	116	David	113	400,000	1:49.45	.117
2001	Inlcude	4	J.D. Bailey	118	Sir Bear	117	Broken Vow	116	300,000	1:48.61	.117
2002	Macho Uno	4	G.L. Stevens	117	Evening Attire	114	Include	120	300,000	1:50.52	.110

Not run 1990-94, 2003

Beyer Index: 116.63

W.L. McKNIGHT HANDICAP, 1 1/2 Miles (Turf),
3-Year-Olds and Up, Calder Race Course, 2003 Purse: $200,000

Year	Winner	Age	Jockey	Wt.	Second	Wt.	Third	Wt.	Win Value	Time	Beyer
1973	Getajetholme	4	J. Imparato	121	Daring Young Man	120	Outdoors	116	38,700	1:47.20	
1974	Shane's Prince	4	E. Maple	116	Star Envoy	125	Return to Reality	119	35,700	1:46.00	
1975	Snurb	5	G. St. Leon	119	Buffalo Lark	121	Lord Rebeau	116	37,800	1:46.00	
1976	Toonerville	5	G. St. Leon	119	Ameri Flyer	117	Emperor Rex	115	55,800	1:44.60	
1977	H'll of Reason	4	M. Solomone	119	Visier	120	Lightning Thr'st	116	52,200	1:47.20	
1978	Practitioner	4	J.S. Rodriguez	118	Fort Prevel	111	Bob's Dusty	118	56,250	1:48.80	
1979	Bob's Dusty	5	R. Depass	119	Prince Misko	116	Bridewell	112	55,800	1:48.00	
1980	Old Crony	5	D. Brumfield	117	Once Over Lightly	114	Houdini	125	35,565	1:48.40	
1980	Drum's Captain	5	J. Fell	118	Lot O' Gold	125	Scythian Gold	116	34,875	1:48.00	
1981	El Barril	5	J. Vasquez	118	Lord Bawimer	115	Lobsang II	117	51,630	2:28.40	
1981	Buckpoint	5	J.D. Bailey	122	Scythian Gold	116	Proud Manner	112	52,230	2:28.00	
1982	Ghazwan	5	C. Hernandez	120	Gleaming Channel	116	Beyond Recall	110	61,920	2:28.80	
1982	Russian George	6	M.A. Rivera	114	Euphrosyne	117	Nar		61,320	2:29.80	
1983	Current Blade	5	J.D. Bailey	114	Half Iced	122	Leader Jet	113	70,220	2:29.20	
1984	Open Call	6	J. Velasquez	120	Dom Cimarosa	114	Bold Frond	113	63,075	2:30.20	
1984	Nijinsky's Secret	6	J.A. Velez Jr	124	Dom Menotti	112	Four Bases	114	63,675	2:31.20	
1985	Jack Slade	5	G. Gallitano	120	Rake	116	Rilial	120	69,900	2:26.20	
1985	Flying Pidgeon	4	J.A. Santos	114	Pass the Line	114	Selous Scout	110	70,800	2:25.80	
1986	Flying Pidgeon	5	J.A. Santos	117	Creme Fraiche	115	Amerilad	112	120,000	2:39.60	
1987	Creme Fraiche	5	E. Maple	115	Flying Pidgeon	120	Akabir	113	120,000	2:27.00	
1988	All Sincerity	6	C. Hernandez	111	Blazing Bart	118	Creme Fraiche	118	120,000	2:25.40	
1989	Mataji	5	D. Valiente	113	Mi Selecto	118	Creme Fraiche	118	90,000	2:25.60	
1990	Drum Taps	4	J.A. Santos	114	Black Tulip	112	Turfah	115	60,000	2:29.80	99
1991	Stolen Rolls	5	P.A. Rodriguez	115	Runaway Raja	112	Gallant Mel	110	60,000	2:27.00	105
1992	Bye Union Ave.	6	R.R. Douglas	113	Crockadore	113	Skate on Thin Ice	111	90,000	2:27.20	102
1993	Antartic Wings	5	R.R. Douglas	113	Cigar Toss	112	Luv U. Jodi	110	60,000	2:33.40	102
1994	Cobblestone Road	5	J.C. Ferrer	113	Daarik	113	Fraise	126	90,000	2:27.80	104
1995	Flag Down	5	J.A. Santos	116	Mecke	118	Green Means Go	115	90,000	2:24.00	106
1996	Diplomatic Jet	4	J.F. Chavez	123	Marcie's Ensign	123	(DH) Identity	114	90,000	2:24.20	106
1997	Panama City	3	P. Day	117	Slicious	114	Skillington	113	90,000	2:27.00	103
1998	Wild Event	5	S.J. Sellers	116	N B Forrest	114	Glok	114	90,000	2:26.80	104
1999	Wicapi*	7	C. Velasquez	114	Special Coach	114	King's Jewel	112	90,000	2:26.20	95
2000	A Little Luck	6	M.E. Smith	114	Stokosky		Whata Brainstorm	113	90,000	2:29.01	100
2001	Profit Option	6	M. Guidry	114	Deeliteful Irving	113	Eltawaasul	114	90,000	2:27.95	96
2002	Man From Wicklow	5	J.D. Bailey	118	Serial Bride	114	Rochester	117	120,000	2:28.05	102
2003	Balto Star	5	J.R. Velazquez	121	Continuously	116	Rowans Park	114	120,000	2:24.87	105

Beyer Index: 102.07

MEADOWLANDS BREEDERS' CUP STAKES, 1 1/8 Miles,
3-Year-Olds and Up, The Meadowlands, 2003 Purse: $400,000

Year	Winner	Age	Jockey	Wt.	Second	Wt.	Third	Wt.	Win Value	Time	Beyer
1977	Pay Tribute	5	A. Cordero Jr	117	Father Hogan	112	Super Boy	110	114,920	2:02.60	
1978	Dr. Patches	4	A. Cordero Jr	119	Do Tell George	114	Niteange	115	104,878	2:01.60	
1979	Spectacular Bid	3	W. Shoemaker	126	Smarten	120	Valdez	121	234,650	2:01.20	
1980	Tunerup	4	J. Vasquez	117	Dr. Patches	116	Dewan Keys	115	196,500	2:00.40	
1981	Princelet	3	W. Nemeti	110	Niteange	114	Peat Moss	121	202,080	2:02.40	
1982	Mehmet	4	E. Delahoussaye	118	Thirty Eight Paces	113	John Henry	129	240,000	2:01.40	
1983	Slewpy	3	A. Cordero Jr	116	Deputy Minister	118	Water Bank	117	240,000	2:02.40	
1984	Wild Again	4	R. Migliore	115	Canadian Factor	114	Inevitable Leader	116	300,000	2:00.60	
1985	Bounding Basque	5	R.G. Davis	113	Wild Again	120	Al Mamoon	115	300,000	2:00.40	
1986	Broad Brush	3	J.L. Samyn	117	Skip Trial	122	Little Missouri	116	300,000	2:01.60	
1987	Creme Fraiche	5	L. Pincay Jr	123	Afleet		Cryptoclearance	123	360,000	2:01.80	
1988	Alysheba	4	C.J. McCarron	127	Slew City Slew	116	Pleasant Virginian	123	360,000	1:58.80	
1989	Mi Selecto	4	J.A. Santos	115	Make the Most	110	Master Speaker	114	300,000	2:00.20	
1990	Great Normand	5	C. Lopez	113	Norquestor	116	Beau Genius	122	300,000	1:47.20	117
1991	Twilight Agenda	5	C.J. McCarron	121	Scan	116	Sea Cadet	115	300,000	1:46.60	116
1992	Sea Cadet	4	A. Solis	120	Valley Crossing	111	American Chance	109	300,000	1:48.00	108
1993	Marquetry	6	K.J. Desormeaux	120	Michelle Can Pass	110	Northern Trend	112	300,000	1:47.20	115
1994	Conveyor	6	M.E. Smith	113	Personal Merit	109	Bruce's Mill	114	300,000	1:47.80	105
1995	Peaks and Valleys	3	J.A. Krone	116	Poor but Honest	116	Concern	122	300,000	1:48.00	108
1996	Dramatic Gold	5	K.J. Desormeaux	119	Formal Gold	112	Mt. Sassafras	114	450,000	1:48.00	111
1998	K.J.'s Appeal	4	J.R. Velazquez	112	Hal's Pal	116	Sir Bear	119	300,000	1:46.00	107
1999	Pleasant Breeze	4	J.F. Chavez	110	Jazz Club	118	Vision and Verse	112	300,000	1:47.00	110
2000	North East Bound	4	J.A. Velez Jr.	116	Lord Sterling	115	Where's Taylor	113	240,000	1:48.84	106
2001	Gander	5	J.R. Velazquez	114	Broken Vow	120	Include	121	300,000	1:47.11	104
2002	Burning Roma	4	E.M. Coa	115	Volponi	116	Windsor Castle	112	240,000	1:48.95	107
2003	Bowman's Band	5	R.A. Dominguez	119	Dynever		Volponi	123	240,000	1:46.84	109

Unforgettable Max finished third but was disqualified and placed fourth

Beyer Index: 109.46

MRS. REVERE, 1 1/16 Miles (Turf),
3-Year-Old Fillies, Churchill Downs, 2003 Purse: $175,650

Year	Winner	Age	Jockey	Wt.	Second	Wt.	Third	Wt.	Win Value	Time	Beyer
1991	Spanish Parade	3	P. Day	117	Liz Cee		Savethelastdance		37,400	1:46.00	97
1992	Mckaymackenna	3	J. Velasquez	119	Spinning Round	122	Aquilegia	117	56,200	1:45.04	95
1993	Weekend Madness	3	C. Woods Jr.	117	Flower Circle	117	Amal Hyati	122	74,685	1:46.32	94
1994	Mariah's Storm	3	R. Lester	122	Avie's Fancy	119	Bear Truth	119	75,400	1:43.99	96
1995	Petrouchka	3	D. Penna	122	Christmas Gift	122	Ms. Isadora	117	75,725	1:44.20	96
1996	Maxzene	3	J.A. Krone	117	Fasta	117	Turkappeal	119	72,354	1:43.78	92
1997	Parade Queen	3	P. Day	122	Mystery Code	117	Starry Dreamer	122	108,624	1:45.46	98
1998	Anguilla	3	P. Day	119	Darling Alice	119	White Beauty	119	107,601	1:45.60	93
1999	Silver Comic	3	L. Melancon	115	St. Clair Ridge	119	Circle of Gold	119	108,345	1:45.00	95
2000	Megans Bluff	3	M. Guidry	122	Uncharted Haven	119	Impending Bear	119	107,973	1:43.37	97
2001	Snow Dance	3	C. Perret	122	Stylish	115	Cozy Island	111	106,950	1:42.86	93
2002	Caught in the Rain	3	E.L. King Jr.	119	Glia	119	Bedanken	122	107,694	1:46.25	95
2003	Hoh Buzzard	3	R. Fogelsonger	120	Aud	120	Gamble to Victory	116	108,903	1:45.01	95

Beyer Index: 95.08

NASSAU COUNTY BREEDERS' CUP, 7 Furlongs,
3-Year-Old Fillies, Belmont Park, 2003 Purse: $184,000

Year	Winner	Age	Jockey	Wt.	Second	Wt.	Third	Wt.	Win Value	Time	Beyer
1996	Star de Lady Ann	3	J.F. Chavez	114	Stop Traffic	114	JJ'sdream	121	49,590	1:22.00	89
1997	Alyssum	3	J.A. Santos	116	Screamer	121	Sinclara	112	49,515	1:22.80	98
1998	Jersey Girl	3	M.E. Smith	121	Countess Diana	118	Foil	114	48,832	1:22.60	97
1999	Oh What a Windfall	3	M.E. Smith	118	Paved in Gold	118	Things Change	118	66,480	1:23.59	83
2000	C'est L'Amour	3	E.S. Prado	115	Tugger	114	Miss Inquistive	119	90,000	1:23.46	97
2001	Cat Chat	3	J.R. Velazquez	114	Xtra Heat	122	Shooting Party	114	90,000	1:23.02	95
2002	Nonsuch Bay	3	J.J. Castellano	116	Wopping	116	Wilzada	116	120,000	1:23.90	91
2003	House Party	3	J.A. Santos	122	Cyber Secret	122	City Sister	116	120,000	1:23.28	93

Beyer Index: 92.88

NATIONAL MUSEUM OF RACING HALL OF FAME HANDICAP, 1 1/8 Miles (Turf),
3-Year-Olds, 2003 Purse: $150,000

Year	Winner	Age	Jockey	Wt.	Second	Wt.	Third	Wt.	Win Value	Time	Beyer
1987	Drachma	3	R.G. Davis	115	Crown the Leader	115	Major Beard	115	51,480	1:49.80	
1988	Posen	3	J.D. Bailey	122	Blew by Em	119	Harp Islet	115	55,710	1:47.00	
1989	Orange Sunshine	3	J. Cruguet	117	Past 'n' Gold	115	Expensive Decision	122	55,980	1:49.00	
1990	Social Retiree	3	M.E. Smith	115	Go Dutch	115	Divine Warning	119	54,720	1:48.20	99
1991	Lech	3	A. Cordero Jr	122	Sultry Song	117	Fourstars Allstar	122	73,920	1:49.00	100
1992	Paradise Creek	3	M.E. Smith	115	Smiling and Dancin	119	Spectacular Tide	122	72,600	1:46.60	100
1993	A in Sociology	3	C.W. Antley	115	Strolling Along	117	Palashall	117	73,080	1:48.80	97
1994	Islefaxyou	3	E. Maple	113	Jaggery John	122	Lahint	115	70,200	1:48.60	99
							Mr. Impatience	119			
1995	Flitch	3	M.E. Smith	113	Diplomatic Jet	120	Nostra	112	83,700	1:48.00	102
1996	Sir Cat	3	J.D. Bailey	113	Fortitude	113	Optic Nerve	120	68,340	1:40.40	101
1997	Rob 'N Gin	3	J. D. Bailley	120	River Squall	114	Subordination	120	66,000	1:42.00	99
1998	Parade Ground	3	S.J. Sellers	120	Vergennes	115	Stay Sound	115	90,000	1:47.80	104
1999	Marquette	3	J.D. Bailey	119	Phi Beta Doc	118	Good Night	118	90,000	1:49.20	99
2000	Turnofthecentury	3	A.T. Gryder	118	Aldo	118	Polish Miner	123	90,000	1:52.35	88
2001	Baptize	3	J.D. Bailey	122	Strategic Partner	120	Saint Verre	113	90,000	1:47.94	101
2002	Quest Star	3	P. Day	117	Union Place	115	Patrol	120	90,000	1:49.66	95
2003	Stroll	3	J.D. Bailey	117	Urban King	115	Saint Stephen	115	90,000	1:49.34	102

Beyer Index: 99

NEW ORLEANS HANDICAP, 1 1/8 Miles,
4-Year-Olds and Up, Fair Grounds, 2003 Purse: $500,000

Year	Winner	Age	Jockey	Wt.	Second	Wt.	Third	Wt.	Win Value	Time	Beyer
1925	Quatrain	3	E. Legere	105	Prince James	110	President	106	22,100	1:44.60	
1926	Nurmi	3	J. Thomas	101	Scratch	111	Dazzler	112	32,000	1:47.00	
1927	Cotlogomor	5	C. Allen	107	Shark	104	Banton	112	5,000	1:50.20	
1928	Justice F.	4	A. Pascuma	123	Jock	126	Sea Rocket	114	48,975	1:45.80	
1929	Vermajo	3	A. Pascuma	104	Solace	122	Wellet	104	35,537	1:46.40	
1930	Donnay	4	E. Steffen	112	Uncommon Gold	108	Star o' Morn	101	12,225	1:45.40	
1931	Jimmy Moran	4	E. James	115	Rocket Glare	98	Playtime	111	10,775	1:45.80	
1932	Spanish Play	4	C. Landolt	123	Glastonbury	105	Prince Ath'ng	107	1,530	1:54.80	
1933	Rocky News	5	J. Kacala	108	El Puma	100	War Plane	110	1,680	1:52.60	
1934	Slapped	4	B. Haas	107	Uncle Donald	105	War Plane	114	1,655	1:53.60	
1935	Jesting	5	S. Young	111	Learoyd	111	D'ntless Miss	102	435	1:39.40	
1936	Julia Grant	4	H. Spears	100	Palm Island	107	Cristate	109	750	1:47.40	

Year	Winner	Age	Jockey	Wt.	Second	Wt.	Third	Wt.	Win Value	Time	Beyer
1937	Skeeter	3	F. Ritz	106	Magnolia Cash	104	Sir Midas	115	1,180	1:41.80	
1938	Novelette	3	V. Nodarse	103	Bunny Baby	110	Robber Bold	105	1,485	1:47.00	
1939	Chance Sweet	4	J.E. Oros	109	Hope Eternal	102	Whipowill	103	1,000	1:46.80	
1940	Rough Diamond	8	A. Sorsen	107	Endy	98	Spillway	108	850	1:49.20	
1943	Marriage	7	A. Craig	115	Rounders	124	Moscow II	108	18,575	1:43.80	
1944	Marriage	8	J. Higley	124	Rounders	122	First Fiddle	120	18,775	1:45.00	
1946	Hillyer Court	4	W.L. Johnson	118	Pique	115	King Dorsett	124	19,650	1:45.00	
1947	Earshot	4	F. Moon	112	Jack S.L.	112	Brown Mogul	115	19,150	1:44.80	
1948	Star Reward	4	S. Brooks	115	Jack S.L.	117	Carolyn A.	111	19,800	1:48.80	
1949	My Request	4	S. Brooks	115	Isigny	106	Miss Request	113	20,150	1:44.40	
1950	Red Camelia	4	P. Milligan	104	Blue Thanks	113	Dart By	122	21,600	1:49.40	
1951	Mount Marcy	6	K. Church	119	Lotowhite	124	Thwarted	116	21,150	1:44.80	
1952	Oil Capitol	5	K. Church	111	Greek Ship	120	Light Broom	118	20,700	1:44.00	
1953	Smoke Screen	4	G. Porch	120	Happy Go Lucky	121	Oil Capitol	123	45,100	1:44.00	
1954	Grover B.	5	P.J. Bailey	114	Smoke Screen	117	Capeador	121	46,700	1:52.00	
1955	Sea O Erin	4	K. Church	114	Wise Margin	115	Spur On	121	44,300	1:50.20	
1956	Find	6	E. Guerin	119	Happy Go Lucky	110	Sea O Erin	119	45,300	1:52.40	
1957	Kingmaker	4	S. Boulmetis	115	Full Flight	111	Speed Rouser	122	42,000	1:50.20	
1958	Tenacious	4	R. Broussard	120	Ezgo	109	Oh Johnny	125	43,400	1:51.00	
1959	Tenacious	5	R. Broussard	120	Pete's Folly	112	Hare Raising	110	43,900	1:50.20	
1960	Tudor Era	7	R.L. Stevenson	123	Noble Sel	112	Day Court	117	40,300	1:50.80	
1961	Greek Star	6	R. Broussard	122	Road House	110	All Hands	121	40,650	1:49.80	
1962	Yorktown	5	J. Nichols	113	Hillsborough	113	Carry Back	129	47,000	1:50.60	
1963	Endymion	4	J. Nichols	115	Loyal Son	118	Hoop Bound	123	45,100	1:51.40	
1964	Green Hornet	5	R. Broussard	115	Bold Commander	119	Tollway	113	44,000	1:50.20	
1965	Valiant Man	5	R. Ussery	116	Tenacle	108	Suspicious	121	46,500	1:49.20	
1966	Just About	4	L. Moyers	115	R. Thomas	120	Benetero	119	50,200	1:48.80	
1967	Cabildo	4	J. Combest	118	I Owe	114	Mike's Red	115	46,600	1:49.60	
1968	Diplomat Way	4	L. Moyers	124	Cabildo	123	High Tribute	115	41,300	1:49.20	
1969	Miracle Hill	5	D.E. Whited	123	San Roque	113	Spring Double	114	45,700	1:51.80	
1970	Etony	5	P. Rubbicco	118	Vif	119	Otomano II	113	50,000	1:49.20	
1971	Rio Bravo	5	F. Valdizan	113	Joe Frazier	114	Herbalist	113	50,000	1:48.80	
1972	Urgent Message	4	G. St. Leon	119	Helio Rise	112	No No Billy	117	50,000	1:49.80	
1973	Combat Ready	4	L. Moyers	111	Hustlin Greek	111	Guitar Player	114	50,000	1:51.00	
1974	Smooth Dancer	4	L. Adams	116	Trupan	108	Rastaferian	115	56,300	1:50.60	
1975	Lord Rebeau	4	C.H. Marquez	116	Warbucks	113	Diam'nd Bl'ck	110	61,000	1:50.60	
1976	Master Derby	4	D.G. McHargue	127	Hatchet Man	118	Promised City	116	61,000	1:50.00	
1977	T'd'r Tambourine	4	A.J. Trosclair	112	Inca Roca	113	Soy Numero Uno	127	65,000	1:49.80	
1978	Life's Hope	5	C.J. McCarron	112	Silver Series	125	Inca Roca	111	77,550	2:02.20	
1979	A Letter to Harry	5	E. Delahoussaye	126	Prince Majestic	117	Johnny's Image	112	84,050	2:02.60	
1980	Pool Court	5	R. Ardoin	111	Five Star General	112	Book of Kings	113	84,500	2:04.60	
1981	Sun Catcher	4	A. Guajardo	123	Prince Majestic	118	Yosi Boy	112	103,550	2:03.40	
1982	It's the One	4	W.A. Guerra	124	Boys Nite Out	116	Aspro	113	112,000	2:01.80	
1983	Listcapade	4	E.J. Perrodin	121	Bold Style	113	Aspro	114	112,000	2:03.20	
1984	Wild Again	4	P. Day	112	Explosive Bid	112	Crazy Moon	110	112,000	2:02.00	
1985	Westheimer	4	L. Snyder	112	Inevitable Leader	116	Vornorco	108	112,000	2:01.80	
1986	Herat	4	R.Q. Meza	116	Hopeful Word	120	Inevitable Leader	116	112,000	2:01.80	
1987	Honor Medal	6	R.A. Baze	116	Dramatic Desire	117	Inevitable Leader	116	71,040	1:52.20	
1988	Honor Medal	7	P. Day	121	New York Swell	114	Manzotti	115	60,000	1:50.00	
1989	Galba	5	A.L. Castanon	115	Honor Medal	123	Position Leader	116	60,000	1:51.20	
1990	Festive	5	B.J. Walker Jr	117	Majesty's Imp	116	De Roche	116	60,000	1:50.40	
1991	Silver Survivor	5	L. Melancon	120	El Zorzal	110	Sangria Time	115	60,000	1:50.00	
1992	Jarraar	5	B.J. Walker Jr	113	Irish Swap	120	Bayou Reality	113	60,000	1:48.80	107
1993	Latin American	5	G.K. Gomez	112	Delafield	115	West by West	119	90,000	1:49.20	104
1994	Brother Brown	4	P. Day	118	Far Out Wadleigh	112	Eequalsmcsquared	116	120,000	1:48.80	108
1995	Concern	4	M.E. Smith	125	Fly Cry	118	Tossofthecoin	117	120,000	1:49.40	108
1996	Scott's Scoundrel	4	Ardoin R.	116	Knockadoon	113	Patio de Naranjos	114	162,540	1:49.80	106
1997	Isitingood	6	Flores D. R.	121	Western Trader	114	Scott's Scoundrel	113	180,000	1:48.40	107
1998	Phantom On Tour	4	Melancon L.	114	Precocity	114	Lord Cromby	116	300,000	1:48.00	111
1999	Precocity	5	Martin E. M. Jr.	118	Real Quiet	122	Allen's Oop	108	320,640	1:49.00	103
2000	Allen's Oop	5	W. Martinez	112	Take Note of Me	116	Ecton Park	117	300,000	1:48.80	112
2001	Include	4	J.D. Bailey	114	Nite Dreamer	112	Valhol	116	300,000	1:49.18	112
2002	Parade Leader	5	C.J. Lanerie	115	Olmodavor	117	Strive	114	300,000	1:48.92	116
2003	Mineshaft	4	R.J. Albarado	115							

Beyer Index: 109

NEW YORK HANDICAP, 1 1/4 Miles (Turf),
Fillies and Mares, 3-Year-Olds and Up, Belmont Park, 2003 Purse: $250,000

Year	Winner	Age	Jockey	Wt.	Second	Wt.	Third	Wt.	Win Value	Time	Beyer
1940	Shot Put	4	W. Garner	106	Equitable	94	High Fidelity	97	42,400	3:48.80	
1941	Fenelon	4	J. Stout	119	Market Wise	118	Corydon	109	93,500	3:47.00	
1942	Alsab	3	C. Bierman	121	Obash	106	Whirlaway	130	21,450	3:47.20	

Year	Winner	Age	Jockey	Wt.	Second	Wt.	Third	Wt.	Win Value	Time	Beyer
1943	Bolingbroke	6	S. Brooks	124	Fairy Manhurst	116	Vagrancy	112	19,400	3:52.20	
1944	Caribou	5	T. Atkinson	104	Bolingbroke	126	Great Rush	110	18,485	3:53.00	
1945	Reply Paid	3	W. Mehrtens	105	Pot o' Luck	119	Momo Flag	117	21,055	3:53.80	
1946	Stymie	5	B. James	128	Rico Monte	121	Athenia	109	41,200	3:51.20	
1947	Rico Monte	5	E. Arcaro	126	Talon	122	Phalanx	116	73,700	3:48.40	
1948	Miss Grillo	6	C. McCreary	120	Donor	119	Fire Point	104	19,600	3:53.60	
1949	Donor	5	W. Mehrtens	126	Stymie	122	Chains	110	20,450	3:51.20	
1950	Pilaster	6	R.J. Martin	112	Going Away	115	First Nighter	109	19,250	3:52.60	
1951	Hill Prince	4	E. Arcaro	128	One Hitter	117	Sudan	105	20,700	1:49.00	
1952	Battlefield	4	E. Arcaro	118	General Staff	113	Combat Boots	109	20,250	1:48.40	
1953	Crafty Admiral	5	E. Arcaro	125	Flaunt	105	Jampol	113	20,500	1:48.80	
1954	Bicarb	4	T. Atkinson	111	Trusting	110	Cold Command	118	20,400	1:48.60	
1955	Chevation	4	E. Guerin	116	Queens Beeches	113	Guardian II	106	17,100	2:24.80	
1956	Nearque II	7	I. Valenzuela	118	Prince Morvi	126	Jabneh	115	19,450	2:18.80	
1958	Anxious Moment	4	W. Shoemaker	114	One-Eyed King	117	Mystic II	114	18,745	2:17.20	
1959	Amerigo	4	W. Hartack	112	One-Eyed King	116	Marlow Road	104	19,687	1:47.00	
1960	Nickel Boy	5	I. Valenzuela	118	Sheild Bearer	119	Four Fathoms	113	13,691	1:51.00	
1960	Wolfram	4	E. Nelson	116	King Grail	119	Ambergris	113	13,691	1:50.40	
1961	Wise Ship	4	H. Gustines	113	Art Market	116	Nasomo	113	19,435	2:14.00	
1962	Honey Dear	4	J. Sellers	112	Barnesville Miss	114	Cat Call	113	19,305	2:03.80	
1963	Goofed	3	J. Vasquez	112	Doll Ina	120	Lady Provost	108	14,381	1:56.80	
1963	Blue Thor	3	E. Monacelli	110	Jazz Queen	109	Prodana Neviesta	110	14,381	1:57.00	
1964	Batteur	4	L. Adams	112	Intervene	117	Gay Serenade	113	19,760	1:55.60	
1965	Blue Thor	5	W. Blum	115	Margarethen	113	Monivea	109	15,291	1:42.40	
1965	Batteur	5	M. Ycaza	123	Good Jane	110	Straight Deal	116	15,129	1:42.60	
1966	Indian Sunlite	3	L. Adams	115	Native Street	119	Mount Regina	120	15,080	1:43.40	
1966	Swinging Mood	3	E. Fires	119	Short Fall	112	What a Treat	121	15,080	1:44.00	
1967	Politely	4	R. Broussard	122	Swinging Mood	128	Princessnesian	113	19,272	1:43.20	
1968	Ludham	4	J. Vasquez	123	Mount Regina	117	Who Cabled	113	19,142	1:57.20	
1969	Drumtop	4	L. Adams	114	Helen Jennings	108	Ludham	116	15,080	1:54.40	
1969	Klassy Poppy	4	M. Hole	113	Desert Law	118	Sarita	111	15,242	1:55.40	
1970	Marchandeuse	4	H. Gustines	114	Turn 'n Turn About	113	A.T's Olie	109	15,096	1:58.00	
1970	Last of the Line	3	L. Pincay Jr	115	Arachne	112	Tudor M'lle	109	14,609	1:57.40	
1971	Telly	3	J.E. Arellano	109	Dee Dee Luxe	113	Careerist	108	16,920	1:55.20	
1971	Princess Pout	5	J. Cruguet	127	Specious	114	Street Dancer	116	16,920	1:56.00	
1972	Barely Even	3	R. Broussard	127	Bold Bikini	108	Mindy Malone	112	17,940	1:23.40	
1976	Sugar Plum Time	4	A. Cordero Jr	113	Desee du Val	120	Dos a Dos	111	33,780	2:03.20	
1977	Fleet Victress	5	R. Hernandez	115	Lady Singer	113	Welsh Pearl	119	33,333	1:39.20	
1978	Pearl Necklace	4	R. Hernandez	122	Waya	116	Dottie's Doll	118	33,360	1:40.00	
1978	Late Bloomer	4	J. Velasquez	115	Island Kiss	108	Fia	113	33,810	1:41.20	
1979	La Soufriere	4	J. Cruguet	111	Navajo Princess	118	Emerald Hill	120	33,600	1:41.20	
1980	Just a Game II	4	D. Brumfield	121	Poppycock	112	Please Try Hard	113	33,720	2:00.40	
1981	Mairzy Doates	5	A. Cordero Jr	120	Love Sign	114	Wayward Lassie	107	33,960	2:04.00	
1982	Noble Damsel	4	J. Velasquez	114	Office Wife	113	Castle Royale	111	34,620	2:07.00	
1983	Sabin	3	E. Maple	111	If Winter Comes	113	Doodle	115	53,010	2:01.00	
1984	Annie Edge	4	J. Velasquez	112	Thirty Flags	114	Geraldine's Store	121	58,950	2:02.20	
1985	Powder Break	4	J.D. Bailey	115	Annie Edge	112	Pull the Wool	107	53,280	2:03.60	
1986	Possible Mate	5	J.L. Samyn	123	Lucky Touch	110	Perfect Point	113	51,750	2:02.40	
1987	Anka Germania	5	C. Perret	117	Videogenic	117	Lead Kindly Light	109	83,580	2:01.00	
1988	Beauty Cream	5	P. Day	119	Antique Mystique	109	Key to the Bridge	114	70,200	2:03.00	
1989	Miss Unnameable	5	R.I. Rojas	108	Love You by Heart	119	Gaily Gaily	113	72,000	2:05.80	
1990	Capades	4	A. Cordero Jr	119	Laugh and Be Merry	114	Key Flyer	109	71,640	1:58.40	105
1991	Foresta	5	A. Cordero Jr	121	Crockadore	112	Flaming Torch	110	72,360	1:59.20	102
1992	Plenty of Grace	5	J.A. Krone	111	Dancing Devilette	111	Flaming Torch	115	72,720	2:00.60	98
1993	Aquilegia	4	J.A. Krone	114	Via Borghese	117	Ginny Dare	108	74,760	1:59.00	101
1994	You'd Be Surprised	5	J.D. Bailey	118	Dahlia's Dreamer	112	Aquilegia	115	65,340	1:59.60	101
1995	Irish Linnet	7	J.R. Velazquez	118	Danish	116	Market Booster	116	65,520	1:59.80	105
1996	Electric Society	5	J.F. Chavez	115	Danish	115	Chelsey Flower	116	90,000	2:03.60	102
1997	Maxzene	4	M.E. Smith	116	Memories Of Silver	122	Shemozzle	114	120,000	1:59.80	106
1998	Auntie Mame	4	J.R. Velazquez	118	Tresoriere	115	Cuando	113	120,000	1:59.40	103
1999	Soaring Softly	4	M.E. Smith	117	Tampico	116	Anguilla	119	120,000	2:02.20	102
2000	Perfect Sting	4	J.D. Bailey	122	Snow Polina	116	Pico Teneriffe	115	150,000	2:05.36	101
2001	England's Legend	4	C.S. Nakatani	115	Gaviola	119	Spook Express	117	150,000	1:59.63	102
2002	Owsley	4	E.S. Prado	114	Volga	116	Janet	119	150,000	1:59.81	98
2003	Snow Dance	5	R. Migliore	116	Pertuisane	115	Riskaverse	119	150,000	1:59.63	104

Beyer Index: 102.14

NORFOLK, 1 1/16 Miles,
2-Year-Olds, Santa Anita, 2003 Purse: $250,000

Year	Winner	Age	Jockey	Wt.	Second	Wt.	Third	Wt.	Win Value	Time	Beyer
1970	June Darling	2	W. Mahorney	115	Jeanenes Lark	118	American Girl	118	45,765	1:43.00	
1971	MacArthur Park	2	W. Shoemaker	118	D.B. Carm	118	Solar Salute	118	59,445	1:41.80	
1972	Groshawk	2	W. Shoemaker	118	Autry	118	Bottle Brush	118	59,025	1:42.20	

Year	Winner	Age	Jockey	Wt.	Second	Wt.	Third	Wt.	Win Value	Time	Beyer
1973	Money Lender	2	J. Lambert	118	Merry Fellow	118	Holding Pattern	118	58,050	1:42.60	
1974	George Navonod	2	D. Pierce	118	Diabolo	118	Fleet Velvet	118	77,370	1:42.20	
1975	Telly's Pop	2	F. Mena	118	Imacornishprince	118	Thermal Energy	118	74,295	1:43.60	
1976	Habitony	2	W. Shoemaker	118	Replant	118	Hey Hey J.P.	118	79,290	1:42.00	
1977	Balzac	2	W. Shoemaker	118	Misrepresentation	118	Noble Bronze	118	157,230	1:45.40	
1978	Flying Paster	2	D. Pierce	118	Golden Act	118	Knights Choice	118	118,860	1:42.20	
1979	The Carpenter	2	C.J. McCarron	118	Rumbo	118	Idyll	118	119,280	1:41.60	
1980	Sir Dancer	2	F. Olivares	118	Chiaroscuro	118	Partez	118	100,980	1:43.80	
1980	High Counsel	2	L. Gilligan	118	Regalberto	118	Cogency	118	99,780	1:42.80	
1981	Stalwart	2	C.J. McCarron	118	Racing is Fun	118	Gato del Sol	118	140,900	1:42.20	
1982	Roving Boy	2	E. Delahoussaye	118	Desert Wine	118	Aguila	118	181,110	1:41.60	
1983	Fali Time	2	S. Hawley	118	Life's Magic	117	Artichoke	118	168,930	1:44.20	
1984	Chief's Crown	2	D. MacBeth	118	Matthew T. Parker	118	Viva Maxi	118	201,960	1:42.40	
1985	Snow Chief	2	A. Solis	118	Lord Allison	118	Darby Fair	118	167,340	1:44.60	
1986	Capote	2	L. Pincay Jr.	118	Gulch	118	Gold on Green	118	193,680	1:45.20	
1987	Saratoga Passage	2	J.J. Steiner	118	Purdue King	118	Bold Second	118	181,140	1:45.00	
1988	Hawkster	2	P.A. Valenzuela	118	Bold Bryn	118	Double Quick	118	187,740	1:43.40	
1989	Grand Canyon	2	C.J. McCarron	118	Single Dawn	118	Due to the King	118	166,440	1:43.20	
1990	Best Pal	2	P.A. Valenzuela	118	Pillaring	118	Formal Dinner	118	178,620	1:42.80	
1991	Bertrando	2	A. Solis	118	Zurich	118	Bag	118	164,820	1:42.80	95
1992	River Special	2	K.J. Desormeaux	118	Imperial Ridge	118	Devil Diamond	118	120,000	1:43.40	93
1993	Shepherd's Field	2	C.J. McCarron	118	Ramblin Guy	118	Ferrara	118	120,000	1:43.00	87
1994	Supremo	2	G.L. Stevens	118	Desert Mirage	118	Strong Ally	118	120,000	1:43.40	87
1995	Future Quest	2	K.J. Desormeaux	118	Odyle	118	Exetera	118	120,000	1:43.20	94
1996	Free House	2	K.J. Desormeaux	118	Zippersup	118	Swiss Yodeler	118	120,000	1:43.60	92
1997	Souvenir Copy	2	G.L. Stevens	118	Old Trieste	118	Double Honor	118	120,000	1:36.00	100
1998	Buck Trout	2	E. Delahoussaye	118	Eagleton	118	Daring General	118	120,000	1:37.40	87
1999	Dixie Union	2	A. Solis	118	Forest Camp	118	Anees	118	120,000	1:35.60	104
2000	Flame Thrower	2	V. Espinoza	118	Street Cry	118	Mr Freckles	118	120,000	1:34.86	105
2001	Essence of Dubai	2	A. Solis	118	Ibn Al Haitham	118	Ecstatic	118	150,000	1:37.16	93

Roman Dancer finished third but was disqualified and placed fourth

Year	Winner	Age	Jockey	Wt.	Second	Wt.	Third	Wt.	Win Value	Time	Beyer
2002	Kafwain	2	V. Espinoza	120	Bull Market	120	Listen Indy	120	120,000	1:42.75	92
2003	Ruler's Court	2	A. Solis	120	Capitano	120	Perfect Moon	120	150,000	1:41.27	102

Beyer Index: 94.69

OAK LEAF STAKES, 1 1/16 Miles, 2-Year-Old Fillies,
Santa Anita, 2003 Purse: $250,000

Year	Winner	Age	Jockey	Wt.	Second	Wt.	Third	Wt.	Win Value	Time	Beyer
1969	Opening Bid	2	R. Rosales	115	Sailors Mate	115	Loved	115	69,855	1:43.60	
1970	June Darling	2	W. Mahorney	115	Sapose Speed	115	Our Madam Lucky	115	44,520	1:43.20	
1971	Sporting Lass	2	F. Alvarez	115	Goldian	115	Miss Lady Bug	115	60,645	1:44.00	
1972	Fresh Pepper	2	J. Lambert	115	Sphere	115	Sleek and Fleet	115	60,045	1:43.80	
1973	Divine Grace	2	S. Valdez	115	Chalk Face	115	Round Rose	115	59,940	1:43.60	
1974	Cut Class	2	F. Toro	115	Double You Lou	115	Sweet Old Girl	115	84,300	1:42.80	
1975	Answer	2	M. Hole	115	Queen to Be	115	Awaken	115	84,720	1:44.20	
1976	Any Time Girl	2	R. Schacht	115	Lady T.V.	115	Glenaris	115	73,140	1:44.00	
1977	B. Thoughtful	2	D.G. McHargue	115	Grenzen	115	High Pheasant	115	73,530	1:43.80	
1978	It's in the Air	2	E. Delahoussaye	115	Caline	115	Spiffy Laree	115	75,570	1:41.20	
1979	Bold 'n Determined	2	A. Cordero Jr	115	Hazel R.	115	Arcades Ambro	115	82,440	1:46.20	
1980	Astrious	2	T. Lipham	115	Irish Arrival	115	Bee a Scout	115	90,180	1:43.80	
1981	Header Card	2	D.G. McHargue	115	A Kiss for Luck	117	Model Ten	115	144,390	1:43.00	
1982	Landaluce	2	L. Pincay Jr	117	Sophisticated Girl	115	Granja Reina	115	155,610	1:41.80	
1983	Life's Magic	2	C.J. McCarron	117	Althea	117	Persistent	115	164,310	1:44.40	
1984	Folk Art	2	L. Pincay Jr	117	Pirate's Glow	115	Wayward Pirate	115	183,540	1:42.60	
1985	Arewehavingfunyet	2	P.A. Valenzuela	115	Trim Colony	115	Laz's Joy	115	192,420	1:44.60	
1986	Sacahuista	2	C.J. McCarron	115	Silk's Lady	115	Delicate Vine	115	187,050	1:44.60	
1987	Dream Team	2	C.J. McCarron	115	Lost Kitty	117	Tomorrow's Child	115	158,910	1:44.40	
1988	One of a Klein	2	C.J. McCarron	115	Stocks Up	115	Lady Lister	115	168,090	1:44.00	
1989	Dominant Dancer	2	E. Delahoussaye	116	Bel's Starlet	115	Materco	115	153,870	1:44.60	
1990	Lite Light	2	R.A. Baze	115	Garden Gal	115	Beyond Perfection	115	148,320	1:42.80	
1991	Pleasant Stage	2	E. Delahoussaye	116	Soviet Sojourn	116	La Spia	115	156,540	1:43.53	89
1992	Zoonaqua	2	C.J. McCarron	115	Turkstand	115	Madame L'Enjoleur	115	120,000	1:43.91	83
1993	Phone Chatter	2	L. Pincay Jr	117	Sardula	116	Tricky Code	115	120,000	1:41.78	98
1994	Serena's Song	2	C.S. Nakatani	115	Call Now	115	Mama Mucci	115	120,000	1:41.83	90
1995	Tipically Irish	2	L. Pincay Jr	117	Ocean View	115	Gastronomical	117	120,000	1:42.60	85
1996	City Band	2	J.A. Garcia	115	Clever Pilot	115	Wealthy	115	120,000	1:44.57	80
1997	Vivid Angel	2	E. Delahoussaye	116	Love Lock	116	Balisian Beauty	115	120,000	1:37.33	90
1998	Excellent Meeting	2	K.J. Desormeaux	115	Antahkarana	115	Stylish Talent	115	120,000	1:37.71	84
1999	Chilukki	2	D.R. Flores	118	Abby Girl	118	Spain	118	120,000	1:36.12	94
2000	Notable Career	2	D.R. Flores	118	Euro Empire	118	Cindy's Hero	118	120,000	1:36.34	90
2001	Tali'sluckybusride	2	J. Valdivia Jr.	117	Imperial Gesture	117	Ms Louisett	117	150,000	1:37.77	85
2002	Composure	2	M.E. Smith	119	Buffythecenterfold	119	Sea Jewel	119	120,000	1:42.65	93
2003	Halfbridled	2	J.A. Krone	119	Tarlow	119	Hollywood Story	119	150,000	1:43.72	98

Beyer Index: 89.15

Distance 1 mile 1997-2001

OAK TREE BREEDERS' CUP MILE, 1 Mile (Turf),
3-Year-Olds and Up, Santa Anita, 2003 Purse: $300,000

Year	Winner	Age	Jockey	Wt.	Second	Wt.	Third	Wt.	Win Value	Time	Beyer
1986	Palace Music	5	G.L. Stevens	122	Skywalker	122	Mangaki	116	59,350	1:35.00	
1987	Double Feint	4	F. Toro	117	Deputy Governor	118	Vilzak	115	64,810	1:37.00	
1988	Mohammed Abdu	4	G.L. Stevens	120	Mazilier	116	Deputy Governor	121	65,550	1:34.40	
1989	Political Ambition	5	E. Delahoussaye	122	Mister Wonderful I	118	Sabona	117	67,800	1:33.40	
1990	Notorious Pleasure	4	L. Pincay Jr	117	Kanatiyr	114	Fly Till Dawn	114	68,700	1:33.00	107
1991	Ibero	4	A. Solis	115	Val des Bois	118	Tokatee	116	67,000	1:33.60	105
1992	Twilight Agenda	6	C.J. McCarron	120	Luthier Enchanteur	117	Bourgogne	115	65,300	1:33.36	104
1993	Johann Quatz	4	E. Delahoussaye	119	Myrakalu	114	The Tender Track	117	62,350	1:36.28	103
1994	Bon Point	4	Delahoussaye E	116	Journalism	120	Johann Quatz	117	62,050	1:33.86	109
1995	Ventiquattrofogli	5	G.F. Almeida	116	Megan's Interco	119	Debutant Trick	115	76,850	1:35.30	108
1996	Urgent Request	6	C.J. McCarron	115	Megan's Interco	119	Felon	116	110,300	1:32.44	106
1997	Fantastic Fellow	3	A. Solis	115	Magellan	119	Taiki Blizzard	119	165,000	1:36.23	112
1998	Hawksley Hill	5	A. Solis	123	Mr. Lightfoot	119	Magellan	119	166,200	1:36.72	106
1999	Silic	4	C.S. Nakatani	121	Bouccaneer	119	Brave Act	119	150,000	1:33.76	109
2000	War Chant	3	G.L. Stevens	117	Road to Slew	119	Sharan	119	150,000	1:33.75	107
2001	Val Royal	5	J. Valdivia Jr.	119	Thady Quill	119	I've Decided	119	120,000	1:33.21	111
2002	Night Patrol	6	J. Valdivia Jr.	119	Kachamandi	119	Nicobar	119	150,000	1:32.93	103
2003	Designed for Luck	6	P.A. Valenzuela	119	Sarafan	119	Century City	119	180,000	1:32.61	107

Beyer Index: 106.93

OAK TREE DERBY, 1 1/8 Miles (Turf),
3-Year-Olds, Santa Anita, 2003 Purse: $150,000

Year	Winner	Age	Jockey	Wt.	Second	Wt.	Third	Wt.	Win Value	Time	Beyer
1969	Tell	3	W. Shoemaker	130	Noholme Jr.	118	Neutral	113	35,000	1:46.80	
1970	Mickey McGuire	3	W. Shoemaker	124	Woodie Can	117	Mayhedo	120	17,200	1:47.40	
1971	Vegas Vic	3	H. Grant	122	Struck Out	114	Artaxerxes	115	20,050	1:48.20	
1972	Bicker	3	G. Brogan	120	Woodland Pines	116	Queen's Hustler	115	19,650	1:48.20	
1974	Within Hail	3	W. Shoemaker	124	Orders	117	Chief Pronto	113	27,250	1:48.40	
1975	Messenger of Song	3	J. Lambert	119	Larrikin	123	Forceten	125	25,450	1:46.80	
1976	Today 'n Tomorrow	3	L. Pincay Jr	121	Pocket Park	115	Kings Cliffe	115	19,450	1:46.80	
1977	Kulak	3	W. Shoemaker	123	Hill Fox	114	Kaskee	110	19,800	1:46.80	
1978	Wayside Station	3	L. Pincay Jr	117	April Axe	122	John Henry	122	34,600	1:47.80	
1979	Hyannis Port	3	W. Shoemaker	118	Red Crescent	115	Relaunch	126	32,300	1:47.60	
1980	Pocketful of Vail	3	F. Toro	115	Son of a Dodo	118	Always Best	117	39,400	1:47.80	
1981	Seafood	3	M. Castaneda	118			High Counsel	117	33,350	1:49.00	
	Waterway Drive	3	J.D. Bailey	120							
1982	Lamerok	3	L. Pincay Jr	117	Craelius	118	Sari's Dreamer	113	66,300	1:46.20	
1983	Mamaison	3	C.J. McCarron	117	Sunny's Halo	126	Fifth Division	118	63,900	1:49.80	
1984	Tights	3	C.J. McCarron	121	Tsunami Slew	120	Blind Spot	115	65,500	1:46.60	
1985	Justoneoftheboys	3	A. Solis	115	Floating Reserve	118	Schiller	113	65,000	1:47.60	
1986	Air Display	3	G.L. Stevens	114	Armada	117	Vernon Castle	124	64,700	1:48.00	
1987	The Medic	3	S. Hawley	119	Temperate Sil	122	Hot and Smoggy	115	63,800	1:47.80	
1988	Coax Me Clyde	3	P.A. Valenzuela	116	Bel Air Dancer	117	Undercut	120	81,500	1:48.40	
1989	Seven Rivers	3	R.G. Davis	115	Bruho	117	Raise a Stanza	121	66,100	1:45.80	
1990	In Excess	3	G.L. Stevens	117	Warcraft	118	Barton Dene	113	65,300	1:46.60	
1991	General Meeting	3	K.J. Desormeaux	116	Dominion Gold	115	Eternity Star	120	69,500	1:46.60	98
1992	Blacksburg	3	A. Solis	118	Siberian Summer	117	Star Recruit	115	67,700	1:48.00	95
1993	Eastern Memories	3	J.D. Bailey	113	Cigar	118	Snake Eyes	120	66,800	1:48.00	102
1994	Run Softly	3	L. Pincay Jr	117	Alphabet Soup	114	Powis Castle	118	64,800	1:49.80	103
1995	Helmsman	3	C.J. McCarron	115	Virginia Carnival	118	Mr Purple	121	75,650	1:48.80	103
1996	Odyle	3	C.J. McCarron	118	Lago	111	Rainbow Blues	120	80,250	1:46.80	101
1997	Lasting Approval	3	A. Solis	118	Voyagers Quest	118	Early Colony	118	150,000	1:50.80	96
1998	Ladies Din	3	G.L. Stevens	120	Dr Fong	120	Bouccaneer	118	150,000	1:50.20	104
1999	Mula Gula	3	G.L. Stevens	118	Eagleton	118	Super Quercus	118	150,000	1:46.60	100
2000	Sign of Hope	3	A. Solis	118	David Copperfield	118	El Gran Papa	118	150,000	1:47.71	100
2001	No Slip	3	K.J. Desormeaux	118	Sligo Bay	118	Romanceishope	122	90,000	1:46.56	94
2002	Johar	3	A. Solis	118	Rock Opera	118	Mananan McLir	120	90,000	1:46.00	100
2003	Devious Boy	3	J.A. Krone	118	Sweet Return	118	Urban King	118	90,000	1:48.82	94

Beyer Index: 99.08

OAKLAWN HANDICAP, 1 1/8 Miles, 4-Year-Olds and Up,
Oaklawn Park, 2003 Purse: $500,000

Year	Winner	Age	Jockey	Wt.	Second	Wt.	Third	Wt.	Win Value	Time	Beyer
1946	Lights Abeam	5	D. Adams	117	Baruna	112	Rockwood Lou	110	3,720	1:45.00	
1947	Sugar Beet	4	H. Feathston	113	Bymeabond	120	Late Thread	112	3,685	1:43.20	

Year	Winner	Age	Jockey	Wt.	Second	Wt.	Third	Wt.	Win Value	Time	Beyer
1948	Dinner Hour	4	R. Camp	108	Cid Play	105	Boden's Pal	118	3,570	1:44.40	
1949	Fancy Flyer	4	P. Milligan	116	Mr. Tuck	103	Cacomo	109	3,520	1:44.60	
1950	Tharted	7	C. Beasy	119	Provocative	126	Bullish	122	3,455	1:43.60	
1951	Boo Boo Shoo	5	A. Skoronski	111	Kings Hope	106	Virtue	102	3,250	1:43.40	
1952	Spur On	4	J. Adams	112	Ruhe	117	Gloriette	105	3,125	1:46.40	
1953	Our Challenge	4	F. Kaelin	118	Joe Graves	113	Old Mason	113	3,125	1:43.60	
1954	Andros	4	H. Trent	105	Peu-a-Peu	112	Phil D.	120	3,125	1:43.60	
1963	Wa-Wa-Cy	4	E. Van Hook	117	Loyal Son	126	Gay Revoke	114	14,820	1:43.00	
1964	Gay Revoke	6	R.J. Campbell	110	Country Squire	119	Rob Roy III	112	19,321	1:43.80	
1965	Gay Revoke	7	C. Stone	117	Prince Reaper	109	El Bora	116	25,050	1:43.60	
1967	Mike's Red	5	J. Lopez	119	Actor II	113	BF's Own	114	35,460	1:42.00	
1968	Diplomat Way	4	L. Moyers	126	Barbs Delight	125	Hy Frost	118	34,050	1:42.80	
1969	Listado	5	R.L. Baird	116	Missouri Gent	110	Old Dudley	110	35,400	1:45.00	
1970	Charlie Jr.	4	L. Snyder	112	Vif	119	Traffic Mark	118	35,160	1:43.60	
1971	Rio Bravo	5	F. Valdizian	117	Sado	116	Great Mystery	121	33,990	1:42.20	
1972	Gage Line	4	L. Spindler	117	Errullah	110	Elegant Heir	122	34,320	1:44.60	
1973	Prince Astro	4	D.W. Whited	116	Herbalist	116	Gage Line	118	34,470	1:43.60	
1974	Royal Knight	4	I. Valenzuela	123	Crimson Falcon	122	Visualizer	121	38,070	1:43.40	
1975	Warbucks	5	D. Gargan	121	Hey Rube	112	Eastern Pageant	115	37,380	1:42.80	
1976	Master Derby	4	D.G. McHargue	125	Royal Glint	128	Dragset	113	70,890	1:41.60	
1977	Soy Numero Uno	4	R. Broussard	123	Romeo	119	Dragset	114	80,610	1:42.40	
1978	Cox's Ridge	4	E. Maple	128	Prince Majestic	115	All the More	120	80,190	1:43.20	
1979	San Juan Hill	4	D. Brumfield	114	Alydar	127	A Letter to Harry	125	101,730	1:43.40	
1980	Unccol	5	J. Velasquez	116	Hold Your Tricks	111	Braze and Bold	118	103,110	1:44.40	
1981	Temperence Hill	4	E. Maple	126	Suncatcher	123	Unccol	114	128,310	1:43.40	
1982	Eminency	4	P. Day	116	Reef Searcher	117	Thirty Eight Paces	120	166,740	1:44.00	
1983	Bold Style	4	P. Day	113	Eminency	123	Listcapade	123	165,180	1:43.00	
1984	Wild Again	4	P. Day	115	Win Stat	114	Dew Line	118	173,940	1:46.80	
1985	Imp Society	4	P. Day	125	Strength in Unity	109	Pine Circle	118	168,540	1:48.40	
1986	Turkoman	4	C.J. McCarron	123	Gate Dancer	123	Red Attack	114	159,180	1:47.40	
1987	Snow Chief	4	A. Solis	123	Red Attack	112	Vilzak	108	163,020	1:46.60	
1988	Lost Code	4	C. Perret	126	Cryptoclearance	122	Gulch	120	300,000	1:47.00	
1989	Slew City Slew	5	A. Cordero Jr	118	Stalwars	113	Homebuilder	115	240,000	1:49.00	
1990	Opening Verse	4	C.J. McCarron	118	De Roche	114	Silver Survivor	116	300,000	1:47.20	
1991	Festin	5	E. Delahoussaye	115	Primal	115	Jolie's Halo	120	300,000	1:48.00	108
1992	Best Pal	4	K.J. Desormeaux	125	Sea Cadet	120	Twilight Agenda	123	300,000	1:48.00	121
1993	Jovial	6	E. Delahoussaye	117	Lil E. Tee	123	Best Pal	123	450,000	1:48.60	111
1994	The Wicked North	5	K.J. Desormeaux	119	Devil His Due	120	Brother Brown	116	450,000	1:47.80	111
1995	Cigar	5	J.D. Bailey	120	Silver Goblin	119	Concern	122	450,000	1:47.20	121
1996	Geri	4	J.D. Bailey	115	Wekiva Springs	119	Scott's Scoundrel	113	450,000	1:47.40	116
1997	Atticus	5	S.J. Sellers	114	Isitingood	120	Tejano Run	115	450,000	1:48.20	114
1998	Precocity	4	C.V. Gonzalez	114	Frisk Me Now	117	Phantom on Tour	117	450,000	1:48.28	114
1999	Behrens	5	J.F. Chavez	116	Littlebitlively	112	Precocity	119	450,000	1:47.77	117
2000	K One King	4	C.H. Borel	113	Almutawakel	117	Cat Thief	118	360,000	1:48.02	115
2001	Traditonally	4	P. Day	112	Mr Ross	117	Wooden Phone	118	360,000	1:48.15	116
2002	Kudos	5	E. Delahoussaye	117	Bowman's Band	114	Dollar Bill	114	300,000	1:48.34	113
2003	Medaglia d'Oro	4	J.D. Bailey	122	Slider	112	Kudos	117	300,000	1:47.66	111

Beyer Index: 114.46

For 3–year–olds and up prior to 1980. Distance 1 1/16 miles prior to 1984.

PAT O'BRIEN HANDICAP, 7 Furlongs,
3-Year-Olds and Up, Del Mar, 2003 Purse: $150,000

Year	Winner	Age	Jockey	Wt.	Second	Wt.	Third	Wt.	Win Value	Time	Beyer
1990	Sensational Star	6	R.Q. Meza	116	Frost Free	116	Earn Your Stripes	116	49,275	1:20.60	113
1991	Bruho	5	C.S. Nakatani	118	Burn Annie	115	Due to the King	116	46,350	1:21.40	105
1992	Light of Morn	6	E. Delahoussaye	116	Three Peat	116	Slerp	114	66,025	1:20.60	110
1993	Slerp	4	A.D. Lopez	117	Porto Ferraio	114	Cardmania	116	47,850	1:21.20	104
1994	D'Hallevant	4	Nakatani CS	115	Minjinsky	117	J.F. Williams	115	59,725	1:20.20	112
1995	Lit de Justice	5	Nakatani CS	118	D'Hallevant	117	Pembroke	119	60,400	1:20.00	113
1996	Alphabet Soup	5	C.W. Antley	118	Boundless Moment	116	Lit de Justice	123	65,450	1:20.60	114
1997	Tres Paraiso	5	G.L. Stevens	115	High Stakes Player	119	Gold Land	114	68,200	1:21.40	108
1998	Old Topper	3	E. Delahoussaye	116	Son of a Pistol	123	Uncaged Fury	115	95,220	1:21.40	108
1999	Regal Thunder	5	C.W. Antley	116	Christmas Boy	118	Bet On Sunshine	116	90,000	1:21.13	117
2000	Love That Red	4	C.S. Nakatani	118	Cliquot	117	Son of a Pistol	117	90,000	1:20.42	119
2001	El Corredor	4	V. Espinoza	119	Swept Overboard	117	Ceeband	114	90,000	1:21.89	105
2002	Disturbingthepeace	4	V. Espinoza	119	Hot Market	115	I Love Silver	117	90,000	1:21.89	105
2003	Disturbingthepeace	5	V. Espinoza	116	Rushin' to Altar	117	Full Moon Madness	119	90,000	1:21.53	106

Beyer Index: 109.93

OHIO DERBY, 1 1/8 Miles,
3-Year-Olds, Thistledown, 2003 Purse: $300,000

Year	Winner	Age	Jockey	Wt.	Second	Wt.	Third	Wt.	Win Value	Time	Beyer
1876	Bombay	3	Walker	100	Harry Hill		Preston		1,000	2:46.00	
1877	McWhirter	3	James	100	Oddfellow		Commodore Parisot		975	2:40.00	
1878	Harper	3	McClellan	105	J.R. Swiney		Stella		1,025	2:40.50	
1879	Ben Hill	3	Shauer	105	Cash Clay		Enterprise		750	2:54.50	
1880	Mary Anderson	3		102	Brooklyn	105	Pat Farrell	105	600	2:51.75	
1881	Bootjack	3	Allen	105	Windrush		King Nero		550	2:41.00	
1882	Babcock	3	Kelso	110	Katie Creel	105	Effie H.	105	950	2:45.50	
1883	Pilot	3	Watkins	107	Orange Blossom	105	Standiford Keller	110	1,100	2:55.00	
1924	Black Gold	3	J.D. Mooney	126	Payman	112	Dunoon	108	4,000	1:57.40	
1925	Millwick	3	K. Noe	111	Almadel	115	Kentucky Cardinal	120	7,320	1:50.80	
1926	Boot to Boot	3	A. Johnson	122	Bolton	114	Brazen	114	7,320	1:57.00	
1928	Sunfire	3	R. Leonard	121	Easter Stockings	119	Golden Racket	115	7,320	1:57.00	
1929	Thistle Fyrn	3	V. Smith	113	Dinah Did Upset	113	Voltear	121	11,880	1:51.60	
1930	Culloden	3	P. Gross	118	Tonto Rock	118	Dark Entry	121	10,480	1:51.60	
1931	A La Carte	3	F. Catrone	118	Spanish Play	121	Up	121	11,580	1:58.00	
1932	Economic	3	F. Horn	118	Springsteel	118	Our Fancy	118	7,760	1:51.60	
1935	Paradisical	3	L. Hardy	114	Clang	116	Whopper	116	4,250	1:51.20	
1952	Carter's Pride	3	S. Bielen	113	Scrub	118	Dr. Noddy	118	3,733	1:54.40	
1953	Find	3	E. Guerin	118	Buck 'n Gee	118	Dictar	126	18,989	1:48.00	
1954	Timely Tip	3	P.A. Ward	122	Rustic Billy	118	Sea o Erin	122	18,704	1:49.80	
1955	Traffic Judge	3	E. Arcaro	126	Selinsgrove	118	Honeys Alibi	126	29,939	1:50.20	
1956	Born Mighty	3	J. Choquette	116	Fabius	124	Toby R.	124	29,041	1:55.80	
1957	Manteau	3	K. Church	120	Shan Pac	116	Air Wonder	112	18,980	1:49.00	
1958	Terra Firma	3	L.C. Cook	118	A Dragon Killer	118	Plion	122	19,710	1:54.20	
1959	On-and-On	3	S. Brooks	120	Sir Hawley	116	Marless	112	19,730	1:49.40	
1960	Playgoer	3	C. Meaux	111	Dress Blue	111	Money Now	117	11,757	1:47.80	
1961	Gay's Pal	3	G. Smithson	115	First Monday	111	Up Scope	111	12,477	1:43.60	
1962	Gushing Wind	3	R.L. Baird	114	Times Roman	110	Submerge	110	15,616	1:42.80	
1963	Lemon Twist	3	S. LeJeune	120	The Baron	110	Grand Stand	113	20,572	1:44.40	
1964	National	3	P. Anderson	115	Morning Cast	111	Roseberry	108	19,435	1:44.60	
1965	Terri Hi	3	R.J. Campbell	120	Victorian Era	116	Little Gray Pet	113	21,020	1:50.00	
1966	War Censor	3	D. Kassen	120	Eladio	120	Squadron E.	113	22,320	1:52.20	
1967	Out the Window	3	B. Wall	113	English Muffin	112	Royal Malabar	124	21,000	1:52.00	
1968	Te Vega	3	M. Manganello	116	Funny Fellow	116	Campion Kid	120	19,075	1:51.00	
1969	Berkley Prince	3	J. Giovanni	124	Mr. Clinch	116	Polar Traffic	116	22,450	1:50.60	
1970	Climber	3	H. Gustines	116	Son Excellence	112	High Quotient	112	25,641	1:50.60	
1971	Twist the Axe	3	R. Woodhouse	122	Spotted Kid	118	Eastern Fleet	122	36,256	1:52.40	
1972	Freetex	3	J. Moseley	122	True Knight	115	Ladiga	115	64,134	1:50.40	
1973	Our Native	3	A. Rini	122	Hearts of Lettuce	112	Arbees Boy	115	63,882	1:50.20	
1974	Stonewalk	3	M.A. Rivera	120	Better Arbitor	122	Sharp Gary	122	63,000	1:53.20	
1975	Brent's Prince	3	B.R. Felciano	115	Sylvan Place	112	Canvasser	115	66,780	1:49.40	
1976	Return of a Native	3	G. Patterson	115	Cojak	122	Dream'n Be Lucky	115	75,000	1:49.80	
1977	Silver Series	3	L. Snyder	122	Cormorant	122	Pruneplum	115	90,000	1:49.20	
1978	Special Honor	3	R. Breen	115	Batonnier	122	Star de Naskra	120	90,000	1:47.80	
1979	Smarten	3	S. Maple	124	Bold Ruckus	115	Picturesque	122	90,000	1:47.40	
1980	Stone Manor	3	P. Day	123	Colonel Moran	123	Hilbizon	114	90,000	1:52.00	
1981	Pass the Tab	3	A. Graell	120	Paristo	123	Classic Go Go	123	90,000	1:49.20	
1982	Spanish Drums	3	J. Vasquez	123	Air Forbes Won	126	Lejoli	114	90,000	1:49.60	
1983	Pax Nobiscum	3	R. Platts	120	Bet Big	114	Fightin Hill	114	90,000	1:50.20	
1984	At the Threshold	3	G. Patterson	123	Biloxi Indian	123	Perfect Player	120	120,000	1:49.60	
1985	Skip Trial	3	J.L. Samyn	114	Encolure	123	Jacque l'Heureux	114	120,000	1:49.00	
1986	Broad Brush	3	G.L. Stevens	126	Bolshoi Boy	123	Forty Kings	114	150,000	1:51.20	
1987	Lost Code	3	G. St. Leon	126	Proudest Duke	117	Homebuilder	114	150,000	1:50.60	
1988	Jim's Orbit	3	S.P. Romero	123	Primal	114	Intensive Command	114	150,000	1:50.60	
1989	King Glorious	3	C.J. McCarron	120	Roi Danzig	114	Caesar	114	180,000	1:50.40	
1990	Private School	3	J. Vasquez	120	Restless Con	123	Real Cash	123	180,000	1:50.20	
1991	Private Man	3	J.R. Velazquez	114	Richman	126	Shudanz	114	180,000	1:51.20	
1992	Majestic Sweep	3	E. Fires	117	Technology	126	Always Silver	117	180,000	1:50.20	.104
1993	Forever Whirl	3	A.R. Toribio	122	Boundlessly	120	Mighty Avanti	114	180,000	1:50.00	.105
1994	Exclusive Praline	3	W. Martinez	118	Concern	122	Smilin Singin Sam	122	180,000	1:49.40	.104
1995	Petionville	3	P. Day	122	Dazzling Falls	124	Is Sveikatas	116	180,000	1:48.80	.97
1996	Skip Away	3	J.A. Santos	122	Victory Speech	118	Clash By Night	118	180,000	1:47.80	.110
1997	Frisk Me Now	3	E.L. King Jr.	122	Anet	122	Mr. Groush	118	180,000	1:48.20	.111
1998	Classic Cat	3	S.J. Sellers	122	Old Bold Stroke	118	Hot Wells	118	180,000	1:49.80	.100
1999	Stellar Blush	3	M.J. McCarthy	119	Ecton Park	116	Valhol	114	180,000	1:49.20	.103
2000	Milwaukee Brew	3	M.J. McCarthy	116	Brave Quest	113	Kiss a Native	116	180,000	1:50.40	.104
2001	Western Pride	3	D.G. Whitney	119	Woodmoon	113	Macho Uno	119	180,000	1:50.71	.105
2002	Magic Weisner	3	R.Migliore	116	Wiseman's Ferry	120	The Judge Sez Who	114	180,000	1:49.96	.106
2003	Wild and Wicked	3	S.J. Sellers	114	Hackendiffy		Midway Road	114	180,000	1:50.08	.101

Beyer Index: 103.92

ORCHID HANDICAP, 1 1/2 Miles (Off the turf),
Fillies and Mares, 3-Year-Olds and Up, Gulfstream Park, 2003 Purse: $200,000

Year	Winner	Age	Jockey	Wt.	Second	Wt.	Third	Wt.	Win Value	Time	Beyer
1954	Queen Hopeful	3	J. Adams	121	Garb	106	Trisong	110	6,700	1:12.00	
1965	Vassar Grad	3	K Knapp	112	Money to Burn	116	Special T.	112	10,050	1:46.20	
1966	Chalina	3	K. Knapp	114	Lady Pitt	114	Native Street	118	9,700	1:43.40	
1967	Indian Sunlite	4	H. Grant	117	Turn to Talent	113	Shim'g G'd	113	1,317	1:34.60	
1967	Straight Deal	5	J. Velasquez	122	Cologne	111	Pollen	117	13,387	1:35.20	
1968	Chriscinca	4	E. Fires	109	Ring Francis	109	Forest Nan	113	14,725	1:35.80	
1969	Spire	5	R. Broussard	118	Crystal Palace	116	Ludham	123	23,950	1:43.00	
1970	Pattee Canyon	5	E. Fires	119	Klassy Poppy	120	Blue Rage	115	36,950	1:43.00	
1971	Swoon's Flower	4	C. Marquez	115	Stolen Base	115	Toter Back	112	27,915	1:41.60	
1972	Evending Bag	7	W. Gavidia	111	Aladancer	119	Painted Pony	116	29,760	1:41.60	
1972	Toter Back	5	J. Tejeira	114	Gem Wood Betty	113	Flor de S'bra	114	29,760	1:41.60	
1973	Deb Marion	3	F. Ianelli	106	Tico's Donna	113	Barely Even	125	27,240	1:42.60	
1974	Dogtooth Violet	4	D. Brumfield	113	Dove Creek Lady	124	Shearwater	115	38,420	1:41.00	
1975	Protectora	6	H. Gustines	114	Zippy Do	118	Lorraine Edna	116	26,100	1:41.20	
1976	Deessee du Val	5	C. Marquez	116	Redundancy	120	K D Princess	110	28,785	1:41.80	
1977	Copano	5	M. Solomone	122	Jabot	117	Carolina Moon	114	43,400	1:41.40	
1978	Time for Pleasure	4	T. Barrow	115	Late Bloomer	113	Rich Soil	116	37,800	1:41.00	
1979	Sans Arc	5	E. Fires	116	Terpsichorist	122	Time for Pleasure	119	86,093	1:41.40	
1980	Just a Game II	4	D. Brumfield	119	La Soufriere	115	La Rouquine II	114	80,340	1:40.40	
1981	Honey Fox	4	J. Vasquez	115	The Very One	125	Solo Haina	114	88,530	1:41.20	
1982	Blush	4	J. Vasquez	114	Pine Flower	114	Honey Fox	125	76,500	1:41.00	
1983	Sweetest Chant	5	E. Fires	116	Betty Money	114	Norsan	115	53,040	1:43.60	
1983	Larida	4	E. Maple	118	Syrianna	116	Promising Native	115	53,640	1:44.80	
1984	Sabin	4	E. Maple	125	Jubilous	114	Sulemeif	115	70,680	1:41.40	
1985	Pretty Perfect	5	G. Gallitano	120	Early Lunch	113	Trinado	112	61,980	1:41.60	
1985	Aspen Rose	5	J. Velasquez	116	Over Your Shoulder	114	Dictina	117	63,180	1:42.00	
1986	Videogenic	4	R.G. Davis	121	Powder Break	118	Devalois	117	118,440	2:27.20	
1987	Anka Germania	5	C. Perret	117	Singular Bequest	116	Ivor's Image	119	90,000	2:31.40	
1988	Beauty Cream	5	P. Day	115	Ladanum	112	Green Oasis	112	120,000	2:28.40	
1989	Gaily Gaily	6	J.A. Krone	110	Anka Germania	120	Laugh and Be Merry	110	120,000	2:26.80	
1990	Coolawin	4	J.D. Bailey	112	Laugh and Be Merry	113	Gaily Gaily	121	120,000	2:24.20	
1991	Star Standing	4	C.W. Antley	114	Coolawin	118	Peinture Bleue	119	120,000	2:25.00	105
1992	Crockadore	5	M.E. Smith	112	Indian Fashion	112	Sardaniya	114	120,000	2:28.20	100
1993	Fairy Garden	5	W.S. Ramos	115	Rougeur	115	Trampoli	115	120,000	2:25.60	104
1994	Trampoli	5	M.E. Smith	121	Good Morning Smile	110	Northern Emerald	112	120,000	2:25.40	103
1995	Exchange	7	L. Pincay Jr	120	Market Booster	116	Northern Emerald	115	120,000	2:29.00	102
1996	Memories	5	J.A. Santos	114	Caromana	112	Curtain Raiser	113	120,000	2:31.40	98
1997	Golden Pond	4	W.H. McCauley	116	Tocopilla	115	Miss Caerleona	114	120,000	2:26.80	104
1998	Colonial Play	4	R.G. Davis	113	Almost Skint	114	Gastronomical	113	120,000	2:24.60	96
1999	Coretta	5	J.A. Santos	118	Delilah	117	Almost Skint	113	120,000	2:23.80	103
2000	Lisieux Rose	5	J.A. Santos	114	Champagne Royal	114	Fly for Avie	114	120,000	2:25.64	97
2001	Innuendo	6	J.D. Bailey	116	Windsong	113	Aiglonne	114	120,000	2:25.24	104
2002	Julie Jalouse	4	J.A. Santos	114	Sweetest Thing	115	Refugee	110	120,000	2:25.89	96
2003	Tweedside	5	R.R. Douglas	116	San Dare	119	Hi Tech Honeycomb	115	120,000	2:32.36	91

Beyer Index: 100.23

PALOMAR BREEDERS' CUP HANDICAP, 1 1/16 Miles (Turf),
Fillies and Mares, 3-Year-Olds and Up, Del Mar, 2003 Purse: $191,000

Year	Winner	Age	Jockey	Wt.	Second	Wt.	Third	Wt.	Win Value	Time	Beyer
1955	Robinar	3	J. Longden	115	Royal Grace	110	Madam Jet	114	6,550	1:09.00	
1956	In Reserve	4	J. Longden	122	Baby Alice	112	Chargers Gal	110	8,375	1:09.40	
1957	Myrtle	4	I. Valenzuela	115	Bettyanbull	110	Mateka	104	8,375	1:09.40	
1958	Camloc	3	P. Moreno	115	Ballet Khal	122	Sweet Land	113	8,375	1:09.80	
1959	Sweet June	3	R. York	110	Boston Again	125	Peeress	108	9,200	1:09.20	
1960	Perizade	4	R. Campas	107	Sweet June	122	Boston Again	121	9,025	1:09.20	
1961	Nascania	4	E. Ohayon	116	Cherokee Miss	112	Ypres	112	9,075	1:09.00	
1962	Sunday Slippers	3	J. Leonard	116	Spark Plug	121	Edie Belle	117	8,875	1:09.20	
1963	Sabina Louise	3	J. Lambert	113	Corolla	114	Kea	115	8,725	1:12.20	
1964	Soldier Girl	3	J. Longden	126	Jam n Jellie	121	C'li's'm h'n'y	113	8,675	1:09.40	
1965	Jam n Jellie	5	W. Hartack	116	Sari's Song	119	Pretty Bubbles	111	8,850	1:08.80	
1966	Fleet Treat	3	F. Alvarez	115	Admirably	127	Maintain	115	9,050	1:08.80	
1967	Admirably	5	J. Lambert	130	Roman Heiress	113	Francine M.	111	10,225	1:08.60	
1968	Pacific Cross	4	J. Sellers	115	Mira Femme	125	Peggy's World	118	8,725	1:09.00	
1969	Time to Leave	4	D. Velasquez	129	Talking Barb	114	Fast Dish	122	20,900	1:08.20	
1970	Lynn's Orphan	4	D. Tierney	117	Hi Q.	116	Poona Downs	116	7,925	1:29.60	
1970	La Sevillana	4	A. Pineda	114	Windy Mama	116	Everything Lovely	117	7,925	1:29.20	
							Boughs o' Holly	117			
1971	Street Dancer	4	W. Shoemaker	118	Shelf Talker	114	Ancient Silk	112	8,500	1:29.20	
1971	Opening Bid	4	J. Lambert	118	Dumpty's Lady	112	Hi Q.	121	8,400	1:29.80	
1972	Minstrel Miss	5	D. Pierce	118	Street Dancer	121	Balcony's Babe	118	10,175	1:28.40	

Year	Winner	Age	Jockey	Wt.	Second	Wt.	Third	Wt.	Win Value	Time	Beyer
1973	Meilleur	3	D. Pierce	114	Lady Debbie	116	Probation	113	10,775	1:28.80	
1973	Belle Marie	3	W. Shoemaker	114	Best Go	115	Chargerette	116	9,975	1:28.80	
1974	Sphere	4	S. Valdez	114	Lt.'s Joy	121	Modus Vivendi	122	14,050	1:28.40	
1975	Modus Vivendi	4	F. Toro	122	Move Abroad	113	Tizna	124	14,100	1:28.80	
1976	Just a Kick	4	L. Pincay Jr	120	Our First Delight	114	Effusive	113	15,900	1:29.40	
1977	Dancing Femme	4	D. Pierce	120	Swingtime	121	Dacani	115	17,250	1:35.60	
1978	Drama Critic	4	D. Pierce	118	Afifa	119	Fact	115	26,550	1:36.40	
1979	More So	4	W. Shoemaker	115	Giggling Girl	119	Wishing Well	118	34,150	1:35.40	
1980	A Thousand Stars	5	E. Delahoussaye	115	Wishing Well	121	Devon Ditty	120	34,150	1:34.80	
1981	Kilijaro	5	M. Castaneda	129	Lisawan	115	Satin Ribera	118	40,700	1:35.40	
1982	Northern Fable	4	S. Hawley	114	Sangue	124	Princess Gayle	116	33,500	1:35.20	
1982	Star Pastures	4	W. Shoemaker	117	Honey Fox	122	Cannon Boy	114	34,000	1:35.40	
1983	Triple Tipple	4	C.J. McCarron	118	Castilla	121	First Advance	115	52,050	1:35.60	
1984	Moment to Buy	3	T.M. Chapman	115	L'Attrayante	120	Royal Heroine	125	50,550	1:35.20	
1985	Capici	5	R.A. Baze	116	L'Attrayante	119	Gala Event	115	50,150	1:35.20	
1986	Aberuschka	4	P.A. Valenzuela	118	Sauna	118	Fran's Valentine	119	62,750	1:34.40	
1987	Festivity	4	A. Solis	115	Adorable Micol	117	Secuencia	117	64,850	1:35.80	
1988	Chapel of Dreams	4	E. Delahoussaye	117	Short Sleeves	121	Davie's Lamb	117	78,000	1:42.60	
1989	Claire Marine	4	R.G. Davis	122	Galunpe	118	Daring Doone	116	64,800	1:43.20	
1990	Jabalina Brown	5	J.A. Garcia	112	Stylish Star	116	Nikishka	117	64,200	1:42.60	
1991	Guiza	4	G.L. Stevens	114	Agirlfromars	114	Run to Jenny	113	49,300	1:42.00	
1991	Somethingmerry	4	L. Pincay Jr	117	Countus In	117	Sweet Roberta	115	48,800	1:41.80	.103
1992	Super Staff	4	C.J. McCarron	114	Odalea	114	Only Yours	115	64,900	1:42.40	.101
1993	Heart of Joy	6	D.R. Flores	119	Kalita Melody	114	Amal Hayati	114	63,000	1:42.00	.104
1994	Shir Dar	4	C.S. Nakatani	114	Baby Diamonds	110	Prying	117	63,600	1:42.80	.95
1995	Morgana	4	G.L. Stevens	118	Yearly Tour	118	Lady Affirmed	117	74,450	1:42.40	.103
1996	Yearly Tour	5	C.J. McCarron	116	Slewvera	115	Real Connection	114	81,350	1:42.40	.101
1997	Blushing Heiress	5	C.J. McCarron	117	Traces of Gold	115	Listening	120	83,200	1:43.20	.96
1998	Tuzla	4	C.S. Nakatani	117	Ecoute	114	Call Me	116	80,970	1:42.20	.98
1999	Happyanunoit	4	B. Blanc	113	Tuzla	123	Ile de France	118	80,520	1:41.28	.101
2000	Tranquility Lake	5	E. Delahoussaye	121	Tout Charmant	121	Miss Of Wales	114	82,170	1:41.01	.104
2001	Tranquility Lake	6	E. Delahoussaye	123	La Ronge	116	Al Desima	113	90,000	1:41.94	.101
2002	Voodoo Dancer	4	K.J. Desormeaux	120	I'm the Business	114	Skywriting	114	90,000	1:41.56	.102
2003	Spring Star	4	A. Solis	116	Magic Mission	117	Garden in the Rain	114	120,000	1:40.78	.101

Beyer Index: 100.77

PALOS VERDES HANDICAP, 6 Furlongs, 4-Year-Olds and Up, Santa Anita, 2003 Purse: $150,000

Year	Winner	Age	Jockey	Wt.	Second	Wt.	Third	Wt.	Win Value	Time	Beyer
1951	Northern Star	3	T. Atkinson	118	Admiral Drake	113	Phil D.	113	14,150	1:10.40	
1952	First Glance	5	E. Guerin	119	Reighs Bull	121	Stranglehold	112	13,300	1:10.20	
1953	Heliowise	5	P. Moreno	107	Cyclotron	122	Phil D.	113	14,950	1:09.40	
1954	Imbros	4	J. Longden	128	Berseem	124	Hour Regards	110	14,650	1:09.00	
1955	History Book	5	R. Neves	113	Karim	115	Hour Regards	111	14,050	1:10.80	
1956	Porterhouse	6	E. Arcaro	125	Johnie Mike	119	Scent	119	13,300	1:10.20	
1957	Nashville	3	W. Shoemaker	115	El Khobar	118	Noredski	112	14,100	1:09.60	
1958	Golden Notes	4	E. Arcaro	115	Seaneen	119	The Searcher	113	13,350	1:09.60	
1959	Clandestine	4	W. Shoemaker	113	Fleet Nasrullah	126	Caronat	112	12,750	1:09.20	
1960	Ole Fols	4	W. Shoemaker	117	Henrijan	114	Finnegan	118	14,700	1:09.40	
1961	Revel	5	A. Maese	127	Ole Fols	119	Windy Sands	113	14,250	1:09.80	
1962	Crozier	4	I. Valenzuela	122	Olden Times	126	Songman	110	14,150	1:09.20	
1963	Cyrano	4	M. Ycaza	122	Sledge	118	Olden Times	126	13,450	1:08.40	
1964	Native Diver	5	J. Lambert	122	Viking Spirit	120	Sledge	125	14,350	1:10.20	
1965	Native Diver	6	J. Lambert	129	Isle of Greece	114	Sledge	121	13,800	1:09.00	
1966	Pretense	3	W. Shoemaker	114	Hoist Bar	116	Aurelius II	115	17,950	1:09.20	
1967	Kissin' George	4	W. Mahorney	126	Hoist Bar	114	Suteki	114	16,950	1:09.20	
1968	Rising Market	4	L. Pincay Jr	124	Tumiga	123	Baffle	117	17,650	1:10.40	
1971	King of Cricket	4	H. Grant	120	Brazen Brother	122	Tower East	112	19,900	1:11.00	
1971	Jungle Savage	5	J. Lambert	117	Ack Ack	129	King of Cricket	119	19,350	1:08.60	
1972	Crusading	4	F. Toro	117	Single Agent	122	Grey Papa	115	21,900	1:08.60	
1973	Woodland Pines	4	D. Pierce	115	Tragic Isle	117	Ancient Title	112	20,800	1:09.00	
1974	Ancient Title	4	L. Pincay Jr	126	Princely Native	116	King o't'Bl's	113	20,900	1:08.80	
1975	Messenger of Song	3	J. Lambert	125	Wilmar	115	Rise High	118	19,800	1:08.60	
1976	Maheras	3	L. Pincay Jr	119	Sure Fire	116	Ancient Title	126	29,400	1:08.60	
1977	Impressive Luck	4	S. Hawley	119	Maheras	120	Curr'nt Concept	117	26,000	1:10.40	
1978	Little Reb	3	F. Olivares	116	Crash Program	112	Bad 'n Big	125	33,900	1:08.60	
1979	Beau's Eagle	3	S. Hawley	122	Always Gallant	124	Charley Sutton	115	32,750	1:10.00	
1980	To B. or Not	4	M. Castaneda	121	Unalakleet	115	Syncopate	113	34,000	1:08.20	
1981	I'm Smokin'	5	P.A. Valenzuela	119	To B. or Not	121	Solo Guy	119	39,200	1:08.00	
1982	Chinook Pass	3	L. Pincay Jr	120	General Jimmy	112	Unpredictable	122	40,050	1:07.60	
1983	Fighting Fit	4	E. Delahoussaye	122	Expressman	115	Gemini Dreamer	117	38,150	1:09.00	

Year	Winner	Age	Jockey	Wt.	Second	Wt.	Third	Wt.	Win Value	Time	Beyer
1984	Debonaire Junior	3	C.J. McCarron	120	Charging Falls	112	Premiership	117	51,700	1:10.20	
1985	Phone Trick	3	L. Pincay Jr	121	Five North	112	Debonaire Junior	123	50,100	1:08.00	
1986	Bedside Promise	4	G.L. Stevens	123	Bolder Than Bold	116	Rocky Marriage	115	60,000	1:08.40	
1987	High Brite	3	G.L. Stevens	116	Hilco Scamper	117	Zany Tactics	123	62,500	1:09.00	
1988	On the Line	4	G.L. Stevens	124	Claim	118	Basic Rate	115	62,700	1:07.60	
1989	Sunny Blossom	4	G.L. Stevens	115	Olympic Prospect	123	Sam Who	122	62,400	1:07.20	
1990	Frost Free	5	C.J. McCarron	119	Valiant Pete	117	Kipper Kelly	112	61,400	1:08.60	
1992	Individualist	4	L. Pincay Jr	117	High Energy	114	Rushmore	114	65,600	1:08.60	111
1993	Music Merci	7	D.R. Flores	114	Star of the Crop	119	Cardmania	117	63,700	1:08.80	104
1994	Concept Win	4	Stevens GL	115	J.F. Williams	117	Scherando	116	62,100	1:07.60	112
1995	D'Hallevant	3	Nakatani CS	117	Cardmania	120	Subtle Trouble	115	94,400	1:08.40	107
1996	Lit De Justice	6	E. Delahoussaye	122	Siphon	119	Lakota Brave	115	135,100	1:08.80	112
1997	High Stakes Player	5	C.S. Nakatani	114	Rotsaluck	114	Larry the Legend	116	131,600	1:08.40	109
1998	Funontherun	4	G.F. Almeida	116	Red	116	Elmhurst	119	120,000	1:08.80	107
1999	Big Jag	6	J. Valdivia Jr.	116	Kona Gold	121	Swiss Yodeler	114	120,000	1:08.00	115
2000	Kona Gold	6	A. Solis	121	Big Jag	121	Freespool	115	120,000	1:08.55	112
2001	Men's Exclusive	8	L. Pincay Jr.	116	Big Jag	120	Freespool	116	120,000	1:08.33	112
2002	Snow Ridge	4	M.E. Smith	116	Squirtle Squirt	122	Ceeband	117	90,000	1:07.70	117
2003	Avanzado	6	T.C. Baze	116	Mellow Fellow	117	Disturbingthepeace	120	90,000	1:07.85	117

Beyer Index: 111.25

PAN AMERICAN HANDICAP, 1 1/2 Miles (Turf), 3-Year-Olds and Up, Gulfstream Park, 2003 Purse: $200,000

Year	Winner	Age	Jockey	Wt.	Second	Wt.	Third	Wt.	Win Value	Time	Beyer
1962	Shirley Jones	6	L. Gilligan	121	Aeroflint	118	Deton	109	11,800	1:51.20	
1963	Sensitivo	6	H. Grant	120	Valetine	118	Tin God	114	11,800	1:50.00	
1964	Babington	5	R. Broussard	117	Totem II	113	Flying Johnnie	114	14,500	1:51.60	
1965	Cool Prince	5	W. Hartack	114	Babington	117	Barbaron	115	45,200	2:26.40	
1966	Pillanlebun	5	F. Toro	117	Cedar Key	122	Rob't's Fl'g	111	40,600	2:26.40	
1967	War Censor	4	E. Fires	120	Voluntario III	113	Ginger Fizz	118	46,500	2:26.00	
1968	Irish Rebellion	4	A. Cordero Jr	114			Pillan'ebun	114	28,850	2:26.40	
	Estreno II	7	D. Hidalgo	109							
1969	Hibernian	4	P. Anderson	114	Irish Rebellion	112	N'dles Stitch	112	42,600	2:28.60	
1970	One for All	4	C. Perret	114	Snow Sporting	122	Eaglesham	113	67,600	2:26.80	
1971	Chompion	6	M. Hole	116	Snow Sporting	119	One for All	114	63,600	2:25.60	
1972	Unanime	5	H. Gustines	110	Double Entry	112	Gleaming	124	74,360	2:26.60	
1973	Lord Vancouver	5	W. Blum	112	Life Cycle	118	Windtex	116	43,520	2:26.60	
1974	London Company	3	A. Cordero Jr	119	Outdoors	112	Bush Fleet	113	84,720	2:26.40	
1975	Buffalo Lark	5	L. Snyder	120	London Company	123	Duke Tom	115	84,120	2:27.60	
1976	Improviser	4	J. Cruguet	114	Green Room	109	P'p'r'd j'bn'h	113	86,880	2:26.60	
1977	Gravelines	5	J.D. Bailey	124	Le Cypriote	110	Gay Jitterbug	124	80,400	2:24.80	
1978	Bowl Game	4	J. Velasquez	117	That's a Nice	116	Court Open	112	100,000	2:30.20	
1979	Noble Dancer II	7	J. Vasquez	124	Fleet Gar	116	Warfever	113	100,000	2:25.20	
1980	Flitalong	4	R.I. Encinas	110	Morning Frolic	119	Novel Notion	117	100,000	2:28.40	
1981	Little Bonny	4	E. Maple	114	Lobsang II	115	Buckpoint	124	121,030	2:32.40	
1982	Robsphere	5	J. Velasquez	117	Come Rain or Shine	110	The Bart	124	102,150	2:26.00	
1983	Highland Blade	5	J. Vasquez	121	Tonzarun	108	Dhausli	113	80,295	2:29.20	
1983	Field Cat	6	J.L. Samyn	110	Pin Puller	112	Santo's Joe	109	82,095	2:29.60	
1984	Tonzarun	6	W.H. McCauley	112	Ayman	114	Nassipour	110	109,275	2:26.80	
1985	Selous Scout	4	R. Platts	112	Norclin	111	Nassipour	115	185,280	2:25.20	
1986	Powder Break	5	S.B. Soto	112	Uptown Swell	116	Flying Pidgeon	118	180,000	2:25.00	
1987	Iroko	5	E. Fires	112	Akabir	113	Glaros	112	150,000	2:26.40	
1988	Carotene	6	D.J. Seymour	115	Ladanum	110	Salem Drive	117	180,000	2:25.00	
1989	Mi Selecto	4	J.A. Santos	114	Pay the Butler	121	Fabulous Indian	112	180,000	2:01.60	
1990	My Big Boy	7	H. Castillo Jr	112	Marksmanship	113	Turfah	115	180,000	2:29.20	101
1991	Phantom Breeze	5	J.A. Krone	116	Dr. Root	114	Runaway Raja	110	180,000	2:29.40	
1992	Wall Street Dancer	4	J. Velasquez	114	Passagere du Soir	116	Missionary Ridge	115	210,000	2:25.40	100
1993	Fraise	5	P.A. Valenzuela	117	Stagecraft	117	Futurist	115	180,000	2:32.80	107
1994	Fraise	6	M.E. Smith	124	Summer Ensign	113	Fairy Garden	115	180,000	2:24.60	104
1995	Awad	5	E. Maple	114	Misil	120	Frenchpark	117	180,000	2:29.40	110
1996	Celtic Arms	5	M.E. Smith	115	Broadway Flyer	116	Flag Down	117	180,000	2:25.60	109
1997	Flag Down	7	J.A. Santos	117	Lassigny	117	Awad	117	180,000	2:27.00	108
1998	Buck's Boy	5	E. Fires	115	African Dancer	115	Royal Strand	114	150,000	2:23.40	108
1999	Unite's Big Red	5	M.E. Smith	114	African Dancer	116	Panama City	115	150,000	2:23.00	106
2000	Buck's Boy	7	E.S. Prado	120	Thesaurus	113	Epistolaire	114	150,000	2:24.80	101
	Beautiful Dancer finished third but was disqualified and placed sixth										
2001	Whata Brainstorm	4	J.R. Velazquez	114	Subtle Power	115	Craigsteel	114	150,000	2:23.75	106
2002	Deeliteful Irving	4	C.P. DeCarlo	113	Cetewayo	118	Mr. Livingston	114	120,000	2:24.14	105
2003	Quest Star	4	E.S. Prado	113	Man From Wicklow	122	Reduit	114	120,000	2:28.45	104

Beyer Index: 105.31

PETER PAN, 1 1/8 Miles,
3-Year-Olds, Belmont Park, 2003 Purse: $200,000

Year	Winner	Age	Jockey	Wt.	Second	Wt.	Third	Wt.	Win Value	Time	Beyer
1975	Singh	3	E. Maple	114	Majestic One	114	Sir Paulus	115	33,420	1:35.20	
1976	Sir Lister	3	J. Velasquez	114	Jamming	117	El Portugues	114	34,620	1:36.00	
1977	Spirit Level	3	A. Graell	114	Sanhedrin	114	Lynn Davis	114	32,910	1:49.20	
1978	Buckaroo	3	J. Velasquez	114	Darby Creek Road	117	Star de Naskra	123	32,520	1:48.00	
1979	Coastal	3	R. Hernandez	120	Lucy's Axe	123	Pianist	117	32,820	1:47.00	
1980	Comptroller	3	R.I. Encinas	114	Bar Dexter	117	Suzanne's Star	114	34,080	1:49.20	
1981	Tap Shoes	3	R. Hernandez	126	Willow Hour	117	West on Broad	120	34,080	1:48.40	
1982	Wolfie's Rascal	3	A. Cordero Jr	120	John's Gold	114	Illuminate	117	34,020	1:48.80	
1983	Slew o' Gold	3	A. Cordero Jr	126	I Enclose	123	Foyt	117	34,380	1:46.80	
1984	Back Bay Barrister	3	D. MacBeth	117	Gallant Hour	114	Romantic Tradition	114	57,330	1:50.00	
1985	Proud Truth	3	J. Velasquez	126	Cutlass Reality	114	Salem Drive	114	67,050	1:47.60	
1986	Danzig Connection	3	P. Day	117	Clear Choice	123	Parade Marshal	117	85,380	1:48.40	
1987	Leo Castelli	3	J.A. Santos	114	Gone West	126	Shawklit Won	114	132,360	1:48.00	
1988	Seeking the Gold	3	P. Day	120	Tejano	125	Gay Rights	117	140,880	1:47.60	
1989	Imbibe	3	A. Cordero Jr	117	Irish Actor	126	Pro Style	117	110,160	1:48.60	
1990	Profit Key	3	J.A. Santos	117	Country Day	114	Paradise Found	114	106,560	1:47.20	
1991	Lost Mountain	3	C. Perret	114	Man Alright	114	Scan	126	106,380	1:49.40	.104
1992	A.P. Indy	3	E. Delahoussaye	126	Colony Light	114	Berkley Fitz	114	106,380	1:47.40	.108
1993	Virginia Rapids	3	E. Maple	114	Colonial Affair	117	Itaka	114	90,000	1:48.40	.109
1994	Twining	3	J.A. Santos	122	Lahint	112	Gash	119	90,000	1:49.00	.103
1995	Citadeed	3	E. Maple	112	Pat n Jac	113	Treasurer	115	90,000	1:50.00	.99
1996	Jamies First Punch	3	J.R. Velazquez	118	Unbridled's Song	123	Diligence	118	90,000	1:47.20	.110
1997	Banker's Gold	3	E. Maple	113	Zede	120	Prince Guistino	114	90,000	1:48.60	.101
1998	Grand Slam	3	J.D. Bailey	120	Rubiyat	113	Parade Ground	120	90,000	1:49.00	.100
1999	Best of Luck	3	J.L. Samyn	113	Treasure Island	114	Lemon Drop Kid	120	90,000	1:47.94	.107
2000	Postponed	3	E.S. Prado	113	Unshaded	123	Globalize	123	120,000	1:49.71	.99
2001	Hero's Tribute	3	J.F. Chavez	117	E Dubai	123	Dayton Flyer	115	120,000	1:47.47	.112
2002	Sunday Break	3	G.L. Stevens	121	Puzzlement	115	Deputy Dash	115	120,000	1:48.10	.99
2003	Go Rockin' Robin	3	S.X. Bridgmohan	117	Alysweep	123	Supervisor	115	120,000	1:48.47	.93

Beyer Index: 103.38

MOLLY PITCHER BREEDERS' CUP HANDICAP, 1 1/8 Miles,
Fillies and Mares, 3-Year-Olds and Up, Monmouth Park, 2003 Purse: $2891,000

Year	Winner	Age	Jockey	Wt.	Second	Wt.	Third	Wt.	Win Value	Time	Beyer
1946	Mahmoudess	4	M.A. Buxton	113	Fair Ann	100	Elpis	116	13,500	1:46.60	
1947	Elpis	5	F. Moon	113	Proverb	112	Lawless Miss	108	13,250	1:45.00	
1948	Camargo	4	C. Kirk	115	Imprudence II	113	Halsgal	107	11,900	1:45.40	
1949	Allie's Pal	4	J. Gilbert	116	My Emma	114	Irisen	109	12,300	1:46.20	
1950	Danger Ahead	4	H. Lindberg	111	My Celeste	110	Allie's Pal	112	12,750	1:46.20	
1951	Marta	4	C. McCreary	108	My Celeste	108	Leading Home	111	12,650	1:46.20	
1952	Dixie Flyer	5	P. Roberts	116	My Celeste	112	Valadium	117	17,000	1:45.40	
1953	My Celeste	7	L. Batchellor	110	Atalanta	117	Grandma Josie	106	19,550	1:47.60	
1954	Shady Tune	4	W. Blum	106	Miss Joanne	110	Winning Stride	111	19,900	1:44.00	
1955	Misty Morn	3	S. Boulmetis	112	Clear Dawn	120	Manotick	111	21,650	1:45.40	
1956	Blue Sparkler	4	O. Scurlock	120	Rico Reto	117	Another World	110	18,450	1:44.60	
1957	Manotick	5	J. Choquette	118	Rare Treat	120	Stolen Hour	108	17,835	1:42.80	
1958	Searching	6	H. Keene	120	Rare Treat	112	Pardala	117	18,452	1:44.20	
1959	Miss Orestes	4	L. Gilligan	110	Mlle. Dianne	117	Polamby	114	18,712	1:45.60	
1960	Royal Native	4	W. Hartack	127	Quill	122	Miss Orestes	114	18,517	1:43.80	
1961	Shirley Jones	5	H. Grant	121	Secret Honor	114	Chalvedele	104	20,020	1:43.20	
1962	Primonetta	4	B. Baeza	126	Shirley Jones	123	Dreamflower	112	18,070	1:42.40	
1963	Patrol Woman	4	S. Brooks	113	Frimanaha	118	Decline and Fall	110	14,446	1:44.40	
1964	Spicy Living	4	M. Ycaza	124	Snow Scene II	112	Old Hat	119	19,110	1:43.20	
1965	Miss Cavandish	4	H. Grant	121	Beautiful Day	112	Snow Scene II	116	18,752	1:44.60	
1966	Discipline	4	R. Broussard	117	Straight Deal	120	Lovejoy	112	25,187	1:43.60	
1967	Politely	4	W. Boland	115	Straight Deal	126	Indian Sunlite	117	25,041	1:44.20	
1968	Politely	5	A. Cordero Jr	122	Mac's Sparkler	123	Green Glade	114	25,350	1:45.00	
1969	Singing Rain	4	R. Broussard	119	Gay Sailorette	114	C'ms F'ry G'd	117	25,480	1:43.80	
1970	Double Ripple	5	E. Nelson	112	What a Dream	115	Deb's Darling	114	29,087	1:44.00	
1971	Double Delta	5	K. Knapp	121	Cathy Honey	118	Peaceful Union	113	30,144	1:42.80	
1972	Out in Space	5	C. Barrera	113	Chou Croute	124	Secret Retreat	112	29,429	1:43.80	
1973	Light Hearted	4	E. Nelson	120	Wanda	118	Alma North	121	28,259	1:41.40	
1974	Lady Love	4	M. Hole	117	Ponte Vecchio	116	Belle Marie	117	28,908	1:43.80	
1975	Honky Star	4	J. Tejeira	123	Twixt	126	Bundler	119	36,156	1:43.00	
1976	Garden Verse	4	F. Lovato	112	Spring Is Here	111	Vodka Time	112	26,432	1:46.00	
1977	Dotties Doll	4	C. Perret	113	Proud Delta	123	Mississippi Mud	115	37,180	1:41.80	
1978	Creme Wave	4	D. MacBeth	114	Pearl Necklace	123	Flame Lily	110	36,530	1:45.20	
1979	Navajo Princess	5	C. Perret	120	Frosty Skater	121	Water Malone	116	36,335	1:43.40	
1980	Plankton	4	V. Bracciale Jr	120	Doing It My Way	114	Whose Bid	113	34,950	1:44.20	

Year	Winner	Age	Jockey	Wt.	Second	Wt.	Third	Wt.	Win Value	Time	Beyer
1981	Weber City Miss	4	R. Hernandez	119	Jameela	118	Wistful	121	49,455	1:44.00	
1982	Jameela	6	J.L. Kaenel	120	Pukka Princess	114	Prismatical	117	67,620	1:42.60	
1983	Ambassador of Luck	4	A. Graell	117	Kattegat's Pride	122	Dance Number	115	67,830	1:41.20	
1984	Sultry Sun	4	M. Solomone	116	Quixotic Lady	118	Nany	114	68,640	1:41.60	
1985	Sefa's Beauty	6	P. Day	119	Mitterand	119	Dowery	115	69,090	1:42.60	
1986	Lady's Secret	4	P. Day	126	Chaldea	110	Key Witness	112	95,610	1:41.20	
1987	Reel Easy	4	W.H. McCauley	112	Lady's Secret	125	Catatonic	117	99,300	1:42.00	
1988	Personal Ensign	4	R.P. Romero	125	Grecian Flight	119	Le L'Argent	117	90,000	1:41.80	
1989	Bodacious Tatas	4	R. Wilson	111	Make Change	112	Grecian Flight	122	90,000	1:42.40	
1990	A Penny Is a Penny	5	A.T. Gryder	120	Leave It Be	116	Bodacious Tatas	117	90,000	1:43.40	97
1991	Valay Maid	4	M. Castaneda	116	Train Robbery	112	Toffeefee	116	90,000	1:43.80	91
1992	Versaillles Treaty	4	M.E. Smith	120	Quick Mischief	120	Cozzene's Wish	113	90,000	1:43.00	105
1993	Wilderness Song	5	D. Clark	119	Quilma	117	Looie Capote	116	90,000	1:44.60	102
1994	Hey Hazel	4	R.C. Landry	114	Ann Dear	113	Future of Gold	110	120,000	1:46.40	92
1995	Inside Information	4	M.E. Smith	124	Jade Flush	115	Halo America	118	90,000	1:43.80	106
1996	Halo America	6	P. Day	117	Rogues Walk	116	Why Be Normal	112	120,000	1:41.60	112
1997	Rare Blend	4	M.E. Smith	116	Top Secret	116	Chip	115	120,000	1:43.60	102
1998	Relaxing Rhythm	4	P. Day	116	Minister's Melody	117	Glitter Woman	120	120,000	1:42.20	107
1999	Heritage of Gold	5	C.T. Lambert	114	Harpia	116	Tap to Music	116	180,000	1:41.76	111
2000	Lu Ravi	5	P. Day	116	Silverbulletday	118	Bella Chiarra	116	180,000	1:43.17	110
2001	March Magic	4	M.J. Luzzi	113	Vivid Sunset	112	Shine Again	113	180,000	1:43.79	100
2002	Atelier	5	E.M. Coa	115	Summer Colony	119	Spain	122	180,000	1:48.63	105
2003	Summer Colony	5	G.L. Stevens	120	She's Got the Beat	112	Call an Audible	110	180,000	1:51.83	93

Beyer Index: 102.36

POTRERO GRANDE BREEDERS' CUP HANDICAP, 6 1/2 Furlongs, 4-Year-Olds and Up, Santa Anita, 2003 Purse: $134,000

Year	Winner	Age	Jockey	Wt.	Second	Wt.	Third	Wt.	Win Value	Time	Beyer
1983	Chinook Pass	4	L. Pincay Jr	123	Haughty but Nice	115	The Captain	114	37,050	1:14.60	
1984	Honeyland	5	W. Shoemaker	117	American Legion	113	Shecky Blue	116	40,450	1:15.40	
1985	Fifty Six Ina Row	4	L. Pincay Jr	117	Hula Blaze	120	Coyotero	114	44,650	1:15.40	
1986	Halo Folks	5	C.J. McCarron	124	Bozina	111	American Legion	112	43,050	1:15.60	
1987	Zabaleta	4	L. Pincay Jr	117	Zany Tactics	120	Bedside Promise	125	44,850	1:15.00	
1988	Gulch	4	E. Delahoussaye	123	Very Subtle	120	Gallant Sailor	112	44,050	1:15.00	
1989	On the Line	5	G.L. Stevens	125	Ron Bon	116	Jamoke	114	66,500	1:14.00	
1990	Olympic Prospect	6	P.A. Valenzuela	121	Raise a Stanza	118	Doncareer	114	60,400	1:14.20	121
1991	Jacodra	4	C.S. Nakatani	111	Answer Do	118	Bruho	117	62,300	1:15.00	109
1992	Cardmania	5	E. Delahoussaye	117	Frost Free	117	Answer Do	123	60,200	1:17.16	101
1993	Gray Slewpy	5	K.J. Desormeaux	118	Cardmania	117	Star of the Crop	119	64,700	1:14.91	118
1994	Sir Hutch	4	Valenzuela PA	117	Concept Win	117	Furiously	117	61,100	1:14.48	104
1995	Lit de Justice	5	Nakatani CS	115	Cardmania	119	Phone Roberto	116	63,000	1:14.65	104
1996	Abaginone	5	G.L. Stevens	115	Dramatic Gold	117	Kingdom Found	118	124,400	1:14.59	116
1997	First Intent	8	R.R. Douglas	114	Hesabull	117	Northern Afleet	118	64,250	1:14.75	108
1998	Son Of A Pistol	6	G.K. Gomez	114	White Bronco	114	Gold Land	115	66,420	1:13.71	116
1999	Big Jag	6	K.J. Desormeaux	119	Gold Land*	111	Son Of A Pistol	120	123,720	1:15.09	112
2000	Kona Gold	6	A. Solis	122	Old Topper	116	Your Halo	116	123,060	1:14.75	119
2001	Kona Gold	7	A. Solis	126	Hollycombe	114			123,000	1:15.03	112
					Explicit	116					
2002	Kalookan Queen	6	A. Solis	116	Ceeband	116	Elaborate	115	130,620	1:15.31	108
2003	Bluesthestandard	6	M.E. Smith	115	Joey Franco	116	Kona Gold	121	72,000	1:14.86	105

Beyer Index: 110.93

PRINCESS ROONEY HANDICAP, 6 Furlongs, Fillies and Mares, 3-Year-Olds and Up, Calder Race Course, 2003 Purse: $500,000

Year	Winner	Age	Jockey	Wt.	Second	Wt.	Third	Wt.	Win Value	Time	Beyer
1985	Birdie Belle	4	J. Santiag	121	Private Secretary	119	T.V. Snow	118	32,240	1:24.40	
1986	Classy Tricks	3	R. Lester	112	Fleur de Soleil	113	Southern Velvet	113	28,130	1:25.00	
1987	Classy Tricks	4	M. Suckie	115	Sheer Ice	117	Spirit of Fighter	123	32,040	1:25.00	
1988	Spirit of Fighter	5	O. Londono	121	Stanleys Run	111	Sheer Ice	117	32,550	1:24.60	
1989	Ana T.	4	R. Lester	113	Ells Once Again	111	My Sweet Replica	112	48,990	1:24.80	
1990	Sweet Proud Polly	3	P. Rodriguez	112	Legend One	110	Love's Exchange	117	32,040	1:25.00	
1991	Magal	4	R. Hernandez	112	Joyce Azalene	110	We Ride Run	112	32,550	1:24.60	90
1992	Magal	5	R. Hernandez	117	Fortune Forty Four	111	My Own True Love	116	30,000	1:23.60	95
1993	Lady Sonata	4	M. Lee	115	Fortune Forty Four	112	Treasured	116	30,000	1:23.00	96
1994	Roamin Rachel	4	W. Ramos	119	Sigrun	113	Goldarama	110	60,000	1:24.00	96
1995	Miss Gibson County	4	G.Boulanger	115	Goldarama	113	Sigrun	116	60,000	1:23.00	103
1996	Chaposa Springs	4	L.Pincay, Jr.	126	Reign Dancer	113	Supah Jess	113	60,000	1:23.40	94
1997	Vivace	4	R.Romero	117	Ashboro	119	Special Request	115	150,000	1:10.80	108
1998	U Can Do It	5	E.Coa	117	Closed Escrow	116	Colonial Minstrel	118	150,000	1:10.00	111
1999	Princess Pietrina	5	Homeister R. B.	114	Hurricane Bertie	118	U Can Do It	119	180,000	1:10.40	96
2000	Hurricane Bertie	5	P. Day	117	Bourbon Belle	116	Cassidy	116	240,000	1:11.43	104

Year	Winner	Age	Jockey	Wt.	Second	Wt.	Third	Wt.	Win Value	Time	Beyer
2001	Dream Supreme	4	P. Day	122	Hidden Assets	114	Sugar N spice	114	240,000	1:10.48	111
2002	Gold Mover	4	J.D. Bailey	115	Xtra Heat	127	Fly Me Crazy	112	240,000	1:10.21	112
2003	Gold Mover	5	J.D. Bailey	118	Vision in Flight	113	Harmony Lodge	116	294,000	1:11.31	103

Beyer Index: 101.46

RAMPART HANDICAP, 1 1/8 Miles,
Fillies and Mares, 3-Year-Olds and Up, Gulfstream Park, 2003 Purse: $200,000

Year	Winner	Age	Jockey	Wt.	Second	Wt.	Third	Wt.	Win Value	Time	Beyer
1976	Moon Glitter	4	E. Fires	110	Regal Quillo	112	K D Princess	111	9,960	1:22.20	
1981	Wistful	4	D. Brumfield	117	Lillian Russell	109	Deby's Willing	112	54,180	1:44.60	
1982	Sweetest Chant	4	E. Fires	117	Deby's Willing	115	Pretorienne	114	25,662	1:43.40	
1983	Flag Waver	4	A. Solis	108	Prime Prospect	118	Our Darling	112	57,960	1:44.00	
1984	Thinghatab	4	C. Perret	118	National Banner	117	Vestris	112	36,870	1:43.80	
1985	Isayso	6	E. Maple	113	Pretty perfect	122	Basie	114	70,080	1:44.20	
1986	Endear	4	E. Maple	113	Isayso	118	Natania	112	103,080	1:45.80	
1987	Life at the Top	4	R.P. Romero	122	I'm Sweets	119	Natania	113	97,440	1:44.00	
1988	By Land By Sea	4	F. Toro	118	Queen Alexandra	120	Bound	113	120,000	1:43.80	
1989	Colonial Waters	4	W.H. McCauley	112	Savannah's Honor	113	Haiati	112	120,000	1:44.80	
1990	Barbarika	5	C. Perret	113	Fit for a Queen	112	Natala	112	120,000	1:44.20	100
1991	Charon	4	C. Perret	121	Wortheroatsingold	112	Train Robbery	113	120,000	1:43.00	102
1992	Fit for a Queen	6	J.D. Bailey	119	Firm Stance	111	Nannerl	113	120,000	1:43.60	108
1993	Girl on a Mission	4	J.D. Bailey	112	Luv Me Luv Me Not	116	Haunting	114	120,000	1:45.40	92
1994	Nine Keys	4	M.E. Smith	113	Educated Risk	120	Traverse City	113	120,000	1:42.00	97
1995	Educated Risk	5	M.E. Smith	126	Recognizable	117	Jade Flush	113	120,000	1:43.00	105
1996	Investalot	5	S.J. Sellers	114	Queen Tutta	113	Alcovy	117	120,000	1:43.80	99
1997	Chip	4	J. Bravo	114	Rare Blend	122	Hurricane Viv	116	120,000	1:42.40	96
1998	Dance for Thee	4	J. Bravo	113	Escena	119	Glitter Woman	121	120,000	1:44.60	106
1999	Banshee Breeze	4	J.D. Bailey	122	Glitter Woman	119	Timely Broad	114	120,000	1:42.80	108
2000	Bella Chiarra	5	S.J. Sellers	116	Lines of Beauty	114	Up We Go	113	120,000	1:43.27	106
2001	De Bertie	4	J.F. Chavez	116	Apple of Kent	114	Scratch Pad	116	120,000	1:50.48	103
2002	Forest Secrets	4	P. Day	117	Summer Colony	118	Happily Unbridled	114	120,000	1:49.83	103
2003	Allamerican Bertie	4	J.R. Velazquez	122	Smok'n Frolic	118	Softly	115	120,000	1:47.92	104

Beyer Index: 102.07

REMSEN, 1 1/8 Miles,
2-Year-Olds, Aqueduct, 2003 Purse: $200,000

Year	Winner	Age	Jockey	Wt.	Second	Wt.	Third	Wt.	Win Value	Time	Beyer
1904	Dandelion	2	W. Davis	103	Gamara	110	Pasadena	117	1,535	1:06.80	
1905	Jacobite	2	J. Jones	126	Hermitage	95	Yalagal	100	1,810	1:07.40	
1906	Frank Gill	2	J. Notter	107	Oraculum	115	Killaloe	114	1,635	1:08.00	
1907	King Cobalt	2	E. Dugan	99	Arasee	104	Bellwether	95	1,525	1:07.40	
1909	The Turk	2	C.H. Shilling	108	Grasmere	120	Cherryola	114	1,050	1:08.20	
1918	War Pennant	2	J. Loftus	122	Lord Brighton	119	Sweep On	120	1,925	1:13.20	
1919	Pilgrim	2	C. Fairbrother	110	St. Allan	111	Head Over Heels	117	2,675	1:12.80	
1920	Grey Lag	2	L. Ensor	123	Knobbie	122	Care Free	109	3,625	1:13.00	
1921	Missionary	2	A. Schuttinger	108	Mustard Seed	112	Surf Rider	120	4,450	1:13.60	
1922	Tall Timber	2	J. Butwell	109	Aladdin	106	Blanc Seing	110	4,125	1:12.00	
1923	Ladkin	2	H. Thurber	122	Bracadale	122	Sun Pal	119	4,075	1:12.00	
1924	Master Charlie	2	G. Babin	130	Swope	122	Faddist	106	4,675	1:11.60	
1925	Timmara	2	H. Thurber	109	Sarmaticus	122	Flat Iron	109	4,175	1:13.40	
1926	Sweepster	2	L. Fator	124	Saxon	118	Cheops	114	4,500	1:12.60	
1927	Excalibur	2	G. Ellis	114	Ariel	124	Leonard B.	101	4,950	1:12.00	
1928	Chatford	2	C. Watters	102	Comstockery	112	African	106	4,250	1:12.80	
1929	Flying Heels	2	W. Kelsay	125	Dunsany	108	Polygamous	123	4,350	1:12.80	
1930	Vander Pool	2	A. Abel	124	Rollin In	115	Timely	114	5,100	1:13.80	
1931	Cambal	2	E. Ambrose	114	Regula Baddun	108	Lucky Tom	125	2,895	1:13.00	
1932	Quel Jeu	2	J. Long	122	Balios	118	Kerry Patch	126	1,425	1:11.80	
1933	Sgt. Byrne	2	A. Robertson	114	Peace Chance	117	Slapdash	119	1,690	1:12.60	
1934	Esposa	2	E. Porter	107	Mantanga	109	Below Zero	112	3,660	1:13.40	
1935	The Fighter	2	E. Arcaro	122	Teufel	112	Postage Due	124	3,885	1:12.00	
1936	Clodion	2	J. Gilbert	110	Night Bud	110	Dogaway	119	3,065	1:12.60	
1937	Bourbon King	2	C. Kurtsinger	117	Mountain Ridge	119	The Chief	118	7,500	1:12.40	
1938	Johnstown	2	J. Stout	126	Lovely Night	122	Beau James	120	7,100	1:11.00	
1939	Camp Verde	2	D. Meade	118	Fenelon	112	Jacomar	119	6,600	1:11.80	
1940	Harvard Square	2	L. Haas	112			Signator	110	6,425	1:11.20	
	Mettlesome	2	A. Robertson	115							
1941	Apache	2	J. Stout	110	Devil Diver	124	Contradiction	119	8,950	1:12.80	
1942	Blue Swords	2	C. Bierman	123	Ocean Wave	117	Joe Burger	110	8,250	1:12.80	
1943	Bellwether	2	J. Longden	117	Dance Team	122	Tropea	114	7,912	1:13.20	
1943	Black Badge	2	W.D. Wright	118	Lucky Draw	126	Sweeping Time	112	8,112	1:11.40	

Year	Winner	Age	Jockey	Wt.	Second	Wt.	Third	Wt.	Win Value	Time	Beyer
1944	War Jeep	2	A. Snider	121			Plebiscite	116	5,395	1:12.40	
	Great Power	2	E. Arcaro	116							
1945	Lord Boswell	2	E. Guerin	119	They Say	108	Marine Victory	122	8,595	1:11.20	
1946	Phalanx	2	R. Donoso	117	Tavistock	116	Donor	126	18,000	1:45.80	
1947	Big If	2	C. Givens	117	Escadru	122	My Request	126	17,450	1:47.00	
1948	Eternal World	2	T. Atkinson	122	Eternal Dream	117	Transfluent	117	14,300	1:00.60	
1949	Lights Up	2	O. Scurlock	114	Cornwall	115	Selector	112	8,875	1:13.40	
1950	Repetoire	2	K. Church	112	Rough'n Tumble	120	Pictus	118	8,575	1:11.20	
1953	Galdar	2	J. Nichols	115	By Jeepers	119	Swift Sword	114	19,550	1:46.60	
1954	Roman Patrol	2	D. Dodson	122	Grandpaw	112	Ever Best	122	37,250	1:48.00	
1955	Nail	2	H. Woodhouse	122	Prince John	122	Noorsaga	122	64,425	1:45.20	
1956	Ambehaving	2	L. Batcheller	122	Missile	122	Finlandia	112	64,975	1:45.60	
1957	Misty Flight	2	E. Arcaro	113	Whitley	112	Rose Trellis	120	20,100	1:45.00	
1958	Atoll	2	J. Ruane	117	Rico Tesio	114	Derrick	114	18,322	1:44.60	
1959	Victoria Park	2	E. Guerin	124	Progressing	111	Fleet Greek	114	23,050	1:37.20	
1960	Carry Back	2	J. Sellers	120	Vapor Whirl	111	Ambiopoise	113	22,822	1:36.40	
1961	Figaro Bob	2	J.L. Rotz	113	Daddy R.	111	Melanion	115	19,240	1:36.80	
1962	Rocky Link	2	J.L. Rotz	114	Duc de Thor	113	Ornamento	117	19,305	1:36.40	
1963	Northern Dancer	2	M. Ycaza	124	Lord Date	112	Repeating	111	18,427	1:35.60	
1964	Sum Up	2	D. Pierce	113	Sparkling Johnny	112	Flag Raiser	111	18,427	1:33.80	
1965	Gary G.	2	B. Baeza	119	Amberoid	117	Native Pitt	117	18,460	1:36.00	
1966	Damascus	2	W. Shoemaker	117	Native Guile	117	Reflected Glory	119	19,695	1:37.00	
1967	Salerno	2	M. Ycaza	119	Verbatim	115	Mr. Hasty	119	19,890	1:38.00	
1968	Palauli	2	L. Adams	119	Distinctive	117	I Found Gold	117	18,980	1:36.40	
1969	Protanto	2	J. Velasquez	117	Needles n Pens	115	Fried Eggs Over	117	19,792	1:35.60	
1970	Jim French	2	A. Cordero Jr	119	Win Desmond	119	Misty Moon	115	18,360	1:36.80	
1971	Key to the Mint	2	B. Baeza	119	Determined Cosmic	119	Traffic Cop	117	21,570	1:36.60	
1972	Kinsman Hope	2	E. Maple	115	Restless Jet	115	Imperator	119	18,045	1:37.00	
1973	Heavy Mayonnaise	2	C. Baltazar	112	Hegemony	112	Flip Sal	112	17,925	1:51.40	
1974	El Pitirre	2	M. Venezia	112	Bombay Duck	118	Circle Home	115	34,380	1:49.40	
1975	Hang Ten	2	L. Pincay Jr	116	Dance Spell	113	Play the Red	113	52,290	1:49.20	
1976	Royal Ski	2	J. Kurtz	122	Nostalgia	122	Hey Hey J.P.	116	49,545	1:50.40	
1977	Believe It	2	E. Maple	122	Alydar	122	Quadratic	116	48,015	1:47.80	
1978	Instrument Landing	2	J. Fell	119	Lucy's Axe	117	Picturesque	117	48,375	1:50.20	
1979	Plugged Nickle	2	B. Thornburg	122	Googolplex	117	Proctor	113	64,560	1:50.40	
1980	Pleasant Colony	2	V. Bracciale Jr	116	Foolish Tanner	113	Akureyri	117	67,920	1:50.20	
	Akureyri finished first but was disqualified and placed third										
1981	Laser Light	2	E. Maple	113	Real Twister	115	Wolfie's Rascal	113	103,500	1:50.80	
1982	Pax in Bello	2	J. Fell	113	Chumming	115	Primitive Pleasure	113	141,300	1:50.20	
1983	Dr. Carter	2	J. Velasquez	113	Secret Prince	117	Hail Bold King	113	134,700	1:49.00	
1984	Mighty Appealing	2	G. Smith	122	Hot Debate	117	Bolting Holme	115	178,680	1:53.20	
	Stone White finished first but was subsequently disqualified from the purse money										
1985	Pillaster	2	A. Cordero Jr	119	Mr. Classic	113	Dance of Life	113	175,800	1:49.00	
1986	Java Gold	2	P. Day	114	Talinum	115	Drachma	113	172,680	1:49.60	
1987	Batty	2	J.A. Santos	113	Old Stories	114	Three Engines	113	176,400	1:52.40	
1988	Fast Play	2	A. Cordero Jr	122	Fire Maker	115	Silver Sunsets	122	197,400	1:50.60	
1989	Yonder	2	E. Maple	115	Roanoke	122	Armed for Peace	113	145,680	1:51.20	
1990	Scan	2	J.D. Bailey	119	Subordinated Debt	115	Kyle's Our Man	113	106,560	1:52.40	
1991	Pine Bluff	2	C. Perret	113	Offbeat	113	Cheap Shades	122	120,000	1:50.80	93
1992	Silver of Silver	2	J. Vasquez	122	Dalhart	115	Wild Gale	115	120,000	1:50.20	96
1993	Go for Gin	2	J.D. Bailey	117	Arrovente	113	Linkatariat	113	120,000	1:52.60	95
1994	Thunder Gulch	2	G.L. Stevens	115	Western Echo	119	Mighty Magee	114	120,000	1:53.80	89
1995	Tropicool	2	J.F. Chavez	112	Skip Away	112	Crafty Friend	113	170,000	1:50.20	94
1996	The Silver Move	2	R. Migliore	114	Jules	122	Accelerator	122	120,000	1:53.40	91
1997	Coronado's Quest	2	M.E. Smith	122	Halory Hunter	115	Brooklyn Nick	115	120,000	1:52.20	91
1998	Comeonmom	2	J. Bravo	113	Millions	122	Wondertross	113	120,000	1:49.80	94
1999	Greenwood Lake	2	J.L. Samyn	122	Un Fino Vino	113	Polish Miner	113	120,000	1:50.60	91
2000	Windsor Castle	2	R.G. Davis	116	Ommadon	122	Buckle DownBen	122	120,000	1:51.92	92
2001	Saarland	2	J.R. Velazquez	116	Nokoma	116	Silent Fred	116	120,000	1:51.28	87
2002	Toccet	2	J.F. Chavez	122	Bham	116	Empire Maker	116	120,000	1:50.40	101
2003	Read the Footnotes	2	J.D. Bailey	122	Master David	116	West Virginia	116	120,000	1:50.62	105

Beyer Index: 93.77

RICHTER SCALE BREEDERS' CUP HANDICAP, 7 Furlongs, 3-Year-Olds and Up, Gulfstream Park, 2003 Purse: $200,000

Year	Winner	Age	Jockey	Wt.	Second	Wt.	Third	Wt.	Win Value	Time	Beyer
1972	Close Decision	4	M. Castaneda	110	Insubordination	118	Intensitivo	115	27,240	1:22.60	
1974	Cheriepe	4	J. Velasquez	115	Shecky Greene	127	Gay Pierre	112	25,236	1:22.40	
1977	Yamanin	5	W. Gavidia	122	Full Out	119	Rexson	114	37,860	1:22.80	
1981	King's Fashion	6	J.L. Samyn	122	Jaklin Klugman	124	Joanie's Chief	108	34,920	1:22.60	
1983	Deputy Minister	4	D. MacBeth	122	Wipe 'Em Out	109	Center Cut	118	38,040	1:22.80	

Year	Winner	Age	Jockey	Wt.	Second	Wt.	Third	Wt.	Win Value	Time	Beyer
1984	Number One Special	4	E. Fires	116	Ward Off Trouble	116	El Perico	114	..23,793	1:21.80	
1985	Key to the Moon	4	R. Platts	122	For Halo	123	Northern Ocean	112	..42,552	1:22.60	
1986	Hot Cop	4	J.L. Samyn	115	Dwight D.	114	Opening Lead	115	..45,324	1:22.80	
1987	Dwight D.	5	R.N. Lester	116	Splendid Catch	113	Uncle Ho	112	..27,816	1:10.80	
1988	Royal Pennant	5	J.A. Santos	113	Grantley	112			..45,612	1:23.20	
					Real Forest	113					
1989	Claim	4	C. Perret	115	Position Leader	117	Prospector's Halo	115	..41,904	1:23.40	
1990	Dancing Spree	5	A. Cordero Jr	126	Pentelicus	114	Shuttleman	111	..30,000	1:10.00	..106
1991	Gervazy	4	W.S. Ramos	115	Shuttleman	114	Swedaus	110	..60,000	1:21.40	..117
1992	Groomstick	6	W.S. Ramos	112	Ocala Flame	111	Cold Digger	113	..60,000	1:23.80	..107
1993	Binalong	4	J.D. Bailey	112	Loach	114	Richman	113	..60,000	1:21.20	..109
1994	I Can't Believe	6	Maple E	113	American Chance	114	British Banker	114	..60,000	1:22.40	..108
1995	Cherokee Run	5	M.E. Smith	122	Waldoboro	113	Evil Bear	116	..60,000	1:21.60	..114
1996	Patton	5	R.G. Davis	113	Forty Won	115	Our Emblem	115	..100,140	1:21.80	..107
1997	Frisco View	4	J.D. Bailey	116	El Amante	114	Templado	114	..98,160	1:23.00	..113
1998	Rare Rock	5	P. Day	117	Irish Conquest	114	Frisco View	118	..120,000	1:22.00	..111
1999	Frisk Me Now	5	E.L.King Jr	117	Young At Heart	113	Good and Tough	115	..60,000	1:22.80	..104
2000	Richter Scale	6	R. Migliore	118	Forty One Carats	116	Kelly Kip	120	..120,000	1:23.30	..111
2001	Hook and Ladder	4	R. Migliore	115	Trippi	120	Rollin With Nolan	116	..120,000	1:21.85	..109
2002	Dream Run	4	P. Day	113	Binthebest	114	Burning Roma	118	..120,000	1:22.30	..104
2003	Tour of the Cat	5	A. Cabassa Jr	116	Burning Roma	116	Highway Prospector	114	..120,000	1:21.15	..107

Beyer Index: 109.07

Run as Gulfstream Park Sprint Championship Handicap prior to 2003

RIVA RIDGE BREEDERS' CUP, 7 Furlongs,
3-Year-Olds, Belmont Park, 2003 Purse: $200,000

Year	Winner	Age	Jockey	Wt.	Second	Wt.	Third	Wt.	Win Value	Time	Beyer
1988	Evening Kris	3	L. Pincay Jr	117	Perfect Spy	122	King's Nest	115	..69,120	1:22.80	
1989	Is It True	3	C.W. Antley	122	Mr. Nickerson	115	Fierce Fighter	115	..70,200	1:22.20	
1990	Adjudicating	3	J. Vasquez	122	Silent Generation	115	Bayou Blurr	115	..68,040	1:23.80	..99
1991	Fly So Free	3	J.D. Bailey	122	Formal Dinner	122	Dodge	122	..74,040	1:23.00	..98
1992	Superstrike	3	J.A. Santos	115	Three Peat	122	Windundermywings	115	..70,560	1:22.40	..103
1993	Montbrook	3	C.J. Ladner III	117	As Indicated	122	Forever Whirl	122	..74,160	1:23.20	..99
1994	You and I	3	McCarron CJ	122	End Sweep	114	Slew Gin Fizz	122	..67,080	1:20.20	..108
1995	Western Larla	3	Stevens GL	119	Mr. Greeley	122	Blu Tusmani	122	..66,960	1:24.20	..101
1996	Gold Fever	3	M.E. Smith	118	Gameel	114	Bright Launch	120	..67,620	1:23.20	..94
1997	Smoke Glacken	3	C. Perret	123	Trafalger	123	Wild Wonder	120	..66,060	1:20.80	..114
1998	Coronado's Quest	3	M.E. Smith	123	Mellow Roll	113	Flashing Tammany	120	..82,050	1:22.40	..111
1999	Yes It's True	3	J.D. Bailey	123	Lion Hearted	114	Silver Season	113	..90,000	1:22.20	..103
2000	Trippi	3	J.D. Bailey	123	Bevo	120	Sun Cat	116	..90,000	1:23.68	..101
2001	Put It Back	3	N.A. Wynter	120	Flame Thrower	120	Touch Tone	123	..90,000	1:21.76	..106
2002	Gygistar	3	P. Day	119	Draw Play	115	True Direction	119	..120,000	1:22.61	..105
2003	Posse	3	C.J. Lanerie	123	Midas Eyes	123	Halo Homewrecker	123	..120,000	1:22.03	..111

Beyer Index: 103.79

SAN ANTONIO HANDICAP, 1 1/8 Miles,
4-Year-Olds and Up, Santa Anita, 2003 Purse: $250,000

Year	Winner	Age	Jockey	Wt.	Second	Wt.	Third	Wt.	Win Value	Time	Beyer
1935	Head Play	5	C. Kurtsinger	128	Fleam	121	Azucar	128	..5,950	1:52.40	
1936	Time Supply	5	T. Luther	116	Pompeys Pillar	105	Ariel Cross	106	..6,000	1:49.40	
1937	Rosemont	5	H. Richards	122	Star Shadow	106	Special Agent	117	..6,825	1:50.20	
1938	Aneroid	5	C. Rosengarten	118	Seabiscuit	130	Indian Broom	108	..7,125	1:50.00	
1939	Whichcee	5	B. James	109	Today	112	Congressman	105	..10,950	1:49.40	
1940	Seabiscuit	7	J. Pollard	124	Kayak II	128	Viscounty	110	..10,000	1:42.40	
1941	Mioland	4	L. Haas	128	Hysterical	111	Bay View	105	..9,460	1:45.40	
1946	First Fiddle	7	J. Longden	123	Autocrat	112	Paperboy	115	..44,710	1:50.00	
1947	El Lobo	6	W. Bailey	111	Hank H.	116	Pere Time	108	..42,450	1:49.20	
1948	Talon	6	E. Arcaro	122	Double Jay	118	On Trust	126	..47,300	1:49.40	
1949	Dinner Gong	4	J. Westrope	114	Autocrat	112	Paperboy	115	..36,700	1:49.60	
1950	Ponder	4	S. Brooks	128	Citation	130	Noor	114	..37,800	1:50.20	
1951	All Blue	4	W. Shoemaker	111	Sudan	109	Next Move	119	..44,850	1:49.40	
1952	Phil D.	4	R. York	117	Intent	118	Bed o' Roses	120	..17,450	1:49.80	
1953	Trusting	5	W. Shoemaker	114	Don Rebelde	112	First Glance	120	..16,250	1:49.20	
1954	Mark-Ye-Well	5	E. Arcaro	130	Rejected	116	Decorated	114	..36,300	1:52.00	
1955	Gigantic	4	R. Summ	109	Imbros	124	Correspondent	112	..36,900	1:48.40	
1956	Mister Gus	5	W. Boland	118	Honeys Alibi	116	Bobby Brocato	124	..36,300	1:49.00	
1957	Terrang	4	I. Valenzuela	118	Honeys Alibi	121	Social Climber	121	..34,700	1:47.40	
1958	Round Table	4	W. Shoemaker	130	Mystic Eye	108	Promised Land	116	..33,300	1:46.80	
1959	Bug Brush	4	A. Valenzuela	113	Hillsdale	120	Terrang	116	..3,500	1:46.40	
1960	Bagdad	4	W. Shoemaker	123	First Landing	124	How Now	118	..34,400	1:48.20	
1961	American Comet	5	W. Harmatz	113	How Now	116	Grey Eagle	113	..35,300	1:48.60	

Year	Winner	Age	Jockey	Wt.	Second	Wt.	Third	Wt.	Win Value	Time	Beyer
1962	Olden Times	4	A. Maese	113	Juanro	105	British Roman	110	37,550	1:53.60	
1963	Physician	6	D. Pierce	117	Crimson Satan	127	Game	107	35,500	1:51.00	
1964	Gun Bow	4	W. Shoemaker	125	Cyrano	124	Quita Dude	114	36,200	1:47.40	
1965	Gun Bow	5	M. Ycaza	129	Candy Spots	127	George Royal	113	35,000	1:47.80	
1966	Hill Rise	5	M. Ycaza	125	Teddy's Secret	122	Bold Bidder	125	34,000	1:47.00	
1967	Pretense	4	W. Shoemaker	121	Drin	119	Native Diver	128	35,000	1:48.60	
1968	Rising Market	4	L. Pincay Jr	115	Quicken Tree	117	Suteki	115	54,250	1:48.40	
1969	Praise Jay	5	M. Yanez	113	Racing Room	116	Estambul II	114	53,800	1:49.60	
1970	Dewan	5	L. Pincay Jr	117	Rising Market	123	Comtal	112	50,600	1:47.60	
1971	Ack Ack	5	W. Shoemaker	124	Good Manners	115	Hanalei Bay	117	54,450	1:47.00	
1972	Unconscious	4	A. Cordero Jr	123	Triple Bend	117	Cougar II	128	52,300	1:47.40	
1973	Kennedy Road	5	D. Pierce	119	Crusading	119	Big Spruce	117	49,400	1:47.60	
1974	Prince Dantan	4	L. Pincay Jr	116	Forage	119	Dancing Papa	116	51,550	1:47.60	
1975	Cheriepe	5	A. Santiago	120	First Back	117	Ancient Title	128	52,850	1:46.80	
1976	Lightning Mandate	5	A. Cordero Jr	118	Dancing Papa	117	Messenger of Song	122	54,350	1:48.20	
1977	Ancient Title	7	S. Hawley	119	Double Discount	115	Properantes	114	72,500	1:47.80	
1978	Vigors	5	D.G. McHargue	121	Ancient Title	120	Double Discount	114	67,100	1:46.20	
1979	Tiller	5	A. Cordero Jr	121	Painted Wagon	114	Life's Hope	120	65,800	1:47.00	
1980	Beau's Eagle	4	D. Pierce	121	Relaunch	117	Double Discount	114	79,650	1:48.40	
1981	Flying Paster	5	C.J. McCarron	126	Doonesbury	121	King Go Go	119	91,700	1:46.60	
1982	Score Twenty Four	5	P.A. Valenzuela	115	Super Moment	124	High Counsel	114	124,200	1:47.80	
1983	Bates Motel	4	T. Lipham	114	Time to Explode	121	It's the One	124	132,200	1:47.00	
1984	Poley	5	C.J. McCarron	120	Water Bank	117	Danebo	122	156,900	1:48.00	
1985	Lord at War	5	W. Shoemaker	122	Al Mamoon	114	Hail Bold King	122	125,200	1:48.20	
1986	Hatim	5	L. Pincay Jr	117	Right Con	117	Nostalgia's Star	118	128,700	1:47.40	
1987	Bedside Promise	5	G.L. Stevens	121	Hopeful Word	118	Bruiser	114	129,600	1:47.20	
1988	Judge Angelucci	5	E. Delahoussaye	122	Ferdinand	128	Crimson Slew	115	156,700	1:48.60	
1989	Super Diamond	9	L. Pincay Jr	121	Frankly Perfect	116	Cherokee Colony	120	159,600	1:48.80	
1990	Criminal Type	5	A. Solis	117	Stylish Winner	113	Ruhlmann	122	190,500	1:49.00	
1991	Farma Way	4	G.L. Stevens	118	Anshan	116	Louis Cyphre	111	196,750	1:47.20	.113
							Festin	116			
1992	Ibero	5	A. Solis	115	In Excess	123	Cobra Classic	114	189,750	1:47.00	.117
1993	Marquetry	6	E. Delahoussaye	117	Sir Beaufort	120	Reign Road	116	155,500	1:48.80	.101
1994	The Wicked North	5	K.J. Desormeaux	116	Region	117	Hill Pass	116	155,500	1:47.40	.115
1995	Best Pal	7	C.J. McCarron	121	Slew of Damascus	119	Tossofthecoin	117	148,500	1:47.40	.111
1996	Alphabet Soup	5	C.W. Antley	119	Soul of the Matter	121	Dare and Go	119	184,900	1:49.80	.108
1997	Gentlemen	5	G.L. Stevens	122	Alphabet Soup	122	Kingdom Found	116	180,300	1:47.20	.116
1998	Gentlemen	6	G.L. Stevens	124	Da Bull	115	Refinado Tom	120	180,000	1:47.60	.109
1999	Free House	5	C.J. McCarron	119	Malek	119	Dramatic Gold	116	180,000	1:48.40	.110
2000	Budroyale	7	G.K. Gomez	121	Cat Thief	120	Elaborate	116	180,000	1:48.70	.108
2001	Guided Tour	5	L. Melancon	115	Lethal Instrument	116	Moonlight Charger	113	180,000	1:48.26	.107
2002	Reddatore	7	A. Solis	116	Euchre	119	Irisheyesareflying	119	150,000	1:48.66	.106
2003	Congaree	5	J.D. Bailey	123	Milwaukee Brew	120	Pleasantly Perfect	117	150,000	1:47.60	.118

Beyer Index: 110.69

SAN CLEMENTE HANDICAP, 1 Mile (Turf),
3-Year-Old Fillies, Del Mar, 2003 Purse: $150,000

Year	Winner	Age	Jockey	Wt.	Second	Wt.	Third	Wt.	Win Value	Time	Beyer
1970	Loved	3	J. Lambert	114	Likely Lark	113	Beja	115	9,775	1:43.80	
1971	Gowran Green	3	R. Rosales	117	At Twillight	117	Fleetaglo	117	9,350	1:43.60	
1972	Bert's Tryst	3	R. Rosales	112	Homespun	115	Ground Song	117	9,600	1:43.00	
1973	Button Top	3	S. Valdez	112	Merry Madeleine	120	Gourmet Lark	117	12,750	1:43.80	
1974	Bold Ballet	3	F. Toro	121	Shah's Envoy	121	Sweet Ramblin Rose	116	13,350	1:44.00	
1975	Miss Francesca	3	D.G. McHargue	113	Summer Evening	115	Bradley's Pago	113	10,275	1:43.80	
1975	Princess Papulee	3	F. Toro	121	Mia Amore	121	Miracolo	113	10,275	1:43.80	
1976	Go March	3	D. Pierce	114	Granja Sueno	112	I Going	115	13,150	1:42.80	
1977	Teisen Lap	3	D.G. McHargue	113	Goldfilled	112	Lullaby	120	12,850	1:44.80	
1978	Miss Magnetic	3	M. Castaneda	117	Secala	112	Agree	114	13,550	1:44.20	
1978	Joe's Bee	3	L. Pincay Jr	120	Fairy Dance	117	Carrie's Angel	115	13,150	1:44.40	
1979	Ancient Art	3	F. Toro	121	Our Suiti Pie	116	Double Deceit	117	23,550	1:44.20	
1980	Plenty O'Toole	3	T. Lipham	116	Potter	115	Swift Bird	113	26,850	1:44.20	
1981	French Charmer	3	D.G. McHargue	118	Tap Dancer II	113	I Got Speed	121	32,100	1:43.40	
1982	Northern Style	3	M. Castaneda	114	Mama Tia	116	Marl Lee Ann	115	32,100	1:43.40	
1983	Eastern Bettor	3	L. Pincay Jr	113	Nice n Proper	117	Olympic Bronze	116	25,875	1:44.00	
1983	Lituya Bay	3	L. Pincay Jr	121	Corselette	116	Capitalization	115	25,375	1:43.80	
1984	Fashionably Late	3	C.J. McCarron	114	Auntie Betty	117	Patricia James	114	32,800	1:43.20	
1985	Mint Leaf	3	C.J. McCarron	122	Queen of Bronze	115	Stakes to Win	117	33,650	1:42.60	
1986	Our Sweet Sham	3	S.B. Soto	114	Mille et Une	115	T.V. Residual	115	33,450	1:43.20	
1987	Davie's Lamb	3	F. Toro	115	Develop		Wild Manor	115	25,500	1:42.80	
1987	Future Bright	3	P.A. Valenzuela	114	Chapel of Dreams	114	Down Again	116	25,300	1:44.60	
1988	Do So	3	A. Solis	121	Affordable Price	115	Variety Baby	117	50,650	1:35.80	

Year	Winner	Age	Jockey	Wt.	Second	Wt.	Third	Wt.	Win Value	Time	Beyer
1989	Darby's Daughter	3	G.L. Stevens	120	Sticky Wile	117	Bel Darling	116	66,000	1:36.60	
1990	Nijinsky's Lover	3	G.L. Stevens	118	Bimbo II	113	Slew of Pearls	116	50,300	1:36.40	
1990	Lonely Girl	3	P.A. Valenzuela	116	Bel's Starlet	114	Bidder Cream	113	50,300	1:36.20	91
1991	Flawlessly	3	C.J. McCarron	120	Gold Fleece	114	Miss High Blade	117	64,600	1:34.80	96
1992	Golden Treat	3	K.J. Desormeaux	121	Morriston Belle	118	Alysbelle	118	49,350	1:35.20	91
1993	Hollywood Wildcat	3	E. Delahoussaye	120	Miami Sands	116	Beal Street Blues	117	49,950	1:34.80	107
1994	Work the Crowd	3	C.J. McCarron	120	Pharma	116	Dancing Mirage	115	48,550	1:36.00	99
1995	Jewel Princess	3	C.J. McCarron	115	Auriette	119	Scratch Paper	119	59,650	1:36.00	97
1996	True Flare	3	C.S. Nakatani	116	Gastronomical	119	Najecam	114	67,200	1:35.40	100
1997	Famous Digger	3	B. Blanc	120	Cozy Blues	116	Really Happy	119	71,725	1:36.00	95
1998	Sicy D'Alsace	3	C.S. Nakatani	115	Miss Hot Salsa	117	Tranquility Lake	114	67,500	1:34.80	92
1999	Sweet Ludy	3	C.S. Nakatani	118	Caffe Latte	115	Sweet Life	117	90,000	1:35.00	99
2000	Uncharted Haven	3	A. Solis	116	Automated	117	Islay Mist	118	90,000	1:35.13	96
2001	Reine de Romance	3	E. Delahoussaye	116	Gabriellina Giof	116	La Vida Loca	116	90,000	1:34.88	91
2002	Little Treasure	3	K.J. Desormeaux	117	Pina Colada	115	Arabic Song	118	90,000	1:33.97	93
2003	Katdogawn	3	J.A. Krone	116	Atlantic Ocean	120	Buffythecenterfold	118	90,000	1:33.62	92

Beyer Index: 95.64

SAN DIEGO HANDICAP, 1 1/16 Miles,
3-Year-Olds and Up, Del Mar, 2003 Purse: $250,000

Year	Winner	Age	Jockey	Wt.	Second	Wt.	Third	Wt.	Win Value	Time	Beyer
1937	Clean Out	5	D. Smith	107	Illeanna	105	Bollermaker	115	750	1:12.00	
1938	King Saxon	7	J. Adams	110	Count Atlas	116	Advocator	111	2,005	1:45.20	
1945	High Resolve	4	W. Bailey	123	Ended	124	Deer	111	5,245	1:10.00	
1946	Lovonsite	3	N. Wall	106	Pride of Hygro	120	Ended	112	5,150	1:10.40	
1947	Ended	8	J. Nichols	118	Be Fearless	126	Darby D-Day	107	4,700	1:11.00	
1948	Prevaricator	5	A. Gray	122	Iron Maiden	110	Coast Invasion	104	6,475	1:42.60	
1949	Prevaricator	6	M. Caffarella	111	Moonrush	108	Top's Boy	120	6,600	1:42.00	
1950	Manyunk	5	G. Moore	119	Amarillo Kid	118	Frankly	122	6,775	1:42.40	
1951	Blue Reading	4	B. Pearson	120	Home Free	107	Pete Silver	105	6,575	1:41.60	
1952	Moonrush	6	R. Neves	112	Blue Reading	124	Stormy C'd	109	6,275	1:42.20	
1953	Goose Khal	4	W. Shoemaker	107	Chanlea	112	Bernwood	108	6,375	1:42.80	
1954	Stranglehold	5	B. Pearson	122	Golden Abbey	118	Blue Trumpeter	106	6,275	1:41.80	
1955	Trigonometry	4	R. Trejos	111	Arrogate	110	Karim	115	12,500	1:41.20	
1956	Honeys Alibi	4	R. York	115	Poona II	122	Beau Busher	110	12,700	1:41.40	
1957	Eddie Schmidt	4	I. Valenzuela	122	Gigantic	113	Pirnie	109	12,600	1:42.00	
1958	How Now	5	W. Harmatz	125	Swirling Abbey	118	Noredski	111	12,100	1:42.00	
1959	Twentyone Guns	4	G. Taniguchi	115	Find	121	Solid Fleet	113	12,000	1:42.00	
1960	Eddie Schmidt	7	A. Maese	118	King's Marshall	109	Honeys Gem	113	13,050	1:41.20	
1961	New Policy	4	R. Mundorf	119	Nagea	113	First Balcony	122	12,400	1:41.00	
1962	Windy Sands	5	R. York	122	Typhoon II	118	Cadiz	121	13,350	1:40.00	
1963	Native Diver	4	R. Neves	123	Rob Roy II	118	Cadiz	121	12,400	1:40.60	
1964	Native Diver	5	J. Lambert	122	Final Command	109	Drill Site	117	12,550	1:41.80	
1965	Native Diver	6	J. Lambert	131	Nearco Blue	110	Carang	111	12,500	1:40.00	
1966	Old Mose	4	D. Pierce	115	Whit's Pride	114	Silk Hat	114	12,650	1:41.40	
1967	French Fox	5	D.C. Hall	110	Sharp Decline	103	Bern Book	112	15,450	1:41.60	
1968	Rivet	4	M. Yanez	116	Vale of Tears	122	Title Game	113	12,300	1:40.80	
1969	Kissin' George	6	W. Mahorney	122	Rivet	118	Fiddle Isle	117	11,825	1:41.40	
1970	T.V. Commercial	5	D. Pierce	118	Imaginative	118	Quicken Tree	124	12,950	1:41.40	
1971	Advance Guard	5	W. Shoemaker	124	Far to Reach	114	The Field	113	13,400	1:41.00	
1972	Figonero	7	F. Alvarez	114	War Heim	120	Jeff David	117	13,600	1:40.80	
1973	Kennedy Road	5	W. Shoemaker	126	Imaginative	117	New Pr'pect	120	15,700	1:41.40	
1974	Matun	5	W. Shoemaker	121	Chesapeake	113	Imaginative	115	16,150	1:41.00	
1975	Chesapeake	6	F. Olivares	116	Top Command	116	Against the Snow	123	16,800	1:40.60	
1976	Good Report	6	L. Pincay Jr	116	Austin Mittler	117	Holding Pattern	115	19,000	1:42.40	
1977	Mark's Place	5	W. Shoemaker	124	Austin Mittler	113	C'nf. Yankee	114	18,450	1:40.60	
1978	Vic's Magic	5	F. Toro	116	Mr. Redoy	119	Clout	117	25,300	1:40.20	
1979	Always Gallant	5	D.G. McHargue	118	Bad 'n Big	120	Bl'die's Dancer	117	32,050	1:41.00	
1980	Island Sultan	5	M. Castaneda	114	Summer Time Guy	116	Borzoi	120	38,000	1:41.80	
1981	Summer Time Guy	5	S. Hawley	115	Shamgo	117	Exploded	115	48,550	1:41.00	
1982	Wickerr	5	E. Delahoussaye	117	Cajun Prince	117	Drouilly	114	50,350	1:41.40	
1983	Bates Motel	4	T. Lipham	122	The Wonder	123	Runaway G'm	117	47,650	1:41.00	
1984	Ancestral	4	E. Delahoussaye	116	Retsina Run	117	Slew's Royalty	117	60,550	1:41.20	
1985	Super Diamond	6	R.Q. Meza	115	M. Double M.	119	French Leg'naire	115	48,550	1:41.40	
1986	Skywalker	4	L. Pincay Jr	121	Nostalgia's Star	118	Epidaurus	113	65,350	1:40.80	
1987	Super Diamond	7	L. Pincay Jr	123	Nostalgia's Star	116	Good Command	114	48,050	1:40.80	
1988	Cutlass Reality	6	G.L. Stevens	123	Simply Majestic	115	Nostalgia's Star	116	63,700	1:41.40	
1989	Lively One	4	R.G. Davis	120	Mi Preferido	115	Hot Operator	114	76,200	1:40.80	
1990	Quiet American	4	K.J. Desormeaux	115	Bayakoa	122	Bosphorus	112	89,800	1:40.40	109
1991	Twilight Agenda	5	C.S. Nakatani	118	Roanoke	118	Louis Cyphre	118	90,900	1:47.60	

Year	Winner	Age	Jockey	Wt.	Second	Wt.	Third	Wt.	Win Value	Time	Beyer
1992	Another Review	4	L. Pincay Jr	120	Claret	116	Quintana	114	76,050	1:47.00	105
1993	Fanatic Boy	6	C.J. McCarron	114	Memo	116	Missionary Ridge	116	74,450	1:48.40	107
1994	Kingdom Found	4	C.J. McCarron	116	Tossofthecoin	117	Rapan Boy	115	75,850	1:41.20	107
1995	Blumin Affair	4	C.J. McCarron	116	Rapan Boy	116	Luthier Fever	115	87,200	1:41.20	101
1996	Savinio	6	Antley C. W.	116	Misnomer	118	Nonproductiveasset	118	95,350	1:40.80	105
1997	Northern Afleet	4	McCarron C. J.	118	Benchmark	117	New Century	114	100,300	1:41.80	106
1998	Mud Route	4	McCarron C. J.	117	Hal's Pal	113	Benchmark	117	150,300	1:41.20	111
1999	Mazel Trick	4	McCarron C. J.	117	River Keen	116	Tibado	116	150,000	1:40.60	118
2000	Skimming	4	G.K. Gomez	112	Prime Timber	116	National Saint	117	150,000	1:41.06	113
2001	Skimming	5	G.K. Gomez	120	Futural	120	Captain Steve	122	150,000	1:41.62	116
2002	Grey Memo	5	E. Delahoussaye	116	Euchre	116	Congaree	120	150,000	1:43.48	107
2003	Taste of Paradise	4	V. Espinoza	113	Gondolieri	117	Reba's Gold	116	150,000	1:42.62	102

Beyer Index: 108.23

SAN FELIPE, 1 1/16 Miles,
3-Year-Olds, Santa Anita, 2003 Purse: $250,000

Year	Winner	Age	Jockey	Wt.	Second	Wt.	Third	Wt.	Win Value	Time	Beyer
1935	Ted Clark	5	C. Turk	104	Jabot	111	Wacoche	94	2,060	1:37.60	
1936	Azucar	8	A. Robertson	115	Ariel Cross	115	Scotch Bun	107	2,100	1:36.00	
1937	Boxthorn	5	G. Woolf	115	Accolade	117	Stand Pat	120	3,425	1:23.60	
1938	Speed to Spare	5	R. Workman	114	Mr. Blaze	106	Woodberry	114	4,525	1:12.40	
1939	Specify	4	J. Adams	118	Main Man	117	Airflame	120	10,000	1:10.20	
1940	Our Mat	4	R. Neves	106	Lassator	104	Sun Egret	117	10,050	1:10.40	
1941	Bull Reigh	3	B. James	117	After Dawn	117	Porter's Cap	126	10,600	1:24.00	
1945	Sir Bim	3	J. Longden	119	Quick Reward	119	Gold Bolt	119	19,235	1:11.80	
1946	Galla Damion	3	R. Neves	116	Hampden	116	Darby D-Day	116	17,505	1:10.20	
1947	Owners Choice	3	J. Longden	118	Yankee Valor	118	On Trust	118	37,950	1:23.60	
1948	May Reward	3	E. Arcaro	123	Solidarity	120	Salmagundi	120	41,400	1:23.60	
1949	Olympia	3	W. Garner	126	Hayseed	120	Admiral Lee	120	51,950	1:22.80	
1950	Your Host	3	J. Longden	126	Great Circle	120	Blue Reading	123	45,000	1:23.40	
1951	Phil D.	3	R. York	122	Gold Note	114	Rough'n Tumble	118	40,700	1:22.80	
1952	Windy City II	3	E. Arcaro	126	Indian Land	118	Marcador	114	18,000	1:44.00	
1953	Decorated	3	J. Longden	120	Chanlea	122	Social Outcast	115	16,950	1:44.20	
1954	Determine	3	R. York	120	Travertine	113			17,800	1:42.40	
					Mr. Mustard	113					
1955	Jean's Joe	3	W. Boland	115	Beau Busher	112	Trentonian	123	17,800	1:43.00	
1956	Social Climber	3	L. Gilligan	108	Count Chic	120	Terrang	124	18,200	1:44.40	
1957	Joe Price	3	G. Glisson	115	Sir William	118	Blue Spruce	111	18,500	1:43.40	
1958	Carrier X.	3	G. Taniguchi	108	Aliwar	119	Furyvan	113	16,350	1:45.60	
1959	Finnegan	3	W. Harmatz	115	Tomy Lee	124	Royal Orbit	118	32,900	1:43.40	
1960	Flow Line	3	W. Boland	118	T.V. Lark	120	John William	121	35,200	1:42.40	
1961	Flutterby	3	J. Longden	122	Olden Times	124	Wire Us	111	36,700	1:42.20	
1962	Doc Jocoy	3	W. Harmatz	113	Royal Attack	119	Admiral's Voyage	122	40,400	1:44.20	
1963	Denodado	3	R. Campas	110	Might and Main	114	Doolin Point	112	42,750	1:45.00	
1964	Hill Rise	3	D. Pierce	124	Wil Rad	114	Real Good Deal	120	38,950	1:41.40	
1965	Jacinto	3	M. Ycaza	126	Lucky Debonair	120	Isle of Greece	118	35,400	1:41.80	
1966	Saber Mountain	3	W. Shoemaker	124	Exhibitionist	119	Hill Clown	112	40,400	1:42.40	
1967	Rising Market	3	L. Pincay Jr	118	Ruken	117	Field Master	113	40,050	1:42.80	
1968	Prince Pablo	3	J. Sellers	118	Aley Fighter	114	Poleax	112	23,900	1:42.40	
1968	Dewan	3	J. Lambert	119	Don B.	122	Proper Proof	115	24,400	1:42.40	
1969	Elect the Ruler	3	E. Belmonte	116	Lonny's Secret	117	Mr. Joe F.	122	36,050	1:44.20	
1970	Cool Hand	3	J. Lambert	115	Plenty Old	117	Sir Wiggle	117	30,050	1:41.80	
1970	Terlago	3	W. Shoemaker	118	George Lewis	122	Willowick	114	29,550	1:41.80	
1971	Unconscious	3	L. Pincay Jr	122	Steal a Dance	114	Fast Fellow	118	36,150	1:42.60	
1972	Solar Salute	3	L. Pincay Jr	121	Quack	117	Indian	114	41,800	1:41.80	
1973	Linda's Chief	3	B. Baeza	126	Ancient Title	120	Out of the East	115	42,700	1:41.80	
1974	Aloha Mood	3	D. Pierce	118	Money Lender	124	Triple Crown	124	43,700	1:42.40	
1975	Fleet Velvet	3	F. Toro	120	George Navonod	122	Diabolo	124	33,200	1:42.40	
1976	Crystal Water	3	W. Shoemaker	117	Beau Talent	117	Double Discount	113	34,000	1:42.60	
1977	Smasher	3	S. Hawley	115	Habitony	122	Miami Sun	115	32,850	1:42.60	
1978	Affirmed	3	S. Cauthen	126	Chance Dancer	117	Tampoy	118	38,100	1:42.60	
1979	Pole Position	3	S. Hawley	119	Switch Partners	114	Flying Paster	127	48,500	1:41.20	
1980	Raise a Man	3	W. Shoemaker	119	The Carpenter	123	Rumbo	119	64,300	1:41.60	
1981	Stancharry	3	F. Toro	118	Splendid Spruce	116	Flying Nashua	121	69,500	1:42.00	
1982	Advance Man	3	C.J. McCarron	117	Gato del Sol	118	Cassaleria	123	77,550	1:42.20	
1983	Desert Wine	3	W. Shoemaker	124	Naevus	117	Fifth Division	120	62,900	1:41.60	
1984	Fali Time	3	S. Hawley	122	Gate Dancer	117	Commemorate	117	103,450	1:42.60	
1985	Image of Greatness	3	L. Pincay Jr	120	Skywalker	120	Nostalgia's Star	117	106,350	1:43.20	
1986	Variety Road	3	C.J. McCarron	120	Big Play	114	Dancing Pirate	116	7,535	1:45.40	

Year	Winner	Age	Jockey	Wt.	Second	Wt.	Third	Wt.	Win Value	Time	Beyer
1987	Chart the Stars	3	E. Delahoussaye	116	Alysheba	120	Temperate Sil	122	107,450	1:43.00	
1988	Mi Preferido	3	C.J. McCarron	119	Purdue King	119	Tejano	122	96,300	1:42.20	
1989	Sunday Silence	3	P.A. Valenzuela	119	Flying Continental	118	Music Merci	124	91,800	1:42.60	
1990	Real Cash	3	A. Solis	113	Warcraft	117	Music Prospector	117	102,600	1:42.00	
1991	Sea Cadet	3	C.J. McCarron	119	Scan	119	Compelling Sound	116	124,200	1:41.80	
1992	Bertrando	3	A. Solis	122	Arp	116	Hickman Creek	116	120,800	1:42.60	97
1993	Corby	3	C.J. McCarron	116	Personal Hope	116	Devoted Brass	122	121,100	1:42.00	100
1994	Soul of the Matter	3	K.J. Desormeaux	116	Brocco	119	Valiant Nature	119	118,500	1:44.60	106
1995	Afternoon Deelites	3	K.J. Desormeaux	119	Timber Country	122	Lake George	116	117,200	1:42.00	99
1996	Odyle	3	C.S. Nakatani	116	Smithfield	116	Cavonnier	122	152,400	1:42.40	101
1997	Free House	3	D.R. Flores	119	Silver Charm	122	King Crimson	116	152,400	1:42.40	103
1998	Artax	3	C.J. McCarron	122	Real Quiet	119	Prosperous Bid	116	150,000	1:41.60	108
1999	Prime Timber	3	D.R. Flores	116	Exploit	122	High Wire Act	116	150,000	1:42.00	106
2000	Fusaichi Pegasus	3	K.J. Desormeaux	116	The Deputy	122	Anees	119	150,000	1:42.66	106
2001	Point Given	3	G.L. Stevens	122	I Love Silver	116	Jamaican Rum	119	150,000	1:41.94	105
2002	Medaglia d'Oro	3	L. Pincay Jr.	116	U S S Tinosa	116	Siphonic	122	150,000	1:41.95	107
2003	Buddy Gil	3	G.L. Stevens	119	Atswhatimtalknbout	116	Brancusi	116	150,000	1:43.64	102

Beyer Index: 103.33

SAN FERNANDO BREEDERS' CUP, 1 1/16 Miles, 4-Year-Olds, Santa Anita, 2003 Purse: $219,600

Year	Winner	Age	Jockey	Wt.	Second	Wt.	Third	Wt.	Win Value	Time	Beyer
1952	Counterpoint	4	D. Gorman	118	Phil D.	115	Intent	114	14,300	1:45.20	
1953	Mark-Ye-Well	4	E. Arcaro	122	Stranglehold	112	Southarlington	109	15,550	1:44.20	
1954	By Zeus	4	J. Westrope	112	Resistance	112	Joe Jones	114	16,350	1:49.40	
1955	Poona II	4	W. Shoemaker	112	Miz Clementine	113	Duke's Lea	112	16,550	1:40.80	
1956	Beau Busher	4	J. Westrope	118	Traffic Judge	122	Honeys Alibi	122	17,400	1:43.60	
1957	Holandes II	4	W. Shoemaker	115	Family Album	112	More Glory	112	17,400	1:43.20	
1958	Round Table	4	W. Shoemaker	130	The Searcher	114	Seaneen	124	15,750	1:42.20	
1959	Hillsdale	4	T. Barrow	124	Jewel's Reward	120	Gleeman	114	16,700	1:42.40	
1960	King o' Turf	4	A. Valenzuela	113	First Landing	117	Civic Pride	113	32,100	1:50.00	
1961	Prove It	4	W. Shoemaker	113	Tompion	123	Prince Blessed	113	31,900	1:47.60	
1962	Four-and-Twenty	4	J. Longden	126	Olden Times	120	Obsession	114	31,900	1:48.80	
1963	Crimson Satan	4	H. Hinojosa	117	Native Diver	120	Pirate Cove	114	36,300	1:47.20	
1964	Nevada Battler	4	M. Ycaza	114	B. Major	120	Big Raff	114	26,125	1:48.80	
1964	Gun Bow	4	W. Shoemaker	114	Lamb Chop	115	Win-Em-All	111	26,125	1:47.80	
1965	Hill Rise	4	D. Pierce	123	Pelegrin	114	Canadian B.	113	39,050	1:48.40	
1966	Isle of Greece	4	W. Blum	121	Terry's Secret	121	Bold Bidder	121	36,000	1:48.60	
1967	Buckpasser	4	B. Baeza	124	Fleet Host	121	Pretense	118	34,050	1:48.20	
1968	Damascus	4	W. Shoemaker	126	Most Host	113	Ruken	120	34,450	1:48.80	
1969	Cavamore	4	E. Belmonte	113	Dignitas	117	Dewan	120	36,950	1:49.00	
1971	Willowick	4	E. Belmonte	113	Hanalei Bay	120	War Heim	114	40,600	1:48.80	
1972	Autobiography	4	E. Belmonte	113			Good Counsel	117	35,300	1:47.20	
	Triple Bend	4		117							
1973	Bicker	4	G. Brogan	120	Royal Owl	120	Commoner	114	56,350	1:48.20	
1974	Ancient Title	4	L. Pincay Jr	120	Linda's Chief	123	Mariache II	114	50,250	1:47.60	
1975	Stardust Mel	4	W. Shoemaker	120	Century's Envoy	120	Princely Native	120	36,700	1:48.60	
1975	First Back	4	J. Vasquez	114	Lightning Mandate	120	Confederate Yankee	117	37,700	1:46.80	
1976	Messenger of Song	4	J. Lambert	120	Avatar	123	Larrikin	120	54,350	1:48.20	
1977	Kirby Lane	4	L. Pincay Jr	120	Double Discount	117	Rajab	114	39,000	1:47.60	
1977	Pocket Park	4	S. Cauthen	114	Properantes	114	Crystal Water	123	38,500	1:48.60	
1978	Text	4	F. Toro	120	J.O. Tobin	123	Centennial Pride	114	65,500	1:49.40	
1979	Radar Ahead	4	D.G. McHargue	123	Affirmed	126	Little Reb	120	69,200	1:48.00	
1980	Spectacular Bid	4	W. Shoemaker	126	Flying Paster	126	Relaunch	120	63,300	1:48.00	
1981	Doonesbury	4	S. Hawley	120	Raise a Man	120	Idyll	117	74,300	1:47.00	
1982	It's the One	4	W.A. Guerra	120	Princelet	123	Rock Softly	114	84,650	1:47.60	
1983	Wavering Monarch	4	E. Delahoussaye	123	Water Bank	120	Prince Spellbound	126	88,400	1:50.00	
1984	Interco	4	P.A. Valenzuela	123	Desert Wine	123	Paris Prince	120	92,850	1:48.60	
1985	Precisionist	4	C.J. McCarron	126	Greinton	120	Gate Dancer	126	123,350	1:47.40	
1986	Right Con	4	R.Q. Meza	117	Nostalgia's Star	120	Fast Account	114	101,800	1:48.40	
1987	Variety Road	4	L. Pincay Jr	123	Broad Brush	126	Snow Chief	126	96,300	1:49.00	
1988	On the Line	4	J. Santos	120	Candi's Gold	123	Grand Vizier	114	122,400	1:49.00	
1989	Mi Preferido	4	C.J. McCarron	123	Speedratic	120	Perceive Arrogance	120	138,200	1:47.40	
1990	Flying Continental	4	C.A. Black	120	Splurger	114	Secret Slew	114	128,600	1:47.20	
1991	In Excess	4	G.L. Stevens	120	Warcraft	120	Go and Go	123	128,800	1:46.60	
1992	Best Pal	4	K.J. Desormeaux	122	Olympio	122	Dinard	122	130,000	1:48.20	121
1993	Bertrando	4	C.J. McCarron	120	Star Recruit	120	The Wicked North	116	127,800	1:51.20	109
1994	Zignew	4	C.J. McCarron	116	Nonproductiveasset	116	Pleasant Tango	116	135,400	1:47.80	107
1995	Wekiva Springs	4	K.J. Desormeaux	116	Dramatic Gold	120	Dare and Go	116	126,800	1:48.40	105
1996	Helmsman	4	C.J. McCarron	118	Gold and Steel	120	The Key Rainbow	116	134,500	1:48.80	103
1997	Northern Afleet	4	C.J. McCarron	116	Ambivalent	116	Ready to Order	116	194,400	1:48.40	96

Year	Winner	Age	Jockey	Wt.	Second	Wt.	Third	Wt.	Win Value	Time	Beyer
1998	Silver Charm	4	G. L. Stevens	122	Mud Route	116	Lord Grillo	120	125,520	1:41.80	112
1999	Dixie Dot Com	4	D. R. Flores	116	Event of the Year	122	Old Topper	118	190,800	1:41.00	114
2000	Saint's Honor	4	K.J. Desormeaux	117	Cat Thief	122	Mr. Broad Blade	118	190,200	1:41.94	105
2001	Tiznow	4	C.J. McCarron	122	Walkslikeaduck	120	Wooden Phone	116	98,880	1:42.05	107
2002	Western Pride	4	G.K. Gomez	122	Orientate	120	Fancy As	120	134,640	1:41.30	110
2003	Pass Rush	4	C.S. Nakatani	116	Tracemark	116	Tizbud	116	131,760	1:42.37	106

Beyer Index: 107.92

SAN FRANCISCO BREEDERS' CUP MILE HANDICAP, 1 Mile (Turf), 3-Year-Olds and Up, Bay Meadows, 2003 Purse: $177,500

Year	Winner	Age	Jockey	Wt.	Second	Wt.	Third	Wt.	Win Value	Time	Beyer
1948	Prevaricator	5	J. Longden	118	Hemet Squaw	109	Shannon II	122	12,390	1:34.40	
1949	Dinner Gong	4	J. Westrope	124	Miche	109	Cover Up	117	12,690	1:36.00	
1950	Citation	5	S. Brooks	128	Bolero	123	On Trust	116	14,550	1:33.60	
1951	Pension Plan	4	R. York	111	Star Fiddle	114	Bullreigh Jr	110	6,800	1:38.20	
1952	Lights Up	5	R. Neves	120	Phil D.	124	Boomerang Boy	109	17,150	1:35.60	
1953	Goose Khal	4	W. Shoemaker	125	High Scud	113	Fleet Bird	122	15,800	1:36.40	
1954	Golden Abbey	4	J. Westrope	119	Strangehold	120	Imbros	128	9,625	1:35.00	
1955	Determine	4	R. York	128	Poona II	123			29,325	1:38.00	
1956	Arrogate	5	R. Neves	126	Grey Tower	116	Battle Dance	107	12,750	1:34.80	
1957	Battle Dance	5	H. Moreno	125	North End	112	Hi Pardner	111	8,400	1:35.20	
1958	Battle Dance	6	H. Moreno	117	Social Climber	121	Bailarin	113	12,850	1:37.40	
1959	The Searcher	5	G. Lanoway	116	ShahJehan II	116	Battle Dance	120	8,725	1:35.20	
1961	Sea Orbit	5	A. Valenzuela	122	Roman Incense	112	Sparrow C'stle	115	6,100	1:36.60	
1962	Chase Eddie	5	J. Longden	114	Woodhaven	111	Novalook	115	6,250	1:36.40	
1963	Native Diver	4	W. Shoemaker	125	More Megaton	118	Aeroflint	115	9,200	1:35.20	
1964	Switchback	4	R. Neves	110	More Megaton	114	Slegde	116	6,875	1:35.80	
1964	Mustard Plaster	5	D. Hall	115	Upper Half	110	Native Diver	123	6,875	1:34.80	
1965	Viking Spirit	5	K. Church	119	Native Diver	128	Honored Sir	113	8,875	1:36.80	
1966	Lush Life	4	E. Medina	113	Travel Orb	114	Sir Bolco	117	6,350	1:34.20	
1966	Gamin	6	A. Pineda	116	Zulu Lad	113	Sen'r Grande	120	6,350	1:34.40	
1967	Native Diver	8	J. Lambert	133	Perris	113	Triple Tux	113	9,125	1:35.20	
1968	Bi G.	6	R. Peniche	108	Lucky P.J.	116	Little Matador	112	15,850	1:37.00	
1969	Wingover	6	R. Cespedes	114	Glory Hallelujah	120	Fiddler's Gr'n	112	15,950	1:36.80	
1970	Field Master	6	M. Valenzuela	119	Lonny's Secret	115	Baffle	122	16,700	1:37.80	
1971	Figonero	6	A. Pineda	123	Fighting	110	Long Position	111	19,100	1:34.60	
1972	Imaginative	6	W. Mahorney	115	Long Position	116	Quiet Star	116	12,850	1:34.60	
1972	Panzer Chief	5	V. Tejada	119	Against the Wind	117	Du Call	115	12,725	1:36.20	
1973	New Prospect	4	J. Sellers	118	Masked	116	Rock Bath	113	22,150	1:43.20	
1974	Visualizer	4	F. Mena	114	Roka Zaca	117	Larkal II	110	21,900	1:38.00	
1975	Whoa Boy	4	G. Baze	113	Ocala Boy	113	Star of Kuwait	116	18,100	1:39.00	
1977	Crafty Native	4	M. James	112	Cojak	122	Money Lender	119	26,350	1:38.40	
1978	Jumping Hill	6	J. Lambert	121	Boy Tike	115	Dr. Henry K.	109	32,500	1:38.40	
1979	Struttin' Geo	5	T.M. Chapman	117	Crafty Native	111	Foreign Power	115	32,950	1:37.40	
1980	Don Alberto	5	R.M. Gonzalez	114	Saboulard	116	Capt. Don	121	33,300	1:33.40	
1981	Opus Dei	6	F. Olivares	119	Drouilly	116	His Honor	117	41,850	1:34.80	
1982	Silveyville	4	D. Winick	121	Visible Pole	110	A Sure Hit	113	51,050	1:36.80	
1983	King's County	4	E. Munoz	112	Police Inspector	118	Silveyville	121	48,950	1:37.60	
1984	Drumalis	4	E. Delahoussaye	117	Silveyville	117	Ten Below	115	43,275	1:35.60	
1984	Ice Hot	4	M. Castaneda	115	Major Sport	117	Otter Slide	114	34,275	1:35.40	
1985	Truce Maker	7	J.A. Garcia	112	Lina Cavalieri	115	Baron O'Dublin	116	69,500	1:35.20	
1986	Hail Bold King	5	M. Castaneda	117	Right Con	119	Lucky n Green	114	69,900	1:36.40	
1987	Dormello	6	A.L. Diaz	113	Air Display	116	Barbery	115	82,500	1:36.20	
1988	Ifrad	6	T.M. Chapman	115	The Medic	118	Blanco	117	82,500	1:36.20	
1989	Patchy Groundfog	6	F. Olivares	116	No Commitment	113	Mazilier	115	110,000	1:38.20	
1990	Colway Rally	6	C.A. Black	116	River Master	115	Miswaki Tern	117	110,000	1:35.80	
1991	Forty Niner Days	4	T.T. Doocy	113	Exbourne	116	Blaze O'Brien	116	110,000	1:38.80	
1992	Tight Spot	5	L. Pincay Jr	125	Notorious Pleasure	116	Forty Niner Days	116	55,000	1:35.40	108
1993	The Wicked North	4	A. Solis	114	The Tender Track	117	Slew of Damascus	115	110,000	1:41.80	104
1994	Gothland	5	C.S. Nakatani	116	Emerald Jig	113	The Tender Track	116	110,000	1:35.40	105
1995	Unfinished Symph	4	C.W. Antley	118	Vaudeville	119	Torch Rouge	114	120,000	1:34.00	110
1996	Gold And Steel	4	A. Solis	114	Savinio	115	Debutant Trick	117	120,000	1:35.00	105
1997	Wavy Run	6	B. Blanc	116	Savinio	118	Romarin	118	120,000	1:32.00	106
1998	Hawksley Hill	5	G.L. Stevens	119	Fantastic Fellow	121	Uncaged Fury	117	120,000	1:34.20	109
1999	Tuzla	5	B. Blanc	112	Poteen	116	Rob 'n Gin	117	180,000	1:35.40	104
2000	Ladies Din	5	K.J. Desormeaux	120	Fighting Falcon	116	Self Feeder	116	150,000	1:35.46	107
2001	Redattore	6	J. Lumpkins	115	Hawksley Hill	119	Kerrygold	116	137,500	1:35.14	106
2002	Suances	5	D.R. Flores	116	Decarchy	121	The Tin Man	116	110,000	1:35.19	106
2003	Ninebanks	5	R.J. Warren Jr	117	Nicobar	116	National Anthem	116	110,000	1:37.20	103

Beyer Index: 106.08

SAN GABRIEL HANDICAP, 1 1/8 Miles (Turf), 3-Year-Olds and Up, Santa Anita, 2003 Purse:$150,000

Year	Winner	Age	Jockey	Wt.	Second	Wt.	Third	Wt.	Win Value	Time	Beyer
1938	Morning Breeze	2	N. Merritt	119	Montecito	119	Alex the Great	122	5,920	0:33.40	
1945	Vain Prince	6	G. Woolf	117	Orion	114	Phar Song	117	19,890	1:11.40	
1946	Sun Lady	4	H. Trent	107	High Resolve	122	Jean Miracle	118	17,890	1:10.40	
1952	Windy City II	3	E. Arcaro	114	A Gleam	108	Hill Gail	119	13,350	1:22.40	
1953	Decorated	3	J. Longden	114	Chanlea	122	Boo Who	111	13,100	1:23.00	
1954	Determine	3	R. York	118	Mr. Mustard	114	Brighter Days	118	14,050	1:24.40	
1955	St. Vincent	4	J. Longden	116	Star of the Forest	122	Novarullah	119	19,750	2:00.00	
1956	Star of Ross	4	R. Trejos	110	Mintaka	114	Dictar	111	16,500	2:01.20	
1957	Corn Husker	4	G. Taniguchi	107	High Button	115	Posadas	117	17,450	2:00.20	
1958	Tall Chief II	6	W. Harmatz	117	Ekaba	119	Whatitoldyou	116	17,650	1:59.80	
1959	MacBern	4	H. Moreno	113	Andrew Alan	116	Hakuchikara	119	16,500	2:00.40	
1960	Eddie Schmidt	7	A. Maese	120	Sisters Prince	113	Greek Star	120	16,900	1:49.60	
1961	Geechee Lou	5	J. Longden	112	How Now	125	Sundown II	113	18,050	1:46.60	
1962	Art Market	4	I. Valenzuela	120	Grey Eagle	117	The Axe II	115	17,000	1:48.40	
1963	Dusky Damion	6	I. Valenzuela	117	Rablero	114	Pardao	120	16,300	1:48.40	
1964	Marlin Bay	4	M. Ycaza	116	Gay Challenger II	122	Mr. Consistency	120	17,550	1:48.40	
1965	Biggs	5	W. Harmatz	113	Polizonte	115	Colorado King	125	17,000	1:49.00	
1966	Perfect Sky	4	A. Pineda	111	Or et Argent	118	Cedar Key	123	17,100	1:55.00	
1967	Flag	7	W. Blum	117	Quicken Tree	111	Ultimate	116	18,370	1:47.60	
1968	Rivet	4	M. Volzke	113	Most Host	113	Moontrip	113	18,050	1:50.60	
1969	Easy Mark	4	E. Belmonte	113	Deck Hand	117	Biggs	118	16,800	1:49.00	
1971	Cougar II	5	W. Shoemaker	120	Suerte al Cobre	111	Try Sheep	112	20,500	1:52.60	
1972	Big Shot II	7	E. Belmonte	117	Vegas Vic	120	Far to Reach	118	27,050	1:48.60	
1973	Astray	4	J. Vasquez	115	Golden Doc Ray	115	Kirrary	117	26,250	1:48.20	
1973	Kentuckian	4	D. Pierce	114	Artaxerxes	113	Harkville	112	26,950	1:47.60	
1974	Fair Test	6	A. Santiago	113	Indefatigable	118	Montmartre	118	25,750	1:50.20	
1975	Zanthe	6	S. Hawley	117	Copper Mel	115	Riot in Paris	124	26,550	1:47.40	
1977	Riot in Paris	6	W. Shoemaker	125	Distant Land	115	Ribot Grande	113	34,000	1:50.00	
1978	Mr. Redoy	4	S. Hawley	110	Dr. Krohn	116	Papelote	113	33,100	1:48.40	
1979	Fluorescent Light	5	A. Cordero Jr	118	As de Copas	118	Tiller	127	32,200	1:47.60	
1980	Premiere Ministre	4	L. Pincay Jr	118	Galaxy Libra	117	Fast	118	28,250	1:48.20	
1980	John Henry	5	D.G. McHargue	123	Smasher	111	As de Copas	117	39,300	1:49.80	
1981	The Bart	5	E. Delahoussaye	125	Irish Heart	115	Forlion	114	48,040	1:48.00	
1983	Greenwood Star	8	D. Pierce	119	Tell Again	118	Western	115	51,500	1:47.20	
1984	Prince Fl'r'm'nd	6	P.A. Valenzuela	118	Ten Below	113	Ginger Brink	118	40,225	1:48.20	
1984	Beldale Lustre	5	L. Pincay Jr	118	I'll See You	112	Color Bearer	111	39,425	1:48.80	
1985	Dahar	4	F. Toro	120	Paris Prince	116	Massera	116	50,750	1:47.60	
1986	Yashgan	5	C.J. McCarron	124	Tights	118	Rivlia	116	51,800	1:49.60	
1987	Nostalgia's Star	5	L. Pincay Jr	118	Inevitable Leader	112	Spellbound	116	61,550	1:51.20	
1988	Simply Majestic	4	J.D. Bailey	120	Payant	118	Dr. Death	116	66,150	1:47.40	
1988	Conquering Hero	5	G.L. Stevens	115	Hot and Smoggy	117	Ten Key	116	66,500	1:50.60	
1989	Wretham	4	L. Pincay Jr	117	Patchy Groundfog	117	In Extremis	117	67,700	1:46.20	
1990	In Excess	3	G.L. Stevens	117	Rouvignac	113	Kanatiyr	115	68,100	1:47.20	
1992	Classic Fame	6	E. Delahoussaye	118	Super May	119	Defensive Play	116	64,300	1:46.60	.108
1993	Star of Cozzene	5	G.L. Stevens	118	Bistro Garden	114	Leger Cat	115	66,100	1:48.20	.107
1994	Earl of Barking	5	C.J. McCarron	118	Fanmore	116	Navarone	119	65,300	1:48.60	.104
1995	Romarin	5	C.S. Nakatani	119	Inner City	116	Ianomami	116	62,900	1:49.20	.104
1996	Romarin	6	C.S. Nakatani	119	Virginia Carnival	116	Silver Wizard	117	82,050	1:49.60	.104
1997	Rainbow Blues	6	G.L. Stevens	119	River Deep	116	Via Lombardia	116	81,500	1:46.80	.104
1997	Martiniquais	5	C.S. Nakatani	116	Bienvenido	115	Da Bull	115	99,180	1:48.40	.100
1998	Brave Act	4	G.F. Alemeida	118	Mash One	116	Fabulous Guy	113	90,000	1:46.60	.108
2000	Brave Act	6	A. Solis	120	Native Desert	116	Manndar	116	97,470	1:49.25	.109
2001	Irish Prize	5	K.J. Desormeaux	117	Manndar	121	Here Comes Big C	110	90,000	1:47.88	.102
2002	Grammarian	4	J. Valdivia Jr.	117	David Copperfield	117	Decarchy	119	90,000	1:48.12	.106
2003	Redattore	8	A. Solis	122	Continental Red	116	Denied	116	90,000	1:48.17	.107

Beyer Index: 105.25

SAN GORGONIO HANDICAP, 1 1/8 Miles (Turf), Fillies and Mares, 4-year-Olds and Up, Santa Anita, 2003 Purse: $150,000

Year	Winner	Age	Jockey	Wt.	Second	Wt.	Third	Wt.	Win Value	Time	Beyer
1968	Tumble Wind	4	J. Sellers	122	Sky Gipsy II	118	Poona Khan	113	14,150	1:13.60	
1969	Jimmy Peanuts	4	W. Blum	118	Security Check	119	Royal Come'n	122	15,900	1:52.00	
1971	Never Confuse	5	L. Pincay Jr	120	Pleasant Harbour	122	Gallant Policy	114	18,300	1:51.60	
1972	Tradesman	8	E. Belmonte	114	Delaware Chief	119	Quiet Star	115	23,600	1:49.20	
1973	Extra Hand	7	L. Pincay Jr	118	Timoteo	122	Dundee Marmalade	115	23,200	1:49.00	
1974	Margum	5	W. Shoemaker	115	Harbor Point	117	Expediter	115	22,500	1:50.60	
1975	Madison Place	7	D. Pierce	119	Grotonian	115	At the D'ne	115	21,400	1:48.40	
1976	Tizna	7	F. Alvarez	132	Miss Tokyo	120	Charger's Star	121	25,800	1:47.20	
1977	Lucie Manet	5	W. Shoemaker	121	Theia	116	Claire Valentine	115	32,250	1:54.00	
1977	Merry Lady III	5	L. Pincay Jr	119	Our First Delight	117	Pacara	114	36,200	1:50.80	

Year	Winner	Age	Jockey	Wt.	Second	Wt.	Third	Wt.	Win Value	Time	Beyer
1979	Via Maris	4	A. Cordero Jr	113	Drama Critic	122	Donna Inez	114	33,500	1:52.60	
1980	Miss Magnetic	5	L.E. Ortega	111	Maytide	112	Persona	113	39,700	1:50.00	
1981	Kilijaro	5	W. Shoemaker	128	Queen to Conquer	122	Refinish	117	36,300	1:49.20	
1982	Track Robbery	6	E. Delahoussaye	123	Rainbow Connection	117	Targa	114	45,700	1:52.60	
1983	Castilla	4	C.J. McCarron	122	Star Pastures	119	Cat Girl	115	50,800	1:46.40	
1984	First Advance	5	M. Castaneda	115	Avigaition	120	L'Attrayante	121	53,950	1:48.80	
1985	Fact Finder	6	F. Toro	118	Capichi	118	Comedy Act	119	62,500	1:48.20	
1986	Mount'n Bear	5	E. Delahoussaye	118	Royal Regatta	115	Justicara	117	67,150	1:48.40	
1987	Frau Altiva	5	L. Pincay Jr	117	Auspiciante	122	Solva	119	63,100	1:50.20	
1988	Miss Alto	5	E. Delahoussaye	116	Top Corsage	119	My Virginia Reel	115	63,200	1:49.20	
1989	No Review	4	R.Q. Meza	117	Annoconnor	122	White Mischief II	116	79,950	1:48.80	
1990	Invited Guest	6	R.A. Baze	117	White Mischief II	115	Oeilladine	115	83,750	1:46.40	102
1991	Royal Touch	6	C.J. McCarron	118	Countus In	119	Marshua's Dancer	113	83,850	1:47.80	101
1992	Paseana	5	C.J. McCarron	118	Laura Ly	112	Reluctant Guest	117	77,250	1:53.80	97
1993	Southern Truce	5	C.S. Nakatani	114	Laura Ly	114	Lite Light	115	67,100	1:51.20	104
1994	Hero's Love	6	L. Pincay Jr	119	Skimble	118	Miss Turkana	118	66,800	1:47.60	101
1995	Queens Court Queen	6	C.S. Nakatani	117	Wende	117	Vinista	115	62,000	1:48.60	103
1996	Wandesta	5	C.S. Nakatani	119	Matiara	118	Yearly Tour	117	80,550	1:49.00	106
1997	Sixieme Sens	5	C.S. Nakatani	116	Alpride	120	Grafin	116	82,950	1:47.00	106
1998	Golden Arches	4	C.J. McCarron	120	Ecoute	115	Real Connection*	116	96,870	1:49.40	103
1999	See You Soon	5	K.J. Desormeaux	118	Sonja's Faith	118	Verinha	115	90,000	1:49.00	105
2000	Lady at Peace	4	G.K. Gomez	115	Spanish Fern	119	Riboletta	116	90,000	1:48.75	101
2001	Uncharted Haven	4	A. Solis	115	Brianda	110	Beautiful Noise	116	90,000	1:50.02	98
2002	Tout Charmant	6	C.J. McCarron	120	Janet	119	Vencera	115	90,000	1:47.22	104
2003	Tates Creek	5	P.A. Valenzuela	121	Megahertz	117	Double Cat	114	90,000	1:46.91	103

Beyer Index: **102.43**

SAN LUIS OBISPO HANDICAP, 1 1/2 Miles (Turf), 4-Year-Olds and Up, Santa Anita, 2003 Purse: $200,000

Year	Winner	Age	Jockey	Wt.	Second	Wt.	Third	Wt.	Win Value	Time	Beyer
1968	Dr. Isby	4	W. Blum	113	Biggs	118	Deck Hand	115	25,825	2:27.80	
1968	Tumble Wind	4	J. Sellers	120	Model Fool	118	Jungle Road	117	25,825	2:27.00	
1969	Quicken Tree	6	W. Hartack	124	Red Vandal	105	Rivet	120	36,800	2:37.60	
1970	Quilche	6	J. Lambert	115	Royal Dynasty	116	Society II	115	35,600	1:58.00	
1971	Daryl's Joy	5	J. Sellers	128	Cougar II	127	Onandaga	110	38,300	2:29.20	
1972	Practicante	6	W. Shoemaker	118	Golden Eagle II	118	Y'low Zorker	114	35,050	2:26.40	
1972	Lord Derby	5	W. Shoemaker	112	Dendron	115	Moomba Fox	112	35,050	2:27.40	
1973	Queen's Hustler	4	R. Rosales	112	China Silk	115	River Buoy	117	40,800	2:27.20	
1974	Captain Cee Jay	4	F. Alvarez	113	Court Ruling	112	El Rey	112	28,150	2:23.80	
1974	Astray	5	J. Vasquez	118	Scantling	112	Wichita Oil	115	28,150	2:24.40	
1975	Madison Palace	7	L. Pincay Jr	120	Toujours Pret	121	Barclay Joy	118	40,100	2:30.20	
1976	Announcer	4	F. Toro	118	Top Crowd	123	Zanthe	121	38,200	2:30.80	
1977	Royal Derby II	8	W. Shoemaker	126	Gallivantor	115	Anne's Pretender	123	41,700	2:24.80	
1978	Copper Mel	6	S. Hawley	115	Avodire	110	Tacitus	115	42,300	2:28.00	
1979	Fluorescent Light	5	L. Pincay Jr	124	As de Copas	118	Alpha Boy	112	48,950	2:28.20	
							Nostalgia	113			
1980	Silver Eagle	6	W. Shoemaker	120	Balzac	123	Friuli	114	65,100	2:30.20	
1981	John Henry	6	L. Pincay Jr	127	Galaxy Libra	119	Zor	115	62,800	2:24.00	
1982	Regal Bearing	6	J.J. Steiner	114	Le Duc de Bar	114	Goldiko	119	80,450	2:27.20	
1983	Pelerin	6	W. Shoemaker	116	Western	118	Massera	118	67,200	2:24.60	
1984	Sir Pele	5	R.Q. Meza	118	Lucence	115	Debonair Herc	114	79,375	2:27.40	
1985	Western	7	G.L. Stevens	114	Scrupules	121	Strong Dollar	117	89,250	2:26.00	
1986	Talakeno	6	P.A. Valenzuela	115	Foscarini	117	Strawberry Road II	126	123,750	2:33.20	
1987	Louis le Grand	5	W. Shoemaker	118	Zoffany	125	Schiller	115	96,600	2:28.40	
1988	Great Communicator	5	R. Sibille	117	Trokhos	116	Ivor's Image	114	133,800	2:27.60	
1989	Great Communicator	6	R. Sibille	124	Vallotton	117	Roberto's Dancer	114	122,800	2:30.20	
1990	Frankly Perfect	5	C.J. McCarron	124	Delegant	116	Just as Lucky	114	171,100	2:28.00	101
1991	Rial	6	J. Velasquez	118	Intelligently	113	Royal Reach	113	163,400	2:24.00	107
1992	Quest for Fame	5	G.L. Stevens	121	Cool Gold Mood	114	Miss Alleged	121	158,500	2:28.60	111
1993	Kotashaan	5	K.J. Desormeaux	114	Carnival Baby	113	The Name's Jimmy	115	129,600	2:27.60	108
1994	Fanmore	6	K.J. Desormeaux	116	Bien Bien	124	Navire	114	131,400	2:27.00	108
1995	Square Cut	6	C.W. Antley	114	Ianomami	115	River Rhythm	111	133,200	2:26.00	103
1996	Windsharp	5	E. Delahoussaye	115	Wandesta	114	Virginia Carnival	115	130,800	2:30.20	108
1997	Shanawi	5	B. Blanc	111	Rainbow Dancer	117	Bon Point	117	132,100	2:24.40	101
1998	Bienvenido	5	C.J. McCarron	115	Prize Giving	116	Callisthene	115	120,000	2:29.20	104
1999	Kessem Power	7	G.L. Stevens	115	Brave Act	121	Lazy Lode	120	120,000	2:28.00	106
2000	Dark Moondancer	5	C.J. McCarron	120	The Fly	115	Casino King	116	120,000	2:39.61	106
2001	Persianlux	5	T. Baze	113	Devon Deputy	114	Falcon Flight	116	120,000	2:27.70	105
2002	Nazirali	5	B. Blanc	112	Continental Red	116	Bonapartiste	116	120,000	2:26.09	103
2003	The Tin Man	5	M.E. Smith	121	Special Matter	113	Harrisand	116	120,000	2:31.22	111

Beyer Index: **105.86**

SAN LUIS REY HANDICAP, 1 1/2 Miles (Turf), 4-Year-Olds and Up, Santa Anita, 2003 Purse: $250,000

Year	Winner	Age	Jockey	Wt.	Second	Wt.	Third	Wt.	Win Value	Time	Beyer
1952	Dark Count	3	G. Glisson	114	Stranglehold	114	Grey Tower	114	11,200	1:24.20	
1953	Tee Dee Gee	3	J. Longden	118	Hour Regards	118	Book Circle	111	10,750	1:11.20	
1954	Allied	3	R. York	109	Fault Free	115	El Drag	109	13,150	1:35.60	
1955	Alidon	4	R. Lumm	106	Ole Travis	113	Salmon Peter	104	17,950	2:26.40	
1956	Blue Volt	7	W. Shoemaker	113	Lychnus	113	Allied	108	17,500	2:28.00	
1957	Posadas	6	W. Shoemaker	113	Infantry	114	Prince of Greine	110	17,300	2:27.60	
1958	Solid Son	5	R. York	120	Roscoe Maney	118	Whatitoldyou	115	17,350	2:30.60	
1959	Infantry	6	G. Taniguchi	113	Lookout Point	112	Whatitoldyou	118	17,200	2:31.80	
1960	Lookout Point	7	D. Pierce	113	Nickel Boy	126	Turin	114	18,250	2:33.40	
1961	Don't Alibi	5	W. Shoemaker	118	Odd Fellow	111	Prince Blessed	119	17,350	2:26.20	
1962	Vinci	4	R. Campas	108	Mr. Erdley	114	Chimorro	111	17,550	2:36.60	
1963	The Axe II	5	P. Moreno	124	Rablero	120	Dr. Kacy	114	33,100	2:34.60	
1964	Inclusive	4	R. Campas	104	Mr. Consistency	127	Dusky Damion	120	36,800	2:25.20	
1965	Cedar Key	5	M. Ycaza	125	Polizonte	116	Or et Argent	117	35,000	2:24.20	
1966	Polar Sea	6	W. Hartack	115	Tudor Fame	116	Ask Father	110	26,525	2:26.40	
1966	Cedar Key	6	W. Shoemaker	122	Plaque	113	O'Hara	116	27,025	2:25.20	
1967	Niarkos	7	W. Shoemaker	120	Poker	113	Moontrip	118	26,175	2:26.00	
1967	Fleet Host	4	J. Lambert	117	Flit-To	114	Hill Clown	114	27,675	2:23.80	
1968	Biggs	8	J. Lambert	117	Tobin Bronze	123	Ole Bob Bowers	113	21,250	2:26.00	
1968	Quicken Tree	5	J. Lambert	119	Rivet	114	Finance World	114	22,250	2:24.60	
1969	Taneb	6	W. Shoemaker	124	Petrone	121	Quicken Tree	125	35,200	2:29.40	
1970	Fiddle Isle	5	W. Shoemaker	124	Hitchcock	118	Noholme Atoll	115	32,650	2:23.00	
1970	Quilche	6	J. Lambert	116	Quicken Tree	124	Royal Dynasty	116	32,650	2:25.40	
1971	Try Sheep	5	F. Alvarez	118	Tampa Trouble	118	Bacuco	124	48,250	2:26.00	
1972	Nor II	5	D. Velasquez	118	Hill Run	118	Rinconcito	114	50,900	2:25.80	
1973	Big Spruce	4	D. Pierce	126	Cicero's Court	126	Cougar II	126	66,800	2:27.60	
1974	Astray	5	J. Tejeira	126	Big Spruce	126	Quack	126	67,000	2:24.40	
1975	Trojan Bronze	4	J. Tejeira	126	Okavango	126	Montmartre	126	63,500	2:29.60	
1976	Avatar	4	L. Pincay Jr	126	Top Crowd	126	Top Command	126	64,300	2:24.80	
1977	Caucasus	5	F. Toro	126	King Pellinore	126	Top Crowd	126	64,400	2:25.60	
1978	Noble Dancer	6	S. Cauthen	126	Properantes	126	Text	126	64,400	2:24.00	
1979	Noble Dancer	7	J. Vasquez	126	Tiller	126	Good Lord	126	95,300	2:34.60	
1980	John Henry	5	D.G. McHargue	126	Relaunch	126	Silver Eagle	126	94,800	2:23.00	
1981	John Henry	6	L. Pincay Jr	126	Obraztsovy	126	Fiestero	126	93,900	2:25.20	
1982	Perrault	5	L. Pincay Jr	126	Exploded	126	John Henry	126	116,200	2:24.00	
1983	Erins Isle	5	L. Pincay Jr	126	Prince Spellbound	126	Majesty's Prince	126	120,900	2:26.20	
1984	Interco	4	P.A. Valenzuela	126	Gato Del Sol	126	John Henry	126	127,200	2:26.80	
1985	Prince True	4	C.J. McCarron	126	Western	126	Dahar	126	147,300	2:25.40	
1986	Dahar	5	A. Solis	126	Strawberry Road II	126	Alphabatim	126	148,600	2:26.40	
1987	Zoffany	7	E. Delahoussaye	126	Louis Le Grand	126	Long Mick	126	121,200	2:27.20	
1988	Rivlia	6	C.J. McCarron	126	Great Communicator	126	Swink	126	158,400	2:27.20	
1989	Frankly Perfect	4	C.J. McCarron	126	Great Communicator	126	Payant	126	152,400	2:32.80	
1990	Prized	4	E. Delahoussaye	126	Hawkster	126	Frankly Perfect	126	180,000	2:25.20	109
1991	Pleasant Variety	7	G.L. Stevens	126	Royal Reach	126	Mashkour	126	188,250	2:24.40	105
1992	Fly Till Dawn	6	L. Pincay Jr	124	Provins	124	Quest for Fame	124	179,000	2:27.26	110
1993	Kotashaan	5	K.J. Desormeaux	124	Bien Bien	124	Fast Cure	124	148,250	2:23.91	108
1994	Bien Bien	5	C.J. McCarron	124	Navire	124	Grand Flotilla	124	149,500	2:26.65	111
1995	Sandpit	6	C.S. Nakatani	124	River Rhythm	124	Square Cut	124	155,000	2:27.15	107
1996	Windsharp	5	E. Delahoussaye	117	Wandesta	117	Silver Wizard	122	161,900	2:27.91	108
1997	Marlin	4	C.J. McCarron	122	Sunshack	122	Peckinpah's Soul	122	166,600	2:28.14	107
1998	Kessem Power	6	L. Dettori	122	Storm Trooper	122	Star Performance	122	150,000	2:28.40	103
1999	Single Empire	5	K.J. Desormeaux	122	Kessem Power	122	Alvo Certo	122	150,000	2:27.97	105
2000	Dark Moondancer	5	C.J. McCarron	122	Single Empire	122	Bonapartiste	122	150,000	2:26.00	105
2001	Blueprint	6	G.L. Stevens	116	Devon Deputy	114	Kerryold	116	150,000	2:28.57	103
2002	Continental Red	6	P.A. Valenzuela	116	Keemoon	115	Speedy Pick	112	150,000	2:26.81	103
2003	Champion Lodge	6	A. Solis	116	Special Matter	113	Adminniestrator	116	150,000	2:33.48	108

Beyer Index: 106.57

SAN MARCOS, 1 1/4 Miles (Turf), 4-Year-Olds and Up, Santa Anita, 2003 Purse: $150,000

Year	Winner	Age	Jockey	Wt.	Second	Wt.	Third	Wt.	Win Value	Time	Beyer
1952	Hill Prince	5	E. Arcaro	126	Bryan G.	122	Be Fleet	117	14,750	1:35.80	
1953	Grover B.	4	E. Arcaro	122	Trusting	120	First Glance	126	13,350	1:36.80	
1954	Mark-Ye-Well	5	E. Arcaro	126	Thirteen of Diamon	120	Nothirdchance	112	18,200	2:00.20	
1955	Great Captain	6	W. Boland	110	Poona II	124	High Scud	115	17,700	2:03.80	
1956	Bobby Brocato	5	G. Taniguchi	124	Turk's Delight	117	Jet Stream	111	16,450	2:03.60	
1957	Alidon	6	J. Longden	114	Battle Dance	116	Corn Husker	114	17,200	2:05.80	
1958	Ekaba	4	W. Shoemaker	121	Solid Son	109	Promised Land	125	16,750	2:01.20	
1959	Round Table	5	W. Shoemaker	132	Eddie Schmidt	116	Andrew Alan	115	16,700	1:58.40	

Year	Winner	Age	Jockey	Wt.	Second	Wt.	Third	Wt.	Win Value	Time	Beyer
1960	Whodunit	5	R. Neves	114	Anisado	113	Twentyone Guns	109	16,950	2:01.40	
1961	Anisado	7	I. Valenzuela	113	Scotland	116	How Now	120	18,000	1:59.60	
1962	The Axe II	4	R. Yanez	113	Oink	124	Dress Up	114	16,700	2:03.00	
1963	Rablero	5	J. Longden	115	Hy-Nat	115	The Axe II	123	18,150	2:00.40	
1964	Mr. Consistency	6	K. Church	119	Dusky Damion	119	Marlin Bay	120	17,200	2:02.40	
1965	Desert Chief III	9	D. Ross	116	Polizonte	114	Cadiz	114	17,450	2:01.00	
1966	Or et Argent	5	W. Blum	119	Switchback	114	Cedar Key	124	17,250	2:01.60	
1967	Rehabilitate	4	W. Shoemaker	113	Flag	120	Attention III	114	18,350	1:59.80	
1968	Biggs	8	J. Lambert	114	French Fox	109	Deck Hand	114	21,150	2:04.40	
1969	Deck Hand	6	D. Pierce	118	Rivet	118	Noble House	113	19,800	2:05.80	
1971	Cougar II	5	W. Shoemaker	124	Staunch Eagle	115	S'te al C'bre	114	25,100	2:02.00	
1972	Aggressively	5	D. Pierce	114	Lord Derby	114	Bold Inquiry	115	20,725	2:00.60	
1972	Big Shot II	7	E. Belmonte	122	Golden Eagle II	118	The Pruner	116	20,325	1:59.80	
1973	Tuqui II	6	L. Pincay Jr	114	Soudard	115	Aggressively	114	27,000	2:02.20	
1974	Triangular	7	D. Pierce	118	Big Spruce	124	Kentuckian	118	33,000	2:04.80	
1975	Trojan Bronze	4	W. Shoemaker	117	Indefatigable	115	El Botija	114	34,550	1:59.80	
1976	Announcer	4	F. Toro	115	Zanthe	122	Top Crowd	123	32,800	1:58.40	
1977	Royal Derby II	8	W. Shoemaker	124	Anne's Pretender	123	Teddy's Courage	116	34,150	1:58.20	
1978	Vigors	5	D.G. McHargue	121	Pay Tribute	122	Jumping Hill	123	33,350	1:46.60	
1979	Tiller	5	A. Cordero Jr	126	Palton	121	How Curious	112	37,700	1:58.80	
1980	John Henry	5	D.G. McHargue	124	El Fantastico	113	Commemorativo	110	37,350	2:01.60	
1981	Galaxy Libra	5	A. Cordero Jr	116	Bold Tropic	127	Mike Fogarty	116	40,300	2:00.20	
1982	Super Moment	5	L. Pincay Jr	125	Forlion	114	Le Duc de Bar	111	45,900	2:00.60	
1983	Western	5	C.J. McCarron	116	Handsome One	116	Tell Again	117	47,950	2:04.00	
1984	Lucene	5	P.A. Valenzuela	114	Ginger Brink	117	Sir Pele	114	54,200	2:01.80	
1985	Dahar	4	F. Toro	121	Scrupules	122	Alphabatim	124	61,900	2:01.20	
1986	Silveyville	8	C.J. McCarron	120	Strawberry Road II	125	Nasib	115	63,200	2:00.80	
1987	Zoffany	7	E. Delahoussaye	123	Louis le Grand	117	Strawberry Road II	122	64,100	2:00.80	
1988	Great Communicator	5	R. Sibille	115	Schiller	113	Bello Horizonte	113	100,400	2:02.60	
1989	Trokhos	6	L. Pincay Jr.	117	Vallotton	117	Roberto's Dancer	113	97,200	2:02.00	
1990	Putting	7	C.A. Black	114	Colway Rally	115	Live the Dream	119	105,600	1:58.20	
1991	Fly Till Dawn	5	L. Pincay Jr	120	Vaguely Hidden	115	The Medic	115	97,350	1:58.60	108
1992	Classic Fame	6	E. Delahoussaye	120	Fly Till Dawn	120	French Seventyfive	115	90,600	1:58.00	109
1993	Star of Cozzene	5	G.L. Stevens	120	Kotashaan	116	Carnival Baby	112	77,650	2:01.60	107
1994	Bien Bien	5	L. Pincay Jr	122	Explosive Red	116	Myrakalu	113	75,850	2:00.40	107
1995	River Flyer	4	C.W. Antley	118	Silver Wizard	117	Savinio	116	92,200	2:05.60	110
1996	Urgent Request	6	C.W. Antley	115	Bon Point	114	Virginia Carnival	116	97,000	2:02.20	113
1997	Sandpit	8	C.S. Nakatani	123	River Deep	116	Shanawi	112	99,000	2:00.60	108
1998	Prize Giving	5	A. Solis	114	Bienvenido	115	Martiniquais	118	97,380	2:04.40	101
1999	Brave Act	5	G.F. Alemeida	120	Ferrari	117	Native Desert	117	90,000	2:04.20	108
2000	Public Purse	6	A. Solis	119	Dark Moondancer	120	The Fly	114	98,280	1:59.58	108
2001	Bienamado	5	C.J. McCarron	122	Kerrygold	116	Northern Quest	122	90,000	2:02.75	107
2002	Irish Prize	6	G.L. Stevens	122	Continental Red	116	Cagney	119	90,000	2:01.27	105
2003	Johar	4	A. Solis	120	The Tin Man	122	Grammarian	122	90,000	1:57.92	106

Beyer Index: **107.46**

SAN PASQUAL HANDICAP, 1 1/16 Miles,
4-Year-Olds and Up, Santa Anita, 2003 Purse: $150,000

Year	Winner	Age	Jockey	Wt.	Second	Wt.	Third	Wt.	Win Value	Time	Beyer
1935	Bluebeard	3	H. Richards	114	Polish Beau	120	Moonson	122	2,190	1:12.80	
1936	Proclivity	3	T. Luther	112	Indian Broom	110	Jubilee Jim	106	2,370	1:12.00	
1937	Special Agent	5	B. James	114	Chanceview	111	Sangreal	110	3,325	1:42.80	
1938	Sun Egret	3	J. Adams	104	Clingendaal	118	Speed to Spare	110	5,050	1:23.40	
1939	Gosum	5	A. Gray	110	No Dice	108	Quick Devil	108	10,100	1:50.00	
1940	Don Mike	6	L. Balaski	112	Can't Wait	106	Woodberry	100	8,650	1:59.00	
1941	Mioland	4	L. Haas	130	Gen'l Manager	112	V'na Groom	100	8,900	1:51.60	
1945	Thumbs Up	6	J. Longden	125	Bizerte	109	Texas Sandman	119	19,065	1:44.60	
1946	Lou-Bre	5	R. Permane	108	Sirde	123	Bull Reigh	120	41,930	1:42.40	
1947	Lets Dance	5	J. Gilbert	117	Olhaverry	116	Texas Sandman	122	40,900	1:43.60	
1948	Olhaverry	9	M. Peterson	116	Autocrat	117	V-Boy	112	45,000	1:44.00	
1949	Shim Malone	5	R. Neves	110	On Trust	124	Autocrat	122	37,450	1:45.60	
1950	Solidarity	5	R. Neves	121	Noor	112	Ponder	125	44,100	1:43.80	
1951	Moonrush	5	F.A. Smith	103	Manyunk	105	Repeluz	106	38,550	1:42.40	
1952	Be Fleet	5	J. Longden	113	Bryan G.	124	Stormy Cloud	109	15,150	1:44.00	
1953	Moonrush	7	R. Neves	122	Trusting	113	Horsetr'r-Ed	112	15,550	1:43.40	
1954	Phil D.	6	M. Volzke	112	Indian Hemp	117	High Scud	113	16,700	1:41.60	
1955	Rejected	5	W. Shoemaker	128	Tordito	105	Great Captain	114	16,300	2:04.60	
1956	Bobby Brocato	5	G. Taniguchi	123	Nagpuni	116	Prince Hill	112	16,250	1:42.60	
1957	Battle Dance	4	G. Taniguchi	110	Honeys Alibi	120	Porterhouse	126	16,150	1:42.20	
1958	Terrang	5	W. Boland	122	Find	121	Porterhouse	125	16,400	1:41.40	
1959	Tempest II	5	W. Shoemaker	120	The Searcher	111	Eddie Schmidt	120	16,250	1:42.60	

Year	Winner	Age	Jockey	Wt.	Second	Wt.	Third	Wt.	Win Value	Time	Beyer
1960	Fleet Nasrullah	5	J. Longden	117	Linmold	110	Crasher	115	16,450	1:41.40	
1961	New Policy	4	I. Valenzuela	120	Free Copy	112	Oink	115	17,300	1:41.60	
1962	Micarlo	6	A. Valenzuela	116	Free Copy	111	Nagea	113	16,800	1:47.80	
1963	Olden Times	5	W. Shoemaker	125	Native Diver	125	Physician	117	16,250	1:42.20	
1964	Olden Times	6	W. Shoemaker	120	Doc Jocoy	118	Donut King	113	17,250	1:44.40	
1965	Candy Spots	5	W. Shoemaker	124	Viking Spirit	118	Bonjour	114	16,300	1:42.20	
1966	Native Diver	7	J. Lambert	128	Cupid	118	Isle of Greece	119	17,250	1:41.00	
1967	Pretense	4	W. Shoemaker	118	Aurelius II	114	Native Diver	132	15,800	1:43.00	
1968	Kings Favor	5	J. Sellers	116	Mr. Right	118	Suteki	119	29,550	1:44.20	
1969	Kings Favor	6	J. Leonard	116	Most Host	118	Jimmy P'nuts	112	28,500	1:45.60	
1970	Nodouble	5	J. Tejeira	128	Field Master	116	Dewan	120	28,650	1:40.40	
1971	Ack Ack	5	W. Shoemaker	129	Delaware Chief	118	Figonero	121	33,300	1:41.40	
1972	Western Wagon	5	L. Pincay Jr	115	Cougar II	128	Star of Kuwait	114	35,100	1:41.20	
1973	Single Agent	5	J. Lamber	119	Kennedy Road	119	Autobiography	125	33,850	1:41.80	
1974	Tri Jet	5	W. Shoemaker	121	Forage	121	Susan's Girl	119	36,550	1:41.40	
1975	Okavango	5	F. Toro	114	Tallahto	118	Cheriepe	114	38,400	1:41.40	
1976	Lightning Mandate	5	S. Hawley	118	Guards Up	113	Ga Hai	116	32,250	1:48.40	
1977	Uniformity	5	F. Toro	117	Distant Land	116	Pisistrato	117	35,500	1:41.00	
1978	Ancient Title	8	D.G. McHargue	124	Mark's Place	120	Double Discount	120	30,250	1:40.20	
1979	Mr. Redoy	5	A. Cordero Jr	117	Life's Hope	116	Big John Taylor	115	38,900	1:42.20	
1980	Valdez	4	L. Pincay Jr	125	Prenotion	111	Balzac	122	46,350	1:40.20	
1981	Flying Paster	5	C.J. McCarron	127	King Go Go	117	Fiestero	113	47,150	1:41.20	
1982	Five Star Flight	4	L. Pincay Jr	120	Tahitian King	122	King Go Go	119	65,000	1:40.80	
1983	Regal Falcon	5	E. Delahoussaye	115	Time to Explode	121	West on Broad	113	53,900	1:43.20	
1984	Danebo	5	L. Pincay Jr	120	Water Bank	118	Honeyland	116	91,900	1:41.80	
1985	Hula Blaze	5	P.A. Valenzuela	115	Video Kid	117	Tennessee Rite	112	95,300	1:42.00	
1986	Precisionist	5	C.J. McCarron	126	Bare Minimum	113	My Habitony	116	90,000	1:41.20	
1987	Epidaurus	5	G. Baze	116	Ascension	114	Nostalgia's Star	120	90,800	1:42.40	
1988	Super Diamond	8	L. Pincay Jr	125	Judge Angelucci	122	He's a Saros	114	92,300	1:43.00	
1989	On the Line	5	G.L. Stevens	123	Mark Chip	114	Stylish Winner	113	93,300	1:41.00	
1990	Criminal Type	5	C.J. McCarron	114	Lively One	122	Present Value	121	96,300	1:41.00	
1991	Farma Way	4	G.L. Stevens	116	Flying Continental	122	Stylish Stud	114	93,100	1:40.80	111
1992	Twilight Agenda	6	K.J. Desormeaux	125	Ibero	116	Answer Do	118	22,500	1:42.20	110
1993	Jovial	6	M.K. Walls	115	Marquetry	118	Provins	115	91,400	1:41.80	107
1994	Hill Pass	5	C.J. McCarron	115	Best Pal	122	Lottery Winner	116	87,800	1:41.00	105
1995	Del Mar Dennis	5	A. Solis	118	Slew of Damascus	120	Tossofthecoin	117	116,100	1:41.20	108
1996	Alphabet Soup	5	C.W. Antley	118	Luthier Fever	115	Cezind	114	130,100	1:41.60	108
1997	Kingdom Found	7	G.L. Stevens	115	Savinio	117	Eltish	114	122,200	1:40.60	108
1998	Hal's Pal	5	B. Blanc	112	Malek	116	Flick	116	120,000	1:41.80	103
1999	Silver Charm	5	G.L. Stevens	125	Malek	119	Crafty Friend	118	120,000	1:41.60	109
2000	Dixie Dot Com	5	P.A. Valenzuela	118	Budroyale	122	Six Below	116	120,000	1:40.95	116
2001	Freedom Crest	5	G.L. Stevens	116	Bosque Redondo	114	Sultry Substitute	114	120,000	1:41.94	107
2002	Wooden Phone	5	D.R. Flores	119	Euchre	120	Red Eye	112	120,000	1:41.83	104
2003	Congaree	5	J.D. Bailey	121	Kudos	119	Hot Market	116	90,000	1:41.04	115

Beyer Index: 109

SAN RAFAEL, 1 Mile,
3-Year-Olds, Santa Anita, 2003 Purse: $200,000

Year	Winner	Age	Jockey	Wt.	Second	Wt.	Third	Wt.	Win Value	Time	Beyer
1975	Donna B Quick	4	W. Shoemaker	114	In Prosperity	115	Take Powder	122	11,300	1:09.60	
1976	Vagabonda	5	W. Shoemaker	114	Bastonera II	122	Mia Amore	117	16,825	1:48.20	
1978	Little Happiness	4	S. Cauthen	116			Up to Juliet	118	16,975	1:35.40	
1981	Johnlee n' Harold	3	M. Castaneda	119	Minnesota Chief	115	A Run	119	51,500	1:36.00	
1982	Prince Spellbound	3	M. Castaneda	119	Muttering	121	Unpredictable	119	68,200	1:34.40	
1983	Desert Wine	3	C.J. McCarron	119	Naevus	114	Balboa Native	116	65,900	1:35.60	
1984	Precisionist	3	C.J. McCarron	120	Fali Time	122	Commemorate	118	91,600	1:35.00	
1985	Smarten Up	3	R.Q. Meza	122	Fast Account	122	Stan's Bower	118	94,500	1:36.20	
1986	Variety Road	3	C.J. McCarron	116	Ferdinand	116	Dancing Pirate	116	68,300	1:35.60	
1987	Masterful Advocate	3	L. Pincay Jr	122	Chart the Stars	116	Hot and Smoggy	116	90,500	1:35.80	
1988	What a Diplomat	3	G.L. Stevens	115	Flying Victor	121	Success Express	121	79,350	1:38.00	
1989	Music Merci	3	G.L. Stevens	121	Manastash Ridge	118	Past Ages	118	76,300	1:34.80	
1990	Mister Frisky	3	G.L. Stevens	115	Tight Spot	115	Land Rush	115	80,300	1:36.60	107
1991	Dinard	3	C.J. McCarron	118	Apollo	118	Best Pal	121	91,900	1:35.80	110
1992	A.P. Indy	3	E. Delahoussaye	121	Treekster	116	Prince Wild	118	90,300	1:35.41	100
1993	Devoted Brass	3	K.J. Desormeaux	115	Union City	115	Stuka	118	90,000	1:35.13	106
1994	Tabasco Cat	3	P. Day	121	Powis Castle	115	Shepherd's Field	121	89,700	1:36.39	102
1995	Larry the Legend	3	K.J. Desormeaux	122	Fandarel Dancer	118	Timber Country	121	88,600	1:37.61	100
1996	Honour and Glory	3	G.L. Stevens	121	Halo Sunshine	115	Matty G	121	122,000	1:36.45	103
1997	Funontherun	3	G.F. Alameida	115	Inexcessivelygood	115	Hello	121	121,800	1:36.01	101
1998	Orville N Wilbur's	3	C.S. Nakatani	115	Souvenir Copy	121	Futuristic	115	120,000	1:35.96	108
1999	Desert Hero	3	C.S. Nakatani	116	Prime Timber	115	Capsized	115	120,000	1:36.45	95
2000	War Chant	3	K.J. Desormeaux	116	Archer City Slew	118	Cocky	115	120,000	1:36.45	103

Year	Winner	Age	Jockey	Wt.	Second	Wt.	Third	Wt.	Win Value	Time	Beyer
2001	Crafty C.T.	3	E. Delahoussaye	116	Palmeiro	117	Early Flyer	118	..120,000	1:35.79	..111
2002	Came Home	3	C.J. McCarron	..118	Easy Grades	116	Werblin	115	..120,000	1:36.24	..106
2003	Rojo Toro	3	J.D. Bailey	115	Spensive	118	Crowned Dancer	...118	..120,000	1:35.89	..94

Beyer Index:103.29

SAN VICENTE, 7 Furlongs,
3-Year-Olds, Santa Anita, 2003 Purse: $150,000

Year	Winner	Age	Jockey	Wt.	Second	Wt.	Third	Wt.	Win Value	Time	Beyer
1935	Trumpery	4	R. Workman	112	Marooned	106	Rock X.	101	...4,800	1:10.00	
1936	Time Supply	5	T. Luther	120	Rosemont	118	Singing Wood	126	...4,475	1:10.20	
1937	Merry Maker	3	J. Longden	108	Coramine	112	Upper Birth	108	...3,915	1:27.40	
1938	Sun Egret	3	A. Shelhamer	...125	Legal Light	118	Sir Raleigh	118	...5,125	1:25.40	
1939	Impound	3	S. Coucci	112	Our Mat	118	Porter's Mite	126	...10,300	1:23.00	
1940	Gallahadion	3	B. James	113	Sweepida	107	Exarch	113	...11,650	1:38.80	
1941	Good Turn	3	C. Bierman	118	Porter's Cap	126	Valdina Groom	114	...12,950	1:38.20	
1945	Busher	3	J. Longden	121	Sea Sovereign	121	Bismarck Sea	121	...19,300	1:36.60	
1946	Air Rate	3	H. Pratt	122	Favorito	113	Darby D–Day	111	...18,550	1:37.80	
1947	Hubble Bubble	3	B. Layton	113	Hormone	109	On Trust	122	...38,050	1:43.40	
1948	Salmagundi	3	J. Longden	122	Call Bell	122	Solidarity	122	...37,600	1:44.20	
1952	Hill Gail	3	S. Brooks	122	Haltafire	122	Tiger Sir	122	...15,950	1:10.00	
1953	Chanlea	3	E. Arcaro	119	Hour Regards	122	Silverado	119	...10,600	1:10.60	
1954	James Session	3	J. Phillippi	120	Determine	116	Larks Music	116	...13,900	1:09.40	
1955	Swaps	3	W. Shoemaker	..116	Trentonian	120	Jean's Joe	114	...13,650	1:24.00	
1956	Terrang	3	W. Shoemaker	..122	Fathers Risk	122	Bold Bazooka	124	...15,500	1:22.80	
1957	Buford	3	I. Valenzuela	116	Seaneen	110	Golden One	117	...13,350	1:22.00	
1958	Old Pueblo	3	R. Neves	124	Disdainful	117	Strong Bay	115	...13,250	1:22.60	
1959	Ole Fols	3	M. Ycaza	118	Tomy Lee	126	Finnegan	118	...13,550	1:22.40	
1960	John William	3	I. Valenzuela	114	New Policy	120	T.V. Lark	120	...13,850	1:22.00	
1961	Captain Fair	3	D. Pierce	120	Olden Times	122	Wire Us	114	...13,850	1:22.40	
1962	Black Sheep	3	R. Campas	109	Rattle Dancer	118	Killoqua	112	...13,900	1:23.60	
1963	Mr. Thong	3	A. Maese	112	Olympiad King	116	Viking Spirit	112	...13,700	1:23.80	
1964	Wil Rad	3	W. Shoemaker	..120	Perris	120	Real Good Deal	121	...15,000	1:22.60	
1965	Lucky Debonair	3	W. Shoemaker	..118	Isle of Greece	120	Gummo	122	...14,900	1:22.00	
1966	Saber Mountain	3	W. Shoemaker	..115	Ri Tux	113	Wingover	121	...21,000	1:22.40	
1967	Tumble Wind	3	W. Shoemaker	..114	Don B.	124	Disciplarian	118	...16,950	1:22.20	
1968	Dignitas	3	M. Ycaza	115	Rising Market	112	Proper Proof	112	...18,350	1:22.00	
1969	Majestic Prince	3	W. Hartack	121	Elect the Ruler	115	Inverness Drive	113	...17,400	1:25.60	
1971	Diplomatic Agent ...	3	L. Pincay Jr	114	Steal a Dance	112	Tower East	121	...20,100	1:21.60	
1971	....						Crimson Clem	121			
1972	Solar Salute	3	L. Pincay Jr	118	D.B. Carm	121	Andrew Feeney	115	...25,250	1:21.20	
1973	Ancient Title	3	F. Toro	122	Linda's Chief	122	Out of the East	114	...28,150	1:21.00	
1974	Triple Crown	3	B. Baeza	114	El Espanoleto	114	Destroyer	114	...28,000	1:22.60	
1975	Boomie S.	3	S. Hawley	114	George Navonod ...	122	Udonegood	114	...21,350	1:22.00	
1976	Thermal Energy	3	W. Shoemaker	..117	Stained Glass	122	Bold Forbes	119	...20,200	1:21.80	
1977	Replant	3	D.G. McHargue	.117	Current Concept	122	Smasher	122	...27,750	1:21.20	
1978	Chance Dancer	3	R. Culberson	122	O Big Al	122	Reb's Golden Ale ...	114	...25,600	1:22.20	
1979	Flyting Paster	3	D. Pierce	124	Oats and Corn	119	Infusive	122	...37,300	1:21.20	
1980	Raise a Man	3	W. Shoemaker	..117	Super Moment	115	Bold 'n Rulling	117	...39,550	1:21.40	
1981	Flying Nashua	3	A. Cordero Jr	114	Minnesota Chief	117	Torso	117	...40,450	1:23.40	
1982	Unpredictable	3	E. Delahoussaye	122	Prince Spellbound ..	122	Sepulveda	119	...50,700	1:21.20	
1983	Shecky Blue	3	S. Hawley	114	Full Choke	119	Naevus	115	...48,200	1:22.40	
1984	Fortunate Prospect ..	3	D. Haire	119	Precisionist	122	Tights	117	...49,700	1:22.80	
1985	The Rogers Four	3	C.J. McCarron	...122	Teddy Naturally ...	119	Michadilla	122	...49,400	1:22.80	
1986	Grand Allegiance ...	3	R. Hernandez	114	Royal Treasure	114	Dancing Pirate	119	...51,050	1:23.20	
1987	Stylish Winner	3	G.L. Stevens	119	Prince Sassafras	116	Mount Laguna	116	...46,750	1:23.80	
1988	Mi Preferido	3	A. Solis	120	No Commitment	120	Success Express ...	123	...45,900	1:22.60	
1989	Gum	3	L. Pincay Jr	117	Yes I'm Blue	120	Roman Avie	114	...47,600	1:22.40	
1990	Mister Frisky	3	G.L. Stevens	118	Tarascon	120	Top Cash	120	...47,250	1:22.60	..108
1991	Olympio	3	E. Delahoussaye	120	Dinard	118	Scan	123	...61,075	1:21.40	
1992	Mineral Wells	3	P.A. Valenzuela	116	Star of the Crop	116	Prince Wild	118	...61,450	1:21.28	..104
1993	Yappy	3	P.A. Valenzuela	116	Denmars Dream	118	Devoted Brass	116	...63,100	1:22.33	..94
1994	Fly'n J. Bryan	3	C.A. Black	114	Gracious Ghost	114	Cois Na Tine	116	...60,700	1:22.32	..95
1995	Afternoon Deelites ..	3	K.J. Desormeaux	120	Mr Purple	116	Fandarel Dancer ...	117	...59,725	1:21.35	..103
1996	Afleetaffair	3	C.S. Nakatani	...116	Honour and Glory ..	123	Ready to Order	120	...63,850	1:22.28	..103
1997	Silver Charm	3	C. J. McCarron	..120	Free House	120	Funontherun	114	...66,400	1:21.07	..110
1998	Sea of Secrets	3	K.J. Desormeaux	116	Late Edition	115	Yes It's True	123	...90,000	1:22.00	..93
1999	Exploit	3	C.J. McCarron	...123	Aristotle	116	Yes It's True	123	...90,000	1:22.00	..104
2000	Archer City Slew	3	K.J. Desormeaux	117	Joopy Doopy	116	Gibson County	120	...90,000	1:22.18	..103
2001	Early Flyer	3	C.J. McCarron	...114	Lasersport	120	D'wildcat	117	...90,000	1:21.51	..108
2002	Came Home	3	C.J. McCarron	...123	Jack's Silver	116	Werblin	116	...90,000	1:21.12	..115
2003	Kafwain	3	V. Espinoza	123	Sum Trick	120	Southern Image ...	117	...90,000	1:21.40	..109

Beyer Index: 103.77

SANFORD, 6 Furlongs,
2-Year-Olds, Saratoga Race Course, 2003 Purse: $150,000

Year	Winner	Age	Jockey	Wt.	Second	Wt.	Third	Wt.	Win Value	Time	Beyer
1913	Little Nephew	2	T. Killingworth	116	Undaunted	110	Trumps	116	2,650	1:14.80	
1914	Regret	2	J. Notter	127	Solly	113	Dinah Do	107	2,675	1:13.40	
1915	Bulse	2	C. Ganz	127	Marse Henry	110	Jacoba	119	2,675	1:16.80	
1916	Campfire	2	J. McTaggart	125	Rickety	108	The Knocker	107	2,850	1:13.40	
1917	Papp	2	L. Allen	130	Kashmir	118	Escoba	127	3,825	1:15.60	
1918	Billy Kelly	2	E. Sande	130	Lion d'Or	115	Col. Livingston	122	3,925	1:14.60	
1919	Upset	2	W. Knapp	115	Man o' War	130	Golden Broom	130	3,925	1:11.20	
1920	Pluribus	2	J. Rodriguez	127	Serapis	115	Gen. J.G. G'z	112	4,425	1:15.20	
1921	Sir High	2	M. Garner	115	Bigheart	115	Column	130	3,925	1:13.00	
1922	Bo McMillan	2	F. Smith	115	Dan E. O'Sullivan	115	Tall Timber	118	4,425	1:18.00	
1923	Parasol	2	E. Sande	114	Elvina	112	Big Blaze	110	5,425	1:12.80	
1924	Nicholas	2	L. McAtee	123	Crumple	115	Marcellus	110	4,100	1:15.60	
1925	Canter	2	C. Turner	122	Powhatan	115	Fiddlesticks	115	4,925	1:12.60	
1926	Northland	2	J. Maiben	115	Lord Chaucer	115	Bostonian	115	5,175	1:13.00	
1927	Nassak	2	L. Fator	115	Finite	115	Peter Simple	112	4,875	1:12.40	
1928	Chestnut Oak	2	J.H. Burke	115	Holiday	112	Bargello	115	4,275	1:13.00	
1929	Hi-jack	2	L. McAtee	115	Polygamous	115	Grattan	125	5,100	1:12.00	
1930	Sun Meadow	2	E. Watters	118	Surf Board	125	Condescend	118	5,800	1:12.60	
1931	Mad Pursuit	2	T. Malley	118	Ha Ha	112	Lucky Tom	118	5,025	1:12.20	
1932	Sun Archer	2	R. Workman	118	Grand Time	122	Sarada	112	4,025	1:12.80	
1933	First Minstrel	2	R. Jones	113	Cavalcade	123	Soon Over	116	2,675	1:15.00	
1934	Psychic Bid	2	M. Garner	113	Omaha	113	Boxthorn	122	2,525	1:12.20	
1935	Crossbow II	2	E. Arcaro	113	Bow to Me	113	Sangreal	113	3,600	1:12.40	
1936	Maedic	2	E. Liztenberger	117	Third Count	110	Privileged	110	2,750	1:13.00	
1937	Spillway	2	D. Dubois	113	Maetall	119	Quick Devil	110	2,650	1:14.00	
1938	Birch Rod	2	W.D. Wright	112	Trailer	115	Get Off	107	4,725	1:14.20	
1939	Boy Angler	2	F.A. Smith	113	Epatant	117	Corydon	112	5,125	1:12.20	
1940	Good Turn	2	B. James	110	Grand Party	109	Omission	122	4,300	1:13.20	
1941	Devil Diver	2	D. Meade	114	Ramillies	110	Colchis	117	5,375	1:12.80	
1942	Devil's Thumb	2	C. McCreary	122	Noonday Sun	114	Tip-Toe	110	4,575	1:12.80	
1943	Rodney Stone	2	T. Atkinson	114	Ravenala	117	Free Lance	114	5,700	1:11.20	
1944	The Doge	2	F. Zufelt	114	War Jeep	122	Maransart	116	8,245	1:10.40	
1945	Pellicle	2	C. McCreary	108	Diri	108	Chevalier	108	7,830	1:10.80	
1946	Donor	2	J. Jessop	126	Cornish Knight	116	Lucky Reward	114	8,375	1:11.60	
1947	Inseparable	2	J. Jessop	120	Energetic	113	Faraway	113	8,475	1:11.80	
1948	Slam Bang	2	W. Mehrtens	108	Blue Counselor	113	Swords Town	114	8,250	1:12.00	
1949	Detective	2	T. Atkinson	120	Keep Right	113	Endurable	115	7,450	1:12.80	
1950	Big Stretch	2	E. Arcaro	114	Nullify	126	Silver Wings	120	7,900	1:11.60	
1951	Tom Fool	2	T. Atkinson	113	First Refusal	116	Secant	108	8,800	1:12.60	
1952	Bradley	2	J. Nichols	122	Belfaster	114	Fighting Cock	114	7,975	1:14.60	
1953	Bobby Brocato	2	O. Scurlock	114	War Piper	114	Way Thorn	114	10,200	1:13.20	
1954	Brother Tex	2	C. McCreary	122	Dark Ruler	122	Feast	118	10,325	1:12.80	
1955	Head Man	2	P.J. Bailey	113	Prince John	118	Nan's MInk	118	10,500	1:11.80	
1956	Thin Ice	2	T. Atkinson	116	Clem	116	Bora	116	12,500	1:12.60	
1957	Louis d'Or	2	R. Sterling	116	Deadeye Dick	119	Wing Jet	119	12,600	1:13.20	
1958	Pilot	2	E. Arcaro	119	Royal Anthem	126	Lake Erie	111	11,720	1:13.40	
1959	Weatherwise	2	J. Ruane	114	Tompion	115	Persian Spy	114	24,132	1:12.40	
1960	Hail to Reason	2	R. Ussery	124	Busher's Beauty	114	Apple	114	23,157	1:11.00	
1961	Rash Prince	2	I. Valenzuela	114	Ornamento	114	Valiant Skoal	120	25,301	1:04.60	
1962	Delirium	2	B. Baeza	114	Traffic	114	Golden Louis	114	23,010	1:05.40	
1963	Cornish Prince	2	D. Pierce	114	New Act	120	Tanistair	114	22,685	1:04.60	
1964	Flame Tree	2	R. Ussery	120	Spring Double	115	Impressive	115	23,969	1:04.60	
1965	Yorkville	2	J.L. Rotz	115	Sir Winzalot	115	Top Bid	115	22,490	1:05.00	
1966	Exclusive Native	2	A. Cordero Jr	115	Vitriolic	116	Forward Pass	120	22,474	1:03.60	
1967	King Emperor	2	B. Baeza	115	Hey Good Lookin	115	Winnies Choice	113	23,514	1:03.40	
1968	Walker's	2	A. Cordero Jr	115	High Echelon	115	Very High	124	23,579	1:10.40	
1969	Executioner	2	J. Vasquez	115	Raise Your Glass	120	Dundee Marmalade	115	27,430	1:09.40	
1970	Cohasset Tribe	2	M. Ycaza	120	Tarboosh	124	Buck the System	115	25,500	1:10.60	
1971	Secretariat	2	R. Turcotte	121	Linda's Chief	121	Northstar Dancer	121	16,650	1:10.00	
1972	Az Igazi	2	M. Venezia	121	Prince of Reason	121	Totheend	121	16,680	1:10.60	
1973	Ramahorn	2	C. Baltazar	121	Prop Man	121	Knightly Sport	121	17,205	1:11.00	
1974	Turn to Turia	2	E. Maple	121	Iron Bit	121	Gentle King	121	22,575	1:10.80	
1975	Turn of Coin	2	A. Cordero Jr	122	Hey Hey J.P.	115	Super Joy	115	22,395	1:10.20	
1976	Affirmed	2	S. Cauthen	124	Tilt Up	122	Jet Diplomacy	124	22,290	1:09.60	
1977	Fuzzbuster	2	J. Velasquez	115	Make a Mess	115	Turn Buckle	115	22,230	1:10.80	
1978	I Speedup	2	J. Fell	122	Muckraker	122	My Pal Jeff	117	26,175	1:10.40	
1979	Tap Shoes	2	R. Hernandez	115	Triocala	115	Painted Shield	117	34,260	1:10.00	
1980	Mayanesian	2	J. Vasquez	115	Shipping Magnate	115	Lejoli	115	35,280	1:11.20	
1981	Copelan	2	J.D. Bailey	115	Smart Style	115	Safe Ground	117	33,660	1:10.40	
1982	Big Walt	2	J. Fell	115	Fill Ron's Pockets	122	Agile Jet	115	34,260	1:11.00	
1983	Tiffany Ice	2	G. McCarron	115	Vindaloo	115	Fortunate Dancer	113	51,300	1:10.80	

Year	Winner	Age	Jockey	Wt.	Second	Wt.	Third	Wt.	Win Value	Time	Beyer
1985	Sovereign Don	2	J. Velasquez	122	Roy	115	Cause for Pause	119	54,000	1:10.60	
1986	Persevered	2	A. Cordero Jr	115	Perdition's Son	115	Bucks Best	115	51,120	1:10.60	
1987	Forty Niner	2	E. Maple	115	Once Wild	115	Velvet Fog	115	65,340	1:10.00	
1988	Mercedes Won	2	R.G. Davis	119	Leading Prospect	115	Fire Maker	115	55,440	1:10.00	
1989	Bite the Bullet	2	J.A. Santos	115	Graf	115	For Really	113	54,720	1:09.80	
1990	Formal Dinner	2	J.A. Santos	115	Beadaspic	115	Link	117	55,260	1:10.20	
1991	Caller I.D.	2	J.D. Sellers	122	Pick up the Phone	119	Money Run	115	69,000	1:10.80	.98
1992	Mountain Cat	2	P. Day	119	Satellite Signal	115	Rule Sixteen	115	73,440	1:10.60	.84
1993	Dehere	2	C.J. McCarron	122	Prenup	115	Distinct Reality	122	68,520	1:10.40	.90
1994	Montreal Red	2	Santos JA	115	Boone's Mill	115	De Niro	122	64,620	1:10.80	.93
1995	Maria's Mon	2	Davis RG	115	Seeker's Reward	115	Frozen Ice	112	68,340	1:10.80	.90
1996	Kelly Kip	2	J.L. Samyn	118	Boston Harbor	118	Say Florida Sandy	115	66,840	1:10.20	.107
1997	Polished Brass	2	P. Day	116	Double Honor	116	Jigadee	116	65,520	1:10.20	.92
1998	Time Bandit	2	P. Day	119	Prime Directive	117	Texas Glitter	117	66,480	1:11.40	.89
1999	More Than Ready	2	J.R. Velazquez	122	Mighty	114	Bulling	114	64,560	1:09.60	.105
2000	City Zip	2	J.A. Santos	119	Yonaguska	119	Scorpion	115	65,220	1:10.69	.90
2001	Buster's Daydream	2	J.R. Velazquez	122	Seeking the Money	117	Heavyweight Champ	117	64,680	1:10.55	.96
2002	Whywhywhy	2	E.S. Prado	122	Wildcat Heir	118	Spite the Devil	118	90,000	1:10.40	.93
2003	Chapel Royal	2	J.R. Velazquez	122	Blushing Indian	118	Flushing Meadows	118	90,000	1:10.74	.100

Beyer Index: 94.38

SANTA ANA HANDICAP, 1 1/8 Miles (Turf), Fillies and Mares, 4-Year-Olds and Up, Santa Anita, 2003 Purse: $150,000

Year	Winner	Age	Jockey	Wt.	Second	Wt.	Third	Wt.	Win Value	Time	Beyer
1968	Gabby Abby	5	J. Lambert	118	Pink Pigeon	120	Luz Del Sol	115	17,250	1:47.60	
1969	Miss Ribot	4	D. Pierce	122	Desert Law	119	Third Market	111	16,450	1:48.60	
1970	Boughs o'Holly	5	J. Lambert	115	Luz Del Sol	122	Gay Year	115	19,550	1:47.20	
1971	Mizzle	5	J. Lambert	114	Tipping Times	120	Sight to See	110	19,300	1:48.20	
1972	Street Dancer	5	W. Shoemaker	124	Minstrel Miss	115	Balcony's Babe	117	15,600	1:47.00	
1973	Bird Boots	4	E. Belmonte	115	Best Go	119	Resolutely	115	15,300	1:46.80	
1973	Minstrel Miss	6	D. Pierce	119	Rich Return II	118	Hill Circus	124	26,800	1:46.60	
1974	Belle Marie	4	W. Shoemaker	118	Grasping	114	Flying Fur	115	19,500	1:51.40	
1975	Move Abroad	4	S. Hawley	115	Joli Vert	114	Bold Ballet	122	19,600	1:48.40	
1976	Sun Festival	7	D. Pierce	116	Quaze Quilt	122	Cut Class	117	25,450	1:48.40	
1977	Up to Juliet	4	L. Pincay Jr	120	Quintas Fannie	114	Belle o' Reason	115	27,550	1:48.00	
1978	Kittyluck	5	F. Toro	115	Innuendo	111	Belle o' Reason	120	26,750	1:53.00	
1979	Waya	5	A. Cordero Jr	127	Amazer	123	Shua	115	38,450	1:48.20	
1980	The Very One	5	C. Cooke	117	Sisterhood	118	Mairzy Doates	116	37,300	1:48.40	
1981	Queen to Conquer	5	L. Pincay Jr	121	Track Robbery	119	Ack's Secret	123	46,900	1:48.00	
1982	Track Robbery	6	E. Delahoussaye	123	Manzanera	117	Ack's Secret	123	65,100	1:47.20	
1983	Happy Bride	5	C.J. McCarron	116	Avigaition	121	Miss Huntington	115	63,400	1:47.80	
1984	Avigaition	5	W. Shoemaker	118	Pride of Rosewood	116	L'Attrayante	122	93,600	1:48.40	
1985	Estrapade	5	F. Toro	123	Fact Finder	119	Air Distingue	116	67,100	1:47.00	
1986	Videogenic	4	R.G. Davis	120	Capichi	118	Water Crystals	114	62,800	1:48.40	
1987	Reloy	4	W. Shoemaker	116	Northern Aspen	119	North Sider	120	91,300	1:48.00	
1988	Pen Bal Lady	4	E. Delahoussaye	118	Fitzwilliam Place	119	Galunpe	119	94,900	1:47.20	
1989	Maria Jesse	4	G.L. Stevens	116	Fieldy	117	Claire Marine	115	97,100	1:47.20	
1990	Annoconnor	6	C.A. Black	119	Royal Touch	121	Brown Bess	123	94,500	1:47.80	.103
1991	Noble and Nice	5	K.J. Desormeaux	113							
	Annual Reunion	4	G.L. Stevens	116			Bequest	117	63,400	1:46.60	.103
1992	Gravieres	4	G.L. Stevens	116	Appealing Missy	117	Explosive Ele	115	94,900	1:47.60	.104
1993	Exchange	5	L. Pincay Jr	120	Party Cited	116	Villandry	116	89,700	1:46.20	.103
1994	Possibly Perfect	4	K.J. Desormeaux	119	Hero's Love	120	Lady Blessington	120	91,000	1:51.00	.103
1995	Wandesta	4	C.S. Nakatani	115	Yearly Tour	116	Aube Indienne	120	90,700	1:50.00	.104
1996	Pharma	5	C.J. McCarron	116	Angel in My Heart	120	Matiara	120	95,650	1:49.00	.105
1997	Windsharp	6	E. Delahoussaye	121	Wheatly Special	114	Donna Viola	120	97,750	1:49.40	.100
1998	Fiji	4	K.J. Desormeaux	115	Shake The Yoke	116	Golden Arches	120	96,480	1:49.80	.106
1999	See You Soon	5	K.J. Desormeaux	119	Blending Element	116	La Madame	116	90,000	1:49.40	.103
2000	Spanish Fern	5	V. Espinoza	119	Virginie	120	Country Garden	116	97,830	1:49.30	.98
2001	Beautiful Noise	5	C.J. McCarron	115	High Walden	114	Matiere Grise	113	90,000	1:47.27	.100
2002	Golden Apples	4	G.K. Gomez	119	Starine	122	Astra	122	90,000	1:47.05	.105
2003	Noches de Rosa	5	M.E. Smith	115	Garden in the Rain	116	Megahertz	117	90,000	1:48.31	.100

Beyer Index: 102.64

SANTA BARBARA HANDICAP, 1 1/4 Miles (Turf), Fillies and Mares, 4-Year-Olds and Up, Santa Anita, 2003 Purse: $250,000

Year	Winner	Age	Jockey	Wt.	Second	Wt.	Third	Wt.	Win Value	Time	Beyer
1937	Balking	2	L. Knapp	119	Mainstay	122	Inhale	119	3,580	0:33.20	
							Roy T.	122			
1938	Galley Slave	2	R. Workman	119	Batter	122	Likely Lad	122	5,450	0:34.40	
1941	Chiquita Mia	2	L. Haas	119	Bold Lucy	119	Doctor Reder	122	6,795	0:33.80	
1941	Black Raider	2	L. Balaski	117	Thumbs Up	122	Hooks	122	6,345	0:33.60	

Year	Winner	Age	Jockey	Wt.	Second	Wt.	Third	Wt.	Win Value	Time	Beyer
1946	Whirlabout	5	T. Atkinson	118	Blue Alibi	112	Canina	112	18,200	1:23.00	
1952	Last Greetings	3	E. Arcaro	119	Season's Best	110	Wild Glory	110	10,900	1:24.60	
1953	De Anza	3	R. Neves	122	Hour Regards	119	Singan	117	12,350	1:10.40	
1954	Frosty Dawn	3	E. Arcaro	116	Sweet as Honey	110	Heather Khal	119	9,350	1:09.60	
1955	Berseem	5	J. Longden	120	Joe Jones	117	Dawn Lark	107	16,700	1:42.00	
1956	Porterhouse	5	E. Arcaro	116	Colonel Mack	113	Cycoltron	109	15,700	1:43.00	
1957	Pylades	4	R. Sterling	107	Terrang	124	Duc de Fer	120	16,500	1:42.00	
1958	Golden Notes	4	H. Moreno	117	Vino Supremo	112	How Now	117	13,300	1:13.60	
1962	Cat Call	5	B. Baeza	110	Tritoma	116	Barnesville Miss	119	17,350	2:03.00	
1963	Chicha	5	M. Ycaza	115	Barnesville Miss	116	Errcountess	114	17,150	2:02.60	
1964	Oil Royalty	6	J. Longden	121	Glory Hill	117	Curious Clover	121	18,400	2:00.60	
1965	Batteur	5	M. Ycaza	121	Curious Clover	121	Kisco Gal	110	21,200	1:58.40	
1966	Straight Deal	4	W. Shoemaker	122	Miss Rincon	107	Petticoat	113	28,350	1:58.80	
1967	April Dawn	5	W. Shoemaker	114	Pixy Gal II	113	Check Bye	114	20,750	2:01.20	
1967	Ormea	6	I. Valenzuela	114	Maintain	116	Miss Rincon	110	25,800	2:00.80	
1968	Amerigo's Fancy	6	J. Lambert	118	Gamely	128	Lady Pitt	115	25,800	2:02.40	
1968	Princessnesian	4	L. Pincay Jr	124	Amerigo Lady	122	Courageously	114	25,800	2:00.80	
1969	Pink Pigeon	5	D. Pierce	123	Desert Law	117	Gamely	129	34,550	1:58.20	
1970	Sallarina	4	W. Mahorney	112	Drumtop	121	Luz Del Sol	117	33,500	1:59.20	
1971	Manta	5	L. Pincay Jr	128	Hi Q.	113	TippingTime	117	38,700	2:00.20	
1972	Hail the Grey	5	E. Fires	112	Manta	125	Street Dancer	118	38,500	1:58.60	
1973	Susan's Girl	4	L. Pincay Jr	129	Veiled Desire	110	Gray Mirage	112	37,600	2:03.60	
1974	Tallahto	4	L. Pincay Jr	118	La Zanzara	120	Tizna	127	39,600	1:59.20	
1975	Gay Style	5	W. Shoemaker	125	Move Abroad	113	La Zanzara	117	316,000	2:01.40	
1976	Stravina	5	W. Shoemaker	109	Katonka	122	Tizna	127	38,600	1:59.60	
1977	Desiree	4	V. Centeno	110	Swingtime	120	Charger's Star	113	38,100	2:02.60	
1978	Kittyluck	5	L. Pincay Jr	116	Countess Fager	117	Sensational	120	40,400	2:00.60	
1979	Waya	4	A. Cordero Jr	131	Petron's Love	117	Island Kiss	112	49,100	2:01.00	
1980	Sisterhoos	5	L. Pincay Jr	118	Petron's Love	114	Relaxing	118	67,600	2:00.40	
1981	The Very One	6	J. Velasquez	122	Mairzy Doates	117	Ack's Secret	121	65,900	2:01.20	
1982	Ack's Secret	6	L. Pincay Jr	122	Landresse	116	Plenty O'Toole	114	78,550	2:00.60	
1983	Avigaition	4	E. Delahoussaye	121	Happy Bride	120	Comedy Act	116	78,650	1:59.80	
1984	Comedy Act	5	C.J. McCarron	116	L'Attrayante	122	Lido Isle	114	121,200	2:00.40	
1985	Fact Finder	6	G.L. Stevens	118	Love Smitten	117	Salt Spring	114	116,600	2:01.60	
1986	Mountain Bear	5	C.J. McCarron	119	Estrapade	124	Royal Regatta	116	119,300	2:01.00	
1987	Reloy	4	W. Shoemaker	120	Northern Aspen	119	Ivor's Image	119	97,600	2:00.00	
1988	Pen Bal Lady	4	E. Delahoussaye	119	Carotene	121	Galunpe	119	95,800	1:59.60	
1989	No Review	4	E. Delahoussaye	116	Galunpe	117	Annoconnor	121	128,800	2:02.60	
1990	Brown Bess	8	J.L. Kaenel	123	Royal Touch	121	Double Wedge	111	122,000	1:58.40	103
1991	Bequest	5	E. Delahoussaye	117	Noble and Nice	114	Annual Reunion	117	126,400	1:57.40	103
1992	Kostroma	6	K.J. Desormeaux	124	Miss Alleged	124	Free at Last	117	152,700	1:59.60	106
1993	Exchange	5	L. Pincay Jr	121	Trishyde	120	Revasser	114	120,400	2:02.20	105
1994	Possibly Perfect	4	K.J. Desormeaux	121	Pracer	115	Waitryst	114	122,800	2:00.40	103
1995	Wandesta	4	C.S. Nakatani	118	Yearly Tour	116	Morgana	116	126,400	2:01.60	104
1996	Auriette	4	K.J. Desormeaux	116	Angel In My Hart	119	Wandesta	121	190,900	2:02.00	107
1997	Donna Viola	5	G.L. Stevens	120	Fanjica	114	Windsharp	122	197,200	1:59.80	105
1998	Fiji	4	K.J. Desormeaux	119	Pomona	115	Ecoute	114	150,000	2:01.00	102
1999	Tranquility Lake	5	E. Delahoussaye	116	Virginie	118	Midnight Line	118	150,000	2:00.20	107
2000	Caffe Latte	4	C.S. Nakatani	116	Happyanunoit	121	Country Garden	116	150,000	2:00.51	107
2001	Astra	5	K.J. Desormeaux	118	Beautiful Noise	116	Uncharted Haven	116	150,000	2:01.33	106
2002	Astra	6	K.J. Desormeaux	121	Golden Apples	121	Polaire	115	150,000	2:01.40	100
2003	Megahertz	4	A. Solis	117	Trekking	111	Noches de Rosa	117	150,000	2:00.08	102

Beyer Index: 104.29

SANTA CATALINA, 1 1/16 Miles,
3-Year-Olds, Santa Anita, 2003 Purse: $150,000

Year	Winner	Age	Jockey	Wt.	Second	Wt.	Third	Wt.	Win Value	Time	Beyer
1990	Music Prospector	3	F. Olivares	114	Senegalaise	114	Tsu's Dawning	120	46,950	1:43.60	
1991	Mane Minister	3	D.R. Flores	114	Conveyor	114	Famed Devil	114	48,375	1:42.60	93
1992	Vying Victor	3	C.A. Black	115	Turbulent Kris	114	Al Sabin	117	51,000	1:43.33	92
1993	Art of Living	3	G.L. Stevens	115	Tossofthecoin	115	Glowing Crown	115	45,900	1:43.48	91
1994	Wekiva Springs	3	K.J. Desormeaux	121	Gracious Ghost	116	Dream Trapp	117	45,900	1:41.94	97
1995	Larry the Legend	3	K.J. Desormeaux	118	In Character	115	Awesome Thoughts	119	45,975	1:42.93	95
1996	Prince of Thieves	3	G.L. Stevens	114	Smithfield	116	Matty G	124	64,250	1:42.94	103
1997	Hello	3	C.J. McCarron	120	Bagshot	116	Carmen's Baby	120	65,950	1:42.60	97
1998	Artax	3	C.J. McCarron	114	Souvenir Copy	120	Allen's Oop	117	64,320	1:42.32	109
1999	General Challenge	3	G.L. Stevens	117	Buck Trout	120	Brilliantly	115	63,900	1:42.93	95
2000	The Deputy	3	C.J. McCarron	115	High Yield	117	Captain Steve	123	64,380	1:43.04	103
2001	Millennium Wind	3	C.J. McCarron	114	Palmeiro	115	Denied	116	64,620	1:42.38	98
2002	Labamta Babe	3	K.J. Desormeaux	115	Siphonic	123	Cottonwood Cowboy	115	90,000	1:42.50	104
2003	Domestic Dispute	3	D.R. Flores	113	Our Bobby V.	113	Scrimshaw	115	90,000	1:42.20	103

For prior runnings, refer to 1990 Manual

Beyer Index: 98.46

SANTA YNEZ, 7 Furlongs,
3-Year-Old Fillies, Santa Anita, 2003 Purse: $150,000

Year	Winner	Age	Jockey	Wt.	Second	Wt.	Third	Wt.	Win Value	Time	Beyer
1952	Lap Full	2	E. Arcaro	119	Hug-Me-Tight	115	Khalati	119	10,900	1:11.60	
1952	Last Greetings	3	E. Arcaro	119	A Gleam	119	Season's Best	119	14,700	1:11.20	
1954	Sweet as Honey	3	J. Longden	119	Frosty Dawn	113	Quillo Maid	111	10,550	1:23.00	
1955	In Reserve	3	J. Longden	113	Miss Arlette	119	Solid Rae	116	13,300	1:22.40	
1956	Neva T.	3	G. Taniguchi	116	Mrs. Muriel L.	116	Yutta	116	10,350	1:11.00	
1957	Sully's Trail	3	G. Taniguchi	116	Market Basket	116	Tourbillonte	116	10,400	1:10.20	
1958	Zevs Joy	3	G. Taniguchi	113	Well Away	116	Winking Louise	116	11,550	1:17.40	
1959	Silver Spoon	3	R. York	116	Gun Box	116	Pardal Lassie	113	11,000	1:17.00	
1960	Solid Thought	3	W, Shoemaker	116	Miss Imbros	112	Julie Kate	116	11,200	1:18.00	
1961	Het's Pet	3	W. Shoemaker	119	Bully's Lady	116	Kantankerous K'ty	111	10,550	1:16.80	
1962	Don't Linger	3	W. Shoemaker	115	Jet Parade	115	Pixie Erin	114	10,300	1:17.60	
1963	Nalee	3	K. Church	117	Lamb Chop	117	Delhi Maid	111	13,850	1:16.40	
1964	Face the Facts	3	M. Ycaza	117	Leisurely Kin	120	Roman Goddess	113	13,900	1:15.40	
1965	Respected	3	M. Ycaza	113	Ardell C.	117	Hock Me Not	113	21,200	1:16.20	
1966	Spearfish	3	D. Pierce	117	Be Suspicious	113	Premise	120	17,750	1:16.20	
1967	Mira Femme	3	W. Blum	121	Forgiving	114	Ellen Gruder	114	16,300	1:24.20	
1968	Allie's Serenade	3	L. Pincay Jr	115	Miss Ribot	118	Fish Net	118	17,600	1:22.60	
1969	Poona Downs	3	W. Shoemaker	112	Dumptys Lady	113	Lover's Quarrel	118	18,300	1:24.00	
1970	Opening Bid	3	D. Pierce	121	Loved	113	Top Frolic	112	20,400	1:22.20	
1971	Turkish Trousers	3	W. Shoemaker	112	Ulla Britta	115	Sapose Speed	114	20,300	1:23.60	
1972	Susan's Girl	3	V. Tejada	118	Foreseer	115	Impressive Style	118	29,200	1:21.80	
1973	Tallahto	3	J. Tejeira	117	Waltz Fan	117	Windy's Daughter	121	25,800	1:21.40	
1974	Modus Vivendi	3	D. Pierce	119	Donna Chere	114	Special Team	121	28,500	1:22.40	
1975	Raise Your Skirts	3	W. Mahorney	117	Fascinating Girl	115	Miss Francesca	117	23,350	1:22.40	
1976	Daisy Do	3	S. Hawley	114	Girl in Love	115	Windy Welcome	117	20,300	1:22.40	
1977	Wavy Waves	3	L. Pincay Jr	121	Don's Music	119	Any Time Girl	121	29,550	1:22.80	
1978	Grenzen	3	D.G. McHargue	119	Extravagant	121	Happy Kin	114	27,600	1:22.20	
1979	Terlingua	3	L. Pincay Jr	121	Caline	119	It's in the Air	121	37,900	1:21.20	
1980	Table Hands	3	W. Shoemaker	124	Street Ballet	119	Hazel R.	119	38,700	1:22.40	
1981	Past Forgetting	3	S. Hawley	119	Rosie Doon	119	Nell's Briquette	121	41,800	1:22.40	
1982	Flying Partner	3	R. Sibille	115	Skillful Joy	124	Carry a Tune	114	49,300	1:22.80	
1983	A Lucky Sign	3	C.J. McCarron	121	Sophisticated Girl	116	Fabulous Notion	124	49,050	1:23.40	
1984	Gene's Lady	3	L. Pincay Jr	117	Kennedy Express	115	Natural Summit	117	41,600	1:23.80	
1984	Boo La Boo	3	L. Pincay Jr	122	Personable Lady	122	Costly Array	117	39,900	1:23.20	
1985	Wising Up	3	E. Delahoussaye	119	Rascal Lass	122	Reigning Countess	119	52,700	1:23.40	
1986	Sari's Heroine	3	A. Solis	119	An Empress	117	Life at the Top	115	52,000	1:23.40	
1987	Very Subtle	3	W. Shoemaker	122	Chic Shirine	119	Young Flyer	122	46,200	1:22.60	
1988	Goodbye Halo	3	J. Velasquez	123	Bolchina	116	Floral Magic	114	46,950	1:22.80	
1989	Hot Novel	3	E. Delahoussaye	121	Fantastic Look	114	Agotaras	121	46,950	1:22.80	
1990	Fit to Scout	3	C.J. McCarron	118	Bright Candles	118	Heaven for Bid	116	60,625	1:23.80	
1991	Brazen	3	C.J. McCarron	121	Fowda	116	Ifyoucouldseemenow	121	46,050	1:23.60	91
1992	Looie Capote	3	K.J. Desormeaux	114	Icy Eyes	118	Soviet Sojourn	121	61,450	1:23.42	97
1993	Fit to Lead	3	C.S. Nakatani	116	Nijivision	114	Booklore	114	62,500	1:22.55	93
1994	Tricky Code	3	Nakatani CS	121	Fancy 'n Fabulous	114	Sophisticatedcielo	116	59,575	1:22.16	89
1995	Serena's Song	3	Nakatani CS	123	Cat's Cradle	121	Call Now	121	59,800	1:21.45	102
1996	Raw Gold	3	C.W. Antley	121	Pareja	121	Hidden Lake	116	64,550	1:22.66	90
1997	Queen Of Money	3	D.R. Flores	116	Goodnight Irene	116	High Heeled Hope	121	65,650	1:22.55	89
1998	Nijinsky's Passion	3	C.A. Black	121	Well Chosen	115	Vivid Angel	123	64,980	1:23.15	87
1999	Honest Lady	3	K.J. Desormeaux	115	Rayelle	118	Controlled	123	63,240	1:21.67	105
2000	Penny Blues	3	E. Delahoussaye	118	Classic Olympio	121	Mean Imogene	117	63,600	1:23.38	89
2001	Golden Ballet	3	C.J. McCarron	123	Affluent	114	Warren's Whistle	116	90,000	1:22.30	99
2002	Dancing	3	G.L. Stevens	116	Respectful	116	Lady George	123	90,000	1:23.07	84
2003	Elloluv	3	P.A. Valenzuela	121	Watching You	116	Himalayan	116	90,000	1:23.03	94

Beyer Index: 93

SARATOGA BREEDERS' CUP HANDICAP, 1 1/4 Miles,
3-Year-Olds and Up, Saratoga Race Course, 2003 Purse: $294,000

Year	Winner	Age	Jockey	Wt.	Second	Wt.	Third	Wt.	Win Value	Time	Beyer
1865	Kentucky	4	Gilpatrick	104	Captain Moore	104	Rhinodyne	114	1,850	4:01.00	
1866	Kentucky	5	C. Littlefield	114	Beacon	114	Delaware	114	2,250	4:04.00	
1867	Muggins	4	Clark	118	Onward	114	Delaware	114	1,850	4:03.00	
1868	Lancaster	5	Hayward	114	J.A. Connolly	108	F. Cheath'm	105	1,960	4:14.00	
1869	Bayonet	4	Miller	108	Nellie McDonald	105	Vauxhall	108	2,250	4:10.00	
1870	Helmbold	4	Robinson	108	Hamburg	90	Glenelg	108	1,850	4:03.75	
1871	Longfellow	4	Swim	108	Kingfisher	108			1,550	4:02.75	
1872	Harry Bassett	4	J. Rowe	108	Longfellow	114	Defender	114	1,550	3:59.00	
1873	Joe Daniels	4	McCabe	108	Harry Bassett	114	True Blue	108	1,700	4:10.75	
1874	Springbok	4	Barbee	108	Preakness	114	Katie Pease	105	2,450	4:11.75	
1875	Springbok	5	W. Clark				Grinstead	108	2,250	2:56.25	
	Preakness	6	Hayward	114							

Year	Winner	Age	Jockey	Wt.	Second	Wt.	Third	Wt.	Win Value	Time	Beyer
1876	Tom Ochiltree	4	Barbee	118	Parole	97	Big Sandy	118	1,850	4:06.50	
1877	Parole	4	Barrett	115	Tom Ochiltree	124	Athlene	115	2,150	4:04.50	
1878	Parole	5	Barrett	121	Joe	118	Gen. Phillips	118	1,700	4:08.50	
1879	Bramble	4	J. McLaughlin	118	Wilful	100	Lou Lanier	115	1,500	4:11.75	
1880	Long Taw	5	Wolfe	125	Franklin	121			1,300	4:08.00	
1881	Checkmate	6	I. Murphy	120	Monitor	119	Irish King	122	1,800	4:09.75	
1882	Thora	4	Brophy	113	Carley B.	101	Alta B.	96	1,850	4:05.50	
1883	Gen. Monroe	5	Fitzpatrick	122	Boatman	115			1,950	4:21.50	
1884	Gen. Monroe	6	Blaylock	123	Compensation	120	L. Stanhope	118	1,650	4:05.00	
1885	Bob Miles	4	Fitzpatrick	118	Boatman	120	Powh'n III	118	2,150	4:02.00	
1886	Volante	4	I. Murphy	118	Aretino	118			1,700	4:25.00	
1891	Los Angeles	6	I. Lewis	121	Vallera	111	Ind. Rubber	107	2,900	3:43.50	
1901	Blues	3	Shaw	113	Bayou Pepper	113	Imp	122	3,350	2:52.40	
1902	Advance Guard	5	McCue	127	Wyeth	113	A. Williams	113	3,350	3:01.80	
1903	Africander	3	Fuller	113	Heno	126	Waterboy	126	3,350	2:58.00	
1904	Beldame	3	F. O'Neill	108	Africander	126	The Picket	126	8,100	3:03.80	
1905	Caughnawaga	6	Redfern	127	Beldame	121	Cairngorm	113	5,800	3:00.80	
1906	Go Between	5	Shaw	127	Sir Huon	113	Samson	113	6,050	3:05.40	
1907	Running Water	4	W. Miller	121	Nealon	126	Frank Gill	113	6,050	3:06.20	
1909	Olambala	3	Butwell	113	Wintergreen	113	P. and Needl's	122	2,175	2:58.00	
1910	Countless	3	V. Powers	113	Olambala	126	Am' Jenks	108	4,100	2:58.60	
1913	Sam Jackson	5	Loftus	124	Ringling	108	Lahore	124	1,650	3:08.40	
1914	Star Gaze	3	J. McCahey	126	San Vega	113	Flying Fairy	121	2,175	3:10.00	
1915	Roamer	4	J. Butwell	123	Virile	124	Star Gaze	127	2,225	3:01.80	
1916	Friar Rock	3	J. McTaggart	113	Roamer	127	The Finn	126	3,375	3:03.00	
1917	Omar Khayyam	3	J. Butwell	113	Spur	126	Fair Mac	127	5,050	3:07.80	
1918	Johren	3	F. Robinson	113	Roamer	127			5,250	3:02.20	
1919	Exterminator	4	A. Schuttinger	126	Purchase	126	The Trump	116	5,600	2:58.00	
1920	Exterminator	5	C. Fairbrother	126	Cleopatra	111			4,950	2:56.40	
1921	Exterminator	6	W. Kelsay	126					4,750	3:04.60	
1922	Exterminator	7	A. Johnson	126	Mad Hatter	126	Bon Homme	126	6,800	3:00.40	
1923	My Own	3	E. Sande	116	Bunting	126	Prince James	126	6,850	2:57.20	
1924	Mr. Mutt	3	H. Thurber	116	My Play	126	Aga Khan	116	8,550	3:00.80	
1925	Mad Play	4	L. Fator	126	Swope	116	Flames	126	7,150	2:59.40	
1926	Espino	3	L. Fator	116	Display	116	Princess Doreen	121	7,650	3:00.40	
1927	Chance Play	4	J. Maiben	126	Forever and Ever	126	Espino	126	7,100	3:03.60	
1928	Reigh Count	3	C. Lang	118	Display	126			6,500	2:55.00	
1929	Diavolo	4	J. Maiben	126	Double Play	126	African	116	7,350	2:58.00	
1930	Gallant Fox	3	E. Sande	118	Frisius	126	Gone Away	116	9,275	2:56.00	
1931	Twenty Grand	3	L. McAtee	118	Sun Beau	126	Sir Ashley	118	8,250	3:01.20	
1932	War Hero	3	J. Gilbert	118	Blenheim	126	Dark Secret	118	7,825	2:59.20	
1933	Equipoise	5	R. Workman	126	Gusto	126	Keep Out	118	6,050	3:00.00	
1934	Dark Secret	5	C. Kurtsinger	126	Faireno	126	Cleves	118	5,525	2:59.20	
1935	Count Arthur	3	W.D. Wright	116	Esposa	111	Faireno	126	7,145	2:58.40	
1936	Granville	3	J. Stout	116	Discovery	126			6,520	3:00.80	
1937	Count Arthur	5	L. Balaski	126	Matey	116	Esposa	121	6,425	3:02.20	
1938	War Admiral	4	M. Peters	126	Esposa	121	Anaflame	111	6,600	2:55.80	
1939	Isolater	6	J. Stout	126	Cravat	126			6,400	2:56.20	
1940	Fenelon	3	J. Longden	116							
	Isolater	7	J. Stout						4,650	3:02.00	
1941	Dorimar	4	C. McCreary	121	Welcome Pass	116	Fairymant	116	9,850	2:58.40	
1942	Bolingboke	5	H. Lindberg	126	Trierarch	116	Buckskin	116	9,550	2:58.20	
1943	Princequillo	3	S. Brooks	116	Bolingboke	126	Dark Discovery	121	18,200	2:56.60	
1944	Bolingbroke	7	R. Permane	126	Bounding Home	118	Eurasian	126	17,950	2:57.60	
1945	Stymie	4	J. Longden	126	Olympic Zenith	126	Bankrupt	126	18,645	2:58.00	
1946	Stymie	5	B. James	126					5,975	3:07.40	
1947	Talon	5	J. Adams	126	Hachazo	126	Eb	126	12,300	2:58.40	
1948	Snow Goose	4	J. Jessop	121	Miss Grillo	121	Word of Honor	116	11,000	2:57.80	
1949	Doubtless II	5	T. Atkinson	126	Shackleton	116	Quemadito	126	11,650	2:57.40	
1950	Cochise	4	E. Arcaro	126	Double Brandy	126	Escador	126	11,900	2:57.60	
1951	Busanda	4	E. Guerin	121	Lone Eagle	126	Bit o' Fate	126	10,950	2:59.00	
1952	Busanda	5	T. Atkinson	121	Lone Eage	126	Kiss Me Kate	121	11,325	2:59.80	
1953	Alerted	5	C. McCreary	126	Bit o' Fate	126	Great Captain	126	10,875	3:01.20	
1954	Great Captain	5	E. Arcaro	126	Impulsivo	126	Kazmaier	117	11,075	3:02.40	
1955	Chevation	4	E. Guerin	126	Mark's Puzzle	117	Let's Fly II	126	10,525	3:02.60	
1963	Will I Rule	3	H. Woodhouse	107	Quick Pitch	110	David K.	119	18,622	2:39.80	
1994	Thunder Rumble	5	Migliore R	112	West by West	113	Wallenda	117	150,000	1:48.40	.116
1995	L'Carriere	4	J.D. Bailey	113	Yourmissinthepoint	108	Unaccounted For	120	120,000	2:02.80	.116
1996	L'Carriere	5	J.F. Chavez	114	Peaks and Valleys	121	Mahogany Hall	116	130,000	2:01.60	.116
1997	Cairo Express	5	J.L. Samyn	111	Golden Larch	111	Instant Friendship	108	180,000	2:03.80	.106
1998	Awesome Again	4	P. Day	120	Concerto	114	Early Warning	110	180,000	2:03.00	.110
1999	Running Stag	5	S.J. Sellers	122	Catienus	115	Golden Missile	115	180,000	2:01.00	.116
2000	Pleasant Breeze	5	J.F. Chavez	116	Catienus	114	Gander	114	180,000	2:02.17	.109

Year	Winner	Age	Jockey	Wt.	Second	Wt.	Third	Wt.	Win Value	Time	Beyer
2001	Aptitude	4	J.D. Bailey	122	Perfect Cat	115	A Fleets Dancer	115	180,000	2:01.55	116
2002	Evening Attire	4	S.X. Bridgmohan	115	Abreeze	113	Dollar Bill	117	180,000	2:02.95	113
2003	Puzzlement	4	J.F. Chavez	113	Volponi	122	Iron Deputy	115	180,000	2:03.54	113

Beyer Index: 113.10

SARATOGA SPECIAL, 6 1/2 Furlongs,
2-Year-Olds, Saratoga Race Course, 2003 Purse: $150,000

Year	Winner	Age	Jockey	Wt.	Second	Wt.	Third	Wt.	Win Value	Time Beyer
1901	Goldsmith	2	N. Turner	122	Blue Girl	119	Masterman	122	14,500	1:08.20
1902	Irish Lad	2	N. Turner	122	Dazzling	119	Blue Ribbon	122	18,000	1:08.20
1903	Aristocracy	2	F. O'Neill	122	Broomstick	122	Stalwart	122	21,500	1:11.80
1904	Sysonby	2	Redfern	122	Hot Shot	122	Britisher	122	14,000	1:07.00
1905	Mohawk II	2	Redfern	122	Voorhees	122	Tangle	119	16,500	1:07.00
1906	Salvidere	2	Sewell	119	McCarter	122	Peter Pan	122	15,000	1:12.40
1907	Colin	2	W. Miller	122	Uncle	122			13,000	1:12.00
1908	Sir Martin	2	C.H. Shilling	122	Wedding Bells	119	Mediant	119	9,250	1:18.80
1909	Waldo	2	Nicol	122	Sweep	122	Herkimer	122	4,875	1:15.80
1910	Novelty	2	C.H. Shilling	122	Iron Mask	122	Naushon	122	6,500	1:13.00
1913	Roamer	2	Byrne	119	Gainer	122	Black Toney	122	6,500	1:13.00
1914	Regret	2	J. Notter	119	Pebbles	122	Paris	122	5,125	1:11.60
1915	Dominant	2	T. McTaggart	122	Puss in Boots	119	Friar Rock	122	5,125	1:16.00
1916	Campfire	2	J. McTaggart	122	Tom McTaggart	122	Hourless	116	5,625	1:13.20
1917	Sun Briar	2	W. Knapp	122	Rosie O'Grady	119	Papp	122	11,750	1:15.00
1918	Hannibal	2	L. Ensor	122	Terentia	119	Yurucari	122	11,000	1:16.20
1919	Golden Broom	2	E. Ambrose	122	Wildair	122	King Thrush	122	8,500	1:12.80
1920	Tryster	2	J. Rodriguez	122	Prudery	122	Dimmesdale	122	9,500	1:12.60
1921	Morvich	2	F. Keogh	122	Kal-Sang	122	Whiskaway	122	10,500	1:12.20
1922	Goshawk	2	L. McAtee	122	McKee	122	Bud Lerner	122	12,750	1:12.20
1923	St. James	2	E. Sande	122	Sun Flag	122	Diogenes	122	12,750	1:11.60
1924	Sunny Man	2	L. Fator	122	Voltaic	122	Cloudland	112	13,000	1:12.40
1925	Haste	2	E. Sande	122	Pompey	122	Flight of Time	122	12,000	1:12.40
1926	Chance Shot	2	E. Sande	122	Scapa Flow	122	Osmand	122	15,750	1:13.00
1927	Ariel	2	L. Fator	122	Sun Edwin	122	Distraction	122	18,000	1:12.60
1928	Blue Larkspur	2	A. Pascuma	122	Jack High	122	Too High	119	16,750	1:13.60
1929	Whichone	2	L. McAtee	122	Pansy Walker	119	Sarazen II	122	16,500	1:13.80
1930	Jamestown	2	L. McAtee	122	Equipoise	122	Sun Meadow	122	14,050	1:11.40
1931	Top Flight	2	R. Workman	119	Indian Runner	122	Curacao	122	11,000	1:12.00
1932	Happy Gal	2	T. Malley	119	Ladysman	122	Caterwaul	122	9,250	1:13.00
1933	Wise Daughter	2	J. Gilbert	119	Singing Wood	119	Hadagal	122	8,500	1:12.60
1934	Boxthorn	2	D. Meade	122	Plat Eye	122	Today	122	6,750	1:12.20
1935	Red Rain	2	R. Workman	122			Bien Joli	122	3,500	1:13.00
	Coldstream	2	E. Arcaro	122						
1936	Forty Winks	2	R. Workman	122	Flying Scot	122	Galsun	122	7,000	1:13.80
1937	Pumpkin	2	J. Gilbert	122	Maetall	122	Bull Lea	122	8,000	1:12.60
1938	El Chico	2	N. Wall	122	Eight Thirty	122	Third Degree	122	8,000	1:10.40
1939	Bimelech	2	F.A. Smith	122	Briar Sharp	122	Andy K.	122	9,000	1:10.80
1940	Whirlaway	2	J. Longden	122	New World	122	Good Turn	122	9,750	1:11.20
1941	Amphitheatre	2	A. Robertson	122	Shut Out	122	Black Raider	122	11,250	1:11.60
1942	Halberd	2	G. Woolf	122	Collect Call	122	Bourmont	122	8,000	1:13.00
1943	Cocopet	2	C. McCreary	119	Mrs. Ames	119	Dustman	122	5,500	1:10.60
1944	Pavot	2	G. Woolf	122	Plebiscite	122	Jeep	122	4,945	1:10.20
1945	Mist o' Gold	2	W.D. Wright	122	Our Bully	122	Condiment	122	6,435	1:13.40
1946	Grand Admiral	2	J. Jessop	122	Loyal Legion	122	Khyber Pass	122	14,250	1:12.80
1947	Better Self	2	E. Arcaro	122	Relic	122	Star Bout	122	10,500	1:13.00
1948	Blue Peter	2	E. Guerin	122	Sport Page	122	Entrust	122	12,750	1:13.80
1949	More Sun	2	G. Glisson	122	Suleiman	122	Navy Chief	122	11,500	1:11.20
1950	Battlefield	2	E. Arcaro	122	Northern Star	122	Battle Morn	122	13,000	1:12.00
1951	Cousin	2	E. Guerin	122	Old Ironsides	122	Mr. Turf	122	17,500	1:13.20
1952	Native Dancer	2	E. Guerin	122	Doc Walker	122	South Point	122	17,250	1:12.80
1953	Turn-to	2	H. Moreno	122	Permian	122	Sir Boss	122	15,000	1:12.20
1954	Royal Coinage	2	E. Arcaro	122	Pyrenees	122	Summer Tan	122	15,000	1:11.40
1955	Polly's Jet	2	E. Arcaro	122	Reneged	122	Noorsaga	122	15,250	1:13.00
1956	Nearctic	2	G. Walker	122	Clem	122	Amarullah	122	13,800	1:13.60
1957	Grey Monarch	2	J. Nichols	122	Jester	122	Don't Alibi	122	13,800	1:12.80
1958	First Landing	2	E. Arcaro	122	Pilot	122	Udaipur	122	38,725	1:12.00
1959	Irish Lancer	2	E. Arcaro	116	Tompion	122	Udaipur	122	22,822	1:11.60
1960	Bronzerullah	2	R. York	116	Ambiopoise	116	Chinchilla	119	24,814	1:10.00
1961	Battle Joined	2	M. Ycaza	114	Jaipur	120	Cavalanche	114	25,837	1:12.60
1962	Mr. Cold Storage	2	J. Sellers	114	Aim n Fire	114	Bold Tim	114	21,417	1:10.80
1963	Duel	2	B. Baeza	114	Count Bud	114	Traffic	114	20,995	1:10.60
1964	Sadair	2	M. Ycaza	120	Cornish Prince	124	O'Hara	114		

Year	Winner	Age	Jockey	Wt.	Second	Wt.	Third	Wt.	Win Value	Time	Beyer
1965	Impressive	2	B. Baeza	114	Flame Tree	124	Irish Ruler	114	22,945	1:10.20	
1966	Favorable Turn	2	R. Ussery	116	Bold Hour	120	Top Bid	114	21,547	1:10.60	
1967	Vitriolic	2	B. Baeza	114	Exclusive Native	122	Pappa Steve	114	22,977	1:10.40	
1968	Reviewer	2	B. Baeza	122	Hey Good Lookin	114	Buck Run	122	21,710	1:10.40	
1969	Pontifex	2	P. Anderson	120	Foggy Road	114	High Echelon	114	21,045	1:11.60	
1970	Three Martinis	2	A. Cordero Jr	120	Raise Your Glass	120	Tamtent	120	22,945	1:10.80	
1971	Tarboosh	2	E. Maple	120	Loquacious Don	114	Rest Your Case	122	2,064	1:10.40	
1972	Stop the Music	2	J. Vasquez	117	Step Nicely	117	Macadamian	117	17,145	1:11.20	
1973	Az Igazi	2	M. Venezia	117	Gusty O'Shay	117	Lakeville	117	17,025	1:11.00	
1974	Our Talisman	2	M. Venezia	117	Valid Appeal	117	Knightly Sport	120	17,430	1:10.40	
1975	Bold Forbes	2	J. Velasquez	120	Family Doctor	117	Gentle King	120	22,680	1:09.80	
1976	Banquet Table	2	J. Vasquez	122	Turn of Coin	122	May I Rule	117	22,455	1:11.60	
1977	Darby Creek Road	2	A. Cordero Jr	117	Jet Diplomacy	122	Quadratic	117	22,470	1:10.00	
1978	General Assembly	2	D.G. McHargue	117	Smarten	117	Turn Buckle	117	22,350	1:09.00	
1979	J.P. Brother	2	E. Maple	122	Native Moment	117	Muckraker	122	25,365	1:12.00	
1980	Well Decorated	2	M. Venezia	117	Tap Shoes	117	Motivity	119	34,320	1:10.20	
1981	Conquistador Cielo	2	E. Maple	117	Herschelwalker	117	Timely Writer	122	33,900	1:10.60	
1982	Victorious	2	A. Cordero Jr	122	Pappa Riccio	124	Safe Ground	119	33,960	1:10.60	
1983	Swale	2	E. Maple	117	Shuttle Jet	117	Big Walt	117	33,720	1:12.60	
1984	Chief's Crown	2	D. MacBeth	117	Do It Again Dan	117	Sky Command	122	42,060	1:10.20	
1985	Sovereign Don	2	J. Velasquez	122	Hagley Mill	117	Bullet Blade	117	43,200	1:11.40	
1986	Gulch	2	A. Cordero Jr	122	Jazzing Around	117	Java Gold	117	54,990	1:10.00	
1987	Crusader Sword	2	R.G. Davis	117	Tejano	117	Endurance	119	66,420	1:10.20	
1988	Trapp Mountain	2	J.D. Bailey	117	Bio	122	Leading Prospect	117	66,240	1:10.80	
1989	Summer Squall	2	P. Day	124	Dr. Bobby A.	117	Graf	117	53,370	1:09.80	
1990	To Freedom	2	A. Cordero Jr	124	Fighting Affair	117	Eugene Eugene	117	52,710	1:11.40	
1991	Caller I.D.	2	J.D. Bailey	117	Pick Up the Phone	122	Coin Collector	122	71,040	1:09.40	103
1992	Tactical Advantage	2	J.A. Krone	117	Strolling Along	117	Mi Cielo	117	72,600	1:10.40	87
1993	Dehere	2	E. Maple	117	Slew Gin Fizz	117	Whitney Tower	117	71,760	1:09.80	89
1994	Montreal Red	2	J.A. Santos	122	Flitch	115	Law of the Sea	115	64,800	1:17.80	87
1995	Bright Launch	2	J.A. Santos	112	Devil's Honor	114	Severe Clear	113	66,540	1:17.80	79
1996	All Chatter	2	J.F. Chavez	113	Gray Raider	114	Just a Cat	113	84,375	1:16.20	90
1997	Favorite Trick	2	P. Day	122	Case Dismissed	114	K.O. Punch	119	90,000	1:17.00	97
1998	Prime Directive	2	J.F. Chavez	114	Silk Broker	114	Tactical Cat	114	90,000	1:17.00	100
1999	Bevo	2	E.S. Prado	117	Afternoon Affair	114	Settlement	114	90,000	1:17.60	85
2000	City Zip	2	J.A. Santos	122	Scorpion	114	Standard Speed	117	90,000	1:16.88	91
2001	Jump Start	2	P. Day	115	Heavyweight Champ	115	Booklet	117	90,000	1:17.35	86
2002	Zavata	2	J.D. Bailey	122	Lone Star Sky	122	Spite the Devil	116	90,000	1:17.65	101
2003	Cuvee	2	J.D. Bailey	122	Pomeroy	118	Limehouse	122	90,000	1:15.97	103

Beyer Index: 92.15

SCHUYLERVILLE, 6 Furlongs,
2-Year-Old Fillies, Saratoga Race Course, 2003 Purse: $150,000

Year	Winner	Age	Jockey	Wt.	Second	Wt.	Third	Wt.	Win Value	Time	Beyer
1918	Tuscaloosa	2	G. Walls	107	Herodias	104	Terentia	124	3,300	1:04.60	
1919	Homely	2	W. Kelsay	107	Constancy	127	Miss Jemima	127	2,325	1:06.40	
1920	Careful	2	W. Kelsay	127	Nancy Lee	122	Charity	106	2,950	1:05.60	
1921	Miss Joy	2	M. Garner	127	Second Thoughts	124	Nancy Shanks	106	3,175	1:05.60	
1922	Edict	2	L. Fator	107	Miss Smith	110	Great Luck	104	3,400	1:08.80	
1923	Befuddle	2	L. Lyke	112	Sunny Sal	107	Fluvanna	126	3,925	1:05.80	
1924	Royalite	2	L. Fator	112	Blue Warbler	112	Extra Dry	114	3,925	1:08.40	
1925	Taps	2	A. Johnson	114	Ruthenia	112	Martha Washington	119	3,925	1:07.00	
1926	Aromagne	2	E. Ambrose	107	Bonnie Pennant	112	Candy Star	112	3,925	1:07.40	
1927	Pennant Queen	2	J. Maiben	112	Bateau	122	Anita Peabody	124	4,175	1:07.00	
1928	Atlantis	2	L. McAtee	112	Pennant Lass	111	Brown Elf	115	3,925	1:07.40	
1929	Flying Gal	2	D. McAuliffe	111	Conclave	115	Erin	119	4,925	1:05.40	
1930	Pansette	2	R. Workman	115	Blind Lane	115	Ladana	122	6,075	1:06.00	
1931	Polonaise	2	M. Garner	122	Dinner Time	111	Parry	119	3,925	1:08.00	
1932	Volette	2	R. Workman	115	Notebook	111	Cutie Face	113	3,350	1:07.60	
1933	Slapdash	2	H. Mills	122	Rhythmic	115	Proud Girl	112	2,900	1:06.00	
1934	Uppermost	2	L. Humphries	112	Vicaress	115	Bird Flower	112	2,550	1:05.60	
1935	Parade Girl	2	L. Fallon	112	Beanie M.	112	High Fleet	112	2,475	1:06.20	
1936	Maecloud	2	E. Litzenberger	110	Magic Circle	110	Pepium	110	2,725	1:07.60	
1937	Creole Maid	2	H. Richards	111	Jacola	113	Merry Lassie	120	2,900	1:05.80	
1938	Soldierette	2	L. Dupps	110	Grey Nurse	110	Dinner Date	110	4,600	1:05.60	
1939	Teacher	2	J. Westrope	120	War Beauty	110	Little Risque	110	4,625	1:05.60	
1940	Nasca	2	R. Donoso	110	Tangled	120	Traffic Court	110	3,725	1:05.20	
1941	Romping Home	2	J. Skelly	113	Mar-Kell	113	Pony Ballet	119	4,800	1:06.40	
1942	Brittany	2	C. McCreary	113	High Bit	113	Flight	113	4,400	1:06.80	
1943	Boojiana	2	T. Atkinson	116	Thread o' Gold	116	Everget	116	5,075	1:04.40	
1944	Ace Card	2	G. Woolf	119	Silver Smoke	112	Leslie Grey	119	7,315	1:04.60	

Year	Winner	Age	Jockey	Wt.	Second	Wt.	Third	Wt.	Win Value	Time	Beyer
1945	Red Shoes	2	H. Lindberg	112	Bonnie Beryl	112	Boojie	112	7,385	1:04.40	
1946	Bright Song	2	P. Miller	112	Pipette	122	Maid of Harlem	112	9,250	1:07.40	
1947	Spats	2	E. Guerin	114	Bellesoeur	113	Red Risque	112	9,325	1:04.80	
1948	Gaffery	2	A. Kirklan	112	Greek Blond	115	Gay Mood	112	7,900	1:07.00	
1949	Striking	2	E. Arcaro	115	Sunday Evening	112	Nazma	115	8,000	1:05.40	
1950	Atalanta	2	H. Woodhouse	112	Rose Fern	115	Ruddy	115	8,025	1:06.00	
1951	Rose Jet	2	E. Guerin	115	Star-Enfin	122	Landmark	113	8,375	1:06.20	
1952	Grecian Queen	2	R. York	111	Cold Heart	114	Piedmont Lass	114	9,525	1:07.40	
1953	Evening Out	2	O. Scurlock	123	Riant	119	Incidentally	123	9,400	1:05.40	
1954	Two Stars	2	W. Lester	111	Misty	111	Bless Pat	114	10,150	1:05.80	
1955	Dark Charger	2	A. DeSpirito	119	Pet Child	111	Recherche	111	9,800	1:05.60	
1956	Miss Blue Jay	2	E. Guerin	122	Snow White	119	Tourbillonte	115	11,525	1:06.40	
1957	Pocahontas	2	E. Arcaro	116	Bridgework	119	Gleaming Star	112	12,775	1:07.40	
1958	Rich Tradition	2	W. Boland	116	Lady Be Good	122	Quill	116	11,639	1:07.60	
1959	Irish Jay	2	E. Arcaro	119	Heavenly Body	116	Roving Mary	116	14,065	1:06.00	
1959	Make Sail	2	M. Ycaza	116	Undulation	116	Affection	116	14,390	1:06.20	
1960	Shuette	2	S. Boulmetis	116	Little Tumbler	122	Really Sumthin	116	19,655	1:11.80	
1961	Cicada	2	L. Adams	119	Batter Up	122	Bramalea	116	19,402	1:11.00	
1962	Bold Princess	2	H. Woodhouse	116	Barbwolf	116	Majesta	112	19,012	1:06.00	
1963	Gallatia	2	E. Guerin	116	Hasty Matelda	112	Mechanicville	116	18,980	1:06.80	
1964	Marshua	2	R. Ussery	116	Candalita	116	What a Treat	112	19,890	1:04.80	
1965	Prides Profile	2	D. Pierce	116	Lady Pitt	116	Never in Paris	119	15,177	1:05.00	
1965	Amerala	2	W. Blum	116	Thirty Lima	116	Hula Girl	116	15,502	1:05.40	
1966	Vanilla	2	L. Loughry	116	Northeast Trades	119	Great Era	116	19,532	1:05.00	
1967	Idealistic	2	R. Ussery	116	Copper Canyon	116	Ave Valeque	116	20,150	1:04.60	
1968	Golden Or	2	J.L. Rotz	116	Repercussion	116	Shoo Fly	116	19,272	1:05.60	
1969	Bright Sun	2	E. Belmonte	116	Stolen Base	116	Meritus	116	18,460	1:12.00	
1970	Patelin	2	B. Baeza	116	Bid High	116	Caroline G.	116	19,955	1:10.80	
1971	Numbered Account	2	B. Baeza	119	Bendara	114	Vichy	114	20,220	1:12.60	
1972	La Prevoyante	2	J. LeBlanc	119	Sparkalark	116	Sweet Sop	116	17,850	1:11.40	
1973	Talking Picture	2	B. Baeza	116	Imajoy	116	Celestial Lights	119	17,760	1:10.80	
1974	Our Dancing Girl	2	V. Bracciale Jr	116	Secret's Out	119	But Exclusive	116	16,575	1:11.20	
1974	Laughing Bridge	2	B. Baeza	117	Molly Ballantine	116	Fair Wind	119	16,500	1:09.80	
1975	Nijana	2	J. Velasquez	112	Future Tense	116	Crown Treasure	116	22,680	1:12.20	
1976	Mrs. Warren	2	E. Maple	114	Tickle My Toes	116	Spy Flag	112	22,980	1:11.80	
1977	L'Alezane	2	R. Turcotte	121	Akita	121	Lakeville Miss	114	22,350	1:11.80	
1978	Palm Hut	2	R.I. Velez	114	Hermanville	114	Please Try Hard	114	22,215	1:10.40	
1979	Damask Fan	2	E. Maple	114	Jet Rating	114	Lovin' Lass	112	25,860	1:10.20	
1980	Sweet Revenge	2	J. Velasquez	114	Companionship	114	Heavenly Cause	114	34,980	1:10.40	
1981	Mystical Mood	2	J. Vasquez	114	Aga Pantha	114	Trove	116	34,320	1:11.80	
1982	Weekend Surprise	2	J. Velasquez	114	Share the Fantasy	114	Flying Lassie	114	34,620	1:11.00	
1983	Bottle Top	2	D. Brumfield	114	Officer's Ball	114	Ark	114	34,020	1:11.40	
1984	Weekend Delight	2	C.R. Wood Jr.	119	Resembling	114	Winter's Love	114	4,240	1:11.60	
1985	I'm Splendid	2	A. Cordero Jr.	114	Musical Lark	114	Famous Speech	114	41,820	1:10.80	
1986	Sacahuista	2	C.J. McCarron	115	Our Little Margie	114	Collins	114	44,540	1:10.60	
1987	Over All	2	A. Cordero Jr.	119	Joe's Tammie	116	Flashy Runner	119	68,850	1:10.60	
1988	Wonders Delight	2	J.A. Santos	114	Coax Chelsie	114	Attu	112	67,680	1:09.80	
1989	Golden Reef	2	J.A. Santos	114	Lucy's Glory	119	Miss Cox's Hat	114	54,360	1:10.40	
1990	Meadow Star	2	C.W. Antley	114	Garden Gal	119	Prayerful Miss	114	52,590	1:11.20	
1991	Turnback the Alarm	2	D. Carr	114	Speed Dialer	119	Teddy's Top Ten	114	7,200	1:12.00	
1992	Distinct Habit	2	J.D. Bailey	119	Tourney	114	Lily La Belle	114	72,480	1:11.00	.80
1993	Strategic Maneuver	2	J.A. Santos	114	Astas Foxy Lady	119	She Rides Tonite	114	73,560	1:11.00	.79
1994	Changing Ways	2	M.E. Smith	114	Unacceptable	119	Artic Experience	114	67,980	1:12.60	.73
1995	Golden Attraction	2	D.M. Barton	121	Daylight Come	112	Westerm Dreamer	121	65,940	1:10.80	.90
1996	How About Now	2	R. Migliore	115	Exclusive Hold	115	City College	115	68,280	1:12.20	.79
1997	Countess Diana	2	S.J. Sellers	116	Love Lock	119	Sequence	116	64,800	1:10.20	.99
1998	Call Me Up	2	J.F. Chavez	117	Brittons Hill	117	Fantasy Lake	117	66,060	1:12.80	.82
1999	Magicalmysterycat	2	P. Day	122	Circle Of Life	114	Regally Appealing	114	65,700	1:10.80	.87
2000	Gold Mover	2	C. Perret	122	Seeking It All	114	Miss Doolittle	114	64,920	1:10.33	.93
2001	Touch Love	2	J.F. Chavez	119	Lakeside Cup	117	Lost Expectations	117	65,460	1:11.12	.74
2002	Freedom's Daughter	2	J.R. Velazquez	118	Miss Mary Apples	118	Mymich	116	90,000	1:12.14	.84
2003	Ashado	2	E.S. Prado	118	Maple Syrple	122	Hermione's Magic	118	90,000	1:12.12	.81

Beyer Index: 83.42

SHEEPSHEAD BAY HANDICAP, 1 3/8 Miles (Turf),
Fillies and Mares, 3-Year-Olds and Up, Belmont Park, 2003 Purse: $150,000

Year	Winner	Age	Jockey	Wt.	Second	Wt.	Third	Wt.	Win Value	Time	Beyer
1959	Greek Star	4	H. Woodhouse	110	Whitley	115	Oh Johnny	119	17,867	1:42.20	
1960	Tharp	5	R. York	116	Misty Flight	117	Shield Bearer	117	18,907	1:49.00	
1961	Wolfram	5	I. Valenzuela	130	Wise Ship	109	Shield Bearer	120	18,330	1:50.60	
1962	Rose O'Neill	4	M. Ycaza	124	Seven Thirty	123	Play Time	117	18,655	1:34.20	
1963	Cicada	4	L. Adams	128	Nubile	109	Doll Ina	117	18,232	1:42.40	
1964	Intervene	4	M. Ycaza	116	Nubile	112	Princess Arle	114	19,435	1:46.40	

Year	Winner	Age	Jockey	Wt.	Second	Wt.	Third	Wt.	Win Value	Time	Beyer
1965	Snow Scene II	5	B. Baeza	115	Treachery	115	Steeple Jill	126	37,765	1:56.80	
1966	Straight Deal	4	W. Blum	122	Mount Regina	120	Treachery	111	37,115	1:55.40	
1967	Indian Sunlite	4	H. Gustines	118	Mount Regina	117	Amerivan	119	37,440	1:54.80	
1968	Ludham	4	J. Vasquez	119	Hail the Queen	117	Lady Diplomat	113	30,420	1:54.80	
1968	Politely	5	A. Cordero	125	Mount Regina	115	Treacherous	114	30,095	1:55.40	
1969	Symona II	3	J. Velasquez	109	Harem Lady	116	Swiss Cheese	108	38,480	1:55.80	
1970	Princess Pout	4	J. Cruguet	108	A.T.;s Olie	109	Klassy Poppy	116	29,640	1:56.40	
1970	Pattee Canyon	5	J.L. Rotz	132	Top Round	115	Jungle Fire II	109	29,640	1:57.40	
1971	Princess Pout	5	J. Cruguet	124	Tanagra	113	Joans Paris	113	35,340	1:56.60	
1972	Sydneys Nurse	4	J. Vasquez	113	Ziba Blue	109	Flor de S'bra	112	27,510	1:57.00	
1972	Inca Queen	4	G. Patterson	122	Kittiwake	118	Society Column	109	27,810	1:56.40	
1973	Shearwater	4	A. Cordero Jr	122	Inca Queen	118	Aglimmer	115	35,610	1:59.80	
1974	North Broadway	4	A. Cordero Jr	116	Lorraine Edna	117	Gnome Home	109	35,190	1:56.20	
1975	Gems and Roses	5	M. Venezia	112	Hinterland	113	Carolerno	110	34,740	2:01.60	
1976	Glowing Tribute	4	J. Velasquez	118	Bubbling	119	Carmelize	109	50,700	1:49.20	
1976	Fleet Victress	4	P. Day	115	Redundancy	123	Summertime Promise	119	51,600	1:49.00	
1977	Glowing Tribute	3	J. Velasquez	118	Fleet Victress	119	Dottie's Doll	116	65,700	1:59.60	
1978	Late Bloomer	4	J. Velasquez	118	Waya	115	Pearl Necklace	124	68,880	2:01.00	
1979	Terpsichorist	4	E. Maple	117	Late Bloomer	123	Warfever	110	67,200	2:01.60	
1980	The Very One	5	C. Cooke	116	Euphrosyne	114	Baby Sister	115	71,520	2:13.00	
1981	Love Sign	4	R. Hernandez	114	Rokeby Rose	115	Mairzy Doates	122	67,680	2:13.00	
1982	Dana Calqui	4	A. Cordero Jr	110	If Winter Comes	110	Noble Damsel	115	66,060	2:14.20	
1983	Sabin	3	E. Maple	112	First Approach	118	Mintage	114	67,920	2:13.80	
1984	Sabin	4	E. Maple	125	Thirty Flags	114	Double Jeux	111	71,880	2:12.80	
1985	Persian Tiara	5	J. Velasquez	116	Key Dancer	118	Dictina	112	86,820	2:16.00	
1986	Possible Mate	5	J.L. Samyn	124	Tremulous	112	Dawn's Curtsey	112	75,480	2:14.00	
1987	Steal a Kiss	4	E. Maple	111	Videogenic	117	Graceful Darby	112	87,180	2:23.80	
1988	Nastique	4	R.G. Davis	111	Princely Proof	115	Anka Germania	124	71,040	2:16.40	
1989	Love You by Heart	4	J. Cruguet	118	Nastique	117	Laugh and Be Merry	112	72,480	2:12.60	
1990	Destiny Dance	4	J.A. Santos	111	Key Flyer	108	Yestday's Kisses	112	55,080	2:19.20	93
1991	Crockadore	4	M.E. Smith	112	Rigamajig	114	Star Standing	114	71,760	2:14.80	104
1992	Ratings	4	J. Cruguet	112	Ristna	110	Dancing Devilette	113	75,000	2:15.00	97
1993	Trampoli	4	M.E. Smith	116	Aquilegia	116	Revasser	114	67,680	2:14.00	98
1994	Market Booster	5	J.A. Santos	114	Irish Linnet	115	Fairy Garden	120	66,960	2:11.60	103
1995	Duda	4	J.D. Bailey	112	Danish	116	Chelsey Flower	112	65,700	2:13.60	105
1996	Chelsey Flower	5	R.G. Davis	114	Look Daggers	114	Transient Trend	113	67,320	2:12.60	101
1997	Maxzene	4	M.E. Smith	117	Fanjica	117	Future Act	112	90,000	2:11.40	106
1998	Maxzene	5	J.A. Santos	121	Sweetzie	111	Colonial Play	115	90,000	2:14.00	101
1999	Soaring Softly	4	M.E. Smith	114	Starry Dreamer	114	Pinafore Park	113	90,000	2:15.00	101
2000	Lisieux Rose	5	J.A. Santos	116	Melody Queen	113	La Ville Rouge	113	90,000	2:14.16	98
2001	Critical Eye	4	M.J. Luzzi	122	Playact	115	Janet	116	90,000	2:18.18	100
2002	Tweedside	4	J.R. Velazquez	114	Sweetest Thing	119	Golden Corona	114	90,000	2:13.63	95
2003	Mariensky	4	J.R. Velazquez	114	Owsley	119	Silent Crystal	112	90,000	2:28.19	106

Beyer Index: 100.57

SHUVEE HANDICAP, 1 Mile,
Fillies and Mares, 3-Year-Olds and Up, Belmont Park, 2003 Purse: $200,000

Year	Winner	Age	Jockey	Wt.	Second	Wt.	Third	Wt.	Win Value	Time	Beyer
1976	Proud Delta	4	J. Velasquez	122	Snooze	108	Let Me Linger	115	33,810	1:35.00	
1977	Mississippi Mud	4	J. Vasquez	113	Sweet Bernice	109	Secret Lanvin	111	32,760	1:43.60	
1978	One Sum	4	R. Hernandez	121	Sparkling Topaz	107	Charming Story	113	31,830	1:44.00	
1979	Pearl Necklace	5	J. Fell	121	Tingle Stone	120	Kit's Double	109	32,280	1:41.40	
1980	Alada	4	J. Fell	115	Lady Lonsdale	115	Blitey	116	32,460	1:43.00	
1981	Chain Bracelet	4	R. Hernandez	117	Weber City Miss	118	Wistful	120	32,700	1:42.80	
1982	Anti Lib	4	J. Vasquez	113	Tina Tina Too	112	Funny Bone	108	33,420	1:41.60	
1983	Dance Number	4	A. Cordero Jr	113	Number	117	May Day Eighty	113	49,500	1:40.40	
1984	Queen of Song	5	S. Maple	117	Try Something New	121	Narrate	116	86,340	1:43.00	
1985	Life's Magic	4	J. Velasquez	117	Heatherten	126	Some for All	109	83,820	1:42.40	
1986	Lady's Secret	4	P. Day	126	Endear	115	Ride Sally	125	81,780	1:41.80	
1987	Ms. Eloise	4	R.G. Davis	117	North Sider	120	Clemanna's Rose	114	107,820	1:41.80	
1988	Personal Ensign	4	R.P. Romero	121	Clabber Girl	118	Bishop's Delight	111	102,060	1:41.60	
1989	Banker's Lady	4	A. Cordero Jr	122	Rose's Cantina	117	Grecian Flight	117	104,580	1:40.80	
1990	Tis Juliet	4	R. Migliore	113	Survive	119	Dreamy Mimi	114	102,780	1:43.00	102
1991	A Wild Ride	4	M.E. Smith	119	Buy the Firm	122	Degenerate Gal	117	103,140	1:42.40	101
1992	Missy's Mirage	4	E. Maple	116	Harbour Club	110	Versailles Treaty	119	102,960	1:40.60	100
1993	Turnback the Alarm	4	C.W. Antley	117	Shared Interest	113	Vivano	112	90,000	1:43.00	93
1994	Sky Beauty	4	M.E. Smith	125	For All Seasons	113	Looie Capote	112	90,000	1:40.60	111
1995	Inside Information	4	J.A. Santos	119	Sky Beauty	126	Restored Hope	115	80,220	1:35.00	111
1996	Clear Mandate	4	J.A. Krone	111	Smooth Charmer	111	Restored Hope	115	90,000	1:35.00	97
1997	Hidden Lake	4	R. Migliore	115	Flat Fleet Feet	120	Escena	116	90,000	1:35.20	107

Year	Winner	Age	Jockey	Wt.	Second	Wt.	Third	Wt.	Win Value	Time	Beyer
1998	Colonial Minstrel	4	J.R. Velazquez	117	Dixie Flag	120	Hidden Reserve	113	90,000	1:36.20	109
1999	Catinca	4	R. Migliore	121	Sister Act	117	Tap to Music	115	90,000	1:34.20	110
2000	Beautiful Pleasure	5	J.F. Chavez	122	Biogio's Rose	115	Up We Go	114	120,000	1:35.65	113
2001	Apple of Kent	5	R. Migliore	114	March Magic	113	Country Hideaway	118	120,000	1:35.16	102
2002	Shiny Band	4	R.G. Davis	113	Raging Fever	121	Victory Ride	118	120,000	1:34.95	106
2003	Wild Spirit	4	J.J. Castellano	115	Smok'n Frolic	119	You	120	120,000	1:34.51	106

Beyer Index: 104.86

SILVERBULLETDAY, 1 1/16 Miles,
3-Year-Old Fillies, Fair Grounds, 2003 Purse: $150,000

Year	Winner	Age	Jockey	Wt.	Second	Wt.	Third	Wt.	Win Value	Time	Beyer
1982	Linda North	3	R. Franklin		Mickey's Echo		Rose Bouquet			1:42.80	
1983	Duped	3	J. Espinoza		Shamivor		Juliet's Pet			1:43.00	
1984	Texas Cowgirl Nite	3	K. Borque		Only Bid		Runny Nose			1:42.00	
1985	Marshua's Echelon	3	R. Franklin		Turn to Wilma		Not Again Debbie			1:45.20	
1986	Tiffany Lass	3	R. Frazier		Super Set		Port of Departure			1:46.00	
1987	Out of the Bid	3	K. Borque		Trapped		Quick Closing			1:47.20	
1988	False Glitter	3	S. Romero		Part Native		Quite a Gem			1:47.40	
1989	Exquisite Mistress	3	C.H. Borel	114	Jewel Bid	117	Lunar Princess	112		1:46.80	
1990	Windansea	3	R. Romero	119	Everlasting Lady	119	A Hula	114		1:46.40	
1991	Nalees Pin	3	K. Borque	122	Oxford Screen	112	Lady Blockbuster	119		1:46.40	80
1992	Prospector's Delite	3	B. Walker Jr.	117	Royal Med	112	Glitzi Bj	119		1:43.80	
1993	Bright Penny	3	R. Ardoin	114	She's A Little Shy	122	Wakerup	112	19,095	1:44.80	85
1994	Playcaller	3	R. Ardoin	119	Two Altazano	112	Briar Road	112	30,000	1:44.20	85
1995	Legendary Princess	3	C.Emigh	113	Broad Smile	122	Hero's Valor	114	25,875	1:44.80	87
1996	Up Dip	3	C.Bourque	114	Brush With Tequila	113	Not Likely	122	37,635	1:44.60	84
1997	Blushing KD	3	L.Meche	122	Tomisue's Delight	114	Morelia	122	60,000	1:42.40	103
1998	Cool Dixie	3	R.Ardoin	122	Lu Ravi	114	Silent Eskimo	112	75,000	1:43.20	102
1999	Silverbulletday	3	G.Stevens	122	Brushed Halory	114	On a Soapbox	119	75,000	1:44.36	100
2000	Shawnee Country	3	D.Meche	122	Chilukki	122	Humble Clerk	122	75,000	1:45.11	91
2001	Lakenheath	3	C. Lanerie	119	Morning Sun	112	Beloved by All	114	75,000	1:46.09	83
2002	Take Charge Lady	3	A.J. D'Amico	122	Charmed Gift	119	Chamrousse	115	90,000	1:42.09	109
2003	Belle of Perintown	3	C.H. Borel	122	Afternoon Dreams	112	Rebridled Dreams	117	90,000	1:44.48	99

Beyer Index: 92.33

Run as the Davona Dale through 2000.

RED SMITH HANDICAP, 1 3/8 Miles (Turf),
3-Year-Olds and Up, Aqueduct, 2003 Purse: $150,000

Year	Winner	Age	Jockey	Wt.	Second	Wt.	Third	Wt.	Win Value	Time	Beyer
1960	North Pole II	4	S. Boulmetis	114	King o' Turf	114	Crasher	112	18,550	2:15.00	
1961	Wolfram	5	I. Valenzuela	128	Our Jeep	115	Disperse	113	18,492	2:15.00	
1962	Wise Ship	5	H. Gustines	122	Shield Bearer	120	Dead Center	111	18,460	2:16.00	
1963	Vimy Ridge	4	S. Boulmetis	118	Prego	110	Shield Bearer	120	18,395	1:59.40	
1964	Will I Rule	5	B. Baeza	116	Marlin Bay	122	Irish Dandy	110	18,557	1:59.40	
1965	Tenacle	5	R. Ussery	115	Hot Dust	119	Purser	114	19,337	1:55.80	
1966	Spoon Bait	4	J.L. Rotz	113	Paoluccio	112	Knightly Manner	116	18,557	1:54.40	
1967	Ginger Fizz	5	F. Toro	117	Chinatower	114	Handsome Boy	111	19,825	1:55.00	
1968	High Hat	4	E. Belmonte	126	Ruffled Feathers	120	Primo Richard	106	18,330	2:20.20	
1969	Majetta	5	A. Cordero Jr	114	Liaison	114	Fort Marcy	126	18,915	2:19.00	
1970	Drumtop	4	A. Cordero Jr	121	Tradesman	113	Chompion	113	19,110	2:20.40	
1971	Drumtop	5	C. Baltazar	124	Kling Kling	113	Practicante	116	19,560	2:16.60	
1972	New Alibhai	4	F. Ianelli	113	Kling Kling	115	Golden Eagle II	120	16,935	2:02.40	
1973	Red Reality	7	J. Velasquez	122	Malwak	114	New Hope	113	16,890	2:13.20	
1974	Take Off	5	R. Turcotte	117	Jogging	112	Red Reality	112	23,070	2:00.40	
1975	Telefonico	5	C. Perret	120	Drollery	114	Barcas	114	17,400	2:03.00	
1976	Erwin Boy	5	R. Turcotte	116	Clout	111	Quick Card	110	28,110	2:01.20	
1977	Clout	5	G. Martens	114	Chati	117	Gay Jitterbug	122	25,928	1:40.00	
1977	Quick Card	4	A. Cordero Jr	112	Bemo	115	Noble Dancer II	119	25,688	1:39.60	
1978	Tiller	4	J. Fell	114	True Colors	116	Tacitus	113	33,960	2:00.20	
1980	Marquee Universal	4	H. Pilar	121	Match the Hatch	114	Lyphard's Wish	122	68,160	1:58.80	
1981	Match the Hatch	5	K. Skinner	114	Passing Zone	108	Great Neck	114	68,160	1:59.60	
1982	Highland Blade	4	J. Vasquez	124	Dom Menotti	109	Open Call	124	69,000	2:06.40	
1983	Super Sunrise	4	C. Perret	114	Mariacho	116	Field Cat	111	67,200	2:06.80	
1983	Thunder Puddles	4	J.L. Samyn	117	John's Gold	112	Open Call	124	67,200	2:06.40	
1984	Hero's Honor	4	J.D. Bailey	117	Win	114	Eskimo	112	102,900	2:02.20	
1985	Sharannpour	5	A. Cordero Jr	112	Inevitable Leader	116	Cold Feet II	110	114,600	2:04.20	
1986	Divulge	4	J. Cruget	116	Tri for Size	113	Island Sun	118	88,950	1:59.00	
1986	Equalize	4	W.A. Guerra	114	Palace Panther	116	Entitled To	112	103,650	2:02.20	
1987	Theatrical	5	P. Day	122	Dance of Life	122	Equalize	122	116,460	2:00.80	
1988	Pay the Butler	4	R.G. Davis	108	Equalize	116	Yankee Affair	120	118,620	2:01.40	

Year	Winner	Age	Jockey	Wt.	Second	Wt.	Third	Wt.	Win Value	Time	Beyer
1989	Rambo Dancer	5	J.A. Santos	113	El Senor	113	Salem Drive	116	72,360	2:01.00	
1990	Yankee Affair	8	J.A. Santos	122	Hodges Bay	116	Phantom Breeze	112	70,560	2:00.20	102
1991	Who's to Pay	5	J.D. Bailey	117	Simili	114	Solar Splendor	114	71,160	1:58.00	108
1992	Montserrat	4	J.A. Krone	118	Preferences	110	First Rate	111	70,920	2:00.20	101
1993	Royal Mountain Inn	4	J.A. Krone	110	Spectacular Tide	113	Share the Glory	111	71,760	1:59.80	106
1994	Franchise Player	5	D.V. Beckner	109	Red Bishop	119	Same Old Wish	112	72,120	2:20.40	105
1995	Flag Down	5	J.A. Santos	114	Party Season	116	Proceeded	110	69,900	2:22.00	103
1996	Mr. Bluebird	5	M.E. Smith	116	Ops Smile	116	Raintrap	117	87,750	2:15.20	106
1997	Instant Friendship	4	J.R. Velazquez	123	Demi's Bret	117	Trample	112	90,000	2:17.00	107
1998	Musical Ghost	6	J.R. Velazquez	115	Rice	115	Plato's Love	109	90,000	2:15.40	105
1999	Monarch's Maze	3	J. Bravo	113	Williams News	114	Gritty Sandie	114	90,000	2:14.40	103
2000	Cetewayo	6	R. Migliore	114	Understood	113	Val's Prince	118	90,000	2:17.93	104
2001	Mr. Pleasentfar	4	J.A. Santos	115	Eltawaasul	114	Regal Dynasty	113	90,000	2:16.94	100
2002	Evening Attire	4	S.X. Bridgmohan	126	Fisher Pond	116	Pleasant Breeze	120	90,000	2:14.81	109
2003	Balto Star	5	J.R. Velazquez	120	Macaw	118	Cetewayo	116	90,000	2:18.86	105

Run on main track in 2002

Beyer Index: 104.57

SORRENTO, 6 1/2 Furlongs,
2-Year-Old Fillies, Del Mar, 2003 Purse: $150,000

Year	Winner	Age	Jockey	Wt.	Second	Wt.	Third	Wt.	Win Value	Time	Beyer
1967	Windsor Honey	2	J. Sellers	112	Y. So	114	Free Sample	112	13,125	1:30.60	
1970	June Darling	2	W. Mahorney	119	Ulla Britta	113	Sapose Speed	114	7,737	1:10.80	
1970	Countess Market	2	A. Pineda	113	Balcony's Babe	115	Tried Wings	114	7,837	1:10.40	
1971	Chargerette	2	F. Olivares	113	Miss Lady Bug	116	Impressive Style	113	9,750	1:09.20	
1972	Windy's Daughter	2	W. Shoemaker	113	Bold Liz	119	Sleek and Fleet	114	9,125	1:09.00	
1973	Fleet Peach	2	D. Pierce	113	Calaki	116	Poona's Double	116	12,600	1:09.20	
1974	Spout	2	A. Pineda	115	Just a Kick	115	Cut Class	113	14,000	1:36.80	
1975	Queen to Be	2	D.G. McHargue	113	T.V. Terese	114	Pet Label	116	13,350	1:36.80	
1976	Telferner	2	L. Pincay Jr	117	Lullaby	117	Asterisca	115	16,150	1:36.60	
1977	My Little Maggie	2	W. Shoemaker	114	Extravagant	114	Short Stanza	114	16,150	1:36.40	
1978	Beauty Hour	2	M. Castaneda	114	Hand Creme	117	Top Soil	114	19,150	1:37.00	
1979	Hazel R.	2	C.J. McCarron	117	Arcades Ambo	113	Princess Karenda	114	19,100	1:35.80	
1980	Native Fancy	2	L. Pincay Jr	117	Raja's Delight	115	Wedding Reception	114	22,950	1:38.80	
1981	First Advance	2	W. Shoemaker	113	Merry Sport	115	Skillful Joy	113	26,100	1:38.60	
1982	Time for Sale	2	W. Shoemaker	113	Sharili Brown	117	Infantes	115	32,300	1:38.40	
1983	Leading Ladybug	2	P.A. Valenzuela	115	Bright Orphan	118	Lapidist	116	31,150	1:40.20	
1984	Wayward Pirate	2	W. Shoemaker	114	Doon's Baby	120	Trunk	116	31,350	1:37.20	
1985	Arewehavingfunyet	2	P.A. Valenzuela	120	Life at the Top	116	Python	117	34,250	1:37.00	
1986	Brave Raj	2	P.A. Valenzuela	117	Breech	117	Footy	121	33,250	1:22.60	
1987	Hasty Pasty	2	L. Pincay Jr	121	Lost Kitty	121	Torch of the Track	117	37,200	1:23.00	
1988	Stocks Up	2	G.L. Stevens	117	Approved to Fly	116	Lea Lucinda	117	48,350	1:23.40	
1989	Cheval Volant	2	L. Pincay Jr	117	Breezing Dixie	115	Dancing Jamie	115	46,575	1:23.80	
1990	Lite Light	2	R.A. Baze	115	Beyond Perfection	117	Dragonetta	117	47,100	1:22.00	
1991	Soviet Sojourn	2	C.S. Nakatani	121	La Spia	117	She's Tops	117	44,475	1:22.20	92
1992	Zoonaqua	2	E. Delahoussaye	117	Eliza	117	Medici Bells	117	49,125	1:22.40	88
1993	Phone Chatter	2	L. Pincay Jr	117	Rhapsodic	121	Noassemblyrequired	117	45,900	1:16.20	85
1994	How So Oiseau	2	P.A. Valenzuela	117	Ski Dancer	117	Serena's Song	121	47,100	1:15.80	92
1995	Batroyale	2	G.L. Stevens	119	Cosmic Fire	117	Waycross	117	59,200	1:15.60	90
1996	Desert Digger	2	E. Delahoussaye	116	Silken Magic	117	Montecito	117	65,950	1:16.00	90
1997	Career Collection	2	C.S. Nakatani	117	Griselle	117	Bent Creek City	121	67,825	1:17.80	74
1998	Silverbulletday	2	G.L. Stevens	121	Excellent Meeting	117	Colorado Song	117	64,980	1:17.40	84
1999	Chilukki	2	D.R. Flores	121	November Slew	117	She's Classy	117	90,000	1:16.40	98
2000	Give Praise	2	L. Pincay Jr.	116	Sea Reef	115	Fort Lauderdale	117	90,000	1:17.88	79
2001	Tempera	2	D.R. Flores	117	Respectful	115	Roaring Blaze	117	90,000	1:16.13	95
2002	Buffythecenterfold	2	M.S. Garcia	121	Tricks Her	115	Indy Groove	117	90,000	1:17.39	84
2003	Tizdubai	2	D.R. Flores	118	Dirty Diana	122	Solar Fire	118	90,000	1:17.15	79

Beyer Index: 86.92

STRUB, 1 1/8 Miles,
4-Year-Olds, Santa Anita, 2003 Purse: $400,000

Year	Winner	Age	Jockey	Wt.	Second	Wt.	Third	Wt.	Win Value	Time	Beyer
1948	Flashco	4	J. Westrope	113	On Trust	125	Double Jay	118	83,500	2:03.20	
1949	Ace Admiral	4	J. Westrope	113	Rose Beam	112	Dinner Gong	114	85,200	2:02.20	
1950	Ponder	4	S. Brooks	126	Two Lea	116	Mocopo	112	75,200	2:02.40	
1951	Great Circle	4	W. Shoemaker	115	Lotowhite	116	Bed o' Roses	110	144,325	2:00.40	
1952	Intent	4	E. Arcaro	113	Gold Capitol	114	Black Douglas	113	112,750	2:02.80	
1953	Mark-Ye-Well	4	E. Arcaro	126	Fleet Bird	112	Happy Go Lucky	114	85,600	2:03.40	
1954	Apple Valley	4	M. Volzke	113	By Zeus	114	Cerise Reine	115	85,025	2:08.00	
1955	Determine	4	R. York	126	Miz Clementine	117	James Session	113	87,000	2:00.40	
1956	Trackmaster	4	R. Neves	114	Traffic Judge	123	Honeys Alibi	119	79,600	2:04.80	

Year	Winner	Age	Jockey	Wt.	Second	Wt.	Third	Wt.	Win Value	Time	Beyer
1957	Spinney	4	W. Harmatz	113	Beam Rider	112	Lucky G.L.	113	93,870	2:04.80	
1958	Round Table	4	W. Harmatz	126	Seaneen	117	Promised Land	125	80,360	2:01.80	
1959	Hillsdale	4	T. Barrow	123	Royal Living	112	Jewel's Reward	116	91,150	2:02.40	
1960	First Landing	4	E. Arcaro	116	Bagdad	118	Linmold	117	80,490	2:00.60	
1961	Prove It	4	W. Shoemaker	116	Prince Blessed	113	Grey Eagle	113	93,370	2:01.00	
1962	Four-and-Twenty	4	J. Longden	126	Garwol	111	Olden Timems	114	79,910	2:01.00	
1963	Crimson Satan	4	H. Hinojosa	118	Pirate Cove	114	Dr. Kacy	112	92,400	2:00.60	
1964	Gun Bow	4	W. Shoemaker	117	Rocky Link	114	Win-em-All	113	87,000	1:59.80	
1965	Duel	4	M. Ycaza	112	Or Et Argent	113	Pelegrin	114	79,600	2:00.60	
1966	Bold Bidder	4	W. Shoemaker	119	Isle of Greece	120	Terry's Secret	125	89,500	1:59.60	
1967	Drin	4	L. Pincay Jr.	117	Quicken Tree	115	Kings Favor	116	84,800	2:02.00	
1968	Most Host	4	W. Harmatz	114	Damascus	126	Ruken	117	73,700	2:04.00	
1969	Dignitas	4	F. Alvarez	115	Nodouble	123	Cavamore	117	81,300	2:02.00	

Nodouble finished first but was disqualified and placed second

Year	Winner	Age	Jockey	Wt.	Second	Wt.	Third	Wt.	Win Value	Time	Beyer
1970	Snow Sporting	4	L. Pincay Jr.	114	Might	116	Comtal	114	84,500	1:48.80	
1971	War Helm	4	J. Sellers	115	Hanalei Bay	118	Mickey McGuire	117	87,100	2:00.60	
1972	Unconscious	4	W. Shoemaker	121	Triple Bend	118	Good Counsel	116	85,300	2:00.40	
1973	Royal Owl	4	J. Sellers	116	Big Spruce	117	New Prospect	117	82,800	2:04.00	
1974	Ancient Title	4	L. Pincay Jr.	121	Dancing Papa	116	Prince Dantan	115	85,200	2:00.80	
1975	Stardust Mel	4	W. Shoemaker	120	Confederate Yankee	116	Rube the Great	122	86,300	2:04.20	
1976	George Navonod	4	F. Toro	115	Larrikin	118	Dancing Gun	115	76,900	2:12.00	
1977	Kirby Lane	4	S. Hawley	118	Properantes	114	Double Discount	115	90,900	2:00.40	
1978	Mr. Redoy	4	D. McHargue	116	Text	121	J.O. Tobin	122	140,200	2:01.00	
1979	Affirmed	4	L. Pincay Jr.	126	Johnny's Image	115	Quip	115	142,500	2:01.00	
1980	Spectacular Bid	4	W. Shoemaker	126	Flying Paster	121	Valdez	122	124,500	1:57.80	
1981	Super Moment	4	F. Toro	116	Exploded	116	Doonesbury	118	145,000	2:01.20	
1982	It's the One	4	W.A. Guerra	118	Dorcaro	116	Rock Softly	115	172,700	2:00.40	
1983	Swing Till Dawn	4	P.A. Valenzuela	115	Wavering Monarch	121	Water Bank	117	178,000	2:02.00	
1984	Desert Wine	4	E. Delahoussaye	117	Load the Cannons	115	Silent Fox	114	221,400	2:02.20	
1985	Precisionist	4	C.J. McCarron	125	Greinton	117	Gate Dancer	126	189,300	2:00.20	
1986	Nostalgia's Star	4	F. Toro	116	Roo Art	117	Fast Account	115	314,250	2:03.60	
1987	Snow Chief	4	P.A. Valenzuela	126	Ferdinand	126	Broad Brush	126	291,750	2:00.00	
1988	Alysheba	4	C.J. McCarron	126	Candi's Gold	117	On The Line	119	275,000	2:00.40	
1989	Nasr El Arab	4	P.A. Valenzuela	123	Perceive Arrogance	117	Silver Circus	120	275,000	2:02.20	
1990	Flying Continental	4	C.A. Black	119	Quiet American	114	Hawkster	126	275,000	2:01.40	
1991	Defensive Play	4	J.A. Santos	122	My Boy Adam	117	In Excess	121	275,000	2:00.80	
1992	Best Pal	4	K.J. Desormeaux	124	Dinard	120	Reign Road	118	275,000	1:59.95	.119
1993	Siberian Summer	4	C.S. Nakatani	118	Bertrando	122	Major Impact	118	275,000	2:00.78	.114
1994	Diazo	4	L. Pincay Jr	120	Nonproductiveasset	118	Stuka	118	275,000	2:00.33	.110
1995	Dare and Go	4	A. Solis	118	Dramatic Gold	124	Wekiva Springs	122	275,000	2:00.15	.110
1996	Helmsman	4	C.J. McCarron	122	Afternoon Deelites	120	Mr Purple	118	300,000	2:02.76	.106
1997	Victory Speech	4	J.D. Bailey	124	The Barking Shark	118	Ambivalent	118	300,000	2:01.50	.108
1998	Silver Charm	4	G.L. Stevens	123	Mud Route	117	Bagshot	117	300,000	1:47.27	.113
1999	Event of the Year	4	C.S. Nakatani	119	Dr Fong	121	Hanuman Highway	117	300,000	1:47.65	.115
2000	General Challenge	4	C.S. Nakatani	123	Luftikus	117	Saint's honor	121	300,000	1:48.81	.112
2001	Wooden Phone	4	C.S. Nakatani	117	Tiznow	123	Jimmy Z	117	300,000	1:48.43	.107
2002	Mizzen Mast	4	K.J. Desormeaux	121	Giant Gentleman	117	Fancy As	119	240,000	1:47.25	.117
2003	Medaglia d'Oro	4	J.D. Bailey	123	Olmodavor	117	Tracemark	117	240,000	1:48.04	.119

Beyer Index: 112.5

SUNSET HANDICAP, 1 1/2 Miles (Turf), 3-Year-Olds and Up, Hollywood Park, 2003 Purse: $150,000

Year	Winner	Age	Jockey	Wt.	Second	Wt.	Third	Wt.	Win Value	Time	Beyer
1940	Kayak II	5	J. Adams	131	Specify	116	Big Flash	109	13,750	2:30.20	
1941	King Torch	4	J. Deering	105	Mioland	128	W. and Wing	105	18,950	2:44.40	
1946	Historian	5	O. Scurlock	121	Paperboy	110	Triplicate	122	37,150	2:40.80	
1947	Cover Up	4	R. Permane	122	Burning Dream	117	Lets Dance	113	32,000	2:41.20	
1948	Drumbeat	3	T. Williams	100	On Trust	126	Shannon II	124	33,100	2:41.00	
1949	Ace Admiral	4	J. Longden	122	Natural	102	Dinner Gong	117	34,650	2:39.80	
1950	Hill Prince	3	E. Arcaro	128	Next Move	114	Great Circle	109	35,300	1:48.60	
1951	Alderman	4	J. Westrope	112	Mocopo	106	Stormy Cloud	105	34,400	2:42.00	
1952	Great Circle	5	R. Heather	112	Stormy Cloud	108	Wistful	112	31,700	2:41.80	
1953	Lights Up	6	J. Westrope	114	Endowment	106	Fleet Bird	120	60,400	2:41.20	
1954	Fleet Bird	5	R. Neves	115	Rejected	128	Six Fifteen	107	63,200	2:40.80	
1955	Social Outcast	5	E. Guerin	121	Rejected	122	Alidon	119	64,400	2:40.60	
1956	Swaps	4	W. Shoemaker	130	Honeys Alibi	108	Blue Volt	108	64,400	2:38.20	
1957	Find	7	R. Neves	119	Eddie Schmidt	109	Porterhouse	122	66,000	2:40.00	
1958	Gallant Man	4	W. Shoemaker	132	Eddie Schmidt	110	St. Vincent	111	61,500	2:41.00	
1959	Whodunit	4	R. York	110	Day Court	114	Find	118	63,700	2:40.80	
1960	Dotted Swiss	4	E. Burns	120	Nickel Boy	112	Turin	112	63,100	2:40.20	
1961	Whodunit	6	M. Ycaza	117	Dress Up	113	Prince Blessed	122	52,800	2:39.00	
1962	Prove It	5	W. Shoemaker	129	Windy Sands	112	Notable II	107	55,000	2:39.60	

Year	Winner	Age	Jockey	Wt.	Second	Wt.	Third	Wt.	Win Value	Time	Beyer
1963	Arbitrage	5	P. Moreno	110	Mr. Consistency	117	Cadiz	122	50,350	2:41.20	
1964	Colorado King	5	W. Shoemaker	124	Drill Site	113	Viking Spirit	111	50,650	2:40.80	
1965	Terry's Secret	3	A. Maese	116	Ramant	108	Ask Father	110	48,000	2:41.80	
1966	O'Hara	4	D. Pierce	113	Rehabilitate	106	Silk Hat	109	52,650	2:40.40	
1967	Hill Clown	4	W. Shoemaker	109	Pretense	129	Niarkos	121	63,500	2:27.80	
1968	Fort Marcy	4	L. Pincay Jr	122	Quicken Tree	122	Fiddle Isle	108	73,500	2:26.60	
1969	Petrone	5	J. Sellers	124	Society II	112	Off	109	61,450	3:18.00	
1970	One for All	4	L. Pincay Jr	114	Onandaga	113	Over the Counter	111	75,350	3:21.80	
1971	Over the Counter	7	J. Lambert	114	Cougar II	130	Typecast	110	80,650	3:19.20	
1972	Typecast	6	J. Sellers	120	Over the Counter	112	Violonor	114	78,350	3:20.60	
1973	Cougar II	7	W. Shoemaker	128	Life Cycle	120	Rock Bath	114	80,100	2:26.00	
1974	Greco II	5	W. Shoemaker	113	Big Whippendeal	120	Scantling	118	69,600	2:27.00	
1975	Barclay Joy	5	W. Shoemaker	117	Captain Cee Jay	118	Top Crowd	115	50,450	2:26.80	
1975	Cruiser II	6	F. Olivares	114	Pass the Glance	119	Kirrary	116	49,450	2:27.00	
1976	Caucasus	4	F. Toro	121	King Pellinore	124	Riot in Paris	123	81,350	2:26.40	
1977	Today 'n Tomorrow	4	W. Shoemaker	116	Hunza Dancer	122	Copper Mel	117	104,450	2:27.60	
1978	Exceller	5	W. Shoemaker	130	Diagramatic	122	Effervescing	122	96,600	2:27.00	
1979	Sirlad	5	D.G. McHargue	122	Ardiente	115	Inkerman	119	103,000	2:24.00	
1980	Inkerman	5	W. Shoemaker	115	Balzac	120	Obraztsovy	121	94,700	2:24.40	
1981	Galaxy Libra	5	W. Shoemaker	119	Caterman	122	The Bart	117	136,050	2:25.80	
1982	Erins Isle	4	A. Cordero Jr	118	Don Roberto	117	Exploded	119	129,600	2:25.60	
1983	Craelius	4	C.J. McCarron	118	Palikaraki	115	Decadrachm	115	137,600	2:26.40	
1984	John Henry	9	C.J. McCarron	126	Load the Cannons	118	Pair of Deuces	113	129,800	2:24.80	
1985	Kings Island	4	F. Toro	116	Greinton	122	Val Danseur	114	148,800	2:25.80	
1986	Zoffany	6	E. Delahoussaye	122	Dahar	125	Flying Pidgeon	121	161,500	2:24.40	
1987	Swink	4	W. Shoemaker	112	Forlitano	122	Rivlia	122	165,300	2:25.00	
1988	Roi Normand	5	F. Toro	114	Putting	117	Circus Prince	114	170,000	2:24.60	
1989	Pranke	5	P.A. Valenzuela	117	Frankly Perfect	123	Pleasant Variety	117	157,200	2:28.00	
1990	Petite Ile	4	C.A. Black	115	Live the Dream	116	Soft Machine	110	163,600	2:25.60	102
1991	Black Monday	5	C.S. Nakatani	112	Super May	117	Razeen	116	158,400	2:26.00	107
1992	Qathif	5	A. Solis	114	Seven Rivers	114	Stark South	116	153,600	2:26.60	103
1993	Bien Bien	4	C.J. McCarron	122	Emerald Jig	114	Beyton	117	154,300	2:25.40	106
1994	Grand Flotilla	7	G.L. Stevens	119	Semillon	116	Emerald Jig	115	158,000	2:26.20	105
1997	Marlin	4	D.R. Flores	120	Flyway	117	Percutant	118	240,000	2:25.20	107
1998	River Bay	5	A. Solis	121	Lazy Lode	115	Devonwood	114	210,000	2:27.40	106
1999	Plicck	6	D.R. Flores	116	River Bay	121	Lazy Lode	120	150,000	2:26.80	106
2000	Bienamado	4	C.J. McCarron	122	Deploy Venture	115	Single Empire	120	150,000	2:25.06	105
2001	Blueprint	6	G.L. Stevens	116	Kudos	116	Northern Quest	116	120,000	2:26.16	103
2002	Grammarian	4	B. Blanc	112	Continental Red	116	Lord Flasheart	115	150,000	2:26.59	99
2003	Puerto Banus	4	V. Espinoza	113	Cagney	116	Continental Red	116	90,000	2:26.95	101

Beyer Index: 104.17

SUPER DERBY, 1 1/8 Miles, 3-Year-Olds,
Louisiana Downs, 2003 Purse: $500,000

Year	Winner	Age	Jockey	Wt.	Second	Wt.	Third	Wt.	Win Value	Time	Beyer
1980	Temperence Hill	3	E. Maple	126	First Albert	126	Cactus Road	126	300,000	2:06.60	
1981	Island Whirl	3	L. Pincay Jr	126	Summing	126	Willow Hour	126	300,000	2:03.20	
1982	Reinvested	3	J. Velasquez	126	El Baba	126	Drop Your Drawers	126	300,000	2:01.60	
1983	Sunny's Halo	3	L. Pincay Jr	126	Play Fellow	126	My Habitony	126	300,000	2:01.60	
1984	Gate Dancer	3	L. Pincay Jr	126	Precisionist	126	Big Pistol	126	300,000	2:00.20	
1985	Creme Fraiche	3	E. Maple	126	Encolure	126	Government Corner	126	300,000	2:02.80	
1986	Wise Times	3	E. Maple	126	Cheapskate	126			300,000	2:04.00	
					Southern Halo	126					
1987	Alysheba	3	C.J. McCarron	126	Candi's Gold	126	Parochial	126	600,000	2:03.20	
1988	Seeking the Gold	3	P. Day	126	Happyasalark Tomas	126	Lively One	126	600,000	2:03.80	
1989	Sunday Silence	3	P.A. Valenzuela	126	Big Earl	126	Awe Inspiring	126	600,000	2:03.20	
1990	Home at Last	3	J.D. Bailey	126	Unbridled	126	Cee's Tizzy	126	600,000	2:02.00	
1991	Free Spirit's Joy	3	C.H. Borel	126	Olympio	126	Zeeruler	126	600,000	2:00.80	
1992	Senor Tomas	3	A. Gryder	126	Count the Time	126	Orbit's Revenge	126	450,000	2:04.00	96
1993	Wallenda	3	W.H. McCauley	126	Saintly Prospector	126	Peteski	126	450,000	2:02.60	101
1994	Soul of the Matter	3	K.J. Desormeaux	126	Concern	126	Bay Street Star	126	450,000	2:03.40	101
1995	Mecke	3	J.D. Bailey	126	Pineing Patty	126	Scott's Scoundrel	126	450,000	2:00.20	110
1996	Editor's Note	3	G.L. Stevens	126	The Barking Shark	126	Devil's Honor	126	450,000	2:00.20	106
1997	Deputy Commander	3	C.J. McCarron	126	Precocity	126	Blazing Sword	126	300,000	2:00.80	111
1998	Arch	3	C.S. Nakatani	126	Classic Cat	126	Sir Tiff	126	300,000	2:01.51	103
1999	Ecton Park	3	A. Solis	126	Menifee	126	Pineaff	126	300,000	2:00.59	117
2000	Tiznow	3	C.J. McCarron	126	Commendable	126	Mass Market	126	300,000	1:59.84	114
2001	Outofthebox	3	L.J. Meche	126	E Dubai	126	Quadrophonic Sound	126	300,000	2:06.20	101
2002	Essence of Dubai	3	J.F. Chavez	124	Walk in the Snow	124	A.P. Five Hundred	124	300,000	1:49.43	105
2003	Ten Most Wanted	3	P. Day	124	Soto	124	Crowned King	124	300,000	1:50.77	107

Distance 1 1/4 miles prior to 2002

Beyer Index: 106

SWAPS STAKES, 1 1/8 Miles, 3-Year-Olds,
Hollywood Park, 2003 Purse: $400,000

Year	Winner	Age	Jockey	Wt.	Second	Wt.	Third	Wt.	Win Value	Time	Beyer
1974	Agitate	3	W. Shoemaker	123	Stardust Mel	120	Master Music	114	66,300	1:59.60	
1975	Forceten	3	D. Pierce	120	Sibirri	114	Diabolo	123	119,800	1:59.80	
1976	Majestic Light	3	S. Hawley	114	Crystal Water	123	Double Discount	115	98,200	1:59.20	
1977	J.O. Tobin	3	W. Shoemaker	120	Affiliate	117	Text	120	194,900	1:58.60	
1978	Radar Ahead	3	D. McHargue	120	Batonnier	123	Poppy Popowich	115	133,300	2:00.00	
1979	Valdez	3	L. Pincay Jr.	120	Shamgo	114	Paint King	114	124,250	1:59.40	
1980	First Albert	3	F. Mena	123	Amber Pass	123	Mr. Mud	114	162,200	2:00.80	
1981	Noble Nashua	3	L. Pincay Jr.	123	Dorcaro	115	Stancharry	123	127,000	2:01.20	
1982	Journey at Sea	3	C.J. McCarron	120	West Coast Native	114	Casselaria	123	91,300	2:00.20	
1983	Hyperborean	3	F. Toro	115	My Habitony	120	Tanks Brigade	120	97,500	2:01.00	
1984	Precisionist	3	C.J. McCarron	123	Prince True	120	Majestic Shore	114	121,300	1:59.80	
1985	Padua	3	P.A. Valenzuela	115	Turkoman	115	Don't Say Halo	120	123,500	2:01.40	
1986	Clear Choice	3	C.J. McCarron	120	Southern Halo	114	Jota	116	137,000	2:03.60	
1987	Temperate Sil	3	W. Shoemaker	123	Candi's Gold	123	Pledge Card	115	124,400	2:02.20	
1988	Lively One	3	W. Shoemaker	120	Blade of the Ball	114	Iz a Saros	123	13,200	2:01.00	
1989	Prized	3	E. Delahoussaye	120	Sunday Silence	126	Endow	123	232,400	2:01.80	
1990	Jovial	3	G.L. Stevens	120	Silver Ending	126	Stalwart Charger	126	120,000	2:01.20	108
1991	Best Pal	3	P.A. Valenzuela	116	Corporate Report	114	Compelling Sound	123	120,000	2:00.60	111
1992	Bien Bien	3	C.J. McCarron	119	Treekster	123	Sevengreenpairs	119	123,400	2:02.80	102
1993	Devoted Brass	3	L. Pincay Jr.	123	Future Storm	119	Codified	123	124,000	2:00.60	103
1994	Silver Music	3	C.W. Antley	119	Dramatic Gold	119	Valiant Nature	121	123,800	2:00.60	106
1995	Thunder Gulch	3	G.L. Stevens	126	Da Hoss	118	Petionville	120	275,000	1:49.00	101
1996	Victory Speech	3	J.D. Bailey	118	Prince of Thieves	118	Hesabull	118	300,000	1:48.20	104
1997	Free House	3	K. Desormeaux	122	Deputy Commander	118	Wild Rush	122	300,000	1:45.80	115
1998	Old Trieste	3	C.J. McCarron	118	Grand Slam	120	Old Topper	117	300,000	1:47.00	116
1999	Cat Thief	3	P. Day	120	General Challenge	122	Walk That Walk	117	300,000	1:47.87	107
2000	Captain Steve	3	C.S. Nakatani	120	Tiznow	118	Spacelink	118	300,000	1:48.01	111
2001	Congaree	3	G.L. Stevens	122	Until Sundown	118	Jamaican Rum	118	300,000	1:48.61	106
2002	Came Home	3	M.E. Smith	122	Like a Hero	114	Fonz's	116	300,000	1:48.28	108
2003	During	3	J.D. Bailey	115	Ten Most Wanted	122	Eye of the Tiger	118	240,000	1:49.38	96
							Outta Here	120			

Beyer Index: 106.71

Distance 1 1/4 miles prior to 1995

TOM FOOL HANDICAP, 7 Furlongs,
3-Year-Olds and Up, Belmont Park, 2003 Purse: $150,000

Year	Winner	Age	Jockey	Wt.	Second	Wt.	Third	Wt.	Win Value	Time	Beyer
1975	Kinsman Hope	5	J. Ruane	116	Lonetree	125	Right Mind	113	26,925	1:21.40	
1976	El Pitirre	4	A. Cordero Jr	114	Nalees Knight	110	Honorable Miss	118	26,550	1:24.40	
1977	Mexican General	4	C. Perret	115	Full Out	119	Sticky Situation	110	22,605	1:22.00	
1978	J.O. Tobin	4	J. Fell	129	White Rammer	119	It's Freezing	116	25,950	1:20.80	
1979	Cox's Ridge	5	E. Maple	119	Nice Catch	121	Tilt Up	119	25,500	1:22.20	
1980	Plugged Nickle	3	J. Fell	121	Dr. Patches	119	Isella	119	33,060	1:22.20	
1981	Rise Jim	5	A. Cordero Jr	119	Proud Appeal	121	Rivalero	119	32,820	1:21.20	
1982	Rise Jim	6	A. Cordero Jr	119	Maudlin	119	And More	119	32,940	1:23.80	
1983	Deputy Minister	4	D. MacBeth	126	Fit to Fight	119	Maudlin	126	52,020	1:22.20	
1984	Believe the Queen	4	J. Velasquez	126	A Phenomenon	119	Cannon Shell	121	70,680	1:22.40	
1985	Track Barron	4	A. Cordero Jr	123	Mt. Livermore	126	Cannon Shell	126	82,260	1:22.00	
1986	Groovy	3	J.A. Santos	112	Phone Trick	126	Basket Weave	119	80,460	1:21.60	
1987	Groovy	4	A. Cordero Jr	128	Sun Master	121	Moment of Hope	119	81,900	1:22.40	
1988	King's Swan	8	A. Cordero Jr	128	Gulch	128	Abject	119	100,980	1:22.40	
1989	Sewickley	4	R.P. Romero	119	Houston	114	Crusader Sword	119	67,920	1:24.00	
1990	Quick Call	6	J.F. Chavez	119	Sewickley	123	Traskwood	119	52,680	1:21.40	
1991	Mr. Nasty	4	A. Cordero Jr	119	Rubiano	121	Senor Speedy	119	67,800	1:21.60	
1992	Rubiano	5	J.A. Krone	126	Take Me Out	119	Arrowtown	119	70,920	1:21.60	108
1993	Birdonthewire	4	C. Perret	119	Fly So Free	119	Take Me Out	119	67,680	1:20.80	111
1994	Virginia Rapids	4	J.L. Samyn	124	Cherokee Run	121	Boundary	119	64,380	1:22.20	112
1995	Lite the Fuse	4	J.A. Krone	117	Our Emblem	115	Evil Bear	118	65,220	1:21.60	116
1996	Kayrawan	4	R. Migliore	113	Cold Execution	112	Lite the Fuse	122	64,869	1:22.80	105
1997	Diligence	4	J.A. Santos	116	Royal Haven	119	Elusive Quality	114	90,000	1:22.40	106
1998	Banker's Gold	4	J.F. Chavez	115	Boundless Moment	115	Partner's Hero	114	90,000	1:21.00	113
1999	Crafty Friend	6	R. Migliore	116	Affirmed Success	119	Aratx	117	90,000	1:20.60	114
2000	Trippi	3	J.D. Bailey	112	Cornish Snow	113	Sailor's Warning	111	90,000	1:21.69	106
2001	Exchange Rate	4	J.D. Bailey	114	Say Florida Sandy	117	Here's Zealous	112	90,000	1:21.24	109
2002	Left Bank	5	J.R. Velazquez	121	Affirmed Success	120	Summer Note	113	90,000	1:20.17	121
2003	Aldebaran	5	J.D. Bailey	122	Peeping Tom	117	State City	118	90,000	1:22.54	105

Beyer Index: 110.5

TOP FLIGHT HANDICAP, 1 Mile,
Fillies and Mares, 3-Year-Olds and Up, Aqueduct, 2003 Purse: $150,000

Year	Winner	Age	Jockey	Wt.	Second	Wt.	Third	Wt.	Win Value	Time	Beyer
1940	True Call	3	D. Meade	107	Piquet	106	Dolly Val	120	6,200	1:43.60	
1941	Tangled	3	C. McCreary	110	Misty Isle	112	Dipsy Doodle	114	4,800	1:44.60	
1942	Level Best	4	D. Meade	123	Up the Hill	114	Transient	112	5,325	1:42.80	
1943	Mar-Kell	4	B. Thompson	122	Yarrow Maid	110	Stefanita	106	4,700	1:44.40	
1944	Boojiana	3	T. Atkinson	106	Mar-Kell	126	Silvestra	112	8,165	1:43.40	
1945	Miss Keeneland	4	A. Snider	122	Legend Bearer	122	Bertie S.	109	7,585	1:45.00	
1946	Sicily	4	E. Arcaro	113	Surosa	113	Recce	118	17,400	1:43.20	
1947	Rytina	4	T. Atkinson	104	Miss Grillo	123	Be Faithful	121	18,550	1:43.60	
1948	Honeymoon	5	D. Dodson	124	Red Shoes	108	Gallorette	126	16,950	1:43.00	
1949	But Why Not	5	D. Gorman	126	Paddeluck	119	Allie's Pal	114	11,450	1:43.60	
1950	Nell K.	4	G. Hettinger	126	Lithe	116	Roman Candlee	116	12,200	1:43.80	
1951	Busanda	4	E. Guerin	120	How	113	Leading Home	107	12,650	1:42.40	
1952	Renew	5	W. Boland	115	Valadium	115	Blue Moon	111	16,850	1:43.80	
1953	Marta	6	C. McCreary	119	Sunshine Nell	112	No Score	110	22,350	1:42.80	
1954	Sunshine Nell	6	E. Guerin	125	Spinning Top	112	La Corredora	125	24,750	1:43.40	
1955	Parlo	4	E. Guerin	126	Gainsboro Girl	114	Spinning Top	113	21,700	1:41.80	
1956	Searching	4	C. McCreary	121	Parlo	124	Rico Reto	107	19,400	1:42.60	
1957	Plotter	4	P. Anderson	116	Outer Space	112	Sorceress	104	19,950	1:42.60	
1958	Plucky Roman	4	H. Grant	114	Outer Space	117	Happy Princess	119	17,672	1:43.00	
1959	Big Effort	4	W. Shoemaker	123	Endine	118	Tempted	118	17,575	1:42.80	
1960	Royal Native	4	W. Hartack	126	Quill	123	Bug Brush	120	36,385	1:43.00	
1961	Make Sail	4	M. Ycaza	116	Funny Bone	112	Rash Statement	114	35,945	1:51.00	
1962	Pepper Patch	5	D. Pierce	113	Counter Call	111	Honey Dear	108	37,050	1:50.20	
1963	Firm Policy	4	M. Ycaza	125	Tamarona	111	Cicada	128	35,880	1:48.60	
1964	Oil Royalty	6	H. Grant	122	Tona	114	Smart Deb	122	37,180	1:50.80	
1965	Affectionately	5	W. Blum	120	Steeple Jill	123	Old Hat	127	37,180	1:49.80	
1966	Summer Scandal	4	G. Patterson	117	Malhoa	113	Straight Deal	119	35,945	1:49.40	
1967	Straight Deal	5	A. Cordero Jr	126	Mac's Sparkler	122	Malhoa	112	36,075	1:49.60	
1968	Amerigo Lady	4	J. Velasquez	119	Serene Queen	111	Muse	109	37,830	1:49.00	
1969	Amerigo Lady	5	M. Ycaza	123	Harem Lady	108	Treacherous	113	35,620	1:50.40	
1970	Shuvee	4	B. Baeza	120	Singing Rain	122	Swiss Cheese	110	37,375	1:48.60	
1971	Shuvee	5	R. Turcotte	127	Cathy Honey	118	Office Queen	127	32,340	1:49.60	
1972	Inca Queen	4	G. Patterson	112	Polly Piper	110	Aladancer	117	33,900	1:50.00	
1973	Poker Night	3	R. Woodhouse	110	Summer Guest	123	Roba Bella	113	33,420	1:48.20	
1974	Lady Love	4	E. Maple	114	Krislin	111	Penny Flight	115	33,120	1:48.60	
1975	Twixt	6	W.J. Passmore	125	Heloise	109	Something Super	116	33,240	1:50.60	
1976	Proud Delta	4	J. Velasquez	120	Let Me Linger	116	Spring Is Here	108	49,455	1:49.00	
1977	Shawi	4	M. Venezia	111	Proud Delta	124	Mississippi Mud	114	48,285	1:49.80	
1978	Northernette	4	J. Fell	121	One Sum	121	Dottie's Doll	116	48,330	1:49.40	
1979	Waya	5	A. Cordero Jr	128	Pearl Necklace	120	Island Kiss	112	64,680	1:50.80	
1980	Glorious Song	4	J. Velasquez	123	Misty Gallore	126	Blitey	117	66,360	1:49.60	
1981	Chain Bracelet	4	R. Hernandez	115	Lady Oakley	115	Weber City Miss	118	64,680	1:49.60	
1982	Andover Way	4	J. Velasquez	121	Anti Lib	113	Discorama	116	66,360	1:50.00	
1983	Adept	4	K.L. Rogers	109	Broom Dance	122	Dance Number	115	65,160	1:50.00	
1984	Sweet Missus	4	R.J. Thibeau	103	Lady Norcliffe	115	Adept	110	104,040	1:50.20	
1985	Flip's Pleasure	5	J.L. Samyn	117	Sintrillium	119	Some for All	110	101,160	1:51.00	
1986	Ride Sally	4	W.A. Guerra	123	Squan Song	124	Leecoo	107	148,140	1:49.20	
1987	Ms. Eloise	4	R.G. Davis	116	Beth's Song	111	Clemenna's Rose	115	138,480	1:50.20	
1988	Clabber Girl	5	J.A. Santos	117	Psyched	112	Cadillacing	112	141,840	1:49.40	
1989	Banker's Lady	4	A. Cordero Jr	121	Colonial Waters	114	Aptostar	117	133,680	1:51.20	
1990	Dreamy Mimi	4	J.D. Bailey	111	She Can	108	Survive	120	136,800	1:50.40	
1991	Buy the Firm	5	J.A. Krone	119	Colonial Waters	118	Sharp Dance	113	120,000	1:52.20	.93
1992	Firm Stance	4	P. Day	114	Haunting	112	Lady d'Accord	117	120,000	1:50.40	.92
1993	You'd Be Surprised	4	J.D. Bailey	112	Looie Capote	115	Shared Interest	114	90,000	1:48.80	.103
1994	Educated Risk	4	M.E. Smith	120	Triumph at Dawn	111	Imah	111	90,000	1:34.80	.108
1995	Twist Afleet	4	M.E. Smith	123	Chaposa Springs	118	Lotta Dancing	114	90,000	1:35.20	.106
1996	Flat Fleet Feet	3	M.E. Smith	116	Queen Tutta	114	Miss Golden Circle	116	90,000	1:37.00	.91
1997	Dixie Flag	3	M.J. Luzzi	117	Aldiza	112	Mil Kilates	117	90,000	1:35.20	.106
1998	Catinca	3	R. Migliore	119	Furlough	115	Glitter Woman	120	90,000	1:35.80	.106
1999	Belle Cherie	3	J.R. Velazquez	113	Furlough	118			90,000	1:35.40	.104
					Harpia	117					
2000	Reciclada	5	J.D. Bailey	116	Country Hideaway	120	Critical Eye	120	90,000	1:35.54	.106
2001	Cat Cay	4	J.R. Velazquez	117	Tugger	116	Atelier	120	90,000	1:35.45	.101
2002	Sightseek	3	J.D. Bailey	113	Zonk	116	Nasty Storm	116	90,000	1:35.46	.101
2003	Randaroo	3	H. Castillo Jr.	116	Beauty Halo	115	Pocus Hocus	116	90,000	1:36.49	.102

Beyer Index: 101.31

TRUE NORTH BREEDERS' CUP HANDICAP, 6 Furlongs,
3-Year-Olds and Up, Belmont Park, 2003 Purse: $190,000

Year	Winner	Age	Jockey	Wt.	Second	Wt.	Third	Wt.	Win Value	Time	Beyer
1979	Moleolus	4	J.L. Samyn	110	Jet Diplomacy	118	Northern Prospect	116	25,335	1:10.40	
1980	Syncopate	5	L. Pincay Jr	120	Isella	117	Double Zeus	116	33,000	1:09.20	
1981	Joanie's Chief	4	J.L. Samyn	109	Proud Appeal	117	Guilty Conscience	113	33,480	1:09.00	
1982	Shimatoree	3	M. Pino	117	Pass the Tab	121	Will of Iron	112	49,590	1:08.60	
1983	Gold Beauty	4	D. Brumfield	121	Singh Tu	111	Fit to Fight	113	50,760	1:10.40	
1984	Believe the Queen	4	J. Velasquez	114	Muskoka Wyck	112	Cannon Shell	115	52,110	1:09.80	
1985	Cannon Shell	6	D.J. Murphy	114	Basket Weave	114	Mt. Livermore	126	52,200	1:10.80	
1986	Phone Trick	4	J. Velasquez	127	Love That Mac	117	Cullendale	111	66,480	1:09.00	
1987	Groovy	4	A. Cordero Jr	123	King's Swan	120	Sun Master	117	78,780	1:07.80	
1988	High Brite	4	A. Cordero Jr	120	Irish Open	115	King's Swan	122	81,300	1:10.00	
1989	Dancing Spree	4	A. Cordero Jr	113	Dr. Carrington	109	Pok Ta Pok	118	68,160	1:09.40	
1990	Mr. Nickerson	4	C.W. Antley	119	Sewickley	117	Dancing Spree	123	51,360	1:10.40	.116
1991	Diablo	4	J.A. Krone	112	Sunny Blossom	120	Bravely Bold	119	69,720	1:08.20	.117
1992	Shining Bid	4	E. Maple	112	Arrowtown	113	To Freedom	117	71,880	1:08.20	.105
1993	Lion Cavern	4	J.A. Krone	116	Arrowtown	115	Lady's Key	111	69,120	1:10.20	.105
1994	Friendly Lover	6	R. Wilson	114	Boundary	117	Birdonthewire	119	67,380	1:09.60	.106
1995	Waldoboro	4	E. Maple	112	Corma Ray	111	Mining Burrah	117	66,300	1:09.60	.108
1996	Not Surprising	6	R.G. Davis	121	Prospect Bay	113	Forest Wildcat	114	66,720	1:09.00	.113
1997	Punch Line	7	R.G. Davis	122	Cold Execution	112	Jamies First Punch	116	66,180	1:08.80	.107
1998	Richter Scale	4	J.D. Bailey	119	Trafalger	114	Kelly Kip	122	83,160	1:08.80	.116
1999	Kashatreya	5	J.L. Samyn	110	Artax	119	The Trader's Echo	111	90,000	1:09.60	.105
2000	Intidab	7	R.G. Davis	117	Brutally Frank	119	Oro de Mexico	113	90,000	1:10.22	.109
2001	Say Florida Sandy	7	A.T. Gryder	116	Wake At Noon	117	Explicit	115	90,000	1:08.77	.111
2002	Explicit	5	L.J. Meche	119	Entepreneur	115	Late Carson	114	150,000	1:09.98	.106
2003	Shake You Down	5	M.J. Luzzi	118	Highway Prospector	115	Vodka	114	90,000	1:09.59	.108

Beyer Index: 109.43

VAGRANCY HANDICAP, 6 1/2 Furlongs,
Fillies and Mares, 3-Year-Olds and Up, Belmont Park, 2003 Purse: $136,500

Year	Winner	Age	Jockey	Wt.	Second	Wt.	Third	Wt.	Win Value	Time	Beyer
1948	Conniver	4	T. Atkinson	121	Harmonica	120	Casa Camara	105	20,150	1:43.60	
1952	Marta	5	C. McCreary	117	Renew	118	Valadium	115	19,200	1:45.00	
1953	Home-Made	3	E. Guerin	114	Atalanta	123	Aesthete	108	17,100	1:24.60	
1954	Canadiana	4	C. O'Brien	115	Clear Dawn	113	Dispute	112	23,375	1:23.40	
1955	Searching	3	C. McCreary	111	Blue Banner	114	Parlo	129	19,675	1:23.60	
1955	Talora	4	H. Moreno	111	Tremor	107	Smart Devil	108	19,675	1:24.60	
1956	Miz Clementine	5	E. Arcaro	125	Searching	125	Happy Princ's	110	15,950	1:23.40	
1957	Plotter	4	P. Anderson	120	Searching	126	Nasrina	111	16,450	1:24.20	
1958	Outer Space	4	E. Nelson	121	Mlle. Dianne	113	Alanesian	121	18,940	1:23.80	
1959	Dandy Blitzen	4	P.I. Grimm	113	Honeys Gem	118	Idun	112	18,972	1:22.60	
1960	Mommy Dear	4	W. Boland	120	Wiggle II	121	Craftiness	107	18,680	1:22.60	
1961	Sun Glint	4	S. Cole	116	Undulation	116	Refute	113	16,022	1:23.60	
1962	Rose O'Neill	4	M. Ycaza	123	Play Time	114	Funloving	114	15,145	1:23.60	
1963	Cicada	4	L. Adams	127	Bramalea	120	My Portrait	114	14,137	1:22.80	
1964	No Resisting	4	J.L. Rotz	112	Oil Royalty	125	Look Ma	110	18,622	1:23.80	
1965	Affectionately	5	W. Blum	130	Sought After	111	Face the Facts	119	38,285	1:23.00	
1966	Queen Empress	4	B. Baeza	123	Petite Rouge	113	M'nt Regina	113	17,647	1:23.20	
1967	Triple Brook	5	B. Baeza	116	Mac's Sparkler	121	Cestrum	111	17,940	1:23.80	
1968	Mac's Sparkler	6	W. Boland	121	Plucky Pan	112	Amerigo Lady	121	18,232	1:22.60	
1969	Grey Slacks	4	E. Belmonte	113	Heartland	125	Sarita	113	18,297	1:23.20	
1970	Process Shot	4	C. Baltazar	127	Powder Mountain	104	Native Partner	110	18,232	1:23.80	
1971	Golden Or	5	J.L. Rotz	114	Process Shot	124	Gay Missile	112	19,740	1:23.00	
1972	Chou Croute	4	R. Kotenko	124	Cyanome	115	Wire Chief	113	17,490	1:22.60	
1973	Krislin	4	M. Castaneda	113	Numbered Account	120	Fairway Flyer	115	16,845	1:22.60	
1974	Coraggioso	4	D. Brumfield	119	Ponte Vecchio	114	Lady Love	118	35,940	1:22.40	
1975	Honorable Miss	5	J. Vasquez	120	Viva la Vivi	126	Coraggioso	121	34,020	1:22.20	
1976	My Juliet	4	J. Velasquez	127	Shy Dawn	119	Kudara	116	32,790	1:22.00	
1977	Shy Dawn	6	A. Cordero Jr	119	Reasonable Win	118	Secret Lanvin	111	31,590	1:23.80	
1978	Dainty Dotsie	4	B. Phelps	124	What a Summer	127	Navajo Princess	110	32,160	1:21.80	
1979	Frosty Skater	4	D. MacBeth	119	Hagany	114	Skipat	126	33,240	1:23.20	
1980	Lady Lonsdale	5	L. Saumell	114	Peaceful Banner	108	Worthy Poise	112	32,700	1:24.40	
1981	Island Charm	4	R. Migliore	110	Contrary Rose	112	The Wheel Turns	114	32,520	1:23.60	
1982	Westport Native	4	J. Velasquez	115	Tell a Secret	115	Raise 'n Dance	113	32,580	1:22.60	
1983	Broom Dance	4	G. McCarron	121	Syrianna	114	Sprouted Rye	115	33,480	1:22.80	

Year	Winner	Age	Jockey	Wt.	Second	Wt.	Third	Wt.	Win Value	Time	Beyer
1984	Grateful Friend	4	A. Cordero Jr	114	Pleasure Cay	118	Sweet Laughter	108	52,470	1:24.00	
1985	Nany	5	J. Velasquez	121	Sugar's Image	120	Brindy Brindy	113	52,020	1:23.80	
1986	Le Slew	5	J.A. Santos	113	Clocks Secret	121	Willowy Mood	114	54,630	1:23.80	
1987	North Sider	5	A. Cordero Jr	121	Storm and Sunshine	117	Funistrada	114	64,440	1:24.20	
1988	Grecian Flight	4	C. Perret	121	Nasty Affair	114	Tappiano	123	66,240	1:20.80	
1989	Aptostar	4	A. Cordero Jr	118	Toll Fee	110	Lambros	111	51,570	1:22.80	
1990	Mistaurian	4	W.H. McCauley	113	Feel the Beat	118	Fantastic Find	116	50,040	1:25.20	99
1991	Queena	5	M.E. Smith	115	Missy's Mirage	109	Gottagetitdone	111	55,080	1:22.00	99
1992	Nannerl	5	J.A. Santos	116	Serape	115	Makin Faces	112	51,210	1:22.40	96
1993	Spinning Round	4	J.F. Chavez	112	Reach Forever	114	Nannerl	118	52,740	1:24.40	102
1994	Sky Beauty	4	M.E. Smith	122	For All Seasons	114	Pamzig	107	48,855	1:21.60	97
1995	Sky Beauty	5	M.E. Smith	125	Aly's Conquest	111	Through the Door	110	47,865	1:21.40	105
1996	Twist Afleet	4	Krone J. A.	122	Smooth Charmer	111	Lottsa Talc	120	66,300	1:20.80	100
1997	Inquisitive Look	4	Chavez J. F.	111	Flat Fleet Feet	123	Mama Dean	114	64,800	1:22.00	108
1998	Chip	5	Bravo J.	115	Furlough	114	Parlay	115	48,945	1:15.60	97
1999	Gold Princess	4	Velazquez J. R.	114	Hurricane Bertie	114	Delta Music	113	63,840	1:16.40	97
2000	Country Hideaway	4	J.D. Bailey	117	Hurricane Bertie	118	Imperfect World	115	65,640	1:17.05	103
2001	Dat You Miz Blue	4	J.R. Velazquez	116	Dream Supreme	122	Katz Me If You Can	115	64,080	1:15.32	112
2002	Xtra Heat	4	H. Vega	127	Gold Mover	115	Shine Again	117	90,000	1:16.44	107
2003	Shawklit Mint	4	R. Migliore	115	Shine Again	121	Gold Mover	118	90,000	1:15.38	105

Beyer Index: 101.93

Run at 1 1/6 miles 1948, 1952; at 7 furlongs, 1953–1997

ALFRED G. VANDERBILT HANDICAP, 6 Furlongs,
3-Year-Olds and Up, Saratoga Race Course, 2003 Purse: $200,000

Year	Winner	Age	Jockey	Wt.	Second	Wt.	Third	Wt.	Win Value	Time	Beyer
1990	Prospectors Gamble	5	J.A. Garcia	122	Sewickley	115	Mr. Nickerson	122	50,400	1:09.20	113
1991	Kid Russell	5	R. Mojica Jr	115	Mr. Nasty	122	To Freedom	117	71,400	1:09.40	
1992	For Really	5	P. Day	115	Burn Fair	115	Drummond Lane	122	71,520	1:08.60	109
1993	Gold Spring	5	P. Day	119	Friendly Lover	122	Detox	115	70,680	1:09.20	108
1994	Boundary	4	J.R. Velazquez	117	Cherokee Run	120	I Can't Believe	113	65,880	1:08.60	113
1995	Not Surprising	5	R.G. Davis	115	Chimes Band	119	Mining Burrah	116	67,140	1:09.60	114
1996	Prospect Bay	4	J.D. Bailey	113	Honour and Glory	119	Lite the Fuse	123	65,760	1:08.20	123
1997	Royal Haven	5	R. Migliore	116	Cold Execution	116	Punch Line	120	65,220	1:09.60	114
1998	Kelly Kip	4	J.L. Samyn	114	Trafalger	114	Receiver	113	82,545	1:09.60	113
1999	Intidab	6	R.G. Davis	113	Artax	117	Yes It's True	117	90,000	1:09.00	120
2000	Successful Appeal	4	E.S. Prado	118	dq-Intidab	120	Chasin' Wimmin	112	120,000	1:09.21	120
	Intidab finished first but was disqualified and placed second										
2001	Five Star Day	5	G.K. Gomez	117	Delaware Township	116	Bonapaw	117	120,000	1:08.57	111
2002	Orientate	4	J.D. Bailey	121	Say Florida Sandy	115	Multiple Choice	112	120,000	1:09.72	112
2003	Private Horde	4	J. Lumpkins	115	Mountain General	118	Mike's Classic	114	120,000	1:09.18	117

Beyer Index: 114.38

Run as A Phenomenon prior to 2000

WASHINGTON PARK HANDICAP, 1 3/16 Miles,
3-Year-Olds and Up, Arlington Park, 2003 Purse: $400,000

Year	Winner	Age	Jockey	Wt.	Second	Wt.	Third	Wt.	Win Value	Time	Beyer
1926	Smiling Gus	3	L. Edwards	97	Cudgeller	103	Arabian	96	10,710	2:10.60	
1927	Girl Scout	5	S. Cooper	104	Sanola	109	Pr. of Wales	129	6,490	1:15.00	
1929	Misstep	4	C. McCrossen	124	Golden Prince	117	Cayuga	112	5,510	1:12.20	
1930	Misstep	5	E. Shropshire	126	Brown Wisdow	123	My Dandy	120	6,410	1:12.40	
1931	Tannery	4	R. Heigle	112	Don Leon	111	Stock Market	108	6,210	1:13.00	
1932	Gold Step	5	H. Schutte	107	Silverdale	118	Ladder	112	5,290	1:12.00	
1933	No More	5	E. Arcaro	109	Mr. Sponge	122	Isaiah	111	2,295	1:12.60	
1934	Isaiah	4	J. Kacala	110	Some Pomp	102	Advancing Anna	112	2,240	1:12.00	
1935	Late Date	6	A. Robertson	111	Calumet Dick	102	Watch Him	110	4,220	2:06.80	
1936	Where Away	4	C. Corbett	115	Count Arthur	114	Black Gift	110	8,080	2:03.00	
1938	Dora May	5	K. McCombs	108	Mad Money	114	Chance Ray	106	1,650	1:12.00	
1939	Star Border	3	A. Bodiou	105	Viscounty	117	Some Count	112	4,350	1:50.20	
1940	War Plumage	4	N. Wall	110	Viscounty	118	Burning Star	109	24,800	2:04.00	
1941	Big Pebble	5	J. Westrope	120	Bushwhacker	110	Haltal	115	25,500	2:03.20	
1942	Marriage	6	C. Corbett	114	Alsab	121	Thumbs Up	102	25,200	2:02.40	
1943	Thumbs Up	4	O. Grons	120	Royal Nap	107	Marriage	124	25,950	2:05.00	

Year	Winner	Age	Jockey	Wt.	Second	Wt.	Third	Wt.	Win Value	Time	Beyer
1944	Equifox	7	A. Bodiou	113	Daily Trouble	105	Some Chance	109	40,700	2:03.00	
1945	Busher	3	J. Longden	115	Armed	120	Take Wing	112	40,200	2:01.80	
1946	Armed	5	D. Dodson	130	Challenge Me	112	Take Wing	110	39,300	2:01.00	
1947	Armed	6	D. Dodson	130	Honeymoon	111	With Pleasure	123	37,500	2:02.00	
1948	Fervent	4	N.L. Pierson	120	Eternal Reward	119	Stud Poker	118	36,000	2:04.80	
1949	Coaltown	4	S. Brooks	130	Armed	110	Lithe	103	34,800	2:03.80	
1950	Inseparable	5	K. Church	110	Fervent	107	Curandero	113	33,000	2:06.20	
1951	Curandero	5	A. Gomez	115	Oil Capitol	116	County Delight	123	113,950	1:34.60	
1952	Crafty Admiral	4	E. Guerin	128	To Market	123	Sickle's Image	110	119,900	1:36.80	
1953	Sickle's Image	5	W.M. Cook	106	Ruhe	116	Indian Hemp	114	108,500	1:36.80	
1954	Pet Bully	6	W. Hartack	119	Good Call	108	Spur On	115	110,900	1:34.40	
1955	Jet Action	4	W. Shoemaker	120	Duke's Lea	117	Helioscope	130	96,000	1:34.00	
1956	Swaps	4	W. Shoemaker	130	Summer Tan	115	Sea O Erin	112	85,750	1:33.40	
1957	Pucker Up	4	W. Shoemaker	111	Find	122	Swoon's Son	130	80,800	1:34.80	
1958	Clem	4	J. Sellers	110	Round Table	131	Nadir	114	94,175	1:34.00	
1959	Round Table	5	W. Shoemaker	132	Dunce	114	Belleau Chief	112	72,650	1:47.20	
1960	T.V. Lark	3	J. Sellers	116	Dotted Swiss	123	Talent Show	118	68,600	1:34.20	
1961	Chief of Chiefs	4	C. Meaux	112	Talent Show	110	Run for Nurse	112	72,900	1:34.60	
1962	Prove It	5	W. Shoemaker	131	Try Cash	114	Cadiz	115	68,450	1:33.80	
1963	Crimson Satan	4	H. Hinojosa	126	Piper's Son	110	B. Major	117	68,150	1:49.60	
1964	Gun Bow	4	W. Blum	132	Lemon Twist	111	Going Aboad	114	69,750	1:51.00	
1965	Take Over	4	L. Kunitake	110	Chieftain	126	Gallant Romeo	120	68,600	1:35.20	
1966	Bold Bidder	4	P. Anderson	120	Tom Rolfe	128	Tronado	117	64,200	1:32.80	
1967	Handsome Boy	4	E. Belmonte	122	Pretense	128	Bold Tactics	116	68,000	1:37.60	
1968	Dr. Fager	4	B. Baeza	134	Racing Room	116	Info	112	67,700	1:32.20	
1969	Night Invader	3	D.E. Whited	112	Out the Window	112	Rising Market	121	68,050	1:36.20	
1970	Doc's T.V.	4	D.E. Whited	114	Famed Prince	115	Strong Strong	114	33,900	1:36.60	
1972	Well Mannered	4	M. Solomone	120	No No Billy	116	Intensitivo	112	33,500	1:34.60	
1973	Burning On	5	D. Richard	114	New Hope	113	Vegas Vic	109	32,800	2:02.20	
1974	Super Sail	6	W. Gavidia	118	Smooth Dancer	112	J'a D'm Aw'y	111	38,300	2:03.00	
1975	Hasty Flyer	4	H. Arroyo	115	Group Plan	116	Yaki King	113	38,100	1:48.60	
1976	Double Edge Sword	6	H. Arroyo	116	Zografos	113	Proponent	109	70,400	1:48.20	
1977	Majestic Light	4	M. Venezia	120	Fifth Marine	122	Improviser	122	54,180	1:48.00	
1978	That's a Nice	4	D. Richard	116	Court Open	115	Improviser	117	53,100	1:50.60	
1979	That's a Nice	5	I.J. Jimenez	117	Calderina	113	Me Good Man	112	52,320	1:50.00	
1980	Spectacular Bid	4	W. Shoemaker	130	Hold Your Tricks	119	Architect	119	155,880	1:46.20	
1981	Rossi Gold	5	P. Day	119	John's Monster	112	Lord Gallant	114	81,870	1:48.60	
1982	Summer Advocate	5	P. Day	115	Mythical Ruler	112	Law Me	112	64,920	1:49.80	
1983	Harham's Sizzler	4	J.L Diaz	112	Listcapade	122	Stage Reviewer	112	67,620	1:49.80	
1984	Thumbsucker	5	S. Maple	115	Timeless Native	122	Le Cou Cou	122	80,940	1:48.60	
1985	Par Flite	4	E. Fires	112	Big Pistol	122	Timeless Native	122	78,300	1:47.60	
1987	Taylor's Special	6	J. Lively	118	Blue Buckaroo	120	Fuzzy	114	61,965	1:51.60	
1989	Blushing John	4	P. Day	124	Grantley	112	Paramount Jet	113	48,030	1:50.80	
1990	Lay Down	6	W.H. McCauley	115	Sir Wesley	112	Mercedes Won	112	64,680	1:48.40	108
1991	Black Tie Affair	5	S.J. Sellers	120	Summer Squall	119	Secret Hello	114	150,000	1:49.40	117
1992	Irish Swap	5	B.E. Poyadou	118	Clever Trevor	119	Barkerville	113	90,000	1:47.80	114
1993	Powerful Punch	4	C.C. Bourque	114	Memo	115	Northern Trend	113	120,000	1:50.00	105
1994	Brother Brown	4	P. Day	117	Eequalsmcsquared	113	Antrim Rd.	113	120,000	1:49.60	110
1996	Polar Expedition	5	M. Guidry	115	Knockadoon	115	Tejano Run	117	120,000	1:49.80	111
1997	Beboppin Baby	4	G.K. Gomez	112	City By Night	116	Stephanotis	118	90,000	1:49.00	109
2000	Blazing Sword	6	J.A. Rivera II	113	Mula Gula	114	Nite Dreamer	116	150,000	1:50.59	106
2001	Guided Tour	5	L. Melancon	116	A Fleets Dancer	115	Duckhorn	114	240,000	2:00.76	117
2002	Tenpins	4	R.J. Albarado	116	Generous Rosi	115	Bonus Pack	115	240,000	1:55.07	108
2003	Perfect Drift	4	P. Day	120	Aeneas	115	Flatter	114	240,000	1:55.49	112

Beyer Index: 110.64

WINSTAR GALAXY, 1 3/16 Miles (Turf), Fillies and Mares, 3-Year-Olds and Up, Keeneland Race Course, 2003 Purse: $500,000

Year	Winner	Age	Jockey	Wt.	Second	Wt.	Third	Wt.	Win Value	Time	Beyer
1998	Witchful Thinking	4	C.J. McCarron	115	Memories of Silver	120	Starry Dreamer	115	169,415	1:54.20	102
1999	Happyanunoit	4	B. Blanc	119	Pleasant Temper	119	Fiji	117	346,270	1:53.80	109
2000	Tout Charmant	4	C.J. McCarron	117	Perfect Sting	121	License Fee	119	343,480	1:54.74	104
2001	Spook Express	7	M.E. Smith	120	Solvig	118	Veil of Avalon	118	349,370	1:54.24	102
2002	Owsley	3	E.S. Prado	122	Snow Dance	120	Surya	118	337,590	1:56.72	100
2003	Bien Nicole	5	D.R. Pettinger	121	Approach	116	New Economy	121	310,000	1:55.87	100

Beyer Index: 102.83

Histories of Grade 3 Stakes Events

ACK ACK HANDICAP, 7 1/2 Furlongs,
3-Year-Olds and Up, Churchill Downs, 2003 Purse: $165,450

Year	Winner	Age	Jockey	Wt.	Second	Wt.	Third	Wt.	Win Value	Time	Beyer
1991	Seven Spades	4	D. Cox	108	Discover		Senator to Be		38,510	1:37.60	100
1994	Lost Pan	4	D. Barton	114	Sir Vixen		Groovy Jett		54,795	1:30.27	108
1995	Mystery Storm	3	C.V. Gonzalez	112	I'm Very Irish		Tarzan's Blade		75,600	1:29.10	109
1996	Western Trader	5	C.H. Borel	113	Top Account		Strategic Intent		70,308	1:29.84	112
1997	Cat's Career	4	W. Martinez	108	Rare Rock	112	Victor Cooley	122	69,160	1:32.06	104
1998	Distorted Humor	5	C.H. Borel	120	Crafty Friend	113	Chindi	113	68,262	1:29.61	102
1999	Littlebitlively	5	C.H. Borel	119	Run Johnny	117	Tactical Cat	117	71,672	1:28.97	111
2000	Chindi	6	T.T. Doocy	113	Smolderin Heart	113	Millencolin	113	70,494	1:29.30	107
2001	Illusioned	3	P. Day	118	Strawberry Affair	112	Fappie's Notebook	116	70,866	1:28.63	106
2002	Twilight Road	5	P. Day	113	Mountain General	116	Binthebest	113	69,874	1:29.39	105
2003	Cappuchino	4	J.K. Court	117	Pass Rush	116	Twilight Road	116	102,579	1:31.66	99

Beyer Index: 105.73

AEGON TURF SPRINT, 5 Furlongs (Turf),
3-Year-Olds and Up, Churchill Downs, 2003 Purse: $115,300

Year	Winner	Age	Jockey	Wt.	Second	Wt.	Third	Wt.	Win Value	Time	Beyer
1995	Long Suit	4	W. Martinez	114	Bold N' Flashy		Scottish Fantasy		57,086	:56.90	99
1996	Danjur	4	J.D. Bailey	114	Hello Paradise		Linear		57,281	:56.09	108
1997	Sandtrap	4	A. Solis	123	Appealing Skier		G H's Pleasure		71,734	:56.51	102
1998	Indian Rocket	5	G.L. Stevens	116	G H's Pleasure		Claire's Honor		75,950	:57.32	100
1999	Howbaddouwanit	4	M.E. Smith	123	Mr Festus		Three Card Willie		71,486	:57.03	100
2000	Bold Fact	5	R. Migliore	120	Howbaddouwanit		Fantastic Finish		75,330	:56.37	101
2001	Morluc	5	R.J. Albarado	122	Testify	119	Texas Glitter	122	70,494	:56.60	106
2002	Testify	5	E. Delahoussaye	119	Texas Glitter	122	Gone Fishin	116	75,206	:57.39	104
2003	Fiscally Speaking	4	J.K. Court	114	Morluc	122	Testify	122	71,486	:56.01	102

Beyer Index: 102.44

AFFECTIONATELY HANDICAP, 1 1/16 Miles,
Fillies and Mares, 3-Year-Olds and Up, Aqueduct, 2003 Purse: $109,600

Year	Winner	Age	Jockey	Wt.	Second	Wt.	Third	Wt.	Win Value	Time	Beyer
1976	Proud Delta	4	J. Velasquez	114	Mary Queenofscots	119	Shy Dawn	119	34,640	1:37.40	
1977	Shy Dawn	6	D. Montoya	115	Double Quester	115	Shawi	108	31,620	1:45.20	
1977	Illiterate	5	S. Cauthen	113	Quintas Vicki	113	Secret Lanvin	118	31,770	1:45.20	
1978	One Sum	4	R. Hernandez	117	Keep It Secret	103	Passage Way	113	32,910	1:44.80	
1979	Kit's Double	6	A. Graell	110	Whodatorsay	111	Sue Me Not	116	33,150	1:48.60	
1980	Plankton	4	R. Hernandez	116	Worthy Poise	112	Propitiate	112	35,100	1:45.00	
1981	Plankton	5	R. Hernandez	120	Sweet Maid	114	The Wheel Turns	114	34,380	1:45.40	
1982	Perfect Poppy	5	V.H. Molina	106	Hitting Irish	112	Andover Way	123	33,960	1:48.60	
1983	Adept	4	K.L. Rogers	108	Princess Oola	118	Debonair Dancer	113	32,880	1:43.40	
1983	Polite Rebuff	4	F. Lovato Jr	110	Nafees	107	Cheap Seats	121	32,880	1:43.80	
1984	Am Capable	4	A. Cordero Jr	118	Far Flying	121	Sintrillium	115	59,760	1:46.20	
1985	Descent	5	R.J. Thibeaux J	106	Sweet Missus	112	Bracalena	114	52,110	1:45.60	
1985	Sintrillium	7	R.G. Davis	116	Emphatic	104	Far Flying	116	52,830	1:45.60	
1986	Lady on the Run	4	A. Cordero Jr	118	Satch	112			52,110	1:46.20	
					Squan Song	124					
1987	Squan Song	6	J.A. Santos	124	Clemanna's Rose	107	Ms. Eloise	120	69,840	1:46.20	
1988	Tricky Squaw	5	J.A. Santos	123	With a Twist	111	Seriously	111	52,740	1:45.20	
1989	Rose's Cantina	5	E. Maple	114	Tops in Taps	114	Thirty Eight Go Go	116	54,720	1:42.80	
1990	Naskra's Return	4	M.E. Smith	113	Bold Wench	118	Dreamy Mimi	115	51,480	1:43.80	111
1991	My Treasure	4	C. Lopez	115	Buy the Firm	122	Personal Business	116	54,360	1:44.20	
1992	Get Lucky	4	M.E. Smith	113	My Treasure	114	Haunting	114	52,650	1:46.00	96
1993	Hilbys Brite Flite	4	J.R. Velasquez	111	My Treasure	112	Lady Lear	117	52,470	1:44.60	95
1994	Poolesta	5	Lovato F Jr	115	Hey Baba Lulu	117	Groovy Feeling	123	49,425	1:44.80	96
1995	Sea Ditty	4	Madrid A Jr	113	Beloved Bea	114	Acting Proud	111	50,190	1:46.80	93
1996	Lotta Dancing	5	H. Castillo Jr	120	Winner's Edge	109	Vinista	114	39,024	1:42.40	97
1997	Mil Kilates	4	J.F. Chavez	113	Whaleneck	110	Shoop	120	39,996	1:44.60	96
1998	Sweetzie	6	Pezua J. M	113	Shoop	116	Gold Colony	112	50,700	1:41.80	102
1999	Biding Time	5	Gryder A. T.	118	Shoop	113	Daily Reflection	116	50,220	1:44.60	111
2000	Theresa the Teacha	5	H. Castillo Jr	114	Roaring Twenties	114	Two Fer Boston	118	51,855	1:46.42	91
2001	Pentatonic	6	A.T. Gryder	117	Strolling Belle	121	Pompei	116	66,300	1:43.17	95
2002	Zonk	4	C.C. Lopez	116	People's Princess	115	Search Party	114	68,040	1:42.58	95
2003	Zonk	5	C.C. Lopez	118	Wishful Splendor	112	Kiss a Miss	113	65,760	1:44.58	94

Beyer Index: 97.85

AFFIRMED HANDICAP, 1 1/16 Miles,
3-Year-Olds, Hollywood Park, 2003 Purse: $103,096

Year	Winner	Age	Jockey	Wt.	Second	Wt.	Third	Wt.	Win Value	Time	Beyer
1979	Valdez	3	L. Pincay Jr	119	Pole Position	118	Beau's Eagle	123	37,500	1:47.40	
1980	Score Twenty Four	3	D.G. McHargue	114	First Albert	116			37,200	1:48.20	
					Loto Canada	119					
1981	Stancharry	3	P.A. Valenzuela	117	Dusty Hula	116	Seafood	117	47,150	1:51.00	
1982	Journey at Sea	3	C.J. McCarron	122	Cassaleria	120	Guachan	112	49,600	1:46.80	
1983	My Habitony	3	D. Pierce	115	Tanks Brigade	119	Hyperborean	115	47,250	1:48.60	
1984	Tights	3	L. Pincay Jr	119	M. Double M.	116	Precisionist	121	46,850	1:48.60	
1985	Pancho Villa	3	L. Pincay Jr	118	Proudest Doon	118	Nostalgia's Star	118	64,050	1:33.80	
1986	Melair	3	P.A. Valenzuela	115	Southern Halo	113	Snow Chief	127	220,000	1:32.80	
1987	Candi's Gold	3	G.L. Stevens	116	On the Line	116	The Medic	116	93,000	1:47.60	
1988	Iz a Saros	3	A.T. Gryder	113	Stalwars	119	Bel Air Dancer	117	95,900	1:49.00	
1989	Raise a Stanza	3	C.A. Black	115	Broke the Mold	112	Prized	116	102,200	1:48.40	
1990	Stalwart Charger	3	L. Pincay Jr	120	Toby Jug	112	Kentucky Jazz	120	91,100	1:48.40	104
1991	Compelling Sound	3	G.L. Stevens	118	Best Pal	123	Caliche's Secret	117	91,300	1:47.80	107
1992	Natural Nine	3	L. Pincay Jr	117	Prospect for Four	114	Never Round	117	95,500	1:49.40	94
1993	Codified	3	G.L. Stevens	117	Roman Image	117	Future Storm	118	94,100	1:48.80	99
1994	R Friar Tuck	3	J.D. Bailey	113	Pollock's Luck	114	Wild Invader	115	96,100	1:49.00	95
1995	Mr Purple	3	Nakatani CS	120	Pumpkin House	115	Oncefortheroad	114	77,050	1:42.20	95
1996	Hesabull	3	E. Delahoussaye	117	Benton Creek	116	Semoran	118	61,050	1:43.20	93
1997	Deputy Commander	3	C.S. Nakatani	117	Hello	121	Holzmeister	121	61,500	1:42.80	107
1998	Old Trieste	3	C.J. McCarron	118	Old Topper	117	Kraal	116	62,340	1:41.80	105
1999	General Challenge	3	D.R. Flores	124	Desert Hero	120	Crowning Storm	116	75,000	1:40.83	111
2000	Tiznow	3	C.J. McCarron	111	Dixie Union	122	Millencolin	117	80,550	1:42.40	103
2001	Until Sundown	3	G.L. Stevens	117	Top Hit	114	Bayou the Moon	118	60,000	1:43.10	96
2002	Came Home	3	C.J. McCarron	124	Tracemark	120	Calkins Road	117	64,500	1:41.99	107
2003	Eye of the Tiger	3	A. Solis	119	Ministers Wild Cat	118	Bullistic	115	63,120	1:42.30	107

Beyer Index: **101.64**

ALL ALONG BREEDERS' CUP, 1 1/8 Miles (Turf),
Fillies and Mares 3-Year-Olds and Up, Colonial Downs, 2003 Purse: $190,000

Year	Winner	Age	Jockey	Wt.	Second	Wt.	Third	Wt.	Win Value	Time	Beyer
1988	Ravinella	3	G. Guignard	119	Chapel of Dreams	120	Betty Lobelia	116	150,000	1:49.80	
1989	Lady Winner	3	K.J. Desormeaux	112	Capades	116	Betty Lobelia	116	180,000	1:53.60	
1990	Foresta	4	A. Cordero Jr	116	Miss Josh	120	Vijaya	114	180,000	1:49.40	101
1991	Sha Tha	3	M.E. Smith	113	Julie La Rousse	113	Once in My Life	114	180,000	1:52.40	106
1992	Marble Maiden	3	T. Jarnet	114	Wedding Ring	112	Sheba Dancer	114	180,000	1:49.80	100
1993	Lady Blessington	5	C.A. Black	116	Via Borghese	118	Logan's Mist	116	150,000	1:51.40	102
1994	Alice Springs	4	R.R. Douglas	120	Via Borghese	116	Mz. Zill Bear	116	150,000	1:47.20	107
1996	Another Legend	4	C.O. Klinger	115	Brushing Gloom	119	Short Time	115	60,000	1:58.80	96
1997	Beyrouth	5	D. S. Rice	115	Hero's Pride	117	Palliser Bay	122	67,830	1:49.20	98
1998	Bursting Forth	4	E.S. Prado	122	The Unforgiven	117	Be Elusive	115	60,000	1:48.00	89
2000	Idle Rich	5	A.T. Gryder	115	Emanating	115	Orange Sunset	115	60,000	1:55.95	90
2001	Colstar	5	J.K. Court	121	Lucky Lune	119	Crystal Sea	119	90,000	1:47.53	102
2002	Secret River	5	H.A. Karamanos	117	Golden Corona	117	Cayman Sunset	117	90,000	1:50.76	88
2003	Dress to Thrill	4	E.S. Prado	117	Lady Linda	117	Lady of the Future	117	120,000	1:49.16	95

Beyer Index: **97.83**

ANNE ARUNDEL, 1 1/8 Miles,
3-Year-Old Fillies, Laurel, 2003 Purse: $100,000

Year	Winner	Age	Jockey	Wt.	Second	Wt.	Third	Wt.	Win Value	Time	Beyer
1974	Pinch Pie	3	C. Baltazar	114	Sailingon	111	Enchanted Native	112	17,595	1:37.40	
1975	My Juliet	3	D.G. McHargue	123	Funny Cat	114	Gala Lil	119	20,070	1:36.80	
1976	What a Summer	3	C.J. McCarron	122	Turn the Guns	114	Avum	114	16,560	1:38.20	
1977	Worrisome Thing	3	H. Hinojosa	112	Northern Sea	121	Luck Penny	121	26,610	1:37.40	
1978	The Very One	3	C. Cooke	110	Silver Ice	121	Dr. Penny Binn	113	26,970	1:40.00	
1979	Jameela	3	W.J. Passmore	113	Sentencia	111	Contrary Rose	111	32,580	1:38.00	
1980	Caught in Amber	3	D.R. Wright	115	Fair Hit	113	Running Around	115	33,330	1:35.60	
1981	Up the Flagpole	3	M.G. Pino	118	Privacy	125	Zvetlana	111	34,080	1:36.20	
1982	Kattegat's Pride	3	D.A. Miller Jr	119	Wedding Party	117	Delicate Ice	115	34,020	1:37.40	
1983	Quixotic Lady	3	G. McCarron	122	Bemissed	119	Batna	117	33,210	1:36.80	
1984	Dowery	3	A.S. Black	118	Basie	115	Dumdedumdedum	114	35,400	1:37.00	
1985	Classy Cut	3	D.A. Miller Jr	116	A Joyful Spray	115	Little Brooks Mesa	106	37,180	1:36.80	
1986	Burt's Dream	3	R. Wilson	114	Now Your Teapottin	110	Vacherie	114	49,900	1:36.00	
1986	Toes Knows	3	D.R. Wright	121	Foot Stone	106	Notches Trace	107	36,400	1:36.40	
1987	Doubles Partner	3	A. Cordero Jr	119	Ruling Angel	122	Arctic Cloud	113	47,330	1:37.20	
1988	Empress Tigere	3	G. McCarron	114	Lost Kitty	119	North Watch	110	58,244	1:49.80	

Year	Winner	Age	Jockey	Wt.	Second	Wt.	Third	Wt.	Win Value	Time	Beyer
1989	Misty Ivor	3	M.T. Hunter	115	Under Oath	112	Slew a Native	107	45,000	1:49.60	
1990	McKilts	3	J. Rocco	114	Trumpet's Blare	115	Secreto's Glory	113	32,760	1:50.40	
1991	Devilish Touch	3	M. Castaneda	115	Get Lucky	112	Far Out Nurse	113	30,000	1:24.20	
1992	Avian Assembly	3	L.C. Reynolds	112	Gammy's Alden	117	Singing Ring	115	30,000	1:50.60	
1993	By Your Leave	3	M.G. Pino	114	Tennis Lady	121	Double Sixes	114	33,030	1:52.40	
1994	Miss Slewpy	3	Reynolds LC	114	Cherokee Wonder	114	Churchbell Chimes	121	45,000	1:51.00	
1995	Blue Sky Princess	3	Pino MG	122	Substantial	115	Blonde Actress	115	45,000	1:51.40	
1996	Hay Let's Dance	3	Martinez S. B.	115	Double Stake	115	Mesabi Maiden	122	45,000	1:50.80	91
1997	G. O' Keefe	3	Johnston M. T.	115	Snit	122	Cotton Carnival	122	60,000	1:51.20	97
1998	Merengue	3	Johnston M. T.	122	Queen of Oz	115	Manoa	115	60,000	1:51.80	90
1999	Undermine	3	Melancon L.	115	Gold From The West	115	Batique	115	60,000	1:49.20	100
2000	Gin Talking	3	R.A. Dominguez	122	Tax Affair	115	A.O.L. Hayes	115	60,000	1:50.21	103
2002	Martha's Music	3	S. Elliott	122	Pass the Virtue	122	Shop Till You Drop	115	60,000	1:50.84	92
2003	Smooth Maneuvers	3	M.G. Pino	115	Devotion Unbridled	117	Alchemist	117	60,000	1:51.56	88

Beyer Index: **94.43**

AQUEDUCT HANDICAP, 1 1/16 Miles,
3-Year-Olds and Up, Aqueduct, 2003 Purse: $107,400

Year	Winner	Age	Jockey	Wt.	Second	Wt.	Third	Wt.	Win Value	Time	Beyer
1902	Glenwater	3	McIerney	117	Andy Williams	110	Carbuncle	116	1,060	1:48.80	
1903	Wild Thyme	3	Redfern	98	Embarrassment	102	Ahumada	98	2,705	1:49.20	
1904	Israelite	3	Shilling	99	Dolly Spanger	120	Agile	97	2,750	1:45.40	
1905	Bedouin	3	O.Neill	114	Coy Maid	108	S. Catalina	106	3,315	1:46.60	
1906	Rye	3	Finn	102	Bad News	109	Oxford	119	3,020	1:46.00	
1907	Brookdale Nymph	4	Notter	116	Monfort	95	Gret.' Green	107	2,760	1:47.00	
1908	Monfort	4	D.McCarthy	100	Royal Tourist	104	The Squire	105	650	1:46.00	
1909	Firestone	4	C.H. Shilling	113	Maskette	126	Olambala	119	1,925	1:48.40	
1917	Roamer	6	A. Schuttinger	127	Manister Toi.	108	Runes	101	2,225	1:50.20	
1918	Corn Tassel	4	F. Robinson	113	Ticket	102	Papp	108	2,625	1:52.80	
1919	Lucullite	4	L. Fator	133	Corn Tassel	110	Star Master	122	3,200	1:49.80	
1920	John P. Grier	3	C. Kummer	120	Cleopatra	104			4,550	2:12.00	
1921	Damask	4	L. Penman	108	Mad Hatter	129	Kingdom II	105	4,950	2:11.80	
1922	Prince James	4	E. Taplin	105	Captain Alcock	109	Sedgefield	95	7,600	2:11.00	
1923	My Play	4	A. Schuttinger	121	Sunsini	100	Homest'tch	107	5,150	2:11.60	
1925	Dazzler	4	B. Thompson	98	Dangerous	108	Sunsini	108	5,050	2:12.00	
1926	Black Maria	3	J. Callahan	112	Pompey	118	Dazzler	100	5,950	1:51.40	
1927	Black Maria	4	L. Fator	122	Light Carbine	106	Flippant	107	5,900	1:49.80	
1928	Chance Play	5	H. Thurber	123	Byrd	105	Glade	102	6,550	1:52.00	
1929	Sun Beau	4	F. Coltiletti	116	Diavolo	127	Live Oak	104	5,650	1:50.00	
1930	Black Mammy	3	J. Passero	98	Khara	97	Sun Mission	97	6,100	1:52.20	
1931	Curate	4	M. Garner	114	Blenheim	108	Reveille Boy	126	3,020	1:50.60	
1932	Blenheim	4	T. Malley	120	Apprentice	116			1,700	1:50.40	
1933	Golden Way	3	J. Stout	110	Union	107			1,660	1:45.00	
1934	Coequal	3	E. Litzenberger	102	Indian Runner	120	Go'd Advice	118	3,340	1:45.00	
1935	Good Gamble	3	S. Renick	112	Count Arthur	109	Vicaress	100	5,110	1:43.60	
1936	Action	7	J. Gilbert	116	Rosemont	125	Tatterdem'n	107	4,910	1:44.00	
1937	Caballero II	5	A. Robertson	122	No Dice	106	Thorson	121	5,100	1:43.60	
1938	Isolater	5	J. Longden	114	Idle Miss	113	Fighting Fox	124	4,450	1:43.60	
1939	Volitant	3	D. Meade	113	Stands Alone	110	Opera Hat	115	4,650	1:42.60	
1940	War Dog	4	D. Meade	110	Roman Flag	111	Sickle T.	114	6,200	1:44.00	
1941	Ponty	5	N. Wall	105	Foxbrough	126	Market Wise	114	7,900	1:43.60	
1942	Pictor	5	G. Woolf	114	Blue Pair	110	The Rhymer	114	7,900	1:44.20	
1943	With Regards	4	J. Longden	122	Apache	122	First Fiddle	122	7,850	1:43.60	
1944	Alex Barth	4	F. Zufelt	117	Famous Victory	106	Tex Martin	104	7,535	1:45.00	
1945	New Moon	5	J. Gilbert	112	Eurasian	107	Rick's Raft	109	7,940	1:44.80	
1946	Coincidence	4	T. Atkinson	118	Lets Dance	112	King Dorsett	126	12,100	1:44.40	
1947	Stymie	6	C. McCreary	132	Gallorette	122	Elpis	114	20,050	1:44.40	
1948	Stymie	7	R. Permane	130	Conniver	117	Double Jay	126	19,750	1:45.40	
1949	Wine List	3	T. Atkinson	114	Riverlane	107	Mount Mary	113	16,625	1:46.00	
1950	Wine List	4	T. Atkinson	108	Steel Blue	105	De Luxe	103	15,975	1:43.60	
1951	Bryan G.	4	J. Nichols	120	Moonrush	118	Post Card	105	15,025	1:44.40	
1952	Bryan G.	5	B. Green	114	Hall of Fame.	123	Tocoli	105	19,450	1:44.00	
1953	First Aid	3	A. Catalano	109	Combat Boots	117	Elixir	113	19,050	1:44.60	
1954	Crash Dive	4	E. Guerin	121	G.R. Petersen	106	Level Lea	119	20,200	1:44.40	
1955	Icarian	4	A. Valenzuela	109	Fabulist	116	Paper Tiger	117	19,600	1:44.80	
1959	Hillsdale	4	T. Barrow	132	Bald Eagle	122	Tick Tock	119	37,880	1:36.40	
1960	Bald Eagle	5	M. Ycaza	130	Intentionally	125	Warhead	113	35,930	1:34.80	
1961	Tompion	4	J.L. Rotz	118	Whodunit	121	Black Th'mper	108	36,660	1:47.40	
1962	Crozier	4	B. Baeza	114	Guadalcanal	114	Ridan	123	69,095	1:48.80	
1963	Kelso	6	I. Valenzuela	134	Crimson Satan	129	Garwol	116	71,890	1:49.80	
1964	Kelso	7	I. Valenzuela	128	Gun Bow	128	Saidam	119	70,005	1:48.60	
1965	Malicious	4	R. Ussery	116	Pluck	116	Roman Brother	121	70,330	1:49.00	
1966	Tom Rolfe	4	W. Shoemaker	127	Pluck	114	Big R'ck Candy	110	74,295	1:52.20	

Year	Winner	Age	Jockey	Wt.	Second	Wt.	Third	Wt.	Win Value	Time	Beyer
1967	Damascus	3	W. Shoemaker	125	Ring Twice	119	Straight Deal	116	69,420	1:48.20	
1968	Damascus	4	B. Baeza	134	More Scents	114	Fort Drum	114	70,330	1:48.40	
1973	Cannonade	2	P. Anderson	126	Roger's Dandy	112	Flip Sal	116	34,080	1:51.60	
1976	Right Mind	5	R. Turcotte	114	General Beauregard	119	Our Hero	115	34,670	1:38.80	
1977	Magnetizer	4	A. Santiago	112	Turn and Count	126	Due Diligence	112	32,580	1:45.40	
1978	Wise Philip	5	J. Vasquez	117	Gallivantor	119	Vanistorio	112	33,060	1:43.80	
1980	Charlie Coast	5	J. Miranda	112	Pole Position	126	Pirate's Bounty	112	35,400	1:44.80	
1981	Irish Tower	4	J. Fell	114	Dr. Blum	116	Lark Oscillation	108	32,760	1:44.60	
1982	Reef Searcher	5	A. Cordero Jr	114	Deedee's Deal	107	Alla Breva	114	35,760	1:48.40	
1983	Fort Monroe	6	V.H. Molina	108	Lark Oscillation	113	Fabulous Find	116	33,420	1:42.40	
1984	Moro	5	J.L. Samyn	120	Jacksboro	120	Ask Muhammad	117	45,120	1:43.40	
1985	Fight Over	4	A. Cordero Jr	118	Imp Society	113	Verbarctic	112	55,260	1:42.60	
1986	Aggressive Bid	5	M. Venezia	109	Badwagon Harry	120	Carjack	114	50,850	1:43.80	
1987	King's Swan	7	J.A. Santos	118	Raja's Revenge	111	Cost Conscious	112	54,990	1:41.80	
1988	Clever Secret	4	C.W. Antley	112	Proud Debonair	114	Native Wizard	112	54,810	1:45.20	
1989	Lord of the Night	6	W.H. McCauley	114	Its Acedemic	110	True and Blue	113	52,110	1:42.80	
1990	Congeleur	5	A. Cordero Jr	116	Silver Survivor	118	King's Swan	116	52,020	1:44.80	
1991	Sports View	5	J.D. Bailey	115	I'm Sky High	115	Lost Opportunity	112	51,750	1:43.40	109
1992	Formal Dinner	4	A. Cordero Jr	113	Shots are Ringing	113	Island Edition	110	51,750	1:43.60	107
1993	Shots Are Ringing	6	J.R. Velazquez	118	A Call to Rise	111	Federal Funds	110	52,650	1:44.40	100
1994	As Indicated	4	Davis RG	121	Primitive Hall	113	Jacksonport	112	48,690	1:45.60	104
1995	Danzig's Dance	6	Chavez JF	111	Key Contender	115	Golden Larch	112	50,010	1:41.00	112
1996	Mighty Magee	4	M.J. Luzzi	118	May I Inquire	113	More to Tell	115	39,780	1:43.80	109
1997	Pacific Fleet	5	J.F. Chavez	112	More to Tell	116	Admiralty	116	39,924	1:43.40	109
1998	Star of Valor	4	A.T. Gryder	113	Christian Soldier	113	Mr. Sinatra	117	82,875	1:42.40	104
1999	Mr. Sinatra	5	A.T. Gryder	118	Brushing Up	112	Wouldn't We All	117	49,335	1:43.11	106
2000	Sky Approval	6	C. Velasquez	115	Parental Pressure	115	Phone the King	114	49,770	1:44.45	104
2001	Liberty Gold	7	J. Bravo	115	Coyote Lakes	115	Talk Is Cheap	116	66,300	1:42.20	102
2002	Evening Attire	4	S.X. Bridgmohan	116	Ground Storm	115	Tempest Fugit	114	65,520	1:42.69	112
2003	Snake Mountain	5	M.J. Luzzi	120	Ground Storm	117	Cat's at Home	114	64.440	1:44.17	104

Beyer Index: 106.31

ARISTIDES HANDICAP, 6 1/2 Furlongs,
3-Year-Olds, Churchill Downs, 2003 Purse: $109,000

Year	Winner	Age	Jockey	Wt.	Second	Wt.	Third	Wt.	Win Value	Time	Beyer
1994	Never Wavering	5	S.Sellers	116	Demaloot Demashoot	119	American Chance	117	53,479	1:17.17	111
1995	Boone's Mill	3	D.Barton	106	Ojai	113	Hot Jaws	118	69,924	1:16.16	105
1996	Lord Carson	4	D.Barton	115	Criollito-Arg	117	Bet On Sunshine	110	70,525	1:16.16	107
1997	High Stakes Player	5	S.Sellers	119	Traflagar	106	Bet On Sunshine	112	67,580	1:16.16	106
1998	Thisnearlywasmine	4	S.Sellers	115	Partner's Hero	115	El Amante	118	67,518	1:16.16	114
1999	Run Johnny	7	P. Day	116	Squall Valley	112	Neon Shadow	114	68,572	1:16.20	103
2000	Bet On Sunshine	8	F.C. Torres	119	Proven Cure	111	Sun Bull	111	68,014	1:15.11	107
2001	Bet On Sunshine	9	C.H. Borel	120	Alannan	119	Dash for Daylight	110	67,208	1:14.79	113
2002	Orientate	4	R.J. Albarado	118	Binthebest	114	No Armistice	116	66,650	1:14.41	115
2003	Mountain General	5	C.J. Lanerie	116	Beau's Town	123	Pass Rush	118	67,580	1:16.01	102

Beyer Index: 108.3

ARLINGTON HANDICAP, 1 1/4 Miles (Turf),
3-Year-Olds and Up, Arlington Park, 2003 Purse: $250,000

Year	Winner	Age	Jockey	Wt.	Second	Wt.	Third	Wt.	Win Value	Time	Beyer
1929	Misstep	4	C. McCrossen	123	Display	115	B'dy Bauer	114	22,075	1:50.40	
1930	Pigeon Hole	5	R. Finnerty	105	Curate	108	The Nut	114	34,400	2:07.60	
1931	Sun Beau	6	C. Phillips	128	Satin Spar	105	Plucky Play	109	27,300	2:03.20	
1932	Plucky Play	5	G. Woolf	111	Equipoise	134	Pittsburger	105	22,000	2:02.20	
1933	Equipoise	5	R. Workman	135	Watch Him	106	Gallant Sir	125	9,260	2:02.60	
1934	Riskulus	3	D. Meade	108	Watch Him	106	Hadagal	114	9,580	2:02.40	
1935	Discovery	4	J. Bejshak	135	Stand Pat	115	Riskulus	116	8,640	2:01.20	
1936	Sun Teddy	3	B. James	98	Where Away	106	Count Morse	102	8,480	2:02.00	
1937	Dellor	3	S. Young	107	Infantry	118	Giant Killer	110	15,375	2:03.20	
1938	Cardinalis	4	J.G. Wilson	106	Arabs Arrow	112	Grey Gold	118	4,000	2:05.00	
1939	Count d'Or	4	J. Longden	112	Some Count	101	Stands Alone	113	4,050	2:05.00	
1941	Equifox	4	A. Craig	113	Idle Sun	110	Cherry Trifle	100	6,895	1:58.80	
1942	Rounders	3	F.A. Smith	103	Whirlaway	130	Staretor	104	22,000	2:04.00	
1943	Marriage	7	G. Burns	120	Thumbs Up	118	Anticlimax	113	40,950	2:03.60	
1944	War Knight	4	C. Corbett	109	Georgie Drum	121	Daily Trouble	104	37,850	2:02.00	
1945	Busher	3	J. Longden	113	Take Wing	110	Sirde	114	36,900	2:09.80	
1946	Historian	5	O. Scurlock	112	Armed	130	Take Wing	111	38,700	2:01.00	
1947	Armed	6	D. Dodson	130	Bridal Flower	111	Challenge Me	114	37,400	2:02.40	
1948	Stud Poker	5	R.L. Baird	110	Star Reward	113	Fervent	124	38,000	2:04.40	
1949	Coaltown	4	S. Brooks	130	Star Reward	116	Armed	113	36,100	2:03.40	

Year	Winner	Age	Jockey	Wt.	Second	Wt.	Third	Wt.	Win Value	Time	Beyer
1950	Ponder	4	S. Brooks	128	Aegina	102	Inseparable	110	46,800	2:01.60	
1951	Cochise	5	O. Scurlock	120	Oil Capitol	108	County Delight	124	98,550	2:03.80	
1952	To Market	4	W. Boland	118	Oil Capitol	113	Ruhe	112	107,150	1:52.20	
1953	Oil Capitol	6	C. McCreary	120	Sub Fleet	118	Brush Burn	108	49,650	2:03.40	
1954	Stan	4	E. Nelson	114	Brush Burn	113	Sir Mango	125	99,050	1:57.00	
1955	Platan	5	J. Adams	117	Impasse	110	Mark-Ye-Well	116	104,650	1:54.60	
1956	Mister Gus	5	I. Valenzuela	118	Summer Tan	122	Sir Tribal	122	97,900	1:54.20	
1957	Manassas	4	D. Dodson	121	Swoon's Son	128	St. Vincent	120	88,800	1:55.40	
1958	Round Table	4	W. Shoemaker	130	Clem	109	St. Vincent	111	54,100	1:54.40	
1959	Round Table	5	W. Shoemaker	132	Manassas	112	Noureddin	109	75,760	1:53.40	
1960	One-Eyed King	6	M. Ycaza	118	King Grail	109	Martini II	109	32,100	1:58.60	
1961	Tudorich	4	S. Hernandez	115	Oink	126	Prince Blessed	118	35,900	1:57.80	
1962	El Bandito	5	R. Broussard	115	Crimson Satan	122	Rablero	109	34,900	1:58.60	
1963	Bounding Main	4	J. Nichols	113	B. Major	115	Hellenic Hero	114	34,300	1:36.20	
1964	Master Dennis	4	D. Brumfield	112	Parka	118	Carteret	116	33,750	1:55.80	
1965	Chieftain	4	W. Shoemaker	123	Suspicious	112	Ampose	122	31,650	1:49.40	
1966	Tronado	6	B. Moreira	114	Hedevar	120	Time Tested	123	31,500	1:35.80	
1967	Stupendous	4	L. Pincay Jr	119	Bold Tactics	116	R. Thomas	113	32,900	1:35.00	
1968	Tumiga	4	W. Blum	120	Info	116	Lightning Orphan	114	20,300	1:20.40	
1972	Cloudy Dawn	3	W. Hartack	116	Viewpoise	109	Our Papa Joe	112	63,350	2:31.00	
1973	Dubasoff	4	J. Vasquez	117	Jogging	114	Red Reality	118	72,750	1:58.60	
1974	Buffalo Lark	4	L. Snyder	118	Royal Glint	112	Spot T.V.	111	91,800	1:54.40	
1975	Royal Glint	5	J. Tejeira	125	Zografos	113	Buffalo Lark	122	87,400	1:55.80	
1976	Victorian Prince	6	R. Platts	118	Improviser	118	Bold Roll	112	90,000	1:58.20	
1977	Cunning Trick	4	B. Fann	110	Vadim	108	No Turning	118	72,480	2:33.80	
1978	Romeo	5	E. Fires	116	Fluorescent Light	118	Improviser	118	73,080	2:32.00	
1979	Bowl Game	5	J. Velasquez	124	Young Bob	110	L've'ntes'nshe	105	79,260	2:32.20	
1980	Yvonand	4	E. Beitia	111	Rossi Gold	120	Lyphard's Wish	121	71,700	2:31.40	
1981	Spruce Needles	4	J.C. Espinoza	115	Summer Advocate	117	Sea Chimes	116	72,060	2:35.00	
1982	Flying Target	5	R. Cox	115	Rossi Gold	125	Don Roberto	118	71,640	2:32.40	
1983	Paliraki	5	W. Shoemaker	116	Rossi Gold	122	Late Act	113	76,200	2:35.80	
1984	Who's for Dinner	5	M. Venezia	109	Nijinsky's Secret	127	Star Choice	112	70,800	2:04.00	
1985	Pass the Line	4	J.L. Diaz	113	The Noble Player	118	Executive Pride	113	82,050	2:00.40	
1986	Mourjane	6	J.A. Santos	117	Will Dancer	115	Clever Song	118	112,350	2:01.40	
1987	Ifrad	5	G. Baze	114	Storm on the Loose	115	Grey Classic	114	90,360	2:12.20	
1989	Unknown Quantity I	4	J. Velasquez	112	Frosty the Snowman	122	Delegant	113	120,000	2:11.20	
1990	Pleasant Variety	6	E. Fires	115	Double Booked	114	Ten Keys	121	180,000	2:04.00	
1991	Filago	5	P.A. Valenzuela	112	Super Abound	113	Izvestia	116	150,000	2:01.40	110
1992	Sky Classic	5	P. Day	125	Buck'roo	112	Glity	116	150,000	2:00.60	102
1993	Evanescent	6	A.T. Gryder	114	Split Run	113	Magesterial Cheer	112	150,000	2:00.80	105
1994	Fanmore	6	P. Day	119	Marastani	114	Split Run	114	150,000	2:00.20	104
1995	Manilaman	4	R.P. Romero	114	Snake Eyes	117	Bluegrass Prince	117	120,000	2:02.80	106
1996	Torch Rouge	5	M.Guidry	116	Sentimental Moi	113	Volochine	115	120,000	2:03.20	105
1997	Wild Event	4	M. Guidry	114	Storm Trooper	114	Chorwon	113	90,000	2:01.40	103
2000	Northern Quest	5	R.J. Albarado	115	Profit Option	112	Where's Taylor	114	90,000	2:02.13	104
2001	Make No Mistake	6	R.J. Albarado	116	Takarian	116	El Gran Papa	115	150,000	2:02.53	101
2002	Falcon Flight	6	R.R. Douglas	115	Kappa King	117	Gretchen's Star	115	135,000	2:03.13	103
2003	Honor in War	4	D.R. Flores	120	Better Talk Now	115	Mystery Giver	118	150,000	2:02.71	100

Beyer Index: 103.91

ARLINGTON MATRON HANDICAP, 1 1/8 Miles,
Fillies and Mares 3-Year-Olds and Up, Arlington Park, 2003 Purse: $150,000

Year	Winner	Age	Jockey	Wt.	Second	Wt.	Third	Wt.	Win Value	Time	Beyer
1930	Valenciennes	3	E. Steffen	107	Beaming Over	105	Alcibiades	112	7,900	1:35.80	
1931	Risque	3	E. Steffen	108	Manta	118	Cousin Jo	113	10,850	1:42.20	
1932	Tred Avon	4	J.H. Burke	122	Con Amore	117	Fr. Duchess	98	8,475	1:37.40	
1937	Marica	4	R. Dotter	122	Shatterproof	109	Schoolmom	105	4,810	1:36.80	
1938	Idle Miss	4	P. Ryan	118	Dolly Val	108	Jewell Dorsett	109	5,010	1:42.20	
1939	Flying Lill	3	J. Longden	107	Unerring	108	Lady Maryland	120	4,360	1:36.60	
1940	Shine O'Night	3	B. Thompson	103	Montsin	110	Ma'nie O'Hara	109	6,565	1:36.20	
1941	Shine O'Night	4	S. Brooks	110	Pink Gal	112	Montsin	112	6,875	1:38.20	
1942	Blue Delight	4	R. Neves	110	Emolument	102	Inscolassie	105	9,960	1:38.40	
1943	Askmenow	3	C. Bierman	109	Mar-Kell	126	Pomayya	118	8,950	1:38.20	
1944	Harriet Sue	3	N. Jemas	103	Traffic Court	112	Happy Issue	114	11,450	1:36.60	
1945	War Date	3	O. Grohs	113	Whirlabout	120	Durazna	117	18,800	1:39.40	
1946	Good Blood	4	N.L. Pierson	120	Jack's Jill	114	Athene	116	22,850	1:36.80	
1947	But Why Not	3	W. Mehrtens	114	Say Blue	111	Camargo	112	24,250	1:37.60	
1948	Four Winds	3	S. Brooks	119	Brownian	111	Happy Issue	114	23,650	1:36.00	
1949	Lithe	3	F.A. Smith	102	Bewitch	121	Danada Gift	112	18,700	1:36.20	
1950	Lithe	4	E. Nelson	108	Wistful	118	Evanstep	107	15,275	1:34.80	
1951	Sickle's Image	3	B. Fisk	120	Aunt Jinny	107	War Talk	109	53,925	1:36.20	

Year	Winner	Age	Jockey	Wt.	Second	Wt.	Third	Wt.	Win Value	Time	Beyer
1952	Real Delight	3	E. Arcaro	126	Belle Figura	112	Whirla Lea	113	37,800	1:36.60	
1953	Real Delight	4	E. Arcaro	124	Fulvous	107	Bella Figura	119	25,250	1:35.40	
1954	Lavender Hill	5	C. McCreary	115	Vixen Fixit	105	Rosemary B.	111	20,880	1:36.60	
1955	Arab Actress	5	W.M. Cook	117	Clear Dawn	124	C'ry the News	113	37,100	1:35.80	
1956	Delta	4	S. Brooks	119	Amoret	113	Queen Hopeful	120	34,500	1:36.80	
1957	Pucker Up	4	W. Shoemaker	120	Bornastar	111	Lady Swords	108	34,250	1:37.00	
1958	Estacion	5	J. Combest	109	Munch	116	Rosewood	111	32,400	1:50.40	
1959	Wiggle II	4	R.L. Barnett	116	Honey's Gem	118	Born Rich	111	34,050	1:53.00	
1960	Royal Native	7	W. Hartack	128	Woodlawn	110	Silver Spoon	128	33,750	1:50.40	
1961	Shirley Jones	5	H. Grant	124	Call Card	110	Equifun	111	28,600	1:48.00	
1962	Kootenai	4	W. Shoemaker	116	Shirley Jones	123	Fluoresee	108	33,250	1:52.80	
1963	Smart Deb	3	W. Hartack	116	Solabar	113	Nubile	114	50,500	1:50.00	
1964	Tosmah	3	S. Boulmetis	117	Old Hat	116	Nubile	111	49,050	1:49.40	
1965	Old Hat	6	R. Gallimore	126	Swoonalong	122	Miss Cav'ndish	125	46,200	1:49.40	
1966	Swinging Mood	3	E. Fires	112	Margarethen	124	Amerivan	114	33,250	1:48.60	
1967	May's Guide	5	C. Perret	113	Grand Coulee	111	Gabby Abby	113	26,050	1:49.40	
1967	Swinging Mood	4	E. Fires	121	April Dawn	116	Amerivan	114	25,850	1:49.40	
1968	Ludham	4	J. Vasquez	122	Pattee Canyon	110	Harem Lady	110	31,700	1:52.60	
1969	Pink Pigeon	5	W. Harris	123	Egloga	110	Miss Ribot	118	32,400	1:49.80	
1970	Pattee Canyon	5	D.E. Whited	129	Drumtop	126	Not Too Shy	120	30,900	1:47.60	
1971	Toter Back	4	J.R. Anderson	110	Away	117	Ziba Blue	114	34,300	1:51.20	
1972	Kittiwake	4	R. Woodhouse	122	Blade o' War	110	Barely Even	118	33,200	1:51.20	
1973	Last Home	4	F. Alvarez	112	North Broadway	115	Ziba Blue	114	35,800	1:50.00	
1974	Sixty Sails	4	D.E. Whited	121	Protectora	113	What Will Be	118	46,300	1:50.60	
1975	Polynesienne	4	L. Snyder	110	Princess Grey	110	Pass a Glance	116	45,050	1:51.80	
1975	Sixty Sails	5	L. Snyder	114	Victorian Queen	118	Pr'c's Ormea	110	45,050	1:52.80	
1976	Nicosia	4	W. Gavidia	118	B.J. King	111	H'pe of Glory	109	45,450	1:49.40	
1976	Cycylya Zee	3	H. Arroyo	110	Sugar Plum Time	115	True Reality	109	46,200	1:49.60	
1977	Javamine	4	J. Velasquez	119	Star Ball	110	Ivory Castle	110	52,620	1:53.20	
1978	Rich Soil	4	C.H. Silva	117	Satan's Cheer	112	Sans Arc	113	38,340	1:51.20	
1979	Amerigirl	4	B. Swatuk	115	Frosty Skater	118	Calderina	122	52,800	1:51.20	
1980	Impetuous Gal	5	E. Fires	115	Sal;zburg	112	Liv'nthesunshine	108	67,200	2:01.40	
1981	La Bonzo	5	J. Lively	110	Wistful	123	Weber City Miss	123	66,360	2:02.60	
1982	Sweetest Chant	4	E. Fires	115	Miss Huntington	119	Turnablade	115	48,960	2:02.60	
1983	May Day Eighty	4	J. Vasquez	115	Sefa's Beauty	125	Stay a Leader	113	50,355	2:04.40	
1984	Ch'se a Partner	4	D. Brumfield	116	First Flurry	113	Silvered Silk	117	62,595	2:04.00	
1985	Heatherten	6	R.P. Romero	126	Solo Skater	112	Mr. T.'s Tune	114	49,410	2:04.00	
1986	Queen Alexandra	4	D. Brumfield	122	Mr. T.'s Tune	113	Bessarabian	121	92,220	1:48.40	
1987	Family Style	4	S. Hawley	123	Royal Cielo	113	Tide	113	49,320	1:52.20	
1989	Between the Hedges	5	P.A. Johnson	112	Topicount	116	Stoneleigh's Hope	114	65,010	1:48.60	
1990	Degenerate Gal	5	R.P. Romero	117	Evangelical	115	Confirmed Dancer	113	48,555	1:49.20	
1991	Lucky Lady Lauren	4	J. Velasquez	112	Beth Believes	113	Bungalow	112	45,000	1:49.20	95
1992	Lemhi Go	4	E. Fires	114	Beth Believes	112	Diamond City	112	45,000	1:49.60	99
1993	Erica's Dream	5	W. Martinez	115	Pleasant Jolie	114	Meafara	123	60,000	1:23.00	99
1994	Hey Hazel	4	Pino MG	115	Passing Vice	114	Pennyhill Park	116	60,000	1:49.40	99
1995	Mariah's Storm	4	Lester RN	117	Mysteriously	117	Minority Dater	114	60,000	1:50.80	101
1996	Belle Of Cozzene	4	Pettinger D. R.	115	War Thief	113	Your Ladyship	116	75000	1:49.20	101
1997	Omi	4	Guidry M.	114	Gold Memory	115	Trick Attack	114	60000	1:51.80	100
2000	Megans Bluff	3	C.R. Woods Jr.	111	On a Soapbox	115	Tutorial	113	90,000	1:51.41	97
2001	Humble Clerk	4	L. Melancon	114	Maltest Superb	115	Lakenheath	115	90,000	1:51.53	96
2002	Lakenheath	4	C.A. Emigh	115	With Ability	116	Your Out	115	90,000	1:50.78	105
2003	Take Charge Lady	4	S.J. Sellers	123	Lakenheath	116	To the Queen	117	90,000	1:50.19	107

Beyer Index: 99.91

ARLINGTON-WASHINGTON FUTURITY, 1 Mile, 2-Year-Olds, Arlington Park, 2003 Purse: $150,000

Year	Winner	Age	Jockey	Wt.	Second	Wt.	Third	Wt.	Win Value	Time	Beyer
1962	Candy Spots	2	W. Shoemaker	122	Never Bend	122	Rash Prince	122	142,250	1:21.80	
1963	Golden Ruler	2	H. Hinojosa	122	Chieftain	122	Dunfee	122	112,500	1:24.80	
1964	Sadair	2	W. Shoemaker	122	Umbrella Fella	122	Royal Gunner	122	134,925	1:23.40	
1965	Buckpasser	2	B. Baeza	122	Fathers Image	122	Flame Tree	122	190,475	1:23.00	
1966	Diplomat Way	2	W. Shoemaker	122	Wilbur Clark	122	Lightning Orphan	122	195,200	1:22.60	
1967	T.V. Commercial	2	P. Anderson	122	Gin-Rob	122	Royal Cap	122	105,875	1:23.80	
1967	Vitriolic	2	W. Shoemaker	122	Exclusive Native	122	Royal Trace	122	105,875	1:24.00	
1968	Strong Strong	2	D. Gargan	122	King Emperor	122	Night Invader	122	212,850	1:22.80	
1969	Silent Screen	2	J.L. Rotz	122	Insubordination	122	Windy Tide	122	206,075	1:22.60	
1971	Hold Your Peace	2	C. Marquez	122	Heisanative	122	Pokachief	122	45,000	1:11.00	
1971	Governor Max	2	C. Perret	122	Chevron Flight	122	Danahoney	122	45,000	1:11.20	
1972	Shecky Greene	2	C. Marquez	122	Sunny South	122	Sailors Night Out	122	103,020	1:10.40	
1973	Lover Johm	2	R. Ussery	122	Beau Groton	122	Hula Chief	122	97,470	1:11.60	
1974	Greek Answer	2	M. Castaneda	122	Colonel Power	122	The Bagel Prince	122	122,505	1:17.80	

Year	Winner	Age	Jockey	Wt.	Second	Wt.	Third	Wt.	Win Value	Time	Beyer
1975	Honest Pleasure	2	D.G. McHargue	122	Khyber King	122	Rule the Ridge	122	140,610	1:18.40	
1976	Run Dusty Run	2	D.G. McHargue	122	Royal Ski	122	Eagletar	122	120,465	1:16.40	
1977	Sauce Boat	2	S. Cauthen	122	Gonquin	122	Forever Casting	122	130,665	1:16.60	
1978	Jose Binn	2	A. Cordero Jr	122	Exuberant	122	Strike Your Colors	122	120,660	1:17.40	
1979	Execution's Reason	2	E. Delahoussaye	122	Preemptive	122	Brent's Trans Am	122	89,790	1:22.40	
1980	Well Decorated	2	L. Pincay Jr	122	Lord Avie	122	Fairway Phantom	122	240,885	1:23.80	
1981	Lets Dont Fight	2	J. Lively	122	Tropic Ruler	122	Music Leader	122	305,385	1:29.20	
1982	Total Departure	2	E. Fires	122	Coax Me Matt	122	Highland Park	122	271,515	1:23.60	
1983	All Fired Up	2	R.D. Evans	122	Holme on Top	122	Smart n Slick	122	330,135	1:27.00	
1984	Spend a Buck	2	C. Hussey	122	Dusty's Darby	122	Viva Maxi	122	355,320	1:38.00	
1985	Meadowlake	2	J.L. Diaz	122	Bar Tender	122	Papal Power	122	286,320	1:16.80	
1986	Bet Twice	2	C. Perret	122	Conquistarose	122	Jazzing Around	122	300,420	1:37.20	
1987	Tejano	2	J. Vasquez	122	Jim's Orbit	122	Native Stalwart	122	247,080	1:36.20	
1989	Secret Hello	2	A.T. Gryder	122	Richard R	122	Bite the Bullet	122	220,860	1:35.80	
1990	Hansel	2	P. Day	122	Walesa	122	Discover	122	220,440	1:36.40	
1991	Caller I.D.	2	J.D. Bailey	121	Count the Time	121	West by West	121	188,880	1:36.00	91
1992	Gilded Time	2	C.J. McCarron	121	Boundlessly	121	Rockamundo	121	200,580	1:37.80	91
1993	Polar Expedition	2	C.C. Bourque	121	Gimme Glory	121	Delicate Cure	121	120,000	1:39.20	82
1994	Evansville Slew	2	P. Compton	121	Valid Wager	121	Mr Purple	121	120,000	1:37.80	82
1996	Night in Reno	2	M. Guidry	121	Flying With Eagles	121	Thisnearlywasmine	121	120,000	1:36.60	83
1997	Cowboy Dan	2	D. Kutz	121	Captain Maestri	121	Fiamma	121	90,000	1:37.60	90
2000	Trailthefox	2	S.J. Sellers	121	Stabury	121	Blame It On Ruby	121	90,000	1:37.25	91
2001	Publication	2	R. Meier	122	It'sallinthechase	122	Dubai Squire	122	90,000	1:38.78	78
2002	Most Feared	2	M. Guidry	122	Anasheed	122	Unleash the Power	122	90,000	1:37.52	79
2003	Cactus Ridge	2	E.M.Martin Jr	117	Glittergem	117	Texas Deputy	119	90,000	1:35.44	95

Beyer Index: 86.2

ARLINGTON-WASHINGTON LASSIE, 1 Mile,
2-Year-Old Fillies, Arlington Park, 2003 Purse: $100,000

Year	Winner	Age	Jockey	Wt.	Second	Wt.	Third	Wt.	Win Value	Time	Beyer
1929	Capture	2	E. Shropshire	117	Ma Yerkes	117	Thistle Down	124	9,175	1:06.00	
1930	Risque	2	E. Steffen	117	Glidelia	115	Panasette	113	6,650	1:05.80	
1931	Top Flight	2	A. Robertson	120	Modern Queen	118	Princess Camelia	117	19,125	1:05.20	
1932	Hilena	2	R. Workman	119	Edelweiss	117	Swivel	119	17,900	1:10.40	
1933	Mata Hari	2	R. Jones	117	Far Star	119	Dabchick	117	21,670	1:12.00	
1934	Motto	2	R. Workman	119	Toro Nancy	115	Bye Lo	117	22,510	1:13.40	
1935	Forever Yours	2	D. Meade	117	Parade Girl	117	Balcony	117	25,790	1:12.80	
1936	Apogee	2	E. Steffen	122	Jewell Dorsett	117	Oddesa Girl	117	21,020	1:13.20	
1937	Theen	2	I. Anderson	117	Inhale	122	Well Rewarded	122	15,630	1:11.80	
1938	Inscoelda	2	C. Rollins	117	Dinner Date	117	Unerring	119	17,540	1:11.60	
1939	Now What	2	R. Workman	122	War Beauty	117	Piquet	117	18,820	1:13.00	
1940	Blue Delight	2	A. Snider	119	Misty Isle	122	Valdina Myth	122	17,250	1:12.80	
1941	Petrify	2	R. Donoso	117	Lotopoise	119	Court Manners	117	17,200	1:12.60	
1942	Fad	2	A. Craig	117	Askmenow	117	Miss Barbara	117	25,980	1:13.60	
1943	Twilight Tear	2	N. Jemas	113	Miss Keeneland	113	Music Hall	110	26,460	1:13.20	
1944	Expression	2	F. Zufelt	119	Twosy	119	Blue Alibi	119	28,900	1:12.40	
1945	Beaugay	2	J. Adams	119	Enfilade	119	Aladear	119	35,900	1:12.20	
1946	Four Winds	2	I. Anderson	119	Musical Lady	119	War Fan	119	51,000	1:12.00	
1947	Bewitch	2	D. Dodson	119	Boswell Lady	119	Lea Lark	119	47,150	1:10.80	
1948	Pail of Water	2	W. Mehrtens	119	Alsab's Day	119	Stole	119	40,350	1:12.40	
1949	Duchess Peg	2	S. Brooks	119	Baby Comet	119	Bed o' Roses	119	45,125	1:15.60	
1950	Shawnee Squaw	2	A.D. Rivera	119	Red Cross	119	Hasty Request	119	43,865	1:12.00	
1951	Princess Lygia	2	K. Church	119	Hadn't Orter	119	Aesthete	119	45,580	1:11.20	
1952	Fulvous	2	S. Brooks	119	Aerolite	119	Hula	119	53,275	1:13.80	
1953	Queen Hopeful	2	J. Adams	119	Miz Clementine	119	Beanir	119	66,565	1:10.60	
1954	Delta	2	S. Brooks	119	Lea Lane	119	Alspal	119	62,750	1:10.40	
1955	Judy Rullah	2	D. Erb	119	Guard Rail	119	Waikiki	119	57,335	1:13.80	
1956	Leallah	2	W. Hartack	119	Splendored	119	Frank's Flower	119	56,010	1:11.60	
1957	Poly Hi	2	E. Guerin	119	Delnita	119	Hasty Doll	119	65,025	1:10.60	
1958	Dark Vintage	2	J. Heckmann	119	Little Kid	119	Debbie Lorraine	119	64,000	1:10.80	
1959	Monarchy	2	S. Brooks	119	My Dear Girl	119	Heavenly Baby	119	61,950	1:10.00	
1960	Colfax Maid	2	S. Brooks	119	Caps and Bells	119	Apatontheback	119	59,350	1:11.80	
1961	Rudoma	2	W. Hartack	116	Cherry Laurel	116	Song of Glory	116	38,500	1:11.40	
1962	Smart Deb	2	M. Ycaza	119	Honey Bunny	119	Fast Luck	119	44,900	1:16.20	
1963	Sari's Song	2	W. Shoemaker	119	Ye-Cats	119	Castle Forbes	119	61,505	1:18.20	
1964	Admiring	2	W. Hartack	119	Privileged	119	Mr. B's Sister	119	77,815	1:18.00	
1965	Silver Bright	2	J. Nichols	119	Ole Liz	119	Prides Profile	119	111,265	1:18.20	
1966	Mira Femme	2	I. Valenzuela	119	Teacher's Art	119	Woozem	119	96,525	1:16.80	
1967	Shenow	2	L. Pincay Jr	119	Ave Valeque	119	Lucretia Bori	119	92,500	1:18.40	
1968	Process Shot	2	C. Baltazar	119	Kahoolawe	119	Lynne's Orphan	119	80,000	1:17.40	
1969	Clover Lane	2	W. Shoemaker	119	Belle Noire	119	Dixie Wind	119	80,000	1:18.40	
1972	Double Your Fun	2	L. Melancon	119	Crosstie	119	Greek Lovliness	119	35,160	1:12.00	

Year	Winner	Age	Jockey	Wt.	Second	Wt.	Third	Wt.	Win Value	Time	Beyer
1972	Natural Sound	2	J. Tejeira	119	Vaguely Familiar	119	Felane	119	35,610	1:11.60	
1973	Special Team	2	A. Pineda	119	Thirty One Jewels	119	Two Timing Lass	119	59,574	1:11.00	
1974	Hot n Nasty	2	D.G. McHargue	119	Sharm a Sheikh	119	Mystery Mood	119	64,386	1:11.40	
1975	Dearly Precious	2	M. Hole	119	Free Journey	119	Head Spy	119	67,938	1:11.20	
1976	Special Warmth	2	S. Maple	119	Wavy Waves	119	Drama Critic	119	68,700	1:10.40	
1977	Stub	2	R. Turcotte	119	Rainy Princess	119	Go Line	119	70,329	1:10.40	
1978	It's in the Air	2	E. Delahoussaye	119	Angel Island	119	Bequa	119	71,394	1:09.60	
1979	Sissy's Time	2	E. Fires	119	Ellie Milove	119	Vogue Folks	119	63,399	1:11.00	
1980	Truly Bound	2	W. Shoemaker	119	Safe Play	119	Masters Dream	119	83,022	1:25.20	
1981	Milingo	2	R. Sibille	119	Maniches	119	Justa Litte One	119	129,798	1:25.20	
1982	For Once'n My Life	2	E. Maple	119	Some Kinda Flirt	119	How Clever	119	106,461	1:23.40	
1983	Miss Oceana	2	E. Maple	119	Life's Magic	119	Bottle Top	119	112,146	1:23.40	
1984	Contredance	2	P. Day	119	Tiltalating	119	Miss Delice	119	211,560	1:26.00	
1985	Family Style	2	L. Pincay Jr	119	Deep Silver	119	Pamela Kay	119	250,200	1:18.00	
1986	Delicate Vine	2	G.L. Stevens	122	Sacahuista	122	Ruling Angel	122	165,660	1:23.40	
1987	Joe's Tammie	2	C. Perret	122	Tomorrow's Child	122	Pearlie Gold	122	186,840	1:25.00	
1989	Trumpet's Blare	2	L. Pincay Jr	122	Special Happening	122	Puffy Doodle	122	128,040	1:38.60	
1990	Through Flight	2	J.M. Johnson	120	Good Potential	120	Wolf for Traci	120	138,870	1:39.00	76
1991	Speed Dialer	2	P. Day	119	Cadillac Women	119	Mystic Hawk	119	141,390	1:36.40	79
1992	Eliza	2	P.A. Valenzuela	119	Banshee Winds	119	Tourney	119	134,850	1:39.40	84
1993	Mariah's Storm	2	R.N. Lester	119	Shapely Scrapper	119	Minority Dater	119	90,000	1:38.80	73
1994	Shining Light	2	J.L. Diaz	119	She's a Lively One	119	Alltheway Bertie	119	90,000	1:41.60	68
1996	Southern Playgirl	2	R. P. Romero	119	Leo's Gypsy Dancer	119	Broad Dynamite	119	90,000	1:38.20	79
1997	Silver Maiden	2	B.S. Laviolette	119	Artic Lady	119	So Generous	119	60,000	1:37.40	81
2000	Thunder Bertie	2	J.A. Beasley	119	Caressing	119	Zahwah	119	60,000	1:36.91	87
2001	Joanies Bella	2	M. St. Julien	121	Brief Bliss	121	First Again	121	60,000	1:39.34	80
2002	Moonlight Sonata	2	B.S. Laviolette	121	Parting	121	Souris	121	60,000	1:37.82	76
2003	Zosima	2	P. Day	118	Everyday Angel	116	Cryptos' Best	118	60,000	1:36.02	89

Beyer Index: 79.27

ATHENIA HANDICAP, 1 1/16 Miles (Turf),
Fillies and Mares 3-Year-Olds and Up, Aqueduct, 2003 Purse: $113,000

Year	Winner	Age	Jockey	Wt.	Second	Wt.	Third	Wt.	Win Value	Time	Beyer
1978	Terpsichorist	3	M. Venezia	114	Consort	110	Bonnie Blue Flag	110	33,300	2:03.20	
1979	Poppycock	3	J. Velasquez	114	Fourdrinier	114	Six Crowns	114	52,470	2:05.60	
1980	Love Sign	3	R. Hernandez	121	Rokeby Rose	111	Classic Curves	111	50,490	2:00.40	
1981	De la Rose	3	E. Maple	125	Noble Damsel	111	Andover Way	113	51,120	2:00.40	
1982	Mintage	3	J.L. Samyn	114	Doodle	119	Street Dance	112	32,790	2:17.80	
1982	Middle Stage	3	J. Miranda	112	Realms Reason	114	Vocal	115	32,790	2:17.40	
1983	Rose Crescent	4	R.G. Davis	108	Lady Norcliffe	111	Infinite	112	34,380	2:22.00	
1984	Key Dancer	3	A. Cordero Jr	111	Surely Georgie's	107	Rossard	123	56,700	2:14.80	
1985	Videogenic	3	J. Cruguet	114	Persian Tiara	119	Key Witness	108	61,020	2:15.40	
1986	Dawn's Curtsey	4	E. Maple	111	Festivity	113	Perfect Point	115	55,440	2:16.00	
1987	Lead Kindly Light	4	J.M. Pezua	110	Barbara's Moment	111	Spectacular Bev	114	70,920	2:23.80	
1988	High Browser	3	P. Day	108	Miss Unnameable	109	Gaily Gaily	110	57,780	2:18.60	
1989	Capades	3	A. Cordero Jr	115	Miss Unnameable	114	Key Flyer	110	54,360	2:13.20	
1990	Buy the Firm	4	J.D. Bailey	111	Rigamajig	111	Igmaar	111	52,650	2:18.20	
1991	Flaming Torch	4	P.A. Valenzuela	113	Plenty of Grace	114	Highland Penny	116	55,800	2:13.80	
1992	Fairy Garden	4	J.A. Krone	112	Passagere du Soir	117	Seewillo	113	52,020	2:13.60	97
1993	Trampoli	4	M.E. Smith	117	Kirov Premiere	110	Dahlia's Dreamer	110	54,000	2:17.00	105
1994	Lady Affirmed	3	Chavez JF	111	Irving's Girl	110	Cox Orange	116	52,245	1:48.60	98
1995	Caress	4	Davis RG	114	Manila Lila	115	Vinista	119	69,340	1:54.00	82
1996	Sixieme Sans	4	J.D. Bailey	116	Rapunzel Runz	115	Fashion Star	113	66660	1:37.80	103
1997	Rapid Selection	4	Bravo J	113	Dynasty	114	Preachersnightmare	111	65940	1:47.00	105
1998	Tampico	5	Bravo J	114	Irish Daisy	113	Rumpipumpy	115	51210	1:42.80	96
1999	Antoniette	4	J.F. Chavez	119	Dominique's Joy	113	Prospectress	115	66,840	1:41.89	102
2000	Wild Heart Dancing	4	J.F. Chavez	115	Fickle Friends	114	Silken	114	67,500	1:43.40	95
2001	Verruma	5	J.R. Velazquez	114	Siringas	112	Freefourracing	113	82,725	1:42.09	94
2001	Babae	5	J.F. Chavez	116	Batique	114	Sweet Prospect	110	82,725	1:40.53	108
2002	Babae	6	J.F. Chavez	120	Strawberry Blonde	116	Silver Rail	112	70,020	1:44.90	100
2003	Caught in the Rain	4	R. Migliore	115	Lojo	114	Coney Kitty	113	67,800	1:47.05	93

Beyer Index: 98.31

AZALEA BREEDERS' CUP, 6 Furlongs,
3-Year-Old Fillies, Calder Race Course, 2003 Purse: $291,525

Year	Winner	Age	Jockey	Wt.	Second	Wt.	Third	Wt.	Win Value	Time	Beyer
1972	Mr. Brick's Image	4	J. Salinas	112	First Bloom	122	M's Gunflint	117	16,200	1:46.80	
1976	Forty Nine Sunsets	3	G. St. Leon	122	Head Spy	113	Noble Royalty	113	13,560	1:11.80	
1977	Countess Pruner	3	J.S. Rodriguez	116	Delphic Oracle	113	White Goddess	119	13,440	1:11.20	
1978	Lucy Belle	3	A. Smith Jr	113	We Believe in You	113	Wings of Destiny	122	14,040	1:25.20	

Year	Winner	Age	Jockey	Wt.	Second	Wt.	Third	Wt.	Win Value	Time	Beyer
1979	Burn's Return	3	M.A. Rivera	115	Solo Haina	120	Speier's Hope	115	16,860	1:24.00	
1980	She Can't Miss	3	W.A. Guerra	122	Nice and Sharp	115	Karla's Enough	119	16,515	1:11.20	
1981	Ange Gal	3	G. Cohen	113	Float Upstream	115	Whoop It	114	16,515	1:26.00	
1981	Kaylem Ho	3	A. Smith Jr	115	Toga Toga	119	Secret Kingdom	115	16,515	1:25.80	
1982	Here's to Peg	3	J.A. Velez Jr	116	Cut	114	Bad Dancin Rita	116	16,905	1:26.00	
1983	Current Gal	3	E. Cardone	112	Silvered Silk	115	Paris Roulette	115	17,295	1:25.60	
1984	Birdie Belle	3	H.A.Valdivieso	120	Sugar's Image	120	Scorched Panties	120	33,990	1:25.80	
1985	Jackie McCleaf	3	C. Hussey	120	Nahema	118	Nyama	118	33,840	1:25.80	
1986	Classy Tricks	3	M.C. Suckie	112	Janjac	112	Thirty Zip	119	30,410	1:25.40	
1987	My Sweet Replica	3	S.B. Soto	115	Shot Gun Bonnie	114	Ches Pie	116	33,990	1:25.20	
1988	Grand Splash	3	R.N. Lester	114	Myfavorite Charity	114	Hi Maudie	116	46,500	1:25.60	
1989	Princess Mora	3	S. Gaffalione	112	Georgies Doctor	118	Silk Stocks	117	32,790	1:25.60	
1990	Sweet Proud Polly	3	P.A. Rodriguez	115	Highway Lady	115	Bald Cat	112	32,790	1:26.20	
1991	Ranch Ragout	3	E.O. Nunez	113	Parisian Flight	115	Foolishly Wild	110	33,120	1:18.40	
1992	C.C.'s Return	3	R.J. Thibeau Jr	113	Fortune Forty Four	114	Subtle Dancer	113	30,000	1:25.20	90
1993	Kimscountrydiamond	3	J. Vasquez	115	Nijivision	113	Hollywood Wildcat	117	60,000	1:23.40	80
1994	Cut the Charm	3	Castillo H Jr	121	Just a Little Kiss	114	Tasso Bee	112	60,000	1:25.40	83
1995	Lucky Lavender Gal	3	Douglas RR	116	Chaposa Springs	117	Dancin Renee	116	60,000	1:23.40	99
1996	J J's Dream	3	Castillo H. Jr	118	Supah Avalanche	112	Race Artist	114	65100	1:23.80	89
1997	Little Sister	3	Lovato F. Jr	116	Princess Pietrina	112	Maggie Answer	114	120000	1:13.00	98
1998	Cassidy	3	Rivera J. A. II	114	Holy Capote	114	Fantasy Angel	118	75000	1:11.80	98
1999	Show Me the Stage	3	R.J. Courville	116	Could Be	116	Exact	116	75,000	1:11.91	91
2000	Swept Away	3	P.Day	116	Precious Feather	112	Watchfull	116	120,000	1:11.53	103
2001	Hattiesburg	3	M. Guidry	116	Southern Tour	114	Spanish Glitter	116	150,000	1:11.81	93
2002	Bold World	3	C.H. Borel	118	Willa on the Move	114	Tchula Miss	114	105,000	1:10.86	102
2003	Ebony Breeze	3	C. Velasquez	118	Storm Flag	116	Crafty Brat	116	176,025	1:10.82	102

Beyer Index: 94

BALDWIN, about 6 1/2 Furlongs (Turf), 3-Year-Olds, Santa Anita, 2003 Purse: $114,550

Year	Winner	Age	Jockey	Wt.	Second	Wt.	Third	Wt.	Win Value	Time	Beyer
1968	Royal Fols	3	W. Harmatz	120	Pinjara	114	Key Rulla	114	9,600	1:12.80	
1968	Fiddle Isle	3	J. Sellers	114	Right or Wrong	117	Baffle	117	9,500	1:13.40	
1969	Tell	3	W. Shoemaker	114	Modern Spirit	114	Might	114	15,200	1:12.80	
1970	Smugglin George	3	J. Lambert	114	Rancho Lejos	120	Cum Shane	114	13,850	1:13.00	
1971	Restless Runner	3	E. Belmonte	117	Triple Bend	120	Long Term	114	18,450	1:13.20	
1972	Finalista	3	L. Pincay Jr	114	Impressive Style	114	Torquemada	114	21,500	1:13.80	
1973	Bensadream	3	D. Pierce	115	Princely Axe	114	Gold Bag	115	21,350	1:14.00	
1974	Battery E	3	L. Pincay Jr	116	Wedge Shot	117	Ride Off	117	19,150	1:14.00	
1975	Uniformity	3	S. Hawley	114	Crumbs	114	Wine Nipper	114	20,050	1:13.20	
1976	Gaelic Christian	3	R. Rosales	114	El Portugues	117	Grandaries	114	20,750	1:13.60	
1977	Current Concept	3	S. Hawley	120	Bad 'n Big	117	Text	120	24,900	1:13.20	
1978	B.W. Turner	3	D. Pierce	117	O Big Al	120	Princely Lark	114	27,550	1:14.00	
1979	To B. or Not	3	C. Baltazar	114	Debonair Roger	116	Young Driver	114	27,000	1:15.60	
1980	Corvette Chris	3	F. Toro	115	Executive Counsel	114	Moorish Star	114	28,550	1:13.60	
1981	Descaro	3	D.G. McHargue	115	Motivity	120	Steelinctive	114	36,700	1:14.60	
1982	Remember John	3	E. Delahoussaye	117	Time to Explode	120	Crystal Star	114	39,200	1:15.20	
1983	Total Departure	3	L. Pincay Jr	117	Paris Prince	114	Morry's Champ	114	40,950	1:15.20	
1984	Debonaire Junior	3	C.J. McCarron	114	Fortunate Prospect	119	Distant Ryder	117	41,700	1:14.40	
1985	Knighthood II	3	G.L. Stevens	114	Full Honor	117	Infantryman	114	39,900	1:14.80	
1986	Jetting Home	3	D.G. McHargue	116	Royal Treasure	114	El Corazon	114	38,350	1:17.40	
1987	Chime Time	3	P.A. Valenzuela	116	Sweetwater Springs	117	McKenzie Prince	114	40,750	1:15.00	
1988	Exclusive Nureyev	3	E. Delahoussaye	116	Prospectors Gamble	117	Mehmetski	114	39,162	1:14.40	
1988	Dr. Brent	3	A. Solis	117	Accomplish Ridge	117	Glad Music	114	39,262	1:15.00	
1989	Tenacious Tom	3	E. Delahoussaye	119	Mountain Ghost	122	Gum	119	51,900	1:14.80	
1990	Farma Way	3	R. Sibille	115	Iam the Iceman	117	Robyn Dancer	117	52,975	1:13.80	
1991	What a Spell	3	D.R. Flores	117	Broadway's Top Gun	122	Shining Prince	114	49,875	1:16.20	
1992	Reckless Ruckus	3	P.A. Valenzuela	116	Fabulous Champ	114	Slerp	115	49,850	1:17.20	102
1993	Future Storm	3	K.J. Desormeaux	117	Concept Win	119	Siebe	117	51,550	1:15.00	92
1994	Silver Music	3	C.W. Antley	114	Eagle Eyed	117	Makinanhonestbuck	117	48,375	1:13.60	93
1995	Sierra Diablo	3	Delahoussaye E	116	Raji	117	Huge Gator	116	47,300	1:15.20	96
1996	Sandtrap	3	C.S. Nakatani	114	Strangelove	115	Benton Creek	117	64,300	1:15.00	99
1997	Latin Dancer	3	C.A. Black	117	King of Swing	117	Swiss Yodeler	122	67,850	1:14.40	99
1998	Wrekin Pilot	3	E. Delahoussaye	116	Commitisize	122	Tenbyssimo	117	66,240	1:13.20	101
1999	American Spirit	3	E. Ramsammy	114	Chomper	115	Impressive Grades	119	69,300	1:13.93	89
2000	Fortifier	3	B. Blanc	114	Performing Magic	116	Joopy Doopy	117	66,870	1:16.79	93
2001	Skip to the Stone	3	C.S. Nakatani	117	Trailthefox	122	Bills Paid	114	66,000	1:16.29	101
2002	Shuffling Kid	3	P.A. Valenzuela	117	Red Briar	116	Dark Sorcerer	114	68,640	1:13.30	89
2003	Buddy Gil	3	G.L. Stevens	117	King Robyn	116	Flirt With Fortune	116	68,730	1:12.56	106

Beyer Index: 96.67

BALLSTON SPA BREEDERS' CUP HANDICAP, 1 1/16 Miles (Turf), Fillies and Mares 3-Year-Olds and Up, Saratoga, 2003 Purse: $120,000

Year	Winner	Age	Jockey	Wt.	Second	Wt.	Third	Wt.	Win Value	Time	Beyer
1989	Wakonda	5	A. Cordero Jr.	116	Foresta	108	Toll Fee	111	93,900	1:33.80	
1990	Fire the Groom	3	L. Dettori	114	Sally Rous	114	Christiecat	115	95,820	1:35.20	109
1991	Paris Opera	5	G.L. Stevens	116	Daring Doone	114	La Famo	114	94,470	1:37.40	98
1992	Aurora	4	C. Perret	114	Olden Rijn	112	Irish Linnet	113	93,870	1:36.80	96
1993	One Dreamer	5	E. Fires	116	Eenie Meenie Miney	111	Irish Linnet	116	94.440	1:39.20	102
1994	Weekend Madness	5	S.Sellers	115	You'd Be Surprised	120	Heed	111	93,510	1:44.44	104
1995	Weekend Madness	6	S.Sellers	117	Irish Linnet	120	Allez Les Trois	115	93,300	1:40.40	104
1996	Danish	5	J.A. Santos	115	Apolda	121	Caress	113	126,360	1:41.40	105
							Upper Noosh	111	126,360	1:41.40	
1997	Valor Lady	5	J.R. Velazquez	112	Antespend	116	Rumpipumpy	114	130,200	1:39.40	98
1998	Memories of Silver	5	J.D. Bailey	122	Witchful Thinking	118	Ashford Castle	114	126,600	1:40.80	104
1999	Pleasant Temper	5	J.D. Bailey	118	Cuanto Es	113	Lets Get Cozzy	114	124,680	1:41.80	100
2000	License Fee	5	P. Day	116	Pico Teniriffe	116	Hello Soso	114	125,700	1:44.44	99
2001	Penny's Gold	4	J.D. Bailey	118	Babae	114	Chaste	113	126,120	1:40.69	102
2002	Surya	4	J.D. Bailey	114	Shooting Party	118	Solvig	114	126,409	1:52.29	95
2003	Stylish	5	J.R. Velazquez	116	Snow Dance	117	Cozzy Corner	112	120,000	1:41.03	98

Beyer Index: 101

BALTIMORE BREEDERS' CUP HANDICAP, 1 1/8 Miles, 3-Year-Olds and Up, Pimlico, 2003 Purse: $112,000

Year	Winner	Age	Jockey	Wt.	Second	Wt.	Third	Wt.	Win Value	Time	Beyer
1986	Salem Drive	4	V. Bracciale Jr.	115	Little Bold John	115	Roo Art	116	101,530	1:44.00	
1987	Bagetelle	5	K.J. Desormeaux	107	Fobby Forbes	115	Little Bold John	117	36,628	1:43.40	
1988	Little Bold John	6	D.A. Miller Jr	124	Ron Stevens	113	Bagetelle	112	101,400	1:42.60	
1989	Homebuilder	5	J. Rocco	113	Slew City Slew	120	Baldski's Choice	112	92,280	1:48.60	
1990	Shy Tom	4	M.G. Pino	113	Doc's Leader	114	Overnight Hero	113	107,970	1:49.60	
1991	Runaway Stream	4	R. Wilson	111	Silver Survivor	113	Tricky Creek	113	109,350	1:48.00	
1992	Excellent Tipper	4	E.S. Prado	112	Sunny Sunrise	117	Out of Place	113	105,000	1:47.60	106
1993	Sunny Sunrise	6	M.T. Johnson	120	Snappy Landing	114	Baron Mathew	115	108,750	1:48.80	105
1994	Taking Risks	4	M.T. Johnson	117	Conte di Savoya	115	Frottage	114	65,880	1:49.20	100
1995	Poor but Honest	5	D.P. Butler	109	Mary's Buckaroo	112	Rugged Bugger	113	126,120	1:49.00	110
1996	Pyramid Peak	4	W.H. McCauley	122	Coup d'Argent	108	Personal Merit	113	124,350	1:47.60	111
1997	Pyramid Peak	5	P. Day	118	Wild Deputy	115	Tam's Armada	110	125,520	1:48.80	110
1998	Testafly	4	G.W. Hutton	115	Hot Brush	115	Proud and True	114	60,000	1:49.80	111
1999	Testafly	5	G.W. Hutton	114	Rod And Staff	114	Willing	114	60,000	1:49.80	108
2000	Leave It to Beezer	7	T.L. Dunkelberger	115	Eastern Daydream	114	Thunder Flash	114	60,000	1:49.02	109
2001	Lightning Paces	4	G.W. Hutton	114	Milwaukee Brew	114	Grundlefoot	113	60,000	1:50.52	103
2002	Grundlefoot	5	M.G. Pino	116	Lyracist	114	Private Ryan	114	60,000	1:49.65	107
2003	P Day	8	R. Fogelsonger	118	Changeintheweather	114	Full Brush	115	75,000	1:48.94	102

Beyer Index: 106.83

BASHFORD MANOR, 6 Furlongs, 2-Year-Olds, Churchill Downs, 2003 Purse: $162,750

Year	Winner	Age	Jockey	Wt.	Second	Wt.	Third	Wt.	Win Value	Time	Beyer
1902	Von Rouse	2	Winkfield	118	Pericles	113	Captain Arnold	113	1,335	:55.25	
1903	J.P. Mayberry	2	H. Booker	118	Copperfield	113	Paris	118	1,485	:55.00	
1904	Oiseau	2	Munro	121	Florentine	118	Rebounder	113	1,360	:54.50	
1905	George C. Bennett	2	Nicol	118	Charlie Eastman	120	Hermitage	118	1,600	:56.20	
1906	Zal	2	Obert	118	Warner Griswell	118	Fair Fagot	118	1,720	:56.00	
1907	John Marrs	2	Troxler	118	Great Pirate	118	Honest	118	1,570	:54.00	
1908	Fundamental	2	Heidel	118	French Cook	114	Woolwinder	118	1,415	:54.40	
1909	Joe Morris	2	Page	118	King Solomon	118	Donau	118	1,690	:53.40	
1910	La U Mexican	2	E. Griffin	118	Jack Denman	118	Incision	118	1,800	:54.20	
1911	Worth	2	T. Koerner	121	Buckhorn	113	Presumption	115	1,990	:54.80	
1912	Hawthorn	2	Fain	120	Forward	118	Yankee Notions	118	1,940	:54.00	
1913	Little Nephew	2	Loftus	118	Old Rosebud	118	Black Toney	118	700	:53.00	
1914	Luke	2	W.W. Taylor	121	Marion Goosby	113	Dr. Carmen	113	2,710	:53.00	
1915	Ellison	2	R. Goose	113	Marse Henry	118	Heir Apparent	118	2,350	:54.20	
1916	Harry Kelly	2	G. Garner	121	Sedan	113	Berlin	121	2,190	:53.60	
1917	Escoba	2	J. Hanover	121	Jas. T. Clark	118	Big Enough	118	2,920	:54.00	
1918	Billy Kelly	2	R. Simpson	118	Col. Taylor	118	Col. Livingston	115	2,910	:54.00	
1919	Sam Freedman	2	J. Morys	113	Westwood	113	Best Pal	118	4,680	:54.20	
1920	United Verde	2	L. Ensor	117	Oriole	117	East'eside	122	7,075	:55.60	
1921	Casey	2	D. Connelly	122	Rekab	125	Braedalbane	117	5,900	:55.20	
1922	Triumph	2	A. Johnson	117	Dan E. O'Sullivan	122	Jack Bauer	117	6,980	:53.80	
1923	Black Gold	2	D. Connelly	122	T.S. Jordan	122	Digit	122	7,520	:53.00	
1924	Reputation	2	E. Smallwood	122	Step Along	122	Ocean Current	122	6,280	:53.00	
1925	Take a Chance	2	H. Hamilton	122	Sanction	122	Percentage	117	7,860	:54.00	
1926	Torchilla	2	E. Legere	122	General Haldeman	126	Jock	117	7,740	1:00.60	

Year	Winner	Age	Jockey	Wt.	Second	Wt.	Third	Wt.	Win Value	Time	Beyer
1927	Typhoon	2	A. Johnson	122	Toro	122	Misstep	117	7,820	1:00.20	
1928	Roguish Eye	2	J. Heupel	117	The Okah	122	Yermajo	122	7,580	1:00.20	
1929	All Upset	2	R. Zucchini	122	High Foot	122	Sydney	117	7,400	1:00.00	
1930	Back Log	2	H. Fisher	122	Don Leon	125	La Salle	122	7,260	1:00.40	
1931	Proteus	2	J. Smith	125	Liberty Limited	122	Tellico	122	7,030	1:01.00	
1932	In High	2	C. McCrossen	117	Red Whisk	122	Levaal	122	5,710	1:00.40	
1933	Miss Patience	2	G. Elston	119	New Deal	122	Speedy Skippy	122	5,590	1:01.80	
1934	St. Bernard	2	H. Schutte	122	Fraidy Cat	122	Byo Lo	119	3,165	1:00.60	
1935	Coldstream	2	P. Keester	122	Bright Light	125	Lemont	122	3,035	:59.40	
1936	Murph	2	E. Arcaro	122	Foolish Moment	119	Prairie Dog	117	6,015	:59.20	
1937	Sky Larking	2	A. Robertson	122	Teddy's Comet	122	Knee Deep	117	5,460	1:01.60	
1938	Royal Pam	2	I. Hanford	119	Unerring	119	Cherry Jam	122	5,390	:59.00	
1939	Roman	2	W. Yarberry	125	Black Brummel	122	Charitable	122	2,615	:59.40	
1940	Air Brigade	2	T. Marshall	122	My Bill	122	Blue Pair	122	2,525	1:01.20	
1941	Black Raider	2	A. Craig	127	Omathon	122	Bayridge	117	2,655	:59.60	
1942	Navy Cross	2	J. Richard	117	Take Away	122	Hoosier	122	3,045	:59.60	
1943	Black Swan	2	M. Caffarella	122	Civil Liberty	117	Black Badge	117	2,735	1:00.80	
1944	Best Effort	2	M. Caffarella	122	Dockstader	122	Black Pepper	122	3,005	1:01.80	
1945	Fighting Frank	2	G. South	117	Inroc	122	Bold Regard	117	5,050	1:00.40	
1946	Tweet's Boy	2	P. Roberts	125	Colonel O'F	125	Black Knave	122	10,300	1:01.60	
1947	Phar Mon.	2	S. Brooks	127	Loujac	122	Circus Clown	122	10,153	1:00.40	
1948	Ky. Colonel	2	S. Brooks	122	Olympia	122	Commodore Lea	122	10,050	1:00.20	
1949	Old Tom	2	J. Duff	122	Curtice	117	Black Sambo	125	10,225	1:00.00	
							Shadows Start	122			
1950	Kings Hope	2	R.L. Baird	122	Robust	122	Pur Sang	122	10,625	1:01.20	
1951	Red Curtice	2	J.D. Jessop	122	Smoke Screen	117	Very Special	117	10,250	:58.80	
1952	Ace Destroyer	2	T. Barrow	122	Prince Marque	122	Happy Carrier	125	9,187	1:01.60	
1953	Mr. Prosecutor	2	J. Adams	122	Everett Jr.	127	Portray	117	13,150	:59.60	
1954	Royal Note	2	H. Moreno	125	Texas Bulldog	117	Prince Eric	122	13,100	1:00.20	
1955	Swoon's Son	2	D. Erb	117	Mr. Jay Gee	122	Night Intruder	117	10,425	1:01.00	
1956	Jet Sub	2	R.L. Baird	122	All Speed	122	Implement	117	13,200	:59.20	
1957	Little Reaper	2	J. Sellers	122	Lord Jan	122	Unique Commando	122	10,650	:58.80	
1958	Tribalove	2	F.A. Smith	117	I Step	122	Wet Back	122	8,812	:58.80	
1959	Maxinkuckee	2	W.B. Williams	122	Pawhuska Sam	122	Dickie Don	122	9,560	:59.00	
1960	He's a Pistol	2	K. Church	122	Ok Chief	122	Arab Road	122	8,634	:58.60	
1961	Mike G.	2	W.M. Cook	122	Jetting Home	122	Loil Roil	117	9,409	:58.40	
1962	Keeper's Choice	2	J. Vasquez	122	Dontstopnow	122	Goer	117	9,100	1:00.40	
1963	Amastar	2	J. Nichols	125	Mom's Request	122	Dancing Brave	122	12,317	:58.20	
1964	Loom	2	J. Nichols	125	Mahjubill	122	Dark Clover	122	12,480	:58.40	
1965	He Jr.	2	J. Fieselman	125	Seaman Sinbad	122	Hard Track	122	12,122	:58.60	
1966	Willow Cage	2	B. Phelps	122	Big Tim	117	Zip Line	122	13,114	:58.60	
1967	T.V. Commercial	2	M. Manganello	125	Royal Exchange	122	Rhythmic	122	12,724	:58.20	
1968	Santiago Road	2	M. Manganello	125	Traffic Mark	122	Campbellsville	122	12,772	:57.80	
1969	Spotted Line	2	D.E. Whited	122	Buptedo	117	Whiskey Romeo	122	12,447	:59.60	
1970	Hook It Up	2	J. Nichols	122	Satan's Story	122	Laughing Dancer	122	16,087	:58.40	
1971	Whitesburg	2	T. Sisum	125	Elmer L. Brown	122	Busted	125	16,315	:58.60	
1972	Pleasure Castle	2	D.E. Whited	122	Gallant Agent	122	Game Lad	122	17,160	:58.20	
1973	Tisab	2	M. Manganello	122	No Advance	122	To the Rescue	122	16,965	:58.80	
1974	Pac Quick	2	G. Patterson	125	Paris Dust	127	Kaanapali	122	16,607	:59.60	
1975	Khyber King	2	E. Delahoussaye	122	Bold Laddie	122	Right on Mike	122	15,632	:58.60	
1976	Judge John Boone	2	E. Delahoussaye	122	Wishem Well	122	Golden Trade	117	14,625	:58.60	
1977	Going Investor	2	B. Sayler	122	Old Jake	117	Chwesboken	122	14,235	:58.40	
1978	Spy Charger	2	G. Mahon	127	Uncle Fudge	122	Vennie Redberry	122	14,089	:58.40	
1979	Rajohn Greco	2	J.C. Espinoza	122	Egg's Dynamite	122	Native Amber	122	19,451	1:00.20	
1980	Golden Derby	2	J.C. Espinoza	117	Wrong Impression	122	Stubilem	117	19,338	:59.00	
1981	T.V. Mark	2	P. Nicolo	122	Shilling	122	Good Ole Master	122	18,103	:59.60	
1982	Willow Drive	2	W.J. Neagle	115	Stepping E.J.	118	Mindboggling	115	20,264	1:05.00	
1983	Betwixt n' Between	2	P. Day	115	Real Sharp Dancer	112	Biloxi Indian	118	22,896	1:05.00	
1984	Jerry F.	2	P. Day	112	Storm Scope	115	Wet My Whistle	115	17,241	1:05.80	
1985	Tile	2	L. Melancon	115	Tug	115	Sir Grandeur	115	30,896	1:04.40	
1986	Faster Than Sound	2	C. Perret	118	Renumeration	115	Arunti	121	46,648	1:11.20	
1987	Blair's Cove	2	S.J. Sellers	114	Endurance	118	Mr. Igloo	116	37,310	1:11.80	
1988	Bio	2	P.A. Johnson	118	Revive	112	Curtis John	114	37,148	1:11.80	
1989	Summer Squall	2	P. Day	121	Table Limit	118	Appealing Breeze	121	35,068	1:12.20	
1990	To Freedom	2	J.C. Espinoza	121	Richman	121	Discover	116	35,555	1:10.20	
1991	Pick up the Phone	2	J.C. Espinoza	116	Sprintmaster	116	Thanatopsis	112	35,815	1:12.00	78
1992	Mountain Cat	2	C.R. Woods Jr	116	Tempered Halo	121	Storm Flight	116	53,869	1:10.60	85
1993	Miss Ra He Ra	2	W. Martinez	113	Ramblin Guy	116	Riverinn	112	76,180	1:12.80	72
1994	Hyroglyphic	2	Gomez GK	116	Boone's Mill	116	Hobgoblin	116	75,660	1:10.20	91
1995	A.V. Eight	2	Trosclair AJ	115	Aggie Southpaw	115	Seeker's Reward	115	71,630	1:11.40	97
1996	Boston Harbor	2	M.J. Luzzi	115	Prairie Junction	115	Nobel Talent	115	72,150	1:09.80	97
1997	Favorite Trick	2	P. Day	121	Double Honor	115	Cowboy Dan	118	68,696	1:09.80	97
1998	Time Bandit	2	C.R. Woods Jr	115	Yes It's True	121	Haus of Dehere	115	68,262	1:10.60	85

Year	Winner	Age	Jockey	Wt.	Second	Wt.	Third	Wt.Win Value	Time Beyer
1999	Dance Master	2	B.D. Peck	115	Sky Dweller	115	Snuck In	115 .. 89,280 .. 1:10.20 .. 92
2000	Duality	2	C.H. Borel	115	Strait Cat	114	Take Arms	115 .. 86,258 .. 1:10.09 .. 85
2001	Lunar Bounty	2	F. Lovato Jr.	115	Binyamin	115	Storm Passage	115 .. 82,925 .. 1:09.90 .. 80
2002	Lone Star Sky	2	M. Guidry	115	Posse	121	Cooper Crossing	115 .. 84,475 .. 1:09.68 .. 95
2003	Limehouse	2	R.J. Albarado	121	First Money	117	Cuvee	121 .. 100,905 .. 1:10.62 .. 86

Beyer Index: 86.92

BAY MEADOWS BREEDERS' CUP HANDICAP, About 1 1/8 Miles (Turf), 3-Year-Olds and Up, Bay Meadows, 2003 Purse: $142,500

Year	Winner	Age	Jockey	Wt.	Second	Wt.	Third	Wt.Win Value	Time Beyer
1934	Time Supply	3	T. Luther	123	Dark Winter	107	Fleam	105 .... 21,100 . 1:53.80
1935	Head Play	5	C. Kurtsinger	118	Time Supply	116	Gusto	110 .... 20,300 . 2:00.60
1936	Special Agent	4	G. Burns	117	Azucar	124	Uppermost	106 .... 8,100 . 1:43.00
1937	Seabiscuit	4	J. Pollard	127	Exhibit	105	Watersplash	103 .... 7,530 . 1:44.60
1938	Seabiscuit	5	G. Woolf	133	Gosum	113	Today	112 .... 11,270 . 1:49.00
1939	Specify	4	C. Corbett	121	Stands Alone	113	Sweepalot	112 .... 7,150 . 1:45.80
1940	Sweepida	3	R. Neves	123	Omelet	115	Mr. Grundy	110 .... 7,380 . 1:51.60
1941	No Comp'tion	5	F. Weidaman	115	Mount Vernon II	110	G. M'ager	114 .... 7,710 . 1:50.80
1942	Stinging Bee	3	J. Longden	110	Sir Jeffrey	112	Step By	111 .... 7,940 . 1:54.20
1943	Put In	4	G. Woolf	115	Jerry Lee	108	Kind Sir	112 .... 12,830 . 1:50.00
1944	Okana	3	A. Bassett	126	Shut Up	111	Jade Boy	121 .... 18,450 . 1:52.00
1945	No Wrinkles	5	R. Summers	112	Wise Eagle	115	S'my Angott	120 .... 20,930 . 2:00.80
1946	Adrogue	6	F. Zufelt	112	Autocrat	113	Olhaverry	120 .... 44,500 . 1:52.40
1946	Occupy	5	C. Corbett	124	Mediterranean	112	Stitch Again	124 .... 19,000 . 1:49.20
1947	Artillery	4	H. Lindberg	121	Adrogue	115	Happy Issue	113 .... 42,800 . 1:49.00
1948	Mafosta	6	J. Longden	126	Faucon	117	Hemet Squaw	109 .... 41,600 . 1:51.00
1949	Moonrush	3	B. Pearson	108	Solidarity	120	Colosal	116 .... 40,600 . 1:49.00
1950	Frankly	5	W. Shoemaker	122	Coma	108	Sun State	115 .... 12,320 . 1:49.40
1951	Moonrush	5	W. Shoemaker	121	Mocopo	110	Be Fleet	121 .... 43,700 . 1:51.20
1952	Moonrush	6	R. Neves	115	Two Lea	126	Grantor	118 .... 33,350 . 2:01.60
1953	Stranglehold	4	B. Pearson	120	Goose Khal	124	Indian Hemp	117 .... 16,150 . 1:51.80
1954	Decorated	4	J. Longden	113	Cyclotron	117	Southarlingt'n	111 .... 16,500 . 1:43.80
1955	Arrogate	4	J. Longden	120	Bobby Brocato	117	Bassanio	112 .... 13,700 . 1:42.00
1956	Holandes II	3	W. Shoemaker	122	Eugenio	118	Arrogate	122 .... 15,350 . 1:47.80
1957	Count Chic	4	M. Volzke	116	Fleet Charge	110	Battle Dance	118 .... 12,700 . 1:45.60
1958	Battle Dance	6	R. Neves	121	Ordained	113	More Glory	115 .... 10,150 . 1:42.20
1959	Promised Land	5	I. Valenzuela	122	Eddie Schmidt	120	The Searcher	111 .... 16,750 . 1:48.60
1960	Prize Host	5	W. Harmatz	112	Sea Orbit	116	Quidico	114 .... 13,100 . 1:41.40
1961	Mr. Wag	4	J. Longden	117	Typhoon II	111	Jewelsmith	113 .... 14,450 . 1:48.00
1962	Sea Orbit	6	R. York	129	My Rx	112	Mr. Wag	117 .... 13,050 . 1:44.80
1963	Mustard Plaster	4	M. Volzke	112	Dusky Damion	118	Little Juan	115 .... 13,400 . 1:43.00
1964	Biggs	4	W. Harmatz	115	Honored Sir	118	Hello Uncle	113 .... 9,125 . 1:41.60
1965	Maker's Mark	4	F. Costa	121	Gainstrive	112	By the Way II	112 .... 9,025 . 1:49.80
1966	Diamond Lou	4	P. Frey	120	Black Pool	116	Quicken Tree	113 .... 13,425 . 1:42.80
1967	No Host	4	A. Maese	116	Aqua Vite	121	Plimenek	117 .... 16,500 . 1:41.60
							Father Dino	118	
1968	Praise Jay	4	A. Pineda	114	His Boy II	114	Kings Favor	119 .... 17,650 . 1:42.40
1969	Field Master	5	I. Valenzuela	115	Royal Fols	119	True Balcony	114 .... 18,550 . 1:41.80
1970	Traffic Beat	5	M. Volzke	115	Try Sheep	110	Dizzy Babe	124 .... 15,650 . 1:50.60
1971	Silver Double	5	L. Wall	120	Dagmar's Boy	112	Domineering	114 .... 19,000 . 1:49.40
1972	Timoteo	4	F. Alvarez	113	Vitenpost	113	Ipse	114 .... 18,000 . 1:47.40
1973	Partner's Hope	4	A.L. Diaz	117	Ipse	116	Woodland Pines	118 .... 17,525 . 1:43.20
1974	Indefatigable	4	D. Pierce	117	Star of Kuwait	116	Confederate Yankee	115 .. 31,900 . 1:41.40
1975	Bahia Key	5	F. Olivares	122	Fleet Velvet	120	Holding Pattern	120 .. 31,700 . 1:43.00
1976	Life's Hope	3	D.G. McHargue	118	Fighting Bill	113	Podium	117 .. 31,400 . 1:43.40
1977	Painted Wagon	4	M.S. Sellers	120	Sudanes	117	Mark's Place	123 .. 51,000 . 1:41.40
1978	Bywayofchicago	4	F. Toro	122	Noble Bronze	113	As de Copas	119 .. 72,000 . 1:50.80
1979	Leonotis	6	M. Gonzalez	118	John Henry	123	Capt. Don	117 .. 69,900 . 1:49.60
1980	Super Moment	3	F. Toro	116	Fleet Tempo	114	Mike Fogarty	118 .. 68,600 . 1:46.20
1981	Super Moment	4	L. Pincay Jr	124	Tahitian King	121	The Bart	126 .. 98,400 . 1:53.60
1982	Super Moment	5	R.A. Baze	120	Buchanette	113	Les Aspres	112 .. 132,400 . 1:51.60
1983	Interco	3	J.C. Judice	116	Super Sunrise	116	Floriano	114 .. 179,200 . 1:55.40
1984	Scrupules	4	E. Delahoussaye	117	Raami	120	Both Ends Burning	123 .. 178,500 . 2:17.20
1985	Drumalis	4	R.Q. Meza	116	Silveyville	121	Talakeno	115 .. 165,000 . 1:47.00
1986	Palace Music	5	F. Toro	123	Nugget Point	113	Barberry	116 .. 165,000 . 1:50.60
1987	Show Dancer	5	M. Castaneda	113	Skip out Front	114	Exclusive Partner	116 .. 165,000 . 1:47.80
1988	Wait Til Monday	4	R. Dominguez	113	Miswaki Tern	113	Skip out Front	117 .. 137,500 . 1:46.00
1989	Ten Keys	5	K.J. Desormeaux	118	Colway Rally	116	Nediym	113 .. 137,500 . 1:46.60
1990	Robinski	7	J. Velasquez	112	Sekondi	113	Rushing Raj	113 .. 137,500 . 1:50.80
1991	French Seventyfive	4	G. Boulanger	112	Forty Niner Days	116	Batshoof	116 .. 137,500 . 1:49.40 .. 104
1992	Forty Niner Days	5	C.S. Nakatani	115	Bistro Garden	115	Luthier Enchanteur	118 .. 137,500 . 1:46.40 .. 104
1993	Slew of Damascus	5	T.M. Chapman	114	Fast Cure	115	Lissitki	112 .. 110,000 . 1:45.80 .. 102

Year	Winner	Age	Jockey	Wt.	Second	Wt.	Third	Wt.	Win Value	Time	Beyer
1994	Blues Traveller	4	Stevens GL.	116	Fastness	116	Wharf	114.	110,000	1:46.00	105
1995	Caesour	5	Baze RA.	115	Johann Quatz	115	Canaska Dancer.	113.	110,000	1:45.40	107
1996	Gentlemen	4	C.S. Nakatani	117	Party Season	116	Petit Poucet	119.	110,000	1:45.80	106
1997	El Angelo	5	A. Solis.	119	Via Lombardia	115	Dreamer	115.	110,000	1:45.40	110
1998	Hawksley Hill	5	A. Solis.	120	Magellan	117	Floriselli	114.	110,000	1:45.40	109
1999	Kirkwall.	5	V. Espinoza	114	Special Quest.	115	Game Ploy	113.	110,000	1:47.13	100
2000	Devine Wind	4	G.K. Gomez	114	Irish Prize	115	Deploy Venture	117.	110,000	1:47.19	103
2001	Super Quercus	4	R.A. Baze	117	Most Likely	112	Sign of Hope	116.	55,000	1:47.50	102
2002	David Copperfield.	5	J. Lumpkins	117	Ninebanks	115	Little Ghazi	115.	110,000	1:48.95	101
2003	Mister Acpen.	5	R.M. Gonzalez	116	Fateful Dream	117	Ninebanks	118.	55,000	1:46.94	105

Beyer Index: 104.46

BAY MEADOWS BREEDERS' CUP SPRINT HANDICAP, 6 Furlongs, 3-Year-Olds and Up, Bay Meadows, 2003 Purse: $142,500

Year	Winner	Age	Jockey	Wt.	Second	Wt.	Third	Wt.	Win Value	Time	Beyer
1995	Lucky Forever	6	G.Almeida	116	Wild Gold	115	Uncaged Fury.	115.	117,700	1:08.60	102
1996	Boundless Moment	4	K.Desormeaux	116	Concept Win	115	Paying Dues	119.	110,000	1:08.80	102
1997	Tres Paraiso	5	C.Nakatani	116	Mshk's Pride	112	Boundless Moment	117.	110,000	1:07.80	107
1998	Musafi	4	D.Flores	116	The Barking Shark.	116			110,000	1:08.40	103
					Mr. Doubledown	116					
1999	Big Jag.	6	J.Valdivia	118	Men 's Exclusive.	115	Lexicon	116.	110,000	1:08.80	110
2000	Lexicon	5	R.Baze	115	Men 's Exclusive.	115	Dixie Dot Com	116.	110,000	1:09.09	105
2001	Lexicon	6	R.A. Baze	117	Swept Overboard	117	You and You Alone	115.	82,500	1:07.94	106
2002	Mellow Fellow	7	R.A. Baze	119	Explicit	120	Swept Oveboard	122.	110,000	1:08.35	108
2003	El Dorado Shooter	6	C.P. Schvaneveldt	120	Halo Cat.	118	Radar Contact	116.	82,500	1:08.61	102

Beyer Index: 105

BAY MEADOWS DERBY, 1 1/8 Miles (Turf), 3-Year-Olds, Bay Meadows, 2003 Purse: $100,000

Year	Winner	Age	Jockey	Wt.	Second	Wt.	Third	Wt.	Win Value	Time	Beyer
1954	Determine	3	R. York.	126	Allied	120	Fault Free	114.	15,800	1:49.20	
1957	Round Table	3	R. Neves	122	Swirling Abbey	122	Irisher	122.	24,375	1:41.60	
1978	Quip	3	T. Lipham	115	Shagbark	115	Kamehameha	123.	34,250	1:45.20	
1979	Nain Bleu	3	C. Baltazar	113	Bends Me Mind.	118	Gummaka	115.	32,300	1:45.40	
1980	Fleet Tempo	3	R.M. Gonzalez.	114	Super Moment	123	Aliyoun	112.	32,750	1:44.60	
1981	Silveyville.	3	D. Winick	120	Sunshine Swag	115	Tempo's Tiger	117.	67,000	1:48.20	
1982	Ask Me.	3	F. Toro	120	Water Bank	120	Take the Floor	121.	66,100.		
1983	Interco.	3	J.C. Judice	116	Bang Bang Bang.	112	Baron o'Dublin.	120.	63,500	1:49.60	
1984	Mangaki	3	C. Lamance	115	Refueled	117	Foscarini	120.	68,400	1:52.00	
1985	Minutes Away	3	C.R. Hummel	115	Charming Duke	124	Lucky n Green	115.	56,800	1:51.40	
1986	Le Belvedere	3	W. Shoemaker.	113	Santella Mac	115	Grand Exchange	116.	81,300	1:47.60	
1987	Hot and Smoggy	3	J. Vasquez.	117	Wolsey	116	Lucky Harold H.	115.	66,400	1:48.60	
1988	Coax Me Clyde	3	R.J. Warren Jr.	118	Gran Judgement.	116	Literati	117.	68,500	1:49.00	
1989	Irish	3	M.A. Espindola.	115	Polar Boy	115	Two Moccasins	113.	55,000	1:48.20	
1990	Sekondi.	3	R.M. Gonzalez.	114	Courtesy Title.	115	Appealing Missy	113.	55,000	1:48.80	97
1991	Bistro Garden	3	M. Castaneda	120	Dominion Gold	116	Fraise	115.	82,500	1:46.60	102
1992	Star Recruit.	3	R.D. Hansen	115	Siberian Summer	116	Fax News	115.	55,000	1:49.00	108
1993	Ranger	3	G. Boulanger	114	El Atroz	113	Guide	120.	55,000	1:48.80	98
1994	Marvin's Faith	3	Castaneda M.	116	Western Trader.	116	Turbo Fan	115.	55,000	1:48.80	101
1995	Virginia Carnival	3	Warren RJ Jr.	115	Helmsman.	114	Tabor	115.	55,000	1:46.00	100
1996	Ocean Queen	3	J.A. Garcia	110	Mateo	115	Mystic Knight	116.	110,000	1:47.80	99
1997	Shellbacks	3	R.Q. Meza	113	Brave Act	122	Zippersup.	122.	82,500	1:49.00	101
1998	Takarian	3	C.A. Black.	116	I.M. Bzy	115	Prevalence.	114.	82,500	1:46.80	99
1999	Mula Gula.	3	R.Q. Meza	117	Miss Chryss	111	Fighting Falcon.	120.	82,500	1:45.34	100
2000	Walkslikeaduck	3	E. Delahoussaye	122	Jokerman	119	Calamari.	115.	82,500	1:46.57	101
2001	Blue Steller	3	A. Solis.	119	Sir Alfred.	116	Sea to See	116.	55,000	1:46.81	94
2002	Royal Gem	3	R.A. Baze	119	Aly Bubba	114	Century City.	122.	55,000	1:48.38	89
2003	Stanley Park	3	E. Saint-Martin	116	Bis Repetitas	118	Kewen	116.	55,000	1:48.97	96

Beyer Index: 98.93

BAY SHORE, 7 Furlongs, 3-Year-Olds, Aqueduct, 2003 Purse: $150,000

Year	Winner	Age	Jockey	Wt.	Second	Wt.	Third	Wt.	Win Value	Time	Beyer
1960	Francis S.	3	H. Moreno.	119	Don Rickles	118	Count Amber	116.	18,842	1:36.00	
1961	Merry Ruler	3	R.L. Gilbert.	115	Hy-Nat.	111	Stan the Man	111.	18,850	1:36.40	
1962	Duc d'Or	3	I. Valenzuela	113	Sidluck.	113	Lucky Uncle	112.	14,137	1:36.40	
1962	Western Warrior	3	L. Adams	111	MIster Pitt	110	Dedimoud	112.	14,137	1:36.40	
1963	Jet Traffic	3	R. Ussery.	120	Top Gallant.	112	Bonjour	123.	18,322	1:34.20	
1964	Determined Man	3	J. Ruane.	110	Lord Date	112	Alphabet.	113.	18,687	1:23.20	
1965	Flag Raiser	3	I. Valenzuela	114	Turn to Reason	111	Tom Rolfe	120.	18,915	1:23.60	
1966	Quinta	3	W. Blum.	114	Impressive	128	Buffle	113.	18,785	1:22.80	

Year	Winner	Age	Jockey	Wt.	Second	Wt.	Third	Wt.	Win Value	Time	Beyer
1967	Damascus	3	W. Shoemaker	115	Disciplinarian	117	Nehoc's Bullet	110	18,590	1:25.80	
1968	Verbatim	3	J.L. Rotz	118	Wellpoised	112	Sir Beau	115	14,576	1:24.20	
1968	Clever Foot	3	J. Culmone	124	Irish Chief	113	Czar Alexander	110	14,576	1:26.00	
1969	Reviewer	3	R. Ussery	130	Hey Good Lookin	113	I Found Gold	111	17,972	1:22.80	
1970	Sunny Tim	3	C. Baltazar	117	Native Royalty	110	Delaware Chief	111	19,435	1:24.20	
1971	Hoist the Flag	3	J. Cruguet	126	Droll Role	117	Jim French	121	20,640	1:21.00	
1972	Explodent	3	M. Venezia	120	Eager Exchange	120	Gay Gallant	112	17,175	1:23.40	
1973	Secretariat	3	R. Turcotte	126	Champagne Charlie	118	Impecunious	126	16,650	1:23.20	
1974	Hudson County	3	M. Miceli	113	Frankie Adams	119	Instead of Roses	116	34,680	1:22.60	
1975	Laramie Trail	3	M. Venezia	113	T.V. Charger	113	Ascetic	121	26,910	1:23.60	
1975	Lefty	3	R. Turcotte	113	Tass	113	Gallant Bob	118	27,360	1:23.80	
1976	Bold Forbes	3	A. Cordero Jr	119	Eustace	121	Full Out	124	33,780	1:20.80	
1977	Cormorant	3	D. Wright	121	Medieval Man	119	Hey Hey J.P.	114	32,460	1:10.80	
1978	Piece of Heaven	3	R. Hernandez	119	Just Right Classi	114	Slap Jack	114	32,460	1:11.00	
1979	Belle's Gold	3	G. Martens	114	Screen King	121	General Assembly	123	32,040	1:21.80	
1980	Colonel Moran	3	J. Velasquez	121	Son of a Dodo	115	Dunham's Gift	114	34,260	1:23.80	
1981	Proud Appeal	3	J. Fell	121	Willow Hour	114	Royal Pavilion	114	32,940	1:22.20	
1982	Shimatoree	3	A. Cordero Jr	114	Big Brave Rock	114	John's Gold	114	33,000	1:23.20	
1983	Strike Gold	3	E. Maple	114	Assault Landing	114	Chas Conerly	114	34,620	1:22.60	
1984	Secret Prince	3	C. Perret	114	The Wedding Guest	126	I'm a Rounder	114	65,580	1:11.20	
1985	Pancho Villa	3	F. Lovato Jr	114	El Basco	114	Spend a Buck	123	97,020	1:22.20	
1986	Zabaleta	3	D.G. McHargue	115	Groovy	117	Belocolus	114	95,250	1:22.00	
1986	Buck Aly	3	N. Santagata	117	Landing Plot	119	Raja's Revenge	119	95,250	1:23.80	
1987	Gulch	3	J.A. Santos	123	High Brite	119	Shawklit Won	114	124,800	1:23.20	
1988	Perfect Spy	3	R.G. Davis	119	Success Express	123	Proud and Valid	117	98,460	1:22.60	
1989	Houston	3	L. Pincay Jr	116	Mr. Nickerson	114	Wee Stark	119	69,000	1:22.40	
1990	Richard R.	3	J.A. Santos	117	For Really	114	Dangerous Dawn	114	70,080	1:22.80	98
1991	Stately Wager	3	J.F. Chavez	119	Mineral Ice	119	Vouch for Me	117	71,040	1:23.80	97
1992	Three Peat	3	C.W. Antley	114	Goldwater	117	Best Decorated	114	75,600	1:21.60	105
1994	Prank Call	3	J.R. Velazquez	113	Mr. Shawklit	117	Popol's Gold	122	65,940	1:09.80	93
1995	Blissful State	3	M.J Luzzi	118	Northern Ensign	113	Pat n Jac	115	64,680	1:23.80	89
1996	Jamies First Punch	3	J.R. Velazquez	115	Gold Fever	115	Firey Jennifer	115	67,220	1:22.00	102
1997	Hawks Landing	3	R. Migliore	114	Adverse	113	Standing on Edge	113	66,480	1:22.00	95
1998	Limit Out	3	J.L. Samyn	115	Good and Tough	113	Diamond Studs	113	65,460	1:20.40	116
1999	Perfect Score	3	E.S. Prado	118	Royal Ruby	114	Prince Monty	116	66,120	1:22.98	88
2000	Precise End	3	J.F. Chavez	116	Turnofthecentury	114	Port Herman	114	66,000	1:22.27	99
2001	Skip to the Stoe	3	V. Espinoza	120	Multiple Choice	116	Friday's A Comin'	120	90,000	1:22.46	96
2002	Roman Dancer	3	K.J. Desormeaux	120	Warners	116	Monthir	116	90,000	1:22.21	101
2003	Halo Homewrecker	3	J.R. Velazquez	116	Don Six	116	Stanislavsky	116	90,000	1:23.19	96

Beyer Index: 98.08

BEAUGAY HANDICAP, 1 1/16 Miles (Turf), Fillies and Mares 3-Year-Olds and Up, Aqueduct, 2003 Purse: $112,400

Year	Winner	Age	Jockey	Wt.	Second	Wt.	Third	Wt.	Win Value	Time	Beyer
1978	Shukey	3	J. Velasquez	113	Sans Critique	118	Whodatorsay	109	25,755	1:45.20	
1979	Plankton	3	R. Hernandez	113	Miss Baja	114	Reflection Pool	112	25,612	1:46.00	
1979	Heavenly Ade	3	S. Solomone	114	Propitiate	112	Gladiolus	122	25,612	1:45.60	
1980	Samarta Dancer	4	L. Saumell	114	Plankton	121	Bien Fait	109	33,540	1:43.60	
1981	Andover Way	4	A. Cordero Jr	120	Water Dance	117	Tournament Star	109	34,440	1:44.00	
1982	Cheap Seats	3	A. Cordero Jr	113	Tina Tina Too	115	Fancy Naskra	112	33,780	1:45.20	
1983	Trevita	6	J. Velasquez	119	Beech Island	108	Top of the B'rr'l	105	37,020	1:47.80	
1984	Thirty Flags	4	A. Cordero Jr	113	Jubilous	114	Nany	111	45,840	1:42.00	
1985	Possible Mate	4	J. Vasquez	119	Make the Magic	109	Annie Edge	114	42,600	1:40.60	
1986	Duty Dance	4	J. Cruguet	115	Possible Mate	124	Lucky Touch	109	55,800	1:40.20	
1987	Give a Toast	4	R.G. Davis	111	Videogenic	117	Small Virtue	113	68,940	1:44.20	
1988	Key to the Bridge	4	E. Maple	109	Mrimascus	112	Just Class	115	65,160	1:51.80	
1989	Summer Secretary	4	J.L. Samyn	109	Far East	110	Fieldy	116	56,880	1:43.40	
1990	Fieldy	7	C. Perret	119	Summer Secretary	114	Lady Talc	110	52,740	1:45.80	99
1991	Summer Secretary	6	J. Velasquez	116	Virgin Michael	113	Christiecat	115	54,270	1:40.00	102
1992	Christiecat	5	J.L. Samyn	116	Metamorphose	113	Navarra	109	56,520	1:46.80	105
1993	McKaymackenna	4	J. Velasquez	113	Aurora	115	Chinese Empress	114	57,240	1:44.80	97
1994	Cox Orange	4	J.D. Bailey	112	Irish Linnet	116	Statuette	116	49,395	1:43.20	99
1995	Caress	4	Davis RG	113	Shir Dar	113	Statuette	116	49,905	1:42.00	101
1996	Christmas Gift	4	J.D. Bailey	118	Caress	119	Aucilla	113	50,805	1:42.80	98
1997	Careless Heiress	4	J. Bravo	116	Song of Africa	113	Gastronomical	115	65,760	1:46.20	100
1998	National Treasure	5	R. Migliore	117	Aspiring	113	Dixie Ghost	111	67,740	1:37.80	90
1999	Tampico	6	J.R. Velazquez	114	U R Unforgetable	115	Shashobegon	114	67,020	1:44.32	101
2000	Perfect Sting	4	J.D. Bailey	119	License Fee	114	Fictitious	114	65,820	1:42.30	101
2001	Gaviola	4	J.D. Bailey	120	Truebreadpudding	113	Efficient Frontier	114	65,940	1:41.74	98
2002	Voodoo Dancer	4	J.D. Bailey	119	Golden Corona	115	Babae	116	67,920	1:43.10	102
2003	Delta Princess	4	M.J. Luzzi	113	Wonder Again	118	Voodoo Dancer	120	67,440	1:42.36	99

Beyer Index: 99.43

BED O' ROSES BREEDERS' CUP HANDICAP, 1 Mile,
Fillies and Mares 3-Year-Olds and Up, Aqueduct, 2003 Purse: $155,100

Year	Winner	Age	Jockey	Wt.	Second	Wt.	Third	Wt.	Win Value	Time	Beyer
1957	Little Pache	4	C. McCreary	121	Gay Life	112	Manotick	118	18,900	1:47.00	
1958	Outer Space	4	W. Boland	113	Lori-El	110	Searching	123	17,575	1:43.80	
1959	Big Effort	4	E. Nelson	122	A Glitter	120	Mlle. Dianne	117	18,257	1:44.20	
1960	Chistosa	5	H. Woodhouse	106	Royal Native	128	Craftiness	110	17,542	1:36.40	
1961	Prince's Gate	4	E. Arcaro	113	Make Sail	117	Teacation	119	18,297	1:36.60	
1962	Seven Thirty	4	L. Adams	121	Epitome	108	Rose O'Neill	121	19,240	1:36.20	
1963	Royal Patrice	4	I. Valenzuela	119	Cyclopavia	117	Nubile	109	18,492	1:39.20	
1964	Spicy Living	4	M. Ycaza	123	Look Ma	108	Oil Royalty	122	13,959	1:38.60	
1964	Beauful	5	W. Mayorga	110	Pams Ego	122	Smart Deb	127	13,959	1:37.80	
1965	Steeple Jill	4	J. Ruane	118	Petticoat	114	Treachery	116	18,590	1:35.80	
1966	Straight Deal	4	R. Ussery	117	What a Treat	126	Queen Empress	123	18,167	1:35.80	
1967	Straight Deal	5	R. Ussery	122	Indian Sunlite	116	Kerensa	110	18,297	1:37.60	
1968	Too Bald	4	M. Ycaza	123	Amerigo Lady	120	Treacherous	114	18,362	1:35.00	
1969	Heartland	4	J.L. Rotz	123	A Pleasant Sort	111	Treacherous	114	18,590	1:35.80	
1970	Watch Fob	5	H. Gustines	111	Process Shot	128	Someday	114	18,525	1:36.80	
1971	Office Queen	4	C. Baltazar	125	Shuvee	127	Royal Fillet	110	19,680	1:36.80	
1972	Red Shoes	4	A. Loguercio	118	Aladancer	119	Dares J.	113	16,680	1:36.40	
1973	Poker Night	3	R. Woodhouse	108	Numbered Account	123	Ferly	114	16,605	1:35.40	
1974	Klepto	4	D. Montoya	123	Ladies Agreement	112	Summer Guest	122	16,410	1:35.40	
1975	Shy Dawn	4	D. Montoya	121	Something Super	118	Flo's Pleasure	115	16,860	1:36.20	
1976	Imminence	4	E. Maple	115	Spring Is Here	108	Land Girl	114	23,040	1:35.40	
1977	Shawi	4	M. Venezia	109	Proud Delta	125	Secret Lanvin	111	25,770	1:45.80	
1978	Fearless Queen	5	M. Venezia	108	Notably	110	One Sum	123	25,785	1:46.20	
1979	Lady Lonsdale	4	C.B. Asmussen	111	Hagany	113	Back to Stay	107	31,980	1:36.80	
1979	One Sum	5	J. Fell	118	Reflection Pool	113	Pearl Necklace	121	31,980	1:37.80	
1980	Misty Gallore	4	D. MacBeth	125	Propitiate	115	Gueniviere	111	33,600	1:36.40	
1981	Chain Bracelet	4	F. Lovato Jr	114	Lady Oakley	116	Contrary Rose	115	33,960	1:35.40	
1982	Who's to Answer	4	E. Beitia	108	Real Prize	114	Faisana	110	33,180	1:36.60	
1983	Broom Dance	4	G. McCarron	118	Adept	109	Viva Sec	112	33,420	1:35.40	
1984	Pleasure Cay	4	R.G. Davis	115	Sweet Missus	103	Sintrillium	113	54,090	1:42.00	
1985	Nany	5	J. Vasquez	120	Flip's Pleasure	118	Sintrillium	120	50,850	1:36.00	
1986	Chaldea	6	J.L. Samyn	115	Add Mint	112	Lady on the Run	120	75,120	1:36.00	
1987	Ms. Eloise	4	R.G. Davis	115	Spring Beauty	116	Tricky Squaw	115	84,660	1:36.60	
1988	Aptostar	3	J.A. Krone	103	Clabber Girl	117	Psyched	114	70,680	1:35.40	
1989	Banker's Lady	4	A. Cordero Jr	118	Aptostar	118	Avie's Gal	114	68,400	1:35.40	
1990	Survive	6	J.A. Santos	117	Amy Be Good	114	Warfie	111	68,640	1:34.20	
1991	Devil's Orchid	4	R. Baez	120	Colonial Waters	119	Sharp Dance	114	68,520	1:35.80	104
1992	Nannerl	5	J.A. Krone	115	English Charm	111	Spy Leader Lady	115	68,100	1:37.20	102
1992	Lady D'Accord	4	J.F. Chavez	110	My Treasure	112	Crystal Vous	112	68,580	1:37.80	96
1993	Lady D'Accord	6	J.D. Chavez	111	Missy's Mirage	123	Buck Some Belle	106	67,320	1:36.60	96
1994	Classy Mirage	4	R.G. Davis	117	For All Season	115	Dispute	122	64,680	1:34.00	108
1995	Incinerate	5	F. Leon	113	Imah	114	Beckys Shirt	113	63,960	1:35.80	96
1996	Punkin Pie	6	J. Trejo	110	Incinerate	115	Lottsa Talc	121	65,220	1:35.00	95
1997	Flat Fleet Feet	4	M.E. Smith	121	Mama Dean	113	Ashboro	116	95,940	1:34.00	103
1998	Dixie Flag	4	M.J. Luzzi	117	Hidden Reserve	113	U Can Do It	118	96,780	1:33.60	109
1999	Catinca	4	R. Migliore	110	Foil	113	License Fee	113	94,620	1:34.95	99
2000	Ruby Rubles	5	C.C. Lopez	113	Up We Go	114	Go To The Ink	111	65,580	1:36.96	103
2001	Country Hideaway	5	J.R. Velazquez	117	Critical Eye	115	Jostle	117	95,520	1:34.98	102
2002	Raging Fever	4	J.R. Velazquez	121	Atelier	119	Shiny Band	112	94,980	1:34.96	98
2003	Raging Fever	5	A.T. Gryder	119	Smok'n Frolic	120	Nonsuch Bay	117	93,960	1:34.86	101

Beyer Index: 100.86

BEN ALI, 1 1/8 Miles,
4-Year-Olds and Up, Keeneland Race Course, 2003 Purse: $106,991

Year	Winner	Age	Jockey	Wt.	Second	Wt.	Third	Wt.	Win Value	Time	Beyer
1917	Colonel Vennie	4	W. Crump	125	Embroidery	108	Marion Goosby	110	1,941	1:46.00	
1918	Opportunity	4	E. Pool	111	Arriet	107	Bribed Voter	104	1,710	1:53.80	
1919	Exterminator	4	J. Morys	124	American Ace	99	Midway	120	2,615	1:50.40	
1920	General Haig	4	M. Garner	110	Regalo	106	Pictor	114	3,460	1:50.00	
1921	Best Pal	4	L. Lyke	116	Ginger	112	Pluribus	107	3,630	1:46.60	
1922	United Verde	4	M. Garner	112	Advocate	108	Rouleau	112	3,280	1:45.60	
1937	Count Morse	4	I. Anderson	117	Dellor	108	White Tie	105	2,700	1:46.20	
1938	Main Man	4	W.F. Yard	120	Old Nassau	110	Galsun	110	2,800	1:45.00	
1939	Burning Star	5	W. Yarberry	120	Birthday	114	Arabs Arrow	117	2,550	1:47.00	
1940	Arabs Arrow	6	C. Bierman	116	Shot Put	106	Easy Mon	122	2,625	1:48.80	
1941	Red Dock	4	A. Bodiou	114	Viscounty	117	Blue Pair	106	2,675	1:46.00	
1942	Steel Heels	6	J. George	116	Aonbarr	116	Get Off	115	2,700	1:46.40	
1943	Aletern	4	J. Adams	114	Valdina Orphan	123	Corydon	113	2,375	1:46.20	
1944	Alquest	4	J. Adams	113	Anticlimax	115	Parasang	110	4,025	1:45.60	

Year	Winner	Age	Jockey	Wt.	Second	Wt.	Third	Wt.	Win Value	Time	Beyer
1945	Pot o' Luck	3	D. Dodson	110	Colonel Read	105	Cold Crack	111	3,800	1:46.60	
1946	Bull Play	4	R. Campbell	110	Letmenow	114	South Dakota	116	4,475	1:44.40	
1947	Pot o' Luck	5	D. Dodson	121	Jack S.L.	112	Bymeabond	115	8,600	1:44.00	
1948	Fervent	4	N.L. Pierson	124	Colosal	116	Star Reward	115	9,350	1:43.80	
1949	Shy Guy	4	C. McCreary	120	Pellicle	106	Free America	114	8,250	1:45.00	
1950	Mount Marcy	5	K. Church	117	Commodore Lea	112	Flying Disc	103	8,850	1:43.80	
1951	Wistful	5	D. Dodson	112	Counterpoint	105	Little Imp	110	8,250	1:45.00	
1952	Seaward	7	S. Brooks	113	Ruhe	114	Hedgewood	110	8,280	1:45.00	
1953	Oil Capitol	6	C. McCreary	119	Seaward	112	Breeze By	104	7,880	1:44.00	
1954	Mister Black	5	J. Adams	122	Second Avenue	113	Greatest	112	8,442	1:27.00	
1955	Sea O Erin	4	S. Brooks	122	Smoke Screen	113	Mister Black	122	8,012	1:27.40	
1956	Timely Tip	5	J.L. Rotz	110	Sea O Erin	124	Breakers	113	8,800	1:27.80	
1957	Star Rover	5	J. Heckmann	118	Sea O Erin	118	Tommy's Jet	113	8,070	1:25.60	
1958	Safe Message	4	D. Dodson	113	Shan Pac	115	Ezgo	121	8,037	1:26.40	
1959	Greek Chief	4	W. Hartack	113	Nadir	125	Gleeman	112	8,395	1:26.60	
1960	Fulcrum	5	S. Brooks	111	Dunce	118	Shan Pac	112	7,591	1:25.40	
1961	Cactus Tom	4	L. Hansman	114	Eight Again	117	Careless John	120	7,979	1:26.80	
1962	Run for Nurse	5	S. Brooks	118	Bluescope	122	Editorialist	122	7,735	1:25.60	
1963	Decidedly	4	J. Nichols	121	Times Roman	115	Gun Glory	114	7,199	1:41.40	
1964	Copy Chief	4	D. Brumfield	117	Choker	118	Lemon Twist	115	11,505	1:42.00	
1965	Gallant Romeo	4	W. Knapp	114	Alphabet	112	Big Brigade	112	14,950	1:42.80	
1966	Swift Ruler	4	L. Spraker	124	Big Brigade	117	Charolero	114	14,690	1:42.80	
1967	Francis U.	4	R.J. Campbell	119	Swift Ruler	120	Moccasin	116	15,080	1:45.00	
1968	Miracle Hill	4	R. Gallimore	121	Gay Flight	114	Air Boat	113	14,300	1:42.60	
1969	Court Recess	4	E. Guerin	116	Miracle Hill	119	Gleaming Sw'd	115	15,015	1:44.60	
1970	Gallant Moment	6	D. Kassen	110	True North	114	Bold Favorite	118	15,047	1:42.60	
1971	Great Mystery	4	P.I. Grimm	117	Early Fall	112	True North	121	14,560	1:41.80	
1972	Knight Counter	4	D. Brumfield	114	No No Billy	115	Tribal Line	117	15,405	1:43.40	
1973	Knight Counter	5	D. Brumfield	120	Guitar Player	118	Introductivo	114	18,785	1:43.00	
1974	Knight Counter	6	E. Fires	119	Model Husband	117	Jim's Alibhi	113	17,647	1:41.80	
1975	Navajo	5	J. Nichols	122	L. Grant Jr.	118	Hasty Flyer	115	19,419	1:43.80	
1976	My Friend Gus	4	D.G. McHargue	114	Packer Captain	116	Dragset	113	18,119	1:42.40	
1977	Honest Pleasure	4	C. Perret	124	Inca Roca	118	Packer Captain	113	18,623	1:42.40	
1978	Prince Majestic	4	E. Delahoussaye	118	Inca Roca	114	All the More	122	21,824	1:41.80	
1979	Kodiack	5	G. Gallitano	114	Hot Words	113	Morning Frolic	115	31,054	1:49.60	
1980	Architect	4	S.A. Spencer	120	Revivalist	116	All the More	116	27,999	1:48.80	
1981	Withholding	4	B. Sayler	113	Summer Advocate	113	Two's a Plenty	115	34,986	1:50.20	
1982	Withholding	5	L. Melancon	121	Aspro	122	Swinging Light	113	35,880	1:49.60	
1983	Aspro	5	V. Bracciale Jr.	115	Thirty Eight Paces	116	Rivalero	121	35,588	1:49.60	
1984	Aspro	6	D. Brumfield	116	Play Fellow	123	Jack Slade	115	34,564	1:50.80	
1985	Bello	4	G. Gallitano	116	Silent King	117	Hi Pi	113	35,295	1:48.80	
1986	Czar Nijinsky	4	W.H. McCauley	119	Little Missouri	114	Minneapple	117	43,541	1:50.20	
1987	Intrusion	5	S. Hawley	111	Coaxing Mark	114	Blue Buckaroo	117	34,678	1:49.60	
1988	Homebuilder	4	D. Brumfield	119	Bet Twice	126	Blue Buckaroo	117	52,293	1:51.40	
1989	Classic Account	4	P. Day	114	Regal Classic	117	Brian's Time	121	53,885	1:50.60	
1990	Master Speaker	5	J.D. Bailey	121	Lac Ouimet	114	Silver Survivor	119	54,890	1:49.00	
1991	Sports View	4	C. Perret	119	Bright Again	113	Exemplary Leader	112	53,490	1:49.60	114
1992	Profit Key	5	S. Sellers	119			Out of Place	119	34,210	1:49.80	110
	Loach	4	P.A. Valenzuela	117							105
1993	Sunny Sunrise	6	R. Wilson	119	Conte di Savoya	113	Prize Fight	112	50,933	1:48.80	103
1994	Pistols and Roses	5	M.E. Smith	123	Sunny Sunrise	119	Compadre	113	50,251	1:51.60	105
1995	Wildly Joyous	4	Walls MK	114	Danville	117	Powerful Punch	113	50,406	1:49.60	99
1996	Knockadoon	4	J.D. Bailey	112	Halo's Image	117	Thorny Crown	113	66,216	1:48.80	106
1997	Louis Quatorze	4	P. Day	119	Knockadoon	113	King James	113	66,526	1:49.60	115
1998	Storm Broker	4	R.J. Albarado	114	Delay of Game	119	Gator Dancer	114	67,208	1:48.20	106
1999	Jazz Club	4	P. Day	115	Smile Again	115	Early Warning	115	67,456	1:48.16	104
2000	Midway Magistrate	6	S.J. Sellers	116	Liberty Gold	116	Early Warning	118	67,518	1:49.15	101
2001	Broken Vow	4	E.S. Prado	116	Perfect Cat	116	Jadada	116	66,216	1:48.47	116
2002	Duckhorn	5	J.F. Chavez	116	Parade Leader	120	Connected	118	66,464	1:50.18	114
2003	Mineshaft	4	R.J. Albarado	120	American Style	116	Metatron	116	68,386	1:48.52	116

Beyer Index: 108.14

BERKELEY HANDICAP, 1 Mile,
3-Year-Olds and Up, Golden Gate Fields, 2003 Purse: $100,000

Year	Winner	Age	Jockey	Wt.	Second	Wt.	Third	Wt.	Win Value	Time	Beyer
1981	Head Hawk	5	D. Sorenson	111	His Honor	115	Beau Moro	117	25,750	1:45.60	
1982	Foyt's Ack	7	R.M. Gonzalez	115	Borrego Sun	118	Pleasant Power	112	25,650	1:38.00	
1983	Pleasant Power	5	J.R. Anderson	115	Lord Advocate	117	Red Crescent	119	27,800	1:40.60	
1984	Songhay	5	J.C. Judice	114	Grand Balcony	113	The Jandy Man	113	27,300	1:35.40	
1985	Nak Ack	4	J.C. Judice	114	Holmbury	113	Chum Salmon	116	26,600	1:36.20	
1986	Sun Master	5	M. Castaneda	117	Beldale Lear	123	Prairie Breaker	114	25,400	1:34.60	

Year	Winner	Age	Jockey	Wt.	Second	Wt.	Third	Wt.	Win Value	Time	Beyer
1987	Rocky Marriage	7	R. Baze	116	Dormello	115	Bagdad Dawn	112	32,250	1:36.80	
1988	Sanger Chief	5	T.T. Doocy	114	Lucky Harold H.	114	Power Forward	119	31,900	1:35.60	
1989	Ongoing Mister	4	T.T. Doocy	114	Present Value	113	Lucky Harold H.	110	33,600	1:34.20	
1990	On the Menu	4	C.L. Davenport	112	Crackedbell	116	Ongoing Mister	117	31,600	1:34.80	99
1991	High Energy	4	R. Warren Jr.	115	Bold Current	114	Beau's Alliance	115	32,800	1:35.60	90
1992	Music Prospector	5	R.D. Hansen	118	Michael's Flyer	115	Flying Continental	124	31,450	1:35.20	97
1993	Infamous Deed	5	R. Warren Jr.	115	Misty Wind	116	J.F. Williams	115	25,960	1:35.67	91
1994	River Special	4	T. Chapman	115	He's Illustrious	116	Misty Wind	114	32,600	1:34.33	106
1995	Double Jab	4	R.Baze	115	Corslew	116	Cleante		49,725	1:35.18	103
1996	Houston Fleet M D	2	D.Carr	118	Slew'a Doop	116	Big Find	116	26,600	1:36.67	86
1998	Wild Wonder	4	R.Baze	115	General Royale	115	March Of Kings	116	51,450	1:35.18	111
1999	Hal's Pal	4	B.Blanc	117	Wild Wonder	122	Worldly Ways	115	75,000	1:34.96	112
2000	Voice Of Destiny	4	R. Meza	113	Mr.Doubledown	115	Twilight Affair	115	75,000	1:35.67	108
2001	Blade Prospector	6	O. Berrio	116	Dixie Dot Com	119	Milkwood	115	55,000	1:34.18	109
2002	Irisheyesareflying	6	J. Valdivia Jr.	120	Boss Ego	116	Palmeiro	116	55,000	1:35.41	98
2003	I'madrifter	5	R.M. Gonzalez	115	Palmeiro	117	Skip to the Stone	116	55,000	1:35.13	98

Beyer Index: 100.62

For previous runnings, refer to 1980 Manual

BEWITCH, 1 1/2 Miles (Turf), Fillies and Mares
4-Year-Olds and Up, Keeneland Race Course, 2003 Purse: $112,100

Year	Winner	Age	Jockey	Wt.	Second	Wt.	Third	Wt.	Win Value	Time	Beyer
1962	Bonnie's Girl	2	C. Meaux	114	Nalee	111	The Smoocher	114	9,766	0:48.20	
1963	Royal Bund	2	A. Gomez	114	Cadabra	114	Vera T.	114	8,547	0:49.40	
1964	Mississippi Mama	2	R. Baldwin	114	Swoon's Tune	114	Wing Revoked	114	8,872	0:48.20	
1965	Justakiss	2	K. Knapp	114	Hurry Star	114	Balla Fib	114	8,182	0:53.00	
1965	Ole Liz	2	W. Shoemaker	119	Champagne Women	114			8,052	0:52.40	
					Sturdy Gerty	115					
1966	Shore	2	J. Nichols	115	Lotta Miss	114	Lady Goldie	113	7,735	0:52.00	
1966	Furl Sail	2	E. Fires	114	Idle Dreamer	119	Ritanita	114	7,800	0:52.60	
1967	Jet to Market	2	G. Overton	119	Blue Carbon	114	Shenow	114	9,051	0:51.60	
1968	Royalty Note	2	M. Manganello	114	Alert Princess	114	Artist Johanna	114	15,112	0:51.00	
1969	Little Tudor	2	D.E. Whited	114	Glenary	114	Pussy Footing	112	15,242	0:52.80	
1970	Fancy Road	2	N. Menard	119	Mistq Joy	114	Holda	111	14,105	0:52.20	
1971	Sidle	2	D. Kassen	114	Swing Step	116	Miss Beaustark	114	12,967	0:52.20	
1971	Cautious Bidder	2	J. Nichols	115	Apple Jackie	114	Little Queensw're	114	13,032	0:52.00	
1972	Gallant Davelle	2	J. Nicholas	119	All in Fun	111	Greek Loveliness	114	13,536	0:52.40	
1972	Bosun Strike	2	A. DeSpirito	114	Barrister Girl	114	Say Cheesecake	111	13,731	0:53.20	
1973	Me and Connie	2	J. Nichols	121	Lady Bahla	115	Bundler	115	12,603	0:52.40	
1974	Dancing Home	2	A. Patterson	116	Semi Princess	119	Spark	116	11,793	0:53.60	
1974	Secret's Out	2	D. Brumfield	119	Floral Princess	116	Ain't Easy	119	11,727	0:53.20	
1975	Pink Jade	2	E. Delahoussaye	116	Old Goat	119	T.V. Vixen	119	12,139	0:51.60	
1976	Olden	2	R. Breen	116	Bagiorix	116	Foreverness	116	11,030	0:52.00	
1976	Fun and Tears	2	L. Melancon	119	Miss Cigarette	119	Every Move	116	11,290	0:51.40	
1977	Crystalan	2	G. Patterson	119	No No-Nos	119	Surprise Trip	119	11,947	0:53.00	
1978	Twenty One Inch	2	E. Delahoussaye	119	All's Well	119	Satan's Pride	116	11,846	0:52.60	
1979	Miss Baja	4	E. Maple	119	Likely Exchange	110	Plains and S'mple	113	23,285	1:43.00	
1980	Jolie Dutch	4	R.P. Romero	113	Miss Baja	112	Mi Muchacha	113	29,039	1:43.00	
1981	Bold 'n Determined	4	E. Delahoussaye	116	Likely Exchange	113	Save Wild Life	110	38,236	1:43.80	
1982	Expressive Dance	4	D. Brumfield	116	Mean Martha	115	Really Royal	116	36,416	1:43.40	
1983	Try Something New	4	P. Day	110	Kattegat's Pride	119	Number	119	37,001	1:44.20	
1984	Heatherten	5	S. Maple	119	Any Spray	110	Marisma	119	36,628	1:45.80	
1985	Sintra	4	K.K. Allen	119	Electric Fanny	110	Switching Trick	110	43,964	1:43.60	
1986	Devalois	4	E. Maple	118	Debutant Dancer	113	Natural Approach	113	35,685	1:54.00	
1987	Gerrie Singer	6	R.L. Frazier	113	Innsbruck	110	Debutant Dancer	110	36,221	1:52.60	
1988	Beauty Cream	5	P. Day	121	Native Mommy	121	Fraulein Lieber	113	55,933	1:51.60	
1989	Gaily Gaily	6	J.A. Krone	122	Chez Chez Chez	114	Bl'ss'm'ngB'ty	113	53,853	1:50.00	
1990	Coolawin	4	J.D. Bailey	122	To the Lighthouse	114	Ann Alleged	122	54,048	1:49.20	
1991	Miss Unnameable	7	P. Day	112	Cheerful Spree	117	The Caretaker	114	56,220	1:50.00	97
1992	La Gueriere	4	B.D. Peck	114	Indian Fashion	117	Plenty of Grace	112	54,430	1:48.20	100
1993	Miss Lenora	5	J.A. Krone	112	Hero's Love	117	Radiant Ring	119	51,367	1:50.60	93
1994	Freewheel	5	P. Day	114	Key Chance	114	Amal Hayati	119	50,871	1:50.20	94
1995	Market Booster	6	P. Day	119	Memories	113	Abigailthewife	114	50,731	2:29.20	101
1996	Memories	5	S.J. Sellers	117	Future Act	117	Curtain Raiser	116	66,030	2:30.00	100
1997	Cymbala	5	P. Day	113	Noble Cause	113	Last Approach	113	69,130	2:28.80	95
1998	Maxzene	5	J.A. Santos	113	Cuando	113	Gastronomical	113	69,626	2:30.40	104
1999	Bursting Forth	5	J.F. Chavez	114	Moments of Magic	114	Pinafore Park	114	68,758	2:27.54	97
2000	The Seven Seas	4	A. Solis	116	Innuendo	116	Hollywood Baldcat	116	70,122	2:29.31	99
2001	Keemoon	5	J.D. Bailey	120	Playact	116	Krisada	116	124,000	2:30.28	99
2002	Sweetest Thing	4	M. Guidry	120	Lapuma	116	Lady Upstage	116	68,634	2:31.97	99
2003	Lilac Queen	5	J.D. Bailey	116	Beyond the Waves	116	San Dare	118	69,503	2:29.70	99

Beyer Index: 98.23

BOILING SPRINGS HANDICAP, 1 1/16 Miles (Turf),
3-Year-Old Fillies, The Meadowlands, 2002 Purse: $194,000

Year	Winner	Age	Jockey	Wt.	Second	Wt.	Third	Wt.	Win Value	Time	Beyer
1977	Council House	3	C. Perret	116	Rich Soil	119	Pressing Date	115	28,633	1:42.40	
1977	Critical Cousin	3	A. Cordero Jr.	119	Sans Arc	116	Small Raja	123	28,243	1:42.40	
1978	Key to the Saga	3	J.L. Samyn	118	Terpsichorist	117	Amerigirl	112	28,519	1:41.40	
1978	Sisterhood	3	B. Gonzalez	112	Island Kiss	108	White Star Line	122	28,519	1:41.40	
1979	Jameela	3	V. Bracciale Jr.	118	Fanny Saperstein	119	Whydidju	119	27,934	1:41.60	
1979	Gala Regatta	3	E. Maple	122	Record Acclaim	114	Tweak	113	27,934	1:41.00	
1980	Champagne Ginny	3	J. Velasquez	114	Qui Royalty	112	Classic Curves	111	26,505	1:42.00	
1980	Refinish	3	C.J. McCarron	113	Keep Off II	111	Cannon Boy	113	26,505	1:41.60	
1981	Irish Joy	3	C.C. Lopez	114	First Approach	113	Dance Forth	114	26,925	1:42.40	
1981	Wings of Grace	3	J. Velasquez	112	Andover Way	114	Pukka Princess	120	26,385	1:41.40	
1982	Sunny Sparkler	3	J.L. Samyn	113	Fact Finder	113	Milingo	117	26,895	1:41.40	
1982	Larida	3	E. Maple	119	Doodle	115	Distinctive Moon	114	27,075	1:41.40	
1983	Sabin	3	E. Maple	124	Aspen Rose	114	Propositioning	117	33,480	1:47.80	
1984	Possible Mate	3	D. MacBeth	116	Distaff Magic	113	Miss Audimar	112	33,930	1:41.80	
1985	Jolly Saint	3	J.A. Santos	114	Miss Hardwick	115	Dawn's Curtsey	115	49,620	1:41.00	
1986	Small Virtue	3	J.A. Santos	114	Sweet Velocity	115	Country Recital	121	47,985	1:41.60	
1986	Small Fir	3	D.B. Thomas	119	Ala Mahlik	116	Spring Innocence	113	47,985	1:41.60	
1987	Rullah Runner	3	W.A. Guerra	109	Tappiano	119	Key Bid	120	35,460	1:41.40	
1988	Siggebo	3	R. Wilson	119	Flashy Runner	115	Lusty Lady	113	51,930	1:43.20	
1989	Darby Shuffle	3	J.A. Krone	116	To the Lighthouse	116	Warranty Applied	115	53,730	1:40.60	
1990	Memories of Pam	3	J.D. Bailey	112	Hot Marshmellow	114	Baltic Chill	118	41,550	1:41.00	
1990	Plenty of Grace	3	J.D. Bailey	112	Southern Tradition	120	Sabina	114	40,950	1:42.20	
1991	Dance o'My Life	3	C.W. Antley	114	Monica Faye	111	Verbasle	115	45,000	1:41.40	97
1992	Captive Miss	3	J. Bravo	120	Logan's Mist	116	Aquilegia	113	45,000	1:40.60	94
1993	Tribulation	3	J.L. Samyn	110	Exotic Sea	114	Bright Penny	115	45,000	1:42.60	92
1994	Avie's Fancy	3	Ferrer JC	119	Teasing Charm	113	Knocknock	115	45,000	1:41.40	98
1995	Christmas Gift	3	W.H. McCauley	116	Ring by Spring	114	Transient Trend	114	48,000	1:43.40	94
1995	Class Kris	3	Wilson R	118	Twilight Encounter	112	Appointed One	114	48,000	1:43.20	96
1996	Careless Heiress	3	C. Perret	118	Briarcliff	114	Dathuil	115	60,000	1:50.40	94
1997	Stoneleigh	3	J.A. Santos	114	Majestic Sunlight	114	Dancing Water	115	60,000	1:41.00	94
1997	Victory Chime	3	M.E. Smith	114	Miss Pop Carn	111	Colonial Play	113	60,000	1:41.80	87
1998	Mysterious Moll	3	J.L. Espinoza	116	Who Did It and Run	120	Thunder Kitten	116	120,000	1:40.00	99
1999	Wild Heart Dancing	3	J.F. Chavez	116	Confessional	118	Petunia	114	120,000	1:43.08	94
2000	Storm Dream	3	J.L. Samyn	116	Watch	117	Lady Dora	114	60,000	1:47.09	98
2001	Mystic Lady	3	E.M. Coa	120	Shooting Party	114	Plunderthepeasants	114	120,000	1:42.63	94
2002	Showlady	3	E.M. Coa	114	Dreamers Glory	116	With Patience	117	120,000	1:42.27	92

Beyer Index: 94.50

Run on main track in 2001; Not run in 2003

BOLD RULER HANDICAP, 6 Furlongs,
3-Year-Oids and Up, Belmont Park, 2003 Purse: $108,400

Year	Winner	Age	Jockey	Wt.	Second	Wt.	Third	Wt.	Win Value	Time	Beyer
1976	Chief Tamanaco	3	A. Cordero Jr.	114	Relent	114	Jacks'n Square	116	21,750	1:09.80	
1977	Jaipur's Gem	4	J.L. Samyn	113	Expletive Deleted	107	Cojak	126	22,050	1:09.60	
1978	Half High	5	A. Santiago	115	Great Above	121	Cruise on In	110	25,665	1:09.40	
1979	Star de Naskra	4	J. Fell	119	Vencedor	126	Big John Taylor	119	48,420	1:09.20	
1980	Dave's Friend	5	V. Bracciale Jr.	123	Tilt Up	121	Double Zeus	121	48,690	1:09.80	
1981	Dave's Friend	6	A.S. Black	123	Naughty Jimmy	119	Fappiano	119	48,510	1:09.60	
1982	Always Run Lucky	4	J. Miranda	123	King's Fashion	119	Band Practice	119	49,050	1:09.40	
1983	Maudlin	5	J.D. Bailey	119	Top Avenger	123	Singh Tu	121	49,500	1:11.60	
1984	Top Avenger	6	A. Graell	121	Believe the Queen	119	Au Point	123	55,350	1:09.80	
1985	Rocky Marriage	5	A. Cordero Jr.	119	Entropy	121	Majestic Venture	119	51,390	1:08.80	
1986	Phone Trick	4	J. Velasquez	123	Love That Mac	119	Rexson's Bishop	121	70,680	1:08.80	
1987	Pine Tree Lane	5	A. Cordero Jr.	118			Play the King	121	103,680	1:09.00	
1988	King's Swan	8	C.W. Antley	123	Seattle Knight	119	Faster Than Sound	123	103,680	1:10.20	
1989	Pok Ta Pok	4	R. Migliore	121	Teddy Drone	119	Claim	119	67,560	1:09.80	
1990	Mr. Nickerson	4	C.W. Antley	119	Dancing Pretense	119	Diamond Donnie	119	66,240	1:09.20	113
1991	Rousing Past	4	N. Santagata	119	True and Blue	121	Sunshine Jimmy	119	67,200	1:09.80	107
1992	Jolies Appeal	4	W.H. McCauley	119	Reappeal	119	Fiercely	119	67,560	1:09.20	110
1993	Slerp	4	J.A. Santos	119	Argyle Lake	121	Big Jewel	121	70,200	1:09.00	107
1994	Chief Desire	4	Velazquez JR	117	Boom Towner	120	Won Song	112	66,300	1:08.60	107
1995	Rizzi	4	Beckner DV	112	Lite the Fuse	111	Evil Bear	116	64,560	1:08.80	112
1996	Lite the Fuse	5	J.A. Krone	119	Cold Execution	115	Splendid Sprinter	115	64,500	1:09.40	116
1997	Punch Line	7	R.G. Davis	122	Golden Tent	111	Blissful State	116	64,980	1:08.80	103
1998	Kelly Kip	4	J.L. Samyn	117	Say Florida Sandy	111	Johnny Legit	114	66,120	1:07.60	121
1999	Kelly Kip	5	J.L. Samyn	123	Artax	115	Brushed On	115	64,440	1:07.54	120
2000	Brutally Frank	6	S.X. Bridgmohan	115	Kelly Kip	121	Kashatreya	115	65,880	1:08.64	112
2001	Say Florida Sandy	7	J. Bravo	117	Delaware Township	117	Lake Pontchartrain	113	65,520	1:08.67	111
2002	Left Bank	5	J.R. Velazquez	121	Silky Sweep	114	Say Florida Sandy	116	63,646	1:09.30	109
2003	Shake You Down	5	M.J. Luzzi	115	Here's Zealous	114	Peeping Tom	117	65,040	1:08.47	113

Beyer Index: 111.5

BROWN BESS HANDICAP, 1 1/16 Miles (Turf),
Fillies and Mares, 4-Years-old and Up, Golden Gate, 2003 Purse: 100,000

Year	Winner	Age	Jockey	Wt.	Second	Wt.	Third	Wt.	Win Value	Time	Beyer
1995	Work The Crowd	5	R.Baze	118	Watch Rachel	115	Zoonaqua	120	32,450	1:41.40	107
1996	Traces of Gold	4	R.Baze	115	Luzette	116	Just A Wish	115	55,000	1:42.00	100
1997	Traces of Gold	5	R.Baze	115	Notagoldbrick	115	Princess Kali	115	55,000	1:44.40	100
1998	Traces of Gold	6	R.Baze	118	Taurus Forus	116	La Soberbia	116	55,000	1:43.00	96
1999	Call Me	6	R.Meza	115	Curitibia	115	Plus	115	50,475	1:49.16	95
2000	Guinevere	5	J. Matias	115	Royal Terminal	112	Blended Element	118	55,000	1:47.75	99
2001	Out of Reach	4	R. Baze	115	Miss of Wales	114	Keld	114	55,000	1:46.78	100
2002	Janet	5	D.R. Flores	123	Impeachable	115	Alexine	117	55,000	1:44.14	100
2003	Lindsay Jean	5	C.P. Schvaneveldt	116	Bush Triumph	116	Crazy Ensign	118	55,000	1:44.35	97

Beyer Index: 99.33

CARLETON F. BURKE HANDICAP, 1 1/2 Miles (Turf),
3-Year-Olds and Up, Santa Anita, 2003 Purse: $139,250

Year	Winner	Age	Jockey	Wt.	Second	Wt.	Third	Wt.	Win Value	Time	Beyer
1969	Fiddle Isle	4	W. Shoemaker	115	Pink Pigeon	117	Gamelight	110	30,000	1:59.80	
1970	Fiddle Isle	5	W. Shoemaker	129	Daryl's Joy	123	Mickey McGuire	111	30,000	1:58.80	
1971	Kobuk King	5	H. Grant	110	Over the Counter	118	Figonero	115	34,400	1:59.60	
1972	Cougar II	5	D. Pierce	128	Kentuckian	110	Tetrack	114	34,600	2:00.20	
1973	Kentuckian	4	D. Pierce	117	Wing Out	119	Le Cle	116	33,400	1:59.00	
1974	Tallahto	4	L. Pincay Jr	120	High Protein	117	Scantling	117	32,300	1:59.00	
1975	Top Command	4	W. Shoemaker	113	Against the Snow	116	Top Crowd	116	24,875	2:01.20	
1975	Kirrary	5	F. Mena	114	Buffalo Lark	121	Dulcia	117	24,875	2:00.40	
1976	King Pellinore	4	W. Shoemaker	124	Royal Derby II	116	George Navonod	115	33,300	1:57.60	
1977	Double Discount	4	F. Mena	116	No Turning	118	Vigors	120	33,000	1:57.40	
1978	Star of Erin II	4	W. Shoemaker	113	Improviser	115	Mr. Redoy	118	38,400	1:59.00	
1978	Palton	5	H.E. Moreno	122	Star Spangled	118	Lunar Probe	114	38,400	1:59.00	
1979	Silver Eagle	5	F. Toro	115	John Henry	118	Shagbark	118	50,200	1:59.20	
1980	Bold Tropic	5	W. Shoemaker	125	Balzac	121	Shagbark	121	49,300	1:58.20	
1981	Spence Bay	6	F. Toro	120	Providential II	121	Super Moment	121	67,200	2:00.60	
1982	Mehmet	4	E. Delahoussaye	117	Craelius	114	It's the One	124	63,600	1:58.60	
1983	Bel Bolide	5	T. Lipham	117	Travelling Victor	118	Bold Run	118	64,200	2:01.20	
1984	Silveyville	6	C.J. McCarron	117	Gordian	115	Gato del Sol	121	64,100	1:59.60	
1985	Tsunami Slew	4	G.L. Stevens	121	Yashgan	121	Best of Both	115	78,500	1:59.60	
1986	Louis le Grand	4	W. Shoemaker	115	Schiller	114	Silveyville	120	133,700	2:01.20	
1987	Rivlia	5	L. Pincay Jr	121	Captain Vigors	116	Circus Prince	115	102,500	2:03.20	
1988	Nasr el Arab	3	G.L. Stevens	121	Northern Provider	112	Trokhos	115	133,000	2:01.00	
1989	Alwuhush	4	J.A. Santos	120	Frankly Perfect	122	Speedratic	115	134,400	1:58.00	
1990	Ultrasonido	5	C.J. McCarron	114	Rial	118	Eradicate	117	129,400	1:59.80	106
1991	Super May	5	C.S. Nakatani	117	Algenib	121	Pride of Araby	112	103,700	1:58.40	106
1992	Missionary Ridge	5	K.J. Desormeaux	117	Carnival Baby	112	Myrakalu	113	98,000	2:00.80	105
1993	Know Heights	4	K.J. Desormeaux	117	Fanmore	117	Myrakalu	114	96,000	2:00.80	107
1994	Savinio	4	C.J. McCarron	114	Square Cut	114	Sir Mark Sykes	117	95,700	2:02.60	105
1995	Varadavour	4	A. Solis	115	Patio de Naranjos	117	Raintrap	116	90,350	2:30.20	100
1996	Dernier Empereur	6	C.J. McCarron	118	Bon Point	118	Party Season	116	158,750	2:24.20	108
1997	Prussian Blue	5	K.J. Desormeaux	117	Embraceable You	116	Kessem Power	114	75,000	2:31.20	102
1998	Perim	5	B. Blanc	113	Single Empire	116	Rate Cut	114	75,000	2:29.20	103
1999	Public Purse	5	A. Solis	119	Star Performance	115	Achilles	115	90,000	2:25.83	103
2000	Timboroa	4	D.R. Flores	114	Kerrygold	116			84,990	2:27.91	100
					Res Judicata	115					
2001	Cagney	4	M.E. Smith	116	Kerrygold	116	Northern Quest	118	90,000	2:26.10	105
2002	Special Matter	4	T.C. Baze	110	Alyzig	113	Dance Dreamer	117	90,000	2:28.47	101
2003	Runaway Dancer	4	M.E. Smith	112	Labirinto	116	Senor Swinger	114	83,550	2:28.38	99

Beyer Index: 103.57

CALDER DERBY, 1 1/8 Miles (Turf),
3-Year-Olds, Calder Race Course, 2003 Purse: $200,000

Year	Winner	Age	Jockey	Wt.	Second	Wt.	Third	Wt.	Win Value	Time	Beyer
1972	First Bloom	4	C. Stone	116	Hickory Gray	117	The Republican	117	6,540	1:25.80	
1973	Wilmar	5	G. St. Leon	122	Sea Phantom	118	Hickory Gray	115	7,020	1:25.20	
1974	Amberbee	6	J. Garrido	117	Enchanted Ruler	112	Seminole Joe	113	14,280	1:46.60	
1975	Rimsky II	4	A. Haldar	116			Plagiarization	121	12,400	1:42.20	
	Strand of Gold	5	P. Nicolo	122							
1976	Chilean Chief	5	J. Imparato	118	El Rosillo	112	L. Grand Jr.	116	17,700	1:45.80	
1977	What a Threat	5	R. Gaffflione	117	Noble Royalty	116	Lightning Thrust	122	17,400	1:42.60	
1978	Ole Wilk	4	L. Jimenez	114	America Behave	110	Classy State	115	18,600	1:42.40	
1979	Breezy Fire	4	M. Rivera	118	Abba Cap	115	Selma's Boy	117	16,665	1:52.00	
1980	J. Rodney G.	5	F. Verardi	113	Two's a Plenty	109	Cherry Pop	125	23,040	1:53.20	
1981	Poking	5	G. Cohen	122	Yosi Boy	114	Pair of Deuces	112	23,415	1:53.40	
1982	Gorious Past	3	A. Smith Jr	115	Court Rebeau	115	Ell's New Canaan	112	19,905	1:45.80	
1983	Opening Lead	3	B. Gonzalez	117	The Cerfer	112	Neutral Player	112	20,640	1:48.20	
1984	Opening Lead	4	J. Santos	114	Ward off Trouble	114	Darn That Alarm	114	34,860	1:47.60	

Year	Winner	Age	Jockey	Wt.	Second	Wt.	Third	Wt.	Win Value	Time	Beyer
1985	Gray Haze	3	F. Pennisi	115	Alfred	115	Jeblar	115	33,780	1:46.00	
1986	Annapolis John	3	J. Velez Jr	120	Kid Colin	115	Real Forest	118	28,160	1:46.20	
1987	Schism	3	R. Lester	117	Slewdonza	112	Fabulous Devotion	114	32,640	1:47.20	
1988	Frosty the Snowman	3	D. Valiente	116	In the Slammer	116	Distinctintentions	112	30,750	1:44.40	
1989	Silver Sunsets	3	M. Gonzalez	114	Compuquine	114	Run for Your Honey	111	32,190	1:45.80	
1990	Zalipour	3	D. Acevedo	118	County Isle	115	Rowdy Regal	114	32,580	1:46.60	
1991	Scottish Ice	3	R. Lester	113	Chihuahua	120	Jackie Wackie	121	33,450	1:46.00	
1992	Birdonthewire	3	M. Hunter	112	Shahpour	113	Ponche	111	30,000	1:44.20	106
1993	Medieval Mac	3	M. Russ	113	Raise an Alarm	113	Fight for Love	116	30,000	1:41.60	100
1994	Halo's Image	3	Boulanger G.	117	Honest Colors	117	Rocky's Halo	117	90,000	1:52.20	100
1995	Pineing Patty	3	Melancon L	122	Sea Emperor	122	Mucha Mosca	117	60,000	1:51.40	102
1996	Laughing Dan	3	P. Rodriguez	117	Sea Horse	117	Flying Concery	114	66,300	1:50.60	103
1997	Blazing Sword	3	G. Boulanger	117	Topaz Runner	117			90,000	1:53.00	102
					Royal Tuneup	117					
1998	Crowd Pleaser	3	J.L. Samyn	122	Stay Sound	122	The Kaiser	117	120,000	1:47.60	102
1999	Isaypete	3	J.C. Ferrer	122	Rhythmean	117	Phi Beta Doc	122	120,000	1:50.01	92
2000	Whata Brainstorm	3	R.B. Homeister Jr	122	Muntel	122	Womble	117	120,000	1:47.80	98
2001	Western Pride	3	D.G. Whitney	122	Tour of the Cat	113	Built Up	117	120,000	1:51.12	108
2002	Union Place	3	E.M. Coa	115	Miesque's Approval	122	The Judge Sez Who	122	120,000	1:47.76	
2003	Stroll	3	J.D. Bailey	122	Certifiably Crazy	115	Super Frolic	119	120,000	1:48.39	97

Beyer Index: **100.91**

CANADIAN TURF HANDICAP, 1 1/16 Miles (Turf), 3-Year-Olds and Up, Gulfstream Park, 2003 Purse: $100,000

Year	Winner	Age	Jockey	Wt.	Second	Wt.	Third	Wt.	Win Value	Time	Beyer
1967	Chinatower	5	H. Gustines	114	Snow Dance	112	Circus	112	2,300	1:41.20	
1968	Flit-to	5	J. Vasquez				Out the Window	115	15,575	1:41.20	
	War Censor	5	E. Fires	115							
1969	Go Marching	4	M. Ycaza	123	Out the Window	114	Jean-Pierre	112	26,550	1:43.80	
1970	Jungle Cove	4	L. Adams	114	Zarco	112	Elegant Heir	112	34,650	1:52.80	
1971	Broker's Tip II	6	M. Hole	115	Tudor Reward	112	North Flight	110	31,305	1:41.80	
1972	Speedy Zephyr	4	R. Turcotte	117	Knight Counter	113	Mr. Pow Wow	123	43,560	1:43.60	
							Super Sail	112			
1973	Windtex	4	J.L. Rotz	116	Dubasoff	117	Getajetholme	112	23,835	1:41.40	
1973	Life Cycle	4	F. Ianelli	115	Roundhouse	113	Hope Eternal	112	23,415	1:42.80	
1974	Baccalaureate	4	R. Woodhouse	110	Rey Maya	112	Jogging	117	43,800	1:42.20	
1975	Sir Jason	4	M.A. Rivera	113	Westgate Mall	109	Mr. Door	114	30,675	1:40.80	
1976	Step Forward	4	M. Solomone	117	Lord Henham	112	Conesaba	113	40,320	1:40.20	
1977	Gravelines	5	J.D. Bailey	122	Proponent	114	Lord Layabout	112	33,420	1:44.40	
1977	Gay Jitterbug	4	L. Saumell	121	Riverside Sam	110	Blacksmith	110	32,820	1:44.00	
1978	Practitioner	5	J.S. Rodriguez	119	Haverty	112	That's a Nice	116	29,820	1:41.60	
1978	Court Open	4	R. Woodhouse	109	All Friends	114	Oilfield	114	29,520	1:40.80	
1979	Roan Star	6	C. Perret	115	Fleet Gar	117	Family Doctor	114	31,590	1:40.80	
1979	Noble Dancer II	7	J. Vasquez	128	Scythian Gold	118	River Warrior	114	31,290	1:41.00	
1980	Morning Frolic	4	A. Cordero Jr	118	Pearlescent	114	Dickens Hill	122	41,220	1:41.20	
1981	Proctor	4	C. Perret	119	Imperial Dilemma	113	Foretake	115	61,290	1:41.00	
1982	Robsphere	5	D. Brumfield	115	Dom Menotti	111	King of Mardi Gras	115	39,690	1:41.00	
1983	Data Swap	6	M. Solomone	115	Northrop	118	Wicked Will	116	42,105	1:47.20	
1983	Super Sunrise	4	E. Maple	112	Summer Advocate	118	Pin Puller	112	40,755	1:46.60	
1984	Ayman	4	J. Cruguet	112	Smart and Sharp	110	Guston	114	57,555	1:40.00	
1985	Nepal	5	J.D. Bailey	112	Dr. Schwartzman	116	Roving Minstrel	120	61,410	1:40.00	
1986	Amerilad	5	J.A. Velez Jr	113	Flying Pidgeon	119	Uptown Swell	118	57,060	1:40.20	
1986	Vanlandingham	5	D. MacBeth	126	Ends Well	115	Dr. Schwartzman	118	56,460	1:40.00	
1987	Racing Star	5	S.B. Soto	112	Glaros	112	Salem Drive	113	54,420	1:40.80	
1987	New Colony	4	V.H. Molina	109	Tri for Size	110	Trubulare	111	55,020	1:42.00	
1988	Equalize	6	J.D. Bailey	112	Yankee Affair	118	Sans the Shadow	117	99,180	1:41.20	
1989	Equalize	7	J.A. Santos	126	Sunshine Forever	126	Mi Selecto	116	71,280	1:41.00	
1990	Youmadeyourpoint	4	D. Valiente	114	Wanderkin	116	Maceo	113	60,000	1:44.60	106
1991	Izvestia	4	R. Platts	122	Miss Josh	112	Bye Union Ave	113	60,000	1:41.40	100
1992	Buckhar	4	J. Cruguet	113	Tin Can Ali	113	Archies L'ghter	114	60,000	1:48.40	102
1993	Stagecraft	6	J.D. Bailey	112	Roman Envoy	121	Carterista	114	60,000	1:47.80	106
1994	Paradise Creek	5	M.E. Smith	123	Glenfiddich Lad	113	Nijinsky's Gold	113	60,000	1:47.00	108
1995	The Vid	4	J.D. Bailey	117	Star of Manila	118	Country Coy	113	60,000	1:47.00	108
1996	The Vid	6	W.H. McCauley	124	Gone for Real	114	Warning Glance	115	60,000	1:47.00	107
1997	Devil's Cup	4	R. Wilson	114	Da Bull	113	Green Means Go	115	60,000	1:47.00	107
1998	Subordination	4	J.D. Bailey	112	Cimarron Secret	117	Tour's Big Red	113	60,000	1:50.80	99
1999	Federal Trial	4	R.G. Davis	114	Deep Dive	114	Unite's Big Red	116	60,000	1:47.90	103
2000	Shamrock City	5	E.S. Prado	114	Rhythmean	113	Sharp Appeal	115	60,000	1:47.15	104
2001	Inexplicable	6	J.A. Santos	115	Band Is Passing	118	David Copperfield	114	90,000	1:39.43	107
2002	North East Bound	6	J.A. Velez Jr	116	Capsized	114	Fyling Avie	116	90,000	1:44.01	101
2003	Political Attack	4	M. Guidry	114	Miesque's Approval	116	Strategic Partner	114	60,000	1:40.43	102

Beyer Index: **104.43**

Run on main track in 1998, 2002

CARDINAL HANDICAP, 1 1/8 Miles (Turf),
Fillies and Mares 3-Year-Olds and Up, Churchill Downs, 2003 Purse: $175,200

Year Winner	Age	Jockey	Wt.	Second	Wt.	Third	Wt.	Win Value	Time	Beyer
1974 Cut the Talk	3	D. Brown	116	Holding Pattern		Sturdy Steel			1:45.20	
1975 Visier	3	R. Riera	116	Slade's Prospect		Ski Run			1:45.80	
1976 Hope of Glory	4	D. Brumfield	113	Bronze Point		Straignt			1:25.00	
1976 Vivacious Meg	4	R. Breen	113	Regal Gal		Regal Humor			1:25.40	
1977 Likely Exchange	3	J. McKnight	114	My Complements		My Bold Beauty			1:25.80	
1977 Famed Princess	4	C. Ledezma	113	Chatta		Leigh Simms			1:24.80	
1978 Love to Tell	3	E. Delahoussaye	116	Selari's Choice		Bit of Sunshine			1:24.40	
1978 Unreality	4	L. Suire	123	Navajo Princess		Irish Agate			1:24.20	
1979 Impetuous Gal	4	E. Fires	113	Billy Jane		Cookie Puddin			1:24.60	
1979 Gap Axe	4	D. Brumfield	115	Unreality		Honey Blonde			1:24.80	
1980 Vite View	4	D. Brumfield	120	Doing It My Way		Jeanie's Fancy			1:24.60	
1980 Champagne Ginny	3	D. Brumfield	119	Impetuous Gal		Red Chiffon			1:24.80	
1981 Knight's Beauty	4	T. Hightower	115	Deuces Over Seven		Roger's Turn			1:24.80	
1981 Safe Play	3	S. Spencer	122	Lillian Russell		La Vue			1:24.20	
1982 Betty Money	3	B. Sayler	116	Raja's Delight		Mezimica			1:38.80	
1982 Promising Native	3	S. Maple	114	What Glitter		Sweetest Chant			1:39.60	
1983 Charge My Account	4	P. Day	112	Heatherten		Etoile du Matin			1:47.20	
1984 Electric Fanny	3	J. Espinoza	112	Straight Edition		Mickey's Echo			1:48.00	
1985 Mrs. Revere	4	L. Melancon	112	Wealthy and Wise		My Inheritance			1:48.20	
1985 Mr. T's Tune	4	K. Allen	118	Gerrie Singer		Adaptable			1:47.00	
1986 Oriental	4	K. Allen	123	Kapalua Butterflu		Glorious View			1:45.80	
1987 Lake Champlain	4	P. Day	119	Marianna's Girl		Shot Gun Bonnie			1:46.20	
1988 Top Corsage	5	P. Valenzuela	118	Savannah's Honor		Graceful Darby			1:52.40	
1989 Townsend Lass	4	K. Allen	114	Bangkok Lady		Bearly Cooking			1:52.00	
1990 Dance for Lucy	4	D. Penna	113	Betty Lobelia		Phoenix Sunshine		39,270	1:51.80	93
1990 Lady in Silver	4	P. Day	122	Coolawin	121	Splendid Try		38,780	1:51.40	97
1991 Christiecat	4	A. Cordero Jr	118	Super Fan	115	Screen Prospect	113	75,010	1:51.00	99
1992 Auto Dial	4	S.J. Sellers	113	Radiant Ring	119	Red Journey	114	73,125	1:52.04	84
1993 River Ball	7	J.R. Parsley	109	Marshua's River	112	Logan's Mist	118	74,945	1:55.79	99
1994 Bold Ruritana	4	P. Day	116	Eternal Reve	117	Monaassabaat	113	76,375	1:48.25	99
1995 Apolda	4	P. Day	114	Alive With Hope	114	Lady Reiko	115	75,530	1:49.59	100
1996 Miss Caerleona	4	L. Melancon	114	Bail Out Becky	121	Striesen	113	72,850	1:47.81	105
Bail Out Becky finished first but was disqualified and placed second										
1997 Colcon	4	J.D. Bailey	114	Dancer Clear	112	Sagar Pride	113	108,903	1:51.89	100
1998 B.A. Valentine	5	J.F. Chavez	115	Mingling Glances	112	Cuando	116	111,693	1:48.62	102
1999 Pratella	4	B. Peck	114	Mingling Glances		Uanme		106,299	1:48.88	101
2000 Illiquidity	4	J. Court	115	License Fee	118	Miss of Wales	114	109,182	1:49.72	100
2001 Watch	4	C. Perret	114	Sitka	111	Gino's Spirits	118	104,997	1:49.12	97
2002 Quick Tip	4	R.J. Albarado	114	Sun Dare	114	Bien Nicole	118	107,322	1:51.08	98
2003 Riskaverse	4	C.H. Velasquez	118	Bien Nicole	120	Firth of Lorne	116	108,624	1:50.53	102

Beyer Index: 98.4

ROBERT F. CAREY MEMORIAL HANDICAP, 1 Mile (Turf),
3-Year-Olds and Up, Hawthorne Race Course, 2003 Purse: $150,000

Year Winner	Age	Jockey	Wt.	Second	Wt.	Third	Wt.	Win Value	Time	Beyer
1983 Sir Pele	4	O. Vergara	112	John's Gold	120	Energetic King	111	64,800	1:55.00	
1984 Ronbra	4	C. Marquez	115	Grazie	115	Bold Run	115	66,540	2:03.80	
1985 River Lord	6	R. Meier	112	Harham's Sizzler	118	Attaway to Go	112	63,370	2:06.20	
1986 Pass the Line	5	J.L. Diaz	117	Explosive Darling	117	Salem Drive	116	94,500	2:01.00	
1987 The Sassman	4	K.D. Clark	113	Zaizoom	115	Zuppardo's Love	111	89,130	2:05.40	
1988 New Colony	5	R.R. Douglas	114	Rio's Lark	115	Bank Fast	116	93,900	1:47.60	
1989 Iron Courage	5	D. Penna	121	Saint Oxford	112	Do Loop	109	94,080	1:47.00	
1990 Allijeba	4	K.D. Clark	118	Wave Wise	114	Expensive Decision	118	87,070	1:39.20	
1991 Slew the Slewor	4	G.K. Gomez	114	Jalajel	118	The Great Carl	118	96,090	1:38.60	105
1992 Double Booked	7	J.C. Ferrer	115	Evanescent	113	That's Sunny	114	60,000	1:39.80	98
1993 High Habitation	5	G.C. Retana	114	Beau Fasa	114	Glenfiddich Lad	114	60,000	1:35.20	96
1994 Recoup the Cash	4	J.L. Diaz	119	Road of War	115	Glenfiddich Lad	114	60,000	1:40.80	109
1995 Homing Pigeon	5	R.J. Albarado	114	Gilder		Rare Reason	119	60,000	1:38.00	98
1996 Homing Pigeon	6	R.J. Albarado	114	Joker	115	Why Change	115	90,000	1:36.40	104
1997 Trail City	4	J.D. Bailey	119	Power of Opinion	113	Da Bull	114	90,000	1:36.00	105
1998 Soviet Line	8	S.J. Sellers	115	Fun To Run	110	Wild Event	115	90,000	1:33.40	103
1999 Ray's Approval	6	E. Fires	114	Stay Sound	115	Inkatha	115	90,000	1:37.01	103
2000 Where's Taylor	4	C.J. Lanerie	117	Dernier Croise	113	Associate	115	90,000	1:36.31	103
2001 Galic Boy	6	R. Sibille	115	Where's Taylor	121	Good Journey	115	90,000	1:35.10	105
2002 Kimberlite Pipe	6	C.A. Emigh	115	Aslaaf		Major Omansky	115	90,000	1:35.94	98
2003 Mystery Giver	5	C.H. Marquez Jr	120	Al's Dearly Bred	118	Major Rhythm	116	90,000	1:34.70	98

Beyer Index: 101.92

Run at 1 3/16 miles, turf, in 1983; 1 1/4 miles, turf, 1984, 1986-87; 1 1/4 miles, 1985; 1 1/8 miles, turf, 1988-89, 1 mile 70 yards, 1994

CARRY BACK, 6 Furlongs
3-Year-Olds, Calder Race Course, 2003 Purse: $300,000

Year	Winner	Age	Jockey	Wt.	Second	Wt.	Third	Wt.	Win Value	Time	Beyer
1975	Precipitory	2	J. Salinas	116	Chic Ruler	116	Upper Current	119	14,400	1:06.80	
1976	Winner's Hit	2	R. Broussard	119	My Budget	119	Time for Fun	116	14,640	1:07.00	
1977	Chwesboken	2	D. Hidalgo	119	Noon Time Spender	122	Ski's Never Bend	116	13,320	1:05.40	
1978	Admiral Rix	2	T. Barrow	116	Tartan Tam	116	Cherry Pop	116	14,160	1:07.40	
1979	Breezy Fire	4	M. Rivera	120	Cherry Pop	113	Noble Heart	111	16,770	1:24.60	
1980	Diplomatic Note	3	J. Bailey	112	Buck'n Shoe	115	Fast Fast Freddie	113	16,785	1:12.00	
1981	Face the Moment	3	E. Cardone	115	Toga Toga	113	Incredible John	118	16,530	1:11.00	
1982	Rex's Profile	3	E. Cardone	115	Libra Moon	118	Center Cut	123	16,395	1:11.40	
1983	Opening Lead	3	B. Gonzalez	112	El Perico	117	Neutral Player	112	16,785	1:25.80	
1984	Bowmans Express	3	O. Londono	119	Mo Exception	114	No Room	119	19,305	1:25.40	
1985	Smile	3	J. Vasquez	123	Paravon	112	Hickory Hill Flyer	114	46,260	1:23.80	
1986	Kid Colin	3	G. St. Leon	116	Big Jolt	116	Lucky Rebeau	116	38,610	1:25.80	
1987	You're No Bargain	3	O. Londono	117	Right Rudder	112	Jilsie's Gigalo	118	44,010	1:25.60	
1988	In the Slammer	3	M. Gonzalez	114	Lover's Trust	122	Ashmint	115	32,220	1:23.50	
1989	Big Stanley	3	D. Valiente	120	Valid Space	114	Jabotinsky	117	32,610	1:23.60	
1990	Country Isle	3	H. Castillo Jr	114	Run Turn	120	Ultimate Swale	112	33,840	1:24.80	
1991	Ocala Flame	3	R. Lester	113	Sunny and Pleasant	113	Jacquelyn's Groom	113	33,180	1:19.00	
1992	Always Silver	3	M. Lee	116	Appealtothechief	114	Dr Arne	114	30,000	1:25.00	101
1993	Humbugaboo	3	M. Russ	112	Signoir Valery	112	Kassec	113	60,000	1:22.74	98
1994	Score a Birdie	3	H. Castillo Jr	115	Fortunate Joe	112	Ali'lbito'reality	114	60,000	1:24.09	100
1995	Sonic Signal	3	R. Douglas	115	Leave'm Inthedark	117	Too Great	113	60,000	1:24.79	92
1996	Fortunate Review	3	A. Toribio	117	Betweenhereorthere	115	Night Runner	113	60,000	1:23.27	97
1997	Renteria	3	E. Coa	115	Red	122	Willow Skips Trial	115	120,000	1:11.28	108
1998	Mint	3	E. Coa	115	Diamond Studs	115	Mt. Laurel	112	120,000	1:11.38	110
1999	Silver Season	3	E. Coa	112	Deep Gold	117	Night Patrol	117	120,000	1:11.32	103
2000	Caller One	3	C.S. Nakatani	122	Fappie's Notebook	115	Malagot	115	120,000	1:10.35	116
2001	Illusioned	3	J.F. Chavez	117	Beyond Brilliant	117	Gallant Frolic	115	150,000	1:11.08	102
2002	Royal Lad	3	J.D. Bailey	117	Captain Squire	122	Friendly Frolic	114	150,000	1:10.73	105
2003	Valid Video	3	J. Bravo	122	Cajun Beat	117	Super Fuse	117	177,000	1:10.15	110

Beyer Index: 103.5

Run as Carry Back Handicap, 1981-1993; For 2-year-olds, 1975-1978; For 3-year-olds and up, 1979; At 5 1/2 furlongs, 1975-1978; At 6 1/2 furlongs in 1991; At 7 furlongs in 1979, 1983-1990, 1992-1996

CHAPOSA SPRINGS HANDICAP, 7 Furlongs
Fillies and mares 3-Year-Olds and Up, Calder Race Course, 2003 Purse: $100,000

Year	Winner	Age	Jockey	Wt.	Second	Wt.	Third	Wt.	Win Value	Time	Beyer
1983	Florida Jig	4	R. Danjean	119	Voo Doo Dance	113	Amber's Desire	115	35,340	1:25.60	
1984	Hiusoanso	4	B. Gonzalez	114	Birdie Belle	119	Queen of Song	123	35,550	1:25.00	
1985	Birdie Belle	4	J.A. Santiago	118	Gyspy Prayer	114	Really Flashy	115	35,010	1:24.20	
1986	Jose's Bomb	3	R.N. Lester	112	Algenib	114	Thirty Zip	118	30,570	1:25.60	
1988	Tappiano	4	C. Perret	122	Le L'Argent	117	Easter Mary	111	52,995	1:24.00	
1988	Thirty Zip	5	R. Breen	115	Behind the Scenes	118	Triple Wow	118	66,120	1:25.00	
1990	Love's Exchange	4	H. Castillo Jr	127	Spirit of Fighter	118	Fit for a Queen	114	33,720	1:23.20	
							Ana T.	115			
1990	Ells Once Again	6	M.A. Lee	111	Banbury Fair	113	Storm of Glory	111	52,380	1:24.40	89
1992	Magal	5	R. Hernandez	115	Gene Propp's Dream	113	My Own True Love	113	51,675	1:24.20	100
1993	Maggies Pistol	4	J.A. Bracho	112	My Own True Love	118	Luv Me Luv Me Not	118	45,000	1:23.80	100
1994	Educated Risk	4	M.E. Smith	122	Goldarama	115	Floramera	110	60,000	1:23.00	112
1995	Chaposa Springs	3	J.D. Bailey	119	Investalot	115	Easter Doll	114	60,000	1:25.20	95
1996	Race Artist	4	Boulanger G.	112	La Nina De Orumila	113	Flat Fleet Feet	119	60,000	1:25.20	95

Chaposa Springs finished first but was disqualified and placed seventh

1997	Flashy n Smart	4	P. Day	118	U Can Do It	115	Special Request	114	60,000	1:26.60	94
1998	Openstock	6	J.A. Garcia	113	Lily O'Gold	111	U Can Do It	119	60,000	1:24.84	89
2000	Could Be	4	P. Day	115	Extended Applause	114	Class On Class	114	60,000	1:24.97	91
2000	England's Rose	4	J.R. Velazquez	112	Swept Away	118	Sugar N Spice	114	60,000	1:24.82	97
2001	Vague Memory	4	J.A. Garcia	113	Gold Mover	117	Platinum Tiara	114	60,000	1:24.15	90
2002	Chispiski	3	J.A. Garcia	115	Abundantly Blessed	114	Away	117	60,000	1:25.14	86
2003	Barbara O'Brien	4	E. Coa	114	Holy Bubbette	114	Splasha	114	60,000	1:23.51	104

Beyer Index: 95.54

CHICAGO BREEDERS' CUP HANDICAP, 7 Furlongs,
Fillies and Mares 3-Year-Olds and Up, Arlington Park, 2003 Purse: $145,750

Year	Winner	Age	Jockey	Wt.	Second	Wt.	Third	Wt.	Win Value	Time	Beyer
1986	Lazer Show	3	P. Day	115	Balladry	115	Gene's Lady	122	93,360	1:21.40	
1987	Lazer Show	4	P. Day	123	Very Subtle	120	M'nngm McQ'en	111	46,275	1:22.80	
1989	Rose's Record	5	J. Velasquez	114	Sunshine Always	114	Daloma	116	93,120	1:24.60	
1990	Fit for a Queen	4	P. Day	112	Channel Three	114	Sexy Slew	113	94,650	1:23.00	
1991	Safely Kept	5	C. Perret	126	Nurse Dopey	115	Token Dance	114	93,060	1:23.00	102

Year	Winner	Age	Jockey	Wt.	Second	Wt.	Third	Wt.	Win Value	Time	Beyer
1992	Withallprobability.	4	G.L. Gomez	115	Fit for a Queen	120	Madam Bear	114	93,450	1:21.20	99
1993	Meafara	4	J.L. Diaz	121	Shared Interest	115	Real Display	114	93,870	1:22.00	100
1994	Minidar	4	Belvoir VT	116	Spinning Round	118	Traverse City	113	93,960	1:22.40	106
1995	Low Key Affair	4	A.T. Gryder	113	Morning Meadow	115	Marina Park	120	93,840	1:24.60	94
1996	Bunbeg	4	M.K. Walls	119	Morris Code	118	Rhapsodic	114	102,990	1:23.80	101
1997	J J'sdream	4	M. Guidry	118	Capote Belle	120	Eseni	117	101,625	1:22.20	106
2000	Saoirse	4	D. Clark	118	The Happy Hopper	115	Dif a Dot	114	102,195	1:23.09	101
2001	Trip	4	C. Perret	114	Hidden Assets	115	Rose of Zollern	115	99,312	1:22.18	97
2002	Mandy's Gold	4	R.R. Douglas	116	Cat and the Hat	116	Caressing	115	98,664	1:22.86	94
2003	For Rubies	4	C. Perret	116	Raging Fever	120	Oglala Sue	113	69,450	1:24.21	95

Beyer Index: 99.55

(CITGO) DISTAFF TURF MILE, 1 Mile (Turf),
Fillies and Mares 3-Year-Olds and Up, Churchill Downs, 2003 Purse: $117,000

Year	Winner	Age	Jockey	Wt.	Second	Wt.	Third	Wt.	Win Value	Time	Beyer
1983	Le Cou Cou		D. Howard	121	High Honors		Common Sense			1:49.60	
1987	Fast Forward		P. Day	115	Sooner Showers		Homebuilder			1:43.20	
	High Honors finished first but was disqualified and placed second										
1988	Buoy		P. Day	123	Frosty the Snowman		Cougarized			1:43.40	
1989	Classic Account	4	P. Day	116	Fast Forward		R.B. McCurry			1:51.20	
1990	Foresta	4	A. Cordero Jr.	114	Saros Brig		Bearly Cooking		36,200	1:37.20	103
1991	Foresta	5	A. Cordero Jr.	123	Coolawin		Primetime North		38,870	1:36.20	100
1992	Quilma	5	E. Delahoussaye	120	Behaving Dangeer		Raidant Ring		38,200	1:35.36	100
1993	Lady Blessington	5	P. Day	120	You'd Be Surprised		Wassifa		37,570	1:34.96	96
1994	Weekend Madness	4	C. Woods Jr.	123	Russian Bride		Suspect Terrain		55,770	1:38.58	98
1995	Bold Ruritana	5	P. Day	123	Icy Warning	114	Rapunzel Runz	116	56,111	1:34.64	101
1996	Apolda	4	J.D. Bailey	123	Country Cat	123	Bold Ruritana	123	55,283	1:36.50	103
1997	B.A. Valentine	4	S.J. Sellers	114	Striesen	116	Romy	123	71,796	1:36.98	100
1998	Witchful Thinking	4	S.J. Sellers	120	Colcon	123	Swearingen	123	74,896	1:37.23	97
1999	Shires End	4	J. Velazquez	118	Ashford Castle	120	Sophie My Love	123	74,152	1:35.43	98
2000	Don't Be Silly	5	J.F. Chavez	116	Really Polish	114	Pricearose	116	71,548	1:34.78	100
2001	Iftiraas	4	J.D. Bailey	118	Gino's Spirits	118	Solvig	120	70,432	1:36.69	100
2002	Sylish	4	J.D. Bailey	116	La Recherche	123	Dianehill	123	71,424	1:35.72	95
2003	Heat Haze	4	J. Valdivia Jr	123	Quick Tip	123	Sentimental Value	121	72,540	1:33.96	99

Beyer Index: 99.29

CICADA, 7 Furlongs,
3-Year-Old Fillies, Aqueduct, 2003 Purse: $108,300

Year	Winner	Age	Jockey	Wt.	Second	Wt.	Third	Wt.	Win Value	Time	Beyer
1993	Personal Bid	3	J.A. Santos	118	Sheila's Revenge	118	In Excelcis Deo	116	31,800	1:23.40	100
1994	Our Royal Blue	3	Wilson R	113	Sovereign Kitty	118	Princess Joanne	113	48,375	1:22.20	89
1995	Lucky Lavender Gal	3	Davis RG	114	Stormy Blues	118	Dancin Renee	116	48,870	1:23.40	98
1996	J J'sdream	3	G. Boulanger	121	Dahl			114	50,310	1:23.40	98
1997	Vegas Prospector	3	M.J. McCarthy	116	Ormsby County	112	Valid Affect	118	48,375	1:26.20	70
1998	Jersey Girl	3	R. Migliore	116	Vienna Blues	114	Babai Danzig	116	50,175	1:22.80	93
1999	Potomac Bend	3	M.T. Johnston	118	Carleaville		Jane	112	48,915	1:23.18	91
2000	Finder's Fee	3	J.D. Bailey	118	Apollo Cat	116	Southern Sandra	116	65,100	1:23.07	92
2001	Xtra Heat	3	R. Wilson	122	Erin Moor		Chasm	116	63,770	1:23.39	89
2002	Proper Gamble	3	J.J. Castellano	122	Short Note	118	Forest Heiress	120	65,160	1:23.32	97
2003	Cyber Secret	3	S.X. Bridgmohan	122	Roar Emotion	116	Boxer Girl	118	64,980	1:22.55	88

Beyer Index: 91.36

CINEMA BREEDERS' CUP HANDICAP, 1 1/8 Miles (Turf),
3-Year-Olds, Hollywood Park, 2003 Purse: $184,550

Year	Winner	Age	Jockey	Wt.	Second	Wt.	Third	Wt.	Win Value	Time	Beyer
1946	Honeymoon	3	J. Westrope	128	Don Peppino	107	Eiffel Tower	117	20,050	1:44.00	
1947	Yankee Valor	3	N. Richardson	115	On Trust	129	Stepfather	120	17,750	1:42.80	
1948	Drumbeat	3	O. Webster	112	Belle Jolie	108	Solidarity	122	19,600	1:44.00	
1949	Pedigree	3	J. Longden	124	Rhodes Bull	109	Blue Dart	120	19,250	1:42.80	
1950	Great Circle	3	R. Neves	121	Valquest	115	Akimbo	109	15,150	1:36.00	
1951	Mucho Hosso	3	F. Chojnacki	110	Tuzado	106	Gold Capitol	125	18,450	1:43.60	
1952	A Gleam	3	H. Moreno	124	Alate	115	Horsetrader-Ed.	108	17,500	1:42.80	
1953	Ali's Gem	3	W. Shoemaker	120	Rejected	112	Imbros	126	16,350	1:42.00	
1954	Miz Clementine	3	I. Valenzuela	113	Fault Free	116	War Tryst	108	14,050	1:42.60	
1955	Guilton Madero	3	I. Valenzuela	114	Brooksickle	110	Mr. Sullivan	115	15,750	1:41.80	
1956	Social Climber	3	I. Valenzuela	121	Blen Host	109	Terrang	124	16,150	1:48.20	
1957	Round Table	3	W. Shoemaker	130	Joe Price	114	Seaneen	109	26,350	1:47.80	
1958	The Shoe	3	W. Shoemaker	117	Strong Bay	111	El Cajon	108	20,900	1:49.60	
1959	Silver Spoon	3	W. Boland	120	Friar Roach	111	Civic Pride	105	29,990	1:47.60	
1960	New Policy	3	W. Shoemaker	123	Tempestuous	113	T.V. Lark	126	34,450	1:46.60	

Year	Winner	Age	Jockey	Wt.	Second	Wt.	Third	Wt.	Win Value	Time	Beyer
1961	Bushel-n-Peck	3	E. Burns	117	Songman	111	Double Lea	114	32,675	1:48.00	
1961	Four-and-Twenty	3	J. Longden	126	Mr. America	122	We're Hoping	110	32,175	1:47.00	
1962	Black Sheep	3	J. Longden	114	Indian Blood	113	Doc Jocoy	125	33,800	1:48.40	
1963	Y Flash	3	E. Burns	120	Missilery	116	Bre'r Rabbit	116	27,075	1:50.00	
1963	Quita Dude	3	J. Leonard	113	Sky Gem	117	Olympiad King	126	27,075	1:49.80	
1964	Close By	3	W. Shoemaker	119	Real Good Deal	122	Pelegrin	114	34,750	1:49.00	
1965	Arksroni	3	W. Hartack	116	Easy Lime	114	Charger's Kin	115	36,000	1:47.80	
1966	Drin	3	W. Shoemaker	115	Tragniew	115	Fleet Host	110	33,800	1:48.80	
1967	Dr. Roy E.	3	W. Mahorney	116	Ruken	123	Tumble Wind	123	35,250	1:48.60	
1968	Pinjara	3	L. Pincay Jr	112	American Tiger	115			32,400	1:49.00	
					Distinctly	112					
1969	Noholme Jr.	3	L. Pincay Jr	117	Tell	128	Makor	113	32,150	1:48.40	
1970	D'Artagnan	3	L. Pincay Jr	113	Top the Market	114	Hanalei Bay	115	33,850	1:47.40	
1971	Niagara	3	F. Toro	114	Crimson Clem	116	Triple Bend	122	40,400	1:48.20	
1972	Finalista	3	L. Pincay Jr	120	Quack	124	Woodland Pines	114	38,300	1:48.00	
1973	Amen II	3	E. Belmonte	115	Kirrary	114	Card Table	110	52,350	1:49.00	
1975	Terrete	3	W. Shoemaker	113	Larrikin	125	Dusty County	117	46,400	1:48.60	
1976	Majestic Light	3	S. Hawley	121	L'Heureux	120	Bynoderm	116	67,200	1:48.20	
1977	Bad 'n Big	3	L. Pincay Jr	121	Iron Constitution	124	Minnesota Gus	112	96,450	1:48.00	
1978	Kamehameha	3	T.M. Chapman	120	El Fantastico	114	Singular	118	102,800	1:47.40	
1979	Beau's Eagle	3	S. Hawley	121	Ibacache	122	Paint King	113	64,500	1:47.00	
1980	First Albert	3	F. Mena	113	Big Doug	115	Kenderboun	117	68,800	1:48.00	
1981	Minnesota Chief	3	C.J. McCarron	119	Stancharry	117	Splendid Spruce	125	69,900	1:40.60	
1982	Give Me Strength	3	J.L. Samyn	121	Journey at Sea	122	Bargain Balcony	118	64,600	1:40.60	
1983	Baron O'Dublin	3	E. Delahoussaye	115	Tanks Brigade	119	Re Ack	116	56,300	1:43.00	
1984	Prince True	3	P.A. Valenzuela	117	M. Double M.	116	Majestic Shore	115	63,700	1:40.20	
1985	Don't Say Halo	3	D.G. McHargue	116	Derby Dawning	115	Emperdori	115	65,800	1:47.60	
1986	Manila	3	F. Toro	117	Vernon Castle	120	Mazaad	121	80,400	1:47.00	
1987	Something Lucky	3	L. Pincay Jr	119	The Medic	117	Savona Tower	115	62,400	1:46.80	
1988	Peace	3	A. Solis	117	Blade of the Ball	113	Roberto's Dancer	115	78,400	1:46.80	
1989	Raise a Stanza	3	L. Pincay Jr	114	Exemplary Leader	116	Notorious Pleasure	120	62,100	1:47.80	
1990	Jovial	3	G.L. Stevens	115	Mehmetori	113	Itsallgreektome	117	67,400	1:47.80	97
1991	Character	3	G.L. Stevens	114	River Traffic	117	Kalgrey	114	62,600	1:47.00	97
1992	Bien Bien	3	C.J. McCarron	114	Fax News	114	Prospect for Four	114	65,600	1:47.00	97
1993	Earl of Barking	3	C.J. McCarron	121	Manny's Prospect	115	Minks Law	113	61,100	1:47.40	95
1994	Unfinished Symph.	3	Baze G	118	Vaudeville	115	Fumo di Londra	121	63,100	1:46.40	102
1995	Via Lombardia	3	Delahoussaye E	119	Bryntirion	113	Oncefortheroad	115	65,400	1:47.20	102
1996	Let Bob Do It	3	K.J. Desormeaux	120	Dr. Sardonica	115	Winter Quarters	120	81,660	1:47.40	98
1997	Worldly Ways	3	C.S. Nakatani	115	P.T. Indy	118	Brave Act	120	66,180	1:48.40	97
1998	Commitisize	3	D.R. Flores	118	Killer Image	115	Lord Smith	116	65,220	1:48.00	100
1999	Fighting Falcon	3	B. Blanc	119	Eagleton	120	Major Hero	113	66,000	1:48.06	98
2000	David Copperfield	3	V. Espinoza	116	Duke of Green	117	Silver Axe	115	64,560	1:47.73	98
2001	Sligo Bay	3	L. Pincay Jr	118	Learing at Kathy	117	Marine	119	65,160	1:48.40	98
2002	Inesperado	3	K.J. Desormeaux	116	Regiment	122	Johar	118	97,560	1:47.63	99
2003	Just Wonder	3	K.J. Desormeaux	117	Bis Repetitas	115	Slew City Citadel	115	98,730	1:47.41	100

Beyer Index: 98.43

CLIFF HANGER HANDICAP, 1 1/16 Miles (Off the turf), 3-Year-Olds and Up, The Meadowlands, 2002 Purse: $145,000

Year	Winner	Age	Jockey	Wt.	Second	Wt.	Third	Wt.	Win Value	Time	Beyer
1977	Dan Horn	5	D. MacBeth	125	Shore Patrol	113	Popular Victory	118	34,873	1:43.60	
1978	Mr. Lincroft	4	V. Bracciale Jr.	117	Telly Hill	119	Forbidden Isle	109	36,270	1:44.20	
1979	Exclusively Mine	3	W. Nemeti	114	Telly Hill	126	Picturesque	114	34,678	1:44.20	
1980	Quality T.V.	4	J. Velasquez	114	Conservatoire	109	Bill Wheeler	112	32,640	1:43.80	
1981	Bill Wheeler	4	W.H. McCauley	119	Mannerism	113	Brahmin	114	33,510	1:43.60	
1982	Erin's Tiger	4	J. Velasquez	114	Santo's Joe	116	Dew Line	114	26,295	1:44.60	
1982	Acaroid	4	A. Cordero Jr	114	North Course	114	Thirty Eight Paces	116	26,115	1:44.60	
1983	Erin's Tiger	5	J. Velasquez	112	Who's for Dinner	113	Kentucky River	112	33,450	1:41.20	
1984	Late Act	5	E. Maple	113	Sitzmark	112	Quick Dip	114	46,020	1:40.80	
1984	Cozzene	4	W.A. Guerra	115	Ayman	112	Pin Puller	114	45,300	1:40.40	
1985	Late Act	5	E. Maple	113	Silver Surfer	116	Pax Nobiscum	116	47,790	1:45.00	
1986	Explosive Darling	4	R.P. Romero	118	Equalize	114	Lieutenant's Lark	120	48,360	1:40.00	
1987	Foligno	5	J.A. Santos	115	Cost Conscious	116	Air Display	114	46,995	1:41.40	
1987	Silver Comet	4	W.H. McCauley	117	Broadway Tommy	112	Prince Daniel	114	31,830	1:43.80	
1988	Wanderkin	5	R.G. Davis	118	Salem Drive	117	Sans the Shadow	117	53,730	1:39.40	
1989	Ten Keys	5	K.J. Desormeaux	114	Wanderkin	121	Soviet Lad	112	52,290	1:42.40	
1990	Chas' Whim	3	A.T. Stacy	115	Kali High	115	Royal Ninja	116	45,000	1:46.40	
1991	Finder's Choice	6	R.B. Aviles	116	Royal Rue	113	Great Normand	117	45,000	1:40.20	
1992	Roman Envoy	4	C. Perret	116	Futurist	116	Royal Ninja	115	45,000	1:39.80	103
1993	Excellent Tipper	5	C. Perret	117	Rinka Das	115	First and Only	115	45,000	1:43.60	98
1994	Binary Light	5	Samyn JL	112	Brazany	114	Burst of Applause	109	45,000	1:41.40	98
1995	Mighty Forum	4	W.H. McCauley	114	Joker	106	Fourstars Allstar	120	60,000	1:41.00	98

Year	Winner	Age	Jockey	Wt.	Second	Wt.	Third	Wt.	Win Value	Time	Beyer
1996	Thorny Crown	5	M.J. Luzzi	115	Ihtiraz	111	Winnetou	112	60,000	1:44.60	100
1997	Dixie Bayou	4	J.R. Velazquez	114	Brave Note	115	Joker	116	60,000	1:39.40	98
1998	Mi Narrow	4	J Bravo	111	Treat Me Doc	114	Boyce	114	60,000	1:43.40	97
1999	Virginia Carnival	7	J.L. Samyn	114	Star Connection	114	Grapeshot	116	90,000	1:42.44	99
2000	North East Bound	4	J.A. Velez Jr.	118	Johnny Dollar	114	Swamp	120	90,000	1:41.78	104
2001	Crash Course	5	R. Wilson	114	Solitary Dancer	114	Union One	114	90,000	1:43.14	103
2002	Saint Verre	4	J.L. Samyn	113	Pinky Pizwaanski	116	Spruce Run	115	90,000	1:42.40	106

Off the turf in 2002; Not run in 2003

Beyer Index: 100.36

COMELY, 1 Mile,
3-Year-Old Fillies, Aqueduct, 2003 Purse:$107,900

Year	Winner	Age	Jockey	Wt.	Second	Wt.	Third	Wt.	Win Value	Time	Beyer
1945	Moon Maiden	7	W.D. Wright	113	Darby Delilah	106	Elpis	115	15,615	1:45.40	
1946	Bonnie Beryl	3	H. Woodhouse	114	Hypnotic	114	Bridal Flower	116	16,700	1:44.20	
1947	Elpis	5	L. Hansman	113	Risolator	121	War Date	118	19,225	1:44.20	
1948	Conniver	4	E. Guerin	123	Miss Request	120	Carolyn A.	118	20,200	1:45.00	
1949	Lithe	3	H. Lindberg	107	But Why Not	116	Gaffery	116	20,700	1:45.20	
1950	Siama	3	O Scurlock	112	Antagonism	114	September	118	20,150	1:45.00	
1951	Bed o' Roses	4	E. Guerin	127	Nothirdchance	112	Regal	111	19,500	1:44.60	
1952	Devilkin	3	W. Boland	118	Enchanted Eve	112	Th'lma B'gar	112	20,250	1:44.60	
1953	La Corredora	4	I. Hanford	122	Canadiana	116	Arab Actress	121	19,237	1:45.20	
1953	Home-Made	3	E. Guerin	116	Gay Grecque	116	Sunshine Nell	121	18,987	1:45.20	
1959	Bally Ache	2	D. Erb	122	Tufanhai	122	Progressing	122	11,362	0:59.20	
1960	Irish Jay	3	E. Arcaro	121	Improve	115	Staretta	112	18,680	1:23.00	
1961	Seven Thirty	3	H. Woodhouse	112	Apatontheback	115	Shuette	115	15,112	1:24.20	
1962	Upswept	3	B. Baeza	115	First Dark	113	White Gown	114	15,437	1:24.60	
1963	Pams Ego	3	I. Valenzuela	115	Fashion Verdict	115	Vast Scope	112	11,456	1:23.80	
1963	Lamb Chop	3	B. Baeza	118	Spicy Living	112	Fool's Play	115	11,326	1:24.40	
1964	Face the Facts	3	M. Ycaza	118	Petticoat	112	Miss Cavandish	112	18,525	1:23.80	
1965	What a Treat	3	J.L. Rotz	118	Equiria	113	Adorable	112	17,680	1:24.60	
1966	Swift Lady	3	J.L. Rotz	115	Good Queen Bess	113	Tagend	118	18,785	1:23.60	
1967	Gala Honors	3	B. Baeza	113	Just Kidding	118	Lake Chelan	116	18,947	1:25.00	
1968	Best in Show	3	H. Gustines	112	Heartland	113	Gay Matelda	115	19,240	1:22.40	
1969	Ta Wee	3	E. Belmonte	118	Shuvee	121	Hasty Hitter	118	18,492	1:22.60	
1970	Predictable	3	R. Ussery	116	Princess Roycraft	118	Capercaillie	112	14,852	1:24.00	
1970	Royal Signal	3	B. Baeza	118	Office Queen	118	Luci Tee	112	15,015	1:24.00	
1971	Forward Gal	3	M. Hole	121	Sea Saga	118	Deceit	115	20,460	1:23.40	
1972	Stacey d'Ette	3	J. Ruane	115	Numbered Account	121	Candid Catherine	118	16,290	1:21.60	
1973	Java Moon	3	A. Cordero Jr	116	Windy's Daughter	121	Voler	116	17,610	1:22.80	
1974	Clear Copy	3	D. Montoya	113	Shy Dawn	118	Chris Evert	118	17,670	1:24.40	
1975	Ruffian	3	J. Vasquez	113	Aunt Jin	113	Point in Time	113	16,755	1:21.20	
1976	Tell Me All	3	J. Ruane	113	Dearly Precious	121	Worthyana	113	22,080	1:23.20	
1977	Bring out the Band	3	D. Brumfield	118	Cum Laude Laurie	113	Emmy	113	22,650	1:23.60	
1978	Mashteen	3	R. Hernandez	113	Tempest Queen	118	Mucchina	113	25,665	1:23.00	
1979	Countess North	3	A. Cordero Jr	113	Palm Hut	116	Run Cosmic Run	113	25,725	1:23.40	
1980	Cybele	3	C.B. Asmussen	113	Punta Punta	113	Kashan	113	27,225	1:22.60	
1981	Expressive Dance	3	D. MacBeth	113	Tina Tina Too	118	Explosive Kingdom	114	35,220	1:23.40	
1982	Nancy Huang	3	J. Velasquez	113	Broom Dance	113	Dance Number	113	34,860	1:24.40	
1983	Able Money	3	A. Graell	113	Stark Drama	113	Idle Gossip	113	35,580	1:23.80	
1984	Wild Applause	3	P. Day	113	Suavite	113	Proud Clarioness	116	52,110	1:23.20	
1985	Mom's Command	3	A. Fuller	121	Majestic Folly	113	Clocks Secret	121	55,170	1:22.20	
1986	Misty Drone	3	J. Vasquez	113	I'm Splendid	121	Storm and Sunshine	114	59,940	1:24.00	
1987	Devil's Bride	3	R. Meza	116	Oh So Precious	116	Valid Line	114	65,790	1:23.60	
1988	Avie's Gal	3	J. Velasquez	114	Topicount	116	Ready Jet Go	114	53,280	1:22.40	
1989	Surging	3	A. Cordero Jr	118	Nite of Fun	112	Luv That Native	112	52,290	1:23.00	
1990	Fappaburst	3	J. Vasquez	114	Miss Spentyouth	114	Bundle Bits	118	49,770	1:21.60	112
1991	Meadow Star	3	C.W. Antley	121	Do It With Style	114	I'm a Thriller	118	67,560	1:38.00	95
1992	Saratoga Dew	3	W.H. McCauley	114	City Dance	112	Looking for a Win	114	69,480	1:37.20	93
1993	Private Light	3	R.G. Davis	112	Russian Bride	113	True Affair	118	68,280	1:44.00	91
1994	Dixie Luck	3	Leon F	116	Penny's Reshoot	116	Our Royal Blue	112	66,240	1:37.00	88
1995	Nappelon	3	Chavez JF	112	Stormy Blues	121	Incredible Blues	114	64,440	1:36.20	88
1996	Little Miss Fast	3	J.F. Chavez	118	J J'sdream	118	Stop Traffic	112	65,940	1:36.40	95
1997	Dixie Flag	3	J.L. Samyn	114	Global Star	114	How About Now	114	66,120	1:36.80	94
1998	Fantasy Angel	3	J.F. Chavez	114	Hansel's Girl	116	Best Friend Stro	118	69,300	1:37.40	85
1999	Madison's Charm	3	J.L. Samyn	112	Better Than Honour	121	Oh What a Windfall	121	65,520	1:35.54	92
2000	March Magic	3	R. Migliore	114	Jostle	121	Finder's Fee	121	65,460	1:36.79	92
2001	Two Item Limit	3	R. Migliore	122	Mandy's Gold	118	It All Adds Up	116	66,060	1:36.17	90

Mandy's Gold (Beyer: 89) finished first but was disqualified and placed second

Year	Winner	Age	Jockey	Wt.	Second	Wt.	Third	Wt.	Win Value	Time	Beyer
2002	Bella Bellucci	3	G.L. Stevens	122	Short Note	116	Nonsuch Bay	116	64,920	1:35.50	103
2003	Cyber Secret	3	S.X. Bridgmohan	122	Storm Flag Flying	122	Bonay	116	64,740	1:35.97	89

Beyer Index: 93.36

COUNT FLEET SPRINT HANDICAP, 6 Furlongs,
3-Year-Olds and Up, Oaklawn Park, 2003 Purse: $150,000

Year	Winner	Age	Jockey	Wt.	Second	Wt.	Third	Wt.	Win Value	Time	Beyer
1974	Barbizon Streak	6	R. Wilson	114	Pleasure Castle	120	Pesty Jay	122	17,370	1:11.00	
1975	Prince Astro	6	D.W. Whited	123	Silver Doctor	117	Faneuil Boy	112	18,030	1:10.00	
1976	Brets Kicker	5	J.D. Bailey	111	Silver Doctor	118	Mr. Barb	110	17,640	1:10.00	
1977	Silver Hope	6	R.L. Turcotte	120	Dr's Enjoy Dollars	116	Brets Kicker	113	18,480	1:10.40	
1978	Last Buzz	5	A. Rini	126	Best Person	110	Sucha Pleasure	118	33,390	1:11.00	
1979	Amadevil	5	T.G. Greer	114	Little Reb	120	Sean's Song	114	34,890	1:11.20	
1980	Silent Dignity	4	S. Maple	114	Gustoso	111	J. Burns	115	34,680	1:11.00	
1981	General Custer	4	L. Snyder	111	Avenging Gossip	111	Be a Prospect	112	34,470	1:10.40	
1982	Sandbagger	4	D. Haire	114	Blue Water Line	117	Lockjaw	116	39,240	1:12.00	
1983	Dave's Friend	8	L. Snyder	124	General Jimmy	117	Liberty Lane	113	70,320	1:10.00	
1984	Dave's Friend	9	E. Delahoussaye	122	All Sold Out	114	Lucky Salvation	114	70,260	1:09.00	
1985	Taylor's Special	4	R.P. Romero	123	Mt. Livermore	119	T.H. Bend	110	98,280	1:08.40	
1986	Mister Gennaro	5	F. Olivares	115	Beveled	114	Charging Falls	125	71,100	1:08.80	
1987	Sun Master	6	G.L. Stevens	117	Rocky Marriage	116	Chhief Steward	118	69,540	1:09.40	
1988	Salt Dome	5	L. Snyder	116	Pewter	113	Bold Pac Man	112	60,000	1:08.60	
1989	Twice Around	4	C.H. Borel	116	Be a Agent	117	Never Forgotten	114	60,000	1:09.20	
1990	Malagra	4	V.L. Smith	117	Pentelicus	115	Sunny Blossom	120	60,000	1:08.80	106
1991	Overpeer	7	P. Day	122	Silent Reflex	113	Peaked	118	60,000	1:08.20	108
1992	Gray Slewpy	4	K.J. Desormeaux	117	Potentiality	116	Hidden Tomahawk	115	60,000	1:08.80	116
1993	Approach	6	P. Day	116	Ponche	113	Never Wavering	110	90,000	1:09.60	109
1994	Demaloot Demashoot	4	M.E. Smith	115	Honor the Hero	117	Sir Hutch	118	90,000	1:08.20	113
1995	Hot Jaws	5	Borel CH	113	Demaloot Demashoot	116	Mr. Cooperative	114	90,000	1:09.40	110
1996	Concept Win	4	G.L. Stevens	116	Roythelittleone	114	Spiritbound	113	90,000	1:09.00	102
1997	High Stakes Player	5	K.J. Desormeaux	120	Capote Belle	116	Victor Avenue	116	90,000	1:08.80	107
1998	Chindi	4	D.R. Pettinger	113	E J Harley	113	Western Fame	115	75,000	1:09.60	104
1999	Reraise	4	C.S. Nakatani	122	Run Johnny	114	E J Harley	115	75,000	1:08.59	109
2000	Show Me the Stage	4	D.R. Flores	116	Smolderin Heart	115	Vinnie's Boy	114	75,000	1:09.62	102
2001	Bonapaw	5	G. Melancon	118	Chindi	114	Bidis	117	75,000	1:08.18	119
2002	Explicit	5	L.J. Meche	116	Entepreneur	115	Junior Deputy	113	90,000	1:08.60	114
2003	Beau's Town	5	H.J. Theriot II	122	Honor Me	116	Sand Ridge	114	90,000	1:09.01	106

Beyer Index: 108.93

CROWN ROYAL AMERICAN TURF, 1 1/16 Miles, (Turf),
3-Year-Olds, Churchill Downs, 2003 Purse: $121,400

Year	Winner	Age	Jockey	Wt.	Second	Wt.	Third	Wt.	Win Value	Time	Beyer
1992	Senor Tomas	3	M.E. Smith	118	Coaxing Matt		Black Question		37,440	1:43.10	94
1993	Desert Waves	3	S.J. Sellers	118	Compadre		Super Snazzle		36,620	1:42.64	84

Compadre finished first but was disqualified and placed second

Year	Winner	Age	Jockey	Wt.	Second	Wt.	Third	Wt.	Win Value	Time	Beyer
1994	Jaggery John	3	M.Smith	123	Milt's Overture		Zuno Star		56,452	1:45.05	96
1995	Unanimous Vote	3	G.Stevens	120	Nostra		Native Regent		76,700	1:42.07	99
1996	Broadway Beau	3	C.McCarron	114	Trail City	123	Gotcha	114	76,375	1:41.87	99
1997	Royal Strand	3	P.Day	116	Rob 'n Gin	118	Deputy Commander	115	71,796	1:40.93	96
1998	Dernier Croise	3	G.Stevens	116	Tenbyssimo	123	Silver Lord	114	78,120	1:44.28	99
1999	Air Rocket	3	J.Bailey	120	Haus of Dehere	116	Conserve	118	71,548	1:42.65	92
2000	King Cugat	3	J.Bailey	123	Lendell Ray	116	Go Lib Go	123	73,222	1:41.25	99
2001	Strategic Partner	3	J.R. Velazquez	116	Baptize	123	Dynameaux	120	73,098	1:42.89	94
2002	Legislator	3	E.S. Prado	116	Stage Call	123	Orchard Park	123	72,106	1:44.43	92
2003	Senor Swinger	3	P. Day	117	Remind	117	Foufa's Warrior	117	75,268	1:41.38	97

Beyer Index: 95.08

DEBUTANTE, 5 1/2 Furlongs,
2-Year-Old Fillies, Churchill Downs, 2003 Purse: $110,900

Year	Winner	Age	Jockey	Wt.	Second	Wt.	Third	Wt.	Win Value	Time	Beyer
1895	Amanda	2	N. Turner	120	Marquise	110	Stella	110	1,640	49.40	
1896	Cleophus	2	Simms	110	Eugenia Wickes	110	Ethel Lee	115	1,640	48.00	
1897	Mary Black	2	Corner	110	Sophronia D.	118	Uarda	115	945	50.50	
1898	Rush	2	J. Hill	115	Anna Bain	110	Gay Parisienne	115	945	51.00	
1899	Mollie Newman	2	N. Turner	115	Bab	115	Honeywood	115	945	50.00	
1900	Sinfi	2	Howell	115	Rose Apple	110	Bonnie Lissak	116	945	48.00	
1901	Autumn Leaves	2	Gilmore	110	The Esmond	110	The Boston	115	945	47.60	
1902	Olefiant	2	R. Williams	120	Mary Lavanna	110	Eva Russell	115	1,735	48.75	
1903	White Plume	2	J. Winkfield	110	Nannie Hodge	118	Sararose	110	1,560	48.25	
1904	Miss Inez	2	Helgesen	110	Lady Savoy		Frances Dillon	110	1,530	48.25	
1905	Beautiful Bess	2	Nicol	110	Ohiyesa	118	Lady Carol	110	1,585	50.00	
1906	Lillie Turner	2	D. Austin	118	Wing Ting	118	Alanie	115	1,845	49.60	
1907	Ancient	2	Troxler	115	Woodlane	118	Black Mary	118	1,715	49.40	
1908	Crystal Maid	2	Heidel	110	Elizabeth Harwood	118	Neoga	110	1,455	50.20	
1909	Ethelburg	2	Hannan	115	Placide		My Gal	110	1,635	47.80	

1330

THE AMERICAN RACING MANUAL

Year Winner	Age	Jockey	Wt.	Second	Wt.	Third	Wt.	Win Value	Time Beyer
1910 Round the World	2	A. Walsh	115	Golden Egg	115	Princess Industry	115	1,440	48.00
1911 Calisse	2	T. Rice	118	Rose of Jeddah	115	Mary Emily	118	1,990	48.40
1912 Briar Path	2	Ganz	110	Christmas Star	115	Oneida	115	1,910	48.00
1913 Robinetta	2	Goose	110	Birdie Williams	115	Aunt Mamie	115	700	47.80
1914 Climber	2	J. Kederis	120	Waterblossom	115	Aunt Josie	115	2,740	47.40
1915 Little Sister	2	W. Andress	110	Margaret N.	115	Lucky R.	115	2,590	48.00
1916 Rosabel	2	F. Cooper	110	Jocular	115	Believe Me Boys	110	2,410	48.40
1917 Ocean Sweep	2	D. Connelly	110	Violet Bonnie	110	Atalanta	110	2,790	47.80
1918 Regalo	2	D. Connelly	115	Jap	110	Madras	110	2,610	48.80
1919 Talisman	2	J. Groth	110	Ruby	111	Busy Signal	112	5,000	47.80
1920 Bit of White	2	L. Lyke	110	MIss Muffins	122	Miss Fontaine	114	6,115	47.40
1921 Fair Phantom	2	L. Lyke	114	Martha Fallon	119	Aloft	114	6,770	46.60
1922 Sympathy	2	B. Kennedy	119	Sweetheart	119	Belphrizonia	114	6,840	48.00
1923 Edna V.	2	G. Yeargin	122	Paloma	114	Lady Longridge	114	7,200	55.00
1924 Kitty Pat	2	L. McDermott	119	Little Visitor	119	Cream Puff	119	7,280	53.40
1925 Epsomite	2	F. Coltiletti	119	Belle	119	Panola	119	8,040	54.00
1926 Thirteen Sixty	2	E. Legere	119	Ethel Dear	119	Krick	114	8,060	54.00
1927 Anita Peabody	2	G. Johnson	119	Miss Fire	119	Pink Lily	114	7,700	1:01.80
1928 Port Harlem	2	H. Thurber	119	Ben Machree	114	That's It	114	7,540	1:03.00
1929 Alcibiades	2	W. Fronk	119	Lucile	122	Pansy Walker	114	6,920	59.80
1930 Betty Derr	2	C. McCrossen	119	Purple Lady	119	Martha Jones	114	6,620	1:01.20
1931 Butter Beans	2	C.E. Allen	119	At Sunrise	119	Princess Ivre	122	6,550	1:00.00
1938 Dolly Whisk	2	W. Garner	114	Espania	119	Oddesa Beulah	124	2,415	1:01.00
1939 Downy Pillow	2	J.E. Oros	119	Lynn	114	Drury Lane	119	2,690	59.80
1940 Wise Moss	2	J.E. Oros	119	Blue Lily	119	Misty Isle	122	2,435	1:01.40
1941 Royal Martha	2	G. King	119	Valdina Melia	119	My Choice	119	2,535	59.60
1942 Trustee	2	W. Eads	114	Burgoolette	114	Su nJesting	114	2,740	1:00.60
1943 Whirlabout	2	J. Adams	114	Miss Valor	114	Red Wonder	119	2,660	1:01.20
1944 Flyweight	2	R. Eccard	119	Misweet	114	Valdina Jane	119	2,600	1:00.80
1945 Breezy Louise	2	G. South	114	Calmara	114	Donna M.G.	119	4,810	1:02.00
1946 Blue Grass	2	D. Padgett	114	Jeannie Pie	119	Gayest	114	10,650	1:02.00
1947 Bewitch	2	D. Dodson	119	Pelt	114	Loriot	119	9,700	1:00.60
1948 Acoma	2	W. Garner	119	Blue Note	119	Jetrose	119	9,650	1:01.60
1949 Aunt Jayne Z.	2	N. Cartwright	119	Lady Marquest	119	Duchess Peg	119	9,700	59.60
1950 Juliets Nurse	2	K. Church	122	Flyamanita	119	Romanda	114	10,500	59.20
1951 Crownlet	2	R.L. Baird	122	Mutation	119	Hadn't Orter	119	11,050	59.60
1952 Bubbley	2	E. Arcaro	119	Biddy Jane	119	Lillal	119	11,125	59.00
1953 Golly	2	J. Adams	119	Spy Magic	119	Beanir	119	13,350	1:00.00
1954 Gambetta	2	E. Arcaro	119	Serry	114	Timely Story	119	13,800	:59.20
1955 Cherry	2	J. Heckmann	119	Babcha	119	Guard Rail	114	13,550	1:00.40
1956 Delamar	2	K. Church	119	Doris Hart	119	Romanita	119	13,600	58.40
1957 Margaretta	2	V. Guajardo	119	Errard's Isle	119	Hasty Doll	119	10,925	59.20
1958 Patty's Choice	2	J. Heckmann	119	Pinecrest Miss	119	Battle Heart	119	8,894	1:00.20
1959 Airmans Guide	2	E. Gross	119	Greek Top	119	Sandy's Sis W.	119	9,267	58.60
1960 Bright Silver	2	J.L. Rotz	122	Honey Dear	119	Double Sun	119	8,796	59.80
1961 Helfersartin	2	J. Bev	119	Volunteer State	119	Miss Sum'r Time	119	9,132	59.80
1962 Speedwell	2	W. Shoemaker	119	Girl Artist	114	Royal Wayfarer	119	8,905	58.80
1963 Wood Nymph	2	J.L. Rotz	119	Danville Miss	122	Busy Bird	119	9,230	58.40
1964 Mississippi Mama	2	W. Shoemaker	122	Amerivan	119	Gracie May	119	9,181	58.20
1965 Ole Liz	2	W. Shoemaker	122	Justakiss	122	Balafib	119	12,724	58.00
1966 Furl Sail	2	W. Shoemaker	122	Popping Mary	119	Your It	114	12,642	59.20
1967 Jet to Market	2	G. Overton	124	Owe Everything	119	Penny Mart	119	12,724	58.80
1968 Alert Princess	2	I. Valenzuela	119	Royalty Note	122	Jest Come	119	13,292	58.80
1969 Little Tudor	2	D.E. Whited	122	Dixie Wind	122	Colorado Coed	114	13,000	58.60
1970 Misty Joy	2	J.L. Rotz	119	Bid High	119	Amber Pudding	119	12,740	59.80
1971 Cautious Bidder	2	J. Nichols	122	Excitable Miss	119	Levee Flash	119	16,819	58.80
1972 Sylva Mill	2	R. Martinez Jr	114	Fish Wife	117	Fairway Fancy	119	17,485	58.60
1973 Me and Connie	2	J. Nichols	124	Bundler	119	Shanjar	114	16,835	58.20
1974 Sun and Snow	2	E. Guerin	119	Floral Princess	114	Classy Note	119	17,794	59.40
1975 Answer	2	M. Hole	119	Pink Jade	122	Turn Over	119	16,282	58.20
1976 Olden	2	R. Breen	122	Jungle Angel	119	Every Move	114	14,950	58.80
1977 Sweet Little Lady	2	R. Turcotte	122	Sahsie	119	Crystalan	122	14,706	58.00
1978 Nervous John	2	C.J. McCarron	122	Porpourie	114	Rainbow Streak	122	14,658	58.40
1979 Lissy	2	M.S. Sellers	114	Barbizon's Flower	119	Happy Hollie	119	20,426	59.80
1980 Excitable Lady	2	D. Brumfield	119	Masters Dream	119	Bend the Times	119	19,448	58.60
1981 Pure Platinum	2	P. Day	119	Miss Preakness	119	Cypress Bay	119	19,939	58.80
1982 Ice Fantasy	2	P.A. Johnson	115	Wrong Answer	115	Fifth Affair	121	20,735	1:04.60
1983 Arabizon	2	L. Moyers	115	Ark	115	Starafar	115	22,181	1:05.80
1984 Knot	2	K.K. Allen	115	Don't Joke	112	Off Shore Breeze	115	22,393	1:06.40
1985 Tricky Fingers	2	L. Melancon	115	Likker Is Quikker	118	Time for Honor	115	31,013	1:05.20
1986 Burnished Bright	2	P. Day	121	Before Sundown	118	Shivering Gal	115	46,810	1:11.20
1987 Bold Lady Anne	2	J. Davidson	118	Over All	118	Penny's Growl	114	25,773	1:11.60
1987 Dark Silver	2	M. McDowell	116	She's Freezing	116	Saved by Grace	116	26,260	1:12.60

Year	Winner	Age	Jockey	Wt.	Second	Wt.	Third	Wt.	Win Value	Time	Beyer
1988	Seaquay	2	R.M. Ehrlinspie.	114	Weekend Spree	118	Coax Chelsie	112	35,718	1:11.20	
1989	Ice Folly	2	K.K. Allen	118	Hard Freeze	118	Lucy's Glory	118	37,993	1:11.20	
1990	Barbara's Nemesis	2	J.C. Deegan	116	Gracielle	112	Cosmic Music	112	36,690	1:12.00	65
1991	Greenhaven Lane	2	K. Tsuchiya	112	Moment of Grace	113	One for Smoke	116	36,950	1:06.20	65
1992	Hollywood Wildcat	2	F.A. Arguello J	116	Cosmic Speed Queen	118	Dixie Band	115	38,480	1:06.02	79
1993	Fly Love	2	B.E. Bertram	116	Miss Ra He Ra	116	Astas Foxy Lady	121	37,635	1:05.23	74
1994	Chargedupsycamore	2	P. Day	121	Phone Bird	116	Our Gem	116	54,405	1:05.24	82
1995	Golden Attraction	2	D.M. Barton	115	Western Dreamer	121	Tipically Irish	115	70,947	1:04.19	82
1996	Move	2	P. Day	121	Sarah's Prospector	115	Live Your Best	115	73,840	1:05.74	78
1997	Love Lock	2	P. Day	115	Countess Diana	115	Quick Lap	115	72,478	1:03.84	92
1998	Silverbulletday	2	W. Martinez	115	The Happy Hopper.	115	Mancari's Rose	115	69,502	1:04.71	87
1999	Chilukki	2	W. Martinez	121	Miss Wineshine	112	Cecilia's Crown	115	69,998	1:03.66	98
2000	Gold Mover	2	C. Perret	121	Princess Belle	115	Tricky Elaine	115	69,626	1:03.79	86
2001	Cashier's Dream	2	D.J. Meche	118	Lakeside Cup	115	Colonial Glitter	115	68,510	1:02.52	97
2002	Awesome Humor	2	C.H. Borel	115	Vibs	115	Attemptress	115	67,890	1:03.45	93
2003	Be Gentle	2	C. Velasquez	117	Renaissance Lady	117	Sweet Jo Jo	117	68,758	1:03.96	83

Beyer Index: 82.93

DELAWARE OAKS, 1 1/16 Miles,
3-Year-Old Fillies, Delaware Park, 2003 Purse: $500,000

Year	Winner	Age	Jockey	Wt.	Second	Wt.	Third	Wt.	Win Value	Time	Beyer
1996	Like A Hawk	3	R.Colton	114	Mercedes Song	118	Winter Melody	118	30,000	1:37.00	84
1997	Runup The Colors	3	P.Day	116	Timely Broad	113	City Band	113	90,000	1:44.20	95
1998	Nickel Classic	3	C.Borel	119	Lu Ravi	122	Taffy Davenport	117	120,000	1:42.80	99
1999	Brushed Halory	3	E.Martin, Jr.	115	Gold From The West	115	Queen's Word	115	150,000	1:43.42	96
2000	Sincerely	3	M.McCarthy	117	Trip	119	Valleydar	117	150,000	1:43.83	100
2001	Zonk	3	M.J. McCarthy	115	Mystic Lady	122	Lady Andromeda	115	151,000	1:45.27	98
2002	Allamerican Bertie	3	L. Melancon	115	Alternate	117	Pass the Virtue	119	150,000	1:43.81	101
2003	Island Fashion	3	I.L. Puglisi	122	Awesome Humor	115	Ladyecho	115	300,000	1:44.95	94

Beyer Index: 95.88

Not run 1983-95. For previous runnings, refer to 1983 Manual

DEPUTY MINISTER HANDICAP, 6 1/2 Furlongs,
3-Year-Olds and Up, Gulfstream Park, 2003 Purse: $100,000

Year	Winner	Age	Jockey	Wt.	Second	Wt.	Third	Wt.	Win Value	Time	Beyer
1990	Beau Genius	5	C. Perret	118	The Red Rolls		Joel		30,000	1:23.00	104
1991	Unbridled	4	P. Day	119	Housebuster		Shuttleman		30,000	1:21.80	117
1992	Take Me Out	4	J.D. Bailey	118	Drummond Lane		Frozen Runway		30,000	1:22.60	108
1993	Loach	5	J.A. Santos	114	Hidden Tomahawk		British Banker		30,000	1:22.40	108
1994	I Can't Believe	6	E. Maple	113	Demaloot Demashoot.		Devil On Ice		30,000	1:08.00	108
1995	Chimes Band	4	J.Bailey	120	Distinct Reality	112	Ponche	113	30,000	1:09.00	106
1996	Jess C's Whirl	6	J.Krone	115	Buffalo Dan	117	Patton	114	30,000	1:10.60	106
1997	Templado	6	J.Bailey	113	Sea Emperor	114	Punch Line	119	45,000	1:09.60	106
1998	Irish Conquest	5	E.Coa	113	Frisk Me Now		Oro de Mexico		60,000	1:22.40	106
1999	Good And Tough	4	S.Sellers	115	Western Boreders	113	Mint	113	60,000	1:21.60	116
2000	Deep Gold	4	J.R.Velasquez	112	Forty One Carats	116	Klabin's Gold	114	60,000	1:15.89	103
2001	Instintaj	5	J.D. Bailey	118	Fappie's Notebook	113	Fantastic Finish	114	60,000	1:16.08	106
2002	Fappie's Notebook	5	J.F. Chavez	116	Twilight road	113	Binthebest	114	60,000	1:16.19	106
2003	Native Heir	5	C. Velasquez	114	Binthebest	115	Fire and Glory	114	60,000	1:15.17	109

Beyer Index: 107.79

DERBY TRIAL, 1 Mile,
3-Year-Olds, Churchill Downs, 2003 Purse: $167,400

Year	Winner	Age	Jockey	Wt.	Second	Wt.	Third	Wt.	Win Value	Time	Beyer
1938	The Chief	3	G. Woolf	117	Lawrin	118	Stagehand	118	2,145	1:35.80	
1939	Viscounty	3	C. Bierman	110	Technician	118	Steel Heels	110	2,150	1:38.40	
1940	Bimelech	3	F.A. Smith	118	Gallahadion	115	Sirocco	112	2,170	1:38.00	
1941	Blue Pair	3	J. Richard	115	Whirlaway	118	Cadmium	110	2,045	1:36.60	
1942	Valdina Orphan	3	C. Bierman	111	Sun Again	118	Alsab	118	23,050	1:36.80	
1943	Ocean Wave	3	W. Eads	112	Slide Rule	115	No Wrinkles	115	2,290	1:38.20	
1944	Broadcloth	3	F. Zufelt	110	Broad Grin	112	Rockwood Boy	110	4,400	1:37.20	
1945	Burning Dream	3	D. Dodson	111	Best Effort	118	Foreign Agent	112	4,570	1:38.20	
1946	Rippey	3	F. Zufelt	110	Spy Song	118	With Pleasure	118	9,775	1:40.20	
1947	Faultless	3	D. Dodson	118	Star Reward	110	Cosmic Bomb	118	9,075	1:37.60	
1948	Citation	3	E. Arcaro	118	Escadru	118	Eagle Look	118	8,525	1:37.40	
1949	Olympia	3	E. Arcaro	118	Ponder	110	Capot	118	9,000	1:37.40	
1950	Black George	3	E. Nelson	112	Middleground	118	Sunglow	118	9,850	1:40.00	
1951	Fanfare	3	D. Dodson	112	Bernwood	110	King Clover	110	10,250	1:36.60	
1952	Hill Gail	3	E. Arcaro	118	Arroz	110	Shag Tails	112	9,775	1:35.40	
1953	Dark Star	3	H. Moreno	115	Money Broker	118	Spy Defense	112	11,650	1:36.00	

Year	Winner	Age	Jockey	Wt.	Second	Wt.	Third	Wt.	Win Value	Time	Beyer
1954	Hasty Road	3	J. Adams	118	Determine	118	Allied	115	11,700	1:35.00	
1955	Flying Fury	3	C. McCreary	118	Jean's Joe	118	Nabesna	112	11,200	1:38.00	
1956	Fabius	3	W. Hartack	112	Countermand	118	Head Man	118	13,050	1:36.60	
1957	Federal Hill	3	W. Carstens	122	Gen. Duke	122	Better Bee	116	10,500	1:36.20	
1958	Tim Tam	3	I. Valenzuela	122	Ebony Pearl	116	Flamingo	112	10,380	1:39.60	
1959	Open View	3	K. Korte	116	Finnegan	122	Royal Orbit	119	10,385	1:35.60	
1960	Beau Purple	3	E. Guerin	116	Cuvier Relic	116	Pied d'Or	116	10,770	1:35.60	
1961	Crozier	3	B. Baeza	122	Four-and-Twenty	122	Dr. Miller	116	10,627	1:34.60	
1962	Roman Line	3	J. Combest	122	Lee Town	116	Sharp Count	119	10,432	1:37.20	
1963	Bonjour	3	W. Shoemaker	122	Gray Pet	116	On My Honor	122	10,530	1:36.40	
1964	Hill Rise	3	W. Shoemaker	122	Roman Brother	122	Mr. Moonlight	122	10,432	1:35.20	
1965	Bold Lad	3	W. Hartack	122	Carpenter's Rule	116	Bugler	116	10,237	1:35.20	
1966	Exhibitionist	3	E. Belmonte	122	Duc d'Eclair	116	Williamston Kid	122	10,237	1:36.00	
1967	Barbs Delight	3	W. Hartack	116	Cool Reception	122	Lightning Orphan	122	10,627	1:35.40	
1968	Proper Proof	3	J. Sellers	122	Jig Time	116	Verbatim	122	10,627	1:36.00	
1969	Ack Ack	3	M. Ycaza	122	Indian Emerald	122	Fleet Allied	122	10,432	1:34.40	
1970	Admiral's Shield	3	J. Nichols	119	George Lewis	122	Panicum Repens	117	10,725	1:37.20	
1971	Vegas Vic	3	H. Grant	119	Jr's Arrowhead	116	On the Money	114	13,910	1:37.00	
1972	Key to the Mint	3	B. Baeza	122	No Le Hace	122	Dr. Neale	116	14,560	1:36.20	
1973	Settecento	3	L. Adams	116	Mr. Prospector	116	I'm Guaranteed	119	13,650	1:37.00	
1974	Ga Hai	3	M. Manganello	122	Perfect Aim	122	To the Rescue	116	13,650	1:38.00	
1975	Round Stake	3	M. Hole	116	Rushing Man	116	Naughty Jake	122	13,650	1:36.40	
1976	Justa Bad Boy	3	W. Gavidia	116	Pastry	122	Here Comes Jo	116	13,520	1:38.00	
1977	Kodiack	3	R.L. Turcotte	116	Model Sailor	119	Castle Call	116	13,910	1:25.20	
1978	Braze and Bold	3	J. McKnight	119	Silver Nitrate	122	As in Elbow	116	13,780	1:25.40	
1979	Dreamy Prospect	3	D. Haire	119	Zuppardo's Prince	116	Great Redeemer	112	16,900	1:24.40	
1980	Royal Sporan	3	D. Brumfield	119	Real Emperor	122	Stutz Blackhawk	122	17,290	1:25.60	
1981	What It Is	3	J.C. Espinoza	116	Vodika Collins	119	Cornish Music	119	18,785	1:24.60	
1982	Listcapade	3	D. Haire	116	Star Gallant	122	Royal Roberto	122	40,853	1:38.20	
1983	Caveat	3	L. Pincay Jr	122	Total Departure	122	Pax in Bello	116	39,553	1:37.80	
1984	Devil's Bag	3	E. Maple	122	Biloxi Indian	122	Secret Prince	122	35,425	1:35.60	
1985	Creme Fraiche	3	R.P. Romero	119	Fast Account	122	Nordic Scandal	113	38,285	1:37.40	
1986	Savings	3	P.A. Johnson	113	Trobio	113	Sumptious	113	38,188	1:35.60	
1987	On the Line	3	P. Day	118	No More Flowers	116	Contractor's Tune	113	36,855	1:36.60	
1988	Jim's Orbit	3	S.P. Romero	122	Kingpost	122	Lover's Trust	119	36,953	1:38.60	
1989	Houston	3	L. Pincay Jr	122	Belek	119	Affirmed's Image	119	54,698	1:36.20	
1990	Housebuster	3	C. Perret	122	Private School	119	Falling Sky	117	54,454	1:37.60	
1991	Alydavid	3	P. Day	114	Honor Grades	117	Formal Dinner	122	57,760	1:36.40	97
1992	Alydeed	3	C. Perret	119	Binalong	117	Dignitas	119	56,200	1:36.20	110
1993	Cherokee Run	3	P. Day	122	Darien Deacon	114	Ground Force	117	56,355	1:37.40	103
1994	Numerous	3	C.J. McCarron	115	Dynamic Asset	114	Exclusive Praline	119	72,540	1:37.20	101
1995	Peaks and Valleys	3	P. Day	122	Our Gatsby	122	Strategic Intent	114	73,515	1:36.40	109
1996	Valid Expectations	3	D.R. Pettinger	119	Great Southern	114	Storm Creek	117	77,025	1:36.81	98
1997	Richter Scale	3	S.J. Sellers	114	Trafalger	122	Precocity	113	70,122	1:36.17	112
1998	Souvenir Copy	3	D.R. Flores	122	Yarrow Brae	114	Black Cash	122	70,246	1:35.80	105
1999	Patience Game	3	C.S. Nakatani	112	Prime Directive	122	Straight Man	114	71,176	1:37.86	105
2000	Performing Magic	3	P. Day	114	Sun Cat	117	Valiant Halory	114	70,680	1:35.99	102
2001	Meetyouathebrig	3	R.J. Albarado	122	Dream Run	114	One By the Knows	119	72,602	1:36.44	98
2002	Sky Terrace	3	C. Perret	114	Cashel Castle	122	Ide Be Spencers	114	69,936	1:36.87	101
2003	Midas Eyes	3	J.D. Bailey	122	Champali	122	Desert Warrior	118	103,788	1:36.22	105

Beyer Index: 103.54

DESERT STORMER HANDICAP, 6 Furlongs, Fillies and Mares, 3-Year-Olds and Up, Hollywood Park, 2003 Purse: $106,800

Year	Winner	Age	Jockey	Wt.	Second	Wt.	Third	Wt.	Win Value	Time	Beyer
1997	Advancing Star	4	K.J. Desormeaux	119	Stop Traffic	118	Tiffany Diamond	114	60,000	1:14.20	109
1998	Corona Lake	4	E. Delahoussaye	118	Lavender	116	Grab the Prize	116	64,020	1:14.60	101
1999	A.P. Assay	5	E. Delahoussaye	122	Woodman's Dancer	116	Corona Lake	118	63,600	1:08.60	106
2000	Theresa's Tizzy	6	L. Pincay Jr.	118	Hookedonthefeelin	117	Seth's Choice	114	64,980	1:09.30	105
2001	Go Go	4	E. Delahoussaye	122	Kalookan Queen	117	Wired to Fly	113	63,600	1:08.09	113
2002	Slewsbox	5	L. Pincay Jr.	117	Kalookan Queen	123	Rolly Polly	117	64,260	1:09.57	104
2003	Madame Pietra	6	P.A. Valenzuela	121	Bear Fan	116	Jetinto Houston	116	64,080	1:09.71	94

Beyer Index: 104.57

Run at 6 1/2 furlongs, 1997–98

DISCOVERY HANDICAP, 3-Year-Olds, 1 1/8 Miles, Aqueduct, 2003 Purse: $111,800

Year	Winner	Age	Jockey	Wt.	Second	Wt.	Third	Wt.	Win Value	Time	Beyer
1945	War Jeep	3	A. Kirkland	122	Chief Barker	116	Buzfuz	114	20,010	1:51.40	
1946	Mighty Story	3	B. James	115	Mahout	112	Assault	126	20,050	1:51.80	
1947	Cosmic Bomb	3	O. Scurlock	126	Double Jay	115	Phalanx	128	19,750	1:51.20	

Year	Winner	Age	Jockey	Wt.	Second	Wt.	Third	Wt.	Win Value	Time	Beyer
1948	Better Self	3	D. Gorman	123	Mount Marcy	117	Loser Weeper	109	20,850	1:53.80	
1949	Prophet's Thumb	3	D. Gorman	113	One Hitter	114	Curandero	109	15,650	1:52.20	
1950	Sunglow	3	D. Dodson	113	Steel Blue	106	Bit o' Fate	104	15,100	1:49.00	
1951	Alerted	3	O. Scurlock	114	Battlefield	126	Vulcania	108	15,225	1:50.40	
1952	Ancestor	3	T. Atkinson	107	Flaunt	107	Marcador	110	19,550	1:50.80	
1953	Level Lea	3	B. Green	112	Dictar	120	Landlocked	126	19,075	1:52.00	
1954	Chevation	3	E. Guerin	122	Kope's Baby	115	Guayana	109	20,500	1:50.00	
1955	Westward Ho	3	C. McCreary	113	Illusionist	111	Power	110	19,300	1:52.80	
1956	Reneged	3	I. Valenzuela	122	Riley	114	Oh Johnny	122	20,600	1:48.20	
1957	Ben Lomond	3	E. Arcaro	116	Harmonizing	110	Bureaucracy	118	21,600	1:49.20	
1958	Warhead	3	E. Arcaro	124	Grey Monarch	118	Backbone	124	19,330	1:51.20	
1959	Middle Brother	3	E. Arcaro	116	Demobilize	117	Intentionally	129	18,777	1:50.60	
1960	Kelso	3	E. Arcaro	124	Careless John	116	Count Amber	116	18,290	1:48.40	
1961	Ambiopoise	3	W. Shoemaker	123	Garwol	112	Wise Flushing	111	18,297	1:48.80	
1962	Comic	3	L. Adams	111	Dedimoud	116	Black Beard	120	19,012	1:48.60	
1963	Quest Link	3	W. Shoemaker	115	Outing Class	123	Hot Dust	117	19,305	1:49.80	
1964	Roman Brother	3	F. Alvarez	125	Lt. Stevens	113	Twice as Gay	109	18,135	1:49.00	
1965	Sammyren	3	H. Gustines	110	Selari	112	Royal Gunner	117	18,492	1:49.00	
1966	Deck Hand	3	W. Shoemaker	114	Yonder	110	Irish Ruler	113	18,557	1:49.60	
1967	Bold Hour	3	W. Shoemaker	119	Successor	119	Gala Performance	118	18,525	1:48.40	
1968	Ardoise	3	E. Belmonte	113	Balustrade	122	Pamir	111	18,557	1:49.20	
1969	Hydrologist	3	D.B. Thomas	111	Red Reality	112	Say Not So	111	18,492	1:47.60	
1970	Burd Alane	3	J. Velasquez	114	Buzkashi	115	Captain Nash	120	18,492	1:47.40	
1971	Autobiography	3	L. Pincay Jr	115	Minsky	114	Boone the Great	109	20,550	1:50.40	
1972	Forage	3	E. Maple	113	Sunny and Mild	120	Festive Mood	112	17,055	1:48.60	
1973	Forego	3	H. Gustines	127	My Gallant	122	Arbees Boy	114	33,300	1:47.20	
1974	Rube the Great	3	A. Cordero Jr	119	Holding Pattern	126	Sharp Gary	118	33,270	1:48.20	
1974	Green Gambados	3	A. Cordero Jr	120	Best of It	116	Jolly Johu	121	33,570	1:48.20	
1975	Dr. Emil	3	B. Baeza	115	Rushing Man	125	Syllabus	113	33,630	1:48.60	
1976	Wise Phillip	3	D. Montoya	107	Teddy's Courage	115	Patriot's Dream	112	32,460	1:48.60	
1977	Cox's Ridge	3	E. Maple	126	Broadway Forli	123	Papelote	107	32,670	1:48.60	
1978	Sorry Lookin	3	R.I. Velez	110	Silent Cal	115	Judge Advocate	114	31,740	1:49.60	
1979	Belle's Gold	3	A. Cordero Jr	121	Smarten	122	Gallant Best	115	33,270	1:48.00	
1980	Fappiano	3	A. Cordero Jr	114	Reef Searcher	114	Royal Hierarchy	111	35,280	1:50.00	
1981	Princelet	3	E. Maple	113	Accipiter's Hope	118	Pass the Tab	126	33,240	1:51.00	
1982	Trenchant	3	J.L. Samyn	113	Dew Line	113	Exclusive Era	112	32,880	1:50.80	
1983	Country Pine	3	J.D. Bailey	115	Jacque's Tip	115	Father Don Juan	112	33,420	1:49.60	
1984	Key to the Moon	3	D. Beckon	120	Silver Stark	112	Raja's Shark	124	42,300	1:50.00	
1985	Proud Truth	3	J. Velasquez	126	Important Business	113	Romancer	110	51,750	1:49.20	
1986	Moment of Hope	3	M. Venezia	108	Gold Alert	109	Clear Choice	112	54,000	1:49.60	
1987	Parochial	3	J.A. Krone	117	Homebuilder	112	Forest Fair	115	109,620	1:51.20	
1988	Dynaformer	3	A. Cordero Jr	116	Star Attitude	113	Congeleur	112	104,580	1:50.00	
1989	Tricky Creek	3	C. Perret	117	Traskwood	113	Farewell Wave	110	71,280	1:50.00	
1990	Sports View	3	J.A. Santos	113	Chief Honcho	117	Killer Diller	116	52,830	1:48.60	
							Out of Place	112			
1991	Upon My Soul	3	J.L. Samyn	112	Excellent Tipper	114	Honest Ensign	110	75,960	1:49.60	105
1992	New Deal	3	R.G. Davis	111	Offbeat	114	Dodsworth	113	74,880	1:48.00	98
1993	Prospector's Flag	3	J.F. Chavez	114	Virginia Rapids	118	Living Vicariously	114	70,320	1:52.20	103
1994	Serious Spender	3	Chavez JF	113	Unaccounted For	121	Malmo	112	63,540	1:51.20	97
1995	Michael's Star	3	J.A. Krone	112	Hunting Hard	113	Reality Road	114	67,380	1:50.20	99
1996	Gold Fever	3	M.E. Smith	121	Crafty Friend	115	Early Echoes	111	66,720	1:49.00	106
1997	Mr. Sinatra	3	M.E. Smith	116	Concerto	121	Twin Spires	116	64,620	1:49.40	102
1998	Early Warning	3	J.F. Chavez	115	Deputy Diamond	117	Gulliver	115	50,010	1:48.80	111
1999	Adonis	3	J.R. Velazquez	118	Best of Luck	118	Waddaan	113	64,980	1:50.11	103
2000	Left Bank	3	J.R. Velazquez	119	Perfect Cat	114	Open Sesame	115	64,020	1:47.30	103
2001	Evening Attire	3	S.X. Bridgmohan	111	Street Cry	118	Free of Love	115	65,580	1:48.62	103
2002	Saint Marden	3	J.D. Bailey	117	Regency Park	115	No Parole	117	68,400	1:49.13	106
2003	During	3	J.A. Santos	120	Unforgettable Max	114	Inamorato	114	67,080	1:51.18	106

Beyer Index: 103.23

DOGWOOD, 1 1/16 Miles,
3-Year-Old Fillies, Churchill Downs, 2003 Purse: $109,000

Year	Winner	Age	Jockey	Wt.	Second	Wt.	Third	Wt.	Win Value	Time	Beyer
1975	My Juliet	3	A. Hill	121	Snow Dolly	118	Hope She Does	118	14,999	1:24.00	
1976	T.V. Vixen	3	M. Maganello	121	Sunny Romance	116	Old Goat	121	14,154	1:23.40	
1977	Unreality	3	M. Fromin	121	Shady Lou	115	Time for Pleasure	118	15,031	1:25.40	
1978	Bold Rendezvous	3	A. Rini	121	Step in the Circle	118	Timeforaturn	118	14,446	1:23.40	
1979	Split the Tab	3	D. Haire	121	Shawn's Gal	121	Safe	121	19,663	1:24.00	
1980	Quality Corner	3	M.S. Haire	121	Forever Cordial	121	No No Nona	121	19,403	1:24.00	
1981	Savage Love	3	P. Nicolo	116	Westport Native	118	Brian's Babe	116	19,053	1:24.80	
1981	Fancy Naskra	3	J. Lively	118	Contrefaire	121	Solo Disco	118	17,948	1:25.20	

Year	Winner	Age	Jockey	Wt.	Second	Wt.	Third	Wt.	Win Value	Time	Beyer
1982	Amazing Love	3	L. Melancon	117	Sefa's Beauty	117	Bold Siren	113	23,546	1:46.60	
1983	Bon Gout	3	P. Day	117	Andthebeatgoeson	112	Workin Girl	112	36,368	1:53.00	
1984	Mrs. Revere	3	L. Melancon	121	Rambling Rhythm	119	Robin's Rob	115	49,510	1:51.20	
1985	Foxy Deen	3	D. Montoya	118	Weekend Delight	120	Clouhalo	112	35,945	1:50.00	
1986	Hail a Cab	3	P.A. Johnson	119	Tall Poppy	111	Marshesseaux	114	46,810	1:46.60	
1987	Lady Gretchen	3	M. McDowell	112	Super Cook	122	Jonowo	122	46,193	1:44.00	
1988	Darien Miss	3	D. Brumfield	121	Stolie	118	Most Likely	116	35,848	1:43.80	
1989	Luthier's Launch	3	P. Day	118	Motion in Limine	116	Dreamy Mimi	121	36,465	1:45.20	
1990	Patches	3	K.K. Allen	118	Mrs. K.	116	Mirth	114	34,870	1:46.60	88
1991	Be Cool	3	A.T. Gryder	121	Barri Mac	114	Saratoga Dame	121	36,560	1:46.40	79
1992	Hitch	3	B.E. Bartram	121	Bionic Soul	121	Secretly	114	36,070	1:47.60	83
1993	With a Wink	3	C.R. Woods Jr.	114	Lovat's Lady	112	Unlaced	116	36,010	1:44.20	89
1994	Briar Road	3	L. Melancon	114	Stella Cielo		Shadow Miss		53,186	1:44.78	94
1995	Gal In A Ruckus	3	W. McCauley	121	Country Cat	116	Naskra Colors	114	53,527	1:43.88	104
1996	Ginny Lynn	3	L. Melancon	121	Everhope	121	Hidden Lake	114	53,576	1:43.22	99
1997	Leo's Gypsy Dancer	3	P. Day	116	Buckeye Search		Flying Lauren		68,696	1:44.95	93
1998	Really Polish	3	P. Day	116	Beat The Play	114	Victorica	114	67,642	1:44.60	94

Nickel Classic finished second but was disqualified and placed fifth

Year	Winner	Age	Jockey	Wt.	Second	Wt.	Third	Wt.	Win Value	Time	Beyer
1999	Golden Temper	3	S.J. Sellers	116	Boom Town Girl	121	Honey Hill Lil	116	69.068	1:43.73	94
2000	Welcome Surprise	3	F.C. Torres	112	Lady Melesi	114	Vivid Sunset	114	68,014	1:46.80	86
2001	Nasty Storm	3	L.J. Meche	114	Love at Noon	114	Golly Greeley	116	68,014	1:43.41	98
2002	Take Charge Lady	3	A.J. D'Amico	121	Charmed Gift	116	Allamerican Bertie	114	67,890	1:42.73	98
2003	Golden Marlin	3	S.J. Sellers	115	Double Scoop	114	Throne	114	67,580	1:45.96	91

Beyer Index: 92.14

EATONTOWN HANDICAP, 1 1/16 Miles (Turf), Fillies and Mares
3-Year-Olds and Up, Monmouth Park, 2003 Purse: $100,000

Year	Winner	Age	Jockey	Wt.	Second	Wt.	Third	Wt.	Win Value	Time	Beyer
1971	Flor de Sombra	6	H. Hinojosa	111	Ziba Blue	115	Sea Force	114	18,769	1:43.20	
1972	Telly	4	V. Bracciale Jr.	115	Tico's Donna	111	Jolly Fox	114	14,454	1:42.40	
1972	Best Go	4	V. Bracciale Jr.	110	Irish Party	115	Joans Paris	112	14,617	1:42.40	
1973	Telly	5	V. Bracciale Jr.	113	Lightning Lucy	110	Wire Chief	111	14,763	1:43.60	
1973	Cathy Baby	4	M.A. Rivera	116	Aglimmer	116	Bold Place	117	14,633	1:42.60	
1974	Bird Boots	5	B. Thornburg	119	Belle Marie	117	Shaya	108	19,207	1:46.80	
1975	Hinterland	5	C. Perret	114	Ringmistress	114	Kudara	119	18,135	1:43.60	
1976	Collegiate	4	J.W. Edwards	113	Copano	119	Double Ack	114	14,950	1:43.60	
1976	Stage Luck	4	J.W. Edwards	118	Hinterland	114	D'sse du Val	121	14,787	1:43.20	
1977	Jolly Song	5	J. Nied Jr.	112	T.V. Genie	112	All Biz	117	18,590	1:47.20	
1978	Huggle Duggle	4	B. Gonzalez	113	All Biz	118	Navajo Princess	114	22,116	1:42.60	
1979	The Very One	4	C. Cooke	116	Frosty Skater	120	Municipal Bond	113	25,236	1:46.20	
1980	Riddle's Reply	4	E. Cardone	113	Sharp Zone	111	Newmarket Lady	112	20,078	1:44.20	
1980	Nasty Jay	5	R.E. McKnight	111	T.V. Highlights	119	O'Connell Street	113	20,288	1:44.00	
1981	Wayward Lassie	4	D. Montoya	112	Earlham	114	Paris Press	114	16,958	1:44.60	
1981	Endicotta	5	D. Brumfield	116	Dance Troupe	115	Farewell Letter	113	16,717	1:44.80	
1982	Kuja Happa	4	D.R. Wright	114	Qui Silent	113	Suave Princess	113	27,465	1:44.80	
1983	Doodle	4	J. Miranda	118	Olamic	110	Bright Choice	112	28,410	1:44.00	
1984	Jubilous	4	G. McCarron	118	Maidenhead	113	High Schemes	118	36,060	1:43.40	
1985	Agacerie	4	A. Cordero Jr.	116	Meddlin Maggie	115	Naturela Grace	114	34,830	1:44.20	
1986	Mazatleca	6	C. Perret	117	Cope of Flowers	114	Darbrielle	113	27,960	1:43.20	
1986	Bharal	5	J. Velasquez	114	Thirteen Keys	114	Dawn's Curtsey	118	28,200	1:43.80	
1987	Bailrullah	5	N. Santagata	111	Princely Proof	116	Krotz	118	28,590	1:44.00	
1987	Cadabra Abra	4	W.H. McCauley	118	Treasure Map	115	Spruce Fir	121	28,110	1:43.80	
1988	Hear Music	5	M. Castaneda	115	Fancy Pan	112	Antique Mystique	111	34,440	1:49.80	
1989	Highland Penny	4	D. Carr	112	Starofanera	113	River Memories	114	34,770	1:50.00	
1990	Miss Unnameable	6	L. Saumell	113	Lip Service	116	Perfect Coin	112	34,110	1:48.00	
1991	Jacuzzi Boogie	4	N. Santagata	119	Hear the Bells	113	Be Exclusive	113	21,000	1:41.60	
1992	Red Journey	4	N. Santagata	114	Hot Times Are Here	113	Flashing Eyes	113	21,000	1:45.00	89
1993	Topsa	6	L. Rivera Jr.	113	Naked Royalty	115	Suspect Terrain	115	21,000	1:46.20	87
1994	Verbal Volley	5	R. Colton	119	Irving's Girl	114	Uptown Show	113	24,000	1:44.60	92
1995	Symphony Lady	5	J. Bravo	119	Cox Orange	122	Grafin	119	30,000	1:43.60	93
1996	Gail's Brush	5	Boulanger G.	116	Plenty Of Sugar	117	Lady Affirmed	116	45,000	1:40.40	96
1997	B. A. Valentine	4	McCarron C. J.	122	Everhope	112	Vashon	112	41,460	1:41.20	96
1998	Gastronomical	5	Stevens G. L.	115	Tampico	117	Dance Clear	112	41,400	1:43.20	100
							Poopsie	114			
1999	Formal Tango	4	J.D. Bailey	113	Proud Owner	115	Natalie Too	122	60,000	1:42.62	99
2000	Reciclada	5	A. Solis	115	Mumtaz	122	Dominique's Joy	117	60,000	1:44.34	104
2001	Cousin Gigi	4	R. Wilson	115	Quidnaskra	116	Crystal Sea	113	60,000	1:47.50	101
2002	Clearly a Queen	5	E.M. Coa	119	Laurica	114	Presumed Innocent	117	60,000	1:44.02	97
2003	Stylish	5	H. Castillo Jr	118	Something Ventured	117	Sweet Deimos	113	60,000	1:41.69	95

Beyer Index: 95.75

EL CAMINO REAL DERBY, 1 1/16 Miles,
3-Year-Olds, Golden Gate, 2003 Purse: $200,000

Year	Winner	Age	Jockey	Wt.	Second	Wt.	Third	Wt.	Win Value	Time	Beyer
1982	Cassaleria	3	D.G. McHargue	120	Crystal Star	120	Tropic Ruler	120	76,100	1:42.80	
1983	Knightly Rapport	3	F. Toro	120	Croeso	120	Twilight Career	120	96,700	1:44.80	
1984	French Legionaire	3	R.A. Baze	120	Gate Dancer	120	Heavenly Plain	120	126,200	1:42.40	
1985	Tank's Prospect	3	J. Velasquez	120	Right Con	120	Dan's Diablo	120	151,000	1:41.00	
1986	Snow Chief	3	A. Solis	120	Badger Land	120	Darby Fair	120	137,500	1:42.60	
1987	Masterful Advocate	3	L. Pincay Jr	120	Fast Delivery	120	Hot and Smoggy	120	137,500	1:42.40	
1988	Ruhlmann	3	P. Day	117	Havanaffair	117	Chinese Gold	119	137,500	1:39.40	
1989	Double Quick	3	A. Solis	115	Rob an Plunder	119	Hawkster	122	165,000	1:43.60	
1990	Silver Ending	3	G.L. Stevens	115	Individualist I	115	Single Dawn	122	165,000	1:43.00	
1991	Sea Cadet	3	T.M. Chapman	117	General Meeting	118	Mizter Interco	122	165,000	1:40.60	
1992	Casual Lies	3	A. Petterson	117	Seahawk Gold	115	Silver Ray	122	165,000	1:42.00	90
1993	El Atroz	3	R.Q. Meza	117	Offshore Pirate	117	Lykatill Hil	119	110,000	1:43.60	85
1994	Tabasco Cat	3	P. Day	113	Flying Sensation	115	Robannier	115	110,000	1:42.60	90
1995	Jumron	3	G.F. Almeida	113	Snow Kidd'n	115	American Day	114	110,000	1:43.60	103
1996	Cavonnier	3	M.A. Pedroza	115	Sergeant Stroh	113	E C's Dream	115	110,000	1:43.40	90
1997	Pacificbounty	3	K.J. Desormeaux	120	Wild Wonder	115	Carmen's Baby	117	110,000	1:41.80	98
1998	Event of the Year	3	R.A. Baze	115	Post a Note	117	Clover Hunter	120	110,000	1:40.20	105
1999	Cliquot	3	D.R. Flores	115	Charismatic	115	No Cal Bread	117	110,000	1:43.29	95
2000	Remember Sheikh	3	F.T. Alvarado	117	True Confidence	116	Country Coast	115	110,000	1:43.47	92
2001	Hoovergetthekeys	3	R. Warren	120	Startac	120	Mo Mon	115	110,000	1:40.85	103
2002	Yougottawanna	3	J. Lumpkins	120	Danthebluegrassman	117	Lusty Latin	115	110,000	1:43.48	87
2003	Ocean Terrace	3	M.E. Smith	115	Ministers Wild Cat	117	Ten Most Wanted	115	110,000	1:42.26	93

Beyer Index: 94.25

EL CONEJO HANDICAP, 5 1/2 Furlongs,
4-Year-Olds and Up, Santa Anita, 2003 Purse: $108,800

Year	Winner	Age	Jockey	Wt.	Second	Wt.	Third	Wt.	Win Value	Time	Beyer
1981	To B. Or Not	5	P.A. Valenzuela	122	Summer Time Guy	119	Cool Frenchy	115	35,500	1:02.40	
1982	To B. Or Not	6	C.J. McCarron	122	Belfort	116	Terresto's Singer	115	39,350	1:02.20	
1983	Pompeii Court	6	L. Pincay Jr	123	General Jimmy	115	Kangroo Court	120	39,350	1:02.80	
1984	Premiership	4	R.A. Meza	115	Haughty But Nice	116	Chip o' Lark	117	30,425	1:03.40	
1984	Night Mover	4	E. Delahoussaye	117	Dave's Friend	120	Bara Lass	117	30,525	1:03.20	
1985	Debonaire Junior	4	C.J. McCarron	126	Much Fine Gold	112	Fifty Six Ina Row	119	38,950	1:02.60	
1986	Take My Picture	4	G.L. Stevens	119	Rosie's K.T.	119	Five North	114	64,300	1:03.00	
1988	Sylvan Express	5	E. Delahoussaye	119	Carload	117	High Brite	120	48,100	1:03.80	
1989	Sunny Blossom	4	F.H. Valenzuela	114	Sensational Star	115	Prospector's Gamble	116	47,100	1:04.60	
1990	Frost Free	5	C.J. McCarron	115	Sunny Blossom	119	Prospector's Gamble	114	45,900	1:03.00	
1991	Black Jack Road	7	G.L. Stevens	115	Laurens Quest	110	Lee's Tanthem	117	61,975	1:05.20	
1992	Gray Slewpy	4	K.J. Desormeaux	114	Frost Free	119	Cardmania	116	61,270	1:02.01	111
1993	Fabulous Champ	4	C.J. McCarron	115	Arrowtown	117	Slerp	117	63,800	1:02.66	105
1994	Gundaghia	7	E. Delahoussaye	116	Sir Hutch	114	Davy Be Good	118	64,800	1:02.01	108
1995	Phone Roberto	6	C.J. McCarron	114	Lost Pan	115	Rotsaluck	112	65,000	1:02.34	101
1996	Lit de Justice	6	C.S. Nakatani	119	A.J. Jett	112	Fu Man Slew	116	64,250	1:01.85	114
1997	High Stakes Player	5	C.S. Nakatani	116	Kern Ridge	113	Subtle Trouble	114	63,850	1:02.89	107
1998	The Exeter Man	6	G.K. Gomez	114	Tower Full	117	Red	114	64,020	1:02.23	107
1999	Kona Gold	5	A. Solis	119	Big Jag	117	Mr. Doubledown	118	64,380	1:01.74	115
2000	Freespool	4	C.J. McCarron	114	Mellow Fellow	115	Old Topper	116	64,200	1:03.33	106
2001	Freespool	4	C.J. McCarron	114	Men's Exclusive	117	Lexicon	118	65,220	1:02.50	107
2002	Snow Ridge	4	M.E. smith	114	Explicit	117	Rio Oro	117	65,700	1:03.05	102
2003	Kona Gold	9	A. Solis	123	Radiata	115	No Armistice	116	65,280	1:02.63	109

Beyer Index: 107.67

The 2001 running took place in Dec. 2000

ELKHORN, 1 1/2 Miles (Turf),
4-Year-Olds and Up, Keeneland Race Course, 2003 Purse: $150,000

Year	Winner	Age	Jockey	Wt.	Second	Wt.	Third	Wt.	Win Value	Time	Beyer
1988	Yankee Affair	6	P. Day	123	Stormonthel'se	118	Blazing Bart	123	56,485	1:49.60	
1989	Exclusive Partner	7	F. Toro	120	Yankee Affair	120	Pappas Swing	120	54,958	1:50.40	
1990	Ten Keys	6	R.P. Romero	123	Yankee Affair	123	Maceo	118	71,460	1:51.80	105
1991	Itsallgreektome	4	R.A. Baze	123	Pirate Army	113	Spark O'Dan	113	71,143	1:51.20	
1992	Fourstars Allstar	4	J.D. Bailey	113	Slew the Slewor	120	Rainbows for Life	120	79,490	1:47.60	100
1993	Coaxing Matt	4	P. Day	118	Cleone	113	Maxigroom	118	68,572	1:47.60	104
1994	Lure	5	M.E. Smith	123	Buckhar	120	Pride of Summer	120	66,526	1:53.60	109
1995	Marvin's Faith	4	C. Perret	113	Hasten to Add	120	Opera Score	120	70,680	1:47.00	101
1996	Vladivostok	6	P. Day	112	Penn Fifty Three	114	Party Season	119	68,262	2:30.80	102
1997	Chief Bearhart	4	J.A. Santos	114	Snake Eyes	113	Lassigny	122	68,324	2:28.40	104
1998	African Dancer	6	J.D. Bailey	114	Chief Bearhart	122	Chorwon	114	66,712	2:31.60	104
1999	African Dancer	7	J.D. Bailey	114	Magest	114	Chorwon	113	68,138	2:27.84	104
2000	Drama Critic	4	J.D. Bailey	116	Craigsteel	116	Dixie's Crown	116	69,750	2:28.03	101

Year	Winner	Age	Jockey	Wt.	Second	Wt.	Third	Wt.	Win Value	Time	Beyer
2001	Williams News	6	R.J. Albarado	116	Gritty Sandie	116	Craigsteel	116	70,308	2:29.13	102
2002	Kim Loves Bucky	5	J.F. Chavez	116	Rochester	116	Cetewayo	118	93,000	2:32.49	98
2003	Kim Loves Bucky	6	K.J. Desormeaux	117	Man From Wicklow	123	Williams News	116	93,000	2:29.39	105

Beyer Index: 103

ENDINE HANDICAP, 6 Furlongs,
3-Year-olds and Up, Fillies and Mares, Delaware Park, 2003 Purse: $200,000

Year	Winner	Age	Jockey	Wt.	Second	Wt.	Third	Wt.	Win Value	Time	Beyer
1971	Royal Signal	4	M. Hole	119	I'm for Mama	119	Faneuil Hall	112	19,272	1:10.80	
1972	Main Pan	4	W.J. Passmore	114	Alma North	120	Secret Retreat	113	18,850	1:11.20	
1973	Light Hearted	4	E. Neilson	118	Barely Even	125	Levee Night	113	18,525	1:10.00	
1974	Miss Rebound	6	B. Baeza	123	Flo's Pleasure	116	Gallant Davelle	116	19,045	1:10.00	
1975	Honky Star	4	J. Tejeira	119	Laraka	117	Sailingon	114	18,655	1:11.00	
1976	Donetta	5	J.W. Moseley	118	Susie's Last	112	Crackerfax	115	17,145	1:12.00	
1977	My Juliet	5	A.S. Black	127	Debby's Turn	115	Catabias	113	17,973	1:09.60	
1978	Dainty Dotsie	4	B. Phelps	127	Spot Two	123	Debby's Turn	115	21,450	1:09.60	
1979	Quatre Saisons	4	V. Bracciale Jr.	115	Shanachie	112	Order in Court	115	21,580	1:12.00	
1980	Candy Eclair	4	J.D. Bailey	126	Wonderous Me	108	Grecian Victory	112	29,803	1:09.80	
1981	Veiled Look	5	W.J. Passmore	120	Rejuvanate	113	Tequila Sheila	109	17,875	1:08.80	
1982	Wading Power	4	H. Pilar	107	Bravo Native	108	Lady Dean	123	14,723	1:10.80	
1996	Hay Hanne	4	J.A. Velez Jr.	114	Know B's	116	Ayrial Delight	122	22,770	1:10.20	95
1997	Dancin Renee	3	J.A. Velez Jr.	122	Two Punch Lil	122	Ana Belen	113	30,000	1:10.00	101
1998	Soverign Lady	4	M.E. Smith	115	Weather Vane	122	Little Sister	117	45,000	1:09.40	106
1999	Hurricane Bertie	4	P. Day	117	Little Sister	119	Bourbon Belle	119	60,000	1:08.75	109
2000	Superduper Miss	4	T. Turner	114	Debby d'Or	119	Cassidy	119	60,000	1:10.22	95
2001	Xtra Heat	3	R. Wilson	118	Ivy's Jewel	118	Big Bambu	121	90,000	1:09.64	117
2002	Xtra Heat	4	H. Vega	121	Outstanding Info	118	Urban Dancer	118	90,000	1:10.91	100
2003	House Party	3	J.A. Santos	117	Vision in Flight	114	Mooji Moo	115	120,000	1:08.35	108

Beyer Index: 103.88

ESSEX HANDICAP, 1 1/16 Miles
4-Year-Olds and Up, Oaklawn Park, 2003 Purse: $100,000

Year	Winner	Age	Jockey	Wt.	Second	Wt.	Third	Wt.	Win Value	Time	Beyer
1976	Navajo	6	J. Nichols	123	My Friend Gus	121	Bold Trap	113	34,950	1:41.00	
1977	Go to the Bank	5	G. Patterson	111	Romeo	119	Limited Ad't'n	114	37,260	1:42.40	
1978	Cisk	5	G. Patterson	117	Forever Casting	114	Oui Henry	117	36,570	1:41.60	
1980	J. Burns	5	J. McKnight	113	Convenient	114	Dar'ng Damacus	115	35,220	1:42.80	
1981	Prince Majestic	4	G. Patterson	117	Blue Ensign	114	Uncool	115	34,650	1:42.40	
1982	Plaza Star	4	R.P. Romero	118	Vodika Collins	118	Tally Ho the Fox	116	37,950	1:42.80	
1983	Eminency	5	W. Nemeti	121	Dance Pavilion	113	Majestys Prince	125	38,670	1:42.40	
1984	Le Cou Cou	4	D.L. Howard	119	Hi Pi	120	Double Ready	114	36,480	1:41.80	
1985	Star Choice	6	J. McKnight	121	Plaza Star	115	Shamtastic	112	49,260	1:40.60	
1986	Double Ready	6	D.E. Whited	113	Red Attack	112	Kohzaam	112	51,060	1:41.60	
1987	Sun Master	6	R.L. Frazier	116	Royal Troon	112	Lyphard's Ridge	111	36,750	1:41.00	
1988	Savings	4	P.A. Johnson	117	Entitled To	117	Red Attack	115	43,680	1:42.60	
1989	Proper Reality	4	J.D. Bailey	120	Contact Game	111	Lyphard's Ridge	112	34,530	1:44.00	
1990	Forli Light	4	D. Guillory	115	Momsfurrari	115	Traskwood	115	36,930	1:42.80	113
1991	Greydar	4	P. Day	117	Silent Survivor	120	The Great Carl	112	34,770	1:42.00	107
1992	Allijeba	6	P. Day	118	On the Edge	113	Bedeviled	116	34,500	1:43.80	98
1993	Delafield	4	P. Day	113	Famed Devil	117	Yukon Robbery	116	33,900	1:42.00	103
1994	Greatsilverfleet	4	Gomez GK	116	Prize Flight	113	All Gone	111	32,250	1:42.00	106
1995	Silver Goblin	4	Cordova DW	122	Prince of the Mt.	113	Golden Gear	113	33,150	1:42.00	110
1996	Classic Fit	6	C.V. Gonzalez	114	Judge TC	122	Juliannus	113	47,700	1:42.80	107
1997	No Spend No Glow	5	R.N. Lester	113	Illesam	113	Auggie My Dad	111	45,000	1:45.80	100
1998	Relic Reward	4	C.H. Borel	113	Phnatom on Tour	119	Brush With Pride	116	45,000	1:43.80	108
1999	Brush With Pride	7	T.T. Doocy	116	Littlebitlively	115	Treat Me Doc	114	45,000	1:43.26	103
2000	Maysville Slew	4	L.S. Quinonez	115	Sand Ridge	112	Mr Ross	116	45,000	1:44.12	94
2001	Mr Ross	6	D. Pettinger	117	Remington Rock	114	Maysville Slew	118	45,000	1:43.59	101
2002	Crafty Shaw	4	J. Lopez	116	Kiss of Lion	113	Remington Rock	116	45,000	1:43.14	113
2003	Colorful Tour	4	L.S. Quinonez	116	Ask the Lord	118	Premeditation	117	60,000	1:46.62	99

Beyer Index: 104.71

EXCELSIOR BREEDERS' CUP HANDICAP, 1 1/8 Miles,
3-Year-Olds and Up, Aqueduct, 2003 Purse: $170,000

Year	Winner	Age	Jockey	Wt.	Second	Wt.	Third	Wt.	Win Value	Time	Beyer
1903	Blackstock	4	G.C. Fuller	98	Heno	116	Yel. Tail	100	6,730	1:46.60	
1904	Rostand	4	H. Phillips	105	Red Knight	112	Lord Barge	99	6,600	1:45.60	
1905	Santa Catalina	3	W. Miller	95	Rapid Water	119	Sinister	94	6,450	1:46.40	

Year Winner	Age	Jockey	Wt.	Second	Wt.	Third	Wt.	Win Value	Time	Beyer
1906 Merry Lark	4	W. Miller	106	Ormonde's Right	111	Eug. Burch.	110	7,350	1:47.20	
1907 Dr. Gardner	4	J. Martin	123	Glorifier	115	Cairngorm	115	7,350	1:48.20	
1908 McCarter	4	J. Notter	113	Jack Atkin.	119	Rifleman.	111	6,850	1:46.00	
1910 Guy Fisher	4	E. Taplin	100	Fayette.	112	Arasee.	106	1,925	1:46.00	
1913 Meridian	5	J. Glass	120	Cock o' the Walk	114	Lahore.	113	2,575	1:44.60	
1915 Addie M.	3	J. McCahey	97	Stromboli	122	Short Grass	123	1,925	1:45.80	
1916 Sand Marsh	4	J. Butwell	111	Flying Fairy	111	Slumber II	113	2,425	1:46.00	
1917 Roamer	6	A. Schuttinger	123	Borrow.	117	Old Koenig.	112	2,825	1:45.40	
1918 George Smith	5	W. Kelsay	117	Roamer	120	W. Hogan	122	3,850	1:45.40	
1919 Naturalist	5	C. Fairbrother.	122	Star Master	119	Boniface.	108	3,850	1:45.40	
1920 Boniface	5	E. Sande	117	Lanius.	112	Naturalist.	122	4,850	1:45.20	
1921 Blazes.	4	T. Rice	118	Exterminator.	120	Naturalist.	126	8,550	1:47.20	
1922 Sennings Park.	6	C. Fairbrother.	115	Mad Hatter.	129	Vel. Hand.	126	5,850	1:44.80	
1923 Grey Lag.	5	L. Fator	130	Exodus	111	Prince James	112	5,850	1:45.00	
1924 Rialto	4	J. Corcoran.	115	Sunsini.	102	Zev	133	5,850	1:46.00	
1925 Sting.	4	B. Breuning	106	Cherry Pie.	111	Mad Play	124	5,850	1:42.60	
1926 Turf Idol	4	S. Hebert.	108	Cherry Pie.	107	Wilderness.	111	6,400	1:45.60	
1927 Amberjack	4	J. McCoy	102	Cherry Pie.	110	Navigator.	108	6,200	1:44.00	
1928 Brown Flash.	4	V. Peterson	114	Herodian	105	Grey Lag.	118	6,200	1:46.40	
1929 Mowlee	4	L. Fator	115	Son o' Battle	106	Mi Vida.	108	7,200	1:45.20	
1930 Minotaur.	4	C. Kurtsinger.	106	Sandy Ford.	114	Comstockery	107	5,950	1:45.80	
1931 Mokatam	4	W. Kelsay	126	Flaming	107	Maya	110	5,700	1:46.00	
1932 Pompeius	3	L. Knapp	105	Mountain Elk	114	Light. Bolt	116	4,850	1:45.20	
1934 Watch Him.	5	S. Steffen	108	Caesars Ghost	112	Mr. Khayyam	123	2,450	1:46.00	
1935 King Saxon.	4	C. Rainey.	120	Okapi	109	Coequel	102	5,430	1:43.80	
1936 King Saxon.	5	C. Landolt.	121	Good Harvest.	108	Esposa	102	5,400	1:45.20	
1937 Thorson.	5	W. Ray	107	Memory Book	116	Whopper	127	6,950	1:43.80	
1938 Caballero II	6	W.D. Wright.	114	Tatterdemalion.	112	Teufel	112	6,650	1:45.40	
1939 Thanksgiving.	4	R. Workman.	120	Fighting Fox	120	Tatterdemalion	114	6,950	1:44.20	
1940 The Chief	5	I. Anderson.	112	Sandy Boot.	108	Anthology	108	6,200	1:44.20	
1941 Robert Morris	3	N. Wall.	100	Olympus.	102	Corydon	112	8,275	1:44.60	
1942 Olympus	7	C. Wahler	105	Boysy	114	Sir Jeffrey	106	8,775	1:46.80	
1943 Riverland	5	S. brooks.	124	Minee-Mo.	108	Marriage.	121	9,300	1:44.40	
1944 Alex Barth	4	N. Jemas	105	Grey Wing	109	Boysy.	114	7,375	1:46.40	
1945 Saguaro.	4	M. Caffarella	108	Dockstader.	106	Rounders	113	7,070	1:44.60	
1946 Fighting Step	4	J. Adams	123	King Dorsett	115	Lets Dance.	111	12,750	1:45.00	
1947 Coincidence	5	T. Atkinson.	115	Polynesian	126	Lets Dance.	112	15,900	1:44.00	
1948 Knockdown	4	F. Zufelt.	114	Double Jay	125	Stymie.	128	20,750	1:46.00	
1949 My Request	4	C. Erickson.	126	Vulcan's Forge	123	Nearway	113	16,700	1:44.80	
1950 Arise.	4	D. Dodson.	116	Olympia.	126	Delegate.	119	17,200	1:43.80	
1951 Lotowhite.	4	E. Arcaro.	116	Ferd.	123	Great Circle.	119	20,750	1:44.20	
1952 Spartan Valor	4	J. Stout	126	Greek Ship	122	Sonic	108	18,950	1:44.60	
1953 First Glance.	6	E. Guerin.	118	Bryan G.	119	Dark Count	106	20,500	1:44.00	
1954 Find	4	E. Guerin.	121	Count Cain	112	Capeador	119	21,250	1:44.00	
1955 Fisherman	4	H. Woodhouse.	126	Joe Jones	119	Gold'n Gloves	112	20,450	1:45.00	
1956 Find	6	E. Guerin.	116	Joe Jones	119	Fisherman	122	19,800	1:43.20	
1957 Midafternoon	5	E. Arcaro.	126	Beam Rider.	110	Pylades	112	19,750	1:43.60	
1958 Kingmaker	5	R. Ussery.	126	Third Brother.	124	Beam Rider	114	18,615	1:43.60	
1959 Whitley	4	S. Boulmetis	116	Mystic II	118	Grey Monarch	118	18,485	1:43.80	
1960 Talent Show.	5	R. Broussard	119	Nimmer	115			18,745	1:34.80	
1961 Mail Order	5	L. Adams	120	Disperse.	114	All Hands	118	19,110	1:49.20	
1962 Hitting Away	4	R. Ussery.	116	Up Scope.	113	Manassa Mauler	114	18,557	1:50.00	
1963 Greek Money.	4	J.L. Rotz	115	Misty Day	112	Rebellious	108	18,265	1:48.60	
1964 Uppercut.	5	J. Sellers	112	Rocky Link	116	Morry E.	115	17,875	1:50.00	
1965 Tenacle	4	W. Mayorga	110	Tibaldo.	118	Quita Dude.	114	35,750	1:49.40	
1966 Choker.	6	R. Ussery.	115	Point du Jour.	113	Quita Dude.	116	36,010	1:49.20	
1968 Peter Piper	5	J. Velasquez.	112	Straight Deal.	115	Grace Born	112	35,945	1:48.00	
1969 San Roque	4	H. Gustines.	119	Tropic King II	120	Juvenile John	120	37,310	1:49.60	
1970 Hydrologist	4	C. Baltazar	119	Never Bow	119	Gaelic Dancer	118	37,570	1:48.80	
1971 Loud	4	J. Vasquez.	116	Personality	126	Knight in Armor	110	34,200	1:50.80	
1972 Autobiography	4	A. Cordero Jr.	123	Native Royalty	115	Urgent Message	119	34,860	1:49.00	
1973 Key to the Mint	4	R. Turcotte.	126	King's Bishop	115	North Sea.	120	32,640	1:47.80	
1974 Everton II.	5	M. Castaneda	117	Prince Dantan	123	Three or Less	108	33,840	1:49.00	
1975 Step Nicely	4	A. Cordero Jr.	126	Monetary Principle	113	Jolly Johu	119	33,990	1:48.40	
1976 Double Edge Sword	6	A. Cordero Jr.	112	Northerly.	115	Sharp Gary.	119	51,120	1:48.20	
1977 Turn and Count	4	S. Cauthen	123	Festive Mood.	115	Gabe Benzur	112	48,150	1:51.00	
1978 Cox's Ridge	4	E. Maple	129	Pumpkin Moonshine	108	Nearly on Time.	113	49,005	1:50.60	
1979 Special Tiger.	4	G. Martens.	113	Mister Brea.	125	Coverack	112	63,600	2:03.80	
1980 Ring of Light.	5	C.B. Asmussen	114	Silent Cal.	122	Rivalero	118	67,560	2:01.40	
1981 Irish Tower.	4	J. Fell	127	Ring of Light	113	Relaxing	125	64,680	2:00.80	
1982 Globe	5	M. Venezia	112	Accipiter's Hope.	116	Bar Dexter	118	66,480	2:03.40	
1983 Fast Gold	4	J.L. Samyn	114	Turn Bold	107	Sing Sing	124	67,200	2:04.00	
1984 Canadian Factor	4	J. Velasquez	117	Luv a Libra	117	Canadian Calm.	108	102,150	2:03.00	

Year Winner	Age	Jockey	Wt.	Second	Wt.	Third	Wt.	Win Value	Time	Beyer
1985 Morning Bob	4	J. Vasquez	112	Lord of the Manor	112	Last Turn	110	67,750	2:04.20	
1986 Garthorn	6	R.Q. Meza	124	Nordance	110	Broadway T'mmy	107	101,340	2:02.40	
1987 Lac Ouimet	4	E. Maple	114	Alioth	113	Proud Debonair	115	106,380	2:02.00	
1988 Lac Ouimet	5	J.D. Bailey	116	Personal Flag	117	Talinum	116	140,880	2:00.20	
1989 Forever Silver	4	J.A. Krone	111	Its Acedemic	113	Jack of Clubs	113	99,720	2:02.60	
1990 Lay Down	6	C.W. Antley	112	Lac Ouimet	113	Doc's Leader	112	100,980	2:02.20	108
1991 Chief Honcho	4	M.E. Smith	117	I'm Sky High	115	Apple Current	115	102,060	2:02.60	113
1992 Defensive Play	5	D.R. Flores	117	Alyten	111	Will to Reign	108	102,780	2:01.80	112
1993 Devil His Due	4	M.E. Smith	117	Exotic Slew	109	Bill of Rights	112	72,120	2:03.00	110
1994 Colonial Affair	4	J.A. Santos	121	Contract Court	109	West by West	116	90,000	1:49.80	110
1995 Iron Gavel	5	J.R. Martinez J	111	Electrojet	114	Danzig's Dance	115	90,000	1:49.20	115
1996 May I Inquire	7	J. Bravo	111	Personal Merit	114	Ormsby	115	120,000	1:50.60	105
1997 Ormsby	5	C.C. Lopez	116	Greatsilverfleet	112	Circle of Light	111	120,000	1:47.60	121
1998 Sir Bear	5	E.M. Jurado	117	K.J.'s Appeal	117	Accelerator	111	120,000	1:49.20	108
1999 Smart Coupons	6	R.R. Douglas	114	Archers Bay	118	Pasay	112	120,000	1:49.71	102
2000 Lager	6	H. Castillo Jr	113	Best of Luck	114	Chester House	117	120,000	1:49.76	109
2001 Cat's at Home	4	F. Leon	115	Top Official	113	Boston Party	115	120,000	1:48.92	112
2002 John Little	4	N. Arroyo Jr	111	Windsor Castle	113	Ground Storm	118	120,000	1:49.25	109
2003 Classic Endeavor	5	C.C. Lopez	113	Balto Star	119	Tempest Fugit	114	90,000	1:48.10	105

Beyer Index: 109.93

FALL HIGHWEIGHT HANDICAP, 6 Furlongs, 3-Year-Olds and Up, Aqueduct, 2003 Purse: $108,300

Year Winner	Age	Jockey	Wt.	Second	Wt.	Third	Wt.	Win Value	Time	Beyer
1914 Comely	2	J. McCahey	110	Forum	120	Surprising	124	1,275	1:12.00	
1915 Harmonicon	5	J. Notter	140	Flittergold	128	H. Prynne	124	1,195	1:10.80	
1916 Mount d'Or	5	J. Notter	133	Short Grass	135	Hidden Star	112	1,230	1:13.20	
1917 Ima Frank	4	J. McTaggart	111	Hank O'Day	126	H'wfa	100	1,410	1:11.80	
1918 Hollister	4	J. Loftus	123	Ima Frank	108	Papp	120	2,100	1:10.00	
1919 Naturalist	5	C. Fairbrother	140	Billy Kelly	108	Enfilade	116	2,900	1:11.60	
1920 Lion d'Or	4	E. Sande	134	On Watch	124	Naturalist	145	3,100	1:09.80	
1921 Crocus	3	Coltiletti	122	Krewer	128	Step Lightly	107	2,725	1:11.20	
1922 Careful	4	J. Butwell	126	Prodigious	108	Exodus	128	3,300	1:12.60	
1923 Fair Phantom	4	E. Sande	122	Runviso	115	Dunlin	123	3,275	1:10.40	
1924 Worthmore	3	S. O'Donnell	126	Shuffle Along	125	Sarazen	135	4,225	1:11.60	
1925 Superlette	3	L. Fator	124	Wild Aster	122	McAuliffe	121	3,400	1:12.40	
1926 Powhatan	3	J. Maiben	115	Croydon	117	Pompey	132	3,800	1:12.00	
1927 Happy Argo	4	S. O'Donnell	134	Byrd	118	What'll I Do	116	4,050	1:11.20	
1928 Finite	3	F. Moon	123	Extreme	127	Byrd	120	3,700	1:12.60	
1929 Osmand	5	W. Garner	140	Balko	118	Finite	119	3,600	1:10.60	
1930 Balko	5	J. Bejshak	136	The Heathen	129	Finite	129	3,375	1:09.40	
1931 Mr. Sponge	4	W. Garner	126	Helianthus	115	Balko	138	3,025	1:11.60	
1932 Larranga	3	R. Workman	126	Halcyon	127	Black Jacket	119	2,450	1:10.40	
1933 Microphone	4	S. Coucci	110	Pairbypair	120	B'd Bo'boy	117	1,485	1:11.00	
1934 Miss Merriment	3	E. Steffen	119	Kievex	123	Halcyon	118	2,750	1:10.40	
1935 Sation	5	J. Hunter	140	Whopper	117	Cycle	111	3,075	1:10.20	
1936 Miss Merriment	5	R. Workman	127	Fraidy Cat	113	Cycle	124	3,200	1:09.60	
1937 Preeminent	5	E. Arcaro	128	He Did	130	Crossbow II	130	2,975	1:10.80	
1938 The Fighter	5	R. Workman	131	Go Home	120	Preeminent	140	4,750	1:10.00	
1939 Rough Time	5	F. Faust	129	Golden Voyage	130	Preeminent	120	6,100	1:09.40	
1940 T.M. Dorsett	4	R. Workman	125	Pictor	129	Joe Schenck	126	4,500	1:11.40	
1941 Roman	4	D. Meade	140	Speed to Spare	124	The Chief	120	4,500	1:10.00	
1942 Imperatrice	4	C. McCreary	119	Tola Rose	119	Doublrab	140	5,925	1:10.20	
1943 Cassis	4	T. Atkinson	126	Tellmenow	109	True North	117	6,725	1:11.20	
1944 Ariel Lad	5	E. Arcaro	125	Tellmenow	117	True North	136	7,285	1:08.40	
1945 True North	5	T. Atkinson	140	Armed	135	Breezing Home	120	7,370	1:08.80	
1946 Cassis	7	B. James	116	True North	130	Buzfuz	132	16,750	1:08.80	
1947 Rippey	4	O. Scurlock	131	Pipette	114	Ben Lewis	103	21,300	1:10.80	
1948 First Flight	4	E. Arcaro	123	Big Story	124	Blue Border	124	22,650	1:08.60	
1949 Royal Governor	5	E. Guerin	129	Royal Blood	132	Tea-Maker	127	17,150	1:12.00	
1950 Arise	4	D. Dodson	133	Delegate	128	Royal Governor	129	17,800	1:08.80	
1951 Guillotine	4	T. Atkinson	134	Squared-Away	126	Ferd	128	18,700	1:09.00	
1952 Hitex	3	E. Arcaro	130	Tea-Maker	140	Papoose	117	17,300	1:08.40	
1953 Kaster	4	A. Catalano	121	Jet Master	114	Dutch Lane	118	16,600	1:09.80	
1954 Pet Bully	6	W. Hartack	136	Dutch Lane	135	Dark Peter	125	17,800	1:11.20	
1955 Sailor	3	H. Woodhouse	120	I Appeal	124	Tahiti	130	21,550	1:09.00	
1956 Impromptu	4	C. McCreary	127	Decimal	122	Gay Warrior	114	21,550	1:09.00	
1957 Itobe	4	E. Nelson	124	Commendation	116	Gay Warrior	117	20,600	1:09.40	
1958 Bull Strength	4	E. Arcaro	120	Reneged	136	Cohoes	127	19,135	1:10.00	
1959 Mystic II	5	M. Sorrentino	122	Discard	125	Silver Ship	140	18,095	1:11.00	

Year	Winner	Age	Jockey	Wt.	Second	Wt.	Third	Wt.	Win Value	Time	Beyer
1960	Four Lane	3	S. Boulmetis	125	Yes You Will	125	Tick Tock	122	18,192	1:09.00	
1961	Smashing Gail	3	R. Ussery	117	Tick Tock	129	Gyro	122	18,655	1:10.00	
1962	Be on Time	3	P. Anderson	120	Crozier	126	Jets Pat	124	18,752	1:09.40	
1963	Accordant	3	P. Kallai	124	For the Road	132	Merry Ruler	130	14,787	1:10.20	
1964	Delta Judge	4	J.L. Rotz	138	Uppercut	129	Third Martini	137	18,005	1:10.80	
1965	Pack Trip	5	M. Ycaza	131	Determined Man	129	Flag Raiser	140	18,167	1:13.80	
1966	Impressive	3	K. Knapp	132	Brooklyn Bridge	128	Hoist Bar	123	18,752	1:10.40	
1967	Indulto	4	J.L. Rotz	132	Full of Fun	134	Flag Raiser	137	18,200	1:12.60	
1968	More Scents	4	A. Cordero Jr	136	Gaylord's Feather	133	Taipan	125	18,460	1:11.80	
1969	Ta Wee	3	J.L. Rotz	130	King Emperor	131	Gaylord's Feather	129	18,622	1:10.20	
1970	Ta Wee	4	J.L. Rotz	140	Towzie Tyke	121	Distinctive	134	18,935	1:10.40	
1971	Shut Eye	5	A. Cordero Jr	135	Flight Topic	119	Naskra	124	20,280	1:10.80	
1972	Chou Croute	4	J.L. Rotz	131	Icecapade	135	Saxony Warrior	132	17,340	1:10.00	
1973	King's Bishop	4	E. Maple	129	Shecky Greene	137	Aljamin	125	17,310	1:09.40	
1974	Piamem	4	M.A. Rivera	133	Lonetree	140	Rastaferian	124	22,575	1:10.40	
1975	Honorable Miss	6	W. Shoemaker	130	No Bias	130	Lonetree	132	54,720	1:09.80	
1976	Relent	5	R. Hernandez	120	Kirby Lane	124	Soy Numero Uno	137	39,105	1:09.80	
1976	Honorable Miss	6	W. Shoemaker	130	Lachesis	126	Rush'g Man	129	39,780	1:10.00	
1977	What a Summer	4	J. Vasquez	134	Broadway Forli	123	Piamem	129	50,490	1:10.00	
1978	What a Summer	5	A. Cordero Jr	134	Buckfinder	129	White Rammer	128	48,195	1:09.40	
1979	Whatsyourpleasure	6	A. Cordero Jr	127	Dewan Keys	130	Tilt Up	130	49,095	1:09.60	
1980	King's Fashion	5	J.L. Samyn	136	Double Zeus	135	J.P. Brother	118	51,120	1:10.60	
1981	Piedmont Pete	5	K. Black	128	Miswaki	130	Turbulence	120	50,490	1:10.40	
1982	Gold Beauty	3	D. Brumfield	126	Engine One	131	Osorno	125	50,940	1:09.20	
1983	Chas Conerly	4	J. Miranda	136	Singh Tu	124	Let Burn	134	50,670	1:10.40	
1984	Mamaison	4	C.J. McCarron	130	Timeless Native	138	Muskoka Wyck	131	77,040	1:10.20	
1985	Mt. Livermore	4	J. Velasquez	140	Fighting Fit	139	Ziggy's Boy	134	89,460	1:10.60	
1986	Funistrada	4	R.G. Davis	117	Raja's Shark	137	Love That Mac	133	82,140	1:09.40	
1987	Purple Mountain	5	R. Migliore	123	Banker's Jet	125	Moment of Hope	129	85,500	1:08.80	
1988	Parlay Me	3	R.P. Romero	125	Well Selected	121	High Brite	135	69,000	1:09.60	
1989	Sewickley	4	R.P. Romero	131	Once Wild	129	Dancing Spree	133	68,880	1:09.60	
1990	Senor Speedy	4	J.F. Chavez	131	Sunshine Jimmy	131	Diablo	131	51,030	1:09.80	
1992	Salt Lake	3	M.E. Smith	128	Burn Fair	126	Belong to Me	122	68,520	1:09.00	107
1993	Fly So Free	5	J.D. Bailey	135	Demaloot Demashoot	126	Take Me Out	134	72,360	1:09.40	110
1994	Chimes Band	3	J.D. Bailey	135	Golden Pro	128	Boom Towner	131	65,940	1:11.20	107
1995	Jess C's Whirl	5	J.F. Chavez	126	Classy Mirage	134	Demaloot Demashoot	134	66,180	1:09.80	105
1996	Victor Avenue	4	J.F. Chavez	127	Splendid Sprinter	133	Stalwart Member	128	67,440	1:09.20	109
1997	Royal Haven	5	R. Migliore	136	King Roller	129	Kelly Kip	135	65,820	1:10.60	111
1998	Punch Line	8	J.F. Chavez	126	American Champ	131	Golden Tent	126	66,840	1:10.00	103
1999	Richter Scale	5	J.F. Chavez	134	Aristotle	130	Bought in Dixie	128	66,060	1:09.00	116
2000	Kashatreya	6	O. Vergara	131	Exciting Story	131	Oro de Mexico	130	67,140	1:11.03	92
2001	Yonaguska	3	J.A. Santos	131	Big E E	129	Voodoo	123	67,320	1:09.60	103
2002	True Direction	3	J.J. Castellano	134	Crossing Point	133	Gold I.D.	127	66,960	1:09.62	106
2003	Bossanova	3	E.S. Prado	128	Papua	132	Savoy Special	127	64,980	1:10.06	101

Beyer Index: 105.83

FAYETTE, 1 1/8 Miles,
3-Year-Olds and Up, Keeneland Race Course, 2003 Purse: $163,800

Year	Winner	Age	Jockey	Wt.	Second	Wt.	Third	Wt.	Win Value	Time	Beyer
1959	Terra Firma	4	K. Church	123	Hymient	119	Dru Away	123	10,865	1:51.40	
1960	Little Fitz	5	W.A. Peake	117	Toby's Brother	108	Better Bee	118	11,255	1:49.60	
1961	Zumbador II	4	R. Broussard	116	Bluescope	118	Tompion	126	10,887	1:47.60	
1962	Blue Cro'n	4	N. Cox	117	Gushing Wind	122	Loyal Son	118	11,407	1:48.80	
1963	Choker	3	K. Church	114	Port of Mecca	115	Jet Clipper	114	11,765	1:41.40	
1964	Swoonen	4	K. Knapp	113	City Line	119	Lemon Twist	116	18,590	1:42.00	
1965	Old Hat	6	R. Gallimore	119	Lt. Stevens	122	Big Brigade	114	18,330	1:42.80	
1966	Yumbel	5	H. Pilar	113	Road Hog	109	Come On II	117	18,525	1:43.60	
1967	Swoonaway	6	B. Phelps	119	Hy Frost	116	Miracle Hill	115	19,012	1:42.60	
1968	Yorkville	4	D.E. Whited	119	War Censor	115	Monitor	114	18,362	1:42.00	
1969	Royal Harmony	5	M. Solomone	117	Otomano II	115	Miracle Hill	116	18,557	1:42.60	
1970	Royal Harmony	6	E.J. Knapp	118	Dust Commander	113	Fast Hilarious	122	17,826	1:42.80	
1971	Royal Harmony	7	D.E. Whited	119	New Round	112	Mariuco	111	19,402	1:42.60	
1972	Chou Croute	4	J.L. Rotz	123	Sensitive Music	117	Chateauvira	114	18,899	1:44.00	
1973	Chateauvira	6	G. Gallitano	112	Grocery List	116	O So Big	115	19,094	1:42.80	
1974	Jesta Dream Away	4	A. Rini	115	Super Sail	121	Joyous Jester	112	18,119	1:41.60	
1975	Warbucks	5	J. Nichols	120	Hasty Flyer	119	Mr. Door	114	18,460	1:44.40	
1976	Silver Badge	5	G. Patterson	111	Easy Gallop	117	Topinabee	112	17,981	1:44.60	
1976	Yamanin	4	G. Patterson	114	Run for Clem	111	Faneuil Boy	119	17,899	1:43.20	
1977	Bob's Dusty	3	R. Depass	117	Man's Man	115	Packer Captain	118	18,395	1:42.80	
1978	Silver Series	4	D. Brumfield	121	Buckfinder	121	Romeo	118	20,768	1:41.20	

Year Winner	Age	Jockey	Wt.	Second	Wt.	Third	Wt.	Win Value	Time	Beyer
1979 Architect	3	S.A. Spencer	117	Coverack	121	Trimlea	120	35,699	1:49.60	
1980 Hurry Up Blue	3	G. Gallitano	112	Marcy Road	111	All the More	116	39,423	1:49.00	
1981 Ironworks	3	P. Day	117	Two's a Plenty	116	Sun Catcher	118	39,861	1:49.20	
1982 Rivalero	6	R.P. Romero	115	Cad		Recusant	114	35,563	1:50.40	
1982 El Baba	3	D. Brumfield	118	Vodika Collins	120	Hechizado	115	38,813	1:50.20	
1983 Frost King	5	R. Platts	123			Bold Style	120	22,663	1:48.80	
1984 Star Choice	5	J. McKnight	112	Explosive Wagon	117	Bright Baron	113	47,492	1:47.40	
1985 Wop Wop	3	D.E. Foster	112	Banner Bob	117	Exclusive Greer	114	36,530	1:51.40	
1986 Harham's Sizzler	7	R. Meier	120	Derby Wish	119	Pirate's Skiff	112	34,792	1:49.20	
1987 Good Command	4	D. Brumfield	118	Minneapple	120	Savings	115	73,921	1:46.80	
1988 Homebuilder	4	D. Brumfield	121	Blue Buckaroo	120	Ile de Jinsky	112	68,315	1:51.20	
1989 Drapeau Tricolore	4	J.E. Bruin	114	Air Worthy	116	Blue Buckaroo	118	71,695	1:48.20	
1990 Lac Ouimet	7	R.P. Romero	119	Din's Dancer	121	Secret Hello	116	70,233	1:47.20	111
1991 Summer Squall	4	P. Day	122	Unbridled	122	Secret Hello	115	69,810	1:48.80	109
1992 Barkerville	3	S.J. Sellers	114	Medium Cool	117	Majesterian	114	70,680	1:48.40	112
1993 Grand Jewel	3	J.D. Bailey	120	Split Run	120	Secreto's Hideaway	114	68,634	1:46.80	108
1994 Sunny Sunrise	7	J.D. Carle	120	Key Contender	117	Powerful Punch	117	67,766	1:50.00	111
1995 Judge T C	4	J.M. Johnson	114	Powerful Punch	120	Sir Vixen	114	104,625	1:49.00	109
1996 Isitingood	5	D.R. Flores	120	Distorted Humor	114	Strawberry Wine	117	120,110	1:50.40	110
1997 Whiskey Wisdom	4	W. Martinez	115	City by Night	123	Pyramid Peak	120	101,184	1:48.60	118
1998 Arch	3	S.J. Sellers	123	Touch Gold	115	Wild Tempest	115	98,394	1:53.80	111
1999 Social Charter	4	M. St. Julien	120	Master O Foxhounds	118	Early Warning	118	135,904	1:55.28	100
2000 Jadada	5	S.J. Sellers	118	Mojave Moon	118	Get Away With It	118	214,800	1:54.92	99
2001 Connected	4	M. St. Julien	119	Broken Vow	123	Outofthebox	122	103,509	1:50.05	106
2002 Tenpins	4	C. Perret	123	X Country	119	Crafty Shaw	121	99,789	1:51.17	110
2003 M B Sea	4	C. Perret	119	Tenpins	121	Seattle Fitz	119	101,556	1:50.30	103
						Changeintheweather	119			

Run at 1 1/16 miles, 1963–78; at 1 3/16 miles, 1998–2000

Beyer Index: 108.36

FIFTH SEASON, 1 1/16 Miles,
4-Year-Olds and Up, Oaklawn Park, 2003 Purse: $100,000

Year Winner	Age	Jockey	Wt.	Second	Wt.	Third	Wt.	Win Value	Time	Beyer
1994 Nelson	7	S.P. Romero	117	Punch Line	117	Senor Tomas	114	41,640	1:43.00	95
1995 Tyus	6	C. Borel	114	Prince of the Mt.	114	Joseph's Robe	114	26,760	1:42.80	105
1996 No Spend No Glow	5	R. Lester	117	Bucks Nephew	117	Groovy Jett	117	47,880	1:42.80	98
1997 Krigeorj's Gold	5	J. Johnson	119	Bucks Nephew	117	Prince of the Mt.	116	49,500	1:43.20	103
1998 Acceptable	4	A. Solis	117	Littlebitlively	117	Brush With Pride	124	60,000	1:42.40	106
1999 Truluck	4	L. Melancon	114	Slide to the Left	114	Rock and Roll	114	60,000	1:42.20	108
2000 Mr. Ross	5	E. Perner	115	Relic Reward	114	Crimson Classic	114	60,000	1:42.93	106
2001 Remington Rock	7	D.E. Simington	114	Kombat Kat	114	Da Devil	114	45,000	1:43.13	102
2003 Patton's Victory	5	A.E. Birzer	117	Colorful Tour	122	Makors Mark	118	60,000	1:43.26	107

Not run in 2002

Beyer Index: 103.33

FIRST LADY HANDICAP, 6 Furlongs,
Fillies and Mares 3-Year-Olds and Up, Gulfstream Park, 2003 Purse: $100,000

Year Winner	Age	Jockey	Wt.	Second	Wt.	Third	Wt.	Win Value	Time	Beyer
1981 Island Charm	4	J. Velasquez	113	La Voyageuse		Lacey		22,536	1:10.60	
1983 Prime Prospect	5	D. MacBeth	118	Miss Hitch		Mrs. Roberts		28,282	1:10.80	
1985 Nany	5	G. St. Leon	120	Micky's Echo		Birdie Bell		29,352	1:09.80	
1986 Sugar's Image	5	J. Velez Jr	115	Summer Mood		Mr. T's Tune		29,736	1:11.20	
1987 One Fine Lady	5	R. Danjean	114	Fleur de Soleil		Sheer Ice		24,045	1:10.40	
1988 Funistrada	5	W. Guerra	120	Easter Mary		Cadillacing		29,232	1:10.20	
1989 Waggley	6	J.L. Samyn	112	Damality		My Peace		27,288	1:11.00	
1990 Sez Fourty	4	M. Gonzalez	114	Classic Value		Fit for a Queen		22,760	1:11.20	95
1991 Spirit of Fighter	8	J. Velez	118	Mistaurian		Love's Exchange		30,000	1:11.60	
1992 Withallprobability	4	C. Perret	118	Christina Czarina		Spirit of Fighter		30,000	1:11.00	100
1993 Si Si Sezyo	5	R. Hernandez	112	Illeria		Jeano		30,000	1:11.20	97
1994 Santa Catalina	6	J.D. Bailey	114	Insight to Cope	119	Capture the Crown	113	30,000	1:11.20	100
1995 Recognizable	4	M.E. Smith	113	Insight to Cope		Maison de Reve	114	30,000	1:09.60	104
1996 Chaposa Springs	4	J.D. Bailey	122	Phone the Doctor	117	Market Slide	113	45,000	1:10.20	98
1997 Chip	4	J. Bravo	113	Phone the Doctor	116	Surprising Fact	113	45,000	1:09.60	101
1998 U Can Do It	5	S.J. Sellers	115	Start at Once	113	Vivace	118	45,000	1:09.80	102
1999 Scotzanna	7	R. Migliore	114	U Can Do It	118	Foil	116	45,000	1:10.17	110
2000 Hurricane Bertie	5	P. Day	118	Marley Vale	118	Cassidy	113	45,000	1:10.22	99
2001 Another	4	E.S. Prado	113	Curious Treasure	114	Dynamite Diablo	115	60,000	1:10.41	90
2002 Raging Fever	4	J.R. Velazquez	118	Cat Cay	118	Mandy's Gold	116	60,000	1:10.36	106
2003 Harmony Lodge	5	J.R. Velazquez	113	Fly Me Crazy	114	Haunted Lass	114	60,000	1:10.31	98

Beyer Index: 100

FLASH, 5 Furlongs,
2-Year-Olds, Belmont Park, 2003 Purse: $103,400

Year	Winner	Age	Jockey	Wt.	Second	Wt.	Third	Wt.	Win Value	Time	Beyer
1981	Ringaro	2	A. Cordero Jr.	119	Lead Astray	119	Prince Westport	115	33,300	1:04.60	
1982	Victorious	2	J.D. Bailey	115	Satan's Charger	119	Great Ending	119	33,420	1:04.20	
1999	More Than Ready	2	J.R. Velazquez	119	Diablo's Addition	115	Bevo	115	49,200	57.00	102
2000	Yonaguska	2	J.D. Bailey	115	The Goo	115	City Zip	115	49,200	57.80	97
2001	Buster's Daydream	2	E.S. Prado	115	Harmony Hall	115	Huber Woods	115	49,365	56.93	94
2002	Whywhywhy	2	E.S. Prado	114	Presence	115	Down Play	114	65,460	57.10	85
2003	Chapel Royal	2	J.R. Velazquez	114	Hasslefree	114	Juventus	114	63,955	57:02	99

Beyer Index: 95.4

Run at 5 1/2 furlongs, 1981–1982. Not run from 1972–1980, 1983–1998. For runnings previous to 1972, refer to 1972 Manual

FLORAL PARK HANDICAP, 6 Furlongs, Fillies and Mares,
3-Year-Olds and Up, Belmont Park, 2003 Purse: $108,500

Year	Winner	Age	Jockey	Wt.	Second	Wt.	Third	Wt.	Win Value	Time	Beyer
1995	Twist Afleet	4	G.L. Stevens	120	For All Reason	115	Regal Solution	113	32,490	1:09.20	109
1996	Lottsa Talc	6	F.T. Alvarado	119	Fresa	113	Culver City	113	38,736	1:09.80	95
1997	Creamy Dreamy	4	R.G. Davis	118	Silent City	113	Secret Prospect	118	47,835	1:10.40	93
1998	Blue Begonia	5	J.F. Chavez	114	Dixie Flag	117	Soverign Lady	116	48,570	1:10.20	100
1999	Positive Gal	3	J.D. Bailey	113	Final Proposal	113	Flamingo Way	113	49,125	1:09.23	102
2000	Big Bambu	3	R.G. Davis	114	Tropical Punch	114	Cash Run	114	64,620	1:09.81	104
2001	Gold Mover	3	E.S. Prado	114	Dat You Miz Blue	119	Finder's Fee	115	65,040	1:10.00	100
2002	Carson Hollow	3	J.R. Velazquez	117	Gold Mover	117	Shiny Band	115	63,955	1:10.25	107
2003	Bauhauser	5	R. Migliore	115	Shine Again	120	Literary Light	113	65,100	1:10.84	94

Beyer Index: 100.44

FLORIDA OAKS, 3-Year-Old Fillies,
1 1/16 Miles, Tampa Bay Downs, 2003 Purse: $150,000

Year	Winner	Age	Jockey	Wt.	Second	Wt.	Third	Wt.	Win Value	Time	Beyer
1984	Sure Too Explode	3	R.D. Luhr	114	April Sonnett	116	Northern Jazz	111	38,940	1:25.40	
1985	Ertswhile	3	C. Hussey	113	Erin's Dunloe	112	Flickering Match	119	39,270	1:48.00	
1986	Noranc	3	H. McCauley	122	Man a Stan	112	An Affirmation	115	64,980	1:44.60	
1987	Single Blade	3	J.M. Pezua	112	Without Feathers	119	Merry Mercedes	112	76,200	1:45.60	
1988	Colonial Waters	3	V.H. Molina	112	Tomorrow's Child	119	Tilt My Halo	119	65,400	1:44.80	
1989	She's Scrumptious	3	R.M. Adkins	113	Iron and Silver	119	Georgies Doctor	119	60,000	1:46.00	
1990	Dance Colony	3	W.H. McCauley	122	Premier Question	119	Sun Luck	113	60,000	1:45.20	
1991	Designated Dancer	3	W. Martinez	119	Car Gal	115	Fantastic Morning	115	60,000	1:45.40	
1992	Luv Me Luv Me Not	3	W. Martinez	121	New Dance	114	Foxy Persuasion	113	60,000	1:45.60	
1993	Star Jolie	3	E.O. Nunez	111	Hollywood Wildcat	121	Jacody	121	60,000	1:46.40	81
1994	Cavada	3	Whitley K	118	Come on Joy	113	Strategic Maneuver	121	60,000	1:46.40	83
1995	Sneaky Quiet	3	M.E. Smith	121	Commando Dancer	118	Smooth Quest	113	60,000	1:45.40	83
1996	Mindy Gayle	3	J.A. Guerra	118	Plum Country	121	Weekend in Seattle	114	60,000	1:45.80	81
1997	Anklet	3	S.J. Sellers	118	Global Star	114	Screamer	111	60,000	1:45.00	89
1998	Pantufla	3	P. Day	114	Puddlejump	114	Try N Sue	111	60,000	1:45.40	82
1999	Crown Jewel	3	L. Martinez	118	Madison's Charm	111	Here I Go	118	60,000	1:46.69	89
2000	Secret Status	3	P. Day	118	March Magic	114	Musical	111	75,000	1:45.05	82
2001	Quick Tip	3	R. Migliore	116	Southern Ficton	116	Emery Board	116	90,000	1:45.36	85
2002	French Satin	3	R.A. Dominguez	118	Romancin Dixie	120	Ciudad de Carson	116	90,000	1:45.49	85
2003	Ebony Breeze	3	M. Guidry	120	Dakota Light	122	Crimson and Roses	116	90,000	1:45.20	89

Beyer Index: 84.45

FORT MARCY HANDICAP, 1 Mile (Off the Turf),
3-Year-Olds and Up, Aqueduct, 2003 Purse: $117,500

Year	Winner	Age	Jockey	Wt.	Second	Wt.	Third	Wt.	Win Value	Time	Beyer
1975	Apollo Nine	8	M. Venezia	110	Silver Badge	112	Bold Play	112	24,630	1:23.00	
1975	Beau Bugle	5	J. Cruguet	113	Ribot Grande	112	New Alibhai	112	24,510	1:22.40	
1978	True Colors	4	E. Maple	114	Proud Arion	112	Cinteelo	119	25,410	1:42.80	
1978	Tiller	4	J. Fell	112	Noble Dancer II	127	Arachnoid	111	25,410	1:41.80	
1979	Uncle Pokey	5	J. Cruguet	113	Alias Smith	114	Proud Arion	111	32,550	1:45.60	
1980	Sten	4	C.B. Asmussen	115	Native Courier	126	Told	113	35,460	1:44.00	
1981	Masked Marvel	5	R.I. Encinas	112	Blue Ensign	116	Freeo	113	33,300	1:44.80	
1981	Key to Content	4	J. Fell	117	Ghazwan	114	Contare	107	33,060	1:46.00	
1982	Folge	4	J. Velasquez	110	Johnny Dance	114	St. Brendan	116	36,060	1:42.80	
1983	John's Gold	4	A. Graell	108	Acaroid	115	Beagle	105	36,600	1:47.40	
1984	Hero's Honor	4	J.D. Bailey	115	Super Sunrise	126	Reinvested	115	54,270	1:43.60	
1985	Forzando II	4	J. Velasquez	114	Native Raid	115	Solidified	113	54,180	1:46.00	
1986	Onyxly	5	J.A. Santos	117	Equalize	114	Lieutenant's Lark	117	55,890	1:42.20	
1987	Dance of Life	4	R.P Romero	120	Regal Flier	113	Iroko	118	84,240	1:45.00	
1987	Glaros	5	E. Maple	114	Onyxly		Expl'sive Dancer	111	85,200	1:45.00	
1988	Equalize	6	J.A. Santos	115	All Hands on Deck	109	Glaros	111	89,340	1:42.60	
1989	Arlene's Valentine	4	J.A. Krone	112	Fourstardave	113	Sunshine Forever	126	52,920	1:50.20	

Year	Winner	Age	Jockey	Wt.	Second	Wt.	Third	Wt.	Win Value	Time	Beyer
1990	Crystal Moment	5	J.F. Chavez	113	Impersonator	112	Wanderkin	117	53,010	1:43.40	
1991	Stage Colony	4	C. Perret	115	Chenin Blanc	114	Scottish Monk	116	54,630	1:42.20	
1992	Maxigroom	4	J.A. Krone	111	Colchis Island	111	Buchman	111	56,460	1:42.60	102
1993	Adam Smith	5	J.L. Samyn	112	Kiri's Clown	114	Casino Magistrate	113	55,260	1:42.20	102
1994	Adam Smith	6	M.E. Smith	118	Halissee	113	Nijinsky's Gold	115	49,650	1:42.40	105
1995	Fourstars Allstar	7	Santos JA	118	Chief Master	112	A in Sociology	118	50,250	1:41.60	105
1996	Warning Glance	5	M.E. Smith	119	Shahid	115	Grand Continental	113	51,690	1:42.40	106
1997	Influent	6	J.L. Samyn	117	Slicious	115	Montjoy	117	67,140	1:47.40	106
1998	Subordination	4	J.F. Chavez	118	Fortitude	116	Crimson Guard	110	67,620	1:35.20	111
1999	Wised Up	4	M.J. Luzzi	112	N B Forrest	116	La-Faah	114	69,660	1:45.03	100
2000	Spindrift	5	J.L. Samyn	115	Middlesex Drive	118	Wised Up	114	67,680	1:40.88	109
2001	Strategic Mission	6	R. Migliore	118	Pine Dance	116	Legal Jousting	114	67,740	1:41.62	104
2002	Pyrus	4	E.S. Prado	113	Proud Man	116	Capsized	113	67,260	1:44.53	98
2003	Saint Verre	5	J.L. Espinoza	117	Windsor Castle	119	Judge's Case	115	70,500	1:33.77	112

Off the turf in 2003.

Beyer Index: 105

(STONERSIDE) FORWARD GAL, 7 Furlongs, 3-Year-Old Fillies, Gulfstream Park, 2003 Purse: $100,000

Year	Winner	Age	Jockey	Wt.	Second	Wt.	Third	Wt.	Win Value	Time	Beyer
1981	Dame Mysterieuse	3	J.L. Samyn	118	Heavenly Cause	121	Master's Dream	113	26,040	1:22.20	
1982	Trove	3	L. Saumell	116	Here's to Peg	112	Wendy's Ten	113	17,828	1:22.80	
1982	All Manners	3	O.J. Londono	116	Acharmer	114	Smart Heiress	112	17,978	1:23.00	
1983	Unaccompanied	3	R. Woodhouse	114	Lisa's Capital	114	Quixotic Lady	113	28,203	1:23.40	
1984	Miss Oceana	3	E. Maple	121	Katrinka	112	Scorched Panties	121	24,108	1:22.40	
1985	Lucy Manette	3	C. Perret	114	Grand Glory	112	Boldly Dared	112	39,690	1:23.40	
1986	Noranc	3	W.H. McCauley	116	Dancing Danzig	112	I'm Sweets	121	36,000	1:23.80	
1987	Added Elegance	3	J. Vasquez	121	Beau Love Flowers	112	Easter Mary	112	37,380	1:24.60	
1988	On to Royalty	3	C. Perret	114	Social Pro	112	Most Likely	112	37,020	1:23.20	
1989	Open Mind	3	A. Cordero Jr	121	Surging	114	Georgies Doctor	118	36,780	1:24.20	
1990	Charon	3	E. Fires	112	Trumpet's Blare	121	De La Devil	121	36,180	1:24.80	
1991	Withallprobability	3	C. Perret	114	Private Treasure	118	Far Out Nurse	112	48,240	1:22.40	
1992	Spinning Round	3	J.A. Santos	118	Patty's Princess	116	Super Doer	118	44,551	1:24.80	83
1993	Sum Runner	3	E. Fires	118	Boots 'n Jackie	121	Lunar Spook	118	45,250	1:23.60	95
1994	Mynameispanama	3	M. Castaneda	113	Frigid Coed	116	Wonderlan	114	45,960	1:22.80	82
1995	Chaposa Springs	3	H. Castillo Jr	114	Culver City	113	Mackenzie Slew	114	44,580	1:24.00	101
1996	Mindy Gayle	3	J.A. Krone	112	Marfa's Finale	113	Supah Jen	114	45,000	1:24.40	92
1997	Glitter Woman	3	M.E. Smith	114	City Band	121	Southern Playgirl	121	45,000	1:21.60	105
1998	Uanme	3	S.J. Sellers	113	Diamond on the Run	114	Holy Capote	112	45,000	1:24.40	86
1999	China Storm	3	P. Day	114	Three Ring	121	Extended Applause	112	45,000	1:23.69	90
2000	Miss Inquistive	3	T.G. Turner	114	Swept Away	118	Regally Appealing	118	45,000	1:22.25	98
2001	Gold Mover	3	J.D. Bailey	121	Hazino	114	Thunder Bertie	118	60,000	1:22.43	95
2002	Take the Cake	3	R.R. Douglas	117	A New Twist	121	Cherokee Girl	117	60,000	1:25.47	81
2003	Midnight Cry	3	E.S. Prado	117	Final Round	117	Chimichurri	121	60,000	1:22.55	91

Beyer Index: 91.58

GALLORETTE HANDICAP, 1 1/16 Miles (Turf), Fillies and Mares 3-Year-Olds and Up, Pimlico Race Course, 2003 Purse: $100,000

Year	Winner	Age	Jockey	Wt.	Second	Wt.	Third	Wt.	Win Value	Time	Beyer
1952	La Corredora	3	I. Hanford	112	Kiss Me Kate	123	Marta	117	20,225	1:52.40	
1953	Sabette	3	J. Higley	111	Sunny Dale	117	Canadiana	114	10,975	1:51.60	
1954	Mlle. Lorette	4	A. Catalano	114	Dispute	114	Another World	114	11,900	1:50.20	
1955	Searching	5	D. Erb	117	Brightest Star	111	June Fete	114	10,975	1:53.60	
1956	Little Pache	3	A. Kirkland	112	Blue Banner	117	Searching	120	9,750	1:52.40	
1957	Searching	5	D. Erb	117	Mlle. Dianne	111	Snow White	113	9,725	1:51.20	
1958	Hoosier Honey	4	J. Ruane	117	Alanesian	120	Cousin Con	114	13,799	1:52.40	
1959	High Bid	3	H. Moreno	120	Polamby	115	A Glitter	120	14,660	1:51.00	
1960	Sister Antoine	3	R. York	111	Loyal Lady II	114	My Dear Girl	117	11,329	1:52.80	
1961	Barnesville Miss	3	P. Anderson	114	Colony Flyer	111	Miss Melis'de	114	11,716	1:53.80	
1962	Waltz Song	4	S. Mellon	117	Cyclopavia	114	Royal Patrice	120	19,289	1:52.00	
1963	Double Heritage	4	T. Lee	114	Abby's Crown	111	Doll Ina	117	20,166	1:52.60	
1964	Gay Serenade	4	F. Alvarez	117	Open Fire	111	My Card	117	19,402	1:51.20	
1965	Gold Digger	3	L. Adams	114	Gallarush	111	Lovejoy	114	19,711	1:53.20	
1966	Gold Digger	4	B. Phelps	117	Alondra II	114	Petticoat	114	21,190	1:51.20	
1967	Lady Diplomat	4	F. Toro	112	Straight Deal	126	Indian Sunlite	117	21,612	1:42.60	
1968	Serene Queen	4	F. Lovato	109	Straight Deal	122	Politely	122	21,645	1:44.80	
1969	Back in Paris	5	C. Baltazar	114	Singing Rain	116	Pers'n Intrigue	110	21,385	1:42.80	
1970	Singing Rain	5	F. Lovato	119	Shuvee	122	Miss F'l River	109	21,417	1:43.60	
1971	Cold Comfort	4	M. Venezia	117	Daring Step	114	Lum'n's L'g'n	110	21,222	1:43.40	
1972	Sun Colony	4	C. Jimenez	110	Tico's Donna	109	Alma North	122	21,970	1:45.00	
1973	Deb Marion	3	A. Agnello	107	Groton Miss	115	Aglimmer	115	22,067	1:44.00	

Year	Winner	Age	Jockey	Wt.	Second	Wt.	Third	Wt.	Win Value	Time	Beyer
1974	Sarre Green	6	T. Lee	113	Unknown Heiress	103	Out Cold	112	22,295	1:44.60	
1975	Gulls Cry	4	E. Maple	117	Sarah Percy	115	Twixt	127	37,960	1:46.20	
1976	Redundancy	5	R. Broussard	119	Dos a Dos	119	Margravine	112	29,575	1:42.20	
1976	Deesse de Val	5	C. Marquez	119	Summertime Promise	117	Jabot	114	29,835	1:42.20	
1977	Summertime Promise	5	L. Moyers	121	Summer Session	111	Siz Ziz Zit	112	37,050	1:43.60	
1978	Huggle Duggle	4	B. Gonzalez	113	Council House	118	Nanticious	112	37,765	1:44.20	
1979	Calderina	4	C. Perret	121	Dottie O.	105	Warfever	116	56,875	1:44.80	
1980	Jamila Kadir	6	M.G. Pino	109	The Very One	122	Wild Bidder	108	57,428	1:44.40	
1981	Exactly So	4	G. McCarron	112	Crimson April	110	Ernestine	111	55,998	1:47.20	
1982	Island Charm	5	N. Santagata	117	Lovely Lei	112	Vibro Vibes	115	57,168	1:46.40	
1983	Wedding Party	4	C. Perret	119	Sunny Sparkler	122	Bemissed	110	56,648	1:50.00	
1984	Kattegat's Pride	5	D.A. Miller Jr	118	Amanti	114	Bright Choice	110	55,770	1:42.80	
1985	La Reine Elaine	4	G.W. Hutton	115	Stufida	115	Lady Emerald	107	58,013	1:41.60	
1986	Natania	4	J.W. Edwards	114	Scotch Heather	115	Valid Doge	108	71,448	1:45.60	
1987	Scotch Heather	5	M.G. Pino	113	Catatonic	117	Foot Stone	113	54,600	1:44.40	
1988	Just Class	4	C. Perret	115	Landaura	115	Hangin Ona Star	119	54,145	1:42.80	
1989	Dance Teacher	4	J.L. Samyn	115	Arcroyal	114	Fortunate Facts	118	60,000	1:44.00	
1990	Highland Penny	5	R.I. Rojas	116	Saphaedra	112	Channel Three	112	60,000	1:42.40	
							Double Bunctious	113			
1991	Miss Josh	5	E.S. Prado	121	Splendid Try	113	Highland Penny	115	60,000	1:41.80	103
1992	Brilliant Brass	5	E.S. Prado	113	Spanish Dior	112	Stem the Tide	112	60,000	1:44.80	102
1993	You'd Be Surprised	4	J.D. Bailey	113	Captive Miss	117	Dior's Angel	112	60,000	1:43.40	98
1994	Tribulation	4	Samyn JL	117	Mckaymackenna	118	Fleet Broad	115	60,000	1:41.60	96
1995	It's Personal	5	J.A. Krone	112	Churchbell Chimes	112	Open Toe	113	60,000	1:43.60	96
1996	Aucilla	5	M.E. Smith	114	Julie's Brilliance	114	Brushing Groom	114	60,000	1:44.80	88
1997	Palliser Bay	5	C.H. Marquez Jr.	113	Elusive	114	Sangria	117	60,000	1:43.80	93
1998	Tresoriere	6	J.A. Santos	114	Bursting Forth	114	Starry Dreamer	114	60,000	1:45.20	100
1999	Winfama	6	E.S. Prado	114	Pleasant Temper	119	Earth to Jackie	119	60,000	1:43.31	101
2000	Colstar	4	A. Delgado	120	Melody Queen	115	Terreavigne	118	60,000	1:43.60	95
2001	License Fee	6	P. Day	118	Starine	114	Crystal Sea	113	60,000	1;42,81	97
2002	Quidnaskra	7	C.J. McCarron	116	De Aar	111	Step With Style	115	60,000	1:46.73	88
2003	Carib Lady	4	P.A. Valenzuela	116	Affirmed Dancer	113	Lady of the Future	114	60,000	1:50.69	97

Beyer Index: 96.46

GARDENIA HANDICAP, 1 1/8 Miles,
Fillies and Mares 3-Year-Olds and Up, Ellis Park, 2003 Purse: $200,000

Year	Winner	Age	Jockey	Wt.	Second	Wt.	Third	Wt.	Win Value	Time	Beyer
1982	Sweetest Chant	4	E. Fires	121	Muriesk	111	Run Tulle Run	112	43,778	1:49.80	
1983	Migola	3	G. Patterson	115	Kitchen	117	Run Tulle Run	113	42,315	1:51.60	
1984	Rambling Rhythm	3	L. Martinez	114	Run Tulle Run	114	Queen of Song	122	39,325	1:50.20	
1985	Crimson Orchid	3	S.E. Miller	114	Electric Fanny	114	Dusty Gloves	116	41,535	1:49.80	
1986	Queen Alexandra	4	D.E. Foster	123	Fleet Secretariat	119	Sherizar	113	63,000	1:49.20	
1987	No Choice	4	C.R. Woods Jr	113	Layovernite	112	Firgie's Jule	112	94,500	1:49.20	
1988	Lt. Lao	4	D. Brumfield	123	Saucy Deb	118	Silk's Lady	112	90,000	1:47.60	
1989	Lawyer Talk	5	M.E. Doser	114	Gallant Ryder	120	Miss Barbour	112	90,000	1:50.00	
1990	Evangelical	4	L. Melancon	113	Degenerate Gal	117	Anitas Surprise	113	90,000	1:49.80	91
1991	Summer Matinee	4	C.A. Black	113	Blissful Union	113	Beth Believes	113	90,000	1:50.40	97
1992	Bungalow	5	F.C. Torres	118	Forever Fond	113	Fappies Cosy Miss	112	120,000	1:48.60	101
1993	Erica's Dream	5	W. Martinez	113	Fappies Cosy Miss	111	Hitch	114	120,000	1:49.80	94
1994	Alphabulous	5	Thorwalth JO	112	Added Asset	115	Hey Hazel	116	120,000	1:50.00	95
1995	Laura's Pistolette	4	Martin EM Jr.	115	Sadie's Dream	112	Cat Appeal	116	120,000	1:50.80	102
1996	Country Cat	4	D.M. Barton	115	Bedroom Blues	111	Alcovy	116	120,000	1:49.60	99
1997	Three Fanfares	4	F.A. Arguello Jr.	113	Gold N Delicious	119	Birr	116	120,000	1:49.00	96
1998	Meter Maid	4	P.A. Johnson	119	Proper Banner	114	ThreeFanfares	113	120,000	1:51.00	106
1999	Lines of Beauty	4	F.C. Torres	112	Roza Robata	113	Castle Blaze	109	120,000	1:49.60	102
2000	Silent Eskimo	5	J. Lopez	116	Roza Robata	119	Tap to Music	116	120,000	1:50.56	101
2001	Asher	4	M. Guidry	115	Zenith	112	Royal Fair	116	120,000	1:50.16	97
2002	Minister's Baby	4	C. Perret	117	Lakenheath	115	Softly	114	120,000	1:49.73	109
2003	Bare Necessities	4	R.R. Douglas	119	Desert Gold	114	So Much More	115	120,000	1:50.09	106

Beyer Index: 98.07

GENEROUS, 1 Mile (Turf),
2-Year-Olds, Hollywood Park, 2003 Purse: $100,000

Year	Winner	Age	Jockey	Wt.	Second	Wt.	Third	Wt.	Win Value	Time	Beyer
1982	Fifth Division	2	L. Pincay Jr	117	Dominating Dooley	116	Mezzo	116	33,450	1:35.60	
1983	Artichoke	2	W. Shoemaker	120	Nagurski	114	Fortune's Kingdom	115	50,100	1:38.40	
1983	Precisionist	2	C.J. McCarron	116	Fali Time	120	Tights	115	50,100	1:37.40	
1984	Overtrump	2	C.J. McCarron	120	Right Con	120	Herat	120	123,350	1:41.80	
1985	Darby Fair	2	A.L. Castanon	120	Snow Chief	120	Acks Lika Ruler	114	119,400	1:37.00	
1986	Persevered	2	G.L. Stevens	120	Wilderness Bound	120	Quietly Bold	115	86,050	1:41.80	
1986	Sweettuc	2	G.L. Stevens	113	Savona Tower	116	Lord Duckworth	114	68,050	1:41.60	

Year	Winner	Age	Jockey	Wt.	Second	Wt.	Third	Wt.	Win Value	Time	Beyer
1987	Purdue King	2	C.J. McCarron	121	Chinese Gold	121	Blade of the Ball	115	47,500	1:36.00	
1987	White Mischief	2	J.A. Santos	115	King Alobar	115	Texas Typhoon	115	68,750	1:35.40	
1988	Music Merci	2	G.L. Stevens	121	Double Quick	121	Crown Collection	115	58,220	1:36.40	
1988	Shipping Time	2	C.A. Black	114	Super May	115	Past Ages	116	58,220	1:37.20	
1989	Single Dawn	2	A. Solis	114	Pleasant Tap	118	Doyouseewhatisee	121	69,600	1:35.60	
1990	Satis	2	C.A. Black	115	What a Spell	115	Ev for Shir	114	67,800	1:35.20	86
1991	Silver Ray	2	M.A. Pedroza	114	Thinkernot	115	African Colony	117	74,775	1:35.00	78
1992	Earl of Barking	2	A. Solis	114	Devil's Rock	115	Corby	118	137,500	1:34.40	95
1993	Delineator	2	R. Baze	118	Devon Port	116	Ferrara	114	137,500	1:34.60	86
1994	Native Regent	2	Penna D.	121	Dangerous Scenario	116	Claudius	121	137,500	1:37.00	91
1995	Old Chapel	2	Stevens GL.	121	Ayrton S	116	Heza Gone West	117	137,500	1:35.00	88
1996	Hello	2	McCarron C.J.	121	Steel Ruhlr	114	Divine Insight	114	150,000	1:34.60	90
1997	Mantles Star	2	McCarron C.J.	114	F J's Pace	116	Commitisize	121	150,000	1:36.60	96
1998	Incurable Optimist	2	Velazquez J.R.	121	Company Approval	114	Brave Gun	117	150,000	1:37.60	101
1999	Jokerman	2	P. Day	118	Purey Cozzene	121	Kleofus	121	120,000	1:35.20	92
2000	Startac	2	A. Solis	118	Broadway Moon	116	Deeliteful Irving	114	120,000	1:34.76	89
2001	Mountain Rage	2	D.R. Flores	116	Miesque's Approval	121	National Park	117	120,000	1:40.31	88
2002	Peace Rules	2	V. Espinoza	118	Lismore Knight	121	Outta Here	115	120,000	1:35.49	92
2003	Castledale	2	J.A. Krone	116	Dealer Choice	116	Lucky Pulpit	116	60,000	1:35.43	92

Beyer Index: 90.29

GLENS FALLS HANDICAP, 1 3/8 Miles (Turf), Fillies and Mares
3-Year-Olds and Up, Saratoga Race Course, 2003 Purse: $113,100

Year	Winner	Age	Jockey	Wt.	Second	Wt.	Third	Wt.	Win Value	Time	Beyer
1996	Ampulla	5	S.J. Sellers	113	Look Daggers	118	Electric Society	120	67,500	2:16.40	102
1997	Shemozzle	5	J.D. Bailey	115	Picture Hat	115	Last Aproach	113	64,740	2:12.80	98
1998	Auntie Mame	4	J.R. Velazquez	120	Yvecrique	115	Makethemostofit	111	66,000	2:13.00	106
1999	Idle Rich	4	J.D. Bailey	115	Adrian	114	Bundling	114	65,760	2:12.81	99
2000	I'm Indy Mood	5	H. Castillo Jr.	114	Idle Rich	114	Cybil	114	66,120	2:07.41	87
2001	Irving's Baby	4	J.D. Bailey	126	New Assmebly	113	Caveat's Shot	114	65,995	2:07.56	91
2002	Owsley	4	E.S. Prado	116	Mot Juste	116	Sunstone	114	68,100	2:15.99	96
2003	Sixty Seconds	5	J.A. Santos	115	Primetimevalentine	113	Alternate	116	67,860	2:13.96	97

Beyer Index: 97

Run at 1 1/4 miles on main track in 2000, 2001

GOLDEN GATE BREEDERS' CUP HANDICAP, 1 1/8 Miles (Turf),
3-Year-Olds and Up, Golden Gate Fields, 2003 Purse: $136,250

Year	Winner	Age	Jockey	Wt.	Second	Wt.	Third	Wt.	Win Value	Time	Beyer
1947	Triplicate	6	J. Longden	115	Bymeabond	112	Autocrat	112	52,450	2:05.20	
1948	Shannon II	7	J. Westrope	124	See-tee-See	116	Stepfather	111	61,000	1:59.80	
1949	Solidarity	4	R. Neves	119	Stepfather	119	Roman In	112	38,200	2:00.00	
1950	Noor	5	J. Longden	127	Citation	126	On Trust	103	32,950	1:58.20	
1951	Palestinian	5	W. Shoemaker	124	Simonsez	107	Moonrush	119	15,250	1:48.00	
1952	Lights Up	5	R. Neves	123	Intent	126	Conversion	104	34,800	1:59.80	
1953	Fleet Bird	4	J. Longden	123	High Scud	112	Goose Khal	124	32,700	1:52.60	
1954	Determine	3	R. York	125	Poona II	104	Blue Trump't'r	106	15,150	1:50.60	
1955	Alidon	4	J. Longden	112	Determine	129	Novarullah	111	29,325	1:59.40	
1956	Battle Dance	4	J. Ruggeri	106	Ole Travis	110	Count Chic	115	12,750	1:49.60	
1957	Barouche	3	M. Volzke	112	Tall Chief II	113	Golden Notes	122	12,750	1:47.60	
1958	Ekaba	4	P. Moreno	116	Social Climber	122	Eddie Schmidt	117	25,500	1:47.40	
1959	Sisters Prince	4	J. Longden	112	Sweet Revenge	109	Mr. Eiffel	121	15,350	2:00.60	
1960	Prince Cohen	4	J. Longden	113	Honk	113	Whiz Bam	110	13,150	2:00.60	
1961	Gem Town	4	J. Longden	119	Fighting Hodge	115	Sea Rover	113	12,650	2:01.40	
1962	Mandate	4	J. Longden	114	Sea Orbit	126	Nite Shift	114	12,950	1:42.00	
1963	Native Diver	4	W. Shoemaker	130	Friendly Fred	112	Ol' Bleu	106	12,200	1:44.80	
1964	Real Good Deal	3	J. Longden	124	Carang	116	Second Honeymoon	104	13,200	1:42.00	
1965	Real Luck	5	D. Ross	118	Carang	116	Mangayte	122	15,875	1:47.40	
1966	Ask Father	4	M. Valenzuela	112	Sheldrake	117	Whit's Pride	117	18,500	1:47.20	
1967	Carang	6	M. Volzke	119	Lucky P.J.	110	Ask Father	114	18,650	1:47.80	
1968	Lucky P.J.	5	B. Jennings	120	Most Host	124	Mainsheet	117	18,700	1:41.40	
1969	Diego Security	4	D. Tierney	118	Most Host	118	Dizzy Babe	115	19,400	1:42.00	
1970	Governors Party	4	J. Leonard	119	Diego Security	118	Figonero	126	18,050	1:41.20	
1971	Imaginative	4	M. Volzke	112	Most Host	115	Inverness Drive	122	23,300	1:41.40	
1972	Panzer Chief	5	H. Grant	122	On the Track	123	Fair Test	119	36,600	1:42.60	
1973	Wing Out	5	R. Schacht	124	Fair Test	116	Yvetot	116	30,800	1:43.80	
1974	Acclimatization	6	S. Valdez	119	Yvetot	118	Wild World	111	46,350	2:27.80	
1975	Pass the Glass	4	F. Olivares	115	Confederate Yankee	116	Ga Hai	118	33,150	1:41.80	
1976	Pass the Glass	5	F. Olivares	119	Willie Pleasant	111	Barrydown	117	31,250	1:41.40	
1977	Announcer	5	M. Castaneda	115	The Fop	114	Sir Jason	116	71,700	1:40.40	
1978	Bad 'n Big	4	A. Diaz	120	Effervescing	115	Jumping Hill	124	65,500	1:44.80	
1979	As de Copas	6	H.E. Moreno	120	True Statement	115	Bywayofchicago	123	62,600	1:43.40	

Year	Winner	Age	Jockey	Wt.	Second	Wt.	Third	Wt.	Win Value	Time	Beyer
1980	Eagle Toast	6	P.A. Valenzuela.	113	Daranstone	108	Saboulard	116	63,200	1:41.00	
1981	Caterman	5	M. Castaneda	123	Opus Dei	121	His Honor	118	77,000	1:41.40	
1982	Regal Bearing	4	R.A. Baze	117	Visible Pole	110	Score Twenty Four	121	73,900	1:46.00	
1983	Silveyville	5	D. Winick	115	Ask Me	115	Majesty's Prince	122	165,800	2:16.40	
1984	John Henry	9	C.J. McCarron	125	Silveyville	117	Lucence	116	184,200	2:13.00	
1985	Fatih	5	T. Lipham	119	Fact Finder	115	Semillero	114	171,770	2:15.40	
							Nak Ack	115			
1986	Val Danseur	5	G.L. Stevens	117			Complice II	115	100,375	2:15.40	
	Le Solaret	4	M. Castaneda	113							
1987	Rivlia	5	C.J. McCarron	116	Air Display	115	Reco	113	165,000	2:14.20	
1988	Great Communicator	5	R. Sibille	120	Putting	117	Rivlia	120	165,000	2:15.40	
1989	Frankly Perfect	4	E. Delahoussaye	122	Pleasant Variety	114	Brown Bess	114	165,000	2:15.00	
1990	Petite Ile	4	C.A. Black	113	Valdali	114	Pleasant Variety	116	220,000	2:15.60	107
1991	Forty Niner Days	4	R.Q. Meza	115	Aksar	115	Missionary Ridge	114	220,000	2:17.20	
1992	Algenib	5	L. Pincay Jr	120	Missionary Ridge	114	Never Black	113	220,000	2:13.80	106
1993	Val des Bois	7	P.A. Valenzuela	119	Norwich	116	Never Black	116	165,000	1:48.20	108
1994	Alex the Great	5	P.A. Valenzuela	118	Fanmore	117	Emerald Jig	113	165,000	2:15.00	105
1995	Special Price	6	E. Delahoussaye	122	Bluegrass Prince	122	Sans Ecocide	122	110,000	2:15.00	110
1996	Time Star	5	C.A. Black	116	Sand Reef	116	Bon Point	117	120,000	2:16.20	105
1997	Irish Wings	5	D. Carr	114	Savinio	117	Mufattish	114	120,000	1:49.60	102
1998	Dushyantor	5	C.S. Nakatani	118	Eternity Range	114	Star Performance	116	150,000	2:15.20	103
1999	Sayarshan	4	B. Blanc	124	Alvo Certo	117	Plicck	115	120,000	2:15.56	106
2000	Deploy Venture	4	R.A. Baze	115	Single Empire	121	Bonapartiste	119	120,000	2:19.12	102
2001	Northern Quest	6	V. Espinoza	118	Eagleton	114	Entorchado	115	137,500	1:58.58	102
2002	No Slip	4	K.J. Desormeaux	117	Kerrygold	116	Sumitas	119	82,500	1:49.41	103
2003	Ninebanks	5	R.J. Warren Jr	116	Surprise Halo	115	Royal Gem	118	82,500	1:50.07	97

Beyer Index: 104.31

GOLDEN GATE DERBY, 1 1/16 Miles,
3-Year-Olds, Golden Gate Fields, 2003 Purse: $100,000

Year	Winner	Age	Jockey	Wt.	Second	Wt.	Third	Wt.	Win Value	Time	Beyer
1947	Cutty Hunk	3	F. Zufelt	114	Pretty Mggie	111	Triskelion	117	16,450	1:54.80	
1948	Henpecker	3	J. Longden	117	Smoke Tree	114	Grandpere	123	16,650	1:47.80	
1949	Pedigree	3	J. Westrope	120	Blue Dart	114	Smart Count	114	17,950	1:49.00	
1950	Sir Butch	3	G. Glisson	113	Great Circle	122	War Poppy	113	15,520	1:48.00	
1952	Maracador	3	R.L. Baird	117	Steel	110	Alate		15,900	1:48.40	
1955	Golden Land	3	R. York	126	Beau Busher	126	Bequeath	126	29,325	1:48.60	
1958	Furyvan	3	A. Maese	121	Brief Interlude	110	Harcall	118	25,700	1:42.60	
1959	Mr. Eiffel	3	G. Taniguchi	122	Cellyar		Trumpet	112	15,950	1:42.20	
1997	Pacificbounty	3	KJ. Desormeaux	118	Dancer's Kolo	118	Esteemed Friend.	118	120,000	1:43.00	91
1998	Clover Hunter	3	R. Baze	120	Mantles Star	120	Allen's Oop	120	120,000	1:43.33	98
1999	Epic Honor	3	L.J. Meche	120	Blue Tune	120	Brave Gun	120	90,000	1:43.58	96
2000	New Advantage	3	A.D. Lopez	120	Nurdlinger	120	Shake Loose	120	90,000	1:42.66	81
2001	Hoovergetthekeys.	3	R. Warren Jr.	120	High Cascade	120	Media Mogul	120	90,000	1:42.88	90
2002	Danthebluegrassman	3	J.J. Steiner	120	Cappuchino	120	USS Tinosa	120	68,750	1:43.87	91
2003	Standard Setter	3	R.M. Gonzalez	120	Ozzie Cat	120	Pine for Java	120	55,000	1:43.76	84

Beyer Index: 90.14

GOTHAM, 1 Mile 70 Yards,
3-Year-Olds, Aqueduct, 2003 Purse: $200,000

Year	Winner	Age	Jockey	Wt.	Second	Wt.	Third	Wt.	Win Value	Time	Beyer
1953	Native Dancer	3	E. Guerin	120	Magic Lamp	120	Sickle's Sound	120	24,500	1:44.20	
1953	Laffango	3	N. Shuk	120	Invigorator	120	Fly Wheel	120	24,500	1:44.00	
1954	Fisherman	3	H. Woodhouse	120	Galdar	120	Mel Leavitt	120	27,150	1:46.20	
1955	Go Lightly	3	J. Culmone	120	Mr. Al L	120	Bangborough	126	21,250	1:46.60	
1956	Career Boy	3	E. Guerin	122	Jean Baptiste	122	Nail	126	20,200	1:45.60	
1957	Mister Jive	3	H. Woodhouse	118	Promised Land	122	Clem	122	21,400	1:45.60	
1958	Oh Johnny	5	W. Boland	114	Paper Tiger	114	Tick Tock	112	18,257	1:43.60	
1959	Atoll	3	E. Arcaro	122	Intentionally	122	Open View	114	18,290	1:43.00	
1960	John William	3	S. Boulmetis	118	New Commander	115	Count Amber	114	18,257	1:36.40	
1961	Ambiopoise	3	R. Ussery	114	Globemaster	114	Merry Ruler	114	37,895	1:35.80	
1962	Jaipur	3	W. Shoemaker	122	Sunrise County	118	Sidluck	114	38,025	1:37.00	
1963	Debbysman	3	L. Adams	114	Bonjour	122	Crewman	122	37,375	1:34.60	
1964	Mr. Moonlight	3	J. Combest	114	Traffic	122	Mr. Brick	122	37,895	1:37.20	
1965	Flag Raiser	3	R. Ussery	118	Dapper Dan	114	Dependability	118	37,310	1:36.60	
1966	Stupendous	3	P. Anderson	114	Impressive	118	Handsome Boy	118	38,480	1:34.60	
1967	Dr. Fager	3	M. Ycaza	122	Damascus	122	Reason to Hail	114	37,570	1:35.20	
1968	Verbatim	3	J.L. Rotz	118	Wise Exchange	126	What a Pleasure	122	39,000	1:34.00	
1969	Dike	3	J. Velasquez	122	Rooney's Shield	114			37,700	1:34.80	
					Reviewer	122					

Year	Winner	Age	Jockey	Wt.	Second	Wt.	Third	Wt.	Win Value	Time	Beyer
1970	Native Royalty	3	A. Cordero Jr.	114	Delaware Chief	114	Silent Screen	126	37,765	1:36.20	
1971	Good Behaving	3	R. Turcotte	118	Droll Role	114	Sound Off	114	34,080	1:36.00	
1972	Freetex	3	C. Baltazar	126	Eager Exchange	122	Upper Case	126	36,750	1:36.40	
1973	Secretariat	3	R. Turcotte	126	Champagne Charlie	117	Flush	117	33,330	1:33.40	
1974	Stonewalk	3	M.A. Rivera	116	L'Amour Rullah	116	Wing South	119	27,570	1:36.00	
1974	Rube the Great	3	M.A. Rivera	119	Hosiery	116	Cumulo Nimbus	116	27,420	1:35.20	
1975	Laramie Trail	3	M. Venezia	121	Lefty	121	Kalong	116	27,180	1:38.00	
1975	Singh	3	A. Cordero Jr.	121	Round Stake	116	Mr. Duds	116	27,630	1:37.00	
1976	Zen	3	J. Vasquez	116	Cojak	124	Play the Red	114	34,740	1:35.60	
1977	Cormorant	3	D. Wright	123	Fratello Ed	121	Papelote	114	22,065	1:43.60	
1978	Slap Jack	3	J. Velasquez	114	Quadratic	123	Shelter Half	121	33,210	1:38.60	
1979	General Assembly	3	J. Velasquez	123	Belle's Gold	123	Screen King	123	49,680	1:43.60	
1980	Colonel Moran	3	J. Velasquez	123	Dunham's Gift	114	Bucksplasher	115	53,370	1:37.00	
1981	Proud Appeal	3	J. Fell	123	Cure the Blues	126	Noble Nashua	123	50,040	1:33.60	
1982	Air Forbes Won	3	M. Venezia	114	Shimatoree	123	Big Brave Rock	114	50,750	1:35.60	
1983	Assault Landing	3	V. Bracciale Jr.	114	Bounding Basque	123	Jacque's Tip	123	50,895	1:35.80	
1983	Chas Connerly	3	J. Fell	123	Elegant Life	123	Law Talk	114	50,535	1:36.60	
1984	Bear Hunt	3	D. MacBeth	114	Lt. Flag	123	On the Sauce	114	136,440	1:40.40	
1985	Eternal Prince	3	R. Migliore	114	Pancho Villa	121	El Basco	114	147,840	1:34.40	
1986	Mogambo	3	J. Vasquez	121	Tasso	123	Zabaleta	121	214,200	1:34.40	
1987	Gone West	3	R.G. Davis	114	Shawklit Won	114	Gulch	123	190,200	1:34.60	
1988	Private Terms	3	C.W. Antley	126	Seeking the Gold	114	Perfect Spy	121	181,500	1:34.80	
1989	Easy Goer	3	P. Day	123	Diamond Donnie	114	Expensive Decision	118	168,300	1:32.40	
1990	Thirty Six Red	3	M.E. Smith	114	Senor Pete	121	Burnt Hills	114	182,400	1:33.80	
1991	Kyle's Our Man	3	A. Cordero Jr.	121	King Mutesa	118	Another Review	118	150,000	1:34.60	106
1992	Lure	3	M.E. Smith	114			Best Decorated	114	102,500	1:35.60	100
	Devil His Due	3	W.H. McCauley	114							
1993	As Indicated	3	C.V. Bisono	114	Itaka	114	Strolling Along	121	120,000	1:36.20	100
1994	Irgun	3	J.D. Bailey	114	Bit of Puddin	117	Jesse F	114	150,000	1:36.20	105
1995	Talkin Man	3	M.E. Smith	122	Da Hoss	117	Devious Course	117	150,000	1:36.80	110
1996	Romano Gucci	3	J.A. Krone	119	Tiger Talk	117	Feather Box	114	120,000	1:34.40	103
1997	Smokin Mel	3	J.R. Velazquez	112	Ordway	122	Wild Wonder	119	120,000	1:34.20	101
1998	Wasatch	3	J.D. Bailey	117	Dr J		Late Edition	114	150,000	1:36.40	97
1999	Badge	3	S.X. Bridgmohan	120	Apremont	120	Robin Goodfellow	113	90,000	1:34.72	104
2000	Red Bullet	3	A. Solis	113	Aptitude	113	Performing Magic	114	120,000	1:34.27	100
2001	Richly Blended	3	R. Wilson	116	Mr. John	116	Voodoo	116	120,000	1:35.14	100
2002	Mayakovsky	3	E.S. Prado	116	Saarland	120	Parade of Music	116	120,000	1:34.90	102
2003	Alysweep	3	R. Migliore	120	Grey Comet	120	Spite the Devil	116	120,000	1:40.60	103

Beyer Index: 102.38

GRAVESEND HANDICAP, 6 Furlongs,
3-Year-Olds and Up, Aqueduct, 2003 Purse: $109,000

Year	Winner	Age	Jockey	Wt.	Second	Wt.	Third	Wt.	Win Value	Time	Beyer
1959	Silver Ship	4	E. Arcaro	126	Discard	115	Besomer	114	17,380	1:10.20	
1960	Brush Fire	3	R. Ussery	118	Vendetta	116	Rick City	126	17,867	1:09.60	
1961	Bolinas Boy	3	J.L. Rotz	115	Four Lane	122	Chief of Chiefs	126	14,072	1:09.40	
1962	Merry Ruler	4	J. Sellers	123	Rullah Red	115	Hellenic Hero	113	18,200	1:21.40	
1963	Ahoy	3	H. Grant	123	For the Road	120	Merry Ruler	121	14,755	1:08.80	
1964	Delta Judge	4	D. Pierce	122	Valentine	110	Rainy Lake	117	18,167	1:09.40	
1965	Determined Man	4	M. Venezia	109	Kilmoray	113	Dark King	116	18,167	1:10.40	
1966	Winnie	4	E. Belmonte	113	Malicious	124	Understudy	111	17,647	1:09.80	
1967	Tumiga	3	B. Feliciano	120	Beaupy	116	Smooth Seas	109	17,745	1:09.00	
1968	Jim J.	4	A. Cordero Jr.	124	Our Michael	114	Royal Exchange	111	18,167	1:10.20	
1969	Royal Exchange	4	A. Cordero Jr.	119	Grey Slacks	116	Godspeed	110	1,742	1:09.80	
1970	Distinctive	4	W. Blum	114	Ta Wee	134	Tyrant	121	18,395	1:08.80	
1971	Summer Air	4	A. Cordero Jr.	118	Silver Mallet	106	Eastern Fleet	117	20,010	1:10.00	
1972	Silver Mallet	4	B. Baeza	115	Close Decision	111	Rollicking	121	16,425	1:09.20	
1973	Petrograd	4	A. Cordero Jr.	120	Full Pocket	120	Delta Oil	111	16,635	1:08.60	
1974	Mr. Prospector	4	J. Vasquez	124	Infuriator	112	Lonetree	119	22,830	1:09.00	
1975	Honorable Miss	5	J. Vasquez	123	Queen City Lad	111	Piamem	118	16,485	1:10.00	
1976	Christopher R.	5	W.J. Passmore	131	Mac Corkle	115	Gallant Bob	120	26,940	1:09.80	
1977	Full Out	4	A. Cordero Jr.	116	Great Above	114	Jackson Square	114	22,065	1:10.20	
1978	Half High	5	A. Santiago	113	Intercontinent	114	B'ld and Stormy	107	25,755	1:09.60	
1979	Shelter Half	4	S.A. Boulmetis	116	Double Zeus	114	Tanthem	125	26,220	1:11.00	
1980	Clever Trick	4	J. Vasquez	117	Rise Jim	119	Dr. Blum	114	32,460	1:09.00	
1981	Lines of Power	4	D. MacBeth	116	Stiff Sentence	112	Bayou Black	115	32,760	1:09.60	
1982	Chan Balum	3	J.L. Samyn	108	Maudlin	126	In From Dixie	120	34,320	1:11.20	
1983	Main Stem	5	V. Lopez	109	Havagreatdate	119	In From Dixie	113	34,440	1:14.00	
1984	Elegant Life	4	J. Velasquez	115	Tarantara	120	Top Avenger	126	42,180	1:09.40	
1985	Love That Mac	3	J. Velasquez	111	Raja's Shark	126	Aggressive Bid	110	40,860	1:11.00	
1986	Comic Blush	3	A. Graell	106	King's Swan	122	Cutlass Reality	117	41,100	1:09.40	

Year	Winner	Age	Jockey	Wt.	Second	Wt.	Third	Wt.	Win Value	Time	Beyer
1987	Vinnie the Viper	4	J.A. Krone	116	King's Swan	122	Best by Test	117	54,360	1:09.60	
1988	High Brite	4	A. Cordero Jr	122	King's Swan	119	Matter of Hon'r	111	48,540	1:10.60	
1989	Never Forgotten	5	A. Madrid Jr	117	Proud and Valid	111	Garemma	113	40,980	1:12.60	
1990	Mr. Nasty	3	J.D. Bailey	113	Senor Speedy	114	Dargai	113	41,220	1:09.80	
1991	Shuttleman	5	A. Cordero Jr	113	Senor Speedy	120	Gallant Step	112	52,830	1:10.20	113
1992	Hidden Tomahawk	4	J.F. Chavez	111	Smart Alec	113	Miner's Dream	114	52,920	1:08.60	105
1993	Astudillo	3	F.A. Arguello J	112	Fabersham	113	Ferociously	113	51,300	1:11.80	94
1994	Mining Burrah	4	Velazquez JR	111	Golden Pro	115	Won Song	113	51,270	1:10.80	101
1995	Cold Execution	4	Pezua JM	116	Crafty Alfel	117	Golden Tent	111	50,820	1:09.40	103
1996	Victor Avenue	3	J.F. Chavez	119	Royal Haven	117	Stalwart Member	114	50,325	1:09.20	109
1997	Royal Haven	5	R. Migliore	122			Laredo	115	32,670	1:10.00	112
	Stalwart Member	4	A. T. Gryder	118					32,670	1:10.00	
1998	Say Florida Sandy	4	S. X. Bridgmohan	117	Esteemed Friend	114	Home On the Ridge	117	50,220	1:11.00	100
1999	Cowboy Cop	5	A. T. Gryder	115	Brushed On	112	Unreal Madness	116	50,370	1:09.40	109
2000	Say Florida Sandy	5	J. Bravo	116	Liberty Gold	115	Lake Pontchartrain	116	51,450	1:09.80	104
2001	Here's Zealous	4	E.S. Prado	114	Peeping Tom	120	Say Florida Sandy	120	64,740	1:10.37	108
2002	Multiple Choice	4	V. Carrero	118	Sing Me Back Home	114	Gold I.D.	113	65,520	1:09.26	107
2003	Shake You Down	5	M.J. Luzzi	124	Way to the Top	114	Gators n Bears	115	65,400	1:09.55	110

Beyer Index: 105.77

HAL'S HOPE HANDICAP, 1 1/16 Miles,
3-Year-Olds and Up, Gulfstream Park, 2003 Purse: $100,000

Year	Winner	Age	Jockey	Wt.	Second	Wt.	Third	Wt.	Win Value	Time	Beyer
1990	Big Sal	5	E. Fires	119	Twice Too Many		Groomstick		20,340	1:24.80	
1991	New York Swell	8	J. Alferez	111	Rhythm		Mercedes Won		45,000	1:42.40	
1992	Peanut Butter Onit	6	J.A. Santos	114	Sunny Sunrise		Honest Ensign		45,000	1:43.40	
1993	Classic Seven	5	C. Lopez	116	Devil on Ice		Keratoid		60,000	1:43.40	
1994	Forever Whirl	4	W.H. McCauley	113	Northern Trend	113	Royal n Gold	113	45,000	1:41.80	106
1995	Warm Wayne	4	J.D. Bailey	112	Meadow Monster	113	Silent Lake	113	45,000	1:43.00	100
1996	Geri	4	J.D. Bailey	114	Halo's Image	120	Second Childhood	113	45,000	1:41.40	113
1997	Louis Quatorze	4	P. Day	121	Strawberry Wine	113	Exalto	108	45,000	1:43.40	110
1998	K.J.'s Appeal	4	J.R. Velazquez	114	Powerful Goer	112	Tour's Big Red	114	45,000	1:42.20	114
1999	Jazz Club	4	P. Day	114	Rock and Roll	113	Hanarsaan	113	45,000	1:42.76	114
2000	Dancing Guy	5	J.D. Bailey	120	Yankee Victor	113	Midway Magistrate	117	45,000	1:44.94	106
2002	Hal's Hope	5	R.I. Velez	112	American Halo	113	Windsor Castle	112	60,000	1:42.40	108
2003	Windsor Castle	5	E.M. Coa	115	Saint Verre	114	Najran	114	60,000	1:42.33	109

Beyer Index: 108.89

Run as Creme Fraiche Handicap prior to 2003

HANSHIN CUP HANDICAP, 1 Mile,
3-Year-Olds and Up, Arlington Park, 2003 Purse: $100,000

Year	Winner	Age	Jockey	Wt.	Second	Wt.	Third	Wt.	Win Value	Time	Beyer
1941	Equifox	4	A. Craig	112	Technician	110	Dog House	103	4,190	1:38.20	
1942	Best Seller	4	H. Litzenberger	118	Woof Woof	118	Heartman	109	7,265	1:36.00	
1943	Best Seller	5	F.A. Smith	113	Thumbs Up	113	Some Chance	109	9,800	1:37.00	
1944	Sun Again	5	C. McCreary	127	Georgie Drum	113	Anticlimax	104	9,350	1:36.20	
1945	Equifox	8	A. Bodiou	119	St. Jock	107	Vald'a Lamar	106	18,550	1:38.00	
1945	Daily Trouble	7	F.A. Smith	109	Take Wing	110	Signator	115	18,550	1:37.20	
1946	Witch Sir	4	R. Campbell	110	Old Kentuck	106	Armed	132	24,200	1:37.20	
1947	With Pleasure	4	W. Garner	116	Armed	130	Mighty Story	114	23,150	1:35.00	
1948	Fervent	4	N.L. Pierson	124	Mighty Story	109	Loujac	105	23,000	1:35.20	
1949	Star Reward	5	R.L. Baird	116	Coaltown	132	Carrara Marble	112	18,800	1:35.00	
1950	Oil Capitol	3	K. Church	111	Shy Guy	123	Prop	113	19,700	1:35.00	
1951	Curandero	5	J. Westrope	114	Prop	108	Inseparable	118	18,745	1:40.20	
1952	Woodchuck	4	E. Arcaro	122	Ruhe	112	Andy B.W.	114	22,300	1:37.20	
1953	Ruhe	5	J. Adams	113	Sub Fleet	116	Hill Gail	128	36,000	1:35.40	
1954	Smoke Screen	5	D. Scurlock	116	First Aid	113	Spur On	115	36,000	1:38.60	
1955	Platan	5	J. Adams	111	Smoke Screen	112	Jet Action	120	38,500	1:35.00	
1956	Bardstown	4	W. Hartack	114	Skipper Bill	122	Sir Tribal	124	37,300	1:35.60	
1957	Swoon's Son	4	D. Erb	132	Call Me Lucky	108	Fabius	123	34,900	1:36.80	
1958	Swoon's Son	5	D. Erb	129	Bardstown	122	Indian Creek	107	87,675	1:34.80	
1959	Better Bee	5	J. Choquette	115	Belleau Chief	114	Round Table	132	33,450	1:37.00	
1960	Intentionally	4	W. Hartack	126	Dunce	121	Little Tytus	113	32,200	1:34.40	
1961	Run for Nurse	4	K. Church	115	Pied d'Or	120	John William	114	20,425	1:36.80	
1962	Intervener	5	B. Sorenson	111	Oink		Natego	108	19,625	1:37.80	
1963	Wa-Wa Cy	4	W.M. Cook	111	Editorialist	124	B'nding Main	113	27,700	1:36.20	
1964	Tamao	6	R. Broussard	124	Spanish Fort	117	Wa-Wa Cy	114	28,750	1:33.20	
1965	Pia Star	4	J. Sellers	112	Quita Dude	118	Troy Our Boy	112	32,550	1:33.20	
1966	Hedevar	4	W. Blum	116	Tosmah	119	Bold Bidder	124	25,300	1:37.00	
1967	Renewed Vigor	4	M. Heath	111	Estreno II	111	Errante II	114	25,300	1:37.00	
1968	R. Thomas	7	J. Nichols	119	Info		Out the Window	114	26,900	1:35.00	

Year	Winner	Age	Jockey	Wt.	Second	Wt.	Third	Wt.	Win Value	Time	Beyer
1969	Promise	4	R. Ussery	118	Info	120	Renewed Vigor	113	32,700	1:35.00	
1979	Bask	5	M.R. Morgan	112	Bold Standard	111	Hold Your Tricks	120	22,605	1:33.20	
1980	Prince Majestic	6	G. Patterson	113	Sea Ride	114	Braze and Bold	118	69,300	1:39.20	
1981	J. Burns	6	J.D. Bailey	115	Summer Advocate	115	Brent's Trans Am	114	68,340	1:35.80	
1982	Summer Advocate	5	R.P. Romero	117	Prince Freddie	109	Fabulous Find	110	49,860	1:36.40	
1983	Hale Herk	4	R.D. Evans	113	Thumbsucker	116	Spoonf'l of H'n'y	115	52,560	1:36.00	
1984	Win Stat	7	D. Pettinger	117	Le Cou Cou	116	Harham's Sizzler	111	49,860	1:37.80	
1985	Timeless Native	5	J. Tejeira	122	Par Flite	115	Harham's Sizzler	115	49,275	1:33.80	
1986	Smile	4	J. Vasquez	121	Taylor's Special	124	Red Attack	114	69,180	1:34.00	
1987	Red Attack	5	M.E. Smith	116	Taylor's Special	127	Come Summer	114	48,570	1:34.20	
1989	Present Value	5	P. Olivares	114	Paramount Jet	114	Sutter's Prospect	110	50,310	1:34.40	
1990	Black Tie Affair	4	J. Velasquez	119	Bio	112	New Plymouth	110	47,923	1:36.00	
1991	Bright Again	4	P. Day	112	Secret Hello	115	Irish Swap	112	45,000	1:35.20	
1992	Katahaula County	4	C.C. Bourque	114	The Great Carl	113	Stalwars	116	45,000	1:37.20	103
1993	Split Run	5	E. Fires	114	Gee Can He Dance	114	Danc'n Jake	114	60,000	1:34.80	111
1994	Slerp	5	Fires E	117	Seattle Morn	116	Dancing Jon	113	60,000	1:35.40	99
1995	Tarzans Blade	5	P. Day	115	Swank	114	Come on Flip	113	45,000	1:35.60	103
1996	Golden Gear	5	M. Guidry	122	Exclusive Garth	113	Prospect for Love	113	105,000	1:36.00	107
1997	Announce	5	C.C. Borque	116	Victor Cooley	117	Hunk of Class	116	60,000	1:36.80	106
2000	Yankee Victor	4	H. Castillo Jr.	122	Bright Valour	114	Desert Demon	113	60,000	1:34.97	105

Yankee Victor [114] finished first but was subsequently disqualified from the purse (Battle Mountain placed third)

Year	Winner	Age	Jockey	Wt.	Second	Wt.	Third	Wt.	Win Value	Time	Beyer
2001	Bright Valour	5	R.J. Albarado	115	Apt to Be	114	Castlewood	116	60,000	1:36.21	100
2002	Bonapaw	6	G. Melancon	121	Slider	115	Discreet Hero	116	60,000	1:34.00	109
2003	Apt to Be	6	E. Razo Jr	117	There's Zealous	116	San Pedro	116	60,000	1:34.40	110

Beyer Index: 105.3

HAWTHORNE DERBY, 1 1/8 Miles (Turf)
3-Year-Olds, Hawthorne, 2003 Purse: $250,000

Year	Winner	Age	Jockey	Wt.	Second	Wt.	Third	Wt.	Win Value	Time	Beyer
1965	Bold Bidder	3	E. Nelson	115	Gummo	118	Slystitch	117	37,100	1:43.40	
1966	Handsome Boy	3	L. Moyers	115	Francis U.	116	Whisper Jet	119	37,750	1:41.60	
1967	Gentleman James	3	R. Nono	114	Royal Speed	113	High Tribute	117	36,650	1:48.60	
1968	Te Vega	3	L. Pincay Jr	120	Foreign Comet	117	Francsull	113	34,300	1:41.80	
1969	Oil Power	3	J. Cruguet	113	Fast Hilarious	120	North Flight	124	30,950	1:40.60	
1970	Well Mannered	3	F. Verardi	120	Sarasota Bay	111	Coaltown Cat	118	54,450	1:41.80	
1971	Northfields	3	M. Ycaza	122	New Round	115	Saltwell	111	42,100	1:40.80	
1972	Feloniously	3	E. Fires	118	Sensitive Music	116	Suspected	114	28,750	1:42.40	
1973	Golden Don	3	M. Manganello	116	Impecunious	123	Cades Cove	114	40,600	1:41.20	
1974	Stonewalk	3	R. Turcotte	123	Tytus Casella	116	Mr. Door	114	63,150	1:40.60	
1975	Winter Fox	3	B. Fann	119	Intrepid Hero	125	American History	117	93,800	1:49.20	
1976	Wardlaw	3	J. Tejeira	117	Practitioner	112	Hurricane Ed	117	82,200	1:42.80	
1977	Silver Series	3	L. Snyder	114	Courtly Haste	114	Affiliate	112	100,800	1:41.20	
1978	Sensitive Prince	3	J. Vasquez	118	Gordie H.	112	Esops Foibles	124	73,680	1:39.60	
1979	Architect	3	S.A. Spencer	115	Incredible Ease	112	Door King	112	48,360	1:44.60	
1980	Jaklin Klugman	3	C.J. McCarron	121	Summer Advocate	115	Hurry Up Blue	121	64,440	1:40.80	
1981	Jeremy Jet	3	C. Silva	112	Loose Thoughts	112	Recusant	112	67,200	1:45.60	
1982	Drop Your Drawers	3	P. Day	118	Harham's Sizzler	118	Northern Majesty	118	64,830	1:42.80	
1983	St. Forbes	3	E. Fires	117	His Flower	117	Saverton	117	67,200	1:44.40	
1984	Pass the Line	3	C. Marquez	117	Mr. Japan	117	Bet Blind	115	66,750	1:57.60	
1985	Derby Wish	3	R.P. Romero	123	Day Shift	115	Explosive Darling	123	64,320	2:00.20	
1986	Autobot	3	E. Fires	120	Spellbound	117	Son of the Desert	115	96,360	2:00.40	
1987	Zaizoom	3	E. Fires	119	Sir Bask	114	Rio's Lark	116	89,280	2:09.80	
1988	Pappa's Swing	3	E.S. Prado	119	Djedar	115	Foolish Intent	117	94,200	1:55.80	
1989	Broto	3	S.J. Sellers	115	Joey Jr.	117	Chenin Blanc	115	94,350	1:53.00	
1990	Tutu Tobago	3	P.A. Johnson	113	Take That Step	122	Seti I.	115	64,710	1:53.60	
1991	Rainbows for Life	3	D. Penna	122	Drummer Boy	117	Kiltartan Cross	115	65,370	1:44.60	101
1992	Bantan	3	C.C. Bourque	117	Words of War	114	Gee Can He Dance	117	60,000	1:48.00	99
1993	Snake Eyes	3	G.K. Gomez	122	Lt. Pinkerton	117	Ft. Bent	115	90,000	1:50.20	102
1994	Chrysalis House	3	Guidry M.	115	Unfinished Symph.		Marvin's Faith	122	90,000	1:51.80	99
1995	Cuzzin Jeb	3	Lopez CC	117	Hawk Attack	122	Seven n Seven	114	90,000	1:48.80	93
1996	Jaunatxo	3	Diaz J. L.	122	Trail City	122	Canyon Run	122	120,000	1:47.00	101
1997	River Squall	3	C. Perret	119	Honor Glide	122	Blazing Sword	115	120,000	1:48.20	107
1998	Stay Sound	3	D'Amico A. J.	115	El Mirasol	111	Yankee Brass	114	150,000	1:47.40	99
1999	Minor Wisdom	3	Zimmerman R.	115	Air Rocket	119	Fred of Gold	113	150,000	1:49.00	102
2000	Hymn	3	L. Pincay Jr.	115			Lonely Place	113	100,000	1:53.79	95
	Rumsontheontheriver	3	A.J. Juarez Jr.	115							
2001	Kalu	3	J.A. Santos	115	Proud Man	119	Rahy's Secret	115	150,000	1:50.49	93
2002	Flying Dash	3	V. Espinoza	119	Scooter Roach	115	Quest Star	115	150,000	1:58.88	90
2003	False Promises	3	C.H. Marquez Jr	115	Megoman	115	Beau Classic	113	150,000	1:48.48	91

Beyer Index: 97.85

HAWTHORNE HANDICAP, 1 1/16 Miles,
Fillies and Mares 3-Year-Olds and Up, Hollywood Park, 2003 Purse: $103,292

Year	Winner	Age	Jockey	Wt.	Second	Wt.	Third	Wt.	Win Value	Time	Beyer
1974	Tallahto	4	L. Pincay Jr	119	Sister Fleet	116	Lt.'s Joy	119	23,200	1:20.60	
1975	Tizna	6	J. Lambert	122	Modus Vivendi	121	Lucky Spell	121	22,600	1:20.60	
1976	Swingtime	4	W. Shoemaker	118	Call Me Proper	116	Tuscarora	113	19,150	1:41.80	
1976	Mia Amore	4	F. Toro	116	Bastonera II	118	Sometime Promise	119	19,950	1:41.80	
1977	Cascapedia	4	S. Hawley	123	Bastonera II	124	Star Ball	121	26,850	1:40.80	
1978	Sensational	4	L. Pincay Jr	119	Up to Juliet	114	Grand Luxe	117	27,300	1:41.80	
1979	Country Queen	4	L. Pincay Jr	118	Grande Brisa	113	Sisterhood	120	26,600	1:41.20	
1980	Country Queen	5	L. Pincay Jr	122	Devon Ditty	117	Wishing Well	112	30,800	1:40.60	
1981	Save Wild Life	4	C.J. McCarron	113	Princess Karenda	122	Spiffy Laree	113	37,400	1:42.80	
1982	Weber City Miss	5	S. Hawley	122	Miss Huntington	117	Aduana	115	31,750	1:42.40	
1983	Marisma	5	K. Black	115	Sierva	115	Matching	121	30,700	1:44.80	
1984	Adored	4	F. Toro	117	Holiday Dancer	116	Princess Rooney	123	36,200	1:41.80	
1985	Adored	5	L. Pincay Jr	124	Mitterand	124	Her Royalty	118	45,350	1:34.80	
1986	Dontstop Themusic	6	L. Pincay Jr.	121	Till You	115	Fran's Valentine	122	46,950	1:35.40	
1987	Seldom Seen Sue	4	C.J. McCarron	114	Clabber Girl	116	Tiffany Lass	123	59,900	1:33.60	
1988	Integra	4	G.L. Stevens	120	Invited Guest	118	Behind the Scenes	117	59,400	1:36.00	
1989	Bayakoa	5	L. Pincay Jr	122	Goodbye Halo	123	Behind the Scenes	114	61,400	1:32.80	
1990	Bayakoa	6	L. Pincay Jr	125	Stormy but Valid	119	Fantastic Look	115	61,400	1:34.00	.100
1991	Brought to Mind	4	P.A. Valenzuela	116	Fantastic Look	118	Fit to Scout	118	62,300	1:41.40	
1992	Sacramentada	6	K.J. Desormeaux	117	Brought to Mind	120	Re Toss	116	61,600	1:43.00	.97
1993	Freedom Cry	5	A. Solis	117	Vieille Vigne	114	Miss High Blade	114	67,600	1:41.00	.110
1994	Golden Klair	4	K.J. Desormeaux	118	Likeable Style	119	Andestine	117	60,000	1:41.40	.100
1995	Paseana	8	C.J. McCarron	122	Pirate's Revenge	117	Top Rung	117	63,300	1:42.40	.98
1996	Borodislew	6	C.S. Nakatani	119	Jewel Princess	120	Urbane	118	64,200	1:41.20	.104
1997	Twice The Vice	6	C.J. McCarron	120	Chile Chatte	115	Listening	117	64,860	1:42.60	.101
1998	I Ain't Bluffing	4	C.J. McCarron	114	Fun in Excess	117	Tomorrows Sunshine	115	63,720	1:41.40	.106
1999	Victory Stripes	5	C.J. McCarron	115	Magical Allure	118	Housa Dancer	115	90,000	1:41.60	.105
2000	Riboletta	5	C.J. McCarron	117	Excellent Meeting	122	Speaking of Time	111	90,000	1:42.33	.105
2001	Printemps	4	C.J. McCarron	116	Feverish	119	Brianda	109	90,000	1:43.21	.97
2002	Queen of Wilshire	6	P.A. Valenzuela	115	Alexine	119	Verruma	116	63,660	1:43.16	.98
2003	Keys to the Heart	4	J. Valdivia Jr	115	Rhiana	116	Alexine	117	63,240	1:42.97	.94

Se Me Acabo finished third but was disqualified and placed fourth

Beyer Index: 101.15

HERECOMESTHEBRIDE, 1 1/16 Miles (Turf),
3-Year-Old Fillies, Gulfstream Park, 2003 Purse: $100,000

Year	Winner	Age	Jockey	Wt.	Second	Wt.	Third	Wt.	Win Value	Time	Beyer
1984	Delta Mary	3	F. Pennisi	112	Vast Domain		Ingot Way		14,955	1:42.00	
1984	Oakbrook Lady	3	J. Velez Jr.	112	Illaka		Rain Devil		14,655	1:42.80	
1985	Debutante Dancer	3	G. Gallitano	113	One Fine Lady		Affirmance		38,640	1:42.80	
1986	Judy's Red Shoes	3	G. St. Leon	114	Tea for Top		Minstress		35,740	1:43.00	
1987	Sum	3	R. Woodhouse	112	Easter Mary		Dawandeh		25,410	1:43.20	
1988	Topicount	3	J.L. Samyn	112	Aquaba		Above Special		40,350	1:43.20	
1989	Darby Shuffle	3	C. Perret	121	Seattle Meteor		Imago		36,510	1:42.80	
1992	Morriston Belle	3	D. Penna	118	Snazzle Dazzle		Miss Jealski		30,000	1:42.20	.87
1993	Sigrun	3	R. Douglas	116	So Say All of Us		Supah Gem		30,000	1:45.60	.85
1994	Cut the Charm	3	W. Ramos	116	Mynameispanama		Tambien Me Voy		30,000	1:43.60	.87
1995	Clever Thing	3	C. Perret	114	Transient Trend		Palliser Bay		30,000	1:53.00	.73
1996	Lulu's Ransom	3	J.D. Bailey	116	Cymbala		Vashon		30,000	1:47.40	.92
1997	Auntie Mame	3	J.Bailey	114	Witchful Thinking	116	Classic Approval	114	45,000	1:46.40	.97
1998	Rashas Warning	3	M.E. Smith	118	Quick Lap	116	Runaway Dream	116	45,000	1:51.40	.87
1999	Pico Teneriffe	3	J.D. Bailey	118	European Rose	112	Wild Heart Dancing	114	45,000	1:48.80	.89
2000	Gaviola	3	J.D. Bailey	114	Solvig	121	Are You Up	114	45,000	1:47.28	.93
2001	Mystic Lady	3	J.D. Bailey	116	Open Minded	114	Ruff	118	60,000	1:46.73	.80
2002	Cellars Shiraz	3	C. Velasquez	117	August Storm	121	She's Vested	115	60,000	1:43.21	.89
2003	Gal O Gal	3	C.P. DeCarlo	117	Formal Miss	117	Devil at the Wire	117	60,000	1:42.38	.87

Beyer Index: 87.17

Run on main track in 2001

HILL PRINCE, 1 1/8 Miles (Off the Turf),
3-Year-Olds, Belmont Park, 2003 Purse: $113,100

Year	Winner	Age	Jockey	Wt.	Second	Wt.	Third	Wt.	Win Value	Time	Beyer
1975	Don Jack	3	G. Martens	110	Annie's Brat		Rapid Invader	113	34,650	2:23.20	
1976	Fifth Marine	3	R. Turcotte	126	Quick Card	120	Drover's Dawn	121	27,405	1:41.20	
1977	Forward Charger	3	J. Vasquez	115	Stir the Embers	112	Winter Wind	112	22,575	1:34.40	
1978	Darby Creek Road	3	A. Cordero Jr	121	John Henry	111	Scythian Gold	111	22,605	1:35.20	
1979	Bends Me Mind	3	J. Velasquez	114	Crown Thy Good	115	T.V. Series	110	34,470	1:46.00	

Year	Winner	Age	Jockey	Wt.	Second	Wt.	Third	Wt.	Win Value	Time	Beyer
1980	Ben Fab	3	J. Cruguet	126	Vatzka	113	Don Daniello	117	34,800	1:43.40	
1981	Summing	3	A. Cordero Jr	114	Stage Door Key	114	Sportin' Life	114	35,700	1:42.40	
1982	Majesty's Prince	3	R. Hernandez	114	A Real Leader	115	Honed Edge	109	33,180	1:43.40	
1982	Larida	3	E. Maple	112	Dew Line	117	John's Gold	114	33,180	1:42.60	
1983	Domynsky	3	J.D. Bailey	114	White Birch	114	Macho Duck	114	36,660	1:48.80	
1984	A Gift	3	D. MacBeth	114	Is Your Pleasure	126	Jesse's Hope	117	43,680	1:48.40	
1985	Danger's Hour	3	D. MacBeth	114	Foundation Plan	119	Exclusive Partner	114	59,310	1:40.60	
1986	Double Feint	3	J.A. Santos	121	Glow	121	Jack of Clubs	114	53,190	1:41.40	
1987	Forest Fair	3	J.A. Santos	119	Kindly Court	117	First Patriot	121	86,220	1:42.80	
1988	Sunshine Forever	3	A. Cordero Jr	114	Posen	121	Kris Green	114	85,620	1:41.20	
1989	Slew the Knight	3	C.W. Antley	121	Orange Sunshine	117	Expensive Decision	121	56,520	1:41.00	
1990	Solar Splendor	3	E. Maple	114	Divine Warning	119	Bismarck Hills	114	57,870	1:41.20	
1991	Young Daniel	3	A. Cordero Jr	114	Share the Glory	119	Lech	114	58,050	1:39.80	102
1992	Free at Last	3	J.D. Bailey	126	Casino Magistrate	123	Kiri's Clown	114	53,190	1:41.00	95
1993	Halisee	3	J.A. Krone	121	Proud Shot	117	Logroller	114	52,020	1:40.80	95
1994	Pennine Ridge	3	J.D. Bailey	112	Check Ride	119	Add the Gold	114	50,925	1:39.80	100
1995	Green Means Go	3	J.D. Bailey	117	Smells and Bells	114	Debonair Dan	119	68,160	1:40.20	101
1996	Optic Nerve	3	Santos J. A.	114	Fortitude	117	Allied Forces	119	66,420	1:39.60	103
1997	Subordination	3	Velazquez J. R.	113	Rob 'n Gin	119	Tekken	119	67,200	1:45.60	101
1998	Recommended List	3	J.F. Chavez	119	Daniel My Brother	119	Availability	119	68,100	1:49.20	94
1999	Time Off	3	Samyn J. L.	119	Hoyle	113	Lenny's Ransom	113	66,720	1:47.40	91
2000	Promontory Gold	3	E.S. Prado	119	Rob's Spirit	113	Avezzano	115	66,540	1:49.15	100
2001	Proud Man	3	R.R. Douglas	122	Package Store	114	Navesink	118	68,760	1:48.25	95
2002	Van Minister	3	M.J. Luzzi	114	Miesque's Approval	120	Westcliffe	114	65,580	1:54.42	92
2003	Happy Trails	3	S.X. Bridgmohan	120	Traffic Chief	114	Chilly Rooster	114	67,860	1:50.13	91

Off the turf in 2003.

Beyer Index: 96.92

HOLLYWOOD JUVENILE CHAMPIONSHIP, 6 Furlongs, 2-Year-Olds, Hollywood Park, 2003 Purse: $102,500

Year	Winner	Age	Jockey	Wt.	Second	Wt.	Third	Wt.	Win Value	Time	Beyer
1938	Unerring	2	J. Adams	119	Kenty Miss	113	Valley Lass	116	2,015	1:06.00	
1939	Polymelior	2	R. Neves	118	Loreby	115	Ted's Clover	118	8,320	1:13.00	
1940	Flying Choice	2	J. Longden	115	Lady Bos'n	115	Tin Pan Alley	122	7,600	1:11.60	
1941	Madie Greenock	2	P. Martinez	119			Zaca Rosa	119	6,200	1:12.40	
	Phar Rong	2	G. Woolf	122							
1944	Post Graduate	2	H. Woodhouse	115	Sea Swallow	115	Gold Bolt	115	15,650	1:23.20	
1944	Realization	2	R. Neves	115	War Allies	115	Bismark Sea	115	17,750	1:24.20	
1945	Favorito	2	J. Craigmyle	114	Widow's Peak	115	Please Me	114	21,540	1:24.20	
1946	U Time	2	L. Balaski	114	Stepfather	117	Hemet Squaw	114	21,900	1:10.20	
1947	Zenoda	2	R. Neves	111	Grandpere	118	Solidarity	114	16,800	1:10.00	
1948	Star Fiddle	2	H. Trent	118	Audacious Man	118	Top Turrett	118	21,050	1:12.60	
1949	Thanks Again	2	F. Chojnacki	116	Great Circle	113	Sturdy One	119	31,100	1:11.00	
1950	Gold Capitol	2	R. Neves	114	Frendswood	113	Good Loser	114	28,600	1:43.80	
1951	Prudy's Boy	2	G. Lasswell	114	Alate	114	Big Noise	114	24,900	1:10.80	
1952	Little Request	2	J. Longden	122	Decorated	112	Chanlea	112	20,350	1:10.60	
1953	Arrogate	2	E. LeBlanc	114	Larks Music	116	James Session	119	44,500	1:10.80	
1954	Blue Ruler	2	S. Brooks	113	Colonel Mack	119	Modern World	113	45,700	1:10.80	
1955	Bold Bazooka	2	R. York	116	Blen Host	119	Fortuneway	116	47,200	1:09.80	
1956	Lucky Mel	2	J. Longden	122	Nashville	116	Joe Price	116	61,450	1:09.40	
1957	Old Pueblo	2	E. Arcaro	116	Fleet Nasrullah	119	Strong Ruler	111	49,900	1:10.20	
1958	Tomy Lee	2	W. Shoemaker	122	Finnegan	118	Monk's Hood	122	52,500	1:10.40	
1959	Noble Noor	2	D. Pierce	113	Tompion	116	Warfare	112	118,850	1:10.00	
1960	Pappa's All	2	G. Taniguchi	122	Sullivan's Bud	116	Big Smoky	116	98,200	1:10.00	
1961	Rattle Dancer	2	R. Yanez	116	Doc Jocoy	116	Indian Blood	122	102,800	1:09.80	
1962	Y Flash	2	R. Campas	116	Slipped Disc	116	Court Tower	116	69,100	1:10.40	
1962	Noti	2	E. Burns	116	Copper Student	116	Honey Bunny	116	69,100	1:10.20	
1963	Malicious	2	I. Valenzuela	119	Wil Rad	119	Close BY	119	65,150	1:09.60	
1963	Nevada Bin	2	R. York	116	Nevada P.J.	119	Leisurely Kin	116	66,150	1:10.60	
1964	Charger's Kin	2	P. Moreno	122	Azure Te	116	Gummo	116	86,075	1:09.80	
1964	Neke	2	L. Gilligan	116	Donson	116	Old Mose	116	86,075	1:09.80	
1965	Port Wine	2	W. Shoemaker	122	Ri Tux	122	Flame Tree	122	111,500	1:10.20	
1966	Forgotten Dreams	2	A. Maese	122	Tumble Wind	122	Wilbur Clark	122	101,300	1:09.40	
1967	Jim White	2	W. Hartack	122	Poleax	122	Broad Shadows	122	120,050	1:09.80	
1968	Fleet Kirsch	2	A. Pineda	122	One More Chorus	122	Fleet Allied	122	125,850	1:09.20	
1969	Insubordination	2	L. Pincay Jr	122	With Evidence	122	Windy Tide	122	101,850	1:09.20	
1970	Fast Fellow	2	D. Tierney	122	Kfar Tov	122	Moonsplash	122	106,400	1:10.00	
1971	Royal Owl	2	W. Shoemaker	122	MacArthur Park	122	Wind'n Sand	122	101,000	1:09.20	
1972	Bold Liz	2	J. Tejeira	119	Doc Marcus	122	Bottle Brush	122	83,000	1:09.40	
1973	Century's Envoy	2	J. Lambert	122	Such a Rush	122	Tinsley's Image	122	78,550	1:09.00	
1974	Dimaggio	2	L. PIncay Jr	122	The Bagel Prince	122	George Navonod	122	74,500	1:08.60	
1975	Restless Restless	2	S. Hawley	122	Imacornishprince	122	Telly's Pop	122	79,350	1:09.80	
1976	Fleet Dragoon	2	F. Olivares	122	Grey Moon Runner	122	Red Sensation	117	103,250	1:09.60	

Year	Winner	Age	Jockey	Wt.	Second	Wt.	Third	Wt.	Win Value	Time	Beyer
1977	Affirmed	2	L. Pincay Jr	122	He's Dewan	122	Esops Foibles	122	60,975	1:09.20	
1978	Terlingua	2	D. McHargue	119	Flying Paster	122	Exuberant	122	77,000	1:08.80	
1978	Noble Bronze	2	S. Hawley	117	Little Reb	122	Tally Ho the Fox	122	62,225	1:09.80	
1979	Parsec	2	W. Shoemaker	122	Doonesbury	122	Encino	122	89,350	1:10.00	
1980	Loma Malad	2	L. Pincay Jr	122	Motivity	122	Bold Ego	122	101,150	1:10.00	
1981	The Captain	2	L. Pincay Jr	117	Rember John	115	Helen's Beau	120	64,000	1:10.40	
1982	Desert Wine	2	F. Olivares	117	Ft. Davis	117	Full Choke	120	57,900	1:09.60	
1983	Althea	2	L. Pincay Jr	117	Rejected Suitor	117	Auto Commander	117	66,200	1:09.40	
1984	Saratoga Six	2	A. Cordero Jr	117	Ten Grand	117	Spectacular Love	117	90,500	1:10.20	
1985	Hilco Scamper	2	G. Stevens	120	Little Red Cloud	117	Exuberant's Image	117	64,400	1:09.80	
1986	Captain Valid	2	C. McCarron	117	Qualify	117	Jazzing Around	117	73,600	1:11.60	
1987	Mi Preferido	2	A. Solis	117	Mixed Pleasure	120	Purdue King	117	75,900	1:10.00	
1988	King Glorious	2	C. McCarron	120	Bruho	117	Mountain Ghost	117	64,200	1:08.80	
1989	Magical Mile	2	E. Delahoussaye	117	Forty Niner Days	117	Willing Worker	117	61,200	1:10.00	
1990	Deposit Ticket	2	G. Stevens	117	Avenue of Flags	117	Stone God	117	56,500	1:09.00	
1991	Scherando	2	F. Mena	117	Prince Wild	117	Burnished Bronze	120	56,400	1:09.60	101
1992	Altazarr	2	E. Delahoussaye	117	Tatum Canyon	117	Just Sid	117	58,700	1:10.00	90
1993	Ramblin Guy	2	E. Delahoussaye	117	Swift Walker	117	Individual Style	117	57,600	1:10.00	86
1994	Mr Pruple	2	C.J. McCarron	117	Serena's Song	117	Cyrano	117	57,600	1:10.00	86
1995	Hennessy	2	G.L. Stevens	117	Reef Reef	117	Desert Native	117	57,400	1:09.80	91
1996	Swiss Yodeler	2	A. Solis	120	Red	117	Vermillion	117	61,470	1:09.60	94
1997	K. O. Punch	2	Stevens G. L.	120	Old Topper	117	Majorbigtimesheet	120	66,120	1:09.80	86
1998	Yes It's True	2	J.D. Bailey	120	O' Rey Fantasma	117	Worldly Manner	117	61,620	1:09.40	97
1999	Dixie Union	2	A. Solis	117	Exchange Rate	117	High Yield	115	63,780	1:09.80	88
2000	Squirtle Squirt	2	L. Pincay Jr	120	Legendary Weave	117	Drumcliff	117	63,540	1:09.98	93
2001	Came Home	2	C.J. McCarron	117	Metatron	117	A Major Pleasure	117	64,440	1:09.20	105
2002	Crowned Dancer	2	A. Solis	120	Outta Here	117	Chief Planner	117	64,980	1:10.10	92
2003	Perfect Moon	2	P.A. Valenzuela	117	Blairs Roarin Star	117	Ruler's Court	117	61,500	1:10.39	82

Beyer Index: 91.62

(JACK DANIEL'S) HOLLYWOOD PREVUE, 7 Furlongs, 2-Year-Olds, Hollywood Park, 2003 Purse: $100,000

Year	Winner	Age	Jockey	Wt.	Second	Wt.	Third	Wt.	Win Value	Time	Beyer
1981	Sepulveda	2	C.J. McCarron	112	Gato del Sol	122	Desert Envoy	112	44,625	1:22.00	
1982	Copelan	2	J.D. Bailey	122	R. Awacs	115	Desert Wine	122	62,850	1:21.40	
1983	So Vague	2	P.J. Cooksey	115	Country Manor	115	French Legionaire	115	76,300	1:22.20	
1984	First Norman	2	W. Shoemaker	112	Teddy Naturally	122	Dan's Diablo	122	63,700	1:22.20	
1985	Judge Smells	2	C.J. McCarron	117	Raised on Stage	112	Old Bid	115	46,850	1:23.00	
1986	Exclusive Enough	2	W. Shoemaker	112	Persevered	122	Gold on Green	116	45,900	1:23.00	
1988	King Glorious	2	C.J. McCarron	122	Past Ages	116	Shipping Time	115	47,150	1:21.20	
1989	Individual'st I	2	R.G. Davis	115	Top Cash	122	Tarascon	115	46,600	1:22.20	
1990	Olympio	2	E. Delahoussaye	116	Barrage	115	General Meeting	114	62,600	1:21.80	
1991	Star of the Crop	2	G.L. Stevens	114	Seahawk Gold	121	Salt Lake	121	57,700	1:22.20	94
1992	Stuka	2	P.A. Valenzuela	118	Codified	114	Altazarr	121	62,350	1:21.80	99
1993	Individual Style	2	C.W. Antley	121	Egayant	117	Soul of the Matter	115	46,100	1:21.00	89
1994	Afternoon Deelites	2	Desormeaux KJ	115	Valid Wager	114	Hunt for Missouri	114	57,500	1:20.80	94
1995	Cobra King	2	C.J. McCarron	121	Hennessy	121	Exetera	116	58,800	1:21.20	103
1996	In Excessive Bull	2	Nakatani C. S.	115	Thisnearlywasmine	118	Constant Demand	116	61,120	1:21.40	106
1997	Commitisize	2	Flores D. R.	116	Buttons N Moes	119	Search Me	117	60,000	1:21.60	94
1998	Premier Property	2	Flores D. R.	119	Select Few	114	American Spirit	115	60,000	1:23.20	89
1999	Grey Memo	2	Garcia M. S.	115	Magical Dragon	115	Cameron Pass	116	60,000	1:24.40	86
2000	Proud Tower	2	V. Espinoza	122	Chinook Cat	116	Yonaguska	122	60,000	1:23.01	95
2001	Fonz's	2	L. Pincay Jr	117	Popular	113	Labamta Babe	113	60,000	1:22.03	97
2002	Roll Hennessy Roll	2	A. Solis	119	Red Apache	115	Hell Cat	114	75,000	1:22.68	95
2003	Lion Heart	2	M.E. Smith	114	Cooperation	116	Voladero	113	60,000	1:20.63	103

Beyer Index: 95.69

HOLLYWOOD TURF EXPRESS HANDICAP, 5 1/2 Furlongs (Turf), 3-Year-Olds and Up, Hollywood Park, 2003 Purse: $150,000

Year	Winner	Age	Jockey	Wt.	Second	Wt.	Third	Wt.	Win Value	Time	Beyer
1987	Lord Ruckus	4	L. Pincay Jr	117	Bundle of Iron	114	Faro	115	49,600	1:08.20	
1988	On the Line	4	G.L. Stevens	121	Little Red Cloud	115	Faro	118	47,650	1:09.20	
1989	Summer Sale	3	B.A. Hernandez	114	Ofanto	117	Oraibi	120	51,000	1:07.80	
1990	Answer Do	4	R.A. Baze	115	Waterscape	115	Yes I'm Blue	118	51,200	1:07.00	
1991	Gundaghia	4	C.S. Nakatani	114	Club Champ	116	Sun Brandy	115	61,875	1:01.40	103
1991	Answer Do	5	E. Delahoussaye	120	Apollo	115	Cardmania	116	61,875	1:01.40	103
1992	Answer Do	6	E. Delahoussaye	121	Repriced	118	Gundaghia	117	110,000	1:02.00	104
1993	Wild Harmony	4	C.J. McCarron	117	Robin des Pins	119	Monde Bleu	119	110,000	1:01.80	104
1994	Rotsaluck	4	F.H. Valenzuela	118	Marina Park	116	D'Hallevant	117	82,500	1:02.20	106
1995	Cyrano Storme	5	R.R. Douglas	116	Lakota Brave	115	Pembroke	121	110,000	1:01.60	106

Year	Winner	Age	Jockey	Wt.	Second	Wt.	Third	Wt.	Win Value	Time	Beyer
1996	Sandtrap	3	A. Solis	114	Cyrano Storme	118	Suggest	114	120,000	1:01.40	102
1997	Advancing Star	4	K.J. Desormeaux	119	Latin Dancer	116	Surachai	117	240,000	1:02.60	109
1998	Soldier Field	3	R. Wilson	117	Surachai	118	Bodyguard	115	120,000	1:02.00	99
1999	Mr. Doubledown	5	V. Espinoza	115	Howbaddouwantit	120	Champ's Star	115	120,000	1:01.80	101
2000	El Cielo	6	C.S. Nakatani	122	Texas Glitter	117	Full Moon Madness	121	120,000	1:01.73	107
2001	Swept Overboard	4	E. Delahoussaye	122	Speak In Passing	117	Blu Air Force	118	120,000	1:01.86	111
2002	Texas Glitter	6	J.R. Velazquez	119	Rocky Bar	114	Malabar Gold	118	120,000	1:01.52	106
2003	King Robyn	3	T. Baze	120	Geronimo	116	Golden Arrow	115	90,000	1:02.08	102

Beyer Index: 104.50

HOLY BULL, 1 1/16 Miles, 3-Year-Olds, Gulfstream Park, 2003 Purse:$100,000

Year	Winner	Age	Jockey	Wt.	Second	Wt.	Third	Wt.	Win Value	Time	Beyer
1990	Home at Last	3	J.D. Bailey	118	Run Turn	122	Sound of Cannons	118	140,160	1:53.20	
1991	Shoot to Kill	3	W.S. Ramos	112	Shotgun Harry J.	114	Cahill Road	114	120,000	1:43.40	99
1992	Waki Warrior	3	E. Fires	114	Scream Machine	112	Careful Gesture	113	78,258	1:44.20	92
1993	Pride of Burkaan	3	J.D. Bailey	112	Kassec	112	Jetting Along	114	45,000	1:44.60	88
1994	Go for Gin	3	J.D. Bailey	119	Halo's Image	114	Senor Conquistador	112	45,000	1:41.60	100
1995	Suave Prospect	3	J.D. Bailey	119	Bullet Trained	114	Rush Dancer	112	45,000	1:44.00	100
1996	Cobra King	3	C.J. McCarron	117	Editor's Note	119	Tilden	114	45,000	1:43.40	107
1997	Arthur L.	3	J.R.Velazquez	122	Acceptable	114	Captain Bodgit	119	60,000	1:42.80	107
1998	Cape Town	3	J.D. Bailey	119	Comic Strip	114	Sweetsouthernsaint	119	60,000	1:44.00	101
1999	Grits'n Hard Toast	3	R.G. Davis	114	Doneraille Court	119	Mountain Range	119	60,000	1:45.20	100
2000	Hal's Hope	3	R.I. Velez	112	Personal First	117	Megacles	113	60,000	1:44.52	100
2001	Radical Riley	3	E. Nunez	119	Buckle Down Ben	119	Cee Dee	117	60,000	1:46.06	90
2002	Booklet	3	E.M. Coa	122	Harlan's Holiday	122	Thiscannonsloaded	116	60,000	1:46.16	101
2003	Offlee Wild	3	M. Guidry	116	Powerful Touch	116	Bham	118	60,000	1:43.00	99

Run as Preview Stakes, 1990-95

Beyer Index: 98.77

HONEY FOX HANDICAP, 1 1/16 Miles (Turf), Fillies and Mares 3-Year-Olds and Up, Gulfstream Park, 2003 Purse: $100,000

Year	Winner	Age	Jockey	Wt.	Second	Wt.	Third	Wt.	Win Value	Time	Beyer
1985	One Fine Lady	3	V. Molina	116	Foxy Deen		Boldly Dared		19,257	1:34.60	
1985	Affirmance	3	E. Maple	116	Miss Delice		Deceit Dancer		19,617	1:35.60	
1986	One Fine Lady	4	J. Velez	112	Shocker T.		Donna's Dolly		29,655	1:22.00	
1986	Gypsy Prayer	5	R. Lester	116	Four Flings		Isayso		29,985	1:21.00	
1987	Small Virtue	4	J. Vasquez	114	Thirty Zip		Chaldea		27,915	1:37.00	
1987	Top Socialite	5	C. Perret	119	Give a Toast		Judy's Red Shoes		27,615	1:37.40	
1988	Allegedum	5	A. Cordero Jr.	114	Autumn Glitter		Fama		31,515	1:35.20	
1988	Shaughnessy Road	4	J. Velez	112	Rally for Justice		Fieldy		31,215	1:36.00	
1989	Fieldy	6	C. Perret	114	Miss Unnameable		Aquaba		30,135	1:35.80	
1989	Vana Turns	4	R.P. Romero	113	For Kicks		Stolie		30,435	1:36.00	
1990	Fieldy	7	J.D. Bailey	120	Betty Lobelia		Leave It Be		30,000	1:37.60	100
1991	Vigorous Lady	5	M. Lee	116	Joyce Azalene		Stacie's Toy		30,000	1:40.20	
1992	Explosive Kate	5	D. Penna	113	Indian Fashion		Belleofbasinstreet		30,000	1:43.20	97
1993	Hero's Love	5	E. Fires	114	Quilma		Lady Blessington		30,000	1:42.80	99
1994	Sambacarioca	5	J.D. Bailey	121	Tiney Toast	114	Marshua's River	114	36,000	1:43.40	90
1995	Regal Joy	4	D. Penna	113	Sambacarioca	119	Sovereign Kitty	119	36,000	1:44.60	96
1996	Apolda	5	J.D. Bailey	116	Class Kris	116	Alice Springs	121	45,000	1:41.40	102
1997	Rare Blend	4	J.D. Bailey	118	Queen Tutta	114	Hurricane Viv	121	45,000	1:44.20	103
1998	Parade Queen	4	P. Day	118	Dispersion	113	Dance Clear	114	45,000	1:42.00	99
1999	Colcon	6	J.D. Bailey	119	Lovers Knot	115	Tampico	114	45,000	1:41.60	104
2000	Dominique's Joy	5	J.D. Bailey	113	Circus Charmer	114	Pico Teneriffe	117	45,000	1:39.91	99
2001	Spook Express	7	M.E. Smith	115	Please Sign In	116	Lady Dora	115	60,000	1:35.60	87
2002	Batique	4	J.F. Chavez	117	My Sweet Westly	115	Silver Bandana	114	60,000	1:49.32	100
2003	San Dare	5	M. Guidry	115	Calista	118	Laurica	114	60,000	1:46.19	99

Run at 7 furlongs on main track, 1986; at 1 1/16 miles 1991-2000. Run as Joe Namath Handicap prior to 2001.

Beyer Index: 98.08

HONORABLE MISS HANDICAP, 6 Furlongs, 3-Year-Olds and Up, Fillies and Mares, Saratoga Race Course, 2003 Purse: $107,600

Year	Winner	Age	Jockey	Wt.	Second	Wt.	Third	Wt.	Win Value	Time	Beyer
1993	Nannerl	6	J.D. Bailey	117	Vivano	117	Via Dei Portici	117	29,040	1:15.00	93
1994	Classy Mirage	4	J.A. Krone	122	Spinning Round	119	For All Seasons	117	48,675	1:09.60	104
1995	Low Key Affair	5	P. Day	115	Classy Mirage	123	Twist Afleet	120	48,195	1:09.60	102
1996	Twist Afleet	5	M.E. Smith	119	Broad Smile	119	In Conference	113	49,455	1:09.80	101
1997	Dancin Renee	5	R. Migliore	116	Ashboro	116	Vivace	113	48,465	1:09.00	107
1998	Furlough	4	M.E. Smith	113	Angel's Tearlet	114	Dixie Flag	119	48,765	1:11.20	90

Year	Winner	Age	Jockey	Wt.	Second	Wt.	Third	Wt.	Win Value	Time	Beyer
1999	Bourbon Belle	4	Johnson P. A.	116	Gold Princess	116	License Fee	114	67,560	1:09.40	106
2000	Debby d'Or	5	S.J. Sellers	114	Tropical Punch	115	Katz Me If You Can	113	66,450	1:10.11	101
2000	Bourbon Belle	4	W. Martinez	116	Cassidy	114	Go to the Ink	114	65,850	1:08.93	115
2001	Big Bambu	4	J.D. Bailey	118	Country Hideaway	118	Dat You Miz Blue	120	63,708	1:09.64	104
2002	Mandy's Gold	4	E.S. Prado	116	Shine Again	116	Dat You Miz Blue	114	65,100	1:09.24	108
2003	Willa on the Move	4	E.S. Prado	114	Shine Again	120	Smok'n Frolic	117	64,560	1:09.92	105

Beyer Index: 103

FRED W. HOOPER HANDICAP, 1 1/8 Miles,
3-Year-Olds and Up, Calder Race Course, 2003 Purse: $100,000

Year	Winner	Age	Jockey	Wt.	Second	Wt.	Third	Wt.	Win Value	Time	Beyer
1994	Take Me Out	6	M.E. Smith	115	Migrating Moon	119	Meena	114	60,000	1:51.80	104
1994	Halo's Image	3	G. Boulanger	117	Fight For Love	114	Migrating Moon	120	60,000	1:51.40	109
1995	Bound by Honor	4	J.A. Krone	112	Bay Street Star	113	Halo's Image	121	60,000	1:51.80	105
1996	Cimarron Secret	5	Velez J.A. Jr	115	Laughing Dan	114	Wicapi	116	60,000	1:52.60	101
1997	Shrike	5	J.D. Bailey	113	Wicapi	112	Sir Bear	113	60,000	1:38.60	105
1998	Wicapi	4	J. Bravo	113	Smuggler's Prize	111	Best of the Rest	115	60,000	1:52.00	99
1999	Dancing Guy	4	J.C. Ferrer	120	Wicapi	118	Loon	112	60,000	1:50.83	100
2000	American Halo	4	C. Hunt	111	General Grant	112	Sir Bear	118	60,000	1:51.68	108
2001	Kiss a Native	4	C. Velasquez	116	Hal's Hope	115	Groomstick Stock's	113	60,000	1:51.05	106
2002	The Judge Sez Who	3	C. Velasquez	116	Best of the Rest	121	Dancing Guy	112	60,000	1:50.53	106
2003	Predawn Raid	4	J.F. Chavez	112	Best of the Rest	122	Deeliteful Guy	112	60,000	1:52.47	102

Beyer Index: 104.09

Run as Tropical Park Handicap prior to 1997. For previous runnings, refer to 1994 Manual

INDIANA BREEDERS' CUP OAKS, 1 1/16 Miles,
3-Year-Old Fillies, Hoosier Park, 2003 Purse: $306,900

Year	Winner	Age	Jockey	Wt.	Second	Wt.	Third	Wt.	Win Value	Time	Beyer
1998	French Braids	3	W. Martinez	116	Remember Ike	121	Barefoot Dyana	118	124,080	1:43.00	97
1999	Brushed Halory	3	E.M. Martin Jr.	121	The Happy Hopper	116	Chelsea's House	116	124,140	1:44.64	89
2000	Humble Clerk	3	L. Melancon	114	Megans Bluff	121	Miss Seffens	116	92,580	1:42.40	101
2001	Scoop	3	R.J. Albarado	122	Gold Huntress	115	Caressing	121	123,480	1:44.06	93
2002	Bare Necessities	3	J. Valdivia Jr.	118	Erica's Smile	121	Tarnished Lady	118	183,840	1:45.83	94
2003	Awesome Humor	3	R. Albarado	116	Cloakof Vagueness	114	Shot Gun Favorite	118	184,140	1:45.75	96

Beyer Index: 95

INDIANA DERBY, 1 1/16 Miles,
3-Year-Olds, Hoosier Park, 2003 Purse: $411,800

Year	Winner	Age	Jockey	Wt.	Second	Wt.	Third	Wt.	Win Value	Time	Beyer
1995	Peruvian	3	D. Kutz	117	I Still Believe	117	Mine Inspector	119	66,900	1:43.00	99
1996	Canyon Run	3	F.C. Torres	115	Broadway Bit	113	Hunk of Class	117	64,560	1:41.40	94
1997	Dubai Dust	3	S.P. LeJeune Jr.	113	Frisk Me Now	122	Tansit	119	127,440	1:44.00	97
1998	One Bold Stroke	3	R.J. Albarado	122	Dixie Dot Com	117	Da Devil	122	188,700	1:43.00	110
1999	Forty One Carats	3	J.F. Chavez	115	Zanetti	111	First American	122	188,100	1:42.24	105
2000	Mister Deville	3	L.S. Quinonez	119	Performing Magic	122	One Call Close	119	184,500	1:41.80	99
2001	Orientate	3	R.J. Albarado	115	Saratoga Games	121	Trion Georgia	124	188,460	1:42.22	105
2002	Perfect Drift	3	J.K. Court	124	Easyfromthegitgo	124	Premeditation	121	248,820	1:43.50	106
2003	Excessivepleasure	3	J.K. Court	124	Grand Hombre	124	Wando	124	247,080	1:43.48	103

Beyer Index: 102

INGLEWOOD HANDICAP, 1 1/16 Miles (Off the Turf),
3-Year-Olds and Up, Hollywood Park, 2003 Purse: $103,782

Year	Winner	Age	Jockey	Wt.	Second	Wt.	Third	Wt.	Win Value	Time	Beyer
1938	Ligaroti	6	N. Richardson	119	No Dice	106	Sweepalot	115	4,250	1:38.80	
1939	Specify	4	C. Corbett	118	Main Man	118	Flying Wild	102	6,975	1:36.40	
1940	Hysterical	4	L. Balaski	116	Specify	122	Wed'g Call	113	7,475	1:43.40	
1941	Sir Jeffrey	4	J. Westrope	113	Woof Woof	120	Mr. Grundy	109	7,975	1:42.40	
1945	High Resolve	4	C. Corbett	126	Prince Ernest	111	Challenge Me	110	11,600	1:22.00	
1946	Quick Reward	4	A. Skoronski	122	Canina	116	Vanslam	109	20,200	1:23.60	
1947	Artillery	4	H. Lindberg	112	Texas Sandman	115	See-tee-see	117	18,900	1:22.00	
1948	With Pleasure	5	J. Westrope	125	Mafosta	126	Fair Truckle	123	18,900	1:11.20	
1949	Ace Admiral	4	F. Zufelt	124	Pretal	110	Amble In	112	18,400	1:42.80	
1950	Miche	5	J. Westrope	122	Dharan	110	Frankly	112	17,550	1:49.00	
1951	Sturdy One	4	R. Neves	109	All Blue	111	Be Fleet	123	17,950	1:42.20	
1952	Sturdy One	5	R. Neves	111	Stormy Cloud	105	Admiral Drake	116	15,700	1:42.20	
1953	Pet Bully	5	R. Neves	123	Royal Serenade	116	Fleet Bird	122	16,250	1:42.00	
1954	High Scud	5	R. Trejos	113	Curragh King	113	Fleet Bird	118	14,900	1:42.00	
1955	Determine	4	R. York	124	Mister Gus	114	Alidon	117	15,250	1:40.80	
1956	Swaps	4	W. Shoemaker	130	Mister Gus	115	Bobby Brocato	121	29,450	1:39.00	

Year	Winner	Age	Jockey	Wt.	Second	Wt.	Third	Wt.	Win Value	Time	Beyer
1957	Find	7	R. Neves	118	Eddie Schmidt	112	Pit Boss	109	30,200	1:40.80	
1958	Eddie Schmidt	5	A. Maese	117	How Now	122	Social Climber	117	31,650	1:41.60	
1959	Bug Brush	4	A. Valenzuela	123	Amerigo	110	How Now	112	31,000	1:40.80	
1960	Bagdad	4	W. Shoemaker	121	Sea Orbit	118	Prize Host	110	31,300	1:40.80	
1961	Sea Orbit	5	A. Valenzuela	120	Dress Up	112	First Balcony	124	32,350	1:41.00	
1962	Prove It	5	J. Moreno	122	Sea Orbit	112	Rablero	109	33,450	1:41.00	
1963	Native Diver	4	R. Neves	121	Pirate Cove	115	Aldershot	114	32,450	1:42.20	
1964	Native Diver	5	J. Lambert	116	Mustard Plaster	118	Mr. Consistency	124	32,700	1:41.60	
1965	Tronado	5	J. Baze	113	Hill Rise	120	Quadrangle	124	32,800	1:40.40	
1966	Native Diver	7	J. Lambert	125	Sledge	115	Tronado	113	35,650	1:41.60	
1967	Quicken Tree	4	F. Alvarez	113	Hill Clown	112	Niarkos	124	26,750	1:41.60	
1967	Pretense	4	J. Sellers	128	Biggs	117	Aurelius II	111	26,250	1:39.80	
1968	Gamely	4	W. Harris	119	Rising Market	120	Hill Shine	118	34,550	1:47.20	
1969	Rising Market	5	L. Pincay Jr	120	Dewan	114	Rivet	114	32,850	1:46.60	
1970	Baffle	5	J. Lambert	122	Pleasure Seeker	111	T.V. Com'l	111	31,650	1:47.20	
1971	Advance Guard	5	W. Shoemaker	118	Manta	119	Far to Reach	111	44,850	1:48.00	
1972	War Heim	5	V. Tejada	112	Kennedy Road	119	Figonero	113	46,600	1:47.40	
1973	Ancient Title	3	F. Toro	122	Groshawk	122	Pontoise	114	32,550	1:21.00	
1974	Shirley's Champion	3	H. Grant	118	Rocket Review	117	Such a Rush	121	20,100	1:14.80	
1975	El Botija	5	J. Tejeira	116	Kirrary	115	Against the Snow	117	25,475	1:41.60	
1975	Gay Style	4	W. Shoemaker	120	Out of the East	116	June's Love	116	26,475	1:41.60	
1976	Riot in Paris	5	J. Lambert	121	Absent Minded	114	Pa's'ate Pi'te	113	25,750	1:41.60	
1976	King Pellinore	4	W. Shoemaker	118	Antique	114	Big Band	117	26,250	1:42.00	
1977	Today 'n Tomorrow	4	S. Hawley	117	Anne's Pretender	122	Sir Jason	118	32,300	1:41.00	
1978	Star Spangled	4	A. Cordero Jr	116	Bad 'n Big	122	No Turning	116	26,800	1:39.80	
1978	Star of Erin II	4	W. Shoemaker	117	Landscaper	113	Life's Hope	117	26,300	1:40.60	
1979	Johnny's Image	4	C.J. McCarron	117	Rich Cream	117	Smoggy	112	26,875	1:40.60	
1979	Star Spangled	5	L. Pincay Jr	119	Bywayofchicago	122	As de Copas	121	25,875	1:40.00	
1980	Red Crescent	4	C.J. McCarron	112	Henschel	118	Numa Pompilius	115	31,300	1:40.60	
1981	Bold Tropic	6	W. Shoemaker	124	The Bart	117	Adraan	117	52,250	1:40.00	
1982	Maipon	5	D.G. McHargue	115	Spence Bay	122	Wickerr	116	68,900	1:40.20	
1983	Bold Style	4	P. Day	115	Noalto	115	Western	118	65,400	1:41.40	
1984	Royal Heroine	4	F. Toro	116	Bel Bolide	120	Vin St. Benet	118	71,500	1:40.20	
1985	Al Mamoon	4	E. Delahoussaye	116	The Noble Player	118	Swoon	114	62,900	1:40.40	
1986	Zoffany	6	E. Delahoussaye	117	Palace Music	124	Truce Maker	112	63,300	1:45.60	
1987	Le Belvedere	4	W. Shoemaker	113	Sharrood	118	Barberty	114	65,100	1:40.40	
1988	Steinlen	5	G.L. Stevens	119	Deputy Governor	120	Galunpe	115	66,200	1:40.40	
1989	Steinlen	6	G.L. Stevens	120	Pasakos	115	Mi Preferido	117	63,400	1:39.60	
1990	Mohamed Abdu	6	G.L. Stevens	117	Peace	117	Classic Fame	117	64,800	1:39.40	107
1991	Tight Spot	4	L. Pincay Jr	121	Somethingdifferent	116	Razeen	114	63,400	1:40.20	110
1992	Golden Pheasant	6	G.L. Stevens	121	Blaze O'Brien	114	Native Boundary	116	64,900	1:39.80	102
1993	The Tender Track	6	E. Delahoussaye	117	Journalism	118	Johann Quatz	117	62,500	1:40.00	106
1994	Gothland	5	C.S. Nakatani	117	Rapan Boy	117	Johann Quatz	117	60,700	1:39.60	110
1995	Blaze O'Brien	8	C.A. Black	116	Savinio	118	Stoller	117	79,800	1:39.40	109
1996	Fastness	6	C.S. Nakatani	122	Helmsman	120	Tyconic	120	79,470	1:39.40	112
1997	El Angelo	4	C.S. Nakatani	115	Irish Wings	114	Tyconic	118	63,900	1:40.20	102
1998	Fantastic Fellow	4	C.S. Nakatani	118	Via Lombardia	116	Sharekann	113	64,740	1:38.60	112
1999	Brave Act	5	G.F. Almeida	120	Lord Smith	119	Expressionist	116	66,420	1:39.00	113
2000	Montemiro	6	V. Espinoza	117	Bonapartiste	118	Takarian	116	66,300	1:40.71	104
2001	Fateful Dream	4	D.R. Flores	114	National Anthem	115	Casino King	115	64,260	1:41.65	99
2002	Night Patrol	6	V. Espinoza	113	Redattore	120	Seinne	117	65,820	1:39.35	107
2003	Gondolieri	4	F.T. Alvarado	116	Truly a Judge	114	Freefourinternet	116	63,540	1:40.32	108

Off the turf in 2003.

Beyer Index: 107.21

IROQUOIS, 1 Mile,
2-Year-Olds, Churchill Downs, 2003 Purse: $113,700

Year	Winner	Age	Jockey	Wt.	Second	Wt.	Third	Wt.	Win Value	Time	Beyer
1990	Richman	2	P. Day	121	Speedy Cure	114	Honor Grades	116	36,628	1:36.60	
1991	Portroe	2	M.E. Smith	114	Walkie Talker	121	Richard of England	121	76,570	1:37.80	85
1992	Shoal Creek	2	B.E. Bartram	114	Saw Mill	116	Demaloot Demashoot	116	76,375	1:37.40	89
1993	Tarzans Blade	2	B.E. Bartram	121	Dove Hunt	121	Amathos	114	74,945	1:37.00	91
1994	Peruvian	2	J.A. Santos	121	Our Gatsby	116	Super Jeblar	116	77,025	1:36.60	84
1995	Ide	2	C. Perret	121	El Amante	116	City by Night	114	73,645	1:36.80	89
1996	Global View	2	K. Borque	112	Partner's Hero	112	Haint	121	68,200	1:36.40	96
1997	Keene Dancer	2	P. Day	121	Yarrow Brae	113	Dawn Exodus	113	68,882	1:37.80	93
1998	Exploit	2	C.J. McCarron	114	Crowning Storm	114	Olympic Journey	114	71,114	1:36.20	98
1999	Mighty	2	M. St. Julien	112	Ifitstobeitsuptome	113	Nature	114	68,758	1:35.80	94
2000	Meetyouathebrig	2	G.L. Stevens	118	Hero's Tribute	114	Keats	112	77,066	1:35.24	91
2001	Harlan's Holiday	2	A.J. D'Amico	121	Request for Parole	121	Gold Dollar	116	70,184	1:35.01	97
2002	Champali	2	P. Day	118	Alke	116	What a Bad Day	118	70,804	1:37.06	82
2003	The Cliff's Edge	2	S.J. Sellers	117	Korbyn Gold	121	Grand Score	117	70,494	1:35.57	101

Beyer Index: 91.54

PHILIP H. ISELIN BREEDERS' CUP HANDICAP, 1 1/8 Miles,
3-Year-Olds and Up, Monmouth Park, 2003 Purse: $189,000

Year	Winner	Age	Jockey	Wt.	Second	Wt.	Third	Wt.	Win Value	Time	Beyer
1884	Drake Carter	4	Hayward	120	Heel-and-Toe	108	Kinglike	120	3,460	2:37.60	
1885	Richmond	3	J. McLaughlin	110	Louisette	116	War Eagle	102	4,025	2:38.20	
1886	Hidalgo	4	Spellman	123	Bonanza	114	Maumee	104	3,570	2:39.20	
1887	Kaloolah	4	Church	107	Rupert	103	Eurus	112	3,570	2:42.20	
1888	Firenzi	4	Garrison	123	Exile	118	Belvidere	121	5,385	2:36.00	
1889	Eurus	6	Hayward	124	Senorita	104	Firenzi	124	4,715	2:50.00	
1890	Tea Tray	5	Moore	110	Rhono	118	Lavinia Belle	110	5,335	2:34.00	
1891	Banquet	4	Lamley	113	Peter	101	English Lady	103	5,055	2:40.00	
1892	Reckon	4	Penn	100	Lamplighter	115	Banquet	124	3,770	2:33.20	
1893	Gloaming	6	A. Clayton	100	The Pepper	114	Picknicker	106	3,955	2:33.00	
1946	Lucky Draw	5	C. McCreary	111	Stymie	126	Aonbarr	100	22,970	2:01.80	
1947	Round View	4	L. Hildebrandt	112	Talon	112	Gallorette	119	19,700	2:01.20	
1948	Tide Rips	4	P. Roberts	108	Vertigo II	109	Bug Juice	108	19,850	2:03.20	
1949	Three Rings	4	H. Woodhouse	110	Round View	112	Splash	104	20,200	2:03.60	
1950	Greek Ship	3	J. Culmone	107	Hypocrite II	108	Three Rings	121	21,250	2:02.40	
1951	Arise	5	S. Boulmetis	122	Post Card	117	Why Not Now	106	19,200	2:04.80	
1952	One Hitter	6	T. Atkinson	114	Combat Boots	108	County Delight	124	18,750	2:04.20	
1953	My Celeste	7	L. Batchellor	110	Again II	104	Devilkin	111	23,500	2:05.20	
1954	Bassanio	4	S. Cole	109	Closed Door	115	Level Lea	118	40,700	2:02.20	
1955	Helioscope	4	S. Boulmetis	131	High Gun	135	Punkin Vine	111	56,400	2:02.20	
1956	Nashua	4	E. Arcaro	129	Mr. First	110	Mielleux	107	78,200	2:02.80	
1957	Dedicate	5	E. Arcaro	124	Third Brother	119	Rockcastle	109	72,625	2:01.80	
1958	Bold Ruler	4	E. Arcaro	134	Sharpsburg	113	Bill's Sky Boy	105	70,772	2:01.60	
1959	Sword Dancer	3	W. Shoemaker	120	Amerigo	116	Talent Show	124	72,787	2:05.00	
1960	First Landing	4	E. Arcaro	123	Manassa Mauler	117	Talent Show	117	71,650	2:02.80	
1961	Don Poggio	5	S. Boulmetis	122	Our Hope	117	Black Thumper	108	72,995	2:02.40	
1962	Carry Back	4	J.L. Rotz	124	Kelso	130	Beau Purple	117	70,947	2:00.40	
1963	Decidedly	4	M. Ycaza	120	Mongo	126	Guadalcanal	113	72,345	2:02.00	
1964	Mongo	5	W. Chambers	127	Kelso	130	Gun Bow	124	69,875	2:01.80	
1965	Repeating	4	H. Woodhouse	110	Tenacle	114	Ampose	119	70,395	2:04.20	
1966	Bold Bidder	4	P. Anderson	122	Paoluccio	115	Pluck	114	74,392	2:03.60	
1967	Handsome Boy	4	J. Vasquez	115	Amberoid	118	Good Knight	113	73,060	2:02.00	
1968	Bold Hour	4	W. Boland	116	Mr. Right	114	Damascus	131	72,150	2:03.00	
1969	Verbatim	4	P. Anderson	116	San Roque	113	Chompion	111	73,970	2:02.20	
1970	Gladwin	4	H. Gustines	110	Charles Elliott	112	My Dad George	116	75,660	2:02.60	
1971	Jontilla	4	J. Giovanni	115	Never Bow	122	Pass Catcher	113	75,140	2:01.00	
1972	West Coast Scout	4	J.L. Rotz	113	Hitchcock	114	Eastern Fleet	117	73,775	2:02.20	
1973	West Coast Scout	5	L. Adams	114	Tentam	118	Windtex	113	74,295	2:01.20	
1974	True Knight	5	M.A. Rivera	124	Ecole Etage	112	Hey Rube	111	72,215	2:02.00	
1975	Royal Glint	5	C. Perret	121	Proper Bostonian	118	Stonewalk	121	70,947	2:00.60	
1976	Hatchet Man	5	V. Bracciale Jr	112	Intrepid Hero	119	Forego	136	71,792	2:00.60	
1977	Majestic Light	4	S. Hawley	124	Capital Idea	108	Peppy Addy	116	71,143	2:00.40	
1978	Life's Hope	5	C. Perret	115	Wise Philip	114	Father Hogan	115	72,183	2:03.20	
1979	Text	5	W. Shoemaker	118	Cox's Ridge	120	Silent Cal	115	70,948	1:47.40	
1980	Spectacular Bid	4	W. Shoemaker	132	Glorious Song	117	The Cool Virginian	112	158,160	1:48.00	
1981	Amber Pass	4	C.B. Asmussen	117	Joanie's Chief	108	Ring of Light	114	170,580	1:47.40	
1982	Mehmet	4	E. Delahoussaye	115	Pukka Princess	108	Summer Advoate	117	174,240	1:48.20	
1983	Bates Motel	4	T. Lipham	124	Island Whirl	124	Linkage	115	167,520	1:47.20	
1984	Believe the Queen	4	D.A. Miller Jr	120	World Appeal	121	Bet Big	117	194,040	1:48.20	
1985	Spend a Buck	3	L. Pincay Jr	118	Carr de Naskra	120	Valiant Lark	115	162,180	1:46.80	
1986	Roo Art	4	W. Shoemaker	117	Precisionist	125	Lady's Secret	120	188,280	1:48.60	
1987	Bordeaux Bob	4	C.W. Antley	115	Silver Comet	114	Lost Code	117	163,920	1:48.20	
1988	Alysheba	4	C.J. McCarron	124	Bet Twice	123	Gulch	122	300,000	1:47.80	
1989	Proper Reality	4	J.D. Bailey	119	Bill E. Shears	112	Mi Selecto	114	150,000	1:48.00	
1990	Beau Genius	5	R.D. Lopez	122	Tricky Creek	112	De Roche	115	150,000	1:48.20	.114
1991	Black Tie Affair	5	P. Day	119	Farma Way	122	Chief Honcho	115	300,000	1:47.80	.112
1992	Jolie's Halo	5	E.S. Prado	116	Out of Place	113	Valley Crossing	111	300,000	1:46.80	.106
1993	Valley Crossing	5	C.W. Antley	113	Devil His Due	123	Bertrando	119	300,000	1:49.20	.113
1994	Taking Risks	4	M.T. Johnston	115	Valley Crossing	117	Proud Shot	112	150,000	1:48.20	.113
1995	Schossberg	4	D. Penna	118	Poor But Honest	115	Mickeray	114	180,000	1:49.20	.111
1996	Smart Strike	4	C. Perret	115	Eltish	116	Serena's Song	115	180,000	1:41.40	.115
1997	Formal Gold	4	K.J. Desormeaux	121	Skip Away	124	Distorted Humor	115	250,000	1:40.20	.124
1998	Skip Away	5	J.D. Bailey	131	Stormin Fever	113	Testafly	114	300,000	1:47.20	.114
1999	Frisk Me Now	5	E.L. King Jr	117	Call Me Mr. Vain	110	Black Cash	112	210,000	1:49.00	.109
2000	Rize	4	J.C. Ferrer	112	Sir Bear	118	Talk's Cheap	114	210,000	1:48.42	.111
2001	Broken Vow	4	R.A. Dominguez	119	First Lieutenant	115	Sir Bear	117	210,000	1:49.55	.108
2002	Cat's at Home	5	J.A. Velez Jr.	116	Bowman's Band	117	Runspastum	114	210,000	1:49.10	.107
2003	Tenpins	5	R.J. Albarado	119	Aeneas	114	Jersey Giant	115	120,000	1:50.35	.110

Beyer Index: 111.93

JAIPUR HANDICAP, 7 Furlongs (Off the Turf),
3-Year-Olds and Up, Belmont Park, 2003 Purse: $112,100

Year	Winner	Age	Jockey	Wt.	Second	Wt.	Third	Wt.	Win Value	Time	Beyer
1984	Cannon Shell	5	D.J. Murphy	115	Chan Balum	115	Believe the Queen	115	35,280	1:09.20	
1985	Mt. Livermore	4	J. Velasquez	119	Main Top	117	Cozzene	117	49,020	1:09.20	
1986	Red Wing Dream	5	J.D. Bailey	117	Creme Fraiche	122	Roy	109	48,510	1:23.60	
1986	Basket Weave	5	R. Migliore	117	Alev	117	Judge Costa	117	48,330	1:22.80	
1987	Raja's Revenge	4	M. Venezia	117	Trubulare	117	Give a Toast	114	52,200	1:25.20	
1988	Real Courage	5	J. Vasquez	117	Tinchen's Prince	117	Spectacularphantom	117	60,570	1:22.00	
1989	Harp Inlet	4	C. Perret	117	Fourstardave	119	Down Again	114	57,150	1:27.00	
1990	Fourstardave	5	M.E. Smith	122	Harperstown	117	Wanderkin	119	57,240	1:21.00	
1991	Kanatiyr	5	J.D. Bailey	117	Senor Speedy	117	Fourstardave	122	54,630	1:23.80	103
1992	To Freedom	4	J.A. Krone	117	Fourstardave	122	Smart Alec	117	55,710	1:22.80	102
1993	Home of the Free	5	J.D. Bailey	117	Wind Symbol	117	Fourstardave	117	55,080	1:20.60	106
1994	Nijinsky's Gold	5	Santos JA	114	Dominant Prospect	114	Home of the Free	122	34,905	1:20.00	109
1994	A in Sociology	4	Maple E	119	Roman Envoy	114	Halissee	119	34,905	1:20.20	106
1995	Inside the Beltway	4	Chavez JF	114	Gabr		Golden Cloud	114	49,245	1:21.20	99
1995	Mighty Forum	4	Stevens GL	117	Dominant Prospect	117	City Nights	111	49,995	1:21.00	102
1996	Grand Continental	5	R. Migliore	114	Inside The Beltway	115	Goldmine	111	51,720	1:23.60	107
1997	Atraf		Velazquez J. R.	114	Mighty Forum	114	Play Smart	113	49,635	1:23.60	90
1998	Elusive Quality	5	J.D. Bailey	115	Bristling		Optic Nerve	115	51,750	1:20.80	103
1999	Notoriety	6	Espinoza J. L.	115	Optic Nerve	116	Cryptic Rascal	117	52,335	1:21.20	98
2000	Gone Fishin	4	J.R. Velazquez	114	Weatherbird	113	French Envoy	113	52,290	1:21.73	103
2001	Affirmed Success	7	J.D. Bailey	123	Texas Glitter	116	Bought in Dixie	114	66,475	1:21.69	107
2002	Shibboleth	5	J.D. Bailey	121	Malabar Gold	121	Cozzy Corner	111	67,140	1:20.08	107
2003	Garnered	5	V. Carrero	116	Speightstown	121	Whitewaterspritzer	115	67,260	1:23.49	85

Run at 6 furlongs on dirt, 1984, 1985. Off the turf in 2001, 2003

Beyer Index: 101.8

JEFFERSON CUP, 1 1/8 Miles (Turf),
3-Year-Olds, Churchill Downs, 2003 Purse: $220,600

Year	Winner	Age	Jockey	Wt.	Second	Wt.	Third	Wt.	Win Value	Time	Beyer
1977	Old Jake	3	J. Espinoza	122	Boldero's Orphan	122	Set in My Ways	122	14,219	1:04.80	
1978	Future Hope	3	A. Rini	125	Backstabber	125	Amber White	117	14,073	1:05.20	
1979	Rockhill Native	3	J. Oldham	122	Earl of Odessa	122	Egg's Dynamite	122	19,581	1:05.20	
1980	Golden Derby	3	J. Espinoza	125	Plain Speaking	119	Bold Tyson	125	19,257	1:04.20	
1981	Talent Town	3	B. Sayler	122	Helen's Tip	122	Ken's Revenge	122	19,858	1:05.40	
1982	Wavering Monarch	3	R.P. Romero	111	Forli's Jet	117	Noted	111	23,026	1:44.20	
1983	Pron Regard	3	C. Woods Jr.	116	Le Cou Cou	125	Whitesburg Lark	112	36,303	1:51.60	
1984	Coax Me Chad	3	W.H. McCauley	114	Fairly Straight	114	Last Command	114	48,958	1:50.60	
1985	Avey's Brother	3	D. Montoya	110	La Marseillaise	110	Hollywood Hackett	113	50,420	1:50.00	
1986	Buffalo Beau	3	J. McKnight	110	Clear Choice	124	Sumptious	113	53,040	1:52.80	
1987	Fast Forward	3	R. Frazier	120	Unleavened	118	Gretna Green	112	63,109	1:50.00	
1988	Stop the Stage	3	M. McDowell	115	Cold Cathode	114	Bates Fay	115	62,310	1:51.60	
1989	Shy Tom	3	E. Fires	120	Captain Savy	116	Ruszhinka	112	52,114	1:49.20	
1990	Divine Warning	3	J. Deegan	117	Super Abound	115	Bioblast	110	36,238	1:52.20	
1991	Hanging Curve	3	J. Johnson	119	Wall Street Dancer	119	Air Force	112	36,360	1:50.80	94
1992	Senor Tomas	3	P. Day	122	Coaxing Matt	113	Black Question	122	35,945	1:49.80	95
1993	Lt. Pinkerton	3	T. Hebert	115	Snake Eyes		Mi Cielo		35,555	1:48.27	90
1994	Milt's Overture	3	P. Day	112	Jaggery John		Camptown Dancer		53,527	1:48.21	97
1995	Ago	3	S. Sellers	115	Michael's Star		Lemon Drop		56,550	1:49.48	94
1996	Unruled	3	C. Perret	119	Broadway Beau		Trail City		54,201	1:50.07	101
1997	Greed Is Good	3	W. Martinez	115	Royal Strand		Crimson Classic		69,068	1:49.47	98
1998	Buff	3	C. Borel	122	Keene Dancer		Ladies Din		175,770	1:50.80	104
1999	Special Coach	3	C. Velasquez	122	Silver Chadra		Air Rocket		180,110	1:49.82	98
2000	King Cugat	3	R.J. Albarado	122	Four on the Floor	122	Field Cat	122	177,940	1:47.27	106
2001	Indygo Shiner	3	L.J. Meche	113	Strategic Partner	119	Fast City	114	175,150	1:48.81	97
2002	Orchard Park	3	M. Guidry	119	Mr. Mellon	112	Quest Star	113	172,050	1:48.53	93
2003	Senor Swinger	3	R.J. Albarado	120	Remind	116	Rapid Proof	120	136,772	1:47.54	103

Beyer Index: 97.69

JENNY WILEY, 1 1/16 Miles (Turf), Fillies and Mares 4-Year-Olds and Up,
Keeneland Race Course, 2003 Purse: $113,300

Year	Winner	Age	Jockey	Wt.	Second	Wt.	Third	Wt.	Win Value	Time	Beyer
1989	Native Mommy	6	C. Perret	121	Blossoming Beauty	113	Here's Your Silver	115		1:43.60	
1990	Regal Wonder	6	R. Lopez	121	Majestic Legend	121	Phoenix Sunshine	115	36,040	1:46.20	92
1991	Foresta	5	A. Cordero Jr.	121	Dance for Lucy	121	The Caretaker	115	37,110	1:43.80	100
1992	Indian Fashion	5	J.A. Santos	115	Spanish Parade	121	Radiant Ring	121	39,760	1:41.20	100
1993	Lady Blessington	5	P. Day	118	Radiant Ring	118	Super Fan	118	34,844	1:42.40	95
1994	Misspitch	4	M.E. Smith	118	Park Dream	112	Sh Band	118	34,658	1:43.80	96
1995	Romy	4	FC Torres	118	Weekend Madness	121	Bold Ruritana	121	52,173	1:43.20	100
1996	Apolda	5	J.D. Bailey	121	Mediation	118	Luzette-BR	121	69,006	1:40.60	104

Year	Winner	Age	Jockey	Wt.	Second	Wt.	Third	Wt.	Win Value	Time	Beyer
1997	Thrilling Day	4	W. Martinez	115	Romy	121	Gastronomical	115	68,634	1:41.00	102
1998	Maxzene	5	J. A. Santos	114	Parade Queen	121	Rumpipumpy	114	69,192	1:42.80	104
1999	Pleasant Temper	5	J.D. Bailey	117	Mingling Glances	114	Red Cat	117	70,246	1:40.80	103
2000	Astra	4	C.S. Nakatani	118	Pratella	118	Ronda	116	69,688	1:42.48	101
2001	Penny's Gold	4	J.A. Santos	116	License Fee	118	Solvig	116	70,618	1:40.93	101
2002	Tates Creek	4	K.J. Desormeaux	116	Snow Dance	123	Step With Style	116	70,432	1:42.27	95
2003	Sea of Showers	4	J.D. Bailey	116	Magic Mission	116	Snow Dance	116	70,246	1:41.89	101

Beyer Index: 99.57

JERSEY DERBY, 1 1/16 Miles (Off the Turf), 3-Year-Olds, Monmouth Park, 2003 Purse: $100,000

Year	Winner	Age	Jockey	Wt.	Second	Wt.	Third	Wt.	Win Value	Time	Beyer
1942	Salto	3	W. Mehrtens	106	Trierarch	111	Air Current	110	8,450	1:49.80	
1943	Eurasian	3	F. Zehr	116	Royal Nap	110	Water Pearl	118	8,900	1:50.40	
1944	Lucky Draw	3	W.D. Wright	121	Megogo	103	Tex Martin	111	25,300	1:50.40	
1945	Trymenow	3	H. Linberg	118	Buzfuz	115	Turbine	114	25,850	1:51.80	
1946	Mahout	3	W.D. Wright	114	Assault	126	Blue Yonder	113	24,200	1:49.20	
1947	Double Jay	3	J. Gilbert	114	Fervent	125	Lighthouse	109	24,550	1:49.60	
1948	Citation	3	E. Arcaro	126	Macbeth	114	Faraway	111	43,300	2:03.00	
1949	Palestinian	3	H. Woodhouse	114	Olympia	126	Colonel Mike	111	40,700	2:01.80	
1950	Ferd	3	C. McCreary	118	Greek Song	114	Passemon	111	21,850	2:02.80	
1951	Steadfast	3	H. Woodhouse	110	Alerted	119	Joey Boy	112	23,900	2:04.40	
1952	King Jolie	3	J. Stout	111	Primate	118	Topside	111	25,850	2:03.60	
1953	Royal Bay Gem	3	J. Combest	118	Park Dandy	111	Better Goods	112	25,450	1:53.20	
1954	War of Roses	3	J. Westrope	111	Red Hannigan	111	High Gun	111	46,800	1:51.60	
1955	Dedicate	3	S. Boulmetis	118	Saratoga	118	Simmy	113	44,700	1:48.20	
1956	Fabius	3	W. Hartack	126	Kingmaker	111	Career Boy	118	44,700	1:48.80	
1957	Iron Liege	3	W. Hartack	126	Clem	118	We Trust	111	44,300	1:48.00	
1958	Lincoln Road	3	C. Rogers	111	Talent Show	118	Li'l Fella	118	37,865	1:49.00	
1959	Waltz	3	L. Gilligan	111	Scotland	114	Lake Erie	111	37,670	1:49.60	
1960	Bally Ache	3	R. Ussery	126	Tompion	126	Celtic Ash	126	77,995	1:49.00	
1961	Ambiopoise	3	R. Ussery	126	Crozier	126	Globemaster	126	80,600	1:49.20	
1962	Jaipur	3	L. Adams	126	Admiral's Voyage	126	Crimson Satan	126	84,955	1:49.00	
1963	Candy Spots	3	W. Shoemaker	126	Get Around	126	Sky Wonder	126	78,715	1:50.00	
1964	Roman Brother	3	F. Alvarez	126	Mr. Brick	126	National	126	81,445	1:49.60	
1965	Hail to All	3	J. Sellers	126	Reverse	126	Selari	128	86,905	1:48.60	
1966	Creme Dela Creme	3	D. Brumfield	126	Indulto	126	Fathers Image	126	89,635	1:49.60	
1967	In Reality	3	E. Fires	126	Air Rights	126	Gallant Moment	126	77,480	1:48.00	
1968	Out of the Way	3	E. Belmonte	126	Captain's Gig	126	Iron Ruler	126	87,555	1:49.00	
1969	Al Hattab	3	M. Hole	126	Ack Ack	126	Rooney's Shield	126	89,115	1:48.00	
1970	Personality	3	E. Belmonte	126	Corn off the Cob	126	Silent Screen	126	83,460	1:48.20	
1971	Bold Reasoning	3	J. Vasquez	126	Pass Catcher	126	Twist the Axe	126	87,360	1:49.60	
1972	Smiling Jack	3	F. Iannelli	126	Second Bar	126	Halo	126	89,180	1:50.60	
1973	Knightly Dawn	3	J. Arellano	122	Pvt. Smiles	122	Step Nicely	122	85,280	1:53.20	
1974	Better Arbitor	3	C. Barrerra	122	Stonewalk	122	Christoforo	122	104,000	1:50.40	
1975	Singh	3	A. Cordero Jr.	122	Honey Mark	122	Bombay Duck	122	88,140	1:50.80	
1976	Life's Hope	3	M.A. Rivera	122	Cojak	122	Strawberry L'd'g	122	86,905	1:52.60	
1977	Cormorant	3	D.R. Wright	122	Iron Constitution	122	Hey Hey J.P.	122	80,730	1:50.40	
1981	Five Star Flight	3	C. Perret	118	Tap Shoes	126	Silver Express	118	107,775	1:50.00	
1982	Aloma's Ruler	3	A. Cordero Jr.	126	Star Choice	126	Spanish Drums	126	90,000	1:49.60	
1983	World Appeal	3	J. Vasquez	118	Parfaitement	121	Princilian	121	60,000	1:46.60	
1984	Birdie's Legend	3	W.A. Guerra	118	Key to the Moon	126	Light Spirits	123	60,000	1:49.00	
1985	Spend a Buck	3	L. Pincay Jr	126	Creme Fraiche	126	El Basco	126	2,600,000	2:02.60	
1986	Snow Chief	3	A. Solis	126	Mogambo	126	Tasso	126	600,000	2:03.00	
1987	Avie's Copy	3	M. Solomone	126	Proudest Duke	126	Templar Hill	126	300,000	2:03.40	
1988	Dynaformer	3	C. Perret	126	Tsarbaby	126	Cefis	126	300,000	2:02.80	
1989	Awe Inspiring	3	C. Perret	126	Halo Hansom	126	Faultless Ensign	126	300,000	2:03.00	
1990	Yonder	3	J.D. Bailey	126	Video Ranger	126	Real Cash	126	300,000	2:04.40	
1991	Greek Costume	3	M.E. Smith	126	Subordinated Debt	126	Private Man	126	180,000	1:51.40	93
1992	American Chance	3	P. Day	126	Majestic Sweep	126	Palace Line	126	180,000	1:50.80	100
1993	Llandaff	3	J.A. Krone	116	Logroller	116	Forest Wins	116	90,000	1:42.40	98
1994	Zuno Star	3	M.E. Smith	116	Seattle Rob	116	Mr. Angel	126	90,000	1:43.80	91
							Warn Me	116			
1995	Da Hoss	3	J.A. Krone	119	Claudius	119	Crimson Guard	123	90,000	1:43.00	95
1996	More Royal	3	J.A. Krone	123	Optic Nerve	116	Value Investor	116	90,000	1:42.40	103
1997	Rob 'N Gin	3	J.D. Bailey	119	Tekken	123	Keep It Strait	121	90,000	1:40.80	96
1998	Who Did It and Run	3	F.L Ortiz	116	Essential	116	Cryptic Rascal	126	90,000	1:41.20	107
1999	Swamp	3	R. Migliore	124	Crash Course	117	Good Skate	117	90,000	1:40.80	100
2000	Lendell Ray	3	A.T. Gryder	114	Powerful Appeal	114	Cogburn	113	60,000	1:42.96	96
2001	Mystic Lady	3	F. Leon	114	Sir Brian's Sword	117	What's Your Wish	117	60,000	1:44.31	88
2002	Emergency Status	3	R. Alvarado Jr.	122	Kris's Prayer	114	Rapadash	114	60,000	1:42.26	87
2003	Happy Trails	3	A.R. Toribio	114	Stone Canyon	114	Angelic Aura	115	60,000	1:45.40	89

Beyer Index: 95.62

Run on dirt prior to 1991. Run at 1 1/8 miles, 1942-47, 1953-84; at 1 1/4 miles, 1948-52, 1985-90. Off the turf, in 2001, 2003.

JERSEY SHORE BREEDERS' CUP, 6 Furlongs,
3-Year-Olds, Monmouth Park, 2003 Purse: $97,250

Year	Winner	Age	Jockey	Wt.	Second	Wt.	Third	Wt.	Win Value	Time	Beyer
1992	Surely Six	3	R. Wilson	112	Superstrike	122	Salt Lake	119	64,230	1:21.80	103
1993	Montbrook	3	C.J. Ladmer III	122	Evil Bear	114	Shu Fellow	114	63,420	1:21.00	102
1994	End Sweep	3	M.E. Smith	115	Meadow Flight	122	Foxie G	115	63,300	1:21.20	95
1995	Ft. Stockton	3	J. Bravo	115	Jealous Crusader	115	Gala Knockout	115	64,050	1:22.60	89
1996	Swing and Miss	3	T.G. Turner	112	Seacliff	119	Dixie Connection	115	60,000	1:10.00	96
1997	Smoke Glacken	4	C. Perret	122	Partner's Hero	115	King Buck	115	30,000	1:08.40	117
1998	Good and Tough	3	W.H. McCauley	115	Klabin's Gold	117	El Mirasol	112	45,000	1:10.00	94
1999	Yes It's True	3	J.D. Bailey	122	Erlton	122	Flying Griffoni	112	60,000	1:08.40	106
2000	Disco Rico	3	J. Bravo	115	Max's Pal	122	Stormin Oedy	117	60,000	1:09.05	99
2001	City Zip	3	J.C. Ferrer	119	Sea of Green	117	Songandaprayer	122	60,000	1:09.02	102
2002	Boston Common	3	E.M. Martin Jr.	117	Listen Here	117	It's a Monster	115	60,000	1:09.35	103
2003	Gators n Bears	3	C.C. Lopez	115	Mt. Carson	122	Don Six	115	60,000	1:09.80	106

Beyer Index: 101

JUST A GAME BREEDERS' CUP HANDICAP, 1 Mile (Turf)
Fillies and Mares 3-Year-Olds and Up, Belmont Park, 2003 Purse: $214,500

Year	Winner	Age	Jockey	Wt.	Second	Wt.	Third	Wt.	Win Value	Time	Beyer
1995	Caress	5	R.Davis	119	Coronation Cup	119	Grafin	117	49,320	1:32.40	108
1996	Caress	6	R.Davis	117	Class Kris	122	Upper Noosh	112	94,890	1:33.20	106

Class Kris finished first but was disqualified and placed second

Year	Winner	Age	Jockey	Wt.	Second	Wt.	Third	Wt.	Win Value	Time	Beyer
1997	Memories of Silver	4	J.Bailey	120	Dynasty	113	Elusive	115	95,370	1:33.33	104
1998	Witchful Thinking	4	McCarron C.J.	118	Sopran Mariduff	117	Dixie Ghost	111	95,745	1:33.40	101
1999	Cozy Blues	5	J.F. Chavez	112	U R Unforgetable	114	Mysterious Moll	115	94,620	1:33.20	101
2000	Peerfect Sting	4	J.D. Bailey	121	Ronda		Snow Polina	116	111,800	1:34.48	101
2001	License Fee	6	P. Day	118	Shopping for Love	114	Veil of Avalon	115	114,780	1:32.62	105
2002	Babae	6	J.F. Chavez	115	Tates Creek	117	Stylish	116	67,920	1:34.57	102
2003	Mariensky	4	J.A. Santos	116	Riskaverse	119	Wonder Again	119	128,700	1:43.28	108

Beyer Index: 104

KENT BREEDERS' CUP, 1 1/8 Miles (Turf),
3-Year-Olds, Delaware Park, 2003 Purse: $250,000

Year	Winner	Age	Jockey	Wt.	Second	Wt.	Third	Wt.	Win Value	Time	Beyer
1982	Cagey Cougar	3	V. Bracciale Jr.	113	King's Dusty		Big Shot		14,600	1:44.20	
1996	Sir Cat	3	J.Bailey	113	Optic Nerve	122	Fortitude	116	60,000	1:52.80	108
1997	Royal Strand	3	P. Day	122	Subordination	122	Broad Choice	113	90,000	1:48.00	94
1998	Keene Dancer	3	P. Day	117	Red Reef		Danielle's Gray		120,000	1:50.60	97
1999	North East Bound	3	J.A. Velez Jr.	114	Courtside	113	Swamp	119	150,000	1:51.80	96
2000	Three Wonders	3	P. Day	115	Field Cat	117	Dawn of the Condor	115	150,000	1:48.95	98
2001	Navesink	3	R.A. Dominguez	115	Bowman Mill	115	Harrisand	115	151,000	1:49.98	95
2002	Miesque's Approval	3	J.D. Bailey	115	Regal Sanction	115	Quest Star	115	150,000	1:48.81	99
							Coco's Madness	115			
2003	Foufa's Warrior	3	R.A. Dominguez	115	Remind	115	Lismore Knight	119	150,000	1:47.44	95

Beyer Index: 97.75

For previous runnings, refer to 1980 Manual

KENTUCKY BREEDERS' CUP, 5 1/2 Furlongs,
2-Year-Olds, Churchill Downs, 2003 Purse: $174,200

Year	Winner	Age	Jockey	Wt.	Second	Wt.	Third	Wt.	Win Value	Time	Beyer
1988	Island Esccape	2	C. Woods Jr.	115	One That Got Away		Papa Leonard			1:04.60	
1989	Summer Squall	2	C. Woods Jr.	118	Dr. Bobby A.		Wink Road			1:05.00	
1990	To Freedom	2	J. Espinoza	118	St. Alegis		Maxwell Street			1:05.00	
1991	Hippomenes	2	P. Day	112	Cold Gate		It's Chemistry			1:06.20	
1992	Tempered Halo	2	P. Johnson	121	Mountain Cat		Secret Bundle		50,320	1:05.39	73

Exclusive Zone finished second but was disqualified and placed fourth

Year	Winner	Age	Jockey	Wt.	Second	Wt.	Third	Wt.	Win Value	Time	Beyer
1993	Asta's Foxy Lady	2	T. Hebert	118	Dish It Out		Riverinn		68,737	1:05.51	77
1994	My My	2	S.J. Sellers	116	Wise Affair		Hyroglyphic		37,310	1:05.96	69
1995	Miraloma	2	D.M. Barton	112	Great Southern		A.V. Eight		68,932	1:04.04	82
1996	Move	2	S.J. Sellers	113	Prairie Junction	115	Live Your Best	112	71,175	1:05.74	91
1997	Favorite Trick	2	P. Day	121	Jess M	115	Cutie Luttie	112	68,882	1:04.80	91
1998	Yes It's True	2	S.J. Sellers	121	Tactical Cat	115	Alannan	115	85,948	1:03.61	97
1999	Chilukki	2	Albarado R. J.	112	Barrier	115	Sky Dweller	115	106,485	1:04.01	93
2000	Gold Mover	2	C. Perret	113	City Zip	115	Unbridled Time	121	101,091	1:03.67	94
2001	Leelanau	2	J.K. Court	115	Gygistar	115	Lakeside Cup	112	100,812	1:03.11	89
2002	Posse	2	D.J. Meche	115	Del Diablo	115	Blackjack Boy	115	102,300	1:03.73	85
2003	Cuvee	2	L.J. Meche	117	First Money	117	Exploit Lad	117	109,554	1:04.45	93

Beyer Index: 86.17

KENTUCKY CUP JUVENILE, 1 1/16 Miles,
2-Year-Olds, Turfway Park, 2003 Purse: $100,000

Year	Winner	Age	Jockey	Wt.	Second	Wt.	Third	Wt.	Win Value	Time	Beyer
1986	Rainbow East	2	O.B. Aviles	120	Alysheba	120	David L.'s Rib	120	78,500	1:37.20	
1987	Jim's Orbit	2	P. Day	120	Kingpot	120	Delightful Doctor	120	81,250	1:37.80	
1988	Light Crude	2	R. Frazier	120	Bravoure	120	Revive	120	81,250	1:44.80	
1989	Fighting Fantasy	2	D.W. Cox	120	Top Snob	120	Hardburly	120	81,250	1:48.40	
1990	Fire in Ice	2	J.A. Garcia	120	Wall Street Dancer	120	Gold Shoulder	120	81,250	1:46.60	
1991	Star Recruit	2	R.D. Lopez	120	Pick up the Phone	120	Battenburg	120	97,500	1:45.60	94
1992	Mountain Cat	2	C.R. Woods Jr	120	Saw Mill	120	Shoal Creek	120	97,500	1:43.40	86
1993	Bibury Court	2	S.T. Saito	120	Moving Van	120	Durham	120	81,250	1:47.60	78
1994	Tejano Run	2	J.D. Bailey	120	Gold Miner	120	Bick	120	65,000	1:46.00	80
1995	Editor's Note	2	Stevens GL.	115	Devil's Honor	118	Never to Squander	110	65,000	1:45.00	87
1996	Boston Harbor	2	D.M. Barton	120	Play Waki for Me	118	Dr. Spine	112	65,000	1:42.80	90
1997	Laydown	2	M.E. Smith	114	Time Limit	118	Da Devil	114	62,600	1:43.00	92
1998	Aly's Alley	2	P.A. Johnson	118	Time Bandit	120	Mac's Rule	116	62,600	1:45.60	78
1999	Millencolin	2	P. Day	114	Personal First	118	Deputy Warlock	118	62,600	1:47.00	86
2000	Point Given	2	S.J. Sellers	114	Holiday Thunder	114	The Goo	116	62,600	1:47.01	81
2001	Repent	2	A.J. D'Amore	114	French Assault	118	Gold Dollar	114	62,750	1:43.78	90
2002	Vindication	2	M.E. Smith	116	Private Gold	118	Tito's Beau	114	62,750	1:46.70	87
2003	Mr. Jester	2	R. Bejarano	118	The Cliff's Edge	114	Pomeroy	116	62,000	1:46.61	85

Pomeroy finished first but was disqualified and placed third

Beyer Index: 85.69

KENTUCKY CUP SPRINT, 6 Furlongs,
3-Year-Olds, Turfway Park, 2003 Purse: $100,000

Year	Winner	Age	Jockey	Wt.	Second	Wt.	Third	Wt.	Win Value	Time	Beyer
1994	End Sweep	3	C.J. McCarron	120	Exclusive Praline	122	Chimes Band	122	97,500	1:09.80	104
1995	Lord Carson	3	M.E. Smith	116	Ft. Stockton	122	Evansville Slew	116	97,500	1:08.60	119
1996	Appealing Skier	3	M.E. Smith	118	Capote Belle	119	Delay of Game	114	97,500	1:08.20	109
1997	Partner's Hero	3	P. Day	114	Oro de Mexico	116	Prosong	114	74,400	1:09.00	100
1998	Reraise	3	C.S. Nakatani	114	Copelan Too	114	Mr. Bert	114	93,900	1:08.40	119
1999	Successful Appeal	3	E.S. Prado	122	Five Star Day	114	American Spirit	118	74,400	1:09.40	119
2000	Caller One	3	K.J. Desormeaux	120	Millencolin	116	Kings Command	116	93,750	1:09.46	117
2001	Snow Ridge	3	P. Day	114	City Zip	122	Dream Run	117	94,500	1:09.22	103
2002	Day Trader	3	P. Day	118	Premier Performer	114	Ecstatic	114	94,500	1:10.01	108
2003	Cajun Beat	3	C. Velasquez	122	Clock Stopper	116	Champali	122	62,000	1:09.54	113

Beyer Index: 111.1

KENTUCKY CUP TURF HANDICAP, 1 1/2 Miles,
2-Year-Olds, Kentucky Downs, 2003 Purse: $200,000

Year	Winner	Age	Jockey	Wt.	Second	Wt.	Third	Wt.	Win Value	Time	Beyer
2000	Down the Aisle	7	R.J. Albarado	102	Crowd Pleaser	113	Royal Strand	115	186,000	2:27.60	102
2001	Chorwon	8	J.K. Court	113	The Knight Sky	114	Man From Wicklow	114	186,000	2:28.68	104
2002	Rochester	6	E.M. Martin Jr.	115	Nowrass	112	Continental Red	117	186,000	2:38.28	107
2003	Rochester	7	E.M. Martin Jr.	116	Quest Star	116	Art Variety	111	124,000	2:31.39	97

Art Variety finished first but was disqualified and placed third

Beyer Index: 102.5

LA JOLLA HANDICAP, 1 1/16 Miles (Turf),
3-Year-Olds, Del Mar, 2003 Purse: $150,000

Year	Winner	Age	Jockey	Wt.	Second	Wt.	Third	Wt.	Win Value	Time	Beyer
1937	Topsy Omar	5	T. Sena	108	Grey Count	118	Distribute	108	1,180	1:45.40	
1938	Dogaway	4	E. Yager	122	Capt. Cal	114	Gray Jack	111	1,660	1:37.20	
1940	Justice M.	3	E. Rodriguez	114	Exarch	120	Bachelor Tom	116	1,625	1:37.20	
1941	Vain Grove	3	F. Zufelt	118	Vegas Justice	107	Brown China	113	1,625	1:37.80	
1945	Gold Boom	3	F. Zehr	114	Inflammable	116	Orion	122	3,730	1:37.60	
1946	First to Fight	5	H. Trent	122	Montanes	109	Nanby Pass	109	5,150	1:37.40	
1947	Handlebars	3	L. Balaski	124	Sparky Cannon	112	Winsir	118	4,675	1:38.20	
1948	Henpecker	3	J. Gilbert	122	Lady Zev	107	Belle Jolie	119	6,375	1:37.80	
1949	Dinner Gong	3	R. Neves	126	Challenging	116	Prevaricator	114	6,625	1:36.00	
1950	Blue Reading	3	B. Pearson	115	Manyunk	122	Mercenary	116	6,925	1:36.00	
1951	Oats	3	G. Glisson	117	Grantor	124	Mucho Hosso	120	6,500	1:37.80	
1952	Arroz	3	W. Shoemaker	116	Stranglehold	114	Horsetrader-Ed.	110	6,775	1:37.40	
1953	Threesome	3	J. Phillippi	116	Smart Barbara	109	Six Fifteen	112	6,600	1:36.40	
1954	Leterna	3	W. Harmatz	107	War Tryst	119	Indian Red	112	6,500	1:36.00	
1955	Hillary	3	G. Glisson	110	Damocles	116	Valiant Ace	119	6,725	1:35.40	
1956	Blen Host	3	R. Neves	119	Pit Boss	120	Lucky G.L.	122	8,900	1:37.00	
1957	No Bumps	3	W. Ferguson	108	Mystic Eye	116	Redi-Reading	112	8,875	1:36.80	
1958	Sir Ruler	3	G. Taniguchi	119	The Shoe	122	Foreverett	111	8,550	1:36.60	
1959	Sir Ara	3	D. Pierce	117	Chevalate	111	Mr. Eiffel	110	8,450	1:35.40	
1960	Our Rulla	3	J. Longden	120	Nagea	119	First Balcony	117	8,925	1:35.00	

Year	Winner	Age	Jockey	Wt.	Second	Wt.	Third	Wt.	Win Value	Time	Beyer
1961	Apple	3	E. Ohayon	115	Speak John	117	Songman	118	9,075	1:35.20	
1962	Testum	3	D. Hallman	119	Olympiarco	112	Gallant Host	113	8,525	1:35.60	
1963	Top Light	3	J. Leonard	111	Real Luck	121	Broom II	111	7,360	1:36.20	
1963	Big Raff	3	R. Campas	109	Nevada Battler	119	Ahora	111	7,360	1:35.40	
1964	Royal Eiffel	3	J. Lambert	120	War Helmet	114	Pop's Harmony	111	8,950	1:35.80	
1965	Mr. Payne	3	J. Lambert	114	Parking Ticket	110	Nasharco	119	7,350	1:35.40	
1965	Hoist Bar	3	W. Hartack	116	Tivoli	114	Terry's Secret	126	7,350	1:34.80	
1966	Embassy	3	R. Menell	115	Ri Tux	120	Hill Clown	117	9,125	1:35.40	
1967	Jungle Road	3	J. Robinson	119	Charlie Boots	112	Space Ruler	110	10,900	1:34.60	
1968	Baffle	3	W. Hartack	117	Traffic Beat	107	Bargain Day	106	9,650	1:35.40	
1969	Eagle Fly	3	M. Volzke	115	Juliet's Dream	115	Little Scrib	117	9,825	1:35.40	
1970	Sugar Loaf	3	F. Toro	113	Terra Berry	111	War Heim	114	13,400	1:35.40	
1971	Petes Ruler	3	W. Mahorney	113	Niagara	120	Jeff David	114	9,875	1:35.20	
1971	Great Career	3	J. Lambert	115	My Little Man	115	Struck Out	113	9,875	1:35.60	
1972	Solar Salute	3	W. Mahorney	123	New Prospect	121	Woodland Pines	115	15,400	1:34.40	
1973	Groshawk	3	W. Shoemaker	125	Dancing Papa	115	Expression	123	16,300	1:34.20	
1974	Lightning Mandate	3	A. Pineda	125	Within Hail	120	Sea Aglo	113	15,800	1:34.40	
1975	Larrikin	3	D. Pierce	123	Wood Carver	115	Sibirri	119	16,850	1:35.00	
1976	Today 'n Tomorrow	3	D. Pierce	114	Noble Envoy	114	Wood Green	115	19,400	1:35.20	
1977	Stone Point	3	M. Castaneda	114	Pay the Toll	114	Windy Dancer	114	18,850	1:35.80	
1978	Singular	3	D.G. McHargue	114	Misr'presentation	119	Sea Ride	114	23,150	1:35.80	
1979	Relaunch	3	L. Pincay Jr	117	Hyannis Port	122	Pole Position	124	25,600	1:35.40	
1980	Aristocratical	3	C.J. McCarron	117	Son of a Dodo	117	Exploded	117	32,850	1:36.20	
1981	Minnesota Chief	3	C.J. McCarron	122	High Counsel	117	Stancharry	124	40,950	1:35.20	
1982	Hugabay	3	K. Black	115	Bargain Balcony	118	The Captain	118	33,050	1:35.60	
1982	Take the Floor	3	C.J. McCarron	115	Craelius	116	Sword Blade	115	33,050	1:35.60	
1983	Tanks Brigade	3	E. Delahoussaye	120	Dr. Daly	121	Pair of Aces	116	50,150	1:35.80	
1984	Tights	3	C.J. McCarron	120	Ocean View	113	Refueled II	115	59,150	1:35.60	
1985	Floating Reserve	3	P.A. Valenzuela	117	First Norman	116	Derby Dawning	119	62,750	1:34.60	
1986	Vernon Castle	3	E. Delahoussaye	120	First Norman	116	Derby Dawning	119	64,650	1:35.20	
1987	The Medic	3	C.J. McCarron	116	Something Lucky	120	Savona Tower	117	66,250	1:42.20	
1988	Perfecting	3	G.L. Stevens	116	Roberto's Dancer	115	Prove Splendid	115	64,800	1:41.60	
1989	River Master	3	C.J. McCarron	115	Tokatee	113	Art Work	114	65,100	1:42.60	
1990	Tight Spot	3	E. Delahoussaye	118	Itsallgreektome	119	Music Prospector	118	62,100	1:41.80	100
1991	Track Monarch	3	P.A. Valenzuela	116	Soweto	116	Persianalli	115	61,400	1:41.80	93
1992	Blacksburg	3	K.J. Desormeaux	119	Free at Last	121	Fax News	116	64,700	1:41.60	94
1993	Manny's Prospect	3	C.J. McCarron	115	Golden Slewpy	116	Hawk Spell	116	64,700	1:42.00	93
1994	Marvin's Faith	3	C.W. Antley	114	Unfinished Symph.	120	Ocean Crest	114	62,800	1:42.20	97
1995	Petionville	3	Nakatani CS	120	Private Interview	115	Beau Temps	115	74,600	1:44.20	92
1996	Ambivalent	3	Douglas R. R.	116	The Barking Shark	114	Caribbean Pirate	117	82,850	1:43.20	100
1997	Fantastic Fellow	3	Solis R.	118	Worldly Ways	119	Falkenham	115	85,450	1:43.40	105
1998	Ladies Din.	3	G.L. Stevens	120	Success And Glory	116	Lucayan Indian	116	81,810	1:41.80	103
1999	Eagleton	3	I.D. Enriquez	119	In Frank's Honor	117	Zanetti	117	90,000	1:41.80	97
2000	Purely Cozzene	3	D.R. Flores	120	Duke of Green	117	Sign of Hope	115	90,000	1:41.50	105
2001	Marine	3	C.S. Nakatani	117	Romanceishope	118	Mister Approval	113	90,000	1:41.72	95
2002	Inesperado	3	E. Delahoussaye	118	Regiment	121	Mountain Rage	119	90,000	1:43.92	98
2003	Singletary	3	P.A. Valenzuela	118	Devious Boy	117	Senor Swinger	120	90,000	1:40.39	99

Beyer Index: 97.93

LA TROIENNE, 7 Furlongs,
3-Year-Old Fillies, Churchill Downs, 2003 Purse: $111,800

Year	Winner	Age	Jockey	Wt.	Second	Wt.	Third	Wt.	Win Value	Time	Beyer
1994	Packet	3	J. Johnson	113	Golden Braids		Miss Ra He Ra		55,770	1:24.14	80
1995	Dixieland Gold	3	D.Penna	121	Daylight Ridge		Ivorilla		55,087	1:22.74	96
1996	Rare Blend	3	P.Day	121	Ruby Baby		Prissy One		55,673	1:23.75	93
1997	Star Of Goshen	3	A.Solis	115	Pearl City	115	Flying Lauren	116	70,370	1:22.75	101
1998	Sister Act	3	C. H. Borel	113	Bourbon Belle	118	Marie J	114	69,874	1:24.40	96
1999	Sapphire n' Silk	3	P. Day	113	English Bay	116	Grand Deed	121	69,936	1:23.80	102
2000	Roxelana	3	L. Melancon	116	Magicalmysterycat	121	Watchfull	116	70,308	1:21.97	105
2001	Caressing	3	P. Day	121	Sweet Nanette	121	Golly Greeley	116	75,020	1:22.90	90
2002	Cashier's Dream	3	D.J. Meche	121	Shameful	113	Colonial Glitter	121	69,812	1:24.83	91
2003	Final Round	3	J.D. Bailey	116	Lovely Sage	116	Fast Cookie	118	69,316	1:22.13	93

Beyer Index: 94.7

For previous runnings, refer to 1994 Manual

LADIES HANDICAP, 1 1/4 Miles,
Fillies and Mares 3-Year-Olds and Up, Aqueduct, 2003 Purse: $112,100

Year	Winner	Age	Jockey	Wt.	Second	Wt.	Third	Wt.	Win Value	Time	Beyer
1868	Bonnie Braes	3	Hennessey	107	Australia	107	Fanny Ludlow	107	1,850	3:06.75	
1869	Tasmania	3	Miller	107	Invercauld	107	Rapture	107	2,150	3:07.75	
1870	Annette	3	Wilson	107	Midway	107	Nellie James	107	2,800	3:02.00	
1871	Nellie Gray	3	Swim	107	Mary Clark	107	Mary Louise	107	3,400	3:03.00	

Year	Winner	Age	Jockey	Wt.	Second	Wt.	Third	Wt.	Win Value	Time Beyer
1872	Victoria	3	Gradwell	107	Elsie	107	Experience Oaks	107	2,800	3:11.00
1873	Katie Pease	3	J. Rowe	107	Sally Watson	107	Annie Hall	107	3,150	2:58.25
1874	Bonaventure	3	A. Lakeland	107	Lava	107	Countess	107	2,850	2:42.25
1875	Olitipa	3	Evans	107	Mattie A.	107	Invoice	107	2,850	2:42.75
1876	Sultana	3	Hayward	107	Merciless	107	Patience	107	2,950	2:46.00
1877	Idalia	3	G. Barbee	107	Zoo Zoo	107	Oriole	107	3,300	2:41.00
1878	Invermore	3	Sparling	113	Balance All	113	Favorite	113	3,000	2:46.75
1879	Ferida	3	Costello	113	Magnetism	113	Bonnie Leaf	113	2,900	2:47.00
1880	Carita	3	Hayward	113	Edelweiss	113	Queen's Own	113	2,350	2:44.50
1881	Aella	3	Costello	113	Bliss	113	Spark	113	2,400	2:51.00
1882	Hiawasse	3	Feakes	113	Rica	113	Olivia	113	2,800	2:44.00
1883	Miss Woodford	3	J. McLaughlin	113	Carnation	113	Fairview	113	3,040	2:43.50
1884	Duchess	3	W. Donahue	113	Economy	113	Nonage	113	2,360	2:46.00
1885	Miss Palmer	3	J. McLaughlin	113	Punka	113	Brita	113	2,120	2:47.50
1886	Bandala	3	J. McLaughlin	113	Charity	113	Long Stop	113	2,270	2:12.50
1887	Firenze	3	F. Littlefield	113	Flageoletta	113	Almy	113	2,670	2:14.75
1888	Bella B.	3	J. McLaughlin	113	Golden Reel	113	Inverwick	113	2,970	2:14.50
1889	Fides	3	Garrison	115	Auricoma	115			4,040	2:00.50
					Senorita	113				
1890	Sinaloa II	3	Barnes	103	Gloaming	104	Bibelot	103	5,670	1:19.00
1891	Castalia	3	Taral	117	Equity	117	Graylock	117	3,420	1:20.50
1892	Yorkville Belle	3	I. Murphy	117	Madrid	117	Ada Blue	117	3,530	1:56.50
1893	Naptha	3	Simms	117	Lillian Russell	110	Grace Brown	117	3,445	1:42.20
1894	Nahma	3	Littlefield	120	Lightfoot	109	Kentigerna	117	4,600	1:49.00
1896	Intermission	3	Littlefield	109	Cassette	113	St. Agnes	109	1,425	1:43.50
1897	Divide	3	Taral	114	Lady Mitchell	114	Min. Alphonse	114	2,550	1:44.00
1898	Geisha	3	T. Sloan	117	Miss Miriam	117	Kenmore Queen	117	2,240	1:43.00
1899	Prestidigitatrice	3	Littlefield	117	Lady Madge	117	Lady Lindsey	117	2,340	1:43.00
1900	Oneck Queen	3	Maher	121	Indian Fairy	121	Motley	121	2,600	1:40.75
1901	Janice	3	Piggott	121	Lady of the Valley	121	La Valliere	121	2,485	1:45.25
1902	Blue Girl	3	T. Burns	121	Hataso	121	Hanover Queen	121	2,395	1:42.00
1903	Girdie	3	T, Burns	121	Stolen Moment	121	Gravina	121	3,445	1:42.20
1904	Beldame	3	Hildebrand	121	Audience	121	Marjoram	121	4,870	1:41.20
1905	Flinders	3	Lyne	121	Gold Ten	121	Coy Maid	121	5,345	1:42.40
1906	Perverse	3	Lyne	121			Edna Jackson	121	5,000	1:39.80
1907	Yankee Girl	3	Radtke	121	Adoration	121	Court Dress	121	5,405	1:40.60
1908	Stamina	3	E. Dugan	121	Anonyma	121	Laughing Eyes	121	6,385	1:40.80
1909	Maskette	3	Butwel	121	Lady Bedford	121	Field Mouse	121	6,630	1:39.00
1910	Ocean Bound	3	G. Garner	121	Indian Maid	121	Mexoana	121	1,520	1:43.00
1913	Flamma	4	H. Radtke	101	Hedge	108	Flying Fairy	117	1,720	1:39.60
1914	Flying Fairy	4	T. Davies	126	Cadeau	109	Tarts	112	2,110	1:38.00
1915	Addie M.	4	G. Byrne	106	Lady Rotha	106	Comely	113	1,450	1:39.20
1916	Celandria	3	M. Garner	113	Capra	124	Fenmouse	111	1,610	1:41.00
1917	Rhine Maiden	5	R. Ball	108	Wistful	108	Celandria	111	2,060	1:41.00
1918	Eyelid	3	M. Rowan	110	Priscilla Mullens	117	Dorcas	112	2,130	1:40.00
1919	Salvestra	4	E. Taplin	117	Enfilade	125	Lady G'trdue	112	1,955	1:37.60
1920	Milkmaid	4	E. Sande	126	Cleopatra	115	Banksia	111	3,175	1:38.20
1921	Pen Rose	5	L. Fator	122	La Rablee	114	Lady G'trude	116	1,745	1:40.60
1922	Many Smiles	3	C. Fairbrother	113	Chateau Thierry	120	Polly Ann	117	3,475	1:37.20
1923	Solisa	3	B. Marinelli	104	Careful	123	Story Teller	112	3,325	1:38.80
1924	Relentless	3	J. Maiben	105	Outline	114	Sunayr	105	3,725	1:38.00
1925	Whetstone	4	A. Johnson	120	Nellie Morse	122	Extra Dry	112	3,400	1:37.80
1926	Black Maria	3	L. Fator	120	Extra Dry	119	Rapture	122	3,175	1:38.80
1927	Black Maria	4	F. Coltiletti	127	Jumbo	110	Corvette	111	3,500	1:39.80
1928	Twitter	3	R. Workman	114	Nixie	110	Bateau	114	3,275	1:40.40
1929	Lace	4	L. Fator	114	Bateau	126	B'ldey's P'y	107	3,750	1:38.20
1930	Snowflake	3	L. Schaefer	116	Dustemall	112	Flimsy	114	4,375	1:40.00
1931	Valenciennes	4	C. Kurtsinger	116	Risque	126	Polly Play	118	2,725	1:37.40
1932	Top Flight	3	R. Workman	126	Parry	114	Risque	118	2,275	1:37.80
1933	White Lies	3	M. Garner	110	Sweet Scent	107	Notebook	107	1,030	1:38.40
1934	Coequal	3	E. Litzenberger	106	Black Queen	105	Slapdash	114	2,030	1:37.40
1935	Vicaress	3	E. Arcaro	111	Alberta	116	Kate	114	2,325	1:37.40
1936	Rust	4	E. Yager	113	Maecloud	102	Fortification	111	2,395	1:38.40
1937	Genie Palatine	4	C. Kurtsinger	119	Rust	117	Sparta	120	2,405	1:38.00
1938	Idle Miss	3	A. Robertson	123	Jacola	117	Rust	109	5,400	1:37.60
1939	Red Eye	3	B. James	116	Bass Wood	115	Savage Beauty	111	5,900	1:36.40
1940	Salaminia	3	D. Meade	115	Pretty Pet	114	Fairy Chant	123	12,250	2:30.00
1941	Up the Hill	3	C. McCreary	107	Dark Discovery	102	Pretty Pet	115	11,800	2:30.00
1942	Vagrancy	3	J. Stout	126	Dark Discovery	108	Loveday	117	11,075	2:31.20
1943	Stefanita	3	C. McCreary	116	Vagrancy	123	Dark Discovery	106	11,025	2:31.80
1944	Donitas First	3	T. Atkinson	115	Letmenow	112	Moon M'den	113	11,040	2:31.20
1945	War Date	3	A. Kirkland	124	Surosa	121	Letmenow	113	11,730	2:34.40
1946	Athenia	3	T. Atkinson	116	Riskolator	109	Rosa Blanca	107	16,700	2:30.60

Year	Winner	Age	Jockey	Wt.	Second	Wt.	Third	Wt.	Win Value	Time	Beyer
1947	Snow Goose	3	T. Atkinson	113	But Why Not	121	Gallorette	123	42,600	2:29.60	
1948	Miss Request	3	T. Atkinson	114	Gallorette	121	Honeymoon	123	40,600	2:30.00	
1949	Gaffery	3	E. Guerin	114	Miss Request	119	Adile	115	24,800	2:29.80	
1950	Next Move	3	E. Guerin	120	My Celeste	106	Wistful	124	20,700	2:29.40	
1951	Marta	4	C. McCreary	111	Bed o' Roses	126	Kiss Me Kate	120	31,250	2:30.20	
1952	How	4	N. Shuk	112	Marta	122	Enchanted Eve.	112	40,900	2:31.40	
1953	La Corredora	4	I. Hanford	118	Nothirdchance	111	How	118	40,900	2:30.40	
1954	Lavender Hill	5	S. Small	122	Ming Yellow	113	Riverina	114	43,400	2:32.20	
1955	Manotick	3	A. Valenzuela	117	Misty Morn	124	Countess Fleet.	117	43,900	2:31.40	
1956	Flower Bowl	4	W. Shoemaker	116	Dotted Line	111	Bright't Star	107	40,100	2:29.80	
1957	Rare Treat	5	P.J. Bailey	118	Gay Life	107	Snow White	113	40,800	2:31.60	
1958	Endine	4	E. Nelson	114	Dotted Line	123	An'e-Lu-San.	108	37,165	2:30.40	
1959	Tempted	4	E. Nelson	128	High Bid.	112	Big Effort	115	36,580	2:09.00	
1960	Berlo	3	E. Guerin	124	Woodlawn	112	Who's Ahead.	105	38,205	2:30.60	
1961	Mighty Fair	3	P.J. Bailey	115	Craftiness	120	Tritoma	116	37,050	2:11.80	
1962	Royal Patrice	3	H. Grant	114	Waltz Song	115	Oil Royalty.	113	37,245	2:10.60	
1963	Goofed	3	J.L. Rotz	113	Suiti	112	Dupage Lady.	110	37,765	2:29.40	
1964	Steeple Jill	3	J. Ruane	109	Dupage Lady	109	Tona.	115	38,415	2:29.60	
1965	Straight Deal	3	J. Sellers	114	Steeple Jill	126	Yes Please	109	36,335	2:03.60	
1966	Destro	3	B. Baeza	115	Straight Deal	118	Miss Dickey.	113	36,725	2:02.40	
1967	Sweet Folly	4	H. Gustines	114	Harem Lady	108	Muse	106	38,090	2:04.60	
1968	Politely	5	A. Cordero Jr.	128	Amerigo Lady	118	Raison d'Etre	110	36,335	2:02.60	
1969	Shuvee	3	J. Davidson	117	Amerigo Lady	121	Obeah	121	37,830	2:03.00	
1970	Cathy Honey	3	A. Cordero Jr.	115	Manta	116	Taken Aback.	122	36,010	2:02.20	
1971	Sea Saga	3	C.H. Marquez.	117	Helen Jennings	110	Aqua Belle	109	34,680	2:02.60	
1972	Graf'itti	4	M. Venezia	109	Sea Saga	112	Hill Circus	116	32,250	2:04.80	
1973	Wakefield Miss.	5	A. Cordero Jr.	113	Roba Bella.	112	Ferly	113	33,180	2:03.80	
1974	Coraggioso	4	E. Maple	118	Poker Night	117	Twixt	124	33,300	2:02.00	
1975	Tizna	6	F. Alvarez	124	Pass a Glance.	113	Susan's Girl	126	51,390	2:03.60	
1976	Bastonera II	5	A. Cordero Jr.	122	Proud Delta	125	Sugar Plum Time	114	65,220	2:01.40	
1977	Sensational	3	M. Venezia	114	Dottie's Doll	114	Charming Story.	116	64,560	2:02.80	
1978	Ida Delia	4	A. Santiago.	110	Water Malone	122	Cum Laude Laurie	115	65,820	2:02.40	
1979	Spark of Life	4	J. Cruguet	116	Catherine's Bet.	113	Six Crowns	117	64,740	2:02.80	
1980	Plankton	4	C.B. Asmussen	119	Sugar and Spice	114	Weber City Miss.	119	65,400	2:03.00	
1981	Jameela	4	A. Cordero Jr.	120	Discorama	115	Tina Tina Too	112	66,240	2:01.80	
1982	Tina Tina Too	4	D. MacBeth	110	Weber City Miss.	124	Mademoiselle Forli	114	65,520	2:03.00	
1983	Mademoiselle Forli	4	G. McCarron	113	Quixotic Lady	119	Mochila.	113	67,320	2:03.40	
1984	Heatherten	5	R.P. Romero	123	Solar Halo.	112	Key Dancer	113	71,400	2:04.00	
1985	Videogenic	3	R.G. Davis	114	Basie	113	Alabama Nana	119	67,800	2:02.00	
1986	Life at the Top	3	R.P. Romero	118	Coup de Fusil.	116	Steal a Kiss	114	167,160	2:03.80	
1987	Nastique	3	R.G. Davis	110	Tricky Squaw.	117	No Choice	113	146,880	2:04.40	
1988	Banker's Lady.	3	A. Cordero Jr.	120	Make Change.	114	Thirty Eight Go Go	115	138,960	2:02.00	
1989	Dance Teacher	4	J.A. Santos	113	Whose Doubt.	110	Warfie	112	141,120	2:05.80	
1990	Colonial Waters.	3	J.A. Santos	121	Buy the Firm	118	Jessi Jessi	113	104,400	2:05.80	104
1991	Wortheroatsingold	4	E. Maple	114	Summer Matinee	115	Lady D'Accord.	116	150,000	2:02.40	99
1992	Brilliant Brass.	5	E.S. Prado	120	Low Tolerance.	111	Lady Lear.	111	150,000	2:03.40	104
1993	Groovy Feeling.	4	W.H. McCauley	111	Turnback the Alarm	121	Avie's Daisy.	113	120,000	2:05.80	100
1994	Tara Roma	4	F.T. Alvarado.	114	Beloved Bea	113	Dancer's Gate.	112	84,300	2:06.60	87
1995	Transient Trend.	3	J.L. Samyn	111	Lotta Dancing	117	Manila Lila.	114	67,800	2:01.40	96
1996	Miss Slewpy.	5	L.C. Reynolds	120	Hooded Dancer	109	Very True.	114	66,600	2:03.20	95
1997	Prophet's Warning	4	J.F. Chavez.	112	Mil Kilates	117	Biogio's Rose.	112	67,620	2:06.20	94
1998	Unbridled Hope	4	R. Migliore	114	Manoa	114	Sazarac Jazz	111	85,250	2:03.44	105
1999	Strolling Belle.	3	H. Castillo Jr.	116	Maiden Fair	112	Sazarac Jazz	115	65,640	2:04.72	95
2000	Strolling Belle.	4	H. Castillo Jr.	120	dq-Pentatonic.	117	Reine Amandine	114	66,000	2:06.60	93

Pentatonic finished first but was disqualified and placed second

2001	Summer Colony.	3	J.R. Velazquez.	114	Stop for Schnapps.	113	Strolling Belle	118	66,600	2:05.80	94
2002	Critical Eye	5	M.J. Luzzi	116	Ellie's Moment	114	With Ability.	118	64,440	2:04.19	96
2003	Savedbythelight.	3	R. Migliore	115	Queen's Triomphe	113	Retroactive	113	67,260	2:05.99	88

Beyer Index: 96.43

LAFAYETTE, 7 Furlongs,
3-Year-Olds, Keeneland Race Course, 2003 Purse: $107,900

Year	Winner	Age	Jockey	Wt.	Second	Wt.	Third	Wt.	Win Value	Time	Beyer
1937	Chic Maud	2	I. Anderson	114	Green Bottle	117	Knee Deep	114	4,225	:47.20	
1938	Oddesa Beulah	2	M. Calvert	119	Cherry Jam	117	Batter	117	3,600	:45.00	
1939	Roman	2	W. Yarberry	117	Flying Mary	114	Charitable	114	3,550	:47.60	
1940	Misty Isle	2	K. McCombs	114	Blue Lily	114	Blue Pair	117	3,950	:47.00	
1941	Black Raider	2	A. Craig	122	Fade	119	My Choice	114	4,050	:46.40	
1942	Menex	2	E. Arcaro	122	Ogma	114	Sun Jesting	111	4,450	:46.60	
1943	Ogham	2	J. Longden	117	Whirlabout	112	Sweetest Girl	114	4,700	:54.80	
1944	Poca Mas	2	G. Seabo	117	Best Effort	117	Roi Rouge	117	6,475	:53.80	
1946	Colonel O'F	2	W. Bailey	117	Rhodelin	114	Etnom	117	5,750	:46.40	

Year	Winner	Age	Jockey	Wt.	Second	Wt.	Third	Wt.	Win Value	Time	Beyer
1947	Phar Mon	2	A. LoTurco	122	Tiger Flash	117	Pelt	114	13,500	:46.20	
1948	Irish Sun	2	A. LoTurco	117	Acoma	114	Olympia	117	11,950	:46.20	
1949	Black Sambo	2	R.L. Baird	117	Wisconsin Boy	117	Go Jeep Go	122	14,050	:47.40	
1950	Mals Boy	2	J.D. Jessop	117	Dydamic	122	Flyamanita	114	15,150	:45.40	
1951	Recover	2	D. Dodson	114	Free for Me	114	Hudgens	117	13,125	:46.60	
1951	Crownlet	2	R.L. Baird	114	Red Curtice	117	Very Special	114	13,125	:46.60	
1952	Happy Carrier	2	G. Porch	117	Ace Destroyer	117	Orofino	111	10,126	:46.20	
1952	Aerolite	2	D. Dodson	114	Bubbley	114	Fighting Eagle	117	9,964	:45.80	
1953	Everett Jr.	2	A. Popara	122	Terrebonne	117	Beanir	114	13,035	:45.40	
1954	Royal Note	2	H. Moreno	117	Smart Devil	114	Tricky Homer	117	12,417	:49.40	
1955	First Lap	2	J.D. Jessop	117	Tiger Wander	114	Skeptical Kid	122	13,425	:50.00	
1956	Round Table	2	S. Brooks	117	Jet Colonel	117	Chookoss	117	12,677	:49.60	
1957	Bumpy Road	2	W. Hartack	117	Alliance	117	Red Hot Pistol	117	9,955	:48.40	
1958	Grand Wizard	2	V. Guajardo	117	Matisse	117	Goshen	114	8,899	:50.80	
1958	Bagdad	2	J. Heckmann	117	Severn	117	Subway Strike	114	8,834	:50.60	
1959	Vital Force	2	J. Sellers	117	Neshenun	117	Rock Age	117	10,069	:49.00	
1959	Chuckabuck	2	W. Hartack	117	Careless John	114	Pensive Sun	114	10,069	:49.80	
1960	Bright Silver	2	J.L. Rotz	114	Fading Sky	114	Cyclobob	117	8,355	:49.60	
1960	Sal's Beau	2	B. Baeza	117	He's a Pistol	117	Chinchilla	117	8,160	:48.80	
1961	Crimson Satan	2	W. Carstens	117	Mike G.	117	Jetting Home	117	10,221	:49.00	
1962	Donstopnow	2	M. Duhon	122	Sound Trick	117	Bora Bora	117	10,270	:48.60	
1963	Amastar	2	J. Nichols	117	Delirium	117	Doubly Fare	114	8,726	:48.20	
1964	Loom	2	J. Nichols	117	Mahjubill	117	Ramflow	117	8,840	:48.00	
1965	He Jr.	2	J. Fielselman	117	Highest Alp	117	Fearless Knight	117	9,327	:52.00	
1966	Quick Swoon	2	E. Fires	117	Better Bee's Jr.	114	Nascourt	114	8,937	:51.40	
1967	T.V. Commercial	2	K. Knapp	117	Caribbean Line	117	Rhythmic	117	8,905	:52.00	
1968	Santiago Road	2	K. Knapp	117	Star o' Victory	114	February Fun	117	12,106	:52.00	
1968	Traffic Mark	2	M. McDowell	117	Jay Ray	117	Gage Line	114	12,301	:52.60	
1969	Spotted Line	2	D.E. Whited	117	Dee Dee Tees	117	Irish Loom	117	13,877	:51.80	
1970	Seen Alot	2	M. Manganello	117	Beauty's Son	122	Surya	117	14,690	:53.00	
1971	Busted	2	M. Solomone	117	One Nation	117	Rest Your Case	117	15,210	:51.60	
1972	Cari County	2	P. Rubbicco	117	Entity	117	Slander	117	15,665	:52.00	
1973	Mr. A.Z.	2	R. Ussery	118	Hudson County	115	Best of It	116	12,808	:52.60	
1974	Paris Dust	2	C. Perret	122	Commercial Pilot	119	Master Derby	119	12,379	:51.80	
1975	Inca Roca	2	T. Warner	116	Joseph Daniel	116	Khyber King	119	11,927	:52.80	
1976	United Holme	2	W. Gavidia	119	Marve	119	Golden Gossip	119	11,125	:52.00	
1977	Fiddle Faddle	2	W. Gavidia	116	Old Crony	119	Bye Bye Bud	116	11,356	:52.80	
1978	Spy Charger	2	G. Mahon	122	It's a Rerun	119	Trip Over	116	11,278	:53.20	
1979	Raised Socially	2	M.R. Morgan	119	Native Moment	119	Landing Stripes	119	16,380	:52.20	
1980	Firm Boss	2	M.R. Morgan	122	Bend the Times	116	Silver Dollar Boy	122	14,723	:53.00	
1981	Grey Bucket	2	J. Oldham	119	Talent Town	116	Lady Ann's Key	116	15,356	:53.20	
1982	Jungle Blade	3	W.J. Neagle	115	Talk of the Times	118	Baraco	112	39,794	1:10.20	
1983	Freezing Rain	3	D. Brumfield	118	Harry 'n Bill	118	Hamlet	112	36,546	1:11.20	
1984	Delta Trace	3	K.K. Allen	118	Patch of Sun	112	Soybean Trader	112	37,489	1:10.00	
1985	Proudest Hour	3	R.P. Romero	121	Felter on the Quay	112	Don't Hesitate	121	35,133	1:10.80	
1986	Numero Uno Pass	3	C. Perret	113	Color Me Smart	121	Friendly Blue	112	35,945	1:23.60	
1987	Trick Card	3	D.A. Miller Jr	118	War	118	Contractor's Tune	112	35,084	1:23.80	
1988	Forty Niner	3	P. Day	121	Buoy	121	Aloha Prospector	121	46,306	1:22.00	
1989	Belek	3	S.P. Romero	112	Notation	118	Mr. Sea Sanders	118	35,051	1:23.00	
1990	Housebuster	3	C. Perret	121	Sacra Hoxen	114	Critical Choice	113	52,215	1:22.80	
1991	To Freedom	3	C.W. Antley	121	Romiano	114	Broadway's Top Gun	121	54,958	1:22.80	
1992	American Chance	3	P. Day	115	Capitalimprovement	118	Mon Capitan	114	56,770	1:22.00	104
1993	Cherokee Run	3	P. Day	118	Poverty Slew	112	Williamstown	121	52,328	1:21.20	103
1994	Exclusive Praline	3	J.A. Santos	121	Dynamic Asset	115	End Sweep	113	49,321	1:23.80	99
1995	Mr. Greeley	3	J.A. Krone	121	Peaks and Valleys	118	Tethra	121	51,429	1:21.40	109
1996	Wire Me Collect	3	K.L. Chapman	112	Appealing Skier	121	Irish Conquest	112	69,192	1:21.80	99
1997	Trafalger	3	J.D. Bailey	113	Open Forum	118	Muchacho Fino	113	67,456	1:21.60	101
1998	Dontletthebigonego	3	W. Martinez	114	Flashing Tammany	114	Swear By Dixie	114	67,394	1:23.00	100
1999	Yes It's True	3	J.D. Bailey	123	Trickey Crew	118	Fort La Roca	115	66,340	1:22.00	104
2000	Caller One	3	R.G. Davis	120	Sun Cat	117	Littleexpectations	120	70,370	1:21.73	108
2001	Griffinito	3	J.A. Santos	116	Sam Lord's Castle	118	Yonguska	117	68,820	1:22.61	104
2002	Cashel Castle	3	P. Day	116	Governor Hickel	116	Sky Terrace	116	69,006	1:24.47	93
2003	Posse	3	C.J. Lanerie	118	Roll Hennessy Roll	118	Bossanova	116	66,898	1:23.14	108

Beyer Index: 102.67

LAKE GEORGE, 1 1/16 Miles (Turf), 3-Year-Old Fillies,
Saratoga Race Course, 2003 Purse: $114,500

Year	Winner	Age	Jockey	Wt.	Second	Wt.	Third	Wt.	Win Value	Time	Beyer
1996	Memories Of Silver	3	J.Bailey	112	Clamorosa	118	Captive Number	113	33,780	1:42.80	96
1996	Dynasty	3	J.Bailey	112	River Antoine	113	Vashon	116	33,630	1:42.20	89
1997	Auntie Mame	3	J.Bailey	121	Crab Grass	114	Innovate	116	51,120	1:42.80	90

Year	Winner	Age	Jockey	Wt.	Second	Wt.	Third	Wt.	Win Value	Time	Beyer
1998	Tenski	3	R. Migliore	114	Pratella	114	Camella	114	50,070	1:40.80	97
1998	Caveat Competitor	3	J.R. Velazquez	116	Mysterious Moll	114	Recording	121	50,060	1:41.00	94
1999	Nani Rose	3	S.J. Sellers	122	Perfect Sting	122	Intrigued	122	67,680	1:40.00	100
2000	Millie's Quest	3	J.R. Velazquez	114	Shopping for Love	117	Battenkill	114	70,080	1:44.52	90
2001	Light Dancer	3	M. Guidry	117	Owsley	115	Cozzy Corner	115	67,050	1:41.06	94
2001	Voodoo Dancer	3	J.D. Bailey	122	Sadler's Sarah	117	O K to Dance	122	67,350	1:41.45	94
2002	Nunatall	3	J.F. Chavez	115	Guana	117	Mariensky	117	69,000	1:40.71	95
2003	Film Maker	3	E.S. Prado	115	Ocean Drive	119	Gal O Gal	122	68,700	1:41.80	95

Beyer Index: **94.09**

LANDALUCE, 6 Furlongs,
2-Year-Old Fillies, Hollywood Park, 2003 Purse: $100,300

Year	Winner	Age	Jockey	Wt.	Second	Wt.	Third	Wt.	Win Value	Time	Beyer
1945	Widow's Peak	2	J. Longden	116	Me Again	116	Sweet Arline	112	14,035	1:12.00	
1946	U Time	2	L. Balaski	114	Hemet Squaw	119	Hubble Bubble	114	19,650	1:10.20	
1947	Nursery School	2	J. Longden	115	Star Beauty	115	Song Fest	115	20,200	1:05.20	
1948	Brenton Light	2	J. Longden	119	Cosmopolite	119	Sleepers Jinx	119	19,800	1:06.00	
1949	Fleet Rings	2	J. Westrope	119	Dew of June	115	Imago	119	28,850	1:06.40	
1950	Sickle's Image	2	W. Fisk	112	Ruth Lily	107	Worn Out	108	21,750	1:10.00	
1951	Thataway	2	D. Erb	119	Dugout	119	Princess Rita	119	20,850	1:06.00	
1952	Fleet Khal	2	R. Heather	115	Haunted	119	Speedy Ace	115	15,500	1:04.60	
1953	Chorus Khal	2	L. Leon	116	Lady Cover Up	110	Heather Khal	116	17,400	1:05.20	
1954	Fair Molly	2	R. Tejos	111	Madam Jet	111	First Aid Kit	111	18,450	1:04.60	
1955	Miss Todd	2	R. York	115	Doc Upton	111	Carmel	115	18,000	1:04.60	
1956	Darling Adelle	2	J. Longden	119	Royal Rasher	113	Molly Maid	113	16,500	1:04.20	
1957	Sally Lee	2	J. Longden	119	Camloc	113	Pie Face	116	16,300	1:04.80	
1958	Khalita	2	R. York	115	Tassle Dancer	119	Kiddie Book	111	16,800	1:05.80	
1959	Echoic	2	W. Shoemaker	111	Miss Imbros	111	Linita	119	17,200	1:04.00	
1960	Het's Pet	2	G. Taniguchi	111	Regal Weather	111	Never More	119	16,450	1:04.00	
1961	Sunday Slippers	2	P. Moreno	111	Spark Plug	119	Lady's Matinee	112	15,800	1:03.60	
1962	Honey Bunny	2	W. Shoemaker	119	Lanabu	111	Brev Hostess	111	17,650	1:04.00	
1963	Sari's Song	2	J. Leonard	111	Sweet and Fleet	111	Pretty Bubbles	111	17,500	1:04.00	
1964	Getaway Maid	2	S. Trevino	113	Real Sweet Deal	119	Candyean	119	59,275	1:04.80	
1965	Premise	2	M. Yanez	119	Roman Heiress	119	Prides Profile	119	56,800	1:04.00	
1966	Mira Femme	2	I. Valenzuela	119	Native Honey	119	Indovina	119	50,650	1:03.60	
1967	Morgaise	2	W. Shoemaker	119	Hula Bend	119	Esquimau Pie	119	51,050	1:03.80	
1968	Lynne's Orphan	2	J. Sellers	119	Jan Jessie	119	O'Lucky You	119	46,075	1:03.40	
1969	Consider Me Lucky	2	L. Pincay Jr	119	Emmania	119	Court Gem	119	41,500	1:09.80	
1970	June Darling	2	W. Mahorney	119	Sea Frolic	119	Wicked Fairy	119	38,125	1:10.20	
1971	Cautious Bidder	2	J.L. Rotz	119	Miss Lady Bug	119	Bright Bright	119	54,825	1:09.20	
1972	Windy's Daughter	2	W. Shoemaker	119	Protest	119	Rosalie Mae Wynn	119	35,725	1:09.60	
1972	Bold Liz	2	J. Tejeira	119	Kedesh	119	Lucky Jen	119	35,225	1:09.40	
1973	Special Goddess	2	L. Pincay Jr	119	Calaki	119	Fleet Peach	119	53,125	1:09.60	
1974	Hot n Nasty	2	D.G. McHargue	119	Miss Tokyo	119	Angle	119	55,225	1:09.00	
1975	Walk in the Sun	2	F. Olivares	119	Pet Label	119	Doc Shah's Siren	119	56,025	1:10.40	
1976	Wavy Waves	2	L. Pincay Jr	119	Lullaby	114	Any Time Girl	119	55,225	1:10.20	
1977	B. Thoughtful	2	D. Pierce	119	Sweet Little Lady	119	Ubetido	119	53,475	1:10.20	
1978	Terlingua	2	D.G. McHargue	119	Joi'ski	119	Caline	119	48,725	1:08.80	
1979	Table Hands	2	E. Munoz	119	Open Gate	119	Jet Rating	119	54,475	1:10.40	
1980	Native Fancy	2	L. Pincay Jr	119	Icy Pop	115	Lead Us	119	54,425	1:10.00	
1981	Ticketed	2	D.G. McHargue	119	Orphan's Art	119	First Advance	116	46,200	1:11.40	
1982	Landaluce	2	L. Pincay Jr	117	Bold Out Line	115	Barzell	119	43,750	1:08.00	
1983	Simple Magic	2	E. Delahoussaye	116	Althea	117	Reb's Gateau	116	46,300	1:10.60	
1984	Window Seat	2	E. Delahoussaye	114	Raise a Prospector	119	Full o Wisdom	114	64,550	1:10.00	
1985	Arewehavingfunyet	2	W. Shoemaker	119	Fashion Dynasty	116	La Codorniz	117	59,700	1:10.00	
1986	Delicate Vine	2	G.L. Stevens	116	Anything for Love	114	Purdue Queen	119	58,850	1:10.00	
1987	Over All	2	G.L. Stevens	116	Blue Jean Baby	116	Tomorrow's Child	116	63,400	1:10.60	
1988	Distinctive Sis	2	A. Solis	116	Lea Lucinda	116	Executive Row	116	62,250	1:10.80	
1989	Dominant Dancer	2	E. Delahoussaye	116	Cheval Volant	116	Autumn Beauty	115	60,100	1:10.40	
1990	Garden Gal	2	M. Pedroza	116	Perky Slew	116	Lite Light	116	60,900	1:10.40	
1991	Fluttery Danseur	2	M. Pedroza	116	Soviet Sojourn	116	Prospector's Dame	117	56,200	1:09.40	100
1992	Zealous Connection	2	M. Pedroza	116	Medici Bells	119	Sweet Mama	117	58,500	1:09.80	89
1993	Rhapsodic	2	E. Delahoussaye	116	Miss Gibson County	119	Becky's Appeal	116	59,800	1:10.40	81
1994	Serena's Song	2	G.L. Stevens	116	Embroidered	116	Cat's Cradle	116	66,800	1:10.00	86
1995	Raw Gold	2	A. Solis	116	Wasmi Song	116	Liberty Nite	117	59,600	1:10.60	74
1996	Starry Ice	2	E. Delahoussaye	119	Trav n' Kris	114	Montecito	116	20,720	1:11.20	85
1997	Career Collection	2	C.S. Nakatani	116	Bent Creek City	119	Unreal Squeal	119	62,820	1:10.40	78
1998	Hookedonthefeelin	2	G.L. Stevens	116	Box Office Girl	116	Excellent Meeting	116	62,760	1:09.60	90
1999	Magicalmysterycat	2	C.W. Antley	116	She's Classy	116	Princess Melissa	116	63,120	1:11.00	73
2000	Notable Career	2	C.S. Nakatani	116	Sea Reel	116	Starrer	115	65,040	1:11.10	83
2001	Georgia's Storm	2	C.J. McCarron	119	Respectful	114	Who Loves Aleyna	116	65,040	1:10.45	85
2002	Buffythecenterfold	2	M.S. Garcia	116	Tricks Her	115	Little Bit a Swiss	116	66,360	1:10.51	90
2003	Wacky Patty	2	J. Valdivia Jr	119	Cherish Destiny	116	Platinum Princess	116	65,040	1:10.28	86

Beyer Index: **84.62**

LAS CIENEGAS HANDICAP, About 6 1/2 Furlongs (Turf), Fillies and Mares 4-Year-Olds and Up, Santa Anita, 2003 Purse: $110,000

Year	Winner	Age	Jockey	Wt.	Second	Wt.	Third	Wt.	Win Value	Time	Beyer
1974	Woodland Pines	5	D. Pierce	120	Pataha Prince	112	Single Agent	116	18,650	1:13.00	
							Pontoise	116			
1976	Life's Hope	3	L. Pincay Jr	116	Sure Fire	119	Private Signal	114	20,100	1:09.40	
1977	Dancing Femme	4	W. Shoemaker	117	Winter Solstice	123	Katonka	120	24,600	1:13.60	
1978	Drama Critic	4	D.G. McHargue	119	Perils of Pauline	118	Litt'e Happiness	120	27,800	1:14.00	
1979	Pressing Date	5	A. Cordero Jr	114	Country Queen	121	Critic	114	27,500	1:16.40	
1980	Great Lady M.	5	P.A. Valenzuela	116	Wishing Well	120	Billie Bets	115	28,100	1:14.80	
1981	Wishing Well	6	F. Toro	122	Back at Two	114	Peppy's Lucky Girl	113	24,250	1:13.40	
1982	Excitable Lady	4	E. Delahoussaye	119	Peppy's Lucky Girl	117	Glitter Hitter	116	37,450	1:14.40	
1983	Faneuil Lass	4	L. Pincay Jr	120	Queen of Song	115	Waving	117	41,200	1:17.40	
1984	Tangent	4	G. Barrera	120	Irish O'Brien	118	Frieda Frame	118	39,600	1:15.00	
1985	Danzadar	4	D.A. Lozoya	114	Pampas	120	Nat'l Summit	116	37,250	1:14.00	
1986	Shywing	4	L. Pincay Jr	120	Reigning Countess	114	Her Royalty	121	37,550	1:18.00	
1987	Lichi	7	G. Baze	115	An Empress	119	Aromacor	112	38,150	1:14.40	
1988	Hairless Heiress	5	G.L. Stevens	117	Chick or Two	115	Aromacor	113	52,050	1:15.00	
1989	Imperial Star	5	R.G. Davis	115	Down Again	117	Serve n' Volley	115	50,450	1:15.60	
1990	Stylish Star	4	C.J. McCarron	117	Stormy but Valid	120	Hot Novel	118	47,100	1:13.00	104
1991	Flower Girl	4	E. Delahoussaye	116	Mahaska	117	Survive	117	49,650	1:13.20	104
1992	Heart of Joy	5	C.J. McCarron	123	Sheltered View	114	Crystal Gazing	119	63,470	1:12.60	107
1993	Glen Kate	6	C.A. Black	121	Heart of Joy	121	Worldly Possesssio	115	61,225	1:12.60	102
1994	Mamselle Bebette	4	C.J. McCarron	120	Cool Air	122	Bel's Starlet	122	45,975	1:13.00	103
1995	Marina Park	4	A. Solis	119	Pirate's Revenge	116	Rabiadella	118	63,175	1:13.60	101
1996	Ski Dancer	4	G.L. Stevens	117	Klassy Kim	117	Igotrhythm	117	64,300	1:14.40	102
1997	Advancing Star	4	G.L. Stevens	115	Ski Dancer	118	Grab The Prize	116	96,550	1:12.40	105
1998	Dance Parade	4	K.J. Desormeaux	119	Advancing Star	121	Imroz	116	64,800	1:13.60	100
1999	Desert Lady	4	C.S. Nakatani	118	Hula Queen	112	Bella Chiarra	115	65,640	1:13.60	98
2000	Evening Promis	4	D. Sorenson	114	La Madame	116	Reciclada	113	63,840	1:13.66	99
2001	Go Go	4	E. Delahoussaye	118	Separata	118	Dianehill	116	65,700	1:13.54	105
2002	Rolly Polly	4	K.J. Desormeaux	119	Penny Marie	119	Twin Set	116	65,100	1:12.55	99
2003	Heat Haze	4	J. Valdivia Jr	114	Icantgoforthat	114	Paga	116	66,000	1:13.11	97

Beyer Index: 101.86

LAS FLORES HANDICAP, 6 Furlongs, Fillies and Mares 4-Year-Olds and Up, Santa Anita, 2003 Purse: $135,500

Year	Winner	Age	Jockey	Wt.	Second	Wt.	Third	Wt.	Win Value	Time	Beyer
1951	Next Move	4	E. Guerin	124	Special Touch	122	Sickle's Image	117	12,250	1:09.80	
1952	Spanish Cream	4	E. Guerin	117	Great Dream	112	A Gleam	126	12,900	1:10.60	
1954	Vickie Blue	4	W. Shoemaker	114	Smart Barbara	118	Fleet Khal	122	14,900	1:09.40	
1955	Miz Clementine	4	R. Neves	126	Alibhai Lynn	121	Lap Full	116	13,500	1:10.00	
1956	On the Move	3	D. Lewis	112	Scansion	109	Island Queen	106	15,200	1:10.20	
1957	Miss Todd	4	E. Arcaro	116	Our Betters	119	Mary Machree	120	12,750	1:09.80	
1958	Ballet Khal	4	W. Shoemaker	112	Coverit	121	Betty Rose		13,600	1:10.00	
1959	Bug Brush	4	A. Valenzuela	112	Gleaming Star	111	Nushie	113	15,100	1:09.40	
1960	Linita	3	M. Ycaza	116	My Dear Girl	119	Swiss Roll	119	15,000	1:10.20	
1960	Margaretta	5	I. Valenzuela	117	Khalita	115	Indian Maid	120	13,750	1:09.60	
1961	Bright Holly	3	B. Baeza	118	Linita	120	Oil Royalty	116	14,450	1:09.80	
1962	Oil Royalty	4	W. Shoemaker	117	My Portrait	117	Rose O'Neil	123	14,500	1:10.00	
1963	Chop House	3	B. Baeza	113	Red Belle	120	Savaii	117	10,925	1:09.60	
1963	Shimmering Star	3	R. Campas	112	Hi Rated	115	Pixie Erin	120	10,925	1:09.80	
1964	Affectionately	4	W. Shoemaker	125			Curious Clover	120	9,775	1:10.00	
	Chop House	4	I. Valenzuela	119							
1965	Poona Queen	5	I. Valenzuela	117	Respected Way	116	Fairway Fun	116	17,200	1:10.00	
1966	Natashka	3	W. Shoemaker	122	Admirably	121	Miss Moona	114	16,250	1:09.40	
1967	Sharp Curve	3	W. Harris	114	Nevada Marga	118	Peggy's World	109	15,050	1:09.60	
1968	Time to Leave	3	D. Velasquez	125	Morgaise	121	Francine M.	117	14,700	1:10.20	
1970	Everything Lovely.	5	L. Pincay Jr	118	Undercover Miss	114	Dumpty Ann	118	17,800	1:09.20	
1972	Chou Croute	4	J.L. Rotz	126	Generous Portion	116	Minstrel M's	114	22,200	1:09.20	
1972	Crowning Glory	4	J. Lambert	116	Goddess Special	113	Minstrel M's	112	23,500	1:09.00	
1973	Sandy Blue	3	D. Pierce	120	Market Again	112	Impressive Style	122	22,150	1:08.60	
1975	Lucky Spell	4	J. Tejeira	120	Tizna	123	Impressive Style	121	21,700	1:09.60	
1976	Just a Kick	4	E. Munoz	114	Raise Your Skirts	121	Mismoyola	115	21,550	1:09.20	
1977	Winter Solstice	5	D.G. McHargue	120	Squander	114	Don's Music	115	26,100	1:11.80	
1977	My Juliet	4	A.S. Black	128	Just a Kick	121	Juliana F.	115	26,750	1:10.20	
1978	Sweet Little Lady	3	D.G. McHargue	117	Grenzen	122	Great Lady M.	114	33,200	1:09.00	
1979	Terlingua	3	D.G. McHargue	121	Powder Room	113	Ideal Exchange	116	32,800	1:08.40	
1981	Shine High	5	T. Lipham	114	Image of Reality	119	Parsley	117	32,600	1:08.60	
1982	Back at Two	5	C.J. McCarron	117	Abisinia	116	Excitable Lady	120	37,750	1:12.40	
1983	Matching	5	L. Pincay Jr	122	Bara Lass	115	Past Forgetting	122	38,650	1:09.00	
1984	Bara Lass	5	P.A. Valenzuela	122	Champagne Isle	116	Bally Knockan	114	40,100	1:09.40	

Year Winner	Age	Jockey	Wt.	Second	Wt.	Third	Wt.	Win Value	Time	Beyer
1985 Foggy Nation	5	L. Pincay Jr	117	Lovlier Linda	124	Tangent	122	37,250	1:09.60	
1986 Baron's Direct	5	E. Delahoussaye	120	Her Royalty	120	Aerturas	113	38,850	1:08.40	
1987 Pine Tree Lane	5	A. Cordero Jr	124	Rangoon Ruby	117	Her Royalty	120	38,350	1:09.80	
1989 Very Subtle	5	L. Pincay Jr	124	Sadie B. Fast	113	Comical Cat	116	44,350	1:08.60	
1990 Stormy but Valid	4	E. Delahoussaye	117	Survive	117	Warning Zone	119	47,850	1:08.20	106
1991 Classic Value	5	G.L. Stevens	116	Devil's Orchid	116	Hasty Pasty	116	60,325	1:10.20	105
1992 Forest Fealty	5	M.A. Pedroza	116	Middleford Rapids	118	Phil's Illusion	113	49,350	1:08.80	99
1993 Bountiful Native	5	P.A. Valenzuela	121	Freedom Cry	119	Forest Fealty	112	60,325	1:09.40	92
1994 Mamselle Bebette	4	Nakatani CS	118	Arches of Gold	120	Aspasante	114	47,475	1:08.20	105
1995 Desert Stormer	5	Desormeaux KJ	117	Velvet Tulip	114	Flying in the Lane	114	59,725	1:08.40	104
1996 Igotrhythm	4	Nakatani C.S.	115	Miss L Attack	115	Little Blue Sheep	115	81,100	1:08.80	110
1997 Our Summer Bid	5	Silva J. G.	114	Track Gal	120	Advancing Star	116	80,100	1:09.00	105
1998 Funallover	4	Solis A.	112	Advancing Star	122	Zenda's Diablo	109	79,800	1:09.20	97
1999 Enjoy The Moment	4	Pincay L. Jr.	117	Tomorrows Sunshine	114	Closed Escrow	116	78,720	1:08.40	111
2000 Show Me the Stage	4	K.J. Desormeaux	118	Theresa's Tizzy	117	Woodman's Dancer	115	79,440	1:08.54	110
2001 Go Go	4	E. Delahoussaye	116	La Feminn	120	Cover Gal	119	80,400	1:08.83	103
2002 Above Perfection	4	C.S. Nakatani	117	Kalookan Queen	122	Enchanted Woods	117	78,642	1:08.65	111
2003 Spring Meadow	4	C.S. Nakatani	117	Brisquette	116	Wild Tickle	117	81,300	1:10.20	94
						September Secret	116			

Beyer Index: 103.71

LAUREL FUTURITY, 1 1/16 Miles,
2-Year-Olds, Laurel, 2003 Purse: $100,000

Year Winner	Age	Jockey	Wt.	Second	Wt.	Third	Wt.	Win Value	Time	Beyer
1921 Morvich	2	A. Johnson	122	Lucky Hour	119	Runantell	122	42,750	1:42.00	
1922 Blossom Time	2	A. Johnson	119	Donges	119	Little Celt	122	41,015	1:39.80	
1922 Sally's Alley	2	A. Johnson	116	Martingale	122	My Own	122	41,015	1:39.20	
1923 Beau Butler	2	G.W. Carroll	122	Rustic	122	Aga Khan	117	54,030	1:39.80	
1924 Stimulus	2	H. Thurber	122	Star Lore	119	Candy Kid	122	49,220	1:39.80	
1925 Canter	2	C. Turner	117	Bubbling Over	122	Display	119	53,350	1:40.80	
1926 Fair Star	2	O. Bourassa	119	Jopagan	122	Whiskery	119	59,660	1:40.60	
1927 Glade	2	L. Morris	114	Petee-Wrack	119	Eugene S.	122	53,310	1:41.80	
1928 High Strung	2	L. McAtee	122	Dr. Freeland	122	Neddie	119	50,750	1:39.00	
1929 Flying Heels	2	W. Kelsay	117	Spinach	119	Galaday	116	55,810	1:47.00	
1930 Equipoise	2	R. Workman	119	Twenty Grand	119	Mate	119	50,360	1:48.60	
1931 Top Flight	2	R. Workman	119	Tick On	119	Burgoo King	119	56,170	1:44.80	
1932 Swivel	2	J. Gilbert	116	Golden Way	122	Repaid	119	62,430	1:46.80	
1935 Hollyrood	2	S. Coucci	122	Grand Slam	122	Ned Reigh	119	45,850	1:46.60	
1936 Matey	2	H. Richards	119	Brooklyn	122	Billionaire	122	25,300	1:46.80	
1937 Nedayr	2	W.D. Wright	122	Jacola	119	Dauber	122	28,140	1:45.20	
1938 Challedon	2	G. Seabo	119	Third Degree	119	Gilded Knight	122	28,770	1:45.80	
1939 Bimelech	2	F.A. Smith	122	Rough Pass	122	Straight Lead	122	33,230	1:45.20	
1940 Bold Irishman	2	J. Gilbert	122	Our Boots	119	Whirlaway	122	33,830	1:49.80	
1941 Contradiction	2	K. McCombs	122	Devil Diver	119	Chiquita Mia	119	33,910	1:47.40	
1942 Count Fleet	2	J. Longden	119	Occupation	122	Vincentive	122	30,820	1:43.40	
1943 Platter	2	C. McCreary	119	By Jimminy	119	Smolensko	122	33,440	1:47.60	
1944 Pot o' Luck	2	D. Dodson	122	Plebiscite	122	Recce	119	35,130	1:46.40	
1945 Star Pilot	2	A. Kirkland	122	Billy Bumps	119	Colony Boy	117	36,365	1:47.80	
1946 Jet Pilot	2	J. Gilbert	122	Fervent	122	Bastogne	119	37,615	1:46.00	
1947 Citation	2	D. Dodson	119	Better Self	119	Ace Admiral	122	36,675	1:48.80	
1948 Capot	2	T. Atkinson	119	Slam Bang	122	Sun Bahram	122	47,325	1:45.80	
1949 Oil Capitol	2	E.J. Knapp	122	Lot o Luck	122	Striking	119	48,755	1:44.20	
1950 Big Stretch	2	T. Atkinson	122	Bold	117	General Staff	122	45,090	1:45.40	
1951 Cajun	2	N. Shuk	122	Lord Priam	119	Inyureye	119	46,450	1:47.60	
1952 Isasmoothie	2	B. Mitchell	119	Count Cain	119	County Clare	122	59,410	1:46.60	
1953 Errard King	2	S. Boulmetis	122	War Doings	122	Nirgal Lad	119	61,450	1:45.20	
1954 Thinking Cap	2	D. Dodson	122	Flying Fury	119	Saratoga	122	53,870	1:46.80	
1955 Nail	2	H. Woodhouse	122	Liberty Sun	122	Countermand	122	67,980	1:47.00	
1956 Missile	2	P. Anderson	122	Cohoes	122	Ambehaving	122	71,235	1:45.00	
1957 Jewel's Reward	2	W. Shoemaker	122	Nala	122	Staysail	122	115,347	1:44.20	
1958 Intentionally	2	W. Shoemaker	122	Rico Tesio	122	Black Hills	122	119,571	1:46.00	
1959 Progessing	2	H. Woodhouse	122	All Hands	122	Catapult	122	71,635	1:45.40	
1960 Garwol	2	I. Valenzuela	122	Bal Musette	122	Sherluck	122	67,046	1:45.80	
1961 Crimson Satan	2	W. Shoemaker	122	Green Ticket	122	Endymion	122	72,585	1:46.40	
1962 Right Proud	2	J. Leonard	122	Delta Judge	122	Master Dennis	122	72,637	1:47.00	
1963 Quadrangle	2	W. Hartack	122	Breakspear	122	Bupers	122	110,012	1:47.20	
1964 Sadair	2	M. Ycaza	122	Hail to All	122	Umbrella Fella	122	110,913	1:43.40	
1965 Spring Double	2	H. Hinojosa	122	Fathers Image	122	Amberoid	122	134,543	1:44.80	
1966 In Reality	2	J.L. Rotz	122	Successor	122	Proviso	122	121,667	1:45.80	
1967 Vitriolic	2	B. Baeza	122	T.V. Commercial	122	Gin-Rob	122	113,015	1:45.20	
1968 King Emperor	2	E. Belmonte	122	Dike	122	Mr. Leader	122	114,380	1:44.00	
1969 High Echelon	2	M. Ycaza	122	Toasted	122	Brave Emperor	122	114,803	1:44.20	
1970 Limit to Reason	2	J. Cruguet	122	New Round	122	Droll Role	122	123,526	1:44.80	

Year	Winner	Age	Jockey	Wt.	Second	Wt.	Third	Wt.	Win Value	Time	Beyer
1971	Riva Ridge	2	R. Turcotte	122	Festive Mood	122	Drum Fire	122	90,733	1:43.40	
1972	Secretariat	2	R. Turcotte	122	Stop the Music	122	Angle Light	122	83,395	1:42.80	
1973	Protagonist	2	A. Santiago	122	Hasty Flyer	122	Prince of Reason	122	79,911	1:43.20	
1974	L'Enjoleur	2	S. Hawley	122	Wajima	122	Bombay Duck	122	75,564	1:42.60	
1975	Honest Pleasure	2	B. Baeza	122	Whatsyourpleasure	122	Dance Spell	122	91,662	1:42.80	
1976	Royal Ski	2	J. Kurtz	122	For the Moment	122	Medieval Man	122	86,046	1:44.00	
1977	Affirmed	2	S. Cauthen	122	Alydar	122	Star de Naskra	122	82,290	1:44.20	
1978	Spectacular Bid	2	R.J. Franklin	122	General Assembly	122	Clever Trick	122	84,237	1:41.60	
1979	Plugged Nickle	2	B. Thornburg	122	Gold Stage	122	New Regent	122	108,630	1:43.80	
1980	Cure the Blues	2	R.L. Turcotte	122	Matching Gift	122	Kan Reason	122	91,116	1:44.40	
1981	Deputy Minister	2	D. MacBeth	122	Laser Light	122	Majesty's Prince	122	110,190	1:44.60	
1982	Cast Party	2	J. Velasquez	122	Pax in Bello	122	Primitive Pleasure	122	145,293	1:45.00	
1983	Devil's Bag	2	E. Maple	122	Hail Bold King	122	Pied a' Tierre	122	138,150	1:42.20	
1984	Mighty Appealing	2	G.P. Smith	122	Cutlass Reality	122	Rhoman Rule	122	169,485	1:43.00	
1985	Southern Appeal	2	J. Davidson	122	Papal Power	122	Miracle Wood	122	130,770	1:44.20	
1986	Bet Twice	2	C. Perret	122	Pledge Card	122	Grand Rol	122	146,145	1:45.00	
1987	Antiqua	2	C.B. Asmussen	122	Mister Modesty	122	Kohen Witha K	122	150,000	1:46.00	
1988	Luge II	2	J.A. Santos	122	Ringerman	122	Downtown Davey	122	150,000	1:45.20	
1989	Go and Go	2	C. Perret	122	Robyn Dancer	122	Super Cholo	122	180,000	1:44.00	
1990	River Traffic	2	C.B. Asmussen	122	Fourstars Allstar	122	Share the Glory	122	180,000	1:44.80	
1991	Smiling and Dancin	2	R. Migliore	122	Free at Last	122	Older but Smarter	122	120,000	1:48.60	
1992	Lord of the Bay	2	R. Wilson	122	Glorieux Dancer	122	Halisee	122	120,000	1:45.40	
1993	Dove Hunt	2	R.G. Davis	122	Lotsa Chile	122	Thrilla in Manila	122	81,000	1:49.00	81
1994	Western Echo	2	Prado ES	122	Old Tascosa	122	Shimmering Prince	122	60,000	1:30.80	85
1995	Appealing Skier	2	Wilson A	122	Liberty Road	122	Pirate Performer	122	60,000	1:30.60	87
1996	Captain Bodgit	2	F.G. Douglas	122	Concerto	122	Carrolls Favorite	122	60,000	1:49.40	101
1997	Fight For M'Lady	2	C.H.Marquez Jr.	122	Victory Gallop	122	Essential	122	60,000	1:53.60	93
1998	Millions	2	Prado E. S.	122	Raire Standard	122	More Better	122	60,000	1:51.40	84
1999	Scottish Halo	2	Turner T. G.	122	Un Fino Vino	122	Grundlefoot	122	60,000	1:49.20	96
2000	Buckle Down Ben	2	M.J. McCarthy	122	Gift of the Eagle	122	Niner's Echo	122	60,000	1:51.93	88
2002	Toccet	2	J.F. Chavez	122	Ironton	122	Cherokee's Boy	122	60,000	1:46.10	96
2003	Tapit	2	R.A. Dominguez	122	Polish Rifle	122	Ghost Mountain	122	60,000	1:43.81	98

Beyer Index: 90.9

LAWRENCE REALIZATION HANDICAP, 1 1/2 Miles (Turf), 3-Year-Olds, Belmont Park, 2003 Purse: $150,000

Year	Winner	Age	Jockey	Wt.	Second	Wt.	Third	Wt.	Win Value	Time	Beyer
1889	Salvator	3	J. McLaughlin	122	Tenny	109	Long Dance	112	34,100	2:51.00	
1890	Tournament	3	W. Hayward	113	Her Highness	116	Banquet	119	25,300	2:51.00	
1891	Potomac	3	A. Hamilton	119	Montana	109	Strathmeath	116	30,850	2:51.00	
1892	Tammany	3	E. Garrison	119	The Pepper	115	Patron	119	28,470	2:51.40	
1893	Daily America	3	W. Simms	107	St. Leonards	118	Sir Walter	122	24,150	2:50.60	
1894	Dobbins	3	W. Simms	122	Hornpipe	122	Rey el Santa Anita	119	33,400	2:55.00	
1895	Bright Phoebus	3	L. Reiff	115	Keenan	122	King Arthur II	112	29,700	2:51.40	
1896	Requital	3	A. Clayton	119	Peep o' Day	107	Merry Prince	110	17,365	2:49.40	
1897	The Friar	3	F. Littlefield	115	Rennssalaer	112	Buddha	118	18,125	2:48.40	
1898	Hamburg	3	T. Sloan	122	Plaudit	122	George Boyd	112	13,875	2:51.20	
1899	Ethelbert	3	H. Spencer	118	Lothario	122	Filton d'Or	119	12,890	2:51.40	
1900	Prince of Melbourn	3	H. Spencer	126	Ildrim	126	Kilogram	119	14,325	2:49.80	
1901	The Parader	3	P. McCue	126	Commando	121	Mortallo	116	13,555	2:49.80	
1902	Major Daingerfield	3	G. Odom	123	The Rival	111	Goldsmith	123	12,875	2:47.60	
1903	Africander	3	J. Bullman	126	Golden Maxim	126	Savable	126	18,635	2:45.20	
1904	Ort Wells	3	F. O'Niell	126	Mercury	113	Graziallo	122	20,945	2:47.60	
1905	Sysonby	3	D. Nicol	126	Tanya	121	Migraine	116	17,935	2:47.00	
1906	Accountant	3	J. Martin	126	Entree	119	Bull's Eye	116	16,260	2:48.00	
1907	Dinna Ken	3	G. Mountain	123	Frank Gill	126	Salvidere	123	16,880	2:48.00	
1908	Fair Play	3	E. Dugan	126	King James	126	Dorante	126	17,685	2:46.20	
1909	Fitz Herbert	3	V. Powers	122	Olambala	122	Fayette	126	14,900	2:45.00	
1910	Sweep	3	J. Notter	126	Suffragist	116	Hindoo Star	116	9,755	2:53.00	
1913	Rock View	3	T. McTaggart	127	Monocacy	110	Rock Fish	90	2,475	2:51.00	
1916	Star Hawk	3	H.H. Phillips	117	Spur	126	Crimper	111	2,775	2:32.60	
1917	Omar Khayyam	3	M. Buxton	126	Hourless	126	Buckboard	116	5,950	2:33.40	
1918	Johren	3	F. Robinson	126	Whippoorwill	116			10,725	2:55.20	
1919	Vexatious	3	W. Knapp	126	Dunboyne	126	Thunderstorm	116	20,540	2:47.60	
1920	Man o' War	3	C. Kummer	126	Hoodwink	116			15,040	2:40.80	
1921	Touch Me Not	3	F. Coltiletti	126	Grey Lag	126	Sporting Blood	121	17,850	2:43.20	
1922	Kai-Sang	3	E. Sande	126	Bunting	126	Rockminister	122	21,400	2:42.40	
1923	Zev	3	E. Sande	126	Untidy	123	Rialto	119	24,410	2:44.60	
1924	Aga Khan	3	J. Maiben	116	Transmute	126	Mr. Mutt	126	25,120	2:48.40	
1925	Marconi	3	K. Noe	116	Swope	126	Chantley	126	26,500	2:43.80	
1926	Espino	3	L. Fator	126	Crusader	126	Mars	126	26,100	2:42.60	
1927	Nimba	3	H. Thurber	123	Brown Bud	126	Flippant	119	29,470	2:45.00	
1928	Reigh Count	3	C. Lang	126	Diavolo	126	Sortie	126	28,430	2:44.60	

Year	Winner	Age	Jockey	Wt.	Second	Wt.	Third	Wt.	Win Value	Time	Beyer
1929	The Nut	3	M. Garner	119	African	119	Beacon Hill	126	31,760	2:45.60	
1930	Gallant Fox	3	E. Sande	126	Questionnaire	123	Yarn	116	29,610	2:41.20	
1931	Twenty Grand	3	C. Kurtsinger	126	Sun Meadow	123	Sir Ashley	123	29,700	2:41.20	
1932	Faireno	3	T. Malley	126	Over Time	116	War Hero	126	24,985	2:43.60	
1933	War Glory	3	J. Gilbert	123	Pomposity	116	Sarada	123	21,400	2:44.60	
1934	Carry Over	3	T. Malley	116	Observant	126	Good Goods	116	18,110	2:44.00	
1935	Firethorn	3	E. Arcaro	119	Count Arthur	119	Purple Knight	116	16,780	2:42.20	
1936	Granville	3	J. Stout	126	Giant Killer	116	Memory Book	126	19,550	2:43.60	
1937	Unfailing	3	F. Koepel	112	Privileged	119	Moonton	112	19,590	2:44.20	
1938	Magic Hour	3	J. Longden	112	Roseretter	109	Dan He	112	16,800	2:45.00	
1939	Hash	3	E. Arcaro	119	Chip In	112	Shining One	123	18,750	2:42.60	
1940	Fenelon	3	J. Stout	123	Your Chance	123	Romanov	112	18,070	2:44.80	
1941	Whirlaway	3	A. Robertson	126	Alaking	112	Time Counts	112	23,050	2:44.20	
1942	Alsab	3	G. Woolf	126	Vagrancy	115	Trierarch	110	7,900	2:42.00	
1943	Fairy Manhurst	3	J. Longden	109	Eurasian	122	Famous Victory	111	7,475	2:43.00	
1944	By Jimminy	3	G. Woolf	126	Bounding Home	126			13,805	2:43.20	
1945	Pot o' Luck	3	D. Dodson	126	Chief Barker	108	Michaelo	108	20,060	2:43.60	
1946	School Tie	3	T. Atkinson	110	Alamond	114			18,300	2:43.60	
1947	Cosmic Bomb	3	O. Scurlock	114	Phalanx	126	Snow Goose	115	19,050	2:42.80	
1948	Ace Admiral	3	T. Atkinson	114	Noble Hero	114	Shy Guy	112	20,400	2:44.20	
1949	Ponder	3	S. Brooks	126	Blue Hills	110	Prophets Thumb	116	15,500	2:42.60	
1950	Bed o' Roses	3	N. Combest	107	Greek Ship	118	Theory	110	15,600	2:42.60	
1951	Counterpoint	3	D. Gorman	126	Saxony	110	Alerted	114	15,700	2:43.40	
1952	Mark-Ye-Well	3	E. Arcaro	118	One Count	126	Marcador	114	20,000	2:42.00	
1953	Platan	3	C. McCreary	110	Dictar	118	Level Lea	118	20,150	2:43.40	
1954	Fisherman	3	H. Woodhouse	122	Full Flight	122	Privacy	110	18,900	2:44.60	
1955	Thinking Cap	3	P.J. Bailey	114	Westward Ho	122	Sweet Chariot	110	18,250	2:44.40	
1956	Riley	3	T. Atkinson	120	Third Brother	114	Oh Johnny	120	18,450	2:43.40	
1957	Promised Land	3	H. Woodhouse	114	Assemblyman	117	Jocko's Walk	114	19,800	2:43.20	
1958	Martins Rullah	3	W. Shoemaker	117	Warhead	120	Plion	120	17,900	2:43.00	
1959	Middle Brother	3	E. Arcaro	120	Polylad	114	Nasomo	114	18,225	2:44.40	
1960	Kelso	3	E. Arcaro	120	Tompion	123	Tooth and Nail	116	35,800	2:40.80	
1961	Sherluck	3	B. Baeza	123	Ambiopoise	120	Carry Back	123	35,490	2:43.80	
1962	Battle Joined	3	M. Ycaza	116	Smart	116	Comic	120	37,245	2:42.60	
1963	Dean Carl	3	R. Ussery	120	B. Major	120	Master Dennis	116	36,530	2:42.00	
1964	Quadrangle	3	M. Ycaza	126	Roman Brother	123	Knightly Manner	116	35,165	2:45.00	
1965	Munden Point	3	S. Boulmetis	116	Selari	116	Sammyren	120	35,880	2:43.60	
1966	Buckpasser	3	B. Baeza	126	Ring Twice	116	Poker	116	35,490	2:44.20	
1967	Successor	3	B. Baeza	126	Gentleman James	116	Irish Rebellion	116	35,620	2:44.60	
1968	Funny Fellow	3	B. Baeza	116	Draft Card	116	Chompion	123	36,595	2:41.20	
1969	Oil Power	3	J. Cruguet	116	Red Reality	120	Pollution	116	34,970	2:42.20	
1970	Kling Kling	3	J. Cruguet	114	Loud	123	Naskra	120	37,310	2:27.60	
1971	Specious	3	E. Maple	111	Yellow Zorker	114	Gleaming	120	34,740	2:36.80	
1972	Halo	3	B. Baeza	114	Betsy Be Good	112	Ruritania	114	35,280	2:28.20	
1973	Amen II	3	E. Belmonte	128	Big Whippendeal	117	Expropriate	117	34,590	2:26.80	
1974	Prod	3	J. Velasquez	117	Prince of Reason	117	The Scotsman	117	34,050	2:35.00	
1975	Gab Bag	3	J. Cruguet	117	One on the Aisle	117	Martial Law	117	34,590	2:31.60	
1976	Great Contractor	3	P. Day	117	Teddy's Courage	117	Crackle	117	26,130	2:27.60	
1976	L'Heureux	3	D. Pierce	121	Banghi	117	Chati	117	26,130	2:27.80	
1977	Zinov	3	A. Graell	117	Poor Man's Bluff	117	Johnny D	117	32,500	2:29.20	
1978	Mac Diarmida	3	J. Cruguet	123	Native Courier	114	Robin's Song	114	32,970	2:27.20	
1979	Golden Act	3	S. Hawley	126	Smarten	126	T.V. Series	114	50,355	2:27.60	
1980	Rumbo	3	W. Shoemaker	114	Proctor	117	Pirate Law	114	50,580	2:26.00	
1981	Our Captain Willie	3	A. Cordero Jr.	114	Change the Patch	114	Open Call	114	49,050	2:27.40	
1982	Ten Below	3	J. Miranda	114	Majesty's Prince	123	Khatango	121	51,030	2:26.40	
1983	Moon Spirit	3	A. Cordero Jr.	114	Win	114	Tough Mickey	114	53,100	2:28.40	
1984	Roving Minstrel	3	K. Skinner	114	Vision	123	Solidified	114	55,530	2:28.00	
1985	Danger's Hour	3	J.D. Bailey	123	Silent Slander	114	Regal Diplomat	114	66,915	2:30.40	
1985	Noisy When Hot	3	J.A. Santos	114	Broadway Tommy	114	Ctutlass Reality	114	54,135	2:30.60	
1986	The Lone Ranger	3	C.J. McCarron	114	Southjet	123	Dark Flood	114	72,600	2:37.40	
1987	Tertiary Zone	3	S. Hawley	114	Major Beard	114	Sport Royal	114	92,100	2:30.00	
1988	Blew by Em	3	C.W. Antley	114	Colchis Island	114	Face Nord	114	86,100	2:27.20	
1989	Caltech	3	R.R. Douglas	123	Pach to Batan	114	Fast 'n' Gold	114	74,280	2:26.00	
1990	Baylis	3	L. Dettori	114	Cozzene's Prince	114	Libor	114	76,920	2:29.00	102
1991	Jaded Dancer	3	J.L. Samyn	117	Pitch In	114	Silvardara	114	72,240	2:32.00	96
1992	Timber Cat	3	R.G. Davis	114	Tomorrow's Spirit	114	Gainzer	113	76,560	2:28.80	91
1993	Strolling Along	3	C.J. McCarron	114	Scattered Steps	113	Noble Sheba	114	75,480	2:32.60	98
1994	Personal Merit	3	Chavez JF	113	Kristen's Baby	111	Holy Mountain	116	67,260	2:29.20	96
1995	Flitch	3	M.E. Smith	117	Look Daggers	109	Diplomatic Jet	118	69,300	2:34.40	103
1996	Da Dean	3	R. Migliore	113	Senor Senor	113	Value Investor	116	68,880	2:39.00	102
1997	Renewed	3	Leon F	112	Devonwood	112	Belgravia	113	67,320	2:27.20	93
1998	Parade Ground	3	P. Day	121	Pay Zone	112	Vergennes	112	83,595	2:25.80	99
1999	Gritty Sandie	3	M.E. Smith	114	Monkey Puzzle	116	Just Listen	115	90,000	2:28.60	98

Year	Winner	Age	Jockey	Wt.	Second	Wt.	Third	Wt.	Win Value	Time	Beyer
2000	Ciro	3	J.A. Santos	123	Whata Brainstorm	115	Lodge Hill	115	90,000	2:31.48	107
2001	Sharp Performance	3	J.R. Velazquez	120	Tiger Trap	116	Whitmore's Conn	114	90,000	2:27.04	102
2002	Fisher Pond	3	J.R. Velazquez	116	Irish Colonial	116	Extra Check	116	90,000	2:30.34	100
2003	Kicken Kris	3	J. Castellano	121	Rowans Park	115	Fortune Writers	113	90,000	2:27.98	99

Beyer Index: 99

LECOMTE STAKES, 1 Mile,
3-Year-Olds, Fair Grounds, 2003 Purse: $100,000

Year	Winner	Age	Jockey	Wt.	Second	Wt.	Third	Wt.	Win Value	Time	Beyer
1943	Valdina Orphan	4	F. Zufelt	122	Moscow II	109	Yankee Dandy	108	3,330	1:51.00	
1944	First Fiddle	5	J. Westrope	118	Pops Pick	115	Rounders	120	2,315	1:45.60	
1946	King Dorsett	4	C. LeBlanc	120	Bold Salute	110	Pique	113	3,345	1:44.60	
1947	Jack S.L.	7	S. Brooks	111	Earshot	114	Republican	112	6,500	1:45.20	
1948	Jack S.L.	8	R.L. Baird	114	Seven Hearts	125	Noble One	118	6,500	1:49.20	
1949	Caillou Rouge	4	J. West	105			Rabies	115	4,780	1:50.80	
	My Request	4	O. Scurlock	123							
1950	Johns Joy	4	D. Scurlock	121	Blue Thanks	113	Red Camelia	104	8,620	1:45.20	
1951	Thelma Berger	4	K. Stuart	107	Little Flower	110	Riverlane	118	9,350	1:45.80	
1952	False	4	E. Van Hook	107	Light Broom	125	The Gink	110	8,050	1:45.60	
1953	Smoke Screen	4	G. Porch	114	Spur On	123	Shy Guy	113	9,850	1:47.80	
1954	Futuresque	7	E. Jenkins	109	Bugledrums	110	Money Broker	111	9,925	1:45.60	
1955	Spur On	7	P.J. Bailey	118	Bobby Brocato	119	Epic King	120	10,850	1:44.40	
1956	Galdar	5	E. Van Hook	114	Nonnie Jo	113	Ja Ja	115	9,900	1:44.00	
1957	Speed Rouser	5	J. Heckmann	121	Big Sweep	110	Ramrod	116	8,975	1:46.60	
1958	Speed Rouser	6	A. Popara	115	Ezgo	112	Tenacious	120	8,625	1:45.40	
1959	Tenacious	5	R. Broussard	119	Shoerullah	112	Jet Colonel	121	8,450	1:43.00	
1960	Tenacious	6	R. Broussard	120	Sun Better	107	Matinal	111	8,350	1:48.40	
1961	Tenacious	7	C. Meaux	113	Tony Graff	112	Road House	115	8,575	1:45.00	
1962	Treasury Note	3	B. Phelps	113	Touch Bar	111	For the Road	114	9,400	1:46.40	
1963	City Line	3	R.L. Baird	123	Lemon Twist	122	Top Gallant	120	8,950	1:42.40	
1964	Susan's Gent	3	R.L. Baird	123	Whit's Pride	121	Gordon W.	109	9,225	1:45.20	
1965	Dapper Delegate	3	J. Heckmann	123	Saber Dance	112	The Dancer	115	10,175	1:43.40	
1966	Sails Pride	3	L. Moyers	120	Royal Franklin	114	Royal Okie	122	9,825	1:50.60	
1967	Grand Premiere	3	J. Combest	119	Jalo Bond	116	Tom's Favor	115	11,600	1:44.60	
1968	Port Digger	3	M. Heath	111	Judge Kilday	120	Forever	115	11,275	1:46.80	
1969	Foolish Prince	3	D.E. Whited	118	Cangirod	114	Rush Date	114	10,625	1:45.80	
1970	Action Getter	3	M. Venezia	117	Herbalist	116	Tenacious Jr.	115	12,500	1:44.20	
1971	Helio Rise	3	P. Rubbicco	121	Felonious	114	List	116	11,950	1:45.00	
1972	No Le Hace	3	P. Rubbicco	122	Feloniously	119	Breakozone	117	14,900	1:44.40	
1973	Vodika	3	T. Barrow	119	Navajo	120	Rocket Pocket	123	15,825	1:46.00	
1974	Crimson Ruler	3	K. LeBlanc	118	Don't Be Late Jim	116	Heavy Mayonnaise	120	17,650	1:43.80	
1975	Colonel Power	3	P. Rubbicco	123	Davey Dan	113	Rustic Ruler	119	18,625	1:40.60	
1976	Tudor Tambourine	3	D. Copling	117	Glassy Dip	112	Go East Young Man	117	18,000	1:46.20	
1977	Clev Er Tell	3	R. Broussard	119	A Letter to Harry	118	Sea Defier	110	16,725	1:44.80	
1978	Dragon Tamer	3	R. Sibille	118	Batonnier	110	Traffic Warning	114	22,050	1:44.60	
1979	Fuego Seguro	3	M.R. Morgan	116	Bo	114	Will Henry	116	21,175	1:46.60	
1980	Withholding	3	B. Fann	108	Brent's Trans Am	120	Bold Source	107	23,650	1:44.20	
1981	Law Me	3	J. McKnight	113	Brazen Ruler	119	Corsicana	114	24,800	1:46.40	
1982	Linkage	3	G.P. Smith	120	Soy Emperor	113	Mid Yell	109	23,350	1:45.00	
1983	Explosive Wagon	3	C. Mueller	116	Found Pearl Harbor	116	Pronto Forli	120	26,900	1:45.00	
1984	Silent King	3	C. Mueller	115	Taylor's Special	122	Fairly Straight	111	24,150	1:45.20	
1985	Encolure	3	A. Doin	114	Northern Bid	119	Ten Times Ten	116	33,450	1:45.80	
1986	Timely Albert	3	P. Rubbicco	109	Irish Irish	114	New Plymouth	117	34,200	1:43.60	
1987	One Tough Cat	3	K.P. LeBlanc	114	Authentic Hero	118	French 'n Irish	113	17,250	1:48.20	
1988	Pastourelles	3	B.J. Walker Jr.	113	Risen Star	122	Run Paul Run	114	16,275	1:46.60	
1989	Majesty's Imp	3	S.R. Rydowski	116	Nooo Problema	119	Esker Island	113	16,455	1:45.60	
1990	Martha's Buck	3	B. Walker	113	Axe It	115	Arrowhead Al	112	16,050	1:47.00	
1991	Big Courage	3	T.L. Fox	116	Near the Limit	118	Slick Groom	111	19,725	1:48.20	
1992	Line in the Sand	3	S.P. Romero	115	Greinton's Dancer	113	Best Boy's Jade	116	19,215	1:39.80	88
1993	Dixieland Heat	3	E.J. Perrodin	116	Apprentice	117	Masters Windfall	112	19,995	1:37.60	85
1994	Fly Cry	3	R. Ardoin	119	Smilin Singin Sam	114	Sweet Wager	115	19,905	1:39.29	100
1995	Moonlight Dancer	3	L. Melancon	112	Beavers Nose	114	Timeless Honor	120	25,725	1:40.13	93
1996	Boomerang	3	E. Martin Jr.	116	Commanders Palace	116	Playing to Win	115	25,845	1:39.49	82
1997	Cash Deposit	3	R. Ardoin	120	Stroke	114	Kalispell	113	36,000	1:37.97	96
1998	Western City	3	R. Albarado	112	Captain Maestri	116	Slick Report	112	60,000	1:37.84	89
1999	Some Actor	3	E. Martin Jr.	114	Desert Demon	114	Silver Chadra	114	60,000	1:38.59	84
2000	Noble Ruler	3	L. Melancon	114	Mighty	122	Peninsula	119	60,000	1:39.11	96
2001	Sam Lord's Castle	3	R. Albarado	122	Wild Hits	122	McMahon	119	60,000	1:37.98	93
2002	Easyfromthegitgo	3	D. Meche	114	Sky Terrace	119	It'sallinthechase	122	60,000	1:37.98	90
2003	Saintly Look	3	S.J. Sellers	122	Call Me Lefty	122	Winning Fans	114	60,000	1:37.62	95

Beyer Index: 90.92

Run at 1 mile 40 yards in 1975, 1994-1995; 1 mile 70 yards in 1944, 1946; Run at 1 1/16 miles in 1947-1948, 1950-1974, 1976-1991; Run at 1 1/8 miles in 1943, 1949; Not run in 1945.

LEXINGTON, 1 1/4 Miles (Turf),
3-Year-Olds, Belmont Park, 2003 Purse: $150,000

Year	Winner	Age	Jockey	Wt.	Second	Wt.	Third	Wt.	Win Value	Time	Beyer
1961	Wise Ship	4	H. Gustines	120	Our Jeep	125	Art Market	115	36,335	2:41.80	
1962	Mongo	3	C. Burr	118	Dedimoud	117	In Force	117	18,850	1:34.20	
1963	Marlin Bay	3	J. Sellers	114	Running Bowline	117	Wild Card	115	18,752	1:41.20	
1964	Laugh Aloud	3	R. Turcotte	113	Gun Boat	114	National	124	19,142	1:43.00	
1969	Eaglesham	3	P. Anderson	119	Red Reality	110	Larceny Kid	119	18,720	1:46.60	
1970	Roman Scout	3	J. Vasquez	111	On the Track	113	Flying Brick	111	14,771	1:43.20	
1970	Naskra	3	J. Cruguet	115	Tumble Lark	112	Hubbub	116	15,096	1:43.40	
1971	Bold Reason	3	J.L. Rotz	120	Gleaming	126	Northfields	120	33,840	1:54.80	
1972	Big Spruce	3	R. Cespedes	115	Ruritana	113	Tentam	114	34,740	1:56.80	
1973	London Company	3	L. Pincay Jr	125	Rapid Sage	112	Bold Nix	116	35,760	1:56.00	
1974	Jack Sprat	3	R. Turcotte	112	Kin Run	115	Never Explain	116	28,020	1:56.40	
1974	Hasty Tudor	3	V. Bracciale Jr.	112	R. Tom Can	115	Splitting Headache	118	27,870	1:56.80	
1975	Dr. Emil	3	M. Venezia	109	Martial Law	109	Le Cypriote	112	27,270	2:07.00	
1975	Brian Boru	3	B. Baeza	116	Rapid Invader	111	Clout	113	27,270	2:07.60	
1976	Fabled Monarch	3	J. Vasquez	114	Fighting Bill	113	Effervescing	112	27,450	1:50.00	
1976	Modred	3	C. Perret	117	Dream'n Be Lucky	112	Spanish Dagger	116	27,300	1:49.40	
1977	Swoon Swept	3	L. Melancon	112	Stir the Embers	112	Lynn Davis	116	32,400	1:41.20	
1977	Johnny D.	3	A. Cordero Jr	113	Forward Charger	117	Best Person	112	32,100	1:41.00	
1978	Mac Diarmida	3	J. Cruguet	126	John Henry	112	Ashikaga	110	34,110	1:41.00	
1979	Virilify	3	R.I. Velez	108	T.V. Series	113	Crown Thy Good	114	50,895	2:02.40	
1980	Good Bid	3	J.L. Samyn	112	Proctor	116	Don Daniello	122	50,310	2:01.00	
1981	Acaroid	3	C.B. Asmussen	114	De la Rose	121	Wicked Will	117	52,380	2:00.20	
1982	Majesty's Prince	3	E. Maple	126	Lamerok	114	Flamingo Two	114	50,310	2:03.00	
1982	Royal Roberto	3	J. Fell	126	Otter Slide	117	Royal Ring	114	5,031	2:01.80	
1983	Kilauea	3	J. Cruguet	114	Fortnightly	126	Top Competitor	114	34,800	2:00.60	
1984	Onyxly	3	J.D. Bailey	114	Dr. Schwartzman	126	Vision	126	58,770	2:01.20	
1985	Danger's Hour	3	J.D. Bailey	123	Foundation Plan	123	Exclusive Partner	114	71,370	2:00.40	
1986	Manila	3	J.A. Santos	126	Glow	123	Dance Card Filled	114	88,980	2:03.20	
1987	Milesius	3	E. Maple	114	Yucca	117	Rio's Lark	114	89,580	2:03.20	
1988	Sunshine Forever	3	A. Cordero Jr	123	Hodges Bay	114	Ask Not	114	85,500	2:03.00	
1989	Coosaragga	3	R. Migliore	114	Valid Ordinate	114	Orange Sunshine	119	69,720	2:00.80	
1990	Solar Splendor	3	E. Maple	123	Rouse the Louse	123	Apple Current	114	56,640	2:01.80	
1991	Lech	3	A. Cordero Jr	114	Fourstars Allstar	123	Lucky Mathieu	114	71,160	1:59.40	100
1992	Spectacular Tide	3	J.A. Krone	114	Preferences	121	Casino Magistrate	123	69,120	2:02.20	96
1993	Llandaff	3	J.A. Krone	123	Strolling Along	114	Eastern Memories	114	52,380	2:02.80	99
1994	Holy Mountain	3	Velazquez JR	112	Islefaxyou	112	Check Ride	117	50,850	1:59.60	96
1995	Green Means Go	3	J.D. Bailey	119	Nostra	112	Flitch	112	66,960	2:01.60	95
1996	Ok by Me	3	J.F. Chavez	122	Value Investor	117	Alzeus	113	68,160	2:03.40	98
1997	Private Buck Trout	3	J.F. Chavez	119	Red Castle	112	Renewed	112	90,000	2:01.20	90
1998	Parade Ground	3	M.E. Smith	117	Ay Rouge	113	La Reine's Terms	113	84,060	2:00.40	99
1999	Mythical Gem	3	J.F. Chavez	117	Monkey Puzzle	113	Bugatti	114	90,000	2:01.20	95
2000	Rob's Spirit	3	J.D. Bailey	113	Plato	113	Rumsonontheriver	115	90,000	2:02.87	104
2001	Sharp Performance	3	J.R. Velazquez	114	Package Store	114	Whitmore's Conn	114	90,000	1:58.93	101
2002	Chiselling	3	J.D. Bailey	114	Finality	114	Irish Colonial	114	90,000	2:00.42	96
2003	Sharp Impact	3	R. Migliore	114	Hidden Truth	118	Urban King	114	90,000	2:02.62	96

Beyer Index: 97.31

LOCUST GROVE HANDICAP, 1 1/8 Miles,
Fillies and Mares 3-Year-Olds and Up, Churchill Downs, 2003 Purse: $164,400

Year	Winner	Age	Jockey	Wt.	Second	Wt.	Third	Wt.	Win Value	Time	Beyer
1982	Excitable Lady	4	D. McHargue	120	Dawn's Beginning		Sweetest Fantasy			1:37.20	
1983	Try Something New	4	P. Day	117	Kitchen		Naskra Magic			1:45.20	
1984	Heatherten	5	S. Maple	122	Mickey's Echo		Forest Maiden			1:43.20	
1985	Sintra	4	K. Allen	123	Sweet Missus		Switching Trick			1:43.40	
1986	Glorious View		C. Woods Jr	113	Zenobia Empress		Tide			1:44.20	
1987	Luckiest Girl	4	D. Soto	114	Slipping 'n Slyding		Marianna's Girl			1:51.60	
1988	Chez Chez Chez	4	J. Garcia	111	Lt. Lao		How I Wish			1:45.20	
1989	Jungle Gold	4	C. Woods Jr	111	Here's Your Silver		Heretic			1:43.20	
1990	Dibs	4	A. Gryder	111	City Crowds		Phillipa Rush			1:50.60	
1991	Nice Serve	4	J. Johnson	111	Super Fan		Behaving Dancer		73,840	1:51.20	101
1992	Behaving Dancer	5	D. Howard	117	Firm Stance		Olden Rijn		74,750	1:47.27	101
1993	Lady Blessington	4	C. Black	121	Gone Seeking		Cruise		74,425	1:50.16	94
1994	Life Is Delicious	4	J.Martinez, Jr.	113	Eurostorm		Obtain		70,850	1:53.87	83
1995	Memories	4	S.Sellers	114	Market Booster	120	Thread	115	71,760	1:47.48	101
1996	Bail Out Becky	4	C.Perret	121	Ms. Isadora		Memories	117	72,850	1:47.80	105
1997	Romy	6	F.Torres	121	Yokama	112	Cymbala	116	68,634	1:48.89	97
1998	Colcon	5	Sellers S. J.	118	Leo's Gypsy Dancer	113	Mingling Glances	112	103,974	1:48.40	102
1999	Shires Ende	4	Martinez W.	117	Formal Tango	116	Uanme	112	107,508	1:49.00	97
2000	Colstar	4	A. Delgado	121	Pricearose	113	Histoire Sainte	113	102,300	1:47.44	102
2001	Colstar	5	J.K. Court	121	Solvig	115	Megans Bluff	119	107,136	1:48.79	100
2002	Voodoo Dancer	4	J.A. Santos	120	Blue Moon	116	Solvig	116	104,718	1:46.91	102
2003	Ipi Tombe	5	P. Day	123	Kiss the Devil	116	Quick Tip	117	101,928	1:47.70	99

Beyer Index: 98.77

LONE STAR DERBY, 1 1/8 Miles,
3-Year-Olds, Lone Star Park, 2003 Purse: $500,000

Year	Winner	Age	Jockey	Wt.	Second	Wt.	Third	Wt.	Win Value	Time	Beyer
1997	Anet	3	D.R. Flores	122	Frisk Me Now	122	Holzmeister	122	140,000	1:40.80	105
1998	Smolderin Heart	3	T.T. Doocy	122	Shot of Gold	122	Troy's Play	122	145,000	1:46.20	89
1999	T. B. Track Star	3	E.M. Martin Jr.	122	Desert Demon	122	Congratulate	122	165,000	1:42.92	103
2000	Tahkodha Hills	3	E.M. Coa	122	Jeblar Sez Who	122	Big Number	122	180,000	1:44.05	90
2001	Percy Hope	3	J.K. Court	122	Fifty Stars	122	Gift of the Eagle	122	292,500	1:50.27	93
2002	Wiseman's Ferry	3	J.F. Chavez	122	Tracemark	122	Peekskill	122	277,500	1:49.92	104
2003	Dynever	3	E.S. Prado	122	Most Feared	122	Commander's Affair	122	277,500	1:50.43	98

Beyer Index: 97.43

LONE STAR PARK HANDICAP, 1 1/16 Miles,
3-Year-Olds and Up, Lone Star Park, 2003 Purse: $300,000

Year	Winner	Age	Jockey	Wt.	Second	Wt.	Third	Wt.	Win Value	Time	Beyer
1997	Connecting Terms	4	L. Melancon	113	Humble Seven	112	Isitingood	122	120,000	1:41.80	104
1998	Mocha Express	4	M.St. Julien	114	Prince of the Mt.	114	Dickey Rickey	114	123,000	1:42.17	103
1999	Mocha Express	5	M. St. Julien	108	Littlebitlively	116	Nite Dreamer	113	183,300	1:43.20	108
2000	Luftikus	4	D.R. Flores	114	Nite Dreamer	118	Sultry Substitute	114	180,000	1:40.87	109
2001	Dixie Dot Com	6	D.R. Flores	118	Fan the Flame	113	Big Numbers	114	180,000	1:40.53	111
2002	Congaree	4	P. Day	119	Prince Iroquois	115	Mercenary	115	180,000	1:42.96	109
2003	Pie n Burger	5	H.J. Theriot II	117	Bluesthestandard	120			180,000	1:42.03	107
					Maysville Slew	114					

Beyer Index: 107.29

LONG BRANCH BREEDERS' CUP, 1 1/16 Miles,
3-Year-Olds, Monmouth Park, 2003 Purse: $100,000

Year	Winner	Age	Jockey	Wt.	Second	Wt.	Third	Wt.	Win Value	Time	Beyer
1994	Meadow Flight	3	J. Bravo	120	Red Tazz	114	Don's Sho	114	47,370	1:43.80	111
1995	Pyramid Peak	3	W.H. McCauley	120	Suave Prospect	120	Mighty Magee	118	47,250	1:44.00	108
1996	Dr. Caton	3	J. Bravo	112	Devil's Honor	122	Clash by Night	114	45,000	1:41.80	102
1997	Jules	3	A. Gryder	114	Leestown	120	Capture the Gold	114	60,000	1:42.40	105
1998	Favorite Trick	3	P. Day	116	Tomorrows Cat	113	Arctic Sweep	114	60,000	1:43.20	101
1999	Ghost Story	3	R.G. Davis	112	Unbridled Jet	114	Clever Gem	114	60,000	1:42.60	100
2000	Thistyranthasclass	3	J.A. Velez Jr.	114	Graeme Hall	120	Summinitup	114	60,000	1:43.60	105
2001	Burning Roma	3	R. Wilson	122	This Fleet Is Due	114	Thunder Blitz	122	60,000	1:43.28	99
2002	Puck	3	M. Aguilar	122	Shah Jehan	114	Stephentown	114	60,000	1:44.35	97
2003	Max Forever	3	J.C. Ferrer	113	Christine's Outlaw	115	Chilly Rooster	112	60,000	1:43.56	99

Beyer Index: 102.70

For previous runnings, see 1994 Manual

LONGACRES MILE HANDICAP, 1 Mile,
3-Year-Olds and Up, Emerald Downs, 2003 Purse: $250,000

Year	Winner	Age	Jockey	Wt.	Second	Wt.	Third	Wt.	Win Value	Time	Beyer
1993	Adventuresome Love		G. Baze	117	Sneakin Jake	118	For the Children	116	48,050	1:34.60	93
1994	Want a Winner		V. Belvoir	119	Sneakin Jake	118	Forgotten Days	114	48,250	1:35.20	87
1995	L.J. Express		M. Allen	119	Funboy	121	Secret Damascus	115	50,350	1:34.60	94
1996	Isitingood	5	D.R. Flores	117	Cleante	121	Humpty's Hoedown	114	110,000	1:35.60	105
1997	Kid Katabatic	4	C. Loseth	113	Hesabull	119	Liberty Road	114	110,000	1:34.20	105
1998	Wild Wonder	4	E. Delahoussaye	121	Mocha Express	114	Hal's Pal	117	110,000	1:33.20	111
1999	Budroyale	6	G.K. Gomez	119	Mike K	117	Kid Katabatic	116	137,500	1:34.60	106
2000	Edneator	4	G.V. Mitchell	111	Big Ten	119	Crafty Boy	114	137,500	1:33.20	104
2001	Irisheyesareflying	5	I.L. Puglisi	117	Handy N Bold	119	Makors Mark	116	137,500	1:34.60	96
2002	Sabertooth	4	N.J. Chaves	114	Moonlight Meeting	119	San Nicolas	115	137,500	1:35.40	100
2003	Sky Jack	7	R.A. Baze	123	Poker Brad	116	Lord Nelson	116	137,500	1:33.00	105

Beyer Index: 100.55

For previous runnings, refer to 1992 Manual; Run at Yakima, 1993–1995; Run at Longacres prior to 1993

LOS ANGELES TIMES HANDICAP, 6 Furlongs,
3-Year-Olds and Up, Hollywood Park, 2003 Purse: $200,000

Year	Winner	Age	Jockey	Wt.	Second	Wt.	Third	Wt.	Win Value	Time	Beyer
1955	Karim	5	G. Glisson	112	History Book	110	The Character	109	15,850	1:09.20	
1956	Colonel Mack	4	R. Neves	119	Stranglehold	103	Poona II	117	15,150	1:09.00	
1957	Porterhouse	6	J. Longden	123	Flight History	110	Corn Husker	119	32,700	1:20.80	
1958	How Now	5	W. Harmatz	114	Golden Notes	113	The Searcher	109	31,150	1:21.60	
1959	Hillsdale	4	T. Barrow	124	Seaneen	117	Amerigo	116	32,300	1:21.00	
1960	Finnegan	4	R. Neves	113	Clandestine	116	Dotted Swiss	108	31,400	1:20.80	
1961	T.V. Lark	4	J. Longden	121	New Policy	117	First Balcony	111	33,100	1:21.20	
1962	Winonly	5	W. Harmatz	118	Crazy Kid	106	Windy Sands	110	33,550	1:21.60	
1963	Doc Jocoy	4	W. Harmatz	117	Crazy Kid	116	Winonly	123	32,850	1:20.80	
1964	Cyrano	5	J.L. Rotz	124	Quita Dude	114	Admiral's Voyage	121	32,900	1:21.40	

Year	Winner	Age	Jockey	Wt.	Second	Wt.	Third	Wt.	Win Value	Time	Beyer
1965	Native Diver	6	J. Lambert	126	Viking Spirit	126	Tronado	115	32,800	1:20.00	
1966	Nasharco	4	B. Jennings	113	Pelegrin	116	Aurelius II	111	32,200	1:21.60	
1967	Native Diver	8	J. Lambert	128	Shebason	111	Chiclero	114	32,150	1:21.00	
1968	Rising Market	4	L. Pincay Jr	117	Aurelius II	113	Pedrinho	112	32,050	1:20.60	
1968	Kissin' George	5	W. Mahorney	128	Dr. Roy E.	115	Son Jack	112	32,050	1:21.20	
1969	Indulto	6	D. Pierce	122	Rising Market	124	Dewan	121	33,850	1:20.60	
1970	Ack Ack	4	D. Pierce	126	Right or Wrong	114	Baffle	123	31,250	1:20.60	
1971	Fleet Surprise	5	D. Pierce	114	Inverness Drive	115	Master Hand	111	38,900	1:20.80	
1972	Triple Bend	4	D. Pierce	123	Single Agent	122	Miles Tyson	119	37,600	1:19.80	
1973	Soft Victory	5	D. Pierce	118	Crusading	124	Convenience	117	31,850	1:21.00	
1974	Ancient Title	4	L. Pincay Jr	126	Woodland Pines	118	Soft Victory	118	32,200	1:20.40	
1975	Big Band	5	L. Pincay Jr	117	Century's Envoy	121	Shirley's Ch'n	120	32,300	1:20.60	
1976	Century's Envoy	5	S. Hawley	123	Home Jerome	116	Sport'ng Goods	120	31,950	1:20.80	
1977	Beat Inflation	4	D.G. McHargue	120	Full Out	117	Mark's Place	126	30,500	1:20.20	
1978	J.O. Tobin	4	S. Cauthen	130	Maheras	125	Drapier	121	30,200	1:21.40	
1979	Hawk'ns Special	4	D.G. McHargue	117	White Rammer	117	Whatsyourpleasure	117	31,350	1:08.40	
1980	Beau's Eagle	4	L. Pincay Jr	123	Real Soul	116	Minstrel Grey	114	32,400	1:08.20	
1981	Doonesbury	4	S. Hawley	121	Reb's Golden Ale	115	Summer Time Guy	122	37,900	1:08.80	
1982	T'rr'sto's Singer	5	P.A. Valenzuela	113	Remember John	115	Petro D. Jay	116	47,800	1:09.20	
1983	Mr. Prime Minister	7	M.A. Pedroza	115	Poley	118	Unreal Zeal	107	45,500	1:09.80	
1984	Night Mover	4	E. Delahoussaye	118	Debonaire Junior	113	Croeso	117	47,150	1:08.40	
1985	Charging Falls	4	W. Shoemaker	114	Fifty Six Ina Row	117	Premiership	115	48,650	1:08.80	
1986	Rosie's K.T.	5	P.A. Valenzuela	116	Mane Magic	116	Much Fine Gold	112	47,050	1:10.00	
1987	Bedside Promise	5	G.L. Stevens	126	Bolder Than Bold	117	Lincoln Park	115	46,200	1:08.40	
1988	Olympic Prospect	4	A. Solis	116	Happy in Space	113	Sylvan Express	119	47,700	1:08.80	
1989	Sam Who	4	L. Pincay Jr	118	Prospectors Gamble	114	Mi Preferido	119	46,200	1:09.40	
1990	Timeless Answer	4	R.G. Davis	114	Prospectors Gamble	116	Sam Who	120	64,500	1:08.80	108
1991	Black Jack Road	7	R.A. Baze	117	Sunny Blossom	121	Tanker Port	116	62,000	1:09.00	112
1992	Cardmania	6	E. Delahoussaye	118	Gray Slewpy	119	Robyn Dancer	119	61,200	1:08.60	109
1993	Star of the Crop	4	G.L. Stevens	119	Fabulous Champ.	116	Wild Harmony	116	63,200	1:08.60	105
1994	J.F. Williams	5	C.J. McCarron	115	Gundaghia	118	Thirty Slews	120	61,900	1:09.00	108
1995	Forest Gazelle	4	Desormeaux KJ	116	Lucky Forever	114	Cardmania	119	83,650	1:07.80	113
1996	Abaginone	5	Stevens G. L.	119			Score Quick	115	53,480	1:08.20	111
	Paying Dues	4	Antley C. W.	115					53,480	1:08.20	
1997	Men's Exclusive	4	Pincay L. Jr.	117	First Intent	117	Gold Land	115	80,970	1:08.80	117
1998	Gold Land	4	Desormeaux K. J.	116	Mr. Doubledown	119	The Exeter Man.	114	64,800	1:08.00	114
1999	Son of a Pistol	7	A. Solis	122	Men's Exclusive	118	Ray of Sunshine.	118	63,300	1:08.00	109
2000	Highland Gold	5	C.J. McCarron	115	Mellow Fellow	113	Your Halo.	114	64,260	1:09.11	106
2001	Caller One	4	C.S. Nakatani	124	Stormy Jack	115	Rapidough	115	64,380	1:08.35	116
2002	Kona Gold	8	A. Solis	125	No Armistice	116	Komax	114	64,500	1:08.72	113
2003	Hombre Rapido	6	J. Valdivia Jr.	116	Publication	116	Giovannetti	116	120,000	1:08.49	107

Beyer Index: 110.57

LOUISVILLE HANDICAP, 1 3/8 Miles (Turf),
3-Year-Olds and Up, Churchill Downs, 2003 Purse: $112,000

Year	Winner	Age	Jockey	Wt.	Second	Wt.	Third	Wt.	Win Value	Time	Beyer
1994	L'Hermine	5	L. Melancon	110	Llandaff	116	Snake Eyes	118	70,525	1:48.36	100
1995	Lindon Lime	5	C. Perret	114	Caesour	116	Snake Eyes	116	72,800	1:48.12	108
1996	Nash Terrace	4	D. Barton	105	Vladivostok	117	Hawkeye Bay	110	71,760	2:18.82	106
1997	Chorwon	4	C.H. Borel	113	Down the Aisle	111	Snake Eyes	116	67,952	2:19.45	100
1998	Chorwon	5	P. Day	114	African Dancer	114	Thesaurus	110	69,812	2:17.10	103
1999	Chorwon	6	C.H. Borel	114	Buff	117	Keats and Yeats.	115	67,890	2:14.15	102
2000	Buff	5	F.C. Torres	113	Williams News	116	Royal Strand.	115	71,734	2:14.31	105
2001	With Anticipation	6	J.K. Court	112	Profit Option	112	Gritty Sandie	115	68,138	2:16.28	109
2002	Pisces	5	R.J. Albarado	116			Red Mountain.	114	47,335	2:15.82	101
	Classic Par	4	D.J. Meche	114							

Two Point Two Mill finished first but was disqualified and placed eighth

2003	Kim Loves Bucky	6	S.J. Sellers	117	Rochester	117	Dr. Kashnikow	117	69,440	2:14.09	104

Beyer Index: 103.80

For previous runnings, refer to 1994 Manual

MAC DIARMIDA HANDICAP, 1 3/8 Miles (Turf),
3-Year-Olds and Up, Gulfstream Park, 2003 Purse: $100,000

Year	Winner	Age	Jockey	Wt.	Second	Wt.	Third	Wt.	Win Value	Time	Beyer
1995	Kings Fiction	3	R.G. Davis	112	Ops Smile	112	Mecke	113	30,000	1:43.00	87
1996	A Real Zipper	3	A.T. Gryder	114	Tour's Big Red	114	Shananie's Finale	114	30,000	1:42.60	91
1997	Mecke	5	J.D. Bailey	122	Fabulous Frolic	114	Spicilege	111	45,000	2:05.80	101
1998	Copy Editor	6	J.D. Bailey	114	Inkatha	114	Lafitte The Pirate	112	60,000	2:16.60	105
1999	Panama City	5	J.D. Bailey	114	The Kaiser	113	Notoriety	111	60,000	2:20.60	105
2000	Unite's Big Red	6	J.F. Chavez	113	Thesaurus	112	Carpenter's Halo.	113	60,000	2:12.14	97
2002	Crash Course	6	J.D. Bailey	114	Unite's Big Red	112	Eltawaasul.	112	60,000	2:12.67	102
2003	Riddlesdown	6	R.I. Velez	113	Macaw	114	Just Listen.	113	60,000	2:14.75	104

Beyer Index: 99

SENATOR KEN MADDY JR. HANDICAP, About 6 1/2 Furlongs (Turf), Fillies and Mares 3-Year-Olds and Up, Santa Anita, 2003 Purse: $112,000

Year	Winner	Age	Jockey	Wt.	Second	Wt.	Third	Wt.	Win Value	Time	Beyer
1994	Starolamo	5	K.J. Desormeaux	117	Sophisticatedcielo	114	Beautiful Gem	115	47,475	1:16.07	100
1995	Denim Yenem	3	C.J. McCarron	115	Miss L Attack	116	Jacodra's Devil	116	60,400	1:14.92	105
1996	Dixie Pearl	4	E. Delahoussaye	116	Ski Dancer	119	Cat's Cradle	118	66,400	1:12.33	105
1997	Madame Pandit	4	E. Delahoussaye	118	Advancing Star	120	Highest Dream	116	60,000	1:13.82	105
1998	Dance Parade	4	K.J. Desormeaux	120	Advancing Star	121	Green Jewel	116	60,000	1:13.87	99
1999	Hula Queen	5	A. Solis	116	Desert Lady	121	Ecudienne	117	67,740	1:13.05	100
2000	Evening Promise	4	K.J. Desormeaux	118	Strawberry Way	114	Southern House	114	67,020	1:13.05	95
2001	A La Reine	4	A. Solis	115	Nanogram	111	Global	113	66,240	1:13.27	93
2002	Rolly Polly	4	P.A. Valenzuela	119	I'm the Business	117	Nanogram	113	68,460	1:12.86	99
2003	Belleski	4	V. Espinoza	117	Buffythecenterfold	116	Icantgoforthat	115	67,200	1:12.37	99

Beyer Index: 100

Run as Autumn Days Handicap prior to 1999. For previous runnings, refer to 1994 Manual.

MARYLAND BREEDERS' CUP HANDICAP, 6 Furlongs, 3-Year-Olds and Up, Pimlico Race Course, 2003 Purse: $120,000

Year	Winner	Age	Jockey	Wt.	Second	Wt.	Third	Wt.	Win Value	Time	Beyer
1987	Purple Mountain	5	E. Ortiz Jr	111	Little Bold John	120	Berngoo	106	100,100	1:24.40	
1988	Fireplug	5	J.F. Hampshire	116	Harriman	117	High Brite	121	35,620	1:10.60	
1989	King's Nest	4	J. Rocco	120	Silano	115	Regal Intention	119	92,760	1:09.60	
1990	Norquestor	4	C. Perret	115	Kechi	115	Amerrico's Bullet	112	93,540	1:09.40	111
1991	Jew'ler's Choice	6	C.J. McCarron	115	Shuttleman	116	Hadif	118	92,610	1:10.20	104
1992	Potentiality	6	P. Day	117	Smart Alec	114	Boom Towner	117	93,300	1:10.20	106
1993	Senor Speedy	4	J.D. Bailey	117	He Is Risen	115	Who Wouldn't	113	93,390	1:09.60	110
1994	Secret Odds	4	E.S. Prado	119	Honor the Hero	117	Linear	119	93,615	1:10.20	109
1995	Commanche Trail	4	M.E. Smith	113	Goldminer's Dream	116	Marry Me Do	114	92,850	1:09.20	109
1996	Forest Wildcat	5	J. Bravo	109	Kayrawan	113	Demaloot Demashoot	115	129,720	1:09.00	109
1997	Cat Be Nimble	5	J. Rocco	118	Political Whit	116	Excelerate	114	127,560	1:10.00	105
1998	Richter Scale	4	J.D. Bailey	117	Trafalger	115	Original Gray	112	120,000	1:09.40	106
1999	Yes It's True	3	J.D. Bailey	113	The Trader's Echo	109	Purple Passion	114	120,000	1:09.20	118
2000	Dr. Max	4	S.J. Sellers	113	Moon Over Prospect	114	Crucible	113	60,000	1:10.91	101
2001	Disco Rico	4	H. Vega	118	Flame Thrower	114	Istintaj	116	120,000	1:10.40	106
2002	Snow Ridge	4	M.E. Smith	120	Smile My Lord	113	Clever Gem	116	120,000	1:10.06	114
2003	Pioneer Boy	5	J. Rose	113	Sassy Hound	113	Highway Prospector	115	60,000	1:10.35	105
							Tasty Caberneigh	114			

Beyer Index: 108.07

MATCHMAKER HANDICAP, 1 1/8 Miles (Turf), Fillies and Mares 3-Year-Olds and Up, Monmouth Park, 2003 Purse: $100,000

Year	Winner	Age	Jockey	Wt.	Second	Wt.	Third	Wt.	Win Value	Time	Beyer
1967	Politely	4	R. Broussard	118	Straight Deal	123	Gamely	114	30,000	1:55.20	
1968	Politely	5	A. Cordero Jr	123	Green Glade	115	Amerigo Lady	118	30,000	1:55.20	
1969	Gallant Bloom	3	J.L. Rotz	117	Gamely	123	Singing Rain	118	30,000	1:55.40	
1970	Dedicated to Sue	4	M. Hole	113	Cold Comfort	108	Office Queen	121	30,000	1:56.40	
1971	Deceit	3	J.L. Rotz	113	Sea Saga	114	Double Delta	125	30,000	1:56.80	
1972	Numbered Account	3	L. Pincay Jr	115	Honestous	110	Alma North	115	30,000	1:57.60	
1973	Alma North	4	F. Lovato	118	Light Hearted	121	Susan's Girl	125	30,000	1:55.20	
1974	Desert Vixen	4	L. Pincay Jr	123	Coraggioso	115	Twixt	123	3,000	1:55.20	
1975	Susan's Girl	6	R. Broussard	121	Aunt Jin	114	Pink Tights	114	20,000	1:54.20	
1976	Dancers Countess	4	C.J. McCarron	119	Vodka Time	114	Garden Verse	119	20,000	1:56.00	
1977	Mississippi Mud	4	J. Tejeira	119	Vodka Time	114	Lucie Manet	124	30,000	1:54.20	
1978	Queen Lib	3	D.MacBeth	112	Debby's Turn	114	Dottie's Doll	115	25,000	1:56.40	
1979	Warfever	4	J.L. Samyn	113	Smooth Journey	106	La Soufriere	118	25,000	2:03.20	
1980	Just a Game II	4	D. Brumfield	120	La Soufriere	115	Record Acclaim	115	25,000	1:57.60	
1981	Mairzy Doates	5	C.B. Asmussen	120	Honey Fox	120	Little Bonny	120	35,000	1:56.00	
1982	Hunston	4	J.L. Samyn	114	Trevita	118	Kuja Happa	115	35,000	1:58.60	
1983	Luminaire	4	B. Thornburg	113	Vestris	113	Lonely Balladier	113	25,000	1:56.80	
1984	Sabin	4	E. Maple	123	Doblique	113	Virgin Bride	113	30,000	1:53.80	
1985	Key Dancer	4	J.D. Bailey	118	Forest Maiden	118	Dictina	115	30,000	2:02.40	
1986	Lake Country	5	V. Bracciale Jr	118	Capo di Monte	120	Top Socialite	120	60,000	1:54.60	
1987	Carotene	4	D.J. Seymour	118	Spruce Fir	115	Cadabra Abra	120	73,500	1:56.60	
1988	Magdelaine	5	E. Maple	120	Spruce Fir	115	Carotene	120	60,000	1:56.20	
1989	Spruce Fir	6	D.B. Thomas	113	Ravinella	120	Native Mommy	120	90,000	1:53.40	
1990	Capades	4	A. Cordero Jr	120	Gaily Gaily	115	Summer Secretary	118	90,000	1:53.60	105
1991	Miss Josh	5	L. Pincay Jr	123	Whip Cream	113	Le Famo	113	90,000	1:54.00	104
1992	Radiant Ring	4	R.E. Colton	115	Highland Crystal	118	La Gueriere	118	60,000	1:55.80	100
1993	Fairy Garden	5	M.E. Smith	118	Saratoga Source	118	Logan's Mist	118	60,000	1:47.80	91
1994	Alice Springs	4	J.A. Krone	118	Hero's Love	118	Cox Orange	118	60,000	1:55.20	105

Year	Winner	Age	Jockey	Wt.	Second	Wt.	Third	Wt.	Win Value	Time	Beyer
1995	Avie's Fancy	4	W.H. McCauley	113	Plenty of Sugar	118	Northern Emerald	113	60,000	1:54.00	100
1996	Powder Bowl	4	D.S. Rice	113	Class Kris	120	Turkish Tryst	114	60,000	1:54.60	102
1998	Bursting Forth	4	M.E. Verge	116	French Buster	116	Gastronomical	113	60,000	1:48.40	97
1999	Natalie Too	5	J. Bravo	116	Saralea	116	U R Unforgetable	120	60,000	1:46.81	103
2000	Horatia	4	J.A. Santos	114	Camella	120	Champagne Royal	114	60,000	1:47.52	95
2001	Batique	5	J.C. Ferrer	113	Melody Queen	114	Lucky Lune	114	60,000	1:46.19	99
2002	Clearly	5	E.M. Coa	115	Siringas	116	Platinum Tiara	115	60,000	1:47.76	95
2003	Volga	5	J. Bravo	116	Something Ventured	117	Cocktailsandreams	115	60,000	1:48.22	97

Beyer Index: 99.46

MEMORIAL DAY HANDICAP, 1 1/16 Miles,
3-Year-Olds and Up, Calder Race Course, 2003 Purse: $100,000

Year	Winner	Age	Jockey	Wt.	Second	Wt.	Third	Wt.	Win Value	Time	Beyer
1971	Anchorage	4	J. Moseley	108	Caw King	113	Black Pipe	119	6,600	1:39.00	
1972	Willmar	4	K. Knapp	121	Tall Fellow	117	Asher	111	9,600	1:45.20	
1973	Correbtoso	6	R. Danjean	116	Great Divide	121	Asher	104	10,620	1:47.80	
1974	Snurb	4	G. St. Leon	121	Stariway to Stars	113	Somewhat Striking	113	14,040	1:46.20	
1975	Plagiarize	4	G. St. Leon	118	Rimsky II.	115	Trusted	115	13,800	1:45.80	
1976	Freepet	6	R. Broussard	117	Chilean Chief	119	Rastaferian	112	20,700	1:53.80	
1977	Lightning Thrust	4	G. St. Leon	121	Jatski	110	What a Threat	116	21,780	1:45.80	
1978	One Moment	5	J. Giovanni	114	Out Door Johnny	115	Haverty	112	21,240	1:52.20	
1979	Great Sound	5	W. Guerra	115	Raymond Earl	123	Prince Misko	116	20,835	1:45.40	
1980	Poverty Boy	5	M. Fromin	119	J. Rodney G.	115	Irish Swords	117	20,565	1:45.60	
1982	Two's a Plenty	5	A. Smith Jr.	122	Catch That Pass	114	Poking	117	19,470	1:45.40	
1983	Bolivar	6	S. Soto	116	Dallas Express	114	Gray Adorn	115	23,700	1:46.00	
1985	Rexson's Hope	4	G. Bain	113	Brother Liam	121	Amerilad	115	33,660	1:43.60	
1988	Billie Osage	4	G. St. Leon	116	Fabulous Devotion	110	Engrupido II	114	33,150	1:46.20	
1989	Hotting Star	4	J. Velez Hr.	116	Val D'enchere	116	Bright Baloon	111	33,300	1:41.20	
1990	Primal	5	H. Castillo Jr.	122	Eagle Watch	114	Public Account	113	33,180	1:47.40	
1991	S.W. Wildcard	5	P. Rodriguez	110	So Dashing	119	Bold Circle	113	34,110	1:46.80	
1992	Jodi's Sweetie	4	J. Duarte	114	Scottish Ice	114	Bidding Proud	113	30,000	1:44.20	96
1993	Boots 'n Buck	4	M. Russ	116	Yankee Axe	119	Darian's Reason	112	30,000	1:53.80	95
1994	Final Sunrise	4	P. Rodriguez	113	Crucial Trial	114	Bill Mooney	112	30,000	1:51.80	94
1995	Mr. Light Tres	6	K. Chapman	113	Fabulous Frolic	112	Flying American	116	30,000	1:47.00	92
1996	Marcie's Ensign	3	E.M. Coa	115	Derivative	114	Halo Bird	110	30,000	1:50.00	108
1997	Vilhelm	5	J.C. Ferrer	114	Sir Bear	113	Donthelumbertrader	118	30,000	1:40.80	100
1998	Born Mighty	4	J.A. Rivera II	114	Hard Rock Ridge	114	Auroral	114	30,000	1:40.80	94
1999	Wicapi	7	E.M. Coa	116	Dancing Guy	114	Golf Game	112	30,000	1:46.60	98
2000	Danmcing Guy	5	J.C. Ferrer	121	Reporter	111	Groomstick Stock's	111	45,000	1:46.28	108
2001	Hal's Hope	4	R.I. Velez	115	American Halo	115	Tahkodha Hills	118	45,000	1:45.81	107
2002	Best of the Rest	7	C. Velasquez	123	High Ideal	112	Hal's Hope	117	60,000	1:44.75	109
2003	Dancing Guy	8	R.I. Velez	113	Shotgun Fire	110	High Ideal	113	60,000	1:45.56	92

Beyer Index: 99.42

MIAMI MILE BREEDERS' CUP HANDICAP, 1 Mile (Off the Turf),
3-Year-Olds and Up, Calder Race Course, 2003 Purse: $150,000

Year	Winner	Age	Jockey	Wt.	Second	Wt.	Third	Wt.	Win Value	Time	Beyer
1987	Blazing Bart	3	J.A. Santos	117	Silver Voice	115	New Colony	114	93,630	1:44.20	
1988	Simply Majestic	4	J.D. Bailey	117	Sal d'Enchere	116	Racing Star	115	93,900	1:43.60	
1989	Simply Majestic	5	H. Castillo Jr.	117	Maceo	113	Bold Circle	110	93,510	1:48.60	
1990	Public Account	5	P. Rodriguez	115	Bold Circle	112	Primal	126	93,300	1:52.00	107
1991	Run Turn	4	G. St. Leon	120	Scottish Ice	116	Hidden Tomahawk	112	93,150	1:52.80	98
1992	Jodi's Sweetie	4	J.D. Bailey	115	Walkie Talker	114	Futurist	117	94,140	1:43.80	104
1993	Carterista	4	M. Lee	117	Wild Forest	112	Mr. Explosive	112	95,610	1:47.40	96
1994	The Vid	4	R.R. Douglas	114	Mr. Angel	118	Carterista	116	94,350	1:48.20	104
1995	Elite Jeblar	5	E. Fires	113	Myrmidon	117	Fabulous Frolic	114	94,200	1:47.60	96
1996	Satellite Nealski	3	J.C. Ferrer	112	Marcie's Ensign	115	Copy Editor	117	95,805	1:47.60	94
1997	Vilhelm	5	J.C. Ferrer	114	Marcie's Ensign	114	Elite Jeblar	113	120,000	1:36.60	103
1998	Unite's Big Red	4	E. Nunez	115	Fig Fest	113	Ensign Ray	113	120,000	1:36.60	100
							Copy Editor	117			
1999	Sharp Appeal	6	J.J. Castellano	114	Shamrock City	114	Hurrahy	115	135,000	1:35.60	102
2000	Band Is Passing	4	E.M. Coa	115	Hurrahy	115	Tiger Shark	112	90,000	1:37.28	100
2001	Mr. Livingston	4	A. Castellano Jr.	115	Honorable Pic	114	Pisces	112	90,000	1:33.75	100
2002	Band Is Passing	6	C.H. Velasquez	117	Pisces	116	Doowaley	113	90,000	1:37.78	105
2003	Tour of the Cat	5	A. Cabassa Jr.	115	Last Stand	113	Lavender's Lad	114	90,000	1:38.65	102

Beyer Index: 100.79

Run at 1 1/8 miles on turf, 1987-89, 1992-96; Run at 1 1/8 miles on main track, 1990-91; Off the turf in 2003.

MIESQUE, 1 Mile (Turf),
2-Year-Old Fillies, Hollywood Park, 2003 Purse: $100,000

Year	Winner	Age	Jockey	Wt.	Second	Wt.	Third	Wt.	Win Value	Time	Beyer
1991	More Than Willing	2	E. Delahoussaye	118	Stormagain	115	Looie Capote	114	61,875	1:35.40	93
1991	Hopeful Amber	2	D.R. Flores	114	Storm Ring	115	Crownette	114	61,875	1:36.60	81
1992	Creaking Board	2	K.J. Desormeaux	115	Ask Anita	117	Zoonaqua	121	137,500	1:32.80	82
1993	Tricky Code	2	C.S. Nakatani	116	Irish Forever	121	Roget's Fact	114	137,500	1:35.00	83
1994	Bail out Becky	2	Desormeaux KJ	121	Miss Union Avenue	121	Makin Whopee	117	110,000	1:37.20	89
1995	Antespend	2	C.W. Antley	121	Wheatly Special	121	Platinum Blonde	121	110,000	1:34.20	90
1996	Ascutney	2	E. Delahoussaye	116	Wealthy	116	Clever Plot	118	120,000	1:35.00	80
1997	Star's Proud Penny	2	G.K. Gomez	116	Superlative	121	Ransom the Dreamer	121	120,000	1:37.40	87
1998	Here's To You	2	E. Delahoussaye	116	Sweet Lady	118	Nausicaa	116	120,000	1:36.40	88
1999	Prairie Princess	2	Solis A	116	She's Classy	118	Mary Kies	121	120,000	1:37.20	85
2000	Fantastic Filly	2	G.K. Gomez	116	Smart Timing	115	Eminent	118	120,000	1:35.11	98
2001	Forty On Line	2	C.S. Nakatani	117	Riskaverse	121	Daisyago	118	120,000	1:36.38	85
2002	Atlantic Ocean	2	D.R. Flores	121	Tangle	114	Major Idea	121	120,000	1:34.63	89
2003	Mambo Slew	2	M.E. Smith	116	Ticker Tape	116	Winendynme	116	60,000	1:36.17	81

Beyer Index: 86.5

(EARLY TIMES) MINT JULEP HANDICAP, 1 1/16 Miles (Turf),
Fillies and Mares 4-Year-Olds and Up, Churchill Downs, 2003 Purse: $168,300

Year	Winner	Age	Jockey	Wt.	Second	Wt.	Third	Wt.	Win Value	Time	Beyer
1977	Satan's Cheer	5	M. Maganello	115	Comfort Zone	117	Decided Lady	115	14,300	1:24.00	
1978	Time for Pleasure	4	T. Barrow	120	Don't Cry Barbi	119	Dear Irish	119	14,609	1:23.40	
1979	Bold Rendezvous	4	A. Fernandez	115	Likely Exchange	116	Popped Corn	116	17,908	1:25.00	
1980	Likely Exchange	6	D.E. Whited	118	Nauti Lass	119	Dearyouloveme	117	19,728	1:24.40	
1981	Lillian Russell	4	R. Hirdes Jr	118	Run Ky. Run	121	Salud	114	19,468	1:23.20	
1982	Kate's Cabin	4	E. Snell	115	Mean Martha	112	Forever Cordial	114	23,855	1:25.20	
1983	Naskra Magic	4	P. Rubbicco	114	Excitable Lady	120	Charge My Account	112	23,433	1:36.60	
1984	Lass Trump	4	G. Patterson	111	Lady Hawthorn	114	Delhousie	111	26,267	1:37.00	
1985	Stave	4	C. Woods Jr	112	Gerrie Singer	120	Switching Trick	117	21,694	1:35.00	
1986	Zenobia Empress	5	E. Fires	120	Donuts Pride	120	Ante	117	28,418	1:35.80	
1987	Thunderdome	4	S. Bass	119	Acquire	119	No Choice	119	26,247	1:37.80	
1987	Innsbruck	4	S. Hawley	114	Fantasy Lover	114	Marianna's Girl	122	21,470	1:38.00	
1988	How I Wish	4	E. Fires	113	Gaily Gaily	113	No Choice	114	36,660	1:51.00	
1989	Here's Your Silver	4	M. McDowell	115	Lt. Lao	117	Danzig's Bride	114	37,115	1:50.40	
1990	Tunita	5	R. Thibeau	114	Port St. Mary	113	Flags Waving	112	25,821	1:43.80	89
1990	Phoenix Sunshine	5	J. Deegan	116	Vanna Turns	111	Carousel Baby	111	31,476	1:43.20	
1991	Dance for Lucy	5	L. Melancon	116	Welsh Muffin	113	Super Fan	118	37,148	1:43.00	102
1992	Lady Shirl	5	P. Johnson	123	Topsa	112	Behaving Dancer	119	37,083	1:41.41	104
1993	Classic Reign	4	F.A. Arguello Jr.	115	Tap Routine	113	Liz Cee	114	37,538	1:42.84	94
1994	Words of War	5	C. Marquez	117	Freewheel	116	Eurostorm	112	55,672	1:40.98	99
1995	Romy	4	J. Diaz	118	Olden Lek	114	Memories	113	54,941	1:42.69	102
1996	Bail Out Becky	4	C. Perret	118	Country Cat	117	Fluffkins	115	54,698	1:41.86	102
1997	Valor Lady	5	R.J. Albarado	114	My Secret	114	Everhope	114	71,238	1:41.20	96

Romy (Beyer: 96) finished first but was disqualified and placed fourth

Year	Winner	Age	Jockey	Wt.	Second	Wt.	Third	Wt.	Win Value	Time	Beyer
1998	B.A. Valentine	5	F. Torres	116	Lordy Lordy	113	Mingling Glances	112	70,804	1:41.42	96
1999	Mingling Glances	5	L. Melancon	113	Formal Tango	115	Red Cat	116	70,928	1:42.59	101
2000	Pratella	5	L. Melancon	118	Silver Comic	115	Histoire Sainte	113	69,378	1:43.08	99
2001	Megans Bluff	4	C. Perret	118	Sitka	109	Good Game	116	70,432	1:42.88	97
2002	Megans Bluff	5	C. Perret	118	Cozy Island	112	Solvig	117	69,998	1:42.87	98
2003	Kiss the Devil	5	L.J. Meche	115	Quick Tip	119	Cellars Shiraz	120	104,346	1:41.73	93

Beyer Index: 98

MISS PREAKNESS, 6 Furlongs,
3-Year-Old Fillies, Pimlico Race Course, 2003 Purse: $100,000

Year	Winner	Age	Jockey	Wt.	Second	Wt.	Third	Wt.	Win Value	Time	Beyer
1986	Marion's Madel	3	C.J. McCarron	115	Zigbelle		Babbling Brook		21,060	1:12.80	
1987	Cutlasee	3	C.J. McCarron	116	I'm Out		Pelcian Bay		21,158	1:12.60	
1988	Caromine	3	C.J. McCarron	115	Light Beat		Saved by Gracer		24,911	1:13.00	
1989	Montoya	3	L. Pincay Jr	118	Another Boom				22,470	1:10.60	
					Cojinx						
1990	Love Me a Lot	3	C.J. McCarron	115	Dixie Landera		Tabs		19,170	1:11.40	
1991	Missy's Music	3	M. Pino	114	Dixie Rouge		Accent Knightly		15,975	1:11.40	
1992	Toots La Mae	3	J. Bravo	113	Missy White Oak	118	Jazzy One	121	26,505	1:11.80	75
1993	My Rosa	3	E.S. Prado	113	Fighting Jet	121	Cole Blum	121	32,175	1:11.20	89
1994	Foolish Kisses	3	E.S. Prado	113	Aly's Conquest	114	Platinum Punch	113	32,730	1:12.40	93
1995	Lilly Capote	3	G.L. Stevens	122	Broad Smile	122	Norstep	122	32,640	1:10.80	88
1996	Nic's Halo	3	R. Wilson	115	Palette Knife	115	Crafty but Sweet	122	32,655	1:11.60	86
1997	Weather Vane	3	M. Pino	122	Move	122	Cayman Sunset	122	64,740	1:11.80	84

Year	Winner	Age	Jockey	Wt.	Second	Wt.	Third	Wt.	Win Value	Time	Beyer
1998	Storm Beauty	3	C.R. Woods Jr.	119	Brac Drifter	115	Hair Spray	122	45,000	1:10.80	93
1999	Hookedonthefeelin	3	G.L. Stevens	122	Silent Valay	122	Paula's Girl	122	60,000	1:11.20	90
2000	Lucky Livi	3	R. Wilson	119	Big Bambu	117	Swept Away	119	60,000	1:10.00	96
2001	Kimbralata	3	T. Dunkelberger	117	Carafe	117	Stormy Pick	122	60,000	1:11.20	93
2002	Vesta	3	M. Pino	117	Willa on the Move	117	Shameful	119	60,000	1:10.25	99
2003	Belong to Sea	3	J.J. Castellano	117	Chimichurri	122	Forever Partners	119	60,000	1:11.10	88

Beyer Index: 89.5

MODESTY HANDICAP, 1 3/16 Miles (Turf),
Fillies and Mares 3-Year-Old and Up, Arlington Park, 2003 Purse: $150,000

Year	Winner	Age	Jockey	Wt.	Second	Wt.	Third	Wt.	Win Value	Time	Beyer
1942	Lotopoise	3	S. Brooks	113	Questvive	113	Waygal	113	2,910	1:37.80	
1943	Burgoo Maid	3	G. Burns	111	Mar-Kell	125	Jerry Lee	109	4,475	1:27.40	
1944	Gold Princess	5	J. Higley	110	Night Shadow	112	Happy Issue	112	10,850	1:39.40	
1945	War Date	3	J. Adams	110	Night Shadow	114	Durazna	120	15,225	1:38.80	
1946	Athene	3	W. Mehrtens	111	Jack's Jill	112	Twosy	121	19,400	1:36.00	
1947	Sea Snack	4	M.N. Gonzalez	117	Miss Kimo	109	Blue Grass	115	19,600	1:11.60	
1948	Bewitch	3	H. Woodhouse	107	Tre Vit	113	Bogle	109	20,850	1:10.20	
1949	No Strings	4	F.A. Smith	101	Two Lea	111	Dandilly	108	19,150	1:10.00	
1950	Myrtle Charm	4	G. Laswell	121	Alsab's Day	121	Fabulous Shake	102	14,400	1:10.00	
1951	Sickle's Image	3	C. Swain	120	Asphalt	105	Two Rainbows	104	16,900	1:10.80	
1952	Real Delight	3	E. Arcaro	126	Sickle's Image	117	Dickie Sue	111	29,600	1:35.60	
1953	Belle Figura	4	D. Wagner	117	Gala Fete	116	Night-Phara	110	10,450	1:10.20	
1954	Sickle's Image	6	D. Dodson	118	Mimi Mine	112	Vixen Fixit	103	13,950	1:10.00	
1955	Insouciant	3	B. Fisk	111	Cajole	110	Queen Hopeful	120	13,850	1:43.40	
1956	Queen Hopeful	5	J. Adams	116	Blue Hawaii	109	Amoret	112	13,450	1:44.80	
1957	Grecian Ayr	4	L. Gilligan	109	Tremor	111	Estacion	116	13,475	1:43.60	
1958	Melody Mine	3	R.L. Barnett	108	Beautillion	118	Market Basket	122	13,500	1:10.80	
1959	A Glitter	4	C. Rogers	118	Tinkalero	120	Wayward Bird	107	9,925	1:10.00	
1960	Indian Maid	4	J.L. Rotz	123	Equifun	112	Judy Jump-Up	113	8,900	1:09.60	
1961	Indian Maid	5	J. Sellers	126	Equifun	111	Our Special Jet	109	9,325	1:09.80	
1962	Goldflower	4	H. Hinojosa	120	Gerts Image	114	Cherry Laurel	112	10,375	1:10.40	
1963	Hushaby	4	W. Hartack	117	Lucky Viola	112	Road Maid	112	9,925	1:23.00	
1964	Alecee	5	W. Blum	118	Abrogate	120	Hushaby	112	9,450	1:23.00	
1965	Isaduchess	4	K. Knapp	119	Tuzana	112	Abrogate	120	24,000	1:23.20	
1966	Margarethen	4	J. Nichols	118	Miss Rincon	114	Bea Hasty	114	12,525	1:37.40	
1966	Treasure Chest	3	J. Beebe	112	Lady Amigo	108	May's Guide	118	12,525	1:37.20	
1967	Amerivan	5	R. Turcotte	119	Ice Water	113	Turn to Talent	113	16,850	1:46.20	
1968	Ludham	4	J. Vasquez	117	Gabby Abbey	123	Doc Nan	113	13,800	1:44.40	
1981	Innocent Victim	3	R. Cox	108	Passolyn	113	Touch of Glamour	112	35,040	1:59.00	
1982	Office Wife	4	E. Fires	113	Sprite Flight	112	Touch of Glamour	117	33,750	1:58.20	
1983	Dana Calqui	5	F. Lovato Jr	114	Unknown Lady	113	Sar'h's Beauty	115	34,470	2:01.40	
1984	Jay's Sue	5	P. Day	123	Dictina	109	Pretty Perfect	113	43,719	2:01.20	
1985	Kapalua Butterfly	4	R.P. Romero	115	Trinado	116	Another Penny	111	44,265	1:55.00	
1986	Zenobia Empress	5	E. Fires	118	Navarchus	112	Flying Girl	118	53,580	1:44.00	
1987	Spruce Luck	6	D. Brumfield	114	Dancing on a Cloud	120	Autumn Glitter	114	34,080	1:51.60	
1989	Gaily Gaily	6	J.A. Krone	123	Baba Cool	117	Coolawin	115	52,740	1:58.20	
1990	Gaily Gaily	7	M.E. Smith	114	Coolawin	123	M'rsha's Dancer	114	51,405	1:55.40	98
1991	Lady Shirl	4	S.J. Sellers	120	Lyphover	114	Country Casual	114	45,000	1:56.40	97
1992	Tango Charlie	3	A.G. Sorrows Jr	114	Alcando	114	Hero's Love	117	45,000	1:58.60	95
1993	Hero's Love	5	E. Fires	120	Villandry	114	Silvered	120	60,000	1:55.20	93
1994	Assert Oneself	4	Valenzuela FH.	115	One Dreamer	117	Seventies	115	60,000	1:56.00	98
1996	Belle Of Cozzene	4	Pettinger D.R.	114	Trick Attack	112	Naskra Colors	114	60,000	1:58.20	105
1997	War Thief	5	Sellers S.J.	116	My Secret	114	Bog Wild	117	60,000	1:57.40	101
2000	Wade for Me	5	C.A. Emigh	116	Candleinthedark	113	Wild Heart Dancing	115	60,000	1:57.06	97
2001	Ioya Two	6	M. Guidry	115	Megans Bluff	118	Solvig	116	90,000	1:55.47	98
2002	England's Legend	5	R.R. Douglas	121	Quick Tip	114	Innit	116	90,000	1:55.69	101
2003	Owsley	5	R.R. Douglas	120	Bien Nicole	119	Beret	115	90,000	1:55.06	100

Beyer Index: 98.45

MONROVIA HANDICAP, About 6 1/2 Furlongs (Turf),
Fillies and Mares 3-Year-Olds and Up, Santa Anita, 2003 Purse: $109,300

Year	Winner	Age	Jockey	Wt.	Second	Wt.	Third	Wt.	Win Value	Time	Beyer
1968	Mellow Marsh	5	M. Vanenzuela	113	Pink Pigeon	115	Telepathy	112	16,900	1:13.40	
1969	Morgaise	4	D. Pierce	121	Desert Law	118	Grey Cricket	110	13,500	1:22.20	
1970	Beautiful Dream	5	J. Lambert	118	Pacific Cross	114	Lovers Quarrel	120	14,750	1:16.20	
1971	Atomic Wings	4	R. Kilborn	112	Formal Marriage	116	Sh'ke a Sh'd'w	114	17,850	1:13.40	
1972	Mia Mood	4	V. Tejada	113	Crowning Glory	119	Generous Portion	118	20,350	1:13.00	
1973	Tizna	4	F. Toro	119	Generous Portion	120	Soul Mate	120	22,700	1:13.80	
1974	Viva la Vivi	4	D. Pierce	118	Impressive Style	120	Charger's Star	113	17,800	1:15.00	
1975	Special Goddess	4	S. Hawley	116	Charger's Star	115	Miss Musket	124	20,700	1:13.80	

Year	Winner	Age	Jockey	Wt.	Second	Wt.	Third	Wt.	Win Value	Time	Beyer
1976	Winter Solstice	4	J. Lambert	117	Miss Tokyo	121	Exotic Age	115	20,300	1:17.60	
1977	Winter Solstice	5	M. Sellers	119	Nana Lee	116	Olive Wreath	113	27,600	1:13.60	
1978	Little Happiness	4	L. Pincay Jr	116	Perils of Pauline	115	Harvest Girl	119	26,200	1:16.00	
1979	Camarado	4	W. Shoemaker	119	Pet Label	115	Sister Julie	115	22,900	1:15.40	
1979	Palmistry	4	C.J. McCarron	114	Sing Back	113	Pressing Date	114	22,500	1:15.20	
1980	Fondre	5	F. Olivares	113	Powder Room	117	Celine	118	27,500	1:15.20	
1981	Kilijaro	5	M. Castaneda	127	Love You Dear	115	She Can't Miss	119	34,950	1:12.40	
1982	Cat Girl	4	C.J. McCarron	117	Excitable Lady	122	Chateau Dancer	117	41,250	1:14.60	
1983	Matching	5	R. Sibille	123	Irish O'Brien	115	Night Fire	115	40,600	1:13.20	
1984	Tangent	4	J.A. Garcia	117	Irish O'Brien	115	Frieda Frame	119	41,750	1:14.60	
1985	Lina Cav'leri	5	E. Delahoussaye	121	Air Distingue	117	Tangent	121	39,650	1:14.00	
1986	Water Crystals	5	G.L. Stevens	116	Baroness Direct	120	Solva	116	40,100	1:15.60	
1987	Sari's Heroine	4	P.A. Valenzuela	117	Lichi	116	Aberuschka	124	38,400	1:15.00	
1988	Aberuschka	6	G.L. Stevens	121	Pen Bal Lady	118	Acromacor	114	50,050	1:14.60	
1989	Daloma	5	F.H. Valenzuela	114	Valdemosa	116	Sadie B. Fast	116	49,550	1:16.20	
1990	Down Again	6	C.A. Black	117	Sexy Slew	111	Hot Novel	116	50,520	1:13.00	101
1991	Wedding B'guet	4	K.J. Desormeaux	115	Linda Card	118	Flower Girl	116	51,875	1:13.80	
1992	Middlef'rk Rapids	4	P.A. Valenzuela	116	Remarkably Easy	115	Crystal Gazing	121	51,150	1:12.40	100
1993	Glen Kate	6	C.A. Black	118	Bel's Starlet	122	Heart of Joy	121	48,650	1:12.80	103
1994	Mamselle Bebette	4	C.S. Nakatani	117	Shuggleswon	114	Kalita Melody	117	49,650	1:15.20	95
1995	Rabiadella	4	P.A. Valenzuela	117	Dezibelle's Star	114	Las Meninas	120	47,450	1:14.80	99
1996	Klassy Kim	5	G.F. Almeida	116	Ski Dancer	116	Baby Diamonds	114	65,650	1:14.40	97
1997	Grab The Prize	5	A. Solis	116	Finite E. F.	111	Evil's Pic	116	66,900	1:16.80	95
1998	Madame Pandit	5	E. Delahoussaye	118	Ski Dancer	115	Dixie Pearl	117	65,700	1:15.80	101
1999	Desert Lady	4	C.S. Nakatani	116	Sweet Mazarine	118	Supercilious	119	65,100	1:14.40	89
1999	Show Me The Stage	3	K.J. Desormeaux	117	Chinchim	116	Honest Lady	114	64,140	1:15.00	100
2000	Evening Promise	4	K.J. Desormeaux	120	Squall Linda	113	New Heaven	119	68,640	1:12.62	99
2001	Paga	4	M.E. Smith	117	Twin Set	115	Impeachable	115	70,890	1:15.09	97
2002	Lil Sister Stich	5	L. Pincay Jr	115	Pina Colada	115	I'm the Business	116	68,820	1:13.81	94
2003	Icantgoforthat	4	T. Baze	114	Polygreen	116	Spring Star	119	65,580	1:13.07	97

Beyer Index: 97.64

MORVICH HANDICAP, About 6 1/2 Furlongs (Turf), 3-Year-Olds and Up, Santa Anita, 2003 Purse: $110,800

Year	Winner	Age	Jockey	Wt.	Second	Wt.	Third	Wt.	Win Value	Time	Beyer
1994	Rotsaluck	3	F. Valenzuela	115	D'Hallevant	118	Didyme	115	47,925	1:13.66	115
1995	Score Quick	4	G. Almeida	113	Dramatic Gold	120	Fu Man Slew	114	60,700	1:14.60	111
1996	Comininalittlehot	5	K. Desormeaux	117	Wild Zone	116	Wavy Run	116	65,100	1:11.57	107
1997	Reality Road	5	C. Nakatani	115	Latin Dancer	116	Torch Rouge	115	60,000	1:13.60	107
1998	Musafi	4	G. Gomez	117	Fabulous Guy	114	Expelled	119	60,000	1:14.54	104
1999	Riviera	5	E. Ramsammy	118	Kahal	114	Howmaddouwantit	121	66,840	1:12.80	98
2000	El Cielo	6	J. Valdivia Jr	115	Kahal	119	Montemiro	116	67,020	1:12.00	107
2001	El Cielo	7	J. Valdivia Jr	123	Speak in Passing	116	Islander	115	64,680	1:11.46	111
2002	Master Belt	4	T.C. Baze	114	I Love Silver	116	Kachamandi	117	67,020	1:12.26	104
2003	King Robyn	3	A. Solis	117	Medicis	116	Geronimo	115	66,480	1:13.22	102

Beyer Index: 106.60

For previous runnings, refer to 1994 Manual

MR. PROSPECTOR HANDICAP, 6 Furlongs, 3-Year-Olds and Up, Gulfstream Park, 2003 Purse: $100,000

Year	Winner	Age	Jockey	Wt.	Second	Wt.	Third	Wt.	Win Value	Time	Beyer
1994	Binalong	5	J.D. Bailey	116	I Can't Believe		Golden Pro		30,000	1:09.60	108
1995	Sweet Beast	5	M.Smith	118	Exclusive Praline		Sweet Reality		30,000	1:09.20	110
1996	Meadow Monster	5	R.Wilson	114	Lord Carson	119	Ponche	118	30,000	1:09.40	117
1997	Punch Line	7	P.Day	116	Appealling Skier	122	Western Warrior	113	45,000	1:08.40	114
1998	Rare Rock	5	P.Day	116	Heckofaralph	115	Banjo	116	45,000	1:08.60	112
1999	Cowboy Cop	5	P. Day	114	Good and Tough	115	Mint	115	45,000	1:08.80	113
2000	Mountain Top	5	J.A. Santos	115	Lifeisawhirl	112	Silver Season	115	45,000	1:10.80	96
2001	Instintaj	5	J.D. Bailey	116	Miners Gamble	115	Smokin Pete	115	60,000	1:09.63	105
2002	Hook and Ladder	5	J.R. Velazquez	116	Kipperscope		Red's Honor	114	60,000	1:09.69	111
2003	Baileys Edge	6	G. Boulanger	114	Friendly Frolic		Out of Fashion	115	60,000	1:09.95	99

Beyer Index: 108.5

Run as Hallandale Handicap, 1946-2000. For previous runnings, refer to 1994 Manual

MY CHARMER HANDICAP, 1 1/8 Miles (Turf), Fillies and Mares 3-Year-Olds and Up, Calder Race Course, 2003 Purse: $100,000

Year	Winner	Age	Jockey	Wt.	Second	Wt.	Third	Wt.	Win Value	Time	Beyer
1984	Our Reverie	3	G. St. Leon	114	Id Am Fac	114	Break In		13,927	1:47.20	
1984	Burst of Colors	4	J.A. Santos	116	Ava Romance	111	Cosmic Sea Queen	115	13,928	1:47.60	
1985	Power Break	4	J.A. Santos	116	Duty Dance	117	Dictina	117	20,555	1:47.50	

Year	Winner	Age	Jockey	Wt.	Second	Wt.	Third	Wt.	Win Value	Time	Beyer
1985	Shocker T.	3	G. St. Leon	119	Erin's Dunlop	117	Spruce Luck	112	20,675	1:48.80	
1986	Donna's Dolly	4	M. Lee	112	Fritzie Bay	114	Thirty Zip	113	31,010	1:55.00	
1988	Princely Proof	5	R. Breen	113	Travelin Lieber	112	Judy's Red Shoes	114	33,870	1:46.20	
1988	Fama	5	J. Pezua	111	Singular Bequest	116	Ladanum	115	24,570	1:44.50	
1989	Sunny Issues	3	W. Guerra	109	Beauty Cream	119	Miss Unameable		28,830	1:45.40	
1989	Judy's Red Shoes	5	D. Valiente	117	Orange Motif	113	Chores at Dawn	113	29,130	1:45.60	
1990	Princess Mora	3	M. Gonzalez	111	Coolawin	118	Yestday's Kisses	115	36,000	1:47.60	
1991	Homeland	4	H. Castillo Jr	111	Seaquay	112	Calm Dancer	114	27,975	1:45.40	
1991	Primetime North	3	W. Ramos	112	Igmaar	112	Be Exclusive	113	27,825	1:45.60	
1992	Lady Shirl	5	E. Fires	120	Ratings	115	Seaquay	111	51,150	1:44.60	97
1993	Explosive Kate	5	D. Penna	118	Mia Bird Too	113	Kiwi Mint	114	30,000	1:46.40	93
1993	Julie La Rousse	4	J.D. Bailey	120	Marshua's River	114	Highland Crystal	115	30,000	1:45.60	98
1994	Chickasha	4	R. Lopez	115	Marshua's River	113	Always Nettie	114	30,000	1:47.20	94
1994	Caress	3	R.G. Davis	114	Putthepowdertoit	114	Cox Orange	116	60,000	1:50.60	101
1995	Danish	4	J.Santos	116	Cox Orange	119	Alice Springs	123	60,000	1:46.40	96
1996	Romy	5	F.Torres	114	Delta Love	114	Ms. mostly	115	60,000	1:45.60	96
1997	Overcharger	5	J.Rivera II.	116	Dance Clear	113	Hero's Pride	116	60,000	1:48.00	99
1998	Colcon	5	J.Bailey	118	Cuando	117	Winfama	117	60,000	1:50.51	101
1999	Crystal Symphony	3	C. Velazquez	114	Winfama	114	Khumba Mela	120	60,000	1:47.60	90
2000	Wild Heart Dancing	4	J.F. Chavez	116	Megans Bluff	116	Orange Sunset	114	60,000	1:47.58	98
	Megans Bluff finished first but was disqualified and placed second										
2001	Batique	5	J.F. Chavez	116	Please Sign In	114	Wander Man	114	60,000	1:49.85	95
2002	Wander Mom	4	E.M. Coa	114	Strawberry Blonde	114	Babae	121	60,000	1:48.43	96
2003	New Economy	5	R.B. Homeister Jr	115	Something Ventured	116	Ivanavinalot	113	60,000	1:46.97	96

Beyer Index: 96.43

NASHUA, 1 Mile,
2-Year-Olds, Aqueduct, 2003 Purse: $113,100

Year	Winner	Age	Jockey	Wt.	Second	Wt.	Third	Wt.	Win Value	Time	Beyer
1975	Lord Henribee	2	E. Maple	115	Cojak	120	Expletive Deleted	115	33,030	1:35.80	
1976	Nearly on Time	2	J. Vasquez	114	Ruthie's Native	114	Upper Nile	114	22,005	1:35.60	
1977	Quadratic	2	E. Maple	119	No Sir	114	Quip	114	21,975	1:35.40	
1978	Instrument Landing	2	J. Fell	114	Miroman	114	Bold Ruckus	117	26,520	1:37.00	
1979	Googolplex	2	L. Pincay Jr	117	Thanks to Tony	114	Comptroller	114	32,550	1:36.40	
1980	A Run	2	C.J. McCarron	114	Copper Mine	114	Triocala	114	35,460	1:37.20	
1981	Our Escapade	2	D. MacBeth	114	John's Gold	114	Hostage	114	35,460	1:37.60	
1982	I Enclose	2	R. Hernandez	114	Loose Cannon	114	Moment of Joy	114	35,280	1:36.80	
1983	Don Rickles	2	A. Cordero Jr	114	Arabian Gift	114	Raja's Shark	114	34,800	1:38.40	
1984	Stone White	2	R.G. Davis	119	Banner Bob	117	Old Main	114	71,550	1:38.20	
1985	Raja's Revenge	2	R.G. Davis	117	Royal Doulton	117	Bordeaux Bob	114	56,610	1:44.40	
1986	Bold Summit	2	C.W. Antley	114	Drachma	114	Perdition's Son	114	72,360	1:12.40	
1987	Cougarized	2	J.A. Santos	117	Blew By Em	119	Chicot County	117	104,160	1:46.00	
1988	Traskwood	2	A. Cordero Jr	117	Doc's Leader	119	Triple Buck	117	63,240	1:45.20	
1989	Champagneforashley	2	J. Vasquez	119	Armed for Peace	114	Flathorn	114	66,480	1:45.20	
1990	Kyle's Our Man	2	J.D. Bailey	114	Oregon	114	Vouch for Me	117	55,980	1:45.40	93
1991	Pine Bluff	2	C. Perret	124	Speakerphone	114	Best Decorated	114	75,960	1:46.00	98
1992	Dalhart	2	M.E. Smith	114	Rohwer	114	Peace Baby	114	74,640	1:44.60	99
1993	Popol's Gold	2	W.H. McCauley	114	Personal Merit	117	Sonny's Bruno	114	74,880	1:46.60	84
1994	Devious Course	2	F.T. Alvarado	114	Mighty Magee	112	Old Tascosa	122	65,580	1:37.40	88
1996	Jules	2	J. A.Santos	114	Shammy Davis	114	Sal's Drifter	114	68,340	1:36.80	95
1997	Coronado's Quest	2	M.E. Smith	122	Not Tricky	117	Dice Dancer	119	65,100	1:37.00	89
1998	Doneraile Court	2	J.D. Bailey	115	Successful Appeal	122	Exiled Groom	113	66,600	1:36.00	97
1999	Mass Market	2	M.E. Smith	117	Polish Miner	114	Parade Leader	117	67,020	1:38.60	88
2000	Ommadon	2	A.T. Gryder	115	Windsor Castle	115	Griffinite	115	67,920	1:36.74	90
2001	Listen Here	2	J.D. Bailey	117	Monthir	115	Thunder Days	115	65,680	1:37.61	95
2002	Added Edge	2	P. Husbands	122	Outer Reef	116	Boston Bull	122	65,820	1:36.77	98
2003	Read the Footnotes	2	J.D. Bailey	118	Paddington	120	Who Is Chris G.	116	67,860	1:36.48	92

Beyer Index: 93.46

NATIONAL JOCKEY CLUB HANDICAP, 1 1/8 Miles,
3-Year-Olds and Up, Hawthorne, 2003 Purse: $250,000

Year	Winner	Age	Jockey	Wt.	Second	Wt.	Third	Wt.	Win Value	Time	Beyer
1956	Better Goods	6	H. Viera	115	Jimmy the One	115	Key Biscayne	110	20,500	1:45.00	
1957	Point of Order	4	J. Fiesel,am	114	Bernburgoo	116	River Gate	109	20,050	1:52.20	
1958	Racetracker	5	J. Fieselman	114	Pete's Folly	118	Estacion	116	20,750	1:45.00	
1959	Easy Spur	3	J. Nichols	126	Redbird Wish	118	Pete's F'lly	117	18,650	1:49.40	
1960	American Comet	4	B. Walt	115	Rose's Gem	118	Redbird Wish	111	19,900	1:45.60	
1961	Currock	4	L. Spraker	118	Get Lucky	113	Santiago	113	21,250	1:51.60	
1962	Hoop Bound	5	L.C. Cook	109	K'rri San	112	Santiago	113	19,300	1:49.00	
1963	Tollway	5	L. Spraker	120	Kur'i San	117	Sonny Fleet	120	19,500	1:44.60	

Year	Winner	Age	Jockey	Wt.	Second	Wt.	Third	Wt.	Win Value	Time	Beyer
1964	Grand Stand	4	E. Coffman	113	Quita Dude	115	Barbaron	117	18,395	1:43.60	
1965	Ramblin Road	4	E. Coffman	119	Take Over	122	Untested	113	15,565	1:45.20	
1966	Sammyren	4	E. Fires	120	Eladio	115	Wild Card	111	20,900	1:45.00	
1967	Royal Course	4	J.R. Lopez	128	Hy Frost	116	Casing Tools	113	21,230	1:46.00	
1968	Hy Frost	5	T. Barrow	115	Road to Rock	116	Abe's Hope	114	18,425	1:46.20	
1969	Bold Favorite	4	D. Richard	115	Happy Intellectual	111	Mr. Swinger	113	17,985	1:48.00	
1970	High Rover	5	J. Lively	115	Terrible Tiger	120	Royal Harmony	133	14,685	1:46.00	
1971	Terrible Tiger	6	D.W. Whited	117	Royal Harmony	128	Elegant Heir	114	15,180	1:45.00	
1972	Full Pocket	3	J.R. Anderson	119	Moonsplash	121	Insubordination	116	21,120	1:16.40	
1973	Fame and Power	4	A. Rini	118	Full Pocket	122	Chateauvira	113	21,285	1:37.80	
1974	Tom Tulle	4	L. Snyder	120	Smooth Dancer	111	Chateauvira	117	37,800	1:43.40	
1975	Zografos	7	H. Arroyo	120	Sr. Diplomat	116	Sharp Gary	118	34,410	1:44.20	
1976	Honey Mark	4	R. Sibille	124	Heathen Ways	114	Chateauvira	111	46,680	1:46.80	
1977	Yallah Native	4	J. Powell	112	Dare to Command	119	Brown Cabildo	111	31,860	1:37.80	
1978	Auberge	5	O. Sanchez	112	Bill Bonbright	121	Brown Cabildo	116	19,305	1:41.00	
1979	Once Over Lightly	6	S.A. Spencer	113	Batonnier	114	Hold Your Tricks	114	46,800	1:45.60	
1980	All the More	7	L. Snyder	119	Hold Your Tricks	114	Young Bob	117	46,890	1:46.20	
1981	Dusky Duke	5	G.E. Louviere	118	Boyne Valley	117	Good and Early	112	46,350	1:49.00	
1982	Frost King	4	R. Platts	127	Dusky Duke	114	Recusant	115	66,150	1:49.80	
1983	Determined Bidder	4	C.H. Silva	114	Thumbsucker	117	John's Gold	115	64,710	1:52.00	
1984	Price Forli	4	R. Meier	118	Full Flame	119	Spare Card	117	64,080	1:52.60	
1985	Norwick	6	K. Skinner	117	Harham's Sizzler	121	Badwagon Harry	115	81,696	1:51.20	
1986	Magic North	4	J.L. Diaz	117	Rocky Knave	121	Tuner Jr.	113	85,220	1:50.00	
1987	Honor Medal	6	L.E. Ortega	118	Blue Buckaroo	115	Coffer Dam	113	95,490	1:49.80	
1988	Lost Code	4	C. Perret	124	Honor Medal	122	Outlaws Sham	114	125,640	1:49.60	
1989	Present Value	5	W. Shoemaker	112	Super Roberto	113	Honor Medal	121	126,510	1:49.20	
1990	Dual Elements	4	J.L. Diaz	118	Tricky Creek	120	Blue Buckaroo	115	143,730	1:49.60	
1991	Allijeba	5	S.J. Sellers	116	Whiz Along	110	Sound of Cannons	115	157,680	1:50.40	
1992	Stalwars	7	M. Guidry	115	Richman	122	Sunny Prince	113	156,300	1:48.00	105
1993	Stalwars	8	J.L. Diaz	118	Count the Time	115	Richman	119	150,000	1:49.40	99
1994	Recoup the Cash	4	J.L. Diaz	113	Dread Me Not	114	Danc'n Jake	112	150,000	1:49.00	106
1995	Dusty Screen	7	E. Maple	116	Come on Flip	114	Adhocracy	113	150,000	1:51.40	106
1996	Prory	4	C.H. Silva	113	Polar Expedition	116	Shed Some Light	114	150,000	1:50.80	102
	Bucks Nephew finished first but was disqualified and placed fourth										
1997	Bucks Nephew	7	G.K. Gomez	118	Natural Selection	114	Gotha	112	120,000	1:49.80	103
1998	Polar Expedition	7	M. Guidry	117	Bucks Nephew	115	Shed Some Light	114	120,000	1:49.80	106
1999	Baytown	5	M. Guidry	114	Precocity	120	Fred Bear Claw	116	120,000	1:47.60	106
2000	Take Note of Me	6	R.J. Albarado	120	Glacial	113	Nite Dreamer	118	120,000	1:49.91	106
2001	Chicago Six	6	A.J. Juarez Jr.	117	Guided Tour	118	Glacial	114	120,000	1:48.28	106
2002	Hail the Chief	5	J.F. Chavez	114	E Z Glory	115	Ubiquity	115	120,000	1:51.72	110
2003	Fight for Ally	6	E. Razo Jr.	116	Colonial Colony	114	Parrott Bay	115	150,000	1:53.46	97

Beyer Index: 104.33

NATIVE DIVER HANDICAP, 1 1/8 Miles,
3-Year-Olds and Up, Hollywood Park, 2003 Purse: $100,000

Year	Winner	Age	Jockey	Wt.	Second	Wt.	Third	Wt.	Win Value	Time	Beyer
1979	Life's Hope	6	L. Pincay Jr	117	Hawkin's Special	117	White Rammer	116	31,500	1:35.00	
1980	Replant	6	W. Shoemaker	111	Relaunch	120	Flying Paster	124	63,000	1:34.20	
1981	Syncopate	6	C.J. McCarron	117	King Go Go	115	Wickerr	121	63,500	1:38.80	
1982	Native Tactics	4	E. Delahoussaye	116	Belfort	116	Rock Softly	115	67,000	1:41.60	
1983	Menswear	5	F. Toro	115	Fighting Fit	117	Major Sport	115	63,200	1:42.40	
1984	Lord at War	4	W. Shoemaker	120	Fighting Fit	118	Video Kid	118	62,700	1:35.40	
1985	Innamorato	4	S. Hawley	107	Beldale Lear	116	Lord at War	125	87,900	1:33.40	
1986	Hopeful Word	5	L. Pincay Jr	117	Epidaurus	115	Nostalgia's Star	118	90,800	1:47.80	
1987	Epidaurus	5	P.A. Valenzuela	116	Midwest King	116	He's a Saros	116	91,200	1:47.60	
1988	Cutlass Reality	6	G.L. Stevens	124	Precisionist	123	Payant	116	63,000	1:48.60	
1989	Ruhlmann	4	C.J. McCarron	121	Lively One	122	Stylish Winner	116	63,100	1:48.00	
1990	Warcraft	3	C.J. McCarron	117	Pleasant Tap	115	Go and Go	115	63,500	1:47.40	104
1991	Twilight Agenda	5	C.J. McCarron	124	Ibero	117	Cobra Classic	114	60,600	1:49.00	109
1992	Sir Beaufort	5	C.J. McCarron	119	Memo	115	Berillo	115	61,700	1:47.80	109
1993	Slew of Damascus	5	C.S. Nakatani	118	Lottery Winner	117	L'Express	115	63,300	1:47.40	107
1994	Best Pal	6	C.J. McCarron	121	Tossofthecoin	117	Royal Chariot	114	109,000	1:48.40	110
1995	Alphabet Soup	4	C.W. Antley	117	El Florista	118	Regal Rowdy	116	61,400	1:47.00	116
1996	Gentlemen	4	G.L. Stevens	121	Dramatic Gold	122	Don't Blame Rio	112	63,840	1:45.20	118
1997	Refinado Tom	4	G.L. Stevens	119	Steel Ruhlr	112	Boggle	114	60,000	1:47.80	104
1998	Puerto Madero	4	K.J. Desormeaux	121	Musical Gambler	117	River Keen	114	60,000	1:48.40	112
1999	General Challenge	3	C.J. McCarron	123	Moore's Flat	117	Koslanin-AR	113	60,000	1:49.00	109
2000	Sky Jack	4	L. Pincay Jr.	118	Lethal Instrument	116	Grey Memo	113	60,000	1:46.81	122
2001	Momentum	3	C.S. Nakatani	117	Euchre	121	Last Parade	117	60,000	1:48.24	107
2002	Piensa Sonando	4	L. Pincay Jr.	117	Fleetstreet Dancer	112	Nose the Trade	116	60,000	1:48.43	104
2003	Olmodavor	4	A. Solis	117	Nose the Trade	115	Chinkapin	118	60,000	1:49.16	102

Beyer Index: 109.5

NEXT MOVE HANDICAP, 1 1/8 Miles,
Fillies and Mares 3-Year-Olds and Up, Aqueduct, 2003 Purse: $108,000

Year	Winner	Age	Jockey	Wt.	Second	Wt.	Third	Wt.	Win Value	Time	Beyer
1975	My Juliet	3	D.G. McHargue	125	Channelette	117	Spring Is Here	113	33,660	1:35.60	
1976	Yes Dear Maggie	4	R. Hernandez	119	Pass a Glance	115	Mary Queenofscots	110	48,360	1:49.40	
1977	Forty Nine Sunsets	4	J. Vasquez	116	Double Quester	115	Shark's Jaws	116	48,915	1:51.00	
1978	One Sum	4	R. Hernandez	121	Crab Grass	121	Sweet Bernice	114	48,690	1:52.80	
1979	One Sum	5	R. Hernandez	116	Kit's Double	111	Municipal Bond	111	48,105	1:53.00	
1980	Water Lily	4	M. Castaneda	113	Plankton	121	Propitiate	116	49,410	1:51.00	
1981	Plankton	5	R. Hernandez	123	Nalee's Fantasy	107	Ms. Balding	109	50,130	1:53.40	
1982	Andover Way	4	J. Velasquez	122	Autumn Glory	112	Who's to Answer	109	50,940	1:50.20	
1983	Chieft'n's Command	4	A. Smith Jr	116	Noble Damsel	115	Pert	113	32,880	1:53.20	
1984	Adept	5	M. Venezia	109	Far Flying	120	Ch'ft'n's Command	123	67,860	1:57.80	
1985	Flip's Pleasure	4	J.L. Samyn	112	Sintrillium	121	Emphatic	104	52,380	1:58.20	
1986	Cherry Jubilee	4	C.H. Marquez Jr	110	Madame Called	109	Lady on the Run	121	68,220	1:56.00	
1987	Tricky Squaw	4	C.W. Antley	110	Ms. Eloise	115	Videogenic	121	70,440	1:58.40	
1988	Triple Wow	4	R. Migliore	116	With a Twist	112	Cuantalamera	104	66,120	1:57.60	
1989	Rose's Cantina	5	E. Maple	118	To the Hunt	111	No Butter	108	49,950	1:59.80	
1990	Bold Wench	5	J. Velasquez	117	Buy the Firm	112	Dactique	113	53,280	1:58.40	
1991	Buy the Firm	5	W.H. McCauley	119	Overturned	115	Won Scent	112	68,850	1:56.40	100
1992	Spy Leader Lady	4	M.E. Smith	112	Haunting	117	Grecian Pass	115	67,560	2:00.20	100
1993	Low Tolerance	4	M.E. Smith	114	Hilbys Brite Flite	112	Lady Lear	114	67,470	1:55.80	102
1994	Groovy Feeling	5	M.J. Luzzi	123	Broad Gains	116	Megaroux	112	63,735	1:59.60	95
1995	Restored Hope	4	M.J. Luzzi	118	Cherokee Wonder	114	Sterling Pound	114	48,975	1:52.20	94
1996	Madame Adolphe	4	F. Leon	110	Shoop	114	Lotta Dancing	122	49,080	1:51.20	95
1997	Full And Fancy	5	R. Migliore	115	Shoop	117	Prophet's Warning	117	49,500	1:51.20	97
1998	Panama Canal	4	S.X. Bridgmohan	113	Endowment	110	Dewars Rocks	116	40,455	1:51.20	90
1999	Diggins	5	Espinoza J. L.	113	Biogio's Rose	116	Powerful Nation	114	48,915	1:48.80	96
2000	Biogio's Rose	6	N. Arroyo Jr.	117	Up We Go	115	Perlinda	114	49,875	1:51.32	96
2001	Atelier	4	E.S. Prado	117	Pompeii	117	Tax Affair	114	64,264	1:50.65	98
2002	With Ability	4	J.J. Castellano	113	Irving's Baby	117	Diversa	113	65,160	1:49.88	105
2003	Smok'n Frolic	4	J.R. Velazquez	120	Ellie's Moment	116	Pupil	113	64,800	1:49.11	95

Beyer Index: 97.15

NOBLE DAMSEL HANDICAP, 1 Mile (Turf),
Fillies and Mares 3-Year-Olds and Up, Belmont Park, 2003 Purse: $150,000

Year	Winner	Age	Jockey	Wt.	Second	Wt.	Third	Wt.	Win Value	Time	Beyer
1996	Perfect Arc	4	Velazquez J. R.	125	Fashion Star	112	Tough Broad	112	60,160	1:42.40	103
1997	Colcon	4	J.D. Bailey	113	Antespend	118	Tiffany's Taylor	113	69,360	1:32.80	104
1998	Oh Nellie	4	Velazquez J. R.	116	Heaven's Command	116	Irish Daisy	114	50,400	1:32.80	105
1999	Khumba Mela	4	Santos J. A.	118	Uanme	114	Cyrillic	116	67,740	1:34.40	102
2000	Gino's Spirits	4	E.S. Prado	114	La Ville Rouge	115	Solar Bound	114	66,720	1:36.61	105
2001	Tugger	4	J.D. Bailey	119	Shine Again	123	Tippity Witch	113	68,280	1:35.18	98
2002	Tates Creek	4	J.D. Bailey	119	Amonita	117	Dat You Miz Blue	114	68,640	1:32.79	105
2003	Wonder Again	4	E.S. Prado	117	Dancal	114	Something Ventured	115	90,000	1:33.07	102

Beyer Index: 103

OAKLAWN BREEDERS' CUP, 1 1/16 Miles,
Fillies and Mares 3-Year-Olds and Up, Oaklawn Park, 2003 Purse: $200,000

Year	Winner	Age	Jockey	Wt.	Second	Wt.	Third	Wt.	Win Value	Time	Beyer
1994	Morning Meadow	4	S.Romero	116	Gravette	113	Her Valentine	113	94,650	1:44.60	96
1995	Halo America	5	C.H. Borel	115	Heavenly Prize	121	Biolage	111	90,000	1:42.40	108
1996	Belle of Cozzene	4	D.R. Pettinger	113	Hamo America	120	Little May	115	90,000	1:43.20	95
1997	Halo America	7	C.H. Borel	109	Gold N Delicious	112	Capote Belle	117	90,000	1:42.00	109
1998	Turn to the Queen	5	T.T. Doocy	112	Danzalert	112	Leo's Gypsy Dancer	118	90,000	1:44.60	92
1999	Sister Act	4	C.H. Borel	113	Glitter Woman	114	Mil Kilates	114	120,000	1:42.00	112
2000	Heritage of Gold	5	S.J. Sellers	112	Lu Ravi	112	Light Line	112	120,000	1:44.15	103
2001	Heritage of Gold	6	R.J. Albarado	116	Lu Ravi	118	Ive Gota Bad Liver	114	120,000	1:44.30	95
2002	Ask Me No Secrets	4	M.E. Smith	116	Red n'Gold	116	Descapate	118	120,000	1:44.56	100
2003	Bien Nicole	5	D.R. Pettinger	122	Red n'Gold	117	Mandy's Gold	117	120,000	1:44.19	94

Beyer Index: 100.4

For previous runnings refer to 1994 Manual

OCEANPORT HANDICAP, 1 1/16 Miles (Off the Turf),
3-Year-Olds and Up, Monmouth Park, 2003 Purse: $100,000

Year	Winner	Age	Jockey	Wt.	Second	Wt.	Third	Wt.	Win Value	Time	Beyer
1947	Polynesian	5	W.D. Wright	134	Misleader	105	Gallant Bull	104	8,195	1:10.40	
1948	Yankee Hill	4	W.J. Passmore	109	Mangohick	116	Brown Mogul	114	8,900	1:12.40	
1949	Rippey	6	J. Gilbert	125	Cacique	104	Mangohick	125	7,875	1:11.40	

Year	Winner	Age	Jockey	Wt.	Second	Wt.	Third	Wt.	Win Value	Time	Beyer
1950	Imacomin	4	M. Basile	113	Cacique	109	Noble Impulse	116	8,575	1:11.20	
1951	Tuscany	3	S. Boulmetis	107	War King	113	Call Over	119	7,925	1:10.20	
1952	General Staff	4	W.J. Passmore	112	Hi Billee	112	Northern Star	113	12,100	1:11.40	
1953	Cinda	4	J. Stout	113	Indian Land	118	Squared Away	127	13,700	1:12.00	
1954	Master Ace	5	J. Renick	106	White Skies	136	Eatontown	113	13,000	1:09.00	
1955	Dark Peter	7	S. Boulmetis	118	I Geegee	112	Bobby Brocato	122	13,050	1:10.00	
1956	Decathlon	3	G.R. Martin	116	I Appeal	113	Royal Briar	108	12,250	1:09.40	
1957	Decathlon	4	W. Hartack	130	Itobe	116	Nahodah	122	10,517	1:08.40	
1958	True Verdict	4	H. Grant	115	Sand Boy	112	Beau Pilot	115	11,151	1:10.60	
1959	Itobe	6	S. Boulmetis	117	Isendu	122	Li'l Fella	117	11,281	1:09.60	
1960	Besomer	7	H. Woodhouse	115	Itobe	116	Seven Corners	112	11,005	1:09.80	
1961	Careless John	4	W. Boland	116	Winonly	120	Watch Your Step	118	11,277	1:09.00	
1962	Jets Pat	4	S. Boulmetis	116	Beau Admiral	117	Will Ye	115	10,936	1:09.60	
1963	Accordant	3	P. Kallai	110	Bull Story	114	Merry Ruler	120	10,920	1:09.20	
1964	Turbo Jet II	4	S. Brooks	111	Thanks Doc	110	Uncle Percy	115	11,619	:59.20	
1965	Uncle Percy	7	E. McIvor	119	Isaduchess	115	Lucky Turn	114	11,391	:58.20	
1966	Canal	5	W. Mayorga	119	Deutron	114	Finance King	111	10,977	:57.40	
1966	Country Friend	4	J. Velasquez	115	Meistersinger	112	Welshwyn	112	10,847	:57.80	
1967	Canal	6	W. Mayorga	121	Valiant Bull	113	Caligerro	113	14,397	:58.00	
1967	County Monaghan	6	J. Leonard	112	Chicot	122	Country Friend	119	14,430	:57.80	
1968	Country Friend	6	J. Vasquez	116	Burning Bridges	111	Vis-a-Vis	109	18,046	1:36.60	
1968	Quite an Accent	5	B. Thornburg	113	More Scents	117	Tornum	112	18,046	1:36.40	
1969	Mara Lark	4	F. Toro	112	Kentucky Kin	112	A Latin Spin	110	15,210	1:37.00	
1969	Swoonland	6	R. Turcotte	113	Palace Ruler	117	Monitor	117	15,145	1:36.20	
1970	Mr. Leader	4	C. Baltazar	114	Good Manners	112	A Latin Spin	110	19,419	1:39.40	
1971	Red Reality	5	F. Ianelli	114	Mister Diz	118	Well Mannered	117	15,080	1:36.60	
1971	Tudor Reward	4	C.H. Marquez	117	Charney	114	Double Gee	113	15,047	1:37.60	
1972	Native Heir	6	V. Bracciale Jr.	111	Real Note	115	Red Reality	119	19,354	1:36.20	
1973	Lexington Park	6	J. Imparato	118	Prince of Truth	116	Halo	117	15,056	1:45.20	
1973	Dartsum	4	M. Cedeno	110	Dundee Marmalade	114	Return to Reality	111	14,893	1:46.20	
1974	Mo Bay	5	W. Tichenor	118	Shane's Prince	118	Barbiz'n Streak	116	18,541	1:42.40	
1975	R. Tom Can.	4	D. Brumfield	115	Prod	117	Royal Glint	119	15,291	1:49.80	
1975	Haraka	5	J. Velasquez	113	London Company	124	East Sea	115	15,096	1:49.80	
1976	Toujours Pret	7	J.W. Edwards	114	Hat Full	114	Our Hermis	113	15,072	1:43.00	
1976	Break up the G'me.	5	E. Delahoussaye	114	Expropriate	120	L'roft'e Bid	118	14,682	1:44.20	
1977	Quick Card	4	M. Solomone	115	Bemo	115	Star of the Sea	115	19,516	1:42.60	
1978	Mr. Red Wing	4	W.H. McCauley	110	Chati	118	Dan Horn	116	23,514	1:43.20	
1979	Revivalist	5	W. Nemeti	117	Horatius	117	Gristle	112	18,866	1:38.00	
1979	Alias Smith	6	M. Solomone	114	Qui Native	114	Fed Funds	114	18,671	1:38.00	
1980	North Course	5	B. Thornburg	114	Horatius	119	Lucy's Axe	116	24,210	1:44.00	
1981	Winds of Winter	4	G. McCarron	113	Foretake	116	No Bend	115	24,225	1:43.40	
1982	McCann	4	J. Fell	114	Sprink	108	Lord Carn'von	111	27,555	1:43.60	
1982	Erin's Tiger	4	K. Skinner	114	Dom Menotti	111	War of Words	114	27,555	1:43.00	
1983	Fray Star	5	O. Vergara	114	Domynsky	112	And More	117	35,190	1:43.40	
1984	World Appeal	4	C. Perret	120	Rocco Reale	109	Castle Guard	120	34,950	1:42.80	
1985	Cozzene	5	W.A. Guerra	121	Stay the Course	119	Roving Minstrel	118	34,470	1:42.40	
1986	Salem Drive	5	D.B. Thomas	115	Exclusive Partner	120	Spellbound	117	34,650	1:42.60	
1987	Sovereign Song	5	J.A. Krone	106	Feeling Gallant	120	Spellbound	117	35,100	1:41.60	
1988	Feeling Gallant	6	C.W. Antley	119	Copper Cup	111	Sovereign Song	107	41,820	1:45.20	
1989	Yankee Affair	7	P. Day	121	River of Sin	116	Primino	110	51,870	1:43.40	
1990	Bill E. Shears	5	R. Wilson	118	Pete the Chief	115	Timely Warning	113	53,910	1:42.80	97
1991	Fiftysevenvette	4	J.C. Ferrer	113	Great Normand	118	Thunder Regent	112	45,000	1:44.80	
1992	Maxigroom	4	R.G. Davis	113	Rocket Fuel	112	Go Dutch	112	45,000	1:41.60	98
1993	Furiously	4	J.D. Bailey	119	Adam Smith	120	Rocket Fuel	114	45,000	1:39.60	106
1994	Nijinsky's Gold	5	Davis RG	120	Winnetou	116	Marco Bay	116	45,000	1:41.60	106
1995	Boyce	4	Black AS	113	Myrmidon	117	Rocket City	112	45,000	1:40.80	102
1997	Boyce	6	J.A. Krone	118	Foolish Pole	113	Jambalaya Jazz	116	60,000	1:40.20	101
1998	Daylight Savings	4	H. Castillo Jr.	115	Mi Narrow	121	Rob 'n Gin	120	60,000	1:42.20	102
1999	Mi Narrow	5	J. Bravo	113	Hurrahy	114	Forbidden Apple	111	60,000	1:39.40	106
2000	North East Bound	4	J.A. Velez Jr.	114	Rize	112	Selective	114	60,000	1:44.60	98
2001	Key Lory	7	C.C. Lopez	111	North East Bound	121	Crash Course	115	60,000	1:40.39	100
2002	Tempest Fugit	5	J.A. Velez Jr.	115	Runspastum	112	One Eyed Joker	114	60,000	1:42.72	110
2003	Runspastum	6	J. Pimentel	113	Balto Star	119	Saint Verre	118	60,000	1:42.31	101

Beyer Index: 102.25

Off the turf in 2002, 2003

OKLAHOMA DERBY, 1 1/8 Miles,
3-Year-Olds, Remington Park, 2003 Purse: $159,000

Year	Winner	Age	Jockey	Wt.	Second	Wt.	Third	Wt.	Win Value	Time	Beyer
1989	Clever Trevor	3	D.R. Pettinger	122	Gauntlett Boy	122	Launch a Ruler	118	152,500	1:43.00	
1990	Wicked Destiny	3	J. Lively	122	Seasabb	118	Penthouse E.	118	150,000	1:43.00	

Year	Winner	Age	Jockey	Wt.	Second	Wt.	Third	Wt.	Win Value	Time	Beyer
1991	Queen's Gray Bee.	3	P.W. Steinberg	118	Lanyons Star	122	Near the Limit	118	150,000	1:44.20	
1992	Vying Victor	3	R.D. Hansen	122	Ecstatic Ride	122	Capitalimprovement	122	150,000	1:43.60	
1993	Marked Tree	3	G.K. Gomez	122	Brother Brown	122	Ragtime Rebel	122	180,000	1:43.80	
1994	Smilin Singin Sam.	3	L. Melancon	122	Blumin Affair	118	Silver Goblin	122	180,000	1:43.20	112
1995	Dazzling Falls	3	G.Gomez	122	Our Gatsby	122	Capote's Promise	118	180,000	1:42.80	104
1996	Semoran	3	R.Baze	122	Connecting Terms	118	Devil's Honor	122	180,000	1:46.60	95
1997	Wild Rush	3	G.Stevens	121	Blazing Sword	119	Precocity	117	180,000	1:53.60	100
1998	Classic Cat	3	S.Sellers	124	Leave A Legacy	121	Sir Tiff	117	180,000	1:48.00	100
1999	Temperence Time	3	T.Doocy	119	Answer Lively	115	Stellar Brush	124	180,000	1:49.40	102
2000	Performing Magic.	3	S.Sellers	124	Mister Deville	124	Del Mar Denny	124	180,000	1:50.20	96
2001	Top Hit	3	G.K. Comez	114	Unbridled Time	118	Compendium	118	180,000	1:49.79	102
2002	The Judge Sez Who	3	C. Velasquez	115	Easyfromthegitgo	121	A.P. Five Hundred	115	177,000	1:49.34	101
2003	Comic Truth	3	M. Berry	115	Excessivepleasure	124	Morning Merry	112		1:49.59	111

Beyer Index: 102.3

PALM BEACH, 1 1/8 Miles (Turf),
3-Year-Olds, Gulfstream Park, 2003 Purse: $100,000

Year	Winner	Age	Jockey	Wt.	Second	Wt.	Third	Wt.	Win Value	Time	Beyer
1990	Dawn Quixote	3	C. Perret	119	Rowdy Regal	119	Always Running	115	30,000	1:23.40	94
1991	Magic Interlude	3	C.W. Antley	114	Island Delay	117	Explosive Jeff	114	38,310	1:43.00	90
1992	Preferences	3	J.C. Duarte	114	Doo You	112	Stress Buster	114	38,940	1:42.60	95
1993	Kissin Kris	3	D. Penna	113	Pride Prevails	112	Awad	119	38,760	1:46.40	87
1994	Mr. Angel	3	W.H. McCauley	112	Clint Essential	114	Fabulous Frolic	119	30,000	1:44.40	91
1995	Admiralty	3	J.A. Krone	114	Nostra	112	Smells and Bells	114	30,000	1:51.00	94
1996	Harrowman	3	M.E. Smith	114	A Real Zipper	117	Ok by Me	119	45,000	1:49.20	90
1997	Unite's Big Red	3	Hernandez R.	117	Trample	112	Tekken	117	45,000	1:47.20	92
1998	Cryptic Rascal	3	M.E. Smith	119	The Kaiser	113	American Odyssey	114	45,000	1:55.00	93
1999	Swamp.	3	R. Migliore	114	Marquette	114	Valid Reprized	119	45,000	1:48.20	96
2000	Mr. Livingston	3	S.J. Sellers	114	Powerful Appeal	114	Gateman	117	45,000	1:48.04	96
2001	Proud Man	3	R.R. Douglas	114	One Eyed Joker	114	Strategic Partner	112	60,000	1:48.32	91
2002	Orchard Park	3	J.D. Bailey	118	Lord Juban	118	Red's Top Gun	116	60,000	1:49.80	90
2003	Nothing to Lose	3	J.D. Bailey	122	White Cat	118	Imitation	118	60,000	1:48.28	93

Beyer Index: 92.29

PEBBLES HANDICAP, 1 1/8 Miles (Turf),
3-Year-Old Fillies, Belmont Park, 2003 Purse: $110,300

Year	Winner	Age	Jockey	Wt.	Second	Wt.	Third	Wt.	Win Value	Time	Beyer
1993	Statuette	3	M.E. Smith	121	Tricky Princess	114	Belle Nuit	115	45,060	1:40.60	86
1994	Saxuality	3	J.A. Krone	114	Lady Affirmed	118	Tensie's Pro	118	41,580	1:34.00	95
1995	Queen Tutta	3	G.Stevens	115	Transient Trend	114	Nappelon	118	53,820	1:43.20	90
1996	Rare Blend	3	G.Stevens	115	Polish Spring	114	Inner Circle	114	52,110	1:44.40	90
1997	Heaven's Command	3	J.Santos	116	Wollastina	110	Colonial Minstrel	116	51,375	1:42.80	95
1998	Sophie My Love	3	J.R.Velazquez	118	Appealing Kris	111	Proud Owner	116	51,150	1:52.20	91
1999	Eze	3	Davis R. G.	113	Colstar	115	Jazz	114	49,950	1:52.80	94
2000	Lady Dora	3	J.R. Velazquez	114	De Aar	114	Tippity Witch	117	52,245	1:48.76	94
2001	Heads Will Roll	3	E.S. Prado	115	New Economy	114	Salty You	115	66,060	1:47.75	88
2001	Love N' Kiss S.	3	J.A. Santos	114	Calista	118	Shooting Part.	115	66,360	1:47.50	90
2002	Glia	3	J.J. Castellano	113	Nonsuch Bay	123	Delta Princess	113	68,580	1:49.68	91
2003	Betty's Wish	3	J.R. Velazquez	116	Mystery Itself	112	Andover Lady	114	66,180	1:51.00	97

Beyer Index: 91.75

PENNSYLVANIA DERBY, 1 1/8 Miles,
3-Year-Olds, Philadelphia Park, 2003 Purse: $750,000

Year	Winner	Age	Jockey	Wt.	Second	Wt.	Third	Wt.	Win Value	Time	Beyer
1979	Smarten	3	S. Maple	122	Incredible Ease	122	Incubator	122	68,880	1:49.20	
1980	Lively King	3	C.J. Baker	122	Mutineer	122	Stutz Blackhawk	122	99,480	1:48.80	
1981	Summing	3	G. Martens	122	Sportin' Life	122	Classic Go Go	122	100,380	1:49.00	
1982	Spanish Drums	3	J. Vasquez	122	Air Forbes Won	122	A Magic Spray	122	101,460	1:49.00	
1983	Dixieland Band	3	W.J. Passmore	122	Jacques Tip	122	Intention	122	136,500	1:49.40	
1984	Morning Bob	3	G. McCarron	122	At the Threshold.	122	Biloxi Indian	122	132,240	1:49.40	
							Raja's Shark	122			
1985	Skip Trial	3	J.L. Samyn	122	El Basco	122	Jacque L'Heureux	119	180,000	1:50.20	
1986	Broad Brush	3	A. Cordero Jr.	122	Sumptious	122	Glow	122	180,000	1:50.80	
1987	Afleet	3	G. Stahlbaum	122	Lost Code	122	Homebuilder	119	180,000	1:48.20	
1988	Cefis	3	L. Saumell	122	Congeleur	119	Ballindaggin	119	180,000	1:49.60	
1989	Western Playboy	3	K. Clark	122	Roi Danzig	122	Tricky Creek	122	180,000	1:47.60	
1990	Summer Squall	3	P. Day	122	Challenge My Duty	122	Sports View	122	180,000	1:48.20	
1991	Valley Crossing	3	A.J. Seefeldt	119	Gala Spinaway	122	Riflery	117	90,000	1:50.00	

Year	Winner	Age	Jockey	Wt.	Second	Wt.	Third	Wt.	Win Value	Time	Beyer
1992	Thelastcrusade....	3	V.H. Molina	114	Ecstatic Ride	114	Nines Wild	117.	90,000	1:49.40	107
1993	Wallenda.........	3	W.H. McCauley.	114	Press Card	117	Saintly Prospector	122.	120,000	1:49.20	100
1994	Meadow Flight....	3	J. Bravo	122	Red Tazz	117	Kandaly	122.	120,000	1:49.00	106
1995	Pineing Patty	3	L. Melancon	122	Royal Haven	117	Tenants Harbor	117.	120,000	1:48.00	108
1996	Devil's Honor	3	A.S. Black	122	Formal Gold	117	Clash by Night	119.	120,000	1:48.40	114
1997	Frisk Me Now	3	E. L. King Jr.	122	Envy of the Crown.	114	Christian Soldier.	114.	120,000	1:48.00	114
1998	Rock and Roll	3	H. Castillo Jr	114	Tomorrows Cat.	114	Black Blade	119.	150,000	1:47.60	110
1999	Smart Guy	3	R. E. Colton	119	Ghost Ring	114	Pineaff	122.	180,000	1:49.40	109
2000	Pine Dance.......	3	M.J. McCarthy	122	Mass Market	122	Cherokeeinthehills	114.	180,000	1:49.03	105
2001	Macho Uno.......	3	G.L. Stevens....	116	Unbridled Elaine.	119	Touch Tone	122.	300,000	1:49.69	104
2002	Harlan's Holiday ..	3	E.S. Prado	122	Essence of Dubai .	122	Make the Bend.	119.	300,000	1:51.10	96
2003	Grand Hombre	3	J. Bravo	114	Gimmeawink	122	Ashmore	114.	450,000	1:49.03	108

Beyer Index: 106.75

PHILADELPHIA PARK BREEDERS' CUP HANDICAP, 6 Furlongs, 3-Year-Olds and Up, Philadelphia Park, 2002 Purse: $183,000

Year	Winner	Age	Jockey	Wt.	Second	Wt.	Third	Wt.	Win Value	Time	Beyer
1986	Lazer Show	3	P. Day	112	I Am the Game	114	Purple Mountain.	114.	92,610	1:22.20	
1987	High Brite.	3	J.L. Kaenel	116	Vinnie the Viper	115	Foligno	115.	92,550	1:21.60	
1988	Claramount	4	N. Santagata	117	Quick Call	114	Flourescent Gem.	112.	93,780	1:21.40	
1989	Flourescent Gem.	6	J.F. Chavez	113	Quick Call	116	Whiz Along	107.	93,390	1:09.20	
1990	Glitterman	5	W.A. Guerra	119	Mr. Nickerson	121	Quick Call	119.	93,120	1:09.40	111
1991	Key Spirit.......	5	R.E. Colton.	118	Hadif	115	Pulverizing	113.	92,760	1:09.40	105
1992	Smart Alec.......	4	M.G. Pino	113	Megas Vukefalos .	119	Arrowtown	114.	92,820	1:09.60	105
1993	Blushing Julian...	3	R.E. Colton	111	Thelastcrusade	114	Bruksbookie	112.	92,640	1:09.60	107
1994	King Ruckus	4	Kabel TK.	122	Friendly Lover	120	Demaloot Demashoot	117.	92,580	1:09.00	107
1995	Friendly Lover ...	7	Wilson R	122	Buffalo Dan	119	Goldminer's Dream	115.	93,420	1:08.40	106
1996	Friendly Lover ...	8	McCauley W. H.	118	Elajjud	113	Goldminer's Dream	114.	90,000	1:09.40	104
1997	Cat Be Nimble....	5	Rocco J.	122	Wire Me Collect	114	Score A Birdie	113.	90,000	1:09.20	106
1998	Buffalo Dan......	7	Elliott S.	117	Western Fame.	115	Inajam	113.	120,000	1:08.80	100
1999	Loaded Gun......	4	Flores J. L.	114	Artax	119	Power by Far	115.	60,000	1:08.40	107
2000	Iron Punch.......	6	C. Cruz	114	Say Florida Sandy .	117	Just Call Me Carl.	118.	60,000	1:07.89	108
2001	Say Florida Sandy .	7	A.T. Gryder	118	Wake At Noon	119	Max's Pal	118.	120,000	1:08.51	112
2002	True Passion	4	A.S. Black	115	Late Carson	118	Really Irish	114.	120,000	1:10.72	104

Beyer Index: 106.31

Not run in 2003

PHOENIX BREEDERS' CUP, 6 Furlongs, 3-Year-Olds and Up, Keeneland Race Course, 2003 Purse: $264,000

Year	Winner	Age	Jockey	Wt.	Second	Wt.	Third	Wt.	Win Value	Time	Beyer
1994	Lost Pan	4	D. Barton	114	Pacific West.	116	Fort Chaffe	119.	33,728	1:09.40	108
1995	Golden Gear......	5	C.Perret	124	Hello Paradise	115	Mississippi Chat .	113.	67,456	1:08.80	109
1996	Forest Wildcat....	5	J.Bravo	121	Valid Expectations	119	Bet On Sunshine .	115.	101,246	1:09.40	114
1997	Bet On Sunshine ..	5	F.Torres.	122	Receiver.	117	Valid Expectations	117.	97,464	1:08.60	111
1998	Partner's Hero ...	4	C.Borel.	117	Pyramid Peak	123	High Stakes Player	123.	100,533	1:09.20	109
1999	Richter Scale.....	5	K.J. Desormeaux	117	Bet On Sunshine.	117	Vicar	121.	166,780	1:08.40	102
2000	Five Star Day.....	4	G.K. Gomez	119	Istintaj	119	Bet On Sunshine .	123.	167,245	1:07.90	116
2001	Bet On Sunshine ..	9	C.H. Borek	123	Robin De Nest	121	Erlton	119.	166,470	1:09.65	104
2002	Xtra Heat	4	H. Vega	123	Day Trader	120	Touch Tone	119.	155,000	1:10.13	107
2003	Najran	4	J. Castellano	122	Ethan Man	118	Take Achance on Me	118.	169,880	1:08.32	111

Beyer Index: 109.1

For previous runnings, refer to 1994 Manual

PIMLICO BREEDERS' CUP DISTAFF HANDICAP, 1 1/16 Miles, Fillies and Mares 3-Year-Olds and Up, Pimlico Race Course, 2003 Purse: $145,500

Year	Winner	Age	Jockey	Wt.	Second	Wt.	Third	Wt.	Win Value	Time	Beyer
1992	Wilderness Song ..	4	C. Perret	121	Harbour Club	110	Brilliant Brass .	117.	150,000	1:49.00	103
1993	Deputation.......	4	C.W. Antley	114	D. Theatrical Gal.	112	Low Tolerance.	115.	120,000	1:49.00	97
1994	Double Sixes	4	Prado ES.	112	Broad Gains	118	Mz. Zill Bear	118.	120,000	1:51.00	94
1995	Pennyhill Park ...	5	M.E. Smith	115	Halo America	117	Calipha	121.	120,000	1:49.20	98
1996	Serena's Song....	4	Stevens G. L.	123	Shoop	116	Churchbell Chimes	114.	120,000	1:49.60	103
1997	Rare Blend.......	4	J.D. Bailey	114	Scenic Point.	114	Aileen's Countess	114.	120,000	1:51.40	92
1998	Ajina............	4	J.D. Bailey	120	Naskra Colors	112	Pocho's Dream Girl	113.	120,000	1:48.60	106
1999	Mil Kilates	6	Sellers S. J.	113	Merengue	121	Unbridled Hope.	116.	120,000	1:49.00	103
2000	Roza Robata	5	P. Day	114	Bella Chiarra	118	On a Soapbox	116.	120,000	1:49.82	105
2001	Serra Lake	4	P. Day	112	Jostle	119	Prized Stamp	114.	120,000	1:50,22	99
2002	Summer Colony ..	4	J.R. Velazquez.	119	Dancethruthedawn	119	Happily Unbridled	115.	90,000	1:42.90	110
2003	Mandy's Gold	5	J.D. Bailey	117	Summer Colony	121	Stormy Frolic....	114.	90,000	1:46.32	86

Beyer Index: 99.67

POKER HANDICAP, 1 Mile (Turf),
3-Year-Olds and Up, Belmont Park, 2003 Purse: $116,200

Year	Winner	Age	Jockey	Wt.	Second	Wt.	Third	Wt.	Win Value	Time	Beyer
1988	Wanderkin	5	J.A. Santos	122	Kings River	122	My Prince Charming	117	54,720	1:35.60	
							Silver Voice	117			
1989	Fourstardave	4	J.A. Santos	117	Feeling Gallant	117	Valid Fund	117	56,610	1:33.20	
1990	Scottish Monk	7	A. Cordero Jr.	117	Quick Call	117	Yankee Affair	122	52,110	1:33.40	
1991	Who's to Pay	5	J.D. Bailey	117	Scott the Great	117	Senor Speedy	117	56,160	1:33.40	103
1992	Scott the Great	6	J.L. Samyn	117	Kate's Valentine	117	Cigar Toss	117	54,810	1:33.40	101
1993	Fourstardave	8	R. Migliore	117	Adam Smith	122	Lech	117	53,190	1:33.00	107
1994	Dominant Prospect	4	Chavez JF	114	Fourstardave	114	Nijinsky's Gold	114	49,905	1:32.60	109
1995	Caress	4	Davis RG	117	Fourstars Allstar	119	Pennine Ridge	119	51,030	1:34.20	110
1996	Smooth Runner	5	Krone J. A.	113	Mighty Forum	116	Da Hoss	119	51,600	1:33.60	111
1997	Draw Shot		Antley C. W.	118	Val's Prince	114	Fortitude	112	51,345	1:33.00	105
1998	Elusive Quality	5	J.D. Bailey	117	Za-Im	114	Fortitude	114	51,240	1:31.60	112
1999	Rob 'n Gin	5	J.F. Chavez	118	Bomfim	115	Wised Up	115	69,120	1:32.80	108
2000	Affirmed Success	6	J.F. Chavez	117	Rabi	114	Weatherbird	113	68,280	1:34.06	108
2001	Affirmed Success	7	J.D. Bailey	121	In Frank's Honor	114	Union One	114	66,240	1:34.60	109
2002	Volponi	4	S.X. Bridgmohan	115	Saint Verre	112	Navesink	117	66,720	1:32.24	109
2003	War Zone	4	J.J. Castellano	117	Trademark	114	Saint Verre	112	69,720	1:32.81	100

Beyer Index: 107.08

PRAIRIE MEADOWS CORNHUSKER BREEDERS' CUP HANDICAP, 1 1/8 Miles,
3-Year-Olds and Up, Prairie Meadows, 2003 Purse: $350,000

Year	Winner	Age	Jockey	Wt.	Second	Wt.	Third	Wt.	Win Value	Time	Beyer
1966	Royal Gunner	4	W. Hartack	121	Sammyren	118	Just About	122	31,075	1:43.00	
1967	Single Needle	4	L.J. Durousseau	110	Tenzing II	112			30,772	1:46.80	
					Lucky Hour	110					
1968	Ninfalo	5	C. Stone	114	Air Boat	111	BF's Own	112	24,764	1:41.80	
1968	Vale of Tears	5	L.J. Durousseau	117	R. Thomas	124	Romanullah	110	24,764	1:41.20	
1969	Vale of Tears	6	L.J. Durousseau	124	Romanullah	109	Zorba II	117	30,827	1:42.20	
1970	Blazing Silk	6	L.J. Durousseau	116	Zorba II	117	Two Bobbs	107	31,432	1:42.60	
1971	Action Getter	4	K. Jones	114	Tripsville	123	Prince Hemp	113	31,034	1:44.00	
1972	Joey Bob	4	L. Moyers	115	Royal Harmony	124	Road Man	117	31,212	1:42.60	
1973	Joey Bob	5	L. Moyers	118	Haveago	121	Prince Astro	114	30,827	1:42.80	
1974	Blazing Gypsy	5	S. Burgos	114	Tom Tulle	122	Super Sail	117	57,963	1:49.60	
1975	Stonewalk	4	R. Turcotte	120	Sharp Gary	115	Rooter	114	59,290	1:48.40	
1976	Dragset	5	S. Maple	112	Sharp Gary	113	Methdioxya	114	60,500	1:49.00	
1977	Private Thoughts	4	R. Perez	118	Latimer	114	Dragset	113	62,783	1:48.00	
1978	True Statement	4	B. Fann	118	Big John Taylor	115	Giboulee	116	60,912	1:48.20	
1979	Star de Naskra	4	J. Fell	125	Prince Majestic	119	Quiet Jay	117	90,613	1:48.40	
1980	Hold Your Tricks	5	D. Pettinger	116	Overskate	126	Daring Damascus	117	88,688	1:49.20	
1981	Summer Advocate	4	K. Jones	118	Sun Catcher	121	Brent's Trans Am	116	93,143	1:48.20	
1982	Recusant	4	R.J. Hirdes Sr	118	Plaza Star	121	Vodika Collins	118	92,895	1:51.60	
1983	Win Stat	6	D. Pettinger	111	Bersid	116	Aspro	121	92,978	1:53.20	
1984	Timeless Native	4	D. Brumfield	122	Inevitable Leader	120	Wild Again	121	90,000	1:49.40	
1985	Gate Dancer	4	C.J. McCarron	126	Badwagon Harry	114	Eminency	119	100,800	1:48.60	
1986	Gourami	4	T.T. Doocy	116	Honor Medal	114	Smile	120	150,000	1:49.40	
1987	Bolshoi Boy	4	C.W. Antley	117	Forkintheroad	112	Honor Medal	119	120,000	1:48.40	
1988	Palace March	4	J.A. Krone	118	Outlaws Sham	114	Galba	112	120,000	1:49.00	
1989	Blue Buckaroo	6	S.J. Sellers	115	Henbane	115	Advancing Ensign	112	120,000	1:49.40	
1990	Dispersal	4	J. Velasquez	122	No More Cash	114	Protect Yourself	113	90,000	1:50.00	97
1991	Black Tie Affair	5	P. Day	124	Bedeviled	117	Whodam	113	75,000	1:48.60	110
1992	Irish Swap	5	B.E. Poyadou	117	Zeeruler	115	Stalwars	116	75,000	1:47.80	106
1993	Link	5	R. Ardoin	114	Rapid World	115	Flying Continental	117	75,000	1:50.40	98
1994	Zeeruler	6	Lester RN	116	Powerful Punch	118	Dancing Jon	114	75,000	1:50.20	104
1995	Powerful Punch	6	Bourque CC	115	All Gone	115	Glaring	116	90,000	1:49.80	98
1997	Semoran	4	D.R. Flores	117	Mister Fire Eyes	115	Come On Flip	114	120,000	1:48.40	108
1998	Beboppin Baby	5	J.M. Campbell	114	Acceptable	116	Pacificbounty	113	150,000	1:46.60	109
1999	Nite Dreamer	4	R.J. Albarado	113	Mocha Express	117	Worldly Ways	116	231,000	1:48.85	110
2000	Sir Bear	7	E.M. Coa	116	Skimming	111	Ecton Park	117	240,000	1:48.49	111
2001	Euchre	5	G.K. Gomez	116	Dixie Dot Com	119	Sure Shot Biscuit	115	240,000	1:47.72	118
2002	Mr. John	4	M. Guidry	114	Unshaded	115	Fajardo	113	240,000	1:47.97	110
2003	Tenpins	5	R.J. Albarado	118	Bowman's Band	116	Woodmoon	116	210,000	1:48.39	111

Beyer Index: 106.92

PUCKER UP, 1 1/8 Miles (Turf),
3-Year-Old Fillies, Arlington Park, 2003 Purse: $175,000

Year	Winner	Age	Jockey	Wt.	Second	Wt.	Third	Wt.	Win Value	Time	Beyer
1961	Kootenai	3	A. Skoronski	119	My Portrait	122	Play Time	119	13,800	1:38.80	
1962	Royal Patrice	3	I. Valenzuela	112	Polylady	114	Dinner Partner	115	39,300	1:48.80	
1963	Vitamin Shot	3	R. Nono	110	Delhi Maid	119	Solabar	114	33,600	1:49.80	
1964	Sceree	3	W. Hartack	119	Donamus	121	Sabemar	117	33,600	1:49.40	
1965	Mine Lovely	3	W. Shoemaker	118	Nellie D.	110	Amerivan	116	33,250	1:49.40	

Year	Winner	Age	Jockey	Wt.	Second	Wt.	Third	Wt.	Win Value	Time	Beyer
1966	Swinging Mood	3	E. Fires	110	Cologne	110	Aunt Tilt	112	33,800	1:35.20	
1967	Gay Sailorette	3	G. Overton	112	Court Circuit	112	Grand Coulee	113	34,500	1:35.40	
1968	Another Nell	3	C. Perret	119	Foggy Note	117	Miss Ribot	121	34,700	1:34.00	
1969	Double Delta	3	C. Perret	120	Nutty Donut	118	Mrs. Jo Jo	114	34,900	1:35.20	
1970	New Leaf	3	H. Arroyo	110	Princess Roycraft	123	Predictable	118	35,300	1:35.20	
1971	Main Pan	3	G. McCarron	122	Sonny Says Quick	121	Gray's Little Girl	119	21,700	1:36.60	
1972	Barely Even	3	R. Broussard	128	Knightly Belle	115	Bridget o' Brick	118	20,000	1:35.40	
1973	Eleven Pleasures	3	H. Arroyo	112	Princess Doubleday	121	Guided Missile	112	16,150	1:37.60	
1974	Tappahannock	3	W. Gavidia	113	Pot Roast Billie	112	Miss Indian Chief	115	22,350	1:47.60	
1975	Kissapotanmus	3	D. Stover	118	Miami Game	118	Be Victorious	113	21,400	1:45.60	
1976	T.V. Vixen	3	M. Manganello	122	Three Colors	119	True Reality	113	36,600	1:48.40	
1977	Rich Soil	3	M.A. Rivera	122	New Scent	114	Ivory Castle	122	34,530	1:50.40	
1978	Key to the Saga	3	J.L. Samyn	119	Pretty Delight	119	Xandu	122	34,650	1:51.40	
1979	Allison's Girl	3	M.R. Morgan	112	Safe	121	Cup of Honey	116	34,500	2:00.40	
1980	Ribbon	3	P. Day	114	Satin Ribera	121	Cannon Boy	113	35,550	1:52.20	
1981	Melanie Frances	3	R. Sibille	116	Safe Play	121	Touch of Glamour	116	33,660	1:51.80	
1982	Rose Bouquet	3	R.P. Romero	121	Stay a Leader	116	Smart Heiress	121	34,710	1:53.60	
1983	Decision	3	E. Fires	121	Narrate	118	W'n'ty'c'meh'me	116	35,310	1:51.20	
1984	Witwatersrand	3	E. Fires	112	Madam Flutterby	118	Mr. T's Tune	112	48,885	1:52.40	
1984	Dictina	3	J.L. Diaz	112	Nettie Cometti	121	Princess Moran	116	48,285	1:51.40	
1985	Itsagem	3	K.K. Allen	118	Miss Ultimo	121	Tide	112	35,520	1:57.60	
1986	Top Corsage	3	S. Hawley	120	Marianna's Girl	115	Innsbruck	114	34,620	1:44.20	
1987	Sum	3	E. Fires	118	Spectacular Bev	118	Lucie's Bower	113	47,790	1:51.80	
1989	Oczy Czarnie	3	C.A. Black	112	Adira	112	Vanities	115	67,680	1:55.00	
1990	Southern Tradition	3	E. Fires	116	Virgin Michael	116	Slew of Pearls	116	71,040	1:49.20	
1991	Jinski's World	3	A. Madrid Jr	111	Ms. Aerosmith	116	Radiant Ring	121	60,000	1:47.40	101
1992	Ziggy's Act	3	G. Boulanger	116	Bernique	111	Luv Me Luv Me Not	121	60,000	1:48.60	96
1993	Amal Hayati	3	W.S. Ramos	113	Warside	113	Future Starlet	111	60,000	1:53.20	91
1994	Work the Crowd	3	A.T. Gryder	118	Irish Forever	116	Looking for Heaven	116	60,000	1:49.20	96
1995	Grand Charmer	3	P. Day	116	Upper Noosh	116	Set Me Straight	114	60,000	1:49.40	89
1996	Ms. Mostly	3	R P Romero	114	Mountain Affair	116	Clamorosa	121	90,000	1:51.00	87
1997	Witchful Thinking	3	G.K. Gomez	121	Swearingen	116	Cozy Blues	116	75,000	1:48.80	94
2000	Solvig	3	P. Day	121	Zoftig	118	Impending Bear	118	90,000	1:52.40	91
2001	Snow Dance	3	C. Perret	122	Kiss the Devil	116	Twilite Tryst	116	90,000	1:47.93	90
2002	Little Treasure	3	R.R. Douglas	122	Cellars Shiraz	122	Kathy K D	116	90,000	1:49.92	93
2003	Aud	3	B.D. Peck	118	Hail Hillary	116	Julie's Prize	120	105,000	1:49.16	93

Beyer Index: 92.82

QUEENS COUNTY HANDICAP, 1 3/16 Miles,
3-Year-Olds and Up, Aqueduct, 2003 Purse: $108,300

Year	Winner	Age	Jockey	Wt.	Second	Wt.	Third	Wt.	Win Value	Time	Beyer
1902	Margraviate	4	O. Wonderly	112	Colonel Padden	119	Oom Paul	120	1,050	1:46.00	
1903	Yellow Tail	6	W. Shaw	108	Dr. Saylor	101	Injunction	101	1,725	1:45.20	
1904	Rosetint	4	T. Burns	105	Colonsay	101	Ostrich	100	1,855	1:39.20	
1905	St. Valentine	4	M. Crimmins	112	Rapid Water	125	Sinister	104	1,715	1:39.20	
1906	Ram's Horn	4	Perrine	118	Batts	90	Race King	101	1,710	1:39.40	
1907	W.H. Carey	4	Mountain	115	Pretension	112	Good Luck	115	1,795	1:40.00	
1908	Jack Atkin	4	P. Musgrave	124	Rifleman	104	Spooner	98	1,555	1:39.00	
1910	Arasee	5	J. Glass	109	Prince Ahmed	118	Magazine	109	1,050	1:39.80	
1914	Flying Fairy	4	T. Davies	120	Meridian	120	Leo Skolny	107	1,190	1:42.80	
1915	Roamer	4	J. Butwell	127	Stromboli	125	Harmonicon	121	2,300	1:39.40	
1916	Short Grass	8	F. Keogh	114	Roamer	129	Gainer	108	0	1:36.40	
1917	Old Rosebud	6	F. Robinson	125	Roamer	129	Chiclet	110	3,825	1:37.60	
1918	Roamer	7	L. Lyke	123	Tom McTaggart	109	H'd Grenade	105	3,775	1:36.60	
1919	Star Master	5	M. Buxton	116	Naturalist	130	Crimper	104	3,825	1:37.40	
1920	Cirrus	4	L. Ensor	120	Wildair	116	Lion d'Or	124	4,050	1:38.00	
1921	John P. Grier	4	F. Keogh	127	Audacious	126	Yellow Hand	112	6,555	1:36.00	
1922	Grey Lag	4	L. Fator	127	Sennings Park	120	Capt. Alcock	112	6,450	1:38.00	
1923	Zev	3	E. Sande	117	Dunlin	107	Nedna	103	7,100	1:37.00	
1924	Mad Hatter	8	E. Sande	127	Rialto	111	Dunlin	111	6,900	1:36.40	
1925	Mad Play	4	L. Fator	128	Shuffle Along	116	Whetstone	111	7,700	1:36.60	
1926	Macaw	4	L. McAtee	110	Navigator	100	Nedana	114	8,150	1:37.00	
1927	Light Carbine	4	J. McCoy	103	Chance Play	123	Mars	128	7,650	1:36.80	
1928	Kentucky II	4	G. Schreiner	115	Black Panther	107	Tantivy	100	8,650	1:38.80	
1929	Comstockery	3	S. Hebert	97	Sortie	117	Mi Vida	108	8,850	1:39.60	
1930	Kildare	4	J. Passero	95	Kai Feng	109	Balko	123	7,350	1:38.60	
1931	Halcyon	3	G. Rose	100	St. Brideaux	100	Mr. Sponge	114	7,500	1:38.60	
1932	Halcyon	4	H. Mills	108	Pompeius	109	Ormesby	108	5,800	1:38.00	
1933	Kerry Patch	3	R. Wholey	108	Okapi	108	Dark Secret	114	2,980	1:38.00	
1934	Singing Wood	3	R. Jones	114	War Glory	118	Burgoo King	115	22,000	1:38.60	
1935	King Saxon	4	C. Rainey	118	Only One	116	Singing Wood	113	3,700	1:37.20	

Year	Winner	Age	Jockey	Wt.	Second	Wt.	Third	Wt.	Win Value	Time	Beyer
1936	Good Gamble	4	S. Renick	112	Clang	110	Good Harvest	113	4,050	1:37.20	
1937	Snark	4	J. Longden	116	Memory Book	117	Scotch Bun	105	4,225	1:37.40	
1938	War Admiral	4	C. Kurtsinger	132	Snark	126	D'ger Point	112	4,425	1:36.80	
1939	Lovely Night	3	J. Longden	106	Heelfly	113	Fighting Fox	121	4,725	1:36.40	
1940	He Did	7	E. Arcaro	118	War Dog	112	The Chief	114	4,600	1:43.20	
1941	Salford II	5	D. Meade	116	Can't Wait	120	Corydon	112	4,270	1:44.40	
1942	Waller	4	B. Thompson	112	Dit	117	Can't Wait	118	4,675	1:44.00	
1943	The Rhymer	5	C. McCreary	112	Kingfisher	105	Boysy	114	4,425	1:45.00	
1944	First Fiddle	5	J. Longden	126	Tola Rose	106	Alex Barth	117	7,780	1:44.20	
1945	Olympic Zenith	4	C. McCreary	108	Stymie	120	Haile	106	7,630	1:45.60	
1946	Helioptic	4	P. Miller	111	Lets Dance	112	Alison Peters	108	7,750	1:43.20	
1947	Gallorette	5	J. Jessop	119	Stymie	129	Mangoneo	104	14,950	1:45.40	
1948	Knockdown	4	F. Zufelt	118	Stymie	132	Gasparilla	107	15,025	1:44.60	
1949	Three Rings	4	T. Atkinson	110	Conniver	114	Bug Juice	107	15,700	1:47.40	
1950	Three Rings	5	H. Woodhouse	126	Mount Marcy	119	Piet	121	15,200	1:44.60	
1951	Sheilas Reward	4	O. Scurlock	113	Lights Up	121	Piet	121	15,000	1:44.60	
1952	County Delight	5	D. Gorman	121	Quiet Step	104	Auditing	113	14,975	1:43.60	
1953	Flaunt	4	S. Cole	105	Indian Land	114	Count Turf	110	20,300	1:44.20	
1954	Find	4	E. Guerin	122	Invigorator	114	Cold Command	118	21,300	1:44.00	
1955	Fabulist	4	T. Atkinson	111	Red Hannigan	111	First Aid	114	20,400	1:43.60	
1956	Blessbull	5	W. Lester	111	Midafternoon	122	Joe Jones	121	20,300	1:42.00	
1957	Bold Ruler	3	E. Arcaro	133	Promised Land	111	Greek Spy	114	19,350	1:42.80	
1958	Oh Johnny	5	W. Boland	120	Whititoldyou	112	Eddie Schmidt	123	18,127	1:43.40	
1959	Whitley	4	E. Guerin	115	Rick City	125	Promised Land	117	18,095	1:36.40	
1960	Cranberry Sauce	3	H. Gustines	110	Promised Land	117	Talent Show	124	19,232	1:36.20	
1961	Manassa Mauler	5	B. Baeza	113	Mail Order	115	Black Th'per	117	19,955	1:36.20	
1962	Grid Iron Hero	3	M. Ycaza	117	Misty Day	120	Nimmer	114	18,980	1:34.00	
1963	Uppercut	4	M. Ycaza	114	Tropical Breeze	111	Get Around	121	19,370	1:35.40	
1964	Third Martini	5	W. Boland	116	Smart	112	Fan Jet	108	36,335	1:50.60	
1965	Prairie Schooner	4	E. Belmonte	112	Tibaldo	112	Just About	113	38,350	1:50.20	
1966	Amberoid	3	W. Blum	121	Exhibitionist	113	Flag Raiser	122	38,025	1:50.60	
1967	Mr. Right	4	H. Gustines	115	Proud Clarion	125	Successor	116	36,140	1:49.60	
1968	Irish Dude	4	S. Hernandez	112	Chompion	113	Ribereno	111	38,025	1:49.60	
1969	Vif	4	L. Adams	113	Misty Run	113	Mr. Right	124	37,505	1:49.20	
1970	Best Turn	4	L. Adams	118	Irurzun	112	Judgable	119	39,130	1:50.00	
1971	Red Reality	5	J. Velasquez	114	Peace Corps	117	Tunex	116	35,880	1:49.60	
1972	Sunny and Mild	3	M. Venezia	109	Chartered Course	111	Rule by Reason	112	35,490	1:54.40	
1973	True Knight	4	A. Cordero Jr	126	Triangular	110	North Sea	117	35,070	1:55.00	
1974	Free Hand	4	J. Amy	109	Arbees Boy	121	Group Plan	123	33,780	1:55.00	
1975	Hail the Pirates	5	R. Turcotte	111	Sharp Gary	110	Herculean	111	34,560	1:55.60	
1976	It's Freezing	4	J. Vasquez	113	Distant Land	111	Nalees Rialto	108	32,640	1:56.60	
1977	Cox's Ridge	3	E. Maple	126	Father Hogan	111	Popular Victory	115	32,670	1:55.80	
1978	Cum Laude Laurie	4	A. Cordero Jr	114	Wise Philip	112	Do Tell George	112	32,580	1:55.80	
1979	Dewan Keys	4	E. Maple	112	Mr. International	108	Gallant Best	116	32,940	1:56.80	
1980	Fool's Prayer	5	J. Velasquez	112	Ring of Light	115	Picturesque	114	33,360	1:56.00	
1981	French Cut	4	D. MacBeth	112	Bar Dexter	110	Alla Breva	109	35,040	1:56.40	
1982	Bar Dexter	5	J. Fell	112	Castle Knight	111	Nice Pirate	110	32,880	1:58.20	
1983	Country Pine	3	J.D. Bailey	118	Count Normandy	108	Megaturn	113	33,240	1:58.00	
1984	Puntivo	4	R.G. Davis	114	High Honors	114	Moro	121	44,640	1:58.00	
1985	Late Act	6	E. Maple	118	Lightning Leap	110	Morning Bob	113	52,380	1:55.40	
1986	Pine Belt	4	E. Maple	111	Scrimshaw	108	Cost Conscious	111	55,260	1:57.20	
1987	Personal Flag	4	R.P. Romero	116	Easy n Dirty	113	Gold Alert	114	64,170	1:59.00	
1988	Lay Down	4	J.L. Samyn	109	Nostalgia's Star	113	Pleasant Virginian	113	64,980	1:57.20	
1989	Its Acedemic	5	J.D. Bailey	115	Homebuilder	113	Ole Atocha	113	52,290	1:58.00	
1990	Sports View	3	C. Perret	114	I'm Sky High	115	Killer Diller	115	53,550	1:57.00	
							Lost Opportunity	112			
1991	Nome	5	E. Maple	112	Runaway Stream	116	Challenge My Duty	114	51,390	1:56.00	109
1992	Shots Are Ringing	5	J.R. Velazquez	117	A Call to Rise	111	Jacksonport	111	51,120	1:54.80	100
1993	Repletion	4	M.E. Smith	111	Dibbs n' Dubbs	111	Primitive Hall	113	53,010	1:44.20	96
1994	Federal Funds	5	D. Carr	111	Jacksonport	110	Contract Court	116	49,665	1:56.40	101
1995	Aztec Empire	5	J.L. Samyn	113	Mighty Magee	115	More to Tell	115	50,340	1:55.40	109
1996	Topsy Robsy	4	P. Keim-Bruno	111	More To Tell	114	Colonial Secretary	116	48,705	1:55.20	103
1997	Mr. Sinatra	3	R. Migliore	115	Delay of Game	118	Draw	113	49,725	1:55.60	105
1998	Fire King	5	F. .Lovato Jr	113	Las Vegas Ernie	112	Mr. Sinatra	119	49,140	1:56.80	103
1999	Early Warning	4	J.F. Chavez	110	Doc Martin	112	Yankee Victor	114	49,230	1:55.00	105
2000	Boston Party	4	N. Arroyo Jr	115	Talk's Cheap	115	Turnofthecentury	116	50,340	1:56.32	103
2001	Evening Attire	3	S.X. Bridgmohan	113	Balto Star	118	Top Official	113	67,140	1:55.08	105
2002	Snake Mountain	4	J.A. Santos	117	Docent	115	Cat's at Home	115	66,000	1:56.84	106
2003	Thunder Blitz	5	J.F. Chavez	114	Evening Attire	123	Seattle Fitz	115	64,980	1:55.90	110

Beyer Index: 104.23

RAILBIRD, 7 Furlongs,
3-Year-Old Fillies, Hollywood Park, 2003 Purse: $107,200

Year	Winner	Age	Jockey	Wt.	Second	Wt.	Third	Wt.	Win Value	Time	Beyer
1963	Well Ordered	3	A. Maese	113	Bre'r Rabbit	123	Sheereen's Porter	120	14,600	1:22.20	
1964	Fran La Femme	3	M. Yanez	112	Lil's Nite Out	112	Roman Goddess	114	13,800	1:22.00	
1965	Mine Lovely	3	J. Baze	113	Cut It Up	112	Quick Win	112	15,625	1:22.60	
1965	Gala Host	3	M. Valenzuela	112	Ardell C.	121	Bubble Bath	113	15,875	1:21.60	
1966	Fleet Treat	3	A. Pineda	112	Mellow Marsh	112	What a Charmer	118	16,000	1:22.00	
1967	Forgiving	3	J. Lambert	118	Gamely	113	Francine M.	113	17,500	1:22.20	
1968	Morgaise	3	J. Lambert	118	Time to Leave	118	Toe Shoes	112	13,250	1:21.20	
1969	Tipping Time	3	M. Valenzuela	114	Marjorie's Girl	115	Dumpty's Lady	121	13,350	1:21.40	
1970	Bold Jil	3	W, Shoemaker	118	Opening Bid	121	Amber Light	115	12,750	1:21.40	
1971	Turkish Trousers	3	W. Shoemaker	121	Convenience	115	Countess Market	115	17,200	1:21.80	
1972	Impressive Style	3	L. Pincay Jr	121	Cautious Bidder	118	Crimson Saint	118	16,600	1:21.00	
1973	Sandy Blue	3	D. Pierce	118	Sphere	113	Goddess Roman	113	20,250	1:21.80	
1974	Modus Vivendi	3	D. Pierce	121	Fleet Peach	118	Fresno Star	118	19,800	1:21.60	
1975	Raise Your Skirts	3	W. Mahorney	118	Miss Tokyo	117	Fascinating Girl	119	19,350	1:20.80	
1976	Hail Hilarious	3	D. Pierce	114	Doc Shah's Siren	119	I Going	115	20,550	1:21.40	
1977	Taisez Vous	3	F. Toro	114	Wavy Waves	122	Silent Wisdom	114	22,650	1:22.60	
1978	Eximious	3	W. Shoemaker	119	B. Thoughtful	122	Joe's Bee	114	25,550	1:22.20	
1979	Eloquent	3	D. Pierce	122	Celine	122	Joy's Jewel	114	26,800	1:20.60	
1980	Cinegita	3	T. Lipham	114	Thundertee	122	Back at Two	119	31,450	1:20.80	
1981	Cherokee Frolic	3	G. Cohen	119	Strangeways	119	Terra Miss	115	32,400	1:22.20	
1982	Faneuil Lass	3	T. Lipham	117	Jones Time Machine	119	Hasty Hannah	119	32,400	1:23.20	
1983	Ski Goggle	3	C.J. McCarron	122	Madam Forbes	115	Gatita	117	33,150	1:23.40	
1984	Mitterand	3	E. Delahoussaye	115	Gene's Lady	122	Lucky Lucky Lucky	122	40,000	1:22.20	
1985	Reigning Countess	3	G.L. Stevens	122	Window Seat	122	Charming Susan	115	38,300	1:22.40	
1986	Melair	3	P.A. Valenzuela	115	Comparability	119	Silent Arrival	122	48,600	1:22.40	
1987	Very Subtle	3	W. Shoemaker	122	Joey the Trip	117	Sacahuista	122	45,750	1:22.60	
1988	Sheesham	3	L. Pincay Jr	122	Affordable Price	114	Super Avie	116	49,700	1:22.60	
1989	Imaginary Lady	3	G.L. Stevens	122	Kiwi	114	Stormy but Valid	122	47,800	1:21.40	
1990	Forest Fealty	3	J.A. Garcia	114	Patches	122	Golden Reef	122	48,950	1:21.60	
1991	Suziqcute	3	C.J. McCarron	119	Zama Hummer	117	Ifyoucouldseemenow	122	62,800	1:21.80	100
1992	She's Tops	3	K.J. Desormeaux	114	Race the Wild Wind	121	Magical Maiden	121	66,500	1:22.60	94
1993	Afto	3	P. Atkinson	114	Fit to Lead	121	Nijivision	113	64,500	1:22.40	93
1994	Sportful Snob	3	P.A. Valenzuela	118	Pirate's Revenge	121	Accountable Lady	116	61,400	1:21.80	96
1995	Sleep Easy	3	C.S. Nakatani	113	Texinadress	118	Laguna Seca	115	64,600	1:22.40	94
1996	Supercilious	3	C.S. Nakatani	121	Tiffany Diamond	118	Raw Gold	121	64,260	1:22.60	91
1997	I Ain't Bluffing	3	E. Delahoussaye	118	Really Happy	121	Montecito	114	65,100	1:22.60	95
1998	Brulay	3	G.L. Stevens	115	Gourmet Girl	119	Unreal Squeal	116	64,260	1:20.80	104
1999	Olympic Charmer	3	C.J. McCarron	115	Dianehill	115	Fee Fi Foe	116	90,000	1:21.00	106
2000	Abby Girl	3	C.S. Nakatani	119	Cover Gal	122	Wired to Fly	122	90,000	1:22.57	96
2001	Golden Ballet	3	C.J. McCarron	123	Starrer	115	Pretty 'n Smart	115	90,000	1:21.57	101
2002	Spetember Secret	3	P.A. Valenzuela	118	Affairs of State	118	Fun House	118	63,780	1:22.95	95
2003	Buffythecenterfold	3	V. Espinoza	123	Honest Answer	117	Dash for Money	115	64,320	1:22.54	88

Beyer Index: 96.38

RANCHO BERNARDO HANDICAP, 6 1/2 Furlongs,
Fillies and Mares 3-Year-Olds and Up, Del Mar, 2003 Purse: $150,000

Year	Winner	Age	Jockey	Wt.	Second	Wt.	Third	Wt.	Win Value	Time	Beyer
1967	Sharp Decline	5	R. Bianco	114	Bern Book	116	Gueenie	116	7,475	1:33.80	
1967	Quicken Tree	4	W. Hartack	116	Blazing Silk	112	Het's Cadet	115	7,475	1:34.80	
1973	Fairly Certain	4	S. Valdez	121	Tannyhill	117	Norm'ndy Glory	115	10,400	1:42.80	
1973	Dollar Discount	4	S. Valdez	119			Dr. Kerlan	118	6,400	1:43.20	
	D.B. Carm	4	F. Toro	119							
1974	Impressive Style	5	R. Rosales	117	Fleet Peach	115	Lt's Joy	120	16,300	1:08.60	
1975	Mama Kali	4	J. Lambert	120	Hooley Ruler	117	Modus Vivendi	124	17,050	1:08.40	
1976	Mama Kali	5	L. Pincay Jr	117	Mismoyola	120	Vol au Vent	120	16,400	1:09.20	
1977	Lullaby Song	4	L. Pincay Jr	120	Miss Rising Marke	113	Honeyhugger	117	16,550	1:09.00	
1978	Happy Holme	4	C.J. McCarron	120	Telferner	117	Dallas Deb	113	18,200	1:13.00	
1979	Fantastic Girl	3	W. Shoemaker	112	Happy Holme	120	Delice	122	22,850	1:09.20	
1980	Great Lady M.	5	L. Pincay Jr	121	Sal's High	118	Western Hand	110	25,800	1:08.60	
1981	Forluvofiv	4	E. Delahoussaye	118	Untamed Spirit	122	Ack's Secret	118	31,400	1:09.40	
1982	Lucky Lady Ellen	3	L. Pincay Jr	117	Glitter Hitter	118	Excitable Lady	125	31,850	1:08.60	
1983	Bara Lass	4	C.J. McCarron	120	Excitable Lady	124	Milingo	113	31,800	1:09.40	
1984	Pleasure Cay	4	L. Pincay Jr	121	Lovlier Linda	120	Pride of Rosewood	115	32,250	1:08.60	
1985	Take My Picture	3	F. Olivares	114	Sales Bulletin	118	Mimi Baker	112	33,200	1:09.20	
1986	Bold n Special	3	C.J. McCarron	115	Rangoon Ruby	116	Eloquack	117	30,850	1:14.60	
1987	Julie the Flapper	3	C.J. McCarron	114	Clabber Girl	117	Sari's Heroine	119	33,200	1:15.00	
1988	Clabber Girl	5	L. Pincay Jr	120	Queen Forbes	113	Behind the Scenes	117	38,750	1:14.60	
1989	Kool Arrival	3	L. Pincay Jr	117	Super Avie	117	Survive	116	47,625	1:15.20	
1990	Hot Novel	4	K.J. Desormeaux	118	Sexy Slew	116	Down Again	115	62,875	1:14.60	106
1991	Cascading Gold	5	L. Pincay Jr	117	Survive	120	Suziqcute	114	60,100	1:15.40	103

Year	Winner	Age	Jockey	Wt.	Second	Wt.	Third	Wt.	Win Value	Time	Beyer
1992	Bountiful Native	4	P.A. Valenzuela.	117	Devil's Orchid	120	She's Tops	114.	63,400	1:15.20	100
1993	Knight Prospector	4	K.J. Desormeaux	119	Interactive	119	Bountiful Native.	120.	45,675	1:16.40	96
1994	Desert Stormer	4	Delahoussaye E	116	Magical Maiden	120	Booklore	117.	62,800	1:14.80	103
1995	Track Gal	4	C.J. McCarron.	118	Desert Stormer	119	Lakeway	122.	58,650	1:14.20	107
1996	Track Gal	5	McCarron C. J.	122	Tricky Code	116	Evil's Pic	117.	63,550	1:14.60	110
1997	Track Gal	6	Stevens G. L.	120	Madame Pandit.	118	Advancing Star	116.	69,125	1:15.60	107
1998	Advancing Star	5	McCarron C. J.	120	Closed Escrow.	115	Tiffany Diamond.	116.	64,140	1:14.60	110
1999	Enjoy The Moment	4	Flores D. R.	119	Snowberg	117	Stop Traffic	121.	90,000	1:15.80	100
2000	Theresa's Tizzy	6	L. Pincay Jr.	117	Nany's Sweep	117	Hookedonthefeelin	119.	90,000	1:16.23	103
2001	Kalookan Queen	5	A. Solis.	119	Go Go	125	Warren's Whistle	111.	90,000	1:15.52	103
2002	Kalookan Queen	6	A. Solis.	123	Warren's Whistle	116	Fancee Bargain	112.	90,000	1:16.40	98
2003	Secret Liaison	5	C.S. Nakatani	116	Lacie Girl	116	Spring Meadow	117.	90,000	1:15.53	102

Beyer Index: 103.43

RAVEN RUN, 7 Furlongs,
3-Year-Old Fillies, Keeneland, 2003 Purse: $174,450

Year	Winner	Age	Jockey	Wt.	Second	Wt.	Third	Wt.	Win Value	Time	Beyer
1999	Dreamy Maiden	3	P. Day	117	Golden Illusion	117	Cosmic Wing	117.	37,706	1:22.64	91
2000	Darling My Darling	3	M.E. Smith	117	Surfside	123	Cat Cay	117.	51,104	1:20.88	105
2001	Nasty Storm	3	P. Day	123	Hattiesburg	123	Forest Secrets	117.	68,138	1:23.30	100
2002	Sightseek	3	J.D. Bailey	117	Miss Lodi	123	Respectful	117.	106,578	1:23.98	98
2003	Yell	3	P. Day	123	Ebony Breeze	123	Tina Bull	117.	108,159	1:21.75	102

Beyer Index: 99.2

RAZORBACK HANDICAP, 1 1/16 Miles,
4-Year-Olds and Up, Oaklawn Park, 2003 Purse: $100,000

Year	Winner	Age	Jockey	Wt.	Second	Wt.	Third	Wt.	Win Value	Time	Beyer
1976	Royal Glint	6	J. Tejeira	126	Marauding	114	Heaven Forbid	112.	35,550	1:42.40	
1977	Dragset	4	J. Kunitake.	120	Romeo	120	Last Buzz	115.	35,910	1:44.40	
1978	Cox's Ridge	4	E. Maple	125	Dr. Riddick	116	Mark's Place	124.	37,110	1:43.00	
1979	Cisk	5	G. Patterson	120	Droll's Reason	113	Prince Majestic.	121.	53,700	1:45.40	
1980	All the More.	7	L. Snyder	114	Prince Majestic	116	Br'ker Br'ker.	117.	56,400	1:45.40	
1981	Temperence Hill.	4	E. Maple	124	Blue Ensign	113	Belle's Ruler	112.	11,110	1:44.20	
1982	Eminency	4	P. Day	111	Reef Searcher	119	Tally Ho the Fox	115.	76,200	1:45.20	
1983	Eminency	5	P. Day	120	Cassaleria	115	Bold Style	113.	70,740	1:43.60	
1984	Dew Line	5	S. Maple	116	Passing Base	112	Win Stat	115.	74,520	1:41.60	
1985	Imp Society	4	P. Day	126	Introspective	113	Strength in Unity	109.	97,740	1:42.60	
1986	Red Attack	4	L. Snyder	111	Vanlandingham.	125	Inevitable Leader	111.	96,900	1:42.00	
1987	Bolshoi Boy	4	R.P. Romero	119	Lyphard's Ridge.	110	Sun Master	115.	86,520	1:40.80	
1988	Lost Code.	4	C. Perret	123	Red Attack	112	Demons Begone.	121.	73,500	1:40.40	
1989	Blushing John.	4	P. Day	117	Lyphard's Ridge.	111	Proper Reality	123.	60,000	1:43.00	
1990	Opening Verse	4	P. Day	116	Primal.	121	Silver Survivor.	118.	90,000	1:41.40	
1991	Bedeviled	4	D.L. Howard.	115	Din's Dancer.	117	Black Tie Affair.	118.	90,000	1:42.40	
1992	Tokatee	6	G.K. Gomez	115	On the Edge	112	Total Assets	110.	90,000	1:42.80	
1993	Lil E. Tee.	4	P. Day	123	Zeeruler	115	Senor Tomas.	114.	90,000	1:41.40	116
1994	Prize Fight	5	P.A. Johnson	113	Brother Brown	120	Country Store	113.	90,000	1:43.60	111
1995	Silver Goblin	4	D.W. Cordova	124	Joseph's Robe	111	Wooden Ticket	115.	120,000	1:42.60	113
1996	Juliannus	7	R.J. Albarado.	113	Judge TC	121	Dazzling Falls	118.	90,000	1:43.20	98
1997	No Spend No Glow	5	R.N. Lester	115	Illesam	114	Come On Flip	115.	90,000	1:43.20	102
1998	Brush With Pride.	6	T.T. Doocy	115	Littlebitlively.	112	Krigeorj's Gold.	115.	75,000	1:43.40	105
1999	Desert Air	4	C.J. Lanerie	113	Magnify	113	Black Tie Dinner.	112.	75,000	1:44.75	101
2000	Well Noted.	5	T.T. Doocy	112	Crimson Classic	115	Mr Ross	115.	75,000	1:43.21	105
2001	Mr. Ross	6	D. Pettinger	119	Graeme Hall	120	Maysville Slew.	117.	75,000	1:42.60	109
2002	Mr. Ross	7	D. Pettinger	120	Remington Rock.	115	Big Numbers.	116.	60,000	1:44.13	105
2003	Colorful Tour	4	L.S. Quinonez	118	Crafty Shaw	119	Windward Passage	118.	60,000	1:43.53	98

Beyer Index: 105.73

RED BANK HANDICAP, 1 Mile (Off the Turf),
3-Year-Olds and Up, Monmouth Park, 2003 Purse: $97,000

Year	Winner	Age	Jockey	Wt.	Second	Wt.	Third	Wt.	Win Value	Time	Beyer
1974	Mystery Mood	2	J. Tejeira	115	Molly Ballantine.	121	Lucky Leslie	117.	18,672	1:45.20	
1975	Kudara	4	D. MacBeth	118	Enchanted Native.	111	Twixt	121.	18,850	1:42.20	
1976	Collegiate	4	J.W. Edwards.	116	Shoe Me How.	110	Four Bells	114.	25,919	1:40.20	
1977	Playin' Footsie.	4	R. Ardoin.	110	Desiree	110	Artfully	112.	29,510	1:44.20	
1978	Love Jenny	4	M.A. Gomez	108	Table Hopper	111	Chanctonbury	114.	28,308	1:46.20	
1979	Navajo Princess	5	J. Vasquez.	122	La Soufriere	116	Sans Arc	115.	22,441	1:43.20	
1980	Horatius	5	D. MacBeth	117	Pipedreamer	116	North Course	114.	24,495	1:35.00	
1981	Colonel Moran	4	G.W. Donohue.	116	Dan Horn	115	Contare	108.	24,570	1:35.20	
1982	Alhambra Joe	5	W. Nemeti.	111	Pepper's Segundo.	117	Timely Counsel.	112.	23,265	1:38.60	
1983	Sun and Shine	4	J. Terry	115	St. Brendan.	116	Mr. Dreamer	113.	24,480	1:36.60	

Year	Winner	Age	Jockey	Wt.	Second	Wt.	Third	Wt.	Win Value	Time	Beyer
1984	Tough Mickey	4	K. Skinner	118	Fortnightly	117	Roman Bend	108	28,470	1:36.40	
1984	Castle Guard	5	J.C. Ferrer	118	Super Sunrise	123	Fray Star	117	28,530	1:35.80	
1985	Castelets	6	V. Bracciale Jr.	115	Evzone	117	Gothic Revival	112	27,885	1:37.00	
1985	Ends Well	4	M.R. Morgan	116	Domynsky	117	Bold Southerner	115	26,065	1:35.40	
1986	Mazatleca	6	C.W. Antley	112	Feeling Gallant	114	Hi Ideal	113	34,800	1:35.80	
1987	Feeling Gallant	5	C.W. Antley	117	Hi Ideal	114	Racing Star	117	35,610	1:37.20	
1988	Iron Courage	4	W.H. McCauley	118	Spellbound	112	Ioskeha	113	42,210	1:35.40	
1989	Arlene's Valentine	4	J.C. Ferrer	115	Yankee Affair	121	Alwasmi	114	52,290	1:40.20	
1990	Norquestor	4	J.L. Samyn	118	Master Speaker	120	Grande Jette	111	52,980	1:36.00	109
1991	Double Booked	6	J.C. Ferrer	122	Great Normand	118	Now Listen	112	45,000	1:33.20	110
1992	Daarik	5	L. Saumell	114	Leger Cat	116	Kate's Valentine	114	45,000	1:34.00	98
1993	Adam Smith	5	J.L. Samyn	116	Fourstars Allstar	116	Rinka Das	115	45,000	1:34.20	103
1994	Adam Smith	6	J.A. Krone	120	Discernment	113	Fourstardave	118	45,000	1:34.40	110
1995	Dove Hunt	4	W.H. McCauley	118	Rare Reason	115	Winnetou	113	45,000	1:33.80	104
1996	Joker	4	Velez A. J. Jr	113	Rare Reason	118	Diplomatic Jet	116	60,000	1:35.80	106
1997	Basqueian	4	Wilson R.	118	Wild Night Out	111	Jambalaya Jazz	117	60,000	1:35.80	103
1998	Statesmanship	4	Santos J. A.	115	Rob 'n Gin	120	Bomfim	114	60,000	1:35.00	104
1999	Inkatha	5	Castillo H. Jr.	114	Rob 'n Gin	119	Soviet Line	118	90,000	1:33.80	104
2000	Mi Narrow	6	C. Velasquez	114	Deep Gold	114	Inkatha	117	90,000	1:34.84	105
2001	Pavillon	7	J. Bravo	112	Western Summer	114	Runspastum	114	90,000	1:36.38	96
2002	Key Lory	8	H. Vega	117	Sardaukar	113	Spruce Run	113	60,000	1:35.92	100
2003	Just le Facts	4	J. Bravo	111	Saint Verre	118	Runspastum	114	60,000	1:37.73	93

Beyer Index: 103.21

Off the turf in 2003.

REGRET, 1 1/8 Miles (Turf),
3-Year-Old Fillies, Churchill Downs, 2003 Purse: $231,000

Year	Winner	Age	Jockey	Wt.	Second	Wt.	Third	Wt.	Win Value	Time	Beyer
1994	Packet	3	J.Johnson	117	Thread	122	Slew Kitty Slew	112	54,551	1:42.14	90
1995	Christmas Gift	3	C.Woods	122	Bail Our Becky	122	Grand Charmer	117	54,210	1:45.00	94
1996	Daylight Come	3	C.Bourque	117	Fleur de Nuit	112	Esquive	115	55,526	1:45.72	89
1997	Starry Dreamer	3	W.Martinez	122	Cozy Blues	115	Swearingen	122	69,378	1:42.77	94
1998	Formal Tango	3	C.Woods	115	Adel	122	Pratella	112	105,927	1:43.73	90
1999	Nani Rose	3	S.J. Sellers	115	Solar Bound	122	Suffragette	115	104,439	1:42.40	102
2000	Solvig	3	P. Day	122	Trip	117	Miss Chief	115	104,439	1:42.95	89
2001	Casual Feat	3	L. Melancon	115	Amaretta	117	La Vida Loca	119	103,695	1:42.75	95
2002	Distant Valley	3	J.D. Bailey	119	Peace River Lady	115	Styleistick	122	104,811	1:42.71	92
2003	Sand Springs	3	M. Guidry	118	Personal Legend	116	Achnasheen	116	143,220	1:48.78	92

Beyer Index: 92.7

For previous runnings, refer to 1994 Manual

LEONARD RICHARDS, 1 1/16 Miles,
3-Year-Olds, Delaware Park, 2003 Purse: $250,000

Year	Winner	Age	Jockey	Wt.	Second	Wt.	Third	Wt.	Win Value	Time	Beyer
1997	Leestown	3	J. Velez Jr.	116	Universe		Bleu Madura		90,000	1:43.40	
1998	Scatmandu	3	R. Migliore	114	Hot Wells		True Silver		90,000	1:42.40	
1999	Stellar Brush	3	M. McCarthy	114	Smart Guy		Successful Appeal		120,000	1:42.78	
2000	Grundlefoot	3	T. Dunkelberger	113	Perfect Cat		Mercaldo		120,000	1:44.04	96
2001	Burning Roma	3	R. Wilson	122	Marciano		Bay Eagle		120,000	1:42.41	114
2002	Running Tide	3	R.A. Dominguez	115	Nothing Flat	115	The Sewickley Kind	115	150,000	1:45.10	97
2003	Awesome Time	3	A.S. Black	115	Christine's Outlaw	115	Cherokee's Boy	122	150,000	1:43.26	95

Beyer Index: 100.5

For previous runnings, refer to 1983 Manual

RISEN STAR, 1 1/16 Miles,
3-Year-Olds, Fair Grounds, 2003 Purse: $150,000

Year	Winner	Age	Jockey	Wt.	Second	Wt.	Third	Wt.	Win Value	Time	Beyer
1988	Risen Star	3	S. Romero	120	Pastourelles	115	Jim's Orbit	122	12,000	1:40.00	
1989	Nooo Problema	3	S. Romero	117	Alota Strawberry	114	Majesty's Imp	119	12,000	1:42.40	
1989	Dispersal	3	B.J. Walker	114	Island Alibi	114	Major Prospect	114	12,000	1:42.20	
1990	Genuine Meaning	3	R.J. Hirdes	122	Very Formal	114	Diamond Prospector	114	15,000	1:40.80	
1991	Big Courage	3	T.L. Fox	119	Slick Groom	114	Denizen	115	18,000	1:46.60	
1992	Line in the Sand	3	S. Romero	119	Hill Pass	119	Sheik to Sheik	114	19,210	1:45.00	88
1993	Dixieland Heat	3	R.P. Romero	119	O'Star	114	Gold Angle	114	19,995	1:43.20	85
1993	Dry Bean	3	A. Gryder	117	Apprentice	119	Grand Jewel	114	16,020	1:43.80	87
1994	Fly Cry	3	R. Ardoin	122	Smilin Singin Sam	122	Little Jazz Boy	114	31,155	1:43.00	100
1995	Knockadoon	3	W. Martinez	114	Key to Milagra	114	Scott's Scoundrel	122	31,882	1:45.40	90
1995	Beavers Nose	3	K. Bourque	117	Moonlight Dancer	122	Fuzzy Me	114	31,792	1:45.20	92
1996	Zarb's Magic	3	E.J. Perrodin	122	Imminent First	114	Palikar	122	37,950	1:42.80	100
1997	Open Forum	3	D.M. Barton	117	Crypto Star	117	Cash Deposit	122	60,000	1:44.20	91
1998	Comic Strip	3	S.J. Sellers	119	Captain Maestri	122	Time Limit	122	75,000	1:44.20	91
1999	Ecton Park	3	S.J. Sellers	114	Answer Lively	122	Kimberlite Pipe	122	75,000	1:44.80	95

Year	Winner	Age	Jockey	Wt.	Second	Wt.	Third	Wt.	Win Value	Time	Beyer
2000	Exchange Rate	3	C.S. Nakatani	119	Mighty	122	Ifitstobeitsuptome	114	75,000	1:44.20	97
2001	Dollar Bill	3	C.J. McCarron	122	Gracie's Dancer	114	Rahy's Secret	122	75,000	1:43.40	102
2002	Repent	3	A.J. D'Amico	122	Bob's Image	115	Easyfromthegitgo	122	90,000	1:43.17	102
2003	Badge of Silver	3	R.J. Albarado	116	Lone Star Sky	122	Defrere's Vixen	114	90,000	1:42.99	108

Beyer Index: 94.86

RIVER CITY HANDICAP, 1 1/8 Miles (Turf), 3-Year-Olds and Up, Churchill Downs, 2003 Purse: $172,800

Year	Winner	Age	Jockey	Wt.	Second	Wt.	Third	Wt.	Win Value	Time	Beyer
1978	Inca Roca	5	J.C. Espinoza	118	Perplext	114	Raymond Earl	115	17,859	1:10.40	
1979	Go With the Times	3	G. Gallitano	120	Cossett Charlie	112	Bask	117	19,435	1:10.20	
1980	Tinsley's Hope	6	J.C. Espinoza	114	Go With the Times	122	Withholding	114	19,208	1:11.00	
1981	Suliman	4	L. Snyder	113	Tiger Lure	121	Senate Chairman	113	20,199	1:10.60	
1982	Pleasing Times	3	P. Day	110	Hechizado	115	Rackensack	118	20,719	1:38.20	
1983	Northern Majesty	4	S. Maple	120	Shot n' Missed	123	Straight Flow	115	18,249	1:37.00	
1984	Eminency	6	P. Day	115	Thumbsucker	123	Boyou Hebert	116	18,103	1:38.40	
1985	Banner Bob	3	K.K. Allen	118	Rapid Gray	123	Cullendale	116	29,348	1:36.60	
1986	Taylor's Special	5	P. Day	123	Doonesbear	116	Sumptious	121	30,007	1:36.20	
1987	King's River II	5	M.E. Smith	114	Lord Grundy	119	Boulder Run	117	37,148	1:45.40	
1988	Ile de Jinsky	4	E.J. Sipus Jr	113	Stop the Stage	114	Herakles	117	44,618	1:53.20	
1989	Spark O'Dan	4	J.M. Johnston	113	Exclusive Greer	115	Air Worthy	118	55,429	1:50.80	
1990	Silver Medallion	4	C. Perret	118	Blair's Cove	114	Rushing Raj	114	56,550	1:50.80	
1991	Spending Record	4	P. Day	114	Stage Colony	113	Silver Medallion	118	75,075	1:50.20	105
1992	Cozzene's Prince	5	D. Penna	117	Lotus Pool	118	Stagecraft	114	73,060	1:49.20	103
1993	Secreto's Hideaway	4	W. Martinez	110	Little Bro Lantis	115	Ganges	113	72,670	1:53.80	99
1994	Lindon Lime	4	Sellers SJ	113	Torch Rouge	114	Jaggery John	115	75,660	1:49.20	106
1995	Homing Pigeon	4	Romero RP	114	Hawk Attack	115	Dusty Asher	111	73,320	1:51.00	99
1996	Same Old Wish	6	Sellers S. J.	119	Jet Freighter	113	Franchise Player	112	70,122	1:49.20	105
1997	Same Old Wish	7	Sellers S. J.	117	Aboriginal Apex	113	Joyeus Danseur	114	106,578	1:50.80	103
1998	Wild Event	5	Sellers S. J.	116	Buff	113	Floriselli	114	116,436	1:49.00	109
1999	Comic Strip	4	P. Day	119	Keats and Yeats	112	Aboriginal Apex	114	106,113	1:50.60	105
2000	Brahms	3	P. Day	112	Vergennes	115	Super Quercus	116	111,879	1:48.09	107
2001	Dr. Kashnikow	4	R.J. Albarado	116	Tijiyr	117	Strategic Mission	115	109,926	1:47.90	104
2002	Dr. Kashnikow	5	R.J. Albarado	116	Foster's Landing	109	Roxinho	115	108,903	1:51.44	100
2003	Hard Buck	4	B. Blanc	118	Warleigh	117	Rowans Park	114	107,136	1:51.60	103

Beyer Index: 103.69

WILL ROGERS, 1 Mile (Turf), 3-Year-Olds, Hollywood Park, 2003 Purse: $112,600

Year	Winner	Age	Jockey	Wt.	Second	Wt.	Third	Wt.	Win Value	Time	Beyer
1938	Dogaway	4	A. Gray	121	Speed to Spare	122	Faithful Maud	114	2,025	1:23.80	
1939	Time Alone	3	E. Tucker	122	Roman Hero	116	Teddy Kerry	115	5,400	1:23.80	
1940	Sweepida	3	R. Neves	122	Weigh Anchor	119	Last Gold	115	7,625	1:23.80	
1941	Battle Colors	3	G. Woolf	124	Strong Arm	113	Painted Veil	114	7,925	1:23.60	
1944	Phar Rong	5	O. Grohs	114	Appleknocker	119	Happy Issue	120	11,200	1:24.20	
1945	Quick Reward	3	A. Skoronski	112	Busher	123	War Allies	110	19,750	1:37.60	
1946	Burra Sahib	3	C. Corbett	115	Enfilade	116	Going With Me	108	20,100	1:24.40	
1947	On Trust	3	J. Longden	126	Handlebars	108	Sullivan	115	20,100	1:22.60	
1948	Speculation	3	F. Chojnacki	115	Stage Glitter	120	Solidarity	124	19,050	1:11.00	
1949	Blue Dart	3	J. Westrope	112	Terry's Man	114	Spotted Bull	111	19,250	1:10.20	
1951	Gold Note	3	W. Shoemaker	114	Ruth Lily	116	Gold Capitol	125	15,650	1:10.20	
1952	Forelock	3	R.L. Baird	110	Alate	110	Warcos	118	17,250	1:09.80	
1953	Imbros	3	R. York	110	Atomic Speed	110	Karim	110	16,450	1:10.00	
1954	Don McCoy	3	I. Valenzuela	110	Rolyat	112	Arrogate	122	16,550	1:09.60	
1955	Swaps	3	W. Shoemaker	126	Bequeath	122	Mr. Sullivan	118	14,850	1:35.00	
1956	Terrang	3	W. Shoemaker	126	Tecolotito	114	Social Climber	118	17,400	1:35.20	
1957	Round Table	3	R. Neves	122	Joe Price	118	Miquelet	111	16,150	1:34.40	
1958	Hillsdale	3	R. York	110	Prize Host	114	Sir Ruler	110	15,600	1:36.20	
1959	Ole Fols	3	I. Valenzuela	118	Frair Roach	110	Tramore II	110	15,000	1:35.20	
1960	Flow Line	3	J. Longden	123	Natego	114	First Balcony	114	16,000	1:34.80	
1961	Four-and-Twenty	3	J. Longden	126	Olden Times	123	Sonofagun	114	16,000	1:34.40	
1962	Wallet Lifter	3	A. Maese	114	Pirate Cove	114	Drill Site	114	15,425	1:35.00	
1962	Prince of Liberty	3	A. Valenzuela	114	Royal Attack	126	Doc Jocoy	123	15,675	1:34.60	
1963	Viking Spirit	3	J. Longden	114	Y Flash	120	Beekeeper	114	16,675	1:36.60	
1963	Bre'r Rabbit	3	R. York	114	Doolin Point	114	On My Honor	123	16,375	1:36.00	
1964	Count Charles	3	M. Yanez	120	Royal Eiffel	114	Pelegrin	114	20,700	1:36.00	
1965	Terry's Secret	3	A. Maese	120	Easy Lime	114	Arksroni	114	35,000	1:35.20	
1966	Ri Tux	3	I. Valenzuela	113	Drin	114	Galanomad	112	23,925	1:35.80	
1966	Aqua Vite	3	D. Ross	112	Vague Image	116	Postage	112	24,425	1:35.60	
1967	Jungle Road	3	J. Lambert	113	Pagan Gem	113	Tumiga	120	35,450	1:36.40	
1968	Poleax	3	L. Pincay Jr	113	Right or Wrong	116	Glory Hallelujah	114	20,450	1:34.40	

Year	Winner	Age	Jockey	Wt.	Second	Wt.	Third	Wt.	Win Value	Time	Beyer
1969	Tell	3	W. Shoemaker	115	Modern Spirit	114	Greek Static	115	19,250	1:35.20	
1970	Lime	3	L. Gilligan	113	Sugar Loaf	112	Sir Wiggle	115	26,200	1:35.80	
1970	Whittingham	3	D. Pierce	114	Colorado King Jr.	115	Rancho Lejos	115	26,200	1:36.00	
1971	Dr. Knighton	3	I. Valenzuela	115	Smooth It	112	Restless Runner	115	32,675	1:35.80	
1971	Fast Fellow	3	L. Pincay Jr	118	Authorize	115	Triple Bend	115	33,175	1:34.80	
1972	Quack	3	W. Shoemaker	112	Finalista	115	Royal Owl	121	32,450	1:34.60	
1973	Groshawk	3	W. Shoemaker	123	Ancient Title	124	Mug Punter	113	33,600	1:35.60	
							Out of the East	118			
1974	Stardust Mel	3	F. Toro	120	Agitate	122	El Seetu	114	32,800	1:40.80	
1975	Uniformity	3	W. Shoemaker	115	Dusty County	117	Exact Duplicate	114	32,150	1:42.00	
1976	Madera Sun	3	L. Pincay Jr	116	An Act	126	Today 'n Tomorrow	115	32,100	1:42.00	
1977	Nordic Prince	3	S. Hawley	117	Sonny Collins	119	Bad 'n Big	123	33,950	1:41.40	
1978	April Axe	3	C.J. McCarron	115	Poppy Popwich	115	He's Dewan	117	33,100	1:41.60	
1979	Ibacache	3	D.G. McHargue	118	Beau's Eagle	121	David's Gotcha	111	32,350	1:40.80	
1980	Stiff Diamond	3	T. Lipham	113	Naked Sky	117	Big Doug	115	34,300	1:41.40	
1981	Splendid Spruce	3	D.G. McHargue	123	Seafood	119	Surprise George	115	38,900	1:41.40	
1982	Give Me Strength	3	D.G. McHargue	123	Ask Me	115	Accoustical	113	26,550	1:40.00	
1982	Sword Blade	3	D.G. McHargue	115	Art Director	114	Lucky Ship	114	26,050	1:41.80	
1983	Barberstown	3	F. Toro	116	Lover Boy Leslie	117	Tanks Brigade	120	35,200	1:41.40	
1984	Tsunami Slew	3	L. Pincay Jr	119	Swinging Scobie	115	Tights	122	37,550	1:39.80	
1985	Pine Belt	3	R.Q. Meza	113	Rich Earth	119	Academy Road	116	40,700	1:41.00	
1986	Mazaad	3	W. Shoemaker	120	Autobot	119	He;s a Saros	115	48,800	1:42.40	
1987	Something Lucky	3	L. Pincay Jr	117	The Medic	115	Persevered	119	49,600	1:43.00	
1988	Word Pirate	3	E. Delahoussaye	119	Perfecting	115	Roberto's Dancer	116	50,400	1:40.20	
1989	Notorious Pleasure	3	L. Pincay Jr	117	Advocate Training	115	First Play	116	66,900	1:40.20	
1990	Itsallgreektome	3	C.S. Nakatani	114	Warcraft	120	Balla Cove	116	66,500	1:40.20	
1991	Compelling Sound	3	P.A. Valenzuela	119	Stark South	116	Persianelli	117	66,100	1:40.60	96
1992	The Name's Jimmy	3	D. Sorenson	116	Bold Assert	117	Prospect for Four	114	63,600	1:40.80	88
1993	Future Storm	3	K.J. Desormeaux	116	Lykatill Hil	119	Earl of Barking	122	68,900	1:40.40	94
1994	Unfinished Symph.	3	G. Baze	116	Silver Music	118	Valiant Nature	122	64,600	1:40.60	99
1995	Via Lombardia	3	E. Delahoussaye	114	Mr Purple	119	Bee El Tee	117	63,650	1:34.00	99
1996	Let Bob Do It	3	K.J. Desormeaux	118	Nightcapper	114	Dr. Sardonica	116	67,140	1:34.00	102
1997	Brave Act	3	C.J. McCarron	117	P.T. Indy	118	Without Doubt	116	68,520	1:34.00	96
1998	Magical	3	R.R.Douglas	114	Commitisize	119	Son's Corona	114	65,820	1:33.80	102
1999	Eagleton	3	C.A. Black	118	Hidden Magic	115	Mr. Reignmaker	115	67,800	1:34.20	97
2000	Purely Cozzene	3	V. Espinoza	120	Duke of Green	116	Silver Axe	115	66,000	1:34.67	98
2001	Media Mogul	3	A. Solis	116			Learing at Kathy	116	43,920	1:35.10	91
	Dr. Park	3	T.C. Baze	117					43,920		
2002	Doc Holiday	3	D.R. Flores	116	Johar	119	Golden Arrow	115	63,900	1:34.64	99
2003	Private Chef	3	V. Espinoza	115	Banshee King	115	Singletary	117	67,560	1:35.57	94

Beyer Index: 96.54

ROYAL HEROINE, 1 Mile (Turf),
Fillies and Mares 3-Year-Olds and Up, Hollywood Park, 2003 Purse: $112,200

Year	Winner	Age	Jockey	Wt.	Second	Wt.	Third	Wt.	Win Value	Time	Beyer
1986	Mircaulous	3	G.L. Stevens	118	Seldom Seen Sue	115	Miss Alto	115	22,000	1:41.80	
1998	Tuzla	4	C.S. Nakatani	115	Sonja's Faith	119	Plus	115	42,990	1:34.20	99
1999	Tuzla	5	C.S. Nakatani	123	Isle de France	119	Chime After Chime	113	42,240	1:34.20	103
2000	Tranquility Lake	5	E. Delahoussaye	121	Dianehill	119	Reciclada	119	46,590	1:33.98	104
2001	Kalatiara	4	C.J. McCarron	114	Dianehill	119	Al Desima	116	65,940	1:34.41	94
2002	Surya	4	K.J. Desormeaux	117	Angel Gift	117	Reine de Romance	121	68,880	1:34.73	97
2003	Magic Mission	5	C.S. Nakatani	115	Little Treasure	121	Belleski	115	67,320	1:34.25	100

Beyer Index: 99.5

SABIN HANDICAP, 1 1/16 Miles,
Fillies and Mares 3-Year-Olds and Up, Gulfstream Park, 2003 Purse: $100,000

Year	Winner	Age	Jockey	Wt.	Second	Wt.	Third	Wt.	Win Value	Time	Beyer
1991	Fit for a Queen	5	J.D. Bailey	114	Trumpet's Blare		Express Star		46,020	1:42.40	
1992	Lemhi Go	4	R. Lester	113	Trumpet's Blare		Tappanzee		45,000	1:44.60	99
1993	Now Dance	4	M. Guidry	113	Spinning Round		Luv Me Luv Me Not		30,000	1:41.60	98
1994	Hunzinga	5	Felix JE	113	Nine Keys	114	Pleasant Jolie	112	45,000	1:39.40	95
1995	Recognizable	4	M.E. Smith	115	Jade Flush	113	Sambacarioca	118	45,000	1:42.40	101
1996	Lindsay Frolic	4	P. Day	117	Investalot	114	Queen Tutta	113	45,000	1:43.60	91
1997	Rare Blend	4	J.D. Bailey	120	Golden Gale	113	Termly	112	45,000	1:41.20	101
1998	Radiant Megan	5	J.A. Krone	113	Escena	119	Biding Time	113	45,000	1:41.60	95
1999	Timely Broad	5	N.J. Petro	115	Highfalutin	116	Mudslinger	116	45,000	1:42.40	101
2000	Brushed Halory	4	M.E. Smith	115	Roza Robata	115	Mop Squeezer	113	45,000	1:41.84	104
2001	De Bertie	4	J.F. Chavez	115	Royal Fair	113	Frankly My Dear	116	60,000	1:44.74	91
2002	Miss Linda	5	R. Migliore	119	Forest Secrets	117	Tap Dance	113	60,000	1:42.61	108
2003	Allamerican Bertie	4	J.D. Bailey	120	Small Promises	112	Redoubled Miss	114	60,000	1:42.49	105

Beyer Index: 99.08

SAFELY KEPT BREEDERS' CUP, 6 Furlongs,
3-Year-Old Fillies, Pimlico, 2003 Purse: $150,000

Year	Winner	Age	Jockey	Wt.	Second	Wt.	Third	Wt.	Win Value	Time	Beyer
1986	Debtor's Prison	...3	D. Byrnes	108	Night Above		Bea Quaility		28,178	1:11.40	
1987	Endless Surprise	..3	K.J. Desormeaux	118	Bea Quality		Miracle Wood		28,340	1:17.40	
1988	Clever Power	3	J.A. Krone	120	Lake Valley		Ready Jet Go		65,000	1:16.40	
1989	Safely Kept	3	C. Perret	122	Cojinx		Kathleen the Queen		60,000	1:11.20	
1990	Voodoo Lily	3	K.J. Desormeaux	117	Miss Spentyouth		Catchamenot		60,000	1:10.60	
1991	Missy's Mirage	3	W.H. McCauley	119	Withallprobability	....	Corporate Fund		60,000	1:10.40	
1992	Meafara	3	B. Swatuk	119	Squirm		Super Doer		60,000	1:10.40	
1993	Miss Indy Anna	...3	D. Thomas	119	Ann Dear		Lily of the North		60,000	1:10.00	
1994	Twist Afleet	3	D.Carr	117	Penny's Reshoot	117	Our Royal Blue	113	60,000	1:10.80	97
1995	Broad Smile	3	J.Brown	117	Scotzanna	122	Shebatim's Trick	115	60,000	1:10.20	91
1996	J J's Dream	3	Pino M. G.	122	Flat Fleet Feet	119	Rare Blend	119	60,000	1:09.40	103
1997	Weather Vane	3	Pino M. G.	119	Vegas Prospector	117	Requesting More	115	64,800	1:10.20	90
1998	Hair Spray	3	Velez J. A. Jr.	117	Expensive Issue	115	Ninth Inning	119	66,390	1:10.60	91
1999	Godmother	3	Pino M. G.	117	Superduper Miss	117	Rills	113	60,000	1:09.20	102
2000	Swept Away	3	J.A Beasley	122	Another	115	Cat Cay	117	60,000	1:09.51	102
2002	Miss Lodi	3	R. Fogelsonger	117	For Rubies	117	Wilzada	117	60,000	1:11.20	99
2003	Randaroo	3	H. Castillo Jr.	119	Follow Me Home	117	Awesome Charm	115	90,000	1:10.54	95

Beyer Index: 96.67

Run as Columbia Stakes prior to 1996. Run at 6 1/2 furlongs in 1987 and 1988.

SALVATOR MILE HANDICAP, 1 Mile,
3-Year-Olds and Up, Monmouth Park, 2003 Purse: $100,000

Year	Winner	Age	Jockey	Wt.	Second	Wt.	Third	Wt.	Win Value	Time	Beyer
1948	Vertigo II	7	A. Kirklan	112	Coincidence	115	Bright Sword	115	9,425	1:39.00	
1949	Istan	4	H. Mora	114	High Trend	112	Royal Governor	119	9,375	1:37.60	
1950	Noble Impulse	4	W. Downs	114	Faraway	112	Curt'n Time	112	8,600	1:39.00	
1951	Call Over	4	M. Peterson	118	Overexposed	112	Ferd	122	8,225	1:38.80	
1952	General Staff	4	J. Stout	122	Senator Joe	118	Joey Boy	122	18,000	1:39.20	
1953	Tuscany	5	J. Stout	112	Larry Ellis	114	Scobeyville	114	13,950	1:37.40	
1954	Closed Door	5	W. Hartack	114	Resilient	114	Kaster	118	14,200	1:37.00	
1955	Helioscope	4	S. Boulmetis	126	Ifabody	118			12,200	1:36.80	
1956	Skipper Bill	6	J.A. Regalbuto	123	Cedar Hill	113	Sol-Hi	115	14,550	1:37.00	
1957	Nahodah	4	J. Culmone	118	Skipper Bill	115	Tudor Era	111	10,729	1:34.60	
1958	Sonny Dan	4	W. Blum	112	Hicks Error	111	True Verdict	112	10,989	1:37.20	
1959	Li'l Fella	4	W. Hartack	114	Cohoes	114	Talent Show	126	10,810	1:37.20	
1960	Im Willing	4	W. Hartack	114	Open View	114	Pen Bolero	114	10,875	1:37.00	
1961	Careless John	4	W. Boland	122	Black Thumper	113	Francis S.	114	11,294	1:35.00	
1962	Towson	4	D. French	111	Invigor	114	Narokan	111	11,066	1:40.20	
1963	Dedimoud	4	J. Culmone	118	Mongo	126	Narokan	114	11,066	1:36.80	
1964	Inbalance	6	J. Culmone	118	Cool Prince	113	City Line	118	18,557	1:37.00	
1965	Twice As Gay	4	P.I. Grimm	114	Why Lie	114	Prairie Sch'r	120	18,606	1:38.80	
1966	Tom Rolfe	4	W. Shoemaker	126	Steel Pike	113	Twin Teddy	112	17,842	1:37.00	
1967	Swoonaway	6	J. Vasquez	113	Steel Pike	115	Spring Double	116	18,606	1:37.80	
1968	R. Thomas	7	J. Nichols	123	Spring Double	119	Besieger	113	18,557	1:37.00	
1969	Addy Boy	4	M. Hole	116	Irish Dude	115	Iron Ruler	120	18,232	1:37.40	
1970	Tyrant	4	W. Hartack	119	Royal Comedian	114	Futura Bold	115	18,362	1:37.40	
1971	Well Mannered	4	M. Solomone	122	Royal Comedian	114	Tyrant	121	18,330	1:38.80	
1972	Red Reality	6	B. Baeza	116	Towzie Tyke	116	Twin Time	115	21,970	1:37.00	
1973	Prince of Truth	5	W. Blum	117	Windtex	116	New Alibhai	115	17,761	1:35.80	
1974	Okavango	4	W. Blum	117	Hey Rube	114	Escaped	113	18,265	1:35.80	
1975	Proper Bostonian	.5	M. Miceli	117	Rastaferian	113	Orbit Round	100	14,576	1:36.20	
1975	Mongogo	6	B. Thornburg	119	Good John	114	Silver Hope	116	14,576	1:36.20	
1976	Royal Glint	6	J. Tejeira	126	Talc	113	Peppy Addy	118	18,395	1:35.20	
1977	Peppy Addy	5	B. Phelps	120	Resound	115	Break up the Game	117	18,168	1:36.00	
1978	Do Tell George	5	W.E. Mize	113	Buckfinder	118	Get Permission	114	17,664	1:36.40	
1979	Revivalist	5	D. MacBeth	122	Horatius	120	Nice Catch	120	25,578	1:35.40	
1980	Convenient	4	V. Bracciale Jr.	114	Tunerup	113	Foretake	113	26,640	1:36.60	
1981	Colonel Moran	4	C. Perret	117	Sun Catcher	120	Pikotazo	117	35,190	1:35.60	
1982	Count His Fleet	4	W. Nemeti	116	Explosive Bid	117	Accipiter's Hope	116	35,070	1:35.40	
1983	Naughty Jimmy	...6	L. Saumell	114	Castle Guard	115	Star Gallant	120	33,510	1:37.00	
1984	Rumptious	4	W.H. McCauley	115	English Master	111	World Appeal	122	34,260	1:34.60	
1985	Valiant Lark	5	V. Bracciale Jr.	114	Pat's Addition	115	Rumptious	114	33,990	1:36.00	
1986	Jyp	5	J. Rocco	115	Minneapple	119	Valiant Lark	117	33,300	1:35.80	
1987	Moment of Hope	..4	M. Venezia	118	Owens Troupe	117	Entitled To	116	33,270	1:34.60	
1988	Slew City Slew	4	M. Castaneda	116	Bet Twice	125	Matthews Keep	116	38,880	1:35.00	
1989	Bill E. Shears	4	R. Hernandez	112	Festive	110	Mi Selecto	117	49,890	1:35.40	
1990	Shy Tom	4	J.A. Krone	115	Bill E. Shears	121	Pete the Chief	115	49,020	1:36.00	

Year	Winner	Age	Jockey	Wt.	Second	Wt.	Third	Wt.	Win Value	Time	Beyer
1991	Peanut Butter Onit	5	W.S. Ramos	115	Private School	114	Run'way Stream	116	45,000	1:34.40	
1992	Peanut Butter Onit	6	A.T. Gryder	120	Root Boy	114	He Is Risen	118	45,000	1:36.20	107
1993	Dusty Screen	5	E.L. King Jr	117	Count New York	112	Root Boy	118	45,000	1:35.80	113
1994	Storm Tower	4	R. Wilson	119	Cold Digger	113	Koluctoo Jimmy Al	114	45,000	1:36.20	109
1995	Schossberg	5	D. Penna	116	Cast Iron	110	Relentless Star	111	45,000	1:35.80	109
1996	Smart Strike	4	S. Hawley	113	Cozy Drive	113	November Sunset	115	60,000	1:36.20	108
1997	Distorted Humor	4	J.A. Krone	114	Wild Deputy	114	Smooth the Loot	113	60,000	1:36.00	112
1998	El Amante	5	J.A. Krone	119	Stormin Fever	117	Gold Token	114	60,000	1:34.80	116
1999	Truluck	4	J. Bravo	115	Rock and Roll	119	Siftaway	114	90,000	1:35.00	104
2000	Leave It to Beezer	7	R. Alvarado Jr.	120	Delaware Township	112	Prime Directive	114	90,000	1:37.29	106
2001	Sea of Tranquility	5	J.C. Ferrer	115	Knock Again	112	Hal's Hope	117	90,000	1:36.74	100
2002	Sea of Tranquility	6	J.C. Ferrer	120	Free of Love	117	First Lieutenant	114	60,000	1:36.12	99
	First Lieutenant finished first but was disqualified and placed third										
2003	Vinemeister	4	J.A. Velez Jr.	114	Jersey Giant	117	Highway Prospector	113	60,000	1:35.89	98

Beyer Index: 106.75

SAN BERNARDINO HANDICAP, 1 1/8 Miles,
4-Year-Olds and Up, Santa Anita, 2003 Purse: $150,000

Year	Winner	Age	Jockey	Wt.	Second	Wt.	Third	Wt.	Win Value	Time	Beyer
1957	Lightning Jack	3	M. Peterson	112	Mystic Eye	111	Royal Heir	115	16,500	1:49.20	
1958	Terrang	5	W. Boland	125	Porterhouse	123	Seaneen	115	16,550	1:42.00	
1959	Terrang	6	W. Boland	126	How Now	117	Bug Brush	123	29,550	1:42.00	
1960	Restless Wind	4	E. Arcaro	118	Seaneen	117	Top Charger	111	16,650	1:42.20	
1961	New Policy	4	W. Shoemaker	122	Finnegan	118	Resolved	121	16,600	1:42.00	
1962	Four-and-Twenty	4	J. Longden	127	Macdan	112	Juanro	107	17,350	1:48.20	
1963	Crozier	5	B. Baeza	128	Pirate Cove	114	Mr. Consistency	113	30,900	1:41.60	
1964	Cyrano	5	M. Ycaza	126	Drill Site	111	Colorado King	118	16,700	1:42.20	
1965	Real Good Deal	4	D. Pierce	118	Pelegrin	114	Calgary Br'k	113	16,500	1:41.80	
1966	Native Diver	7	J. Lambert	130	Real Good Deal	116	Prairie Schooner	114	15,750	1:40.60	
1967	Sermon	4	L. Pincay Jr	114	Biggs	117	Hill Clown	114	18,450	1:47.40	
1968	Tiltable	4	L. Pincay Jr	113	Model Fool	119	Gamely	118	16,750	1:49.00	
1969	Pinjara	4	W. Shoemaker	121	Laughing Gull	113	Poleax	119	17,850	1:46.40	
1970	Governors Party	4	W. Harris	118	Pinjara	122	Figonero	125	17,050	1:49.60	
1971	Bargain Day	6	L. Pincay Jr	115	Efa	114	Lonny's Secret	117	24,975	1:46.60	
1971	Dendron	4	J. Lambert	114	Batitu	112	Society II	115	24,725	1:47.20	
1972	Golden Eagle II	7	J. Lambert	118	Panzer Chief	118	Dendron	112	38,500	1:46.80	
1973	Quack	4	D. Pierce	125	River Buoy	119	Curious C'se	112	36,500	1:49.00	
1974	Court Ruling	4	B. Baeza	117	Captain Cee Jay	119	Accl'tization	115	25,900	1:48.40	
1974	Wichita Oil	6	L. Pincay Jr	116	Madison Palace	117	Woodland Pines	118	25,800	1:47.60	
1975	Royal Glint	5	W. Shoemaker	120	Against the Snow	115	June's Love	115	34,800	1:45.80	
1976	Zanthe	7	S. Hawley	118	Riot in Paris	121	Mateor	114	34,300	1:45.80	
1977	Today 'n Tomorrow	4	S. Hawley	112	Exact Duplicate	115	Rajab	114	35,300	1:46.40	
1978	J.O. Tobin	4	S. Cauthen	123	Henschel	115	Riot in Paris	119	31,950	1:47.80	
1979	Star Spangled	5	L. Pincay Jr	117	Farnesio	118	State Dinner	118	46,650	1:45.80	
1980	Peregrinator	5	C.J. McCarron	115	Lunar Probe	116	Henschel	120	65,300	1:47.80	
1981	Borzoi	5	W. Shoemaker	118	Shamgo	117	King Go Go	122	64,700	1:46.20	
1982	Super Moment	5	C.J. McCarron	124	Mehmet	116	It's the One	126	75,450	1:48.60	
1983	The Wonder	5	W. Shoemaker	122	Konewah	112	Swing Till Dawn	119	62,500	1:49.20	
1984	Journey at Sea	5	W.A. Guerra	122	My Habitony	118	Fighting Fit	121	102,050	1:48.00	
1985	Greinton	4	L. Pincay Jr	120	Precisionist	127	Al Mamoon	115	117,300	1:47.00	
1986	Precisionist	5	C.J. McCarron	126	Greinton	126	Encolure	116	148,200	1:47.60	
1987	Judge Angelucci	4	W. Shoemaker	115	Iron Eyes	116	Grecian Wonder	113	129,400	1:48.40	
1988	Alysheba	5	C.J. McCarron	127	Ferdinand	127	Good Taste	113	350,000	1:47.20	
1989	Ruhlmann	4	L. Pincay Jr	119	Lively One	120	Saratoga Passage	116	185,600	1:47.20	
1990	Ruhlmann	5	G.L. Stevens	123	Criminal Type	119	Stylish Winner	113	240,800	1:47.20	119
1991	Anshan	4	C.S. Nakatani	115	Louis Cyphre	112	Pleasant Tap	116	158,900	1:47.00	113
1992	Another Review	4	K.J. Desormeaux	114	Defensive Play	115	Loach	116	163,100	1:47.20	114
1993	Memo	6	P. Atkinson	114	Charmonnier	117	Marquetry	118	125,800	1:47.40	113
1994	Del Mar Dennis	4	S. Gonzalez Jr	114	Hill Pass	115	Tinners Way	115	129,400	1:48.20	105
1995	Del Mar Dennis	5	C.W. Antley	117	Wharf	113	Stoller	115	130,000	1:47.20	114
1996	Del Mar Dennis	6	K.J. Desormeaux	118	Just Java	116	Regal Rowdy	115	96,650	1:48.20	108
1997	Benchmark	6	C.J. McCarron	114	Kingdom Found	115	Private Song	122	97,650	1:48.20	105
1998	Budroyale	5	M.S. Garcia	112	Don't Blame Rio	114	Bagshot	116	100,530	1:48.40	108
1999	Classic Cat	5	G.L. Stevens	122	Budroyale	119	Klinsman	115	90,000	1:47.77	112
2000	Early Pioneer	5	M.S. Garcia	113	David	113	General Challenge	123	95,490	1:49.08	112
2001	Futural	5	G.K. Gomez	115	Irisheyesareflying	117	Tribunal	117	90,000	1:47.87	109
2002	Bosque Redondo	5	C.J. McCarron	114	Mysterious Cat	111	Freedom Crest	116	90,000	1:49.11	104
2003	Western Pride	5	P.A. Valenzuela	116	Total Impact	113	Fleetstreet Dancer	112	90,000	1:48.56	112

Beyer Index: 110.57

SAN MIGUEL, 6 Furlongs,
3-Year-Olds, Santa Anita, 2003 Purse: $107,800

Year	Winner	Age	Jockey	Wt.	Second	Wt.	Third	Wt.	Win Value	Time	Beyer
1994	Mr. Cooperative	3	M.A. Pedroza	114	Subtle Trouble	118	Rambling Guy	121	48,300	1:09.53	92
1995	Petionville	3	C.W. Antley	114	Regal Fighter	114	Cold N Calculating	116	45,225	1:09.16	98
1996	Honour and Glory	3	G.L. Stevens	121	Afleetaffair	118	Valid Expectations	118	64,350	1:08.93	102
1997	Thisnearlywasmine	3	C.J. McCarron	118	Smokin Mel	114	Renteria	116	64,350	1:08.55	106
1998	Rio Oro	3	D. Lozoya	118	Iron Cat	114	Cat Doctor	114	66,180	1:08.60	105
1999	Cape Canaveral	3	D.R. Flores	118	Aristotle	114	Actin Time	116	62,760	1:09.00	100
2000	Swept Overboard	3	E. Delahoussaye	116	Forest Camp	121	Joopy Doopy	118	64,320	1:08.99	106
2001	Lasersport	3	C.S. Nakatani	116	Early Flyer	114	Bills Paid	114	64,500	1:08.60	104
2002	Popular	3	V. Espinoza	114	Roman Dancer	118	Royal Moro	114	64,740	1:09.00	105
2003	Omega Code	3	M.A. Pedroza	121	Only the Best	121	Jimmy O	118	64,680	1:08.65	103

Beyer Index: 102.1

For previous runnings, refer to 1994 Manual

SAN SIMEON HANDICAP, About 6 1/2 Furlongs (Turf),
4-Year-Olds and Up, Santa Anita, 2003 Purse: $137,500

Year	Winner	Age	Jockey	Wt.	Second	Wt.	Third	Wt.	Win Value	Time	Beyer
1968	Poona Khan	7	M. Yanez	114	Dr. Roy E.	118	Dizzy Babe	113	14,000	1:22.00	
1969	Ottawa Hills	6	L. Pincay Jr.	117	First Mate	120	Indulto	120	14,850	1:22.20	
1970	Right Cross	4	L. Pincay Jr	116	First Mate	120	Canterbury Road.	118	14,050	1:21.40	
1971	Long Position	5	J. Sellers	114	Earl of Milldale	116	Page	118	16,400	1:21.80	
1972	Single Agent	4	H. Grant	122	Long Position	114	Indulto	114	21,200	1:21.00	
1973	Soft Victory	5	D. Pierce	115	Selecting	115	Andrew F'ney	116	23,050	1:21.40	
1974	Matun	5	S. Valdez	115	Selecting	115	Forage	123	21,200	1:21.20	
1975	Century's Envoy	4	J. Tejeira	121	First Back	121	Rocket Rev'ew	120	19,700	1:22.40	
1976	Pay Tribute	4	L. Pincay Jr	118	Against the Snow	118	King Pellinore	122	25,650	1:35.20	
1977	Mark's Place	5	S. Hawley	122	Maheras	118	Painted Wagon	114	26,250	1:21.00	
1978	Maheras	5	L. Pincay Jr	122	Yu Wipi	114	Bad 'n Big	119	25,650	1:22.80	
1979	Bywayofchicago	5	D.G. McHargue	120	Maheras	118	Whatsyourpleasure	117	33,850	1:21.80	
1980	Dragon Comm'd	6	E. Delahoussaye	118	Numa Pompilius	115	Bywayofchicago	115	29,050	1:12.60	
1981	Syncopate	6	D. Pierce	119	Parsec	117	Matsad'ns Honey	115	31,450	1:16.40	
1982	Shagbark	7	L. Pincay Jr	122	Shanekite	118	Belfort	116	39,850	1:13.00	
1983	Chinook Pass	4	L. Pincay Jr	124	Shanekite	118	Earthquack	121	39,100	1:15.40	
1984	Champagne Bid	5	R. Sibille	121	Retsina Run	115	Famous Star	115	53,350	1:14.40	
1985	Champagne Bid	6	R. Sibille	121	Forzando II.	122	Smart and Sharp.	118	52,150	1:13.60	
1986	Estate	7	A.L. Castanon	114	Will Dancer	118	Exclusive Partner	116	52,150	1:13.80	
1987	Bolder Than Bold	5	G. Baze	117	Prince Bobby B.	122	Lichi	112	49,800	1:13.60	
1988	Caballo de Oro	4	R.Q. Meza	112	Gallant Sailor	112	Sylvan Express.	121	46,700	1:15.40	
1989	Mazilier	5	P.A. Valenzuela	116	Imperial Star	112	Caballo de Oro	116	48,750	1:15.80	
1990	Coastal Voyage	6	A. Solis	118	Patchy Groundfog.	117	Raise a Stanza	119	60,000	1:12.20	107
1991	Forest Glow	4	J.A. Garcia	116	Answer Do	119	Shirkee	117	63,900	1:12.40	111
1992	Heart of Joy	5	C.J. McCarron	119	Regal Groom	115	Time Gentlemen	117	69,600	1:12.80	105
1993	Exemplary Leader	7	M.A. Pedroza	113	Prince Ferdinand	119	Wild Harmony	117	64,300	1:13.80	102
1994	Rapan Boy	6	G.L. Stevens	114	The Berkeley Man	115	Artistic Reef	116	63,100	1:13.00	103
1995	Finder's Fortune	6	P.A. Valenzuela	117	Rotsaluck	117	Pembroke	117	64,550	1:13.60	107
1996	Ski Dancer	4	G.L. Stevens	114	Daggett Peak	115	Boulderdash Bay	118	64,200	1:13.80	104
1997	Sandtrap	4	A. Solis	117	Daggett Peak	113	Tyconic	120	96,850	1:12.40	104
1998	Labeeb	6	K.J. Desormeaux	118	Surachai	118	Captain Collins	115	67,860	1:12.80	103
1999	Naninja	6	C.J. McCarron	115	Expressionist	116	Indian Rocket	119	65,220	1:13.20	104
2000	El Cielo	6	J. Valdivia Jr.	117	King Slayer	116	Scooter Brown	117	79,440	1:12.66	104
2001	Lake William	5	V. Espinoza	114	Macward	117	Touchofthe Blues	116	80,175	1:12.34	106
2002	Malabar Gold	5	C.J. McCarron	117	Astonished	117	Nuclear Debate	118	82,825	1:11.73	100
2003	Speak in Passing	6	D.R. Flores	118	Spinelessjellyfish	115	Rocky Bar	116	82,500	1:12.87	100

Beyer Index: 104.71

SANDS POINT, 1 1/8 Miles (Off the Turf),
3-Year-Old Fillies, Belmont Park, 2003 Purse: $114,600

Year	Winner	Age	Jockey	Wt.	Second	Wt.	Third	Wt.	Win Value	Time	Beyer
1995	Perfect Arc	3	J.R.Velazquez	117	Miss Union Avenue	123	Transient Trend	110	49,395	1:43.00	106
1996	Merit Wings	3	R.Davis	120	Unify	113	Turkappeal	117	51,945	1:45.80	86
1997	Auntie Mame	3	J.Bailey	121	Hoochie Coochie	114	Sagacious	113	66,720	1:46.60	94
1998	Recording	3	J.F. Chavez	113	Royal Ransom	114	Naskra's de Light	116	69,600	1:48.80	89
1999	Perfect Sting	3	P. Day	118	Pico Teneriffe	121	Illiquidity	113	65,160	1:46.80	95
2000	Gaviola	3	J.D. Bailey	121	Shopping for Love	121	Millie's Quest	113	66.780	1:47.77	100
2001	Tweedside	3	R. Migliore	119	Owsley	114	Platinum Tiara	122	66,674	1:50.43	82
2002	Riskaverse	3	R.G. Davis	119	Cyclorama	115	She's Vested	115	69,660	1:51.63	91
2003	Savedbythelight	3	R. Migliore	115	Virgin Voyage	117	Little Bonnet	115	68,760	1:49.18	94

Beyer Index: 93

Off the turf in 2003.

SANTA YSABEL, 1 1/16 Miles,
3-Year-Old Fillies, Santa Anita, 2003 Purse: $110,900

Year	Winner	Age	Jockey	Wt.	Second	Wt.	Third	Wt.	Win Value	Time	Beyer
1994	Princess Mitterand	3	C.J. McCarron	119	Dianes Halo	115	Jacodra's Devil	115	44,925	1:43.25	90
1995	Ski Dancer	3	K.J. Desormeaux	115	Dixie Pearl	117	Wilga	115	45,750	1:44.24	83
1996	Antespend	3	C.W. Antley	120	Dancing Prism	114	Rumpipumpy	116	64,950	1:43.87	85
1997	Sharp Cat	3	C.S. Nakatani	120	Clever Pilot	115	Guthrie	116	64,300	1:41.34	94
1998	Love Lock	3	K.J. Desormeaux	120	Nonies Dancer Ali	114	Mamaison Miss	116	63,660	1:44.14	83

Love Lock was subsequently disqualified for post-race positive; Continental Lea, 4th, placed third

Year	Winner	Age	Jockey	Wt.	Second	Wt.	Third	Wt.	Win Value	Time	Beyer
1999	Holywood Picture	3	O. Vergara	115	Exbourne Free	115	Gleefully	116	64,860	1:43.48	90
2000	Surfside	3	P. Day	123	Rings a Chime	115	She's Classy	118	62,882	1:43.53	103
2001	Collect Call	3	A. Solis	115	Irguns Angel	115	Eminent	115	65,580	1:44.69	85
2002	Bella Bella Bella	3	C.J. McCarron	115	Tamarack Bay	116	No Turbulence	116	64,550	1:44.14	85
2003	Atlantic Ocean	3	D.R. Flores	120	Sea Jewel	115	SummerWindDancer	120	66,540	1:43.25	90

Beyer Index: 88.8

For previous runnngs, refer to 1994 Manual

SAPLING, 6 Furlongs,
2-Year-Olds, Monmouth Park, 2003 Purse: $100,000

Year	Winner	Age	Jockey	Wt.	Second	Wt.	Third	Wt.	Win Value	Time	Beyer
1883	Duchess	2	W. Donohue	107	Blossom	100	Thackery	110	3,255	1:18.75	
1884	Brookwood	2	Feakes	110	Goano	103	Cholula	110	3,905	1:15.50	
1885	Savanac	2	Onley	108	Quito	115	Salisbury	105	4,120	1:17.00	
1886	Hanover	2	McLaughlin	115	Spendthrift-Kapang	108	Austriana	105	5,500	1:17.50	
1887	Fitz James	2	Garrison	109	Now or Never	105	Fordham	110	5,825	1:16.50	
1888	Tipstaff	2	Eilke	105	Sensation-Faverdal	115	Tom Ochiltree-Cade	108	6,350	1:15.25	
1889	Devotee	2	Hayward	115	Cayuga	129	Grammercy	105	6,850	1:15.25	
1890	Sorcerer	2	Reagan	113	Russell	123	Foxford	109	6,450	1:16.25	
1891	Air Plant	2	Hamilton	118	Fremont	118	Falsetto	111	5,990	1:12.75	
1892	Don Alonzo	2	Taral	118	Hammie	118	Tom Watson	115	4,640	1:13.75	
1893	Senator Daly	2	Midgley	111	Hyder Abad	118	Henry of Navarre	111	7,510	1:05.00	
1946	Donor	2	J. Jessop	115	Lookout Son	111	Milk Pact	111	11,890	1:12.20	
1947	Task	2	R.J. Martin	111	Itsabet	116	Picture Card	111	10,825	1:11.60	
1948	Blue Peter	2	E. Guerin	122	Harbourton	111	Razzmatazz	111	10,325	1:12.80	
1949	Casemate	2	J. Gilbert	122	Hill Prince	115	Thorn	113	9,900	1:11.60	
1950	Battlefield	2	E. Arcaro	122	Uncle Miltie	115	Lord Putnam	125	10,400	1:10.80	
1951	Landseair	2	J. Stout	111	War Age	111	Master Fiddle	115	11,300	1:12.60	
1952	Landlocked	2	F. Fernandez	113	Game Gene	122	Jamie K.	113	21,275	1:13.00	
1952	Laffango	2	F. Pannell	122	Sun Warrior	113	Chief Fanelli	113	21,525	1:12.80	
1953	Artismo	2	J. Stout	113	Permian	116	Passembud	116	30,200	1:11.00	
1954	Royal Coinage	2	J. Skelly	122	Royal Note	124	Impromptu	113	28,050	1:11.00	
1955	Needles	2	J. Choquette	116	Decathlon	124	Polly's Jet	124	27,000	1:10.60	
1956	King Hairan	2	E. Arcaro	124	Ben Lomond	113	Burma Charm	113	44,700	1:10.80	
1957	Plion	2	N. Shuk	119	Li'l Fella	124	A Dragon Killer	119	37,945	1:11.40	
1958	Watch Your Step	2	E. Guerin	114	Intentionally	124	Restless Wind	124	37,685	1:10.60	
1959	Sky Clipper	2	W. Harmatz	122	Bally Ache	122	Big Biz	122	82,617	1:11.40	
1960	Hail to Reason	2	R. Ussery	122	He's a Pistol	122	Carry Back	122	80,925	1:10.40	
1961	Sir Gaylord	2	I. Valenzuela	122	Battle Joined	122	Green Ticket	122	74,046	1:10.60	
1962	Delta Judge	2	R. Broussard	122	Bonjour	122	Never Bend	122	64,833	1:10.60	
1963	Mr. Brick	2	L. Adams	122	Big Pete	122	Bold Sultan	122	62,976	1:10.60	
1964	Bold Lad	2	B. Baeza	122	Native Charger	122	Sadair	122	61,545	1:09.40	
1965	Buckpasser	2	B. Baeza	122	Quinta	122	Our Michael	122	67,311	1:10.60	
1966	Great Power	2	W. Shoemaker	122	In Reality	122	Disciplinarian	122	62,691	1:09.40	
1967	Subpet	2	R. Broussard	122	What a Pleasure	122	Iron Ruler	122	72,423	1:10.40	
1968	Reviewer	2	B. Baeza	122	Night Invader	122	Al Hattab	122	68,835	1:10.40	
1969	Ring for Nurse	2	M. Miceli	122	Rollicking	122	Hard Work	122	67,548	1:11.80	
1970	Staunch Avenger	2	D.E. Whited	122	Pass Catcher	122	Raise Your Glass	122	81,522	1:11.40	
1971	Chevron Flight	2	M. Fromin	122	Chauffeur	122	King of Cornish	122	70,530	1:11.80	
1972	Assagai Jr.	2	J. Imparato	122	Little Big Chief	122	Swift Courier	122	66,804	1:10.80	
1973	Tisab	2	W. Blum	122	Wedge Shot	122	Go for Love	122	77,721	1:10.20	
1974	Foolish Pleasure	2	J. Vasquez	122	The Bagel Prince	122	Bombay Duck	122	86,997	1:10.40	
1975	Full Out	2	B. Thornburg	122	Riverside Sam	122	Eustace	122	82,227	1:11.60	
1976	Ali Oop	2	L. Saumell	122	Ahoy Mate	122	First Ambassador	122	84,636	1:09.80	
1977	Alydar	2	E. Maple	122	Noon Time Spender	122	Dominant Ruler	122	65,829	1:10.60	
1978	Tim the Tiger	2	J. Fell	122	Groton High	122	Spartan Emperor	122	86,682	1:11.80	
1979	Rockhill Native	2	J. Oldham	122	Antique Gold	122	Gold Stage	122	75,366	1:08.80	
1980	Travelling Music	2	C. Perret	122	Lord Avie	122	Timeless Event	122	78,438	1:11.00	
1981	Out of Hock	2	D. Brumfield	122	T. Dykes	122	What a Wabbit	122	90,591	1:10.20	
1982	O.K. by You	2	C. Perret	122	Willow Drive	122	Love to Laugh	122	79,032	1:10.80	
1983	Smart n Slick	2	D.A. Miller Jr	122	Tonto	122	Triple Sec	122	120,615	1:10.80	
1984	Doubly Clear	2	J.R. Garcia	122	Tiltalating	122	Do It Again Dan	122	120,150	1:10.40	
1985	Hilco Scamper	2	G.L. Stevens	122	Danny's Keys	122	Mr. Spiffy	122	114,555	1:10.80	

Year	Winner	Age	Jockey	Wt.	Second	Wt.	Third	Wt.	Win Value	Time	Beyer
1986	Bet Twice	2	C.W. Antley	122	Faster Than Sound	122	Homebuilder	122	120,000	1:10.20	
1987	Tejano	2	J. Vasquez	122	Unzipped	122	Jim's Orbit	122	111,600	1:09.00	
1988	Bio	2	P.A. Johnson	122	Truely Colorful	122	Light My Fuse	122	111,600	1:10.40	
1989	Carson City	2	J.A. Krone	122	Mr. Nasty	122	Adjudicating	122	120,000	1:10.40	96
1990	Deposit Ticket	2	G.L. Stevens	122	Alaskan Frost	122	Hansel	122	120,000	1:11.00	
1991	Big Sur	2	R. Migliore	122	Never Wavering	122	Dr. Fountainstein	122	120,000	1:10.80	102
1992	Gilded Time	2	C.J. McCarron	122	Wild Zone	122	Great Navigator	122	120,000	1:07.80	85
1993	Sacred Honour	2	C. Lopez Sr.	122	Meadow Flight	122	Solly's Honor	117	120,000	1:11.00	85
1994	Boone's Mill	2	P. Day	122	Enlighten	122	Western Echo	122	120,000	1:10.40	92
1995	Hennessy	2	D.M. Barton	122	Built for Pleasure	122	Cashier Coyote	122	120,000	1:10.80	77
1996	Smoke Glacken	2	C. Perret	122	Harley Tune	122	Country Rainbow	122	120,000	1:10.20	86
1997	Double Honor	2	J. Bravo	122	Jigadee	122	E Z Line	122	120,000	1:09.60	95
1998	Yes It's True	2	S.J. Sellers	122	Eriton	122	Heroofthegame	122	120,000	1:10.00	90
1999	Dont Tell the Kids	2	J. Tejeira	122	Outrigger	122	House Burner	122	120,000	1:10.18	80
2000	Shooter	2	J. Bravo	119	Snow Ridge	119	T P Louie	119	120,000	1:10.63	88
2001	Pure Precision	2	E.M. Coa	120	Truman's Raider	120	Wild Navigator	120	90,000	1:10.82	89
2002	Valid Video	2	C.C. Lopez	120	Farno	120	Boston Park	120	60,000	1:09.88	95
2003	Dashboard Drummer	2	J.C. Ferrer	120	Deputy Storm	120	Charming Jim	120	60,000	1:10.84	85

Beyer Index: 88.93

SARANAC HANDICAP, 1 3/16 Miles (Turf),
3-Year-Olds, Saratoga Race Course, 2003 Purse: $108,800

Year	Winner	Age	Jockey	Wt.	Second	Wt.	Third	Wt.	Win Value	Time	Beyer
1901	Dublin	3	Shaw	113	Baron Pepper	104	Choctanunda	109	3,850	1:52.60	
1902	Hermis	3	Rice	122	Whiskey King	104	Cunard	115	5,150	1:51.40	
1903	Molly Brant	3	J. Martin	100	Shorthose	120	Grey Friar	112	5,675	1:55.20	
1904	Dolly Spanker	3	Shaw	115	St. Valentine	112	Fort Hunter	126	3,850	1:53.20	
1905	Dandelion	3	O'Niell	110	Merry Lark	112	Bedouin	118	3,850	1:53.80	
1906	Gallavant	3	Miller	119	Tiptoe	118			3,850	1:56.60	
1907	Vails	3	Miller	113	Rio Grande	90	Don Enrique	102	3,850	1:53.40	
1908	Golconda	3	D. McCarthy	97	Thomas Calhoun	100	Crack Shot	94	350	1:57.40	
1909	Field Mouse	3	E. Dugan	111	Wintergreen	112	Gliding Belle	102	1,410	1:37.60	
1910	Martinez	3	S. Davis	112	Lovetie	107	Starbottle	105	2,315	1:52.20	
1913	Ten Point	3	Loftus	124	Nightstick	106	Leochares	116	1,855	1:39.00	
1914	Stromboli	3	A. Neylon	113	Punch Bowl	114	Gainer	119	1,495	1:38.60	
1915	Regret	3	J. Notter	123	Trial by Jury	114	Lady Rotha	106	1,050	1:42.00	
1916	Dodge	3	F. Murphy	125	Spur	127	Tea Caddy	107	1,500	1:38.00	
1917	Midway	3	J. Butwell	118	Corn Tassel	118	Hollister	116	2,650	1:39.40	
1918	Motor Cop	3	W. Knapp	119	The Porter	118	Tippity Witchet	115	2,575	1:36.80	
1919	Purchase	3	W. Knapp	133	Passing Shower	107	The Trump	105	2,325	1:42.20	
1920	Dinna Care	3	C. Kummer	110	Dr. Clark	120	Busy Signal	112	6,400	1:38.60	
1921	Crocus	3	L. Fator	120	Bit of White	119	Idle Dell	110	5,225	1:37.80	
1922	Little Chief	3	L. Fator	114	Kai-Sang	133	Horologe	111	5,900	1:37.80	
1923	Cherry Pie	3	J. Corcoran	114	Untidy	114	The Clown	116	8,250	1:38.00	
1924	Sarazen	3	J. Maiben	120	Klondyke	114	Wise Counsellor	122	8,250	1:37.60	
1925	Peanuts	3	F. Coltiletti	110	Silver Fox	128	Senalado	110	8,250	1:39.00	
1926	Mars	3	C. Turner	120	Rock Star	120	Croydon	108	9,300	1:39.00	
1927	Osmand	3	E. Sande	123	Valorous	123	Cheops	120	9,400	1:39.60	
1928	Sun Edwin	3	H. Thurber	117	Sunfire	110	Bobashela	117	8,450	1:41.60	
1929	Hard Tack	3	J.H. Burke	114	Vermajo	106	Dr. Freeland	117	10,100	1:37.40	
1931	Danour	3	S. Renick	103	A la Carte	110	Surf Board	111	8,500	1:40.20	
1932	Morfair	3	R. Workman	124	Pompeius	112	Sunmelus	114	7,050	1:41.40	
1933	War Glory	3	J. Gilbert	125	Kerry Patch	120	Okapi	119	3,900	1:38.60	
1934	Kievex	3	W.D. Wright	110	Bazaar	116	Observant	112	3,850	1:37.20	
1935	Good Gamble	3	S. Renick	118	Black Gift	110	Esposa	103	4,675	1:38.40	
1936	Sun Teddy	3	E. Arcaro	112	Pullman	112	Sangreal	112	5,250	1:40.20	
1937	Burning Star	3	H. Richards	117	Forty Winks	114	Rex Flag	113	5,175	1:39.40	
1938	Thanksgiving	3	L. Dupps	113	Encore	106	Lucky Omen	110	3,725	1:38.80	
1939	Heather Broom	3	B. James	113	Golden Voyage	112	Nitro	112	4,025	1:38.80	
1940	Parasang	3	B. James	118	Call to Colors	105	The Finest	110	4,200	1:38.20	
1941	Whirlaway	3	A. Robertson	130	War Relic	117	Omission	112	3,800	1:38.00	
1942	Bless Me	3	S. Young	116	Star Beacon	107	Lochinvar	115	4,100	1:37.20	
1948	Mount Marcy	3	E. Arcaro	116	Better Self	126	Ace Admiral	111	16,000	1:44.80	
1949	Sun Bahram	3	E. Arcaro	120	Eatontown	112	Arise	114	11,950	1:45.00	
1950	Sunglow	3	E. Arcaro	115	Lights Up	126	Bit o' Fate	105	10,825	1:43.60	
1951	Bold	3	E. Arcaro	125	Loridale	111	Mandingo	105	10,950	1:43.60	
1952	Golden Gloves	3	N. Wall	116	Hitex	120	Count Flame	113	16,600	1:45.40	
1953	First Aid	3	A. Catalano	106	Beachcomber	121	Fly Wheel	113	16,450	1:43.80	
1954	Full Flight	3	J. Higley	114	Paper Tiger	111	Red Hannigan	114	21,700	1:44.80	
1955	Saratoga	3	N. Shuk	126	Misty Morn	112	Nance's Lad	123	20,000	1:44.00	
1956	Ricci Tavi	3	P.J. Bailey	122	Bill's Sky Boy	114	Pertshire	115	18,500	1:43.40	

Year	Winner	Age	Jockey	Wt.	Second	Wt.	Third	Wt.	Win Value	Time	Beyer
1957	Cohoes	3	T. Atkinson	120	Bureaucracy	113	St. Amour II	116	21,350	1:42.20	
1958	Nasco	3	R. Broussard	113	Nisht Amool	113	Isendu	114	18,225	1:44.40	
1959	Mail Order	3	P.J. Bailey	113	The Irishman	122	Seven Corners	113	18,095	1:41.80	
1960	Divine Comedy	3	M. Sorrentino	113	John William	121	Brush Fire	120	17,867	1:34.60	
1961	Globemaster	3	J.L. Rotz	125	Dr. Miller	118	Hi Greco	110	18,687	1:36.60	
1962	David K.	3	R. Ussery	119	Rainy Lake	114	Subtle	110	18,427	1:35.80	
1963	Outing Class	3	B. Baeza	120	Choker	113	Ahoy	122	18,557	1:36.80	
1964	Lt. Stevens	3	T. Barrow	114	Bupers	116	Lord Date	116	19,045	1:36.40	
1965	La Cima	3	R. Ussery	114	Eurasian	111	Hail to All	127	38,660	1:34.40	
1966	Alexville	3	M. Ycaza	113	Flame Tree	116	Sense of Rhythm	111	37,570	1:36.40	
1967	Bold Hour	3	J.L. Rotz	123	Tumiga	123	Reason to Hail	119	36,530	1:36.00	
1968	Stage Door Johnny	3	H. Gustines	126	Out of the Way	124	Iron Ruler	122	36,205	1:35.40	
1969	Best Turn	3	E. Belmonte	112	Prevailing	118	Buck Run	112	37,830	1:35.60	
1970	Silent Screen	3	J.L. Rotz	123	Aggressively	112	Naskra	117	36,985	1:36.00	
1971	Salem	3	J. Vasquez	121	Farewell Party	117	Highbinder	114	33,960	1:34.80	
1972	Icecapade	3	E. Maple	117	Tentam	114	Traffic Cop	114	34,290	1:33.60	
1973	Linda's Chief	3	B. Baeza	126	Step Nicely	123	Illbrightback	117	33,150	1:34.00	
1974	Accipiter	3	A. Santiago	123	Best of It	117	Hosiery	117	34,980	1:36.40	
1975	Bravest Roman	3	E. Maple	114	Wajima	114	Valid Appeal	114	34,380	1:34.80	
1976	Dance Spell	3	A. Cordero Jr.	114	Zen	123	Quiet Little Table	114	33,030	1:34.20	
1977	Bailjumper	3	A. Cordero Jr.	114	Lynn Davis	114	Gift of Kings	114	39,910	1:35.20	
1978	Buckaroo	3	J. Velasquez	123	Junction	123	Quadratic	123	31,950	1:35.00	
1979	Told	3	J. Cruguet	114	Crown Thy Good	114	Quiet Crossing	123	35,250	1:34.40	
1980	Key to Content	3	G. Martens	114	Current Legend	114	Ben Fab	123	36,300	1:33.80	
1981	De la Rose	3	E. Maple	112	Stage Door Key	114	Color Bearer	112	35,400	1:34.40	
1982	Prince Westport	3	J.D. Bailey	114	Four Bases	114	A Real Leader	114	35,040	1:39.00	
1983	Sabin	3	E. Maple	113	Fortnightly	117	Domynsky	123	36,600	1:39.40	
1984	Is Your Pleasure	3	A. Cordero Jr.	114	Onyxly	114	Loft	123	61,470	1:35.20	
1985	Equalize	3	R.G. Davis	114	Verification	114	Danger's Hour	114	71,820	1:39.00	
1986	Glow	3	E. Maple	114	Manila	114	Pillaster	120	72,270	1:34.60	
1987	Lights and Music	3	E. Maple	114	Forest Fair	114	First Patriot	117	73,560	1:34.80	
1988	Posen	3	D. Brumfield	123	Sunshine Forever	114	Blew by Em	117	73,560	1:38.40	
1989	Expensive Decision	3	J.L. Samyn	114	Ninety Years Young	114	Valid Ordinate	114	55,140	1:36.00	
1989	Slew the Knight	3	J.L. Samyn	114	Verbatree	114	Luge II	123	55,620	1:36.00	
1990	Rouse the Louse	3	J.D. Bailey	114	My Girl Jeannie	118	V.J.'s Honor	114	78,600	1:37.00	
1991	Club Champ	3	A. Cordero Jr.	114	Share the Glory	117	Young Daniel	114	81,480	1:34.20	92
1992	Casino Magistrate	3	E. Maple	120	Restless Doctor	114	Smiling and Dancin	117	76,440	1:39.20	
1993	Halisee	3	J.A. Krone	114	Forest Wind	117	Compadre	114	74,280	1:34.20	95
1994	Casa Eire	3	Bravo J	114	Warn Me	114	Presently	117	66,480	1:34.60	93
1995	Debonair Dan	3	Chavez JF	112	Crimson Guard	122	Treasurer	114	50,400	1:33.60	109
1996	Harghar	3	P. Day	113	Sir Cat	123	Defacto	115	68,880	1:48.40	105
1997	River Squall	3	C. Perret	114	Daylight Savings	114	Inkatha	114	68,460	1:52.80	106
1998	Crowd Pleaser	3	Samyn J. L.	115	Parade Ground	122	Reformer Rally	115	66,060	1:53.40	98
1999	Phi Beta Doc	3	Dominguez R. A.	118	Monarch's Maze	114	Big Rascal	113	67,020	1:51.60	105
2000	Rob's Spirit	3	J.D. Bailey	120	Whata Brainstorm	117	Dawn of the Condor	117	68,280	1:55.47	99
2001	Blazing Fury	3	J.J. Castellano	113	Fast City	114	Rapid Ryan	114	67,500	1:54.88	102
2002	Ibn Al Haitham	3	R. Migliore	114	Finality	116	Irish Colonial	115	66,900	1:55.30	97
2003	Shoal Water	3	J.R. Velazquez	116	Urban King	115	Sharp Impact	116	65,280	1:55.43	99

Beyer Index: **100**

WILLIAM DONALD SCHAEFER HANDICAP, 1 1/8 Miles,
3-Year-Olds and Up, Pimlico, 2003 Purse: $100,000

Year	Winner	Age	Jockey	Wt.	Second	Wt.	Third	Wt.	Win Value	Time	Beyer
1987	Brilliant Stepper	5	A. Stacy	108	Bagetelle		Fobby Forbes		36,335	1:58.20	
1988	Little Bold John	6	D.A. Miller Jr.	124	Along Came Jones		Entertain		35,571	1:50.40	
1989	Private Terms	4	K.J. Desormeaux	122	Instensive Command		New York Swell		32,025	1:47.20	
1990	Flaming Emperor	4	C.J. Ladner III	112	Loyel Pal		Jet Stream		32,730	1:49.60	
1991	Senator to Be	4	P. Day	112	Flaming Emperor		Challenge My Duty		33,540	1:42.20	
1992	Senator to Be	5	P. Day	114	Fiftysevenette	119	Medium Cool	113	34,260	1:42.60	
1993	Root Boy	5	W.H. McCauley	114	Late Guest	109	Forry Cow How	114	45,000	1:42.60	102
1994	Taking Risks	4	M. Johnston	117	Frottage	115	Super Memory	112	45,000	1:49.40	101
1995	Tidal Surge	5	J.D. Carle	112	Mary's Buckaroo	113	Ameri Valay	119	60,000	1:48.00	110
1996	Canaveral	5	S.J. Sellers	115	Michael's Star	114	Rugged Bugger	114	45,000	1:49.00	108
1997	Western Echo	5	E.S. Prado	116	Suave Dancer	114	Mary's Buckaroo	120	60,000	1:49.40	108
1998	Acceptable	4	J.D. Bailey	118	Littlebitlively	118	Testafly	114	63,000	1:48.60	106
1999	Perfect to a Tee	7	A.C. Cortez	112	Allen's Oop	113	Smile Again	114	60,000	1:49.20	102
2000	Ecton Park	4	P. Day	116	The Groom Is Red	111	Crosspatch	116	60,000	1:49.21	110
2001	Perfect Cat	4	J.D. Bailey	115	Rize	115	Judge's Case	115	60,000	1:49.55	105
2002	Tenpins	4	R.J. Albarado	114	Bowman's Band	117	Tactical Side	113	60,000	1:50.20	104
2003	Windsor Castle	5	J.A. Santos	117	Changeintheweather	113	Tempest Fugit	116	60,000	1:50.08	104

Beyer Index: **105.45**

SEABISCUIT HANDICAP, 1 1/16 Miles,
3-Year-Olds and Up, Bay Meadows, 2003 Purse: $100,000

Year	Winner	Age	Jockey	Wt.	Second	Wt.	Third	Wt.	Win Value	Time	Beyer
1968	Lucky P.J.	5	B. Jennings	122	Speedy King	114	Nasharco	114	12,700	1:09.00	
1969	Royal Fols.	4	W. Mahorney	120	Damage Control	115	Speedy King	117	12,950	1:09.80	
1970	Royal Fols.	5	W. Mahorney	119	Snappy Nashville	111	Tanfo Gold	119	12,250	1:08.80	
1971	Dizzy Babe	7	J.T. Gonzalez	116	Little Scrib	114	Court Clown	117	12,000	1:09.80	
1972	Long Position	6	J. Sellers	118	Galea Pass	116	Indulto	122	15,050	1:09.20	
1973	Selecting	4	R. Yaka	112	I'm Ed.	111	Goalie	120	15,150	1:09.00	
1974	Tragic Isle	5	F. Mena	124	Prince Rameses	113	Times Rush	113	15,000	1:08.80	
1975	Cherry River	5	W. Mahorney	126	El Potrero	115	Black Tornado	116	16,200	0:56.80	
1976	Shirley's Champion	5	F. Olivares	114	King Charly	113	Oriental Magic	114	15,800	0:56.80	
1977	L'Natural	4	R. Cabellero	114	Maheras	126	Sporting Goods	122	15,800	0:56.00	
1978	Maheras	5	W. Mahorney	132	Charley Sutton	115	Oriental Magic	113	15,550	0:56.20	
1979	Str'ttn Geo	5	T.M. Chapman	122	Don Alberto	119	Charley Sutton	114	13,100	1:28.00	
1980	California Express.	5	J. Aragon	113	Kamehameha	121	Miami Sun	120	19,000	1:29.60	
1981	Borrego Sun	4	R.A. Baze	114	Prenotion	116	Kane County	113	25,550	1:29.60	
1982	Crews Hill	6	R.A. Baze	116	Shagbark	122	Hallowed Envoy.	116	64,800	1:29.40	
1983	Major Sport	6	T.M. Chapman	115	Aristocratical	114	Take the Floor	115	50,300	1:29.40	
							Famous Star	115			
1984	Ancestral	4	R. Sibille	115	Otter Slide	116	Silveyville	124	49,750	1:29.20	
1985	Hegemony	4	D.G. McHargue	121	Champion Pilot	121	Nack Ack	117	71,740	1:28.60	
1986	Clever Song	4	F. Toro	122	Truce Maker	114	Ocean View	117	63,000	1:28.00	
1987	Mangaki	6	T.T. Doocy	115	Barbery	116	Santella Mac	115	79,550	1:34.40	
1988	Ifrad	6	T.M. Chapman	117	Stop the Fighting.	115	Nickle Band	113	5,500	1:43.40	
1989	Simply Majestic	5	R.D. Hansen	121	Ongoing Mister	113	Astronaut Pr'nce.	115	5,500	1:42.40	
1990	River Master	4	R.G. Davis	116	Miswaki Tern	116	Exclusive Partner	117	55,000	1:43.20	101
1991	Forty Niner Days	4	T.T. Doocy	115	Neptuno	116	Trebizond	115	55,000	1:43.60	
1992	Gum	6	G. Boulanger	112	Forty Niner Days	116	Prudent Manner	115	55,000	1:41.60	108
1993	Never Black	6	C.S. Nakatani	115	Stark South	115	Daros	114	55,000	1:42.40	107
1994	Slew of Damascus.	6	T.M. Chapman	122	Fast Cure	114	The Tender Track	116	55,000	1:43.60	106
1995	Bluegrass Prince	4	T.M. Chapman	114	Lord Shirldor	116	Kinema Red.	113	68,750	1:49.00	101
1996	Tzar Rodney	4	T.M. Chapman	114	Joy of Glory	115	Opera Score	115	60,000	1:49.60	102
1997	Mister Fire Eyes.	5	R.J. Warren Jr.	115	Region	115	Tolomeo	113	60,000	1:41.20	99
1998	Wild Wonder	4	Baze R. A.	121	Crypto Star.	118	General Royal.	115	60,000	1:41.20	99
1999	Worldly Ways	5	Baze R. A.	116	Barter Town	112	Highland Gold	115	60,000	1:40.60	104
							Scooter Brown	114	60,000	1:40.60	
2000	Peach Flat	6	J. Valdivia Jr.	114	Boss Jo	115	Casey Girffin	115	75,000	1:42.48	105
2001	Euchre	5	J. Lumpkins	114	Irisheyesareflying	118	Moonlight Charger	115	82,500	1:41.69	103
2002	Palmeiro	4	J. Lumpkins	115	Moonlight Meeting	116	Prodigious	116	82,500	1:42.31	97
2003	Reba's Gold	6	C.J. Rollins	118	Free Corona	116	Truly a Judge	117	55,000	1:41.63	100

Beyer Index: 102.46

Run as the All-American Handicap prior to 2003.

SENORITA, 1 Mile (Turf),
3-Year-Old Fillies, Hollywood Park, 2003 Purse: $113,500

Year	Winner	Age	Jockey	Wt.	Second	Wt.	Third	Wt.	Win Value	Time	Beyer
1968	Time to Leave	3	D. Velasquez	118	Toe Shoes	112	Saipan	114	14,300	1:36.00	
1969	Prove It Girl.	3	W. Mahorney	112	Ynez Queen.	114	Sallarina	112	12,850	1:36.40	
1969	Commissary	3	A. Pineda	114	Marjorie's Theme.	112	Fourth Round.	115	13,050	1:36.40	
1970	Night Staker	3	J. Sellers	115	Tanta Bella	114	Shoosh	112	16,800	1:36.40	
1971	Shelf Talker	3	J. Lambert	114	Lady Debbie	112	Mariways	115	19,400	1:36.00	
1971	Turkish Trousers.	3	W. Shoemaker.	118	Aladancer	118	Lady of Rome.	112	18,800	1:35.80	
1972	Impressive Style	3	L. Pincay Jr	114	Pallisima	112	Logistic	112	20,400	1:35.80	
1973	Cellist.	3	J.L. Rotz	119	Jungle Princess.	120	Meilleur	119	20,250	1:42.20	
1975	Raise Your Skirts.	3	W. Mahorney	119	Fresno Flyer.	117	Vol Au Vent.	117	19,050	1:36.40	
1976	Raise Pending.	3	D. Pierce	114	Cascapedia	115	Queen to Be.	115	20,650	1:35.80	
1977	Glenaris	3	W. Shoemaker.	114	Countess Fager.	119	Shop Windows	114	19,300	1:36.00	
1978	Blue Blood	3	D. Pierce	117	Equanimity.	122	Eximious	119	25,000	1:37.00	
1979	Variety Queen	3	R. Rosales.	117	Top Soil	119	Whydidju	122	25,850	1:37.00	
1980	Ballare	3	P.A. Valenzuela.	114	Street Ballet	122	Cinegita	114	31,600	1:35.00	
1981	Shimmy	3	P.A. Valenzuela.	114	Queen of Prussia	117	Bee a Scout.	114	37,450	1:36.20	
1982	Skillful Joy.	3	C.J. McCarron.	119	Phaedra	122	Faneuil Lass	122	31,050	1:34.00	
1983	Stage Door C'n'n.	3	C.J. McCarron.	114	I'm Prestigious	116	O'Happy Day.	115	25,675	1:35.60	
1983	Preceptress.	3	M. Castaneda	115	Madam Forbes	114	Toga.	116	25,675	1:36.60	
1984	Heartlight.	3	L. Pincay Jr	117	Table Ten	115	Dear Carrie	115	38,900	1:35.60	
1985	Akamini.	3	F. Toro.	117	Charming Susan.	115	Sharp Ascent	114	32,250	1:36.60	
1985	Shywing	3	T. Lipham	117	Delaware Ginny.	117	Savannah Dancer	113	33,450	1:35.60	
1986	Nature's Way	3	C.J. McCarron.	117	An Empress	115	Miraculous	119	39,200	1:42.60	
1987	Pen Bal Lady.	3	E. Delahoussaye	117	Sweettuc.	119	Dave's Lamb.	115	61,350	1:35.40	
1988	Do So	3	A. Solis.	117	Pattern Step	119	Sheesham	117	45,950	1:34.20	
1989	Reluctant Guest.	3	C.J. McCarron.	114	Formidable Lady	119	General Charge	117	50,200	1:34.00	

Year	Winner	Age	Jockey	Wt.	Second	Wt.	Third	Wt.	Win Value	Time	Beyer
1990	Brought to Mind	3	A. Solis	114	Tasteful T.V.	119	She's a V.P.	117	62,600	1:34.40	
1991	Paula Revere	3	J.A. Santos	117	Shy Trick	114	Island Shuffle	119	61,850	1:35.40	93
1992	Charm a Gendarme	3	R.Q. Meza	116	Moonlight Elegance	116	Morriston Belle	118	67,250	1:33.60	89
1993	Likeable Style	3	K.J. Desormeaux	121	Adorydar	113	Icy Warning	118	61,250	1:34.40	97
1994	Rabiadella	3	L. Pincay Jr.	118	Magical Avie	116	Fancy 'n Fabulous	118	60,800	1:34.80	98
1995	Top Shape	3	C.S. Nakatani	114	Artica	118	Auriette	116	63,900	1:34.60	92
1996	To B. Super	3	C.W. Antley	118	Gastronomical	118	Ribot's Secret	116	68,940	1:34.80	96
1997	Kentucky Kaper	3	R.R. Douglas	114	Ascutney	120	Ava Knowsthecode	115	66,780	1:34.20	90
1998	Dancing Rhythm	3	K.J. Desormeaux	118	Phone Alex	115	Star's Proud Penny	122	64,920	1:35.20	83
1999	Coracle	3	K.J.Desormeaux	116	Aviate	116	Dianehill	115	67,740	1:34.00	93
2000	Islay Mist	3	D.R. Flores	116	Fire Sale Queen	118	Miss Pixie	114	67,080	1:34.16	88
2001	Fantastic Filly	3	G.K. Gomez	123	Innit	115	Blushing Bride	115	65,880	1:35.13	97
2002	Adoration	3	G.K. Gomez	117	High Society	115	Nunatall	115	64,380	1:34.91	92
2003	Makeup Artist	3	V. Espinoza	117	Rutters Renegade	117	Shapes and Shadows	117	68,100	1:36.54	90

Beyer Index: 92.15

SHAKERTOWN, 5 1/2 Furlongs (Turf),
3-Year-Olds and Up, Keeneland, 2003 Purse: $113,700

Year	Winner	Age	Jockey	Wt.	Second	Wt.	Third	Wt.	Win Value	Time	Beyer
1997	G.H.'s Pleasure	5	J.A. Santos	114	Louie the Lucky	114	Parklo	117	34,410	1:03.00	97
1998	Sesaro	6	S.J. Sellers	123	Brave Pancho	114	Claire's Honor	114	43,850	1:02.35	99
1999	Prankster	6	S.J. Sellers	115	Tyaskin	120	Howbaddouwantit	123	43,850	1:02.43	99
2000	Bold Fact	5	R. Migliore	115	Howbaddouwantit	118	Claire's Honor	115	46,800	1:02.61	101
2001	Airbourne Command	6	J.F. Chavez	118	Final Row	118	Grangeville	118	52,824	1:02.71	100
2002	Morluc	6	R. Albarado	118	Mighty Beau	116	Grangeville	118	52,731	1:02.35	103
2003	No Jacket Required	6	B. Blanc	118	Testify	120	Abderian	120	70,494	1:03.25	100

Beyer Index: 99.86

SHIRLEY JONES HANDICAP, 7 Furlongs,
Fillies and Mares 3-Year-Olds and Up, Gulfstream Park, 2003 Purse: $100,000

Year	Winner	Age	Jockey	Wt.	Second	Wt.	Third	Wt.	Win Value	Time	Beyer
1976	Regal Quillo		C. Baltazar	114	Forty Nine Sunsets	112	Tristana	112	10,200	1:42.20	
1979	Candy Eclair		A.S. Black	122	Davona Dale	122	Drop Me a Note	114	17,766	1:08.60	
1981	Sober Jig	4	J.P. Souter	112	Likely Exchange	116	Island Charm	115	27,153	1:23.20	
1982	Bushmaid	4	J.D. Bailey	112	Expressive Dance	124	Sweetest Chant	117	19,470	1:23.20	
1983	Meringue Pie	5	J. Velasquez	115	Cherokee Frolic	118	Mara Mia	109	24,717	1:24.20	
1983	Secrettame	5	J. Vasquez	116	Prime Prospect	120	Miss Hitch	114	25,158	1:23.60	
1984	Chic Belle	4	C. Perret	114	Promising Native	114	First Flurry	115	25,578	1:22.40	
1985	Mickey's Echo	6	W.A. Guerra	117	Sugar's Image	117	Nany	122	37,110	1:23.60	
1986	Soli	4	J.D. Bailey	113	Bessarabian	123	Nany	117	39,390	1:23.80	
1987	Life at the Top	4	R.P. Romero	121	I'm Sweets	120	Jose's Bomb	112	35,640	1:22.80	
1988	Tappiano	4	J. Cruguet	115	Cadillacing	111	Bound	115	52,110	1:23.00	
1989	Social Pro	4	J.F. Chavez	110	Haiati	113	Costly Shoes	114	35,640	1:23.60	
1990	Love's Exchange	4	E. Fires	112	Fantastic Find	113	Fit for a Queen	114	36,720	1:23.60	
1991	Love's Exchange	5	H. Castillo Jr	126	Peach of It	116	Tipsy Girl	114	35,820	1:23.20	104
1992	Nannerl	5	J.A. Krone	111	Withallprobability	120	Fit for a Queen	119	36,600	1:23.20	97
1993	Jeano	5	S.J. Sellers	113	Santa Catalina	115	Miss Jealski	111	39,060	1:23.40	94
1994	Santa Catalina	6	P. Day	115	Jeano	113	Traverse City	113	60,000	1:21.80	98
1995	Educated Risk	5	M.E. Smith	125	Elizabeth Bay	115	Clever Act	114	60,000	1:22.80	112
1996	Dust Bucket	5	R.G. Davis	112	Russian Flight	110	Culver City	115	60,000	1:25.80	90
1997	Chip	4	Bravo J.	114	Steady Cat	113	Flat Fleet Feet	117	60,000	1:22.20	101
1998	U Can Do It	5	Sellers S. J.	116	Glitter Woman	123	Flashy n Smart	118	60,000	1:23.20	110
1999	Harpia	5	R. Migliore	118	Scotzanna	115	Memories of Gold	113	60,000	1:22.00	102
2000	Marley Vale	4	J.R. Velazquez	118	Cassidy	113	Class on Class	115	60,000	1:22.24	103
2001	Hidden Assets	4	J.D. Bailey	114	Another	115	Dream Supreme	120	60,000	1:22.40	95
2002	Cat Cay	5	P. Day	118	Raging Fever	120	Vague Memory	112	60,000	1:22.31	102
2003	Harmony Lodge	5	J.R. Velazquez	114	Gold Mover	117	Nonsuch Bay	117	60,000	1:22.35	104

Beyer Index: 100.92

SINGAPORE PLATE, 1 1/8 Miles,
3-Year-Old Fillies, Arlington Park, 2003 Purse: $100,000

Year	Winner	Age	Jockey	Wt.	Second	Wt.	Third	Wt.	Win Value	Time	Beyer
1930	Alcibiades	3	J. Smith	121	Dustemall	118	Valenciennes	116	12,975	1:52.80	
1931	Canfli	3	P. Dyer	116	Tambour	121	Blind Lane	118	14,875	1:51.80	
1932	Top Flight	3	R. Workman	121	Evening	121	Parry	118	13,475	1:50.80	
1980	Ribbon	3	P. Day	121	Save Wild Life	121	All a Dream	114	50,400	1:50.00	
1981	Sweetest Chant	3	E. Fires	116	Fancy Naskra	114	Contrefaire	115	67,380	1:49.60	
1982	Hurry Renee	3	E. Fires	116	Rose Bouquet	121	Sefa's Beauty	116	50,760	1:50.40	

Year	Winner	Age	Jockey	Wt.	Second	Wt.	Third	Wt.	Win Value	Time	Beyer
1983	Choose a Partner	3	K.D. Clark	114	Narrate	116	Bon Gout	121	49,365	1:48.20	
1984	Lucky Lucky Lucky	3	R.G. Davis	121	Mrs. Revere	121	Basie	115	76,590	1:49.80	
1985	Just Anything	3	J.L. Diaz	114	Hope U. Win	116	Front Room	121	49,680	1:50.40	
1986	Top Corsage	3	G. Stevens	120	Lady Gallant	112	Pamela Paul	112	67,500	1:49.40	
1987	Shot Gun Bonnie	3	C.H. Marquez Jr	112	Royal Cielo	112	Acting Sue	114	63,810	1:53.40	
1989	Confirmed Dancer	3	M.E. Smith	112	Etoile Eternelle	112	Flags Waving	112	50,475	1:52.60	
1990	Overturned	3	R.P. Romero	114	Train Robbery	118	Mercedes Miss	116	51,795	1:50.40	89
1991	Til Forbid	3	S.J. Sellers	112	Auto Dial	116	Ms. Aerosmith	116	45,000	1:49.60	
1992	Pleasant Baby	3	G.K. Gomez	111	Low Tolerance	114	Pleasureconnection	116	45,000	1:55.00	89
1993	Added Asset	3	J.S. Sellers	116	Dream Mary	113	Princess Polonia	112	60,000	1:50.00	92
1994	Mariah's Storm	3	R.N. Lester	118	Stellarina	116	Minority Dater	111	60,000	1:49.60	100
1995	Niner's Home	3	T.J. Hebert	111	A Goodlookin Broad	114	Strawberry Reason	114	45,000	1:52.00	79
1996	Cuando Puede	3	R.J. Albarado	113	Ginny Lynn	121	Effectiveness	114	75,000	1:51.20	99
1997	Minister's Melody	3	G.K. Gomez	112	Lady of Blue	115	Dawn's Black Tie	116	60,000	1:51.20	93
2000	Megans Bluff	3	M. Guidry	114	Instinct	115	My Turn Kissin	111	75,000	1:50.20	92
2001	Caressing	3	R.R. Douglas	120	Gal on the Go	120	Scoop	122	75,000	1:50.74	89
2002	Lost at Sea	3	R.R. Douglas	122	See How She Runs	122	Strikes No Spares	116	60,000	1:50.58	91
2003	Sue's Good News	3	T.T. Doocy	120	Keeping the Gold	122	Meet Me at Midnite	118	60,000	1:50.53	90

Beyer Index: 91.18

SIXTY SAILS HANDICAP, 1 1/8 Miles,
Fillies and Mares 3-Year-Olds and Up, Hawthorne, 2003 Purse: $250,000

Year	Winner	Age	Jockey	Wt.	Second	Wt.	Third	Wt.	Win Value	Time	Beyer
1976	Enchanted Native	5	L. Snyder	115	Honky Star	121	Regal Rumor	118	31,650	1:40.00	
1977	Kissapotamus	5	G. Baze	115	Kittyluck	116	Lady B Gay	116	22,470	1:38.80	
1978	Drop the Pigeon	4	J.L. Diaz	118	Evelyn's Time	113	Creation	119	16,320	1:39.40	
1979	Strate Sunshine	5	R. Lindsay	113	Timeforaturn	114	Century Type	112	46,830	1:40.80	
1980	Doing It My Way	4	R.J. Hirdes Jr	115	Powerless	118	Cookie Puddin	116	40,335	1:40.20	
1980	Conga Miss	4	G. Gallitano	118	Century Type	120	Royal Villa	115	40,215	1:40.20	
1981	Karla's Enough	4	E. Fires	120	Favorite Prospect	117	Romantic Mood	113	46,890	1:37.60	
1981	Gold Treasure	4	J.L. Diaz	118	Sissy's Time	120	Satin Ribera	120	47,040	1:38.00	
1982	Targa	5	R.D. Evans	116	Really Royal	115	Knights Beauty	115	98,040	1:45.00	
1983	Queen of Song	4	R.J. Hirdes Jr	115	Bersid	121	Sefa's Beauty	120	96,630	1:43.80	
1984	Queen of Song	5	R.J. Hirdes Jr	122	Frosty Tail	120	Herb Wine	118	97,710	1:46.60	
1985	Sefa's Beauty	6	P. Day	122	Farer Belle Lee	115	Princess Moran	113	113,580	1:52.60	
1986	Sefa's Beauty	7	R.P. Romero	124	Flying Heat	122	Farer Belle Lee	118	112,290	1:50.60	
1987	Queen Alexandra	5	D. Brumfield	123	My Gallant Duchess	116	Happy H'll'w Miss	113	126,330	1:49.60	
1988	Top Corsage	5	P.A. Valenzuela	118	Yukon Dolly	114	Inspiracion II	110	125,010	1:52.00	
1989	Valid Vixen	4	J.L. Diaz	116	Scorned Lass	115	Arcroyal	116	156,480	1:52.60	
1990	Leave It Be	5	H.A. Sanchez	119	Anitas Surprise	114	Degenerate Gal	116	156,510	1:53.40	
1991	Balotra	4	R. Meier	112	Charon	122	Beth Believes	113	157,860	1:50.80	
1992	Peach of It	6	E.T. Baird	114	Bungalow	115	Zend to Aiken	113	162,090	1:51.20	91
1993	Pleasant Baby	4	J.L. Diaz	112	Miss Jealski	113	Steff Graf	115	180,000	1:49.20	95
1994	Princess Polonia	4	W.S. Ramos	113	Eskimo's Angel	115	Joyous Melody	113	180,000	1:51.80	95
1995	Eskimo's Angel	6	M. Guidry	114	Little Buckles	113	Norfolk Lavender	112	180,000	1:51.40	93
1996	Alcovy	6	W. Martinez	118	Shoop	118	Lotta Dancing	120	180,000	1:50.60	100
1997	Top Secret	4	C. Perret	115	Hurricane Viv	119	Gold n Delicious	114	180,000	1:49.60	100
1998	Glitter Woman	4	G.L.Stevens	118	Top Secret	115	I'm Out First	112	180,000	1:50.40	102
							Tuxedo Junction	115			
1999	Crafty Oak	5	R. Sibille	114	Highfalutin	115	Lines Of Beauty	114	180,000	1:46.60	97
2000	Lu Ravi	5	P. Day	116	Tap to Music	120	Batuka	116	180,000	1:49.15	104
2001	License Fee	6	L. Melancon	116	Lady Melesi	116	Megans Bluff	116	180,000	1:49.11	98
2002	With Ability	4	J.J. Castellano	115	Lakenheath	115	Katy Kat	116	180,000	1:51.37	92
2003	Bare Necessities	4	R.R. Douglas	118	Jaramar Rain	114	Lakenheath	114	150,000	1:52.84	102

Beyer Index: 97.42

SKIP AWAY HANDICAP, 1 1/16 Miles,
3-Year-Olds and Up, Gulfstream Park, 2003 Purse: $100,000

Year	Winner	Age	Jockey	Wt.	Second	Wt.	Third	Wt.	Win Value	Time	Beyer
1955	Swaps	4	W. Shoemaker	130	Galdar		Our Gob		14,100	1:39.60	
1987	Big Blowup	6	C. Baltazar	115	Micanopy Boy		JIm Bowie		34,290	1:44.40	
1990	Primal	5	E. Fires	120	Ole Atocha	113	Wonderloaf	113	60,000	1:43.40	
1991	Chief Honcho	4	M.E. Smith	116	No Marker	112	Barkada	114	45,000	1:48.00	
1992	Honest Ensign	4	J. Cruguet	109	Peanut Butter Onit	114	Strike the Gold	117	45,000	1:49.40	109
1993	Technology	4	J.D. Bailey	118	Barkerville	117	Bidding Proud	115	45,000	1:42.40	107
1994	Devil His Due	5	M.E. Smith	121	Migrating Moon	116	Northern Trend	111	45,000	1:43.00	103
1995	Fight for Love	5	J.D. Bailey	113	Danville	113	Pride of Burkaan	113	45,000	1:43.80	106

Northern Trend finished second but was disqualified and placed fifth

| 1996 | Halo's Image | 5 | P. Day | 119 | Wekiva Springs | 119 | Flying Chevron | 116 | 45,000 | 1:42.60 | 114 |
| 1997 | Crafty Friend | 4 | M.E. Smith | 114 | Diligence | 116 | Ghostly Moves | 114 | 45,000 | 1:42.20 | 109 |

Year	Winner	Age	Jockey	Wt.	Second	Wt.	Third	Wt.	Win Value	Time	Beyer
1998	Sir Bear	5	E.M. Jurado	112	Black Forest	113	Kiridashi	116	60,000	1:43.20	106
1999	Sir Bear	6	J.D. Bailey	119	Behrens	113	Hanarsaan	119	60,000	1:43.66	109
2000	Horse Chestnut	5	M.E. Smith	117	Isaypete	116	Rock and Roll	120	60,000	1:42.78	110
2001	American Halo	5	R.G. Davis	114	Vision and Verse	114	Pleasant Breeze	118	60,000	1:42.31	108
2002	Sir Bear	9	E.S. Prado	116	Red Bullet	118	Hal's Hope	114	60,000	1:43.98	109
2003	Best of the Rest	8	E.M. Coa	121	Consistency	114	Roger E.	114	60,000	1:42.72	105

Beyer Index: 107.92

Run as Broward Handicap through 2000. Run for 3-year-olds at about 1 1/16 miles on turf in 1987; Run at 1 1/8 miles in 1991 and 1992; Run as overnight handicap at 1 mile 70 yards in 1955.

SMILE SPRINT HANDICAP, 6 Furlongs,
3-Year-Olds and Up, Calder Race Course, 2003 Purse: $500,000

Year	Winner	Age	Jockey	Wt.	Second	Wt.	Third	Wt.	Win Value	Time	Beyer
1984	I Really Will	4	G. St. Leon	120	Mo Exception	120	El Kaiser	122	33,984	1:12.00	
1985	Opening Lead	5	J. Pezua	117	Rexson's Hope	121	King of Bridlewood	115	32,760	1:24.00	
1986	Jeblar	4	J. Velez Jr.	123	Power Plan	116	Mugatea	115	32,790	1:24.80	
1987	Princely Lad	4	B. Green	116	Rilial	113	Ward Off Trouble	114	32,580	1:23.80	
1988	Position Leader	3	D. Valiente	112	Medieval Victory	112	Hooting Star	113	49,635	1:24.80	
1989	Glitterman	4	W. Guerra	119	Doodle Bug Mel	112	Proud and Valid	112	32,970	1:10.40	
1990	Groomstick	4	P. Rodriguez	113	Country Isle	113	Medieval Victory	119	49,170	1:24.20	
1991	Greg at Bat	6	J. Vasquez	114	Sunny and Pleasant	113	Perfection	115	51,105	1:24.20	
1992	My Luck Runs North	3	R. Lopez	114	Groomstick	119	Cigar Toss	112	45,000	1:17.40	
1993	Song of Ambition	4	R. Lopez	116	Coolin It	113	Daniel's Boy	117	45,000	1:22.40	
1994	Exclusive Praline	3	W. Ramos	117	Migrating Moon	118	Fortunate Joe	114	60,000	1:22.20	
1995	Request a Star	4	A. Toribio	113	Thats Our Buck	113	Halo's Image	118	60,000	1:23.60	
1996	Constant Escort	4	R. Nunez	114	Honest Colors	114	Excelerate	113	60,000	1:21.80	
1997	Vivace	4	R. Romero	114	Score a Birdie	113	Valid Expectations	117	150,000	1:10.60	
1998	Heckofaralph	5	W. Ramos	115	Thunder Breeze	113	Nicholas Ds	115	180,000	1:11.40	
1999	Silver Season	3	E. Coa	112	Son of a Pistol	119	My Jeff's Mombo	116	180,000	1:10.03	107
2000	Forty One Carats	4	J. Castellano	116	Personal First	114	Alice's Notebook	111	180,000	1:08.95	115
2001	Fappie's Notebook	4	J.F. Chavez	116	Thrillin Discovery	112	Salty Glance	115	120,000	1:09.89	101
2002	Orientate	4	M.E. Smith	119	Echo Eddie	117	Crafty C. T.	117	240,000	1:09.98	115
2003	Shake You Down	5	M.J. Luzzi	119	Private Horde	113	My Cousin Matt	116	294,000	1:10.03	121

Beyer Index: 111.8

Run as Miami Beach Handicap 1984-1993; Run as Miami Beach Sprint Handicap 1994-1998; Run at 6 1/2 furlongs in 1992; Run at 7 furlongs in 1985-1988, 1990-1991, 1993-1996

SORORITY, 6 Furlongs,
2-Year-Old Fillies, Monmouth Park, 2003 Purse: $100,000

Year	Winner	Age	Jockey	Wt.	Second	Wt.	Third	Wt.	Win Value	Time	Beyer
1956	Marullah	2	W. Boland	116	Herb's Miss	116	Alpenrose	112	15,700	1:10.40	
1957	Bridgework	2	E. Guerin	114	Maraja	112	Sweet Mandy	112	15,722	1:12.80	
1958	Mommy Dear	2	S. Boulmetis	112	Royal Native	114	Flying Josie	114	14,895	1:13.40	
1959	Evening Glow	2	H. Grant	114	Rose of Serro	119	Boston Princess	110	18,517	1:12.20	
1960	Apatontheback	2	R. Broussard	119	Princess Leeyan	119	Honey Dear	119	67,890	1:11.60	
1961	Batter Up	2	H. Woodhouse	119	Polylady	119	Laurel Mae	119	60,000	1:12.00	
1962	Affectionately	2	I. Valenzuela	119	Fashion Verdict	119	Nalee	119	60,264	1:10.00	
1963	Castle Forbes	2	W. Hartack	119	Petite Rouge	119	Behaving Deby	119	66,792	1:11.60	
1964	Bold Experience	2	R. Ussery	119	Rhodie	119	Queen Empress	119	60,000	1:09.60	
1965	Native Street	2	M. Ycaza	119	Shimmering Gold	119	Lovely Gypsy	119	74,448	1:10.40	
1966	Like a Charm	2	J. Velasquez	119	Just Kidding	119	Rhubarb	119	64,449	1:12.60	
1967	Queen of the Stage	2	B. Baeza	119	Cockey Miss	119	Gay Matelda	119	62,190	1:10.00	
1968	Big Advance	2	B. Baeza	119	Alert Princess	119	White Xmas	119	60,000	1:11.00	
1969	Box the Compass	2	J. Vasquez	119	Royal Crisis	119	Ashua	119	70,368	1:12.00	
1970	Forward Gal	2	F. Ianelli	119	Unity Hall	119	Deceit	119	63,066	1:11.60	
1971	Brenda Beauty	2	R. Woodhouse	119	Dance Partner	119	Rondeau	119	63,868	1:10.00	
1972	Sparkalark	2	A. Cordero Jr	119	Juke Joint	119	Bold Memory	119	69,717	1:11.00	
1973	Irish Sonnet	2	B. Baeza	119	Honky Star	119	In Hot Pursuit	119	62,982	1:10.40	
1974	Ruffian	2	J. Vasquez	119	Hot n Nasty	119	Stream Across	119	62,688	1:09.00	
1975	Dearly Precious	2	M. Hole	119	Optimistic Gal	119	Totie Fields	119	63,123	1:10.40	
1976	Squander	2	A. Cordero Jr	119	Sensational	119	Miss Cigarette	119	73,740	1:10.80	
1977	Stub	2	R. Turcotte	119	Sunny Bay	119	Sweeping View	119	62,874	1:11.20	
1978	Mongo Queen	2	W.W. Rice	119	Fine Prospect	119	Whisper Fleet	119	72,567	1:10.60	
1979	Love Street	2	J. Tejeira	119	Daisy Miller	119	Bluer Than Blue	119	75,723	1:11.40	
1980	Fancy Naskra	2	L. Snyder	119	Sue Babe	119	Cherokee Frolic	119	79,068	1:12.00	
1981	Apalachee Honey	2	M.R. Morgan	119	Distinctive Moon	119	Laughing Gull	119	91,872	1:12.40	
1982	Singing Susan	2	W.J. Passmore	119	For Once'n My Life	119	Wings of Joy	119	82,635	1:11.60	
1983	Officers Ball	2	C. Perret	119	Terrible Terri T.	119	Dash of Hope	119	119,850	1:11.80	
1984	Tiltalating	2	P. Valenzuela	119	Raise a Q	119	Schematic	119	117,450	1:10.80	

Year	Winner	Age	Jockey	Wt.	Second	Wt.	Third	Wt.	Win Value	Time	Beyer
1985	Lazer Show	2	C.W. Antley	119	Act of Magic	119	Storm and Sunshine	119	112,470	1:10.40	
1986	Delicate Vine	2	G.L. Stevens	119	Burnished Bright	119	Easter Mary	119	120,000	1:09.60	
1987	Blue Jean Baby	2	C.J. McCarron	119	Tomorrow's Child	119	Granny's Portrait	119	111,600	1:10.20	
1988	Divine Answer	2	R. Wilson	119	Seaquay	119	Lea Lucinda	119	113,520	1:11.80	
1989	Fuerza	2	R.E. Colton	119	Icy Folly	119	Victory Party	119	120,000	1:11.60	
1990	Good Potential	2	E. Fires	119	Royal Summit	119	Flashing Eyes	119	120,000	1:11.40	76
1991	Fluttery Danseur	2	M.A. Pedroza	119	Miss Legality	119	Capture the Crown	119	120,000	1:10.60	85
1992	Hollywood Wildcat	2	F.A. Arguello J	119	Family Enterprize	119	D'Accordress	119	120,000	1:10.80	86
1993	Cat Attack	2	R.G. Davis	119	Shapely Scrapper	119	At the Half	119	120,000	1:11.40	90
1994	Stormy Blues	2	J.A. Krone	119	Cat Appeal	119	A Real Eye Opener	119	120,000	1:11.00	89
1995	Crafty but Sweet	2	Santagata N.	119	Golden Attraction	119	Careless Heiress	119	120,000	1:10.80	82
1996	Annie Cake	2	W.H. McCauley	119	Corporate Vision	199	Little Sister	119	90,000	1:11.60	73
1997	Unky And Ally	2	J.R. Martinez Jr.	119	Tipperary Melody	119	Love in the Hills	119	90,000	1:11.40	75
1998	Appealing Phylly	2	C.C. Lopez	119	Paved in Gold	119	Betty's Star	119	90,000	1:10.80	85
1999	Sister Fiona	2	J. Bravo	119	Katz Me If You Can	112	Mycatcandance	119	90,000	1:09.60	87
2000	Stormy Pick	2	J.C. Ferrer	119	Zonk	119	With Ability	119	90,000	1:10.96	85
2001	Forest Heiress	2	D.V. Beckner	119	Haunted Lass	119	Divine Angel	119	90,000	1:11.61	87
2002	Wild Snitch	2	E.M. Coa	119	Grand Natalie Rose	119	Runaway Chanel	119	60,000	1:11.09	79
2003	Feline Story	2	J.C. Ferrer	119	Whirlwind Charlott	119	Stand on Top	119	60,000	1:10.93	85

Beyer Index : 83.14

SPECTACULAR BID, 6 Furlongs,
3-Year-Olds, Gulfstream Park, 2003 Purse: $100,000

Year	Winner	Age	Jockey	Wt.	Second	Wt.	Third	Wt.	Win Value	Time	Beyer
1981	Jiggs Alarm	3	P. Day	112	Dame Mysterieuse		Spirited Boy		21,600	1:10.40	
1982	Sharp Future	3	E. Fires	113	Marshaller		Broad Minded		19,425	1:46.60	
1983	Freezing Rain	3	D. Brumfield	114	Write Off		Total Departure		22,194	1:10.00	
1984	Klaytone	3	G. St. Leon	114	Amerilad		Marine		25,851	1:42.60	
1985	Cherokee Fast	3	J.A. Santos	112	Vindalee		Secretary General		30,072	1:10.40	
1986	Groovy	3	C. Perret	113	Kenny Lane		Limited Practice		27,792	1:11.80	
1987	Spectacular Phanto	3	J. Velez	114	Micanopy Boy		Superceded		39,840	1:35.60	
1988	Cook's Brown Rice	3	A. Smith Jr	114	Evening Kris		Riff		35,481	1:11.00	
1989	Halrose	3	D. Valiente	117	Jabotinsky		Winners Laugh		34,770	1:12.00	
1990	Housebuster	3	C. Perret	114	Fit Contender		Stalker		30,000	1:11.40	
1991	To Freedom	3	A. Cordero Jr	119	Dark Brew		Here He Goes		32,817	1:10.40	
1992	Return to Quarters	3	W. Ramos	114	Scream Machine		Majestic Sweep		45,100	1:10.00	106
1993	Great Navigator	3	J.A. Santos	119	Demaloot Demashoot		Hidden Trick		45,078	1:09.40	89
1994	Halo's Image	3	J. Vasquez	114	Distinct Reality	119	Senor Conquistador	113	44,811	1:10.20	97
1995	Mr. Greeley	3	J.A. Krone	114	Make Me	112	Sea Emperor	119	44,823	1:10.60	99
1996	Seacliff	3	R.R. Douglas	122	Built for Pleasure	112	Gomtuu	119	45,000	1:11.80	92
1997	Confide	3	M.E. Smith	114	Kelly Kip	119	Crown Ambassador	117	45,000	1:09.80	94
1998	Time Limit	3	J.D. Bailey	117	Sejm Run	114	Governor Hicks	117	45,000	1:10.40	100
1999	Texas Glitter	3	J.R. Velazquez	114	Valid Trefaire	112	Lifeisawhirl	114	45,000	1:09.80	115
2000	B L's Appeal	3	M.E. Smith	114	American Bullet	114	Tour the Hive	112	45,000	1:10.68	82
2001	Icanseetherain	3	J.A. Santos	114	Diablo's Choice	112	American Century	114	60,000	1:11.04	90
2002	Maybry's Boy	3	J.R. Velazquez	116	Showmeitall	118	Harmony Hall	116	60,000	1:12.19	96
2003	First Blush	3	J.F. Chavez	116	Crafty Guy	120	Silver Squire	120	60,000	1:10.97	93

Beyer Index: 96.08

Run at 1 1/16 miles 1982, 1984, 1987

SPEND A BUCK HANDICAP, 1 1/16 Miles,
3-Year-Olds and Up, Calder Race Course, 2003 Purse: $100,000

Year	Winner	Age	Jockey	Wt.	Second	Wt.	Third	Wt.	Win Value	Time	Beyer
1991	Higgler	3	D. Nied	112	Jodie's Sweetie	115	Treblestaff	112	50,505	1:48.20	
1992	Poulain d'Or	3	P. Rodriguez	112	Ponche	112	Sir Stephenmichael	113	14,000	1:42.20	
1994	Daniel's Boy	6	P. Rodriguez	111	It'sali'Iknownfact	110	Aggressive Chief	115	60,000	1:52.68	107
1995	Pride of Burkaan	5	R. Douglas	119	Crafty Chris	114	Dauntless Gem	114	60,000	1:51.96	104
1996	King Rex	4	R. Lopez	116	Derivative	113	Leave'm Inthedark	114	48,945	1:52.80	96
1997	Derivative	6	J. Ferrer	116	Shan's Ready	114	Sur Irish's Secret	114	30,000	1:45.65	99
1998	Unruled	5	G. Boulanger	116	Sir Bear	124	Laughing Dan	113	60,000	1:45.68	107
1999	Best of the Rest	4	E. Coa	114	Dancing Guy	113	High Security	114	60,000	1:44.67	107
2000	Groomstick Stock's	4	R. Homeister Jr.	111	Reporter	113	Broadway Tune	113	60,000	1:44.82	101
2001	Best of the Rest	6	E. Coa	116	Dancing Guy	117	Sir Bear	117	60,000	1:42.59	106
2002	Pay the Preacher	4	C. Velasquez	114	Best of the Rest	121	Built Up	112	60,000	1:44.91	105
2003	Tour of the Cat	5	A. Cabassa Jr.	116	Best of the Rest	122	Dancing Guy	116	60,000	1:46.30	99

Beyer Index: 103.1

Run as Spend a Buck Breeders' Cup Handicap in 1996; Run as Spend a Buck Overnight Handicap in 1992; For 3-year-olds in 1992; Run at 1 mile 70 yards in 1992; Run at 1 1/8 miles in 1994–1996; Not run 1993

SPORT PAGE HANDICAP, 7 Furlongs,
3-Year-Olds and Up, Belmont Park, 2003 Purse:$112,700

Year	Winner	Age	Jockey	Wt.	Second	Wt.	Third	Wt.	Win Value	Time	Beyer
1953	White Skies	4	J. Stout	130	Hilarious	114	Joe Jones	107	15,500	1:11.60	
1954	Joe Jones	4	C. McCreary	118	Canadiana	114	Game Chance	122	19,250	1:12.00	
1955	Squared Away	8	E. Arcaro	119	Dark Peter	119	Gandharva	112	20,100	1:11.00	
1956	Jo Jones	6	C. McCreary	125	Decathlon	126	History Book	111	16,900	1:10.80	
1957	Tick Tock	4	R. Ussery	122	St. Amour II	117	Portersville	121	15,950	1:11.00	
1958	Nahodah	5	J. Culmone	118	Bumpy Road	118	Nan's Mink	110	19,135	1:10.20	
1959	Ole Fols	3	W. Boland	125	Nahodah	116	Tick Tock	125	17,770	1:10.80	
1960	April Skies	3	J. Leonard	118	Mail Order	120	Four Lane	124	17,575	1:10.20	
1961	Intentionally	5	M. Ycaza	129	Windy Sands	112	Gyro	119	15,535	1:10.00	
1962	Misty Day	4	W. Boland	115	Nassau Hall	113	Surfer	114	15,600	1:10.80	
1963	Merry Ruler	5	J. Sellers	118	Uppercut	112	Excl'e Nashua	116	14,690	1:10.00	
1964	Affectionately	4	W. Shoemaker	117	Red Gar	113	Macedonia	116	18,655	1:10.40	
1965	Ornamento	5	W. Boland	112	Affectionately	127	R. Thomas	119	18,362	1:10.40	
1966	Impressive	3	R. Turcotte	126	Vitencamps	110	Hoist Bar	113	18,135	1:09.80	
1967	R. Thomas	6	E. Belmonte	121			Flag Raiser	124	11,900	1:09.60	
	Sun Gala	3	L. Pincay Jr	112							
1968	Kissin' George	5	B. Baeza	124	Jim J.	126	Royal Exchange	115	18,362	1:09.20	
1969	King Emperor	3	B. Baeza	119	Coup Landing	122	Jaikyl	112	18,622	1:09.40	
1970	Fresh 'n Foolish	4	J. Velasquez	110	Ocean Bar	112	True North	116	19,305	1:10.00	
1971	Lonesome River	5	R. Woodhouse	112	Brazen Brother	121	Coup Landing	119	20,940	1:11.00	
1972	Petrograd	3	E. Maple	113	North Sea	116	Tap the Tree	117	17,055	1:10.20	
1973	Timeless Moment	3	B. Baeza	116	Tap the Tree	122	North Sea	124	16,350	1:09.20	
1974	Startahemp	4	J. Velasquez	114	Nostrum	114	Fr'nkie A'ms	121	22,950	1:09.60	
1975	Lonetree	5	E. Maple	122	Petrograd	119	Piamem	114	26,805	1:09.40	
1976	Amerrico	4	S. Hawley	111	Honorable Miss	115	Relent	113	32,610	1:09.80	
1977	Affiliate	3	A. Cordero Jr	124	Intercontinent	112	Gitchee Gumee	117	31,560	1:10.00	
1978	Topsider	3	M. Venezia	109	What a Summer	124	Affiliate	118	32,400	1:10.20	
1979	Amadevil	5	W.H. McCauley	113	Tanthem	123	Dave's Friend	119	32,580	1:09.40	
1980	Dave's Friend	5	V. Bracciale Jr	126	Tilt Up	114	Hawkin's Spec'l	114	34,380	1:08.20	
1981	Well Decorated	3	R. Hernandez	117	Engine One	116	Guilty Conscience	126	32,760	1:10.60	
1982	Mauldin	4	J.D. Bailey	115	Top Avenger	115	Duke Mitchell	115	34,200	1:09.40	
1983	Fast As the Breeze	4	M. Toro	110	Maudlin	120	Swelegant	117	33,180	1:10.60	
1984	Tarantara	5	R. Migliore	117	Muskoka Wyck	114	New Connecti'n	113	46,140	1:10.80	
1985	Raja's Shark	4	A. Cordero Jr	120	Love That Mac	113	Whoop Up	115	51,120	1:09.60	
1986	Best by Test	4	F. Lovato Jr	112	King's Swan	118	Sun Master	117	66,870	1:08.80	
1987	Vinnie the Viper	4	J.A. Krone	115	King's Swan	123	Banker's Jet	118	67,500	1:10.40	
1988	High Brite	4	A. Cordero Jr	120	Proud and Valid	111	Born to Shop	117	64,980	1:09.60	
1989	Garemma	3	J.F. Chavez	111	Proud and Valid	111	Born to Shop	117	51,120	1:10.20	
1990	Senor Speedy	3	A. Santiago	113	Brave Adventure	116	Dargai	115	53,190	1:10.00	
1991	Senor Speedy	4	J.F. Chavez	119	Shuttleman	113	Gallant Step	113	55,080	1:09.20	110
1992	R.D. Wild Whirl	4	R.G. Davis	114	Senor Speedy	122	Burn Fair	114	51,570	1:09.80	103
1993	Boom Towner	5	F. Lovato Jr	117	Raise Heck	115	Fabersham	113	53,730	1:10.60	116
1994	Man's Hero	4	M.J. Luzzi	111	Itaka	117	Storm Tower	118	51,045	1:22.00	113
1995	Siphon	4	K.J. Desormeaux	117	In Case	113	Ft. Stockton	113	74,160	1:22.00	106
1996	Valid Expectations	3	C.B. Asmussen	117	Diligence	116	Blissful State	117	68,040	1:21.80	112
1997	Stalwart Member	4	A.T. Gryder	114	Basqueian	116	Why Change	115	68,640	1:22.00	109
1998	Stormin Fever	4	R. Migliore	120	Olympic Cat	113	Adverse	113	50,115	1:21.40	112
1999	Scatmandu	4	A.T. Gryder	115	Aristotle	114	Watchman's Warning	112	50,250	1:22.60	103
2000	Stalwart Member	7	N. Arroyo Jr	117	Istintaj	117	Mister Tricky	112	48,690	1:21.97	108
2001	Yonaguska	3	C.J. McCarron	116	Silky Sweep	116	Big E E	114	65,640	1:15.54	107
2002	Multiple Choice	4	V. Carrero	113	Bowman's Band	118	Sing Me Back Home	113	66,840	1:23.28	108
2003	Voodoo	5	J.F. Chavez	114	Bowman's Band	120	Highway Prospector	114	67,620	1:22.18	111

Beyer Index: **109.08**

Run at 6 furlongs 1963-93; at 6 1/2 furlongs, 2001

STARS AND STRIPES BREEDERS' CUP TURF HANDICAP, 1 1/2 Miles (Turf),
3-Year-Olds and Up, Arlington Park, 2003 Purse: $219,200

Year	Winner	Age	Jockey	Wt.	Second	Wt.	Third	Wt.	Win Value	Time	Beyer
1929	Dowagiac	4	A. Pascuma	108	Misstep	125	Sun Beau	120	15,550	1:50.60	
1930	Blue Larkspur	4	J. Smith	121	Misstep	124	Sun Beau	125	26,050	1:49.40	
1931	Plucky Play	4	D. Trivett	105	Mike Hall	116	The Nut	114	24,650	1:50.80	
1932	Equipoise	4	R. Workman	129	Tred Avon	107	Dr. Freeland	110	22,300	1:54.80	
1933	Indian Runner	4	A. Tipton	114	Gallant Sir	124	Watch Him	103	10,440	1:51.40	
1934	Indian Runner	5	A. Tipton	118	Advising Anna	102	Ladysman	120	10,760	1:49.80	
1935	Discovery	4	J. Bejshak	126	Chief Cherokee	106	Riskulus	118	9,000	1:50.80	
1936	Stand Pat	5	C. McTague	116	Corinto	108	Whopper	122	9,520	1:49.60	
1937	Corinto	5	J. Westrope	109	Infantry	116	Sir Jim Ja's	105	9,000	1:50.60	
1938	War Minstrel	4	I. Hanford	107	Seabiscuit	130	Arabs Arrow	111	9,060	1:54.20	
1939	Count d'Or	4	J. Longden	107	Drudgery	116	Taxes	107	8,620	1:50.80	

Year Winner	Age	Jockey	Wt.	Second	Wt.	Third	Wt.	Win Value	Time	Beyer
1940 Advocator	6	J.E. Oros	118	Joe Schenck	114	Yale o' Nine	109	9,260	1:50.00	
1941 Steel Heels	5	A. Snider	110	Equifox	114	Gallahadion	116	9,900	1:49.80	
1942 Take Wing	4	F.A. Smith	103	Marriage	116	Equifox	116	8,600	1:58.60	
1943 Rounders	4	F. Zufelt	116	Thumbs Up	113	Marriage	116	42,050	1:53.60	
1944 Georgie Drum	5	G. Woolf	113	Equifox	107	Rounders	115	41,000	1:49.80	
1945 Devalue	7	S. Brooks	108	Thumbs Up	130	Sirde	115	40,000	1:51.60	
1946 Witch Sir	4	R. Campbell	115	Richmond Jac	109	Old Kentuck	108	40,100	1:49.40	
1947 Armed	6	D. Dodson	130	With Pleasure	117	Mighty Story	114	37,600	1:49.20	
1948 Citation	3	E. Arcaro	119	Eternal Reward	116	Pellicle	106	38,000	1:49.20	
1949 Coaltown	4	S. Brooks	130	Armed	110	Star Reward	121	36,700	1:48.40	
1950 Inseparable	5	K. Church	114	Seaward	118	Colosal	114	20,375	1:52.20	
1951 Royal Governor	7	E. Arcaro	115	Volcanic	124	Miche	116	41,950	1:49.20	
1952 Royal Mustang	4	P.J. Bailey	109	Cuore	112	Going Away	112	18,625	1:49.20	
1953 Abbe Sting	5	R. Baldwin	110	Armageddon	118	Iceberg II	122	16,675	1:48.40	
1954 Sir Mango	4	D. Erb	124	Iceberg II	123	Stan	114	17,300	1:49.40	
1955 Mark-Ye-Well	6	D. Erb	114	Ruhe	111	Blue Choir	117	16,700	1:48.40	
1956 Sir Tribal	5	W. Hartack	121	Mahan	115	Blue Choir	124	16,875	1:49.00	
1957 Manassas	4	C. Burr	115	Bryn	105	Bernburgoo	112	17,150	1:50.60	
1958 Terra Firma		L.C. Cook	118	Lincoln Road	124	Judge	114	54,800	1:50.60	
1959 Round Table	5	W. Shoemaker	132	Noureddin	110	Tudor Era	117	54,700	1:47.20	
1960 Dunce	4	B. Baeza	121	Martini II	109	King Grail	111	32,200	1:57.60	
1961 Oink	4	J. Sellers	126	Noholme II	117	Resolved	120	21,025	1:50.60	
1962 Porvenir II	8	A. Gomez	122	Oink	120	Gung Ho! II	114	26,875	1:51.20	
1963 Hard Rock Man	4	W. Blum	120	Wa-Wa Cy	113	Intercepted	118	20,100	1:48.20	
1964 Spanish Fort	4	D. Brumfield	112	Irish Dandy	110	Rob Roy III	106	28,500	1:48.60	
1965 Marlin Bay	5	H. Hinojosa	114	Or et Argent	117	Hard Rock Man	114	35,550	1:49.40	
1966 Climax II	5	W. Hartack	115	The Dancer	114	Miss Rincon	110	35,400	1:50.20	
1967 Climax II	6	L. Pincay Jr	113	Dominar	114	Toro Charger	110	33,800	1:49.60	
1968 Out the Window	4	H. Moreno	112	War Censor	117	Irish Rebellion	125	26,100	1:50.40	
1968 Fort Marcy	4	C.H. Marquez	119	The Knack II	110	Nashua Pilot	114	26,000	1:50.60	
1969 Hawaii	5	M. Ycaza	118	Great Cohoes	114	Quilche	112	35,100	1:49.80	
1970 Mr. Leader	4	J. Tejeira	116	Kerry's Time	115	Ribofilio	117	34,900	1:47.40	
1971 Knight in Armor	4	M. Venezia	115	Colorado City	115	Red Bayou	118	33,700	1:51.20	
1972 Unanime	5	W. Gavidia	113	Wing Out	125	Kling Kling	115	34,600	1:51.20	
1973 Triumphant	4	A. Rini	119	Super Sail	116	Vegas Vic	114	36,400	1:34.80	
1974 Zografos	6	W. Gavidia	113	Smooth Dancer	111	Fun Co K	109	45,600	1:50.80	
1975 Buffalo Lark	5	L. Snyder	121	Kuryakin	111	Zografos	115	40,600	1:43.00	
1976 Passionate Pirate	5	H. Arroyo	114	Improviser	122	Zografos	115	39,500	1:43.00	
1977 Quick Card	4	M. Solomone	118	Proponent	116			35,640	1:43.00	
				Emperor Rex	116					
1978 Old Frankfort	6	R. Turcotte	112	Capt. Stevens	114	That's a Nice	122	34,380	1:50.20	
1979 Overskate	4	R. Platts	125	That's a Nice	119	Bold Standard	111	33,360	1:44.00	
1980 Told	4	J.L. Samyn	114	Rossi Gold	111	Overskate	130	66,960	1:43.00	
1981 Ben Fab	4	G. Stahlbaum	122			Opus Dei	116	48,600	1:43.80	
Rossi Gold	5	P. Day	123							
1982 Rossi Gold	6	P. Day	124	Johnny Dance	115	Don Roberto	118	70,560	1:46.00	
1983 Rossi Gold	7	P. Day	122	Who's for Dinner	110	Lucence	115	70,860	1:48.80	
1984 Tough Mickey	4	J.L. Samyn	119	Fortnightly	115	Jack Slade	113	80,460	1:41.40	
1985 Drumalis	5	P. Day	118	Best of Both	115	Lofty	117	91,920	1:42.20	
1986 Explosive Darling	4	E. Fires	115	Clever Song	120	Forkintheroad	113	70,560	1:48.40	
1987 Sharrood		F. Toro	120	Explosive Darling	121	Santella Mac	115	52,080	1:56.20	
1989 Salem Drive	7	P. Day	116	Green Barb	115	Delegant	115	69,660	1:55.20	
1990 Mistery Sicy	4	C.A. Black	114	Silver Medallion	115	Careafolie	113	69,900	1:54.40	
1991 Blair's Cove	6	G.K. Gomez	115	Opening Verse	118	Cameroon	112	60,000	1:55.80	99
1992 Plate Dancer	7	E. Fires	114	Little Bro Lantis	114	Stark South	114	60,000	1:55.00	102
1993 Little Bro Lantis	5	C.C. Bourque	114	Stark South	119	Coaxing Matt	115	60,000	1:56.80	101
1994 Marastani	4	A.T. Gryder	113	Snake Eyes	117	The Vid	113	60,000	1:54.60	101
1995 Snake Eyes	5	R.J. Alborado	116	Coaxing Matt	115	Bucks Nephew	114	45,000	1:56.40	104
1996 Vladivostok	5	C. Perret	116	Raintrap	118	Special Price	118	138,075	2:30.20	107
1997 Lakeshore Road	4	C.H. Borel	113	Chief Bearhart	119	Awad	119	140,025	2:29.40	105
2000 Williams News	5	R.J. Albarado	115	Profit Option	110	Buff	114	148,425	2:31.22	104
2001 Falcon Flight	5	R.R. Douglas	114	Langston	114	Williams News	116	96,300	2:27.86	101
2002 Cetewayo	8	R.R. Douglas	118	Private Son	115	Pisces	117	137,475	2:27.50	102
2003 Ballingarry	4	R.R. Douglas	121	Dr. Brendler	118	Jack's Own Time	112	131,520	2:28.30	100

Beyer Index: 102.36

STUYVESANT HANDICAP, 1 1/8 Miles,
3-Year-Olds and Up, Aqueduct, 2003 Purse: $110,300

Year Winner	Age	Jockey	Wt.	Second	Wt.	Third	Wt.	Win Value	Time	Beyer
1916 Fernrock	3	E. Haynes	107	Mustard	102	Dad's Choice	100	2,350	1:13.00	
1917 Julialeon	3	R. Troxler	113	Woodtrap	114	Straight Forward	117	3,175	1:14.20	
1918 Motor Cop	3	J. Loftus	115	Flags	113	Jack Hare Jr	129	2,825	1:12.20	

Year	Winner	Age	Jockey	Wt.	Second	Wt.	Third	Wt.	Win Value	Time	Beyer
1919	Purchase	3	J. Loftus	129	Eternal	125	Ophelia	107	3,850	1:38.80	
1920	Man o' War	3	C. Kummer	135	Yellow Hand	103			3,850	1:41.60	
1921	Sedgefield	3	F. Coltiletti	100	Knobbie	112	Muskallonge	114	4,650	1:39.60	
1922	Snob II	3	E. Sande	117	Galantman	115	Pirate Gold	116	4,650	1:39.60	
1923	Dot	3	E. Sande	110	Moonraker	107	Great Man	117	4,650	1:39.40	
1924	Ordinance	3	E. Legere	108	Laurano	105	Samaritan	105	4,650	1:38.40	
1937	Chicolorado	3	E. Arcaro	115	Vamoose	102	Guy Fawkes	117	4,425	1:13.00	
1938	Merry Lassie	3	J. Stout	116	Steel Knight	100	Nedayr	126	3,700	1:11.00	
1939	T.M. Dorsett	3	L. Haas	116	Star Runner	109	Entracte	114	3,925	1:12.20	
1963	Rocky Link	3	S. Hernandez	112	Sunrise Flight	117	Yorky	110	18,297	1:49.20	
1964	Macedonia	4	H. Gustines	111	Bonjour	112	Piave	114	18,622	1:37.20	
1965	Flag Raiser		R. Ussery	121	Turn to Reason	115	Cupid	112	39,780	1:35.60	
1966	Understanding	3	A. Cordero Jr.	110	Mr. Right	116	Advocator	114	37,765	1:36.00	
1967	Sun Gala	3	R. Turcotte	111	Understanding	110	R. Thomas	119	37,180	1:36.80	
1968	Spring Double	5	C. Baltazar	114	Mile's Fancy	113	Principe	107	38,480	1:36.20	
1969	King Emperor	3	C.H. Marquez	116	Dewan	116	Jaikyl	112	39,520	1:34.40	
1970	Never Bow	4	E. Belmonte	114	Gleaming Light	114	Protanto	112	36,420	1:35.80	
1971	Red Reality	5	L. Pincay Jr	116	Silver Mallet	113	Summer Air	117	36,420	1:35.80	
1972	Icecapade	3	E. Maple	119	Sunny and Mild	108	Tentam	114	36,570	1:34.00	
1973	Riva Ridge	4	E. Maple	130	Forage	116	True Knight	122	34,320	1:47.00	
1974	Crafty Khale	5	J. Cruguet	121	Stop the Music	120	True Knight	121	34,890	1:48.00	
1975	Festive Mood	6	H. Hinojosa	115	Step Nicely	124	Stonewalk	122	33,210	1:48.40	
1976	Distant Land	4	H. Gustines	111	Blue Times	114	It's Freezing	115	32,610	1:49.00	
1977	Cox's Ridge	3	E. Maple	124	Wise Philip	114	Gentle King	112	32,760	1:48.40	
1978	Seattle Slew	4	A. Cordero Jr.	134	Jumping Hill	115	Wise Phillip	113	62,310	1:47.40	
1979	Music of Time	5	J. Fell	114	What a Gent	111	Dewan Keys	112	65,220	1:50.40	
1980	Plugged Nickle	3	C.B. Asmussen	122	Dr. Patches	115	Ring of Light	116	68,880	1:50.20	
1981	Idyll	4	C.B. Asmussen	114	Spoils of War	113	Silver Buck	112	68,280	1:48.80	
1982	Engine One	4	R. Hernandez	123	Bar Dexter	112	Fit to Fight	118	67,200	1:49.60	
1983	Fit to Fight	4	J.D. Bailey	117	Deputy Minister	119	Sing Sing	115	70,080	1:51.40	
1984	Valiant Lark	4	V. Bracciale Jr.	114	Puntivo	112	Bounding Basque	117	70,080	1:51.40	
1985	Garthorn	5	R.Q. Meza	112	Morning Bob	114	Waitlist	118	70,320	1:48.40	
1986	Little Missouri	4	R.G. Davis	116	Waquoit	115	Let's Go Blue	118	125,280	1:50.00	
1987	Moment of Hope	4	M. Venezia	118	Wind Chill	110	I Rejoice	111	109,080	1:49.60	
1988	Talinum	4	M. Castaneda	112	Nostalgia's Star	113	Pleas'nt Virginian	113	111,240	1:51.20	
1989	Its Acedemic	5	J.D. Bailey	111	Congeleur	115	Homebuilder	114	70,560	1:48.80	
1990	I'm Sky High	4	M.E. Smith	111	Silver Survivor	113	Lost Opportunity	111	71,760	1:48.20	111
1991	Montubio	6	J.M. Pezua	111	Mountain Lore	112	Timely Warning	114	72,480	1:48.20	108
1992	Shots are Ringing	3	J.R. Velazquez	114	Key Contender	111	Timely Warning	115	69,120	1:49.20	104
1993	Michelle Can Pass	5	J.R. Velazquez	115	Key Contender	115	Primitive Hall	113	70,200	1:51.00	103
1994	Wallenda	4	W.H. McCauley	118	Lost Soldier	110	Pistols and Roses	117	64,560	1:50.60	103
1995	Silver Fox	4	M.E. Smith	113	Yourmissinthepoint	111	Earth Colony	114	68,940	1:48.00	100
1996	Poor But Honest	6	J.F. Chavez	116	Flitch	115	Admirality	117	66,480	1:49.40	108
1997	Delay of Game	4	Samyn J. L.	114	Concerto	118	Mr. Sinatra	117	66,060	1:47.60	108
1998	Mr. Sinatra	4	Gryder A. T.	115	Rock and Roll	114	Accelerator	114	65,280	1:48.00	109
1999	Best of Luck	5	M.E. Smith	114	Wild Imagination	115	Durmiente	113	67,200	1:49.60	108
2000	Lager	6	H. Castillo Jr.	116	Top Official	113	Fire King	115	64,860	1:50.03	97
2001	Graeme Hall	4	J.R. Velazquez	119	Country Be Gold	115	Cat's at Home	114	64,620	1:47.95	113
2002	Snake Mountain	4	J.A. Santos	115	Windsor Castle	115	Docent	115	68,040	1:50.56	103
2003	Presidentialaffair	4	R. Migliore	115	Thunder Blitz	114	Gander	115	66,180	1:50.86	106

Beyer Index: 105.79

SUWANNEE RIVER HANDICAP, 1 1/8 Miles (Turf), Fillies and Mares 3-Year-Olds and Up, Gulfstream Park, 2003 Purse: $100,000

Year	Winner	Age	Jockey	Wt.	Second	Wt.	Third	Wt.	Win Value	Time	Beyer
1947	Ariel Song	4	D. Dodson	114	Nance's Ace	120	Kay Gibson	118	4,100	1:24.20	
							Edified	112			
1948	Buzfuz	6	A. Snider	122	Delegate	114	Gestapo	111	8,200	1:11.20	
1950	Theory	3	E. Nelson	106	John's Joy	120	Beau Dandy	118	3,250	1:09.00	
1951	Circus Clown	6	J. Stout	117	Lextown	119	All at Once	120	4,750	1:10.20	
1952	Penson		K. Church	118	Woodford Sir		Swamp Son		1,875	1:44.60	
1953	Sunny Dale	5	K. Church	118	Mad Hare	112	Blue Kay	103	10,800	1:44.60	
1954	Atalanta	6	H.B. Wilson	122	Lavender Hill	110	Intencion	107	10,650	1:43.60	
1955	Queen Hopeful	4	J. Adams	118	Clear Dawn	115	Rosemary B.	115	10,950	1:43.60	
1956	Tremor	4	W. Shoemaker	106	Flower Bowl	106	Queen Hopeful	116	10,505	1:43.00	
1957	Estacion	4	W.M. Cook	109	Amoret	121	Pucker Up	114	17,050	1:42.40	
1958	Rosewood	4	C. Burr	108	Pink Velvet	113	Ficha	106	17,425	1:45.80	
1959	Oil Rich	4	J. Sellers	109	Happy Princess	112	Rosewood	120	9,600	1:44.00	
1960	Royal Native	4	W. Hartack	130	Meadow Miss	107	Woodlawn	110	9,075	1:42.00	
1961	Airmans Guide	4	W. Hartack	120	Shirley Jones	119	Indian Maid	119	9,650	1:22.40	
1962	Coup d'Etat	5	W. Hartack	114	Prim Flower	110	Shirley Jones	122	9,625	1:23.40	
1963	Old Hat	4	H. Grant	117	Cicada	126	Coup d'Etat	111	9,350	1:23.20	

Year	Winner	Age	Jockey	Wt.	Second	Wt.	Third	Wt.	Win Value	Time	Beyer
1964	Smart Deb	4	W. Blum	123	Lady Karachi	116	Yes Please	111	9,600	1:23.00	
1965	Old Hat	6	D. Brumfield	125	Abrogate	112	Money to Burn	110	12,775	1:23.00	
1966	Wild Note	4	R. Broussard	116	Clown Around	112	Alondra II	115	13,575	1:22.80	
1967	Cologne	4	L. Moyers	112	Kerensa	115	Indian Sunlite	122	22,200	1:47.00	
1968	Ludham	4	K. Knapp	110	Farest Nan	113	Ring Francis	111	23,300	1:41.80	
1969	Spire	5	R. Broussard	115	Crystal Palace	114	Treacherous	114	14,550	1:39.40	
1970	Blue Rage	4	M. Solomone	112	Director	117	Dark Stream	113	22,300	1:43.20	
1970	Starstrand	4	D. MacBeth	110	Klassy Poppy	120	Thai Silk	112	22,800	1:43.60	
1971	Delta Sal	5	W. Blum	113	Dedicated to Sue	117	Evening Bag	112	15,690	1:35.60	
1971	Sign of the Times	4	J. Velasquez	108	Stolen Base	116	S'nd Speculation	110	15,990	1:36.00	
1972	Irish Party	4	R. Woodhouse	114	Ruth's Edition	113	Glenary	114	16,470	1:37.20	
1972	Stay out Front	6	J. Vasquez	112	Aladancer	121	Wilderness	110	16,620	1:37.20	
1973	Ziba Blue	6	M. Miceli	110	Cathy Baby	113	Barely Even	127	21,270	1:35.80	
1974	Dove Creek Lady	4	M.A. Rivera	121	North Broadway	120	North of Venus	119	21,960	1:36.40	
1975	Deesse du Val	4	M. Hole	115	North of Venus	118	Lorraine Edna	118	20,400	1:35.40	
1976	Jabot	4	H. Gustines	112	Redundancy	119	Deesse du Val	117	21,330	1:34.60	
1977	Bronze Point	4	H. Arroyo	120	Funny Peculiar	114	Collegiate	114	21,390	1:24.20	
1978	Len's Determined	4	J. Cruguet	119	What a Summer	122	Late Bloomer	113	19,260	1:35.60	
1979	Navajo Princess	5	C. Perret	124	La Soufriere	119	Unreality	121	19,650	1:35.20	
1979	Calderina	4	J. Fell	117	Terpsichorist	122	She Can Dance	113	19,200	1:36.20	
1980	Ouro Verde	4	R.I. Encinas	112	No Disgrace	110	Anna Yrrah D.	112	18,870	1:37.20	
1980	Just a Game II.	4	D. Brumfield	117	La Soufriere	113	La Voyageuse	120	18,870	1:35.20	
1981	Honey Fox	4	J.L. Samyn	111	Racquette	115	Pompoes	110	22,568	1:35.20	
1981	Exactly So	4	J.L. Samyn	109	Draw In	114	Champagne Ginny	118	22,567	1:35.80	
1982	Pine Flower	4	C. Perret	113	Sweetest Chant	116	Fair Davina	110	27,000	1:35.40	
1982	Teacher's Pet	5	C. Marquez	114	Shark Song	114	Blush	113	27,300	1:35.20	
1983	Norsan	4	J.D. Bailey	113	Dana Calqui	114	Colatina	111	28,890	1:38.20	
1983	Syrianna	4	J. Vasquez	114	Meringue Pie	115	Plenty O'Toole	114	27,390	1:24.20	
1983	Promising Native.	4	D. MacBeth	113	Avowal	117	Our Darling	112	27,060	1:23.80	
1984	Sulemeif	4	J.D. Bailey	113	Jubilous	115	M'lanie Francis	113	39,330	1:36.80	
1985	Early Lunch	4	W.A. Guerra	112	Eva G.	114	Maidenhead	111	28,521	1:35.60	
1985	Sherizar	4	J. McKnight	113	Madam Flutterby	114	Melanie Franc's	115	28,820	1:36.40	
1985	Burst of Colors	5	J.A. Santos	117	Queen of Song	121	Silver in Flight	115	28,820	1:35.60	
1986	Cheshire Kitten	4	J.L. Samyn	112	Chaldea	111	Four Flings	113	30,990	1:44.80	
1986	Videogenic	4	R.G. Davis	120	Contredance	117	Verbality	112	30,690	1:44.60	
1987	Fieldy	4	C. Perret	114							
	Fama	4	R.P. Romero	114			Navarchus	114	17,810	1:44.20	
1987	Singular Bequest	4	E. Fires	114	Cadabra Abra	114	Duckweed	112	26,415	1:43.60	
1988	Go Honey	5	J.M. Pezua	110	Princely Proof	115	Fieldy	118	38,490	1:41.80	
1988	Anka Germania	6	C. Perret	122	Sum	114	Fama	112	39,090	1:41.80	
1989	Love You by Heart	4	R.P. Romero	117	Native Mommy	117	Aquaba	115	37,275	1:41.60	
1989	Fieldy	6	C. Perret	116	Summer Secretary	110	Chapel of Dreams	122	36,975	1:41.60	
1990	Princess Mora	4	M.A. Gonzalez	111	Fieldy	121	Northling	113	38,970	1:41.20	100
1991	Vigorous Lady	5	M.A. Lee	119	Yen for Gold	110	Pr'mier Question	114	36,120	1:45.00	
1992	Julie la Rousse	4	J.D. Bailey	115	Christiecat	117	Grab the Green	120	38,670	1:48.40	102
1993	Via Borghese	4	J.D. Bailey	116	Marshua's River	113	Blue Daisy	114	40,230	1:48.20	103
1994	Marshua's River	7	Santos JA	114	Sheila's Revenge	118	Icy Warning	115	45,000	1:46.60	99
1995	Cox Orange	5	J.D. Bailey	116	Irving's Girl	113	Alice Springs	120	45,000	1:47.40	103
1996	Class Kris	4	P. Day	116	Apolda	118	Majestic Dy	113	45,000	1:49.80	101
1997	Golden Pond	4	J.D. Bailey	114	Rumpipumpy	114	Elusive	113	45,000	1:47.80	98
1998	Seebe	4	Rice D.S.	114	Colcon	115	Parade Queen	119	45,000	1:47.40	102
1999	Winfama	6	R. Migliore	114	Circus Charmer	113	Colcon	120	45,000	1:52.20	101
2000	Pico Teneriffe	4	J.F. Chavez	115	Dominique's Joy	114	Crystal Symphony	115	45,000	1:47.83	97
2001	Spook Express	7	M.E. Smith	116	Gaviola	120	Windsong	113	60,000	1:47.28	96
2002	Snow Dance	4	P. Day	119	Step With Style	114	Windsong	113	60,000	1:49.04	97
2003	Amonita	5	J.L. Samyn	117	What a Price	114	Calista	118	60,000	1:47.90	98

Beyer Index: 99.77

SWALE, 7 Furlongs,
3-Year-Olds, Gulfstream Park, 2003 Purse: $150,000

Year	Winner	Age	Jockey	Wt.	Second	Wt.	Third	Wt.	Win Value	Time	Beyer
1985	Chief's Crown	3	D. MacBeth	122	Creme Fraiche		Cherokee Fast		30,792	1:22.40	
1986	One Magic Moment	3	C. Perret	113	Admiral's Mirage		Two Punch		31,230	1:22.40	
1988	Seeking the Gold	3	R.P. Romero	114	Above Normal		Perfect Spy		35,100	1:21.60	
1989	Easy Goer	3	P. Day	122	Trion		Tricky Creek		34,290	1:22.20	
1990	Housebuster	3	C. Perret	122	Summer Squall	122	Thirty Six Red	113	34,350	1:22.20	
1991	Chihuahua	3	J.D. Alferez	112	To Freedom	119	Greek Costume	114	51,060	1:23.40	97
1992	D.J. Cat	3	J.D. Bailey	114	Binalong	114	Always Silver	112	71,250	1:23.20	115
1993	Premier Explosion	3	D. Penna	114	Demaloot Demashoot	113	Cherokee Run	114	53,520	1:23.20	100
1994	Arrival Time	3	C.J. McCarron	115	Senor Conquistador	113	Meadow Monster	112	45,000	1:22.40	97
1995	Mr. Greeley	3	J.A. Krone	114	Devious Course	119	Pyramid Peak	114	45,000	1:22.00	103
1996	Roar	3	M.E. Smith	113	Gomtuu	119	Dixie Connection	112	45,000	1:22.40	94

Year	Winner	Age	Jockey	Wt.	Second	Wt.	Third	Wt.	Win Value	Time	Beyer
1997	Confide	3	M.E. Smith	117	Country Rainbow	112	The Silver Move	119	45,000	1:23.20	107
1998	Favorite Trick	3	P. Day	122	Good and Tough	114	Dice Dancer	113	60,000	1:22.80	104
1999	Yes It's True	3	J.D. Bailey	122	Texas Glitter	117	Lucky Roberto	119	60,000	1:22.20	103
2000	Trippi	3	J.D. Bailey	113	Ultimate Warrior	117	Harlan Traveler	114	60,000	1:23.43	98
2001	D'wildcat	3	C.S. Nakatani	116	Tarek	112	Yonaguska	122	90,000	1:22.25	110
2002	Ethan Man	3	P. Day	116	Listen Here	120	Governor Hickel	116	90,000	1:22.29	98
2003	Midas Eyes	3	J.D. Bailey	116	Posse	120	Whywhywhy	122	90,000	1:21.06	110

Beyer Index: 102.77

SYCAMORE BREEDERS' CUP, 1 1/2 Miles (Turf),
3-Year-Olds and Up, Keeneland, 2003 Purse: $138,200

Year	Winner	Age	Jockey	Wt.	Second	Wt.	Third	Wt.	Win Value	Time	Beyer
1995	Lindon Lime	5	C. Perret	123	Hyper Shu	114	Lordly Prospect	114	39,098	2:42.11	100
1996	Gleaming Key	4	R. Albarado	114	Nash Terrace	120	Hawkeye Bay	114	32,860	2:44.49	99
1997	Gleaming Key	5	S.J. Sellers	116	Double Leaf	116	Seattle Blossom	116	33,015	2:45.86	96
1998	Royal Strand	4	S.J. Sellers	116	Thesaurus	116	Lakeshore Road	116	33,015	2:41.93	100
1999	Royal Strand	5	P. Day	117	Arizona Storm	117	Magest	117	42,315	2:38.68	103
2000	Crowd Pleaser	5	C. Borel	118	Dixie's Crown	122	Kim Loves Bucky	114	44,439	2:44.00	101
2001	Rochester	5	P. Day	119	Chorwon	125	Regal Dynasty	119	103,044	2:31.29	98
2002	Rochester	6	P. Day	125	Roxinho	120	Lord Flasheart	120	101,928	2:30.48	101
2003	Sharbayan	5	P. Day	120	Cetewayo	122	Deputy Strike	120	73,904	2:29.55	104

Beyer Index: 100.22

TAMPA BAY DERBY, 1 1/16 Miles,
3-Year-Olds, Tampa Bay Downs, 2003 Purse: $250,000

Year	Winner	Age	Jockey	Wt.	Second	Wt.	Third	Wt.	Win Value	Time	Beyer
1981	Paristo	3	D.C. Ashcroft	112	Bravestofall	120	Darby Gillic	122	43,560	1:45.40	
1982	Reinvested	3	R.D. Luhr	114	Stage Reviewer	120	Real Twister	120	40,140	1:45.20	
1983	Morganmorganmorgan	3	W. Rodriguez	118	Slew o' Gold	118	Quick Dip	118	60,000	1:47.20	
1984	Bold Southerner	3	W. Crews	116	Rexson's Hope	122	Stickler	120	95,400	1:44.60	
1985	Regal Remark	3	J. Fell	122	Verification	122	Sport Jet	118	95,400	1:46.80	
1986	My Prince Charming	3	G. Perret	122	Lucky Rebeau	120	Major Moran	116	98,100	1:46.60	
1987	Phantom Jet	3	K.K. Allen	122	Homebuilder	116	You're No Bargain	116	90,000	1:43.80	
1988	Cefis	3	E. Maple	116	Buck Forbes	118	Twice Too Many	118	90,000	1:44.40	
1989	Storm Predictions	3	S. Gaffalione	120	With Approval	120	Mercedes Won	122	90,000	1:43.80	
1990	Champagneforashley	3	J. Vasquez	122	Slew of Angels	120	Always Running	116	90,000	1:44.60	
1991	Speedy Cure	3	R.D. Lopez	118	Link	118	Shudanz	116	90,000	1:46.20	
1992	Careful Gesture	3	R.N. Lester	118	Chief Speaker	116	Clipper Won	116	120,000	1:45.93	89
1993	Marco Bay	3	R. Allen Jr.	120	Thriller Chiller	116	Tunecke Charlie	118	90,000	1:44.40	93
1994	Prix de Crouton	3	M. Walls	120	Able Buck	120	Parental Pressure	122	90,000	1:46.60	82
1995	Gadzook	3	G. Boulanger	116	Composer	116	Bet Your Bucks	116	90,000	1:45.20	87
1996	Thundering Storm	3	J. Guerra	118	El Amante	118	Natural Selection	116	90,000	1:43.80	100
1997	Zede	3	J.D. Bailey	118	Brisco Jack	116	Favorable Regard	118	90,000	1:44.80	91
1998	Parade Ground	3	P. Day	118	Middlesex Drive	118	Rock and Roll	116	90,000	1:44.20	94
1999	Pineaff	3	J.A. Santos	122	Menifee	120	Doneraile Court	122	90,000	1:45.33	102
2000	Wheelaway	3	R. Migliore	116	Impeachment	116	Perfect Cat	116	90,000	1:43.90	94
2001	Burning Roma	3	R. Migliore	123	American Prince	123	Paging	116	120,000	1:44.30	95
2002	Equality	3	R. Dominguez	118	Tails of the Crypt	123	Political Attack	123	120,000	1:43.66	103
2003	Region of Merit	3	E.M. Coa	120	Aristocat	118	Hear No Evil	123	150,000	1:44.61	95

Beyer Index: 93.75

TEMPTED, 1 Mile,
2-Year-Old Fillies, Aqueduct, 2003 Purse: $110,700

Year	Winner	Age	Jockey	Wt.	Second	Wt.	Third	Wt.	Win Value	Time	Beyer
1975	Secret Lanvin	2	J. Cruguet	117	Free Journey	121	Imaflash	113	33,600	1:35.40	
1976	Pearl Necklace	2	A. Cordero Jr.	114	Our Mims	113	Road Princess	113	22,380	1:39.60	
1977	Caesar's Wish	2	G. McCarron	116	Itsamaza	116	Lucinda Lea	114	22,635	1:36.20	
1978	Whisper Fleet	2	A. Cordero Jr.	119	Run Cosmic Run	114	Distinct Honor	113	25,665	1:36.20	
1979	Genuine Risk	2	J. Vasquez	114	Street Ballet	117	Tell a Secret	115	33,060	1:36.00	
1980	Tina Tina Too	2	C.B. Asmussen	114	Prayers'n Promises	121	Explosive Kingdom	114	32,580	1:38.40	
1981	Choral Group	2	J. Velasquez	122	Michelle Mon Amour	114	Middle Stage	113	33,000	1:38.00	
1982	Only Queens	2	M.A. Rivera	114	Future Fun	113	Blue Garter	116	33,180	1:37.00	
1983	Surely Georgie's	2	R. Hernandez	113	Baroness Direct	114	Dumdedumdedum	114	34,320	1:39.60	
1984	Willowy Mood	2	J. Velasquez	121	Koluctoo's Jill	114	Easy Step	116	57,330	1:46.20	
1985	Cosmic Tiger	2	E. Maple	121	Tracy's Espoir	114	Roses for Avie	114	68,580	1:46.80	
1986	Silent Turn	2	C.W. Antley	119	Grecian Flight	119	Chase the Dream	119	74,400	1:46.20	
1987	Thirty Eight Go Go	2	K.J. Desormeaux	121	Best Number	114	Dangerous Type	116	100,920	1:44.60	
1988	Box Office Gold	2	J.A. Santos	116	Dreamy Mimi	116	Surging	116	57,600	1:46.20	

Year	Winner	Age	Jockey	Wt.	Second	Wt.	Third	Wt.	Win Value	Time	Beyer
1989	Worth Avenue	2	R.P. Romero	113	Crown Quest	119	Voodoo Lily	114	69,480	1:46.80	
1990	Flawlessly	2	J.D. Bailey	121	Debutant's Halo	121	Slept Thru It	114	56,250	1:46.60	
1991	Deputation	2	D.W. Lidberg	114	Turnback the Alarm	121	Bless Our Home	114	72,600	1:46.60	87
1992	True Affair	2	J. Bravo	121	Broad Gains	121	Touch of Love	114	68,520	1:47.40	87
1993	Sovereign Kitty	2	J.R. Velazquez	112	Seeking the Circle	113	Her Temper	112	69,720	1:46.80	81
1994	Special Broad	2	J.A. Krone	114	Carson Creek	114	Golden Bri	114	66,000	1:37.20	88
1996	Ajina	2	J.D. Bailey	112	Glitter Woman	114	Aldiza	114	66,240	1:36.40	86
1997	Dancing With Ruth	2	T.G. Turner	118	Soft Senorita	118	Aunt Anne	116	65,340	1:37.40	84
1998	Oh What a Windfall	2	J.D. Bailey	121	La Ville Rouge	114	Honour a Bull	114	66,120	1:39.80	65
1999	Shawnee Country	2	J.F. Chavez	116	To Marquet	114	Marigalante	116	65,460	1:38.60	88
2000	Two Item Limit	2	R. Migliore	117	Celtic Melody	115	Twining Star	115	65,520	1:38.53	80
2001	Smok'n Frolic	2	J.R. Velazquez	119	Saintly Action	115	Wopping	117	66,900	1:37.77	89
2002	Chimichurri	2	J.R. Velazquez	119	Reheat	115	Bonay	115	66,240	1:37.52	83
2003	La Reina	2	J.R. Velazquez	115	Eye Dazzler	115	Sisti's Pride	115	66,420	1:36.15	90

Beyer Index: 84

TEXAS MILE, 1 Mile,
3-Year-Olds and Up, Lone Star Park, 2003 Purse: $300,000

Year	Winner	Age	Jockey	Wt.	Second	Wt.	Third	Wt.	Win Value	Time	Beyer
1997	Isitingood	6	D.R. Flores	123	Spiritbound	116	Skip Away	116	150,000	1:34.40	106
1998	Littlebitlively	4	C.V. Gonzalez	118	Anet	116	Scott's Scoundrel	118	150,000	1:37.07	113
1999	Littlebitlively	5	C.V. Gonzalez	116	Real Quiet	116	Allen's Oop	113	145,000	1:35.60	110
2000	Sir Bear	7	E.M. Coa	116	Lexington Park	116	Luftikus	118	170,000	1:35.98	105
2001	Dixie Dot Com	6	D.R. Flores	116	Mr Ross	120	Five Straight	115	180,000	1:34.72	110
2002	Unrullah Bull	5	A.J. Lovato	116	Reba's Gold	118	Compendium	116	170,000	1:37.78	107
2003	Bluesthestandard	6	M.A. Pedroza	120	Bonapaw	116	Compendium	116	170,000	1:35.68	108

Beyer Index: 108.43

THE VERY ONE HANDICAP, 1 3/8 Miles (Turf)
Fillies and Mares 3-Year-Olds and Up, Gulfstream Park, 2003 Purse: $100,000

Year	Winner	Age	Jockey	Wt.	Second	Wt.	Third	Wt.	Win Value	Time	Beyer
1987	First Prediction	5	J.M. Pezua	114	Thirty Zip		Lady of the North		37,620	1:35.20	
1990	Storm of Glory	6	J.D. Bailey	113	Tukwila		Topicount		30,000	1:25.00	
1991	Rigamajig	5	R.P. Romero	116	Star Standing		Ahead		30,000	2:15.00	
1992	Bungalow	5	S.J. Sellers	114	Raffinerte		Lover's Quest		30,000	2:05.60	92
1993	Fairy Garden	5	W. Ramos	113	Trampoli		Tango Charlie		30,000	2:14.60	99
1994	Russian Tango	4	J.D. Bailey	112	Maxamount		Camiunch		30,000	2:02.40	95
1995	P.J. Floral	6	S.J. Sellers	113	Trampoli		Memories		30,000	2:14.40	100
1996	Electric Society	5	M.E. Smith	113	Northern Emerald	114	Chelsey Flower	114	30,000	2:15.20	97
1997	Tocopilla	7	B. Peck	114	Ampulla	123	Beyrouth	113	45,000	2:14.20	105
1998	Shemozzle	5	J.R. Velazquez	114	Turkappeal	114	Yoakama	119	45,000	2:19.00	100
1999	Delilah	5	J.D. Bailey	116	Starry Dreamer	114	Beyrouth	113	45,000	2:13.45	97
2000	My Sweet Westly	4	P. Day	110	I'm Indy Mood	114	Manoa	114	45,000	2:06.79	86
2001	Innuendo	6	J.D. Bailey	115	Lucky Lune	114	Silver Bandana	114	60,000	2:13.62	104
2002	Moon Queen	4	J.D. Bailey	118	Jennasietta	114	Sweetest Thing	114	60,000	2:18.38	103
2003	San Dare	5	M. Guidry	116	Tweedside	115	Hi Tech Honeycomb	113	60,000	2:13.76	100

Beyer Index: 98.17

Run at one mile on turf in 1987; at seven furlongs on main track in 1990; at 1 1/4 miles on the main track in 1992, 1994, and 2000.

THOROUGHBRED CLUB OF AMERICA, 6 Furlongs, Fillies and Mares
3-Year-Olds and Up, Keeneland Race Course, 2003 Purse: $125,000

Year	Winner	Age	Jockey	Wt.	Second	Wt.	Third	Wt.	Win Value	Time	Beyer
1988	Tappiano	4	J. Vasquez	123	Bound	117	Pine Tree Lane	123	48,750	1:10.20	
1989	Plate Queen	4	R.P. Romero	117	Degenerate Gal	114	Social Pro	123	48,750	1:11.20	
1990	Safely Kept	4	C. Perret	123	Volterra	112	Medicine Woman	117	48,750	1:10.40	
1991	Avie Jane	7	C. Perret	117	Amen	114	Hoga	114	48,750	1:10.20	89
1992	Ifyoucouldseemenow	4	C. Perret	120	Harbour Club	117	Madam Bear	117	48,750	1:09.60	104
1993	Jeano	5	P. Day	120	Apelia	117	Fluttery Danseur	120	46,500	1:09.20	94
1994	Tenacious Tiffany	4	Perret C	113	Roamin Rachel	120	Jeano	120	46,500	1:11.00	98
1995	Cat Appeal	3	D.M. Barton	116	Russian Flight	113	Traverse City	118	46,500	1:10.00	104
1996	Suprising Fact	3	P. Day	110	Morris Code	118	Mama's Pro	113	62,000	1:10.00	104
1997	Sky Blue Pink	3	P. Day	111	Bluffing Girl	114	Mama's Pro	116	62,000	1:10.00	97
1998	Bourbon Belle	3	Martinez W.	111	J J's Dream	121	Meter Maid	121	62,000	1:08.60	107
1999	Cinemine	4	Martin E. M. Jr.	120	Bourbon Belle	122	Lucky Again	114	62,000	1:08.80	96
2000	Katz Me If You Can	3	J.F. Chavez	115	Hurricane Bertie	123	My Alibi	117	67,394	1:09.42	99
2001	Cat Cay	4	P. Day	118	Spanish Glitter	120	Another	124	67,580	1:09.24	111
2002	French Riviera	3	D.J. Meche	116	Don't Countess Out	120	Away	122	77,500	1:09.75	108
2003	Summer Mis	4	R.R. Douglas	122	Don't Countess Out	122	Born to Dance	122	77,500	1:09.77	90

Beyer Index: 100.08

TOBOGGAN HANDICAP, 6 Furlongs,
3-Year-Olds and Up, Aqueduct, 2003 Purse: $109,100

Year	Winner	Age	Jockey	Wt.	Second	Wt.	Third	Wt.	Win Value	Time	Beyer
1890	Fides	4	Hamilton	116	Geraldine	122	Blue Rock	120	6,900	1:10.20	
1892	Madstone	6	Garrison	124	Tournament	122	Russell	125	2,215	1:13.00	
1893	Prince George	3	Lamley	109	Yemen	122	G.W. Johnson	112	3,900	1:11.40	
1894	Correction	6	Littlefield	117	Roche	107	Stonell	130	3,900	1:10.40	
1896	Hastings	3	Griffin	114	Hanwell	110	Sherlock	102	1,425	1:12.60	
1897	Octagon	3	Hewitt	107	Irish Reel	119	Lithos	111	1,150	1:12.00	
1898	Octagon	4	Simms	125	Irish Reel	119	Cleophus	126	1,425	1:15.20	
1899	Banastar	4	Maher	116	Sanders	121	Octagon	130	1,820	1:09.00	
1900	Voter	6	Spencer	128	Maribert	110	Contestor	105	1,375	1:12.20	
1901	Banastar	6	Odom	130	King Pepper	103	Unmasked	110	1,210	1:13.40	
1902	Old England	3	J. Woods	105	Arsenal	106	Cervera	120	1,700	1:12.60	
1903	Mizzen	3	Bullman	112	Illyria	93	Invincible	97	2,620	1:11.40	
1904	Hurst Park	4	Odom	111	Kohinoor	96	Gay Boy	120	2,790	1:14.00	
1905	Roseben	4	F. O'Neill	112	Sparkling Star	87	Pasadena	105	2,670	1:13.00	
1906	Clark Griffith	3	W. Miller	100	Tiptoe	102	Oxford	107	3,510	1:11.60	
1907	Ben Ban	4	Garner	95	Pantoufle	100	Red River	109	3,990	1:16.40	
1908	Berry Maid	4	Shreve	100	Baby Wolf	118	Restigouche	105	3,940	1:11.60	
1909	De Mund	5	Butwell	125	Field Mouse	103	Harrigan	108	1,010	1:11.00	
1910	Mary Davis	4	J. Glass	114	Dreamer	104	Field Mouse	101	1,150	1:13.00	
1913	Iron Mask	5	Troxler	130	Spring Board	105	Hes Prynne	99	2,065	1:10.00	
1914	Rock View	4	J. Butwell	126	Figinny	100	Ten Point	128	2,610	1:12.40	
1915	High Noon	3	C. Borel	108	Stromboli	127	Y. Notions	114	1,450	1:09.60	
1916	High Noon	4	J. Loftus	124	Benevolent	108	Phosphor	119	1,990	1:10.80	
1917	Campfire	3	J. McTaggart	115	Stromboli	133	Rickety	111	4,275	1:11.20	
1918	Naturalist	4	M. Buxton	107	Motor Cop	113	Old Koenig	120	3,875	1:10.00	
1919	Billy Kelly	3	J. Loftus	116	Lucullite	127	Papp	114	3,450	1:10.80	
1920	Lion d'Or	4	E. Ambrose	107.5	Motor Cop	128	Naturalist	126	3,325	1:09.60	
1921	Gladiator	4	C. Kummer	125	Sennings Park	111	Mad Hatter	135	6,950	1:08.80	
1922	Rocket	3	L. Penman	106	Dunboyne	130	Tryster	127	7,500	1:11.00	
1923	Mad Hatter	7	E. Sande	128	Runantell	104	Cyclops	109	8,150	1:10.60	
1924	Sheridan	3	L. Fator	105.5	Worthmore	110	Mad Hatter	128	8,750	1:11.60	
1925	Worthmore	4	A. Johnson	125	Silver Fox	112	Noah	111	8,700	1:11.00	
1926	Sarmaticus	3	H. Richards	107	Rock Star	105	Sun Pal	106	9,050	1:12.20	
1927	Chance Play	4	E. Sande	128	Sarmaticus	114	Pompey	120	8,200	1:11.00	
1928	Osmand	4	E. Sande	124	Scapa Flow	124	Happy Argo	108	8,650	1:11.40	
1929	Osmand	5	W. Garner	129	Polydor	123	Finite	108	8,250	1:10.60	
1930	Balko	5	J. Bejshak	111	Flying Heels	117	High Strung	124	8,650	1:11.40	
1931	Caruso	4	J.C. Meek	120	Balko	130	Happy Scot	111	8,250	1:14.80	
1932	Equipoise	4	R. Workman	129	Ironclad	108	Helianthus	110	6,550	1:09.60	
1933	Okapi	3	D. Bellizzi	104	Parry	105	Good Advice	103	3,515	1:11.40	
1934	Okapi	4	M. Garner	117	Kawagoe	105	High Glee	104	3,250	1:10.60	
1935	Identify	4	S. Renick	108	Ajaccio	116	Pompeys Pillar	102	4,225	1:11.60	
1936	Singing Wood	5	J. Gilbert	120	Sation	135	Whopper	123	3,875	1:10.80	
1937	Preeminent	5	H. Richards	113	Snark	114	Tintagel	119	3,625	1:11.20	
1938	Deliberator	5	W.D. Wright	124	Parmelee T.	106	Jay Jay	125	5,350	1:11.00	
1939	Entracte	3	N. Wall	103	Fighting Fox	126	He Did	122	5,500	1:11.00	
1940	Eight Thirty	4	H. Richards	127	War Dog	113	Our Matt	109	6,100	1:09.80	
1941	Eight Thirty	5	H. Richards	129	Dr. Whinny	119	Doubt Not	115	5,275	1:11.20	
1942	Omission	4	J. Gilbert	119	Overdrawn	120	Rosetown	115	5,425	1:10.80	
1943	Devil Diver	4	G. Woolf	116	With Regards	118	Thumbs Up	116	5,650	1:10.00	
1944	Devil Diver	5	E. Arcaro	134	Signator	120	Brownie	114	5,030	1:12.60	
1945	Apache	6	J. Stout	129	Devil Diver	135	Mrs. Ames	107	10,995	1:11.00	
1946	Polynesian	4	W.D. Wright	124	Cassis	113	King Dorsett	117	11,650	1:13.00	
1947	Buzfuz	5	B. James	121	Degage	114	Polynesian	134	17,900	1:11.00	
1948	Rippey	5	O. Scurlock	129	Owners Choice	114	Buzfuz	121	20,650	1:09.60	
1949	Rippey	6	E. Guerin	129	Pipette	108	Up Beat	120	16,850	1:09.40	
1950	Piet	5	J. Nichols	118	Olympia	126	Nell K.	116	17,250	1:10.60	
1951	Hyphasis	4	R. Bernhardt	110	Tea-Maker	123	Casemate	119	17,650	1:09.40	
1952	Dark Peter	4	A. Widman	108	Crafty Admiral	118	Tea-Maker	120	16,150	1:09.20	
1953	Tuscany	5	N Shuk	122	Hyphasis	116	Dark Peter	122	21,450	1:10.00	
1954	White Skies	4	E. Arcaro	132	Caesar Did	109	Hilarious	116	21,600	1:09.20	
1955	Sailor	3	H. Woodhouse	106	Bobby Brocato	116	White Skies	132	18,950	1:08.80	
1956	Nance's Lad	4	J. Choquette	126	Switch On	124	War Command	118	17,350	1:08.40	
1957	Decimal	5	W. Lester	124	Jovial Jove	126	Gay Warrior	115	15,200	1:08.40	
1958	Bold Ruler	4	E. Arcaro	133	Clem	117	Tick Tock	116	18,582	1:09.00	
1959	Tick Tock	6	R. Ussery	122	Cohoes	125	Warhead	122	18,680	1:10.80	
1960	Intentionally	3	W. Hartack	128	Rick City	122	Vendetta	115	17,835	1:10.60	
1961	Chief of Chiefs	4	J. Leonard	113	April Skies	128	Sweet William	113	14,560	1:10.00	
1962	Merry Ruler	4	I. Valenzuela	116	Rullah Red	113	Hitting Away	120	14,885	1:11.20	
1963	Kilmoray	4	J.L. Rotz	116	For the Road	118	Misty Day	115	14,885	1:10.60	

Year	Winner	Age	Jockey	Wt.	Second	Wt.	Third	Wt.	Win Value	Time	Beyer
1964	Scythe	4	W. Hartack	116	Third Martini	115	Exclusive Nashua	115	17,842	1:10.20	
1965	Affectionately	5	W. Blum	124	Chieftain	126	Exclusive Nashua	115	18,167	1:09.40	
1966	Time Tested	4	B. Baeza	126	Beaupy	115	Hoist Bar	125	18,070	1:09.80	
1967	Advocator	4	L. Pincay Jr.	118	Bold and Brave	117	Beaupy	112	18,395	1:10.20	
1968	Jim J.	4	A. Cordero Jr.	119	Air King II.	115	Mr. Washington	124	18,200	1:09.80	
1969	Beaukins	4	J. Cruguet	111	Gaylord's Feather	118	Pappa Steve	128	17,550	1:09.80	
1970	Duck Dance	3	J. Ruane	110	Master Hand	115	Jaikyl	115	17,615	1:09.60	
1971	Shut Eye	5	L. Adams	113	Tyrant	122	Cut the Comedy	113	19,860	1:10.60	
1972	Leematt	4	E. Nelson	115	Invested Power	117	Highbinder	113	16,185	1:09.40	
1973	Tentam	4	J. Velasquez	122	Spanish Riddle	115	Tap the Tree	118	16,710	1:09.40	
1974	Mike John G.	4	V. Bracciale Jr.	112	Tap the Tree	115	Delta Champ	113	16,575	1:08.60	
1975	Honorable Miss	5	J. Vasquez	117	Frankie Adams	116	Startahemp	121	16,350	1:09.00	
1976	Due Diligence	4	J. Vasquez	111	Pompini	113	Gallant Bob	129	34,740	1:10.20	
1977	Great Above	5	S. Cauthen	112	Full Out	117	Patriot's Dream	126	32,490	1:09.40	
1978	Barrera	5	R. Hernandez	126	Pumpkin Moonshine	106	Fratello Ed	121	31,890	1:08.80	
1979	Vencedor	5	M.A. Rivera	127	Jet Diplomacy	113	Al Battah	125	32,280	1:10.00	
1980	Tilt Up	5	J. Fell	116	Ardaluan	111	Double Zeus	123	33,660	1:11.00	
1981	Dr. Blum	5	R. Hernandez	123	Guilty Conscience	115	Dunham's Gift	118	32,340	1:11.20	
1982	Always Run Lucky	4	J. Miranda	110	Swelegant	113	In From Dixie	125	33,180	1:10.00	
1983	Mouse Corps	5	R. Alvarado Jr.	111	Top Avenger	123	Prince Valid	115	33,000	1:09.40	
1984	Top Avenger	6	A. Graell	120	Main Stem	109	Elegant Life	116	43,080	1:10.40	
1985	Fighting Fit	5	R. Migliore	123	Entropy	123	Shadowmar	107	51,210	1:09.60	
1986	Rexson's Bishop	4	R. Baez	114	Green Shekel	126	Cullendale	116	50,760	1:11.40	
1987	Play the King	4	R. Hernandez	112	Comic Blush	117	Best by Test	124	50,400	1:09.60	
1988	Afleet	4	G. Stahlbaum	123	Pinecutter	115	Vinnie the Viper	122	66,480	1:09.20	
1989	Lord of the Night	6	J. Velasquez	114	Teddy Drone	117	Vinnie the Viper	115	52,290	1:10.40	
1990	Sunny Blossom	5	E. Maple	117	Diamond Donnie	112	Once Wild	123	51,300	1:09.60	
1991	Bravely Bold	5	M.E. Smith	115	True and Blue	116	Proud and Valid	110	52,020	1:10.60	
1992	Boom Towner	4	D. Nelson	115	Real Minx	112	Gallant Step	114	52,740	1:10.03	115
1993	Argyle Lake	7	D. Carr	109	The Great M.B.	111	Regal Conquest	110	55,530	1:10.11	103
1994	Blare of Trumpets	5	D. Carr	112	Preporant	117	Fabersham	115	49,200	1:09.70	105
1995	Boom Towner	7	F. Lovato Jr.	117	Virginia Rapids	113	Won Song	112	49,080	1:23.77	102
1996	Placid Fund	4	J. Chavez	112	Valid Wager	116	Pat n Jac	112	51,480	1:22.92	111
1997	Royal Haven	5	R. Migliore	115	Jamies First Punch	115	Cold Execution	113	48,600	1:22.47	105
1998	Home on the Ridge	4	W.H. McCauley	114	Wire Me Collect	118	King Roller	116	49,650	1:23.01	104
1999	Wouldn't We All	5	R. Migliore	114	Brushed On	115	Esteemed Friend	120	48,900	1:20.95	110
2000	Brutally Frank	6	S.X. Bridgmohan	114	Master o Foxhounds	114	Watchman's Warning	113	49,410	1:20.77	103
2001	Peeping Tom	4	S.X. Bridgmohan	118	Say Florida Sandy	117	Lake Pontchartrain	110	64,380	1:21.25	110
2002	Affirmed Success	8	R. Migliore	119	Vodka	114	Multiple Choice	111	64,920	1:22.87	109
2003	Affirmed Success	9	R. Migliore	118	Peeping Tom	117	Captain Red	115	65,460	1:09.09	110

Beyer Index: 107.25

Run as Toboggan Slide Handicap prior to 1896. Not run in 1891, 1895, 1911 and 1912. Distance 3–4 mile over old straight course prior to 1942; Widener Course from 1928 to 1940, inclusive, and from 1942 to 1958, inclusive; main course from 1922 to 1927, inclusive, and in 1941, in 1961 the purse was taken away from Chief of Chiefs and awarded to April Skies; second, Sweet William; third, Mito. Run at Belmont Park prior to 1962.

TRANSYLVANIA, 1 Mile (Turf),
3-Year-Olds, Keeneland, 2003 Purse: $100,000

Year	Winner	Age	Jockey	Wt.	Second	Wt.	Third	Wt.	Win Value	Time	Beyer
1989	Shy Tom	3	R. Romero	121	Once Over Knightly	118	Ringerman	121	35,133	1:50.00	
1990	Izvestia	3	R. Romero	112	Scattered	115	Divine Warning	112	36,043	1:43.80	
1991	Eastern Dude	3	S.J. Sellers	121	Magic Interlude	121	January Man	116	36,514	1:42.80	
1992	Casino Magistrate	3	R. Lopez	121	Coaxing Matt	112	Trans Caribbean	115	35,636	1:46.62	89
1993	Proud Shot	3	W.H. McCauley	118	Explosive Red	121	Awad	121	34,364	1:44.17	89
1994	Star of Manila	3	S.J. Sellers	121	Prix de Crouton	118	Carpet	118	33,635	1:42.87	96
1995	Crimson Guard	3	M.E. Smith	118	Dixie Dynasty	114	Nostra	118	42,259	1:44.04	93
1996	More Royal	3	J.A. Krone	112	Defacto	121	Rough Opening	121	43,202	1:35.92	103
1997	Near the Bank	3	P. Day	118	Daylight Savings	114	Song for James	114	44,349	1:36.53	88
1998	Dog Watch	3	R. Davis	116	Reformer Rally	118	American Odyssey	114	45,781	1:34.65	92
1999	Good Night	3	S.J. Sellers	114	Air Rocket	114	Make Your Mark	114	70,308	1:35.00	95
2000	Field Cat	3	M.E. Smith	116	Lendell Ray	116	Go Lib Go	123	70,618	1:35.19	96
2001	Baptize	3	J.D. Bailey	120	Dynameaux	116	Act of Reform	116	70,556	1:35.28	92
2002	Flying Dash	3	J.D. Bailey	116	Back Packer	116	Political Attack	120	62,000	1:35.69	103
2003	White Cat	3	S.J. Sellers	116	Deep Shadow	118	Christmas Away	116	62,000	1:34.98	94

Beyer Index: 94.17

TREMONT, 5 1/2 Furlongs,
2-Year-Olds, Belmont Park, 2003 Purse: $110,200

Year	Winner	Age	Jockey	Wt.	Second	Wt.	Third	Wt.	Win Value	Time	Beyer
1887	Guarantee	2	Fitzpatrick	122	Now or Never	115	Fordham	115	2,605	1:15.50	
1888	Oregon	2	J. McLaughlin	116	Harebell	122	Lucerne	112	4,560	1:22.75	
1889	Padisha	2	Garrison	115	Cayuga	115	Banquet	112	6,620	1:16.00	

Year	Winner	Age	Jockey	Wt.	Second	Wt.	Third	Wt.	Win Value	Time	Beyer
1890	Chatham	2	Garrison	118	Bolero	118	Correction	118	6,400	1:15.75	
1891	Spinalong	2	F. Littlefield	115	Air Plant	118	Osric	118	7,280	1:18.25	
1892	Don Alonzo	2	Doggett	118	Miles Standish	118	Prince George	118	5,740	1:17.50	
1893	Dobbins	2	Lamley	118	Declare	118	Hurlingham	118	5,620	1:16.50	
1894	Gotham	2	Garrison	123	Waltzer	123	Sir Gallahad	118	5,640	1:15.75	
1895	Handspring	2	Doggett	111	Refugee	115	Applegate	123	7,800	1:15.00	
1896	Don de Oro	2	Griffin	118	Bowling Brook	111	Rhodesia	115	8,525	1:15.25	
1897	Handball	2	Simms	118	The Friar	111	Varus	111	7,750	1:15.00	
1898	Jean Bereaud	2	T. Sloan	125	Frohsinn	115	Kingdom	122	8,895	1:15.00	
1899	Maribert	2	Maher	112	Modrine	112	Missionary	112	12,645	1:15.00	
1900	Blues	2	Maher	115	Prince Pepper	115	Tommy Atkins	125	7,750	1:15.80	
1901	Whiskey King	2	Odom	115	Blue Girl	126	Golden Cottage	115	7,750	1:10.80	
1902	Artvis	2	Doggett	115	Whitechapel	115	Fire Easter	115	9,910	1:12.00	
1903	Magistrate	2	Bullman	129	Gettysburg	115	Dimple	112	7,300	1:13.80	
1904	Merry Lark	2	J. Martin	112	Veto	112	Britisher	115	9,800	1:10.80	
1905	Bohemian	2	Lyne	115	Voorhees	115	Jacobite	119	9,500	1:10.60	
1906	Water Peal	2	J. Jones	129	Saracinesca	115	Golf Ball	115	10,200	1:12.00	
1907	King James	2	Radtke	115	Ben Fleet	115	Beaucoup	115	13,200	1:13.40	
1908	Fayette	2	W. Miller	115	Sir Martin	129	Bobbin	115	12,500	1:09.60	
1909	Waldo	2	Nicol	129	Dullcare	115	Glennadeane	112	1,925	1:11.60	
1910	Footprint	2	E. Dugan	115	Blackfoot	115	Babbler	126	6,480	1:11.20	
1914	Ed Crump	2	J. Butwell	115	Lady Barbary	115	Trial by Jury	106	1,925	1:15.20	
1915	Tea Caddy	2	C. Turner	107	Achievement	109	Slipshod	99	2,325	1:15.00	
1916	Ticket	2	J. Butwell	107	Stargazer	107	Hourless	127	3,900	1:13.40	
1917	Gold Tassel	2	A. Collins	112	War Machine	115	Lucullite	125	5,250	1:12.40	
1918	Lord Brighton	2	L. Lyke	125	Sweep On	115	War Pennant	112	5,800	1:12.80	
1919	Man o' War	2	J. Loftus	130	Ralco	115	Ace of Aces	112	4,800	1:13.00	
1920	Inchcape	2	A. Johnson	115	Broomspun	112	Jeg	115	5,400	1:12.00	
1921	Olympus	2	C. Kummer	112	Mustard Seed	115	William A.	127	7,600	1:13.60	
1922	Martingale	2	C. Kummer	115	Bud Lerner	125	Goshawk	130	7,600	1:12.40	
1923	Transmute	2	L. McAtee	125	Lord Baltimore II	115	Diogenes	115	7,600	1:12.60	
1924	Young Martin	2	E. Sande	115	Swope	130	Goldbeater	112	7,600	1:13.80	
1925	Flight of Time	2	J. Maiben	115	Sarmaticus	125	Mars	115	7,600	1:13.00	
1926	Draconis	2	J. Maiben	125	Bostonian	115	Saxon	115	11,300	1:12.80	
1927	Diavolo	2	E. Sande	115	Folamile	112	Congress	110	11,200	1:12.20	
1928	Jack High	2	L. McAtee	110	Hypoluxo	115	Donnay	115	12,050	1:13.00	
1929	Sarazen II	2	W. Garner	125	Mokatam	125	Prometheus	115	13,550	1:14.80	
1930	Polydorus	2	L. Fator	115	Phantom Star	112	Condescend	115	12,300	1:14.00	
1931	Economic	2	F. Catrone	115	Irene's Bob	125			11,150	1:13.40	
1932	Balios	2	H. Mills	115	Dynastic	115	Orphean	112	8,050	1:13.00	
1936	Airflame	2	S. Renick	117	Fairy Hill	112	Fencing	112	4,650	0:59.80	
1937	Perpetuate	2	J. Stout	119	Indian Lodge	115	Gayset	112	4,750	0:59.00	
1938	Maeline	2	J. Westrope	119	Ariel Toy	112	Selmalad	117	4,250	0:59.00	
1939	Gannet	2	R. Nash	117	Dodger	108	Cockerel	118	4,125	0:58.60	
1940	Chicuelo	2	R. Eccard	108	War Result	112	Omission	117	4,500	1:05.40	
1941	Requested	2	A. Robertson	119	Rodney	113	Sun Again	119	6,200	1:05.40	
1942	Supermont	2	J. Gilbert	113	Hygrohour	117	Four Freedoms	115	6,400	1:05.80	
1943	Lucky Draw	2	C. McCreary	122	Ravenala	117	Grant Rice	112	5,150	1:05.80	
1944	Burg-El-Arab	2	T. Atkinson	112	Esteem	110	Hillyer Court	112	7,755	1:05.80	
1945	Degage	2	C. McCreary	112	Islam Prince	114	Manipur	112	7,370	1:05.00	
1946	Jet Pilot	2	E. Guerin	122	Useless	118	Eternal War	122	9,375	1:05.80	
1947	Inseparable	2	J. Jessop	114	Saggy	118	Royal Blood	114	17,125	1:05.00	
1948	The Admiral	2	R. Permane	108	Foray Vina	118	Arise	118	17,250	1:05.00	
1949	Fox Time	2	E. Guerin	114	Navy Chief	118	Detective	113	9,000	1:07.80	
1950	Battlefield	2	E. Arcaro	126	Patch	117	Nullify	117	9,625	1:05.00	
1951	Pintor	2	H. Woodhouse	117	Jet Master	126	Count Flame	117	8,450	1:05.40	
1952	Hilarious	2	E. Guerin	122	Belfaster	116	Fort Salonga	122	9,975	1:05.40	
1953	Quick Lunch	2	N. Wall	122	War Piper	116	Full Flight	122	10,300	1:05.60	
1954	Right Down	2	J. Nichols	122	Blackway	116	Dark Ruler	116	9,925	1:05.80	
1955	Getthere Jack	2	H. Woodhouse	122	Eiffel Blue	116	Bob-O-Bob	116	9,350	1:05.20	
1956	King Hairan	2	E. Arcaro	122	Gavel	114	Little Hermit	114	14,950	1:05.00	
1957	Jewel's Reward	2	W. Blum	114	Li'l Fella	122	Louis d'Or	118	16,050	1:04.80	
1958	Restless Wind	2	E. Arcaro	120	Dark Prince	113	Royal Anthem	120	14,830	1:04.40	
1959	Vital Force	2	W. Hartack	122	Ouija Board	122	Bally Ache	122	23,092	1:05.20	
1960	Hail to Reason	2	R. Ussery	118	Bronzerullah	118	Nashua Blue	114	24,295	1:05.00	
1961	Clover Leaf	2	R. Ussery	114	I'm for More	122	Stewvard	118	24,489	1:05.00	
1962	Bonjour	2	M. Ycaza	118	Near Man	118	Delta Judge	115	24,489	1:04.00	
1963	Chieftain	2	W. Hartack	118	Delirium	118	Mighty Mark	114	23,005	1:04.40	
1964	Bold Lad	2	M. Ycaza	122	Joust	114	Turn to Reason	114	24,472	1:06.20	
1965	Buckpasser	2	B. Baeza	118	Spring Double	118	Hospitality	118	22,344	1:03.80	
1966	Successor	2	B. Baeza	114	Bold Hour	114	Favorable Turn	114	23,952	1:04.20	
1967	Wise Exchange	2	R. Turcotte	114	Iron Ruler	122	T.V. Commercial	122	22,961	1:04.40	
1968	Buck Run	2	H. Gustines	114	Top Knight	114	Virginia Del'gate	114	22,051	1:03.20	

Year	Winner	Age	Jockey	Wt.	Second	Wt.	Third	Wt.	Win Value	Time	Beyer
1969	Very High	2	F. Toro	114	King's Mantle	114	Fried Eggs Over	114	22,604	1:05.20	
1970	Raise Your Glass	2	J. Velasquez	114			Helio Rise	122	15,597	1:05.00	
	Tamtent	2	E. Belmonte	118							
1971	Chauffeur	2	E. Belmonte	118	Plum Bold	122	Abdicating	114	25,200	1:04.40	
1972	Linda's Chief	2	B. Baeza	120	Dust the Plate	117	Macadamion	114	16,545	1:03.60	
1973	Raise a Cup	2	C. Baltazar	120	As Igazi	117	Big Latch	112	16,800	1:03.60	
1974	Foolish Pleasure	2	C. Baltazar	120	What a Sketch	114	Ricks Jet	115	17,280	1:10.80	
1975	Bold Forbes	2	L. Pincay Jr	120	Iron Bit	114	Peerless McGrath	114	16,170	1:09.40	
1976	Turn of Coin	2	A. Cordero Jr	115	To the Quick	122	Judge J'hn B'ne	122	22,590	1:12.40	
1977	Alydar	2	E. Maple	124	Believe It	117	Jet Diplomacy	124	21,975	1:10.00	
1978	Tim the Tiger	2	J. Fell	124	Jose Binn	124	Fuzzbuster	117	22,485	1:10.00	
1979	I Speedup	2	A. Cordero Jr	115	J.P. Brother	122	Blues Alley	122	25,950	1:11.80	
1980	Golden Derby	2	D.G. McHargue	122	Great Prospector	115	Lord Avie	122	33,720	1:11.40	
1981	Regal Stone	2	J. Velasquez	115	Minced Words	115			34,740	1:10.40	
					Ring Proud	115					
1982	Laus' Cause	2	J. Tejeira	122	Ruling Gold	115	Sunny's Halo	122	32,760	1:10.20	
1983	Track Barron	2	J. Cruguet	115	Tonto	115	Supporting Cast	115	33,840	1:10.40	
1984	Beat Me Daddy	2	E. Maple	113	Lord Carlos	117	Mount Reality	113	40,140	1:12.20	
1985	Sovereign Don	2	J. Velasquez	115	Mr. Classic	113	Bullet Blade	115	42,300	1:13.60	
1986	Gulch	2	A. Cordero Jr	115	Shawklit Won	117	Bucks Best	115	40,620	1:10.40	
1987	Morgan's Levee	2	R.G. Davis	113	Endurance	117	Eon	115	42,600	1:11.40	
1988	Mr. Sea Sanders	2	J. Velasquez	115	Fire Maker	115			53,730	1:11.40	
					Leading Prospect	115					
1989	Eternal Flight	2	R.P. Romero	115	Dr. Bobby A	115	Eastern Chill	115	53,640	1:06.00	
1990	Hansel	2	R.P. Romero	115	Vermont	115	Stately Wager	115	67,650	1:04.40	
1991	Salt Lake	2	R.P. Romero	115	Treasure Man	115	Caller I.D.	115	68,190	1:03.00	
1992	England Expects	2	J.D. Bailey	115	Peace Baby	115	Linear	115	69,900	1:03.20	98
1993	Distinct Reality	2	J.D. Bailey	115	Gusto Z	115	Slew Gin Fizz	115	67,470	1:04.60	76
1994	De Niro	2	E. Maple	114	Jump the Shadow	114	Mane Ingredient	114	63,240	1:05.00	80
1995	Rosie O'Greta	2	J.A. Santos	115	Busheta Buck	114	Victory Speech	114	32,400	1:07.20	69
1996	Kelly Kip	2	J.L. Samyn	114	Say Florida Sandy	114	Leestown	114	33,210	1:04.60	94
1997	Time Limit	2	J. Bravo	114	Torgan	118	Jigadee	114	32,100	1:06.60	79
1998	Tactical Cat	2	J.D. Bailey	115	Lucky Roberto	115	King's Crown	115	49,600	1:03.20	98
1999	More Than Ready	2	J.R. Velazquez	119	Afternoon Affair	115	King Kokand	115	65,040	1:02.40	105
2000	City Zip	2	J.A. Santos	116	The Goo	116	Scorpion	116	64,320	1:03.81	95
2001	Buster's Daydream	2	J.R. Velazquez	120	Draw Play	116	Day Trader	116	63,780	1:03.96	84
2002	Zavata	2	J.D. Bailey	114	Hussar	114	Desert Warrior	114	63,960	1:02.66	102
2003	Heckle	2	J.R. Velazquez	114	Adage	114	Hasslefree	114	66,120	1:04.70	88

Beyer Index: 89

TROPICAL PARK DERBY, 1 1/8 Miles (Turf),
3-Year-Olds, Calder Race Course, 2003 Purse: $100,000

Year	Winner	Age	Jockey	Wt.	Second	Wt.	Third	Wt.	Win Value	Time	Beyer
1976	Star of the Sea	3	C. Perret	115	Controller Ike	114	Great Contractor	121	55,800	1:44.00	
1977	Ruthie's Native	3	L. Saumell	112	Fort Prevel	121	Dreaming of Moe	112	55,800	1:44.40	
1978	Dr. Valeri	3	R. Rieri Jr	116	Quadratic	119	Galimore	119	73,200	1:45.20	
1979	Bishop's Choice	3	D. MacBeth	111	Lot o' Gold	119	Smarten	119	74,400	1:44.20	
1980	Superbity	3	J. Vasquez	121	Ray's Word	121	Irish Tower	121	69,600	1:45.60	
1981	Double Sonic	3	A. Smith Jr	121	Akureyri	121	Might Be Home	121	70,740	1:46.40	
1982	Victorian Line	3	A. Smith Jr	121	North Cat	121	Sandy Bee's Baby	121	68,280	1:45.40	
1983	My Mac	3	D. MacBeth	121	Caveat	121	Blink	121	100,350	1:46.60	
1984	Morning Bob	3	E. Maple	121	Don Rickles	121	Papa Koo	121	89,310	1:46.00	
1985	Irish Sur	3	J.A. Santos	121	Artillerist	121	Banner Bob	121	107,370	1:45.60	
1986	Strong Performance	3	J. Cruguet	117	Dr. Dan Eyes	114	Real Forest	117	143,760	1:54.40	
1987	Baldski's Star	3	C. Perret	117	Manhattan's Woody	112	Schism	117	139,920	1:54.80	
1988	Digress	3	E. Maple	117	Intensive Command	117	Granacus	117	176,460	1:54.60	
1989	Big Stanley	3	J. Vasquez	114	Appealing Pleasure	114	Prized	114	100,170	1:52.40	
1990	Run Turn	3	E. Fires	117	Country Day	112	Shot Gun Scott	119	66,420	1:52.40	
1991	Jackie Wackie	3	H. Castillo Jr	119	Gizmo's Fortune	119	Paulrus	114	69,120	1:51.80	
1992	Technology	3	J.D. Bailey	119	Majestic Sweep	114	Always Silver	114	134,160	1:53.00	105
1993	Summer Set	3	M.A. Gonzalez	112	Duc d'Sligovil	112	Silver of Silver	122	60,000	1:53.80	89
1994	Fabulous Frolic	3	Cruguet J	112	Wake Up Alarm	117	Gator Back	119	60,000	1:46.80	87
1995	Mecke	3	Castillo H Jr	117	Val's Prince	112	Claudius	119	60,000	1:51.00	88
1996	Ok by Me	3	J.D. Bailey	117	Darn That Erica	114	Tour's Big Red	117	60,000	1:47.20	93
1997	Arthur L	3	Coa E. M	119	Unite's Big Red	117	Keep It Strait	117	60,000	1:46.80	94
1998	Draw Again	3	Bravo J	119	Buddha's Delight	115	Daddy's Dream	117	60,000	1:51.20	84
1999	Vaild Reprized	3	Castellano J. J.	115	Mr. Roark	115	Wertz	119	60,000	1:53.40	93
2000	Go Lib Go	3	J.A. Santos	119	Mr. Livingston	115	Granting	115	60,000	1:46.60	91
2001	Proud Man	3	R.R. Douglas	115	Mr Notebook	119	Cee Dee	119	60,000	1:47.95	88
2002	Political Attack	3	M. Guidry	119	The Judge Sez Who	115	Deeliteful Guy	114	60,000	1:51.71	95
2003	Nothing to Lose	3	J.D. Bailey	115	Millennium Storm	119	Supah Blitz	115	60,000	1:50.45	90

Beyer Index: 91.42

TROPICAL TURF HANDICAP, 1 1/8 Miles, (Turf),
3-Year-Olds and Up, Calder Race Course, 2003 Purse: $100,000

Year	Winner	Age	Jockey	Wt.	Second	Wt.	Third	Wt.	Win Value	Time	Beyer
1935	Golden Rock II	5	W.D. Wright	112	Top Dog	116	Chasar	117	1,100	1:37.40	
1936	Paradisical	4	G. Seabo	112	Jinnee	100	Two Bob	112	1,200	1:42.80	
1937	Mucho Gusto	5	E. Arcaro	114	Paradisical	110	Bulwark	106	1,000	1:44.00	
1938	Sandy Boot	5	I. Hanford	109	Court Scandal	106	Bob's Boys	110	850	1:44.20	
1946	Statesman	4	O. Scurlock	117	Bel Reigh	112	Crack Reward	115	8,600	1:43.40	
1948	Marchons II	4	W. Saunders	119	Bright Sword	112	Bug Juice	116	5,950	1:43.60	
1949	Irisen	5	J. Robertson	119	Bolo Mack	110	Loriot	115	3,250	1:12.20	
1952	Crystal Boot	6	C. Errico	120	Elixir	115	Recline	119	7,900	1:50.60	
1953	Marked Game	4	W.B. Williams	109	Quick Fire	107	Gulf Stream	110	6,375	1:50.20	
1954	Precious Stone	4	W.M. Cook	115	Scimitar	112	French Bleu	110	7,850	1:50.80	
1955	Marked Game	6	L. Parent	106	Shimke	109	Full Flight	112	7,825	1:50.80	
1956	Dru Away	4	R. Ussery	114	Mr. First	114	Fabricator	117	7,775	1:50.20	
1957	Gray Phantom	4	J. Ruane	124	Juamario	106	Rockcastle	114	7,625	1:49.60	
1958	Hoop Band	5	H. Grant	124	Air Pilot	118	Little Porter	106	6,790	1:50.00	
1959	Stratmat	5	G. Gibb	110	Rare Rice	115	M'ners G'de	110	7,350	1:47.40	
1960	Eurasia	5	S. Boulmetis	114	Heroshogala	122	Moony	119	7,610	1:43.00	
1961	Humane Leader	4	B. Baeza	113	Eurasia	120	Level Flight	114	7,589	1:44.00	
1962	Intercepted	3	W. Hartack	116	Rob Roy III	116	Aw'y With You	113	7,832	1:44.40	
1963	Frankie's Nod	3	K. Korte	112	Deton	115	Sky Wonder	119	7,605	1:42.40	
1964	Somali Bird	6	H. Wajda	112	Suspicious	117	Demigod	113	7,288	1:42.60	
1964	Tronado	4	C. Gonzalez	120	Doctor Hank K.	117	S'alesman Pr'r	119	7,288	1:42.60	
1965	Turn to Reason	3	R. Ussery	118	Abdul	116	First Family	116	11,099	1:42.20	
1966	Naughty Jester	3	N. Mercier	114	Fathers Image	120	Steel Pike	114	10,839	1:41.40	
1967	Crafty Look	3	C.H. Marquez	115	Peace Pipe	115	Tequillo	115	9,214	1:43.00	
1967	Wild Card	7	A. Cordero Jr.	115	Sacramento	117	Aczay	115	9,214	1:43.60	
1968	Abe's Hope	5	R. Grubb	116	Valam	117	Subpet	118	10,425	1:41.40	
1969	Dorileo	5	D. Richard	115	Great Cohoes	122	Elegant Heir	114	10,425	1:41.40	
1969	Barely Even	3	G. Gallitano	119	Vif	121	Ocean Bar	115	10,485	1:41.60	
1970	Irurzun	6	C. Marquez	117	Coaltown Cat.	120	Lanzerac	118	15,210	1:43.80	
1971	French Corners	5	D. MacBeth	112	Handsome Kid.	113	Jet a Bit	114	18,210	1:41.20	
1972	Prince of Truth	4	J. Vasquez	117	Rastaferian	114	Glazed D'nut	114	17,700	1:46.00	
1973	Proud and Bold	4	R. Woodhouse	121	Outatholme	116	Seminole Joe	1120	17,100	1:45.60	
1974	L. Grant Jr.	4	J. Combest	121	Super Sail	118	El Tordillo	115	18,300	1:45.80	
1979	Lot o' Gold	3	D. Brumfield	123	King Celebrity	117	J. Rodney G.	114	33,330	1:52.60	
1980	Yosi Boy	4	A. Smith Jr	111	Two's a Plenty	120	Von Clausewitz	119	33,180	1:51.80	
1981	The Liberal Member	6	J.D. Bailey	115	Jayme G.	116	Recusant	112	35,130	1:51.80	
1982	Rivalero	6	J. Vasquez	120	Current Blade	115	In All Honesty	110	33,270	1:53.60	
1983	Eminency	5	P. Day	122	World Appeal.	118	Ready to Prove	110	34,770	1:51.20	
1984	Biloxi Indian	5	B. Fann	114	Key to the Moon.	122	Di Roma Feast	114	32,700	1:54.00	
1985	Ban the Blues	6	G. St. Leon	114	Jim Bracken	112	Bold Southerner	112	34,140	1:53.20	
1986	Arctic Honeymoon	3	R.N. Lester	111	Lover's Cross	121	Darn That Alarm	112	32,550	1:54.00	
1988	Equalize	6	J.A. Santos	122	Val d'Enchere	116	Racing Star	114	35,010	1:45.00	
1989	Vaguely Double	4	W.A. Guerra	118	Mr. Adorable	113	Highland Springs	120	35,490	1:48.80	
1990	Stolen Rolls	4	P.A. Rodriguez	112	Gay's Best Boy	111	Seasabb	111	35,700	1:45.20	
1992	Carterista	3	M.A. Lee	112	Rinka Das	114	Pidgeon's Promise	110	30,000	1:46.20	100
1992	Bidding Proud.	3	J.A. Santos	115	Buckhar	118	Plate Dancer	116	30,000	1:46.00	102
1993	Carterista	3	W.S. Ramos	121	Rinka Das	113	Daarik	114	45,000	1:44.80	97
1994	The Vid	4	R.R. Douglas	116	Country Coy.	113	Gone for Real	113	60,000	1:49.00	104
1995	The Vid	5	W.H. McCauley	120	Elite Jeblar	114	Scannapieco	113	60,000	1:44.80	112
1996	Mecke	4	R.G.Davis	124	Satellite Nealski	113	Elite Jeblar	114	60,000	1:46.40	102
1997	Sir Cat	4	J.A. Rivera II	116	Foolish Pole	115	Written Approval	112	60,000	1:54.00	102
1998	Unite's Big Red	4	E.O. Nunez	115	N B Forrest	115	Glok	115	60,000	1:48.80	103
1999	Hibernian Rhapsody	4	R.R. Douglas	117	Garbu	117	Shamrock City	114	60,000	1:46.00	98
2000	Stokosky	4	C.A. Hernandez	114	Special Coach	114			60,000	1:48.77	100
					Band Is Passing	119					
2001	Band Is Passing	5	C.V. Gonzalez	118	Crash Course	116	Groomstick's Stock	114	60,000	1:46.90	109
2002	Krieger	4	E.M. Coa	113	Stokosky	113	Serial Bride	114	60,000	1:47.02	101
2003	Political Attack	4	R.R. Douglas	116	Millennium Dragon	116	Sforza	115	60,000	1:45.81	103

Beyer Index: 102.54

TURFWAY BREEDERS' CUP, 1 1/16 Miles,
Fillies and Mares 3-Year-Olds and Up, Turfway Park, 2003 Purse: $175,000

Year	Winner	Age	Jockey	Wt.	Second	Wt.	Third	Wt.	Win Value	Time	Beyer
1988	Darien Miss	3	P.A. Johnson	115	Integra	123	Ms. Eloise	120	101,758	1:43.60	
1989	Winning Colors	4	C.J. McCarron	115	Grecian Flight	123	Lawyer Talk	123	101,368	1:44.80	
1990	Barbarika	5	A.T. Gryder	123	Colonial Waters	114	Luthier's Launch.	112	117,015	1:44.00	107
1991	Fit for a Queen	5	R.D. Lopez	123	Til Forbid	118	Screen Prospect.	114	117,358	1:43.20	108
1992	Fit for a Queen	6	R.D. Lopez	123	Auto Dial	120	Hitch	112	117,975	1:43.20	109
1993	Gray Cashmere	4	D. Kutz	117	Deputation	120	November Snow.	113	117,130	1:43.20	105

Year	Winner	Age	Jockey	Wt.	Second	Wt.	Third	Wt.	Win Value	Time	Beyer
1994	Pennyhill Park	4	C. McCarron	123	Roamin Rachel	123	Hey Hazel	123	118,072	1:44.20	97
1995	Mariah's Storm	5	R. Lester	117	Serena's Song	119	Alcovy	117	116,415	1:41.60	120
1996	Golden Attraction	3	G.L. Stevens	114	Bedroom Blues	117	Betty Van	119	205,920	1:42.40	94
1997	Feasibility Study	5	M.E. Smith	119	City Band	114	Gold n Delicious	121	160,022	1:42.40	98
1998	Biding Time	4	C.S. Nakatani	117	Meter Maid	121	Dancing Gulch	119	162,266	1:43.00	102
1999	Ruby Surprise	4	Martinez W.	118	Let	118	French Braids	114	162,886	1:44.80	97
2000	Spain	3	P. Day	118	Ruby Surprise	118	Undermine	118	156,500	1:44.85	101
2001	Trip	4	C. Perret	118	Precious Feather	114	Spain	122	125,500	1:42.47	102
2002	Trip	5	P. Day	116	Mystic Lady	118	Red n'Gold	118	125,500	1:43.01	109
2003	Smok'n Frolic	4	E.S. Prado	122	Awesome Humor	112	So Much More	118	108,500	1:44.98	100

Beyer Index: 103.5

TURFWAY PARK FALL CHAMPIONSHIP, 1 Mile,
3-Year-Olds and Up, Turfway Park, 2003 Purse: $100,000

Year	Winner	Age	Jockey	Wt.	Second	Wt.	Third	Wt.	Win Value	Time	Beyer
1919	Mad Hatter		L. Fator		Sway		Stockwell			3:06.00	
1920	Cleopatra		C. Fairbrother		On Watch		Damask			2:56.80	
1921	Sporting Blood		F. Keogh		Black Servant		Hymphrey			3:05.60	
1922	Rockminster		M. Garner		Lucky Hour		Surf Rider			2:55.60	
1923	In Memoriam		M. Garner		Zev		My Own			3:00.80	
1924	Chilhowee		M. Garner		Mad Play		Aga Khan			2:54.60	
1925	King Nadi		E. Sande		Old Slip		Drowsy Waters			3:06.40	
1926	Display		J. Maiben		Boot to Boot		Helen's Babe			2:58.80	
1927	Rolled Stocking		W. Crump		Wooldridge		Brown Bud			2:55.60	
1928	Sun Beau		J. Craigmyle		Sortie		Lawley			3:00.60	
1929	The Nut		J. Smith		Curate		Ben Machree			3:26.00	
1930	Spinach		G. Ellis		Yarn		Star Lassie			2:59.60	
1931	St. Brideaux		C. Kurtsinger		Rocky News		Dixie King			3:01.40	
1932	Gallant Sir		G. Woolf		Mad Frump		Gusto			3:12.40	
1933	Pomposity		J. Bejshak		Caesars Ghost		Contraband			3:02.00	
1964	Sought After		J. Warner		Godessa		Renepache			1:58.00	
1965	Busking		J. Lynch		Will Dance		Dandy K			1:51.60	
1966	Brochaza		M. Manganello		Grand Central		Big Darby			1:52.20	
1967	Likely Swap		M. Manganello		Hy Frost		Great Chip			1:51.00	
1968	T.V.'s Princess		M. Manganello		Reigning Count		Swift Gem			1:45.40	
1969	DeMito		M. Manganello		Danton II		Larry's Reward			1:46.60	
1970	Tort-Feazor		O. Torres		Mistong		Broadcloth			1:44.20	
1971	Man of Parts		J. McIntosh		Sea O Joe		Jay Lea			1:44.20	
1971	Tesart		M. Manganello		Second Adventure		Gold Flake			1:44.20	
1973	Knight Counter		D. Brumfield		Divorce Trial		On the Money			1:46.80	
1974	Bootlegger's Pet		G. Solomon		Lesters Jester		Babingtons Image			1:47.60	
1975	Eager Wish		C. Bramble		Zografos		Princess Jilo			1:44.40	
1976	Brustigert		A. Herrera		Faneuil Boy		Visier			1:45.40	
1977	Certain Roman		M. McDowell		The Pepe		Payne Street			1:44.80	
1978	Likely Exchange		M. Sellers		Pirogue		Mr. Pitty Pat			1:45.60	
1979	Lotta Honey		J. Espinoza		Penalty Declined		One Lucky Devil			1:42.40	
1980	Silver Shears		R.R. Matias		Penalty Declined		One Lucky Devil			1:43.20	
1981	Exterminate		D. Foster		Kentucky Scout		Withholding			1:44.40	
1982	Leader Jet		C. Woods Jr.		Rock Steady		Diverse Dude			1:44.00	
1983	Cad		D. Brumfield		His Flower		Noted			1:44.00	
1984	Immediate Reaction		M. McDowell		Fairly Straight		Never Company			1:43.80	
1985	Country Hick		J. Espinoza		Turn Here		McShane			1:43.00	
1986	Big Pistol		L. Melancon		Exit Five B.		Something Cool			1:42.80	
1987	Lord Glacier		M. Solomone		Aggie's Best		Ten Times Ten			1:43.60	
1988	Mr. Odie		S. Neff		Boyish Charm		Government Corner			1:52.40	
1989	Currentsville Lane		W.J. Neagle		Air Worthy		Loyal Pal			1:51.60	
1990	Aly Mar		D. Kutz		Cefis		Cantrell Road			1:49.20	
1991	Allijeba		J. Bruin	116	D.C. Tenacious		Discover		41,420	1:49.60	106
1992	Flying Continental		J. Velasquez	122	Alyten		Regal Affair		27,510	1:48.60	105
1993	Powerful Punch		C. Borque	116	Medium Cool		Benburb		41,047	1:50.40	105
1994	Meena		W. Martinez	114	Powerful Punch		It'sal'ilknownfact		27,284	1:52.80	104
1995	Bound by Honor	5	R.P. Romero	113	Lord Gordon	113	Lordly Prospect	112	42,600	1:51.40	104
1996	Strawberry Wine	4	B. Peck	114	Kiridashi	121	Prospect for Love	114	65,000	1:50.00	111
1997	Tejano Run	5	W. Martinez	122	Short Stay	114	Thesaurus	112	46,950	1:49.40	101
1998	Acceptable	4	C. Perret	118	Magnify	114	Muchacho Fino	118	62,600	1:51.80	108
1999	Phil the Grip	5	R.J. Albarado	112	Part the Waters	111	Metatonia	110	49,600	1:52.15	95
2000	Mount Lemon	6	R.J. Albarado	117	Unloosened	114	Phil the Grip	117	62,600	1:51.14	98
2001	Generous Rosi	6	L.J. Meche	115	Storm Day	117	Jadada	117	46,500	1:49.83	108
2002	Crafty Shaw	4	J. Lopez	117	Rock Slide	117	Deferred Comp	115	62,750	1:52.29	102
2003	Crafty Shaw	5	C. Perret	117	Cat Tracker	117	Cappuchino	119	62,500	1:36.89	103

Beyer Index: 103.85

TURNBACK THE ALARM HANDICAP, 1 1/8 Miles,
Fillies and Mares 3-Year-Olds and Up, Aqueduct, 2003 Purse: $107,500

Year	Winner	Age	Jockey	Wt.	Second	Wt.	Third	Wt.	Win Value	Time	Beyer
1995	Incinerate	6	F.Leon	115	Lotta Dancing	115	Pretty Discreet	110	49,005	1:48.80	103
1996	Shoop	5	J.Bailey	121	Queen Tutta	116	Madame Adolphe	113	48,940	1:51.20	92
1997	Mil Kilates	4	J.Bravo	116	Radiant Megan	110	Shoop	114	48,380	1:49.40	89
1998	Snit	4	J.R.Velazquez	117	Manoa	112	Shoop	114	49,740	1:51.20	94
1999	Belle Cherie	3	Velazquez J. R.	112	Brushed Halory	114	Sweet Misty	116	66,000	1:50.00	97
2000	Atelier	3	E.S. Prado	115	Tap to Music	119	Pentatonic	115	67,920	1:48.95	106
2001	Rochelle's Terms	4	R.G. Davis	113	Resort	113	Strolling Belle	118	65,100	1:51.19	87
2002	Svea Dahl	5	R. Migliore	114	Mystic Lady	119	Critical Eye	115	64,800	1:50.42	105
2003	Pocus Hocus	5	J.A. Santos	114	Nonsuch Bay	115	Miss Linda	118	64,500	1:50.67	101

Beyer Index: 97.11

VERNON O. UNDERWOOD, 6 Furlongs,
3-Year-Olds and Up, Hollywood Park, 2003 Purse: $100,000

Year	Winner	Age	Jockey	Wt.	Second	Wt.	Third	Wt.	Win Value	Time	Beyer
1981	Shanekite	3	S. Hawley	114	Syncopate	122	Big Presentation	114	50,500	1:08.20	
1981	Smokite	5	D.C. Hall	116	I'm Smokin	120	Stand Pat	114	50,500	1:08.60	
1982	Mad Key	5	E. Delahoussaye	116	Shanekite	120	Dave's Friend	114	70,600	1:08.20	
1982	Unpredictable	3	K. Black	120	Remember John	120	Chinook Pass	112	69,100	1:08.60	
1983	Fighting Fit	4	E. Delahoussaye	120	Expressman	112	Matching	119	101,950	1:09.60	
1984	Fifty Six Ina Row	3	S. Hawley	112	Debonaire Junior	120	Charging Falls	112	91,975	1:09.40	
1984	Lovlier Linda	4	W. Shoemaker	121	Sonrie Jorge	116	Fali Time	121	89,475	1:10.00	
1985	Pancho Villa	3	L. Pincay Jr	122	Charging Falls	122	Temerity Prince	122	121,900	1:08.80	
1986	Bedside Promise	4	G.L. Stevens	122	Bolder Than Bold	114	Pine Tree Lane	117	127,200	1:08.80	
1987	Hilco Scamper	4	C.A. Black	114	Reconnoitering	112	Zabaleta	122	62,800	1:09.60	
1988	Gallant Sailor	5	F. Olivares	116	Reconnoitering	116	Very Subtle	117	63,400	1:09.60	
1989	Olympic Prospect	5	A. Solis	120	Sam Who	122	Order	122	60,200	1:08.80	
1990	Frost Free	5	C.J. McCarron	120	Timebank	112	Sam Who	114	65,300	1:08.20	
1991	Individualist	4	K.J. Desormeaux	114	Thirty Slews	117	Cardmania	120	64,500	1:08.80	105
1992	Gundaghia	5	G.L. Stevens	116	Gray Slewpy	124	Cardmania	124	61,300	1:09.20	113
1993	Meafara	5	G.L. Stevens	119	Arches of Gold	121	Davy Be Good	116	60,900	1:10.00	108
1994	Wekiva Springs	3	K.J. Desormeaux	118	Cardmania	120	Gundaghia	120	63,750	1:08.20	107
1995	Powis Castle	4	G.L. Stevens	114	Lucky Forever	122	Plenty Zloty	116	62,300	1:08.40	108
1996	Paying Dues	4	P. Day	124	Men's Exclusive	114	Kern Ridge	114	64,860	1:08.20	114
1997	Tower Full	5	C.S. Nakatani	118	Trafalger	118	Swiss Yodeler	114	60,000	1:08.00	106
1998	Love That Jazz	4	K.J. Desormeaux	117	Peyrano–AR	116	Swiss Yodeler	120	60,000	1:08.60	103
1999	Five Star Day	3	A. Solis	120	Your Halo	122	Son of a Pistol	122	60,000	1:09.80	109
2000	Men's Exclusive	7	L. Pincay Jr	116	Love All the Way	117	Lexicon	122	60,000	1:09.02	108
2001	Men's Exclusive	8	L. Pincay Jr	120	Tavasco	114	Caller One	124	60,000	1:09.04	102
2002	Debonair Joe	3	J.A. Krone	112	F J's Pace	116	American System	116	60,000	1:08.93	101
2003	Watchem Smokey	3	J.A. Krone	112	Our New Recruit	114	Hasty Kris	116	60,000	1:08.93	101

Beyer Index: 106.15

VALLEY STREAM, 6 Furlongs,
2-Year-Old Fillies, Aqueduct, 2003 Purse: $112,200

Year	Winner	Age	Jockey	Wt.	Second	Wt.	Third	Wt.	Win Value	Time	Beyer
1995	Oxford Scholar	2	J.D. Bailey	112	Zee Lady	120	Stormy Krissy	112	32,430	1:12.00	85
1996	Dixie Flag	2	J.L. Samyn	116	Alyssum	114	Nimble Thread	114	32,490	1:10.00	102
1997	Cotton House Bay	2	J.F. Chavez	114	Foil	116	Kate Again	116	33,990	1:10.00	89
1998	Paula's Girl	2	J.R. Velazquez	116	President's Girl	114	Godmother	121	38,700	1:11.80	81
1999	Magicalmysterycat	2	M.E. Smith	121	Sahara Gold	121	Silentlea	121	49,800	1:10.40	86
2000	Astrapi	2	D. Nelson	116	Major Wager	116	Look of the Lynx	118	48,570	1:10.66	88
2001	Forest Heiress	2	R. Migliore	122	A New Twist	116	On Parade	116	48,465	1:08.66	105
2002	Randaroo	2	J.R. Velazquez	116	House Party	116	Fast Cookie	116	66,780	1:09.46	105
2003	Smokey Glacken	2	J.A. Santos	118	Baldomera	118	Stoic	118	67,320	1:11.18	77

Beyer Index: 90.89

VALLEY VIEW, 1 1/16 Miles (Turf),
3-Year-Old Fillies, Keeneland Race Course, 2003 Purse: $112,900

Year	Winner	Age	Jockey	Wt.	Second	Wt.	Third	Wt.	Win Value	Time	Beyer
1991	La Gueriere	3	B. Peck	121	Dance o' My Life	121	Spanish Parade	121	29,250	1:43.40	97
1992	Spinning Round	3	F. Arguello Jr	121	Shes Just Super	121	Enticed	121	23,870	1:41.40	89
1993	Weekend Madness	3	C. Woods Jr	121	Life Is Delicious	121	Augusta Springs	121	23,870	1:43.00	91
1994	Pharma	3	C.W. Antley	121	Mariah's Storm	121	Thread	121	50,747	1:42.40	102
1995	Country Cat	3	D.M. Barton	121	Appointed One	121	Petrouchka	121	50,840	1:44.80	101
1996	Turkappeal	3	D.M. Barton	117	Inner Circle	113	Mariuka	117	52,126	1:46.00	96
1997	Mingling Glances	3	J. Bravo	117	Majestic Sunlight	117	Fluid Move	113	52,592	1:44.40	101
1998	White Beauty	3	C. Borel	113	Shires Ende	117	Leaveemlaughing	117	56,591	1:43.00	91
1999	Gimmeakissee	3	Cooksey P. J.	115	The Happy Hopper	119	Celestialbutterfly	119	70,122	1:42.00	90
2000	Good Game	3	P. Day	119	Impending Bear	119	Soccory	119	71,176	1:45.69	92

Year	Winner	Age	Jockey	Wt.	Second	Wt.	Third	Wt.	Win Value	Time	Beyer
2001	Cozzy Corner	3	L.J. Meche	119			Quick Tip	123	46,576	1:42.93	90
	Chausson Poire	3	R.W. Woolsey	119							
2002	Bedanken	3	D.R. Pettinger	119	Mariensky	119	High Maintenance	119	71,734	1:44.24	95
2003	Dyna da Wyna	3	P. Day	119	Mexican Moonlight	116	Derrianne	123	69,998	1:43.54	94

Beyer Index: 94.54

VIOLET HANDICAP, 1 1/16 Miles (Turf),
Fillies and Mares 3-Year-Olds and Up, The Meadowlands, 2003 Purse: $150,000

Year	Winner	Age	Jockey	Wt.	Second	Wt.	Third	Wt.	Win Value	Time	Beyer
1977	Lady Singer	4	A. Cordero Jr.	113	Sans Arc	111	Jolly Song	112	35,035	1:48.40	
1978	Navajo Princess	4	C. Perret	115	Pressing Date	114	Fun Forever	118	35,360	1:44.00	
1979	Terpsichorist	4	M. Venezia	122	Spark of Life	111	Sisterhood	117	36,010	1:43.20	
1980	Producer	4	J. Fell	119	Champagne Ginny	116	Cannon Boy	113	26,325	1:41.60	
1980	The Very One	5	J. Velasquez	117	Hey Babe	115	Poppycock	113	26,145	1:42.40	
1981	Honey Fox	4	J.L. Samyn	120	Adlibber	117	Hemlock	116	33,690	1:41.40	
1982	Pat's Joy	4	J.D. Bailey	114	Prismatical	115	Kuja Happa	113	26,670	1:42.20	
1982	Dearly Too	4	J.L. Samyn	114	Tableaux	112	Dance Troupe	114	26,670	1:42.20	
1983	Twosome	4	J.D. Bailey	113	Princess Roberta	115	Svarga	112	26,535	1:41.20	
1983	Geraldine's Store	4	J.L. Samyn	117	Maidenhead	110	Mistretta	116	26,355	1:40.60	
1984	Rash but Royal	4	J.L. Kaenel	114	High Schemes	115	Candlelight Affair	110	49,020	1:42.20	
1984	Aspen Rose	4	J. Velasquez	114	It's Fine	112	If Winter Comes	113	49,020	1:42.00	
1985	Possible Mate	4	J.L. Samyn	119	Eastern Dawn	112	Carlypha	116	52,665	1:42.20	
1985	Vers la Caisse	4	R. Migliore	116	Cato Double	117	Forest Maiden	117	63,240	1:43.00	
1986	Lake Country	5	V. Bracciale Jr.	118	Buckweed	111	Anka Germania	114	68,310	1:41.20	
1987	Videogenic	5	J. Cruguet	118	Spruce Fir	119	Cadabra Abra	120	45,180	1:42.00	
1987	Dismasted	5	J.L. Samyn	118	Small Virtue	118	Country Recital	113	44,790	1:41.60	
1988	Just Class	4	C.W. Antley	117	Shadowfay	109	Flying Katuna	115	53,400	1:40.20	
1988	Graceful Darby	4	R.P. Romero	115	Mystical Lass	112	Kim Kimmie	111	42,900	1:41.00	
1989	Gather the Clan	4	C. Perret	117	Sweet Blow Pop	119	Summer Secretary	117	55,260	1:39.60	
1990	Miss Josh	4	M.G. Pino	116	Summer Secretary	117	Leave It Be	118	54,750	1:40.00	101
1991	Southern Tradition	4	J.A. Santos	116	Songlines	115	Memories of Pam	113	45,000	1:43.60	98
1992	Highland Crystal	4	E.S Prado	116	Irish Actress	116	Navarra	111	45,000	1:41.20	96
1993	Mz. Zill Bear	4	E.S. Prado	113	Vivano	115	Topsa	113	45,000	1:44.40	97
1994	It's Personal	4	J.R. Velazquez	111	Carezza	115	Artful Pleasure	109	45,000	1:42.60	97
1995	Symphony Lady	5	J. Bravo	116	Kira's Dancer	115	Irish Linnet	122	60,000	1:45.40	95
1996	Plenty Of Sugar	5	R.E. Colton	117	Brushing Gloom	121	Hello Mom	115	60,000	1:48.60	96
1997	Sangria	4	R. Wilson	114	Fasta	113	Shemozzle	117	60,000	1:42.00	91
1998	Heaven's Command	4	R. Migliore	115	Maxzene	123	Oh Nellie	116	60,000	1:40.60	101
1999	Tookin Down	4	E.S. Prado	113	Proud Run	115	Darling Alice	113	90,000	1:42.20	94
2000	Follow the Money	4	C.J. McCarron	116	Melody Queen	116	Fickle Friends	114	90,000	1:42.65	97
2001	Clearly a Queen	4	C.C. Lopez	119	Salina's Gift	119	Smart as Scot	115	90,000	1:36.40	100
2002	Babae	6	J.F. Chavez	119	Platinum Tiara	115	Stylish	119	90,000	1:41.17	105
2003	Dancal	5	J. Castellano	116	Madeira Mist	116	Something Ventured	116	90,000	1:43.69	99

Beyer Index: 97.64

MARTHA WASHINGTON BREEDERS' CUP, 1 1/16 Miles (Turf)
3-Year-Old Fillies, Pimlico, 2003 Purse: $147,000

Year	Winner	Age	Jockey	Wt.	Second	Wt.	Third	Wt.	Win Value	Time	Beyer
1982	Smart Heiress	3	M. Venezia	115	Ring Dancer		Zvetlana		14,445	1:41.40	
1982	Party Bonnet	3	J. Walford	110	Susie Cherie		Dancing Secret		15,075	1:43.00	
1984	Berkeley Court	3	J.L. Samyn	113	La Reine Elaine		Tagalog		34,200	1:43.20	
1985	Duty Dance	3	J. Cruguet	114	Jolly Saint		A Joyful Spray		37,765	1:49.20	
1986	Toes Knows	3	D. Wright	124	Spruce Fir		CountryRecital		38,740	1:47.20	
1987	Cutlasee	3	A. Stacy	109	Doubles Partner		Kerygma		37,229	1:45.80	
1988	Timely Business	3	T. Vega	112	Quaff	115	Siggebo	119	62,250	1:43.60	
1989	Yestday's Kisses	3	F. Lovato Jr	114	Whip Cream	110	Tia Juanita	114	45,000	1:46.20	
1990	Southern Tradition	3	E.S. Prado	120	Starfield	113	Secret Advice	115	45,000	1:40.40	
1991	Polish Holiday	3	M.G. Pino	113	Fashion Miss	114	Monica Faye	115	45,000	1:49.20	
1992	Mz. Zill Bear	3	S.D. Hamilton	112	Star Minister	120	Tootsie	112	45,000	1:48.60	
1993	Tennis Lady	3	A.J. Seefeldt	113	Putthepowdertoit	113	Missymooiloveyou	113	45,000	1:42.80	95
1994	Tee Kay	3	Wilson R	115	Avie's Fancy	119	Lady Ellen	115	60,000	1:45.20	97
1995	Strawberry Reason	3	Prado ES	117	Blue Sky Princess	122	Rosebud	117	30,000	2:15.20	85
1996	Silent Greeting	3	Reynolds L. C.	119	Rare Blend	122	Stop That Broad	115	60,000	1:43.40	102
1997	Cotton Carnival	3	Pino M. G.	122	Romantic Notions	115	Bursting Forth	115	60,000	1:46.20	83
1998	Mysterious Moll	3	Wilson R.	118	Wolfer	114	Proud Owner	117	90,000	1:42.20	94
1999	Colstar	3	Delgado A.	119	Polaire	122	Jazz	115	60,000	1:45.60	95
2000	Tippity Witch	3	J.L. Espinoza	119	Senza Paura	117	Windsong	117	60,000	1:42.20	95
2002	Martha's Music	3	H. Vega	115	Bells for Marlin	122	Restraining Order	115	90,000	1:45.62	82
2003	Derrianne	3	B. Blanc	122	Chic Joy	115	Twining and Dining	115	90,000	1:46.53	77

Beyer Index: 92

WEST VIRGINIA DERBY, 1 1/8 Miles,
3-Year-Olds, Mountaineer Park, 2003 Purse: $600,000

Year	Winner	Age	Jockey	Wt.	Second	Wt.	Third	Wt.	Win Value	Time	Beyer
1958	Sea Hymn	3	J. Contreras	117	Dixie Hill	119	Entangler	114	9,750	1:5520	
1959	Redbird Wish	3	W. Chamber	119	Royal Border	111	Idle Time	117	9,500	1:52.80	
1961	Dip and Whirl	3	B. Walt	114	Besteater	114	Royal Case	114	2,410	1:54.60	
1963	Etimota	3	F. Green	116	Count John	105	Dr. Scott	117	3,570	1:52.00	
1964	Peter Le Grand	3	F. Green	124	A.J.'s Winn	114	Navy Rocket	118	3,025	1:53.00	
1965	Pantuity	3	F. Green	115	Cloud Chief	118	Jayell	115	5,559	1:53.00	
1966	Kerensa	3	F. Green	119	Bellofthefleet	113	Dear Mike	118	5,472	1:50.40	
1967	Miracle Hill	3	R.C. Gallimore	121	More of Mort	126	Air Boat	115	5,498	1:53.20	
1968	Chargertown	3	R. Nakama	115	Son I Rob	118	Frosty Hal	115	10,273	1:54.40	
1969	Roman Partner	3	M. Solomone	121	Polar Traffic	124	Silver Alley	121	17,794	1:51.80	
1970	Two Joys	3	J. Imparato	118	Captain Nash	124	Delicate John	118	18,167	1:53.00	
1971	Trico O'Erin	3	T. DePalo	118	Spoiled Kid	126	Comedy Hour	116	18,785	1:52.20	
1972	Family Table	3	M. Solomone	118	Extra Man	121	Rollin Roman	118	13,000	1:50.60	
1972	Bold Nobleman	3	J. Kelly	118	Aerodrome	118	Prince Selari	115	13,325	1:49.40	
1973	Blue Chip Dan	3	M. Solomone	118	Dr. Pantano	121	Double Edge Sword	124	20,930	1:49.20	
1974	Park Guard	3	B.M. Feliciano	124	Sea Songster	126	Sahib Nearco	124	32,500	1:47.40	
1975	At the Front	3	A. Santiago	117	My Friend Gus	117	Packer Captain	117	32,500	1:48.60	
1976	Wardlaw	3	J. Tejeira	121	American Trader	115	Joachim	121	32,500	1:47.60	
1977	Best Person	3	V. Bracciale Jr.	115	Swoon Swept	115	A Letter to Harry	115	32,500	1:48.60	
1978	Beau Sham	3	P. Day	115	Silent Cal	115	Morning Frolic	115	32,500	1:48.60	
1979	Architect	3	S.A. Spencer	115	Sir Prince P	115	Lt. Bert	115	32,500	1:51.00	
1980	Summer Advocate	3	W.L. Floyd	115	Lucky Pluck	115	Foolish Move	115	32,500	1:50.80	
1981	Park's Policy	3	J.S. Lloyd	115	Diverse Dude	115	Iron Gem	115	22,750	1:49.60	
1981	Johnny Dance	3	F. Lovato Jr.	115	Master Tommy	115	Amasham	115	22,750	1:47.80	
1988	Old Stories	3	R. Hernandez	114	Viva Deputy	117	Rising Colors	112	60,000	1:52.20	
1989	Doc's Leader	3	W. Fox Jr.	114	Halo Hansom	120	Downtown Davey	117	60,000	1:50.00	
1990	Challenge My Duty	3	L. Ayarza	113	My Other Brother	115	Gay's Best Boy	115	60,000	1:49.60	
1998	Da Devil	3	J. Court	113	One Bold Stroke	122	Jess M	115	120,000	1:48.80	99
1999	Stellar Brush	3	J. Stokes	122	American Spirit	113	Harry's Halo	119	150,000	1:49.02	108
2000	Mass Market	3	R. Wilson	115	Hal's Hope	122	Bet on Red	122	180,000	1:49.94	100
2001	Western Pride	3	D. Whitney	113	Saratoga Games	115	Thunder Blitz	119	300,000	1:47.20	102
2002	Wiseman's Ferry	3	J.F. Chavez	122	The Judge Sez Who	115	Captain Squire	115	360,000	1:49.63	104
2003	Soto	3	R.A. Dominguez	111	Dynever	117	Colita	111	360,000	1:46.29	114

Beyer Index: 104.50

WESTCHESTER HANDICAP, 1 Mile,
3-Year-Olds and Up, Belmont Park, 2003 Purse: $109,700

Year	Winner	Age	Jockey	Wt.	Second	Wt.	Third	Wt.	Win Value	Time	Beyer
1918	George Smith	5	F. Robinson	127	Star Master	118	Corn Tassel	107	2,150	1:51.60	
1919	Star Master	5	C. Kummer	125	Blairgowrie	95	W. Machine	95	2,275	2:09.20	
1920	Mad Hatter	4	E. Sande	126	War Note	95	Cromwell	100	4,550	2:07.40	
1921	Yellow Hand	4	C.H. Miller	132	Bon Homme	110	Thunder Clap	123	4,850	2:05.60	
1922	Prince James	4	E. Taplin	119	Mad Hatter	126	Horologe	99	5,150	1:53.00	
1923	Hephaistos	4	M. Fator	100	Cherry Pie	112	Nedna	103	4,860	1:53.40	
1924	Mad Play	3	L. Fator	124	Horologe	105	Wilkes Br'e	98	5,510	1:51.60	
1925	Aga Khan	4	F. Stevens	129	Catalan	106	Turf Idol	107	4,990	1:51.80	
1926	Cloudland	4	L. Fator	109	Laura Dianti	104	Copiapo	109	4,970	1:53.80	
1927	Light Carbine	4	C. Zoeller	106	Herodian	106	Cloudland	106	5,390	1:53.60	
1928	Arcturus	3	G. Schreiner	100	Onecalibur	114	Wee Burn	103	4,970	1:53.00	
1929	Genie	4	W. Kelsay	110	Sud Edwin	124	Low Gear	105	4,930	1:52.00	
1930	Questionnaire	3	C. Kurtsinger	129	Sun Edwin	118	Sun Mission	115	4,650	1:53.60	
1931	Dr. Freeland	5	J. Bethel	120	Reveille Boy	126	Mad Career	118	2,880	1:53.60	
1934	King Saxon	3	T. Mailey	118	Halcyon	103			1,985	1:54.40	
1935	Good Harvest	4	S. Renick	106	Spanish Way	105	Vicares	107	4,550	1:51.80	
1936	Thorson	4	E. Arcaro	112	Piccolo	107	Seabiscuit	119	4,790	1:52.00	
1937	Thorson	5	E. Roberts	116	Busy K	105	Da'ger Point	107	7,550	1:54.00	
1938	Great Union	3	S. Renick	107	Esposa	124	Idle Miss	115	6,550	1:52.00	
1939	Third Degree	3	E. Arcaro	123	Don Mike	116	Thanksgiving	118	7,250	1:51.40	
1940	Mioland	3	L. Haas	119	Foxbrough	110	Hash	122	15,950	2:00.20	
1941	Gramps	4	H. Lindberg	105	Tola Rose	107	Boysy	113	19,650	1:59.80	
1942	Riverland	4	A. Robertson	114	Tola Rose	108	Alsab	124	19,850	1:56.40	
1943	Slide Rule	3	J. Westrope	119	Boysy	115	First Fiddle	114	22,700	1:57.60	
1944	Seven Hearts	4	P. Keiper	124	Good Morning	109	Stymie	109	23,515	1:58.00	
1945	Stymie	4	R. Permane	125	Buzfuz	116	Olympic Zenith	117	38,765	1:56.80	
1946	Assault	3	E. Arcaro	122	Lucky Draw	128	Lets Dance	104	38,600	1:56.40	
1947	Bridal Flower	4	W. Mehrtens	108	With Pleasure	130	Donor	112	39,700	1:57.80	
1948	Better Self	3	D. Gorman	119	War Trophy	110	Phalanx	126	39,600	1:57.80	
1949	Three Rings	4	H. Woodhouse	116	Delegate	120	Royal Governor	123	20,200	1:56.80	
1950	Palestinian	4	S. Boulmetis	123	Sunglow	113	Chicle II	121	25,100	1:57.20	
1951	Bryan G.	4	O. Scurlock	117	County Delight	124	Bed o' Roses	116	21,100	1:49.20	
1952	Battlefield	4	A. Schmidl	123	Tom Fool	125	Alerted	125	38,350	1:50.20	

Year	Winner	Age	Jockey	Wt.	Second	Wt.	Third	Wt.	Win Value	Time	Beyer
1953	Cold Command	4	H. Woodhouse	112	Crafty Admiral	128	Jampol	112	38,150	1:49.60	
1959	Mystic II	5	M. Sorrentino	110	Whitley	110	Slaipner	119	18,452	1:43.60	
1960	Vendetta	4	J. Leonard	112	Big Effort	109	Mystic II	116	19,005	1:35.20	
1961	Mail Order	5	L. Adams	114	Pied d'Or	115	Talent Show	116	18,655	1:34.00	
1962	Globemaster	4	J.L. Rotz	125	Rideabout	113	Merry Ruler	118	18,687	1:34.60	
1963	Sunrise County	4	J.L. Rotz	111	Key Issue	112	Dedimoud	111	18,005	1:34.20	
1964	Rocky Link	4	D. Pierce	113	Bonjour	115	Morry E.	114	18,947	1:35.20	
1965	Tibaldo	5	B. Baeza	116	Quita Dude	113	P'r of Destiny	115	39,130	1:36.60	
1966	R. Thomas	5	L. Adams	116	Cupid	117	Seaman	114	37,375	1:36.20	
1967	Advocator	4	M. Ycaza	114	Our Michael	116	Model Fool	112	35,815	1:35.20	
1968	R. Thomas	7	J. Nichols	118	Peter Piper	117	Grace Born	111	36,335	1:35.40	
1969	Iron Ruler	4	A. Cordero Jr.	117	Beaukins	113	Sky Count	114	36,335	1:35.00	
1970	Dewan	5	E. Belmonte	119	Gaelic Dancer	114	Gleaming Light	117	37,440	1:34.20	
1971	Never Bow	5	V. Tejada	124	Knight in Armor	111	Dan Patch	113	35,580	1:36.40	
1972	Autobiography	4	A. Cordero Jr.	119	Tunex	119	Native Royalty	118	34,560	1:34.20	
1973	North Sea	4	R.C. Smith	117	Forage	116	Summer Guest	118	33,990	1:33.60	
1974	Dundee Marmalade	6	M. Hole	113	Infuriator	113	Prove Out	126	32,940	1:36.00	
1975	Step Nicely	5	J. Velasquez	126	Tambac	116	Onion	119	33,900	1:34.00	
1976	Double Edge Sword	6	A. Cordero Jr.	114	Dr. Emil	116	Bold and F'y	111	34,170	1:33.40	
1977	Cinteelo	4	E. Maple	113	Turn and Count	124	Cojak	120	33,090	1:43.40	
1978	Pumpkin Moonshine	4	D.A. Borden	105	Lynn Davis	115	Sharpstone	111	32,250	1:44.40	
1979	Vencedor	5	R. Hernandez	126	Don Aronow	108	Coverack	114	33,060	1:44.00	
1980	Nice Catch	4	J. Fell	120	Ardaluan	119	Lark Oscillation	115	34,020	1:36.80	
1981	Dunham's Gift	4	M. Venezia	115	Ring of Light	114	Dr. Blum	124	33,000	1:35.00	
1982	John Casey	5	J. Fell	114	Brasher Doubloon	111	Accipiter's Hope	120	33,090	1:38.00	
1982	Fabulous Find	4	J.O. Cintron	109	In From Dixie	122	Princelet	126	33,330	1:38.00	
1983	Singh Tu	4	J.L. Samyn	109	Master Digby	114	Fabulous Find	114	33,780	1:35.20	
1984	Jacque's Tip	4	A. Cordero Jr.	114	Minstrel Glory	111	Havagreatdate	112	55,440	1:41.80	
1985	Verbarctic	5	G. McCarron	114	Moro	122	Fighting Fit	124	53,460	1:36.60	
1986	Garthorn	6	R. Meza	120	Ends Well	115	Grand Rivulet	110	75,240	1:33.80	
1987	King's Swan	7	J.A. Santos	122	Cutlass Reality	114	Landing Plot	115	69,120	1:36.20	
1988	Faster Than Sound	4	J.A. Krone	113	Ron Stevens	109	King's Swan	133	108,000	1:34.40	
1989	Lord of the Night	6	J. Velasquez	115	Dancing Spree	112	Congeleur	112	71,040	1:35.60	
1990	Once Wild	5	A. Cordero Jr.	121	Its Acedemic	116			67,800	1:35.00	107
					King's Swan	113					
1991	Rubiano	4	J.D. Bailey	111	Senor Speedy	113	Killer Diller	115	71,520	1:34.80	114
1992	Rubiano	5	J.A. Santos	117	Out of Place	115	Wild Away	111	68,880	1:34.80	107
1993	Bill of Rights	4	J.L. Samyn	110	Fly So Free	118	Loach	113	72,720	1:34.60	107
1994	Virginia Rapids	4		116	Colonial Affair	121	Cherokee Run	119	65,640	1:34.40	107
1995	Mr. Shawklit	4	Luzzi MJ	112	Devil His Due	124	Our Emblem	110	65,760	1:34.60	107
1996	Valid Wager	4	Pezua J. M.	115	Pat N Jac	111	More To Tell	118	66,240	1:34.60	107
1997	Pacific Fleet	4	Alvarado F. T.	114	Circle of Light	110	Stalwart Member	114	65,940	1:33.80	111
1998	Wagon Limit	4	Samyn J. L.	114	Draw	113	Lucayan Prince	116	66,420	1:34.00	118
1999	Mr. Sinatra	5	Lopez C. C.	114	Laredo	114	Brushing Up	113	64,202	1:35.00	105
2000	Yankee Victor	4	H. Castillo Jr.	115	Golden Missile	116	Watchman's Warning	113	66,000	1:34.37	110
2001	Cat's at Home	4	F. Leon	114	Little Hans	113	Milwaukee Brew	117	64,920	1:33.60	106
2002	Free Of Love	4	J.D. Bailey	114	Dayton Flyer	112	Country Be Gold	114	67,500	1:35.56	102
2003	Najran	4	E.S. Prado	113	Saarland	114	Justification	113	65,820	1:32.24	111

Beyer Index: 108.5

WHIRLAWAY HANDICAP, 1 1/16 Miles,
4-Year-Olds and Up, Fair Grounds, 2003 Purse: $125,000

Year	Winner	Age	Jockey	Wt.	Second	Wt.	Third	Wt.	Win Value	Time	Beyer
1973	Guitar Player	5	T. Barrow	118	Holy Land	116	Grocery List	114	12,000	1:41.40	
1974	Tom Tulle	4	C. Perret	119	Navajo	115	Native Cadet	108	12,000	1:38.80	
1975	Burglar Alarm		P. Rubbicco		Faneuil Boy		Sr. Diplomat			1:39.20	
1975	Hearts of Lettuce		A. LeBlanc		Fame and Power		Aerodrome			1:38.80	
1976	Master Derby		D.G McHargue		Strictly Business		Native Drone			1:38.80	
1977	Cylinder		R. Sibille		Minnie Bus		Almost Grown			1:39.60	
1981	Occasionally Monday		A. Trosclair	114	Selma's Boy	115	Dr. Riddick	115		1:40.20	
1985	Rapid Gray	6	R. Romero	122	Hopeful Word	113	Silver Diplomat	118	19,250	1:43.00	
1992	Irish Swap	5	B. Poyadou	118	Jarraar	113	Wild and Tingley	113	18,975	1:43.00	100
1993	West by West	4	J.L. Samyn	117	Place Dancer	112	Genuine Meaning	113	18,885	1:43.80	98
1994	Cool Quaker	5	E. Martin Jr.	114	Dixie Poker Ace	121	Dixieland Heat	114	31,005	1:42.55	99
1995	Adhocracy	5	L. Melancon	112	Dynamic Brush	111	Cool Quaker	113	31,530	1:43.10	101
1996	Bucks Nephew	4	C. Perret	116	Prory	114	Vast Joy	114	38,025	1:43.40	101
1997	Byars	4	C. Bourque	114	Bucks Nephew	117	Clash by Night	113	60,000	1:44.47	91
1998	Moonlight Dancer	6	C. Bourque	114	Precocity	117	Hot Brush	113	75,000	1:44.34	109
1999	Precocity	5	E. Martin Jr.	117	Prory	114	Take Note of Me	117	75,000	1:43.42	108
2000	Take Note of Me	6	R. Albarado	118	Crimson Classic	114	Nite Dreamer	115	75,000	1:42.94	105
2001	Include	4	L. Meche	112	Connected	112	Kombat Kat	113	75,000	1:42.94	105
2002	Valhol	6	R. Albarado	115	Parade Leader	115	Fight for Ally	113	75,000	1:44.01	105
2003	Balto Star	5	E.M. Martin Jr.	118	Mineshaft	116	Bonapaw	115	75,000	1:43.74	111

Run at 1 mile 40 yards in 1973–1981; Not run 1982–1984, 1986–1991

Beyer Index: 103

WILSHIRE HANDICAP, 1 Mile (Turf),
Fillies and Mares 3-Year-Olds and Up, Hollywood Park, 2003 Purse: $111,000

Year	Winner	Age	Jockey	Wt.	Second	Wt.	Third	Wt.	Win Value	Time	Beyer
1953	Ria Rica	3	B. Pearson	110	Laska	108	Mary Be Good	109	9,925	1:37.20	
1963	Edie Belle	6	W. Shoemaker	110	Pixie Erin	119	Mountain Glory	107	13,200	1:26.40	
1964	Researcher	4	P. Moreno	110	Star Maggie	115	Curious Clover	124	13,850	1:26.40	
1965	Jalousie II.	6	J. Longden	112	Savaii	117	Gala Host	112	16,550	1:21.00	
1966	Poona Queen	6	W. Shoemaker	117	Jalousie II	113	Gala Host	115	16,500	1:22.20	
1967	Romanticism	5		119	Admirably	124	Mellow Marsh	110	14,700	1:22.40	
1968	Gamely	4	W. Harris	125	Romanticism	119	Nev'da M'rga	114	14,150	1:21.00	
1969	Gamely	5	W. Harris	128	Time to Leave	123	Ind'n Love C'l.	120	13,150	1:21.00	
1970	Tanta Bella	3	J. Lambert	115	Last of the Line	113	Thoroly Blue	113	13,300	1:48.80	
1971	New Leaf	4	D. Tierney	113	Sallarina	121	Thoroly Blue	121	17,700	1:49.00	
1972	Manta	6	F. Toro	113	Tico's Donna	112	Minstrel Miss	118	16,100	1:48.80	
1973	Balcony's Babe	5	J. Lambert	116	Ground Song	118	Dating	111	17,250	1:48.60	
1973	Convenience	5	J.L. Rotz	124	Pallisima	120	Veiled Desire	109	16,900	1:49.00	
1974	Tallahto	4	L. Pincay Jr	121	Ready Wit	113	Dogtooth Violet	119	33,650	1:47.60	
1975	Tizna	6	J. Lambert	123	Susan's Girl	123	Dulcia	120	33,300	1:48.60	
1976	Miss Toshiba	4	F. Toro	117	Charger's Star	116	Swingtime	120	32,300	1:49.20	
1977	Now Pending	4	R. Campas	114	Swingtime	116	Up to Juliet	116	33,550	1:48.80	
1978	Lucie Manet	5	C.J. McCarron	119	Swingtime	119	Drama Critic	119	30,950	1:49.00	
1979	Country Queen	4	L. Pincay Jr	121	Giggling Girl	116	Camarado	119	33,100	1:40.40	
1980	Wishing Well	5	F. Toro	120	Sisterhood	119	Love You Dear	113	38,500	1:41.60	
1981	Track Robbery	5	P.A. Valenzuela	118	Luth Music	115	Save Wild Life	116	47,550	1:40.80	
1982	Miss Huntington	5	P.A. Valenzuela	115	Mi Quimera	117	French Charmer	116	51,250	1:41.40	
1983	Mademoiselle Forli	4	P.A. Valenzuela	118	Night Fire	117	Nan's Charger	115	47,300	1:44.80	
1984	Triple Tipple	5	L. Pincay Jr	117	Comedy Act	122	Nan's Dancer	116	48,900	1:41.20	
1985	Johnica	4	C.J. McCarron	114	Tamarinda	119	Salt Spring	113	63,100	1:40.60	
1986	Outstandingly	4	G.L. Stevens	117	La Koumia	118	Estrapade	124	75,600	1:41.60	
1987	Galunpe	4	F. Toro	118	Top Socialite	119	Perfect Match	116	75,900	1:41.00	
1988	Chapel of Dreams	4	G.L. Stevens	115	Fitzwilliam Place	119	Invited Guest	116	64,700	1:39.40	
1989	Claire Marine	4	C.J. McCarron	117	Fitzwilliam Place	119	Galunpe	119	62,700	1:39.00	
1990	Reluctant Guest	4	R.G. Davis	114	Beautiful Melody	115	Estrella Fuega	114	62,400	1:39.40	
1991	Fire the Groom	4	G.L. Stevens	118	Odalea	115	Agirlfromars	114	63,000	1:40.00	107
1992	Kostroma	6	K.J. Desormeaux	123	Danzante	114	Appealing Missy	116	62,500	1:41.20	102
1993	Toussaud	4	K.J. Desormeaux	116	Visible Gold	117	Wedding Ring	115	63,500	1:40.00	100
1994	Skimble	5	E. Delahoussaye	118	Bel's Starlet	118	Miami Sands	116	62,800	1:41.20	99
1995	Possibly Perfect	5	K.J. Desormeaux	121	Morgana	116	Aube Indienne	119	76,600	1:40.20	103
1996	Pharma	5	C.S. Nakatani	118	Didina	116	Matiara	120	79,770	1:40.80	107
1997	Blushing Heiress	5	C.J. McCarron	115	Real Connection	115	De Puntillas	117	65,040	1:40.80	100
1998	Shake The Yoke	5	E. Delahoussaye	118	Traces of Gold	116	Cozy Blues	115	66,240	1:34.00	104
1999	Sapphire Ring	4	G.L. Stevens	119	Bella Chiarra	116	Green Jewel	118	65,160	1:33.86	102
2000	Tout Charmant	4	C.J. McCarron	121	Penny Marie	117	Perfect Copy	117	64,740	1:33.86	99
2001	Tranquility Lake	6	E. Delahoussaye	123	Dianehill	116	Out of Reach	117	65,160	1:34.69	97
2002	Eurolink Raindance	5	C.J. McCarron	115	Crazy Ensign	118	Impeachable	115	63,960	1:34.31	97
2003	Dublino	4	K.J. Desormeaux	120	Southern Oasis	116	Final Destination	118	66,600	1:33.62	106

Beyer Index: 101.77

WINSTAR DISTAFF HANDICAP, 1 Mile (Turf),
Fillies and Mares 3-Year-Olds and Up, Lone Star Park, 2003 Purse: $200,000

Year	Winner	Age	Jockey	Wt.	Second	Wt.	Third	Wt.	Win Value	Time	Beyer
2000	Mumtaz	4	V. Espinoza	113	Evening Promise	117	Really Polish	114	120,000	1:37.28	100
2001	Voladora	6	M. Berry	114	Dyna Likes Bingo	109	Iftiraas	118	120,000	1:42.23	99
2002	Queen of Wilshire	6	D.R. Flores	117	Pleasant State	115	Blushing Bride	115	120,000	1:38.96	98
2003	Eagle Lake	5	G. Melancon	116	Little Treasure	117	Magic Mission	116	120,000	1:43.02	95

Beyer Index: 98

WITHERS, 1 Mile,
3-Year-Olds, Aqueduct, 2003 Purse: $150,000

Year	Winner	Age	Jockey	Wt.	Second	Wt.	Third	Wt.	Win Value	Time	Beyer
1874	Dublin	3	Ponton	110	Vandalite	107	Reform	110	3,200	1:50.00	
1875	Aristides	3	Swim	110	Rhadamanthus	110	Ozark	110	4,150	1:45.75	
1876	Fiddlesticks	3	Feakes	110	Charley Howard	110	Merciless	107	3,500	1:46.50	
1877	Bombast	3	Barrett	110	Cardinal Wolsey	110	Glen Dudley	110	4,200	1:46.00	
1878	Duke of Magenta	3	Hughes	118	Bramble	118	Danicheff	118	3,500	1:48.00	
1879	Dan Sparling	3	Kelly	118	Spendthrift	118	Report	118	5,395	1:48.00	
1880	Ferncliffe	3	Barrett	118	Grenada	118	Oden	118	3,800	1:49.00	
1881	Crickmore	3	Hughes	115	Prism	118	Filette	113	4,275	1:48.00	
1882	Forester	3	J. McLaughlin	118	Marsh Redon	118	Rica	113	4,600	1:46.50	
1883	Geo. Kinney	3	J. McLaughlin	118	Pizarro	118	Trombone	118	2,990	1:45.00	
1884	Panique	3	Fitzpatrick	118	Richmond	118	Pampero	118	3,240	1:48.00	
1885	Tyrant	3	P. Duffy	118	Himalaya	118	Tecumseh	118	3,070	1:45.25	
1886	Biggonet	3	Maynard	113	Repartee	118	Headland	118	3,260	1:48.00	
1887	Hanover	3	J. McLaughlin	118	Stockton	118	Belvidere	118	3,490	1:46.50	

Year	Winner	Age	Jockey	Wt.	Second	Wt.	Third	Wt.	Win Value	Time	Beyer
1888	Sir Dixon	3	Fitzpatrick	118	Prince Royal	118	Tea Tray	119	3,620	1:47.00	
1889	Diablo	3	Godfrey	121	Eric	118	Reporter	118	5,380	1:45.00	
1890	King Eric	3	Garrison	110	Magnate	113	Cayuga	113	8,140	1:41.00	
1891	Picknicker	3	F. Littlefield	117	Montana	117	Laurestan	114	4,190	1:40.75	
1892	Tammany	3	Garrison	122	Patron	122	Yorkville Belle	117	7,460	1:40.00	
1893	Dr. Rice	3	Taral	122	Rainbow	122	Sir Walter	122	9,470	1:42.00	
1894	Domino	3	Taral	122	Henry of Navarre	122	Dobbins	122	7,100	1:40.00	
1895	Lucania	3	Reiff	109	Brandywine	105	Gotham	111	2,700	1:41.75	
1896	Handspring	3	Simms	122	Hastings	122	Sherlock	112	2,550	1:41.00	
1897	Octagon	3	Simms	119	Ogden	122	Regulator	119	2,550	1:43.00	
1898	The Huguenot	3	Spencer	122	Mr. Baiter	122	Handball	122	3,815	1:43.00	
1899	Jean Bereaud	3	Clawson	122	Filon d'Or	119	The Bouncer	122	4,450	1:42.25	
1900	Kilmarnock	3	N. Turner	126	Mesmerist	126	Ildrim	126	5,470	1:41.25	
1901	The Parader	3	Landry	126	Bonnibert	126	Bellario	126	5,020	1:42.50	
1902	Compute	3	Shaw	126	Old England	123	King Hanover	126	4,815	1:42.00	
1903	Shorthose	3	Haack	126	Mexican	126	Injunction	126	6,395	1:41.00	
1904	Delhi	3	Odom	126	Bryn Mawr	126	Conjurer	126	5,750	1:40.00	
1905	Blandy	3	W. Davis	126	Hot Shot	126	Sparkling Star	126	6,220	1:44.60	
1906	Accountant	3	J. Martin	126	Bohemian	126	Clark Griffith	126	6,850	1:38.80	
1907	Frank Gill	3	Notter	126	Peter Pan	126	Saracinesca	123	7,775	1:40.00	
1908	Colin	3	Notter	126	Fair Play	126	King James	126	12,090	1:41.00	
1909	Hilarious	3	Butwell	126	Joe Madden	126	Fayette	126	11,070	1:41.20	
1910	The Turk	3	M. McGee	126	Prince Imperial	126	Grasmere	126	3,000	1:40.00	
1913	Rock View	3	Butwell	118	Prince Eugene	118	Yan'e Notions	118	2,325	1:39.40	
1914	Charlestonian	3	C. Burlingame	115	Gainer	118	Roamer	115	2,900	1:39.80	
1915	The Finn	3	G. Byrne	118	Sharpshooter	115	Half Rock	118	1,425	1:39.40	
1916	Spur	3	J. Loftus	118	Churchill	118	Friar Rock	118	2,900	1:38.40	
1917	Hourless	3	J. Butwell	118	Rickety	118	Skeptic	118	5,475	1:39.00	
1918	Motor Cop	3	E. Taplin	118	Cum Sah	118	Tr. La Mort	118	7,100	1:39.60	
1919	Sir Barton	3	J. Loftus	118	Eternal	118	Pastoral Swain	118	8,075	1:38.80	
1920	Man o' War	3	C. Kummer	118	Wildair	118	David Harum	118	4,825	1:35.80	
1921	Leonardo II	3	A. Schuttinger	118	Sporting Blood	118	Grey Lag	118	5,475	1:37.40	
1922	Snob II	3	C. Kummer	118	Pillory	118	June Grass	118	17,050	1:35.80	
1923	Zev	3	E. Sande	118	Martingale	118	Barbary Bush	118	18,300	1:37.40	
1924	Bracadale	3	E. Sande	118	Sun Pal	118	Sheridan	118	19,000	1:39.00	
1925	American Flag	3	A. Johnson	118	Silver Fox	118	Gold Stick	118	19,600	1:38.20	
1926	Haste	3	E. Sande	118	Crusader	118	Espino	118	22,800	1:37.60	
1927	Chance Shot	3	E. Sande	118	Sweepster	118	Boise de Rose	118	23,250	1:39.80	
1928	Victorian	3	R. Workman	118	Mowlee	118	Polydor	118	22,300	1:39.00	
1929	Blue Larkspur	3	M. Garner	118	Chestnut Oak	118	Jack High	118	28,250	1:36.00	
1930	Whichone	3	R. Workman	118	Swinfield	118	Starpatic	118	26,150	1:38.20	
1931	Jamestown	3	L. McAtee	118	Ladder	118	Clock Tower	118	27,300	1:36.60	
1932	Boatswain	3	A. Robertson	118	Osculator	118	Pairbypair	118	21,600	1:39.80	
1933	The Darb	3	A. Robertson	118	Golden Way	118	Dark Winter	118	20,550	1:39.00	
1934	Singing Wood	3	R. Jones	118	Roustabout	118	Chicstraw	118	16,000	1:37.80	
1935	Rosemont	3	W.D. Wright	118	Omaha	118	Plat Eye	118	11,250	1:36.60	
1936	White Cockade	3	E. Litzenberger	118	Brevity	118	Teufel	118	18,200	1:37.20	
1937	Flying Scot	3	J. Gilbert	118	Charing Cross	118	Mosawtre	118	15,050	1:37.40	
1938	Menow	3	C. Kurtsinger	118	Thanksgiving	118	Redbreast	118	15,000	1:37.40	
1939	Johnstown	3	J. Stout	118	Hash	118	Porter's Mite	118	15,750	1:35.80	
1940	Corydon	3	E. Arcaro	118	Bimelech	118	Roman	118	16,650	1:37.20	
1941	King Cole	3	J. Gilbert	118	Robert Morris	118	Porter's Cap	118	20,300	1:38.20	
1942	Alsab	3	B. James	126	Lochinvar	126	Fairaris	126	15,500	1:36.20	
1943	Count Fleet	3	J. Longden	126	Slide Rule	126	Tip-Toe	126	12,700	1:36.00	
1944	Who Goes There	3	J. Longden	126	By Jimminy	126	Boy Knight	126	16,150	1:38.00	
1945	Polynesian	3	W.D. Wright	126	Pavot	126	King Dorsett	126	19,125	1:39.80	
1946	Hampden	3	E. Arcaro	126	Natchez	126	Perfect Bahram	126	20,320	1:36.00	
1947	Faultless	3	D. Dodson	126	Brabancon	126	Stage Kid	126	20,950	1:38.20	
1948	Vulcan's Forge	3	D. Dodson	126	Coaltown	126	Better Self	126	20,100	1:37.40	
1949	Olympia	3	E. Arcaro	126	Ocean Drive	126	One Hitter	126	21,150	1:36.80	
1950	Hill Prince	3	E. Arcaro	126	Middleground	126	Ferd	126	20,700	1:35.80	
1951	Battlefield	3	E. Arcaro	126	Jumbo	126	Nullify	126	20,600	1:35.80	
1952	Armageddon	3	R. York	126	One Count	126	Primate	126	22,000	1:37.00	
1953	Native Dancer	3	E. Guerin	126	Invigorator	126	Real Brother	126	23,050	1:36.20	
1954	Jet Action	3	R. Contreras	126	Buttevant	126	High Gun	126	26,250	1:36.60	
1955	Traffic Judge	3	E. Arcaro	126	Nance's Lad	126	Portersville	126	21,850	1:36.00	
1956	Oh Johnny	3	H. Woodhouse	126	Eiffel Blue	126	Lawless	126	20,100	1:45.20	
1957	Clem	3	C. McCreary	126	Cohoes	126	Tenacious	126	19,100	1:36.80	
1958	Sir Robby	3	E. Guerin	126	Clandestine	126	Misty Flight	126	19,362	1:36.20	
1959	Intentionally	3	M. Ycaza	126	Manassa Mauler	126	Bagdad	126	58,072	1:35.60	
1960	John William	3	H. Woodhouse	126	Count Amber	126	Francis S.	126	74,950	1:35.40	
1961	Hitting Away	3	H. Woodhouse	126	Up Scope	126	Nashua Blue	126	38,935	1:35.20	
1962	Jaipur	3	W. Shoemaker	126	Green Ticket	126	Cyrano	126	38,090	1:35.60	
1963	Get Around	3	B. Baeza	126	Sky Wonder	126	Top Gallant	126	39,650	1:36.60	
1964	Mr. Brick	3	R. Ussery	126	National	126	Alphabet	126	40,105	1:35.60	
1965	Flag Raiser	3	R. Ussery	126	Gallant Lad	126	Record Dash	126	39,000	1:34.20	

Year Winner	Age	Jockey	Wt.	Second	Wt.	Third	Wt.	Win Value	Time	Beyer
1966 Indulto............	3	J.L. Rotz	126	Creme Dela Creme.	126	Fathers Image ...	126....	38,935	.1:35.00	
1967 Dr. Fager.........	3	B. Baeza........	126	Tumiga............	126	Reason to Hail ...	126....	37,895	.1:33.80	
1968 Call Me Prince ...	3	W. Boland......	126	Salerno............	126	Verbatim	126....	38,220	.1:35.20	
1969 Ack Ack........	3	M. Ycaza	126	Tyrant............	126	Rooney's Shield..	126....	37,765	.1:34.80	
1970 Hagley...........	3	R. Turcotte.....	126	Delaware Chief ...	126	Tatoi	126....	38,805	.1:34.80	
1971 Bold Reasoning ..	3	J. Vasquez......	126	Highbinder	126	Salem	126....	35,100	.1:35.80	
1972 Key to the Mint ..	3	B. Baeza........	126	Icecapade	126	Zulu Tom	126....	35,400	.1:34.80	
1973 Linda's Chief.....	3	J. Velasquez....	126	Stop the Music ...	126	Forego	126....	33,120	.1:34.80	
1974 Accipiter........	3	A. Santiago.....	126	Best of It.........	126	Hosiery	126....	36,240	.1:35.60	
1975 Sarsar...........	3	W. Shoemaker..	121	Laramie Trail......	126	Ramahorn........	126....	36,360	.1:34.60	
1976 Sonkisser	3	B. Baeza........	126	El Portugues	126	Full Out..........	126....	32,760	.1:35.00	
1977 Iron Constitution .	3	J. Velasquez....	126	Cormorant	126	Affiliate	126....	33,360	.1:37.00	
1978 Junction	3	M. Solomone....	126	Star de Naskra....	126	Buckaroo	126....	32,520	.1:36.80	
1979 Czaravich	3	J. Cruguet......	126	Instrument Landing	126	Strike the Main ..	126....	34,200	.1:34.40	
1980 Colonel Moran ...	3	J. Velasquez....	126	Temperence Hill ..	126	J.P. Brother......	126....	33,600	.1:36.80	
1981 Spirited Boy	3	A. Cordero Jr...	126	Willow Hour......	126	A Run............	126....	33,300	.1:35.40	
1982 Aloma's Ruler	3	J.L. Kaenel.....	126	Spanish Drums ...	126	John's Gold......	126....	52,380	.1:35.60	
1983 Country Pine	3	J.D. Bailey......	126	I Enclose	126	Megaturn.........	126....	69,750	.1:36.40	
1984 Play On	3	J.L. Samyn	126	Morning Bob	126	Back Bay Barrister	126....	72,990	.1:36.60	
1985 El Basco	3	J. Vasquez......	126	Another Reef	126	Concert..........	126....	71,550	.1:35.60	
1986 Clear Choice	3	J. Velasquez....	126	Tasso	126	Landing Plot......	126....	82,620	.1:36.40	
1987 Gone West	3	E. Maple	126	High Brite........	126	Mr. S.M..........	126....	69,360	.1:35.20	
1988 Once Wild.......	3	P. Day..........	126	Tejano	126	Perfect Spy......	126....	73,800	.1:36.40	
1989 Fire Maker	3	J.D. Bailey......	126	Imbibe	126	Sunny Serve	126....	71,040	.1:34.80	
1990 Housebuster	3	C. Perret.......	126	Profit Key........	126	Kyle's Our Man ..	126....	73,920	.1:34.00	.. 102
1991 Subordinated Debt	3	J.A. Krone......	126	Scan	126	Superstrike.......	126....	73,080	.1:33.60	.. 108
1992 Dixie Brass.......	3	J.M. Pezua	126	Big Sur..........	124	Farmonthefreeway	124....	76,800	.1:32.60	.. 104
1993 Williamstown	3	C. Perret.......	126	Virginia Rapids ...	124	Presently	123....	67,140	.1:34.60	.. 102
1994 Twining.........	3	J.A. Santos	123	Able Buck	123	Northern Ensign .	123....	67,260	.1:35.00	.. 91
1995 Blu Tusmani.....	3	J.A. Santos	123	Pat n Jac........	123	Roar.............	123....	66,120	.1:35.00	.. 104
1996 Appealing Skier ..	3	R Wilson.......	123	Jamies First Punch	123	Stormin Fever ...	123....	67,140	.1:35.20	.. 95
1997 Statesmanship ...	3	W.H. McCauley.	123	Cryp Too	123	Limit Out	123....	90,000	.1:34.40	.. 114
1998 Dice Dancer.....	3	J.F. Chavez.....	123	Rubiyat	123	Treasure Island ..	116....	90,000	.1:35.00	.. 96
1999 Successful Appeal.	3	J.L. Espinosa...	120	Best of Luck......	116	Port Herman.....	116....	90,000	.1:35.69	.. 93
2000 Big E E..........	3	H. Castillo Jr....	116	Precise End	123	Telescam	116....	90,000	.1:35.66	.. 97
2001 Richly Blended...	3	R. Wilson.......	123	Le Grande Dansuer	120	Listen Here	120....	90,000	.1:36.41	.. 100
2002 Fast Decision	3	J.A. Santos	116	Shah Jehan.......	118	Stanislavsky	116....	90,000	.1:35.89	.. 96
2003 Spite the Devil ...	3	L. Chavez	116	Alysweep..........	123					

Beyer Index: 100.15

YERBA BUENA BREEDERS' CUP HANDICAP, About 1 1/8 Miles (Turf), Fillies and Mares 3-Year-Olds and Up, Bay Meadows, 2003 Purse: $107,500

Year Winner	Age	Jockey	Wt.	Second	Wt.	Third	Wt.	Win Value	Time	Beyer
1973 Live Forever	4	J.T. Gonzalez ...	112	Fleet Ahead	112	Homespun.......	111...	12,050	.2:19.60	
1974 Merry Madeleine ..	4	F. Mena........	113	Hurry Countess....	110	Hum Dum.......	111...	17,625	.2:31.40	
1975 Joli Vert	4	F. Olivares	115	Lucky Spell.......	122	Gentleweave.....	106...	31,000	.2:16.80	
1976 Our First Delight ..	4	E. Munoz.......	120	Graceful Banner ...	112	L'rking Party	113...	33,400	.2:16.40	
1977 Star Ball	5	J.L. Vargas	121	Bastonera II......	124	Up to Juliet......	117...	48,350	.2:14.80	
1978 Star Ball	6	D.G. McHargue..	124	Up to Juliet......	114	Surera..........	112...	63,800	.2:13.60	
1980 Mairzy Doates....	4	F. Mena........	116	Sisterhood	121	Smaller Bicker...	113...	66,900	.2:15.00	
1981 Mairzy Doates....	5	F. Mena........	120	Princess Karenda..	123	Princess Toby....	117...	78,550	.2:15.80	
1982 Sangue..........	4	T.M. Chapman..	117	Berry Bush	119	Mademoiselle Ivor	112...	78,400	.2:16.40	
1983 Dilmoun.........	4	J.J. Steiner	111	Latrone	112	Berry Bush......	119...	82,350	.2:31.60	
1984 Fact Finder	5	M. Castaneda ...	115	Lido Isle.........	114	Her Decision	115...	107,200	.2:30.20	
1985 Salt Spring.......	6	T.M. Chapman..	115	High Spruce......	111	L'Attrayante.....	120...	95,800	.2:30.20	
1986 Scythe..........	5	T.M. Chapman..	113	Heat Spell........	115	Lock's Dream....	114...	85,000	.2:32.20	
1987 Ivor's Image	4	C.J. McCarron..	119	Micenas.........	115	Royal Regatta....	114...	82,500	.2:29.60	
1988 Magdelaine	5	T.T. Doocy	113	Sweet Roberta....	115	Top Corsage.....	118...	82,500	.2:14.40	
1989 Brown Bess	7	J.L. Kaenel.....	119	Carmenetta	114	Flattering News..	111...	82,500	.2:15.60	
1990 Petite Ile........	4	C.A. Black......	118	Double Wedge....	112	Brown Bess......	124...	82,500	.2:15.60	
1991 Free at Last	4	R.D. Hansen....	120	Noble and Nice...	117	Louve Bleue	114...	82,500	.2:15.00	
1992 Flaming Torch	4	R.A. Baze.......	114	Indian Chris	116	Silvered	114...	82,500	.2:16.20	... 96
1993 Party Cited	4	R.J. Warren Jr..	117	Silvered.........	115	Rougeur	115...	55,000	.2:15.00	.. 102
1994 Ask Anita	4	Belvoir VT	116	Miami Sands	115	Oxava...........	115...	55,000	.2:15.40	.. 100
1995 Work the Crowd...	4	Baze RA........	123	Late Sailing	116	Ask Anita.......	117...	68,750	.1:49.20	... 95
1996 Fanjica..........	4	Carr D.........	114	Nimble Mind	115	Dynatar.........	113...	60,000	.2:17.40	.. 100
1997 De Puntillas......	5	Espinoza V.	116	Dynatar.........	117	Tricky Code......	116...	60,000	.1:46.60	... 98
1998 Miss Universal ...	5	Mercado P......	114	Proud Fillie......	115	Squeak	118...	75,000	.2:15.60	... 99
1999 Blending Element .	6	Gomez G. K.....	117	Queen Douna	113	Midnight Line....	117...	120,000	.2:17.20	... 95
2000 Gleefully........	4	R.Q. Meza	113	Country Garden ...	116	Marie de Bayeux .	113...	110,000	.2:15.99	... 96
2001 Janet	4	D.R. Flores	115	Keemoon.........	121	Alexine..........	119...	82,500	.2:17.09	... 99
2002 Peu a Peu	4	R.A. Baze.......	115	Janet............	122	Racene..........	115...	55,000	.2:16.39	... 98
2003 Chiming..........	5	C.S. Nakatani...	116	Noches de Rosa....	119	Lindsay Jean.....	118...	55,000	.1:45.41	.. 108

Beyer Index: 98.83

American Match Races

Match races are scheduled for two horses, usually a winner-take-all, or skewered purse distribution. In 1999, there was only one official Match Race, at Les Bois racetrack in Boise, Idaho. Two-horse races are those in which three or more were entered, but only two actually ran.

MATCH RACES

Contestants	Location	Date
American Eclipse – Sir Charles	Washington D. C.	November 20, 1822
American Eclipse – Henry	Union Course, Long Island, New York	May 27, 1823
Ariel – Lafayette	Union Course, Long Island, New York	October 6, 1825
Flirtilla – Ariel	Union Course, Long Island, New York	October 31, 1825
Arietta – Ariel	Union Course, Long Island, New York	May 8, 1830
Portsmouth – Boston	Petersburg, Virginia	April, 16, 1839
Black Maria – Brilliant	Union Course, Long Island, New York	October 23, 1839
Boston – Gano	Augusta, Georgia	December 7, 1840
Fashion–Boston	Union Course, Long Island, New York	May 10, 1842
Peytona – Fashion	Union Course, Long Island, New York	May 13, 1845
Fashion – Peytona	Camden, New Jersey	May 27, 1845
Lexington – Sallie Waters	New Orleans, Louisiana	December 2, 1853
Lexington – Le Comte	New Orleans, Louisiana	April 14, 1855
Kentucky – Aldebaran	Paterson, New Jersey	September 17, 1864
Norfolk – Lodi	San Francisco, California	May 23, 1865
Norfolk – Lodi	Sacramento, California	September 18, 1865
Norfolk – Lodi	Sacramento, California	September 23, 1865
Flora – Pele	San Francisco, California	January 6, 1866
Ooltawa – Muggins	Nashville, Tennessee	April 7, 1866
Lewis E. Smith – Maiden	New Orleans, Louisiana	April 20, 1866
Mike Edwards – Red Oak	St. Louis, Mo.	May 15, 1866
Maid of Honor – Redwing	Jerome Park, New York	October 3, 1866
Derringer – Susie B. Moore	San Francisco, California	January, 14, 1867
Tornado – Minnie C.^	New Orleans, Louisiana	January 22, 1867
De Courcy – Maid of Honor	Jerome Park, New York	May 25, 1867
Raquette – Redwing	Jerome Park, New York	November 9, 1867
Maid Of Honor – Trovatore	Jerome Park, New York	November 7, 1868
Nannie McNairy – Le Noir	New Orleans, Louisiana	December 7, 1868
Nannie McNairy – Lewis E. Smith	New Orleans, Louisiana	April 8, 1869
Miss Alice – The Gloamin colt	Jerome Park, New York	June 3, 1869
Glenelg – Rapture	Jerome Park, New York	June 3, 1869
Intrigue – El Dorado	Jerome Park, New York	June 6, 1869
Finesse – Intrigue*	Saratoga Springs, New York	July 31, 1869
Pasta Filly – Miss Alice*	Saratoga Springs, New York	July 31, 1869
Finesse – Intrigue	Jerome Park, New York	October 6, 1869
Nannie McNairy – Sarah McDonald	New Orleans, Louisiana	December 4, 1869
By the Sea – The Gloamin colt*	Jerome Park, New York	October 13, 1870
Vigil – Chalmette	New Orleans, Louisiana	May 20, 1871
Alarm – Inverary	Saratoga Springs, New York	August 16, 1871
Thad Stevens – Nettie Brown	San Francisco, California	February 22, 1873
Thad Stevens – Ben Wade	Oakland, California	June 28, 1873
Nell Flaherty – Abi	Oakland, California	June 28, 1873
Survivor – Aerolite	Monmouth, New Jersey	July 21, 1873
Girl of the Period – Ophelia	Jerome Park, New York	October 4, 1873
Shylock – M. A. B.	Jerome Park, New York	October 4, 1873
Joe Daniels – Nell Flaherty	San Francisco, California	December 25, 1873
Limestone – Revenge**	Charleston, South Carolina	March 9, 1874
Shylock – Vaultress	Monmouth, New Jersey	July 18, 1874
Bullet – Trouble***	Jerome Park, New York	June 10, 1875
Shirley – Resolute	Pimlico, Maryland	October 28, 1876
Basil – Cloverbrook	Jerome Park, New York	June 18, 1877
Rappahannock – Kilburn	Pimlico, Maryland	October 26, 1877
Jake – Madge Duke	San Francisco, California	November 29, 1877

Contestants	Location	Date
Mollie McCarthy - Jake	Sacramento, California	March 2, 1878
Ten Broeck - Mollie McCarthy	Louisville, Kentucky	July 4, 1878
Spartan - Bramble	Monmouth Park, New Jersey	July 6, 1878
Rocco - Fibbertigibbet	Jerome Park, New York	June 10, 1879
Jallop - Kester	Riverside, California	June 22, 1880
Luke Blackburn - Uncas	Sheepshead Bay, Long Island, New York	September 14, 1880
Maggie May - Lilla G.	Dallas, Texas	November 22, 1880
Marathon - Geranium	Jerome Park, New York	June 4, 1881
Geranium - Marathon	Sheepshead Bay, Long Island, New York	June 23 1881
Onondaga - Sachem	Sheepshead Bay, Long Island, New York	June 25, 1881
Eole - Getaway	Saratoga Springs, New York	August 12, 1881
Hiawasse - Memento	Monmouth Park, New Jersey	August 20, 1881
Crickmore - Hindoo	Sheepshead Bay, Long Island, New York	September 17,1881
Sisterly - Clifton Bell	Denver, Colorado	April 29, 1882
Ida - Duke of Montrose	Monmouth Park, New Jersey	May 3, 1882
Pearl Jennings - Cinderella	Denver, Colorado	May 6, 1882
Red Boy - Wildmoor	Salt Lake City, Utah	June, 17, 1882
Wildmoor - Euchre	Salt Lake City, Utah	July 5, 1882
Corsair - Hospodar	Monmouth Park, New Jersey	July 8, 1882
Pearl Jennings - Maria F.	Salt Lake City, Utah	July 17, 1882
Longstride - Belle of the West	Salt Lake City, Utah	July 19, 1882
Pearl Jennings - Red Boy	Salt Lake City, Utah	July 22, 1882
Wildmoor - Red Boy	Salt Lake City, Utah	August 2, 1882
Vampire - Hospodar	Monmouth Park, New Jersey	August 2, 1882
Adams Mare - Jim Douglas	Sacramento, California	May 21, 1883
Premium- Kelpie	Sacramento, California	Sept. 15, 1883
Pitchfork Johnnie - Tom Green	Trinidad, Colorado	June 3, 1884
East Lynne - Cricket	Monmouth Park, New Jersey	July 24, 1884
Wallflower - Eulogy	Saratoga Springs, New York	August 2, 1884
Miss Woodford - Drake Carter	Sheepshead Bay, Long Island, New York	September 18, 1884
Marmosette - Sungleam	Lexington, Kentucky	November 18, 1884
Dundee - Hobson's Choice	Jerome Park, New York	May 28, 1885
General Harding - Shelby Barnes	Brighton Beach, Long Island, New York	June 19, 1885
Miss Woodford - Freeland	Monmouth Park, New Jersey	August 20, 1885
Blue Bird - Lela B	Fort Worth, Texas	November 20, 1885
Billy Johnson - Albemarle	San Francisco, California	January 9, 1886
Boomerang - Red Girl	Denver, Colorado	May 26 1886
Volante - Tyrant*	St. Louis, Mo.	June 17, 1886
Troubadour - Miss Woodford	Coney Island, New York	June 29, 1886
Salvatore - Tenny	Sheepshead Bay, Long Island, New York	June 25, 1890
Long Street - Tenny	Morris Park, New York	August 1, 1891
Kingston - Van Buren	Garfield Park, Chicago, Illinois	August 31, 1891
Domino - Dobbins^^	Sheepshead Bay, Long Island, New York	August 31, 1893
Domino - Henry of Navarre^^	Gravesend, Brooklyn, New York	September 15, 1894
Cleophas - Suisun	Churchill Downs, Louisville, Kentucky	May 14, 1896
Admiration - May Hempstead	Sheepshead Bay, Long Island, New York	July 1, 1899

*Walkover; ** Over Hurdles; *** Steeplechase; ^ Winning owner took loser's horse; ^^ Dead Heat*

MATCH RACES SINCE 1900

Winner	Age	Wt.	Winrs Lead	Second	Age	Wt.	Track	Distance	Date	Net Value	Time
Ethelbert	4	126	10	Jean Bereud	4	126	Gravesend	1 1/4 m	June 2 1900	$6,005	2:08 1/5
End'ce by Right	2	112	1	Heno	2	115	Gravesend	about 6f	Sept. 28 1901	1,775	1:08 3/5
Dick Welles	3	112	1	Grand Opera	4	115	Harlem	1 m	Aug. 14 1903	1,000	1:37 2/5
Novelty	2	122	3	Textile	2	122	Saratoga	6 f	Aug. 17 1910	5,005	1:13 1/5
Iron Mask	6	115	5	Pan Zereta	4	110	Juarez	6 f	Jan. 4 1914	400	1:09 3/5
Hourless	3	126	1	Omar Khayyam	3	126	Laurel	1 1/4 m	Oct. 18 1917	10,200	2:02
Eternal	2	122	head	Billy Kelly	2	122	Laurel	6 f	Oct. 28 1918	20,000	1:12
Man O' War	3	120	7	Sir Barton	4	126	Kenilworth	1 1/4 m	Oct. 12 1920	80,000*	2:03
Zev	3	126	5	Papyrus	3	126	Belmont	1 1/2 m	Oct. 20 1923	85,000*	2:35 2/5
Sarazen	2	118	2	Happy Thoughts	2	115	Laurel	6 f	Oct. 26 1923	15,025	1:14

Winner	Age	Wt.	Winrs Lead	Second	Age	Wt.	Track	Distance	Date	Net Value	Time
Zev	3	126	nose	In Memoriam	4	115	Churchill	1 1/4 m	Nov. 17 1923	25,000	2:06 3/5
Marietta	3	105	2 1/2	Liberty	4	114	Smithville, Mo.	1 1/16 m	Sept. 30 1927	500	1:54 3/5
Winooka	5	120	4 1/2	Onrush	3	105	Longacres	6 f	Sept. 16 1933	5,000	1:14
Dirigible	4	112	4	Suitor	9	117	Agua Caliente	6 f	April 14 1935	400	1:12 3/5
Myrtlewood	3	110	nose	Clang	3	110	Hawthorne	6 f	Sept. 25 1935	2,000	1:10 4/5
Clang	3	110	nose	Myrtlewood	3	110	Coney Island	6 f	Oct. 12 1935	2,000	1:09 1/5
Myrtlewood	4	118	3	Miss Merriment	5	118	Keeneland	6 f	Oct. 24 1936	No Purse	1:11 4/5
Rought Time	3	108	2	Appealing	3	115	Suffolk	6 f	Aug. 14 1937	1,000	1:10 2/5
Seabiscuit	5	130	nose	Ligaroti	6	115	Del Mar	1 1/8 m	Aug. 12 1938	25,000	1:49
Sky Pirate	5	111	1 1/2	Susi Q	3	107	Longacres	6 f	Sept. 18 1938	No Purse	1:10 3/5
Seabiscuit	5	120	4	War Admiral	4	120	Pimlico	1 3/16 m	Nov. 1 1938	15,000	1:56 3/5
Little Cartago	2	122	3	Mar Quick	2	122	Agua Caliente	4 f	May 7 1939	500	:46 4/5
Unerring	3	110	2	Flying Lill	3	110	Wash. Park	1 m	Aug. 31 1939	6,250	1:37 4/5
Beaver Lake	8	112	1 1/2	Miss Monte	5	107	Fairmont	6 f	June 5 1940	Gold Cup	1:13 3/5
Annibal	7	140	1 1/2	Ossabaw	6	140	Belmont	abt 2 m	June 6 1940	3,000	3:41 2/5
Bonnie Sea	5	114	nose	Rushaway	7	114	Agua Caliente	1 1/2 m	June 30 1940	1,000	2:30 3/5
Soup and Fish	4	112	3/4	Betty Main	3	106	Beulah	1 m	Sept. 20 1941	1,000	1:37 4/5
Alsab	2	122	3 1/2	Requested	2	122	Belmont	6 1/2 f	Sept. 23 1941	10,000	1:16
Lee Torch	6	125	nose	Abide	5	125	Agua Caliente	1 m	Oct. 5 1941	700	1:41 2/5
Lee Torch	6	125	7	Abide	5	125	Agua Caliente	1 m	Oct. 12 1941	1,000	1:42
Wise Moss	3	108	2 3/4	Sweet Willow	4	118	Rockingham	6 f	Nov. 2 1941	5,000	1:11 1/5
Wanche	2	110	3	Cabecilla	2	110	Havana	3 f	Feb. 24 1942	2,000	:37 2/5
Sir Winsome	4	115	4	Urge Me	7	115	Agua Caliente	6f	July 19 1942	700	1:12
Lavengro	7	115	2 1/2	Sir Winsome	4	110	Longacres	6 f	Aug. 16 1942	2,005	1:10
Alsab	3	119	nose	Whirlaway	4	126	Narragansett	1 3/16 m	Sept. 19 1942	25,000	1:56 2/5
Grayce P.	2	115	5	Dandy Day	2	118	Mexico City	5 1/2 f	Oct. 12 1944	1,547	1:08
Busher	3	115	3/4	Durazna	4	115	Wash. Park	1 m	Aug. 29 1945	25,000	1:37 4/5
Here's How	2	116	3 1/2	Lady Gunner	2	116	Narragansett	6 f	Sept. 15 1945	7,500	1:12 4/5
Dinner Party	6	120	1	Float Me	5	120	Rockingham	1 1/8 m	Nov. 23 1946	10,000	1:57 3/5
Armed	6	126	8	Assault	4	126	Belmont	1 1/4 m	Sept. 27 1947	100,000	2:02 4/5
Tardado	3	117	4	Pretencioso	3	112	Mexico City	6 f	Feb. 12 1949	No Purse	1:14 1/5
Capot	3	120	12	Coaltown	4	126	Pimlico	1 3/16 m	Oct. 28 1949	15,000	1:56 4/5
Virginia Fair	2	121	1/2	Virden	2	118	Edmonton	abt 5 f	Aug. 15 1952	1,000	1:00 2/5
Coquetona	2	115	1 1/4	Bandara Negra	2	115	Mexico City	4 f	May 15 1954	800	:49
Vicious Vixen	7	113	10	Calolet	8	119	Mexico City	7 1/2 f	May 23 1954	800	1:32 4/5
Manzanero	7	118	3	Katy's Prince	3	112	Mexico City	6 f	Jan. 23 1955	800	1:12 1/5
La Mexicana	2	115	2	Don Nico	2	117	Mexico City	2 f	Feb. 15 1955	650	:22 1/5
Nashua	3	126	6 1/2	Swaps	3	126	Washington	1 1/4 m	Aug. 31 1955	100,000	2:04 1/5
Queen Doris	3	115	12	Molly Darling	4	120	Centennial	5 1/2 f	July 28 1956	2,500	1:05 3/5
Noorahge	4	120	4 1/4	Early Bull	7	120	Wheeling Downs	6 1/2 f	Sept. 14 1957	2,000	1:24
Wildoath	3	108	2 1/4	War Marshal	4	112	Fresno, Calif.	1 1/16 m	Oct. 12 1957	1,200	1:43 3/5
Alumni	3	115	2 1/2	Rogation	5	115	Oriental Park	6 f	Oct. 13 1957	1,000	1:41
Lori Lynn	4	115	1 1/2	Salmon Peter	9	120	Centennial	1 1/4 m	Aug. 22 1959	1,200	2:05
Roman Colonel	4	126	neck	Benedicto	5	115	Detroit	6 f	June 11 1960	12,000	1:10 2/5
Matisse	4	111	1 1/2	Tondi	4	111	Albuquerque	5 1/2 f	Sept. 24 1960	2,000	1:03
Routeen	2	119	8	Modest Step	2	110	Latonia	6 f	Oct. 1 1960	1,000	1:13 3/5
Witchita Maid	4	112	3/4	Gilhooley	5	112	Centennial	5 1/2 f	Aug. 19 1961	1,200	1;04 2/5
Cesca	2	119	5 3/4	Aim n Fire	2	122	Woodbine	5 1/2 f	July 7 1962	15,000	1:04 3/5
Short Nail	2	115	6	Florida Cracker	2	115	Garden State	6 f	Dec. 4 1962	1,500	1:13 2/5
Poplar	3	115	4	Tono	3	115	Mexico City	6 f	March 10 1963	800	1:13 1/5
Try It	8	115	2 3/4	Spinney	10	115	Turf Paradise	1 1/2 m	April 14 1963	2,250	2:30 2/5
Before Sun	2	115	head	Princess Cloud	2	115	Hazel Park	4 f	June 2 1964	No Purse	:47
Over Current	5	115	3 1/2	Golden Briar	5	115	Exhibition	6 f	June 27 1964	1,500	1:13 3/5
Wandering Boy	6	115	2 3/4	Mr. McCoy	5	115	Turf Paradise	2 f	April 11 1965	5,739	:21 2/5
Wandering Boy**	6	118	nose	Air Space	3	118	Turf Paradise	2 f	Dec. 5 1965	4,500	:21 1/5
Nancycee	4	113	1	Nasharco	4	118	Turf Paradise	5 f	Mar. 20 1966	2,500	:56 1/5
Nasharco	4	118	4 3/4	Nancycee	4	113	Turf Paradise	5 1/2 f	April 10 1966	2,500	1:10 1/5
Permano	4	114	7	Frannie	5	114	Exhibition	6 1/2 f	Sept. 7 1966	1,000	1:17
Christopher G.	3	120	neck	Moroni Joe	6	125	Prescott	5 1/2 f	Aug. 27 1967	525	1:06 2/5
Pocomoke	5	120	3	Murata San	6	115	Agua Caliente	6 f	Feb. 2 1969	500	1:11 2/5
Mr. Longwait	6	115	neck	Sunday Cruz	5	115	Thistledown	1 m	Mar. 22 1969	No Purse	1:44
Rowdy Lad	4	115	nose	Tebbad	6	120	Sunland Park	5 f	Mar. 29 1969	No Purse	:59 2/5
Emerald Chief	4	129	5	High Nail	6	140	Shenandoah	3 1/2 f	Nov. 15 1969	1,000	:40
Princess Khal	4	127	1	Off to Market	5	108	Centennial	1 m70 yds	Aug. 16 1970	3,000	1:41 3/4
Convenience	4	120	head	Typecast	6	120	Hollywood	1 1/8 m	June 17 1972	250,000	1:47 3/5

Jovial John	4	115	1	Blunt Man	9	115	Cahokia Downs 5 f	Nov. 16 1972	1,000	1:00 4/5
Ponderosa Jane	5	118	2 1/2	Distant U	6	118	Calder 6 f	Oct. 10 1973	2,000	1:13 2/5
Distant U	6	118	1/2	Ponderosa Jane	5	118	Calder 6 f	Oct. 20 1973	2,000	1:14
Bob Twinklet's**	4	117	1 1/2	Deleterious	4	117	Latonia 1 m	April 4 1974	2,500	1:44 4/5
Chris Evert	3	121	50	Miss Musket	3	121	Hollywood 1 1/4 m	July 20 1974	350,000	2:02
Dennis Beau	5	115	nose	Scottish Time	4	120	Lincoln Downs 1 m	Oct.10 1974	4,000	1:39 3/5
Scottish Time	4	120	1 1/4	Dennis Beau	6	118	Lincoln Downs 1 m	Oct. 17 1974	4,000	1:42 1/5
Foolish Pleasure^	3	126	1	Ruffian	3	121	Belmont Park 1 1/4 m	July 6 1975	225,000	2:02
Jobim	4	121	1 1/4	Bitache	5	121	Mexico City 4 1/2 f	Mar. 7 1976	4,000	:52 4/5
Fleet and Ready	6	120	1 1/2	Moms Freddy	7	120	Agua Caliente 6 f	Dec. 12 1976	5,000	1:10
Keen Traveler	3	114	neck	Graphic Miss	3	114	Centennial 5 f	June 7 1981	6,000	:57 4/5
Mr. McMoose	4	115	nose	Hail Satan	5	115	Agua Caliente 1 1/4 m	June 19 1982	7,500	2:02 3/5
Baltanas	8	115	5	Skillful Look	4	115	Agua Caliente 1 1/2 m	Nov. 23 1985	2,500	2:33
Who Doctor Who	5	125	3 1/2	Explosive Girl	4	120	Ak-Sar-Ben 1 m70 yds	July 23 1988	40,000	1:42
Slash Adder	5	122	4 1/2	Win Your Heart	4	122	Les Bois Park 4 1/2 f	Sept. 18 1988	2,000	:51 2/5

Winner	Second	Track	Distance	Date	Race	Surf
Soviet Problem	Lazor	Golden Gate	6 f	May 12 1994	6	Dirt
Soviet Problem	Mamselle Bebette	Del Mar	5 f	Aug. 21 1994	10	Turf
Busy Banana	Richard Of England	Santa Anita	1 1/2 m	Mar. 23 1996	11	Dirt
Isthataclaimgirl	Calico Rose	Prairie Meadows	6 f	June 24 1996	8	Dirt
Maybe Jack	Pro On Ice	Suffolk	1 m	Dec. 14 1997	7	Dirt
Rosy Way	Howthewestwaswon	Boise	6 1/2 f	July 21 1999	9	Dirt
Call Me Mr. Vain	Diplomatical	Suffolk Downs	6 f	Oct. 22, 2003	6	Dirt
Chester's Choice	Woke Up Dreamin	Del Mar	1 1/16 m	Sep. 7, 2003	4	Dirt

* Includes 5,000 Gold Cup; ** Three-horse match race; On Dec. 5, 1965 at Turf Paradise, Madabet (3), 118 finished 3rd beaten by 2 1/2 length: on April 4, 1974, at Latonia, Quipid (4) 112 finished 3rd, beaten by 1 1/2 lengths. ^ After completing three and one half furlongs, Ruffian broke down and could not finish.

2-HORSE RACES SINCE 1993

Track	Date	Race	Dis	Surf	Winner	Place
PIM	08/06/93	3	1 1/8	D	Sleek N Graceful	Ebonizer
TET	08/28/93	11	7	D	Persuasive Murr	Meritip
FL	11/06/93	1	6	D	Explosive Kiss	Princess Stacy
DEL	07/19/94	5	5	D	Hafef	Don't Blush Doctor
MTH	06/14/95	7	1 1/16	D	November Sunset	Trucking Baron*
MD	08/20/95	3	6 1/2	D	Burst Of Autumn	Butterscotchripple
PIM	09/26/95	6	1 1/16	D	Java Royal	Dr. Chicollini
PRE	08/17/96	2	5 1/2	D	Quintons Fan Club	Darting Garanda
PHA	09/22/96	7	1 1/8	D	Sansue's Castle	Wishful Dream
PHA	09/23/96	8	1M 70Y	D	Manassa Station	Light Crusader
PRE	09/01/97	12	7	D	Tio Saros	Littlefield
DEL	10/25/97	7	1M	D	Select Session	Tote Dancer
PRE	09/07/98	5	5 1/2	D	Real Dancer	Covered Wells
MD	09/13/98	2	1 1/16	D	Rouge Royale	Glue Stick
CNL	09/26/98	9	1 1/8	T	Kerfoot Corner	Poncho Duck
MTH	08/26/99	9	1 1/16	D	Sunny Stutz	Essential
TAM	12/18/99	1	5	D	Belle Of The South	Doasyouaretold
MNR	02/07/00	9	1M 70Y	D	Bow Legged Honey	War Genie
PHA	05/20/00	5	5 1/2F	D	Dark Tag	Bessie
PHA	05/27/00	5	6F	D	Trastevere	Dr. Marvel
MID	10/08/00	4	Ab.3 miles	Timber	Holzmann	IvorgorianNO
WRD	4/15/01	7	2	D	Avenue of Style	Mr. Debernardo
PHA	3/30/01	2	5 1/2	D	Dashing Patriot	Nicks Hope
ATH	4/14/01	5	2 3/8 M	T	Dalton River (CHI)	Crowned Crane
BOI	5/19/01	5	5	D	Im Ok So Far	Hodson
OXM	5/27/01	5	3 M	T	Fast Steppin Man	De Laurentis (CHI)
TIL	8/11/01	4	5	D	Bubba's T K O	Running Justice
YAV	8/13/01	6	1M	D	Spitfire Dancer	Savannah Smiles
SJ	9/16/01	6	5 1/2	D	Cathedral Miss	Huddled
UN	6/8/02	2	5 1/2F	D	Mr Juan Sock	Afta David
PHA	6/15/02	8	1M 70Y	D	Run for Joy	Als Delight
FAX	9/21/02	6	About3M	T	Complete Verdict	Temperence Night
ELP	7/10/03	3	1M	D	Heldinhighesteem	If You Believe
ELK	8/31/03	1	5 1/2F	D	Thats Final	Seanster
DEL	9/23/03	7	6F	D	Boston Common	Sing Me Back Home

*Trucking Baron was placed 1st due to disqualification

Record of Walkovers

The walkover, one of racing's rarities these days, typically consists of a horse going over the course alone as the only starter in a race. The 1997 Bayakoa Handicap, in which only Sharp Cat ran, was the first walkover in a major event since Horse of the Year Spectacular Bid concluded his career with a solo gallop under Bill Shoemaker in the 1980 Woodward at Belmont Park. Prior to that, the last walkover in a major event came in 1949 when Coaltown faced no rivals in the Edward Burke Handicap at Havre de Grace.

Another kind of walkover is a race in which the horses competing all belong to the same interest or individual. The last known instance of this extreme oddity occurred in 1943 when stablemates Azogue Speed and Clara C. were the only entrants in the Juvenile Debut Stakes at Havana in Cuba.

Walkovers since 1913

Horse	Name of Stakes where applicable	Track	Date
Web Carter	Gracefield Cup Steeplechase	Great Neck, NY	Nov. 8, 1913
Roamer	Autumn Stakes	Belmont Park, NY	Sep. 19, 1914
Napier		Saratoga, NY	Aug. 13, 1915
Purchase	Jockey Club Stakes	Belmont Park, NY	Sep. 13, 1919
Reliance		Belmont Park Term	May 22, 1920
Royce Rools	Gramatan Handicap	Empire City, NY	Jly. 15, 1921
Exterminator	Saratoga Cup	Saratoga, NY	Aug. 31, 1921
Doublet		Belmont Park Term	Sep. 1, 1921
Millwick	Hempstead Highweight Handicap	Belmont Park, NY	May 24, 1927
Saguenay	King's Plate	Blue Bonnets, Que	Aug. 5, 1927
Maelstrom	Waverly Purse	Saratoga, NY	Sep. 2, 1927
Crack Willow	United Hunts Double Event (2nd)	Belmont Park, NY	Nov. 5, 1929
Questionnaire	Mount Kisco Stakes	Empire City, NY	Jly. 23, 1930
Awake *(entrymate of Questionnaire)*			
Little Nap	West Point Claiming Handicap	Empire City, NY	Oct. 29, 1930
Sun Meadow	Sysonby Purse	Belmont Park, NY	Jun. 9, 1931
Pilate	Waterboy Handicap	Saratoga, NY	Aug. 14, 1933
St. Francis	Old Glory Steeplechase Handicap	Aqueduct, NY	Jly. 2, 1936
Isolater	Saratoga Cup	Saratoga, NY	Aug. 31, 1940
Fenelon *(entrymate of Isolater)*			
Whirlaway	Pimlico Special	Pimlico, MD	Oct. 28, 1942
Azogue Speed	Juvenile Debut Stakes	Havana, Cuba	Jan. 31, 1943
Clara C. *(entrymate of Azogue Speed)*			
Star of Padula		Jamaica, NY	Apr. 10, 1944
Stymie	Saratoga Cup	Saratoga, NY	Aug. 31, 1946
Casa Camara	Diamond Ring Stakes	Long Branch, Ont	Oct. 26, 1946
Canada's Teddy	King's Plate Trial	Blue Bonnets, Que	Jly. 21, 1948
Citation	Pimlico Special	Pimlico, MD	Oct. 29, 1948
Coaltown	Edward Burke Handicap	Havre de Grace, MD	Apr. 23, 1949
Foxy Fighter	The Colonel Purse	Oxmoor, KY	Jun. 2, 1956
Appointed Hour	H.P. Stewart Memorial Challenge Cup	Media, PA	Oct. 13, 1962
Spectacular Bid	Woodward Stakes (G1)	Belmont Park, NY	Sep. 20, 1980
Chinese Export		Ligonier, PA	Sep. 18, 1982
Hawa		Middleburg, VA	Oct. 5, 1986
Quico		Middleburg, VA	Oct. 5, 1986
Alylad		Marquis Downs, Sask	Oct. 4, 1992
Impatient You		Atokad Park, NE	Jly. 2, 1995
Sharp Cat	Bayakoa Handicap (G2)	Hollywood Park, CA	Dec. 7, 1997
Young Dubliner		Foxfield, VA	Sep. 27, 1998

Triple Dead-Heats for Win

The most famous triple dead-heat to win in North American racing came in the 1944 running of the Carter Handicap at Aqueduct on June 10, when Brownie, Bossuet and Wait a Bit were deadlocked at the end of the seven-furlong event run over a sloppy track.

Triple dead-heats for win since 1940

Date	Track	Winners		
Sep. 21, 1940	Willows Park	My Debut	Margery Daw	Saucy Maid
Oct. 6, 1942	Detroit Fairgrounds	Sabra	Cutloose	Queen Echo
Jun. 10, 1944	Aqueduct	Brownie	Bossuet	Wait a Bit
Oct. 3, 1945	Wheeling Downs	Second Thought	Idle Knight	Palkin
Oct. 22, 1955	Caliente Race Track	Stormsorno	Beaufair	Chance Speed
Jly. 3, 1957	Hollywood Park	Joe's Pleasure	Challenger Tom	Leaful
Aug. 10, 1963	Arlington Park	Royal Redress	Livingston	Mr. S. Chance
Nov. 18, 1965	Sportsman's Park	Paddy o' Rock	Me Willwin	Miss Brendy
Aug. 27, 1966	Fairmount Park	Noholts Bard	Turn Tattle	Off Short
Sep. 5, 1966	Scarborough Downs	Around the Moon	Gold Bomb	Rebel Cheer
May 2, 1968	Beulah Park	Payola Joy	City Market	Equicharge
Mar. 22, 1974	Latonia	Deleterious	Quipid	Bob Twinkletoes
Feb. 9, 1975	Sunland Park	Flying Envoy	Ronny J.	Reserve Clause
Jun. 11, 1980	Santa Fe Downs	Pantaroni	Prince Kukui	Iron Hulk
Jun. 17, 1980	Northlands Park	Anne Ivers	Slightly Shady	Naughty Cage
Nov. 9, 1980	Sunland Park	Moon Barb	Teddy's Table	Grins Spirit
Oct. 23, 1981	Lincoln (Neb)	I Will Be	One Way	El Lark Rise
Dec. 31, 1981	Suffolk Downs	Great Combination	Dawn's Count	Needachant
May 20, 1990	Arlington	All Worked Up	Marshua's Affair	Survival
Oct. 7, 1991	Belmont Park	Space Appeal	Scorecard Harry	Cafe Lex
May 12, 1996	Yakima Meadows	Terri After Five	Allihavonztheradio	Fly Like a Angel
Dec. 7, 1997	Hollywood Park	Tina Celesta	Chans Pearl	Cool Miss Ann

Steeplechase and Hurdle Racing – 2003

By KAREN M. JOHNSON

McDynamo made the most of his three starts in 2003, and his flawless performances in the country's most important jump races earned him the Eclipse Award as the top steeplechase horse.

McDynamo, a 6-year-old gelding, won three Grade 1's: the Royal Chase Hurdle at Keeneland on April 25; the Breeders' Cup Steeplechase at Far Hills, N.J. on Oct. 19; and the Marion du Pont Scott Colonial Cup at Springdale Race Course in Camden, S.C. on Nov. 16. His combined margin of victory in those races was 26 3/4 lengths.

Heading into his final race of the season, the Colonial Cup, McDynamo had appeared to have sewn up the championship with his 15 1/4-length win in the Breeders' Cup four weeks earlier. If there were any doubts, McDynamo put them to rest with his four-length win in course-record time in the Colonial Cup. McDynamo covered the distance in 5:05.40 for the 2 3/4 miles over 17 fences.

Trained by Sanna Hendriks, McDynamo is owned by Michael Moran. Moran bought the son of Dynaformer as a yearling at Keeneland and ran him on the flat before switching him to the jumps in 2001. Craig Thornton was aboard for each of McDynamo's wins in 2003.

McDynamo topped the year-end earnings list with $252,025, which is $104,537 more than the runner-up, Trebizond, who won a pair of Grade 1 races for novices, the Hard Scuffle at Churchill Downs and the Meadow Brook at Belmont Park.

Other Grade 1 winners in 2003 were Praise the Prince, winner of the New York Turf Writers Handicap at Saratoga; Pelagos, who won the Iroquois at Percy Warner Park in Nashville; and Al Skywalker, the winner of the Carolina Cup at Springdale Race Course.

Hendriks, who is married to fellow steeplechase trainer, Ricky Hendriks, led trainers in money won for the second time in three years with $587,907 in earnings. In addition to McDynamo, Hendriks also trained Praise the Prince. Jack Fisher topped trainers in races won with 25 victories for his first year-end title.

George Strawbridge, whose horses run in the name of Augustin Stables, led owners in purses won for a record 22nd time with $335,882.

David Bentley and Matthew McCarron shared the riding title with 16 wins apiece. The title was the second for Bentley and the first for McCarron, who is the nephew of Hall of Fame flat jockey Chris McCarron. Tom Foley earned his first title by leading riders in money won with $543,605.

FOREIGN RACING

Year in Review

Timeform Ratings

International Classifications

Stakes Histories

2003 Stakes Results

2003 Leaders

Major European Track Profiles

Racing in Europe – 2003

By Alan Shuback

While lacking the fireworks provided in recent years by Rock Of Gibraltar, Johannesburg, Sakhee or Sinndar, the 2003 European season threw up more than its fair share of thrills through some very solid efforts by Dalakhani, Alamshar, Falbrav, Oasis Dream and Bago.

The absence of a clear-cut champion was reflected in the questionable choice of Hawk Wing as the highweight on the International Classification. His single 11-length romp in a subpar Lockinge Stakes in which every other horse was running well below his best not only calls the criteria and the judgment of the Classification Committee into question, but also denied the very deserving Dalakhani of his well-deserved distinction as the best horse to race in Europe in 2003.

A product of the Aga Khan's superb breeding operation, Dalakhani faltered just once in six starts, that when his talented but cocksure young rider Christophe Soumillon sent him to the front too soon in the Irish Derby, thus allowing another of the Aga Khan's proteges, Alamshar, to snatch the victory.

Those two dominated the mile and a half scene, Dalakhani having earlier won the Prix du Jockey-Club (French Derby) and later following with an impressive score in the Prix de l'Arc de Triomphe. Alamshar would next trounce Sulamani, Epsom Derby winner Kris Kin, and Falbrav in the King George VI and Queen Elizabeth Diamond Stakes, and while he didn't win after that, he was clearly in the same league as Dalakhani.

Trained in France by Alain de Royer-Dupre, Dalakhani was lauded after his rather handy three-quarter length Arc win over the ever-improving Mubtaker as one of the best horses in memory. He was not quite that but the Darshaan colt did merit the 2003 world championship. Sadly, for the racing game but happily for the breeding world, he was retired a week after the Arc to stand at the Aga Khan's Stud in Ireland for a fee of 45,000 euros ($56,000).

At about the same time, the Aga announced that Alamshar, who first sidestepped the Arc to avoid another conflict with Dalakhani, and then was rerouted from the Canadian International to the Champion Stakes, had been sold to stand in Japan. The late season shenanigans of the John Oxx-trained Irish-bred proves that even a top-class outfit like that of the Aga Khan's can mismanage a campaign, or at least the tail end of one.

Alamshar's last two runs were unplaced efforts over an inadequate 10 furlongs in the Irish Champion Stakes and the Newmarket equivalent. A run by the Key of Luck colt in the Breeders' Cup Turf over his preferred mile and a half might have given a different look to everyone's year-end analyses.

The dominance that we have come to expect from the yards of Aidan O'Brien and Saeed bin Suroor was missing in 2003 as they both found the Group 1 winners' enclosure a more difficult club to crack. Godolphin did win the Dubai World Cup on its home ground at Nad Al Sheba with Moon Ballad and the Grosser Preis von Baden with second stringer Mamool, but it was the far-flung empire of Khalid Abdullah which posted a most remarkable succession of international triumphs at the top level.

The Saudi prince has long played his racing cards for the highest stakes. Racing a stable that, like the Aga Khan's, consists exclusively of home-breds, Abdullah, winner of Eclipse Awards as both leading owner and breeder, led the owners' lists in both Britain and France, narrowly beating out the Aga Khan on the final day of the French season. His totals in Britain, France and Ireland showed 139 victories from 607 starts, a .229 win percentage for earnings of $6,180,259. Added to his 33 North American tallies in 122 starts for $6,265,030, the Juddmonte juggernaut went 172-for-729 in the world's four most highly competitive markets for earnings of $12,445,289. That comes to an average of $17,071 per start.

In America, where Bobby Frankel routinely provides a smooth entry into graded race company for Juddmonte's European imports, Abdullah had Grade 1 winners in Aldebaran, Empire Maker, Heat Haze, Megahertz and Tates Creek. In France, Andre Fabre engineered Nebraska Tornado's victories in the Prix de Diane (French Oaks) and the Prix du Moulin de Longchamp, while Criquette Head-Maarek trained American Post to win the Prix Jean-Luc Lagardere (formerly the Grand Criterium) prior to sending him to Doncaster to land the Racing Post Trophy.

In England, Oasis Dream, trained for Prince Khalid by John Gosden, proved himself to be the smartest sprinter seen in Europe since Dayjur's championship season in 1990. His victory in the July Cup over Australia's two-time Royal Ascot sprint winner Choisir established the 2002 European juvenile champ as Europe's leading sprinter. His Nunthorpe Stakes win, achieved in the most impressive manner and in just .04 seconds off Dayjur's York track record for five furlongs, briefly had people talking of the Green Desert colt as a horse of the year candidate.

The classic season in Europe, i.e., the series of Guineas, Derbies and Oaks that run from late April through mid-July, produced Dalakhani and Alamshar from the top drawer in the Derby category, as well as German Derby winner Dai Jin, who cannot be rated too far behind. However, with the exception of 1000 Guineas winner Russian Rhythm, there was a sense of equality about the rest of the classic generation.

Michael Stoute did not present Russian Rhythm for her seasonal debut until May 4 at Newmarket when she held off a late rush by the unlucky Six Perfections to land the 1000 Guineas. The Kingmambo filly followed with a sharp score at Royal Ascot in the Coronation Stakes before stepping up to 10 furlongs to beat older fillies in the Nassau Stakes. Her second-place finish behind Falbrav in the Queen Elizabeth II Stakes only added luster to her accomplishments.

But in the long run, Six Perfections probably had an edge on Russian Rhythm and must certainly rate higher than 2000 Guineas winner Refuse to Bend. After her luckless run at Newmarket, the Pascal Bary-trained daughter of Celtic Swing was an unfortunate nose second to Yesterday in the Irish 1000 Guineas. Following yet another runner-up finish in the Prix d'Astarte, this time to the very good 4-year-old filly Bright Sky, Bary must have been wondering what it would take to get his talented filly into the winners' circle again.

Six Perfections rose to the occasion with a game neck score over stablemate and defending Breeders' Cup Mile champ Domedriver in Deauville's Prix Jacques le Marois. Bary then gambled on holding her out of action for 10 weeks prior to the Mile. His patience was rewarded as she turned in a career-best effort to win under new rider Jerry Bailey.

Somehow, this brilliant filly was overlooked by both the mavens on the International Classification Committee and the voters for the Eclipse Awards. Six Perfections, who will race again in 2004, may be one of the best horses not to win a championship in the last half-century.

Casual Look's victory in the English Oaks was more noteworthy for the fact that she is owned by Will Farish, America's ambassador to Great Britain. It was a banner year for Farish on both sides of the Atlantic. His Mineshaft, a mere maiden winner in England in 2002, was Horse of the Year in North America, while Place Rouge won the Group 3 Lancashire Oaks for Mineshaft's former trainer, John Gosden.

Casual Look, however, never recaptured the form that gave her the Oaks by a neck from Yesterday. And that Aidan O'Brien-trained full sister to the three-time classic runner-up Quarter Moon was even more unlucky than Six Perfections. After her Irish 1000 Guineas heroics, Yesterday was winless in five starts, finishing a close second in both the Prix Vermeille (to Mezzo Soprano) and the Prix de l'Opera (to Zee Zee Top) before chasing home Islington and stablemate L'Ancresse in the Breeders' Cup Filly & Mare Turf.

Islington was without question the best older filly or mare in Europe in 2003. While her one-length victory over Ocean Silk in the Yorkshire Oaks was less than convincing, it was her second

straight in that mile and a half Group 1. She was at her best when a fast-closing third behind High Chaparral and Falbrav, beaten just a neck and a head, in the Irish Champion Stakes, but concluded her career with an unplaced effort in the Japan Cup without ever having won a race against colts, something Six Perfections has already done twice at the Group 1 level.

Like Nebraska Tornado, who beat older colts in the Prix du Moulin de Longchamp, fillies and mares have long been rather successful against males in European Group 1s, simply because there have been so few such races restricted to their sex. In future years we may be seeing fewer distaffers winning races against older colts and horses. The European Pattern Race Committee has embarked on a program to upgrade races for fillies and mares, from the listed level up to Group 1s. One of the reasons for this move is an effort, especially on the part of the British Horseracing Board, to stem the steady flow of fillies from Europe to America. With more good races restricted to females in Europe, it is believed that the dollars of American owners will be less appealing to European owners of fillies who are racing for relatively low purses at home.

To a certain extent, European racing will always be at the mercy of richer nations like America and Japan, simply because of the relative amounts of prize money available. Europe not only lost Alamshar to stud duty in Japan, it also lost the redoubtable Falbrav.

The 4-year-old Irish-bred son of Fairy King was perhaps the most accomplished horse in the world in 2003. He was certainly the best at 10 furlongs, counting the Eclipse Stakes, the Juddmonte International and the Hong Kong Cup among his five Group 1 tallies.

Had he not been squeezed out of the Irish Champion Stakes by High Chaparral, Falbrav would have claimed the distinction of having won Group 1 races in five different countries, as he had also won the 1 1/8-mile Prix d'Ispahan at Chantilly. He also just failed to last 12 furlongs when beaten a head by High Chaparral and Johar in the Breeders' Cup Turf. An impressive example of Thoroughbred horseflesh, Falbrav was as sound as a bell throughout his racing career and could become the replacement the Japanese breeding industry has been seeking since the death of Sunday Silence.

On the European 2-year-old front, the late season program in France again appears to have produced the leading contender for classic glory in 2004. The remarkable six-length cakewalk of Bago in the one-mile Group 1 Criterium International at Saint-Cloud on Nov. 1 was the best performance by a 2-year-old anywhere in the world. Trained by Jonathan Pease for the Niarchos Family, the undefeated Nashwan colt looks set to follow in the footsteps of last year's Criterium International winner, Dalakhani.

Khalid Abdullah appears ready for a 2004 campaign that could be the equal of his glorious 2003 season. Three Valleys is a prominent 2000 Guineas candidate despite having been stripped of his victory in the Middle Park Stakes due to a drug positive.

Even more promising for Juddmonte is American Post. The Criquette Head-Maarek-trained son of Bering was explosive in winning the 7-furlong Prix Jean-Luc Lagardere (formerly the Grand Criterium) by four lengths at Longchamp on Oct. 5. He followed that just 20 days later with a 1 3/4-length score in the one-mile Racing Post Trophy at Doncaster. American Post has the speed necessary to win the Poule d'Essai des Poulains (French 2000 Guineas) and the breeding to win races like the Grand Prix de Paris at 1 1/4 miles, although a European Derby might be a bit too long for him.

Aidan O'Brien will take the Guineas route with One Cool Cat, a Storm Cat colt who landed a pair of Group 1's in the 6-furlong Phoenix Stakes and the 7-furlong National Stakes. Milk It Mick, trained by ex-jump jockey Jamie Osborne, concluded a 12-race juvenile campaign with a neck victory over Three Valleys in the 7-furlong Dewhurst Stakes and is another leading Guineas candidate, as is 7-furlong Group 2 Champagne Stakes winner Lucky Story.

Attraction, trained like Lucky Story in England by Mark Johnston, was the highweight juvenile filly on the European Classification, on which she was rated just two pounds beneath Bago and on equal terms with Grey Swallow, the Dermot Weld-trained Daylami colt who won his only two races by a combined 17 lengths, the second of them coming in the Group 3 Killavullan Stakes. Attraction capped a perfect five-for-five season with a last-to-first five-length romp in the Group 2 Cherry Hinton Stakes in July but later suffered a cracked pedal bone. If she recovers fully she could challenge Denebola in one of the myriad Group 1 miles for 3-year-old fillies.

On a purely international front, the ever-increasing influence upon American racing of foreign imports and foreign invaders demands attention.

European invaders High Chaparral and Islington both won Eclipse Awards in 2003, and Six Perfections was denied the 3-year-old filly title by just two votes. European re-imports Mineshaft and Aldebaran were also Eclipse Award winners while

juvenile filly champ Halfbridled is a homebred owned by the French-based Wertheimer Brothers.

Add Group 1 winners like the Argentine-bred Candy Ride and the Chilean-bred Wild Spirit, plus major winners like Dimitrova and the first three finishers from the French 1000 Guineas - Musical Chimes, Maiden Tower and Etoile Montante - all of whom ran in the Matriarch Stakes, and a disturbing picture emerges.

American racing and breeding continues to lose ground to its foreign rivals, be they European, Arab or Japanese. Not only does the Japanese breeding industry pick up the services of Falbrav and Alamshar, outfits like Coolmore Stud, Juddmonte Farms, Flaxman Holdings, Wertheimer & Frere, Ecurie Wildenstein, Darley, Shadwell and Gainsborough are producing the lines of Thoroughbred power which once lay in the hands of the Phippses, Whitneys, Vanderbilts, Mellons, Hancocks and Taylors.

If, as Karl Marx theorized, the future will be controlled by those who control the means of production, than the future of racing rests in Newmarket, County Kildare, Chantilly, Hokkaido and those regions of Kentucky that have been colonized by foreign breeding interests. That surmise is illuminated by a comparison of the relative merits of Europe's 3-year-old champion, the Aga Khan's Irish-bred Dalakhani, who slammed a field of Europe's best older horses in his season finale, the Prix de l'Arc de Triomphe, and his American counterpart, the New York-bred gelding Funny Cide who, in his season finale, was beaten 20 lengths into ninth in America's Arc equivalent, the Breeders' Cup Classic.

If further evidence is required to support this theory, note that seven of the 10 runners in two of America's most important year-end races, the Woodward and the Jockey Club Gold Cup, were either foreign imports or foreign invaders. None of those 10 horses had ever run in a Triple Crown race, an indication that once the foreigners arrive, they tend to knock the American classic generation out of the picture.

The deplorable rise of statebred racing in America, our increasing focus on short-term gain plus our obsessions with exotic and internet wagering have undermined what was until 1980 the strongest racing and breeding industry in the world. Meanwhile, the Arabs, Europeans and Japanese are concentrating on that aspect of the game, quality breeding, that has secured for them the dominant positions in racing's future.

Richest Stakes Races in the World in 2003

Race Rank/Name	Track	Conditions	Purse
1-Dubai World Cup-G1	Nad Al Sheba (UAE)	1/4m(D) 4yo+	$6,000,000
2-Japan Cup-G1	Tokyo (Jpn)	1 1/2m(T) 3yo+	4,403,982
3-Breeders' Cup Classic-G1	**Santa Anita (USA)**	**1 1/4m(D) 3yo+**	**3,668,200**
4-Melbourne Cup Hcp-G1	Flemington (Aus)	2m(T) 3yo+	3,231,960
5-Arima Kinen (Grand Prix)-G1	Nakayama (Jpn)	1 9/16m(T) 3yo+	3,221,892
6-Tokyo Yushun (Japanese Derby)-G1	Tokyo (Jpn)	1 1/2m(T) 3yo	2,919,185
7-Kikuka Sho (Japanese St Leger)-G1	Kyoto (Jpn)	1 7/8m(T) 3yo c&f	2,512,849
8-Epsom Derby-G1	Epsom (GB)	1 1/2m(T) 3yo c&f	2,416,974
9-Autumn Tenno Sho-G1	Tokyo (Jpn)	1 1/4m(T) 3yo+	2,343,922
10-Hong Kong Cup-G1	Sha Tin (HK)	1 1/4m(T) 3yo+	2,318,400
11-Japan Cup Dirt-G1	Tokyo (Jpn)	1 5/16m(D) 3yo+	2,312,657
12-Spring Tenno Sho-G1	Kyoto (Jpn)	2m(T) 4yo+	2,163,885
13-Takarazuka Kinen-G1	Hanshin (Jpn)	1 3/8m(T) 3yo+	2,142,377
14-W S Cox Plate-G1	Moonee Valley (Aus)	1 1/4m,65y(T) 3yo+	2,128,194
15-Dubai Duty Free-G1	Nad Al Sheba (UAE)	1 1/8m(T) 4yo+	2,000,000
15-Dubai Golden Shaheen-G1	Nad Al Sheba (UAE)	6f(D) 4yo+	2,000,000
15-Dubai Sheema Classic-G1	Nad Al Sheba (UAE)	1 1/2m(T) 4yo+	2,000,000
15-UAE Derby-G2	Nad Al Sheba (UAE)	1 1/4m(D) 3yo	2,000,000
19-Yushun Himba (Japanese Oaks)-G1	Tokyo (Jpn)	1 1/2m(T) 3yo f	1,957,557
20-Satsuki Sho (Japanese 2000 Guineas)-G1	Nakayama (Jpn)	1m(T) 3yo	1,950,099
21-Breeders' Cup Turf-G1	**Santa Anita (USA)**	**1 1/2m(T) 3yo+**	**1,944,040**
22-Prix de l'Arc de Triomphe-G1	Longchamp (Fr)	1 1/2m(T) 3yo+ c&f	1,874,880
23-Breeders' Cup Distaff-G1	**Santa Anita (USA)**	**1 1/8m(D) 3yo+ f&m**	**1,834,000**
24-Golden Slipper Stakes-G1	Rosehill (Aus)	6f(T) 2yo	1,825,785
25-Hong Kong Mile-G1	Sha Tin (HK)	1m(T) 3yo+	1,803,200
25-Hong Kong Sprint-G1	Sha Tin (HK)	5f(T) 3yo+	1,803,200
25-Hong Kong Vase-G1	Sha Tin (HK)	1 1/2m(T) 3yo+	1,803,200
28-Hong Kong Derby-G1	Sha Tin (HK)	1 1/2m(T) 4yo	1,794,800
28-Queen Elizabeth II Cup-G1	Sha Tin (HK)	1 1/4m(T) 4yo+	1,794,800
30-Oka Sho (Japanese 1000 Guineas)-G1	Hanshin (Jpn)	1m(T) 3yo f	1,751,614
31-Caulfield Cup-G1	Caulfield (Aus)	1 1/2m(T) 3yo+	1,738,871
32-Mile Championship-G1	Kyoto (Jpn)	1m(T) 3yo+	1,691,807
33-Sprinters Stakes-G1	Nakayama (Jpn)	6f(T) 3yo+	1,661,288
34-Shuka Sho-G1	Kyoto (Jpn)	1 1/4m(T) 3yo+	1,591,010
35-February Stakes-G1	Nakayama (Jpn)	1 1/8m(T) 4yo+	1,565,622
36-Takamatsunomiya Kinen-G1	Chukyo (Jpn)	6f(T) 4yo+	1,564,746
37-Yasuda Kinen-G1	Tokyo (Jpn)	1m(T) 3yo+	1,564,608
38-NHK Mile Cup-G1	Tokyo (Jpn)	1m(T) 3yo+	1,545,790
39-JBC Classic-G1	Ohi (Jpn)	1 1/4m(D) 3yo+	1,529,150
40-Irish Derby-G1	Curragh (Ire)	1 1/2m(T) 3yo c&f	1,496,950
41-Derby Italiano-G1	Capannelle (Ity)	1 1/2m(T) 3yo c&f	1,426,180
42-Breeders' Cup Juvenile-G1	**Santa Anita (USA)**	**1 1/16m(D) 2yo**	**1,375,500**
42-Breeders' Cup Mile-G1	**Santa Anita (USA)**	**1m(T) 3yo+**	**1,375,500**
44-Prix du Jockey-Club (French Derby)-G1	Chantilly (Fr)	1 1/2m(T) 3yo c&f	1,292,610
45-JBC Sprint-G1	Ohi (Jpn)	6f(D) 3yo+	1,223,320
46-BMW Classic-G1	Rosehill (Aus)	1 1/2m(T) 3yo+	1,219,830
47-King George VI & Queen Elizabeth Diamond Stakes-G1	Ascot (GB)	1 1/2m(T) 3yo+	1,219,275
48-AJC Derby-G1	Randwick (Aus)	1 1/2m(T) 3yo	1,209,800
48-Doncaster Hcp-G1	Randwick (Aus)	1m(T) 3yo+	1,209,800
50-Teio Sho-G1	Ohi (Jpn)	1 1/4m(D) 4yo+	1,152,872

Race Rank/Name	Track	Conditions	Purse
51-Canadian International-G1	**Woodbine (Can)**	1 1/2m(T) 3yo+	**1,136,550**
52-CBC Sho-G2	Chukyo (Jpn)	6f(T) 3yo+	1,149,015
53-Stayers Stakes-G2	Nakayama (Jpn)	2 1/4m(T) 3yo+	1,133,012
54-Mainichi Okan-G2	Tokyo (Jpn)	1 1/8m(T) 3yo+	1,130,669
55-Kyoto Daishoten-G2	Kyoto (Jpn)	1 1/2m(T) 3yo+	1,129,567
56-Irish Champion Stakes-G1	Leopardstown (Ire)	1 1/4m(T) 3yo+	1,110,600
57-Sankei Sho All-Comers-G2	Nakayama (Jpn)	1 3/8m(T) 3yo+	1,105,438
58-Kentucky Derby-G1	**Churchill Downs (USA)**	1 1/4m(D) 3yo	**1,100,200**
59-Breeders' Cup Sprint-G1	**Santa Anita (USA)**	6f(D) 3yo+	**1,082,060**
60-Asahi Hai Futurity Stakes-G1	Nakayama (Jpn)	1m(T) 2yo c&g	1,076,100
61-Hanshin Himba Stakes-G2	Hanshin (Jpn)	1m(T) 3yo+ f&m	1,075,080
62-Hanshin Juvenile Fillies-G1	Hanshin (Jpn)	1m(T) 2yo f	1,067,889
63-Sapporo Kinen-G2	Sapporo (Jpn)	1 1/4m(T) 3yo+	1,049,550
64-Kyoto Kinen-G2	Kyoto (Jpn)	1 3/8m(T) 4yo+	1,049,007
65-Nakayama Kinen-G2	Nakayama (Jpn)	1 1/8m(T) 4yo+	1,048,250
66-Nikkei Shinshun Hai-G2	Kyoto (Jpn)	1 1/2m(T) 4yo+	1,045,769
67-American Jockey Club Cup-G2	Nakayama (Jpn)	1 3/8m(T) 4yo+	1,041,729
68-Nikkei Sho-G2	Nakayama (Jpn)	1 9/16m(T) 4yo+	1,041,303
69-Kinko Sho-G2	Chukyo (Jpn)	1 1/4m(T) 3yo+	1,041,216
70-Swan Stakes-G2	Kyoto (Jpn)	7f(T) 3yo+	1,040,362
71-Copa Republica Argentina Hcp-G2	Tokyo (Jpn)	1 9/16m(T) 3yo+	1,031,784
72-Sankei Osaka Hai-G2	Hanshin (Jpn)	1 1/4m(T) 4yo+	1,030,286
73-Hanshin Daishoten-G2	Hanshin (Jpn)	1 7/8m(T) 4yo+	1,025,714
74-Hong Kong Champions & Chater Cup-G1	Sha Tin (HK)	1 1/2m(T) 3yo+	1,025,600
74-Hong Kong Classic Mile-G1	Sha Tin (HK)	1m(T) 4yo	1,025,600
74-Hong Kong Gold Cup-G1	Sha Tin (HK)	1 1/4m(T) 3yo+	1,025,600
74-Stewards Cup-G1	Sha Tin (HK)	1m(T) 3yo+	1,025,600
78-Arlington Million-G1	**Arlington Park (USA)**	1 1/4m(T) 3yo+	**1,000,000**
78-Belmont Stakes-G1	**Belmont Park (USA)**	1 1/2m(D) 3yo	**1,000,000**
78-Delta Jackpot	**Delta Downs (USA)**	1 1/16m(D) 2yo	**1,000,000**
78-Florida Derby-G1	**Gulfstream Park (USA)**	1 1/8m(D) 3yo	**1,000,000**
78-Godolphin Mile-G2	Nad Al Sheba (UAE)	1m(D) 4yo+	1,000,000
78-Haskell Invitational Hcp-G1	**Monmouth Park (USA)**	1 1/8m(D) 3yo	**1,000,000**
78-Jockey Club Gold Cup-G1	**Belmont Park (USA)**	1 1/4m(D) 3yo+	**1,000,000**
78-Preakness Stakes-G1	**Pimlico (USA)**	1 3/16m(D) 3yo	**1,000,000**
78-Santa Anita Hcp-G1	**Santa Anita (USA)**	1 1/4m(D) 4yo+	**1,000,000**
78-Travers Stakes-G1	**Saratoga (USA)**	1 1/4m(D) 3yo	**1,000,000**
88-Keio Hai Spring Cup-G2	Tokyo (Jpn)	7f(T) 4yo+	983,840
89-Pacific Classic-G1	**Del Mar (USA)**	1 1/4m(D) 3yo+	**980,000**
90-Breeders' Cup Filly & Mare Turf-G1	**Santa Anita (USA)**	1 1/4m(T) 3yo+ f&m	**972,020**
91-Grosser Preis von Baden-G1	Baden-Baden (Ger)	1 1/2m(T) 3yo+	966,222
92-Meguro Kinen Hcp-G2	Tokyo (Jpn)	1 9/16m(T) 3yo+	960,892
93-Hai Tokai Stakes-G2	Chukyo (Jpn)	1 7/16m(D) 3yo+	960,036
94-Yomiuri Milers Cup-G2	Hanshin (Jpn)	1m(T) 4yo+	958,534
95-Kobe Shimbun Hai-G2	Hanshin (Jpn)	1 1/4m(T) 3yo c&f	944,189
96-Japanese St Leger Trial-G2	Nakayama (Jpn)	1 3/8m(T) 3yo	936,568
97-Mile Championship Nambu Hai-G1	Morioka (Jpn)	1m(D) 3yo+	936,258
98-Breeders' Cup Juvenile Fillies-G1	**Santa Anita (USA)**	1 1/16m(D) 2yo f	**917,000**
99-Derby Grand Prix-G1	Morioka (Jpn)	1 1/4m(D) 3yo	908,616
100-Kyoto Shimbun Hai-G2	Kyoto (Jpn)	1 3/8m(T) 3yo	898,592

Bold-faced type indicates races in North America.

2003 Timeform Ratings

2-YEAR-OLDS

Horse	Rating	Horse	Rating	Horse	Rating
Bago (Fr)	121p	f-Denebola (USA)	113p	Simplex (Fr)	110
Milk It Mick (GB)	120	Imperial Stride (GB)	113p	f-Carry On Katie (USA)	109p
Lucky Story (USA)	119p	Fantastic View (USA)	113	Duke Of Venice (USA)	109p
Three Valleys (USA)	119	f-Much Faster (Ire)	113	Azarole (Ire)	109
American Post (GB)	118p	Nevisian Lad (GB)	113	Barbajuan (Ire)	109
One Cool Cat (USA)	118p	Voix du Nord (Fr)	113	Moscow Ballet (Ire)	109
f-Attraction (GB)	118	Wathab (Ire)	113	Mutahayya (Ire)	109
Whipper (USA)	118	Magritte (Ire)	112p	Old Deuteronomy (USA)	109
Balmont (USA)	117	Grand Reward (USA)	112	Rule Of Law (USA)	109
Grey Swallow (Ire)	116p	f-Green Noon (Fr)	112	Top Seed (Ire)	109
Majestic Missile (Ire)	116p	Peak To Creek (GB)	112	Azamour (Ire)	108p
Bayeux (USA)	116	Pearl Of Love (Ire)	112	Boogie Street (GB)	108p
Bachelor Duke (USA)	115p	Apsis (GB)	111p	Charming Prince (Ire)	108
Diamond Green (Fr)	115p	Snow Ridge (Ire)	111p	f-Majestic Desert (GB)	108
Haafhd (GB)	115¶	Byron (GB)	111	Tahreeb (Fr)	108
Fokine (USA)	115	Chineur (Fr)	111	The Mighty Tiger (USA)	108
Holborn (UAE)	115	Howick Falls (USA)	111	f-Punctilious (GB)	107p
Russian Valour (Ire)	115	Spirit Of Desert (Ire)	111	f-Sundrop (Jpn)	107p
Auditorium (GB)	114	f-Latice (Ire)	110p	f-Nyramba (GB)	107
Colossus (Ire)	114	Pastoral Pursuits (GB)	110p	Relaxed Gesture (Ire)	107
Kheleyf (USA)	114	f-Red Bloom (GB)	110p	Sabbeeh (USA)	107
Troubadour (Ire)	114	Cape Fear (GB)	110		

3-YEAR-OLDS

Horse	Rating	Horse	Rating	Horse	Rating
Alamshar (Ire)	133	Super Celebre (Fr)	121	Balestrini (Ire)	117
Dalakhani (Ire)	133	f-Airwave (GB)	120	Checkit (Ire)	117
Oasis Dream (GB)	129	The Great Gatsby (Ire)	120	Hawk Flyer (USA)	117
Kalaman (Ire)	126	Weightless (GB)	120	Hold That Tiger (USA)	117
Kris Kin USA)	126	Arakan (USA)	119	Kalabar (GB)	117
Somnus (GB)	125	Baron's Pit (GB)	119	Maharib (USA)	117
Vespone (Ire)	125	f-Dimitrova (USA)	119	f-Mezzo Soprano (USA)	117
Brian Boru (GB)	124	f-Etoile Montante (USA)	119	Mingun (USA0	117
Ikhtyar (Ire)	124	Indian Haven (GB)	119	f-Musical Chimes (USA)	117
Magistretti (USA)	124	Le Vie dei Colori (GB)	119	Policy Maker (Ire)	117
Refuse To Bend (Ire)	124	Martillo (Ger)	119	Ransom O'War (USA)	117
f-Six Perfections (Fr)	124	Membership (USA)	119	f-Vintage Tipple (Ire)	117
Trade Fair (GB)	124	f-Ocean Silk (USA)	119	Westmoreland Road (USA)	117
Dai Jin (GB)	123	Sabre d'Argent (USA)	119	Alberto Giacometti (Ire)	116
f-L'Ancresse (Ire)	123	f-Spanish Sun (USA)	119	Avonbridge (GB)	116
f-Nebraska Tornado (USA)	123	f-Yesterday (Ire)	119	Clodovil (Ire)	116
Roosevelt (Ire)	123	Leporello (Ire)	118p	Deportivo (GB)	116
f-Russian Rhythm (USA)	123	Big Bad Bob (Ire)	118	f-Itnab (GB)	116
Zafeen (Fr)	123	Muqbil (USA)	118	Lateen Sails (GB)	116
Doyen (Ire)	122p	Norse Dancer (Ire)	118	Look Honey (Ire)	116
Phoenix Reach (Ire)	122p	f-Pleasure Place (Ire)	118	f-Maiden Tower (GB)	116
High Accolade (GB)	122	f-Soviet Song (Ire)	118	Rimrod (USA)	116
Powerscourt (GB)	122	Tarjman (GB)	118	Stormont (Ire)	116

Timeform Codes
f-Filly or mare
p-Likely to improve

4-YEAR-OLDS & UP

Horse	Rating	Horse	Rating	Horse	Rating
Hawk Wing (USA)	136	Leadership (GB)	124	f-Bright Sky (Ire)	120
Candy Ride (Arg)	133	Mr Dinos (Ire)	124	Dano-Mast (GB)	120
Falbrav (Ire)	133	Patavellian (Ire)	124	Desert Deer (GB)	120
High Chaparral (Ire)	132	Special Kaldoun (Ire)	124	Far Lane (USA)	120
Mineshaft (USA)	132	Asian Heights (GB)	123	Just James (GB)	120
Mubtaker (USA)	132	Bollin Eric (GB)	123	My Risk (Fr)	120
Symboli Kris S (USA)	132	Fair Mix (Ire)	123	Persian Punch (Ire)	120
Moon Ballad (Ire)	131	Imperial Dancer (GB)	123	The Tatling (Ire)	120
Domedriver (Ire)	128	Mamool (Ire)	122	The Trader (Ire)	120
Nayef (USA)	128	Tillerman (GB)	122	Victory Moon (SAf)	120
Sulamani (Ire)	128	f-Aquarelliste (Fr)	121	Grandera (Ire)	120
Dubai Destination (USA)	127	Black Sam Bellamy (Ire)	121	Darasim (Ire)	119
Choisir (Aus)	126	Carnival Dancer (GB)	121	First Charter (GB)	119
f-Ipi Tombe (Zim)	126	Ekraar (USA)	121	Indian Creek (GB)	119
Nayyir (GB)	126	Gamut (Ire)	121	In Time's Eye (GB)	119
Rakti (GB)	126	Highest (Ire)	121	Jardines Lookout (Ire)	119
Silent Witness (Aus)	126	Kaieteur (USA)	121	Parasol (Ire)	119
Lohengrin (Jpn)	125	Millenary (GB)	121	Short Pause (GB)	119
Storming Home (GB)	125	Next Desert (Ire)	121	Sights On Gold (Ire)	119
Telegnosis (Jpn)	125	Olden Times (GB)	121	Sunstrach (Ire)	119
Vinnie Roe (Ire)	125	Paolini (Ger)	121	Zipping (Ire)	119
Ange Gabriel (Fr)	124	Warrsan (Ire)	121		
f-Islington (Ire)	124	Westerner (GB)	121		

2003 International Classification

Includes horses from Europe and North America plus horses from Japan, Hong Kong, Australia and the UAE which have competed in major international races. The 2-year-old ratings, which only include horses trained in Europe, was in 2003 renamed the European Classification.

2-YEAR-OLDS (European-trained horses only.)

Horse	Rating	Horse	Rating	Horse	Rating
Bago (Fr)	121	Apsis (GB)	113	Magritte (Ire)	111
f-Attraction (GB)	119	Auditorium (GB)	113	f-Majestic Desert (GB)	111
Grey Swallow (Ire)	119	Chineur (Fr)	113	Nevisian Lad (GB)	111
Lucky Story (USA)	118	Colossus (Ire)	113	Peak To Creek (GB)	111
Milk It Mick (GB)	118	Diamond Green (Fr)	113	Simplex (Fr)	111
One Cool Cat (USA)	118	Fantastic View (USA)	113	Barbajuan (Ire)	110
Three Valleys (USA)	118	f-Green Noon (Fr)	113	Cape Fear (GB)	110
American Post (GB)	117	Imperial Stride (GB)	113	Carrizo Creek (Ire)	110
Whipper (USA)	117	f-Much Faster (Ire)	113	Glad Lion (Ger)	110
Majestic Missile (Ire)	116	f-Red Bloom (GB)	113	Moscow Ballet (Ire)	110
Balmont (USA)	115	Russian Valour (Ire)	113	Pastoral Pursuits (GB)	110
Haafhd (GB)	115	Snow Ridge (Ire)	113	f-Punctilious (GB)	110
Bachelor Duke (USA)	114	Troubadour (Ire)	113	Rule Of Law (USA)	110
f-Denebola (USA)	114	f-Carry On Katie (USA)	112	Sabbeeh (USA)	110
Fokine (USA)	114	Howick Falls (USA)	112	f-Sundrop (Jpn)	110
Holborn (UAE)	114	The Mighty Tiger (USA)	112	f-Tulipe Royale (Fr)	110
Old Deuteronomy (USA)	114	Spirit of Desert (Ire)	112	f-Villadolide (Fr)	110
Pearl of Love (Ire)	114	Byron (GB)	111		
Voix du Nord (Fr)	114	Grand Reward (USA)	111		

International Classification codes:

f-filly or mare
Italics-Rating earned on dirt

S-Sprints
M-Mile
I-Intermediate
L-Long distance
E-Stayers

3-YEAR-OLDS

Horse	Cat	Rating	Horse	Cat	Rating	Horse	Cat	Rating
Dalakhani (Ire)	L	132	f-Airwave	S	118	Stroll (USA)	M	116
Alamshar (Ire)	L	132	Atswhatimtalknabout	I	118	f-Vintage Tipple (Ire)	L	116
Oasis Dream (GB)	S	125	f-Bird Town (USA)	M	117	f-Yesterday (Ire)	M	116
Dai Jin (GB)	L	122	Brian Boru (GB)	E	117	Clodovil (Ire)	M	115
Empire Maker (USA)	L	122	Ikhtyar (Ire)	I	117	f-Dimitrova (USA)	I	115
Funny Cide (USA)	I	122	Indian Haven (GB)	M	117	France (GB)	M	115
Kris Kin (USA)	L	122	f-Nebraska Tornado (USA)	M	117	Gallant Arrow (Jpn)	M	115
Alamshar (Ire)	I	122	Neo Universe (Jpn)	L	117	Hold That Tiger (USA)	M	115
Doyen (Ire)	L	121	Norse Dancer (Ire)	L	117	Indian Express (USA)	M	115
Magistretti (USA)	I	121	Powerscourt (Ire)	L-E	117	Kalabar (GB)	L	115
Zafeen (Fr)	M	121	Ransom O'War (USA)	I	117	f-Lady Tak (USA)	S-M	115
Cajun Beat (USA)	S	120	f-Russian Rhythm (USA)	M-I	117	Look Honey (USA)	I	115
Empire Maker (USA)	M	120	f-Six Perfections (Fr)	M	117	f-Mezzo Soprano (USA)	L	115
Peace Rules (USA)	M	120	Somnus (GB)	S	117	Mingun (USA)	I	115
Roosevelt (Ire)	L	120	Strong Hope (USA)	M	117	f-Ocean Silk (USA)	L	115
Ten Most Wanted (USA)	I-L	120	Balestrini (Ire)	L	116	Osorio (Ger)	L	115
Trade Fair (GB)	M	120	Buddy Gil (USA)	M	116	Phoenix Reach (Ire)	L	115
Dynever (USA)	I	119	f-Composure (USA)	M	116	Policy Maker (Ire)	L	115
Kalaman (Ire)	M	119	f-Elloluv (USA)	M	116	Rhythm Mad (Fr)	L	115
f-L'Ancresse (Ire)	I	119	Ghostzapper (USA)	S	116	Soto (USA)	M	115
The Great Gatsby (Ire)	L	119	High Accolade (GB)	L	116	f-Spoken Fur (USA)	M	115
Vespone (Ire)	I	119	Le Vie dei Colori (GB)	M	116	Valid Video (USA)	D	115
Refuse To Bend (Ire)	M	118	f-Maiden Tower (GB)	M	116	Zenno Rob Roy (Jpn)	I-L	115
Super Celebre (Fr)	L	118	Martillo (Ger)	M	116			

4-YEAR-OLDS & Up

Horse	Cat	Rating	Horse	Cat	Rating	Horse	Cat	Rating
Hawk Wing (USA)	M	133	Durandal (Jpn)	M	120	Admire Don (Jpn)	M-I	117
Mubtaker (USA)	L	130	Hishi Miracle (Jpn)	L	120	f-Adoration (USA)	M	117
Candy Ride (Arg)	I	127	f-Islington (Ire)	I	120	Affluent (USA)	S	117
Falbrav (Ire)	I	127	Lonhro (Aus)	M	120	Carnival Dancer (GB)	I	117
High Chaparral (Ire)	L	127	Perfect Drift (USA)	M	120	Fleetstreet Dancer (USA)	I	117
Johar (USA)	L	127	Redattore (Brz)	M	120	Gamut (USA)	E	117
Mineshaft (USA)	M	127	f-Sightseek (USA)	M	120	f-Golden Apples (Ire)	M	117
Moon Ballad (Ire)	I	126	Special Ring (USA)	M	120	Imperial Dancer (GB)	I	117
Dubai Destination (USA)	M	125	Denon (USA)	L	119	Indian Creek (GB)	L	117
Nayef (USA)	I	125	Domedriver (Ire)	M	119	Kaieteur (USA)	I	117
Sulamani (Ire)	L	125	f-Ipi Tombe (Zim)	M	119	Lucky Owners (NZ)	M	117
Pleasantly Perfect (USA)	I	124	Leadership (GB)	L	119	Millenary (GB)	L	117
Symboli Kris S (USA)	L	124	Lohengrin (Jpn)	M	119	National Currency (SAf)	S	117
Ange Gabriel (Fr)	L	123	Mamool (Ire)	L	119	Nayyir (GB)	M	117
f-Azeri (USA)	M	123	Mr Dinos (Ire)	E	119	Olden Times (GB)	I	117
Tap Dance City (USA)	L	123	Tsurumaru Boy (Jpn)	I-L	119	Paolini (Ger)	I	117
Congaree (USA)	M-I	122	Vinnie Roe (Ire)	I-L	119	Special Kaldoun (Ire)	M	117
Good Journey (USA)	M	122	f-Wild Spirit (Chi)	M-I	119	Telegnosis (Jpn)	M	117
Medaglia d'Oro (USA)	M-I	122	f-Xtra Heat (USA)	S	119	Tillerman (GB)	M	117
Storming Home (GB)	L	122	Black Sam Bellamy (Ire)	I-L	118	Touch Of The Blues (Fr)	M	117
Aldebaran (USA)	S	121	Eishin Preston (USA)	I	118	Volponi (USA)	M-I	117
Bollin Eric (GB)	L	121	Ekraar (USA)	L	118	f-Voodoo Dancer (USA)	M	117
Choisir (Aus)	S	121	Harlan's Holiday (USA)	I	118	Warrsan (Ire)	L	117
Congaree (USA)	S	121	Next Desert (Ire)	L	118	Westerner (GB)	E	117
Silent Witness (Aus)	S	121	f-Tates Creek (USA)	M	118			
Rakti (GB)	I	121	The Tin Man (USA)	L	118			

Foreign Stakes Histories

Australia

MELBOURNE CUP. 2 Miles. 3-year-olds and upward.
(Flemington, Melbourne, Victoria)

FIRST RUN IN 1851

Year	First	Age	Jockey	Wt	Second	Age	Wt	Third	Age	Wt	Time	Win Value
1955	Taparoa	7	N Sellwood	106	Rising Fast	6	140	Sir William	5	108	3:28 1/4	$22,625
1956	Evening Peal	4	G Podmore	112	Red Craze	6	143	Caranna	4	124	3:19 1/2	33,600
1957	StraighT Draw	5	N McGrowdie	117	Prince Darius	3	104	Pansie Sun	5	119	3:24 1/2	49,550
1958	Baystone	6	M Schumaker	121	Monte Carlo	5	132	Red Pine	4	102	3:21 1/4	30,000
1959	Mac Dougal	6	P Glennon	123	Nether Gold	7	104	white Hills	6	112	3:23	33,600
1960	Hi Jinx	5	W Smith	108	Howsie	5	118	Illumquh	5	118	3:23 4/5	56,000
1961	Lord Fury	4	R Selkrig	105	Grand Print	4	110	Dhaulagiri	5	131	3:19	46,480
1962	Even Stevens	5	L G. Coles	117	Comicquita	5	108	Aquanita	5	130	3:21 2/5	31,500
1963	Gatum Gatum	5	J Johnson	110	Illumquh	8	124	Grand Print	6	128	3:21.1	43,120
1964	Polo Prince	6	R Taylor	115	Elkayah	6	119	Welltown	4	105	3:19 3/5	43,023
1965	Light Fingers	4	R Higgins	116	Ziema	4	118	Midlander	3	95	3:21.1	46,652
1966	Galilee	4	J Miller	125	Light Fingers	5	127	Duo	5	113	3:21.9	41,300
1967	Red Handed	7	R Higgins	121	Red Crest	7	118	Floodbird	5	105	3:20 1/5	46,251
1968	Rain Lover	4	J Johnson	114	Fileur	4	119	Fans	6	118	3:19.1	41,300
1969	Rain Lover	5	J Johnson	133	Alsop	4	104	Ben Lomond	5	129	3:21 1/2	51,100
1970	Bagdad Note	5	E J Disham	119	Vanisittart	4	112	Clear Prince	3	96	3:19.7	51,100
1971	Silver Knight	4	R B Marsh	121	Igloo	4	115	Tails	6	126	3:19 1/2	69,900
1972	Piping Lane	6	J Letts	106	Maginfique	4	115	Gunsynd	5	133	3:19.3	72,900
1973	Gala Supreme	4	F Reys	108	Glengowan	6	125	Daneson	5	106	3:19 1/2	67,900
1974	Think Big	4	H White	117	Leilani	4	122	Captain Peri	6	115	3:23 1/5	108,900
1975	Think Big	5	H White	129	Holiday Waggon	4	110	Medici	7	101	3:23 3/5	110,000
1976	Van Der Hum	5	R J Skelton	120	Gold and Black	4	110	Kythera	6	112	3:34.1	129,097
1977	Gold and Black	5	J Duggan	126	Reckless	7	125	Hyperno	4	115	3:18 2/5	126,779
1978	Arwon	5	H White	111	Dandeleith	6	111	Karu	7	107	3:24.3	149,890
1979	Hyperno	6	H White	123	Salamander	6	122	Red Nose	4	113	3:21.8	214,012
1980	Beldale Ball	5	J Letts	109	My Blue Denim	5	118	Love Bandit	6	112	3:19.8	228,481
1981	Just A Dash	4	P Cook	118	El Laurena	5	115	Flashing Light	4	108	3:21.2	223,080
1982	Gurner's Lane	4	L Dittman	123	Kingston Town	6	130	Noble Comment	5	109	3:21	182,247
1983	Kiwi	6	J Cassidy	115	Noble Comment	6	111	Mr. Jazz	4	110	3:18.9	178,249
1984	Black Knight	5	P Cook	110	Chagemar	5	120	Mapperley Heights	4	112	3:18.9	280,475
1985	What A Nuisance	7	P Hyland	116	Koiro Corrie May	6	113	Tripsacum	4	108	3:23	435,175
1986	At Talaq	5	M Clarke	120	Rising Fear	4	117	Sea Ledgend	4	108	3:21.7	417,105
1987	Kensei	5	L Olsen	113	Empire Rose	5	110	Rosedale	5	123	3:22	551,687
1988	Empire Rose	6	T Allan	118	Natski	5	121	Na Botto	4	112	3:19.9	879,986
1989	Tawrrific	5	R S Dye	119	Super Impose	5	123	Kudz	6	116	3:17.1	925,160
1990	Kingston Rule	5	D Breadman	117	The Phantom	5	120	Mr. Brooker	5	117	3:16.3	1,024,400
1991	Let's Elope	4	S King	112	Shiva's Revenge	4	118	Magnolia Hall	5	116	3:18.9	1,043,970
1992	Subzero	4	G Hall	120	Veandercross	3	120	Casteltown	7	126	3:243/5	904,670
1993	Vintage Crop	7	M J Kinane	122	Te Akau Nick	5	123	Mercator	7	119	3:252/5	870,408
1994	Jeune	6	W Harris	125	Paris Lane	4	122	Oompala	6	116	3:19.80	962,780
1995	Doriemus	5	D M Oliver	120	Nothin' Leica Dane	3	105	Vintage Crop	9	130	3:27.60	1,015,001
1996	Saintly	4	D Beadman	122	Count Chivas	5	126	Skybeau	4	110	3:18.8	1,152,955
1997	Might and Power	4	J Cassidy	123	Doriemus	7	127	Markham	4	116	3:18.33	1,030,774
1998	Jezabeel	6	C J Munce	112	Champagne	4	112	Persian Punch	6	125	3:18.59	1,070,503
1999	Rogan Josh	7	J Marshall	110	Central Park	5	127	Zazabelle	4	108	3:19.64	1,175,318
2000	Brew	6	K McEvoy	108	Yippyio	5	115	Second Coming	6	116	3:18.68	1,077,940
2001	Ethereal	3	S Seamer	114	Give The Slip	4	121	Persian Punch	8	126	3:21.08	944,656
2002	Media Puzzle	6	D M Oliver	116	Mr Prudent	8	115	Beekeeper	4	117	3:16.97	1,139,439
2003	Makybe Diva	6	G Boss	112	She's Archie	4	110	jardines Lookout	6	122	3:19.90	1,655,844

Canada

ATTO MILE-GRADE 1

1 Mile (turf), 3-year-olds and up, Woodbine.

FIRST RUN IN 1997

Year	First	Age	Jockey	Wt	Second	Age	Wt	Third	Age	Wt	Time	Win Value
1997	Geri		C. Antley	117	Helmsman			Crown Attorney			1:36.30	300,000
1998	Labeeb		K. Desormeaux	121	Jim and Tonic			Poteen			1:33.00	450,000
1999	Quiet Resolve*		R. Landry	117	Rob'n Gin			Jim and Tonic			1:33.19	630,000
2000	Riviera		J. Velazquez	117	Arkadian Hero			Affirmed Success			1:33.18	600,000
2001	Numerous Times		P. Husbands	117	Affirmed Success			Quiet Resolve			1:32.79	600,000
2002	Good Journey	6	P. Day	121	Chopinina	9	114	Nuclear Debate	7	121	1:33.27	600,000
2003	Touch of the Blues	6	K.J. Desormeaux	119	Soaring Free	4	121	Perfect Soul	5	121	1:33.39	600,000

*Hawksley Hill finished first, but was disqualified and placed fourth.

CANADIAN INTERNATIONAL-G1
1-1/2 miles(turf), 3-year-olds & up, Woodbine
FIRST RUN IN 1938.

Year	First	Age	Jockey	Wt	Second	Age	Wt	Third	Age	Wt	Time	Win Value
1994	Raintrap		R. Davis	126	Alywow			Volochine			2:36.40	606,900
1995	Lassigny		P. Day	126	Mecke			Hasten to Add			2:29.90	653,250
1996	Singspiel		G. Stevens	126	Chief Bearhart			Mecke			2:33.30	600,000
1997	Chief Bearhart		J. Santos	126	Down the Aisle			Romanov			2:29.00	600,000
1998	Royal Anthem		G. Stevens	119	Chiefbearhart			Parade Ground			2:29.60	630,000
1999	Thornfield		R. Ros Ramos	126	Fruits of Love			Courteous			2:32.39	936,000
2000	Mutafaweg		L. Dettori	126	William News			Daliapour			2:27.62	900,000
2001	Mutamam		R. Hills	126	Paolini			Lodge Hill			2:28.46	900,000
2002	Ballingarry	3	M. Kinane	118	Falcon Flight	6	126	Yavanas	10	126	2:31.68	900,000
2003	Phoenix Reach	3	D. Martin	119	Macaw	4	126	Brian Boru	3	119	2:33.62	900,000

For previous runnings see the 1994 Manual

E.P. TAYLOR-G1
1-1/4miles(turf), 3-year-olds & up fillies and mares, Woodbine
FIRST RUN IN 1956.

Year	First	Age	Jockey	Wt	Second	Age	Wt	Third	Age	Wt	Time	Win Value
1994	Truly a Dream		C. McCarron	118	Bold Ruritana			Hero's Love			2:01.60	207,180
1995	Timarida		L. Dettori	117	Matiara			Bold Ruritana			2:03.60	213,120
1996	Wandering Star		H. McCauley	118	Flame Valley			Carling			2:04.60	204,120
1997	Kool Kat Katie		O. Peslier	118	Mousse Glacee			L'Annee Folle			2:02.00	206,460
1998	Zomaradah		G. Stevens	118	Tresoriere			Griselda			2:02.40	273,600
1999	Insight		M. Smith	123	Cerulean Sky			Midnight Line			2:05.34	300,000
2000	Fly For Avie		T. Kabel	123	Lady Upstage			Innuendo			2:02.78	300,000
2001	Choc Ice		J. Murtagh	119	Volga			Spring Oak			2:03.01	300,000
2002	Fraulein	3	K. Darley	117	Alasha	3	117	Volga	4	123	2:10.03	502,650
2003	Volga	5	R. Migliore	123	Tigertail	4	123	Hi Dubai	3	118	2:05.68	450,000

For previous runnings see the 1994 Manual

QUEEN'S PLATE
1-1/4 miles, 3-year-olds, Woodbine
FIRST RUN IN 1860.

Year	First	Age	Jockey	Wt	Second	Age	Wt	Third	Age	Wt	Time	Win Value
1860	Don Juan											
1861	Wild Irishman											
1862	Palermo											
1863	Touchstone											
1864	Brunette											
1865	Lady Norfolk											
1866	Beacon											
1867	Wild Rose											
1868	Nettie											
1869	Bay Jack											
1870	John Bell											
1871	Floss											
1872	Fearnaught											
1873	Mignonette											
1874	Swallow											
1875	Trumpeter											
1876	Norah P.											
1877	Amelia											
1878	King George											
1879	Moss Ross											
1880	Bonnie Bird	4	Leary	107	Fanny Wiser	3	94	King Tom	4	110	2:47	300
1881	Vice Chancellor	4	Brown	115	Jessie McCullough	6	118	Athlete	6	119	2:53	340
1882	Fanny Wiser	5	A.E. Gates	112	Williams	4	115	Tullamore	5	119	2:51	400
1883	Rhody Pringle	3	Smith	97	Williams	5	120	P'cess Louise	3	95	2:52.5	420
1884	Williams	6	Martin	121	Marquis	5	121	Modjeska	5	118	2:50.75	415
1885	Willie W.	4	Jamieson	115	Fred Henry	a	121	Edmonton	4	120	2:58	470
1886	Wild Rose	4	C. Butler	113	Fred Henry	a	121	Wild Bruce	3	97	2:48.25	490
1887	Bonnie Duke	5	Wise	119	Fred Henry	a	122	Aunt Alice	7	117	2:19	357
1888	Henry Cooper	4	C. O'Leary	118	Evangeline	4	113	Cast Off	5	117	2:18.5	487
1889	Colonist	3	R. O'Leary	106	Bonnie Ino	3	101	Long Shot	6	126	2:16	322
1890	Kite String	3	Coleman	105	La Blanche	4	117	Flip Flop	4	117	2:22	327
1891	Victorious	3	Gorman	106	La Blanche	5	121	Moyama	3	101	2:14.5	407
1892	O'Donohue	3	Horton	106	Queen Mary	3	101	H'ther Bl'm	3	101	2:22	422
1893	Martello	4	Blaylock	119	Athalo	3	103	H'ther Bl'm	4	117	2:14	830
1894	Joe Miller	4	Booker	122	Bel Demonio	5	126	Maj. General	3	106	2:28.5	785

Year	First	Age	Jockey	Wt	Second	Age	Wt	Third	Age	Wt	Time	Win Value
1895	Bonniefield	3	Booker	106	Millbrook	3	106	Lochinvar	4	119	2:17.5	995
1896	Millbrook	4	Lewis	122	Springal	3	102	Dictator	5	126	2:19	975
1897	Ferdinand	3	Lewis	106	Bon Ino	3	101	Wicker	3	106	2:13	1,015
1898	Bon Ino	4	R. Williams	117	Dalmoor	4	122	Maritana II	3	101	2:15.5	1,010
1899	Butter Scotch	3	Mason	101	Dalmoor	5	126	Toddy Ladle	3	103	2:15.5	1,331
1900	Dalmoor	6	Lewis	126	The Provost	3	108	Bellcourt	4	117	2:14	1,395
1901	John Ruskin	3	Vititoe	105	Bellcourt	5	121	Fernietickle	3	101	2:18.75	1,570
1902	Lyddite	3	Wainwright	101	Fly-in-Amber	4	117	Opuntia	3	129	2:15	1,725
1903	Thessalon	3	Castro	104	Nesto	3	103	Gold'n Crest	4	117	2:15.5	1,960
1904	Sapper	3	J. Walsh	103	Nimble Dick	3	106	War Whoop	3	106	2:12	1,975
1905	Inferno	3	H. Phillips	106	Will King	3	106	H. Seas Over	3	106	2:15	2,092
1906	Slaughter	3	Trebel	106	Court Martial	3	106	Haruko	3	101	2:11.6	3,395
1907	Kelvin	3	Foley	106	Half-a-Crown	3	106	Bilbery	5	123	2:12.6	3,707
1908	Seismic	3	Fairbrother	106	Shimonese	3	101	Half-a-Crown	4	122	2:11	3,650
1909	Shimonese	4	Gilbert	119	Tollendal	3	108	For Garry	3	108	2:10.4	3,250
1910	Parmer	3	J. Wilson	105	Commola	3	104	Jane Shore	3	103	2:12.4	3,332
1911	St. Bass	3	E. Dugan	108	Powderman	3	105	Jane Shore	4	119	2:08.8	3,395
1912	Heresy	3	Small	108	Amberite	3	103	Rustling	3	103	2:11	4,535
1913	Hearts of Oak	3	J. Wilson	113	Maid of Frome	3	108	Gold Bud	4	119	2:09.2	4,335
1914	Beehive	3	G. Burns	113	Dark Rosaleen	3	108	Sea Lord	3	105	2:10.6	4,735
1915	Tartarean	3	H. Watts	108	Fair Montague	3	108	Pepper S'ce	3	113	2:09.2	4,310
1916	Mandarin	3	A. Pickens	113	Gala Water	3	108	Gala Day	3	113	2:12	4,015
1917	Belle Mahone	3	F. Robinson	108	Tarahera	3	108	Gala Dress	3	108	2:08.8	6,125
1918	Springside	3	L. Mink	113	Ladder of Light	4	119	May Bloom	3	108	2:08.8	2,540
1919	Ladder of Light	5	L. Lyke	122	Doleful	3	108	Hong Kong	3	113	2:09.4	2,750
1920	St. Paul	3	R. Romanelli	105	Bugle March	4	121	Prime	4	108	2:09	6,050
1921	Herendesy	3	J. Butwell	113	Royal Visitor	3	113	M. Cutpurse	3	103	2:10	5,070
1922	South Shore	4	K. Parrington	122	Paddle	3	113	El Jesmar	3	113	2:12	7,565
1923	Flowerful	3	T. Wilson	113	Cheechako	3	124	Trail Blazer	3	105	2:11	7,745
1924	Maternal Pride	3	G. Walls	110	Thorndyke	3	109	Maypole	4	127	1:57.6	7,825
1925	Fairbank	3	C. Lang	122	Duchess	3	112	Jean Crest	3	112	1:56.4	7,835
1926	Haplite	3	H. Erickson	117	Attack	3	113	Taurus	3	112	1:59.6	7,550
1927	Troutlet	3	F. Horn	112	Mr. Gaiety	3	112	Gems to Let	3	117	1:55.8	10,820
1928	Young Kitty	3	L. Pichon	112	Bonnington	3	112	H'na Deebe	3	107	1:57	10,775
1929	Shorelint	3	J.D. Mooney	117	Ichitaro	4	132	Lindsay	3	108	1:57.6	10,960
1930	Aymond	3	H. Little	117	Whale Oil	3	117	Ichitaro	5	133	1:57.2	10,980
1931	Froth Blower	3	F. Mann	117	Bronze	3	112	Skygazer	3	112	1:59.2	8,100
1932	Queensway	3	F. Mann	112	King O'Connor	3	112	Spey Crest	3	112	1:55.2	5,870
1933	King O'Connor	4	E. Legere	127	Easter Hatter	4	132	Syngo	3	117	1:56.4	6,360
1934	Horometer	3	F. Mann	117	Speygold	3	117	Papalico	4	132	1:54.2	5,650
1935	Sally Fuller	3	M. Lindberg	107	Chickpen	3	112	Gay Sy'athy	3	109	1:55.4	4,290
1936	Monsweep	3	D. Brammer	117	Stormblown	3	112	Epicurus	4	132	1:55	5,360
1937	Goldlure	3	S. Young	117	Cease Fire	3	117	Siler Jubilee	3	117	1:55.4	6,180
1938	Bunty Lawless	3	J.W. Bailey	117	Mona Bell	3	112	Cabin Gal	3	112	1:54.4	7,030
1939	Archworth	3	S.D. Birley	117	Sea General	3	117	Skyrunner	3	117	1:54.4	8,970
1940	Willie the Kid	3	R. Nash	112	Curwen	3	117	Hood	3	117	1:55.8	6,720
1941	Budpath	3	R. Watson	117	Undisturbed	3	117	Attrisius	3	112	1:56.8	6,670
1942	Ten to Ace	3	C.W. Smith	117	Cossack Post	3	117	Depressor	3	117	1:57.8	6,680
1943	Paolita	3	P. Remillard	112	Arbor Vita	3	117	Tulachmore	3	117	2:02.6	6,640
1944	Acara	3	R. Watson	107	Ompalo	3	117	Korafloyd	3	117	1:54.8	9,350
1945	Uttermost	3	R. Watson	119	Tarian	3	119	Ferry Pilot	3	118	1:54.6	9,695
1946	Kingarvie	3	J. Dewhurst	119	David T.	3	119	Bluesweep	3	119	1:55.6	9,850
1947	Moldy	3	C. McDonald	119	Burboy	3	119	Watch Wrack	3	119	1:54.2	10,335
1948	Last Mark	3	H.R. Bailey	119	Lord Fairmond	3	110	Joey Bomber	3	119	1:52	11,260
1949	Epic	3	C. Rogers	119	Speedy Irish	3	119	Filsis	3	114	1:52.2	11,060
1950	McGill	3	C. Rogers	119	Sir Strome	3	119	Unionville	3	119	1:52.4	14,290
1951	Major Factor	3	A. Bavington	119	Libertine	3	119	Bear Field	3	119	1:53	16,152
1952	Epigram	3	G. Robillard	119	Genthorn	3	114	Latin Lad	3	114	1:58.6	17,022
1953	Canadiana	3	E. Arcaro	114	Blue Scooter	3	119	Lively Action	3	114	1:52.2	20,592
1954	Collisteo	3	C. Rogers	119	Queen's Own	3	119	King Maple	3	119	1:52	22,452
1955	Ace Marine	3	G. Walker	119	Baffin Bay	3	114	Senator Jim	3	119	1:52.4	25,514
1956	Canadian Champ	3	D. Stevenson	119	Argent	3	119	London Calling	3	119	1:55	25,430
1957	Lyford Cay	3	A. Gomez	126	Chopadette	3	126	Flying Atom	3	126	2:02.6	26,210
1958	Caledon Beau	3	A. Coy	126	White Apache	3	126	Stole the Ring	3	121	2:04.2	26,151
1959	New Providence	3	R. Ussery	126	Major Flight	3	126	Winning Shot	3	126	2:04.8	51,767
1960	Victoria Park	3	A. Gomez	126	Quintain	3	126	Champagne Velv't	3	126	2:02	42,750
1961	Blue Light	3	H. Dittfach	126	Just Don't Shove	3	126	Ramblin Wreck	3	126	2:05	46,475
1962	Flaming Page	3	J. Fitzsimmons	121	Choperion	3	126	Peter's Chop	3	126	2:04.6	51,225
1963	Canebora	3	M. Ycaza	126	Son Blue	3	126	Warriors Day	3	126	2:04	54,850
1964	Northern Dancer	3	W. Hartack	126	Langcrest	3	126	Grand Garcon	3	126	2:02.2	49,234
1965	Whistling Sea	3	T. Inouye	126	Flyalong	3	126	Blue Mel	3	126	2:03.8	47,852
1966	Titled Hero	3	A. Gomez	126	Bye and Near	3	126	Bright Monarch	3	126	2:03.6	52,274
1967	Jammed Lovely	3	J. Fitzsimmons	121	Pine Point	3	126	Come By Chance	3	126	2:03	51,979

Year	First	Age	Jockey	Wt	Second	Age	Wt	Third	Age	Wt	Time	Win Value
1968	Merger	3	W. Harris	126	Big Blunder	3	126	Rouletabille	3	126	2:05.4	53,775
1969	Jumpin Joseph	3	A. Gomez	126	Fanfaron	3	126	Fire n Desire	3	126	2:04.2	55,157
1970	Almoner	3	S. Hawley	126	Fanfreluche	3	121	Top Call	3	126	2:04.8	57,525
1971	Kennedy Road	3	S. Hawley	126	Fabe Count	3	126	Great Gabe	3	126	2:03	54,518
1972	Victoria Song	3	R. Platts	126	Barachois	3	126	Gentleman Conn	3	126	2:03.2	56,278
1973	Royal Chocolate	3	T. Colangelo	126	Sinister Purpose	3	126	My Archie Bald	3	126	2:08	80,834
1974	Amber Herod	3	R. Platts	126	Native Aid	3	126	Rushton's Corsair	3	126	2:09.2	96,671
1975	L'Enjoleur	3	S. Hawley	126	Near the High Sea	3	126	Mystery Time	3	126	2:02.6	95,465
1976	Norcliffe	3	J. Fell	126	Military Bearing	3	126	Confederation	3	126	2:05	89,804
1977	Sound Reason	3	R. Platts	126	Northernette	3	121	Giboulee	3	126	2:06.6	86,538
1978	Regal Embrace	3	S. Hawley	126	Overskate	3	126	L'Alezane	3	121	2:02	107,091
1979	Steady Growth	3	B. Swatuk	126	Bold Agent	3	126	Ram Good	3	126	2:06.6	106,542
1980	Driving Home	3	W. Parsons	126	Someolio Man	3	126	Allan Blue	3	126	2:04.2	119.555
1981	Fiddle Dancer Boy	3	D. Clark	126	Wayover	3	126	Frost King	3	126	2:04.8	119,616
1982	Son of Briartic	3	J.P. Souter	126	Runaway Groom	3	126	Le Danseur	3	126	2:04.6	141,504
1983	Bompago	3	L. Attard	126	Sir Khaled	3	126	Rockcliffe	3	126	2:04.2	151,386
1984	Key to the Moon	3	R. Platts	126	Let's Go Blue	3	126	Ten Gold Pots	3	126	2:03.8	164,352
1985	La Lorgnette	3	D. Clark	121	Imperial Choice	3	126	Pre Emptive Strike	3	126	2:04.6	174,504
1986	Golden Choice	3	V. Bracciale Jr	126	Cool Halo	3	126	Steady Effort	3	126	2:07.2	174,465
1987	Market Control	3	K. Skinner	126	Afleet	3	126	One From Heaven	3	121	2:03.6	204,219
1988	Regal Intention	3	J.M. Lauzon	126	Regal Classic	3	126	Granacus	3	126	2:06.2	199,497
1989	With Approval	3	D.J. Seymour	126	Most Valiant	3	126	Domasca Dan	3	126	2:03	257,660
1990	Izvestia	3	D.J. Seymour	126	Very Formal	3	126	Iskandar Elakbar	3	126	2:01.8	235,200
1991	Dance Smartly	3	P. Day	121	Wilderness Song	3	121	Shudanz	3	126	2:03.4	234,840
1992	Alydeed	3	C. Perret	126	Grand Hooley	3	126	Benburb	3	126	2:04.6	228,900
1993	Peteski	3	C. Perret	126	Cheery Knight	3	126	Janraffole	3	126	2:04.2	218,600
1994	Basqueian	3	C. Perret	126	Bruce's Mill	3		Parental Pressure	3		2:03.40	267,942
1995	Regal Discovery	3	T. Kabel	126	Freedom Fleet	3		Mt. Sassafras	3		2:03.90	261,660
1996	Victor Cooley	3	M. Frostad	126	Stephanotis	3		Kristy Krunch	3		2:03.90	255,480
1997	Awesome Again	3	M. Smith	126	Cryptocloser	3		Sovereign Storm	3		2:04.30	255,420
1998	Archers Bay	3	K. Desormeaux	126	Brite Adam	3		Kinkennie	3		2:02.30	300,000
1999	Woodcarver	3	G. Schickedanz	126	Gandria	3		Euchre	3		2:03.13	300,000
2000	Scatter the Gold	3	T. Kabel	126	I and I	3		For Our Sake	3		2:05.53	600,000
2001	Dancethruthedawn	3	G. Boulanger	126	Win City	3		Brushing Bully	3		2:03.78	600,000
2002	T J's Lucky Moon	3	S. Bahen	126	Anglian Prince	3	126	Forever Grand	3	126	2:06.88	600,000
2003	Wando	3	P. Husbands	126	Mobil	3	126	Rock Again	3	126	2:02.48	800,000

Britain

ASCOT GOLD CUP-G1
2-1/2 miles, 4-year-olds & up, Royal Ascot
FIRST RUN IN 1807.

Year	1st (Age)	Jockey	Trainer	Owner	2nd	3rd	Time
1970	Precipice Wood (4)	J. Lindley	Mrs R. Lomax	R. McAlpine	Blakeney	Clairon	4:27.4
1971	Random Shot (4)	G. Lewis	A. Budgett	Mrs G. Benskin	Orosio	Charlton	4:41.4*
1972	Erimo Hawk (4)	Pat Eddery	G. Barling	Y. Yamamoto	Rock Roi	Irvine	4:28.6
1973	Lassalle (4)	J. Lindley	R. Carver	Z Yoshida	Celtic Cone	The Admiral	4:33.4
1974	Ragstone (4)	R. Hutchinson	J. Dunlop	Duke of Norfolk	Proverb	Lassalle	4:35
1975	Sagaro (4)	L. Piggott	F Boutin	G. Oldham	Le Bavard	Kambalda	4:48
1976	Sagaro (5)	L. Piggott	F Boutin	G. Oldham	Crash Course	Sea Anchor	4:26
1977	Sagaro (6)	L. Piggott	F Boutin	G. Oldham	Buckskin	Citoyen	4:28.4
1978	Shangamuzo (5)	G. Starkey	M. Stoute	Mrs E Charles	Royal Hive	Hawkberry	4:27.4
1979	Le Moss (4)	L. Piggott	H Cecil	C. d'Alessio	Buckskin	Arapahos	4:25.2
1980	Le Moss (5)	J. Mercer	H Cecil	C. d'Alessio	Ardross	Vincent	4:27.6
1981	Ardross (5)	L. Piggott	H Cecil	C. St George	Shoot A Line	Ayyabaan	4:51.2
1982	Ardross (6)	L. Piggott	H Cecil	C. St George	Tipperary Fixer	El Badr	4:35.2
1983	Little Wolf (5)	W. Carson	W. R. Hern	Lord Portchester	Khairpour	Indian Prince	4:24.2
1984	Gildoran (4)	S. Cauthen	B. Hills	R. Sangster	Ore	Condeil	4:18.8
1985	Gildoran (5)	B. Thomson	B. Hills	R. Sangster	Longboat	Destroyer	4:25.2
1986	Longboat (5)	W. Carson	W. R. Hern	R. D. Hollingsworth	Eastern Mystic	Spicey Story	4:22
1987	Paean (4)	S. Cauthen	H Cecil	H de Walden	Sadeem	Saronicos	4:33.2
1988+	Sadeem (5)	G. Starkey	G. Harwood	Sheikh Mohammed	Sergeyevich	Chauve Souris	4:15.6
1989	Sadeem (6)	W. Carson	G. Harwood	Sheikh Mohammed	Mazzacano	Lauries Crusader	4:22.6
1990	Ashal (4)	R. Hills	H T Jones	H Al Maktoum	Tyrone Bridge	Thethingaboutitis	4:28.4
1991	Indian Queen (6f)	W. R. Swinburn	Lord Huntingdon	G. Brunton	Arazanni	Warm Feeling	4:23.8
1992	Drum Taps (5)	L. Dettori	Lord Huntingdon	Y. Asakawa	Arcadian Heights	Turgeon	4:18.2
1993	Drum Taps (7)	L. Dettori	Lord Huntingdon	Y. Asakawa	Assessor	Turgeon	4:32.57
1994	Arcadian Heights (6)	M. Hills	G. Wragg	J. Pearce	Vintage Crop	Sonus	4:27.67

1995	Double Trigger (4)	J. Weaver	M. Johnston	R. Huggins	Moonax	Admiral's Well	4:20.25
1996	Classic Cliche (4)	M. J. Kinane	S. bin Suroor	Godolphin	Double Trigger	Nononito	4:23.2
1997	Celeric (5)	Pat Eddery	D. Morley	C. Spence	Classic Cliche	Election Day	4:26.19
1998	Kayf Tara (4)	L. Dettori	S. bin Suroor	Godolphin	Double Trigger	Three Cheers	4:32.36
1999	Enzeli (4)	J. P Murtagh	J. Oxx	Aga Khan	Invermark	Kayf Tara	4:18.85
2000	Kayf Tara (6)	M J Kinane	S bin Suroor	Godolphin	Far Cry	Compton Ace	4:24.53
2001	Royal Rebel (5)	J P Murtagh	M Johnston	P D Savill	Persian Punch	Jardines Lookout	4:18.92
2002	Royal Rebel (6)	J P Murtagh	M Johnston	P D Savill	Vinnie Roe	Wareed	4:25.64
2003	Mr Dinos (4)	K Fallon	P Cole	C Shiacolas	Persian Punch	Pole Star	4:20.15

*Rock Roi finished first but was disqualified from purse money.
+Royal Gait finished first but was disqualified and placed last.

CHAMPION STAKES-G1
1-1/4 miles, 3-year-olds & up, Newmarket (Rowley Mile Course)
FIRST RUN IN 1877

Year	1st (age)	Jockey	Trainer	Owner	2nd	3rd	Time
1970	Lorrenzaccio (5)	G Lewis	N Murless	C St George	Nijinsky II	Hotfoot	2:05.8
1971	Brigadier Gerard (3)	J Mercer	W R Hern	Mrs J Hislop	Rarity	Welsh Pageant	2:17.8
1972	Brigadier Gerard (4)	J Mercer	W R Hern	Mrs J Hislop	Riverman	Lord David	2:07.4
1973	Hurry Harriet (3f)	J Cruguet	P Mullins	M Thorp	Allez France	Sharp Edge	2:08.4
1974	Giacometti (3)	L Piggott	H Price	C St George	Northern Gem	Pitcairn	2:09.4
1975	Rose Bowl (3f)	W Carson	R J Houghton	Mrs C Engelhard	Allez France	Ramirez	2:05.2
1976	Vitiges (3)	Pat Eddery	P Walwyn	Mme M Laloun	Rose Bowl	Northern Treasure	2:09.6
1977	Flying Water (3)	Y Saint-Martin	A Penna	D Wildenstein	Relkino	North Stoke	2:06.8
1978	Swiss Maid (3f)	G Starkey	P Kelleway	M Fine	Hawaiian Sound	Gunner B	2:03.8
1979	Northern Baby (3)	P Paquet	F Boutin	Mme A d'Estainville	Town And Country	Haul Knight	2:03.8
1980	Cairn Rouge (3f)	A Murray	M Cunningham	D Brady	Master Willie	Nadjar	2:05.6
1981	Vayraan (3)	Y Saint-Martin	F Mathet	H H Aga Khan	Cairn Rouge	Amyndas	2:08
1982	Time Charter (3f)	W Newnes	H Candy	R Barnett	Prima Voce	Noalto	2:10.6
1983	Cormorant Wood (3f)	S Cauthen	B Hills	R McAlpine	Flame Of Tara	Miramar Reef	
1984	Palace Music (3)	Y Saint-Martin	P-L Biancone	N B Hunt	Pebbles	Raft	2:01
1985	Pebbles (4f)	Pat Eddery	C Brittain	Sheikh Mohammed	Slip Anchor	Palace Music	2:04.6
1986	Triptych (4f)	A Cruz	P-L Biancone	A Clore	Celestial Storm	Park Express	2:09.4
1987	Triptych (5f)	A Cruz	P-L Biancone	A Clore	Most Welcome	Saint Andrews	2:10.8
1988	Indian Skimmer (4f)	M Roberts	H Cecil	Sheikh Mohammed	Persian Heights	Doyoun	2:10.4
1989	Legal Case (3)	W R Swinburn	L Cumani	G White	Dolpour	Ile de Chypre	2:02.8
1990	In The Groove (3f)	S Cauthen	D Elsworth	B Cooper	Linamix	Legal Case	2:05.6
1991	Tel Quel (3)	T Jarnet	A Fabre	Sheikh Mohammed	Cruachan	In The Groove	2:01.8
1992	Rodrigo de Triano (3)	L Piggott	P Chapple-Hyam	R Sangster	Lahib	Environment Friend	2:02.4
1993	Hatoof (4f)	W R Swinburn	C Head	M Al Maktoum	Ezzoud	Dernier Empereur	2:06.8
1994	Dernier Empereur (4)	S Guillot	A Fabre	G Tanaka	Grand Lodge	Muhtarram	2:05.65
1995	Spectrum (3)	J Reid	P Chapple-Hyam	Lord Weinstock	Riyadian	Montjoy	2:02.55
1996	Bosra Sham (3f)	Pat Eddery	H Cecil	W Said	Halling	Timarida	2:03.71
1997	Pilsudski (5)	M J Kinane	M Stoute	Lord Weinstock	Loup Sauvage	Bahhare	2:05.46
1998	Alborada (3f)	G Duffield	M Prescott	K Rausing	Insatiable	Daylami	2:03.69
1999*	Alborada (4f)	G Duffield	M Prescott	K Rausing	Shiva	Kabool	2:05.57
2000	Kalanisi (4)	J P Murtagh	J Oxx	HH Aga Khan	Montjeu	Distant Music	2:05.59
2001	Nayef (3)	R Hills	M Tregoning	H Al Maktoum	Tobougg	Indian Creek	2:07.72
2002	Storming Home (4)	M Hills	B Hills	M Al Maktoum	Moon Ballad	Noverre	2:01.42
2003	Rakti (4)	P Robinson	M Jarvis	G A Tanaka	Carnival Dancer	Indian Creek	2:03.34

*Run on the July Course.

CHEVELEY PARK STAKES-G1
6 furlongs, 2-year-old fillies, Newmarket (Rowley Mile Course)
FIRST RUN IN 1899.

Year	1st	Jockey	Trainer	Owner	2nd	3rd	Time
1970	Magic Flute	A Barclay	N Murless	H de Walden	Ballet	Francais Melodina	1:12.63
1971	Waterloo	E Hide	J Watts	Mrs R Stanley	Marisela	Miss Paris	1:13.6
1972	Jacinth	J Gorton	B Hobbs	Lady Butt	Caspian	Marble Arch	1:12.6
1973	Gentle Thoughts	W Pyers	T Curtin	N B Hunt	Red Berry	Lady Tan	1:15
1974	Cry Of Truth	J Gorton	B Hobbs	P Johnston	Delmora	Rose Bowl	1:15.2
1975	Patsy	Pat Eddery	P Walwyn	G Williams	Dame Foolish	Solar	1:15
1976	Durtal	L Piggott	B Hills	R Sangster	Be Easy	Rings	1:14.4
1977	Sookera	W Swinburn	D K Weld	R Sangster	Fair Salinia	Smarten Up	1:11.4
1978	Devon Ditty	G Starkey	H T Jones	E McAlpine	Kilijaro	Do Be Darling	1:12
1979	Mrs Penny	J Matthias	I Balding	E Kronfeld	Millingdale Lillie	Abeer	1:13.4
1980	Marwell	L Piggott	M Stoute	E Loder	Welshwyn	Pushy	1:12.6
1981	Woodstream	Pat Eddery	M V O'Brien	R Sangster	On The House	Admiral's Princess	1:14.2
1982	Ma Biche	F Head	C Head	Mme A Head	Favoridge	Super Entente	1:14.6

Year	1st	Jockey	Trainer	Owner	2nd	3rd	Time
1983	Desirable	S Cauthen	B Hills	Mrs J Corbett	Pebbles	Prickle	1:14.8
1984	Park Appeal	D Gillespie	J Bolger	P Burns	Polly Daniels	Al Bahathri	1:13.8
1985	Embla	A Cordero Jr	L Cumani	C St George	Kingscote	Rose Of The Sea	1:12.4
1986	Minstrella	J Reid	C Nelson	E P Evans	Canadian Mill	Shaikiya	1:12.4
1987	Ravinella	G Moore	C Head	Ecurie Aland	First Waltz	Ela Romara	1:14.2
1988	Pass The Peace	T R Quinn	P Cole	B Bell	Dancing Tribute	Jaljuli	1:11.8
1989	Dead Certain	C Asmussen	D Elsworth	G Marten	Line Of Thunder	Chimes Of Freedom	1:14.8
1990	Capricciosa	J Reid	M V O'Brien	R Sangster	Imperfect Circle	Divine Danse	1:12.2
1991	Marling	W R Swinburn	G Wragg	E Loder	Absurde	Basma	1:11.6
1992	Sayyedati	W R Swinburn	C Brittain	M Obaida	Lyric Fantasy	Poker Chip	1:11.8
1993	Prophecy	Pat Eddery	J Gosden	K Abdullah	Risky	Lemon Souffle	1:14.68
1994	Gay Gallanta	Pat Eddery	M Stoute	Cheveley Park Stud	Tanami	Harayir	1:11.08
1995	Blue Duster	M J Kinane	D Loder	Sheikh Mohammed	My Branch	Najiya	1:12.78
1996	Pas de Reponse	F Head	C Head	Wertheimer & Frere	Moonlight Paradise	Ocean Ridge	1:11.16
1997	Embassy	K Fallon	D Loder	Sheikh Mohammed	Crazee Mental	Royal Shyness	1:12.26
1998	Wannabe Grand	Pat Eddery	J Noseda	B McAllister	Imperial Beauty	Subeen	1:12.4
1999*	Seazun	T R Quinn	M Channon	J Breslin	Torgau	Crimplene	1:12.92
2000	Regal Rose	L Dettori	M Stoute	Cheveley Park Stud	Toroca	Mala Mala	1:13.75
2001	Queen's Logic	S Drowne	M Channon	Jaber Abdullah	Sophisticat	Good Girl	1:12.34
2002	Airwave	C Rutter	H Candy	H Candy & Partners	Russian Rhythm	Danaskaya	1:10.72
2003	Carry On Katie	L Dettori	J Noseda	Mohammed Rashid	Majestic Desert	Badminton	1:13.03

*Run on the July Course.

CORONATION CUP-G1
1-1/2 miles, 4-year-olds & up, Epsom
FIRST RUN IN 1902

Year	1st (Age)	Jockey	Trainer	Owner	2nd	3rd	Time
1970	Caliban (4)	A. Barclay	N. Murless	S. Joel	Park Top	Shoemaker	2:49.2
1971	Lupe (4f)	G. Lewis	N. Murless	Mrs S. Joel	Stintino	Quayside	2:37.6
1972	Mill Reef (4)	G. Lewis	I Balding	P Mellon	Homeric	Wenceslas	2:34.8
1973	Roberto (4)	L. Piggott	M. V O'Brien	J. Galbreath	Attica Meli	Baragoi	2:34.4
1974	Buoy (4)	J. Mercer	W. R. Hern	R. Hollingsworth	Tennyson	Dahlia	2:36.4
1975	Bustino (4)	J. Mercer	W. R. Hern	Lady Beaverbrook	Ashmore	Mil's Bomb	2:33.4
1976	Quiet Fling (4)	L Piggott	J. Tree	J. H Whitney	Libra's Rib	Major Green	2:38
1977	Exceller (4)	G. Dubroeucq	F Mathet	N. B. Hunt	Quiet Fling	Smuggler	2:36.8
1978	Crow (5)	P. Eddery	P Walwyn	D. Wildenstein	Balmerino	Smuggler	2:34.4
1979	Ile de Bourbon (4)	J. Reid	R. J. Houghton	P Oppenheimer	Frere Basile	Gay Mecene	2:43.4
1980	Sea Chimes (4)	L Piggott	J.. Dunlop	J. Thursby	Niniski	Soleil Noir	2:35.8
1981	Master Willie (4)	P. Waldron	H Candy	R. Barnett	Prince Bee	Vielle	2:44.4
1982	Easter Sun (5)	B. Raymond	M.. Jarvis	Lady Beaverbrook	Glint Of Gold	Critique	2:35
1983	Be My Native (4)	L. Piggott	R. Armstrong	K. Hsu	Electric	Old Country	2:45.2
1984	Time Charter (5f)	S. Cauthen	H Candy	R. Barnett	Sun Princess	Lovely Dancer	2:40.6
1985	Rainbow Quest (4)	P. Eddery	J. Tree	K. Abdullah	Old Country	Long Pond	2:35.8
1986	Saint Estephe (4)	P. Eddery	A. Fabre	Y. Houyvet	Triptych	Petoski	2:34.8
1987	Triptych (5f)	A. Cruz	P-L Biancone	A. Clore	Rakaposhi King	Acatenango	2:35.8
1988	Triptych (6f)	S. Cauthen	P-L Biancone	P Brant	Infamy	Moon Madness	2:34.8
1989	Sheriff's Star (4)	R. Cochrane	Lady Herries	Duchess of Norfolk	Ile de Chypre	Green Adventure	2:35.4
1990	In the Wings (4)	C. Asmussen	A. Fabre	Sheikh Mohammed	Observation Post	Ibn Bey	2:36.4
1991	In The Groove (4f)	S. Cauthen	D. Elsworth	B. Cooper	Terimon	Rock Hopper	2:36.2
1992	Saddlers' Hall (4)	W. R. Swinburn	M. Stoute	Lord Weinstock	Rock Hopper	Terimon	2:35.6
1993	Opera House (4)	M. Roberts	M. Stoute	Sheikh Mohammed	Environment Friend	Apple Tree	2:35.13
1994	Apple Tree (5)	T Jarnet	A. Fabre	Sultan Al Kabeer	Environment Friend	Blush Rambler	2:35.43
1995	Sunshack (4)	Pat Eddery	A. Fabre	K. Abdullah	Only Royale	Time Star	2:35.85
1996	Swain (4)	L Dettori	A. Fabre	Sheikh Mohammed	Singspiel	De Quest	2:40.27
1997	Singspiel (5)	L Dettori	M. Stoute	Sheikh Mohammed	Dushyantor	Le Destin	2:37.72
1998	Silver Patriarch (4)	P. Eddery	J. Dunlop	P Winfield	Swain	Ebadiyla	2:37.6
1999	Daylami (5)	L Dettori	S. bin Suroor	Godolphin	Royal Anthem	Dream Well	2:40.26
2000	Daliapour (4)	K Fallon	M Stoute	HH Aga Khan	Fantastic Light	Border Arrow	2:41.63
2001	Mutafaweq (5)	L Dettori	S bin Suroor	Godolphin	Wellbeing	Millenary	2:36.70
2002	Boreal (4)	K Fallon	P Schiergen	Gestut Amerland	Storming Home	Zindabad	2:45.01
2003	Warrsan (5)	P Robinson	C E Brittain	S Manana	Highest	Black San Bellamy	2:35.68

DEWHURST STAKES-G1
7 furlongs, 2-year-old colts & fillies, Newmarket (Rowley Mile Course)
FIRST RUN IN 1875

Year	1st	Jockey	Trainer	Owner	2nd	3rd	Time
1974	Grundy	Pat Eddery	P Walwyn	C Vittadini	Steel Heart	Baldur	1:33.6
1975	Wollow	G Dettori	H Cecil	C d'Alessio	Malinowski	All Hope	1:25.8
1976	The Minstrel	L Piggott	M V O'Brien	R Sangster	Saros	Crown Bowler	1:28.2
1977	Try My Best	L Piggott	M V O'Brien	R Sangster	Sexton Blake	Camden Town	1:28.6
1978	Tromos	J Lynch	B Hobbs	G Cambanis	More Light	Warmington	1:24.6

Year	1st	Jockey	Trainer	Owner	2nd	3rd	Time
1979	Monteverdi	L Piggott	M V O'Brien	R Sangster	Tyrnavos	Romeo Romani	1:26
1980	Storm Bird	Pat Eddery	M V O'Brien	R Sangster	To-Agori-Mou	Miswaki	1:29
1981	Wind And Wuthering	P Waldron	H Candy	R Cyzer	Be My Native	Tender King	1:26.6
1982	Diesis	L Piggott	H Cecil	H de Walden	Gordian Tough	Commander	1:27.4
1983	El Gran Senor	Pat Eddery	M V O'Brien	R Sangster	Rainbow Quest	Siberian Express	1:24.8
1984	Kala Dancer	G Baxter	B Hanbury	R Tikkoo	Law Society	Local Suitor	1:27.6
1985	Huntingdale	M Hills	J Hindley	Mrs P Threlfall	Bakharoff	Sure Blade	1:26.2
1986	Ajdal	W R Swinburn	M Stoute	Sheikh Mohammed	Genghiz	Mister Majestic	1:28.8
1987	RACE NOT RUN						
1988	Prince Of Dance*	W Carson	N Graham	M Sobell			
1988	Scenic *	M Hills	B Hills	Sheikh Mohammed	–	Saratogan	1:27.6
1989	Dashing Blade	J Matthias	I Balding	J C Smith	Call To Arms	Anshan	1:25.4
1990	Generous	T R Quinn	P Cole	Prince F Salman	Bog Trotter	Surrealist	1:28.4
1991	Dr Devious	W Carson	P Chapple-Hyam	L Gaucci	Great Palm	Thourios	1:23.4
1992	Zafonic	Pat Eddery	A Fabre	K Abdullah	Inchinor	Firm Pledge	1:23.6
1993	Grand Lodge	Pat Eddery	W Jarvis	H de Walden	Stonehatch	Nicolotte	1:28.27
1994	Pennekamp	T Jarnet	A Fabre	Sheikh Mohammed	Green Perfume	Eltish	1:25.41
1995	Alhaarth	W Carson	W R Hern	H Al Maktoum	Danehill Dancer	Tagula	1:24.64
1996	In Command	M Hills	B Hills	M Al Maktoum	Musical Pursuit	Air Express	1:25.93
1997	Xaar	O Peslier	A Fabre	K Abdullah	Tamarisk	Impressionist	1:24.81
1998	Mujahid	R Hills	J Dunlop	H Al Maktoum	Auction House	Stravinsky	1:25.31
1999+	Distant Music	M Hills	B Hills	K Abdullah	Brahms	Zentsov Street	1:26.84
2000	Tobougg	C Williams	M Channon	Ahmed Al Maktoum	Noverre	Tempest	1:27.93
2001	Rock Of Gibraltar	M J Kinane	A P O'Brien	Ferguson & Magnier	Landseer	Tendulkar	1:28.70
2002	Tout Seul	S Carson	R JhnsnHoughton	Eden Racing	Tomahawk	Trade Fair	1:23.99
2003	Milk It Mick	D Hollandq	J Osborne	P J Dixon	Three Valleys	Haafhd	1:25.22

*Prince Of Dance and Scenic finished in a deadheat in 1988.
+Run on the July Course.

ECLIPSE STAKES-G1
1-1/4 miles, 3-year-olds & up, Sandown Park
FIRST RUN IN 1886. RUN AT KEMPTON PARK IN 1973.

Year	1st (Age)	Jockey	Trainer	Owner	2nd	3rd	Time
1970	Connaught (5)	A Barclay	N Murless	H Joel	Karabas	Nor	2:06
1971	Mill Reef (3)	G Lewis	I Balding	P Mellon	Caro	Welsh Pageant	2:05.4
1972	Brigadier Gerard (4)	J Mercer	W R Hern	Mrs J Hislop	Gold Rod	Home Guard	2:20.2
1973	Scottish Rifle (4)	R Hutchison	J Dunlop	A Struthers	Moulton	Sun Prince	2:12.4
1974	Coup de Feu (5)	Pat Eddery	D Sasse	F Sasse	Ksar	Mount Hagen	2:08.8
1975	Star Appeal (5)	G Starkey	T Grieper	W Zeitelhack	Taros	Royal Manacle	2:06
1976*	Wollow (3)	G Dettori	H Cecil	C d'Alessio	Radetzky	Ann's Pretendre	2:05.4
1977	Artaius (3)	L Piggott	M V O'Brien	Mrs G Getty II	Lucky Wednesday	Arctic Tern	2:05.4
1978	Gunner B (5)	J Mercer	H Cecil	Mrs P Barratt	Balmerino	Radetzky	2:05
1979	Dickens Hill (3)	A Murray	M O'Toole	Mme J Binet	Crimson Beau	Northern Baby	2:06.2
1980	Ela-Mana-Mou (4)	W Carson	W R Hern	S Weinstock	Hello Gorgeous	Gregorian	2:10
1981	Master Willie (4)	P Waldron	H Candy	R Barnett	Vielle	Fingal's Cave	2:07.4
1982	Kalaglow (4)	G Starkey	G Harwood	A Ward	Lobkowiez	Rocamadour	2:08.8
1983	Solford (3)	Pat Eddery	M V O'Brien	R Sangster	Muscatite	Tolomeo	2:06.2
1984	Sadler's Wells (3)	Pat Eddery	M V O'Brien	R Sangster	Time Charter	Morcon	2:04.4
1985	Pebbles (4f)	S Cauthen	C Brittain	Sheikh Mohammed	Rainbow Quest	Bob Back	2:07.21
1986	Dancing Brave (3)	G Starkey	G Harwood	K Abdullah	Triptych	Teleprompter	2:06
1987	Mtoto (4)	M Roberts	A Stewart	Al Maktoum	Reference Point	Triptych	2:04.2
1988	Mtoto (5)	M Roberts	A Stewart	A Al Maktoum	Shady Heights	Triptych	2:06
1989	Nashwan (3)	W Carson	W R Hern	H Al Maktoum	Opening Verse	Indian Skimmer	2:07.2
1990	Elmaamul (3)	W Carson	W R Hern	H Al Maktoum	Terimon	Ile de Chypre	2:04.
1991	Environment Friend (3)	G Duffield	J Fanshawe	W Gredley	Stagecraft	Sanglamore	2:07.6
1992	Kooyonga (4f)	W O'Connor	M Kauntze	M Haga	Opera House	Sapience	2:10.8
1993	Opera House (5)	M J Kinane	M Stoute	Sheikh Mohammed	Misil	Tenby	2:06.25
1994	Ezzoud (5)	W R Swinburn	M Stoute	M Al Maktoum	Bob's Return	Erhaab	2:04.7
1995	Halling (4)	W R Swinburn	S bin Suroor	Godolphin	Singspiel	Red Bishop	2:05.32
1996	Halling (5)	J Reid	S bin Suroor	Godolphin	Bijou d'Inde	Pentire	2:08.05
1997	Pilsudski (5)	M J Kinane	M Stoute	Lord Weinstock	Benny the Dip	Bosra Sham	2:12.51
1998	Daylami (4)	L Dettori	S bin Suroor	Godolphin	Faithful Son	Central Park	2:06.82
1999	Compton Admiral (3)	D Holland	G Butler	E Penser	Xaar	Fantastic Light	2:06.42
2000	Giant's Causeway (3)	G Duffield	A P O'Brien	Mrs J Magnier/M Tabor	Kalanisi	Shiva	2:05.32
2001	Medicean (4)	K Fallon	M Stoute	Cheveley Park Stud	Grandera	Bach	2:04.65
2002	Hawk Wing (3)	M J Kinane	A P O'Brien	Mrs J Magnier	Sholokhov	Equerry	2:13.34
2003	Falbrav (5)	D Holland	L Cumani	Scuderia Rencati	Nayef	Kaieteur	2:05.59

*Trepon finished first but was disqualified from purse money.

ENGLISH OAKS-G1
1-1/2 miles, 3-year-old fillies, Epsom
FIRST RUN IN 1779

Year	1st	Jockey	Trainer	Owner	2nd	3rd	Time
1970	Lupe	A. Barclay	N. Murless	Mrs S Joel	State Pension	Arctic Wave	2:41.4
1971	Altesse Royale	G. Lewis	N. Murless	F Hue-Williams	Maina	La Manille	2:36.8
1972	Ginerva	A Murray	H Price	C St George	Regal Exception	Arkadina	2:39.4
1973	Mysterious	G. Lewis	N. Murless	G Pope Jr	Where You Lead	Aureoletta	2:36.4
1974	Polygamy	P. Eddery	P Walwyn	L Freedman	Furioso	Matuta	2:39.4
1975	Juliette Marny	L Piggott	J. Tree	J Morrison	Val's Girl	Moonlight Night	2:39
1976	Pawneese	Y. Saint-Martin	A. Penna	D Wildenstein	Roses For The Star	African Dancer	2:35.2
1977	Dunfermline	W. Carson	W. R. Hern	The Queen	Freeze The Secret	Vaguely Deb	2:36.4
1978	Fair Salinia	G. Starkey	M. Stoute	S Hanson	Dancing Maid	Suni	2:36.8
1979	Scintillate	Pat Eddery	J. Tree	J Morrison	Bonnie Isle	Britannia's Rule	2:43.6
1980	Bireme	W. Carson	W. R. Hern	R D Hollingsworth	Vielle	The Dancer	2:34.2
1981	Blue Wind	L Piggott	D. K. Weld	Mrs B Firestone	Madam Gay	Leap Liveley	2:40.8
1982	Time Charter	W. Newnes	H Candy	R Barnett	Slightly Dangerous	Last Feather	2:34.2
1983	Sun Princess	W. Carson	W. R. Hern	M Sobell	Acclimatise	New Coins	2:40.8
1984	Circus Plume	L Piggott	J. Dunlop	R McAlpine	Media Luna	Poquito Queen	2:38.8
1985	Oh So Sharp	S. Cauthen	H Cecil	Sheikh Mohammed	Triptych	Dubian	2:41.2
1986	Midway Lady	R. Cochrane	B. Hanbury	H Ranier	Untold	Maysoon	2:35.6
1987	Unite	W. R. Swinburn	M. Stoute	Sheikh Mohammed	Bourbon Girl	Three Tails	2:38
1988	Diminuendo	S. Cauthen	H Cecil	Sheikh Mohammed	Sudden Love	Animatrice	2:35
1989	Snow Bride	S. Cauthen	H Cecil	M Al Maktoum	Roseate Tern	Mamaluna	2:34.2*
1990	Salsabil	W. Carson	J. Dunlop	H Al Maktoum	Game Plan	Knight's Baroness	2:38.6
1991	Jet Ski Lady	C. Roche	J. Bolger	M Al Maktoum	Shamshir	Shadayid	2:37.2
1992	User Friendly	G. Duffield	C. Brittain	W Gredley	All At Sea	Pearl Angel	2:39.6
1993	Intrepidity	M. Roberts	A. Fabre	Sheikh Mohammed	Royal Ballerina	Oakmead	2:34.19
1994	Balanchine	L Dettori	H Ibrahim	Godolphin	Wind In Her Hair	Hawajiss	2:40.37
1995	Moonshell	L Dettori	S. bin Suroor	Godolphin	Dance A Dream	Pure Grain	2:35.44
1996	Lady Carla	Pat Eddery	H Cecil	W. Said	Pricket	Mezzogiorno	2:35.55
1997	Reams Of Verse	K. Fallon	H Cecil	K. Abdullah	Gazelle Royale	Crown Of Light	2:35.59
1998	Shahtoush	M. J. Kinane	A P O'Brien	Nagle & Magnier	Bahr	Midnight Line	2:38.23
1999	Ramruma	K. Fallon	H Cecil	Prince F Salman	Noushkey	Zahrat Dubai	2:38.72
2000	Love Divine	T R Quinn	H Cecil	Lordship Stud	Kalypso Katie	Melikah	2:43.11
2001	Imagine	M J Kinane	A P O'Brien	Magnier & Nagle	Flight Of Fancy	RelishTheThought	2:36.70
2002	Kazzia	L Dettori	S bin Suroor	Godolphin	Quarter Moon	Shadow Dancing	2:44.52
2003	Casual Look	M Dwyer	A Balding	W S Farish III	Yesterday	Summitville	2:38.07

*Aliysa finished first but was disqualified from purse money.

DERBY STAKES (EPSOM DERBY)-G1
1-1/2 miles, 3-year-old colts & fillies, Epsom
FIRST RUN IN 1780. RUN AT 1 MILE 1780-1784.
Run at Newmarket (July Course) as the New Derby 1915-1918 and 1940-1945.

Year	1st	Jockey	Trainer	Owner	2nd	3rd	Time
1780	Diomed	S Arnull	R Teasel	Sir C Bunbury	Boudrow	Spitfire	
1781	Young Eclipse	C Hindley	D O'Kelly		Crop	Prince Of Orange	
1782	Assassin	S Arnull	F Neale	Earl of Egremont	Sweet Robin	Fortunio	
1783	Saltram	C Hindley	F Neale	J Parker	Dungannon	Parlington	
1784	Serjeant	J Arnull	D O. Kelly	Carlo Khan	Dancer	-	
1785	Aimwell	C Hindley	J Pratt	Earl of Clermont	Grantham	Verjuice	
1786	Noble	J White	F Neale	T Panton	Meteor	Claret	
1787	Sir Peter Teazle	S Arnull	Saunders	Earl of Derby	Gunpowder	Bustler	
1788	Sir Thomas	W South	F Neale	Prince of Wales	Aurelius	Feenow	
1789	Skyscraper	S Chifney Sr	M Stephenson	Duke of Bedford	Sir George	Skylark	
1790	Rhadamanthus	J Arnull	J Pratt	Lord Grosvenor	Asparagus	Lee Boo	
1791	Eager	M Stephenson	M Stephenson	Duke of Bedford	Vermin	Proteus	
1792	John Bull	F Buckle	J Pratt	Lord Grosvenor	Speculator	Bustard	
1793	Waxy	W Clift	R Robson	Sir F Poole	Gohanna	Triptolemus	
1794	Daedalus	F Buckle	J Pratt	Lord Grosvenor	Ragged Jack	Leon	
1795	Spread Eagle	A Wheatley	R Prince	Sir F Standish	Caustic	Pelter	
1796	Didelot	J Arnull	R Prince	Sir F Standish	Stickler	Leviathan	
1797	c by Fidget	J Singleton Jr	M Stephenson	Duke of Bedford	Esculus	Plaistow	
1798	Sir Harry	S Arnull	F Neale	J Cookson	Telegraph	Young Spear	
1799	Archduke	J Arnull	R Prince	Sir F Standish	Gislebert	Eagle	
1800	Champion	W Clift	T Perren	C Wilson	Tag	Mystery	
1801	Eleanor (f)	J Saunders	J Frost	Sir C Bunbury	by Fidget	Remnant	
1802	Tyrant	F Buckle	R Robson	Duke of Grafton	by Young Eclipse	Orlando	
1803	Ditto	W Clift	J Lonsdale	Sir H Williamson	Sir Oliver	c by Sir Peter Teazle	
1804	Hannibal	W Arnull	F Neale	Earl of Egremont	Pavilion	Hippocampus	

Year	1st (Age)	Jockey	Trainer	Owner	2nd	3rd	Time
1805	Cardinal Beaufort	D Fitzpatrick	D Boyce	Earl of Egremont	Plantagenet	Goth	
1806	Paris	J Shepherd	R Prince	Baron Foley	Trafalgar	Hector	
1807	Election	J Arnull	D Boyce	Earl of Egremont	Giles Scroggins	Coriolanus	
1808	Pan	F Collinson	J Lonsdale	Sir H Williamson	Vandyke	Chester	
1809	Pope	T Goodisson	R Robson	Duke of Grafton	Wizard	Salvator	
1810	Whalebone	W Clift	R Robson	Duke of Grafton	The Dandy	Eccleston	
1811*	Phantom	F Buckle	J Edwards	Sir J Shelley	Magic	-	
1812	Octavius	W Arnull	D Boyce	R Ladbroke	Sweep	Comus	
1813	Smolensko	T Goodisson	Crouch	Sir C Bunbury	Caterpillar	Illusion	
1814*	Blucher	W Arnull	D Boyce	Baron Stawell	Perchance	-	
1815	Whisker	T Goodisson	R Robson	Duke of Grafton	Raphael	Busto	
1816	Prince Leopold	W Wheatley	W Butler	Duke of York	Nectar	Pandour	
1817*	Azor	J Robinson	R Robson	J Payne Young	Wizard	-	
1818	Sam	S Chifney Jr	T Perren	T Thornhill	Raby	Prince Paul	
1819*	Tiresias	W Clift	R Prince	Duke of Portland	Sultan	-	
1820	Sailor	S Chifney Jr	W Chifney	T Thornhill	Abjer	Tiger	
1821	Gustavus	S Day	Crouch	J Hunter	Reginald	Sir Huldibrand	
1822	Moses	T Goodisson	W Butler	Duke of York	Figaro	Hampden	
1823*	Emilius	F Buckle	R Robson	J Udney	Tancred	-	
1824*	Cedric	J Robinson	J Edwards	Sir J Shelley	Osmond	-	
1825	Middleton	J Robinson	J Edwards	Earl of Jersey	Rufus	Hogarth	
1826*	Lap-Dog	G Dockeray	Bird	Earl of Egremont	Shakspeare	-	
1827	Mameluke	J Robinson	J Edwards	Earl of Jersey	Glenartney	Edmund	
1828*	Cadland	J Robinson	D Boyce	Duke of Rutland	The Colonel	-	
1829*	Frederick	J Forth	J Forth	G Gratwicke	The Exquisite	-	
1830	Priam	S Day	W Chifney	W Chifney	Little Red Rover	Mahmoud	
1831	Spaniel	W Wheatley	J Rogers	Viscount Lowther	Riddlesworth	Incubus	
1832	St Giles	W Scott	J Webb	R Ridsdale	Perion	Trustee	
1833	Dangerous	J Chapple	I Sadler	I Sadler	Connoisseur	Revenge	
1834	Plenipotentiary	P Conolly	G Payne	S Batson	Shilelagh	Glencoe	
1835*	Mundig	W Scott	J Scott	J Bowes	Ascot	-	
1836*	Bay Middleton	J Robinson	J Edwards	Earl of Jersey	Gladiator	-	
1837*	Phosphorus	G Edwards	J Doe	Baron Berner	Caravan	-	
1838	Amato	J Chapple	R Sherwood	Sir G Heathcote	Ion	Grey Momus	
1839*	Bloomsbury	S Templeman	W Ridsdale	W Ridsdale	Deception	-	
1840	Little Wonder	W Macdonald	J Forth	D Robertson	Launcelot	Discord	
1841*	Coronation	P Conolly	Painter	A Rawlinson	Van Amburgh	-	
1842*	Attila	W Scott	J Scott	G Anson	Robert De Gorham	-	
1843*	Cotherstone	W Scott	J Scott	J Bowes	Gorhambury	-	
1844	Orlando	N Flatman	W Cooper	J Peel	Ionian	Bay Momus	
1845	The Merry Monarch	F Bell	J Forth	G Gratwicke	Annandale	Old England	
1846	Pyrrhus The First	S Day	J Day	J Gully	Sir Tatton Sykes	Brocardo	2:55
1847	Cossack	S Templeman	J Day Jr	T H Pedley	War Eagle	Van Tromp	2:52
1848	Surplice	S Templeman	J Kent	Viscount Clifden	Springy Jack	Shylock	2:48
1849	The Flying Dutchman	C Marlow	J Fobert	Earl of Eglinton	Hotspur	Tadmor	3:00
1850	Voltigeur	J Marson	R Hill	Earl of Zetland	Pitsford	Clincher	2:50
1851	Teddington	J Marson	A Taylor Sr	Sir J Hawley	Marlborough Buck	Neasham	2:51
1852	Daniel O'Rourke	F Butler	J Scott	J Bowes	Barbarian Chief	Baron Nicholson	3:02
1853	West Australian	F Butler	J Scott	J Bowes	Sittingbourne	Cineas	2:55
1854	Andover	A Day	J Day Jr	J Gully	King Tom	The Hermit	2:52
1855	Wild Dayrell	R Sherwood	J Rickaby	F Popham	Kingstown	Lord Of The Isles	2:54
1856	Ellington	T Aldcroft	T Dawson	O Harcourt	Yellow Jack	Cannobie	3:04
1857	Blink Bonny (f)	J Charlton	W I'Anson	W I'Anson	Black Tommy	Adamas	2:45
1858	Beadsman	J Wells	G Manning	Sir J Hawley	Toxophilite	The Hadji	2:54
1859	Musjid	J Wells	G Manning	Sir J Hawley	Marionette	Trumpeter	2:59
1860	Thormanby	H Custance	M Dawson	J Merry	The Wizard	Horror	2:55
1861	Kettledrum	R Bullock	G Oates	C Towneley	Dundee	Diophantus	2:45
1862	Caractacus	J Parsons	R Smith	C Snewing	The Marquis	Buckstone	2:45.5
1863	Macaroni	T Chaloner	J Godding	R Naylor	Lord Clifden	Rapid Rhone	2:50.5
1864	Blair Athol	J Snowden	W I'Anson	W I'Anson	General Peel	Scottish Chief	2:43
1865	Galdiateur	H Grimshaw	T Jennings	Comte F de Lagrange	Christmas Carol	Eltham	2:56
1866	Lord Lyon	H Custance	J Dover	R Sutton	Savernake	Rustic	2:50
1867	Hermit	J Daley	G Bloss	H Chaplin	Marksman	Vauban	2:52
1868	Blue Gown	J Wells	J Porter	Sir J Hawley	King Alfred	Speculum	2:43.5
1869	Pretender	J Osborne	T Dawson	J Johnstone	Pero Gomez	The Drummer	2:52.5
1870	Kingcraft	T French	M Dawson	Viscount Falmouth	Palmerston	Muster	2:45
1871	Favonius	T French	J Hayhoe	M de Rothschild	Albert Victor	King Of The Forest	2:50
1872	Cremorne	C Maidment	W Gilbert	H Savile	Pell Mell	Queens Messenger	2:45.5
1873	Doncaster	F Webb	R Peck	J Merry	Gang Forward	Kaiser	2:50
1874	George Frederick	H Custance	T Leader	W Cartwright	Couronne de Fer	Atlantic	2:46
1875	Galopin	J Morris	J Dawson	Prince G Batthyany	Claremont	Remorse	2:48
1876	Kisber	C Maidment	J Hayhoe	A Baltazzi	Forerunner	Julius Caesar	2:44
1877	Silvio	F Archer	M Dawson	Viscount Falmouth	Glen Arthur	Rob Roy	2:50

Year	1st	Jockey	Trainer	Owner	2nd	3rd	Time
1878	Sefton	H Constable	A Taylor Sr	W S Crawfurd	Insulaire	Childeric	2:56
1879	Sir Bevys	G Fordham	J Hayhoe	L N de Rothschild	Palmbearer	Visconti	3:02
1880	Bend Or	F Archer	R Peck	Duke of Westminster	Robert The Devil	Mask	2:46
1881	Iroquois	F Archer	J Pincus	P Lorillard	Peregrine	Town Moor	2:50
1882	Shotover (f)	T Cannon	J Porter	Duke of Westminster	Quicklime	Sachem	2:45.6
1883	St Blaise	C Wood	J Porter	Sir F Johnstone	Highland Chief	Galliard	2:48.4
1884^	Harvester	S Loates	J Jewitt	Sir J Willoughby			
1884^	St Gatien	C Wood	R Sherwood	J Hammond	–	Queen	2:46.2
1885	Melton	F Archer	M Dawson	Baron Hastings	Paradox	Royal Hampton	2:44.2
1886	Ormonde	F Archer	J Porter	Duke of Westminster	The Bard	St Mirin	2:45.6
1887	Merry Hampton	J Watts	M Gurry	G Baird	The Baron	Martley	2:43
1888	Ayrshire	F Barrett	G Dawson	Duke of Portland	Crowberry	Van Dieman's Land	2:43
1889	Donovan	T Loates	G Dawson	Duke of Portland	Miguel	El Dorado	2:44.4
1890	Sainfoin	J Watts	J Porter	Sir J Miller	Le Nord Orwell	Sir J Miller	2:49.8
1891	Common	G Barrett	J Porter	Sir F Johnstone	Gouverneur	Martenhurst	2:56.8
1892	Sir Hugo	F Allsopp	T Wadlow	Earl of Bradford	La Fleche	Bucentaure	2:44
1893	Isinglass	T Loates	J Jewitt	H McCalmont	Ravensbury	Raeburn	2:43
1894	Ladas	J Watts	M Dawson	Earl of Roseberry	Matchbox	Reminder	2:45.8
1895	Sir Visto	S Loates	M Dawson	Earl of Roseberry	Curzon	Kirkconnel	2:43.4
1896	Persimmon	J Watts	R Marsh	Prince of Wales	St Frusquin	Earwig	2:42
1897	Galtee More	C Wood	S Darling	J Gubbins	Velasquez	History	2:44
1898	Jeddah	O Madden	R Marsh	J Larnach	Batt	Dunlop	2:47
1899	Flying Fox	M Cannon	J Porter	Duke of Westminster	Damocles	Innocence	2:42.8
1900	Diamond Jubilee	H Jones	R Marsh	Prince of Wales	Simon Dale	Disguise	2:42
1901	Volodyovski	L Reiff	J Huggins	W C Whitney	William The Third	Veronese	2:40.8
1902	Ard Patrick	S Martin	S Darling	J Gubbins	Rising Glass	Friar Tuck	2:42.2
1903	Rock Sand	D Maher	G Blackwell	Sir J Miller	Vinicius	Flotsam	2:42.8
1904	St Amant	K Cannon	A Hayhoe	L de Rothschild	John O'Gaunt	St Denis	2:45.4
1905	Cicero	D Maher	P Peck	Earl of Roseberry	Jardy	Signorino	2:39.6
1906	Spearmint	D Maher	P Gilpin	E Loder	Picton	Troutbeck	2:36.8
1907	Orby	J Reiff	F MacCabe	R Croker	Wool Winder	Slieve Gallion	2:44
1908	Signorinetta (f)	B Bullock	O Ginistrelli	O Ginistrelli	Prime	Llangwm	2:39.8
1909	Minoru	H Jones	R Marsh	King Edward VII	Louviers	William The Fourth	2:42.4
1910	Lemberg	B Dillon	A Taylor	A Cox	Greenback	Charles O'Malley	2:35.2
1911	Sunstar	G Stern	C Morton	J B Joel	Stedfast	Royal Tender	2:36.8
1912	Tagalie (f)	J Reiff	D Waugh	W Raphael	Jaeger	Tracery	2:38.8
1913+	Aboyeur	E Piper	T Lewis	A Cunliffe	Louvois	Great Sport	2:37.6
1914	Durbar	M MacGee	T Murphy	H Duryea	Hapsburg	Peter The Hermit	2:38.4
1915	Pommern	S Donoghue	C Peck	S B Joel	Let Fly	Rossendale	2:32.6
1916	Fifinella (f)	J Childs	D Dawson	Sir E Hulton	Kwang-Su	Nassovian	2:36.6
1917	Gay Crusader	S Donoghue	A Taylor	A Cox	Dansellon	Dark Legend	2:40.6
1918	Gainsborough	J Childs	A Taylor	Lady J Douglas	Blink	Treclare	2:33.2
1919	Grand Parade	F Templeman	F Barling	Baron Glanely	Buchan	Paper Money	2:35.8
1920	Spion Kop	F O'Neill	P Gilpin	G Loder	Archaic	Orpheus	2:34.8
1921	Humorist	S Donoghue	C Morton	J B Joel	Craig An Eran	Lemonora	2:36.2
1922	Captain Cuttle	S Donoghue	F Darling	Baron Woolavington	Tamar	Craigangower	2:34.6
1923	Papyrus	S Donoghue	B Jarvis	B Irish	Pharos	Parth	2:38
1924	Sansovino	T Weston	G Lambton	Earl of Derby	St Germans	Hurstwood	2:46.6
1925	Manna	S Donoghue	J Maher	H Morriss	Zionist	The Sirdar	2:40.6
1926	Coronach	J Childs	F Darling	Baron Woolavington	Lancegaye	Colorado	2:47.8
1927	Call Boy	C Elliott	J Watts	F Curzon	Hot Night	Shian Mor	2:34.4
1928	Felstead	H Wragg	O Bell	Sir H Cunliffe-Owen	Flamingo	Black Watch	2:34.4
1929	Trigo	J Marshall	D Dawson	W Barnett	Walter Gay	Brienz	2:36.4
1930	Blenheim	H Wragg	D Dawson	Aga Khan	Iliad	Diolite	2:38.2
1931	Cameronian	F Fox	F Darling	J A Dewar	Orpen	Sandwich	2:36.6
1932	April The Fifth	F Lane	G Whitelaw	T Walls	Dastur	Miracle	2:43
1933	Hyperion	T Weston	G Lambton	Earl of Derby	King Salmon	Statesman	2:34
1934	Windsor Lad	C Smirke	M Marsh	Maharaja of Rajpipla	Easton	Colombo	2:34
1935	Bahram	F Fox	F Butters	Aga Khan	Robin Goodfellow	Field Trial	2:36
1936	Mahmoud	C Smirke	F Butters	Aga Khan	Taj Akbar	Thankerton	2:33.8
1937	Mid-Day Sun	M Beary	F Butters	L Miller	Sandsprite	Le Grand Duc	2:37.6
1938	Bois Roussel	C Elliott	F Darling	P Beatty	Scottish Union	Pasch	2:39.2
1939	Blue Peter	E Smith	J Jarvis	Earl of Roseberry	Fox Cub	Heliopolis	2:36.8
1940	Pont l Eveque	S Wragg	F Darling	F Darling	Turkhan	Lighthouse	2:30.8
1941	Owen Tudor	B Nevett	F Darling	C Macdonald-Buchanan	Morogoro	Firoze Din	2:32
1942	Watling Street	H Wragg	W Earl	Earl of Derby	Hyperides	Ujiji	2:29.6
1943	Straight Deal	T Carey	W Nightingall	D Paget	Umiddad	Nasrullah	2:30.4
1944	Ocean Swell	B Nevett	J Jarvis	Earl of Roseberry	Tehran	Happy Landing	2:31
1945	Dante	B Nevett	M Peacock	Sir E Ohlson	Midas	Court Martial	2:26.6
1946	Airborne	T Lowrey	D Perryman	J Ferguson	Gulf Stream	Radiotherapy	2:44.6
1947	Pearl Diver	G Bridgland	P Carter	Baron G de Waldner	Migoli	Sayajirao	2:38.4
1948	My Love	R Johnstone	R Carver	Aga Khan	Royal Drake	Noor	2:40
1949	Nimbus	C Elliott	G Colling	M Glenister	Amour Drake	Swallow Tail	2:42

Year	1st	Jockey	Trainer	Owner	2nd	3rd	Time
1950	Galcador	R Johnstone	C Semblat	M Boussac	Prince Simon	Double Eclipse	2:36.8
1951	Arctic Prince	C Spares	W Stephenson	J McGrath	Sybil s Nephew	Signal Box	2:39.4
1952	Tulyar	C Smirke	M Marsh	Aga Khan	Gay Time	Faubourg	2:36.4
1953	Pinza	G Richards	N Bertie	Sir V Sassoon	Aureole	Pink Horse	2:35.6
1954	Never Say Die	L Piggott	J Lawson	R S Clarke	Arabian Night	Darius	2:35.8
1955	Phil Drake	F Palmer	F Mathet	S Volterra	Panaslipper	Acropolis	2:39.8
1956	Lavandin	R Johnstone	A Head	P Wertheimer	Montaval	Roistar	2:36.4
1957	Crepello	L Piggott	N Murless	Sir V Sassoon	Ballymoss	Pipe Of Peace	2:35.4
1958	Hard Ridden	C Smirke	J M Rogers	Sir V Sassoon	Paddy's Point	Nagani	2:41.2
1959	Parthia	H Carr	C Boyd-Rochfort	Sir H de Trafford	Fidalgo	Shantung	2:36
1960	St Paddy	L Piggott	N Murless	Sir V Sassoon	Alcaeus	Kythnos	2:35.6
1961	Psidium	R Poincelet	H Wragg	E Plesch	Dicta Drake	Pardao	2:36.4
1962	Larkspur	N Sellwood	M V O'Brien	R Guest	Arcor	Le Cantilien	2:37.6
1963	Relko	Y Saint-Martin	F Mathet	F Dupre	Merchant Venturer	Ragusa	2:39.4
1964	Santa Claus	A Breasley	J M Rogers	J Ismay	Indiana	Dilettante	2:41.98
1965	Sea-Bird	P Glennon	E Pollet	J Ternynck	Meadow Court	I Say	2:38.41
1966	Charlottown	A Breasley	G Smyth	Lady Z Wernher	Pretendre	Black Prince	2:37.63
1967	Royal Palace	G Moore	N Murless	J Joel	Ribocco	Dart Board	2:38.36
1968	Sir Ivor	L Piggott	M V O'Brien	R Guest	Connaught	Mount Athos	2:38.73
1969	Blakeney	E Johnson	A Budgett	A Budgett	Shoemaker	Prince Regent	2:40.3
1970	Nijinsky II	L Piggott	M V O'Brien	C Engelhard	Gyr	Stintino	2:34.68
1971	Mill Reef	G Lewis	I Balding	P Mellon	Linden Tree	Irish Ball	2:37.14
1972	Roberto	L Piggott	M V O'Brien	J Galbreath	Rheingold	Pentland Firth	2:36.09
1973	Morston	E Hide	A Budgett	A Budgett	Cavo Doro	Freefoot	2:35.92
1974	Snow Knight	B Taylor	P Nelson	S Phillips	Imperial Prince	Giacometti	2:35.04
1975	Grundy	Pat Eddery	P Walwyn	C Vittadini	Nobiliary	Hunza Dancer	2:35.34
1976	Empery	L Piggott	M Zilber	N B Hunt	Relkino	Oats	2:35.69
1977	The Minstrel	L Piggott	M V O'Brien	R Sangster	Hot Grove	Blushing Groom	2:36.44
1978	Shirley Heights	G Starkey	J Dunlop	Earl of Halifax	Hawaiian Sound	Remainder Man	2:35.3
1979	Troy	W Carson	W R Hern	M Sobell	Dickens Hill	Northern Baby	2:36.59
1980	Henbit	W Carson	W R Hern	E Plesch	Master Willie	Rankin	2:34.77
1981	Shergar	W R Swinburn	M Stoute	Aga Khan	Glint Of Gold	Scintillating Air	2:44.21
1982	Golden Fleece	Pat Eddery	M V O'Brien	R Sangster	Touching Wood	Silver Hawk	2:34.27
1983	Teenoso	L Piggott	G Wragg	E Moller	Carlingford Castle	Shearwalk	2:49.07
1984	Secreto	C Roche	D V O'Brien	L Miglietti	El Gran Senor	Mighty Flutter	2:39.12
1985	Slip Anchor	S Cauthen	H Cecil	H de Walden	Law Society	Damister	2:36.23
1986	Shahrastani	W R Swinburn	M Stoute	Aga Khan	Dancing Brave	Mashkour	2:37.13
1987	Reference Point	S Cauthen	H Cecil	L Freedman	Most Welcome	Bellotto	2:33.9
1988	Kahyasi	R Cochrane	L Cumani	Aga Khan	Glacial Storm	Doyoun	2:33.84
1989	Nashwan	W Carson	W R Hern	H Al Maktoum	Terimon	Cacoethes	2:34.9
1990	Quest For Fame	Pat Eddery	R Charlton	K Abdullah	Blue Stag	Elmaamul	2:37.26
1991	Generous	A Munro	P Cole	Prince F Salman	Marju	Star Of Gdansk	2:34
1992	Dr Devious	J Reid	P Chapple-Hyam	S Craig	St. Jovite	Silver Wisp	2:36.19
1993	Commander In Chief	M J Kinane	H Cecil	K Abdullah	Blue Judge	Blues Traveller	2:34.51
1994	Erhaab	W Carson	J Dunlop	H Al Maktoum	King's Theatre	Colonel Collins	2:34.16
1995	Lammtarra	W R Swinburn	S bin Suroor	S M Al Maktoum	Tamure	Presenting	2:32.31
1996	Shaamit	M Hills	W Haggas	K A Dasman	Dushyantor	Shantou	2:35.05
1997	Benny The Dip	W Ryan	J Gosden	L Knight	Silver Patriarch	Romanov	2:35.77
1998	High-Rise	O Peslier	L Cumani	M O Al Maktoum	City Honours	Border Arrow	2:33.88
1999	Oath	K Fallon	H Cecil	The Thoroughbred Corp	Daliapour	Beat All	2:37.43
2000	Sinndar	J P Murtagh	J Oxx	HH Aga Khan	Sakhee	Beat Hollow	2:36.75
2001	Galileo	M J Kinane	A P O'Brien	Magnier & Tabor	Golan	Tobougg	2:33.27
2002	High Chaparral	J P Murtagh	A P O'Brien	Tabor & Magnier	Hawk Wing	Moon Ballad	2:39.45
2003	Kris Kin	K Fallon	M R Stoute	S Suhail	The Great Gatsby	Alamshar	2:33.35

*No horse was officially placed third.
^Harvester and St Gatien finished in a deadheat in 1884.
+Craganour finished first but was disqualified and placed last.

FILLIES' MILE-G1
1m, 2-year-old fillies, Ascot
FIRST RUN IN 1973.
Run as the Green Shield Stakes in 1973. Run as the Argos Stakes 1975-1977.

Year	1st	Jockey	Trainer	Owner	2nd	3rd	Time
1973	Escorial	L Piggott	I Balding	The Queen	Evening Venture	Gaily	1:51.37
1974	RACE NOT RUN						
1975	Icing	C Roche	P Prendergast	Lady Iveagh	Bedfellow	Gliding	1:46.6
1976	Miss Pinkie	L Piggott	N Murless	H J Joel	Dunfermline	Triple First	1:45.31
1977	Cherry Hinton	L Piggott	H Wragg	R B Moller	Tartan Pimpernel	Watch Out	1:42.52
1978	Formulate	J Mercer	H Cecil	Mrs D Butler	Odoon	Rimosa's Pet	1:43.61
1979	Quick As Lightning	W Carson	J Dunlop	O M Phipps	Viollo	Sharp Castan	1:43.17
1980	Leap Lively	J Matthias	I Balding	P Mellon	Exclusively Raised	Fiesta Fun	1:41.80
1981	Height Of Fashion	J Mercer	W R Hern	The Queen	Stratospheric	Zinzara	1:44.72

Year	1st	Jockey	Trainer	Owner	2nd	3rd	Time
1982	Acclimatise	A Murray	B Hobbs	J Hembro	Dancing Meg	Alligatrix	1:47.28
1983	Nepula	B Crossley	G Huffer	A Al Qemias	Nonesuch Bay	Circus Plume	1:44.68
1984	Oh So Sharp	L Piggott	H Cecil	Shaikh Mohammed	Helen Street	Morning Devotion	1:42.44
1985	Untold	W R Swinburn	M Stoute	R H Cowell	Moonlight Lady	Sue Grundy	1:40.92
1986	Invited Guest	S Cauthen	R Armstrong	Kinderhill Corp	Mountain Memory	Shining Water	1:43.47
1987	Diminuendo	S Cauthen	H Cecil	Sheikh Mohammed	Haiati	Ashayor	1:43.10
1988	Tessla	Pat Eddery	H Cecil	C St George	Pick Of The Pops	Rain Burst	1:43.96
1989	Silk Slippers	M Hills	B Hills	R Sangster	Moon Cactus	Fujaiyrah	1:42.49
1990	Shamshir	L Dettori	L Cumani	Shaikh Mohammed	Safa	Atlantic Flyer	1:43.27
1991	Midnight Air	Pat Eddery	P Cole	C Wright	Culture Vulture	Mystery Play	1:46.11
1992	Ivanka	M Roberts	C Brittain	A Saeed	Ajfan	Iviza	1:46.65
1993	Fairy Heights	C Asmussen	N Callaghan	F Golding	Dance To The Top	Kissing Cousin	1:44.44
1994	Aqaarid	W Carson	J Dunlop	H Al Maktoum	Jural	Snowtown	1:44.70
1995	Bosra Sham	Pat Eddery	H Cecil	W Said	Bint Shadayid	Matiya	1:43.13
1996	Reams Of Verse	M J Kinane	H Cecil	K Abdullah	Khassah	Sleepytime	1:44.32
1997	Glorosia	L Dettori	L Cumani	R H Smith	Jibe	Exclusive	1:42.31
1998	Sunspangled	M J Kinane	A O'Brien	Tabor & Magnier	Calando	Edabiya	1:44.79
1999	Teggiano	L Dettori	C Brittain	A S Bul Hab	Britannia	My Hansel	1:49.69
2000	Crystal Music	L Dettori	J Gosden	A Lloyd-Webber	Summer Symphony	Hotelgenie Dot Com	1:44.44
2001	Gossamer	J P Spencer	L Cumani	G W Leigh	Maryinsky	Esloob	1:46.40
2002	Soviet Song	O Urbina	J Fanshawe	Elite Racing Club	Casual Look	ReachForTheMoon	1:42.32
2003	Red Bloom	K Fallon	M R Stoute	Cheveley Park Stud	Sundrop	Punctilious	1:40.81

JUDDMONTE INTERNATIONAL STAKES-G1
1 mile, 2 furlongs, 85 yards, 3-year-olds & up, York
FIRST RUN IN 1972.
Run as the Benson & Hedges Gold Cup through 1985.
Matchmaker International 1986-7. International Stakes in 1988.

Year	1st (age)	Jockey	Trainer	Owner	2nd	3rd	Time
1972	Roberto (3)	B Baeza	M V O'Brien	J Galbreath	Brigadier Gerard	Gold Rod	2:07.0
1973	Moulton (4)	G Lewis	H Wragg	R Moller	Scottish Rifle	Rheingold	2:20.4
1974	Dahlia (4f)	L Piggott	M Zilber	N B Hunt	Imperial Prince	Snow Knight	2:09.6
1975	Dahlia (5f)	L Piggott	M Zilber	N B Hunt	Card King	Star Appeal	2:10.8
1976	Wollow (3)	G Dettori	H Cecil	C d'Alessio	Crow	Patch	2:11.6
1977	Relkino (4)	W Carson	W R Hern	Lady Beaverbrook	Artaius	Orange Bay	2:09.2
1978	Hawaiian Sound (3)	L Piggott	B Hills	R Sangster	Gunner B	Jellaby	2:09.8
1979	Troy (3)	W Carson	W R Hern	M Sobell	Crimson Beau	Lyphard's Wish	2:13.4
1980	Master Willie (3)	P Waldron	H Candy	W Barnett	Cairn Rouge	Cracaval	2:13.2
1981	Beldale Flutter (3)	Pat Eddery	M Jarvis	M Kelly	Kirtling	Master Willie	2:13.2
1982	Assert (3)	Pat Eddery	D V O'Brien	R Sangster	Norwick	Amyndas	2:09.0
1983	Caerleon (3)	Pat Eddery	M V O'Brien	R Sangster	Hot Touch	John French	2:16.2
1984	Cormorant Wood(4)	S Cauthen	B Hills	R McAlpine	Tolomeo	Chief Singer	2:09.8
1985	Commanche Run (4)	L Piggott	L Cumani	I Allan	Oh So Sharp	Triptych	2:18.6
1986	Shardari (4)	W R Swinburn	M Stoute	Aga Khan	Triptych	Damister	2:08.2
1987	Triptych (5f)	S Cauthen	P-L Biancone	A Clore	Ascot Knight	Sir Harry Lewis	2:15.4
1988	Shady Heights (4)	W Carson	R Armstrong	G Tong	Indian Skimmer	Persian Heights	2:06.2
1989	Ile de Chypre (4)	A Clark	G Harwood	G Christodoulou	Cacoethes	Shady Heights	2:06.8
1990	In The Groove (3f)	S Cauthen	D Elsworth	B Cooper	Elmaamul	Batshoof	2:08.6
1991	Terimon (5)	M Roberts	C Brittain	Lady Beaverbrook	Quest For Fame	Stagecraft	2:16
1992	Rodrigo de Triano (3)	L Piggott	P Chapple-Hyam	R Sangster	All At Sea	Seattle Rhyme	2:07
1993	Ezzoud (4)	W R Swinburn	M Stoute	M Al Maktoum	Sabrehill	Spartan Shareef	2:12.16
1994	Ezzoud (5)	W R Swinburn	M Stoute	M Al Maktoum	Muhtarram	King's Theatre	2:08.85
1995	Halling (4)	W R Swinburn	S bin Suroor	Godolphin	Bahri	Annus Mirabilis	2:06.42
1996	Halling (5)	L Dettori	S bin Suroor	Godolphin	First Island	Bijou d'Inde	2:06.88
1997	Singspiel (5)	L Dettori	M Stoute	Sheikh Mohammed	Desert King	Benny the Dip	2:12.1
1998	One So Wonderful(4)	Pat Eddery	L Cumani	Helena Springfield Ltd	Faithful Son	Chester House	2:06.46
1999	Royal Anthem (4)	G Stevens	H Cecil	Thoroughbred Corp	Greek Dance	Chester House	2:06.91
2000	Giant's Causeway (3)	M J Kinane	A P O'Brien	Mrs J Magnier/M Tabor	Kalanisi	Lear Spear	2:09.13
2001	Sakhee (4)	L Dettori	S bin Suroor	Godolphin	Grandera	Medicean	2:08.27
2002	Nayef (4)	R Hills	M Tregoning	H Al Maktoum	Golan	Noverre	2:08.74
2003	Falbrav (5)	D Holland	L Cumani	Scuderia Rencati	Magistretti	Nayef	2:06.84

KING GEORGE VI AND QUEEN ELIZABETH DIAMOND STAKES-G1
1-1/2 miles, 3-year-olds & up, Ascot
First run in 1951.

Year	1st (Age)	Jockey	Trainer	Owner	2nd	3rd	Time
1954	Aureole (4)	E Smith	C Boyd-Rochfort	The Queen	Vamos	Darius	2:44
1955	Vimy (3)	R Poincelet	A Head	P Wertheimer	Acropolis	Elopement	2:33.6
1956	Ribot (4)	E Camici	U Penco	Marchese Incisa	High Veldt	Todrai	2:40.24
1957	Montaval (4)	F Palmer	G Bridgland	R Strassburger	Al Mabsoot	Tribord	2:41.02
1958	Ballymoss (4)	A Breasley	M V O'Brien	J McShain	Almeria	Doutelle	2:36.33

Year	1st (Age)	Jockey	Trainer	Owner	2nd	3rd	Time
1959	Alcide (4)	W Carr	C Boyd-Rochfort	H de Trafford	Gladness	Balbo	2:31.39
1960	Aggressor (5)	J Lindley	J Gosden	H Wernher	Petite Etoile	Kythnos	2:35.21
1961	Right Royal (3)	R Poincelet	E Pollet	Mme E Couturie	St Paddy	Rockavon	2:40.34
1962	Match (4)	Y Saint-Martin	F Mathet	F Dupre	Aurelius	Arctic Storm	2:32.02
1963	Ragusa (3)	G Bougoure	P Prendergast	J Mullion	Miralgo	Tarqogan	2:33.8
1964	Nasram (4)	W Pyers	E Fellows	Mrs H Jackson	Santa Claus	Royal Avenue	2:33.15
1965	Meadow Court (3f)	L Piggott	P Prendergast	G Bell	Soderini	Oncidium	2:33.27
1966	Aunt Edith (4f)	L Piggott	N Murless	J Hornung	Sodium	Prominer	2:35.06
1967	Busted (4)	G Moore	N Murless	S Joel	Salvo	Ribocco	2:33.64
1968	Royal Palace (4)	A Barclay	N Murless	H Joel	Felicio	Topyo	2:33.22
1969	Park Top (5f)	L Piggott	B van Cutsem	Duke of Devonshire	Crozier	Hogarth	2:32.46
1970	Nijinsky II (3)	L Piggott	M V O'Brien	C Engelhard	Blakeney	Crepellana	2:36.16
1971	Mill Reef (3)	G Lewis	I Balding	P Mellon	Ortis	Acclimitization	2:32.56
1972	Brigadier Gerard (4)	J Mercer	W R Hern	Mrs J Hislop	Parnell	Riverman	2:32.91
1973	Dahlia (3f)	W Pyers	M Zilber	N B Hunt	Rheingold	Our Mirage	2:30.43
1974	Dahlia (4f)	L Piggott	M Zilber	N B Hunt	Highclere	Dankaro	2:33.03
1975	Grundy (3)	Pat Eddery	P Walwyn	C Vittadini	Bustino	Dahlia	2:26.98
1976	Pawneese (3f)	Y Saint-Martin	A Penna	D Wildenstein	Bruni	Orange Bay	2:29.36
1977	The Minstrel (3)	L Piggott	M V O'Brien	R Sangster	Orange Bay	Exceller	2:30.48
1978	Ile de Bourbon (3)	J Reid	J F Houghton	D McCall	Hawaiian Sound	Montcontour	2:30.53
1979	Troy (3)	W Carson	W R Hern	M Sobell	Gay Mecene	Ela-Mana-Mou	2:33.75
1980	Ela-Mana-Mou (4)	W Carson	W R Hern	S Weinstock	Mrs Penny	Gregorian	2:35.39
1981	Shergar (3)	W R Swinburn	M Stoute	Aga Khan	Madam Gay	Fingals Cave	2:35.4
1982	Kalaglow (4)	G Starkey	G Harwood	A Ward	Assert	Glint Of Gold	2:31.58
1983	Time Charter (4f)	J Mercer	H Candy	R Barnett	Diamond Shoal	Sun Princess	2:30.78
1984	Teenoso (4)	L Piggott	G Wragg	E Moller	Sadler's Wells	Tolomeo	2:27.95
1985	Petoski (3)	W Carson	W R Hern	Lady Beaverbrook	Oh So Sharp	Rainbow Quest	2:27.61
1986	Dancing Brave (3)	Pat Eddery	G Harwood	K Abdullah	Shardari	Triptych	2:29.49
1987	Reference Point (3)	S Cauthen	H Cecil	L Freedman	Celestial Storm	Triptych	2:34.63
1988	Mtoto (5)	M Roberts	A Stewart	A Al Maktoum	Unfuwain	Tony Bin	2:37.33
1989	Nashwan (3)	W Carson	W R Hern	H Al Maktoum	Cacoethes	Top Class	2:32.27
1990	Belmez (3)	M J Kinane	H Cecil	Sheikh Mohammed	Old Vic	Assatis	2:30.76
1991	Generous (3)	A Munro	P Cole	Prince F Salman	Sanglamore	Rock Hopper	2:28.99
1992	St. Jovite (3)	S Craine	J Bolger	V K Payson	Saddlers' Hall	Opera House	2:30.85
1993	Opera House (5)	M Roberts	M Stoute	Sheikh Mohammed	White Muzzle	Commander In Chief	2:33.94
1994	King's Theatre (3)	M J Kinane	H Cecil	Sheikh Mohammed	White Muzzle	Wagon Master	2:28.92
1995	Lammtarra (3)	L Dettori	S bin Suroor	S M Al Maktoum	Pentire	Strategic Choice	2:31.01
1996	Pentire (4)	M Hills	G Wragg	Mollers Racing	Classic Cliche	Shaamit	2:28.11
1997	Swain (5)	J Reid	S bin Suroor	Godolphin	Pilsudski	Helissio	2:36.45
1998	Swain (6)	L Dettori	S bin Suroor	Godolphin	High-Rise	Royal Anthem	2:29.06
1999	Daylami (5)	L Dettori	S bin Suroor	Godolphin	Nedawi	Fruits Of Love	2:29.35
2000	Montjeu (4)	M J Kinane	J Hammond	M Tabor	Fantastic Light	Daliapour	2:29.98
2001	Galileo (3)	M J Kinane	A P O'Brien	Magnier & Tabor	Fantastic Light	Hightori	2:27.71
2002	Golan (4)	K Fallon	M Stoute	Est of Lord Weinstock	Nayef	Zindabad	2:29.70
2003	Alamshar (3)	J P Murtagh	J Oxx	H H Aga Khan	Sulamani	Kris Kin	2:33.26

MIDDLE PARK STAKES-G1
6 furlongs, 2-year-old colts, Newmarket (Rowley Mile Course)
FIRST RUN IN 1866

Year	1st	Jockey	Trainer	Owner	2nd	3rd	Time
1970	Brigadier Gerard	J Mercer	W R Hern	Mrs J Hislop	Mummy's Pet	Swing Easy	1:15.1
1971	Sharpen Up	W Carson	B van Cutsem	Mrs B van Cutsem	Philip Of Spain	Sun Prince	1:13.4
1972	Tudenham	J Lindley	D Smith	L Holliday	Quentillian	Wohurst	1:15.6
1973	Habat	Pat Eddery	P Walwyn	C Vittadini	Pitcairn	Boots Green	1:13.7
1974	Steel Heart	L Piggott	D K Weld	R Tikkoo	Royal Manacle	Auction Ring	1:15.7
1975	Hittite Glory	F Durr	A Breasley	R Tikkoo	Duke Ellington	Patris	1:17.4
1976	Tachypous	G Lewis	B Hobbs	G Cambanis	Nebbiolo	Mandrake Major	1:16.3
1977	Formidable	Pat Eddery	P Walwyn	P Goulandris	Persian Bold	Labienus	1:11.2
1978	Junius	L Piggott	M V O'Brien	S Fraser	Young Generation	Lightning Label	1:11
1979	Known Fact	W Carson	J Tree	K Abdullah	Sonnen Gold	Lord Seymour	1:13.2
1980	Mattaboy	L Piggott	R Armstrong	R Tikkoo	Bel Bolide	Poldhu	1:11.4
1981	Cajun	L Piggott	H Cecil	J Stone	Lucky Hunter	Wattlefield	1:16.4
1982	Diesis	L Piggott	H Cecil	H de Walden	Orixo	Krayyan	1:13.2
1983	Creag-An-Sgor	S Cauthen	C Nelson	Mrs W Tulloch	Superlative	Vacarme	1:13.2
1984	Bassenthwaite	Pat Eddery	J Tree	S Niarchos	Doulab	Primo Dominie	1:13.4
1985	Stalker	J Mercer	P Walwyn	P Fetherston-Godley	Silvino	Laird o' Montrose	1:12
1986	Mister Majestic	R Cochrane	R Williams	D A Johnson	Risk Me	Genghiz	1:13.6
1987	Gallic League	S Cauthen	B Hills	R Sangster	Rahy	Persian Heights	1:13.8
1988	Mon Tresor	M Roberts	R Boss	Mrs P Fitsall	Pure Genius	Northern Tryst	1:12.2
1989	Balla Cove	S Cauthen	R Boss	H Cohen	Rock City	Cordoba	1:11
1990	Lycius	C Asmussen	A Fabre	Sheikh Mohammed	Distinctly North	Majlood	1:10
1991	Rodrigo de Triano	W Carson	P Chapple-Hyam	R Sangster	Lion Cavern	River Falls	1:11

Year	1st	Jockey	Trainer	Owner	2nd	3rd	Time
1992	Zieten	S Cauthen	A Fabre	Sheikh Mohammed	Pips Pride	Factual	1:11.2
1993	First Trump	M Hills	G Wragg	Mollers Racing	Owington	Redoubtable	1:13.74
1994	Fard	W Carson	D Morley	H Al Maktoum	Green Perfume	Fallow	1:11.36
1995	Royal Applause	W R Swinburn	B Hills	M Al Maktoum	Woodborough	Kahir Almaydan	1:11.4
1996	Bahamian Bounty	L Dettori	D Loder	M Al Maktoum	Muchea	In Command	1:11.95
1997	Hayil	R Hills	D Morley	H Al Maktoum	Carrowkeel	Designer	1:12.39
1998	Lujain	L Dettori	D Loder	Sheikh Mohammed	Bertolini	Vision Of Night	1:14.74
1999*	Primo Valentino	Pat Eddery	P Harris	Primo Donnas	Fath	Brahms	1:12.83
2000	Minardi	M J Kinane	A P O'Brien	Magnier & Tabor	Endless Summer	Red Carpet	1:12.75
2001	Johannesburg	M J Kinane	A P O'Brien	Tabor & Magnier	Zipping	Doc Holiday	1:11.73
2002	Oasis Dream	J Fortune	J Gosden	K Abdulla	Tomahawk	Elusive City	1:09.61
2003¶	Balmont	Pat Eddery	J Noseda	S R Robertson	Holborn	Auditorium	1:10.68

*Run on the July Course
¶Three Valleys finished first but was disqualified form purse money.

NUNTHORPE STAKES-G1
5 furlongs, 2-year-olds & up, York
FIRST RUN IN 1903

Year	1st (age)	Jockey	Trainer	Owner	2nd	3rd	Time
1970	Huntercombe (3)	A Barclay	A Budgett	H Renshaw	The Brianston	Raffingora	1:04
1971	*Swing Easy (3)	L Piggott	J Tree	J H Whitney	Green God	Native Bazaar	1:00.8
1972	Deep Diver (3)	W Williamson	P Davey	D Robinson	Stilvi	Parsimony	:57.7
1973	Sandford Lad (3)	A Murray	H Price	C Olley	Balliol	The Go-Between	1:00.6
1974	Blue Cashmere (4)	E Hide	M Stoute	R Clifford-Turner	Rapid River	Saritamer	:59.21
1975	Bay Express (4)	W Carson	P Nelson	P Cooper	Willy Willy	Polly Poachum	:58.99
1976	Lochnager (4)	E Hide	M Easterby	C Spence	Faliraki	Polly Poachum	:58.92
1977	Haverold (3)	E Hide	N Adam	T Newton	Godswalk	Lady Constance	1:01.47
1978	Solinus (3)	L Piggott	M V O'Brien	D Schwartz	Smarten Up	Epsom Imp	:59.23
1979	Ahonoora (4)	G Starkey	F Durr	E Alkhalifa	Abdu	Double Form	1:00.58
1980	Sharpo (4f)	Pat Eddery	J Tree	Miss M Sheriffe	Valariga	Abdu	1:01.2
1981	Sharpo (4f)	Pat Eddery	J Tree	Miss M Sheriffe	Marwell	Moorestyle	1:00.86
1982	Sharpo (5f)	S Cauthen	J Tree	Miss M Sheriffe	Chellaston Park	Kind Music	:58.68
1983	Habibti (3f)+	W Carson	J Dunlop	M Mutawa	Fine Edge	Chellaston Park	:57.99
1984	Committed (4f)	B Thomson	D K Weld	R Sangster	Jonacris	Habibti	:57.24
1985	Never So Bold (5)	S Cauthen	R Armstrong	K Kessly	Primo Dominie	Storm Warning	:59.81
1986	Last Tycoon (3)	Y Saint-Martin	R Collet	R Strauss	Double Schwartz	Green Desert	:57.47
1987	Ajdal (3)	W R Swinburn	M Stoute	Sheikh Mohammed	Sizzling Melody	Perion	:58.48
1988	Handsome Sailor (5)	M Hills	B Hills	R Sangster	Silver Fling	Perion	:58.73
1989	Cadeaux Genereux (4)	Pat Eddery	A Scott	M Al Maktoum	Silver Fling	Statoblest	:57.67
1990	Dayjur (3)	W Carson	W R Hern	H Al Maktoum	Statoblest	Pharaoh's Delight	:56.16
1991	Sheikh Albadou (3)	Pat Eddery	A Scott	H Salem	Paris House	Blyton Lad	:58.21
1992	Lyric Fantasy (2f)	M Roberts	R Hannon	Lord Carnarvon	Mr Brooks	Diamonds Galore	:57.39
1993	Lochsong (5f)	L Dettori	I Balding	J C Smith	Paris House	College Chapel	:58.12
1994	Blue Siren (3)	M Hills	M Channon	J Mitchell	Piccolo	Mistertopogigo	:57.61
1995	So Factual (5)	L Dettori	S bin Suroor	Godolphin	Ya Malak	Hever Golf Rose	:57.47
1996	Pivotal (3)	G Duffield	M Prescott	Cheveley Park Stud	Eveningperformance	Hever Golf Rose	:56.53
1997	Coastal Bluff (5)	K Darley	T Barron	Mrs D Sharp	Ya Malak	Averti	:59.58
1998	Lochangel (4f)	L Dettori	I Balding	J C Smith	Sainte Marine	Dashing Blue	:56.83
1999	Stravinsky (3)	M J Kinane	A P O'Brien	Tabor & Magnier	Sainte Marine	Proud Native	:59.33
2000	Nuclear Debate (5)	G Mosse	J Hammond	J R Chester	Bertolini	Pipalong	:57.83
2001	Mozart (3)	M J Kinane	A P O'Brien	Tabor & Magnier	Nuclear Debate	Bishops Court	:57.27
2002	Kyllachy (4)	J P Spencer	H Candy	Thurloe Thrghbrds	Malhub	Indian Prince	:58.10
2003	Oasis Dream (3)	R Hughes	J Gosden	K Abdulla	The Tatling	Acclamation	:56.20

*In 1971 Green God finished first but was disqualified and placed second.
+In 1983 Soba finished first but was disqualified and placed last.

1000 GUINEAS STAKES-G1
1 mile, 3-year-old fillies, Newmarket (Rowley Mile Course)
FIRST RUN IN 1814.

Year	1st	Jockey	Trainer	Owner	2nd	3rd	Time
1970	Humble Duty	L Piggott	P Walwyn	Lady Ashcombe	Gleam	Black Satin	1:42.13
1971	Altesse Royale	Y Saint-Martin	N Murless	F Hue-Williams	Super Honey	Catherine Wheel	1:40.90
1972	Waterloo	E Hide	J Watts	Mrs R Stanley	Marisela	Rose Dubarry	1:39.49
1973	Mysterious	G Lewis	N Murless	G Pope	Jacinth	Shellshock	1:42.12
1974	Highclere	J Mercer	W Hern	The Queen	Polygamy	Mrs Twiggywinkle	1:40.32
1975	Nocturnal Spree	J Roe	S Murless	Mrs D O'Kelly	Girl Friend	Joking Apart	1:41.65
1976	Flying Water	Y Saint-Martin	A Penna	D Wildenstein	Konafa	Kesar Queen	1:37.83
1977	Mrs McArdy	E Hide	M Easterby	Mrs E Kettlewell	Freeze The Secret	Sanedtki	1:40.07
1978	Enstone Spark	E Johnson	B Hills	R Bonnycastle	Fair Salinia	Seraphima	1:41.56
1979	One In A Million	J Mercer	H Cecil	Helena Springfield Ltd	Abbeydale	Yanuka	1:43.06
1980	Quick As Lightning	B Rouse	J Dunlop	O Phipps	Our Home	Mrs Penny	1:41.89
1981	Fairy Footsteps	L Piggott	H Cecil	H Joel	Tolmi	Go Leasing	1:40.43
1982	On The House	J Reid	H Wragg	P Oppenheimer	Time Charter	Dione	1:40.45

Year	1st	Jockey	Trainer	Owner	2nd	3rd	Time
1983	Ma Biche	F Head	C Head	M Al Maktoum	Favoridge	Habibti	1:41.71
1984	Pebbles	P Robinson	C Brittain	M Lemos	Meis El-Reem	Desirable	1:38.18
1985	Oh So Sharp	S Cauthen	H Cecil	Sheikh Mohammed	Al Bahathri	Bella Colora	1:36.85
1986	Midway Lady	R Cochrane	B Hanbury	H Ranier	Maysoon	Sonic Lady	1:41.54
1987	Miesque	F Head	F Boutin	S Niarchos	Milligram	Interval	1:38.48
1988	Ravinella	G Moore	C Head	Ecurie Aland	Dabaweyaa	Diminuendo	1:40.88
1989	Musical Bliss	W R Swinburn	M Stoute	Sheikh Mohammed	Kerrera	Aldbourne	1:42.69
1990	Salsabil	W Carson	J Dunlop	H Al Maktoum	Heart Of Joy	Negligent	1:38.06
1991	Shadayid	W Carson	J Dunlop	H Al Maktoum	Kooyonga	Crystal Gazing	1:38.18
1992	Hatoof	W R Swinburn	C Head	M Al Maktoum	Marling	Kenbu	1:39.45
1993	Sayyedati	W R Swinburn	C Brittain	M Obaida	Niche	Ajfan	1:37.34
1994	Las Meninas	J Reid	T Stack	R Sangster	Balanchine	Coup de Genie	1:36.71
1995	Harayir	R Hills	W R Hern	H Al Maktoum	Aqaarid	Moonshell	1:36.72
1996	Bosra Sham	Pat Eddery	H Cecil	W Said	Matiya	Bint Shadayid	1:37.75
1997	Sleepytime	K Fallon	H Cecil	Greenbay Stables Ltd	Oh Nellie	Dazzle	1:37.66
1998	Cape Verdi	L Dettori	S bin Suroor	Godolphin	Shahtoush	Exclusive	1:37.86
1999*	Wince	K Fallon	H Cecil	K Abdullah	Wannabe Grand	Valentine Waltz	1:37.91
2000	Lahan	R Hills	J Gosden	Hamdan Al Maktoum	Princess Ellen	Petrushka	1:36.38
2001	Ameerat	P Robinson	M Jarvis	A Al Maktoum	Muwakleh	Toroca	1:38.36
2002	Kazzia	L Dettori	S bin Suroor	Godolphin	Snowfire	Alasha	1:37.85
2003	Russian Rhythm	K Fallon	M R Stoute	Cheveley Park Stud	Six Perfections	Intercontinental	1:38.43

*Run on the July Course.

QUEEN ELIZABETH II STAKES-G1
1 mile, 3-year-olds & up, Ascot
First run in 1955.

Year	1st	Jockey	Trainer	Owner	2nd	3rd	Time
1970	Welsh Pageant (4)	A Barclay	N Murless	H J Joel	Gold Rod	Prince de Gellos	1:42.08
1971	Brigadier Gerard (3)	J Mercer	W R Hern	Mrs J Hislop	Dictus	Ashleigh	1:41.39
1972	Brigadier Gerard (4	J Mercer	W R Hern	Mrs J Hislop	Sparkler	Redundent	1:39.96
1973	Jan Ekels (4)	J Lindley	G Harwood	A E Bodie	Pompous	Loyal Manzer	1:47.20
1974	RACE NOT RUN						
1975	Rose Bowl (3)	W Carson	R Houghton	Mrs C Engelhard	Gay Fandango	Anne's Pretender	1:48.97
1976	Rose Bowl (4)	W Carson	R Houghton	Mrs C Engelhard	Ricco Boy	Dominion	1:43.49
1977	Trusted (4)	W Carson	J Dunlop	Duchess of Norfolk	Air Trooper	Radetzky	1:41.40
1978	Homing (3)	W Carson	W R Hern	Lord Rotherwick	Stradavinsky	Caro Bambino	1:40.39
1979	Kris (3)	J Mercer	H Cecil	H de Walden	Fovoros	Jellaby	1:40.69
1980	Known Fact (3)	W Carson	J Tree	K Abdullah	Kris	Gift Wrapped	1:40.02
1981	To-Agori-Mou (3)	L Piggott	G Harwood	Mrs A Muinos	Kittyhawk	Cracaval	1:48.76
1982	Buzzards Bay (4)	W R Swinburn	H Collingridge	Mrs B McKinney	Noalcoholic	Achieved	1:44.98
1983	Sackford (3)	G Starkey	G Harwood	A E Bodie	Adonijah	Montekin	1:39.85
1984	Teleprompter (4)	W Carson	J Watts	Lord Derby	Katies	Sackford	1:42.96
1985	Shadeed (3)	W R Swinburn	M Stoute	M Al Maktoum	Teleprompter	Zaizafon	1:38.80
1986	Sure Blade (3)	B Thomson	B Hills	Sheikh Mohammed	Teleprompter	Efisio	1:41.71
1987	Milligram (3f)	Pat Eddery	M Stoute	Helena Springfield Ltd	Miesque	Sonic Lady	1:40.04
1988	Warning (3)	Pat Eddery	G Harwood	K Abdullah	Salse	Persian Heights	1:40.51
1989	Zilzal (3)	W R Swinburn	M Stoute	M Al Maktoum	Polish Precedent	Distant Relative	1:40.57
1990	Markofdistinction(4)	L Dettori	L Cumani	G Leigh	Distant Relative	Green Line Express	1:39.7
1991	Selkirk (3)	R Cochrane	I Balding	G Strawbridge	Kooyonga	Shadayid	1:44.34
1992	Lahib (3)	W Carson	J Dunlop	H Al Maktoum	Brief Truce	Selkirk	1:44.50
1993	Bigstone (3)	Pat Eddery	E Lellouche	D Wildenstein	Barathea	Kingmambo	1:42.89
1994	Maroof (3)	R Hills	R Armstrong	H Al Maktoum	Barathea	Bigstone	1:42.75
1995	Bahri (3)	W Carson	J Dunlop	H Al Maktoum	Ridgewood Pearl	Soviet Line	1:40.54
1996	Mark Of Esteem (3)	L Dettori	S bin Suroor	Godolphin	Bosra Sham	First Island	1:40.95
1997	Air Express (3)	O Peslier	C Brittain	M Obaida	Rebecca Sharp	Faithful Son	1:40.61
1998	Desert Prince (3)	O Peslier	D Loder	Lucayan Stud	Dr Fong	Second Empire	1:39.63
1999	Dubai Millennium (3	L Dettori	S bin Suroor	Godolphin	Almushtarak	Gold Academy	1:46.24
2000	Observatory (3)	K Darley	J Gosden	K Abdullah	Giant's Causeway	Best Of The Bests	1:41.40
2001	Summoner (4)	R Hills	S bin Suroor	Godolphin	Noverre	Hawkeye	1:44.54
2002	Where Or When (3)	K Darley	T G Mills	John Humphreys Ltd	Hawk Wing	Tillerman	1:41.37
2003	Falbrav (5)	D Holland	L Cumani	Scuderia Rencati	Russian Rhythm	Tillermqn	1:38.99

RACING POST TROPHY-G1
1 mile, 2-year-old colts & fillies, Doncaster
FIRST RUN IN 1961.
Run as the Timeform Gold Cup 1961-1964. Run as the Observor Gold Cup 1965-1975.
Run as the William Hill Futurity 1976-1988. Run at Newcastle in 1989.

Year	1st	Jockey	Trainer	Owner	2nd	3rd	Time
1970	Linden Tree	D Keith	P Walwyn	Mrs D McCalmont	Minsky	Fine Blade	1:39.4
1971	High Top	W Carson	B Van Cutsem	Sir J Thorn	Steel Pulse	Pentland Firth	1:40.8
1972	Noble Decree	L Piggott	B van Cutsem	N B Hunt	Ksar	Stanleyville	1:42.8
1973	Apalachee	L Piggott	M V O'Brien	J Mulcahy	Mississipian	Alpine Nephew	1:43.6

Year	1st (Age)	Jockey	Trainer	Owner	2nd	3rd	Time
1974	Green Dancer	F Head	A Head	Mme P Wertheimer	Dea Break	No Alimony	1:45.2
1975	Take Your Place	G Dettori	H Cecil	C d'Alessio	Earth Spirit	Gallapiat	1:40.00
1976	Sporting Yankee	Pat Eddery	P Walwyn	William Hill Racing	Sultan's Ruby	Orchestra	1:45.6
1977	Dactylographer	Pat Eddery	P Walwyn	S Niarchos	Julio Mariner	Home Run	1:43.8
1978	Sandy Creek	C Roche	C Collins	A McClean	Warmington	Lyphard's Wish	1:38.4
1979	Hello Gorgeous	J Mercer	H Cecil	D Wildenstein	Choucri Moomba	Masquerade	1:42.4
1980	Beldale Flutter	Pat Eddery	M Jarvis	A Kelly	Shergar	Sheer Gift	1:43.4
1981	Count Pahlen	G Baxter	B Hobbs	Mrs A Villar	Paradis Terrestre	Jalmood	1:42.4
1982	Dunbeath	L Piggott	H Cecil	M Riordan	Cock Robin	Lyphard's Special	1:44.00
1983	Alphabatim	G Starkey	G Harwood	K Abdullah	Mendez	Ilium	1:41.2
1984	Lanfranco	L Piggott	H Cecil	C St George	Damister	Brave Bambino	1:43.8
1985	Bakharoff	G Starkey	G Harwood	K Abdullah	Nomrood	Water Cay	1:41.2
1986	Reference Point	Pat Eddery	H Cecil	L Freedman	Bengal Fire	Love The Groom	1:45.00
1987	Emmson	W Carson	W R Hern	M Sobell	Sheriff's Star	Salse	1:42.6
1988	Al Hareb	W Carson	N Graham	H Al Maktoum	Zalazi	Frequent Flyer	1:40.6
1989	Be My Chief	S Cauthen	H Cecil	P Burrell	Baligh	Qathil	1:42.99
1990	Peter Davies	S Cauthen	H Cecil	C St George	Mukaddamah	Marcham	1:46.00
1991	Seattle Rhyme	C Asmussen	D Elsworth	H J Senn	Mack The Knife	Assessor	1:39.58
1992	Armiger	Pat Eddery	H Cecil	K Abdullah	Ivanka	Zind	1:39.70
1993	King's Theatre	W Ryan	H Cecil	M Poland	Fairy Heights	Bude	1:41.04
1994	Celtic Swing	K Darley	Lady Herries	P Savill	Annus Mirabilis	Juyush	1:40.04
1995	Beauchamp King	J Reid	J Dunlop	E Penser	Even Top	Mons	1:38.89
1996	Medaaly	G Hind	S bin Suroor	Godolphin	Poteen	Benny The Dip	1:41.12
1997	Saratoga Springs	M J Kinane	A P O'Brien	Tabor & Magnier	Mudeer	Mutamam	1:40.36
1998	Commander Collins	J Fortune	P Chapple-Hyam	Sangster & Collins	Magno	Housemaster	1:47.80
1999	Aristotle	G Duffield	A P O'Brien	Mrs J Magnier	Lermontov	Ekraar	1:45.60
2000	Dilshaan	J P Murtagh	M Stoute	S Suhail	Tamburlaine	Bonnard	1:45.87
2001	High Chaparral	K Darley	A P O'Brien	Tabor & Magnier	Castle Gandolfo	Redback	1:45.39
2002	Brian Boru	K Darley	A P O'Brien	Mrs J Magnier	Powerscourt	Illustrator	1:46.01
2003	American Post	C Soumillon	C Head-Maarek	K Abdullah	Fantastic View	Magritte	1:39.57

ST. LEGER STAKES-G1
1 mile, 6 furlongs, 132 yards, 3-year-old colts & fillies, Doncaster
FIRST RUN IN 1776.
Run at Ayr in 1989.

Year	1st	Jockey	Trainer	Owner	2nd	3rd	Time
1970	Nijinsky II	L Piggott	M V O'Brien	C Engelhard	Meadowville	Politico	3:06.4
1971	Athens Wood	L Piggott	H T Jones	Mrs J Rogerson	Homeric	Falkland	3:14.9
1972	Boucher	L Piggott	M V O'Brien	O Phipps	Our Mirage	Ginerva	3:28.71
1973	Peleid	F Durr	W Elsey	W Behrens	Buoy	Duke Of Ragusa	3:08.21
1974	Bustino	J Mercer	W R Hern	Lady Beaverbrook	Giacometti	Riboson	3:09.02
1975	Bruni	A Murray	R Price	C St George	King Pellinore	Libra's Rib	3:09.02
1976	Crow	Y Saint-Martin	A Penna	D Wildenstein	Secret Man	Scallywag	3:13.17
1977	Dunfermline (f)	W Carson	W R Hern	The Queen	Alleged	Classic Example	3:05.17
1978	Julio Mariner	E Hide	C Brittain	M Lemos	Le Moss	M-Lolshan	3:04.94
1979	Son of Love	A Lequeux	R Collet	A Rolland	Soleil Noir	Niniski	3:09.02
1980	Light Cavalry	J Mercer	H Cecil	H Joel	Water Mill	World Leader	3:11.48
1981	Cut Above	J Mercer	W R Hern	J Astor	Glint Of Gold	Bustomi	3:11.60
1982	Touching Wood	P Cook	H T Jones	M Al Maktoum	Zilos	Diamond Shoal	3:03.53
1983	Sun Princess (f)	W Carson	W R Hern	M Sobell	Esprit du Nord	Carlingford Castle	3:16.65
1984	Commanche Run	L Piggott	L Cumani	I Allan	Baynoun	Alphabatim	3:09.93
1985	Oh So Sharp (f)	S Cauthen	H Cecil	Sheikh Mohammed	Phardante	Lanfranco	3:07.13
1986	Moon Madness	Pat Eddery	J Dunlop	Duchess of Norfolk	Celestial Storm	Untold	3:05.03
1987	Reference Point	S Cauthen	H Cecil	L Freedman	Mountain Kingdom	Dry Dock	3:05.91
1988	Minster Son	W Carson	N Graham	Lady Beaverbrook	Diminuendo	Sheriff's Star	3:06.80
1989	Michelozzo	S Cauthen	H Cecil	C St George	Sapience	Roseate Tern	3:20.72
1990	Snurge	T R Quinn	P Cole	M Arbib	Hellenic	River God	3:08.78
1991	Toulon	Pat Eddery	A Fabre	K Abdullah	Saddlers' Hall	Micheletti	3:03.12
1992	User Friendly (f)	G Duffield	C Brittain	W Gredley	Sonus	Bonny Scot	3:05.48
1993	Bob s Return	P Robinson	M Tompkins	Mrs G Smith	Armiger	Edbaysaan	3:07.85
1994	Moonax	Pat Eddery	B Hills	Sheikh Mohammed	Broadway Flyer	Double Trigger	3:04.19
1995	Classic Cliche	L Dettori	S bin Suroor	Godolphin	Minds Music	Istidaad	3:09.74
1996	Shantou	L Dettori	J Gosden	Sheikh Mohammed	Dushyantor	Samraan	3:05.10
1997	Silver Patriarch	Pat Eddery	J Dunlop	P Winfield	Vertical Speed	The Fly	3:06.92
1998	Nedawi	J Reid	S bin Suroor	Godolphin	High And Low	Sunshine Street	3:05.61
1999	Mutafaweq	R Hills	S bin Suroor	Godolphin	Ramruma	Adair	3:02.75
2000	Millenary	T R Quinn	J Dunlop	L N Jones	Air Marshall	Chimes At Midnight	3:02.58
2001	Milan	M J Kinane	A P O'Brien	Tabor & Magnier	Demophilos	Mr Combustible	3:05.16
2002	Bollin Eric	K Darley	T Easterby	N Westbrook	Highest	Bandari	3:02.92
2003	Brian Boru	J P Spencer	A P O'Brien	Mrs J Magnier	High Accolade	Phoenix Reach	3:04.64

SUSSEX STAKES-G1
1 mile, 3-year-olds & up, Goodwood
FIRST RUN IN 1878.

Year	1st	Jockey	Trainer	Owner	2nd	3rd	Time
1970	Humble Duty (3f)	D Keith	P Walwyn	Lady Ashcombe	Gold Rod	Joshua	1:40.6
1971	Brigadier Gerard (3)	J Mercer	W R Hern	Mrs J Hislop	Faraway Son	Joshua	1:41.8
1972	Sallust (3)	J Mercer	W R Hern	M Sobell	High Top	Sparkler	1:37.4
1973	Thatch (3)	L Piggott	M V O'Brien	J Mulcahy	Jacinth	Sun Prince	1:39.4
1974	Ace of Aces (4)	J Lindley	M Zilber	N B Hunt	Habat	Mount Hagen	1:41.2
1975	Bolkonski (3)	G Dettori	H Cecil	C d'Alessio	Rose Bowl	Lianga	1:39.4
1976	Wollow (3)	G Dettori	H Cecil	C d'Alessio	Free State	Poacher's Moon	1:39.6
1977	Artaius (3)	L Piggott	M V O'Brien	Mrs G Getty II	Free State	Relkino	1:39.4
1978	Jaazeiro (3)	L Piggott	M V O'Brien	R Sangster	Radetzky	Formidable	1:40.4
1979	Kris (3)	J Mercer	H Cecil	H de Walden	Swiss Maid	Alert	1:41.6
1980	Posse (3)	Pat Eddery	J Dunlop	O Phipps	Final Straw	Star Way	1:41.6
1981	King's Lake (3)	Pat Eddery	M V O'Brien	Mme J Binet	To-Agori-Mou	Noalto	1:39.4
1982	On The House (3)	J Reid	H Wragg	P Oppenheimer	Sandhurst Prince	Achieved	1:37.6
1983	Noalcoholic (6)	G Duffield	G Pritchard-Gordon	W du Pont III	Tolomeo	Wassl	1:37.4
1984	Chief Singer (3)	R Cochrane	R Sheather	J C Smith	Creag-An-Sgor	Wassl	1:38.2
1985	Rousillon (4)	G Starkey	G Harwood	K Abdullah	Bairn	King Of Clubs	1:41.0
1986	Sonic Lady (3f)	W R Swinburn	M Stoute	Sheikh Mohammed	Scottish Reel	Pennine Walk	1:39.6
1987	Soviet Star (3)	G Starkey	A Fabre	Sheikh Mohammed	Star Cutter	Hadeer	1:38.8
1988	Warning (3)	Pat Eddery	G Harwood	K Abdullah	Then Again	Most Welcome	1:39.8
1989	Markofdistinction	R Cochrane	L Cumani	Mana Al Maktoum	Most Welcome	Opening Verse	1:36.77
1990	Distant Relative (4)	W Carson	B Hills	W Said	Green Line Express	Shavian	1:36.0
1991	Second Set (3)	L Dettori	L Cumani	R Duchossois	Shadayid	Priolo	1:40.4
1992	Marling (3f)	Pat Eddery	G Wragg	E Loder	Selkirk	Second Set	1:36.6
1993	Bigstone (3)	D Boeuf	E Lellouche	D Wildenstein	Sayyedati	Inchinor	1:40.19
1994	Distant View (3)	Pat Eddery	H Cecil	K Abdullah	Barathea	Grand Lodge	1:35.71
1995	Sayyedati (5f)	B Doyle	C Brittain	M Obaida	Bahri	Darnay	1:36.17
1996	First Island (4)	M Hills	G Wragg	Mollers Racing	Charnwood Forest	Alhaarth	1:37.75
1997	Ali-Royal (4)	K Fallon	H Cecil	Greenbay Stables Ltd	Starborough	Allied Forces	1:37.98
1998	Among Men (4)	M J Kinane	M Stoute	Tabor & Magnier	Almushtarak	Lend A Hand	1:40.23
1999	Aljabr (3)	L Dettori	S bin Suroor	Godolphin	Docksider	Almushtarak	1:35.66
2000	Giant's Causeway (3)	M J Kinane	A P O'Brien	Mrs J Magnier/M Tabor	Dansili	Medicean	1:38.65
2001	Noverre (3)	L Dettori	S bin Suroor	Godolphin	No Excuse Needed	Black Minnaloushe	1:37.12
2002	Rock Of Gibraltar (3)	M J Kinane	A P O'Brien	Ferguson & Magnier	Noverre	Reel Buddy	1:38.29
2003	Reel Buddy (5)	Pat Eddery	R Hnnon	Speedith Group	Statue Of Liberty	Norse Dancer	1:40.00

2000 GUINEAS STAKES-G1
1 mile, 3-year-old colts & fillies, Newmarket (Rowley Mile Course)
FIRST RUN IN 1809

Year	1st	Jockey	Trainer	Owner	2nd	3rd	Time
1970	Nijinsky II	L Piggott	M V O'Brien	C Engelhard	Yellow God	Roi Soleil	1:41.54
1971	Brigadier Gerard	J Mercer	W Hern	Mrs J Hislop	Mill Reef	My Swallow	1:39.2
1972	High Top	W Carson	B van Cutsem	J Thorn	Roberto	Sun Prince	1:40.82
1973	Mon Fils	F Durr	R Hannon	Mrs B Davis	Noble Decree	Sharp Edge	1:42.97
1974	Nonoalco	Y Saint-Martin	F Boutin	Mme M Berger	Giacometti	Apalachee	1:39.53
1975	Bolkonski	G Dettori	H Cecil	C d'Alessio	Grundy	Dominion	1:39.53
1976	Wollow	G Dettori	H Cecil	C d'Alessio	Vitiges	Thieving Demon	1:38.09
1977	Nebbiolo	G Curran	K Prendergast	N Schibbye	Tachypous	The Minstrel	1:38.54
1978	Roland Gardens	F Durr	D Sasse	J Hayter	Remainder Man	Weth Nan	1:47.33
1979	Tap On Wood	S Cauthen	B Hills	A Shead	Kris	Young Generation	1:43.6
1980	Known Fact+	W Carson	J Tree	K Abdullah	Posse	Alert	1:40.46
1981	To-Agori-Mou	G Starkey	G Harwood	Mrs A Muinos	Mattaboy	Bel Bolide	1:41.43
1982	Zino	F Head	F Boutin	G Oldham	Wind And Wuthering	Tender King	1:37.13
1983	Lomond	Pat Eddery	M V O'Brien	R Sangster	Tolomeo	Muscatite	1:43.87
1984	El Gran Senor	Pat Eddery	M V O'Brien	R Sangster	Chief Singer	Lear Fan	1:37.41
1985	Shadeed	L Piggott	M Stoute	M Al Maktoum	Bairn	Supreme Leader	1:37.41
1986	Dancing Brave	G Starkey	G Harwood	K Abdullah	Green Desert	Huntingdale	1:40
1987	Don't Forget Me	W Carson	R Hannon	J Horgan	Bellotto	Midyan	1:36.74
1988	Doyoun	W R Swinburn	M Stoute	Aga Khan	Charmer	Bellefella	1:41.73
1989	Nashwan	W Carson	W R Hern	H Al Maktoum	Exbourne	Danehill	1:36.44
1990	Tirol	M J Kinane	R Hannon	J Horgan	Machiavellian	Anshan	1:35.84
1991	Mystiko	M Roberts	C Brittain	Lady Beaverbrook	Lycius	Ganges	1:37.83
1992	Rodrigo de Triano	L Piggott	P Chapple-Hyam	R Sangster	Lucky Lindy	Pursuit Of Love	1:38.37
1993	Zafonic	Pat Eddery	A Fabre	K Abdullah	Barathea	Bin Ajwaad	1:35.32
1994	Mister Baileys	J Weaver	M Johnston	G R Bailey Ltd	Grand Lodge	Colonel Collins	1:35.08
1995	Pennekamp	T Jarnet	A Fabre	Sheikh Mohammed	Celtic Swing	Bahri	1:35.16
1996	Mark Of Esteem	L Dettori	S bin Suroor	Godolphin	Even Top	Bijou d'Inde	1:37.59
1997	Entrepreneur	M J Kinane	M Stoute	Tabor & Magnier	Revoque	Poteen	1:35.64
1998	King Of Kings	M J Kinane	A O'Brien	Tabor & Magnier	Lend A Hand	Border Arrow	1:39.25

Year	1st (Age)	Jockey	Trainer	Owner	2nd	3rd	Time
1999*	Island Sands	L Dettori	S bin Suroor	Godolphin	Enrique	Mujahid	1:37.14
2000	King's Best	K Fallon	M Stoute	S Suhail	Giant's Causeway	Barathea Guest	1:37.77
2001	Golan	K Fallon	M Stoute	Lord Weinstock	Tamburlaine	Frenchmans Bay	1:37.48
2002	Rock Of Gibraltar	J P Murtagh	A P O'Brien	Ferguson & Magnier	Hawk Wing	Redback	1:36.50
2003	Refuse To Bend	P J Smullen	D K Weld	Moyglare Stud Farm	Zafeen	Norse Dancer	1:37.98

+Nureyev finished first but was disqualified and placed last.
*Run on the July Course

FRANCE

CRITERIUM DE SAINT-CLOUD-G1
2000 meters (1-1/4 miles), 2-year-old colts & fillies, Saint-Cloud

Year	1st	Jockey	Trainer	Owner	2nd	3rd	Time
1970	Rheffic	Y Saint-Martin	F Mathet	Mme F Dupre	Toulon	Sigisbee	2:11.7
1971	Gay Saint	A Barclay	F Boutin	Mrs A Manning	Pardner	Lassalle	2:12.7
1972	Simbir	W Pyers	F Mathet	A Plesch	Robertino	Ben Trovato	2:14.4
1973	Ribecourt	Y Saint-Martin	F Boutin	Mme J Couterie	La Tulipe	Exceptionnel	2:19.6
1974	Easy Regent	W Pyers	G Delloye	Mme P de Moussac	Olmeto	Roses Market	2:23.8
1975	Kano	G Rivases	R Poincelet	M Boussac	Loredo	La Girouette	2:17.4
1976	Conglomerat	P Paquet	F Boutin	J Ternynck	Seguro	Istre	2:17.5
1977	Tarek	Y Saint-Martin	A Hawa	M Fustok	Orange Marmelade	Kutuzov	2:16.3
1978	Callio	A Badel	J Sens	J Bossuyt	Echion	Lord Zara	2:10.8
1979	Providential	F Head	F Boutin	B R Firestone	Belgio	Kareliaan	2:22.7
1980	The Wonder	A Gibert	J de Chevigny	Mme A du Breil	Mont Pelion	Brinkbero	2:18.7
1981	Bon Sang	A Gibert	M Saliba	M Fustok	Marcao	Coussika	2:17.6
1982	Escaline (f)	M Philipperon	J Fellows	Mme J Fellows	White Spade	Pietru	2:26.9
1983	Darshaan	Y Saint-Martin	A de Royer-Dupre	Aga Khan	Grand Orient	Real Gold	2:07.4
1984	Mouktar	Y Saint-Martin	A de Royer-Dupre	Aga Khan	Hello Bill	Siberian Hero	2:25
1985	Fast Topaze	A Badel	G Mikhalides	M Fustok	Flying Trio	Manetho	2:15.5
1986	Magistros	E Legrix	G Bonnaventure	P Coudert	Sir David	Groom Dancer	2:23.9
1987	Waki River	A Lequeux	B Secly	J Clerico	Hours After	Blushing John	2:20.6
1988	Miserden	Pat Eddery	A Fabre	K Abdullah	Louis Cyphre	Plein d'Esprit	2:16.4
1989	*Intimiste	G Mosse	F Boutin	I della Rochetta	Snurge	Guiza	2:19.3
1990	Pistolet Bleu	D Boeuf	E Lellouche	D Wildenstein	Pigeon Voyageur	Fortune's Wheel	2:17.8
1991	Glaieul	D Boeuf	E Lellouche	D Wildenstein	Calling Collect	Contested Bid	2:20.3
1992	Marchand de Sable	D Boeuf	E Lellouche	L De Angeli	Infrasonic	Arinthod	2:19.4
1993	Sunshack	T Jarnet	A Fabre	K Abdullah	Zindari	Tikkanen	2:15.2
1994	Poliglote	F Head	C Head	J Wertheimer	Solar One	Highest Cafe	2:19.4
1995	Polaris Flight	J Reid	P Chapple-Hyam	R Kaster	Ragmar	Oliviero	2:13.7
1996	Shaka	J-R Dubosc	J-C Rouget	R Bousquet	Daylami	Sendoro	2:15.8
1997	Special Quest	O Doleuze	C Head	Wertheimer & Frere	Asakir	Daymarti	2:11.9
1998	Spadoun	D Boeuf	C Laffon-Parias	J Gonzalez	Bienamado	Cupid	2:21.5
1999	Goldamix (f)	D Boeuf	C Laffon-Parias	Wertheimer & Frere	Petroselli	Cosmographe	2:15.7
2000	Sagacity	O Peslier	A Fabre	J-L Lagardere	Reduit	Sligo Bay	2:17.80
2001	Ballingarry	J P Spencer	A P O'Brien	Magnier & Tabor	Castle Gandolfo	Black Sam Bellamy	2:24.60
2002	Alberto Giacometti	M J Kinane	A P O'Brien	Mrs J Magnier	Summerland	Marshall	2:25.90
2003	Voix du Nord	D Boeuf	D Smaga	Zuylen de Nyevelt	Simplez	Day or Night	2:16.00

*Snurge finished first but was disqualified and placed second.

PRIX JEAN-LUC LAGARDERE-G1
1400 meters (7 furlongs), 2-year-old colts & fillies, Longchamp
Run at 1600 meters (1 mile) through 2000
Run as the Grand Criterium through 2002

Year	1st	Jockey	Trainer	Owner	2nd	3rd	Time
1970	My Swallow	L Piggott	P Davey	D Robinson	Bonami	Marche Persan	1:43.2
1971	Hard to Beat	W Pyers	R Carver	S Sokolow	Steel Pulse	Prodice	1:41.1
1972	Satingo	H Samani	A Head	Mme Wertheimer	Ben Trovato	Thyratron	1:44.6
1973	Mississippian	W Pyers	M Zilber	N B Hunt	Nonoalco	Mount Hagen	1:39.7
1974	Mariacci	G Rivases	J-M de Choubersky	G de Rothschild	Val de l'Orne	Free Round	1:46.2
1975	Manado	P Paquet	F Boutin	Mme S Vanian	Comeram	French Swandee	1:40.4
1976	Blushing Groom	H Samani	F Mathet	Aga Khan	Amyntor	J.O. Tobin	1:44.7
1977	Super Concorde	P Paquet	F Boutin	W Haefner	Pyjama Hunt	Acamas	1:43.93
1978	Irish River	M Phillipperon	J Cunnington Jr	Mme R Ades	Inshalla	Boitron	1:39
1979	Dragon	A Goldsztejn	M Saliba	M Fustok	Nice Havrais	Princesse Lida	1:41.3
1980	Recitation	G Starkey	G Harwood	A Bodie	Critique	Dunphy	1:44.2
1981	Green Forest	A Gibert	M Saliba	M Fustok	Norwick	Rollins	1:46.2
1982	Saint Cyrien	F Head	C Head	Mme A Head	L'Emigrant	The Noble Player	1:46.5

Year	1st (Age)	Jockey	Trainer	Owner	2nd	3rd	Time
1983	Treizieme (f)	G Dubroeucq	M Zilber	T Tatham	Truculent	Mendez	1:38.8
1984	Alydar's Best (f)	C Roche	D V O'Brien	A Clore	River Drummer	No Pass No Sale	1:49
1985	Femme Elite (f)	A Lequeux	M Zilber	S Fradkoff	Bold Arrangement	Kadrou	1:40
1986	Danishkada (f)	Y Saint-Martin	A de Royer-Dupre	Aga Khan	Lockton	Fotitieng	1:40.7
1987	Fijar Tango	A Gibert	G Mikhalides	M Fustok	Pasakos	Most Precious	1:45.2
1988	Kendor	M Phillipperon	R Touflan	A Bader	Along All	Ecossais	1:40.8
1989	Jade Robbery	C Asmussen	A Fabre	Z Yoshida	Linamix	Honor Rajana	1:40.6
1990	Hector Protector	F Head	F Boutin	S Niarchos	Masterclass	Beau Sultan	1:41.1
1991	Arazi	G Mosse	F Boutin	A E Paulson	Rainbow Corner	Seattle Rhyme	1:41.4
1992	Tenby	Pat Eddery	H Cecil	K Abdullah	Blush Rambler	Basim	1:46.9
1993	Lost World	O Peslier	E Lellouche	D Wildenstein	Signe Divin	Psychobabble	1:45.9
1994	Goldmark	S Guillot	A Fabre	Sheikh Mohammed	Walk on Mix	Montjoy	1:43.4
1995	Loup Solitaire	O Peslier	A Fabre	D Wildenstein	Manninamix	Eternity Range	1:37.6
1996	Revoque	J Reid	P Chapple-Hyam	R Sangster	Majorien	King Sound	1:37.7
1997	Second Empire	M J Kinane	A P O'Brien	Tabor & Magnier	Charge d'Affaires	Alboostan	1:47.76
1998	Way of Light	C Asmussen	P Bary	Niarchos Family	Red Sea	Glamis	1:52.5
1999	Ciro*	M J Kinane	A P O'Brien	Tabor & Magnier	Barathea Guest	Ocean of Wisdom	1:50.5
2000	Okawango	O Doleuze	C Head	Wertheimer & Frere	King's County	Honours List	1:41.80
2001	Rock Of Gibraltar	M J Kinane	A P O'Brien	Ferguson & Magnier	Bernebeau	Dobby Road	1:22.98
2002	Hold That Tiger	K Fallon	A P O'Brien	Tabor & Magnier	Le Vie dei Colori	Intercontinental	1:20.40
2003	American Post	R Hughes	C Head-Maarek	K Abdullah	Charming Prince	Ximb	1:24.50

*Barathea Guest finished first but was disqualified and placed second.

GRAND PRIX DE PARIS-G1
2000 meters (1-1/4 miles), 3-year-old colts & fillies, Longchamp
FIRST RUN IN 1863
Run at 3000 meters (1-7/8 miles) until 1987

Year	1st	Jockey	Trainer	Owner	2nd	3rd	Time
1970	Roll of Honour	L Piggott	R Carver	E Scheib	Fontarabal	High Moon	3:23.9
1971	Rheffic	W Pyers	F Mathet	Mme F Dupre	Point de Rhiz	Valdrague	3:27.5
1972	Pleben	M Depalmas	G Watson	Baron de Rede	Sukawa	Talleyrand	3:23.6
1973	Tennyson	A Gibert	P Head	F Burmann	Authi	Rasgavor	3:17.7
1974	Sagaro	L Piggott	F Boutin	G Oldham	Bustino	Kamaraan	3:27.6
1975	Matahawk	R Jallu	H Van de Poele	Mme E Stern	Citoyen	Avance	3:17.9
1976	Exceller	Y Saint-Martin	F Mathet	N B Hunt	Secret Man	Caron	3:20.5
1977	Funny Hobby	P Paquet	J de Chevigny	Mme T Caralli	Valinsky	Midshipman	3:21.7
1978	Galiani	A Lequeux	M Zilber	A Ben Lassim	Roi de Mai	Whitstead	3:18.2
1979	Soleil Noir	H Samani	F Mathet	G de Rothschild	Son of Love	Stout Fellow	3:21.7
1980	Valiant Heart	A Gibert	B Secly	A Michel	What a Joy	Water Mill	3:25.1
1981	Glint Of Gold	J Matthias	I Balding	P Mellon	Tipperary Fixer	Vayrann	3:25.5
1982	Le Nain Jaune	H Samani	F Mathet	G de Rothschild	Chem	Rhoecus	3:18.4
1983	Yawa	P Waldron	G Lewis	Elisha Holdings	Fubymam du Tenu	Jasper	3:24
1984	At Talaq	A Murray	H T Jones	H Al Maktoum	Woolskin	Spicy Story	3:14
1985	Sumayr	Y Saint-Martin	Aga Khan	A de Royer-Dupre	Exactly Right	Montecito	3:20
1986	Swink	W Swinburn	J Pease	N B Hunt –	War Hero	Silver Word	3:19.3
1987	Risk Me	S Cauthen	P Kelleway	L Norris	Seattle Dancer	Trempolino	2:08.3
1988	Fijar Tango	A Cruz	G Mikhalides	M Fustok	Pasakos	Welkin	2:05.8
1989	Dancehall	C Asmussen	A Fabre	T Wada	Norberto	Creator	2:03.6
1990	Saumarez	S Cauthen	N Clement	B McNall	Priolo	Tirol	2:07.5
1991	Subotica	T Jarnet	A Fabre	O Lecerf	Sillery	Kotashaan	2:05.2
1992	Homme de Loi	T Jarnet	A Fabre	P de Moussac	Kitwood	Guislaine	2:03.9
1993	Fort Wood	S Guillot	A Fabre	Sheikh Mohammed	Bigstone	Siam	2:01.6
1994	Millkom	J-R Dubosc	J-C Rouget	J-C Gour	Solid Illusion	Celtic Arms	2:04.4
1995	Valanour	G Mosse	A de Royer-Dupre	Aga Khan	Singspiel	Diamond Mix	2:02.2
1996	Grape Tree Road	T Jarnet	A Fabre	M Tabor	Glory of Dancer	Android	2:02.3
1997	Peintre Celebre	O Peslier	A Fabre	D Wildenstein	Ithaki	Shaka	2:08.4
1998	Limpid	O Peslier	A Fabre	Sheikh Mohammed	Almutawakel	Croco Rouge	2:03.2
1999	Slickly	T Jarnet	A Fabre	J-L Lagardere	Indian Danehill	Sardaukar	2:03.9
2000	Beat Hollow	T R Quinn	H Cecil	K Abdullah	Premier Pas	Rhenium	2:03.70
2001	Chichicastenango	A Junk	P Demercastel	Mme B Brunet	Mizzen Mast	Bonnard	2:01.00
2002	Khalkevi	C Soumillon	A de Royer-Dupre	HH Aga Khan	Shaanmer	WithoutConnexion	2:02.40
2003	Vespone	C-P Lemaire	N Clement	Ecurie Mister Ess A S	Magistretti	Look Honey	2:01.10

GRAND PRIX DE SAINT-CLOUD-G1
2400 meters (1-1/2 miles), 3-year-olds & up, colts & fillies, Saint-Cloud
FIRST RUN IN 1903

Year	1st (age)	Jockey	Trainer	Owner	2nd	3rd	Time
1970	Gyr (3)	W Williamson	E Pollet	W Guest	Grandier	Hallez	2:36.8
1971	Ramin (4)	H Samani	G Watson	Baron de Zuylen	Hokkaio	Tarbes	2:43.7
1972	Rheingold (3)	Y Saint-Martin	B Hills	H Zeizel	Arlequino	Hard to Beat	2:41.9
1973	Rheingold (4)	Y Saint-Martin	B Hills	H Zeizel	Direct Flight	Roybet	2:35.6

Year	1st	Jockey	Trainer	Owner	2nd	3rd	Time
1974	Dahlia (4f)	Y Saint-Martin	M Zilber	N B Hunt	On My Way	Direct Flight	2:39.4
1975	Un Kopeck (4)	M Philipperon	J Cunnington Jr	J Marx	Ashmore	On My Way	2:38
1976	Riverqueen (3f)	F Head	C Datessen	Mme A Head	Ashmore	Tip Moss	2:34.9
1977	Exceller (4)	F Head	F Mathet	N B Hunt	Riboboy	Iron Duke	2:32.8
1978	Guadanini (4)	H Samani	R Carver	J Kaida	Trillion	Noir et Or	2:41.7
1979	Gay Mecene (4)	F Head	A Head	J Wertheimer	Ela-Mana-Mou	Gain	2:33.4
1980*	Dunette (4f)	G Doleuze	E Chevalier du Fau	Mme Love			
1980*	Shakapour (4)	Y Saint-Martin	F Mathet	Aga Khan	–	Policeman	2:39.8
1981	Akarad (3)	Y Saint-Martin	F Mathet	Aga Khan	Bikala	Lancastrian	2:38.9
1982	Glint Of Gold (4)	Pat Eddery	I Balding	P Mellon	Lancastrian	Real Shadai	2:41.4
1983	Diamond Shoal (4)	S Cauthen	I Balding	P Mellon	Lancastrian	Zalataia	2:34.9
1984	Teenoso (4)	L Piggott	G Wragg	E Moller	Fly Me	Esprit du Nord	2:34.5
1985	Strawberry Road (6)	Y Saint-Martin	P-L Biancone	D Wildenstein	Seismic Wave	Treizieme	2:34.5
1986	Acatenango (4)	S Cauthen	H Jentzsch	Haras Fahrhof	Saint Estephe	Noble Fighter	2:37.2
1987	Moon Madness (4)	Pat Eddery	J Dunlop	Duchess of Norfolk	Tony Bin	Grand Pavois	2:26.5
1988	Village Star (5)	C Asmussen	A Fabre	A J Richards	Saint Andrews	Frankly Perfect	2:36.3
1989	Sheriff's Star (4)	T Ives	Lady Herries	Duchess of Norfolk	Golden Pheasant	Boyatino	2:35.8
1990	In the Wings (4)	C Asmussen	A Fabre	Sheikh Mohammed	Ode	Zartota	2:29.6
1991	Epervier Bleu (4)	D Boeuf	E Lellouche	D Wildenstein	Rock Hopper	Passing Sale	2:28.1
1992	Pistolet Bleu (4)	D Boeuf	E Lellouche	D Wildenstein	Magic Night	Subotica	2:30.3
1993	User Friendly (4f)	G Duffield	C Brittain	W Gredley	Apple Tree	Modhish	2:28.5
1994	Apple Tree (5)	T Jarnet	A Fabre	Sultan Al Kabeer	Muhtarram	Zimzalabim	2:30
1995	Carnegie (4)	T Jarnet	A Fabre	Sheikh Mohammed	Luso	Only Royale	2:35.2
1996	Helissio (3)	O Peslier	E Lellouche	E Sarasola	Swain	Poliglote	2:27.4
1997	Helissio (4)	C Asmussen	E Lellouche	E Sarasola	Magellano	Riyadian	2:29.5
1998	Fragrant Mix (4)	O Peslier	A Fabre	J-L Lagardere	Romanov	Gazelle Royale	2:31.3
1999	El Condor Pasa (4)	M Ebina	Y Ninomiya	T Watanabe	Tiger Hill	Dream Well	2:28.8
2000	Montjeu (4)	C Asmussen	J Hammond	M Tabor	Daring Miss	Sagamix	2:31.40
2001	Mirio (4)	C Soumillon	J de Choubersky	E Soderberg	Perfect Sunday	Egyptband	2:29.30
2002	Ange Gabriel (4)	T Jarnet	E Libaud	Mme H Devin	Polish Summer	Aquarelliste	2:28.60
2003	Ange Gabriel (5)	T Jarnet	E Libaud	Mme H Devin	Polish Summer	Loxias	2:30.90

*Dunette and Shakapour finished in a deadheat in 1980.

POULE D'ESSAI DES POULAINS (French 1000 Guineas)–G1
1600 meters (1 mile), 3-year-old colts, Longchamp
FIRST RUN IN 1883

Year	1st	Jockey	Trainer	Owner	2nd	3rd	Time
1970	Caro	W Williamson	A Klimscha	Comtesse Batthyany	Breton	Faraway Son	1:41.3
1971	Zug	J-C Desaint	J Cunnington	W Hawn	Tarbes	Breeders Dream	1:37.6
1972	Riverman	J-C Desaint	A Head	Mme Wertheimer	Gift Card	Daring Display	1:38.6
1973	Kalamoun	H Samani	F Mathet	Aga Khan	Bally Game	Satingo	1:41.8
1974	Moulines	M Philipperon	R Carver	J Kashiyama	Mississippian	Contraband	1:43.9
1975	Green Dancer	F Head	A Head	J Wertheimer	Condorcet	Dandy Lute	1:39.3
1976	Red Lord	F Head	A Head	J Wertheimer	Roan Star	Comeram	1:42.3
1977	Blushing Groom	H Samani	F Mathet	Aga Khan	Pharly	Hasty Reply	1:41.8
1978	Nishapour	H Samani	F Mathet	Aga Khan	Rusticaro	Pyjama Hunt	1:46.1
1979	Irish River	M Philipperon	J Cunnington Jr	Mme Ades	Sharpman	Nadjar	1:39.8
1980	In Fijar	G Doleuze	M Saliba	M Fustok	Moorestyle	Argument	1:38.4
1981	Recitation	G Starkey	G Harwood	A Bodie	Redoutable	Cresta Rider	1:40.7
1982	Melyno	Y Saint-Martin	F Mathet	S Niarchos	Tampero	Day is Done	1:38.6
1983	L'Emigrant	C Asmussen	F Boutin	S Niarchos	Crystal Glitters	Margouzed	1:46.3
1984	Siberian Express	A Gibert	A Fabre	M Fustok	Green Paradise	Mendez	1:35.8
1985	No Pass No Sale	Y Saint-Martin	R Collet	R C Strauss	Candy Stripes	Synefos	1:38.1
1986	Fast Topaze	C Asmussen	G Mikhalides	M Fustok	Highest Honor	Art Francais	1:48.3
1987	Soviet Star	G Starkey	A Fabre	Sheikh Mohammed	Noble Minstrel	Glory Forever	1:36.2
1988	Blushing John	F Head	F Boutin	A E Paulson	French Stress	Tay Wharf	1:37.2
1989	Kendor	M Philipperon	R Touflan	A Bader	Goldneyev	Ocean Falls	1:36.1
1990	Linamix	F Head	F Boutin	J-L Lagardere	Zoman	Funambule	1:35.9
1991	Hector Protector	F Head	F Boutin	S Niarchos	Acteur	Francais Sapieha	1:37.6
1992	Shanghai	F Head	F Boutin	S Niarchos	Rainbow Corner	Lion Cavern	1:38.2
1993	Kingmambo	C Asmussen	F Boutin	S Niarchos	Bin Ajwaad	Hudo	1:39.1
1994	Green Tune	O Doleuze	C Head	J Wertheimer	Turtle Island	Psychobabble	1:37.4
1995	Vettori	L Dettori	S bin Suroor	Godolphin	Atticus	Petit Poucet	1:40.4
1996	Ashkalani	G Mosse	A de Royer-Dupre	Aga Khan	Spinning World	Tagula	1:37.6
1997	Daylami	G Mosse	A de Royer-Dupre	Aga Khan	Loup Sauvage	Visionary	1:42.6
1998	Victory Note	J Reid	P Chapple-Hyam	Magnier & Sangster	Muhtathir	Desert Prince	1:34.5
1999	Sendawar	G Mosse	A de Royer-Dupre	Aga Khan	Dansili	Kingsalsa	1:36.2
2000	Bachir	L Dettori	S bin Suroor	Godolphin	Berine's Son	Valentino	1:39.40
2001*	Vahorimix	C Soumillon	A Fabre	J-L Lagardere	Clearing	Denon	1:35.40
2002	Landseer	M J Kinane	A P O'Brien	Tabor & Magnier	Medecis	Bowman	1:36.80
2003	Clodovil	C Soumillon	A Fabre	Famille Lagardere	Catcher In The Rye	Krataios	1:36.40

*Noverre finished first but was disqualified from purse money.

POULE D'ESSAI DES POULICHES (French 1000 Guineas)–G1
1600 meters (1 mile), 3-year-old fillies, Longchamp
FIRST RUN IN 1883

Year	1st (age)	Jockey	Trainer	Owner	2nd	3rd	Time
1970	Pampered Miss	M Philipperon	J Cunnington Jr	N B Hunt	Prudent Miss	Popkins	1:40.6
1971	Bold Fascinator	W Williamson	J Fellows	W Rosso	Malva	Tawny Owl	1:39.7
1972	Mata Hari	J Cruguet	A Penna	Comtesse Batthyany	Bisaltis	If	1:44.7
1973	Allez France	Y Saint-Martin	A Klimscha	D Wildenstein	Princess Arjumand	Dahlia	1:44.6
1974	Dumka	A Lequeux	J de Chevigny	C Bauer	Hippodamia	Curtain Row	1:47.5
1975	Ivanjica	F Head	A Head	J Wertheimer	Nobiliary	Broadway Dancer	1:38.4
1976	Riverqueen	F Head	C Datessen	Mme A Head	Suvannee	Sky's Sunny	1:38.6
1977	Madelia	Y Saint-Martin	A Penna	D Wildenstein	Beaune	Durtal	1:39.9
1978	Dancing Maid	F Head	A Head	J Wertheimer	Fruhlingstag	A Thousand Stars	1:45.3
1979	Three Troikas	F Head	C Head	Mme A Head	Nonoalca	Waterway	1:46.00
1980	Aryenne	M Philipperon	J Fellows	D Volkert	Safita	Princesse Lida	1:43.6
1981	Ukraine Girl	Pat Eddery	R Collet	Mme J Mullion	Star Pastures	Ionian Raja	1:41.00
1982	River Lady	L Piggott	F Boutin	R Sangster	Typhoon Polly	Vidor	1:39.6
1983	L'Attrayante	A Badel	O Douieb	Mme Theriot	Mysterieuse Etoile	Maximova	1:42.5
1984	Masarika	Y Saint-Martin	A de Royer-Dupre	Aga Khan	Boreale	Speedy Girl	1:39.3
1985	Silvermine	F Head	C Head	Mme A Head	Top Socialite	New Bruce	1:40.7
1986	Baiser Vole	G Guignard	C Head	R Sangster	Secret Form	River Dancer	1:39.9
1987	Miesque	F Head	F Boutin	S Niarchos	Sakura Reiko	Libertine	1:38.1
1988	Ravinella	G Moore	C Head	Ecurie Aland	Duckling Park	Sacre Look	1:38.3
1989	Pearl Bracelet	A Gibert	R Wojtowiez	Ecurie Fustok	Pass the Peace	Golden Opinion	1:37.1
1990	Houseproud	Pat Eddery	A Fabre	K Abdullah	Pont Aven	Gharam	1:38.5
1991	Danseuse du Soir	D Boeuf	E Lellouche	D Wildenstein	Sha-Tha	Caerlina	1:38.6
1992	Culture Vulture	T R Quinn	P Cole	C Wright	Hydro Calido	Guislaine	1:37.00
1993	Madeleine's Dream	C Asmussen	F Boutin	A E Paulson	Ski Paradise	Gold Splash	1:36.4
1994	East of the Moon	C Asmussen	F Boutin	S Niarchos	Agathe	Bella Argentine	1:37.1
1995	Matiara	F Head	C Head	Ecurie Aland	Carling	Shaanxi	1:42.4
1996	Ta Rib	W Carson	E Dunlop	H Al Maktoum	Shake the Yoke	Sagar Pride	1:38.7
1997	Always Loyal	F Head	C Head	M Al Maktoum	Seebe	Red Camellia	1:40.2
1998	Zalaiyka	G Mosse	A de Royer-Dupre	Aga Khan	Cortona	La Nuit Rose	1:35.7
1999	Valentine Waltz	R Cochrane	J Gosden	Kirby Maher Synd	Karmifira	Calando	1:36.00
2000	Bluemamba	S Guillot	P Bary	Ecurie Skymarc Farm	Peony	Alshakr	1:40.20
2001	Rose Gypsy	M J Kinane	A P O'Brien	Magnier & Tabor	Banks Hill	Lethals Lady	1:36.70
2002	Zenda	R Hughes	J Gosden	K Abdullah	Firth of Lorne	Sophisticat	1:37.00
2003	Musical Chimes	C Soumillon	A Fabre	M Al Maktoum	Maiden Tower	Etoile Montante	1:36.00

PRIX DE DIANE (French Oaks)–G1
2100 meters (1-5/16 miles), 3-year-old fillies, Chantilly
FIRST RUN IN 1843

Year	1st	Jockey	Trainer	Owner	2nd	3rd	Time
1970	Sweet Mimosa	W Williamson	S McGrath	S McGrath	Highest Hopes	Pampered Miss	2:11
1971	Pistol Packer	F Head	A Head	Mme A Head	Cambrizzia	Dixie	2:12.2
1972	Rescousse	Y Saint-Martin	G Watson	Baron de Rede	Prodice	Paysanne	2:10.3
1973	Allez France	Y Saint-Martin	A Klimscha	D Wildenstein	Dahlia	Virunga	2:07.5
1974	Highclere	J Mercer	W R Hern	The Queen	Comtesse de Loir	Odisea	2:07.7
1975	RACE NOT RUN						
1976	Pawneese	Y Saint-Martin	A Penna	D Wildenstein	Riverqueen	Lagunette	2:09
1977	Madelia	Y Saint-Martin	A Penna	D Wildenstein	Trillion	Fabuleux Jane	2:10.3
1978	Reine de Saba	F Head	A Head	J Wertheimer	Cistus	Calderina	2:09.4
1979	Dunette	G Doleuze	E Chevalier de Fau	Mme H Love	Three Troikas	Producer	2:08.6
1980	Mrs Penny	L Piggott	I Balding	E Kronfeld	Aryenne	Paranete	2:10.1
1981	Madam Gay	L Piggott	P Kelleway	G Kaye	Val d'Erica	April Run	2:06.5
1982	Harbour	F Head	C Head	Ecurie Aland	Akiyda	Paradise	2:16.8
1983	Escaline	G Moore	J Fellows	Mme J Fellows	Smuggly	Air Distingue	2:07.8
1984	Northern Trick	C Asmussen	F Boutin	S Niarchos	Grise Mine	Pampa Bella	2:11.6
1985	Lypharita	L Piggott	A Fabre	L T Al Swaidi	Fitnah	Persona	2:05.90
1986	Lacovia	F Head	F Boutin	G Oldham	Secret Form	Galunpe	2:07.00
1987	Indian Skimmer	S Cauthen	H Cecil	Sheikh Mohammed	Miesque	Masmouda	2:11.4
1988	Resless Kara	G Mosse	F Boutin	J-L Lagardere	Riviere d'Or	Raintree Renegade	2:07.5
1989	Lady in Silver	A Cruz	R Wojtowiez	A Karim	Louveterie	Premier Amour	2:10.6
1990	Rafha	W Carson	H Cecil	Prince A Faisal	Moon Cactus	Air de Rien	2:11.7
1991	Caerlina	E Legrix	J de Roualle	K Nitta	Magic Night	Louve Romaine	2:10.5
1992	Jolypha	Pat Eddery	A Fabre	K Abdullah	Sheba Dancer	Verveine	2:09.5
1993	Shemaka	G Mosse	A de Royer-Dupre	Aga Khan	Baya	Dancienne	2:16.00
1994	East of the Moon	C Asmussen	F Boutin	S Niarchos	Her Ladyship	Agathe	2:07.9
1995	Carling	T Thulliez	C Barbe	Ecurie Delbart	Matiara	Tryphosa	2:07.7
1996	Sil Sila	C Asmussen	B Smart	L Alvarez-Cervera	Miss Tahiti	Matiya	2:07.3
1997	Vereva	G Mosse	A de Royer-Dupre	Aga Khan	Mousse Glace	Brilliance	2:08.2
1998	Zainta	G Mosse	A de Royer-Dupre	Aga Khan	Abbatiale	Insight	2:11.2

Year	1st (Age)	Jockey	Trainer	Owner	2nd	3rd	Time
1999	Daryaba	G Mosse	A de Royer-Dupre	Aga Khan	Star of Akkar	Visionnaire	2:16.1
2000	Egyptband	O Doleuze	C Head	Wertheimer & Frere	Volvoreta	Goldamix	2:08.50
2001	Aquarelliste	D Boeuf	E Lellouche	D Wildenstein	Nadia	Time Away	2:09.50
2002	Bright Sky	D Boeuf	E Lellouche	Ecurie Wildenstein	Dance Routine	Ana Marie	2:07.60
2003	Nebraska Tornado	R Hughes	A Fabre	K Abdullah	Time Ahead	Musical Chimes	2:08.10

PRIX DE L'ABBAYE DE LONGCHAMP-G1
1000 meters (5 furlongs), 2-year-old & up, colts & fillies, Longchamp

Year	1st (age)	Jockey	Trainer	Owner	2nd	3rd	Time
1970	Balidar (4)	L Piggott	J Winter	D Prenn	Huntercombe	Raffingora	:58.40
1971	Sweet Revenge 4)	G Lewis	T Corbett	Mrs Attenborough	Swing Easy	Calahorra	1:02.00
1972	Deep River (3)	W Williamson	P Davey	D Robinson	Home Guard	Primaticcio	:57.00
1973	Sandford Lad (3)	A Murray	H Price	C Olley	Abergwaun	Supreme Gift	:59.20
1974	Moubariz (3)	H Samani	F Mathet	Aga Khan	Ace of Aces	La Poesie	:59.70
1975	Lianga (4f)	Y Saint-Martin	A Penna	D Wildenstein	Primo Rico	Mendip Man	:59.20
*1976	Mendip Man (4)	A Gibert	A Paus	Mme J Davis			
*1976	Gentilhombre (3)	T McKeown	N Adam	T Robson	-	Raga Navarro	1:00.30
1977	Gentilhombre (4)	P Cook	N Adam	J Morrell	Madang	Haverold	:58.00
1978	Sigy (2f)	F Head	C Head	Mme A Head	Solinus	Double Form	:59.00
1979	Double Form	J Reid	R J Houghton	Baronne	Thyssen Kilijaro	Greenland Park	:56.70
1980	Moorestyle (4)	L Piggott	R Armstrong	M J Furman Ltd	Sharpo	Valeriga	:56.30
1981	Marwell (3f)	W R Swinburn	M Stoute	E Loder	Sharpo	Rabdan	:58.70
1982	Sharpo (5)	Pat Eddery	J Tree	Mlle Sheriffe	Fearless Lad	King Music	1:00.20
1983	Habibti (3f)	W Carson	J Dunlop	M Mutawa	Soba	Sicyos	:54.30
1984	Committed (4f)	S Cauthen	D K Weld	R Sangster	Habibti	Anita's Prince	:59.80
1985	Committed (5f)	M J Kinane	D K Weld	A E Paulson	Vilikaia	Parioli	:55.20
1986	Double Schwartz (5)	Pat Eddery	C Nelson	R Sangster	Parioli	Hallgate	:56.80
1987	Polonia (3f)	C Roche	J Bolger	H deKwiatkowski	La Grande Epoque	Tenue de Soiree	:56.70
1988	Handsome Sailor (5)	M Hills	B Hills	R Sangster	Caerwent	Silver Fling	:57.00
1989	Silver Fling (4f)	J Matthias	I Balding	G Strawbridge	Zadracarta	Nabeel Dancer	:59.90
1990	Dayjur (3)	W Carson	W R Hern	H Al Maktoum	Lugana Beach	Pharaoh's Delight	:58.70
1991	Keen Hunter (4)	S Cauthen	J Gosden	Sheikh Mohammed	Sheikh Albadou	Magic Ring	:59.40
1992	Mr Brooks (5)	L Piggott	R Hannon	P C Greem	Keen Hunter	Elbio	1:02.30
1993	Lochsong (5f)	L Dettori	I Balding	J C Smith	Stack Rock	Monde Bleu	:59.70
1994	Lochsong (6f)	L Dettori	I Balding	J C Smith	Mistertopogigio	Spain Lane	:57.20
1995	Hever Golf Rose (4f)	J Weaver	T J Naughton	M Hanson	Cherokee Rose	Eveningperformance	:57.70
1996	Kistena (3f)	O Doleuze	C Head	Wertheimer & Frere	Anabaa	Hever Golf Rose	:59.30
1997	Carmine Lake (3f)	J Reid	P Chapple-Hyam	R Sangster	Pas de Reponse	Royal Applause	:56.90
1998	My Best Valentine(8)	R Cochrane	V Soane	The Valentines	Averti	Sainte Marine	:58.90
1999	Agnes World (4)	Y Take	H Mori	T Watanabe	Imperial Beauty	Keos	1:01.40
2000	Namid (4)	J P Murtagh	J Oxx	Lady Clague	Superstar Leo	Pipalong	:55.10
2001	Imperial Beauty (5f)	Y Take	J Hammond	Mrs J Magnier	Bahamian Pirate	Pipalong	:58.88
2002	Continent (5)	D Holland	D Nicholls	Lucayan Stud	Slap Shot	Zipping	:57.20
2003	Patavellian	S Drowne	R Charlton	D J Deer	The Trader	The Tatling	:59.30

*Mendip Man and Gentilhombre finished in a deadheat in 1976.

PRIX DE L'ARC DE TRIOMPHE-G1
2400 meters (1-1/2 miles), 3-year-olds & up colts & fillies, Longchamp
FIRST RUN IN 1920

Year	1st (age)	Jockey	Trainer	Owner	2nd	3rd	Time
1950	Tantieme (3)	J Doysabere	F Mathet	F Dupre	Alizier	L'Amiral	2:34.22
1951	Tantieme (4)	J Doysabere	F Mathet	F Dupre	Nuccio	Le Tyrol	2:32.84
1952	Nuccio (4)	R Poincelet	A Head	Aga Khan	La Mirambule	Dynamiter	2:39.8
1953	La Sorellina (3f)	M Larraun	E Pollet	P Duboscq	Sinet	Worden	2:31.9
1954	Sica Boy (3)	W Johnstone	P Pelat	Mme J Cochery	Banassa	Philante	2:36.4
1955	Ribot (3)	E Camici	U Penco	Marchese Incisa	Beau Prince	Picounda	2:35.6
1956	Ribot (4)	E Camici	U Penco	Marchese Incisa	Talgo	Tanerko	2:34.8
1957	Oroso (4)	S Boullenger	D Lescalle	R Meyer	Denisy	Balbo	2:33.4
1958	Ballymoss (4)	A Breasley	M V O'Brien	J McShain	Fric	Cherasco	2:37.9
1959	Saint Crespin (3)	G Moore	A Head	Prince Aly Khan	Midnight Sun	Le Loup Garou	2:33.3
1960	Puissant Chief (3)	M Garcia	C Bartholomew	H Aubert	Hautain	Point d'Amour	2:43.9
1961	Molvedo (3)	E Camici	A Maggi	E Verga	Right Royal	Misti	2:38.4
1962	Soltikoff (3)	M Depalmas	R Pelat	Mme C Del Duca	Monade	Val de Loir	2:30.9
1963	Exbury (4)	J Deforge	G Watson	G de Rothschild	Le Mesnil	Misti	2:34.9
1964	Prince Royal II (3)	R Poincelet	G Bridgland	R Ellsworth	Santa Claus	La Bamba	2:35.5
1965	Sea-Bird (3)	P Glennon	E Pollet	J Ternynck	Reliance	Diatome	2:35.5
1966	Bon Mot (3)	F Head	W Head	F Burmann	Sigebert	Lionel	2:39.8
1967	Topyo (3)	W Pyers	M Bartholomew	Mme L Volterra	Salvo	Ribocco	2:38.2
1968	Vaguely Noble (3)	W Williamson	E Pollet	Mrs R Franklyn	Sir Ivor	Carmarthen	2:35.2
1969	Levmoss (4)	W Williamson	S McGrath	C McGrath	Park Top	Grandier	2:29.00

Year	1st (Age)	Jockey	Trainer	Owner	2nd	3rd	Time
1970	Sassafras (3)	Y Saint-Martin	F Mathet	A Plesch	Nijinsky II	Miss Dan	2:29.7
1971	Mill Reef (3)	G Lewis	I Balding	P Mellon	Pistol Packer	Cambrizzia	2:38.3
1972	San San (3f)	F Head	A Penna	Comtesse Batthyany	Rescousse	Homeric	2:28.3
1973	Rheingold (4)	L Piggott	B Hills	H Zeizel	Allez France	Hard to Beat	2:35.8
1974	Allez France (4f)	Y Saint-Martin	A Penna	D Wildenstein	Comtesse de Loir	Margouillat	2:36.9
1975	Star Appeal (5)	G Starkey	T Grieper	W Zeitelhack	On My Way	Comtesse de Loir	2:33.6
1976	Ivanjica (4f)	F Head	A Head	J Wertheimer	Crow	Youth	2:39.4
1977	Alleged (3)	L Piggott	M V O'Brien	R Sangster	Balmerino	Crystal Palace	2:30.6
1978	Alleged (4)	L Piggott	M V O'Brien	R Sangster	Trillion	Dancing Maid	2:36.1
1979	Three Troikas (3f)	F Head	C Head	Mme A Head	Le Marmot	Troy	2:28.9
1980	Detroit (3f)	Pat Eddery	O Douieb	R Sangster	Argument	Ela-Mana-Mou	2:28.00
1981	Gold River (4f)	G Moore	A Head	J Wertheimer	Bikala	April Run	2:35.2
1982	Akiyda (3f)	Y Saint-Martin	F Mathet	Aga Khan	Ardross	Awaasif	2:37.00
1983	All Along (4f)	W R Swinburn	P-L Biancone	D Wildenstein	Sun Princess	Luth Enchantee	2:28.1
1984	Sagace (4)	Y Saint-Martin	P-L Biancone	D Wildenstein	Northern Trick	All Along	2:39.1
1985*	Rainbow Quest (4)	Pat Eddery	J Tree	K Abdullah	Sagace	Kozana	2:29.5
1986	Dancing Brave (3)	Pat Eddery	G Harwood	K Abdullah	Bering	Triptych	2:27.7
1987	Trempolino (3)	Pat Eddery	A Fabre	P de Moussac	Tony Bin	Triptych	2:26.3
1988	Tony Bin (5)	J Reid	L Camici	Mme V Gaucci del Bono	Mtoto	Boyatino	2:27.3
1989	Carroll House (4)	M J Kinane	M Jarvis	A Balzarini	Behera	Saint Andrews	2:30.8
1990	Saumarez (3)	G Mosse	N Clement	B McNall	Epervier Bleu	Snurge	2:29.8
1991	Suave Dancer (3)	C Asmussen	J Hammond	H Chalhoub	Magic Night	Pistolet Bleu	2:31.4
1992	Subotica (4)	T Jarnet	A Fabre	O Lecerf	User Friendly	Vert Amande	2:39.00
1993	Urban Sea (4f)	E Saint-Martin	J Lesbordes	D Tsui	White Muzzle	Opera House	2:37.9
1994	Carnegie (3)	T Jarnet	A Fabre	Sheikh Mohammed	Hernando	Apple Tree	2:31.1
1995	Lammtarra (3)	L Dettori	S bin Suroor	S M Al Maktoum	Freedom Cry	Swain	2:31.8
1996	Helissio (3)	O Peslier	E Lellouche	E Sarasola	Pilsudski	Oscar Schindler	2:29.9
1997	Peintre Celebre (3)	O Peslier	D Wildenstein	A Fabre	Pilsudski	Borgia	2:24.6
1998	Sagamix (3)	O Peslier	A Fabre	J-L Lagardere	Leggera	Tiger Hill	2:34.5
1999	Montjeu (3)	M J Kinane	J Hammond	M Tabor	El Condor Pasa	Croco Rouge	2:38.5
2000	Sinndar (3)	J P Murtagh	J Oxx	HH Aga Khan	Egyptband	Volvoreta	2:25.80
2001	Sakhee (4)	L Dettori	S bin Suroor	Godolphin	Aquarelliste	Sagacity	2:35.87
2002	Marienbard (5)	L Dettori	S bin Suroor	Godolphin	Sulamani	High Chaparral	2:26.70
2003	Dalakhani (3)	C Soumillon	A de Royer-Dupre	HH Aga Khan	Mubtaker	High Chaparral	2:32.30

*Sagace finished first in 1985 but was disqualified and placed second.

CRITERIUM INTERNATIONAL-G1
1600 meters (1 mile), 2-year-old colts & fillies, Saint-Cloud
Replaced the Prix de la Salamandre (7 furlongs, Longchamp) in 2001

Year	1st	Jockey	Trainer	Owner	2nd	3rd	Time
1970	My Swallow	L Piggott	P Davey	D Robinson	La Mie au Roy	Swing Easy	1:22.2
1971	Our Mirage	L Piggott	B Hills	Mrs S Enfield	Trait d'Union	Citheron	1:26
1972	Zapoteco	A Barclay	F Boutin	Mme M-F Berger	Thyratron	Ruling	1:24.8
1973	Nonoalco	L Piggott	F Boutin	Mme M-F Berger	Lion du Nord	Moulines	1:26.8
1974	Delmora (f)	F Head	F Boutin	G Oldham	Free Round	Sky Commander	1:20.7
1975	Manado	P Paquet	F Boutin	Mme S Vanian	Vitiges	Comeran	1:22.9
1976	Blushing Groom	H Samani	F Mathet	Aga Khan	Assez Cuite	Alpherat	1:24.8
1977	John de Coombe	G Baxter	P Cole	H Warren	Bilal	Kenmare	1:22.5
1978	Irish River	M Philipperon	J Cunnington Jr	Mme R Ades	Boitron	Nadjar	1:22.3
1979	Princesse Lida (f)	F Head	A Head	J Wertheimer	Choucri	Koboko	1:21.8
1980	Miswaki	P Paquet	F Boutin	Mme A Plesch	Prince Mab	Silver Express	1:22.7
1981	Green Forest	A Gibert	M Saliba	M Fustok	Zino	Star Princess	1:24.3
1982*	Deep Roots	W Carson	P Bary	C Barbe	–	Crystal	1:23.2
1982*	Maximova (f)	F Head	C Head	Haras d'Etreham	–	Crystal	1:23.2
1983	Seattle Song	C Asmussen	F Boutin	S Niarchos	Siberian Express	Blushing Scribe	1:24.3
1984	Noblequest	Y Saint-Martin	R Collet	Prince Al Kabir	Northern Walker	No Pass No Sale	1:29.2
1985	Baiser Vole (f)	F Head	C Head	R Sangster	Regal State	Bold Arrangement	1:22.1
1986	Miesque (f)	F Head	F Boutin	S Niarchos	Sakura Reiko	Whakilyric	1:25.5
1987	Common Grounds	F Head	F Boutin	S Niarchos	Most Precious	Miss Boniface	1:21.8
1988	Oczy Czarnie (f)	G Moore	J-M Beguigne	G de Rothschild	Kendor	Star Touch	1:25
1989	Machiavellian	F Head	F Boutin	S Niarchos	Qirmazi	Ernani	1:24.8
1990	Hector Protector	F Head	F Boutin	S Niarchos	Lycius	Booming	1:20.8
1991	Arazi	G Mosse	F Boutin	A E Paulson	Made of Gold	Silver Kite	1:20.9
1992	Zafonic	Pat Eddery	A Fabre	K Abdullah	Kingmambo	Splendent	1:23.3
1993	Coup de Genie (f)	C Asmussen	F Boutin	S Niarchos	Majestic Role	Volochine	1:23.1
1994	Pennekamp	T Jarnet	A Fabre	Sheikh Mohammed	Montjoy	Bin Nashwan	1:22.9
1995	Lord Of Men	L Dettori	J Gosden	Sheikh Mohammed	With Fascination	Woodborough	1:27
1996	Revoque	J Reid	P Chapple-Hyam	R Sangster	The West	Zamindar	1:20.9
1997	Xaar	O Peslier	A Fabre	K Abdullah	Charge d'Affaires	Speedfit Too	1:21.6
1998	Aljabr	L Dettori	S bin Suroor	Godolphin	Kingsalsa	Zirconi	1:24

Year	1st	Jockey	Trainer	Owner	2nd	3rd	Time
1999	Giant's Causeway	M J Kinane	A O'Brien	Tabor & Magnier	Race Leader	Bachir	1:22.9
2000	Tobougg	C Williams	M Channon	Ahmed Al Maktoum	Honours List	Wooden Doll	1:22.20
2001	Act One	T Gillet	J Pease	G W Leigh	Landseer	Guys And Dolls	1:47.10
2002	Dalakhani	C Soumillon	A de Royer-Dupre	HH Aga Khan	Chevalier	Governor Brown	1:52.00
2003	Bago	T Gillet	J Pease	Niarchos Family	Top Seed	Acropolis	1:47.00

*Deep Roots and Maximova finished in deadheat for first in 1982.

PRIX DU JOCKEY-CLUB (French Derby)-G1
2400 meters (1-1/2 miles), 3-year-old colts & fillies, Chantilly
FIRST RUN IN 1836

Year	1st	Jockey	Trainer	Owner	2nd	3rd	Time
1952	Auriban	W Johnstone	C Semblat	M Boussac	Corindon	Silnet	2:29.4
1953	Chamant	M Garcia	C Bartholomew	H Letellier	Sephiros	Marly Known	2:29.8
1954	Le Petit Prince	R Bertiglia	C Semblat	L Lawrence	Antares	Sica Boy	2:43.6
1955	Rapace	F Palmer	R Wallon	Comte de Ganay	Vimy	Beignet	2:37.8
1956	Philius	S Boullenger	C Elliot	M Boussac	Saint-Raphael	Tanerko	2:45.2
1957	Amber	M Garcia	R Carver	Mme A Mariotti	Guard's Tie	Le Haar	2:34
1958	Tamanar	J Deforge	J Cunnington	R Beaumonte	Bella Paola	Pepin le Bref	2:34.8
1959	Herbager	G Chancelier	P Pelat	Mme Del Duca	Dan Cupid	Midnight Sun	2:34
1960	Charlottesville	G Moore	A Head	Aga Khan	Night and Day	Bonjour	2:34.8
1961	Right Royal	R Poincelet	E Pollet	Mme J Couturie	Match	My Prince	2:31.6
1962	Val de Loir	F Palmer	M Bonaventure	Marquise du Vivier	Picfort	Exbury	2:29.4
1963	Sanctus	M Larraun	E Pollet	J Ternynck	Nycros	Duc de Gueldre	2:33.4
1964	Le Fabuleux	J Massard	W Head	Mme Weisweiller	Trenel	Djel	2:32.4
1965	Reliance	Y Saint-Martin	F Mathet	F Dupre	Diatome	Carvin	2:36.2
1966	Nelcius	Y Saint-Martin	M Clement	P Duboscq	Bon Mot	Behistoun	2:36.8
1967	Astec	A Jezequel	A Lieux	Baron de la Rochette	Minamote	Taj Dewan	2:29.8
1968	Tapalque	Y Saint-Martin	F Mathet	A Plesch	Timmy My Boy	Val d'Aoste	2:32.2
1969	Goodly	F Head	W Head	M Lehmann	Beaugency	Djakao	2:30.4
1970	Sassafras	Y Saint-Martin	F Mathet	A Plesch	Roll of Honour	Caro	2:31.1
1971	Rheffic	W Pyers	F Mathet	Mme F Dupre	Nymbio	Tarbes	2:32
1972	Hard to Beat	L Piggott	R Carver	J Kashiyama	Sancy	Flair Path	2:27.1
1973	Roi Lear	F Head	A Head	Mme Wertheimer	Tennyson	Gunter	2:34.2
1974	Caracolero	P Paquet	F Boutin	Mme M Berger	Dankaro	Kamaraan	2:32.1
1975	Val de l'Orne	F Head	A Head	J Wertheimer	Patch	Marriacci	2:35.2
1976	Youth	F Head	M Zilber	N B Hunt	Twig Moss	Malacate	2:27.4
1977	Crystal Palace	G Dubroeucq	F Mathet	G de Rothschild	Artaius	Concertino	2:29.6
1978	Acamas	Y Saint-Martin	G Bonnaventure	M Boussac	Frere Basile	Turville	2:32.3
1979	Top Ville	Y Saint-Martin	F Mathet	Aga Khan	Le Marmot	Sharpman	2:25.3
1980	Policeman	W Carson	C Milbank	F Tinsley	Shakapour	Providential	2:27.3
1981	Bikala	S Gorli	P-L Biancone	J Ouaki	Akarad	Gap of Dunloe	2:29.5
1982	Assert	C Roche	D V O'Brien	R Sangster	Real Shadai	Bois de Grace	2:29.5
1983	Caerleon	Pat Eddery	M V O'Brien	R Sangster	L'Emigrant	Esprit du Nord	2:27.3
1984	Darshaan	Y Saint-Martin	A de Royer-Dupre	Aga Khan	Sadler's Wells	Rainbow Quest	2:32.2
1985	Mouktar	Y Saint-Martin	A de Royer-Dupre	Aga Khan	Air de Cour	Premier Role	2:34
1986	Bering	G Moore	C Head	Mme A Head	Altayan	Bakharoff	2:24.1
1987	Natroun	Y Saint-Martin	A de Royer-Dupre	Aga Khan	Trempolino	Naheez	2:30.8
1988	Hours After	Pat Eddery	P-L Biancone	Marquise de Moratall	Ghost Buster's	Emmson	2:33.4
1989	Old Vic	S Cauthen	H Cecil	Shaikh Mohammed	Dancehall	Galetto	2:28.7
1990	Sanglamore	Pat Eddery	R Charlton	K Abdullah	Epervier Bleu	Erdelistan	2:24.6
1991	Suave Dancer	C Asmussen	J Hammond	H Chalhoub	Subotica	Cudas	2:27.4
1992	Polytain	L Dettori	A Spanu	Mme Houillion	Marignan	Contested Bid	2:30.3
1993	Hernando	C Asmussen	F Boutin	S Niarchos	Dernier Empereur	Hunting Hawk	2:27.2
1994	Celtic Arms	G Mosse	P Bary	J-L Bouchard	Solid Illusion	Alriffa	2:31.3
1995	Celtic Swing	K Darley	Lady Herries	P Savill	Poliglote	Winged Love	2:32.8
1996	Ragmar	G Mosse	P Bary	J-L Bouchard	Polaris Flight	Le Destin	2:27.2
1997	Peintre Celebre	O Peslier	A Fabre	D Wildenstein	Oscar	Astarabad	2:29.6
1998	Dream Well	C Asmussen	P Bary	Niarchos Family	Croco Rouge	Sestino	2:39.3
1999	Montjeu	C Asmussen	J Hammond	M Tabor	Nowhere to Exit	Rhagaas	2:33.5
2000	Holding Court	P Robinson	M Jarvis	J R Good	Lord Flasheart	Circus Dance	2:31.80
2001	Anabaa Blue	C Soumillon	C Lerner	C Mimouni	Chichicastenango	Grandera	2:27.90
2002	Sulamani	T Thulliez	P Bary	Niarchos Family	Act One	Simeon	2:25.00
2003	Dalakhani	C Soumillon	A de Royer-Dupre	HH Aga Khan	Super Celebre	Coroner	2:26.70

PRIX DU MOULIN DE LONGCHAMP-G1
1600 meters (1 mile), 3-year-olds & up, colts & fillies, Longchamp

Year	1st (age)	Jockey	Trainer	Owner	2nd	3rd	Time
1970	Gold Rod (3)	L Piggott	R Ackekure	Mrs C Dick	Faraway Son	Prudent Miss	1:37.8
1971	Faraway Son (4)	Y Saint-Martin	M Zilber	D Wildenstein	Gold Rod	Blinis	1:38.3
1972	Sallust (3)	J Mercer	W R Hern	M Sobell	Lyphard	Daring Display	1:35.7
1973	Sparkler (5)	L Piggott	R Armstrong	Mme Mehl-Mulhens	Kalamoun	Princess Arjumand	1:41.7
1974	Mount Hagen (3)	P Paquet	A Penna	D Wildenstein	Northern State	Liunga	1:48.5
1975	Delmora (3f)	P Paquet	F Boutin	G Oldham	Son of Silver	Riot in Paris	1:41
1976	Gravelines (4)	Y Saint-Martin	A Penna	D Wildenstein	Dona Barod	Manado	1:42
1977	Pharly (3)	M Philipperon	J Cunnington Jr	A Blasco	Monseigneur	Sanedtki	1:40.6

Year	1st	Jockey	Trainer	Owner	2nd	3rd	Time
1978	Sanedtki (4f)	A Lequeux	O Douieb	S Fradkoff	Homin	Nishapour	1:37.9
1979	Irish River (3)	M Philipperon	J Cunnington Jr	Mme R Ades	Lyphard's Wish	Boitron	1:38.8
1980	Kilijaro (4f)	F Head	O Douieb	S Fradkoff	Nadjar	Katowice	1:36.9
1981	North Jet (4)	F Head	O Douieb	S Fradkoff	Hilal	The Wonder	1:35.2
1982	Green Forest (3)	A Gibert	M Saliba	M Fustok	The Wonder	Sandhurst Prince	1:34.9
1983	Luth Enchantee (3f)	M Philipperon	J Cunnington Jr	P de Moussac	L'Emigrant	Wassl	1:38.9
1984	Mendez (3f)	C Asmussen	F Boutin	S Niarchos	Lear Fan	Meis El Reem	1:43.4
1985	Rousillon (4)	G Starkey	G Harwood	K Abdullah	Kozana	Procida	1:39
1986	Sonic Lady (3f)	W Swinburn	M Stoute	Sheikh Mohammed	Thrill Show	Lirung	1:35.8
1987	Miesque (3f)	F Head	F Boutin	S Niarchos	Soviet Star	Grecian Urn	1:37.5
1988	Soviet Star (4)	C Asmussen	A Fabre	Sheikh Mohammed	Miesque	Gabina	1:40.3
1989	Polish Precedent (3)	C Asmussen	A Fabre	Sheikh Mohammed	Squill	Cadeaux Genereux	1:38.5
1990	Distant Relative (4)	Pat Eddery	W Said	B Hills	Linamix	Priolo	1:38.38
1991	Priolo (4)	G Mosse	F Boutin	Ecurie Skymarc Farm	Mukaddamah	Lycius	1:38.4
1992	All At Sea (3f)	Pat Eddery	H Cecil	K Abdullah	Brief Truce	Hatoof	1:40.7
1993	Kingmambo (3)	C Asmussen	S Niarchos	F Boutin	Ski Paradise	Bigstone	1:37.6
1994	Ski Paradise (4f)	Y Take	A Fabre	T Yoshida	East of the Moon	Green Tune	1:37.8
1995	Ridgewood Pearl(3f)	J P Murtagh	J Oxx	A Coughlan	Shaanxi	Missed Flight	1:36.9
1996	Ashkalani (3)	G Mosse	A de Royer-Dupre	Aga Khan	Spinning World	Shake the Yoke	1:37.2
1997	Spinning World (4)	C Asmussen	J Pease	Niarchos Family	Helissio	Daylami	1:37.1
1998	Desert Prince (3)	O Peslier	D Loder	Lucayan Stud	Gold Away	Second Empire	1:40.9
1999	Sendawar (3)	G Mosse	A de Royer-Dupre	Aga Khan	Gold Away	Dansili	1:35.2
2000	Indian Lodge (4)	C Asmussen	A Perrett	S Cohn & E Parker	Kingsalsa	Diktat	1:40.80
2001	Slickly (5)	L Dettori	S bin Suroor	Godolphin	Banks Hill	Hawkeye	1:39.00
2002	Rock Of Gibraltar(3)	M J Kinane	A P O'Brien	Ferguson & Magnier	Banks Hill	Gossamer	1:39.30
2003	Nebraska Tornado(3f)	R Hughes	A Fabre	K Abdullah	Lohengrin	Bright Sky	1:38.70

PRIX GANAY-G1
2100 meters (1-5/16 miles), 4-year-olds & up, colts & fillies, Longchamp

Year	1st	Jockey	Trainer	Owner	2nd	3rd	Time
1970	Grandier (6)	M Philipperon	J Cunnington Jr	Mme P Ribes	Yelapa	Prince Regent	2:14.2
1971	Caro (4)	M Philipperon	A Klimscha	Comtesse Batthyany	Amadou	Stintino	2:08.6
1972	Mill Reef (4)	G Lewis	I Balding	P Mellon	Amadou	El Toro	2:16.2
1973	Rheingold (4)	Y Saint-Martin	B Hills	H Zeisel	Bog Road	Citheron	2:17.2
1974	Allez France (4f)	Y Saint-Martin	A Penna	D Wildenstein	Tennyson	Gombos	2:23.2
1975	Allez France (5f)	Y Saint-Martin	A Penna	D Wildenstein	Card King	Comtesse de Loir	2:12
1976	Infra Green (4f)	J Taillard	E Bartholomew	Mme Pochna	Kasteel	Ivanjica	2:14.8
1977	Arctic Tern (4)	M Philipperon	J Fellows	Mrs J Knight	Exceller	Infra Green	2:11.6
1978	Trillion (4f)	L Piggott	M Zilber	E Stephenson	Monseigneur	Sirlad	2:18.2
1979	Frere Basile (4)	J-L Kessas	B Secly	J-P Binet	Trillion	Pevero	2:17.2
1980	Le Marmot (4)	P Paquet	F Boutin	R Schafer	Three Troikas	Northern Baby	2:15
1981	Argument (5)	A Lequeux	M Zilber	B McNall	Armistice Day	In Fijar	2:12.2
1982	Bikala (4)	S Gorli	P-L Biancone	J Ouaki	Lancastrian	Al Nasr	2:09.7
1983	Lancastrian (6)	A Lequeux	D Smaga	M Sobell	Cadoudal	Welsh Tern	2:16.9
1984	Romildo (4)	C Asmussen	F Boutin	G Oldham	Sagace	Adonijah	2:12
1985	Sagace (5)	Y Saint-Martin	P-L Biancone	D Wildenstein	Romildo	Careillor	2:10.3
1986	Baillamont (4)	F Head	F Boutin	S Niarchos	Mersey	Saint Estephe	2:11.7
1987	Triptych (5f)	A Cruz	P-L Biancone	A Clore	Takfa Yahmed	Highest Honor	2:15.1
1988	Saint Andrews (4)	A Badel	J-M Beguigne	Mme Volterra	Grand Fleuve	Triptych	
1989	Saint Andrews (5)	A Badel	J-M Beguigne	Mme Volterra	Star Lift	Mansonnien	2:20.8
1990	Creator (4)	C Asmussen	A Fabre	Sheikh Mohammed	In the Wings	Ibn Bey	2:13
1991	Kartajana (4f)	W Mongil	A de Royer-Dupre	Aga Khan	Passing Sale	Dear Doctor	2:18.4
1992	Subotica (4)	T Jarnet	A Fabre	O Lecerf	Pistolet Bleu	Suave Dancer	2:09.3
1993	Vert Amande (5)	D Boeuf	E Lellouche	E Sarasola	Opera House	Misil	2:02.1
1994	Marildo (7)	G Guignard	D Smaga	D Smaga	Intrepidity	Urban Sea	2:11.9
1995	Pelder (5)	L Dettori	P Kelleway	O Pedroni	Alderbrook	Richard of York	2:20.7
1996	Valanour (4)	G Mosse	A de Royer-Dupre	Aga Khan	Luso	Swain	2:10.9
1997	Helissio (4)	O Peslier	E Lellouche	E Sarasola	Le Destin	Pilsudski	2:12.1
1998	Astarabad (4)	G Mosse	A de Royer-Dupre	Aga Khan	Que Belle	Taipan	2:21.5
1999	Dark Moondancer (4)	G Mosse	A de Royer-Dupre	B Arbib	Dream Well	Croco Rouge	2:11.3
2000	Indian Danehill (4)	O Peslier	A Fabre	Baron E de Rothschild	Greek Dance	Chelsea Manor	2:27.20
2001	Golden Snake (5)	Pat Eddery	J Dunlop	The National Stud	Egyptband	With the Flow	2:16.70
2002	Aquarelliste (4f)	D Boeuf	E Lellouche	Ecurie Wildenstein	Execute	Sensible	2:11.40
2003	Fair Mix (5)	O Peslier	M Rolland	Ecurie Week-End	Execute	Falbrav	2:13.00

PRIX JACQUES LE MAROIS-G1
1600 meters (1 mile), 3-year-olds & up, colts & fillies, Deauville

Year	1st (age)	Jockey	Trainer	Owner	2nd	3rd	Time
1970	Priamos (6)	A Gibert	H Jentzsch	V Oppenheimer	Faster	Yellow God	1:41.3
1971	Dictus (4)	Y Saint-Martin	R de Mony-Pajol	J-M Soriano	Sparkler	Roi Soleil	1:37.4
1972	Lyphard (3)	F Head	A Head	Mme P Wertheimer	High Top	Jan Ekels	1:38.2
1973	Kalamoum (3)	H Samani	F Mathet	Aga Khan	Rose Laurel	Sparkler	1:36
1974	Nonoalco (3)	L Piggott	F Boutin	Mme M-F Berger	El Toro	Coup de Feu	1:37.2

Year	1st (Age)	Jockey	Trainer	Owner	2nd	3rd	Time
1975	Lianga (4)	Y Saint-Martin	A Penna	D Wildenstein	Sky Commander	Delmora	1:34.6
1976	Gravelines (4)	G Moore	A Penna	D Wildenstein	Radetzky*	Vitiges*	1:35.1
1977	Flying Water (4)	Y Saint-Martin	A Penna	D Wildenstein	Blushing Groom	Trepan	1:44.2
1978	Kenmare (3)	A Badel	F Mathet	G de Rothschild	Sanedtki	Faraway Times	1:38.6
1979	Irish River (3)	M Philipperon	J Cunnington Jr	Mme R Ades	Bellypha	A Thousand Stars	1:35.5
1980	Nadjar (4)	A Lequeux	A Paus	A D Rogers	Final Straw	Manjam	1:38.4
1981	Northjet (4)	F Head	O Douieb	S Fradkoff	To-Agori-Mou	King's Lake	1:34.5
1982	The Wonder (4)	Pat Eddery	J de Chevigny	Marquise de Moratalla	Green Forest	Zino	1:35.5
1983	Luth Enchantee (3f)	M Philipperon	J Cunnington Jr	P de Moussac	L'Emigrant	Montekin	1:35.9
1984	Lear Fan (3)	Pat Eddery	G Harwood	A Salman	Palace Music	Siberian Express	1:34.9
1985	Vin de France (3)	E Legrix	P-L Biancone	D Wildenstein	Vertige	River Mist	1:38.2
1986	Lirung (4)	S Cauthen	H Jentzsch	Haras Fahrhof	Regal State	Efisio	1:36.4
1987	Miesque (3f)	F Head	F Boutin	S Niarchos	Nashmeel	Hadeer	1:35
1988	Miesque (4f)	F Head	F Boutin	S Niarchos	Warning	Gabina	1:38.6
1989	Polish Precedent (3	C Asmussen	A Fabre	Sheikh Mohammed	French Stress	Magic Gleam	1:37.3
1990	Priolo (3)	A Lequeux	F Boutin	Ecurie Skymarc Farm	Linamix	Distant Relative	1:38.2
1991	Hector Protector (3)	F Head	F Boutin	S Niarchos	Lycius	Danseuse du Soir	1:39.4
1992	Exit to Nowhere (4)	C Asmussen	F Boutin	S Niarchos	Lahib	Cardoun	1:40.8
1993	Sayyedati (3f)	W Swinburn	C Brittain	M Obaida	Ski Paradise	Kingmambo	1:39.8
1994	East of the Moon(3f)	C Asmussen	F Boutin	S Niarchos	Sayyedati	Mehthaaf	1:35.7
1995	Miss Satamixa (3f)	S Guillot	A Fabre	J-L Lagardere	Sayyedati	Shaanxi	1:35.7
1996	Spinning World (3)	C Asmussen	J Pease	Niarchos Family	Vetheuil	Shaanxi	1:39.1
1997	Spinning World (4)	C Asmussen	J Pease	Niarchos Family	Daylami	Neuilly	1:34.4
1998	Taiki Shuttle (4)	Y Okabe	K Fujisawa	Taiki Farm Inc	Among Men	Cape Cross	1:37.4
1999	Dubai Millennium(3)	L Dettori	S bin Suroor	Godolphin	Slickly	Dansili	1:44.3
2000	Muhtathir (5)	L Dettori	S bin Suroor	Godolphin	Sendawar	Kingsalsa	1:34.60
2001¶	Vahorimix (3)	O Peslier	A Fabre	J-L Lagardere	Banks Hill	Noverre	1:38.80
2002	Banks Hill (4f)	O Peslier	A Fabre	K Abdullah	Domedriver	Best Of The Bests	1:35.19
2003	Six Perfections (3f)	T Thulliez	P Bary	Niarchos Family	Domedriver	Telegnosis	1:38.30

*Radetzky and Vitiges finished in a deadheat for second in 1976.
¶Proudwings finished first but was disqualified and placed last.

PRIX MARCEL BOUSSAC-G1
1600 meters (1 mile), 2-year-old fillies, Longchamp

Year	1st	Jockey	Trainer	Owner	2nd	3rd	Time
1970	Two to Paris	J-C Desaint	J Cunnington	L Doherty	Tawny Owl	Bold Fascinator	1:42.1
1971	Dark Baby	G Doleuze	J Laumain	M Fournier	Paysanne	Rose de Saron	1:39.5
1972	Allez France	Y Saint-Martin	A Klimscha	D Wildenstein	Kerlande	Fiery Diplomate	1:38
1973	Hippodamia	W Pyers	M Zilber	N B Hunt	Comtesse de Loir	La Tulipe	1:43
1974	Oak Hill	Y Josse	G Bridgland	Mme S Houyvet	Margravine	Harmonise	1:47.8
1975	Theia	Y Saint-Martin	R Touflan	Baronne Lopez-Tarrag	Suvanee	Luna Real	1:44.3
1976	Kamicia	F Flachi	J Laumain	Mme H Rabatel	Doha	Orchid Miss	1:49.7
1977	Tarona	P Paquet	F Boutin	G Oldham	Cistus	Praise	1:41.9
1978	Pitasia	A Gibert	A Paus	D Clague	Minstrel Girl	Cheerfully	1:48.3
1979	Aryenne	Y Saint-Martin	J Fellows	D Volkert	Pompoes	Teacher's Pet	1:41.3
1980	Tropicaro	A Lequeux	M Zilber	B Coates	Coral Dance	Salmana	1:43.4
1981	Play It Safe	L Piggott	F Boutin	Mrs B Firestone	River Lady	Perlee	1:46.9
1982	Goodbye Shelley	J Lowe	S Norton	Mrs S Brook	Mysterieuse Etoile	L'Attrayante	1:47.4
1983	Almeira	D Vincent	J-C`Cunnington	Comtesse Batthyany	Masarika	Feerie Boreale	1:38.8
1984	Triptych	A Lequeux	D Smaga	A Clore	Silvermine	Coup de Folie	1:46.7
1985	Midway Lady	L Piggott	B Hanbury	H Ranier	Fieldy	Riverbride	1:37.9
1986	Miesque	F Head	F Boutin	S Niarchos	Milligram	Sakura Reiko	1:37.5
1987	Ashayer	W Carson	J Dunlop	H Al Maktoum	Riviere d'Or	Harmless Albatross	1:37.4
1988	Mary Linoa	A Lequeux	D Smaga	D Smaga	Rose de Crystal	Reine du Ciel	1:41.2
1989	Salsabil	W Carson	J Dunlop	H Al Maktoum	Houseproud	Alchi	1:40.3
1990	Shadayid	W Carson	J Dunlop	H Al Maktoum	Caerlina	Sha-Tha	1:40.7
1991	Culture Vulture	T R Quinn	P Cole	C Wright	Hatoof	Verveine	1:40.6
1992	Gold Splash	G Mosse	C Head	J Wertheimer	Kindergarten	Love of Silver	1:44.9
1993	Sierra Madre	G Mosse	P Bary	J-L Bouchard	Flagbird	Mehthaaf	1:45.4
1994	Macoumba	F Head	C Head	Haras d'Etreham	Piquetnol	Chrysalu	1:43.8
1995	Miss Tahiti	O Peslier	A Fabre	D Wildenstein	Shake the Yoke	Solar Crystal	1:40.2
1996	Ryafan	L Dettori	J Gosden	K Abdullah	Yashmak	Family Tradition	1:39.8
1997	Loving Claim	O Doleuze	C Head	M Al Maktoum	Isle de France	Plaisir des Yeux	1:37.6
1998	Juvenia	O Doleuze	C Head	Wertheimer & Frere	Crystal Downs	Blue Cloud	1:43.0
1999	Lady of Chad	O Peslier	R Gibson	J D Martin	New Story	Lady Vettori	1:44.9
2000	Amonita	T Jarnet	P Bary	Mme P de Moussac	Karasta	Choc Ice	1:36.30
2001	Sulk	L Dettori	J Gosden	J Wigan	Danseuse d'Etoile	Kournakova	1:41.95
2002	Six Perfections	T Thulliez	P Bary	Niarchos Family	Etoile Montante	Luminata	1:37.90
2003	Denebola	C-P Lemaire	P Bary	Niarchos Family	Green Noon	Tulipe Royale	1:40.90

PRIX MORNY-G1
1200 meters (6 furlongs), 2-year-old colts & fillies, Deauville

Year	1st	Jockey	Trainer	Owner	2nd	3rd	Time
1970	My Swallow	L Piggott	P Davey	D Robinson	Impertinent	Tarbes	1:17.7

Year	1st (Age)	Jockey	Trainer	Owner	2nd	3rd	Time
1971	Daring Display	F Head	W Head	Lady Granard	Rose de Saron	Pompous	1:13.7
1972	Filiberto	J Cruguet	A Penna	Comtesse Batthyany	Zapoteco	El Rastro	1:10.8
1973	Nonoalco	L Piggott	F Boutin	Mme M-F Berger	Insistance	Cake	1:10.8
1974	Broadway Dancer (f)	Y Saint-Martin	A Penna	D Wildenstein	Janthina	Princesse Lee	1:11.7
1975	Vitiges	G Rivases	G Philippeau	Mme Laloum	Imogene	Wood Green	1:11.4
1976	Blushing Groom	H Samani	F Mathet	Aga Khan	Water Boy	Alpherat	1:12.4
1977	Super Concorde	P Paquet	F Boutin	W Haefner	Little Love	El Muleta	1:12.0
1978	Irish River	M Philipperon	J Cunnington Jr	Mme R Ades	Pitasia	Young Generation	1:12.7
1979	Princesse Lida (f)	F Head	A Head	J Wertheimer	Varingo	Firyal	1:11.7
1980	Ancient Regime (f)	M Philipperon	J Fellows	R Scully	Miswaki	Prince Mab	1:10.1
1981	Green Forest	A Gibert	M Saliba	M Fustok	Maelstrom Lake	River Lady	1:11.9
1982	Deep Roots	W Carson	P Bary	C Barbe	On Stage	Ma Biche	1:11.1
1983	Siberian Express	A Gibert	M Saliba	M Fustok	Ti King	Masarika	1:10.1
1984	Seven Springs (f)	G Moore	J Fellows	R Scully	Gallanta	Noblequest	1:09.9
1985	Regal State (f)	D Beadman	J Fellows	R Scully	River Dancer	Baiser Vole	1:12.6
1986	Sakura Reiko (f)	E Legrix	P-L Biancone	E Zen	Shy Princess	Miesque	1:14.5
1987	First Waltz (f)	M Philipperon	E Bartholomew	R McAlpine	Common Grounds	Balawaki	1:12.8
1988	Tersa (f)	G Mosse	F Boutin	Ecossais	A E Paulson	Money Movers	1:15.6
1989	Machiavellian	F Head	F Boutin	S Niarchos	Qirmazi	Mill Lady	1:12.8
1990	Hector Protector	F Head	F Boutin	S Niarchos	Divine Danse	Acteur Francais	1:14.4
1991	Arazi	G Mosse	F Boutin	A E Paulson	Kenbu	Lion Cavern	1:13.3
1992	Zafonic	Pat Eddery	A Fabre	K Abdullah	Secrage	Marina Park	1:14.8
1993	Coup de Genie (f)	C Asmussen	F Boutin	S Niarchos	Psychobabble	Spain Lane	1:13.1
1994	Hoh Magic (f)	M Hills	M Bell	D Allport	Bruttina	Tereshkova	1:11.7
1995	Tagula	W R Swinburn	I Balding	Mr & Mrs R Hitchens	With Fascination	Barricade	1:11.6
1996	Bahamian Bounty	L Dettori	D Loder	Lucayan Stud Ltd	Zamindar	Pas de Reponse	1:11.0
1997	Charge d'Affaires	G Mosse	A de Royer-Dupre	Marquise de Moratalla	Xaar	Heeremandi	1:12.7
1998	Orpen	M J Kinane	A P O'Brien	Tabor & Magnier	Exeat	Golden Silca	1:10.5
1999	Fasliyev	M J Kinane	A P O'Brien	Tabor & Magnier	Warm Heart	Bachir	1:11.00
2000	Bad As I Wanna Be	G Mosse	B Meehan	J Allbritton	Endless Summer	Noverre	1:10.30
2001	Johannesburg	M J Kinane	A P O'Brien	Tabor & Magnier	Zipping	Meshaheer	1:10.40
2002	Elusive City	K Fallon	G Butler	Thoroughbred Corp	Zafeen	Loving Kindness	1:10.40
2003	Whipper	S Maillot	Robert Collet	E Zaccour	Much Faster	Denebola	1:14.00

PRIX VERMEILLE-G1
2400 meters (1-1/2 miles), 3-year-old fillies, Longchamp

Year	1st	Jockey	Trainer	Owner	2nd	3rd	Time
1970	Highest Hopes	J Mercer	W R Hern	L Holliday	Miss Dan	Parmelia	2:29.2
1971	Pistol Packer	F Head	A Head	Mme A Head	Cambrizzia	Pink Pearl	2:34.7
1972	San San*	J Cruguet	A Penna	D Wildenstein			
1972	Paysanne*	H Samani	G Watson	G de Rothschild -	–	Decigale	2:35.6
1973	Allez France	Y Saint-Martin	A Klimscha	D Wildenstein	Hurry Harriet	Fi Mina	2:43.4
1974	Paulista	Y Saint-Martin	A Penna	D Wildenstein	Comtesse de Loir	Gaily	2:33.6
1975	Ivanjica	G Moore	A Head	J Wertheimer	Nobiliary	May Hill	2:34.7
1976	Lagunette	P Paquet	F Boutin	M Berghgracht	Sarah Siddons	Floressa	2:40.2
1977	Kamicia	A Badel	J Laumain	Mme H Robatel	Royal Hive	Fabuleux Jane	2:30.5
1978	Dancing Maid	F Head	A Head	J Wertheimer	Relfo	Amazer	2:34.0
1979	Three Troikas	F Head	C Head	Mme A Head	Salpinx	Pitasia	2:30.3
1980	Mrs Penny	J Matthias	I Balding	E Kronfeld	Little Bonny	Detroit	2:34.9
1981	April Run	P Paquet	F Boutin	Mrs B Firestone	Leandra	Madam Gay	2:32.9
1982	All Along	G Starkey	P-L Biancone	D Wildenstein	Akiyda	Grease	2:29.9
1983	Sharaya	Y Saint-Martin	A de Royer-Dupre	Aga Khan	Estrapade	Vosges	2:42.1
1984	Northern Trick	C Asmussen	F Boutin	S Niarchos	Circus Plume	Treizieme	2:40.9
1985	Walensee	E Legrix	P-L Biancone	D Wildenstein	Fitnah	Galla Placidia	2:32.7
1986	Darara	Y Saint-Martin	A de Royer-Dupre	Aga Khan	Reloy	Lacovia	2:38.7
1987	Bint Pasha	Pat Eddery	P Cole	Prince F Salman	Three Tails	Something True	2:31.7
1988	Indian Rose	A Cruz	J-M Beguigne	G de Rothschild	Sudden Love	Light the Lights	2:28.8
1989	Young Mother	A Badel	J-M Beguigne	J-M Beguigne	Sierra Roberta	Colorado Dancer	2:33.1
1990	Salsabil	W Carson	J Dunlop	H Al Maktoum	Miss Alleged	In The Groove	2:29.6
1991	Magic Night	A Badel	P Demercastel	Mme P Demercastel	Pink Turtle	Crnagora	2:27.8
1992	Jolypha	Pat Eddery	A Fabre	K Abdullah	Cunning	Urban Sea	2:32.8
1993	Intrepidity	T Jarnet	A Fabre	Sheikh Mohammed	Wemyss Bight	Bright Moon	2:36.8
1994	Sierra Madre	G Mosse	P Bary	J-L Bouchard	Yenda	State Crystal	2:35.3
1995	Carling	T Thulliez	C Barbe	Ecurie Delbart	Valley of Gold	Larrocha	2:32.8
1996	My Emma	C Asmussen	R Guest	Matthews Breeding&Racng	Papering	Miss Tahiti	2:31.3
1997	Queen Maud	O Peslier	J de Roualle	G Tanaka	Gazelle Royale	Brilliance	2:28.2
1998	Leggera	T R Quinn	J Dunlop	Mrs A Focke	Cloud Castle	Zainta	2:41.4
1999	Daryaba	G Mosse	A de Royer-Dupre	Aga Khan	Etizaaz	Cerulean Sky	2:30.6
2000	Volvoreta	M J Kinane	C Lerner	Mme M S Vidal	Reve d'Oscar	Egyptband	2:26.30
2001	Aquarelliste	D Boeuf	E Lellouche	D Wildenstein	Diamilina	Mare Nostrum	2:27.95
2002	Pearly Shells	C Soumillon	F Rohaut	6C Racing Ltd	Ana Marie	Bright Sky	2:26.00
2003	Mezzo Soprano	L Dettori	S bin Suroor	Godolphin	Yesterday	Fidelite	2:26.10

*San San and Paysanne finished in a deadheat in 1972.

IRELAND

IRISH CHAMPION STAKES-G1
1-1/4 miles, 3-year-olds & up, Leopardstown
FIRST RUN IN 1984
Run as the Phoenix Champion Stakes at Phoenix Park prior to 1991.

Year	1st	Jockey	Trainer	Owner	2nd	3rd	Time
1984	Sadler's Wells	Pat Eddery	M V O'Brien	R Sangster	Seattle Song	Princess Pati	2:00.9
1985	Commanche Run	L Piggott	L Cumani	I Allan	Bob Back	Damister	2:09.2
1986	Baillamont	F Head	J Bolger	P H Burns	Sharrood	Supreme Leader	2:02.5
1987	Triptych	A S Cruz	P-L Biancone	A Clore	Entitled	Cockney Lass	2:06.7
1988	Indian Skimmer (4f)	M Roberts	H Cecil	Sheikh Mohammed	Shady Heights	Triptych	2:06.5
1989	Carroll House (4)	M J Kinane	M Jarvis	A Balzarini	Citidancer	Petrullo	2:04.0
1990	Elmaamul (3)	W Carson	W R Hern	H Al Maktoum	Sikeston	Kostroma	2:02.9
1991	Suave Dancer (3)	C Asmussen	J Hammond	H Chalhoub	Environment Friend	Stagecraft	2:06.8
1992	Dr Devious (3)	J Reid	P Chapple-Hyam	S Craig	St. Jovite	Alflora	2:10
1993	Muhtarram (4)	W Carson	J Gosden	H Al Maktoum	Opera House	Lord Of The Field	2:06.1
1994	Cezanne (5)	M J Kinane	M Stoute	Godolphin	Del Deya	Grand Lodge	2:07.9
1995	Pentire (3)	M Hills	G Wragg	Mollers Racing	Freedom Cry	Flagbird	2:04.4
1996	Timarida (4f)	J P Murtagh	J Oxx	Aga Khan	Dance Design	Glory Of Dancer	2:06.2
1997	Pilsudski (5)	M J Kinane	M Stoute	Lord Weinstock	Desert King	Alhaarth	2:04.7
1998	Swain (6)	L Dettori	S bin Suroor	Godolphin	Alborada	Xaar	2:10.2
1999	Daylami (5)	L Dettori	S bin Suroor	Godolphin	Dazzling Park	Dream Well	2:08.4
2000	Giant's Causeway (3)	M J Kinane	A P O'Brien	Mrs J Magnier/M Tabor	Greek Dance	Best Of The Bests	2:03.10
2001	Fantastic Light (5)	L Dettori	S bin Suroor	Godolphin	Galileo	Bach	2:01.80
2002	Grandera (4)	L Dettori	S bin Suroor	Godolphin	Hawk Wing	Best Of The Bests	2:04.70
2003	High Chaparral (4)	M J Kinane	A P O'Brien	M Tabor/Mrs J Magnier	Falbrav	Islington	2:03.30

IRISH DERBY-G1
1-1/2 miles, 3-year-old colts & fillies, The Curragh
FIRST RUN IN 1866

Year	1st	Jockey	Trainer	Owner	2nd	3rd	Time
1950	Dark Warrior	J Thompson	P Prendergast	F M O'Ferrall	Eclat	Pardal	2:37.6
1951	Fraise du Bois II	C Smirke	H Wragg Begum	Aga Khan	Signal Box	Bolivar	2:33
1952	Thirteen Of Diamonds	J Mullane	P Prendergast	A. Hawkins	Prince Of Fairfield	D.C.M.	2:31.67
1953	Chaumier*	W Rickaby	M V O'Brien	Mrs F Vickerman	Sea Charger	Clonleason	2:34.6
1954	Zarathustra	P Powell Jr	M Hurley	T Gray	Hidalgo	Tale Of Two Cities	2:34.8
1955	Panaslipper	J Eddery	S McGrath	J McGrath	Hugh Lupus	Ann s Kuda	2:37.84
1956	Talgo	E Mercer	H Wragg	G Oldham	Roistar	No Comment	2:30.92
1957	Ballymoss	T Burns	M V O'Brien	J McShain	Hindu Festival	Valentine Slipper	2:39.12
1958	Sindon	L Ward	M Dawson	Mrs A Biddle	Paddy's Point	Royal Highway	2:58.9
1959	Fidalgo	J Mercer	H Wragg	G Oldham	Bois Belleau	Anthony	2:33.5
1960	Chamour	G Bougoure	A S O'Brien	F Burmann	Alcaeus	Prince Chamier	2:37.5
1961	Your Highness	H Holmes	H Cottrill	G Bell	Soysambu	Haven	2:33.5
1962	Tambourine	R Poincelet	E Pollet	Mrs H Jackson	Arctic Storm	Sebring	2:28.8
1963	Ragusa	G Bougoure	P Prendergast	J Mullion	Vic Mo Chroi	Tiger	2:45.6
1964	Santa Claus	W Burke	J M Rogers	J Ismay	Lionhearted	Sunseeker	2:35.6
1965	Meadow Court	L Piggott	P Prendergast	G Bell	Convamore	Wedding Present	2:46.8
1966	Sodium	F Durr	G Todd	R Sigtia	Charlottown	Paveh	2:31.5
1967	Ribocco	L Piggott	R J Houghton	C Engelhard	Sucaryl	Dart Board	2:32.4
1968	Ribero	L Piggott	R J Houghton	C Engelhard	Sir Ivor	Val d Aoste	2:33.9
1969	Prince Regent	G Lewis	E Pollet	Comtesse de la Valdene	Ribofilio	Reindeer	2:36.1
1970	Nijinsky II	J Ward	M V O'Brien	C Engelhard	Meadowville	Master Guy	2:33.6
1971	Irish Ball	A Gibert	P Lallei	E Littler	Lombardo	Guillemot	2:36.6
1972	Steel Pulse	W Williamson	A Breasley	R Tikkoo	Scottish Rifle	Ballymore	2:39.8
1973	Weavers' Hall	G McGrath	S McGrath	S McGrath	Ragapan	Buoy	2:32.0
1974	English Prince	Y Saint-Martin	P Walwyn	Mrs V Hue-Williams	Imperial Prince	Sir Penfro	2:33.4
1975	Grundy	Pat Eddery	P Walwyn	C Vittadini	King Pellinore	Anne's Pretender	2:31.1
1976	Malacate	P Paquet	F Boutin	Mme M-F Berger	Empery	Northern Treasure	2:31.2
1977	The Minstrel	L Piggott	M V O'Brien	R Sangster	Lucky Sovereign	Classic Example	2:31.9
1978	Shirley Heights	G Starkey	J Dunlop	Lord Halifax	Exdirectroy	Hawaiian Sound	2:32.3
1979	Troy	W Carson	W R Hern	M Sobell	Dickens Hill	Bohemian Grove	2:30.6
1980	Tyrnavos	A Murray	B Hobbs	G Cambanis	Prince Bee	Ramian	2:34.8
1981	Shergar	L Piggott	M Stoute	Aga Khan	Cut Above	Dance Bid	2:32.6
1982	Assert	C Roche	D V O'Brien	R Sangster	Silver Hawk	Patcher	2:33.2
1983	Shareef Dancer	W R Swinburn	M Stoute	M Al Maktoum	Caerleon	Teenoso	2:29.4
1984	El Gran Senor	Pat Eddery	M V O'Brien	R Sangster	Rainbow Quest	Dahar	2:31.4
1985	Law Society	Pat Eddery	M V O'Brien	S Niarchos	Theatrical	Damister	2:29.8

Year	1st (Age)	Jockey	Trainer	Owner	2nd	3rd	Time
1986	Shahrastani	W R Swinburn	M Stoute	Aga Khan	Bonhomie	Bakharoff	2:32.0
1987	Sir Harry Lewis	J Reid	B Hills	H Kaskel	Naheez	Entitled	2:40.2
1988	Kahyasi	R Cochrane	L Cumani	Aga Khan	Insan	Glacial Storm	2:32.4
1989	Old Vic	S Cauthen	H Cecil	Sheikh Mohammed	Observation Post	Ile de Nisky	2:29.8
1990	Salsabil (f)	W Carson	J Dunlop	H Al Maktoum	Deploy	Belmez	2:33.0
1991	Generous	A Munro	P Cole	Prince Fahd Salman	Suave Dancer	Star Of Gdansk	2:33.3
1992	St. Jovite	C Roche	J Bolger	V K Payson	Dr Devious	Contested Bid	2:25.6
1993	Commander In Chief	Pat Eddery	H Cecil	K Abdullah	Hernando	Foresee	2:31.2
1994	Balanchine (f)	L Dettori	H Ibrahim	Godolphin	King's Theatre	Colonel Collins	2:32.7
1995	Winged Love	O Peslier	A Fabre	Sheikh Mohammed	Definite Article	Annus Mirabilis	2:30.1
1996	Zagreb	P Shanahan	D K Weld	A E Paulson	Polaris Flight	His Excellence	2:30.6
1997	Desert King	C Roche	A O'Brien	Tabor & Magnier	Dr Johnson	Loup Sauvage	2:32.5
1998	Dream Well	C Asmussen	P Bary	Niarchos Family	City Honours	Desert Fox	2:44.3
1999	Montjeu	C Asmussen	J Hammond	M Tabor	Daliapour	Tchaikovsky	2:30.1
2000	Sinndar	J P Murtagh	J Oxx	HH Aga Khan	Glyndebourne	Ciro	2:33.90
2001	Galileo	M J Kinane	A P O'Brien	Magnier & Tabor	Morshdi	Golan	2:27.10
2002	High Chaparral	M J Kinane	A P O'Brien	Tabor & Magnier	Sholokhov	Ballingarry	2:32.20
2003	Alamshar	J P Murtagh	J Oxx	HH Aga Khan	Dalakhani	Roosevelt	2:28.20

*Premonition finished first but was disqualified and placed last.

IRISH OAKS-G1
1-1/2 miles, 3-year-old fillies, The Curragh
FIRST RUN IN 1895

Year	1st	Jockey	Trainer	Owner	2nd	3rd	Time
1970	Santa Tina	L Piggott	C Milbanks	S O'Flaherty	Parmella	Sweet Mimosa	2:34.9
1971	Altesse Royale	G Lewis	N Murless	F Hue-Williams	Vincennes	Lavendula Rose	2:32
1972	Regal Exception	M Philipperon	J Fellows	R Scully	Arkadina	Pidget	2:32
1973	Dahlia	W Pyers	M Zilber	N B Hunt	Mysterious	Hurry Harriet	2:43.8
1974	Dibidale	W Carson	B Hills	N Robinson	Gaily	Polygamy	2:35.2
1975	Juliette Marny	L Piggott	J Tree	J Morrison	Tuscarora	Nobiliary	2:29.8
1976	Lagunette	P Paquet	F Boutin	M Berghgarcht	Sarah Siddons	I've A Bee	2:33
1977	Olwyn	J Lynch	R Boss	S Vanian	Sassabunda	Nanticious	2:35
1978	Fair Salinia	G Starkey	M Stoute	S Hanson	Sorbus	Relfo	2:35.2
1979	Godetia	L Piggott	M V O'Brien	R Sangster	Producer	Queen To Conquer	2:33.6
1980	Shoot A Line	W Carson	W R Hern	A Budgett	Little Bonny	Racquette	2:39.4
1981	Blue Wind	W R Swinburn	D K Weld	B R Firestone	Condessa	Stracomer Queen	2:35.8
1982	Swiftfoot	W Carson	W R Hern	Lord Rotherwick	Prince's Polly	Rosananti	2:33.8
1983	Give Thanks	D Gillespie	J Bolger	Mrs O White	High Hawk	Green Lucia	2:32.2
1984	Princess Pati	P Shanahan	C Collins	Mrs J Mullion	Circus Plume	Marble Run	2:28.6
1985	Helen Street	W Carson	W R Hern	M Sobell	Alydar's Best	Dubian	2:39.8
1986	Colorspin	Pat Eddery	M Stoute	Helena Springfield Ltd	Fleur Royale	Untold	2:40.8
1987	Unite	W R Swinburn	M Stoute	Sheikh Mohammed	Bourbon Girl	Eurobird	2:34.8
1988	Diminuendo*	S Cauthen	H Cecil	Sheikh Mohammed			
1988	Melodist*	W R Swinburn	M Stoute	Sheikh Mohammed	-	Silver Lane	2:36.4
1989	Alydaress	M J Kinane	H Cecil	Sheikh Mohammed	Aliysa	Petite Ile	2:31..0
1990	Knight's Baroness	T R Quinn	P Cole	Prince F Salman	Atoll	Assertion	2:31.6
1991	Possessive Dancer	S Cauthen	A Scott	A Al Maktoum	Jet Ski Lady	Eileen Jenny	2:31.0
1992	User Friendly	G Duffield	C Brittain	W Gredley	Market Booster	Arrikala	2:33.7
1993	Wemyss Bight	Pat Eddery	A Fabre	K Abdullah	Royal Ballerina	Oakmead	2:35.8
1994	Bolas	Pat Eddery	B Hills	K Abdullah	Hawajiss	Gothic Dream	2:37.6
1995	Pure Grain	J Reid	M Stoute	R Barnett	Russian Snows	Valley Of Gold	2:33.6
1996	Dance Design	M J Kinane	D K Weld	Moyglare Stud Farm	Shamadara	Key Change	2:29.7
1997	Ebadiyla	J P Murtagh	J Oxx	HH Aga Khan	Yashmak	Brilliance	2:33.7
1998	Winona	J P Murtagh	J Oxx	Lady Clague	Kitza	Bahr	2:39.8
1999	Ramruma	K Fallon	H Cecil	Prince F Salman	Sunspangled	Sister Bella	2:33.00
2000	Petrushka	J P Murtagh	M Stoute	Highclere Thor. Racing	Melikah	Inforapenny	2:31.20
2001	Lailani	L Dettori	E Dunlop	M Al Maktoum	Mot Juste	Karsavina	2:30.50
2002	Margarula	K J Manning	J Bolger	Mrs J Bolger	Quarter Moon	Lady's Secret	2:37.40
2003	Vintage Tipple	L Dettori	P Mullins	P J O'Donovan	L'Ancresse	Casual Look	2:28.30

*Diminuendo and Melodist finished in a deadheat in 1988.

IRISH 1000 GUINEAS-G1
1 mile, 3-year-old fillies, The Curragh
FIRST RUN IN 1922

Year	1st	Jockey	Trainer	Owner	2nd	3rd	Time
1970	Black Satin	R Hutchinson	J Dunlop	W Reynolds	Lovely Kat	Miralife	
1971	Favoletta	L Piggott	H Wragg	R Moller	Mariel	Spring Garden	
1972	Pidget	W Swinburn	K Prendergast	N Butler	Arkadina	Klairlone	
1973	Cloonagh	G Starkey	H Cecil	A Boyd-Rochfort	Annerbelle	Desert Nymph	

Year	1st	Jockey	Trainer	Owner	2nd	3rd	Time
1974	Gaily	R Hutchinson	W R Hern	M Sobell	Northern Gem	Pepi Image	
1975	Miralla	R Parnell	F Nugent	Lady Lister-Kaye	Silky	Highest Trump	
1976	Sarah Siddons	C Roche	P Prendergast	Mrs J Mullion	Clover Princess	Lady Singer	
1977	Lady Capulet	T Murphy	M V O'Brien	R Sangster	Bold Fantasy	Lady Mere	
1978	More So	C Roche	P Prendergast	L Gelb	Sorbus	Ridaness	
1979	Godetia	L Piggott	M V O'Brien	R Sangster	La Samanna	Fair Davina	
1980	Cairn Rouge	A Murray	M Cunningham	D Brady	Millingdale Lillie	Mrs Penny	
1981	Arctique Royale	G Curran	K Prendergast	J Binet	Blue Wind	Martinova	
1982	Princess Polly	W R Swinburn	D K Weld	T Nicholson	Woodstream	On The House	1:40.4
1983	L'Attrayante	A Badel	O Douieb	Mme C Theriot	Maximova	Annie Edge	1:49.2
1984	Katies	P Robinson	M Ryan	T Ramsden	Alianna	So Fine	1:38.6
1985	Al Bahathri	A Murray	H T Jones	H Al Maktoum	Vilikaia	Top Socialite	1:41.2
1986	Sonic Lady	W R Swinburn	M Stoute	Sheikh Mohammed	Lake Champlain	Asteroid Field	1:44.8
1987	Forest Flower	T Ives	I Balding	P Mellon	Milligram	Taking Steps	1:43.6
1988	Trusted Partner	M J Kinane	D K Weld	Moyglare Stud	Dancing Goddess	Jingle Gold	1:39.8
1989	Ensconse	R Cochrane	L Cumani	Sheikh Mohammed	d Aldbourne	Run To Jenny	1:38.4
1990	In The Groove	S Cauthen	D Elsworth	B Cooper	Heart Of Joy	Performing Arts	1:41.2
1991	Kooyonga	W O'Connor	M Kauntze	M Haga	Julie La Rousse	Umniyatee	1:37.2
1992	Marling	W R Swinburn	G Wragg	E Loder	Market Booster	Tarwiya	1:41.4
1993	Nicer	M Hills	B Hills	Mrs J Corbett	Goodnight Kiss	Danse Royale	1:44.2
1994	Mehthaaf	W Carson	J Dunlop	H Al Maktoum	Las Meninas	Relatively Special	1:49
1995	Ridgewood Pearl	C Roche	J Oxx	A Coughlan	Warning Shadows	Khaytada	1:43.9
1996	Matiya	W Carson	B Hanbury	H Al Maktoum	Dance Design	My Branch	1:39.8
1997	Classic Park	S Craine	A O'Brien	S Burns	Strawberry Roan	Caiseal Ros	1:42.2
1998	Tarascon	J P Spencer	T Stack	Mrs J Rowlinson	Kitza	La Nuit Rose	1:38.4
1999	Hula Angel	M Hills	B Hills	J R Fleming	Golden Silca	Dazzling Park	1:38.8
2000	Crimplene	P Robinson	C E Brittain	Marwan Al Maktoum	Amethyst	Storm Dream	1:39.80
2001	Imagine	J A Heffernan	A P O'Brien	Magnier & Nagle	Crystal Music	Toroca	1:41.10
2002	Gossamer	J P Spencer	L Cumani	G Leigh-Cancerbacup	Quarter Moon	Starbourne	1:45.50
2003	Yesterday	M J Kinane	A P O'Brien	Mrs J Magnier	Six Perfections	Dimitrova	1:40.80

IRISH 2000 GUINEAS-G1
1 mile, 3-year-old colts & fillies, The Curragh
FIRST RUN IN 1921

Year	1st	Jockey	Trainer	Owner	2nd	3rd	Time
1970	Decies	L Piggott	B van Cutsem	N B Hunt	Great Heron	Mon Plaisir	
1971	King's Company	F Head	G Robinson	B R Firestone	Sparkler	King's View	
1972	Ballymore	C Roche	P Prendergast	Mrs J Mullion	Martinmas	Flair Path	
1973	Sharp Edge	J Mercer	W R Hern	J Astor	Midsummer Star	Dapper	
1974	Furry Glen	G McGrath	S McGrath	P McGrath	Pitcairn	Cellini	
1975	Grundy	Pat Eddery	P Walwyn	C Vittadini	Monsanto	Mark Anthony	
1976	Northern Treasure	G Curran	K Prendergast	A Brennan	Comeran	Lucky Wednesday	
1977	Pampapaul	G Dettori	H Murless	H Paul	The Minstrel	Nebbiolo	
1978	Jaazeiro	L Piggott	M V O'Brien	R Sangster	Strong Gale	Columbanus	
1979	Dickens Hill	A Murray	A O'Toole	Mme J Binet	Brother Philips	Mister Niall	
1980	Nikoli	C Roche	P Prendergast	Lord Iveagh	Last Fandango	Final Straw	
1981	Kings Lake	Pat Eddery	M V O'Brien	Mme J Binet	To-Agori-Mou	Prince Echo	
1982	Dara Monarch	M J Kinane	L Browne	Mrs L Browne	Tender King	Red Sunset	1:41.8
1983	Wassl	A Murray	J Dunlop	A Al Maktoum	Lomond	Parliament	
1984	Sadler's Wells	G McGrath	M V O'Brien	R Sangster	Procida	Secreto	1:38.2
1985	Triptych (f)	C Roche	D V O'Brien	A Clore	Celestial Bounty	Sun Valley	1:42.8
1986	Flash Of Steel	M J Kinane	D K Weld	B R Firestone	Mr John	Sharrood	1:53.4
1987	Don't Forget Me	W Carson	R Hannon	Jim Horgan	Entitled	Stately Don	1:38
1988	Prince Of Birds	D Gillespie	M V O'Brien	R Sangster	Caerwent	Intimidate	1:39.8
1989	Shaadi	W R Swinburn	M Stoute	Sheikh Mohammed	Great Commotion	Distant Relative	1:37.4
1990	Tirol	Pat Eddery	R Hannon	John Horgan	Royal Academy	Lotus Pool	1:39.2
1991	Fourstars Allstar	M E Smith	L O'Brien	R Bomze	Star Of Gdansk	Lycius	1:38.6
1992	Rodrigo de Triano	L Piggott	P Chapple-Hyam	R Sangster	Ezzoud	Brief Truce	1:41.6
1993	Barathea	M Roberts	L Cumani	Sheikh Mohammed	Fatherland	Massyar	1:43
1994	Turtle Island	J Reid	P Chapple-Hyam	R Sangster	Guided Tour	Ridgewood Ben	1:50.1
1995	Spectrum	J Reid	P Chapple-Hyam	Lord Weinstock	Adjareli	Bahri	1:40.3
1996	Spinning World	C Asmussen	J Pease	Niarchos Family	Rainbow Blues	Beauchamp King	1:38.8
1997	Desert King	C Roche	A P O'Brien	M Tabor	Verglas	Romanov	1:38.3
1998	Desert Prince	O Peslier	D Loder	Lucayan Stud	Fa-Eq	Second Empire	1:36.25
1999	Saffron Walden	O Peslier	A P O'Brien	Tabor & Magnier	Enrique	Orpen	1:38.1
2000	Bachir	L Dettori	S bin Suroor	Godolphin	Giant's Causeway	Cape Town	1:39.80
2001	Black Minnaloushe	J P Murtagh	A P O'Brien	Magnier & Tabor	Mozart	Minardi	1:41.40
2002	Rock Of Gibraltar	M J Kinane	A P O'Brien	Ferguson & Magnier	Century	Della Frnacesca	1:47.20
2003	Indian Haven	J F Egan	P D'Arcy	Gleeson/Smith/Conway	France	Tout Seul	1:41.50

GERMANY

GROSSER PREIS VON BADEN-G1
1-1/2 miles, 3-year-olds & up, Baden-Baden (Ger)

Year	1st	Jockey	Trainer	Owner	2nd	3rd	Time
1970	Alpenkonig (3)	F Dreschler	H Jentzsch	Gestut Schlenderhan	Cortez	Snraceno	2:34
1971	Cortez (6)	O Langner	S von Mitzlaff	Gestut Zoppenbroich	Segnes	Spirit	2:32.2
1972	Caracol (3)	O Langner	S von Mitzlaff	Gestut Fahrhof	Experte	Arratos	2:30.5
1973	Athenagoras (3)	H Remmert	S von Mitzlaff	Gestut Zoppenbroich	Arratos	Telemach	2:32
*1974	Meautry (4)	E Sauvaget	G Pezerll	F Baral	Bakuba	Recupere	2:34.6
*1974	Marduk (3)	P Remmert	H Bollow	Comtesse Batthyany	Card King	Athenagoras	2:34.8
1975	Marduk (4)	P Remmert	H Bollow	Comtesse Batthyany	Lord Udo	Card King	2:41
1976	Sharper (3)	W Carson	A Hecker	A van Kaick	Windwurf	Tutlinger	2:38
1977	Windwurf (5)	G Lewis	H Gummelt	Gestut Ravensberg	Stuyvesant	Casaque	2:32.4
1978	Valour (3)	J Reid	R J Houghton	G Ward	Tip Moss	Marzvogel	2:38.4
1979	M-Loishan (4)	B Taylor	R Price	E Alkhalifa	Konigsstuhl	Perougos	2:30.9
1980	Nebos (4)	L Mader	H Bollow	Comtesse Batthyany	Cherubin	Marraci	2:37.6
1981	Pelerin (4)	G Starkey	H Wragg	Sir P Oppenheimer	Hohritt	Maivogel	2:27.6
1982	Glint Of Gold (4)	Pat Eddery	I Balding	P Mellon	Orofino	Ti amo	2:29.1
1983	Diamond Shoal (4)	S Cauthen	I Balding	P Mellon	Abary	Prima Voce	2:28
1984	Strawberry Road (5)	B Thomson	J Nicholls	R F Stehr	Esprit du Nord	Abary	2:29.6
1985	Gold And Ivory (4)	S Cauthen	I Balding	P Mellon	Daun	Crazy	2:37.8
1986	Acatenango (4)	G Bocskai	H Jentzsch	Gestut Fahrhof	St Hilarion	Daun	2:28.3
1987	Acatenango (5)	G Bocskai	H Jentzsch	Gestut Fahrhof	Moon Madness	Winwood	2:34.7
1988	Carroll House (3)	B Raymond	M Jarvis	A Balzarini	Helikon	Boyatino	2:52.7
1989	Mondrian (3)	K Woodburn	U Stoltefuss	Stall Hanse	Per Quod	Summer Trip	2:29.6
1990	Mondrian (4)	M Hofer	U Stoltefuss	Stall Hanse	Ibn Bey	Per Quod	2:34.6
1991	Lomitas (3)	P Schiergen	A Wohler	Gestut Fahrhof	Temporal	Wajd	2:28.8
1992	Mashaallah (4)	J Reid	J Gosden	A Al MAktoum	Platini	Sapience	2:37.8
1993	Lando (3)	A Tylicki	H Jentzsch	Gestut Haus Ittlingen	Platini	George Augustus	2:28.2
1994	Lando (4)	P Schiergen	H Jentzsch	Gestut Haus Ittlingen	Monsun	Kornado	2:27.3
1995	Germany (4)	L Dettori	B Schutz	J Abdullah	Lecroix	Right Win	2:37.7
1996	Pilsudski (4)	W R Swinburn	M Stoute	Lord Weinstock	Germany	Sunshack	2:26.7
1997	Borgia (3f)	K Fallon	B Schutz	Gestut Ammerland	Luso	Predappio	2:28.5
1998	Tiger Hill (3)	A Suborics	P Schiergen	Baron G von Ullmann	Caitano	Public Purse	2:40.1
1999	Tiger Hill (4)	T Hellier	P Schiergen	Baron G von Ullmann	Flamingo Road	Belenus	2:29.9
2000	Samum (3)	A Starke	A Schutz	Stall Balnkenese	Catella	Fruits Of Love	2:38.95
2001	Morshdi (3)	P Robinson	M Jarvis	Darley Stud Mngmnt	Boreal	Sabiango	2:31.27
2002	Marienbard (4)	L Dettori	S bin Suroor	Godolphin	Salve Regina	Noroit	2:34.93
2003	Mamool (4)	L Dettori	S bin Suroor	Godolphin	Black Sam Bellamy	Dano-Mast	2:32.75

*Run in two divisions in 1974.

PREMIER ASIAN STAKES

DUBAI WORLD CUP-G1
2000 meters (1-1/4 miles) (Dirt), 4-year-olds & up, Nad Al Sheba
FIRST RUN IN 1996

Year	1st	Jockey	Trainer	Owner	2nd	3rd	Time
1996	Cigar (6)	J D Bailey	W I Mott	A E Paulson	Soul of the Matter	L'Carriere	2:03.84
1997	Singspiel (5)	J D Bailey	M Stoute	Sheikh Mohammed	Siphon	Sandpit	2:01.91
1998	Silver Charm (4)	G Stevens	B Baffert	R & B Lewis	Swain	Loup Sauvage	2:04.29
1999	Almutawakel (4)	R Hills	S bin Suroor	H Al Maktoum	Malek	Victory Gallop	2:00.65
2000	Dubai Millennium (4)	L Dettori	S bin Suroor	Godolphin	Behrens	Public Purse	1:59.50
2001	Captain Steve (4)	J D Bailey	B Baffert	M E Pegram	To The Victory	Hightori	2:00.40
2002	Street Cry (4)	J D Bailey	S bin Suroor	Godolphin	Sei Mi	Sahkee	2:01.18
2003	Moon Ballad (4)	L Dettori	S bin Suroor	Godolphin	Harlan's Holiday	Nayef	2:00.48

HONG KONG CUP-G1
2000 meters (1-1/4 miles), 3-year-olds & up, Sha Tin
FIRST RUN IN 1990
Run twice in 1993, in April and December.
Run as Hong Kong International Cup at 1800 meters (1-1/8 miles) 1990-1998.

Year	1st (age)	Jockey	Trainer	Owner	2nd	3rd	Time
1990	Kessem (5)	K Moses	B J Smith	Durcan & Smith	Livistona Lane	Colonial Chief	1:48.4
1991	River Verdon (4)	G Mosse	D Hill	O Cheung	Prudent Manner	Majestic Boy	1:49.8

Year	1st (Age)	Jockey	Trainer	Owner	2nd	3rd	Time
1992	RACE NOT RUN						
1993	Romanee Conti (4)	G Childs	L K Laxson	P J & P M Vela	Fraar	Charmonnier	1:48.2
1993	Motivation (5)	J Marshall	J Moore	S Hui	Verveine	Stark South	1:49.2
1994	State Taj (5)	D Oliver	J Riley	H & Mrs L Croll	River Majesty	Volochine	1:48.4
1995	Fujiyama Kenzan (7)	M Ebina	H Mori	T Fujimoto	Ventquattrofogli	Jade Age	1:47.0
1996	First Island (4)	M Hills	G Wragg	Mollers Racing	Seascay	Kingston Bay	1:48.2
1997	Val's Prince (5)	C Asmussen	J Picou	Martin & Weiner	Oriental Express	Wixim	1:47.2
1998	Midnight Bet (4)	H Kawachi	H Nagahama	Shadai Racehorse Co	Johan Cruyff	Almushtarak	1:46.9
1999	Jim and Tonic (5)	G Mosse	F Doumen	J D Martin	Running Stag	Lear Spear	2:01.4
2000	Fantastic Light (4)	L Dettori	S bin Suroor	Godolphin	Greek Dance	Jim and Tonic	2:02.20
2001	Agnes Digital (4)	H Shii	T Shirai	T Watanabe	Tobougg	Terre a Terre	2:02.80
2002	Precision (4)	M J Kinane	D Oughton	Wu Sai Wing	Paolini	Dano-Mast	2:07.10
2003	Falbrav (5)	L Dettori	L Cumani	Scuderia Rencati	Rakti	Elegant Fashion	2:00.90

JAPAN CUP-G1
2400 meters (1-1/2 miles), 3-year-olds & up, Tokyo
FIRST RUN IN 1981

Year	1st	Jockey	Trainer	Owner	2nd	3rd	Time
1981	Mairzy Doates (5f)	C Asmussen	J Fulton	A Schefler	Frost King	The Very One	2:25.3
1982	Half Iced (3)	D MacBeth	S Hough	B R Firestone	All Along	April Run	2:27.1
1983	Stanerra (5f)	B Rouse	F Dunne	F Dunne	Kyoei Promise	Esprit du Nord	2:27.6
1984	Katsuragi Ace (4)	K Nishiura	K Domon	I Node	Bedtime	Symboli Rudolf	2:26.3
1985	Symboli Rudolf (4)	Y Okabe	Y Nohira	Symboli Bokujo	Rocky Tiger	The Filbert	2:28.8
1986	Jupiter Island (7)	Pat Eddery	C Brittain	Marquess of Tavistock	Allez Milord	Miho Shinzan	2:25
1987	Le Glorieux (3)	A Lequeux	R Collet	Mme S Wolf	Southjet	Dyna Actress	2:24.9
1988	Pay the Butler (4)	C McCarron	R Frankel	E Gann	Tamamo Cross	Oguri Cap	2:25.5
1989	Horlicks (6f)	L O'Sullivan	D O'Sullivan	G de Gruchy	Oguri Cap	Pay the Butler	2:22.2
1990	Better Loosen Up (5)	M Clarke	D Hayes	G Farrah	Ode	Cacoethes	2:23.2
1991	Golden Pheasant (5)	G Stevens	C Whittingham	B McNall	Magic Night	Shaftesbury Avenue	2:24.7
1992	Tokai Teio (4)	Y Okabe	S Matsumoto	M Uchimura	Naturalism	Dear Doctor	2:24.6
1993	Legacy World (4)	H Kawachi	H Mori	Y Souma	Kotashaan	Winning Ticket	2:24.4
1994	Marvelous Crown (4)	K Minai	M Osawa	S Sasahara	Paradise Creek	Royce And Royce	2:23.6
1995	Lando (5)	M Roberts	H Jentzsch	Gestut Ittlingen	Hishi Amazon	Hernando	2:24.6
1996	Singspiel (4)	L Dettori	M Stoute	Sheikh Mohammed	Fabulous la Fouine	Strategic Choice	2:23.8
1997	Pilsudski (5)	M J Kinane	M Stoute	Lord Weinstock	Air Groove	Bubble Gum Fellow	2:25.8
1998	El Condor Pasa (3)	M Ebina	Y Ninomiya	T Watanabe	Air Groove	Special Week	2:25.9
1999	Special Week (4)	Y Take	T Shirai	H Usuda	Indigenous	High-Rise	2:25.5
2000	T.M. Opera O (4)	R Wada	I Iwamoto	M Takezono	Meisho Doto	Fantastic Light	2:26.10
2001	Jungle Pocket (3)	O Peslier	S Watanabe	Y Saito	T.M. Opera O	Narita Top Road	2:23.80
*2002	Falbrav (4)	L Dettori	L Brogi	Scuderia Rencati	Sarafan	Symboli Kris S	2:12.20
2003	Tap Dance City	T Sato	S Sasaki	Yushun Horse	That's The Plenty	Symboli Kris S	2:28.70

*Run at Nakayama at 1 3/8 miles.

MAJOR JUMP RACES

CHAMPION HURDLE-G1
2-1/16 miles (8 hurdles), 5-year-old & up, Cheltenham (GB)
FIRST RUN IN 1927

Year	1st	Jockey	Trainer	Owner	2nd	3rd	Time
1968	Persian War (5)	J Uttley	C Davies	H Alper	Chorus	Black Justice	4:03.8
1969	Persian War (6)	J Uttley	C Davies	H Alper	Drumikill	Privy Seal	4:41.8
1970	Persian War (7)	J Uttley	C Davies	H Alper	Major Rose	Escalus	4:13.8
1971	Bula (6)	P Kelleway	F Winter	E Edwards	Persian Rose	Major Rose	4:22.2
1972	Bula (7)	P Kelleway	F Winter	E Edwards	Boxer	Lyford Cay	4:25.2
1973	Comedy Of Errors (6)	W Smith	F Rimell	E Wheatley	Easby Abbey	Captain Christy	4:07.8
1974	Lanzarote (6)	R Pitman	F Winter	H de Walden	Comedy Of Errors	Yenisei	4:17.7
1975	Comedy Of Errors (8)	K White	F Rimell	E Wheatley	Flash Imp	Tree Tangle	4:28.5
1976	Night Nurse (5)	P Broderick	M Easterby	R Spencer	Birds Nest	Flash Imp	4:05.9
1977	Night Nurse (6)	P Broderick	M Easterby	R Spencer	Monksfield	Dramatist	4:24.0
1978	Monksfield (6)	T Kinane	D McDonogh	M Mangan	Sea Pigeon	Night Nurse	4:12.7
1979	Monksfield (7)	D T Hughes	D McDonogh	M Mangan	Sea Pigeon	Beacon Light	4:27.0
1980	Sea Pigeon (10)	J J O'Neill	M Easterby	P Muldoon	Monksfield	Birds Nest	4:06.9
1981	Sea Pigeon (11)	J Francome	M Easterby	P Muldoon	Pollardstown	Daring Run	4:11.4
1982	For Auction (6)	C Magnier	M Cunningham	P Heaslip	Broadsword	Ekbalco	4:12.4

Year	1st (Age)	Jockey	Trainer	Owner	2nd	3rd	Time
1983	Gaye Brief (6)	R Linley	M Rimell	A Abu Khamsin	Boreen Prince	For Auction	3:57.08
1984	Dawn Run (6f)	J J O'Neill	P Mullins	Mrs C D Hill	Cima	Very Promising	3:52.6
1985	See You Then (5)	S Smith Eccles	N Henderson	Stype Wood Stud	Robin Wonder	Stans Pride	3:51.7
1986	See You Then (6)	S Smith Eccles	N Henderson	Stype Wood Stud	Gaye Brief	Nohalmdun	3:53.3
1987	See You Then (7)	S Smith Eccles	N Henderson	Stype Wood Stud	Flatterer	Barnbrook Again	3:57.3
1988	Celtic Shot (6)	P Scudamore	F Winter	D Horton	Classical Charm	Celtic Chief	4:14.4
1989	Beech Road (7)	R Guest	G Balding	A Geake	Celtic Chief	Celtic Shot	4:02.1
1990	Kribensis (6)	R Dunwoody	M Stoute	Sheikh Mohammed	Nomadic Way	Past Glories	3:50.7
1991	Morley Street (7)	J Frost	G Balding	M Jackson	Nomadic Way	Ruling	3:54.6
1992	Royal Gait (9)	G McCourt	J Fanshawe	Sheikh Mohammed	Oh So Risky	Ruling	3:57.2
1993	Granville Again (7)	P Scudamore	M Pipe	E Scarth	Royal Derbi	Halkopous	3:51.6
1994	Flakey Dove (8)	M Dwyer	R Price	J Price	Oh So Risky	Large Action	4:02.0
1995	Alderbrook (6)	N Williamson	K Bailey	E Pick	Large Action	Danoli	4:03.0
1996	Collier Bay (6)	G Bradley	J Old	W Stuart	Alderbrook	Pridwell	3:59.0
1997	Make A Stand (6)	A P McCoy	M Pipe	P A Deal	Theatreworld	Space Trucker	3:48.4
1998	Istabraq (6)	C Swan	A P O'Brien	J P McManus	Theatreworld	I'm Supposin	3:49.1
1999	Istabraq (7)	C Swan	A P O'Brien	J P McManus	Theatreworld	French Holly	3:56.8
2000	Istabraq (8)	C Swan	A P O'Brien	J P McManus	Hors La Loi III	Blue Royal	3:48.10
2001	RACE NOT RUN						
2002	Hors La Loi III (7)	D Gallagher	J Fanshawe	P Green	Marble Arch	Bilboa	3:53.80
2003	Rooster Booster (9)	R Johnson	P J Hobbs	T Warner	Westender	Rhinestone Cowboy	3:54.70

CHELTENHAM GOLD CUP STEEPLECHASE-G1
3-1/4 miles (22 fences), 6-year-olds & up, Cheltenham (GB)
FIRST RUN IN 1924

Year	1st	Jockey	Trainer	Owner	2nd	3rd	Time
1970	L'Escargot (7)	T Carberry	D Moore	R Guest	French Tan	Spanish Steps	6:47.4
1971	L'Escargot (8)	T Carberry	D Moore	R Guest	Leap Frog	The Dikler	8:00.6
1972	Glencaraig Lady (8f)	F Berry	F Flood	P Doyle	Royal Toss	The Dikler	7:17.8
1973	The Dikler (10)	R Barry	F Walwyn	Mrs D August	Pendil	Charlie Potheen	6:37.2
1974	Captain Christy (7)	H Beasley	P Taafe	Mrs J Samuel	The Dikler	Game Spirit	7:05.5
1975	Ten Up (8)	T Carberry	J Dreaper	Dchss of Westminster	Soothsayer	Bula	7:51.4
1976	Royal Frolic (7)	J Burke	F Rimell	E Hanmer	Brown Lad	Colebridge	6:40.1
1977	Davy Lad (7)	D Hughes	M O'Toole	Mrs J McGowan	Tied Cottage	Summerville	7:13.8
1978	Midnight Court (7)	J Francome	F Winter	Mrs O Jackson	Brown Lad	Master H	6:57.3
1979	Alverton (9)	J J O'Neill	M Easterby	Snailwell Stud	Royal Mail	Aldaniti	7:01
*1980	Master Smudge (8)	R Hoare	A Barrow	A Barrow	Mac Vidi	Approaching	7:14.2
1981	Little Owl (7)	Mr A Wilson	M Easterby	R Wilson	Night Nurse	Silver Buck	7:09.9
1982	Silver Buck (10)	R Earnshaw	M Dickinson	Mrs C Feather	Bregawn	Sunset Cristo	7:11.3
1983	Bregawn (9)	G Bradley	M Dickinson	J Kennelly	Captain John	Wayward Lad	6:57.6
1984	Burrough Hill Lad (8)	P Tuck	J Pitman	R Riley	Brown Chamberlain	Drumlargan	6:41.4
1985	Forgive 'N' Forget (8)	M Dwyer	J FitzGerald	T Kilroe & Sons	Righthand Man	Earls Brig	6:48.3
1986	Dawn Run (8f)	J J O'Neill	P Mullins	Mrs C D Hill	Wayward Lad	Forgive'N' Forget	6:35.3
1987	The Thinker (9)	R Lamb	W Stephenson	T McDonagh Ltd	ybrandian	Door Latch	6:56.1
1988	Charter Party (9)	R Dunwoody	D Nicholson	Mrs C Smith	Cavvies Clown	Beau Ranger	6:58.9
1989	Desert Orchid (10)	S Sherwood	D Elsworth	R Burridge	Yahoo	Charter Party	7:17.6
1990	Norton's Coin (9)	G McCourt	S Griffiths	S Griffiths	Toby Tobias	Desert Orchid	6:30.9
1991	Garrison Savannah (8)	M Pitman	J Pitman		The Fellow	Desert Orchid	6:49.8
1992	Cool Ground (10)	A Maguire	G Balding	Whitcombe Manor	The Fellow	Docklands Express	6:47.5
1993	Jodami (8)	M Dwyer	P Beaumont	J Yeardon	Rushing Wild	Royal Athlete	6:34.4
1994	The Fellow (9)	A Kondrat	F Doumen	Marquise de Moratalla	Jodami	Young Hustler	6:40.6
1995	Master Oats (9)	N Williamson	K Bailey	P Matthews	Dubacilla	Minnehoma	6:56.1
1996	Imperial Call (7)	C O'Dwyer	F Sutherland	Lisselan Farm	Rough Quest	Couldnt Be Better	6:42.5
1997	Mr Mulligan (9)	A P McCoy	N Chance	M & G Worcester	Barton Bank	Dorans Pride	6:35.5
1998	Cool Dawn (10)	A Thornton	R Alner	Miss D Harding	Strong Promise	Dorans Pride	6:39.5
1999	See More Business (9)	M FitzGerald	P Nicholls	Barber & Keighley	Go Ballistic	Florida Pearl	6:41.9
2000	Looks Like Trouble (8)	R Johnson	N Chance	T Collins	Florida Pearl	Strong Promise	6:30.30
2001	RACE NOT RUN						
2002	Best Mate (7)	J Culloty	J Lewis	H C Knight	Commanche Court	See More Business	6:50.10
2003	Best Mate (8)	J Culloty	J Lewis	H C Knight	Truckers Tavern	Harbour pilot	6:39.00

*Tied Cottage finished first in 1980 but was disqualified from purse money.

GRAND NATIONAL STEEPLECHASE HANDICAP-G3
4-1/2 miles (30 fences), 7-year-olds & up, Aintree (GB)
FIRST RUN IN 1839

Year	1st (age)	Jockey	Trainer	Owner	2nd	3rd	Time
1950	Freebooter (9)	J Power	R Renton	Mrs L Brotherton	Wot No Sun	Acthon Major	9:24.2
1951	Nickel Coin (9)	J Bullock	J O'Donaghue	J Royle	Royal Tan	Derrinstown	9:48.8

Year	1st (Age)	Jockey	Trainer	Owner	2nd	3rd	Time
1952	Teal (10)	A Thompson	N Crump	H Lane	legal Joy	Wot No Sun	9:21.5
1953	Early Mist (8)	B Marshall	M V O'Brien	J Griffin	Mont Tremblant	Irish Lizard	9:22.8
1954	Royal Tan (10)	B Marshall	M V O'Brien	J Griffin	Tudor Line	Irish Lizard	9:32.8
1955	Quare Times (9)	P Taafe	M V O'Brien	Mrs W Welman	Tudor Line	Carey's Cottage	10:19.2
1956	E.S.B. (10)	D Dick	F Rimell	Mrs L Carver	Gentle Moya	Royal Tan	9:21.4
1957	Sundew (11)	F Winter	F Hudson	Mrs G Kohn	Wyndburgh	Tiberetta	9:42.4
1958	Mr What (8)	A Freeman	T Taafe	D J Coughlan	Tiberetta	Green Drill	9:59.8
1959	Oxo (8)	M Scudamore	W Stephenson	J Bigg	Wyndburgh	Mr What	9:37.8
1960	Merryman II (9)	G Scott	N Crump	Miss W Wallace	Badanloch	Clear Profit	9:26.2
1961	Nicolaus Silver (9)	H Beasley	F Rimell	C Vaughan	Merryman II	O'Malley Point	9:22.6
1962	Kilmore (12)	F Winter	R Price	N Cohen	Wyndburgh	Mr What	9:50
1963	Ayala (9)	P Buckley	K Piggott	P Raymond	Carrickbeg	Hawa s Song	9:35.8
1964	Team Spirit (12)	G Robinson	F Walwyn	J Goodman	Purple Silk	Peacetown	9:46.8
1965	Jay Trump (8)	Mr T C Smith	F Winter	Mrs M Stephenson	Freddie	Mr Jones	9:30.6
1966	Anglo (8)	T Norman	F Winter	S Levy	Freddie	Forest Prince	9:52.8
1967	Foinavon (9)	J Buckingham	J Kempton	C Watkins	Honey End	Red Alligator	9:49.6
1968	Red Alligator (9)	B Fletcher	D Smith	J Manners	Moidore's Token	Different Class	9:28.8
1969	Highland Wedding(12)	E P Harty	G Balding	T McCoy Jr	Steel Bridge	Rondetto	9:30.8
1970	Gay Trip (8)	P Taafe	F Rimell	A J Chambers	Vulture	Miss Hunter	9:38
1971	Specify (9)	J Cook	J Sutcliffe	F Pontin	Black Secret	Astbury	9:34.2
1972	Well To Do (9)	G Thorner	T Forster	T Forster	Gay Trip	Black Secret	10:08.4
1973	Red Rum (8)	B Fletcher	D McCain	N Le Mare	Crisp	L'Escargot	9:01.9
1974	Red Rum (9)	B Fletcher	D McCain	N Le Mare	L'Escargot	Charles Dickens	9:20.3
1975	L'Escargot (12)	T Carberry	D Moore		Red Rum	Spanish Steps	9:31.1
1976	Rag Trade (10)	J Burke	F Rimell	P Raymond	Red Rum	Eyecatcher	9:20.9
1977	Red Rum (12)	T Stack	D McCain	N Le Mare	Churchtown Boy	Eyecatcher	9:30.3
1978	Lucius (9)	B Davies	G W Richards	Mrs D Whitaker	Sebastian V	Drumroan	9:33.9
1979	Rubstic (10)	M Barnes	J Leadbetter	J Douglas	Zongalero	Rough And Tumble	9:52.9
1980	Ben Nevis (12)	Mr C Fenwick	T Forster	R Stewart Jr	Rough And Tumble	The Pilgarlic	10:17.4
1981	Aldaniti (11)	R Champion	J Gifford	S Embiricos	Spartan Missile	Royal Mail	9:47.2
1982	Grittar (9)	Mr C Saunders	F Gilman	F Gilman	Hard Outlook	Loving Words	9:12.6
1983	Corbiere (8)	B De Haan	J Pitman	B Burrough	Greasepaint	Yer Man	9:47.4
1984	Hallo Dandy (10)	N Doughty	G W Richards	R Shaw	Greasepaint	Corbiere	9:21.4
1985	Late Suspect (11)	H Davies	T Forster	Dchss of Westminster	Mr Snugfit	Corbiere	9:42.7
1986	West Tip (9)	R Dunwoody	M Oliver	P Luff	Young Driver	Classified	9:33.0
1987	Maori Venture (11)	S Knight	A Turnell	H Joel	The Tsarevich	Lean Ar Aghaidh	9:19.3
1988	Rhyme N' Reason (9)	B Powell	D Elsworth	Miss J Reed	Durham Edition	Monanore	9:53.5
1989	Little Polveir (12)	J Frost	G Balding	E Harvey	West Tip	The Thinker	10:06.8
1990	Mr Frisk (11)	Mr M Armytage	K Bailey	Mrs H Duffey	Durham Edition	Rinus	8:47.8
1991	Seagram (11)	N Hawke	D Barons	E Parker	Garrison Savannah	Auntie Dot	9:29.9
1992	Party Politics (8)	C Llewellyn	N Gaselee	Mrs D Thompson	Romany King	Laura's Beau	9:06.3
1993	RACE VOID						
1994	Minnehoma (11)	R Dunwoody	M Pipe	F Starr	Just So	Moorcroft Boy	10:18.8
1995	Royal Athlete (12)	J F Titley	J Pitman	G & L Johnson	Party Politics	Over the Deel	9:04.1
1996	Rough Quest (10)	M Fitzgerald	T Casey	A Wates	Encore Un Peu	Superior Finish	9:00.8
1997	Lord Gyllene (9)	A Dobbin	S Brookshaw	S Clarke	Suny Bay	Camelot Knight	9:05.9
1998	Earth Summit (10)	C Llewellyn	N Twiston-Davies	Summit Prtnrshp	Suny Bay	Samlee	10:51.4
1999	Bobby Jo (9)	P Carberry	T Carberry	R Burke	Blue Charm	Call It A Day	9:14.1
2000	Papillon (9)	R Walsh	T M Walsh	Mrs B Moran	Mely Moss	Niki Dee	9:09.70
2001	Red Marauder (11)	R Guest	N B Mason	N B Mason	Smarty	Blowing Wind	11:00.1
2002	Bindaree (8)	J Culloty	N Twiston-Davies	H R Mould	What's Up Boys	Blowing Wind	9:08.60
2003	Monty's Pass (10)	B J Geraghty	J J Mangan	Dee Racing Syndicate	Supreme Glory	Amberleigh House	9:21.70

GRAND STEEPLECHASE DE PARIS-G1
5800 meters (3-5/8 miles) (23 obstacles), 6-year-olds & up, Auteuil (Fr)

Year	1st (age)	Jockey	Trainer	Owner	2nd	3rd	Time
1970	Huron (6)	C Drieu	A Adele	B Larrouse	Haroue	Karcimont	8:02.00
1971	Pot d'Or (5	J-J Declercq	M Wallon	R Weill	Haroue	Morgex	8:09.00
1972	Morgex (6)	J-P Ciravegna	J Sens	Mme M Marie	Vaillance	Tirizano	8:12.00
1973	Giquin (6)	J-P Creveuil	A Adele	Mme M-F Berger	Silvery Moon	Spoleto	8:18.00
1974	Chic Type (7)	J-P Renard	J-J Beaume	G Murray	hasty Love	Lucky Boy	8:28.00
1975	Air Landais (5)	P Beyer	G Pelat	Mme C Frolich	Captain Christy	Hasty Love	8:58.00
1976	Piomares (5)	G Negrel	D Perea	J Kalda	Air Landais	Royal Exile	8:39.00
1977	Corps a Corps (5)	A Fabre	A Adele	Baron T de Zuylen	Le Pompier	Mentocha	8:41.00
1978	Mon Filleul (5)	J-L Llorens	B Secly	J-C Weill	Piomares	Chinco	8:43.00
1979	Chinco (7)	P Brame	J-P Gallorini	G Campanella	Mon Filleul	Fiasquito	8:20.00
1980	Fondeur (7)	M Legrand	A Fabre	A Bezard	Tanlas	Lapo d'Or	8:28.00
1981	Isopani (7)	A Chelet	A Fabre	P David	Carmont	Ardiera	7:02.00
1982	Metatero (9)	B Jollivet	A Fabre	G Margogne	Azmi	Lord Gag	7:02.00
1983	Jasmin II (8)	M Chirol	A Fabre	M Thibault	Altimetre	Brodi Dancer	7:03.00
1984	Brodi Dancer (6)	D Leblond	P-L Biancone	Mme C Diallo	V'a Parame	Le Pontif	7:18.00

	1st (age)	Jockey	Trainer	Owner	2nd	3rd	
1985	Sir Gain (6)	S Berard	L Gaumondy	Mme L Belotti	Le Pontif	Lamie Bleue	7:38.00
1986	Otage du Perche (6)	S Berard	P Lamotte d'Argy	P Lamotte d'Argy	Nupsala	Le Pontif	7:33.00
1987	Oteuil (7)	B Jollivet	R Cherruau	Mme R Soulais	Otage du Perche	Mister Sy	7:51.00
1988	Katko (5)	D Vincent	B Secly	Comte de Montesson	Nupsala	Cyborg	7:09.00
1989	Katko (6)	J-Y Beaurain	B Secly	Comte de Montesson	Oteuil	Ouragan Collonges	7:09.00
1990	Katko (7)	J-Y Beaurain	B Secly	Comte de Montesson	Sabre d'Estruval	The Fellow	7:15.00
1991	The Fellow (6)	D Vincent	F Doumen	Marquise de Moratalla	Sabre d'Estruval	Oteuil	7:14.00
1992	El Triunfo (6)	D Vincent	F Rohaut	Mme M Montauban	Ucello II	Ubu III	7:20.00
1993	Ucello II (7)	C Aubert	F Doumen	Marquise de Moratalla	Al Capone II	Vorentin	7:16.00
1994	Ucello II (8)	C Aubert	F Doumen	Marquise de Moratalla	Venus de Mirande	Arenice	7:07.00
1995	Ubu III (9)	P Chevalier	F Doumen	Marquise de Moratalla	Val d'Alene	Bannkipour	7:20.00
1996	Arenice (8)	P Sourzac	G Macaire	Mme M Montauban	Al Capone II	Bannkipour	7:07.00
1997	Al Capone II (9)	J-Y Beaurain	B Secly	R Fougedoire	Cand'Or	Gracky	7:42.00
1998	First Gold (5)	T Doumen	F Doumen	Marquise de Moratalla	Saint-Quenin	Chamberko	7:10.00
1999	Mandarino (6)	P Chevalier	M Rolland	Mme D Ricard	Al Capone II	Chant Royal	7:43.00
2000	Vieux Beaufai (7)	P Bigot	F Danloux	Ecurie Siklos	Or Jack	First Gold	7:19.00
2001	Kotkijet (6)	T Majorcryk	J-P Gallorini	D Wildenstein	Ilare	El Paso III	7:13.00
2002	Double Car (6)	C Cheminaud	B de Watrigant	J Biraben	El Paso III	Batman Senora	7:31.00
2003	Line Marine (6f)	C Pieux	C Aubert	Mme G Vuillard	Batman Senora	Urga	7:37.00

GRANDE COURSE DE HAIES D'AUTEUIL (French Champion Hurdle)–G1
5100 meters (3-3/16 miles) (16 obstacles), 5-year-olds & up, Auteuil (Fr)

Year	1st (age)	Jockey	Trainer	Owner	2nd	3rd	
1970	Samour (5)	C Mabe	J Laumain	Mme H Seutet	Saboulo	Francois Saubaber	
1971	Le Pontet (6)	F Bonni	G Philippeau	Mlle J Rossi	Depou	Next Time	
1972	Hardatit (6)	C Fornaroli	R Pelat	C Sweeny	Marco Polo	Next Time	
1973	Hardatit (7)	P Costes	R Pelat	C Sweeny	Boniface	Yaxilio	
1974	Baby Taine (5)	R Dupon	A Adele	G Blizniansky	Porto Rafti	Boniface	
1975	Mazel Tov (5)	S Roux	A Adele	Mme J Decrion	Dom Helion	Itau	
1976	Les Roseaux (7)	D Merle	G Boeuf	Mlle N Sarmant	Acreon	Endless	
1977	Top Gear (5)	D Costard	G Pelat	D Wildenstein	Sampietro	Schoeller	
1978	Roselier (5)	S Berard	L Gaumondy	Mme L Gaumondy	Great Mist	Holm Oak	
1979	Paiute (6)	M Blackshaw	G Pelat	D Wildenstein	El Condor	Rosator	
1980	Paiute (7)	D Costard	J-H Barbe	D Wildenstein	Carmont	Nellio	
1981	Bison Fute (5)	D Costard	J de Chevigny	Mme J Couturie	Paiute	Val d'Ajol	
1982	World Citizen (5)	N Peguy	P Rago	D Wildenstein	Tell Harmall	Gaye Chance	
1983	Melinoir (5)	D Bailliez	J-H Barbe	F Wintz	World Citizen	For Auction	
1984	Dawn Run (6f)	A Mullins	P Mullins	Mrs C D Hill	Mister Jack	Salute	
1985	Le Rheusois (5)	R Duchene	P Rago	C Ouyoucef	Video Tape	Point Vernal	
1986	Le Rheusois (6)	D Leblond	P Rago	C Ouyoucef	Flatterer	Gacko	
1987	Claude le Lorrain (8)	P-A Sauvat	L Audon	A Bergalet	Gacko	Petite Fortune	
1988	Goodea (8)	B Marie	J-P Gallorini	P Elmoznino	Marly River	Rocarvin	
1989	Sire Rochelais (5)	L Manceau	G Cherel	J-C Evain	Frappeuse	Afkal	
1990	Tongan (7)	D Vincent	G Collet	W Nikolic	Isabey	Ma Puce	
1991	Rose Or No (7)	V Sartori	P Demercastel	Ecurie Ouaki	Ubu III	March On	
1992	Ubu III (6)	A Kondrat	F Doumen	Marquise de Moratalla	Roi d'Ecajeul	Crystal Spirit	
1993	Ubu III (7)	A Kondrat	F Doumen	Marquise de Moratalla	True Brave	Gabarret	
1994	Le Roi Thibault (5)	Y Fouin	G Doleuze	Haras du Reuilly	Ubu III	Bog Frog	
1995	Matchou (6)	D Mescam	J Lesbordes	Mlle Montauban	Royal Chance	Chinese Gordon	
1996	Earl Grant (7)	J-Y Beaurain	B Secly	L Gautier	Mysilv	Montperle	
1997	Bog Frog (8)	J-Y Beaurain	B Secly	Mme Scarisbrick	Alpha Tauri	Royal Chance	
1998	Mantovo (6)	F Benech	M Rolland	F A McNulty	Earl Grant	Nononito	
1999	Vaporetto (6)	T Majorcryk	J-P Gallorini	D Wildenstein	Mon Romain	Asolo	
2000	Le Sauvignon (6)	T Majorcryk	J Bertran de Balanda	D J Jackson	Full of Ambition	Vaporetto	6:09.00
2001	Le Sauvignon (7)	D Bressou	J Bertran de Balanda	D J Jackson	Gilder	Bounce Back	6:19.00
2002	Laveron (7	T Doumen	F Doumen	D Grauert	Vic Toto	Galant Moss	6:19.00
2003	Nobody Told Me (5f)	D J Casey	W Mullins	Amber Syndicate	Karly Flight	Katiki	6:25.00

Results of 2003 Group Races in Europe and Asia

BRITAIN

DATE	TRACK	RACE	CONDITIONS	1st	2nd	3rd
Apr12	Newbury	John Porter S-G3	1 1/2m 4yo+	Warrsan	Asian Heights	Compton Bolter
Apr12	Newbury	Greenham S-G3	7f 3yo c&g	Muqbil	Zafeen	Mister Links
Apr12	Newbury	Fred Darling S-G3	7f 3yo f	Tante Rose	Crystal Star	Rag Top
Apr15	Newmarket	Nell Gwyn S-G3	7f 3yo f	Khulood	Cala	Hector's Girl
Apr16	Newmarket	Earl of Sefton S-G3	1 1/8m 4yo+	Olden Times	Desert Deer	Priors Lodge
Apr17	Newmarket	Craven S-G3	1m 3yo c&g	Hurricane Alan	Lundy's Lane	Splendid Era
Apr25	Sandown	Classic Trial-G3	1 1/4m 3yo	Shield	Inch Again	Strength 'n Honour
Apr26	Sandown	Sandown Mile-G2	1m 4yo+	Desert Deer	Smirk	Reel Buddy
Apr26	Sandown	Gordon Richards S-G3	1 1/4m 4yo+	Indian Creek	Bourgainville	Imperial Dancer
Apr26	Leicester	Leicestershire S-G3	7f 4yo+	Tillerman	Gateman	Millennium Force
Apr30	Ascot	Sagaro S-G3	2m,45y 4yo+	Alcazar	Savannah Bay	Pole Star
May2	Newmarket	Jockey Club S-G2	1 1/2m 4yo+	Warrsan	Millenary	Highest
May3	Newmarket	2000 Guineas S-G1	1m 3yo c&f	Refuse To Bend	Zafeen	Norse Dancer
May3	Newmarket	Palace House S-G3	5f 3yo+	Needwood Blade	Bahamian Pirate	Smokin Beau
May4	Newmarket	1000 Guineas S-G1	1m 3yo f	Russian Rhythm	Six Perfections	Intercontinental
May6	Chester	Chester Vase-G3	a1 9/16m 3yo c/g	Dutch Gold	Summerland	Risk Taker
May8	Chester	Ormonde S-G3	a1 5/8m 4yo+	Asian Heights	Compton Bolter	Razkalla
May8	Chester	Dees S-G3	a1 1/4m 3yo c&g	Kris Kin	Big Bad Bob	Private Charter
May10	Lingfield	Derby Trial-G3	a1 1/2m 3yo c&g	Franklins Gardens	Let Me Try Again	Shanty Star
May13	York	Duke of York S-G2	6f 3yo+	Twilight Blues	Just James	Polar Way
May13	York	Musidora S-G3	a1-5/16m 3yo f	Cassis	Geminiani	Irtahal
May14	York	Dante S-G2	a1 5/16m 3yo	Magistretti	Tuning Fork	Dunhill Star
May15	York	Yorkshire Cup-G2	1 3/4m 4yo+	Mamool	Warrsan	Bollin Eric
May17	Newbury	Lockinge S-G1	1m 4yo+	Hawk Wing	Where Or When	Olden Times
May26	Sandown	Temple S-G2	5f 3yo+	Airwave	Repertory	Acclamation
May26	Sandown	Henry II S-G3	2m78y 4yo+	Mr Dinos	Pole Star	Kasthari
May27	Sandown	Brigadier Gerard S-G3	1 1/4m 4yo+	Sights On Gold	Parasol	Indian Creek
Jun6	Epsom	English Oaks-G1	1 1/2m 3yo f	Casual Look	Yesterday	Summitville
Jun6	Epsom	Coronation Cup-G1	1 1/2m 4yo+	Warrsan	Highest	Black Sam Bellamy
Jun7	Epsom	Epsom Derby-G1	1 1/2m 3yo c&f	Kris Kin	The Great Gatsby	Alamshar
Jun7	Epsom	Diomed S-G3	1 1/16m 3yo+	Gateman	Reel Buddy	King Of Happiness
Jun17	Royal Ascot	St James's Palace S-G1	1m 3yo c	Zafeen	Kalaman	Martillo
Jun17	Royal Ascot	Queen Anne S-G2	1m 3yo+	Dubai Destination	Right Approach	Where Or When
Jun17	Royal Ascot	King's Stand S-G2	5f 3yo+	Choisir	Acclamation	Oasis Dream
Jun17	Royal Ascot	Coventry S-G3	6f 2yo	Three Valleys	Botanical	Privy Seal
Jun18	Royal Ascot	Prince of Wales'sS-G1	1 1/4m 4yo+	Nayef	Rakti	Islington
Jun18	Royal Ascot	Jersey S-G3	7f 3yo	Membership	Arakan	Rimrod
Jun18	Royal Ascot	Queen Mary S-G3	5f 2yo f	Attraction	Catstar	Majestic Desert
Jun19	Royal Ascot	Ascot Gold Cup-G1	2 1/2m 4yo+	Mr Dinos	Persian Punch	Pole Star
Jun19	Royal Ascot	Ribblesdale S-G2	1 1/2m 3yo f	Spanish Sun	Ocean Silk	Mezzo Soprano
Jun19	Royal Ascot	Norfolk S-G3	5f 2yo	Russian Valour	Kheleyf	Nevisian Lad
Jun20	Royal Ascot	Coronation S-G1	1m 3yo f	Russian Rhythm	Soviet Song	Mail The Desert
Jun20	Royal Ascot	King Edward VII S-G2	1 1/2m 3yo c&g	High Accolade	Delsarte	Summerland
Jun20	Royal Ascot	Queen's Vase-G3	2m,45y 3yo	Shanty Star	Singleton	Cruzspiel
Jun21	Royal Ascot	Golden Jubilee S-G1	6f 3yo+	Choisir	Airwave	Baron's Pit
Jun21	Royal Ascot	Hardwicke S-G2	1 1/2m 4yo+	Indian Creek	Bollin Eric	Zindabad
Jun28	Newcastle	Chipchase S-G3	6f 3yo+	Orientor	Country Reel	Danger Over
Jun28	Newmarket	Criterion S-G3	7f 3yo+	Trade Fair	Just James	King Of Happiness
Jly5	Sandown	Eclipse S-G1	1 1/4m 3yo+	Falbrav	Nayef	Kaietear
Jly5	Haydock	Lancashire Oaks-G3	1 1/2m 3yo+f&m	Place Rouge	Flying Wanda	New Orchid
Jly8	Newmarket	Cherry Hinton S-G2	6f 2yo f	Attraction	Pearl Grey	Birthday Suit
Jly8	Newmarket	Princess of Wales's S-G2	1 1/2m 3yo+	Millenary	Bandari	Gamut
Jly9	Newmarket	Falmouth S-G2	1m 3yo+f&m	Macadamia	Waldmark	Walzerkoenigin
Jly9	Newmarket	July S-G2	6f 3yo c&g	Nevisian Lad	Cape Fear	Byron
Jly10	Newmarket	July Cup-G1	6f 3yo+	Oasis Dream	Choisir	Airwave
Jly10	Newmarket	Superlative S-G3	7f 2yo	Kings Point	Chester Le Street	King Hesperus
Jly11	York	Summer S-G3	6f 3yo+ f&m	Torosay Spring	Khulood	Golden Nun
Jly12	Ascot	Silver Trophy-G3	1m 4yo+	Tillerman	Beauchamp Pilot	Right Approach
Jly21	Ayr	Scottish Derby-G2	1 1/4m 3yo+	Princely Venture	Sights On Gold	Delsarte
Jly25	Chepstow	Golden Daffodil S-G3	1 1/4m 3yo+ f&m	Chorist	Favourable Terms	Monturani
Jly26	Ascot	King Geo/Queen. Eliz S-G1	1 1/2m 3yo+	Alamshar	Sulamani	Kris Kin
Jly26	Ascot	Princess Margaret S-G3	6f 2yo f	River Belle	Rosehearty	Voile
Jly29	Goodwood	Richmond S-G2	6f 2yo c&g	Carrizo Creek	Old Deuteronomy	Cedarberg
Jly29	Goodwood	Gordon S-G3	1 1/2m 3yo	Phoenix Reach	High Accolade	Hawk Flyer
Jly29	Goodwood	Lennox S-G3	7f 3yo+	Nayyir	Arakan	Tante Rose
Jly30	Goodwood	Sussex S-G1	1m 3yo+	Reel Buddy	Statue Of Liberty	Norse Dancer
Jly30	Goodwood	Vintage S-G2	7f 2yo	Lucky Story	The Mighty Tiger	Devil Moon
Jly31	Goodwood	Goodwood Cup-G2	2m 3yo+	Persian Punch	Jardines Lookout	Savannah Bay
Jly31	Goodwood	Molecomb S-G3	5f 2yo	Majestic Missile	Nights Cross	Dallaah
Jly31	Goodwood	King George S-G3	5f 3yo+	The Tatling	Dragon Flyer	Slap Shot
Aug2	Goodwood	Nassau S-G1	1 1/4m 3yo+f&m	Russian Rhythm	Ana Marie	Ze Zee Top
Aug9	Haydock	Rose of Lancaster S-G3	15/16m 3yo+	Sabre d'Argent	Far Lane	Izdiham
Aug16	Newbury	Geoffrey Freer S-G2	a1 5/8m	Mubtaker	Systematic	Mamool
Aug16	Newbury	Hungerford S-G3	7f 3yo+	With Reason	Tarjman	Ashdown Express
Aug19	York	Juddmonte Intl S-G1	a1 5/16m	Falbrav	Magistretti	Nayef
Aug19	York	Great Voltigeur S-G2	1 1/2m 3yo c&g	Powerscourt	Brian Boru	Hawk Flyer
Aug19	York	Lonsdale S-G3	2m 3yo+	Bollin Eric	Cover Up	Zindabad

DATE	TRACK	RACE	CONDITIONS	1st	2nd	3rd
Aug20	York	Yorkshire Oaks-G1	1 1/2m 3yo+ f/m	Islington	Ocean Silk	Summitville
Aug20	York	Gimcrack S-G2	6f 2yo c&g	Balmont	Fokine	Grand Reward
Aug21	York	Nunthorpe S-G1	5f 2yo+	Oasis Dream	The Tatling	Acclamation
Aug21	York	Lowther S-G2	6f 2yo f	Carry On Katie	Badminton	Dunloskin
Aug23	Goodwood	Celebration Mile-G2	1m 3yo+	Priors Lodge	Passing Glance	Tillerman
Aug23	Windsor	Winter Hill S-G3	1 1/4m 3yo+	Leporello	Bourgainville	Island House
Aug24	Goodwood	Prestige S-G3	7f 2yo f	Gracefully	Ithaca	Dubaian Duel
Aug30	Sandown	Solario S-G3	7f 2yo	Barbajuan	Milk It Mick	Matloob
Sep3	York	Strensall S-G3	1 1/8m 3yo+	Naheef	Eventuail	Akshar
Sep6	Haydock	HaydockPkSprintCup-G	6f 3yo+	Somnus	Oasis Dream	Airwave
Sep6	Kempton	September S-G3	1 1/2m 3yo+	Mubtaker	First Charter	Indian Creek
Sep6	Kempton	Sirenia S-G3	6f 2yo	Pastor Of Pursuits	Diospyros Blue	Cartography
Sep10	Doncaster	Park Hill S-G3	1 13/16m3yo+ f&mDiscreet Brief		Floreeda	Singleton
Sep11	Doncaster	Doncaster Cup-G2	2 1/4m 3yo+	Persian Punch	Dusky Warbler	Hugs Dancer
Sep11	Doncaster	May Hill S-G2	1m 2yo f	Kinnaird	Hathrah	Lucky Pipit
Sep11	Doncaster	Park S-G3	1m 3yo+	Polar Ben	With Reason	Tarjman
Sep12	Doncaster	Champagne S-G2	7f 2yo c&g	Lucky Story	Auditorium	Haafhd
Sep13	Goodwood	Select S-G3	1-1/4m 3yo+	Leporello	Muqbil	Kaieteur
Sep13	Doncaster	St Leger S-G1	a1 13/16m 3yo c&f	Brian Boru	High Accolade	Phoenix Reach
Sep13	Doncaster	Flying Childers S-G2	5f 2yo	Howick Falls	China Eyes	Nights Cross
Sep19	Newbury	Mill Reef S-G3	6f 2yo	Byron	Grand Reward	Tahreeb
Sep20	Newbury	Dubai Airport Trophy-G3	5f,34y 3yo+	Ratio	Mornin Reserves	Dragon Flyer
Sep25	Goodwood	Supreme S-G3	7f 3yo+	With Reason	Monsieur Bond	Tantina
Sep27	Ascot	Queen Elizabeth II S-G1	1m 3yo+	Falbrav	Russian Rhythm	Tillerman
Sep27	Ascot	Fillies Mile-G1	1m 2yo f	Red Bloom	Sundrop	Punctilious
Sep27	Ascot	Royal Lodge S-G2	1m 2yo c&g	Snow Ridge	Moscow Ballet	Rule Of Law
Sep27	Ascot	Diadem S-G2	6f 3yo+	Acclamation	Polar Way	Lochridge
Sep28	Ascot	Cumberland Lodge-G3	1 1/2m 3yo+	High Accolade	Compton Bolter	Indian Creek
Oct2	Newmarket	Cheveley Park S-G1	6f 2yo f	Carry On Katie	Majestic Desert	Badminton
Oct2	Newmarket	Somerville Tattersalls-G3	7f 2yo	Milk It Mick	Bayeux	Bachelor Duke
Oct3	Newmarket	Middle Park S-G1	6f 2yo c	*Balmont	Holborn	Auditorium
Oct3	Newmarket	Joel S-G3	1m 3yo+	Splendid Era	Kalaman	Muqbil
Oct4	Newmarket	Sun Chariot S-G2	1m 3yo+f&m	Echoes In Eternity	Macadamia	Almond Mousse
Oct11	Ascot	Princess Royal S-G3	1 1/2m 3yo+f/m	Itnab	Summitville	Chorist
Oct11	Ascot	Cornwallis S-G3	5f 2yo	Majestic Missile	Nights Cross	Fast Heart
Oct11	Ascot	Autumn S-G3	1m 2yo	Fantastic View	Menokee	Temple Place
Oct17	Newmarket	Bentinck S-G3	6f 3yo+	Ashdown Express	Royal Millennium	Colonel Cotton
Oct18	Newmarket	Champion S-G1	1 1/4m 3yo+	Rakti	Carnival Dancer	Indian Creek
Oct18	Newmarket	Dewhurst S-G1	7f 2yo c&f	Milk It Mick	Three Valleys	Haafhd
Oct18	Newmarket	Challenge S-G2	7f 3yo+	Just James	Nayyir	Arakan
Oct18	Newmarket	Rockfel S-G2	7f 2yo f	Cairns	Snow Goose	Kelucia
Oct18	Newmarket	Jockey Club Cup-G3	2m 3yo+	Persian Punch	Millenary	Kasthari
Oct24	Newbury	Horris Hill S-G3	7f 2yo c&g	Peak To Creek	Josephus	Millbag
Oct25	Newbury	St Simon S-G3	1-1/2m 3yo+	Imperial Dancer	High Accolade	Dubai Success
Oct25	Doncaster	Racing Post Trophy-G1	1m 2yo c&f	American Post	Fantastic View	Magritte

*Three Valleys finished first but was disqualified from purse money.

FRANCE

DATE	TRACK	RACE	CONDITIONS	1st	2nd	3rd
Mar8	Saint-Cloud	Prix Exbury-G3	1 1/4m 4yo+	Aquarelliste	Caesarion	Border Arrow
Mar29	Saint-Cloud	Prix Edmond Blanc-G3	1m 4yo+	Salselon	Almond Mousse	Massigann
Mar30	Longchamp	Prix d'Harcourt-G2	1-1/4m 4yo+	Ana Marie	Fiar Mix	Valentino
Apr6	Longchamp	Prix Noailles-G2	1 3/8m 3yo c&f	Super Celebre	Coroner	Jipapibaquigrafo
Apr8	Saint-Cloud	Prix Penelope-G3	1 5/16m 3yo f	Humouresque	Sweet Folly	Commercante
Apr17	Longchamp	Prix d'Hedouville-G3	1 1/2m 4yo+	Martaline	Loxias	Craig's Falcon
Apr20	Longchamp	Prix Greffulhe-G2	1 5/16m 3yo c&f	Dalakhani	Jipapibaquigrafo	Fairly Ransom
Apr20	Longchamp	Prix de Fontainebleau-G3	1m 3yo c	Clodovil	Shuttle Diplomacy	Snipewalk
Apr20	Longchamp	Prix de la Grotte-G3	1m 3yo f	Maiden Tower	Fdelio's Miracle	Welcome Millenium
Apr27	Longchamp	Prix Ganay-G1	1 5/16m 4yo+	Fair Mix	Execute	Falbrav
Apr27	Longchamp	Prix Vanteaux-G3	a1 1/8m 3yo f	Campsie Fells	Mystic Melody	Liska
Apr27	Longchamp	Prix de Barbeville-G3	1 15/16m 4yo+	Morozov	Clety	L'Impatient
May1	Saint-Cloud	Prix du Muguet-G2	1m 4yo+	Dandoun	Domedriver	Bernbeau
May5	Saint-Cloud	Prix La Force-G3	1 1/4m 3yo	Vespone	Vadalix	Kalabar
May8	Longchamp	Prix Hocquart-G2	1-1/2m 3yo c&f	Coroner	Touch Of Land	Risk Seeker
May11	Longchamp	Poule d'Essai P'lains-G1	1m 3yo c	Clodovil	Catcher In The Rye	Krataios
May11	Longchamp	Poule d'Essai P'liches-G1	1m 3yo f	Musical Chimes	Maiden Tower	Etoile Montante
May11	Longchamp	Prix Lupin-G1	1 5/16m 3yo c&f	Dalakhani	Super Celebre	Alberto Giacometti
May11	Longchamp	Prix de Saint-Georges-G3	5f 3to+	Best Walking	Zipping	Ela Merici
May12	Saint-Cloud	Prix Cleopatre-G3	1-5/16m 3yo f	Sweet Folly	Baie	Vallee Enchantee
May15	Longchamp	Prix de Guiche-G3	a1 1/8m 3yo c	Marshall	Jipapibaquigrafo	Art Moderne
May18	Longchamp	Prix d'Ispahan-G1	a1 1/8m 4yo+	Falbrav	Bright Sky	Carnival Dancer
May18	Longchamp	Prix Saint-Alary-G1	1 1/4m 3yo f	Fidelite	Hi Dubai	Arvada
May18	Longchamp	Pr Vicomtesse Vigier-G2	1 15/16m 4yo+	Cut Quartz	Morozov	Terrazzo
May21	Saint-Cloud	Pr Jean de Chaudenay-G2	1-1/2m 4yo+	Loxias	Millenary	Martaline
May22	Longchamp	Prix du Palais-Royal-G3	7f 3yo+	Saratan	Meshaheer	Mount Abu
May31	Chantilly	Prix de Royaumont-G3	1-1/2m 3yo f	Diasilixa	Aynthia	Suborneuse
Jun1	Chantilly	Prix du Jockey-Club-G1	1-1/2m 3yo c&f	Dalakhani	Super Celebre	Coroner
Jun1	Chantilly	Prix Jean Prat-G1	1-1/8m 3yo c&f	Vespone	Prince Kirk	Tashkandi
Jun1	Chantilly	Prix de Sandringham-G2	1m 3yo f	Maiden Tower	Acago	Intercontinental

DATE	TRACK	RACE	CONDITIONS	1st	2nd	3rd
Jun1	Chantilly	Prix du Gros-Chene-G2	5f 3yo+	Porlezza	Zipping	The Trader
Jun8	Chantilly	Prix de Diane-G1	1 5/16m 3yo f	Nebraska Tornado	Time Ahead	Musical Chimes
Jun8	Chantilly	Grand Prix de Chantilly-G2	1 1/2m 4yo+	Ange Gabriel	Martaline	Balakheri
Jun8	Chantilly	Pr Chemin de Fer Nord-G3	1m 4yo+	Tripat	Special Kaldoun	Bernbeau
Jun9	Saint-Cloud	Prix Corrida-G3	1 1/4m 4yo+ f&m	Trumbaka	Bonne Gargotte	Amathia
Jun16	Chantilly	Prix de la Jonchere-G3	1m 3yo c&g	King's Drama	Mister Charm	Balin's Sword
Jun19	Longchamp	La Coupe-G3	1 1/4m 4yo+	Carnival Dancer	Naheef	Victorian Order
Jun22	Longchamp	Grand Prix de Paris-G1	1 1/4m 3yo c&f	Vespone	Magistretti	Look Honey
Jun22	Longchamp	Prix du Lys-G3	1 1/2m 3yo c&g	Doyen	Policy Maker	Mosogno
Jun22	Longchamp	Pr de la Porte Maillot-G3	7f 3yo+	Lucky Strike	Millennium Force	Saratan
Jun24	Longchamp	Prix Chloe-G3	1 1/8m 3yo f	Acago	Garlinote	Precious Pearl
Jun28	Chantilly	Prix du Bois-G3	5f 2yo	Ela Merici	Zinziberine	On Line
Jun29	Saint-Cloud	Grand Prix de St-Cloud	1 1/2m 3yo+	Ange Gabriel	Polish Summer	Loxias
Jun29	Saint-Cloud	Prix de Malleret-G2	1 1/2m 3yo f	High Praise	Underwater	Sweet Folly
Jly5	Deauville	Prix du Bois-G3	5f 2yo	Much Faster	Leila	Sister Moonshine
Jly6	Deauville	Prix de Ris-Orangis-G3	6f 3yo+	Swedish Shave	Vasywait	Blanche
Jly13	Deauville	Prix Messidor-G3	1m 3yo+	Special Kaldoun	Tashkandi	Bernebeau
Jly13	Deauville	Prix Berteux-G3	1 7/8m 3yo	Risk Seeker	Clear Thinking	Rotheram
Jly14	M-Laffitte	Prix Eugene Adam-G2	1 1/4m 3yo	Look Honey	Kalabar	Ridaar
Jly19	M-Laffitte	Prix Maurice de Nieuil-G2	1 3/4m 4yo+	Martaline	Westerner	Clety
Jly23	Vichy	Grand Prix de Vichy-G3	1 1/4m 3yo+	Vangelis	Labirinto	Almond Mousse
Jly27	M-Laffitte	Prix Daphnis-G3	1 1/8m 3yo c&g	Lateen Sails	Shakis	Streamix
Jly27	M-Laffitte	Prix Robert Papin-G2	5 1/2f 2yo c&f	Much Faster	Colossus	Leila
Aug2	Deauville	Prix de Cabourg-G3	6f 2yo	Denebola	Bonaire	Via Milano
Aug4	Deauville	Prix d'Astarte-G2	1m 3yo+ f&m	Bright Sky	Six Perfections	Marbye
Aug9	Deauville	Prix de Psyche-G3	1 1/4m 3yo f	Commercante	Baie	Mezzo Soprano
Aug10	Deauville	Prix Maurice de Gheest-G1	6-1/2f 3yo+	Porlezza	Etoile Montante	Avonbridge
Aug10	Deauville	Prix de Pomone-G2	1 11/16m 3yo+ f/m	Vallee Enchantee	Treble Heights	Mandela
Aug15	Deauville	Prix Guillaume d'Ornano-G2	1 1/4m 3yo	Kalabar	Saturn	Prince Kirk
Aug16	Deauville	Prix Gontaut-Biron-G3	1 1/4m 4yo+	Carnival Dancer	Without Connexion	Sunstrach
Aug17	Deauville	Prix Jacques le Marois-G1	1m 3yo+ c&f	Six Perfections	Domedriver	Telegnosis
Aug23	Deauville	Prix du Calvados-G3	7f 2yo f	Green Swallow	Via Milano	Leila
Aug24	Deauville	Prix Kergorlay-G2	1 7/8m 3yo+	Darasim	Westerner	Swing Wing
Aug24	Deauville	Prix de la Nonette-G3	1 1/4m 3yo f	State of Art	Hoh Buzzard	Felicity
Aug26	Deauville	Prix Minerve-G3	1 9/16m 3yo f	Whortleberry	Monetary	Sovana
Aug29	Deauville	Prix Quincey-G3	1m 3yo+	My Risk	Star Valley	Mister Charm
Aug31	Deauville	Prix Morny-G1	6f 2yo c&f	Whipper	Much Faster	Denebola
Aug31	Deauville	Grand Prix de Deauville-G2	1 9/16m 3yo+	*Policy Maker	Polish Summer	Craig's Falcon
Aug31	Deauville	Prix de Meautry-G3	6f 3yo+	Blanche	Zinziberine	Crystal Castle
Sep7	Longchamp	Prix du Moulin-G1	1m 3yo+	Nebraska Tornado	Lohengrin	Bright Sky
Sep7	Longchamp	Prix du Petit Couvert-G3	5f 3yo+	Repertory	Traou Mad	Melkior
Sep10	M-Laffitte	Prix d'Arenberg-G3	5-1/2f 2yo	Villadolide	Needles And Pins	Peak To Creek
Sep11	Longchamp	Prix de Lutece-G3	1 7/8m 3yo	Risk Seeker	Grey Glitters	Clear Thinking
Sep11	Longchamp	Prix La Rochette-G3	7f 2yo	Diamond Green	Charming Prince	Ershaad
Sep14	Longchamp	Prix Vermeille-G1	1 1/2m 3yo f	Mezzo Soprano	Yesterday	Fidelite
Sep14	Longchamp	Prix Niel-G2	1 1/2m 3yo c&f	Dalakhani	Doyen	Kris Kin
Sep14	Longchamp	Prix Foy-G2	1 1/2m 4yo+ c&f	Ange Gabriel	Martaline	Imperial Dancer
Sep14	Longchamp	Prix d'Aumale-G3	1m 2yo f	Green Noon	Laila	Anabaa Republic
Sep14	Longchamp	Prix Gladiateur-G3	1 15/16m 4yo+	Darasim	Westerner	Soreze
Sep16	M-Laffitte	La Coupe de M-Laffitte-G3	1 1/4m 3yo+	Gruntled	Highdown	Secret Singer
Sep20	Longchamp	Pr du Prince d'Orange-G3	1 1/4m 3yo	Weightless	Shakis	Touch Of Land
Sep20	Longchamp	Prix des Chenes-G3	1m 2yo c&g	Bago	Valixir	Happy Crusader
Oct1	M-Laffitte	Prix Eclipse-G3	6f 2yo	Bonaire	Viladolide	Chineur
Oct4	Longchamp	Pr Daniel Wildenstein-G2	1m 3yo+	Special Kaldoun	My Risk	Gateman
Oct4	Longchamp	Prix Dollar-G2	1 3/16m,55y 3yo+	Weightless	Short Pause	Execute
Oct4	Longchamp	Prix de Royallieu-G2	1 9/16m 3yo+ f/m	Moon Search	Whortleberry	Ocean Silk
Oct4	Longchamp	Prix Hubert de Chaudenay-G2	1 7/8m 3yo	Behkara	Risk Seeker	Clear Thinking
Oct5	Longchamp	Prix de l'Arc de Triomphe-G1	1 1/2m 3yo+ c&f	Dalakhani	Mubtaker	High Chaparral
Oct5	Longchamp	Prix de l'Opera-G1	1 1/4m 3yo+ f&m	Zee Zee Top	Yesterday	Bright Sky
Oct5	Longchamp	Prix de l'Abbaye-G1	5f 2yo+	Patavellian	The Trader	The Tatling
Oct5	Longchamp	Prix Marcel Boussac-G1	1m 2yo f	Denebola	Green Noon	Tulipe Royale
Oct5	Longchamp	Pr JeanLuc Lagardere-G1	7f 2yo c&f	American Post	Charming Prince	Ximb
Oct5	Longchamp	Prix du Cadran-G1	2 1/2m 4yo+	Westerner	Germinis	Darasim
Oct12	Longchamp	Prix de la Foret-G1	7f 3yo+	Etoile Montante	Royal Millennium	Saratan
Oct14	Saint-Cloud	Prix Thomas Bryon-G3	1m 2yo	Apsis	Gwaihir	Always King
Oct16	Lyon-Parilly	Prix Andre Baboin-G3	1-1/4m 3yo+	Sign of the Wolf	Millennium Mambo	Arnathia
Oct19	Longchamp	Prix du Conseil de Paris-G2	1 1/2m 3yo+	Vallee Enchantee	Kalabar	Vangelis
Oct19	Longchamp	Prix de Conde-G3	1 1/8m 2yo	Latice	Voix du Nord	Prospect Park
Oct21	Deauville	Prix des Reservoirs-G3	1m 2yo f	Via Milano	Colony Band	Agata
Oct26	Longchamp	Prix Royal-Oak-G1	1 15/16m 3yo+	Westerner	Alcazar	Behkera
Oct27	Saint-Cloud	Prix de Flore-G3	1-5/16m 3+ f&m	Visorama	Commercante	Actrice
Oct31	M-Laffitte	Criterium de M-Laffitte-G2	6f 2yo	Whipper	Chineur	Black Escort
Oct31	M-Laffitte	Prix de Seine-et-Oise-G3	6f 3yo+	Soave	Welsh Emperor	Amazon Beauty
Nov1	Saint-Cloud	Criterium International-G1	1m 2yo c&f	Bago	Top Seed	Acropolis
Nov1	Saint-Cloud	Prix Perth-G3	1m 3yo+	My Risk	Execute	Saratan
Nov4	M-Laffitte	Prix Miesque-G3	7f 2yo f	Dalna	Malaica	La Ina
Nov8	Saint-Cloud	Criterium de St-Cloud-G1	1-1/4m 2yo c&f	Voix du Nord	Simplex	Day or Night
Nov11	Toulouse	Prix Fille de l'Air-G3	1-5/16m 3+ f&m	Walkamia	Monturani	Handria

*Polish Summer finished first but was disqualified and placed second.

IRELAND

DATE	TRACK	RACE	CONDITIONS	1st	2nd	3rd
Apr6	Curragh	Gladness S-G3	7f 3yo+	Millennium Force	One More Round	Marino Marini
Apr13	Leopardstown	Ballysax S-G3	1 1/4m 3yo	Balestrini	Alamshar	Alberto Giacometti
Apr27	Curragh	Tetrarch S-G3	7f 3yo c&f	France	Al Turf	Dalcassian
Apr27	Curragh	Athasi S-G3	7f 3&4yo f	Walayef	Vintage Tipple	Bon Expresso
Apr27	Curragh	Mooresbridge S-G3	1 1/4m 4yo+	Nysaean	Mkuzi	Miss Honorine
May11	Leopardstown	Derrinst'n Stud Derby Tr.-G2	1 1/4m 3yo	Alamshar	The Great Gatsby	Brian Boru
May11	Leopardstown	1000 Guineas Trial-G3	1m 3yo f	Cat Belling	Flamelet	Hymn Of Love
May24	Curragh	Irish 2000 Guineas-G1	1m 3yo c&f	Indian Haven	France	Tout Seul
May24	Curragh	Greenlands S-G3	6f 3yo+	Miss Emma	Captain Rio	Red Carpet
May25	Curragh	Irish 1000 Guineas	1m 3yo f	Yesterday	Six Perfections	Dimitrova
May25	Curragh	Tattersalls Gold Cup-G1	1 5/16m 4yo+	Black Sam Bellamy	Highdown	Narrative
Jun8	Curragh	Gallinule S-G3	1 1/4m 3yo+	Nysaean	Handel	Tipperary All Star
Jun11	Leopardstown	Ballycorus S-G3	7f 3yo+	Abunawwas	One More Round	Miss Emma
Jun15	Cork	Ballyogan S-G3	5f 3yo+	Miss Anabaa	Belle du Jour	Marino Marini
Jun28	Curragh	Pretty Polly S-G2	1 1/4m 3yo+ f&m	Hanami	Snippets	Zee Zee Top
Jun28	Curragh	Curragh Cup-G3	1 3/4m 3yo+	Maharib	Arundel	Rayshan
Jun29	Curragh	Irish Derby-G1	1 1/2m 3yo c&f	Alamshar	Dalakhani	Roosevelt
Jun29	Curragh	Railway S-G3	6f 2yo	Antonius Pius	Spanish Ace	Il Pirata
Jly5	Leopardstown	Brownstown S-G3	7f 3yo+ f&m	Perfect Touch	Irrestible	Dixie Evans
Jly12	Curragh	International S-G2	1m 3yo+	Sea Dart	Al Turf	France
Jly13	Curragh	Irish Oaks-G1	1 1/2m 3yo f	Vintage Tipple	L'Ancresse	Casual Look
Jly13	Curragh	Anglesey S-G3	6f,63y 2yo	One Cool Cat	Leicester Square	Mokabra
Jly13	Curragh	Minstrel S-G3	7f 3yo+	Avorado	D'Anjou	Millennium Force
Jly26	Leopardstown	Meld S-G3	1 1/4m 3yo+	Mingun	Carnival Dancer	In Time's Eye
Aug10	Curragh	Phoenix S-G1	6f 2yo c&f	One Cool Cat	Old Deuteronomy	Three Valleys
Aug10	Curragh	Phoenix Sprint S-G3	6f 3yo+	Bonus	Sun Slash	Anna Frid
Aug10	Curragh	Royal Whip S-G2	1 1/4m 3yo+	High Chaparral	Imperial Dancer	In Time's Eye
Aug10	Curragh	Debutante S-G3	7f 2yo f	Necklace	Caldy Dancer	Red Feather
Aug17	Leopardstown	Desmond S-G3	1m 3yo+	Refuse To Bend	Latino Magic	Middlemarch
Aug23	Curragh	Futurity S-G2	7f 2yo	Pearl Of Love	Tumblebrutus	The Mighty Tiger
Aug31	Curragh	Moyglare Stud S-G1	7f 2yo f	Necklace	Red Feather	Menhoubah
Aug31	Curragh	Flying Five-G3	5f 2yo+	Deportivo	Daganya	Cool Cousin
Sep6	Leopardstown	Irish Champion S-G1	1 1/4m 3yo+	High Chaparral	Falbrav	Islington
Sep6	Leopardstown	Matron S-G2	1m 3yo+ f&m	Favourable Terms	Perfect Touch	Dossier
Sep13	Curragh	Irish St Leger-G1	1 3/4m 3yo+	Vinnie Roe	Gamut	Powerscourt
Sep13	Curragh	Ridgewood Pearl S-G3	6f 3yo+	Fayr Jag	Hanabad	Avonbridge
Sep14	Curragh	National S-G1	7f2yo c&f	One Cool Cat	Wathab	Pearl Of Love
Sep14	Curragh	Blandford S-G3	1 1/4m 3yo+ f&m	Chorist	Place Rouge	Dossier
Sep21	Curragh	Park S-G3	7f 2yo f	Venturi	Misty Heights	Opera Comique
Oct5	Tipperary	Concorde S-G3	7f 3yo+	Sheppard's Watch	Latino Magic	Perfect Touch
Oct12	Curragh	Beresford S-G2	1m 2yo	Azamour	Relaxed Gesture	Mustameet
Oct27	Leopardstown	Killavullan S-G3	7f 2yo	Grey Swallow	Newton	Takice

GERMANY

DATE	TRACK	RACE	CONDITIONS	1st	2nd	3rd
Apr6	Cologne	GP der Bremer Wirtschaft-G3	1 3/8m 4yo+	Aolus	Epalo	Olaso
Apr13	Krefeld	Dr Busch-Memorial-G3	1 1/16m 3yo	Soldier Hollow	Ransom O'War	Checkit
Apr27	Frankfurt	Fruhjhars Dreijahrigen-G3	1 1/4m 3yo	Flambo	Corriolanus	Minley
May5	Cologne	Gerling-Preis-G2	1 1/2m 4yo+	Aolus	Levirat	Olaso
May11	Dusseldorf	Henkel-Rennen-G2	1m 3yo f	Diacada	White Rose	Finora
May18	Cologne	Mehl-Mulhens-Rennen-G2	1m 3yo c&f	Martillo	Royal Price	Ransom O'War
May24	Baden-Baden	Betty Barclay-Rennen-G3	2m 4yo+	Olaso	Tomster	Levirat
May25	Baden-Baden	Badener-Meile-G3	1m 3yo+	Zarewitsch	Areias	Chan Chan
May30	Baden-Baden	Benazet-Rennen-G3	6f 3yo+	Ingolf	Gold Type	Traou Mad
Jun1	Baden-Baden	Grosser Mercedes-Benz-G2	1 3/8m 4yo+	Epalo	Salve Regina	Next Desert
Jun8	Mulheim	Preis der Diana-G1	1 3/8m 3yo f	Next Gina	White Rose	Mandela
Jun9	Munich	Grosse Muller Brot Pr-G2	1 1/4m 3yo	Ransom O'War	Winning Dash	Silver Spur
Jun15	Cologne	Oppenheim-Union-Rennen-G2	1 3/8m 3yo	Dai Jin	North Lodge	Palmridge
Jun22	Dortmund	Dortmunder Wirtschaft-G3	1m,165y 3yo+	War Blade	Royal Price	Arlecchina
Jun22	Bremen	W J Jacobs-Rennen-G3	1 5/16m 3yo	Wild Passion	Rajpute	Lomicelli
Jun28	Hamburg	Deutscher Herold-Preis-G3	1 3yo+	Up And Away	Horeion Directa	Royal Dubai
Jun29	Hamburg	Idee Hansa-Preis-G2	1 3/8m 3yo+	Aolus	Epalo	Sabiango
Jly4	Hamburg	Grssr Jubilaumspreis-G3	1 3/8m 3yo+ f&m	Lysuna	Luttje Lage	
Jly5	Hamburg	Holsten-Trophy-G3	6f 3yo+	Capricho	Welsh Emperor	Fiepes Shuffle
Jly6	Hamburg	Deutsches Derby-G1	1 1/2m 3yo c&f	Dai Jin	Ransom O'War	Storm Trooper
Jly13	Hoppegarten	Berlin-Brndnburg Trphy-G2	1m 3yo+	Martillo	Mail The Desert	Bear King
Jly20	Frankfurt	Hessen-Pokal-G3	1-1/4m 3yo+	Picotee	Caluna	Corriolanus
Jly27	Dusseldorf	Deutschlandpreis-G1	1-1/2m 3yo+	Sabiango	Storm Trooper	Leviart
Aug3	Cologne	Otto Wolff-Meile-G3	1m 3yo+	Scapolo	Saratan	Dupont
Aug3	Munich	Bayerisches Zuchtrennen-G1	1 1/4m 3yo+	Ransom O'War	dh-Highdown	dh-Epalo
Aug10	Hoppegarten	GP von Berlin-G3	6-1/2f 3yo+	Fiepes Shuffle	Topkamp	Toylsome
Aug17	Cologne	Credit Suisse Pokal-G1	1 1/2m 3yo+	Dai Jin	Next Desert	Warrsan
Aug29	Baden-Baden	Spreti-Rennen-G3	1 1/4m 4yo+	Diamante	Picotee	Longridge
Aug31	Baden-Baden	Furstenberg-Rennen-G3	1 1/4m 3yo	Big Bad Bob	Senex	Winning Dash
Sep2	Baden-Baden	Oettingen-Rennen-G2	1m 3yo+	Passing Glance	Bear King	Zarewitsch
Sep3	Baden-Baden	Golden Peitsche-G2	6f 3yo+	Stormont	Soave	Lucky Strike
Sep5	Baden-Baden	Maurice Lacroix-Trophy-G2	6f 2yo	Mokabra	Slawomira	Marabout Directa

Sep7	Baden-Baden	Grosser Preis von Baden-G1	1 1/2m 3yo+	Mamool	Black Sam Bellamy	Dano-Mast
Sep21	Frankfurt	Euro-Cup-G2	1-1/4m 3yo+	Fruhlingssturm	Naheef	Fruhtau
Sep27	Cologne	Deutscher Stutenpreis-G3	1 1/2m 3yo+f&m	Anzasca	Fleurie Domaine	Perima
Sep28	Cologne	Grosse Europa-Meile-G2	1m 3yo+	Peppercorn	Peppershot	Diacada
Sep28	Cologne	Preis von Europa-G1	1 1/2m 3yo+	Mamool	Albanova	Well Made
Oct3	Mulheim	Preis der Winterkonigin-G3	1m 2yo f	Night Lagoon	Vallera	La Ina
Oct3	Hoppegarten	Prs Deutschen Einheit-G3	1 1/4m 3yo+	Terre de l'Homme	Winning Dash	Royal Experiment
Oct5	Dortmund	Deutsches St Leger-G2	1 3/4m 3yo c&f	Royal Fantasy	Western Devil	Wild Passion
Oct12	Dusseldorf	GP von Dusseldorf-G3	1 1/16m 3yo+	Medici	Peppercorn	Larana
Oct12	Munich	Buchmacher Sprngr Sprint-G3	6 1/2f 3yo+	Konig Shuffle	Glad To Be Fast	Toylsome
Oct19	Cologne	Pr des Winterfavoriten-G3	1m 2yo	Glad Lion	Pepperstorm	Er
Oct27	Bremen	GP von Bremen-G3	1m 3yo+	Capital Secret	Blueberry Forest	Berber
Nov2	Frankfurt	Frankfurt-Trophy-G3	1 3/8m 3yo+	Royal Fantasy	Anani	El Dessert

ITALY

DATE	TRACK	RACE	CONDITIONS	1st	2nd	3rd
Apr27	Capannelle	Premio Parioli-G2	1m 3yo c	Le Vie dei Colori	Prince Kirk	Royal Dignitary
Apr27	Capannelle	Premio Regina Elena-G2	1m 3yo f	Golden Nepi	Vale Mantovani	Kiralik
May12	Capannelle	Pr Pres Della Repubblica-G1	1 1/4m 4yo+ c&f	Rakti	Tigertail	Altieri
May18	San Siro	Oaks d'Italia-G1	1 3/8m 3yo f	Meridiana	Lady Catherine	Vale Mantovani
May18	San Siro	Premio Emilio Turati-G2	1m 3yo+	Walzerkoenigin	Salselon	Gateman
May25	Capannelle	Derby Italiano-G1	1 1/2m 3yo c&f	Osorio	Private Charter	Lundy's Lane
May25	Capannelle	Premio Carlo d'Alessio-G2	1 3/4m 4yo+	Maktub	Desirao	Rainer
May25	Capannelle	Premio Tudini-G3	6f 3yo+	Pleasure Place	Dream Chief	Sopran Foldan
Jun22	San Siro	Gran Premio di Milano-G1	1 1/2m 3yo+ c&f	Leadership	Warrsan	Maktub
Jun22	San Siro	Premio Primi Passi-G3	6f 2yo	Clifden	Golden Pivotal	Flint Fly
Jun22	San Siro	Premio Mario Incisa-G3	1 1/2m 3yo+ f&m	Aynthia	Discreet Brief	Vale Mantovani
Jly13	Naples	GP Citta di Napoli-G3	5f 3yo+	Slap Shot	Sopran Foldan	Regina Saura
Oct4	San Siro	Premio Federico Tesio-G3	1-3/8m 4yo+	Maktub	Capitano Corelli	Serenus
Oct12	San Siro	Pr Vittorio di Capua-G1	1m 3yo+ c&f	Le Vie dei Colori	Blatant	Salselon
Oct12	San Siro	Premio Dormello-G3	1m 2yo f	Mamela	Saldentigerin	Kate Winslet
Oct19	San Siro	GP del Jockey Club-G1	1 1/2m 3yo+ c&f	Ekraar	Maktub	Warrsan
Oct19	San Siro	Gran Criterium-G1	1m 2yo c&f	Pearl Of Love	Spirit of Desert	Barbajuan
Oct19	San Siro	Premio Sergio Cumani-G3	1m 3yo+ f&m	Marbye	Monturani	Arlecchina
Oct19	San Siro	Premio Omenoni-G3	5f 3yo+	Pleasure Place	Slap Shot	Regina Saura
Oct26	Capannelle	Pr Guido Berardelli-G3	1 1/8m 2yo	Groom Tesse	Vol de Nuit	Noble Stella
Oct26	Capannelle	Premio Lydia Tesio-G2	1 1/4m 3yo+f&m	Whortleberry	Templerin	Aubonne
Nov2	San Siro	Premio Chiusura-G3	7f 2yo+	Salselon	Glad To Be Fast	Dream Chief
Nov16	Capannelle	Premio Roma-G1	1 1/4m 3yo+ c&f	Imperial Dancer	Altieri	Sunstrach
Nov16	Capannelle	Premio Ribot-G2	1m 3yo+	Duca d'Atri	Romaldo	Marbye
Nov16	Capannelle	Premio Umbria-G3	6f 2yo+	Glad To Be Fast	Fairy Beauty	Golden Pivotal

UNITED ARAB EMIRATES

DATE	TRACK	RACE	CONDITIONS	1st	2nd	3rd
Mar29	Nad Al Sheba	Dubai World Cup-G1	1 1/4m 4yo+	Moon Ballad	Harlan's Holiday	Nayef
Mar29	Nad Al Sheba	Dubai Duty Free-G1	a1 1/8m 4yo+	Ipi Tombe	Paolini	Royal Tryst
Mar29	Nad Al Sheba	Dubai Sheema Classic-G1	1 1/2m 4yo+	Sulamani	Ange Gabriel	Ekraar
Mar29	Nad Al Sheba	Dubai Golden Shaheen-G1	6f 3yo+	State City	Avanzado	Captain Squire
Mar29	Nad Al Sheba	UAE Derby-G2	1 1/8m 3yo	Victory Moon	Songlark	Inamorato
Mar29	Nad Al Sheba	Godolphin Mile-G2	1m 3yo+	Firebreak	Grey Memo	Estimraar

JAPAN

DATE	TRACK	RACE	CONDITIONS	1st	2nd	3rd
Nov29	Tokyo	Japan Cup Dirt-G1	1 1/8m 3yo+	Fleetstreet Dancer	Admire Don	Hagino High Grade
Nov30	Tokyo	Japan Cup-G1	1 3/8m 3yo+	Tap Dance City	That's The Plenty	Symboli Kris S

HONG KONG

DATE	TRACK	RACE	CONDITIONS	1st	2nd	3rd
Apr27	Sha Tin	Queen Eliz II Cup-G1	1-1/4m 3yo+	Eishin Preston	Elegant Fashion	Paolini
Dec14	Sha Tin	Hong Kong Cup-G1	1 1/4m 3yo+	Falbrav	Rakti	Elegant Fashion
Dec14	Sha Tin	Hong Kong Vase-G1	1 1/2m 3yo+	Vallee Enchantee	Polish Summer	Warrsan
Dec14	Sha Tin	Hong Kong Mile-G1	1m 3yo+	Lucky Owners	Bowman's Crossing	Lohengrin
Dec14	Sha Tin	Hong Kong Sprint-G1	5f 3yo+	Silent Witness	National Currency	Cape Of Good Hope

SINGAPORE

DATE	TRACK	RACE	CONDITIONS	1st	2nd	3rd
May10	Kranji	Singapore Air Intl Cup-G1	1-1/4m 3yo+	RACE NOT RUN		

European Leaders in 2003

LEADING JOCKEYS IN BRITAIN-2003

Jockey	Mts	1st	2nd	3rd	W%	Earnings
Fallon K	1055	221	162	144	.209	$8,503,128
Holland D	989	158	135	109	.160	5,211,082
Darley K	870	125	114	97	.144	3,029,366
Hughes R	750	122	89	80	.163	3,618,843
Culhane A	862	112	107	88	.130	1,498,469
O'Neill Dane	1019	110	109	111	.108	2,179,279
Drowne S	1022	108	105	99	.106	2,118,079
Ahern E	851	108	103	91	.127	2,308,876
Spencer J P	597	102	96	62	.171	3,050,671
Dettori L	495	102	89	61	.206	4,541,170
Other notables						
Sanders S	860	101	105	91	.117	1,704,073
Dwyer Martin	790	90	87	73	.114	3,188,003
Quinn T R	587	82	80	66	.140	2,127,644
Eddery Pat	620	77	63	51	.124	3,163,354
Hills R	373	75	58	32	.201	2,291,730
Robinson P	486	70	53	60	.144	2,534,589
Hills M	433	58	49	50	.134	1,542,323
Fortune J	381	46	55	46	.121	1,220,935
Jones, Lisa	519	43	32	46	.083	516,018
Murtagh J P	50	12	5	7	.240	1,898,795
Soumillon C	33	5	2	2	.152	470,561
Kinane M J	88	3	10	12	.034	963,742
Stevens G L	13	1	1	0	.077	106,929
Peslier O	12	0	0	0	.000	47,163
Thulliez T	6	0	2	0	.000	138,196

LEADING TRAINERS IN BRITAIN-2003

Trainer	Sts	1st	2nd	3rd	W%	Earnings
Stoute M R	482	115	73	69	.239	$6,044,403
Johnston M	758	139	105	72	.183	3,322,192
Channon M R	1136	143	124	152	.126	3,254,411
Hannon R	1031	122	118	101	.118	2,745,013
Hills B W	640	107	72	76	.167	2,372,491
Tregoning M P	260	56	47	22	.215	2,256,129
Gosden J H M	391	72	69	49	.184	2,205,881
O'Brien A P	58	6	10	7	.103	2,015,530
Easterby T D	829	58	80	66	.070	1,916,126
Cumani L M	268	57	29	33	.213	1,880,414
Other notables						
Balding A M	521	54	55	56	.104	1,855,628
Loder D R	225	70	50	19	.311	1,769,917
Dunlop J L	569	86	68	50	.151	1,764,380
Brittain C E	397	41	43	38	.103	1,613,890
Suroor S bin	98	23	17	8	.235	1,599,971
Charlton R	270	57	42	16	.211	1,552,690
Meehan B J	522	56	73	57	.107	1,534,435
Noseda J	191	37	32	14	.194	1,403,006
Butler G A	406	63	45	46	.155	1,381,385
Cole P F I	408	56	50	50	.137	1,331,928
Oxx J M	9	1	0	2	.111	1,000,703
Cecil H R A	156	25	36	22	.160	575,201
Weld D K	13	2	2	1	.154	475,449
Head-Maarek C	1	1	0	0	1.000	256,883
Mourier F	7	0	3	1	.000	32,941
Morse R L	1	0	0	0	.000	0

LEADING OWNERS IN BRITAIN-2003

Owner	Sts	1st	2nd	3rd	W%	Earning
Abdullah K	357	79	61	53	.221	$3,182,708
Al Maktoum H	524	103	79	49	.197	2,811,478
Cheveley Pk Stud	237	48	31	28	.203	2,277,754
Sheikh Mohammed	366	96	76	46	.262	2,227,000
Suhail Saeed	57	17	5	13	.298	1,920,412
Godolphin	98	23	17	8	.235	1,599,971
H H Aga Khan	51	15	4	7	.294	1,411,330
Magnier Mrs J	21	5	5	0	.238	1,378,186
Scuderia Rencati	20	5	1	1	.200	1,184,208
Smith J C	179	23	19	21	.128	1,050,517
Other notable						
Manana Saeed	120	15	12	9	.125	902,185
Exors of late						
Lord Weinstock	50	14	9	4	.280	830,073
Al Maktoum M	233	32	31	32	.137	811,075
Al Maktoum A	215	43	37	30	.202	727,587
Tabor M	66	9	8	11	.136	576,860
Tanaka G A	5	1	1	0	.200	507,162
Farish W S III	16	4	4	0	.250	487,789
Niarchos Family	38	10	10	4	.263	445,745
Sangster R E	45	8	5	3	.178	370,402
Moyglare Stud Farm	5	2	0	1	.400	357,949
Lucayan Stud	144	10	13	11	.069	335,357
The Queen	73	11	7	10	.151	238,525
Tabor M &						
Magnier Mrs J	23	0	3	3	.000	229,547
Strawbridge G	42	7	6	9	.167	145,879
The T'bred Corp	9	3	2	2	.333	42,271

LEADING JOCKEYS IN IRELAND-2003

Jockey	Mts	1st	2nd	3rd	W%	Earnings
Kinane M J	382	103	60	54	.270	$4,161,580
Smullen P J	494	84	62	55	.170	2,207,296
Murtagh J P	285	68	42	31	.239	2,773,596
Heffernan J A	498	44	49	47	.088	1,130,880
Berry F M	506	44	63	36	.087	1,019,801
McDonogh D P	394	41	36	42	.104	1,072,371
O'Shea T P	536	34	38	42	.063	857,693
McCullagh N G	508	33	45	47	.065	817,305
Cosgrave P	428	31	30	29	.072	587,870
Manning K J	439	31	41	56	.071	1,016,696
Other notables						
Gannon, Catherine	328	28	26	28	.085	563,787
Shanahan P	380	25	32	29	.066	651,951
O'Donoghue C	230	11	23	16	.048	393,368
Hughes R	25	5	3	2	.200	369,133
Fallon K	19	4	3	2	..211	424,897
Spencer J P	31	3	7	0	.097	325,714
Holland D	6	2	2	1	.333	400,682
Fortune J	6	2	0	1	.333	117,379
Culhane A	2	1	0	0	.500	42,770
Soumillon C	5	1	2	2	.200	366,023
Dettori L	5	1	1	0	.200	275,097
Darley K	8	1	1	2	.125	84,325
Ahern E	20	1	1	0	.050	24,949
Drowne S	3	0	1	1	.000	10,666

LEADING TRAINERS IN IRELAND-2003

Trainer	Sts	1st	2nd	3rd	W%	Earnings
O'Brien A P	235	73	37	35	.311	$4,022,590
Oxx J M	404	79	45	51	.196	2,942,320
Weld D K	562	90	73	61	.160	2,390,718
Prendergast K	345	43	47	38	.125	1,325,729
Bolger J S	403	31	34	53	.077	982,650
Halford M	427	29	41	28	.068	785191
Gerassick M J	223	26	29	24	.117	532,465
Lynam E	245	25	21	20	.102	462,709
Wachman D	170	24	15	12	.141	422,357
Rogers H	221	13	14	17	.059	400,197
Other notables						
Channon M R	12	3	3	2	250	306,356
Royer-Dupre A	1	0	1	0	.000	299,390
Stoute M R	6	1	1	2	.167	266,016
Stack T	102	10	15	9	.098	259,938
Collins C	153	10	14	13	.065	259,891
Hannon R	12	3	2	0	.250	222,507
Cumani L M	1	0	1	0	.000	222.110
Johnston M	4	1	2	1	.250	137,094
Loder D R	2	1	0	0	.500	105,815
Suroor S bin	3	0	1	1	.000	96,944
Easterby T D	4	1	1	1	.250	89,024
Bary P	1	0	1	0	.000	81,526
Meehan B	1	1	0	0	1.000	80,998

LEADING OWNERS IN IRELAND-2003

Owner	Sts	1st	2nd	3rd	W%	Earnings
Tabor M	81	29	21	9	.178	$1,833,812
H H Aga Khan	140	29	32	16	.207	1,824,919
Magnier Mrs J	136	34	15	23	.250	1,772,856
Sheikh Mohammed	102	21	15	11	.206	783,840
Moyglare Stud Farm	130	26	15	18	.200	631,485
Al Maktoum H	108	19	11	19	.176	615,095
Lady O'Reilly	195	20	21	26	.103	518,251
Dobson D H W	107	8	7	17	.075	279,829
Higgins J	55	11	7	6	.200	270,779
McStay G	30	6	1	4	.250	256,432
Other notables						
Smurfit M W J	47	5	10	6	.106	223,637
Scuderia Rencati	1	0	1	0	.000	222,110
Niarchos Family	4	3	1	0	.750	209,877
Abdullah K	6	2	0	1	.333	188,397
Weld Mrs C L	29	4	5	3	.138	185,060
Ballylinch Stud	50	8	4	5	.160	183,883
Bolger Mrs J S	139	6	11	8	.043	178,967
Exors of the late						
Lord Weinstock	7	1	2	1	.143	173,349
Magnier Mrs J &						
Tabor M	8	4	0	1	.500	122,648
Cheveley Pk Stud	4	1	2	1	.250	113,736
Al Maktoum M	13	2	2	4	154	105,900
Sangster R E	38	5	3	5	.132	102,002
Godolphin	3	0	1	1	.000	96,944
Firestone B R	42	2	7	6	.048	76,093
Farish W S III	2	0	1	1	.000	61,346
Ramsey K L	14	1	2	0	071	17,541

LEADING JOCKEYS IN FRANCE-2003

Jockey	Mts	1st	Plc	W%	Earnings
Soumillon C	1017	207	451	.204	$8,162,166
Mendizabal I	821	165	366	.201	2,941,003
Boeuf D	1113	149	499	.134	5,243,918
Peslier O	746	109	307	.146	3,873,394
Jarnet T	712	94	283	.132	2,968,921
Thulliez T	782	75	296	.096	2,936,680
Lemaire C-P	750	75	300	.100	2,863,179
Pasquier S	881	74	366	.084	2,806,767
Bonilla D	760	73	326	.096	2,302,441
Gillet T	640	72	243	.113	2,364,683
Other notables					
Blondel F	597	69	265	.116	1,259,973
Androuin M	488	59	219	.121	1,275,042
Blancpain M	529	45	178	.085	1,054,680
Maillot S	523	39	176	.075	1,094,038
Lerner Y	498	37	178	074	1,058,912
Marchelli R	575	26	172	.045	955,315
Placais O	430	24	150	.056	876,656
Thomas R	396	22	130	.056	738,599
Hughes R	20	6	7	.300	1,041,384
Dettori L	36	5	19	.139	768,464
Fallon K	21	2	11	.095	682,649
Drowne S	8	1	4	.125	155,760
Mosse G	8	1	2	.125	33,438
Fortune J	9	1	4	.111	109,879
Holland D	9	1	4	.111	59,087
Eddery Pat	10	1	3	.100	82,220
Kinane M J	16	0	9	.000	391,174

LEADING TRAINERS IN FRANCE-2003

Trainer	Sts	1st	Plc	W%	Earnings
Fabre A	399	98	194	.231	$4,119,383
Royer-Dupre A de	383	66	173	.172	3,525,229
Rouget J-C	625	167	306	.267	2,711,696
Pantall-H-A	817	123	397	.151	2,615,249
Lellouche E	408	47	192	.115	2,581,721
Head-Maarek C	428	77	191	.180	2,512,757
Collet Robert	1013	75	363	.074	2,423,934
Bary P	227	39	103	.172	1,736,082
Laffon-Parias C	367	58	175	.158	1,578,007
Smaga D	187	30	84	.190	1,176,692
Other notables					
Rohaut F	425	62	196	.146	1,157,657
Gibson R	223	34	103	.152	1,007,690
Libaud E	195	45	13	.231	969,136
Pease J	206	28	120	.136	937,98
Clement N	209	24	87	.115	936,584
Hammond J	190	30	80	.158	856,429
Sepulchre D	335	44	149	.131	697,271
O'Brien A P	31	0	14	.000	594,323
Head F	196	19	85	.097	575,767
Demercastel P	227	11	89	.048	532,222
Roualle J de	169	13	84	094	499,264
Doumen F	292	21	85	.072	470,030
Tregoning M P	3	0	1	.000	412,833
Suroor S bin	22	3	9	.136	391,529

Trainer	Sts	1st	Plc	W%	Earnings	Owner	Sts	1st	Plc	W%	Earnings
Dunlop J L	19	3	9	.158	314,061	Head A	59	12	33	.203	417,247
Gosden J H M	31	3	15	.097	287,113	Ecurie Chalhoub	78	8	37	.103	413,172
						Strawbridge G	110	13	63	.118	393,973
LEADING OWNERS IN FRANCE-2003						Godolphin	22	3	9	.136	391,529
Abdullah K	244	58	129	.238	$2,809,154	Ecurie Bader	108	10	49	093	358,898
H H Aga Khan	196	41	96	.209	2,808,945	Ecurie J-L Bouchard	33	9	15	273	352,211
Ecurie Wildenstein	278	50	145	.180	2,198,504	Ecurie Fabien Ouaki	94	10	49	.106	301,250
Sheikh Mohammed	243	46	132	.189	1,484,805	Head Mme A	72	11	26	.153	259,488
Marquise de Moratalla	403	65	168	.161	2,388,707	Tabor M &					
Wertherimer & Frere	296	48	134	.162	1,361,929	Magnier Mrs J	12	0	3	.000	248,337
SNC Lagardere Elevage	134	41	59	306	1,148,447	Magnier Mrs J	13	2	4	.154	188,865
Niarchos Family	91	16	42	.176	1,087,305	Rothschild Baron E de	56	10	29	.179	188,162
Al Maktoum M	137	23	60	.168	880,138	Tanaka G A	26	4	15	.154	183,115
Seroul J-C	319	59	138	.185	778,306	Cheveley Park Stud	12	5	1	417	175,677
Other notables						Magnier Mrs J &					
Al Maktoum H	60	13	34	.217	706,295	Tabor M	9	0	5	.000	166,461
Devin Mme H	62	15	26	.242	539,338	Tabor M	6	1	5	.167	159,034
Barbe Corine	218	13	84	.060	489,624	Lady O'Reilly	42	7	15	167	147,013
Strauss R C	90	9	42	.100	464,392	Moussac Mme Paul de	56	9	26	.161	137,250
Collet Robert	223	18	84	.081	424,730						

European Track Diagrams

ASCOT, ENGLAND

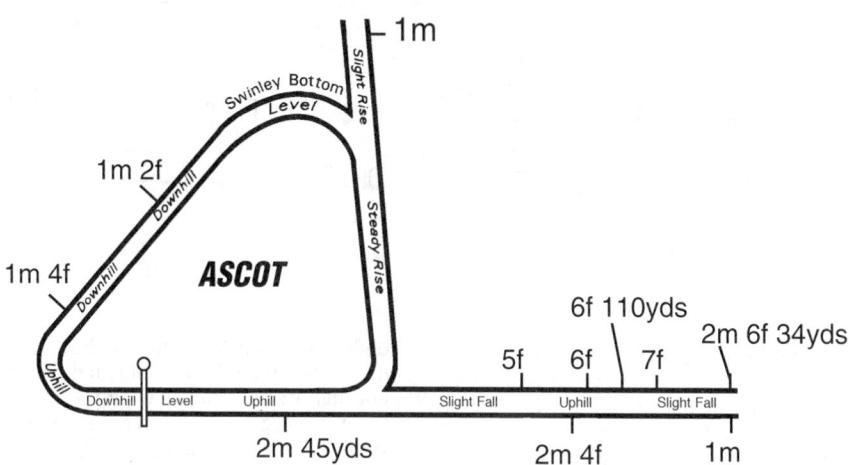

Course Discription Ascot is a right-handed, triangular course, 1 3/4 miles around with a stretch of 2-1/2 furlongs. There is also a one-mile straight course which joins the triangular course at the head of the stretch.

Races at 1 1/2 miles, e.g., the King George VI and Queen Elizabeth Diamond Stakes, begin with a downhill run of half a mile to Swinley Bottom, a right-hand bend at the lowest point in the track. From the mile pole it is almost entirely uphill past the 90-degree turn into the stretch. The final furlong is level. The straight course is mildly undulating throughout.

One-mile races are run from two different starting points. Those on the Old Mile, e.g., Queen Elizabeth II Stakes, St. James's Palace Stakes, Coronation Satkes, start from a chute near Swinley Bottom and are almost entirely uphill until the final furlong. Other mile races, e.g., the Queen Anne Stakes and big handicpas like the Royal Hunt Cup Handicap, are run on the straight course. All races shorter than a mile are run on the straight course.

Ascot places a premium on stamina and is ideal for long-striding gallopers. The Old Mile, over which the Queen Elizabeth II Stakes is run in late September, is hardly an ideal prep for the Breeders' Cup Mile as its uphill nature makes it a stayers mile as opposed to the near sprint that is the BC Mile. No winner of the QEII has ever won the BC Mile. The ground at Ascot can be very testing when soft or heavy, especially in the lower regions at Swinley Bottom.

History: Ascot was founded in 1711 by Queen Anne after she bought the property following a stag hunt. It has been in the hands of the Royal Family ever since. That first meeting, held on August 13, was the premier Royal Meeting. It would develop into the four-day Royal Ascot festival held annually during the third week of June. Outside of those four days of Royal Ascot, the track is referred to as simply Ascot. The racecourse conducts 22 days of racing annually, 13 on the flat and nine over jumps.

CHANTILLY, FRANCE

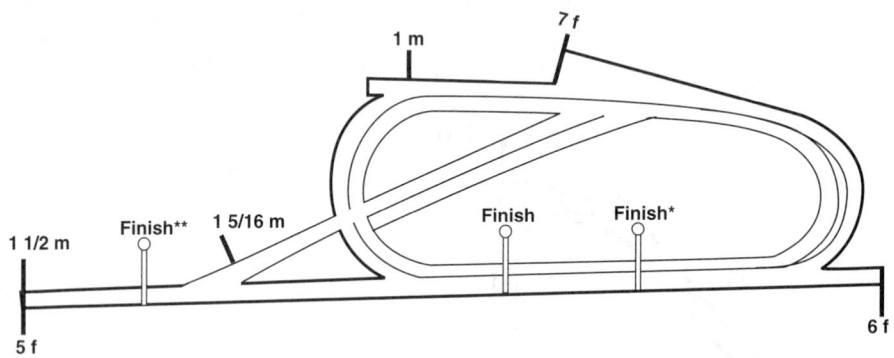

Course Description: Chantilly is a right-handed track with a number of configurations. The Piste du Jockey-Club, over which is run the Prix du Jockey-Club (French Derby), is 1 1/2 miles in length. After the first furlong, there is a mild left-handed bend onto the backstretch. On the turn for home there is a decline followed by a rise midway through the right-handed turn which lasts until the horses reach the stretch, three frulongs from the line.

The Prix de Diane (French Oaks) is run over the same course, but starts 1 1/2 furlongs later on the backstretch. Five-furlong races start in the same place as the French Derby and are run past the stands on the level straight course. Six-furlong races are also run on the straight course in front of the grandstand, but in the opposite direction.

There is also a right-handed inner course, or petite piste.

History: The first races at Chantilly were run under the auspices of the Duc d'Orleans. The first Prix du Jockey-Club was was organized by the Englishman Lord Seymour in 1836, with the premier Prix de Diane following in 1843. The current racecourse was founded by the Duc d'Aumale in 1886 on property owned by the Duc de Conde.

Racing at Chantilly is provided with perhaps the most beautiful backdrop of any course in the world. On what we in America would call the far turn there sits the Chateau de Conde, ancestral home of the Ducs de Conde. One such 18th century duke was convinced he would be reincarnated as a Thoroughbred. So that he would be able to live in suitable digs upon his return, he built the Grandes Ecuries (Grand Stables), the palatial barn on the Chantilly backstretch. Both the chateau and the ecuries are now museums, open to the public on racedays and dark days.

Chantilly holds much the same place in French racing that Newmarket does in England. The town and nearby Lamorlaye contain the yards of most of France's leading trainers. This year there were 2,558 horses-in-training at Chantilly, accounting for 70 percent of all the runners on the Parisian circuit: Chantilly, Longchamp, Saint-Cloud, Maisons-Laffitte and Deauville. This high concentration of top class Thoroughbred bloodstock is the reason why racing on the Parisian circuit possesses the highest concentration of class in the world. The gallops, or training tracks, cut through the local forest, and are perhaps the world's most beautiful, topped by the unparalled Les Aigles.

Until eight years ago, Chantilly held just six days of racing per year, all of them in June around the running of the Prix du Jockey-Club on the first Sunday in June and the Prix de Diane on the second Sunday of that month. There were 14 days of racing this season, which was curtailed after June for the refurbishment of the outdated fin-de-siecle grandstand. Next year Chantilly will return to its full complement of 26 days.

THE CURRAGH, IRELAND

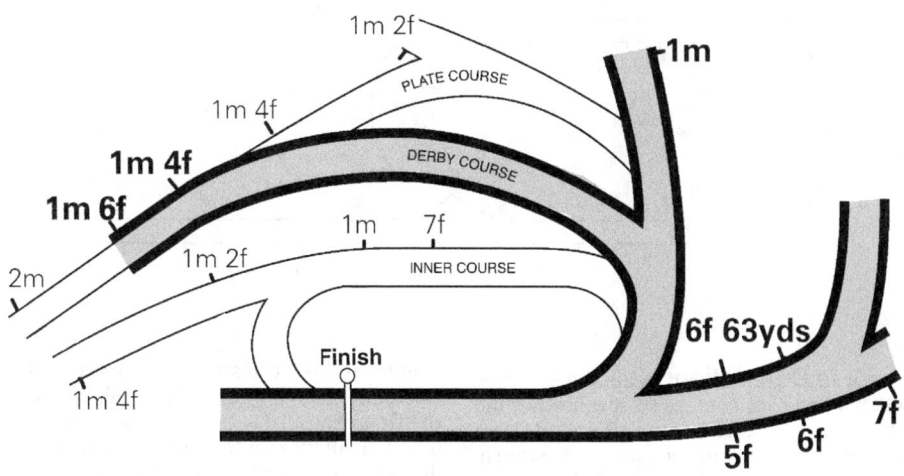

Course Description: The Curragh is an undulating, right-handed track. The round course is horseshoe-shaped and 1 3/4 miles in length, the last 1 1/2 miles of which is the Irish Derby course, the first two furlongs of which are straight, followed by a mild right-hand bend. Then comes another two-furlong straight followed by a sweeping right-hand turn into the uphill three-furlong stretch. There is also a one-mile track that is virtually straight but includes a mild righ-hand bend after 2-1/2 furlongs. It meets the round course at the head of the stretch, three furlongs from the line and is the track over which both the Irish 1000 and 2000 Guineas are run.

As Ireland receives considerably more rain than even England, the ground at the Curragh is more likely to be yielding, soft or heavy than good or firm. Stamina is at a premium here and it is essential that horses possess the ability to see out the trip, especially given the uphill finish. A preponderance of the country's best group races are run at the Curragh, so a horse that does well in good company here can be expected to acquit himself well in America, but only if he finds the same ground in the U.S. that he is used to running on in Ireland. It must also be noted that two trainers, Aidan O'Brien and Dermot Weld, have a majority of the best horses in Ireland, with Jim Bolger and Kevin Prendergast the only others who can compete with them on anything approaching a regular basis.

History: Curragh is the Gaelic word for course, or racecourse. Racing has been conducted there in one form or another since the 12th century. The first recorded match was run in 1679, with organized races becaming commonplace in the early 18th century. From time to time racing was abandoned due to the itroublesî. The Irish Turf Club was founded at the Curragh in 1790 and has ben in charge of the sport ever since.

By that time the Curragh had become the unquestioned center of Irish racing, in much the same way that Newmarket serves English racing. Many of Ireland's leading trainers have their stables nearby.

All five of Ireland's classic races are run at the Curragh. The first Irish Derby was run in 1866, the first Irish Oaks in 1895, and the first Irish St. Leger in 1915. The two Guineas both had their inaugural runnings in 1921.

The Curragh conducts 15 days of racing a year, all on the flat.

DEAUVILLE, FRANCE

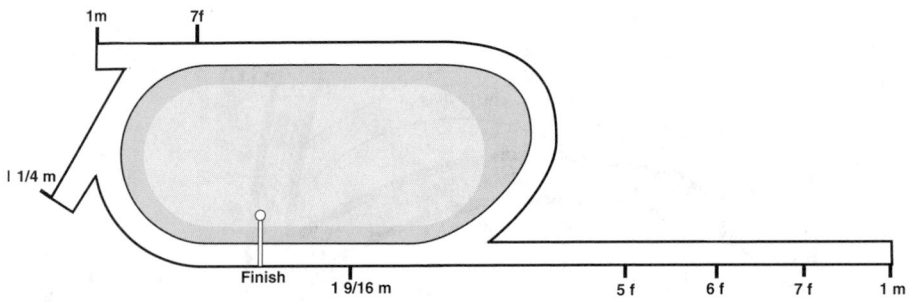

Course Description: Deauville is a level, right-handed oval course, 1 3/8 miles around with a three-furlong stretch. Races at 1 1/4 miles start from a chute beyond the first turn. The turns are very mild. Indeed, they are so mild that they make those on Belmont's main track seem tight by comparison. There is a one-mile straight course which is very mildly undulating until it joins the oval course three furlongs from the finish. There is also a less frequently used course inside the main track called the petite piste.

Deauville is a very wide as well as a very fair course that does not confer an advantage on any particular type of horse. It always yields a number of 3-year-olds who later run with success at Del Mar and at the Hollywood Turf Festival.

History: The racecourse at Deauville was founded by the Duc de Morny in 1864, the same year that Saratoga opened, but the two tracks share more than a founding date.

Deauville serves the same purpose vis-a-vis Parisian racing that Saratoga does for racing in New York. That is to say, the entire racing community in Paris, including the bulk of the training centers at Chantilly and Maisons-Laffitte, pull up stakes on or about the first of August and relocates north for the month to Deauville. Like Saratoga, Deauville is host to the first exposure of many of the best 2-year-olds. Late in the month, Agence Francaise conducts France's most important yearling sale in the town.

As a diversion, there is a second racecourse about two miles up the road from Deauville at Clairefontaine. On days in August when Deauville is dark, Calirefontaine is likely to be open. In addition to flat racing of a slightly lower standard, Clairefontaine, a 1 1/4-mile right-handed oval with a 3-furlong stretch, offers hurdle and steeplechase racing on a course inside its flat track, thus bringing similarities to Saratoga full circle.

The charms of Deauville are many. Before racing there are the attractions of one of the world's most fashionable beaches. Apres piste, for those who have any money left, there are the temptations of the famous beachfront casino.

Deauville conducts 24 days of racing annually, sixteen during its prestigious August meeting, five days in July, and three days in late October. During the August meeting, Clairefontaine runs eight mixed meetings (flat and jumps).

EPSOM, ENGLAND

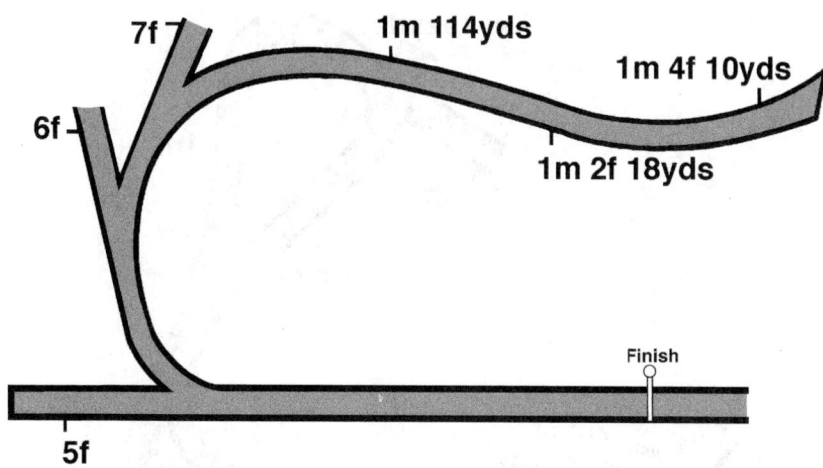

Course Description: Epsom is a left-handed, horseshoe-shaped track, its 1 1/2-mile circumference being the distance of the Derby and the Oaks The Derby course is stiffly uphill for the first six furlongs with a very mild right-hand bend 1-1/2 furlongs after the start. The course levels off at the top of the hill at halfway, or six furlongs from the line, after which there is a descent around an unbanked left-handed turn. That descent is at its steepest half a mile from home at Tattenham Corner, where the horses turn into the 3-1/2-furlong stretch which, while continuing downhill, is banked towards the inner rail. The final 110 yards is a slight rise to the finish.

Races at six and seven furlongs start from chutes at the top of the hill. There is also a five-furlong straight course that joins the Derby course at the head of the stretch. It is entirely and steeply downhill until the final sixteenth.

It takes an athletic type to successfully manouver Epsom's hills, unbanked turns and the infamous switchback, the term used to describe what happens when speeding horses being constrained to keep a straight line through Tattenham Corner suddenly meet the stretch with its ground cambered towards the inner rail. Horses with a high action or big, long striding gallopers frequently have trouble at Epsom.

History: It would be difficult to overestimate the importance of Epsom's 1 1/2-mile course in the history of racing. From the inception of the Derby in 1780 until the middle of the 20th century, it was the testing ground over which the best of the Thoroughbred breed was determined in both the Derby and the Oaks. During that period Derby winners routinely sired Derby winners and winners of other major races in England and the rest of the world. While the great race was challenged in mid-century by the Kentucky Derby and the French Derby, and while it suffered a decline in the 1990's, it still ranks as one of the world's most important Thoroughbred contests, especially from a breeder's point of view.

Epsom conducts eight days of racing a year, all on the flat.

GOODWOOD, ENGLAND

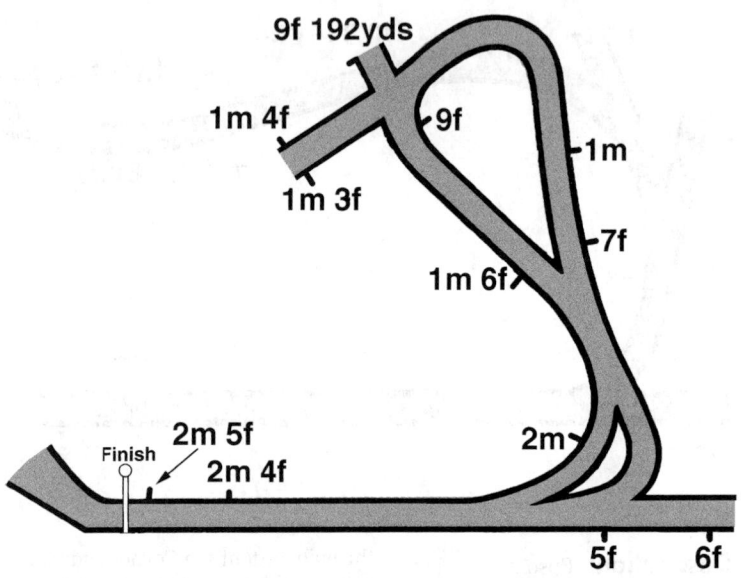

Course Description: No racecourse in the world differs more from America's standardized ovals than Goodwood. There is a six-furlong straight course which is slightly uphill at the start, then generally downhill until the final sixteenth, which is level. What separates Goodwood from all other tracks is its triangular right-handed loop built on the edge of a ridge. Races at 1 1/2 miles start from a chute with the horses running away from the finish line. They go uphill for 2-1/2 furlongs before turning right. The remainder of the course is undulating.

Races between two and 2 1/2 miles start in the stretch with the horses running away from the finish towards the loop. To complicate matters, there are two spurs used for entry into the stretch. Races at 1 1/8 miles and 1 1/4 miles, which go uphill in the opposite direction used in two-mile races, take the outer spur onto a 4-furlong stretch. All other races of seven furlongs or longer use the inner spur into a 3-furlong stretch.

Goodwood favors handy types who can manouver its undulations and rather sharp turns, although at races of nine furlongs or longer, there is no advantage to any given type. As a isharpî track where speed is at a premium, Goodwood should generally produce runners able to adapt to American tracks with their tight turns, this in spite of the vast differences in configuration between it an places like Hollywood or Keeneland. A singular example would be Tolomeo, who used the Sussex Stakes to vault to victory in the Arlington Million.

History: Goodwood was founded by the third Duke of Richmond in 1801. In 1839 it became the first racecourse to incorporate post position draws. The great undefeated (54-for-54) Hungarian mare Kincsem won the Goodwood Cup there in 1878, by which time the track's five-day late July, early August meeting, now dubbed Glorious Goodwood, had become part of the English social season along with Royal Ascot, the Henley Regatta, Wimbledon and the British Open.

Goodwood conducts thirteen days of racing a year, all on the flat.

LEOPARDSTOWN, IRELAND

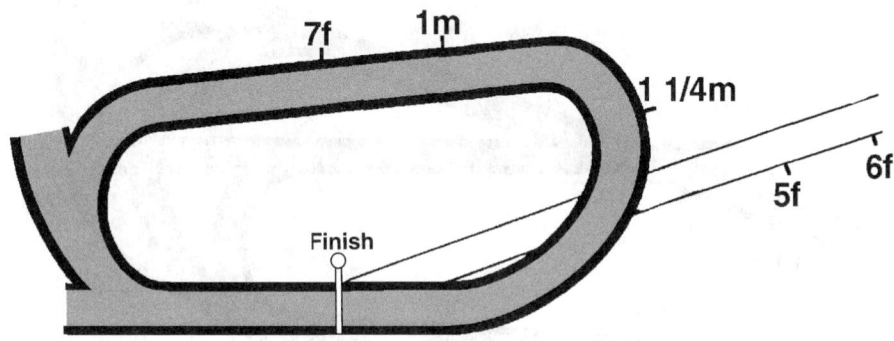

Course Description: Leopardstown is a left-handed oval, 1 3/4 miles in length and is virtually level except for an uphill finish. The turns are mild and the stretch is slightly longer than two furlongs. There is also a six-furlong straight course that dissects the oval course in much the same fashion as the old Widener Chute did at Belmont Park. Leopardstown is a very wide track that seems to suit gallopers a bit more than close-actioned types. The track is also used for jump racing from November through March.

History: Leopardstown is patterned after England's Sandown Park, which was the first enclosed track in Europe. It was opened on August 27, 1888, its name derived from its medieval title, Lepers Town, as the area had become known due to the lepers' hospital that had long been situated there. With the demise of Phoenix Park in central Dublin after the 1990 season, Leopardstown became the capital area's only racecourse.

At that time the 1 1/4-mile Irish Champion Stakes was moved to Leopardstown. The stakes record of 2:01.80 was set by Fantastic Light in his tremendous duel with Galileo in 2001.

While the quality of the flat racing is undoubtedly high- the same horses that run at the Curragh can always be seen at Leopardstown- the jump racing there takes precedence in a country that is first and foremost in love with the jumpers. The 4-day jump race meeting held at Leopardstown between Christmas and New Year's is one of the world's best.

Leopardstown conducts 30 days of racing a year, 15 on the flat and 15 over jumps.

LONGCHAMP, FRANCE

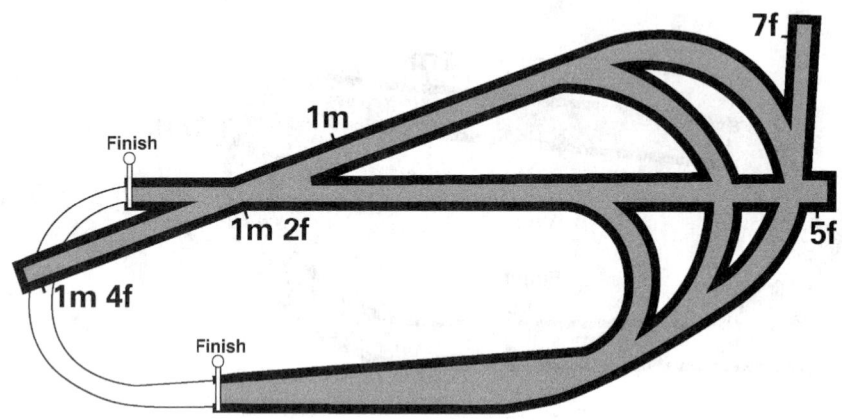

Course Description: Longchamp is a right-handed track with five separate courses, some of which share parts of others.

The grande piste is 1 5/8 miles, 55 yards around. It is on this course that the 1 1/2-mile Prix de l'Arc de Triomphe is run. That race starts from a short chute at the head of the backstretch. It is steadily uphill for the first six furlongs where the long right-handed, downhill turn begins. The course levels off after a mild bend into the one-furlong ïfalse straightî, so called because many an inexperienced rider has mistaken it for the actual straight, which follows after another mild right-hand bend and is 2-1/2 furlongs in length.

The 1 9/16-mile moyenne piste, or middle course, occupies the same ground as the grande piste until breaking off a furlong earlier for a downhill descent of its own to midway on the false straight.

The nouveau piste, or new course, starts behind the far turn. It is used primarily for seven-furlong races and is slightly downhill for the first two furlongs before joining the grande piste. Seven-furlong races at Longchamp finish at the deuxieme poteau, or second finish line, 100 meters past the premier poteau, or first finish line, which is used for a majority of races, including the Arc. Even with its downhill start, the nouveau piste produces unusually fast times for seven furlongs. The course is perhaps 20 meters short of its officially listed 1400 meters, a distance that is already seven yards short of seven furlongs.

The rarely used 1 5/16-mile, 55-yard petite piste lies inside the moyenne piste but shares the stretch with the two larger courses. Five-furlong races are run right to left on the ligne droite, or straight course.

Longchamp is an eminently fair course with what is, at 2-1/2 furlongs, a stretch that is short by most European standards. As in most French races, the early pace can be painfully slow, with the field bunching up on the approach to the final turn, after which horses fan out in their search for running room. The racing at Longchamp is high class. Horses that succeed there at any level- allowance, handicap, listed or group race- not infrequently find success at least one level higher in America.

History: The first races were run at Longchamp in 1857 with Emperor Napoleon III present as master of ceremonies. From the mid 1860's until the start of World War II, the Grand Prix de Paris routinely attracted up to 100,000 Parisians on the last Sunday in June. On April 4, 1943, the track was bombed by American reconaissance planes after they were fired upon by a jittery German artillery gunner who was manning one of the occupying forces' defense weapons deployed on the racecourse infield. Seven racegoers perished in the bombing.

The first Prix de l'Arc de Triomphe was run in 1920 in celebration of France's victory in World War I. Since 1955, the year of Ribot's first Arc triumph, it has reigned supreme as Europe's championship event.

Longchamp conducts 30 days of racing annually, all on the flat.

NEWMARKET, ENGLAND

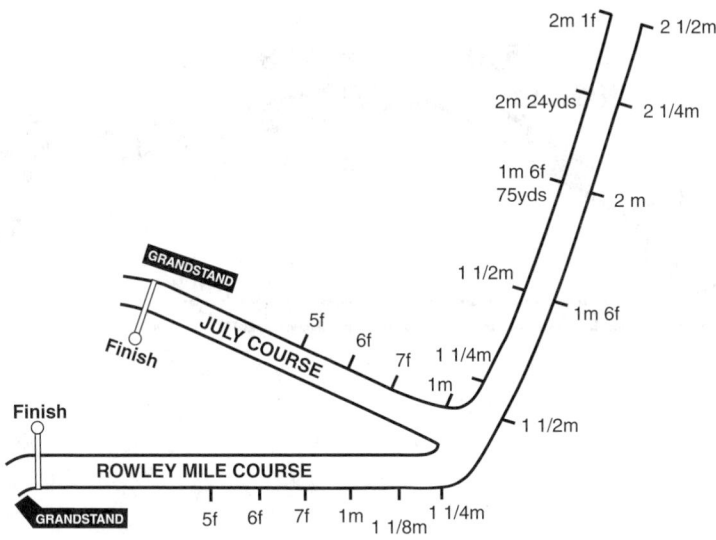

Course Description: Newmarket is, in reality, two courses in one. The Rowley Mile Course, used in April, May, September, October and November, shares a one-mile spur with the July Course, which is used in June, July and August.

That spur creates a 2 1/2-mile course used in the spring and fall. The spur is generally downhill until meeting a sharp rise about furlong before the right-handed turn into the Rowley Mile Course, which is a straight 1 1/4 miles, the last mile of which is used for both the 1000 and 2000 Guineas. It is undulating throughout with the penultimate furlong a pronounced downhill prior to The Dip, which is followed by an uphill run to the finish.

Including the spur it shares with the Rowley Mile Course, the July Course is 2 1/8 miles in length with a straight one-mile stretch known as the Bunbury Mile, which is similar to the proportions of the Rowley Mile.

The two tracks with their separate grandstands are separated by Devil's Dyke, a prehistoric manmade embankment. Both courses are very wide and ideal for long striding gallopers with the stamina necessary to see out every inch of the trip. Like the Guineas, the 1 1/4-mile Champion Stakes is run entirely on the straight, placing a premium on stamina and an ability to change leads when required without the signposts built into American ovals.

With so many trainers nearby, Newmarket attracts large fields and runs some of the most important maiden races in the world. A horse that wins a Newmarket maiden first time out usually possesses a touch of class which can translate into a certain success in America.

History: Racing on the broad, windswept plains of Newmarket has been conducted since the reign of James I in the early 17th century, but the first officially recorded race there was run on March 8, 1622. When Charles II was restored to the throne in 1660, Newmarket became a racing and social center, as all and sundry flocked to imitate the king, who, before and after racing, would dally in the town with his mistress Nell Gwyn, after whom a key April prep for the 1000 Guineas is named.

For nearly 300 years Newmarket has been the headquarters of British racing. In addition to its two tracks, it is home to at least 50 trainers' yards and numerous training tracks, or gallops. Tattersalls, the leading British sales company, is based in Newmarket, as is the British Racing Museum, the headqurters of the Jockey Club, and various other offical racing bodies.

Newmarket holds 33 days of racing per year, all on the flat. Eighteen of those are run on the Rowley Mile Course, eight in the spring and ten in the autumn. The other fifteen days are held on the July Course.

YORK, ENGLAND

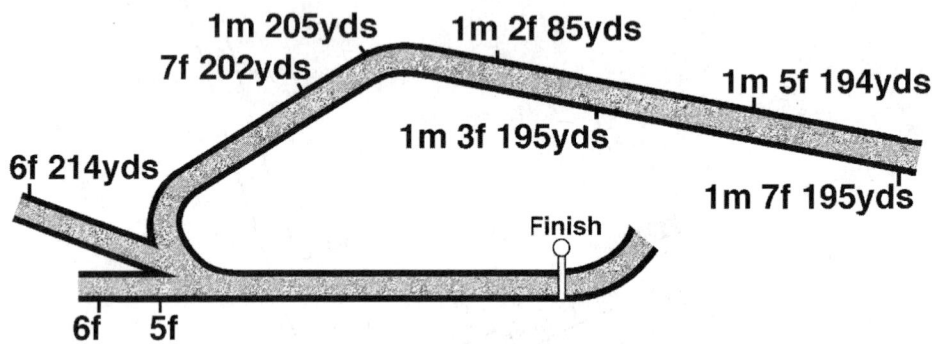

Course Description: York is a left-handed, perfectly level, horseshoe shaped course, two miles in length. Five and six-furlong races are run on a straight course that meets the left-handed course at the top of its 4-1/2-furlong stretch. Seven furlong races start from a chute, after which there is a mild left-handed bend at the head of the stretch.

Long striding gallopers will take to the long straights and mild turns of York, but in fact, the track really does not confer advantages to any particular type of horse. It is considered one of the fairest tracks in England, unlike a track like Chester, with its almost continual left-handed bends and realtively short two-furlong stretch.

But although York is left-handed and level, that does not translate into automatic success in America for winners there, especially as many of York winners have been given plenty of time to find room and crank up through the long stretch. By comparison, even the longest stretches in America are less than half the length of York's.

History: The earliest recorded race in York was run in 1530, although the course as we know it today did not see competition until 1709. The track is built on an ancient mudheap near the banks of the River Ouse known as the Knavesmire, so-called as it was so adept at slowing the progress of escaped criminals. As one of England's oldest racecourses, York now drains well and the track dries out rather quickly after rain.

York was the site of one of the most famous match races in history on May 13, 1851 when 1850 Derby and St. Leger winner The Flying Dutchman defeated the 1849 Derby and St. Leger winner Voltigeur. In the inaugural Benson & Hedges Gold Cup (now the Juddmonte International) in 1972, Braulio Baeza gave British jockeys a lesson in pace when he guided John Galbreath's Roberto to a pillar-to-post victory over the undefeated Brigadier Gerard. Roberto set a course record for 1 1/4 miles, 85 yards that stood for sixteen years.

The most important track in the north of England, York conducts fifteen days of racing a year, all on the flat. Its two best meetings are the three-day May Meeting, when key preps for the Derby and Oaks are run.

Top Money-Winning European Runners in 2003

Horse	Age	Sex	Starts	1st	2d	3d	Earn. US $	Horse	Age	Sex	Starts	1st	2d	3d	Earn. US $
Dalakhani (IRE)	3	C	6	5	1	0	$2,312,908	Ange Gabriel (FR)	5	H	4	3	0	0	362,726
Alamshar (IRE)	3	C	7	3	1	1	1,985,961	Milk It Mick (GB)	2	C	12	5	1	2	357,629
Kris Kin	3	C	5	2	0	2	1,633,448	Persian Punch (IRE)	10	G	9	4	1	0	351,637
Falbrav (IRE)	5	H	8	4	1	1	1,466,885	Pearl of Love (IRE)	2	C	6	4	1	1	348,831
High Chaparral (IRE)	4	C	3	2	0	1	953,924	Mr Dinos (IRE)	4	C	3	2	0	0	338,395
Russian Rhythm	3	F	5	3	1	0	879,972	Le Vie Dei Colori (GB)	3	C	5	4	1	0	334,874
Mamool (IRE)	4	C	5	3	0	1	855,026	Reel Buddy	5	H	7	1	1	1	329,312
Rakti (GB)	4	C	3	2	1	0	805,777	Whipper	2	C	7	3	0	1	326,468
Warrsan (IRE)	5	H	8	3	2	2	669,478	Karly Flight (FR)	5	M	7	3	4	0	324,872
Dai Jin (GB)	3	C	6	3	2	0	613,315	Westerner (GB)	4	C	8	3	3	0	322,010
The Great Gatsby (IRE)	3	C	3	0	2	0	600,352	Great Love (FR)	5	G	10	4	2	1	318,529
Mubtaker	6	H	4	3	1	0	580,768	Patavellian (IRE)	5	G	5	4	0	0	315,354
Osorio (GER)	3	C	3	2	1	0	575,792	Imperial Dancer (GB)	5	H	15	4	1	2	313,770
Yesterday (IRE)	3	F	6	1	3	0	573,191	Musical Chimes	3	F	5	2	0	1	313,103
Nebraska Tornado	3	F	5	4	0	0	558,240	Balmont	2	C	6	4	1	0	309,238
Nayef	5	H	5	1	1	1	556,761	Indian Creek (GB)	5	H	8	2	0	4	309,083
Monty's Pass (IRE)	10	G	5	1	0	0	543,873	Vinnie Roe (IRE)	5	H	4	2	0	0	303,496
Oasis Dream (GB)	3	C	4	2	1	1	524,836	Meridiana (GER)	3	F	2	2	0	0	303,478
American Post (GB)	2	C	4	3	1	0	508,482	Clodovil (IRE)	3	C	6	3	0	0	302,266
Brian Boru (GB)	3	C	5	1	1	1	499,844	Indian Haven (GB)	3	C	5	2	0	0	295,744
Vespone (IRE)	3	C	6	4	1	0	490,152	Peak To Creek (GB)	2	C	12	7	2	2	295,207
Six Perfections (FR)	3	F	5	2	3	0	476,076	Macadamia (IRE)	4	F	7	3	2	0	292,534
Choisir (AUS)	4	C	3	2	1	0	467,685	Batman Senora (FR)	7	G	5	2	2	0	292,503
Best Mate (IRE)	8	G	3	2	1	0	465,045	Sulamani (IRE)	4	C	2	0	1	0	290,242
High Accolade (GB)	3	C	9	4	3	0	460,441	Carnival Dancer (GB)	5	H	8	3	2	1	279,933
Magistretti	3	C	5	2	2	0	458,559	Nobody Told Me (IRE)	5	M	8	5	1	0	279,170
One Cool Cat	2	C	5	4	0	0	458,491	Native Upmanship (Ire)	10	G	5	2	1	1	276,871
Black Sam Bellamy (Ire)	4	C	9	2	1	1	457,090	Loumie (FR)	4	F	13	3	4	1	274,297
Casual Look	3	F	5	1	0	1	449,835	Vale Mantovani (GB)	3	F	8	4	1	2	273,988
Moscow Flyer (IRE)	9	G	6	5	0	0	440,013	Sacundai (IRE)	6	H	8	5	2	0	273,212
Line Marine (FR)	6	M	7	6	1	0	417,679	Martillo (GER)	3	C	5	3	0	1	273,188
Zafeen (FR)	3	C	5	1	2	0	417,141	Airwave (GB)	3	F	6	1	1	2	273,169
Islington (IRE)	4	F	4	1	0	2	403,942	Vintage Tipple (IRE)	3	F	4	1	1	0	272,890
Maktub (ITY)	4	C	10	6	1	1	401,744	Cape Fear (GB)	2	C	6	2	1	1	272,225
Super Celebre (FR)	3	C	3	1	2	0	393,471	Somnus (GB)	3	G	8	3	1	0	271,568
Rooster Booster (GB)	9	G	5	2	2	0	385,611	Dubai Destination	4	C	4	2	0	0	271,080
Refuse To Bend (IRE)	3	C	5	3	0	0	383,998								
Nickname (FR)	4	C	7	4	1	1	373,399								
Ransom O'War	3	C	6	2	2	1	365,041								

Earnings for races in England, France, Germany, Ireland and Italy only.

Top Money–Winning Runners in England in 2003

Horse	Age	Sex	Starts	1st	2d	3d	Earn. US $	Horse	Age	Sex	Starts	1st	2d	3d	Earn. US $
Kris Kin	3	C	3	2	0	1	$1,620,410	Islington (IRE)	4	F	3	1	0	1	305,099
Falbrav (IRE)	5	H	5	3	0	0	1,138,855	Refuse To Bend (IRE)	3	C	2	1	0	0	297,832
Alamshar (IRE)	3	C	3	1	0	1	983,803	Macadamia (IRE)	4	F	7	3	2	0	292,534
Russian Rhythm	3	F	5	3	1	0	879,972	Peak To Creek (GB)	2	C	11	7	2	1	284,106
Nayef	5	H	5	1	1	1	556,761	Airwave (GB)	3	F	5	1	1	2	273,169
Monty's Pass (IRE)	10	G	1	1	0	0	543,228	Cape Fear (GB)	2	C	6	2	1	1	272,225
The Great Gatsby (Ire)	3	C	1	0	1	0	537,555	Somnus (GB)	3	G	7	3	1	0	271,568
Oasis Dream (GB)	3	C	4	2	1	1	524,836	Sulamani (IRE)	4	C	1	0	1	0	267,399
Rakti (GB)	4	C	2	1	1	0	518,402	Nyramba (GB)	2	F	5	3	1	0	265,162
Warrsan (IRE)	5	H	5	3	1	0	496,038	Dubai Destination	4	C	3	2	0	0	259,812
Choisir (AUS)	4	C	3	2	1	0	467,685	American Post (GB)	2	C	1	1	0	0	256,883
High Accolade (GB)	3	C	9	4	3	0	460,441	Carry On Katie	2	F	3	3	0	0	251,226
Brian Boru (GB)	3	C	3	1	1	0	437,132	Baracouda (FR)	8	G	3	3	0	0	248,193
Zafeen (FR)	3	C	4	1	2	0	417,141	Far Lane	4	C	8	3	1	3	246,219
Casual Look	3	F	3	1	0	0	407,795	Bollin Eric (GB)	4	C	6	1	1	1	244,754
Rooster Booster (GB)	9	G	5	2	2	0	385,611	Acclamation (GB)	4	C	7	3	1	2	244,050
Milk It Mick (GB)	2	C	12	5	1	2	357,629	Unleash	4	C	10	4	1	2	243,490
Persian Punch (IRE)	10	G	8	4	1	0	351,637	Norse Dancer (IRE)	3	C	6	0	0	2	240,273
Best Mate (IRE)	8	G	2	1	1	0	343,862	Strong Flow (IRE)	6	G	7	6	1	0	231,440
Mr Dinos (IRE)	4	C	2	2	0	0	338,395	New Seeker (GB)	3	C	6	3	1	2	230,263
Moscow Flyer (IRE)	9	G	2	2	0	0	334,141	Native Upmanship (Ire)	10	G	2	1	1	0	224,506
Reel Buddy	5	H	6	1	1	1	329,312	Leporello (IRE)	3	C	7	6	0	1	223,924
Magistretti	3	C	4	2	1	0	325,891	Saint Alebe (GB)	4	G	6	2	1	0	218,110
Balmont	2	C	6	4	1	0	309,238	Truckers Tavern (IRE)	8	G	6	1	2	1	215,855
Indian Creek (GB)	5	H	8	2	0	4	309,083	The Tatling (IRE)	6	G	14	2	4	2	215,547

Top Money–Winning Runners in France in 2003

Horse	Age	Sex	Starts	1st	2d	3d	Earn. US $	Horse	Age	Sex	Starts	1st	2d	3d	Earn. US $
Dalakhani (IRE)	3	C	5	5	0	0	$2,025,901	Bago (FR)	2	C	4	4	0	0	228,321
Nebraska Tornado	3	F	5	4	0	0	558,240	Maiden Tower (GB)	3	F	4	3	1	0	216,824
Vespone (IRE)	3	C	5	4	1	0	490,152	High Chaparral (IRE)	4	C	1	0	0	1	211,610
Mubtaker	6	H	1	0	1	0	423,221	Maia Eria (FR)	3	F	7	3	0	1	209,341
Line Marine (FR)	6	M	7	6	1	0	417,679	Doyen (IRE)	3	C	5	3	1	0	205,549
Super Celebre (FR)	3	C	3	1	2	0	393,471	Prince des Ifs (FR)	4	G	8	7	0	0	197,858
Nickname (FR)	4	C	7	4	1	1	373,399	Much Faster (IRE)	2	F	5	4	1	0	197,289
Ange Gabriel (FR)	5	H	4	3	0	0	362,726	Katiki (FR)	6	G	9	1	0	2	191,655
Karly Flight (FR)	5	M	7	3	4	0	324,872	Psychee Du Berlais (FR)	3	F	13	3	2	0	180,303
Westerner (GB)	4	C	8	3	3	0	322,010	Ice Mood (FR)	4	G	6	3	0	1	179,218
Great Love (FR)	5	G	10	4	2	1	318,529	Urga (FR)	12	G	8	0	0	2	175,493
Musical Chimes	3	F	5	2	0	1	313,103	Bright Sky (IRE)	4	F	4	1	1	2	175,032
Whipper	2	C	6	3	0	1	311,349	Katoune (FR)	4	F	11	1	1	5	173,036
Clodovil (IRE)	3	C	5	3	0	0	290,893	Mezzo Soprano	3	F	2	1	0	1	172,440
Batman Senora (FR)	7	G	4	1	2	0	286,655	Look Honey (IRE)	3	C	8	3	1	1	171,401
Loumie (FR)	4	F	13	3	4	1	274,297	Ty Benjam (FR)	7	G	6	2	1	0	169,036
Six Perfections (FR)	3	F	3	2	1	0	271,777	Policy Maker (IRE)	3	C	6	4	1	0	168,196
Ladykish (FR)	4	F	6	3	2	0	259,227	Touch of Land (FR)	3	C	7	2	1	2	167,547
Rougenoir (FR)	10	G	10	1	1	4	255,924	Porlezza (FR)	4	F	5	2	0	0	167,241
Kotkijet (FR)	8	G	5	4	0	0	252,867	Voix Du Nord (FR)	2	C	6	2	3	0	166,950
American Post (GB)	2	C	3	2	1	0	251,599	Zee Zee Top (GB)	4	F	1	1	0	0	165,292
Coroner (IRE)	3	C	5	3	1	1	250,057	Nobody Told Me (IRE)	5	M	2	1	0	0	161,711
Northerntown	7	G	8	5	1	0	245,204	Martaline (GB)	4	C	5	2	2	1	160,355
Etoile Montante	3	F	6	3	1	1	240,719	My Risk (FR)	4	C	7	5	1	0	160,291
Denebola	2	F	4	2	0	1	237,155	Kapgarde (FR)	4	C	7	2	2	1	160,007

Top Money–Winning Runners in Germany in 2003

Horse	Age	Sex	Starts	1st	2d	3d	Earn. US $	Horse	Age	Sex	Starts	1st	2d	3d	Earn. US $
Mamool (IRE)	4	C	2	2	0	0	$695,332	Picotee (GER)	6	G	7	2	1	2	64,385
Dai Jin (GB)	3	C	5	3	2	0	613,315	Olaso (GER)	4	C	4	1	0	3	64,072
Ransom O'War	3	C	6	2	2	1	365,041	Fiepes Shuffle (GER)	3	C	6	2	0	1	62,739
Next Gina (GER)	3	F	6	2	0	1	263,129	Capital Secret	6	G	9	3	1	2	61,960
Martillo (GER)	3	C	3	3	0	0	223,146	Flambo (GER)	3	C	3	1	0	0	61,818
Epalo (GER)	4	C	5	2	3	0	185,071	Nureus (GER)	3	C	6	3	0	0	61,197
Pepperstorm (GER)	2	C	4	3	1	0	171,688	Medici (GER)	3	C	8	2	2	0	59,117
Aolus (GER)	4	C	5	3	1	0	164,271	Mokabra (IRE)	2	C	1	1	0	0	58,862
Storm Trooper (GER)	3	C	6	2	1	1	156,683	Albanova (GB)	4	F	1	0	1	0	58,538
Black Sam Bellamy (Ire)	4	C	2	0	1	0	155,484	Mandela (GER)	3	F	3	2	0	1	58,291
Diacada (GER)	3	F	2	1	0	1	140,802	Fruhlingssturm (GB)	3	C	5	2	0	1	57,142
Royal Fantasy (GER)	3	F	8	4	1	0	140,546	Nocino (IRE)	2	C	3	1	2	0	56,233
White Rose (GER)	3	F	4	0	2	0	133,283	Zarewitsch (IRE)	4	C	3	1	0	1	55,771
Sabiango (GER)	5	H	3	1	0	1	128,563	King of Boxmeer (Ger)	4	G	5	2	0	0	55,764
Glad Lion (GER)	2	C	2	2	0	0	103,291	Longridge (GER)	5	G	7	2	2	1	55,277
Next Desert (IRE)	4	C	3	0	1	1	86,238	Fair Dream (GER)	2	F	3	1	0	0	54,950
Night Lagoon (GER)	2	F	3	2	1	0	84,892	Passing Glance (GB)	4	C	1	1	0	0	54,085
Dano-Mast (GB)	7	H	1	0	0	1	83,295	Australian Dreams (GB)	4	F	9	5	0	0	54,072
Peppercorn (GER)	6	G	6	3	2	1	82,089	Bear King (GER)	6	H	7	1	2	2	53,615
Royal Price (GER)	3	C	5	0	3	1	73,694	Fleur (GER)	3	F	6	3	0	0	53,263
Wild Passion (GER)	3	G	7	2	2	2	73,215	Winning Dash (GER)	3	C	7	1	2	1	50,580
Stormont (IRE)	3	C	1	1	0	0	70,467	Koonunga Hill (GER)	2	F	2	1	1	0	50,222
Capricho (IRE)	6	G	1	1	0	0	68,934	Konig Shuffle (GER)	7	H	9	1	3	1	49,179
Soave (GER)	4	C	7	1	2	0	68,541	Russian Samba (IRE)	4	F	10	6	0	2	49,000
Avenir Rubra (GER)	3	F	9	3	1	0	65,074	Soldier Hollow (GB)	3	C	2	1	0	0	48,299

Top Money–Winning Runners in Ireland in 2003

Horse	Age	Sex	Starts	1st	2d	3d	Earn. US $	Horse	Age	Sex	Starts	1st	2d	3d	Earn. US $
Alamshar (IRE)	3	C	4	2	1	0	$1,002,158	L'Ancresse (IRE)	3	F	4	1	2	0	155,271
High Chaparral (IRE)	4	C	2	2	0	0	742,314	Roosevelt (IRE)	3	C	3	1	0	1	151,094
One Cool Cat	2	C	4	3	0	0	446,317	Cloone River (IRE)	7	G	7	3	3	0	142,846
Yesterday (IRE)	3	F	2	1	0	0	290,793	Mingun	3	C	3	3	0	0	139,559
Dalakhani (IRE)	3	C	1	0	1	0	287,007	Arctic Copper (IRE)	9	G	10	1	5	1	138,485
Vintage Tipple (IRE)	3	F	4	1	1	0	272,890	Sacundai (IRE)	6	H	7	4	2	0	137,405
Indian Haven (GB)	3	C	1	1	0	0	266,412	Kadoun (IRE)	6	G	11	5	2	0	134,327
Livadiya (IRE)	7	M	14	5	1	3	259,608	Perfect Touch	4	F	8	1	3	1	132,970
Beef Or Salmon (IRE)	7	G	6	4	0	2	255,189	Native Performance (Ire)	8	G	12	2	3	1	132,737
Necklace (GB)	2	F	3	2	1	0	241,018	Nearly A Moose (IRE)	7	G	10	2	2	1	131,787
Vinnie Roe (IRE)	5	H	2	2	0	0	240,446	Timbera (IRE)	9	G	4	1	1	0	124,307
Black Sam Bellamy (Ire)	4	C	2	2	0	0	225,738	Best Mate (IRE)	8	G	1	1	0	0	121,183
Falbrav (IRE)	5	H	1	0	1	0	209,903	World Wide Web (IRE)	7	G	1	1	0	0	120,810
Newmill (IRE)	5	G	7	4	2	0	182,916	Alexander Goldrun (Ire)	2	F	8	3	2	1	119,152
Latino Magic (IRE)	3	C	9	4	3	0	177,827	Central House (GB)	6	G	7	2	3	1	118,766
France (GB)	3	C	5	1	1	1	174,334	Pearl of Love (IRE)	2	C	2	1	0	1	118,137
Back In Front (IRE)	6	G	7	4	2	0	171,746	Nysaean (IRE)	4	C	2	2	0	0	118,032
Sabadilla	9	H	9	4	0	1	167,539	Nobody Told Me (IRE)	5	M	6	4	1	0	117,459
Avorado (IRE)	5	G	9	3	2	1	167,419	Zimbabwe (GB)	3	G	6	3	1	0	116,459
Holy Orders (IRE)	6	G	8	3	1	1	164,961	Azamour (IRE)	2	C	2	2	0	0	114,409
Glenelly Gale (IRE)	9	G	9	2	2	2	161,506	Sea Dart	3	C	3	2	0	0	112,593
Majestic Desert (GB)	2	F	1	1	0	0	160,098	Sutter's Fort (IRE)	2	C	1	1	0	0	112,474
Deportivo (GB)	3	C	2	2	0	0	160,017	Blue Corrig (IRE)	3	G	14	3	1	1	112,007
Wathab (IRE)	2	C	10	2	4	1	159,486	Desert Fantasy (IRE)	4	C	4	3	0	0	111,699
King Carew (IRE)	5	H	24	6	3	1	157,445	Antonius Pius	2	C	2	2	0	0	111,431

Top Money–Winning Runners in Italy in 2003

Horse	Age	Sex	Starts	1st	2d	3d	Earn. US $
Osorio (GER)	3	C	3	2	1	0	$575,792
Maktub (ITY)	4	C	10	6	1	1	401,744
Le Vie Dei Colori (GB)	3	C	5	4	1	0	334,874
Meridiana (GER)	3	F	1	1	0	0	289,350
Rakti (GB)	4	C	1	1	0	0	287,375
Vale Mantovani (GB)	3	F	8	4	1	2	273,988
Private Charter (GB)	3	C	1	0	1	0	234,234
Leadership (GB)	4	C	1	1	0	0	232,140
Marbye (IRE)	3	F	9	4	3	1	216,711
Golden Nepi (IRE)	3	F	6	2	2	1	193,048
Spirit of Desert (IRE)	2	C	5	4	1	0	188,897
Pleasure Place (IRE)	3	F	6	6	0	0	186,676
Golden Pivotal (GB)	2	C	10	5	3	1	184,142
Sopran Foldan (IRE)	5	G	14	6	3	1	181,904
Ekraar	6	H	1	1	0	0	175,125
Pearl of Love (IRE)	2	C	1	1	0	0	175,125
Prince Kirk (FR)	3	C	6	2	2	1	169,109
Golden Devious (IRE)	3	C	7	4	2	0	155,785
Duca d'Atri (IRE)	4	C	8	5	2	0	151,125
Salselon (GB)	4	C	6	1	2	2	147,641
Miss Vegas (IRE)	2	F	6	5	0	1	147,602
Rosa Delle Alpi	4	F	16	4	3	3	146,935
Warrsan (IRE)	5	H	2	0	1	1	144,172
Giovane Imperatore (GB)	5	H	8	5	1	0	140,555
Altieri (GB)	5	H	4	1	1	1	139,678
Frottola (GB)	5	M	7	4	1	1	139,606
Sciur Renato (IRE)	2	C	10	3	3	2	137,611
Rumba Loca (IRE)	2	F	8	4	0	2	131,853
Darrel (GB)	5	G	12	6	3	0	130,206
Rekindled Applause (GB)	2	F	10	3	4	1	129,333
Lundy's Lane (IRE)	3	C	1	0	0	1	128,829
Lindholm (GER)	4	C	7	3	2	1	128,589
Lady Catherine (GB)	3	F	1	0	1	0	127,314
Sunstrach (IRE)	5	H	4	1	1	1	126,831
Tigertail (FR)	4	F	1	0	1	0	126,445
Caluki (GB)	6	H	10	4	3	1	125,112
Montesino (ITY)	5	G	17	4	8	1	124,832
Nonno Carlo (IRE)	3	C	7	3	1	0	124,321
Imperial Dancer (GB)	5	H	1	1	0	0	117,820
Bening (FR)	3	C	8	3	1	1	115,186
Nice Look (IRE)	3	C	9	4	1	1	113,652
Tenero Giacomo (IRE)	7	G	21	5	4	4	112,446
Scabiun (IRE)	5	H	11	5	4	1	111,202
Tea Garden (IRE)	3	C	15	4	3	1	110,357
Flint Fly (IRE)	2	C	10	2	4	1	107,792
Regina Saura (GB)	5	M	10	2	2	3	106,018
Klaus Boy (GB)	4	G	14	5	2	2	105,954
Romaldo (GER)	3	C	8	2	3	2	103,281
Fielding (IRE)	3	C	10	2	4	1	102,673

Italian racing complete through 11/30/03

Top Money–Winning Runners in Japan in 2003

Horse	Age	Sex	Starts	1st	2d	3d	Earn. US $
Neo Universe (JPN)	3	C	9	5	0	2	$4,560,373
Tap Dance City	6	H	6	4	0	1	3,939,138
Still in Love (JPN)	3	F	7	4	2	0	3,651,145
Symboli Kris S	4	C	4	2	0	1	3,627,007
That's the Plenty (JPN)	3	C	7	1	1	1	2,744,906
Hishi Miracle (JPN)	4	C	5	2	1	0	2,517,311
Zenno Rob Roy (JPN)	3	C	8	4	1	2	2,312,462
Star King Man	4	C	14	4	2	3	2,309,742
Admire Don (JPN)	4	C	5	3	1	0	2,297,108
Admire Groove (JPN)	3	F	6	3	1	1	2,131,684
Durandal (JPN)	4	C	5	3	0	1	2,080,307
Win Marvelous (JPN)	6	H	8	6	1	1	1,952,572
Tsurumaru Boy (JPN)	5	H	7	0	3	1	1,718,125
Believe (JPN)	5	M	7	2	2	0	1,682,576
Ingrandire (JPN)	4	C	9	4	0	0	1,628,544
Big Wolf (JPN)	3	C	12	6	1	0	1,626,016
Lincoln (JPN)	3	C	6	2	2	0	1,596,068
Biwa Shinseiki (JPN)	5	H	11	2	4	2	1,516,375
Gallant Arrow (JPN)	3	C	9	3	2	1	1,508,671
South Vigorous	7	H	4	3	1	0	1,468,155
Lohengrin (JPN)	4	C	5	2	1	1	1,409,027
Camphor Best (JPN)	4	C	11	3	3	2	1,389,748
Air Eminem (IRE)	5	H	6	2	1	2	1,354,398
Sterling Rose (JPN)	6	H	7	3	2	1	1,346,481
Sakura President (JPN)	3	C	7	1	3	0	1,343,522
Kanetsu Fleuve (JPN)	6	H	7	3	0	0	1,332,959
Utopia (JPN)	3	C	7	2	2	0	1,316,732
Meisho Domenica (JPN)	6	G	17	5	2	2	1,285,114
Precise Machine (JPN)	4	C	12	6	1	1	1,277,098
Balance of Game (JPN)	4	C	6	1	2	0	1,247,097
Cosmo Sunbeam (JPN)	2	C	7	4	2	0	1,246,892
Tagano My Bach (JPN)	4	C	6	4	1	0	1,241,879
D S Thunder (JPN)	4	C	12	3	3	2	1,241,112
She is Tosho (JPN)	3	F	8	1	2	2	1,231,445
Win Kluger (JPN)	3	C	8	3	0	0	1,229,270
Name Value (JPN)	5	M	8	2	0	2	1,228,066
Fleetstreet Dancer	5	G	1	1	0	0	1,217,026
Tenshino Kiseki (JPN)	5	M	8	3	1	0	1,179,241
Gold Allure (JPN)	4	C	3	2	0	0	1,176,440
Strong Blood (JPN)	4	C	9	4	2	0	1,175,547
Lady Pastel (JPN)	5	M	5	2	2	0	1,167,570
Daitaku Bertram (JPN)	5	H	5	2	0	2	1,113,373
Big Taste (JPN)	5	H	5	3	1	1	1,082,895
Yamakatsu Lily (JPN)	3	F	7	1	1	1	1,078,362
Fine Motion (IRE)	4	F	4	1	2	0	1,070,930
Silent Deal (JPN)	3	C	8	2	1	0	1,063,114
Vita Rosa (JPN)	3	C	11	4	0	2	1,052,821
Meisho Bowler (JPN)	2	C	5	4	1	0	1,050,914
Meiner Select (JPN)	4	C	4	3	1	0	1,048,554
Agnes Digital	6	H	7	1	1	0	1,026,354

Top Money–Winning Runners in Puerto Rico in 2003

Horse	Age	Sex	Starts	1st	2d	3d	Earn. US $	Horse	Age	Sex	Starts	1st	2d	3d	Earn. US $
D' Wildcat Speed	3	F	12	12	0	0	$290,815	Grandson Gabe	2	C	11	4	3	1	77,244
Despreciado	3	C	10	6	1	1	270,418	Kud'zu Magic	4	F	14	4	7	1	73,718
Monoestrellado	3	C	11	3	4	2	202,051	Mi Abogada	3	F	14	6	4	2	73,657
Cafajeste (PAN)	3	C	1	1	0	0	180,000	Malcadi	2	F	6	4	1	0	70,060
Coordinadora	2	F	8	5	2	1	158,005	Forbidden King	3	C	12	6	2	2	68,777
Imbuias Son	3	C	17	5	5	3	139,735	Paso Palma	6	M	10	3	1	3	68,047
Uno Numero	3	C	15	3	4	5	139,089	Padre Valeriano	4	C	15	9	1	2	63,270
Mi Pradera	5	M	8	4	1	1	138,091	Divac	2	C	11	4	3	2	62,995
Andiroba	3	F	9	6	1	0	137,186	Tropical Concerto	3	C	10	5	1	1	62,095
Mister Fanucci	2	C	8	7	1	0	136,105	Little Franky Boy	2	C	10	2	2	2	61,068
Dr Arbatach	4	C	13	9	1	1	127,296	Chilenito	2	C	12	5	2	1	61,050
Starlet in Motion	6	M	16	5	6	3	126,248	Hunters Walk	2	F	9	4	3	0	60,872
Panimetro	4	C	10	5	4	1	112,550	Fascinatin Lady	4	F	16	4	4	3	60,824
Don Piero	6	H	10	6	3	0	101,407	Palmera	3	F	5	1	2	0	60,240
Omar Alejandro	2	C	7	6	1	0	101,060	My Own Business (Ven)	6	H	1	1	0	0	60,000
Madero de Marfin	3	C	13	4	3	4	99,669	Lady Wanda Iris	3	F	18	2	3	3	56,545
Mi Jesuse	4	C	13	6	4	1	99,275	Friskys Show	6	H	28	6	8	9	56,250
Dona Ingrid	4	F	17	3	6	4	97,168	Sr. Eddie B.	5	H	21	8	5	4	56,241
Miss Caimito	2	F	10	4	3	2	93,740	Voice of Destiny	7	H	13	3	2	3	54,859
Alanita	3	F	9	5	1	2	93,620	Kaoma	3	F	13	7	3	1	54,166
Forbidden Queen	2	F	4	2	1	1	91,144	My Favorite Dream	4	C	8	2	3	2	53,409
Voluntariosa	3	F	14	3	3	2	88,741	Wild for Speed	3	C	15	4	3	3	53,294
Estrellero	5	H	10	4	1	2	88,245	Bancada	3	F	14	1	3	3	53,085
Westmoreland Girl	3	F	18	7	6	4	85,032	Mi Amigo Cesar	3	C	22	7	7	5	53,057
Blancamaya	3	F	3	2	0	1	79,880	Bullet Breeze	3	C	10	3	3	1	52,840

Top Money–Winning Runners in United Arab Emirates in 2003

Horse	Age	Sex	Starts	1st	2d	3d	Earn. US $	Horse	Age	Sex	Starts	1st	2d	3d	Earn. US $
Moon Ballad (IRE)	4	C	2	2	0	0	$3,657,183	Eventuail (ARG)	5	G	1	0	0	0	100,000
Victory Moon (SAF)	4	C	3	2	1	0	1,390,000	Outta Here	3	C	1	0	0	0	100,000
Ipi Tombe (ZIM)	5	M	3	3	0	0	1,314,345	Feet So Fast (GB)	4	G	3	2	0	1	94,624
State City	4	C	4	2	0	0	1,259,088	Tangeriano (ARG)	4	C	5	2	1	0	93,094
Sulamani (IRE)	4	C	1	1	0	0	1,200,000	Dubai Honor (GB)	4	C	8	4	1	1	91,244
Harlan's Holiday	4	C	1	0	1	0	1,200,000	Bourbonnais (IRE)	3	C	2	0	0	1	85,000
Firebreak (GB)	4	C	2	1	1	0	619,061	Grand Ekinoks (TUR)	5	H	2	0	1	0	79,054
Nayef	5	H	1	0	0	1	600,000	Baaridd (GB)	5	H	7	3	1	0	71,710
Avanzado (ARG)	6	H	1	0	1	0	400,000	Nowrass (GB)	7	G	4	1	0	1	69,405
Paolini (GER)	6	H	1	0	1	0	400,000	Dancal (IRE)	5	M	5	1	1	0	68,211
Ange Gabriel (FR)	5	H	1	0	1	0	400,000	Seattle Fitz (ARG)	4	C	4	1	0	0	65,881
Songlark (GB)	3	C	1	0	1	0	400,000	Ashraaf	3	F	2	0	1	1	65,000
Grandera (IRE)	5	H	2	1	0	0	357,162	Al Ash Hab	4	C	8	5	0	1	64,616
Inamorato	3	C	2	1	0	1	320,000	Masterful	5	H	2	0	0	0	61,906
Danuta	3	F	2	2	0	0	270,000	Akinfeet (SAF)	4	F	5	1	1	1	61,742
Royal Tryst	6	H	5	1	2	1	251,736	Conroy	5	G	4	1	0	0	60,021
State Shinto	7	H	3	0	1	0	203,825	My Cousin Matt	4	G	1	0	0	0	60,000
Ekraar	6	H	1	0	0	1	200,000	Sights On Gold (IRE)	4	C	2	0	1	0	59,054
Grey Memo	6	H	1	0	0	0	200,000	Kayseri (IRE)	4	C	3	1	0	0	58,204
Captain Squire	4	G	1	0	0	1	200,000	Mamool (IRE)	4	C	1	1	0	0	57,183
Estimraar	6	G	4	1	1	1	168,211	Naheef (IRE)	4	C	3	1	0	0	57,183
Mezzo Soprano	3	F	1	1	0	0	150,000	Imtiyaz	4	C	2	1	0	0	57,162
Grundlefoot	6	H	2	0	0	0	139,054	Highest (IRE)	4	C	2	1	0	0	57,162
Belle Du Jour (AUS)	6	M	1	0	0	0	100,000	Desert Glow (IRE)	3	F	7	0	1	1	57,011
Polish Summer (GB)	6	H	1	0	0	0	100,000	Emteyaz (GB)	5	H	7	2	0	1	54,228

2003

RECORDS OF HORSES

The record of each thoroughbred who
raced in the United States and Canada
during 2003 appears in this section,
showing the sex, age, number of starts,
firsts, seconds and thirds, as well as the
total amount of money earned.
If any record shows either first, second
or third placings but no money earned,
trophies were awarded instead.

Horse	Age	Sex	Sts	1st	2d	3d	Won
A B C Cat	2	F	1	0	0	0	0
A B Noodle	4	F	6	0	1	0	16,200
A Bag a Day	2	G	4	1	0	0	6,450
A Bag of Porpourie	4	F	7	0	0	1	1,652
A Bag On Top	2	F	5	0	1	0	13,120
A Barry Good Act	5	M	10	2	3	0	60,385
A Barry Good Actor	4	G	14	1	3	0	9,576
A Beautiful Heart	3	G	7	0	1	1	4,990
A Bet of Honey	2	F	3	0	0	0	564
A Big Tip	2	G	2	0	0	0	0
A Bit Foolish	3	F	7	0	1	1	7,433
A Bit O'Gold	2	G	4	3	0	0	230,029
A Bit Private	4	F	3	0	0	0	0
A Blaze of Fury	4	C	6	1	1	0	12,850
A Boy Name Sue	7	G	2	0	0	0	60
A Boy Named Luke	4	G	12	0	1	2	5,083
A Buccaneer's Life	2	F	2	0	0	0	0
A Buck for Kimbell	4	F	8	0	0	0	2,270
A Buck Forty Nine	3	C	6	1	0	1	6,760
A Buck Onthe Black	5	G	1	0	0	0	0
A Bud's Hope	4	F	1	0	0	0	217
A C Key	4	F	4	0	0	1	1,442
A Call for Gertie	2	F	6	1	1	1	21,826
A Call to Post	7	G	16	1	0	2	4,688
A Case of Class	2	F	4	0	2	0	12,150
A Certain Rapport	4	G	9	1	3	1	8,610
A Champ for Sara	2	C	2	0	0	0	0
A Classic	3	F	14	1	3	5	18,070
A Coady Moment	3	F	7	1	0	1	3,880
A C's Nurse	4	F	1	0	0	0	582
A Dance a Day	2	C	2	0	0	0	0
A Date With Ruby	2	F	3	0	0	0	250
A Dee Double You	3	F	7	1	1	1	10,580
A Delightful Day	4	F	17	2	1	4	13,547
A Devils Life	4	G	6	0	0	2	2,639
A Diligent Ruckus	3	C	1	0	1	0	3,200
A Diller a Dollar	5	M	11	2	3	1	29,176
A Diplomat Manor	4	C	1	0	0	0	0
A Dream Come True	2	F	1	0	1	0	2,735
A Dream of Mine	4	G	11	1	4	1	11,325
A F Repson	4	G	7	1	0	0	10,400
A Familiar Face	2	F	1	0	1	0	4,370
A Feu Bucks	4	F	1	0	0	0	0
A Few Z's	2	F	5	0	0	0	685
A Fine Cat	4	C	13	0	3	3	13,198
A Fine Irish Son	3	C	3	0	0	0	0
A Fine One	2	F	1	0	0	1	1,200
A Firm Warning	4	G	6	0	0	0	0
A Flash of Green	2	G	2	0	0	0	88
A Fleet Badger	3	F	10	2	1	2	12,540
A Fleet Peach	3	F	6	2	1	0	39,757
A Funny Story	3	G	4	0	0	0	0
A G Kat	3	F	4	0	0	0	2,745
A Genius for Place	3	C	7	2	2	0	43,700
A Gentle Man	3	G	15	0	1	2	12,820
A Genuine Honour	7	H	1	0	0	0	2,994
A Ghostly Tale	4	F	7	0	1	0	3,655
A Gift of Bull	3	C	4	0	0	0	211
A Glory Holme	6	G	8	0	0	2	2,310
A Gold Moment	3	F	1	0	0	0	0
A Good Day to Run	4	G	11	1	1	2	27,222
A Good Plan	2	F	4	1	1	0	15,025
A Grade Above	4	G	5	0	1	0	9,655
A Great Hunt	2	C	2	0	0	0	780
A Great Team	3	C	6	3	1	1	98,620
A Groom With Class	2	F	1	0	0	0	0
A Hero Like Me	3	F	11	1	1	1	5,245
A Huevo	7	G	3	2	0	0	204,000
A J and George	2	G	2	0	0	0	1,085
A J Dustdevil	5	H	14	0	0	2	4,270
A J Flyer	7	G	17	0	2	2	1,943
A J's Gone	2	G	4	0	0	1	8,275
A J's Lady Slew	4	F	5	0	0	2	3,228
A J's Pick	5	G	5	0	1	1	3,410
A J's Ticket	2	G	3	0	1	1	3,428
A Kismet Story	4	F	3	0	1	0	3,000
A Knight Mission	5	G	10	3	2	1	16,186
A Known Feu	8	M	5	2	0	1	3,642
A Kours Mood	6	M	4	0	0	0	435
A K's Barron	4	G	18	3	3	3	17,567
A K's Quest	2	G	6	0	2	1	5,870
A Lady's Caress	3	F	11	2	1	2	26,375
A Laknada	4	F	7	1	0	1	1,936
A Lil Excess	6	M	5	3	0	0	108,960
A Lil Sweet	5	G	3	0	0	1	550
A Little Gin	3	F	1	0	0	0	0
A Little Gold	3	F	7	2	1	0	59,479
A Little Magic	7	M	4	0	0	0	173
A Little Respect	7	M	9	0	0	3	2,422
A Little Smooch	4	F	13	1	3	2	16,820
A Little Syn	6	M	14	2	0	1	9,521
A Little Western	4	F	10	1	3	0	5,790
A Long Comedy	6	G	2	0	0	0	110
A Loose Kisser	4	F	13	2	2	4	41,957
A Lot of Mary	8	M	1	0	0	0	360
A Lot of Try	4	F	8	3	0	0	38,364
A Lotta Lad	2	C	2	0	0	0	425
A Lulu Ofa Menifee	2	F	3	0	2	0	10,780
A Ma Guise	3	F	3	0	0	0	0
A Magical Touch	6	G	4	0	0	0	457
A Major Pleasure	4	G	5	1	1	1	8,410
A Major Star	6	H	4	0	2	0	4,260
A Man Called Sue	3	C	1	0	0	0	0
A Mandolin	3	F	11	1	0	1	9,015
A May Zing Devil	4	C	8	2	2	1	13,084
A Memo for Avie	3	G	4	2	0	1	30,450
A Midnight Sheik	4	C	3	1	0	0	2,420
A Million Up	4	F	1	0	1	0	3,200
A Name to Remember	2	F	4	0	0	0	380
A New Twist	4	F	3	2	1	0	116,463
A Newlove	2	F	4	0	0	0	200
A Nice Splash	3	G	17	2	3	3	56,526
A Nicer Fleet	2	F	1	0	0	0	1,302
A Nip of Vodka	3	F	8	0	0	0	930
A One Rocket	4	G	4	2	0	0	14,490
A P Credit	3	G	5	0	1	1	5,470
A P Illini	2	G	2	0	0	0	140
A Pachee Girl	4	F	11	2	2	1	11,893
A Patch of Jade	6	G	4	0	0	1	2,430
A Penny At a Time	3	F	10	0	6	2	34,680
A Penny Maid	6	M	2	0	0	1	1,450
A Perfect Dream	2	C	1	0	0	0	0
A Perfect Wood	2	C	3	0	0	0	3,876
A Perfectredransom	9	G	7	0	0	1	2,848
A Pitch From Bklyn	4	C	1	0	0	0	370
A Pizza for Nick	3	G	5	0	0	0	1,740
A Point Well Made	10	G	7	0	0	1	924
A Prince in Court	2	G	2	0	0	0	450
A Proven Fact	4	C	4	0	1	0	1,080
A P's Belek	2	C	3	1	0	0	6,795
A P's Rebel	4	G	14	2	1	0	8,840
A Queen's Smile	3	F	8	2	1	1	58,978
A Queens Tale	3	F	4	0	3	0	27,860
A R Crackers	2	C	4	0	0	0	1,200
A R Spun	4	G	13	1	2	1	26,381
A Rack of Bengies	4	G	8	2	2	4	8,536
A Rainbow Princess	2	F	1	0	0	0	700
A Ram Sam Sam	2	C	5	0	0	1	550
A Rare Book	5	G	2	1	0	0	13,400
A Rare Brunswick	5	M	9	0	1	1	6,682
A Rash Inski	3	C	12	3	2	0	69,310
A Ray of Magic	5	M	12	0	3	2	26,790
A Real Bad Pain	4	C	3	0	0	0	0
A Real Fancy Gal	2	F	3	1	1	0	28,400
A Real Gem	3	F	8	2	1	1	39,890
A Real King	4	G	12	0	2	4	11,260
A Real Knockout	5	M	8	2	0	1	7,842
A Real Lady	2	F	3	0	1	2	14,140
A Real Nor'easter	6	M	7	0	2	1	16,107
A Reel Tizzy	3	F	5	1	1	1	22,010
A Regal Reflection	3	F	12	4	0	1	25,629
A River Ran Slewit	4	C	2	0	0	0	190
A Rizzi Rueben	2	C	4	1	0	0	6,620
A Rod Genius Jones	3	G	9	1	0	4	3,972
A Rose an Excluse	3	G	1	0	0	0	0
A Rose for Delaine	6	M	5	0	0	0	348

Horse	Age	Sex	Sts	1st	2d	3d	Won
A Royal Imp	6	M	8	1	0	1	5,198
A Royal Scam	2	G	6	0	0	0	935
A Royale Tizzy	7	G	11	2	1	1	17,138
A Ruff Way to Go	4	G	17	0	2	4	11,532
A Run for My Money	3	F	3	0	0	0	350
A Runnin Coyote	8	G	1	0	0	0	38
A Runyon Story	4	G	10	0	0	0	1,065
A Secret Scoop	4	G	12	4	1	2	33,640
A Shaky Start	3	F	9	6	2	0	173,931
A Sharp	4	C	1	0	0	0	0
A Shortt Tour	3	F	4	0	0	0	1,282
A Silent Greek	2	C	1	0	0	0	0
A Slew of Eagles	4	G	9	0	0	2	3,412
A Slew of Scotts	5	G	9	1	1	2	2,482
A Smart Punch	4	F	4	3	0	0	17,640
A Smashing Bull	3	C	4	0	0	0	1,827
A Smile Per Mile	5	M	13	5	2	2	124,020
A Song for Nick	3	G	10	1	0	1	9,255
A Song in A Minor	2	F	2	0	1	1	15,080
A Special Chic	4	F	9	1	0	0	1,178
A Special Romance	8	H	5	0	0	0	523
A Spire a Dream	2	F	2	0	0	0	252
A Spot of Greatnes	2	C	3	0	1	0	5,590
A Star Above	5	M	10	1	4	2	55,148
A Star Has Risen	4	F	2	0	0	2	6,500
A Star I Are	4	F	5	0	0	0	244
A Star in Time	3	F	10	2	0	1	30,793
A Step Beyond	5	M	5	1	2	1	3,329
A Storm Is Brewing	6	G	6	0	0	1	3,500
A Stroke of Luck	5	H	2	0	0	0	220
A T Secondairborne	3	C	1	0	0	0	2,640
A Table for Three	4	C	17	2	1	1	24,662
A Tad Early	4	F	7	1	1	1	31,204
A Tale to Remember	4	C	5	1	0	0	2,869
A Team Leader	2	C	7	1	2	1	9,058
A Tempting Light	6	M	9	1	4	1	10,335
A Time to Run	4	G	18	0	0	1	2,940
A Timeless Lady	2	F	4	0	0	0	162
A to the Z	3	C	3	0	0	0	263
A Touch of Grey	8	G	1	0	0	0	0
A Trick for Sarah	3	F	4	0	0	0	875
A Twist of Sherree	3	F	8	2	3	0	44,208
A View Indeed	4	F	6	1	1	0	38,705
A Vision in Gray	3	F	11	2	2	4	71,370
A Walk With Class	2	F	7	0	1	0	4,330
A Western Queen	3	F	3	0	0	0	720
A Wheaties Girl	6	M	15	3	1	1	15,895
A Whole Force	5	H	1	0	0	0	0
A Wild Tour	3	F	2	0	0	1	400
A Wish for Travis	3	F	6	1	0	0	4,725
A Younger Brother	4	G	2	0	2	0	4,360
A. B. Cry	6	H	1	0	0	0	0
A. B. May	3	C	6	0	0	0	1,144
A. B. Mutah	5	G	6	0	0	1	1,116
A. C. Danzer	3	C	9	1	1	0	13,344
A. C. Rhapsody	4	F	4	0	0	0	478
A. Caterina	3	F	8	1	4	1	29,947
A. F. Annsel	3	F	5	0	0	0	692
A. G. Dreams	5	M	4	0	0	1	970
A. J. Melini	2	C	3	0	2	0	7,215
A. J. the Great	2	C	4	1	0	0	6,150
A. J.'s Express	2	G	9	1	0	1	6,698
A. J.'s Luck	7	G	16	1	5	3	11,891
A. J's Cafe	3	G	6	1	0	1	25,220
A. K. A. Diamond	2	F	5	1	0	0	15,210
A. K. A. Market	4	C	2	0	0	0	7,000
A. P. Adventure	2	F	1	1	0	0	27,000
A. P. Agenda	5	G	11	1	2	2	16,015
A. P. Amazon	4	F	5	1	0	0	13,100
A. P. Andie	5	M	6	1	0	0	57,522
A. P. Aspen	4	G	10	2	3	2	44,700
A. P. Brownie	2	G	3	0	0	0	1,950
A. P. Carson	2	C	1	0	1	0	4,000
A. P. Delta	6	H	2	0	0	0	420
A. P. Devlin	4	G	3	0	0	0	219
A. P. Jetta	3	F	9	1	1	1	7,295
A. P. Junior	4	G	4	0	1	1	12,710
A. P. Lax	2	C	1	0	0	0	137
A. P. Leo	6	G	7	0	0	0	238

Horse	Age	Sex	Sts	1st	2d	3d	Won
A. P. Mountain	3	C	13	2	2	4	17,916
A. P. Slew	4	C	3	0	0	1	8,280
A. P. Thunder	5	H	10	1	0	2	11,093
A. P. Trapp	5	H	11	1	2	1	8,429
A. Peezing Gina	3	F	6	2	1	0	11,095
A. T.'s Plaything	10	G	4	0	0	0	180
A. V. Eight Queen	2	F	1	0	0	0	0
A. V. Eight Tee	2	G	5	0	0	1	1,335
A. V. Seven	2	G	1	0	0	0	0
Aaron's Favorite	6	G	13	2	3	0	43,454
Aaron's Magic	6	H	9	0	1	2	6,528
Aaron's Prospect	6	G	13	0	2	1	19,040
Aaron's to Run	6	G	11	1	3	0	16,607
Aaron's Trick	3	C	5	0	0	0	388
Aat Falt	5	M	14	6	3	1	73,215
Aba Daba Doo	3	G	11	1	3	2	63,908
Abadbaddude	5	G	7	0	1	0	1,843
Abagfullofit	4	G	2	0	0	0	0
Abagintime	4	F	2	0	0	0	0
Abagintwo	4	C	8	2	1	1	15,800
Abagofmagic	3	G	3	0	0	1	1,764
Abarouge	4	G	18	2	2	5	20,421
Abatares	3	G	5	0	3	2	10,390
Abatement	4	C	14	1	2	2	18,460
Abba Do	4	C	12	4	1	2	52,850
Abba Gold	5	M	8	0	1	0	12,992
Abba Gooba Gail	3	F	13	1	3	2	17,838
Abbaboo	4	F	5	1	1	0	4,280
Abbadaba	4	G	4	1	0	2	4,215
Abbadance	4	F	12	2	4	2	8,920
Abbandando	3	C	4	0	1	0	8,200
Abbey Bridge	5	M	7	2	2	0	78,260
Abbeys Runner	2	F	2	1	0	0	7,740
Abbeywood	4	F	8	1	0	0	1,210
Abbie's Gale	2	F	2	1	0	0	8,400
Abbi's Choice	5	G	10	2	2	2	50,212
Abby Coole	6	M	14	1	2	2	12,919
Abby Lake	5	M	1	0	0	0	38
Abby O	3	F	3	0	0	0	0
Abby's Magic	4	F	2	0	0	0	244
Abby's Not Normal	3	F	4	1	1	1	58,680
Abbys Silverdream	3	G	11	0	2	1	8,230
Abby's Sister	3	F	3	0	0	0	980
Abderian (IRE)	6	H	11	0	2	5	86,182
Abduction	5	H	1	1	0	0	21,600
Abe	4	C	1	0	0	0	100
Abeam	4	G	15	1	3	4	24,690
Abellezza	3	F	7	1	0	0	8,840
Abel's Luck	5	M	6	0	0	1	1,235
Abel's Prince	4	C	11	1	0	1	4,510
Abenaki	9	G	4	0	0	1	1,650
Abernathy's Deed	3	G	9	0	0	1	1,040
Aberration	6	G	1	0	0	0	0
Abesi	3	F	4	1	1	1	6,800
Abidjar (GER)	5	G	2	0	0	0	0
Abigale's Wing	4	F	3	0	0	0	120
Ability Springs	2	G	2	0	0	0	360
Abirdinthehand	5	M	6	0	0	2	4,778
Abita Please	5	M	10	1	1	0	8,806
Abitofadandy	5	M	2	0	0	1	1,155
Ablazing Grace	3	F	3	0	0	0	2,790
Able Ally	5	M	3	0	0	1	983
Able Cielo	6	G	6	0	0	0	1,043
Able Hero (AUS)	6	G	7	2	0	1	12,730
Abo Cat	2	F	1	0	0	0	115
Abobe	5	M	10	3	1	0	12,142
Abottleinfrontofme	4	G	4	0	0	0	807
Abou Ben Adhem	3	C	3	0	0	0	0
Abounding Love	4	F	14	1	4	1	8,448
Abounding Truth	3	F	6	4	0	1	53,200
About Love	4	F	2	0	0	0	0
About Respect	5	M	3	0	0	1	1,532
Above All Others	2	F	9	0	1	3	9,667
Above Cause	8	G	4	0	0	2	4,196
Above Justice	4	C	5	2	1	1	109,050
Above Par	5	H	4	1	0	0	4,830
Above Perfection	5	M	1	0	0	0	0
Above the Crowd	10	G	8	3	1	1	21,175
Above the Devil	2	F	5	1	0	1	29,330

Horse	Age	Sex	Sts	1st	2d	3d	Won
Above the Harbor	5	M	10	3	1	2	66,905
Above the Knowl	8	G	5	0	0	0	294
Above the Roar	3	F	1	0	0	0	0
Above the Storm	4	G	5	1	2	0	16,960
Above the Wind	6	G	7	2	1	1	59,023
Abovo	4	F	8	1	1	0	9,147
Aboynamedguinevere	4	G	11	0	1	0	2,718
Abradan of April	3	G	6	0	0	0	1,458
Abreeze	8	G	10	3	1	1	173,810
Abrigail	7	M	2	1	0	0	1,133
Abri's Lilly	11	M	6	0	0	2	465
Abroad	2	C	6	0	2	2	14,560
Abs	4	C	1	0	0	0	0
Absent Answer	4	F	1	0	0	0	89
Absent Ashlee	5	M	15	2	2	1	13,109
Absent Friend	3	C	7	2	0	0	68,122
Absent Lover	3	G	10	2	1	2	30,480
Absentlee	4	C	13	3	4	2	21,520
Absobootly	4	F	2	0	1	1	3,280
Absolute Ability	2	C	1	0	0	0	45
Absolute Advantage	5	G	11	1	0	1	23,210
Absolute Blue	4	F	7	0	1	1	2,530
Absolute Charmer (IRE)	4	F	2	0	1	0	11,200
Absolute Jack	3	C	8	1	1	0	20,150
Absolute Jewel	6	M	5	0	1	0	2,692
Absolute Jo	3	F	7	0	0	0	5,040
Absolute Kris	3	G	14	3	0	1	20,993
Absolute Lee	6	H	1	0	0	0	90
Absolute Nectar	2	F	5	2	0	1	50,886
Absolute Pleasure	3	G	10	0	0	4	22,832
Absolute Reward	4	F	2	0	0	0	576
Absolute Rocks	2	F	9	2	1	2	47,817
Absolutely Active	6	M	6	1	1	1	2,590
Absolutely Certain	3	F	1	0	0	0	0
Absolutely Chilito	3	F	2	0	0	0	2,460
Absolutely Citron	3	F	11	1	0	0	15,024
Absolutely Crystal	3	F	1	0	0	0	0
Absolutely Gifted	5	M	5	1	0	2	6,062
Absolutely Joe	2	C	2	1	0	0	24,600
Absolutely Lovely	4	F	3	0	0	1	7,220
Absolutely Nothing	9	G	7	0	1	0	1,457
Absolutely True	3	G	8	3	2	0	46,278
Absolutism	4	F	1	0	0	0	0
Absolutly Belongs	7	M	4	0	0	0	550
Absolutly Orange	4	F	10	0	1	2	5,619
Absterous	5	H	9	2	2	0	10,134
Abstract Image	5	M	12	6	1	2	12,450
Abu Leil	7	G	11	3	3	1	29,470
Abuela Esther (URU)	6	M	3	0	0	0	1,110
Abuelo	5	M	7	0	1	1	1,352
Abulous	2	G	5	0	0	0	90
Abundantly Blessed	4	F	9	0	3	3	56,480
Abundo	6	H	4	0	0	0	308
Abyss	4	F	5	2	0	0	34,742
Abyssal Storm	4	G	18	3	1	3	33,800
Abyssinian	3	G	13	2	0	1	13,101
Acacian Express	5	G	6	0	1	1	4,587
Acacian Song	7	M	9	0	0	0	587
Academic	6	G	9	0	0	1	27,859
Academic Angel	4	F	9	4	2	0	136,730
Academic Ash	4	G	7	0	0	1	10,100
Academic Lass	2	F	1	0	0	0	780
Academically Right	9	G	9	0	2	2	9,134
Academician	8	G	5	0	0	1	1,686
Academy	2	C	1	0	0	0	0
Academy Bay	4	G	6	1	0	1	5,040
Academy Lass	2	F	5	0	1	0	8,125
Academy Minister	4	F	1	0	0	1	700
Academy Road	7	M	1	0	0	1	420
Academy Spy	4	G	4	1	0	0	36,040
Acadian	4	G	1	0	0	0	0
Acadian Style	3	F	1	1	0	0	4,200
Acadiana Belle	6	M	5	0	0	1	3,473
Acago	3	F	8	2	1	0	110,291
Acalady	4	F	6	1	1	0	6,860
Acall to Persevere	5	G	4	1	1	0	6,770
Acaroids Jewel	2	C	1	0	0	0	60
Acatatlast	3	C	10	1	2	3	40,560
Acca	5	G	14	1	2	1	16,270
Accelerant	5	H	1	0	0	0	1,380
Accelerating Star	4	F	11	0	0	1	622
Accent of Gold	5	M	11	0	2	2	8,076
Accept	5	H	6	0	1	1	12,590
Accept Domra	3	F	9	3	3	0	13,962
Accept for Ryan	2	G	1	0	0	0	750
Acceptable Venture	3	C	12	2	7	0	189,750
Acceptional	3	C	7	1	0	0	4,032
Acceptor	4	G	13	3	0	0	22,869
Access Agenda	5	G	5	0	1	1	10,240
Access Approved	4	G	12	4	1	1	53,075
Accidental Magic	2	G	2	0	0	1	2,596
Accionario (ARG)	7	G	10	1	1	2	5,496
Acclaimed Honour	4	C	3	0	0	1	5,880
Acclimate	2	C	7	2	1	2	51,815
Accomodator	8	G	15	1	0	3	9,374
Accomplish	2	C	6	0	0	0	1,050
Accomplished	3	F	2	0	0	0	0
Accord	4	C	9	1	5	1	63,124
Accordian Man	2	C	7	2	0	3	18,610
Account	2	C	7	1	0	0	17,199
Account Executive	3	G	3	0	0	0	449
Account for Me	5	G	14	3	4	1	77,520
Account of Bette	4	F	13	1	3	2	21,687
Account Paid	2	G	4	0	1	0	2,040
Account Renewed	4	G	13	0	2	2	7,351
Accountable Boy	7	G	9	0	1	1	9,379
Accounted For	6	G	11	3	3	0	72,346
Accountmein	4	F	1	0	0	0	0
Ace Connection	5	H	3	0	0	0	260
Ace in Place	3	F	3	0	0	1	5,334
Ace My Style	3	C	3	1	0	1	6,340
Ace of Club	3	G	5	0	0	0	165
Ace of Suedes	6	G	11	0	0	0	3,596
Ace the Experts	3	F	2	0	0	0	642
Ace Up the Sleeve	4	F	1	0	0	0	120
Aceface	2	G	2	0	0	0	0
Aceinthebag	3	G	15	1	2	1	8,608
Acemeifyoudare	5	M	5	2	2	0	8,013
Ace's Angel	8	M	3	0	0	0	133
Ace's Cappella	2	F	5	0	0	1	9,195
Ace's Crystal	4	F	5	0	0	0	150
Ace's High	2	F	1	0	0	0	216
Aces of Gold	3	G	8	2	0	4	24,418
Aces Sunny Dee	6	G	2	0	0	0	120
Aces Up	4	G	1	0	0	0	45
Ace's Valentine	5	M	12	2	3	0	56,950
Aces Wild	3	M	3	0	1	1	5,580
Achancetoshine	2	F	1	0	1	0	3,200
Achari	5	M	9	3	0	4	67,410
Achill	4	G	8	2	2	1	23,240
Achilles	3	G	17	1	0	0	6,298
Achnasheen	3	F	11	2	1	3	96,702
Achoo	5	H	7	0	0	0	1,016
Achromatic	4	C	1	0	0	0	0
Acid Rain	7	G	10	1	2	4	12,978
Ack Eyes	7	G	10	1	0	1	5,885
Ack's Best	3	F	5	1	1	1	22,106
Acks Like a Devil	5	M	1	0	0	0	0
Acks Like Dusty	5	H	12	4	1	4	50,175
Ack's of War	2	F	1	0	0	0	0
Ackybacky	6	M	14	2	1	1	9,838
Aclare	6	G	1	0	0	0	0
Aclevershadeofjade	3	F	12	2	3	1	92,850
Aconarkbuilder	5	G	12	0	1	1	3,875
Aconcagua	3	G	1	0	0	0	240
Aconfirmedtornado	5	H	17	0	3	4	6,385
Acotte Run	3	G	7	0	4	0	4,170
Acountforthecash	7	G	6	1	1	2	11,246
Acqualina	3	F	7	0	0	0	2,010
Acquiescent	3	F	10	3	1	0	13,598
Acquila	3	F	11	0	1	1	3,992
Acraduck	3	F	5	0	1	0	1,960
Acres	6	G	5	1	0	0	20,410
Acrolect	6	G	7	3	1	2	121,725
Across the Creek	5	M	12	1	0	2	13,616
Across the Line	8	G	1	0	0	0	0
Acrostic	4	G	7	0	2	0	10,740
Ac's Blackcat	3	F	5	1	0	0	18,960

Horse	Age	Sex	Sts	1st	2d	3d	Won
Act Classy	2	G	2	0	0	0	217
Act Foolish	4	F	1	0	1	0	2,900
Act Like a Lady	3	F	9	1	0	0	7,895
Act Nice	3	G	6	1	2	1	10,325
Act of Reform	5	H	14	1	4	5	84,490
Act of War	5	H	9	2	1	1	116,407
Act Special	4	F	13	1	0	0	5,400
Act With Pride	5	G	11	0	1	2	5,951
Actaeon	2	C	5	1	0	1	33,780
Actalittle	2	F	3	0	0	0	715
Actalot	6	G	13	1	1	1	10,295
Actceed	4	C	4	1	2	1	2,214
Actcelerate	2	C	8	0	1	1	8,170
Actcellent	3	F	9	2	4	1	105,590
Actcentric	2	F	6	1	0	1	14,215
Actcentuate	4	F	5	2	0	0	27,870
Actcess	4	F	8	4	1	1	19,980
Actcolades	3	C	4	0	0	0	1,900
Actin Like a Pro	5	G	7	0	0	1	4,705
Actin Time	7	G	4	0	0	0	285
Acting Class	4	G	7	1	0	0	5,070
Acting Decision	2	C	4	0	0	0	0
Acting Deputy	4	F	8	2	0	3	146,155
Acting Foolish	3	F	7	1	1	2	27,390
Acting Maudlin	4	F	17	2	5	3	29,630
Acting Report	2	C	2	1	0	0	4,640
Acting Tips	8	G	17	1	1	3	8,814
Acting Tricky	3	F	4	0	0	2	3,435
Acting Up	5	H	13	1	1	4	13,884
Action Attraction	4	F	11	3	1	1	40,136
Action Cat	2	C	1	0	0	0	0
Action for Real	8	G	7	0	0	0	877
Action Forthe Year	6	M	9	1	3	2	20,300
Action Request	5	H	5	0	2	0	12,900
Action Talk	4	F	7	1	0	0	7,361
Action This Day	2	C	3	2	1	0	817,200
Action Tonight	3	G	6	0	0	3	8,425
Action West	5	M	4	0	0	2	6,765
Activado's Image	3	G	2	0	0	0	192
Activate	5	G	15	1	1	1	5,697
Active Angel	6	M	7	0	3	0	1,330
Active Radium	5	G	16	1	2	0	4,024
Actor	3	C	2	0	0	0	1,700
Acts Well	4	F	4	0	0	0	180
Actscape	4	F	1	0	0	0	220
Actsclamation	5	M	10	4	2	0	16,749
Actsclusive	3	F	10	1	1	0	13,675
Actscuse	3	C	15	1	5	1	22,355
Actslikechamp	3	G	11	1	2	0	10,569
Actsposure	5	M	9	1	1	2	10,194
Acttractive	3	F	14	3	3	1	17,396
Actual Illusion	4	G	16	3	2	3	39,655
Actual Trapp	4	F	8	1	0	0	2,940
Actuary's Son	5	G	6	1	0	1	12,711
Actxotic	6	M	8	1	1	0	12,929
Actxpedite	2	C	1	0	0	0	195
Actxpress	5	G	12	1	1	4	6,247
Actxpressive	3	G	15	1	4	1	45,320
Actxquisite	5	M	13	0	0	1	2,916
Actxtravagant	3	F	11	0	0	2	6,325
Acuff	3	F	1	0	0	0	0
Acumen	6	G	9	2	1	3	86,136
Acupuncture	2	G	2	0	0	0	651
Acure for Geri	4	F	3	0	0	0	564
Acute Vision	3	F	4	0	0	0	0
Aczar	9	G	6	0	2	1	3,410
Ad Astra	3	F	2	0	0	0	0
Ad Hoc	4	F	5	0	0	0	505
Ada Flower	6	M	4	0	1	0	2,235
Adage	2	C	6	1	3	0	71,575
Adagio Twinkles	7	G	12	1	1	0	10,948
Adalgisa	4	F	10	1	1	3	81,238
Adaline Plantation	8	G	3	0	0	0	120
Adam in Eden	6	H	1	0	0	0	0
Adam Lets Share	8	M	12	0	1	0	2,826
Adam Man	3	G	5	3	1	0	61,120
Adam T	6	G	7	0	1	1	2,918
Adamandia's Girl	5	M	5	0	0	0	144
Adamant Victor	3	C	2	0	0	1	970
Adamic	3	G	8	2	1	1	8,264
Adams	4	C	3	0	0	0	280
Adam's Able	5	G	10	2	0	0	11,400
Adam's Bratt	4	G	7	0	0	0	1,804
Adams Castle	4	F	8	2	1	1	58,280
Adam's Jag	3	C	4	4	0	0	50,700
Adams Peak	4	G	10	3	3	0	40,100
Adam's Pullet	5	M	7	0	2	1	13,278
Adam's R Pic	3	G	6	0	0	0	805
Adam's Reality	7	G	8	0	1	1	2,291
Adams Tribe	4	C	11	0	3	1	35,482
Adam's Way	3	G	10	1	0	3	14,630
Adanac	6	G	10	0	1	4	13,303
Adance for Corinne	3	F	5	0	0	0	185
Adaptation	2	C	1	0	0	0	137
Adar	3	C	10	1	1	0	6,150
Adbass Dancer	8	G	9	0	0	4	1,192
Add a Moment	3	G	14	1	1	1	22,536
Add It Up	4	C	7	2	1	1	63,624
Add the Numbers	5	G	8	1	0	0	12,988
Adda Devil	3	F	11	0	0	3	2,825
Adda Drums	4	G	16	3	2	1	11,265
Addakiss	5	H	12	4	0	3	42,931
Added Annuity	3	F	10	0	3	1	15,911
Added Edge	3	C	4	0	0	3	41,723
Added Fun	2	G	1	0	0	0	0
Addicious	3	C	2	0	0	0	361
Addicks	4	C	10	1	1	2	50,410
Addie Anne	3	F	7	0	0	1	753
Addie Go	2	F	3	0	0	1	1,255
Addie's Native	4	C	10	3	2	0	14,704
Addieville	3	C	1	0	0	0	330
Addinson	7	G	2	0	0	0	0
Addy's Hoedown	5	M	13	4	1	1	15,127
Adee	6	H	9	0	5	3	12,245
Adelantada	5	M	1	0	0	0	625
Adele Lucille	2	F	7	0	1	2	8,320
Adella	4	F	7	0	2	3	7,830
Adequate Statement	3	C	1	0	0	0	170
Adham (CHI)	5	G	8	0	0	1	5,180
Adhesive	4	G	9	2	3	3	5,340
Adieu and Farewell	3	F	13	3	1	4	21,618
Adif	6	M	9	1	3	0	14,160
Adina's Star	7	M	7	3	0	2	24,500
Adinatha	3	F	5	1	2	1	30,280
Adine	2	F	4	1	0	0	6,165
Adios Amigo	7	G	1	0	0	0	40
Adios Birdie	4	F	12	2	3	0	12,977
Adios Meadowlake	3	F	10	1	2	2	46,440
Adios Muchachos	7	H	7	0	0	1	954
Adios Nonino (URU)	5	H	5	0	1	0	2,575
Adiostra	2	C	2	0	0	0	120
Adirondack Counsel	3	G	13	2	0	2	9,210
Adirun	5	M	6	2	0	0	6,660
Adjalah	4	C	8	0	3	3	68,332
Adjalon	3	G	12	2	0	1	10,715
Adjust	7	G	7	1	2	1	31,070
Adjutant	7	G	9	2	2	2	7,911
Adjutant (GB)	8	G	5	1	0	1	13,272
Adlib	5	M	9	0	1	2	4,641
Administration	3	C	3	1	0	0	13,426
Adminniestrator	6	G	3	1	0	1	292,900
Admiral Albert	4	G	16	4	4	1	89,589
Admiral Bo	10	G	7	0	1	3	6,735
Admiral Canaris	3	C	9	0	1	1	3,905
Admiral Dewey	6	G	10	1	1	0	6,282
Admiral Fox	3	G	19	3	4	4	22,984
Admiral Lance	3	G	8	1	0	0	38,313
Admiral Nelson	4	G	4	0	0	0	185
Admiral Picket	2	C	7	1	1	1	6,799
Admiral Roxbury	9	H	9	3	2	3	6,546
Admiral Slew	4	C	12	2	4	2	97,095
Admiral Zimbobby	5	G	6	2	1	1	15,210
Admiralinthenavy	2	C	3	0	0	0	0
Admirality Drive	4	F	4	0	0	0	567
Admiral's Cap	5	G	8	0	0	0	1,475
Admiral's Cup (IRE)	6	H	7	3	0	0	18,113
Admiral's Pride	8	M	6	0	0	2	2,435
Admiralty Arch	3	C	8	2	3	0	87,930

Horse	Age	Sex	Sts	1st	2d	3d	Won
Admiralty Inlet	2	C	1	0	0	0	0
Admiration	4	C	11	0	3	1	13,980
Admired	3	F	3	0	0	0	241
Admit	4	G	5	0	0	0	504
Admo Jr.	4	G	13	4	2	2	36,438
Ado	3	C	1	0	0	0	0
Adobe Canyon	5	M	15	2	1	1	35,624
Adobe M	5	G	2	0	0	0	0
Adobe Runner	4	G	18	3	3	3	10,070
Adopted Daughter	3	F	6	1	1	2	121,820
Adopting Habit	3	G	1	0	1	0	3,400
Adorable	3	F	1	0	0	0	195
Adorable Audrey	4	F	9	1	0	3	30,800
Adorable Cielo	4	F	10	2	1	0	22,783
Adorable Julie	4	F	5	0	2	1	6,750
Adorable One	5	M	2	0	0	0	8,892
Adorable Racer	11	G	1	0	0	0	471
Adorable Rose	5	M	1	0	0	0	0
Adoration	4	F	5	2	1	1	1,160,750
Adoremus	4	C	6	0	2	0	2,494
Adoring	4	F	3	0	0	0	381
Adoublecause	10	G	10	1	3	1	12,238
Adreality	3	F	5	1	0	1	22,095
Adreamisborn	4	C	7	0	4	0	28,940
Adrenalin Running	2	F	4	0	0	0	2,640
Adrian's Way	4	C	11	1	2	4	11,580
Adrienne K	3	F	9	0	0	1	983
Adrinkinseattle	5	M	11	2	1	2	11,846
Adroitly Superb	5	G	9	1	3	1	35,479
Advance to Go	2	G	3	0	0	1	1,990
Advanced Edition	6	G	1	0	0	1	684
Advanced Notice	3	F	15	2	2	2	29,992
Advancewithcaution	5	M	17	1	1	4	23,637
Advantage (CHI)	6	H	1	0	0	0	100
Advantage Miss	5	M	4	0	0	0	860
Advantage Plus	7	M	11	2	2	1	24,084
Advantageoverbrook	6	G	11	1	0	0	3,729
Adventurette	3	F	1	0	0	0	0
Adventurous	9	G	5	1	0	1	2,881
Adventurous Guy	3	G	4	1	0	0	5,475
Adversary	4	G	14	2	5	1	25,985
Advisarial	3	G	1	0	0	0	0
Advocate Annie	4	F	10	1	2	2	17,470
Advocate General	3	C	12	2	2	0	13,078
Aeneas	4	C	9	0	4	2	336,300
Aer Afrik	5	G	15	2	1	3	18,305
Aeras	4	G	14	1	4	6	29,200
Aerial Command	3	G	5	0	0	2	9,740
Aerial Empress	4	F	7	1	0	0	6,073
Aerialist	4	F	13	1	1	0	10,254
Aerie Bayadere	6	M	10	2	0	1	8,670
Aerojack	2	C	5	0	0	1	7,380
Aerolass	3	F	1	0	0	0	0
Aeronotica	4	F	7	2	0	1	18,985
Aeropeter	2	C	4	1	0	0	11,760
Aesthete Approval	5	M	4	0	0	0	2,993
Aesthetic	7	G	8	0	0	0	310
Aetha	5	M	5	1	0	0	10,660
Afar	2	C	1	0	0	0	1,350
Afastfast	3	C	2	0	0	0	846
Aferds Finale	2	F	3	0	0	0	378
Aferds Key	2	G	2	0	0	0	252
Aferds Legacy	2	C	2	0	0	0	252
Affable	3	C	7	0	1	0	12,608
Affair in the Air	5	G	5	0	2	0	22,360
Affair Play	4	G	3	1	1	0	14,892
Affair Promise	3	G	7	2	0	2	11,270
Affair to Be	7	G	3	0	2	0	2,480
Affairoftherose	3	F	6	0	0	2	2,811
Affancy Affair	6	M	4	0	0	1	1,153
Affectation	2	F	4	0	1	0	3,075
Affectionate Gal	3	F	7	1	0	0	11,888
Affectionate Girl	2	F	8	1	1	1	8,445
Affirm	3	G	4	1	1	0	7,649
Affirm Cat	4	G	10	1	1	3	12,155
Affirm Challenge	6	H	11	1	2	2	5,752
Affirm Miss	4	F	1	1	0	0	34,200
Affirm Rail	3	G	7	1	0	0	3,788
Affirm Strategy	3	C	4	0	0	0	720
Affirm Trump	9	G	3	0	0	0	0
Affirmative	4	C	1	0	0	0	2,880
Affirmed Admiral	5	H	8	2	1	1	3,285
Affirmed Dancer	4	F	10	3	1	1	126,928
Affirmed Destiny	2	G	7	0	0	0	1,400
Affirmed Doe	6	M	4	0	1	0	1,523
Affirmed Feeling	4	G	6	3	1	1	153,329
Affirmed Manner	2	F	4	0	1	0	4,033
Affirmed Perfect	4	C	15	1	1	3	15,314
Affirmed Pleasure	4	G	4	1	1	1	22,160
Affirmed Reality	5	G	10	2	0	1	19,550
Affirmed Success	9	G	4	2	0	1	114,300
Affirming Storm	4	G	7	1	0	1	5,439
Affirmlode	2	G	10	1	2	1	26,219
Affirm's Image	5	G	4	0	0	1	660
Affixed	4	C	12	2	2	3	13,230
Affliction	3	C	6	0	0	0	140
Affluent	5	M	4	1	0	1	184,236
Afforce of Course	3	F	2	1	0	0	14,074
Affordable Fun	5	G	7	0	2	1	10,661
Afiddleintheband	3	F	5	0	1	0	875
Afieromeno	3	G	2	0	0	0	250
A'fire	6	G	14	1	2	4	24,940
Aflame	2	F	4	1	1	0	7,705
Afleet Angel	3	F	4	2	0	1	20,262
Afleet Buck	4	G	15	3	2	1	65,892
Afleet Cat	2	F	3	0	0	0	0
Afleet Command	2	C	5	0	1	2	14,350
Afleet Diablo	3	F	9	2	1	2	17,700
Afleet Loyd	4	C	11	1	3	2	38,520
Afleet Shawklit	2	C	3	1	0	0	8,220
Afleetilation	3	F	7	1	0	0	7,150
Afleetkitty	3	F	13	1	3	3	25,771
Afoolandhismoney	4	G	5	0	0	0	668
Afortunado	3	C	9	0	2	0	14,595
African Chatter	3	C	10	2	0	2	7,902
African Gold	6	G	8	0	1	2	3,013
African Nights	3	F	6	1	1	0	10,200
African Princess	4	F	15	2	4	2	70,440
African Skyline	4	F	10	3	3	2	64,870
African Wildfire	3	C	4	0	1	0	2,410
Afro Look (ARG)	4	F	2	0	0	0	0
After Five	3	G	5	0	0	0	100
After My Heart	4	F	9	1	1	2	40,680
After Sunset	3	F	9	2	3	0	7,524
After Tea	3	F	6	0	0	0	1,770
After the Fact	4	F	2	0	0	0	0
After the Race	6	G	3	0	0	1	1,210
After the Run	6	G	8	2	1	2	45,262
After the Tone	2	F	6	0	2	0	25,080
Afterdinnerdrink	3	G	13	1	1	1	7,180
Afterdinnerthunder	2	G	4	0	0	0	1,437
Aftermath	3	G	4	0	0	2	6,750
Afternoon Amour	5	M	20	1	2	1	8,643
Afternoon Bride	3	F	2	0	0	0	0
Afternoon Charlie	2	C	5	1	3	0	41,821
Afternoon Clinic	2	G	5	1	2	1	25,935
Afternoon Dreams	3	F	8	1	1	0	51,840
Afternoon Edition	3	C	1	0	0	0	0
Afternoon in Rio	2	G	4	1	2	0	24,500
Afternoon Jewel	3	G	4	0	1	0	2,280
Afternoon Magick	4	F	15	4	3	2	53,232
Afternoon Martini	2	G	9	0	1	2	7,770
Afternoon Pleasure	5	G	11	2	1	3	46,120
Afternoon Reward	3	G	17	0	1	1	2,715
Afternoon Sun	6	H	12	1	2	3	17,972
Afternoon Tea	5	M	17	2	3	2	39,243
Afternoonbuzz	3	C	12	0	2	0	10,160
Afterthreemartinis	5	G	9	0	1	3	2,457
Aftica	3	F	7	1	1	1	60,139
Ag 'n Max	3	F	2	0	0	0	0
Againadevil	4	G	10	0	0	0	1,006
Against Odds	8	G	3	0	0	0	0
Agame	3	G	13	0	4	2	27,840
Agapanther	3	G	13	3	0	1	11,622
Agata Slew	4	F	3	0	0	0	230
Agate's Saint	5	H	4	0	0	0	148
Agave	3	F	4	1	0	1	17,074
Agbayani	4	F	6	1	1	0	22,321

RECORDS OF HORSES

Horse	Age	Sex	Sts	1st	2d	3d	Won	Horse	Age	Sex	Sts	1st	2d	3d	Won
Age of Flight	11	G	3	0	1	0	1,725	Ain't No Bullzip	3	G	3	1	0	0	13,980
Agean Winds	3	C	5	0	0	0	1,125	Aint No Connection	5	H	3	1	2	0	2,795
Agenda Preciosa	5	M	18	2	4	2	13,992	Ain't No Sunshine	3	G	8	2	0	1	46,167
Agenda's Trouble	3	G	10	2	0	1	9,672	Ain't No Yank	9	G	1	0	0	0	40
Agent Bradley J	3	C	9	0	1	0	1,787	Ain't She a Beauty	2	F	2	1	0	0	24,708
Agent Danseur	2	C	7	1	3	2	23,630	Ain't She Awesome	3	F	1	0	1	0	11,760
Agent Talk	3	G	7	1	1	0	6,422	Ain't She Quaint	3	F	3	0	0	0	320
Aggadan	4	C	11	3	2	2	243,230	Aint She Something	3	F	6	0	0	0	728
Aggie Grit	2	C	3	1	1	0	10,400	Ain't Talkin	3	F	7	3	0	0	51,780
Aggie Minister	4	F	11	2	0	1	17,541	Ain't Tellin'	3	F	4	0	0	0	150
Aggie Peach	3	F	7	0	1	1	2,662	Ainthatrighthoney	3	G	4	0	1	1	8,607
Aggie Roo	4	F	6	0	0	1	841	Aintthisamess	3	G	2	0	0	1	800
Aggieblitz	4	F	4	1	0	0	4,110	Air Academy	2	C	3	0	0	1	5,980
Aggies Hideaway	6	M	12	3	2	3	28,465	Air Adair	3	F	3	0	0	0	596
Aggie's Storm	3	F	12	2	2	1	27,558	Air American	2	C	6	0	2	0	8,868
Aggies Style	4	F	10	2	1	0	7,730	Air Annie	6	M	15	2	2	4	17,811
Aggressive	6	G	1	0	0	0	0	Air Bag	10	G	8	2	0	2	8,912
Aggressive Action	6	G	11	2	0	1	21,477	Air Base	4	G	7	1	1	2	45,430
Aggressive Dixie	4	F	9	2	1	0	24,170	Air Brush	2	C	5	0	1	0	10,830
Aggressive Man	3	G	6	1	0	0	5,624	Air Cactus Lil	2	F	2	0	0	0	0
Aggressive Nanny	4	G	8	0	1	0	4,440	Air Cadet	6	H	10	0	0	1	2,066
Aggrevating Amy	4	F	4	0	0	0	240	Air Command	2	C	1	0	0	0	91
Agile Aly	5	M	5	1	1	1	8,960	Air Cool	9	H	13	3	3	3	60,620
Agilena	2	F	3	1	0	0	6,720	Air Cop	8	G	5	0	0	1	763
Agincourt	4	F	13	3	2	2	48,599	Air Cowgirl	4	F	3	0	0	0	0
Agitated Attitude	6	G	11	0	4	2	13,100	Air Driver	3	F	9	2	2	1	34,771
Agnes Rose	4	F	5	1	0	0	6,390	Air Fever	4	F	3	0	1	0	2,380
Ago Ruhles	3	F	5	2	0	0	7,807	Air Flyer	4	G	7	1	0	1	3,900
Agolo	5	M	7	2	1	1	119,790	Air Forbes	4	G	13	2	0	1	15,440
Agone	3	G	6	2	0	2	24,386	Air Forbes Jones	2	F	5	1	0	0	4,185
Agora	6	M	9	1	1	0	8,320	Air Forbes Too	6	H	14	6	2	4	18,368
Agorein	3	C	4	0	2	1	25,800	Air Hadif	2	C	6	1	1	1	9,150
Agree	6	H	14	0	2	0	2,954	Air Janalex	5	M	14	2	0	2	15,497
Agree to Disagree	3	F	4	1	0	2	10,770	Air Karakorum	5	M	8	2	3	1	40,911
Agreement	4	C	5	0	0	0	630	Air King	3	G	9	1	0	2	23,034
Agretta Darling	2	F	1	0	0	0	0	Air Kiss	4	G	5	0	0	1	1,467
Agricola	3	C	1	0	0	0	0	Air Lass One	5	M	1	0	0	0	160
Agrivating General	4	G	13	2	8	1	145,350	Air Lode	3	G	7	0	1	0	1,300
Agro	2	G	3	1	0	0	12,540	Air Lordan	3	C	7	2	1	0	19,590
Agua Fria Express	5	G	3	0	0	0	0	Air Marshall	3	F	7	0	2	3	37,790
Agua Frio	6	H	12	4	1	2	36,206	Air Naevus	6	G	2	0	0	0	106
Aguara	3	F	8	1	2	0	32,470	Air of Excellence	6	M	6	0	0	0	632
Ah Boo	3	C	4	0	0	2	3,600	Air Raid Two	5	G	1	0	0	0	42
Ah Shutup	5	H	5	0	2	1	3,740	Air Rail	4	G	1	1	0	0	5,730
Ah Still Suits Me	4	F	9	1	2	0	13,999	Air Storm	5	M	4	1	0	1	6,902
Ah Struck	4	F	1	0	0	0	0	Air Tech	5	G	13	0	3	1	6,303
Ah Wilderness	3	C	7	2	0	0	44,300	Air the Flag	7	M	1	0	0	0	40
Ahhsome Explosion	4	G	8	0	0	1	5,886	Air Turbulence	4	G	12	4	3	1	25,940
Ahimsa	4	F	8	3	1	0	58,753	Airbill	11	G	1	0	0	0	0
Ahknow a Story	3	C	5	0	0	0	315	Airborne Shuttle	10	G	10	0	2	1	7,742
Ahmagooden	6	H	4	0	0	0	0	Airbourne Command	8	G	5	0	1	0	13,651
Ahmee's Best	4	F	13	0	1	2	6,286	Aireslew	2	G	4	0	1	0	8,558
Aho Acre	2	C	6	1	1	0	15,160	Airialissue	3	F	8	0	0	0	6,864
Ahoy	2	F	3	0	0	1	2,600	Airiasaffair	6	G	7	0	1	2	17,155
Ahoy El Paso	2	G	2	0	1	0	2,730	Airingout	5	H	8	0	1	0	1,920
Ahpo Here	6	G	4	1	0	0	27,970	Air'nsea	7	G	8	0	1	0	6,458
Ahsogroovy	3	F	7	1	1	1	11,055	Airship	5	G	14	7	1	3	33,350
Ahuriri Hikawai (NZ)	4	F	4	0	1	1	15,750	Airspeed Alive	2	C	1	0	0	0	145
Aibrean	4	C	1	0	0	0	450	Airtight Alibi	8	G	10	1	0	0	9,047
Aidan's Turn	3	G	4	0	0	0	700	Airtune	6	G	7	0	1	0	2,531
Aiken to Be	5	G	11	0	0	1	7,910	Aislamiento	4	F	12	1	1	0	11,794
Aileen's Derby	3	C	6	0	1	1	3,800	Aisle Light	3	F	1	0	0	1	4,200
Aileen's Valay	5	M	10	1	1	1	14,032	Aislebeseeinya	3	F	9	1	0	1	3,168
Aileesh	4	F	13	0	5	2	23,827	Aj Cielo	4	C	2	0	0	0	185
Aim High Flier	5	H	5	0	2	0	5,280	Ajax Jet	3	F	6	1	1	0	7,700
Aim of the Game	8	M	1	0	0	0	0	Ajedrez (ARG)	4	C	4	3	0	0	58,800
Aim to Win	5	H	9	1	0	4	12,325	Ajergabead	4	G	9	0	0	0	1,660
Aima (IRE)	6	G	6	0	0	1	840	Aj's Here to Win	3	G	12	0	2	1	7,802
Aime Moi Toujour	3	F	12	3	2	1	14,086	Aj's Honor	4	G	10	0	1	1	4,173
Aimee	3	F	12	1	1	3	9,490	Aka Remy	4	G	11	0	2	1	7,078
Aimees Pride	3	G	7	0	0	0	5,740	Akalacor	4	C	3	0	0	0	280
Aimer	2	F	1	0	0	0	1,020	Akamai	3	G	2	0	0	0	1,020
Aimless Breeze	8	G	13	2	1	0	6,391	Akanti (IRE)	3	G	4	0	0	0	3,300
Aint	3	G	16	1	3	1	12,388	Akatsakat	3	C	8	3	2	0	97,500
Aint Dat Right Ted	2	F	3	0	0	0	1,081	Akbar	4	C	14	1	0	0	20,211
Ain't Hazel	4	F	15	1	2	2	10,969	Akimboalogo	3	G	8	1	1	1	8,263
Ain't I Kool	3	F	2	1	0	0	4,975	Akin Breakin'	5	H	12	1	2	0	3,070
Ain't It Sweep	3	F	3	0	0	0	1,405	Akins Alibi	3	F	7	1	2	0	6,302
Ain't No Big Deal	8	M	5	2	0	0	16,473	Akissifyouwin	3	F	10	2	3	3	11,773

Horse	Age	Sex	Sts	1st	2d	3d	Won
Aknightinbrooklyn	2	F	4	1	1	1	7,850
Akram's Rudy	4	G	5	0	2	0	4,996
Akram's Weehee	5	M	4	0	0	0	0
Akron Avenue	3	F	8	3	2	1	92,860
Akron Blue	4	F	1	0	0	0	0
Al Anoosh	2	C	1	0	0	0	0
Al Barrak	5	G	4	0	0	0	281
Al Berto	9	G	11	1	1	0	10,200
Al Better	5	H	3	0	0	0	225
Al Cory Lucas	6	G	2	0	0	0	490
Al Dente	4	C	16	1	1	2	18,780
Al Hajji	7	G	19	0	0	2	2,792
Al Khaaser	5	H	9	1	0	0	21,880
Al Mamaaliq	6	G	1	0	0	0	0
Al Prospector	6	H	22	1	1	4	12,030
Al Rock	5	G	7	1	0	1	6,625
Al Safeer	3	C	2	0	0	0	0
Al Sami	2	C	1	0	0	0	0
Al Saqaar	3	C	6	1	2	1	28,573
Al Skywalker	10	G	7	3	0	1	126,385
Al Tony O's Babe	3	G	4	1	0	0	4,595
Al Turf (IRE)	3	C	8	0	2	0	47,522
Alabaster	3	C	2	1	0	0	3,696
Alabastrino	3	C	12	2	0	1	12,234
Aladdin's Lamp	2	C	3	1	0	1	27,885
Aladin Sane	4	G	12	2	1	1	18,858
Alafia	3	F	2	0	0	0	0
Alagold	5	H	1	0	0	0	0
Alajwad	3	C	6	2	2	1	77,445
Alakayfa	5	M	15	2	1	0	11,390
Alaki's Jet	3	C	2	0	0	0	1,400
Alalila	3	F	6	1	0	1	15,320
Alameda Duke	6	H	16	0	4	1	10,964
Alamo Rose	4	F	1	0	0	0	0
Alamo Slew	4	C	2	0	0	0	186
Alamomiss	3	F	1	0	0	0	0
Alamotta	3	F	3	0	1	0	5,160
Alandem	5	G	8	0	0	0	472
Alannadontstop	3	F	7	1	0	0	12,480
Alan's Plum Frozen	2	C	2	0	0	0	666
Alantacana	4	F	1	0	0	0	91
Alar	4	G	12	1	3	1	7,812
Alarkandadove	2	F	7	1	2	3	41,295
Alarm Code	7	G	16	2	1	2	19,360
Alarm On the Farm	2	C	1	0	0	0	975
Alarm System	2	G	8	0	2	2	5,030
Alarm the C. E. O.	4	G	15	4	2	2	54,570
Alarming Billy	5	G	14	0	1	0	2,430
Alarming Leader	9	G	12	2	1	1	12,610
Alarmist	6	H	11	4	0	3	30,981
Alashir's World	3	F	2	1	0	0	34,800
Alaska Ash	2	F	5	0	3	0	18,038
Alaska Gold	3	F	3	0	0	0	318
Alaska Beau	3	G	3	0	0	0	773
Alaskan Belle	9	M	8	0	0	1	1,500
Alaskan Buck	12	G	2	0	0	0	136
Alaskan Gambler	6	G	2	0	1	0	900
Alaskan Glory	6	M	11	0	0	0	1,946
Alaskan Gold	4	C	14	3	4	3	55,804
Alaskan Hill	6	G	9	1	0	0	3,752
Alaskan Lights	9	G	10	2	3	0	12,171
Alaskan Moon	2	G	4	0	0	0	1,260
Alaskan Nights	6	H	13	1	4	3	9,306
Alaskan Star	5	H	1	0	0	0	630
Alaskan Twins	5	G	8	1	1	2	32,090
Alaskan Vodka	8	G	11	3	1	2	13,929
Alaskee	7	G	6	1	0	0	1,610
Alayna's Louski	6	M	4	0	0	0	0
Alba Idol	8	M	3	0	0	0	228
Albaaz	3	C	7	2	0	1	56,097
Albany Boy	5	G	11	0	1	1	2,488
Albarino	2	G	4	0	0	0	1,077
Albatros (ARG)	6	H	11	2	3	3	106,520
Albert and Baby	3	C	1	0	0	0	110
Albert E.	3	G	15	4	5	1	85,650
Albert F	2	C	5	0	0	0	725
Albert G	4	G	5	0	1	2	20,100
Albert Slewsky	3	G	16	2	2	0	36,528
Alberta Brass	3	F	8	2	1	2	13,384
Alberta Cafe	3	G	1	0	0	0	0
Alberta Devil	2	G	5	1	0	0	6,676
Alberta Energy	3	G	12	3	1	0	21,534
Alberta Oak	5	G	6	0	1	0	8,229
Albertmyman	5	H	9	2	2	1	4,031
Alberto Giacometti (IRE)	3	C	6	0	0	2	26,482
Albert's Crossing	3	G	8	0	0	2	11,150
Alberts Dance	6	G	11	0	0	1	1,750
Albino Aligator	3	G	14	1	1	3	7,576
Albrannon	8	G	7	1	0	3	6,940
Alchema	2	F	1	0	1	0	7,200
Alchemilla	4	F	7	1	1	1	91,296
Alchemist	3	F	6	3	1	1	104,800
Alcres George	2	G	3	0	0	0	980
Aldaro	4	C	8	1	0	0	8,550
Aldebaran	5	H	8	5	1	1	1,110,606
Alden's Card	5	G	9	1	0	1	13,610
Alderbaron	4	G	1	1	0	0	5,560
Aldergroovy	6	G	1	0	0	0	278
Aldina From Medina	5	M	12	1	2	5	10,031
Aldo	6	H	6	0	1	1	8,650
Aldoc	5	H	2	0	0	0	428
Alecks	4	F	7	0	0	1	1,740
Aledo Affair	3	F	6	0	2	0	2,920
Aledo Pass	3	G	15	4	2	0	51,665
Aleef	6	G	1	0	0	0	500
Alegorico (ARG)	5	G	18	1	2	4	38,900
Alegrita	3	F	9	2	1	1	13,351
Aleke	3	G	10	1	0	1	10,092
Alena's Boy	2	C	6	1	2	1	27,090
Alena's Tornado	6	G	7	2	3	1	32,083
Alencino	3	G	3	0	0	0	0
Alert	4	C	4	4	0	0	56,400
Alert and Ready	7	G	5	2	0	0	7,320
Alert Cat	3	G	10	0	0	0	195
Alert David	9	G	17	1	0	3	16,650
Alert to Go (FR)	9	H	9	0	0	0	459
Alert Woman	3	F	7	0	1	0	1,949
Alerting	3	F	4	1	0	0	8,280
Alesia Gold Boy	5	G	13	1	0	2	3,752
Alesias Affair	4	G	10	1	1	1	26,208
A'leuring Star	5	G	21	3	5	4	38,515
Aleutian Frost	4	G	22	2	6	2	35,630
Alex Dancer (VEN)	5	H	1	0	0	0	73
Alex Legreat	5	G	7	0	0	0	654
Alex Marie	11	M	2	0	0	1	208
Alex Programmer	6	G	9	1	0	1	4,901
Alex the Gray	5	G	12	0	0	0	1,533
Alex the Mad Dog	4	C	1	0	0	0	0
Alexa Grace	3	F	11	1	3	2	16,710
Alexander Looker	6	M	9	0	0	1	1,670
Alexander Springs	5	H	2	0	0	0	244
Alexander T	3	C	3	0	0	0	521
Alexander's Belle	2	F	2	0	0	1	1,350
Alexanders Charm	6	H	8	4	0	0	12,594
Alexander's Peak	4	G	1	0	0	0	91
Alexander's Sword	5	G	4	0	1	0	2,441
Alexandria	3	F	17	3	3	7	87,170
Alexandrite	2	F	1	1	0	0	6,600
Alexi Dancer	2	F	3	0	0	0	1,380
Alexine (ARG)	7	M	6	0	1	2	42,033
Alexis Pony	4	G	12	3	1	2	9,840
Alexis Pride	4	F	4	0	0	0	0
Alexisourdestiny	2	F	1	0	0	0	50
Alex's Angel	6	M	4	0	0	0	0
Alex's Castledream	4	G	2	0	0	0	180
Alex's Dream	4	G	2	0	0	0	0
Alex's Hot Fudge	3	F	8	1	2	2	32,720
Alex's Love	5	G	20	5	4	2	66,244
Alex's Pal	4	C	7	2	0	1	52,380
Alex's Sister	3	F	2	0	0	0	270
Alexspike	3	G	6	0	0	0	322
Alextrician	4	G	3	0	0	0	601
Aleyeska	3	G	7	1	1	1	20,240
Alfaari Highway	3	C	9	1	2	0	18,955
Alfaari's Lass	4	F	10	1	0	2	4,943
Alfaari's Magic	4	G	4	1	1	1	23,072
Alfaari's Reign	4	G	12	1	2	2	10,658
Alfaari's Solo	4	G	5	0	0	2	7,326

Horse	Age	Sex	Sts	1st	2d	3d	Won
Alfarri's Ringer	4	G	7	0	0	1	1,139
Alfayiz	5	G	6	1	2	1	25,320
Alferrari	4	G	7	1	1	0	6,022
Alfie	5	M	10	2	0	1	12,352
Alfir's Ace	3	F	1	0	0	0	180
Alfredo	3	C	12	3	2	0	20,118
Alfred's Bluff	9	G	15	2	2	4	8,009
Alfurune	5	G	10	1	3	5	101,150
Algezir	4	G	4	0	1	0	6,840
Algonquin	5	H	3	1	0	1	18,750
Algonquin Farewell	4	G	14	0	0	2	4,235
Algonquin Flag	2	C	1	0	0	1	4,100
Algorhythm	4	G	15	1	1	1	19,035
Alhorsesgotoheaven	5	G	11	1	0	1	12,115
Ali Be Contender	4	G	9	0	0	0	649
Ali Be Warned	4	G	1	0	0	0	48
Ali Brocco	5	G	3	0	0	0	147
Ali Dare Me	4	F	9	0	0	0	1,277
Ali Dove	4	F	8	0	0	0	900
Ali G.	7	M	10	2	1	0	6,944
Ali Olah	3	F	6	1	0	0	16,143
Ali On the Sly	3	F	1	0	0	0	0
Ali Online	3	F	7	0	0	1	6,640
Ali Oop Geni	5	M	11	1	4	2	8,737
Ali P Slick	2	F	3	0	0	1	1,550
Ali the Cat	2	F	6	0	0	1	899
Ali Won	2	C	2	0	0	1	1,997
Alias Blackout	4	G	9	0	0	1	1,260
Alias Special	5	M	1	0	0	1	880
Alibi Expert	6	M	7	2	2	2	8,866
Alibob	3	F	13	1	3	3	62,980
Alic From Dallas	2	F	5	1	1	0	7,685
Alice From Marigny	5	G	12	3	2	3	87,340
Alice in Wonder	4	F	2	0	0	0	250
Alice Nevada	6	M	13	4	3	3	45,934
Alice Rose	5	M	6	0	0	1	4,225
Alice's Blue Gown	4	F	17	2	4	4	25,444
Alice's Notebook	7	G	15	5	2	3	73,445
Alices Silver Lady	4	F	10	1	1	4	53,980
Alicia (PER)	4	F	10	1	0	1	12,230
Alicias Quick Draw	4	G	4	0	0	0	0
Alicita My Love	3	F	3	2	1	0	31,426
Alicnator	3	G	12	1	1	1	4,511
Alidanjay	3	F	8	0	0	0	648
Alien	5	G	6	0	0	0	1,380
Alienated	4	F	9	3	1	2	81,625
Alienist	5	G	4	0	0	1	3,672
Alie's Code Red	3	C	2	0	0	0	108
Alie's Del Prado	2	C	3	0	1	1	7,130
Alii Kai	2	F	2	1	0	0	7,458
Alii Kat Al	2	F	7	1	0	1	4,466
Alilbitofhope	5	M	1	0	0	0	0
Alina Alina	4	F	14	2	1	3	62,170
Alipalooza	3	F	15	2	2	4	18,980
Ali's Glori	4	F	5	1	4	0	5,460
Ali's Gold	3	G	2	1	0	0	11,000
Ali's Honor	2	C	3	0	0	0	0
Ali's Miss Leader	3	F	9	0	3	3	13,996
Ali's Pride	3	C	7	1	0	1	20,020
Ali's Rose	5	M	8	0	2	1	6,240
Ali's Shadow	4	G	1	0	0	0	0
Alishowest	3	G	14	2	1	0	14,442
Alison Kate	6	M	8	0	0	2	3,870
Alison's Winner	6	M	8	3	1	1	105,644
Alitabithot	2	F	1	0	0	0	120
Alittle Bit Spunky	4	C	5	0	0	0	1,259
Alittlebitbrassy	5	M	9	0	1	4	26,630
Alittlebitofheaven	3	F	9	0	2	0	3,841
Alittlebitofkash	5	M	6	1	0	0	3,020
Alittlegirlsdance	3	F	5	0	0	0	2,145
Alittlehardtohold	4	F	10	1	1	0	4,596
Alittlemoresauce	5	M	1	0	0	0	0
Aljeson's Prospect	6	H	3	0	0	0	0
Alkali Ike	5	H	5	0	0	1	2,750
Alkarnak	6	G	9	1	2	2	13,180
Alke	3	C	4	2	1	0	77,600
Alki Run	6	G	9	3	2	2	20,702
Alkris Baby	2	F	1	0	0	0	455
All a Blur	5	M	16	0	1	3	5,776
All Ablaze	3	F	9	2	1	1	64,925
All About Conner	4	G	1	0	0	0	651
All About Elsie	3	F	15	1	3	1	13,318
All About Eve	3	F	9	3	0	0	23,032
All About Mary	2	F	8	0	3	0	4,720
All About Me	4	C	13	3	0	3	26,008
All About Money	5	H	1	0	0	0	86
All About You Bob	4	G	12	2	0	2	14,320
All Academic	3	C	2	0	0	0	1,560
All Access	5	H	1	0	0	0	100
All Ahead Full	3	C	6	0	0	0	584
All American Blond	2	F	2	0	0	0	500
All American Blue	3	G	8	2	2	1	70,558
All American Chris	4	G	6	2	1	0	42,764
All American Ernie	2	G	12	2	2	2	19,105
All American Girl	4	F	7	0	0	0	300
All and All	3	G	12	1	3	2	14,608
All Apologies	5	M	6	2	1	1	17,071
All Around Town	3	C	5	0	2	1	9,080
All Ashore	2	C	2	0	0	0	0
All At Once	3	F	4	1	1	0	25,010
All Best Wishes	6	M	6	0	1	1	3,640
All Bluff	2	C	1	0	0	0	0
All by Chance	3	F	12	3	0	3	20,168
All Canadian Kid	5	G	14	1	1	1	2,178
All Cat	3	G	8	0	1	1	7,000
All Circuits Go	2	F	2	0	0	0	1,775
All Class	6	G	7	1	0	0	6,534
All Dash	5	M	14	1	1	2	7,223
All Day All Night	2	F	3	0	0	0	135
All Day Long	5	G	16	3	4	3	18,979
All Disco	2	C	2	2	0	0	16,500
All Ears	4	F	12	1	2	0	8,235
All Electric	2	F	2	1	0	0	27,815
All for Me	6	M	6	1	0	0	8,470
All for Now	2	C	1	0	0	0	105
All for One	5	M	11	1	1	1	3,878
All for Sunny	5	M	5	0	0	0	180
All for the Game	3	F	6	2	0	1	6,852
All Four Chads	4	F	10	0	0	1	2,136
All Geared Up	4	G	13	0	1	2	4,635
All Glitter	3	G	3	1	0	1	10,700
All Gone Cat	4	G	6	1	0	0	12,321
All Gone John	2	G	6	1	1	0	14,050
All Gong (GB)	9	G	2	0	0	0	9,231
All Great	5	G	11	1	0	0	4,442
All Hail Stormy	2	C	2	0	0	1	4,950
All Hyped Up	3	F	5	0	0	0	740
All I Got	5	G	6	4	0	1	32,770
All in Favor	4	G	11	1	2	2	32,200
All in the Book	11	G	4	0	0	0	839
All in the Gate	8	G	9	1	1	2	7,514
All Initials	8	G	7	0	0	0	654
All Inspired	3	G	12	1	2	3	29,433
All Irish	2	G	7	0	2	0	9,710
All Is Bright	5	M	2	0	0	0	0
All Is Calm	2	C	1	0	0	1	1,573
All Is Gold	4	C	1	0	0	0	330
All Is Rosey	6	M	11	0	1	1	4,425
All It Is	3	C	6	0	0	1	1,570
All Knight Music	3	G	15	0	0	3	15,122
All Line	4	G	13	1	5	0	26,340
All Majick	2	G	1	0	0	0	156
All My Dreams	8	M	8	0	0	0	711
All My Yesterdays	3	F	9	0	0	1	5,193
All N the Game	3	G	10	2	2	2	15,168
All Net	3	C	9	0	0	0	1,372
All Night Party	3	C	8	0	1	0	4,441
All of Me	4	F	8	0	4	1	27,553
All Okie	5	H	12	0	0	3	1,833
All Or Nothing	7	M	6	1	1	0	10,951
All Out Springs	4	G	9	0	0	2	5,836
All Over the Citi	6	H	18	2	0	4	21,933
All Over the World	3	G	5	0	0	1	929
All Pent Up	5	G	13	0	1	1	2,884
All Power	2	G	9	2	0	2	21,675
All Prayers	3	F	1	0	0	0	118
All Pride	4	F	4	0	0	0	309
All Purpose	4	G	5	2	2	0	19,558

Horse	Age	Sex	Sts	1st	2d	3d	Won	Horse	Age	Sex	Sts	1st	2d	3d	Won
All Quacked Up	7	M	6	0	3	2	8,358	Alleynedale	5	M	1	0	0	0	155
All Right Kathy	2	F	2	0	0	0	232	Alleyquoit	8	H	1	0	0	0	0
All Rumor	10	G	15	0	4	4	20,134	Alley's Derby	4	G	9	3	1	0	29,411
All Said and Done	6	G	11	0	0	0	524	Alley's Princess	4	F	1	0	0	0	0
All Sams Jazz	8	G	8	1	1	1	6,010	Alley's Rainbow	3	F	12	1	1	1	21,800
All Seymoura	3	F	12	2	2	1	22,820	Allez Chris	4	C	10	1	0	2	7,160
All Souped Up	2	G	5	0	0	0	2,640	Algonoquit	5	G	10	0	1	0	1,643
All Star Frank	3	G	6	1	1	1	42,120	Allgoodtogo	4	C	4	0	1	0	11,060
All Star Girl	3	F	6	0	3	0	6,258	Allie Boy	4	G	7	1	0	0	3,330
All Star Lover	4	G	10	1	3	1	115,304	Allie Ohlee	4	F	12	2	3	0	19,996
All Star Player	3	C	1	0	0	0	0	Allied Wonder	3	F	4	0	0	0	1,780
All Sweetness	5	M	1	0	0	0	504	Allie's Angel	3	F	4	0	1	0	1,825
All Talk	3	C	2	0	0	1	6,400	Allie's Excavator	5	G	13	2	2	1	52,871
All Teed Up	3	C	3	1	1	0	18,400	Allie's Fund	3	F	8	3	3	1	64,367
All Terrain	3	G	8	1	1	0	5,960	Allie's Hope	4	F	5	3	0	1	27,940
All That and More	7	M	5	1	1	0	5,320	Allies Love	5	M	11	1	2	2	9,114
All That Glitters	9	M	7	3	0	1	95,716	Allie's Punch	4	C	2	0	0	0	2,880
All That Magic	4	G	4	0	0	0	960	Allie's Star	4	F	6	0	0	0	454
All That Sass	3	F	6	0	0	2	3,140	Allie's Warrior	4	G	15	3	0	1	12,868
All the Boys	6	G	4	2	2	0	151,400	Allieslildiamond	3	F	1	0	0	0	100
All the Gears	6	H	2	0	0	1	11,700	Alliesunrun	6	M	12	1	3	2	22,324
All the Girls	6	M	11	3	1	0	11,550	Alligator Mouth	2	G	1	0	0	1	1,092
All the Honor	3	F	10	4	0	2	93,354	Alligator Pattie	5	M	14	2	0	0	5,525
All the Loot	5	G	11	5	0	2	73,080	Allinduetime	7	M	1	0	0	0	47
All the Marbles	8	G	6	0	1	0	1,492	Allino	6	M	9	3	1	1	27,365
All the Numbers	3	C	3	1	0	0	13,890	Alli's Dream	2	F	9	0	4	0	7,990
All the Tricks	3	F	7	1	1	1	12,000	Allison's Cat	3	F	12	2	1	1	13,254
All the Way	3	C	3	0	0	2	10,310	Allison's Eyes	4	F	5	0	1	2	11,460
All Things French	4	G	7	1	4	0	28,636	Allison's Hope	2	F	2	0	0	0	195
All to True	2	G	2	0	0	0	0	Allisons Smile	4	G	14	1	1	1	38,769
All too Groovy	4	F	1	0	1	0	600	Allnall	3	C	8	1	1	1	9,700
All too Often	4	F	8	0	0	0	491	Allocation	4	F	11	1	1	1	32,305
All True	2	C	5	1	2	0	41,800	Allofeverything	2	F	4	1	0	0	16,440
All We Can Stand	7	G	3	0	0	0	0	Allondra	6	M	9	2	0	1	9,851
All We Have	3	F	7	2	1	1	11,945	Allonym	8	M	2	0	0	0	0
All Weekend Long	3	F	8	2	0	3	57,010	Allou	3	F	5	0	1	0	6,600
All Winner (ARG)	4	G	3	0	2	0	12,700	Allourwishes	2	F	5	2	1	1	13,622
All Wound Up	6	M	3	0	0	0	0	Allover	4	C	4	2	1	0	72,800
All Y'all	4	G	13	1	0	1	3,922	Allovertheplace	5	G	10	1	0	2	4,598
Alla Breve	3	G	9	0	0	0	271	Already	4	G	8	2	4	0	23,870
Alla Tigger	6	H	7	2	0	0	5,905	Allrightea	3	G	6	3	0	0	9,677
Allai	5	G	8	0	5	1	12,889	Allrightjack	3	G	8	0	0	1	2,273
Allamerican Beauty	2	F	6	1	1	2	43,170	All's Quiet	5	H	1	0	0	0	0
Allamerican Bertie	4	F	3	2	0	0	180,000	All's Well Slewpy	3	G	6	1	2	1	5,512
Allan G.	3	G	10	3	0	1	15,310	Allspice	3	F	4	0	1	1	49,302
Allans Money	5	H	14	0	2	2	8,010	Allstar Blues	4	G	6	0	1	3	7,100
Alldafax	2	G	1	0	0	0	145	Allstate Performer	4	G	16	0	2	3	7,349
Alleged Feu	8	G	15	7	2	1	10,940	Allswellendswell	3	F	14	2	1	2	21,150
Alleged Force	5	H	5	1	0	0	3,980	Alltappedout	4	F	11	3	2	2	61,104
Alleged Halo	2	F	2	0	0	0	0	Allthat N Thensome	2	F	2	0	0	0	0
Alleged Light	3	F	15	2	1	1	22,792	Allthatnabagochips	3	G	6	0	1	0	4,860
Alleged Storm	6	H	8	1	0	3	4,694	Allthatwhite	3	C	1	0	0	0	0
Alleged Style	5	G	7	1	0	0	3,460	Allthechips	3	C	9	1	0	3	9,170
Alleged Wager	3	C	3	0	0	0	0	Allthewayalydeed	3	C	2	0	0	0	280
Alleged Whisper	3	F	11	3	2	1	97,070	Allthewaygone	3	G	5	0	0	0	375
Allegedly an Angel	5	M	2	0	0	0	120	Allthewaytothemint	4	F	1	0	0	0	0
Allegra's Affair	2	F	3	0	0	1	1,575	Alltime Blues	5	G	11	1	0	3	4,164
Allegro Lady	2	F	3	0	1	0	5,615	Alltroienne	4	F	4	0	1	1	7,580
Allen Eugene	6	G	13	0	1	0	796	Alluded	4	G	11	1	0	2	6,652
Allen O Allen	6	G	20	1	1	1	6,769	Allurable	4	F	8	4	0	1	19,705
Allen's Angel	3	F	6	0	1	0	4,615	Allure l'Amour	5	M	8	0	0	1	1,827
Allens Blessing	3	F	11	5	3	3	85,100	Alluring	4	F	7	0	4	1	45,140
Allen's Goldgorian	6	G	11	1	1	2	10,130	Alluring Trapp	4	F	18	0	1	3	4,076
Allen's Heiress	3	F	8	0	0	0	593	Allwood	3	C	7	3	0	1	76,025
Allen's Jet	3	F	8	0	0	0	0	Ally McSqueal	3	F	4	0	0	1	1,260
Allen's Last	4	C	1	0	0	0	0	Ally Prospector	6	H	5	1	0	0	1,176
Allen's Ms	4	F	8	0	1	1	2,884	Ally Scats	4	F	7	2	1	2	14,730
Allen's Navigator	2	C	2	0	0	0	0	Allynn's Deal	2	C	4	0	0	2	6,020
Allen's On a Roll	3	G	5	0	0	0	787	Allys Thunder	3	G	4	1	0	0	5,370
Allen's Protege	5	G	7	0	0	0	0	Ally's Valentine	5	M	5	0	0	0	1,032
Allen's Sphinx	6	H	5	0	1	0	4,706	Alma Dancer	9	G	9	1	2	3	8,231
Allensky	3	C	6	0	2	0	9,880	Alma Mater	6	M	2	0	0	0	598
Allenswood	3	C	8	2	1	0	21,680	Alma's Mill	3	F	9	1	0	0	11,052
Aller Baby	3	G	18	1	1	3	13,702	Almaty	5	M	4	0	1	0	3,427
Allerooyah	5	G	13	2	0	0	10,320	Almaz	4	C	5	0	0	0	769
Alley Ack	4	F	4	0	0	0	340	Almenora	6	M	14	1	1	2	18,821
Alley Creek	2	F	1	0	0	1	1,375	Almiddina (IRE)	6	M	1	0	1	0	9,600
Alley Gal	4	F	2	0	0	0	188	Almighty Above	4	G	11	2	4	1	12,286
Alleycat Coat	5	M	3	0	0	0	1,240	Almighty Cochise	4	G	14	1	2	1	7,291

RECORDS OF HORSES

Horse	Age	Sex	Sts	1st	2d	3d	Won
Almitra	4	F	6	1	0	1	1,139
Almond Blossom	3	F	4	1	1	1	11,625
Almond Eyes	3	G	12	4	3	3	32,921
Almost a Scandal	6	M	6	0	0	0	111
Almost a Valentine	5	M	9	4	2	0	24,309
Almost Allegend	2	G	3	0	0	0	1,381
Almost Amos	2	G	1	0	0	0	0
Almost Aprom Queen	3	F	4	1	1	0	23,890
Almost Dancing (IRE)	2	F	5	1	0	0	12,455
Almost Dissuaded	3	F	13	0	1	1	18,112
Almost Fooled	3	F	2	1	1	0	12,540
Almost Golden	9	G	12	3	0	2	27,826
Almost Holy	3	C	10	1	3	0	18,795
Almost Home	5	H	4	0	0	2	11,324
Almost Justice	3	F	1	0	0	0	0
Almost Magic	5	M	15	3	5	3	66,930
Almost Misty	4	F	6	1	0	2	6,772
Almost Plum	5	M	11	2	3	3	18,453
Almost There	7	M	6	1	2	1	22,902
Almostagentleman	2	G	7	0	1	0	4,360
Almostashar	5	H	1	0	0	0	1,020
Almuhathir	5	H	10	2	1	2	97,658
Almungid	4	C	15	1	2	1	12,165
Alnaab the Gold	5	G	6	0	2	0	5,400
Alnaabadancer	6	G	8	0	0	1	1,362
Alnahaam (IRE)	5	H	5	1	0	0	22,500
Alnaskra	5	G	8	3	0	1	15,355
Alnbill	4	G	6	1	0	0	8,250
Alnoba	4	G	3	0	0	1	907
Aloe Cat	3	F	2	0	0	0	0
Aloesha	7	G	8	1	1	0	1,902
Aloha Bold	5	H	5	2	1	2	62,560
Aloha Bound	3	G	1	0	0	0	0
Aloha Carol	5	M	1	0	0	1	1,045
Aloha Class	3	F	16	1	1	0	8,979
Aloha Hagan	4	G	10	2	1	1	4,491
Aloha Hula	4	F	2	0	0	0	0
Aloha I Got Gold	4	G	7	0	0	0	432
Aloha Lola	3	F	10	3	4	1	12,746
Aloha Motel	5	M	3	0	1	0	3,179
Aloha Mya	2	C	6	1	3	1	43,400
Aloha Rosa	3	F	11	0	1	2	13,050
Aloha Seven	3	F	2	0	0	0	825
Aloha Superity	9	G	5	1	1	1	6,393
Alohalani	3	F	8	1	1	1	10,939
Aloha's Girl	6	M	10	1	3	1	16,760
Aloma's Cobra	4	C	7	0	4	1	7,268
Aloma's Daisey	2	F	2	0	0	0	140
Alone At Home	5	G	12	0	2	3	11,645
Alone At the Alter	4	F	6	1	0	1	6,910
Along Came George	6	M	3	1	1	0	4,392
Along Came Jules	3	C	1	0	0	0	0
Along Came Mary	5	M	6	1	2	0	66,260
Alongcameachance	2	F	3	0	0	0	780
Alongcameaspider	3	F	1	0	0	0	0
Alongcametheprince	10	G	7	0	0	0	910
Alosa	4	F	4	0	0	0	620
Alota Cat	3	G	8	0	2	3	6,435
Alota Green	3	G	13	1	0	3	11,238
Alotaboo	4	F	1	0	0	0	0
Alotacherokee	2	F	3	1	0	0	7,770
Alotawanna	4	G	6	1	5	0	35,110
Alotta Numbers	5	G	12	2	4	3	67,880
Alotta Spirit	3	F	9	2	1	0	31,999
Alotta Threshold	3	G	12	1	2	4	7,426
Alotta Tomfoolery	2	C	3	0	1	0	1,660
Alottadar	2	C	5	0	0	1	10,920
Alottafunfortherun	4	F	11	0	0	1	4,390
Alovut	7	G	11	1	3	1	6,183
Aloween	7	G	3	1	0	0	4,088
Alowmdah	5	H	9	0	0	4	8,520
Alozaina (IRE)	4	F	9	1	2	1	72,880
Alpena Magic	13	G	14	1	1	2	9,060
Alpenfest	2	G	3	2	0	0	86,205
Alpenwald	2	F	9	1	0	0	38,234
Alpha Capo	2	G	4	0	1	1	10,860
Alpha Heat	4	F	5	3	2	0	199,370
Alpha King	3	G	3	1	0	0	36,360
Alpha Lady	3	F	6	1	0	1	2,830
Alpha Light	3	F	1	0	1	0	11,760
Alpha Mama	4	F	2	0	0	1	6,600
Alpha Max	3	G	13	1	0	1	8,218
Alpha Ray	4	F	5	0	0	0	0
Alpha Saphire	3	F	8	2	1	1	211,470
Alpha Star Omega	2	C	8	0	0	0	2,880
Alpha Strike	5	G	14	1	2	4	18,300
Alpha Traders	8	G	3	0	0	0	450
Alphabet Gold	3	F	5	0	2	1	7,410
Alphabet Song	4	F	9	2	0	1	29,940
Alphabet Storm	2	G	5	0	0	1	2,340
Alphabetic	3	G	4	2	1	0	33,220
Alphabetical	4	C	11	2	5	1	86,320
Alphabetizing	4	C	7	0	1	3	4,185
Alphabetty	4	F	11	0	0	1	1,788
Alphacat	4	F	12	1	1	2	10,390
Alphagirl	3	F	7	1	0	1	6,485
Alpha's Halo	8	G	4	0	0	0	160
Alpha's Target	4	C	13	0	2	0	2,128
Alpine Creek	2	F	3	0	0	0	580
Alpine Mountain	3	C	7	1	1	2	28,240
Alpine Pass	4	F	4	1	2	1	34,740
Alpine Ridge	9	G	9	0	1	1	1,480
Alpine Silver	5	M	12	1	3	0	8,960
Alpine Singer	3	F	10	2	2	2	77,020
Alpine Walk	4	F	5	0	3	1	12,600
Alpler	3	G	3	1	0	0	17,977
Already Taken	2	G	5	2	0	0	28,920
Alright Already	5	G	9	1	0	1	19,335
Alroyed	4	G	6	2	0	0	16,980
Al's Dearly Bred	6	G	7	3	2	0	125,300
Als Dream Boy	5	G	11	1	0	1	7,707
Al's Gamble	3	G	2	0	0	1	2,430
Al's Gift	4	G	4	0	0	0	165
Al's Little Squaw	3	F	15	2	1	1	11,711
Al's Music	6	G	3	1	0	1	1,960
Al's Odds	5	G	12	2	1	3	29,022
Al's Silver Ghost	2	C	6	0	0	1	2,280
Alsace	3	G	2	0	0	0	320
Alsaleet	5	H	2	0	0	0	0
Alsalsa	3	C	15	2	2	1	54,155
Alstemeria (IRE)	4	F	4	0	2	0	19,720
Alston Fair	6	G	5	2	0	1	10,640
Alstott	3	G	10	1	1	0	9,306
Alta Aire	2	F	2	2	0	0	42,084
Alta Clocker	4	F	11	1	3	2	22,263
Altamira	3	F	7	1	0	0	6,124
Altamont Pass	4	G	3	0	0	0	226
Alter Ego	6	G	10	2	1	2	58,335
Alternate	4	F	8	2	3	1	164,591
Alternate Verse	2	F	4	1	1	0	25,040
Alternative	3	G	3	0	0	0	755
Altiro	2	G	3	0	0	0	856
Altitune	4	G	1	0	0	0	320
Alto Maestro (FR)	5	G	3	1	1	0	7,200
Alton Bay	3	C	9	0	4	0	35,760
Altria	3	F	1	0	0	0	0
Altruistic	3	F	3	1	1	0	18,560
Altura	7	G	15	2	0	4	13,028
Alumadog	3	G	7	0	0	1	1,273
Alumni	6	G	16	3	5	3	80,450
Alunite	5	H	7	2	1	1	36,012
Alvaro Al	3	C	1	0	0	0	0
Alvin P.	4	G	4	0	2	0	1,983
Alvis	4	G	9	1	1	3	8,533
Alwajd	2	C	2	0	0	0	0
Always a Fox	4	F	9	0	0	0	878
Always a Gamble	4	F	16	1	1	0	9,871
Always a Gem	2	F	1	0	0	0	370
Always a Player	4	G	15	3	2	3	22,488
Always A. E.	7	G	8	0	0	2	1,534
Always Alert	2	G	2	1	0	0	14,950
Always Annie's	3	F	8	1	3	1	34,234
Always Awesome	3	F	4	1	0	0	42,900
Always Be Sunny	3	F	4	0	0	0	3,225
Always Clever	6	M	6	0	0	0	0
Always Colleen	2	F	1	0	0	0	0
Always Crown Royal	4	F	9	1	0	0	6,465
Always Daring	3	F	3	0	1	0	1,450

Horse	Age	Sex	Sts	1st	2d	3d	Won
Always Devilish	3	F	12	1	3	1	15,037
Always Dreaming	3	F	11	1	1	3	18,778
Always Excessive	3	F	1	0	0	1	6,600
Always Fancy	3	F	2	0	0	0	264
Always Fighting	3	G	16	1	3	1	10,544
Always Fire	4	F	4	0	0	0	380
Always First	4	G	7	0	0	3	4,015
Always Friendly	4	G	5	1	0	0	18,180
Always Game	6	H	3	1	2	0	28,140
Always Giving	5	M	3	0	1	0	1,247
Always Honorable	3	C	7	1	1	2	11,665
Always Hope	2	F	2	0	0	0	0
Always in Action	4	C	2	0	0	0	350
Always in Front	4	F	11	3	2	2	24,450
Always in the Red	3	G	16	2	4	2	45,297
Always Indy Mood	3	G	14	0	3	5	12,361
Always Lisa	5	M	11	3	2	0	18,215
Always Love	5	M	2	0	0	0	0
Always Meggie	5	M	1	0	0	0	0
Always My Lady	3	F	12	3	0	0	13,765
Always On	10	G	1	0	0	0	0
Always On Time	5	G	15	2	0	0	28,675
Always On Top	4	F	4	0	2	0	4,655
Always Original	2	G	3	0	0	2	16,993
Always Precious	4	F	17	2	1	3	13,664
Always Present	2	C	2	0	0	0	720
Always Ready	4	F	3	1	1	1	22,280
Always Remember	3	G	7	0	0	2	15,550
Always Smiling	3	F	3	0	0	1	1,000
Always Softly	4	F	3	1	0	1	5,713
Always Split Aces	4	F	7	0	3	1	28,757
Always Stormin	5	H	1	0	0	0	190
Always Surprizing	3	C	4	0	0	0	0
Always Take Cash	4	G	5	1	0	0	8,855
Always the Winner	4	G	12	2	1	1	42,314
Always Timely	5	M	11	0	2	4	10,251
Always Tool Time	5	H	8	1	1	1	12,105
Always Twining	5	M	6	0	0	1	6,140
Always Valiant	3	C	4	0	1	0	3,655
Always You	7	M	10	0	1	1	3,858
Alwaysacontender	6	G	10	0	2	2	31,462
Alwaysanet	5	G	12	0	1	3	5,000
Alwaysbepleasant	3	F	1	1	0	0	6,840
Alwaysinbloom	4	F	2	1	0	1	13,490
Alwaysintrouble	4	G	6	0	0	0	670
Alwaysonmymind	2	F	2	0	0	0	600
Alwayswantmore	2	C	1	0	0	0	0
Aly Aly	5	M	2	0	0	0	0
Aly Aly Free	5	M	14	0	0	2	5,201
Aly Aly O	6	G	14	3	0	2	69,952
Aly Aly Oxen Free	8	G	8	3	1	1	10,674
Aly Babble	3	F	5	1	1	0	7,038
Aly Baghdad	6	M	3	0	0	0	2,580
Aly Bid Six	6	G	2	0	0	1	210
Aly Boom Ah Yea	6	H	9	0	0	0	1,083
Aly Bubba	4	G	6	1	1	1	53,135
Aly Champ	5	M	8	1	1	1	18,109
Aly Kathy	9	M	5	0	0	0	252
Aly Mania	6	H	14	3	3	1	25,226
Aly Order	5	G	15	4	2	2	20,707
Aly Performer	7	M	9	1	1	1	8,831
Aly Queen	4	F	14	2	3	1	22,152
Aly Rally	4	G	7	0	1	1	9,030
Aly Ron	5	G	9	2	1	4	25,090
Aly Victory	4	G	14	0	4	1	30,125
Aly Vita	5	G	7	0	2	1	4,244
Alyazuli	2	C	10	1	2	0	29,050
Alybea	5	M	8	0	2	0	3,048
Alyblues	4	C	7	0	0	0	900
Alybri	7	G	6	1	0	2	4,120
Alybull	6	G	2	0	0	0	0
Alybye	3	F	9	4	2	0	29,240
Alycheq	4	C	8	1	2	1	22,950
Alychois	6	M	5	0	0	1	2,315
Alydarling	4	G	6	1	0	1	8,000
Alydars Lost Child	2	C	1	0	0	0	126
Alydeed's Deal	4	F	11	1	1	0	4,416
Alydeed's Leader	4	G	13	1	7	2	21,534
Alydelta	5	G	13	1	1	2	36,770
Alyforce	8	G	9	0	0	1	1,238
Alygo	3	F	3	0	0	0	103
Alygrey	4	F	8	2	1	1	17,210
Alyharp	3	F	3	0	0	0	359
Alyjeb	7	H	5	0	1	0	3,646
Alyjon	5	G	3	0	0	0	83
Alylivia	6	M	5	0	0	0	5,400
Alylouis	4	G	6	1	1	0	5,274
Alymill	7	G	6	1	2	0	6,151
Alymir	8	G	6	0	0	1	2,300
Alyode	2	G	3	0	0	0	202
Alyou	5	H	10	0	3	1	10,982
Alyplace	4	G	14	2	5	2	12,103
Alyria	5	M	1	0	0	0	0
Alyrida's Storm	2	F	1	0	0	0	0
Alyround the Flag	4	F	7	0	1	0	3,100
Alyrunj	6	M	9	0	0	0	215
Aly's Alley	7	H	1	0	0	0	0
Aly's Alpha Boy	2	C	3	0	0	0	1,370
Aly's Fever	5	G	5	0	0	2	2,080
Alys Good Deed	5	M	10	3	3	1	16,810
Alys Island Charm	5	M	6	2	2	0	12,020
Aly's Java Gold	3	F	1	0	0	0	0
Aly's Leader	6	M	14	5	1	3	61,626
Aly's Little Star	3	F	9	0	0	1	2,032
Aly's Magic	4	G	3	0	0	0	146
Aly's Martini	3	C	1	0	0	1	2,399
Aly's Open	2	F	1	0	0	0	100
Aly's Ticonderoga	3	F	1	0	0	0	0
Aly's War Lady	3	F	4	0	0	1	952
Alys Wildcat	3	G	3	0	0	0	360
Alysage	7	M	14	0	4	4	8,566
Alysanna	6	M	4	0	0	0	218
Alysara Dandi	8	M	4	0	0	0	242
Alyshar	4	G	11	1	0	1	16,561
Alysheba Storm	3	C	4	0	0	0	0
Alysheba's Angel	4	F	7	0	1	0	1,508
Alyshebagood	4	F	8	1	0	0	5,580
Alyson Rambles On	5	M	9	0	3	0	10,210
Alysweep	3	R	8	3	2	0	263,680
Alyswell	8	G	17	3	5	5	49,430
Alytress	5	M	11	0	1	0	1,658
Alyvia	3	F	5	1	0	0	30,300
Alyzig	6	H	3	1	1	0	60,290
Am a Dancer	7	G	21	0	4	5	9,415
Am a Pal	12	G	2	0	0	0	0
Am a Ranch	3	C	4	0	0	0	678
Am a Silver Thread	9	G	11	1	0	0	2,809
Am All Jazzed Up	4	G	8	1	0	1	6,862
Am I Too	9	G	5	0	1	1	4,234
Ama Missprint	2	F	4	2	0	0	21,557
Ama Ray	3	F	4	1	1	0	17,425
Amachance	3	F	7	1	1	0	10,504
Amador	2	C	1	0	1	0	6,600
Amafastbaby	4	G	10	2	2	1	11,615
Amamia	2	F	1	0	0	0	460
Amanda Louise (IRE)	3	F	6	1	1	2	15,420
Amanda Lynn	2	F	6	1	1	1	14,088
Amanda Marie	2	F	3	1	0	0	7,040
Amanda Mia	5	M	9	3	0	1	10,530
Amanda Rules	5	M	3	0	0	0	2,850
Amandancer	3	F	6	1	1	0	19,160
Amanda's Babe	2	G	3	0	0	0	0
Amanda's Crown	4	F	6	1	1	0	12,654
Amanda's Deelite	4	F	3	1	0	1	13,895
Amanda's Fancy	2	C	1	1	0	0	13,461
Amanda's First	7	G	1	0	0	0	0
Amanda's Rose	3	F	1	0	0	0	0
Amandasgoldngliter	4	F	5	0	1	0	4,062
Amanuensis	2	F	5	0	0	3	13,960
Amapola Star	4	F	1	0	0	0	0
Amapola's Wish	4	F	1	0	0	0	0
Amaral A. B. C.	3	G	1	0	0	0	0
Amaras	2	F	6	2	2	0	29,616
Amarelle	4	F	2	2	0	0	43,200
Amarettiornot	4	G	9	0	1	0	2,479
Amarettorumble	5	G	6	0	0	1	1,950
Amaretto	3	F	12	1	1	2	51,420
Amarillo Star	6	G	13	1	2	4	14,202

RECORDS OF HORSES

Horse	Age	Sex	Sts	1st	2d	3d	Won
Amarodeo	3	C	4	0	1	0	1,800
Amasoldier	3	G	3	1	0	0	12,940
Amateur Hour	2	G	5	0	0	1	4,680
Amazem Grace	2	F	6	1	1	1	17,080
Amazement	3	G	9	1	0	1	22,400
Amazer	2	F	5	1	3	1	55,300
Amazing Ben	6	G	13	1	3	2	5,565
Amazing Capt. Mike	5	G	1	0	0	0	0
Amazing G	2	C	7	0	0	2	5,030
Amazing Glace	3	F	5	1	0	0	8,730
Amazing Glory	3	F	4	0	0	0	900
Amazing Harmony	4	F	1	0	0	0	0
Amazing Lady	4	F	6	1	3	0	49,320
Amazing Linda	5	M	3	0	0	0	164
Amazing Max	4	G	6	4	0	0	19,325
Amazing Ruckus	4	G	5	0	0	0	0
Amazing Secret	3	F	4	0	0	0	450
Amazing Silver	6	M	2	0	0	0	134
Amazing Slew	5	H	7	0	0	0	482
Amazing Story	3	F	18	1	1	1	12,900
Amazing Sue	4	F	9	2	0	1	21,558
Amazing Thunder	3	F	8	3	0	2	39,922
Amazing Truth	8	M	7	0	2	1	7,026
Amazinglygraced	4	F	17	2	4	5	13,146
Amazon Ace	6	H	6	1	0	1	17,689
Amazon Adam	5	M	10	1	0	1	10,091
Amazon Court	5	H	4	0	0	2	6,155
Amazon Mist	5	M	6	0	0	1	440
Amazon River	5	G	2	0	0	0	0
Amazonian Brand On	3	F	3	0	0	0	311
Amazonian Jade	4	G	6	3	0	2	76,470
Amazonian Stalker	3	F	7	1	0	0	10,236
Amazonian Wish	4	C	9	0	2	1	10,300
Ambe	8	H	11	1	3	1	17,704
Ambe Two	4	G	17	3	1	2	12,536
Amber Ale	5	G	14	2	6	1	46,511
Amber Blue	3	F	4	0	0	0	521
Amber Comet	6	M	12	0	2	1	17,735
Amber Hills	3	F	10	3	0	1	144,900
Amber Jule	3	F	8	2	0	5	41,411
Amber Myth	3	F	2	0	0	0	0
Amber Note	3	F	5	1	1	2	10,005
Amber On the Run	3	F	16	1	0	2	8,464
Amber Quick	6	M	11	1	1	1	2,914
Amber Run	4	F	9	0	0	3	2,980
Amber Sky	5	G	7	4	0	1	32,800
Amber Song	4	F	4	1	0	1	8,693
Amber Tides	4	F	3	1	2	0	2,660
Amber Token	4	F	4	2	0	1	37,430
Amber Twilight	3	F	5	2	1	0	31,040
Amber Waves	2	F	1	0	0	0	0
Amberall	3	F	12	2	2	3	34,141
Amber's County	5	M	8	0	0	0	394
Amber's Glow	6	M	17	0	1	3	26,476
Amber's Mischief	4	C	7	1	2	2	14,040
Amber's Way	5	M	7	0	1	1	19,100
Ambersent	5	M	5	1	0	2	23,688
Ambessa Belle	4	F	4	0	0	0	1,228
Ambi's Bro	7	G	15	4	4	3	29,316
Ambition Unbridled	2	F	3	0	2	1	15,100
Ambition's End	6	G	6	1	0	2	4,099
Ambitious	2	G	3	1	0	0	5,460
Ambitious Alibi	5	M	4	1	0	0	6,247
Ambitious Buster	4	G	6	1	1	1	8,278
Ambitious Choice	7	M	12	4	2	4	52,166
Ambitious Dancer	7	G	19	0	1	0	2,784
Ambitious Gulch	2	F	4	0	1	0	2,555
Ambivilent Force	11	G	9	1	0	1	3,320
Ambusher	8	G	4	1	0	1	4,900
Amdor's Nick	7	G	15	2	3	2	11,656
Amedeo	2	F	4	2	0	0	28,720
Amego Mel	5	H	5	1	1	0	3,060
Amelia	5	M	3	0	0	0	2,129
Amelia E.	2	F	1	0	0	0	0
Amen Amen	4	C	5	0	0	0	0
Amen Ben	7	H	1	0	0	0	0
Amen Brother	2	C	5	1	1	1	10,700
Amended Return	3	C	10	1	0	0	8,670
Amere	5	G	17	1	3	1	17,295

Horse	Age	Sex	Sts	1st	2d	3d	Won
Ameri Brass	5	M	1	0	0	0	0
Ameri Brilliance	4	G	10	5	1	0	106,808
Ameri Dream	3	C	5	1	1	0	15,600
Ameri Holly	5	M	5	1	3	0	11,590
Ameri Lady	2	F	1	0	1	0	4,600
Ameri Princess	4	F	4	0	0	1	1,491
Ameribrill	3	G	8	0	1	4	5,450
America	6	G	1	0	0	0	0
America Alive	2	C	4	2	0	0	33,300
America America	2	F	17	3	6	3	298,640
America Reprized	3	C	6	0	0	2	3,144
America the Brave	3	G	6	0	1	0	4,525
America West	3	G	1	0	0	0	582
American All Star	3	G	5	1	2	0	27,734
American Allusion	3	F	1	0	0	0	0
American Anthem	3	F	8	1	4	2	57,400
American Approval	2	G	2	0	0	0	0
American Avenger	2	F	5	0	0	0	1,035
American Band	4	C	5	2	0	0	9,960
American Boundary	3	G	6	0	0	2	5,476
American Boy	3	G	16	2	1	3	26,880
American Bull	3	G	17	3	4	1	21,777
American Byline	2	G	5	0	0	0	3,471
American Cadillac	12	G	2	0	0	1	355
American Candidate	2	C	3	0	0	0	2,460
American Car	8	G	12	1	1	0	9,700
American Cat	3	C	7	0	0	0	2,573
American Century	5	H	4	2	0	0	69,120
American Challenge	3	F	6	1	0	0	15,440
American Charmer	5	G	1	0	0	0	150
American Choice	2	G	2	1	0	0	8,700
American Class	6	H	13	2	3	1	41,035
American Czar	5	G	8	1	0	0	2,926
American Czarina	5	M	3	0	0	0	2,420
American Del Siglo	2	F	1	0	0	0	0
American Deputy	4	C	8	1	2	3	39,681
American Diamond	2	F	5	2	1	0	29,230
American Don	3	G	13	1	3	3	7,565
American Dot Com	6	G	10	4	0	3	17,428
American Dreamer	5	M	8	0	0	0	6,569
American Dreams	2	F	2	0	0	0	390
American Fable	2	G	2	0	0	1	1,425
American Falcon	7	G	1	0	0	0	270
American Fighter	7	G	2	0	0	0	0
American Flagship	3	C	4	0	0	0	257
American Flame	4	F	5	0	0	0	316
American Flash	4	F	1	0	0	0	0
American Forum	4	G	11	1	3	2	53,017
American Freedom	5	G	10	1	2	5	91,500
American Fury	3	C	10	2	2	1	95,376
American Grace	3	F	2	0	0	0	103
American Guy	3	G	4	0	0	0	2,360
American Hero	7	G	13	0	0	4	3,549
American Honey	3	F	2	0	0	0	0
American Hope	2	G	1	0	0	0	0
American in Paris	6	M	7	0	0	1	12,577
American Ingot	3	F	14	2	1	1	12,746
American Jade	2	G	2	0	0	0	390
American Jazz	3	G	3	1	0	0	3,965
American Jewel (NZ)	5	M	5	0	0	1	2,250
American Knockout	3	F	2	0	0	0	125
American Lady	5	M	16	2	2	1	9,981
American Liberty	3	C	7	0	1	3	27,340
American Link	2	C	2	0	0	0	1,144
American Llave	4	F	6	0	0	0	1,144
American Maude	5	M	11	1	0	3	9,689
American Miss	2	F	8	1	1	2	20,910
American Mon	3	C	5	1	1	1	43,900
American Money	4	F	9	0	2	1	19,631
American Moud	2	F	4	0	0	0	365
American Moxie	3	G	7	3	2	1	26,738
American Music	3	G	14	1	2	5	39,380
American Myth	6	G	7	1	0	1	11,432
American Original	3	G	3	0	0	0	400
American Outlaw	3	G	16	1	3	4	17,652
American Pace	9	H	13	3	2	1	12,591
American Pass	7	H	15	2	0	4	16,711
American Pastime	5	G	2	0	0	1	3,855
American Power	2	C	2	0	0	0	1,195

Horse	Age	Sex	Sts	1st	2d	3d	Won
American Prince	5	G	11	0	3	3	33,600
American Profit	4	F	6	0	1	1	6,430
American Proud	3	G	9	3	1	0	25,310
American Quest	3	C	6	1	1	1	42,570
American Red	3	C	1	0	0	0	348
American Resolve	3	C	7	1	1	2	5,254
American Saga	3	F	2	0	1	0	8,800
American Skipper	4	F	8	2	1	1	116,830
American Son	3	C	4	2	1	0	42,160
American Song	3	C	10	0	2	2	28,245
American Star	2	C	3	0	1	0	7,325
American Strike	4	F	8	0	3	1	6,562
American Style	4	C	10	1	3	1	87,050
American Sweets	2	F	2	1	0	0	3,060
American System	4	C	5	0	0	1	11,440
American Thunder	2	C	4	1	1	0	21,410
American Toga	2	C	1	0	0	0	900
American Up There	7	G	15	5	1	2	29,887
American Vision	3	C	5	1	1	1	11,158
American Warrior	4	C	2	0	1	0	8,000
American Winner	3	G	13	0	1	5	8,510
American Writer	4	G	4	0	1	0	3,405
Americas Amazing	6	H	18	1	4	3	10,520
America's Dream	3	G	1	0	0	0	360
America's Dutchess	2	F	2	0	0	0	0
America's Guy	5	H	3	0	1	0	7,200
Americas Hope	2	G	5	1	2	0	14,580
Americas Pride	2	F	11	4	2	1	60,049
America's Princess	3	F	6	1	0	0	3,660
America's Punch	2	F	2	0	0	0	1,850
America's Queen	4	F	5	0	1	1	13,280
America's Roar	3	G	11	1	1	0	17,875
America's Spirit	2	F	3	0	0	0	0
America's Storm	4	C	8	3	1	1	70,770
America's Team	3	G	1	0	0	0	0
Americelebration	4	F	8	1	1	2	12,040
Amerikiss	2	F	7	1	0	0	7,410
Amerikite	7	M	12	0	0	1	1,560
Amerindio (ARG)	6	H	5	1	0	1	31,860
Ameriway	4	F	4	0	0	1	4,970
Amersham	6	H	10	0	0	1	2,287
Amethyst Flight	4	F	11	0	0	0	1,260
Amherst Wildcat	4	G	9	2	1	0	48,468
Amiable Amy	3	F	4	1	1	0	39,660
Amicure	4	F	3	1	0	0	4,554
Amidst Storm	3	F	1	0	0	0	0
Amie de Naskra	4	F	8	1	1	2	22,950
Amien	3	F	5	0	0	1	3,830
Amiga	3	F	2	0	1	0	7,800
Amiran	3	C	3	0	0	0	244
Amirror Ghazi	2	C	1	0	0	1	1,800
Amiwain (FR)	5	H	1	0	0	0	400
Amjaad	5	H	5	0	1	1	16,110
Ammann	2	C	5	0	0	1	2,500
Ammo Bag	6	H	10	1	1	3	9,698
Ammodio	4	G	12	3	2	2	12,693
Ammoexcavate	3	F	5	0	0	0	1,401
Amo Ava'	3	F	1	0	0	0	0
Amo Ebaci	3	G	15	4	1	5	88,958
Amodeed	3	F	13	2	1	2	34,901
Amok	5	H	2	0	0	2	1,000
Amon	3	C	14	3	3	3	76,182
Among My Souvenirs	2	F	1	1	0	0	14,250
Among the Best	5	G	5	0	0	0	220
Amongtheprivileged	4	F	9	2	2	1	26,905
Amonita (GB)	5	M	3	1	0	0	65,665
Amorama (FR)	2	F	6	2	0	1	34,046
Amoreena	2	F	7	0	1	2	6,729
Amores Peregrinos	2	F	2	0	0	0	150
Amoriah	5	M	13	3	4	2	47,075
Amorini	2	F	4	0	0	1	1,540
Amorphous	7	G	4	1	1	0	4,296
Amos's Savage	3	F	9	0	1	1	3,145
Amoure King (IRE)	4	C	1	0	0	0	1,818
Ampersand	3	C	8	1	1	1	12,165
Amphorae	4	F	7	0	0	0	1,500
Ampita	5	M	1	0	0	1	620
Ample's Star	5	M	9	0	0	3	5,000
Amplitude	3	C	5	1	0	1	14,270
Ampsterdam	3	F	1	0	0	0	140
Amptitude	3	F	6	1	0	1	3,340
Amstel River	3	F	5	0	0	0	1,350
Amsterdam Ave	2	C	4	0	0	1	4,620
Amtodd	2	C	5	1	2	0	8,215
Amuffintogo	2	F	6	1	0	1	16,290
Amurado (COL)	3	C	1	0	0	0	0
Amusingly	3	F	9	2	3	0	73,164
Amy 'n Jill	5	M	6	0	0	0	2,550
Amybdancing	5	M	6	0	1	3	16,475
Amygotherway	3	F	12	1	1	1	9,062
Amy's Aces	3	F	1	0	0	0	47
Amy's Believer	6	M	17	1	4	0	17,727
Amy's Falcon	4	F	4	0	0	2	24,268
Amy's First	3	F	8	0	0	0	346
Amy's Hannah	3	F	2	0	0	1	1,260
Amy's Jet	4	C	3	1	0	0	7,990
Amy's Lady	3	F	8	0	0	0	543
Amy's Pearl	4	F	12	0	2	2	4,607
Amys Punch	4	G	5	0	1	0	1,620
Amy's Starr	5	M	3	2	0	0	3,345
Amy's Three	6	M	12	0	2	4	4,728
Amyscharmingway	3	F	8	0	0	0	900
Amzac	3	G	11	2	1	1	19,625
An American Idol	2	G	2	0	1	0	5,250
An Annika Moment	2	F	2	0	1	0	9,400
An Ecstatic Double	8	G	3	0	0	0	763
An Naabi	7	G	12	3	1	3	11,100
An Oscar for Bert	6	G	10	1	2	1	17,240
An Unreal Sham	4	F	3	0	0	0	255
Ana	6	M	12	1	0	0	4,731
Anabatic	3	F	7	1	2	1	31,116
Anabeltaylor	3	F	5	0	4	0	34,860
Anacosta	3	F	9	2	1	1	22,460
Anadarko W Q	4	G	1	0	0	0	0
Anahi	9	M	14	2	1	2	11,705
Analyze	4	F	7	1	2	1	13,090
Anand	5	H	3	0	1	1	3,685
Anapest	2	F	4	2	0	1	38,100
Ana's Lady Bird	2	F	4	2	0	1	65,190
Anasham	2	F	2	0	0	1	2,530
Anasheed	3	C	7	1	0	2	45,980
Anatole's Las Hope	3	G	9	0	0	0	691
Anaturalbluff	4	G	18	1	1	2	7,528
Anatwine	3	F	3	0	0	0	0
Anazeha (CHI)	7	M	3	0	1	1	7,325
Anbar	5	G	12	5	0	4	57,995
Ancestry	3	F	7	0	3	2	16,080
Anchor Alert	4	G	19	3	2	1	35,420
Ancient Beauty	4	F	11	0	2	1	6,222
Ancient City	6	G	9	1	3	0	6,872
Ancient Hill	3	G	13	3	5	0	15,020
Ancient Myth	2	C	3	0	0	2	5,460
Ancient Remedy	3	G	7	1	1	0	25,042
Ancient Ritual	3	G	3	1	1	0	6,400
Ancient Ruins	3	C	3	0	0	0	408
Ancient Ruler	3	G	14	1	2	1	11,852
Ancient Traveler	6	G	4	1	0	0	3,891
Ancient Ways	4	G	14	0	0	1	2,251
And Blues	4	C	6	1	0	0	4,650
And Herecumdejudge	4	G	9	1	0	4	5,666
And Heres to You	3	G	10	1	0	2	5,790
And I	5	G	5	1	0	2	8,579
And Nobody Knows	3	F	11	2	3	1	44,750
And She Hits Me	3	F	4	0	1	0	3,950
And So It Goes	2	G	7	0	1	1	7,260
And That's It	2	F	3	0	0	0	0
And Thats My Story	4	F	9	1	2	0	39,000
Andale Pronto	4	G	6	1	0	3	10,375
Andean Jewel	2	F	1	0	0	0	0
Andean Orchid	4	F	6	0	1	0	420
Andele	5	G	5	0	1	0	1,726
Andelegend	4	C	10	2	1	0	41,260
Andeleisha	4	F	6	0	0	0	414
Andes Pride	5	M	5	0	0	1	1,087
Andimon	8	H	10	3	0	1	19,028
Andonetime	3	F	1	0	0	0	0
Andora Springs	4	F	2	0	0	0	1,220
Andover Boy	2	C	2	0	1	0	2,420

RECORDS OF HORSES

Horse	Age	Sex	Sts	1st	2d	3d	Won
Andover Forest	3	C	9	1	0	2	17,506
Andover Lady	3	F	5	2	1	1	76,533
Andoverend	6	M	5	1	0	1	8,550
Andra's Memory	5	M	8	1	2	0	8,547
Andrea	2	F	7	1	1	2	9,082
Andrea Allstar	5	M	12	3	0	1	13,206
Andrea Jeanne	4	F	15	2	1	2	18,515
Andrea Star	5	M	15	2	2	2	14,338
Andrea's Jet	3	F	10	1	1	1	6,366
Andrea's Mustang	3	G	6	0	1	1	2,876
Andrea's Nurse	5	M	1	0	0	0	0
Andrew C.	3	G	17	2	2	2	8,794
Andrew J	3	C	8	1	0	0	4,870
Andrew the Man	6	G	8	2	1	0	15,069
Andriana	2	F	1	0	0	0	0
Andshe'soff	5	M	4	1	1	0	7,940
Andthe Angels Sing	5	M	4	0	0	0	339
Andy Boy	3	G	2	0	1	0	9,200
Andy Dufresne (GB)	8	G	2	0	0	0	0
Andy Man	2	G	3	1	0	0	4,566
Andy's Candi	3	F	6	0	0	0	0
Andy's Gray Lady	3	F	8	1	2	0	7,892
Andy's Jet	8	G	8	1	0	1	8,445
Andy's Silver	3	F	1	0	0	0	0
Andy'struleymissed	4	G	7	1	2	1	5,590
Anearlyfil	2	F	2	0	0	0	0
Aneat Amaani	2	F	6	0	1	1	7,368
Anegada	2	F	2	0	0	0	145
Anewcat	4	C	8	1	2	2	5,372
Aneysar (IRE)	9	H	1	0	0	0	43
Angel Aglo	2	G	1	0	0	0	651
Angel Approval	4	G	15	2	0	0	33,770
Angel Be Great	4	F	10	2	1	1	19,135
Angel by Day	3	G	9	2	0	1	19,250
Angel Connection	4	F	1	0	0	0	0
Angel Deelite	2	F	1	0	0	0	306
Angel Falls	3	F	1	0	0	0	0
Angel Flash	6	H	6	1	3	0	19,675
Angel for a Judge	3	F	19	3	6	2	16,767
Angel for Tiffany	3	F	3	0	0	0	720
Angel Gift	5	M	6	1	0	2	69,434
Angel Ice	3	F	1	0	0	0	0
Angel in Style	3	F	2	1	0	0	2,700
Angel in the Cloud	4	F	3	0	0	0	0
Angel in the Wind	3	F	7	0	2	0	7,728
Angel in Tights	3	F	9	2	0	2	66,953
Angel Layne	3	F	6	1	0	0	4,499
Angel Luck	3	F	9	0	1	2	4,568
Angel of Fire	9	G	10	0	3	1	2,609
Angel of Goliad	3	F	10	1	1	2	7,764
Angel of Justice	3	C	1	0	0	0	402
Angel of Mercy	3	F	4	0	0	0	83
Angel of Sharacco	6	M	11	2	0	1	7,547
Angel of the Sea	5	M	4	0	1	0	12,085
Angel On Board	4	F	2	0	0	1	1,155
Angel On the Wing	4	G	8	3	3	1	152,719
Angel On Tour	3	F	2	0	0	1	3,220
Angel On Track	3	F	10	1	2	2	26,420
Angel Orders	5	H	2	0	0	0	202
Angel Punch	3	F	4	2	0	0	31,400
Angel Road	6	M	4	0	0	0	259
Angel Saint Claire	5	M	13	2	0	3	31,286
Angel Slipper	5	M	8	2	1	0	15,821
Angel Springs	5	G	5	1	0	1	9,185
Angel Street	4	F	2	0	0	0	1,170
Angel Tree	2	F	2	0	0	0	140
Angel Wine	4	F	9	2	5	0	20,138
Angel With Wings	9	M	2	0	0	0	480
Angela L	4	F	13	4	2	2	25,575
Angelano	3	F	6	0	2	1	3,603
Angelas Butterfly	4	F	12	1	1	2	6,230
Angela's Diary	5	M	12	1	1	0	11,063
Angela's Love	3	F	5	3	0	0	66,340
Angela's Pride	2	F	3	0	0	0	780
Angela's Tune	7	M	9	4	0	0	19,346
Angela'stoughwater	4	G	12	2	1	3	52,960
Angelic	2	F	4	0	1	1	6,435
Angelic Aura	3	G	10	4	2	3	117,690
Angelic Gal	3	F	17	0	3	3	7,583
Angelic Halo	4	F	18	0	2	2	8,220
Angelic Hero	4	G	12	0	2	3	15,952
Angelic Hope	2	F	1	0	0	0	0
Angelic Jewel	4	F	9	2	5	1	31,760
Angelic Light	2	F	2	0	0	0	0
Angelic Mist	3	F	6	0	0	1	1,605
Angelica Facci	5	M	5	0	0	1	737
Angelina Doll	4	F	3	0	0	0	0
Angelina Love	3	F	3	2	0	0	9,300
Angeline	5	M	7	0	2	0	13,000
Angeline W	3	F	5	1	0	0	10,557
Angelo the Jet	5	G	3	0	0	0	1,710
Angelo'sport	4	G	9	1	0	0	4,810
Angelrose	4	F	7	1	2	1	9,100
Angel's Advice	4	F	7	1	0	2	8,678
Angel's All	4	F	3	0	0	0	0
Angels Believer	3	F	7	0	0	0	225
Angels Blessed	3	F	4	0	0	0	0
Angel's Bull	4	G	7	0	0	0	981
Angels Cut	4	F	2	0	0	0	190
Angel's Dowry	3	F	2	1	1	0	10,850
Angels Dream	7	M	11	0	0	1	1,310
Angel's Family	4	F	3	0	0	0	224
Angel's Hero	4	G	12	5	1	1	33,116
Angel's Manner	4	C	6	1	0	1	13,616
Angels Playboy	7	G	12	1	2	1	13,574
Angels Rage	6	G	3	0	0	0	496
Angel's Refrain	3	F	8	1	1	0	6,335
Angels Ruse	7	G	7	3	1	0	16,150
Angel's Sing	6	M	10	2	2	2	13,560
Angels Surprise	3	F	5	2	1	0	18,120
Angel's Sweep	4	G	3	1	0	1	24,193
Angels Valentine	6	M	8	0	1	0	2,970
Angel's Victor E	5	G	14	1	2	2	6,738
Angels View	9	H	11	1	0	1	4,400
Angel's Wisdom	3	G	13	0	6	2	42,811
Angelsaver	3	F	2	0	0	0	0
Angelswatchnoverme	2	C	1	0	0	0	195
Angeltona	4	F	14	1	0	5	5,567
Angie A	5	M	10	1	0	0	4,114
Angie Wont Tell	3	G	8	0	0	0	0
Angie's Cat	4	F	9	0	0	0	3,900
Angies First Shot	3	G	13	3	2	1	12,362
Angie's Lass	6	M	2	0	0	0	0
Angie's Legacy	3	F	9	2	2	1	12,557
Angie's Picture	5	H	4	0	2	0	4,300
Angie's Reason	5	G	6	0	0	0	0
Angies Storm Creek	3	F	6	3	1	0	18,086
Angiesbrotherdanny	8	M	9	0	0	1	1,266
Angisse (GB)	2	F	3	1	0	1	23,898
Angle of Pursuit	11	G	13	3	3	0	19,040
Anglian Prince	4	G	12	1	2	4	152,545
Angliana Dancer	3	F	7	1	1	1	30,280
Angora	2	C	3	0	0	0	0
Angryarguingalex	3	G	10	0	2	1	5,739
Anguished Thespian	4	C	2	0	0	0	0
Angus Halo	4	G	9	0	0	3	2,648
Angus the Guts	3	G	5	1	0	0	5,465
Anikawi	3	F	3	0	0	0	420
Anima Mundi (IRE)	4	F	8	1	2	0	40,730
Animal Quackers	2	F	6	0	0	1	1,065
Animator	8	G	1	0	0	0	0
Animperial Win	2	C	8	1	1	2	18,048
Anita Clearone	6	M	8	0	0	0	630
Anita Cocktail	5	M	12	5	1	3	113,055
Anita Doreen	4	F	11	2	2	2	11,625
Anita Garibaldi	3	F	6	0	0	1	8,430
Anita Rocket	2	G	2	0	0	1	900
Anita Xanax	2	F	2	1	0	0	4,500
Anita's Dance Slew	3	C	11	1	3	2	35,608
Anita's Golden Boy	2	C	2	0	0	1	1,100
Anita's Niner	3	F	2	0	0	0	0
Anita's Slew	4	F	11	4	2	0	33,980
Anja	4	F	2	0	0	0	0
Anja (IRE)	3	F	4	1	1	0	28,519
Anjikahn	7	G	1	0	0	0	136
Anjiz Dream	6	M	6	0	0	0	509
Anjiz'halo	6	M	15	1	1	4	7,645
Anjiz's Prospect	7	G	12	0	2	2	10,240

Horse	Age	Sex	Sts	1st	2d	3d	Won	Horse	Age	Sex	Sts	1st	2d	3d	Won
Anjo's Legend	2	G	10	1	1	2	12,910	Anofferucantrefuse	6	G	5	2	0	1	83,780
Anklesocks	3	F	5	0	1	1	775	Anoiden Time	4	F	7	0	0	0	1,240
Ann August	4	F	8	1	2	0	4,655	Anointed One	4	F	14	2	1	0	26,620
Ann Dear	3	F	12	4	1	2	87,975	Another Account	5	M	5	0	0	0	2,725
Ann Michelle	4	F	9	1	1	2	5,583	Another Alphabet	2	C	8	2	0	0	26,580
Ann the Fan	3	F	2	1	0	0	4,877	Another Altitude	5	M	10	0	0	2	1,360
Anna Begins	8	M	12	1	0	2	8,025	Another Angelica	4	F	3	0	0	0	195
Anna Capri	4	F	17	5	3	2	52,849	Another Angie	3	F	7	0	1	1	1,627
Anna Em	2	F	3	0	1	0	5,200	Another Birdie	3	F	10	0	2	3	11,210
Anna K.	3	F	8	1	1	2	17,659	Another Brianna	2	F	4	0	0	0	1,820
Anna Rose	2	F	2	0	0	0	0	Another Cafe	4	F	10	1	0	0	7,537
Annabelle's Song	2	F	1	0	1	0	6,600	Another Career	4	F	13	3	2	1	33,151
Annabelly	3	F	5	3	0	0	77,100	Another Carson	2	C	5	1	2	0	31,490
Annagreta	3	F	4	0	2	0	14,720	Another Chaka	5	G	2	0	0	0	0
Annahlee J.	3	F	4	0	0	0	1,440	Another Chance	3	F	1	0	0	0	0
Annamae'swillpower	4	C	21	1	4	2	16,230	Another Chapter	3	F	4	0	0	0	980
Annamoriah	8	M	7	3	1	1	14,398	Another Chukker	4	G	15	2	2	5	10,815
Annapurna	3	F	1	0	0	0	0	Another Crypto	4	G	9	0	0	0	676
Anna's Advice	4	F	5	0	0	1	1,379	Another Dance	5	M	7	0	0	2	1,499
Anna's Birthday	6	M	6	0	0	0	145	Another Day	3	F	8	1	1	1	13,926
Anna's Cat	3	F	4	1	0	1	13,515	Another Dream	4	C	8	1	1	1	11,634
Anna's Code	5	M	13	1	0	1	8,455	Another Elusive	3	C	3	1	0	0	18,110
Anna's Girl	2	F	1	0	0	0	0	Another Episode	4	F	7	1	1	0	14,510
Anna's Hannah	3	F	2	0	0	0	0	Another Flavor	3	F	14	3	2	2	22,154
Anna's Pro	3	F	2	0	0	0	619	Another Fortune	4	G	1	0	0	0	140
Annasterian	4	F	9	2	2	2	11,415	Another Freddy	2	C	9	1	2	1	29,768
Annatoga	6	M	5	2	1	0	83,640	Another Gear	5	G	4	0	1	0	4,097
Anncloatkey	4	F	4	0	0	1	1,437	Another Gem	3	C	6	0	0	0	1,460
Anne English	5	M	10	1	2	1	9,440	Another George	3	G	9	3	0	3	61,055
Anneofgreengables	3	F	8	2	0	1	30,159	Another Grey Lady	7	M	2	0	0	0	0
Anne's Choice	6	M	21	3	2	3	14,525	Another Hi	5	G	14	0	2	1	9,996
Anne's Girl	4	F	2	0	0	0	0	Another Houston	4	F	1	0	0	0	360
Annette's Star	4	F	3	1	1	0	4,840	Another Ivory	5	M	13	6	3	1	95,130
Annettos Prize	4	F	7	0	0	1	5,800	Another Kahuna	2	C	2	0	0	0	0
Annexcel	2	G	1	0	0	0	0	Another Laugh	2	F	2	0	0	0	0
Anney's Trick	6	G	15	0	0	5	1,466	Another Lovelysong	2	F	4	1	0	0	12,013
Anniano	3	F	9	1	0	2	29,024	Another Misty Morn	6	M	16	0	0	4	6,005
Annie Anny	7	M	15	5	1	2	22,938	Another Moochie	2	F	9	0	3	1	16,295
Annie Fitch	3	F	8	1	1	0	14,771	Another Natural	5	M	2	0	0	0	78
Annie Flo	6	M	4	2	1	0	6,640	Another Nephew	5	G	6	0	0	0	162
Annie Go	4	F	10	0	0	3	5,304	Another One	3	G	2	0	0	0	990
Annie Hawk	3	F	1	0	0	0	0	Another Prince (ARG)	9	G	2	1	0	0	3,300
Annie Jones	5	M	4	0	1	0	1,006	Another Quatorze	4	C	3	0	0	0	206
Annie Lee	2	F	7	0	1	0	2,750	Another Quest	5	M	13	2	1	2	19,792
Annie N Me	3	F	4	0	1	0	5,860	Another Red Wind	7	M	2	0	1	0	2,400
Annie N Will	5	M	10	4	2	1	6,181	Another Reply	4	F	6	0	0	0	564
Annie Pannie	3	F	10	1	1	0	9,653	Another Rocket	3	G	19	0	8	4	32,424
Annie Pokely	3	F	1	0	0	0	0	Another Show	3	G	4	0	0	0	2,700
Annie Potcake	4	F	9	2	1	1	90,539	Another Sis	2	F	2	0	0	0	500
Annie Sweet	3	F	3	2	0	0	11,034	Another Skip	2	C	2	1	0	0	5,540
Annie T	4	F	3	1	0	0	23,595	Another Story	2	C	3	0	0	0	290
Annie Too	3	F	1	0	0	0	0	Another True Manor	2	F	2	0	0	1	2,170
Annie Up	5	M	8	0	0	1	2,560	Another Variety	3	F	5	0	0	1	10,502
Annie Warbucks	9	M	11	0	0	1	1,100	Another Wager	5	G	5	2	1	1	13,738
Annie's Future	6	M	8	1	0	0	2,842	Anotherbagman	4	G	7	2	0	1	5,578
Annie's Got a Gun	2	F	4	2	0	0	24,900	Anothercrookeddeal	4	C	5	0	0	0	144
Annie's Honor	6	M	10	2	2	0	27,510	Anotherpretty One	6	M	13	2	4	2	14,609
Annie's No Orphan	7	M	10	0	1	2	2,623	Ansky	6	G	10	0	1	2	5,718
Annie's Pal	4	G	6	1	2	1	15,730	Anstar (GB)	6	G	11	6	3	1	120,300
Annie's Ponytails	3	F	11	1	1	1	9,732	Answer From Above	5	M	18	2	4	1	22,363
Annie's Pride	4	F	4	0	1	0	2,040	Answer Me Al	8	G	8	2	1	2	12,218
Annies Prospect	3	F	2	0	1	0	4,991	Answer the Storm	3	F	7	2	2	1	41,630
Annie's Runaway	3	F	16	2	1	3	30,014	Answer This	5	G	16	0	0	3	5,567
Annies Shadow	5	M	10	0	2	0	15,880	Answerback	5	M	7	1	1	1	6,495
Annie's Sister Ida	4	F	5	1	0	0	7,800	Answermykiss	6	G	6	1	1	0	6,009
Annie's Winner	3	G	6	0	1	0	2,170	Answertoeverything	4	C	1	0	0	0	546
Anniversary Waltz	8	H	6	0	0	0	2,746	Ant Cara	4	F	7	2	0	0	12,390
Anniversary Year	7	G	6	0	0	1	1,100	Ant Sami	4	M	12	0	0	1	1,639
Announce Me	3	C	7	1	0	3	29,845	Antaeus (NZ)	5	G	3	0	0	0	2,280
Announce of Charm	2	F	4	0	0	2	2,740	Antagonist	5	M	1	0	0	0	0
Announce of Gold	2	G	6	1	1	1	13,901	Antara	3	C	2	0	0	0	315
Announcement	3	C	5	1	0	0	16,260	Ante Oaklee	3	F	3	0	0	1	632
Ann's Emblem	5	M	12	1	0	0	11,788	Ante Up Eva	3	F	9	1	1	2	10,188
Ann's Glory	4	C	7	1	0	1	8,810	Ante Up Pete	2	G	7	0	1	2	11,880
Annslee	3	F	4	1	1	1	23,340	Anthem Hill	4	G	5	1	0	0	5,400
Annual Challenge	3	C	7	0	0	3	5,974	Antherium	8	M	6	1	0	0	5,285
Annuity	4	G	3	0	1	0	1,342	Anthonia	3	F	12	3	1	3	120,530
Annulet	8	G	4	0	0	1	400	Anthony B.	7	H	7	1	2	0	9,775
Annunciation	4	C	12	3	0	0	13,300	Anthony Eats	2	G	9	1	4	1	41,840

Horse	Age	Sex	Sts	1st	2d	3d	Won
Anthony Ruhls	4	G	7	0	4	2	11,555
Anthony Soprano	4	G	8	2	0	0	17,909
Anthony's Gem	3	F	8	0	0	1	1,600
Anthony's Nockover	2	G	2	0	0	0	1,230
Anthony's Only Way	2	F	2	0	0	0	990
Anthonys Toy	7	H	3	0	0	0	554
Anti Social	3	F	4	0	0	2	4,050
Anti Versary	5	M	1	0	0	0	175
Anticipate Magic	5	G	11	1	1	3	4,804
Antics Upstairs	8	M	4	0	1	0	1,950
Anties Boy	6	G	15	0	0	0	1,545
Antietam	4	C	13	2	4	2	28,013
Anting Anting	3	C	6	2	1	1	4,591
Antique	4	G	12	1	0	0	8,785
Antique Crystal	2	F	2	0	0	1	1,512
Antique Freak	5	M	16	1	1	4	6,359
Antique Land	3	C	4	0	0	0	0
Antoinette's Joy	4	F	3	0	0	0	0
Antonio Star	7	H	4	0	0	0	2,100
Anton's Memory	4	G	4	1	1	1	9,915
Ants	5	M	9	0	1	1	3,262
Antsy	3	G	12	2	1	2	49,793
Anvil Dancer	3	F	9	0	0	4	2,700
Anwar	2	C	2	0	1	0	11,900
Anxious Alex	4	F	10	1	2	1	10,075
Anxious Axie	3	F	3	0	0	0	225
Anxious Otto	11	H	1	0	0	0	0
Anxious Prospect	6	H	1	0	0	0	0
Any for Love (ARG)	5	M	5	0	2	0	23,480
Any Lie's Better	3	F	1	0	0	0	0
Any Old Disk	3	C	7	0	0	2	3,185
Any One Wish	3	G	11	0	0	1	1,624
Any Place But Home	4	F	4	0	0	1	3,390
Any Questions	2	G	5	0	0	3	21,756
Any Reason	4	F	2	1	1	0	30,780
Any Scoop	5	M	2	0	0	0	3,390
Any Way At All	4	C	1	1	0	0	36,960
Any Wonder	4	F	7	1	2	0	5,226
Anybuddee	4	F	11	0	2	0	4,686
Anyone Wood	4	G	2	0	0	0	0
Anyones Guess	3	F	5	0	2	1	1,890
Anyplace Anytime	3	F	9	0	2	4	28,345
Anything for You	6	M	3	0	0	1	5,730
Anytime Eddie	3	G	8	2	1	0	22,305
Anywhere Anytime	5	M	8	1	1	0	3,185
Anza	3	G	13	2	4	3	42,164
Anziyan Royalty	3	C	6	4	0	1	96,700
Ap to Be Duff	4	G	11	0	1	2	1,456
Ap to Cash	10	G	8	0	0	0	346
Apache Bee	3	F	7	1	3	0	14,111
Apache Brave	2	G	3	1	0	0	12,410
Apache Bride	5	M	4	0	0	0	0
Apache Corner	3	F	5	0	0	0	1,355
Apache Dance	3	G	12	2	3	1	18,505
Apache Dancer	4	F	1	0	0	0	113
Apache Dispatch	4	G	7	2	1	1	11,860
Apache Flame	4	F	14	2	5	1	20,321
Apache Flyer	2	C	6	1	1	1	24,985
Apache King	5	H	7	1	0	1	10,209
Apache Lady	5	M	8	0	2	1	6,667
Apache Pass	7	H	10	0	0	0	309
Apache Signal	3	F	5	0	0	0	0
Apache Son	4	C	1	0	0	0	300
Apache Spirit	3	F	5	1	1	1	11,830
Apache Surprise	3	G	10	0	4	2	28,550
Apache Thunder	4	C	9	2	2	1	28,103
Apache Tribe	3	G	9	0	2	4	29,440
Apache Twist (IRE)	10	G	3	0	1	2	3,800
Apache Wildcat	3	F	11	2	4	0	29,040
Apache Wings	5	G	4	1	0	0	39,000
Apache Woman	3	F	3	0	0	0	183
Apachee Lion	6	H	4	0	0	0	274
Apak	10	G	4	0	2	1	5,985
Apalabity	3	F	6	0	0	1	1,155
Apalachee Cola	2	C	5	1	1	0	54,973
Apalachee Island	6	G	13	1	3	1	9,503
Apalachee Man	3	C	1	0	0	0	0
Apalachee Money	4	F	4	0	0	0	180
Apalachee Special	8	H	4	0	1	0	10,240
Apalachee's Native	6	G	8	0	3	2	9,710
Apalachian Thunder	3	C	4	1	1	1	115,473
Apaneca	3	F	2	0	0	0	713
Aparecida	2	F	2	1	0	1	21,070
Apartfromanna	2	F	3	0	0	0	180
Apasionata Sonata	5	M	4	2	0	0	85,380
Apeak	8	G	13	3	2	1	6,990
Apello	3	F	13	1	2	1	7,914
Apenitas	2	C	8	0	2	0	4,485
Aperfectladydoctor	5	M	8	0	0	1	2,590
Aphonic	3	G	9	0	3	2	20,395
Aphrodites	3	F	7	1	0	1	5,344
Apian Way	8	G	4	0	0	0	597
Apical	3	F	3	0	1	1	3,540
Apico	7	G	3	1	0	0	1,051
Apleasantworld	5	G	10	1	0	3	6,966
Aplomado	10	G	16	1	0	1	4,496
Apocalyptic	5	M	4	0	0	0	367
Apolla Eleven	2	F	5	1	1	1	11,642
Apollicee	4	G	19	1	0	3	11,965
Apollo Charm	3	F	8	0	2	2	8,338
Apollo Jack	2	C	1	0	0	1	2,400
Apollo Suelto	7	H	1	0	0	0	0
Apollo Treasure	4	F	3	0	1	1	3,175
Apollo Uno	3	C	5	2	0	0	34,710
Apollo Willfool'ya	5	M	8	2	2	1	25,800
Apollon	4	G	7	0	1	0	1,509
Apollonea	3	F	6	2	2	1	23,550
Apollonian	3	G	7	1	3	2	58,515
Apollo's Music	7	M	3	0	0	0	410
Apollo's Rooks	2	C	1	0	0	0	540
Apostle	4	G	5	0	1	1	13,020
Apotheotic	4	G	2	0	0	0	310
Appalachian Sunset	5	H	1	0	0	0	370
Appas Tappas	3	G	7	0	3	2	47,383
Appawling	9	G	13	0	1	3	4,041
Appeal Review	3	F	5	0	0	0	0
Appeal to Reality	6	H	4	0	0	0	225
Appeal to Reason	7	G	14	0	0	1	2,768
Appealing Action	3	F	4	0	0	0	960
Appealing Class	2	F	5	0	1	2	10,670
Appealing Command	7	H	2	0	0	1	1,615
Appealing Dancer	4	F	9	0	0	0	696
Appealing Fella	4	G	16	1	0	2	8,570
Appealing Grades	3	C	11	2	3	0	10,190
Appealing Greeley	4	F	16	1	1	1	10,265
Appealing Jet	5	M	12	0	5	2	16,375
Appealing Jewel	4	F	1	0	0	0	0
Appealing Lauren	3	F	4	1	0	1	10,070
Appealing Liaison	2	C	3	0	3	0	31,600
Appealing Melody	4	F	7	0	1	2	21,741
Appealing Pinky	3	F	6	2	1	1	14,210
Appealing Promise	6	H	10	2	0	1	4,494
Appealing Reality	3	C	1	0	0	0	0
Appealing Secret	2	C	8	4	0	0	69,960
Appealing Song	3	F	2	1	0	0	5,399
Appealing Space	3	F	1	0	0	0	140
Appealing Star	4	C	3	0	0	1	918
Appealing Tasso	7	G	5	0	0	0	900
Appealing to Us	3	F	1	0	0	0	40
Appealing Trick	3	F	1	0	0	0	0
Appealing Turk	5	H	4	0	1	1	840
Appealing Wind	4	F	2	0	0	0	109
Appealing Wolf	3	G	24	2	5	4	27,280
Appealingfire	2	F	5	0	0	0	1,040
Appealingly Bold	6	M	7	3	1	1	24,175
Append	3	F	5	1	0	0	6,600
Apple Appeal	3	F	6	1	1	1	6,235
Apple Boyd	3	G	9	1	0	0	10,503
Apple Butter Annie	4	F	17	7	2	2	33,689
Apple Cart	3	C	6	0	0	1	6,055
Apple Creek	2	F	1	0	0	0	195
Apple Juice	3	F	3	1	0	1	21,880
Apple Juice Tea	3	F	4	2	0	0	46,720
Apple Krisp	2	C	9	1	3	2	52,440
Apple o' Dale	4	C	2	1	0	0	13,336
Apple Rose	2	F	3	0	0	1	3,580
Appleby Gardens	3	F	3	1	0	0	41,940
Apple's Delight	5	M	12	2	1	2	19,981

Horse	Age	Sex	Sts	1st	2d	3d	Won
Apple's Hero	3	F	2	0	0	0	103
Apples Hoss	5	M	8	1	0	0	7,060
Appleton (MEX)	5	G	7	1	3	1	10,822
Appleturnover Mike	6	G	11	1	0	0	4,640
Applied Economics	9	M	6	0	0	1	770
Appointed	4	G	3	1	0	0	5,314
Appro	3	F	3	1	0	1	20,780
Approach	5	G	15	2	3	0	15,438
Approach (GB)	3	F	5	1	1	0	138,563
Approvable	4	C	9	0	0	2	3,515
Approval Pending	4	F	7	0	1	0	1,490
Approved Code	4	F	7	0	0	3	10,148
Approximate Odds	4	G	15	2	0	2	17,098
Appsolutely	7	G	10	1	2	1	4,446
Appygolucky	6	G	6	3	0	1	11,898
Apres Minuit	5	M	2	1	0	1	15,018
Aprice	4	F	7	1	1	0	17,749
April Afternoon	3	F	6	1	1	1	12,305
April and Kansas	4	F	7	1	0	2	9,717
April Baby	5	G	13	2	2	2	39,497
April Bay	2	F	2	0	0	0	366
April Blues	4	G	17	2	0	1	21,779
April Cap	2	C	8	0	0	0	1,285
April Does It	5	M	2	0	0	0	300
April Eyes	3	F	5	2	0	0	19,920
April Fool Girl	8	M	7	0	1	0	1,262
April Foolish	4	F	6	1	0	1	21,257
April Fun	2	F	6	1	1	0	10,265
April Lilly	4	F	11	1	0	2	7,582
April Morning	6	M	13	0	0	1	3,870
April On Time	3	F	11	1	6	0	13,554
April Rose	5	M	20	1	4	2	13,426
April Runner	7	M	12	1	2	0	9,395
April Russian	7	H	2	0	0	0	225
April Serenade	2	F	2	0	0	1	1,400
April Seven	4	F	15	0	0	2	1,494
April Springs	2	F	2	0	0	0	390
April Steel (FR)	5	G	7	1	0	0	35,460
April Sunshine	6	G	7	1	1	0	9,270
April Surprise	7	G	12	1	2	2	17,958
April Talent	4	F	7	0	0	1	2,262
April Trust	4	F	4	1	0	2	35,870
April Who	6	G	6	1	2	0	3,905
April's Bold Baby	3	F	7	1	1	0	10,710
April's Explosion	2	C	2	0	0	0	0
April's Louve	4	F	9	1	1	5	13,747
April's Lucky Boy	4	G	9	2	2	2	65,980
April's Miss Thing	2	F	3	0	0	1	1,443
April's Prince	2	C	9	2	0	0	30,080
April's Project	6	G	15	2	0	1	7,475
April's Whirlwind	4	F	4	0	0	0	1,419
Aprizedslew	6	G	2	0	0	0	4,210
Apt Contender	6	G	7	1	0	0	3,665
Apt Prelude	3	F	14	4	2	0	39,283
Apt to Be	6	G	5	3	0	0	110,880
Apt to Please	3	F	3	0	0	1	1,268
Aptlyput	3	C	3	0	0	1	480
Apto Fire	2	G	1	0	0	0	700
Aquaduck	4	F	9	1	3	0	13,125
Aquaduct Charlie	4	F	18	2	2	1	20,609
Aquarium	3	F	6	1	0	0	5,616
Aquatic Gap	3	F	8	0	0	1	10,450
Aquiess	3	G	6	1	0	0	7,226
Aquina's Rose	3	F	14	0	6	3	21,876
Aquita	3	F	5	0	0	1	12,816
Aquitania	4	F	3	0	0	0	530
Aquitted	4	C	2	0	0	0	0
Ar Jay (NZ)	8	G	5	1	0	0	6,235
Arab Bride	2	F	5	1	0	0	8,450
Arab Influence	2	F	1	0	0	0	540
Arab Miss	3	F	9	0	1	3	29,340
Arab Verse	2	F	3	0	0	0	0
Arab Warning	6	G	15	1	6	2	10,768
Arabian Diablo	6	M	11	1	2	3	12,755
Arabian Secret	3	F	11	0	0	1	1,820
Arabian Wager	5	H	1	0	0	0	0
Arabic Song (IRE)	4	F	4	1	1	2	75,745
Arabica's Boy	6	G	12	2	1	1	13,708
Arabis	4	F	9	2	1	0	90,007
Aran Island	9	G	10	1	3	1	6,073
Aran Narayan	4	C	15	2	2	2	21,343
Aranjuez Amor	6	H	3	0	0	0	455
Aranmore	4	G	6	1	0	1	11,387
Aran's Lad	4	G	9	2	4	1	31,977
Araz	5	M	1	0	0	0	0
Arbee's Love	6	M	6	0	0	0	675
Arbitrage	3	F	1	0	0	0	150
Arbitrageuse	2	F	3	0	0	0	60
Arbitrary Andrew	4	G	5	0	0	1	1,140
Arbitrate	3	C	13	2	1	2	66,170
Arbor Day	6	G	14	2	1	2	10,524
Arbroath	4	G	4	0	0	0	860
Arcadia Light	4	G	12	0	0	0	1,810
Arcadia Street	7	H	5	1	1	0	7,775
Arcana	2	F	5	0	0	1	3,925
Arcanine	4	F	7	1	1	1	6,984
Arcanum	4	F	3	0	0	0	141
Arcatec	2	C	1	1	0	0	15,720
Arch Ability	3	F	7	1	2	1	27,520
Arch Angel Gabriel	4	G	5	0	0	0	385
Arch Hall	2	C	5	0	0	1	12,694
Arch Lady	3	F	15	3	3	5	63,639
Arch of Triumph	3	F	7	1	1	0	27,280
Archabella	2	F	5	0	1	1	14,636
Archbishop	3	G	6	1	0	0	5,538
Archdiesis	7	G	5	1	0	0	5,945
Archer County	8	G	2	0	0	0	280
Archer Fleet	2	C	2	0	0	0	3,528
Archers Angel	2	F	1	0	0	0	0
Archers Bow	2	C	4	0	1	1	31,270
Archers Gal	5	M	18	2	3	5	107,040
Archetype	3	C	4	0	2	0	6,660
Archeval	3	G	8	1	1	1	13,656
Archie B	2	C	5	1	0	1	31,845
Archiehitthegold	2	C	3	0	0	0	0
Architecture	3	G	8	2	0	0	13,420
Archness	2	C	2	0	0	0	760
Archy	5	H	12	2	2	1	28,258
Arcola Lane	4	C	13	3	2	2	38,314
Arcola Playboy	4	C	17	0	1	3	11,327
Arco's Gold	3	C	6	1	1	1	164,218
Arctic Annie	2	F	3	1	1	0	7,768
Arctic Boy	5	H	7	0	0	0	3,870
Arctic Dove	3	F	6	0	0	1	7,330
Arctic Drift	3	F	5	1	2	0	39,882
Arctic Fox	4	C	4	1	1	1	8,500
Arctic Frost	4	C	6	0	0	1	1,140
Arctic Horizon	7	G	9	3	1	2	18,791
Arctic Ice	2	F	3	0	0	0	611
Arctic Knight	6	H	8	0	0	1	1,085
Arctic Lightning	5	H	9	0	0	0	623
Arctic Pleasures	4	F	10	2	0	2	3,537
Arctic Prize	8	G	14	1	3	4	21,015
Arctic River	6	G	10	1	2	1	27,003
Arctic Roar	3	G	5	1	0	0	4,472
Arctic Rose	3	F	3	0	1	1	12,910
Arctic Rumble	3	C	13	1	2	2	21,856
Arctic Sand	4	G	13	2	4	1	30,510
Arctic Sleigh	4	C	6	2	2	0	17,312
Arctic Snow	4	F	9	0	0	1	2,323
Arctic Sparkle	5	M	3	0	0	0	0
Arctic Sweep	8	G	10	1	1	0	7,790
Arctic Trail	4	F	3	0	0	0	667
Arctic Warning	3	C	6	2	0	0	9,552
Arctic Wish	6	M	1	0	0	0	240
Arctic Wood	6	H	2	0	0	0	0
Arcus	2	G	3	1	0	0	16,380
Ardennes	3	F	1	0	1	0	4,780
Ardent Arab	11	G	3	0	0	0	0
Ardent Eddy	3	G	12	2	2	0	35,657
Ardent Lover	5	M	5	0	1	0	2,900
Ardum Relaunch	4	F	11	2	2	4	115,024
Are You Blue	5	G	17	3	3	2	38,013
Are You Down	4	G	10	2	4	2	95,356
Are You Home	3	F	8	3	1	1	49,245
Are You Irish	3	F	5	2	1	1	32,556
Are You Joking	3	F	3	0	0	0	427

Horse	Age	Sex	Sts	1st	2d	3d	Won
Are You Lookn	3	G	4	0	2	1	18,000
Are You There	2	F	1	0	1	0	3,150
Areacode Twoonetwo	7	G	2	0	0	0	200
Areafiftyone	7	H	3	0	0	0	136
Areallyniceguy	6	G	2	0	0	0	190
Areasonforfreedom	4	C	1	0	0	0	0
Arel	2	G	1	0	0	0	0
Areyouamused	3	C	11	0	1	1	11,045
Areyoukidding Me	5	G	11	0	0	3	3,680
Areyoutalkintome	2	G	3	1	0	2	14,640
Arf	6	H	7	0	0	1	1,792
Argent Francais (FR)	3	F	1	1	0	0	26,400
Argentum	4	F	5	1	0	2	22,310
Argonne	3	C	1	0	0	0	0
Argosy North	5	G	11	0	3	0	5,215
Argue	5	H	6	2	0	0	26,040
Argyl Rose	3	F	3	1	0	1	1,672
Argyle	3	C	2	0	0	0	0
Argyrotoxos	5	H	9	0	4	3	16,002
Arianna's Song	6	M	12	0	0	2	6,308
Arianne	3	F	11	2	1	3	5,324
Aria's Diva	6	M	4	2	1	0	9,913
Ariel Chief	7	H	5	0	0	0	510
Ariel's Melody	4	F	5	0	2	0	38,984
Ariesdotcom	5	G	8	2	1	2	10,670
Arikara	3	F	4	0	0	0	3,705
Arimonas Agenda	3	F	2	0	0	0	0
Arion Sands	2	G	6	1	0	1	6,505
Arions Gal	4	F	2	0	0	0	107
Arirang Champion	3	F	3	0	0	0	651
Arisen Angel	3	F	3	0	0	1	1,526
Aristas	3	F	3	0	0	0	118
Aristide the Great	4	G	15	3	2	4	21,952
Aristocat	3	C	4	1	2	0	78,060
Aristocrat Cat	2	G	5	0	0	1	3,103
Aristona	3	F	1	0	0	0	70
Aritelli	6	G	10	2	1	0	15,980
Ariveradechy Ruby	3	F	6	1	0	0	5,520
Arizona Bay Cat	3	C	9	1	0	1	6,242
Arizona City Bob	2	G	3	0	0	0	0
Arizona Creek	4	F	5	1	2	1	5,802
Arizona Express	4	G	5	0	0	0	740
Arizona Gold	8	G	11	1	0	0	5,826
Arizona Irishman	8	G	12	0	0	0	297
Arizona Lady	5	F	5	1	0	0	4,620
Arizona Lil	4	F	6	0	1	1	5,109
Arizona Orphan	3	F	2	0	0	0	310
Arizona Sheik	3	H	3	1	1	0	1,275
Arizona Sky	2	G	5	1	3	0	11,119
Arizona Slew	4	F	14	1	2	0	3,387
Arizona Storm	8	G	3	0	0	0	0
Arizona Superstar	6	G	11	3	3	3	35,773
Arjay's Flag	3	C	19	1	1	3	46,525
Arjumad	2	F	2	0	0	0	0
Ark Maker	4	C	1	0	0	0	0
Ark Mo	5	H	8	2	1	0	2,770
Arkansas Gold	2	C	3	0	0	0	194
Arkansas Queen	3	F	9	1	1	0	6,600
Arkansas Red	2	F	5	0	0	0	200
Arkansas Swinger	2	F	1	0	0	0	0
Arkie's Nozetta	3	F	13	1	1	2	21,733
Arkon (CHI)	7	G	15	1	2	0	11,780
Arkoudi	4	F	4	1	1	1	14,280
Arkwin	4	G	5	1	0	0	3,850
Arky Holler	8	G	6	1	2	1	12,559
Arlines Only Angel	4	F	1	0	0	0	50
Arlington Pond	2	F	2	0	2	0	6,400
Arlo	7	G	7	1	0	0	6,960
Armada Missy	4	F	7	3	2	0	5,092
Armado	4	G	2	0	0	0	0
Arman	4	G	3	0	0	0	800
Armed 'n Crafty	5	G	4	0	0	2	3,240
Armed Response	5	M	10	5	0	0	31,109
Armedwith Patience	6	M	7	0	0	0	1,516
Armee Rouge	4	F	7	1	2	1	32,810
Armenian Aghcheek	6	M	2	0	0	0	0
Armistice Day	6	M	8	1	1	2	10,011
Armourette	3	F	6	0	0	0	660
Arms Control	4	F	2	0	0	1	9,600
Arms Talk	4	F	6	1	0	2	9,160
Arms Wide Open	4	G	7	1	1	1	15,739
Armsofanangel	5	M	14	1	1	3	10,445
Armstrong	6	H	7	1	0	0	7,540
Armstrong (GER)	9	H	3	0	0	0	480
Army Boots	2	C	5	0	1	0	8,230
Army Cat	4	C	9	2	0	0	15,320
Army Discharge	2	F	4	1	0	0	5,895
Army Games	3	F	12	1	0	1	11,690
Army General	4	G	9	1	1	2	12,061
Army Hero	3	G	10	0	0	4	7,762
Army of One (GB)	9	G	2	0	0	0	1,020
Arnchew Gorgeous	4	F	4	1	0	0	4,967
Arnie Starlet	7	G	1	0	0	0	0
Arnie the King	7	H	1	0	0	0	0
Arnold's Candle	5	G	5	0	0	0	2,750
Arogos	4	G	10	2	1	5	5,385
Aron's Matzoballs	2	C	1	0	0	0	2,460
Aroseformygirls	4	F	16	1	3	0	7,578
Around Marry Lou	7	M	1	0	0	0	282
Around the Ring	5	G	7	0	0	0	783
Around the Sea	7	G	7	0	0	0	413
Arpege	3	F	3	2	0	1	36,680
Arpeggio	8	M	7	0	1	2	9,510
Arpent	3	C	10	1	3	0	19,790
Arrabell Rose	3	F	3	0	0	0	510
Arran Pilot (GB)	3	G	4	0	1	1	11,300
Arrangement	3	F	9	1	2	0	9,106
Arremlee	6	M	3	0	0	1	3,271
Arrest Me Red	4	F	13	1	1	1	7,971
Arrestare	6	G	10	5	0	2	18,775
Arresting Beauty	3	F	3	0	1	0	2,285
Arrival Time	3	F	2	0	1	0	6,000
Arriviste	4	F	6	0	0	0	336
Arrogance	3	F	10	3	1	0	104,098
Arrogant Leader	4	C	8	1	1	0	5,858
Arrow Angel (NZ)	6	M	12	1	1	1	15,462
Arrowwood	5	G	5	2	0	0	6,660
Arroyo Bay	4	F	3	0	0	1	616
Arsen	4	G	10	2	2	4	114,660
Arsen Annie	3	F	10	4	1	1	79,296
Art Contemporain (FR)	5	G	5	1	1	1	12,488
Art Deco Lady	5	M	3	0	0	0	1,032
Art Fair	4	F	7	1	1	2	23,282
Art Fan	2	F	5	2	0	1	52,364
Art Form	3	F	3	0	0	0	440
Art of Dance	2	F	4	0	0	1	9,769
Art of Gold	5	M	9	1	1	3	3,909
Art of War	4	C	16	1	3	1	13,703
Art Thou a Winer	5	H	5	0	0	0	404
Art Thou Glory	6	G	12	3	3	1	6,064
Art to Rain	8	G	11	1	1	0	17,495
Art Variety (BRZ)	5	H	7	1	0	2	57,248
Artanis	4	G	4	0	0	1	880
Artax Dancer	2	F	3	0	1	2	18,150
Artax Too	4	C	1	0	0	0	0
Artaxes At Work	2	C	3	1	0	0	27,440
Artech	2	C	1	0	0	0	810
Artemio	7	G	12	0	1	2	4,628
Artemus Eagle	3	G	6	1	0	1	5,764
Artemus Sunrise	2	C	3	1	1	0	38,495
Artful Aviator	3	F	13	1	3	1	19,459
Artful Lady	3	F	11	1	2	1	15,329
Artful Way	3	G	12	1	0	3	10,399
Artfulnesse	5	M	3	0	0	1	2,730
Arthel	3	F	13	3	6	0	31,962
Arthur	5	H	5	1	0	0	5,299
Arthur Roy	6	G	15	2	4	1	14,634
Arthuron	3	C	5	0	1	0	2,955
Arthur's Dream	5	G	3	1	0	1	23,369
Artic Bella	2	F	2	0	0	0	550
Artic Breeze	5	G	8	1	1	2	14,102
Artic Deputy	3	C	7	0	0	0	252
Artic Destroyer	10	G	6	1	1	2	6,444
Artic Dream	2	G	3	0	1	1	11,920
Artic Express	5	H	2	0	0	0	468
Artic Fox	4	F	12	2	1	2	9,864
Artic Gamble	3	C	2	0	0	0	696
Artic Ice	4	G	10	1	0	2	33,827

Horse	Age	Sex	Sts	1st	2d	3d	Won
Artic Jazz	2	F	1	0	0	0	0
Artic Party	5	M	11	5	2	2	92,330
Artic Sonnet	5	M	11	5	1	1	29,236
Artic Squire	7	G	2	0	0	0	0
Artic Stage	3	G	2	0	0	0	0
Artie Schiller	2	C	5	2	1	1	88,275
Artie Takes Two	2	G	4	1	1	1	9,645
Arties Lady	6	M	8	2	1	2	26,526
Artie's Pride	3	G	5	0	1	0	1,513
Artillery Man	3	C	7	2	1	1	40,205
Artillery Punch	5	H	12	0	1	1	4,692
Artist Johanna (ARG)	5	M	6	2	1	1	80,000
Artistic Awareness	4	C	9	0	3	0	37,800
Artistic Cat	3	F	1	0	0	0	350
Artistic Design	4	G	7	3	3	0	42,455
Artistic Dreamer	3	F	12	0	1	3	5,210
Artistic John	8	G	24	3	1	6	14,303
Artistic License	5	G	7	1	1	0	9,337
Artistry On Ice	4	F	7	1	1	1	6,825
Artist's Meeting	3	G	8	1	3	0	11,730
Artist's Studio	3	F	7	0	0	3	28,008
Artoo Run	4	F	12	2	3	1	5,808
Arts	4	F	9	1	1	1	13,780
Artsy	2	F	2	0	0	0	410
Arturo	3	C	5	1	2	0	46,840
Artwork	5	G	6	0	0	0	2,120
Artyme	3	G	3	0	0	0	0
Arvalany	4	F	10	2	1	2	13,066
Arvida	4	F	1	0	0	0	0
Arvilla Priscilla	2	F	5	1	0	3	33,829
Arzo	3	F	1	0	0	0	700
A's an B's	5	G	10	2	0	3	12,480
A's Anchorman	4	G	17	0	7	2	20,346
As de Corazones	3	G	9	1	0	0	3,258
As de Oro	8	H	5	4	0	0	22,258
As Expected	4	G	10	0	2	2	44,513
As If I Care	6	G	10	0	0	1	2,876
As We Play	3	F	4	1	0	1	22,075
As Wicked	5	G	10	3	1	0	66,840
As You Were	3	F	2	0	0	0	170
Asa Diamonds	4	G	9	2	1	1	6,382
Asa Un Fuegos	4	C	6	2	1	0	11,288
Asailortoremember	3	G	9	0	4	2	31,866
Asaja	2	F	6	1	0	0	5,360
Asbury Lane	4	G	10	0	1	0	2,851
Asbury Park	3	F	3	2	0	0	33,250
Ascending Light	9	M	8	0	0	0	985
Ascertain Groom	5	H	11	0	3	2	5,824
Asclepius	2	G	3	1	0	0	7,100
Ascorbicus	2	C	7	1	1	1	21,306
Ascot Doll	9	G	16	3	2	1	16,356
Ascot From Heaven	9	G	8	0	1	1	2,325
Ascot in the Gate	2	F	1	0	0	0	0
Ascribe	2	C	1	0	0	0	217
Asfarasyoucansea	4	F	7	2	0	1	71,482
Ash Grove	3	G	10	2	0	1	37,833
Ash the Flash	4	F	10	0	2	0	2,226
Ashado	2	F	6	4	1	0	610,800
Ashagio	5	G	16	8	4	0	149,331
Ashar	8	G	6	0	0	2	12,643
Ashary (GER)	3	F	4	0	0	0	3,405
Ashbecca	4	F	2	0	0	0	900
Ashburn Rd	2	F	3	1	0	0	42,911
Ashdown's Dream	5	M	17	2	5	1	13,340
Ashe Ole'	3	G	11	1	4	3	15,640
Asheville	5	M	8	1	2	1	45,842
Ashford Eclipse	4	F	3	0	1	0	1,132
Ashford Seven	4	G	3	0	0	0	1,260
Ashinni	5	M	1	0	0	0	0
Ashlar	3	F	15	3	1	2	28,912
Ashlee's Bella	2	F	2	1	0	0	21,540
Ashlee's Royal	4	F	3	0	0	0	0
Ashley B	3	F	9	1	1	0	6,528
Ashley Brook	4	G	4	1	0	0	7,800
Ashley County	2	F	5	0	0	3	6,091
Ashley Kate	5	M	12	3	4	1	6,820
Ashley 'n Robert	2	F	2	0	0	0	780
Ashley Oaks	7	M	6	0	1	0	699
Ashley Springs	7	M	4	0	0	0	0
Ashley's Affair	4	F	5	1	1	1	10,517
Ashley's Alibi	5	M	2	0	0	0	450
Ashleys Attitude	4	F	9	1	5	1	5,000
Ashley's Caper	4	F	6	0	1	1	8,520
Ashley's Charm	5	H	9	0	0	0	1,350
Ashley's Clan	3	F	8	0	0	0	1,980
Ashley's Folly	3	F	4	0	2	1	25,158
Ashley's Joy	4	F	13	0	1	0	2,620
Ashley's Luck	3	F	10	2	1	1	11,452
Ashleys Paige	3	F	5	0	0	0	1,800
Ashleys' Pride	5	M	18	3	1	2	9,608
Ashley's Summer	5	G	11	0	2	2	16,745
Ashley'ssummergold	3	F	2	0	0	0	0
Ashmore	3	G	11	3	2	4	182,750
Ashoka	3	C	3	1	1	1	43,340
Ashraaf	3	F	7	1	3	2	118,100
Ashtons Dreams	3	G	8	0	1	0	7,977
Ashwell Springs	4	F	1	0	0	0	285
Ashwood C C	5	M	10	5	4	0	184,164
Asian Knight	2	G	2	1	0	0	17,640
Asian Native	4	F	8	5	1	0	31,765
Asian Son	3	G	7	1	1	0	6,376
Asia's Class	3	F	5	1	2	2	19,314
Asiceit	4	G	11	5	1	0	22,021
Asilmottamrich	10	G	1	0	0	0	0
Asiyu	5	M	4	0	0	1	1,795
Ask a Devil	5	G	4	1	2	0	8,750
Ask Dorothy	4	F	15	3	0	7	66,270
Ask Dr. Dave	2	G	4	1	0	1	12,033
Ask Linda	3	F	14	2	3	2	44,865
Ask Me Again	7	M	13	2	2	0	36,340
Ask Nadine	4	F	1	0	0	0	0
Ask Nancy	5	G	9	1	0	3	4,244
Ask Not	4	F	9	3	0	0	88,968
Ask Queenie	2	F	5	3	0	2	56,100
Ask Skip's Tigress	6	M	11	0	2	1	1,924
Ask Slew	12	G	7	3	1	1	4,908
Ask the Doc	7	H	3	0	0	2	2,676
Ask the Lord	6	G	11	5	1	2	204,120
Aska Ba Ba	5	G	10	0	1	1	3,310
Aska Sailor	4	C	2	0	1	0	620
Askabb	9	H	8	0	0	0	484
Askara	6	M	10	3	3	1	82,895
Askforaraise	3	F	10	1	2	1	58,683
Askham	5	H	5	1	0	1	22,518
Askim (NZ)	7	G	2	2	0	0	36,000
Asking for Luck	9	G	10	0	3	1	15,382
Askmetofly	4	F	2	0	0	0	150
Aslaaf	5	H	4	1	0	0	18,910
Aslan	5	M	4	1	0	1	1,555
Asmokeafterdinner	3	F	16	3	0	4	70,827
Asoleado	4	F	3	0	0	0	0
Asong for Billy	4	G	6	2	2	1	126,691
Asp	3	C	1	1	0	0	4,260
Aspen Bud	5	H	1	0	0	0	0
Aspen Falls	2	F	4	0	0	0	5,540
Aspen Flower	4	F	16	3	4	2	80,190
Aspen Gal	2	F	5	4	0	0	75,840
Aspen Hill	4	F	4	1	2	1	29,500
Aspen Leaf	2	F	2	0	0	0	100
Aspen Moon	2	C	2	1	0	0	9,750
Aspen Ridge	4	C	12	3	0	4	110,385
Aspen Skier	3	G	13	1	0	1	7,415
Aspenmagic	5	M	6	2	2	1	10,159
Aspersal	4	G	6	0	0	0	833
Aspirante	3	C	1	0	0	0	0
Aspirin	5	G	5	2	1	0	19,290
Aspirring George	6	H	2	0	0	0	0
Assaggini	4	F	10	1	0	0	9,940
Assault Commander	2	C	4	1	1	0	11,000
Assault Princess	6	M	6	1	1	0	4,024
Assaulting Ride (BRZ)	8	G	10	0	1	3	6,301
Assembly	7	H	1	0	0	0	750
Assert N Advantage	3	G	3	0	0	2	8,660
Assert Yourself	9	G	7	1	0	0	7,635
Asserted	3	C	5	0	0	1	5,260
Assertive One	3	F	7	2	0	1	13,965
Assertive Winner	5	M	13	1	1	4	14,151
Assess	3	F	4	0	0	1	3,520

Horse	Age	Sex	Sts	1st	2d	3d	Won	Horse	Age	Sex	Sts	1st	2d	3d	Won
Assets of Gold	3	F	11	4	1	0	35,370	Atiba	10	G	3	0	1	0	3,441
Assets of Luck	2	C	2	0	0	1	594	Atirador (BRZ)	3	G	3	0	0	0	0
Assignation	4	C	2	0	0	0	1,764	Atish	4	F	11	2	3	2	24,262
Assignment	4	F	6	3	1	1	28,193	Atitudeofgratitude (IRE)	2	F	4	0	1	1	8,690
Assistant	3	G	4	1	1	1	28,170	Atlanta Rose	3	F	7	1	1	2	26,645
Assmar	5	H	8	0	0	3	13,210	Atlantic Affair	2	F	1	0	0	1	2,860
Associate	8	H	3	1	0	0	13,800	Atlantic Ave	3	C	7	2	1	2	20,900
Assumed Risk	5	G	19	1	4	3	30,150	Atlantic Frost	2	F	3	0	0	2	7,280
Assumption	5	G	13	0	1	0	3,059	Atlantic Fury	4	F	4	1	0	0	21,720
Assured	2	F	5	0	0	0	555	Atlantic Hero	2	F	1	0	0	0	0
Assuring Touch	4	F	10	2	1	1	7,514	Atlantic Kid	2	C	3	0	1	1	6,440
Astaire Danseur	2	F	4	1	0	0	6,840	Atlantic Lover	3	F	1	0	0	0	106
Astaires Tipallade	4	C	3	0	0	0	1,850	Atlantic Mist	3	F	4	0	0	0	171
Astana	3	F	3	0	0	0	1,251	Atlantic Ocean	3	F	9	2	3	1	443,430
Astapay	2	C	5	0	1	2	2,326	Atlantic Patrol	2	F	4	1	1	0	16,080
Astarinmyeye	6	M	3	0	0	0	938	Atlantic Romance	2	F	1	0	0	0	266
Astartorember	6	G	14	1	2	3	11,044	Atlantic Snow	2	F	7	1	0	2	18,548
Asti Casino	5	M	6	1	0	2	4,513	Atlantic Wind	3	F	4	3	1	0	71,400
Astonish	4	C	12	2	3	0	14,830	Atlantic Zone	2	C	5	0	0	1	1,565
Astonishingmemory	3	C	1	0	0	0	0	Atlantis Crusader	4	G	9	6	1	0	39,900
Astor Bar	3	C	4	0	0	0	368	Atlantis Dream	4	C	10	0	2	2	8,232
Astor Street	3	G	12	1	5	0	17,345	Atlas Hugged	4	C	6	0	0	1	700
Astorbilt	4	F	8	1	0	1	21,670	Atlas Peak	2	C	3	0	1	0	2,400
Astra Ridge	8	H	12	0	1	2	10,321	Atlasta	5	G	8	0	1	1	1,788
Astral	2	C	2	0	0	0	895	Atlasta Crypto	5	M	11	0	0	1	1,620
Astral Journey	5	G	17	0	2	1	4,610	Atliata	5	M	3	0	0	0	569
Astral Plane	3	C	4	2	1	0	41,958	Atm Angie's Rodeo	2	F	1	0	0	0	240
Astral Victor	2	C	3	0	0	0	660	Atom Skier	3	C	13	1	1	2	12,774
Astraphisgal	3	F	3	0	0	0	70	Atomic	5	H	1	0	0	0	107
Astra's Sister	2	F	4	1	0	0	15,120	Atomic Connection	3	F	2	0	0	0	244
Astrickyas	4	F	12	2	0	2	7,528	Atomic Dawg	3	G	4	0	0	0	295
Astrid	5	M	5	2	0	1	86,510	Atomic Energy	3	C	7	1	0	1	8,330
Astro Flight	5	G	11	0	1	0	1,230	Atomic Sub	4	G	7	1	2	0	33,020
Astro Rex (ARG)	6	H	8	1	2	1	11,368	Atonement	5	G	1	0	0	0	0
Astrocyte	2	C	1	0	0	0	0	Atouratoura	3	G	10	3	1	2	81,180
Astrologist	5	H	4	0	1	0	7,800	Atru Dancer	5	M	5	0	0	0	123
Astrology	7	G	14	2	3	3	9,652	Atsa Pretty Muffin	4	F	1	0	0	0	840
Astronian Sound	4	C	11	2	0	1	21,560	Atsa Slew	6	H	2	0	0	0	0
Astronic	2	F	1	0	0	0	1,035	Atswhatimtalknbout	3	C	6	2	1	1	209,120
Astronomer	3	G	2	0	0	0	600	Atta Boy Bo	9	G	17	3	3	4	18,347
Astros Choice	3	F	10	0	0	3	4,919	Atta Boy David	7	H	5	1	0	0	4,500
Astuta	3	F	10	1	0	2	7,946	Atta Mom	4	F	3	0	1	1	7,250
Astuto	2	G	2	0	1	0	3,600	Attababe	3	F	4	1	0	0	11,890
Asummerforwindy	6	M	5	0	0	2	3,765	Attaboy Eskimo	7	H	8	0	0	1	1,450
Asun	4	F	7	0	2	0	7,858	Attabrook	4	G	6	1	0	2	19,395
At a Boy Harry	2	G	1	0	0	0	0	Attack Alert	2	C	2	1	1	0	38,200
At a Boy Luther	4	G	16	6	3	1	61,475	Attack Force	3	G	3	1	0	0	22,825
At a Glance	3	F	2	0	0	0	0	Attack the Books	4	C	10	2	1	2	67,153
At a Premium	5	M	14	3	1	2	19,900	Attack Zak	4	F	11	1	6	3	15,166
At Bat	3	G	4	0	1	0	1,562	Attacksum	5	G	9	3	4	1	52,270
At Dawn	3	G	10	1	1	1	55,964	Attackux	4	G	12	0	0	2	3,529
At Ease Diablo	4	F	9	0	1	1	7,920	Attainable	3	G	10	4	3	0	124,890
At Jimmy D's	3	C	9	1	0	2	9,610	Attakapa	5	G	12	0	1	2	6,103
At Presidents Day	2	C	7	0	0	0	174	Attalid	3	G	7	0	1	1	4,999
At Sword's Points	6	G	1	0	0	0	51	Attasta	5	M	9	2	1	2	7,137
At the Ball	4	F	2	1	0	0	3,720	Attawapiskat	6	G	10	1	1	1	9,836
At the Bell	3	G	3	0	0	0	0	Attaway	3	G	2	0	0	1	5,010
At the Copa	4	F	7	3	0	0	54,750	Attempt	3	C	4	0	0	0	895
At the Dock	5	G	11	1	2	2	17,493	Atten Hut	2	C	7	2	0	0	49,765
At the Mine	3	C	2	0	0	0	200	Attend to Me	3	F	7	1	0	0	2,756
At the Moment	3	C	11	1	0	1	11,840	Attention Sir	3	C	1	0	0	0	375
At the Money	3	F	7	0	0	0	910	Attenuate	3	C	5	0	1	1	3,690
At the Wheel	4	G	2	0	0	0	1,380	Atterbury	4	G	11	3	1	2	38,158
At the Wire	8	G	1	0	0	0	61	Attest	7	G	8	0	2	2	66,630
Ata Slew	4	G	1	0	0	0	150	Atti Girl Fergie	2	F	2	1	1	0	15,500
Atahualpa	9	G	8	2	1	0	8,930	Attic	3	C	7	2	4	0	47,760
Ataka Brite	5	H	14	0	1	3	2,746	Attic Sale	4	G	9	1	0	0	9,078
Ataka Cue	4	G	17	2	1	1	11,063	Attico	4	F	6	1	0	1	41,325
Ataka Go Go	5	G	5	0	0	0	508	Atticus Finch	4	G	6	0	1	2	6,640
Ataka Ridge	5	H	5	1	0	0	4,668	Atticus Forever	4	G	5	1	1	0	39,940
Atanarjuat	3	F	11	2	2	2	13,628	Atticus' Goddess	3	F	7	0	1	1	10,505
Atardecer	5	H	5	1	1	1	1,820	Atticus Kristy	2	G	2	0	0	1	5,460
Atascaderan	3	G	7	0	2	2	6,916	Atticus Lace	3	C	6	0	1	1	12,216
Atatick	2	C	1	0	0	0	105	Atticus Lady	2	F	1	0	0	0	0
Atchafalaya	3	F	7	1	2	1	24,056	Atticus River	2	C	1	0	0	0	180
Atempt Snooker	6	G	8	1	0	1	1,890	Atticus Star	3	G	7	2	2	0	69,780
Atfirst Blush	3	C	7	1	0	1	44,610	Attiki	4	F	11	2	2	1	108,283
Athena Girl	2	F	1	0	0	0	0	Attitana	4	C	5	1	1	0	1,376
Athena Starwoman	4	F	2	0	0	1	5,520	Attitudal	3	F	3	0	0	0	590

Horse	Age	Sex	Sts	1st	2d	3d	Won	Horse	Age	Sex	Sts	1st	2d	3d	Won
Attitude City	3	F	1	0	0	0	0	Auntie T	4	F	2	0	0	0	0
Attitude E. Ree	3	G	11	3	3	2	25,600	Auntie's Bag	3	F	9	2	2	3	42,558
Attitude Kate	6	M	1	0	0	0	0	Auriferous	4	G	7	0	0	0	846
Attitude Princess	2	F	1	0	0	0	130	Auriga Star	6	H	2	0	0	0	161
Attnine	4	G	4	1	0	0	5,798	Aurora G.	3	F	5	0	0	0	215
Attobigboy	5	H	9	1	1	1	11,712	Aurora Gold	3	F	10	4	2	1	19,330
Attol Costs	4	F	7	0	1	1	3,897	Aurora Guadalupe	3	F	10	3	3	1	57,704
Attonotauto	4	G	8	1	2	1	23,769	Aurora Regina	6	M	2	0	0	0	0
Attorney At Law	2	C	8	0	0	3	7,470	Aurora Tiger	3	G	1	0	0	0	0
Attractive Brass	3	G	7	2	0	0	8,893	Aurora's Charm	2	F	2	0	0	0	145
Attribution	2	C	1	0	0	0	0	Aurum	5	M	3	0	0	1	2,563
Atwaar	6	H	4	0	0	0	0	Auser Blue	4	F	10	2	2	3	14,859
Atwater	5	H	6	1	1	1	9,060	Auspicious Temper	5	M	5	0	0	0	582
Atwinkleinhereye	5	M	2	1	0	0	3,840	Auspiciously	5	G	1	1	0	0	6,380
Atylia	2	F	1	0	0	0	135	Aussie Girl	6	M	16	3	3	1	50,465
Atys Pistol	4	F	5	1	1	1	2,107	Aussie Playgirl	2	F	1	0	0	0	95
Au Fait	4	F	1	0	0	0	0	Aussie's Crown	4	C	1	0	0	0	0
Au Journee	3	F	3	0	0	0	0	Austere	2	F	1	0	0	0	0
Au Point Sauce	3	G	12	1	0	4	11,515	Austin Barber	2	G	13	2	2	0	29,870
Au Poivre	8	G	4	0	1	2	2,790	Austin L.	2	C	3	0	0	0	1,908
Auat	5	G	23	2	4	1	13,353	Austin Richard	6	H	8	1	1	3	7,446
Aubee's Prospect	3	G	6	0	1	1	8,280	Austin W	2	C	2	0	0	0	2,660
Aubrey's Hope	8	M	2	0	0	0	0	Austin's Ace	3	F	6	1	0	1	5,224
Aubrianna	5	M	13	0	2	1	4,454	Austin's Assassin	3	G	1	0	1	0	2,050
Aud	3	F	11	4	2	0	228,045	Austin's Awesome	4	G	15	0	2	2	34,929
Audacious Alice	5	M	5	0	1	2	2,334	Austin's Belle	3	F	12	4	2	3	110,350
Audacious Explorer	7	G	15	3	2	1	51,770	Austin's Charm	6	G	13	3	1	2	27,976
Audacious Girl	3	F	9	1	0	0	4,014	Austin's Mom	3	F	10	4	1	0	105,190
Audacious Kid	7	M	2	0	0	0	0	Austin's Victory	4	G	8	0	0	0	651
Audax Minor	4	G	10	2	2	0	18,995	Auston's Chief	7	G	6	0	0	1	1,400
Audio Express	3	F	11	2	2	1	23,239	Australis	4	F	4	0	0	3	18,056
Audio Player	4	C	2	0	0	0	0	Austrian Devil	5	G	15	1	4	2	23,096
Audioslave	2	C	2	0	0	0	214	Austyn's Rose	5	M	3	2	0	0	4,400
Audit Exception	4	F	4	0	1	0	8,762	Authenic	3	F	3	0	0	1	1,345
Audrey Hep	3	F	5	2	2	0	77,374	Authentic	5	G	10	2	0	1	4,775
Audreys Dream	4	F	5	0	0	1	1,496	Authentic Lady	4	F	1	0	0	0	1,230
Audrey's Hope	4	F	13	0	0	3	6,043	Authentic Luck	10	M	1	0	0	0	0
Audrey's Quest	3	F	1	0	0	0	0	Authentic Prince	10	G	1	0	0	0	0
Aufluential	9	M	13	2	2	1	15,419	Authenticated	3	F	4	0	1	0	873
Auguri Shardae	4	F	12	0	1	1	11,817	Autistic Angel	2	F	1	0	0	0	0
August Game	3	F	13	2	1	1	12,906	Autistic Girl	3	F	15	2	1	3	84,794
August Moon Dancer	4	F	9	0	1	1	8,658	Auto Be a Chuto	2	G	2	0	0	0	0
August Song	4	C	7	3	0	0	71,400	Auto Be Del	2	F	4	0	1	2	4,332
August West	3	G	6	0	1	2	7,680	Auto City	3	C	11	1	5	2	67,820
Augusta Lady	4	F	6	0	0	1	1,527	Auto Drive	3	C	6	0	0	1	1,546
Augustan	4	C	16	2	1	0	18,558	Auto Pilot	2	C	3	0	0	2	11,500
Augusta's Slew	5	G	1	0	0	0	0	Autobesarah	5	M	12	2	2	3	94,472
Augustness	3	F	8	1	0	4	17,780	Autocrat	2	C	7	0	1	1	5,120
Augustus Gold	2	C	1	0	0	0	0	Autocry	4	C	1	0	0	0	0
Augustus McGee	4	G	1	0	0	0	45	Automatic O. D.	6	H	20	2	4	3	14,404
Augustus the Roman	3	G	1	0	0	0	0	Automatic Teller	5	G	12	1	2	0	11,169
Aukbar	3	G	2	0	0	1	4,609	Automatic Tie	4	F	3	0	0	0	616
Auke Bay	3	C	15	1	1	3	18,630	Automatic Weapon	2	C	3	1	0	0	9,000
Aunt Bertie	3	F	2	0	0	0	570	Autonomy (IRE)	6	H	8	0	1	3	30,008
Aunt Beth	3	F	1	0	1	0	5,600	Autopscot	3	G	2	0	1	1	7,920
Aunt Celie	4	F	2	1	0	0	5,130	Autowinner	2	C	1	0	0	0	0
Aunt Chick	5	M	8	2	2	2	10,118	Autum Pie	2	F	3	0	0	0	1,301
Aunt Connie	3	F	12	1	0	0	21,533	Autumn Accent	2	F	1	1	0	0	28,200
Aunt Eller	3	F	7	2	0	0	10,813	Autumn Ayr	3	F	6	0	0	0	80
Aunt Emily	3	F	1	0	0	0	120	Autumn Bliss	2	F	4	1	0	1	14,878
Aunt Emma	6	M	2	0	0	0	0	Autumn Colors	3	F	9	1	1	3	24,975
Aunt Emma's Magic	7	M	14	0	0	2	5,500	Autumn Creek	4	F	4	2	0	0	31,560
Aunt Eva	5	M	8	0	0	2	643	Autumn Due	4	C	10	1	1	0	25,950
Aunt Filomena	4	F	13	1	2	3	10,772	Autumn Flame	4	C	3	0	0	0	1,200
Aunt Gemma	2	F	2	0	0	0	0	Autumn Glow	4	F	9	1	1	2	34,680
Aunt Ike	3	F	19	3	2	3	29,175	Autumn Prospect	3	F	7	2	5	0	45,650
Aunt Imo	4	F	3	0	0	0	0	Autumn Runner	6	G	11	2	2	1	28,205
Aunt Jewell	6	M	3	2	0	0	2,481	Autumn Sky	3	F	5	0	0	0	0
Aunt Laura	5	M	5	0	0	1	1,400	Autumn Two	3	F	6	0	0	0	600
Aunt Lilly	6	M	2	0	0	0	0	Autumn Ty	3	F	1	0	0	0	224
Aunt Louise	5	M	2	0	0	1	1,870	Autumn Weekend	5	G	11	0	1	2	2,176
Aunt Lynnie	8	M	8	0	0	0	558	Autumn's Molly	2	F	5	0	0	0	840
Aunt Marguerite	5	M	1	0	0	0	42	Ava Anne	3	F	5	1	0	1	35,730
Aunt Minerva	3	F	5	0	0	1	1,675	Ava Jayne	4	F	4	0	0	0	570
Aunt Pansy	4	F	12	1	1	2	7,551	Ava Marisa	4	F	10	1	3	1	16,873
Aunt Shee Shee	4	F	7	0	2	1	2,607	Avail	4	G	3	0	0	0	560
Aunt Sophie	5	M	4	2	0	1	67,250	Available	5	G	8	2	1	0	6,852
Aunt Tizzy	2	F	4	1	0	1	15,046	Available Katie	3	F	15	0	1	0	3,795
Auntie Laura	4	F	2	0	0	0	103	Avalanche Alert	2	G	4	0	0	0	2,100

Horse	Age	Sex	Sts	1st	2d	3d	Won	Horse	Age	Sex	Sts	1st	2d	3d	Won
Avalanche Bay	2	F	2	0	1	0	6,000	Awesome Aggie	4	F	4	0	0	0	0
Avalancher	11	G	15	3	4	4	18,635	Awesome Alarm	2	C	6	2	1	1	18,734
Avalino	2	C	3	0	1	1	6,540	Awesome Alec	4	G	7	0	1	1	3,710
Avalos	4	F	7	2	1	2	58,131	Awesome Allen	2	C	2	0	0	0	160
Avanzado (ARG)	6	H	8	2	2	0	602,645	Awesome American	5	H	8	1	0	0	4,422
Avaricity	2	F	5	0	1	0	6,360	Awesome Anew	2	F	2	0	0	0	2,000
Avary too Step	4	F	4	1	0	1	12,300	Awesome Asher	3	G	1	0	0	0	0
Ava's Delight	5	M	2	0	0	2	1,930	Awesome Attorney	2	C	4	1	1	1	34,096
Ava's Future	2	F	8	1	0	0	5,210	Awesome Audrey	8	M	8	3	1	0	23,695
Avast	5	M	8	1	0	1	5,092	Awesome Beginning	2	F	6	0	2	1	28,000
Avastro	3	F	6	0	0	0	288	Awesome Cannonball	3	C	2	1	0	0	15,940
Avatar Moon	2	G	2	0	0	0	744	Awesome Charm	3	F	8	4	1	1	93,160
Ave Atque Vale	3	G	11	2	1	0	35,113	Awesome Charmer	3	F	9	1	2	4	9,844
Ave de Rapina	7	G	10	1	1	1	13,820	Awesome Dancer	5	G	6	2	0	1	2,422
Ave of Excess	2	F	2	0	0	0	176	Awesome Dancing	3	G	7	0	0	1	13,220
Avec Toi (FR)	4	F	7	2	2	0	39,985	Awesome Deduction	2	F	1	0	0	0	0
Avenella's Dancer	6	M	2	0	0	1	1,760	Awesome Deed	5	M	3	0	0	0	1,428
Avengin Annie	3	F	1	0	0	0	82	Awesome Devil	2	C	1	1	0	0	6,879
Avenging Bullet	3	C	9	0	0	2	4,130	Awesome Dividend	3	C	2	0	0	1	6,300
Avenging Eagle	8	G	10	1	0	0	3,551	Awesome Echo	3	C	2	0	0	0	0
Avenging Hill	8	G	15	1	1	3	4,652	Awesome Feu	3	C	3	1	0	1	8,564
Avenging Passion	6	M	12	4	4	1	97,440	Awesome Find	4	G	2	0	0	0	0
Avenida Del Cielo	4	F	4	1	0	0	2,590	Awesome for Sure	3	F	13	0	1	3	15,669
Avenida Lady	4	F	3	0	0	1	4,785	Awesome Form	3	C	4	0	1	2	3,379
Aventura	4	G	11	0	2	2	3,877	Awesome Fox	4	F	7	1	2	0	3,370
Aventura Place	3	C	9	2	0	2	59,780	Awesome Frances	3	F	5	1	1	0	20,481
Aventurous Sword	3	G	3	1	0	0	15,600	Awesome Gal	3	F	8	0	1	3	28,310
Avenue of Magic	3	G	8	0	0	4	14,109	Awesome Here	4	G	10	1	2	1	17,911
Avenue of Rich's	4	G	1	0	0	0	250	Awesome Humor	3	F	7	2	4	0	539,835
Avenue of Royalty	4	G	5	1	1	0	15,750	Awesome Image	2	F	2	0	0	0	360
Avenue of Siam	4	G	8	4	1	0	21,425	Awesome Joy	2	F	2	1	0	0	26,350
Avenueofknowledge	4	G	4	0	0	0	760	Awesome Knight	8	G	3	0	0	0	205
Average Down	6	H	9	0	0	0	2,201	Awesome Lad	2	G	5	0	1	0	2,655
Average Star	2	F	2	0	1	0	1,820	Awesome Lady	2	F	5	1	0	1	25,160
Averill Park	3	F	4	2	0	0	10,940	Awesome Look	2	C	2	0	0	0	0
Avert	2	G	2	0	0	0	0	Awesome Mass	2	F	2	0	0	0	480
Avery's Rebel	5	M	3	0	0	0	204	Awesome Minister	3	G	6	0	0	1	1,323
Ave's Princessa	3	F	8	1	0	1	34,860	Awesome Missile	5	G	10	0	0	0	405
Avian	6	M	8	3	1	2	38,630	Awesome of Course	3	C	8	2	0	0	60,230
Aviation Vacation	5	M	5	2	0	1	8,912	Awesome Out West	5	H	1	0	0	0	113
Aviatress	3	F	4	0	1	0	14,380	Awesome Powers	3	F	16	1	3	4	29,895
Avid Achiever	4	G	6	0	0	0	1,812	Awesome Prospect	2	G	3	0	0	1	1,970
Avid David	4	G	15	2	2	1	14,641	Awesome Reef	3	F	10	0	0	3	14,620
Avid Skier	2	C	2	2	0	0	20,295	Awesome Royale	3	G	10	0	3	2	6,266
Avid Spell	2	C	7	1	2	0	10,713	Awesome Rush	3	G	8	1	4	1	102,600
Avie Cielo	6	G	2	0	0	0	320	Awesome Time	3	C	9	2	1	1	189,610
Avie Street	4	G	6	0	0	1	2,100	Awesome Touch	3	F	8	1	1	1	57,521
Avies Blue Max	3	C	2	0	0	0	1,370	Awesome Weapon	3	G	9	1	1	1	24,457
Avies Halo	3	C	6	1	0	0	1,960	Awesomebabyawesome	2	C	4	0	0	0	570
Avies Perfect Copy	3	F	2	0	0	0	0	Awesomewithbroads	2	C	4	1	0	0	20,456
Avie's Princess	4	F	8	2	0	0	53,575	Awestruck	2	C	2	0	0	0	43
Avimora	3	F	2	1	0	0	19,800	Awful Tricky	2	C	5	0	0	0	1,162
Aviso	4	C	10	2	0	2	42,460	Awfully Awesome	5	H	7	0	1	2	3,295
Avranches (FR)	4	F	10	0	0	1	10,084	Awhim	4	F	10	0	1	1	3,045
Avril Ann	2	F	3	0	0	0	325	Awholelotanothin	2	F	3	0	1	0	5,689
Awad of Bills	3	G	5	1	0	0	15,030	Awholelotofmalarky	5	H	4	0	1	1	9,520
Awad of Money	3	G	8	0	0	1	2,495	Awininthepipeline	2	C	2	0	0	0	0
Awadawin	3	C	1	0	0	0	0	Awishandaprayer	2	F	4	1	0	1	18,950
Awadist	3	F	3	0	0	0	0	Awol	4	F	5	1	0	0	12,970
Awads Award	3	C	10	1	0	2	12,266	Awol Honey	7	G	9	0	0	1	3,625
Awad's Jackie	3	F	10	1	2	1	15,154	Awol Soldier	4	G	8	1	0	0	12,763
Awaiting Good News	3	F	7	1	0	0	7,220	Awsom Light	2	C	2	0	0	0	1,200
Awake America	4	F	12	0	0	1	1,752	Awsome Cause	4	F	3	0	2	0	5,880
Awake At the Gate	5	G	1	0	0	0	89	Awsumsausum	3	C	16	1	1	2	13,650
Awaken the Dragon	3	C	5	1	1	2	46,260	Awtair	3	C	4	1	1	1	10,950
Awanda	3	F	7	1	2	1	30,610	Axe Maggie Mae	6	M	7	0	0	1	632
Award Winning Team	3	C	1	0	0	0	0	Axe N Ice	8	M	1	0	0	0	0
Aware (GB)	8	H	2	0	0	0	0	Axe's Fancy Blaze	3	F	3	0	0	0	0
Away	6	M	1	0	0	0	0	Axis	4	C	15	1	4	0	46,990
Away to Boston	2	C	1	1	0	0	14,810	Axle	3	C	12	2	2	1	38,260
Away to Go	3	F	7	0	0	0	4,140	Axle Lode	12	G	2	0	0	0	80
Away West	2	C	3	0	0	0	795	Axle Powder	4	G	4	0	0	0	165
Awayatcamp	3	F	4	1	0	0	6,370	Axtell G R	4	G	6	0	0	1	2,547
Awayne	3	G	11	2	1	0	13,730	Ay Dee Dee	2	F	3	1	0	0	22,000
Awayo	4	F	12	0	1	0	2,400	Ay Won	5	G	1	0	0	0	0
Awaysaway	3	F	10	1	1	1	8,390	Aya	5	M	1	0	0	0	0
Awe	3	G	14	4	2	1	62,110	Ayanna	4	F	1	0	0	0	0
Awesome Action	3	G	11	2	2	1	140,769	Aye a Hot Shot	3	C	7	1	0	0	13,408
Awesome Adam	3	G	6	0	0	1	1,097	Aye Begor	2	G	1	0	0	0	0

Horse	Age	Sex	Sts	1st	2d	3d	Won	Horse	Age	Sex	Sts	1st	2d	3d	Won
Aye Chihuahua	3	G	8	0	1	1	7,990	B My Slew	2	F	1	0	0	0	120
Aye Glide Along	6	H	13	1	3	1	12,388	B n' Bay	3	F	14	1	1	1	7,305
Aye Trouble	6	H	7	0	1	1	8,360	B N One	2	G	4	0	0	1	1,110
Ayearintime	4	G	3	0	0	0	1,747	B One Bomber	4	F	1	0	0	0	0
Ayita	3	F	9	2	3	2	28,690	B Onefifty	2	C	10	0	0	1	2,355
Aylward	8	H	4	1	0	0	1,370	B R Sweetie	3	F	3	0	0	0	244
Ayr Three Miles	5	G	13	3	2	1	18,215	B Rock	4	G	10	0	0	0	748
Ayres Hall	5	M	10	1	1	2	20,480	B Rules	4	C	3	0	1	0	2,920
Aza	2	G	5	0	0	1	8,615	B T Cruiser	2	C	6	1	0	1	4,205
Azal	5	H	5	0	0	0	517	B T's Birthday	4	F	8	1	1	1	5,367
Azalean	4	F	14	3	2	2	43,270	B W's Pride	4	F	12	0	1	1	3,312
Azazel	5	G	9	1	1	0	18,260	B. a . Tabbie	2	G	3	0	0	0	475
Azdeck	2	F	1	0	0	0	882	B. a Dancer	4	C	1	0	0	0	0
Azer	2	C	5	0	0	0	180	B. A. Way	3	C	6	0	2	0	17,195
Azeri	5	M	8	5	4	1	817,080	B. All Mine	4	C	2	0	0	1	1,380
Azichill	3	F	7	3	0	1	26,520	B. B. Ruckus	2	F	2	1	0	1	9,022
Azillion	5	G	5	1	0	0	4,750	B. B.'s Finest	2	C	2	0	0	0	0
Azillion (IRE)	4	C	3	1	0	1	30,240	B. B.'s Johnny	2	C	2	0	0	0	890
Azimut	4	F	6	0	0	0	1,520	B. B.'s Pride	3	G	8	0	0	0	1,296
Aziorder	3	G	7	3	0	2	34,355	B. C. Manners	2	F	1	0	0	0	0
Aziyan	3	C	3	0	0	1	2,960	B. C. Perseverance	5	H	9	1	3	3	12,709
Azle	5	G	15	0	1	1	3,506	B. C. Taylor	3	C	1	0	0	0	370
Azotus	5	G	2	0	0	0	38	B. C. West	5	G	13	2	1	3	104,506
Aztec	2	F	2	0	0	0	195	B. C.'s Hero	2	G	2	0	0	0	748
Aztec Pearl	4	F	8	1	1	1	46,860	B. D. Cube	11	G	1	0	0	0	0
Aztec Silver	7	G	1	0	0	0	54	B. D. Victor	6	G	9	1	3	1	77,583
Aztec Two	11	H	1	0	0	0	0	B. Extreme	8	G	8	5	0	2	11,614
Azteco de Oro	3	G	7	2	1	0	36,536	B. Fabulous	5	M	5	2	1	0	8,945
Aztek Sky	5	G	17	3	1	0	16,672	B. G. Tiger	4	C	4	1	2	0	39,606
Azure	5	M	12	1	0	2	16,977	B. G.'s Choice	2	F	3	1	0	0	14,130
Azure Blue Angel	5	M	3	0	0	0	130	B. G.'s Dream	2	F	1	0	1	0	5,200
Azure Ciel	7	G	7	1	1	3	23,660	B. G.'s Trix	2	F	1	0	0	0	212
Azure Spring	3	F	4	0	1	1	17,880	B. Geri	4	C	3	0	0	0	580
B an R Money	2	F	1	0	1	0	1,340	B. Good Hero	3	C	8	1	2	1	15,570
B B Blues	6	G	18	0	0	0	924	B. H. Dream	3	F	11	3	0	1	11,145
B B Brite	3	G	11	4	3	2	26,219	B. J. Bear	4	F	5	1	1	0	8,766
B B Choice	2	F	5	0	1	1	8,115	B. J. Burg	6	G	15	0	0	1	2,363
B B Dancer	5	G	11	1	0	1	12,725	B. J. Star	3	G	9	2	1	0	13,996
B B M Xtra	3	G	9	1	0	2	8,789	B. J.'s Baby	4	F	10	0	0	0	1,521
B B Saunter	2	C	5	0	0	0	1,020	B. J.'s Country	5	G	9	1	1	2	4,796
B B Superstar	4	F	3	1	0	0	4,320	B. J.'s Dancer	4	C	4	1	0	1	5,320
B Bop Aloopa	5	M	10	1	5	2	11,812	B. J.'s Miss Belle	3	F	6	0	0	0	412
B B's Account	3	C	12	0	3	2	34,980	B. J.'s Secret	2	C	1	0	0	0	0
B B's Girl	4	F	1	0	0	0	0	B. J.'s Toy	9	H	1	0	0	0	0
B B's Pleasure	4	F	8	2	1	1	19,292	B. K.'s Prince	4	G	5	1	2	1	19,907
B Flat Major	8	G	14	2	2	4	24,165	B. Linda L.	3	F	1	0	0	0	0
B G Drums	4	G	5	0	0	0	400	B. Lucky	3	C	9	2	0	0	38,885
B Gone Blues	3	F	7	1	1	0	32,340	B. Mr. Lucky	9	G	4	0	1	0	2,062
B Great Today	3	F	9	2	1	4	10,785	B. N. Bad	3	G	6	0	0	0	630
B J Bullet	3	F	5	0	1	0	2,870	B. Nile	7	G	11	0	1	4	22,125
B J Hungarian	7	M	2	0	0	0	0	B. Nimble Jak	8	G	10	1	0	2	13,736
B J S Twister	4	C	4	0	0	0	0	B. R. Dream	4	C	6	0	0	1	2,450
B J Valentine	3	C	2	0	1	0	940	B. R. Prospector	6	G	16	0	3	3	7,347
B Jazzy	5	M	2	0	0	0	1,260	B. S. Smoked Duck	6	G	5	0	1	0	808
B J's Bandit	5	H	5	1	2	0	7,250	B. Seger	6	G	12	0	1	2	2,396
B J's Black Gold	4	F	11	2	1	2	10,952	B. T. Hudson	5	G	14	2	2	3	14,106
B J's Classact	5	M	6	1	1	1	4,130	B. W. Bihm	4	G	10	1	0	0	9,417
B J's Classic	5	G	2	0	0	0	225	B. W. Randolph	3	G	2	0	1	0	2,180
B J's Dream	7	G	1	0	0	0	190	B. Z. Jones	4	G	5	2	1	0	46,000
B J's Gypsy	4	G	5	0	0	0	555	Ba Ba Boom	3	C	4	1	0	2	36,045
B J's Me Me	4	F	12	0	3	1	7,990	Ba Ma Mama	4	F	8	1	1	1	8,739
B J's Mon	5	H	5	0	0	0	450	Baba Blue	3	F	10	2	1	1	18,075
B J's Mr Gold	7	G	11	0	1	3	2,640	Baba Gonzo	2	F	5	1	2	0	41,600
B J's On Fire	3	F	5	0	0	0	0	Bababing	3	F	11	0	4	1	5,711
B J's Pistol	4	G	8	2	1	3	24,840	Babarocke	2	C	1	0	0	0	75
B J's Smile	4	G	18	1	2	1	11,637	Baba's Best	3	C	3	0	0	0	0
B J's Star Budget	2	G	1	0	0	0	0	Baba's Pie	4	C	5	0	0	0	584
B J's Verse	5	G	13	2	1	4	13,502	Babay Julep	2	F	3	0	0	0	542
B K Dodger	4	C	1	0	1	0	2,622	Babbler	4	F	7	0	0	2	5,640
B K Stubby	4	G	17	1	7	1	16,358	Babe Ruthie	4	F	1	0	0	0	0
B K's On the Park	2	C	2	0	0	0	0	Babe Too	6	M	2	1	1	0	7,520
B L Cool	2	G	5	0	1	0	2,450	Babe's Baby	2	F	4	0	0	0	264
B L T to Go	3	G	3	0	0	0	50	Babe's Bet	3	C	3	0	0	0	1,962
B L's Banker	2	C	1	0	0	0	0	Babes Blade	5	G	2	0	0	0	138
B L's Booboo	4	F	1	1	0	0	3,480	Babe's Dream	6	G	8	4	2	2	27,510
B L's Gal	4	F	11	0	0	0	675	Babe's Flair	4	F	5	0	0	1	2,110
B L's Secretia	4	F	11	0	1	1	3,540	Babes Glory	2	G	4	0	0	0	310
B L's Sweep	7	G	8	2	0	2	6,168	Babe's Jubilee	5	G	6	1	0	1	22,643
B Mark	4	G	2	0	0	0	91	Babe's Match	4	C	7	1	0	0	2,470

Horse	Age	Sex	Sts	1st	2d	3d	Won
Babes Wont Tell	4	C	10	2	2	1	16,048
Babe'sgremlinpeace	5	G	3	0	0	0	0
Babeth (BRZ)	4	F	5	0	1	0	8,110
Babilicious Bride	2	F	2	1	0	0	7,800
Babinsky	4	G	12	1	0	1	7,133
Baboom	7	M	7	0	1	0	1,516
Babson Business	3	F	5	0	0	0	900
Baby Angel	3	F	6	1	0	0	34,068
Baby Ankles	3	F	9	0	1	0	2,500
Baby B Cool	5	M	5	0	0	1	885
Baby Bayou	9	G	5	0	0	0	470
Baby Bea	4	F	10	0	0	0	330
Baby Beans	5	M	3	0	0	2	4,280
Baby Bear's Soup	3	C	8	1	3	2	31,910
Baby Berk	5	G	3	0	0	0	0
Baby Bird C C	3	F	17	2	1	2	38,996
Baby Book	4	F	7	2	2	1	5,405
Baby Boomer	7	H	4	1	0	1	1,616
Baby Bubbles	4	F	6	0	0	0	912
Baby Butz	9	G	14	1	1	2	7,905
Baby Chips	4	F	9	2	0	1	14,840
Baby Concerto	3	F	8	1	0	1	5,496
Baby Corn	4	F	12	2	2	3	11,012
Baby Doll	4	F	5	1	1	0	4,095
Baby Frank	4	C	1	0	0	0	145
Baby G	8	G	3	0	0	0	350
Baby Girl Paula	2	F	1	0	0	0	0
Baby Hailey	3	F	4	0	1	1	5,351
Baby Helen	5	M	2	1	0	0	5,550
Baby Hold On	2	F	5	0	0	0	660
Baby I'm Ablaze	7	G	3	0	0	0	120
Baby I'm Bad	2	C	2	0	1	0	5,400
Baby I'm Gone	3	G	5	1	1	2	5,200
Baby I'm the One	2	C	1	0	1	0	4,400
Baby I'm Wild	3	F	4	1	1	0	16,190
Baby J	5	M	8	1	2	1	17,624
Baby Jack	5	H	1	0	0	0	122
Baby Jewel	2	F	2	0	0	0	348
Baby Kat	4	F	2	0	0	0	185
Baby Leena	3	F	11	1	2	0	13,910
Baby Lets Cruise	3	F	5	0	1	0	6,790
Baby Let's Groove	2	F	3	2	0	0	9,295
Baby Let's Roll	3	F	8	2	3	1	32,210
Baby Lock	5	M	1	0	0	0	145
Baby Mel	4	F	6	0	0	0	0
Baby Milo	4	G	11	0	3	3	7,570
Baby Poppy	7	G	4	0	1	0	3,780
Baby Shane	4	F	3	0	0	0	225
Baby Shaq	6	G	14	3	2	6	51,045
Baby Shark	5	H	6	2	3	0	126,000
Baby Slew	2	G	2	0	0	0	0
Baby Slippers	3	F	1	0	0	0	410
Baby Star	4	F	4	0	0	3	2,126
Baby Stories	5	M	5	0	1	0	1,724
Baby Supreme	2	F	7	0	2	3	4,332
Baby Trend	6	G	19	5	4	2	31,811
Baby Wallys Joy	3	F	8	1	2	2	4,430
Baby Wave	7	G	2	0	0	1	495
Baby Winalot	5	M	4	0	0	2	1,500
Babybeef	4	C	6	0	0	1	385
Babyletsrocknroll	9	M	3	0	1	0	439
Babypaws	4	C	2	0	0	0	0
Babysgottado	4	F	5	1	0	1	5,450
Baca	6	M	12	3	2	3	35,414
Bacardi Boys	7	G	10	1	1	0	13,621
Baccalaureate	4	C	4	0	1	1	12,960
Bachelor Blues	2	C	8	2	3	0	265,406
Bachelor Forever	4	G	7	1	1	0	9,807
Bachelor Girl	2	F	2	0	0	0	0
Bachelorette	4	F	11	1	1	1	5,360
Bachelorette Party	4	F	7	0	1	1	5,230
Bachelor's Delight	3	F	11	2	5	2	81,540
Bachelor's Gold	3	G	15	1	1	2	22,420
Back Again Ben	2	C	1	0	0	0	0
Back Bay Bea	2	F	10	0	2	3	33,970
Back Bay Boss	3	C	7	1	0	3	9,342
Back Bay Lady	3	F	7	1	3	1	58,110
Back Booth	3	G	14	4	1	4	43,050
Back Door Betsey	6	M	1	0	0	0	37
Back Door Money	4	F	4	0	0	0	462
Back Houser	6	H	4	2	2	0	13,150
Back O Bourke	5	G	3	0	0	0	1,265
Back of the Pack	8	H	12	1	3	1	15,736
Back Peddle	6	G	7	2	3	0	21,680
Back Rae	3	G	3	0	0	0	360
Back Spin	4	G	7	0	0	1	1,204
Back Stage Carl	3	F	4	0	0	0	541
Back Stage Harlot	6	M	10	1	1	4	5,502
Back Street Gal	3	F	8	4	0	1	24,645
Back to Capetown	3	F	4	1	0	0	34,520
Back to Ribot	3	G	11	0	0	1	2,270
Back to Riyadh	6	G	13	1	1	0	5,608
Back to Work	3	G	10	2	0	0	55,224
Back Twacking	5	M	8	1	1	0	6,024
Back With Hope	3	F	4	1	0	1	1,628
Backatitagain	6	G	13	1	1	0	17,484
Backbone	3	C	6	1	2	0	22,380
Backdoorpick	5	G	1	0	0	0	42
Backhaul	6	G	13	4	1	1	30,145
Backinline	6	H	9	3	0	1	10,687
Backinthebusiness	3	F	10	1	2	2	55,590
Backoffboyz	3	F	10	0	1	1	2,445
Backonbabyside	3	C	2	0	1	0	420
Backseat Romance	4	F	9	1	0	2	16,890
Backstreet Music	4	G	10	1	3	1	3,837
Backstretch Boone	4	C	11	1	1	2	7,555
Backthat Thing Up	3	F	1	0	1	0	5,240
Backwater Hope	3	F	10	2	2	1	23,715
Backwater Nikki	6	M	12	0	1	0	3,611
Backwoods Chill	10	G	3	0	0	0	0
Backyard	4	F	2	0	0	0	44
Bad	2	F	1	0	0	0	0
Bad Act	3	G	3	0	0	0	1,430
Bad Bad Brenda	6	M	11	1	0	0	6,270
Bad Bad Dancer	5	G	5	0	0	0	0
Bad Bad Mojo	5	H	2	0	0	0	0
Bad Bad Red	6	M	11	1	1	1	4,333
Bad Bad Rocket	3	G	3	1	1	0	19,440
Bad Betsy	2	F	7	1	1	1	35,585
Bad Billy	4	C	2	0	0	0	0
Bad Bo	3	G	1	0	0	0	0
Bad Bobbie	3	F	2	0	1	0	2,312
Bad Boy Bill	2	G	3	0	0	0	1,060
Bad Boy Bob	5	G	4	0	0	0	119
Bad Boy Eric	8	G	5	0	0	1	1,034
Bad Boy Slew	7	G	1	0	0	0	38
Bad Boy Yankee	6	H	6	3	1	1	19,316
Bad Brad	7	H	7	0	1	0	1,090
Bad Cop Good Cop	4	G	9	1	1	3	17,439
Bad Dog	7	G	9	0	2	3	8,405
Bad Dog Press	5	H	3	1	0	1	6,950
Bad Fox	3	G	15	2	2	2	14,775
Bad Gambler	3	C	6	0	2	1	14,750
Bad Hock Rock	3	C	9	2	0	0	36,165
Bad Hombre	5	G	4	0	0	1	1,790
Bad Kitty	2	F	5	3	1	0	66,036
Bad Little Fellow	4	G	11	2	1	1	35,673
Bad Machine	4	F	3	0	0	0	0
Bad Man's Bride	2	F	1	0	0	0	1,500
Bad Medicine	7	G	2	0	0	0	0
Bad N Beautiful	3	F	2	0	0	0	3,690
Bad Pirate	6	G	2	0	0	0	225
Bad Rule	4	C	5	2	2	1	8,185
Bad to the Bone	5	G	9	0	1	1	5,435
Bad Toda Bone	11	G	8	3	1	0	7,382
Bad White	5	H	8	0	0	2	3,692
Bada Bam Bada Boom	5	G	10	3	0	1	82,239
Bada in Nevada	2	C	2	0	0	1	3,220
Badaboom	4	F	10	0	0	1	4,312
Badasbill	3	C	8	0	0	1	3,016
Badasiwantabe	8	G	8	1	0	1	4,224
Badcopnodonut	4	G	4	0	0	0	1,050
Badfish	2	G	7	1	0	2	9,155
Badge of Glory	2	G	5	0	0	0	110
Badge of Silver	3	C	3	2	0	0	130,500
Badger Bob	3	G	9	3	1	0	37,123
Badger Creek	6	G	3	0	0	0	300
Badger Don	8	G	9	4	0	2	9,573

Horse	Age	Sex	Sts	1st	2d	3d	Won
Badger Gold	7	G	1	0	0	0	0
Badger K. Eli	4	G	9	4	2	1	41,635
Badger Ridge	4	G	10	0	1	3	4,402
Badger's Lass	4	F	9	1	2	1	22,137
Badgerup	3	C	16	0	1	2	19,264
Badgett of Honor	3	G	2	0	1	1	5,950
Badgett's Mandate	2	C	6	1	3	0	78,220
Badgett's Mango	4	F	11	2	1	1	61,272
Badinage	3	F	15	2	2	2	40,300
Badiola	3	G	6	0	2	2	3,653
Badlite	4	F	7	2	1	0	6,347
Badmitton	5	G	9	1	2	1	5,145
Badness	6	H	3	0	0	1	1,345
Badolstory	3	G	6	3	0	1	12,073
Badshot	3	G	11	1	2	1	7,289
Baeled Haye	4	G	3	0	1	0	4,920
Baendaz	7	H	10	0	2	0	1,979
Bag a Bit	6	G	11	1	1	0	7,034
Bag a Buckie	3	C	1	0	0	0	0
Bag 'Em	3	G	10	0	0	1	15,260
Bag 'Em Up	6	G	1	0	0	0	0
Bag It Up	4	G	16	1	2	0	7,918
Bag Me One	4	F	5	0	0	0	765
Bag Me Up	4	C	5	0	0	0	0
Bag N Needle	5	M	3	1	0	0	7,200
Bag of Allusions	3	F	5	1	1	0	13,300
Bag of Gems	3	G	18	4	0	4	33,556
Bag of Jules	3	G	11	2	1	3	26,710
Bag of Mischief	4	C	7	1	1	0	51,140
Bag of Snow	5	G	18	3	4	6	38,644
Bag of Stars	5	M	11	2	1	1	50,690
Bag of Sugar	4	F	2	0	0	0	0
Bag of Tootie's	3	F	3	1	0	0	9,000
Bag That Alarm	6	G	15	3	1	3	18,940
Bag the Crown	5	M	5	0	1	0	2,828
Bag the Gold	3	G	8	1	0	0	6,961
Bag to the Bone	2	G	3	0	1	0	12,140
Bagdad Gambler	3	G	1	0	0	0	320
Bagdad Sands	4	F	6	1	1	1	5,152
Baggage	3	G	1	0	0	0	0
Baggerina	3	F	7	1	1	1	8,193
Baggy Pants	4	F	10	2	1	1	10,803
Baghran	2	G	8	1	0	1	37,117
Bagitdon'tchargeit	2	F	8	1	1	0	38,418
Bagless	5	G	2	0	0	1	1,320
Bagnit	4	G	11	3	2	0	9,300
Bagobucks	4	G	12	1	4	1	33,121
Bagofwhispers	3	F	3	0	0	0	0
Bagonia Bay	4	F	4	2	0	1	16,980
Bags Are Packed	4	G	3	1	0	0	27,150
Bag's Soul	8	G	1	0	0	0	0
Bagyourown	4	C	4	1	0	1	2,565
Bah Humbug	2	C	2	0	0	0	150
Bahama Boy	9	G	9	1	1	1	5,665
Bahama John	3	C	2	1	0	0	28,275
Bahati River	4	F	13	2	3	4	24,406
Bahroba	5	H	6	1	1	1	21,815
Baiana	4	F	2	0	1	0	1,245
Baie (FR)	3	F	8	2	3	0	120,571
Baie Comeau	5	G	4	1	0	0	8,771
Bail Bond	6	M	5	0	0	2	10,670
Bail Me Out Again	2	F	1	0	0	0	0
Bail Money	7	M	2	0	0	0	800
Bail N Out	3	C	2	0	0	0	310
Bail Out the Broad	4	C	7	1	0	0	17,585
Bail Out the King	5	G	9	1	1	1	68,490
Bailadora	6	M	5	2	0	0	13,560
Bailamos	4	G	13	1	3	0	31,220
Bailar	4	F	12	0	2	2	23,480
Bailee's Clue	6	M	14	0	0	1	3,661
Bailey County	4	F	3	0	0	1	1,001
Bailey Marie	4	F	7	3	0	0	7,020
Baileys	6	M	6	0	0	0	150
Baileys Affair	3	F	7	1	2	1	30,620
Baileys Attire	2	C	9	1	1	1	23,085
Baileys Baby	3	F	1	0	0	0	0
Bailey's Best	4	C	6	1	0	0	7,533
Bailey's Chance	3	F	3	1	1	0	7,030
Baileys Eagle	4	F	5	1	0	1	30,878

Horse	Age	Sex	Sts	1st	2d	3d	Won
Baileys Edge	6	G	1	1	0	0	60,000
Baileys Flurry	4	G	1	0	0	0	0
Bailey's Ledge	5	G	11	2	2	2	10,142
Bailey's Reprized	2	F	12	4	1	0	34,610
Baileys Ridge	4	G	5	0	0	1	6,960
Bailey's Toy	3	F	10	0	0	2	2,100
Bailey's Wish	2	F	12	0	1	3	5,410
Baileysontherocks	6	G	7	0	0	0	389
Baileyspet	5	G	13	2	0	4	8,553
Bailie's Band	4	G	9	0	2	2	11,820
Bailing Twine	5	M	2	0	0	0	257
Bailius	3	C	1	0	0	0	0
Baillie's Beauty	3	F	16	0	4	5	18,830
Bailout With Style	2	C	2	0	0	0	145
Baiser d'Amour	4	F	6	2	1	1	46,746
Bait	3	F	6	0	0	0	161
Baits 'Em	5	G	10	1	4	1	15,025
Baja Dancer	3	F	6	0	2	0	9,020
Baja Harri	7	G	15	1	1	3	13,555
Baja Rosa	3	F	14	1	0	5	8,026
Baked Beans	9	H	5	1	0	1	3,620
Baker Road	6	H	9	2	1	2	119,389
Baker Road Joe	4	G	2	0	0	0	251
Baker Sign	3	G	2	0	0	0	270
Baker's Gold Won	2	F	1	0	0	1	1,330
Bakersfield Jack	5	H	2	0	0	0	0
Bakewell Lad	3	G	4	0	1	0	6,660
Bakewell Tart (IRE)	3	F	2	0	0	0	0
Baklava	4	F	14	3	3	1	44,122
Baksheesh (NZ)	8	G	3	0	3	0	11,700
Bal Bay	7	H	11	2	0	0	2,865
Bal Harbour	8	G	10	0	3	2	13,406
Bala	4	F	7	0	1	1	42,803
Baladi	4	G	15	1	4	0	14,714
Balance Sheet	3	G	12	0	0	1	6,442
Balance the Books	3	C	8	3	1	0	32,060
Balanced Bodgit	4	G	10	4	0	2	47,860
Balancetheaccount	7	M	1	0	0	0	24
Balancethebudget	10	H	4	0	0	0	3,163
Balancethecurtain	3	G	1	0	0	1	1,260
Balandra	2	C	4	0	3	0	36,000
Balantrae	5	M	19	3	2	1	33,246
Balarat	6	G	12	1	3	3	44,866
Balatine	4	F	1	0	0	0	46
Balboa Native Jr.	5	H	11	1	1	1	3,971
Balcarres	6	M	13	1	2	2	15,356
Bald Hill Native	7	G	3	0	0	0	0
Bald N Blue	2	F	4	0	0	0	4,650
Baldachino	4	F	8	1	0	0	23,635
Balderdash	5	G	9	0	0	2	3,823
Baldjim	7	G	12	4	1	1	5,796
Baldomera	2	F	8	2	3	2	62,530
Baldski's Image	3	C	12	2	0	2	10,346
Baldski's Line	2	F	1	0	0	0	145
Baldstyle	4	G	11	1	1	0	5,290
Baldwin County	5	G	4	0	1	0	8,280
Baldwina (FR)	5	M	3	0	0	0	0
Baldy Brook	3	F	6	0	1	1	3,105
Baldy's Darlin	3	F	5	1	0	1	8,257
Balenos (BRZ)	5	G	7	0	0	1	4,620
Balentino Boy	12	G	3	0	0	0	300
Bali	5	M	6	0	0	0	693
Balin	5	G	3	0	1	1	3,033
Balineas Lastdance	3	F	2	0	0	0	0
Balin's Sword (IRE)	3	C	7	1	1	1	40,455
Balkan	4	C	9	0	0	1	715
Balko Bay	7	G	9	1	3	2	4,577
Ball of Roses	3	G	5	0	0	0	565
Ball Park	2	G	2	0	0	0	0
Balla Twine	5	M	6	1	1	1	33,700
Balladeer	5	H	13	2	1	1	20,819
Ballade's Magic	3	F	3	0	0	0	4,002
Ballade's Reprise	3	G	7	0	0	0	1,020
Ballado Belle	3	F	3	0	0	0	841
Ballado Breeze	2	C	4	1	1	1	27,980
Ballado Chieftan	3	C	5	1	2	0	58,260
Ballado Hill	3	F	5	1	0	0	19,560
Ballado Melody	4	F	10	1	0	0	13,290
Ballado On Tour	2	F	4	0	1	0	2,010

RECORDS OF HORSES

Horse	Age	Sex	Sts	1st	2d	3d	Won
Ballado Star	6	G	4	0	0	0	228
Ballado's Baby	5	M	14	4	2	2	95,042
Ballado's Devil	5	H	7	3	2	0	56,200
Ballado's Halo	4	F	9	1	3	1	45,500
Ballaghisheen	4	F	15	2	4	1	36,623
Ballen Isle	3	C	9	2	0	0	70,668
Ballence	3	F	2	0	1	0	4,590
Ballerina Prima	2	F	2	0	0	0	0
Ballerina Rose	3	F	4	1	0	0	4,393
Ballerina's Halo	3	G	9	1	0	0	53,342
Ballet Critic	5	H	6	1	0	0	21,240
Ballet Prince	3	C	1	0	0	0	0
Ballingarry (IRE)	4	C	5	1	0	1	194,700
Balli's Bullet	6	G	3	1	0	0	1,474
Ballistic	7	G	11	2	5	1	32,830
Ballistic Angel	3	F	9	1	1	1	18,040
Ballistic Babe	4	F	1	0	0	0	0
Ballistic Ballet	6	G	4	0	0	0	177
Ballistic Echo	3	F	2	0	0	0	610
Ballistic Missile	3	C	9	2	4	1	52,610
Ballonenostrikes	3	G	8	3	2	0	97,270
Balloon Balloon	3	C	1	0	0	0	0
Ballotade	3	F	13	3	1	3	17,522
Ballroom Blitz	2	C	3	0	0	0	0
Ballroom Champ	3	G	9	0	2	2	13,710
Ballroom Deputy	2	F	3	1	0	0	16,345
Balluvial	8	G	4	0	2	1	1,119
Bally Cat	5	M	11	2	3	2	9,923
Ballymaloe	2	F	3	0	0	2	12,936
Ballymena Dancer	5	M	9	0	3	1	9,429
Bally's Fun Guy	3	G	13	2	1	2	9,467
Balmy	4	F	8	4	0	2	140,280
Balsora	2	G	5	0	1	1	1,810
Baltic City	3	F	10	3	1	1	70,239
Baltic Heights	3	C	3	2	0	0	52,800
Baltic Lover	6	G	21	0	2	2	4,896
Baltic Maria	3	F	3	0	0	1	1,975
Baltic Marque	6	H	20	4	1	6	20,743
Baltic Nations	3	F	2	1	0	0	29,400
Baltic Prince	3	C	8	2	4	0	34,764
Balto Star	5	G	13	4	2	1	907,500
Balustrade	3	C	5	2	0	0	56,735
Balvanera	4	F	11	1	2	0	8,014
Balzell	6	H	4	0	1	2	4,885
Bam	8	M	7	0	0	1	1,988
Bam Bam Bahram	5	G	3	0	0	0	0
Bam Bam Ham	2	C	4	0	0	0	757
Bam Good Tune	4	F	1	0	0	0	32
Bam That Martini	3	G	7	0	0	0	662
Bama Belle	6	M	8	1	2	1	8,310
Bama Point	2	F	3	0	0	0	720
Bama Red	5	G	8	3	0	1	10,170
Bama Royal	4	G	8	1	1	0	12,520
Bama Vantage	3	C	4	0	0	1	1,425
Bamagal	2	F	1	0	0	0	0
Bamam	3	F	7	1	1	0	3,198
Bamba	3	F	7	2	2	3	62,050
Bambi Baby	9	M	3	0	0	0	0
Bambi Canyon	4	F	3	0	0	0	496
Bambina	6	M	2	0	0	1	1,870
Bambina Mia	3	F	4	0	0	0	2,235
Bamboo Belle	3	F	6	0	1	3	11,130
Bamboo Orient	2	F	4	1	1	1	23,267
Bamboozle	6	M	10	1	0	0	8,595
Bamboozler	3	G	2	0	0	1	2,090
Bambotto	3	G	13	1	1	3	8,260
Bambury	3	F	6	1	0	1	7,460
Ban Tom Six	4	G	4	1	0	0	4,689
Banami Ma Me	4	F	6	4	0	1	40,570
Banana Wind	8	G	3	0	0	0	33
Bananas	4	C	5	0	0	0	5,178
Banco de Datos	4	F	16	2	4	2	13,764
Banco de Oro	2	C	3	1	0	1	15,300
Band Dixie	2	C	3	0	0	0	0
Band Lady	6	M	2	0	0	0	426
Band Leader	6	H	7	0	2	1	3,012
Band of Gold	5	M	9	1	2	2	18,659
Band of Lilies	2	F	2	0	0	0	4,974
Band of Reflection	5	M	24	1	0	1	5,620
Band of White	4	F	3	1	0	0	8,811
Band Performance	11	G	17	3	5	2	17,392
Band Queen	5	M	4	1	0	1	22,575
Band R Laro	6	H	10	0	0	1	1,862
Bandaid Kid	5	G	4	1	0	0	3,492
Bandana	6	G	7	2	2	2	52,791
Banded One	3	G	4	0	1	0	4,040
Bandera Dude	3	C	11	2	0	2	17,481
Banderberg	3	C	10	0	0	0	6,003
Banderole	2	C	4	1	0	0	8,240
Bandidazo (ARG)	7	G	11	1	0	0	5,519
Bandido Leyenda	4	C	2	0	1	1	2,330
Bandido Rial	4	G	16	2	5	3	16,316
Bandi's Big Red	3	C	6	0	0	0	1,220
Bandi's Boy	6	H	7	0	2	1	14,819
Bandit Nailhead	2	C	3	0	0	0	1,980
Bandito	3	G	8	1	1	1	15,370
Banditti	3	G	3	0	0	1	1,260
Bandy	6	M	10	2	0	1	11,485
Baneful	2	F	1	0	0	0	0
Banff Springs	4	G	12	1	1	0	5,818
Bang	3	G	3	2	0	0	47,333
Bang Bang Rosie	9	G	1	0	0	0	2,520
Bang Slough	3	G	2	0	0	0	106
Bangbangonthedoor	2	F	1	1	0	0	15,600
Bangkok by Night	2	G	1	0	0	0	280
Bangzoom Birdie	5	M	14	0	2	4	8,984
Banish	3	C	3	0	1	0	5,600
Banish Misfortune	2	C	1	0	0	0	126
Banish the Thought	3	G	5	1	0	1	6,720
Banished Lover	5	M	10	1	2	0	33,740
Banjo Gal	2	F	2	0	2	0	3,744
Banjo Picker	3	G	8	1	1	0	22,000
Bank Audit	2	F	4	0	3	0	21,140
Bank Bag	3	G	2	0	0	0	360
Bank Burglar	5	H	11	2	1	2	6,527
Bank Draft	4	G	2	0	1	0	4,750
Bank Me	3	C	9	1	1	0	14,952
Bank of Gold	2	C	2	0	0	0	0
Bank of Kanata	5	G	16	1	0	1	3,865
Bank On Della	2	F	3	0	0	0	227
Bank On Frank	3	C	2	0	0	0	0
Bank On Greida	3	F	7	0	2	1	11,927
Bank On Henry	3	C	2	0	0	0	0
Bank On It	5	G	2	0	0	1	1,260
Bank On Slew	3	F	2	1	0	0	2,250
Bank Onahomerun	3	F	5	0	0	1	3,038
Bank Roll	2	C	1	0	0	0	0
Bank Shot	5	M	16	2	2	3	16,397
Bank Ticket	5	G	10	0	0	1	4,960
Bankable	3	C	1	0	0	0	0
Banker Bert	6	G	7	0	1	0	4,100
Banker Boy	3	G	13	3	2	0	59,725
Banker for Dinner	6	M	9	1	3	1	13,272
Banker Jason	4	G	15	2	5	0	13,694
Banker Jazz	5	G	3	0	0	0	0
Banker Queen	3	F	12	2	4	1	25,805
Banker Wallace	3	C	14	2	1	3	13,910
Bankerette	3	F	8	0	1	2	28,648
Bankers Creek	2	F	2	0	0	0	0
Bankers Heart	4	G	11	1	0	0	3,561
Banker's Hill	2	C	3	0	1	0	4,740
Banker's May West	3	C	3	0	0	1	1,138
Banker's Mint	3	F	5	1	0	0	24,600
Banker's Promise	4	F	2	0	0	1	1,846
Banker's R. N.	3	F	10	2	1	2	9,235
Banker's Touch	6	H	6	2	0	0	17,066
Banker's Trapp	2	C	2	0	0	0	0
Bankers Wish	9	G	5	0	1	0	1,744
Bankin On Blossom	2	F	2	0	0	0	0
Bankrupe	3	F	12	2	1	3	17,815
Bankruptcy Bound	9	G	11	2	1	4	11,117
Bannack	3	C	4	2	0	1	58,600
Bannatyne	4	F	2	0	0	0	214
Banned in Boston	3	C	10	4	2	0	119,870
Banner Boy	9	G	3	0	0	0	1,250
Banner Elk	2	F	3	1	1	0	14,800
Banner Headline	6	G	4	0	2	1	13,040
Banner Key	6	M	11	1	0	2	10,145

Horse	Age	Sex	Sts	1st	2d	3d	Won	Horse	Age	Sex	Sts	1st	2d	3d	Won
Banner Queen	3	F	3	1	0	1	32,680	Barefootin Pollock	4	G	7	1	0	2	6,596
Banner Salute	6	G	3	0	0	1	1,607	Barely Perfect	4	F	8	1	2	2	51,870
Banners Flying	4	G	5	0	1	1	4,100	Barely Sovereign	4	F	9	2	2	0	20,800
Banners Wave	4	F	11	1	1	2	10,275	Barelyinourbodgit	2	C	3	2	0	0	44,881
Bannerstone	4	F	17	3	5	1	22,442	Barfly Babe	3	F	4	0	1	0	1,470
Bannister	6	H	12	0	0	1	709	Barfly Begone	5	G	11	2	0	2	9,340
Bannock Burner	3	G	4	2	0	0	33,360	Bargain	7	G	15	2	2	1	17,613
Bannon's Pick	4	F	12	2	4	0	33,260	Bargain Belle	4	F	2	0	1	0	3,940
Bano's Adil	3	C	3	0	0	0	185	Bargain Betty	4	F	10	0	1	1	2,645
Banquero	5	G	5	1	0	0	3,272	Bargain Dancer	4	F	10	2	1	1	27,215
Banshee Boy	3	G	11	2	2	1	27,782	Bargaining Chip	6	H	4	0	0	0	0
Banshee Brad	5	H	14	4	6	2	72,910	Bargette	3	F	12	0	1	1	6,515
Banshee Bridesmaid	2	F	7	0	2	2	4,740	Bargoonski	3	G	6	1	2	1	5,703
Banshee Connection	5	G	10	1	0	1	28,346	Bark for Mercy	3	C	5	0	0	0	434
Banshee King	3	G	3	1	2	0	62,720	Barkenlor Cat	8	G	13	1	1	3	4,944
Bantamweight	3	C	8	3	0	2	16,417	Barkerman	2	G	2	0	0	0	0
Banyu Dewi (GER)	4	F	4	1	1	1	58,940	Barley Creek	8	G	22	5	7	4	40,386
Baptize	5	H	1	0	0	0	0	Barmara	6	M	8	4	0	0	13,127
Baquera	2	F	5	1	1	1	3,200	Barmascus	3	G	5	0	0	0	553
Bar B John	8	G	6	1	0	0	3,630	Barn Bug	2	G	1	0	0	0	0
Bar Bailey	3	F	6	1	1	1	17,781	Barn Dance	2	F	6	1	2	0	34,200
Bar Buddy	4	C	9	1	0	2	3,152	Barnabus	5	H	5	1	0	0	10,050
Bar Dance	4	C	8	1	1	0	12,969	Barnacle Jim	9	G	4	0	1	0	2,534
Bar Fly	4	F	15	5	4	3	75,110	Barnacle Steve	4	G	9	3	1	2	82,640
Bar Girl	3	F	7	0	0	2	5,460	Barnard Man	4	G	9	4	1	0	68,790
Bar Shoe	6	G	10	3	1	0	9,770	Barnes Creek	4	G	5	1	1	1	12,460
Bar Shot	5	M	1	0	0	0	365	Barney B	3	G	11	0	0	1	2,199
Bar the Hatch	4	F	1	0	0	0	0	Barney Rumble	3	G	1	0	0	0	0
Bar U Anio	3	C	9	0	3	0	35,761	Barney Smith	4	C	12	1	2	3	35,907
Bara Lad	4	G	6	1	0	0	7,347	Barney's Mistress	5	M	13	1	2	2	67,169
Barabara	4	G	14	2	3	4	11,510	Barnhartvale Belle	3	F	9	0	0	3	1,244
Baracuda	3	F	2	0	0	0	0	Barnsy	2	F	3	1	1	0	36,020
Baramundi Jan	2	G	4	0	0	1	6,468	Barnwell	7	G	10	3	0	1	7,900
Barath	4	G	15	6	4	1	72,540	Barometric	4	C	4	2	1	1	73,664
Baravus	7	H	8	0	0	1	2,050	Baron Et All	3	G	1	0	1	0	4,362
Barb At the Wire	3	F	10	1	0	1	9,237	Baron the Big Red	3	G	13	3	2	1	20,327
Barbara D F K	3	F	8	1	0	0	6,330	Baron Von Ruckus	4	G	7	1	1	1	14,490
Barbara Darlin	3	F	3	0	0	0	212	Baron Von Tom	10	G	10	3	0	1	12,534
Barbara Nancy	4	F	4	1	0	0	6,615	Baronage	2	C	7	3	0	1	53,250
Barbara O'Brien	4	F	9	3	4	0	171,035	Baroness Silvia	2	F	5	0	0	0	3,180
Barbara Orr	3	F	2	1	0	0	29,460	Barongin	2	C	5	1	0	0	14,475
Barbaralynnehogan	2	F	2	0	0	0	80	Baronia	7	G	3	1	1	1	1,436
Barbara's Jade	2	F	3	0	0	0	1,750	Barons Hoolie	4	C	4	0	0	1	2,736
Barbara's Jewel	3	G	19	5	5	2	78,474	Baron's Prodigy	6	G	12	0	0	1	2,228
Barbara's Lastlove	6	H	5	0	0	2	5,510	Baron's Rank	3	G	11	2	3	1	40,975
Barbara's Song	4	F	1	0	0	0	0	Barra Steel	2	F	4	0	0	2	4,490
Barbaray's Claim	4	F	10	1	0	1	8,299	Barrage	6	H	4	1	0	0	4,495
Barbarees Hill	5	M	12	1	2	1	42,038	Barraza	4	G	6	0	1	1	1,295
Barbarella	4	F	2	0	0	0	0	Barrel Racer	2	F	5	1	1	0	28,736
Barbarian King	4	G	3	0	0	0	0	Barren	5	G	2	0	1	0	3,780
Barbaric Saint	3	G	1	0	0	1	450	Barren Creek	3	G	8	1	0	1	22,700
Barbaross	5	G	2	0	0	0	360	Barretodo	9	G	15	1	2	2	15,958
Barbeau Ruckus	4	G	7	4	2	0	310,585	Barrett Kathryn	4	F	12	1	0	2	14,721
Barbecue Bob	2	C	3	1	0	0	5,894	Barretta Queen	5	M	2	0	0	0	0
Barber Talk	3	C	7	1	1	1	6,805	Barrett's Babe	3	F	4	1	0	1	7,063
Barber's Magic	2	G	2	0	0	0	0	Barricade Point	3	G	12	2	2	1	19,672
Barbers Pride	3	F	1	0	0	0	0	Barricaded	2	G	3	0	1	0	1,924
Barbie Jo Jo	3	F	8	0	1	1	3,467	Barrington	4	G	8	2	0	2	37,610
Barbie Q	5	M	1	0	0	0	435	Barrington Lady	2	F	7	0	3	0	17,940
Barboura (FR)	3	F	11	1	1	2	40,120	Barron Dan	6	G	12	2	1	2	10,463
Barbs and Bows	3	F	1	0	0	0	0	Barron H	5	G	13	4	3	4	87,350
Barb's Ghazi	2	F	3	0	0	0	175	Barry Bold Dancer	4	C	5	0	0	0	0
Barbs Kipper	6	M	2	0	0	0	113	Barry County	5	G	5	1	0	0	3,634
Barb's Lucky Lady	4	F	10	0	3	0	9,589	Bars of Gold	3	C	1	0	0	1	3,520
Barb's Promise	3	F	14	0	2	6	7,270	Bars Thunder	3	F	3	0	0	0	480
Barb's Speed Dial	2	F	3	0	0	0	352	Barsafire	3	F	11	0	2	5	4,917
Barb's Valentine	2	F	3	0	0	0	165	Barsnit	2	F	1	0	0	0	0
Barb's Word	3	F	6	2	0	0	9,156	Bartax	2	C	2	0	0	1	1,005
Barbwire and Roses	3	F	9	0	0	0	832	Bartee Home Boy	4	C	17	2	2	5	13,757
Barby's Shamrock	2	F	2	1	0	0	13,086	Bartee Pride	5	G	7	0	3	1	9,550
Bardic	7	G	8	0	2	0	3,293	Bartella's Way	3	F	2	0	0	0	217
Bards Miss Quickly	3	F	11	1	0	0	7,335	Bartender	5	G	12	3	0	0	27,325
Bardstale	3	C	6	1	0	0	15,185	Bartending Mike	3	G	5	1	0	1	13,620
Bare Beware	3	F	5	0	0	0	260	Bartendress	5	M	9	2	1	2	14,296
Bare Knuckles	3	G	3	0	0	0	240	Bartholemew	3	G	10	3	3	3	24,770
Bare Legs	6	M	3	0	0	0	91	Bartko	4	G	18	4	6	2	37,012
Bare Necessities	4	F	8	4	0	3	431,175	Bartlett Run	2	F	2	0	0	0	0
Barefoot Hugh	4	G	14	2	3	1	11,218	Bartley	5	M	16	2	4	5	54,700
Barefoot Jerry	4	G	14	2	6	1	31,113	Bartok's Beau	3	F	5	2	0	0	32,600

RECORDS OF HORSES

Horse	Age	Sex	Sts	1st	2d	3d	Won
Bartok's Blithe	3	F	9	3	2	1	229,700
Bartons Barndance	2	G	3	0	1	0	2,262
Barton's Breeze	3	G	7	1	0	2	6,764
Bart's Page	3	G	6	2	2	1	40,525
Bartus Christian	2	G	3	1	0	0	7,906
Baryshnikov's Song	6	G	5	2	1	0	19,300
Barzini	4	C	7	0	1	3	2,510
Bas Giant	2	G	1	0	0	0	0
Basalt	5	G	10	0	1	0	1,224
Base Stealer	3	F	9	0	0	2	6,500
Baseball	6	G	6	1	0	1	10,940
Baseball Champion	5	H	3	0	1	0	10,380
Baseline Road	6	G	10	1	1	2	7,739
Baseport	2	C	4	0	0	1	1,140
Basha's Charm	2	F	4	0	0	1	1,650
Bashful Blue	4	F	13	2	2	2	11,334
Bashful Bob	3	G	12	0	2	2	5,343
Bashful Dancer	4	F	7	1	0	2	8,186
Bashful John	11	G	12	1	1	0	4,691
Bashful Kate	4	F	1	0	0	0	0
Bashi	5	G	2	0	0	0	260
Basic Bug	3	G	4	1	1	0	10,400
Basic Concern	6	H	3	0	0	1	2,125
Basic Magic	3	C	4	0	0	0	415
Basic Power	3	F	2	0	0	0	0
Basic Trainee	8	G	8	1	2	1	9,595
Basically Noble	4	G	13	2	0	1	10,683
Basically Radical	3	G	5	1	1	0	8,364
Basically Sexy	2	F	2	0	0	0	360
Basier Ma Ack	4	G	14	0	1	2	5,078
Basilisk	4	G	14	6	0	1	30,517
Basil's Rhythm	5	H	1	0	0	0	0
Basin of Beauty	5	M	4	0	0	0	183
Basinbob	6	G	10	8	0	0	50,146
Bask in Honor	3	F	1	0	1	0	2,700
Basket Lady	4	F	2	0	0	0	225
Basket of Dreams	2	F	1	0	0	0	1,309
Basketball Court	2	C	7	4	1	0	55,090
Basketfullofposies	3	F	7	0	0	1	2,340
Basking Tiger	3	F	7	1	2	1	5,116
Baskket	4	F	10	1	1	2	11,460
Basque of Love	2	F	2	0	0	0	240
Bass Creek	9	G	4	0	0	0	218
Bass Lake	2	F	3	0	1	0	1,740
Bassam	5	G	11	2	3	0	11,495
Bassant	5	G	12	2	0	3	47,752
Bassmaster	2	C	1	0	0	0	145
Bastante	4	F	6	0	0	1	2,440
Bastaya	3	G	5	1	0	2	6,570
Bastione	3	C	1	0	0	0	95
Bat Lady	3	F	10	0	1	0	4,535
Bat Mobile	3	C	3	2	0	1	52,400
Bat 'n Time	4	G	6	1	1	2	9,450
Batabano	2	C	1	0	0	0	0
Bates	5	G	10	4	2	1	54,012
Bates Again	10	M	12	3	2	2	32,322
Bates Castle	3	C	13	1	1	3	8,693
Bates Choice	4	F	9	0	2	1	4,972
Bates City	3	C	2	0	0	1	1,320
Bates Honor	6	M	14	2	3	4	22,657
Bates of Course	8	M	10	0	0	0	3,705
Bath House Bet	3	F	8	0	2	0	4,165
Bath House Row	4	G	7	2	1	0	7,122
Bathing Expressive	7	G	3	1	1	1	1,396
Bathurst St Blues	6	M	12	0	2	1	6,067
Batiana	3	F	2	0	0	0	100
Batist	5	H	4	0	0	0	226
Battante	4	F	1	0	0	0	440
Battar	4	G	13	0	5	1	11,836
Battenberg	8	G	10	1	0	1	6,215
Batter Up	5	G	7	0	0	1	696
Battier	4	G	6	1	1	0	32,100
Battin' Ghosts	5	G	8	1	3	1	15,750
Battle	5	H	8	2	2	1	40,521
Battle Boots	3	G	12	1	3	1	4,337
Battle Bunker	2	F	1	0	0	0	372
Battle Countess	4	F	3	0	0	2	4,860
Battle Ghost	6	G	11	0	0	0	749
Battle God	6	H	4	0	1	1	5,720
Battle Group	3	G	3	2	1	0	22,532
Battle Hero	2	C	4	1	0	1	14,770
Battle Mountain	9	G	7	0	2	1	8,030
Battle of a Lion	4	G	6	0	0	1	650
Battle Prospect	3	C	5	1	0	0	4,674
Battle Red	2	C	1	0	0	0	0
Battle Royale	8	G	12	2	1	1	10,686
Battle Search	6	M	5	0	0	0	546
Battle Strike	3	C	9	0	1	0	4,711
Battle Tank	3	C	9	0	2	2	36,794
Battle Tap	4	G	14	0	0	1	3,210
Battle Tested	3	C	9	1	0	1	10,548
Battle Tough	4	G	4	0	0	0	179
Battle West	3	C	6	0	0	1	3,210
Battle Won	3	G	5	3	0	0	65,722
Battledar	5	G	10	2	1	3	44,902
Battleground	7	H	9	2	0	0	14,490
Battleing Tigress	7	M	3	1	0	0	2,496
Battleland	3	G	19	2	2	4	18,465
Battlements	3	G	9	4	2	2	265,150
Battler Bob	4	C	6	2	1	0	70,035
Battleriver King	4	G	5	0	1	0	1,089
Battleship Louis	3	G	8	1	0	0	25,110
Battletown	5	G	1	0	0	1	1,000
Battlin Billy	6	G	1	0	0	0	0
Battlin Syke	3	C	3	0	0	0	1,080
Battling Buzz	2	C	10	1	1	2	13,400
Battu Khan	7	G	1	0	0	0	54
Batucada's Spirit	5	M	2	0	0	1	1,700
Batum	5	G	9	2	2	2	35,520
Baturrogivemeluck	3	C	4	0	0	0	0
Bauble a Bit	2	C	3	0	1	0	6,060
Bauhauser (ARG)	5	M	4	2	1	0	113,750
Bavarian Girl	3	F	3	2	0	0	51,600
Bavario	10	G	5	1	1	1	18,950
Baviera (GB)	3	F	4	0	0	2	5,500
Bawl	4	F	10	1	0	0	13,500
Baxter Hall	2	F	1	0	0	1	4,390
Bay Be Rock	3	F	3	2	0	0	2,805
Bay Be Rocker	4	F	8	1	0	1	5,110
Bay Blossom	4	F	1	0	0	0	414
Bay Breezer	3	F	12	1	1	2	31,430
Bay Citi Girl	2	F	1	1	0	0	21,780
Bay Commander	4	G	9	0	1	1	4,600
Bay Day	2	F	4	1	0	1	5,522
Bay Dragon	6	M	8	1	0	0	19,050
Bay Eagle	5	G	5	1	2	1	43,040
Bay Ghost	3	C	10	0	1	1	4,175
Bay Guy	7	H	4	0	2	1	2,660
Bay Harbor Island	2	C	6	1	0	1	6,490
Bay Head King	5	H	3	2	0	0	24,600
Bay Joe	6	H	9	0	0	2	644
Bay Kisses	2	F	1	0	0	0	100
Bay Lizzy	5	M	4	0	0	0	1,212
Bay Marvel	4	G	3	2	1	0	39,200
Bay Not Gray	4	F	13	2	0	0	12,748
Bay of Bulls	2	F	5	1	0	0	10,543
Bay of Love	4	G	12	3	2	2	70,894
Bay Raider	3	G	12	1	1	1	25,880
Bay Shark	4	G	11	2	2	4	19,133
Bay Smoker	2	F	2	0	0	0	1,260
Bay Street Belle	6	M	11	4	3	0	24,171
Bay Street Blues	8	G	14	4	1	2	15,654
Bay Street Boy	2	G	8	0	0	0	430
Bay Street Gal	6	M	8	0	0	2	17,100
Bay Sweetie Babe	2	F	2	1	0	0	38,808
Bay Town Boy	5	G	3	1	1	0	40,600
Bay Wide Total	3	G	9	3	0	0	14,324
Bay Window	2	F	5	0	0	1	5,685
Bayakoa's Image	4	F	7	2	0	1	45,050
Bayamo (IRE)	4	G	2	1	0	1	36,720
Bayani	3	F	9	0	1	4	28,570
Baybe Paces	5	H	6	2	0	0	17,060
Baybee's Prospect	5	M	5	0	0	0	1,140
Bayberry Blue	3	F	8	1	0	1	5,630
Bayboro	5	M	2	0	0	0	200
Bayfront	2	F	3	1	1	1	16,800
Bayjur	3	F	16	0	5	4	20,125
Baylaura	2	F	2	1	0	1	18,680

RECORDS OF HORSES

Horse	Age	Sex	Sts	1st	2d	3d	Won
Baylees Irishdream	4	F	1	0	0	0	0
Bayley Bopp	6	G	3	0	0	1	1,992
Bayli's Beads	7	M	5	2	1	0	13,658
Baymont	2	F	3	0	1	0	4,680
Bayonet Charge	4	G	1	0	0	0	0
Bayou Accacia	4	G	7	2	0	2	47,470
Bayou Babe	5	M	10	0	0	1	844
Bayou Beauty	2	F	2	0	0	0	210
Bayou Boots	3	F	3	0	0	1	6,300
Bayou Buster	4	G	8	0	3	0	25,020
Bayou Cha Cha	6	M	12	0	2	5	24,582
Bayou D' Indre	7	G	17	3	4	0	18,197
Bayou Delight	4	F	3	0	0	0	0
Bayou Deroche	3	G	15	2	2	3	14,773
Bayou Flower	2	F	2	0	0	0	1,572
Bayou Jaguar	5	H	7	0	0	1	2,292
Bayou Joe	3	C	10	1	1	1	9,474
Bayou Miss	5	M	10	0	1	2	3,870
Bayou Mist	3	F	7	2	0	0	53,145
Bayou Moon	3	G	8	3	0	0	68,632
Bayou Queen	4	F	7	1	0	0	3,785
Bayou the Moon	5	H	5	1	1	1	62,680
Bayside Party	6	H	5	0	0	0	144
Bayville	4	F	7	1	2	1	10,980
Baywatcher	6	G	2	0	0	0	126
Bazargan	5	M	6	1	0	2	13,260
Bazooka Blaze	3	C	1	0	0	0	0
Bazooka Joe	3	G	3	1	0	0	808
Bbop Dancer	4	F	4	0	0	0	580
Bbuurrrr	3	G	7	1	0	1	5,064
Bc's Music	2	G	7	1	1	0	18,980
Be a Donor	3	C	3	1	0	0	16,260
Be a Good Dancer	4	F	3	0	0	0	1,595
Be a Hero	3	C	1	0	0	0	0
Be a Hunter	4	G	4	1	0	0	3,495
Be a Leah Mackee	3	F	1	0	0	0	42
Be a Millionaire	5	H	2	0	0	0	565
Be a Saint	4	C	4	0	0	0	0
Be a Smooth Talker	5	G	4	1	1	0	32,520
Be a Winner	4	F	5	0	1	1	1,952
Be Able	2	C	2	0	0	0	195
Be Accountable	8	H	5	0	0	0	719
Be Better	4	G	11	2	0	2	22,471
Be Blessed	5	M	5	0	0	1	847
Be Clever Evelyn	3	F	3	0	0	0	450
Be Concerned	3	F	11	1	1	1	12,047
Be Delightful	5	M	14	2	1	3	10,867
Be Do Have	3	C	11	0	0	2	4,480
Be Factual	4	F	11	3	0	3	54,802
Be Free	2	G	1	0	0	0	640
Be Fuhr Real	3	F	11	1	2	0	1,110
Be Gentle	2	F	7	4	1	0	523,078
Be Happy My Love	3	F	8	1	1	1	15,435
Be He Runs	4	C	1	0	0	0	0
Be Irish	4	G	1	0	0	0	50
Be Like Mike	4	C	7	4	0	2	133,237
Be Like Mom	5	M	1	0	0	0	0
Be Lucky for Me	8	G	4	2	1	0	19,146
Be Mine Sunshine	6	M	17	1	2	3	18,632
Be My Bride	4	F	3	0	2	0	2,220
Be My Friend	6	M	8	1	1	1	19,449
Be My Light	5	G	5	1	0	0	3,702
Be My Lovelysister	4	F	2	0	0	0	0
Be My Molly	3	F	12	2	1	2	24,912
Be My Sun	6	G	11	1	1	1	3,316
Be My Valentine	4	F	8	2	1	2	69,254
Be Naughty With Me	5	G	1	0	0	0	0
Be Not Afraid	3	C	5	0	0	1	880
Be On the Look Out	3	F	3	0	0	0	0
Be Positive	2	F	1	0	0	0	0
Be Quick Drummer	5	M	6	1	0	0	4,760
Be Quicker	4	F	4	0	0	2	1,224
Be Quite Emily	3	F	9	0	0	0	435
Be So Bright	3	F	11	1	0	1	3,624
Be Sorta Bad	4	G	5	0	0	0	540
Be Sovereign	4	C	11	2	1	2	11,518
Be Still My Heart	4	F	11	1	3	2	8,421
Be That Way	4	G	15	3	0	2	42,690
Be the Bunny	7	G	8	2	0	1	10,023

Horse	Age	Sex	Sts	1st	2d	3d	Won
Be the Glory	3	G	9	1	1	1	23,550
Be There Baby	7	G	4	0	0	0	0
Be True Rene	3	F	6	1	0	0	10,874
Be Valiant	7	H	11	1	2	1	14,670
Be Vidgilant	4	F	4	0	0	0	1,770
Bea Careless	3	C	8	0	0	0	517
Bea Minute	6	M	1	0	0	0	0
Bea Princess	3	F	5	0	0	1	1,210
Bea Sassy	2	F	8	0	0	0	1,445
Bea Tuff	6	M	7	0	0	1	722
Beabasque	4	C	9	0	2	1	15,176
Beach Barbicue	3	F	1	0	0	0	0
Beach Bertie	3	F	8	3	1	0	22,776
Beach Bound	3	C	8	1	1	2	10,383
Beach Bunny Blonde	4	F	5	0	0	0	1,350
Beach Fit	3	G	8	1	2	1	14,304
Beach Heat	5	M	9	2	3	0	32,000
Beach of Bali	3	F	2	0	0	0	530
Beach Pizza	2	F	2	1	0	0	15,240
Beach Plum	3	F	14	2	3	1	77,152
Beach Side	2	F	8	0	0	4	9,570
Beach View	3	F	5	0	0	0	2,480
Beach Walker	4	G	14	1	3	0	11,702
Beachbums Dayout	4	C	4	0	0	0	483
Beached	4	F	6	1	2	0	40,495
Beachstreet Boogie	4	F	9	2	2	1	10,770
Beachy Head	4	F	4	0	0	1	2,696
Beacon of Speed	3	F	8	0	3	0	3,932
Beacontree	2	F	9	0	3	1	19,760
Beads of Promise	10	G	6	0	1	2	2,478
Beam n' Reason	11	G	8	1	0	2	4,238
Beam Run	5	G	1	0	0	0	0
Beamer One	2	G	1	0	0	0	780
Beamer'n Glick	2	C	2	1	0	0	9,000
Beamero	3	G	8	0	0	1	976
Beamhit	6	H	5	0	0	1	1,590
Beaming Looker	4	F	1	0	0	0	0
Beaming Star	4	G	13	2	2	2	29,384
Beanie Beemer	6	M	16	1	4	2	11,035
Beanie Genie	5	M	2	0	0	0	0
Beaniegirl	3	F	3	0	0	1	288
Beans in the Teens	5	H	21	0	1	1	7,575
Beans N Quackers	6	G	2	0	0	0	84
Beans On Toast	2	G	3	0	2	1	7,359
Beansandcornbread	4	G	1	0	0	0	100
Bear Arms	5	G	9	2	0	0	7,338
Bear Bluff	2	C	5	0	0	1	4,660
Bear Brass	2	G	2	0	0	0	0
Bear Breakfast	3	G	7	0	0	0	130
Bear Claw	5	M	5	1	0	1	5,777
Bear Cut	6	G	16	2	1	2	14,137
Bear Diamond	3	F	1	0	0	0	0
Bear Down	2	C	2	0	0	0	1,916
Bear Energy	8	G	1	0	0	0	126
Bear Fan	4	F	4	1	2	0	67,170
Bear Force Won	4	G	14	2	2	1	17,762
Bear in the House	4	F	4	1	0	0	5,740
Bear King	2	G	6	1	1	2	10,422
Bear On My Mind	3	C	1	0	0	0	1,680
Bear On Tour	3	C	14	1	1	1	9,822
Bear Trak Jack	9	G	1	0	0	0	42
Bear West	3	F	1	0	0	0	360
Bear With a Flair	8	G	1	0	0	0	48
Bear Witness	3	G	10	0	0	0	3,085
Bearacer	4	G	5	0	0	0	1,570
Bearcat Drive	3	G	5	0	0	0	1,005
Bearcat Jett	7	G	11	1	0	2	6,581
Bearcat Kenyon	3	C	9	2	0	0	11,490
Bearcat Magic	3	G	3	1	0	0	21,600
Bearhouse	7	G	11	0	1	1	2,282
Bearly Castelli	3	G	13	1	3	2	12,371
Bearly Irish	3	F	6	0	1	2	2,320
Bears Little Angel	2	F	6	1	1	3	51,942
Bearspaw	5	H	7	0	0	0	1,120
Beary	4	G	7	1	1	1	13,207
Bea's Reality	6	G	6	1	2	0	4,468
Bea's Thunder	2	F	1	0	0	0	0
Beasue	3	F	4	1	0	0	4,260
Beat the Street	5	M	6	0	0	0	437

Horse	Age	Sex	Sts	1st	2d	3d	Won	Horse	Age	Sex	Sts	1st	2d	3d	Won
Beat the Ticket	3	C	8	0	0	1	1,754	Beautiful Crazy	3	F	10	3	2	2	110,760
Beat the Traffic	2	C	6	1	1	0	23,393	Beautiful Devil	4	F	3	1	1	0	7,300
Beat Your Feet	5	M	12	3	2	2	114,950	Beautiful Emblem	4	F	4	0	0	1	680
Beater	5	M	12	2	0	1	14,473	Beautiful Eyes	4	F	15	2	3	3	15,704
Beating Heart	4	F	8	2	0	1	3,168	Beautiful Flight	8	M	3	0	0	0	346
Beatlestix	2	C	1	0	0	0	0	Beautiful Honor	3	F	2	2	0	0	33,200
Beatnik	6	G	2	0	0	0	375	Beautiful Ingenue	4	F	9	0	0	1	3,592
Beatrix	4	F	8	2	0	2	16,710	Beautiful Kathy	3	F	1	0	0	0	0
Beau Alaric	4	G	5	0	1	0	3,600	Beautiful Lady	4	F	4	0	3	0	9,450
Beau Allure	2	C	2	0	0	0	1,190	Beautiful Lassie	4	F	6	1	1	1	16,710
Beau an Airo	6	G	7	1	0	1	2,673	Beautiful Love	4	F	1	0	0	0	420
Beau Bailey	3	G	9	1	0	0	4,246	Beautiful Mess	2	F	1	0	0	0	0
Beau Brass	3	G	9	2	3	1	83,666	Beautiful Navona	5	M	8	0	1	1	7,425
Beau Bunny	2	F	3	0	0	0	1,320	Beautiful Prize	3	F	9	3	1	0	13,851
Beau Chaffee	4	G	10	0	2	0	2,081	Beautiful Spy	3	F	14	5	0	0	74,030
Beau Classic	3	C	8	0	3	3	54,847	Beautiful Starlet	4	F	18	2	2	3	48,586
Beau Coup	10	G	1	0	0	0	0	Beautiful Stella	2	F	1	0	0	0	0
Beau Creek	3	G	2	0	0	0	207	Beautiful Story	4	G	9	1	0	1	1,803
Beau Dashes	8	G	9	0	0	3	3,042	Beautiful Swan	4	F	11	1	0	1	4,003
Beau Devious	2	G	4	0	0	0	540	Beautiful Treasure	3	F	11	0	0	0	10,210
Beau Emperor	4	C	5	0	0	1	2,923	Beautifuldreamgirl	6	M	10	1	1	0	10,562
Beau Happy	2	F	4	0	0	0	0	Beautify Life	2	G	3	0	0	1	1,859
Beau Jackson	3	C	7	2	2	1	23,780	Beauty and Glory	2	F	1	0	1	0	2,490
Beau Joey	5	G	3	0	1	0	2,655	Beauty Charm	3	F	6	1	1	2	22,176
Beau Kent	2	G	4	0	0	0	182	Beauty Go Leor (IRE)	7	G	13	0	4	1	8,402
Beau Manners	4	G	10	4	1	1	49,610	Beauty Halo (ARG)	4	F	4	2	1	0	89,931
Beau Moro	6	H	3	0	0	0	0	Beauty in Paradise	2	F	3	0	0	2	5,100
Beau On Tour	3	G	10	3	1	0	27,880	Beauty Indeed	4	F	5	0	0	0	0
Beau Pip	4	G	6	0	0	1	3,600	Beauty Legs	5	M	9	1	1	3	24,850
Beau Ring	6	G	8	2	1	0	26,808	Beauty Nina	5	M	8	2	1	1	3,645
Beau Rivage	2	C	1	0	0	0	0	Beauty On Duty	3	F	6	1	0	1	34,420
Beau River Lulu	3	F	2	0	0	0	0	Beauty to Boot	3	F	3	1	0	0	6,180
Beau Ryder	3	C	13	4	2	0	32,773	Beautybyaday	3	F	9	0	3	1	16,934
Beau Soleil	3	C	7	2	3	0	83,280	Beautycanfly	3	C	3	1	0	0	5,280
Beau Tanner	4	C	3	0	0	0	360	Beauty's Boy	7	G	2	0	0	0	238
Beau Tie	6	G	8	1	0	2	38,645	Beauty's Dream	5	M	1	0	0	0	0
Beau Tommie	6	H	1	0	0	0	0	Beauty's Due	6	M	1	0	0	0	0
Beau Toy	3	C	8	0	1	1	3,110	Beauty's Image	4	F	8	1	3	1	10,650
Beau Watch	2	F	4	1	2	0	21,160	Beauty's Kitty	2	F	2	0	0	0	0
Beau Weevil	4	G	8	0	1	2	2,673	Beauty's Outlaw	5	G	7	0	0	1	1,207
Beau Willie	6	G	1	0	0	0	0	Beauvalay	4	C	9	1	1	0	16,272
Beau Zapada	4	F	4	0	0	0	215	Beaux Artes	4	F	7	0	0	0	1,072
Beauallis	5	M	9	2	1	0	24,611	Beauzak	3	G	11	2	1	1	31,275
Beaucatcher	2	F	2	0	0	0	115	Beavenger	3	F	10	0	1	1	3,240
Beauchamp Pilot (GB)	5	G	4	0	1	1	29,255	Beaver Cat	4	G	5	1	3	0	29,031
Beaucoup Bien	4	F	2	0	0	0	328	Beaver Tales	3	G	1	0	0	0	0
Beaucoup Trois	5	M	5	1	1	2	11,220	Beaverton	2	G	3	0	0	0	867
Beaudazzler	7	G	4	0	0	0	2,550	Bebe Betz	3	F	11	2	1	2	25,395
Beaudelair Jones	6	H	11	1	1	3	15,371	Bebe Garcon	3	G	4	1	1	0	27,370
Beaudiggity	5	G	9	1	1	0	22,450	Bebe Sneakers	11	G	1	0	0	0	0
Beaufighter (NZ)	5	G	4	1	0	0	9,900	Bebopping Gold	3	F	13	2	2	0	11,790
Beaufort Scale	2	C	3	0	0	0	390	Becalmed	6	G	10	0	1	1	4,622
Beaufort West	8	H	2	0	0	0	0	Because I Said So	3	C	2	0	0	0	0
Beaugar	3	G	8	1	0	0	17,332	Because of Candy	7	M	9	2	0	1	5,284
Beaugie	7	G	12	0	1	0	1,913	Because Youre Mine	5	M	11	2	3	0	19,102
Beaulena	3	F	6	2	2	0	19,080	Becca's Bambi	6	M	7	1	0	1	8,190
Beaulieu	3	G	11	1	0	2	18,136	Becca's Salut	3	C	8	1	3	0	29,465
Beaumaris	10	H	4	0	0	1	1,761	Beck	6	G	6	0	0	0	1,692
Beaumes de Venise	7	G	11	3	3	1	26,200	Beck Key	7	M	9	0	0	0	684
Beaunaskra	6	M	5	0	0	3	2,207	Beckelman	6	G	13	1	2	2	16,182
Beau's Ace	3	F	14	3	1	1	30,074	Beckham	4	G	18	3	2	5	48,695
Beau's County	2	C	3	1	0	2	28,190	Beckiss	5	M	6	0	0	0	285
Beau's Diva	2	F	2	0	1	0	2,800	Beckon the King	7	G	6	0	1	1	8,992
Beau's Fantasy	5	G	7	1	1	0	41,990	Beckson	2	C	3	1	0	0	8,748
Beau's Halo Man	3	C	3	0	0	1	1,760	Beckstein	3	G	13	3	2	0	19,580
Beau's Regal Gal	4	F	10	1	2	1	10,576	Becky B Mine	4	F	4	3	0	0	23,430
Beau's Surprise	5	G	10	1	1	0	26,681	Becky Beth	3	F	11	0	1	4	3,143
Beau's Town	5	G	6	4	1	0	351,800	Becky in Pink	2	F	4	1	0	1	18,380
Beau's Wager	5	G	10	4	1	0	60,052	Becky's Revenge	6	M	12	2	2	3	16,707
Beausox	4	F	9	0	2	0	8,434	Becky's Rock	4	F	14	1	1	1	12,825
Beautiful America	3	F	7	1	1	1	184,403	Becloud	3	F	5	0	0	0	370
Beautiful Angel	2	C	4	0	0	0	2,340	Bed Pro	3	F	16	6	1	2	50,507
Beautiful Balance	6	G	2	0	0	0	0	Bedanken	4	F	1	0	0	0	36,000
Beautiful Baroness	3	F	9	2	0	0	96,138	Bedazzle 'Em	3	F	11	0	4	2	53,280
Beautiful Beau	4	F	9	2	2	1	19,933	Bedford Boy	2	C	8	1	2	2	29,990
Beautiful Becke	4	F	12	1	1	4	20,437	Bedford Road	3	G	10	6	1	1	34,453
Beautiful Bets	3	F	13	2	2	3	61,340	Bedford's Comet	4	F	5	0	0	1	1,365
Beautiful Blonde	5	M	1	0	0	0	282	Bedillion	2	G	9	4	2	1	30,680
Beautiful Call	3	F	2	0	1	0	1,800	Bedline	2	C	1	0	0	0	180

Horse	Age	Sex	Sts	1st	2d	3d	Won	Horse	Age	Sex	Sts	1st	2d	3d	Won
Bedouin Sheikh	7	H	1	0	0	0	0	Belardinha	3	F	2	0	0	0	800
Bedouina	4	F	9	1	1	0	19,679	Belazar	3	F	3	0	0	0	0
Bedroom Kisser	5	G	13	3	1	3	47,030	Beldean	8	M	1	0	0	0	0
Bedtime Lullaby	4	F	13	1	1	1	5,901	Beledi	6	M	3	0	0	0	129
Bedwarmer	4	G	12	4	3	1	26,612	Beleive a Caper	2	G	1	0	0	0	0
Bee Bee Doubleyou	3	F	3	0	0	0	0	Belenda Back	4	F	17	2	2	2	11,220
Bee Bee Gun	2	C	2	0	0	0	0	Belfast Drive	7	G	17	1	5	2	8,497
Bee Bo's Gal	6	M	3	0	0	0	225	Belgenio	7	G	11	0	0	1	2,070
Bee Eight (GB)	6	G	11	4	1	0	26,503	Belgrade	5	H	10	1	0	3	8,256
Bee Flat	2	F	2	0	0	0	485	Belgravia (GB)	9	G	2	1	0	0	4,020
Bee Fly	4	C	1	0	0	1	1,820	Belibhai	6	G	1	0	0	0	0
Bee Honey	5	G	11	2	4	1	11,381	Belichick	3	C	3	1	0	0	21,560
Bee Line Genius	4	F	12	0	4	3	28,370	Belie	4	F	16	2	3	2	36,141
Bee Mountain	4	C	1	0	0	0	0	Believable Choice	5	G	8	3	0	1	28,618
Bee My Honey	4	F	7	0	2	2	22,880	Believable Copy	2	G	4	2	0	0	40,920
Bee My Selecto	4	F	14	1	0	3	6,209	Believable Host	3	G	9	1	2	1	40,910
Bee 'n Bee	10	G	9	0	1	0	915	Believable Shirley	3	F	14	0	3	0	10,072
Bee On Track	4	F	4	0	1	0	1,654	Believable Trick	3	F	5	0	0	1	993
Beebe Lake	3	F	9	2	4	1	109,380	Believablepleasure	2	F	3	0	1	1	9,811
Beebionic	3	G	3	0	0	0	0	Believably Barton	9	G	1	0	0	0	59
Beebop Tothe Music	9	G	10	2	0	1	2,569	Believe a Countess	3	F	10	3	2	0	24,111
Beeboppin Cousin	2	G	1	0	0	1	1,596	Believe I Can Fly	4	C	9	1	0	1	20,880
Beecher	5	G	10	4	0	2	18,586	Believe Im Special	4	G	6	2	0	2	68,800
Beeda	2	F	1	0	0	0	0	Believe in Dreams	4	F	11	1	0	0	7,313
Beef'n Brew	4	G	11	2	2	1	19,864	Believe in Missy	2	F	4	2	1	0	76,370
Beekman Court	4	G	5	0	0	0	1,080	Believe Its Brooke	2	F	3	0	0	0	308
Beekwik	5	M	1	0	0	0	80	Believe She Can	5	M	8	1	0	1	5,947
Beeline	2	F	2	0	0	0	875	Believe the Chief	6	H	4	0	0	1	1,365
Beeline Express	5	G	1	0	0	0	70	Believe the D J	11	G	6	0	1	0	450
Beelzebub	3	G	8	1	0	1	9,031	Believe the Devil	5	G	14	2	1	2	23,367
Beelzebubba	3	C	5	0	0	0	1,750	Believe the Doctor	3	F	12	0	0	1	1,570
Beemer	5	H	15	2	2	0	3,556	Believe the Sound	6	G	3	0	0	0	136
Been Broke	2	C	1	0	0	0	0	Believe You Me	7	G	13	2	4	1	16,009
Been Done Dat Dare	2	C	1	0	0	0	224	Believeambest	3	F	4	0	0	0	0
Been Refused	3	C	3	0	0	0	518	Believein Mud Bugs	3	G	10	0	2	2	13,953
Been Sent	4	F	4	0	0	0	54	Believeitohko	3	G	3	0	0	0	0
Been Wavering	4	C	2	0	0	0	1,200	Believemewenitellu	3	C	19	0	1	4	9,766
Beenaloha	6	G	1	0	0	0	0	Believen It	3	F	1	0	0	0	0
Beenonabender	3	G	2	0	0	0	0	Believer's Dolly	4	F	11	1	3	1	24,893
Beep and Go	4	G	13	0	1	3	5,923	Believer's Lucky	4	G	12	2	2	3	49,990
Beep Bandit	2	F	3	0	1	0	2,580	Believer's Miss	5	M	12	2	0	0	14,835
Beep Beep Beep	3	C	9	1	0	2	37,446	Believer's Queen	1	M	1	0	0	0	0
Beep Me	9	G	17	6	4	2	28,729	Believer's Ruckus	2	G	6	0	0	0	3,918
Beep Zone	2	F	2	0	1	0	4,560	Beligerent Lady	5	M	1	0	0	0	1,800
Beer Belly	3	G	8	0	0	0	407	Beliveau	2	G	4	1	2	0	12,190
Beer Goggles	5	G	16	2	3	2	9,843	Belize Vacation	2	G	6	0	0	0	536
Beer Run	3	G	1	0	0	0	170	Bell Bottom	6	H	7	0	0	0	1,331
Beerbellys Sister	4	F	16	1	0	1	8,337	Bell Boy	4	C	11	1	3	1	12,048
Beermeathebit	4	G	14	1	1	1	4,992	Bell Captain	3	G	14	1	3	2	13,440
Beetrap	3	C	10	1	3	2	18,020	Bell Express	4	G	4	1	0	0	4,508
Beeville	3	F	13	3	5	0	63,360	Bell Power	4	C	7	1	2	1	14,382
Beezly	6	M	6	0	0	0	135	Bell Sara	2	F	1	0	0	0	0
Before Sunset	2	F	1	0	0	0	2,500	Bella and Whistles	2	F	4	0	0	0	1,260
Beganet	3	C	2	0	0	0	745	Bella Anna	4	F	5	0	2	2	3,425
Begborrowanddeal	2	G	4	2	1	1	100,559	Bella Baloosa	3	F	3	0	1	0	2,534
Begin the Beguine	3	F	9	2	1	1	54,283	Bella Bambola	4	F	13	2	0	1	35,404
Begintodance	3	F	1	0	0	0	0	Bella Bandita	3	F	5	1	0	0	6,670
Begone Quick	3	G	9	0	1	3	2,600	Bella Bella Bailey	4	F	9	3	1	2	31,327
Begonebydaylight	2	F	1	0	0	0	0	Bella Belle	6	M	6	0	0	1	565
Begoodatit	6	G	3	0	1	0	1,153	Bella Bellucci	4	F	3	0	1	2	90,000
Behind Bars	4	F	5	1	0	0	3,609	Bella Bianca	2	F	1	0	0	0	1,050
Behind Enemy Lines	4	C	11	1	5	1	55,260	Bella Bimba	3	F	1	0	0	0	0
Behind On Points	3	G	9	0	0	0	3,390	Bella Boo	2	F	2	0	0	0	400
Behind the Bluff	4	F	7	1	2	0	34,050	Bella Bourie	2	F	5	1	0	2	17,987
Behkat	3	G	2	0	0	0	120	Bella Can't Stop	6	G	7	1	0	2	4,658
Behler's Beauty	3	F	11	1	0	2	25,475	Bella Cara	3	F	5	0	1	0	1,245
Behold the Storm	3	G	3	0	0	0	0	Bella Cat	4	F	9	2	1	3	11,692
Behrnik	3	F	8	2	3	1	91,000	Bella Cobra	2	F	6	0	1	1	6,505
Being Green	6	G	9	0	0	1	1,933	Bella Coola Bebe	4	F	5	0	0	0	1,227
Being With You	3	F	10	1	2	3	17,685	Bella Cosa	3	F	4	0	0	0	2,520
Beirut	3	C	5	1	0	1	4,065	Bella Cruella	2	F	4	1	0	1	8,530
Bej Dor	7	M	1	0	0	0	0	Bella de Fattoria	3	F	8	2	1	3	20,860
Beknown to Me	7	G	10	0	2	6	54,440	Bella Diablo	4	F	9	1	0	2	7,720
Bel Air Belle	5	M	2	1	0	0	13,200	Bella Faccia	6	M	1	0	0	0	0
Bel Baie	4	F	9	0	1	2	25,480	Bella Favola	4	F	12	0	2	0	8,012
Bel Chateau	3	F	3	1	0	1	5,460	Bella Fumatori	3	F	8	2	0	0	34,225
Bela Carol	2	F	3	0	1	0	2,120	Bella Giorno	3	F	9	1	2	1	40,510
Belal	8	G	16	6	2	1	20,786	Bella Girl	4	F	8	0	1	2	14,978
Belanso	3	G	13	1	2	1	6,658	Bella Grand Slam	6	M	4	0	0	0	900

Horse	Age	Sex	Sts	1st	2d	3d	Won
Bella Isabella	2	F	2	0	0	0	740
Bella Katrina	3	F	3	0	0	0	1,764
Bella La Ghosi	2	F	3	0	0	0	900
Bella Lauren	3	F	6	2	1	0	52,056
Bella Luce	4	F	3	0	1	1	12,230
Bella Nunzi	4	F	4	0	2	1	27,560
Bella Rouge	5	M	6	3	0	1	57,410
Bella Rubia	2	F	1	0	0	0	0
Bella Savella	3	F	21	3	5	6	54,930
Bella Sheba	3	F	5	1	0	0	4,905
Bella Siena	3	F	2	0	0	0	700
Bella Sierra	3	F	7	0	3	2	9,270
Bella Sunrise	2	F	1	0	0	0	45
Bella Tizzy	5	M	6	3	1	0	17,048
Bella Tusa (IRE)	3	F	4	0	0	0	4,281
Bella Villa	7	M	4	0	1	0	5,450
Bella Volare	5	M	13	2	1	1	77,500
Bellachos	3	F	1	0	0	0	0
Bellacuzin	2	F	1	0	0	0	160
Belladumaani	2	C	7	1	2	1	52,440
Bellamanga	4	F	14	2	2	4	11,226
Bellanique	2	F	1	0	1	0	8,200
Bellanova	3	F	1	0	0	0	0
Bellaral	3	F	3	0	0	0	610
Bellarama	2	F	1	0	0	0	2,100
Bellaroma	4	F	8	1	1	2	6,445
Bellas Legacy	2	C	1	0	0	1	4,000
Bellasultress	4	F	7	0	2	0	6,580
Bellavena	3	F	12	2	4	1	17,200
Belle a Versailles	3	F	1	1	0	0	8,680
Belle American	5	M	8	3	0	1	16,941
Belle Angel	3	F	16	4	1	2	31,860
Belle Artiste	5	M	12	1	3	1	91,096
Belle City Boy	2	C	1	0	0	0	0
Belle de La France	2	F	4	0	0	0	240
Belle de Naskra	4	F	12	0	2	1	39,593
Belle de Sand	3	F	5	0	0	0	770
Belle Flamme	4	F	13	0	2	1	2,841
Belle Fourche	2	F	4	1	2	0	7,628
Belle Gully	2	C	2	0	0	0	350
Belle of Indiana	2	F	8	1	1	3	28,403
Belle of Liberty	6	M	3	0	0	0	510
Belle of Livorno	3	F	5	1	0	0	14,053
Belle of Perintown	3	F	5	1	0	3	141,390
Belle of Portugal	3	F	5	2	1	1	46,120
Belle of Rio	4	F	5	0	0	1	1,023
Belle Quick	3	F	3	0	0	0	0
Belle Rapids	3	F	1	1	0	0	20,460
Belle Rebelle	3	F	11	1	1	3	18,260
Belle Riviere	7	M	7	0	0	1	2,254
Belle Rosia	3	F	3	0	0	0	0
Belle Sherri	4	F	10	1	2	0	7,790
Belle Toujours	3	F	3	0	0	0	1,770
Belleciela	3	F	2	0	0	0	1,818
Belleek	5	M	3	0	0	0	0
Bellefontaine	5	M	12	2	4	3	15,798
Bellengrath	3	F	4	1	0	0	13,420
Belle's Beast	2	C	2	0	0	0	0
Belle's Best Baby	2	F	3	0	0	0	120
Belles Bibianna	4	F	5	0	1	1	1,093
Belle's Deed	4	F	20	2	0	5	14,730
Belle's Eryn	2	F	2	0	0	1	1,050
Belle's Halo	4	F	6	1	1	1	3,826
Belles Honor	4	F	6	0	1	0	3,476
Belles Lettres	4	F	9	1	2	2	57,440
Belles of Syn	4	G	6	1	3	0	8,745
Belle's Secret	3	F	7	2	0	1	14,027
Belle's Star	3	F	3	0	0	1	1,748
Belle's Trick	2	F	6	0	0	0	555
Belleski	4	F	7	4	1	1	195,059
Belleview Lady	3	F	4	0	0	0	664
Belleview Rattler	3	G	11	1	2	0	7,065
Bellicose Papa	7	G	1	0	0	0	0
Bellicosity	4	G	11	0	0	0	345
Bellini Gal	3	F	3	1	0	0	9,378
Bellini Martini	2	F	2	1	0	0	38,808
Bellisa	7	M	9	1	2	2	2,868
Bellisimo	5	G	7	1	0	0	8,144
Belljar	3	C	19	3	1	2	36,514

Horse	Age	Sex	Sts	1st	2d	3d	Won
Bellman Wilson	4	C	3	0	0	0	771
Bello Bambino	2	G	3	0	1	0	1,360
Bello Cozza	5	H	1	0	0	0	0
Bello Ragazzo	3	G	8	1	0	0	4,450
Bells Fool	3	G	6	0	1	2	1,865
Bell's Lass	2	F	1	0	0	0	3,528
Bell's Miracle	8	G	7	0	2	2	3,007
Bells O Fun	4	F	2	0	1	0	652
Bells 'o Joy	3	F	14	1	2	0	12,185
Bells of Thunder	5	G	7	1	1	2	23,140
Bells On Her Toes	3	F	10	3	0	1	30,596
Bellus	3	F	3	0	0	0	328
Bellwether	7	H	8	2	3	0	18,970
Bellwood Girl	5	M	8	0	3	2	5,762
Belmont Babe	2	F	2	0	0	1	4,100
Belmont Blues	4	F	12	1	2	2	25,850
Belmont Bob	3	G	3	0	0	1	638
Belmont Groovy	2	G	1	1	0	0	9,600
Belmont Harbor	2	F	2	1	0	0	7,200
Belong to Sea	3	F	6	3	0	0	113,460
Belong to Who	6	G	8	1	0	1	3,714
Belongs Fast	6	M	10	2	2	2	66,130
Belongs to J D	5	M	5	2	0	1	14,090
Belongs to Mony	7	M	2	1	0	0	15,600
Belong's to Three	3	G	21	2	5	6	48,545
Below Freezing	5	M	5	2	0	0	10,365
Belt	4	G	9	1	2	1	11,660
Belt Driven	6	G	9	1	0	2	5,435
Belted Dawn	3	F	1	0	0	0	0
Belterra	4	F	1	0	0	1	11,000
Beltway	2	C	2	0	0	0	1,080
Belusko's Babe	2	F	3	0	0	1	1,750
Belva Casey	3	F	8	1	0	1	8,115
Belvedere Miss	4	F	9	2	2	2	44,000
Belvedere Rocks	3	G	2	0	1	0	1,800
Bemo	5	G	12	2	3	2	13,388
Bemybabytonite	2	F	1	0	0	0	120
Bemywildestdream	3	F	3	0	0	0	100
Ben	6	G	9	0	1	1	3,428
Ben a Lover	3	G	5	0	0	1	3,260
Ben and Me	2	G	5	0	1	1	7,520
Ben Ben	6	H	5	0	0	0	128
Ben Gunn	3	G	3	0	0	0	0
Ben H	3	G	8	0	1	1	6,985
Ben J	3	C	9	1	0	1	6,372
Ben Saw San	7	G	3	0	2	0	7,820
Ben Speedin	6	H	3	0	1	0	1,428
Ben the Man	6	G	8	1	2	1	38,480
Ben Told	9	G	1	0	0	0	1,045
Bench Atara	3	F	4	1	1	1	7,301
Bench Confrence	4	G	9	4	1	1	47,840
Bench Maker	3	C	1	1	0	0	12,586
Bench Mench	3	G	13	2	2	3	17,119
Bench Press	2	C	1	1	0	0	11,400
Benchmark Bargain	3	F	12	1	0	1	6,248
Benchrun	2	F	2	0	0	0	206
Bencivenga	6	H	1	0	0	0	0
Bend a Little	2	F	1	0	0	1	2,700
Bend the Track	5	H	14	2	6	2	18,822
Bendalee	4	F	3	1	1	1	4,540
Benden Weyr	8	G	10	1	1	2	28,500
Benderosa	4	C	2	0	0	0	0
Bendette	3	F	1	0	0	0	0
Bending Strings	2	F	3	2	1	0	39,150
Bending the Rules	2	F	4	0	0	0	240
Bendito	3	C	7	0	0	1	355
Bendo Line	6	M	1	0	0	0	58
Bene Hill (IRE)	2	C	2	0	0	0	0
Benedict A. Kite	5	G	16	3	1	2	25,419
Beneficial Bartok	2	F	4	0	0	2	13,128
Benefit Party	4	F	4	1	0	1	18,003
Benelli	8	G	1	0	0	0	0
Beneteau	6	G	6	0	0	0	957
Benevolent Prince	3	C	7	1	0	2	11,705
Benewin	2	G	1	1	0	0	5,700
Bengal Boy	4	G	8	1	0	2	3,736
Bengalesa (ARG)	5	M	3	0	0	1	6,690
Bengaly	7	H	2	0	0	1	1,134
Benge B	5	G	14	0	0	4	7,514

Horse	Age	Sex	Sts	1st	2d	3d	Won
Bengoa	3	G	5	0	0	0	1,100
Beniamino	3	C	9	0	3	3	8,750
Benicia Storm	4	F	7	1	0	0	3,305
Beniflower	2	F	1	0	0	0	960
Benigni	5	G	6	0	0	0	712
Benita	2	F	1	0	0	0	0
Benjamin Bag	5	G	9	1	1	0	4,200
Benjamin Swanson	3	G	2	0	0	0	305
Benjamin's Foxy	6	M	9	0	1	0	3,072
Benji	9	H	1	0	0	0	61
Benji'special Blue	3	G	18	2	3	1	26,185
Bennett of Bologna	4	F	7	1	0	0	1,825
Bennie Ben Benny	3	G	9	1	1	0	32,598
Bennington	2	F	4	0	0	1	3,855
Benny and Bert	3	G	2	0	0	0	660
Benny Benz	3	G	6	1	0	0	2,410
Benny G	2	G	4	1	0	0	7,130
Benny the Hawk	4	G	14	3	0	1	20,657
Benny the Lip	4	G	17	3	4	1	24,850
Benny's Atlas	2	G	1	0	0	0	0
Benny's Boy	3	G	2	0	0	0	415
Benny's Gem	3	F	6	1	0	1	12,190
Bennys Lady	3	F	4	0	0	0	1,041
Benny's Little Dip	3	G	4	0	2	1	8,540
Bennys Tune	4	G	8	1	0	0	8,391
Benoit	3	G	4	0	0	3	14,960
Benray's Flash	6	M	7	0	0	1	4,984
Ben's Bluesman	7	G	8	0	1	0	6,160
Ben's Charm	2	F	1	0	0	0	0
Ben's Choice	4	G	6	0	0	1	3,042
Bens Corker	4	C	10	1	2	1	3,564
Ben's Courage	2	G	5	2	0	1	31,320
Ben's Florida Lady	2	F	2	0	0	0	1,560
Ben's Good Deed	4	G	4	0	0	0	875
Ben's Hammer	3	C	15	0	5	2	8,728
Ben's Lady	3	F	9	1	2	0	4,460
Ben's Reflection	3	G	8	5	2	0	101,362
Bensalem	6	G	12	8	0	4	161,066
Bensonhurst's Best	5	M	3	0	0	0	795
Bensquito	2	C	3	2	0	0	19,982
Benswaki	6	H	4	0	2	1	2,385
Bent for Glory	3	G	9	1	0	2	7,680
Bent On Speed	3	G	7	3	1	0	11,540
Bent Suze	2	F	1	0	0	0	0
Bent Tree	3	C	3	0	0	0	0
Bent Tree Miracle	4	F	5	2	2	0	28,360
Bentley Pride	3	F	3	1	1	1	31,540
Bentley Ten	4	G	9	0	1	0	6,910
Benton	3	C	8	1	2	0	8,522
Benton Cookie	3	F	2	0	0	0	59
Bentucky	3	C	9	2	2	1	40,568
Ben'z Mercedes	7	H	3	0	0	0	0
Benza Winner	10	G	3	0	0	1	440
Beoangel	3	C	1	0	0	0	0
Beppe	3	G	2	0	1	0	5,980
Bequeathed	4	C	1	0	1	0	546
Bequia Tequila	5	M	3	0	1	0	3,614
Bequoit	5	G	9	1	1	0	9,855
Berani	4	G	4	0	1	0	2,611
Beranjiz	3	F	12	1	4	0	15,990
Berarducci	5	G	9	0	0	0	555
Bereft	4	G	7	1	3	1	10,243
Beret	4	F	6	2	0	1	56,575
Berfy	3	G	13	2	3	1	18,525
Berg	3	G	1	0	0	0	0
Berglerized	5	H	7	1	0	1	4,852
Bering Strait	4	F	10	1	3	0	7,055
Beringly	2	F	1	0	0	0	75
Beriskaio (IRE)	6	G	8	1	1	0	8,525
Berkelhammer	2	C	7	1	1	0	13,300
Berkley's Gold	4	F	12	1	3	1	8,529
Berkshire Eagle	3	C	8	2	1	1	24,940
Berkshire Princess	2	F	7	0	0	1	8,310
Berlanga	3	G	6	0	1	2	5,330
Berlin (IRE)	5	G	9	1	1	0	9,289
Berliner	7	H	4	1	1	1	8,645
Bermuda Blizzard	2	G	2	0	1	0	3,640
Bermuda Isle	2	F	1	0	0	0	1,500
Bernard's Candy	4	G	1	0	0	1	2,880
Bernie B	4	C	2	0	0	0	700
Bernie's Gold	5	M	8	2	0	1	55,987
Berry Berry	2	F	3	2	0	1	46,600
Berry Berry Funny	4	F	10	1	0	2	3,422
Berry Bid	10	G	1	0	0	0	58
Berry Brick	2	F	3	1	0	1	5,885
Berry Divine	5	M	8	0	0	2	1,703
Berry Funny	7	G	6	0	0	1	616
Berry Good	2	F	1	0	0	0	360
Berry Hill	7	H	2	0	0	0	0
Berry Southern	3	F	3	0	0	0	0
Berry Springs	4	F	2	0	0	0	725
Berry Viva	2	F	7	1	2	0	12,667
Berry's a Smoking	5	H	15	2	2	5	40,889
Bertha's Bikini	7	M	1	0	0	0	650
Berthon (BRZ)	7	G	1	0	0	0	300
Bertie's Dream	2	G	4	0	0	0	0
Bertie's Halo	4	F	10	1	0	2	6,274
Bertl	4	F	1	0	0	0	0
Bertology	3	G	4	0	0	0	0
Bertrando Russell	3	G	1	0	0	1	900
Bertrando's Dare	3	F	4	1	0	0	24,350
Bertrando's Model	4	F	6	2	0	0	55,740
Bert's Bar	3	C	7	2	0	0	40,043
Bert's Best	2	C	2	0	0	0	556
Bert's House	2	G	4	1	0	0	4,244
Bert's Nicky	4	G	13	4	3	0	63,540
Bertshero	4	C	6	1	2	2	7,091
Beryl Bear	3	F	1	0	0	0	465
Beryl's Quest	3	F	10	1	0	1	6,220
Besheft	3	G	3	0	0	0	600
Besige	4	F	5	0	0	0	540
Beso Del Sol	5	M	15	1	5	2	42,305
Bess Wing	12	G	2	0	0	0	80
Bessame	7	M	1	0	0	0	87
Bessie's Angel	6	M	2	0	0	0	0
Bessiesimage	2	F	2	0	0	0	0
Bess's Donaldo	8	G	6	0	0	0	0
Best Advantage	4	F	10	3	1	0	21,963
Best Alert	4	G	12	3	3	2	44,894
Best and Proud	2	F	3	0	1	0	2,350
Best Bet	5	M	6	0	0	0	725
Best Bird	2	G	4	1	0	0	8,318
Best Block	2	G	4	0	0	0	2,230
Best Caper	2	C	4	1	2	0	15,369
Best Card	4	F	6	0	0	1	2,640
Best Cat	4	G	10	1	0	1	4,460
Best Chum	2	C	6	0	0	2	6,720
Best Contest	2	F	1	0	0	0	1,275
Best Dispersion (IRE)	5	H	1	0	0	0	0
Best Echo	3	C	7	2	1	2	28,770
Best Epic	5	G	11	0	3	2	5,238
Best Essence	4	C	7	0	0	0	240
Best Foot Forward	4	F	10	1	0	5	34,395
Best Friend	4	F	10	4	1	1	44,020
Best From the West	7	G	16	1	0	2	12,296
Best Game in Town	2	G	4	1	1	1	7,300
Best Girl Yet	5	M	9	1	2	1	8,162
Best in the Storm	2	F	6	1	1	0	20,510
Best Interview	3	F	9	0	1	3	23,480
Best Jest B a Lady	5	M	12	1	2	0	9,842
Best Kept Secret	4	F	12	1	2	2	8,567
Best Line	6	G	4	0	0	0	0
Best Love	2	C	2	0	0	0	0
Best Minister	3	C	6	2	2	0	123,170
Best o' Prince	7	H	5	1	0	0	1,317
Best of Change	2	G	5	0	0	1	1,651
Best of Class	3	C	12	1	0	0	7,500
Best of D West	4	C	1	0	0	0	0
Best of Glory	3	G	5	0	0	0	981
Best of Jazz	5	M	2	0	0	0	0
Best of K C	6	G	8	0	1	2	15,160
Best of the Duck	7	G	11	4	2	0	36,916
Best of the East	4	F	12	2	1	1	17,929
Best of the Rest	8	H	6	3	2	0	753,500
Best On Tap	3	G	7	1	1	2	23,700
Best Pick	2	C	2	0	1	0	1,017
Best Pine Yet	5	G	12	3	0	2	8,493
Best Play	3	G	3	0	0	0	1,220

Horse	Age	Sex	Sts	1st	2d	3d	Won
Best Practices	3	F	12	2	3	1	25,880
Best Prize	5	M	8	2	2	2	38,410
Best Quality	3	G	11	2	1	1	48,232
Best Return	4	G	8	0	0	1	3,187
Best Shot Yet	7	G	2	0	0	0	2,100
Best Storm	3	G	11	2	1	3	11,481
Best Surprise	3	G	9	0	1	1	4,872
Best to Be King	2	C	3	1	1	0	34,275
Best to Best	4	G	9	0	3	3	4,269
Best Turn Me Loose	2	F	4	1	0	1	3,500
Best World	4	G	18	0	0	1	1,625
Bestabayou	5	M	11	1	1	1	26,525
Bestbandintheland	7	H	3	0	0	0	68
Bestrongspeaktrue	2	C	3	0	0	1	1,020
Besttobeabachelor	8	G	14	3	1	1	26,016
Bet a Bargann	5	G	11	5	1	4	31,353
Bet a Heather	3	F	5	0	0	0	598
Bet a Whirl	8	G	2	0	0	0	183
Bet Awad	3	G	4	1	0	0	3,300
Bet Brick	7	G	10	1	4	0	5,351
Bet Double	3	G	3	0	0	0	0
Bet Gold	3	G	15	2	3	4	29,720
Bet Me Best	7	G	5	1	0	0	30,000
Bet Me Jack	5	G	4	0	0	0	661
Bet On a Vision	3	F	17	1	2	3	9,261
Bet On Bam-Bam	3	G	1	0	0	0	110
Bet On Boston	3	C	10	2	0	1	33,132
Bet On Brad	4	G	17	1	1	4	11,846
Bet On Joe	5	H	6	2	1	0	61,860
Bet On Lori	5	M	10	2	1	0	10,940
Bet On the Rainbow	3	F	4	0	0	1	3,080
Bet Or Believe Her	3	F	2	0	0	0	248
Bet Shes Supreme	3	F	3	0	0	0	0
Bet the Breeze	3	G	11	1	0	0	13,266
Bet the Farm	3	F	3	0	0	0	140
Bet the House	4	C	3	0	0	0	0
Bet the Line	10	G	5	0	0	0	1,362
Bet the Ranch	3	C	6	3	0	1	40,080
Bet the Rock	4	G	16	2	1	1	11,231
Bet Whom	6	M	15	2	4	3	12,673
Bet Your Stars	5	G	8	2	6	0	21,644
Betabet On Betty	3	F	9	0	0	0	553
Betairai	4	F	6	0	0	0	150
Betake	4	F	2	0	0	0	5,727
Betcha's Brat	3	C	11	1	1	2	15,570
Betchawanakeephim	5	G	9	1	1	2	4,214
Bethel Heights	2	G	4	0	0	0	713
Bethel Road	5	G	11	0	1	1	11,581
Bethestar	4	G	9	0	1	1	15,680
Beths Baby	4	G	9	0	0	4	3,099
Beth's Bo	7	H	12	0	2	1	5,585
Beth's Choice	5	H	11	1	3	3	13,453
Beth's Expectation	4	F	8	2	0	1	31,368
Betido	3	F	10	1	3	1	17,612
Betimfantastique	5	G	19	2	0	1	6,097
Betkatjo	3	F	5	1	1	0	6,768
Betonbuddy	3	C	1	0	0	0	94
Betondegray	2	C	1	0	0	0	0
Betonslew	4	F	10	0	0	3	2,376
Betonsmells	8	G	4	0	0	0	100
Betray	5	M	14	0	1	2	11,040
Betshe Hath a Way	3	F	1	1	0	0	16,830
Betsy Bewild	3	F	11	1	0	1	7,458
Betsy Boo	5	M	7	0	0	1	1,630
Betsy N	3	F	10	3	2	0	50,249
Betsy's Forum	6	G	10	0	0	1	2,358
Betta Bing	3	G	4	0	0	0	0
Bette	6	M	6	2	0	0	10,914
Better	6	M	8	0	1	2	9,548
Better Be Now	5	M	12	2	1	0	13,086
Better Choice	9	G	10	0	3	1	11,420
Better Dan	8	G	7	1	0	0	5,288
Better Daze	3	F	1	0	0	0	0
Better Guess Again	4	F	9	1	2	4	2,804
Better Half	3	F	6	0	0	1	4,422
Better Idol	4	G	5	1	0	1	31,615
Better Place	3	F	15	1	2	5	25,895
Better Quality	2	C	4	1	0	3	27,680
Better Road	6	G	3	1	0	0	11,585
Better Senorita	4	F	16	3	3	2	26,572
Better Talk Now	4	G	7	3	1	2	240,152
Better Than That	6	G	12	2	2	4	17,327
Better Zbetter	3	C	3	0	0	2	6,225
Betterbegoodtome	6	G	17	1	3	1	12,288
Bettermaid	4	F	11	1	1	1	7,581
Betters Best Bet	5	G	2	0	0	0	500
Betterthanaverage	6	G	4	0	0	0	272
Betterthanexpected	4	G	7	1	0	1	4,990
Bette's Half Dozen	4	F	7	1	0	0	5,670
Bette's Shell Cat	3	F	9	1	2	3	29,930
Bettie's Dancer	5	M	2	0	0	0	600
Betting Lady	3	F	10	1	2	0	8,144
Bettor by Farr	4	G	7	1	0	0	9,086
Bettor Cote	7	G	17	0	4	1	8,475
Bettor Knot	2	F	4	0	0	0	3,074
Bettor Met	5	M	6	1	0	1	8,045
Bettor Royalty	5	G	15	3	3	1	56,550
Bettorbeleveawoman	3	F	6	1	1	0	9,060
Bettors Delight	3	F	2	1	0	0	6,013
Bettors Faith	2	F	3	0	0	0	255
Betty B	4	F	9	1	1	1	22,135
Betty C	6	M	14	3	2	3	52,442
Betty Lee	3	F	18	3	3	4	36,715
Betty Mae A	7	M	9	2	1	2	19,329
Betty Shea Miller	2	F	2	0	0	0	0
Betty Spaghetti	3	F	11	5	2	2	58,249
Betty Sue	4	F	16	2	1	2	12,396
Bettybird	4	F	1	0	0	1	3,410
Bettylou's Badboy	3	C	8	0	0	0	125
Betty's Boop	3	F	3	1	0	0	4,686
Betty's Grand Bet	2	F	2	0	0	0	0
Betty's Hat	7	M	6	0	0	0	6,900
Betty's Little Bit	3	F	1	0	1	0	1,500
Betty's Solutions	3	F	14	2	2	0	27,234
Betty's Time Bomb	7	M	2	0	0	0	66
Betty's Wish	3	F	9	5	2	1	209,440
Betuitscold	3	F	8	2	1	1	13,175
Betunome	3	C	1	1	0	0	3,120
Between Two Blues	4	C	2	0	0	0	192
Betwick	6	H	1	0	0	0	0
Betwineyouandme	4	F	15	5	3	1	94,725
Betyourbucksonrio	5	M	3	1	0	0	944
Beverley Minster	3	F	4	1	0	0	5,727
Beverly Greedy	8	G	12	4	0	3	86,260
Beverly Kay	4	F	14	0	1	1	2,114
Beverly Lady	5	M	6	0	0	0	624
Beverly Tricks	3	F	18	0	2	4	7,037
Beverly's Best	3	F	13	2	2	5	12,423
Beverlys Gold	4	F	4	0	0	1	1,087
Beverly's Halo	3	F	4	0	0	1	2,293
Bevie's Dare	4	G	18	2	3	2	30,138
Bevmar	5	M	11	1	2	2	13,471
Bev's Bully	3	F	10	3	1	1	3,520
Bevys Affair	3	F	12	3	3	2	37,041
Bevys Boy	2	C	2	0	0	0	60
Beware Avalanche	7	G	11	2	1	1	81,120
Beware the Ides	8	G	11	3	2	1	9,723
Beweave in Spirits	2	F	2	0	0	0	137
Bewitching Bartok	2	C	7	1	0	1	50,082
Bewitching Briar	5	M	4	0	1	2	4,744
Bewitching Eyes	9	M	10	2	0	1	19,549
Bewitchury	4	F	8	2	3	2	7,050
Bexley	2	F	3	0	1	0	4,660
Beyers Fortune	7	M	8	3	0	0	21,090
Beyers Real Deal	5	G	7	0	2	2	2,766
Beyond all Limits	10	G	4	0	0	0	152
Beyond Brilliant	5	G	8	1	1	2	37,835
Beyond Chance	4	C	13	1	1	1	43,625
Beyond Control	3	C	1	0	0	0	75
Beyond Infinity (FR)	3	G	11	2	2	2	74,240
Beyond Joy	4	F	11	1	0	2	8,805
Beyond Our Wildest	4	G	2	1	0	0	10,680
Beyond Reach	4	F	6	0	2	3	1,760
Beyond Reasoning	3	F	9	2	1	1	9,762
Beyond the Horizon	2	F	4	1	1	0	51,768
Beyond the Light	3	G	5	0	0	0	0
Beyond the Limit	3	F	3	0	0	0	0
Beyond the Sea	3	G	8	1	0	0	4,725

Horse	Age	Sex	Sts	1st	2d	3d	Won
Beyond the Waves	6	M	8	1	3	1	78,698
Beyond the West	6	M	1	0	0	0	100
Beyond Time	4	C	9	0	1	1	4,395
Beyond Winnie	5	M	9	1	2	1	17,549
Beyond Worth	5	G	6	0	0	0	100
Bguygian	5	G	5	0	0	0	1,596
Bh Whata Challenge	5	G	2	1	0	0	600
Bham	3	C	1	0	0	1	11,000
Bhaskar	9	G	19	1	3	2	7,145
Biagio	4	G	8	1	1	1	20,825
Bianco Appeal	5	G	16	1	2	1	17,690
Bianconi Baby	2	F	3	1	1	0	11,203
Biangood	2	F	4	1	0	2	10,390
Biaplayer	2	C	2	0	0	0	180
Bibda Love	2	F	1	0	0	0	145
Bibelot	3	F	12	2	0	3	11,362
Biblical	5	H	15	1	3	0	17,895
Bibye	5	H	11	1	2	2	17,039
Bicentennial	5	H	1	0	0	0	0
Bicol Express	5	M	8	0	1	0	4,309
Bic's Pick	2	F	3	0	0	0	817
Bid for Boston	4	G	19	0	1	3	4,711
Bid Her Sweet	4	F	3	1	1	0	15,353
Bid N Battle	3	G	8	0	0	0	455
Bid On Love	5	M	1	0	0	0	270
Bid On Me	3	F	3	0	0	0	1,290
Bid On My Basket	5	M	17	1	2	1	5,135
Bid the Zeal	9	G	17	3	1	1	20,395
Bid Wild	6	G	12	1	0	0	14,248
Bid Zup	3	C	9	2	1	0	14,245
Bidagainben	6	G	9	1	1	1	3,752
Bidder	5	G	4	1	1	0	4,537
Bidders Champ	7	H	17	0	1	0	2,365
Bidders Out	5	G	19	1	1	1	7,130
Bidding Pro	3	F	5	0	1	0	9,630
Biddy Biddy	9	G	9	1	1	0	5,118
Biddy's Lad	3	G	7	1	1	2	91,904
Bideflyck	3	G	11	1	1	2	3,437
Bidforakiss	4	F	4	1	0	1	17,488
Bidic	5	H	1	0	0	0	0
Bidis	6	G	1	0	0	0	3,000
Bidless	2	C	2	0	0	2	9,900
Bid's Fame	4	G	1	0	0	0	0
Bid's for Gold	4	C	10	1	0	2	5,668
Biedermeier	2	C	3	1	1	1	8,573
Bieganow	2	C	2	0	1	0	2,400
Bien Amie	4	F	5	0	0	0	1,955
Bien Bati	6	G	14	1	2	2	4,285
Bien Blushing	5	G	13	1	2	1	12,900
Bien Dancing	8	G	2	1	1	4	14,100
Bien Nicole	5	M	10	4	3	0	690,540
Biennale	9	G	9	0	2	2	5,180
Bienvenue	4	C	3	1	0	0	3,828
Bierstadt	3	C	7	1	0	0	26,580
Biff	4	G	12	2	2	3	27,070
Biff America	3	C	5	0	0	0	0
Bifocal	7	G	1	0	0	0	0
Big Adam J.	5	H	8	0	1	3	2,215
Big Al T.	5	G	17	4	4	5	18,456
Big Alex	5	G	10	2	1	1	13,314
Big Alley Cat	2	G	5	0	0	0	252
Big Al's Pal	6	G	1	0	0	0	0
Big American Force	3	C	11	2	3	2	43,630
Big Ankle Ben	2	G	3	0	0	0	250
Big Aristotle	5	G	13	1	2	0	5,311
Big Arthur's Joy	2	C	1	0	0	0	0
Big Bad Al	5	H	1	0	0	1	2,400
Big Bad Bue	4	G	14	4	6	1	36,538
Big Bad Diamond	3	C	1	0	0	0	73
Big Bad George	6	H	4	1	0	0	23,820
Big Bad Girl	3	F	2	0	0	0	0
Big Bad Juan	5	G	1	0	0	1	450
Big Bad Louie	2	C	1	0	0	0	0
Big Bad Sally	4	F	12	3	2	0	41,820
Big Band Man	3	C	4	0	0	0	633
Big Banker	3	C	13	2	2	3	45,508
Big Bay Brite	2	G	2	0	0	0	0
Big Becker	8	G	18	5	2	3	65,824
Big Bid	9	G	14	2	1	2	15,195
Big Big Bert	3	C	8	1	0	2	7,414
Big Big Stanley	4	G	6	0	0	1	4,623
Big Bill	4	G	4	0	1	0	888
Big Bing	8	G	14	0	1	2	2,620
Big Bizkit	3	C	1	0	0	0	0
Big Bloke	4	C	2	0	0	0	273
Big Blue Adventure	3	C	1	0	0	0	0
Big Bluff	9	G	14	0	0	1	1,922
Big Board (ARG)	7	G	1	1	0	0	36,600
Big Bob Sr.	4	C	2	0	0	0	0
Big Bobastar	2	G	7	1	1	1	16,759
Big Bobby Joe	3	F	3	0	0	0	0
Big Bold Rush	2	G	1	0	0	0	1,560
Big Bold Sweep	3	G	9	3	2	0	69,340
Big Bonus	4	G	14	4	3	1	38,270
Big Booster	2	C	3	1	0	0	40,386
Big Boss Man	5	H	7	0	1	0	3,640
Big Boy Jesse	7	G	14	3	3	2	24,916
Big Boy Looker	4	C	2	0	0	0	328
Big Boy Roy	5	G	4	0	0	0	348
Big Boy Slew	2	G	1	0	0	0	0
Big Brass Band	3	F	5	0	0	1	4,200
Big Broken Straw	5	G	4	1	0	0	23,980
Big Brother Don	3	G	9	1	1	0	6,479
Big Brown Bear	5	G	9	2	3	1	34,348
Big Brown Punch	3	C	2	0	0	0	100
Big Brush	7	G	1	0	0	0	1,200
Big Burner	4	C	7	0	0	0	1,935
Big Buster	4	G	4	0	0	0	520
Big Cajun Cat	2	G	1	0	0	0	0
Big Cam	3	G	7	0	0	0	2,095
Big Cat Reno	3	C	6	0	0	0	757
Big Chad	8	G	7	0	1	2	880
Big Change	7	G	6	1	0	0	4,380
Big Cheque	3	F	7	5	0	0	188,916
Big Chestnut	2	C	2	0	0	0	0
Big Chris	4	G	1	0	0	0	0
Big City	4	G	3	1	0	0	22,640
Big City Boy	5	G	18	3	3	3	17,488
Big City Bull	3	C	5	1	1	0	13,397
Big City Lover	3	F	2	0	0	0	720
Big City Money	3	C	9	1	1	2	25,589
Big Country	3	C	8	2	1	2	73,260
Big Creek	4	G	15	0	3	4	22,697
Big Dad Jones	2	C	1	0	0	0	105
Big Daddy Dave	6	G	8	2	0	1	12,997
Big Daddy Longlegs	6	G	9	2	0	1	64,161
Big Daddy Tee	5	G	5	2	0	0	29,880
Big Decision	3	G	5	0	0	1	11,234
Big Deed	4	G	14	3	3	1	86,492
Big Delta	5	G	1	0	0	0	546
Big Disaster	6	G	9	1	1	0	6,021
Big Dividend	5	H	14	3	2	2	49,789
Big Dog Diamond	4	C	2	0	0	0	525
Big E E	6	H	1	0	0	0	1,680
Big E Flying	3	C	6	0	0	0	0
Big E W	7	G	2	0	0	0	263
Big Ears	5	G	4	0	0	0	0
Big Easy Blues	3	G	4	1	0	0	7,410
Big Ed Benko	7	H	6	0	0	0	2,240
Big Feathers	2	C	1	0	0	0	0
Big Feeler	3	G	8	1	3	0	19,200
Big Fish Marlin	4	C	8	1	3	2	21,000
Big Frank	4	C	3	1	1	1	11,145
Big Fun	5	H	4	1	0	0	4,080
Big Future (GB)	6	H	7	1	1	1	39,440
Big Glori	3	C	15	2	0	1	45,770
Big Gold	7	G	9	3	0	1	9,836
Big Gold Martini	6	G	14	1	1	0	7,285
Big Gun	3	C	3	1	0	1	31,900
Big Gun Annie	5	M	9	0	1	1	1,916
Big Harry Deal	4	C	1	0	0	0	0
Big Harry Smacker	3	C	2	0	0	0	0
Big Head Phil	4	G	8	1	1	0	6,889
Big Hearted Wayne	4	G	5	0	1	1	14,250
Big Hero	2	C	4	0	0	2	5,157
Big Hope	5	G	4	0	1	0	1,950
Big Hoss	5	G	6	1	1	1	2,772
Big Hubie	5	H	4	0	0	1	6,940

RECORDS OF HORSES

Horse	Age	Sex	Sts	1st	2d	3d	Won	Horse	Age	Sex	Sts	1st	2d	3d	Won
Big Hy Five	3	G	3	0	0	0	990	Big Swed	3	G	19	3	0	3	19,968
Big Ide	4	F	7	4	0	1	46,780	Big Swinger	3	G	14	0	1	1	6,874
Big Ike	7	H	7	0	0	1	1,063	Big Talkin Man	5	G	4	0	1	0	16,550
Big Impact	5	G	4	0	0	0	255	Big Tam	7	G	3	0	1	0	899
Big Interview	4	F	7	1	0	0	8,549	Big Tater	10	G	7	2	2	0	13,645
Big Is	6	H	2	0	0	1	870	Big Team Spirit	6	G	14	4	5	0	78,915
Big Jack	3	C	5	0	2	1	11,250	Big Tease	3	F	9	5	1	0	44,458
Big Jim	3	C	2	0	0	0	339	Big Tex	2	C	1	1	0	0	7,560
Big Joe Reggie	3	G	1	0	0	0	86	Big Thunder	6	H	8	0	1	2	9,930
Big Joe Zee	2	G	2	0	0	0	1,680	Big Ticker	4	G	6	0	2	1	6,810
Big Joes Account	2	G	3	0	0	1	1,495	Big Time Flyer	7	G	15	1	6	2	11,660
Big Joes Girl	3	F	14	3	4	1	47,582	Big Time Fox	4	G	6	0	0	0	783
Big John Henry	2	C	3	0	0	0	442	Big Time Luck	7	M	11	3	1	1	26,949
Big Johnny	4	C	11	3	1	3	24,441	Big Time Pete	4	G	1	0	0	0	107
Big Kahuna	3	C	3	1	0	1	27,020	Big Time Spender	5	G	12	1	1	2	7,560
Big Komotion	2	F	2	0	0	0	2,574	Big Tom	3	G	14	1	0	2	6,318
Big L. L. B.	3	C	9	1	1	0	5,366	Big Top	5	H	1	0	0	0	46
Big League	5	H	13	4	2	3	93,450	Big Top Star	9	G	12	0	1	0	2,502
Big League Lady	3	F	3	1	0	0	14,760	Big Town	4	G	11	1	2	2	12,067
Big Lonesome Train	3	G	6	1	0	0	16,089	Big Wagner	2	G	10	1	1	1	8,542
Big Lord Nelson	3	G	5	1	1	0	31,290	Big Wells	8	G	14	1	3	5	10,573
Big Lucky	3	G	9	1	1	1	12,422	Big Whinnyings	5	G	18	4	0	4	27,563
Big Mac Attack	4	G	7	0	1	0	1,998	Big Whiskey	3	G	1	0	0	0	0
Big Mac Mtn.	5	G	13	1	4	2	9,632	Big Will	5	G	8	1	0	2	25,417
Big Mag	4	F	13	3	2	3	28,267	Big Wolf	3	F	7	1	1	1	18,510
Big Mama Pearl	3	F	9	0	0	2	3,610	Big Woodrow	6	H	1	0	0	0	0
Big Man	4	G	8	0	0	1	1,400	Big Yankee Fan	3	C	11	1	2	1	5,974
Big Matt	2	C	4	0	0	1	1,960	Bigado	8	H	3	0	0	0	0
Big Meadow	2	F	5	0	0	0	840	Bigamo (URU)	5	G	18	1	3	3	30,474
Big Meany	5	G	13	2	3	1	51,914	Bigandscarlet	3	G	2	0	0	0	0
Big Meeko's G. T.	4	C	7	1	0	0	6,049	Bigboystoy	4	F	5	3	1	0	38,000
Big Mig	9	G	4	0	1	1	4,292	Bigbucksnowhammies	3	G	2	0	1	1	2,880
Big Miss	7	M	13	2	3	0	60,774	Bigcuz	5	M	4	0	0	1	1,186
Big Momma B	3	F	3	0	0	0	570	Biggen	8	H	6	1	1	0	1,568
Big Money Maker	3	C	1	0	0	0	0	Bigger N Bettor	6	M	8	1	0	0	2,715
Big Mountain	4	G	9	2	0	0	22,380	Biggerthanthese	2	C	2	0	0	0	400
Big Nana's Boy	2	C	2	0	0	0	5,160	Biggieandbellboy	5	H	7	0	0	1	1,401
Big Numbers	6	H	9	0	0	4	20,705	Biggly Slew	3	C	5	0	0	0	2,280
Big Otto	7	G	1	0	0	1	336	Biggly Star	4	C	8	1	0	1	5,532
Big Oxx	7	G	10	0	0	2	1,694	Bigmike Littlemike	2	C	6	0	0	1	1,349
Big Pain	4	C	3	1	1	0	9,930	Bigmixes Boy	4	C	3	0	0	0	330
Big Papa	5	G	12	2	1	3	15,170	Bigolcountryboy	5	G	12	2	2	1	15,310
Big Pete	4	G	16	2	4	2	18,970	Bigoneontheend	4	G	14	1	2	3	17,625
Big Pete's Rib	3	C	2	0	0	0	184	Bigredcoup	3	G	15	2	3	2	19,029
Big Punch	4	G	2	0	0	1	1,080	Bigshotangie	2	F	1	0	0	0	0
Big Queen	4	F	2	0	0	2	2,013	Bigtimeaffair	2	F	4	1	0	1	14,650
Big Quest	6	H	12	1	2	4	21,555	Bigtimesentence	5	G	14	1	0	0	3,379
Big R	4	C	7	2	2	0	13,215	Bigwinedrinker	6	G	2	0	0	0	0
Big Rascal	7	G	7	1	1	0	14,100	Bijou	4	F	4	1	1	0	38,360
Big Red Chunk	4	C	7	2	1	0	8,788	Bijou Basin	3	G	8	2	4	0	23,210
Big Red Fan	7	G	7	0	1	2	2,241	Bijou Belle	4	F	9	4	3	0	99,900
Big Red Irishman	11	G	8	1	0	2	8,232	Bijou Queen	3	F	4	0	1	3	26,000
Big Red Rascal	7	G	1	0	0	0	0	Biker's Sis	4	F	6	1	3	0	26,540
Big Red Robyn	5	H	8	1	2	2	38,610	Bikini Wiggle	2	F	3	1	0	1	33,400
Big Red Ruler	2	C	5	1	1	2	11,066	Bikinisandmartinis	3	F	5	1	1	0	7,931
Big Reflection	3	C	1	0	0	0	0	Bilbaino	7	G	8	0	1	3	4,446
Big Rocket	4	C	7	0	0	0	471	Bilbo Baggins	3	G	4	1	0	0	8,199
Big Ruby K	4	G	7	1	0	0	32,660	Bilini North	8	G	5	1	0	0	1,155
Big Rush	3	F	1	0	0	0	0	Bill and Jim	3	C	11	3	1	0	25,115
Big Rut	10	G	12	4	1	0	26,906	Bill Heinz	2	C	5	0	1	1	5,030
Big Sancho	2	G	2	0	0	0	0	Bill Is in Love	3	G	16	2	3	4	21,442
Big Sand	4	G	3	1	0	0	14,220	Bill the Banker	5	G	5	1	1	0	21,950
Big Sandy	5	G	19	1	1	4	13,681	Bill the Great	3	C	1	1	0	0	36,360
Big Scoop	10	G	1	0	0	0	109	Billanetta	3	F	13	1	3	1	9,401
Big Score	3	F	5	1	0	0	24,528	Billanksphonetrick	4	G	13	3	3	1	25,875
Big Sexy	6	G	3	0	0	0	165	Billet Doux	3	F	8	1	0	0	11,060
Big Shakespeare	5	G	3	0	0	0	4,000	Billie Dove	4	F	8	1	2	0	11,490
Big Shot	5	H	1	0	0	0	47	Billie's Kaye	4	F	2	0	0	0	87
Big Shoulders	2	G	5	0	0	0	291	Billnchar	6	M	2	0	0	0	144
Big Show	5	H	9	0	0	3	10,056	Billow	5	M	5	1	0	1	10,257
Big Sid's Party	5	G	7	2	3	1	81,330	Bills Bull	2	G	1	0	0	0	0
Big Sis	5	M	1	0	0	0	40	Bill's Lady	3	F	4	0	0	1	693
Big Sky Blue	2	C	6	0	0	0	450	Bill's Lil Fappi	4	F	9	1	0	3	13,250
Big Sky River	3	G	3	2	0	0	2,365	Bill's Miracle	2	F	2	0	0	0	180
Big Smoothy	2	C	4	1	1	1	9,610	Bills Paid	5	G	2	0	0	0	0
Big Stew	5	H	12	2	1	2	13,693	Bills Royal Honey	3	F	14	0	0	3	3,335
Big Stone Gap	3	C	7	0	0	0	920	Billstown	7	G	21	1	3	4	15,915
Big Storm Comin	5	G	5	0	0	0	564	Billy Angel	3	C	11	3	3	0	43,023
Big Sur	5	G	9	1	1	3	7,782	Billy Be Normal	4	G	17	2	3	4	21,670

Horse	Age	Sex	Sts	1st	2d	3d	Won
Billy Beguile	3	G	7	1	0	1	5,455
Billy Big Rigger	5	G	10	1	2	1	23,500
Billy Bill Flash	4	G	9	3	1	0	15,450
Billy Bird	3	C	4	0	1	1	2,566
Billy Bob's Jolie	3	F	7	0	1	1	6,320
Billy Bowlegs	4	G	16	3	0	3	16,817
Billy C	5	G	4	1	0	0	14,220
Billy D. Kid	3	G	5	0	0	1	2,960
Billy Dixon	2	C	5	0	1	2	14,205
Billy Etbauer	2	C	2	1	0	0	6,600
Billy Gilman	3	C	4	2	1	0	39,640
Billy Gumbo	4	C	6	0	0	0	230
Billy Haggard	8	H	6	1	0	0	8,420
Billy Idel	3	G	10	2	2	1	68,097
Billy Jeans Bag	6	M	8	1	0	2	11,044
Billy Mac	3	G	2	0	2	0	6,400
Billy Spruce	7	G	3	0	0	0	158
Billy Sundance	7	G	1	0	0	0	0
Billy White Shoes	3	G	15	3	2	3	13,130
Billyball	5	G	13	2	2	0	11,104
Billybob Bly	2	C	7	2	2	0	17,680
Billy's Ace	2	G	1	0	0	0	360
Billy's Echo	5	G	7	1	2	2	62,920
Billy's for Real	3	F	8	2	2	0	42,490
Billy's Plan	2	C	2	0	1	0	2,800
Billys Wild	4	G	4	0	0	0	0
Billysberry	4	F	4	0	1	1	1,074
Biloxi Pride	2	C	3	1	0	0	21,444
Biloxi Prospect	3	F	1	0	0	0	0
Biloxi Purple Haze	2	G	2	2	0	0	12,240
Bimbo's Kiss	8	M	5	0	0	0	1,514
Bimini Rose	4	F	8	2	1	1	19,437
Bimis Call	4	F	1	0	0	0	160
Bim's Baby Bun	3	C	8	1	1	1	48,943
Bin Rockin'	6	H	11	3	2	1	26,953
Bin to D. C.	4	G	7	0	0	0	1,613
Bin to Miami	5	M	8	2	2	0	9,464
Bin Working	3	C	11	1	1	0	19,310
Bin Zin	2	F	1	0	0	0	55
Binabee	4	F	5	0	0	0	103
Binahoni	4	F	6	2	0	0	6,257
Binalong Summer	3	F	5	1	0	1	3,055
Binalonglongday	2	G	7	0	1	1	3,683
Binalongtimecom'en	4	F	12	5	1	1	78,165
Binandgone	3	F	6	0	0	0	1,110
Binary	5	G	2	0	0	1	728
Binary Code	5	M	1	0	0	0	201
Binawhile	7	H	13	1	2	3	12,539
Binbo	4	C	9	1	0	0	21,147
Binder	4	G	19	1	3	3	13,150
Bing an a Prayer	3	C	1	0	0	0	375
Bing Girl	4	F	8	1	1	1	21,950
Bingo	7	G	7	0	0	0	0
Bingo Baby's Best	4	F	4	1	0	0	6,160
Bingo Brat	7	G	6	0	1	1	1,985
Bingo Card	5	G	10	1	0	0	22,200
Bingo Helen	3	F	2	0	0	1	530
Bingo Liz	3	F	12	2	1	0	19,340
Bingo McGruder	4	F	3	0	0	0	439
Bingo Queen	3	F	2	0	0	0	86
Bingobear	2	G	4	0	0	0	110
Bingo's Orphan	3	G	11	2	1	1	9,910
Binks'belle	2	F	2	0	0	0	0
Binn Tin Tin (FR)	7	G	7	0	1	2	10,500
Binoche	3	F	7	0	0	1	1,648
Bint Jumeriah	4	F	2	0	0	0	96
Bint Sahara	3	F	8	0	2	0	4,137
Bint Tell	3	F	7	0	0	0	600
Binthebest	6	G	4	0	1	0	33,688
Biogio's Beauty	3	F	14	4	2	2	153,332
Biogio's Dream	3	F	3	0	1	0	9,548
Biometal	3	G	11	1	2	0	8,664
Bionic Angel	4	F	10	0	1	1	5,532
Bionic Bold	6	M	4	1	0	1	3,834
Bionic Jean	5	M	6	1	1	0	2,799
Bionic Lad	3	G	2	0	0	0	340
Bionic Showgirl	4	F	9	1	1	0	6,518
Bionic Slew	3	C	3	0	0	0	0
Bionic Star	4	F	2	0	0	0	87
Bionic Toddy	9	M	3	0	0	0	126
Bionic Whirl	8	G	4	0	0	0	228
Biorhythm	4	C	14	3	0	2	44,035
Bippy d'Or	3	F	10	1	1	1	7,965
Bird Call	3	C	3	0	0	0	1,430
Bird Chatter	2	F	1	0	1	0	1,900
Bird Dog Bill	3	C	6	1	0	1	21,700
Bird in Spring	3	F	5	1	1	0	17,020
Bird Key	3	F	14	3	2	2	35,956
Bird of Courage	5	M	10	1	1	4	29,512
Bird On the Rise	4	F	3	0	0	0	769
Bird Town	3	F	8	3	4	0	815,976
Birdatthewire	5	H	3	1	0	0	8,805
Birdcee	4	F	14	2	0	1	12,541
Birdie Barrage	2	F	2	1	0	0	19,092
Birdie in the Dark	4	F	12	2	1	3	10,472
Birdie Putt	5	M	12	7	1	0	73,470
Birdie Shooter	3	F	2	0	1	1	4,104
Birdieonthewire	5	G	7	0	0	1	2,014
Birdies Rocket	3	C	2	0	0	0	0
Birdies Secret	2	F	7	1	0	0	4,700
Birdie's World	4	F	16	2	0	1	9,158
Birdland	3	G	17	2	3	2	31,575
Birdonthehighwire	5	H	3	1	0	0	2,980
Bird's Advantage	4	F	9	3	2	2	23,695
Birdsinhere	3	F	1	0	0	0	47
Birdstone	2	C	3	2	0	0	339,000
Birth Sign	5	G	6	0	1	1	9,394
Birthday Boy Louie	2	C	2	0	0	0	455
Birthday Gift	6	H	5	2	1	1	26,345
Birthday Song	2	F	4	1	1	0	38,055
Bis Repetitas	3	C	7	1	2	0	114,270
Bisbee's Prospect	3	F	4	2	0	2	39,865
Biscay Appeal	4	G	16	1	3	3	11,692
Bishoftu	5	H	9	3	1	1	44,278
Bishop Court Hill	3	C	10	4	1	0	138,700
Bishop to King	3	G	1	0	0	0	0
Bishop Wins	4	G	10	1	1	2	6,185
Bishop's Gate	3	F	14	1	2	1	12,762
Bishops Pay Master	7	H	4	0	0	0	868
Bishops Tree	3	G	5	1	0	3	11,150
Bishop's Vine	4	F	10	0	2	1	3,839
Bishop's Wood (IRE)	4	C	3	0	0	0	0
Biskuits	4	G	3	0	0	0	0
Bisque d'Jour	4	C	3	0	0	1	4,250
Bisti Badlands	3	C	12	3	2	3	40,526
Bistro Mathematics	3	G	6	1	1	1	12,864
Bit Moody	2	F	2	0	0	0	160
Bit o' Mortlock	2	G	4	0	1	0	3,060
Bit of Dixie	2	F	1	0	0	0	0
Bit of Luck (GB)	4	G	4	2	0	0	55,910
Bit Shee Believer	3	F	8	2	0	0	39,009
Bitdaboss	4	F	4	0	0	0	865
Bite My Bumpers	3	F	10	0	1	1	7,732
Bite N Red	3	F	1	0	0	0	0
Bite Vernon	12	G	7	0	3	0	1,560
Biterman	2	G	1	0	0	0	0
Bithynian	5	G	10	1	3	0	12,257
Bitingly Cold	6	M	8	1	0	1	25,620
Bitofbutter	2	F	2	0	0	0	0
Bitsy's Double Z	2	F	1	0	0	0	0
Bitter Luck	3	C	3	0	0	0	0
Bitter Truth	3	C	3	1	0	1	6,075
Bitterroot River	3	F	5	1	0	0	15,340
Bittersweet Bonnie	2	F	2	0	0	0	0
Bittersweet Rain	3	F	9	2	1	0	81,711
Bittersweetreality	3	F	11	1	3	3	35,235
Bittersweetsymfony	6	G	6	0	0	0	696
Bitting Boy	2	G	1	0	0	0	0
Bitty Bou	5	H	2	0	0	1	710
Bity Rose	4	F	9	1	3	1	9,397
Bix	3	G	7	1	2	1	6,075
Bixby	3	F	3	0	0	0	60
Bixby Knolls	4	C	14	2	2	3	15,754
Biz Man	3	C	1	0	0	0	0
Bj's Brave	4	C	3	0	0	1	3,020
Bk's Dippybroad	3	F	11	0	1	0	6,795
Bk's Double Jade	3	G	6	0	0	0	722
Bk's Tricky Native	6	G	17	1	3	2	27,409

RECORDS OF HORSES

Horse	Age	Sex	Sts	1st	2d	3d	Won	Horse	Age	Sex	Sts	1st	2d	3d	Won
Blabby B.	4	F	1	0	0	0	575	Blackburg	5	G	6	0	0	0	159
Black Banana	3	F	7	0	0	0	438	Blackcatsnladyluck	4	F	4	0	0	0	0
Black Barry Velvet	4	F	6	1	1	0	2,694	Blackchesters (GB)	10	G	5	0	0	0	2,250
Black Bart	4	G	7	1	1	0	19,380	Blackeyed Special	2	F	1	0	0	0	156
Black Beard	4	C	1	1	0	0	7,800	Blackfoot Maiden	3	F	2	0	0	0	651
Black Box	5	G	13	2	0	1	14,370	Blackhawk Knight	3	G	4	0	0	1	970
Black Bullet	6	H	10	0	0	4	2,752	Blackhawk Special	6	H	11	1	0	1	6,970
Black Butler	3	C	5	0	0	0	900	Blackhawk's Double	4	F	9	1	1	2	2,176
Black Caddie	2	G	4	0	2	1	5,896	Blackhearted	6	G	10	1	0	2	6,992
Black Canyon	4	C	20	1	9	3	6,212	Blackie Baby	3	F	10	0	0	0	649
Black Canyon Bart	3	G	6	1	1	0	1,782	Blackinton	3	C	8	2	1	2	58,510
Black Cloud	5	H	5	0	0	1	595	Blackjack Boy	3	C	9	1	1	1	23,740
Black Cougar	5	G	12	2	1	0	17,481	Blackjack Canyon	2	C	1	0	0	0	750
Black Cove	7	G	12	3	0	2	12,722	Blackjacks Rollin	3	G	2	0	0	0	0
Black Creek Angel	4	F	1	1	0	0	12,586	Blackmailer	2	C	1	0	1	0	4,600
Black Dakota	5	G	3	0	0	0	0	Black's Legacy	4	G	4	0	0	0	50
Black Diva	4	F	1	0	0	0	104	Blacksher	8	M	11	0	3	2	6,689
Black Dragon	5	H	4	0	0	0	278	Blackstone Clock	5	M	1	0	0	0	0
Black Ego	10	G	3	2	0	1	2,037	Blackstone Dreamer	5	G	5	0	1	0	3,157
Black Eyed Girl	3	F	5	1	0	0	12,540	Blackstone Drummer	3	C	1	0	0	0	80
Black Eyed Lilly	4	F	4	0	0	0	1,630	Blacktail	4	F	5	0	0	0	1,210
Black Forest	9	G	14	3	4	2	32,017	Blacktiesndiamonds	3	F	9	1	0	1	7,947
Black Gear	4	F	2	0	0	1	470	Blackwood Chief	5	H	1	0	0	0	0
Black Havoc	10	G	7	0	0	0	653	Blade Ae	9	G	8	1	1	0	7,670
Black Heart	3	F	9	1	1	0	37,402	Blades Flyer	5	G	11	3	2	1	21,383
Black Hole	6	G	1	0	0	0	0	Blaine County High	5	G	2	1	0	0	3,135
Black Horse Money	2	C	6	1	3	0	53,200	Blaine Elegant	3	F	10	1	1	0	19,009
Black It Out	6	M	4	0	0	2	5,720	Blaine's Secret	2	F	3	0	0	0	1,560
Black Jack Attack	2	C	1	0	0	0	0	Blaine's Song	6	M	2	0	0	0	0
Black Jack Jaws	6	M	9	3	0	1	14,654	Blaine's Storm	2	C	4	0	1	1	9,180
Black Jet	3	G	13	1	1	5	27,000	Blair Zepa	4	F	2	0	0	0	0
Black Joe	3	C	12	3	3	1	35,821	Blairs General	3	G	10	1	1	3	63,049
Black Keys	1	F	1	0	0	0	49	Blairs Roarin Star	2	C	4	1	1	0	46,900
Black Label	3	G	11	0	0	3	15,158	Blaise Pascale	3	C	9	0	2	2	29,790
Black Lace	4	F	1	0	0	0	280	Blake the Snake	3	G	9	1	0	1	6,508
Black Lace Sam	2	F	3	0	0	1	8,040	Blakelock	3	C	7	2	1	0	65,955
Black Lagoon	4	C	8	1	0	3	23,536	Blake's Groomstick	6	G	1	0	0	0	0
Black Legend	5	H	7	1	0	2	15,445	Blakes Pistol	6	H	12	0	0	4	3,640
Black Licorice	4	C	14	1	0	0	5,280	Blake's Tricky	3	G	4	0	0	0	412
Black Lightning	4	F	13	1	3	1	12,884	Blakesmyboy	4	G	6	1	1	0	6,300
Black Lilly	3	F	3	1	0	0	11,360	Blakestone	5	G	9	0	1	3	7,694
Black Magic Damsel	4	F	10	1	0	1	4,762	Blame It On Beau	4	G	5	1	1	1	16,240
Black Magic Lady	2	F	3	1	0	1	15,960	Blame It On Ruby	5	H	6	0	3	1	10,370
Black Magic Woman	4	F	2	0	1	0	4,500	Blameitonblake	3	G	4	0	0	2	4,050
Black Mambo	2	C	9	1	3	0	53,800	Blameitontherain	4	G	3	0	0	0	1,950
Black Market	4	G	10	0	1	1	18,650	Blameitonthewine	3	G	3	0	0	0	0
Black Mercury	7	G	6	0	1	1	2,350	Blanc	5	H	1	0	0	0	0
Black Midnite	5	M	2	0	0	2	520	Blanc Gold	6	H	1	0	0	0	0
Black Molly	9	M	12	2	3	1	13,318	Blanchetta	2	F	3	0	0	1	2,340
Black Montecarlo	3	G	15	1	0	2	13,185	Blanchita	3	F	5	0	1	1	14,660
Black n' Tan	4	G	4	0	0	0	458	Blandish	2	F	4	0	1	0	6,500
Black Porsche	7	G	1	0	0	0	0	Blankets	7	G	16	0	4	3	15,387
Black Powder Smoke	2	C	1	0	0	1	820	Blantyre	5	G	10	1	0	2	5,064
Black Rainbow	5	G	18	4	2	1	44,859	Blare That Music	4	G	10	2	2	0	10,235
Black Ransom	2	C	3	0	2	0	3,052	Blarney Bay	3	G	3	2	0	1	11,355
Black Raptor	2	C	2	1	1	0	15,210	Blarney Boy	4	G	4	1	0	0	26,520
Black Rat Snake	4	F	7	0	0	0	394	Blarney Stream	5	G	4	1	1	0	38,607
Black Raven	2	F	4	1	0	0	5,700	Blasphemous	3	F	4	0	1	0	3,875
Black Sea	5	M	5	1	1	0	13,694	Blast	3	G	12	1	1	2	4,965
Black Seraphim	7	M	18	0	0	2	3,776	Blast of Class	10	G	12	1	2	1	8,525
Black Silk	6	H	8	1	1	0	6,900	Blasted	3	G	11	1	2	3	40,128
Black Silk (GB)	7	G	8	1	3	2	68,850	Blather Skite	2	G	6	0	0	0	425
Black Sugar	3	F	7	1	0	1	5,995	Blaze Lado	5	M	2	0	0	0	0
Black Tast	4	F	9	1	1	0	1,930	Blaze McQ	5	M	9	0	3	1	26,661
Black Tejano	3	F	15	0	6	0	14,665	Blaze of Honor	5	H	2	1	0	0	3,805
Black Tie Classic	2	G	1	0	0	0	0	Blaze of Light	3	C	1	0	0	0	250
Black Tie Dinner	10	G	4	0	0	1	877	Blaze to Glory	3	F	3	0	0	1	1,095
Black Tie Joe	2	C	1	0	0	0	0	Blaze Too	3	C	5	0	1	1	12,746
Black Tie Justice	5	G	10	0	3	1	21,394	Blazen Beau	5	G	11	0	0	1	3,265
Black Tie Queen	6	M	3	0	0	0	317	Blaze'n Blake	3	C	2	0	0	0	50
Black Tie Trick	5	G	15	1	2	5	14,948	Blazen Ice	3	G	7	0	0	0	650
Black Ties Ferrari	7	G	10	0	0	2	1,980	Blaze'n Light	3	F	9	2	1	1	7,300
Black Topper	3	F	11	3	3	0	37,966	Blazer Mania	2	G	2	0	0	0	722
Black Twenty Nine	2	G	2	0	0	0	0	Blazetobo	3	G	10	1	1	1	11,116
Black Velvet Lady	4	F	2	0	0	0	237	Blazin Brian	2	G	1	0	0	0	100
Black Velvet Miss	3	F	4	1	0	1	4,050	Blazin Dar	3	C	3	0	0	0	520
Blackberry	4	F	2	0	0	1	1,400	Blazin Spades	4	G	10	1	1	1	18,035
Blackberry Rain	3	C	8	0	0	1	174	Blazin Sunrise	2	F	4	0	2	1	17,792
Blackberry Springs	3	C	12	3	0	0	74,480	Blazing Bartok	3	F	1	0	0	0	0
								Blazing Bonnie							

Horse	Age	Sex	Sts	1st	2d	3d	Won	Horse	Age	Sex	Sts	1st	2d	3d	Won
Blazing Boo Kay	3	F	5	2	2	0	3,652	Blissful Kiss	4	F	4	0	0	0	4,056
Blazing Buckeroo	3	F	1	0	0	0	94	Blissful Morning	6	M	11	1	2	1	14,710
Blazing Cat	3	F	8	0	4	0	29,060	Blisteringfraction	5	H	11	2	2	1	10,120
Blazing Chaak	2	G	1	0	0	0	0	Blitz Away	3	C	2	0	0	0	0
Blazing Colors	7	G	3	1	1	0	13,200	Blitz the Star	7	G	7	0	1	0	704
Blazing Count	6	H	8	3	1	1	76,090	Blitz Wedding	3	F	3	0	0	1	1,170
Blazing Countess	3	F	5	2	1	1	12,240	Blitzen Tucker	3	C	3	0	1	0	3,600
Blazing Deputy	4	F	6	0	0	1	4,035	Blizzard Bliss	2	C	3	0	0	0	410
Blazing Devil	8	G	16	3	3	2	14,881	Blizzard of Oz	3	G	10	0	1	2	10,235
Blazing Dove	3	F	8	1	0	1	2,232	Blkice	5	G	11	1	1	1	11,014
Blazing Element	3	G	13	0	1	3	29,321	Block N Tackle	7	G	2	0	0	1	1,700
Blazing Exit	6	G	4	0	0	0	0	Block the Deal	3	G	2	1	0	1	3,780
Blazing Forest	4	C	14	3	4	4	39,866	Blockade Runner	5	G	18	4	4	1	67,740
Blazing Freedom	3	C	6	0	1	0	9,795	Blocked Call	3	C	16	4	3	2	36,580
Blazing Fury	5	G	4	0	1	0	13,520	Blocked Kick	2	C	2	0	2	0	4,800
Blazing Genius	7	G	7	1	1	0	1,722	Blond Dancer	5	M	6	2	0	4	78,258
Blazing Halo	4	F	13	0	2	1	7,432	Blond Del	7	M	2	0	0	0	825
Blazing Intrusion	9	G	5	0	0	0	434	Blondage	5	M	11	1	3	1	4,020
Blazing Mama	2	F	2	0	0	1	770	Blonde Dynamite	4	F	18	1	4	5	87,417
Blazing Maple	2	F	1	0	0	0	0	Blonde Executive	2	F	7	3	1	1	196,328
Blazing Maxi	4	G	1	0	0	0	64	Blonde Okie	5	M	9	1	2	2	9,940
Blazing Miss	5	M	6	0	0	1	800	Blonde Roots	3	F	3	0	0	0	764
Blazing Paul	8	G	6	1	1	1	5,779	Blondel de Nesle	4	G	4	0	0	0	5,046
Blazing Road	5	G	6	0	1	0	12,870	Blondie Ona Budget	6	M	2	0	0	0	140
Blazing Roberto	5	G	14	2	2	5	35,701	Blondie's Poohbear	7	M	16	1	1	0	5,672
Blazing Seven	5	G	11	2	1	0	18,993	Blondy's Honor	6	M	20	1	1	3	12,932
Blazing Sharp	3	F	2	0	0	0	0	Blondz Away	2	F	8	1	1	1	37,400
Blazing Song	3	C	6	0	1	1	13,940	Blood	3	C	11	2	1	1	8,294
Blazing Star	8	F	8	0	1	1	6,680	Blood Brother	3	G	14	1	0	2	7,384
Blazing Starlight	4	F	4	0	0	0	330	Bloodshot	3	F	4	0	1	0	9,275
Blazing Sun	5	H	6	0	0	0	399	Bloody Baron	4	C	14	3	2	1	10,473
Blazing Trail Mix	3	F	3	0	0	0	0	Bloody Liz	4	F	11	4	1	2	46,002
Blazing Tune	3	F	13	1	1	5	55,690	Bloomin Bird	4	C	3	0	0	0	0
Blazing Whiskey	4	C	8	1	0	0	6,743	Bloomin Justice	2	F	1	0	0	0	360
Blazing Wind	6	G	12	2	2	2	23,029	Blooming Bluff	5	M	4	0	2	2	6,040
Blazinmint's Lady	4	F	5	0	1	2	4,000	Blooming Colors	3	C	7	2	1	0	14,241
Blaz'n Penny	4	F	6	1	1	0	5,270	Blooming Grove	4	G	4	0	1	0	8,800
Blazonry	3	C	3	1	0	1	96,720	Blossom Belle	3	F	8	0	1	3	3,931
Blazy Lou	4	F	5	0	1	0	2,500	Blossom Hill	4	F	8	2	3	2	33,191
Bleached	3	G	12	3	2	2	24,045	Blossom	4	F	7	1	1	1	27,670
Bled too Red	6	M	13	0	1	2	4,602	Blossom Girl	3	F	2	0	0	0	0
Blend of Devil	4	F	1	0	0	1	2,090	Blow a Kiss	4	F	2	1	0	0	28,458
Blending Swords	7	G	12	2	2	1	48,590	Blow Em Away	4	G	7	1	1	0	9,021
Blendon Woods	5	G	1	0	0	0	45	Blowin in the Wind	4	G	9	1	3	2	53,019
Blendor	10	M	2	0	0	0	0	Blowin the Gold	2	G	2	0	0	0	1,072
Blennerhassett	4	F	7	2	0	2	15,670	Blowing Bartok	2	F	8	0	2	3	66,935
Bless Him	5	G	13	2	1	3	15,740	Blown Away	3	F	3	0	0	0	0
Bless Me	3	C	1	0	0	0	0	Blown Fuze	4	F	4	0	0	0	180
Bless My Soles	4	F	4	0	1	2	4,435	Blown Overboard	3	G	5	0	0	0	265
Bless Our Nation	3	C	2	0	0	1	1,700	Blown Surprise	3	F	13	4	2	3	56,505
Bless Thismess	3	F	7	0	2	1	3,225	Blown to Sea	4	F	4	1	0	0	3,459
Blessed Conquista	3	C	5	1	0	0	6,322	Blu Spur	4	F	7	1	1	2	57,085
Blessed Fager	2	C	1	0	0	0	95	Blu Starr Lady	3	F	14	1	1	5	19,211
Blessed Peace	3	F	14	0	0	1	3,326	Blue Afleet	3	C	2	1	0	1	18,360
Blessed Sun	4	G	10	2	1	1	7,965	Blue Agave	2	G	2	0	0	0	713
Blessing Angelica	4	F	4	1	1	0	6,450	Blue and Bold	4	F	3	0	0	1	1,231
Blessings	4	F	15	3	4	1	62,690	Blue Angel's Echo	5	G	6	3	1	1	46,202
Bleu Glace	4	F	4	0	0	0	711	Blue Atlantis	3	F	10	2	0	1	11,015
Bleu Victoriate	7	G	6	0	1	0	3,277	Blue Barrel	5	G	10	0	1	2	4,239
Bleuesville	2	F	1	0	0	0	100	Blue Barrett	3	F	6	2	1	0	18,800
Bleu's Apparition	2	F	1	0	0	0	0	Blue Blood Boot	3	G	5	1	0	0	43,650
Blewpy	7	G	3	0	0	0	250	Blue Blue Sea	4	G	18	4	1	2	36,959
Blind Ambition	5	M	6	3	2	0	206,640	Blue Boar Ten	3	C	4	1	0	0	7,800
Blind Canyon	2	F	9	1	3	1	18,720	Blue Boat	4	C	7	3	0	2	95,840
Blind Falcon	10	G	7	0	0	0	0	Blue Bodgit	4	F	9	2	0	0	6,540
Blind Reality	5	M	16	1	1	2	4,470	Blue Book	3	F	1	0	0	0	0
Blinded by Love	5	M	1	0	0	0	16,370	Blue Boundary	3	G	1	0	0	0	2,760
Blindfold	2	F	6	0	0	0	450	Blue Bug	8	G	9	1	0	0	6,164
Blinding Splash	6	M	14	1	3	2	6,462	Blue Bull	4	C	2	0	0	0	0
Blink His Gone	3	C	9	0	0	1	1,685	Blue Burn	4	C	5	1	2	0	33,940
Blink N Miss Me	3	F	17	1	2	2	21,259	Blue Burner	4	C	4	1	0	1	39,960
Blink of an Eye	4	G	13	2	5	4	12,945	Blue by Slew	2	G	7	1	1	0	12,935
Blink Twice	3	F	4	1	1	1	43,250	Blue Camay	7	M	9	0	0	3	1,206
Blinkandshesgone	4	F	12	0	1	4	5,887	Blue Cay	2	F	2	0	1	0	4,600
Blinkers Off	3	G	3	0	0	0	302	Blue Champagne	3	G	4	0	0	1	3,920
Blinkit	2	F	5	0	0	0	405	Blue Chapeau	4	F	3	0	0	0	345
Blip On the Screen	4	F	1	0	0	0	0	Blue Chief	3	F	4	0	0	0	500
Bliss Landing	3	G	7	1	0	2	6,367	Blue Chip Gal	4	F	11	0	1	2	3,938
Bliss to Rage	3	C	7	0	1	0	5,100	Blue Cinder	12	G	11	0	1	2	1,212

Horse	Age	Sex	Sts	1st	2d	3d	Won	Horse	Age	Sex	Sts	1st	2d	3d	Won
Blue Cliff	5	G	7	0	0	0	1,618	Blue Souvie	3	G	3	0	0	1	7,440
Blue Clues	4	F	9	0	1	0	1,286	Blue Spade	3	C	2	0	0	0	0
Blue Cobalt	3	C	11	0	0	2	10,379	Blue Spruce	9	G	11	1	0	0	6,866
Blue Conn	3	C	4	0	0	0	882	Blue Starlite	2	F	5	0	0	0	852
Blue Copy	3	F	9	1	0	1	5,851	Blue Steel Band	3	C	3	0	0	2	15,690
Blue Craft	3	G	4	0	0	1	635	Blue Steel High	9	G	9	2	0	1	5,884
Blue Creek	4	F	9	0	1	2	17,680	Blue Steller (IRE)	5	H	3	1	0	0	49,000
Blue Creek Bart	4	G	8	1	0	1	1,344	Blue Submarine	3	G	4	0	0	1	3,170
Blue Creeker	4	F	8	0	0	2	15,051	Blue Tejano	9	G	5	1	1	2	20,320
Blue Dancer	4	G	7	0	3	1	11,938	Blue Tesseract	10	M	1	0	0	0	70
Blue Daze	4	F	5	0	1	0	5,086	Blue Tiger	3	C	2	1	0	0	6,500
Blue Deal	5	M	1	0	0	0	0	Blue Two	3	F	10	1	2	2	11,948
Blue Desert	2	G	2	0	0	1	1,855	Blue Voyage	4	G	7	0	0	0	410
Blue Explosion	6	G	13	2	1	0	11,492	Blue Warrior	4	G	14	3	1	1	9,818
Blue Express	6	M	1	0	0	0	320	Blue West	6	M	1	0	0	0	0
Blue Eyed Buck	5	G	2	0	0	0	0	Blue Without You	5	H	9	1	0	1	4,650
Blue Eyed Kayla	3	F	5	0	1	1	4,236	Blue Zepher	4	F	7	0	0	0	511
Blue Eyed Tiger	4	C	8	1	1	4	10,050	Blueasarobinseggs	3	F	9	1	0	3	23,345
Blue Eyes	5	M	6	0	0	1	2,027	Bluebayouman	4	C	5	1	3	0	6,655
Blue Eyes Princess	2	F	2	0	2	0	8,400	Bluebell Lassie	4	F	7	3	0	0	11,632
Blue Finally	3	C	8	2	2	1	64,410	Blueberry Pie	2	F	1	0	0	0	195
Blue Frosty Mug	8	M	12	0	1	3	8,276	Bluebird Day (IRE)	4	F	3	0	0	0	3,840
Blue Ginger	3	F	2	1	0	0	5,596	Bluebird's Song	3	F	10	0	1	0	3,780
Blue Girl	4	F	11	0	4	0	2,345	Bluecheesedressing	5	H	7	0	0	0	413
Blue Grass Angel	3	F	7	1	1	0	6,218	Bluefinger	2	C	2	0	1	0	12,120
Blue Grass Blues	10	G	10	0	0	4	5,139	Bluegrass Belle	3	F	7	2	0	2	68,510
Blue Grass Dancer	2	F	3	0	1	0	4,095	Bluegrass Brass	8	G	1	0	0	0	38
Blue Grey	7	G	8	0	0	1	6,733	Bluegrass Sara	2	F	5	3	0	0	140,652
Blue Guru	5	M	9	3	2	1	103,380	Bluegrass Spirit	3	C	2	0	0	0	4,260
Blue Hill Ave	5	G	4	0	0	0	540	Bluegrass Ted	4	G	10	1	0	1	13,965
Blue Hills	5	M	7	1	1	3	46,675	Bluegrayday	6	H	3	1	1	0	1,290
Blue Holiday	6	M	3	0	1	0	4,200	Bluehue	4	F	3	0	0	0	1,176
Blue Imp	3	F	13	2	1	4	14,560	Blueisjr'sfavorite	3	C	3	0	0	0	550
Blue Iris	6	M	3	0	0	0	1,155	Blueknob	4	C	13	2	1	1	12,591
Blue Jean Princess	5	M	6	0	0	2	1,613	Blues At Sunrise	3	F	11	1	1	3	14,780
Blue Jean Racer	7	H	2	0	0	0	0	Blues Away	9	G	11	1	1	1	21,735
Blue Jeans Man	3	G	4	0	0	0	0	Blues Begone	7	G	1	0	0	0	228
Blue Krismas	7	G	6	0	0	1	1,650	Blues City Kitty	3	F	12	1	1	2	7,278
Blue Label	3	G	5	0	0	0	0	Blue's First Baby	2	F	3	0	0	1	980
Blue Lake	2	F	1	0	0	0	0	Blues Highway	3	C	8	2	3	0	81,960
Blue Launch	6	G	5	0	1	1	5,938	Blues in Advance	3	F	7	0	0	0	625
Blue Lou	3	C	7	0	2	3	5,579	Blues in Seattle	3	F	6	0	2	1	16,820
Blue Lupin	2	F	1	0	0	0	0	Blues Mobile	4	G	19	3	3	3	17,795
Blue Magnolia	4	F	2	1	0	0	4,202	Blues New Image	6	G	4	0	0	0	152
Blue Mail Box	6	M	4	0	0	1	1,398	Blues Night Out	2	G	2	0	0	0	0
Blue Mambo	4	G	12	2	3	0	23,586	Blue's Prospector	3	G	12	2	0	3	42,245
Blue Martinis	3	F	7	1	1	0	8,234	Blue's Secret	2	C	2	0	0	0	426
Blue Mill	3	G	9	1	0	1	2,984	Blues Snoop	6	M	10	0	1	0	1,598
Blue Mint	4	F	11	1	1	5	9,237	Blueseeker	2	C	2	0	0	0	252
Blue Moon Bay	3	F	1	0	0	0	0	Blueskiesfromnowon	4	F	7	0	0	1	951
Blue Moon Night	5	M	5	0	1	0	1,465	Bluesman	2	C	6	0	2	0	11,120
Blue Moon Rising	4	F	7	0	1	2	10,650	Bluesnclues	3	C	1	1	0	0	16,800
Blue Moon Special	4	F	8	1	5	1	43,835	Bluespeedwhitelite	2	F	2	0	0	0	320
Blue Moonray	5	M	14	3	3	1	27,537	Bluesthestandard	6	G	10	4	2	2	631,975
Blue Mound	3	G	1	0	0	0	375	Bluestoreggae	7	M	2	0	0	0	324
Blue N Beyond	7	M	10	1	3	1	19,680	Bluewaters	2	G	3	0	0	0	960
Blue Native	5	M	1	0	0	0	0	Bluff No More	4	F	1	0	0	0	0
Blue Puffette	3	F	10	1	0	0	11,791	Bluff to Win	4	G	4	0	0	0	270
Blue Rapids	4	F	8	2	0	0	7,776	Bluffer	7	M	8	2	2	2	45,075
Blue Ray	3	G	3	0	0	0	390	Bluffie Slew	3	F	15	0	5	3	50,240
Blue Reality	5	M	15	2	4	1	14,271	Bluffin Rail	3	F	13	2	2	1	16,406
Blue Red Bullet	3	G	4	1	0	0	20,388	Bluffing Fast	6	G	12	0	1	2	6,501
Blue Ribbon Time	3	F	13	2	1	1	8,637	Blufflette	3	F	9	0	1	2	10,521
Blue Ridge Robbery	4	C	8	0	0	0	1,815	Bluledo	4	F	8	2	2	3	48,920
Blue Rob	3	C	6	1	1	1	2,272	Blumin Easy	5	G	3	0	0	0	0
Blue Rouge	4	F	2	0	0	0	106	Blumin Exuberant	5	M	6	1	0	0	4,655
Blue Russian	7	G	8	0	0	0	600	Blumin Harris	5	G	7	0	1	1	5,329
Blue Safari	3	F	1	0	0	0	258	Blumin Henry	3	G	2	0	0	0	0
Blue Sage	5	G	1	0	0	0	0	Blumin Nasty	3	F	2	0	0	0	0
Blue Scarf	2	F	1	0	0	0	330	Blumurr	4	F	16	2	1	0	6,027
Blue Senorita	3	F	1	0	0	0	182	Blurr City Bandit	9	G	4	1	1	0	5,219
Blue Seti	3	G	14	0	3	4	38,315	Blurrs Got a Halo	4	C	13	0	1	2	1,278
Blue Silver Dollar	5	G	4	0	0	0	241	Blurrs the Word	4	C	16	2	1	0	8,938
Blue Skies Ahead	3	C	8	1	1	2	46,690	Blurry Dawn	8	G	5	1	0	0	13,942
Blue Sky Baby	5	M	7	2	1	1	57,940	Blush	2	F	2	0	0	0	0
Blue Sky's Coyota	3	F	4	0	0	0	487	Blush of Red	6	H	10	3	0	1	10,990
Blue Slew	3	G	5	1	1	1	2,931	Blushadif	5	M	2	0	0	0	80
Blue Slew's Shoes	4	C	14	1	1	1	24,400	Blushes Beauty	3	F	13	2	1	1	17,775
Blue Song	2	F	4	2	0	1	12,750	Blushing Ava	4	F	3	0	0	0	0

Horse	Age	Sex	Sts	1st	2d	3d	Won
Blushing Babe	2	F	2	0	0	0	217
Blushing Banannie	6	M	5	0	1	0	2,897
Blushing Barbie	3	F	5	1	0	1	7,526
Blushing Bride (GB)	5	M	1	0	0	0	0
Blushing Bull	3	F	1	0	0	1	5,280
Blushing Caller	7	M	18	2	3	3	23,545
Blushing Ciel	3	G	19	2	5	1	54,660
Blushing Frisco	3	G	1	0	0	0	0
Blushing Gal	3	F	3	0	0	0	900
Blushing Girl	6	M	4	1	1	0	6,606
Blushing Hattie	6	M	3	0	0	0	118
Blushing Indian	2	C	6	1	1	2	83,366
Blushing Jabar	6	M	4	0	0	2	1,570
Blushing Judith	4	G	7	0	3	3	17,716
Blushing Maiden	5	M	5	0	0	1	1,615
Blushing Queen	2	F	1	0	0	0	990
Blushing Rahy	5	M	2	1	0	0	17,400
Blushing Rainbow	4	F	6	0	2	0	9,040
Blushing Richard	10	G	1	0	0	0	0
Blushing Sam	6	G	11	1	1	1	4,966
Blushing Starlite	2	F	3	1	1	0	13,895
Blushing Valleys	3	F	16	2	4	2	73,550
Blushing Wildly	2	F	1	0	0	0	0
Blushing Witness	5	M	5	0	2	0	5,060
Blushingkittentale	2	F	8	1	1	1	16,425
Blush'n Frolic	4	F	15	4	3	1	42,530
Bluvalley Tiger	2	G	2	0	0	1	1,540
Blythewood	3	F	9	2	1	2	23,760
Bmyholy One	4	C	2	0	0	0	122
Bo Barley	7	G	4	1	0	0	10,680
Bo Bo's Vice	3	G	7	3	0	1	222,259
Bo Dee Man	3	G	6	0	0	0	1,050
Bo Dippity	3	F	14	0	1	3	2,470
Bo Jingles	5	M	1	0	0	0	0
Bo Knows	3	C	1	0	0	0	110
Bo n' Aero	4	G	4	0	0	0	0
Bo Naskra	11	G	2	0	0	0	219
Bo of Leed's	7	H	1	0	0	0	66
Bo Peaks	4	F	5	0	0	0	300
Bo Simpson	10	G	9	2	3	0	33,040
Bo Tangles	5	H	1	0	0	0	120
Bo Wonder Can Run	2	G	4	0	0	0	435
Boalex Party	5	H	9	2	1	1	31,710
Boana (GER)	5	M	8	2	3	0	62,710
Board Elligible	3	F	17	3	4	0	132,080
Board Games	4	G	12	0	2	1	4,126
Board to Run	3	G	11	0	0	2	2,488
Boardroom Banter	5	G	10	0	1	0	591
Boardroom Drama	4	G	12	2	0	1	33,055
Boast	2	F	3	0	2	0	12,000
Boastful	5	H	7	2	2	0	60,220
Boat Drinks	2	F	1	1	0	0	23,760
Boat Ride	4	F	9	0	2	4	16,060
Boat Show	5	M	2	0	0	0	0
Boathouse Symphony	5	G	5	0	0	0	437
Boatswain	2	C	2	0	0	0	1,420
Bob Adababyitzaboy	3	C	5	0	0	0	389
Bob Davenport	4	G	3	1	0	0	28,860
Bob F. M.	4	C	2	0	0	0	0
Bob Jo	5	M	13	2	1	5	23,012
Bob Loblaw	4	C	3	0	0	0	0
Bob 'n Velma	2	G	2	0	0	0	562
Bob Ridge	4	G	2	0	0	0	0
Bob Roy	6	G	14	3	2	2	15,688
Bob Shanklin	5	G	2	0	0	0	0
Bob Stories	7	G	12	3	4	0	19,513
Bob Watson	4	C	11	2	0	1	8,590
Bobbiblue Bayou	6	H	8	5	1	1	12,667
Bobbie Gene	3	F	14	4	1	3	46,671
Bobbie Lou	3	F	7	1	0	0	11,240
Bobbie Use	2	F	4	1	1	0	44,540
Bobbie Wagner	2	F	1	0	0	1	1,590
Bobbieonemoretime	5	G	8	0	0	0	590
Bobbies Bad Boy	8	G	4	0	0	0	184
Bobbie's Beauty	3	F	4	0	1	0	5,185
Bobbies Sunrise	4	F	4	1	0	0	1,595
Bobbiessette	3	F	1	0	0	0	55
Bobbinjean	3	F	6	1	0	1	20,269
Bobby Blurr	7	H	11	2	1	0	37,710
Bobby Dazzler	3	C	5	0	0	0	3,940
Bobby Luvs P. R.	3	C	13	3	3	1	20,058
Bobby McGee	3	G	10	1	1	0	8,116
Bobby Naz	5	G	14	2	2	1	14,670
Bobby Told	6	G	5	1	0	1	10,440
Bobby Twice	10	G	7	0	1	1	751
Bobby Two	4	C	2	0	0	0	122
Bobby Z	5	H	14	0	3	1	2,786
Bobby's Buckaroo	7	G	9	2	3	0	67,970
Bobby's Bullet	3	G	3	0	0	1	749
Bobbys Day	2	G	2	0	0	1	1,331
Bobby's Gem	3	C	3	0	0	0	0
Bobby's Red Jet	4	C	2	0	0	0	564
Bobcat Logic	3	F	1	0	0	0	270
Bobi Cat	2	F	2	1	1	0	11,620
Bobs Big Idea	6	G	4	0	0	0	660
Bob's Lady	4	F	2	1	0	0	55,000
Bob's Luck	6	G	14	0	2	2	3,590
Bob's Moment	4	G	3	0	0	0	123
Bobs Peak a Boo	9	G	5	2	1	0	5,942
Bob's Proud Moment	2	C	4	0	0	0	1,770
Bob's Retired	4	G	20	2	2	4	22,657
Bob's Rockn'	4	C	6	2	2	0	3,480
Bob's Shadow	3	C	8	3	0	1	25,092
Bob's Silver	3	F	1	0	0	0	90
Bobs Spunky Girl	2	F	6	0	2	2	6,084
Bobs the Result	4	G	4	0	0	0	0
Bob's Toy	4	F	5	0	0	4	6,160
Bob's Valentine	2	F	6	1	2	0	24,500
Bobsingstheblues	7	H	4	0	0	1	1,900
Bobski	2	C	3	0	0	0	0
Bobsthebigdog	3	G	4	1	0	0	5,685
Bobsway	4	G	13	1	3	4	26,715
Boca Bound	3	G	10	2	0	2	34,980
Boca Dream	7	M	10	0	4	2	45,680
Boca Flyer	4	G	1	0	0	0	0
Boca Rose	4	F	15	0	0	4	3,877
Bocage	2	G	2	0	0	1	3,080
Bocca Al Lupo	3	C	4	3	1	0	53,910
Bocciolo	4	G	25	5	1	2	16,560
Bocelli	3	G	5	1	0	0	4,568
Bocelli (IRE)	6	G	14	3	1	2	27,553
Bodacious Bubba	9	G	15	1	2	1	20,358
Bodacious Cat	3	F	10	1	2	1	14,200
Bodacious Dream	5	G	10	1	1	3	8,145
Bodacious Justin	3	G	9	0	0	0	323
Bodacious Shooter	5	G	6	0	0	1	2,090
Bodgit Be Tru	2	G	3	1	0	1	17,266
Bodgit Dancer	3	F	9	1	1	2	9,409
Bodgiteer	3	G	8	3	0	0	57,765
Bodgit's Girl	3	F	4	0	1	0	4,250
Bodi's Buddy	5	G	23	1	0	3	11,320
Body Building	5	H	6	1	0	0	5,324
Body Image	4	F	7	1	2	2	9,218
Bodyguard (GB)	8	G	3	0	0	0	1,850
Boeing (CHI)	7	G	3	0	1	0	4,850
Boeotia	2	F	1	0	0	0	909
Boeufprairie Jerry	6	M	7	0	0	0	1,500
Bog Hunter	4	G	7	0	0	2	7,344
Bogangles	2	C	7	2	2	1	74,575
Bogart	6	G	14	3	1	2	33,753
Bogey Free	4	G	9	2	0	1	24,415
Bogey's Stogey	6	G	4	0	1	0	453
Boggs Creek	4	G	9	0	3	0	4,468
Bogie Lights	4	C	2	0	0	0	192
Bogner Regis	5	G	10	2	2	3	6,852
Bogota Bill	2	G	1	0	1	0	3,000
Bogus Plan	4	F	2	0	1	0	870
Bohemia Slew	6	G	12	2	2	1	20,360
Bohemian Cru	7	M	4	0	0	0	0
Bohemian Lady	2	F	1	1	0	0	24,600
Bohunk	3	C	8	1	4	2	47,560
Boiling Point	3	G	10	2	2	3	42,701
Boink	4	G	15	1	1	1	4,178
Bois D' Arc	6	G	15	1	1	1	5,258
Bojack	6	G	4	0	0	1	775
Bojangle's Cat	2	F	3	1	0	0	29,255
Boji Breeze	3	F	11	1	4	1	19,244
Boji's At Six	2	C	4	0	0	3	12,392

Horse	Age	Sex	Sts	1st	2d	3d	Won
Bokhara	4	G	4	0	0	0	91
Bokonon	3	G	6	2	0	2	14,675
Bolarity's Fuse	5	G	9	0	1	3	16,738
Bolaro	3	F	1	0	0	0	3,000
Bolchina's Prize	9	G	1	0	0	0	1,020
Bold Action	2	C	2	0	0	0	95
Bold Actor	3	C	4	1	1	0	6,750
Bold Airman	4	G	2	0	0	0	675
Bold America	3	C	4	1	1	2	36,293
Bold American	3	F	5	0	0	1	12,060
Bold and Able	4	F	6	0	1	1	3,599
Bold and Blue	4	G	7	1	0	0	1,366
Bold and Brassy	7	H	6	1	0	0	8,680
Bold and Burley	5	H	2	0	0	0	165
Bold and Fiery	8	M	9	1	0	0	2,254
Bold and Lively	10	G	4	0	0	0	175
Bold and Royal	2	C	9	0	1	1	5,700
Bold Aries	3	G	8	1	3	1	19,750
Bold Armageddon	5	G	10	1	0	0	5,956
Bold Artic Ice	3	F	9	0	4	3	79,138
Bold as Angie	7	M	2	0	0	0	340
Bold Attack	5	M	3	0	0	0	450
Bold B	5	G	10	2	2	0	7,448
Bold Bailey	4	C	5	0	0	1	4,620
Bold Bambino	3	G	4	0	0	1	1,700
Bold Banker	3	C	5	2	0	2	18,860
Bold Bastion	6	G	11	1	1	0	6,256
Bold Bayou Baby	2	F	3	0	1	0	6,040
Bold Bluff	5	M	5	0	1	1	23,470
Bold Blush	5	M	9	0	3	0	1,450
Bold Bobo	2	G	1	0	0	0	0
Bold Brigade	3	C	9	0	0	1	2,690
Bold Brush	6	G	6	1	0	1	6,306
Bold Bryan	4	C	1	0	1	0	3,200
Bold Buster	7	H	8	2	1	1	11,315
Bold Caleb	7	H	10	0	1	1	4,574
Bold Caller	4	C	9	3	2	4	76,800
Bold Carma	3	F	4	0	0	0	232
Bold Cascade	5	M	10	2	4	1	19,125
Bold Cat Dancer	4	F	7	0	0	0	364
Bold Cause	6	H	5	1	1	1	8,740
Bold Cesar	3	G	5	0	0	2	2,852
Bold Chant	7	G	3	1	0	0	2,355
Bold Choice	6	G	2	0	0	0	122
Bold Civette	3	F	4	0	2	1	9,720
Bold Clu	2	G	2	0	0	0	0
Bold Composition	5	G	7	0	0	2	7,260
Bold Connection	3	G	6	0	0	0	4,170
Bold Contender	8	H	14	0	3	3	5,673
Bold Cooler	2	F	2	0	0	0	0
Bold Corsair	3	G	10	2	1	0	7,590
Bold Creek	3	G	10	3	0	0	15,489
Bold Crypto	3	G	12	1	2	2	23,470
Bold Cup	5	M	6	1	1	0	3,517
Bold Cursor	6	H	1	0	0	0	0
Bold Dare	6	H	4	1	0	0	1,390
Bold Daygata	2	C	5	0	2	1	4,839
Bold Days	4	G	11	3	1	1	63,905
Bold Demarche	3	F	3	0	0	0	0
Bold Demi	5	G	27	0	3	6	9,318
Bold Diva	5	M	3	0	0	2	8,030
Bold Edshar	12	G	3	0	0	0	174
Bold Emblem	2	G	4	0	0	0	300
Bold Executress	3	F	12	1	1	1	38,030
Bold Expectations	2	F	5	0	0	0	3,120
Bold Explorer	2	C	1	0	0	0	0
Bold Fascination	7	H	4	0	0	0	124
Bold Fever	5	G	16	3	0	4	15,166
Bold Gale	5	M	3	0	0	0	0
Bold Glare	4	G	3	0	0	0	4,146
Bold Glory	5	M	2	0	0	0	225
Bold Green	2	F	4	1	0	2	32,221
Bold Groom	4	C	7	1	0	0	5,760
Bold Groton	3	G	14	1	0	0	5,721
Bold Guest (IRE)	6	G	4	1	0	1	1,226
Bold Gypsy	3	F	1	0	0	0	0
Bold Hickory	4	C	3	1	1	0	3,670
Bold Honoree	3	F	11	4	0	0	40,560
Bold Hush	2	C	3	1	0	1	15,770
Bold in a Storm	2	G	6	0	0	1	7,100
Bold Information	6	H	3	0	0	0	135
Bold Intent	2	C	3	0	1	0	1,913
Bold Irishman	3	C	5	0	0	0	1,000
Bold Italic	7	H	3	1	1	0	1,125
Bold Jerry	4	G	10	1	2	0	6,080
Bold Jest	6	G	6	2	0	0	5,067
Bold Jet	7	G	16	1	1	1	3,829
Bold Josh Sally	6	M	2	1	0	0	4,500
Bold Jubilation	2	F	5	1	0	1	32,464
Bold Kris	4	G	8	0	0	2	15,575
Bold Leo	4	G	7	1	2	0	12,598
Bold Line	6	M	7	3	2	0	26,938
Bold Lisa	3	F	3	0	0	0	0
Bold Little Lass	2	F	5	1	1	1	30,502
Bold Love	2	C	4	0	2	1	24,810
Bold Lover	3	C	7	0	1	3	7,005
Bold Mango	4	G	5	0	0	1	10,290
Bold Mark	5	M	12	3	2	0	19,761
Bold Match	6	H	2	0	0	0	102
Bold Merge	5	G	8	0	0	0	612
Bold Merit	2	G	4	3	0	1	49,440
Bold Mind	4	G	16	3	1	1	26,705
Bold Minister	2	G	2	1	0	0	16,297
Bold Minskya	4	F	2	0	0	0	348
Bold Missy	3	F	19	2	4	5	17,109
Bold Moro	3	G	6	0	1	0	1,525
Bold Move	3	C	5	0	1	0	2,620
Bold 'n Bashful	5	M	2	0	0	2	440
Bold N Broke	3	G	4	0	0	0	4,056
Bold 'n Clever	8	G	7	1	2	1	6,360
Bold N Dark	2	F	1	0	0	0	0
Bold n' Elegant	2	F	2	0	0	0	214
Bold n' Fancy	6	G	7	0	1	0	9,162
Bold 'n Keen	4	C	6	2	2	1	77,943
Bold N Klassy	3	G	3	0	0	0	100
Bold N Old	5	G	17	5	2	2	56,485
Bold n' Perfect	4	G	12	0	2	3	23,283
Bold n' Pretty	5	M	11	2	1	1	21,560
Bold Nxs	2	C	8	4	1	0	45,586
Bold Offer	3	G	6	0	1	0	3,786
Bold Oka	11	G	1	0	0	0	0
Bold Parisian	6	G	9	3	0	0	24,782
Bold Passer	6	G	8	0	0	0	954
Bold Patches	4	F	10	1	3	0	11,540
Bold Performer	3	F	12	2	1	1	10,953
Bold Perfume	5	M	1	0	0	0	0
Bold Pete	5	G	21	3	3	1	22,320
Bold Philosopher	5	M	2	0	1	0	462
Bold Pilot	8	G	8	0	1	3	18,320
Bold Pistol	4	G	2	0	0	0	0
Bold Playmate	4	F	10	1	0	1	5,498
Bold Prospect	4	G	10	1	0	1	20,550
Bold Quest	4	C	7	1	1	1	7,780
Bold Raffie	2	G	2	0	0	0	210
Bold Ranger	4	G	2	1	0	0	40,260
Bold Reackion	5	M	2	0	0	0	158
Bold Reality	2	C	3	1	0	1	18,030
Bold Reply	5	H	19	5	2	5	38,832
Bold Rhapsody	5	M	22	0	1	3	4,168
Bold Rhythm	3	G	12	3	1	2	48,820
Bold Richard	3	C	4	0	0	0	44
Bold Rita	3	F	12	3	0	2	14,131
Bold Roberta	5	M	14	3	3	3	211,198
Bold Round Trip	3	G	7	0	0	0	678
Bold Rush	3	G	3	0	1	0	3,112
Bold Score	3	F	5	1	0	0	12,600
Bold Seahawk	5	G	6	0	0	0	348
Bold Seduction	2	G	3	0	0	0	434
Bold Selecto	7	G	8	0	1	3	5,969
Bold Shadante	2	F	1	0	0	0	100
Bold Shamrock	5	M	2	0	0	0	0
Bold Sheik	4	C	6	2	2	0	27,612
Bold Shenigans	6	H	3	0	0	0	117
Bold Siete	6	H	7	0	0	0	0
Bold Sparkle	4	G	1	0	0	0	44
Bold Speculator	6	G	1	0	1	0	2,180
Bold Starlet	2	F	2	0	0	0	3,636
Bold Starter	4	C	5	0	0	0	985

Horse	Age	Sex	Sts	1st	2d	3d	Won
Bold Sterling	2	C	1	0	0	0	0
Bold Stranger	3	F	2	0	0	0	1,110
Bold Stripes	5	H	10	4	1	1	15,642
Bold Stroke	2	G	3	0	1	0	4,090
Bold Sunset	3	G	9	2	1	0	8,236
Bold Swinger	5	G	4	0	0	1	240
Bold Tactician	4	C	7	1	1	0	5,072
Bold Tena	2	F	3	0	0	0	367
Bold Texas	3	G	7	3	1	1	50,980
Bold Tizzy	3	F	2	0	2	0	3,160
Bold to Gold	6	M	6	0	1	0	1,820
Bold Trader	2	G	6	1	2	1	43,169
Bold Trick	3	G	7	1	0	1	13,770
Bold Truth	4	C	5	0	0	3	23,910
Bold Turn	2	G	2	0	1	0	3,620
Bold Victoress	6	M	7	0	0	0	700
Bold Vigor	4	G	3	1	1	0	19,788
Bold William	4	G	1	0	0	0	0
Bold Wind	3	C	4	0	0	0	1,292
Bold Xena	3	F	1	0	0	0	0
Boldandahalf	3	G	2	0	0	1	1,552
Boldanzar	5	G	8	3	2	3	53,850
Bolder Diamonds	2	C	1	0	0	0	355
Boldest Challenge	7	M	2	0	0	0	91
Boldest Heart	4	G	7	1	0	1	17,680
Boldfalcon	4	G	12	3	1	1	10,462
Boldini (MEX)	8	H	2	0	0	0	138
Boldly Certain	6	M	12	0	0	4	6,386
Boldly Clever	5	G	10	1	0	0	12,483
Boldly Inspired	6	G	10	0	0	0	1,854
Bold'n Cheatin	3	F	4	0	0	1	180
Boldness	3	F	19	2	7	4	48,600
Boldsea	4	F	2	0	0	0	2,760
Boldshannon	5	M	7	0	1	2	5,960
Bolele's Billy	2	C	4	0	0	0	930
Bolero At Eight	6	H	4	0	0	0	0
Bolero Type	9	G	4	0	0	0	220
Bolivar	6	G	13	1	1	1	20,363
Bollix	4	G	7	1	0	2	18,865
Bolo Blurr	4	C	4	0	0	1	266
Bologna Sandwich	6	G	1	0	0	0	0
Bolshoi Ballet	2	F	3	0	0	0	125
Bolt	6	H	5	0	1	1	8,825
Bolt Action	2	C	1	0	0	0	110
Bolted Heart	2	C	9	2	2	1	31,050
Bolting Jake	8	H	5	0	0	0	1,055
Boltoflighting	9	G	9	0	0	0	631
Bolton Landing	2	F	2	0	0	0	118
Bolton Nina	5	M	10	1	1	0	5,532
Boltonia	3	F	3	0	0	0	203
Bolywood	4	C	8	1	1	2	5,618
Bom Luna (ARG)	6	M	13	0	2	0	9,962
Bomanicious	3	C	4	0	0	1	1,430
Bomar Key	7	G	7	0	1	0	4,970
Bomartini	3	G	8	1	2	0	17,865
Bomb Site	3	G	6	1	2	0	23,610
Bomb Squad	4	G	12	3	5	0	16,856
Bombay Blues	4	F	8	0	0	0	5,175
Bombay Casey	4	G	9	0	0	1	748
Bombay Lad	3	G	5	1	2	0	49,295
Bomber	7	G	3	0	0	0	284
Bomber Ace	3	G	5	0	0	0	150
Bombofalooker	2	C	5	0	1	0	4,750
Bombs Away Nickie	3	C	9	0	0	1	6,410
Bomby	4	G	13	1	0	0	3,420
Bon Amigo	6	H	7	3	1	0	47,925
Bon Appeal	3	F	4	0	1	0	4,800
Bon Fille	3	F	7	1	0	0	14,740
Bon Fleur	3	C	3	1	0	0	20,580
Bon Giorno	3	F	2	0	0	0	70
Bon Jour Paris	3	F	15	4	2	1	41,045
Bon Lil	3	F	4	0	0	0	1,980
Bon Marie	2	C	4	1	0	0	46,959
Bon Place	5	M	11	0	1	1	3,980
Bon to Run	11	G	22	4	6	2	16,924
Bona Fide Bauble	3	F	7	0	0	0	1,710
Bona Fide Rebel	3	G	14	1	0	4	14,301
Bonafide Lady	8	M	5	0	0	0	626
Bonaguil	6	G	8	1	1	1	53,620
Bonair Lake	5	H	1	0	0	0	0
Bonanza Jellybean	2	F	3	0	0	0	1,860
Bonaparte	3	G	9	3	0	2	50,694
Bonapaw	7	G	10	1	1	2	116,616
Bonay	3	F	13	2	2	2	78,109
Bonberry	3	F	3	0	1	0	2,600
Bonche	3	G	9	0	2	0	3,124
Boncherie	4	F	4	0	0	1	1,350
Bond Arbitrage	2	C	4	1	1	1	51,230
Bond Bird	3	F	2	0	0	0	140
Bond James Bond	8	H	6	0	0	0	245
Bond Midnight (IRE)	3	F	13	0	0	0	8,060
Bonded	5	G	7	0	0	0	815
Bondi Beach	6	G	14	1	1	0	4,833
Bondsman	3	C	14	2	5	1	60,036
Bone Collector	3	G	5	0	0	0	1,073
Bone Daddy	2	G	1	1	0	0	5,880
Bone Dog	3	G	5	2	1	0	66,480
Bonefide Reason	5	M	11	0	2	4	71,419
Bonegilla Tom (AUS)	9	G	1	0	0	0	0
Bonehead	2	G	1	0	0	0	320
Boney Fingers	3	C	1	0	0	0	0
Bonfire of Soul	3	F	3	0	1	0	3,050
Bonfo	3	C	7	1	0	3	34,446
Bongee	3	F	2	0	0	0	200
Bongo Kitty	2	F	7	1	0	4	19,610
Bongsilver	5	H	17	1	1	0	6,444
Bonhomme Hill Deb	4	F	8	1	1	0	6,060
Bonilla	4	C	6	1	2	1	22,406
Bonita Gata	3	F	3	1	0	0	2,320
Bonita Lady	3	F	1	0	0	0	0
Bonita Mexicana	4	F	10	1	0	1	4,042
Bonita Rose	5	M	4	0	1	1	7,100
Bonita Tyger	3	F	11	2	1	0	15,259
Bonitajima	4	F	6	0	0	0	178
Bonito Bandido	5	M	3	0	0	0	0
Bonjoiu	4	F	5	1	1	0	3,482
Bonjour	5	M	7	3	1	2	7,750
Bonjourno My Lady	2	F	3	0	0	1	630
Bonkers	9	G	16	2	2	0	10,202
Bonne Idee	3	F	10	3	1	1	18,401
Bonne Roberto	4	F	6	0	0	0	378
Bonnechere	5	M	14	3	6	1	58,340
Bonneville Flash	4	G	3	0	0	0	178
Bonney Lake	3	F	1	0	0	0	0
Bonnie	7	M	1	0	0	0	0
Bonnie and Brave	4	F	6	1	0	1	5,058
Bonnie Be Quick	3	F	12	0	2	2	8,841
Bonnie Belle	7	M	17	0	3	2	6,160
Bonnie Bo	6	M	9	2	1	1	5,130
Bonnie Brighton	3	F	11	1	0	2	47,700
Bonnie Clyde	4	F	8	0	0	0	873
Bonnie Expectation	4	F	10	0	2	1	5,430
Bonnie J.	3	F	9	2	1	2	36,450
Bonnie Mae	4	F	16	2	0	3	14,891
Bonnie Pancho	5	M	9	0	4	1	11,513
Bonnie's Bag	9	G	8	2	3	0	48,250
Bonnies Blushing	7	M	8	2	1	0	12,506
Bonnie's Dancer	4	F	12	2	0	2	7,939
Bonnies Kaper	2	F	5	2	1	0	18,100
Bonnieview Miss	3	F	2	0	0	1	4,250
Bonnvilla Dancer	4	F	3	0	0	0	76
Bonny Banker	3	F	4	0	0	1	955
Bonny Be Yours	3	F	4	0	0	0	0
Bonny Go Lightly	2	F	4	0	1	0	5,731
Bonny Johnny	4	G	7	0	3	1	3,900
Bono Striker	5	G	15	3	2	2	49,904
Bonobo	7	H	14	1	1	0	3,982
Bonspiel	2	G	1	0	0	0	515
Bonton	2	F	6	0	0	1	2,376
Bontrando	4	F	6	2	0	0	36,190
Bonus Bid	4	F	15	1	3	3	34,130
Bonus Bonnie	3	F	2	0	0	0	94
Bonus Dessert	2	G	11	1	0	1	11,177
Bonus Extra	3	F	11	3	3	1	70,966
Bonus Factor	4	G	4	0	0	0	258
Bonus Move	3	F	12	3	2	4	29,315
Bonus Pack	5	G	12	2	3	1	119,955
Bonus Paid	5	M	4	0	0	0	1,324

Horse	Age	Sex	Sts	1st	2d	3d	Won	Horse	Age	Sex	Sts	1st	2d	3d	Won
Bonus Pay Day	5	G	8	1	2	2	124,060	Booneomatic	3	C	5	0	0	0	75
Bonus Royal	2	F	4	1	0	0	20,400	Boone's Best	3	G	3	0	0	0	350
Bonusita	5	M	7	4	1	0	14,520	Boone's Big Boy	4	C	3	1	0	1	6,912
Bonyev	2	C	3	0	0	0	0	Boone's Creek	6	G	11	4	2	1	17,186
Bonzai Bay	4	F	10	1	2	2	32,970	Boone's Dad	3	F	9	0	0	0	5,237
Boo Aahhhh	3	C	6	0	0	0	3,470	Boone's Diamond	4	F	6	0	3	0	24,570
Boo Boo Honey	3	F	2	0	0	0	200	Boone's Gate	5	M	2	0	0	0	323
Boo Boo N Moo Moo	4	G	4	0	0	0	450	Boone's Gold	5	M	13	2	4	2	48,280
Boo La Babe	4	F	6	0	1	0	870	Boone's Lake	3	G	9	0	0	2	2,495
Boo Ray	5	G	2	0	0	0	115	Boone's Mask	4	F	1	0	0	1	3,575
Boo Roo	6	G	6	0	0	0	714	Boone's Silent	3	C	3	1	0	0	8,100
Boo Yeah	4	G	8	1	2	1	9,297	Boonesboro Beach	4	F	8	4	0	0	74,600
Boobanell	3	G	8	0	0	1	1,155	Booneslittledancer	3	F	16	2	2	1	32,918
Boogaylynn	4	F	6	0	0	0	1,947	Boone'ssimplydbest	3	G	12	1	0	3	12,383
Booggie Cat	2	G	7	0	1	1	6,540	Boonesville	6	G	9	1	1	3	11,743
Boogie Bill	5	G	1	0	0	0	0	Booneton	5	M	16	4	3	2	27,898
Boogie Board	4	C	4	1	0	1	4,210	Booney	3	F	5	1	1	1	7,823
Boogie Demon	4	F	2	0	0	0	0	Booney B	3	G	16	1	0	2	4,926
Boogie Girl	2	F	5	0	0	0	255	Boo's Boy	7	G	8	2	0	3	13,732
Boogie Lill	3	F	3	0	0	0	64	Boo's Brass Lady	7	M	4	1	1	0	7,800
Boogie Motel	7	M	2	1	0	0	4,428	Booster	3	C	10	2	1	1	46,400
Boogie On	3	C	6	2	0	0	45,270	Boot Hill	6	G	18	0	2	3	14,155
Boogie Power	3	F	11	0	0	3	4,550	Boot It Home	7	G	1	0	0	0	47
Boogie Rhythmn	2	G	2	0	0	0	360	Boot Scooter	2	F	4	0	1	2	4,300
Boogie Woogie Man	3	G	14	2	0	2	23,993	Boot Scootin' Okie	2	G	3	0	2	0	4,245
Boogie Woogie Type	5	G	8	0	2	3	17,300	Boot Scootin Storm	7	G	3	0	0	0	174
Boogieboogieboy	4	C	5	0	1	1	1,893	Boot Scootn Austin	5	G	3	1	0	0	8,100
Boogieboom	4	F	9	2	3	1	22,990	Boot Special	3	F	8	1	1	2	6,672
Boogieforjoy	3	G	5	0	0	0	2,570	Boot Strap	2	F	1	0	0	0	0
Booh	3	F	11	2	0	3	7,836	Boot Tree	5	M	5	0	0	2	3,948
Book Club	3	C	11	1	0	1	7,475	Boot Up	3	C	2	0	0	0	0
Book Note	3	C	7	3	3	0	67,640	Boothbay Harbor	4	F	4	0	0	0	840
Book of Kells	4	G	5	2	0	0	17,440	Booties	4	F	12	2	0	1	5,800
Book of the Month	2	C	1	1	0	0	25,200	Bootillion	6	G	7	2	1	0	9,679
Book of the Year	3	C	15	3	3	2	75,400	Bootleg and Susy	4	F	10	3	2	0	20,477
Book Review	7	G	1	0	0	0	250	Boots a Flyin'	2	F	2	0	0	0	280
Book Seven	4	G	14	2	1	4	22,219	Boots and Saddles	5	G	2	0	0	0	218
Book Smart	6	M	8	1	0	1	4,125	Boots Are Walking	2	C	2	1	1	0	21,000
Book the Bet	3	C	6	0	0	1	8,210	Boots Malone	7	G	2	0	0	0	420
Book the Cat	4	F	16	4	4	2	36,716	Booze Hound	3	C	2	0	0	0	0
Book the Devil	3	F	6	2	1	1	42,900	Boozhoo Niji	6	H	6	1	0	0	5,936
Bookem Carl	4	C	10	2	3	1	13,931	Boozin Blonde	2	F	8	1	3	1	134,539
Booker D	8	G	9	2	3	2	35,080	Boozin' Susan	4	F	8	2	0	3	71,640
Bookin It	3	F	13	0	3	2	17,353	Bop	6	H	3	2	0	0	75,000
Bookkillrr	7	H	4	0	0	0	640	Bop She Bop	2	F	3	0	1	0	2,265
Bookle Bo	7	H	18	2	2	3	20,427	Bora Bora	3	F	1	0	0	0	0
Booklet	4	C	2	0	1	0	224,000	Borabadura	3	F	4	2	1	1	75,434
Bookmaster	3	C	6	2	1	1	52,970	Borasca	4	F	5	1	2	0	26,480
Bookmylaunch	5	G	13	0	2	6	19,771	Borboleta	3	F	15	1	2	3	11,398
Boolean Query	5	H	8	0	0	0	0	Border Blues	3	F	6	1	0	1	26,140
Boom a Cat a Boom	2	C	1	0	0	0	780	Border Bound	3	F	8	2	1	0	73,400
Boom Baby	2	F	4	1	0	0	6,000	Border Bum	6	H	2	0	0	0	115
Boom Bah Yay	3	F	14	1	4	1	59,740	Border Call	5	G	4	0	0	0	2,260
Boom Boom Braude	3	F	6	0	1	0	2,685	Border Raider	3	G	17	1	3	2	9,895
Boom Boom Cha Cha	5	M	11	1	5	1	20,525	Border Reiver	3	G	7	1	0	0	8,076
Boom Chicka Boom	3	F	3	1	1	0	1,260	Border Runner	3	G	5	0	0	0	1,477
Boom City	4	C	6	1	0	0	7,080	Borderline Angel	3	F	4	0	1	0	1,300
Boom Shakalaka	2	F	3	0	0	0	0	Borderline Crazy	2	F	1	0	0	0	2,240
Boom Time	4	C	10	1	1	1	6,410	Borders Edge	3	C	2	0	0	0	214
Boomboomgirl	4	F	8	1	2	0	20,450	Bordgonmagnificent	2	F	6	0	0	1	2,095
Boomer Creek	3	G	11	2	1	4	41,870	Boreal	2	C	1	0	0	0	118
Boomerang Billilea	4	F	1	0	0	0	145	Boreas	7	G	2	0	0	0	138
Boomer's Boot	2	F	1	0	0	0	0	Borgia Basket	5	M	12	0	0	3	2,898
Boomer's Bunny	6	M	1	0	0	0	0	Borgie Girl	5	M	1	0	0	0	0
Boomer's Express	3	C	6	1	1	0	14,911	Boris the Blade	3	C	7	1	1	1	18,810
Boomers in Town	3	G	7	0	0	2	1,559	Boris the Rocket	5	H	1	0	0	0	0
Boomette	3	F	4	0	0	0	0	Born a Roman	2	G	5	0	2	0	10,960
Boomin	4	G	11	1	3	1	11,141	Born Again	5	H	1	0	0	0	126
Boomin Bobbie	3	F	6	0	0	0	1,860	Born Again Slew	5	M	6	0	0	0	258
Booming Sound	2	C	7	0	0	2	4,625	Born Blonde	2	F	4	0	0	0	4,140
Boomslang	4	G	12	2	3	4	72,380	Born Dusty	2	C	2	0	0	0	248
Boomtown Red	3	G	1	0	0	0	1,077	Born Gifted	3	F	4	0	0	0	1,100
Boomzeeboom	2	C	4	0	3	0	27,820	Born Golden	4	F	5	0	0	0	775
Boondock	4	G	7	0	0	1	1,958	Born in the Ghetto	8	M	7	2	1	1	16,210
Boone Avie	6	G	12	2	1	4	12,868	Born in Time	4	F	2	0	0	0	106
Boone County	6	G	4	0	0	0	946	Born Instep	6	M	5	1	1	1	3,980
Boone Time	3	G	2	0	0	0	0	Born Something (IRE)	5	M	7	2	2	2	90,491
Boone Town Lady	4	F	9	2	1	2	11,297	Born to Be Classy	3	F	10	1	2	3	6,660
Boone Vita	3	G	8	1	2	0	6,456	Born to Be Zak	4	G	9	2	1	2	21,339

Horse	Age	Sex	Sts	1st	2d	3d	Won
Born to Bop	6	M	8	0	2	2	7,605
Born to Dance	4	F	10	3	1	5	183,842
Born to Lead	4	G	11	0	0	1	1,601
Born to Pic	6	G	8	2	3	1	54,515
Born to Run Fast	5	G	16	0	2	1	3,792
Born Wild Again	3	G	11	1	1	0	9,060
Borntobealeader	4	G	9	1	0	2	21,735
Borntobeloved	4	F	11	0	1	0	27,967
Borntobelucky	3	C	9	2	1	1	10,342
Borntoberegal	6	G	2	0	0	1	4,268
Bornwithit	2	G	2	1	0	0	11,780
Borrego	2	C	4	2	0	0	63,300
Borrowed Angel	3	F	8	0	1	2	3,488
Borstal Boy	5	G	10	0	0	1	3,432
Borzov	3	G	4	1	1	1	5,794
Bo's a Ten	3	F	19	2	3	6	27,280
Bo's Brat	3	G	1	0	0	0	46
Bo's Bursting Star	7	H	4	1	2	0	2,260
Bo's Quest	6	M	2	1	0	0	926
Bo's Sand Tunnel	2	C	5	1	2	1	10,555
Bo's Sister	4	F	8	5	1	1	121,035
Bo's Vixen	10	M	2	0	0	0	325
Boschee	4	G	9	1	2	2	10,121
Bosefa	2	G	1	0	0	0	0
Boshonto	10	G	9	0	0	1	1,111
Bosia	3	F	3	0	0	0	0
Bosko's Crown	3	C	3	1	0	0	5,918
Boss Daddy	3	C	4	0	2	1	11,800
Boss Ego	7	H	10	3	1	2	90,560
Boss Gable	3	G	5	0	0	0	410
Boss Hogg	7	H	3	0	2	0	2,720
Boss Man	3	C	2	0	0	0	1,280
Boss Nass	2	C	4	0	0	0	4,798
Boss of the Moss	5	M	11	0	0	2	3,405
Boss Owen	8	G	15	1	1	4	9,234
Bossanova	3	C	7	3	1	1	204,906
Bossie D J	6	M	1	1	0	0	7,500
Bossman Gone	4	G	5	0	0	0	180
Bosssaidwin	4	F	2	0	0	0	0
Bossy Gun	4	C	5	0	1	0	2,196
Bostic Hill	8	G	11	1	1	1	13,520
Boston Bar	2	G	2	0	1	0	3,940
Boston Bay	5	G	6	0	0	1	3,360
Boston Bean	2	G	5	1	0	1	8,180
Boston Blackie	6	H	1	0	0	0	65
Boston Brahmin	2	C	8	1	1	1	55,765
Boston Brat	6	G	7	3	2	0	67,790
Boston Bull	3	C	2	0	0	0	3,750
Boston Common	4	G	8	4	1	0	105,930
Boston Fox	3	G	13	8	3	0	146,740
Boston Lady	3	F	5	0	0	0	140
Boston Lass	3	F	1	0	0	0	0
Boston Navigator	2	C	1	0	0	1	3,300
Boston Nova	3	F	1	0	0	0	87
Boston Park	3	C	6	2	0	0	83,025
Boston Post Road	2	F	2	0	0	0	0
Boston Shuttle	3	G	4	1	0	1	16,920
Boston Song	2	F	6	1	3	0	50,725
Boston Spirit	4	F	2	0	0	0	520
Boston Storm	3	F	11	2	1	0	13,393
Boston Symphony	2	F	3	0	0	0	145
Boston Tea Party	3	F	3	0	0	1	6,105
Bostwick	5	H	2	0	0	1	378
Bosworth Field	3	C	2	0	0	0	214
Botanic Man	5	G	7	0	2	1	4,142
Both Guns	11	G	2	0	1	1	980
Botime	2	F	2	0	0	0	190
Bottom Bay	3	G	3	1	0	0	37,221
Botzworth	3	G	4	1	0	0	7,325
Boublitchky	2	F	4	0	0	1	3,088
Bouchart	4	C	4	0	0	0	320
Bought in Dixie	7	H	6	0	0	3	6,950
Boula Boula	2	F	3	1	0	0	11,490
Boulder Boy	7	G	14	2	1	0	7,211
Boulder Chief	3	C	2	0	0	0	528
Boulder Excess	5	G	2	0	0	0	238
Boule	3	G	14	2	2	2	24,300
Bouncing Coyote	3	F	1	0	0	0	84
Bound Along	2	C	5	0	0	2	7,900
Bound by a Legacy	4	G	2	0	0	0	0
Bound by Honour	5	G	5	0	0	0	110
Bound by the Heart	5	G	5	1	1	1	2,600
Bound for Freedom	3	G	9	2	1	0	36,536
Bound for Memphis	9	M	1	0	0	0	35
Bound for Riches	3	G	3	0	0	0	132
Bound On Bi	6	M	9	1	0	2	37,864
Bound to Be a Pro	3	G	10	0	1	1	10,962
Bound to Be Easy	3	C	1	0	0	0	233
Bound to Be Great	5	H	16	1	3	3	13,610
Bound to Be Lucky	3	F	2	0	0	0	0
Bound to Be Sunny	2	G	3	1	0	0	9,114
Bound to Bea Lover	5	M	4	0	0	0	153
Bound to Comet	4	F	4	0	0	0	0
Bound to Cover	5	G	6	1	0	0	7,770
Bound to Entertain	3	G	5	0	0	0	553
Bound to Run	7	G	2	0	0	0	336
Bound to Win	5	H	8	1	1	1	12,732
Bound Two Punch	6	M	4	0	0	0	708
Bound With Honour	4	C	9	0	2	0	28,115
Boundanddetermined	5	M	6	1	4	1	75,220
Boundary Bay	2	C	1	0	1	0	8,200
Boundary Creek	3	G	6	0	0	2	4,501
Boundary Hunter	7	G	9	1	0	0	4,498
Boundary Stone	3	G	1	1	0	0	10,800
Boundforthetop	3	C	11	2	0	0	15,330
Bounding Cat	3	C	5	0	0	0	636
Bounding Charm	3	F	4	1	1	0	37,830
Bounding Rail	5	G	5	1	2	1	14,010
Bounding Smoocher	5	M	7	0	0	1	2,340
Bounding Surprise	4	F	1	0	0	0	300
Bounding Two	5	G	8	0	2	1	4,585
Boundless Endeavor	4	C	2	0	0	0	282
Boundless Joy	3	F	13	1	1	0	6,461
Boundless Spirit	3	F	3	0	0	0	123
Bountiful Me	4	F	11	1	0	0	7,465
Bounty Bill	3	C	11	3	2	2	21,072
Bounty Miss	3	F	4	1	1	0	5,760
Bounty Moon	5	M	9	0	0	1	1,365
Bounty Moses	5	G	2	0	0	0	109
Bounty of Spring	3	F	1	0	1	0	800
Bounzuz	3	F	8	4	2	1	78,643
Bourbon	6	G	10	2	1	3	34,990
Bourbon Ambassador	3	F	4	0	0	1	2,520
Bourbon Brownie	4	F	10	4	3	0	30,800
Bourbon County	4	C	12	2	0	2	100,816
Bourbon Creek	3	G	13	2	4	0	17,330
Bourbon Jack	3	G	5	0	0	0	540
Bourbon Lane	4	G	10	1	1	3	9,787
Bourbon N Blues	2	C	2	1	0	0	10,450
Bourbon N Coke	5	H	8	1	0	0	6,150
Bourbon Party	3	G	8	0	0	0	4,080
Bourbon Ridge	3	G	7	2	2	0	19,306
Bourbon St. Dance	3	F	6	1	0	0	5,558
Bouree	5	M	7	1	0	2	16,406
Bourgeoisie (IRE)	5	M	3	0	1	0	3,400
Bourn a Cowboy	8	G	7	1	0	2	3,430
Bourne Ruler	7	G	7	3	1	1	18,317
Bournmouth	5	H	4	1	0	3	6,156
Boussac Lake	6	M	10	1	2	1	11,970
Boutit Boutit	6	H	1	0	0	0	0
Bow Ante	5	M	4	0	1	1	8,320
Bow Confide	2	C	3	0	0	0	225
Bow Down	3	G	1	0	0	0	0
Bow Legged Honey	9	M	14	0	1	0	1,455
Bow Out	3	C	9	1	3	2	41,000
Bow Spray	5	G	13	0	1	2	5,180
Bowdeck	4	F	8	0	0	1	1,390
Bowditch	5	H	8	0	1	3	4,956
Bowdoin	2	C	4	1	0	1	15,030
Bowen Hill	3	G	5	0	0	0	2,880
Bowerman Road	3	C	3	0	0	0	134
Bowkeen	5	M	4	1	0	0	17,196
Bowl of Fire	4	F	9	0	1	4	7,210
Bowman Mill	5	H	5	1	2	0	327,682
Bowman Too	3	G	13	1	1	1	17,510
Bowman's Band	5	H	9	2	3	1	432,240
Bowman's Crossing	10	H	2	0	0	1	6,500
Bowsprit	5	M	1	0	1	0	1,100

Horse	Age	Sex	Sts	1st	2d	3d	Won
Box Cutter	2	F	6	1	0	1	10,495
Box of Moonlight	3	F	11	0	1	3	6,150
Box Office	4	C	4	1	0	1	12,904
Box Office Smash	3	F	12	0	0	2	3,889
Box Seat Lover	9	G	13	2	3	0	15,483
Boxarox	4	G	10	3	1	0	8,698
Boxcar Bertha	2	F	3	0	0	0	438
Boxer Girl	3	F	5	2	0	1	62,879
Box's Girl	4	F	10	1	0	0	4,365
Boy Cor	5	G	14	1	2	3	9,429
Boy Genius	9	G	12	3	1	0	25,928
Boy Power	2	C	4	1	1	0	17,097
Boy Willy	6	G	6	1	2	0	10,964
Boydston	3	C	5	1	0	0	6,390
Boyers Junction	4	G	7	1	1	0	5,198
Boyfriend	3	G	12	3	2	0	26,650
Boyisdue	9	G	13	0	0	0	1,450
Boyish Dancer	3	G	8	1	0	0	5,534
Boylan	3	G	7	3	1	3	32,225
Boyle Heights Kid	5	G	5	2	0	0	22,110
Boynton	3	C	4	1	1	2	19,280
Boy's in Trouble	6	G	5	1	1	0	3,692
Boys Night Out	5	G	5	1	0	0	6,620
Boys Revenge	12	G	5	1	2	0	7,150
Boy's Trouble	4	C	11	3	0	4	10,176
Boyson Berry	7	G	1	0	0	0	0
Boystownbag	4	G	3	0	0	0	0
Boyum	6	G	11	3	1	0	37,700
Boywhataboy	2	G	2	0	0	0	0
Bozman	5	G	5	0	0	0	0
Braak's Biz	7	G	4	0	0	0	105
Braak's Bizzy Boy	5	G	7	0	0	2	1,846
Braak's Indianmiss	6	M	1	0	0	0	120
Braaks Love	8	G	8	0	0	1	740
Braak's Plain	3	F	4	0	0	0	220
Braak's Special	7	H	10	1	0	1	5,515
Braces Loded	11	G	2	0	0	0	0
Bracey's Prospect	4	F	9	1	2	1	22,688
Bracing Beauty	4	F	11	3	3	0	68,510
Brackenber	2	F	5	1	1	0	20,140
Brackets	4	F	6	2	3	0	25,220
Brad Man	4	G	15	2	1	1	16,946
Brad Z	5	G	22	2	4	1	15,229
Braden's Best	2	C	3	0	0	1	1,640
Braden's Hope	3	F	2	0	0	0	0
Bradford	2	G	4	1	2	0	17,200
Bradley Brave	6	G	9	0	1	1	3,520
Bradley County	6	H	1	0	0	0	164
Bradley McGee	5	G	9	2	1	3	9,102
Bradleys Son	3	G	4	1	2	0	5,220
Brad's Brat	5	G	14	1	2	1	15,072
Brad's On Patrol	3	G	14	1	4	0	22,400
Brady	5	H	11	1	1	1	14,780
Braetta	4	F	10	2	1	1	31,475
Brag Bag	2	F	2	0	0	1	6,090
Bragg Power	8	G	5	0	0	0	369
Braggs Little Mag	8	G	12	1	2	1	5,033
Brahma	2	C	2	0	0	0	0
Brahma Bull	3	C	3	1	0	0	29,280
Brainwash	3	G	9	0	0	0	1,260
Brak	3	G	4	2	1	0	33,020
Bramble Bush	3	C	6	1	2	0	38,577
Brambledown (IRE)	12	M	1	0	0	1	1,000
Brancaster	7	G	12	0	0	1	3,201
Branch Chief	6	G	13	1	1	1	9,486
Branch Office	3	G	6	0	0	0	630
Brancusi	3	C	6	1	1	1	212,580
Brand New Address	2	G	10	1	0	3	10,420
Brand New Ride	6	M	3	0	0	0	90
Brandala	5	M	10	2	1	1	110,936
Brandenburg Gate	2	G	5	1	0	1	7,770
Brandi Drive	5	M	13	0	0	2	2,596
Brandi's Charm	4	G	1	0	0	0	79
Brandish	8	G	7	0	0	1	868
Brando	3	G	3	0	0	1	3,850
Brandon Blaine	3	C	6	0	0	1	825
Brandon Rose	5	M	4	0	0	0	103
Brandon's Award	6	H	3	0	0	0	0
Brandon's Babydoll	4	F	10	1	2	1	12,590
Brandon's Brother	2	C	3	0	0	2	6,791
Brandons Colors	4	G	6	1	2	0	27,920
Brandons Kipperboy	5	H	2	1	0	0	3,720
Brandon's Luck	2	F	2	0	0	0	588
Brandon's Marfa	2	G	2	2	0	0	66,697
Brandon's Starlite	7	H	11	0	2	0	4,825
Brandons Wild Cat	2	F	4	1	0	0	4,825
Brandrews Choice	5	G	12	0	3	2	8,210
Brands Hatch	2	C	2	0	0	0	3,080
Brandski	6	G	4	0	0	0	580
Brandy Creek	3	F	8	1	4	1	7,900
Brandy Doll	4	F	10	3	0	1	13,533
Brandy Vee	4	F	1	0	0	0	0
Brandys Goal	6	M	9	0	0	3	3,044
Branford	4	G	7	0	0	1	1,216
Branjolisa	3	F	1	0	0	0	0
Branscome Hall	6	M	6	0	0	1	12,988
Brant Lake	6	H	5	0	0	0	423
Brant Point	2	F	6	0	0	1	6,795
Brant's Pride	6	G	9	0	4	1	9,749
Brass	4	F	2	0	0	0	1,380
Brass Act	4	G	10	3	0	1	6,755
Brass Arrow	4	G	11	1	2	4	39,340
Brass Bo	7	G	5	0	0	0	0
Brass Boots	3	G	12	0	3	2	17,429
Brass Bull	2	G	1	0	0	0	0
Brass Bunny	2	F	4	1	0	0	7,241
Brass Chime	8	M	10	0	1	0	1,880
Brass Dixie	6	G	8	3	2	2	30,760
Brass Halo	4	G	11	0	2	1	4,063
Brass in Pocket	4	F	7	5	0	1	475,830
Brass Is Class	6	M	3	0	0	1	984
Brass Jazz Band	3	C	1	0	0	0	0
Brass Kat	2	F	5	1	0	2	5,442
Brass Key	7	G	5	1	2	1	15,312
Brass Pendant	3	F	10	3	2	1	37,035
Brass Punch	3	G	11	1	1	2	17,159
Brass Rail	2	F	11	1	2	1	9,155
Brass Robin	4	G	11	0	1	2	3,386
Brass Ruckus	4	C	8	2	3	2	4,720
Brass Ruhler	5	H	9	2	1	1	18,982
Brass Slots	4	F	3	0	0	0	738
Brass Support	7	M	3	1	0	0	17,050
Brass Tango	4	G	4	0	2	1	6,815
Brassy and Sunny	9	G	2	0	0	0	47
Brassy B	4	F	15	0	2	1	15,230
Brassy Babe	5	H	10	1	1	1	22,070
Brassy Fred	9	H	9	3	3	1	60,385
Brassy Karakorum	2	C	3	0	0	0	118
Brassy Kitten	2	F	3	0	0	1	5,740
Brassy Light	2	C	2	1	0	0	19,860
Brassy Nancy	3	F	12	3	3	2	32,797
Brassy Shirley	2	F	3	0	0	1	4,715
Brat	5	M	6	2	0	1	11,626
Brattle Square	4	F	8	1	0	2	9,310
Brattothecore	3	F	8	2	0	0	191,065
Braun Rennen	6	H	2	0	0	0	128
Bravaccio (IRE)	7	G	10	1	1	1	5,580
Brave	5	G	12	0	3	1	21,438
Brave All the Way	8	G	6	0	1	0	2,380
Brave Byars	3	G	10	4	2	0	130,620
Brave Claim	3	F	10	2	0	0	8,600
Brave Columbus	2	C	5	0	0	0	0
Brave Deal	4	F	4	0	0	0	207
Brave Guy	3	G	9	1	2	0	42,230
Brave Heartofclass	6	G	6	0	0	1	572
Brave Joe	3	G	9	1	0	2	16,580
Brave Legacy	10	G	1	0	0	0	260
Brave Miner	9	G	13	2	2	2	9,860
Brave Miss	3	F	7	2	0	2	47,221
Brave 'n Away	3	C	3	0	0	0	220
Brave New Dawn	6	H	7	2	2	1	12,925
Brave Oath	2	G	1	0	0	0	0
Brave One	6	G	13	3	1	3	52,620
Brave Opponent	6	M	19	6	3	1	42,491
Brave Pancho	9	G	8	0	0	0	2,124
Brave Prospect	6	G	11	0	1	3	5,378
Brave Sassafras	3	F	11	0	3	1	7,569
Brave Soldier	8	G	6	0	0	2	1,363

Horse	Age	Sex	Sts	1st	2d	3d	Won	Horse	Age	Sex	Sts	1st	2d	3d	Won
Brave Star	4	G	14	1	1	2	17,475	Brendon's Goal	3	G	11	0	1	3	4,633
Brave Vixen	2	F	4	1	0	0	31,938	Brenita's Princess	5	M	10	1	0	0	5,261
Bravehearted Lady	6	M	13	1	1	3	29,497	Brennan D	5	M	20	6	2	1	51,615
Bravely	4	G	8	2	2	2	128,390	Brennan the Kid	3	C	8	3	0	0	12,814
Bravo Brad	2	C	3	0	0	0	720	Brent Charger Time	2	G	2	0	0	0	235
Bravo Bull	6	H	4	0	0	0	790	Brentahni	4	F	3	0	0	0	436
Bravo Dome Cat	6	G	7	0	0	1	520	Brenta's Prospect	3	F	8	1	0	0	9,165
Bravo Ragasso (IRE)	3	G	13	3	0	1	19,370	Brent's Challanger	4	G	9	1	2	0	17,339
Bravo Romano	2	G	1	0	0	0	100	Brents Mercer	3	C	2	1	0	0	5,472
Bravo Valentino	3	C	10	0	1	0	1,955	Brent's Michael	10	G	13	2	0	3	11,589
Braxton's Yum Yum	4	G	9	1	0	2	4,618	Brent's Tune	6	H	10	1	2	4	12,110
Braytonville	2	F	2	0	0	1	5,000	Brent's Victory	4	G	11	3	2	1	47,145
Brazen Attitude	2	F	1	1	0	0	3,420	Brenzotti	3	F	6	1	0	0	6,015
Brazen Bomber	3	G	2	0	0	0	0	Brereton	5	G	3	2	0	0	35,600
Brazen Brandy	5	H	13	1	3	2	9,397	Bretelyn's Heart	4	F	1	0	0	0	0
Brazen Count	5	H	4	0	1	0	1,460	Brett 'n Butter	3	F	6	1	2	2	15,810
Brazen n' Bold	4	G	7	2	3	1	22,268	Brevard	3	F	9	1	0	0	3,154
Brazen Outlaw	3	C	2	1	0	0	5,934	Brew	7	G	3	0	0	0	1,553
Brazen Prospect	4	G	11	1	1	2	26,613	Brew a Slew	3	G	6	0	0	0	590
Brazen Star	2	C	4	0	0	1	6,930	Brewing Mischief	2	F	1	0	0	0	145
Brazen Virtue	3	F	2	0	0	0	0	Brewton	3	F	9	2	0	1	18,245
Brazil Nut	4	G	12	1	3	3	35,400	Brezing Time	6	G	2	0	0	0	0
Brazilian Mama	4	F	17	1	3	1	12,950	Brian Boru (GB)	3	C	6	1	1	2	664,844
Brazoom	4	F	1	0	0	0	0	Brian Dude	3	C	11	0	2	2	24,500
Brazos Shuttle	4	F	15	1	0	1	4,020	Brian Strikes Back	6	G	7	2	0	1	5,928
Breach of Promise	4	F	1	0	0	0	1,680	Briana's Spirit	2	F	1	0	0	0	50
Bread Basket	3	G	6	0	0	0	252	Brianelle	3	F	11	1	1	3	5,162
Breadknife	7	M	1	0	0	0	0	Brianmeister	3	G	6	1	0	0	2,005
Break of the Day	2	C	2	0	0	0	1,195	Brianna des Pins	6	M	3	1	0	1	4,620
Break Out	2	G	1	0	0	0	525	Briano	5	G	1	0	0	0	0
Break the Barrier	2	C	4	0	1	0	9,630	Brian's a Pro	3	C	2	1	0	0	27,240
Break the Clock	4	C	6	2	1	0	42,058	Brian's Dancer	7	H	13	3	4	0	29,422
Breakable Blush	4	F	14	1	4	1	18,609	Brian's Echo	4	G	12	1	1	1	44,502
Breakaway	2	C	6	1	3	0	48,475	Brians First	3	C	12	0	0	3	2,967
Breakaway Brad	4	G	4	0	0	0	3,851	Brian's Gold	3	G	3	0	0	0	460
Breakaway Quietly	5	G	9	5	2	0	39,762	Brians Joy	6	H	11	1	1	2	12,340
Breaker Boy Jack	5	G	6	1	0	0	7,282	Brian's Lassie	5	M	10	4	1	2	27,683
Breakfast At T's	3	F	11	3	3	1	30,065	Brian's Lil Bud	3	C	5	1	0	1	4,086
Breakfast Bar	3	F	3	0	0	0	0	Brians Move	3	F	10	1	2	1	20,770
Breakfast in Maui	4	G	3	1	0	0	15,340	Brian's Shot	5	G	6	1	0	0	7,066
Breaking News (GB)	5	H	2	0	0	0	122	Brian's Trust	3	G	13	1	1	1	6,835
Breakittomeeasily	6	M	10	1	2	0	11,506	Briar Knight	4	G	2	0	0	0	6,380
Breakneck Bailey	4	G	12	1	1	4	5,736	Briara	5	M	3	3	0	0	37,320
Breaku	3	F	4	0	0	0	0	Briartic Gold	6	G	14	6	2	1	59,248
Breanna's Smile	3	G	15	1	2	6	49,820	Briartic Jade	3	C	1	0	0	0	100
Breathe	3	F	1	0	0	1	935	Briarticslew	3	F	5	0	0	0	115
Breathless	6	G	11	0	5	2	12,245	Bribury	7	M	2	0	0	1	1,493
Breedy Mickey	6	H	13	1	6	2	24,280	Bric n' Bag	6	G	4	0	0	2	3,016
Breesonby	5	M	4	0	0	0	150	Brick Be Rich	4	G	3	0	0	0	0
Breeze Basket	6	M	10	0	2	2	1,624	Brick Cat	4	G	7	0	0	1	1,051
Breeze Catcher	4	C	9	1	1	3	11,595	Brick of Gold	6	G	4	0	0	0	718
Breeze the Weasel	7	M	12	0	1	2	6,846	Brick Salthouse	6	M	9	1	0	1	7,131
Breeze Town	2	F	1	0	0	0	1,572	Brick Um Up	3	G	4	0	0	0	0
Breezeaway	5	H	6	1	0	0	3,535	Brickabrack	6	G	13	3	1	3	32,355
Breezer	2	G	3	0	0	0	0	Brickell	2	C	4	0	0	0	7,620
Breezin Bella	6	H	9	0	2	0	1,185	Brickinthewall	3	C	2	0	0	0	0
Breezin On	5	H	9	1	0	3	11,404	Brick's	3	G	10	1	3	2	49,075
Breezin Tactics	5	H	2	0	0	0	664	Bricks Princess	3	F	16	2	6	1	14,876
Breezing Away	2	G	5	1	1	2	36,115	Bricktona	4	F	3	0	0	0	86
Breezing Bandit	8	G	13	2	3	5	16,411	Brickys First	3	F	10	0	0	0	1,801
Breezing Score	4	G	14	0	2	0	5,943	Bridal Ballad	5	M	10	1	0	2	12,705
Breezing Willow	3	F	1	0	0	0	0	Bridal Creek	3	C	8	0	5	0	3,524
Breeznthru	6	M	2	0	0	0	344	Bridal Gal	3	F	11	1	0	2	11,936
Breezy	3	F	2	0	0	0	2,580	Bridal Gown	6	M	4	0	0	0	103
Breezy Bray	3	F	6	1	0	0	18,030	Bridal Path	2	F	4	1	1	0	19,550
Breezy Bri	5	M	7	0	1	0	7,110	Bride N Groom	3	F	8	0	0	0	567
Breezy Bullette	4	F	19	3	3	6	11,571	Bridestone	3	C	8	1	1	0	14,295
Breezy Launch	3	M	3	0	0	0	228	Bridge	3	C	14	2	0	2	28,811
Breezy's Bay	2	F	1	0	0	0	0	Bridge Builder	3	C	9	2	2	1	44,825
Breezy's Lookin	2	C	1	0	0	0	0	Bridge Creek Bob	4	G	2	0	0	1	3,094
Brenda From Dixie	3	F	1	0	0	0	86	Bridge Jumper	3	C	11	2	1	2	40,130
Brenda n' Buck	7	G	3	0	0	0	150	Bridge Out Again	3	G	5	0	2	0	17,880
Brenda Smoke	4	F	2	0	0	0	120	Bridge Player	3	F	4	0	0	0	360
Brendabettysue	5	M	10	1	3	2	33,425	Bridge Technology	3	G	2	0	0	1	1,350
Brendan Mac	3	G	9	2	1	0	16,560	Bridge to Romance	3	G	4	1	2	0	13,594
Brendan's Aunt	3	F	13	1	0	4	26,019	Bridgepoint	4	C	2	0	0	0	0
Brendan's Gold	4	G	1	0	0	0	0	Bridger	9	G	2	0	1	0	5,460
Brenda's Angel	6	G	7	1	0	0	8,221	Bridges	5	H	9	0	0	0	320
Brendaswhinybrat	6	M	18	4	4	2	39,772	Bridgeside	3	C	1	0	0	0	0

RECORDS OF HORSES

Horse	Age	Sex	Sts	1st	2d	3d	Won	Horse	Age	Sex	Sts	1st	2d	3d	Won
Bridget Says	3	F	10	1	0	1	18,870	Brightest Ice	4	G	6	2	0	0	53,160
Bridgetown	8	G	5	0	0	0	390	Brightest Star	4	F	8	2	0	1	5,955
Bridget's Last	3	F	16	1	4	2	18,149	Brightly Decorated	5	H	7	0	0	1	2,295
Bridgetspoint	2	G	4	1	1	0	17,836	Brightly Victoria	2	F	2	0	0	0	213
Bridgewood	4	F	12	0	2	1	5,272	Brighton Belle	5	M	7	2	1	0	36,354
Bridie's Twist	3	F	14	0	0	2	3,602	Brighton Ridge	3	C	6	1	0	0	36,288
Bridle Bells	3	F	4	0	2	0	4,400	Brightside	3	F	2	0	0	0	2,700
Bridle Registry	2	F	2	0	0	0	260	Brightstar High	2	F	5	0	1	0	3,400
Bridlebit	3	F	6	1	1	0	10,045	Brightstone	4	G	12	2	3	3	40,485
Bridled Gold	4	G	10	1	1	1	4,790	Brightwood Beau	5	H	3	0	0	0	165
Bridlespur	4	G	19	1	4	1	10,825	Brill	3	G	9	0	2	0	4,261
Bridlestone	3	F	6	1	1	3	31,900	Brill Pace	4	C	1	0	0	0	156
Bridletime	4	R	13	3	1	2	13,691	Brilliant Asset	4	F	12	4	2	1	36,015
Brieanna's Boy	3	C	2	1	0	1	16,043	Brilliant Beau	2	C	9	1	1	3	31,165
Brief Affair	3	F	12	2	2	1	14,244	Brilliant Bettina	3	F	6	0	0	3	7,250
Brief Attire	2	F	1	0	0	0	0	Brilliant Blend	5	H	3	0	0	0	500
Brief Blues	7	G	7	1	0	3	14,432	Brilliant Bluff	5	G	4	1	1	1	5,096
Brief Infatuation	3	C	2	0	0	0	0	Brilliant Bride	2	F	2	0	0	0	950
Brief Intoxication	3	F	12	1	1	3	33,210	Brilliant Buffy	3	F	11	2	1	0	9,540
Brief Kiss	6	M	3	0	0	2	1,790	Brilliant Dancer	6	H	1	0	0	0	0
Brief Message	5	G	5	1	0	1	12,840	Brilliant Deniro	6	H	4	0	1	2	3,710
Brief Statement	5	M	6	0	0	0	183	Brilliant End	5	G	5	1	1	1	23,860
Brief Time Machine	5	H	13	1	0	2	4,244	Brilliant for Sure	4	F	5	0	0	1	735
Brief Valentine	7	M	2	0	0	1	1,946	Brilliant Jewel	3	F	9	1	3	2	14,580
Briefcase Girl	4	F	9	0	0	1	4,524	Brilliant Joke	4	G	11	2	0	0	19,075
Briefchic	6	M	16	2	0	4	12,175	Brilliant Mistake	2	F	2	0	0	0	280
Briefdiamond	5	M	17	1	0	0	8,246	Brilliant Move	3	F	4	1	2	0	52,880
Briefly	6	M	10	0	4	1	7,354	Brilliant Music	6	H	13	1	1	2	9,510
Briefly Mythical	5	G	9	0	2	1	7,245	Brilliant Sermon	3	G	17	0	2	4	23,312
Brielle Landing	10	G	7	1	1	1	7,725	Brilliant Storm	7	H	6	1	1	0	4,107
Brier Blaze	5	G	8	1	1	1	7,069	Brilliant Stretch	8	G	4	0	0	1	560
Brigade	7	H	3	2	1	0	12,475	Brilliant Touch	4	F	9	1	1	2	9,559
Brigader	2	C	2	0	0	0	2,442	Brilliantly	7	G	1	0	0	0	0
Brigadier Jones (IRE)	4	G	1	0	0	0	0	Brilliantly Bright	5	M	3	0	0	0	162
Brigadier Star	4	G	7	1	0	0	6,861	Brillig	8	M	5	1	1	0	6,225
Brigadoon	3	F	11	4	3	1	28,172	Brim Storm	4	G	12	0	0	2	3,205
Brigette's Dream	2	F	2	1	0	0	26,705	Brimson	3	C	6	0	1	0	3,500
Brighid	3	F	1	0	0	0	582	Brimstone	4	G	11	2	1	2	55,352
Bright Abraxis	3	F	2	0	0	0	0	Brimstone Tough	5	G	7	1	1	1	10,515
Bright Accent	2	G	6	0	0	1	1,852	Bring Him Gold	2	G	2	1	0	0	8,835
Bright Advised	4	G	12	0	0	0	1,653	Bring Home Thegold	5	G	3	0	1	0	14,500
Bright and Shiny	2	F	4	1	0	0	20,030	Bring On the Crown	2	F	4	0	0	1	2,694
Bright Anna	3	F	2	0	0	1	1,950	Bring On the Music	4	F	3	0	1	0	5,600
Bright Appeal	3	F	4	0	0	2	764	Bring Out the Best	3	C	5	0	0	2	9,430
Bright Big Star	3	G	1	0	0	0	0	Bring to Order	3	F	4	0	0	0	0
Bright Blaze	2	G	6	1	0	0	10,200	Bringdownthehouse	6	G	9	0	2	2	11,790
Bright Briana	3	F	12	3	0	1	33,137	Bringem Jung	4	G	15	1	2	2	28,308
Bright Cat	5	H	1	0	0	0	0	Bringhomethelot	4	F	13	1	3	1	12,069
Bright Day	5	M	4	0	0	0	1,522	Bringmesomemoney	4	G	7	1	2	1	5,670
Bright Diplomat	4	F	21	7	6	1	57,984	Bringontherain	3	F	4	0	0	0	1,395
Bright Flame	3	F	13	4	4	1	27,504	Brini Baby	9	M	4	0	0	1	1,500
Bright Future	2	G	5	0	0	1	850	Brinton Bridge	8	G	9	3	0	4	53,790
Bright Galax	2	G	6	1	0	2	4,535	Briony	2	F	2	0	0	0	990
Bright Gold	3	F	4	1	1	0	21,730	Bri's Bad Boy	4	G	11	3	3	1	15,182
Bright Green	5	G	8	0	1	1	4,380	Brisa	8	M	10	2	1	1	16,748
Bright Harbor	4	C	6	3	0	0	36,100	Brishane	3	G	1	0	0	0	840
Bright Knight	4	F	9	2	4	1	134,269	Brishlin	6	M	9	2	1	0	17,178
Bright Legacy	3	F	9	0	2	0	3,855	Brisk Bartok	2	F	3	0	0	0	1,260
Bright Little Star	4	F	7	0	0	1	2,373	Briskie	2	G	1	0	0	0	0
Bright Mike	2	C	2	0	0	1	5,955	Brisote	5	G	3	0	0	0	0
Bright N Foxy	2	F	1	0	0	0	0	Brisquette	5	M	6	0	1	3	59,355
Bright Path	7	M	5	0	0	0	540	Bristoe Star	4	G	6	0	0	0	576
Bright Poppy	2	C	2	0	0	0	0	Bristolville	7	G	3	0	1	1	7,700
Bright Reagent	2	F	1	0	0	0	0	Brit	3	C	1	0	0	0	0
Bright Reward	10	G	1	0	0	0	0	Brit Kay	5	M	9	1	0	1	10,258
Bright Sea	4	G	3	0	0	1	5,970	Brite Avie	5	M	6	0	0	2	2,485
Bright Shiny Coin	5	H	1	0	0	0	0	Brite Badger	4	G	5	0	1	2	2,449
Bright Sky (IRE)	4	F	6	1	1	2	303,832	Brite Belle	5	G	1	0	0	0	150
Bright Spirit	2	F	5	0	0	0	200	Brite Betty	3	F	7	3	0	1	100,920
Bright Star Busted	2	G	1	0	0	0	0	Brite Bounty	5	G	16	5	0	5	44,030
Bright Stout	5	G	7	1	0	1	2,302	Brite Colony	4	G	1	0	0	0	0
Bright Thunder	9	M	10	0	2	2	7,402	Brite Colors	3	F	7	2	0	2	45,453
Bright Valour	7	H	7	2	2	0	74,208	Brite Dancer	5	M	13	0	0	1	2,770
Bright Village	3	G	11	1	2	1	13,896	Brite Delite	2	F	2	0	0	0	0
Brighten My Day	4	F	8	0	2	1	8,802	Brite Donna	2	F	4	0	2	0	4,665
Brighter Blue	6	M	19	4	2	0	34,560	Brite F X	4	F	17	4	3	2	21,643
Brighter Days	9	G	3	0	0	0	840	Brite Future	6	G	18	2	4	3	19,943
Brighter Than Air	9	M	9	0	1	0	1,305	Brite Hope	5	G	4	2	0	1	15,988
Brightest Hour	3	G	10	0	2	2	12,061	Brite Horizon	5	M	18	1	2	2	8,153

Horse	Age	Sex	Sts	1st	2d	3d	Won
Brite Lark	2	F	1	0	0	0	0
Brite Lassie	2	F	3	0	1	0	5,460
Brite Manner	5	H	2	0	0	2	3,194
Brite Memory	2	C	4	0	1	1	7,480
Brite Message	3	C	7	0	0	1	672
Brite Nite	6	G	4	2	1	0	3,607
Brite Reality	6	G	1	0	0	0	100
Brite Road	6	M	9	2	0	0	22,841
Brite Rock Too	2	G	10	0	1	3	11,267
Brite Roxie	2	F	6	1	1	1	26,600
Brite Steel	3	F	11	4	0	2	10,724
Brite Sunny Day	4	F	9	2	1	2	135,856
Brite Thrill	3	F	9	1	0	3	2,891
Brite Valentin	5	G	16	2	1	2	9,012
Briteliteinthenite	3	G	7	1	0	0	30,469
Britetonzmyday	4	F	2	0	0	0	1,560
British Blue	3	C	1	0	0	1	4,680
Britnee's Bouquet	3	F	12	1	1	0	6,841
Britomartis	2	F	6	0	0	2	4,180
Brit's Belle	4	F	9	1	1	1	8,198
Britt and Brist	5	H	1	0	0	0	0
Brittan	5	G	11	0	0	2	1,433
Brittanic	5	H	2	0	0	0	405
Brittany Bay	2	F	6	2	0	0	14,625
Brittany River	3	F	8	0	0	1	988
Brittany's Buck	5	M	3	0	1	1	3,255
Brittanys First	2	F	8	1	0	3	13,552
Brittney's Secret	4	F	3	0	0	1	630
Britt's Aloha	4	C	10	0	1	0	4,415
Britt's Babe	4	F	7	2	1	1	12,874
Britts Bouquet	5	M	3	0	0	0	136
Britt's Jules	2	G	8	3	0	2	50,898
Britts Signal	2	C	2	0	0	0	600
Britts Xpress	4	C	4	0	1	0	1,080
Brizard	5	G	2	0	0	0	0
Bro Raja	6	G	11	3	1	1	33,233
Broad Breadth	4	F	7	1	2	1	7,752
Broad Concern	4	G	7	0	0	0	1,010
Broad Creek	5	M	16	2	0	3	20,655
Broad Dot Com	6	G	9	1	1	1	4,628
Broad Elegance	4	G	7	3	1	0	21,888
Broad Focus	3	F	6	0	0	0	195
Broad Gale	3	F	8	3	0	1	33,060
Broad Hopes	3	F	8	3	1	1	101,280
Broad Initiative	5	G	8	1	0	3	7,475
Broad N Best	4	C	1	0	0	0	960
Broad Nature	4	G	10	1	2	1	7,027
Broad Picture	4	F	7	1	1	1	47,021
Broad Sanctions	3	G	6	1	1	0	7,920
Broad Scheme	3	F	7	0	0	2	7,080
Broad Spirit	4	C	2	0	0	0	350
Broad Strike	3	F	1	0	0	1	2,750
Broad Stripes	4	F	7	0	1	2	2,865
Broad Sweep	2	G	1	0	0	0	0
Broad Touch	3	G	3	0	0	0	0
Broad Trust	5	H	3	0	0	0	2,355
Broad Victory	6	M	2	1	0	0	5,985
Broad Vision	5	G	13	2	1	3	14,476
Broadside	7	G	10	4	0	1	9,574
Broadway Bernie	2	C	2	1	0	0	7,800
Broadway Bull	3	G	12	1	2	0	17,551
Broadway Buzz	3	C	8	2	1	1	48,340
Broadway Deb	3	F	6	1	0	1	13,860
Broadway Director	4	F	5	1	0	1	9,311
Broadway Flash	3	F	3	2	0	1	2,100
Broadway Jerry	4	G	4	1	0	0	10,800
Broadway Johnny	5	G	15	2	4	0	44,472
Broadway Lady	4	F	6	1	1	2	46,453
Broadway Mac	2	G	3	0	0	0	0
Broadway Mischief	4	G	1	0	0	0	50
Broadway Phill	4	G	4	0	0	0	570
Broadway Show	6	H	6	1	2	0	24,600
Broadway Slew	4	C	4	0	0	1	5,155
Broadway Snowman	6	G	6	0	3	0	19,730
Broadway Stenz	5	H	3	1	0	0	4,245
Broadway View	2	C	7	1	2	0	22,887
Broadway's Niece	9	M	9	0	1	0	4,495
Brobbel	4	G	11	1	0	1	6,326
Brocco Baby	5	M	11	1	0	3	4,932
Brocco Bob	5	G	2	1	0	0	7,200
Brocco Bry	6	G	16	3	2	0	64,865
Brocco Gold Strike	5	G	13	2	2	3	23,225
Broccoboy	5	G	6	1	0	2	13,275
Brocco's Magick	7	G	9	0	1	1	2,535
Brocco's Return	5	M	5	0	0	0	900
Brocco's Rhapsody	5	G	7	1	0	1	4,153
Broccos Secret	5	M	1	0	0	0	320
Brochure	3	C	13	1	1	0	10,406
Brocky's Dream (AUS)	5	M	9	2	1	0	76,631
Brodnicki	2	F	4	1	0	0	12,792
Brodrick	7	G	15	1	1	2	21,520
Brogan's Dragon	5	G	6	0	0	1	1,162
Brogdens Girl	3	F	3	0	0	0	177
Broke Again	3	G	5	0	2	1	19,080
Broke But Stylin	4	G	15	4	2	3	62,165
Broke Egg	5	M	9	1	0	0	3,913
Broke First	3	G	13	2	2	1	27,850
Broke in Blairsden	5	M	8	1	1	3	84,904
Broke Spoke	8	G	14	2	1	1	9,796
Broke the Record	4	G	10	1	2	2	22,445
Broke the Rules	3	F	10	1	0	0	3,127
Broke to Fight	3	C	6	3	0	0	15,940
Broke Trying	2	F	2	0	0	0	45
Broke Us	2	G	3	0	0	1	2,405
Broke Wild	6	M	11	0	1	0	899
Broken Aero	3	G	2	0	0	0	0
Broken Jaw	6	H	12	1	3	3	13,217
Broken Monarch	3	C	7	0	1	0	8,320
Broken Ring	4	F	3	1	0	0	9,000
Broken Star	2	C	1	0	0	0	182
Brokenhearted Cat	2	F	1	1	0	0	13,800
Brokenheartsville	2	F	2	0	0	1	1,100
Broker Assault	3	C	2	0	0	0	500
Brokerage	3	G	12	2	1	3	24,880
Broker's Bonus	2	F	5	1	0	1	5,770
Bronc	3	G	10	0	2	0	13,252
Bronco Billy Bay	9	G	5	1	0	0	1,805
Bronco Brandon	4	G	13	2	2	1	18,385
Bronco Buster	3	C	14	2	2	1	20,027
Bronsonstorm	4	C	1	0	0	0	63
Bronwyn	3	F	14	2	3	2	23,340
Bronx	4	G	3	0	0	0	336
Bronxville Doll	7	M	5	0	0	0	224
Bronxville Express	4	F	6	0	3	1	9,080
Bronze Abe	4	F	9	3	2	1	123,214
Bronze Autumn	4	F	2	0	0	0	2,970
Bronze Bayou	4	G	9	3	2	1	172,146
Bronze Cathedral	6	G	10	1	0	1	5,332
Bronze Defrere	6	G	7	0	0	1	1,759
Bronze Magic	6	G	6	1	0	0	6,814
Bronze Route	2	F	1	1	0	0	26,400
Bronze Sword	2	F	3	0	0	0	900
Bronzed	8	G	1	0	0	0	0
Brook the Wind	4	G	17	3	4	1	44,120
Brookamous	3	F	1	0	0	0	0
Brooke's Bubble	4	F	9	4	1	2	45,500
Brooke's Dancer	2	F	2	0	0	0	2,604
Brookes Trick	4	G	7	2	1	2	24,736
Brookfield Miss	6	M	3	0	0	0	206
Brookland Wood	3	G	2	0	0	0	1,460
Brooklyn Bull	7	G	4	0	1	0	6,130
Brooklyn Farmer	2	G	2	1	0	0	5,604
Brooklyn Way	4	C	5	0	0	1	1,496
Brook's Blaze	3	G	16	1	3	1	26,829
Brooksbobnbucky	6	G	9	3	2	1	9,174
Brookside Drive	4	G	8	1	3	0	11,885
Brookston	6	H	16	0	0	1	11,325
Brookstreet	3	G	12	2	0	0	14,551
Brooksville	2	C	8	0	0	2	3,215
Brookville	3	G	3	0	0	0	230
Broom	4	G	4	0	1	1	4,745
Broom Hilda	4	F	4	0	0	0	192
Broomville	4	F	20	1	3	6	15,547
Brother	6	H	1	0	0	0	0
Brother Andruw	2	G	2	0	0	0	0
Brother Babe	7	G	2	0	0	0	116
Brother Ballado	5	G	1	0	0	0	120
Brother Blaise	8	G	5	0	0	0	510

Horse	Age	Sex	Sts	1st	2d	3d	Won	Horse	Age	Sex	Sts	1st	2d	3d	Won
Brother Blen	3	G	2	0	2	0	6,240	Brushed Charm	4	F	3	0	0	0	840
Brother Bob	6	H	3	1	0	0	7,055	Brushed Ice	3	C	2	0	1	0	11,760
Brother Butch	4	G	5	1	2	1	7,542	Brushed Up	3	G	18	1	2	1	19,501
Brother Darcy	7	G	10	3	3	0	50,101	Brushed With Glory	3	G	4	1	0	1	15,340
Brother Harry	5	H	1	0	0	0	56	Brushedbythebest	6	G	1	0	0	0	0
Brother Huz	8	H	7	2	1	2	7,663	Brusher	6	G	8	0	2	0	3,892
Brother Indy	4	G	10	0	3	2	3,005	Brushher	2	F	2	1	0	0	6,600
Brother Love	7	G	10	1	3	1	29,960	Brushing Bully	5	G	4	0	0	1	12,273
Brother Pat	4	G	5	1	2	0	66,900	Brusque	3	F	3	0	0	0	4,500
Brother Rabbit	7	H	6	1	1	2	8,266	Brutal	4	C	10	3	1	1	41,329
Brother Skip	3	C	6	0	0	1	1,200	Brut's Boomin	3	G	7	1	2	0	9,162
Brother Slocum	4	G	12	4	4	2	23,296	Brutus Maximus	3	G	5	0	0	1	1,445
Brother Steve	3	G	1	0	1	0	1,500	Bruzer Com Stock	3	G	3	0	0	0	288
Brother Tar Heel	3	G	2	0	0	0	87	Bryans Hope	4	C	7	0	0	2	2,205
Brother Walt	4	G	15	0	1	4	6,200	Bryan's Love	2	G	1	0	0	0	0
Brother's Bluff	4	F	1	0	0	0	405	Bryan's Pick	6	G	12	1	0	3	12,421
Brothers Gold	3	G	2	0	0	0	690	Bryanzole'	4	G	11	1	1	1	15,242
Brother's Sister	2	F	10	1	3	1	15,120	Bryce	2	F	2	0	0	0	0
Broughshane	5	M	8	2	1	0	63,200	Bryden's Babe	7	M	4	0	0	1	634
Brown Baron	4	G	2	0	0	0	0	Brymic's Treasure	3	G	11	1	1	3	19,587
Brown Chequer	4	G	10	2	1	2	32,270	Brynes Girls	4	F	9	2	0	1	14,980
Brown Dusty	3	F	5	0	1	1	2,405	Brynhild	6	H	4	0	0	0	390
Brown Eyed Beauty	4	F	10	4	4	2	201,350	Bryns Finale	4	F	3	0	0	0	808
Brown Eyed Lady	5	M	8	1	1	1	18,138	B's Big Boy	3	G	9	1	1	0	3,914
Brown Eyed Major	7	G	9	3	2	1	56,175	B's Choice	5	G	10	1	1	1	9,302
Brown Eyed Mini	3	F	11	2	1	2	23,901	Bs Golden Mop	3	G	3	0	0	0	612
Brown Eyed Miss	3	F	10	1	4	1	52,836	B's Lil Champ	3	G	7	0	1	1	1,836
Brown Eyed Sugar	3	F	9	2	1	0	7,450	B's Playboy	5	H	3	0	1	0	1,263
Brown Gold T I D	4	C	1	0	0	0	0	Bu Bba Be a Star	3	F	2	0	0	0	79
Brown Id Girl	3	M	9	0	1	2	6,601	Bub	3	G	2	0	0	0	2,625
Brown Jet	3	G	10	1	2	2	8,406	Buba's Caper	6	M	14	0	5	5	39,238
Brown Lad (FR)	10	G	4	0	0	3	11,000	Bubba Appeal	5	H	16	2	2	0	5,681
Brown Native	3	G	14	1	0	1	4,697	Bubba Black	3	G	8	1	0	1	3,859
Brown Rouge	4	F	10	2	2	1	33,833	Bubba Boom Boom	4	G	6	0	0	0	388
Brown Screen	4	G	20	2	1	2	16,448	Bubba Gump	10	H	7	0	3	3	2,148
Brown Spanish Eyes	6	M	3	0	0	0	0	Bubba Hyde	3	C	11	2	1	5	66,635
Brown Whiskey	4	C	3	3	0	0	11,748	Bubba Sparks	2	C	5	1	1	0	39,640
Brownbottleflu	7	G	2	0	0	0	0	Bubbah	3	G	4	0	0	0	828
Browneyed Hansuman	2	C	2	1	0	0	7,500	Bubbalou	4	G	4	0	0	1	3,152
Browns Velvet	6	M	14	0	0	2	6,993	Bubba's Colors	5	G	11	0	2	0	21,670
Brownsmill	2	F	5	0	0	0	460	Bubba's Doll House	2	G	2	0	1	0	2,870
Brownstown	3	C	10	1	1	0	6,210	Bubba's Gumby	4	G	2	0	0	0	610
Brrneedfur	2	F	2	0	0	0	460	Bubbasgotadance	4	G	11	1	1	1	3,491
Bruanna	5	M	14	4	2	1	134,408	Bubbawontwork	4	C	5	0	0	0	279
Bruce's Comet	7	H	2	0	0	0	0	Bubbawuzdrinkun	2	F	4	0	0	1	712
Bruce's Way	3	G	4	0	0	1	1,750	Bubbe Bets	3	F	4	0	0	0	1,005
Bruceton	3	C	3	0	1	1	15,680	Bubble Dourbon	3	F	6	2	2	0	23,791
Brucker's Brother	4	G	5	0	0	0	2,390	Bubble Economy	4	G	8	3	1	0	31,950
Bruheria	3	F	2	1	0	1	35,760	Bubblegum Kid	5	G	9	0	1	3	25,909
Bruise Control	5	G	10	3	2	0	27,440	Bubblegum Red	4	F	16	1	3	1	4,454
Bruiser	4	C	10	2	4	1	89,625	Bubbleoni	2	F	5	0	0	0	1,161
Bruja Negra	2	F	6	0	0	1	2,284	Bubbles Cachet	4	F	10	2	0	0	39,880
Brule River	5	G	9	1	3	2	20,760	Bubble's Girl	4	F	7	3	0	0	21,740
Brummy	5	G	17	3	3	4	39,880	Bubbles McGruder	4	F	4	0	0	1	1,587
Brunall	4	G	3	0	0	0	111	Bubbles N Bliss	3	F	8	0	4	2	22,785
Brundy	5	G	4	0	1	1	2,355	Bubbles of Navaron	3	F	3	0	0	0	182
Bruneau Dunes	5	M	9	1	0	1	3,925	Bubbly	3	F	5	0	1	0	2,710
Bruneau Time	5	M	1	0	0	0	1,500	Bubbly Brooke	5	M	7	0	0	1	2,348
Brunella	2	F	2	0	0	0	3,280	Bubby's Bag	3	F	8	2	1	2	14,591
Bruney	3	C	17	1	6	4	60,420	Bub's First Dance	3	G	8	0	2	0	8,622
Brunfelsia	6	M	11	0	0	4	2,911	Bub's Towne Starr	4	F	7	0	0	1	1,530
Bruno Castelli	8	H	2	0	0	0	1,950	Bub's Turn	7	G	9	1	0	1	5,599
Bruno the Dog	8	G	10	0	0	1	1,450	Bubu Cat	2	C	4	0	0	0	1,440
Brunswick Belle	5	M	5	0	0	1	1,763	Bubwiser	2	F	2	1	1	0	5,900
Brunswick Light	6	H	15	2	4	2	13,242	Buc Fan	2	G	6	1	1	1	7,125
Brunswick Sue	6	M	12	1	2	3	7,660	Buccaneer Babe	3	F	15	3	4	2	64,641
Brunswood	4	G	8	1	0	1	13,185	Buccaneer Fever	2	G	3	0	0	0	485
Brush	5	G	10	0	4	1	33,855	Buccaneer Pete	5	G	14	0	2	0	8,599
Brush Ahead	3	C	9	2	0	2	43,380	Buck a Shot	3	F	7	1	0	2	9,800
Brush Arbor	4	F	3	0	0	0	280	Buck and Julio	3	G	9	0	1	0	3,947
Brush Country	3	C	7	1	0	0	2,538	Buck City	5	G	7	3	1	1	8,798
Brush Hour	3	F	7	1	1	1	20,110	Buck for Luck	2	C	4	1	0	0	13,140
Brush Up	3	C	5	1	0	0	16,830	Buck Grove	6	H	10	0	0	0	0
Brush With Destiny	2	F	5	1	0	1	82,610	Buck Henry	3	G	16	1	1	2	10,896
Brush With Glory	9	G	8	1	0	0	4,452	Buck Lucky	10	G	2	0	0	0	125
Brush With Gold	3	G	9	1	1	1	18,040	Buck Magruder	4	C	8	0	3	0	5,751
Brushabybaby	2	F	4	1	0	0	5,370	Buck Mountain	4	F	14	2	3	5	111,900
Brushed Aside	3	C	11	1	0	0	10,765	Buck One	4	G	10	1	0	2	4,655
Brushed by the Law	4	F	5	0	1	0	3,560	Buck Parrish	4	C	8	2	2	1	11,258

Horse	Age	Sex	Sts	1st	2d	3d	Won
Buck Raja	5	G	20	1	2	3	7,054
Buck Snort	3	G	12	2	0	1	3,766
Buck Stops Here	5	G	12	1	2	2	13,441
Buck the Tiger	2	G	8	0	1	2	4,750
Buck Trail	5	G	13	3	3	2	21,413
Buck Trout's Niece	2	F	1	0	0	0	480
Buck Two	5	H	9	0	0	2	1,754
Buck Wild	5	H	1	0	0	0	53
Buckaroo Bandit	6	G	4	0	0	0	0
Buckaroo Boy	3	G	6	1	1	0	8,200
Buckaroo Miss	7	M	7	1	1	0	11,566
Buckaroon	3	C	9	0	0	0	884
Buckaroo's Jazz	5	M	8	2	1	1	12,373
Buckaroo's Magic	7	G	13	4	4	1	54,378
Buckaroot	3	G	3	0	0	0	73
Buckbeak	3	G	3	1	0	1	2,160
Buckdancer	11	G	5	0	0	0	0
Bucket o' Luck	5	H	4	1	0	0	5,700
Buckey Boy	4	C	1	0	0	0	0
Buckeye Bates	6	G	7	4	1	2	54,436
Buckeye Bert	5	G	8	1	3	1	24,216
Buckeye Buckaroo	5	G	5	1	0	0	6,505
Buckeye Bunk	6	H	4	0	0	0	430
Buckeye Fever	2	G	7	0	0	0	3,033
Buckeye Pride	4	F	12	1	0	2	5,517
Buckeye's Regret	7	G	13	1	1	2	11,524
Buckeyhaswings	3	C	3	1	1	1	6,570
Buckhari	6	G	6	0	1	1	13,077
Buckharo	4	G	10	1	1	4	20,364
Buckies Exclusive	4	G	10	0	2	2	2,016
Buckies Lady	7	M	10	0	0	4	3,103
Buckin Bronc	2	G	1	0	0	0	125
Buckingham Tower	5	G	6	0	0	0	459
Buckland Manor	3	C	7	4	1	1	154,320
Buckle Down Ben	5	H	6	2	0	1	26,803
Buckle Up Cart	2	F	11	0	0	1	7,630
Buckmeister	2	G	3	0	0	0	0
Buckmier	6	G	6	0	0	0	310
Buckmont (ARG)	6	G	7	1	1	0	7,730
Buckmountaincreek	5	H	18	3	5	1	42,102
Buck'n and Duck'n	5	G	12	1	2	1	17,381
Buckner Bert	3	G	6	0	1	0	3,666
Buck'n'pearl	4	F	11	0	2	1	3,651
Bucko Wins	6	G	6	0	2	0	5,520
Buck's Appeal	2	C	6	0	0	1	3,640
Bucks Away	3	G	2	0	1	0	546
Buck's Banner	2	G	8	0	0	1	1,491
Buck's Best	5	M	1	0	0	0	0
Buck's Best Boy	7	G	7	0	0	0	1,665
Bucks County Fred	4	G	10	2	1	0	58,200
Bucks for Amos	7	G	2	0	0	0	122
Buck's Glory	7	M	13	1	0	0	7,801
Buck's Home	4	C	8	0	0	1	960
Buck's Jack	3	G	9	0	0	0	1,127
Buck's Lad	4	C	11	2	1	3	11,398
Bucks Little Bean	3	G	7	2	0	0	14,230
Buck's Little Imij	3	G	4	1	0	0	9,130
Buck's Lucky Star	3	F	2	0	0	0	181
Buck's Lullaby	2	F	4	0	0	0	640
Bucks Only	7	G	4	1	0	1	5,126
Buck's Out Again	9	G	6	0	1	1	1,190
Buck's Pal	3	C	11	1	2	1	30,690
Buck's Point	3	C	1	0	0	0	39
Buck's Shar	2	F	11	0	0	0	4,369
Buck's Sunrise	4	G	4	0	0	0	244
Bucks Superstar	6	M	9	1	1	2	7,181
Bucks War	10	G	11	1	0	2	15,580
Buck's Wild Spirit	4	F	1	0	0	0	85
Bucksbrighteststar	4	C	10	2	2	0	57,688
Bucksdancinmalay	3	F	1	0	0	0	0
Bucksemeralddancer	4	F	1	0	0	0	60
Buckshot John	6	G	18	3	0	1	13,956
Buckshot Rabbit	3	C	8	0	0	0	468
Buckskin	3	G	4	0	0	0	1,818
Buckskin Baby	4	F	14	1	1	4	17,405
Bucksome Girl	3	F	9	0	1	2	6,217
Buckstar	6	M	2	0	0	0	135
Bucksweep	4	G	7	2	1	0	17,552
Bucktown Tom	4	C	7	0	1	0	1,741
Buckuphenry	3	G	4	1	1	0	2,175
Buckwheat	2	C	3	0	0	0	420
Bucky Be Fast	3	G	4	0	0	0	579
Bucky Blue	7	G	2	0	0	0	0
Bucky the Bear	3	G	2	0	0	0	0
Bucky the Pirate	4	G	8	1	0	0	4,998
Buckye	3	G	3	0	0	0	0
Buckymikgrif	3	G	12	1	3	2	14,295
Bucky's Lass	2	F	1	0	0	0	0
Bucky's Line	6	M	8	1	1	1	6,076
Buckystrick	2	C	1	0	0	0	55
Bucquista	6	M	9	1	1	1	33,211
Bucsunday	7	H	3	0	0	1	220
Bucyrus	2	C	1	0	0	0	0
Bud Chaffee	3	G	10	4	1	2	76,486
Bud Crainer	2	C	3	0	0	1	2,185
Bud Kin	4	C	2	0	0	0	0
Bud Longneck	3	C	7	0	0	2	1,645
Bud Man Bill	3	G	5	1	0	1	4,216
Bud Wyse Blur	6	G	8	1	1	1	5,390
Budapest Girl	4	F	11	0	1	4	33,100
Budds Landing	3	G	2	0	0	0	0
Buddstark	7	G	2	1	0	0	6,199
Buddy Baby	4	G	4	0	0	0	549
Buddy Baquero	2	G	2	0	0	0	0
Buddy Belle	3	F	7	0	0	0	482
Buddy Gil	3	G	6	3	0	0	668,730
Buddy of Mine	5	G	10	3	1	2	32,648
Buddy Puddy	4	G	13	1	1	6	12,213
Buddy Ug	3	G	2	0	0	0	0
Buddy Victor	4	C	3	0	0	0	0
Buddy Wiser	3	G	9	1	0	0	11,510
Bude 'Em	6	M	14	2	2	1	14,276
Budget Bob	4	G	7	0	1	3	9,225
Bud's Bayou	4	G	22	1	4	0	10,568
Buds Boy	3	G	5	0	0	0	0
Bud's Magic	5	G	10	2	1	3	90,212
Bud's Move	3	G	12	0	0	0	798
Bue Moon	3	F	5	1	1	2	7,796
Buellton	6	G	19	4	5	1	26,676
Buenobambino	3	F	13	1	2	2	13,616
Buenos Dias	9	G	4	0	3	0	37,660
Buff 'n Polish	2	F	3	0	0	0	1,980
Buff Naked	2	C	2	0	0	0	120
Buffalo	5	M	1	0	0	0	620
Buffalo Bob	6	H	5	1	0	1	12,709
Buffalo Boy	8	G	6	1	1	2	1,279
Buffalo Dance	4	F	12	1	1	2	28,070
Buffalo Girl	5	M	13	1	4	3	5,010
Buffalo Jump	3	F	5	0	1	2	53,253
Buffalo River	4	G	9	1	4	1	7,584
Buffalo Soldier	3	C	16	4	2	5	41,250
Buffy Bluegrazz	5	M	1	0	0	0	0
Buffy My Love	2	F	1	0	0	0	0
Buffy the Slayer	2	F	1	0	0	0	0
Buffythecenterfold	3	F	7	2	2	2	228,815
Bufon	3	G	6	0	0	1	3,381
Bug Eyed Misty	3	F	9	3	1	0	14,710
Bug in a Bottle	4	C	13	1	4	2	13,945
Bug River	10	H	3	0	2	0	6,300
Bugalu Girl	5	M	16	1	1	1	7,472
Bugster	5	H	2	1	0	0	6,000
Bugsy Marrone	2	F	7	5	0	1	94,098
Bugsy N Tuff	5	H	7	0	2	1	3,516
Bugwiser	4	F	7	1	0	1	23,530
Bugzy Boy	3	C	1	0	0	0	116
Buhl	7	G	3	0	0	0	215
Buie's Legacy	3	F	8	1	2	0	7,378
Buildaparty	2	C	7	1	0	1	15,424
Built to Last	2	G	7	1	1	2	18,420
Built Up	5	G	9	3	0	1	169,539
Builtforhumanity	2	F	3	1	0	0	18,015
Bujones	8	H	5	0	2	2	3,906
Buju	3	C	2	1	0	1	35,590
Bukat Timah (GB)	3	F	3	2	0	0	49,022
Bukowski	4	G	12	2	2	2	22,927
Bulacan	7	G	11	1	1	0	9,018
Bulette's Bullet	5	G	11	1	0	0	6,644
Bull Bat	7	G	13	3	5	2	35,850

Horse	Age	Sex	Sts	1st	2d	3d	Won
Bull Buster	4	F	12	3	1	1	12,802
Bull Creek	10	G	9	1	0	1	8,492
Bull Halsey	7	G	2	1	1	0	11,700
Bull Head	3	C	7	1	0	2	13,610
Bull Headed Harry	3	C	10	1	1	3	23,360
Bull Leave It	5	G	11	2	0	0	11,468
Bull Moon	3	C	1	0	0	0	220
Bull N Bob	2	G	3	0	0	0	0
Bull O Indiana	4	G	7	0	0	0	383
Bull of Bush	3	C	3	0	0	1	1,100
Bull Pen	4	C	4	0	0	1	1,259
Bull Shooter	4	G	11	2	2	0	19,203
Bull Tai	5	G	16	1	1	4	11,034
Bulldog George	4	G	13	6	2	2	154,515
Bulldozer	4	G	10	1	0	1	8,575
Bullero	5	G	6	0	1	1	1,508
Bullet Again	5	G	18	2	3	0	16,111
Bullet Catcher	4	G	8	0	0	1	1,094
Bullet Gone West	2	C	1	0	0	0	0
Bullet Gulch	2	C	9	1	2	2	34,176
Bullet Jay Bird	4	C	10	2	1	1	29,262
Bullet Proof	9	G	10	2	1	2	9,393
Bullet Rocket	5	H	11	0	2	0	4,831
Bullet Snowrico	3	G	8	1	0	0	6,272
Bulletin Board	6	H	4	1	0	1	996
Bulletman Jack	4	C	4	0	1	1	12,057
Bulletthebluesky	4	C	11	2	1	2	22,335
Bullfinch	10	G	1	0	0	0	0
Bulling	6	G	18	1	1	5	34,410
Bulinsky	5	G	10	3	1	2	20,217
Bullish	3	C	1	0	0	0	220
Bullish Executive	2	G	2	1	0	0	41,640
Bullish Miss	5	M	3	0	0	0	4,500
Bullistic	3	C	7	1	0	3	63,644
Bullistic A. J.	6	G	1	0	0	0	50
Bullistic Flight	4	C	6	1	0	0	11,490
Bullotis	3	G	1	0	0	0	1,500
Bulls Companion	4	F	9	0	1	0	3,760
Bull's Ear	2	F	2	0	0	0	880
Bull's Eye	6	H	3	0	0	0	108
Bull's Revenge	4	G	15	4	3	1	20,121
Bullseye Bess	2	F	4	1	0	0	12,936
Bullseye Bill	3	G	8	1	0	2	26,031
Bullslinger	5	H	7	1	0	0	3,571
Bullwhip	3	C	8	2	2	1	23,100
Bully Baby	3	F	6	2	0	1	12,957
Bully Bully	5	G	7	0	2	1	17,760
Bully Creek	7	G	7	1	1	0	9,180
Bully for Billy	3	G	2	0	0	0	1,980
Bully for Yale	3	G	3	1	0	0	14,580
Bullys Hour	5	M	11	1	1	0	4,987
Bully's North	5	G	12	4	2	2	50,015
Bully's South	6	H	9	3	1	1	3,699
Bumbeling Bert	6	G	8	0	1	1	3,728
Bumkin McGruder	4	G	3	0	0	1	1,346
Bump Run	5	G	10	1	0	1	1,785
Bump Shot	4	G	11	0	0	2	3,265
Bumpawheat	5	G	2	0	0	0	148
Bumper Jack	3	G	1	0	0	0	35
Bumper Sticker	3	G	5	0	0	0	0
Bumper to Bumper	4	F	12	4	2	0	40,655
Bumpin Hub	9	G	7	0	2	1	6,714
Bumpitee	2	G	1	0	0	0	0
Bunches of Silver	5	M	2	0	0	0	0
Bunco Squad	4	G	7	0	2	1	4,495
Bundle Bundle	8	G	2	0	0	0	0
Bundle City	2	C	2	0	0	0	0
Bundle of Emotions	5	G	4	0	1	0	2,892
Bundle of Joy	2	G	9	0	0	1	1,470
Bundle This	3	G	10	3	0	2	12,948
Bundy Rum	5	G	9	0	0	1	3,775
Bungalow Bud	5	H	1	0	0	0	0
Bunigay	3	F	2	1	0	0	5,330
Bunk	2	F	1	0	0	0	0
Bunk N Ted	4	G	2	0	0	0	982
Bunker Buster	2	G	2	0	0	0	0
Bunker Jones	2	C	1	0	0	0	115
Bunkman	8	G	13	3	2	0	28,965
Bunny B.	3	F	5	1	1	0	7,559

Horse	Age	Sex	Sts	1st	2d	3d	Won
Bunny Bugs	4	F	7	1	0	2	10,430
Bunny Dear	8	M	16	0	3	2	6,933
Bunny Run	3	G	9	1	1	0	12,963
Bunny Slope	3	F	10	6	1	2	31,680
Bunnyinthebank	3	F	11	0	0	2	10,440
Bunny's Return	2	G	1	0	0	0	0
Bunratty Castle	5	H	17	0	1	3	4,638
Buper Scooper	7	M	5	0	0	1	2,647
Bupper	5	M	12	4	2	3	32,737
Buppy's Brother	5	H	4	1	0	1	3,800
Buraydas Ticket	4	G	1	0	0	0	762
Burchfield	3	C	9	2	0	1	51,059
Burdakin	4	G	9	0	0	1	3,485
Burdock	4	G	5	1	0	0	6,480
Burgandy Belle	6	M	12	0	1	1	2,142
Burgandy Tower	4	G	13	2	2	2	25,960
Burgeon	3	F	2	0	0	0	0
Burgundy At Last	3	G	5	0	0	0	647
Burkhardt	9	H	3	0	0	0	0
Burkie the Bear	3	G	10	1	0	0	4,545
Burlap	3	G	9	1	0	5	11,770
Burley A	2	G	9	1	1	2	8,945
Burley Girl	4	F	1	0	0	0	250
Burlington Bertie	2	G	3	0	0	0	455
Burlington House	9	H	10	1	1	0	11,120
Burma Jade	3	C	4	1	0	0	15,600
Burn	6	H	6	0	0	2	3,730
Burn a Spark	3	G	15	1	2	3	21,802
Burn Baby Burn	6	M	4	0	1	2	2,255
Burn Dixie Burn	3	F	8	2	2	4	19,463
Burn One Down	11	G	2	0	0	0	0
Burn the Legacy	7	M	5	0	1	0	8,001
Burn the Mortgage	8	G	1	0	0	0	60
Burnemup	3	F	1	0	0	0	0
Burnin Ana Lootin	5	M	11	0	5	2	8,546
Burnin' Memories	4	F	9	2	0	2	43,360
Burning Bay	5	G	8	1	3	1	15,700
Burning Brightly	2	F	1	0	0	0	0
Burning Brite	4	F	14	4	3	2	37,032
Burning Fluid	3	F	1	0	0	0	2,050
Burning Marque	7	H	8	3	1	0	62,760
Burning Memories	5	M	9	4	3	1	56,800
Burning Roma	5	H	5	1	2	0	118,500
Burning Sea	6	M	13	3	2	3	8,700
Burningtobefirst	3	F	5	0	2	0	5,270
Burninit	5	G	4	1	0	2	8,902
Burnished Miss	3	F	9	1	4	2	36,076
Burnrubber	2	C	1	0	0	1	910
Burn's Future	4	C	15	3	5	1	23,396
Burns Hole	3	C	1	0	0	0	0
Burnside Bridge	8	G	4	0	0	0	0
Burnt Bush	3	F	9	1	0	1	7,680
Burnt Foot Brown	2	G	2	0	0	0	360
Burnt Mill Road	9	G	15	5	3	2	73,121
Burnt Pizza	9	G	18	1	2	0	5,131
Burnt Ridge	5	G	5	0	1	0	668
Burnt Umber	4	G	10	0	0	1	2,776
Burnthemupashley	8	M	3	0	1	0	2,622
Burrwood	9	G	3	0	0	0	165
Burson	6	H	1	0	0	0	172
Burst First	9	G	5	0	2	0	6,921
Burst of Dawn	4	F	8	2	0	1	67,218
Burst Your Bubble	4	G	6	1	1	3	24,300
Burt's Cozzene	7	M	11	2	3	2	28,091
Buryurbook	5	G	2	0	0	0	0
Bus Dust	3	G	3	0	0	0	88
Bus Express	2	G	3	1	2	0	6,900
Bus Man Jack	2	G	5	1	1	1	14,330
Buscavida	5	H	9	1	1	2	22,130
Bush	4	G	7	5	0	2	30,409
Bush Cabin	4	G	7	3	0	1	52,706
Bush Time	3	F	1	0	0	0	0
Bush Triumph	5	M	6	2	2	2	119,850
Bush Writer	4	F	9	0	0	1	1,468
Bushel Britches	3	G	9	0	5	1	2,769
Busher's Chad	3	G	12	2	1	2	22,323
Bushes Victory	3	F	2	0	1	0	2,093
Bushwick	3	G	19	4	4	5	54,040
Bushy Park (IRE)	5	H	8	2	1	1	52,000

Horse	Age	Sex	Sts	1st	2d	3d	Won
Bushy's Baby	3	F	2	0	0	0	0
Bushy's Delight	4	F	9	1	1	0	8,910
Bushy's Jay	5	H	15	0	2	1	9,137
Business Decision	10	G	17	1	4	1	9,425
Businessorpleasure	3	C	3	0	0	0	570
Busser	3	G	9	0	2	0	1,942
Bust	3	G	15	2	1	2	27,785
Bust the Must	2	F	7	2	0	2	53,260
Bust the Record	9	G	3	0	0	0	0
Bust Your Bubble	3	G	10	1	0	2	28,020
Busted Flat	3	G	5	1	0	0	3,654
Buster B Bimbo	6	G	6	0	1	0	2,488
Buster Bailey	5	H	8	0	0	0	3,780
Buster the Cat	3	G	2	0	0	0	0
Buster the Vid	3	G	1	0	0	0	0
Buster's Dream	5	H	2	0	0	0	1,350
Bustheroses	2	G	2	0	0	0	0
Bustic	4	F	5	0	1	0	925
Bustin by U	7	G	12	1	4	2	3,435
Bustin Digits	8	G	1	0	0	0	0
Bustin Megan	4	F	1	0	0	0	0
Bustin N the Green	4	F	10	0	0	2	6,087
Bustin' Out	2	C	6	1	0	1	42,238
Bustin Thru	7	G	11	1	0	3	5,881
Bustin'dreams	4	C	10	2	1	3	29,140
Busting Free	4	G	9	0	1	2	8,831
Busy	5	M	9	2	2	0	42,160
Busy Bob	2	G	9	0	2	3	8,288
Busy Bonnie	4	F	11	2	1	2	21,532
Busy Ears	3	F	6	0	0	1	4,327
Busy Falcon	7	M	10	0	1	0	1,567
Busy Lady	3	F	3	0	0	1	720
Busy Line	2	F	1	0	1	0	1,160
But	5	M	1	0	1	0	8,600
But I'm Innocent	3	F	8	0	0	1	2,125
But Mommy	2	F	1	0	0	1	1,650
But of Course	3	G	7	1	1	1	47,600
But Some Girls Doo	3	F	5	0	1	1	1,350
But What Hyacinth	6	M	17	0	2	3	13,140
Butch Pistol	4	G	13	2	1	3	14,340
Butch's Man	3	G	3	0	0	0	0
Butiwillflysomeday	3	F	4	0	0	0	1,040
Butler On Duty	9	G	16	0	1	2	7,122
Butt Out	6	G	12	1	0	0	6,564
Butte City	4	G	12	2	1	1	20,850
Butter Crunch	2	F	2	0	0	1	2,790
Butter Me Up	4	F	11	2	3	0	17,745
Buttercup Express	3	F	16	1	3	1	26,690
Butterface	5	M	16	3	2	2	81,480
Butterfly Boy	5	G	5	0	0	0	740
Butterfly Dancer	4	F	2	0	0	1	620
Buttermilk Slew	4	G	4	0	1	0	1,292
Butternut Red	5	G	13	1	2	1	10,600
Butterscotch Dave	8	G	10	3	1	0	36,400
Buttertart	3	F	8	0	1	0	17,490
Button	6	G	13	1	3	4	9,168
Button Button	3	F	9	0	0	1	1,962
Button Man	3	C	3	1	0	0	10,200
Button Soup	3	F	4	1	0	0	11,713
Button Wood	3	G	10	3	1	3	143,206
Buttonwood Angel	3	F	11	0	0	1	4,596
Buttonwood Ida	4	F	17	2	6	3	34,100
Buttonwood Migtron	7	G	13	1	2	0	7,006
Buttonwood Steve	3	G	1	0	0	0	0
Buttonwood Thunder	3	G	6	0	0	2	4,950
Buy On the Dips	4	F	2	0	0	0	640
Buy Out Time	3	F	9	2	2	0	68,395
Buy the Dips	4	F	3	0	0	1	6,440
Buy the Four N Ten	6	M	13	2	2	0	11,076
Buy the Sport	3	F	7	2	0	1	334,521
Buy You a Bear	7	M	4	0	0	1	690
Buysometime	3	F	7	3	2	1	21,972
Buz Away	3	C	6	1	0	0	7,335
Buzz Around	9	M	12	0	1	1	4,405
Buzz Bar	8	G	1	1	0	0	6,600
Buzz Barton	3	G	10	0	1	1	2,432
Buzz Cat	6	G	9	4	2	1	23,060
Buzz Cut	2	C	2	0	0	0	0
Buzz' Dixie Chick	3	F	2	0	0	0	0
Buzz' Hitman	4	G	2	0	0	0	0
Buzz Me	5	G	2	1	0	0	3,480
Buzz Me Baby	3	C	4	0	1	1	7,380
Buzz of the Party	2	F	4	0	0	0	126
Buzz Off Buzz	3	F	2	1	0	0	9,000
Buzz Oliver	2	G	11	0	1	2	6,940
Buzzard Road	8	G	19	2	3	1	13,696
Buzzer Bob	2	G	3	0	0	1	675
Buzzing B's	5	M	4	1	1	1	19,500
Buzzle Ways	3	G	17	4	1	2	79,176
Buzzword	5	G	2	0	0	0	1,200
Buzzy Bee	2	G	3	0	0	1	5,200
Buzzy O	2	C	1	0	0	0	75
Buzzy's Gold	3	C	9	1	2	2	59,380
Bwana Charlie	2	C	5	0	2	3	31,660
By a County Mile	3	F	10	2	2	2	6,840
By a Mile Baby	4	F	7	1	0	1	3,926
By a Nose	4	G	11	1	2	1	8,220
By Cracky	2	F	1	0	0	0	95
By Daylight	3	F	6	0	2	2	10,200
By Default	2	G	4	1	0	0	8,760
By Design	8	G	8	1	0	1	6,798
By Deuce	3	G	2	0	0	0	105
By Himself	3	G	13	2	5	0	17,225
By Jasper	2	G	2	0	0	0	0
By the Bay	3	G	11	0	0	0	5,139
By the Belle	3	F	5	0	2	0	5,710
By the Slice	10	M	2	0	0	0	0
By the Sword	3	C	8	0	2	2	24,810
By Yourself Lady	5	M	10	1	4	0	5,828
Bya Banana	4	G	10	4	0	2	10,542
Byars and Lookers	3	F	3	0	0	0	1,000
Byars Buzz	2	C	6	1	0	0	3,300
Byars of Gold	2	C	5	1	0	0	5,640
Byasmile	7	G	20	3	1	6	13,568
Byback	4	G	6	2	1	1	73,150
Byby Ike's Cat	3	G	4	2	0	0	1,876
Bybymisamarycanpie	4	F	5	0	1	1	2,704
Bydeed	7	G	12	2	1	1	8,976
Bye Bird	5	G	6	2	0	0	9,076
Bye Bye Ali	2	F	2	0	0	0	3,636
Bye Bye Beylen	4	G	12	5	1	2	48,932
Bye Bye Birdie	4	F	18	2	4	0	44,055
Bye Bye Brickie	2	C	5	0	1	3	8,358
Bye Bye Bunny	3	F	4	0	1	1	4,942
Bye Bye Darlin	2	F	1	0	0	0	651
Bye Bye Hart	5	M	8	2	2	0	11,835
Bye Won	3	G	6	0	0	2	4,392
Byeairmail	2	F	10	2	1	0	15,535
Byestarterhijudge	2	C	4	0	0	0	1,656
Bygeorgeshe'sgotit	2	F	1	0	0	0	0
Byreasonofinsanity	3	G	1	0	0	0	0
Byrneing Passion	5	M	8	0	2	2	12,767
Byro	4	C	2	0	0	0	120
Bythe Grace of God	9	G	1	0	0	0	0
Byzantine	7	M	6	2	0	3	193,955
Byzantium (BRZ)	4	G	1	0	0	0	460
C B Account	10	H	2	0	0	0	208
C B Gold Won	3	G	10	3	3	1	25,571
C B Nute	2	G	2	0	0	0	100
C B Stu	9	G	14	1	3	1	13,287
C Barney Run	10	H	10	0	0	0	1,320
C Brian Run	7	H	13	0	3	0	5,649
C B's Back	9	G	8	0	0	2	1,522
C C Cat	4	G	8	3	0	2	18,148
C C Copy	3	C	5	0	0	0	0
C C Forever	2	F	2	0	0	0	0
C C Red	6	M	15	1	2	2	9,916
C C Sky Dancer	4	F	6	0	2	1	2,102
C Crafty Go	3	G	8	0	0	0	930
C Crafty Peak	2	G	6	1	0	0	3,690
C Crafty Steppin	2	C	2	0	0	0	0
C Cs Candyman	3	C	3	0	0	0	0
C C's Heart	3	G	6	1	1	0	13,430
C Cubed	2	C	2	0	0	0	1,300
C D Cruzer	5	G	4	0	1	1	6,020
C D Gray	5	G	2	1	0	0	2,288
C D World	3	G	9	1	0	1	11,601
C Drive	4	F	4	0	1	1	2,860

Horse	Age	Sex	Sts	1st	2d	3d	Won
C D's Amulet	4	F	19	3	1	4	11,138
C F Slew of Storms	5	G	8	1	1	1	11,091
C Frank	3	G	3	0	0	0	0
C G Regency	3	F	1	0	0	0	1,035
C H Southern Storm	4	C	7	1	1	2	11,877
C J Best	4	F	1	0	0	1	2,882
C J Epping	6	G	4	0	0	1	630
C J Ice	3	G	3	0	0	0	0
C J Pete	5	G	1	0	0	0	0
C J Sirius	2	F	1	0	0	0	630
C Joe Blush	10	G	6	1	1	0	4,559
C J's Lil'frosty	4	G	1	0	0	0	0
C J's Rolex	5	H	8	2	0	0	14,662
C K Jett	2	C	2	1	1	0	22,440
C Kid Blush	3	C	2	0	0	0	468
C L Gray	2	C	1	0	0	0	0
C M U Habit	4	F	9	0	1	2	3,823
C M U Slew	2	F	1	0	0	0	1,713
C Merrill Run	7	G	7	1	1	2	5,455
C'mon Camilla	3	F	4	0	0	0	2,140
C M's Mark	6	G	8	1	3	0	28,842
C R Charm	3	F	3	0	1	0	9,920
C R Fascination	3	F	9	1	0	2	13,449
C R Rocket	5	G	13	0	2	0	2,952
C R Starduster	5	M	12	1	1	0	6,378
C Slew C	4	G	10	1	0	1	4,445
C Squared	4	G	8	0	1	1	3,811
C T King Oftheroad	5	G	17	0	4	0	13,107
C Tallie Run	4	F	5	0	0	0	515
C the Minister	3	G	1	0	0	0	0
C T's Rail	3	F	3	0	0	0	0
C U Around	5	M	10	0	0	0	2,617
C U Glitter	4	F	9	0	2	2	8,983
C U inthe Fastlane	4	G	5	0	0	0	293
C U Later Deviator	2	C	7	1	2	1	9,090
C W Dema Dema Dew	3	G	8	0	0	0	865
C W It's a Breeze	4	C	10	1	4	3	16,382
C Ya	4		14	1	0	1	4,633
C. A. D.'s Combo	4	F	10	2	1	2	19,349
C. Brooke Run	2	F	3	0	0	0	890
C. C. Diamond	4	G	13	1	0	1	9,110
C. C. Integrity	6	G	4	0	0	0	309
C. C. Minister	3	G	3	0	1	0	10,590
C. C. Ruler	6	H	4	0	0	0	490
C. C. Seven	2	F	2	0	0	1	1,925
C. C. Union	3	G	9	1	1	2	15,516
C. C. Water Back	4	G	18	1	4	1	12,860
C. C. Williams	4	F	8	0	1	1	13,880
C. C. With Water	2	F	3	0	0	2	3,868
C. C.'s Crane	3	F	8	2	0	1	3,693
C. C.'s Darling	6	M	2	0	0	0	0
C. C.'s Rocket	2	F	2	1	0	0	7,218
C. D. Haj	4	G	7	1	1	0	10,946
C. D. Palmer	7	G	6	2	0	2	8,160
C. D. Rail	3	F	7	0	1	0	700
C. F. Power Lane	4	G	10	1	1	5	15,318
C. F. Regent	4	G	4	0	0	1	1,140
C. Garrett	3	C	1	0	0	1	1,155
C. J.'s Bitohoney	2	F	2	0	0	0	0
C. J.'s Honour	4	C	5	2	0	1	66,480
C. J.'s Magee	5	G	8	0	1	0	2,704
C. L. Rib	6	G	16	1	3	7	88,840
C. R. Cavalier	5	G	9	3	1	1	13,369
C. R. Daver D.	4	C	3	0	0	0	180
C. R. Flying Sonny	4	G	3	1	1	0	6,735
C. R. Flying Star	3	G	4	1	0	0	11,100
C. R. Pace	6	M	9	0	0	0	1,665
C. R. Slolom Fox	2	G	1	0	0	0	130
C. Russell Run	2	G	3	1	0	1	9,800
C. S. Wells	3	C	2	0	0	0	1,265
C. T. Cruiser	4	F	5	1	0	0	8,745
Ca d'Zan	2	C	1	0	0	0	975
Caballero Negro	2	C	1	0	0	0	975
Caballo de Cielo	5	G	10	1	0	1	4,602
Caballo de Oro	3	G	7	0	2	1	7,925
Cabana Kid	5	G	4	0	0	0	528
Cabaret Dancer	4	G	13	3	2	2	27,382
Cabernet	3	G	7	2	0	2	14,103
Cabert	6	G	7	0	0	0	1,109
Cabeza Prieta	6	H	5	1	0	0	9,520
Cabildo Bag	2	F	4	3	1	0	84,660
Cabin Boy	6	G	12	2	0	1	26,815
Cabin One	4	F	15	2	2	1	22,800
Cabin Stabin	3	G	4	1	0	1	5,100
Cabincreekcassie	2	F	4	0	0	1	1,435
Cabincreekconnie	2	F	4	0	0	0	675
Cable Ready	4	G	10	0	3	0	4,053
Cabo Cat	6	H	6	0	0	0	476
Cabo de Noche	2	F	2	0	0	1	5,780
Cabo Kid	3	C	3	0	0	0	0
Cabo Sunrise	3	F	9	2	1	1	56,910
Cabo Wabo	3	G	7	0	3	2	33,720
Caboret Note	4	F	15	1	2	1	7,531
Cabos	3	C	4	0	1	0	7,730
Cabot Trail	5	G	11	1	1	1	25,090
Cabreo	6	G	6	1	0	0	3,748
Cabri	4	F	3	0	0	0	990
Cabrita Point	7	G	8	0	2	0	5,595
Cache Is King	2	G	1	0	0	0	0
Cache Monster	2	C	6	1	1	0	32,108
Cachet Away	3	G	10	1	0	0	9,699
Cachito's Dancer	3	G	4	0	1	0	5,560
Cachuma's Dancer	3	F	2	0	0	0	0
Cachuma's Lil Man	3	C	11	1	4	1	16,251
Cactus Glacken	4	C	6	0	1	3	3,716
Cactus Gulch	3	C	5	0	1	0	740
Cactus Hill	3	C	5	0	0	0	0
Cactus Ridge	2	C	4	4	0	0	187,850
Cada	6	M	3	0	0	0	126
Cadder	4	G	15	2	2	4	13,363
Caddo	3	C	7	0	0	3	6,480
Caddo Red	2	G	2	0	0	1	1,850
Cadeinator	3	C	4	1	0	1	7,350
Cadenhead	6	G	11	2	4	2	76,124
Cadilac Queen	3	F	2	1	0	0	6,600
Cadillac Bay	5	M	6	0	0	0	0
Cadillac Gold	2	G	2	0	0	1	1,944
Cadillac Jack	3	G	15	2	2	5	24,019
Cadillac Mountain	4	F	9	1	3	0	40,730
Cadillac Sam	7	G	12	1	0	3	11,837
Cadiz	4	G	2	0	0	0	326
Cadron Creek	6	H	8	0	0	1	2,070
Caelly Nethia	2	F	3	0	0	1	3,200
Caesarion (IRE)	4	C	5	0	1	1	36,968
Caesar's Pearl	3	F	1	0	1	0	9,600
Cafe Carefree	2	F	1	0	0	0	0
Cafe de France	8	M	7	0	0	1	1,310
Cafe Del Mar	5	M	4	0	0	0	660
Cafe Espresso	3	F	7	0	2	0	3,352
Cafe Flore	3	F	1	0	0	0	0
Cafe Momus	5	G	13	2	0	2	15,863
Cafe Mystique	7	M	3	1	0	1	7,600
Cafe Noir	3	C	3	2	0	0	13,980
Cafe Photo	2	G	3	0	0	0	1,275
Cafe's Miracle	2	F	1	0	0	0	0
Caffeine and Booze	3	C	7	1	2	1	23,454
Caged	4	F	5	0	0	0	0
Cagey	5	G	6	1	2	1	5,478
Cagey Codger	5	G	4	2	0	0	7,086
Cagey n' Sassy	5	M	5	0	0	0	441
Cagney (BRZ)	6	H	4	0	1	1	75,720
Cahilina	2	F	5	2	0	1	11,725
Cahill Holly	3	F	6	2	2	0	44,720
Cahill in Vogue	2	F	3	0	1	0	960
Cahill Kid	6	H	7	4	1	0	53,600
Cahill Lane	4	G	17	2	1	3	10,723
Cahill Mango	2	C	5	0	1	1	16,580
Cahills Cadillac's	4	F	1	0	0	0	100
Cahill's Catrina	3	F	3	0	0	1	2,079
Cahmonof	7	M	7	0	0	0	675
Cahootin	6	H	7	1	1	0	8,813
Cain's Train	3	C	5	1	0	0	4,149
Cairina Carson	4	F	7	1	1	1	13,090
Cairne	2	G	4	2	1	0	28,200
Caisson	7	G	4	0	2	0	4,573
Cait	4	F	4	1	1	1	29,791
Caities Majesty	3	F	9	2	1	1	5,385
Caitlins Dancer	3	F	5	0	0	0	360

Horse	Age	Sex	Sts	1st	2d	3d	Won
Caitlins Girl	3	F	12	3	1	0	26,704
Caitlin's Idol	3	F	9	2	3	2	79,180
Cajita	3	C	6	0	0	0	1,089
Cajole	3	C	7	2	2	1	39,360
Cajun Addiction	2	G	2	1	1	0	12,560
Cajun Bad Blade	4	C	6	0	2	0	9,390
Cajun Beat	3	G	9	4	2	0	820,000
Cajun Bound	5	G	16	5	3	2	22,123
Cajun Brogue	3	C	1	0	0	0	0
Cajun Cadence	4	G	5	1	0	0	3,000
Cajun Charger	5	H	2	0	0	0	465
Cajun Cocktail	5	G	2	0	0	0	42
Cajun Coed	7	M	4	2	0	0	7,560
Cajun Concert	6	G	13	4	1	1	36,960
Cajun Cotton	3	F	2	0	0	0	45
Cajun Countess	3	F	10	0	3	1	6,599
Cajun Crane	8	G	12	0	3	1	20,408
Cajun Dancer	5	M	10	0	0	0	314
Cajun Deputy	4	G	10	3	1	1	20,043
Cajun Emblem	3	C	7	0	0	1	2,462
Cajun Girl	2	F	3	0	0	0	308
Cajun Kelly	3	F	7	1	3	0	51,840
Cajun Lass	4	F	3	1	0	1	976
Cajun Law	3	G	3	0	1	1	1,580
Cajun Memories	3	G	7	0	2	0	7,730
Cajun Miss	3	F	14	4	2	1	21,160
Cajun Music	3	G	5	0	0	2	3,410
Cajun Peppa	5	G	5	0	0	0	218
Cajun Princess	4	F	4	0	2	2	14,364
Cajun Purchase	2	F	4	1	1	0	16,500
Cajun Razor	5	G	15	2	5	3	18,100
Cajun Rullah	3	G	3	0	0	0	0
Cajun Skier	4	G	8	1	1	1	5,743
Cajun Soup	3	F	8	1	1	1	10,160
Cajun Star	7	G	13	1	4	2	33,376
Cajun Wager	2	F	3	0	0	0	840
Cajuns Crown	3	G	3	1	1	0	22,900
Cal Bread	7	G	7	0	0	0	930
Cal Brite	5	M	12	1	0	3	5,283
Cal Slew	3	C	1	0	0	0	53
Calabar	3	G	7	2	0	2	13,740
Calabres (ARG)	4	C	1	0	0	0	0
Caladium	3	F	3	0	0	0	515
Calahan's Jet	3	F	7	1	2	0	41,850
Calamity Jane	4	F	12	2	2	1	9,511
Calce Clunes	4	F	8	0	1	1	8,015
Calculator	2	C	5	0	0	3	14,760
Calculus	2	G	5	0	0	0	927
Calder Ridge	2	G	2	0	0	0	0
Caledon Bound	4	F	6	0	2	1	28,176
Caledon Colleen	5	M	9	3	0	0	45,266
Caledonia Mission	3	F	1	0	0	0	50
Caledonia Road	2	C	4	1	0	2	17,125
Caledonna	3	F	7	0	0	1	4,276
Calends	4	C	9	2	4	2	91,650
Calformecalifornia	4	F	11	1	1	3	11,644
Calhoon	4	C	23	4	4	2	23,176
Calhoun Bag	3	G	2	0	0	0	0
Cali Cali	2	F	8	0	1	0	2,680
Caliban	6	G	12	3	1	2	72,931
Calibogue Sound	7	M	1	0	0	0	133
Caliboss	3	C	1	0	0	0	0
Calibration	4	F	10	2	2	0	10,631
Calico Creek	6	M	10	2	1	1	27,480
Calico Sioux	5	H	6	0	1	0	4,650
Calidown	5	M	2	0	0	0	0
Caliente Creek	7	M	8	0	0	0	272
Caliente Fuego	4	F	14	4	2	2	37,783
Calif. Native	3	G	4	0	1	1	2,125
Califo	5	G	8	1	0	0	11,728
California Beauty	3	F	3	0	0	0	0
California Casual	4	F	6	1	0	1	23,835
California Chick	3	F	6	1	0	0	955
California Concept	2	F	5	1	0	1	8,895
California Express	6	M	2	0	0	0	52
California Fire	3	F	1	0	0	0	145
California Gal	3	F	6	1	0	0	6,179
California Goal	4	G	3	0	0	1	3,000
California Ivory	3	F	4	0	0	1	3,325
California Kiss	4	C	10	4	1	1	42,390
California Limited	5	M	14	1	1	0	5,222
California Lite	5	G	6	1	2	1	54,160
California Power	4	G	3	1	1	0	31,220
California Season	5	M	7	0	1	0	1,814
California Snow	2	G	3	0	0	0	390
California Storm	4	G	2	0	0	0	1,315
California Valley	3	F	6	2	1	1	9,567
Californian (GB)	3	C	9	3	1	1	149,364
Calin's Belle	3	F	2	0	0	0	0
Calista (GB)	5	M	2	0	1	1	31,000
Calista Regent	3	F	2	0	0	0	0
Calista's Star	4	F	9	0	0	3	23,266
Calisthenic	4	G	5	2	1	1	18,640
Calkins Road	4	C	4	0	0	0	0
Call an Angel	4	F	5	1	2	2	15,600
Call an Audible	4	F	10	2	3	1	119,523
Call an Interview	3	C	10	0	1	2	15,811
Call and Raise	4	G	4	0	1	0	1,418
Call Back	3	G	4	0	0	1	3,344
Call Call	3	F	1	0	0	0	0
Call Carson	2	F	4	1	1	0	20,540
Call Chrystal	6	M	1	0	0	0	0
Call Columbo	3	G	9	1	0	2	11,350
Call Early	2	G	8	0	2	3	16,788
Call Em Lovey	5	G	15	1	2	0	6,823
Call Fiorello	8	G	12	6	1	1	49,135
Call for Freedom	2	C	3	0	0	0	320
Call for Honor	4	F	10	2	0	5	27,210
Call Forwarding	3	F	14	0	0	1	1,577
Call Granny	5	M	14	2	1	2	21,515
Call Her Michele	3	F	3	1	0	0	1,980
Call Him Back Man	5	G	5	2	0	0	10,545
Call Him Wildfire	4	C	3	0	0	0	0
Call His Bluff	4	G	11	1	0	4	14,566
Call Home Now	5	H	3	0	0	0	76
Call It	4	G	5	3	1	0	58,580
Call It a Wrap	9	G	2	0	0	0	40
Call It in the Air	6	G	8	0	0	1	3,596
Call Jim	7	H	7	0	0	1	444
Call Leader	3	G	14	2	1	4	22,734
Call Leo	4	C	7	1	0	1	28,335
Call Man	9	G	3	0	0	0	0
Call Me a Prince	8	G	14	2	0	1	4,194
Call Me Again	6	G	4	0	1	1	3,006
Call Me Awesome	2	C	1	0	1	0	11,760
Call Me Be Be	3	F	1	0	0	0	0
Call Me Bobby	3	G	11	0	0	1	1,155
Call Me C. J.	6	G	10	2	1	1	18,297
Call Me Calhoun	9	G	1	0	0	0	0
Call Me Casanova	6	H	6	1	0	2	10,200
Call Me Cassidy	3	F	4	0	0	0	1,440
Call Me Chester	3	G	1	0	0	0	50
Call Me Chiffie	4	F	3	0	0	0	0
Call Me Cobra	5	G	7	0	0	0	1,104
Call Me Do	3	G	3	1	0	0	2,495
Call Me Dorie	3	F	9	1	1	2	24,100
Call Me First	5	H	2	0	0	0	0
Call Me Frosty	3	G	10	2	0	4	42,867
Call Me Glory	3	G	6	2	0	1	29,156
Call Me Gold	2	G	1	0	0	0	372
Call Me Grace	4	F	3	0	0	1	1,056
Call Me Home	5	G	15	0	3	1	12,350
Call Me Honey	2	F	2	0	0	0	0
Call Me Inky	4	F	11	1	0	1	9,190
Call Me Joyce	4	F	13	1	1	4	11,745
Call Me Kathleen	4	F	2	0	0	0	510
Call Me Kitty	4	F	7	0	0	0	1,266
Call Me Lefty	3	G	7	1	2	1	81,100
Call Me Lightning	4	C	8	3	0	4	34,215
Call Me Loverboy	6	H	6	3	1	0	22,105
Call Me Mac	3	G	2	0	0	0	0
Call Me Madonna	2	F	2	0	0	1	5,550
Call Me Meg	4	F	11	0	1	2	20,600
Call Me Mike	4	G	3	0	0	0	0
Call Me Mister C	3	C	11	2	0	0	16,350
Call Me Moe	2	G	2	1	0	0	21,360
Call Me Mr. Vain	9	G	20	11	4	0	62,162
Call Me Mz Tricky	4	F	5	1	0	0	4,655

RECORDS OF HORSES

Horse	Age	Sex	Sts	1st	2d	3d	Won
Call Me P J	3	C	4	0	1	1	4,456
Call Me Pete	3	G	6	1	1	0	22,510
Call Me Proper	3	G	4	0	0	0	408
Call Me Rosie	5	M	7	0	0	0	644
Call Me Roy	4	C	3	1	1	0	1,304
Call Me Special	4	C	3	0	3	0	1,800
Call Me Sue	4	F	11	2	3	1	79,404
Call Me the Champ	2	G	5	0	0	0	3,750
Call Me Twisted	4	F	6	0	0	0	720
Call Me West	3	C	10	0	1	3	6,010
Call My Alibi	4	F	2	0	0	0	0
Call My Lawyer	3	F	7	2	0	1	15,970
Call Newport	5	H	12	2	4	2	6,820
Call Out	4	F	2	0	0	0	220
Call Shot	6	H	2	0	0	0	0
Call Sign	3	G	9	1	3	0	19,250
Call Sis	3	F	2	0	0	0	85
Call the Ace	3	C	14	0	1	2	5,481
Call the Director	2	G	1	0	0	0	0
Call the Groom	5	G	6	0	0	1	1,418
Call the Lady	5	H	2	0	0	0	202
Call the Lark	2	G	3	0	0	0	4,920
Call the Witness	2	F	5	0	1	1	11,863
Call to Honor	6	H	10	1	0	1	4,238
Call to Order (GB)	8	H	1	0	0	0	0
Call Trace	6	H	12	0	1	1	2,998
Call Waiting	6	G	10	3	1	2	29,310
Callada	4	F	2	0	0	0	2,520
Callbeforeucome	2	G	5	1	1	1	11,550
Callbright	2	C	2	0	0	0	509
Callcan	2	G	7	1	0	1	11,280
Callcat	2	C	3	1	1	0	33,400
Calldara	3	F	6	0	1	1	23,300
Calldownthelaw	5	M	7	0	0	1	1,497
Called to Order	3	F	4	0	1	0	1,800
Caller Back	2	F	2	0	0	0	1,920
Caller Blocked	2	G	3	0	1	1	6,240
Caller Jilly Bean	2	F	4	0	0	0	2,080
Caller Junction	6	G	6	1	1	0	4,988
Caller Pete	7	G	7	1	0	1	6,325
Caller to Post	2	F	2	0	0	0	240
Caller Zi Zi	5	M	11	0	1	0	2,523
Caller's Image	4	F	14	3	2	1	34,740
Calles d'Oro	4	C	8	0	4	0	15,876
Calleybluebayou	3	F	6	1	1	1	77,950
Callfire	2	G	1	0	1	0	4,140
Callforablue	6	H	2	0	0	0	180
Callforme Cheyenne	7	M	7	0	0	1	2,196
Callie Allen	4	F	6	1	1	0	10,928
Callie Mae	4	F	7	1	1	1	5,755
Calliehadaprenup	5	G	13	1	0	1	4,098
Callies Girl	5	M	4	0	0	1	1,211
Callies Remark	3	F	8	2	2	1	37,127
Callin Collect	4	C	10	1	1	2	11,989
Callin Doctor Fran	5	G	15	0	0	2	10,406
Callin Dr Casey	3	F	1	0	0	0	0
Calling	3	F	10	1	0	0	11,860
Calling Again	5	G	6	0	0	0	891
Calling All Angels	2	F	5	0	0	3	10,560
Calling All Forbes	2	G	7	1	2	2	24,010
Calling Angels	2	F	4	0	0	0	1,620
Calling Jonesy	10	M	3	0	0	1	567
Calling Mary Mac	2	F	12	1	2	0	8,815
Calling Nicole	2	F	10	0	1	2	7,315
Calling Randy	3	C	13	3	1	0	25,152
Calling Scarlett	2	F	8	1	2	3	35,847
Calling Ticket	6	M	5	1	2	2	7,864
Callinthetroops	2	F	3	0	1	0	4,200
Calliope Gal	4	F	5	0	0	0	431
Callista Creek	3	F	1	0	1	0	810
Callmeabc	6	M	7	0	0	3	3,781
Callmebrandy	3	F	12	0	1	1	5,899
Callmecountrygirl	3	F	4	0	0	0	0
Callmefrenchie	6	G	8	0	1	1	10,312
Callmegenifur	6	M	1	1	0	0	8,250
Callmeifyouneedme	9	G	7	0	0	0	840
Callmelauryn	2	F	3	0	0	3	10,950
Callmenoshowjones	5	H	4	0	0	0	108
Callnew	2	G	8	1	0	1	13,015
Callone	2	F	3	1	1	0	18,040
Callsports	2	F	10	1	0	2	8,360
Callter	2	F	9	1	1	1	21,035
Callthesheriff	4	G	8	1	2	1	53,470
Callum	2	G	10	1	1	1	12,655
Callvi	2	C	2	0	0	0	220
Callya Later	8	G	12	2	1	1	15,955
Calm in the East	2	F	1	0	0	0	0
Calm Waters	5	G	10	2	2	0	27,600
Calma Prado	5	M	13	1	2	2	46,044
Calmego	2	C	1	0	0	0	0
Calming Effect	5	G	12	3	6	0	25,720
Calomine Loachin	3	C	11	1	2	2	7,740
Cal's Baby	5	M	9	2	0	2	61,380
Cal's Choice	4	F	12	1	2	0	5,896
Cal's Cin	7	M	10	0	0	0	477
Calster	5	G	9	1	1	1	43,220
Calumet Spice (IRE)	5	M	5	0	2	1	3,544
Calvaro	8	G	2	0	1	0	840
Calvary Scout	3	C	6	0	1	0	3,242
Calverstown	4	C	2	0	0	0	1,680
Calvin Clyde	3	G	2	0	0	0	0
Calvin Gene	4	C	1	0	0	0	182
Calvin's Promise	4	G	9	1	0	1	6,100
Calypso Beau	5	H	10	1	1	1	6,572
Calypso Joe	3	C	3	0	0	0	0
Calzada Kid	4	F	3	0	0	1	15,729
Cam a Retta	5	M	2	0	0	1	2,918
Cama Cat	2	F	2	0	0	0	630
Camacho (NZ)	6	G	2	0	0	0	3,630
Camac's Tribute	3	F	8	1	1	1	22,830
Camara Cat	4	F	3	0	0	1	1,730
Camara Gold	3	F	3	0	0	0	632
Cam'a'roney	6	M	1	0	1	0	1,500
Camaron's Harbor	4	G	7	0	2	1	10,742
Camberley	3	F	2	1	0	0	13,763
Camber's American	3	F	4	0	0	0	540
Cambridge Bay	8	G	4	0	1	0	3,000
Camden Bay	3	F	8	0	0	1	10,960
Camden Pine	5	G	7	2	1	0	21,625
Camden Yards	3	C	1	0	0	0	0
Came Calling	6	M	1	0	0	0	0
Came From Paris	2	C	1	0	0	0	0
Camelot Cowboy	6	G	5	0	0	0	0
Camelot Moment	4	F	9	2	1	2	21,388
Camelot Moon	3	C	4	0	0	0	270
Camelot Rose	3	F	3	0	2	0	3,140
Cameo's Covergirl	5	M	16	0	2	4	13,945
Cameragetready	3	G	5	0	0	0	1,650
Cameron	7	G	4	0	0	0	104
Cameron Pass	6	H	2	0	0	0	0
Camerons Chic	6	M	1	0	0	0	0
Cameron's Diamond	5	G	9	0	1	1	2,825
Cameron's Frolic	8	G	2	0	0	0	122
Camerons Lightning	3	C	7	0	0	0	0
Cameron's Way	3	G	4	0	0	0	0
Camford	8	G	23	1	2	3	8,889
Camikaze Cookie	10	G	12	2	0	0	5,493
Camille's Princess	4	F	6	0	0	0	360
Camino	8	G	7	0	1	0	2,422
Camino Cielo	7	H	4	0	0	0	0
Camionette	8	M	8	1	3	1	11,710
Camjack	3	G	7	0	1	0	1,602
Cammy Be Kwik	5	M	10	2	0	3	16,690
Cammy's Jet	3	F	7	2	3	0	48,120
Camoleur	8	G	10	0	0	1	1,397
Camp Clark	3	G	4	0	0	1	3,030
Camp Crescent	3	C	5	1	0	0	20,900
Camp David	4	C	5	0	1	2	22,470
Camp Del Mar Rules	2	F	1	0	0	0	0
Camp Randall	4	G	8	2	1	0	17,012
Camp Sherman	3	G	3	1	0	0	4,875
Camp Takatoka	3	C	6	2	2	1	20,970
Camp Valid	4	F	5	1	2	0	11,315
Campaign Andover	5	M	14	3	3	1	26,702
Campaign Castle	3	C	1	0	0	0	320
Campaign Tactics	3	C	6	1	0	0	4,915
Campaigner	4	G	13	1	2	0	14,180
Campaneronote	5	G	1	0	0	0	44

Horse	Age	Sex	Sts	1st	2d	3d	Won	Horse	Age	Sex	Sts	1st	2d	3d	Won
Campanita	4	F	7	1	3	1	18,660	Candi Man Can	7	G	15	1	1	2	5,092
Camperchano	5	G	16	0	1	1	2,557	Candi Step	4	F	11	0	0	2	927
Campfire Burning	2	G	7	1	3	1	25,790	Candi Story	6	G	3	0	1	0	780
Campfire Ridge	6	G	6	1	1	1	10,716	Candi Twist	8	M	7	0	0	0	534
Campiano	3	G	9	1	1	2	19,108	Candid Ballerina	6	M	12	3	3	1	24,314
Campinout	4	G	13	1	3	3	18,240	Candid Beauty	5	M	13	1	2	0	8,541
Campo de Maniobras	2	F	1	0	0	0	0	Candid Glen	6	G	8	2	0	0	543,300
Campo Lago	2	C	6	1	1	2	70,572	Candid Remark	5	G	14	6	2	1	62,292
Campo Ridge	2	F	7	1	0	3	7,669	Candida	3	F	11	2	3	3	18,215
Campsie Fells (UAE)	3	F	8	1	2	1	117,590	Candi's Dandi	4	G	8	0	0	1	1,890
Camptonville	4	G	4	0	0	1	2,250	Candi's Pleasure	7	G	2	0	1	0	1,221
Campus Corner	2	F	3	0	0	1	1,310	Candi's Soft Touch	2	C	2	0	0	1	2,325
Campus King	4	G	13	0	0	1	1,884	Candi's Treasure	2	F	2	2	0	0	23,870
Cam's Cat	3	F	1	0	0	0	0	Candle Power	6	H	2	0	0	0	0
Cam's Margret	4	F	4	0	0	0	218	Candle Snuffer	8	G	12	4	0	1	26,040
Can Belong	3	G	3	0	1	0	2,994	Candlelight Only	3	G	9	0	0	0	948
Can Dee Corn	3	F	3	0	0	0	385	Candlelight Prince	3	C	5	0	1	0	16,820
Can I	3	F	5	0	0	1	3,040	Candlelighter	3	G	1	0	0	0	53
Can I Call You Dad	3	F	6	2	1	1	62,390	Candler	6	G	14	1	3	1	18,115
Can I Do It	3	G	10	1	4	0	17,020	Cando Cat	3	G	1	0	0	0	0
Can I Kiss You	2	C	2	0	1	1	3,267	Candooz	3	F	5	0	0	0	140
Can I Make It	4	F	9	2	2	1	11,002	Candor	4	F	2	0	0	0	825
Can Ihavethisdance	2	F	4	0	2	1	36,633	Candy Adventure	5	M	14	1	0	0	24,055
Can Keep a Secret	2	C	2	0	1	0	2,250	Candy Basket	3	F	3	1	2	0	15,500
Can Rianne	3	F	4	0	0	0	1,845	Candy Cane C C	3	F	14	2	2	2	37,303
Can Ron	4	F	3	1	0	0	2,832	Candy Clouds	3	F	4	0	0	3	13,094
Can Star	6	G	8	2	0	1	23,132	Candy Factor	6	H	6	1	0	1	4,144
Can Too Dance	4	C	4	1	0	0	1,970	Candy Flame	3	F	5	1	0	0	5,715
Can You Feel It	6	G	10	2	1	4	12,749	Candy Flute	3	F	13	2	1	2	15,392
Can You Hear Me	3	F	5	0	0	0	0	Candy Glide	3	F	2	0	0	1	2,320
Can You See Me Now	2	F	3	1	0	1	15,640	Candy Haze	5	M	5	2	0	0	15,780
Cana Creek	3	G	12	2	1	1	14,966	Candy Kat	8	G	9	1	1	0	2,538
Cana Diesel	3	G	4	0	0	1	1,729	Candy Kisses	4	F	13	3	2	0	18,972
Canaan Land	3	G	6	0	2	1	25,640	Candy Motion	8	M	12	0	1	1	2,847
Canada's Coleman	6	G	6	0	0	0	0	Candy O	4	F	1	0	0	0	73
Canada's Game	4	F	9	1	1	1	3,805	Candy Prize	3	F	4	0	0	0	318
Canadian Alliance	5	M	5	0	2	2	14,774	Candy Ride (ARG)	4	C	3	3	0	0	724,800
Canadian Chic	5	M	2	0	0	1	391	Candy Runner	3	C	13	2	6	1	25,567
Canadian Clipper	4	F	5	1	0	0	2,158	Candy Sprite	5	M	4	0	0	0	0
Canadian Conection	3	G	12	0	1	1	5,719	Candy Stick	4	F	3	0	0	0	3,369
Canadian Currency	4	F	5	0	3	0	15,181	Candy Verse	4	F	8	1	1	2	29,040
Canadian Edition	4	G	11	0	1	2	9,919	Candybag	5	G	10	1	1	1	8,763
Canadian Flyer	6	G	9	1	0	1	20,920	Candybedandy	3	F	9	2	1	2	77,260
Canadian Frontier	4	C	3	1	1	1	36,897	Candyfortheguest	8	M	5	0	0	0	640
Canadian Fury	4	F	6	2	0	0	17,839	Candyman Baker	5	H	7	3	2	0	6,270
Canadian Navy	6	G	23	2	4	1	12,358	Candyndawn	2	F	1	0	0	0	206
Canadian Northern	2	G	1	1	0	0	6,489	Candy's Advantage	4	F	15	0	0	1	9,615
Canadian Peso	4	C	3	1	1	0	32,200	Candys Cannonade	4	G	5	0	0	0	670
Canadian River	2	G	5	1	0	0	24,800	Candys Plan	2	F	4	0	1	1	4,365
Canadian Trick	2	C	4	0	0	0	556	Candy's Prospect	3	G	6	1	0	0	3,070
Canadian Warrior	2	C	2	1	0	0	8,340	Candy's Way	5	M	12	0	1	2	3,925
Canadian Way	2	G	3	0	0	0	858	Cane Ridge	7	G	2	0	0	0	0
Canadian Wrangler	3	C	1	0	0	0	355	Cane River	8	M	2	0	0	0	0
Canajun Cajun	8	G	2	0	0	1	2,649	Cane Vale	4	F	7	2	1	2	29,795
Canal Lake	3	G	13	1	3	3	29,903	Canfield	6	H	9	3	1	2	55,840
Canal Town	6	G	12	1	0	2	9,153	Canna Belle	4	F	12	1	3	0	8,840
Canaletto (GB)	7	G	10	1	1	3	31,119	Canna Lac	2	G	2	0	0	0	0
Canasita (GB)	5	M	3	0	0	0	1,050	Cannacorn	2	G	4	0	0	0	217
Canaska's Princess	3	F	2	0	0	0	525	Canned Heat	3	C	11	1	0	1	6,689
Canasta	3	C	8	0	1	1	13,521	Canned Heat (NZ)	7	G	7	0	4	2	17,705
Canasto Boy	4	G	9	1	1	2	16,912	Cannes' Spring	3	F	4	1	0	0	3,900
Canaverous	4	G	11	3	1	3	76,985	Cannon in G	3	F	13	1	1	0	18,800
Canberra (IRE)	4	C	2	0	0	0	570	Cannon One	3	G	2	0	0	0	0
Canby Dancer	4	F	8	4	2	0	38,800	Cannonball Jo	6	G	10	0	0	0	1,073
Cancel the Suite	3	F	6	2	1	0	29,400	Cannonball Red	4	G	3	0	0	0	1,230
Cancel When Close	10	G	9	0	0	2	1,794	Cannonball Rock	4	G	3	0	1	1	14,280
Canchetta	4	F	15	0	2	3	5,635	Cannonier	5	G	5	3	0	1	43,550
Cancion Alegre	6	G	19	4	2	4	68,741	Cannon's Joker	4	G	15	3	6	3	24,506
Cancione de Amor	3	F	11	1	4	1	14,357	Cannot Chase	2	C	6	1	0	1	13,350
Cancovina	2	F	4	0	0	0	993	Canny Fly (AUS)	6	G	4	0	0	0	1,980
Cande Secret	3	F	6	1	0	1	12,014	Canoe	7	H	12	2	2	1	12,950
Candeelite	3	F	10	2	2	2	43,973	Canoe Creek	5	M	4	0	2	1	5,830
Candeias	8	H	13	1	2	2	8,596	Canoe Maker	4	C	1	0	0	0	79
Candeille	3	F	4	1	0	1	3,450	Canoe Queen	3	F	3	0	0	0	0
Candelotto	10	G	7	1	0	4	11,188	Canonicus	4	G	9	1	4	0	12,375
Candi Art	3	F	2	0	0	0	0	Canoodle	3	C	3	1	1	0	22,400
Candi Corey	3	F	1	0	0	0	135	Canora	3	F	8	2	3	2	29,744
Candi Dancin	4	G	13	1	0	1	5,870	Canought Pass	3	F	3	0	0	0	0
Candi Hour	4	G	4	1	0	1	8,286	Canrock	7	G	11	4	3	0	29,820

Horse	Age	Sex	Sts	1st	2d	3d	Won	Horse	Age	Sex	Sts	1st	2d	3d	Won
Canso	6	G	16	1	1	1	3,730	Caped Crusader	5	G	6	0	0	0	249
Can't Be an Angel	3	F	9	3	0	1	6,485	Capehart (JPN)	2	F	1	0	0	1	5,060
Can't Be Denied	2	F	5	2	0	0	26,880	Capejinsky	2	C	6	2	3	0	110,740
Can't Be Golden	4	G	4	0	2	0	2,210	Caperex	2	C	1	0	0	0	0
Can't Be Wild	3	G	10	1	0	0	3,079	Caperucita Roja	5	M	15	5	3	5	21,150
Can't Buy Class	2	F	1	1	0	0	36,360	Cape's Fury	2	F	2	0	0	0	0
Can't Catch Comet	4	F	1	0	0	0	0	Capeside Lady	2	F	4	3	0	0	149,940
Can't Catch Sandy	4	F	5	0	0	0	249	Capias	2	C	2	0	0	1	2,925
Can't Escape Me	3	F	12	2	1	3	20,325	Capitaine	2	C	1	0	0	0	75
Can't Fool Clyde	4	G	6	0	0	1	2,631	Capital Asset	4	G	11	1	0	0	4,333
Can't Fool Phil	5	G	9	0	0	2	3,195	Capital Charm	2	G	8	2	0	2	29,420
Can't Get Enough	2	F	7	1	1	1	18,750	Capital Dreams	3	F	5	0	1	0	2,912
Can't Get Me	4	G	3	1	0	1	15,020	Capital Geisha	5	M	1	0	0	0	0
Can't Groom Lindy	4	F	9	2	2	2	27,592	Capital Honor	2	F	5	0	0	0	1,515
Can't Hackett	3	F	2	0	1	0	3,680	Capital Hope	5	M	5	1	0	1	4,382
Can't Shake Me	3	F	8	2	0	3	19,927	Capital Market	5	G	4	0	0	1	1,452
Can't Stop Smokin	4	F	4	0	1	0	2,946	Capitalina	3	F	2	0	0	0	260
Can't Tell Ya	4	G	2	1	0	0	6,090	Capitan Cook (CHI)	6	G	7	0	0	0	570
Can't You See	5	M	13	0	1	0	4,215	Capitan El Grande	5	H	8	0	1	2	4,894
Canta Bonita (ARG)	4	F	8	0	1	0	6,155	Capitan Fierro	6	H	1	0	0	0	0
Canta Ke Brave	7	H	2	0	0	0	680	Capitan Takiri	3	G	11	1	0	2	10,352
Can'taffordawreck	5	M	1	0	0	0	0	Capitano	2	C	4	1	2	0	106,400
Cantaloupe	6	M	12	4	1	1	74,080	Capitan's Cowboy	3	G	11	1	1	1	7,500
Cantcatchflashy	5	M	4	0	0	1	3,920	Capitol H	3	G	1	1	0	0	3,480
Can'tcatchme	3	F	1	0	0	0	0	Capitol Man	4	G	7	0	1	0	3,296
Cantey	2	G	2	0	0	0	2,580	Capitol Reality	4	G	7	1	1	1	7,548
Can'tfindmyglasses	4	G	3	0	0	0	1,440	Capitol Society	5	G	14	0	0	0	1,043
Cantilena	3	F	1	0	0	1	3,510	Capitol Won	2	C	7	1	0	0	4,817
Cantkeepfromsingin	5	M	2	0	0	0	6,600	Cap'n Cottontail	3	G	14	4	0	3	44,037
Canton	5	G	1	0	0	0	58	Cap'n Jeff	3	G	12	1	3	1	15,765
Canton Connection	5	G	6	1	2	1	12,013	Cap'n Jerry	5	G	8	0	0	0	1,126
Cantouchis	3	F	6	3	0	2	74,235	Capn Nathan	4	G	6	0	1	0	3,248
Cantus	2	G	4	0	0	0	0	Capo	2	C	5	0	0	0	1,400
Cantyahearmecallin	5	M	2	0	0	0	80	Capo Di Capo	6	G	2	0	0	0	0
Canuck	4	G	3	1	0	0	5,950	Capo Grosso (CHI)	5	G	1	0	0	0	400
Canuto	4	G	19	3	6	0	28,815	Capolaire	4	C	2	1	1	0	6,240
Canvas' Honey	3	F	14	1	1	2	7,570	Capote Dancer	3	C	7	2	0	0	11,362
Canyon Crook	6	G	11	0	1	4	8,460	Capote Express	5	G	18	0	1	2	6,180
Canyon de Oro	4	C	12	3	1	3	48,812	Capote Gold	5	H	1	0	0	0	0
Canyon Key	3	C	3	1	1	0	12,533	Capote Par	7	G	1	0	0	0	0
Canyon Pass	4	G	7	0	0	0	722	Capote Queen	3	F	12	3	0	2	20,060
Canyon Secret	3	F	9	2	1	0	30,498	Capote Slew	3	F	9	2	3	0	25,719
Canyon Turn	3	C	5	0	0	1	5,813	Capote Sun	6	H	4	0	1	1	11,780
Canyon Wish	4	C	2	0	0	0	0	Capote's Native	2	F	3	0	0	0	0
Canyonlake	7	H	9	0	0	0	434	Capow	2	C	1	0	0	0	0
Canyon's First	2	C	1	1	0	0	15,600	Capped	4	F	13	3	4	0	11,959
Canyon's My Honey	2	C	2	0	1	0	5,980	Cappistol	4	G	3	0	1	0	431
Canyoo Sea	6	M	1	0	1	0	1,680	Cappuchino	4	C	10	2	0	3	201,712
Canzady	4	F	5	2	0	2	4,885	Cappucino Carly	2	F	2	0	0	0	428
Canzonetta	3	G	5	0	2	0	6,000	Cappucino Kid	5	G	13	4	2	2	88,730
Cap	5	G	13	1	1	2	45,284	Cappy	9	H	9	0	2	0	2,469
Cap Ferrat (ARG)	6	H	7	1	1	0	25,580	Cappy Cat	4	G	9	0	0	0	2,172
Cap Jaluca	2	F	2	0	0	0	0	Capreta	2	F	1	1	0	0	5,225
Cap 'n America	4	C	3	1	0	1	6,691	Capria	2	F	3	0	0	0	654
Capability	2	C	1	0	0	0	2,135	Capricha	4	F	6	0	1	0	14,512
Capable Capers	4	C	8	2	2	2	15,811	Capricious Charm	2	F	1	0	0	0	0
Capable Dancer	3	G	7	3	3	0	6,650	Capriciousness	6	M	11	0	0	0	1,016
Capable Nila	8	M	7	2	0	1	10,992	Cap's Flying Lady	4	F	1	0	0	1	650
Capable of Gold	5	M	11	1	0	1	2,980	Capsacin	2	F	3	0	0	0	66
Capable Quest	7	G	7	4	2	0	8,095	Capsule	4	G	3	1	2	0	4,015
Capac	2	C	2	1	0	1	31,705	Capt Trops	4	G	2	0	0	0	88
Capazuri	5	G	11	3	2	1	53,676	Capt. Andy	4	C	11	1	2	0	9,679
Cape Breeze	2	F	2	0	0	0	3,000	Capt. Career	3	C	8	1	0	2	13,120
Cape Cod Dancer	4	C	13	0	1	2	4,980	Capt. Defrere	6	G	16	5	3	2	74,046
Cape Cod Gray	3	C	4	0	0	0	150	Capt. Fly Hook	6	G	5	0	0	1	17,400
Cape Colony	5	M	10	2	2	2	20,718	Capt. Jayger	4	G	16	3	1	3	11,227
Cape Crusader	2	G	3	0	0	0	560	Captain Aluppa	4	G	6	0	0	1	2,215
Cape Elizabeth	6	M	12	4	2	2	27,513	Captain Amour	3	G	13	1	4	3	47,446
Cape Fear Fury	4	C	1	0	0	0	0	Captain Andrew	3	C	1	0	0	0	147
Cape Good Hope	3	C	7	3	0	1	68,520	Captain Angel	4	C	7	0	0	0	1,710
Cape Kid	3	C	8	0	0	2	3,244	Captain B Crook	3	G	7	1	0	0	14,895
Cape Montauk	2	F	1	0	0	0	195	Captain Badgett	4	G	8	1	2	3	13,725
Cape Peer	3	G	4	0	0	0	362	Captain Ben	6	G	8	2	0	0	14,055
Cape Pogue	3	C	15	2	3	0	86,100	Captain Binge	2	C	2	0	0	0	1,302
Cape Power	4	C	8	4	3	0	183,301	Captain Blackie	3	G	5	0	0	0	107
Cape Prince	3	G	12	1	0	3	11,076	Captain Blue	2	C	2	0	0	0	300
Cape Town Lass	2	F	3	0	1	0	8,905	Captain Bob	4	C	4	1	0	0	4,830
Cape Verde	2	F	2	0	0	0	9,995	Captain Boo	3	C	7	0	0	0	3,480
Capeable Cat	2	F	2	0	0	0	320	Captain Briggs	3	G	2	0	0	1	2,520

Horse	Age	Sex	Sts	1st	2d	3d	Won	Horse	Age	Sex	Sts	1st	2d	3d	Won
Captain Buck	4	G	9	2	3	2	33,600	Captivator	10	G	7	0	0	2	4,613
Captain C.	3	C	2	0	0	0	0	Captive Forcett	3	F	2	0	0	0	47
Captain Cahill	3	G	7	3	0	0	25,155	Captive Sky	4	F	7	0	1	0	3,237
Captain Calm	3	G	4	0	0	1	940	Capt'nemos	3	C	14	1	3	5	19,805
Captain Capasso	2	C	3	0	0	2	4,640	Capture D' Oro	3	C	2	1	0	0	19,560
Captain Carby	7	G	7	1	0	1	4,368	Capture the Flight	4	F	7	3	2	0	26,692
Captain Carter	4	G	8	1	1	1	6,815	Capture the Silver	4	C	6	1	0	1	8,377
Captain Cause	4	C	6	1	1	0	7,460	Capture the Spirit	8	M	3	1	1	1	6,850
Captain Chessie	4	G	6	1	1	0	27,050	Capture the Wolf	3	C	5	0	2	0	14,460
Captain Colors	7	G	14	2	2	0	14,366	Captured	4	G	8	3	1	1	27,206
Captain Comet	6	H	2	1	0	0	2,275	Captured Cadence	5	G	6	0	0	0	585
Captain Cool	3	C	6	0	1	3	6,462	Capucine	2	F	6	1	0	0	29,163
Captain Craig	9	H	17	3	4	4	32,550	Capwaynesglass	6	G	5	0	0	0	210
Captain Creek	6	G	13	1	7	2	51,216	Car Czar	4	F	2	1	0	0	10,920
Captain Crossgrain	3	C	3	0	0	0	301	Car Keys	5	H	3	0	0	1	7,495
Captain Cummings	5	H	5	1	2	1	6,410	Car Lady	2	F	3	1	0	0	28,785
Captain Cyclops	3	G	3	1	1	0	11,489	Car Salesman	8	G	9	0	1	1	1,815
Captain Dean	4	G	13	1	1	2	6,613	Cara Linda	3	F	10	3	1	0	32,520
Captain Des	5	G	7	0	0	0	2,569	Cara Marisa	5	M	4	0	0	1	1,577
Captain Fancy	2	G	4	0	0	1	2,835	Cara Rubiano	5	G	12	1	1	0	6,092
Captain Fantastic	3	C	17	1	4	2	59,945	Cara Veronica	3	F	7	2	2	0	8,042
Captain Fiddle	3	G	4	1	0	0	2,275	Caralot	7	G	7	0	1	1	2,475
Captain Flash	2	C	3	0	1	0	5,780	Caramel	3	G	10	3	1	2	35,237
Captain Garfield	3	G	6	0	0	1	352	Caramel Prospector	3	F	4	1	0	2	12,335
Captain George	4	G	9	3	2	1	167,215	Caramel Queen (NZ)	5	M	17	3	2	0	34,120
Captain Gill	4	G	5	1	1	1	2,240	Caramel's Express	6	G	4	1	0	1	28,250
Captain Goose	9	G	5	0	0	0	296	Caras Lad	3	C	4	1	0	0	9,990
Captain Greybeard	3	G	9	1	1	3	13,179	Cara's Lassie	5	M	19	2	5	3	42,092
Captain Halo	3	C	4	0	0	0	140	Cara's Native	4	F	2	0	0	0	1,425
Captain Hastings	3	C	16	1	2	0	12,913	Carbinated B B	4	C	7	0	0	0	577
Captain Holloway	4	C	15	6	4	1	102,632	Carbon Comet	7	G	1	0	0	0	220
Captain Jackson	3	C	1	0	0	0	0	Carbon Copy (GB)	5	M	4	0	2	0	33,920
Captain Jim	6	M	10	0	3	2	9,867	Carbonax	4	G	1	0	0	0	0
Captain Jimbob	4	G	10	0	0	1	1,167	Carbonized	8	G	12	1	2	1	2,770
Captain Jinsky	4	G	12	0	0	1	2,357	Card	6	G	10	0	0	1	1,929
Captain Joe	6	G	1	1	0	0	4,800	Card and Flowers	4	F	5	1	0	0	7,530
Captain Keenan	4	G	16	1	5	1	21,720	Card Sound	5	M	13	4	4	1	36,075
Captain Kilo	5	G	9	0	0	1	1,798	Card Traitor	2	F	1	0	0	0	170
Captain Kirby	4	G	8	1	0	0	7,335	Cardenal	3	C	3	0	0	0	595
Captain Larkin	4	G	7	2	0	0	26,009	Cardiac Arrest	3	G	3	0	0	0	185
Captain Leland	6	G	7	0	0	0	0	Cardiff Arms	5	G	8	1	2	2	28,170
Captain Lovely	3	C	9	2	2	1	7,949	Cardigan Bay	3	G	4	1	1	1	10,526
Captain Mac	6	G	11	1	0	5	4,263	Cardinal and Gold	3	G	5	1	1	0	10,450
Captain Malory	4	G	1	0	0	0	0	Cardinal Joe	3	G	9	1	0	3	4,148
Captain Mick	3	G	3	1	1	0	7,875	Cardinal Ryan	4	C	5	1	1	0	16,450
Captain Missy	5	M	6	2	0	1	12,490	Cardinal Verse	6	H	4	0	0	1	1,960
Captain Natural	4	G	3	0	0	0	0	Cardinalli	2	F	5	1	1	1	37,740
Captain Nicholas	5	G	10	2	0	2	50,304	Cardinal's Echo	3	G	1	0	0	0	75
Captain Paul	2	G	5	0	2	0	5,350	Cardiogenic	10	G	9	3	0	2	13,363
Captain Phillip	4	G	6	1	1	1	34,560	Cardtoga Tina	4	F	5	1	0	1	5,587
Captain Popeye	3	C	6	0	1	1	4,250	Care Free Lady	7	M	14	4	0	2	24,737
Captain Red	6	H	7	2	0	0	86,851	Careadancer (ARG)	6	G	4	0	0	0	13,460
Captain Scott	3	G	3	0	0	0	720	Career Advantage	6	G	15	2	0	0	9,475
Captain Smith	4	G	6	0	1	2	17,760	Career Best	4	C	10	1	1	2	12,019
Captain Spaulding	2	C	2	0	0	0	0	Career Day	3	F	2	0	0	0	340
Captain Speed	4	G	11	3	1	2	13,030	Career Party	4	F	8	1	0	2	5,280
Captain Squire	4	G	7	1	2	1	419,625	Career Run	3	C	11	1	2	2	31,388
Captain Stats	5	G	21	1	1	4	19,156	Carefree	6	G	21	3	4	5	33,696
Captain Sventhomas	3	C	5	0	0	1	2,090	Carefree Jim	4	G	11	1	4	0	19,180
Captain Thunder	3	C	4	3	1	0	79,110	Carefull	4	F	6	1	0	0	8,936
Captain Tripps	8	G	1	0	0	0	0	Careless Dream	3	F	3	0	0	1	1,120
Captain Wallstreet	5	H	5	0	1	0	6,435	Careless Gold	5	M	5	0	0	0	0
Captain Weave	3	G	10	2	2	1	10,085	Careless Humor	3	C	7	1	1	0	12,875
Captain Wheat	4	G	14	2	3	1	46,260	Careless Love	2	F	3	1	0	0	6,515
Captain Wild	4	G	2	0	0	1	1,420	Careless Whisper	5	M	3	1	0	0	9,541
Captainbluegrass	3	G	10	2	1	1	8,818	Caress the Wind	6	M	4	0	0	0	2,200
Captainofindustry	4	G	9	1	0	4	37,730	Carey's Blue Mon	4	F	15	3	1	4	7,464
Captain's Daughter	3	F	13	5	3	4	100,415	Carey's Gold	4	C	8	1	0	3	20,416
Captain's Maneuver	3	G	5	2	1	0	18,980	Carey's Lil Boy	4	G	8	1	1	1	3,818
Captains Only	3	C	3	0	0	1	1,885	Carfax Abbey	6	G	13	3	3	2	41,957
Captain's Song	4	F	11	1	2	0	8,193	Cargi	6	G	6	3	1	0	49,719
Captain's Surprise	3	F	14	1	1	1	16,300	Cargo Ship	3	C	8	2	1	2	70,710
Captain's Table	5	G	14	2	1	1	23,986	Cariano	5	M	7	2	0	1	9,664
Captian His Due	3	G	16	4	4	2	37,760	Carib Lady (IRE)	4	F	8	2	1	0	124,703
Captian Literati	3	G	3	1	0	1	3,340	Caribbean Breeze	4	F	3	0	0	0	0
Captilea (IRE)	4	F	9	1	1	0	7,428	Caribbean Code	5	G	7	2	1	0	27,710
Caption	3	G	4	0	0	1	2,370	Caribbean Cutie	6	M	9	2	1	2	3,580
Captiva Cat	3	F	14	2	1	4	94,755	Caribbean Storm	3	G	8	3	0	2	35,051
Captivating Miss	3	F	1	0	0	0	163	Caribben Carnival	7	H	7	1	0	0	4,350

Horse	Age	Sex	Sts	1st	2d	3d	Won
Caribean Boy	2	C	5	0	0	2	5,290
Cariboo Prospector	2	G	4	1	2	0	22,920
Caricature	3	F	7	0	0	2	2,185
Cariel	3	F	3	0	1	0	4,920
Cariful	5	M	3	1	0	0	1,320
Carina	3	F	5	1	0	1	11,350
Carinoso	4	C	4	0	2	1	2,208
Carioca Sunrise	3	F	1	0	0	0	0
Carl	2	G	3	1	1	0	13,608
Carla and Wandy	2	F	3	0	1	0	4,920
Carla Rose	3	F	6	3	0	0	50,820
Carla Sparkles	10	M	16	2	0	2	20,624
Carley Country	3	G	12	1	1	2	4,277
Carley's Call	3	F	8	1	1	0	5,046
Carley's Coin	4	G	3	0	0	0	0
Carleystarlet	4	F	1	0	0	1	1,155
Carline	3	F	8	0	3	0	21,819
Carlingford	5	H	8	2	0	3	4,825
Carli'silver Prize	3	C	8	0	2	1	6,561
Carlo's Gold	11	G	3	0	0	0	294
Carlotta Tendant	4	F	21	1	3	3	10,924
Carl's Accomplice	4	C	7	0	0	0	600
Carls Favorite	3	G	1	0	0	0	0
Carls Tootin Abby	4	F	2	0	0	0	0
Carly Castelli	7	M	8	2	0	4	22,035
Carly Pooh	6	M	13	4	1	2	37,765
Carlyn Road	3	F	7	2	2	0	14,400
Carly's a Twin Too	3	F	3	0	0	0	675
Carmalley	3	F	10	3	3	2	25,400
Carmella	3	F	9	2	1	1	16,277
Carmella Maria	3	F	10	4	1	2	29,871
Carmen Country	5	M	11	1	0	2	6,235
Carmic Delight	2	F	4	0	0	1	1,248
Carmichael's Gold	7	M	5	0	0	0	690
Carmolita's Girl	3	F	1	0	0	0	61
Carney's Prospect	6	G	1	0	0	0	270
Carni Das	3	F	3	0	0	0	900
Carnie's Dancer	4	F	18	3	3	5	136,535
Carnie's Moon	6	M	4	0	0	1	1,765
Carnie's Secret	6	M	6	0	1	0	3,367
Carnie's Thunder	4	G	6	0	0	3	4,010
Carni's Luck	5	M	5	2	0	1	21,900
Carnival Gal	4	F	12	0	4	0	9,483
Carnival Match	5	G	19	0	2	2	7,503
Carnival Sass	3	F	13	1	0	2	8,704
Carnival Trade	4	C	6	1	0	1	7,357
Carnivalkyrie	6	H	1	0	0	0	0
Carny Princess	7	M	3	0	0	0	288
Caro Line Lulu	6	M	15	1	6	1	21,484
Caroca	3	F	4	0	1	0	12,260
Carol Jean	3	F	7	0	2	1	5,960
Caroldean	4	F	4	0	0	1	5,100
Carole's Spirit	4	C	6	1	1	0	6,386
Carolina Cowboy	3	G	4	0	0	0	0
Carolina League	10	G	8	0	1	1	2,913
Carolina Lily	2	F	3	0	0	1	3,775
Carolina Playboy	5	H	1	0	0	1	816
Carolina Storm	3	F	13	2	1	4	30,155
Carolina Sunrise	3	F	9	0	0	2	8,220
Carolina Ties	3	F	4	0	0	0	0
Carolinas Hope	4	F	6	0	0	0	1,355
Carolina's Punch	2	C	3	0	0	0	684
Caroline Island (IRE)	4	F	1	0	0	0	0
Caroline's Candy	3	F	14	2	2	1	32,010
Caroline's Morning	4	F	11	0	0	1	1,615
Caroline's Prince	2	G	8	1	1	2	20,233
Carolinia Miner	3	G	2	0	0	0	70
Carol's Believer	4	F	7	0	0	0	486
Carol's Choice	5	M	8	4	1	0	32,250
Carol's Country	2	F	1	0	0	0	0
Carols Crystal	5	M	11	0	1	3	6,015
Carols Irish Hope	2	C	2	0	0	0	105
Carol's Magic	2	C	6	1	1	1	20,285
Carol's Memories	2	F	2	0	0	0	750
Carols Pic	5	H	7	0	0	2	2,406
Carolyn	3	F	2	0	0	0	700
Carolyn Frances	3	F	8	2	2	3	49,030
Carolyn's Diamond	2	F	3	0	0	0	0
Carolyn's Pride	7	H	2	0	0	0	90

Horse	Age	Sex	Sts	1st	2d	3d	Won
Carolyn's Tour	2	G	6	1	2	1	11,785
Caro's Alley	4	G	15	0	3	1	6,144
Caro's Lady	5	M	7	0	0	0	1,365
Caro's Mark	6	G	17	2	2	1	11,188
Caro's Royalty	10	G	11	3	1	1	45,680
Carouse	4	G	3	0	0	0	830
Carousel's Hope	3	F	2	0	0	0	165
Carpanetto (IRE)	3	C	4	1	1	0	26,361
Carpenter Road	9	G	7	0	0	0	105
Carpenter's Halo	7	G	2	0	0	0	0
Carpet Slipper	6	M	3	1	0	0	15,360
Carr Creek	7	G	3	0	0	0	554
Carr de Bon Bon	6	M	16	1	1	2	10,092
Carr de Great	4	C	1	0	0	0	0
Carr Delicious	3	G	6	0	1	0	6,047
Carr Fourty Four	5	G	11	1	3	1	9,735
Carr On the Run	3	G	19	2	6	3	20,603
Carr Queen	6	M	3	0	0	1	1,650
Carrforthecourse	7	G	12	1	5	2	3,224
Carribean	5	G	3	1	0	0	4,380
Carrickfergus Boy	5	G	6	0	0	1	1,394
Carrie Boone	4	F	7	3	1	1	12,640
Carrie Me Back	3	F	13	2	0	4	27,700
Carrie the Signals	5	H	11	0	2	1	5,682
Carried Away	8	G	17	2	5	4	48,171
Carried Interest	3	C	2	0	0	0	270
Carrier	3	C	10	1	2	0	54,280
Carrie's a Jewel	2	F	1	0	0	1	1,770
Carrie's Luck	2	F	1	1	0	0	5,880
Carrie's Red Rose	2	F	1	0	0	0	230
Carrie's Turn	6	M	9	3	1	0	38,381
Carrie's Wild Girl	4	F	7	2	0	2	7,237
Carrington	2	C	1	1	0	0	35,280
Carriza Planes	5	M	18	2	1	2	12,557
Carrizo Springs	4	G	16	2	5	2	14,052
Carrlana	3	F	1	1	0	0	14,160
Carroll Maker	3	F	2	0	0	0	0
Carroma	3	F	1	0	0	0	0
Carrot Gal	5	M	1	0	0	0	0
Carrot Juice	2	G	6	0	0	2	3,588
Carrots Only	2	C	1	0	0	0	270
Carttiff	3	G	6	1	0	0	8,458
Carry On Carson	5	H	8	3	1	1	12,829
Carry the Cross	9	G	5	0	0	0	110
Carry the Tune	2	F	2	0	0	0	380
Carryabigstick	3	F	6	1	0	0	9,883
Carryon	5	G	2	0	0	0	330
Carseland	5	G	9	2	2	1	31,434
Carson Beach	8	G	4	0	0	1	3,000
Carson Canyon	3	C	1	0	0	0	0
Carson City Blues	3	G	15	4	3	3	67,260
Carson City Kid	9	G	15	2	0	4	19,621
Carson City Limits	5	H	2	0	0	0	370
Carson City Star	3	G	10	2	0	0	17,118
Carson Dealer	5	G	7	0	0	0	0
Carson Grove	4	F	7	0	1	0	2,440
Carson Hollow	4	F	3	1	2	0	164,740
Carson Manor	3	C	5	1	0	1	16,308
Carson Silver	4	F	8	1	0	1	6,570
Carson Unleashed	2	C	7	0	1	3	22,880
Carsonetta	2	F	9	2	2	1	72,333
Carsonic	8	G	13	1	3	3	7,388
Carson's Baby	4	F	10	2	1	0	41,480
Carson's Beauty	2	F	3	0	1	1	5,610
Carson's Cat	3	F	9	2	2	0	26,919
Carson's Girl	3	F	6	1	0	1	17,900
Carson's Lady	2	F	2	0	0	0	0
Cart Dancer	4	C	2	1	0	0	16,800
Cart San	4	G	5	0	0	2	3,191
Carta Gold	2	C	2	0	0	1	3,220
Cartage Agent	2	C	5	0	0	0	45,400
Cartano	4	C	5	1	0	0	6,853
Carte Madera	4	F	6	3	1	1	63,100
Carters Boy	4	C	8	4	1	1	14,470
Carters Place	2	G	4	0	0	0	0
Carthage	3	C	4	1	0	1	27,840
Cartittothebank	4	F	3	0	0	0	120
Cartman	6	G	7	0	0	0	670
Cartoon	6	M	6	0	1	0	1,300

Horse	Age	Sex	Sts	1st	2d	3d	Won	Horse	Age	Sex	Sts	1st	2d	3d	Won
Cartoonist	2	C	2	1	0	0	16,800	Cash Creek	3	G	10	0	0	1	4,806
Cart's Behalf	5	M	4	1	0	1	4,678	Cash Dash	4	C	7	1	1	3	16,186
Cart's Cash	2	G	3	0	0	0	250	Cash Delivery	3	C	12	3	1	1	53,300
Cart's Cutie	2	F	4	1	1	1	9,700	Cash Excess	2	G	1	0	0	1	900
Cart's Exposure	3	G	13	2	3	5	21,130	Cash Fast	3	F	1	0	0	0	145
Cart's Fine Tuned	2	G	3	0	0	0	0	Cash Fever	3	F	8	3	0	1	19,334
Cart's Forty Four	4	G	8	0	0	2	5,601	Cash for Colors	4	F	13	2	3	0	12,067
Carts Forty More	3	G	11	1	2	1	36,640	Cash in Hand	4	C	19	1	1	3	18,190
Cart's Good News	2	F	6	1	2	0	9,595	Cash Instrument	3	F	4	0	0	1	4,030
Cart's Magic	5	G	7	1	1	0	3,613	Cash It Baby	5	M	13	2	4	0	12,585
Cart's Maybe So	2	F	8	1	2	0	30,690	Cash Machine	4	F	1	0	0	0	0
Cart's On Cruise	2	G	6	1	2	1	27,886	Cash Marquet	3	G	1	0	0	0	126
Cart's Plumbob	4	G	9	0	0	3	1,788	Cash On the Run	6	G	12	1	2	0	9,715
Cart's Showoff	2	F	4	0	0	0	263	Cash Only	5	H	8	2	0	0	14,475
Cart's Snappy	5	M	10	1	2	4	16,103	Cash Prospect	5	H	3	2	1	0	4,070
Cart's Upper Crust	4	F	8	1	0	2	10,445	Cash Ransom	3	C	5	0	2	0	3,528
Cartwright's Tish	6	M	10	1	1	2	4,906	Cash Red Jester	9	M	1	0	0	0	216
Cary Creek	3	F	3	0	0	0	244	Cash Reward	6	M	1	0	0	0	0
Caryatid	4	F	3	1	0	0	7,660	Cash Stash	3	G	6	0	1	0	4,750
Cary's Our Man	8	G	14	0	0	0	1,161	Cash the Flash	3	F	6	1	0	0	21,630
Carysfort	5	M	4	0	0	0	339	Cash Trap	3	G	7	0	1	1	1,800
Casa Frio	3	G	16	1	2	2	14,024	Cash Tyme	4	F	1	0	0	0	0
Casa Nekia	2	F	9	2	1	2	29,755	Casha Blanca	2	F	1	0	0	0	95
Casamo	3	G	11	0	2	2	7,020	Cashel Calling	2	F	8	3	1	1	51,460
Casanova Cat	6	H	8	0	0	0	0	Cashel Castle	4	C	4	0	2	1	28,260
Casanova Chris	3	C	7	2	2	0	100,292	Cashem Cheyenne	5	G	15	1	0	1	5,916
Casanova Red	3	C	9	1	0	0	4,290	Cashfromnaevus	5	G	8	1	0	2	5,840
Casanova Slammer	3	G	12	2	4	1	65,710	Cashier's Check	3	G	6	1	0	1	7,275
Casas Caballo	3	C	3	2	1	0	60,200	Cashier's Wager	4	F	14	2	5	1	20,945
Casa's Kids	6	M	2	0	0	0	0	Cashlan (IRE)	3	C	5	1	0	1	19,640
Casca Grossa	2	C	1	0	0	0	75	Cashline	3	G	9	0	0	2	2,625
Cascade Casey	6	G	13	2	2	2	18,420	Cashman	5	H	4	0	0	0	0
Cascade Corona	3	F	3	1	0	0	8,690	Cashmere and Silk	3	F	9	0	4	0	14,130
Cascade Lace	3	F	6	2	1	1	5,070	Cashmere Miss	3	F	12	2	3	4	112,655
Cascade Range	4	G	10	1	3	1	18,873	Cash's Dynamite	2	F	13	0	1	2	7,075
Cascarina	2	F	1	0	0.	0	0	Casimir (IRE)	7	H	7	0	1	1	2,227
Case Charmer	3	C	11	1	1	2	37,870	Casing	4	F	11	2	1	1	45,960
Case Considered	2	F	1	0	0	0	0	Casing the Raw Bar	2	F	1	0	0	0	300
Case He Is	6	G	11	0	0	3	4,520	Casino Bound	3	F	2	0	0	0	195
Case in Thought	5	H	1	0	0	0	364	Casino Casey	3	C	6	1	1	1	23,792
Case Load	5	M	9	2	1	0	24,960	Casino Express	3	F	7	2	2	2	17,325
Case Might Bee	4	F	2	0	2	0	6,090	Casino Gal	2	F	3	0	0	1	1,140
Case N Cure	5	H	2	0	0	0	0	Casino Jack	5	G	12	0	0	1	5,955
Case of Bubbly	2	F	2	0	1	0	12,120	Casino Knight	3	G	10	0	1	1	11,303
Case of Champagne	4	F	10	0	0	1	1,875	Casino Miss	2	F	2	0	1	0	7,620
Case of Nickles	5	H	1	0	0	0	0	Casino Princess	2	F	5	1	1	0	5,550
Case of Pride	4	F	15	1	1	1	20,033	Casino Raider	5	G	10	1	3	1	47,700
Case of the Heart	2	F	1	0	0	0	123	Casino Red	3	C	1	0	0	0	2,000
Case of Wine	3	C	2	0	0	0	261	Casino Wager	3	C	10	1	1	3	25,531
Case Said	5	M	9	1	1	2	22,105	Casper Can Fly	7	H	3	0	0	0	405
Casey B	4	G	5	1	3	1	10,658	Casperino	3	G	8	2	3	0	85,207
Casey Cobalt	3	G	6	0	3	2	51,718	Casperius See	5	G	4	0	0	0	2,056
Casey Darling	2	F	2	0	0	0	1,260	Casper's Ghost	4	C	1	0	0	0	330
Casey House	3	C	10	1	0	2	7,500	Casperuvian	3	G	11	2	2	1	16,315
Casey Mighty Casey	5	G	7	0	0	1	905	Cassa Della	2	F	2	0	0	1	1,020
Casey's Bid	4	F	11	1	2	3	13,651	Cassaforte	4	G	19	4	2	3	36,979
Casey's Bluff	3	G	16	1	0	1	9,690	Cassandra Terms	5	M	4	0	0	0	400
Caseys Call	5	M	2	0	0	0	0	Cassanova Kid	2	G	1	0	0	0	250
Casey's Castaway	3	C	11	1	0	0	7,850	Cassanova Mitch	4	G	5	1	0	1	4,298
Casey's Castle	4	G	10	3	0	0	32,738	Cassa's Affair	3	F	6	3	0	0	18,227
Caseys Charm	3	F	2	0	1	0	4,200	Cassava	4	F	12	1	2	0	8,681
Casey's Cool Cat	2	F	1	0	0	0	0	Cassette Dancer	3	C	5	0	0	0	1,125
Casey's Crimson	3	C	3	0	0	0	410	Cassia	6	M	8	0	1	0	24,549
Caseys Crystal	2	F	2	0	1	1	1,190	Cassidy Jean	3	F	8	2	0	2	5,714
Casey's Our Dream	4	C	3	0	0	0	150	Cassidy Loves You	3	G	7	1	1	1	35,480
Caseys Pride	3	F	17	1	2	1	9,287	Cassidy Princess	3	F	15	3	2	2	23,442
Caseys Storm	2	F	1	0	0	0	130	Cassidy Queen	4	F	6	1	1	2	3,600
Casey's Victory	4	F	4	0	0	0	740	Cassidy's Cat	3	F	8	0	0	0	740
Cash Again	3	F	14	2	1	2	10,430	Cassie Anne	5	M	9	1	0	5	13,157
Cash Attitude	2	C	3	0	0	0	745	Cassie Cat	4	F	10	0	2	3	7,922
Cash Bandit	2	G	4	1	0	1	5,296	Cassie Erin	5	M	8	1	0	3	6,990
Cash Bar	5	G	20	3	6	3	70,075	Cassie the Martyr	2	F	3	0	0	0	0
Cash Button	2	C	8	2	0	1	43,510	Cassie the Slewor	3	F	2	0	0	0	96
Cash Career	4	F	13	2	3	2	25,890	Cassie Vanish	3	F	1	0	0	0	0
Cash Case	3	G	7	2	0	0	26,310	Cassie's Casper	6	G	9	1	2	0	25,282
Cash Clara	3	F	3	0	0	0	262	Cassie's Deer	8	M	11	1	4	0	29,638
Cash Commander	2	C	3	0	1	0	3,573	Cassies Quiet	2	F	3	0	0	1	2,505
Cash Converter	6	M	8	1	0	2	7,990	Cassirer (IRE)	4	G	8	0	1	1	20,592
Cash Coupon	3	C	9	0	0	3	1,881	Cassis	3	F	7	1	0	0	117,995

RECORDS OF HORSES

Horse	Age	Sex	Sts	1st	2d	3d	Won
Cassopolis	3	F	10	4	2	1	63,639
Cassy's Star	2	G	4	0	0	0	300
Cast a Majik Spell	5	M	1	0	0	0	0
Cast a Miracle	3	C	4	0	0	0	282
Cast Call	6	G	1	0	0	1	1,045
Castaic	6	G	6	0	0	0	130
Castelli's Ace	3	F	6	1	1	0	21,905
Castelli's Dance	6	M	1	1	0	0	3,240
Castelli's Gypsy	3	F	6	1	1	2	26,005
Castello Bianco	3	C	4	0	1	0	3,975
Castilian	4	G	2	0	0	0	80
Casting Sun	3	C	14	1	1	1	8,599
Castle Back	7	H	5	0	0	0	450
Castle Comer	6	G	8	1	4	0	38,140
Castle Concert	2	C	11	2	1	3	40,815
Castle Crane	8	G	17	3	1	3	7,513
Castle Dark	3	G	6	1	1	0	10,576
Castle Gandolfo	4	C	4	0	0	2	14,570
Castle Knight	2	G	2	0	0	0	360
Castle Milk	3	F	4	0	0	0	630
Castle Mountain	5	M	5	0	2	1	24,150
Castle Queen	3	F	2	1	0	0	4,950
Castle Racer	9	G	1	0	0	0	0
Castle Rock	5	G	9	1	1	1	6,739
Castle Spring	4	F	3	0	0	1	4,420
Castle Springs (GB)	3	C	3	0	1	1	11,074
Castlebright	5	M	13	3	3	3	55,650
Castlebrook	6	M	1	0	0	0	320
Castledale (IRE)	2	C	8	2	4	1	109,623
Castletown	4	G	5	0	0	1	5,390
Castlewood	6	G	9	4	0	0	86,340
Castling	5	M	5	0	1	0	18,600
Castner	4	G	15	3	4	5	51,828
Castor Troy (IRE)	3	C	4	1	0	0	30,340
Casu	5	M	10	1	1	2	9,461
Casual Attitude	3	F	8	4	0	1	88,940
Casual Conflict	9	G	2	1	0	0	9,150
Casual Country	5	G	10	0	0	1	2,050
Casual Dance	3	F	5	1	1	0	6,675
Casual Gold	3	C	6	1	1	1	1,030
Casual Look	3	F	7	1	0	2	505,104
Casual Smile	4	F	1	0	1	0	900
Casual Thunder	4	G	5	0	1	2	25,280
Casually Urbane	6	G	13	0	2	0	12,230
Casualy Explosive	3	F	6	0	1	2	3,601
Cat Albert	2	C	1	0	0	0	100
Cat Alert	3	F	6	2	2	0	51,380
Cat Ali	4	F	3	1	1	0	13,400
Cat and the Hat	5	M	6	0	0	2	10,300
Cat Ante	4	G	8	1	2	3	40,718
Cat Babu	6	G	12	0	0	1	1,989
Cat Ballew	3	G	3	0	0	0	0
Cat Blade (BRZ)	7	G	1	0	0	0	90
Cat Buster	2	C	4	1	0	1	34,330
Cat Can	4	G	4	0	2	0	751
Cat Charm	3	F	3	1	0	0	25,830
Cat Choo	3	F	6	1	0	0	9,825
Cat Connection	2	G	4	0	0	1	1,354
Cat Creek	8	M	2	0	0	0	129
Cat Creek Christy	4	F	10	1	0	2	8,351
Cat Crossing	4	F	13	2	0	2	15,525
Cat Crusher	4	C	9	2	1	0	34,680
Cat Dreams	2	C	1	1	0	0	27,320
Cat Express	4	G	12	1	2	3	30,312
Cat Fighter	3	F	4	2	2	0	68,800
Cat Five	4	F	1	0	0	0	0
Cat Flap	4	F	1	0	0	1	1,140
Cat Flight	5	G	3	0	0	0	2,580
Cat Genius	3	C	7	2	0	1	79,200
Cat Girls Love	6	M	10	4	1	2	12,070
Cat Gotcha	3	G	2	0	0	0	675
Cat Gun	2	G	11	0	3	1	7,895
Cat in a Tizzy	3	F	2	0	0	0	0
Cat in Deed	3	F	6	2	0	0	34,326
Cat in the Country	3	G	14	0	1	2	11,345
Cat in the Nat	4	F	14	3	3	2	36,475
Cat Is Clean	2	G	2	1	0	0	14,200
Cat Line	3	C	4	0	1	0	4,975
Cat Looker	4	G	16	3	3	2	17,935
Cat Lover	3	F	3	0	0	0	552
Cat Music	2	F	3	0	0	0	125
Cat n' Mouse	4	F	9	0	0	0	959
Cat of Tomorrow	2	G	4	0	1	1	6,970
Cat On a Rail	2	C	3	0	0	0	0
Cat On Guard	4	C	6	0	0	2	4,050
Cat On the Grass	3	C	12	3	3	2	92,880
Cat Out	5	M	1	0	0	0	405
Cat Pass	2	G	2	0	0	0	1,179
Cat Patrol	3	C	4	0	1	0	11,485
Cat Play	4	F	1	0	0	0	340
Cat Ridge	5	H	10	0	2	1	17,010
Cat Royal	4	F	8	3	1	1	20,027
Cat Ruckus	3	F	8	2	0	2	18,510
Cat Scan	7	H	2	0	0	0	1,920
Cat Singer	3	G	8	3	2	1	113,676
Cat Sound	2	C	1	0	0	0	0
Cat Story	3	G	5	1	0	0	28,900
Cat Striker	2	G	11	1	3	3	90,894
Cat Stripe	3	F	6	3	1	0	12,560
Cat Tap	3	C	3	0	0	0	935
Cat Time	4	G	6	0	1	0	1,378
Cat Toy	4	G	2	1	0	0	6,050
Cat Tracker	5	G	6	1	3	0	77,923
Cat Tracks	5	G	14	3	0	0	12,447
Cat Trina D.	3	F	7	1	0	0	3,318
Cat Walkin	5	H	4	0	0	0	0
Cat Woman	4	F	6	0	0	0	0
Catabatic Wind	4	C	1	0	0	0	320
Catahoula Blue	3	F	3	0	1	0	3,075
Catahoula Hope	3	F	4	1	0	1	14,523
Catahoula Huff	3	G	8	0	0	0	1,341
Catahoula Otis	3	G	2	0	0	0	233
Catahoula Rose	5	M	10	1	1	2	35,829
Catale Shine	2	F	3	0	0	0	525
Catalina Cat	3	F	9	1	2	2	56,547
Catalindy	2	F	1	0	0	0	0
Catalissa	3	C	3	1	0	0	21,000
Catalita	4	F	12	2	2	4	73,726
Catalog	6	H	14	1	5	2	15,590
Catalogue Kid	4	C	2	0	0	0	640
Catalone	3	G	6	3	0	0	32,459
Catalyze	3	G	12	1	2	2	22,160
Cataman	2	G	4	0	0	1	4,070
Catarella	3	F	1	0	0	0	214
Cataria	2	F	2	1	0	1	16,500
Catasauqua	4	C	1	0	0	0	480
Catascatcan	2	C	2	0	0	0	2,135
Catawhompus	4	G	12	3	1	0	15,292
Catbaby	2	F	2	0	0	0	0
Catbird Seat	5	G	8	3	0	1	31,106
Catbite	4	G	3	0	0	0	589
Catboat	2	F	3	0	0	1	1,390
Catcantscratchit	2	C	1	0	0	0	100
Catch a Dream	6	G	12	3	3	1	68,584
Catch a Fire	3	F	4	1	0	0	40,854
Catch a Fox	4	C	10	1	3	3	16,045
Catch a Leprechaun	4	C	9	0	1	2	13,720
Catch a Thief	5	G	4	1	0	1	5,585
Catch a Winner	3	F	5	0	1	1	8,812
Catch Bullets	4	G	9	2	0	5	29,566
Catch Catch Can	3	F	11	3	0	1	21,569
Catch Me Deputy	4	F	2	0	0	0	0
Catch Me Eye	5	M	4	0	0	1	2,240
Catch Me First	3	C	2	0	0	0	0
Catch My Cat	2	C	9	3	3	0	65,538
Catch My Ice	3	G	7	1	1	1	4,595
Catch On	2	C	1	0	0	0	105
Catch Simon	3	C	4	0	0	0	2,267
Catch the Bouquet	4	F	6	1	2	0	11,350
Catch the Bullet	2	F	1	0	0	1	2,300
Catch the Crook	4	G	2	0	0	0	78
Catch the Dew	6	H	10	0	1	2	4,493
Catch the Glory	2	C	2	0	0	0	2,760
Catch the Greene	7	M	8	0	0	0	101
Catch the Leader	6	M	3	0	0	0	149
Catch the Spirit	3	F	6	0	2	0	5,473
Catch the Storm	2	G	5	0	0	1	1,899
Catch the Sun	5	G	8	1	1	2	4,588

Horse	Age	Sex	Sts	1st	2d	3d	Won	Horse	Age	Sex	Sts	1st	2d	3d	Won
Catch This Bird	5	M	10	2	1	1	22,480	Cats Cafe	2	F	2	0	0	0	0
Catch This Coin	2	F	2	0	0	0	855	Cat's Cat	3	F	9	2	2	1	76,098
Catch This Jokar	5	G	1	0	0	0	100	Cats' Claws	3	C	3	0	1	1	3,482
Catch Two Thousand	3	G	2	0	0	0	250	Cats Copy	2	F	5	2	1	0	37,655
Catch Up Affair	3	F	7	1	1	0	5,750	Cat's Craft	3	G	12	3	2	2	36,380
Catch Up Fast	3	C	6	0	0	0	612	Cat's Cricket	4	F	1	0	0	0	69
Catchaluckystar	3	F	14	2	2	0	18,035	Cat's Cyclone	2	G	2	0	0	0	170
Catchaser	5	M	8	0	3	0	12,560	Cat's Delight	4	C	13	1	0	3	6,446
Catch'em All	5	G	24	6	5	3	31,762	Cats Fury	4	G	16	1	1	2	39,630
Catchin Some Rays	4	F	3	0	0	0	0	Cat's Gambol	4	G	6	0	2	2	17,006
Catchin Time	6	H	2	0	0	0	0	Cat's Glow	4	F	6	0	1	2	24,060
Catchin' Z's	3	F	7	0	1	1	4,320	Cat's R. N.	4	F	13	2	1	1	7,493
Catching Fire	4	C	3	0	0	0	315	Cat's Roar	2	F	5	0	0	1	7,080
Catching Up	3	G	12	3	0	0	10,496	Cats Rule	2	F	2	0	0	0	1,400
Catchmecat	4	F	8	2	2	0	9,891	Cat's Surprise	4	C	2	0	0	0	0
Catchmeifucan	5	G	7	0	0	0	621	Cat's Theme	4	F	9	2	1	3	16,290
Catchthegroom	2	G	5	1	1	1	24,670	Cat's Touch	3	G	9	2	0	1	17,080
Catchtheroses	4	F	3	0	0	0	0	Cats Tower	3	F	4	2	0	0	34,620
Catchthisjetster	5	M	10	2	2	2	25,836	Catscape	3	G	13	4	2	1	23,512
Catchum	3	G	7	1	0	3	9,077	Catsgotninelives	2	C	2	0	0	0	0
Catchy Music	3	F	10	2	0	1	20,250	Catsuit	3	F	14	2	3	3	54,270
Catchy Phrase	4	C	6	0	2	1	10,890	Catsure	3	C	11	1	2	3	20,830
Catchy Word (GB)	6	G	10	2	0	0	51,735	Cattache	5	M	13	0	0	0	3,695
Catdog	4	F	1	0	0	0	90	Catticus	2	C	5	0	0	1	5,820
Catechol	6	H	9	0	1	2	22,470	Cattle Kate	3	F	10	3	2	1	44,792
Catena	4	F	6	0	1	2	2,124	Catty Laddie	3	G	18	1	2	0	16,650
Cateress	4	F	6	0	3	1	19,970	Catvantageous	6	G	2	0	0	1	1,500
Cate's My Angel	4	F	11	1	3	0	17,576	Catwillcatchyou	4	F	13	1	0	5	10,225
Catessa	3	F	7	2	2	1	65,789	Catylitic Spark	4	G	10	0	1	4	6,442
Catessence	3	F	4	1	0	0	2,750	Catzinga	3	F	9	0	2	2	24,547
Catfish Alley	3	F	10	5	1	1	54,477	Catzzene	5	M	21	2	1	4	29,256
Catfish Charlie	6	G	2	0	0	0	0	Caucus	3	F	8	0	2	1	23,880
Catfish Hunter	3	F	5	0	0	0	458	Caught a Slew	5	M	6	0	1	0	3,168
Catfish Junction	7	H	1	0	0	0	0	Caught Cheatin'	4	F	9	1	0	0	33,150
Catfish Red	4	F	4	0	1	1	1,390	Caught in a Pinch	2	F	1	1	0	0	27,000
Catfit	6	M	1	0	0	0	0	Caught in the Rain	4	F	9	2	0	1	120,708
Cathedra	2	F	4	0	0	1	3,970	Caught Out	5	M	3	0	0	1	5,500
Cathedral Chapel	5	G	4	0	0	0	882	Caught You Running	3	G	5	0	0	1	1,587
Cathedral Friend	6	G	10	0	2	1	6,658	Caught'n	4	C	4	1	2	1	2,153
Cathedral Tower	8	G	7	0	0	1	818	Cause for Concern	3	F	7	0	1	0	3,220
Catherine's Angel	5	H	4	0	0	2	1,240	Cause for Stars	5	H	2	0	0	0	0
Cathrine Marie	3	F	5	0	1	2	4,410	Cause He's Bolger	10	G	17	3	3	4	11,510
Cathy Dear	4	F	7	1	0	0	4,553	Cause I'm a Rebel	3	G	14	1	1	3	10,120
Cathy R	4	F	6	0	1	2	1,487	Cause I'm Fancy	3	F	1	0	0	0	1,430
Cathy Super	4	F	3	0	0	0	0	Cause of Action	2	C	2	0	0	0	1,818
Cathy's Condo	6	M	11	3	0	3	30,671	Causeanative	3	C	2	0	0	0	0
Cathy's Cup	5	M	11	0	2	1	3,321	Causeimacajun	5	H	13	4	1	2	43,086
Cathy's Dream	4	F	12	2	0	1	25,881	Caustic Remark	5	M	8	1	0	1	26,410
Cathy's Luck	2	G	8	0	0	0	189	Caution Beware	4	C	10	3	0	1	36,588
Cathy's Private	5	H	3	0	0	0	2,155	Cautionary	4	F	14	2	1	2	15,301
Cathy's Star	3	M	10	1	1	1	12,246	Cautions	3	C	5	0	0	0	336
Catillac Style	3	C	6	0	1	1	5,117	Cautious Warrior	4	G	5	1	0	0	9,210
Catillacsandlevis	3	F	7	0	2	5	11,250	Cauy	5	M	12	4	3	0	113,616
Catinthedark	4	C	6	2	2	0	7,880	Cavalero	4	G	1	0	0	0	0
Cativa	3	F	11	5	1	0	111,810	Cavalessa	5	M	4	0	0	0	0
Catjur	3	F	9	0	1	1	4,721	Cavalier Billie	4	F	5	1	1	0	58,562
Catlaunch	2	C	5	1	1	0	9,335	Cavallo Grigio	3	F	6	0	2	0	6,138
Catlett Comet	7	G	10	2	1	2	41,930	Cavallo Nero	3	G	12	1	0	4	4,479
Catlike Dancer	3	F	6	1	1	0	30,340	Cave Creek Queen	4	F	12	4	0	2	19,153
Catlike Move	4	C	10	0	1	2	25,020	Caveat Fleet	2	C	1	0	0	0	175
Catmansdream	3	G	17	0	5	4	13,612	Caveats Prospect	4	G	15	4	3	2	73,685
Cat'n Around	3	G	3	0	0	0	480	Caveolin	5	G	1	0	0	0	3,250
Catnabout	4	F	15	0	0	4	17,330	Caviar Emptor	3	F	15	5	3	2	89,888
Catnamedadam	2	F	4	0	0	0	360	Caviar N Diamonds	4	F	1	0	1	0	1,440
Catnapped	4	F	2	0	0	0	119	Cavilling	3	F	3	0	0	1	3,000
Catniro	6	H	16	2	3	6	61,120	Cavish	6	G	1	0	0	0	0
Catomize	4	F	11	1	1	0	5,146	Cavista	2	F	7	1	0	0	6,690
Catonie Time	2	C	3	0	0	0	497	Cavort	4	G	4	0	0	0	408
Caton's Banner	4	F	20	1	4	6	19,294	Cayenne Gold	4	G	4	0	0	0	0
Caton's Boreas	3	G	2	0	0	0	420	Cayenne Pepper	5	M	8	1	0	1	9,024
Caton's Crown	4	G	14	1	0	2	6,751	Cayenne Red	2	G	1	1	0	0	6,600
Caton's Promise	2	F	1	0	0	0	75	Cayenne the Man	2	G	7	1	1	1	22,870
Catpasser	4	G	10	2	0	2	8,635	Cayerless and Bold	3	G	9	2	1	1	26,460
Catrageous	2	C	2	0	0	1	2,750	Cayman Gold	2	F	4	0	1	1	6,720
Cat's a Prowler	2	C	1	0	0	0	0	Caymus	5	G	14	0	1	2	9,396
Cat's Account	2	F	4	1	0	0	17,130	Cayoke (FR)	6	H	4	1	0	0	97,000
Cat's At Bat	3	C	8	1	0	0	6,000	Cazador	7	G	1	0	0	0	0
Cat's At Home	6	H	1	0	0	1	11,814	Cazadotes	3	G	14	1	5	1	18,240
Cats Beauty	3	G	6	2	2	0	38,726	Cbknightspretense	2	C	3	2	0	0	4,814

RECORDS OF HORSES

Horse	Age Sex	Sts	1st	2d	3d	Won	Horse	Age Sex	Sts	1st	2d	3d	Won
Cc's Delight	10M	4	0	0	0	278	Celiac	3 F	3	0	0	1	1,130
Cd's Best Yet	3 F	1	0	0	0	0	Celibate	4 C	2	0	0	2	3,020
Ce Fitzrovia	2 F	5	0	0	2	6,240	Cella Luna	2 F	2	1	0	0	25,830
Ceara 'n Regan	3 F	5	0	0	0	246	Cellamare (FR)	3 F	7	2	0	0	49,455
Cearamic	9 G	11	1	1	1	17,371	Cellars Kiss	3 F	2	0	0	0	660
Ceasar's Fate	3 G	8	1	2	0	13,950	Cellars Merlot	5 H	9	2	0	4	59,403
Ceasar's Ghost	3 G	7	3	0	1	12,770	Cellars Shiraz	4 F	6	1	2	1	155,250
Cease Span	4 F	3	0	0	0	4,120	Cells Bells	4 F	9	5	0	1	60,400
Ceasefire (FR)	4 F	4	0	0	0	676	Cellular Call	6 G	9	0	0	1	3,065
Ceba	2 F	4	0	0	0	1,080	Celona's Girl	6 M	12	0	2	2	8,130
Cecelia Rose	3 F	4	2	1	0	38,680	Celophane Man	2 C	4	0	0	0	1,120
Cecie Baker	3 G	2	0	0	0	70	Celosita Mag (ARG)	4 F	7	1	0	0	10,419
Cecil County	4 G	11	2	1	2	19,375	Celt	4 G	7	4	2	0	77,033
Cecilia's Girl	4 F	10	1	0	1	31,030	Celtic Approval	4 G	13	3	3	2	96,287
Cedar Belle	3 F	10	1	0	1	14,952	Celtic Choice	4 G	3	0	0	0	392
Cedar Dream	3 F	4	0	0	0	263	Celtic Craft	4 F	1	0	0	0	240
Cedar Key	3 G	10	2	1	0	28,570	Celtic Dance	6 M	8	1	0	2	8,379
Cedar Point	2 G	7	2	2	0	40,975	Celtic Eclipse	3 F	7	1	2	0	7,935
Cedar River Bill	4 G	8	1	2	3	11,100	Celtic Fire	3 G	5	0	0	2	8,560
Cedar Run	3 F	5	0	0	0	484	Celtic Fling	4 C	2	1	0	0	4,500
Cedar Runs Case	4 F	8	1	3	1	28,175	Celtic Jet	5 M	9	1	0	2	5,684
Cedar Sea (IRE)	4 F	2	0	0	0	0	Celtic King	6 H	11	1	3	1	9,188
Cedar Slew	2 F	9	0	0	3	9,407	Celtic Memories	3 G	5	1	1	1	45,300
Cedar Summer	2 F	8	1	0	2	35,240	Celtic Moon	5 M	11	0	1	5	4,820
Cedar Top	3 C	7	0	0	0	1,384	Celtic Park	4 C	13	4	2	1	58,335
Cedro Con	5 G	11	0	0	1	1,749	Celtic Prince	6 G	5	0	0	0	900
Cee Cruiser	3 G	7	4	0	2	21,830	Celtic Prospect	8 M	4	0	0	0	156
Cee Dee Riverkamm	2 G	6	0	0	0	165	Celtic Reign	7 G	14	1	3	2	6,886
Cee Double You	4 C	1	0	0	0	35	Celtic Rhapsody	3 F	3	0	0	1	4,100
Cee E T Sing	5 G	15	0	5	1	15,053	Celtic Ride	3 F	12	1	5	3	112,278
Cee El	4 G	11	1	4	1	18,038	Celtic Sin	7 G	4	0	0	0	345
Cee Miss Tizzy	6 M	1	0	0	0	50	Celtic Sky	5 H	5	0	2	1	51,260
Cee Pee	5 G	7	0	0	3	720	Celtic Smoke	6 M	9	1	3	0	23,658
Cee Ruby	6 M	1	0	0	0	0	Celtic Spirit	3 F	11	1	1	2	5,773
Cee the Lead	4 F	3	0	1	1	966	Celtic Susi	3 F	3	0	0	0	365
Cee Till Dawn	4 G	5	1	1	0	15,480	Celtic Way	2 F	1	1	0	0	12,600
Ceebrite	4 G	7	1	1	0	5,662	Cemmec	4 F	7	2	1	0	10,685
Ceecee's Wilddance	2 F	3	1	0	0	8,100	Censor	6 H	8	2	1	1	8,301
Ceecil	3 C	1	0	0	0	282	Centauress's Witch	10 G	2	0	0	0	300
Ceedie Pop	5 H	6	0	2	2	3,025	Center	4 G	6	3	0	0	46,620
Ceehawk	5 M	10	0	3	0	8,323	Center Line	3 C	10	2	2	0	33,790
Ceelinctive	4 G	8	2	4	0	26,350	Center Point Blaze	6 M	8	2	2	0	12,196
Ceely's Classic	4 F	7	0	2	2	17,150	Center Seven	3 F	3	0	0	0	659
Cee's a Cutie	6 M	4	0	1	1	3,938	Center Target	4 F	16	3	3	1	23,375
Cee's a Flirt	2 F	3	0	0	1	2,610	Centerfold Dreamer	6 G	11	4	2	1	48,101
Cee's a Lady	3 F	3	1	1	0	7,140	Centerfold Guy	5 H	3	0	0	0	436
Cee's Cheetah	3 G	1	0	0	0	750	Centerfold Queen	3 F	4	0	0	0	0
Cee's Dancing Now	3 F	3	2	0	0	33,840	Centerofattention	5 M	10	4	1	0	187,962
Cee's Dude	5 G	7	0	1	1	3,178	Centerofthetreat	3 F	11	0	0	0	1,597
Cee's Elegance	6 M	6	2	1	0	398,600	Centerpiece	2 F	3	1	0	0	16,011
Cee's Madness	3 G	6	1	0	1	1,757	Centerstone	4 C	4	0	0	0	38
Cee's Marfa	8 G	18	2	3	5	9,941	Centerton Miss	3 F	21	1	2	2	15,345
Cee's the Moment	3 F	11	2	3	2	36,261	Centerville	5 G	5	1	2	1	12,284
Cee's Valley Girl	4 F	6	1	2	2	94,820	Centi	4 F	7	1	2	1	11,704
Ceesharp	5 G	4	0	0	0	824	Centime	5 M	4	2	1	0	23,260
Ceetart	3 G	3	0	0	1	450	Centra Gold	7 H	6	0	0	0	608
Ceetoit	8 G	9	2	0	2	36,196	Central Market	2 G	7	0	2	2	6,175
Ceetune	4 F	3	0	0	0	0	Centrifucal Motion	5 M	2	1	0	0	8,917
Ceeya Slew	4 F	3	1	0	0	8,010	Cents for Trent	6 G	8	0	2	2	2,817
Cee'z the Dream	3 F	4	0	0	0	400	Centsability	4 F	6	0	1	0	2,946
Cefull	7 M	15	1	0	2	10,807	Centsible Slew	3 G	7	0	2	2	3,495
Celasa	3 F	1	0	0	0	0	Centsible Wager	4 F	14	1	5	3	7,633
Celdif	3 C	3	0	0	1	638	Centurian Man	6 H	4	0	1	0	3,092
Celebrate Away	6 G	1	0	0	0	0	Centurion	11 G	9	0	3	0	5,495
Celebrate the Sun	3 F	10	1	3	0	9,540	Century Boulevard	2 G	7	2	3	1	24,782
Celebration Time	2 C	4	0	0	2	2,310	Century City (IRE)	4 C	9	2	0	2	409,392
Celebrity Alert	5 H	12	0	0	3	6,763	Century Mark	3 F	7	1	2	1	18,611
Celebrity Star	4 C	14	1	0	4	12,113	Century Prospector	4 F	2	1	1	0	16,423
Celebs Boy	4 C	11	0	1	1	6,041	Cepharonious	3 G	16	2	5	1	19,165
Celera	4 C	13	0	0	3	10,340	Ceremonial	3 F	11	2	2	1	70,740
Celerity Boy	3 C	8	1	0	1	7,273	Cerese Sunrise	3 F	2	0	0	0	0
Celestial Journey	3 C	1	1	0	0	7,410	Cerrific	4 F	3	0	0	1	1,035
Celestial Light	4 F	13	0	2	5	5,580	Certain Act	3 G	2	1	0	0	21,600
Celestial Moment	4 F	12	2	0	1	23,758	Certainly a Dilly	4 G	9	2	0	3	25,008
Celestial Prince	3 G	11	0	2	0	4,155	Certainly Appealin	2 G	6	1	0	0	12,760
Celestial Queen	3 F	7	1	0	1	12,675	Certainly Blue	4 G	9	1	0	0	6,520
Celestial Sea	5 M	12	0	4	1	7,902	Certainly Can	4 F	3	0	0	0	500
Celestial Star	2 F	3	0	0	1	3,135	Certainly Regal	2 F	1	1	0	0	10,584
Celestino D	4 G	10	2	0	1	14,124	Certam Sweep	3 G	13	3	1	2	63,750

Horse	Age	Sex	Sts	1st	2d	3d	Won	Horse	Age	Sex	Sts	1st	2d	3d	Won
Certantee	6	G	5	1	1	0	57,750	Champagne Now	2	F	1	0	0	0	0
Certifiable	5	H	1	0	0	0	0	Champagne Punch	3	F	8	1	3	1	34,475
Certifiably Crazy	3	C	6	2	3	0	67,910	Champagne Rep	6	M	7	2	0	0	8,840
Certification	3	G	10	2	0	3	64,902	Champagne Shimmer	4	F	5	0	2	1	5,800
Certified Approval	5	M	15	3	0	2	25,427	Champagne Slew	3	C	1	0	0	0	0
Certified Coin	6	G	12	3	1	4	26,314	Champagne Summer	3	F	16	2	3	2	32,148
Certified Fact	2	G	2	0	0	0	285	Champagne Tony	6	H	3	0	0	1	2,345
Certify	4	G	4	0	0	0	330	Champagne Velvet	4	F	16	2	4	2	21,390
Certin Victory	3	G	2	0	1	0	2,470	Champagne Voyage	8	G	3	0	0	0	0
Cerulean	4	F	12	2	4	1	13,977	Champagne Way	4	G	2	1	0	0	6,630
Cervelo	2	C	3	1	1	0	18,905	Champagne Weekend	7	M	8	0	0	0	0
Cerveza Tom	3	G	8	1	1	1	21,100	Champagneandlace	3	F	9	2	1	2	16,529
Ceside Kiss	5	G	7	0	1	1	9,378	Champagnecelebrity	3	F	1	0	0	0	47
Cetewayo	9	H	6	0	1	1	56,340	Champagnechick	3	F	3	0	0	0	0
Ceviche	5	G	15	1	3	1	58,510	Champagneforalydar	5	G	12	1	2	0	11,975
Ceyenne Ranchero	2	C	4	1	1	1	19,880	Champagneforcarly	5	M	6	1	1	1	2,920
Cf Sparks a Flying	5	M	14	2	3	4	24,958	Champagneforjoanne	9	G	7	0	0	0	1,343
Cha Cha Hedy	9	M	7	0	1	3	4,200	Champagneforshelby	6	M	13	0	0	5	6,770
Chabuka	4	F	1	0	0	0	960	Champagneforwilbur	4	G	12	1	1	2	9,715
Chachacharlie	2	C	2	0	2	0	12,200	Champagnencashmere	3	F	11	1	2	2	13,228
Chaching Chaching	3	G	6	0	1	0	3,805	Champagnen'limos	4	F	4	1	0	1	3,057
Chaco	3	F	1	0	0	0	0	Champagne's Reddy	2	G	1	0	0	0	175
Chaco Primo (ARG)	6	H	5	1	0	1	8,650	Champagns Holiday	4	C	5	2	1	1	7,484
Chad			20	1	1	0	5,689	Champaign Powder	4	F	13	2	1	7	36,165
Chad Counted	3	G	10	0	2	3	9,911	Champali	3	C	10	4	1	3	313,522
Chadbegone	3	C	2	0	0	0	122	Champie G	6	G	16	0	3	1	15,686
Chadbert	4	G	8	0	0	2	1,246	Champignon Du Bois	4	G	8	1	0	0	14,033
Chaddy	7	H	4	0	0	1	1,000	Champion Bones	3	G	12	0	3	2	6,563
Chaddy Jon Jon	4	G	13	1	0	2	6,743	Champion Lodge (IRE)	6	G	4	2	0	1	238,638
Chads Bad Boy	4	G	3	0	0	1	715	Champion Proof	3	F	4	1	1	1	13,374
Chad's Boy R C T	2	C	3	0	0	0	225	Champion Ri	3	C	5	1	1	1	30,260
Chad's Hope	3	C	11	1	3	2	96,754	Champion Slippers	6	H	2	0	0	0	145
Chad's Way	4	C	4	1	1	1	3,210	Championsdaydreams	4	G	7	1	0	1	12,658
Chadsanddimples	4	F	8	2	2	2	10,610	Champman Again	8	H	11	0	0	0	1,075
Chadwicks Well (IRE)	4	G	10	1	2	1	39,200	Champ's Amour	5	G	5	1	2	0	6,434
Chadychadybangbang	3	C	4	1	0	0	4,290	Champ's Gold	3	G	6	0	1	1	7,220
Chaffee's Prospect	6	G	12	3	0	1	21,940	Champ's Jewel	6	M	4	0	0	0	1,050
Chaffery	3	G	11	1	1	0	6,511	Champ's Ole'	3	F	7	1	0	2	22,740
Chagrin River	2	G	9	1	1	2	5,615	Champs Puma	9	G	11	1	1	0	5,835
Chain	4	C	11	2	3	0	42,441	Champ's Rocket	2	F	9	0	3	3	52,940
Chain Blue	4	F	8	0	0	3	8,119	Champ's Star	8	G	2	0	0	0	2,380
Chain Letter	6	M	8	0	2	2	11,858	Champ's Surprise	4	C	12	4	1	3	27,800
Chain Lightning	5	G	8	1	0	3	19,027	Champ's War	6	G	2	0	0	1	600
Chain of Miracles	2	C	3	0	0	0	195	Chamrousse	4	F	6	0	0	3	19,100
Chain Reprisal	5	G	7	0	0	0	1,597	Chan Chan	4	C	6	2	0	2	59,702
Chairman	6	H	7	1	0	4	19,680	Chanago's Classic	7	G	9	0	0	2	3,519
Chairman A. P.	5	G	3	0	0	0	2,660	Chance Aire	5	H	1	0	0	0	0
Chairman Bob	3	C	2	0	0	0	150	Chance Anew	8	G	3	1	0	0	2,500
Chairman Cella	5	G	14	2	4	0	45,510	Chance Arrest	4	F	12	4	2	1	26,117
Chairman of Vice	3	G	11	1	0	3	6,530	Chance Dance	3	F	6	1	1	1	31,510
Chairman's Delight	5	G	9	1	1	2	7,560	Chance Kyl	6	G	13	3	3	0	14,893
Chaka's Jewel	5	M	8	1	1	0	9,188	Chance of Reign	4	G	5	0	1	0	1,871
Chal I Get Them	13	G	1	0	0	0	38	Chance of Sleet	6	G	11	1	0	3	7,278
Chala Mia	5	M	12	3	1	1	10,790	Chance 'ola	3	C	4	0	0	1	4,080
Chalas Cliper	5	G	4	1	1	0	7,923	Chance to Dance	3	C	13	1	0	3	21,675
Chalet Chanteuse	2	F	9	2	1	1	56,320	Chanceisalady	6	M	10	1	0	5	66,272
Chalet Wick	2	C	3	0	1	0	2,500	Chancellor M. H.	6	G	4	0	1	0	4,500
Chalkaholic	3	G	14	3	4	1	15,648	Chances Are I Know	5	G	7	0	0	1	5,560
Chalkupthegold	3	F	1	0	0	0	100	Chances Chiquitin	3	C	2	0	0	0	144
Challenge Cole	6	G	6	0	1	1	7,480	Chance's Domain	3	F	4	1	0	0	17,220
Chalmette	4	F	3	1	0	0	24,700	Chanceto Reminisce	7	M	2	0	0	1	880
Chalouchi	3	F	4	1	0	1	15,446	Chancey Light	2	F	1	0	0	0	130
Chamaco	4	G	4	0	0	1	3,895	Chancier	2	F	4	0	0	0	315
Chambers Creek	3	C	5	0	0	0	291	Chancy Chancy	3	F	14	4	3	1	22,055
Chambord Liqueur	4	G	7	0	0	1	1,662	Chancy Si	2	G	5	1	0	1	15,366
Chameleon	3	G	5	0	1	2	13,040	Chancy Toss	4	F	4	0	0	0	347
Chami Q Too	2	F	2	0	1	0	2,137	Chandler Brooks	4	G	12	1	2	1	5,550
Chamoix	4	F	7	1	0	1	5,812	Chandler Cup (ARG)	5	G	11	3	3	1	71,970
Champagne Account	3	C	7	2	1	0	36,880	Chandler's Midge	3	G	12	0	1	0	3,350
Champagne Alley	4	F	7	1	1	1	6,343	Chandlersthename	4	F	14	3	0	1	14,943
Champagne Cocktail	2	F	1	0	0	0	0	Chandrika	4	F	14	1	1	1	16,639
Champagne Day	5	G	11	4	2	1	36,380	Chanel Number Four	5	M	6	1	1	2	10,855
Champagne Doll	4	F	5	2	0	0	25,560	Chanelles Walk	4	C	1	0	0	0	0
Champagne Edition	3	F	3	0	0	0	75	Chanelly's Dancer	2	F	4	0	0	1	1,470
Champagne Float	4	G	7	0	0	1	1,390	Chanels Star	2	F	2	0	0	0	200
Champagne High	4	F	7	0	0	0	640	Chanel's Valentine	3	C	11	2	1	3	33,955
Champagne Jet	4	F	3	0	0	0	233	Change Course	3	C	2	0	0	1	3,740
Champagne Mountain	6	G	12	3	3	2	12,500	Change in Flight	7	H	3	0	1	0	1,247
Champagne 'n Stars	5	G	8	1	1	4	1,974	Change Me	6	M	1	0	0	0	65

Horse	Age	Sex	Sts	1st	2d	3d	Won
Change of Fortune	2	F	3	1	1	0	17,710
Change of Identity	4	G	5	0	0	2	5,580
Change of Plans	4	G	6	1	1	0	5,075
Change Over Time	8	H	2	0	0	1	869
Change the Locks	5	H	5	0	2	0	2,220
Change the Play	6	M	6	0	1	1	3,262
Change the Record	4	G	17	2	5	0	41,450
Changed	4	G	5	0	1	1	2,240
Changeforafifty	6	M	6	0	3	1	3,710
Changeintheweather	4	C	7	2	4	1	202,245
Changer	4	G	16	3	1	0	24,261
Changesinlattitude	3	F	5	0	1	1	1,164
Changing Light	5	G	15	3	0	4	36,037
Changing Numbers	2	C	3	0	1	1	11,280
Changing Times	4	G	7	0	0	0	1,735
Changing World	3	F	6	3	0	2	120,189
Chango	4	C	5	0	1	1	3,970
Channel Fire	5	M	7	4	1	0	47,348
Channel Surf	5	G	6	0	0	0	150
Channing Way	5	M	1	0	1	0	7,000
Chansel	4	G	2	1	0	0	3,235
Chansonette	4	F	1	0	0	0	0
Chantilly Lad	8	G	6	2	1	1	4,227
Chantilly Light	2	F	8	0	1	1	8,400
Chantilly Philly	4	F	7	1	2	2	14,350
Chantilly Spice	2	F	1	0	0	0	780
Chantre	3	F	7	2	1	1	21,350
Chantress	3	F	10	1	4	1	40,402
Chantz	3	G	4	1	0	0	4,500
Chaos	4	F	6	0	2	2	12,832
Chaos N Confusion	4	G	2	0	0	0	1,740
Chaos Theory	3	F	13	4	0	1	20,259
Chaotica	3	G	4	2	0	0	11,790
Chap Up	4	F	8	0	2	0	9,898
Chapa	4	C	10	1	0	0	3,195
Chapeau	4	F	4	1	1	0	42,400
Chapel Gold	2	C	5	1	1	0	9,236
Chapel Hill	9	G	16	0	2	4	3,880
Chapel Lites	4	F	8	1	1	0	10,919
Chapel Miss	4	F	8	0	0	1	1,050
Chapel Road	4	F	8	2	2	0	26,686
Chapel Royal	2	C	6	3	2	1	484,755
Chaperlaro	3	G	11	2	3	0	10,746
Chapie	9	G	14	0	2	1	4,809
Chapilkim	4	F	10	3	1	4	38,110
Chappaquiddick	3	F	1	0	0	0	0
Chapper Grey	3	G	3	0	0	0	622
Char	4	G	14	2	3	2	40,122
Char Da Valley	5	M	7	0	0	0	735
Character Witness	3	G	7	2	1	0	56,240
Charade	2	F	2	0	0	0	800
Charanne Charlie	4	G	4	1	0	1	5,091
Charanne Park	9	G	6	1	0	0	4,038
Charbar	3	G	10	2	1	3	20,640
Charbon	5	H	1	0	0	0	0
Charbonnier	2	G	4	1	0	0	20,400
Charcoal Bin	6	G	13	1	2	2	14,695
Charcoal Blue	6	H	12	0	1	1	2,621
Charcoal Canyon	4	F	2	0	0	0	675
Charcoal Charm	4	F	2	0	0	0	1,680
Charcot	2	C	3	1	0	0	33,515
Chardonay's Beau	5	G	15	0	1	3	4,072
Charge	3	C	4	2	0	0	69,113
Charge Ahead	2	C	3	0	0	0	210
Charge and Send	4	F	10	2	1	1	25,100
Charge Back	2	G	1	0	0	0	0
Charge n' Reason	4	G	13	3	1	3	20,398
Charged Circuit	4	G	3	0	1	2	940
Charged Up	3	C	10	0	0	1	4,787
Charged Up Cowboy	6	H	4	0	0	0	0
Charged Up Taco	9	G	1	0	0	0	0
Chargeitall	3	C	2	0	0	0	0
Chargeittothegame	2	F	2	0	0	0	0
Chargeout	6	H	1	0	0	0	0
Charging Ruby	3	F	10	5	0	2	49,240
Charginghisway	3	C	7	0	0	1	1,482
Charian	2	F	2	0	0	1	3,993
Charie Sue's Baby	3	F	14	1	3	2	11,697
Chariot	5	H	7	2	0	1	13,000

Horse	Age	Sex	Sts	1st	2d	3d	Won
Charioteer	4	G	7	1	1	3	45,510
Charismatic Appeal	2	F	7	1	0	1	22,243
Charismatic Caller	2	C	4	2	0	0	46,200
Charismatic Kid	2	C	2	0	0	0	1,020
Charismatic Lady	3	F	7	3	0	1	58,539
Charismatic Rob	2	C	5	1	0	1	35,050
Charity Gal	4	F	10	1	1	2	17,040
Charity Girl	2	F	3	1	0	1	36,875
Charity Line	6	G	8	1	4	0	16,650
Charity Man	3	G	12	0	1	0	8,220
Charity's Snowball	3	G	13	0	1	1	2,323
Charla Begone	3	F	2	0	0	0	0
Charla's Norm	2	F	2	0	0	0	210
Charleen's Remark	8	M	12	2	0	0	3,947
Charles	4	G	10	2	1	0	28,475
Charles B.	3	G	1	0	0	0	0
Charles Harbor	3	G	1	0	0	1	1,320
Charleston Cathy	3	F	8	0	2	0	4,810
Charleston Springs	3	F	12	2	0	2	60,050
Charley Bates	4	G	3	1	2	0	52,600
Charley's Bailey	2	F	6	0	2	0	4,910
Charley's Ensign	3	C	3	0	0	1	1,330
Charley's Love	3	G	8	0	1	0	3,660
Charlie Broads	2	C	2	0	1	0	4,020
Charlie Cat	2	G	2	0	0	0	675
Charlie Chapin	3	G	8	2	0	2	25,520
Charlie Go Bear	3	G	4	0	1	2	4,567
Charlie Good Time	5	G	8	0	0	0	0
Charlie Haan	5	G	15	2	1	1	28,604
Charlie Horst	5	G	16	0	2	3	5,283
Charlie Lambert	7	H	10	0	3	2	4,921
Charlie Man	8	G	15	0	2	2	3,698
Charlie Papa	2	F	1	0	0	1	1,625
Charlie Riddell	4	G	11	3	4	1	25,466
Charlie Vaughn	3	C	2	0	0	0	0
Charlie Waller	5	G	20	1	2	4	8,156
Charlies Bandito	3	G	3	1	0	0	5,820
Charlie's Beau	6	H	4	0	1	1	3,685
Charlie's Charmer	3	F	10	2	1	2	12,465
Charlie's Chippy	5	M	3	0	0	0	105
Charlies Cook	4	F	15	1	4	4	7,798
Charlie's Dewan	11	G	6	3	1	1	65,700
Charlie's Gold	3	G	2	0	0	0	720
Charlies Good Girl	4	F	7	0	1	2	14,480
Charlies Indian	3	F	3	2	1	0	18,395
Charlie's Meadow	2	F	2	0	1	0	6,760
Charlie's Never In	4	C	1	0	0	0	0
Charlie's Revenge	3	F	4	0	0	0	570
Charliesfavorite	3	C	7	2	1	1	21,205
Charlie'smydarling	3	F	2	0	0	0	483
Charlomaine	2	F	9	2	1	0	30,935
Charlotte Bay	2	F	5	1	1	1	18,686
Charlotte Forever	5	M	2	0	1	0	5,600
Charlotte Jones	3	F	9	1	1	1	10,550
Charlotte's Ego	9	M	5	1	1	0	13,822
Charlottes Find	7	M	15	3	5	2	22,650
Charlston Blue	6	H	8	1	0	1	6,388
Charm a Song	4	F	5	1	1	1	48,400
Charm Appeal	3	F	14	1	2	2	56,040
Charm Attack	4	G	11	2	1	3	12,934
Charm Boy	3	G	4	1	1	0	4,724
Charm Cat	2	G	9	0	1	2	22,560
Charm Seeker	3	C	1	0	0	0	0
Charm the Angels	4	F	16	2	4	1	13,443
Charmander Char	3	G	1	0	0	0	0
Charmane J.	2	F	2	0	0	0	120
Charmant	5	M	5	0	0	1	220
Charmed Flight	3	G	6	1	0	0	10,800
Charmed Gift	4	F	4	1	1	0	58,732
Charmedandangerous	4	F	1	0	0	0	76
Charmeleon	5	G	12	1	2	7	8,737
Charmer Baron	3	G	13	1	5	1	57,200
Charmer's Image	4	F	1	0	0	0	1,320
Charmico	5	G	7	1	0	2	9,802
Charmie	4	F	8	2	1	2	7,505
Charmie's Secret	3	F	12	0	5	2	19,980
Charmin Chatty	3	F	2	0	0	0	0
Charmin Fifi	5	M	3	0	0	0	446

Horse	Age	Sex	Sts	1st	2d	3d	Won
Charmin' Lil	3	F	5	0	0	0	270
Charmin' Middling	3	G	9	1	1	2	12,593
Charmin' Miss	5	M	10	0	0	0	1,075
Charming Affair	3	F	2	0	0	0	495
Charming Attiude	4	F	14	2	3	0	24,439
Charming Bid	3	F	3	1	2	0	24,560
Charming Boy (ARG)	7	G	12	2	2	1	54,080
Charming Charles	8	G	3	0	1	0	7,370
Charming Cherokee	3	F	12	0	3	3	7,800
Charming Chit Chat	3	F	8	0	2	1	4,518
Charming Clover	3	F	6	1	1	1	25,652
Charming Duchess	4	F	6	0	0	0	1,208
Charming Eyes	7	G	8	1	0	0	6,441
Charming Heiress	7	M	9	0	0	1	954
Charming Hero	5	G	8	0	0	0	853
Charming Home	6	G	16	2	1	1	12,203
Charming Hope	7	H	15	0	2	1	4,420
Charming Humor	2	F	3	0	0	1	6,300
Charming Jim	2	C	7	1	2	1	53,105
Charming John	3	G	11	2	3	2	52,090
Charming Knight	4	F	11	2	4	1	16,306
Charming Lass	6	M	3	0	0	0	190
Charming Naskra	7	G	7	1	1	0	12,680
Charming Native	3	F	4	0	0	0	0
Charming Paige	4	F	6	0	1	0	3,520
Charming Pat	2	F	5	0	0	0	605
Charming Pic	6	H	7	0	0	0	890
Charming Rogue	5	H	2	0	0	0	336
Charming Royalty	4	F	7	1	4	0	16,630
Charming Ruler	4	G	11	0	0	1	880
Charming Sammy	3	C	3	0	1	1	4,035
Charming Shannon	4	F	8	0	0	3	1,910
Charming Skier	4	F	3	0	0	0	192
Charming Socialite	2	G	1	0	0	0	0
Charming Star	5	H	7	0	0	0	0
Charming Terri	3	F	6	1	0	1	11,130
Charming Trip	8	M	3	0	0	0	586
Charminger	6	M	2	0	0	0	56
Charmingintentions	3	G	9	0	0	1	2,188
Charm's Lottery	9	G	5	0	1	1	1,478
Charm's Lucky Lady	4	F	2	0	0	0	115
Charmu	5	H	3	0	1	2	2,027
Charolais	4	G	12	2	0	4	28,360
Charrua's Hill (ARG)	5	H	7	3	2	1	76,100
Char's Bob'n Robin	4	C	14	3	2	4	32,339
Char's Lit'l Girl	4	F	2	0	0	0	182
Chart	2	F	1	0	0	1	1,400
Chart the Course	4	C	9	3	2	0	24,403
Chartbuster	4	F	4	0	0	1	1,138
Chartwell	7	G	9	1	1	1	18,500
Charute	3	F	1	0	0	1	1,430
Chasco Ba Ca	3	F	3	0	0	0	140
Chase a Star	5	M	15	2	3	4	61,552
Chase Bound	3	G	5	0	0	1	2,160
Chase Creek	3	G	11	1	2	1	17,401
Chase Express	4	G	10	1	0	2	9,260
Chase La Vivat	7	G	5	0	0	0	720
Chase Lake	2	F	3	0	0	0	0
Chase the Case	7	H	8	0	0	1	615
Chase the Charmer	3	F	5	1	0	1	5,725
Chase the Sauce	2	F	4	0	0	0	615
Chase This Case	3	G	4	0	2	0	4,400
Chase to Victory	4	C	2	0	0	0	0
Chase You	4	F	9	1	1	1	6,501
Chaseafallenstar	4	F	16	4	2	1	31,638
Chaseaway	5	M	9	0	1	1	4,043
Chase'n Cammie	4	F	8	1	1	0	5,940
Chase'n the Cat	3	C	10	1	1	1	8,624
Chasenthebluesaway	2	F	5	0	1	0	9,100
Chaser	5	H	6	0	0	1	830
Chaserville	8	G	7	1	4	0	2,580
Chases Comet	2	G	4	0	0	0	1,050
Chasethegold	3	F	3	1	1	1	42,900
Chaseur	2	C	2	1	0	1	22,030
Chasin' Bubbly	8	G	2	0	0	0	0
Chasin Jason	3	F	2	0	0	0	0
Chasing a Dream	7	M	9	1	0	1	5,750
Chasing Amy	2	F	2	0	0	0	345
Chasing Julie	6	M	8	1	0	0	6,346
Chasing Lightning	4	F	3	0	0	0	0
Chasing September	3	F	7	1	0	0	6,725
Chasing Shadows	6	G	12	1	1	1	7,270
Chasing Stanley	4	G	10	2	0	1	66,287
Chasing the Dream	3	F	4	0	0	0	439
Chasing the Ghosts	2	G	2	0	0	0	3,180
Chasmo	4	C	11	1	1	2	30,356
Chasnick	5	G	6	0	0	2	2,335
Chasseur's Tresor	7	G	4	1	1	0	4,490
Chassis	3	G	10	1	2	0	20,762
Chaste Fondness	3	F	11	2	4	1	11,242
Chaster	7	M	14	2	2	3	30,916
Chat 'Em Up	3	F	3	0	2	0	5,600
Chat Man	3	G	1	0	0	0	1,020
Chataquos' Chance	3	G	10	2	1	1	28,181
Chateau Beach (IRE)	3	F	5	0	0	0	1,110
Chateau Neuf	5	H	18	3	6	1	23,485
Chattabucktoo	2	G	3	0	0	1	1,416
Chattanooga Choo	3	C	1	0	0	0	260
Chatter Chatter	2	F	7	3	2	1	383,470
Chatter Fox	4	F	14	3	0	3	16,943
Chatterbox Miss	2	F	6	0	1	1	3,846
Chatting	7	G	3	1	0	0	18,000
Chattonugachoochoo	4	G	9	2	1	2	40,462
Chauffe Au Rouge	7	G	9	4	1	1	80,200
Chaun Michael	4	G	9	2	1	0	12,065
Chautauqua	4	F	13	3	2	4	92,500
Chautauqua Native	6	H	10	2	1	2	2,482
Chaya	3	F	6	0	3	1	27,220
Chayotero	4	G	5	0	0	0	964
Che Negrita (ARG)	5	M	2	1	0	0	12,780
Cheadles	3	C	8	0	0	2	12,100
Cheap Charlie	7	G	6	0	2	3	6,845
Cheap Justice	2	C	1	0	0	0	0
Cheap Speed	3	C	5	0	0	0	0
Cheap Talk	4	G	4	1	2	1	71,477
Cheap Trick	9	M	1	0	0	0	42
Cheaperthansandee	3	G	3	0	1	0	1,920
Cheapertokeepher	2	F	2	0	0	2	2,365
Cheater Lady	2	F	1	0	0	0	0
Cheatin Charlie	4	G	5	0	0	1	1,410
Cheatin N Fibbin	3	G	3	1	0	1	1,502
Cheba's Crown	3	F	5	0	0	0	315
Check and Go	4	G	9	1	2	1	8,866
Check Bouncer	3	G	3	0	1	0	1,470
Check by Check	4	G	10	2	0	3	9,220
Check Her Out	4	F	9	2	1	2	21,600
Check It	3	G	13	0	0	0	1,217
Check Memo	4	G	3	0	0	0	208
Check My I. D.	6	H	4	0	1	2	2,205
Check My Luck	3	G	10	0	0	1	418
Check My Pulse	6	M	10	0	1	1	5,501
Check Six	7	G	1	0	0	0	0
Check Station	2	C	3	0	0	0	250
Check This Out	5	M	9	3	1	0	18,738
Checker Boy Coy	10	G	5	0	0	0	131
Checker Flag	2	C	1	0	0	0	0
Checker Hall	4	F	1	0	0	0	1,260
Checker Sue	3	F	8	2	1	3	41,186
Checking In	3	F	8	2	3	1	10,136
Checkmynumber	3	F	4	0	0	0	244
Check'sinthemail	5	M	11	1	1	0	6,336
Checkthisgroove	3	F	4	2	0	1	27,300
Checotah Cat	9	G	12	1	5	2	14,708
Checotah Cowboy	3	C	9	1	0	1	3,585
Checotah Dee	7	G	7	1	0	1	5,925
Checotah Move	4	G	5	0	1	0	1,348
Cheddar	3	C	20	3	1	3	36,610
Chee Chee Favor	3	F	14	2	2	2	11,352
Cheech	6	H	1	0	0	0	300
Cheechako	4	C	9	0	0	1	1,860
Cheeks	5	M	1	0	0	0	130
Cheeks Eightyeight	5	M	15	1	3	1	40,610
Cheeky Miss	5	M	9	3	0	1	12,014
Cheeps	5	M	3	0	0	0	204
Cheer Express	8	M	4	0	0	0	166
Cheer for Molly	6	M	7	0	1	2	4,310
Cheer the Nashua	6	H	1	0	0	0	50
Cheer the Score	3	G	16	2	4	2	23,057

Horse	Age	Sex	Sts	1st	2d	3d	Won	Horse	Age	Sex	Sts	1st	2d	3d	Won
Cheerful Bag	3	F	12	1	1	0	13,105	Cherokee Babe	4	F	13	0	0	2	1,947
Cheerful Charley	3	G	2	0	0	0	100	Cherokee Beau	5	H	2	0	1	0	6,000
Cheerful Cookie	4	C	4	0	0	0	375	Cherokee Charge	3	G	3	0	0	1	510
Cheerful Warrior	2	G	4	1	1	0	6,050	Cherokee Charlie	2	C	3	0	1	0	2,200
Cheerideed	6	G	8	0	1	2	6,462	Cherokee Chocktaw	5	G	2	0	0	0	0
Cheersto Glory	3	G	8	0	0	2	4,620	Cherokee Commander	3	G	6	0	0	0	2,001
Cheery Hour	2	G	2	0	0	0	0	Cherokee Court	5	G	10	0	1	0	3,330
Cheery One	3	F	14	2	3	3	52,830	Cherokee Cutie	7	M	3	0	0	0	450
Cheese Puff	3	F	8	2	2	2	15,726	Cherokee Dash	5	H	14	4	2	3	31,940
Cheeta Is Coming	2	F	5	0	0	0	160	Cherokee Fighter	4	C	6	0	2	0	14,300
Cheetah Reach	4	C	3	0	1	0	7,700	Cherokee Fire	3	F	6	0	0	0	2,433
Cheetah Reta	4	F	13	0	0	1	1,935	Cherokee Flame	5	M	10	2	4	0	20,485
Cheetah Speed	2	C	7	2	0	2	46,850	Cherokee Gold	4	C	1	0	0	0	0
Cheetoe	5	M	3	0	0	0	0	Cherokee Honor	4	C	5	2	1	0	71,970
Chef Bear	4	G	5	1	1	0	11,700	Cherokee Jalapeno	5	M	3	0	0	0	231
Chef Lauren View	4	G	4	0	0	0	293	Cherokee Jolie	7	H	2	0	0	0	115
Chef Vittorina	4	F	11	0	2	1	6,609	Cherokee Junction	3	G	1	0	0	0	120
Chef's Choice	5	M	11	5	2	1	114,573	Cherokee Kelly	4	F	1	0	0	0	0
Chehalis	5	G	15	3	3	2	5,622	Cherokee King	3	G	11	0	2	3	3,527
Cheiron	2	C	4	0	2	0	22,120	Cherokee Lady	5	M	3	0	0	0	525
Cheirourgos	5	G	8	2	3	1	7,870	Cherokee Lee	3	G	9	0	1	2	11,010
Chelatche Prarie	7	G	11	0	0	0	1,130	Cherokee Lightning	4	F	4	1	1	1	14,085
Chelby Cobra	5	G	11	2	1	1	6,546	Cherokee Lite	3	F	8	4	0	0	111,140
Chelcee's Delight	3	F	4	1	0	0	3,093	Cherokee Lover	5	H	2	0	0	0	400
Chelea	6	M	9	1	1	0	3,957	Cherokee Luck	5	M	4	0	1	0	2,520
Chelino	2	C	2	0	0	0	1,560	Cherokee Made	4	F	2	0	0	0	205
Chelsea B	9	M	2	0	0	1	1,364	Cherokee Maiden	4	F	13	1	2	5	25,939
Chelsea Park	2	F	1	0	0	1	1,870	Cherokee Moon	6	M	11	0	2	1	3,508
Chelsea Revenge	2	F	1	0	0	0	0	Cherokee Park	3	C	8	2	0	1	36,294
Chelsea's Gold	3	F	4	0	0	1	3,740	Cherokee Prince	3	C	2	0	1	0	7,420
Chelsea's Night	6	M	1	0	0	0	38	Cherokee Promise	5	M	3	0	1	1	9,000
Chelsea's Pearl	2	F	5	2	0	3	42,050	Cherokee Prospect	6	H	3	0	0	0	840
Chelsey Charmer	3	F	10	1	1	3	12,258	Cherokee Raid	8	G	9	1	2	2	1,850
Chelsey's Bid	2	F	9	1	3	1	28,457	Cherokee Road	4	G	6	0	2	0	7,959
Chelsey's Dyna Sea	3	G	11	3	5	1	37,556	Cherokee Sauce	5	G	7	2	0	0	28,200
Chelyan	2	C	3	1	0	0	13,460	Cherokee Sky	3	F	12	1	3	2	19,214
Chemistry	2	F	3	0	0	0	420	Cherokee Spook	2	C	4	1	2	0	45,000
Chemistry Class	2	C	4	1	0	0	46,181	Cherokee Style	3	G	3	0	0	0	230
Chemold	2	G	2	0	0	0	360	Cherokee Sunrise	2	C	6	3	0	1	45,610
Chemstone	3	G	13	1	1	1	9,685	Cherokee Sunshine	8	M	5	0	0	0	1,428
Chenango Star	11	H	14	3	2	4	13,856	Cherokee Tiara	7	M	2	0	0	0	1,042
Chene Rouge	3	G	3	1	0	0	22,440	Cherokee Tin	4	C	4	0	0	1	3,180
Chenia	2	F	1	0	0	0	400	Cherokee Trail	4	C	6	0	1	1	6,289
Chephron	10	G	14	1	0	0	1,504	Cherokee Wine	4	G	11	1	2	3	9,425
Chepo Star	5	G	13	0	2	6	17,014	Cherokee Wizard	4	G	6	0	0	1	7,028
Chepper	2	F	2	0	0	0	570	Cherokee Women	2	F	4	1	0	1	13,950
Cheq's a Comin	2	G	2	0	1	0	3,200	Cherokee World	4	G	12	2	4	1	21,735
Cheque Out Kristen	3	F	4	0	0	1	1,840	Cherokeeconnection	6	H	5	1	0	0	6,199
Cheque the Green	2	F	1	0	0	0	0	Cherokeeinthehills	6	G	7	1	2	2	46,780
Chequer Account	3	F	2	0	0	0	285	Cherokee's Boy	3	C	7	3	1	1	228,500
Chequer Board	4	F	16	2	3	3	25,715	Cherokee's Disco	3	F	6	1	0	0	35,360
Chequer Street	3	G	3	0	0	0	420	Cherri Knight	4	F	14	0	2	2	7,060
Chequered Love	4	F	14	2	2	2	46,830	Cherry Blend	4	F	2	0	0	0	0
Chequerida	4	F	8	1	2	0	13,061	Cherry Bon Bon	3	F	2	0	0	0	161
Chequer'out	4	F	9	5	1	0	23,660	Cherry Delight	4	F	11	3	0	1	5,460
Chequerpast	4	F	5	0	0	0	358	Cherry Festival	6	M	9	1	2	1	7,790
Chequer's Honey	4	F	7	0	1	1	4,677	Cherry Gold	2	F	1	0	0	0	0
Chequerticket	2	F	3	0	0	0	420	Cherry Ice	3	F	2	0	0	0	100
Cheqydurmove	4	C	6	0	0	0	0	Cherry Martini	4	F	2	1	0	0	916
Cher Ami (ARG)	6	H	1	0	0	0	0	Cherry On Top	5	G	16	4	1	3	47,960
Cheraw	7	H	6	0	0	0	488	Cherry Peppers	4	F	14	2	2	2	53,757
Chercheuse	5	M	3	0	0	1	16,688	Cherry Pie	4	F	6	0	0	0	618
Chere Margot	5	M	5	0	0	0	308	Cherry Point Girl	2	F	2	0	1	0	1,425
Cheri Chardoneigh	3	F	5	1	0	0	5,214	Cherry Rose	3	F	6	0	0	0	1,672
Cherie's Digger	3	C	18	2	5	4	29,835	Cherry Springs	2	F	3	0	0	0	0
Cheri's Dancer	5	M	10	0	1	2	8,581	Cherry Street Gal	6	M	9	0	2	2	4,410
Cheri's Diamond	3	C	10	2	0	1	31,640	Cherry Tree Hill	5	M	3	1	0	1	12,168
Cheris' Jet	3	F	6	2	0	0	14,070	Cherry Wine	5	M	2	0	0	0	225
Cheris' Prospect	6	H	1	0	0	0	53	Cherryblossomroad	2	F	1	0	0	0	45
Cheris' Star	3	C	3	0	1	1	3,454	Cherryhill Champ	5	G	7	2	1	2	12,484
Cheris' Truth	5	M	9	0	2	0	7,479	Cherrys Crane	4	C	7	1	1	1	6,208
Cherish Destiny	2	F	4	1	2	0	55,260	Cherry's Hunter	2	F	3	0	1	0	13,050
Cherish the Groom	2	F	1	0	0	0	0	Cheryl Again Again	3	F	8	1	2	1	11,519
Cherished Bid	2	F	8	2	2	2	90,611	Cheryl's Cookie	2	F	1	0	0	0	80
Cherishing Duke	4	F	15	3	5	2	15,217	Cheryl's Gazelle	8	G	10	2	1	1	12,596
Cherniavsky	2	C	7	0	3	2	27,675	Cheryl's Myth	3	F	5	0	0	0	20,835
Cherokee Act	3	F	7	1	3	0	20,560	Cheryl's Reward	4	F	8	1	4	2	19,140
Cherokee Ambush	2	G	3	0	0	0	172	Cherylville Slew	4	F	12	4	2	3	151,235
Cherokee Apollo	10	M	7	0	1	4	2,539	Chesapeake Charlii	5	G	2	0	0	0	173

Horse	Age	Sex	Sts	1st	2d	3d	Won
Chesapeake Lady	4	F	2	0	0	0	0
Cheshire (GB)	6	G	5	0	0	0	4,510
Chesney Carolina	4	F	8	0	2	0	3,113
Chess Game	5	G	3	0	0	0	0
Chess Play	2	F	2	1	0	0	3,882
Chester Bester	3	G	3	1	1	0	16,456
Chester Cee	4	G	13	0	4	2	5,679
Chester Street	3	C	5	1	0	1	9,165
Chester's Chance	2	G	1	0	0	0	1,920
Chester's Choice	3	C	8	2	1	5	104,320
Chestnut Tree	5	M	5	1	0	1	6,485
Chestnut Way	2	F	1	0	0	0	195
Chet Minty	2	G	3	0	0	1	2,063
Chetsabet	5	G	1	0	0	0	0
Chev Emblem	3	G	5	0	0	1	1,710
Cheval	3	C	4	0	0	0	502
Cheval Blanc	7	G	3	0	0	0	275
Chevalier Bay	4	F	10	0	0	1	3,396
Chevaux	5	M	18	3	3	3	47,910
Chevaux d'Or	3	G	13	1	2	0	11,440
Chevello Creek	3	G	11	0	0	1	1,561
Cheverly Gold	3	C	7	0	2	1	23,060
Chevron Butterfly	3	F	1	0	0	0	0
Chevron Fleet	4	G	5	0	0	0	692
Chevy Up	5	M	3	0	0	0	0
Chex	3	G	4	2	1	0	18,940
Chey	2	F	1	0	0	0	0
Cheyenne Autumn	5	M	4	0	0	2	4,050
Cheyenne Breeze	4	G	10	2	2	2	48,586
Cheyenne Gold (IRE)	7	H	4	1	0	0	3,008
Cheyenne Lil	3	F	2	0	0	1	1,680
Cheyenne Night	5	H	10	0	0	0	555
Cheyenne Owl Woman	2	F	3	0	0	0	240
Cheyenne Rose	4	F	1	0	0	0	0
Cheyenne Spring	3	C	6	0	0	1	17,808
Cheyenne's Boy	5	G	15	3	1	2	23,846
Cheynne Orbit	6	H	4	1	0	0	3,203
Chez Audra	3	F	15	4	2	0	68,670
Chez Black	3	C	1	0	0	0	0
Chez Cherie (GB)	6	M	2	0	0	0	360
Chez La Femme	4	F	7	1	1	2	18,320
Chi Cat	4	G	5	0	0	2	8,340
Chi Chi La Mombo	5	M	3	0	0	0	135
Chi Chi Nette	4	F	3	1	2	0	21,600
Chi O Queen	5	M	14	0	1	3	4,980
Chi Town	2	C	1	0	0	0	0
Chi Town Slew	3	F	4	1	0	1	18,700
Chiacchierone	2	F	5	0	0	1	5,170
Chiado	3	C	2	0	0	0	91
Chianti (IRE)	5	H	3	0	0	1	5,560
Chiave	3	G	12	2	0	3	8,435
Chiawa	3	F	12	0	1	1	1,792
Chic Called Sue	4	F	9	2	1	1	18,708
Chic Crossing	4	F	8	2	1	0	4,626
Chic Dancer	2	F	2	0	0	1	2,860
Chic Domestique	4	F	7	0	2	0	21,611
Chic Joy	3	F	7	1	2	0	66,600
Chic On the Take	4	F	5	1	1	1	16,154
Chic Princess	5	M	3	0	0	2	2,938
Chic Slavique	3	F	5	1	1	1	17,760
Chica Chica	2	F	2	0	0	0	0
Chica Native	3	C	4	0	0	0	52
Chicago Al	2	C	1	0	0	0	0
Chicago Gold	2	C	3	0	0	0	125
Chicago Joe	5	G	6	0	4	1	8,017
Chicago Rock	4	G	15	0	1	3	23,580
Chicago Shark	6	G	11	0	0	0	424
Chicago's Girl	3	F	8	0	1	1	10,790
Chicago's Hope	6	G	5	0	0	2	3,214
Chicamun Jett	4	G	9	1	5	1	7,835
Chicanery	2	G	3	0	0	0	0
Chica's Due	5	M	16	2	1	2	15,844
Chichi Mainus	4	G	7	0	1	0	2,700
Chick Call Me	4	C	1	0	0	0	0
Chick Can Fly	3	F	3	0	0	0	0
Chick Fever	4	G	8	1	1	2	25,545
Chick Flick Cherry	3	F	7	1	1	2	9,850
Chick Power	4	F	6	1	0	0	4,369
Chicka Hermosa	4	F	10	0	2	2	14,623
Chickachoo	4	C	1	0	0	0	0
Chickadee	3	F	16	5	3	0	52,708
Chickadee Creek	5	M	11	0	0	2	3,738
Chickaroo	3	C	2	0	0	1	3,280
Chickee Dasher	4	F	8	0	1	3	1,844
Chicken George	4	C	4	0	0	1	2,087
Chicken Little	3	F	2	1	0	1	7,000
Chicken Man	5	G	9	0	0	0	536
Chicken Soup Kid	3	C	16	1	8	0	84,364
Chickenhouse Slew	5	G	12	0	3	0	4,040
Chick's Big Apple	7	M	3	0	0	0	220
Chick's Frat Boy	4	G	15	3	2	0	32,840
Chick's Hope	6	M	13	1	2	1	6,847
Chico Chico	4	G	5	0	0	0	399
Chico's Gold	4	G	12	3	1	1	10,395
Chidester Rules	10	G	8	4	0	1	12,393
Chidesters Boy	8	G	2	0	0	0	0
Chief Ambassador	4	C	14	1	0	3	5,544
Chief Angel	3	G	3	0	0	0	44
Chief Arias	9	G	6	2	1	0	18,988
Chief Bailey	3	C	1	0	0	0	55
Chief Beauregard	4	G	5	0	0	0	0
Chief Begone	3	G	8	0	1	3	4,383
Chief Black Hawk	4	C	2	0	0	0	0
Chief Blue	5	G	8	0	2	0	5,107
Chief Braveheart	5	H	5	1	0	1	3,115
Chief Cahill	3	G	11	4	0	5	42,050
Chief Caleb	4	G	4	1	0	1	6,869
Chief Cherokee	3	C	2	0	1	1	4,360
Chief Diamond	2	C	2	0	0	0	105
Chief Exchequer	3	C	14	3	2	0	34,520
Chief Forbes	5	G	15	0	0	2	4,699
Chief Four Shoes	3	C	9	2	0	1	10,850
Chief Georgie	6	M	5	0	0	0	236
Chief Gray Wolf	6	G	11	3	1	2	27,089
Chief Inspector	5	G	1	0	0	0	61
Chief Jake	2	C	5	0	1	0	2,720
Chief Joseph	4	G	11	1	1	3	7,020
Chief Koona	5	G	6	2	2	0	3,732
Chief Landscaper	8	G	10	1	0	2	3,700
Chief Little Dan	3	F	2	0	1	1	21,980
Chief Logan	2	C	2	0	0	0	1,982
Chief Magistrate	3	G	8	0	1	1	4,590
Chief Mandu	5	G	10	0	0	1	1,007
Chief Manteo	7	G	3	0	0	0	174
Chief Mathias	3	G	11	1	2	3	10,764
Chief Mtn	2	G	3	1	1	1	11,023
Chief Negotiator	3	G	5	1	0	0	22,190
Chief Okie Dokie	7	H	6	1	0	1	5,113
Chief Omni	2	C	3	1	1	1	39,130
Chief Partner	6	G	8	0	0	1	560
Chief Pawhuska	4	G	14	1	0	6	14,807
Chief Pete	3	C	10	2	1	2	27,577
Chief Planner	3	C	2	1	1	0	160,400
Chief Powhatan	4	C	7	4	1	1	36,747
Chief Problem	5	G	1	0	0	0	77
Chief Rainbow	7	G	10	0	4	3	28,202
Chief Rokeby	5	H	6	0	0	0	949
Chief Runamuck	4	G	8	0	1	1	3,583
Chief Scout	5	H	3	0	0	0	0
Chief Suspect	8	H	3	0	0	2	1,000
Chief Swan	6	G	6	1	1	1	8,515
Chief Truckee	2	G	3	0	1	2	9,900
Chief Tudor	6	G	6	1	0	0	21,230
Chief Two Socks	3	G	8	3	2	0	13,830
Chief White Sox	3	G	9	1	4	1	10,482
Chief Yukon	4	G	12	1	3	1	6,420
Chief's Brother	5	G	13	2	1	1	11,048
Chief's Fire	6	G	9	1	0	1	12,438
Chief's Hogan	6	G	20	1	1	1	13,695
Chiefs Jet	6	G	6	1	0	0	9,325
Chief's Loot	3	F	3	0	0	0	140
Chief's Spokesman	2	G	5	0	1	1	6,840
Chiefs Tam	3	F	3	0	0	0	666
Chieftaincy	5	G	16	1	2	2	8,225
Chiharu	4	F	9	0	2	1	10,022
Chikara	5	M	10	1	3	1	20,695
Chikaskia	6	M	11	0	2	1	4,190
Chilcotin	2	G	1	0	0	0	6,468

Horse	Age	Sex	Sts	1st	2d	3d	Won
Child of Light	2	G	2	1	0	0	8,660
Child of Promise	3	G	1	0	0	0	0
Childhooddream	4	G	16	2	3	3	25,973
Childress	5	M	4	1	0	2	25,270
Child's Fortune	3	F	6	0	0	1	1,230
Chile Bar	6	G	8	0	0	2	4,745
Chile' File'	3	F	7	0	1	1	5,355
Chili Dan	2	C	4	0	1	0	3,485
Chili Doggie	7	H	10	0	0	1	2,533
Chili Express	3	C	4	0	1	2	11,700
Chilipin	5	M	8	0	2	0	8,202
Chill A' Dude	4	C	14	5	6	0	70,025
Chill Factor	4	F	11	0	0	0	1,075
Chill Master	2	G	2	1	0	1	11,606
Chill Phill	4	F	3	1	0	0	12,148
Chill Town	2	F	1	0	0	0	0
Chill Town Banner	2	F	1	0	0	0	254
Chilled Lightning	3	C	10	0	0	2	1,355
Chillin' Chester	3	G	6	0	0	2	7,780
Chilling Effect	4	F	9	4	1	1	83,660
Chilling Sweep	7	H	14	1	1	0	23,270
Chilly A.	7	G	9	1	0	3	20,257
Chilly Bear	9	H	8	0	0	2	1,460
Chilly Bird	4	G	3	0	0	0	451
Chilly Buttons	5	M	10	1	0	0	19,596
Chilly Call	3	F	5	0	1	1	4,910
Chilly Charlie	6	H	3	1	1	0	2,865
Chilly Ending	6	G	3	0	0	0	70
Chilly Gentilly	7	G	14	0	0	1	2,577
Chilly N Slick	8	H	3	1	0	0	5,184
Chilly Reception	3	C	5	1	0	0	7,071
Chilly Rooster	3	G	13	3	4	5	146,741
Chilly Special	3	G	9	1	0	0	3,657
Chilly Wink	3	F	9	3	1	1	17,745
Chilly's Girl	6	M	6	1	0	0	6,813
Chilyev	5	G	6	0	0	0	600
Chimay	6	M	5	0	0	1	2,525
Chimborazo	3	C	4	2	1	0	81,108
Chime Away	4	G	3	0	0	0	600
Chime Choir	5	H	2	0	0	0	0
Chimera Begone	7	M	4	0	0	0	176
Chimes Lady	2	M	2	0	0	0	267
Chimes Motel	5	H	15	1	3	3	8,922
Chimes Rebel	5	G	8	0	1	2	10,990
Chimichurri	3	F	8	0	3	1	120,786
Chiming	8	G	3	0	0	0	125
Chiming (IRE)	5	M	2	1	1	0	66,000
Chimney Fire	7	M	14	1	1	0	11,498
Chimney Slew	3	G	7	0	1	0	6,180
Chimo	4	G	9	1	1	2	36,486
Chimos Brother	4	G	5	0	0	1	2,255
Chin Chin	5	G	11	1	2	1	10,412
Chin Gone	5	G	4	1	0	2	11,501
China Coast	2	C	3	1	0	0	29,398
China Day	4	F	6	0	0	0	650
China Gold	2	C	1	0	0	0	0
China Grind	4	C	2	1	0	0	22,200
China Jewel	5	M	8	0	0	0	11,242
China Kitten	3	F	9	1	0	1	4,261
China Lite	6	M	5	0	0	0	791
China Paint	3	F	20	2	5	1	17,391
China Princess	3	F	9	1	2	1	48,630
China Run	3	G	9	0	0	0	806
China Sea	3	C	6	0	0	0	100
Chinami	5	M	9	1	1	0	5,511
Chinati Gal	4	F	2	0	0	1	780
Chincoteagues Wake	7	G	7	0	1	1	4,423
Chindi	9	G	7	1	2	2	118,931
Chinese	3	C	9	1	1	2	38,436
Chinese Tea	3	F	8	2	1	2	46,290
Chinese Whisper	6	H	6	2	0	0	15,200
Ching a Dara	4	G	15	2	1	5	19,010
Chinkapin	7	G	8	3	2	2	180,450
Chino	3	G	4	1	0	1	16,188
Chino Valley	8	H	6	0	0	1	1,585
Chinoiro	6	H	3	0	1	0	3,520
Chinois	5	G	3	1	0	0	36,180
Chinook Cat	5	G	8	2	1	1	23,120
Chinook to Knight	8	G	14	1	4	1	10,121
Chinooka	3	F	7	1	1	1	17,545
Chinquapin Charlie	6	H	3	0	0	0	150
Chinsegut	5	M	13	1	1	4	23,050
Chip of Gold	5	G	2	1	0	0	7,424
Chip o'When Dancer	4	G	6	0	0	1	1,790
Chip Shot	4	F	3	0	0	0	0
Chip the Vault	2	G	6	0	1	0	4,270
Chipalune	6	G	5	0	0	0	1,350
Chipeak	3	C	2	0	0	1	320
Chipofftheblock	2	G	7	0	0	0	1,998
Chippawama	3	F	5	0	0	0	460
Chipper C	4	C	12	1	6	3	29,962
Chipper Skipper	2	C	4	1	0	0	9,730
Chippewa Day	5	M	6	0	0	2	1,576
Chippewa Slew	5	M	8	2	0	2	4,992
Chippewa Trail	2	G	2	0	2	0	17,560
Chippi Creek	3	C	7	1	0	2	10,267
Chippidale	3	C	1	0	0	0	1,230
Chipping Hammer	6	G	3	0	0	0	205
Chips Damascus	4	F	14	1	1	1	1,943
Chip's N Dip	3	F	2	1	1	0	15,200
Chips N Salsa	5	M	17	2	1	4	12,260
Chips Pride	8	H	1	0	0	0	200
Chip's Sister	5	M	9	5	2	0	27,363
Chipshantinformony	3	G	7	0	0	0	0
Chiquilina	4	F	12	2	4	1	30,640
Chiquita Sweet	3	F	6	1	3	1	24,736
Chiquito	3	G	18	1	1	0	9,305
Chirac At Thetrack	3	C	3	1	0	0	16,950
Chiricahua Chief	6	G	4	1	0	1	1,289
Chirimoya	4	F	15	2	4	5	110,165
Chiris	7	M	1	0	0	1	1,200
Chirundu	4	C	5	1	1	1	10,698
Chisel	3	G	13	3	1	3	18,893
Chiseled	2	C	4	0	0	0	0
Chiseling	4	C	2	0	0	0	4,240
Chisholm	6	G	9	0	2	0	8,100
Chisos Cruiser	5	G	9	1	0	0	2,357
Chisos Free Candy	10	G	5	1	1	1	2,082
Chispass	9	G	5	0	0	0	559
Chispazo	2	C	2	0	1	0	3,705
Chispiro	3	C	3	0	1	1	5,500
Chispiski	4	F	7	3	1	1	136,540
Chit Chat Tee	3	F	7	0	2	0	2,010
Chit Chatter	4	F	7	1	0	2	35,648
Chitchat Chitchat	3	F	5	2	2	0	36,080
Chitter Box	3	F	14	2	2	1	9,434
Chivalry Isnotdead	10	G	4	1	0	2	2,912
Chivann	6	G	5	0	0	0	311
Chivas	3	G	10	1	1	3	75,740
Chloe Pond	7	M	4	0	0	1	3,570
Chloe's Account	4	F	6	0	2	2	22,400
Chloe's Choice	2	F	4	0	1	1	4,720
Chloe's Dream	3	F	9	0	3	0	5,838
Chloe's Edition	3	F	5	0	1	1	4,900
Chloe's Quest	5	M	11	2	1	2	24,550
Chmataja	4	G	3	0	0	0	144
Chocawad	3	F	5	0	0	0	50
Chocolate Almond	4	G	9	0	1	1	5,420
Chocolate Cherry	4	F	4	1	0	1	4,013
Chocolate Coffee	12	G	3	0	0	0	0
Chocolate Cowgirl	9	M	10	3	1	1	9,394
Chocolate Factory	5	M	13	0	1	1	3,219
Chocolate Fix	3	G	1	0	0	0	79
Chocolate Gal	2	F	3	1	0	0	12,192
Chocolate Gem	5	G	12	1	1	0	20,200
Chocolate Knight	3	G	6	0	2	0	10,416
Chocolate Lover	3	F	17	3	3	3	13,449
Chocolate Moose	9	G	2	0	0	0	1,980
Chocolate One	3	G	3	0	0	0	0
Chocolate Pie Togo	5	M	13	0	0	2	3,549
Chocolate Rose	3	F	6	0	2	1	10,516
Chocolate Rules	5	G	2	0	0	1	957
Chocolate Sip	3	F	4	0	1	0	2,877
Chocolate Sox	2	G	4	1	0	0	10,920
Chocolate Sprinkle	3	F	7	1	1	0	11,590
Chocolate Tale	2	F	2	0	0	0	295
Chocolateonhisface	4	C	8	0	0	1	1,100
Chocolatevalentine	5	H	2	0	0	0	480

Horse	Age	Sex	Sts	1st	2d	3d	Won
Chocolateville	3	F	4	0	0	2	2,420
Chocoleta'	2	C	1	0	0	0	78
Chocomount	4	G	7	1	0	0	8,580
Choctaw Bid	2	G	4	1	1	0	9,660
Choctaw Charlie	3	C	2	0	0	0	2,565
Choctaw Lady	3	F	4	0	0	0	0
Choctaw Ridge	5	H	4	1	1	1	28,460
Choctaw Sky	4	F	13	1	0	1	7,100
Chogori	4	C	2	0	0	0	0
Choice Connection	5	G	15	0	1	0	1,420
Choice Paces	3	F	13	2	1	2	26,372
Choice Rumor	3	C	1	0	0	0	0
Choice Slew	4	F	7	1	1	1	4,098
Choice Union	2	G	5	1	1	2	38,770
Choices Are	6	H	4	0	0	0	400
Choir Master	3	G	5	0	0	0	1,160
Choir of Angels	4	C	3	0	0	0	106
Choke Me Again	2	F	3	0	0	0	224
Choke N Go	7	G	23	3	7	4	46,100
Choke the Odds	7	M	2	0	0	0	332
Choker	5	G	2	0	2	0	1,940
Choke's Secret	4	G	17	0	2	4	8,166
Chokettes Pride	4	C	11	0	0	3	4,451
Choktow	4	G	14	1	2	0	11,748
Chola	2	G	1	0	0	0	0
Cholo	3	G	5	0	0	0	2,055
Chomp	5	G	6	0	0	0	1,062
Choo Choo Chad	5	G	10	0	2	1	8,732
Choo Choo Charlie	3	C	2	0	0	0	2,370
Choo Choo Slew	3	F	2	1	0	0	4,660
Choose a Rose	4	F	3	0	0	0	0
Choose Faith	7	M	14	1	2	2	6,050
Choose the Greek	4	G	3	0	1	0	1,500
Choose the Right	2	F	5	2	0	0	19,806
Choose to Differ	9	G	3	0	1	0	3,030
Choose Wisely	5	M	2	0	0	1	852
Choosing Sides	3	G	8	0	2	1	1,908
Chop Chop	4	C	5	0	0	2	8,040
Chop Chop George	6	G	13	1	2	2	14,150
Chop House	2	G	5	0	1	0	1,660
Chopinina	5	M	5	1	1	0	227,070
Chopin's First	3	F	15	1	2	2	9,415
Choppa Toulouse	4	C	13	1	2	2	14,927
Chopper Won	5	H	3	1	1	0	40,800
Choppers Choice	2	G	2	0	0	0	0
Chopt At Dawn	4	C	26	3	1	0	19,155
Chords of Fame	6	M	6	0	1	1	12,318
Choreography	3	G	8	3	3	0	146,330
Chortle	6	G	14	1	0	7	6,605
Chorus Dancer	3	F	7	0	3	1	43,804
Chorus Girl	3	F	10	2	2	0	21,428
Chorus Leader	11	G	3	0	0	0	158
Chorus of Facts	5	M	3	0	1	0	1,850
Chory Four	4	G	6	0	0	0	4,160
Chosen Chief	4	G	9	2	1	1	76,920
Chosen Green	5	H	2	0	0	0	45
Chosen Hero (GB)	2	C	3	0	0	0	0
Chosen Honor	4	F	10	4	2	2	86,300
Chosen Speed	4	F	6	0	0	1	2,445
Chosen Ticket	4	F	3	0	0	0	269
Chotzie	2	C	8	0	2	0	11,997
Chouette Player	6	H	1	0	0	0	59
Chow Down	6	G	13	2	2	1	54,280
Chow Hut	5	G	3	0	1	0	950
Chowder's First	2	C	2	1	0	0	32,100
Chretien's Dawn	7	M	11	2	2	1	11,635
Chris' Best Dancer	5	H	2	0	0	0	0
Chris Can Travy	8	G	9	3	0	1	14,429
Chris Colony	3	C	7	0	0	1	766
Chris Cross Cat	2	C	10	0	3	2	10,940
Chris' Devil	3	C	3	0	0	0	0
Chris' Facts	4	F	7	1	1	0	21,790
Chris Goes West	4	F	10	1	0	0	7,700
Chris Hunts	3	C	6	0	0	1	5,700
Chris My Man	5	H	9	0	2	0	2,085
Chris Run	6	G	7	1	0	0	15,735
Chrisdan	3	C	6	1	1	0	18,744
Chrismet	7	M	10	1	1	0	1,815
Chrismitch	5	M	12	0	1	0	4,694
Chris's Bad Boy	6	G	12	7	2	0	308,099
Chris's Coin	6	H	5	0	0	0	568
Chris's Counter	5	G	8	1	0	0	8,179
Chris's Salty Dog	2	G	6	0	0	2	7,290
Chris's Turn	5	G	11	0	3	0	9,115
Chrissy de Rio	6	M	8	1	2	2	3,150
Chrissy Jay	2	F	2	0	0	0	3,360
Chrissysshadow	2	F	2	0	0	0	0
Christamon	3	G	16	1	4	0	12,035
Christavilla	4	F	8	1	1	2	8,310
Christel Flame (GB)	4	F	6	0	1	2	24,000
Christeph	4	F	14	0	3	1	12,125
Christian Gulch	3	G	10	2	0	2	18,630
Christian Kingdom	2	F	5	0	0	1	993
Christian Ridge	2	G	3	0	0	0	0
Christijeau	5	M	6	1	1	0	6,701
Christina Sanchez	3	F	7	1	1	2	14,939
Christina's Hope	3	F	4	1	0	2	12,347
Christina's Image	2	F	6	0	0	1	993
Christinenicole	5	M	23	2	6	1	17,448
Christine's Baby	6	G	5	0	1	0	8,447
Christine's Outlaw	3	C	10	2	2	1	206,160
Christines Patty	3	F	11	0	0	0	3,028
Christmas Away	3	C	12	0	2	2	41,840
Christmas Boy	10	G	4	2	1	1	13,098
Christmas Card	2	F	1	0	0	0	1,260
Christmas Memory	3	F	12	4	1	2	61,875
Christmas Money	2	F	5	0	0	2	2,745
Christmas Table	3	F	9	3	1	0	26,034
Christmas Time	3	F	8	2	1	0	72,603
Christmas Tree	3	C	6	0	0	1	2,260
Christmas Verse	7	M	5	0	1	1	3,834
Christo Flyaway	5	M	11	0	0	2	3,822
Christo Hallelujah	6	G	21	0	1	0	2,043
Christo Israel	3	G	5	0	0	0	0
Christo Rain	5	G	13	1	0	1	11,500
Christo Star	4	F	2	0	0	0	0
Christo Wings	4	C	11	2	1	3	11,254
Christopher A.	3	C	4	0	0	1	1,830
Christopher J	3	G	6	1	0	1	6,355
Christopher Lee	5	G	3	0	0	0	290
Christophers Boy	2	G	1	0	0	0	0
Christopher's Fire	5	H	8	0	0	0	1,380
Christy de Lit	5	M	3	1	1	0	3,246
Christy Marie	4	F	7	1	0	1	10,961
Christy T.	3	F	13	2	0	4	35,740
Christy's Miracle	2	F	5	1	2	1	11,787
Christy's Secret	4	F	13	3	4	0	23,648
Christy's Spirit	2	F	4	0	0	0	1,418
Chrome Soldier	2	C	6	1	1	1	23,160
Chrome Trim	3	C	5	0	0	1	2,120
Chromeheart	3	G	13	2	3	1	23,915
Chromenall	4	F	5	0	0	0	338
Chromillenium	4	F	1	0	0	0	0
Chronic Iced Tea	3	G	1	0	0	1	1,350
Chronic Tychonic	3	F	13	2	3	2	15,029
Chronicle S.	8	G	12	2	4	2	21,260
Chrusciki	3	F	7	2	1	2	46,800
Chrysalis Court	4	C	12	1	0	0	13,365
Chrysalis Village	4	F	11	1	1	1	4,576
Chu' Rouge	6	M	9	0	1	2	3,357
Chuako	3	G	7	0	1	0	3,091
Chubby Buddy	4	C	11	0	1	2	3,645
Chubby Slic	3	G	1	0	0	0	0
Chuck O Luck	3	C	2	0	0	0	180
Chuck Yeager	3	G	13	2	1	1	18,877
Chuckalee	2	G	3	0	0	0	377
Chuckels	3	C	4	0	1	1	6,860
Chuckie's in Love	3	C	11	4	3	2	42,638
Chuckler	6	H	2	0	0	0	966
Chuck's Angel	3	F	8	1	0	0	6,444
Chucks Playboy	4	G	11	2	2	0	19,276
Chuckygee	5	G	8	1	0	1	5,344
Chuichupa	6	M	6	0	1	1	6,361
Chuky Strode	6	H	6	1	0	1	3,062
Chul Chul	3	F	1	0	1	0	800
Chula	4	F	9	0	0	0	7,421
Chum	4	G	10	1	0	1	11,778
Chump Change	2	C	4	0	1	0	2,790

RECORDS OF HORSES

Horse	Age	Sex	Sts	1st	2d	3d	Won
Chunk Change	3	C	4	0	2	2	4,570
Chunky Cheeks	3	F	7	1	0	2	14,495
Chunters Defense	6	G	11	1	0	0	3,278
Chupacabras	6	G	16	0	0	2	15,090
Chuparosa	4	F	11	0	0	3	2,812
Church Affair	2	F	1	1	0	0	6,710
Church Cross (IRE)	4	G	10	1	0	1	7,582
Church Editor	2	F	5	3	0	2	70,700
Church Gal	3	F	6	1	0	0	1,975
Church Ghost	4	G	5	0	1	1	4,200
Church Goer	3	F	6	1	1	0	2,440
Church Law	3	G	6	0	1	1	6,740
Church Secretary	4	F	15	2	1	1	12,821
Church Street	4	F	6	0	0	1	3,249
Churchbridge	2	G	5	1	3	1	21,106
Churchhill	3	C	1	0	0	0	0
Church's Out	3	F	12	3	3	2	86,212
Churlee Sweet	7	M	4	0	0	0	84
Churn	6	M	3	0	0	0	0
Chute Gate	5	G	9	1	2	0	10,045
Chute the Breeze	3	G	8	1	2	0	45,260
Chy Wolf	6	G	8	0	2	0	2,099
Chynna's Beauty	3	F	4	0	0	0	227
Chyuck	2	G	6	0	0	0	940
Ciano Belle	2	F	3	1	0	0	6,879
Ciano Country	2	G	3	1	0	0	6,771
Ciano Pearl	2	F	1	0	0	0	206
Ciano Silence	2	F	5	0	2	0	3,638
Ciano Warrior	2	G	4	0	0	0	0
Ciano's First	2	F	2	0	0	0	93
Ciano's Six Pack	2	F	5	1	1	0	23,242
Ciao Rhoma	3	G	11	1	1	2	12,962
Cibagof Gold	2	G	6	1	0	2	6,126
Cibo	3	G	10	3	0	1	65,745
Cibolo	4	G	4	0	0	0	840
Cibolo Country	4	C	4	0	0	0	497
Ciccy's Star	2	F	7	0	1	0	6,727
Cicero Grimes	4	C	8	0	1	1	8,430
Cidebar	8	G	4	0	0	1	1,970
Cider	5	G	15	3	1	2	13,796
Cie Club	3	F	3	0	1	0	2,491
Cie Effo	7	G	2	0	0	0	0
Ciehimgo	4	G	4	0	0	0	0
Ciel Avenue	2	G	4	1	0	0	5,462
Ciel Classic	3	F	6	2	0	2	14,390
Ciel d'Or	10	G	4	0	0	1	505
Ciel Noir	7	G	3	0	0	1	980
Cielo Alta	7	M	1	0	0	0	0
Cielo Apache	5	H	5	2	2	0	6,200
Cielo Blincoe	2	G	1	0	0	0	0
Cielo Canosa	8	G	10	1	0	0	6,172
Cielo City	5	H	12	3	1	1	29,612
Cielo de Noche	4	G	10	0	0	1	1,400
Cielo d'Or	5	H	6	1	0	1	11,829
Cielo Girl	4	F	12	5	2	1	180,053
Cielo Halo	3	G	10	0	1	1	4,795
Cielo Moon	5	F	5	2	1	0	62,480
Cielo's Cat	2	F	2	0	0	1	2,310
Cielo's Finest	4	F	2	0	0	0	3,660
Cielo's Garden	4	G	13	2	2	4	25,760
Cielo's Honour	5	G	9	2	4	1	50,160
Cielo's Majesty	4	F	1	0	0	0	61
Cielovation	4	G	7	1	1	0	4,186
Cien	5	M	11	0	1	1	4,268
Cien Memories	6	G	1	0	0	0	0
Cien Seas	6	G	10	0	1	1	2,047
Cien Seattle	5	M	19	2	1	1	10,518
Cien Wins	3	G	8	1	1	0	5,190
Ciens Storm	3	F	14	3	2	1	42,735
Ciento	5	H	6	5	1	0	276,654
Cierra's Junebug	2	F	1	0	0	0	2,340
Cigar Pal	2	C	3	0	0	1	4,560
Cigarette	8	M	5	1	0	0	16,072
Cigi	4	G	7	3	0	2	11,690
Cigno d'Oro	4	F	11	1	1	3	51,100
Ciguapo	4	C	8	1	0	1	6,112
Cilento	3	C	16	3	1	1	24,465
Cimarron Hills	2	F	3	0	1	1	8,440
Cimarron Rain	3	F	5	2	1	0	59,000
Cimarron Summer	2	F	3	0	0	0	103
Cimarron's Jade	2	F	2	1	0	0	5,050
Cimmaron Lady	3	F	2	0	0	0	0
Cin Slew Eve	3	C	4	0	0	0	1,560
Cinamon Sky	3	C	6	0	1	1	1,944
Cinbuster	4	G	10	1	3	0	47,410
Cincinnati Jay	2	G	10	3	1	3	35,010
Cincodemayocaballo	4	C	2	0	2	0	2,000
Cindarullah	2	F	5	0	0	0	1,750
Cindee	6	M	7	1	0	1	2,592
Cinder Cat	7	G	15	3	1	1	17,714
Cinderela	6	M	7	1	0	0	5,148
Cinderella's Coach	4	F	2	0	0	0	300
Cinderella's Fella	5	G	12	0	2	1	2,868
Cinderellaslipper	3	F	1	0	0	0	0
Cinderell's Hope	5	M	2	0	0	0	122
Cindle	5	M	1	0	0	0	0
Cindy Cinda	5	M	9	0	0	0	540
Cindy Lou Slew	5	M	4	0	1	1	4,090
Cindy Lou Two	3	F	11	1	2	3	14,576
Cindy Merindy	5	M	8	0	2	0	2,288
Cindys Devil	5	H	4	0	0	2	1,904
Cindy's Doll	7	M	10	2	2	1	9,475
Cindy's Girl	4	F	22	1	4	2	11,394
Cindy's Hobby	6	M	7	0	0	2	4,443
Cindys Morningstar	3	F	12	3	2	1	15,781
Cindysanticipation	3	F	10	0	1	1	2,094
Cinema Magic	3	C	8	1	0	0	12,116
Cinema Paradisa	3	F	6	2	1	0	40,125
Cinema Star	2	C	2	0	0	0	980
Cinemagic	2	F	5	1	0	1	9,120
Cinnamon Battle	5	G	2	0	0	0	0
Cinnamon Boy	4	G	2	0	0	0	161
Cinnamon Buns	4	F	6	2	0	2	28,135
Cinnamon Cat	6	G	17	2	3	0	20,128
Cinnamon Goose	5	H	5	0	0	0	0
Cinnamon Kiss	2	F	2	0	0	0	0
Cinnamon Light	4	F	9	1	0	2	8,015
Cinnamon Mist	4	F	2	0	0	0	60
Cinnamon Ridge	3	G	14	5	1	3	68,250
Cinnamon Secret	3	F	12	1	3	2	23,908
Cinnamon Silk	3	F	5	0	0	1	6,440
Cinnamonroll	5	M	1	0	0	0	0
Cinnapie	2	F	3	1	1	1	13,874
Cinnful Bride	4	F	7	1	1	2	47,602
Cipriani	2	F	1	0	0	0	0
Circatwothousand	5	H	5	2	1	1	14,160
Circle B Boy	10	G	7	0	0	0	1,540
Circle M Goldie	3	F	10	1	1	0	5,137
Circle M Lighting	3	F	9	1	1	1	16,704
Circle M Midnight	5	G	5	0	0	0	281
Circle of Peace	3	F	14	2	1	4	15,032
Circle the Globe	4	F	9	3	1	0	39,312
Circle Z	3	F	14	1	1	3	16,473
Circleyourpartner	3	F	6	0	0	0	300
Circular Time	3	F	5	0	0	0	455
Circulating Coin	3	C	2	0	0	0	306
Circulating Touch	7	H	12	3	1	1	14,604
Circumstancial	4	F	11	1	1	2	10,260
Circus Boy	4	G	2	0	0	0	654
Circus Du Joy	2	F	1	0	0	0	870
Circus Flyer	4	C	6	1	1	1	3,460
Circus Vision	3	F	5	0	0	1	1,705
Ciribiribin Queen	5	M	6	0	1	1	10,650
Cirilo	6	H	15	2	2	3	12,969
Cirius	3	G	1	0	0	0	91
Cisco Kid	4	G	10	1	2	3	11,900
Cisco Moon	5	G	7	1	1	0	2,985
Cisco 'n' Vic	3	G	12	1	2	3	11,683
Cisco Sis	7	M	10	0	0	1	1,165
Cisco Socks	3	G	7	1	2	0	8,735
Cisco Zesty Sauce	6	M	14	5	1	3	38,390
Ciscolightly	3	G	4	1	1	0	2,490
Cisco's Baby	3	F	8	1	1	3	5,356
Cisco's Beemer	4	C	6	1	0	2	1,870
Cisco's Choice	5	M	1	0	0	1	528
Cisco's Kite	5	G	13	1	1	2	11,320
Cisco's Moonshine	2	F	3	0	0	1	1,005
Cisco's Secretary	4	F	8	1	1	2	7,562

Horse	Age	Sex	Sts	1st	2d	3d	Won
Cisco's Tale	5	M	3	0	0	0	670
Cisne	6	M	4	0	0	1	798
Citadella	2	F	1	0	0	0	320
Citation Jet	9	G	13	0	2	3	5,159
Citi Block	5	M	17	3	5	4	58,738
Citi Buster	2	C	1	1	0	0	5,400
Citi Music	2	F	2	0	0	1	8,232
Citi Rhythm	3	C	8	2	3	1	30,410
Citi State	3	F	12	1	1	2	40,640
Citibid	10	G	3	1	0	0	2,520
Citicentral	2	C	1	0	0	0	600
Citidellino	5	H	15	4	4	2	58,100
Citiflash	4	G	2	0	0	0	0
Citikitti	5	M	6	0	2	0	9,620
Citiparrot	2	C	1	0	0	0	0
Citipower	7	G	7	0	0	0	840
Citiroyal	5	G	17	5	0	3	44,971
Citistar	4	F	2	0	0	0	104
Cititree Diamond	3	C	6	0	0	1	2,062
Citiview	3	F	10	0	4	1	23,877
Citiworld	9	G	9	0	1	1	15,680
Citizen's Arrest	8	G	7	0	0	0	423
Citizenship	2	C	1	0	1	0	8,200
City Academy	3	G	2	1	1	0	28,640
City Appeal	10	G	4	0	1	0	1,291
City Baby	3	F	1	0	0	0	0
City Belle	2	F	1	0	0	1	907
City Blues	3	G	13	5	3	3	112,020
City Boy	3	G	8	1	2	0	15,085
City Brave	3	G	10	1	0	4	6,356
City Celebrations	4	F	11	0	0	3	22,550
City Circle	9	G	4	0	0	0	174
City Clerk	7	G	14	1	2	1	6,774
City Confidential	3	G	12	2	1	0	25,712
City Desk	3	C	9	2	2	0	79,740
City Diamond	2	F	2	0	0	0	180
City Fair	5	M	1	0	0	1	5,980
City Fear	4	C	10	0	2	1	15,570
City Fire	3	F	10	5	1	0	200,549
City Games	6	M	2	0	0	0	122
City Island	5	G	3	0	0	0	0
City Jet	4	G	4	1	0	1	14,580
City Judge	8	G	10	2	1	0	13,580
City Kid	5	G	11	0	3	2	14,375
City Kitty	3	F	10	1	0	3	11,900
City Kowgurl	4	F	7	1	1	0	11,362
City Lights	2	G	1	1	0	0	5,830
City Lights Sonata	5	M	17	1	3	5	10,059
City Limit	2	F	3	1	0	0	6,879
City Line Ave	2	C	5	0	1	0	8,143
City Loot	5	M	3	0	0	0	268
City Mix	3	C	3	0	1	0	2,380
City News	3	G	14	2	4	2	55,270
City of Evansville	2	F	2	0	1	0	2,520
City of Faith	3	G	4	0	0	0	343
City of Peace	6	H	11	3	2	0	69,280
City of Riches	5	G	7	1	3	1	14,858
City Parkway	4	G	17	6	2	2	16,006
City Pilgrim	5	H	13	0	1	2	4,128
City Prayer	3	F	14	3	3	1	18,400
City Prince	2	C	5	1	1	0	11,724
City Radar	4	C	4	1	0	3	3,197
City Rain	3	F	1	1	0	0	28,205
City Rapid	4	C	10	3	1	1	73,605
City Ride	5	G	6	0	0	1	1,346
City Ridge	2	F	10	1	1	0	7,210
City Sharpster	4	G	3	1	0	1	32,880
City Sister	3	F	10	3	2	4	133,330
City Sleeper	3	F	8	4	1	2	91,100
City Styling	3	F	7	2	1	0	31,812
City Trick	2	C	2	0	0	1	1,980
City Zoom	2	F	1	0	0	0	750
City's Honey	2	C	6	0	1	3	13,780
Civil Revolt	5	G	5	0	1	1	2,820
Civil Wars	9	G	18	1	1	2	5,397
Civilian	4	C	5	2	0	0	29,636
Civility Cat	3	F	12	1	4	0	46,360
Cj's Pride	4	G	7	0	3	3	16,326
Claddagh Bay	5	M	10	0	1	1	5,985
Cladhopper	2	C	1	0	0	0	100
Claim Check	7	G	7	1	1	0	10,050
Claim My Love	4	F	6	1	2	0	12,840
Claim's She's Bold	10	M	11	1	1	2	5,787
Claims to Be Good	3	F	14	2	4	2	16,709
Claims to Be Lucky	4	G	13	2	1	0	11,879
Clair de Lune	3	F	5	0	0	2	19,380
Claire	5	M	22	1	1	1	6,228
Claire City	3	F	11	0	1	1	7,675
Claire Ellen	6	M	4	1	1	0	8,844
Claire's Keeper	6	M	1	0	0	0	528
Claire's Rockette	2	F	7	0	0	1	2,130
Claire's Storm Cat	3	G	6	0	3	2	15,850
Clairlyn	4	F	7	0	0	2	8,838
Clairsy Waresy	4	F	1	0	0	0	115
Clairvoyant Gipsy	8	M	15	4	1	2	12,640
Clamato	2	F	2	0	0	0	220
Clang Bang	6	G	8	2	2	2	8,360
Clanton's Dancer	8	G	3	1	1	1	3,904
Clara Allen	4	F	10	2	0	0	16,396
Clara M. D.	7	M	6	0	1	1	1,980
Clara's Boy	3	C	1	0	0	0	150
Clare Cielo	5	M	12	2	1	1	7,390
Claremont Street	4	G	13	1	1	1	11,242
Clare's Bunny	3	F	4	0	1	0	2,184
Clare's Counting	5	M	9	2	3	1	7,387
Clare's Mark	3	F	5	0	0	0	1,240
Claridges	5	M	6	0	0	0	496
Clarins	2	F	2	0	1	0	9,200
Clarion's Star	4	F	10	1	3	2	9,754
Clarissa Lynn	6	M	6	0	1	0	3,057
Clark Fork	7	G	8	0	0	0	3,585
Clark K	4	C	10	0	0	0	180
Clark S Man	4	G	5	1	1	0	12,338
Clark W	3	G	4	0	0	0	504
Clark's Shadow	4	G	4	0	0	1	1,068
Clarksburg	3	C	8	1	0	4	26,380
Clarksburg Queen	2	F	9	1	0	3	58,391
Clarksdale	5	G	13	5	1	2	30,550
Claseybeat	4	C	6	3	1	1	64,500
Clasp	6	G	7	1	1	1	8,219
Class Above	2	F	3	2	0	0	91,400
Class Action	6	G	4	0	0	0	175
Class Adoption	7	G	7	0	0	1	637
Class All Over	6	H	3	0	1	1	3,300
Class Approval	4	F	8	1	0	1	9,609
Class Atack	2	C	1	0	0	0	120
Class Be Ready	3	G	10	0	1	1	2,664
Class Canoe	7	G	4	0	0	1	1,130
Class Carter	7	G	4	0	0	1	440
Class Charmer (GB)	6	G	3	0	0	0	185
Class Choice	3	F	10	2	2	3	37,667
Class Concern	2	G	5	1	0	0	14,850
Class Crimson	3	G	3	0	0	0	0
Class Cutie	3	F	5	0	0	0	348
Class Edition	2	F	3	1	0	1	8,400
Class Halo	3	G	13	0	1	2	5,650
Class of Glass	4	F	3	1	0	1	14,340
Class of Her Own	5	M	10	0	0	0	3,360
Class of Seventy	4	G	3	0	0	0	720
Class Poet	4	G	12	0	2	3	11,610
Class Punch	4	C	3	0	0	2	4,080
Class Reality	3	F	6	0	1	0	4,800
Class Shall Tell	3	F	1	0	0	0	130
Class Shows	4	F	4	0	0	0	792
Class Spree	6	G	1	0	0	0	0
Class Sprite	3	C	2	0	0	0	300
Class Trip	4	F	8	0	1	2	7,366
Class Vigor	2	F	2	0	0	0	0
Class Yankee	5	M	5	0	1	0	12,028
Classa Red Wine	2	F	6	3	1	0	76,615
Classalwayshows	3	G	13	0	1	3	5,340
Classart	3	G	4	0	0	0	0
Classavoy	3	C	3	0	0	0	100
Classiano	4	F	11	3	3	1	13,659
Classic Alliance	8	H	2	0	0	1	1,760
Classic and Regal	2	C	8	0	0	1	2,680
Classic Apollo	3	G	4	1	1	0	8,100
Classic Appeal	6	H	9	2	1	1	141,049

RECORDS OF HORSES

Horse	Age	Sex	Sts	1st	2d	3d	Won
Classic Babe	3	F	1	0	0	0	180
Classic Band	3	C	12	2	3	1	27,935
Classic Beech	3	C	1	0	0	0	0
Classic Bird	5	M	4	0	0	1	5,310
Classic Boom	3	C	9	2	0	3	23,370
Classic Born	3	F	4	0	1	0	11,240
Classic Bounty	7	H	1	0	0	0	82
Classic Brat	6	G	8	1	3	1	11,957
Classic Brief (IRE)	4	G	7	0	1	2	11,870
Classic Brush	8	G	14	2	1	2	9,130
Classic Cal	9	H	1	0	0	0	500
Classic Caller	5	G	15	2	4	3	30,571
Classic Canvas	2	F	1	0	0	0	0
Classic Career	7	G	2	0	0	0	0
Classic Case	4	C	9	1	3	2	26,290
Classic Casey	4	G	10	0	0	1	2,206
Classic Caton	2	C	6	0	0	0	651
Classic Chaps	6	G	10	4	1	0	18,960
Classic Chatter	4	F	11	2	1	2	51,233
Classic Coleen	2	F	8	1	0	0	6,247
Classic Deputy	4	G	15	2	2	0	22,053
Classic Destiny	3	F	3	0	0	1	1,760
Classic Devil	3	F	14	1	3	1	10,385
Classic Display	7	F	1	0	1	1	14,593
Classic Encore	4	F	9	1	0	3	8,385
Classic Endeavor	5	H	11	5	2	0	241,595
Classic Esteem	7	G	3	0	0	1	2,150
Classic Example	2	F	1	1	0	0	27,000
Classic Fantasy	5	H	10	1	1	1	12,278
Classic Fellow	3	G	9	0	0	0	1,490
Classic Fool	4	G	12	1	1	3	64,085
Classic Form	5	G	13	1	0	3	19,350
Classic Gale	4	F	2	0	0	0	1,560
Classic Garbo	6	M	5	0	0	1	5,096
Classic Grata	5	M	2	0	0	0	246
Classic Habit	3	F	16	2	2	4	34,264
Classic Hello	4	C	13	3	2	1	29,437
Classic Hit	3	F	6	0	0	0	75
Classic Hour	2	G	3	1	0	1	19,595
Classic Ingrid	5	M	2	0	0	0	0
Classic Jammer	2	C	2	0	0	0	0
Classic Jazz	3	F	5	1	0	1	5,890
Classic Jourdan	4	F	10	2	1	2	14,645
Classic Kid	3	G	7	3	2	0	24,387
Classic Knight	7	G	3	0	0	1	1,575
Classic La	4	G	12	2	2	3	13,335
Classic Lass	5	M	1	0	0	0	61
Classic Lover	4	F	11	1	2	3	12,171
Classic Man	3	C	11	1	1	2	11,862
Classic Manner	5	G	7	0	1	1	18,051
Classic Mike	4	G	8	1	1	2	80,095
Classic Moment	3	F	9	2	1	3	43,034
Classic Mop	3	F	7	0	0	0	1,675
Classic Motion	3	F	15	1	2	0	13,590
Classic Music	4	F	1	0	0	0	1,572
Classic Nightmare	4	C	9	4	1	0	11,262
Classic Nix	6	M	8	0	0	3	8,651
Classic Onyx	5	G	7	1	3	1	6,426
Classic Par	5	G	8	0	3	1	51,195
Classic Perfection	4	C	7	0	0	0	990
Classic Picnic	3	G	2	0	0	0	370
Classic Place	7	G	1	0	0	0	42
Classic Prince	5	G	9	0	1	1	11,184
Classic Relative	3	C	6	0	2	1	10,760
Classic Rocknroll	3	C	2	0	0	0	0
Classic Royalist	5	G	11	2	1	1	10,336
Classic Run	4	C	7	1	2	0	12,210
Classic Runaway	4	G	17	1	5	2	38,766
Classic Ryder	3	C	5	2	2	0	23,418
Classic Saga	3	G	3	0	1	0	3,350
Classic Saint	4	G	13	1	2	0	12,749
Classic Sands	3	F	2	0	0	0	209
Classic Sauce	5	M	4	0	0	0	0
Classic Sleigh	4	G	1	0	0	0	0
Classic Soldier	3	G	2	0	0	0	227
Classic Solo	6	G	5	1	1	1	4,345
Classic Stag	4	C	7	3	0	0	59,880
Classic Stamp	3	F	8	3	2	2	228,054
Classic Symbol	8	G	3	0	0	0	363
Classic Tee	6	G	1	0	1	0	684
Classic Testamony	4	C	7	0	0	0	2,015
Classic Trouble	3	G	10	1	0	0	14,610
Classic Verse	6	G	4	2	0	0	28,560
Classic Visit	3	F	8	1	0	1	8,585
Classic Wheels	4	F	8	1	0	0	6,489
Classic White Wine	6	M	20	2	1	2	17,586
Classic Wine	2	C	1	1	0	0	15,200
Classic Zone	4	C	9	1	0	1	7,509
Classical Dancer	4	F	11	1	3	1	3,432
Classical Della	3	F	4	0	0	0	1,340
Classical Dice	3	F	5	1	0	1	7,980
Classical Drive	6	G	12	1	4	2	24,180
Classical Event	3	F	5	1	1	0	10,750
Classical Facts	5	M	7	1	0	0	2,897
Classical Guitar	8	H	3	0	0	0	186
Classical Gus	2	F	7	1	1	1	10,250
Classical Hunter	4	G	18	0	4	4	10,346
Classical Money	5	G	8	0	0	1	3,485
Classical Ray	7	G	11	4	4	0	28,692
Classical Ruckus	4	F	11	1	2	1	50,352
Classical Star	4	F	5	0	0	0	351
Classical Tune	4	F	2	0	0	0	170
Classical's First	6	M	6	0	0	1	2,341
Classiccanaveral	4	G	9	2	1	0	18,850
Classie Cassie	3	F	14	3	4	2	41,559
Classie Dancer	8	G	1	0	0	0	68
Classie Drone	5	G	4	1	1	0	4,760
Classie Green	3	F	13	1	3	4	10,704
Classie Smokey	3	G	1	0	0	0	315
Classified Breeze	3	F	4	0	0	0	588
Classified Factor	4	G	5	0	0	0	3,000
Classified Secret	3	G	5	0	2	1	34,127
Classified Special	2	F	2	0	0	0	144
Classifier	3	C	6	1	1	0	7,615
Classikas	4	F	4	1	1	0	9,910
Classky J	9	G	6	0	0	0	422
Classlylilprincess	5	M	14	0	0	1	2,826
Classmate	8	G	3	1	0	1	7,634
Classmate (ARG)	6	G	16	2	2	3	11,702
Classoffiftyseven	4	G	9	2	2	1	44,260
Classwilltell	5	G	15	0	1	0	3,756
Classy Advance	5	M	7	0	3	0	1,493
Classy Anthony	4	C	2	0	0	0	240
Classy Approach	5	M	9	1	0	3	6,679
Classy Barrera	2	F	6	0	1	0	1,964
Classy Bid	4	G	3	0	0	0	495
Classy Boy	3	G	2	0	0	0	0
Classy Brass	4	F	11	2	0	2	15,300
Classy Buckeye	7	M	4	0	0	0	185
Classy Champagne	5	M	1	0	0	0	0
Classy Commander	3	F	9	2	0	0	38,660
Classy Connection	4	F	6	4	1	0	14,540
Classy Conveyor	4	F	13	2	1	3	9,971
Classy Crane	3	G	10	3	0	0	14,124
Classy Creek	5	G	8	1	1	2	5,967
Classy Dan	4	G	5	0	0	1	1,402
Classy Daniela	5	M	10	2	0	1	22,903
Classy Date	4	F	1	0	0	0	960
Classy Diana	2	F	2	0	0	0	65
Classy E. T.	6	H	8	2	1	2	54,880
Classy Fella	4	G	5	1	1	1	36,240
Classy Fellow	3	G	1	0	0	0	0
Classy Flower	3	F	13	2	0	2	34,079
Classy Gaziba	5	M	5	0	0	0	542
Classy Glassie	6	H	1	0	0	0	133
Classy Heroine	3	F	15	3	2	2	32,080
Classy Jack Clark	5	G	12	1	0	1	8,348
Classy Jenna	3	F	2	0	0	0	800
Classy Kay	6	M	9	1	0	1	11,694
Classy Lauren	2	G	2	0	0	0	3,080
Classy Leah	5	M	11	2	0	1	14,044
Classy Legend	2	C	3	0	0	1	1,570
Classy Li'l Fella	3	C	15	1	0	0	3,293
Classy Maid	3	F	11	1	3	1	13,248
Classy Migration	2	C	3	1	1	1	25,240
Classy Miss	6	M	8	0	0	0	0
Classy Miss Alley	5	M	15	0	4	2	7,916
Classy Miss M.	3	F	15	1	1	4	10,575

Horse	Age	Sex	Sts	1st	2d	3d	Won
Classy Moonbeam	2	F	1	0	0	0	0
Classy N Gold	4	F	6	0	0	2	574
Classy Nickie	2	F	3	0	0	0	200
Classy Okie	6	H	4	2	0	1	17,499
Classy Payday	3	F	9	0	0	2	6,391
Classy Pickup	6	M	4	0	0	0	1,583
Classy Prince	5	G	6	1	0	0	10,380
Classy Report	4	F	16	7	2	1	70,833
Classy Retsina	2	G	1	0	0	0	74
Classy Road	3	F	9	2	1	2	34,466
Classy Serenade	4	F	13	0	0	3	6,828
Classy Sheikh	7	G	6	1	2	1	26,910
Classy So n' So	2	C	4	1	0	0	4,784
Classy Solution	5	M	3	0	0	0	5,292
Classy T	5	M	4	0	0	0	476
Classy Wolfe	3	F	1	0	0	0	45
Classy Word	4	F	6	1	0	0	5,581
Classys Half Moon	4	F	1	0	0	0	60
Claudes Favorite	4	C	3	0	0	0	0
Claudia Jane	4	F	13	2	1	2	8,660
Claudia's Agenda	2	F	4	0	0	2	4,180
Claudia's Choice	4	F	4	1	3	0	4,680
Claudia's Secret	5	M	12	2	2	1	14,033
Claudia's Type	3	F	8	1	1	0	16,170
Claudie Rose	2	F	1	0	0	0	95
Claudines Kitten	4	F	8	0	0	1	922
Claudine's Revenge	3	F	10	1	1	1	10,425
Claudio	3	G	10	1	2	2	30,236
Claudius Maximus	3	C	2	0	0	0	150
Clausura	4	F	5	0	0	1	1,380
Claw Hammer	4	G	2	0	0	0	230
Clay City	5	G	12	2	2	1	7,728
Clay Gal	6	M	3	0	0	0	160
Clay Time	4	G	9	3	2	3	15,931
Claydif	4	C	9	3	1	0	15,687
Claymore	4	G	9	1	3	1	20,578
Clays Awesome	3	G	9	1	2	1	32,090
Clay's Rocket	2	F	6	3	1	0	49,020
Clayton	3	G	3	0	0	1	1,046
Clayton's Cat	2	F	1	0	0	1	750
Clayton's Trick	3	C	9	2	1	3	53,755
Clayton's Whirl	5	G	4	0	0	0	183
Clean Break	4	C	1	0	0	0	0
Clean Living	5	G	11	1	1	0	23,725
Cleaning House	3	C	13	3	1	4	72,920
Clear Action M. D.	4	G	1	0	0	0	0
Clear Advantage	2	C	7	1	1	0	9,721
Clear and Cold	2	F	4	1	0	0	13,635
Clear as Daylight	3	F	8	0	1	0	7,860
Clear Creek Canyon	3	G	10	3	2	1	66,355
Clear Denial	4	F	9	4	0	1	19,799
Clear Design	5	G	14	2	1	0	12,609
Clear Destiny	4	F	5	2	2	0	113,532
Clear for Take Off	4	G	18	1	0	2	4,833
Clear in the West	3	F	3	2	0	0	36,000
Clear Panache	2	F	1	0	0	0	126
Clear Path	5	M	3	1	0	0	20,790
Clear Pouch	3	F	1	0	0	0	0
Clear Strike	3	G	3	1	0	0	10,940
Clear Talking Girl	3	F	13	0	0	1	1,193
Clear Terms	3	C	9	3	0	0	29,750
Clear the Bases	2	C	1	0	0	0	2,700
Clear the Benches	3	C	9	0	0	0	800
Clear the Field	10	G	3	0	0	0	240
Clear the Runway	4	F	10	3	3	1	13,767
Clear Tips	3	F	1	0	0	0	0
Clear Title	4	G	2	0	1	1	5,370
Clearance Code	11	G	1	0	0	0	0
Clearance Light	5	M	12	1	2	0	7,629
Clearaway	3	G	3	0	0	0	60
Clearcreek Sassy	3	F	8	1	0	0	11,952
Cleared to Go	4	F	10	1	0	3	30,726
Clearinghouse	4	G	19	1	4	1	10,380
Clearite	5	H	2	0	0	0	34
Clearly a King	2	C	2	0	0	0	252
Clearly Elegant	8	M	2	0	0	0	0
Clearly Irish	5	G	15	3	3	3	18,021
Clearly Nautical	6	G	14	0	2	4	5,642
Clearsoul	2	F	3	0	0	0	75
Cleartalker	2	C	5	1	1	0	23,984
Cleat	7	G	12	2	1	1	33,869
Clef Note	6	G	14	4	3	2	36,248
Clefairy (IRE)	4	F	2	1	0	0	24,000
Clegg	3	G	12	3	4	0	38,940
Cleito	2	F	7	1	0	1	20,650
Clem Da Claimer	2	G	3	0	1	0	1,349
Clem Sky	3	C	9	3	2	0	50,777
Clemency	5	G	9	0	2	1	6,987
Cleo's Bet	4	G	8	0	0	0	378
Clerbuent	4	C	13	1	2	1	6,028
Clergy	4	G	6	1	2	0	59,220
Clerical Error (IRE)	4	F	3	0	0	1	7,308
Clerpark	2	C	1	0	0	0	0
Cleveland Circle	11	G	8	0	1	0	1,798
Clever Affair	2	G	2	0	0	2	3,402
Clever and Fancy	4	C	17	2	1	4	17,939
Clever Anet	3	F	11	0	3	0	5,990
Clever Angelo	10	G	4	0	1	0	1,935
Clever At Midnight	6	G	6	1	1	2	2,338
Clever Ballad	2	F	7	1	2	2	27,240
Clever Bates	4	F	4	2	1	0	7,408
Clever Blonde	4	F	8	0	2	4	36,825
Clever Bluff	3	C	4	0	0	0	0
Clever Book	3	C	15	5	0	0	33,286
Clever Boy	4	G	3	0	0	0	196
Clever Brick	6	G	15	2	6	1	22,037
Clever Bride	2	F	4	0	1	0	2,620
Clever Bull	2	C	8	0	1	1	9,331
Clever Chance	2	C	1	0	0	0	0
Clever Coed	5	M	9	2	2	0	27,740
Clever Colleen	2	F	7	0	0	0	1,620
Clever Comique	2	F	1	0	0	0	0
Clever Concorde	4	F	11	3	1	3	65,140
Clever Connection	2	F	9	0	2	0	7,177
Clever Course	3	C	10	2	0	3	11,813
Clever Cowboy	3	C	2	0	0	0	1,230
Clever Coyote	4	G	14	2	0	3	8,245
Clever Crawford	4	C	18	4	4	2	88,980
Clever Crossing	2	F	4	1	0	0	8,380
Clever Dance	3	G	5	0	0	2	3,400
Clever Deputy	5	G	14	2	1	1	22,934
Clever Edition	3	C	7	0	0	0	1,203
Clever Electrician	4	C	13	2	4	2	89,140
Clever Endeaver	4	G	6	0	1	1	1,717
Clever Envoy	5	G	6	2	0	0	10,200
Clever Eyes	3	F	2	0	0	0	0
Clever Fact	4	F	10	1	0	1	15,526
Clever General	3	G	7	1	0	2	11,855
Clever Gent	8	G	3	0	0	0	1,716
Clever Girl	4	F	12	1	3	2	9,274
Clever Hound	4	G	14	1	1	1	21,425
Clever I Am	4	F	4	1	1	2	5,105
Clever Jack	3	G	15	5	3	0	57,810
Clever Jim	3	G	8	0	0	2	1,770
Clever Jimmy C	3	G	12	2	1	1	31,984
Clever Jove	2	C	2	0	0	0	2,205
Clever June	2	F	6	0	0	1	5,460
Clever Katie	2	F	1	0	0	0	600
Clever Keypsake	3	G	10	1	0	0	6,300
Clever Kiss	2	F	1	0	0	0	0
Clever Legend	3	G	9	1	3	2	3,287
Clever Lil Girl	3	F	8	1	3	0	7,939
Clever Little Dude	5	G	11	2	1	1	11,888
Clever Louis	4	C	10	2	2	1	67,220
Clever Maid	2	F	2	0	0	1	2,390
Clever Maneuver	3	F	1	0	0	0	0
Clever Marlin	4	C	6	0	1	1	1,363
Clever Melody	2	F	6	1	2	2	56,341
Clever Miss Caper	7	M	13	2	5	2	43,080
Clever Miss Trixie	3	F	9	1	1	1	11,460
Clever Moon	3	F	10	2	1	2	100,742
Clever Nureyev	6	G	7	0	0	0	789
Clever Odds	3	G	4	1	0	0	5,880
Clever Pancho	4	C	12	4	1	2	54,215
Clever Peace	2	F	1	0	0	0	0
Clever Play	3	G	6	1	0	3	19,860
Clever Prospector	4	F	8	1	2	2	22,230
Clever Quoit	7	G	8	0	0	1	1,850

Horse	Age	Sex	Sts	1st	2d	3d	Won	Horse	Age	Sex	Sts	1st	2d	3d	Won
Clever Red	3	C	6	3	1	0	9,656	Closing	4	G	5	1	0	0	2,820
Clever Red Head	2	F	4	0	0	0	1,093	Closing Derby	4	G	13	0	3	4	6,380
Clever Revolution	5	G	6	3	0	1	9,045	Closing the Gap	4	F	1	0	0	0	0
Clever Rose	3	F	1	0	0	0	66	Cloud Chief	2	G	4	1	2	0	11,280
Clever Sis	3	F	3	0	0	0	0	Cloud City	6	M	7	0	1	1	9,098
Clever Smile	4	G	23	2	2	1	19,466	Cloud Counting	3	F	8	2	3	1	42,886
Clever Spy	2	G	1	0	0	0	70	Cloud Ghazir	4	F	11	1	1	3	7,170
Clever Tace	4	F	7	1	0	1	5,550	Cloud Harbor	6	M	4	1	1	0	22,400
Clever Thorne	5	H	12	2	1	0	13,189	Cloud Jumper	4	G	12	3	2	1	132,010
Clever to Me	2	F	5	1	3	1	24,890	Cloud Monster	2	C	1	0	0	1	2,990
Clever Too	7	M	13	3	1	4	21,831	Cloud Surfer	3	F	6	1	2	1	23,658
Clever Truce	3	G	6	1	0	1	7,125	Cloud Walker	3	C	1	1	0	0	16,800
Clever Turk	5	M	7	1	0	1	6,520	Cloudier	2	F	1	0	0	0	650
Clever Victor	5	G	13	2	2	2	59,994	Cloudman	10	G	10	2	2	2	36,290
Clever Vixen	5	M	2	0	0	0	225	Clouds Class	9	G	7	0	0	1	1,294
Clever Woman	3	F	2	0	0	0	94	Clouds of Gold	4	F	10	2	1	3	156,785
Cleverandswift	4	F	2	0	0	0	32	Clouds On the Walk	3	C	10	1	2	1	23,550
Cleverbagatricks	3	G	5	1	0	0	12,154	Cloudy Gray	2	F	8	0	2	0	5,155
Cleverita	3	F	3	3	0	0	17,100	Cloudy Mist	4	C	8	0	2	0	2,720
Cleverly Gilded	2	F	2	0	0	0	644	Cloudy Money	2	G	5	0	0	0	950
Clevermen	4	G	10	1	1	1	10,416	Cloudy Morning	2	C	1	0	0	0	205
Clever's Mint	2	F	1	0	0	0	0	Cloudy Sundial	5	M	4	0	0	0	237
Clevertrickyman	2	C	4	0	2	0	5,185	Cloudy's Knight	3	C	4	1	0	0	18,960
Cli Kaori	8	G	7	1	1	1	2,044	Clover Girl	3	F	3	0	0	0	11,430
Clibrig	4	F	8	2	2	1	120,772	Clover Patch Kid	3	C	2	0	0	0	780
Click On Go	3	F	8	0	0	0	223	Clover Situation	3	G	7	0	0	1	14,920
Click On Me	4	F	13	2	2	0	17,878	Clown Prince	2	G	3	0	2	0	4,262
Click On Sleet	6	M	7	0	0	2	1,199	Clownaround	7	G	2	0	0	0	210
Clickety Cat	4	F	12	4	1	3	82,395	Clown's Pleasure	4	C	3	0	0	0	328
Clicksville	4	G	5	0	0	0	565	Clu Too	3	C	7	1	2	0	11,220
Clifden	2	C	7	0	0	0	1,725	Club Forty One	3	G	14	5	1	1	79,765
Clifden Star	5	M	13	2	1	1	23,116	Club Four O Seven	3	F	1	0	0	0	0
Cliff	5	G	3	0	0	0	570	Club Lane	4	G	15	0	1	5	6,081
Cliff Glider	4	C	8	0	1	0	2,605	Club Queen	2	F	2	0	0	0	220
Cliff Notes	5	H	3	0	0	0	18,960	Clubay	5	M	8	2	3	1	145,680
Cliff of Lockport	4	G	1	0	0	0	103	Clubone Carl	7	G	1	0	0	0	50
Cliff's Choice	5	H	7	0	0	1	1,746	Clueless Howie	5	G	7	2	1	1	14,743
Cliffside	4	C	12	2	2	1	9,558	Clutch Player	5	G	7	1	0	3	14,167
Climatic Fever	2	G	5	0	1	1	4,550	Clyde's Cider	2	G	3	1	0	1	6,410
Climay (ARG)	6	H	1	0	0	0	0	Cmego	3	G	9	2	2	1	56,199
Climb	4	F	13	3	3	1	23,970	C'Mon Cat	4	G	4	0	0	0	1,130
Climbeverymountain	5	M	3	0	1	0	2,946	C'Mon Chromie	9	G	1	0	0	0	0
Cling	5	M	13	2	1	2	21,621	C'Mon Cletus	7	H	3	0	0	0	129
Clint	4	C	3	0	0	0	650	Cmonbabylitemyfire	2	F	2	0	0	0	0
Clint Road	2	C	1	0	0	0	756	Cmydust	4	F	2	0	0	0	40
Clinton Hunting	6	H	3	1	0	1	7,344	Cnjs Black Knight	4	G	6	0	2	1	1,639
Clinton's Country	2	C	1	0	0	0	1,572	Co Chief King	3	G	8	0	0	1	3,959
Clints Blue Ribbon	6	G	2	0	0	0	0	Co Co Heart	4	F	6	1	1	2	45,880
Clint's Nature	3	G	3	1	0	0	13,770	Co Twining Niner	4	C	9	1	0	3	9,104
Clints Way	3	G	22	2	5	5	70,750	Coach A. P.	3	G	1	0	0	1	1,920
Clip Joint	6	G	10	1	2	0	4,773	Coach Endres	4	C	7	0	1	0	1,794
Clipboard Eddie	7	G	7	1	0	0	3,778	Coach Gatlin	6	G	1	0	0	0	0
Clipper Cat	2	F	4	0	0	0	570	Coach Gay's Day	5	G	10	2	1	2	11,112
Clippin Avenue	4	F	2	0	0	0	980	Coach Jimi Lee	3	G	11	5	1	2	218,120
Clipping Coins	4	G	8	1	1	2	57,504	Coach Knight	4	C	11	0	0	1	2,785
Cloakof Vagueness	3	F	10	2	5	2	200,145	Coach Numero Uno	2	G	3	1	0	0	9,240
Clobber	3	C	1	0	0	0	0	Coach Rags	7	G	7	1	1	0	40,620
Clock Stopper	3	G	7	4	2	0	177,661	Coach Read	6	G	1	0	0	0	174
Clockwork Orange (AUS)	10	M	5	0	0	1	1,175	Coach Rodger	7	G	11	2	2	0	13,912
Clod Ber Junior (BRZ)	6	H	7	0	0	0	3,834	Coach Roll	4	G	10	0	0	0	980
Clod's Crypto	2	G	4	1	0	0	6,225	Coach Tobacco	5	H	1	0	0	0	230
Cloee Irene	3	F	10	2	1	1	9,902	Coach's Corner	4	G	14	3	1	3	15,692
Cloned Colony	2	G	1	0	0	0	93	Coahoma	4	C	11	0	0	1	18,390
Clonfor	3	F	2	0	0	0	510	Coal Black Rose	3	F	2	0	0	0	230
Clonmany (IRE)	6	G	11	2	2	1	24,425	Coal Creek Slew	5	H	11	0	1	1	1,784
Clooney	6	H	11	1	0	3	21,050	Coal Dust	4	G	3	0	0	0	5,496
Close Clearance	2	F	2	0	0	0	0	Coal Inmy Stocking	3	F	6	1	1	0	7,213
Close Dance	3	G	7	0	3	0	6,749	Coal Smudge	2	C	5	3	1	0	69,906
Close Dancing	2	F	1	0	0	0	40	Coalbank	2	C	1	0	0	0	0
Close On Time	5	H	13	1	2	2	15,280	Coalinzo	4	G	10	1	1	0	1,391
Close the Book	8	G	7	1	1	0	14,350	Coalition	3	C	8	1	2	0	35,960
Close to Accurate	4	C	3	0	1	1	5,700	Coalpepper	3	G	8	1	2	1	29,692
Close to Perfect	2	F	7	0	1	3	16,720	Coast	4	C	1	0	1	0	2,060
Close to Reno	3	C	3	1	0	0	15,600	Coast Line	2	C	1	0	0	0	2,700
Closeeyesfantasize	4	F	12	1	1	2	4,040	Coast Starlight	3	G	3	1	0	0	2,502
Closenuftoperfect	6	H	8	4	0	1	17,280	Coastal Alert	6	G	8	0	0	1	2,530
Closer to Me	6	G	2	0	0	0	116	Coastal Boundary	2	F	4	0	1	1	3,620
Closer Tothe Heart	8	G	4	0	0	0	553	Coastal Candy	2	F	6	1	1	0	15,630
Closets n' Clothes	3	F	6	0	0	0	790	Coastal Cat	4	G	11	2	0	1	36,307

Horse	Age	Sex	Sts	1st	2d	3d	Won
Coastal Colony	3	G	8	0	0	1	3,060
Coastal Crime	5	G	1	1	0	0	4,740
Coastal Display	10	G	7	1	0	0	9,400
Coastal Jig	8	G	13	1	3	2	14,203
Coastal Prince	7	G	2	0	0	1	784
Coastal Rhodes	5	G	3	0	1	0	1,292
Coastal Treasure	5	M	1	0	0	0	0
Coastal War	2	G	2	0	0	0	456
Coastal Wolf	2	F	1	0	0	0	0
Coastalota	6	M	8	1	3	1	64,900
Coastalquicksilver	2	G	3	0	1	1	840
Coasting Barnie	3	G	3	1	0	0	8,321
Coat and Tie	4	G	2	0	0	0	0
Coat of Armor	6	G	12	2	1	3	20,999
Coax	5	H	2	0	0	0	282
Coax a Red Bird	4	G	5	1	1	1	5,911
Coax Kid	3	C	4	0	0	1	17,760
Coax Me Bragg	3	G	1	0	0	0	65
Coax Me Cody	4	G	11	0	2	4	9,624
Coax Me Irish	3	F	3	0	0	0	240
Coax No More	3	C	16	1	0	3	10,761
Coax On Jodi	3	F	1	0	0	0	188
Coaxed	2	C	2	0	0	0	7,650
Coaxing Halo	2	F	6	0	0	1	1,812
Coaxingriches	7	M	5	0	2	0	2,565
Cobalt Casey	2	C	1	0	0	0	220
Cobb County	5	G	3	0	0	0	693
Cobb Road	3	C	4	0	1	0	435
Cobblers Rock	7	G	7	2	1	0	77,411
Cobblestone	5	G	4	0	0	0	130
Cobbley Six	4	G	5	1	0	2	21,296
Cobbley's Jewel	2	F	3	0	0	0	1,980
Cobbley's Mark	6	H	9	3	1	0	20,886
Cobbley's Promise	5	H	4	0	0	1	1,984
Cobb's Prince	4	C	2	0	0	0	163
Cobourg Lodge (IRE)	7	G	4	0	0	1	3,630
Cobra Bay	4	C	1	0	0	0	0
Cobra Devil	5	G	5	0	0	1	440
Cobra Jet	3	C	2	0	0	0	0
Cobra Kid	4	G	3	0	0	1	1,120
Cobra Lady	3	F	8	5	1	2	134,709
Cobra Lips	3	C	9	1	0	0	4,029
Cobra Power	3	G	6	1	1	1	28,920
Cobra Squeeze	4	F	13	0	1	1	3,592
Cobra Star	3	G	9	1	1	1	57,313
Cobra Tongue	4	G	8	1	0	1	7,350
Cobra Torch	3	F	5	1	0	1	5,050
Cobra Trick	4	G	1	0	0	0	48
Cobramaster	4	C	7	0	3	1	1,531
Cobra's Prince	5	G	2	0	0	0	120
Cobra's Princess	3	F	11	2	1	1	14,230
Cobratime	3	F	5	1	0	1	16,124
Coby Appeal	7	G	13	1	1	2	15,075
Cocked	3	G	11	3	0	0	19,030
Cocked N Locked	7	G	14	0	1	1	2,075
Cockle Burr Man	4	G	2	0	0	0	320
Cocktails At Seven	5	M	1	0	0	0	0
Cocktailsandreams	6	M	8	0	1	4	34,922
Cocktalzonthebeach	3	G	12	1	1	0	7,950
Cocky	6	H	3	1	0	0	22,560
Cocky Talk	4	F	9	0	0	1	1,324
Cocky'n Sure	3	G	2	0	0	0	0
Coco Bay	5	M	1	0	0	0	360
Coco de Bentwood	4	F	4	0	0	0	0
Coco Lady	2	F	5	0	1	1	7,120
Coco Mocha	4	F	14	1	2	0	5,134
Coco Rico	4	C	5	0	0	0	353
Coco Vive	7	M	3	1	0	0	15,588
Cocoa Cream	2	F	1	0	0	0	0
Cocoa Latte	2	G	1	0	0	1	720
Cocoa Mio	2	F	5	1	0	0	6,534
Cocoa's Gabriella	4	F	7	1	0	0	3,168
Cocodan	2	G	4	1	1	2	17,068
Cocodrie	4	G	7	1	2	1	7,403
Cocolette	3	F	3	1	0	0	2,718
Coconino	8	G	7	0	0	2	572
Coconut Girl	4	F	6	1	2	1	62,640
Coconut Mango	4	C	10	2	3	0	80,068
Coconut Martini	2	F	2	0	0	0	7,500
Coconut Willamina	3	F	5	0	0	1	1,505
Coconut Willy	6	G	9	1	0	2	12,177
Coconuts Baby	2	C	2	0	0	0	0
Cocopuff	5	M	4	0	0	0	140
Cocorite	3	F	11	0	3	2	20,235
Coco's Clown	3	C	4	0	0	0	140
Coco's for Real	2	F	3	1	0	0	13,290
Coco's Madness	4	G	2	1	0	1	21,460
Coco's Minister	3	G	9	3	2	0	46,240
Coco's My Dream	2	F	5	0	0	0	12,582
Code Ack Moment	4	F	8	1	2	2	19,730
Code Blush	4	G	10	2	1	1	23,660
Code d'Azur	3	F	3	0	0	0	0
Code De	8	G	4	0	0	1	948
Code Found	8	G	15	1	0	1	4,570
Code Hey	3	F	4	0	0	0	122
Code Lady	3	F	12	1	2	1	4,782
Code Man	4	G	9	1	0	1	5,220
Code Name Elmer	3	G	11	1	1	0	21,328
Code Name Flirt	3	F	2	0	0	1	1,560
Code Name Fred	7	G	9	4	0	1	71,180
Code Name Louie	6	H	17	5	3	1	30,147
Code Name Romeo	3	C	9	2	0	1	17,072
Code Name Simon	4	G	13	1	2	3	6,166
Code of Angels	2	C	6	1	2	1	28,700
Code of Conduct	5	G	2	0	0	0	194
Code of Ethics	2	F	1	0	0	0	780
Code of Justice	2	F	4	2	1	0	30,915
Code of the Hills	4	C	11	3	0	1	29,800
Code of the Woods	5	M	2	0	0	0	130
Code One	8	H	11	1	6	1	19,461
Code Song	2	F	2	1	0	0	27,455
Code Sugar	4	G	5	0	0	1	1,984
Code to Justice	3	F	2	0	0	0	0
Code Two High	3	G	7	0	0	1	1,026
Coded Account	4	F	10	1	0	3	10,486
Coded Message	5	G	2	1	0	0	13,200
Codeofmanycolors	2	C	4	1	0	0	3,462
Coder Steve	4	G	6	1	2	0	12,922
Code's Decree	4	F	13	2	1	2	48,477
Codes Miss Doc	2	F	4	1	0	0	7,165
Codes Miss Tex	2	F	3	1	0	2	10,995
Codes Preshisone	5	M	6	0	0	2	10,500
Codes Spit Fire	4	C	7	0	2	0	7,171
Codexs Heiress	5	M	14	0	1	1	2,620
Codger	6	G	12	2	3	3	17,093
Coding	3	F	6	2	2	0	77,654
Cody Coyote	4	C	2	0	0	1	480
Cody Grove	2	C	3	0	2	0	8,700
Cody H.	3	C	9	1	2	2	16,947
Cody Light	5	G	17	3	5	4	44,485
Cody Man West	6	G	12	0	3	2	9,870
Cody Ody	3	G	6	1	0	1	17,309
Cody Steele	4	G	15	0	2	3	4,236
Cody to Reggie	3	G	4	1	1	1	13,885
Cody Wade	2	G	4	0	0	2	1,690
Codyinthelead	3	F	6	2	0	1	13,463
Cody's Account	3	G	7	0	0	0	958
Codys Birthday	6	G	17	2	2	1	10,616
Cody's Con	3	C	2	0	0	0	260
Cody's History	2	C	1	0	0	0	0
Cody's Kisses	2	F	8	0	0	1	5,197
Codys Lucky Appeal	3	C	13	1	1	3	18,232
Cody's Memory	3	C	2	0	0	0	170
Codys My Boy	2	C	1	0	0	0	0
Codys Odds	3	C	7	3	1	0	20,972
Coed Cutie	3	F	8	1	3	0	15,195
Coercion	3	F	14	0	2	4	7,770
Coeur Di Leone	3	G	8	1	0	2	11,520
Coffee and Creme	8	G	4	0	0	1	779
Coffee Bubbles	6	G	7	1	0	2	3,159
Coffee for Me	3	C	10	0	1	0	4,968
Coffee Gully	2	C	1	0	0	0	130
Coffee Joe	5	H	2	0	0	0	84
Coffee Street	3	G	9	2	0	0	33,809
Cogent	9	M	14	4	2	2	72,258
Coggon	5	G	11	0	0	2	22,959
Cognac Supreme	5	G	11	0	3	2	8,972
Cognacs Negotiator	7	G	1	0	0	0	0

Horse	Age	Sex	Sts	1st	2d	3d	Won
Cogs My Man	3	C	2	0	0	1	1,500
Cohassett Rocks	2	C	3	0	0	0	714
Coherent	3	F	1	1	0	0	27,600
Cohiba Connie	4	F	5	1	1	1	9,555
Cohiba Kid	4	G	14	1	3	1	6,605
Coil N Strike	5	G	10	4	2	0	54,225
Coin a Fue	5	G	2	0	0	0	0
Coin Charger	4	G	9	1	1	2	9,009
Coin Collection	2	F	2	0	0	0	0
Coin Machine	5	G	3	0	0	0	306
Coin Maker	2	G	8	0	1	0	9,367
Coin of the Relam	3	F	4	0	0	0	300
Coin Phlip	3	F	2	0	0	0	132
Coin Return	7	G	3	0	0	0	1,361
Coin Treasure	3	G	16	3	2	3	18,587
Coin Trick	3	F	8	0	2	1	15,725
Coincide	4	C	10	1	1	3	33,570
Coincidence	2	F	1	0	0	0	139
Coined for Success	2	C	2	0	1	0	8,200
Cointreau	3	C	6	2	1	2	64,100
Coja	3	C	1	0	0	0	0
Cojet	4	C	8	1	0	0	58,170
Cokaren	4	F	4	0	0	0	0
Coke's Melody	4	F	4	1	0	2	58,920
Coke's Tribute	5	G	12	1	4	3	24,690
Col. Hogan	7	G	8	0	0	0	3,625
Colbegone	4	F	5	0	0	0	491
Colby's Bad Boy	8	G	10	0	1	1	2,255
Colby's Boy	3	C	13	3	0	1	33,844
Colchis	4	C	10	2	1	1	18,389
Cold	5	M	4	0	0	1	900
Cold and Windswept	3	F	13	0	3	2	6,445
Cold Blow Lane	5	G	7	0	1	0	14,260
Cold Call Cowboy	4	G	8	2	0	0	12,433
Cold Cash Reward	4	C	5	1	2	0	12,350
Cold Chill	4	C	3	0	0	0	1,210
Cold Chillin	4	F	13	0	0	0	3,765
Cold Chisel	9	G	10	2	0	1	4,010
Cold Claim	5	G	8	1	1	0	14,060
Cold Cold Facts	5	G	10	2	2	1	10,502
Cold Comfort	2	G	3	0	0	1	1,930
Cold Encounter	3	C	1	0	0	0	
Cold Express	7	G	16	0	6	5	13,492
Cold Game	2	G	6	0	1	2	5,710
Cold Gin	4	C	5	0	0	0	152
Cold Gold	4	G	7	1	0	1	4,340
Cold Hard Truth	8	G	5	0	0	0	374
Cold Heart	6	G	13	2	1	0	12,202
Cold Market	4	G	2	0	0	1	2,520
Cold N Evil	3	G	7	1	0	1	15,940
Cold One	3	F	11	1	3	3	36,766
Cold Outside	5	M	2	0	1	0	1,855
Cold Prospect	4	G	11	3	1	0	15,971
Cold Shot	5	G	9	0	0	2	4,078
Cold Spell	4	C	2	1	0	0	1,200
Cold Spring	5	M	3	1	0	0	3,324
Cold Stone Steve	4	C	8	2	2	1	52,100
Cold Trick	2	C	1	0	0	1	5,000
Cold Truth	3	G	8	1	0	2	27,890
Cold Tudor	2	G	4	0	1	0	1,260
Cold Turkey	5	M	6	1	1	0	25,918
Cold War	2	G	2	0	1	0	11,760
Cold Warrior	3	C	4	1	1	1	26,970
Cold Water	2	G	1	0	0	1	2,390
Cold Wynnter	2	F	4	2	2	0	40,170
Coldbeerathebit	2	F	1	0	0	0	960
Coldblooded Pirate	3	G	9	1	0	1	7,159
Coldiron Slew	4	G	3	1	0	1	16,542
Coldntight	4	F	4	1	1	1	46,280
Coldstream	4	C	9	0	4	1	13,196
Cole	5	G	9	1	1	3	41,487
Cole Younger	4	G	2	0	0	1	4,420
Colebrook Creek	7	G	11	4	2	0	33,482
Colebrook Crusader	5	G	5	0	0	0	0
Colebrook Express	6	G	6	0	0	0	0
Colebrook Fighter	6	M	8	2	1	1	29,042
Colebrook Glory	6	H	2	0	0	0	225
Colebrook Jet	5	H	4	0	0	0	622
Colebrook Red	6	G	8	2	0	2	8,113
Colebrook Ruckus	5	G	12	1	1	1	56,590
Colebrook Striker	3	G	6	0	2	1	18,003
Colebrookadvantage	6	M	8	3	1	0	31,984
Colee Bear	3	F	7	2	0	0	29,880
Coleman Bonner	2	C	5	0	1	3	6,250
Colemans Cheval	6	G	13	2	1	1	19,036
Colero Wildfire	3	F	6	1	0	0	9,600
Coles a Champ	3	G	14	3	2	3	71,170
Coles Choice	5	M	14	2	0	2	10,464
Coles Lad	3	G	8	0	1	1	2,185
Coles Light	3	C	4	0	1	0	3,580
Coles Point	4	C	6	1	2	0	10,537
Colesburg	3	G	18	1	1	1	7,713
Coleslew	3	G	10	2	1	1	20,402
Colette's Tresor	3	F	2	0	0	0	252
Colihan	7	G	10	0	2	1	6,581
Colin and Michael	3	G	3	0	0	0	330
Colin Road	5	G	6	0	0	0	974
Colins Buddy	4	G	6	1	2	1	10,375
Colita	3	C	8	4	0	1	184,050
Collar Button	4	G	5	0	0	0	402
Collateral Damage	3	G	5	0	1	0	13,900
Collateral Maker	2	G	1	0	0	0	0
Colleague	3	F	5	0	1	0	4,690
Collect Deposit	5	H	7	1	0	0	11,482
Collect the Gold	3	G	22	1	2	3	11,074
Collectdance	2	G	3	0	0	0	627
Collecting Coins	3	C	2	0	0	0	0
Collection	4	F	9	1	0	1	13,230
Collectors Edition	4	F	2	0	0	0	0
Colleen's Jackpot	3	F	16	2	2	1	18,790
Colleen's Pidgeon	5	H	4	0	0	0	262
College Dean	8	G	13	1	4	1	33,888
College Honor	3	G	12	6	1	0	110,590
Collier Gold	3	C	10	1	0	1	9,717
Collier Slew	2	G	7	0	2	2	15,745
Collier's Pleasure	5	M	1	0	0	0	0
Collinstown	3	G	12	0	1	3	4,559
Cologny	3	F	15	2	1	4	67,640
Colombard	4	F	12	1	1	1	13,528
Colondelivery	4	G	8	0	2	1	17,999
Colonel Bradshaw	3	C	13	0	4	1	29,480
Colonel Chris	9	G	12	0	1	4	5,636
Colonel Cleator	2	G	6	1	0	0	20,130
Colonel Corn	2	G	2	0	0	1	4,875
Colonel Courtney	3	G	11	2	2	1	36,187
Colonel Dan	3	G	5	1	1	0	3,831
Colonel Day	2	G	1	1	0	0	13,640
Colonel Fordyce	9	H	10	1	4	2	12,650
Colonel Gordon	3	C	1	0	0	0	0
Colonel Jake	3	G	6	0	1	0	2,750
Colonel Kelly	8	G	5	2	0	0	14,615
Colonel Lyle	4	G	4	1	0	0	2,723
Colonel Spike	10	G	11	1	0	1	5,124
Colonel Tap	4	G	2	0	0	0	88
Colonel's Passion	3	G	2	0	0	0	170
Colonel's Secret	9	M	6	0	1	0	3,655
Colonial Asset	5	H	3	0	2	0	5,404
Colonial Bay	4	C	9	2	5	1	110,490
Colonial Billy	3	C	6	1	1	3	16,410
Colonial Boy	6	H	1	0	0	0	750
Colonial Colony	5	H	10	1	3	0	164,665
Colonial Gift	4	C	9	2	3	0	14,460
Colonial Glitter	4	F	7	0	0	2	14,409
Colonial Gray	4	G	7	1	0	0	10,740
Colonial Harbor	3	F	5	0	0	0	656
Colonial Justice	4	C	5	2	0	1	6,478
Colonial Loot	7	H	10	3	0	1	16,096
Colonial Mate	9	G	7	0	0	0	495
Colonial Mint	3	F	14	2	1	1	19,185
Colonial Native	5	G	10	0	1	1	3,503
Colonial Policy	7	G	3	0	0	0	61
Colonial Power	9	H	9	1	3	3	27,568
Colonial Prospect	3	C	6	1	1	1	17,756
Colonial Reign	2	C	2	0	0	0	0
Colonial Secretary	11	G	7	2	0	1	28,421
Colonial Storm	3	F	4	0	0	0	0
Colonial Surprise	3	F	6	2	3	0	88,760
Colonnesse	3	F	4	1	0	0	9,690

Horse	Age	Sex	Sts	1st	2d	3d	Won	Horse	Age	Sex	Sts	1st	2d	3d	Won
Colony Lane	4	G	10	2	1	1	47,126	Come Back Ronnie	8	H	2	0	0	1	5,640
Colony Park	5	G	11	0	1	3	3,243	Come Dance	2	F	4	0	1	0	8,248
Colony Ridge	4	G	10	1	0	1	3,221	Come Dream With Me	4	G	13	5	0	1	49,316
Colony Sands	2	F	3	0	0	0	1,418	Come Fly With Me	10	M	9	1	0	0	7,536
Colony Special	3	F	14	0	1	1	3,940	Come for the Gold	3	F	9	1	1	0	6,620
Color Account	3	G	9	0	1	1	2,286	Come Forth as Gold	3	F	4	0	0	0	293
Color Blind	3	C	6	1	1	0	6,785	Come From Sonora	2	G	1	0	1	0	2,070
Color by d'Or	6	H	8	4	1	1	78,330	Come Hither	4	F	6	2	1	2	31,910
Color Code	3	G	3	0	0	0	0	Come Home Cathy	6	M	3	0	1	0	6,939
Color Copy	5	M	14	4	3	1	26,095	Come Home Friday	3	G	1	0	0	0	0
Color Country	3	G	3	0	0	0	450	Come On Back	4	G	13	0	0	1	6,235
Color Me Bad	3	C	7	0	0	1	2,177	Come On Five	2	F	2	0	0	1	560
Color Me Fast	5	M	4	0	1	1	9,110	Come On Grizz	4	G	8	2	1	0	14,315
Color Me Gifted	6	G	8	0	0	0	720	Come On Jazz	2	C	6	0	0	0	4,020
Color Me Gone	3	C	8	1	0	2	44,930	Come On Nifty	4	C	8	1	2	1	30,054
Color Me Lucky	3	G	13	1	2	1	25,522	Come On Precious	2	F	5	0	1	1	5,740
Color Me Matt C	6	G	7	1	0	1	9,980	Come On Red	2	C	1	0	0	0	0
Color Me Sad	3	F	14	1	2	0	29,610	Come On Reggie	6	M	10	0	0	0	1,375
Color Me Special	5	M	1	0	0	0	0	Come On Smokey	3	G	9	1	1	3	17,401
Color My Rainbow	4	G	22	1	0	3	5,506	Come On Sparkplug	11	G	11	0	0	2	3,369
Color of Roses	3	G	9	0	1	1	8,615	Come On Spider	6	G	9	2	0	1	13,003
Colorado Buckaroo	4	G	3	0	1	0	981	Come September	7	M	5	0	0	1	18,818
Colorado Charmer	2	F	2	0	0	0	0	Come Spring	5	M	2	0	0	0	0
Colorado Cobra	5	M	6	1	0	1	9,652	Come to Cashel	3	F	3	1	0	0	16,460
Coloreado (CHI)	5	G	2	0	0	0	468	Come to Mama	4	F	10	0	2	1	3,131
Colorful Carol	3	F	7	1	0	0	10,314	Come to Pass	4	G	16	1	4	1	16,340
Colorful Consomme'	3	F	4	0	0	0	510	Comealong Charlie	5	G	2	0	0	0	0
Colorful Creek	2	F	1	0	0	0	182	Comearocking	2	F	4	0	0	0	378
Colorful Judgement	3	G	6	2	0	4	184,576	Comeawaywithme	2	F	1	1	0	0	16,800
Colorful Life	3	F	3	0	0	0	219	Comeback to Me	3	F	7	2	0	0	37,660
Colorful One	3	G	13	1	6	1	23,196	Comecatchme	2	F	1	0	0	0	425
Colorful Saint	4	G	12	2	0	1	19,796	Comedy Club	6	G	7	0	0	1	2,087
Colorful Tour	4	C	9	4	2	0	209,525	Comedy Flyer	5	G	5	0	0	0	762
Colorfull Banner	3	C	14	2	4	1	28,180	Comedy Show	3	G	8	1	1	0	14,616
Colormegreen	8	M	5	0	0	0	600	Comeon	4	F	6	1	0	1	7,840
Colors 'n Scents	4	F	12	2	0	1	8,472	Comeon Dixie	3	F	2	0	0	0	1,350
Colors of an Angle	5	M	9	1	0	1	8,771	Comeon Moose	4	G	6	0	0	1	791
Colors of the Wolf	7	G	1	0	0	0	500	Comeoncasey	8	G	1	0	0	0	67
Colorswiththewind	7	G	8	0	1	2	3,060	Comeonthree	5	H	5	0	0	0	700
Colourofmoney	3	F	2	0	0	0	260	Comes a Tide	3	C	14	1	0	1	23,649
Colt Python	3	C	1	0	0	0	360	Comes the Dawn	4	F	5	3	1	0	49,393
Colterkind	5	G	5	0	1	1	14,125	Comes Unglued	2	F	5	0	0	3	6,979
Coltie	6	H	10	0	4	0	2,995	Comesmilewithme	4	F	21	0	1	8	4,621
Colton Creek	4	F	2	1	1	0	4,400	Comet Blue	4	F	8	1	0	3	5,741
Colton's Charm	4	C	3	0	0	0	345	Comet Chaser	6	G	1	0	0	0	0
Coltrane	2	G	1	0	0	0	0	Comet Clash	4	F	1	0	0	0	0
Columba	3	F	6	0	1	2	9,100	Comet Crossing	5	M	8	1	0	1	5,691
Columbia Gorge	8	H	13	1	0	4	4,409	Comet Junior	2	C	4	0	0	1	1,380
Columbia Lion	7	G	3	0	0	0	225	Comet Returns	4	G	13	1	2	0	7,333
Columbian Cat	6	M	8	1	1	2	6,364	Comet Revenge	2	G	9	0	0	0	3,070
Columbus Maid	7	M	9	2	5	0	12,739	Comet Ridge	7	M	2	0	0	0	105
Colway Bobbie	3	F	4	1	0	0	2,090	Comet Surprise	6	G	14	4	0	3	33,700
Comalagold	3	F	8	3	1	0	41,960	Comet Trail	4	F	7	1	1	0	6,615
Comanche Dancer	6	H	13	2	1	4	9,827	Cometary	4	G	10	2	0	1	19,405
Comanche Queen	3	F	10	2	0	2	15,870	Cometeo	6	M	9	2	0	0	13,158
Comanche Star	2	F	1	0	0	0	2,135	Cometes	3	G	8	0	0	1	1,378
Comanche Station	2	C	1	0	0	0	390	Comet's Light	2	F	1	0	0	0	0
Comandante Kyle	3	C	6	0	1	0	1,217	Comets Mystery	6	M	7	1	0	1	10,769
Comander Strodes	4	C	2	0	0	0	431	Comets Point	4	G	12	0	0	2	1,376
Comaoma	3	G	3	0	1	1	13,360	Comfort Me	2	C	4	0	0	0	300
Combahee	7	M	7	0	0	1	1,308	Comfortable Win	4	G	12	0	2	1	2,272
Combanchera	3	F	1	0	0	1	4,950	Comic Ack	2	C	1	0	0	1	1,221
Combat Boots	4	C	10	1	2	0	5,340	Comic Book	3	C	17	2	1	5	13,126
Combat Chief	3	G	12	1	3	2	22,056	Comic Genius	5	H	1	0	0	0	0
Combat Cutie	6	M	11	3	1	0	28,762	Comic Opera	2	F	7	1	3	1	73,439
Combat Mission	3	G	2	0	0	0	2,578	Comic Pride	2	C	2	1	0	0	13,786
Combat Soldier	3	F	5	1	2	0	26,550	Comic Relief	4	F	1	1	0	0	8,360
Combat Zone	2	C	3	0	0	0	585	Comic Truth	3	C	6	1	0	2	140,108
Combeau Tuffy	4	G	17	1	5	2	9,428	Comical Judith	2	F	9	1	1	2	22,787
Combermere	4	F	3	0	0	1	5,000	Comin On Thru	2	G	5	1	2	0	10,000
Combermere Road	2	C	2	0	0	0	0	Comingupforair	3	C	1	0	0	0	180
Combinatorial	3	G	14	1	3	5	9,338	Comkey	2	C	1	0	0	0	220
Combine	4	C	5	0	0	3	4,930	Commack	6	H	12	1	3	2	8,360
Combreezy	5	M	4	0	0	0	370	Commadore Barry	3	C	8	0	0	0	725
Combustion	3	G	10	0	1	3	6,035	Command Power	7	G	11	3	0	1	14,008
Come a Stridin	10	G	9	1	2	1	6,333	Command Respect	2	C	3	1	0	0	15,000
Come About	5	G	2	0	0	1	2,750	Commandeer	4	G	5	1	0	0	5,325
Come Back Madeline	3	F	10	2	1	1	27,187	Commander	4	C	5	1	0	0	5,766
Come Back Now	3	G	4	0	0	0	232	Commander Benno	3	C	15	2	0	2	23,880

RECORDS OF HORSES

Horse	Age	Sex	Sts	1st	2d	3d	Won	Horse	Age	Sex	Sts	1st	2d	3d	Won
Commander Case	3	G	14	2	2	1	7,681	Comprador	3	C	2	0	1	0	7,700
Commander Charge	5	G	1	0	0	0	0	Comprehensively	3	C	1	0	0	0	0
Commander Cody	3	C	3	0	0	0	0	Computer Diana	2	F	3	0	0	3	2,400
Commander Hal	3	G	10	0	2	4	39,153	Computer Gate	4	C	8	0	0	0	2,902
Commander Jag	3	C	4	0	0	0	8,460	Computer Hacker	2	F	3	1	0	0	14,760
Commander Lee	5	G	2	1	0	0	4,950	Computer Whiz	6	M	5	0	0	1	696
Commander Slew	5	G	10	0	1	0	1,760	Comstock Glory	4	F	17	2	5	1	17,558
Commander Spats	4	G	7	0	0	0	379	Comstock King	6	G	4	0	3	0	11,140
Commander Two	3	G	7	0	0	1	3,645	Comte Du Rainier	4	G	15	1	4	1	40,140
Commander's Affair	3	G	8	2	0	2	96,675	Con	6	H	7	0	1	0	1,156
Commander's Flag	4	C	8	2	0	4	137,544	Con Air Won	5	M	12	2	1	2	30,363
Commander's Gal	3	F	6	0	2	1	12,270	Con Quixote	5	G	8	2	1	1	63,630
Commander's Lady	3	F	6	2	2	0	105,340	Conazz	2	F	2	0	0	0	0
Commanding Creek	3	G	11	2	2	3	69,840	Conbest	6	M	11	1	3	2	8,084
Commanding Deputy	3	C	4	0	0	0	0	Conbird	4	F	8	1	1	2	25,755
Commanding Force	2	G	3	0	0	0	654	Concargo	3	G	1	0	0	0	0
Commanding Lady	2	F	1	0	1	0	4,340	Conceal	3	F	4	0	0	0	500
Commanding Link	4	G	10	1	2	1	20,795	Conceal the Deal	2	F	7	2	1	2	39,540
Commandment	2	C	6	1	0	1	27,775	Conceivable	3	F	10	1	2	0	10,320
Comme Il Faut	3	F	10	1	1	1	33,040	Concern Buddy	2	G	4	0	0	0	434
Commemorate's Note	2	F	4	0	1	0	2,175	Concerned Minister	6	G	4	1	1	1	22,730
Commendation	2	C	6	3	0	0	141,120	Concernina	4	F	11	1	0	2	18,860
Commercant Vic	3	C	10	3	3	2	96,745	Concert Classic	4	G	13	0	0	1	1,775
Commercial Kisser	5	M	3	0	0	0	152	Concerta	3	F	9	1	0	1	8,414
Comming Through	4	G	5	0	0	2	1,374	Concerted	5	M	16	0	1	2	4,788
Commodity	3	C	1	0	1	0	5,250	Concerto Cat	2	F	1	0	0	0	500
Commodore Craig	4	G	9	2	2	3	77,540	Concertoville	3	F	4	0	0	0	1,230
Commodore's Flag	3	G	1	0	0	0	0	Concession Speech	3	G	10	2	1	1	26,816
Common Friday	5	G	9	0	0	2	3,516	Concho Honcho	5	H	11	1	3	2	3,637
Common Ground	2	G	5	1	1	2	13,520	Conchy Joe	5	H	3	0	0	1	2,368
Communicate	8	G	3	1	0	0	8,814	Concielo	7	H	3	0	0	1	2,100
Community Honors	3	C	4	1	1	0	26,140	Concisely	3	C	1	1	0	0	6,360
Como Candie	3	F	8	1	1	2	6,080	Concoction	3	F	7	0	0	2	2,750
Comondon	3	G	3	0	0	0	0	Concordance	4	F	10	0	0	1	903
Comp	3	G	5	1	2	1	19,740	Concorde Escapade	4	F	6	1	1	2	45,040
Compadre Dancer	3	G	6	0	0	0	403	Concorde Illusion	8	H	9	2	1	0	9,522
Compadre's Peach	4	F	15	1	4	1	21,781	Concorde Lady	7	M	7	2	0	0	13,154
Companero	2	C	10	0	0	0	2,573	Concorde's Appeal	4	C	11	2	2	0	44,560
Company B	4	F	1	0	0	0	0	Concorde's Term	3	G	16	3	3	2	61,920
Company Clown	9	G	13	1	2	2	5,928	Concord's Melody	7	M	2	1	0	0	7,900
Company Eight	11	H	1	0	0	0	1,250	Concrete Block	3	G	5	0	1	0	6,176
Company Jet	5	H	16	2	2	4	25,756	Concurrent	8	G	8	2	0	2	22,520
Company Man	4	G	11	1	4	5	45,213	Concussion	5	H	3	0	1	0	5,940
Company Memo	3	F	5	1	0	1	5,440	Condearest	5	M	7	0	1	1	3,550
Company of Mary	3	F	11	2	1	1	37,406	Condellone	4	F	3	1	0	0	5,500
Company Storm	5	M	5	1	0	0	22,256	Condemned	6	H	10	0	2	1	5,842
Company's Pleasure	5	G	4	0	1	1	4,290	Condensed Version	5	H	6	0	0	0	1,116
Compassionate Girl	2	F	12	1	3	3	17,463	Condesa	2	F	2	0	0	0	415
Compatable	6	M	13	1	1	5	6,820	Condescending	3	F	7	0	1	0	2,282
Compatriot	4	C	3	0	0	1	759	Conditional Love	4	F	13	1	0	6	18,975
Compeer's Bequest	5	M	10	1	2	1	7,673	Condo Bob	5	G	4	1	0	3	2,890
Compelling Heart	5	G	4	0	2	2	10,200	Condo Prison	4	G	9	1	2	2	33,480
Compelling Launch	6	G	5	1	0	1	5,138	Condor	3	G	8	2	0	0	12,099
Compelling Lights	5	M	2	0	0	0	432	Condor Pasa	8	H	7	4	2	0	5,969
Compelling Moon	5	M	7	1	3	1	30,710	Condotierri	3	G	8	1	3	1	63,670
Compelling Story	4	C	12	1	2	0	17,217	Cones Pride	4	C	5	1	0	0	5,525
Compelling World	5	G	6	0	2	0	43,520	Coney Island King	2	C	6	0	0	1	1,600
Compendium	5	H	8	2	3	3	113,950	Coney Kitty (IRE)	5	M	8	1	0	2	65,540
Compensation	8	G	2	0	0	0	103	Conezdesertglitter	7	M	1	0	0	0	0
Compensator	2	G	6	1	0	0	7,260	Confederacy	4	C	2	0	0	0	0
Compete	3	F	3	1	0	1	20,240	Confederate Jack	4	G	15	5	1	0	36,385
Competitive Edge	3	F	7	1	2	1	15,040	Confederate Symbol	6	G	7	1	1	0	9,415
Competitive Lady	6	M	21	1	2	3	4,916	Confederatesoldier	13	G	8	0	0	0	479
Competitive Nature	4	G	11	1	0	2	7,369	Confer	4	G	3	0	1	0	2,240
Complements	7	M	2	0	0	0	110	Conferee	5	G	1	0	0	0	105
Complete Approval	7	M	16	3	5	4	85,800	Conference	7	H	5	0	0	0	0
Complete Coverage	2	C	4	0	1	0	4,112	Conference Called	3	C	12	0	0	0	1,774
Complete Edition	5	M	6	1	0	2	9,261	Confess	6	G	7	3	0	0	21,862
Complete Package	4	F	3	0	0	1	2,862	Confess to Me	3	C	15	4	0	5	66,390
Complete Tizzy	2	G	2	0	0	1	600	Confessing	2	F	1	0	0	0	0
Complete Verdict	7	G	3	0	0	0	1,000	Confession	3	G	8	2	2	1	19,780
Complete Withdrawl	3	C	4	0	1	1	11,704	Confiance Moi	5	H	18	1	3	3	30,734
Completely Lost	4	F	12	0	0	3	11,398	Confidability	2	F	7	1	0	2	15,970
Completion	2	F	7	0	0	3	8,660	Confidant Jester	5	G	3	0	0	0	161
Compliance Issue	4	F	5	0	0	1	1,224	Confidant Lady	3	F	6	0	0	0	750
Complimentary	4	F	2	0	0	0	0	Confidare	2	C	1	0	0	0	59
Comply With Di	8	G	14	1	2	2	16,118	Confide in Rose	3	F	2	1	0	0	9,600
Composure	3	F	2	2	0	0	300,000	Confide in Tyler	3	G	13	1	2	2	10,885
Compound	2	G	2	0	0	0	220	Confide Star	3	C	2	0	0	0	0

Horse	Age	Sex	Sts	1st	2d	3d	Won	Horse	Age	Sex	Sts	1st	2d	3d	Won
Confidence	7	H	1	0	0	0	234	Conquistador Lad	4	G	10	2	2	0	15,317
Confident	5	M	8	0	1	5	14,665	Conquistador Starr	2	C	4	1	0	0	8,610
Confident Cat	2	C	4	0	2	1	23,370	Conquistadordelite	2	F	6	0	0	3	23,328
Confident Heart	3	F	1	0	0	0	725	Conquistadorluna	7	G	4	0	1	0	1,460
Confident Spirit	2	F	1	0	0	0	124	Conquistador's Joy	2	F	3	0	0	1	4,365
Confidential Sport	3	C	1	0	1	0	5,760	Conquistar Dinero	3	G	15	2	3	1	25,846
Confidenza	3	F	4	1	0	1	6,605	Conroy	5	G	7	1	0	0	60,021
Confiding Winner	3	F	6	2	2	1	63,070	Cons Choice	4	G	6	0	1	2	5,619
Confidital	3	F	5	0	0	0	0	Cons Express	6	G	19	1	2	2	5,521
Confirmed	2	C	2	0	1	0	10,000	Con's Night Flight	8	M	6	0	1	1	4,347
Confirmed Countess	5	M	5	0	0	1	712	Con's Perfectlady	3	F	13	2	1	4	14,299
Confirmed Devil	6	H	6	0	0	0	748	Consabi	4	F	13	2	5	1	24,565
Conflagasion	5	H	11	3	1	1	47,205	Conscious Contact	3	G	14	4	4	2	75,830
Conflagration	7	G	14	0	0	1	3,461	Consecrate	2	C	7	1	0	0	88,340
Conflictingopinion	6	M	6	1	2	0	6,572	Consent	3	C	10	1	2	1	29,330
Confrere	3	F	12	3	2	3	24,956	Consent Agenda	3	C	15	1	5	4	10,084
Confused Genius	4	F	10	3	2	1	13,733	Consenting	2	F	2	0	0	1	1,852
Confused Toni	4	F	9	1	0	1	3,825	Conservation	3	G	11	2	3	1	96,550
Cong Baby	4	C	5	0	1	1	12,784	Conserve	7	G	11	3	4	1	80,840
Congaree	5	H	9	5	2	0	1,608,000	Consfirst	2	F	5	0	0	2	9,085
Congent	3	C	7	0	3	0	9,000	Consider the Night	8	G	3	0	0	0	165
Congi	4	G	14	1	4	3	13,731	Considerable	4	G	9	2	1	0	12,600
Congo Road	7	G	15	2	2	5	18,205	Consiglieres Star	2	G	3	0	1	0	1,680
Congo Swing	3	G	7	1	0	1	4,129	Consigliore	6	G	9	0	1	0	2,571
Congomambo	4	G	12	1	0	2	13,190	Consignada (CHI)	4	F	5	2	2	0	98,060
Congrats	3	C	7	3	0	1	180,388	Consilience	5	M	11	0	1	1	4,880
Congress Gun	6	M	1	0	0	0	0	Consistency	4	G	7	4	1	0	113,220
Congress Park	4	G	7	1	2	1	42,740	Consistently	3	F	7	1	3	0	29,940
Congressional Run	2	G	4	0	1	0	3,800	Consolidated Fact	3	G	2	0	0	1	7,200
Coning Eston	5	M	6	1	0	0	4,297	Consoling Granny	3	F	14	2	1	0	30,000
Conjecture	4	G	5	1	0	0	6,161	Consomme	4	F	17	1	4	6	30,478
Conjuring Creek	3	F	11	1	0	2	6,797	Consort Music	4	F	12	2	0	3	71,969
Conlee	3	G	1	0	1	0	1,800	Constancy	3	F	11	1	2	3	50,988
Conlua	6	M	20	2	3	3	38,430	Constant Commotion	3	G	3	0	0	2	7,844
Conmak	6	G	7	0	2	2	2,318	Constant Pressure	2	C	2	1	0	0	9,240
Conman Cunningham	5	H	7	1	1	1	49,900	Constant Shine	3	G	6	1	1	0	14,560
Conmom	6	G	4	0	2	1	5,859	Constant Star	8	G	3	0	0	1	990
Conneaut	5	M	1	0	0	0	0	Constant Thunder	4	G	4	2	0	0	37,050
Connected	6	G	3	1	0	0	46,708	Constant Touch	3	F	3	1	1	0	28,000
Connected Way	3	C	5	0	1	1	6,680	Constant Vigil	2	G	4	1	2	0	11,845
Connecticut River	7	G	17	0	0	3	3,978	Constantly	5	M	14	4	3	1	17,100
Connecting	5	G	9	0	4	1	42,780	Constituent	4	G	7	2	0	0	26,010
Connectivity	2	C	3	0	0	1	5,330	Constitution	4	C	10	2	0	1	47,920
Conned Again	4	G	8	0	1	1	19,626	Constitutional	3	F	4	0	1	0	4,050
Connell Town	2	F	3	0	0	0	1,818	Constrictor	4	G	21	1	4	5	19,149
Connemara Lass	3	F	7	0	1	0	1,889	Consultant	5	G	6	0	0	0	444
Connie Dar Kid	4	G	5	1	0	0	1,330	Contare's Doll	12	M	1	0	0	0	69
Connie Gail	9	G	3	0	0	0	292	Conte Amour	4	G	11	0	0	1	2,178
Connie One	3	F	9	3	3	0	12,507	Conte Di Dinero	6	H	7	0	1	3	5,892
Connie's Broke	4	F	7	2	0	0	7,690	Contearie Jet	2	C	1	0	0	0	0
Connie's Caboose	3	F	9	1	1	2	9,454	Contemptuous	2	F	1	0	1	0	2,375
Connie's Devil	2	G	1	1	0	0	14,250	Content Cot	2	C	2	0	0	0	0
Connie's Gold	3	G	3	0	0	0	1,300	Contentious Red	3	C	3	1	0	2	5,430
Connie's Hero	2	C	1	0	1	0	3,800	Contessa Beatrice	3	F	1	0	0	0	640
Connie's Hope	4	F	12	2	1	0	15,915	Contessa Slaney	2	F	2	1	0	0	9,000
Connie's Magic	7	G	8	4	2	1	78,750	Contested	4	G	12	2	3	2	39,025
Connies Monster	3	F	14	2	2	3	15,190	Contested Water	3	C	1	0	1	0	1,000
Connie's Passion	4	F	5	2	1	1	42,240	Contexte	6	G	29	3	6	3	65,725
Connie's Rocket	5	M	3	0	0	0	2,838	Continental Bishop	5	H	6	0	0	0	349
Connies Travels	4	F	4	1	0	0	1,300	Continental Boogie	3	G	9	1	1	0	12,620
Conniescharmclass	4	F	10	3	3	1	20,030	Continental Boy	7	G	7	0	0	0	888
Conniption	7	G	4	0	0	0	340	Continental Breeze	4	C	4	0	0	1	580
Conniving Bryan	2	G	3	0	0	1	1,520	Continental Coquet	6	M	13	1	5	2	16,262
Conniving Sal	6	G	9	0	3	0	3,622	Continental Drift	3	G	1	0	1	0	1,680
Connolly	7	G	11	1	2	0	10,318	Continental Guy	6	G	5	0	0	0	382
Connor (IRE)	4	G	2	0	0	1	1,650	Continental Issue	5	M	4	0	0	1	790
Connor's Glory	4	G	12	3	2	2	30,810	Continental Kris	3	F	5	1	1	0	11,474
Connor's Trophy	2	G	1	0	0	0	0	Continental Lady	4	F	4	0	0	0	321
Conny Nell	2	F	1	1	0	0	7,200	Continental Lu	5	M	7	1	2	1	74,760
Connywithay	4	G	15	3	3	3	22,866	Continental Man	5	G	15	3	7	0	13,757
Conowingo	2	F	1	0	0	1	1,430	Continental Miss	6	M	11	1	5	3	48,155
Conquer of Mine	2	F	2	0	0	0	0	Continental Music	6	H	11	1	1	1	3,407
Conquer the Day	4	F	4	1	1	0	12,444	Continental Peak	7	G	8	1	1	1	1,989
Conquer the Devil	3	C	11	2	1	2	54,930	Continental Red	7	G	10	1	3	1	216,705
Conquer the Galaxy	3	G	4	1	1	1	46,800	Continental Stitch	6	G	2	0	1	0	3,100
Conquer This	6	G	8	1	0	1	5,222	Continental Trail	5	M	9	1	1	1	10,975
Conquer's Dancer	4	F	3	1	0	1	3,158	Continental Wine	3	F	7	2	1	0	48,980
Conquestor	4	G	11	1	0	0	5,280	Continentalcolonel	4	G	17	3	1	1	24,006
Conquestress	3	F	9	3	0	1	45,600	Continentalsuccess	7	G	10	0	4	1	55,607

Horse	Age	Sex	Sts	1st	2d	3d	Won
Continuing	3	F	8	0	1	0	1,320
Continuously	4	C	8	3	1	1	293,200
Continuum	3	C	7	2	0	1	30,960
Conto de Natal	5	G	9	4	0	1	51,156
Contract Dispute	4	G	5	0	0	2	1,904
Contraction	4	G	3	1	0	0	9,600
Contradiction	4	G	10	1	1	1	15,800
Contrapuntal	4	G	2	1	0	0	8,100
Contrarianinvestor	8	G	5	0	0	1	798
Control	4	F	2	0	0	0	0
Control Alt Delete	3	F	10	2	1	2	12,510
Control Cat	3	G	7	3	0	0	8,980
Control Signal	5	G	22	3	4	1	40,095
Control Tower	4	C	2	2	0	0	55,200
Controls Free	5	H	4	0	0	0	409
Conundrum	3	G	8	0	0	0	1,416
Convenir	5	G	1	0	0	0	0
Conventionalwisdom	2	C	2	0	0	0	280
Converge	2	C	2	0	0	0	0
Conversano	6	G	9	2	2	1	14,416
Convert N Collect	4	F	8	2	1	0	27,942
Convertible Bond	2	C	5	1	1	0	13,310
Convexity	3	C	6	0	0	0	4,140
Convey the Moment	4	G	15	2	2	1	14,946
Convey This	5	G	14	1	2	1	8,360
Convey to Me	4	F	16	3	5	3	34,805
Conveyors Girl	3	F	3	0	0	0	432
Conveyor's Theme	4	F	11	1	0	0	6,646
Convict	10	H	6	0	2	0	2,530
Conwell	5	G	2	0	0	1	605
Conwiss	4	F	10	0	1	1	8,050
Coo Cold Bird	3	F	18	1	5	0	31,980
Coogamonga	3	G	5	1	0	1	8,799
Cookie Bight Cove	2	F	4	0	0	1	7,820
Cookie Columbis	6	M	4	0	1	0	1,950
Cookie Crumbs	2	F	3	0	0	0	1,103
Cookie Cutouts	3	F	6	1	1	1	16,745
Cookie Marie	5	M	6	1	1	1	9,973
Cookie's Kid	3	C	3	0	0	0	560
Cookies N Cream	6	M	17	0	2	1	7,088
Cookies Pro	4	C	1	0	0	0	0
Cookie's Tigeress	7	M	9	0	0	0	519
Cookie's Toy	2	G	2	0	0	0	0
Cookin Jen	6	M	3	0	0	1	1,100
Cookin Out West	3	F	5	0	0	2	6,320
Cooking Lil	3	F	4	0	0	1	3,610
Cookin's Cast	2	F	6	2	1	0	21,500
Cook'n Light	5	M	11	1	1	1	28,080
Cooks Lane	5	M	12	0	2	0	3,087
Cooky Joe Fletcher	4	C	14	7	0	1	61,370
Cool Advantage	7	H	1	0	0	0	82
Cool Alec	6	H	10	1	1	3	7,043
Cool American	2	F	2	0	0	0	0
Cool and Calm	3	F	9	0	0	1	1,676
Cool and Collect	4	F	10	1	0	0	10,929
Cool and Magic	5	M	5	0	1	1	1,988
Cool Aria	5	M	7	0	2	1	5,690
Cool as Ever	8	H	7	0	0	0	0
Cool Attitude	3	C	9	2	0	2	12,300
Cool Baba	3	G	3	0	0	0	150
Cool Batonic	5	G	8	1	0	2	9,592
Cool Believer	3	G	5	0	0	0	973
Cool Bender	3	G	11	4	2	1	87,537
Cool Bid	4	G	13	4	2	1	46,780
Cool Birdy	2	F	2	0	1	0	2,184
Cool Blush	6	M	6	0	0	0	160
Cool Boots	4	F	9	0	1	1	3,466
Cool Boy	6	H	3	0	1	1	5,280
Cool Breeze Lil	2	F	9	0	1	3	7,784
Cool Brew	4	G	13	0	1	3	4,264
Cool Brook	5	M	4	0	0	2	3,950
Cool Cafe	3	C	6	0	0	4	14,210
Cool Cara	4	F	12	5	1	2	45,556
Cool Cart	2	G	1	0	0	0	0
Cool Cash	5	C	5	0	1	1	6,655
Cool Chaos	3	F	12	1	0	0	4,789
Cool Cinder	4	F	7	0	0	2	3,155
Cool Citidiamond	3	C	6	0	0	1	2,060
Cool Clyde	5	H	1	0	0	0	50
Cool Comet	4	G	5	0	0	0	271
Cool Competitor	2	G	5	1	0	2	26,775
Cool Composure	5	G	12	3	0	2	27,980
Cool Conductor	2	C	4	1	0	1	43,551
Cool Cool Cool	2	F	8	2	3	0	65,180
Cool Country	4	C	3	0	0	1	790
Cool Criminal	2	C	3	0	0	0	1,302
Cool Dancer	6	G	3	0	0	0	0
Cool de Naskra	6	G	7	2	1	0	16,373
Cool Doll	6	M	11	2	1	0	13,550
Cool Drink O Water	4	G	11	2	1	1	13,636
Cool Dude Sam	2	C	1	0	0	0	0
Cool Falstaff	6	G	10	1	1	5	7,607
Cool Fastness	5	M	6	0	0	0	920
Cool Fellow	3	C	2	0	0	0	0
Cool Friday	4	G	7	1	0	2	8,090
Cool Frost	3	G	3	0	1	1	2,625
Cool Gaze	4	F	2	0	0	0	270
Cool Gent	8	G	6	1	1	0	4,730
Cool George	5	G	8	3	1	1	12,615
Cool Ghoul	4	F	1	1	0	0	4,740
Cool Gordy	5	H	15	0	1	3	3,578
Cool Hal	3	C	3	1	0	1	29,440
Cool Heavy Bull	4	G	10	3	2	0	15,412
Cool Honor	2	C	11	2	3	0	29,985
Cool Irony	3	C	3	1	0	0	40,020
Cool Kate	4	F	13	1	2	3	9,585
Cool Kevin	10	G	5	0	0	0	0
Cool Kickin' Lil	5	M	13	1	1	2	10,438
Cool Kitty	4	F	5	1	1	1	25,700
Cool Lad	2	G	3	1	0	2	13,576
Cool Lake	4	G	6	0	0	1	1,126
Cool Lava	4	G	13	1	0	1	6,650
Cool Lonnie	5	G	9	0	0	2	3,072
Cool Love	3	G	8	2	2	1	35,321
Cool Luke	5	H	8	0	3	1	26,350
Cool Man Bragg	4	G	2	0	0	0	224
Cool Man Too	4	C	3	0	0	0	323
Cool Maximus	3	G	9	0	1	0	2,217
Cool Mission	8	G	7	0	4	0	3,330
Cool N Collective	6	G	6	1	3	0	90,145
Cool N Easy	4	F	3	0	0	0	182
Cool N Spunky	3	C	10	1	1	0	6,280
Cool Notes	4	F	2	0	0	0	186
Cool Oasis	2	F	7	1	0	2	9,567
Cool of the Evenin	5	G	10	0	1	0	3,762
Cool One	4	C	9	1	0	0	8,100
Cool Papa Rick	4	G	8	1	0	0	2,244
Cool Pursuit	4	G	3	0	0	0	0
Cool Quip	4	G	3	1	1	0	9,200
Cool Rain Falling	4	C	12	1	1	2	9,606
Cool Rebel	2	F	6	1	1	1	14,868
Cool Red Ninety	4	F	2	0	0	0	206
Cool Rein	5	G	9	2	2	0	10,278
Cool Remark	3	G	7	1	1	1	6,566
Cool Robert	6	G	12	1	2	2	15,377
Cool Ruler	2	C	4	2	0	0	70,032
Cool Runnings	2	C	4	0	0	0	480
Cool Season	4	C	4	0	0	0	4,313
Cool Selection	4	G	8	3	0	1	115,787
Cool Sir	3	G	5	0	0	0	735
Cool Slew	4	F	1	0	0	0	360
Cool Spice	4	C	2	0	0	0	192
Cool Spirit	6	M	12	1	1	3	14,379
Cool Sport	2	C	4	0	1	0	10,350
Cool Striker	8	G	8	1	4	0	11,915
Cool Sundial	4	C	5	1	0	0	7,786
Cool Sweep	6	G	12	3	2	0	46,710
Cool Term	3	F	5	0	0	0	1,163
Cool Testamony	4	F	3	0	0	0	0
Cool Toad	2	G	4	0	0	0	960
Cool Track	7	G	12	1	0	2	4,414
Cool Tsunami	4	F	15	1	1	1	6,651
Cool Up	3	F	5	0	0	0	242
Coola Hula	5	M	4	0	0	1	4,069
Coolandwild	4	F	7	0	0	1	2,062
Coolasacat	4	G	11	3	1	0	76,696
Coole Smoocher	4	C	7	2	0	1	21,821
Coolest Guy	2	C	7	1	3	2	15,022

Horse	Age	Sex	Sts	1st	2d	3d	Won
Cooley Wooley	4	C	1	0	0	0	47
Coolidge	4	G	17	2	6	1	19,625
Coolidge Girl	2	F	1	1	0	0	5,820
Coolie's Son	3	C	3	1	1	1	11,494
Coolin' Down	3	F	1	0	0	0	0
Coolin' With Crown	3	G	2	0	0	1	759
Coolmars	8	G	6	0	0	0	18,633
Coolsteal	5	H	3	0	1	0	3,210
Coolworth	5	G	8	2	1	0	7,732
Cooly Ruler	2	F	3	0	0	1	1,320
Cooper Crossing	3	C	1	0	0	0	230
Cooperation	2	C	7	1	2	0	139,118
Cooper's Song	4	F	10	2	1	1	28,614
Cooperstown	2	C	4	0	0	0	4,100
Coopman	7	G	10	0	0	1	1,949
Coop's Glory	4	G	5	1	1	1	3,837
Coordinate	2	F	3	0	2	0	5,650
Coorsworth	5	G	8	0	0	1	980
Coos Bay	5	M	6	1	0	1	7,961
Cop Out	8	G	7	2	0	1	2,846
Copa	4	F	10	1	2	3	12,190
Copa de Oro	2	F	3	0	1	0	8,800
Copalis	5	M	5	0	0	3	1,040
Copano	5	G	16	3	0	0	25,925
Cope With an Image	4	C	12	0	6	1	19,320
Cope With Dorothy	5	M	3	1	0	0	3,450
Copelan Too	8	H	1	0	0	0	0
Copeland	2	G	2	0	0	0	614
Copelan's Bluff	3	F	1	0	0	0	0
Copelan's Choice	6	G	17	1	2	3	6,026
Copelan's Devilet	5	M	12	6	1	1	53,260
Copelan's Number	8	G	18	3	4	2	45,700
Copelan's Quack	4	G	7	1	0	2	11,353
Copelan's Silver	8	H	4	0	1	0	1,333
Cope's a Wonder	5	H	7	0	0	0	646
Copewithhoneybrown	5	M	6	1	2	1	6,046
Copia	4	G	12	2	0	2	7,668
Coping	4	G	7	1	0	1	36,581
Copper Chevelle	3	C	12	1	0	0	3,041
Copper City	6	G	3	1	0	0	1,540
Copper Classic	3	C	3	1	1	1	10,450
Copper Creek	7	H	14	0	1	3	3,788
Copper Criminal	2	G	5	0	0	0	240
Copper Cup	5	H	4	2	0	1	5,752
Copper Dollar	4	F	6	0	2	0	5,455
Copper Glow	5	G	13	0	2	4	14,509
Copper Gold	4	G	13	1	2	1	7,122
Copper Karat	3	C	3	0	1	0	6,760
Copper Kettle	4	G	12	2	0	2	27,116
Copper Miner	8	H	5	0	0	0	150
Copper Mist	2	G	3	0	0	2	10,740
Copper Moccasin	2	G	1	0	0	0	130
Copper Native	5	M	4	0	0	2	2,982
Copper Ripple	3	C	5	2	0	1	32,710
Copper Shine	5	H	9	0	0	1	1,630
Copper Sparks	2	C	4	1	0	0	6,820
Copper Special	3	F	4	0	0	0	715
Copper Sword	7	G	19	1	5	1	7,866
Copper Trail	4	G	4	2	1	1	162,170
Coppergirl	3	F	1	0	0	0	525
Coppergold'n'silver	3	F	10	2	3	0	19,397
Coppers 'n' Brass	4	C	13	2	0	2	17,980
Copperssweetsecret	7	H	1	0	0	0	150
Copy Bien	4	C	2	0	0	0	470
Copy Cat	10	H	4	0	0	2	3,360
Copy Line	4	C	5	1	0	0	3,355
Copy Me Son	5	G	1	0	0	0	115
Copy Two	8	M	2	0	0	0	70
Coq D' Or	3	F	4	0	0	0	126
Coquelish (ARG)	6	G	5	0	0	0	0
Coquettish	3	F	8	0	3	3	92,183
Coquila Rose	3	F	7	0	1	0	2,019
Coquina Bay	4	F	5	1	0	2	26,790
Coquinerie	2	F	5	2	0	0	34,940
Coquinta Bay	6	M	13	2	0	3	15,568
Coral Castle	3	F	2	0	0	0	0
Coral Cliff	4	F	12	0	2	2	21,599
Coral Creek	2	F	1	0	0	0	237
Coral Gold	2	C	1	0	0	0	0
Coral Key	5	G	7	0	1	1	6,182
Coral Prince	5	H	1	0	0	0	0
Coralann	4	F	11	1	0	0	7,241
Coral's Colony	2	F	2	0	0	0	0
Corarrow	3	F	11	0	2	3	7,598
Cora's Rib	5	M	7	1	1	1	11,939
Cora's Saga	4	F	2	0	0	1	605
Coray (BRZ)	6	M	1	0	0	0	0
Corazon de Acero	2	F	3	0	0	0	400
Corbett	3	G	2	0	0	0	0
Corbin Park	4	F	3	0	0	0	266
Corcovado	6	G	12	3	1	3	15,808
Cordal Bay	6	M	5	0	0	0	480
Cordelia (ARG)	6	M	6	0	0	0	1,693
Cordell	7	H	11	1	0	5	9,205
Cordial Nature	6	M	3	0	0	0	0
Cordon Rouge	5	M	4	1	0	0	3,813
Cords	2	G	5	1	0	0	5,250
Corduroy Road	9	G	12	1	3	1	20,489
Core Idea	9	G	17	2	3	4	30,935
Corella	4	G	20	2	1	4	10,751
Corenn	3	F	5	0	0	0	0
Corey's Bluff	5	M	4	0	1	1	25,863
Corey's Minstrel	9	G	1	0	0	0	0
Corey's Special	3	G	11	1	2	1	5,058
Cori Supreme	3	F	2	0	0	1	780
Corina Kim	6	M	11	1	4	2	16,148
Corinas Poise	9	M	8	3	1	1	24,586
Corinthian Star	2	F	3	1	0	1	26,990
Coriolanus	4	G	17	4	4	1	44,665
Corkie's Princess	4	F	20	1	3	4	7,112
Corky Ridge	7	M	14	3	3	4	21,739
Corleone	5	G	1	0	0	0	0
Corley McKenzie	4	F	4	0	0	0	225
Cormack	3	G	4	0	0	0	1,818
Corn Husk	7	G	3	0	0	0	135
Corn Kicker	6	G	16	3	5	0	38,455
Corn Mash	7	G	10	1	2	1	4,909
Corner Man	7	G	11	0	2	1	4,048
Corner Romance	9	G	10	0	0	1	1,910
Corner Store	4	G	4	0	0	0	66
Cornerback	7	H	5	1	0	2	4,932
Cornerbrook	4	C	13	0	0	3	5,207
Cornerstone	8	G	13	0	0	2	1,960
Cornicopia	3	G	10	0	0	2	16,310
Corning	4	F	5	2	0	0	10,380
Cornish Zeal	7	G	17	1	5	3	9,856
Cornpatch Road	4	G	5	0	2	2	23,551
Corollary	3	C	6	1	0	3	5,580
Corona Classic	4	G	3	1	0	2	46,656
Corona Dorada	3	F	6	0	0	0	0
Corona With Lime	6	G	8	3	0	0	15,480
Coronado Kid	3	G	9	0	0	0	480
Coronado's Lady	3	F	2	0	0	0	300
Coronda Rose	3	F	4	0	0	0	420
Coronis	3	F	3	0	0	0	70
Corp Trip	3	C	4	0	0	0	0
Corp. Jet	2	G	1	0	0	0	0
Corporal Cat	5	G	4	1	0	0	1,696
Corporal Greiner	2	F	9	1	5	1	23,850
Corporal Rules	3	G	13	1	1	1	7,099
Corporate Attitude	5	M	9	0	3	1	3,026
Corporate Cat	9	G	15	0	5	3	5,224
Corporate Chalenge	3	C	13	2	2	4	36,799
Corporate Class	3	F	16	3	4	2	30,988
Corporate Crash	5	G	3	0	0	0	183
Corporate Cure	4	G	8	0	1	4	9,042
Corporate Elation	3	G	8	0	1	0	2,631
Corporate Elegance	5	M	19	0	2	2	7,260
Corporate Emperor	4	G	9	3	2	1	18,586
Corporate Exec	9	G	5	1	0	2	9,130
Corporate Freedom	4	F	2	0	0	0	0
Corporate Intrigue	3	G	24	3	5	5	29,205
Corporate Kitty	3	F	2	0	0	0	300
Corporate Ladder	2	C	6	1	0	1	19,030
Corporate Lady	5	M	11	0	1	1	3,480
Corporate Links	6	G	11	1	0	0	3,172
Corporate Missile	6	G	15	3	1	2	16,080

Horse	Age	Sex	Sts	1st	2d	3d	Won
Corporate Nannie	3	F	1	0	0	0	0
Corporate Plum	4	F	4	0	0	0	0
Corporate Revolt	4	G	3	0	0	0	420
Corporate Runner	8	G	5	0	1	0	1,960
Corporate Shuffle	5	H	1	0	0	0	0
Corporate Storm	7	H	4	0	0	0	1,825
Corporate Teenager	5	M	1	0	0	0	0
Corque	4	G	2	1	0	0	12,540
Corrales Rose	3	F	2	0	0	0	752
Corre Native Corre	3	G	2	0	0	0	0
Corrian	6	G	13	2	2	2	41,910
Corrider's Choice	4	G	7	0	0	1	2,270
Corridor Lil	4	F	4	0	0	0	925
Corrigan	4	F	12	2	2	3	63,880
Corrizo Creek	3	G	13	4	3	0	61,300
Corroboree	5	G	6	0	0	0	2,778
Corruption	5	G	4	0	1	1	9,570
Corsario	4	F	12	0	0	1	3,786
Corsario Tom (ARG)	5	G	10	0	0	0	2,880
Corsita	3	F	4	0	2	1	26,740
Cort Sport	5	M	12	1	0	4	7,524
Cortina	3	F	8	0	1	2	7,073
Cortney	4	F	15	1	2	1	18,291
Cort's P. B.	3	C	18	3	7	3	64,582
Coruscant	2	F	5	0	0	4	5,940
Corvallis	3	F	6	0	0	0	413
Corvallis Dee	2	G	6	2	0	1	76,929
Corvet	6	H	3	0	1	0	2,000
Corwyn Duchess	6	M	14	1	4	2	11,331
Corwyn's Gold	2	C	3	1	0	0	8,220
Cory	3	F	2	0	0	0	244
Corysluckytaz	2	C	1	0	0	0	230
Cosa Rara	5	M	1	0	0	0	0
Cosa Segura	3	F	3	0	1	0	3,560
Cosby	4	F	3	0	1	0	2,820
Cosineros	4	C	3	2	0	1	9,713
Cosmah Star	4	F	2	1	1	0	37,345
Cosmic Account	3	C	6	1	0	0	3,752
Cosmic Dove	3	G	11	1	2	2	9,158
Cosmic Glitter	2	G	3	1	0	0	23,600
Cosmic Gold	3	F	5	1	0	1	4,686
Cosmic Green	4	F	7	0	0	0	5,570
Cosmic High	4	G	9	0	1	1	5,500
Cosmic Jet	3	C	3	0	1	1	13,970
Cosmic Messenger	4	F	8	1	0	0	7,215
Cosmic Rain	6	M	5	1	0	1	18,574
Cosmic Run	3	G	17	0	1	3	6,726
Cosmic Sea	4	G	15	2	5	2	40,641
Cosmic Secrets	7	M	2	0	0	0	80
Cosmic Sky	4	C	5	0	0	0	750
Cosmic Snowman	7	H	11	1	0	0	7,161
Cosmic Train	3	C	2	0	0	0	440
Cosmic Verse	3	C	6	1	2	0	15,820
Cosmic Wish	2	F	4	1	0	0	21,700
Cosmipolitan	6	G	6	1	0	1	9,735
Cosmo	4	G	3	0	1	0	5,560
Cosmo Girl	5	M	2	0	1	0	967
Cosmos Mariner	2	C	1	0	0	0	1,350
Cossack Rose	4	F	12	1	1	0	1,801
Cossatot Falls	4	C	11	0	0	1	2,352
Cossinade	2	F	4	0	0	0	1,110
Cost of Goods	6	H	14	2	1	1	11,086
Costa Nomore	8	G	6	0	0	1	436
Costa Pretty Penny	4	F	7	1	1	0	16,900
Costatoomuch	6	M	13	0	0	2	2,448
Costello	7	G	9	1	1	1	1,690
Costly Castle	2	C	4	1	2	0	41,400
Costly Traits	3	G	6	0	0	0	328
Costly Whim	2	F	1	0	0	0	0
Costume Designer	2	F	1	0	0	1	4,680
Costume Party	4	F	6	0	1	0	6,700
Cosummateconsumer	4	F	1	0	0	0	1,120
Cot Dot Sue	6	M	4	0	0	0	421
Cotive	3	C	2	0	0	0	290
Cottage (ARG)	5	G	14	2	1	2	96,974
Cottage Rose	6	M	7	0	0	1	10,676
Cottage Vale	5	M	9	1	0	0	7,671
Cotte	4	G	4	0	1	0	2,068
Cotton Boll	3	F	13	0	3	2	16,961
Cotton Dreams	3	F	9	2	1	1	11,174
Cotton Eyed Jack	7	H	3	0	0	0	184
Cotton Gin	3	C	3	0	0	1	5,280
Cotton Picker	5	G	2	0	0	0	192
Cotton Valley	4	C	1	0	0	0	0
Cottonuous Peaks	2	F	2	0	2	0	6,800
Couch Man	9	G	10	0	0	2	1,847
Cougar County	4	G	10	0	1	0	1,690
Cougar Slew	4	G	12	0	6	3	6,360
Cougar Streak	3	G	3	0	0	0	0
Cougar Trail	3	F	10	2	1	2	12,191
Coughlin	3	G	4	0	0	0	335
Coul Monet	4	F	3	0	0	1	474
Could Be Good	3	C	2	0	0	0	0
Could Be Icy	5	G	8	1	0	0	4,654
Coulda Shoulda	3	C	8	0	2	0	3,580
Couldbmoonshine	4	G	13	0	1	4	4,750
Coulditbe	2	C	1	0	0	0	300
Coulditbe Satan	3	C	2	0	0	0	136
Couldn't Be	5	M	1	0	0	0	0
Couldthisbemagic	6	H	10	1	1	2	6,833
Couleur d'Amour	3	F	10	0	0	1	1,521
Counsellors Lady	6	M	14	1	1	1	11,816
Counselor Mitchell	6	H	7	1	0	4	3,147
Counselor Neil	6	H	2	1	0	0	6,300
Counselorette	4	F	4	0	0	1	2,063
Count Again	7	G	4	2	0	0	6,480
Count Bailey	6	H	7	1	1	0	14,898
Count Basic	5	G	11	2	1	1	16,801
Count Brocco	6	G	14	0	0	2	6,280
Count Caldiero	2	C	1	0	0	0	0
Count Calypso	4	G	19	2	4	3	14,074
Count Centavos	5	G	14	4	3	2	20,790
Count Crusader	2	C	5	1	0	1	5,750
Count Custodio	5	G	9	2	0	2	9,025
Count Dare	5	G	2	0	0	0	0
Count de Hesse	5	G	8	0	1	0	7,700
Count Dixie	6	H	4	0	0	1	806
Count Greeley	3	C	1	0	0	0	95
Count Henry	3	C	7	2	1	1	8,787
Count Katahaula	4	G	13	1	2	2	14,682
Count Kokand	2	G	6	0	0	1	2,550
Count Manzotti	5	G	7	0	0	0	1,152
Count Me Double	6	M	6	0	0	1	618
Count Montbrook	2	C	6	2	1	0	39,170
Count My Nichols	4	F	10	1	3	1	32,140
Count of Kings	7	G	15	0	4	2	4,699
Count of Macedonia	3	G	14	2	2	7	25,248
Count of One	3	C	10	0	1	0	2,520
Count On Clyde	4	G	2	0	0	0	101
Count On Dacat	3	G	9	1	2	1	24,908
Count On Dolly	6	M	11	2	1	0	34,410
Count On Kris	5	H	3	0	0	0	235
Count On Massimo	2	G	1	0	0	0	0
Count On Mom	3	C	14	1	0	0	9,760
Count On My Word	4	C	7	2	0	2	24,238
Count On Sam	2	C	4	0	0	0	780
Count Orange	2	G	7	2	2	0	36,859
Count Quillo	4	C	12	1	6	3	14,466
Count Remains	3	G	11	1	2	0	10,950
Count Rizzi	2	C	6	0	0	3	8,246
Count Rocky	2	C	2	0	0	0	252
Count Rutledge	4	G	8	2	1	0	30,810
Count Sonna's Time	5	M	9	1	2	0	7,156
Count Stymie	2	G	2	1	0	0	12,803
Count Swish	6	G	16	0	2	2	5,860
Count the Chads	4	G	5	0	0	1	1,275
Count the Money	4	F	10	1	0	1	6,000
Count the Wins	2	C	1	0	0	0	145
Count Them All	6	M	15	7	4	2	15,673
Count This	6	G	1	0	0	0	45
Count to Ten	5	H	2	2	0	0	14,400
Count Trial	3	C	9	2	1	0	15,220
Count V Ullmann	6	G	1	0	0	0	290
Count Xanadu	4	C	16	3	1	0	19,869
Count Your Cards	7	G	1	0	0	0	98
Count Your Nickles	3	F	12	1	2	4	14,622
Countdown	3	F	14	2	1	3	46,922
Counter Bid	5	H	4	0	0	1	1,755

Horse	Age	Sex	Sts	1st	2d	3d	Won	Horse	Age	Sex	Sts	1st	2d	3d	Won
Counter Combo	11	G	13	0	2	3	4,227	County Creek	4	G	8	1	2	3	8,689
Counter Culture	2	F	2	0	0	0	165	County Doctor	5	H	3	0	0	0	234
Counter Punch	3	C	6	1	2	1	25,320	County Favorite	5	H	4	0	0	0	0
Countermeasures	4	F	2	0	0	0	146	County Green	3	G	13	1	3	2	26,420
Countess Ballado	3	F	2	0	0	0	233	County Jail	5	G	19	1	0	1	10,764
Countess Bareeq	2	F	3	0	0	0	0	County Lineman	3	G	17	2	5	1	19,790
Countess Gold	4	F	3	0	0	0	0	County Prince	4	C	4	0	1	0	1,646
Countess I.	3	F	3	0	0	0	697	County Province	3	C	3	0	0	0	0
Countess Judith	7	M	11	1	1	2	13,957	County Recount	4	F	9	0	2	0	6,855
Countess Marq	5	M	1	0	0	0	0	County Road Four	3	G	10	2	2	5	14,781
Countess Rebecca	4	F	4	0	1	0	3,990	County Time Kat	3	G	11	2	1	1	15,480
Countessa	5	M	12	1	1	4	43,180	County Trial	3	C	1	0	0	0	340
Countforjudgement	4	F	9	1	1	0	10,398	Coup	8	G	8	0	4	2	17,590
Countin' Katy	5	M	11	2	0	0	11,780	Coup de Grace	2	C	5	0	0	2	8,830
Counting On Brian	5	G	12	0	0	0	496	Coup de Lafourche	9	G	4	1	0	0	988
Counting Visions	5	M	8	0	0	1	6,756	Coup d'Eclair	3	C	3	0	0	0	285
Countless Moment	5	G	9	1	1	2	12,220	Coupdeville Jack	5	G	8	1	1	1	3,382
Counto	3	G	14	0	0	3	6,635	Couple Whiles	2	F	5	0	0	0	150
Countofmontecristo	4	C	3	0	0	0	259	Courage From Above	7	M	6	0	0	0	345
Country Angel	4	F	15	3	0	2	28,751	Courage Underfire	4	G	5	1	1	0	6,428
Country Be Gold	6	H	7	3	0	0	146,625	Courageous	2	F	1	0	0	0	350
Country Beauty	5	M	8	2	1	2	10,970	Courageous Act	2	C	5	1	1	2	45,160
Country by Nature	4	G	4	0	0	1	1,580	Courageous Brandon	5	G	5	0	0	0	545
Country Casanova	5	G	1	0	0	0	0	Courageous Deputy	5	G	15	2	1	3	15,624
Country Charmer	2	F	3	1	1	0	9,025	Courageous Journey	2	G	2	0	0	0	0
Country Chimes	3	F	5	1	1	0	11,111	Courageous King	2	C	2	0	0	0	2,940
Country Clover	3	G	9	0	1	0	805	Courageous Mode	6	H	2	0	0	0	100
Country Cob	8	G	11	1	2	3	9,016	Courageous Valor	3	F	11	2	2	2	49,462
Country Coursing	5	G	4	0	1	0	1,017	Court a Native	2	F	1	0	0	0	0
Country Cowboy	3	G	6	1	3	0	9,623	Court a Zone	3	C	4	0	0	0	0
Country Creek	3	F	2	0	0	0	0	Court Action	10	G	13	4	4	1	27,215
Country Cutie	3	F	5	0	0	0	300	Court Angel	4	F	1	0	0	0	270
Country Dove	3	C	4	0	0	1	1,050	Court Appointed	4	G	12	3	0	4	13,875
Country Dragon	5	G	8	1	2	0	15,180	Court Costs	8	H	11	1	4	3	9,520
Country Fair	6	G	16	2	1	1	8,959	Court Judge	11	G	3	0	0	1	710
Country Favorite	3	F	4	0	0	1	2,250	Court Key	5	H	3	0	0	1	3,025
Country Flash	4	G	6	1	0	1	3,186	Court Lite Kenny	6	H	13	2	0	1	24,994
Country General	4	G	9	1	2	0	10,690	Court Notes	4	G	13	1	1	2	18,090
Country Gentleman	8	G	2	0	0	0	0	Court of Maximus	3	G	9	0	2	1	14,069
Country Glitz	5	G	5	2	1	2	10,320	Court Recorder	4	F	4	2	0	0	8,370
Country Grand	5	H	3	0	0	0	750	Court Reporter	3	F	6	0	0	0	365
Country Jade	6	M	4	0	0	0	544	Court Savvy	9	G	12	1	2	2	10,928
Country Jeweler	5	H	11	0	1	1	6,099	Court Sense	6	M	8	2	1	0	18,240
Country Joe	7	G	12	4	3	1	33,956	Court Shenanigans	8	G	13	1	3	4	29,980
Country Judge	3	C	3	0	1	1	9,080	Court Talk	2	C	1	0	0	0	180
Country Landing	3	C	10	1	0	1	8,195	Court Verdict	3	C	15	2	1	2	20,150
Country Lawyer	3	C	9	2	2	1	18,760	Courtcase	7	C	7	1	1	1	16,430
Country Legionaire	7	G	15	1	3	3	13,349	Courtenay	5	M	12	2	3	1	12,252
Country Lord	4	C	4	0	1	1	6,956	Courter Man	10	G	2	0	0	0	264
Country Member	4	F	1	0	0	0	0	Courtesan	3	F	11	0	1	1	4,967
Country Moonbeam	2	F	2	0	0	0	0	Courtesan (GB)	7	M	4	1	1	0	14,600
Country Music	6	G	7	0	1	0	8,410	Courthouse	2	C	8	0	1	1	9,710
Country Music Fan	4	F	3	0	0	0	47	Courthouse Junkie	2	G	1	0	0	0	0
Country Native	2	F	11	1	1	1	9,050	Courtier	2	G	3	1	0	1	20,160
Country Only	6	H	6	1	2	0	38,600	Courtin Monica	5	M	12	1	0	3	5,503
Country Paradise	2	F	7	0	0	0	990	Courting Chance	4	G	1	0	0	0	0
Country Park	10	G	12	1	0	0	1,285	Courting Concorde	3	C	8	2	2	2	70,720
Country Prince	3	G	10	0	0	0	980	Courtingaway	3	C	1	0	0	0	0
Country Princess	6	M	9	0	1	3	2,468	Courtly Coin	2	F	1	0	0	0	0
Country Punch	3	C	1	0	0	0	0	Courtly Gal	4	F	2	0	0	0	174
Country Que	5	M	3	0	0	0	330	Courtly Jazz	2	C	2	0	1	0	6,340
Country Ridge	2	F	5	1	0	2	6,006	Courtly Riches	5	G	13	2	3	0	32,279
Country Romance	3	F	10	4	2	1	157,230	Courtnall	2	C	1	0	0	0	2,940
Country' S Best	5	H	7	1	2	0	15,030	Courtney N	3	C	7	1	2	2	8,278
Country Slew	2	C	3	0	0	1	1,425	Courtney's Fighter	2	F	1	0	0	0	90
Country Starlight	4	G	3	0	1	0	2,565	Courtney's Friend	2	F	1	0	0	0	1,085
Country Sunshine	7	M	6	1	0	2	16,953	Courtneys Pleasure	6	M	14	1	2	3	9,799
Country Touch	9	G	3	0	0	0	152	Courtney'sbirthday	2	F	3	1	0	0	9,150
Country Tune	3	C	2	0	0	0	194	Courtricity	4	G	12	2	4	0	28,982
Country Warrior	4	G	11	5	1	0	102,650	Courtroom Drama	6	G	12	4	2	0	32,502
Countrys Finale	4	G	17	1	3	3	8,181	Court's in Session	4	G	6	0	3	2	30,420
Countrystateofmind	6	H	4	0	0	0	49	Courtster	5	M	1	0	0	0	0
Countrywide	5	H	1	0	0	0	0	Courtyard	6	M	4	1	1	1	5,580
Count's Last Reply	2	F	3	0	0	0	400	Courtyard Barbi	4	F	11	0	5	0	10,859
County Cakewalk	3	F	5	0	0	1	1,885	Courvoisier	4	G	2	0	0	0	300
County Cat	6	H	9	1	0	0	7,261	Coushatta	6	G	16	5	1	3	64,341
County Chalk	5	H	1	0	0	0	0	Cousin Bill	2	G	12	1	2	2	13,478
County Chief	6	G	9	0	2	3	6,070	Cousin Charlotte	4	F	7	1	1	0	23,433
County Cork	3	G	3	1	0	0	6,000	Cousin Jim	9	G	4	0	1	0	1,440

Horse	Age	Sex	Sts	1st	2d	3d	Won
Cousin Maggie	8	M	10	1	2	2	10,685
Cousin Montineque	3	F	12	2	3	1	42,820
Cousin 'n Company	7	G	12	2	3	2	51,350
Cousin of Mine	4	F	5	0	0	0	1,192
Cousin Steve	6	H	8	0	1	1	2,532
Cousineau	2	F	2	1	0	0	23,800
Covad	5	G	5	1	0	3	1,543
Cove Hill Missle	4	F	13	1	1	4	34,420
Cove Kat	3	F	5	0	0	1	1,620
Cove Point	5	M	2	0	0	0	0
Cover All Bets	3	G	3	0	0	0	140
Cover Keeper	7	G	6	1	1	2	3,652
Cover Up	2	F	3	0	2	0	3,625
Covered Treasure	4	G	10	1	1	2	10,736
Covering Ground	3	G	10	2	0	0	46,580
Coverly	3	F	3	0	0	0	2,285
Covermewithroses	6	G	5	0	1	1	7,740
Covert	7	M	8	3	0	1	26,978
Covert Tax	3	C	5	0	0	0	970
Covet	2	G	1	0	0	0	0
Covey of Dove	3	F	9	0	0	1	2,240
Covey Roost	5	M	13	2	2	2	29,875
Covington	3	C	4	0	1	0	8,135
Cow Paddy	3	C	2	0	0	0	0
Cowboy Auctioneer	3	G	6	0	1	1	1,941
Cowboy Babe	4	C	1	0	0	0	0
Cowboy Ballad	7	G	2	1	1	0	12,000
Cowboy Brown	2	G	5	0	3	1	13,832
Cowboy Carson	4	C	1	0	0	0	0
Cowboy Cat	4	G	7	1	0	0	17,640
Cowboy Chief	4	F	4	0	0	1	750
Cowboy Classic	2	C	1	0	0	0	180
Cowboy Cobra	3	G	10	1	1	2	16,971
Cowboy Code	2	C	2	0	0	0	780
Cowboy Contender	2	G	1	0	0	0	4,359
Cowboy Court	2	C	1	0	0	0	145
Cowboy Cumbia	5	G	7	1	0	1	7,752
Cowboy Drifter	3	C	11	0	2	2	3,925
Cowboy Gone West			8	0	3	2	5,576
Cowboy Howdy	4	G	6	0	0	0	900
Cowboy Hurricane	3	G	11	0	0	0	1,890
Cowboy in Flight	5	H	18	0	1	0	1,518
Cowboy Jack T	3	C	5	0	2	0	940
Cowboy Jazz	5	G	5	0	2	0	2,072
Cowboy Junction	4	G	6	1	0	1	4,299
Cowboy Justice	4	G	17	0	2	4	9,491
Cowboy Knows	5	M	3	0	0	0	0
Cowboy Kyle	8	G	6	1	1	0	6,377
Cowboy Magic	7	G	10	0	2	1	19,240
Cowboy Rick	3	G	3	1	1	0	4,725
Cowboy Shane	3	G	15	3	2	3	36,189
Cowboy Stuff	4	C	5	2	2	0	74,000
Cowboy Tough	5	G	9	1	0	2	12,950
Cowboy Way	8	G	5	0	0	0	581
Cowboy Wedding	3	F	5	1	0	0	6,544
Cowboyishis Name	5	G	1	0	0	0	40
Cowboys a Flying	4	C	3	0	0	0	0
Cowboy's Limelite	4	G	13	2	0	4	22,337
Cowboys Sissy	3	F	2	0	0	0	90
Cowboys Syn	9	G	5	0	2	1	1,152
Cowgirl in Lace	3	F	6	0	2	0	3,630
Cowgirls Account	4	F	4	2	2	0	26,103
Cowgirls Grit	8	M	11	0	0	1	3,862
Cowgirls n Indians	2	F	1	0	0	0	0
Cowpet Bay	2	C	3	1	0	0	3,240
Cowpoke's Wish	4	G	2	0	0	0	3,480
Cox's Farrara	5	M	9	0	0	2	2,196
Cox's Penny	7	H	10	0	0	0	986
Coy Miss	4	F	1	0	0	0	330
Coyote Ah Go Go	3	C	15	3	2	0	36,500
Coyote Call	5	H	1	0	0	0	0
Coyote Cat	4	G	2	0	0	0	103
Coyote Country	5	G	5	1	1	1	4,777
Coyote Cowgirl	3	F	10	1	1	1	11,001
Coyote Dreamer	3	M	6	0	0	1	685
Coyote Fever	2	C	4	0	0	0	730
Coyote Junction	4	C	8	1	1	0	7,340
Coyote Kid	3	G	9	3	0	1	23,380
Coyote Lakes	9	G	2	0	0	0	3,360
Coyote Message	3	C	12	0	1	0	3,665
Coyote Point	3	C	16	1	2	2	11,109
Coyote Springs	4	F	4	0	0	1	852
Coyote Warning	3	F	1	0	0	0	118
Coyotes Playmate	4	F	9	2	1	2	8,140
Coys Big Geb	2	C	1	0	0	0	0
Coz He's Mean	4	G	6	0	1	0	5,750
Coz Z. Josey	3	C	3	1	0	0	18,099
Cozenza	2	C	5	0	0	0	2,880
Cozie Advantage	4	F	4	1	0	1	34,560
Cozy	6	M	7	1	0	2	40,242
Cozy Anna	2	F	1	0	0	0	120
Cozy B. J.	3	F	7	0	0	0	1,920
Cozy Cat	4	F	11	0	3	2	9,162
Cozy Cay	3	F	3	0	1	0	11,320
Cozy Choice	4	F	4	0	0	0	254
Cozy City	6	M	3	0	0	1	2,300
Cozy Coed	4	F	8	0	1	2	19,340
Cozy Con	4	F	16	2	3	0	32,866
Cozy Cougar	4	G	11	1	0	0	22,865
Cozy Dance	5	G	13	1	0	0	22,449
Cozy Dreams	2	C	9	0	1	3	17,190
Cozy Fellow	3	G	2	1	0	0	4,995
Cozy Fire	7	G	5	0	0	1	760
Cozy Glow	3	F	5	1	2	1	32,800
Cozy Guy	2	G	6	1	1	2	27,720
Cozy Hawk	2	G	1	0	0	0	50
Cozy in Seattle	3	G	12	1	3	1	12,138
Cozy Island	5	M	3	0	1	0	8,000
Cozy Legend	3	F	2	0	1	0	5,460
Cozy Man	6	G	6	2	1	1	35,040
Cozy Maria	4	F	4	0	2	0	17,940
Cozy Meeting	3	G	4	0	0	0	0
Cozy Mite Do	3	C	11	0	0	1	705
Cozy One	3	F	9	2	3	2	78,958
Cozy Spirit	4	C	9	0	1	0	7,533
Cozy Style	2	C	1	0	0	0	285
Cozy Susie	4	F	1	0	0	0	1,020
Cozy Town	3	F	3	1	0	0	2,566
Cozy Up Doc	6	M	3	0	0	0	1,497
Cozy's Mint Julip	7	M	14	0	6	3	17,398
Cozz Star	3	G	12	1	0	1	13,508
Cozzelle's Lady	5	M	6	0	1	0	3,395
Cozzene Along	4	F	6	0	0	1	7,337
Cozzene Appeal	5	H	13	1	2	3	28,685
Cozzene Continued	3	G	15	2	3	2	35,620
Cozzene's Cat	4	G	7	0	2	3	23,880
Cozzene's Devil	4	G	12	0	1	2	5,080
Cozzene's Silver	6	G	14	0	0	1	6,716
Cozzening	4	C	8	0	1	2	11,370
Cozzmic Wonder	3	F	5	0	2	2	23,120
Cozzy Am I	3	F	5	0	0	0	472
Cozzy Corner	5	M	10	0	1	3	53,221
Cozzy Guerra	4	F	9	0	1	1	2,170
Cozzy Temper	3	F	5	2	0	0	42,120
Cr Proud Count	3	G	6	0	0	0	300
Cr Sunny Melba	3	F	16	1	3	3	8,279
Craam Creek Lady	3	F	6	0	0	0	0
Crab Creek	3	G	15	3	0	4	40,423
Crab Man	5	G	9	0	0	0	1,830
Crack of the Bat	4	G	10	3	2	1	41,390
Crack That Whip	3	G	2	0	0	0	180
Crack the Books	4	F	15	5	2	3	62,650
Crack the Vault	5	G	13	0	0	2	10,032
Crack the Veneer	3	G	12	1	2	1	25,640
Crackajack	4	C	6	0	0	0	3,480
Cracked Conch	2	F	4	0	2	0	12,784
Cracker B	7	G	10	0	1	0	1,580
Cracker Day (NZ)	5	G	2	0	1	0	590
Cracker Jack Man	3	G	8	0	2	0	3,960
Crackerbox Palace	4	G	13	3	4	2	25,176
Cracker's Best	7	M	7	1	0	0	460
Cracker's Project	3	G	14	1	2	4	18,156
Cracklin' Ice	6	M	9	1	5	1	3,872
Cracklin Josie	3	F	4	1	0	0	1,230
Crackling	4	G	3	1	0	0	16,710
Crackmeup	2	G	1	0	1	0	4,340
Crackup	3	C	3	0	0	0	9,000
Cradle Snatcher	4	G	2	0	0	0	500

Horse	Age	Sex	Sts	1st	2d	3d	Won	Horse	Age	Sex	Sts	1st	2d	3d	Won
Cradle Will Rock	3	G	4	1	2	0	22,650	Crafty Rocket	3	C	4	2	0	0	40,275
Craft Brewin	8	G	10	1	2	0	2,141	Crafty Route	5	G	1	0	0	0	0
Craftons Leader	4	F	6	0	0	0	0	Crafty Runner	6	H	15	1	3	1	27,670
Crafty Account	4	G	7	1	0	0	4,765	Crafty Saint	3	C	1	0	0	0	130
Crafty Angler	4	G	5	1	0	0	11,111	Crafty Sally	4	F	3	0	1	0	1,000
Crafty Babe	2	F	1	0	1	0	3,800	Crafty Sandi	8	G	7	0	0	1	1,382
Crafty Beau	4	G	11	4	4	0	86,415	Crafty Sarah	2	F	3	0	0	0	1,600
Crafty Blade	3	G	10	1	0	1	10,650	Crafty Schemer	4	G	11	2	0	3	43,910
Crafty Boo	2	C	2	0	0	1	638	Crafty Shaanshu	5	M	9	3	1	2	34,928
Crafty Brat	3	F	11	4	2	2	144,654	Crafty Shaw	5	H	14	4	3	2	351,185
Crafty C. T.	5	H	5	0	2	1	107,807	Crafty Song	3	C	7	2	0	1	55,790
Crafty Captain	4	C	4	0	2	1	17,500	Crafty Spirit	2	F	2	1	0	0	11,895
Crafty Carni	2	F	7	1	1	0	27,804	Crafty Stat	5	M	12	1	0	3	4,642
Crafty Case	8	G	8	1	0	1	8,500	Crafty Taylor	4	F	10	1	1	1	21,770
Crafty Cause	3	F	6	0	0	1	10,973	Crafty Tears	2	F	1	1	0	0	7,800
Crafty Celt	6	G	5	1	0	0	9,500	Crafty Tipie	4	G	2	0	0	0	0
Crafty Charm	3	F	10	0	0	2	2,132	Crafty Valentine	2	F	2	0	0	0	405
Crafty Chatter	3	F	6	3	0	0	12,942	Crafty Value	3	G	10	0	2	0	4,485
Crafty Cindy	5	M	3	0	0	0	1,912	Crafty Wac	3	F	4	0	1	0	3,551
Crafty Cobra	4	G	9	1	1	2	9,659	Crafty War	5	G	1	0	0	0	45
Crafty Comet	2	F	8	1	2	1	12,060	Crafty Who	2	G	2	0	0	0	0
Crafty Comment	7	M	4	0	0	0	1,636	Crafty Wildcat	4	F	11	2	2	1	26,301
Crafty Connection	3	G	4	0	0	0	600	Crafty Zak	4	F	10	4	0	2	72,280
Crafty Conveyor	6	M	5	0	2	0	5,358	Craftyrhonda	2	F	2	0	0	0	570
Crafty Course	4	C	2	0	0	0	0	Crafty's Go Bo	4	C	14	3	2	2	12,666
Crafty Creek	5	M	9	2	1	0	30,990	Crafty's Love	4	C	6	1	0	1	4,040
Crafty Crypto	3	F	4	1	1	0	10,175	Craigs Hope	3	G	10	2	1	2	22,795
Crafty Dame	4	F	8	2	1	0	10,444	Craklin' Suzie	2	F	6	1	1	1	5,542
Crafty Dan	2	G	3	0	0	1	1,639	Cramming	4	G	14	3	2	2	36,359
Crafty Dawn	6	G	18	1	2	1	7,629	Cranberry Red	2	F	1	0	0	0	105
Crafty Deed	6	G	14	3	2	3	14,991	Crane	4	G	9	1	1	2	8,075
Crafty Deer	9	G	9	0	0	0	1,045	Crane Away	4	G	13	3	3	2	6,516
Crafty Demon	8	G	8	1	2	1	7,200	Crane Beach	8	H	1	0	0	0	0
Crafty Desperado	3	G	2	0	0	0	1,736	Cranking George	4	G	1	0	0	0	0
Crafty Diplomat	5	M	10	2	1	0	22,086	Crap Shooter	4	C	5	3	1	0	50,560
Crafty Diva	3	F	17	4	3	3	59,057	Crash Course	7	G	8	2	0	1	38,510
Crafty Dream	4	C	6	1	1	0	4,757	Crash Hot	5	G	3	0	0	0	300
Crafty Dutchman	6	G	7	1	3	0	9,520	Crash McGoon	3	C	4	0	0	1	1,920
Crafty Edition	3	G	4	1	0	0	4,855	Crash the Party	3	C	4	0	0	1	1,753
Crafty Flair	4	F	4	0	0	1	1,038	Crashing Through	6	M	6	1	2	0	5,667
Crafty Fortune	6	H	9	2	0	3	28,286	Crashpad	7	H	11	1	3	1	17,632
Crafty Gender	4	F	6	1	2	1	11,468	Craton (ARG)	6	G	6	0	0	0	5,420
Crafty Guy	3	C	3	0	1	1	37,120	Cravens	3	C	8	1	1	1	44,560
Crafty Hero	3	G	14	3	1	2	30,805	Craving Action	3	G	2	0	0	0	0
Crafty Illusion	6	H	14	3	0	3	8,972	Cravings	2	F	2	0	0	0	1,445
Crafty Jarrett	4	G	18	4	3	1	18,538	Craw Fish	3	C	2	0	0	0	0
Crafty Jay	2	C	2	1	1	0	8,570	Crawfish Etouffee	3	G	8	1	0	1	6,362
Crafty Joanne	5	M	4	0	0	0	60	Crawling	3	F	8	1	1	1	9,645
Crafty Junction	5	H	10	2	2	2	28,489	Crazed	5	G	13	1	1	2	10,589
Crafty Key	3	F	1	0	0	0	0	Crazy Canuck	3	C	2	0	0	0	88
Crafty Kiss	4	F	8	0	0	0	384	Crazy Carpenter	11	G	2	0	0	0	0
Crafty Launch	3	C	7	0	0	0	0	Crazy Daze	8	M	8	2	1	1	3,803
Crafty Lawyer	3	G	6	2	1	0	9,600	Crazy Debutante	3	F	9	1	1	0	9,410
Crafty Line	3	G	5	1	0	0	12,390	Crazy Deputy	4	C	3	0	0	2	3,865
Crafty Loom	4	F	10	3	1	1	27,575	Crazy Ensign (ARG)	7	M	7	3	1	2	231,405
Crafty Lover	4	G	18	1	4	2	14,159	Crazy Grace	2	F	4	0	1	0	8,110
Crafty Luck	4	F	7	1	0	1	19,290	Crazy Hawk	9	M	3	0	0	0	550
Crafty M. D.	5	H	8	1	0	2	9,535	Crazy Horse Saloon	3	C	2	1	0	0	5,795
Crafty Madness	3	F	11	1	3	2	42,750	Crazy Larrys	5	G	13	0	5	2	16,500
Crafty Maid	3	F	5	1	1	0	4,378	Crazy Song	4	G	7	0	2	0	23,460
Crafty Maiden	3	F	7	0	0	0	438	Crazy Talent	4	C	8	3	1	1	16,000
Crafty Maneuvers	4	F	3	0	0	0	815	Crazyboutamercury	4	F	9	2	0	1	19,700
Crafty Maverick	3	C	13	3	0	3	14,320	Crazyluck	2	F	2	0	0	0	0
Crafty Miss	2	F	7	0	0	0	900	Cream Creek	4	F	5	3	2	0	95,000
Crafty Mountain	3	F	1	0	0	0	0	Creamy	5	M	4	0	0	0	247
Crafty Move	3	F	8	1	2	0	46,750	Crease Infraction	5	G	10	1	5	0	126,280
Crafty 'n Smooth	4	F	14	5	3	1	58,465	Create the Case	4	F	12	1	2	0	16,988
Crafty Nat	4	F	6	0	0	0	3,690	Creates	8	G	6	0	1	0	483
Crafty Note	5	H	3	0	1	0	2,460	Creative Ace	3	C	7	1	0	0	7,412
Crafty Notebook	3	F	2	0	0	0	280	Creative Dance	2	C	1	0	1	0	8,200
Crafty Number	7	H	14	2	4	0	21,232	Creative Energy	4	C	7	0	1	0	1,810
Crafty Paces	6	M	9	1	1	1	13,165	Creative Iron	3	G	2	0	0	0	0
Crafty Pal	3	C	12	1	1	0	15,160	Creative Lady	3	F	2	1	1	0	53,000
Crafty Pete	3	F	17	1	1	2	20,637	Creative Patsy	3	F	10	1	0	0	8,394
Crafty Player	2	C	4	1	1	0	37,200	Creative's Dream	3	C	8	2	4	0	100,942
Crafty Purchase	2	G	4	1	0	0	22,801	Crebilly	8	G	7	0	1	0	3,076
Crafty R.	5	H	3	0	0	0	165	Credential	5	M	2	0	0	0	2,280
Crafty Reflection	3	G	14	0	6	4	29,630	Credentials to Fly	7	G	3	0	0	0	450
Crafty Rhythm	6	H	12	2	1	0	5,400	Credit Balance	4	G	12	2	3	2	11,727

Horse	Age	Sex	Sts	1st	2d	3d	Won	Horse	Age	Sex	Sts	1st	2d	3d	Won
Credit Call	6	G	11	4	0	0	29,489	Crimson Dew	3	C	1	0	0	0	0
Credit Gal	5	M	8	0	1	5	17,420	Crimson Hero	4	C	10	1	1	2	61,564
Credit Gold	5	H	10	0	0	2	1,802	Crimson Ide	2	G	4	0	0	0	1,064
Credit Is Due	2	F	4	0	1	1	1,350	Crimson Lake	4	F	8	1	2	0	21,629
Credit Note	7	G	4	0	0	0	920	Crimson Mint	4	G	9	0	2	0	5,158
Credit River	2	G	3	0	0	0	2,868	Crimson N Gold	6	G	8	0	1	1	5,545
Creditcardpurchase	3	F	15	1	2	1	32,570	Crimson Oak	4	G	9	1	0	4	10,950
Creditville	3	F	2	1	0	0	15,625	Crimson Patriot	5	G	17	2	4	4	18,075
Credo	5	M	3	0	0	1	880	Crimson Policy	9	G	1	0	0	0	263
Cree	3	G	13	1	2	3	16,227	Crimson Prospect	7	G	11	2	2	1	20,774
Cree Power	4	C	2	0	1	0	13,520	Crimson Red	8	G	5	0	0	1	1,614
Cree Ridge	5	H	4	0	0	0	0	Crimson Rising	3	F	9	2	0	0	14,700
Creed's Fury	4	F	7	0	1	2	2,472	Crimson Royale	2	F	1	0	1	0	6,000
Creek	4	G	8	0	1	0	1,300	Crimson Satin	3	F	2	0	0	0	174
Creek Bank	4	C	4	0	1	2	2,662	Crimson Summer	6	H	5	0	0	2	440
Creek Code	5	H	9	4	2	0	84,578	Crimson Unlimited	3	G	13	2	3	1	11,600
Creek Connection	4	F	3	0	0	1	462	Crimson Wave	3	G	7	0	1	0	4,460
Creek County	5	H	2	0	0	0	0	Crippen	3	C	17	1	4	2	15,435
Creek Crossing	5	G	13	2	2	1	14,291	Cripple Creek	4	G	2	0	0	0	4,050
Creek 'n Along	4	F	2	0	0	0	0	Criptografo	5	H	2	0	0	0	265
Creekie Cat	2	F	1	0	0	0	100	Criscrosapplesauce	5	M	4	2	2	0	24,500
Creekline	3	G	9	1	1	1	3,820	Crisis Situation	3	G	11	0	1	0	1,775
Creek's Shore	5	G	11	2	3	2	70,150	Crisp Decision	3	C	1	0	0	0	340
Creeky Lane	8	G	9	1	0	1	9,289	Crispy Jet	5	H	5	0	1	0	3,400
Creeque Alley	4	F	7	2	0	2	22,620	Crispys Red	7	M	3	0	0	0	0
Creme Cathexis	4	F	4	0	0	0	563	Crissie's Sweet	5	M	9	0	4	3	5,805
Creme Cee's	4	F	5	1	0	0	14,220	Crissy's Cricket	4	F	3	1	0	0	1,002
Creme D' Argent	4	G	5	1	0	1	16,960	Cristal's Native	2	G	3	0	0	0	288
Creme 'd Lite	4	F	15	0	3	1	8,354	Critic Mood	7	G	7	0	0	0	776
Creme of Champagne	3	C	3	0	1	0	8,800	Critical Battle	5	G	11	0	3	1	41,010
Crenshaw Spot	6	G	5	0	0	0	0	Critical Bull	3	F	11	1	1	2	34,120
Creole Bash	8	G	3	0	0	0	47	Critical Cat	2	F	2	1	0	0	27,600
Creole O Gold	4	F	2	0	0	0	1,085	Critical Link	2	C	3	0	0	0	432
Crepe Da Slew	4	F	1	0	0	0	0	Critical Thinker	6	G	12	2	1	2	7,318
Crescendo	5	H	3	1	1	0	35,060	Critically	5	M	20	1	5	1	35,222
Crescent Chief	4	G	11	1	1	2	21,430	Criticism	3	G	2	0	0	0	0
Crescent Coast	6	M	3	0	1	1	10,500	Crittenden	4	G	8	0	0	1	720
Crescent Remark	4	G	13	1	2	2	23,820	Critter	7	G	7	0	0	2	1,402
Crescent Roll	3	C	6	0	1	0	2,050	Critter Catcher	6	H	6	0	1	1	995
Crescent Street	3	F	1	0	0	0	0	Crocker Road	2	C	1	0	0	0	980
Cresco Big Train	4	G	9	1	2	1	11,923	Crockett	2	C	1	0	0	0	330
Cresco Blaze	5	G	4	0	0	0	0	Crockett's Critter	5	M	14	1	4	1	7,440
Cresco Chief	6	H	2	0	0	0	0	Crocogator	3	G	7	3	0	2	9,048
Cresco Class Act	3	F	11	0	3	1	9,465	Crocrock	6	G	8	2	2	0	51,150
Cresco Dan	3	G	4	1	0	1	8,652	Crocus	3	F	8	0	3	2	7,720
Cresco Jam Runner	4	F	11	2	2	1	7,432	Crocus Rose	2	F	3	1	0	0	36,350
Cresco Jester	3	F	9	0	0	1	1,668	Croftland Hills	5	H	9	0	0	1	1,003
Cresco Night Club	4	G	13	1	2	1	5,710	Croissant	2	F	4	0	1	0	2,725
Cresco Ruler	5	G	15	4	5	1	37,204	Cronkite	4	G	4	0	0	0	0
Cresco Slew Runner	3	F	7	0	0	0	0	Crook	6	G	9	1	2	1	56,240
Cresent City Cat	2	C	4	0	2	1	7,207	Crook On the Run	9	G	14	1	4	2	20,139
Crest Power	6	M	5	0	0	0	443	Crooked Booger	2	F	4	0	1	2	3,686
Cresta Red	8	G	7	0	0	1	195	Crooked Key	4	G	8	0	1	1	12,940
Cresting Tide	4	F	1	1	0	0	2,520	Crooked Root	4	G	11	2	1	1	10,812
Crestofdawn	9	G	4	0	0	0	120	Crooked Sky	3	G	3	0	0	0	270
Cresty's Wild One	4	F	15	1	0	0	3,624	Crooked Wood	4	F	5	1	0	0	24,817
Crete (AUS)	7	G	9	2	0	0	53,216	Crookedlittlemind	3	C	9	1	0	2	4,757
Crew Cut	5	G	13	1	1	2	7,848	Crook's Bullet	3	G	11	0	0	0	615
Crews Cast	2	F	2	0	0	0	180	Crook's Cher	4	F	4	0	1	2	4,185
Crewscut	3	C	3	0	0	0	431	Crook's Cool	4	F	8	1	0	0	4,752
Cri Cry	4	F	6	0	0	0	327	Crook's Jewel	4	F	3	0	0	0	360
Cribsheet	5	M	1	0	0	0	0	Croozer Roo	3	G	2	0	0	0	0
Cricket Wicket	3	F	7	1	0	0	47,562	Crop Angel	4	F	12	1	1	1	15,030
Crimcita	3	F	3	0	0	0	0	Cross Buck	5	G	10	1	0	1	9,873
Crime of Passion	3	F	8	0	1	0	2,226	Cross Canyon	2	C	1	0	0	0	0
Criminal Brain	4	F	11	2	3	0	11,025	Cross Morant	9	H	5	1	0	0	4,423
Criminal Chucky	3	G	11	2	1	3	44,913	Cross Over Please	3	F	7	3	0	0	10,474
Criminal Slew	3	F	1	0	0	0	0	Cross the Border	3	G	7	2	2	0	27,743
Crimsanna	4	F	9	2	0	2	22,423	Cross the Infield	4	F	12	2	1	1	36,777
Crimson	2	F	1	0	0	0	0	Cross the Plate	3	C	1	0	0	0	54
Crimson and Roses	3	F	10	2	3	1	109,800	Crossbar	7	G	6	0	0	1	6,500
Crimson Avenger	9	G	9	2	0	1	7,527	Crosscut	2	C	2	0	0	0	1,080
Crimson B B	3	F	4	1	0	0	5,400	Crossett Light	3	G	14	1	3	2	14,908
Crimson Baghdad	2	F	1	0	0	0	0	Crossfire Trail	3	F	9	3	3	0	19,470
Crimson Clover	2	F	6	0	0	0	0	Crosshatch	3	C	4	0	0	0	1,855
Crimson Comet	5	M	10	1	1	2	15,660	Crossing	3	F	11	3	1	3	35,796
Crimson Commando	3	G	8	0	1	4	8,818	Crossing Creek	4	G	10	3	2	2	73,210
Crimson Courtier	5	M	7	1	1	1	62,661	Crossing Denali	5	M	5	0	0	2	9,960
Crimson Creek	5	G	4	0	0	0	154	Crossing First	7	G	29	3	2	3	19,388

Horse	Age	Sex	Sts	1st	2d	3d	Won
Crossing Lane	4	F	3	0	0	1	1,195
Crossing Piney	2	F	3	0	1	1	7,770
Crossing Point	6	G	11	4	2	1	189,094
Crossledged	7	G	6	0	0	0	0
Crosspoint	3	G	4	0	2	0	11,180
Crosstown Caper	3	C	3	1	0	0	20,760
Crosswicks Creek	3	F	12	2	3	2	31,955
Crossword Clue	5	H	20	0	5	3	8,539
Crouching Thunder	4	F	9	2	0	0	15,352
Crouching Tiger	3	G	12	4	1	2	66,254
Crow Jane	3	F	11	3	2	0	79,998
Crow Territory	3	F	4	0	0	0	600
Crowd	5	H	6	1	0	1	15,760
Crowd Watcher	5	G	11	3	2	0	53,020
Crowded Meadow	5	G	14	2	5	3	51,014
Crowdn Billy	5	G	8	0	1	0	1,610
Crowds a Talkin'	3	G	10	3	0	1	18,294
Crowing Topic	6	H	1	0	0	0	390
Crown Bay	3	F	9	0	1	1	4,120
Crown Butte	7	G	7	2	1	2	9,510
Crown Connection	5	M	8	0	4	2	20,786
Crown Derby	6	G	9	0	2	0	2,879
Crown Diamond	10	G	3	1	0	0	7,980
Crown Fever	2	G	2	0	0	0	0
Crown Me Augie	6	G	23	1	4	3	12,420
Crown Me Later	3	F	3	0	0	0	4,020
Crown Myst	2	C	1	0	0	0	0
Crown N Colors	2	G	3	1	1	0	4,276
Crown N Seven	2	G	3	0	1	0	4,284
Crown of Pearls	3	F	9	2	0	1	5,931
Crown of Will	2	C	2	0	0	0	273
Crown Pacific	2	G	2	0	0	1	1,155
Crown Parisian	2	C	2	0	0	0	1,143
Crown Point Summer	5	G	14	2	0	1	30,390
Crown Prosecutor	2	C	1	0	0	0	0
Crown Rhythm	4	G	2	0	0	0	139
Crown Royal King	3	C	9	0	1	2	36,943
Crown Royalty	2	G	5	2	1	0	16,831
Crown the King	4	C	14	2	2	3	59,281
Crown the Knight	8	G	7	0	0	2	5,828
Crown the Queen	3	F	1	0	1	0	9,000
Crown the Rebel	6	M	10	0	1	3	3,827
Crown the Tiger	6	G	4	2	2	0	2,979
Crownandcoke	6	G	2	0	0	0	0
Crowned Dancer	3	C	10	0	0	3	88,091
Crowned King	3	C	13	3	0	3	351,000
Crowned Kris	9	G	3	0	0	0	235
Crowned Lover	4	G	5	2	1	0	13,504
Crowned Savannah	2	C	2	0	0	0	720
Crowned Star	7	G	3	0	0	0	202
Crowning Adventure	4	F	7	0	3	1	9,160
Crowning Diablo	4	F	13	2	1	1	18,025
Crowning Moment	3	G	12	0	1	0	7,119
Crowning Mystery	5	M	4	0	0	2	3,710
Crowning Point	5	G	5	0	0	0	234
Crowning Prospect	9	G	6	0	1	0	1,632
Crowning Quest	3	F	1	0	0	0	0
Crowning Ruby	7	M	17	1	3	4	4,964
Crowning Sea	3	G	9	2	1	1	4,242
Crowning Step	3	F	13	0	2	2	4,340
Crowning the Queen	3	F	7	1	2	3	5,297
Crowning Thought	4	G	3	0	1	0	5,700
Crown's Justice	3	G	13	2	0	5	64,792
Crown's Prospect	5	G	10	2	0	0	11,593
Crows (ARG)	9	H	13	3	1	0	27,310
Crows Mile	4	C	1	0	0	0	0
Croydons Game	2	F	1	0	0	0	210
Crozet	2	F	4	0	1	1	14,000
Crozier Lex	7	G	7	0	0	1	840
Cruaway	5	M	4	0	0	0	430
Crucial Honor	3	G	11	3	2	2	34,570
Crucial Move	3	G	3	1	0	0	14,193
Crucible	8	G	6	0	1	0	23,035
Crucible of Fire	4	G	12	1	2	0	9,211
Cruel Baron	5	G	4	0	0	0	0
Cruella de Vilzak	5	M	6	1	0	1	1,896
Cruise Along	5	M	6	2	0	0	107,100
Cruise Control	5	M	3	0	0	0	281
Cruise Director	3	C	2	0	0	0	132
Cruise Missle	7	H	13	1	1	2	5,946
Cruisen N Dancin	3	F	11	1	1	2	6,974
Cruisenrightalong	3	G	2	0	0	0	1,320
Cruiseonblue	7	H	2	0	0	0	186
Cruiseship	3	G	8	1	3	1	11,460
Cruisin' Carlos	4	G	4	0	1	1	1,560
Cruisin N	3	G	11	1	3	0	9,433
Cruisin Rio	4	G	2	0	0	0	0
Cruisin Scooter	7	G	10	0	1	1	4,614
Cruisin Together	2	F	2	1	0	0	25,236
Cruising Bullet	5	G	12	2	1	2	14,601
Cruising By	6	G	16	0	3	2	7,012
Cruising Executive	3	F	6	2	0	0	131,037
Cruising Kat	4	G	8	0	0	1	7,475
Crumpet	5	M	3	0	1	1	13,700
Crusader Invader	4	C	5	0	2	0	3,061
Crusader Jo	4	C	8	0	2	1	18,300
Crusader Queen	4	F	7	3	2	0	97,580
Crusader's Belle	7	M	10	0	0	1	1,227
Crusader's Gold	5	H	5	2	1	0	7,934
Crusader's Passage	5	M	13	2	0	0	8,130
Crusading Kip	3	G	14	1	2	2	7,711
Crusading Time	2	F	1	0	0	0	0
Crush On Callie	5	M	12	3	1	1	21,645
Crush This	2	C	2	0	0	0	1,085
Crusin Kris	6	H	3	0	1	0	900
Crutcher	3	C	10	4	2	0	38,635
Crux	2	G	4	1	1	0	7,228
Cruzan Midnight	3	F	8	1	1	0	9,535
Cruzcat	2	C	5	1	1	1	14,170
Cruzenwiththestars	3	F	4	0	0	1	1,735
Cruzin Free	2	G	6	0	0	1	4,310
Cruzing Cruzer	3	C	7	0	1	1	4,078
Cruz'n O. C.	4	F	8	1	0	2	5,156
Cry a Note	4	F	1	0	0	0	150
Cry Baby Cry	9	M	11	1	0	0	2,669
Cry Like Crazy	4	F	5	0	0	0	490
Cry Louder Taylor	8	G	10	0	2	2	8,866
Cry Misty	3	F	9	2	3	0	13,345
Cry of the Banshee	5	H	2	0	0	0	0
Cry of the Cat	3	F	11	1	4	1	53,510
Cryhavoc (GB)	9	G	10	1	0	1	8,270
Crying Out Wild	3	F	7	0	1	0	2,086
Crypt	4	G	4	1	0	1	11,870
Crypt de Chine	8	H	11	7	1	0	98,600
Cryptic Attitude	6	G	9	0	0	0	3,900
Cryptic Code	4	G	4	1	1	0	23,510
Cryptic Devil	5	G	10	3	0	2	69,120
Cryptic John	3	C	8	1	1	3	10,180
Cryptic Lass	3	F	13	0	0	1	1,640
Cryptic Message	4	C	3	0	0	0	450
Cryptic Nite	8	G	2	1	0	1	3,430
Cryptic Skier	2	G	3	1	2	0	39,500
Cryptic Smile	3	C	10	1	2	1	8,345
Cryptic Star	2	F	2	0	0	0	420
Cryptic Storm	4	F	10	0	1	3	3,586
Cryptically	2	F	1	0	0	0	105
Crypto Al	9	G	8	0	0	0	1,345
Crypto Bella	3	G	10	1	0	1	8,500
Crypto Child	6	H	8	0	3	1	5,047
Crypto Comet	8	G	4	0	0	0	198
Crypto Cream	4	F	4	0	0	0	4,230
Crypto Cum Laude	10	G	7	1	4	0	2,047
Crypto Devil	4	G	17	2	4	2	12,932
Crypto Dixie	4	C	11	3	2	3	55,810
Crypto Em	2	F	1	0	1	0	5,600
Crypto Fortune	4	F	7	0	1	2	2,503
Crypto Gal	3	F	10	1	0	2	16,930
Crypto Gold	8	G	4	0	1	1	2,886
Crypto K	5	H	2	0	0	0	336
Crypto Kate	4	F	1	1	0	0	4,740
Crypto Kelly	5	M	4	0	1	0	1,844
Crypto Kiss	4	F	1	0	0	0	135
Crypto 'n Cruise	3	F	6	2	1	1	16,461
Crypto Pool	4	G	18	1	2	1	7,667
Crypto Prince	5	G	15	0	0	3	5,245
Crypto Runs Again	2	C	7	1	1	1	12,080
Crypto Secret	2	F	1	0	0	0	750
Crypto Storm	4	F	17	2	3	4	16,095

Horse	Age	Sex	Sts	1st	2d	3d	Won
Crypto Willie	2	G	4	0	2	0	8,540
Cryptobeat	4	G	10	1	0	3	18,311
Cryptobillie	3	F	11	2	1	1	12,354
Cryptocandie	6	M	9	0	1	3	4,075
Cryptocraft	3	G	12	0	3	4	19,055
Cryptocruiser	3	G	3	0	1	0	1,800
Cryptoeskimo	3	C	5	0	0	2	1,597
Cryptofem	3	F	8	1	2	2	53,305
Cryptograph	2	C	2	1	0	0	6,300
Cryptointhestars	4	F	22	2	4	2	16,608
Cryptologic	5	G	11	2	1	1	6,615
Cryptoman	5	G	23	2	3	0	20,690
Cryptomatic	6	G	10	1	0	1	4,327
Crypton	5	H	10	0	1	2	4,231
Cryptonic Love	4	F	1	0	0	0	106
Cryptorouge	6	M	7	1	0	0	19,003
Cryptorush	4	F	8	0	2	1	3,203
Cryptos' Best	2	F	12	2	1	3	96,345
Crypto's Bid	3	F	5	3	0	1	46,230
Crypto's Cheer	3	C	3	0	0	0	480
Crypto's Friend	3	G	4	0	0	0	1,820
Crypto's Prospect	2	C	5	2	2	0	24,000
Crypto's Silver	3	G	9	0	0	1	6,110
Crypto's Trick	3	F	4	0	0	1	1,287
Crypto's Twinjet	4	F	6	1	0	0	14,995
Cryptoscript	4	F	17	1	1	3	36,460
Crypto'sirishdamsl	4	G	17	0	0	3	6,393
Cryptosummer	2	F	6	2	1	0	18,580
Cryptotoo	3	F	6	2	1	0	49,010
Cryptotune	6	H	12	1	1	3	15,068
Cryptovinsky	2	C	6	0	0	2	16,710
Cry's Sassy Lady	4	F	9	3	0	1	42,950
Crystal Anna	5	M	1	0	0	0	38
Crystal Appeal	5	M	14	0	3	0	11,152
Crystal Billing	4	C	2	1	0	0	3,120
Crystal Charm	3	F	9	0	0	0	1,901
Crystal Charmer	4	F	1	0	0	0	0
Crystal Cinders	9	M	4	2	1	0	4,289
Crystal Clarity	4	F	9	2	0	0	13,290
Crystal Class	3	C	3	0	0	1	4,660
Crystal Clear	3	F	2	0	0	0	100
Crystal Clipper	3	F	15	3	4	4	91,890
Crystal Colony	4	G	3	0	0	1	3,520
Crystal Conquest	4	C	23	3	1	3	21,420
Crystal Cove	3	F	5	0	0	1	6,880
Crystal Crane	10	M	4	0	0	1	1,290
Crystal Dancer	3	F	3	0	0	1	5,780
Crystal Dawn	6	M	15	2	2	3	30,748
Crystal Forest	5	M	9	0	0	1	1,920
Crystal Gail	3	F	15	1	1	2	6,385
Crystal Gala	2	F	2	1	0	0	15,484
Crystal Gate	6	M	4	1	0	0	2,550
Crystal Harmony	5	M	7	2	2	0	91,392
Crystal K. K.	3	F	2	0	0	0	0
Crystal Kate	8	M	6	0	0	0	70
Crystal Lee	5	G	14	4	0	2	34,184
Crystal Lyric	4	F	1	0	0	0	0
Crystal Magic	2	F	1	0	0	0	0
Crystal May	3	F	1	0	0	0	91
Crystal Mt. Stevie	2	F	3	2	0	0	24,885
Crystal n' Reign	6	M	17	4	3	2	21,815
Crystal n'Silver	3	F	6	1	1	0	8,565
Crystal Nugget	7	M	12	0	0	1	3,568
Crystal On Fire	3	C	11	0	0	0	1,875
Crystal Pattern	5	M	14	0	2	2	4,591
Crystal Prediction	8	M	6	0	0	0	822
Crystal Sally	6	M	10	1	0	0	3,039
Crystal Salute	5	M	4	0	0	0	453
Crystal Sea	6	M	11	2	3	1	103,146
Crystal Season	5	H	7	0	0	1	1,519
Crystal Sound	4	G	14	1	1	4	5,197
Crystal Vision	3	G	11	1	1	0	21,864
Crystalaire	4	G	20	1	1	6	11,631
Crystalen Tiffany	4	F	11	0	2	0	9,019
Crystallization	3	G	19	0	5	3	10,839
Crystallo	6	G	13	1	0	3	17,082
Crystals Rally	4	G	3	0	0	1	637
Crystal's Regal	5	G	9	1	2	2	11,925
Crystal's Time	6	H	7	0	1	0	2,185
Cryyoulittledevil	7	G	7	0	0	1	1,001
C's Courser	5	H	8	1	2	1	2,030
C's Victory	2	G	3	0	0	1	3,750
Cu At the Bailey	4	G	21	1	2	7	9,687
Cub Creek	9	H	2	0	1	0	220
Cuban Coffee	3	F	5	0	0	0	595
Cuban Cutie	3	F	5	0	0	0	0
Cuban Leaf	3	C	10	3	2	0	25,440
Cuban Link	4	G	9	1	3	3	15,281
Cuban Mike	9	G	17	1	6	2	12,676
Cubby Bear	3	C	2	0	1	0	2,704
Cube's Cub	4	F	1	0	1	0	2,200
Cube's Kat	5	H	12	3	2	1	10,452
Cubicle	3	F	17	4	2	5	37,771
Cuca	3	F	1	1	0	0	9,600
Cuccinella	4	F	15	2	5	2	65,490
Cuchalian	6	M	11	2	0	1	9,042
Cuchu	3	F	2	0	1	0	1,555
Cucumber	5	H	3	0	0	0	0
Cucuri	7	G	9	1	1	0	4,967
Cucurri Babe	4	F	12	2	1	1	16,647
Cuddley	3	F	5	0	1	0	7,090
Cudo	7	G	4	0	0	0	109
Cued Up	4	G	15	1	3	2	17,817
Cuerdas	6	M	14	2	1	2	21,336
Cuervo Kenny	6	G	1	0	0	0	0
Cuff the Quote	2	C	2	0	0	0	530
Cuffsfatcowboy	2	G	2	0	0	0	0
Cugini Gold	3	C	3	0	0	0	3,931
Cuillin Hills	3	G	5	0	0	1	920
Cukros	5	M	11	2	0	2	9,885
Culaterbye	5	H	1	0	0	0	0
Cullen	2	G	2	0	0	0	2,195
Culley	4	F	14	3	3	3	35,101
Culloden	6	H	5	0	0	0	2,737
Cullowhee	3	F	4	2	0	0	17,480
Culotche Breeze	9	H	14	1	2	1	7,665
Culpeper Moon	2	F	2	1	1	0	14,460
Cultural Blend	3	G	4	0	0	0	0
Cultural Shock	6	M	10	1	0	0	10,566
Cum Laude	4	G	4	0	0	1	1,426
Cumberland Boy	4	G	9	1	0	4	11,469
Cumberland Gap	11	G	10	1	3	2	19,443
Cumberland River	6	G	8	0	1	4	6,489
Cumberland Road	5	M	5	0	0	0	560
Cumby Texas	3	C	7	2	1	0	13,940
Cumulus	4	C	10	1	1	1	14,757
Cunning Casey	3	F	3	0	0	0	0
Cunning Fellow	7	G	7	0	0	1	1,705
Cunning Play	4	F	9	1	0	2	53,380
Cuore d'Oro	3	F	10	1	0	2	5,255
Cup a Spicy Chilly	3	F	6	0	0	1	936
Cup Match	5	M	2	1	0	0	19,494
Cup of Karets	5	M	8	0	0	2	837
Cupalo	4	G	8	2	0	2	9,231
Cupasoup	4	F	4	2	1	0	44,500
Cupcakes and Candy	3	F	7	0	0	1	915
Cupid Season	3	F	10	5	1	1	117,760
Cupidity	4	F	6	1	0	0	3,157
Cupids Angel	2	F	1	0	0	0	0
Cupid's Comet	7	M	12	5	2	0	94,710
Cupid's Honour	4	G	6	0	1	1	4,409
Cupid's Power	3	F	2	0	0	0	87
Cup's Final Shine	2	C	2	0	0	0	200
Cupsky	2	C	3	0	0	0	490
Curb	3	G	11	1	4	2	63,770
Cure Judys Blues	4	F	6	1	0	0	24,600
Cure M	3	C	2	0	0	0	0
Cure the Devil	8	H	4	0	0	0	180
Curicular	3	F	8	0	1	1	2,250
Curiosity	3	F	11	0	3	3	78,089
Curious Conundrum	5	M	12	3	2	0	147,820
Curious Gamble	2	G	6	0	0	3	17,802
Curious Indy	2	C	1	0	0	0	0
Curious Kat	8	M	7	0	0	1	2,572
Curious Kris	5	G	1	0	0	0	0
Curli Babi	2	F	2	0	0	0	0
Curls	3	F	2	0	0	0	438
Curly Carnivalay	8	G	11	2	3	2	8,850

Horse	Age	Sex	Sts	1st	2d	3d	Won	Horse	Age	Sex	Sts	1st	2d	3d	Won
Curly Halo	3	F	8	2	0	2	10,600	Cy	2	C	4	0	0	0	115
Curly Jake	5	G	5	1	0	0	1,552	Cya Baby	2	F	2	0	0	1	4,715
Curly Joe	6	G	17	1	1	4	9,484	Cya Sal	2	F	6	0	0	0	1,285
Curly Spurwink	3	G	7	0	0	0	1,140	Cyalater Ozzie	3	G	3	0	0	0	105
Curly's Pride	2	F	3	0	1	0	7,520	Cyalator	6	G	5	0	0	0	224
Curmudgeon	4	C	9	1	1	4	11,765	Cyane's Thunder	5	H	10	1	3	0	43,860
Curno J. C.	4	G	12	1	2	1	32,394	Cyanne Slew	5	G	3	1	0	0	770
Curragh	3	F	8	0	0	0	521	Cyber Assault	4	C	2	0	0	0	0
Currahee	4	G	7	1	2	1	8,336	Cyber Babe	5	M	10	0	4	0	7,450
Currency Kitty	3	F	8	1	3	0	18,890	Cyber Chat	10	G	4	0	0	1	1,287
Current Affair	4	F	9	1	1	1	15,400	Cyber Cowboy	4	C	2	0	0	0	55
Current Hitter	8	M	8	0	1	0	1,408	Cyber Craze	4	C	1	0	0	0	0
Current Kraze	4	F	4	0	0	0	100	Cyber Hacker	2	C	3	1	1	0	15,245
Current Niner	2	C	6	1	2	0	24,400	Cyber Move	5	M	21	2	4	3	19,346
Current Tirade	3	G	7	0	0	2	2,562	Cyber Secret	3	F	5	3	1	0	214,107
Currently Incharge	5	H	1	0	0	0	300	Cyber Slew	3	F	7	1	2	3	65,000
Currituck	2	C	3	0	0	1	5,580	Cyber Stock	5	H	11	2	0	1	17,080
Currituck Sound	2	F	3	0	0	1	3,060	Cyberdate	4	C	2	0	0	0	165
Currituck Springs	3	G	8	1	1	3	16,025	Cyberdevil	3	G	7	0	1	1	11,739
Cursitor	2	C	1	0	0	0	975	Cyberflash	3	G	1	0	0	0	0
Curtain Queen	3	F	5	0	1	1	8,624	Cybergate	4	C	13	1	5	3	46,630
Curtee	4	G	4	0	0	1	3,689	Cyberkaetzchen	3	C	2	0	0	0	0
Curt's First Bid	4	G	12	4	0	4	53,311	Cyberprince	3	C	8	0	0	1	1,729
Curve Ball	6	G	13	4	0	1	81,467	Cybers' Image	2	C	2	0	0	0	240
Curve Buster	3	F	4	0	0	0	3,000	Cybersimon	3	F	3	0	0	2	2,280
Cuse	2	C	1	0	0	0	2,160	Cybertale	3	F	12	0	0	0	370
Custer's Farewell	3	F	12	1	0	0	4,270	Cyberwiz	3	G	4	0	0	0	152
Custers Last	4	F	9	2	1	0	17,399	Cyberzone	5	M	9	0	0	0	3,801
Custom Built	7	M	12	4	2	1	19,339	Cycic Cyrene	4	F	2	0	0	0	58
Custom Crew	4	C	1	0	0	0	0	Cycle of Life	3	F	4	1	0	0	20,930
Custom Dancer	3	F	1	0	0	0	0	Cyclone Slew	3	F	18	2	6	4	39,405
Custom Framing	3	G	7	3	1	1	61,200	Cyclone Tower	2	G	1	0	0	0	0
Custom Made	5	M	1	0	0	0	380	Cyclorama	4	F	1	0	0	0	0
Custom Made Fellow	4	G	11	0	5	2	11,465	Cyclotron	3	C	2	0	1	0	12,740
Custom Made Jade	2	G	2	0	1	0	2,063	Cymbidium	3	F	11	0	1	4	10,910
Customize	2	F	1	0	0	1	850	Cynar	5	G	3	1	0	1	13,006
Customs	2	F	1	1	0	0	6,960	Cyndaquil	3	F	1	0	0	0	432
Cut a Path	3	F	1	0	0	1	1,700	Cynics Beware	9	G	3	0	0	0	2,600
Cut a Wager	4	F	8	1	0	1	18,289	Cynics Quest	4	G	11	1	2	0	25,541
Cut Ahead	5	G	9	0	0	0	0	Cynthia's Field	3	F	17	2	0	1	10,199
Cut and Shoot	2	C	1	1	0	0	36,360	Cynthus	3	F	5	0	0	0	1,100
Cut Back	2	C	8	0	1	0	3,400	Cypress Cove	3	C	9	2	1	2	89,658
Cut Class	4	G	8	2	2	1	20,930	Cypress Hill	3	F	4	1	1	1	9,950
Cut It Out Rudy	2	C	1	0	0	0	0	Cypress Trail	4	F	8	2	1	0	39,700
Cut Me In	5	H	8	1	0	1	9,313	Cyratoga	5	H	8	2	0	1	15,825
Cut Me Slack Jack	3	G	3	0	0	1	3,180	Cyrgeo	4	G	10	0	1	1	5,585
Cut My Tune	4	F	1	0	0	0	0	Cyrus Noble	4	G	6	1	0	0	6,780
Cut Number	3	F	1	0	0	0	500	Cytherea	2	F	2	0	0	0	0
Cut of Music	3	G	16	4	2	4	68,304	Czar	4	G	10	1	1	2	9,571
Cut Stone	2	G	4	1	0	0	5,100	Czar Kodiack	7	G	11	0	1	1	2,058
Cut the Ace	4	F	3	0	0	0	0	Czar of Cozzene	2	C	2	0	0	0	0
Cut the Ribbon	3	G	2	1	1	0	7,476	Czardas Dancer	7	G	1	0	0	0	80
Cut to the Chase	2	F	5	1	1	1	12,590	Czarist	4	G	1	0	0	0	0
Cut to the Hunt	3	G	6	1	1	1	9,630	Czar's Witch	2	F	1	0	0	0	0
Cutaway	7	G	9	0	0	2	3,330	Czech Mate	3	G	15	3	4	2	62,405
Cute as an Angel	2	F	5	2	1	1	15,110	Czech the Deed	3	F	5	0	0	0	1,530
Cute Connie	2	F	12	3	0	1	45,530	Czech Valentine	2	C	1	0	0	0	0
Cute Cookie	5	M	3	0	0	0	190	D and B Tornado	5	M	3	0	0	0	515
Cute Crafty	3	C	1	0	0	0	0	D Back's Rudy	3	G	7	2	0	0	5,888
Cute N Noble	3	F	9	4	1	1	135,735	D Bandette	9	M	4	0	0	0	111
Cute Rob	5	H	2	0	0	0	0	D C Storm	5	G	11	6	1	0	87,510
Cutie Bye	2	F	1	0	0	0	0	D' Coach	4	C	2	1	0	1	21,300
Cutiecantoo	4	F	16	1	2	1	8,838	D C's Thunder	2	C	4	1	0	1	33,740
Cutie's Fox	6	M	1	0	0	0	0	D C's U S Flag	3	F	2	0	0	0	0
Cutlass Cutie	2	F	2	1	0	0	6,993	D D Dot Comm	6	H	9	4	0	2	13,816
Cutlass Prince	3	G	3	1	0	1	23,050	D D Stormy	5	G	7	0	2	0	2,313
Cutnstyle	4	F	9	1	2	2	16,520	D Day Baby	4	G	1	0	0	0	0
Cutoff Blaze	5	G	4	0	0	0	0	D Diesel	2	C	3	0	0	1	1,100
Cutoffs	3	F	10	3	2	2	66,600	D E Barron	2	G	6	0	0	2	2,370
Cutshin	3	C	11	0	1	3	11,264	D E Intimidator	3	G	7	3	0	0	17,790
Cuttin Cash	3	F	12	1	0	0	2,997	D' Esprit	4	F	12	2	2	2	15,312
Cuttin' Didos	3	C	5	1	1	0	3,460	D Final Answer	3	C	1	0	0	0	0
Cutting a Rug	2	F	2	0	0	0	80	D J Cody	4	G	2	0	0	0	0
Cutting in Line	6	H	5	0	0	0	0	D J North	11	G	8	0	1	0	2,191
Cutting the Rug	4	G	8	2	0	1	25,058	D J's Angel	3	F	3	0	0	0	1,004
Cutty	5	G	10	1	1	2	9,190	D J's Going Places	5	G	3	0	0	2	2,970
Cuvee	2	C	6	4	0	1	360,704	D J's Jubilee	11	G	12	3	3	2	20,865
Cviano	6	G	7	0	0	0	970	D J's Runnaway	2	F	2	0	0	1	780
Cv's Thundrn Heart	5	H	4	0	0	0	0	D J's Show Time	7	G	13	3	4	1	18,528

Horse	Age	Sex	Sts	1st	2d	3d	Won	Horse	Age	Sex	Sts	1st	2d	3d	Won
D J's Tap Dancer	7	G	12	1	2	1	8,683	Daddys Shoes	2	G	5	1	0	0	5,670
D J's Thunderhead	7	G	8	0	0	0	921	Daddyspentdamoney	4	G	7	0	0	0	474
D J's Tridon	4	G	15	0	3	2	7,246	Daddysprideandjoy	4	C	1	0	0	0	0
D J's Wendy's Wish	3	C	3	1	0	0	5,590	Dades Legacy	4	F	5	0	1	1	3,572
D K Dickens	6	G	17	1	1	3	16,474	Dad's Concorde	6	H	1	0	0	0	0
D Lux Chimes	2	G	4	0	0	1	540	Dads Destroyer	3	F	13	2	2	2	61,830
D M Special	3	F	9	2	1	0	13,300	Dad's Indurance	6	G	1	0	0	0	38
D Misterious Angel	4	F	5	0	0	0	0	Dad's Lessons	2	C	3	1	0	0	38,376
D M's Awsum Koko	5	M	8	0	1	1	4,485	Dad's Love	3	F	16	1	5	5	24,126
D' Nile	3	F	13	0	3	3	43,342	Daemon	8	H	1	0	0	0	0
D P Dancer	3	C	7	2	0	2	32,460	Daffodil	6	M	4	0	0	0	206
D Q Buster	5	H	12	1	0	0	3,477	Daffodil Princess	3	F	14	2	2	1	25,866
D Ranger	2	C	1	0	0	0	180	Dafnah Girl	3	F	1	0	0	0	0
D Running Devil	4	C	7	0	0	0	1,050	Dagny Taggert	5	M	13	1	2	0	8,357
D' Special	7	G	12	0	0	1	1,896	Dagonzt	5	G	4	0	0	0	174
D Style	4	G	4	1	0	0	1,222	Dahar Fighter	4	G	2	0	0	0	61
D W's Rose Bud	5	G	3	0	0	0	103	Dahlberg (BRZ)	8	G	4	0	0	0	0
D. A. Way	3	G	9	0	1	2	942	Dahlia Dearest	3	F	7	0	0	0	1,820
D. C. Lady	2	F	2	0	0	0	240	Dahlia's Diamond	2	F	5	1	1	0	10,080
D. C. Ten	3	G	1	0	0	0	200	Dahlias Trempolino	3	G	3	0	0	0	0
D. Cami K.	3	F	2	0	0	0	0	Daily Dance	3	F	10	1	0	1	15,600
D. D.'s Astro	6	G	10	0	1	1	4,934	Daily Flight	6	M	12	2	0	2	9,972
D. J. Fifty-Fifth	6	H	2	0	0	0	128	Daily Report	4	F	15	4	4	1	47,097
D. J. Show Boat	6	G	9	1	1	0	6,177	Daily Sport	4	G	8	0	1	2	6,995
D. J. Tyler	4	G	11	2	2	1	58,554	Daily Total	3	G	16	1	3	1	13,700
D. J.'s Grades	2	G	5	0	0	1	3,160	Daily's Lil Charm	6	M	5	0	0	2	1,080
D. J.'s Hope	6	H	11	3	1	3	68,320	Dainty Cloud	5	G	1	0	0	0	0
D. J.s Last	3	F	11	2	1	0	8,980	Daiquiri Doll	8	M	1	0	1	0	1,460
D. J.'s Slew	2	F	1	0	0	0	93	Dairyman	9	G	2	0	0	0	220
D. L. Renzo	2	C	11	1	2	0	25,830	Daisy Be Good	4	F	14	1	2	3	8,897
D. R. Doug	3	G	2	0	0	0	140	Daisy Cutter	3	F	1	0	0	0	591
D. W. Wheels	7	G	8	1	1	1	7,445	Daisy Daisy	2	F	1	0	0	0	0
Da Beauty	3	F	2	0	0	0	810	Daisy Deluxe	5	M	5	0	1	1	3,995
Da Big Hoss	6	G	2	0	0	0	0	Daisy Double	10	M	10	1	3	1	5,715
Da Birdman	2	C	5	1	0	0	7,480	Daisy Dukes	5	M	1	0	0	0	1,980
Da Blaze	8	G	1	0	0	0	0	Daisy Maid	7	F	6	0	0	1	1,375
Da Boxer	2	C	3	1	1	0	11,936	Daisy Slew	2	F	5	0	0	1	1,172
Da Breeze	5	G	8	1	1	2	8,960	Daisyago	4	F	7	0	1	3	31,360
Da Bull	11	G	2	0	0	0	515	Daisye Duxster	5	M	10	1	2	2	10,011
Da Charm	4	C	3	1	0	0	10,365	Daisy's a Pleasure	3	F	5	0	0	0	3,676
Da Da Rumba	3	G	11	0	0	4	8,950	Daisys Don't Tell	3	F	1	0	0	0	140
Da Dance	3	F	16	3	2	1	30,927	Daisy's Memory	6	G	17	5	1	5	30,904
Da Devil	8	G	5	0	1	1	14,590	Daisy's Mercedes	6	M	10	1	2	2	10,973
Da Diva	4	F	3	0	0	1	1,456	Daisy's Our Dream	3	F	9	2	2	1	20,190
Da Forty Four	2	G	4	0	0	0	246	Daivon Jones	4	C	7	1	3	3	30,318
Da' King	4	G	14	1	2	1	27,383	Dajudge	5	G	24	4	2	4	35,795
Da Lawyer	3	G	10	2	1	3	12,334	Dakini	3	F	5	0	0	1	5,110
Da Legend	3	G	8	1	1	1	52,661	Dakkota's Dream	5	G	3	0	0	0	0
Da Little Guy	2	G	1	0	0	0	100	Dako Rika	7	G	9	0	1	1	1,779
Da Mamboking	2	C	2	0	0	0	201	Dakota Appeal	5	G	10	2	2	0	23,155
Da Meister	5	G	6	0	3	1	11,220	Dakota Bells	2	G	3	0	0	1	1,960
Da Nine	3	G	4	0	0	0	200	Dakota Bullet	4	F	10	0	0	0	664
Da Pillar	2	G	3	1	0	1	5,484	Dakota Cowboy	3	G	3	0	0	0	0
Da Rodeo Man	3	G	2	0	0	0	460	Dakota Danzig	12	G	9	1	0	0	4,665
Da Svedonya	3	F	2	0	0	1	2,040	Dakota Destiny	3	G	13	2	2	1	18,186
Daad's Hot	4	G	15	3	1	4	33,795	Dakota Diamond	4	G	13	3	1	2	57,402
Dab of Wheelock	3	G	9	2	0	1	8,682	Dakota Dixie	2	C	4	0	1	2	11,304
Dabadee	8	G	6	0	0	0	700	Dakota Dolly	4	F	2	0	0	0	0
Dabney Carr	8	G	8	2	0	2	15,321	Dakota Ice	3	G	7	0	0	0	2,432
Dacota Desert	4	G	19	5	3	1	18,210	Dakota Kid	2	C	1	0	0	0	0
Dactique's Quest	3	F	9	2	3	0	41,440	Dakota Light	3	F	13	3	4	1	152,834
Dad Does	5	H	4	0	0	0	46	Dakota Panorama	5	M	7	0	0	0	0
Dad Grands Girl	4	F	3	0	0	0	252	Dakota Prospect	6	G	4	0	0	0	1,155
Dad Gummit Paul	8	G	3	0	0	0	0	Dakota Sage	8	G	3	1	1	0	2,025
Dad Says Yes	2	F	4	0	2	0	4,875	Dakota West	3	G	7	0	1	2	3,888
Dad Smoked Cigar	4	F	8	2	1	2	35,247	Dakota Winter Air	3	C	3	1	0	2	2,472
Dad Strikes Gold	7	H	9	1	0	3	10,561	Dakota Won	3	G	10	1	0	0	2,814
Daddy Cool	5	G	1	0	0	0	1,500	Dakota's Angel	3	F	2	0	0	0	0
Daddy Don't	5	M	1	0	0	0	0	Dal Reo Lad	11	G	5	1	0	1	5,221
Daddy Says No	3	G	4	0	0	0	322	Dalder	6	H	10	1	1	0	4,841
Daddy Who	2	F	3	0	0	0	885	Dales and Glenns	4	G	3	0	1	1	3,620
Daddylovesmetoo	3	F	2	0	0	0	0	Dale's Deluxe	3	G	5	0	3	1	5,883
Daddys Anna	6	M	2	0	0	0	0	Dale's Demon Red	3	C	4	1	0	0	25,100
Daddy's Baby Girl	3	F	4	0	0	0	975	Dale's Irishmelody	5	G	7	0	0	0	1,425
Daddys Bright Star	4	C	13	2	1	3	26,190	Dale's Lil Devil	4	C	3	0	0	0	228
Daddy's Crane	2	C	3	1	0	0	6,150	Dalia Dolly	4	F	2	0	1	0	4,372
Daddy's Destiny	3	F	6	0	0	0	1,085	Dalia's Whirl	5	M	11	0	4	1	9,887
Daddy's Princess	2	F	3	1	0	0	29,400	Dallas	8	G	2	0	0	0	190
Daddy's Punkin	3	F	15	2	3	2	23,060	Dallas Alice	5	M	5	2	1	0	20,340

Horse	Age	Sex	Sts	1st	2d	3d	Won	Horse	Age	Sex	Sts	1st	2d	3d	Won
Dallas Express	3	G	14	3	1	3	46,917	Dance in Fire	4	F	2	0	0	0	150
Dallas K Boy	5	H	1	0	0	0	0	Dance in Flight	3	F	7	0	2	2	17,080
Dalliance	6	H	10	0	1	0	2,633	Dance in the Light	6	G	13	0	1	1	2,751
Dalovaly Linda	2	F	5	0	1	0	3,593	Dance in the Park	5	G	8	0	0	0	656
Dalton Town	6	G	17	1	1	3	8,039	Dance in the Wind	3	F	6	1	1	2	16,977
Dalt's Kingpin	4	C	15	4	4	5	48,428	Dance Instructor	2	F	4	0	1	0	6,950
Dalybuck	3	C	8	2	1	1	9,895	Dance Jane	3	F	1	0	0	0	0
Dam Bustn	3	G	11	3	4	2	38,136	Dance King	5	H	14	2	4	3	24,775
Dam Cat	2	G	5	2	0	0	21,716	Dance Kuntakete	3	F	9	2	1	0	34,987
Dam Scheckel	3	C	6	0	0	0	0	Dance Lead	3	F	2	0	0	0	320
Damar Wayne	4	G	4	1	0	1	16,380	Dance Lessons	4	F	3	1	1	1	53,140
Damariscotta	2	F	4	0	2	0	3,670	Dance Lil Zar	5	G	6	1	0	0	8,400
Damaschino (AUS)	5	M	3	0	0	0	18,660	Dance Lovley	3	F	1	0	0	0	0
Damascus Boy	2	C	1	0	0	0	0	Dance Mary Anne	5	M	16	5	1	2	48,950
Damask Steel (ARG)	6	M	2	0	0	1	2,720	Dance Mattic	3	F	20	4	1	2	39,546
Damavictory	5	M	9	0	0	0	1,024	Dance Me	3	F	11	1	1	1	34,051
Dame Bertie	3	F	11	1	1	2	11,552	Dance Me Free	4	G	10	1	1	0	19,880
Dame Fame	3	F	1	0	0	1	1,920	Dance Me Inside	5	M	1	0	0	0	370
Dame Sylvieguilhem	4	F	3	1	0	0	30,000	Dance Molly Dance	2	F	1	0	0	0	0
Dames Best Man	4	C	8	1	1	0	4,180	Dance Music (ARG)	6	H	10	0	1	2	15,520
Dames I Have Loved	6	M	1	0	0	0	114	Dance My Lady	6	M	9	1	5	1	10,460
Damican	4	C	9	0	4	2	24,847	Dance My Number	3	F	6	1	1	1	9,440
Damiensdelight	3	F	6	0	1	2	6,440	Dance N Kiss	3	G	8	0	2	1	6,730
Damifino	8	G	1	0	0	0	0	Dance N the Blues	3	F	4	1	1	0	1,891
Damn the Torpedoes	6	G	12	3	1	4	56,920	Dance No More	2	C	3	1	0	0	6,750
Damon T	3	G	7	1	1	2	26,752	Dance Note	4	G	14	3	1	1	37,111
Damspicy	5	G	10	0	0	3	1,355	Dance of Creation	4	F	2	0	0	0	419
Damus's Dancer	4	G	14	2	1	1	6,724	Dance of Joy	3	F	10	1	1	2	23,681
Dan D La Kar	8	G	7	0	3	0	3,161	Dance of the Year	2	F	4	1	0	1	34,853
Dan U Devil	5	G	10	0	2	1	2,695	Dance On Home	3	G	13	3	1	1	69,973
Dan Vamp	3	G	10	0	0	1	1,234	Dance Pepper Dance	2	F	1	0	0	0	0
Dana Dragrace	3	F	2	0	0	0	110	Dance Pro	3	G	10	1	1	0	44,537
Danadar	5	G	8	1	1	1	6,401	Dance Proudly	3	G	6	1	2	1	14,980
Danaher	2	C	1	0	0	0	0	Dance Rhythm	5	M	12	5	1	1	47,640
Danaher Steve	5	H	6	2	1	3	66,405	Dance Rocker	4	C	1	0	0	0	0
Danaly Miss	4	F	1	0	0	0	0	Dance Rule	4	G	5	0	0	0	0
Danang	3	G	6	0	0	1	6,117	Dance Saga	3	F	1	0	0	0	240
Danar	8	G	13	1	0	1	9,579	Dance Seeker	3	C	13	0	1	1	3,789
Dana's Dawn	2	F	3	0	1	0	3,980	Dance Sharp	7	M	4	0	0	0	0
Dana's Lucky Lady	2	F	4	2	0	1	80,219	Dance Spark	6	M	1	0	0	0	40
Dana's Promice	3	F	4	0	0	0	144	Dance Star	4	F	4	1	1	0	21,240
Dana's Swish	3	F	4	0	1	0	3,108	Dance Stepper	4	G	1	0	0	0	0
Dana's Wild Gal	4	F	5	0	2	0	1,980	Dance Sweetly	3	F	9	0	0	0	945
Danbuck	12	G	9	0	0	1	1,870	Dance the Green	3	F	10	1	0	1	18,196
Dancal (IRE)	5	M	9	3	2	0	223,011	Dance the Slew	5	M	6	2	1	1	71,420
Dancaway	7	M	11	0	1	0	3,475	Dance Til Morning	9	G	2	0	0	1	583
Dance a Bit	5	G	16	2	2	1	12,832	Dance Til Nine	4	C	2	0	0	1	2,100
Dance Affair	4	G	9	1	2	0	24,770	Dance to Dawn	4	F	6	0	0	0	775
Dance All Night	2	F	2	0	0	1	4,510	Dance to Destiny	4	C	7	3	3	1	150,350
Dance Aly Dance	3	G	11	2	4	1	29,994	Dance West	6	G	4	0	0	0	0
Dance and Dazzle	5	G	7	1	2	1	34,951	Dance Winner	2	F	2	0	0	0	840
Dance and Whirl	5	M	7	2	1	2	8,919	Dance With a Fool	6	G	4	0	0	0	646
Dance Apollo	3	C	5	1	0	1	43,947	Dance With Bo	3	F	4	0	0	1	1,145
Dance Around Table	4	F	3	0	0	0	137	Dance With Genie	3	F	1	0	0	0	103
Dance At Dawn	3	F	11	0	0	0	1,043	Dance With Jenny	4	F	7	0	0	0	0
Dance At Pappas	3	F	4	0	0	0	84	Dance With Kelly	7	H	10	0	0	1	593
Dance Away Home	2	C	8	0	0	1	3,416	Dance With Me Dear	3	F	1	0	1	0	2,520
Dance Dance	4	F	12	4	4	0	53,070	Dance With Pride	3	G	12	2	4	2	15,770
Dance Date	2	F	7	0	1	4	8,500	Dance With Reason	5	M	6	2	0	1	14,820
Dance Delight	6	M	2	0	0	0	261	Dance With Teddi	3	F	6	0	0	0	1,964
Dance Dime	5	M	12	1	2	3	19,182	Dance Withthephone	3	G	2	0	0	0	0
Dance Engagement	3	C	7	2	1	0	155,499	Danceacide	5	M	2	0	0	0	625
Dance Fee	2	F	7	1	2	3	39,950	Danceandbefestive	2	G	7	1	1	0	11,100
Dance Figure	4	F	4	2	0	0	9,500	Danceascore	4	G	1	0	0	0	0
Dance for Debbie	3	F	3	0	0	0	160	Danceaway Dixie	3	F	7	2	1	1	10,670
Dance for Diamonds	5	G	10	1	0	2	9,600	Danceaway Girl	2	F	2	0	0	0	0
Dance for Freedom	3	F	10	2	1	1	10,701	Dancedetide	4	F	4	0	0	1	7,084
Dance for Fun	3	G	13	4	1	0	50,102	Danceforprincessem	3	F	2	0	1	0	1,800
Dance for Gold	6	M	17	3	5	2	37,330	Dancefortyniner	2	C	1	1	0	0	15,600
Dance for John	5	G	15	2	1	3	17,160	Danceing Deano	5	H	17	3	1	2	6,697
Dance for Jove	10	G	1	0	0	1	420	Danceingann	2	F	1	0	0	0	0
Dance for Romeo	3	C	2	0	0	1	3,190	Danceinthecircus	3	F	12	3	0	2	13,354
Dance for Rosel	10	G	5	0	0	2	2,502	Danceinthestreets	3	F	11	7	0	1	175,710
Dance for Sheree	6	M	1	0	0	0	57	Danceinthevalley	4	G	11	0	0	4	5,195
Dance Hall Dandy	3	C	9	0	0	3	4,390	Dancelike a Shadow	8	G	2	0	0	1	1,330
Dance Hall Girl	3	F	10	1	2	4	66,205	Dancemaker	2	C	4	0	0	1	2,569
Dance Hall Hero	3	C	8	1	3	2	37,410	Dance'n in the Red	6	M	10	2	0	1	7,001
Dance Hall Lily	4	F	9	0	0	0	1,758	Dancen in the Sun	5	M	10	1	1	1	69,490
Dance Hall Prize	5	G	5	0	0	0	226	Danceobeahthenight	6	G	8	2	2	1	17,643

Horse	Age	Sex	Sts	1st	2d	3d	Won	Horse	Age	Sex	Sts	1st	2d	3d	Won
Danceoftheflags	4	F	13	1	1	2	29,340	Dancinatthegate	2	F	2	0	0	0	0
Danceonthetable	3	G	7	0	0	1	805	Dancing (GB)	4	F	7	2	0	0	60,625
Dancephone	10	G	4	0	0	0	380	Dancing Air	3	F	2	0	0	0	80
Dancer and You	3	G	12	1	0	3	21,673	Dancing Amelia	5	M	3	0	0	1	2,650
Dancer C C	4	F	9	0	1	1	5,289	Dancing Baba	2	C	2	0	0	0	3,550
Dancer Cielo	4	G	6	0	1	1	11,640	Dancing Bag	4	G	8	1	0	2	8,547
Dancer Dancer	9	M	5	0	0	1	1,386	Dancing Banner	4	G	6	0	0	3	16,020
Dancer Memo	3	F	6	0	1	1	5,145	Dancing Blues	4	F	11	0	1	2	26,080
Dancer Sonata	3	G	21	1	2	2	16,610	Dancing Bonnie	5	M	9	0	0	1	3,001
Dancer's Agenda	3	F	8	0	1	0	1,417	Dancing Bride	4	F	5	0	1	2	2,910
Dancers Blossom	6	M	2	0	0	0	0	Dancing Bull	6	G	15	3	2	3	50,315
Dancer's Code	3	F	1	0	0	1	2,750	Dancing Cajun	4	F	11	1	0	2	5,594
Dancers Dandy	7	M	1	0	0	0	0	Dancing Canaveral	5	M	7	0	0	1	1,849
Dancers Finale	6	M	8	0	0	0	572	Dancing Capote	5	M	8	4	3	0	132,825
Dancer's Flyer	2	C	4	0	0	0	1,416	Dancing Carmela	3	F	2	0	0	0	0
Dancer's Guest	4	G	10	1	3	3	117,268	Dancing Chequer	4	F	19	1	4	6	14,778
Dancer's Hill	2	G	1	0	0	0	0	Dancing Coins	2	F	2	1	0	0	5,462
Dancer's Into It	3	F	5	1	1	1	7,875	Dancing Creek	3	F	7	0	0	1	1,985
Dancer's J B	4	G	1	0	0	0	91	Dancing Crisis	4	F	6	0	0	1	1,060
Dancers Magic	4	G	1	1	0	0	13,424	Dancing Dames	2	F	8	1	1	2	23,480
Dancers Memories	6	G	8	1	0	1	5,270	Dancing Das	4	F	3	0	0	0	690
Dancers Pal	4	F	13	0	0	1	994	Dancing Dee	7	M	9	1	3	0	24,270
Dancer's Pallisade	4	G	8	1	1	1	24,471	Dancing Deer	4	F	18	5	3	1	60,110
Dancer's Prospect	3	F	8	2	3	1	38,670	Dancing Diabla	3	F	2	0	0	0	0
Dancer's Rage	5	G	14	0	4	1	5,736	Dancing Dickie	8	G	15	2	1	0	10,001
Dancer's Truelaugh	7	M	1	0	0	0	122	Dancing Dilemma	4	F	12	1	0	1	14,819
Dancer's Wish	6	G	10	3	0	3	62,160	Dancing Doc	4	G	10	1	0	2	4,956
Dances Alone	4	C	4	0	0	0	230	Dancing Dragon	6	M	1	1	0	0	5,040
Dances Like Velvet	3	F	7	2	0	3	33,800	Dancing Eyes	5	M	5	1	1	1	5,250
Dances On Clouds	3	F	14	1	5	2	31,335	Dancing for Carlos	9	G	9	0	1	1	4,950
Dances With Joy	3	G	9	2	1	2	36,990	Dancing for Dinner	2	F	3	0	0	0	265
Dancethebluesaway	4	F	14	0	0	1	9,125	Dancing Friends	5	M	4	0	0	0	150
Dancethenightrenee	4	F	1	0	0	0	0	Dancing Fruition	3	F	4	1	0	1	8,132
Dancetillmidnight	3	C	1	0	0	0	0	Dancing Gamble	6	H	3	0	0	0	290
Danceville	3	G	2	1	0	0	5,938	Dancing Glory	3	F	4	0	1	0	6,910
Dancewel	6	G	6	1	2	1	26,000	Dancing Guy	8	G	10	1	1	2	103,740
Dancewithadolly	4	F	9	1	3	1	21,600	Dancing Harriett	5	M	1	0	0	0	0
Dancewithasoldier	3	F	8	2	1	2	99,849	Dancing Heniu	4	G	10	1	1	2	9,149
Dancewithavictor	6	G	11	2	3	2	36,640	Dancing Hertfield	3	F	4	0	0	0	1,494
Dancewithavixen	3	F	11	8	2	0	335,921	Dancing Hills	3	F	5	1	0	1	5,490
Dancewithmeashley	5	M	7	2	0	2	7,615	Dancing Hing	2	F	1	1	0	0	4,800
Dancewithmercedes	3	F	7	0	1	2	8,337	Dancing Home	3	G	10	0	1	0	4,125
Dancewithmewesley	4	F	2	0	0	1	625	Dancing Hope	4	G	2	0	0	0	678
Danceyourheartout	3	F	11	2	0	2	24,130	Dancing in Puddles	5	M	9	4	0	0	50,400
Dancin B B	7	M	9	0	0	2	4,078	Dancing in the Fog	4	G	13	3	3	0	50,672
Dancin' Barefoot	4	F	3	0	1	0	2,200	Dancing Indiscreet	5	M	2	0	0	1	4,620
Dancin Beauty	4	F	10	1	0	1	10,137	Dancing Jet G	3	F	3	0	0	0	807
Dancin Candy	2	G	5	1	3	0	20,490	Dancing Jo Jo	3	G	7	0	0	0	263
Dancin' Cat	4	C	2	0	0	0	382	Dancing Jones	3	F	3	0	0	0	555
Dancin Chilly	2	F	3	0	0	0	365	Dancing Julius	2	G	1	0	0	0	182
Dancin Christy	3	F	1	0	0	0	288	Dancing Kack	5	G	4	2	0	0	8,850
Dancin Daddy	5	H	1	0	0	0	0	Dancing Kakie	5	M	8	1	1	1	4,026
Dancin' Daphne	4	F	1	0	0	0	240	Dancing King	3	G	7	3	0	1	44,160
Dancin Daze	4	F	5	0	3	2	7,840	Dancing Knockout	3	C	3	1	1	0	23,680
Dancin' Dickens	3	G	6	0	0	0	0	Dancing Lara	3	F	2	0	0	0	0
Dancin Doll	3	F	12	1	2	0	14,160	Dancing Lass	4	F	5	0	1	1	3,392
Dancin Dottie	2	F	6	0	1	1	14,254	Dancing Laur	3	F	9	1	0	1	20,295
Dancin Dusty	2	C	6	0	2	2	22,290	Dancing Lee	3	F	7	1	0	2	8,092
Dancin Falcon	5	G	10	2	4	0	61,756	Dancing Lehsa	2	F	1	0	0	0	0
Dancin for Gold	3	F	13	1	4	1	45,587	Dancing Lettie	3	F	6	0	0	1	1,730
Dancin Girl	4	F	14	5	1	2	88,150	Dancing Liebling	2	F	1	0	0	0	120
Dancin in Dodge	9	G	2	0	0	0	300	Dancing Madison	4	F	1	0	0	0	255
Dancin in the Dark	4	F	15	1	0	1	6,496	Dancing Manila	7	M	18	5	3	1	8,744
Dancin in the Wind	3	F	13	2	2	3	36,431	Dancing Master (IRE)	5	H	2	1	0	1	16,310
Dancin Jean	4	F	9	1	1	1	5,419	Dancing Meg	2	F	2	0	0	0	125
Dancin Joey	4	G	4	3	1	0	106,960	Dancing Miss	2	F	2	0	0	0	666
Dancin Kaity	5	M	18	2	1	2	11,582	Dancing Missile	5	H	3	0	0	0	1,380
Dancin Kelly Z	2	F	5	1	2	1	19,500	Dancing Nijinsky	6	M	2	0	0	0	93
Dancin Kristina	2	F	6	0	0	0	2,040	Dancing On a Dime	3	F	12	0	0	1	2,116
Dancin Lance	3	G	6	2	1	0	31,882	Dancing On a Star	2	G	2	1	0	0	8,820
Dancin Mortlock	2	G	2	0	0	0	0	Dancing On Air	5	M	3	1	0	1	3,700
Dancin Rahy	3	H	7	3	0	0	29,070	Dancing On the Bar	5	G	4	1	0	0	3,720
Dancin Red Wolf	7	G	7	0	3	0	24,560	Dancing Outloud	4	F	4	0	0	1	330
Dancin Regiment	7	M	12	0	2	0	2,488	Dancing Pits	4	G	5	0	0	0	438
Dancin too Close	3	F	2	0	1	0	560	Dancing Promise	4	F	1	0	0	0	0
Dancin With Motion	2	F	1	0	0	0	100	Dancing Raptor	2	G	3	1	0	1	19,370
Dancin With Tori	3	F	3	0	1	1	9,120	Dancing Rasha	2	F	1	0	0	0	0
Dancinandsingin	2	F	2	0	1	0	8,600	Dancing Rebel	7	G	5	1	1	0	18,130
Dancinasfastasican	2	F	2	0	0	1	3,530	Dancing Sands (NZ)	5	M	11	4	3	0	83,150

Horse	Age	Sex	Sts	1st	2d	3d	Won
Dancing Shawklit	3	F	2	1	0	0	16,800
Dancing Snowflake	6	M	2	0	0	0	206
Dancing Spell	6	M	14	1	0	4	9,763
Dancing Spray	3	F	8	2	1	1	60,946
Dancing Steal	5	G	3	1	0	0	2,640
Dancing Streak	3	F	4	0	0	0	197
Dancing Thief	2	F	5	0	0	0	836
Dancing to Victory	3	F	2	0	0	0	0
Dancing Ty	4	G	12	0	2	1	9,867
Dancing Wager	5	G	5	0	0	0	1,930
Dancing Warren	4	C	8	1	2	2	31,840
Dancing Western	3	F	5	0	1	1	2,912
Dancing With Luck	4	C	4	0	0	1	2,027
Dancing With Me	4	F	9	2	0	0	52,155
Dancing Withthelaw	4	G	16	1	3	3	8,905
Dancingabit	2	G	7	0	0	0	471
Dancinginflorida	3	F	4	1	0	2	8,495
Dancingintheforest	3	C	3	0	0	0	45
Dancingintherain	5	M	9	2	3	0	34,168
Dancinginthesky	2	G	10	0	0	1	6,580
Dancinginthewoods	3	G	6	0	0	0	189
Dancinglion	3	G	2	0	0	0	0
Dancingonthewater	3	F	3	0	0	0	644
Dancingstardiamond	3	F	6	0	1	0	2,500
Dancingwithangel	4	G	5	0	0	0	678
Dancingwithbear	5	H	9	2	1	0	9,746
Dancingwithboots	4	F	2	0	0	0	0
Dancingwithpassion	4	F	20	4	1	2	36,611
Dancininthenight	3	G	16	0	0	1	6,838
Dancinonadare	5	G	4	1	1	1	2,850
Dancinthenightaway	2	C	3	0	0	0	730
Dancinwiththunder	3	C	8	0	0	0	2,395
Danciyan	3	C	3	0	0	0	0
Dancret	4	F	3	0	0	0	174
Dancy Sun	6	M	5	1	0	1	2,590
Dandee's Beau	4	C	6	0	0	0	816
Dandello	7	H	5	0	0	0	312
Dandenong	5	G	9	0	2	2	6,388
Dandi Candi	3	G	22	2	1	0	15,336
Dandione	4	F	13	1	3	1	23,969
Dand'or	6	G	14	2	3	2	22,744
Dandy Alibhai	6	G	10	1	0	0	12,912
Dandy Belle	2	F	13	0	2	1	5,840
Dandy Breeze	4	F	1	0	0	0	172
Dandy Dancer	7	G	2	0	0	0	0
Dandy Dane	3	C	4	0	0	0	3,960
Dandy Devil	5	H	2	0	0	0	294
Dandy Don	6	H	3	0	0	1	314
Dandy Dulce	5	M	11	1	3	3	25,130
Dandy Gentleman	3	C	2	0	0	0	0
Dandy Opportunity	6	G	14	1	2	2	11,800
Dandy Princess	4	F	4	0	0	1	7,265
Dandy Rose	3	F	6	2	0	0	35,650
Dandy Senor	5	H	7	0	1	1	2,033
Dandy Squall	3	G	7	1	2	2	34,340
Dandys to the Bank	7	G	6	0	0	0	0
Dane Again	8	G	5	0	0	0	288
Danehills Grandson	3	G	1	0	0	0	0
Daneleta (IRE)	4	F	5	0	2	0	16,540
Danesbury	2	C	6	1	0	1	32,515
Danesfort	6	G	6	0	1	0	3,930
Danett's Score	3	F	7	0	0	1	2,520
Dangel	3	G	9	2	3	0	26,964
Danger Ahead	3	G	7	1	2	0	9,950
Danger Crocodile	9	G	7	2	1	0	16,295
Danger Point	3	C	8	1	0	0	35,965
Danger Quest	2	C	2	0	1	1	6,360
Danger Ranger	12	H	4	0	0	0	998
Dangerous Delight	5	M	2	1	0	1	12,960
Dangerous Girl	5	M	14	0	1	0	18,358
Dangerous Justice	4	G	9	1	1	0	16,370
Dangerous Thing	3	F	4	1	1	0	5,200
Dangerous Woman	2	F	5	0	0	2	4,800
Dangerously	2	F	5	0	1	1	7,555
Dangler	6	G	4	0	0	0	460
Dangling Dan	4	C	1	0	0	0	262
Dangling Numbers	6	G	3	0	0	0	320
Dangling Prospect	7	H	15	2	2	1	23,227
Dania Bay	5	M	8	0	4	1	30,320
Daniel Alexander	4	C	16	0	1	3	8,166
Daniel Striped Cat	6	G	14	0	1	6	4,399
Daniella F.	8	M	9	0	0	0	552
Danielles Magic	4	C	17	0	2	0	9,771
Danielo	2	G	4	1	0	0	10,934
Daniel's Boy	4	G	16	1	3	2	13,366
Daniel's Gift	2	C	1	0	0	0	0
Daniels Rocks	3	G	12	0	0	2	1,088
Danieltown	2	G	9	1	2	2	31,045
Danio	5	M	1	0	0	0	58
Dani's Bliss	3	C	1	0	0	1	1,155
Dani's Destiny	3	G	13	1	1	2	43,890
Danis Time	3	F	5	0	1	0	3,990
Danish Bonus	3	G	12	1	2	0	12,042
Danish Dancer (ARG)	4	C	2	0	1	0	8,840
Danish Danseur	3	G	8	2	2	1	15,240
Danish Fairytale (DEN)	3	F	8	1	0	1	54,797
Danish Gold	7	H	3	0	0	0	680
Daniz Slavic	3	C	5	0	1	1	3,160
Danjo	5	G	13	1	0	2	11,575
Danjurous	3	C	6	1	0	2	10,724
Danke Schoen	4	G	5	2	0	0	28,500
Danlee	5	H	6	1	0	2	13,469
Danlins World	9	G	3	0	1	1	5,459
Danner	4	C	14	4	0	3	30,500
Dann's Prospect	2	F	1	0	0	0	100
Danny B.	2	G	3	0	1	0	5,600
Danny Boy O'Leary	3	C	10	1	0	3	10,350
Danny C.	4	G	8	1	1	1	29,652
Danny Divver	2	G	2	0	0	0	200
Danny Dream Dancer	6	M	10	1	0	2	5,246
Danny E	5	G	2	0	1	0	5,220
Danny the Blade	3	G	9	2	0	0	14,240
Dannyboys Fortune	3	C	1	0	0	0	0
Danny's Alibi	4	C	8	2	1	1	8,409
Danny's Day	5	G	7	0	1	0	2,277
Danny's Emerald	3	C	5	0	3	1	4,679
Danny's Star	3	G	7	0	0	0	105
Dannys Storey	9	G	9	1	0	2	4,690
Dannys Tiger	6	G	10	0	1	4	5,959
Danny's Turn	6	G	4	0	0	0	60
Danny's Way	3	C	12	2	3	2	16,984
Danny's Wild Lass	3	F	4	0	0	1	2,141
Danotable's Star	4	G	3	0	0	0	0
Dan's Advantage	3	C	6	1	0	2	24,640
Dan's Cowboy	2	G	2	0	0	0	0
Dan's Groovy	7	G	13	5	0	2	62,761
Dan's Hand	6	G	12	5	2	1	15,460
Dans Rambler	7	M	10	1	1	3	5,971
Dan's Report	7	G	8	1	0	1	5,008
Dan's Sweetie	3	F	3	0	0	0	258
Dansalli	3	F	6	1	0	1	1,957
Danse de Sable	3	F	4	1	0	0	22,200
Danse Du Mort	3	F	1	0	0	0	895
Danse Du Sabre	9	M	18	2	1	3	20,321
Dansi	3	G	3	0	0	0	100
Dansil's Angel	4	F	3	1	0	0	4,590
Danswithalexis	2	F	1	0	0	0	0
Dante's Devil	4	C	3	0	0	0	0
Dante's Rocket	4	F	4	0	3	1	19,240
Danthebluegrassman	4	C	5	2	0	0	91,630
Danubio (MEX)	8	H	12	1	0	2	11,600
Danuta	3	F	4	2	1	0	280,000
Danyell Lee	3	F	15	1	0	5	5,605
Danyelle's Court	7	M	9	1	0	1	9,284
Danyelle's Tabby	4	F	14	0	1	3	12,272
Danz	3	G	13	0	2	1	8,144
Danz Music	5	M	4	0	0	1	704
Danza	6	G	6	0	0	0	904
Danzafina	2	C	5	1	0	2	7,530
Danzalnite	2	C	5	0	1	0	4,023
Danzalore	2	F	1	0	0	0	115
Danzaman	6	G	10	2	2	3	39,910
Danzanaskra	3	G	4	0	0	0	417
Danzarina Gaucha	3	F	14	2	3	0	16,844
Danzasouth	3	F	13	1	0	0	33,349
Danzatames Award	3	F	7	0	0	0	1,320
Danzatames Reality	3	F	5	0	1	2	17,470
Danzatore Flag	9	G	6	0	0	1	2,130

Horse	Age	Sex	Sts	1st	2d	3d	Won	Horse	Age	Sex	Sts	1st	2d	3d	Won
Danzette	3	F	3	0	0	0	364	Dark Cloud	2	C	1	0	0	0	145
Danzhound	4	G	12	2	4	1	61,375	Dark Command	3	G	1	1	0	0	22,800
Danziana	2	F	1	0	0	0	540	Dark Demon	3	G	3	0	0	0	274
Danzig Em	8	M	1	0	0	0	0	Dark Denim	2	F	6	1	1	0	10,510
Danzig Good Time	3	G	8	0	1	0	2,400	Dark Devil	7	H	9	2	3	1	13,325
Danzig in the Dark	2	G	3	1	1	0	12,030	Dark Entry	7	G	7	0	0	0	225
Danzigca	6	M	13	1	3	3	32,040	Dark Equation	2	C	2	0	0	0	975
Danzig's Farewell	2	C	4	0	0	0	1,371	Dark Fever	3	G	8	2	1	0	16,780
Danzig's Gold	4	G	8	2	0	2	4,675	Dark Fool	7	G	8	2	0	1	3,690
Danzig's Peace	5	G	11	1	0	0	7,687	Dark Fuse	4	C	13	1	0	0	38,625
Danzig's Snapshot	3	C	2	0	0	0	0	Dark Guest	6	G	1	0	0	0	35
Danzig's Sword	7	G	12	1	0	0	9,978	Dark Harbor	9	G	8	0	2	1	3,328
Danzilation	5	G	1	0	0	0	0	Dark Intent	3	G	10	2	0	2	19,320
Danzin Tyson	2	C	9	1	2	0	11,589	Dark Knight	4	G	3	0	0	0	0
Danzit All	2	F	2	0	0	1	4,200	Dark Lightning	2	C	1	0	0	0	2,160
Dapaciti	4	F	1	0	0	0	47	Dark Magic	5	G	9	4	0	0	10,382
Dapper Dandy	2	C	2	0	0	0	0	Dark Mist	4	F	1	0	0	1	550
Dapper Danny	2	C	2	0	0	0	592	Dark N Wicked	4	G	10	0	1	2	6,107
Dappers Chance	3	C	1	0	0	0	258	Dark Okie	3	G	3	1	0	0	4,840
Dappledan	4	G	15	3	2	0	25,705	Dark Prince	4	C	1	0	0	0	0
Dar You Go	4	F	3	0	0	0	192	Dark Prospect	3	C	7	2	0	2	8,928
Darbie D	4	F	5	1	0	0	8,488	Dark Rain	4	G	9	1	0	0	8,477
Darby Creek Dancer	2	F	4	0	0	0	420	Dark Rapids	4	F	7	1	2	0	18,400
Darby Creek Doc	4	C	11	3	1	2	16,929	Dark Rhodes	4	G	16	0	1	2	2,974
Darby Creek Honey	6	M	14	2	4	1	19,250	Dark Sage	3	F	6	0	0	0	0
Darby Haven	4	F	3	0	1	0	2,813	Dark Sorcerer (GB)	4	G	2	1	0	1	36,960
Darby Lane	4	F	9	2	1	2	20,575	Dark Starling	3	F	3	0	0	1	450
Darby's Boy	4	G	4	0	0	2	3,012	Dark Starlite	3	F	2	0	0	0	0
Darby's Charm	4	F	6	0	3	2	25,950	Dark Tigerlily	6	M	6	0	0	0	288
Darby's Lateststar	4	F	1	0	0	0	0	Dark Token	3	C	4	1	0	0	5,598
Darcellama	2	F	1	0	0	0	0	Dark Torment	4	F	3	1	0	0	7,925
Darcys Sister	5	M	18	2	3	4	30,471	Dark Venture	5	H	10	0	0	1	1,360
Dardanelles	5	M	7	0	0	1	1,500	Dark Whisper	3	C	5	2	0	0	52,980
Dare About	5	M	5	0	1	0	1,740	Darker Than Gold	5	G	4	1	1	0	8,460
Dare Emily	5	M	8	2	1	1	3,642	Darkest Night	3	C	4	0	0	0	252
Dare Erika	3	F	4	0	0	0	330	Darkinvader	6	G	15	5	3	1	32,034
Dare Made Me Go	4	G	11	0	0	0	0	Darklighter	9	G	3	0	0	0	180
Dare My Valentine	4	F	11	1	1	2	6,466	Darkly Noon	3	G	8	2	2	1	48,525
Dare She Goes	5	M	8	0	1	1	12,980	Darkman	6	H	5	0	0	0	510
Dare the Devil	3	C	1	0	0	0	100	Dark'n Debonaire	2	F	1	0	0	0	130
Dare to Be Cool	4	C	3	0	0	0	490	Darkness	2	F	1	1	0	0	11,780
Dare to Be Great	3	G	19	2	5	3	60,330	Darkness At Dawn	4	C	4	0	0	0	0
Dare to Be Wild	5	G	14	1	1	1	11,990	Darknessontheedge	4	G	4	0	1	0	10,960
Dare to Fly	3	G	4	0	0	1	792	Darkus	4	F	11	1	3	3	20,074
Dare to Rum	3	C	6	1	1	0	7,645	Darkworth	8	G	9	0	0	0	244
Dare to Run	5	H	12	1	3	0	13,643	Darla Darla	6	M	5	0	0	0	60
Daredevil Adam	4	C	16	3	2	2	36,452	Darlanda	6	M	15	2	4	2	22,792
Darenda	5	M	3	0	0	1	4,460	Darlene and Nick	5	G	1	0	0	0	0
Darentogo	2	G	5	0	1	1	3,442	Darlene's Daughter	3	F	7	1	0	0	16,432
Dareto	4	C	7	1	1	1	15,450	Darlin Barbie	4	F	2	1	0	0	14,520
Darewood Park	4	C	7	0	1	0	2,028	Darlin Corey	3	F	7	0	2	0	16,046
Darfromaphar	7	M	1	0	0	0	0	Darlin Desire'	4	F	9	1	1	0	6,561
Darien's Approval	2	G	3	0	2	0	5,180	Darlin Maggie	2	F	3	1	0	1	15,820
Daring Bert	4	G	4	0	0	0	445	Darlin Tom	3	C	7	1	0	0	7,890
Daring Bid	5	H	6	1	0	1	10,806	Darlinchil	2	F	2	0	0	0	990
Daring Carolina	4	F	7	0	0	0	0	Darling Aly	6	M	2	1	0	0	3,060
Daring Colors	4	F	13	0	1	3	8,070	Darling Angel	3	F	8	0	1	1	3,223
Daring Daygata	2	G	6	0	0	0	1,152	Darling Betz	7	M	6	0	0	0	1,698
Daring Deeds	7	G	5	1	0	0	4,220	Darling Bobi	7	M	6	1	1	0	11,740
Daring Dennis	6	G	12	2	0	0	21,762	Darling Bride	6	M	2	0	1	1	13,640
Daring Messenger	4	C	3	0	0	0	405	Darling Daphne	4	F	2	0	0	0	94
Daring Mood	2	C	2	1	0	1	8,712	Darling Demon	3	F	7	1	3	0	37,160
Daring Pegasus	5	G	10	2	1	3	48,560	Darling Deputy	5	M	3	0	0	0	3,151
Daring Six	2	C	3	0	0	0	0	Darling Diazo	3	F	1	0	0	0	0
Daring Skipper	3	C	4	0	0	0	909	Darling Edna	3	F	3	0	0	0	0
Daring Smile	4	F	9	3	1	1	40,905	Darling Katey	5	M	5	1	1	1	72,254
Daring Wager	3	G	13	0	0	0	1,348	Darling Kris	5	M	12	2	3	2	39,935
Daring Wit	3	F	7	0	0	0	849	Darling Sandy	3	G	16	2	2	3	10,387
Darinquest	6	M	9	0	3	0	5,114	Darling Stal	6	M	7	0	1	2	2,789
Darios Fire	2	C	1	0	0	0	2,500	Darlyon	3	G	2	0	0	0	0
Dariyoun in Motion	4	F	12	4	0	1	19,854	Darn Bad Cat	3	G	4	0	0	2	1,318
Dariyoun's Command	9	G	9	0	1	2	1,690	Darn Crazy	2	F	1	0	1	0	4,340
Dark Amour	5	G	1	0	0	0	0	Darn That Cat	5	M	17	2	2	3	19,670
Dark Avenue	4	G	2	0	0	0	1,650	Darn That Cobra	2	G	3	1	1	1	13,923
Dark Bark	6	M	10	3	2	1	19,786	Darn That Jack	4	C	12	2	0	1	9,976
Dark Bay	5	M	11	3	2	2	11,083	Darn Tipalarm	10	G	7	2	2	2	36,500
Dark Cape	3	G	2	0	0	0	1,865	Darn Tootin	7	G	8	0	0	2	9,027
Dark Carr	6	H	5	0	1	2	2,358	Darn Wild	2	F	5	2	0	1	28,090
Dark Chocolate	3	G	10	1	0	0	3,420	Darn Yankee	3	G	3	0	0	0	1,260

Horse	Age	Sex	Sts	1st	2d	3d	Won
Darned Alarm	4	G	18	2	4	2	39,927
Darned Bold	4	G	25	6	4	2	47,063
Darnell's Dream	6	M	12	0	0	0	0
Darnestown	4	F	6	0	2	1	33,850
Darnley's Number	3	C	2	0	0	0	0
Darnthatjordan	3	C	3	0	1	1	2,253
Darnthefrost	3	G	3	0	0	1	1,092
D'aroak	4	F	10	4	1	2	41,689
Darrellinthehall	5	G	3	1	1	1	1,664
Darrow's Legacy	10	G	4	1	1	0	4,888
Darsara	4	G	9	1	1	1	3,967
Darsela	4	F	8	1	3	1	30,491
Dart	3	F	4	0	0	1	4,160
Dart for Dough	5	G	9	2	1	2	39,744
Dart Parade (ARG)	5	H	17	2	3	2	58,760
Darth	8	G	16	3	0	1	13,935
Darth Bader	5	G	2	0	0	0	0
Darting Dot	4	F	5	1	0	3	16,330
Daruty	3	G	8	0	1	0	993
Darva's Fling	4	F	4	0	0	0	0
Darwood	5	H	5	0	0	1	1,081
Daryl's Birthday	5	G	9	3	0	1	28,900
Das Clever	6	M	4	1	2	0	6,936
Das Flask	7	H	3	0	0	0	0
Das Is Alles	3	F	9	1	1	3	30,360
Das Wish	4	F	2	0	0	1	1,400
Dash Built	3	C	3	0	0	0	0
Dash Dot	3	F	13	0	2	0	3,660
Dash for Daylight	6	G	11	2	1	3	87,445
Dash for Money	3	F	5	0	1	1	28,602
Dash Home	3	F	7	2	1	0	44,940
Dash Inside	3	F	9	1	0	1	18,178
Dash Man	2	C	1	0	0	0	
Dash 'n Dance	5	H	12	0	0	3	37,540
Dash of Blue	5	M	12	3	3	2	9,844
Dash On Holme	7	M	9	3	1	0	38,372
Dash Rendar	2	C	1	0	0	0	100
Dasha Viking	4	F	10	1	0	2	4,734
Dashanella	3	F	9	0	1	3	3,427
Dashboard Drummer	2	G	4	3	0	1	157,600
Dasheen	4	F	10	0	2	3	24,963
Dasher n' Dancer	3	G	6	0	0	0	583
Dashhound	3	F	16	3	0	3	18,746
Dashigoes	3	F	6	0	0	0	409
Dashin' Devon	6	G	5	1	2	0	2,071
Dashin N Cattin	4	G	9	1	2	1	8,470
Dashincase	3	C	1	0	0	0	0
Dashing	4	G	1	0	0	0	0
Dashing Admiral	2	C	1	1	0	0	22,860
Dashing Ariel	3	F	3	1	0	0	6,345
Dashing Count	3	C	1	0	0	0	0
Dashing Darla	4	F	15	1	1	6	21,988
Dashing Dawn	5	H	4	0	0	0	172
Dashing Deputy	2	C	3	1	0	0	31,050
Dashing Derby	2	C	2	0	0	0	0
Dashing Destiny	3	C	11	0	3	3	21,700
Dashing Diva	2	F	2	0	0	0	0
Dashing Express	2	F	2	1	1	0	9,600
Dashing Girl	5	M	8	0	1	1	6,700
Dashing in Dixie	3	C	3	0	0	0	360
Dashing Knight	3	C	7	0	0	0	998
Dashing Lady	8	F	8	2	1	3	18,805
Dashing Lover	5	M	2	0	0	0	164
Dashing Monty	2	C	2	0	0	0	0
Dashing Princess	2	F	2	0	0	0	243
Dashing Regent	3	C	9	0	0	1	3,176
Dashing Shannan	8	M	3	0	0	0	0
Dash'n Danielle	4	F	7	2	1	0	27,322
Dashof Panache	3	F	9	1	0	2	5,035
Dasini	5	H	6	0	0	1	1,560
Dasl Cammy	2	F	1	0	0	1	3,300
Dastardly Dan	3	C	9	3	1	0	22,853
Data Stream	2	G	3	0	0	1	3,210
Database	4	F	9	3	3	1	106,860
Date	3	F	2	0	0	0	300
Date Me	3	F	9	0	0	0	1,150
Date More Minors	5	H	7	0	1	0	10,496
Date Night	2	F	1	0	0	0	0
Date Tree Bay	3	F	8	3	2	0	48,064

Horse	Age	Sex	Sts	1st	2d	3d	Won
Datebook	2	G	5	0	1	3	7,250
Dating Prospect	9	G	13	2	2	0	21,346
Dation	4	G	10	0	3	0	9,780
Dato Dancer	7	G	3	0	0	0	330
Dats All Folks	4	C	9	2	0	1	9,197
Dats Y	7	H	3	1	0	0	1,300
Datt Way	3	F	8	0	2	1	21,970
Dattt's My Luck	3	C	10	1	1	0	12,440
Daunte	4	G	6	1	1	2	14,703
Daunting	5	G	11	5	1	0	201,405
Daunting Presence	5	G	5	0	0	0	0
Dauntless Hero	3	C	5	0	0	1	2,712
Dauphin	6	G	1	0	0	0	3,660
Dave	2	G	6	0	0	0	4,980
Dave the Dude	2	C	5	2	0	0	112,800
Davene	4	F	10	3	2	1	19,905
Daves Baby	4	F	6	0	3	1	8,837
Dave's Cahill Boy	3	C	4	2	0	0	15,703
Daves Little Girl	6	M	3	0	0	0	70
Dave's Moment	8	G	13	0	2	5	14,325
Davesday	6	G	11	2	1	2	34,400
Davey's Cutlass	7	H	11	2	4	0	67,080
David Strike Back	3	G	4	1	1	0	1,781
Davida's Destiny	3	G	2	0	0	0	0
David's Best Bet	2	G	6	1	0	0	12,069
David's C Biscuit	2	C	4	1	1	1	12,400
David's Destiny	5	M	18	1	4	4	20,720
David's Dignity	3	F	10	2	1	2	23,288
David's Dilemma	3	F	5	1	0	0	25,830
David's Dottie	3	F	2	0	0	0	225
David's Dream	10	G	7	0	1	1	5,032
Davids Expectation	4	C	13	2	3	1	177,976
David's Goal	3	F	6	0	1	1	1,872
David's Groom	6	H	13	3	3	0	15,607
David's Halo	4	G	4	1	0	0	5,145
David's Islander	2	C	1	0	0	0	0
David's Limit	2	G	2	0	0	0	360
David's Melody	3	F	5	1	1	1	7,440
David's Project	4	F	7	3	2	1	17,925
Davis Eyes	4	F	3	0	0	0	0
Davis's Punch	3	F	6	1	1	1	11,723
Davonic (GB)	6	G	12	0	3	2	27,695
Davonnier	3	G	5	0	0	0	922
Davvy	7	G	20	2	0	9	10,891
Davy Jones	5	G	7	0	1	1	6,460
Dawg Fan	3	G	10	2	2	3	18,408
Dawn Charger	5	M	16	2	3	3	28,745
Dawn Edition	5	M	11	1	3	1	90,072
Dawn Exodus	8	G	9	2	1	2	29,706
Dawn Good	7	G	6	0	0	0	0
Dawn of the Condor	6	G	8	0	1	1	15,380
Dawn Renee	4	F	8	1	0	1	4,437
Dawn Till Dust	5	M	6	1	0	1	10,677
Dawn Wan	9	G	5	0	0	0	335
Dawn Watcher	5	G	10	1	1	2	79,004
Dawnabelle	4	F	7	0	0	0	252
Dawnie Wonder	2	F	1	0	0	0	0
Dawn's Amber Light	2	F	3	0	0	0	100
Dawn's Angel	2	F	1	0	0	0	0
Dawn's Baby	3	F	10	1	3	4	17,887
Dawns Ben	5	G	9	4	2	0	8,774
Dawn's Creek	4	C	13	1	1	2	25,538
Dawn's Deed	5	H	7	0	0	2	2,046
Dawns Early Dancer	2	C	5	1	1	0	6,616
Dawn's First Light	6	G	12	3	2	0	20,290
Dawn's Honey	4	F	13	1	2	2	12,947
Dawn's Magic Bag	3	F	2	0	0	0	0
Dawn's Moonlight	7	M	2	0	1	0	2,500
Dawn's Project	3	G	5	0	0	2	2,440
Dawn's Prospect	3	F	11	0	5	2	33,980
Dawn's Revenge	2	C	7	2	1	1	45,886
Dawn's Star	5	H	14	1	3	0	13,672
Dawson	6	G	5	0	0	0	752
Dawson Creek	9	M	7	0	1	1	3,111
Dawson Trail	3	C	3	1	0	0	29,600
Dawsy	7	H	9	1	0	2	2,632
Day At a Beach	4	C	1	0	0	0	0
Day At the Beach	6	M	8	0	1	0	1,176
Day Bue	5	G	12	1	1	0	34,984

Horse	Age	Sex	Sts	1st	2d	3d	Won	Horse	Age	Sex	Sts	1st	2d	3d	Won
Day Classes	4	F	1	1	0	0	6,489	De Braak's Proper	3	F	7	0	0	0	519
Day Court	2	F	3	1	0	0	5,700	De Braak's Special	9	G	3	0	0	0	86
Day Dream Buster	3	G	10	1	3	1	18,370	De Bunny	5	G	3	1	0	0	4,920
Day Flyer	3	C	17	1	0	1	10,171	De Casperis	9	G	3	0	0	0	0
Day Journey	6	H	5	1	1	0	3,175	De Chirrico	2	C	1	0	0	0	720
Day Later	4	F	4	0	1	2	4,520	De Coax	5	H	8	1	3	2	13,903
Day Long Trip	3	C	13	3	1	3	27,081	De Dancer	4	F	19	3	4	3	28,635
Day of Atonement	5	M	14	1	0	6	29,264	De Eat My Dust	4	C	2	0	0	0	0
Day of Infamy	3	G	2	0	0	1	1,560	De Force	3	C	4	0	0	0	339
Day of Judgement	12	G	12	1	0	2	4,033	De Franco	5	G	10	0	0	0	772
Day of Reckoning	3	F	4	0	0	1	1,298	De Gold Stuff	4	F	2	0	0	0	126
Day On the Bay	3	G	11	0	1	3	10,104	De la Cruz	6	H	10	2	1	0	6,876
Day Planner	4	F	2	0	1	0	2,725	De la Mothe	2	C	3	0	0	0	655
Day Secret	3	G	18	1	2	3	21,530	De Lamp	4	C	5	0	0	0	315
Day Trade	7	G	8	1	1	0	13,865	De Laroche (IRE)	4	F	5	1	0	1	33,612
Day Trader	4	C	1	0	0	0	0	De Magic Moment	2	C	3	0	0	1	4,066
Day Willy	3	F	6	0	0	1	4,870	De Mazien	4	G	4	0	0	0	159
Daydream Deelite	2	G	3	0	0	0	71	De Niro's Juel	4	C	10	0	0	1	2,210
Daydreaming	2	F	3	1	0	1	79,000	De Pollock	3	G	18	1	2	5	10,153
Daydreams	3	F	8	3	1	2	18,738	De Real Deal	4	C	2	0	0	0	2,070
Dayja Vu	4	F	6	0	0	1	1,815	De Roma	6	H	16	1	4	1	15,760
Dayjur Can	5	G	11	1	1	1	8,639	De Rose Colony	5	M	1	0	0	0	0
Dayla's Boy	3	G	3	0	0	2	1,610	De Shay	4	F	3	1	0	1	6,428
Daylason	2	G	5	0	2	1	5,705	De Sis	4	F	12	3	1	3	32,259
Daylene Machine	2	F	2	0	0	0	501	De Soto	6	G	5	1	1	0	5,400
Daylight	3	F	7	0	2	1	7,775	De Spike	3	G	11	2	3	0	9,928
Daylight Again	4	C	6	2	3	1	30,460	De Syn	3	F	1	0	0	0	225
Daylight Limited	5	M	2	0	0	0	525	De Troupe	4	G	2	0	0	1	1,210
Daylight Memory	5	M	8	1	1	0	3,903	De Valmont (AUS)	6	G	6	3	1	0	96,898
Daylight Robbery	3	F	16	1	7	1	42,294	De Witt	7	H	6	2	1	1	17,725
Daylightin Dizzy	6	H	7	1	2	1	11,075	Deacon Drive	4	G	7	0	1	0	2,470
Daynnightnightnday	5	G	6	0	0	0	1,990	Deacon Lake	3	F	16	4	4	2	150,237
Day's Sunset	3	F	8	1	0	1	21,280	Deacon Springs	4	G	13	4	3	3	60,190
Daysman	2	F	1	0	0	1	4,510	Dead Broke	3	G	5	0	1	0	5,050
Daytime Edition	2	C	2	0	0	0	0	Dead Centre	4	F	14	4	4	1	30,471
Daytime Riches	5	M	19	1	5	2	10,176	Dead Dog Gorgeous	3	F	6	1	1	1	4,416
Daytime Robbery	7	G	11	4	0	1	81,437	Dead Eye	5	G	2	0	0	0	124
Daytime Style	2	F	2	0	0	0	0	Dead Level	3	G	7	1	0	1	12,350
Dayton Flyer	5	H	5	0	0	0	7,759	Dead of Winter	4	F	19	2	4	2	43,899
Dayton Michael	2	G	2	0	0	0	370	Dead Ringer	2	C	4	0	0	2	6,940
Dayton's Bluff	6	G	9	0	0	1	1,261	Deadline	3	G	12	3	1	1	83,144
Dayvonna Express	5	M	5	0	0	0	2,044	Deadline Dude	9	G	12	0	0	1	13,722
Daz All Folks	5	M	5	0	0	1	858	Deadly Force	8	G	3	0	0	0	0
Dazed	4	F	4	3	0	1	40,300	Deadly Tonic	2	F	1	0	0	0	0
Dazed an Confused	4	F	8	0	1	1	7,320	Deadly Weapon	3	G	3	1	0	0	28,140
Dazu	2	C	7	1	1	1	8,210	Deal 'Em Jack	4	G	3	0	0	1	1,000
Dazzle Baby	5	M	1	0	0	0	0	Deal for the Wine	5	G	6	0	0	0	1,028
Dazzle Cat	3	F	6	2	0	1	5,765	Deal in Spades	3	G	2	0	0	1	3,420
Dazzle N Daze	5	M	13	0	0	0	1,588	Deal Me In	2	C	6	1	1	0	10,400
Dazzle Prince	7	G	6	2	0	0	8,486	Deal Me the Moon	6	M	4	2	0	0	13,940
Dazzle Some	5	H	10	0	4	1	11,702	Deal N Dollars	2	C	3	0	1	1	3,845
Dazzled Bayou	7	M	8	1	0	0	3,834	Deal Withthe Devil	3	F	7	2	1	3	32,800
Dazzlelikethis	4	F	10	2	1	1	23,120	Dealer	8	G	11	1	0	2	6,175
Dazzlem Fast	6	M	3	0	0	0	126	Dealer Choice (FR)	2	C	5	1	4	0	48,717
Dazzling American	2	C	4	1	1	1	14,225	Dealer's Delight	4	F	7	1	0	0	17,640
Dazzling Copies	3	F	10	2	2	1	22,225	Dealer's Dream	4	F	2	0	1	0	2,033
Dazzling Dana	5	M	12	2	4	1	21,359	Dealers Irish Kiss	2	F	3	1	0	0	7,991
Dazzling Deelite	3	F	5	2	1	0	43,870	Dealer's Suprise	4	G	7	1	0	0	7,466
Dazzling Diamonds	7	M	6	0	0	0	1,716	Dealfromtommyhill	3	G	6	0	0	0	405
Dazzling Fluff	4	F	8	1	2	1	10,094	Dealin Jo	5	H	10	2	0	0	7,046
Dazzling Gold	2	F	2	0	1	0	2,400	Dealing Shelby	4	G	12	2	0	1	8,348
Dazzling J. R.	4	C	9	2	2	0	7,868	Dealing With Daisy	3	F	4	0	0	0	2,155
Dazzling Jane	4	F	9	4	1	2	68,550	Dealingwiththeidle	4	G	14	1	2	0	6,536
Dazzling Rubies	4	F	10	1	3	3	58,182	Dealinwithinsanity	3	G	13	2	3	2	53,212
Dazzling Ruckus	5	G	1	0	0	0	105	Dealmenandmakeabuc	2	G	1	0	1	0	4,340
Dazzling Skies	3	F	9	0	1	2	4,700	Deals a Deal	2	G	1	0	0	0	130
Dazzling Spirit	3	G	9	1	1	0	39,280	Deamon's Flight	6	M	8	2	0	0	9,248
Dazzling Sunny	4	G	9	0	0	0	3,791	Dean Sperry	3	G	1	0	0	0	0
Dazzling Tara	5	M	6	0	0	0	300	Dean the Dude	5	G	20	1	0	3	6,780
Dazzling Twist	4	G	7	1	2	3	7,550	Deanie's Bow	6	M	7	0	0	0	368
Dazzling Water	6	G	3	0	0	0	356	Deanies Daydreamer	2	C	3	0	1	0	2,265
Dazzlingexcellence	3	G	12	0	0	0	822	Deanna M	5	M	2	1	0	0	5,325
Dazzlinpersonality	4	G	4	1	0	0	7,356	Deannies Express	2	G	1	0	0	0	0
Dazzmataz	4	G	14	1	2	1	36,343	Deans Alert	3	C	4	0	0	0	182
D'blazr	3	C	3	0	0	0	92	Dean's Baby	9	M	6	0	0	0	313
Dble Diamond Norma	2	F	6	0	0	0	185	Deans Digger	3	G	7	1	2	0	6,418
De Braaks Boy	3	C	5	1	1	1	9,365	Deans Flier	8	G	12	1	2	0	5,278
De Braak's Folly	9	G	7	0	0	0	210	Dean's Rose	2	G	5	0	0	1	1,656
De Braak's Luck	4	F	4	0	0	0	228	Deansdesign	4	F	4	0	0	0	0

Horse	Age	Sex	Sts	1st	2d	3d	Won
Dear Bull	2	C	3	1	1	0	26,012
Dear Daughter (GB)	5	M	1	0	0	0	0
Dear Debbie	4	F	8	0	1	1	1,681
Dear Delilah	2	F	5	1	0	3	24,260
Dear Demetri	8	G	5	0	1	1	4,674
Dear Deputy	3	F	12	3	1	4	35,258
Dear Dixie	2	F	2	0	0	0	0
Dear Emerald	2	F	2	0	0	0	970
Dear Fellow	5	H	6	0	0	0	945
Dear Hailey	6	H	2	0	1	0	882
Dear Hearts	4	F	6	1	0	4	8,524
Dear Hunter	5	G	4	1	0	1	16,843
Dear Jet	3	C	1	0	0	0	0
Dear John	7	H	12	1	2	1	6,085
Dear Me	5	M	5	1	0	0	7,084
Dear Pappa	4	G	5	1	0	1	3,967
Dear Pickles (GB)	5	M	5	1	1	0	11,390
Dear Princess	4	F	12	3	6	0	35,512
Dear Prospector	6	M	12	2	3	0	33,500
Dear Queen	8	M	3	0	0	0	147
Dear Sara	4	F	6	0	1	2	3,549
Dear Silver	2	F	2	0	1	0	9,456
Dear Spirit	3	F	5	0	0	0	780
Dear Stranger	5	M	9	0	0	1	2,812
Dear to Me	3	G	3	1	0	0	11,780
Dear to My Heart	4	F	5	0	0	0	860
Dear Willy	5	H	3	0	0	0	440
Dearest Enemy	4	F	10	2	0	3	8,069
Dearest Heart	2	F	5	1	1	0	45,394
Dearest Jack	5	G	7	1	1	0	11,387
Dearfriendofours	5	M	4	0	0	0	3,990
Deas Island	4	G	7	0	2	1	13,080
Death Trappe	7	G	11	1	2	1	24,500
Death Valley Dolly	8	M	3	0	0	0	408
Deauville Beach	4	C	5	0	0	0	1,017
Debarette	5	M	8	1	0	1	4,649
Debas'cowboypower	6	H	2	0	0	0	0
Debatable	7	H	6	2	2	0	52,661
Debate	6	M	8	2	0	1	8,739
Debate the Issue	3	F	3	0	0	0	0
Debater	3	C	5	0	0	1	705
Debauchery	6	G	18	2	3	6	19,977
Debb Springs	4	C	1	0	0	0	0
Debbie Darlin	3	F	2	0	0	2	3,080
Debbie Sue	2	F	2	0	0	1	4,250
Debbie's Gone	3	F	9	1	4	2	26,771
Debbies Mine	3	F	2	0	0	0	1,155
Debbie's Promise	4	F	11	2	2	0	33,940
Debbies Toy	3	F	10	3	1	1	15,522
Debbie's Turn	2	F	4	1	0	1	16,919
Debbie's Way	3	F	4	1	0	1	29,820
Debbs	7	G	3	0	0	0	144
Debby Do	5	M	8	1	0	3	12,138
Debby's Roar	2	G	1	0	0	0	0
Debbyzz Cat	3	F	6	0	0	0	105
Debi's Sportscar	4	F	11	2	1	3	61,679
Debonair Joe	4	G	7	0	1	1	37,080
Debonair Prince	6	G	2	0	0	0	84
Debonaire Gambler	2	C	1	0	0	0	0
Deborah (CHI)	7	M	6	1	0	0	16,152
Deborah Welsh	3	F	9	3	3	2	50,055
Deborah's Doings	6	M	3	0	0	0	204
Deb's Charm	2	F	3	1	0	2	71,360
Deb's Dawaytogo	4	G	6	1	0	0	8,713
Debs Fantasy	6	M	5	0	1	0	1,182
Deb's Favoite Gift	2	F	4	0	1	1	28,876
Debs Li'l Escapade	4	F	9	1	2	1	10,296
Debs On Stage	4	F	9	1	1	1	4,662
Debt of Honor	4	G	17	4	5	2	32,622
Debt Reduction	2	G	6	0	0	0	674
Debt to Equity	4	G	8	2	1	0	7,781
Debutante Fever	3	F	12	0	1	3	3,582
Decadent Dash	3	F	12	1	0	0	27,303
Decaf	4	G	5	1	1	0	22,500
Decanted	4	F	1	0	1	0	800
Decarchy	6	H	7	0	2	1	166,209
Decathlete	3	C	2	0	0	0	0
Deceit	2	F	5	1	1	0	12,330
Deceitful Darling	3	F	10	2	2	1	31,640
December Miracle	2	F	2	0	0	0	0
Decencia (ARG)	6	M	7	0	0	1	8,745
Decency	4	C	11	3	2	0	23,890
Decent Sara	3	F	16	3	5	3	33,430
Deception Island	6	G	9	0	3	0	5,480
Deceptive	4	F	9	0	4	2	19,130
Deceptive Move	3	F	8	2	3	0	12,408
Decertified	8	G	4	1	2	0	2,990
Decibel	2	C	2	1	0	0	28,950
Decided to Be Wild	4	G	6	0	0	1	2,235
Decidedly Taken	3	C	3	0	0	0	2,640
Decidedlydifferent	2	F	1	0	0	0	1,275
Deciding Factor	2	C	1	0	0	0	0
Decimal	6	G	12	1	2	2	6,570
Decimal Point	4	G	5	1	1	1	10,092
Decimate	4	G	6	0	0	0	7,060
Decipherance	2	C	3	1	0	1	13,446
Decision	5	G	12	5	2	2	46,471
Decision Point	4	G	17	1	2	2	6,831
Decisional	3	C	8	2	0	1	22,550
Decisive	5	G	5	0	0	0	3,576
Deck Game	4	F	11	3	2	0	65,615
Decker	4	G	1	0	1	0	1,460
Declined Amx	6	M	6	1	1	1	29,530
Deco Statis	4	G	3	2	0	0	10,577
Decoder	3	C	5	1	1	1	44,480
Decoding the Gray	7	G	15	4	2	2	38,695
Decorate	3	C	4	1	2	1	12,044
Decorate the Town	5	G	16	2	4	3	16,037
Decorated Admiral	5	H	4	0	0	0	290
Decorated Angel	4	F	7	0	1	0	585
Decorated At Dawn	6	M	12	1	1	2	4,568
Decorated Breeze	2	G	8	0	5	1	12,130
Decorated Cart	3	G	5	0	0	1	1,670
Decorated Drums	9	G	6	1	1	0	10,880
Decorated Heart	3	F	11	1	1	2	6,850
Decorated Hero	4	G	5	0	1	1	12,280
Decorated in Gold	3	F	10	1	1	1	7,675
Decorated Moment	4	C	16	3	0	3	24,230
Decorated Ruler	6	G	1	0	0	0	0
Decorated Storm	7	G	19	1	1	2	6,065
Decoratedmissemma	4	F	3	0	0	0	195
Deco's Secret	3	C	9	2	1	3	53,460
Dedamo	2	G	1	0	0	0	75
Dede's Surprise	5	M	9	0	1	2	3,909
D'edge	3	F	6	0	0	0	0
Dedicated Caper	3	F	9	0	2	1	4,513
Dedicated Moment	8	G	3	1	2	0	6,200
Dedication (FR)	4	F	5	1	1	1	128,450
Dedos Cruzados	6	H	2	0	0	0	0
Deduct Box	4	G	1	0	0	0	0
Deductive Reasonin	5	M	1	0	0	0	52
Dee Be Better	2	F	4	0	2	2	13,540
Dee Da	5	M	1	0	0	0	0
Dee Dee Dancer	4	G	1	0	1	0	1,800
Dee Dee Dee	6	G	10	1	2	2	6,854
Dee Dee's Angel	2	F	1	0	0	0	455
Dee Dee's Cat	2	F	6	0	1	0	6,280
Dee Dee's Diner	3	F	6	2	0	0	57,825
Dee Dee's Dynamite	3	F	8	0	0	0	1,268
Dee Dee's Wildcat	2	F	7	0	0	3	14,040
Dee Double Ya Dan	4	G	18	1	0	6	22,454
Dee Expo	5	M	10	2	1	4	7,103
Dee I Do	4	F	8	1	0	0	6,090
Dee Is a Lady	3	F	8	2	1	3	12,089
Dee Life	5	M	1	0	1	0	1,120
Dee Note	3	G	3	0	0	1	2,072
Dee Ron	3	G	13	1	0	3	12,272
Dee Vid	5	M	6	0	0	0	613
Deebar	4	G	11	0	1	2	3,165
Deed Heads	5	M	1	0	0	0	0
Deed of Gold	6	G	2	0	0	1	650
Deed to the Gate	3	F	10	3	2	1	126,186
Deedarling	3	F	11	1	0	4	35,088
Deeday	4	C	1	0	0	0	300
Deedee	3	F	9	0	1	0	1,868
Deedle E Dee	2	F	3	0	1	0	8,400
Deelasray	4	G	10	0	1	3	5,420
Deelightful Dan	3	G	8	0	0	2	2,927

Horse	Age	Sex	Sts	1st	2d	3d	Won	Horse	Age	Sex	Sts	1st	2d	3d	Won
Deeliteful Guy	4	G	9	2	3	2	82,150	Defy Logic	3	C	11	0	4	4	56,470
Deeliteful Irving	5	H	3	1	1	0	195,000	Defying Angel	6	M	5	0	0	0	401
Deeliteful Shelby	4	F	6	0	0	0	390	Degas	8	G	2	0	0	1	715
Deeliteful Topper	3	F	12	3	0	1	34,978	Degas Vu	6	G	11	3	1	1	31,760
Deelites Love	4	C	5	1	0	0	13,380	Degenerate Gambler	2	C	5	2	0	0	37,560
Deemed Worthy	3	C	13	0	4	2	9,670	Degrove	4	F	4	0	0	1	1,609
Deemie	3	F	5	0	2	1	3,205	Dehere Blues	3	C	12	2	1	2	28,350
Deena's Slew	5	M	2	1	0	0	3,720	Deheres Perky Baby	5	M	1	0	0	0	0
Deep Blue Goodbye	3	G	11	1	0	4	17,949	Dehim	3	C	6	2	3	1	15,605
Deep Dive	8	G	5	0	0	0	0	Deidre Lou	3	F	2	0	0	0	303
Deep Finesse	3	F	14	3	0	2	13,976	Deja	3	F	11	2	2	0	56,742
Deep in My Heart	4	F	4	0	0	0	320	Deja Brew	2	G	9	1	2	2	25,150
Deep in the Woods	2	F	1	0	0	0	2,050	Deja Dancer	3	F	11	1	1	1	9,329
Deep Mischief	7	M	5	0	2	0	4,447	Deja l'Eau	3	C	5	1	0	0	2,904
Deep Roots	3	F	5	1	0	0	15,600	Deja Ne	3	C	3	0	0	0	525
Deep Sea Sailor	8	G	3	0	0	1	690	Deja Vu Diva	4	F	7	1	1	1	7,098
Deep Shadow	3	C	8	1	1	1	59,732	Deja Vue Again	7	G	1	1	0	0	2,280
Deep Sleep	6	H	2	0	0	0	780	Dekalb	4	G	7	2	1	0	22,650
Deep Sun	2	C	2	0	0	0	423	Dekay	2	C	2	0	0	1	1,555
Deep Thunder	4	G	10	1	1	2	7,266	Deke Sweetheart	3	F	16	1	1	2	7,589
Deep Time D. T	5	G	4	0	0	0	55	Deke's Star	3	G	9	2	2	1	9,252
Deepinourpockets	4	G	6	0	0	0	675	Del Carmen	5	M	10	1	3	1	50,493
Deer Be Little	4	C	16	2	0	1	6,711	Del Chiaro	4	G	11	1	3	2	21,104
Deer Creek Lady	2	F	1	0	0	0	0	Del Dancer	4	C	3	0	1	0	950
Deer Danny Boy	3	G	19	1	4	4	31,590	Del Diablo	3	G	6	1	0	0	3,820
Deer in the Wind	3	F	4	1	0	0	7,020	Del Mar Cool	6	G	4	0	1	0	2,200
Deer Lake	4	C	8	4	1	2	150,530	Del Mar Dancer	8	G	5	1	2	1	12,422
Deer Luck	4	C	5	2	0	3	19,000	Del Mar Danny	6	G	6	1	0	1	18,192
Deer Power	3	G	4	1	1	0	9,680	Del Mar Darling	7	M	5	0	0	0	210
Deer Run	6	G	5	0	1	2	35,500	Del Mar Diamond	2	F	5	0	2	0	10,380
Deer Tango	7	G	14	0	4	0	5,766	Del Mar Dreamin'	2	F	5	1	0	2	11,984
Deer Trail	3	C	14	0	0	0	2,850	Del Mar Gray	8	G	5	1	0	0	3,000
Deerfoot	3	C	16	1	2	6	26,254	Del Mar Missy	3	F	2	0	1	1	3,150
Deerhound Angel	4	F	7	0	2	1	9,172	Del Mar Red	2	C	1	0	0	0	580
Deering	6	H	2	0	0	0	100	Del Mar Show	6	H	7	1	1	1	131,698
Deers Rascal	5	M	2	0	0	0	0	Del Norte	3	G	4	0	0	3	7,385
Deerwood Lass	7	M	7	1	1	0	14,850	Del Rae	3	F	6	1	0	1	25,970
Dee's Copycat	2	F	7	0	0	0	562	Delane	2	C	4	0	0	0	1,050
Dee's Dilemma	3	F	13	2	0	1	6,861	Delano's Tricks	3	G	11	1	3	3	13,901
Dee's Echo	3	F	5	0	0	1	2,266	Delante	4	G	12	1	1	1	4,491
Dee's Golden Girl	5	M	2	0	0	0	0	Delavallade	5	M	5	0	2	0	23,120
Dee's Justice	2	F	5	1	1	1	21,620	Delaware Brew	4	G	6	1	1	1	5,522
Dee's Love	3	F	8	1	2	2	59,752	Delaware Line	7	G	14	0	1	1	3,219
Dee's Missy	4	F	9	0	0	1	1,400	Delaware River	2	C	6	1	1	0	21,810
Dee's Profit	3	G	1	0	0	0	0	Delaware Squeeze	2	C	7	0	2	1	7,280
Dee's Rebel	6	G	10	1	1	2	6,756	Delay	5	M	15	0	1	4	12,988
Dee's Seattle Fire	4	F	6	1	0	0	4,455	Delayed Vacation	3	G	2	0	0	0	1,680
Deesalia	3	F	11	1	1	0	38,607	Delbert	5	G	8	2	1	2	8,664
Deeveedee	5	F	5	1	0	0	7,050	Delcastle	3	C	7	4	0	0	64,390
Def	4	G	4	0	0	0	0	Delceda	4	F	4	1	0	1	13,252
Defamation	4	F	11	0	5	1	20,505	Delcrest Idea	4	G	12	0	3	0	8,230
Defend	5	G	2	1	0	0	1,200	Delegate Jones	3	C	2	0	0	0	0
Defend Your Honor	2	C	2	0	0	0	150	Delfinia	8	M	18	3	3	4	20,342
Defendant	3	F	2	0	0	0	540	Delft Buttons	2	F	8	1	0	2	4,775
Defenman	7	G	6	0	2	0	32,998	Delhi Speed	6	G	2	0	0	0	0
Defensive	5	G	9	2	1	1	18,858	Deli Chef	8	H	3	0	0	1	240
Defensive Gem	6	G	14	3	3	6	24,330	Delia Sister	3	F	5	1	2	1	28,413
Defensive Kat	3	G	8	1	3	1	13,135	Delia's Gone	2	F	1	0	0	1	13,750
Defensively	4	C	3	0	0	0	190	Deliberate Attack	5	M	5	1	0	0	1,380
Deferred Comp	5	H	8	2	1	0	60,210	Delicate an Demure	4	F	14	1	1	3	5,539
Defiant Dandy	6	H	10	1	0	0	14,462	Delicate Prince	3	C	19	0	1	2	8,315
Defiant Energy	3	G	8	2	2	1	16,284	Delicatessa	4	F	8	2	2	1	98,516
Defiant Fighter	5	G	11	2	0	1	27,225	Delicious Devil	5	G	9	3	0	0	19,706
Defiant Lord	3	C	1	0	0	0	0	Delicious Dish	2	F	4	0	0	0	1,240
Defiant Prospector	3	C	12	2	2	3	34,311	Delicious Gift	4	F	9	1	3	0	19,587
Defiant Warrior	5	H	16	1	0	1	5,465	Delight At Dawn	3	G	13	1	2	1	19,055
Defiantly Bold	3	C	15	1	4	4	39,509	Delightful Action	2	F	4	0	0	0	1,138
Defibrillator	8	M	12	0	0	2	1,618	Delightful Change	2	F	2	1	0	0	11,540
Definately Cool	3	C	5	0	0	0	600	Delightful Demi	2	C	1	0	0	0	45
Definitely	7	G	17	0	3	1	6,703	Delightful Devil	5	H	2	0	1	0	1,840
Definitely Dear	3	F	5	1	0	0	10,960	Delightful Fire	3	C	3	0	0	0	0
Definitly Social	5	M	7	2	1	0	16,636	Delightful Moment	5	M	1	0	0	1	1,221
Deforestation	3	G	19	1	1	1	8,205	Delightful Reef	7	H	13	0	1	2	4,432
Defrench	3	C	1	0	0	0	0	Delightful Sami	4	F	9	2	0	2	7,909
Defrere's Image	4	F	11	3	3	1	28,422	Delightful Showers	4	F	2	0	0	0	117
Defrere's Venture	2	F	2	1	0	0	9,258	Delightfully Sharp	9	G	8	2	3	1	3,527
Defrere's Vixen	3	C	10	1	0	2	98,350	Delightster	3	G	14	1	4	3	27,740
Defrocked	2	C	2	0	0	0	0	Delila On Line	3	F	1	0	0	0	35
Defuhr	2	F	7	1	3	3	68,535	Delilah Blue	4	C	4	0	0	1	1,398

Horse	Age	Sex	Sts	1st	2d	3d	Won
Delilah's Gold	4	F	3	0	0	0	324
Delineator's Dream	5	G	12	2	2	1	8,596
Delinquenator	2	G	4	0	2	1	7,183
Delirious	9	G	4	0	0	0	175
Delirious Laughter	4	G	11	3	1	4	18,275
Delite D. Devil	4	F	13	0	0	5	5,017
Deliteful Delpha	2	F	5	2	0	1	8,260
Deliver Hope	5	G	11	1	0	3	10,205
Deliver Me	3	F	8	0	0	0	1,457
Deliver Me Quick	2	F	4	0	0	3	5,940
Deliver the Gold	2	F	6	1	2	0	14,336
Delivering Speed	2	C	2	1	0	0	27,280
Delivery	3	C	3	0	0	0	1,200
Dell Place	4	G	8	2	2	1	97,117
Della Francesca	4	C	8	2	1	0	177,360
Della Jhamela	4	F	10	1	0	1	4,075
Della n' Time	2	F	7	0	0	0	2,610
Dellamonte	3	F	4	0	1	0	1,760
Dellasue	2	F	2	0	0	0	170
Delly Elly	3	F	3	0	0	0	300
Delmar Zeal	2	C	1	0	0	0	0
Delmarvelous	4	G	9	1	3	0	40,300
Delmonico Cat	4	F	9	3	4	1	146,764
Deloma Looker	4	F	3	0	0	0	871
Delong	4	G	13	4	1	1	16,520
Delphine	3	F	4	0	0	0	505
Delphiness	4	F	9	2	2	1	20,512
Delray Dancer	4	G	9	2	1	1	19,340
Delray Darling	5	M	8	0	2	0	2,486
Delray Dew	5	M	3	0	0	0	1,275
Delray Dilemma	3	C	3	0	0	1	7,160
Delray Sam	5	G	11	0	0	2	14,021
Delrey Gal	5	M	5	0	0	1	2,239
Del's Angel	6	M	3	0	0	0	604
Del's Delight	6	G	1	0	0	0	114
Delta Command	5	H	3	1	0	0	3,900
Delta Darlin	7	M	1	0	0	0	0
Delta Dawnie	6	M	5	1	1	1	2,709
Delta Dawning	4	F	2	0	0	0	792
Delta Deacon	4	G	5	1	1	0	6,900
Delta Debutante	4	F	10	0	0	2	3,322
Delta Dennis	6	H	5	1	0	0	4,440
Delta Devil	3	G	7	1	1	2	15,552
Delta Dragon	5	G	3	0	0	0	739
Delta Epsilon	5	G	13	1	2	2	25,511
Delta Express	7	M	16	2	2	1	3,734
Delta Form (AUS)	7	G	5	0	0	1	7,440
Delta Ghost	2	C	5	2	0	1	56,367
Delta Junction	7	M	4	1	0	0	1,239
Delta Kat	3	F	15	1	6	2	17,166
Delta Lord	3	C	6	0	2	2	8,020
Delta Mirage	3	F	3	0	0	1	1,350
Delta Miss	2	F	2	0	0	0	0
Delta Pirate	2	G	3	0	0	0	714
Delta Princess	4	F	8	4	0	0	196,110
Delta Rate	7	F	1	1	0	0	4,996
Delta Sea	3	G	10	2	2	0	79,640
Delta Sensation	2	F	1	0	0	0	2,700
Delta Wheel	5	G	5	0	0	0	1,830
Deltaport	4	C	11	1	0	2	7,689
Delta's Snake Eyes	3	C	6	0	0	1	1,885
Deltatron	3	G	2	0	0	0	224
Delusional Lad	3	G	8	0	3	2	9,880
Deluxe Scent	3	G	2	0	0	1	1,320
Dema Wail	5	G	3	0	0	0	400
Demabella	2	F	2	0	0	0	900
Demajake	4	C	14	0	3	3	12,932
Demaloot Dancer	4	C	1	0	0	0	468
Demalootphotoshoot	5	M	8	1	1	1	33,958
Demaloot's Girl	5	M	12	0	2	1	15,111
Demanding Woman	4	F	5	1	1	0	20,160
Demarcus	2	G	3	1	0	0	6,600
Demarest	3	C	6	0	0	0	432
Demarocks	4	F	4	0	0	0	468
Demashoot Demawail	3	F	8	1	0	4	16,992
Demeteor	4	G	8	4	0	0	55,600
Demetra's Love	3	F	7	2	1	0	66,333
Demetrias Brother	3	G	9	1	0	0	7,037
Demi Country	4	F	7	0	0	1	1,713
Demi Deluxe	2	G	1	0	0	0	0
Demi Kat	5	M	13	1	3	2	2,809
Demi Paige	4	F	8	0	1	3	10,580
Demiano	5	H	10	1	4	2	22,025
Demidoff Lilly	3	F	15	0	0	3	2,046
Demidoll	6	M	1	1	0	0	15,000
Demidor	3	G	1	0	0	0	0
Demiparfait	4	F	6	0	1	2	17,369
Demi's Secret	2	F	2	0	1	0	3,465
Demizoe	3	F	4	0	0	0	375
Demo	7	H	7	0	0	0	372
Demo Memo	5	M	1	0	0	0	2,500
Demolition Man	4	G	11	2	2	1	19,624
Demon Bob (ARG)	8	G	3	1	1	0	7,975
Demon Dancer	5	G	17	5	3	1	77,030
Demon Fever	2	F	2	0	0	0	1,275
Demon in the Rough	5	M	1	0	0	1	1,045
Demon Jazz	2	C	1	1	0	0	15,600
Demon Like	4	G	4	0	0	0	480
Demon Rage	4	F	8	0	0	2	613
Demon Tea	3	F	6	0	0	0	563
Demon Tree	6	M	2	0	0	0	149
Demon Warlock	3	C	8	1	1	3	42,170
Demoncrat	4	G	12	0	1	3	7,753
Demondeed	6	G	12	3	2	3	70,370
Demonigal	2	F	3	0	0	1	8,612
Demonite	6	M	1	0	1	0	2,800
Demonously Danced	6	M	8	0	1	0	5,073
Demons and Devils	4	G	6	0	0	1	1,217
Demons Away	3	G	13	0	2	2	4,293
Demons Charmer	4	F	8	0	2	0	2,593
Demons Lad	4	G	6	0	0	1	735
Demon's Prince	5	H	15	1	1	3	10,833
Demopolis	3	C	11	1	1	3	41,330
Demson	2	G	9	2	0	0	17,479
Demus	2	F	3	0	0	1	2,103
Denali Cat	3	F	2	1	0	0	45,850
Denali Miss	4	F	17	1	1	1	10,581
Denali's Shadow	3	C	6	1	1	1	13,169
Dendillo	3	C	6	0	2	1	6,025
Denferstar	3	F	2	0	0	0	130
Denied	5	G	9	4	2	3	214,360
Denim Genes	3	F	3	0	0	0	142
Denim to Diamonds	6	M	7	0	0	2	2,695
Denim Wildcat	2	F	1	0	1	0	7,000
Denimsanddiamonds	3	F	12	5	1	1	95,479
Deniro's Delight	4	F	13	2	2	2	20,505
Deniro's Lad	5	G	9	0	1	0	2,316
Denniebarthedoor	2	C	1	0	0	0	110
Dennis' Demons	4	G	7	3	2	1	90,600
Dennis W County	4	G	10	3	2	1	33,485
Dennisport	2	C	6	1	2	1	21,400
Denny H	3	C	1	1	0	0	3,830
Denny's Devil Baby	4	F	14	0	0	7	10,755
Denny's Victory	2	C	1	0	1	0	3,600
Denon	5	H	7	1	1	1	425,000
Deno's Connection	2	F	4	0	2	1	11,700
Denouncer's Girl	3	F	9	2	2	0	21,330
Densgripinagin	2	C	2	0	0	1	693
Denton County	5	G	14	4	1	3	18,861
Denton Sings Ruby	3	F	5	1	0	1	5,035
Dentons Ruby	5	M	4	0	0	0	1,931
Denver Hi	8	G	2	0	1	0	760
Denver Zephyr	7	M	2	0	0	0	0
Denzil'sfirstbaby	7	M	11	3	5	1	15,465
Deocat	2	G	2	0	0	0	200
Deon	9	M	18	0	5	3	11,550
Deora Store	3	F	3	0	0	1	4,760
Departing Cat	4	F	10	1	3	2	13,575
Departing Dynamo	6	G	21	4	3	4	32,706
Departing South (ARG)	5	M	11	1	1	0	16,320
Departure Time	5	G	2	1	0	1	4,465
Dependable Herbie	3	C	8	2	1	0	39,360
Dependable Will	7	G	5	1	0	0	11,170
Deploy Venture (GB)	7	G	13	2	2	1	57,295
Depop	2	G	6	2	2	0	75,120
Deporte Total (CHI)	6	G	17	3	4	3	42,830
Deportment	5	M	11	0	2	1	13,078
Deposit Dancer	6	H	7	1	0	2	1,949

Horse	Age	Sex	Sts	1st	2d	3d	Won
Deposit E. F.	7	G	2	0	0	0	0
Deposit On Time	3	G	13	5	5	1	76,960
Deposit Thatticket	5	M	19	1	0	1	5,448
Deposit the Cash	6	M	7	0	1	0	5,193
Deposit the Loot	4	F	5	0	1	0	3,027
Depository	3	G	11	1	3	1	42,970
Depurata	3	F	9	0	1	1	4,218
Deputane	6	H	5	0	0	0	525
Deputed Mate	5	M	5	0	0	1	1,190
Deputed Summer	8	M	2	0	0	0	330
Deputies Agent	3	C	13	0	0	0	1,104
Deputy	5	M	3	0	0	1	3,030
Deputy Ambassador	2	G	1	1	0	0	6,120
Deputy Apollo	3	G	11	1	2	0	6,263
Deputy Badman	3	G	10	2	0	2	10,096
Deputy Brawler	2	G	3	0	0	1	1,448
Deputy Call	7	G	14	4	4	1	91,141
Deputy Carson	7	G	6	0	0	0	1,565
Deputy Champ	5	G	12	1	1	5	64,480
Deputy Circle	4	C	17	0	0	0	1,957
Deputy Connor	4	G	17	2	3	2	67,895
Deputy Country	5	H	6	1	4	1	46,800
Deputy Cures Blues	3	F	7	1	0	1	112,800
Deputy Danny Boy	6	H	18	4	6	3	69,740
Deputy Dash	4	C	4	1	0	1	28,560
Deputy Dave	3	C	7	1	1	0	9,023
Deputy David K	3	G	14	2	1	4	53,494
Deputy Dee	3	G	4	0	0	1	830
Deputy Defrere	3	G	13	1	1	3	33,160
Deputy Devil	3	F	1	0	0	0	0
Deputy Diplomat	5	G	3	0	0	0	315
Deputy Director	3	C	5	0	1	1	19,010
Deputy Dirty Deeds	4	G	7	1	3	0	17,551
Deputy Do Right	4	G	3	0	0	0	100
Deputy Doc	3	C	5	1	1	2	29,588
Deputy Doc Renzi	2	C	1	0	0	0	0
Deputy Doo Dah	3	F	4	0	1	1	7,120
Deputy Dude	4	G	11	4	1	1	35,296
Deputy Eagle	4	G	6	0	0	0	475
Deputy Express	2	C	1	0	0	0	0
Deputy Fox	4	G	1	0	0	0	0
Deputy Fudge	3	G	9	2	0	3	38,620
Deputy Halo	3	G	8	0	2	1	7,675
Deputy in Charge	3	G	6	1	2	1	10,630
Deputy Jack	3	C	5	0	0	2	10,985
Deputy Jazz	5	G	15	3	2	1	68,098
Deputy Lad	3	C	7	1	1	0	37,817
Deputy Lou	3	G	11	1	1	3	17,955
Deputy Marshall	5	H	2	0	0	0	339
Deputy Mary	4	F	11	1	4	3	27,029
Deputy Ridge	3	G	6	0	0	1	2,270
Deputy Ring	2	F	2	1	0	0	16,830
Deputy Ruckus	3	G	5	0	0	0	0
Deputy Ruler	5	G	9	1	2	0	20,206
Deputy Rummy	2	C	5	1	1	1	18,220
Deputy Savannah	4	F	6	2	2	1	4,764
Deputy Seabreeze	3	G	10	3	0	0	7,702
Deputy Shaker	5	H	2	1	0	0	5,130
Deputy Sheriff	4	G	7	1	2	2	11,692
Deputy Squealie	2	F	2	0	2	0	17,200
Deputy Storm	2	C	4	2	1	0	78,380
Deputy Strike	5	G	6	0	0	2	36,927
Deputy Stripe	5	G	11	5	1	1	76,990
Deputy Thief	3	G	6	1	1	1	41,460
Deputy Tombe	3	F	5	1	0	2	34,880
Deputy Warrior	3	C	10	2	3	0	14,387
Deputy Wild	3	C	7	0	3	0	4,290
Deputy Woman	4	F	2	0	0	0	500
Deputy's Dan Cin	3	F	4	0	0	0	0
Deputy's Destiny	2	C	2	0	0	0	0
Deputy's Legacy	5	H	4	1	0	0	15,736
Deputy's Reward	4	C	9	0	0	3	13,485
Der He Is	4	C	3	0	0	0	1,560
Der Rock Says	5	H	10	0	0	1	1,050
Der Rosenthing	5	G	16	2	0	2	6,698
Derbster	4	G	9	1	0	0	3,260
Derby Angel	3	F	3	0	0	0	0
Derby Day Brat	10	G	1	0	0	0	0
Derby Day Debut	7	M	16	1	4	4	9,655
Derby Day Hope	3	G	2	0	1	0	800
Derby Doll	3	F	8	0	1	0	2,528
Derby Drive	4	C	6	0	0	0	5,723
Derby Duke	6	G	8	2	0	1	30,763
Derby Fan	3	F	7	1	1	3	7,899
Derby for Darby	2	C	2	0	0	0	0
Derby Gray	5	G	7	0	1	2	5,905
Derby Grifter	4	G	5	0	0	0	435
Derby Joe	3	C	1	0	0	0	0
Derby John	10	G	6	2	0	2	7,639
Derby King Mutesa	5	G	16	3	2	0	12,321
Derby Mc Q	6	G	9	2	1	1	14,655
Derby Our Eagle	4	G	1	0	0	0	0
Derby Time	3	G	6	0	0	0	2,130
Derby World	6	H	8	1	0	0	16,725
Derby's Hellraiser	2	F	1	0	0	0	0
Derby's Moment	4	G	17	2	1	2	9,860
Dereck (ARG)	7	G	10	2	0	1	51,480
Derek's Announced	3	G	4	0	0	0	188
Derek's Cape Town	3	G	8	0	0	0	757
Derek's Magician	8	G	2	0	0	0	141
Derfbobu	3	G	1	0	0	0	50
Deriga Bay	5	G	15	1	0	2	7,318
Derivative	12	G	2	1	1	0	8,580
Derman	6	G	7	1	2	1	21,050
Deroleo	4	G	7	1	2	0	11,436
Derrianne	3	F	7	2	1	2	148,666
Derrick	2	G	8	1	5	0	19,250
Derry Connor	5	H	20	4	4	4	63,721
Derubiano	4	G	6	1	0	2	5,560
Dervorghilla	5	M	11	1	1	2	18,880
Des Arc	4	C	5	0	1	1	12,120
Des Chat	4	F	3	2	0	0	9,320
Des Howl	4	G	5	2	0	0	8,305
Des O Light	8	G	2	0	0	0	116
De's Story	9	G	11	0	1	2	2,467
Descout	7	G	3	0	0	1	1,255
Desdemona's Dream	2	F	4	1	0	1	13,040
Deseo	2	G	2	0	0	0	0
Deseret Honey	4	F	5	0	0	0	331
Desert Air	8	G	6	0	0	1	3,850
Desert Amor	2	F	6	0	1	0	3,335
Desert Best	6	G	2	1	0	0	1,098
Desert Bloom	3	F	7	0	1	1	8,204
Desert Bloomer	7	G	1	0	1	0	2,200
Desert Boom	3	G	8	3	0	0	94,760
Desert Border	2	C	4	1	1	0	19,995
Desert Bounty	3	G	9	1	0	0	3,070
Desert Cactus	3	G	2	0	0	0	0
Desert Call	7	G	5	1	0	0	5,002
Desert Clipper	3	F	1	0	0	0	0
Desert Comet	7	H	1	0	0	0	0
Desert Conquest	4	F	14	3	2	1	46,150
Desert Crank	3	F	5	1	2	0	10,700
Desert Dancer (ARG)	5	H	4	2	0	0	53,212
Desert Darby	6	H	5	2	0	3	77,620
Desert Deed	2	F	2	0	0	0	0
Desert Delight	7	H	11	0	1	1	2,256
Desert Destiny	4	C	2	0	0	0	120
Desert d'Or	6	M	5	0	0	1	2,097
Desert Duty	2	C	1	0	0	0	1,290
Desert Falcon (GER)	5	H	1	0	0	0	90
Desert Fire	3	G	1	0	0	0	440
Desert Flyer	7	G	1	0	0	0	48
Desert Frost	4	F	13	5	3	0	22,458
Desert Gambler	2	G	4	1	0	1	15,575
Desert Gem	3	F	4	0	0	0	845
Desert Girl	3	F	5	1	0	0	17,957
Desert Gold	4	F	5	2	1	0	119,080
Desert Hawk	9	G	8	0	1	4	3,901
Desert King	2	C	3	0	0	1	1,848
Desert Launch	5	H	9	4	0	1	4,875
Desert Lew	7	H	6	0	2	0	1,662
Desert Lightning	5	M	4	0	0	0	1,350
Desert Merlot	4	F	3	0	0	0	466
Desert Monarch	3	G	7	0	1	1	11,370
Desert Nova	2	F	4	2	0	2	36,490
Desert Paran	3	G	10	2	1	2	16,810
Desert Pass	5	M	4	0	0	0	657

Horse	Age	Sex	Sts	1st	2d	3d	Won
Desert Passion	4	F	18	4	1	3	21,213
Desert Patrol	2	C	5	1	0	0	28,380
Desert Pearls	3	F	5	1	2	0	53,320
Desert Place	2	C	2	0	0	0	1,440
Desert Pines	2	C	2	0	0	0	1,440
Desert Place	7	G	18	2	3	1	16,535
Desert Princess (IRE)	3	F	5	0	2	0	5,697
Desert Qui	2	F	5	1	2	0	7,613
Desert Raisin	4	F	5	0	0	0	1,116
Desert Rhythm	4	F	5	0	2	1	3,112
Desert Ruler	3	C	8	1	1	1	4,240
Desert Scholar	4	G	7	0	1	3	13,385
Desert Shadow	4	G	8	0	0	0	1,052
Desert Singer	4	C	2	0	0	0	99
Desert Snow	7	H	9	1	0	1	2,878
Desert Solitaire	2	F	1	0	0	0	214
Desert Star	4	F	11	2	0	4	41,004
Desert Stop In	3	F	3	0	0	0	187
Desert Streak	3	F	1	1	0	0	3,240
Desert Surge	6	G	8	0	0	0	150
Desert Surprise	2	C	1	0	0	0	0
Desert Sword	3	C	10	1	2	3	11,445
Desert Thief	2	C	3	0	0	0	0
Desert View (GB)	3	F	6	1	0	2	47,220
Desert War	2	C	1	0	0	0	125
Desert Warrior	3	C	8	2	0	1	78,737
Desert Wild Fire	5	M	11	0	0	1	1,568
Desert Wise	3	G	3	0	0	0	0
Desert Wolf Girl	4	F	19	7	2	4	35,197
Desertion (IRE)	4	F	1	0	0	0	360
Deserts Memoirs	3	F	3	0	0	0	0
Deserts Miracle	7	M	5	1	0	0	4,518
Deserving	4	G	10	0	1	2	3,919
Desiard	10	G	17	3	2	1	25,153
Designated Winner	3	G	1	0	0	0	72
Designed for Luck	6	G	4	3	0	0	267,735
Designer Boots	3	F	2	0	0	0	300
Designer Dance	4	C	9	1	1	0	6,057
Designer Fashion	4	F	5	0	0	0	477
Designer Genes	5	M	12	1	3	0	10,983
Designer Image	3	F	10	1	1	3	13,140
Designer's Gold	3	F	8	2	1	2	21,890
Designer's Year	2	C	3	0	2	0	4,230
Designs by Vera	4	F	10	0	6	1	19,096
Desilver	4	F	7	0	0	2	1,510
Desirable Fire	8	G	2	0	0	0	0
Desirable Moment	4	F	6	3	1	0	65,480
Desirable Wolf	5	M	10	2	2	1	9,222
Desirabledancer	3	F	11	1	1	3	32,800
Desiraes My Candy	5	M	6	1	1	0	40,000
Desiraes Myhotbaby	3	F	9	1	2	1	15,460
Desi's Lady	3	F	4	0	0	0	0
Desktop	8	H	8	0	2	0	7,701
Desnuda	2	F	4	1	3	0	54,000
Desperate Lady	3	F	3	1	0	0	6,930
Desperate Measures	4	C	1	0	0	0	0
Desperation	4	G	6	1	2	0	10,590
Despite	3	G	14	2	1	2	32,520
Despot	5	M	10	1	1	0	11,433
Dessa's Dream	3	G	19	2	3	3	24,765
Dessert	3	F	6	3	1	1	259,560
Destello del Cielo (CHI)	6	G	6	0	2	0	11,490
Destined to Dance	4	F	4	0	0	0	796
Destined to Win	3	G	9	2	1	4	40,200
Destiny by Chance	2	C	4	0	0	1	1,820
Destiny Calling	5	M	2	0	0	1	1,200
Destiny Calls	3	F	6	3	2	0	85,300
Destiny Chaser	5	M	10	1	0	0	5,490
Destiny Red	3	G	4	1	0	1	48,804
Destiny's Code	5	M	12	0	0	2	1,836
Destiny's Design	3	F	7	1	0	0	10,085
Destiny's Doorstep	2	C	1	0	0	0	120
Destinys Draw	6	M	11	2	0	1	8,729
Destiny's Dream	3	C	4	0	0	0	410
Destiny's Key	4	G	3	0	0	1	550
Destiny's Ruler	3	G	3	0	0	0	182
Desultory	3	G	2	0	0	0	0
Detached	11	G	10	0	2	0	4,945
Detailed Play	7	R	3	0	0	0	225
Detailz	7	H	2	0	0	0	0
Detained	4	G	13	1	0	2	6,316
Detector	6	G	11	2	1	2	16,259
Detente	4	F	5	0	1	1	2,618
Determined	2	G	1	0	0	1	5,880
Determined Destiny	4	C	3	0	0	0	0
Determined Irish	6	M	4	0	0	0	1,870
Determined Lady	2	F	4	0	0	0	409
Determined Will	3	G	4	0	0	0	224
Detramental	4	G	11	3	1	1	20,533
Deuces Galore	5	H	11	2	2	2	9,677
Deuce's Girl	3	F	9	2	4	0	20,730
Deux Mille	4	C	12	2	3	2	42,989
Devant	3	F	14	2	2	2	30,580
Devastating	5	M	3	0	0	0	15,390
Develish S.	5	G	2	0	0	0	0
Develish Turn	5	M	11	0	1	0	3,289
Devil A' Doria	2	F	3	0	0	0	130
Devil Action	2	C	1	0	0	0	74
Devil Anse	5	H	7	3	1	0	20,576
Devil At the Wire	3	F	3	1	1	1	75,520
Devil Badgett	3	G	8	1	1	0	17,532
Devil Boy	5	H	5	0	2	1	3,825
Devil by Choice	3	F	12	1	1	1	9,423
Devil Dancing	4	F	5	1	1	0	38,075
Devil Dear	3	F	9	0	3	0	8,216
Devil Doc's	3	G	6	1	0	1	5,685
Devil Girl	3	F	6	0	1	1	8,230
Devil Hawk	4	F	13	3	2	2	16,916
Devil in Pink	5	M	9	0	0	0	3,535
Devil in Red	5	G	4	0	0	1	2,105
Devil in the Sky	3	G	7	2	3	0	45,027
Devil Indian	3	C	1	0	0	0	0
Devil Lace	2	F	3	1	0	1	6,440
Devil Last	4	F	5	2	1	0	13,575
Devil Man	3	G	6	1	0	2	23,670
Devil Me Care	7	H	13	2	1	0	19,795
Devil Me Too	3	F	1	0	0	0	0
Devil of a Time	3	G	4	0	1	0	3,844
Devil of a Trip	3	C	5	3	0	0	62,034
Devil On Deck	4	C	17	2	4	2	23,524
Devil On the Moon	3	G	7	2	1	2	24,050
Devil On the Run	3	F	20	5	0	4	33,925
Devil One	4	G	11	2	0	2	25,950
Devil Over Due	4	F	7	0	4	2	9,128
Devil Pastdue	3	F	5	0	1	1	2,121
Devil Ray	7	G	12	0	0	1	6,519
Devil Smiles	6	M	2	0	0	0	0
Devil Time	6	G	11	5	0	0	210,460
Devil to Remember	2	C	1	0	0	0	214
Devil Valentine	5	G	11	0	1	1	17,399
Devil Will Do Ya	6	G	20	3	2	5	44,417
Devil With Class	7	H	1	0	0	0	0
Devil Woman	3	F	8	1	0	1	5,350
Devil Women	5	M	6	0	0	0	437
Devil You Say	4	G	8	2	2	0	14,820
Devilastro	6	G	8	3	3	1	47,332
Deviled Ham	3	F	7	0	0	0	1,288
Devilhasasecret	4	F	3	0	0	0	126
Devilin Ruckus	6	G	12	3	4	2	20,511
Devilinahorsesuit	5	M	6	1	0	0	3,480
Devilinbluedenim	4	F	3	0	0	0	2,240
Devilindetail	2	G	3	0	0	0	450
Devilish Amour	3	F	6	1	0	0	7,590
Devilish Dandy	4	C	4	0	0	1	2,330
Devilish Dove	3	G	13	1	1	1	14,090
Devilish Dream	3	G	4	0	1	0	2,330
Devilish Lady	5	M	10	1	0	2	17,083
Devilish Prospect	3	C	5	2	0	1	24,620
Devilishly Unique	2	F	5	1	1	0	11,130
Devilite	2	F	2	0	1	0	2,095
Devillious	6	M	2	0	0	1	4,820
Devilnine	3	G	9	2	4	2	66,542
Devilontheborder	2	C	4	0	0	0	1,218
Devil's Act	2	C	2	0	0	0	0
Devil's Agent	2	C	3	0	0	0	180
Devils Ago Go	3	F	5	0	0	0	0
Devil's Alibi	7	M	6	0	0	1	1,212
Devils Alito	5	G	13	4	0	3	30,455
Devil's Bandit	5	G	10	2	2	1	35,800

Horse	Age	Sex	Sts	1st	2d	3d	Won
Devil's Bid	6	G	18	3	0	5	18,394
Devil's Bro	3	G	13	2	3	3	23,173
Devil's Candy	5	M	1	0	0	0	0
Devil's Case	2	C	1	0	0	0	135
Devil's Cat	3	G	9	1	0	0	15,780
Devil's Chasm	7	M	7	0	0	1	2,165
Devil's Chick	2	F	4	0	0	1	720
Devil's Con	4	G	10	4	0	2	37,260
Devil's Damsel	2	F	6	0	3	0	9,825
Devil's Dandy	5	G	16	2	2	3	29,633
Devil's Dare	4	G	2	0	0	0	0
Devils Day Off	3	C	10	1	1	1	5,885
Devil's Dip	4	F	2	0	0	0	840
Devil's Dixie	2	C	3	0	1	0	2,950
Devil's Domain	5	G	6	3	0	0	44,040
Devil's Duchess	6	M	2	0	1	0	8,360
Devil's Dust	4	C	12	2	3	3	73,930
Devil's Dynasty	6	G	7	0	1	0	2,488
Devil's Echo	4	F	4	0	0	0	507
Devil's Eclipse	2	F	2	0	1	0	4,652
Devil's Edge	4	F	2	0	0	0	0
Devil's Egg	7	G	2	1	0	0	22,200
Devils Fable	4	C	3	0	0	0	500
Devil's Fair	4	G	3	2	1	0	36,470
Devil's Fantasy	5	M	8	0	1	0	2,363
Devil's Flame	3	G	12	2	2	0	27,918
Devil's Formula	5	H	2	0	0	0	400
Devil's Gap	6	M	4	0	0	0	0
Devil's Gate	6	G	19	4	3	1	24,394
Devil's Good Girl	4	F	4	1	0	3	30,500
Devils Grace	3	F	3	0	0	0	210
Devil's Gulch	4	G	10	0	0	2	4,990
Devils Head	4	C	8	1	1	0	6,460
Devil's Honey	4	F	9	4	0	0	26,005
Devil's Horn	6	G	7	0	2	0	31,122
Devil's Iris (PER)	5	M	6	0	0	0	747
Devils Isle	3	G	15	3	1	1	31,680
Devil's Judge	7	G	8	1	3	0	29,315
Devils Knows	4	G	2	0	0	0	0
Devils Lyre	6	G	6	0	0	0	0
Devils Madwoman	7	M	9	3	0	0	49,337
Devil's Mark	5	G	14	2	3	1	25,763
Devils Match	4	C	8	0	0	5	4,670
Devil's Mercenary	7	H	4	0	0	0	362
Devil's Mission	5	H	9	0	0	1	1,238
Devil's Moment	5	H	3	0	0	0	0
Devil's Money	2	C	8	0	2	2	21,980
Devil's Music	6	M	10	0	0	0	687
Devils Partner	7	G	12	0	1	1	2,695
Devil's Passion	5	G	12	0	0	0	666
Devils Peak	3	C	7	1	1	1	50,360
Devil's Playboy	4	C	2	0	0	0	0
Devil's Pledge	3	F	1	0	0	0	455
Devil's Potion	4	G	4	2	1	0	3,080
Devils Proposition	2	C	1	0	0	0	74
Devil's Raise	3	G	1	0	0	0	103
Devil's Ransom	8	G	5	0	0	0	55
Devil's Reason	4	F	6	2	0	1	87,634
Devil's Reflection	3	G	9	2	0	0	6,260
Devil's Reine	7	H	11	1	3	0	10,063
Devils Right Hand	2	G	6	1	0	1	17,098
Devils Rightt	3	C	5	0	1	1	7,945
Devils River	4	F	11	3	1	3	17,265
Devil's Role	5	G	7	0	2	2	4,222
Devil's Run	3	G	1	0	0	0	0
Devil's Scripture	5	G	14	1	1	5	61,344
Devil's Secret Out	3	F	5	0	0	1	2,654
Devil's Shadow	7	G	1	0	0	0	729
Devil's Sky	2	F	2	0	0	0	0
Devil's Snare	3	C	13	3	2	1	19,643
Devil's Triangle	3	C	4	2	0	0	36,073
Devil's Vintage	3	C	7	1	1	0	42,880
Devil's Way	8	G	6	2	1	0	8,207
Devils Wing	3	F	4	0	1	0	3,910
Devils Winner	6	H	1	0	0	0	0
Devil's Wish	7	H	1	0	0	0	0
Devil'sdime	2	C	3	0	1	1	12,337
Devilsfood Cupcake	3	F	8	0	1	0	5,010
Devilsgonnagetcha	2	F	4	2	0	1	30,237
Devilish Intentions	4	C	2	0	0	1	2,016
Devilwithoutacause	4	G	1	0	0	1	640
Devin Is Due	4	G	10	1	0	0	7,643
Devine Dining	2	F	1	0	0	0	1,050
Devine Faith	3	F	7	0	1	2	8,517
Devine Lad	2	G	3	0	0	0	210
Devine Message	7	M	4	0	0	0	188
Devine Premonition	2	C	2	0	0	0	0
Devine Time	4	C	7	0	0	2	4,300
Devine Wind	7	G	7	1	0	0	29,265
Devinedeputy	6	G	15	4	2	2	19,620
Devin's Cash Crop	4	C	9	0	2	3	16,974
Devious Bebe	4	F	14	1	4	2	10,393
Devious Betrayal	4	C	2	0	0	0	0
Devious Boy (GB)	3	G	7	2	2	2	236,480
Devious Dame	3	F	13	2	2	4	31,719
Devious Darren	3	G	9	1	1	3	18,068
Devious Deb	3	F	1	0	0	0	432
Devious Decision	3	F	12	0	2	2	8,580
Devious Deed	4	G	11	0	0	2	1,796
Devious Dezibelle	4	F	2	0	0	0	942
Devious Diva	4	F	19	2	6	1	25,430
Devious Impact	3	F	6	3	0	0	100,360
Devious Indian (IRE)	4	C	3	0	0	1	3,464
Devious Kyle	4	G	3	0	0	0	90
Devious Morn	4	F	14	5	1	3	33,966
Devious Rhome	2	F	3	0	2	0	4,800
Devious Spell	4	C	10	0	0	1	1,618
Devious Thorne	2	C	2	1	0	0	5,685
Devious Ways	4	F	3	2	0	0	65,245
Devious Wish	3	C	8	0	1	0	2,235
Deviouspolitician	2	G	6	0	1	1	9,190
Devise	2	C	5	0	0	0	0
Devlish	4	F	8	4	0	0	61,260
Devoldidit	3	C	12	1	5	1	18,592
Devon Hunt	4	F	8	1	3	2	16,496
Devon Ice	3	F	8	0	1	1	3,337
Devon Princess	3	F	3	1	0	0	5,640
Devon Rose	4	F	8	4	0	1	212,380
Devon Sheer	3	F	1	0	0	0	75
Devon Special	2	C	6	1	0	1	6,279
Devon White Dove	3	G	15	1	1	5	16,157
Devon Wolf	3	F	3	0	0	0	0
Devon Zee	2	F	1	0	0	0	0
Devonairess	2	F	3	0	0	0	1,447
Devonairo	8	G	2	1	0	0	1,960
Devonford	4	C	1	0	0	1	1,386
Devons Bride	3	F	2	0	0	0	0
Devon's Cadillac	3	C	5	0	1	0	2,820
Devon's Diamond	2	C	1	0	0	0	42
Devons Gona Roll	2	C	4	1	0	1	15,367
Devon's Lucky Lady	2	F	1	0	1	0	4,600
Devons Set	2	G	1	1	0	0	13,800
Devons Snow	3	F	1	0	0	0	0
Devon's Song	2	F	2	1	0	1	8,130
Devons Storm	3	G	5	0	2	2	13,631
Devote	3	G	11	1	2	0	48,811
Devoted Fan	3	F	2	0	0	1	837
Devoted Huckster	6	G	6	0	0	1	730
Devoted Lover	2	G	6	1	1	0	26,881
Devotion Motion	3	F	1	0	0	0	795
Devotion Unbridled	3	F	8	4	3	1	152,300
Devout	3	G	7	0	0	1	8,804
Devout Sinner	5	M	7	1	3	1	37,855
Dewan Enclose	7	G	7	0	0	2	2,832
Dewar's Dunit	4	G	11	1	0	0	15,066
Dewars Splash	6	H	12	3	0	2	12,797
Dewey Eyed	4	F	6	0	0	0	318
Dewon and Only	6	M	4	0	0	1	2,619
Dewrag	4	C	8	1	2	1	16,350
Dexcavate	4	G	2	0	0	2	2,266
Dextro Tempore	5	G	9	1	0	0	8,001
Dezibelle's Secret	3	C	3	0	0	0	323
Dhabi's Sweetheart	7	M	1	0	0	0	179
Dhaffir (CHI)	7	G	12	4	2	0	86,050
Dhamma	3	F	2	1	1	0	36,800
D'hanis	3	C	1	0	0	1	660
Dharma Girl	4	F	2	0	0	0	0
Di Grazia Girl	3	F	1	0	0	0	0

Horse	Age	Sex	Sts	1st	2d	3d	Won
Dia Alegre (CHI)	4	G	4	0	0	1	2,735
Dia Del Saros	4	F	3	0	0	0	0
Diablesse	5	M	3	1	1	0	17,445
Diablito	3	G	5	1	0	1	3,773
Diablo Contento	3	G	12	1	3	5	34,776
Diablo de Viernes	2	G	8	0	1	0	16,862
Diablo d'Light	2	G	1	0	0	0	140
Diablo for Certain	6	H	4	0	0	0	0
Diablo His Due	6	G	3	0	0	0	0
Diablo Reigns	5	G	9	3	1	0	28,219
Diablo S Stake	3	C	3	0	0	0	0
Diablo's Aisle	4	G	11	2	1	1	12,410
Diablo's Appealer	4	G	6	0	0	0	1,090
Diablo's Caper	6	G	14	1	3	3	15,537
Diablo's Countess	8	M	23	1	1	1	31,214
Diablo's Crown	6	G	11	1	1	1	11,158
Diablos Crunch	3	F	3	0	0	0	360
Diablo's Deeds	5	M	4	0	0	0	576
Diablo's Donna	5	M	7	0	1	3	4,426
Diablo's Fable	5	G	5	1	1	3	9,990
Diablo's Ghost	7	M	5	0	0	0	253
Diablo's Girl	5	M	6	2	0	0	50,477
Diablo's Gunner	6	H	9	0	0	4	2,314
Diablo's Healer	6	M	1	0	0	0	240
Diablo's Miss	4	F	1	0	0	0	0
Diablo's Ms. Tony	5	M	9	1	1	2	4,814
Diablos Ordination	8	G	7	1	1	0	11,123
Diablo's Peak	6	M	8	2	1	1	48,554
Diablo's Rift	5	G	12	0	1	0	4,700
Diablo's Spirit	7	G	8	1	1	2	11,620
Diablo's Terete	2	C	6	0	0	2	2,955
Diablo's Well	5	H	2	0	0	1	390
Diablosangeleyes	6	M	16	3	4	2	55,924
Diabolique Dancer	6	G	15	2	2	1	11,707
Diadella	6	M	4	0	1	1	58,795
Dial a Dancer	3	C	1	0	0	0	85
Dial a Hero	4	C	10	1	0	5	62,280
Dial a Smile	7	M	1	0	1	0	4,300
Dial for Dollars	7	G	13	0	0	0	1,516
Dial for Speed	2	G	5	2	1	0	13,790
Dial Speed	5	M	10	1	1	1	5,740
Dialemup	3	G	4	0	0	1	1,540
Dialing Delema	8	M	7	0	0	3	4,104
Diamant (ARG)	7	H	7	1	0	4	19,827
Diamon Su	3	F	14	1	0	0	53,424
Diamond a Day	2	G	9	0	0	3	7,825
Diamond Ace	7	G	3	0	0	0	200
Diamond Advantage	2	F	4	0	0	0	950
Diamond Amore	2	F	2	0	0	0	0
Diamond Ballroom	4	C	1	0	0	0	0
Diamond Beau	4	C	1	0	0	0	584
Diamond Blitz	6	G	4	0	0	0	1,100
Diamond Bracelet	5	M	4	0	2	0	12,000
Diamond Britches	3	F	3	0	0	0	35
Diamond Bullet	3	G	8	1	2	2	23,610
Diamond Crusader	7	G	12	1	1	0	8,178
Diamond Cruz	4	C	13	1	2	4	18,820
Diamond Dale	2	C	1	0	0	0	1,085
Diamond Dancer	3	F	9	0	2	0	11,020
Diamond David	2	G	3	0	0	0	1,000
Diamond Dawn	4	G	9	2	1	1	28,732
Diamond Dayjur	3	F	6	0	0	1	1,809
Diamond Days	3	C	7	1	1	3	10,518
Diamond Deal	2	C	1	0	0	0	125
Diamond Decision	3	F	2	0	0	0	210
Diamond Demon	4	G	9	0	0	0	160
Diamond Derby	3	F	13	2	6	2	47,433
Diamond Devon	4	G	7	0	2	0	3,838
Diamond Dinero	2	C	3	0	0	0	0
Diamond Dropper	3	F	10	2	0	0	8,823
Diamond Emblem	5	M	1	0	0	0	0
Diamond Finish	2	F	2	0	0	0	1,309
Diamond Flight	4	F	9	3	1	0	28,086
Diamond Fury	2	C	2	0	0	2	10,560
Diamond Girl	4	F	3	0	0	0	750
Diamond Heirloom	3	F	12	2	3	1	48,121
Diamond Hope	4	G	5	1	1	0	23,880
Diamond Hunter	3	F	13	1	0	3	16,894
Diamond Indy	2	C	2	0	0	1	5,400
Diamond Jack W	2	G	1	0	0	0	0
Diamond Jake	3	G	12	1	0	1	13,100
Diamond Jerry	4	C	9	1	0	0	3,595
Diamond Jill	5	M	5	0	4	0	4,642
Diamond Joe	4	G	11	0	2	1	6,597
Diamond Judy	3	F	7	0	2	1	979
Diamond Ken	4	G	9	1	3	1	4,200
Diamond Kind	2	F	9	0	0	0	990
Diamond Kitty	2	F	2	1	0	0	4,500
Diamond Kylie	3	F	6	1	0	0	4,500
Diamond Laddie	5	H	2	0	0	0	225
Diamond Leap	6	H	11	4	1	2	13,900
Diamond Legend	4	C	5	0	0	0	630
Diamond Life	4	F	3	0	0	0	415
Diamond Little Bit	3	F	8	0	0	3	3,760
Diamond Machine	5	G	10	1	0	0	14,585
Diamond Mama	2	F	1	0	0	0	0
Diamond Mary	2	F	2	0	1	0	2,100
Diamond Mine	4	F	9	0	1	1	6,802
Diamond Moneyhoney	7	M	5	1	0	0	9,261
Diamond Native	4	F	1	1	0	0	3,300
Diamond of Ice	10	G	11	1	1	1	6,531
Diamond of Mine	4	F	15	1	2	1	6,697
Diamond Passer	5	G	11	2	3	0	7,308
Diamond Passion	2	F	3	0	0	1	1,870
Diamond Plate	5	M	1	0	0	0	162
Diamond Point	4	F	10	2	0	0	16,036
Diamond Prince	6	G	6	1	1	0	9,205
Diamond Raiser	5	G	8	0	1	1	4,824
Diamond Rocco	3	C	3	0	0	0	358
Diamond Rock Candy	3	F	8	2	2	1	18,570
Diamond Rocket	3	G	10	1	2	1	10,803
Diamond Roo	5	H	8	1	3	2	17,063
Diamond Saga	3	F	4	1	1	1	17,270
Diamond Sheena	4	F	6	0	0	2	3,122
Diamond Skier	2	F	8	1	0	3	7,030
Diamond Stephanie	3	F	11	1	0	0	8,855
Diamond Supreme	5	H	15	1	5	0	13,949
Diamond T	5	G	19	3	2	3	27,196
Diamond Ten	4	G	1	0	0	0	0
Diamond Terner	2	C	2	0	1	0	1,750
Diamond Tiara	4	F	3	0	0	1	10,740
Diamond Time	3	C	9	2	1	2	30,669
Diamond Trail	5	M	9	3	3	0	27,851
Diamond Treasure	2	F	6	0	1	1	7,246
Diamond Trick	4	F	6	0	1	0	2,475
Diamond Trip	2	C	3	0	0	0	575
Diamond Up	2	F	8	2	0	1	19,440
Diamond Wally	3	G	9	0	1	0	2,181
Diamond Whiz	4	F	1	0	0	0	0
Diamond Willy	4	C	1	0	0	0	540
Diamond Wonder	3	F	2	0	0	0	260
Diamond Year	6	G	5	0	0	0	288
Diamond Zana	9	M	5	0	0	0	0
Diamond Zim	3	G	7	0	0	0	993
Diamondinthebay	5	H	6	0	0	0	448
Diamondintherough	5	G	13	1	1	3	4,331
Diamonds' Adieu	3	G	8	1	0	0	9,098
Diamonds and Curls	2	F	4	0	0	0	285
Diamonds and Fuhr	2	F	7	0	0	1	1,210
Diamonds and Lace	2	F	11	1	1	1	21,231
Diamonds and Notes	6	H	8	4	1	1	31,320
Diamonds Devil	6	M	2	0	0	0	79
Diamonds for Lil	3	F	2	0	0	0	270
Diamonds for Ruth	6	M	1	0	0	0	0
Diamonds in Style	2	G	2	0	0	0	720
Diamonds Jubilee	5	M	4	0	0	0	110
Diamonds N Excess	2	G	1	0	0	0	0
Diamonds Only	3	F	10	3	4	0	57,750
Diamonds R Us	4	G	5	1	0	0	6,584
Diamonds Specs	2	F	4	0	0	1	2,150
Diamonds Trump	4	F	9	0	0	1	705
Diamondsareforever	2	F	3	1	0	0	13,368
Diamondsfordebbi	4	F	1	0	0	0	0
Diamondsnrainbows	2	F	2	0	0	0	0
Diamondsofemblems	2	F	1	0	0	0	0
Diamondsrbueno	2	F	5	0	2	1	14,412
Diamonice	6	G	11	4	0	2	33,665
Diamonique	3	F	13	2	1	2	13,370

Horse	Age	Sex	Sts	1st	2d	3d	Won
Diana Moseley	5	M	10	0	0	0	3,311
Diana of the Woods	3	F	9	2	0	1	30,041
Diana's Angel	3	F	9	1	2	0	4,642
Diana's Count	4	C	8	1	2	2	11,219
Dianas Welcome	2	G	4	1	3	0	18,500
Dianes Angel	4	F	6	0	0	0	400
Diane's Dazzle	6	G	9	0	0	0	0
Diane's Paranoide	3	G	9	0	1	1	2,152
Dianna Cat	4	F	6	1	0	1	13,159
Diannak's Birdie	3	F	5	0	0	0	538
Diano	6	G	6	1	1	1	28,520
Dianthus	2	F	4	1	1	0	27,540
Diaper Rash	4	F	4	0	0	0	309
Diatribe	3	C	9	2	0	0	28,090
Diazo Jo	4	G	11	2	3	1	14,032
Diazo Sport	7	M	2	0	0	1	1,078
Diazolical	5	H	1	0	0	0	0
Diazos Dazzle	4	F	4	1	0	0	7,592
Dice and Slice	2	C	1	0	0	0	1,750
Dice Doctor	5	M	7	0	1	0	7,600
Dick Ford	3	C	5	0	2	0	11,240
Dicken's Storm	6	H	1	0	0	0	1,300
Dickens Too	5	M	9	0	2	1	5,536
Dickey Rickey	10	G	11	0	3	0	15,185
Dickory H Dock	3	G	4	0	1	0	1,980
Dicks Blockbuster	5	G	3	1	1	1	7,925
Dick's Chick	4	F	10	3	1	2	105,010
Dick's Hunter	2	G	3	0	0	0	0
Dick's Last Bear	6	G	4	1	0	0	2,520
Dick's Orphan	4	G	4	0	0	0	104
Dicky	4	G	7	1	0	2	5,882
Dicy Choice	3	F	4	0	0	0	765
Did He Biteyou	4	G	7	4	1	0	71,240
Did We Win	3	F	11	1	1	2	24,845
Didit	5	M	2	0	0	0	0
Diditellyou	3	F	3	1	0	0	7,980
Dieago	8	G	5	0	1	2	5,500
Dienekes	4	G	11	2	3	1	21,260
Diero	3	C	13	2	2	0	9,690
Diesel Annie	3	F	3	0	0	0	1,835
Diesel Earl	3	G	15	2	0	1	15,995
Diesel Electric	6	G	13	1	3	1	7,719
Diesel Fuel	3	C	5	0	0	0	561
Dif a Dot	8	M	1	0	0	0	138
Different Class	4	C	3	2	0	0	21,600
Different Judge	7	G	2	0	0	1	208
Different Kind	3	C	9	1	1	0	15,780
Differentami	5	M	1	0	0	0	210
Difficult Times	4	F	8	0	0	3	2,626
Diffina	3	F	8	2	1	0	15,132
Dig for Diamonds	2	F	3	0	1	0	1,100
Dig for It	8	H	2	0	1	0	12,220
Dig That Angel	5	H	1	0	0	0	0
Dig That Rhythm	2	C	2	0	0	0	0
Dig This Coyote	5	H	9	0	1	2	3,370
Dig This Hoss	4	G	15	2	2	3	15,940
Digger Ben	3	G	1	0	0	0	0
Digger of Diamonds	2	G	4	1	0	0	13,532
Digger's Reply	4	G	12	1	1	1	3,201
Diggers Rest	4	G	6	1	1	0	11,077
Digger's Ridge	3	G	4	0	0	0	149
Diggin After Dark	3	G	2	0	0	0	0
Diggin' Calamity	6	M	10	1	0	3	5,268
Digging for Gold	5	G	7	0	0	0	346
Digging Out	6	G	2	0	0	0	0
Digginginoklahoma	4	G	2	1	1	0	8,440
Diggs	3	G	7	1	0	1	5,433
Diggy's Dream	2	C	1	0	0	0	0
Digimon	3	C	10	2	1	1	37,250
Digit Dancer	4	G	5	1	2	0	14,797
Digital Man	7	H	5	0	0	0	138
Digitech	5	H	6	1	1	2	13,220
Digity Dancer	4	C	6	0	1	3	9,030
Diglett	5	G	3	1	0	0	26,625
Dig'n Summer	2	F	2	0	0	0	0
Dignatario	3	G	13	2	3	2	24,663
Dignibell	2	G	1	0	0	0	0
Dignified Donovan	4	G	13	2	1	7	133,996
Dignified Gal	3	F	4	0	0	1	640
Dignified Pen	3	F	13	4	1	1	16,841
Digniflite	7	G	9	0	0	7	32,975
Dignus	3	G	2	1	0	0	11,400
Digwest	2	C	4	0	1	0	1,930
Dil	3	G	9	1	0	0	18,720
Dileb'sroughgirl	4	F	6	1	0	3	9,192
Dilechance	4	G	6	2	0	0	19,149
Diligent Gal	3	F	9	1	1	0	6,148
Diligent Gambler	2	C	3	0	1	0	7,620
Diligent Manners	5	M	9	4	2	0	46,285
Diligent Princess	3	F	3	2	0	1	35,860
Diligent Spirit	2	G	1	0	0	0	75
Diligent Won	3	G	10	1	0	1	10,024
Dilijinx	3	G	12	0	0	0	1,610
Dill Pickle	2	C	1	0	0	0	0
Dilley Dad Burn It	6	G	1	0	0	0	0
Dillinger	4	G	9	2	3	2	147,817
Dillionaire (GB)	7	G	4	1	0	0	5,093
Dillon R.	3	G	5	2	0	0	12,655
Dilloncovergound	2	C	1	0	0	0	0
Dillonmyboy	6	G	5	1	1	2	33,380
Dillon's Turn	4	G	1	0	1	0	1,300
Dilly Dally	5	M	15	0	4	3	15,497
Dilly Ish	4	F	12	2	1	2	10,330
Dillye	5	M	2	0	2	0	16,600
Dilly's Dragon	4	C	2	0	0	0	111
Diloot	3	F	5	1	1	2	20,020
Dim Sums	5	G	6	0	0	0	840
Dimanno	6	G	4	0	0	0	628
Dimar Briefneedles	4	F	3	0	1	0	650
Dimar Moon Lark	4	C	3	1	0	0	5,640
Dimashq	4	C	1	0	0	0	208
Dime	5	G	8	1	1	1	8,370
Dime Across	5	M	4	0	1	0	3,340
Dime Novel	9	G	12	2	0	2	14,150
Dimeonthewinner	2	F	3	0	0	0	660
Dimilynne	3	F	7	0	3	3	9,485
Dimitri T	6	G	1	0	0	0	100
Dimitrova	3	F	7	4	1	1	1,042,970
Dimmit County	4	G	7	1	1	2	5,967
Dimpled Ballot	5	G	5	0	1	1	10,210
Dimpled Chad	4	F	10	2	2	1	20,935
Dinadoon	3	F	5	0	2	1	4,100
Dinah's Dance	3	F	2	0	0	1	1,190
Dinah's Pearls	3	F	7	0	3	0	24,660
Dinan (ARG)	5	G	9	2	1	0	27,115
Dinapayme	4	F	1	0	0	0	0
Dindi	2	F	1	0	0	0	0
Dine At Tiffany	4	F	4	0	0	0	197
Dinero	4	G	13	3	0	0	13,885
Ding Dang Outlaw	4	G	20	3	4	4	24,612
Dingo Ringo	4	G	10	3	2	2	28,661
Ding's Thing	2	F	4	3	0	0	56,660
Dini Dee	6	M	10	0	0	3	5,630
Dinkers Angel	3	F	12	3	1	4	18,090
Dinkers Cheqmate	4	F	13	2	2	2	14,524
Dinkers Dollar	3	G	12	1	0	3	7,048
Dinkers Forever	2	G	8	0	2	3	7,780
Dinkers Good News	3	G	12	1	3	2	16,270
Dinkers Millennium	4	C	5	1	1	0	8,094
Dinkers Pride	3	F	14	1	5	2	21,757
Dinkers Storm	3	G	9	0	1	1	3,183
Dinky Doo	5	G	3	0	0	1	867
Dinner At Ago's	2	G	5	0	0	0	4,400
Dinner At Jackies	3	F	8	0	1	1	12,499
Dinner At Lido's	4	F	16	3	2	2	20,512
Dinner Axe	4	G	11	1	2	0	9,882
Dinner Band	6	G	11	2	2	0	12,337
Dinner Bound	4	G	11	2	1	3	28,899
Dinner Cider	3	G	10	2	2	0	12,161
Dinner Drums	4	G	13	0	3	2	4,474
Dinner Flight	2	C	4	0	0	0	300
Dinner for Sure	3	F	13	3	5	1	31,020
Dinner Ghost	2	F	1	0	0	0	150
Dinner Mint	2	F	11	2	0	2	18,180
Dinner Music	2	G	2	0	0	0	0
Dinner Soon	4	G	5	1	0	0	4,604
Dinner Sweets	3	F	9	2	2	2	21,950
Dinner Treat	5	M	2	0	0	0	123

Horse	Age	Sex	Sts	1st	2d	3d	Won
Dinner With Ivy	2	F	5	0	0	1	2,640
Dinner Withawinner	3	F	18	3	1	3	35,440
Dinnerathepalms	6	G	9	1	1	0	14,450
Dinner's On Dom	5	M	11	0	1	2	3,320
Dino Bambino	6	G	9	0	1	0	3,509
Dino Blue	3	G	4	1	0	1	6,403
Dino the Immigrant	2	G	5	0	0	0	0
Dino's Dancer	4	G	9	1	0	1	8,724
Din's Got Game	4	G	20	3	5	2	20,457
Din's Punch	2	C	1	0	0	0	45
Diosa Del Sol	4	F	6	0	0	2	8,101
Diplomat	8	G	16	5	2	3	54,345
Diplomate Girl	4	F	2	0	0	0	0
Diplomatic Corps	8	H	10	1	2	4	19,480
Diplomatic Dream	7	M	5	0	0	0	0
Diplomatic Flight	3	F	2	0	0	0	230
Diplomatic Lady	3	F	13	2	2	4	39,219
Diplomatic Lass	4	F	8	1	1	0	3,806
Diplomatic Phil	11	H	9	0	1	0	1,140
Diplomatic Pirate	10	G	4	2	0	0	11,732
Diplomatic Prince	6	H	7	0	2	2	4,216
Diplomatic Ties	3	G	2	1	0	0	7,800
Diplomatical	6	G	19	10	2	0	58,460
Diplomatically	5	G	3	0	0	0	97
Diplomaticdame B B	4	F	2	0	0	0	0
Diplomaticimmunity	5	G	9	0	0	0	682
Diplomats Money	5	G	12	1	0	3	7,531
Diplomat's Reward	8	G	20	1	4	2	21,575
Dipper Doos Voyage	4	F	4	1	0	0	7,587
Dipper's Dancer	4	F	14	1	2	4	32,110
Dipsydoodle Dancer	2	F	2	0	0	2	4,450
Dipthehalk	2	C	1	0	0	0	230
Direct	4	F	12	2	2	2	40,996
Direct Attack	3	F	11	1	2	1	21,155
Direct Charge	7	G	9	1	5	0	22,549
Direct Current	8	G	10	0	0	0	2,490
Direct Deposit	5	M	1	0	0	0	0
Direct Gold	4	G	14	4	3	5	18,719
Direct Hamer	2	C	7	1	0	1	6,480
Direct Investment	11	G	8	0	3	2	4,100
Direct Kick	4	G	8	1	1	0	6,004
Direct Light	6	H	1	0	0	0	0
Direct Male	3	G	5	2	2	0	53,250
Direct Miss	2	F	2	0	0	1	1,778
Direct the Flag	6	H	12	0	0	1	4,368
Directaccess	5	H	8	1	2	3	4,586
Directed Verdict	7	G	10	0	0	1	848
Director of Sports	2	G	2	0	0	0	245
Directors Choice	3	G	5	0	1	1	2,522
Directs Unique One	2	C	1	0	0	0	0
Dirt Ball	2	C	1	0	0	0	126
Dirt Dancer	9	M	10	1	1	2	6,366
Dirt Road Devil	4	G	13	2	2	2	41,190
Dirt Slinger	4	G	1	0	0	0	0
Dirt Storm	5	G	7	0	0	0	1,011
Dirtdobler	5	G	11	2	1	3	14,402
Dirty Bird	5	G	12	2	1	1	20,980
Dirty Blonde	4	F	13	0	1	3	11,066
Dirty Bob	3	G	4	0	0	0	300
Dirty Diana	2	F	5	2	2	0	153,397
Dirty Don	3	G	3	0	0	0	246
Dirty Doug	7	G	20	3	8	1	70,670
Dirty Duke	7	G	13	1	2	4	13,586
Dirty Gerdy	4	F	11	0	0	2	3,990
Dirty Harryette	4	F	13	4	2	1	62,023
Dirty Martini	2	G	1	0	1	0	8,200
Dirty Mike	8	G	15	1	1	5	53,980
Dirty O Harry	2	G	4	0	0	0	330
Dirty Red	6	G	10	5	3	0	62,305
Dirty Secret	3	F	13	2	2	0	16,060
Dirty Shame	5	H	7	1	0	0	5,109
Dirty Tactics	3	G	1	1	0	0	4,260
Dirty Vacation	3	C	2	0	0	0	0
Dirtymoposse	2	C	3	1	1	0	13,275
Di's Delight	3	F	11	2	2	1	54,300
Di's Last Gift	2	C	4	1	0	1	4,718
Di's Little Guy	3	G	1	0	0	0	0
Dis Miss	2	F	2	1	0	0	20,510
Disappearance	5	G	10	2	1	0	31,128
Disappeared	7	G	9	2	1	2	68,385
Disappearing	3	C	7	0	2	0	3,175
Disappearing Dan	3	C	9	0	0	0	1,260
Discern	2	C	2	0	0	0	900
Discernment	3	G	8	3	2	0	61,941
Discipline	6	H	15	1	1	0	7,470
Disco Cowboy	6	H	2	0	0	0	213
Disco Crane	4	F	1	0	0	0	0
Disco John	4	G	14	1	2	1	10,144
Disco Lights	3	C	8	0	0	3	7,924
Disco Robin	5	M	12	1	3	1	28,669
Discomagic	3	F	2	0	0	0	110
Discoman	4	G	8	0	0	0	12,796
Discordant	4	C	7	0	1	0	3,033
Discos Pearl	5	M	8	0	0	2	10,394
Discounted	2	F	7	0	0	0	1,620
Discover Eva	4	F	5	1	0	0	7,444
Discover the Glory	3	C	11	1	5	1	83,545
Discover This	3	G	3	0	0	0	180
Discovered Coin	3	G	1	0	1	0	1,480
Discovering Money	5	G	8	1	0	2	4,659
Discovering You	3	G	14	2	2	0	17,904
Discreet Caper	6	G	2	0	0	0	350
Discreet Hero	5	G	6	0	2	1	37,715
Discreetly Irish	5	M	11	3	0	3	29,591
Disearnment	3	G	16	2	3	3	24,643
Disenfranchised	5	M	11	2	0	1	16,337
Disgruntled	4	G	17	4	3	1	32,692
Disguised	3	C	6	2	2	1	44,030
Disguys Dalimit	8	G	7	3	1	0	61,660
Dish Boggett	3	G	3	0	0	0	455
Disirable Danzig	2	F	3	0	0	0	630
Dismissed a Blurr	3	G	1	0	0	0	0
Dismissedhertouch	2	F	3	1	0	0	5,775
Disorderly Conduct	2	C	5	0	0	0	775
Disorientated Al	5	G	11	1	0	1	6,550
Dispatch Sue	3	F	7	2	0	0	11,410
Dispersal Man	5	H	2	0	0	0	179
Disperse Gold	5	G	22	4	2	3	16,833
Dispersed Reward	5	M	3	0	0	1	5,990
Disputed Intent	4	F	12	3	4	0	12,795
Disqueada (ARG)	8	M	10	0	0	2	3,404
Disrupt	3	F	6	1	1	1	49,550
Disruption	4	G	7	2	0	0	14,350
Dissension	7	G	8	0	0	0	580
Distant Beau	2	F	3	0	0	0	0
Distant Daughter	5	M	5	0	1	0	5,148
Distant Days	5	G	3	1	0	0	6,210
Distant Dibo	6	H	3	0	0	0	0
Distant Echo	5	G	4	0	1	0	1,560
Distant Formation	2	C	1	0	0	0	0
Distant Kid	5	G	16	0	0	2	4,026
Distant Kin	5	M	16	1	4	3	15,756
Distant Moon	6	G	9	5	0	1	39,372
Distant Mountain	3	C	4	1	1	0	13,710
Distant Time	4	C	5	0	1	0	1,339
Distant Valley (GB)	4	F	6	0	1	2	22,340
Distant Venture	8	G	13	2	4	3	14,179
Distant Wizard	2	G	5	1	0	0	3,537
Distante	4	C	10	0	3	2	18,495
Distinct Advantage	4	G	11	1	1	0	18,260
Distinct Diamond	2	G	5	0	0	0	3,410
Distinct Honor	5	G	5	0	0	0	293
Distinct Power	7	G	7	0	0	2	5,100
Distinct Prospect	2	G	2	0	0	0	556
Distinct Vision	3	G	12	6	3	0	138,460
Distinction	4	C	13	3	0	2	68,920
Distinctive Bid	9	G	8	2	3	1	21,910
Distinctive Blues	3	G	12	1	3	0	9,043
Distinctive Cal	4	C	13	1	0	4	14,061
Distinctive Code	4	F	9	4	1	2	171,650
Distinctive Deed	3	F	12	0	6	3	13,162
Distinctive Devil	3	G	2	0	0	0	638
Distinctive Ed	3	G	11	1	1	1	17,210
Distinctive Flyer	4	F	7	0	3	3	17,040
Distinctive Groom	5	H	8	0	0	2	6,290
Distinctive Kitten	3	F	12	3	1	4	80,390
Distinctive Livin	2	F	1	0	0	1	4,510
Distinctive Melody	3	F	2	0	0	0	480

Horse	Age	Sex	Sts	1st	2d	3d	Won	Horse	Age	Sex	Sts	1st	2d	3d	Won
Distinctive Miss	2	F	1	0	0	0	0	Dixie Code Red	3	C	9	0	2	2	7,651
Distinctive Mr. B	7	G	15	1	1	4	44,564	Dixie Colonel	8	G	10	2	1	0	5,620
Distinctive One	5	H	8	0	1	0	1,102	Dixie Colony	3	G	4	1	1	2	13,580
Distinctive Roses	6	M	2	0	0	0	0	Dixie Cup	3	C	13	0	1	2	18,960
Distinctive Speed	4	G	2	0	0	0	420	Dixie D' Or	6	M	5	0	0	0	198
Distinctive Style	3	C	2	0	0	1	1,625	Dixie Dance Band	7	G	12	0	3	3	5,304
Distinctly	4	F	6	2	0	2	13,150	Dixie Decor	2	C	1	0	0	0	126
Distinctly Bold	4	C	1	0	0	0	0	Dixie Dee Dee	3	F	1	0	0	0	0
Distinctly Carotic	8	G	15	3	2	2	15,613	Dixie Do More	4	F	1	0	0	0	0
Distinctly Curious	3	C	7	0	1	2	3,127	Dixie Doree	5	M	7	0	1	2	20,440
Distinctly Perfect	2	G	4	1	1	0	9,058	Dixie Dream	4	F	5	3	0	0	77,400
Distinguish	2	C	3	1	0	0	17,400	Dixie Drifter	6	G	9	6	0	0	11,051
Distinguishable	3	C	12	2	3	2	68,952	Dixie Drummer	5	G	10	2	0	3	41,240
Distinguished Gent	3	C	4	1	0	1	26,780	Dixie Embers	8	G	13	2	0	1	5,364
Distorted Cat	3	G	14	1	3	4	29,423	Dixie Feline	4	F	12	3	0	2	34,250
Distorted Humor Jr	3	G	13	1	1	2	11,135	Dixie G	4	F	8	1	1	0	11,105
Distorted Power	6	G	10	4	0	0	68,820	Dixie Gambler	6	M	5	0	1	1	2,146
Distract	6	G	13	2	0	1	8,106	Dixie Heart	2	F	5	0	1	0	1,875
Distressed Debt	2	C	4	2	0	0	53,400	Dixie High	2	F	5	2	0	1	95,945
Distribute	5	G	8	2	0	1	11,545	Dixie Jane	3	F	9	1	1	1	12,521
District	6	H	8	0	0	1	4,875	Dixie Jazz	3	G	13	1	3	1	9,965
Disturbingthepeace	5	G	6	1	0	2	142,000	Dixie Jig	3	G	8	2	0	1	7,727
Ditch Digger (ARG)	8	G	13	6	0	2	172,440	Dixie Laurel's	7	M	4	1	1	1	27,350
Ditch Witch D	3	F	3	0	0	0	0	Dixie Law	7	G	5	1	0	1	37,420
Ditch'em	4	G	5	0	1	1	6,060	Dixie Lightning	2	F	3	0	0	0	2,220
Ditka	6	G	15	2	3	1	13,435	Dixie Mama	2	F	4	0	0	0	734
Diva Dancer	4	F	4	1	0	0	4,882	Dixie Morning	5	H	6	0	0	0	128
Diva Del Sol	4	F	11	2	0	1	18,867	Dixie of Perth	7	G	2	0	0	1	650
Diva Diver	5	M	2	0	0	0	0	Dixie Preacher	3	G	4	1	1	0	34,030
Diva Girl	4	F	3	0	0	0	2,880	Dixie Pumpkin	4	G	1	0	0	0	140
Diva Star	2	F	9	2	1	1	23,280	Dixie Punch	2	F	3	0	0	1	3,255
Diva's Dividend	5	M	9	0	0	0	2,820	Dixie Ragamuffin	4	F	5	0	0	0	416
Divas Song	5	M	12	1	2	1	8,406	Dixie Rap	3	G	9	1	1	4	21,995
Dive Bomber	7	H	3	0	0	0	280	Dixie Ridge	4	F	13	2	2	1	27,543
Dive for Gold	4	C	12	1	3	2	16,577	Dixie Roll	3	F	4	1	0	0	11,820
Diversification	6	H	1	0	0	0	72	Dixie Run	6	H	8	2	1	2	40,450
Diversifieddiamond	2	C	8	1	2	3	16,425	Dixie Says Goodbye	6	M	15	2	1	3	11,896
Diversionary	2	C	2	0	0	0	285	Dixie Setongo	4	F	16	1	3	2	12,269
Divided Nation	3	G	6	1	1	0	11,464	Dixie Skipper	3	G	10	0	0	0	663
Dividendum	3	G	17	2	6	2	12,520	Dixie Soup	3	F	8	0	3	0	25,369
Divine Assurance	4	G	16	3	3	3	34,620	Dixie Stripes	4	G	6	0	0	0	1,328
Divine Bird	3	F	2	1	0	0	29,820	Dixie Sunset	6	H	5	1	1	1	6,002
Divine Choice	4	F	9	0	2	1	3,861	Dixie T	3	F	6	0	0	1	1,112
Divine Class	4	F	12	0	2	0	13,790	Dixie Tactics	5	M	4	2	0	0	69,535
Divine Climb	3	F	7	0	0	0	2,050	Dixie Thrill	7	G	10	1	2	3	57,080
Divine for Sure	3	G	1	0	0	0	0	Dixie Two Thousand	5	H	3	0	0	0	1,350
Divine Grace	4	F	4	0	0	1	2,253	Dixie Velvet	5	M	2	0	0	0	2,474
Divine Hammer	5	G	10	4	3	0	57,675	Dixie Victory	7	G	9	1	2	1	8,775
Divine Hope	3	F	5	0	2	1	27,373	Dixie Waltz	2	F	5	2	1	1	80,513
Divine Love	3	F	2	1	0	1	31,705	Dixie Whistler	5	G	15	1	2	3	27,807
Divine Luck	6	H	1	0	0	0	0	Dixie Witch	4	F	11	2	0	2	27,156
Divine Madness	4	G	8	0	1	0	3,245	Dixieland Bear	3	C	10	0	0	2	8,640
Divine Miracle	3	C	6	0	0	2	3,260	Dixieland Beat	3	G	3	0	1	2	7,023
Divine Miss N	2	F	4	1	1	1	9,100	Dixieland Creation	9	G	9	2	0	1	8,415
Divine Order	7	G	11	1	0	2	7,646	Dixieland Dixie	2	F	1	0	0	0	320
Divine Prospect	4	F	4	1	2	0	36,900	Dixieland Girl	4	F	2	1	0	0	6,480
Divine Providence	5	H	1	0	0	0	840	Dixieland Gulch	3	F	5	2	1	0	43,500
Divine Quest	2	C	1	0	0	0	130	Dixieland Heater	2	G	5	4	0	0	57,050
Divine Right	4	G	7	0	2	1	7,989	Dixieland King	3	C	1	1	0	0	11,520
Divine Romancer	4	C	1	0	0	0	0	Dixieland Lady	5	M	6	0	2	1	3,222
Divine Spirit	5	H	7	1	2	1	22,400	Dixieland Moon	3	C	1	0	0	0	0
Divino Blanco	2	G	2	0	0	1	540	Dixieland Plan	4	F	15	0	2	3	19,582
Divisional Champ	6	G	5	0	0	2	2,085	Dixieland Rose	3	F	11	0	1	1	4,993
Divorce Lawyer Jay	3	C	7	1	1	3	21,980	Dixieland Shadow	3	F	2	0	0	0	189
Divorce Me C. O. D.	6	G	19	0	1	1	4,576	Dixielander	8	H	5	0	0	0	744
Divot	6	G	8	1	1	1	8,721	Dixielands Devil	5	G	8	2	2	2	37,180
Divvy	3	F	3	0	0	0	500	Dixielandvalentine	5	M	4	0	0	1	787
Divy's Charm	2	F	7	0	0	0	930	Dixieliere	4	F	4	0	0	0	120
Dixey Bull	3	G	7	1	0	1	8,400	Dixieman Blues	5	H	3	1	0	0	6,430
Dixie Baghdad	3	C	1	0	0	0	0	Dixiemore	6	G	27	1	3	5	25,221
Dixie Bar the Door	2	F	5	1	1	1	5,850	Dixie's Band	5	H	9	1	1	0	18,640
Dixie Beauty	8	M	5	1	0	0	6,534	Dixies Eskimo	3	G	3	0	1	0	3,115
Dixie Blue Boy	4	C	7	0	0	0	797	Dixie's Hero	3	G	6	0	2	0	15,980
Dixie Bound	3	F	11	1	3	2	7,252	Dixie's Irish	3	G	14	0	3	2	12,578
Dixie Bourbon	3	C	6	1	1	0	37,780	Dixie's Secret	5	H	2	0	1	0	1,500
Dixie Boy	2	C	5	1	1	0	16,879	Dixietownlady	5	M	12	2	1	3	25,430
Dixie Can Can	3	F	1	1	0	0	24,600	Dizzi Mister Rizzi	3	C	4	3	1	0	36,150
Dixie Charm	4	F	5	0	0	0	603	Dizzy Bend	11	G	1	0	0	0	0
Dixie Chix	3	F	6	1	0	1	8,350	Dizzy Diggy	6	H	23	2	2	7	20,830

Horse	Age	Sex	Sts	1st	2d	3d	Won
Dizzy Miss Lizzy	4	F	2	0	0	0	200
Dj's Bucky Buster	3	C	9	3	0	2	16,987
Dk Gold	2	F	2	0	0	0	2,380
Dlassy Dee	4	F	10	0	0	0	478
Dmitrilynne	2	F	5	0	0	1	2,107
Dm's Dancing Dolly	5	M	5	0	1	0	1,200
Do as I Please	5	M	5	0	0	0	540
Do Da Eisel	7	G	5	0	0	0	407
Do Go Fast	3	F	3	0	0	0	374
Do I Dare	3	C	1	0	0	0	0
Do I Ever	8	G	10	3	2	0	46,900
Do I Make Ya Randi	3	F	4	1	1	0	13,664
Do It Again Blake	4	G	6	0	0	0	415
Do It Again Bragg	4	G	12	4	1	2	16,452
Do It Again Dad	3	G	3	0	0	0	3,780
Do It Again Daisy	3	F	9	1	0	0	2,544
Do It Again Honey	7	M	8	1	1	0	3,934
Do It All	6	H	1	0	0	0	0
Do It Deputy	4	G	21	2	2	5	24,389
Do It My Way	7	G	10	5	0	1	69,920
Do Mark	4	F	10	3	3	1	14,326
Do N Time	5	G	17	2	4	4	16,474
Do No Wrong	2	F	7	1	0	1	12,269
Do Si Darby	3	F	4	0	0	0	844
Do the Dance	4	F	17	0	2	1	3,699
Do the Deal	2	C	1	0	0	0	123
Do the Impossible	2	C	4	0	0	0	1,700
Do the Polka	4	G	2	1	0	0	5,700
Do This Do That	3	G	12	0	4	2	14,969
Do Us Proud	4	F	5	0	0	1	1,319
Do Whats Right	4	G	9	4	2	0	107,370
Do You Love It	2	F	4	0	1	0	32,728
Do You Say	5	G	6	0	0	1	1,015
Doba	6	M	1	0	0	0	0
Dobbie Joe	8	G	14	1	0	3	9,055
Dobies Little Girl	4	F	9	1	3	0	10,480
Doble Aguila (CHI)	6	G	7	1	2	0	24,800
Doc a La Doc	11	G	3	0	2	0	2,737
Doc Art	8	G	3	0	0	0	0
Doc B Quick	5	G	1	0	0	0	0
Doc Baker's Charm	2	G	3	2	0	0	43,200
Doc Christian	5	H	1	0	0	0	1,200
Doc D	4	G	10	1	2	3	71,938
Doc Fee	3	C	1	0	0	1	990
Doc Holiday (IRE)	4	C	4	0	0	0	1,160
Doc Ihnken	8	G	8	0	0	0	3,760
Doc Knows Best	4	F	4	1	1	0	20,200
Doc Magee	4	G	2	0	0	0	0
Doc Murdock	10	G	2	2	0	0	3,100
Doc N Jag	5	G	7	0	2	0	8,400
Doc N Mike	5	H	2	0	0	0	0
Doc On Tour	8	G	2	0	0	1	528
Doc Owens	3	G	10	0	2	2	10,183
Doc Pepper	4	G	9	1	1	2	10,783
Doc Pipe	3	C	3	0	0	0	134
Doc Putnam	3	C	10	0	1	2	2,624
Doc Robbins	3	C	5	1	2	1	51,380
Doc Ron	6	G	14	1	0	3	24,598
Doc Roshon	3	C	6	1	1	0	3,500
Doc Safari	5	G	15	0	2	1	4,924
Doc Senter	5	G	12	2	3	1	24,710
Doc Torry	2	G	10	0	3	1	5,676
Doc Wallace	4	G	11	1	3	2	20,180
Doc Wild	4	G	11	2	3	4	77,930
Doc Wilson	5	G	2	0	0	0	800
Doc Z Do	7	H	1	0	0	0	0
Doc Zotti	5	H	8	1	0	0	2,763
Doce Memoria	2	F	1	0	0	0	0
Docent	5	G	9	6	1	1	292,800
Docile Dame	9	M	1	0	0	0	150
Docket	3	F	3	1	1	0	13,750
Docks Day Off	5	G	18	0	5	2	7,139
Doclange	2	C	3	0	0	0	760
Doc's Allowance	4	G	6	1	0	1	16,050
Doc's Avenger	2	G	5	0	0	1	2,160
Doc's Blaze	3	F	5	0	0	0	0
Docs Boy	7	G	4	0	0	1	466
Doc's Classy Ack	2	F	1	0	0	0	0
Doc's Dingo	6	G	12	1	2	1	7,335
Doc's Doll	3	F	11	3	1	1	102,280
Doc's Fast Ack	5	M	10	1	2	0	5,365
Doc's Golden Bear	7	H	7	1	1	2	11,390
Doc's Got Game	6	G	2	0	0	0	0
Docs Gotta Wish	6	G	3	1	0	0	1,197
Doc's Honey	4	F	12	2	1	1	38,820
Doc's Image	4	G	1	0	0	0	0
Doc's In	6	G	2	0	0	0	0
Doc's Jewel	4	G	16	2	1	4	13,195
Doc's Knot	6	M	15	0	3	0	12,070
Doc's Last Shot	9	G	7	1	0	1	5,705
Doc's Legency	5	M	9	1	0	2	6,118
Doc's Lil' Angel	4	F	4	1	0	0	21,950
Doc's Lil Secret	5	G	1	0	0	0	0
Doc's Live Wire	4	G	6	0	0	0	1,754
Doc's Magic Dream	8	G	14	1	0	1	3,612
Docs Oliver	3	C	5	0	0	0	0
Doc's Option	3	G	12	2	0	2	51,550
Docs Plan	8	G	16	1	0	1	5,851
Doc's Pretty Boy	5	H	4	1	0	0	14,400
Docs Puddin	5	M	13	4	0	1	51,812
Doc's Rasheed	6	G	9	1	2	2	2,980
Doc's Reasoning	2	F	5	0	0	0	216
Doc's Redhead	3	F	2	0	0	0	0
Doc's Rocket	4	G	3	0	1	1	3,510
Doc's Treasure	4	F	10	2	1	1	13,972
Docs Tyrant	5	H	8	2	3	1	7,346
Doctor	4	G	9	1	1	1	12,693
Doctor America	3	F	17	2	2	2	83,170
Doctor Covington	10	G	9	3	1	1	5,050
Doctor D. K.	8	G	16	4	5	2	23,383
Doctor Doctor Mrmd	3	C	4	0	0	1	1,835
Doctor Donnie	3	C	3	0	0	0	208
Doctor Doo Wop	4	G	8	1	4	0	39,970
Doctor Dr Please	3	G	3	0	0	0	220
Doctor Dragon	4	G	5	0	1	0	1,608
Doctor Free	3	F	2	0	0	0	775
Doctor Halsey	7	H	1	0	0	0	46
Doctor Hi	2	C	1	0	0	0	525
Doctor Hilary	3	F	6	0	0	0	3,240
Doctor Ivan	6	H	2	0	1	0	1,400
Doctor Jalili	3	C	4	3	0	0	81,600
Doctor John	9	G	12	3	0	2	9,678
Doctor M	3	G	6	1	0	0	5,400
Doctor Mike	6	H	13	3	1	4	131,075
Doctor of Spin	8	G	9	2	1	1	8,617
Doctor Price	3	G	6	2	1	2	25,050
Doctor Rio	2	G	2	0	0	0	700
Doctor Rock	2	C	1	0	0	0	0
Doctor Suger	5	G	1	0	0	0	0
Doctor Ted	3	C	3	1	0	1	38,400
Doctor Topdog	2	G	3	0	0	0	136
Doctor Turko	3	G	7	0	2	0	8,800
Doctorinthehouse	4	G	10	0	3	0	12,046
Doctor's Approval	4	C	3	0	0	0	573
Doctor's Opinion	3	G	14	0	0	2	9,259
Doctress	3	F	1	0	0	0	350
Document Express	3	G	17	1	2	3	13,370
Documento	8	G	19	3	3	0	24,546
Documoments	3	F	7	0	0	0	549
Dodge City Annie	4	F	8	1	1	1	5,442
Dodge City Girl	3	F	16	1	4	2	12,005
Dodge City Kitty	5	M	5	0	0	0	82
Dodgers Island	6	H	10	1	0	1	2,323
Dodgeumtowin	4	C	4	0	0	0	372
Dodgeville	3	C	5	0	0	0	2,640
Dodi N Me	2	F	2	0	0	0	390
Doeny	5	H	5	2	0	0	37,710
Doeny Rain	4	C	2	0	0	1	4,645
Doeny's Daughter	3	F	5	0	1	0	1,450
Doey Wild	3	F	7	0	1	0	6,888
Dog	3	G	4	1	0	1	5,745
Dog Days	4	C	3	1	0	0	34,760
Dog Gone	6	H	6	0	1	0	3,446
Dog Gone Lucky	2	G	5	1	0	0	14,220
Dog House	4	G	3	0	0	0	0
Dog Soldier	6	H	1	0	0	0	59
Dog Tags	6	H	5	0	2	0	7,808
Dogleg Left	2	C	1	0	0	0	0

Horse	Age	Sex	Sts	1st	2d	3d	Won
Dog's Last Dance	4	F	3	0	0	0	0
D'ohana (ARG)	5	M	8	0	2	3	36,780
Doin Dixie	3	G	2	0	0	0	0
Doin' It Easy	3	F	7	1	0	0	16,020
Doin' Wheelies	6	G	13	3	0	0	17,240
Doinalright	4	C	3	0	0	0	900
Doing It Our Way	2	F	7	0	0	2	7,436
Doingtime	2	F	5	1	0	4	18,950
Doinitforpleasure	8	G	2	1	1	0	4,255
Doitdoitdoit	4	F	7	0	1	4	5,700
Doityourself	3	F	7	1	2	2	8,455
Dokey	5	G	7	0	1	0	2,580
Dolan Bobby	3	F	2	0	0	0	100
Dolan Hill	3	F	8	1	3	1	27,427
Dolce Dawn	6	M	5	1	0	2	9,310
Dolce Latte	2	F	4	1	0	0	2,760
Dolcelina	3	F	14	5	3	1	52,750
Dolcetta	3	F	7	3	0	0	17,662
Dole	6	H	6	1	1	1	15,725
Doll Dance	4	F	3	1	0	0	3,756
Doll Gift	3	F	15	2	1	0	9,402
Doll to Call	3	F	7	0	1	0	1,805
Dollar a Dip	2	C	5	2	1	0	22,620
Dollar a Minute	4	F	11	0	6	1	14,675
Dollar Bill	5	H	1	0	0	1	55,000
Dollar Core	5	G	18	1	2	4	7,688
Dollar Diplomacy	3	G	2	0	0	1	2,030
Dollar for Dollar	3	G	15	1	5	4	23,650
Dollar Signs	5	G	3	1	0	0	12,480
Dollars and Sense	12	G	9	1	2	1	4,770
Dollartongo	6	H	1	0	0	0	0
Dollarwatchcrosing	2	G	6	0	1	1	4,083
Dollarworthofblues	11	G	7	0	0	0	200
Dolley's Goldenboy	6	G	3	1	0	1	8,300
Dolljeta	4	F	4	0	0	0	582
Doll's Forum	4	F	10	1	0	1	8,080
Dolly Dagger	5	M	3	0	1	0	940
Dolly Dynamite	3	F	6	0	2	0	26,988
Dolly M	4	F	15	1	3	3	9,910
Dolly's Delight	3	F	6	1	0	1	7,550
Dolly's Girl	4	F	12	2	0	4	9,139
Dolly's Hit Man	3	G	6	0	2	0	1,440
Dollys Renegade	6	G	8	0	0	2	4,980
Dolly's Threshold	3	G	2	0	0	0	70
Dolly's Wager	5	M	12	2	2	0	49,035
Dolphin Band	3	F	1	0	0	0	1,920
Dolphin Star	3	F	13	1	4	3	9,877
Dolvotto	5	H	5	2	0	1	1,825
Domacho Man	4	G	8	2	0	0	9,180
Domar	3	C	6	0	0	0	540
Domasca Sports	5	M	10	1	0	1	11,144
Domascas Consort	2	G	3	0	0	0	1,070
Domestic Dispute	3	C	8	1	0	1	155,367
Domestic Niner	4	F	9	0	0	0	488
Domesticate Cat	2	G	1	0	0	0	1,080
Dominant Factor	6	G	10	1	0	1	1,463
Dominant Punch B B	3	G	16	1	1	2	6,961
Dominate Jolie	2	F	1	0	0	0	75
Dominated Glory	3	F	2	1	1	0	23,400
Dominated Year	3	F	4	0	0	1	2,670
Domination	7	H	2	0	0	1	5,280
Domingo Juan (ARG)	5	H	4	2	1	0	44,400
Dominic C	3	C	5	1	0	1	7,180
Dominica	5	M	2	0	1	0	9,300
Dominican Doctor	3	G	8	0	0	2	2,590
Dominican Waltz	4	C	13	1	2	2	23,974
Dominique's Prize	3	F	3	0	0	0	651
Domino Theory	6	G	7	0	1	1	5,125
Dominus	6	G	11	3	0	1	12,182
Domnonia	6	M	11	2	1	1	33,662
Dom's Star	3	F	2	0	0	0	0
Don Amin	4	C	3	0	1	0	3,845
Don Double D	6	G	9	1	1	1	3,288
Don E Looker	6	G	12	2	0	0	11,092
Don Gatito	4	G	15	5	2	0	70,122
Don Golden (MEX)	8	G	7	2	2	1	9,658
Don Hector	3	C	13	2	1	1	26,405
Don Honig	6	G	2	0	0	0	0
Don Juan	4	C	6	1	0	2	11,085
Don Julio (MEX)	8	H	4	0	2	0	900
Don Kruse	3	G	11	2	1	0	21,972
Don Luis Felipe	3	G	2	0	0	0	248
Don Lux	4	C	2	0	0	0	1,020
Don Manuel	2	C	10	3	0	2	27,164
Don Pale	3	G	4	0	0	0	452
Don Pan	5	G	3	0	1	1	2,820
Don Ron	5	H	3	1	0	0	3,698
Don Six	3	C	12	4	4	1	193,450
Don Taco	2	C	3	0	0	0	0
Don the Cookster	5	G	7	0	2	3	23,337
Don Wilson	3	G	17	2	5	4	31,124
Dona Petronila C	7	M	3	0	0	0	0
Dona Ridge	5	M	9	0	1	0	2,476
Donadeus	3	F	5	0	1	0	6,900
Donaho Dancer	8	G	6	0	0	1	1,050
Donald David	3	G	6	0	0	0	1,020
Donald Do Right	4	C	8	2	1	0	39,280
Donald Notrump	6	H	5	0	0	1	1,740
Donald's Pride	3	C	10	6	0	2	133,817
Donald's Tomorrow	6	G	18	0	2	4	10,716
Donaldson Flats	2	G	2	1	0	0	16,800
Donandru's Dream	3	F	12	3	2	1	48,580
Donato's Run	5	H	2	0	0	1	3,500
Donazoe	6	M	13	1	0	1	5,629
Donchalisentoumdun	9	G	5	0	0	0	1,058
Donde Estaras	3	F	17	3	3	0	22,045
Done Dreaming	9	G	7	1	0	1	3,051
Done Easy	3	C	2	0	0	0	245
Done Gone Broke	3	G	6	0	1	0	1,555
Donebroke	4	F	11	3	0	1	50,165
Doniphan	7	G	13	0	3	3	11,166
Donivan's Trick	3	G	9	2	1	1	7,843
Donizetti	3	G	10	2	1	2	20,906
Donna C	4	F	6	1	0	2	7,990
Donna Jean	4	F	2	0	0	0	150
Donna Lynn	5	M	1	0	0	0	0
Donna Royalle	4	F	3	2	0	0	16,302
Donnago	3	F	8	1	0	1	3,914
Donnalark	4	F	1	0	0	0	29
Donnaree	5	M	14	4	2	4	107,997
Donnas Destiny	3	F	2	1	0	0	6,972
Donna's Golddigger	3	G	6	2	2	0	40,697
Donna's Honeymoon	3	F	3	0	0	0	240
Donna's Hope	2	F	1	0	0	0	2,100
Donna's Link	5	M	11	1	2	2	55,100
Donna's Mailbag	4	G	4	2	0	0	59,190
Donna's Ruler	3	F	6	1	0	0	5,560
Donna's Tour	6	M	3	0	1	0	8,940
Donnas Trial	2	F	6	1	0	0	34,236
Donner Queen	2	F	2	0	0	0	0
Donnie Armani	6	G	1	0	0	0	40
Donnies Jonnie	7	H	3	0	0	0	450
Donnies Pick	4	G	11	2	4	2	35,917
Donnpour Luck	4	F	2	0	0	0	0
Donny	3	G	12	2	4	2	27,008
Donnys Dimund Slew	4	C	9	4	0	0	7,702
Donovan Scores	5	G	13	3	3	1	10,057
Don's Diamond	7	H	2	0	0	1	605
Don's Fair Share	7	G	11	0	3	2	6,820
Don's Ferrari	5	H	1	0	0	0	627
Dons Hope	3	G	2	2	0	0	10,920
Don's Nell	4	F	16	2	4	4	45,096
Don's Prospector	5	G	4	1	0	1	12,556
Don's Reggin	3	F	7	0	0	0	0
Don't Agitate	3	G	10	1	0	1	20,096
Dont Argue With Me	3	C	4	1	0	0	9,600
Don't Be Cruel	3	C	9	1	0	0	15,520
Don't Be Late Jake	8	H	7	0	0	0	1,080
Don't Be Long Z	7	G	7	0	3	1	14,025
Don't Be Rash	4	F	1	0	1	0	1,500
Don't Blame Bruce	4	F	11	2	2	1	13,875
Dont Bother Me Now	4	G	3	0	0	0	1,054
Don't Box Me In	8	G	5	1	0	1	5,482
Don't Buddy Me	10	G	8	0	0	4	2,475
Don't Call Me	4	C	21	0	1	2	3,522
Don't Call Me Baby	3	F	9	1	1	1	25,185
Don't Catch Me	4	F	13	2	3	2	13,677
Don't Countess Out	4	F	7	3	3	1	164,506

Horse	Age	Sex	Sts	1st	2d	3d	Won	Horse	Age	Sex	Sts	1st	2d	3d	Won
Don't Despair	4	F	9	1	1	0	9,260	Doo Wops Girl	4	F	6	1	1	0	5,700
Don't Digress	6	M	1	0	1	0	2,200	Doodle Nel	4	F	7	1	0	0	5,520
Don't Do It	3	F	8	0	1	0	2,128	Doodles Too	2	F	3	0	0	0	0
Don't Dream	6	G	7	1	0	1	4,101	Doogielosthismind	5	G	12	2	1	2	7,166
Don't Fool J D	7	G	1	0	0	0	60	Doolittleguinevere	4	F	7	1	0	1	4,893
Don't Forget King	2	G	3	0	0	0	460	Doomsday D.	6	G	9	0	1	3	6,130
Don't Hang Up	4	C	4	1	1	0	12,211	Doon Valley Dancer	3	F	6	0	2	0	4,294
Don't Hesitate Boy	4	C	6	0	2	1	5,980	Dooneen	7	M	6	0	0	0	1,625
Dont Hold Me Down	4	G	18	1	2	4	10,755	Doonesbury Lassie	4	F	6	1	2	2	26,794
Don't Holler	4	G	11	1	1	3	15,355	Doonesbury Wine	4	C	8	1	0	0	660
Don't Ignore Her	6	M	12	6	0	1	33,920	Doonies Dancer	5	M	3	1	1	0	3,205
Don't Kiss N Tell	4	C	11	1	2	0	43,263	Doorcrasher	2	F	1	0	0	1	1,030
Dont Knock America	2	C	3	0	1	0	10,500	Doppler Radar	4	G	12	2	2	1	29,320
Don't Know Why	3	F	3	0	0	0	53	Dor V Dor	3	G	2	0	1	0	2,530
Don't Laugh At Me	3	F	7	0	0	1	1,546	Dorado Rules	3	G	12	3	1	1	26,602
Don't Lookatsuesue	8	M	4	0	0	0	0	Doran	9	H	5	1	0	0	11,730
Don't Make a Scene	4	F	2	0	0	0	84	Dora's Daughter	3	F	6	0	1	0	2,325
Dont Make Me Blush	2	F	2	1	0	0	3,809	Dora's Favorite	3	F	8	1	1	3	8,424
Don't Miss Imie	9	M	4	1	0	0	2,899	Dorel	6	M	7	0	1	1	4,946
Don't Not	6	G	12	4	5	1	27,146	Dorella	2	F	1	0	1	0	2,500
Don't Panic Pop	8	G	12	0	0	1	1,174	Dorisee	3	F	4	0	1	0	1,985
Don't Pass	5	G	12	1	1	2	16,990	Dorius (ARG)	5	G	3	0	0	1	2,300
Don't Pass Max	3	C	4	0	0	0	0	Doro's Pet Cat	2	C	3	0	0	0	570
Don't Peek	9	G	2	2	0	0	15,560	Dorothy Star	8	M	4	0	0	0	249
Don't Penny Me	4	F	10	0	1	1	2,286	Dorothys Dream	4	F	2	1	1	0	5,920
Don't Play Me	6	M	12	0	0	0	2,740	Dorothy's Wager	4	F	15	4	3	2	31,105
Don't Quit On Me	5	G	5	1	0	0	4,800	Dorsey	3	G	7	0	1	3	2,666
Dont Run Back	3	F	4	1	0	0	3,984	Dorst	2	G	6	2	1	1	28,085
Dont Run Getthegun	6	M	13	0	1	2	4,860	Dorsy Champ	4	G	12	1	0	3	10,699
Don't Seven Out	7	G	8	2	1	1	118,114	Dorus Daymaker	5	M	7	2	1	1	8,262
Don't Smoke Me	8	G	1	0	0	0	160	Dos Amigos	6	G	4	0	1	0	6,451
Don't Step Back	4	F	5	2	1	0	17,665	Dos Arriba	4	F	7	0	0	0	890
Don't Stop Now	3	F	1	0	0	0	0	Do's Buckshot	5	G	4	1	2	0	20,475
Don't Strike Out	3	G	13	4	3	1	22,195	Dos de Mayo	2	C	4	1	0	2	27,904
Don't Sugah Me	3	F	5	0	1	1	8,580	Dos Deals	5	M	16	5	2	0	29,927
Don't Tell Aly	4	F	1	1	0	0	1,200	Dos Reyes	3	C	1	0	0	0	0
Don't Tell Ashlie	2	F	2	0	0	0	0	Dot	5	M	4	3	0	0	20,126
Dont Tell Jac	3	C	3	1	0	0	40,554	Dot Com Slew	3	F	5	0	0	1	333
Don't Tell Lisa	5	M	3	0	0	0	0	Dot the Page	3	F	6	0	3	0	4,743
Don't Tell Mom	3	F	11	1	0	0	10,270	Dotabar	8	G	7	0	0	0	1,656
Don't Tell Papa	3	F	6	1	2	0	15,580	Dotage	5	H	10	0	0	2	16,140
Don't Tell the Kids	6	G	16	3	0	1	27,456	Dotar Sojet	5	G	8	2	1	1	10,620
Don't Tell Wendy	3	F	16	3	2	2	69,728	Dotcode	4	G	3	0	0	0	0
Don't Touch	5	G	5	1	0	0	7,686	Dothan	2	C	2	1	0	0	9,300
Don't Tread On Me	2	C	2	0	0	0	2,640	Dothedevilin	4	G	3	2	1	0	7,075
Don't Trick Me	8	G	15	0	2	1	4,095	Dothewildthing	2	G	8	1	1	0	18,920
Dont Waver Harvey	6	H	5	0	0	0	0	Dot's Candyman	6	H	6	0	0	1	721
Don't Weave Me	7	G	2	0	0	0	0	Dots Cove	7	G	18	2	1	1	13,818
Dont Ya Like Dat	3	G	4	1	1	1	13,285	Dots N Dashes	4	F	2	0	0	0	233
Don't You Know	3	F	4	0	1	0	580	Dots Question	6	M	3	0	0	0	269
Don't You Tell	6	G	6	1	0	0	14,843	Dotsie's Choice	4	F	2	0	0	0	255
Don'takememints	2	F	6	1	0	1	10,216	Dotted Swiss	3	F	11	1	0	4	25,830
Don'taskdon'ttell	3	G	8	0	1	1	5,650	Dottie Poo	2	F	2	1	0	0	5,490
Don'tasktheprice	5	G	17	2	1	2	13,123	Dottie's Prince	4	G	11	1	1	2	8,915
Dontaskwhy	2	C	4	0	1	0	3,600	Dou Temps	2	C	4	1	1	0	9,370
Dontbotherknocking	5	G	5	3	0	1	53,000	Double Affair	9	G	11	3	1	2	36,502
Don'tcallmeacowboy	8	H	6	0	3	1	5,808	Double Again	3	C	10	2	1	0	47,875
Don'tcallmefrisco	2	C	1	1	0	0	15,500	Double Airs	3	C	7	1	1	1	9,100
Don'tcallmeragun	3	G	5	0	0	0	0	Double Audit	3	F	3	3	0	0	46,800
Dontcounthimout	6	G	6	0	0	0	2,132	Double Barrell	5	G	6	1	0	0	3,982
Dontellannie	3	F	13	0	0	1	948	Double Bars	3	C	1	0	0	0	0
Donthatetheplayer	4	G	6	1	0	1	5,719	Double Belvedere	2	G	2	1	1	0	49,575
Don'timpressmemuch	7	M	7	1	0	2	9,982	Double Beryl	7	F	8	0	0	1	982
Dontjazzmearound	3	G	10	0	2	1	3,950	Double Bid	3	C	9	2	2	1	16,279
Dontmesswithbill	4	C	13	1	1	2	20,780	Double Blue	7	G	13	2	2	2	40,180
Don'tmindifido	4	C	7	2	1	1	19,340	Double Bogey	8	G	2	0	0	0	0
Don'tmissthetrain	9	G	4	1	0	0	8,640	Double Brite	3	F	14	1	1	3	16,099
Dontpineforme	4	F	3	0	0	0	379	Double Bucks G H S	6	G	1	0	0	0	40
Don'tplaywithfire	3	G	11	1	0	1	4,852	Double Buy Buy	4	C	16	2	1	4	25,500
Don'tpraiseme	4	C	4	2	1	0	22,420	Double Candi	3	F	1	0	0	0	0
Don'truinhappy	3	G	3	0	0	0	588	Double Cat	5	M	2	0	0	1	18,000
Dontsayaword	3	F	19	2	3	2	23,356	Double Charlie	3	F	3	0	2	0	7,680
Don'tsellmeshort	2	C	8	4	2	1	294,395	Double Chocolate	4	C	6	1	0	0	27,000
Dontsink	3	F	4	0	0	0	630	Double Choice	3	F	11	3	3	0	16,376
Don'ttrapthemouse	4	C	9	2	1	2	8,069	Double Click	3	G	2	0	0	0	100
Donuts Tomorrow	5	M	17	1	0	5	13,017	Double Coast	2	F	4	0	0	0	315
Donzroar	3	G	2	0	0	0	309	Double Cola	5	G	14	1	2	2	19,050
Doo Bert	3	G	9	1	0	0	5,595	Double Conquest	7	G	15	2	1	2	10,476
Doo Da Do	3	C	8	1	0	1	11,815	Double Crossed	3	C	6	1	1	1	10,145

RECORDS OF HORSES

Horse	Age	Sex	Sts	1st	2d	3d	Won	Horse	Age	Sex	Sts	1st	2d	3d	Won
Double Crown	3	F	6	0	0	0	950	Double Snip	5	H	3	0	1	0	672
Double Cupcake	3	F	9	1	0	1	5,770	Double Storm	3	C	4	1	1	0	16,630
Double D Money	2	G	5	1	1	0	8,507	Double Sweep	4	C	17	2	0	5	12,849
Double 'd' Special	2	F	3	0	0	0	654	Double Talk	3	G	13	1	0	2	10,197
Double Dad	3	C	9	0	0	1	4,190	Double Talkin	7	M	9	2	2	2	43,873
Double Dance	2	F	7	1	1	1	19,036	Double Team	8	G	6	0	1	1	4,225
Double Dare Ya	7	G	3	1	0	0	9,600	Double the Cash	4	F	10	0	0	1	1,304
Double Demons	9	G	9	1	1	2	4,727	Double the Dancers	5	M	1	0	0	0	0
Double Diamond Joe	2	G	2	0	0	0	165	Double the Debt	6	M	5	0	0	2	10,095
Double Didgit Baby	2	F	7	0	0	2	3,490	Double the Love	6	G	6	1	1	1	4,663
Double Digit	4	F	16	3	3	5	36,935	Double the Magic	2	C	2	1	1	0	10,148
Double Doc	3	G	9	3	2	2	74,466	Double the Sauce	5	H	10	0	2	2	7,200
Double Dog Dare Ya	4	G	8	1	2	1	9,936	Double the Speed	2	G	6	0	0	1	2,158
Double Dollar Day	6	G	11	0	1	0	1,518	Double Time	5	G	11	6	2	0	20,120
Double Down Dan	3	G	4	1	1	0	52,116	Double Tower	5	H	7	1	0	0	10,174
Double Down On Red	3	F	11	1	0	1	8,270	Double Two	4	F	3	1	0	2	6,150
Double Dreamin Deb	6	M	15	1	2	4	9,859	Double Warrior	3	C	5	0	1	0	2,277
Double Duces	4	G	14	1	2	2	11,915	Double Well	4	F	5	0	1	1	2,015
Double E Double L	3	C	13	4	1	1	44,130	Double Wild	5	H	1	0	0	0	70
Double Echo	3	C	1	0	0	0	50	Double Your Will	6	G	4	0	0	0	198
Double Eight	2	G	3	0	0	1	2,013	Double Zero Seven	4	C	1	0	1	0	3,200
Double Exuberance	10	G	10	1	2	3	8,577	Doubleback	3	G	6	0	2	0	13,640
Double Fly Pass	6	G	12	1	4	2	24,690	Doubledancindougie	5	M	1	0	0	0	0
Double Foreigner	6	G	5	0	0	1	4,000	Doubledar Diamond	8	G	2	1	0	0	17,662
Double Freeze	3	F	17	2	2	1	18,332	Doubledigitdomedog	4	G	7	0	0	0	437
Double Gloss	10	G	3	0	0	0	0	Doubledownprincess	3	F	4	0	0	0	252
Double Gone	6	G	9	0	1	1	8,625	Doubledriven	5	H	3	0	0	0	109
Double Good Lookin	2	C	3	0	0	1	1,330	Doubleoseven	6	G	4	1	0	0	3,896
Double Grace	3	G	8	2	2	0	27,121	Doublerodeo	2	F	1	0	0	0	0
Double Halo	3	F	7	1	2	0	48,175	Doubleroni	4	F	2	0	1	0	2,266
Double Hat Trick	6	M	9	2	3	2	26,881	Doubletake	2	F	3	0	0	0	180
Double Hi	6	M	13	1	2	7	26,584	Doubletrouble Bear	3	F	5	1	0	2	13,940
Double House	2	C	2	0	0	0	910	Doubly Brite	5	H	12	3	4	1	63,890
Double Image	4	F	1	0	1	0	2,090	Doubly Hard	2	C	1	0	0	1	1,800
Double Impact	2	C	7	1	4	0	13,460	Doubly Irish	3	F	4	0	0	0	2,130
Double Interest	4	C	1	0	0	0	305	Doubt Her Not	4	F	9	0	0	0	305
Double Intrigue	3	C	5	0	0	1	11,382	Doubtful Diva	3	F	7	1	1	0	20,274
Double It	8	H	7	0	0	0	110	Doubtless	3	F	5	1	3	0	39,440
Double J Ranch	3	C	4	0	0	0	670	Douceur	3	G	9	2	2	1	37,892
Double Jab	12	G	5	0	1	2	1,135	Doug the Slug	6	G	10	2	1	3	9,624
Double Jack	7	G	12	2	1	2	7,604	Dough Girl	4	F	3	0	0	1	2,585
Double Jays Slew	3	C	2	0	0	0	0	Doughty	4	F	12	4	1	2	44,735
Double Jeopardy	2	F	1	0	0	0	0	Douglas	4	G	12	2	1	0	18,504
Double K	2	C	3	1	0	0	19,300	Doug's Editorial	3	C	6	1	2	1	12,810
Double Leaf (GB)	10	G	3	0	0	0	310	Doug's Glory	4	F	3	0	0	0	310
Double Lee	3	G	1	0	0	0	0	Doug's Lad	4	G	17	6	2	4	83,838
Double Lock	2	F	2	1	0	0	28,950	Doug's Shadow	8	H	6	2	0	1	14,812
Double Luck	2	G	7	0	0	1	1,300	Dounome	5	G	2	0	0	0	1,360
Double Lyph	2	F	2	0	1	1	5,250	Doux Slew	4	G	1	0	0	0	0
Double M Express	5	G	13	2	3	2	14,832	Dove Above	3	G	10	1	4	1	53,680
Double Milion	3	G	8	2	0	2	9,008	Dove Creek	5	M	6	0	1	0	11,960
Double My Prospect	4	C	4	1	0	0	5,240	Dove Field	2	F	4	0	0	0	675
Double No Trump	6	M	1	0	0	0	0	Dove Flight	3	G	15	0	2	0	3,613
Double O James	6	G	13	2	1	1	13,073	Dove in Flight	4	F	3	1	1	0	1,874
Double O Silver	3	F	2	1	0	0	9,128	Dove Love	2	C	2	0	0	0	0
Double O Snow	3	G	1	0	0	0	0	Dove Mountain	2	C	1	0	0	0	2,160
Double O Special	3	G	11	1	2	0	10,250	Dove Up	3	G	10	1	0	1	7,010
Double Option	4	G	2	0	0	0	0	Dovedale	3	F	12	0	3	1	12,371
Double Our Flag	9	G	15	0	1	0	4,912	Doveena	4	F	11	1	3	1	5,745
Double Oxygen	3	C	17	0	1	5	8,533	Dovenos	3	F	1	0	0	0	0
Double Page	6	H	1	0	0	0	205	Dover Beach	5	G	3	0	0	0	150
Double Perfect	7	G	3	0	0	1	224	Dover Queen	3	F	5	0	1	0	2,599
Double Platinum	8	G	16	1	1	0	13,172	Doveran	6	M	1	0	0	0	0
Double Play	5	G	17	1	0	2	13,910	Dovesahighnote	3	F	1	0	0	1	1,700
Double Powder	4	G	8	0	3	0	4,772	Dovetail	4	F	2	0	0	0	1,680
Double Prince	8	G	7	1	0	1	3,630	Dovey Lovey	4	F	8	0	1	1	13,020
Double Quack	4	F	10	1	1	1	17,080	Dovishness	2	F	1	0	0	0	150
Double Reel Blaze	2	G	6	1	0	1	4,540	Dowdstown Guest (IRE)	6	G	7	0	2	0	7,431
Double Reward	3	F	14	0	1	4	6,879	Down and Out	6	G	14	4	1	1	32,910
Double Ribs	4	C	4	0	1	1	1,460	Down by the Sea	2	F	6	4	1	1	106,580
Double Ridge	2	F	7	0	0	3	6,990	Down East	3	F	4	1	0	0	7,570
Double Salty	8	G	6	2	0	1	6,682	Down Goes Frazier	4	C	7	1	1	1	9,310
Double Scoop	3	F	10	5	2	1	193,744	Down Hill Racer	7	G	5	0	1	0	10,219
Double Screen	10	G	13	1	2	2	18,176	Down in the Dirt	4	G	9	0	0	1	3,650
Double Seeded	3	G	4	1	0	0	6,205	Down Memory Lane	5	M	3	1	2	0	8,550
Double Sherry	3	F	1	0	0	0	0	Down Play	3	G	2	0	1	0	8,500
Double Shotgun	2	C	3	0	0	1	3,780	Down Right Crafty	2	F	12	1	1	2	9,935
Double Six	6	H	6	0	0	0	570	Down Set Hut	2	C	2	0	0	0	660
Double Slam	3	C	9	2	1	2	52,635	Down South Jukin	4	G	2	0	0	0	50

Horse	Age	Sex	Sts	1st	2d	3d	Won	Horse	Age	Sex	Sts	1st	2d	3d	Won
Down the Canyon	4	G	7	1	1	1	14,032	Dr. Ell	8	G	9	0	0	2	1,494
Down the Creek	2	F	7	0	0	0	1,003	Dr. Fixit	6	M	6	0	0	0	142
Down the Shore	5	G	11	1	3	1	37,445	Dr. Foozy	4	G	18	1	2	1	12,006
Down to Dixie	2	F	1	0	0	0	0	Dr. Frank	3	G	10	0	1	0	4,510
Down Up	2	C	2	0	1	0	2,000	Dr. Frosty	5	G	5	1	0	0	23,595
Downhill Skier	2	F	3	1	2	0	15,365	Dr. Game	4	C	3	0	0	1	1,287
Downing's Joker	6	G	3	0	1	1	1,894	Dr. Gary	6	G	16	1	1	1	6,543
Download	7	G	2	0	0	0	66	Dr. Glitter	4	G	2	1	1	0	5,037
Downright	4	C	4	0	0	0	800	Dr. Grayson	8	G	10	0	0	0	300
Downshift N Dustem	3	G	6	0	0	0	834	Dr. G's Hot Sauce	2	F	2	0	1	1	10,769
Downside Risk	4	F	5	1	0	1	7,755	Dr. Guiliani	4	C	8	2	3	0	72,320
Downstream Blues	4	F	1	0	0	0	0	Dr. Hager	4	C	14	2	3	2	19,637
Downtomylastbuck	3	G	7	1	2	0	32,652	Dr. Haste	2	C	1	0	0	0	0
Downtown Dilemma	3	F	4	0	1	0	920	Dr. Hawkrey	4	G	4	0	0	1	838
Downtown Event	2	F	4	0	0	0	868	Dr. Hill (BRZ)	6	G	8	0	1	1	18,300
Downtown Girl	3	F	7	1	1	0	5,752	Dr. Hinni	2	C	6	0	0	1	1,372
Downtown Golfer	2	C	3	0	1	0	6,870	Dr. Holiday	5	G	8	1	0	2	8,437
Downtown Joeybrown	4	G	11	1	0	3	3,435	Dr. Hunter	4	C	8	0	1	1	11,000
Downtown Johnny	3	G	3	0	0	1	935	Dr. J. Bierwith	3	C	11	0	1	1	4,452
Downtown Kid	3	G	4	1	1	2	3,705	Dr. J. M. T.	3	C	8	1	1	2	11,019
Downtown Laddie	5	G	5	0	0	0	222	Dr. Jack K.	6	G	7	0	0	0	1,423
Downtown Man	3	C	2	0	0	0	0	Dr. John T.	2	G	6	0	1	0	5,160
Downtown Suzie	2	F	2	0	0	0	122	Dr. Justy	3	C	5	2	0	3	12,817
Downtownwillybrown	4	G	5	1	0	1	6,375	Dr. Kashnikow	6	G	7	0	1	2	37,280
Downunderthunder (GB)	2	F	3	0	0	0	320	Dr. Kathy	2	F	6	2	0	3	75,485
Doxies Picture	3	F	14	1	1	4	8,807	Dr. Ken	3	G	3	0	0	0	144
D'part	6	H	12	1	1	4	16,161	Dr. Kerby	8	G	3	0	0	0	110
Dr Ante	4	G	2	0	0	0	2,010	Dr. Kitten	9	G	5	0	4	1	1,777
Dr Boo Boo Better	4	F	2	0	0	0	0	Dr. Kris	2	G	3	0	0	0	5,520
Dr Boss	4	G	7	1	0	1	5,856	Dr. L. G. S.	7	G	12	1	0	0	3,280
Dr Carson	6	G	6	2	1	1	35,963	Dr. Lewis	6	H	3	0	1	2	7,140
Dr Castelli's Pet	4	F	6	0	0	1	1,340	Dr. Longlegs	3	C	3	0	1	0	5,200
Dr Chequer	3	C	2	0	0	1	1,540	Dr. Lucado	6	G	19	0	1	4	6,944
Dr Chiang Mai	3	C	11	4	1	2	52,497	Dr. Mary Belle	3	F	6	0	0	0	144
Dr Claire	6	M	5	1	0	0	3,720	Dr. Maturin	2	C	7	0	1	1	4,230
Dr Detroit	4	G	10	1	0	1	21,381	Dr. Miller	3	C	7	1	0	1	32,940
Dr Devil	4	G	10	1	0	2	8,100	Dr. Mo	4	G	12	3	1	2	43,564
Dr Dryuit	3	C	15	2	2	3	9,801	Dr. Mojo	3	G	6	1	1	0	17,900
Dr F Laparco	6	M	17	1	5	1	10,918	Dr. Morehead	3	G	13	3	1	1	21,149
Dr Gold	4	R	7	2	1	3	47,460	Dr. Natalie	6	M	9	0	0	0	1,599
Dr John Martin	4	C	7	1	0	1	12,410	Dr. O.	6	H	3	0	1	0	1,184
Dr Mehta	4	G	6	1	0	1	11,060	Dr. Ormsby	4	C	4	0	0	0	2,640
Dr Noble	4	G	4	1	1	0	11,200	Dr. Pagar	4	G	8	1	1	2	19,220
Dr of Love	5	M	18	4	2	1	16,218	Dr. Park	5	H	5	0	1	1	17,600
Dr Richard Walker	5	H	16	1	2	0	45,279	Dr. Pete	2	C	1	0	0	0	0
Dr Rosie C	7	H	2	0	0	0	0	Dr. Pete Stagg	4	C	4	0	1	0	3,200
Dr Sharen G	4	F	9	2	3	1	25,045	Dr. Phil	3	C	5	0	0	1	5,140
Dr Turchi	2	G	5	1	2	1	13,874	Dr. Pingo (ARG)	6	G	9	1	1	2	14,434
Dr Vetanze	5	H	6	2	1	0	7,802	Dr. Piper	4	F	7	0	1	0	5,075
Dr Wow	3	G	11	1	2	2	68,749	Dr. Precise	2	F	12	1	2	3	16,910
Dr Yaru	3	G	5	0	0	0	900	Dr. Quick	3	F	7	0	2	0	2,867
Dr. Adoue	3	C	2	0	0	0	0	Dr. Ramos	2	G	1	0	0	0	125
Dr. Albert	3	C	4	1	0	2	21,220	Dr. Ramsey	9	G	2	0	1	0	4,600
Dr. Alexander	4	C	1	0	0	0	0	Dr. Rand V.	2	C	2	0	0	0	0
Dr. Altorki	3	F	2	0	0	0	0	Dr. Raymond	5	G	14	2	1	1	15,182
Dr. Anderson	3	C	1	0	0	0	0	Dr. Red Man	6	H	11	1	1	2	6,812
Dr. Banner	2	C	1	0	0	0	230	Dr. Reed	8	G	4	0	0	0	635
Dr. Batonnier	3	G	1	0	0	0	0	Dr. Robbie	6	G	14	1	2	1	13,360
Dr. Big	7	G	4	0	0	1	1,333	Dr. Rockett	4	C	10	0	2	1	34,680
Dr. Bill	4	C	7	1	0	0	10,880	Dr. Sal	7	G	13	3	4	3	28,278
Dr. Bombay	3	C	9	1	2	1	13,724	Dr. Scribble	5	G	7	0	1	1	2,885
Dr. Bones	2	C	1	0	0	0	0	Dr. Seabird	7	G	6	0	1	2	3,242
Dr. Brendler	5	H	8	2	1	1	259,935	Dr. Slew	5	G	18	1	6	0	22,708
Dr. Brick	6	G	10	2	0	2	13,886	Dr. Spellbinder	3	G	6	0	0	0	3,960
Dr. Can Do	4	G	13	2	2	1	13,210	Dr. Stone	3	G	5	1	1	1	11,070
Dr. Cann	5	G	15	2	5	2	19,100	Dr. Sunshine	3	G	11	1	1	1	15,890
Dr. Casola	3	G	7	0	0	0	1,180	Dr. Thunder	5	G	11	2	3	1	37,218
Dr. Clayton	4	G	12	0	0	0	2,045	Dr. Tom B.	4	G	6	2	1	1	3,256
Dr. Cool Beans	5	G	14	2	1	2	40,165	Dr. Tony	3	G	4	0	0	0	2,070
Dr. Coz	3	C	1	0	0	0	0	Dr. Walsh	3	C	3	0	0	0	5,400
Dr. Cruse	6	G	9	0	0	0	2,089	Draco City	3	C	12	2	3	2	27,647
Dr. D. S. D.	8	G	12	0	1	1	2,952	Draco Malfoy	3	G	2	0	0	0	115
Dr. Darkai	3	C	3	1	0	0	12,158	Dracula	6	G	10	0	0	0	4,100
Dr. Donsky	3	G	1	0	0	0	0	Dragon Girl	5	M	10	2	2	3	36,611
Dr. Dorminy	3	C	7	2	0	0	13,014	Dragon Jenny	2	F	2	0	0	0	2,160
Dr. Dreamsteamer	4	F	8	0	0	0	896	Dragon Six	6	G	10	0	0	0	726
Dr. Dubai	3	C	14	5	1	3	99,700	Dragonfly Miss	3	F	4	1	2	0	11,600
Dr. Dude	4	G	3	0	0	0	0	Dragonflyer	2	F	6	0	0	0	900
Dr. E. Claire	3	G	13	1	0	0	15,801	Dragon's Flight	5	G	6	0	0	1	1,907

Horse	Age	Sex	Sts	1st	2d	3d	Won	Horse	Age	Sex	Sts	1st	2d	3d	Won
Dragons Wine	5	H	5	1	0	1	2,602	Dreamer Be There	6	G	10	1	0	0	4,673
Drakensberg	5	H	6	1	1	1	27,253	Dreamer Dreamer	4	F	1	0	0	0	42
Dralion	2	G	4	0	1	2	6,740	Dreamers Glory	4	F	5	1	0	0	33,840
Drama Mama	6	M	3	0	0	0	126	Dreamer's Lad	8	G	13	2	2	3	32,437
Drama Queen	4	F	7	2	1	2	80,886	Dreamers Point	6	G	15	0	1	3	8,315
Drama's Dandy	4	G	8	1	2	0	7,580	Dreamery	5	M	9	0	1	2	2,390
Dramatic Arts	3	C	1	0	0	0	320	Dreametta	6	M	4	0	0	0	279
Dramatic Chance	2	F	7	1	3	0	17,275	Dreamin Big	4	G	8	0	0	0	1,144
Dramatic Copy	2	C	6	1	1	0	31,520	Dreamin Demon	4	G	12	0	1	2	8,340
Dramatic Lion	3	F	1	0	0	0	180	Dreaming Creek	4	F	12	0	1	1	3,420
Dramatic Run	2	G	5	1	0	0	8,710	Dreaming of Roses	3	C	4	1	0	1	4,014
Dramatic Show	6	H	2	0	0	0	0	Dreaming the Blues	4	C	16	0	2	2	45,500
Dramatic Youth	3	G	6	1	0	1	9,790	Dreamingrichard	3	G	19	1	3	3	16,710
Dramatization	4	C	1	0	0	0	0	Dreamland Express	3	F	2	0	0	1	1,390
Drango	3	G	4	0	0	0	2,495	Dreamlin	3	F	11	1	2	2	9,897
Drape	3	C	1	0	0	0	1,700	Dreamon Dearest	2	C	2	0	0	0	104
Drastic Measures	2	C	2	0	0	0	200	Dreamoneir	3	G	5	1	0	1	2,195
Drastic Move	5	G	10	1	1	1	4,485	Dreampark	3	G	2	0	0	0	0
Draupner	7	H	3	0	0	0	223	Dreamport	2	G	3	0	0	0	252
Draven's Fellow	2	G	2	0	0	0	0	Dreams Are Forever	4	F	13	0	0	0	941
Draw Again	8	H	1	0	0	0	230	Dreams At Sunset	3	F	3	0	0	0	5,346
Draw Fire	3	C	10	2	3	0	85,315	Dreams Docome True	5	M	7	0	0	0	344
Draw Nigh	5	M	11	1	0	2	5,084	Dreams Go Bye	5	M	3	0	1	0	23,566
Draw Off	2	C	5	0	0	1	4,080	Dreams Happen	2	C	1	0	0	0	0
Draw Play	4	C	6	1	1	2	41,470	Dreams of Ranco	3	F	7	0	1	2	18,180
Drawing a Blank	7	M	9	2	1	3	72,240	Dreams to Go	2	F	4	1	0	1	9,285
Drawing Away	7	G	1	0	0	0	0	Dreamslingeron	4	G	15	4	1	2	34,666
Dread That Alarm	5	M	7	0	0	0	2,409	Dreamsofthewest	5	M	2	0	0	1	1,100
Dreadnaught	3	G	5	2	0	0	34,280	Dreamsville	5	G	7	1	0	1	9,440
Dream A Dream (GB)	4	F	4	1	0	0	13,062	Dreamy Dream	4	F	3	1	0	1	19,910
Dream About	2	F	5	2	1	0	224,430	Dreamy Lover	3	F	1	0	0	0	1,818
Dream Bear	3	F	2	0	0	0	0	Dreamy Song	3	F	3	0	0	0	6,360
Dream Boldly	3	F	7	1	1	1	23,320	Dreamy Temper	5	M	11	0	3	0	9,596
Dream by Design	3	C	12	3	3	1	21,721	Dreamy Yolanda	2	F	1	0	0	0	600
Dream Chick	5	M	1	0	0	0	79	Dredge	3	C	6	0	0	1	802
Dream City	4	F	11	2	3	2	17,743	Dress to Impress	3	F	7	2	1	2	115,828
Dream Copy	3	F	5	0	0	0	1,260	Dress To Thrill (IRE)	4	F	5	1	0	0	187,780
Dream Counter	6	G	6	2	2	0	49,380	Dress Up	3	F	8	1	0	1	8,590
Dream Dancer	5	M	17	1	6	1	25,200	Dressed for Action	3	F	8	2	3	0	197,104
Dream Day	4	F	9	2	1	2	44,840	Dressy Dress	6	M	8	1	1	0	8,399
Dream Deliverer	3	C	14	2	2	5	68,784	Drew Away	4	F	4	0	0	0	4,400
Dream Dish	3	F	6	2	2	0	16,777	Drewman	5	H	4	2	0	0	66,510
Dream Doll	3	F	12	1	1	2	10,427	Drexel Monorail	4	F	13	2	4	2	142,685
Dream Dust	4	F	7	0	1	0	2,915	Driana	4	F	1	0	0	0	0
Dream Eternal	4	F	5	0	0	0	225	Drifa	5	M	5	0	4	0	23,931
Dream Fleet	2	F	7	1	1	1	15,845	Drift Along	5	M	12	2	1	0	10,593
Dream From Above	2	C	2	0	0	0	1,295	Drifter	2	G	2	0	0	0	540
Dream Landing	5	M	11	2	2	0	9,442	Drifting Free	7	G	13	1	0	1	6,703
Dream Launcher	5	G	5	2	0	0	115,470	Drifting Memory	3	G	11	0	0	3	1,298
Dream Legend	4	F	2	0	0	0	0	Driftwood Lodge	3	G	7	3	1	2	63,040
Dream Machine (FR)	4	G	9	0	2	1	28,780	Driftwood Promise	2	F	1	0	0	0	75
Dream Mussell	3	G	8	1	3	0	6,625	Driftwood Sea	3	G	8	0	0	0	450
Dream No More	3	G	7	2	0	0	10,018	Drill Em'	3	C	10	1	0	0	3,936
Dream of Alleged	5	G	2	0	0	0	166	Drill Hall	4	G	10	2	2	1	54,900
Dream of an Act	2	F	12	1	1	1	7,305	Drill the Hill	5	H	3	0	0	0	0
Dream of Capote	4	G	1	0	0	0	0	Driller	7	G	9	1	2	3	2,870
Dream of Dashing	3	G	14	2	1	2	66,710	Drillmaster	3	G	2	0	0	1	1,800
Dream of Dreams	5	G	4	0	0	1	2,982	Drink a Toast	4	G	6	1	2	1	41,300
Dream of Dust	4	F	11	1	4	1	8,839	Drink Til He Howls	4	F	9	1	0	0	5,520
Dream of Gem	3	C	4	0	0	1	1,220	Drink to B Don	8	M	2	0	0	0	156
Dream of Jenny	3	F	4	0	0	3	4,525	Drinkin Grey Goose	3	F	8	0	2	0	3,460
Dream of Summer	4	F	5	3	1	0	103,500	Drinkin Money	3	G	6	0	0	0	620
Dream of Wealth	3	G	8	1	1	0	11,112	Drinking Time	6	M	3	0	0	0	0
Dream On Doc	2	F	2	0	0	0	720	Drinksatthegrille	3	F	5	1	0	1	6,430
Dream Pirate	3	F	3	0	0	1	2,093	Drinksonme	2	F	6	2	0	0	19,134
Dream Place	2	C	2	1	0	0	25,140	Drip Drop	2	C	3	0	0	0	1,980
Dream Run	5	H	6	0	1	1	11,080	Drislen Jillian	7	H	2	0	0	0	140
Dream Spirit	2	F	1	0	0	0	0	Drive	5	H	7	1	2	1	10,650
Dream State	4	G	7	1	1	0	4,096	Drive Away	4	F	17	1	0	1	5,128
Dream Stream	2	C	3	0	0	1	900	Drive Fast	4	F	5	1	0	2	8,662
Dream Tripper	6	H	8	2	2	1	42,545	Drive in the Lane	3	F	4	0	0	0	884
Dream Walkin	4	F	2	1	0	0	11,292	Drive the Avenue	9	G	6	1	2	2	11,150
Dream Wedding	4	F	9	2	0	0	20,460	Drive Your Stake	4	G	4	1	0	0	1,977
Dream Weekend	7	H	10	4	0	3	71,985	Driven Force	4	G	13	1	0	1	10,281
Dreamadreamforme	2	F	7	2	1	1	37,807	Driven Storm	3	G	14	1	1	1	12,081
Dreamaker's Rhythm	3	C	2	0	0	0	630	Drivenbydesire	3	F	3	0	0	0	0
Dreamalittledream	4	F	3	0	0	0	0	Drivers Seat	4	G	13	2	3	2	11,550
Dreamcast	4	F	4	0	1	1	3,150	Drivinfordough	9	G	11	2	2	1	8,210
Dreamcatcher	3	G	10	1	1	1	4,876	Driving Hennesy	4	G	11	2	1	0	13,880

Horse	Age	Sex	Sts	1st	2d	3d	Won	Horse	Age	Sex	Sts	1st	2d	3d	Won
Driving Miss M	2	F	1	1	0	0	7,563	Ducky Diablo	5	M	8	0	2	3	8,014
Driving Miss Rosie	4	F	17	1	0	0	8,727	Duddly Doo Run	4	G	8	0	2	0	14,418
Driving Miss Susie	3	F	5	0	2	1	11,427	Dude	5	G	13	1	0	1	5,157
Driving Mr. Bert	8	G	1	0	0	0	70	Dude Anonymous	4	G	13	2	0	3	11,461
Driving Music	3	C	10	1	1	3	19,645	Dudeman	4	G	11	2	1	1	13,245
Drivinmetodrink	5	H	1	0	0	0	0	Dudewithanattitude	3	G	10	1	1	1	7,610
Drobney	5	G	10	0	0	2	2,251	Dudgeon	3	F	16	2	1	0	14,290
Droll Dancer	7	G	4	0	0	0	2,569	Dudley Dewfein	6	G	12	0	2	0	5,265
Dromineer	4	G	4	0	1	0	1,900	Due	2	G	3	0	1	1	5,340
Dronero (PAN)	5	H	4	0	0	2	2,166	Due Elegance	5	M	12	1	2	4	15,975
Drop a Twenty	3	F	3	0	0	0	136	Due Season	4	C	8	2	0	0	6,802
Drop Dead Red	2	F	7	0	1	2	13,220	Due the Empress	6	M	11	2	5	0	25,762
Drop of Rain	4	F	9	2	1	0	37,792	Due to Win	8	M	12	0	3	2	37,570
Drop the Buck	7	G	12	1	3	1	9,556	Due to Win Again	5	M	9	1	2	2	59,550
Drop the Gun	9	G	11	2	2	2	20,430	Duelin' Dan	5	G	1	0	0	0	0
Drop Your Veil	3	G	1	0	0	0	270	Dueling Banjo	3	G	4	1	0	0	14,935
Drops of Jupiter	4	G	3	0	1	1	5,862	Dueling Edge	6	G	17	4	1	2	22,239
Drosophila	4	F	9	0	1	2	4,276	Dueling Fool	3	C	1	0	0	1	748
Drought Breaker	2	F	3	0	1	0	7,600	Dueling Roses	7	G	8	0	0	1	2,437
Drouilly's Devil	3	G	7	0	0	0	0	Duel'n Darla	5	M	1	0	0	0	87
Drown the Sorrows	3	F	5	0	1	2	8,850	Dueln Lit'l Joe	6	G	10	1	3	2	6,240
Dr's Cure	3	F	3	0	1	0	13,524	Dues for the Blues	3	G	4	1	0	1	5,857
Drs.tish'n'kinish	8	M	2	0	0	0	113	Duesenberg	4	G	5	2	0	0	15,984
Drum Money	5	M	16	0	1	1	5,021	Duet	2	F	4	1	2	0	104,845
Drum Note	5	G	4	0	0	1	746	Duetherightthing	6	M	5	0	3	0	3,557
Drum Ring	3	C	1	0	0	0	0	Duffer	3	G	3	0	1	0	2,920
Drum Roll Please			14	2	0	3	25,005	Duffy	3	G	11	1	2	1	35,650
Drumcliff	5	G	8	3	2	2	13,469	Duffy's Trick	3	C	3	1	2	0	9,980
Drumlin	3	F	9	1	3	1	36,100	Dugong	6	H	5	0	0	0	624
Drummer Ken	6	G	11	1	2	1	17,756	Dugout Doug	2	G	2	1	0	0	9,173
Drumo	4	G	4	1	0	0	11,400	Duke Crane	7	G	9	1	0	1	3,233
Drumsticks	7	M	8	1	2	0	12,239	Duke of Bellefonte	6	H	5	0	2	0	8,931
Dry County Girl	8	G	8	0	1	2	11,850	Duke of Dutton	4	G	10	3	1	1	29,273
Dry Gulched	5	H	8	0	0	0	494	Duke of Green (GB)	6	H	5	0	3	1	49,800
Dry Humor	2	C	1	0	0	0	780	Duke of Haz	3	C	3	1	0	0	3,760
Dry Ice	5	G	18	3	3	1	38,588	Duke of Hicryflat	6	G	6	0	0	0	1,200
Drysdale	8	G	7	0	0	2	1,226	Duke of Kent	3	G	5	1	0	0	9,700
D's Grand Suprise	3	F	3	0	0	0	1,800	Duke of Paoli	5	G	9	2	4	3	19,364
D's Rocky Ridge	3	F	3	0	0	0	321	Duke of Rosemount	11	G	14	0	0	3	1,768
D's Royal Flush	3	G	4	0	0	0	550	Duke of the Track	7	G	6	0	1	0	3,112
D's Valentine	3	C	10	1	2	1	11,594	Duke Ora	9	G	4	1	1	0	10,140
D'termining	3	G	6	1	0	0	3,547	Duke Wilson	2	C	4	0	0	0	166
Du Nord's Book	10	G	1	0	0	0	120	Duke's Cash Box	9	G	5	0	0	0	390
Du Too	4	C	1	0	0	0	105	Duke's Clone	4	G	6	0	0	0	218
Dual Axle	3	G	6	0	0	0	960	Duke's Crossing	4	G	12	2	2	2	81,640
Dual Doppler	2	F	4	1	1	1	19,141	Dukes Da Man	4	C	1	0	0	0	0
Dual Pep	5	G	1	0	0	0	47	Duke's Hi	3	G	4	0	0	0	500
Dual Wager	2	F	1	0	0	0	85	Dukes Mixture	3	C	12	1	1	3	20,355
Duanes Litlwashita	3	G	1	0	0	0	35	Dukes of Triton	6	H	2	0	0	0	1,920
Duanes Mister Boyd	7	G	4	0	0	0	160	Duke's Phantom	7	G	9	0	0	0	1,920
Duanesdarlingcupie	4	F	3	0	0	0	0	Duke's Power Play	5	H	2	0	0	0	161
Dubai Belle	4	F	3	1	1	0	36,200	Duke's Revenge	3	G	8	2	1	1	27,293
Dubai Cat	4	C	6	0	0	1	7,530	Duke's Show Biz	5	M	12	0	0	0	1,850
Dubai Sheikh	4	G	13	4	3	2	199,820	Duke's Showstopper	7	H	1	0	0	0	0
Dubai Special	4	C	10	2	2	2	12,733	Duke's Tempo	5	H	8	1	0	2	4,304
Dubious Command	4	C	13	0	2	0	8,879	Duke's Tune	5	G	2	1	0	1	2,940
Dubious Destiny	6	H	2	0	0	0	4,487	Duke's Wildcat	8	G	13	4	2	3	18,342
Dublin Darlin	3	F	6	0	0	2	2,983	Dukester	4	G	11	1	2	2	18,485
Dublin Grade	2	G	1	0	0	0	0	Dulce de Leche	4	C	14	2	1	3	50,815
Dublino	4	F	5	1	3	0	266,067	Dulciana	2	F	1	0	1	0	4,340
Dublin's Woodwin	4	G	6	2	0	0	21,719	Dulcinia	3	F	6	0	1	1	4,740
Dubl'nlastchance	10	G	3	0	0	0	216	Dumaaness	5	M	1	0	0	0	0
Dubya	3	G	5	0	0	0	708	Dumaani Deal	4	F	4	0	0	0	0
Ducati Demon	3	G	8	1	0	0	17,440	Dumaani Music	3	G	9	0	1	0	2,240
Duce's Image	2	G	10	3	1	4	48,210	Dumaani of Course	4	C	2	0	2	0	11,380
Duchess' Bid	6	H	5	2	0	0	7,096	Dumaani Star	5	G	6	1	2	0	69,894
Duchess County	3	F	8	1	3	1	51,440	Dumaani Way	5	G	1	0	0	0	110
Duchess Ida Clare	2	F	2	0	0	0	300	Dummy	3	G	1	1	0	0	6,780
Duchess of Cocoa	4	F	15	3	2	4	54,520	Dummy Up	3	C	8	0	1	0	3,840
Duchwonderman	3	G	1	0	0	0	0	Dumtell	2	F	4	1	0	0	15,430
Duck and Frolic	3	G	4	0	0	0	401	Dun Ringill	5	G	8	2	1	0	10,052
Duck Down Under	3	F	3	0	1	1	10,820	Dunbar	2	G	2	0	0	1	2,880
Duck Duck Goose	5	H	9	3	0	3	12,272	Dunbow's Remark	2	G	1	0	0	0	515
Duck for Dinner	5	G	7	1	0	1	8,449	Duncan Flash	11	G	2	0	0	0	0
Duck Grayson	8	H	6	3	0	0	23,160	Duncan Hill	4	G	16	4	3	3	40,655
Duck Shoot	5	H	7	0	0	0	890	Duncan Idaho	4	C	14	1	2	3	38,564
Duck Shot	6	G	3	0	0	0	225	Duncan Miss	6	M	8	2	1	0	10,005
Duck the Punt	5	M	4	0	1	0	3,420	Duncan's Dancer	3	F	12	1	0	3	7,406
Ducktrap Harbor	2	F	3	0	0	0	360	Duncan's Gold	3	G	6	1	1	0	5,440

Horse	Age	Sex	Sts	1st	2d	3d	Won
Dundurn	2	C	2	1	0	0	35,280
Dungeon	4	G	10	1	1	1	14,590
Dunham's Bag	7	H	4	1	0	0	7,800
Dunham's Revenge	7	M	1	0	0	0	55
Dunham's Social	7	M	9	0	1	1	4,120
Dunkaman	6	G	9	1	2	0	6,349
Dunloe Gap	3	C	5	1	1	2	11,391
Dunmore Dame	3	F	7	1	0	0	4,830
Dunne Right	4	G	10	2	0	2	15,716
Dunnewood	2	C	1	0	0	0	0
Dunny's Girl Mary	3	F	7	0	0	0	0
Dunsany	6	M	19	1	0	1	6,364
Dunson	8	G	16	3	3	1	13,792
Dunvegan Ablaze	2	F	1	0	0	0	0
Dupers' Double T	3	C	2	0	0	0	210
Dupes Delight	2	G	2	0	0	1	1,680
Duplicate Award	2	F	3	0	0	0	1,500
Duplicate Copy	4	C	3	1	1	0	18,756
Duplicate Ticket	5	G	7	1	1	1	21,580
Dura Ace	3	G	8	1	0	3	16,320
Durable Mac	2	C	1	1	0	0	3,360
Duracat	2	G	3	1	1	0	17,879
Duradero	4	C	1	0	0	0	0
Durandal	2	C	1	0	0	0	50
Durango	2	C	6	0	1	1	4,248
Durango Sky	3	F	6	1	0	1	12,127
Duration Bob	3	G	12	0	1	2	3,696
Durazo	3	G	5	0	0	0	594
During	3	C	13	5	2	1	514,750
Durkin's Call	2	C	4	0	0	0	7,560
Durmiente (CHI)	9	G	10	2	2	1	58,820
Durvish	6	G	16	2	3	5	16,226
Dusk Till Dawn	3	G	6	0	0	1	1,871
Dusky Devil	6	G	15	0	0	1	5,744
Duson Minstrel	3	G	4	0	0	0	0
Dust Bag	6	H	12	1	1	1	4,561
Dust in Time	4	G	11	1	1	1	8,562
Dust On the Bottle	8	H	9	0	2	0	19,880
Dust Pebble	4	F	11	5	3	0	27,180
Dusthof	5	G	15	2	3	5	6,474
Dustineer	7	G	25	1	1	1	7,436
Dusting of Powder	4	F	5	0	0	2	11,590
Dustinontherun	2	F	3	0	1	0	2,613
Dustin's Dozer	8	G	8	1	3	1	10,319
Dustin's Luckylady	4	F	7	0	0	1	1,593
Dustins Mozart	3	G	13	0	1	3	4,037
Dustinsdestiny	3	G	6	1	1	2	3,622
Dusti's Tune	4	F	4	1	0	0	18,000
Dusty Betsy	5	M	9	0	0	0	1,845
Dusty Call	3	G	2	0	0	0	110
Dusty Cat	4	F	14	2	0	1	15,622
Dusty Chuck	3	C	15	0	1	2	3,042
Dusty Conn	5	G	10	0	3	1	3,030
Dusty Creek	3	G	6	1	1	2	7,134
Dusty Decision	2	G	2	0	0	0	0
Dusty Doc Lou	4	G	2	0	0	0	900
Dusty Evening	3	F	5	1	1	1	40,630
Dusty Guitar	2	G	2	0	0	1	550
Dusty Irish Lass	2	F	3	0	0	0	0
Dusty Jug	3	G	9	1	2	3	9,183
Dusty Mexican	3	F	9	1	3	3	18,978
Dusty Noel	3	F	6	2	1	0	8,660
Dusty Ol' Cognac	3	C	4	1	0	0	7,325
Dusty Pat	2	F	3	0	0	0	100
Dusty Quaker	5	G	22	0	0	2	3,103
Dusty Ridge	9	G	3	1	0	1	2,738
Dusty Road Ahead	4	G	9	2	0	2	7,592
Dusty Slew	5	G	10	2	3	2	6,787
Dusty Spike	9	G	9	3	0	1	157,582
Dusty Tunnel	2	C	8	1	4	0	23,480
Dustys Birthday	4	C	10	2	0	1	41,128
Dusty's Dragster	4	G	11	1	2	1	5,442
Dusty's Express	2	G	3	0	1	0	5,397
Dusty's Gone	3	F	4	0	0	0	0
Dustysarollin	4	G	14	3	2	1	17,476
Dutch Approval	5	M	2	0	0	0	208
Dutch Uncle	8	G	5	0	0	0	104
Dutch Wind Mill	4	G	3	0	0	1	1,455
Dutches's Crown	4	F	6	1	1	0	26,492
Dutchess Dear	3	F	7	2	0	1	6,640
Dutchess Eben	3	F	9	1	2	1	15,564
Dutchess of Win	5	M	3	0	0	0	219
Dutchie	3	F	5	3	0	0	51,300
Duval Town	3	G	2	0	0	0	350
Duvalier	4	G	9	3	2	0	57,902
Duxs Storm	6	G	10	1	1	2	5,168
Dwango	2	C	4	1	2	0	42,200
Dwellerinthevalley	2	G	4	1	0	0	20,460
Dwendi	5	M	13	4	1	1	40,924
D'wildcat	5	H	4	0	0	0	10,400
Dwyerville Giant	7	G	10	0	0	1	963
Dyeledo	5	M	4	0	0	2	858
Dyersburg	3	G	11	0	2	0	4,555
Dyf	4	G	16	6	3	1	37,220
Dyin If I'm Lyin	4	G	3	1	1	0	1,000
Dylan	3	G	12	0	1	1	13,600
Dylans Destiny	2	C	4	0	1	1	14,350
Dylan's Girl	4	F	5	0	0	0	968
Dylan's Grand Paw	5	G	12	0	1	2	4,616
Dylan's My Name	4	G	12	4	2	4	65,513
Dylans Secret	3	G	6	3	1	0	15,415
Dyle Again	5	M	1	0	0	0	0
Dyn O Mite Kid	4	G	8	0	0	0	178
Dyna Color Me Gone	3	C	5	2	1	0	29,294
Dyna Da Wyna	3	F	9	5	0	0	216,517
Dyna Del	2	F	7	2	4	0	62,100
Dyna Flair	2	F	5	0	2	2	7,692
Dyna Flyer	3	F	12	3	0	2	59,603
Dyna King	6	G	18	2	4	4	9,845
Dyna Knight	3	F	1	0	0	0	55
Dyna Low Rider	5	G	13	0	0	2	1,916
Dyna Mae	4	F	4	0	0	1	3,250
Dyna Moe	5	H	6	2	2	0	5,386
Dyna Mojo	3	G	2	0	0	0	368
Dyna Motion	6	M	9	0	1	1	7,623
Dyna My Darlin	4	F	1	0	0	0	86
Dyna Penny	4	F	12	0	3	2	31,370
Dyna Wild	2	F	10	2	1	4	19,885
Dynability	7	G	5	2	1	0	44,500
Dynaboy	8	G	7	0	1	1	4,110
Dynadusty	5	H	3	1	0	0	2,846
Dynafire	2	C	4	1	1	1	54,218
Dynaheart	3	F	3	0	0	0	0
Dynakris	3	F	3	0	0	0	490
Dynalympic	2	C	3	0	0	1	6,165
Dynamation	2	F	2	1	0	0	15,750
Dynameaux	5	H	5	0	2	1	75,670
Dynameesch	6	M	4	0	0	0	2,070
Dynamia	2	F	1	0	1	0	4,180
Dynamic Diva	4	F	12	1	3	1	13,127
Dynamic Dixie	2	F	2	0	0	0	410
Dynamic Gain	3	F	8	1	0	1	8,912
Dynamic Justice	3	F	9	2	1	0	14,471
Dynamic Lady	4	F	7	1	0	1	27,440
Dynamic Light	2	C	9	3	3	1	30,515
Dynamic Lisa	4	F	6	2	1	0	108,830
Dynamic Lord	4	C	9	0	0	2	11,560
Dynamic Performer	7	G	4	0	0	0	0
Dynamic Pic	7	M	18	0	2	0	18,725
Dynamic Prospect	4	G	10	1	1	1	37,058
Dynamic Red	4	F	1	0	0	0	0
Dynamic Ride	4	G	6	0	0	0	220
Dynamic Ruhler	5	M	3	0	1	0	1,138
Dynamic Trick	8	H	1	0	0	0	150
Dynamism	4	F	3	0	0	0	0
Dynamistic	5	M	1	0	0	0	0
Dynamite Cocktail	3	F	10	1	1	1	57,030
Dynamite Dinner	3	G	16	0	3	2	12,511
Dynamite Dot	4	F	7	0	2	0	2,915
Dynamite Dude	4	G	7	0	0	0	0
Dynamite Ghost	4	G	10	2	0	2	6,760
Dynamite Guy	3	C	4	0	0	1	1,760
Dynamite Jimmy	3	C	9	0	0	0	590
Dynamite Miss	4	F	6	1	1	0	39,740
Dynamite On Fire	4	F	1	0	0	0	220
Dynamite Sean	6	G	8	0	0	0	1,429
Dynamite Vic	7	G	8	1	0	2	20,450
Dynamite Wes	3	G	16	2	3	2	11,333

Horse	Age	Sex	Sts	1st	2d	3d	Won
Dynamite Whirlwind	7	G	1	0	0	0	0
Dynamiter	4	F	2	0	0	0	87
Dynamo Don	4	G	8	1	0	4	34,014
Dynamo Ridge	2	F	10	1	1	0	9,536
Dynamometer	3	C	2	1	0	1	30,140
Dynareign	3	C	11	2	2	3	57,855
Dynarhythm	3	F	4	1	0	1	35,640
Dynaruler	3	G	5	1	0	1	31,940
Dynas Cat	4	F	1	0	0	0	0
Dyna's Wicked Ride	4	F	6	2	2	1	25,090
Dynastic Power	3	G	5	0	0	1	3,318
Dynastyle	3	C	7	1	1	0	27,640
Dynasure	3	F	12	3	1	2	62,883
Dynasurf	8	G	13	2	1	5	14,154
Dynatron	8	G	3	1	0	0	2,488
Dynattack	7	M	2	0	1	0	1,638
Dynaville	2	F	4	1	0	3	60,405
Dynavolt	6	G	2	0	0	0	0
Dynawave	4	F	15	2	3	0	36,470
Dynaway	2	G	5	1	0	1	20,369
Dynever	3	C	9	3	3	1	1,154,020
Dyno Dancer	3	F	5	0	0	0	2,520
Dyno Don	2	G	4	1	1	0	9,130
Dysfunctional Lady	2	F	3	0	0	1	1,110
Dyu	5	H	1	0	0	0	73
E Bar El	4	F	9	0	2	1	6,275
E Bar Prospect	4	F	7	0	3	1	8,628
E C Wayne	7	G	3	0	0	0	0
E Core	3	C	2	0	1	0	1,438
E Country	3	C	3	0	0	0	0
E C's Way	3	G	6	1	0	0	4,281
E E Trap	4	C	7	1	2	0	29,270
E J Harley	11	G	5	2	1	1	14,850
E J's Spirit	5	H	3	0	0	0	350
E K's Jet	5	M	3	1	0	0	3,290
E Mail Pat	5	M	9	2	3	0	47,990
E Mail Trail	6	G	9	1	5	1	4,049
E Man	3	G	3	0	0	0	725
E O's Flash	2	C	1	0	0	1	1,650
E T C Mystic	3	F	7	1	1	2	13,320
E T Phone Laura	4	F	8	3	0	0	39,160
E Trade	4	C	10	1	0	2	17,560
E Z Glory	6	H	10	0	4	2	57,138
E Z Goin	4	C	3	0	0	0	454
E Z Line	8	G	1	0	0	1	1,155
E Z Payday	3	F	4	0	0	0	410
E Z Smile	2	F	2	0	0	0	215
E Z Traveler	2	G	2	1	0	0	3,240
E. B. Mitchell	4	C	8	1	3	0	9,632
E. P. Hillary	3	C	2	0	0	0	45
E. R. Nurse	4	F	3	0	0	0	213
E. T.'s Little Sis	5	M	1	0	0	0	100
E. Tee Wanna B.	5	G	11	2	2	1	25,209
E. Z. Bree Z.	3	F	5	0	0	1	1,696
E. Zapata	7	G	5	2	1	1	4,144
Eager Cat	4	C	7	0	2	0	3,196
Eager Intention	7	M	9	2	0	0	11,112
Eager Jarodian	8	G	14	0	0	0	1,291
Eager Lee	4	G	15	1	0	0	8,725
Eagerness	5	G	7	1	2	0	11,760
Eagle Bend	5	G	1	0	0	1	640
Eagle Cat	4	F	18	2	4	5	14,626
Eagle Charger	6	G	10	1	1	0	37,910
Eagle Eagle	3	G	18	0	3	3	7,002
Eagle Eye Fleagle	6	H	3	0	0	0	255
Eagle Eyrie	7	G	7	1	0	0	9,910
Eagle Ize	9	G	7	2	0	3	1,973
Eagle Lake	5	M	11	4	3	0	238,874
Eagle Peak	6	G	16	1	1	3	35,394
Eagle Prospect	4	C	8	1	1	1	14,570
Eagle Reply	8	G	9	0	0	0	300
Eagle Time	6	H	10	2	2	0	80,686
Eagles Bluff	5	H	4	0	0	0	165
Eagle's Buddy	3	C	11	0	1	1	2,801
Eagles Cry	5	G	14	1	3	2	7,375
Eagles Hill	3	C	3	1	0	0	29,280
Eagle's Luck	3	G	18	2	1	3	18,870
Eaglesandbeavers	2	C	1	0	0	0	0
Eaglesfield	6	G	17	1	1	1	9,737
Eagleton	7	G	6	1	1	1	23,868
Eaglewatch	3	F	7	1	0	1	7,493
Eaglez Crown	3	G	9	1	2	1	18,040
Ealing Park	4	C	4	0	0	0	2,340
Earl of Danby	4	C	6	0	2	0	31,592
Earl Penny	4	C	10	1	3	1	13,467
Earl the Pearl	5	G	10	1	1	2	17,263
Earlene	3	F	8	1	0	1	13,672
Earl's Babe	3	F	2	0	0	0	47
Early and Bright	5	M	7	0	2	0	2,083
Early and Often	5	M	3	0	0	2	2,600
Early Arrival	6	M	11	1	1	0	10,680
Early Blessing's	4	F	16	0	3	0	2,930
Early Cotton	3	G	8	2	1	1	36,585
Early Echoes	10	G	6	0	0	1	1,380
Early Fall	6	H	1	0	0	0	369
Early Flyer	5	H	2	1	0	0	20,220
Early Goer	6	G	3	0	0	1	4,335
Early Morning Rain	2	G	4	0	2	0	27,120
Early Package	7	G	11	1	1	2	11,022
Early Primrose	4	F	15	1	2	2	15,095
Early Runningriver	5	M	2	1	0	0	7,200
Early Sensation	8	M	1	0	0	0	0
Early Signal	4	F	5	2	0	0	23,545
Early Snow	3	G	12	2	2	3	86,392
Early Sunday Morn	2	G	5	0	0	2	2,505
Early T Sauce	3	G	15	1	4	3	16,592
Early Term	2	C	4	0	0	0	760
Early Time Diamond	5	H	4	0	0	0	0
Early Wisdom	4	G	2	0	1	0	17,112
Earmark	7	G	5	1	1	1	9,310
Earn a Buck	3	C	8	0	0	0	3,518
Earn My Halo	9	G	6	0	0	2	1,744
Earned Run	2	F	3	0	1	0	11,060
Earnest Storm	5	G	12	5	1	2	82,820
Earnestly	3	G	3	0	0	0	0
Ears	2	F	2	0	0	0	0
Earth Pleasure	4	G	10	1	1	1	7,930
Earth Power	3	C	6	4	2	0	86,305
Earth Shaker	4	F	9	0	3	1	18,180
Earth Shaking	7	G	11	0	1	4	8,960
Earth to Heaven	6	M	11	1	0	1	6,448
Eartha (IRE)	5	M	7	3	0	0	30,660
Earthquake Ride	2	F	6	1	1	1	39,930
Easement Rights	4	F	8	0	0	1	1,528
Easianna	3	F	12	1	1	0	9,265
Easiersaidthandone	4	C	2	0	0	0	462
Easiersgold	3	F	6	0	0	0	881
Easily Assembled	6	H	6	1	1	1	7,610
Easily Recognized	5	M	5	0	0	0	310
East and West	5	G	7	1	0	1	5,655
East Balzac	7	G	4	1	0	1	2,770
East Bay	2	F	2	1	0	0	42,625
East Coker	2	G	1	0	0	0	50
East Goin' West	3	F	11	1	1	1	7,687
East Memory	2	G	2	0	0	0	0
East of Amwell	2	C	12	0	0	3	9,140
East of Seattle	4	F	9	0	0	0	2,297
East River Tatonka	6	G	14	2	2	1	7,627
East Texas Red	3	G	3	1	1	0	30,401
East Texas Sam	4	G	15	1	1	5	13,375
East Vali	4	G	13	1	2	0	8,300
Eastboundrocket	6	G	4	0	0	0	70
Easter Boutinierre	6	M	13	0	2	2	2,103
Easter Buddy	3	F	1	0	0	0	0
Easter Bug	6	G	11	2	3	1	14,023
Easter Cat	5	G	5	0	0	1	3,640
Easter Dawn	3	F	9	1	3	2	14,080
Easter Easter	7	M	13	1	4	0	6,916
Easter Gold	3	F	3	0	0	0	222
Easter Halo	4	G	14	2	2	1	10,922
Easter Lillyhopper	3	F	1	0	0	0	0
Easter Liturgy	4	F	2	1	0	0	26,400
Easter Rebel	4	C	1	0	0	0	0
Easter Saga	4	F	15	0	2	1	9,655
Easter Stitches	4	F	4	0	0	0	48
Easter Sunny	4	G	4	1	0	0	3,372
Easter Treasure	4	G	10	2	2	1	11,822
Easter Tryst	2	F	3	1	0	1	8,400

Horse	Age	Sex	Sts	1st	2d	3d	Won	Horse	Age	Sex	Sts	1st	2d	3d	Won
Easter Weekend	2	F	1	0	0	0	455	Eavesdropper	3	C	5	1	1	1	40,980
Eastern Accent	2	G	4	1	1	1	17,950	Ebb n' Flow	3	F	7	2	2	1	37,090
Eastern All Star	2	G	3	0	0	0	318	Ebben Estoora	5	G	8	0	1	1	12,486
Eastern Bay	2	C	6	2	1	0	32,160	Ebbets	3	G	3	0	0	0	0
Eastern Bid	7	G	4	0	0	0	0	Ebbw Vale	8	G	6	0	0	1	1,487
Eastern Book	6	G	12	0	0	0	1,043	Ebee's	4	G	7	2	1	2	39,490
Eastern Cat	5	G	9	1	1	3	15,570	Eber	5	G	15	1	3	3	20,271
Eastern Comet	7	M	10	1	3	0	7,545	Ebon Storm	2	F	6	0	0	1	2,330
Eastern Crown	3	C	3	0	1	0	14,278	Eboney Oynx	8	M	2	1	0	0	6,380
Eastern Empress	3	F	7	0	1	1	3,580	Ebonist	8	G	9	0	1	0	1,196
Eastern Gale	3	F	11	2	2	3	60,520	Ebonoir	5	M	4	0	1	0	1,253
Eastern Lady	3	F	3	0	0	0	147	Ebony and Ivory	6	H	2	0	0	0	340
Eastern Launch	3	C	2	0	0	0	300	Ebony Angel	5	M	11	0	3	2	27,375
Eastern Memory	3	F	10	1	1	2	35,135	Ebony Boy	5	H	5	0	0	0	1,745
Eastern Mint	9	G	7	0	2	0	1,953	Ebony Breeze	3	F	8	4	1	2	365,887
Eastern Onion	2	F	1	0	0	0	0	Ebony Copy	2	F	8	0	0	0	1,100
Eastern Pilot	2	G	2	0	0	0	0	Ebony Countess	5	M	7	1	0	0	43,923
Eastern Playboy	2	C	1	0	0	0	0	Ebony Eyes	3	G	5	0	0	0	1,102
Eastern Ryder	2	F	2	0	0	0	0	Ebony Gal	7	M	4	1	1	0	4,175
Eastern Storm	3	F	14	1	3	2	16,675	Ebony Post	3	F	12	0	2	1	4,685
Eastern Sun	5	M	4	0	1	0	10,240	Ebony's Atlantian	5	M	6	0	3	0	5,208
Eastern Tale	4	F	8	2	1	2	49,245	Ebony's Opal	4	F	12	1	4	1	8,949
Eastern War Lord	8	G	7	2	1	0	49,638	Ec Lady (GB)	4	F	11	3	2	0	52,515
Eastersonitsway	3	C	1	0	0	0	0	Eccentric	3	C	7	2	0	1	16,050
Eastex Express	6	G	6	0	0	0	316	Eccentric Tycoon	7	G	13	1	2	1	10,065
Eastover	8	G	15	1	3	1	16,197	Eccentric Type	5	G	11	3	1	4	38,660
Eastside Ballad	3	F	5	1	1	2	56,340	Ecclesiastes	3	F	1	0	0	0	220
Eastwood's Song	3	C	9	0	3	3	24,066	Ecclesiastic	2	C	3	0	1	1	14,260
Easy as Abc	2	G	1	0	0	0	120	Ecclesiastical	3	F	1	0	0	0	1,700
Easy as Pie	8	M	6	0	0	0	705	Ech Leebidee Angel	2	F	6	0	3	3	31,829
Easy Bar	4	C	1	0	0	0	455	Echelon	5	G	8	1	0	0	4,905
Easy Buck	4	F	1	0	0	0	650	Echelon Star	8	G	3	1	0	0	4,440
Easy Change	4	G	13	2	3	0	7,600	Echeverria	5	C	9	0	0	0	8,483
Easy Charge	8	G	13	0	0	1	1,384	Echo Away	3	G	13	2	1	0	6,839
Easy Chief	4	G	5	0	0	0	0	Echo Canyon	7	G	10	1	0	3	8,110
Easy Cruiser	3	C	2	0	0	1	4,420	Echo d'Or	3	F	10	2	2	2	47,840
Easy Design	4	C	2	0	0	0	125	Echo Eddie	6	G	8	1	1	0	82,500
Easy E	4	F	4	0	1	0	1,921	Echo Jo	3	F	9	3	1	1	69,180
Easy Edna	2	F	2	0	0	0	0	Echo Lady	3	F	4	0	0	1	2,965
Easy Ellis	2	C	5	1	1	0	10,340	Echo Land	3	F	13	2	3	5	36,455
Easy Enough	4	G	5	3	1	1	38,260	Echo Landing	7	G	3	0	0	0	319
Easy Escapade	4	C	7	1	0	1	5,065	Echo Location	3	F	5	0	0	0	506
Easy Game	4	G	10	2	0	1	46,610	Echo of Freedom	2	G	1	0	0	0	0
Easy Glider	4	F	4	0	0	1	1,320	Echo Prince	2	G	4	0	0	0	0
Easy Grades	4	G	4	0	1	0	36,200	Echo Rocket	3	C	7	1	0	1	10,594
Easy Greeting	4	F	6	1	2	1	11,606	Echo Shane	3	C	4	0	0	0	378
Easy Grinder	2	F	1	0	1	0	1,701	Echo Spring	3	F	13	2	0	2	28,874
Easy Ian	4	G	5	1	0	0	10,320	Echo Test	5	H	5	1	0	0	9,280
Easy Ice Hole	4	C	4	0	0	0	0	Echo Weaver	2	F	6	1	2	0	5,917
Easy Idea	4	F	4	0	0	1	468	Echoe Deniro	4	G	1	0	0	0	240
Easy Investor	4	F	1	0	0	1	1,350	Echoing Cheer	2	F	4	0	0	0	780
Easy Jab	7	G	2	1	0	0	1,825	Echoman	3	G	9	1	3	0	16,437
Easy Lady	4	F	9	1	4	0	4,360	Echo's Charm	4	F	2	0	1	0	2,000
Easy Lassie	3	F	3	0	1	1	9,680	Echo's Delight	5	M	3	0	0	0	162
Easy Lovin	5	G	2	1	0	0	2,365	Echo's Word	4	G	2	0	0	0	0
Easy Million	3	C	5	1	1	1	18,850	Echota	2	C	5	0	2	0	11,960
Easy Mission	5	G	12	3	0	1	21,019	Eckmo	3	C	13	2	3	1	13,306
Easy Operator	2	G	5	0	0	0	180	Eclat	3	G	3	0	0	0	1,240
Easy Orders	5	G	10	1	0	1	4,508	Eclipse Bay	3	F	3	1	0	1	48,240
Easy Partner	4	C	1	0	0	0	0	Eclipse De Luna (CHI)	5	M	3	1	0	0	27,500
Easy Question	2	F	1	0	0	0	0	Eclipsing	2	F	1	0	0	0	336
Easy Rival	4	G	9	2	1	1	10,528	Eclipsio	4	G	10	1	1	1	18,539
Easy Road	3	G	1	0	0	0	52	Ecoli	7	G	2	0	0	0	0
Easy Roany Poney	5	M	7	0	1	2	4,235	Economic	4	F	3	0	0	0	129
Easy Runaway	6	G	8	1	1	0	10,992	Economic Impact	6	M	11	2	5	2	19,900
Easy Step Dancer	5	H	6	1	1	0	7,252	Economic Trend	7	H	10	0	3	2	7,686
Easy Streak	5	G	3	0	0	0	0	Economist At Last	2	C	7	1	1	0	21,350
Easy Thunder	5	H	15	1	0	4	12,558	Economy	3	C	8	1	0	0	5,400
Easy to Apply	6	M	14	0	0	3	1,493	Ecstatic	4	C	13	2	5	3	148,400
Easy to Be Me	3	F	9	2	0	0	7,485	Ecstatic Bunny	4	F	1	0	0	0	70
Easy to Believe	3	G	14	1	2	3	10,280	Ecstatic Force	6	H	2	0	0	0	0
Easy to Please	2	C	3	1	1	0	24,700	Ecstatic Girls	3	F	9	2	2	1	26,635
Easy too Easy	3	G	7	1	0	1	9,219	Ecstatic One	6	M	9	0	0	0	1,637
Easy Whirl	5	M	1	0	0	0	122	Ecumenical	3	G	1	0	0	0	0
Easyfromthegitgo	4	C	6	0	1	0	18,950	Eddie B. Ready	4	C	5	0	1	0	2,328
Eat a Bug	3	F	5	1	0	0	13,185	Eddie K.	4	G	11	1	1	0	5,274
Eat My Dust Buster	5	G	5	1	0	1	3,692	Eddie White Sox	4	G	16	4	4	2	84,715
Eatonville Cruiser	3	G	10	2	1	1	16,878	Eddie Wilson	7	G	16	1	5	1	18,737
Eavesdrop	5	G	1	0	0	0	42	Eddienojado	3	C	7	1	0	2	4,020

Horse	Age	Sex	Sts	1st	2d	3d	Won
Eddies Bad Boy	4	G	6	2	1	0	12,036
Eddiesboysings	2	C	2	0	1	0	5,161
Eddington	2	C	1	0	1	0	9,200
Eddy	3	G	15	1	3	1	10,069
Eddy's Wisdom	2	G	2	0	0	1	4,191
Edeltonga	6	M	2	0	0	0	90
Edelweiss Song	2	F	8	0	0	2	5,220
Eden Fact	4	F	8	0	0	1	2,545
Eden Park	3	F	6	1	0	1	9,635
Edgar Road	4	G	2	0	0	0	0
Edge Creek	3	G	6	1	0	0	5,376
Edge of a Kiss	3	C	15	1	2	1	26,555
Edge Sweep	3	F	5	2	0	0	29,070
Edgefield	7	G	8	0	1	1	15,370
Edgerrin	2	C	3	3	0	0	73,650
Edgestone	7	H	12	3	0	2	8,769
Edgewater Savior	2	F	10	2	2	1	29,405
Edies Memo	4	F	9	1	3	2	15,975
Edie's Rebel	7	M	8	1	1	1	20,613
Edify	3	G	4	1	0	0	4,704
Ediko	4	C	1	1	0	0	8,760
Edile's Spirit	5	M	13	1	4	0	12,375
Edison Lanes	2	F	2	0	0	0	860
Edit	4	F	2	0	0	0	126
Edit It	3	F	6	1	0	1	11,231
Edited	6	G	1	0	0	0	0
Edith Says	5	M	1	0	0	0	103
Editiorial	3	G	11	1	1	1	14,600
Editor's a Natural	3	G	8	1	0	1	4,878
Editor's Cat	3	C	5	0	2	0	12,740
Editors Copy	4	F	14	0	5	2	27,758
Editors Ghost	4	C	4	1	0	0	4,800
Editor's Legacy	4	F	6	0	1	0	18,174
Editors Not	2	F	6	1	2	0	7,289
Editor's Page	2	G	1	0	0	0	130
Editor's Party	4	F	3	0	0	0	600
Editor's Pride	3	F	6	0	1	1	6,600
Editors Shake	3	F	10	2	2	1	36,460
Editress	3	F	12	1	2	2	9,517
Edna Mae	3	F	5	0	0	0	0
Edna Pedna	3	F	7	1	0	0	5,560
Ednaann	3	F	6	0	0	1	922
Edna's Eleven	3	F	7	0	1	1	3,515
Edna's Fancy	4	F	9	2	1	1	13,542
Ed's Best Man	4	G	2	0	0	0	0
Ed's Devil	2	C	2	0	0	0	0
Ed's Party Boy	3	G	12	3	1	1	21,696
Edward the Great	3	C	3	0	0	0	0
Edward'sfancypants	4	F	1	0	0	0	390
Eebay	4	G	2	0	0	0	0
Eecheero	2	G	3	0	0	3	3,170
Eejay	7	H	12	4	1	1	28,580
Eeni Meeni Ibis	5	M	9	2	0	2	9,817
Eff Sixx	4	G	10	1	0	1	13,608
Effective Icarus	4	C	3	0	1	1	2,385
Effectively Wild	3	F	2	0	0	0	3,360
Effervescent	7	M	2	1	1	0	22,600
Efficacious	3	G	5	0	0	0	1,650
Efforts	4	G	11	0	1	0	1,725
Efforts Reward	4	F	1	0	0	0	100
Effrene	5	M	6	1	0	0	8,550
Effusive	5	G	11	4	0	2	17,240
Egads	2	F	4	0	0	1	7,140
Egbert Lad	3	G	9	2	0	1	35,021
Eggbert	6	G	9	1	0	0	40,033
Eggs Galaxy	6	M	9	0	1	0	2,190
Ego Sport	3	C	1	0	0	0	0
Ego Trip	3	F	3	0	0	1	1,067
Egotist	3	G	8	0	0	1	10,012
Egotistical	5	G	10	1	4	1	16,995
Egret Miss	2	F	7	1	0	1	5,426
Egretfully True	4	F	15	1	1	2	12,290
Egri Bikaver	3	G	8	0	0	0	979
Egyptian Cotton	3	G	8	0	0	0	1,474
Egyptian Exile	6	G	12	0	0	1	1,014
Egyptian Eyes	7	M	2	0	1	0	5,400
Egyptian Melody	5	M	5	1	1	0	5,269
Egyptian Runner	4	G	3	0	0	0	0
Ehorseracing	3	C	8	0	3	2	25,450
Eiffelegionaire	5	M	11	2	1	0	12,401
Eight a Lot	3	G	9	0	0	1	1,074
Eight Chimes	5	G	2	0	0	2	1,900
Eight Karat	2	F	4	1	0	1	8,772
Eight Madison Road	3	F	1	0	0	0	0
Eight O Eight	3	G	11	1	1	2	14,635
Eight Stars	11	G	4	0	0	0	152
Eighteen Jewels	5	H	4	0	0	0	792
Eighteenkaratgold	10	G	9	0	0	0	612
Eighties	8	G	9	1	2	0	9,146
Eightsecondstglory	3	C	8	2	2	0	3,388
Eighty Nine	2	F	1	0	0	0	0
Eighty Proof	5	M	7	1	2	1	9,866
Eightyfivebroadst	3	F	10	1	1	1	35,894
Eightysixlane	4	G	3	0	0	0	1,425
Eileen's Crystal	3	F	1	0	0	0	40
Eileen's Glow	4	F	7	1	0	0	3,900
Eilunebs Dream	5	M	5	1	0	0	18,333
Einar	3	G	6	1	1	0	4,506
Eire of Domasca	7	M	12	1	2	1	30,373
Eisel Devil	5	H	5	0	0	0	249
Eisenhower	5	G	9	1	0	2	12,597
Eishin Illini Now	3	F	15	4	2	2	18,400
Eishin's Promise	2	F	1	0	0	0	0
Either Orr	3	C	9	1	3	0	46,056
Ekala	4	F	7	0	0	0	550
Ekati	4	G	10	1	3	1	35,348
Ekim Cielo	4	G	14	1	2	0	19,644
Ekundu	6	H	5	0	0	0	3,288
El Abigeo	4	C	7	0	0	0	1,072
El Aguilio	9	G	15	7	3	3	30,838
El Amuleto (ARG)	6	H	12	1	1	3	21,922
El Arrabal (ARG)	3	G	5	0	0	1	4,695
El Arrabalero (ARG)	6	H	9	0	0	1	1,890
El Arriero	2	C	2	0	0	0	180
El Bambino	3	G	13	1	0	2	6,749
El Barranco	3	G	8	0	1	1	8,467
El Basque	6	G	8	0	0	2	3,687
El Beau	8	G	3	0	0	0	0
El Bille	10	G	4	0	0	0	292
El Bomba	4	G	9	0	1	1	7,180
El Bon	7	G	12	2	3	2	7,201
El Brette	4	G	14	3	4	2	59,154
El Bueno (GB)	5	H	1	0	0	0	0
El Caballito	4	C	1	0	0	0	0
El Campeon	9	G	2	0	0	0	486
El Caress	3	F	4	0	1	0	700
El Case	4	G	11	0	1	0	1,874
El Cassique	2	C	4	2	0	1	18,710
El Caurel (ARG)	5	H	4	1	0	1	2,508
El Charro	2	C	6	1	2	0	22,025
El Chaval	4	G	17	1	1	3	7,722
El Chepo Cosa	4	C	10	1	1	0	5,600
El Chorro	5	H	1	0	0	0	0
El Chubbo	5	H	7	0	0	1	1,066
El Cielo	9	G	2	1	0	1	36,120
El Cimarron	5	H	3	0	0	0	0
El Cisc	3	G	11	1	3	2	21,003
El Citador	5	G	14	1	0	2	7,515
El Cometa	4	C	10	0	0	3	2,522
El Compadre	9	H	1	0	0	0	40
El Condor	4	C	10	1	5	1	52,700
El Courageous	5	G	8	3	0	1	46,664
El Crusader	4	C	9	1	2	2	32,042
El Curioso	6	G	15	0	1	0	22,357
El Dancer	8	G	7	1	0	2	4,526
El Delegado	2	C	2	0	0	0	370
El Depressa (BRZ)	5	G	16	4	2	2	33,530
El Destiny	4	G	4	0	0	0	1,600
El Diago	7	G	12	7	1	1	55,829
El Divinidoso	2	G	10	1	0	3	12,603
El Domenico	4	C	8	2	0	1	21,405
El Dominator	3	C	6	0	0	3	4,930
El Don	2	G	2	1	0	1	26,280
El Dorado Classic	6	M	2	0	0	0	1,400
El Dorado Shooter	6	H	5	3	2	0	211,950
El Duque	2	C	2	0	0	0	845
El Duque's Dream	7	H	2	0	0	0	156
El Duro	4	C	1	0	0	0	46

RECORDS OF HORSES

Horse	Age	Sex	Sts	1st	2d	3d	Won
El End	3	F	2	2	0	0	22,800
El Fabio	3	G	6	1	1	1	13,620
El Fortissimo	3	C	5	0	0	0	0
El Frio	3	C	23	3	4	2	29,615
El Fumar	4	G	10	1	2	0	18,380
El Galante	3	C	2	1	1	0	19,400
El Gallo	2	C	5	0	0	0	1,560
El Gato Rojo	3	C	5	0	1	0	907
El General	4	G	9	0	1	2	33,852
El Ghoste Grande	3	G	8	0	0	1	1,594
El Giuliani	4	G	2	0	0	0	168
El Graduado (CHI)	6	G	23	1	1	4	28,596
El Gran Caesar	5	G	1	0	0	0	50
El Gran Fran (ARG)	6	H	15	3	3	1	21,335
El Gran Habanero	3	C	5	0	0	1	5,440
El Gran Maestro	3	C	12	1	3	1	142,466
El Gran Marco	3	G	16	1	2	6	46,744
El Gran Papa	6	G	7	1	2	0	72,989
El Gran Patagon	4	G	7	2	1	0	15,325
El Grand Bakan	4	G	4	2	0	0	26,145
El Grand Cabillo	3	C	1	0	0	0	100
El Grande Breeze	3	G	9	1	0	1	6,109
El Grande Eloper	3	G	6	0	0	1	1,997
El Guapito (ARG)	6	H	10	2	0	1	23,130
El Guappo	4	G	10	2	0	3	13,585
El Guardaespalda (CHI)	6	G	2	0	0	0	3,000
El Habanero	4	G	3	0	0	0	1,905
El Halcon (ARG)	4	C	11	2	1	1	20,300
El Halito	2	G	9	1	2	3	18,016
El Huichol	4	G	17	1	3	2	12,359
El Insolente	3	C	1	0	0	0	101
El Jai Ton	4	G	12	0	2	5	6,416
El Keep Linda	4	F	6	1	0	1	4,270
El Lapicero (ARG)	5	H	2	0	0	0	210
El Machete	6	H	13	0	0	1	1,894
El Machi (ARG)	4	C	9	2	1	1	12,570
El Malicia	4	C	11	2	1	3	55,440
El Maloso	3	G	1	0	0	0	0
El Master	8	G	15	6	3	0	58,912
El Mat	3	G	6	0	1	1	2,125
El Mirasol	8	H	2	0	0	0	280
El Monstro	4	G	13	1	0	2	2,351
El Nil	2	F	3	0	0	0	369
El Nino Caliente	5	G	22	3	0	4	27,872
El Nino Mi Amor	5	G	11	2	2	2	37,195
El Nino Rial	6	G	1	0	0	0	0
El Noel	2	F	1	0	0	0	0
El Nuki	4	G	4	1	3	0	74,000
El Paso Ed	4	C	4	0	0	3	3,860
El Patron Grande	5	G	12	0	4	1	17,968
El Pequeno	2	G	3	1	0	1	6,650
El Poderoso	4	C	13	1	0	0	8,028
El Portal	5	M	5	0	2	0	7,394
El Possum	6	G	4	0	1	1	2,404
El Prado Diamond	3	F	13	2	3	0	22,130
El Prado Essence	6	M	7	2	2	0	220,108
El Prado in Action	5	G	15	1	1	3	28,720
El Prado Light	5	G	4	0	0	1	2,280
El Prado Rob	2	C	6	2	0	1	93,054
El Prado Star	3	C	2	1	0	0	40,116
El Prado's Delight	5	M	1	0	0	0	0
El Prado's Gal	2	F	5	0	0	0	3,750
El Prado's Plata	3	F	15	3	1	2	34,030
El Prados Treasure	5	G	11	0	0	0	658
El Privado	2	G	2	0	0	0	0
El Progreso	3	R	8	2	1	1	24,460
El Providential	5	G	5	0	2	0	11,400
El Raffy (IRE)	6	M	3	0	0	1	3,149
El Raja	2	C	3	0	0	0	378
El Remolino	2	C	2	0	1	0	4,960
El Reno de Oro	3	G	3	0	0	1	1,426
El Revoso	3	G	8	0	0	0	1,531
El Rio Grande	10	G	11	0	0	0	1,032
El Romantico	4	G	5	0	0	1	2,600
El Ruller	3	C	5	1	1	2	76,838
El S You	2	G	3	0	0	0	0
El Sancho	7	H	2	0	0	0	0
El Segundo Joe	2	C	4	0	0	0	1,107
El Serrucho	7	G	1	0	0	0	0
El Siete O Siete	2	C	5	0	0	0	279
El Silverado	2	C	1	0	0	0	1,290
El Spedito	3	G	3	0	1	0	3,465
El Superhombre	4	C	9	3	2	2	22,790
El Swava	3	F	1	0	0	0	420
El Sysco Kid	2	C	1	0	1	0	22,800
El Tampaino	4	G	11	1	0	2	7,375
El Temperamental	7	G	5	0	0	0	533
El Teporocho	7	G	9	2	2	3	4,071
El Tio Luis	3	C	9	0	0	0	1,415
El Tirador	2	C	2	2	0	0	15,500
El Toto	2	C	4	1	3	0	13,600
El Troppo	4	G	1	0	0	0	0
El Tucan	5	G	7	0	0	0	636
El Unica	2	G	4	0	0	0	0
El Vedado	3	G	3	1	1	0	40,180
El Veneno	3	G	4	0	0	1	2,100
El Vigia (MEX)	8	G	4	1	1	0	1,710
El Waco	4	C	7	1	3	2	9,086
El Yunque	2	C	2	0	0	0	137
Ela Ela	3	F	8	1	1	0	94,581
Elaborate	8	G	3	0	0	1	12,200
Elaboration	3	F	15	2	3	1	38,558
Elaine's Angel	5	M	4	0	0	0	1,690
Elaine's Way	3	F	16	3	4	0	42,162
Elaine's Wolfer	2	C	2	0	1	0	4,340
Elaine's Wolfette	3	F	3	0	0	1	2,915
Elajuud's Gold	3	F	8	2	1	1	15,990
Elakik (GB)	8	H	5	1	1	1	2,114
Elakouklamou	2	F	3	0	1	1	2,405
Elan	3	C	3	2	0	0	58,800
Elana d'Amour	4	F	6	2	0	3	73,394
Elantra	5	M	3	0	0	0	395
Elated Spirit	3	C	4	0	0	1	2,457
Elbader (GB)	5	H	7	0	0	1	11,430
Elberton	6	G	7	0	0	2	19,275
Elberton Ellie	4	F	15	1	2	1	34,655
Elberton Lass	4	G	20	2	3	4	36,787
Elbow Creek	4	G	7	0	2	0	4,500
Elbow Motion	5	M	4	0	0	0	325
Elcoquisound	3	C	3	1	1	0	7,280
Elcriminalpicolino	4	C	2	0	0	0	0
Eldo the Cad	5	G	5	0	0	1	6,355
Eldons Dancer	3	C	11	2	0	2	9,046
Eldorado Belle	7	M	4	0	1	1	1,880
Eldorado Glow	8	G	2	0	0	1	550
Eldorado Gold	7	G	10	0	1	2	7,069
Eldorado Legend	6	M	3	0	1	0	1,580
Eldorado Miss	3	F	9	1	1	0	6,068
Eldoret	8	G	12	0	1	0	3,289
Eleanor's Pet	3	F	3	0	0	0	700
Eleatic	5	M	9	1	4	1	10,978
Election Night	3	G	12	0	1	3	7,985
Election Star	4	F	5	1	0	0	31,130
Electoral College	4	G	8	3	3	0	45,590
Electric Affair	3	F	2	0	0	0	124
Electric Chair	3	F	15	1	2	4	61,960
Electric Fable	3	F	3	0	0	0	1,000
Electric Guitar	3	G	12	1	0	0	16,270
Electric Heat	2	F	3	0	0	1	2,250
Electric Punch	4	G	8	0	1	2	5,382
Electric Salt	4	G	13	0	4	3	5,015
Electric Slide	2	C	1	0	0	1	900
Electric Star	5	M	12	2	3	1	34,420
Electric Wire	2	F	5	1	2	1	40,611
Electrical Carlita	3	F	9	2	5	0	79,160
Electrick City	3	F	6	2	1	1	62,250
Electrisicul	3	G	9	1	2	0	6,308
Electrode	4	G	7	3	2	0	73,360
Elegance by Design	3	F	7	0	2	0	582
Elegant Ambassador	3	C	6	0	0	0	876
Elegant Ambush	5	M	2	0	0	1	583
Elegant Angel	4	F	1	0	0	0	0
Elegant Beau	7	G	12	0	0	2	2,334
Elegant Circle	4	G	5	0	1	0	855
Elegant Colors	6	M	10	1	2	2	16,165
Elegant de Ledo	3	F	2	0	0	1	525
Elegant Designer	3	F	7	3	1	0	119,440
Elegant Fame	2	C	1	0	0	0	840

Horse	Age	Sex	Sts	1st	2d	3d	Won
Elegant Feet	3	F	4	1	0	1	1,561
Elegant Heiress	2	F	3	1	0	0	9,290
Elegant Hunter	4	C	11	4	1	1	100,669
Elegant Lass	6	M	14	2	3	1	16,332
Elegant Magic	7	M	9	0	0	2	2,396
Elegant Mercedes	3	F	11	6	0	2	144,425
Elegant Miss Match	5	M	12	0	0	0	1,386
Elegant Ore	3	F	4	0	0	0	864
Elegant Paradox	2	F	1	0	1	0	8,200
Elegant Prospect	3	F	3	0	0	0	1,680
Elegant Rosey	3	F	5	0	0	2	1,671
Elegant Ryna	9	M	5	0	0	0	612
Elegant Serenade	4	F	7	1	2	0	5,424
Elegant Sunrise	5	M	9	0	3	0	8,140
Elegant Touch	3	F	6	0	0	2	15,170
Elegant Trend	5	H	9	2	3	1	30,065
Elegant Wagon	3	F	9	0	1	3	4,090
Elegante Senor	5	G	14	0	4	2	5,080
Elegantly Wasted	6	M	7	3	1	0	11,210
Elegent Secret	5	H	5	0	1	0	1,675
Elektrona	8	M	3	0	0	1	1,230
Elena's Fame	3	C	3	0	0	0	1,260
Eleven B	3	G	6	1	0	1	9,670
Eleven Stars	2	C	3	0	0	1	6,560
Eleven Sterling	3	C	5	0	2	2	9,600
Eleven Ten Thirty	3	F	3	0	0	0	225
Eleven Twentythree	2	C	3	1	0	0	7,970
Eleven West	5	G	8	0	0	0	920
Elevenlittledevils	4	F	9	0	1	1	5,140
Elevenoclocknews	5	M	3	0	0	0	325
Elfin	3	F	10	1	1	2	16,605
Elgatoesmio (ARG)	5	G	10	0	1	1	12,570
Elgin Park	4	G	2	0	1	0	960
Elhew Henderson	3	C	12	1	2	4	34,480
Elhew Midway	3	F	8	3	1	2	54,692
Eli Banana	7	H	2	0	0	0	0
Eli Lilliput	6	H	7	1	0	1	4,545
Elian	4	G	17	2	1	1	16,560
Eligance	5	M	7	1	1	1	5,756
Eligible Bachelor	3	C	10	0	1	3	20,146
Eligible Receiver	4	G	9	0	0	1	5,481
Elihu	3	G	3	0	0	0	187
Elijah Hill	9	G	9	2	3	3	14,550
Elijah the Profit	8	G	2	0	0	0	0
Elijah's Buck	3	G	5	1	0	2	12,630
Elijan	6	G	1	0	0	0	43
Eliminate	4	G	13	1	2	3	14,223
Elin	4	F	13	1	2	1	12,560
Elio Monti	8	G	2	0	0	0	0
Eli's Dancer	7	G	7	0	0	0	557
Eliseebeau	2	C	1	0	0	0	0
Elise's Notebook	5	M	2	1	0	0	16,580
Elisha Joy	3	F	17	3	5	2	35,870
Elite	2	C	6	0	4	1	24,900
Elite Brother	3	G	17	1	3	3	16,060
Elite Cat	5	M	14	2	0	3	19,450
Elite Eight	2	C	2	0	1	0	7,940
Elite Elion	3	G	1	0	0	0	0
Elite Express	2	F	1	0	0	0	0
Elite Forces	4	G	18	0	0	0	2,215
Elite Guard	4	G	12	2	3	2	12,687
Elite Mercedes	6	H	5	1	0	0	33,300
Elite Nine	3	F	17	1	4	1	7,672
Elite Service	2	G	6	1	1	2	26,777
Elite Spirit	5	G	7	4	1	0	18,922
Elite Tour	3	F	16	2	4	1	26,862
Elitra	3	F	3	0	0	1	545
Elitra Rx	3	F	6	0	0	0	1,595
Eliza Bella	2	F	8	1	1	1	10,675
Eliza's Cat	3	F	8	2	0	0	19,060
Elkhorn Creek	5	H	2	0	0	0	80
Ella Bella	3	F	9	1	1	0	25,500
Ella Eria (FR)	4	F	3	0	0	1	6,600
Ella F.	2	F	5	1	1	1	16,540
Ella Va Wish	3	F	2	0	0	0	91
Ellaroo	3	F	7	0	0	1	700
Ella's Flyer	5	M	7	0	1	1	3,204
Ella's Forum	4	F	14	1	2	3	22,303
Elle Va	4	F	9	0	0	0	540
Ellen in Disguise	4	F	11	1	0	0	4,725
Ellena	3	F	2	0	0	0	0
Ellendales Quest	4	F	1	0	0	0	0
Ellenhighwater	5	M	3	0	0	1	1,920
Ellens Dream	3	F	7	0	0	0	300
Ellens Lucky Star	4	F	10	5	1	3	104,939
Ellen's Souvenir	3	F	10	2	1	2	10,718
Ellensburg	6	M	2	0	1	0	2,532
Ellenton Lass	3	F	12	2	3	4	24,784
Elle's Terms	3	F	16	1	4	2	15,057
Ellie Q	3	F	8	0	1	2	6,848
Ellie Sue	4	F	2	0	0	0	216
Ellieburg	6	M	11	3	0	1	9,146
Ellieonthemarch	2	F	3	1	0	1	39,496
Ellie's Choice	5	G	14	3	0	2	27,995
Ellie's Miss	7	M	5	0	1	0	1,564
Ellie's Moment	5	M	3	1	1	0	84,273
Ellie's Princess	4	F	6	1	0	0	14,741
Ellie's Quest	4	F	11	2	2	1	63,160
Ellie's Rose	6	M	4	0	1	0	19,200
Ellis Basin	3	F	10	2	1	2	82,195
Elloluv	3	F	8	2	3	0	978,775
Ells Editor	2	F	5	1	0	1	16,870
Ells End	6	G	4	2	1	0	13,700
Ellston	6	G	13	0	0	1	1,052
Ellsworth	2	G	1	0	0	1	2,170
Ellusive Quest	3	C	2	0	0	0	970
Elm	2	C	3	0	0	0	1,085
Elm Grove	4	C	7	0	0	0	2,118
Elmer	4	G	2	0	0	0	0
Elmine	3	F	4	0	0	0	1,074
Elm's Legacy	8	G	16	0	2	3	14,106
Eloquent Dawn	2	F	3	0	1	0	2,715
Eloquent Wager	4	G	11	3	1	2	33,245
Elora	3	F	5	0	0	1	6,428
Elrod Petry	3	G	7	0	2	4	12,544
Elron	2	C	4	1	0	0	7,986
Els Belle	5	M	9	0	0	1	1,225
El's Legacy	2	C	1	0	0	0	230
El's Red Cat	3	F	5	1	0	0	11,220
El's Well	3	F	2	1	1	0	6,280
El's Wish	3	F	9	1	0	0	3,494
Elsie Rose	2	F	1	0	0	0	0
Eltawaasul	7	H	3	1	0	0	45,000
Eltish Marengo	3	C	8	3	0	0	23,925
Eltisha	4	F	6	0	1	1	13,670
Elton	3	C	3	0	0	0	1,774
Elton D	7	G	7	0	0	0	183
Elttaes Bay	6	G	6	1	1	0	1,775
Elusion	7	G	11	1	0	1	11,813
Elusive Ashlee	4	F	8	0	1	1	15,927
Elusive Book	3	F	11	1	1	4	13,685
Elusive Crown	4	F	4	1	0	2	18,690
Elusive Figure	3	C	6	1	2	1	38,420
Elusive Fleet	2	F	1	0	0	0	0
Elusive Gentleman	3	C	11	1	0	0	36,230
Elusive Glory	2	C	2	0	0	0	0
Elusive Honey	3	F	6	2	2	1	65,555
Elusive Honor	3	G	11	0	2	1	6,975
Elusive Hour	3	C	3	2	0	0	40,200
Elusive Indian	3	G	5	1	2	0	47,990
Elusive Jazz	2	C	1	0	0	0	0
Elusive Jo Jo	3	F	7	1	0	0	6,744
Elusive Jordan	2	C	2	0	0	0	286
Elusive King	2	G	1	0	0	0	1,800
Elusive Knight	2	C	4	0	0	0	11,661
Elusive Magic	3	G	11	2	3	1	25,713
Elusive Miss	3	F	17	2	1	0	14,649
Elusive Princess	3	F	5	1	1	1	45,880
Elusive Project	2	F	2	0	0	0	1,468
Elusive Reply	6	G	5	0	2	1	4,972
Elusive Road	3	F	8	2	0	1	42,584
Elusive Sara	3	F	5	3	0	0	70,920
Elusive Speed	2	F	8	0	0	0	2,241
Elusive Thought	3	F	8	2	0	2	157,018
Elusive Time	2	C	1	0	0	0	0
Elusive Touch	2	F	3	0	0	2	9,174
Elusive Wolf	5	M	9	0	2	2	7,875
Elvigor	9	G	2	0	1	1	4,200

RECORDS OF HORSES

Horse	Age	Sex	Sts	1st	2d	3d	Won
Elvis Impressme	3	C	2	0	0	0	817
Elvis On Ice	5	G	17	1	1	2	6,970
Elvis Presto	6	G	12	1	1	1	2,719
Elvisvader	3	C	11	0	0	0	1,610
Elway's Way	4	G	2	0	0	0	315
Elwood Blues	9	G	1	0	0	0	0
Elwood's Apple	3	G	13	1	2	0	14,034
Elwood's Wishes	3	C	9	0	2	3	15,433
Ely Hasseen	3	G	11	2	2	2	15,528
Elyon	3	G	8	3	2	2	107,440
Elyse Lane	3	F	5	1	1	1	22,640
Elysian	3	F	4	0	0	0	313
Elysian Elway	5	G	10	1	1	1	24,397
Elysian Springs	4	F	5	0	0	1	1,498
Elzabad	5	H	6	0	0	4	12,688
Em B. Aye	2	C	3	0	1	2	18,460
Em Vee	5	M	7	1	1	1	4,521
Ema Bovary (CHI)	4	F	7	6	0	0	184,340
Ema Dancer	3	F	6	0	1	1	2,850
Emagine That	4	F	12	1	0	3	5,919
Email Eddie	4	G	2	0	1	0	1,000
Emancipate	8	H	3	0	0	0	2,500
Emancipatorempress	2	F	2	1	0	0	8,666
Embank	4	F	4	0	1	0	16,645
Embarassing Moment	2	F	9	2	1	0	14,720
Embarkation	2	C	2	0	0	1	4,750
Embassy Belle (IRE)	5	M	4	0	1	1	33,200
Embassy City	6	H	6	1	1	1	9,851
Embattle	4	C	13	1	3	3	71,676
Embel	2	G	1	0	0	0	570
Emblitterate	3	F	7	2	1	0	22,251
Embon	4	C	12	4	3	1	35,493
Emboss	3	F	6	0	0	0	0
Embracing Monty	4	C	4	0	0	1	815
Embrasse Moi	3	F	1	0	0	0	0
Embroke	5	H	8	0	0	0	150
Embullievable	4	G	10	0	3	3	30,050
Emerald Blue	3	F	4	2	0	1	5,760
Emerald Dixie	4	F	10	3	0	1	96,605
Emerald Drive	6	G	7	4	1	0	20,311
Emerald Earrings	2	F	1	1	0	0	12,840
Emerald Forest	9	G	4	0	0	1	1,377
Emerald Green	4	F	10	0	0	1	10,920
Emerald Hills	4	F	15	4	2	0	19,160
Emerald Irish	2	F	2	0	0	0	0
Emerald Isle	4	F	11	0	1	1	9,477
Emerald Love	5	M	1	0	0	0	0
Emerald Man	5	G	2	0	0	0	155
Emerald N Pearls	2	F	7	0	2	1	12,820
Emerald Pendant	6	M	1	0	0	1	3,600
Emerald Sea	2	F	1	0	0	0	0
Emerald Sky	4	C	17	1	1	1	3,108
Emerald Splash	4	F	6	0	0	0	187
Emerald Verse	6	M	13	2	1	1	14,075
Emerald Vie	3	F	12	1	3	3	14,374
Emeraldforajudge	4	F	2	0	0	1	3,487
Emeralds	3	F	8	1	2	2	7,590
Emerald's Pause	3	F	3	0	0	0	660
Emeraude	2	F	8	0	0	0	1,220
Emergency Exit	6	G	3	0	0	1	702
Emergency Status	4	G	10	1	1	0	32,250
Emerging Spirit	3	G	11	1	5	2	77,300
Emerson Drive	2	G	2	0	0	1	1,900
Emery	3	G	5	0	2	1	2,310
Emilie	3	F	14	3	1	4	15,426
Emilin	2	C	9	1	0	3	2,891
Emil's Account	7	G	3	0	0	0	183
Emily Blaze	2	F	3	0	1	2	9,114
Emily Nicole	3	F	4	1	1	0	8,529
Emily P.	5	M	16	1	3	5	14,243
Emily Q.	6	M	2	0	0	0	0
Emily Ring	5	M	8	1	2	2	66,860
Emilyna	5	M	7	0	1	3	40,382
Emily's Attitude	6	M	3	0	0	0	365
Emilys Dad	9	G	4	1	0	0	3,536
Emily's Gal	3	F	5	1	0	0	6,375
Emily's Get Out	3	F	3	0	1	0	765
Emily's Jubilee	3	F	9	0	0	0	820
Emily's Mark	4	F	8	2	2	0	32,480
Emilys Oyster	2	C	2	1	0	0	11,400
Emily's Rare Trick	4	F	14	1	3	6	36,351
Emily's Reprized	4	F	13	0	1	2	4,675
Emily's Secret	3	F	1	0	0	0	0
Emily's Sugarbear	3	C	7	0	0	1	3,626
Emilysprince	9	G	6	0	0	1	660
Eminent Victory	6	H	7	1	2	1	2,099
Emjay H.	3	F	5	2	0	1	19,718
Emma Bratski	4	F	3	0	1	0	1,152
Emma G	4	F	3	0	0	0	600
Emma Joan	4	F	4	0	0	2	2,278
Emma M.	2	F	4	0	1	1	13,940
Emma Renee	2	F	1	1	0	0	8,950
Emmaria	6	M	3	0	0	0	963
Emma's Delite	5	M	7	0	0	1	3,840
Emma's Dilemma	3	F	5	1	0	0	13,490
Emma's Frown	2	F	2	0	0	0	1,764
Emma's Honor	7	M	7	1	2	0	12,500
Emma's R Hope	2	F	6	0	0	1	1,360
Emma's Wish	2	F	5	0	1	0	2,960
Emmet Square	3	G	11	2	3	1	19,006
Emmies Esperanza	6	M	8	1	2	1	26,805
Emmie's Turn	4	F	5	1	1	0	8,720
Emmitt	7	G	1	0	0	0	54
Emmitts Black Book	3	G	14	0	4	3	19,047
Emo	3	C	17	1	1	5	38,900
Emolument	5	H	9	1	1	4	16,449
Emor	6	G	18	3	4	3	39,295
Emoswa Gold	5	M	5	1	3	0	12,093
Emotional Bluff	2	F	1	0	0	1	1,400
Emotional Ending	3	G	12	1	2	2	14,097
Emotional Era	3	G	13	2	1	0	12,563
Emotional Girl	6	M	11	3	2	4	27,254
Emotional Rosie	3	F	1	0	0	0	0
Emotional Storm	3	F	12	1	4	2	58,640
Emotrin	3	G	8	0	1	1	23,910
Emperor's Victory	6	G	7	0	0	1	1,128
Emphasize	5	G	2	1	0	0	10,800
Emphatic Cayanna	3	F	1	0	0	0	0
Emphatic War	3	G	6	0	0	0	900
Emphatics Path	4	C	1	0	0	0	0
Empire Builder	4	G	18	4	3	3	22,106
Empire Gem	4	F	6	0	0	0	329
Empire Maker	3	C	6	3	3	0	1,936,200
Empire Man (ARG)	4	C	5	0	0	0	0
Empire of Glory (ARG)	5	H	6	1	0	1	9,100
Empire Savannah	6	G	9	1	2	0	12,942
Empire Storm	5	H	1	1	0	0	1,525
Emporia	5	G	17	3	4	3	35,818
Empowered Shark	2	C	4	0	0	0	177
Empress Anna	5	M	5	0	0	0	765
Empress Livia	5	M	11	0	1	2	9,066
Empress of Sheba	3	F	6	0	0	0	3,882
Emptor	2	F	1	0	0	0	164
Empty Portrait	2	F	1	0	0	0	1,680
Empty Promises	3	G	10	2	0	1	4,355
Emptythetill	3	F	7	3	0	2	24,240
Empyreal	8	G	11	1	3	0	12,017
Empyrean Devil	2	F	1	0	0	0	0
Em's Echo	3	C	17	0	2	0	5,775
Emwould	6	G	2	0	0	0	98
Emy Sue	3	F	7	1	1	1	9,809
Emyil's Dreamer	2	C	6	0	0	0	180
En Avant	2	F	3	0	0	0	546
En Ruckus	5	G	8	0	0	0	1,320
En Safari	8	G	8	0	3	0	13,650
Enact	4	F	1	0	0	0	0
Encantador	3	G	3	0	0	0	882
Encanto Oro	2	F	5	0	1	1	2,925
Ence Creek	4	C	3	0	1	2	1,307
Enchanted Castle	6	M	8	0	0	0	1,894
Enchanted Dancer	6	M	3	0	0	0	177
Enchanted Fan	2	C	5	0	0	0	339
Enchanted Ghost	8	H	4	1	1	0	7,820
Enchanted Hope	4	F	1	0	0	0	0
Enchanted Kitten	3	F	8	1	3	2	15,629
Enchanted Knight	5	G	3	0	0	1	780
Enchanted Looker	4	F	3	1	1	0	17,355
Enchanted Magic	2	C	2	0	0	0	240

Horse	Age	Sex	Sts	1st	2d	3d	Won
Enchanted Moment	2	F	12	1	0	0	4,698
Enchanted Prospect	2	F	3	0	0	0	388
Enchanted Trick	3	C	2	0	0	0	0
Enchanting Gal	2	F	7	1	0	0	5,323
Enchanting Gold	3	F	6	0	0	0	0
Enchanting Lass	4	F	9	1	1	2	5,257
Encino Cat	6	H	17	1	3	4	3,746
Encino Ump	4	G	4	1	0	0	23,760
Encore Blade	3	F	2	0	0	0	110
Encore Prince	5	G	7	0	0	1	4,531
Encourage	5	H	5	0	0	0	927
End All	4	G	15	3	4	1	27,093
End Leader	6	G	14	2	0	5	34,682
End O Story	4	F	2	0	0	0	0
End of an Era	2	C	3	2	0	1	25,490
End of the Rainbow	7	H	1	0	0	0	0
End Sweeps Advance	7	G	11	2	0	0	14,327
End Sweep's Gold	3	G	14	1	6	1	20,615
End the Terror	3	G	11	1	2	2	14,871
End the War	3	C	5	0	0	0	774
End Up	6	G	16	4	5	3	27,432
End Wisely	5	G	12	1	3	2	22,890
Endearing Spirit	4	F	14	1	3	2	12,632
Endearment	6	M	7	0	0	2	3,470
Endeavor	5	H	2	1	0	1	36,925
Endeavor Sky	6	M	11	1	1	0	7,337
Endemaj	3	C	3	0	0	1	16,312
Ender Wiggin	7	G	18	5	6	2	40,296
Enderby	2	G	1	0	0	0	300
Ender's Shadow	3	G	7	3	0	1	97,440
Ender's Sister	2	F	5	2	2	0	107,900
Endian Outlaw	4	G	3	0	0	0	1,320
Endicopolis	7	G	5	0	0	2	1,325
Endigo Prince	4	G	1	0	0	1	1,925
Endless Fable	3	G	13	0	0	0	2,795
Endless Good	3	F	1	0	0	0	0
Endless Heat	2	F	2	0	0	0	200
Endless Honour	4	F	5	1	0	1	26,300
Endless Obsession	6	G	6	1	0	2	9,744
Endless Pleasure	3	F	10	1	2	1	23,370
Endless Posibility	4	F	12	1	1	0	5,705
Endless Shadow	4	F	1	0	0	0	0
Endless Song	5	G	8	1	1	0	13,730
Endless Sweep	7	M	8	0	2	0	3,150
Endless Thunder	4	C	9	4	1	0	17,019
Endless Torrential	5	G	1	0	0	0	0
Endofthestorm	4	C	17	3	3	6	32,901
Endoway	3	G	7	0	0	0	1,580
Endowed	10	M	1	0	0	0	100
Endskip	4	F	12	0	1	0	4,970
Endurable	3	C	8	0	2	1	21,069
Endured the Storm	2	F	1	0	1	0	8,080
Enduring Freedom	3	F	8	3	1	0	65,675
Enduring Grace	2	F	1	0	1	0	4,200
Enduring Image	3	G	5	0	1	1	2,410
Enduring Light	2	F	2	1	0	1	4,480
Enduring Storm	5	M	9	1	0	1	4,770
Enemy Number Two	3	F	4	0	0	0	0
Energetic Angel	6	M	6	0	0	0	0
Energetic Storm	2	C	5	1	3	1	28,840
Energized	6	G	21	2	5	5	36,665
Energy Berry	3	F	4	1	0	1	5,810
Energy Bolt	4	C	4	0	0	2	1,540
Energy Lass	2	F	5	0	1	1	6,440
Energy Rush	2	F	3	0	1	0	8,602
Enfatyouated	3	G	2	1	0	0	2,472
Enfield Glen	4	C	1	0	0	0	0
Engagement Ring	4	F	7	0	0	0	720
Engineered	3	C	6	2	1	0	39,800
England Calling	2	G	2	0	0	0	0
England Tower (ARG)	6	G	3	0	0	0	558
English Gentlemen	6	G	16	1	2	3	35,182
English Harbour	3	G	9	3	2	1	54,110
English Sky	4	F	3	0	0	0	0
English Tea	3	F	7	3	0	1	22,250
Engraved	4	G	9	2	0	0	36,190
Engulf	3	G	10	1	3	0	6,676
Enhanced Edition	2	G	1	0	0	0	145
Enjolie	6	M	20	1	1	5	20,896
Enjoy	4	F	6	3	2	0	114,510
Enjoy Idle Time	4	F	9	2	0	0	6,599
Enjoy the Journey	3	F	6	1	1	0	19,390
Enjoy the Wine	3	F	5	1	0	0	9,360
Enka	4	F	4	0	0	0	1,291
Enkidu	3	G	7	0	1	1	6,990
Enlighting	3	F	7	3	1	0	17,750
Enlist	3	G	4	0	0	2	5,774
Ennscho	4	G	10	1	3	1	25,585
Ennui	4	F	5	0	0	1	3,720
Enorme	4	G	6	1	1	1	8,578
Enough Already	6	G	7	1	1	2	11,649
Enough Kissen	3	F	5	2	1	1	49,805
Enough Music	6	H	12	2	0	0	7,738
Enquiry Woman	6	M	1	0	0	1	3,520
Ensenada	2	F	1	0	0	0	1,350
Ensign D C	5	G	13	3	0	4	23,966
Ensign Leon	3	G	2	0	0	0	270
Ensign Pulver	3	C	2	0	0	0	94
Ensign Slew	3	F	9	1	3	1	38,440
Ensigns Babe	5	M	2	0	0	0	0
Ensign's Iron Man	4	G	2	0	0	0	0
Entendu	3	F	9	1	2	1	30,258
Enter Laughing	3	F	2	1	0	0	20,760
Enter Twine	3	G	3	0	0	1	1,950
Entergalatico	5	G	17	2	1	2	20,480
Entice Me	3	F	7	1	2	0	12,425
Enticing Beauty	3	F	10	0	1	2	7,613
Enticing Time	4	F	1	0	0	0	0
Entitledtowin	5	G	10	0	0	2	6,359
Entitlement	4	C	6	1	0	0	34,585
Entour	3	F	18	1	2	2	11,231
Entrancing	4	F	17	2	5	4	34,155
Entrepreneur	6	G	10	1	0	1	30,565
Entrepreneurial	7	G	6	0	0	1	2,123
Entrepreneurship	6	G	14	4	3	1	57,420
Entry Doon	5	M	3	0	1	1	6,400
Entry Point	2	C	5	0	0	3	7,250
Entushab	3	C	10	1	1	1	22,370
Entwiningars	5	G	6	0	2	1	5,886
Enuffdancin	3	G	4	1	1	0	8,412
Enunciate	7	G	14	2	0	1	5,722
Envy Me	5	M	1	0	0	0	0
Eolica	3	F	10	3	1	1	68,283
Eolo (IRE)	5	G	6	1	0	1	4,718
Epee	5	G	9	2	0	2	16,791
Epic	3	C	9	1	1	1	50,510
Epic Beauty	2	F	5	1	0	1	9,495
Epic Drama	2	F	2	0	0	0	474
Epic Fling	2	G	3	0	0	0	713
Epic Gold	2	G	2	0	0	1	480
Epic Hero	4	F	12	1	0	0	3,915
Epic Holiday	2	F	3	0	0	0	450
Epic Honor	7	H	9	0	3	1	25,275
Epic Power	2	G	7	1	0	2	12,100
Epic Wood	5	G	18	4	4	2	21,306
Epica	2	F	4	0	0	2	4,680
Epicentre	4	C	5	1	1	2	82,565
Epona's Destiny	3	F	5	0	0	0	376
Epona's Song	4	F	12	0	3	0	7,755
Epoxy	3	G	4	1	1	1	42,440
Equal Chance	7	G	9	1	1	2	8,189
Equality	4	C	1	0	0	0	3,540
Equality Cat	4	F	4	1	1	0	6,920
Equay	2	F	1	0	0	0	182
Equerry	5	H	4	0	0	1	39,527
Equestria	3	F	4	0	0	0	2,821
Equi Power	4	G	11	2	3	0	36,750
Equideed	8	M	2	0	0	0	580
Equine Affair	4	F	5	0	0	0	0
Equinox	5	H	3	1	0	2	10,710
Equip	5	G	8	0	1	0	3,010
Equity Player	4	F	1	0	0	0	61
Equivalence	4	F	9	2	3	2	9,402
Equivocate	5	G	3	0	3	0	13,100
Equus Maximas	4	G	6	1	0	0	2,470
Era Dynamic	5	M	10	2	0	2	10,801
Era of Chanago	6	G	7	1	0	0	3,036
Eradikate	3	F	7	1	0	4	29,779

Horse	Age	Sex	Sts	1st	2d	3d	Won
Erase	3	F	8	2	2	2	86,190
Erda	4	F	4	1	1	2	46,530
Erewhon	2	C	2	0	0	0	0
Erhard	7	G	10	1	2	1	13,856
Erhu	2	F	3	0	0	1	8,545
Eric C	3	C	1	0	0	0	126
Eric Da Bomb	6	G	1	0	0	0	0
Eric the Grape	3	C	2	0	0	0	0
Erica J	2	F	1	0	0	0	0
Ericas Bad Boy	8	G	2	0	0	0	0
Ericas Bolddestiny	3	F	2	0	0	0	0
Erica's Charm	2	F	1	0	0	0	500
Erica's Money	4	F	8	0	0	2	10,880
Ericas Native	5	M	6	1	0	1	10,265
Erica's Num Num	2	C	2	0	0	0	0
Ericasdellilah	2	F	1	0	0	0	0
Ericka's Eyes	2	F	2	0	0	2	7,500
Ericka's Lass	2	F	3	2	1	0	29,160
Erickson	4	G	18	3	3	2	16,157
Eric's Charmer	3	F	3	0	0	0	0
Eric's Comet	6	H	13	1	3	2	10,071
Eric's Toy	7	H	9	0	0	0	553
Erik the Advisor	5	G	4	0	0	0	488
Erik the Biter	10	G	2	0	0	0	0
Erika Miss Amerika	4	F	9	0	1	1	2,930
Erik's Chance	3	C	15	1	1	0	15,917
Erik's the Charm	2	C	2	0	0	1	5,300
Erimos (IRE)	4	F	10	2	1	2	44,770
Erimos Sheba	4	F	5	0	0	0	340
Erin	3	F	3	0	1	1	18,240
Erin G.	7	M	12	7	2	1	55,672
Erin Go Bragh (NZ)	4	G	3	0	1	0	3,150
Erin Hall	5	M	7	1	1	0	8,468
Erin Heights	3	G	1	0	1	0	1,300
Erin Jane	4	F	3	0	0	0	219
Erin of Wicklow	5	M	16	3	2	4	22,750
Erin Will Win	8	M	2	0	0	0	0
Erin's Dancer	4	G	4	0	0	0	0
Erins Eagle	6	G	13	1	2	4	7,975
Erins Echo	5	M	3	0	0	0	184
Erin's J T	3	G	11	0	1	0	4,927
Erins Jewel	5	M	2	0	0	0	450
Erin's Parade	2	F	2	1	0	0	4,260
Erin's Quest	4	F	6	1	0	0	7,230
Erin's Storm	3	C	11	2	3	1	83,930
Erinsdesertsunrise	4	G	15	2	0	1	8,646
Erin'smalarky	4	F	8	0	1	4	5,412
Ernabel	3	F	4	3	0	0	29,466
Ernestgoestorace	3	G	2	0	0	0	132
Ernie Art	6	G	10	0	1	3	6,017
Eroberer	2	C	1	0	0	0	1,195
Eroica Star	4	F	1	0	1	0	640
Eropa	3	F	2	0	0	0	0
Eros	2	G	2	0	0	0	0
Erotic	3	F	19	1	5	4	14,748
Erotic Flower	10	M	1	0	0	0	0
Erotico	2	C	2	0	1	0	2,980
Erronous	4	G	14	2	2	0	24,795
Erudite	3	C	3	0	0	0	3,120
Erv's Creek	4	G	16	0	1	0	6,759
E's Beautiful	3	F	6	2	1	0	14,600
E's Happy Tune	4	G	17	3	6	1	15,713
Es Muy Stormy	3	F	10	1	1	3	6,729
Es Savoie	2	F	1	0	0	0	0
Es Special	3	C	6	1	0	1	27,804
E's Special Paddok	5	H	10	1	1	1	8,055
Escadilla	4	G	2	0	0	2	9,460
Escalade	6	G	10	0	0	1	1,653
Escalante Drive	4	C	3	0	1	1	1,410
Escalate	3	C	6	0	0	2	4,410
Escalating	4	G	6	1	2	0	13,433
Escalero	3	G	3	0	0	0	0
Escambia County	4	F	2	0	0	0	345
Escape Option	4	C	12	2	1	1	15,185
Escocia (MEX)	5	M	6	0	0	1	988
Escondido	4	G	2	2	0	0	35,100
Escort	6	G	2	0	0	0	122
Escrito	10	H	6	0	1	1	1,880
Eskimo Aly	3	F	2	0	0	0	0
Eskimo Avenue	3	C	3	0	0	0	103
Eskimo Baby	4	F	8	1	2	2	18,612
Eskimo Duke	3	C	1	0	0	0	0
Eskimo Hunter	4	G	10	1	0	0	15,060
Eskimo Ice	3	F	13	1	1	2	12,750
Eskimo Jo	4	C	3	0	0	0	0
Eskimo Passion	7	G	14	4	4	2	53,103
Eskimo Pie Alamode	4	G	5	0	0	1	990
Eskimo Princess	3	F	11	2	1	1	12,135
Eskimobelle	3	F	6	1	1	2	12,660
Eskimo's Deluxe	2	C	2	0	0	0	2,260
Eskimo's Igloo	2	F	3	0	0	1	1,570
Esmay (AUS)	4	F	7	1	1	1	64,808
Esor's Hope	3	G	9	0	0	3	3,556
Espartaco Bob (ARG)	5	G	8	2	1	4	45,290
Especia Magnifica	7	G	3	1	2	0	11,792
Especialista (ARG)	5	G	13	4	3	1	36,875
Especially Nice	2	F	4	0	0	0	97
Especially Royal	2	F	3	1	2	0	8,294
Especially Wild	4	F	15	2	2	1	22,183
Espee Ess	4	G	9	2	2	0	86,934
Espeedo	5	G	19	5	1	2	58,555
Espeedytoo	4	F	2	0	1	0	10,245
Esperanza Gold	7	G	2	0	0	0	0
Esperanza Jazz	2	F	3	0	0	0	652
Esperanza Mambo	10	G	6	0	0	0	1,230
Esperanza Michele	3	F	5	1	1	1	11,431
Esperence	6	H	1	0	0	0	0
Espiga	3	F	19	1	4	2	32,595
Esplanade Star	3	G	4	1	0	0	4,883
Esplendida	2	F	5	1	3	1	31,122
Espresso Oro	8	G	11	2	3	0	19,925
Espresso Song	4	F	1	0	0	0	0
Esprit Kimberly	9	M	6	1	1	0	7,077
Essa's Sharp	3	F	6	0	0	1	3,567
Essay	3	C	4	1	0	0	9,180
Essayons	4	C	2	0	0	0	0
Essence of Cool	2	C	1	1	0	0	5,900
Essence of Snow	3	F	9	1	4	0	14,616
Essential	8	G	1	0	0	0	54
Essex Anne	9	M	1	0	0	1	1,400
Essex Girl	3	F	5	2	2	0	7,604
Essie d'Or	6	M	14	2	2	4	28,352
Essoess	8	G	7	0	0	0	450
Essuvee	3	F	4	1	2	0	2,815
Esta A.	6	M	5	1	0	3	6,500
Establish	5	G	7	1	1	0	13,395
Established Law	4	C	5	0	0	2	10,500
Establishmentcreek	2	F	1	0	0	0	195
Estambul (ARG)	6	H	4	0	0	1	9,020
Estar de Prisa	5	M	3	0	1	0	2,938
Estargee	3	F	2	0	0	0	217
Esta's Diamond	4	G	12	2	3	1	11,093
Esteban Miguel	2	C	5	1	0	2	24,440
Esteemed	4	G	12	2	0	3	23,700
Esteemed Friend	9	G	3	1	0	0	33,120
Esteponia	3	F	7	1	1	1	20,325
Esterhazy	6	G	3	0	0	0	860
Estevan	2	C	5	2	0	1	96,405
Esther Egg	8	G	12	4	3	4	40,972
Estherina	4	F	8	0	1	2	6,880
Esthers Ball	2	F	8	1	2	2	30,822
Esther's Pride	5	M	3	0	0	0	0
Esther's Star	3	F	6	2	0	1	61,970
Estherwood	3	F	8	0	0	1	3,117
Estilo de Cuervo	3	G	17	1	2	1	30,227
Estimated	3	C	2	0	0	0	0
Estimated Prophet	3	G	12	3	2	1	28,960
Estio (CHI)	7	G	5	0	1	1	38,510
Esto Freedom	4	F	12	0	0	1	1,656
Esto Music	3	G	11	0	3	1	6,006
Estonia	6	G	12	1	0	1	34,479
Estrada	4	F	13	5	2	3	84,840
Estravagario	8	G	12	0	3	2	10,985
Estray	3	G	1	0	0	0	0
Estrela	5	M	6	0	0	1	1,030
Estrella Belle	2	F	8	0	1	2	11,245
Estrella Del Sur	4	F	10	2	2	0	15,070
Estrella Prisa	7	G	4	1	0	1	6,060

Horse	Age	Sex	Sts	1st	2d	3d	Won
Estrellita	6	M	2	0	0	0	300
Estrokal	3	F	6	0	0	1	1,566
Et Tu Cleo	4	F	11	0	1	1	6,898
Etbauer's Gift	2	C	1	0	0	0	360
Etcetera Etcetera	5	M	11	3	1	1	37,722
Eternal Affair	5	M	12	0	1	1	4,025
Eternal Cup	3	F	9	2	3	2	76,060
Eternal Dawn	2	F	4	1	1	0	5,710
Eternal Echo	5	G	13	0	3	1	5,728
Eternal Exile	6	H	2	0	0	0	84
Eternal Force	2	G	4	0	1	0	3,667
Eternal Glow	3	C	10	0	1	2	10,442
Eternal Leader	8	G	14	1	0	0	5,234
Eternal Legacy	4	F	9	0	1	0	1,162
Eternal Look	5	G	6	0	3	2	26,532
Eternal Secrecy	6	G	4	1	0	1	31,700
Eternal Secret	4	F	14	1	3	2	17,450
Eternal Spirit	4	F	2	0	0	0	196
Eternal Tune	3	G	17	2	1	1	40,972
Eternally Irish	5	G	17	2	3	3	13,315
Eternally Yours	5	M	9	1	1	1	31,082
Ethan	3	C	11	1	0	3	5,610
Ethan Man	4	G	3	1	1	0	76,400
Ethan's Legend	2	G	2	0	0	0	840
Ethel Marie	5	M	3	0	0	0	286
Ethel N Dave	8	M	13	3	3	0	21,130
Ethel On Tour	5	M	15	4	5	1	25,501
Ethel Redneck	3	G	5	1	0	1	3,119
Ethical Actions	7	G	10	3	0	3	59,400
Ethoria	3	F	4	0	0	0	66
Etoile Montante	3	F	7	3	1	1	240,719
Etoufee	4	F	2	0	0	0	720
Ett Ouimet	3	G	4	1	1	0	4,515
Etta Kay Blackhawk	6	M	3	0	0	0	0
Etta Kitt	6	M	1	0	0	0	0
Etta's Current	9	G	13	4	0	1	30,295
Ette Mae	5	M	1	0	0	0	0
Eucalyptus Hill	5	M	4	1	0	0	10,800
Euchre	7	G	2	0	0	0	0
Euclid Park	3	G	5	1	1	0	7,633
Eufala	5	G	14	2	1	2	22,780
Eugapae	3	F	4	1	1	0	10,670
Eugene's Third Son	3	C	6	3	3	0	292,120
Eulalia	7	M	5	0	0	0	0
Eunever	3	C	3	0	0	0	0
Eureka Gambler	4	G	8	0	0	3	5,968
Eureka Moment	4	F	13	0	0	0	1,503
Eureka Mysteree	5	G	5	1	0	1	6,366
Eureka Valentine	3	F	1	0	1	0	3,402
Eurhrates	4	F	9	3	1	2	12,632
Euribor (IRE)	5	H	5	0	2	0	14,800
Euripides	8	H	3	0	0	0	2,450
Euro Bond	6	G	12	2	3	3	60,370
Euro Liner	2	C	1	1	0	0	21,600
Euroclydon	8	G	11	4	0	0	44,145
European (IRE)	3	C	2	1	0	0	37,359
European Defense	6	G	8	0	1	0	6,901
European Flair	4	F	6	0	2	0	2,594
European Witness	5	G	6	0	1	2	2,953
Eurosilver	2	C	3	2	1	0	284,000
Eurynome	3	F	1	0	0	1	1,155
Evaluation	3	F	10	1	0	1	5,145
Evamar (BRZ)	4	F	3	1	2	0	37,400
Evanders Challenge	8	G	5	1	1	0	27,940
Evanescent	5	H	15	4	3	0	20,681
Evangelista	2	F	2	0	0	0	66
Evanglie	3	C	2	0	0	0	0
Evans	2	C	2	1	0	0	12,300
Evans Catbird	2	F	1	0	0	1	1,540
Evan's Diamond	4	G	7	1	0	1	9,630
Evanwood	3	G	4	0	0	0	409
Eva's Gold	3	F	4	1	0	0	5,181
Eva's Hope	4	F	2	0	0	0	675
Eva's Pegasus	3	F	12	0	1	0	3,020
Eva's Prospector	3	F	12	2	3	0	28,382
Eva's Rainbow	4	F	1	0	0	0	0
Evasive	2	F	1	0	0	0	0
Evasive Decision	5	G	15	1	0	2	6,173
Evasive Fortune	5	G	15	3	4	2	12,595
Evasive Justice	2	F	3	0	0	0	1,500
Evasive Reason	2	G	1	0	0	0	0
Evasive Vision	3	F	3	0	0	0	0
Eve Believes	4	F	1	0	0	0	0
Eve Harrington	7	M	6	2	0	0	23,011
Evelen's Prospect	5	H	1	0	0	0	0
Evelite	6	M	1	0	0	0	0
Evelyn Negri	3	F	1	1	0	0	12,600
Evelyn's Escapades	7	M	3	1	0	0	6,497
Even Flow	3	G	11	3	1	2	55,650
Even Sharper	6	G	4	0	0	1	2,001
Even Temper	6	M	8	0	0	1	1,198
Even the Score	5	H	8	3	0	0	116,408
Eveniano	3	F	6	0	1	1	3,790
Evening After	4	F	8	0	2	2	6,698
Evening Attire	5	G	9	2	2	2	430,160
Evening Clinic	3	G	8	1	1	2	25,220
Evening Dancer	2	C	1	0	1	0	8,170
Evening Edition	2	F	3	1	1	0	34,120
Evening Gents	3	G	7	0	1	0	3,555
Evening Majesty	6	G	3	0	0	0	900
Evening Martinis	7	G	3	0	0	0	522
Evening Mist	3	F	5	0	1	0	7,480
Evening n' Paris	5	M	5	0	1	0	3,190
Evening News	7	G	11	3	0	2	18,407
Evening On Rainier	3	F	4	1	0	1	20,520
Evening Proof	2	F	3	0	1	1	10,170
Evening Puzzles	4	G	10	0	2	4	6,630
Evening Shadows	3	F	4	0	1	0	11,455
Evening Star Rose	4	F	11	3	3	1	38,147
Evening Trial	2	C	2	0	0	0	2,450
Evening Winds	5	M	3	0	1	0	1,193
Eveningchristopher	8	G	7	0	0	1	1,143
Evening's Luck	4	F	1	0	0	0	0
Evensup	5	G	15	2	0	1	8,882
Event	5	G	8	0	0	1	1,784
Eventfull	2	G	5	1	1	0	20,700
Ever Forever	4	F	9	0	1	0	3,628
Ever Quest	4	C	6	0	0	2	440
Ever With You	5	M	3	1	0	0	27,162
Everett Joe	3	C	7	1	2	0	9,878
Everetts Codey	5	M	11	2	1	1	11,962
Everglades City	2	C	1	0	0	0	180
Everheart	2	F	2	1	1	0	40,245
Everlasting Gold	4	G	5	0	0	0	205
Everlasting Life	5	G	7	1	0	1	6,326
Everlasting Night	5	G	7	1	2	1	4,130
Everlasting Suave	4	G	19	3	2	5	56,700
Everviligent	3	G	10	0	2	1	8,040
Everwhat	5	G	14	6	0	3	58,953
Every Advantage	2	C	1	0	0	0	3,080
Every Cloud	4	F	6	1	0	0	23,540
Every Hope	8	G	17	1	1	1	5,794
Every Mountain	3	C	3	1	2	0	46,400
Every Red Cent	4	G	8	1	0	1	5,354
Every Trick	2	F	1	0	0	0	0
Everybodylovesfuzz	6	G	10	3	1	1	29,894
Everybodywantssome	2	C	1	0	0	0	0
Everybottiwins	4	F	7	1	1	1	35,380
Everybuddysbizness	4	F	5	1	1	1	6,510
Everyday Angel	2	F	3	1	2	0	55,720
Everyday Hero	5	G	6	0	0	1	1,047
Everyone Knows	3	G	9	0	2	1	22,412
Everyone's N. V.	3	C	9	0	3	2	2,570
Everything Free	5	H	8	1	1	1	19,050
Everything to Gain	4	G	1	1	0	0	31,270
Everything Wild	2	C	1	0	0	0	0
Everythinguneed	5	M	6	0	2	0	6,229
Eve's Brook	4	F	3	0	0	0	250
Eves Eden	3	F	6	0	0	1	2,090
Eve's World	4	F	4	0	0	0	365
Eviction Notice	2	C	5	0	1	3	12,329
Evie's Appeal	7	M	4	0	0	1	2,114
Evie's Bearcat	6	M	15	2	1	6	31,680
Evil Eye Aly	3	F	9	1	3	1	51,625
Evil Eyes	6	M	12	0	2	3	4,248
Evil Ina	3	F	4	2	0	0	13,516
Evil Lady	4	F	10	5	2	0	64,740
Evil Tricks	6	M	10	1	4	0	19,434

Horse	Age	Sex	Sts	1st	2d	3d	Won	Horse	Age	Sex	Sts	1st	2d	3d	Won
Evil Waters	4	G	5	0	1	0	4,105	Excessively Lucky	4	C	1	0	0	0	254
Evil Weevil	3	C	2	0	0	0	0	Excessively Sarah	3	F	2	0	0	0	0
Evitan Native	4	F	11	2	1	2	39,145	Excessivelycasual	6	M	6	2	1	1	10,968
Eviticus	9	G	4	0	0	0	132	Excessivepleasure	3	G	9	3	4	0	821,782
Evoke	3	C	5	1	0	0	14,999	Exchange Bay	3	F	6	2	1	0	67,520
Evolutionary	5	H	10	1	2	2	10,492	Exchange for Gold	3	C	2	0	0	0	0
Evolving Tactics (IRE)	3	C	6	2	0	2	181,852	Exchangon	3	G	13	0	1	1	2,569
Evora	3	F	2	0	0	0	220	Excitable	2	F	2	0	1	1	13,950
Evrstrive Evrshine	3	F	4	0	0	0	1,185	Excitable Cat	4	G	8	0	0	0	662
Evrybodylvsraymond	3	G	1	0	0	1	980	Excitable Lady	3	F	4	1	0	2	9,920
Ev's Boo Hoo	3	F	7	0	0	0	1,575	Excite Me	3	C	1	0	0	0	0
Evvy	6	M	4	0	0	0	740	Excited At Last	4	G	3	0	0	0	0
Ewer All Wet	7	G	3	0	0	1	3,380	Exciting Flash	6	H	4	0	0	0	0
Ex Federali	6	H	14	3	2	2	67,057	Exciting Jewel	5	M	6	1	0	1	3,557
Ex Kay E	5	G	4	1	1	0	12,482	Exciting Metro	2	C	9	1	3	2	64,940
Ex Pirate	4	G	3	0	1	0	2,360	Exciting Prospect	2	F	3	0	0	0	174
Ex Post Facto	6	G	6	0	3	1	22,160	Exciting Trick	3	G	18	4	7	1	52,260
Ex Smoker	4	C	1	0	0	0	0	Exciting Venture	4	G	9	1	1	1	41,992
Ex Who	5	G	8	1	1	2	23,610	Exclamation	2	C	2	0	0	1	7,200
Exackary	3	G	14	1	2	3	10,255	Exclusive Account	5	M	1	0	0	0	40
Exaggerate This	2	G	2	0	0	0	0	Exclusive Banker	4	G	11	3	1	3	57,309
Exaggeration	4	G	2	0	0	0	282	Exclusive Bud	5	G	16	2	4	2	37,550
Exallent	2	F	3	0	0	0	750	Exclusive Cabin	9	G	4	0	0	0	395
Exaltado	11	G	2	0	0	0	520	Exclusive Chief	3	C	8	1	0	0	3,168
Exanastasis	2	F	4	0	2	1	13,716	Exclusive Dan	5	H	1	0	0	0	40
Exasparate	6	M	4	0	1	1	3,636	Exclusive Dawn	6	H	5	1	0	0	5,113
Excala	4	F	5	0	1	0	2,050	Exclusive Delight	4	F	10	1	2	1	11,456
Excaper	3	C	9	2	1	1	23,065	Exclusive Deposit	4	F	16	2	5	3	48,590
Excavadora	3	F	12	2	3	1	22,269	Exclusive Don Don	3	G	5	0	1	0	1,350
Excavation	4	G	15	3	2	2	41,290	Exclusive Estate	7	G	1	1	0	0	2,520
Excavatress	4	F	3	0	0	0	522	Exclusive Eve	6	M	5	1	0	1	2,940
Exceeding	3	G	8	2	3	0	96,680	Exclusive Glory	2	F	2	0	0	2	5,340
Exceedinlegallimit	6	M	13	3	2	1	35,980	Exclusive Gold	2	C	1	0	0	0	780
Excel for Me Marie	3	F	3	0	0	0	0	Exclusive Honor	3	G	4	0	1	1	4,033
Excel Please	3	G	7	1	0	1	4,180	Exclusive Hopper	3	F	10	2	4	0	43,570
Excel to Accel	2	F	1	0	0	0	140	Exclusive Image	3	F	22	0	1	1	4,958
Excell for Bunty	4	G	4	0	0	0	0	Exclusive Kid	4	G	11	2	1	0	16,086
Excell to Fly	4	G	8	1	2	0	22,520	Exclusive Molly	5	M	11	2	3	1	35,035
Excell Why Not	4	G	4	0	1	0	1,820	Exclusive Moons	4	G	8	0	0	0	286
Excellabet	4	C	8	2	1	1	30,040	Exclusive Pac	3	G	3	0	1	0	3,200
Excellenceinmotion	4	G	13	2	2	1	19,262	Exclusive Pass	6	M	1	0	0	0	35
Excellent Advice	4	F	1	0	0	0	0	Exclusive Print	2	F	1	0	0	1	2,750
Excellent Band	2	C	5	4	1	0	112,080	Exclusive Rio	2	G	2	0	0	0	200
Excellent Blend	2	G	4	2	0	0	37,615	Exclusive Rocket	6	G	7	0	0	0	330
Excellent Charisma	2	F	2	0	0	2	9,020	Exclusive Run	9	G	6	2	1	1	48,350
Excellent Choice	4	F	7	1	1	1	32,890	Exclusive Sainte	3	F	5	0	0	0	300
Excellent Cut (IRE)	3	C	9	0	5	1	64,957	Exclusive Scout	5	H	3	0	1	0	2,600
Excellent Event	2	G	3	0	2	1	22,188	Exclusive Slew	3	G	16	1	1	3	11,275
Excellent Idea	3	F	9	2	0	0	25,530	Exclusive Spa	5	M	12	2	0	1	7,323
Excellent Minute	6	M	10	1	0	0	4,470	Exclusive Storm	3	C	5	0	0	1	1,140
Excellent Play	2	F	2	0	0	0	913	Exclusive Tale	5	G	19	4	0	4	50,793
Excellentcharacter	4	G	9	0	1	1	32,300	Exclusive Talent	4	F	5	1	1	0	2,417
Excellently	4	F	3	1	0	0	6,900	Exclusive Time	4	G	11	0	1	2	3,055
Exceller Lip	4	F	2	0	0	0	0	Exclusiveandcatty	7	M	1	0	0	0	2,025
Excellwithluck	4	C	8	2	0	1	15,612	Exclusively Risque	10	G	11	1	0	2	8,396
Exceptional Chance	3	F	10	1	3	1	22,630	Exclusively Wild	2	F	2	1	0	0	19,972
Exceptional Gift	5	G	20	1	6	4	17,702	Exclusively Yours	4	F	2	0	0	0	40
Exceptional Luck	6	H	6	0	0	0	309	Exclusivelynassau	3	C	4	0	0	0	0
Exceptional Sunset	3	G	6	0	0	0	100	Exclusivenjoyment	2	G	4	0	2	1	31,890
Exceptional Tune	3	F	10	2	2	1	15,170	Exclusivo	9	H	5	0	0	0	0
Exceptional Weave	4	F	17	3	6	2	16,803	Excon	6	G	12	2	0	1	11,915
Exceptionally	2	F	1	0	0	0	1,818	Excuse	4	F	10	1	2	1	11,686
Excess Rouge	4	F	4	0	0	1	2,290	Excuse My French	5	G	11	6	3	1	51,905
Excess Speed	5	G	2	0	0	0	450	Excuseforthejuice	6	G	10	3	1	3	21,987
Excess Star	3	F	9	2	0	0	8,578	Execptional Game	2	G	5	0	0	2	8,912
Excess Summer	3	G	10	6	2	0	294,261	Executioness	6	M	2	0	0	0	170
Excessive Barb	3	C	2	0	0	0	0	Executive Air	4	F	10	2	2	3	16,744
Excessive Behavior	4	C	9	2	3	2	47,186	Executive Attitude	2	F	5	0	0	0	2,154
Excessive Ego	3	F	13	1	4	0	16,310	Executive Belle	3	F	10	3	4	0	48,916
Excessive Hayate	3	G	2	0	1	0	3,400	Executive Brat	4	G	2	0	0	0	1,114
Excessive Noise	5	H	5	1	0	0	7,080	Executive Celtic	4	G	15	1	0	1	18,342
Excessive Reign	2	F	1	0	0	0	230	Executive Charger	2	C	1	0	0	0	130
Excessive Ruhler	5	H	4	1	0	0	2,500	Executive Derby	4	G	4	0	0	0	0
Excessive Spice	2	F	1	0	0	0	0	Executive Jimmy	2	C	3	0	0	1	8,232
Excessive Tab	3	G	7	1	3	0	12,553	Executive Legacy	3	G	11	3	1	1	168,215
Excessive Term	3	G	5	1	0	0	12,940	Executive Mansion	3	F	1	0	1	0	3,400
Excessive Warrior	4	F	1	0	0	0	0	Executive Meeting	3	G	7	0	2	1	7,271
Excessively Bold	2	C	1	0	1	0	9,800	Executive Time	2	F	6	1	2	2	32,419
Excessively Icy	3	F	6	2	0	0	23,129	Executive Willie	2	C	6	1	1	1	66,617

Horse	Age	Sex	Sts	1st	2d	3d	Won
Executive's Gal	5	M	1	0	0	0	0
Exemplary	5	H	12	2	0	5	28,980
Exert	6	H	1	0	0	0	220
Exertion	3	C	9	3	2	1	22,250
Exfirmed	3	G	11	0	0	4	13,497
Exfuseme	3	F	6	0	0	0	3,711
Exhalt	3	G	8	1	2	3	18,250
Exile Lark (BRZ)	6	H	8	2	0	2	33,800
Exile Queen	4	F	2	0	0	1	450
Exist	2	F	6	1	2	0	19,245
Exit Forty One	4	F	6	1	1	0	12,220
Exit Laughing	3	F	10	0	0	1	4,024
Exit Now	2	F	2	0	0	0	2,100
Exitting	7	H	10	1	0	5	19,705
Exmut (ARG)	5	H	11	2	2	3	49,259
Exoctic Gold	4	F	6	4	0	0	14,015
Exorcized	6	M	9	1	1	2	12,969
Exotic Angel	6	M	9	0	2	3	24,045
Exotic Crystal	2	F	6	1	0	0	11,220
Exotic Gem	5	M	14	4	1	3	43,284
Exotic Hoedown	4	G	5	0	1	0	685
Exotic Isle	2	F	2	0	0	0	0
Exotic Monday	6	M	2	0	0	0	0
Exotic Red	5	G	11	0	2	0	16,327
Exotic Sheeba	2	F	4	0	0	0	479
Expandable	3	G	4	1	0	0	12,450
Expansive	3	G	10	1	1	2	8,240
Expect a Mint	4	F	6	2	2	0	55,036
Expect a Ship	4	G	12	3	1	1	89,250
Expect a Star	2	F	1	0	1	0	2,500
Expect a Surprise	2	F	3	0	0	1	2,510
Expect an Angel	3	F	4	2	2	0	33,730
Expect Justice	2	C	4	1	0	0	10,800
Expect Nothing	2	F	3	0	0	0	3,925
Expect Peace	4	G	11	1	3	1	24,340
Expect Roses	3	F	23	2	2	3	25,346
Expect the Best	2	C	6	3	0	3	68,960
Expect the Gold	4	C	3	0	0	0	526
Expect to Jet	3	F	7	2	0	0	6,308
Expectacat	2	C	3	1	0	1	33,480
Expectant	3	F	12	2	5	0	46,814
Expectawildrush	3	F	11	1	2	3	9,790
Expected Command	4	G	11	0	3	3	57,628
Expected Flirt	4	G	10	1	0	2	28,046
Expected Hero	2	F	4	0	3	0	6,120
Expected Hour	4	C	8	0	0	0	5,239
Expected Program	4	C	8	1	1	0	13,910
Expected Rain	4	C	9	1	4	1	32,881
Expected Roll	4	F	1	0	0	0	0
Expected Song	3	F	8	2	3	1	126,635
Expected Temper	4	F	13	2	6	1	21,648
Expected Touch	4	G	8	5	1	0	183,820
Expectedtopeelaway	2	F	4	0	0	0	0
Expecting Joy	4	G	1	0	0	0	91
Expecting Pat	4	G	7	1	1	1	11,246
Expecting Sugar	3	F	13	1	4	4	27,210
Expecting You	4	F	14	3	1	0	15,033
Expedient	2	C	1	0	0	0	0
Expedite It	3	F	15	1	1	3	16,940
Expedition Leader	2	F	1	0	0	1	3,630
Expendable	3	F	12	2	3	3	64,160
Expensive Baby	3	F	2	0	1	0	2,570
Expensive Passion	6	M	10	0	3	2	9,060
Expensive Risk	4	G	10	1	4	1	47,498
Expensive Road	3	C	7	1	0	0	28,980
Expensive Shoes	5	M	3	0	0	0	243
Expensive Verdict	6	M	14	1	1	1	10,840
Expensivo	6	G	12	0	1	3	6,901
Experiencethepower	3	F	10	2	2	1	14,353
Expert	5	G	7	1	2	2	28,940
Expert Design	2	C	2	0	0	1	2,660
Expert's King	9	G	5	0	0	0	49
Experts Only	3	F	8	2	1	0	39,660
Explanation	9	M	11	3	1	2	15,432
Expletive	2	C	1	0	0	0	195
Explicit Action	3	C	3	0	0	1	5,720
Explicitly	2	F	2	0	0	2	6,580
Exploder	5	G	4	0	0	0	238
Exploding Affair	2	G	5	0	0	1	1,645
Exploding Craft	3	C	2	0	0	0	322
Exploding Star	2	F	1	0	0	1	1,950
Explodo Red	9	G	13	0	2	1	6,779
Exploit Choice	2	F	1	0	0	0	0
Exploit Lad	2	C	11	1	2	2	69,841
Exploitation	2	F	5	0	0	1	5,880
Exploited	2	C	6	1	0	1	12,930
Exploited Power	2	C	1	0	0	0	230
Exploited Storm	2	C	6	1	1	0	31,885
Exploit'em	2	C	1	0	0	0	0
Exploiting	2	C	2	0	0	0	0
Exploitive	2	F	8	0	1	0	6,600
Explorationist	4	G	8	4	0	0	45,050
Explosive Action	5	M	9	1	0	1	4,965
Explosive Affair	2	F	2	0	0	1	6,666
Explosive Alliance	4	G	13	1	0	1	5,964
Explosive Asset	3	F	9	3	1	0	26,025
Explosive Attitude	4	F	3	0	0	0	0
Explosive Beauty	3	F	5	2	0	1	67,500
Explosive Bob	5	G	3	0	0	0	300
Explosive Buck	2	G	4	0	0	0	350
Explosive Charade	2	F	9	1	1	1	14,915
Explosive Copy	3	C	1	0	0	0	362
Explosive Count	5	G	12	1	0	2	33,987
Explosive Coyote	2	C	5	0	0	0	730
Explosive Dancing	3	F	3	0	0	1	1,520
Explosive Devil	4	C	2	0	0	0	0
Explosive Doll	4	F	5	2	0	0	5,118
Explosive Doon	2	F	1	0	0	0	0
Explosive Edition	5	M	12	3	2	2	18,487
Explosive Feeling	4	C	2	0	0	1	1,365
Explosive Fury	5	G	7	2	2	0	8,185
Explosive Green	3	C	7	2	1	1	44,380
Explosive Harley	9	G	13	1	4	2	11,655
Explosive Jackie	3	F	8	1	1	2	18,195
Explosive Jasmine	4	F	25	2	3	6	27,689
Explosive Mac	5	G	10	1	3	2	5,370
Explosive Maggie	6	M	1	0	0	0	214
Explosive Meagan	2	F	3	0	0	2	8,610
Explosive Play	5	G	7	2	0	1	15,774
Explosive Reply	7	H	8	2	3	1	7,755
Explosive Revival	2	G	2	0	0	0	1,252
Explosive Starlet	4	F	5	1	0	0	26,361
Explosive Talk	4	F	11	0	0	0	894
Explosive Test	4	C	18	3	2	1	25,780
Explosive Times	6	M	14	1	4	2	20,763
Explosive Truth	4	C	3	0	0	1	3,630
Explosive Vice	3	F	7	1	1	0	4,970
Explosive Vicky	3	F	1	0	0	0	165
Explosive Wish	6	M	5	1	1	1	4,196
Expo Factor	2	F	4	0	0	0	216
Expocito	5	G	8	1	2	1	6,063
Exposer	3	G	12	2	1	0	19,528
Expotential	6	G	5	1	1	0	3,920
Expound	3	C	15	0	0	4	4,465
Express Account	4	F	7	1	0	0	4,290
Express Angel	3	F	3	0	0	0	0
Express Caper	4	G	17	2	0	1	14,510
Express Commander	5	H	2	0	1	0	1,572
Express Jet	5	H	2	0	0	0	82
Express Lover	3	F	17	3	4	2	41,872
Express Male	7	H	1	0	0	0	0
Express Matters	6	H	9	1	2	2	17,942
Express Pointe	8	H	4	0	0	0	67
Express Post	6	H	2	1	1	0	3,120
Express Stat	3	G	3	0	0	0	0
Express Tour	5	H	1	0	0	0	0
Express Trip	6	M	3	0	0	1	
Expressed Desire	4	C	9	0	0	1	2,890
Expressionator	3	G	15	2	3	3	25,413
Expressionist	8	H	17	3	1	7	98,420
Expressive One	5	M	10	0	3	2	7,702
Expressive Word	7	M	9	2	4	2	15,686
Expresso Bay	6	G	10	6	2	0	176,420
Expresso Love	4	F	10	2	1	1	55,439
Expressway	4	F	8	2	1	0	25,360
Exquisite Belief	6	H	1	0	0	0	0
Exquisite Princess	2	F	3	0	0	0	450
Exquisite Ruckus	3	F	1	0	0	0	428

RECORDS OF HORSES

Horse	Age	Sex	Sts	1st	2d	3d	Won	Horse	Age	Sex	Sts	1st	2d	3d	Won
Exspendsive	6	G	10	2	2	5	12,922	Eyeofthestorm	3	F	3	1	0	0	15,924
Exstorminator	3	G	7	0	3	0	13,280	Eyes a Fox	3	F	13	1	1	4	24,805
Extend	5	M	4	0	0	1	10,870	Eyes Are Upon You	2	C	3	0	0	0	100
Extended Credit	3	C	10	0	4	2	5,070	Eyes for Hannah	4	G	10	3	1	1	37,807
Extended View	5	M	1	0	0	0	0	Eyes in Disguise	4	G	16	0	2	1	7,614
Extended Warranty	6	G	2	0	1	0	1,895	Eyes of Berthold	4	F	11	1	7	1	26,002
Extensive Quality	3	G	10	1	0	2	11,135	Eyes of Moscow	3	C	5	0	0	0	840
Extra	3	C	3	0	0	0	0	Eyes of the Critic	3	G	14	3	0	3	52,287
Extra Beat	4	C	2	1	0	0	33,600	Eyes Sucha Delight	6	M	14	0	1	1	2,785
Extra Bold	8	G	1	0	0	0	0	Eyes the Duchess	4	F	7	1	2	0	35,639
Extra Butter	3	G	7	0	0	0	340	Eyes Wide Open	2	F	4	0	0	0	4,110
Extra Check	4	G	5	0	0	0	14,730	Eyes Wide Open (FR)	5	G	9	0	1	1	15,900
Extra Cool	3	G	2	0	0	0	434	Eyesaderbyfantasy	3	C	5	0	0	0	382
Extra Deep	5	G	15	1	4	1	11,315	Eyeseedocgolightly	3	C	13	1	5	0	20,139
Extra Dividend	11	G	2	0	0	0	252	Eyeshadow	3	F	11	3	0	3	24,550
Extra Dry Martini	3	F	5	0	0	1	2,370	Eyestartthemusic	4	G	3	0	0	0	190
Extra Fit	3	C	12	1	1	1	28,600	Ez Money Honey	3	F	1	1	0	0	6,050
Extra Gold	4	G	16	2	2	1	24,367	Ezee Target	2	C	2	0	0	0	114
Extra Kick	2	C	1	1	0	0	13,750	Ezepart	4	C	12	1	2	3	9,086
Extra Olives	3	F	2	0	0	0	222	Ezio	6	G	12	1	1	2	7,713
Extra Pleasant	5	G	4	0	0	1	450	Ezman	4	F	4	0	1	1	4,630
Extra Pockets	2	G	1	0	0	0	0	Ezra	4	G	10	2	3	1	38,825
Extra Secrets	3	C	5	0	0	0	0	F J's Pace	8	G	13	5	1	1	203,840
Extra Spice	3	G	4	1	0	0	6,942	F P Roman Princess	6	M	3	0	0	1	200
Extra Strength	5	M	7	0	1	2	5,635	F. E. Boone	4	G	10	1	0	1	5,913
Extra Sweet	2	F	2	0	0	0	0	F. F. Arada	6	G	12	0	0	1	2,255
Extra Swift	3	F	6	0	0	0	1,404	F. J. Girl	2	F	1	0	0	0	75
Extra Value	4	C	3	0	0	0	708	Fa Vid	3	F	8	0	1	1	8,888
Extra Ying	5	G	17	1	7	1	12,943	Faah Emiss	5	H	4	0	0	0	4,960
Extradyne	2	C	3	0	0	0	0	Fab Do	5	G	10	1	3	1	16,005
Extranet	6	G	16	0	2	2	4,618	Fabaxe	4	F	3	0	0	0	107
Extraordinary Cop	5	H	1	0	0	1	500	Fabeled War	5	H	10	2	2	1	10,092
Extravagant Lady	5	M	8	1	0	0	3,744	Fabiao	8	G	1	0	0	0	0
Extreme Adventure	6	G	4	0	1	0	1,140	Fabia's Flag	3	F	2	0	0	0	590
Extreme Dream	6	M	2	0	0	0	0	Fabled Court	4	G	1	0	0	0	100
Extreme Fighter	3	C	8	3	2	0	43,270	Fabled Fog	7	G	4	1	0	0	5,175
Extreme Hero	2	C	1	0	1	0	2,600	Fabled Wings	3	C	9	1	4	0	6,650
Extreme Machine	3	C	5	0	2	2	27,480	Fablian	6	M	2	0	1	0	2,490
Extreme Miss	7	M	7	0	0	0	650	Fabricator	3	G	1	0	0	0	1,600
Extreme Motion	3	C	1	0	0	0	0	Fabulist (ARG)	4	C	2	0	0	0	1,310
Extreme Pleasure	4	F	1	0	0	0	960	Fabulous Amy	6	M	6	1	1	1	3,862
Extreme Strike	2	F	2	0	0	0	0	Fabulous Blush	5	M	2	0	0	0	415
Extreme Tide	3	G	7	0	0	0	474	Fabulous Bonus	2	F	7	1	0	0	14,500
Extreme Zone	4	G	9	1	1	2	20,399	Fabulous Brew	2	G	4	0	0	0	2,466
Extremeciano	2	F	3	0	0	1	7,169	Fabulous Brush	3	F	9	0	4	3	44,000
Extremely Smart	3	F	10	0	0	0	1,240	Fabulous Caper	3	F	9	0	0	1	1,775
Extremo	3	F	1	0	0	0	80	Fabulous Change	4	G	4	0	0	0	349
Exuberant Pride	4	G	10	1	1	0	11,544	Fabulous Court	3	C	5	2	0	0	12,577
Exuberant Wagon	2	F	5	0	0	0	755	Fabulous Crown	4	G	1	0	0	0	0
Exude	3	G	14	4	2	1	81,385	Fabulous Dasher	3	G	12	1	2	1	20,250
Exultant	8	G	4	0	0	0	1,510	Fabulous Egyptian	3	F	1	0	0	0	100
Exy	4	F	17	1	0	4	15,825	Fabulous Feeling	4	C	1	0	0	0	500
Exzachary	2	C	1	0	0	0	0	Fabulous Fireworks	4	F	2	0	0	0	182
Exzottica	7	M	8	2	1	2	13,194	Fabulous Flame	3	F	4	0	1	2	1,860
Eyad (IRE)	3	G	5	2	0	0	53,500	Fabulous Fortune	5	G	19	1	1	3	28,650
Eye Cant Hear You	10	G	5	1	0	0	4,985	Fabulous Fox	4	F	14	2	3	4	51,632
Eye Con	6	G	8	1	1	1	10,945	Fabulous Fraser	4	G	12	1	1	1	5,365
Eye Dazzler	2	F	5	1	1	2	81,640	Fabulous Friend	6	G	5	0	0	0	1,396
Eye Drink Alone	6	G	9	2	1	0	6,587	Fabulous Fun	4	F	14	4	2	2	15,935
Eye Found It	5	G	17	1	4	1	14,984	Fabulous Fury	4	F	10	3	0	1	39,510
Eye O Wa Dancer	3	G	9	0	2	2	12,309	Fabulous Hawaii	4	F	4	1	1	0	10,180
Eye O Wa Hawk	4	F	11	1	1	1	6,335	Fabulous Idea	4	G	16	2	0	1	9,966
Eye O You	3	G	7	0	0	0	329	Fabulous Jayne	3	F	2	0	0	0	0
Eye of the Artist	2	F	2	0	0	0	180	Fabulous Lady	4	F	3	0	1	1	2,100
Eye of the Comet	4	G	1	0	0	0	0	Fabulous Looker	2	F	3	0	0	1	1,920
Eye of the Hawk	4	F	9	2	0	0	27,894	Fabulous Maid	4	F	8	0	0	0	555
Eye of the Tiger	3	C	8	2	1	2	214,689	Fabulous Notebook	2	F	3	0	0	0	2,395
Eye of Z Storm	3	F	13	2	0	1	15,739	Fabulous Numbers	3	C	1	0	0	0	0
Eye Pea Oh	7	G	6	0	0	3	17,460	Fabulous Offer	3	F	10	0	0	0	745
Eye Slew the City	5	M	2	0	0	0	1,638	Fabulous Passion	3	F	7	1	0	3	29,110
Eye Spy	6	G	14	2	3	1	10,188	Fabulous Peak	4	G	9	0	2	1	15,770
Eye Stopper	2	F	4	0	0	0	0	Fabulous Play	3	F	4	0	0	0	826
Eye Witness	4	C	16	2	1	2	36,300	Fabulous Pride	3	F	11	0	1	2	2,538
Eye You	3	G	7	1	0	0	11,416	Fabulous Punch	4	C	1	0	0	0	381
Eye You Bobbie	4	F	1	0	0	0	35	Fabulous Romp	4	F	7	0	0	0	1,098
Eyebrow Raiser	5	G	11	1	2	2	26,775	Fabulous Slew	3	F	2	0	0	0	150
Eyelash Power	7	M	12	0	0	0	4,995	Fabulous Success	5	G	3	0	0	0	190
Eyena	4	F	10	2	2	1	44,339	Fabulous Sway	2	F	7	0	0	0	1,980
Eyeofthehunter	2	C	4	1	2	0	60,860	Fabulous Wealth	3	G	11	2	2	4	21,961

Horse	Age	Sex	Sts	1st	2d	3d	Won
Fabulous West	3	G	1	0	0	0	960
Fabulous World	3	G	5	1	1	1	24,310
Fabulously Clever	4	F	8	1	0	1	4,340
Fabulously Mine	2	F	7	0	0	1	1,290
Fabuloustilltheend	4	F	9	3	3	0	5,700
Fabutam	2	F	2	0	0	0	665
Faccia Bella	7	M	4	0	0	1	5,698
Face	4	G	2	0	2	0	6,400
Face Card	4	F	1	0	0	0	270
Face It	3	F	2	0	0	0	720
Face of Fortune	3	C	10	1	3	1	14,013
Face the Band	5	H	12	1	2	1	50,067
Face the Facts	4	G	7	1	0	0	4,259
Face the Nation	5	M	9	1	2	1	16,003
Facetious Cat	4	F	1	0	0	0	47
Facial Wager	3	C	2	0	0	0	0
Facile	3	G	6	0	0	0	6,180
Facilita	4	F	3	0	1	0	3,320
Fack Finder	5	M	5	2	1	1	5,865
Fact Based	3	G	9	1	0	1	4,332
Fact Not Fiction	7	G	17	3	4	1	66,495
Fact Royal E	4	C	3	0	1	0	10,654
Factor Fiction	4	F	3	1	0	0	5,233
Factorability	5	G	5	2	0	0	13,862
Factory Mill	4	G	9	2	1	1	7,475
Factory Reject	2	F	2	0	0	0	145
Facts N Figures	5	G	1	0	0	0	40
Facts Related	6	G	10	1	0	2	3,511
Factual Dancer	5	M	3	0	0	0	240
Factual Evidence	6	G	9	0	1	2	1,975
Factual Stan	3	C	7	0	0	1	7,600
Fade Away	3	F	5	1	1	0	7,776
Fade Oraculo (ARG)	6	H	9	0	1	1	11,770
Fade Sabihonda (ARG)	5	M	2	0	0	0	1,200
Fade to Blue	7	G	12	1	1	3	53,770
Faded Love	3	F	1	0	0	0	0
Fading Memories	4	F	5	0	0	0	883
Fadski	6	G	1	0	0	0	0
Faerietaleprincess	3	F	5	0	0	0	1,010
Faeton	3	G	20	1	3	4	14,041
Fafnir	5	M	10	1	2	3	42,556
Fager Chic	4	F	3	0	0	0	660
Fager's Island	4	C	2	0	0	0	1,800
Fager's Valentine	3	G	11	1	1	1	6,469
Fager's Wager	3	C	12	0	3	3	12,425
Fahamore	4	F	1	0	0	0	0
Fahana	7	M	14	0	1	3	4,478
Fail Me Not (ARG)	4	C	10	1	2	1	64,620
Faintly Saintly	5	G	14	0	1	1	6,894
Fair and Grey	5	M	17	4	2	2	30,783
Fair and Lucky	3	F	13	2	3	5	61,090
Fair Believer	3	C	4	1	0	0	21,840
Fair Bianca	4	F	3	0	1	0	11,000
Fair Goer	3	F	10	1	1	2	13,131
Fair Hayley	4	G	8	1	2	0	5,472
Fair Kate	7	M	3	1	0	0	6,310
Fair Lady Camille	4	F	9	1	0	1	9,964
Fair Loom	6	G	1	0	0	0	0
Fair Made Marion	4	F	1	0	0	0	0
Fair Magic	4	F	14	2	0	0	3,072
Fair Millielillie	2	F	3	0	0	0	1,350
Fair Prospect	2	F	4	0	0	0	2,940
Fair Regard	4	F	3	0	1	0	3,289
Fair Reward	2	G	3	0	0	0	58
Fair Smokin (NZ)	6	M	1	0	0	0	0
Fair Trade	5	G	6	0	0	1	1,167
Fair Victory	4	G	7	0	0	0	620
Fair Winds	3	G	8	0	1	1	10,595
Fair Woman	4	F	11	3	1	1	15,091
Fairberry Lady	3	F	11	1	1	0	14,640
Fairchild	3	F	8	1	0	0	4,077
Fairest Riches	5	G	8	1	2	1	13,200
Fairly Crafty	3	C	2	0	0	0	3,042
Fairly Fasty	3	G	20	5	5	2	24,899
Fairly Honest	2	G	1	1	0	0	4,070
Fairly Megan	3	F	2	0	0	0	0
Fairly Ransom	3	C	6	2	2	1	358,819
Fairly Valued	3	G	6	0	0	0	0
Fairly Well Tuned	5	M	6	0	1	0	5,020
Fairly's Dancer	6	G	11	1	2	3	5,861
Fairway Foe	9	G	8	0	0	0	480
Fairway Joey	4	G	15	1	0	3	9,779
Fairway to Heaven	8	G	11	0	3	3	7,498
Fairy	3	F	3	0	0	0	2,770
Fairy Dust	6	M	16	3	1	3	34,344
Fairy Gold	3	F	14	4	2	2	25,572
Fairy Valley	4	F	3	1	1	1	17,745
Fairytale Romance	4	F	15	2	10	1	32,485
Fait Accompli	2	F	6	2	2	1	92,732
Faith Alive	6	M	4	0	0	1	1,249
Faith and Glory	3	G	13	2	0	2	17,375
Faith and Trust	3	F	4	2	0	1	88,626
Faith Forever	6	G	6	0	3	2	3,860
Faith Hall	4	F	9	0	1	1	2,240
Faith Heylin	3	G	15	2	1	3	9,080
Faith in You	3	F	5	0	0	1	2,171
Faith Keeper	3	F	5	1	1	0	36,060
Faitha's Song	3	F	3	0	0	0	169
Faithful Girl	3	F	11	1	1	1	16,903
Faithful Joy	4	F	1	0	0	0	0
Faithful Lad	2	C	1	0	0	1	700
Faiths Hope	4	C	7	4	0	0	25,410
Faiths Wish	5	H	12	3	3	2	31,237
Faithtrustpixidust	2	F	1	0	0	0	0
Fajardo	6	G	3	1	1	0	20,110
Fake I. D.	4	C	2	2	0	0	7,440
Fake It	7	G	15	4	2	1	16,147
Falba	10	G	2	0	0	0	0
Falbrav (IRE)	5	H	10	5	1	2	3,013,845
Falcon Eddie	5	G	18	2	2	3	9,699
Falcon Gentle	3	F	6	0	0	0	1,860
Falcon in Flight	2	C	4	0	0	0	1,560
Falcon Inn	3	F	10	2	1	0	20,970
Falcon Queen	3	F	4	0	1	0	5,980
Falcon Ten	3	C	5	0	0	1	4,465
Falconer (IRE)	4	G	9	0	6	0	44,336
Falconinthenight	5	G	5	0	0	0	342
Falcon's Eye	5	M	6	1	0	0	7,470
Falcons Season	4	F	4	0	0	0	600
Falcon's Wings	7	H	12	1	3	0	6,953
Falconwithahat	3	G	8	3	1	2	24,862
Falhour	8	G	4	0	1	1	554
Falklands Girl	3	F	8	0	1	1	3,760
Fall Affair	5	G	8	1	2	1	16,407
Fall Colors	3	F	5	1	0	0	4,320
Fall Fantasy	2	F	1	0	0	0	4,200
Fall Fashion	2	F	3	1	1	1	18,200
Fall for Me	4	G	5	1	1	0	4,322
Fall in Line	2	C	7	0	1	3	12,550
Fall in Place	3	F	9	2	3	0	26,280
Fall Reign	4	G	16	1	4	2	17,595
Fallen Feather	7	M	6	0	0	0	248
Falling in Luck	5	H	7	0	0	1	1,787
Fallston Vixen	5	M	7	1	1	1	7,616
False Empire	7	M	9	0	1	2	6,634
False Evidence	5	H	5	0	1	0	4,400
False Light	4	C	13	0	2	3	4,021
False Promises	3	G	13	3	3	1	210,740
False Signal	3	F	6	0	1	1	10,180
Falsify	5	M	16	5	1	2	50,013
Falso Testimonio (ARG)	5	H	4	1	0	1	37,080
Falstaffgoldenlady	4	F	5	0	0	0	0
Falstaff's Road	7	G	7	1	0	0	2,043
Falstaffs's Jewel	5	M	9	3	2	3	12,998
Falwyn	5	M	11	3	0	1	53,397
Fame and Fortune	2	G	3	0	0	0	910
Fame and Honour	5	G	9	3	0	1	125,014
Fame Game	2	G	5	0	2	0	16,472
Fame Ina Minute	3	C	8	3	0	2	64,521
Fames Legs	9	G	10	1	1	2	9,157
Fame's Pleasure	3	F	12	1	3	0	7,669
Fame's Star	4	F	12	0	1	1	3,710
Family Album	4	F	8	0	1	0	3,790
Family Book	2	C	5	2	0	2	23,820
Family Code	4	G	4	0	0	1	1,200
Family Covenant	6	M	13	2	2	0	17,525
Family Favorite	2	F	6	1	2	0	52,100
Family Fewd	5	H	13	3	2	7	15,243

RECORDS OF HORSES

Horse	Age	Sex	Sts	1st	2d	3d	Won	Horse	Age	Sex	Sts	1st	2d	3d	Won
Family Fortune	3	C	2	0	0	0	308	Fancy Shmancy	3	F	11	0	0	3	4,780
Family Money	2	G	1	0	0	1	900	Fancy Suenancy	5	M	14	2	3	1	22,140
Family Tales	2	F	2	0	0	1	1,532	Fancy Tal One	3	G	10	0	0	1	4,369
Family Trust	11	H	1	0	0	0	0	Fancy This	3	F	1	0	0	0	1,230
Famous Amos	4	C	13	1	3	2	17,965	Fancy Threat	3	C	6	1	2	0	6,975
Famous Bid	4	F	2	0	0	1	1,365	Fancy Ways	2	F	5	1	0	3	7,224
Famous Call	3	R	17	2	0	2	51,190	Fancy Zone	2	F	6	0	0	0	1,330
Famous Chef	5	H	6	1	0	0	7,200	Fancyghost	2	C	2	0	0	1	4,297
Famous Couch	3	F	4	0	0	1	900	Fancyismyname	4	F	3	0	1	0	260
Famous Dreamin	5	G	10	4	0	1	21,800	Fancyman Jack	3	C	10	1	3	1	25,540
Famous Flame	2	C	1	0	0	0	43	Fancy's Frosty	3	F	1	0	0	0	0
Famous Fury	2	G	2	0	0	0	750	Fancy's Hero	4	G	5	0	0	0	0
Famous Future	5	H	1	0	0	0	186	Faneuil Lad	4	G	1	0	0	0	0
Famous Honoree	3	G	13	0	0	0	1,885	Fankom's Genius	3	F	8	1	0	2	6,216
Famous Hussy	2	F	8	1	1	0	9,899	Fannie Jo	4	F	5	0	0	1	6,130
Famous Minstrel	5	M	13	3	2	1	12,415	Fannie'sgrey Magic	6	G	5	0	0	1	2,288
Famous Olympian	3	G	12	1	3	2	16,540	Fanstar	6	G	9	0	2	0	2,456
Famous Rich	2	C	2	0	0	0	200	Fanstie Doll	4	F	3	0	0	0	0
Famous Roemantic	5	M	2	0	0	0	90	Fantabulous	6	M	7	1	0	2	4,813
Famous Shamus	4	G	6	1	0	1	6,840	Fantana	3	G	10	1	0	0	11,497
Famous Spirit	3	F	4	1	1	1	21,507	Fantasia Di Dolci	4	F	9	2	2	1	18,735
Famous Statesman	2	C	3	0	0	1	1,930	Fantastic Allie	5	M	7	1	1	3	65,208
Famous Woman	3	F	6	3	0	1	56,460	Fantastic Blond	3	F	12	1	2	2	7,361
Famously Free	9	G	20	2	6	6	21,940	Fantastic Caroline	3	F	5	0	1	1	7,280
Famula (ARG)	5	M	11	1	1	0	14,450	Fantastic City	4	F	6	2	0	1	63,105
Fan Appeal	4	F	5	1	0	1	32,320	Fantastic Day	3	G	11	5	3	1	221,456
Fan Attack	2	F	1	0	0	0	95	Fantastic Ed	2	C	3	0	2	1	4,182
Fan Club's Mister	5	H	11	0	0	0	6,170	Fantastic Ego	2	C	4	0	0	0	117
Fan Destiny	3	G	12	1	1	1	21,895	Fantastic Elaine	3	F	6	1	0	0	4,936
Fan Jet Falcon	4	G	7	0	2	3	12,914	Fantastic Fantasy	3	C	9	0	0	2	3,195
Fan Tan Man	5	G	6	0	1	0	3,280	Fantastic Fil	6	G	5	0	0	0	294
Fan the Flame	6	H	12	6	1	2	66,850	Fantastic Finish	7	G	13	3	6	2	55,716
Fanatic Alachee	3	G	9	0	0	0	158	Fantastic Groom	5	G	5	1	0	0	32,880
Fanatic Baby	5	M	12	3	2	1	14,135	Fantastic Joy	3	F	5	1	0	0	10,570
Fanaway	3	C	15	2	0	3	8,108	Fantastic Lover	3	G	13	2	0	2	10,782
Fancatstik	2	C	4	1	1	0	33,060	Fantastic Reality	6	G	11	2	1	0	22,491
Fancebel	4	F	8	1	1	0	4,574	Fantastic Spain	3	C	1	1	0	0	27,600
Fancee Bargain	7	M	8	1	1	1	94,840	Fantastic Vic	2	C	4	0	0	1	3,234
Fanci Frills	7	M	4	0	1	0	1,435	Fantastic Voyage	3	C	2	0	0	0	0
Fancie Boots	5	G	7	1	0	1	3,660	Fantastic Wager	2	C	5	0	1	1	6,440
Fancier Than Thou	3	F	4	0	0	1	1,650	Fantastica	2	F	7	1	0	0	11,725
Fanciwith	6	M	9	1	0	3	12,141	Fantasticat	2	C	4	0	0	3	6,984
Fancy American	4	C	2	0	0	0	0	Fantastisch	7	G	2	0	0	0	76
Fancy As	5	G	2	2	0	0	37,989	Fantasy Boy	7	G	9	0	0	1	808
Fancy B My Name	5	M	9	1	1	0	4,703	Fantasy Jet	4	F	15	1	1	2	16,300
Fancy Batchler	6	G	10	0	1	2	2,091	Fantasy Life	3	G	9	2	0	1	11,209
Fancy Be Quick	4	F	6	0	0	1	1,106	Fantasy On Fire	3	F	10	1	1	3	14,885
Fancy Begining	4	F	19	1	3	5	40,300	Fantasy Quest	3	F	5	0	0	0	2,480
Fancy Bru	3	G	10	3	4	0	83,275	Fantasy Ridge	4	F	10	2	2	0	34,100
Fancy Buckles	3	F	9	7	2	0	165,968	Fantasy Tap	5	H	1	0	0	0	80
Fancy Crown	5	G	3	0	1	0	2,683	Fantasy Valley	5	H	4	0	1	1	3,128
Fancy Dali	6	M	8	0	0	1	2,037	Fantasy Weaver	3	F	12	0	2	1	8,310
Fancy Dealer	3	F	10	1	1	3	8,710	Fantasy's Champ	3	C	4	0	1	0	549
Fancy Drinks	3	F	10	1	2	2	88,252	Fantazmic	2	G	3	1	1	0	9,793
Fancy Feet Stacey	5	M	3	0	0	0	0	Fanteria	2	C	6	0	0	2	1,245
Fancy Firenight	4	C	2	0	0	0	0	Fantino	2	C	3	0	2	1	14,981
Fancy First	4	C	4	0	1	0	3,660	Fantom Fury	7	G	10	4	1	2	23,840
Fancy Flag	3	F	3	0	0	0	195	Fantom of the Keep	5	M	5	0	0	1	980
Fancy Flea	8	G	3	0	0	0	226	Fanzoca	3	F	10	6	0	1	42,234
Fancy Fortune	6	M	1	0	0	0	360	Fappa Fire	6	G	7	1	0	1	17,930
Fancy Forum	3	F	15	3	2	2	32,100	Fappadoon	2	F	3	0	3	0	9,470
Fancy Francie	3	F	7	1	2	0	9,961	Fappi La Boo	5	M	2	0	0	0	0
Fancy Free 'n Such	3	F	6	1	1	0	4,130	Fappiano Lane	2	F	1	0	0	0	120
Fancy Free Playboy	8	G	3	0	0	0	0	Fappiano'srjourney	4	G	7	1	0	1	8,975
Fancy Injun	5	M	10	3	1	1	38,133	Fappilongstockings	4	F	4	0	0	0	360
Fancy Leola	7	M	8	0	1	0	1,455	Fappitune	3	C	4	1	0	1	5,542
Fancy Locket	6	M	7	1	0	1	18,250	Fappy Ending	4	F	10	0	0	1	952
Fancy Looker	3	C	3	0	1	0	5,451	Far Ahead	7	H	10	1	1	1	1,606
Fancy M. D.	4	G	14	6	0	2	64,780	Far and Above	3	F	3	1	0	0	5,200
Fancy Man	2	C	1	0	1	0	2,610	Far and Near	4	F	6	0	1	2	25,806
Fancy Me Yours	4	F	10	0	0	0	3,768	Far Away Bell	4	G	10	2	2	5	37,830
Fancy Mocha	2	F	1	0	0	0	0	Far Better Journey	4	C	11	0	0	1	1,950
Fancy n' Fit	3	F	11	0	1	1	5,097	Far Better Lis	2	F	1	0	0	0	145
Fancy Nancy S	4	F	3	0	0	0	383	Far East of Eden	6	H	11	1	0	1	5,784
Fancy Note	3	F	6	1	0	1	36,293	Far From Frail	3	F	1	0	0	0	0
Fancy Prospector	4	F	7	0	0	0	0	Far North Fire	6	M	2	0	0	0	225
Fancy Retsina	2	C	6	0	0	0	1,552	Far Out	6	G	2	0	0	2	4,400
Fancy Ripsnorton	3	G	4	0	0	1	1,062	Far Out Babe	2	F	9	1	1	1	19,658
Fancy Runmore	5	M	8	0	0	0	1,336	Far Out Chris	3	G	10	0	1	0	10,204

Horse	Age	Sex	Sts	1st	2d	3d	Won
Far Out Fun	4	G	10	1	1	1	5,355
Far Out Gil	4	G	3	0	0	0	1,680
Far Out Slew	10	G	3	2	0	0	5,400
Far Out Wish	5	G	7	0	0	2	988
Far Side	4	C	13	3	1	3	22,925
Far Sighted Sal	5	M	1	1	0	0	35,597
Far the Goodtimes	2	F	1	0	0	0	0
Farah Love	7	M	10	2	2	1	76,240
Farah's Prize	7	M	1	0	0	0	0
Faralong	4	C	5	0	0	0	452
Fara's Passion	3	F	5	0	0	1	4,750
Faraway Legend	4	F	5	1	1	1	43,400
Faraway Places	3	F	2	0	0	0	1,790
Faraway Prospect	6	G	10	3	1	2	31,701
Farber	2	C	1	0	0	0	2,050
Fare Thee Wild	3	F	6	0	0	0	1,310
Farewell Cowboys	2	G	5	0	2	1	9,843
Farewell My Lovely	4	F	5	0	1	0	12,480
Farewell To Arms (GB)	2	F	5	1	2	0	19,340
Farewell to Charm	2	C	6	1	1	1	18,099
Farewell Val	5	G	6	2	1	0	25,577
Farfalla	5	G	4	0	0	0	366
Farfalletto	3	G	1	0	0	0	75
Fargaze Ties	4	F	6	1	0	0	3,312
Fargo Wells	3	G	2	0	0	0	330
Fargo's Freind	2	G	4	1	0	0	15,230
Farhana	2	F	3	1	0	0	17,005
Fariseo	3	G	8	1	1	2	13,660
Farlo	3	C	3	1	1	0	8,540
Farm Fuel	3	C	4	1	0	1	4,240
Farm House	8	G	1	0	0	0	40
Farm Saver	8	G	11	3	0	1	13,442
Farma Jim	4	C	5	1	0	0	18,390
Farma Way Jr.	3	G	13	2	1	1	6,766
Farmadayaway	4	F	1	0	0	0	0
Farmall Red	3	G	1	0	1	0	920
Farmas Best	8	H	8	1	2	1	10,690
Farmas Dream	5	G	1	0	0	0	2,475
Farma's Market	6	M	5	0	0	0	0
Farmer Inthe Dell	3	C	2	2	0	0	22,710
Farmer Jake	5	G	8	3	2	2	104,010
Farmer Jakes Lady	3	F	6	0	0	1	1,237
Farmerjakes Impala	3	F	15	0	5	3	7,827
Farmisist	8	H	7	2	0	0	7,314
Farno	3	C	1	1	0	0	22,200
Farnum Alley	2	C	2	1	0	0	27,455
Faro	3	G	12	2	3	2	45,320
Farragal	2	F	1	0	0	0	450
Farrar	2	F	1	0	0	0	0
Farrelyns' Folly	5	H	2	0	0	0	534
Farrmost	6	M	8	1	1	1	6,494
Farrus' Smile	3	F	8	2	1	0	22,371
Fascio (ARG)	7	H	8	1	1	2	7,690
Faseship	3	F	8	0	1	0	3,102
Fashion Alert	7	M	4	0	0	0	440
Fashion Award	4	G	11	2	3	1	52,739
Fashion Bolt	2	C	4	0	0	1	1,773
Fashion Diamond	3	F	8	0	2	0	3,341
Fashion Expert	6	H	1	0	0	0	204
Fashion Fling	3	F	4	1	0	1	7,330
Fashion Girl	2	F	6	3	0	0	100,165
Fashion Hunter	2	F	4	1	0	2	6,245
Fashion Idol	6	M	10	0	1	4	21,026
Fashion Island	4	F	6	2	0	1	32,600
Fashion Line	2	F	3	0	1	0	3,445
Fashion Proof	3	F	12	1	2	4	44,858
Fashion Secrets	3	F	5	0	1	2	1,595
Fashion Sense	3	F	8	1	2	1	47,779
Fashionable Caton	3	F	6	3	0	0	19,440
Fashionable Kim	3	F	7	2	1	1	41,509
Fashionable Steve	3	C	6	0	2	0	2,128
Fashionista	3	F	8	1	2	0	31,200
Fash's Bull Dog	5	G	6	0	0	0	758
Fasole	4	F	5	0	0	0	630
Fast Access	2	F	2	0	0	0	0
Fast Activation	3	F	9	1	0	0	8,117
Fast Advice	5	M	8	1	1	0	7,506
Fast Agin	3	G	2	0	0	0	300
Fast Aly	3	G	5	0	0	0	325

Horse	Age	Sex	Sts	1st	2d	3d	Won
Fast and Fluid	2	F	5	2	0	0	21,961
Fast and Free	4	F	5	2	0	1	26,497
Fast and Lively	5	H	8	1	1	1	5,368
Fast and Strait	4	C	10	1	2	0	6,905
Fast Announcement	3	F	3	0	0	0	0
Fast Ball	6	G	8	1	1	0	5,821
Fast Baron	4	G	7	1	1	0	19,567
Fast Buck	6	H	3	0	0	0	132
Fast Chacha	3	F	11	1	2	4	3,246
Fast Change	7	M	4	0	0	0	40
Fast City	5	G	3	0	1	0	4,740
Fast Cloud	4	C	4	0	0	0	231
Fast Cookie	3	F	8	4	0	2	255,787
Fast Dancing	5	M	2	0	0	0	100
Fast Dane	3	G	12	0	0	0	1,350
Fast Decision	4	C	4	0	0	2	10,920
Fast Delighter	4	F	6	0	0	0	650
Fast Departure	10	G	19	6	2	1	34,725
Fast Dish	4	G	16	5	1	1	22,944
Fast Dude	3	G	6	0	0	0	570
Fast Easy 'n Free	4	G	13	1	3	3	21,926
Fast Eddie D.	3	C	6	2	0	1	21,752
Fast Entry	2	F	11	0	0	0	3,690
Fast Escape	2	C	1	0	0	0	285
Fast Exercise	2	C	9	0	1	1	6,155
Fast Explosion	3	F	8	0	0	0	1,159
Fast Fast Freddie	4	G	10	0	0	0	1,082
Fast Faster	4	G	13	0	1	0	3,038
Fast Favorite	6	H	4	0	0	1	1,551
Fast Flight Home	3	F	5	2	2	0	12,670
Fast for All	3	F	10	2	1	0	9,760
Fast Force	3	G	11	0	2	1	4,546
Fast Forest	3	G	7	0	0	0	198
Fast Fox Trot	7	G	16	2	1	2	22,315
Fast Getaway	5	H	11	0	1	0	2,727
Fast Girls Joy	4	G	2	0	0	0	0
Fast Goat	5	M	6	0	1	2	14,540
Fast Going	4	F	8	0	0	2	7,109
Fast Gun	5	H	8	1	1	3	2,200
Fast Hurrah	3	F	10	0	0	0	585
Fast in the Dirt	2	F	2	0	0	0	305
Fast Jack	5	G	1	0	0	0	61
Fast Jazz	4	G	13	0	1	1	2,800
Fast Jinks	10	G	15	0	1	2	8,075
Fast Knockout	4	F	14	2	4	1	11,639
Fast Kours	6	M	4	0	0	1	654
Fast Lad	4	G	7	1	1	1	9,985
Fast Lady J	2	F	1	0	0	0	0
Fast Lane Jane	5	M	6	0	0	0	645
Fast Lane Neelie	3	F	6	0	0	0	1,288
Fast Lane Terry	5	M	12	2	0	3	18,253
Fast Laner	2	F	4	2	1	1	35,810
Fast Leroy	4	C	4	0	1	1	1,295
Fast Line	5	G	13	2	1	3	29,242
Fast Lovin Lizzie	3	F	11	0	1	3	11,353
Fast Machine	4	G	2	0	0	0	0
Fast Magic	3	F	2	0	0	0	0
Fast Mary	6	M	7	0	0	0	856
Fast Maybe	5	G	12	2	1	2	13,379
Fast Mouse	3	F	2	0	0	0	450
Fast N Away	7	H	4	0	0	0	195
Fast N Faster	4	F	4	0	0	0	0
Fast N Front	3	G	2	0	0	0	0
Fast Oaks	4	F	4	0	0	1	744
Fast Phil	5	G	1	0	0	0	43
Fast Return	3	F	1	0	0	0	0
Fast River (CHI)	4	G	10	0	1	2	9,040
Fast Senorita	3	F	4	0	0	1	2,575
Fast Set	3	C	1	0	0	0	340
Fast Shack	4	F	11	0	0	0	922
Fast Silver	4	G	1	0	1	0	2,400
Fast Skeeter	3	G	7	1	0	0	1,469
Fast Splash	2	F	7	2	0	2	52,080
Fast Spot	4	G	6	3	0	0	22,880
Fast Steppin Man	7	G	3	0	0	2	4,500
Fast Stitch Gal	2	F	6	1	1	2	17,245
Fast Summer	3	C	1	1	0	0	12,586
Fast Talker	2	G	1	0	0	1	1,800
Fast Talkin Girl	2	F	3	1	0	1	8,030

RECORDS OF HORSES

Horse	Age	Sex	Sts	1st	2d	3d	Won	Horse	Age	Sex	Sts	1st	2d	3d	Won
Fast Track Bob	3	G	7	0	1	0	2,329	Favorite Cross	3	C	3	0	0	0	328
Fast Tracker	4	C	10	1	5	1	31,620	Favorite Dispersal	6	G	12	1	1	2	4,242
Fast Train	2	C	5	1	2	1	49,300	Favorite Ending	6	M	3	1	0	0	14,300
Fast Trapp	5	G	8	1	0	1	8,422	Favorite Friend	5	G	5	1	1	1	3,472
Fast Tude	5	G	10	1	3	0	15,451	Favorite Lil Devil	4	F	7	0	0	0	912
Fast Way Home	3	G	4	0	0	1	782	Favorite Magic	3	G	5	1	0	1	15,580
Fast Willie	4	G	8	1	0	0	3,475	Favorite Miss	6	M	2	0	0	0	1,014
Fastasaspeednbulit	10	G	6	2	1	1	14,825	Favorite Mister	3	G	5	1	1	0	10,600
Fastasiwannabe	4	G	10	0	2	1	1,604	Favorite Moment	2	C	3	0	2	1	13,260
Fastbid	3	C	13	2	0	0	7,608	Favorite Native	3	C	2	0	0	0	136
Fastcash	5	M	8	0	1	1	6,040	Favorite of Mine	3	F	8	2	2	1	31,660
Fastcatlane	4	G	8	1	0	0	6,560	Favorite One	3	G	16	3	3	1	44,690
Faster Master	4	C	7	0	0	1	1,846	Favorite Opening	4	C	7	0	0	3	9,555
Faster Prospect	2	C	6	0	0	0	2,075	Favorite Seat	6	H	12	2	3	1	11,982
Faster Than Light	3	C	10	1	3	1	4,810	Favorite Spy	5	H	1	0	0	0	0
Faster Than Music	7	G	9	1	3	2	2,706	Favorite Sweep	4	C	14	2	1	3	85,680
Faster Than Yours	9	M	6	0	0	2	1,279	Favorite Tune	4	F	3	0	0	3	4,475
Fastest	7	G	14	1	5	2	8,752	Favorite Voice	6	G	6	0	1	0	903
Fastette	3	F	7	0	2	3	19,960	Favoritesweetheart	2	F	3	0	0	0	200
Fastfoot Freddie	8	G	14	3	3	2	4,478	Favour for Joey	3	G	7	3	2	2	39,256
Fastidious	4	G	3	0	0	0	133	Fawazee	3	F	2	0	1	0	12,120
Fastman	5	H	2	0	0	0	1,020	Fax a Freddy	6	G	12	1	1	3	37,342
Fastnfurious	2	F	3	0	0	0	1,280	Fax Blitz	4	F	10	3	1	1	26,220
Fastrak Folly	6	H	1	0	0	0	60	Fax Copy	5	M	10	0	3	1	7,587
Fastrip	3	F	5	0	1	1	13,864	Fax Dance	3	C	13	1	0	2	22,870
Faststeppin Jack	7	G	1	0	0	0	144	Fax Machine	3	C	6	0	0	0	4,100
Fastybutnasty	6	M	2	0	0	0	1,400	Fax Seven Copies	4	F	10	3	1	0	10,096
Faswiga	2	F	5	1	1	0	54,292	Fax the Paige	4	F	10	2	0	1	16,935
Fat Boy Slim	3	G	12	1	1	0	7,333	Faxamillion	4	C	8	1	2	1	35,040
Fat Eddie	6	G	2	0	1	0	1,078	Faxer Than You	3	G	9	1	0	1	7,312
Fat Farm	4	F	9	0	0	0	4,601	Faxin It Down	5	G	3	0	0	0	0
Fat Harry's Girl	2	F	2	0	0	2	1,875	Faxing	5	G	7	1	2	0	19,660
Fat Tuesday	6	H	4	1	0	1	3,050	Faxing the Blues	2	C	2	0	0	0	0
Fatal Affair	3	F	11	1	0	2	6,596	Faxmeback	5	G	8	1	0	1	5,610
Fatal Binge	3	C	12	2	3	2	16,720	Faxxy Sal	4	F	7	0	1	1	7,288
Fatal Caper	3	F	7	1	0	3	56,642	Faye and Howard	2	G	9	2	2	0	27,350
Fatal Instinct	5	M	1	0	0	0	0	Faye Kinitt	2	F	1	0	0	0	95
Fatapiano	3	F	5	1	1	0	5,170	Fayette County	5	M	8	1	3	2	9,983
Fatat Alarab	3	F	4	1	0	2	36,487	Faygo Rocks	3	F	2	0	0	0	1,350
Fate	6	H	1	0	0	0	0	Faylagra	2	G	5	1	0	0	8,578
Fateful Dream	6	H	4	0	2	0	79,135	Fazam Fazam	3	F	4	0	0	0	220
Father Bob	3	G	5	0	1	1	6,256	Fe Fe Gold	7	M	5	0	0	1	865
Father Bryan's Gem	4	G	9	2	0	0	36,030	Fe Fe's Spirits	4	F	16	3	1	1	24,376
Father Confessor	4	G	8	1	3	4	21,272	Fealty	5	G	8	0	1	0	3,668
Father Dan	3	C	12	1	0	2	7,076	Fear Factory	3	C	5	1	0	0	25,398
Father Dooley	2	G	1	0	0	0	0	Fear Nothing	5	G	3	0	2	1	3,771
Father Goose	5	H	1	0	0	0	0	Fearless Anthony	2	G	2	0	0	0	190
Father Judge	3	C	1	0	0	0	0	Fearless Floyd	4	C	5	0	0	0	0
Father Krismas (GB)	8	G	4	1	0	2	8,600	Fearless Peer	9	G	15	5	2	0	54,738
Father Mark	4	G	14	3	1	3	30,230	Fearless Storm	3	F	15	0	0	0	2,535
Father Martin	3	C	3	0	1	0	3,970	Fearless Warrior	3	C	6	1	0	0	8,352
Father Mike	3	G	9	2	1	0	14,575	Fearlessambassador	4	F	7	0	1	0	2,543
Father of All Wins	6	H	2	0	0	1	1,300	Fearnought	5	G	8	0	1	2	5,457
Father Party	2	C	2	0	0	2	9,390	Fearsome	5	G	14	4	1	0	13,532
Father Paul	5	G	3	0	0	0	1,120	Fearsome Foursome	4	G	11	1	1	2	10,175
Father Rheal	4	C	9	1	1	2	7,850	Fearsome Turk	5	H	1	0	0	0	0
Father Steve	4	C	4	1	0	0	14,840	Feather Boa	3	F	8	2	2	0	67,850
Father Thames (GB)	5	H	2	0	0	0	3,480	Feather Maraine	3	F	10	6	0	0	108,021
Father Tony	4	C	6	1	0	1	4,680	Feathered Nest	7	M	9	0	0	2	2,056
Father Val	5	H	2	0	0	0	0	Feathers Lil Devil	3	G	3	0	0	0	0
Father's Air Cargo	4	F	3	0	0	0	370	Featherweight	3	F	7	0	0	0	870
Father's Magic	8	G	9	0	2	0	10,116	Featherweightchamp	4	C	9	2	0	3	3,534
Fathom	4	G	9	1	0	0	3,627	Feature Story	3	G	5	0	0	1	4,100
Fatima's Gold	7	M	12	0	0	1	2,203	Featured Account	5	G	10	2	1	1	8,341
Fatima's Princess	4	F	12	2	2	3	46,730	Featured Singer	5	M	6	0	0	0	650
Fatoul	9	M	1	0	0	0	0	Feb Eleven	2	C	7	1	1	2	36,350
Faultless Cassie	4	F	11	0	0	0	3,896	February Feb	3	F	20	1	0	1	5,953
Fauna	3	F	1	0	0	0	2,135	February Storm	4	C	2	0	0	0	11,018
Faust	4	G	5	1	0	0	8,660	Fed Ex Air Pro	5	G	2	0	0	0	0
Faux Pas	4	F	2	0	0	0	856	Feddlers Bend	7	H	6	0	0	1	480
Favola (GB)	3	F	2	0	0	1	10,002	Federal Case	5	M	8	1	2	0	10,376
Favorable Decision	6	G	15	1	1	3	10,715	Federal Examiner	4	G	12	0	2	0	4,360
Favorable Terms	3	G	15	2	3	6	40,400	Federal Highway	4	G	7	2	1	1	41,100
Favored Sweep	7	G	7	1	0	1	3,388	Federal Number	3	G	1	1	0	0	27,000
Favorite Affair	6	H	2	0	0	0	900	Federal Relief	3	G	1	0	0	0	0
Favorite Angel	3	F	7	0	0	0	820	Federale	3	C	5	0	1	1	3,650
Favorite Brass	7	G	1	0	0	0	0	Feed for Speed	3	F	9	3	1	0	48,840
Favorite Brat	3	F	2	0	0	0	0	Feed the Kitty	3	F	3	1	0	0	14,080
Favorite Companion	3	G	19	1	2	4	10,347	Feel the Dance	3	F	12	2	2	5	41,080

Horse	Age	Sex	Sts	1st	2d	3d	Won
Feel the Felt	6	G	9	0	3	2	5,856
Feel the Wind	4	G	7	1	0	1	17,550
Feelin Free	5	G	10	4	3	1	44,979
Feelin Luck Today	4	F	6	1	0	3	8,420
Feelin Salty	3	C	5	2	0	0	23,405
Feeling Irie	6	G	5	2	0	0	5,914
Feeling Lucky	3	F	6	1	0	1	17,780
Feeling Maudlin	7	M	12	1	2	1	8,405
Feeling Pretty	6	M	6	0	1	0	4,005
Feeling So Pretty	9	M	12	2	0	1	45,660
Feeling Wicked	3	F	7	1	0	0	4,613
Feelinghisoats	7	G	14	3	2	3	37,540
Feelinnopain	5	G	20	2	5	3	17,546
Feelitfirst	4	G	15	1	2	2	18,466
Feels So Right	6	M	5	0	0	0	675
Feet of Fire	5	G	8	1	1	1	14,542
Feet of Flames	5	G	11	1	1	1	17,887
Feets Afire	4	F	5	1	3	0	10,800
Fehr	3	C	7	1	0	2	42,160
Feijoada	3	F	6	0	1	0	4,530
Feisty Bull	3	F	12	4	1	3	134,379
Feisty Cherokee	3	F	17	1	1	1	17,424
Feisty Flirt	4	F	2	0	1	0	2,100
Feisty Fun	3	F	7	0	3	1	11,372
Feisty One	4	F	6	0	2	1	4,810
Feisty Princess	3	F	7	3	1	2	76,213
Feisty Red	2	F	3	1	0	0	7,310
Feisty Snoman	3	G	7	0	1	1	24,003
Feisty Vick	7	G	9	0	1	1	8,151
Fejo	6	G	1	0	0	0	0
Felena	8	M	12	2	2	3	10,538
Felenas Dancescene	8	M	8	0	2	0	3,572
Felica's Ruckus	3	F	3	0	0	0	0
Felicia's N Sync	4	F	1	0	0	0	188
Feline Story	2	F	6	3	1	0	201,780
Felix	3	C	13	3	2	0	47,330
Felix De La Luna	3	G	3	0	1	0	6,980
Felix Legions	4	F	12	0	3	2	11,028
Felix's Fire	3	C	1	0	0	0	0
Felling	2	F	2	1	0	0	17,130
Fellini	3	C	10	3	3	0	42,464
Fellner	3	G	7	1	1	1	27,680
Felo	3	G	22	3	7	1	43,775
Felucca	3	F	4	0	0	1	4,730
Female Accomplice	3	F	9	1	0	0	6,183
Feminine	3	F	3	0	0	1	3,850
Feminine Fury	6	M	1	0	0	0	0
Fence Jumper	3	F	11	1	3	1	15,165
Fencelineneighbor	3	F	12	5	2	2	231,107
Fennel	4	F	6	0	1	0	1,531
Fentastic Pay Day	6	M	5	0	0	0	0
Fenter Again	5	M	1	0	0	0	35
Fenterless	5	M	6	0	3	0	2,497
Fentermore	7	H	11	0	1	3	5,606
Fenter's Luck	4	F	4	0	0	0	255
Fenton Place	10	G	5	0	0	0	300
Fenway	3	C	11	1	0	1	11,080
Fenwise	6	G	6	0	0	0	275
Fenwood	6	G	7	0	0	0	728
Feral Child	3	F	1	0	0	0	0
Ferdinand's Dancer	3	F	3	0	0	0	0
Ferdinand's Quest	3	G	3	1	0	0	6,585
Ferege	5	M	1	0	0	0	0
Ferene	6	H	4	0	0	0	105
Fergie's Showtime	7	G	17	8	3	3	34,821
Fergiesharkattack	3	G	9	1	1	2	11,999
Fernius	3	G	3	0	0	0	400
Ferns Jaakita	6	M	3	0	0	2	1,170
Ferocious	4	G	16	2	7	3	19,210
Ferocity	5	M	3	0	0	1	1,316
Ferrari Frank	3	G	3	0	0	0	246
Ferrazzi	5	G	14	2	2	3	40,481
Ferriday	3	F	12	2	0	1	13,290
Ferrita	2	F	5	1	0	0	4,979
Ferro's Best Yet	3	G	10	1	0	0	6,410
Ferruccio	6	M	11	1	1	0	4,502
Ferrybank	3	F	12	1	1	1	9,552
Fertile	4	F	5	0	0	3	32,082
Fertile Myrtle	4	F	5	0	0	0	330
Fervent Affair	8	G	12	1	1	1	12,477
Fervent Wish (GB)	4	F	6	0	0	1	8,692
Fervid	3	C	3	1	0	0	30,580
Fe's Groom	3	G	7	2	1	1	22,990
Festega	5	M	6	0	3	1	6,630
Festina Famosa (IRE)	6	M	3	0	0	0	0
Festival Chairman	9	G	10	0	1	1	5,454
Festival Lady	3	F	9	1	2	0	19,760
Festival Legs	6	M	1	0	0	0	179
Festival Moon	5	G	7	0	0	1	3,394
Festival Queen (GB)	3	F	3	1	0	0	17,019
Festive Bidder	8	H	12	1	2	0	9,399
Festive Fellow	5	G	4	1	0	0	1,659
Festive Fling	5	M	2	0	0	0	0
Festive Forever	8	G	2	0	0	0	0
Festive Jet	3	G	15	0	1	0	3,120
Festive Lady	5	M	15	6	3	1	136,200
Festive Love	5	G	11	3	1	1	51,843
Festive Madam	5	M	4	0	1	0	7,080
Festive Nicholas	3	G	6	0	3	0	7,225
Festive Ruler	3	G	4	0	0	0	0
Festive Spirit	5	G	9	3	0	0	96,056
Festooned	4	F	13	1	0	2	5,461
Festy Eskimo	3	G	8	1	1	1	42,913
Fetch Dinner	7	H	9	0	1	1	23,216
Fetch Me Cap	3	F	10	1	0	4	20,549
Fetch's Fuse	2	F	3	0	0	0	1,670
Fethard	7	H	10	0	0	3	1,386
Fetzer	7	H	3	0	0	0	750
Feu Green	6	M	7	1	1	2	2,355
Feu Kan Promise	5	M	14	4	4	0	7,308
Feu On Fire	6	M	11	0	0	2	1,943
Feu R Gold	3	G	11	3	1	2	18,795
Feu So Free	5	G	4	1	1	0	2,260
Feudal Lady	3	F	11	4	2	0	23,181
Feu's Bebe	4	F	6	0	0	1	682
Feutoyou	3	G	8	0	1	1	1,127
Fever Fire	2	C	1	0	0	0	0
Fever Like	3	C	13	3	3	1	24,395
Fever N Chills	3	F	18	0	0	2	4,630
Fever of Oneonine	3	C	8	2	1	0	19,042
Fever Time	4	G	12	0	0	2	2,596
Feverinthesouth	4	C	18	4	2	4	25,720
Ffabulous Sandi	3	F	2	0	0	0	630
Fiaafy	3	F	4	0	0	2	6,827
Fickle Factor	3	F	8	3	0	0	64,976
Fickle Fanny	7	M	2	0	0	0	0
Fictitious	3	F	1	1	0	0	4,500
Fidah	2	C	2	0	0	0	0
Fiddle Dee Dee	3	F	1	0	0	0	0
Fiddle McGee	3	F	3	0	0	0	666
Fiddlebid	3	F	2	0	0	0	540
Fiddledee	10	G	3	0	0	0	0
Fiddler On de Hoof	7	H	4	1	2	1	5,839
Fiddlers Fancy	2	F	2	1	0	0	30,180
Fiddlers Sister	2	F	3	0	0	0	0
Fidget	4	F	15	3	5	0	72,265
Field Day	8	G	3	1	2	0	22,200
Field Judge	3	G	1	0	0	0	324
Field of Glory	4	F	8	1	1	1	26,120
Field of Honour	6	M	9	1	3	0	7,896
Field Six	2	C	3	1	0	0	10,800
Fielders Choice	5	M	8	1	0	1	8,800
Fieldes Reward	9	M	5	0	1	2	3,721
Fields Ertel	11	G	6	0	1	0	1,064
Fields of Gail	2	F	6	0	0	1	1,610
Fields of Omagh	8	G	2	0	0	0	0
Fields the Legend	3	G	6	2	0	0	8,915
Fiendel Future	6	H	4	0	0	0	432
Fierce Contender	2	C	3	0	0	0	460
Fierce Flight	2	G	2	0	0	0	80
Fierce Heart	7	G	13	2	2	2	32,885
Fierce Knight	2	G	3	1	1	0	23,440
Fierce Princess	2	F	12	0	1	1	13,564
Fierce Storm	2	C	4	0	1	1	15,370
Fiero Bandera	3	G	12	2	1	2	28,505
Fierrazo (CHI)	9	G	4	1	0	0	2,395
Fiery Colony	4	G	2	0	1	0	1,800
Fiery Diablo	5	H	8	1	3	1	45,190

RECORDS OF HORSES

Horse	Age	Sex	Sts	1st	2d	3d	Won
Fiery Love	3	F	8	0	3	0	4,845
Fiery Salsa	3	F	13	2	1	2	16,200
Fiery Six	8	G	7	0	3	1	5,381
Fiery Sweep	4	G	7	1	0	0	24,160
Fiesta	3	F	11	1	4	0	33,020
Fiesta Spring	4	F	4	0	1	1	1,236
Fiesta Weekend	2	F	8	0	1	1	4,174
Fiesty Amber	3	F	2	0	0	0	312
Fiesty Duke	4	G	16	1	2	3	15,108
Fiesty Fannie	4	F	3	0	1	0	2,345
Fiesty Inez	3	F	9	2	1	2	11,387
Fiesty Irish	4	F	2	0	0	0	252
Fiesty Jones	2	F	3	1	0	0	9,850
Fifi La Slew	7	M	13	0	2	4	6,172
Fifteen Dimes	2	F	2	0	0	0	0
Fifteen Rounds	3	G	6	4	1	0	76,180
Fifteen to Life	9	G	4	0	0	0	152
Fifth Avenue Doll	5	M	19	3	2	3	32,117
Fifth Creek	13	G	2	0	0	1	3,000
Fifth Demension	3	C	7	1	1	0	34,680
Fifth Edition	2	C	1	0	0	0	1,350
Fifth of Hennessy	3	C	8	1	1	2	56,150
Fifth Overture	2	F	1	1	0	0	36,360
Fifthavenuesisu	3	F	1	0	0	0	0
Fifty East	4	G	13	1	2	5	46,590
Fifty Hawken	5	G	10	0	0	1	2,892
Fifty Mission Cap	3	G	3	0	0	0	1,818
Fifty Nine White	8	M	4	1	0	0	1,810
Fifty One Phantom	3	F	1	0	0	0	65
Fifty Second Place	7	G	18	1	2	2	10,125
Fifty Six Diamonds	9	M	4	0	0	0	464
Fifty Six Fan	2	C	1	0	0	0	0
Fifty Stars	5	H	9	1	0	0	30,012
Fifty Three Cards	2	G	7	1	1	1	39,680
Figgy Annette	3	F	4	0	0	0	53
Fight Away	7	G	7	2	0	0	14,326
Fight Em'all	4	C	17	2	3	1	12,502
Fight Festival	3	C	4	0	0	0	0
Fight for a Queen	8	M	18	1	2	2	5,804
Fight for Ally	6	G	5	3	0	0	198,360
Fight for Freedom	5	G	4	1	1	0	7,840
Fight for Life	3	G	6	1	1	2	29,460
Fight for Silver	6	H	13	2	0	1	16,477
Fight Forever	5	M	8	1	1	1	26,696
Fight Night	8	G	16	0	1	3	3,414
Fight Over Sea	4	F	6	1	1	0	7,970
Fight Over's Gold	3	F	3	0	0	0	174
Fight Ya	6	H	6	0	1	0	812
Fighten Beezie	7	H	10	0	2	1	18,720
Fighter Del Diablo	4	G	3	0	0	1	693
Fighter Ray	3	G	15	1	0	1	6,025
Fightin Sixty	2	G	9	0	5	2	17,185
Fighting Deputy	3	C	10	1	1	0	9,255
Fighting Duchess	5	M	2	0	0	0	1,120
Fighting Duke	3	G	2	0	0	0	540
Fighting Fever	3	F	12	3	1	1	69,939
Fighting Forum	2	C	7	1	1	1	16,950
Fighting Indians	4	G	10	0	1	4	43,767
Fighting Jerry	2	C	5	0	0	2	6,560
Fighting Jonny	3	C	7	0	0	0	1,435
Fighting Justice	3	C	13	1	3	1	18,844
Fighting Roy Kelly	3	C	9	2	1	1	68,380
Fighting Sis	3	F	4	0	1	0	2,260
Fighting Skinny	3	F	9	2	1	2	14,893
Fighting Song	5	M	6	1	0	2	14,528
Fighting Spirit	5	H	6	1	1	0	17,250
Fighting Star	5	G	5	1	0	1	27,120
Fighting Wolf	3	C	12	0	3	1	21,160
Fightingtosurvive	3	C	7	0	0	0	711
Fightingupastorm	4	G	5	2	1	1	13,329
Fightrun	6	M	1	0	0	0	78
Fightoverhoney	4	G	4	0	0	0	0
Figure of Speech	4	C	12	1	0	0	10,330
Fiji Girl	4	F	3	0	0	1	1,915
Fiji Rascal	4	F	6	0	0	0	2,640
Fiji Times Express	2	F	2	0	0	0	0
Fil a Buster	3	C	7	1	0	0	1,847
File Corrupted	6	G	9	1	0	1	3,390
Filigree	8	M	2	0	0	0	3,240
Filipino Wind	6	H	15	0	2	2	1,922
Filippone	3	G	16	3	2	3	65,280
Fill the Bucket	2	G	3	0	0	0	700
Filly Chilly	2	F	1	0	0	0	0
Filly Fanatic	2	F	2	1	0	0	11,400
Fillygris	3	F	1	1	0	0	8,550
Fillypasser	4	F	11	0	0	1	6,500
Film Critic	4	F	3	1	0	0	38,558
Film Maker	3	F	9	4	2	2	457,220
Film Star	5	G	11	1	2	0	9,610
Filmore	5	H	10	1	1	1	14,100
Filmos	3	G	13	0	0	0	766
Fin Lady	6	M	10	1	1	2	12,658
Fin Mocha	4	F	6	0	0	0	473
Fina Dur	9	G	7	2	0	0	30,859
Final Adieu	4	F	13	2	3	1	48,036
Final Agenda	4	C	4	0	0	0	309
Final Assault	2	F	4	1	1	1	39,240
Final Attack	3	F	6	2	0	1	27,283
Final Attempt	7	G	20	1	5	9	10,730
Final Bounty	3	G	12	2	1	1	20,347
Final Choice	11	G	3	1	0	0	4,226
Final Course	2	G	2	0	0	0	0
Final Covenant	5	M	9	4	1	1	50,462
Final Debut	7	H	6	0	0	1	448
Final Decision	4	G	10	1	0	1	11,152
Final Destination (NZ)	5	M	2	1	0	1	103,320
Final Discount	3	F	10	3	4	1	104,488
Final Dispersal	5	M	7	4	2	0	66,130
Final Draft	2	C	1	0	1	0	3,000
Final Dream	6	G	10	4	1	0	40,074
Final Drummer	4	F	7	0	1	1	532
Final Edit	4	G	2	0	0	0	120
Final Endeavor	4	G	11	3	0	2	44,804
Final Exam	3	F	5	0	0	0	862
Final Eyes	7	G	10	1	1	1	8,662
Final Finale	3	G	10	1	1	1	7,145
Final Force	3	F	7	1	0	1	5,659
Final Hero	5	G	14	2	0	4	9,788
Final Lover	4	F	17	1	1	1	11,542
Final Marriage	2	F	1	0	0	0	103
Final Movement	3	C	5	0	1	1	5,315
Final Order	2	C	5	2	1	0	12,670
Final Payment	7	G	6	0	0	0	309
Final Prophecy	4	C	12	0	0	3	28,693
Final Rare	7	M	11	0	2	1	4,530
Final Reduction	4	F	1	0	0	0	0
Final Round	3	F	6	1	2	2	172,416
Final Score	4	C	5	0	2	1	9,190
Final Success	2	F	1	0	0	0	330
Final Sweep	5	M	2	1	0	1	7,840
Final Table	4	G	5	0	3	0	28,160
Final Thunder	5	G	7	0	0	0	916
Final Word	5	M	1	0	0	0	150
Finalgame	4	F	9	0	2	1	2,428
Finality	4	C	3	1	0	0	69,120
Finally	6	M	4	0	0	0	675
Finally Happy	3	G	2	0	0	0	115
Finally Here	3	F	8	5	1	1	189,200
Finallytothebank	5	G	14	1	6	3	5,852
Finance the Cat	3	C	8	1	1	0	11,610
Financial	3	C	3	0	0	1	2,860
Financial Aide	4	C	8	0	2	0	2,440
Financial Diplomat	5	H	13	1	0	1	14,515
Financial Editor	4	F	3	0	0	0	1,320
Financial Flag	3	G	1	0	0	0	135
Financial Line	2	G	1	0	0	0	500
Finch Fries	3	G	8	1	0	0	4,330
Find a Way Home	6	G	4	0	0	0	172
Find Me Time	3	G	10	3	1	0	11,755
Find My Halter	4	G	12	2	3	2	54,796
Find Our Star	10	G	14	4	4	0	46,744
Find Sara	2	F	9	0	2	5	14,644
Find the Groom	2	F	2	0	0	0	190
Find the Mine	8	G	7	0	0	0	3,330
Find the Time	6	G	11	0	2	4	20,733
Findaway	7	G	11	1	3	0	14,327
Findee's Keepee's	2	C	1	0	0	0	370
Finder	5	H	3	0	0	1	5,740

Horse	Age	Sex	Sts	1st	2d	3d	Won
Finder's Gold	7	H	1	0	0	0	860
Finding Speed	3	F	7	2	1	0	31,340
Findingbuckriver	6	H	1	0	0	0	56
Findy	5	H	3	0	0	0	114
Fine Affair	8	G	5	0	0	0	239
Fine and Dandy	4	C	2	0	0	0	4,080
Fine Answer	3	C	4	1	1	1	29,420
Fine by Me	3	F	12	1	5	2	16,825
Fine Dance	12	G	2	1	0	0	5,694
Fine Okie	2	F	4	0	0	0	1,780
Fine Results	3	G	14	3	4	3	49,434
Fine Rhythm	4	F	3	0	0	0	0
Fine Ridge	3	F	7	1	0	3	7,469
Fine Stormy	4	G	8	3	2	0	74,739
Fine Strike	2	C	6	1	1	1	23,332
Fine Tuned	8	G	5	0	0	0	465
Fine Tuner	3	C	4	0	0	0	720
Finelytunedmachine	6	G	6	0	0	0	480
Fineonthefarm	3	G	11	5	0	0	46,352
Finer Things	3	G	8	1	2	1	13,304
Finery	3	F	4	2	2	0	72,400
Fines Creek	3	G	11	2	1	4	68,820
Finessable	3	F	7	0	3	1	8,155
Finesse	3	F	8	1	0	1	7,680
Finest	3	F	2	0	0	0	0
Finest Collection	8	M	10	0	0	0	831
Finest Kreem	2	F	2	0	0	0	338
Finest Spell	2	F	2	0	0	0	0
Fingers Cross	6	M	1	0	0	1	715
Finish 'Em Off	5	M	15	2	3	3	49,287
Finish Line	3	C	11	2	0	1	12,854
Finished Smarty	4	F	15	0	0	2	2,012
Fini'slovetower	4	C	1	0	0	0	0
Finisterre Rock	7	G	13	1	2	4	22,720
Finleycreek	4	G	5	1	2	0	5,465
Finn Cantwinatgin	2	C	4	1	0	1	16,520
Finnerty's Frolic	2	F	5	2	1	2	103,812
Fiona Isabella	3	F	10	0	1	1	3,813
Fiorano	4	F	2	0	0	0	0
Fircroft	3	F	7	0	3	0	156,876
Fire	4	G	4	0	1	1	2,482
Fire Again	4	C	14	1	0	4	6,895
Fire Aly	3	G	18	0	2	5	12,627
Fire and Glory	4	G	10	1	1	1	59,266
Fire and Icy	9	G	9	0	0	1	3,300
Fire At Sea	4	F	3	0	0	2	528
Fire At the Wire	12	G	7	0	0	2	2,584
Fire Ball John	9	H	2	1	1	0	2,920
Fire Blitz	4	C	4	0	1	0	15,488
Fire Brigade	5	G	4	1	1	0	3,920
Fire Dance	3	C	4	0	0	1	1,675
Fire Days	3	C	1	1	0	0	5,460
Fire E Mate	3	C	5	0	0	0	480
Fire Emblem	2	F	4	0	1	2	15,266
Fire Fox	5	G	11	2	3	1	22,570
Fire From Ice	4	F	3	0	0	0	0
Fire Hero	2	C	3	0	0	1	3,530
Fire House Slew	2	C	2	0	1	0	1,900
Fire in the Soul	6	G	18	1	2	1	27,215
Fire Inside	3	G	5	0	1	1	2,732
Fire Inu Wire	4	F	7	1	1	0	3,662
Fire Me	7	H	2	1	0	1	4,768
Fire Outa Control	7	G	13	1	2	0	6,909
Fire Pants	3	F	5	0	0	0	573
Fire Place	3	F	1	0	0	0	0
Fire Slam	2	C	3	2	1	0	259,430
Fire Steed	3	F	6	1	3	2	35,430
Fire Strike	2	C	4	1	0	0	14,040
Fire Tac	4	G	12	0	1	0	814
Fire the Bum	7	M	9	1	2	0	16,334
Fire the Firm	4	G	17	2	5	3	51,118
Fire the King	5	G	18	1	2	1	5,071
Fire the Rockets	7	G	13	3	2	4	22,530
Fire the Vet	3	G	6	1	1	0	7,763
Fire Within Fire	3	G	11	2	2	2	15,677
Fire Work	8	H	3	0	0	0	152
Fireballer	4	C	1	0	0	0	390
Firebeacon	4	F	6	2	0	1	12,900
Fireboll	2	F	1	0	0	0	0
Firebolt's Colony	2	C	1	0	0	0	2,280
Fireborne	7	M	13	3	0	2	11,630
Fireboy	4	C	9	0	1	2	3,084
Firecard	5	M	13	3	2	3	92,870
Firedup for Real	2	C	4	0	1	1	3,780
Firefall	7	G	14	6	0	0	17,805
Firefighter Rob	6	H	4	1	1	0	10,763
Firefly Dancer	4	F	14	3	5	1	56,753
Firefree	4	F	6	1	0	2	11,519
Firehouse	4	G	8	0	0	2	2,072
Firehouse Affair	5	M	1	0	1	0	2,340
Fireinthekitchen	3	C	3	0	0	0	580
Firelights Glow	3	G	3	0	0	0	136
Fireman Rahill	3	C	9	1	1	2	11,970
Firenorth	4	F	8	0	0	3	5,380
Fireonthemountain	5	H	5	0	0	0	650
Firespike	2	C	7	2	1	1	30,430
Firestone Special	5	G	6	1	2	0	8,380
Firetail	2	F	2	0	0	0	0
Firetruck	3	C	3	1	0	0	29,460
Firey Dinner	5	M	18	2	2	3	11,350
Firey New Love	2	C	1	0	0	0	90
Firey Nina	3	F	9	1	2	1	11,400
Firey Ridge	6	H	6	0	1	0	2,260
Firing	4	F	13	1	2	2	23,446
Firing Note	4	G	5	0	1	1	6,310
Firm Acceleration	4	G	10	2	2	1	49,650
Firm Affair	5	M	6	1	0	1	7,440
Firm Believer	5	G	7	1	0	2	17,780
Firm Cash	4	G	8	0	1	2	2,520
Firm Command	3	G	9	1	1	2	27,240
Firm Halo	4	F	15	1	1	5	14,077
Firm Kiss	4	F	1	0	1	0	5,600
Firm Reality	3	F	13	3	3	2	60,166
Firmament	4	F	13	1	3	5	18,086
Firmly Done	5	G	7	1	1	2	18,204
First Affair	5	H	5	0	0	2	440
First Again	4	F	6	2	0	2	58,627
First Aly Pie	5	M	12	2	3	2	13,044
First Amendment	6	G	6	1	0	0	23,120
First Armaison	7	G	3	0	0	0	343
First Arrival	7	G	10	0	2	1	18,550
First At Last	2	C	8	0	0	0	5,819
First At War	3	C	3	0	0	0	500
First Away	3	C	8	0	1	2	3,550
First Barrel	4	G	10	0	0	0	1,349
First Blast	4	G	15	2	1	2	5,885
First Blood (GB)	6	G	16	0	2	1	12,210
First Blush	3	C	13	2	3	4	153,750
First Book	5	G	13	2	1	3	7,836
First Boy	3	C	15	1	2	0	7,881
First Class Code	6	M	7	2	0	1	12,330
First Class Honors	4	G	12	1	4	1	34,288
First Class Lady	7	M	18	2	2	3	11,504
First Class Man	3	G	4	0	1	1	1,980
First Class Trip	3	G	6	1	0	1	23,920
First Clu	3	F	7	0	2	2	15,749
First Copy	4	G	11	3	1	1	24,422
First Corinthian	3	G	6	0	0	0	285
First Crack At It	5	M	13	2	1	1	11,024
First Crossing	7	M	5	0	0	0	610
First Curtain Call	4	F	7	0	0	1	691
First Dixie	3	G	16	2	3	4	27,023
First Dollar	3	G	7	0	0	0	322
First Draft	4	F	12	1	4	1	57,955
First Draw	3	C	5	0	0	0	0
First Emperor	7	G	2	1	0	0	9,150
First Encounter	3	F	7	0	0	1	5,880
First Escapade	4	G	12	3	4	0	17,214
First Ever Clever	4	F	4	0	1	0	3,958
First Flash	6	M	3	0	0	0	289
First for Mari	2	F	1	0	0	0	0
First Fuse	5	M	1	0	0	0	255
First Gary	5	G	10	2	1	1	9,070
First Gold	10	G	6	0	0	1	2,117
First Govenor	6	H	10	2	1	0	8,265
First Hit	4	F	4	1	0	0	6,450
First Hoedown	5	G	9	4	0	2	8,838
First Honoree	2	C	8	1	1	1	11,190

RECORDS OF HORSES

Horse	Age	Sex	Sts	1st	2d	3d	Won	Horse	Age	Sex	Sts	1st	2d	3d	Won
First in Flight	4	F	6	1	1	0	7,950	Fistbump	3	G	8	1	1	0	18,516
First Insight	4	G	8	3	0	1	83,148	Fit and Bushy	7	G	7	0	1	0	1,240
First Knighter	7	G	15	2	3	3	10,540	Fit as a Fiddle	6	H	13	1	2	1	4,958
First Lady Luck	3	F	11	1	0	3	5,457	Fit for a King	10	G	2	0	0	0	0
First Lady Patton	4	F	2	0	0	0	200	Fit for Flight	2	C	1	0	0	0	0
First Laugh	3	G	7	1	1	1	12,290	Fit for Glory	2	F	4	1	1	0	6,848
First Lieutenant	6	H	4	0	1	2	28,980	Fit for Silk	5	M	13	3	2	2	27,513
First Mims	3	C	15	0	0	1	3,609	Fit for the Fight	2	C	3	0	0	1	2,086
First Mohican	3	G	7	2	0	2	22,502	Fit Performer	6	M	10	2	3	2	69,850
First Money	2	C	3	1	2	0	92,765	Fit Por Fast	2	F	2	0	0	0	310
First Move	2	F	1	0	0	0	1,350	Fit Queen	3	F	4	0	0	0	800
First Mystery	5	M	5	0	0	1	6,430	Fit Soldier	2	G	4	0	0	1	2,340
First 'n Gold	4	G	3	0	0	0	0	Fit to Battle	4	F	6	0	0	1	975
First Night Alone	3	C	3	0	0	0	205	Fit to Be a Gent	8	G	10	2	0	0	8,838
First October	4	F	12	2	1	0	7,843	Fit to Be Royal	6	G	8	0	1	0	16,095
First Ole	3	G	5	0	0	1	3,835	Fit to Bet	4	G	13	3	1	1	12,364
First On the Moon	3	C	8	0	1	2	7,846	Fit to Cut	3	F	3	0	0	1	2,058
First One Out	5	H	4	0	0	0	997	Fit to Keep	3	G	2	1	0	0	4,520
First Pharme	3	F	3	0	0	0	0	Fit to Kill	3	F	10	5	3	0	91,950
First Picture	5	M	7	1	1	0	8,400	Fit to Skate	3	G	2	0	0	0	0
First Platinum	3	G	2	0	0	0	492	Fit Zun (BRZ)	5	H	8	0	0	1	4,922
First Printing	4	F	10	1	3	2	21,062	Fitadip	3	G	17	1	0	5	12,345
First Quarter	4	F	8	1	1	2	109,122	Fitfull Rage	3	F	1	0	0	0	700
First Row	3	F	8	0	2	1	11,735	Fitstoatee	6	G	7	2	0	2	10,075
First Sargent	7	H	1	0	0	0	185	Fittest	5	M	11	2	2	0	17,654
First Search	4	C	5	0	0	0	165	Fitts Village	3	G	1	0	0	0	375
First Service (GER)	9	G	4	0	2	0	4,060	Fitz Silverstreak	4	G	6	0	0	0	606
First Shot	6	G	15	3	1	2	59,740	Fitzbid	3	F	12	2	3	1	28,274
First Sign	4	C	11	0	1	0	2,360	Fitzgerald	3	G	15	0	2	1	11,299
First Sign of Rain	4	G	5	1	0	1	29,397	Fitzroyal	4	G	7	3	1	0	78,547
First Sip	4	G	9	0	0	0	155	Five Across	5	G	8	0	0	1	1,532
First Snowbound	3	F	3	1	1	0	16,183	Five Bucks	5	G	15	1	2	3	13,021
First Soprano	4	F	9	2	0	1	5,965	Five Card Monty	2	C	3	1	0	1	22,266
First Spear	5	G	11	3	2	0	70,820	Five Cousins	5	H	17	4	3	2	23,665
First Star Deputy	3	C	4	0	0	0	605	Five Diamond Road	3	G	13	1	0	0	15,462
First Starella	3	F	3	0	0	0	517	Five Eighty Four	3	C	8	1	1	4	61,808
First Step House	6	G	11	1	0	2	17,132	Five Elements	2	F	1	0	0	0	0
First Storm	2	F	2	0	0	0	450	Five Fishes (FR)	5	M	7	0	0	2	36,566
First Summing	5	H	6	0	0	0	960	Five Flags	2	C	6	0	0	0	912
First Tango (GER)	6	G	10	1	1	0	4,008	Five Gold Pieces	4	G	1	0	0	0	180
First Time Luck	4	G	16	0	3	2	5,459	Five Moons	3	G	4	0	0	0	0
First Time Viking	5	M	6	0	1	0	1,129	Five More Dreams	6	H	2	1	0	0	1,975
First to Light	5	M	2	0	1	1	4,710	Five Nickels	2	F	1	0	0	0	0
First Trip	5	G	2	0	0	1	990	Five O Five	3	C	7	2	1	1	14,926
First Try	6	G	14	0	0	0	3,522	Five O Nine	7	G	4	0	1	0	2,964
First Up	4	G	11	2	1	2	16,638	Five O Two	2	G	3	0	0	0	360
First Vancouver	6	G	12	1	0	2	2,318	Five Partners	4	G	4	0	0	1	817
First Waltz	2	F	2	0	0	0	527	Five Point Star	3	G	7	3	1	0	60,526
First Wave	5	H	8	0	0	1	2,244	Five Quarters	4	G	11	1	3	1	9,934
First Wolf	6	G	23	3	2	2	17,735	Five Rivers	4	F	4	1	1	0	16,000
First You Dream	3	G	4	0	1	0	12,180	Five Roads (IRE)	3	G	9	0	3	2	11,560
Firstaid Kit	4	C	8	0	1	0	2,149	Five Schillings	7	R	11	5	1	1	121,240
Firstandlast Rose	6	G	8	1	0	1	3,555	Five Secrets	5	M	5	0	0	0	405
Firstclass Upgrade	3	G	2	0	1	0	2,829	Five Star Affair	3	F	11	1	4	1	8,607
Firstgear	2	C	6	0	2	0	27,033	Five Star Award	5	G	11	0	3	0	14,852
Firsthere	2	C	5	0	0	0	0	Five Star Deputy	8	G	1	0	0	0	274
Firstimage	5	M	7	0	2	1	1,394	Five Star Gene	5	G	13	2	2	2	15,870
Firstonehome	3	F	9	0	0	0	192	Five Star General	5	H	3	1	0	0	8,535
Firstoneinthewater	3	F	9	0	1	2	4,352	Five Star Hero	3	F	5	1	1	0	21,120
Firstonthewire	5	G	5	0	1	0	3,618	Five Star Meeting	3	F	8	2	0	1	84,998
Firstround Ko	5	H	5	1	2	0	22,230	Five Star Semoran	2	C	4	0	0	0	365
Firstship	2	G	6	2	1	0	36,010	Five Stars (GB)	4	F	1	0	0	0	360
Firstsonofmachone	4	G	5	1	0	0	8,780	Five Star's Ruby	4	F	11	0	2	2	21,300
Firststatedeposit	5	G	10	0	1	2	16,180	Five Straight	6	H	7	2	1	0	28,380
Firth of Lorne (IRE)	4	F	3	1	0	1	40,550	Five String Banjo	2	G	1	0	0	0	95
Fiscal Nobility	9	G	2	0	0	0	164	Five Swings	3	F	6	0	1	1	3,550
Fiscally Speaking	4	G	8	1	1	1	94,226	Five Tango Charlie	9	G	15	3	4	1	24,524
Fish Cakes	5	M	5	0	0	0	624	Five to Four	5	M	15	2	2	0	11,505
Fish Guys	2	C	3	1	0	1	24,450	Five Travoltas	3	G	10	3	1	1	87,233
Fish Hook	7	G	6	0	2	1	1,292	Five Under	11	G	2	1	1	0	4,640
Fisher Falls	6	H	6	0	0	0	980	Five Wild Cats	2	G	7	1	1	1	22,180
Fisher Peak	5	G	2	0	0	0	0	Five Wishes	4	F	11	1	0	1	3,996
Fisher Pond	4	C	6	0	1	2	25,993	Five Zero Niner	5	G	3	0	0	0	570
Fisherman's Friend	2	C	8	0	2	2	15,020	Fivehundred	5	G	11	0	0	0	880
Fishie's Boy	3	G	13	0	2	1	3,151	Fiveoclock Charley	3	C	2	0	0	0	137
Fishin Bill	6	G	5	0	0	0	738	Fiveoclocksumwhere	2	G	1	0	0	0	0
Fishing Buddy	4	C	5	0	0	1	1,360	Fivefour	4	G	11	0	0	3	6,579
Fision	2	C	3	0	0	1	5,580	Fivestargirl	4	F	16	1	1	3	14,438
Fist Full	4	G	16	0	6	2	17,115	Fivexj	2	G	1	0	0	0	52

Horse	Age	Sex	Sts	1st	2d	3d	Won
Fix the Roof	4	F	2	0	0	0	116
Fix Your Wagon	3	F	1	0	0	0	0
Fixate	5	H	3	0	1	0	1,800
Fixed Image	4	G	24	0	2	2	6,888
Fixin To	3	C	9	1	1	1	13,764
Fixitmiss	3	F	2	0	0	0	400
Fizz	4	G	20	2	2	3	18,455
Flag Angel	3	F	6	1	0	0	7,695
Flag Burner	2	F	7	3	0	1	47,888
Flag Commander	4	C	1	0	0	0	105
Flag Dancer	3	C	5	0	1	0	1,500
Flag Day	3	F	5	0	0	0	675
Flag Em Down	3	C	12	1	0	3	11,057
Flag Flyer	2	G	4	0	1	0	1,716
Flag Girl	3	F	13	1	4	2	20,437
Flag Is Up	3	G	3	0	0	0	0
Flag Lady B	3	F	5	0	0	1	4,980
Flag of Orion	2	C	4	0	0	0	0
Flag Pin	3	F	6	3	0	1	97,436
Flag the Account	3	F	3	0	0	1	708
Flag the Groom	3	C	13	0	3	1	10,456
Flag the Mint Down	3	F	2	0	0	0	1,920
Flag to Fly	3	G	4	1	0	0	10,540
Flag Tower	2	C	3	0	0	0	43
Flager (ARG)	4	F	8	3	1	1	109,222
Flagg's Crossing	6	H	9	1	1	1	9,147
Flags a Flyin	3	F	3	0	0	0	264
Flags At Dawn	5	H	4	0	0	1	1,800
Flagshipenterprise	2	C	4	2	1	0	104,500
Flagstone Blue	3	C	2	0	0	0	53
Flagwave	7	G	11	1	0	2	9,135
Flail	4	F	12	2	3	2	12,884
Flair and Square	4	G	2	0	0	0	624
Flair Play	2	F	6	0	0	0	1,440
Flair to Spare	3	G	5	0	2	0	5,010
Flake O	5	G	10	2	2	0	22,640
Flamante	3	F	15	0	0	2	3,078
Flame Burst	3	C	5	0	0	0	760
Flame Catcher	3	F	12	0	2	2	14,395
Flame in My Heart	3	F	17	2	1	2	17,534
Flame N Go	5	H	2	0	0	0	0
Flame Song	5	M	11	1	3	0	45,039
Flame Tetra	3	F	14	1	3	2	18,492
Flame Winner	4	C	2	0	0	0	0
Flame's Last Game	3	G	4	0	1	1	2,523
Flamethrowintexan	2	G	2	1	1	0	13,775
Flamin' Jolie	6	G	8	1	0	4	27,420
Flamin Lamborghini	3	G	3	0	1	1	2,548
Flaming Bull	3	G	13	2	1	0	12,127
Flaming Cloud	6	M	13	1	0	1	4,909
Flaming Dixie	2	F	3	1	1	0	19,010
Flaming Dot Com	5	M	3	0	0	2	455
Flaming Faith	5	M	6	0	0	3	9,027
Flaming Feu	3	G	10	4	2	1	32,932
Flaming Fire	3	G	9	1	0	1	18,575
Flaming Money	3	F	3	1	0	2	11,200
Flaming Night	4	F	14	3	3	0	21,098
Flaming Phoenix	2	C	2	0	0	1	1,777
Flaming Prospector	3	C	3	0	0	0	82
Flaming Ridge	3	F	8	1	1	1	6,000
Flaming Spare	4	C	15	0	1	4	13,460
Flaming Springs	3	C	6	1	0	0	26,800
Flaming Sword	3	G	10	1	2	2	21,810
Flaming Villa	4	G	4	1	2	0	7,090
Flaming West	9	H	2	0	0	0	0
Flamingo Fantasy	5	M	10	0	0	1	2,400
Flamingo Flash	4	F	1	0	0	0	0
Flamingo Lane	3	F	10	1	0	0	10,690
Flamingo Phil	8	G	7	1	0	0	7,600
Flamingo's World	4	G	11	0	0	0	1,743
Flammabull	3	C	1	0	0	0	360
Flan for You	2	F	3	0	0	0	1,550
Flandins Cat	3	C	4	1	0	1	13,680
Flank Attack	3	C	14	2	1	1	65,610
Flank Stake	3	G	11	3	1	0	14,232
Flanker	2	C	6	0	2	1	4,680
Flannigan	7	H	1	0	0	0	0
Flare Flyer	3	F	8	0	0	0	561
Flaring Moon	8	G	7	0	1	0	1,200
Flarions Flame	3	C	10	1	4	2	41,718
Flash Ante	3	C	6	1	0	0	7,725
Flash At Dawn	3	G	2	0	0	0	0
Flash Buy	4	C	7	0	1	0	1,801
Flash Can Dance	3	G	11	1	1	2	21,230
Flash Forward	4	G	13	1	0	3	20,046
Flash Frame	3	F	7	0	0	2	1,865
Flash From Heaven	4	C	5	0	0	0	565
Flash King	3	C	3	0	0	0	329
Flash Me	5	G	2	0	0	1	528
Flash of Joy	8	G	9	2	0	1	8,326
Flash Run Bepop	3	F	13	0	1	0	5,238
Flash Value	4	G	12	0	1	2	3,602
Flash Your Cash	3	G	10	0	0	2	1,922
Flashback Dancer	2	F	2	0	0	1	2,290
Flashdance Star	2	F	1	0	0	0	0
Flasher	9	G	4	0	0	0	5,514
Flashing Red	3	C	2	0	0	0	180
Flashing Tammany	8	H	3	0	0	1	1,410
Flashinproud	9	G	3	0	0	0	144
Flashlight Lady	6	M	7	0	0	1	1,885
Flashpoint	4	F	3	0	1	0	1,885
Flashthememory	5	M	2	0	0	0	189
Flashy Anna	2	F	3	0	1	1	8,476
Flashy Brass	2	F	4	1	0	1	8,330
Flashy Brew	5	M	7	1	0	4	16,696
Flashy Count	5	H	1	0	0	0	0
Flashy Dreamer	5	H	1	0	0	0	0
Flashy Finale	8	G	13	2	2	1	10,847
Flashy Finish	10	G	2	0	0	0	110
Flashy Furrari	5	G	2	0	1	0	3,500
Flashy Gambler	4	G	3	0	0	1	1,142
Flashy I. D.	5	M	4	0	0	0	513
Flashy in Black	6	M	7	3	1	0	16,404
Flashy Joe	3	C	1	0	0	0	0
Flashy Katherine	4	F	11	1	1	4	32,322
Flashy Lil Sis	4	F	6	0	3	1	7,640
Flashy Lover	4	C	2	0	0	0	428
Flashy Marina	6	M	8	0	0	0	1,064
Flashy Matter	2	C	1	0	0	0	0
Flashy Perfection	5	M	3	0	1	1	1,366
Flashy Player	5	M	11	1	0	1	7,920
Flashy Prospect	6	G	7	2	1	0	8,044
Flashy Roman	3	C	3	0	1	0	2,677
Flashy Silver	4	F	6	3	3	0	123,660
Flashy Thunder	4	F	3	1	0	0	44,172
Flashy Trend	5	G	10	1	3	2	9,965
Flashy Tune	3	C	1	0	0	0	0
Flat Leaver	3	F	11	1	3	2	10,189
Flatfoot Scotty	3	G	7	0	1	0	7,310
Flatland Flyer	8	G	6	0	1	1	1,646
Flatline	5	M	14	2	2	2	46,110
Flattened	7	M	2	0	1	0	2,030
Flatter	4	C	2	1	0	1	82,845
Flawless Diamond	3	F	3	2	0	0	55,200
Flawless Vision	3	C	3	0	0	0	350
Flaxen Flyer	4	F	5	0	2	0	41,075
Flaxton N D	3	G	5	0	0	0	345
Flaxville	6	G	7	0	0	0	0
Flea Powder	3	F	5	1	0	0	5,118
Fle'che Rouge	4	F	16	3	1	3	40,645
Fled	2	G	3	0	1	0	3,640
Flee the Blues	4	G	10	2	4	1	81,447
Fleeing Intent	3	F	9	1	1	0	5,185
Fleet Admiral	8	G	7	0	0	1	1,500
Fleet Aint	3	G	13	2	0	5	52,845
Fleet America	5	G	11	1	1	3	8,806
Fleet and Sweet	3	F	6	1	1	0	6,145
Fleet Andover	3	C	5	0	0	0	0
Fleet Avie	4	G	5	0	0	0	5,195
Fleet Bert	5	M	11	2	1	1	13,402
Fleet Boss	7	G	12	0	3	1	11,335
Fleet Christina	4	F	10	3	1	0	17,155
Fleet Coord	5	G	6	1	1	1	11,062
Fleet Crossing	8	G	1	0	0	0	0
Fleet Deed	6	M	15	5	2	4	69,976
Fleet Deputy	2	C	3	0	0	2	22,142
Fleet Dust	5	G	5	1	0	0	9,015
Fleet Expense	4	G	12	2	1	1	7,252

RECORDS OF HORSES

Horse	Age	Sex	Sts	1st	2d	3d	Won
Fleet Feet Pete	3	G	7	0	0	2	2,978
Fleet Final	4	F	17	3	2	5	17,290
Fleet Flight	4	F	8	1	3	1	9,811
Fleet Flyer	9	G	5	1	2	1	4,235
Fleet Foot	5	H	1	0	0	0	3,300
Fleet Foot Fox	3	C	9	0	2	0	15,570
Fleet Forum	4	G	16	2	3	5	47,237
Fleet Goeen	3	F	17	1	2	2	9,803
Fleet Irish Miss	2	F	1	0	0	0	0
Fleet Man	5	G	14	1	1	1	6,686
Fleet Music	3	G	5	0	1	0	2,756
Fleet Naski	7	M	12	1	1	0	5,397
Fleet of Foot	4	F	2	0	0	2	32,698
Fleet Princess	2	F	1	1	0	0	18,800
Fleet Ridan J. B.	9	G	7	0	0	0	540
Fleet Ruhlmann	7	G	15	1	4	1	9,616
Fleet Sail	9	G	7	0	1	0	956
Fleet Shadow	3	C	11	2	1	1	9,074
Fleet Street	5	G	14	2	1	4	7,265
Fleet Valentine	3	F	3	1	0	1	11,430
Fleet Willy	4	F	14	3	2	1	28,460
Fleet Year	5	G	5	1	0	0	2,400
Fleet Zepphyr	3	F	9	0	3	3	30,264
Fleeta Dif	4	F	4	0	0	1	6,630
Fleetengly	5	M	12	0	3	2	5,912
Fleeting Alliance	3	G	10	5	1	1	23,081
Fleeting Beauty	3	F	14	1	0	3	8,208
Fleeting Encounter	4	C	8	0	0	2	2,155
Fleeting Love	5	M	3	0	0	0	174
Fleeting Term	4	G	6	3	0	0	11,985
Fleetmaster	6	G	11	2	2	2	39,730
Fleetmoon	2	F	5	0	1	0	8,022
Fleetski	4	F	14	4	0	0	33,714
Fleetstreet Dancer	5	G	10	1	4	2	1,519,026
Fleety	6	G	18	1	2	6	55,585
Flemish Cap	5	H	9	2	1	1	37,280
Fleur de Lil	4	G	9	2	0	1	12,345
Fleur de May	3	F	4	0	1	1	8,378
Fleur de Sel	5	M	8	3	1	1	120,409
Fleurdebel	5	M	9	1	0	3	4,810
Flex Jet	5	G	6	1	1	1	11,009
Flick Creek	5	G	7	1	0	0	7,475
Flicka	5	M	7	3	1	1	14,520
Flickering Image	3	F	5	0	0	0	500
Flickering Silk	5	M	10	0	1	1	3,072
Flick's Finale	4	G	5	0	0	0	234
Flies With Eagles	7	G	9	3	1	1	25,950
Flight	4	G	8	2	1	2	54,320
Flight Advisory	6	M	7	0	0	1	2,468
Flight At Eight	5	G	12	1	1	1	3,616
Flight Court	4	F	2	0	0	0	300
Flight Dancer	3	G	10	0	0	0	210
Flight Glide	9	G	5	0	0	0	136
Flight Jab	6	G	22	1	4	5	11,272
Flight Mistress	4	F	1	0	0	0	0
Flight Ninety Nine	4	F	3	2	0	0	13,842
Flight of a Falcon	6	H	13	2	1	1	10,204
Flight of Ego	3	C	1	0	0	0	75
Flight of Ideas	5	M	8	4	0	1	14,078
Flight of Love	2	F	7	0	2	0	4,552
Flight of Time	3	F	13	1	5	1	45,310
Flight One O One	5	H	2	0	0	0	86
Flight Ops	2	F	6	0	3	1	8,231
Flight Path	6	H	18	1	0	3	12,930
Flight Path Girl	4	F	1	0	0	0	0
Flight Quest	4	F	14	1	2	2	6,466
Flight Revue	6	G	2	0	0	1	418
Flight Seven	5	G	9	3	0	4	14,721
Flight to Justice	2	C	7	1	0	1	17,560
Flight Training	3	C	11	3	0	0	38,808
Flight Zone	5	H	2	0	0	0	462
Flightofthebuffalo	4	C	9	2	0	1	16,795
Flight's Moto Kid	5	G	4	1	0	0	3,780
Flighty Forty Nine	6	M	10	0	0	0	1,562
Flinch	4	C	1	0	0	0	0
Fling	3	F	6	0	1	5	11,216
Flint Hall	3	C	1	0	0	0	220
Flintville	2	C	6	1	4	0	38,380
Flip	3	C	3	0	1	2	13,060
Flip and Groovy	3	F	6	1	0	1	8,640
Flip and Stu	3	G	11	0	4	1	33,470
Flip Aswitch	4	F	6	1	1	0	3,408
Flip Tour	2	C	6	0	0	0	3,120
Flipapatty	4	G	9	0	0	2	1,817
Flipette	4	F	3	0	0	0	1,200
Flip's Corner	3	C	1	0	0	0	2,460
Flips Memorial	11	G	7	0	0	0	883
Flipsider	4	F	11	2	3	3	42,058
Flirt	2	F	4	0	0	1	1,760
Flirt to Music	5	G	11	1	4	2	26,515
Flirt With Danger	8	M	14	2	3	0	33,350
Flirt With Fortune	3	C	13	2	4	2	131,306
Flirtation Card	4	F	3	1	1	0	12,480
Flirtatious Class	4	F	7	1	2	0	20,876
Flirtatious Heart	5	M	8	0	1	2	7,274
Flirting	4	F	1	0	0	0	0
Flirting Waltz	4	F	5	2	0	1	16,898
Flirting Ways	3	F	1	0	0	0	2,520
Flirting With Fame	2	F	5	0	0	0	410
Flirting Wolf	7	G	14	3	0	0	7,799
Flirtingwithmagic	4	G	12	0	2	1	3,802
Flirtnwithdisaster	3	F	6	0	0	1	1,100
Flirty Dancer	4	F	7	0	0	0	810
Flitter Bug	5	M	12	1	0	1	3,545
Flitwick's Charms	2	C	1	0	0	0	1,290
Flo	3	F	16	0	3	1	6,785
Flo Jo Express	6	M	2	0	1	0	1,080
Flo Rose 'n Net	2	F	7	2	1	1	31,570
Float and Sting	4	F	9	1	3	1	57,380
Floater	2	G	5	4	0	0	102,926
Floatin On Xtacy	5	M	1	0	0	1	470
Floating Meeting	4	G	9	1	1	1	4,626
Floaway	2	F	5	0	1	1	5,046
Flokey	4	F	8	0	2	1	3,945
Flom N X S	4	F	10	2	0	1	33,306
Flom's Flyer	5	G	15	1	1	1	5,819
Flood Level	3	G	15	2	1	5	15,502
Floor It Man	5	H	15	2	2	3	19,387
Floor Play	8	G	4	0	0	1	4,050
Flopper	4	G	13	1	3	0	24,300
Floppy's Light	3	F	3	0	0	0	214
Flor Del Sol	3	F	7	0	0	0	0
Flor d'Liz	3	F	1	0	0	0	0
Flora de Norte	7	M	3	0	0	0	339
Flora Mac Flimsey	5	M	13	3	2	2	35,066
Floral Avenue	3	G	3	0	0	0	0
Florence	3	F	9	2	1	2	75,298
Flores Dancer	4	G	6	0	0	1	576
Florida Chad	3	G	10	1	0	0	6,937
Florida Express	2	C	4	1	2	0	22,540
Florida Fay	4	F	5	0	1	1	2,170
Florida Jet	3	C	11	1	2	2	12,675
Florida Keys	2	C	1	0	0	0	195
Florida On Fire	5	M	11	0	1	1	9,962
Florida Recount	4	G	7	3	0	0	153,162
Florida Transfer	3	G	12	2	1	0	9,004
Florik's Baby	2	F	1	0	0	0	140
Flo's Bo	4	G	12	1	2	1	39,510
Flo's Gold	5	G	8	1	0	0	6,878
Flo's Lil Lady	5	M	14	1	1	3	6,745
Flo's Wish	8	G	4	0	0	0	350
Flo'ssweetie	4	F	3	0	0	0	360
Flossy Dancer	4	F	1	0	0	0	50
Flotilla	5	G	9	2	0	0	35,898
Flounder	4	F	11	0	0	0	1,152
Flower Cart	4	F	8	0	2	3	17,336
Flower Forest	3	F	5	2	1	1	65,495
Flower Hunter	3	F	5	2	3	0	70,800
Flower Lane	4	G	13	0	1	2	3,361
Flower Mound	3	F	2	0	0	2	4,565
Flower Time	5	M	3	0	0	0	129
Flowers and Fun	3	C	9	1	2	0	12,650
Flowers Isle Bay	4	G	1	0	0	0	0
Flowers My Lady	6	M	17	5	2	4	33,482
Flowers Onthe Wall	4	F	13	2	2	1	46,896
Flowing Rhythm	6	G	11	1	0	0	8,774
Flowing Southward	4	F	17	1	2	1	10,306
Flowington (IRE)	6	M	15	1	3	4	26,933

Horse	Age	Sex	Sts	1st	2d	3d	Won
Flown the Coop	4	F	7	1	2	1	8,143
Fluff My Feathers	3	F	6	1	2	1	9,582
Fluffy Feeling	6	M	6	0	1	2	5,785
Fluid and Fast	3	F	5	0	1	0	5,900
Fluid Gold	11	G	1	0	0	1	360
Fluidly	2	F	1	1	0	0	9,000
Flu's Last Rumble	3	F	5	0	0	0	661
Flush Flush Flush	3	G	6	0	0	0	946
Flushing Meadows	2	C	4	2	0	1	77,100
Flute Song	4	G	21	3	3	2	17,181
Fluted Flame	2	F	1	0	0	0	0
Flutie	6	G	4	0	2	1	3,167
Flutterflies	6	M	10	3	4	0	36,234
Fly Again	3	C	8	1	1	2	12,990
Fly Amery Fly	2	F	4	0	0	0	1,320
Fly and Eagle	4	G	20	0	4	3	58,510
Fly Angel	4	F	10	0	0	1	1,166
Fly Badger Fly	3	G	10	1	0	0	5,168
Fly Beside Me	5	G	9	2	1	1	22,389
Fly Birdie Fly	5	M	17	0	0	0	2,490
Fly Blue Devil	4	G	14	2	3	2	18,052
Fly Borboleta	4	F	7	1	3	0	127,946
Fly by Eli	3	C	4	0	0	0	1,209
Fly by Em	5	M	2	0	0	0	100
Fly by Moonlight	2	C	2	1	0	0	8,658
Fly By Night (NZ)	4	F	1	0	0	1	5,160
Fly by Peru	2	G	5	0	0	0	1,300
Fly by You	5	M	8	1	2	1	55,168
Fly Bye Dawn	6	M	14	0	2	1	8,459
Fly Esteem	2	G	5	2	1	1	57,934
Fly Fire	7	M	6	1	2	1	8,580
Fly Fly Away	3	F	4	0	1	0	613
Fly for Home	6	M	13	0	0	1	1,880
Fly for Jane	9	G	6	0	0	0	1,758
Fly for Less	4	G	4	0	0	0	500
Fly Forever	7	G	12	4	3	1	29,935
Fly Foxy Fly	3	F	3	0	0	0	355
Fly Girl	3	F	11	0	0	1	4,120
Fly Girl Blues	8	M	1	0	0	0	220
Fly Girl Fly	7	M	3	0	0	0	70
Fly Gold Air	4	F	1	0	0	0	0
Fly Harold	7	G	7	1	1	0	4,688
Fly Honor Fly	3	G	6	1	0	1	13,175
Fly Maggie	7	M	14	4	1	0	18,991
Fly Magic Fly	5	G	6	0	0	2	1,800
Fly Man	4	G	10	0	0	0	598
Fly Me Ali	2	F	1	0	1	0	3,510
Fly Me Crazy	5	M	11	1	2	1	89,740
Fly Me Nina	2	F	9	0	3	3	11,965
Fly Nicky Fly	3	F	3	0	0	0	0
Fly On By	7	H	14	1	2	2	5,062
Fly On Home	4	F	1	0	0	0	0
Fly Our Flag	3	F	7	0	0	0	568
Fly Over Early	9	M	8	1	1	1	7,168
Fly Pigeon Fly	4	F	7	1	2	1	30,866
Fly Seattle	5	H	13	3	3	2	22,631
Fly Slama Jama	5	G	9	1	1	1	67,320
Fly Smartly	5	G	4	1	0	2	114,705
Fly So Quick	5	M	10	1	4	0	11,088
Fly Taylor Fly	7	F	13	5	0	3	51,445
Fly to Atlantis	4	C	10	1	4	1	8,403
Fly to Freedom	5	G	7	1	2	3	6,432
Fly to Houston	9	G	3	1	0	0	4,500
Fly to Paradise	4	F	1	0	0	0	0
Fly to the Bank	3	G	18	2	2	7	25,285
Fly to the Lake	6	G	13	3	4	0	76,684
Fly to the Music	3	F	13	0	3	0	4,684
Fly to the Wire	3	G	9	2	6	0	153,545
Fly Tricky	3	G	14	2	2	3	20,470
Fly With Hope	5	H	1	0	0	0	100
Fly With Karakorum	3	F	14	2	3	3	96,875
Fly With Sunny	4	F	3	0	2	0	6,310
Flyhigher	4	F	6	0	0	3	2,456
Flyin Brian	5	H	10	3	3	2	19,631
Flyin Four Shoes	2	C	2	0	0	0	0
Flyin Y	2	F	1	0	0	0	0
Flyindownbaylaurel	3	F	11	1	0	1	35,200
Flying	5	M	10	1	2	0	9,812
Flying Alibi	7	M	13	3	6	2	74,020
Flying all Alona	9	M	6	0	1	0	2,940
Flying Avie	7	G	1	0	0	0	280
Flying Baron	6	H	3	0	0	0	1,761
Flying Birdie	5	M	4	2	1	0	69,421
Flying Biscuit	2	F	1	0	0	0	320
Flying Camila	3	F	3	0	0	0	597
Flying Canuck	3	C	4	0	0	0	9,396
Flying Capote	3	F	3	0	0	0	0
Flying Castelli	4	G	8	1	0	0	8,765
Flying Catman	2	G	5	0	3	0	2,400
Flying Charlotte	7	M	2	0	0	0	280
Flying Chicken	7	M	8	0	0	0	420
Flying Chockli	2	F	2	0	0	0	759
Flying Cisco	3	C	10	0	1	1	1,208
Flying Cobra	3	F	8	2	1	0	14,445
Flying Combat	5	H	10	0	1	0	3,873
Flying Contraption (IRE)	6	G	2	1	1	0	17,700
Flying Cowboy	2	C	3	0	0	0	275
Flying Crusader	4	C	2	0	0	0	105
Flying Dame	5	M	6	1	0	1	7,358
Flying Denouement	8	G	8	2	1	1	14,135
Flying Dove	3	F	3	0	0	0	0
Flying Duck	2	C	4	0	0	1	2,690
Flying Effort	4	G	3	0	0	0	136
Flying Far	3	F	6	0	1	1	3,570
Flying Fast	4	G	4	0	0	0	281
Flying Feathers	3	C	5	0	1	0	6,839
Flying Fire	3	C	3	0	0	0	500
Flying Fleet	9	G	15	0	3	5	16,913
Flying Frederick	7	H	5	0	0	0	579
Flying Free	4	C	4	1	2	0	53,103
Flying Fugitive	4	G	8	0	2	3	13,750
Flying Fury	3	G	11	1	1	2	11,755
Flying Gal	4	F	8	0	0	0	8,915
Flying Garrett	4	C	3	0	0	0	0
Flying General	3	G	9	1	1	0	26,120
Flying Hamer	5	M	9	0	0	0	746
Flying Harley	8	G	13	2	3	2	18,819
Flying Heart	4	F	6	1	1	1	55,340
Flying Hero	5	G	8	2	1	0	9,602
Flying High Again	5	G	7	0	1	0	4,645
Flying Hombre	3	C	4	0	0	0	270
Flying Is Fun	3	C	6	0	0	1	3,121
Flying J. K.s	6	G	12	1	1	3	4,823
Flying Jackie	5	M	16	4	2	1	27,798
Flying Jazz	3	C	6	1	1	0	50,074
Flying Jeb	6	G	14	2	4	4	12,298
Flying Jessie	2	F	9	1	3	0	9,296
Flying Johnny	5	H	12	1	1	2	6,358
Flying Kegan	3	G	8	0	0	1	4,290
Flying King	5	G	8	0	0	2	3,050
Flying Kitty	5	M	12	2	1	4	22,872
Flying Lady Cue	3	F	3	1	0	0	7,891
Flying Lea	3	F	13	2	0	0	22,453
Flying Lingo	3	F	14	3	1	4	15,474
Flying Liz	5	M	10	1	0	3	9,225
Flying Llama	3	G	4	0	1	0	1,940
Flying Marlin	4	F	8	1	1	1	64,576
Flying Memo	2	F	1	1	0	0	7,920
Flying Metro	6	G	8	0	1	0	6,120
Flying Miss Alice	3	F	3	0	0	1	1,045
Flying Moon	4	F	3	1	0	2	2,352
Flying Notes	4	G	1	0	0	1	7,500
Flying Nuggets	3	G	14	3	2	3	59,440
Flying Officer	4	G	12	4	2	1	43,854
Flying Oleta	3	F	14	1	1	0	19,967
Flying Passage	3	F	4	1	0	2	37,250
Flying Past U	4	C	8	1	1	0	1,829
Flying Peacock	3	F	8	1	2	1	61,667
Flying Pembroke	4	G	6	0	1	1	1,504
Flying Penelope	3	F	1	0	0	0	116
Flying Petra	3	F	14	2	2	1	25,579
Flying Pickle	3	F	8	1	0	0	33,032
Flying Pilot	3	G	2	2	0	0	22,800
Flying Piper	3	F	6	1	0	0	4,758
Flying Pro	4	G	15	3	3	6	23,166
Flying Promise	3	G	15	3	3	1	20,213
Flying Pulpit	3	F	6	0	2	0	19,620
Flying Rail	8	M	18	1	1	3	8,294

Horse	Age	Sex	Sts	1st	2d	3d	Won
Flying Reality	4	G	4	0	0	2	3,275
Flying Regina	6	M	6	0	2	0	2,050
Flying Retsina Run	8	G	10	0	3	2	20,542
Flying Robert	3	G	11	0	0	1	3,320
Flying Rocket	3	G	10	1	3	1	18,620
Flying Ruby	3	F	9	1	1	1	5,944
Flying Rudolph	6	G	16	1	7	2	37,230
Flying Scotsman	3	G	8	0	0	1	2,310
Flying Sharon	2	F	2	0	0	0	3,168
Flying Shirttail	3	C	1	0	0	0	41
Flying Singer	7	H	7	3	2	1	46,106
Flying Sissy	6	H	2	0	0	0	210
Flying Soldier	4	G	2	0	0	0	0
Flying Sumo	4	F	4	1	1	1	6,730
Flying Supercon	4	C	10	3	2	2	88,718
Flying Supremo	3	C	2	0	0	0	0
Flying Taz	4	G	17	1	3	2	14,115
Flying to Finish	4	F	14	3	1	4	40,002
Flying to the Moon	2	G	2	0	0	0	0
Flying Tornado	3	F	3	0	0	0	96
Flying Twister	5	G	8	1	0	0	2,291
Flying Vixie Dust	4	F	17	1	0	4	11,995
Flying With Joy	6	M	4	0	0	0	180
Flying With Mimi	5	M	4	1	1	0	14,905
Flyingpaster Power	3	G	10	1	2	1	11,644
Flyingsofine	3	G	3	1	2	0	7,068
Flylikethewind	5	H	1	0	0	0	0
Flymore Willah	6	H	6	2	2	0	55,894
Fly'n Cody	3	C	10	0	2	1	5,065
Flynkus	6	M	20	1	1	2	8,069
Flynn's Flash	5	G	8	0	0	0	810
Fly's to Honey	8	M	8	0	1	0	1,508
Flyswatter	4	F	4	1	0	1	1,400
Focus	4	G	9	0	0	0	564
Focus Factor	2	G	6	1	1	1	10,590
Focus On Marty	7	G	17	1	4	3	19,783
Foe Fives	3	G	15	1	5	2	12,215
Fog Bound	4	F	15	1	2	4	9,674
Fog Buster	3	C	1	0	0	0	0
Fog City Baby	7	M	2	0	0	0	236
Fog City Willy	7	G	11	5	0	2	95,660
Fogerty	5	G	11	1	2	2	10,425
Foggerinthevalley	3	F	3	0	1	0	7,760
Foggia	3	F	16	6	0	1	41,711
Foggy Dew	5	M	8	2	0	0	6,719
Foggy in Seattle	4	F	5	0	0	0	310
Foggy Song	8	G	2	0	0	0	91
Foglifter	3	F	4	0	0	0	200
Foglin	4	F	9	0	2	2	1,726
Foglite Flanker	2	G	1	0	0	0	0
Foiled Again	6	H	4	0	0	0	740
Foist	2	F	2	0	1	0	11,180
Folderol	4	G	5	1	0	0	5,400
Foley's Halo	6	H	17	1	6	2	25,715
Foley's Pub	5	G	10	1	0	1	6,991
Folk Art	2	F	2	0	0	0	0
Folkestone Park	4	C	4	0	0	0	880
Follies Dancer	6	M	10	0	2	1	9,719
Follow Betsy	4	F	6	2	0	1	58,560
Follow Me Home	3	F	12	5	1	1	196,340
Follow My Smoke	4	G	11	3	1	2	21,880
Follow the Queen	3	F	1	0	0	0	0
Following a Notion	5	M	10	1	0	1	8,690
Following Lead	7	H	2	0	0	0	225
Followmefools	3	C	7	0	0	0	305
Folly's Popalolly	5	M	7	0	0	0	310
Folly's Son	7	G	2	0	0	0	183
Folton	3	G	6	1	1	0	4,352
Fon Fon	3	F	4	0	1	1	4,706
Fond	2	F	5	2	1	0	59,250
Fong's Thong	2	C	3	1	1	1	27,400
Fontanero	4	G	11	2	2	1	18,890
Fonzie	6	H	7	0	0	2	2,250
Fonz's	4	G	4	0	2	1	25,660
Food Chain	3	C	5	0	0	0	847
Fool Crazy	4	C	3	0	0	0	1,000
Fool Proof Appeal	3	C	2	1	0	0	4,605
Fool Proof Pursuit	4	G	3	0	1	1	2,400
Fool You	5	H	1	0	0	0	127
Foolah Rullah	3	C	2	0	0	0	784
Fooled Again	7	M	13	2	1	3	10,545
Fooled Ya	4	G	8	0	0	0	2,114
Fooler	3	G	12	2	0	3	22,180
Foolin Type	3	F	14	1	5	3	16,188
Foolish Act	2	C	3	1	0	0	13,536
Foolish Collier	4	C	1	0	0	0	0
Foolish Colors	3	G	2	2	0	0	2,400
Foolish Day	3	G	2	0	0	0	438
Foolish Eyes	8	G	1	0	0	0	54
Foolish Fire	5	M	8	1	1	1	6,999
Foolish Gal	3	F	2	0	0	0	580
Foolish Gamble	4	G	1	0	0	0	0
Foolish Gator	7	M	6	1	0	0	39,396
Foolish Groom	2	G	2	0	1	0	3,600
Foolish Jones	4	G	14	1	2	2	17,134
Foolish Kiss	5	M	2	0	1	0	6,435
Foolish Litigation	4	G	3	0	0	0	155
Foolish McClassic	4	F	2	0	0	0	0
Foolish Megan	5	M	6	0	0	1	5,430
Foolish Moon	2	F	5	0	1	1	6,100
Foolish Paradise	3	G	2	0	0	2	2,750
Foolish Pride	4	C	7	0	0	1	5,240
Foolish Raja	6	G	16	1	1	4	27,552
Foolish Sunny	4	G	3	0	0	0	180
Foolish Times	5	M	11	0	3	0	6,531
Foolish Zeal	4	F	13	2	0	4	8,655
Foolishly	2	F	5	3	0	0	80,456
Foolofit	2	F	2	1	0	0	4,063
Fool's Boy	2	C	3	0	0	0	525
Fools Day	2	C	4	0	1	1	4,820
Fools Day Dream	3	G	3	0	0	0	0
Fool's Detente	3	F	9	0	1	4	3,614
Fool's Game	4	F	8	2	0	1	11,619
Fool's Last Word	5	M	17	2	2	3	13,414
Fools Mate	4	F	16	2	5	5	28,695
Fools Rush In	3	C	8	0	2	0	4,920
Fool's Twister	3	C	2	0	0	0	340
Foolsn Their Money	3	C	2	0	0	0	0
Foot On the Floor	3	G	7	3	0	1	21,135
Foot Trick	2	C	3	0	0	1	5,495
Footlights	3	F	10	1	0	4	38,535
Footloose Louie	3	G	2	0	0	0	50
Foots	6	H	8	0	0	2	10,509
For a Fee	5	H	8	0	1	2	9,700
For a Song	3	F	4	0	0	0	150
For All Who Dream	2	F	3	2	1	0	83,550
For All You Girls	4	F	9	2	2	1	10,447
For Angel	2	G	4	0	1	0	1,875
For Bailey's Sake	5	M	8	2	0	1	14,416
For Cash Only	3	G	11	1	0	1	9,905
For Cindy	3	F	2	0	0	0	0
For Fun	3	F	15	1	1	2	31,570
For Gillian	2	F	2	0	0	0	2,160
For Gold	3	C	5	1	1	2	29,420
For Gold's Sake	4	F	11	1	0	0	15,475
For Liberty	4	G	13	3	0	0	17,398
For Lili	7	M	8	1	0	4	20,695
For Love and Honor	6	G	11	1	0	4	58,890
For Love of Darby	4	F	8	0	0	0	2,188
For Love of Matt	3	F	8	1	0	0	8,611
For Me Too	4	C	2	0	0	0	0
For Midge	5	M	11	2	4	1	26,448
For My Angel	3	F	6	1	2	1	18,800
For My Pleasure	5	M	17	1	3	5	31,770
For My Soul Mate	4	F	2	0	0	0	0
For My Wife	2	F	8	1	3	1	52,660
For Old Times Sake (GB)	9	H	4	1	0	0	3,276
For Paul's Sake	3	G	3	1	1	0	8,981
For Rubies	4	F	9	3	1	0	138,873
For Sale	6	M	2	0	0	0	136
For Tapper	4	C	5	0	0	0	0
For the Dream	5	G	1	0	1	0	1,340
For the Fdny Heros	3	C	14	1	2	2	43,770
For the Love	7	M	3	0	0	1	2,025
For Your Love	2	F	1	0	0	0	500
Forafewdollarsmore	4	C	5	2	0	0	14,160
Foramusementonly	4	F	10	1	1	3	36,885
Foran Gap	3	F	9	0	2	3	5,635

Horse	Age	Sex	Sts	1st	2d	3d	Won
Forawingandaprayer	4	C	1	0	0	0	0
Foray	5	G	19	2	4	5	13,636
Forbes Baby	4	F	5	0	0	0	310
Forbes Creek	3	C	5	1	2	1	28,860
Forbes Falcon	4	F	13	0	0	0	650
Forbes Gunner	3	G	9	0	0	0	585
Forbes Halo	5	G	8	2	0	0	6,111
Forbes Landing	11	G	5	0	1	0	1,008
Forbes Money	5	G	1	0	0	0	0
Forbettysboyz	5	G	10	1	1	4	15,252
Forbid	11	G	3	0	0	1	490
Forbidden Apple	8	H	1	0	0	1	57,360
Forbidden Dance	4	F	6	1	0	2	11,605
Forbidden Fruit	3	F	2	1	0	0	15,360
Forbidden Gold	5	G	16	0	3	5	32,300
Forbidden Horizon	7	H	8	2	1	0	5,745
Forbidden Queen	2	F	8	3	2	1	110,794
Forbidden Star	3	F	1	0	0	0	360
Forbidden Zone	3	F	12	0	2	1	6,816
Forbiddenchocolate	2	F	6	0	0	0	790
Forbidissi Is Easy	4	F	1	0	0	0	81
Force Above	6	M	2	0	0	0	58
Force Five Wind	4	G	5	0	0	0	348
Force Forty Nine	3	G	9	2	3	0	14,340
Force in Excess	5	H	13	2	3	0	4,298
Force King	4	G	12	1	3	3	17,026
Force Ministre	4	G	3	0	0	0	685
Force the Way	3	F	4	0	2	0	11,900
Forced Gump	3	G	5	0	0	0	242
Forcedaccount	3	C	1	0	0	0	0
Forceful Guy	8	G	9	0	0	0	576
Forces Command	2	C	3	0	0	1	4,550
Ford Every Stream	4	C	7	2	1	0	102,110
Ford's Creek	5	H	5	1	0	0	11,790
Fore Payne	4	G	8	3	0	0	10,004
Foreal	4	F	19	5	1	3	28,016
Foreboding	6	G	2	0	0	0	0
Foregone	4	C	2	0	0	0	0
Foregone Reason	7	M	7	0	2	0	3,453
Foreign Accent (GB)	4	G	5	1	0	0	11,300
Foreign Authority	4	G	16	1	2	2	11,334
Foreign Beux	2	G	5	2	0	0	28,215
Foreign Cash	6	M	5	1	1	0	8,255
Foreign Cat	4	F	1	0	0	0	125
Foreign Conspiracy	3	F	8	2	0	0	6,051
Foreign Dance	4	F	1	0	0	0	0
Foreign Episode	3	G	3	0	0	0	120
Foreign Festival	9	G	3	0	0	0	94
Foreign Fighter	5	G	6	1	1	1	4,192
Foreign Flame	7	G	8	2	1	2	16,485
Foreign Image	6	G	10	1	0	1	9,472
Foreign Justice	2	C	8	2	2	2	18,661
Foreign Kiss	4	F	11	0	1	2	2,701
Foreign Mamatwo	4	F	7	1	0	0	6,750
Foreign Melody	3	C	3	0	2	0	5,188
Foreign Money	4	C	7	0	0	0	0
Foreign Princess	3	F	2	0	0	0	0
Foreign Robber	4	F	8	0	0	1	2,832
Foreign Royalty	5	G	2	1	0	0	2,775
Foreign Secretary	6	G	7	3	0	4	69,190
Foreign Slew	3	F	19	1	3	2	6,602
Foreign Vengeance	8	H	9	0	1	1	2,475
Foreing Banker	5	M	14	1	0	0	4,526
Forest Bo K	2	F	2	1	1	0	20,800
Forest City	6	G	16	1	5	1	11,257
Forest Cricket	3	G	10	3	2	0	29,420
Forest Dancer	2	F	1	0	0	1	1,100
Forest Deputy	7	H	8	0	0	0	1,735
Forest Flora	4	F	2	0	0	0	575
Forest Flute	3	F	4	0	1	0	9,945
Forest Grove	2	C	2	0	0	0	350
Forest Heir	5	H	1	0	0	0	693
Forest Heiress	4	F	7	2	1	0	118,003
Forest Kitty	2	F	2	0	0	1	3,500
Forest Landing	3	G	4	3	1	0	84,223
Forest Legend	5	H	5	2	0	0	25,620
Forest Lullaby	3	F	3	0	1	0	6,280
Forest Monarch	6	H	3	0	1	0	462
Forest Music	2	F	4	1	0	1	23,676
Forest Native	3	F	2	0	0	1	7,680
Forest Picnic	3	G	4	1	2	0	33,760
Forest Pine	5	G	11	0	0	0	2,250
Forest Princess	6	M	1	0	0	0	3,000
Forest Prospect	3	F	8	0	0	3	8,054
Forest Rain	3	G	9	0	2	1	14,611
Forest Secrets	5	M	4	0	0	2	30,467
Forest Shadows	3	F	7	3	0	0	105,820
Forest Smoke	7	G	8	1	0	3	7,818
Forest Snitch	4	C	6	1	1	0	31,120
Forest Waltz	4	G	5	1	0	0	4,516
Forest Wild Flower	3	F	8	0	0	3	8,889
Forestier	2	F	1	1	0	0	27,000
Forestina	2	F	2	0	0	0	1,260
Forestville	4	G	9	1	2	2	3,645
Foretell	5	G	17	2	4	2	12,832
Foretold (IRE)	3	G	5	0	1	1	3,308
Forever Amber	4	G	15	1	2	0	30,340
Forever Auburn	4	F	13	2	1	4	26,348
Forever Bad Secret	5	M	3	0	0	1	4,270
Forever Buzzing	3	C	4	0	2	1	5,940
Forever Daisy	5	M	3	0	0	0	651
Forever Diligent	3	F	12	0	2	2	31,490
Forever Eve	2	F	1	0	0	0	217
Forever Flawless	2	F	7	0	0	2	4,208
Forever Gold	5	G	9	0	1	3	4,393
Forever Grand	4	G	10	4	0	3	385,120
Forever Holy	5	M	2	1	0	0	3,630
Forever in Love	5	M	10	6	2	0	75,132
Forever Is Forever	3	F	2	0	0	0	0
Forever Jan	4	F	10	3	5	1	15,086
Forever Joe	3	C	8	0	2	2	23,800
Forever Joy	2	F	5	1	0	3	15,490
Forever Kris	3	F	1	0	0	0	350
Forever Lass	5	M	9	3	0	2	21,555
Forever Loving	3	F	1	0	1	0	1,425
Forever Luck	4	F	4	0	0	0	822
Forever Lucky	4	F	13	2	1	0	17,212
Forever Monteiro	4	G	17	5	5	5	69,170
Forever Naevus	3	F	17	3	0	2	19,704
Forever Now	3	F	7	0	2	2	24,060
Forever Partners	3	F	2	1	0	1	26,960
Forever Phyl	3	G	13	1	3	3	14,438
Forever Plus Two	4	F	2	0	0	0	90
Forever Rafter	3	F	3	1	1	0	15,200
Forever Ready	4	F	8	0	1	3	16,820
Forever Regal	5	M	13	1	4	1	31,110
Forever Running	5	H	11	1	4	3	60,580
Forever Singing	2	F	1	0	0	0	126
Forever Sonic	8	M	4	0	0	0	459
Forever Sunshine	4	C	10	2	2	0	10,742
Forever Talc	9	G	7	0	1	0	2,700
Forever Timeless	5	M	7	2	0	0	6,982
Forever Valid	8	H	11	0	1	3	4,225
Forever Yours	3	C	3	0	0	0	288
Forevercharismatic	2	F	2	0	0	0	120
Foreverinmyheart	3	F	1	0	0	0	0
Foreverme	7	G	10	0	0	0	772
Foreverness	4	G	5	1	1	2	56,580
Forevers Deniro	3	F	3	1	0	0	6,885
Forewarned	3	F	7	1	1	0	13,070
Forfreeit'sforme	4	C	3	0	0	0	348
Forge Away	5	H	4	1	0	1	9,935
Forget the Judge	4	G	8	0	2	0	27,494
Forget the Punch	2	C	7	1	0	2	14,870
Forgin' Ahead	5	G	14	1	2	2	9,162
Forgiveable Sin	2	G	8	1	2	1	20,700
Forgone Conclusion	2	C	3	0	0	0	930
Forgotten Deposit	6	H	4	0	0	0	651
Forgotten Girl	5	M	1	0	0	0	35
Forgotten Photo	7	H	2	0	0	0	81
Forgotten Promise	2	F	3	0	0	0	3,400
Foriegn Deputy	6	G	10	0	2	1	8,079
Fork It Over	3	F	7	0	0	0	4,487
Forlaan	6	G	13	5	1	0	124,200
Forlec	2	C	1	0	0	0	0
Forli Fedora	3	F	12	0	0	2	662
Forli's Chance	3	F	1	0	0	0	42
Forli's Con Man	2	G	8	2	1	1	23,295

RECORDS OF HORSES

Horse	Age	Sex	Sts	1st	2d	3d	Won	Horse	Age	Sex	Sts	1st	2d	3d	Won
Forli's Jig	9	G	6	0	1	2	3,670	Forthelifeofme	3	F	5	2	0	0	52,040
Forli's Mist	6	M	2	0	0	0	250	Fortifier	6	H	1	0	0	0	114
Forli's Pronto	4	F	1	0	0	0	40	Fortify	3	G	9	0	1	0	2,725
Forli's Seminole	4	C	6	2	1	0	10,886	Fortiguns	5	H	3	0	0	0	0
Formada (ARG)	5	M	10	1	3	1	48,901	Fortress Hill	2	F	1	1	0	0	35,280
Formal Affair	5	M	7	0	0	0	780	Fortuitous	3	F	2	0	1	0	15,000
Formal and Fancy	3	F	18	2	4	4	35,660	Fortuna Vena	3	F	12	0	3	2	10,634
Formal Attire	3	C	6	2	2	0	81,200	Fortunate Angel	2	F	10	1	1	1	16,835
Formal Beau	3	C	5	0	0	0	1,416	Fortunate Buy	2	C	3	1	1	0	18,455
Formal Charade	3	C	6	0	1	1	16,945	Fortunate Caitlin	5	M	14	0	5	2	18,540
Formal Cowgirl	3	F	6	1	0	0	11,360	Fortunate Caller	2	C	10	1	2	0	9,365
Formal Dancer	3	F	6	0	0	0	2,250	Fortunate Card	3	F	3	0	0	0	1,440
Formal Deal	3	F	4	0	0	0	1,764	Fortunate Chance	3	F	7	1	1	1	11,140
Formal Decree	3	G	8	2	1	0	43,870	Fortunate Damsel	2	F	3	0	0	1	7,890
Formal Diplomacy	3	G	17	4	2	2	17,450	Fortunate Fastplay	6	M	2	0	0	0	615
Formal Escape	3	C	10	2	1	0	30,870	Fortunate Glory	4	F	12	1	0	1	9,585
Formal Event	3	C	13	5	3	0	85,250	Fortunate Guy	5	H	5	1	0	0	8,400
Formal Fanny	2	F	11	1	4	1	18,135	Fortunate Honor	3	F	9	2	2	1	14,388
Formal Feast	8	G	19	5	3	2	50,128	Fortunate Island	2	C	5	0	3	0	4,825
Formal Finish	2	C	1	0	0	1	3,630	Fortunate Kris	3	C	8	0	2	1	6,212
Formal Green	7	G	10	1	0	3	7,570	Fortunate Match	3	F	13	2	2	1	15,786
Formal Hadif	4	C	2	0	1	0	900	Fortunate Mia	4	F	10	1	1	1	9,759
Formal Jackie	3	F	12	0	0	3	10,835	Fortunate One	5	G	11	4	1	1	30,545
Formal Lady	2	F	11	1	1	2	12,445	Fortunate Romeo	7	H	9	0	1	2	6,900
Formal Lass	3	F	6	1	1	2	11,874	Fortunate Royal	4	C	10	4	0	0	37,750
Formal Meeting	7	H	9	1	2	2	8,526	Fortunate Son	2	C	1	0	0	0	0
Formal Miss	3	F	11	2	3	5	163,690	Fortunate Streak	8	G	4	0	1	0	3,600
Formal Night	3	F	6	0	1	2	10,134	Fortunate Swing	3	F	15	0	5	1	19,771
Formal Odyssey	3	F	4	0	2	0	8,020	Fortunate Winds	6	G	10	2	4	0	23,340
Formal Pass	2	C	8	2	0	0	24,800	Fortune Catcher	2	G	8	1	2	1	24,500
Formal Prince	4	C	6	0	0	1	1,350	Fortune Dane	3	G	13	0	2	1	28,556
Formal Process	4	F	1	0	0	0	0	Fortune n' Fame	5	H	6	0	0	2	3,960
Formal Raise	3	G	20	2	3	1	20,328	Fortune Seeker	2	F	5	0	1	0	2,670
Formal Regards	6	H	6	0	0	0	2,970	Fortune Won	2	F	6	1	0	1	6,207
Formal Salute	5	G	6	0	0	1	3,590	Fortune Writers	3	C	7	1	1	2	60,460
Formal Sportswear	3	F	5	1	0	0	5,130	Fortunes' Bounty	3	G	12	3	2	0	49,997
Formal Tricks	2	F	3	0	0	1	900	Fortune's Fancy	4	C	5	1	1	0	8,181
Formal Victory	3	F	13	1	4	4	12,980	Fortune's Glitter	3	F	5	0	1	1	5,202
Formality	5	G	10	1	1	1	18,438	Fortunes of Gold	8	G	7	2	0	0	5,860
Format	2	F	1	1	0	0	8,700	Fortuoso	9	H	3	0	0	0	260
Formia	4	F	15	2	0	2	13,931	Forty Below Zero	3	F	5	0	0	1	2,146
Formidable Fox	3	C	9	0	1	0	7,120	Forty Dolls	3	F	10	1	0	2	23,106
Formidable Gold	3	C	2	1	0	0	11,460	Forty Durango (ARG)	5	H	9	2	0	2	13,275
Formidable Storm	2	F	2	0	1	1	5,580	Forty Ensign (ARG)	4	C	5	0	1	0	6,440
Formidibull	2	C	2	0	0	0	920	Forty Ensueno (ARG)	4	C	4	1	0	2	29,520
Formosa Strait	3	C	6	1	0	0	13,535	Forty Five	2	C	2	0	0	1	5,255
Form's Illusion	2	F	1	0	0	0	93	Forty Fiver	3	G	12	0	4	0	24,628
Forrer Hall	4	G	3	0	0	1	1,290	Forty Floozies	2	F	2	0	0	0	0
Forrest Gomp	3	G	6	0	0	1	1,940	Forty Foot Fred	4	G	3	1	0	0	5,370
Forrest Lane	6	G	7	2	0	1	13,748	Forty Forth Anna	3	F	11	1	0	3	12,907
Forrore	3	G	3	0	0	0	350	Forty Four	8	G	7	0	0	0	165
Forsberg	7	G	7	5	0	1	26,808	Forty Karats Jade	7	G	14	0	1	1	8,024
Forseeable Future	3	G	17	1	2	2	17,286	Forty Knots	3	G	11	0	0	1	2,550
Fort	4	G	8	1	1	0	15,734	Forty Languido (ARG)	5	H	7	0	0	0	1,740
Fort Alex	3	C	11	0	0	2	4,895	Forty Lengths	4	G	5	1	1	0	26,050
Fort Bragg	3	C	9	2	2	0	19,805	Forty Licks	2	F	2	0	0	0	260
Fort Carson	3	C	5	0	1	3	8,350	Forty Marinesca (ARG)	5	M	10	1	3	1	73,588
Fort City	8	G	2	0	0	0	134	Forty Milito (ARG)	5	H	9	4	1	0	125,640
Fort Conquest	4	C	4	0	0	0	746	Forty Moves	2	F	6	1	3	0	53,200
Fort Coventry	4	C	2	0	0	0	0	Forty Nine Again	6	H	9	1	0	1	6,524
Fort Donna	5	M	1	0	0	0	0	Forty Nine Deeds	4	C	13	1	1	2	49,290
Fort Jill	3	F	11	1	1	1	8,474	Forty Nine Shines	4	F	9	1	1	2	6,806
Fort Kitonia	5	M	2	0	0	0	204	Forty Niner Course	4	G	14	2	1	3	14,183
Fort Masada	3	G	6	0	2	0	12,925	Forty Niner Gold	3	G	13	1	2	0	22,310
Fort Meigs	3	F	3	0	0	0	142	Forty Niner Sweep	5	G	13	0	3	4	7,130
Fort Metfield	9	G	13	2	4	4	29,038	Forty On Line (GB)	4	F	1	0	0	0	0
Fort Monmouth	4	C	5	0	0	0	3,800	Forty One Bucks	4	F	7	0	0	1	577
Fort Nick	3	G	11	0	0	1	1,210	Forty Pureza (ARG)	5	M	17	3	3	2	44,935
Fort Out East	6	G	11	0	1	1	2,255	Forty Rubies	3	F	4	0	0	0	0
Fort Point	4	G	6	1	1	0	13,460	Forty Second St.	3	C	8	0	0	1	10,029
Fort Prado	2	C	2	0	0	1	4,640	Forty Seven	5	M	9	0	3	2	16,359
Fort Rocky	3	C	9	0	0	2	3,160	Forty Si (ARG)	5	M	6	0	0	1	6,036
Fort Ross	7	G	12	3	2	1	13,060	Forty Socks	3	G	1	0	0	0	0
Fort Shananie	6	H	10	2	1	2	14,055	Forty Something	3	G	2	0	0	0	0
Fort Smith	3	C	4	1	0	2	29,140	Forty Star	3	C	4	1	0	0	17,640
Fort Teller	4	C	6	0	0	0	1,770	Forty Sweeps	3	C	9	2	0	2	7,956
Forteyounzer	5	G	12	1	0	1	8,413	Forty Three Steph	5	M	8	2	0	1	9,857
Forthcoming	2	C	3	1	0	0	7,200	Forty Times	4	F	15	3	2	5	12,746
Forthegoodguys	6	M	19	2	3	6	22,225	Forty Two Slew	3	F	17	2	1	2	15,115

Horse	Age	Sex	Sts	1st	2d	3d	Won
Forty Wins	5	G	1	0	0	0	0
Fortynineacrewest	4	C	3	2	1	0	39,170
Fortyninejules	3	F	4	0	0	0	880
Forty's Boy	3	G	3	0	0	0	0
Fortyseven Plus	3	C	2	0	0	0	340
Fortywon Thirtysix	3	G	11	3	3	1	28,910
Forum Rules	2	C	4	1	1	1	23,650
Forum Search	4	F	8	1	3	0	63,432
Forum Way	4	F	9	1	0	0	17,606
Forward Impact	3	F	7	1	0	0	11,130
Forward March	6	R	11	4	2	2	155,616
Fo's Lad	5	H	4	0	0	0	124
Fossie's Chequer	4	F	15	0	2	1	3,682
Fossie's Claire	4	F	10	2	1	1	7,057
Fossie's Jill	4	F	2	1	0	0	4,356
Fosston	5	G	9	0	0	0	1,032
Foster Hill	7	G	5	0	0	0	557
Foster's Landing	5	H	10	1	3	0	76,910
Fostress	3	F	16	6	3	2	70,190
Fotocat	3	C	5	1	0	0	10,416
Fotogenico (ARG)	5	H	3	0	0	1	3,650
Foufa's Warrior	3	G	10	1	1	3	257,358
Foul Rift	10	G	2	0	0	0	116
Foul Weather	6	G	14	1	3	3	18,701
Found a Nickle	6	G	14	1	1	3	9,118
Found Her	3	F	7	1	2	1	30,100
Found My Way	3	G	5	0	0	0	3,680
Founded On Truth	2	C	1	0	0	1	1,485
Founding Chairman	3	G	7	3	2	2	101,005
Fountain Grove	2	C	4	1	2	0	39,346
Fountain Ridge	2	F	5	0	0	1	3,690
Fountain Valley	5	M	6	0	0	0	136
Fountainoffire	5	H	4	0	0	1	1,872
Four Acres	2	G	4	0	0	0	180
Four Alert	6	H	15	2	1	1	93,837
Four and Out	7	H	4	1	1	0	13,720
Four Anne Affair	5	M	10	0	3	2	14,330
Four Bagger	3	C	8	0	3	0	8,580
Four Beers	3	G	2	0	0	0	1,680
Four Bucks N a Doe	4	F	4	0	0	2	280
Four Card Bob	8	G	7	1	2	2	5,670
Four Cards Too	4	G	14	6	2	1	50,491
Four Checker	4	G	10	0	0	0	15,645
Four Columns	2	C	3	1	1	1	26,370
Four Corners	4	G	12	3	2	1	50,373
Four F Regal Bar	6	G	4	0	0	1	396
Four Fifteen	7	H	8	0	0	0	536
Four for Four	6	G	5	1	1	1	5,448
Four Girls	4	F	16	0	4	4	18,846
Four Janet	2	F	4	0	0	2	2,666
Four K's Dream	4	F	9	0	0	0	129
Four Majors	3	C	10	2	2	1	61,040
Four Not Five	3	F	4	1	0	0	4,287
Four Oclock Ruby	4	F	10	1	1	1	21,680
Four On a Match	4	G	13	1	0	4	8,868
Four Pennies	4	F	6	1	1	2	38,559
Four Plus Four	6	M	3	0	1	1	20,500
Four R Approval	3	G	9	1	1	2	33,230
Four Runner	5	G	2	0	0	0	0
Four Seas	4	F	5	0	1	0	3,360
Four Seasons	7	M	3	0	0	0	101
Four Secrets	3	G	8	0	1	1	3,640
Four Song Limit	2	C	5	0	0	3	7,400
Four Speed	3	F	6	1	0	0	7,229
Four Star Admiral	4	C	8	2	1	1	3,218
Four Storms	5	G	4	0	1	0	1,382
Four Sweeper	4	G	3	1	0	0	5,460
Four Tens At Once	3	F	8	1	0	1	4,415
Four Times a Charm	5	M	12	1	1	1	17,485
Four Twenty Seven	3	F	6	2	1	2	14,313
Four Two Won	4	G	4	1	1	0	10,494
Four Winds	4	F	9	1	3	0	11,510
Four Wind's King	5	H	4	0	0	0	425
Fouratsee	6	H	7	0	0	0	330
Fourbaysthenagrey	4	F	3	0	0	0	0
Fourcarrotdiamond	7	M	8	1	2	1	27,533
Fourchon	3	G	6	0	1	0	2,000
Fourforty	4	G	9	0	0	1	985
Fourjaysstormynite	3	G	6	0	1	2	2,945
Fourlitefeet	3	F	3	0	1	0	1,640
Fourpeppermary	3	F	8	0	2	1	7,340
Fours and Tens	6	H	20	2	1	4	10,752
Fourstargeorge	4	G	10	0	1	1	5,742
Fourteen Candles	3	F	7	2	0	0	60,005
Fourteen Ten	6	G	13	1	0	3	7,140
Fourteen Wishes	4	F	6	1	1	1	11,475
Fourth Act	9	G	3	0	0	0	426
Fourth Amendment	4	G	13	2	0	2	8,700
Fourth and Long	3	G	11	3	1	1	36,880
Fourth and Six	9	H	2	1	0	0	5,460
Fourth Commandment	6	G	13	3	2	2	47,901
Fourth Daughter	4	F	6	1	0	0	14,440
Fourth Down Gamble	2	G	4	0	0	1	1,100
Fourth Floor	5	H	11	3	2	2	93,168
Fourth of July	2	G	11	0	0	4	12,035
Fourth Round	5	H	11	2	4	2	12,406
Fourtheboys	3	F	11	0	5	4	14,871
Fourthirteen	2	G	3	1	0	1	13,000
Fourthirty	3	G	3	0	0	0	913
Fourtimesaruler	3	G	11	1	2	3	22,385
Fourty Bucks	5	G	10	1	0	2	7,266
Fourty Four Red	5	G	11	3	1	1	46,430
Fourwalls	3	C	9	0	1	0	2,237
Fourwayinheritance	5	G	21	1	4	4	8,695
Fourwaypress	3	G	10	4	1	3	30,665
Fowl Supper	8	M	13	1	4	1	31,709
Fox Me Not	5	M	5	0	0	0	570
Fox On Tour	5	G	11	1	1	1	13,900
Fox One	7	M	16	3	2	1	32,960
Fox Valley Toots	3	F	15	3	2	2	28,270
Foxann	5	M	2	0	0	0	696
Foxay Illusion	2	F	1	0	0	0	120
Foxboat	4	G	11	1	3	2	31,207
Foxey Jeblar	4	C	5	2	1	0	11,370
Foxey Viking	5	M	4	0	0	0	636
Foxeyfortyniner	4	G	5	0	0	0	904
Foxhat	3	F	8	1	0	0	5,046
Foxhole	5	H	11	0	3	2	7,075
Foxi Attitude	3	F	7	2	0	0	15,748
Foxie Bertie	2	F	7	3	1	0	36,919
Foxlair	3	G	9	2	3	1	39,770
Foxman	4	G	7	1	1	1	7,107
Foxs Bodacious Gal	5	M	7	2	1	0	16,685
Fox's Flyjinsky	9	G	8	1	1	2	20,020
Foxs Gold Digger	3	G	9	2	2	1	31,690
Fox's Grace	9	M	1	0	0	0	0
Fox's Legacy	3	G	12	0	1	2	6,639
Fox's Upper Place	9	G	1	0	0	0	0
Foxtail	4	F	8	1	0	1	4,589
Foxtrot Oscar	2	C	3	2	0	1	23,010
Foxwood Star	5	H	7	0	0	0	360
Foxworthy	3	G	7	1	2	1	76,115
Foxx On Fox	3	F	3	0	0	0	202
Foxy Allure	3	F	13	3	2	0	22,560
Foxy Beau	5	G	2	1	1	0	6,500
Foxy Bid	3	F	7	2	0	0	12,345
Foxy Blue Trail	3	F	11	3	1	1	14,032
Foxy Brick	4	F	2	0	0	0	188
Foxy Captain	3	G	14	6	3	1	91,228
Foxy Clout	3	F	11	0	0	0	1,599
Foxy Dear	4	F	5	1	0	1	5,690
Foxy Elena	2	F	7	1	1	1	9,108
Foxy Email	2	F	5	0	0	0	0
Foxy Feu	2	F	1	0	0	1	1,504
Foxy Fey	3	F	14	1	0	2	4,275
Foxy Friend	2	F	4	0	0	0	0
Foxy Fritzy	5	G	9	1	0	1	4,925
Foxy Frosty	4	F	2	0	0	0	137
Foxy Guy	3	G	10	3	2	1	23,615
Foxy J. R.	6	H	12	1	2	2	26,404
Foxy Jean	2	F	3	0	0	0	7,916
Foxy Jenny	4	F	15	2	4	4	12,937
Foxy Johnny	5	G	10	3	3	0	19,362
Foxy Julie	4	F	1	0	0	0	0
Foxy Kairewich	2	C	5	0	0	1	1,150
Foxy Lover	4	C	2	0	0	0	1,320
Foxy Ole'	4	F	6	1	0	1	3,213
Foxy Power	5	M	13	3	4	3	77,768

Horse	Age	Sex	Sts	1st	2d	3d	Won
Foxy Pro	4	F	7	1	0	2	22,726
Foxy Reason	3	C	1	0	0	0	70
Foxy Roxy	4	F	14	1	0	4	8,192
Foxy Scott	2	C	3	1	0	0	12,642
Foxy Walker	7	G	16	6	0	2	8,428
Foxy Wildcat	5	M	4	1	1	0	8,853
Foxy Woman	4	F	7	1	1	2	19,016
Foxyirish	3	C	6	1	1	0	11,949
Foxzy Lady	3	F	16	5	1	1	57,961
Fra Amici	7	M	8	2	1	1	6,720
Fra Cadfael	7	G	15	1	2	2	14,290
Frabjous Female	3	F	3	0	1	1	3,600
Fractured Sands	3	C	3	0	0	1	1,540
Fragrance	2	F	3	1	0	1	25,840
Fragrant	2	F	3	0	0	1	4,370
Fragrant Cloud	4	F	1	0	0	0	0
Fraidy Cat	2	F	4	1	1	0	10,738
Frajana	5	M	2	0	0	0	420
Frame of Mind	4	F	7	1	0	1	31,180
Fran	5	G	3	0	0	0	510
Fran the Man	3	G	8	0	1	0	7,793
Franbulo (CHI)	7	G	2	0	0	0	0
Franc	7	G	6	2	2	1	49,000
France	2	F	2	0	0	0	45
France (GB)	3	C	8	1	1	1	217,307
France Soir (CHI)	5	M	7	1	1	0	37,416
Frances Durden	3	F	6	1	0	0	5,824
Frances Wren	3	F	1	0	1	0	2,300
Franchise Player	3	C	10	4	2	2	70,725
Franci Dancer	2	F	7	0	1	2	5,910
Francis Albert	11	G	12	0	1	0	4,239
Francis Nolen	8	M	4	1	0	0	4,808
Francis' Tab	6	G	6	0	1	1	1,930
Francisco Villa	5	H	1	0	0	0	0
Franco	4	G	6	1	0	0	4,806
Franco Dinero	3	C	5	0	0	0	483
Franco Lobo	3	G	20	0	3	5	11,733
Francois	8	G	3	1	0	0	2,700
Frandon	2	C	3	0	0	0	216
Franescey	7	M	6	0	0	0	383
Franie Nannie	5	M	7	0	0	1	1,868
Frank Fencepost	3	G	4	0	0	0	0
Frank Headley	5	H	11	1	0	3	15,896
Frank Houser	3	G	13	1	2	2	10,325
Frank J	4	G	2	0	0	0	128
Frank T.	9	G	13	2	0	1	6,291
Frank the Fixer	6	H	5	1	1	0	13,823
Frank the Tank (AUS)	3	C	1	0	0	0	0
Frankatthebank	2	F	1	0	0	0	110
Frankie and Me	3	F	11	1	0	3	12,327
Frankie B	3	G	9	1	0	2	19,790
Frankie Baby	5	H	4	0	0	0	180
Frankie Eyelashes	4	F	1	0	1	0	3,200
Frankie R's Winner	4	G	13	4	5	2	133,138
Frankie the Cat	4	C	8	1	2	1	13,375
Frankiemarie	5	M	9	0	2	4	10,812
Frankie's Fire	3	C	10	0	4	0	41,740
Frankie's Gal	4	F	6	1	0	0	2,763
Frankie's Image	3	F	4	0	0	1	3,260
Frankies Oyster	7	G	13	1	1	2	6,708
Frankie's Star	4	F	14	0	2	1	26,922
Frankies Valentine	3	G	7	0	1	0	7,932
Franklin Manor	3	G	6	0	0	0	369
Franklin's Mint	7	M	2	0	1	1	2,400
Frankly Foolish	4	G	13	3	2	1	12,209
Frankly Tee Riffic	7	G	11	1	1	1	6,297
Franks Green Money	7	G	18	1	2	1	6,690
Frank's Quest	5	H	19	2	1	5	28,859
Frank's Rose	3	F	4	0	0	0	152
Frank's Selection	7	H	9	1	1	1	51,955
Franksgonhollywood	3	C	2	0	0	0	0
Frankston Orleans	5	M	9	0	2	0	7,392
Franny Maguire	5	G	8	0	1	0	8,900
Fran's Glory	4	F	3	0	0	1	2,044
Fran's Jet	2	G	1	0	0	0	0
Fran's Uncle Al	3	C	7	1	0	0	9,600
Franscat	7	F	3	0	0	2	10,060
Frantastic	3	G	11	2	6	1	35,657
Frantic Frenzy	6	M	2	0	0	0	0
Frantic Pace	2	C	3	0	0	1	4,250
Frapper Le Or	8	H	4	0	0	0	204
Frappuccino	7	G	15	2	2	3	8,368
Fraser Charm	6	M	12	2	1	0	12,134
Fraser Laser	5	G	4	0	0	0	203
Fraser Serenade	4	C	7	0	1	1	1,990
Fraserriversspell	3	G	15	3	2	0	21,576
Fraternity	2	G	6	1	0	0	8,740
Fratman	6	H	6	1	2	0	11,600
Frau Blucher	3	F	15	3	1	2	18,216
Fraulien Ruckus	5	M	13	0	3	2	20,751
Frazee's Folly	6	G	13	1	3	5	55,434
Frazzled	5	M	10	0	0	2	6,663
Freaky Feature	4	F	2	0	0	0	197
Freccia	4	F	10	0	0	1	3,772
Freckle Frick	2	F	8	0	2	1	9,760
Freckles Brown	6	G	12	2	3	0	13,515
Frecuente (CHI)	5	G	6	1	3	1	23,950
Fred and Me	3	C	7	0	5	0	18,710
Fred Bear Claw	9	G	5	0	0	1	4,180
Fred C. Dobbs	6	G	7	3	2	1	9,573
Fred Karno (ARG)	6	G	3	0	0	0	107
Fred N Annie	3	C	11	0	1	2	11,669
Fred of Gold	7	H	2	0	0	0	0
Freda Z	3	F	9	1	2	0	8,370
Freda's Diamond	2	F	5	0	1	2	5,174
Fredchens Jet	4	C	2	0	0	0	0
Freddi the Dancer	4	G	7	2	0	0	15,620
Freddie Freeloader	4	G	9	1	1	1	9,688
Freddie the Leader	5	G	10	0	1	1	7,246
Freddie's Folly	4	F	13	2	2	4	54,040
Freddie's Memories	4	C	17	2	3	3	29,125
Freddy Freeforall	5	G	6	0	0	3	1,144
Freddy K.	5	G	7	0	0	0	345
Freddy Kruger	3	C	16	2	3	1	18,173
Freddy Reymarco	4	C	13	1	5	0	18,410
Freddy White Shoes	3	C	6	1	0	0	9,500
Frederick Road	3	F	1	0	0	0	0
Frederick's Finest	5	H	6	0	0	0	546
Fredericksburg	3	C	8	1	0	0	16,375
Fredericktown	4	C	5	3	0	1	88,780
Frederiction	8	G	1	0	0	0	414
Fredexpo	5	G	12	3	2	1	15,529
Fredlea	6	G	9	2	0	3	38,990
Fredlyn	4	F	7	0	0	0	6,300
Fredosstealthcat	4	C	5	0	0	0	104
Fredrico	4	C	5	0	3	0	4,920
Freds Fortune	3	C	1	0	0	0	216
Fred's Notebook	3	G	2	0	0	0	880
Fred's Passion	4	C	9	2	1	1	12,897
Fred's Pentelicus	5	H	3	1	0	1	6,880
Freds Valentine	7	H	1	0	0	0	0
Fred'sniro	5	G	12	1	1	1	7,901
Free	8	H	4	0	0	0	3,120
Free Admission	4	G	1	1	0	0	15,000
Free After Five	2	G	4	0	0	0	350
Free Agent On Ice	6	G	6	0	0	2	9,904
Free and Bold	8	G	5	0	0	0	2,015
Free and Cagey	6	G	7	2	1	0	11,277
Free and Lucky	2	F	3	0	0	0	3,800
Free B's Flying	3	F	15	4	3	4	27,240
Free Cat	4	F	8	1	2	0	8,930
Free Cell	3	G	3	0	0	1	840
Free Chew	4	G	18	2	1	1	9,975
Free Cocktails	2	G	2	0	0	0	2,100
Free Corona	5	G	8	5	2	0	111,720
Free Doctor	2	F	7	0	1	0	6,003
Free Dreamin Kelly	2	F	10	1	1	2	9,903
Free Expresso	4	F	6	3	3	0	67,924
Free Flier	5	M	6	0	0	0	2,475
Free for All	6	M	3	0	0	0	318
Free for the Road	4	G	12	1	4	1	4,292
Free Forever	8	M	3	1	0	1	6,650
Free Hill	4	F	6	1	2	0	26,939
Free Ice	5	H	1	0	0	0	50
Free Jazz	8	G	9	0	1	1	1,837
Free Jet	4	F	7	0	0	0	171
Free Juice	4	F	11	5	1	1	74,577
Free Lance Dancer	5	M	14	1	1	1	7,539

Horse	Age	Sex	Sts	1st	2d	3d	Won
Free Love	2	F	5	0	1	1	2,338
Free Miles	2	F	1	0	1	0	1,540
Free My Soul	3	F	9	1	0	2	15,561
Free 'n Foxy	3	F	10	4	0	1	22,821
Free N Wild	2	C	6	1	0	1	10,216
Free of Love	5	H	12	0	2	5	105,907
Free On Ice	3	G	11	1	0	0	5,438
Free Pass	4	F	7	0	5	1	22,300
Free Play	4	F	12	3	1	1	36,806
Free Pour	3	G	11	3	2	1	43,839
Free Quarter Time	4	F	11	1	5	1	14,400
Free Queen	3	F	4	1	0	0	5,787
Free Rent	2	F	9	1	1	0	23,920
Free Rox	3	C	5	0	1	1	1,550
Free Rules	2	C	6	0	0	0	1,577
Free Runner	5	M	10	2	1	0	10,797
Free Scarlet	3	F	5	0	2	0	17,230
Free Shot	5	M	5	0	0	0	1,040
Free Speech	6	M	4	1	0	1	4,874
Free Spiritess	4	F	10	1	0	2	12,359
Free Strategy	3	G	8	0	0	0	345
Free Strike	2	F	1	0	0	0	195
Free Stylin'	3	F	8	0	2	1	7,809
Free the Mayor	4	G	10	1	0	1	4,057
Free Thinking	2	C	3	1	0	0	44,889
Free Thoughts	5	G	7	0	0	0	4,064
Free Tide	2	F	2	0	0	0	75
Free to Please	2	G	1	0	0	0	0
Free to Run	6	G	9	2	0	0	9,254
Free Will	7	G	3	0	1	0	2,422
Freeable	6	H	12	1	1	5	10,762
Freeaim Ruckus	6	H	11	1	2	1	7,574
Freedom	8	G	1	0	0	0	58
Freedom At Bay	3	C	2	0	0	0	135
Freedom Call's	4	F	10	0	0	0	4,050
Freedom Class	3	C	6	0	1	0	9,640
Freedom Come	4	F	4	2	2	0	126,280
Freedom Counts	2	C	8	2	2	0	47,270
Freedom Crest	7	G	1	0	0	0	3,000
Freedom Fighter	3	C	1	0	0	0	0
Freedom Forever	3	F	7	1	2	0	9,110
Freedom Highway	4	G	15	1	2	1	14,140
Freedom Hill	3	F	4	1	0	0	6,940
Freedom in Flight	2	F	1	1	0	0	4,620
Freedom Land (AUS)	5	G	5	0	0	0	2,160
Freedom Lane	3	C	6	2	1	0	32,075
Freedom Leader	4	G	8	1	3	2	2,978
Freedom March	3	F	10	1	3	1	11,700
Freedom of Depress	6	H	5	0	0	0	0
Freedom of Port	4	F	6	1	2	0	18,315
Freedom Onthe Wind	5	G	10	0	1	0	6,390
Freedom Peaks	2	F	6	0	0	2	3,090
Freedom Rd	6	M	8	1	0	4	7,625
Freedom Rider	3	G	2	0	0	0	225
Freedom Ridge	2	F	2	0	0	0	700
Freedom Roar	4	C	2	0	0	0	315
Freedom Song	3	G	11	2	1	0	22,037
Freedom Stand	2	G	1	0	0	0	123
Freedom Truth	2	C	1	0	0	0	0
Freedom Walk	3	G	14	2	0	0	11,537
Freedom Warrior	3	F	1	0	0	0	0
Freedom's Forum	2	F	7	1	0	2	35,385
Freedom's Honor	3	C	8	3	2	0	108,805
Freedom's Key	3	C	8	0	3	0	20,360
Freedoms Revenge	2	C	3	0	0	0	0
Freefourinternet	5	H	11	2	1	5	418,598
Freei	3	F	2	0	0	1	7,140
Freeland	3	F	13	1	0	1	21,717
Freely Bend	10	G	12	1	1	2	4,018
Freer	5	H	13	0	2	2	3,707
Freeroll	2	F	4	2	1	0	62,400
Free's Lil Lass	2	F	9	1	1	0	30,169
Freesia's Mist	5	M	13	2	4	3	17,893
Freestone	6	H	18	5	3	1	40,815
Freestyle Spirit	4	C	16	2	5	5	33,060
Freetobeme	3	F	7	3	2	0	16,165
Freeway Freddie	5	G	3	0	0	0	195
Freeway Ticket	5	H	2	0	0	1	3,520
Freewheelin Freddy	6	H	7	1	4	0	7,380
Freewheeling	3	F	2	0	0	0	0
Freeze a Roo	4	G	15	2	3	1	12,225
Freeze Alert	6	G	12	4	1	2	97,815
Freeze Bull	5	G	11	3	2	0	20,699
Freeze Em Out	3	F	2	1	0	0	10,614
Freeze the Win	3	G	6	0	1	0	2,653
Freezer	3	C	18	2	1	1	15,256
Freezin Frolic	2	F	4	0	3	0	7,240
Freeznbtweensheets	2	F	4	0	0	0	0
Freidalicious	3	F	3	1	0	0	3,110
Freight Liner	3	C	9	1	1	1	21,970
Freight Train Leo	6	G	2	0	0	0	176
Freire Tail	6	G	9	4	2	1	75,077
Frekle Asset	4	G	8	1	1	0	3,763
Fremont	2	C	1	0	0	0	0
French Account	2	F	3	0	0	0	660
French Affair	6	M	4	0	0	0	423
French Beat	5	M	4	0	1	0	1,792
French Bikini	3	F	1	0	0	0	175
French Bloomers	2	F	1	1	0	0	19,800
French Brandy	3	G	8	0	0	1	2,770
French Charmer	4	G	7	5	0	0	232,800
French Connection	7	G	5	0	1	0	1,800
French Cue	3	F	5	0	0	0	2,098
French Debutante	3	F	2	0	0	1	5,280
French Dish	2	F	3	1	1	1	57,705
French Embassy	2	G	2	0	0	0	125
French Fiction	6	G	5	0	0	0	445
French Flight	2	F	1	1	0	0	25,200
French Flirt	3	G	5	0	0	0	605
French Flower	7	M	9	0	2	0	5,255
French Guzzler	4	C	4	0	0	0	228
French Halo	2	C	4	0	0	0	0
French Hideaway	4	F	3	0	0	0	4,719
French Jeannette	3	F	6	1	1	1	27,642
French Joseph	9	G	6	1	0	0	6,858
French Lick	11	G	4	0	0	2	770
French Lieutenant	3	C	7	3	1	1	121,828
French Miss	5	M	9	1	2	0	13,820
French Packet	6	G	14	3	3	3	27,455
French Passion	6	H	1	0	0	0	360
French Pet	6	G	5	1	1	0	5,970
French Pistol	4	G	7	1	1	0	12,170
French Polo (FR)	3	G	8	3	3	0	78,005
French Prince	3	G	9	1	1	0	9,040
French Rascal	3	G	10	2	0	1	13,933
French Reign	6	M	5	0	0	0	975
French Republic	4	F	11	3	0	3	55,939
French Roast	2	C	5	0	3	0	23,115
French Satin	4	F	5	0	0	0	1,499
French Season	3	G	12	2	3	3	12,276
French Selection	3	G	9	2	0	1	33,650
French Silk	4	F	3	2	0	0	24,510
French Sizzler	4	C	1	0	0	0	77
French Smile (IRE)	5	H	11	3	2	1	50,340
French Snob	3	F	3	0	0	0	980
French Stinger	4	C	4	0	0	2	2,250
French Sunshine	3	F	4	0	0	0	310
French Teacher	7	M	10	3	0	2	40,818
French Toast	3	F	5	1	0	2	10,755
French Twist	5	M	15	6	3	3	43,414
French Victory	4	G	16	1	2	0	11,522
French Village	2	F	4	3	0	0	138,800
French Wedding	4	F	9	2	1	0	21,340
French Wench	3	F	7	1	2	1	7,690
Frenchglen	2	F	1	0	0	0	0
Frenchie	3	F	14	1	2	1	19,064
Frenchmore	3	G	9	1	0	4	8,819
Frenchys Native	5	H	1	0	0	0	44
Freon Flier	5	H	10	2	3	1	59,060
Frequent Meeting	3	F	12	2	0	1	30,445
Frere This	2	G	4	1	0	0	5,110
Fresal	3	F	7	1	1	4	60,332
Fresco	3	F	3	0	1	1	3,844
Fresh and Sassy	3	F	5	2	1	1	32,530
Fresh Believer	6	M	13	1	0	2	30,831
Fresh Broccoli	4	F	8	3	0	0	15,370
Fresh Combatant	9	G	1	0	0	0	1,200
Fresh King	2	G	3	0	1	0	12,940

Horse	Age	Sex	Sts	1st	2d	3d	Won
Fresh Magic	4	F	4	0	0	0	0
Fresh Mary B	8	M	1	0	0	0	110
Fresh Tarte	4	F	4	0	1	1	3,850
Fresh Thunder	4	G	11	3	2	1	57,913
Fresh Tracks	4	F	6	2	2	1	97,231
Fresh Victor	5	G	6	3	1	0	4,668
Freska	2	F	2	0	0	1	8,820
Fresquita	3	F	15	0	0	2	3,295
Freya's Fire	3	F	10	1	3	1	9,275
Friar Tuck	8	G	8	0	0	2	1,270
Fric's Falcon	4	C	7	1	1	1	5,840
Friday Morning	6	M	2	0	0	0	0
Friday's a Comin'	5	G	13	3	3	0	37,228
Fried Beans	9	G	5	0	0	0	559
Friel's for Real	3	F	5	1	0	2	22,770
Friend Forever	4	F	4	0	0	0	0
Friend of Mine	7	G	16	3	2	3	18,078
Friendly Act	2	G	5	1	2	0	9,015
Friendly Affair	2	G	7	1	1	1	17,085
Friendly Beau	3	C	3	0	0	0	502
Friendly Bidder	2	C	4	0	0	0	528
Friendly Bye Bye	2	F	2	0	0	0	175
Friendly Cat	4	F	1	0	0	0	130
Friendly Chad	7	G	1	0	0	0	0
Friendly Change	3	F	3	0	1	0	1,750
Friendly Cop	8	G	14	3	4	2	24,181
Friendly Departure	4	C	8	1	2	0	11,140
Friendly Dorcas	3	F	5	1	1	0	3,975
Friendly Dreamer	3	F	2	0	0	0	912
Friendly Flame	4	F	2	0	0	0	0
Friendly Fortune	3	G	1	0	0	0	56
Friendly Frolic	4	G	10	4	1	1	73,360
Friendly Gal	3	F	3	0	0	0	1,680
Friendly Girl	3	F	8	0	0	1	899
Friendly Heat	3	C	5	0	0	0	5,880
Friendly K J	3	G	6	1	0	0	2,316
Friendly Lass	4	F	13	2	3	3	12,080
Friendly Man	4	G	16	0	3	4	9,532
Friendly Man Do	5	H	3	0	0	0	700
Friendly Matt	4	G	1	0	0	0	100
Friendly Michelle	2	F	3	2	0	0	63,540
Friendly Mickey	3	F	11	3	3	3	27,975
Friendly Mike	3	C	4	0	1	0	11,440
Friendly Nation	5	G	1	0	0	0	0
Friendly Niner	2	G	4	0	0	0	430
Friendly Noble	3	G	4	0	0	0	622
Friendly Party	3	F	6	0	0	1	2,595
Friendly Pioneer	5	M	11	3	3	2	49,144
Friendly Sailor	5	H	12	0	3	3	5,684
Friendly Set	5	G	7	1	3	0	19,074
Friendly Slew	4	F	10	2	1	0	18,149
Friendly Theresa	3	F	14	5	1	3	77,100
Friendofthedevil	3	G	4	1	0	0	7,983
Friendofthefamily	3	F	9	4	1	1	55,010
Friends Lake	2	C	3	2	0	0	84,600
Friends N Family	4	F	1	0	0	0	140
Friendship Avenue	5	G	8	5	1	1	21,035
Friendship Bell	2	F	1	0	0	0	45
Friendship Ring	5	M	6	0	3	0	3,089
Friendship Terrace	2	F	2	0	1	0	8,350
Frigid Pleasure	5	G	1	0	0	1	580
Frigid Witch	3	F	4	0	0	2	2,030
Frigidon	4	G	15	1	2	0	8,357
Frillery	2	F	3	1	0	0	6,045
Frills	3	F	8	0	0	0	0
Frills and Ribbons	5	M	14	1	1	3	14,074
Frills and Thrills	5	M	12	5	1	2	50,226
Frilly Eight	4	F	2	0	0	0	96
Frilly Fun	4	F	14	3	2	1	45,042
Frilly Knight	6	M	4	0	1	1	692
Frilly Miss	4	F	2	2	0	0	8,900
Frilly Wake	5	M	4	1	0	0	3,365
Fringe Comment	3	G	12	1	0	1	10,846
Frio Flag	4	G	5	2	0	1	29,560
Frisby Flyer	2	F	4	0	0	0	172
Frisco	6	H	3	0	0	0	78
Frisco Belle	3	F	9	3	3	0	126,300
Frisco Breeze	4	G	11	0	2	2	1,860
Frisco Fog	2	C	3	1	0	0	5,605
Frisco Frisky	7	G	14	0	0	3	5,705
Frisco Johnny	3	G	12	4	2	1	69,625
Frisco Lady	5	M	5	0	0	0	456
Frisco Light	2	C	5	1	0	0	23,574
Frisco Racer	3	C	6	1	3	0	4,626
Frisco's Tower	3	F	1	0	0	0	0
Frisk for Jade	2	F	5	1	0	0	4,650
Frisk Me Later	2	F	2	0	0	0	95
Frisky Attitude	8	G	6	0	0	0	228
Frisky Boy	4	G	1	0	0	0	1,200
Frisky Devil	4	F	11	1	3	0	16,930
Frisky Kitty	5	M	4	1	0	0	9,000
Frisky Mood	3	F	3	0	1	1	1,419
Frisky Phoebe	5	M	3	1	0	0	12,615
Frisky Spider	2	C	1	1	0	0	13,200
Friskys Profit	2	C	2	0	0	1	1,515
Fritz Blitz	3	G	3	1	0	0	36,360
Fritzie's Prospect	5	M	7	0	2	1	22,886
Fritzi's Michelle	3	F	6	0	0	1	2,480
Fritzl	5	G	10	4	1	2	35,096
Fritzli	3	C	12	2	2	2	18,255
Fritz's Hope	4	G	2	0	0	1	576
Fritzy Hour	3	F	9	3	0	1	32,547
Frivolous Dare	5	G	3	0	0	0	186
Froehlich	7	G	15	1	1	1	8,441
Frog Point	3	G	5	0	0	0	420
Froggywentacourtin	10	G	7	2	0	0	13,780
Frognot	12	G	2	0	0	0	350
Frolic and Detour	4	C	1	0	0	0	0
Frolic Away	2	F	1	0	0	0	1,980
Frolic for Joy	2	C	1	0	0	1	2,145
Frolic in Da Sun	4	G	8	2	0	1	12,449
Frolic's Flash	6	H	2	0	1	0	1,062
Frolics Rumble	3	G	4	0	0	0	0
Frolicus	5	G	9	0	1	4	16,755
From A to Z	4	C	6	0	0	0	8,870
From Away	2	F	4	2	1	0	177,860
From B to B	2	F	7	0	0	0	1,110
From Charlie	3	G	1	0	0	0	123
From Dancin Hills	4	F	2	0	0	0	80
From Heaven Sent	3	F	2	0	0	0	0
From Mars	4	G	13	2	2	4	7,120
From Mike's Heart	4	C	7	1	0	1	7,110
From the Beginning	4	F	4	0	0	0	318
From the Word Go	3	F	1	0	0	0	220
From Your Lips	3	G	11	1	1	0	8,460
Frome	2	G	6	0	1	1	2,725
Fromheretobrazil	3	F	7	0	0	0	477
Fromheretoheaven	4	F	5	0	0	1	7,578
Fromheretothere	5	G	16	1	0	2	9,970
Fromoutoftheclouds	6	H	18	0	3	1	9,521
Fromthebackjack	3	F	10	1	2	3	19,270
Front	3	C	17	3	1	4	21,477
Front Cover Dreams	7	G	3	0	0	0	486
Front Line	2	F	5	1	1	0	26,335
Front Line Dancer	3	F	9	1	0	1	15,451
Front Nine	4	G	10	3	4	1	117,750
Front Paige Fox	4	F	4	2	0	0	3,470
Frontena Cat	4	G	5	1	1	2	7,640
Frontera Power	3	G	11	2	0	0	9,750
Frontier Groom	2	G	1	0	0	0	660
Frontier Image	2	G	4	0	0	0	501
Frontier Justice (IRE)	4	C	1	0	0	0	420
Frontier Man	2	C	5	0	0	0	3,036
Frontier Rider	8	G	5	0	1	0	1,873
Frontier Trail	6	G	6	0	0	0	405
Frontrera One	6	H	10	1	0	0	5,718
Frost N Honey	4	G	5	0	0	1	1,890
Frost Warning	3	C	7	0	1	3	26,470
Frosted Face	2	F	5	0	0	1	1,620
Frosteen	4	F	3	2	0	0	5,640
Frostoria	3	F	8	0	1	0	1,900
Frosty Alibhai	7	G	11	4	1	1	31,840
Frosty Badger	5	G	9	1	0	0	2,340
Frosty Breeze	5	M	7	0	1	0	3,604
Frosty Chick	5	M	3	0	0	0	192
Frosty Coco	5	G	14	4	1	1	19,416
Frosty Court	3	G	1	0	0	0	0
Frosty Delight	3	G	6	0	0	0	0

Horse	Age	Sex	Sts	1st	2d	3d	Won
Frosty Event	2	G	2	0	0	0	0
Frosty Face	2	G	5	1	1	0	9,592
Frosty Favors	4	F	3	0	0	1	615
Frosty Hill	3	C	5	3	0	1	10,420
Frosty Jester	6	M	2	0	0	0	40
Frosty La	7	M	2	0	0	0	326
Frosty Lady	4	F	11	1	1	0	4,625
Frosty Lady Love	9	M	5	0	2	3	6,920
Frosty Naylor	9	G	15	0	1	3	5,201
Frosty Note	4	F	16	4	0	3	41,435
Frosty Paws	3	G	12	0	0	1	9,237
Frosty Pop	3	C	14	1	3	2	12,625
Frosty Prince	4	G	13	3	1	1	16,298
Frosty Prospector	5	M	14	2	0	1	14,751
Frosty Quoit	11	G	1	0	0	0	40
Frosty Reason	2	G	2	0	0	0	0
Frosty Remark	5	M	9	2	2	0	24,554
Frosty Rox	5	M	9	1	0	1	3,696
Frosty Starlight	6	G	7	0	0	0	563
Frosty Tile	5	M	1	0	0	0	435
Frosty Weekend	2	F	2	0	0	1	1,573
Frosty's Babe	3	F	16	1	4	2	18,571
Frosty's Champ	3	G	12	1	1	1	12,333
Frosty's Course	5	C	5	1	0	0	9,510
Frosty's Pleasure	4	F	10	4	0	3	37,711
Frown'n	4	F	4	0	0	0	315
Frozen Account	6	M	1	0	0	1	153
Frozen Chosin	7	H	1	0	0	0	0
Frozen Dream	5	G	8	0	2	2	1,415
Frozen Fax	2	G	6	0	2	0	5,420
Frozen in Time	2	F	3	2	1	0	51,752
Frugal	5	G	4	0	1	1	4,618
Frugality	4	F	2	0	0	1	4,950
Fruit Rapport	6	H	5	1	3	0	3,635
Fruition's First	3	G	1	0	0	0	2,520
Fruition's Jasmine	3	F	7	1	1	0	11,650
Fruits	4	F	14	3	1	2	77,015
Fruits of Labour	3	F	10	1	0	1	35,116
Fruitsoup Olaf	4	G	4	0	2	1	8,631
Ft. Mann	4	F	11	3	3	3	96,406
Ft. Washington	4	G	4	0	0	0	675
Fuddy Buddy	5	G	6	1	1	1	4,600
Fuddy's Dream	2	F	2	0	0	0	57
Fudge	4	F	10	2	2	2	6,721
Fudge Fatale	3	F	11	2	2	1	92,020
Fue Follet Gris	3	G	3	0	0	1	3,300
Fuego Dancer	2	F	6	0	1	0	3,477
Fuego Maximo (ARG)	5	H	2	1	0	0	20,290
Fuego Popular	5	G	20	1	3	2	9,570
Fuelling	2	C	4	0	0	0	2,651
Fuente	4	F	14	3	1	1	14,548
Fugheddaboutit Sid	4	C	14	1	3	4	19,430
Fugitivo	4	C	4	0	0	2	3,181
Fuhr Elise	3	F	13	1	3	3	22,130
Fuhr Ore	3	G	7	1	3	1	31,280
Fuhr Real	3	F	4	0	2	0	6,100
Fuhrfy	3	G	4	0	0	0	268
Fuhrious Fraulein	3	F	1	0	0	0	530
Fuhrline	4	F	5	0	1	2	5,200
Fuhrluck	2	C	2	0	0	0	0
Fuhrmidable	3	F	7	0	1	1	5,190
Fuhry	4	G	18	2	2	4	28,840
Fulfillment	3	F	10	2	2	0	13,501
Fulham	4	G	9	1	5	1	6,794
Full	4	C	1	0	0	0	870
Full Account	4	G	11	0	2	3	3,987
Full Blown Storm	2	F	4	1	2	0	12,944
Full Brush	8	G	11	1	1	1	63,670
Full Carat	3	F	9	3	0	1	19,596
Full Champ	4	G	1	0	0	0	67
Full Clip	6	G	11	0	1	1	3,126
Full Command	8	G	7	0	1	0	2,335
Full Cooler	3	C	2	0	0	1	3,210
Full Cry	3	G	4	1	0	0	8,647
Full Disclosure	3	C	3	0	1	0	3,000
Full Dress Parade	6	G	4	0	0	0	0
Full Flow	6	H	7	0	0	2	13,520
Full Force Gale	6	G	8	1	2	2	23,325
Full Gainer	4	C	7	0	0	0	447
Full Legacy	4	C	1	0	0	0	0
Full Mandate	4	C	8	3	1	0	128,263
Full Moon Dancer	4	C	2	0	2	0	1,660
Full Moon Lady	5	M	4	1	0	0	18,480
Full Moon Madness	8	G	5	1	0	2	93,180
Full Moons Arisin	2	C	8	2	3	0	77,216
Full o' Glee	5	M	2	0	0	1	4,200
Full of Giggles	5	M	11	1	1	1	10,054
Full of Gratitude	4	C	2	0	0	0	180
Full of Luck	4	G	4	1	0	1	32,580
Full of Secrets	2	F	1	0	0	0	0
Full of Wonder	5	H	2	0	0	1	4,070
Full Response	5	H	11	2	0	1	8,347
Full Scream Ahead	7	M	8	1	1	2	32,600
Full Spectrum	4	F	8	2	2	0	109,690
Full Speed Ahead	5	G	14	2	2	1	14,687
Full Strike	5	G	1	0	0	0	0
Full Tank	3	G	5	0	0	2	8,065
Full Tilt	4	F	16	2	1	3	19,840
Full Time Dancer	3	F	7	3	0	0	47,190
Full Time Spirit	6	M	2	0	0	0	160
Full Tithe	4	C	5	0	0	0	380
Full Trick	3	C	7	1	2	0	1,772
Full Value	2	C	2	0	0	1	1,023
Fullajet	4	C	10	1	1	1	7,958
Fullblown Affair	4	C	14	1	2	1	6,170
Fuller's Delight	3	F	7	1	0	0	4,731
Fullpoint	3	G	10	0	0	0	2,966
Fully a King	5	H	2	0	0	0	0
Fully Charged	3	F	4	0	0	0	300
Fully Packed	4	G	15	6	3	2	57,958
Fully Vested	2	G	2	0	0	0	0
Fulmar Pockets	5	M	1	0	0	0	33
Fulton	3	G	4	0	1	1	10,032
Fumar	5	M	2	0	0	0	846
Fumph Around	2	C	8	1	0	2	24,950
Fun	6	M	3	0	0	1	1,158
Fun and Sun	5	H	5	0	1	0	13,260
Fun Forty-Niner	4	F	14	0	0	0	1,393
Fun Fum First	4	G	11	1	1	3	22,119
Fun Habit	2	F	3	0	0	0	900
Fun House	4	F	8	2	3	2	123,340
Fun in Motion	2	C	3	1	1	1	6,348
Fun Loving Jake	3	G	5	0	0	0	740
Fun Maggie	2	F	4	0	0	0	2,160
Fun On Ice	2	C	2	0	0	0	720
Fun Times Ahead	4	G	5	1	0	0	6,184
Fun to Fly	10	G	4	0	1	0	1,086
Funaroundthetable	4	C	7	0	2	2	2,495
Fund of Funds	3	C	5	1	2	1	143,170
Fundable	3	G	8	1	1	0	7,968
Fundamental	4	C	2	0	0	0	0
Funder Jam	2	C	1	0	0	0	180
Funewgie	2	G	3	0	0	0	1,519
Fungee	2	G	2	0	0	0	0
Funicello	3	F	2	0	0	0	0
Funinhawaii	3	G	2	0	0	0	2,100
Funky Cowboy	9	G	7	0	0	0	483
Funky Dancer	5	G	1	0	0	0	0
Funky Dude	5	G	4	1	1	1	11,814
Funky Habit	4	F	8	0	0	0	962
Funlovin	6	M	9	0	0	0	3,947
Funn in the Sunn	3	C	2	0	0	0	0
Fun'ngames Toknite	2	F	4	2	0	1	16,820
Funnin and Runnin	2	C	3	0	0	1	758
Funny Bone	5	M	9	2	0	1	40,950
Funny Cat	2	F	1	1	0	0	13,680
Funny Cide	3	G	8	2	2	2	1,963,200
Funny Colero	4	F	6	0	0	0	315
Funny Comet	5	M	2	0	0	0	186
Funny Farm	3	F	14	2	2	3	23,930
Funny Farmer	4	C	7	2	1	0	8,680
Funny Honey	2	F	3	1	1	0	32,800
Funny Meeting	4	C	7	3	4	0	115,347
Funny Mood (ARG)	4	M	9	3	0	0	68,600
Funny Numbers	6	G	17	4	4	0	19,388
Funny Secret	4	C	7	1	1	0	7,439
Funny Soldier	4	C	8	1	0	1	65,508
Funny Tom (ARG)	8	H	3	1	0	0	6,599

RECORDS OF HORSES

Horse	Age	Sex	Sts	1st	2d	3d	Won	Horse	Age	Sex	Sts	1st	2d	3d	Won
Funny Woman	3	F	5	0	0	0	1,834	G T' S Levendy	2	G	6	0	1	4	26,974
Funracer	3	C	2	0	0	0	1,640	G T'sstillbelievin	4	F	8	1	2	0	14,469
Funtime Freddie	3	G	11	1	2	0	9,295	G U Devil	4	F	14	1	3	2	12,044
Funtotouch	4	G	6	1	0	2	9,670	G W's Capote	6	G	3	0	0	0	0
Funzone	3	F	1	1	0	0	5,050	G. I. Dream	3	F	8	0	0	1	1,590
Fur Gohan	3	C	8	0	1	1	1,185	G. I. Speed	3	G	10	1	0	2	5,572
Furash Alert	4	F	9	2	2	1	10,247	G. P. Glove	7	G	2	1	1	0	1,624
Fureur France (IRE)	6	G	17	2	2	1	15,394	G. R's Dream	8	G	8	1	0	3	11,826
Furious Cat	3	C	4	1	1	0	36,780	G. Starr	4	F	10	3	2	0	42,402
Furious Chad	4	G	11	0	1	1	10,695	G. T.'s Gone West	3	F	12	2	1	2	59,377
Furious Fever	2	C	3	0	0	1	5,800	G. W.'s Deputy	5	G	10	3	2	1	82,320
Furious Flight	5	M	1	0	0	0	51	G. W.'s Skippie	3	C	12	3	2	1	101,960
Furious Victory	7	G	9	2	0	2	3,263	G. W.'s Squall	2	F	1	0	0	1	3,080
Furlegsandatale	5	G	4	0	0	0	285	Gab Bag	2	C	2	0	0	0	118
Furniture Man	12	G	18	0	0	0	2,491	Gabby Blue	3	F	1	0	0	0	126
Further	6	G	1	0	0	0	0	Gabby Dancer	4	F	11	0	0	3	15,828
Furtivo (ARG)	6	G	6	0	1	1	10,060	Gabby Glib	3	G	3	0	0	0	515
Fusaichi's Dance	2	G	5	0	0	0	1,850	Gabby Lou	4	G	6	2	1	1	47,721
Fuse Buster	5	M	13	2	4	0	27,363	Gabbygail	6	M	4	1	0	1	5,068
Fuse It	5	M	13	3	1	3	205,620	Gabe	5	G	7	0	1	0	1,129
Fuse Quick	5	G	5	1	2	0	33,050	Gabianna	3	F	4	1	1	0	20,000
Fuselier	3	G	15	0	1	3	5,539	Gabrieles Princess	4	F	10	4	0	0	45,622
Fussy Fever	4	F	2	0	0	0	206	Gabriellina Giof (GB)	5	M	5	0	0	0	1,080
Fussy Photo	4	G	3	0	0	0	800	Gabriell's Wings	7	G	8	1	1	2	6,126
Fussy's Kid	6	G	8	1	3	2	45,105	Gabriel's Pat	5	G	3	0	0	1	1,410
Fusto	4	C	4	0	0	0	0	Gabriel's Prospect	8	G	9	2	0	1	6,243
Fusty	4	G	8	2	1	0	9,960	Gabriel's Trumpet	2	F	1	0	0	0	93
Futican	4	C	6	0	0	0	1,175	Gabriola	4	F	9	1	3	0	10,766
Futural	7	G	12	2	1	1	62,314	Gaby G	5	M	14	3	1	4	68,340
Future Angel	5	M	10	2	1	2	33,660	Gaby's Dream	8	M	6	0	0	0	1,669
Future Article	4	G	3	0	1	0	2,200	Gad	2	C	5	1	1	0	11,600
Future Blessing	5	M	14	1	3	1	7,746	Gadget Man	2	G	8	0	2	2	11,390
Future Book	4	C	4	0	0	0	780	Gadir	6	H	9	0	1	0	3,690
Future Brass	5	G	6	0	0	0	426	Gaebel's Brew	2	G	1	0	0	1	890
Future Crown	11	G	15	1	3	2	6,240	Gaebel's Gamble	5	M	4	1	0	0	6,585
Future Destiny	3	C	2	0	0	0	50	Gaelic Chief	3	C	1	0	0	0	35
Future Fantasy	2	G	5	0	1	2	9,400	Gaelic Hope	6	G	12	4	2	3	39,342
Future Favorite	4	G	2	0	0	0	130	Gaelic Issue	2	C	5	1	1	2	44,060
Future Flash	2	G	4	1	1	1	43,151	Gaelic Ladd	3	G	14	1	2	3	7,431
Future Justice	2	F	4	0	1	0	3,151	Gaelic Miss	3	F	14	2	3	3	65,080
Future Leader	7	H	7	0	0	2	530	Gaelic Night	5	M	4	0	0	1	669
Future Rainbow	5	M	12	3	0	2	25,844	Gaelic Red	6	G	3	0	0	1	630
Future Settlement	5	G	6	1	1	0	4,043	Gaelic Thunder	6	H	5	0	2	0	3,084
Future Stock	6	H	4	0	0	0	242	Gaelic Vixen	5	M	1	0	0	0	120
Future Thought	4	F	2	0	1	0	10,660	Gaelic Wolf	6	G	3	0	0	0	180
Future Trick	4	G	1	0	0	0	0	Gaelic's a King	5	G	9	3	1	0	3,105
Future Wealth	3	G	3	0	0	0	1,440	Gaelic Warrior	5	G	18	2	1	3	15,799
Fuzz E Delight	3	F	10	2	0	2	26,110	Gaetano's Way	3	C	11	3	1	1	75,180
Fuzz E Love	6	G	14	0	2	2	3,816	Gaffney	4	G	10	1	2	3	15,209
Fuzz E Shine	5	M	5	0	0	0	0	Gai Copper	4	F	8	0	1	0	3,116
Fuzzie's First	3	F	8	1	1	1	9,740	Gai J	3	F	5	0	0	0	246
Fuzzy Abby	5	M	14	2	1	1	16,414	Gailpickedthisone	3	F	3	1	0	1	5,780
Fuzzy Annie	5	M	8	1	0	0	3,841	Gail's Drive	5	G	10	4	0	2	71,345
Fuzzy Dice	3	F	19	0	7	1	12,226	Gail's Last	5	M	3	0	0	0	244
Fuzzy Eagle	8	H	6	0	2	1	3,834	Gail's Melody	4	F	9	3	1	1	8,196
Fuzzy Ferd	6	G	1	0	0	0	58	Gainan Power	3	G	8	1	0	0	3,034
Fuzzy Fund	2	G	5	2	0	0	29,492	Gainango	2	C	2	0	1	1	13,950
Fuzzy Mac	4	G	1	0	0	0	0	Gaining Talent	3	G	3	0	0	0	333
Fuzzy Naevus	7	M	11	0	0	3	1,662	Gairloch	8	G	1	0	0	0	0
Fuzzy Numbers	3	G	7	1	3	0	6,724	Gaiter Girl	6	M	3	0	0	1	1,300
Fuzzy Power	3	F	1	0	0	0	0	Gaitor Ade	8	H	3	0	0	0	162
Fuzzy Star	4	C	9	2	4	1	80,650	Gakkel Ridge	3	C	2	0	0	0	0
Fuzzy Viola	6	M	8	0	2	0	13,211	Gal Friday	3	F	3	1	0	0	6,411
Fynbos	4	F	9	4	3	0	108,643	Gal O Gal	3	F	11	3	0	3	156,957
Fyrbreathingdragon	4	G	11	0	0	2	5,664	Gal On Skis	3	F	14	0	1	2	6,750
G All Day	6	G	13	4	2	0	115,400	Gal On the Go	5	M	2	0	0	0	2,684
G and L Special	5	H	6	1	3	1	6,612	Gal Sally	5	M	5	0	0	0	248
G G Corona	3	C	3	0	0	0	0	Gala Bear	8	G	8	2	0	0	10,559
G G's Millennium	3	F	12	0	1	2	3,019	Gala Cause	2	F	1	0	1	0	5,240
G I Thunder	3	G	8	0	0	2	5,767	Gala Essence	3	F	2	1	0	0	12,175
G Is for Go	2	C	3	0	0	0	0	Gala Gold County	3	G	11	5	1	3	52,480
G J Lost and Found	2	F	1	0	0	0	60	Gala Lady	2	F	1	0	0	0	186
G J M Diablo	5	H	15	1	0	0	9,133	Gala Mag (ARG)	4	F	4	0	1	0	3,790
G L Mickey	3	C	3	0	0	0	0	Gala Reckoning	4	F	6	0	1	0	9,020
G L's Gold Strike	6	G	5	2	2	0	16,760	Galactic Fire	4	G	12	1	0	2	4,681
G M Jake	2	G	4	0	1	0	4,060	Galago	3	G	3	0	0	0	540
G Mans Gal	3	F	16	5	3	2	96,268	Galarus	4	G	9	2	2	1	37,310
G' mornin Donna	7	M	1	0	0	0	0	Gala's Trick	7	H	6	1	0	0	1,385
G P Fleet	3	G	11	3	4	1	109,718	Galatea Cat	4	F	9	1	1	1	54,087

Horse	Age	Sex	Sts	1st	2d	3d	Won	Horse	Age	Sex	Sts	1st	2d	3d	Won
Galatian	4	G	10	1	1	0	4,992	Gamble to Victory	3	F	9	3	1	2	92,203
Galavant	8	G	12	4	2	2	24,545	Gambleemotions	9	G	11	0	0	0	878
Galaxy Belle	6	M	11	4	2	0	58,879	Gamblen Derek	3	C	6	1	1	1	6,948
Galaxy Buddy	4	G	7	0	0	0	583	Gambler's Edge	4	G	9	1	3	1	9,295
Galaxy Gallop	3	C	1	0	0	0	0	Gamblers Ghost	6	H	4	0	1	1	4,000
Galena Summit	3	G	9	1	2	2	16,850	Gambler's Gift	7	M	14	0	1	1	7,293
Galette	3	F	5	1	1	0	9,764	Gambler's Law	2	C	4	0	0	1	1,080
Galic Boy	8	G	7	2	1	1	31,750	Gambler's Mark	3	G	6	1	1	0	29,844
Galindo	7	G	12	0	1	0	7,667	Gamblers Passion	3	F	7	3	0	2	23,932
Galintherain	4	F	6	0	1	1	7,912	Gambler's Prospect	4	G	6	0	0	1	2,712
Galip Home	6	M	3	0	0	0	291	Gambler's Secret	3	G	10	0	0	0	0
Galivantor	4	C	3	0	0	0	0	Gambler's Share	7	G	7	2	0	2	19,570
Gall Bladder	4	G	2	0	0	0	0	Gamble's Answer	4	F	14	1	1	4	47,320
Gallagher	3	G	4	0	0	0	746	Gamble's Ghost	3	F	5	0	0	0	4,180
Gallant (GB)	6	H	6	1	0	0	27,440	Gamblin	2	C	2	0	2	0	15,000
Gallant American	3	C	8	0	0	0	0	Gamblin Annie	3	F	12	2	1	1	20,135
Gallant and Brave	5	G	7	0	0	0	8,325	Gamblin Caper	3	G	5	3	1	0	75,800
Gallant Angel	5	M	20	0	2	3	49,641	Gamblin Cat	5	H	4	1	0	0	1,226
Gallant Beau	6	G	13	2	4	3	13,855	Gamblin Garret	3	G	3	0	0	0	1,425
Gallant Brave	3	C	8	2	2	1	22,185	Gamblin Jake	6	H	9	2	1	1	13,701
Gallant Cat	3	F	6	2	2	0	27,940	Gamblin Town	5	M	3	2	1	0	33,880
Gallant Code	3	F	2	0	0	0	660	Gamblin Woman	6	M	4	0	0	0	263
Gallant Emblem	5	H	4	0	0	0	288	Gambling Bob	5	G	2	0	0	0	110
Gallant Frolic	5	G	2	0	0	0	600	Gambling Cherokee	2	F	4	0	0	0	600
Gallant Gesture	8	G	7	0	0	2	4,136	Gambling Hope	2	F	1	0	0	0	760
Gallant Intern	6	M	7	0	0	1	2,200	Gambling King	4	G	25	2	3	0	27,111
Gallant Jenny	10	M	5	0	0	1	320	Gambling Native	2	C	6	2	1	0	43,420
Gallant Jules	3	G	5	1	0	0	5,182	Gambling Rent	2	C	3	1	1	0	30,400
Gallant Leader	4	C	3	0	1	0	2,106	Gambling Time	2	C	4	0	1	0	1,881
Gallant Manor	6	G	27	1	9	5	23,205	Gambol Gaily	3	F	2	0	0	0	70
Gallant Reign	6	G	5	0	0	0	298	Gambrinus	4	C	2	0	0	0	80
Gallant Robin	4	F	5	2	0	2	13,938	Game Artist	5	H	5	0	0	1	877
Gallant Sioux	5	M	4	0	0	0	810	Game Bag	3	C	6	1	0	0	14,990
Gallant Sir	4	G	8	1	1	3	46,080	Game Bird	7	H	10	2	0	3	38,005
Gallant Skip	6	H	5	0	1	0	2,525	Game Box	3	C	2	0	0	0	1,380
Gallant Slew	9	H	9	0	0	0	1,780	Game Cadillac	4	G	6	2	0	0	7,543
Gallant Snowman	5	G	15	2	3	1	47,139	Game Called	5	G	12	2	0	1	30,189
Gallant Soldier	3	C	3	0	0	0	122	Game Day	3	C	5	0	0	2	9,290
Gallant Spur	4	G	5	0	0	0	0	Game Day Hero	2	C	2	0	1	0	3,200
Gallant Storm	7	H	3	0	0	1	680	Game Day Play	4	G	1	1	0	0	8,800
Gallant Tale	3	C	9	2	1	1	55,684	Game Effort	5	G	8	3	0	1	65,130
Gallant Turk	7	G	2	0	0	0	3,000	Game Fighter	3	G	12	1	1	2	7,216
Gallapiats Cutlass	6	M	1	0	0	0	180	Game Fish	4	G	5	1	0	0	6,619
Gallapiat's Fame	6	M	6	0	0	2	2,470	Game Girl	3	F	6	1	2	0	12,118
Gallapiat's Ghost	3	F	17	0	4	1	9,267	Game I. M.	5	G	11	0	2	1	1,935
Gallapiat'smydaddy	5	G	13	2	2	2	22,496	Game in the Wind	2	F	1	0	0	0	0
Gallatin	5	M	10	1	2	2	14,520	Game Keeper	3	C	1	0	0	0	900
Gallatin Gateway	5	G	4	0	1	1	820	Game Magic	5	G	32	1	2	5	10,785
Gallatin Kid	4	G	9	1	3	1	46,959	Game Master	2	C	6	0	1	2	4,142
Gallelujah	4	F	3	0	0	0	520	Game Planner	3	G	6	0	0	1	1,981
Galleria Daze	3	F	6	2	0	2	17,840	Game Princess	3	F	7	1	3	2	12,935
Galleyhawk	7	M	1	0	0	0	40	Game Prize	2	G	5	0	0	0	206
Galliant	3	G	9	2	1	3	20,987	Game Set Match	4	G	6	0	0	0	890
Gallop Fat Boys	3	G	2	1	0	0	26,400	Game Skipper	11	G	6	1	0	2	4,917
Gallop to Victory	2	C	2	0	0	0	1,260	Game Ticket	5	G	3	0	1	0	2,947
Galloping Christos	3	G	18	2	1	2	7,966	Game Time	3	F	8	1	1	1	15,085
Galloping Dancer	3	F	5	1	1	0	14,750	Game Two	8	G	2	0	0	0	0
Galloping Gal	2	F	5	3	1	0	204,884	Game Warden	3	G	14	1	2	2	7,136
Galloping George	6	G	5	0	0	0	439	Game Within a Game	2	G	9	2	1	1	48,162
Galloping Gourmet	5	H	8	0	0	0	2,655	Gamebri Boy	4	C	12	0	0	3	3,261
Galloping Lu	5	M	7	1	1	0	4,864	Gamely Glittering	4	F	12	3	3	1	45,119
Galloping to Tea	2	F	1	0	0	0	0	Gamer	4	G	19	1	2	3	16,975
Gallop'n Gold	6	G	6	0	1	0	4,822	Games of Chance	5	M	7	0	1	1	4,010
Gallopsey	6	M	6	0	0	3	3,990	Games People Play	2	C	1	0	0	0	52
Galloway Gal	5	M	3	0	0	0	120	Gaming	2	C	7	1	0	1	25,855
Gallys Pearliwhirl	6	M	3	0	0	0	572	Gammagoat Kid	4	G	10	2	1	3	5,330
Galopin Charger	2	C	6	1	2	1	11,095	Gammy Dan	2	C	1	0	0	0	0
Galoriosa	3	F	4	0	0	0	0	Ganadancer	4	C	4	0	2	0	4,750
Galpal	7	M	2	0	1	0	3,200	Ganador	6	G	12	0	0	2	2,168
Galpin's Candi	4	G	3	0	0	0	292	Gander	7	G	7	2	1	2	137,495
Galray	3	G	3	0	1	0	2,185	Ganendyl	3	F	15	6	3	0	85,550
Galson	3	C	12	1	1	1	20,625	Gang	3	G	7	3	0	1	94,010
Galvanizer	3	C	8	2	2	2	45,359	Gangplank	3	G	3	1	0	0	3,720
Galway John	3	C	3	0	0	0	965	Gang's Maxamillion	5	G	5	0	0	0	432
Galway Miner	4	G	12	1	3	1	16,313	Gangsta Rap	6	G	14	2	1	2	24,480
Galway Vixen	4	F	6	0	0	1	1,100	Gangtrous	9	M	11	2	3	5	4,844
Gamble	4	C	7	0	0	2	15,625	Ganharva	3	F	8	0	0	2	9,213
Gamble Les	7	G	7	1	1	0	10,146	Gankster	6	G	10	1	0	0	6,156
Gamble On Me	4	G	13	2	1	3	48,113	Gansta Affair	3	F	8	0	0	0	441

Horse	Age	Sex	Sts	1st	2d	3d	Won
Gar a Lone	2	G	2	0	0	1	762
Garb	4	G	11	1	0	1	11,909
Garces Lady	3	F	2	0	0	0	440
Gardella	9	H	11	0	1	1	2,278
Garden Dance	4	F	5	0	1	1	15,810
Garden Gait	5	G	6	1	0	0	5,748
Garden in the Rain (FR)	6	M	10	2	4	1	189,830
Garden Tracer	5	G	14	1	1	0	5,270
Garden Whimsy	2	F	4	1	1	1	51,900
Garden Wildcat	3	F	6	3	0	0	40,600
Gardeness's Gem	3	F	5	1	0	0	16,926
Gardina	6	M	1	0	0	0	0
Gardner's Heir	4	G	2	0	0	0	82
Garesche	4	C	12	0	3	4	47,368
Garland County	3	F	7	0	0	0	140
Garlax	2	G	8	0	0	0	910
Garlic Country	4	G	9	6	0	2	39,475
Garner Key	7	M	9	0	0	0	1,364
Garner the Roses	3	F	2	0	0	0	0
Garnered	5	H	3	3	0	0	123,660
Garnet Street	4	G	17	2	1	3	9,051
Garnetta	4	F	9	0	1	1	4,413
Garrard	3	C	10	1	0	1	17,510
Garret's Gulch	2	G	2	0	0	0	1,050
Garrett Champ	7	G	17	1	0	2	4,339
Garrett Junior	3	G	9	2	3	0	19,772
Garrett's Girl	2	F	5	2	1	1	29,900
Garrett's Glider	4	G	7	2	1	2	17,465
Garretts Gray	2	G	1	0	0	0	0
Garrett's Tiger	2	G	1	0	0	0	0
Garrettslilnora	5	M	6	3	0	1	55,900
Garrison Hill	4	G	6	1	2	3	22,780
Garrison's Gun	2	F	8	1	0	1	6,850
Gar's Mam	4	F	8	1	0	1	11,105
Garson Rouge	9	G	12	1	2	5	10,070
Garth	2	G	4	0	0	0	500
Gary Battle Wise	3	G	4	0	0	1	1,350
Gary O's Boy	6	G	4	0	0	0	155
Gary the Neighbor	4	G	15	0	1	0	5,175
Garyanna	4	F	5	1	0	0	19,036
Garyisdeceiving	5	G	2	0	0	0	54
Gary's Agenda	4	G	5	1	0	0	3,633
Garys Diamond	4	F	3	0	0	0	0
Garys Dream	5	H	9	0	0	2	4,587
Gary's Key	5	G	8	2	0	0	13,925
Gary's Little Guy	3	G	4	0	0	0	1,950
Gary's Speedy Miss	8	M	17	1	3	1	8,290
Gary's Stuka	4	G	2	0	0	0	54
Garysrappingranny	4	F	10	0	0	2	5,126
Gas House Mouse	4	F	1	0	0	0	0
Gas Me Up	4	F	1	0	0	0	0
Gas Pedal	2	F	1	0	0	0	100
Gaslamp Girl	4	F	2	0	1	1	6,680
Gasparilla Queen	8	M	10	2	2	2	12,614
Gasperillo Daze	6	G	2	0	0	0	4,200
Gassan Colony	3	C	2	0	0	0	5,880
Gassan Rock	2	G	5	1	1	2	23,660
Gassan Royal	3	C	5	1	4	0	68,800
Gastonia	3	C	6	1	0	1	19,270
Gastons Gold	4	C	3	0	0	0	690
Gastown	2	C	2	0	1	0	12,120
Gata Be Patient	3	F	8	2	2	2	77,220
Gata Be Wild	3	F	2	0	0	0	217
Gata Veloz	2	F	2	1	1	0	13,800
Gate Card	5	H	12	3	1	2	18,594
Gate Master	3	G	15	2	5	3	20,220
Gate Opener	5	G	1	0	0	0	38
Gatebuster	9	G	11	3	4	0	18,305
Gated Entrance	3	F	2	0	0	0	700
Gater Power	4	F	13	4	1	5	18,152
Gates Avenue	2	C	3	1	1	0	33,219
Gate's Goal	4	G	16	1	5	3	18,629
Gate's Sunny Boy	5	G	16	2	0	0	5,891
Gather the Roses	7	H	16	1	1	0	18,127
Gathering Storm	2	G	1	0	0	0	0
Gatita	2	F	3	0	0	0	275
Gato Bob	2	C	3	1	0	1	8,946
Gato Del Diablo	3	C	10	1	2	0	11,250
Gato Gato Gato	3	G	11	2	1	1	56,657
Gato Montanes	2	C	3	1	1	1	8,000
Gato Montes	2	C	4	0	1	0	3,146
Gato Negro	3	G	10	1	0	0	6,505
Gato Sol Mitts	3	F	5	0	0	0	640
Gato Twist	2	F	2	1	0	0	13,336
Gatobeanactor	7	G	4	0	0	0	790
Gatopresson	4	G	13	2	1	3	8,369
Gator Chomp	7	G	4	0	1	0	1,240
Gator From Decatur	4	F	6	1	1	1	5,835
Gator Go Getter	6	G	9	1	0	2	4,826
Gator Lake	4	G	3	0	2	1	3,764
Gator Maid	4	F	15	3	1	3	19,592
Gator the Great	2	G	4	0	1	0	2,140
Gators Get	5	G	5	0	1	0	4,174
Gators N Bears	3	C	13	5	3	4	257,270
Gatorzone	4	G	3	0	1	0	4,832
Gatto Fortunato	5	G	9	0	1	0	3,048
Gatto Selvaggio	2	F	4	1	1	2	19,690
Gaucho	6	H	2	0	0	0	480
Gaucho Girl	2	F	4	0	0	0	720
Gauge	3	F	16	2	0	1	4,858
Gauguin Go	4	G	3	0	0	0	50
Gauntlet	6	G	4	0	0	0	0
Gavelock	5	G	5	1	0	1	13,450
Gavin's Sweetie	4	F	8	1	1	1	12,267
Gavins Wish	2	C	5	0	0	1	1,810
Gaviota Pass	6	G	14	1	0	1	5,150
Gavro	3	C	9	1	3	0	84,916
Gavster	4	G	20	0	2	1	4,474
Gay and J Mac	6	M	16	5	3	1	31,785
Gay Mood	3	F	7	3	2	0	31,196
Gay Slewpy	5	G	7	0	0	0	978
Gayla's Storm	2	F	2	0	0	0	190
Gayleharriet	5	M	4	0	0	0	0
Gayles Lioness	3	F	13	1	1	1	7,538
Gaylord Lady	3	F	2	0	0	0	140
Gaynores Special	5	M	3	0	0	0	123
Gaze At Me	6	H	2	0	0	0	204
Gazeemo	4	F	4	0	0	0	101
Gazelle Belle	3	F	10	1	3	1	17,295
Gazillion	4	F	6	3	3	0	137,670
Gear Up	2	F	3	0	0	0	155
Gearbox	2	G	3	2	0	0	31,680
Geardown	3	G	10	2	2	0	36,925
Gearjammer	5	H	2	0	0	0	125
Geaux Bayou Bo	4	G	3	0	0	0	336
Geaux Gabriel	3	G	13	1	1	2	10,008
Geaux Girl Geaux	3	F	7	0	0	0	210
Gebb's Dixie	4	F	6	0	2	0	25,520
Gebb's Flag	3	G	9	1	4	3	18,717
Gebb's Glory	5	M	17	3	3	4	38,812
Gebb's Prince	7	G	11	1	2	4	12,017
Gebb's Princess	5	M	14	1	2	0	15,837
Gee Cashman	3	C	2	0	0	0	0
Gee Don't You Wish	6	M	12	3	2	2	56,730
Gee Dubya	4	G	9	0	0	0	1,379
Gee Dubya Bee	3	G	8	0	0	1	4,330
Gee Gee Belle	3	F	8	0	2	2	9,124
Gee Gee's Grand	5	M	1	0	0	0	0
Gee Wally	8	G	4	0	1	0	2,832
Geebeekay (IRE)	3	G	13	2	0	2	15,893
Geechee Lou	5	M	10	2	1	1	16,642
Gee's Gold	3	F	2	0	0	0	0
Gee's He's Grand	2	C	5	0	0	0	0
Gehrig	4	G	12	2	1	1	43,890
Geiger Tiger	3	C	1	0	0	0	664
Geisha Boo	5	M	3	0	1	0	1,520
Gela	3	G	10	1	0	2	19,074
Geli's Pie	3	F	4	0	0	1	1,782
Gem Gate	5	H	7	0	1	1	2,095
Gem of a Day	2	G	4	0	1	2	8,920
Gem of a Girl	3	F	1	0	0	0	0
Gem of All Jules	2	F	3	0	0	0	0
Gem Royale	3	F	1	0	0	1	5,760
Gem West	3	F	6	1	0	0	4,860
Gemerous	4	G	1	0	0	0	0
Gemhill	4	G	4	0	0	0	810
Gemini Blade	3	G	4	0	1	0	930
Gemini Cruiser	5	H	2	0	0	1	1,121

Horse	Age	Sex	Sts	1st	2d	3d	Won
Gemini Dream	2	C	6	2	1	1	72,905
Gemini Gold	6	M	2	0	0	0	0
Gemjolie	3	G	8	1	0	1	5,347
Gemley	8	M	3	0	1	0	2,084
Gemma Kyle	3	F	14	2	0	1	13,160
Gemma Nunz	4	G	8	2	0	3	16,393
Gemma's Star	4	C	3	0	1	0	8,760
Gems Fella	6	G	11	0	1	0	1,452
Gem's Flora	4	F	14	4	4	1	49,000
Gems of Wisdom	3	F	5	0	0	0	5,688
Gem's Rising Star	6	M	11	1	1	0	12,456
Gem's Wager	4	F	12	1	3	1	55,376
Gemstone's Jewel	3	F	1	0	0	0	0
Gen Fall	4	G	6	2	1	0	25,914
Gen Sterling Price	3	G	4	0	1	0	2,694
Gen. Kennedy	3	F	8	1	1	1	7,204
Genal Syd	4	F	14	2	1	3	19,925
Gender Dance	3	F	9	2	2	0	37,106
Gene	8	G	11	0	1	2	4,109
Geneaudrey	8	G	10	0	0	0	694
General Alexander	3	G	6	1	0	0	10,270
General Approval	2	C	4	1	0	0	5,340
General Ascot	3	G	6	0	0	1	9,278
General Ashby	3	C	1	0	0	0	0
General Athenium	4	G	9	0	2	0	3,663
General Attack	3	C	10	0	0	3	12,270
General Be	3	C	12	2	0	1	42,780
General Biltmore	3	G	6	1	1	0	5,950
General Bull	3	G	11	2	2	3	6,435
General Cara Lee	3	F	4	0	0	0	100
General Challenge	7	G	3	0	0	0	1,160
General Commander	3	C	1	1	0	0	13,800
General Creek	2	G	4	0	1	0	2,690
General Danny	4	G	5	1	0	0	3,120
General Danzer	2	C	4	0	0	0	420
General Delivery	4	C	2	0	0	0	123
General Doonbear	9	G	2	0	0	0	85
General Exceptions	3	F	2	0	0	0	0
General Express	8	G	11	4	1	2	52,440
General Fox	2	C	2	0	0	0	0
General George S	2	G	2	0	0	0	140
General Guidelines	3	C	3	1	0	0	19,440
General Illusion	4	F	2	0	0	0	50
General Insanity	3	C	8	2	3	0	51,478
General Jack	4	G	3	2	0	0	71,040
General Jay	3	C	8	1	1	0	16,220
General Josh	3	G	10	5	1	1	30,047
General Kiridashi	2	C	2	0	0	0	7,056
General Lee	3	C	7	1	0	0	17,160
General Mill	4	G	15	2	1	3	28,280
General Money	2	G	3	0	0	1	2,160
General Moody	2	G	4	1	0	0	35,100
General Naaman	3	C	6	0	2	2	4,022
General Nancy	4	F	1	0	0	0	0
General Obstinate	3	C	4	0	0	0	189
General Pat	5	H	16	4	2	1	31,918
General Plan	2	G	2	0	0	0	700
General Plot	3	G	7	1	0	0	6,747
General Price	2	G	1	0	0	1	1,425
General Roanoke	4	G	18	2	6	3	42,713
General Search	2	C	1	0	0	0	0
General Sheba	4	G	12	1	2	3	31,104
General Silverfoot	3	C	11	1	1	0	6,601
General Store	5	H	4	0	0	1	9,840
General Survivor	3	G	9	1	2	1	10,487
General Tap	3	G	6	0	0	1	1,648
General Tee	2	G	1	0	0	0	240
General Terms	5	G	10	0	0	4	5,916
General Tiff	3	F	2	1	1	0	13,160
General Vassili	8	G	8	1	2	0	6,642
General Villa	8	G	8	0	3	0	4,374
General Waki	4	G	9	1	1	0	8,778
General Will	3	C	11	0	0	2	6,290
General Year	4	G	12	1	1	1	10,639
General Zapata	7	G	8	0	1	1	675
General Zod	3	C	2	0	0	1	4,320
Generalcy	7	M	1	0	0	0	0
Generalito	2	G	3	1	0	0	11,700
Generality	4	C	3	0	2	1	9,960
Generally On	7	G	5	0	2	0	7,401
General's First	6	H	7	0	0	1	1,241
Generals Sword	5	G	8	4	0	0	85,158
Generals'messenger	9	M	5	0	0	0	1,098
Generalsprettygirl	2	F	2	0	0	0	278
Generations	6	H	6	1	0	1	4,549
Generous Gift (GB)	9	H	5	0	0	0	300
Generous Heart	5	M	10	1	2	1	4,787
Generous One	2	C	2	0	0	0	0
Generous Rosi (GB)	8	H	4	1	0	0	30,050
Generously	5	G	13	2	2	1	13,696
Gene's Bid to Win	4	G	14	1	1	2	14,721
Gene's Pride (IRE)	4	G	2	0	0	0	0
Gene's Prospect	3	C	4	0	2	0	8,790
Geneva Cross	3	G	15	3	2	2	21,853
Genevil	3	F	12	1	2	5	66,553
Genie Magic	4	F	19	2	2	5	35,020
Genius Baby	6	M	6	0	1	2	2,740
Genius Rules	7	M	14	3	6	1	35,566
Geniusatwork	2	C	1	0	0	0	0
Geniver	2	F	3	1	0	0	22,062
Genji	4	G	7	0	0	0	965
Gennie's Challenge	4	F	3	0	0	0	951
Genoa Cat	2	F	8	3	2	2	32,676
Genska	4	F	7	1	1	1	63,746
Gent	4	C	3	2	0	0	37,400
Genteel	4	F	12	1	0	2	7,104
Genteel Lady	5	M	14	2	4	3	57,724
Gentille Alouette	5	M	10	1	1	1	44,025
Gentle Bien	4	G	8	1	0	1	24,234
Gentle Breeze Lola	4	F	7	0	2	2	17,640
Gentle Brittney	2	F	5	1	0	0	15,000
Gentle Cielo	4	G	16	2	2	2	30,504
Gentle Dancer	5	M	2	0	0	0	110
Gentle Demi	4	F	5	0	0	0	444
Gentle Ego	2	G	1	0	0	0	0
Gentle Fun	2	F	1	0	0	0	0
Gentle Gem	2	F	4	1	0	0	9,415
Gentle Giant	6	G	2	1	0	0	36,600
Gentle Glide	5	M	10	0	1	2	2,806
Gentle John	3	G	4	0	1	0	3,526
Gentle Magic	2	F	2	0	0	0	424
Gentle Magic (GB)	5	M	1	0	0	0	290
Gentle Moonbeam	3	F	4	2	0	1	7,690
Gentle n'Gold	4	F	4	0	0	0	1,350
Gentle Nudge	3	C	8	0	0	1	6,310
Gentle Point	3	F	1	0	0	0	0
Gentle R	4	F	5	1	1	2	5,782
Gentle Sea	3	F	2	0	0	0	780
Gentleman Ed	4	G	14	4	1	1	18,075
Gentleman Jerry	4	G	11	3	0	1	9,725
Gentleman John	6	G	1	0	0	0	0
Gentleman Jolie	6	G	9	0	0	2	7,220
Gentleman Player	2	G	3	1	0	1	16,378
Gentleman's Girl	2	F	6	1	0	2	28,880
Gentleman's Honor	3	G	6	0	1	0	4,200
Gentleman's Kiss	3	G	7	0	0	0	570
Gentlemen Duel	2	G	8	1	1	1	8,705
Gentlemen J J	3	C	15	4	3	1	113,200
Gentlemen's Club	3	G	3	1	0	0	27,000
Gentlemen's Guest	3	F	6	1	1	2	18,180
Gentlemen's Lady	3	F	4	1	1	1	33,460
Gentlestone	3	G	4	0	0	2	13,260
Gentlman Hawk	3	C	6	1	1	0	13,707
Gentree	8	G	10	3	1	2	17,220
Gent's Advantage	3	C	6	1	0	1	26,770
Gents Big Cat	6	G	11	1	0	2	9,161
Gent's Thunder	6	G	3	0	0	0	186
Genuine Appeal	5	M	1	0	0	0	0
Genuine Blues	5	M	7	2	1	0	10,472
Genuine Count	2	C	4	0	1	1	14,721
Genuine Draft	2	G	2	0	0	0	145
Genuine Dream	6	M	7	2	0	0	9,984
Genuine Fire	3	M	4	0	0	0	1,055
Genuine Lass	5	M	5	1	0	1	3,495
Genuine Pat	2	F	2	0	0	0	174
Genuine Performer	4	F	9	0	0	2	6,650
Genuine Regard	4	G	18	2	5	0	17,580

RECORDS OF HORSES

Horse	Age	Sex	Sts	1st	2d	3d	Won
Genuine Revenue	5	H	7	0	1	0	2,200
Genuine Ruler	4	G	1	0	0	0	0
Genuine Sparky	6	G	6	0	0	1	1,761
Genuine Tact	4	G	8	0	0	0	156
Genuine Tiger	3	G	12	1	3	0	22,950
Genuine Treasure	3	C	6	0	0	0	550
Geodude	5	G	11	0	1	0	1,592
Geomancer	3	F	8	1	1	0	17,683
Geometry	4	G	6	3	0	1	65,915
George Again	5	M	2	0	0	0	214
George Bailey	4	G	6	0	1	1	22,755
George D.	3	C	7	2	0	1	21,643
George Double You	3	G	9	1	0	1	3,399
George Edward	3	G	11	0	1	3	22,060
George George	5	H	4	0	1	1	3,164
George M	6	G	14	1	0	3	4,700
George Taylor	4	G	8	1	0	2	49,319
Georges Best Shot	4	G	7	0	0	1	1,809
George's Boy	3	C	4	0	0	0	0
George's Brother	2	C	4	0	0	1	2,860
George's Gain	3	C	8	2	2	0	27,825
George's Peejays	6	G	12	0	1	2	4,965
George's Starr	4	C	11	1	5	2	21,730
George's Stick	3	G	17	2	1	5	39,990
Georgetown Gal	2	F	2	0	0	0	3,330
Georgia Crown	7	H	11	1	2	2	14,575
Georgia Gentleman	2	G	5	1	1	1	8,395
Georgia Glory	4	G	4	1	1	0	14,040
Georgia Milk Man	7	G	13	1	0	1	5,450
Georgia Ok	2	F	3	1	0	1	7,560
Georgia Time	2	C	4	0	0	1	1,125
Georgian Door	4	G	9	0	2	1	16,486
Georgian Queen	2	F	1	0	0	0	1,764
Georgia's Fancy	3	F	6	1	1	0	16,649
Georgia's Lady	3	F	6	0	0	0	242
Georgie	3	G	2	0	0	0	2,460
Georgie Gem	4	F	10	0	1	3	9,507
Georgie Porgee	5	G	12	2	3	1	15,264
Georgie V Good	3	G	1	1	0	0	2,400
Georgio J.	5	G	11	2	1	0	31,941
Geotex	2	G	5	0	0	1	973
Ger	3	G	3	0	0	0	210
Geraint	7	G	5	1	1	1	75,032
Geranium	3	F	2	0	0	0	400
Geri Gold	3	G	3	0	0	0	0
Geri Lewis	3	C	5	0	1	0	17,520
Geririg	3	G	9	2	1	1	20,446
Geri's Affair	4	G	2	0	0	0	882
Geri's Dancin	3	G	3	0	0	0	0
Germain's Man	7	G	9	0	5	0	7,353
German Village	3	C	2	0	0	0	230
Germanicus	3	C	6	2	1	0	38,930
Germanna Colonies	3	F	1	0	0	0	0
Geronimo	4	G	6	1	0	1	7,609
Geronimo (CHI)	4	G	6	0	2	2	59,896
Geronimos Renegade	2	C	2	0	0	0	0
Gerri's Auto Bee	6	M	3	1	0	0	5,412
Gerri's Rogue	3	G	5	0	0	0	3,900
Gerry Fantasy	2	F	2	0	0	0	60
Gerry Gerry Gerry	2	C	4	0	0	1	11,595
Gerry's Darling	6	M	2	0	0	0	0
Gershom	3	G	3	0	0	0	660
Gert in Vegas	2	F	4	0	0	0	0
Geruase	3	C	7	1	1	1	11,180
Get	3	F	9	0	1	0	6,037
Get Control	7	M	5	1	1	0	5,727
Get Down Wolfie	5	G	8	0	1	2	20,050
Get Festive	2	C	1	0	0	0	75
Get Fiscal	3	C	2	0	0	0	240
Get Going Gracie	2	F	1	0	0	0	0
Get Gone Rabbit	7	G	9	0	1	2	1,930
Get Happy	3	F	12	1	1	1	9,975
Get Home Racso	6	G	13	3	2	2	21,925
Get Inspired	3	F	3	1	0	0	13,560
Get My Drift	5	G	10	1	3	1	8,875
Get My Glitter	11	G	9	0	1	1	3,240
Get N Good	3	G	4	0	1	0	1,925
Get Off the Phone	9	G	9	1	3	0	2,279
Get Outta Dodge	2	C	5	1	0	0	5,695
Get Smarter	3	C	3	1	1	0	37,800
Get the Doc	4	C	4	0	0	0	180
Get the Edge	2	C	1	0	0	0	0
Get the Hook	2	F	1	0	0	0	240
Get the Picture	7	G	5	1	1	0	18,900
Get Tricky	8	G	7	2	0	0	9,256
Get Up and Go	3	G	8	1	0	1	43,238
Getaway Holme	5	H	14	3	2	3	64,350
Getaway in Style	6	G	12	0	1	0	9,180
Getaway Man	2	C	3	0	1	0	4,635
Geteem G. W.	2	G	4	1	0	0	10,960
Getem Frank	4	G	7	0	0	2	5,036
Gethsemane	6	G	5	0	0	0	910
Gethsemani	2	C	7	1	2	3	60,365
Getitgirl	3	F	2	0	0	0	960
Getmefree	4	F	8	1	2	2	3,578
Getnby	7	G	9	0	0	2	1,770
Geton	4	F	12	0	2	0	4,034
Getoutofmyvalay	3	F	1	0	0	0	230
Getoutoftheway	5	M	13	2	3	2	14,414
Getouttamykitchen	2	F	3	0	0	0	1,310
Getta Klew	2	F	1	1	0	0	7,920
Gettarman	3	G	7	1	2	1	30,976
Getten	5	G	2	0	0	0	110
Getthepartystarted	3	F	7	2	1	1	30,955
Gettin Better	3	F	13	2	3	1	12,506
Gettin' Overtime	11	G	3	0	0	0	140
Gettin With It	4	C	3	0	0	0	180
Getting Old	10	G	8	0	1	1	1,944
Getting Tricky	5	G	10	1	0	1	1,818
Getty Up N Go	2	C	1	0	0	0	900
Gettysburg Express	4	F	6	2	0	0	7,672
Getyourbritchesngo	5	H	13	3	1	3	52,640
Ghannam	4	C	6	3	0	0	64,120
Ghaza Run	5	M	2	0	0	0	146
Ghazada	2	F	3	0	0	0	1,625
Ghazelle	5	G	9	2	1	2	58,850
Ghazette	4	F	13	3	7	0	19,325
Ghazi Dust	3	F	11	2	1	0	10,751
Ghazi Gazelle	3	F	9	0	1	0	1,705
Ghazi Girl	6	M	6	0	0	3	2,425
Ghazi Osbourne	2	C	2	0	0	0	520
Ghazi Rose	3	F	14	1	1	3	9,215
Ghazi Strip Dancer	4	F	5	0	0	0	134
Ghazi War	3	G	4	0	0	1	4,477
Ghazibella	2	F	4	0	0	1	1,876
Ghazidora	5	M	2	0	1	0	2,163
Ghazihasit	3	F	3	1	0	0	4,714
Ghazirella	5	M	6	1	1	1	75,074
Ghazi's Delight	4	F	4	1	0	1	14,986
Ghazi's Flight	5	M	16	2	2	1	21,663
Ghazi's Ghost	3	C	9	1	0	2	23,580
Ghazi's Impala	2	G	9	1	1	0	18,122
Ghazi's Lass	5	M	1	0	1	0	1,900
Ghazis Majestic	4	C	4	0	0	0	205
Ghazi's Secret	5	H	3	0	1	0	1,150
Ghazoline	6	H	2	0	0	0	320
Ghetto	2	G	9	0	0	1	1,880
Ghibli's Image	4	G	2	0	0	0	0
Ghoastly Prize	5	G	13	6	2	1	56,927
Ghost Catcher	3	F	4	1	0	0	6,164
Ghost Chatter	3	F	9	4	2	0	121,349
Ghost Fever	7	G	2	0	1	0	5,600
Ghost Flyer	2	F	1	0	0	0	0
Ghost Mate	3	G	10	1	0	2	29,350
Ghost Meadow	3	F	1	0	0	0	0
Ghost Memo	3	G	16	3	1	3	72,085
Ghost Mountain	2	C	6	2	1	1	82,054
Ghost of Earl	6	G	6	1	0	0	1,365
Ghost of Granny	4	G	6	1	0	0	3,319
Ghost Queen	4	F	7	1	0	1	24,465
Ghost Rhythm	6	G	6	2	1	1	25,250
Ghost to the Post	3	C	4	2	1	1	12,517
Ghost Valley	4	G	5	0	1	1	4,550
Ghost Wrestling	4	F	1	0	0	0	93
Ghostly Endeavor	4	C	7	0	1	2	2,620
Ghostly Gate	2	F	4	1	0	2	31,157
Ghostly Image	3	C	13	2	1	0	26,205
Ghostly Maneuvers	2	C	3	1	0	0	9,110

Horse	Age	Sex	Sts	1st	2d	3d	Won
Ghostly Minister	6	H	7	1	1	1	9,350
Ghostly Moon	4	G	5	0	0	0	272
Ghostly Numbers	5	H	9	1	2	0	59,530
Ghostly Victor	3	G	12	2	4	2	12,563
Ghostsong (NZ)	9	G	7	0	1	2	725
Ghostzapper	3	C	4	3	0	1	378,400
Giaco	4	C	6	1	1	0	38,330
Giacobbe	4	G	10	2	3	1	34,425
Giant American	4	G	3	0	0	0	320
Giant Bellyache	3	C	17	2	5	2	53,620
Giant Clam Soup	4	G	8	1	1	0	2,061
Giant Slam	6	H	6	1	0	2	16,428
Giants Party	3	F	15	0	3	2	9,862
Gib Merlin	3	C	8	0	0	1	6,160
Gibbar	2	G	6	0	0	1	2,950
Gibberjabberpitch	4	C	1	0	0	0	118
Gibbs Beach	3	G	9	2	1	0	19,127
Gibford	2	G	8	1	2	1	28,558
Gib's Pal	3	C	3	1	0	0	17,640
Gibson City	4	G	9	2	0	1	9,616
Gibson County	6	H	2	0	0	0	0
Gibson Station	3	G	16	1	1	1	11,345
Gibson Witch	2	F	2	0	0	0	0
Gichy Gichy Yayaya	6	M	3	0	0	0	209
Giddy Lilly	3	F	11	2	3	1	19,150
Giddy Up Bullseye	4	C	11	2	1	1	12,874
Giddy Up Lloyd	7	G	7	0	4	1	2,394
Gideon	5	H	16	3	1	2	54,431
Gifford Road	3	C	4	0	0	0	5,460
Gift Box of Jewels	10	G	6	0	0	0	1,490
Gift of April	2	F	2	0	0	0	290
Gift of Honor	4	F	3	1	1	0	6,975
Gift of Love	5	M	10	2	1	0	25,806
Gift of the Eagle	5	H	2	1	0	0	42,000
Gift of Time	6	M	2	0	0	0	79
Gifted Athlete	6	G	6	3	0	0	16,253
Gifted Daughter	5	M	4	1	0	0	20,625
Gifted Guy	10	G	7	1	1	2	4,663
Gifted Peter	5	G	1	0	0	0	140
Gifted Speaker	4	G	2	0	0	0	860
Gifted Warrior	3	G	4	0	2	0	560
Gigabyte	7	H	8	0	1	1	7,222
Gigahertz	3	F	8	1	0	0	5,100
Gigawatt	3	C	5	0	0	0	52,380
Giggandjogg	3	F	7	1	2	0	10,920
Giggle Box	3	G	8	1	1	1	7,962
Giggle Fit	7	M	3	0	0	0	0
Giggles and Smiles	3	G	9	1	1	0	2,932
Gigha	4	G	3	1	0	2	3,990
Gigi's Skyflyer	4	F	8	1	1	3	33,540
Gigiski	3	F	2	0	0	0	695
Giglet	5	M	1	0	0	0	0
Gigli (BRZ)	5	H	2	0	1	0	12,400
Gilardi's Ace	6	G	1	0	0	0	41
Gilbertslewogold	5	G	16	2	5	1	10,782
Gilded Belle	3	F	7	0	1	1	9,620
Gilded Bertrando	2	C	6	2	1	1	84,839
Gilded Cove	2	C	5	1	0	0	6,915
Gilded Deputy	3	G	14	1	2	0	6,535
Gilded Edition	5	H	3	0	0	0	309
Gilded Emperor	6	G	8	3	0	1	58,010
Gilded Gold	2	F	1	0	0	0	0
Gilded Gold Flyer	3	C	7	2	3	1	46,194
Gilded Graces	2	C	2	0	0	0	100
Gilded Honor	2	G	1	0	0	0	0
Gilded Nip	4	F	11	0	2	2	17,921
Gilded Oreo	3	C	7	0	0	1	2,283
Gilded Pin	3	C	4	1	2	0	15,120
Gilded Queen	4	F	6	0	0	0	0
Gilded Son	9	G	4	0	0	0	250
Gilded Sword	7	G	1	0	0	0	0
Gilded Venture	7	G	14	2	2	1	13,848
Gilded Way	5	H	12	1	1	1	12,195
Gilded Wings	4	F	5	0	3	0	16,660
Gilded Years	3	C	4	0	0	0	0
Gildersleeves	2	C	2	0	0	0	0
Gildmore	4	G	11	2	3	2	39,950
Gillane's Way	4	G	2	0	0	0	0
Gillespie	2	G	5	0	1	0	4,160
Gillys a Ham	3	G	10	1	0	3	6,600
Giltyagain	5	M	3	0	0	0	80
Gimbal	7	M	5	0	1	0	2,945
Gimeone Stall Ples	3	C	6	0	0	0	1,173
Gimme	4	G	5	0	0	1	550
Gimme a Clue	5	M	13	3	1	4	57,052
Gimme a Hint	4	C	11	1	1	0	9,760
Gimme a Vee	2	F	2	0	0	0	0
Gimme an A	4	G	4	1	1	1	24,426
Gimme Dattt	3	C	2	0	0	0	580
Gimme Fever	3	F	5	0	0	3	17,695
Gimme Five	3	F	7	1	1	1	4,844
Gimme Half a Break	4	C	9	0	0	2	8,433
Gimme No Lip	4	G	10	1	2	0	16,913
Gimme Some Love	2	F	1	1	0	0	27,000
Gimme the Willys	5	M	10	0	1	2	9,710
Gimmeawink	3	C	14	6	3	0	456,880
Gimmesumsugar	2	F	2	0	0	0	0
Gin and Sin	3	G	13	3	2	0	67,305
Gin Dandy	4	G	11	0	0	3	8,160
Gin N Ginger	6	M	10	1	3	2	32,735
Gin n' Tychonic	3	F	6	2	2	0	10,300
Gin Real Officer	3	C	6	0	2	0	8,175
Gin Rummy Champ	2	C	7	1	1	2	25,085
Gin Runner	2	F	1	0	0	0	0
Gin Star	3	F	17	1	2	5	18,950
Gin Visions	4	F	7	0	0	0	1,300
Gina Serena	3	F	9	0	1	0	2,880
Gina Z	4	F	5	0	0	2	1,500
Gina's Actress	5	M	6	0	0	0	722
Gina's Eyes	5	G	17	1	1	1	8,198
Ginas Girl	4	F	16	3	3	2	44,751
Ginas Gold	4	F	2	0	0	1	1,050
Gina's Jack	5	G	12	1	3	0	5,279
Gina's Star	2	C	5	0	0	0	350
Gina's Zaroyev	5	M	11	1	0	1	4,387
Gindigo	4	G	9	1	0	2	17,580
Ging	5	G	8	1	1	0	1,604
Ginger	2	F	3	0	0	0	290
Ginger Ale	4	C	13	1	2	3	44,384
Ginger Daddy	7	G	11	2	1	0	13,465
Ginger Dancer	7	M	7	0	0	0	302
Ginger Fish	6	M	2	0	0	0	0
Ginger for Pluck	4	G	8	0	1	1	9,799
Ginger Gold	4	F	9	1	2	0	120,555
Ginger Hoffa	3	F	7	0	0	0	1,432
Ginger Moon	4	F	9	0	1	0	1,828
Ginger N Sugar	2	F	1	1	0	0	24,600
Ginger Roo	5	M	1	0	0	0	82
Ginger Spin	6	M	15	3	2	1	24,703
Ginger Tweak	3	F	13	0	2	3	7,852
Gingerbread House	3	F	10	1	0	3	12,330
Gingerella	3	F	5	1	1	1	20,530
Ginger's Gnash	3	F	15	0	0	2	1,470
Ginger's Honor	3	F	1	0	0	0	0
Ginger's Jet	2	F	3	0	0	0	0
Gingham and Lace	2	F	3	1	1	0	21,600
Gingham Curtains	3	F	11	2	1	1	24,475
Gingi	5	M	5	0	1	1	3,208
Gini Go Go	12	M	1	0	0	0	0
Ginny Hooper	3	F	4	0	0	1	1,860
Ginnypoo	2	F	2	0	1	0	2,617
Ginny's Guy	6	H	1	0	0	0	49
Ginny's Place	6	G	1	0	0	0	38
Gino Massetti	2	C	1	1	0	0	8,400
Ginontherocks	6	H	2	0	0	0	858
Gins Award	3	F	5	0	0	0	313
Ginzano	5	G	7	3	1	1	97,170
Ginzilla	2	F	3	0	0	0	0
Gion	4	F	21	2	3	2	32,319
Giovannetti	4	G	8	2	1	1	163,560
Giovannina	5	M	10	1	3	0	14,820
Gip Jr.	4	G	15	1	2	2	16,098
Gipsy's Noactor	4	G	13	1	1	0	6,591
Girard	4	G	19	5	1	2	45,870
Girded	5	M	2	0	0	0	0
Girl Fever	3	C	8	0	0	1	5,200
Girl Gone Bye Bye	2	F	4	2	0	0	22,200
Girl Gone Crazy	2	F	1	1	0	0	13,800

RECORDS OF HORSES

Horse	Age	Sex	Sts	1st	2d	3d	Won	Horse	Age	Sex	Sts	1st	2d	3d	Won
Girl Gone Wild	3	F	11	2	0	1	11,794	Glade Hunter	2	C	8	1	0	1	11,085
Girl Hunter	2	G	2	0	0	0	0	Gladiator Guy	2	G	5	0	0	1	2,403
Girl of the North	4	F	2	1	0	0	996	Gladiator's Battle	3	G	6	0	0	0	100
Girl On Go	2	F	3	2	1	0	25,710	Gladiator's Drift	3	F	6	1	1	0	50,328
Girl Reporter	3	F	13	2	0	1	16,310	Gladiator's Gold	3	C	17	2	2	2	16,517
Girl Scout	2	F	4	0	0	0	0	Gladies Gold	3	F	3	0	0	0	500
Girl Secrets	2	F	1	0	0	0	0	Gladius	4	C	2	0	0	0	667
Girl Talk	6	M	9	2	0	4	28,860	Gladman	3	C	3	0	0	0	320
Girl Toy	3	F	1	0	0	0	130	Gladpack	4	G	10	0	0	1	2,403
Girl With Attitude	3	F	7	0	5	1	8,656	Gladville	6	M	8	0	0	5	9,465
Girlie Attitude	2	F	1	0	0	0	376	Gladyougottoseeme	3	F	7	3	0	0	38,760
Girls First Love	6	M	15	2	4	2	9,127	Gladys Kravitz	5	M	5	0	0	1	308
Girls' Glory	3	F	10	0	1	0	3,405	Gladys Pembroke	3	F	5	0	0	1	2,159
Girl's Got Rhythm	2	F	3	0	0	0	255	Gladys T.	6	M	1	0	0	0	0
Girls Got Skills	2	F	11	0	3	2	7,380	Glamdring	4	G	9	0	2	2	35,470
Girls Rule	2	F	2	1	0	0	4,980	Glamorama	3	F	3	0	0	1	1,300
Girl's Sport	5	M	9	2	0	0	5,648	Glamorize	3	F	11	1	5	1	31,574
Girlsintheoffice	2	F	2	0	0	1	2,940	Glamorous Life	4	F	2	2	0	0	12,825
Girlsrock	3	F	3	0	0	0	0	Glamour Cat	2	F	1	0	0	0	2,940
Girlyprospect	5	M	4	0	0	0	162	Glamour Gal	3	F	3	1	0	1	9,585
Girusol	3	F	10	0	1	1	17,146	Glamour Puss	3	F	6	0	0	0	1,020
Gisellous	2	F	2	0	0	0	666	Glamour Shot	2	F	2	0	1	0	3,640
Gist	4	F	6	0	1	1	13,360	Glamourus Affair	3	F	4	0	0	1	2,489
Gist of Art	6	G	13	2	0	1	30,453	Glance Again	3	F	2	0	0	0	410
Git Hooked	3	G	2	0	0	0	82	Glance of Glitter	4	G	2	0	0	0	60
Gitano Dancer (ARG)	9	G	2	0	0	0	156	Glance Remark	6	G	13	0	6	2	28,608
Gitem Willie	3	F	5	0	0	1	1,380	Glance Wink Smile	3	F	2	0	1	0	4,960
Gitgo	2	G	1	0	0	0	0	Glancing	3	F	8	1	1	3	11,155
Gitsumyonder	6	M	4	0	0	0	288	Glarenmore	3	G	1	0	1	0	2,600
Giuseppe's Champ	4	G	5	0	0	1	5,735	Glaring Battle	3	G	4	0	0	0	0
Giuseppe's Majesty	5	G	21	2	5	4	19,921	Glaring Bid	5	G	5	0	1	0	5,368
Giuseppe's Ole Pal	3	G	10	0	0	2	1,319	Glaring Ego	3	F	4	0	0	0	0
Giuseppes Rajeanne	5	M	4	0	0	1	1,190	Glaring for a Win	2	G	1	0	0	0	822
Give and Take	4	F	11	1	3	2	57,985	Glaring Jewel	5	G	4	0	0	0	0
Give Away Joe	3	G	20	1	5	5	34,610	Glaring Keyhole	3	C	1	0	0	0	0
Give Faith	2	C	6	0	1	1	22,095	Glaring Senorita	5	M	2	0	0	0	0
Give God the Glory	4	F	6	0	0	1	2,121	Glaring Wistex	3	F	9	0	1	1	2,445
Give It a Go	4	G	2	0	0	0	990	Glaringlory	4	F	1	0	0	0	50
Give It a Shot	6	H	1	0	1	0	1,220	Glass and Glow	3	G	5	0	1	0	1,799
Give Me a Break	4	G	2	0	0	0	0	Glassford Hill	4	F	2	2	0	0	12,780
Give Me a Double	4	C	12	1	1	4	21,049	Glassy Star	3	C	1	0	0	0	0
Give Me a Smile	2	F	1	0	0	0	230	Glastonbury	2	F	1	0	0	0	0
Give Me Cash	4	G	8	0	1	0	1,853	Glazed Gold	4	G	8	1	1	0	5,772
Give Me Five	6	H	13	2	2	1	14,407	Gleam Supreme	4	G	3	1	0	0	5,536
Give Me the Money	6	G	15	0	1	3	4,443	Gleaming Looker	2	F	1	0	0	0	0
Give Up the Cash	4	G	7	0	2	3	5,610	Glean	6	G	9	1	1	0	45,894
Give Us an Encore	7	H	5	0	1	1	3,294	Gleeful Tyler	3	G	8	0	0	0	2,004
Givemeatri	4	F	14	4	1	2	53,653	Gleichen Reserve	5	M	7	1	1	2	21,919
Givemeavector	4	G	2	1	0	0	12,600	Glen Conscience	3	F	14	0	2	0	2,550
Givemeawink	2	G	3	0	0	0	450	Glenbriar Girl	4	F	4	0	0	1	6,000
Givemejustaminute	3	F	4	0	0	0	0	Glencairn	3	C	2	0	1	0	1,880
Givemethejackpot	2	C	5	1	1	1	13,265	Glencreek	6	H	17	4	1	4	22,976
Givemethemine	4	F	4	0	0	1	1,307	Glenda Kay	3	F	16	3	2	4	21,578
Givemethreedimes	5	G	10	0	0	2	11,267	Glenda Smile	8	G	5	0	0	0	0
Givemethreesteps	3	F	2	0	0	1	1,150	Glendas Desertrain	3	F	5	0	1	0	1,129
Given Point	2	F	3	0	0	0	528	Glenleary	2	G	2	0	0	0	0
Given Probation	2	G	1	0	0	0	0	Glenmars Addiction	3	G	18	2	1	2	19,408
Given the Shaft	4	F	8	0	0	2	3,028	Glenmary	4	F	14	5	1	0	19,039
Given to Fly	5	H	10	2	1	3	19,383	Glennascaul	2	F	6	0	0	1	10,454
Givens Road	4	G	4	0	0	0	0	Glenners	2	C	5	0	1	0	5,250
Givensilver	3	G	9	1	1	1	40,210	Glenns Connection	2	C	2	0	1	1	22,555
Givetheboyacigar	3	C	14	1	3	3	36,110	Glens Devil Due	6	H	6	1	0	1	15,840
Giving	6	M	6	0	1	0	1,171	Glen's Love	5	G	13	2	1	1	15,079
Giving Orders	3	G	8	0	2	2	3,829	Glens Muffin	2	G	1	0	0	0	0
Giving Tree	3	G	7	0	1	2	12,672	Glenurla	3	F	3	0	0	0	149
Givonna S	3	F	1	0	0	0	829	Glenville Dottie	5	M	11	0	0	0	829
Giz Anjiz	5	G	8	0	1	1	3,298	Glenwood Springs	6	G	17	5	3	2	32,136
Glace	5	M	11	0	0	0	2,415	Glia	4	F	2	0	0	0	0
Glacier Gal	3	F	7	1	0	1	13,580	Glick	7	H	13	4	2	0	111,330
Glacier Point	7	G	11	2	1	1	22,335	Glide On In	5	H	2	0	0	0	136
Glaciers End	4	C	2	0	0	1	8,400	Glides Emigrant	7	H	17	4	6	2	77,706
Glacken	3	G	6	2	1	1	25,320	Gliding Dancer	9	G	10	1	1	2	9,743
Glad	5	G	1	0	1	0	840	Glifter	3	F	4	0	0	3	17,310
Glad as Knight	2	F	6	0	1	1	14,739	Glimmer Girl	4	F	1	0	0	0	240
Glad It's Holly	7	F	7	1	2	0	9,511	Glimmer of Hope	3	G	2	0	0	0	48
Glad Tidings	6	G	18	3	3	3	17,203	Glimmering Cat	3	F	4	0	1	2	5,310
Glad to Be a Lady	3	F	5	1	0	2	4,465	Glimpse	3	C	8	2	4	1	32,190
Glad to Be Here	3	C	4	2	2	0	21,050	Glimpse of Glamour	3	F	5	0	0	0	0
Glad You Dance	2	C	5	1	0	0	13,800	Glint	4	C	12	3	4	1	47,875

Horse	Age	Sex	Sts	1st	2d	3d	Won
Glint Eastward	6	G	5	1	1	1	4,475
Glit	8	G	10	4	2	0	21,225
Glitgo	9	G	5	0	0	0	80
Glitter Act	3	F	6	2	3	1	86,890
Glitter All Over	4	G	9	3	3	0	16,459
Glitter and Charm	3	G	7	1	0	1	6,298
Glitter B Glitter	3	F	2	0	0	0	0
Glitter Babe	2	F	1	0	0	0	0
Glitter Baby	5	M	14	1	1	2	19,881
Glitter Cat	4	G	8	3	1	0	34,554
Glitter Copy	2	F	2	0	0	0	295
Glitter Cove	3	F	2	1	1	0	14,380
Glitter Gulch	4	F	1	0	0	0	1,950
Glitter in Blue	3	G	14	2	6	2	81,320
Glitter Lil Star	3	F	5	1	0	0	10,380
Glitter Maid	3	F	17	3	3	0	40,860
Glitter Mean	3	G	11	2	4	1	50,257
Glitter Music	5	M	3	0	0	0	1,090
Glitter of Hope	4	G	9	2	1	1	9,728
Glitter Point	3	G	19	2	1	4	33,700
Glitter Queen	2	F	6	1	1	0	26,547
Glitter Storm	3	G	11	3	2	0	25,730
Glitter Time	3	F	3	1	0	0	18,225
Glitter Trapp	4	F	10	0	1	3	4,028
Glitter Twice	4	F	11	2	0	0	15,432
Glitterama	3	G	3	1	0	0	5,663
Glitterbdancing	3	F	5	1	1	0	21,580
Glitterbend	4	G	12	1	1	2	9,940
Glitterberry	5	G	8	1	1	1	7,784
Glitterbug	5	M	6	1	0	0	3,960
Glittergem	2	C	3	1	2	0	58,400
Glittergroup	3	G	3	0	0	0	160
Glittin' Gold	4	F	18	0	3	5	10,607
Glittering Betty	3	F	7	2	0	0	2,722
Glittering Chad	4	F	9	0	0	2	7,066
Glittering Jenna	7	M	13	0	2	1	4,093
Glittering Lady	8	M	4	2	1	0	12,987
Glittering Man	4	G	14	0	1	6	8,840
Glittering Pewter	2	G	5	1	0	0	4,685
Glittering Prize (FR)	2	F	1	0	0	0	217
Glittering Racket	4	F	12	3	6	0	53,680
Glittering Stone	4	G	2	1	0	1	3,710
Glittering Success	3	F	11	2	2	2	40,446
Glitteringmischief	5	M	3	0	0	1	3,100
Glitterjean	4	F	7	2	1	2	14,466
Glitter's Alone	5	H	4	0	0	0	84
Glitterwan	3	C	5	1	0	1	29,140
Glitz and Glitter	5	M	4	1	0	1	3,610
Glo and Go	6	G	4	0	0	0	170
Glo Fer D	4	G	7	1	0	2	7,691
Glo Most Hot	3	F	19	0	1	1	2,374
Glo Pirate	5	M	12	2	2	3	31,262
Gloat	5	H	9	1	1	1	10,640
Global Arena	2	G	3	0	0	0	610
Global Attraction	3	C	1	0	0	0	540
Global Dancer	3	F	4	0	0	2	10,000
Global Dream	5	G	14	3	2	1	28,687
Global Economy	5	G	7	0	0	2	2,425
Global Games	3	G	12	1	1	2	30,078
Global Hawk	3	C	5	1	0	1	16,440
Global Image	4	F	5	2	0	0	23,008
Global Link	4	C	5	0	2	1	7,890
Global Peace	3	C	7	1	0	1	12,820
Global Quest	4	C	3	2	0	0	44,400
Global Risk	3	G	5	0	0	0	286
Global Rullah	3	C	3	1	0	0	3,480
Global Vision	4	F	2	0	0	0	152
Global's Outlaw	10	G	17	2	2	4	10,934
Globel Pine	2	C	1	0	0	0	0
Glorado	6	M	8	1	1	1	31,906
Glori Di Savoya	4	F	2	0	0	0	73
Gloria Gold Cross	4	F	17	2	0	1	10,646
Gloriafrompeoria	3	F	11	0	1	0	2,141
Gloriosa	4	F	7	1	1	0	33,785
Gloriosity	4	F	11	0	2	4	29,775
Glorioso	5	G	7	1	0	0	4,131
Glorious Again	3	F	1	0	1	0	5,250
Glorious Angel	7	G	16	0	0	3	13,622
Glorious Bear	3	C	8	0	0	2	4,025
Glorious Belle	10	M	2	0	0	0	80
Glorious Cat	4	F	3	0	1	1	6,300
Glorious Choice	2	F	3	0	0	0	0
Glorious Dragon	3	F	6	2	1	0	32,605
Glorious Export (BRZ)	5	H	1	0	0	0	0
Glorious Gold	4	G	4	0	0	0	225
Glorious Grace	5	M	10	2	3	0	111,512
Glorious Halo	4	F	9	1	0	2	11,528
Glorious Hero	2	G	1	1	0	0	8,340
Glorious Jenna	3	F	12	2	2	1	80,274
Glorious Jet	6	M	5	0	0	0	2,280
Glorious Jo	4	F	4	0	0	0	350
Glorious King	4	C	8	0	0	3	6,870
Glorious Miss	3	F	5	0	1	2	26,530
Glorious Morn	2	F	3	0	0	0	1,140
Glorious Quest	3	F	7	2	0	1	28,528
Glorious Raj	2	F	8	3	0	2	21,900
Glorious Sandy	3	F	19	0	1	2	3,238
Glorious Survivor	2	G	2	0	0	0	770
Glorious Tune	4	F	10	0	0	1	7,740
Glorita	4	F	1	0	0	0	810
Glory Be Good	3	F	13	4	5	2	93,400
Glory Be to Winloc	3	G	15	3	2	3	113,457
Glory d'Or	5	G	1	0	0	0	90
Glory Glory	5	M	2	0	0	0	2,780
Glory Jean	3	F	13	3	3	2	53,000
Glory of Love	4	F	14	3	2	1	88,260
Glory Queen	5	M	9	1	0	1	5,824
Glory Ride	2	C	1	0	0	0	0
Glory Royale	3	F	11	2	0	1	106,309
Glory Run	2	F	1	0	0	0	780
Glory to God	2	F	1	0	0	0	130
Glory Trail	5	H	4	0	0	1	3,141
Glory Train	3	F	5	1	0	0	3,520
Glory Win	2	F	2	0	1	0	1,520
Glory With Grace	7	G	10	0	0	0	1,120
Glory's Ace	8	G	12	6	1	0	64,600
Glorys Gotcha	5	M	12	1	1	2	9,799
Glory's Wish	3	G	13	0	1	0	2,131
Glo's Moe	8	G	5	3	1	0	8,695
Glow Brook	4	F	3	1	0	2	22,520
Glow of Gold	5	G	3	0	0	1	718
Glow of Love	2	F	1	0	0	1	2,640
Glow Plug	2	C	4	0	0	2	1,804
Glow Ruby Go	4	F	1	0	0	0	0
Glowbulette	5	M	11	0	1	1	1,839
Glowing Breeze	3	F	5	2	0	2	34,250
Glowing Brite	2	F	1	0	0	0	678
Glowing Cat	3	C	1	0	0	0	2,750
Glowing Colors	3	F	7	2	2	2	80,804
Glowing Gold	6	G	10	1	0	0	3,339
Glowing Halo	4	F	1	1	0	0	20,400
Glowing Miss	4	F	11	4	2	0	16,916
Glowing Princess	7	M	2	0	0	0	0
Glowing Review	8	G	3	0	1	1	2,010
Glowing West	3	F	9	1	1	0	7,033
Glows Codetoo	5	G	11	1	0	1	5,750
Glue	4	C	7	1	1	0	6,954
Glycerene	8	G	1	0	0	0	0
Gmork	2	C	1	0	0	0	1,080
Gnarl	11	G	11	0	3	4	4,138
Gnarler	5	H	8	1	1	1	10,940
Gneiss Bonus	2	G	1	0	0	0	0
Gneiss Lady	2	F	6	0	0	0	3,693
Gneiss Limo	2	C	7	0	0	2	6,549
Gneiss Pick	2	F	2	0	1	0	2,800
Gnilpoc	6	M	12	0	2	2	5,005
Gnomes Star	5	G	8	1	3	1	30,338
Go America	2	C	2	0	1	0	4,340
Go and Dare Me	5	G	7	0	0	1	1,508
Go Andsinnomore	6	G	6	0	0	0	0
Go Annika	2	F	6	0	1	2	9,335
Go Ante Go	3	F	11	2	2	0	53,276
Go Ask Alice	5	M	11	3	1	2	7,088
Go Ask Daisy	2	F	4	2	0	1	56,130
Go Avie Go	3	G	6	1	0	0	14,334
Go Baby Geo	4	G	14	2	1	1	8,605
Go Baby Go (IRE)	5	M	2	0	0	0	1,400
Go Baby Go Go	5	M	4	0	0	1	1,884

Horse	Age	Sex	Sts	1st	2d	3d	Won
Go Baby Ice	3	F	1	0	1	0	9,800
Go Baby Slew	4	F	6	1	0	1	3,992
Go Bam Bam Go	5	H	15	5	2	4	26,430
Go Bart Go	3	G	5	0	0	0	522
Go Bear	5	H	8	1	0	0	6,585
Go Betty Jo	4	F	4	0	0	0	277
Go Big Blue	5	G	14	1	2	1	17,120
Go Bob Go	3	F	9	0	0	0	1,305
Go Browns	4	C	9	3	1	1	18,660
Go Bubbles Go	4	F	21	4	2	7	10,448
Go Bug Off	8	H	2	0	0	0	0
Go Bux	10	G	3	0	0	0	468
Go Bye Bye	2	F	3	0	3	0	26,400
Go Cache It	4	G	3	0	0	0	375
Go Calif Go	5	H	5	0	0	1	2,524
Go Cart	4	G	8	0	0	0	937
Go Casper	4	G	5	0	3	0	4,894
Go Cassie Jo	4	F	11	2	1	0	26,999
Go Chandler	10	G	4	0	1	0	1,837
Go Chilean Go	2	G	2	0	1	0	1,360
Go Chloe Go	4	F	10	0	0	1	2,266
Go Coyote	4	G	4	2	1	0	29,780
Go Crystal Go	3	F	6	0	0	1	2,956
Go Dale Go	12	G	5	1	1	0	3,495
Go Deputy	3	C	5	3	1	0	104,200
Go Derby Go	4	F	5	1	1	1	24,513
Go Derek Go	3	G	3	0	0	0	0
Go Diddles Go	4	G	5	0	0	0	0
Go Directlyto Jail	2	C	1	0	0	0	110
Go Doctor Mo	3	G	3	0	0	0	510
Go Figure	5	G	10	1	1	2	56,919
Go Flash Go	3	G	9	3	0	2	11,948
Go Fletch Libby	2	F	2	0	0	0	0
Go for Bust	3	G	17	3	0	2	17,556
Go for Free	3	F	5	1	1	0	7,500
Go for Glamour	3	F	8	2	0	2	120,860
Go for Glitter	5	G	10	4	2	0	35,313
Go for Greed	5	M	3	1	1	0	7,312
Go for Launch	4	F	10	1	1	2	12,727
Go for Leslie	5	M	5	0	0	0	638
Go for Matty	2	F	5	0	0	2	4,190
Go for Now	3	C	3	0	0	1	4,730
Go for Puddin	6	M	11	2	3	0	43,620
Go for Quality	3	F	10	1	1	0	8,280
Go for the Gals	3	G	13	2	0	2	10,487
Go for the Grey	5	M	8	1	3	0	20,130
Go Gal Go	5	M	11	4	1	1	42,460
Go Gavin Go	7	G	10	4	2	0	34,695
Go Get Em Harry	4	G	8	1	1	0	4,561
Go Get It	4	F	1	0	0	0	0
Go Getem Shorty	3	G	4	0	0	0	313
Go Girl Go	4	F	6	1	0	1	24,400
Go Girlfriend Go	2	F	1	0	0	0	95
Go Go Baby Go	4	F	9	4	1	1	70,940
Go Go Chief's	5	G	4	0	0	0	314
Go Go Get Em	5	G	8	0	0	0	261
Go Go Hasty	6	M	10	2	3	2	24,670
Go Go Johnny Go	4	G	1	1	0	0	3,300
Go Go Leslie	4	F	9	3	0	0	13,343
Go Go Okie	3	F	10	4	2	0	41,980
Go Go Pete	4	G	16	5	0	2	16,217
Go Go Rachael	3	F	3	0	0	0	775
Go Go Sassy Sue	2	F	1	0	0	0	0
Go Go Tommy Joe	4	G	11	0	0	2	5,089
Go Go Wiggy	3	F	4	0	0	1	810
Go Going Gone	4	F	7	3	0	2	27,060
Go Go's T K O	5	M	4	0	0	0	484
Go Grace Go	2	F	8	1	1	0	7,346
Go Grant Go	8	G	12	1	0	1	3,158
Go Grey Beu	6	H	3	0	0	0	0
Go Helen Go	4	F	6	0	0	0	1,630
Go High	4	F	5	0	1	0	4,053
Go In	5	M	2	1	0	0	8,820
Go J. S. Go	7	G	3	0	0	0	504
Go Jaylo	2	F	1	0	0	0	0
Go Jeanaie Go	3	F	7	1	0	2	12,165
Go Jelly Bean Go	4	F	9	1	1	2	23,400
Go Jesse Tyler	4	C	12	1	0	2	14,195
Go John	3	G	4	0	0	0	204
Go Johnny Go	2	C	2	2	0	0	17,060
Go Joma	5	G	4	1	0	0	24,600
Go Karina	3	F	10	1	1	2	6,730
Go Kitty Go	2	C	5	0	2	2	39,663
Go Koolla	2	G	1	0	0	0	0
Go Legs Go	4	C	9	3	1	0	25,120
Go Lib Go	6	G	11	2	0	1	9,044
Go Lionel Go	2	C	1	0	0	0	1,560
Go Lite Gold	5	G	18	2	4	2	16,449
Go Little Joe Go	3	C	13	3	4	1	31,450
Go Lively	9	G	16	2	2	3	9,486
Go Man Go	8	G	9	0	2	0	2,626
Go Margo	3	F	11	1	4	0	18,510
Go Max Go	3	G	4	1	0	0	9,750
Go Meem Go	5	M	2	0	0	0	87
Go Mercy Go	4	C	9	2	0	2	10,861
Go Mike	5	G	6	0	3	1	9,636
Go Mikey Go	8	G	5	0	0	0	150
Go Minerva Go	4	F	6	2	1	1	11,627
Go Miss Bag	3	F	8	1	1	3	25,002
Go Mr. Manner	2	G	3	0	0	0	0
Go Natalie Go	5	M	3	0	0	0	920
Go Naz	5	H	1	0	0	0	0
Go Niner	4	F	11	0	1	2	7,295
Go North	3	C	9	1	3	0	73,940
Go North Sammy	3	F	2	0	0	1	1,450
Go Not Whoa	8	G	12	1	1	5	22,373
Go Now	2	C	2	0	0	1	5,350
Go On Baby	5	M	12	2	3	1	115,549
Go On Forever	6	H	11	3	1	5	28,724
Go On Get	3	C	3	0	0	0	368
Go On Green	4	G	4	0	0	2	2,976
Go On Orange	5	H	9	1	1	0	28,049
Go On Red	4	C	8	2	0	0	19,860
Go Peydro Go	3	G	17	3	8	2	25,192
Go Platinum	4	F	13	2	2	1	10,550
Go Polly Ko	4	C	4	0	0	1	620
Go Pui Lai	4	F	1	0	0	0	89
Go Rail Go	5	G	9	2	2	2	69,470
Go Robert Go	3	C	4	0	0	1	1,207
Go Roberta	4	F	3	0	0	1	1,631
Go Rockin' Robin	3	C	11	3	1	2	233,446
Go Rocky Go	5	H	2	0	0	0	108
Go Rolls Go	5	G	7	1	0	2	5,998
Go Rose	3	F	1	0	0	0	1,500
Go Ruby Go	5	M	3	0	0	0	1,200
Go Salem By	6	G	14	2	3	3	5,571
Go Salem Go	6	G	4	0	0	0	0
Go Sammi Go	6	H	8	1	0	1	5,560
Go Scotty	9	G	2	0	0	0	654
Go See Mervin	9	G	11	0	1	1	3,492
Go Sis Go	6	M	2	0	0	2	760
Go Smokey Go	4	F	6	1	0	1	6,262
Go Star Buster	3	G	7	1	1	2	21,130
Go Steady	2	F	2	1	1	0	34,400
Go Steph Go	3	F	14	1	0	3	4,208
Go Tiff Go	3	F	5	1	0	0	10,320
Go to Church	4	F	9	2	1	1	6,660
Go to Guy	8	G	9	1	2	1	7,061
Go to Harvard	5	G	12	0	2	2	7,700
Go Tommy	3	C	6	3	0	1	36,045
Go Too	3	F	3	0	0	0	0
Go Tori Go	3	F	10	1	1	2	9,980
Go Two Gold	4	G	5	0	2	0	5,070
Go Went Gone	6	M	9	0	1	0	6,413
Go West Again	2	G	6	1	2	1	14,937
Go West Jenny	3	F	16	2	2	4	13,110
Go Wild	2	G	5	0	2	0	16,738
Go Willie	4	G	2	0	0	0	720
Go Your Own Way	7	M	7	1	1	2	5,692
Go Yoyo	3	F	9	2	2	1	21,010
Go Zippy Go	6	M	6	0	0	0	3,000
Goal	3	G	10	2	0	0	20,989
Goal Line	5	G	12	0	0	4	5,870
Goal Master	4	G	8	0	0	0	753
Goat Dancer	4	F	8	1	1	0	1,818
Goaway Doctor	4	C	2	0	0	0	0
Gobber	4	G	6	3	1	1	16,626
Gobi Dan	4	C	2	0	1	0	6,200

Horse	Age	Sex	Sts	1st	2d	3d	Won
God Bless Us	5	G	1	1	0	0	2,310
God Sent	5	H	4	1	0	0	6,870
God She's Fast	5	M	1	0	0	0	44
Godchild	5	G	11	0	2	4	14,286
Goddard	4	G	2	0	0	0	0
Goddess Athena	4	F	11	0	2	4	16,212
Goddess of Green	3	F	3	0	0	0	0
Godfrey	3	G	1	0	0	0	160
Godin	3	G	10	0	0	1	5,422
Godiva'n Champagne	3	F	16	2	2	5	11,962
Godolphin Cat	5	H	1	0	0	0	840
Gods Ear	3	F	18	4	2	1	121,473
God's Little Girl	3	F	4	0	0	1	2,225
Godsandodds	2	F	2	0	0	0	247
Godsend	3	G	17	4	2	2	39,470
Goforflo	3	F	12	1	0	1	5,000
Gogarrettgo	5	G	10	1	4	2	12,972
Gogarty's Way	4	G	2	0	1	0	3,375
Gogirlyougo	5	M	7	0	0	0	1,005
Gogo Lilly	3	F	12	1	0	1	7,674
Gohalo	3	G	17	0	4	5	37,790
Goin Deep	6	H	15	1	0	1	3,198
Goin N Style	4	C	10	0	1	0	4,682
Goin On Faith	3	F	2	0	0	0	0
Goin Savin	3	C	5	0	1	0	1,750
Goin' South	7	H	3	0	0	0	562
Goin' Tap City	2	G	2	0	0	0	678
Goin' to Reno	8	M	16	2	2	2	8,901
Goin Wide	4	F	8	1	0	0	7,715
Going Apalachee	8	G	3	1	0	0	3,150
Going Boldly	5	G	11	1	1	1	15,062
Going for Broke	4	G	4	0	0	1	850
Going for Two	4	G	9	1	0	2	3,721
Going Going Going	3	F	1	0	0	0	0
Going Going Gone	3	G	3	1	0	1	8,975
Going Great Guns	4	F	6	1	0	2	6,706
Going On Tour	6	H	14	0	2	1	4,044
Going Out Playin	2	F	2	0	0	0	0
Going Round	4	G	12	6	0	2	46,815
Going Thing	5	G	2	0	0	0	315
Going Twice	5	M	4	0	0	0	476
Gojoetu	3	C	3	0	1	0	6,400
Gol Lee	7	H	2	0	0	0	1,000
Golani (IRE)	6	H	7	1	1	1	27,140
Golazo	2	C	2	0	0	0	0
Golconda	4	G	7	1	3	1	57,860
Gold Act	3	C	5	1	1	1	10,815
Gold Adventure	3	G	9	0	2	0	21,250
Gold and Crystal	2	C	1	0	0	0	780
Gold Aqua	4	C	11	0	0	0	1,360
Gold At Last	4	F	9	2	1	2	13,229
Gold Attache	4	G	11	2	1	1	67,682
Gold Baby	4	C	1	1	0	0	10,200
Gold Baby Gold	3	F	1	0	0	0	0
Gold Ballad	5	H	9	4	3	0	36,820
Gold Band	3	F	13	2	3	2	36,894
Gold Bandit	9	G	14	3	1	2	11,159
Gold Bankers Gold	2	C	8	2	1	1	17,720
Gold Beat	4	G	13	1	1	0	6,826
Gold Bidder	7	G	18	5	5	3	48,508
Gold Binder	3	F	6	0	3	1	6,905
Gold Blue	4	G	15	1	1	2	20,620
Gold Bluff	3	F	13	3	1	3	19,931
Gold Boot	2	C	5	0	0	0	1,600
Gold Buckaroo	3	C	4	0	1	0	3,440
Gold Bull	5	H	3	0	0	1	1,000
Gold Bullion	3	F	12	1	1	0	15,107
Gold Butter	3	F	7	1	1	0	10,823
Gold Call	2	F	2	0	0	0	1,700
Gold Case Pleasure	3	C	11	3	2	1	34,815
Gold Certificate	8	G	7	2	1	1	21,050
Gold Change	4	F	2	0	0	0	83
Gold Charade	4	G	16	2	3	2	20,251
Gold Charter	5	G	7	1	0	1	2,250
Gold Circle	6	G	4	0	0	3	2,061
Gold City Slew	4	C	6	1	1	0	23,049
Gold Clara	3	F	1	0	0	0	0
Gold Commander One	3	G	15	3	2	4	16,810
Gold Conquest	2	C	2	0	0	1	3,488
Gold Coup	7	H	5	1	1	0	6,507
Gold Covergirl	4	F	17	3	3	0	21,967
Gold Crazy	3	F	1	0	0	0	0
Gold Cross	4	F	4	1	0	1	8,146
Gold Crusader	6	G	10	1	1	1	11,637
Gold Dancer	2	F	2	0	0	0	5,400
Gold Dealer	5	G	4	0	0	0	0
Gold Desert	6	M	1	0	0	0	94
Gold Desert Wind	9	G	5	0	0	2	411
Gold Dial	5	G	13	1	3	3	26,034
Gold Digger Gal	3	F	6	0	1	2	5,846
Gold Digger's Cart	5	M	5	1	0	1	3,124
Gold Diggin Darlin	3	F	9	1	0	0	4,350
Gold Doll	4	F	2	0	0	0	0
Gold Dollar	4	C	13	1	0	3	53,385
Gold Dot Supreme	3	F	2	0	0	0	1,519
Gold Emblem	3	F	1	0	0	0	85
Gold Empress	5	M	5	2	1	1	19,120
Gold Envoy	3	C	11	0	1	2	5,714
Gold Explorer	3	C	11	1	1	1	40,820
Gold Fabuleux	4	F	16	4	2	3	38,484
Gold Facts	2	F	4	1	0	0	17,160
Gold Feather	4	F	5	0	3	1	6,040
Gold Felt Blue	3	G	11	1	2	2	55,404
Gold Fevers Gift	5	H	5	1	2	0	11,048
Gold Finale	4	G	2	0	0	0	75
Gold Flash	3	C	3	0	0	0	248
Gold Flinger	2	F	6	1	3	0	48,440
Gold Folley	2	F	9	1	1	0	10,580
Gold Foot	2	F	2	0	0	0	960
Gold for Andrew	2	G	1	0	0	1	1,680
Gold for Ghost	4	G	10	1	0	3	6,712
Gold for Hanta	3	F	3	0	1	0	1,755
Gold for Me	4	F	8	0	3	3	8,765
Gold Fun	2	C	6	0	0	2	3,460
Gold Fund	10	G	9	0	0	0	1,045
Gold Garters	3	F	7	0	3	1	12,720
Gold Ginny	2	F	3	2	1	0	36,000
Gold Glory Won	3	G	14	2	1	1	73,696
Gold Gold Gold	4	F	8	2	1	3	24,970
Gold Goose	3	C	8	1	1	3	15,630
Gold Gunner	2	C	2	0	0	1	21,951
Gold Hunt	4	F	5	0	0	0	1,195
Gold I. D.	4	C	5	0	2	1	31,613
Gold Inside	2	C	7	1	2	1	12,328
Gold Irish	4	F	9	1	0	0	5,843
Gold Is Legal	5	M	2	0	1	0	1,515
Gold Is On Time	6	M	6	1	0	0	6,135
Gold Justice	3	G	8	2	0	1	20,202
Gold Kat	6	M	21	2	2	1	28,863
Gold Kingdom	2	G	2	0	0	0	315
Gold Lad	2	C	5	1	1	0	27,850
Gold Like U	2	F	4	1	0	1	29,110
Gold Linkage	4	F	16	1	3	4	20,767
Gold Lure	2	F	1	0	0	0	3,528
Gold Mantel	8	G	15	2	3	2	9,119
Gold Medal Runs	3	F	3	0	0	0	1,110
Gold Meteor	3	G	6	1	0	0	45,684
Gold Mind	5	M	11	0	4	2	9,318
Gold Mine	4	C	9	0	1	3	22,900
Gold Miner's Find	3	G	13	3	2	1	20,666
Gold Miss	3	F	5	0	0	1	1,287
Gold Mitten	3	F	5	1	0	2	20,140
Gold Mover	5	M	6	2	2	2	462,480
Gold Muff	3	F	6	0	0	0	540
Gold N Deal	7	H	5	0	0	0	296
Gold N Fancy	4	F	10	2	0	2	21,570
Gold 'n Harvest	2	F	3	0	1	0	5,258
Gold N Hollywood	4	F	13	1	0	2	3,555
Gold N Jade	3	G	3	0	0	0	0
Gold N Leeroyal	7	G	15	2	5	2	24,146
Gold 'n Quiet	3	F	11	2	0	0	11,070
Gold 'n Regal	8	G	13	2	1	1	27,765
Gold N Silver	4	G	7	0	1	1	12,640
Gold N Silver Wind	3	G	3	1	0	1	9,940
Gold Not Diamonds	4	F	10	0	1	1	7,781
Gold Nugget	8	G	3	0	0	0	1,080
Gold Occasion	7	G	1	0	0	0	65
Gold Opera	3	C	8	1	2	0	19,360

RECORDS OF HORSES

Horse	Age	Sex	Sts	1st	2d	3d	Won
Gold Options	7	H	10	2	2	0	10,130
Gold Orbit Goldie	9	M	5	0	1	0	1,050
Gold Oxide	4	F	1	0	0	0	2,700
Gold Panic	2	G	2	0	0	0	120
Gold Panning Annie	2	F	5	0	0	0	0
Gold Path	4	G	4	0	0	0	200
Gold Pearl	5	G	2	0	0	1	1,730
Gold Penny	5	M	5	1	0	0	3,370
Gold Pillar	3	G	3	0	0	0	124
Gold Play	4	C	13	2	1	2	14,251
Gold Player	3	F	6	1	0	2	55,660
Gold Point (IRE)	4	G	1	0	0	1	5,060
Gold Prospecting	3	F	6	0	1	0	4,038
Gold Pursuit	3	G	5	0	0	2	2,080
Gold Pyrite	3	C	15	2	2	2	23,551
Gold Queen	7	M	6	0	0	0	1,454
Gold Ray	3	C	14	1	0	1	10,533
Gold Regal	2	G	1	0	0	0	990
Gold Reserve	2	C	4	0	1	1	9,020
Gold Ringer	2	F	4	0	0	0	1,275
Gold Rocket	7	G	13	2	0	0	7,721
Gold Rome	6	M	6	3	0	0	10,661
Gold Ruckus	5	G	6	3	2	0	68,000
Gold Run	8	G	5	0	0	1	1,598
Gold Run Type	3	F	4	0	2	1	15,260
Gold Rush Jones	2	C	2	0	0	1	2,490
Gold Scammer	4	F	2	0	1	0	3,400
Gold Scepter	4	F	3	1	0	0	9,113
Gold Search	3	C	8	0	0	2	4,670
Gold Secret	3	F	10	0	1	1	3,768
Gold Seize	3	G	10	3	0	1	10,826
Gold Sensation	6	G	7	0	0	1	1,120
Gold Shadeed	4	C	9	1	0	1	52,005
Gold Shield	2	C	7	2	1	0	35,520
Gold Shoes	2	C	1	0	0	0	2,387
Gold Sign	3	F	6	0	0	0	510
Gold Slew	2	G	7	1	1	1	12,959
Gold Sneaker	3	C	20	5	1	0	28,127
Gold Socks	4	G	2	1	1	0	2,550
Gold Song	3	C	6	0	0	1	5,090
Gold Souvenir	3	F	2	0	0	1	1,662
Gold Sphinx	4	C	5	2	3	0	90,200
Gold Spike	2	F	6	1	1	0	28,160
Gold Spot	2	F	3	0	0	1	745
Gold Spun Fun	5	G	10	1	3	0	17,260
Gold Squall	2	C	2	0	0	0	40
Gold Star Gum	3	F	1	0	0	0	0
Gold Star Lady	3	F	3	0	0	0	0
Gold Storm	3	C	5	4	0	0	53,700
Gold Sugar	4	F	2	1	0	0	9,600
Gold Summit	8	G	13	1	3	2	22,685
Gold Sunset	3	G	10	2	2	0	45,660
Gold Taker	4	G	5	3	0	1	70,512
Gold Tango	4	C	14	1	4	4	92,520
Gold Target	4	G	1	0	0	0	0
Gold Tempest	6	M	16	0	1	1	4,296
Gold Temptation	3	G	21	0	2	0	4,455
Gold Thief	5	G	5	0	0	0	438
Gold Thunder	3	F	1	0	0	0	345
Gold Tic	4	G	8	0	2	1	4,791
Gold Tracker	4	G	3	0	0	0	140
Gold Trade	3	C	5	1	0	1	15,256
Gold Trick	6	H	19	1	1	1	6,283
Gold Trinket	3	F	2	0	0	0	450
Gold Twine	4	G	14	3	3	2	36,710
Gold Vault	3	F	4	0	0	2	8,280
Gold Will	2	F	1	0	0	0	0
Gold Wings	5	H	8	2	2	1	48,740
Gold Witness	3	C	1	0	0	0	35
Gold Zapper	2	G	7	0	1	0	8,944
Goldasice	2	F	3	0	1	2	10,985
Goldberg	5	H	7	1	1	0	1,561
Goldberger	2	F	1	0	0	1	2,750
Goldbuster	8	G	10	2	2	2	10,144
Goldcappedtooth	3	G	11	1	1	3	5,818
Goldcardmember	2	C	4	0	0	0	755
Goldchild	7	G	12	0	0	3	6,228
Goldderbyday	5	H	4	1	0	0	3,270
Golddigger Beware	3	F	7	1	4	1	43,494
Golden Aberdeen	4	F	12	2	2	0	37,720
Golden Addiction	5	M	9	0	1	1	3,185
Golden Affirmation	3	G	3	0	0	0	75
Golden Amanda	3	F	4	0	0	0	425
Golden Antigua	6	M	1	0	0	1	4,290
Golden Appeal	3	F	12	2	2	0	16,935
Golden Apples (IRE)	5	M	1	0	1	0	50,666
Golden Approval	6	G	15	3	2	1	51,728
Golden Arch	3	G	5	0	2	2	15,980
Golden Aria	7	H	5	0	0	0	724
Golden Arm	5	G	11	3	0	4	38,240
Golden Arrow	4	C	7	1	1	3	86,900
Golden Aura	2	F	4	1	0	0	11,400
Golden Authority	3	F	8	4	1	1	20,202
Golden Bag	4	G	5	0	0	0	1,140
Golden Ballerina	2	F	1	0	0	0	0
Golden Band	4	F	1	0	1	0	11,200
Golden Bangle	4	F	13	1	0	1	13,550
Golden Barbi	3	F	3	1	0	1	6,131
Golden Barroness	2	F	4	1	2	0	6,652
Golden Bee	2	F	5	0	1	0	1,875
Golden Belle	5	M	1	0	0	0	0
Golden Bid	5	M	7	0	4	0	5,340
Golden Blaise	3	C	1	0	0	0	1,230
Golden Bonus	5	G	13	1	6	1	45,802
Golden Bound	6	H	5	2	0	0	12,600
Golden Brass	2	F	3	0	3	0	5,559
Golden Brook	4	G	8	2	2	0	22,827
Golden Butte	3	F	3	0	0	1	2,626
Golden Buzz	2	G	6	2	1	1	24,050
Golden Cab	4	F	13	0	1	0	3,010
Golden Cache	2	F	2	0	1	0	7,000
Golden Carousel	5	M	17	2	3	2	13,359
Golden City Miss	4	F	6	1	1	0	7,462
Golden Coin	3	F	2	0	0	1	1,100
Golden Commander	3	C	7	2	2	0	71,720
Golden Concern	5	M	6	1	0	3	18,381
Golden Concorde	6	G	8	0	0	2	6,290
Golden Contender	5	G	15	3	3	4	59,530
Golden Corona	5	M	4	0	0	1	17,890
Golden Corsage	3	F	7	2	2	0	47,703
Golden Cortez	4	G	3	0	0	0	0
Golden Count	6	G	1	0	0	0	285
Golden Courtney	2	F	4	0	0	1	3,014
Golden Creek	7	G	1	0	0	0	325
Golden Damsel	3	F	9	4	0	2	185,811
Golden Dayjur	3	F	4	0	2	1	14,100
Golden Deception	3	F	1	0	0	0	0
Golden Decree	5	G	10	2	1	0	18,921
Golden Dehere	5	H	7	0	1	0	4,306
Golden Diamond	2	C	7	1	1	1	20,220
Golden Dinner	6	G	12	4	0	0	18,505
Golden Diva	2	F	3	0	1	1	9,030
Golden Doc	2	C	1	0	0	0	0
Golden Dollar	5	M	5	0	0	0	1,090
Golden Domer	3	F	2	0	0	0	0
Golden Donn	2	C	3	0	0	0	3,272
Golden Door	4	G	4	1	0	0	3,060
Golden Dragon (FR)	3	F	3	1	0	0	7,501
Golden Dragon (GB)	5	G	4	1	0	0	41,220
Golden Drive	2	G	2	0	1	0	3,710
Golden Earrings	4	F	9	0	0	1	9,019
Golden Eclipse	2	F	2	0	0	0	0
Golden Egg	3	G	3	0	0	0	360
Golden Ellen	3	F	9	1	1	2	29,780
Golden Embers	3	G	3	0	1	0	10,000
Golden Empress	4	F	1	0	0	0	0
Golden Eyes	6	M	3	0	0	0	254
Golden Fable	5	G	7	0	1	0	4,798
Golden Fantasy	3	F	1	0	0	0	315
Golden Fifty	3	C	11	1	0	2	10,080
Golden Fleet	4	C	8	0	1	2	1,110
Golden Foil	6	H	4	0	0	0	0
Golden Gator	2	C	1	1	0	0	13,200
Golden Gem	6	G	6	0	0	0	503
Golden General	7	G	3	0	0	0	2,940
Golden Genes	7	M	8	0	2	3	9,143
Golden Glacken	4	G	11	3	1	2	64,320
Golden Glen	2	C	5	0	1	1	11,860

Horse	Age	Sex	Sts	1st	2d	3d	Won
Golden Glint	3	F	9	1	1	1	9,870
Golden Gloves	4	F	6	1	1	0	11,100
Golden Glow Two	3	F	2	0	0	1	1,698
Golden Grace	3	F	4	0	0	1	610
Golden Griffin	3	G	4	0	0	0	592
Golden Gus	4	G	4	1	0	0	20,020
Golden Hair	2	F	5	1	0	0	9,365
Golden Halo	5	M	17	3	3	1	44,336
Golden Hare	4	C	4	0	1	0	14,800
Golden Hit	5	G	16	3	1	2	13,076
Golden Honoree	3	F	3	0	0	1	1,990
Golden Idol	2	C	4	0	0	0	2,685
Golden Igloo	7	G	21	2	2	4	13,512
Golden Intelect	3	F	6	1	0	1	12,350
Golden Jackie	4	F	10	0	0	1	1,128
Golden Jenny	3	F	4	1	0	1	17,890
Golden Jet Eye	4	G	10	2	2	0	8,845
Golden Jewel	2	F	1	0	0	0	118
Golden John	3	C	7	2	1	0	8,925
Golden K K	3	F	9	2	4	1	81,440
Golden Karats	7	M	9	1	0	1	2,471
Golden Lark	5	M	12	1	1	2	6,653
Golden Layla	2	F	3	0	0	0	0
Golden Legacy	4	F	6	1	1	2	8,968
Golden Liberty	7	M	11	0	2	0	3,534
Golden Lies	3	G	9	0	0	0	1,491
Golden Lightning	5	G	13	0	3	2	9,910
Golden Loom	3	F	1	0	0	0	35
Golden Louisia	3	F	16	1	3	1	17,910
Golden Made	5	M	7	1	1	2	62,895
Golden Marlin	3	F	11	4	1	0	193,970
Golden Marvel (FR)	7	G	4	0	0	1	7,439
Golden Max	3	F	2	0	0	0	0
Golden Mercy	4	G	15	3	0	0	12,176
Golden Mira	3	F	11	3	0	2	18,202
Golden Monarch	4	F	5	0	1	1	4,060
Golden Monty	2	F	7	1	1	0	9,487
Golden Moon	5	M	5	0	1	1	5,200
Golden Myrrh	2	F	2	0	0	0	0
Golden Mystique	5	M	5	0	0	0	1,216
Golden Nepi (IRE)	3	F	7	2	2	1	193,048
Golden Nest	3	G	4	0	0	0	0
Golden Niblet	3	C	7	1	3	0	16,493
Golden Nicolas	7	G	15	4	3	1	40,620
Golden Night	7	G	1	0	0	0	0
Golden Nugget	4	G	11	1	0	0	11,554
Golden Number	3	F	3	1	1	0	33,950
Golden Oak	4	G	2	0	0	0	460
Golden Oldie	7	H	8	0	1	2	25,200
Golden O's	6	G	17	3	5	4	28,810
Golden Park	2	F	3	0	1	0	8,800
Golden Pass	6	G	4	0	0	0	2,580
Golden Passion	4	G	6	1	1	3	3,685
Golden Paul	6	G	12	0	1	0	1,308
Golden Peace	4	G	15	3	2	2	24,552
Golden Penny	3	F	6	0	0	2	11,420
Golden Peppen	2	F	4	0	0	1	3,060
Golden Pet	4	G	6	0	1	3	2,325
Golden Phoebe	5	M	1	0	0	0	0
Golden Po	2	F	4	0	0	0	1,800
Golden Point	4	C	4	0	0	4	11,000
Golden Prestige	3	F	10	1	2	3	28,272
Golden Promises	2	G	2	0	0	1	660
Golden Prophecy	8	G	18	3	2	3	32,915
Golden Prospect	3	F	1	0	0	1	6,468
Golden Prune	4	C	5	1	0	0	17,280
Golden Rahy	4	G	6	3	0	1	85,320
Golden Rail	2	F	2	0	0	0	372
Golden Raja	4	G	18	1	6	2	16,876
Golden Ram	4	G	13	1	0	2	5,755
Golden Red	6	G	8	0	0	3	2,354
Golden Reputashn	3	F	12	1	4	1	74,450
Golden Returns	7	H	10	1	1	1	31,212
Golden Rhythm	5	M	11	3	1	2	103,780
Golden Romance	3	F	6	0	1	1	4,515
Golden Romani	5	M	14	0	0	5	7,990
Golden Rumor	3	F	8	0	0	1	700
Golden Score	3	C	9	1	1	3	33,460
Golden Scrambler	4	F	9	1	1	2	11,174
Golden Seductress	2	F	1	0	0	0	940
Golden Series	4	C	3	0	0	0	172
Golden Serpent	4	F	8	2	1	0	6,320
Golden Sheika	5	M	12	1	3	1	12,890
Golden Sheriff	4	G	11	1	1	0	24,690
Golden Shoes	3	F	6	1	1	1	4,110
Golden Show	3	F	1	0	0	0	0
Golden Slew	4	C	5	0	0	0	360
Golden Slinkee	5	G	3	0	0	0	868
Golden Smile	7	M	4	0	0	0	545
Golden Sonata	4	F	10	2	3	0	88,575
Golden Sound	6	H	7	0	3	1	6,170
Golden Spats	4	C	7	1	0	0	8,051
Golden Spur	3	C	10	1	5	1	52,900
Golden Starlight	3	G	3	0	0	1	4,200
Golden State Boy	3	G	11	1	1	1	6,746
Golden State Ltd.	5	G	1	0	0	0	67
Golden Style	7	G	5	0	1	2	2,414
Golden Sunshine	3	F	17	6	1	0	41,801
Golden Surge	4	G	12	3	1	0	10,669
Golden Swinger	2	F	7	0	0	0	2,070
Golden Tangle	5	G	7	1	2	1	25,837
Golden Ticket	5	G	8	2	0	1	83,099
Golden Token	2	F	2	0	0	0	0
Golden Tomorrow	3	F	12	1	0	1	19,034
Golden Tones	2	C	3	1	1	0	35,720
Golden Tour	3	F	7	3	2	0	104,930
Golden Trail	3	G	14	0	0	0	1,011
Golden Treasure	5	M	3	1	0	0	6,179
Golden Trevally	4	F	8	3	2	0	72,000
Golden True	3	C	10	0	3	1	7,886
Golden Turquoise	7	G	12	3	0	2	28,112
Golden Unbridled	3	C	1	0	0	0	0
Golden Verse	2	C	4	0	0	0	840
Golden Victory	5	H	7	0	2	1	5,180
Golden View	5	M	6	0	0	1	1,351
Golden Vintage	3	F	8	2	2	2	49,160
Golden Walk	5	M	14	2	3	2	50,929
Golden Wave	3	C	4	0	0	1	2,910
Golden Way	5	G	15	5	2	4	32,176
Golden Wheat	4	C	9	2	1	1	9,169
Golden Works	3	F	1	0	0	0	0
Golden Zak	5	M	2	0	0	0	165
Golden Zodiac	8	G	3	0	0	0	288
Goldenalden's Card	4	G	17	1	2	4	31,265
Goldenberg's Gift	2	C	1	0	0	0	136
Goldendoon	3	F	12	0	1	3	5,432
Goldenita Dancer	3	F	1	0	0	0	0
Goldfellow	4	C	2	1	1	0	21,200
Goldgivespleasure	4	C	5	3	1	1	14,933
Goldglovekid	3	G	13	1	4	2	32,510
Goldharbor Express	3	C	4	2	1	0	7,000
Goldian's Derby	6	H	3	0	0	0	0
Goldie But Goodie	3	F	2	0	0	0	53
Goldie Joy	4	F	11	4	1	0	29,965
Goldie Rio	3	F	5	1	2	1	28,230
Goldie's Claim	5	M	8	0	0	1	1,618
Goldies Legacy	3	C	2	0	0	0	3,180
Goldie's Road	3	F	10	2	1	4	82,031
Goldilocks N Bear	3	F	4	0	0	1	3,203
Goldin Ocala	2	G	5	0	0	2	1,810
Goldin Pawn	3	G	2	0	0	0	0
Goldinrunner	4	G	14	4	8	1	152,008
Goldleafed Mirror	3	F	10	1	3	0	40,370
Goldleha	3	G	3	0	0	1	2,537
Goldman	6	G	11	3	4	0	23,464
Goldmart Queen	4	F	1	0	0	0	0
Goldmember	2	C	2	0	0	1	3,630
Gold'n Grandeur	6	G	8	0	2	1	5,143
Gold'n'regant	3	C	2	0	0	0	273
Goldon	3	C	11	1	1	0	13,500
Goldridge (IRE)	6	G	1	0	0	0	450
Goldrush Girl	4	F	1	0	0	0	0
Gold's First	4	G	4	0	0	0	143
Gold's General	4	G	6	0	0	1	942
Goldsatalking	4	F	10	1	2	1	17,311
Goldshy	2	G	1	0	0	0	0
Goldstar Night	4	F	3	0	0	0	114
Goldswhereyafindit	5	G	9	2	2	2	9,752

RECORDS OF HORSES

Horse	Age	Sex	Sts	1st	2d	3d	Won
Goldtogowith	3	F	4	2	1	0	17,355
Goldverse	6	H	2	0	0	0	0
Goldville Miss	4	F	5	0	0	0	585
Goldwalker	6	M	7	1	1	1	6,442
Goldwaterstribute	5	G	12	1	1	1	5,578
Goldy Gulch	4	F	12	1	1	1	24,104
Goldy Rock	3	F	6	2	1	2	31,760
Goldy Strike	4	F	2	0	0	0	360
Golf Game	8	H	7	1	1	1	10,047
Golf Pro	3	G	10	1	0	0	4,825
Gollie's Gal	4	F	6	0	0	0	281
Golly Why	3	C	4	0	0	0	0
Gollygot	7	M	4	1	0	2	29,184
Golo	4	F	4	1	1	0	1,875
Gomer	3	C	2	0	0	0	540
Gomer Sez Surprise	6	H	3	0	0	0	280
Gomka	7	G	13	3	4	3	23,642
Gona Getcha	11	G	7	0	0	0	545
Gonandunit	5	M	12	2	3	2	31,846
Gondolieri (CHI)	4	G	6	1	2	1	177,218
Gondolier's Song	7	G	14	2	0	0	16,540
Gone Abroad	5	M	13	1	5	0	20,090
Gone Again	3	F	7	0	0	1	1,769
Gone Awry	4	F	15	1	2	1	7,570
Gone Ballistic	3	C	4	1	1	1	29,480
Gone Cattin	3	G	5	0	1	0	4,175
Gone Courting	7	G	8	2	0	0	38,279
Gone Dee	3	G	8	0	0	2	6,270
Gone Exclusive	3	F	3	2	0	0	46,600
Gone Fishin	7	H	13	1	0	2	52,674
Gone for Christmas	3	F	8	2	1	2	73,310
Gone for the Roses	3	F	6	0	2	2	23,360
Gone Golden	4	F	1	0	0	0	0
Gone Golfing	2	F	1	0	0	1	6,468
Gone Gone	6	M	15	3	1	4	11,784
Gone Hunting	5	G	17	2	3	1	25,634
Gone in a Whisper	2	F	5	0	0	0	2,035
Gone Kentucky	4	C	1	0	0	0	0
Gone Mad	2	C	2	0	0	0	0
Gone Majestic	2	F	1	0	0	0	0
Gone Musical	4	F	3	0	0	0	1,955
Gone Off	4	G	13	2	2	1	41,647
Gone On Ahead	3	F	1	0	0	0	0
Gone Skating	4	F	1	1	0	0	13,200
Gone Southwest	2	F	8	0	0	0	993
Gone Sporten	4	G	20	1	4	1	7,659
Gone to Boston	6	M	18	0	2	7	25,355
Gone to Dixie	3	C	11	0	0	2	1,759
Gone to Greece	5	M	3	0	0	1	5,570
Gone to Harvest	4	F	4	2	0	0	7,466
Gone to Party	3	F	5	3	1	0	61,975
Gone to Utah	4	F	4	1	1	0	27,408
Gone to War	3	G	8	1	3	0	53,436
Gone Wish'in	2	G	1	0	0	1	2,090
Gone With the Gold	4	F	5	2	1	0	8,107
Gone With the Win	4	G	8	0	2	3	17,206
Gonefortheweekend	3	F	6	0	1	1	2,320
Gonetorule	3	F	4	2	0	0	36,360
Gonetothedoctor	3	F	9	3	1	0	27,690
Gonetothelake	3	F	4	0	0	2	3,575
Gong	2	C	4	1	1	0	21,810
Gonna Do	3	F	6	1	2	2	19,760
Gonna Get Lucky	4	C	9	1	0	0	2,621
Gonna Gidder	3	G	14	2	2	2	32,275
Gonna Run Over You	4	F	2	0	0	0	0
Gonnabeapartofit	3	F	13	1	2	3	20,200
Gonnabeatchabald	3	C	9	2	1	2	7,135
Gonofasun	6	H	14	3	2	0	8,788
Goo Bye	3	F	7	0	0	2	5,585
Goochiegirl	3	F	4	0	0	0	252
Good Actor	6	H	4	1	0	1	7,928
Good and Gone	3	F	9	0	2	2	14,990
Good and Hot	2	F	2	0	0	0	112
Good and Pesky	9	G	7	1	3	0	2,539
Good Answer	8	H	8	1	0	4	9,696
Good as Silver	2	F	9	1	1	3	33,364
Good Better Best	4	G	16	1	3	0	30,720
Good Bidness	3	F	3	0	1	1	2,700
Good Bit	4	F	3	0	0	0	0
Good Blend	3	C	2	0	0	0	0
Good Boot	4	G	17	4	5	1	26,250
Good Boy Duke	9	G	18	1	2	1	5,041
Good Boy Sam	6	H	9	1	1	1	49,610
Good Boy Yankee	3	C	7	2	0	1	9,837
Good But Testy	5	G	3	0	0	0	0
Good Campagner	2	C	1	0	0	0	0
Good Charlotte	2	F	5	1	0	0	4,713
Good Combination	5	M	10	0	0	1	1,713
Good Company	6	G	12	1	0	3	29,461
Good Conduct Medal	3	C	16	1	1	2	9,006
Good Coochie	5	M	2	0	0	0	0
Good Cop Bad Cop	5	G	5	0	1	3	33,272
Good Date in Park	3	C	9	1	2	0	13,456
Good Day Sir	4	F	11	2	2	0	35,220
Good Day Too (IRE)	3	C	4	1	2	1	54,571
Good Expectation	3	C	12	2	2	2	23,880
Good Faith Gesture	4	G	10	2	1	1	17,661
Good Fella (ARG)	5	H	2	0	0	0	2,845
Good for Me	3	G	18	0	4	3	11,349
Good for You	4	G	9	1	1	2	11,945
Good Future	4	G	10	1	0	2	11,830
Good Going	3	C	3	0	1	1	3,215
Good Gold	3	C	2	1	0	0	24,160
Good Golly James	5	G	7	3	1	0	18,042
Good Grades	5	M	9	0	0	0	1,125
Good Humor Gal	2	F	3	1	0	1	20,460
Good Job	2	C	1	0	0	0	180
Good Journey	7	H	1	0	1	0	80,000
Good Kid	3	C	5	1	0	0	8,221
Good Knight Story	3	F	11	0	2	0	18,714
Good Landing	3	F	3	0	0	2	8,160
Good Lookin'	2	F	4	0	4	0	15,485
Good Lookin Devil	4	G	18	5	2	3	27,618
Good Luck Strikes	2	G	1	0	0	0	0
Good Man Sam	8	G	13	4	2	1	53,408
Good Medicine	3	F	6	0	1	1	3,560
Good Meeting	5	G	11	2	4	2	122,595
Good Night	7	G	9	1	0	1	12,835
Good O Valentine	3	F	21	5	3	1	52,451
Good Ol' Uncle Joe	5	G	1	0	0	0	320
Good Old Days	4	C	4	0	0	0	0
Good Old Sprite	4	G	12	1	3	4	8,275
Good Ole Storm	7	G	21	2	2	4	10,113
Good Print	7	G	4	1	0	1	7,704
Good Reward	2	C	4	1	0	0	33,000
Good Riddance	3	F	1	1	0	0	5,400
Good Talk	3	F	11	1	2	1	28,708
Good Teacher	6	H	13	0	0	1	2,478
Good Terms	4	G	10	1	2	2	16,325
Good Time Gal	3	F	9	2	3	3	11,656
Good Time In' Man	3	C	11	0	3	3	6,024
Good Vibes	4	F	1	0	0	0	360
Good Will Lady	7	M	4	0	0	1	1,014
Goodbar	8	G	5	1	0	1	23,150
Goodbye Baby	4	F	4	0	0	0	102
Goodbye Beautiful	2	F	4	1	0	1	26,091
Goodbye Ben Beau	2	G	5	0	0	4	7,320
Goodbye Big Cat	3	G	1	1	0	0	16,920
Goodbye Cammie	3	F	6	2	2	1	30,725
Goodbye Credit	4	G	15	2	0	2	11,548
Goodbye Gambler	3	F	7	1	2	1	53,632
Goodbye Gear	6	M	6	1	1	1	7,959
Goodbye Heaven	3	C	1	0	1	0	2,660
Goodbye I'm Gone	5	G	17	3	3	0	31,701
Goodbye Lucky	4	F	5	1	1	0	6,050
Goodbye Milady	7	M	6	0	1	1	1,315
Goodbye Mr Goodbye	5	G	10	1	1	2	28,689
Goodbye Note	3	F	1	0	0	0	75
Goodbye Past	3	F	9	1	0	0	10,697
Goodbye Rose	2	F	4	0	1	1	8,900
Goodbyesisterdisco	4	F	13	1	1	1	9,785
Goodbygolddiggers	11	G	13	1	1	1	4,022
Goodfoot	6	G	3	0	0	1	840
Goodgollymissriley	4	F	8	1	1	1	4,278
Goodgoodgood	3	G	5	0	0	0	416
Goodies Galore	2	F	8	1	3	0	50,357
Goodinthehood	3	C	4	0	0	0	400

Horse	Age	Sex	Sts	1st	2d	3d	Won
Goodland Park	2	F	1	0	0	0	75
Goodluck Road	4	G	5	0	0	1	1,640
Goodluckcatchinme	3	G	1	0	0	0	0
Goodman	9	G	1	0	0	0	0
Goodmorningjudge	8	M	5	0	0	0	0
Goodmorninsunshine	3	F	2	0	0	0	2,340
Goodness	4	F	2	0	0	0	271
Goodnews Bay	4	G	9	2	2	3	46,360
Goodnight Trail	6	G	13	0	2	2	17,826
Goodnite My Angel	2	F	6	0	1	0	3,054
Goodnuff	4	G	4	0	0	0	549
Goodoledoctorbob	5	H	1	0	0	0	0
Goodonya	3	F	6	0	0	2	4,040
Goodtime Rocket	6	G	17	3	2	4	33,057
Goodtogonow	4	G	14	1	0	4	8,430
Goodtoknow	4	F	3	0	0	0	315
Goodwin Sands	4	G	1	0	0	0	0
Goody Good	3	G	13	3	1	0	15,565
Goonwithitjones	7	G	3	0	1	2	4,480
Goo's Little Girl	6	M	6	1	1	0	8,745
Goose Dinner	3	F	9	1	0	3	11,665
Goose Feathers	4	F	1	0	0	0	62
Goosey Gander	6	M	7	1	0	0	27,900
Goosey Moose	2	G	3	2	0	0	19,200
Goosie Goosie	3	C	11	1	3	3	39,270
Goost	5	G	16	2	3	5	18,211
Gopher Bowl	2	C	5	0	2	1	9,420
Gopher This One	2	G	5	0	1	1	5,355
Gordon of Eden	4	G	16	0	1	3	4,774
Gordon's Girl	2	F	3	0	0	2	4,400
Gordonzy	5	G	17	1	0	2	4,156
Gordy McCorkell	3	G	8	1	1	3	11,114
Gordy's Our Man	8	G	13	1	2	1	7,174
Gore Road	2	C	3	0	0	0	1,204
Gorge Girl	4	F	2	0	0	0	70
Gorgeous Gabby	4	F	7	1	0	0	11,070
Gorgeous Guest	3	F	11	3	1	1	15,395
Gorgeous Lake	4	F	12	3	3	1	47,820
Gorgeous N Greedy	4	F	9	2	0	2	25,175
Gorgeous Pirate	4	F	9	1	2	2	7,686
Gorin	2	C	1	0	0	0	0
Goshen Pass	3	G	2	0	0	0	0
Goshin's Lad	4	C	7	0	0	2	5,794
Goss the Man	3	C	3	0	0	0	2,322
Gossimore Bay	4	C	12	1	0	0	3,266
Gossip Queen	4	F	3	0	0	0	355
Got a Beep	3	G	6	0	0	1	4,670
Got a Ticket	5	G	9	0	1	1	2,170
Got Attitude	3	F	9	2	0	3	46,230
Got Beer	3	G	12	1	0	1	13,295
Got Brass	4	C	15	3	4	1	38,980
Got Game	6	G	8	0	2	0	3,224
Got Gear	2	F	4	1	1	0	17,426
Got Koko	4	F	6	3	1	1	688,000
Got Luck	7	M	4	0	0	0	273
Got Mercedes	4	F	8	1	0	3	16,633
Got Milk	7	G	6	0	1	1	3,257
Got My Education	5	M	2	1	0	0	8,550
Got My Geht	2	G	2	0	1	0	1,820
Got One for Ya	4	F	4	0	0	0	343
Got Pizazz	2	F	5	0	1	1	8,975
Got Snowed'n	3	F	2	0	0	0	390
Got Soup	2	F	1	0	0	0	0
Got Sum Speed	10	G	1	0	0	0	0
Got Swaped	5	G	6	0	0	0	180
Got That Swing	8	G	12	1	1	0	9,939
Got the Advanatage	3	G	4	0	0	0	0
Got the Beat	3	F	4	1	1	0	18,218
Got the Fever	2	C	4	0	0	2	4,565
Got the Gold	3	C	2	1	0	0	4,135
Got the Goods	2	C	7	1	2	1	34,959
Got the Message	4	G	11	2	2	2	29,240
Got the Rhythm	3	C	2	0	0	2	2,750
Got to Be Magic	2	F	5	1	0	1	7,194
Got to Be Me	3	F	7	1	0	4	27,909
Got Um Smoke Um	5	G	10	0	4	3	8,480
Got You Slew	6	M	12	4	1	1	57,280
Gotabe Inittowinit	10	G	1	0	0	0	0
Gotaghostofachance	2	G	1	0	0	0	350
Gotaloveitbaby	4	F	3	0	0	0	900
Gotcha Baby	3	F	4	0	0	0	450
Gotcha Covered	3	F	14	1	3	2	17,280
Gotcha Goin Mecee	4	G	8	3	2	0	37,377
Gotcha Thinking	6	H	16	2	6	0	17,380
Gotdream (FR)	3	F	1	0	0	0	3,339
Gotham Limited	4	C	11	4	1	3	42,461
Gothenburg	8	G	8	0	0	0	918
Gothic	2	C	1	0	0	0	0
Gothic's Design	3	G	5	0	0	0	0
Gotitgoin	5	H	9	0	1	1	13,720
Gotnomonenmypocket	3	C	1	0	0	0	60
Gotogo Bye	4	F	2	0	0	0	0
Gotoit	5	G	20	1	3	3	14,991
Gotta Ballado	5	G	9	0	1	1	6,577
Gotta Be a Fox	3	F	10	1	0	2	17,117
Gotta Be a Rose	2	F	5	0	1	0	2,577
Gotta Be a Star	5	M	13	1	0	1	11,911
Gotta Beat Em All	3	C	3	0	1	0	1,286
Gotta Believe	3	C	4	0	0	0	0
Gotta Get It	4	C	3	0	0	0	360
Gotta Get Movin	5	H	8	1	1	2	2,135
Gotta Git Gone	3	G	4	0	0	1	998
Gotta Go to Work	5	G	7	0	1	2	25,700
Gotta Have Fun	3	C	8	2	3	1	33,428
Gotta Have Magic	2	G	10	0	1	2	8,900
Gotta Jiboo	4	F	12	2	4	3	33,396
Gotta Lotta Speed	2	F	2	0	0	0	333
Gotta Match	4	C	4	1	0	0	3,009
Gotta Motion	8	M	10	2	0	1	3,485
Gotta Pay the Lady	3	F	3	0	0	1	1,880
Gotta Ridan	7	M	14	1	2	3	9,279
Gotta Stacked Deck	6	G	9	1	0	3	6,870
Gotta Temper	4	F	8	2	2	0	25,360
Gottabeachboy	3	C	10	1	0	2	32,408
Gottacatchemall	4	C	4	0	0	1	440
Gottagetherefirst	2	G	4	0	0	1	875
Gottagetthecash	11	G	4	0	0	1	688
Gottagoodnotion	5	M	4	1	0	0	3,465
Gottahavit	2	F	1	0	0	0	822
Gottalottagas	7	M	11	1	1	1	11,738
Gottalovefaith	4	C	9	2	1	0	31,595
Gottaluvme	3	F	2	0	0	0	0
Gottaparticipate	3	C	4	0	0	0	960
Gotthard	6	G	10	1	0	3	21,230
Gotthemoneyhoney	2	F	7	0	0	1	2,755
Gottobadandy	6	M	13	1	1	4	9,982
Gottodoit	5	M	8	0	2	0	4,710
Gouglyearly	2	G	8	0	0	1	3,168
Gourmet Delight	3	C	3	0	0	0	300
Govans	6	G	13	1	2	3	27,225
Govenors Baba	6	G	7	1	1	1	6,129
Govenors Beele Boy	2	C	2	0	0	0	0
Govenors Mist	3	F	8	2	2	1	11,744
Govenors Sunshine	2	F	3	0	0	0	0
Govenors Trixie	3	F	14	4	3	2	21,078
Govern Game	5	H	4	0	0	0	96
Governer's Heat	5	H	1	0	0	0	0
Governor Bennett	3	C	5	1	2	1	33,540
Governor Brown	3	C	1	0	0	0	380
Governor Hickel	4	C	6	1	0	0	7,960
Governor Jeb	4	G	17	4	4	4	24,311
Governor Joe	6	H	7	0	0	0	870
Governor Roy	3	G	7	0	0	0	1,080
Governor Vasquez	3	C	16	3	4	3	53,790
Governors Gold	2	C	2	0	0	0	810
Governors Intern	2	F	4	0	0	0	0
Governor's Pride	6	G	1	0	0	0	0
Gov's Ace	2	C	2	0	0	0	150
Gowhereyouwannago	4	C	13	1	2	1	10,723
Gowithfate	2	F	4	2	0	1	40,800
Gowrie House	3	G	10	2	2	2	13,625
Gowrie Lass	5	M	6	0	0	0	0
Grab Bag	4	F	4	1	2	1	84,750
Grab N Gears	5	H	12	1	3	1	2,294
Grab the Buck	4	F	4	0	2	0	12,680
Grab the Lady	6	M	14	2	2	4	16,912

RECORDS OF HORSES

Horse	Age	Sex	Sts	1st	2d	3d	Won
Grace and Beauty	5	H	4	0	0	0	408
Grace and Style	4	F	6	3	1	0	35,467
Grace Bay	3	F	5	2	0	2	73,570
Grace Course	4	C	4	1	1	1	41,880
Grace for You	4	F	4	0	0	0	2,999
Grace Line	2	F	4	1	0	0	4,892
Grace of Windsor	3	F	2	0	0	0	2,100
Grace the Stage	3	F	5	2	1	0	15,060
Graced	4	F	11	0	1	3	5,240
Graceful Balance	4	F	5	0	0	0	272
Graceful Cady	3	F	4	1	0	0	8,535
Graceful Cat	5	M	2	0	0	0	1,220
Graceful Devil	5	G	15	5	0	1	41,036
Graceful Exit	5	M	7	1	2	1	7,253
Graceful Gal	5	M	6	1	1	2	71,298
Graceful Gretel	3	F	3	0	0	0	497
Graceful Majesty	4	F	1	0	0	0	0
Graceful Rain	3	F	8	1	1	2	11,690
Graceful Rose	4	F	3	1	0	1	5,550
Graceful Stepper	4	F	4	1	0	1	6,575
Graceful Treasure	6	M	4	0	0	0	675
Gracefulciti	4	F	2	1	0	0	13,924
Gracefully Yours	3	F	6	0	1	0	2,695
Gracewithapproval	3	F	2	0	0	0	525
Gracie B.	2	F	4	0	0	0	315
Gracie's Dancer	5	H	6	0	0	0	7,350
Gracies Mint	2	F	2	0	0	0	100
Gracies Trick	3	F	2	0	0	1	1,380
Gracile	2	F	4	1	0	0	16,500
Gracility	4	F	11	1	3	0	83,163
Gracious Assault	4	F	5	0	0	0	4,260
Gracious Brevity	6	M	5	0	3	0	19,964
Gracious Gift	5	M	9	2	1	1	17,849
Gracious Girl	2	F	2	0	1	0	2,613
Gracious Humor	3	G	6	4	1	1	82,500
Gracious Lady	3	F	6	0	0	2	13,890
Gracious Megan	6	M	19	3	0	1	25,735
Gracy Rules	4	F	10	1	0	1	4,279
Grad School	2	C	5	0	0	1	1,631
Grade Nine	4	F	4	0	0	0	2,000
Grade One	7	G	5	0	0	0	2,900
Grade Three	6	H	2	0	0	0	0
Graded by Results	2	C	1	0	0	0	2,100
Gradepoint	2	C	2	1	0	1	36,285
Grader Blade	4	G	10	1	0	1	8,947
Grades Gold	3	G	9	2	0	1	32,211
Grades of Honor	3	F	12	4	2	2	38,690
Grady	8	G	11	2	0	2	17,225
Grady N	2	C	1	0	0	0	0
Grady's Boy	2	C	3	0	0	1	1,238
Graeme's Gal	3	F	13	2	2	1	12,859
Grafton	3	G	3	1	0	1	30,860
Graham Cracker	2	C	2	0	0	0	1,230
Graham's Surprise	4	G	16	2	3	2	21,520
Gralley	3	G	2	0	0	0	233
Gramar Love	3	F	8	0	1	1	4,825
Gramercy Park	2	C	2	0	1	1	8,000
Gramma Jo's Pride	3	F	14	1	4	3	21,770
Grammarian	5	G	1	0	0	0	18,000
Gramma's Gold	4	F	6	1	0	0	4,940
Gramma's Miracle	3	F	1	0	0	0	61
Grammy Award	4	F	11	2	3	2	11,862
Grammy's Delight	4	F	9	0	0	3	3,485
Grampa	4	C	5	0	0	0	1,511
Gram's Belle	5	M	4	0	0	0	4,400
Gram's Delight	3	F	10	3	1	1	15,760
Gram's Folly	5	G	16	3	4	1	54,880
Gram's Sparkle	4	C	1	0	0	0	0
Gran Amiga (ARG)	4	F	6	0	0	2	4,870
Gran Cesare (ARG)	4	C	10	2	2	1	56,960
Gran Chaco	3	C	4	0	1	1	2,881
Gran Lady Jade	2	F	3	0	0	0	225
Gran Prospect	2	C	5	1	2	1	89,875
Gran Sasso	4	G	9	1	0	2	7,060
Granada Dancer	5	G	10	2	1	2	24,879
Granat	3	F	1	0	1	0	2,060
Granbury	5	G	7	0	0	2	4,812
Granburys Brigade	2	C	1	0	0	0	0
Granby	3	C	1	0	0	0	500
Grand	7	G	5	0	0	1	349
Grand (IRE)	3	C	5	0	1	3	19,230
Grand and Fancy	8	G	17	2	6	3	16,458
Grand and Great	3	C	10	2	3	1	14,430
Grand Ann	2	F	1	0	0	0	0
Grand Appointment	5	H	6	2	1	1	94,380
Grand Canyon	6	G	8	3	2	2	4,711
Grand Cap D	2	F	6	1	1	2	24,520
Grand Caro Lynn	4	F	12	2	1	2	43,190
Grand Chance	3	C	8	1	1	2	26,960
Grand Chief	10	G	2	0	0	0	55
Grand Circus Shark	3	G	5	2	0	0	20,010
Grand Code	4	F	3	1	1	0	13,530
Grand Commemorate	3	G	9	1	0	1	6,279
Grand Coolee	3	G	1	0	0	0	0
Grand Council	2	C	1	0	0	0	0
Grand County	6	G	7	0	1	1	1,924
Grand Desire	4	F	13	3	1	0	15,750
Grand Destiny	3	F	3	1	0	0	27,172
Grand Fan	3	F	6	1	3	0	46,610
Grand Flash	3	C	4	1	1	2	13,590
Grand Fund	3	F	2	0	0	0	0
Grand Gamble	4	F	3	0	0	0	380
Grand General	3	G	5	0	1	0	2,025
Grand Heritage	2	C	6	2	0	2	92,210
Grand Hombre	3	G	5	4	1	0	598,360
Grand Horizon	4	G	7	0	0	0	1,529
Grand Illusion	2	F	2	0	0	0	0
Grand Island	4	G	11	2	1	1	12,168
Grand Kids	3	G	4	0	0	0	0
Grand Lucenci	3	C	7	0	1	1	19,710
Grand Mister	9	G	6	0	0	1	617
Grand Model	3	F	6	0	1	1	10,830
Grand Mystery	4	F	5	1	0	0	4,440
Grand Na Na	3	F	5	0	0	0	100
Grand Natalie Rose	3	F	3	0	0	0	2,760
Grand Old Diamond	4	F	3	0	0	0	0
Grand Particulier	4	F	17	0	1	2	3,498
Grand Piano	2	F	7	2	2	3	17,725
Grand Player	3	C	8	1	2	0	22,970
Grand Prayer	2	F	2	0	2	0	18,000
Grand Prize Winner	3	F	1	0	0	0	700
Grand Rapids Miss	2	F	2	0	1	0	3,528
Grand Red	2	C	6	1	2	1	23,660
Grand Review	3	F	1	0	0	0	195
Grand Runner	3	G	9	1	0	2	4,502
Grand Scam	3	C	7	0	2	1	21,910
Grand Scheme	3	F	12	1	1	6	32,455
Grand Score	2	C	3	1	0	2	47,545
Grand Sequoia	4	F	12	3	3	2	26,093
Grand Sham	3	C	1	0	0	0	50
Grand Skieur	3	G	7	1	0	1	7,658
Grand Slam Jake	3	G	11	1	1	1	14,395
Grand Sorcerer	3	G	11	1	1	2	9,975
Grand Stan	6	H	3	0	0	0	120
Grand Steal	3	G	10	2	2	2	95,148
Grand Strand	5	M	8	4	1	0	8,240
Grand Style	4	F	7	0	0	1	1,314
Grand Targhee	4	F	2	0	0	0	66
Grand Tiara	3	F	1	0	0	0	125
Grand Tomorrow	3	F	4	0	0	0	750
Grand V.	4	F	4	0	0	1	700
Grand Valley	6	M	1	0	0	0	0
Grand Victor	3	G	3	2	0	0	49,484
Grand View Girls	2	F	6	1	0	0	16,560
Grand Visions	4	G	2	0	0	1	6,240
Grand Warrior	2	C	3	0	0	3	14,610
Grand Way	3	F	6	3	0	1	23,468
Granddaughter	2	F	6	0	1	3	19,665
Grandcarol	3	F	2	0	0	0	0
Granddaddy King	3	G	6	0	0	0	525
Grande Blue Streak	3	G	5	0	0	0	1,069
Grande Cache	4	G	12	2	0	2	12,548
Grande Jete	3	F	17	0	3	3	30,680
Grande Mocha	4	F	11	1	2	0	13,876
Grande Paranoid	4	F	8	3	1	1	8,680
Grande Premio	3	G	5	1	1	0	11,676
Grande's Grandslam	2	C	3	0	1	0	7,795
Grandiser (AUS)	5	G	2	1	0	0	49,960

Horse	Age	Sex	Sts	1st	2d	3d	Won
Grandma Grace	3	F	6	1	0	0	15,730
Grandma Nena	3	F	10	1	1	1	13,860
Grandma Sandy	3	F	1	0	0	0	61
Grandma's Ltd	4	F	14	0	1	2	3,696
Grandma's Money	4	F	4	0	0	1	3,570
Grandpa Cat	4	G	4	0	2	1	7,370
Grandpa Chan	3	G	10	2	2	2	57,350
Grandpa Halo	5	M	5	0	0	3	3,719
Grandpa Hillis	10	G	3	1	0	1	4,300
Grandpa P. D.	7	G	2	0	0	0	0
Grandpa Said Yes	3	G	2	0	0	0	187
Grandpa Two	6	G	8	0	4	1	12,386
Grandpa's Dreams	3	G	10	0	2	0	12,866
Grandpa's Gray	6	M	13	0	1	1	7,134
Grandpa's Mandy	4	F	2	0	0	0	136
Grandpashomeatlast	3	F	2	0	1	0	2,550
Grandpawroteyes	3	G	2	0	0	0	115
Grandson Zach	3	G	4	0	1	1	3,335
Grandstand Girl	9	M	10	0	0	0	224
Grandstand Parade	2	F	4	0	0	0	2,485
Grange	4	G	11	0	1	3	6,075
Grangeville	8	G	3	1	0	0	30,960
Granite Head	3	C	9	2	1	0	47,677
Granite Peak	5	H	3	0	0	0	0
Granite Ridge	4	G	20	1	4	3	15,375
Granja Oculta	4	F	2	0	0	0	140
Granja Vivo	4	F	16	3	4	0	64,691
Granjacita	9	M	2	0	0	0	88
Granny Jo	3	F	6	0	0	0	100
Granny Sure Shot	4	F	8	0	0	0	2,521
Granny's Annie	2	F	3	1	1	0	7,470
Granny's Dream	2	F	2	0	0	0	0
Granny's Flurry	7	G	5	0	0	0	352
Granny's Gold	3	G	2	0	0	0	0
Granny's Gun	5	G	8	0	2	1	2,466
Granny's Hope	5	M	11	0	1	0	1,987
Grannys Rosie	4	F	4	1	0	0	4,428
Granny's Store	5	G	21	0	2	6	10,018
Grano de Oro	3	G	6	0	2	0	8,080
Grant	4	G	3	1	0	0	7,915
Grant Marty a Wish	4	F	8	3	2	1	123,615
Grantcor	5	M	4	0	0	0	1,056
Granting	6	G	12	2	4	1	45,580
Grantley	2	C	3	0	0	0	540
Grantmeatrophy	3	F	8	0	0	1	12,880
Grants a Rascal	3	G	1	0	0	0	0
Grant's Moon	2	F	6	2	1	1	60,370
Grant's Our Boy	7	G	4	0	0	0	602
Grant's Vic	4	G	16	2	2	1	31,455
Granville Grant	8	G	8	0	0	2	1,609
Grape Juice	9	G	3	0	0	1	1,725
Grapevine	5	H	7	0	1	0	4,880
Graphic Avenue	4	C	11	4	1	0	23,882
Grasias Sam	5	G	16	1	0	2	4,813
Grasp It All	3	F	13	3	1	4	16,370
Grasp the Moment	4	F	8	1	1	1	13,410
Grass Roots (IRE)	9	G	4	0	2	0	7,914
Grasshopper Flats	5	G	5	1	0	0	8,236
Grassy Butte	4	F	11	0	0	1	2,149
Grateful Symph	4	G	11	1	1	1	4,996
Gratefully	3	F	9	2	0	1	18,380
Gratiaen	6	H	13	3	1	0	83,090
Gratitude Attack	3	C	7	3	1	3	41,180
Gratteau	8	G	2	0	0	0	362
Gratz Park	2	C	3	0	2	1	20,600
Gravano	5	G	19	2	1	5	27,339
Grave Digger	2	C	4	0	0	0	2,990
Gravel Gertie	4	F	11	1	2	1	10,749
Gravellona T	4	F	11	0	3	0	17,320
Graven	4	C	13	3	1	2	9,758
Gravitate	4	C	7	0	1	2	13,200
Gravitating Comet	3	G	10	0	2	1	13,660
Gravy and Bisquits	3	F	2	0	0	0	420
Gray Aggie	4	F	8	0	1	2	4,457
Gray Apple	5	M	4	0	0	1	780
Gray Aras	7	G	5	0	0	1	13,119
Gray Badger	4	C	2	0	0	0	315
Gray Black N White	2	G	1	0	0	0	1,500
Gray Cache	3	F	7	1	2	1	32,090
Gray Coupon	3	F	1	0	0	0	0
Gray Falcon	5	H	9	1	0	0	6,620
Gray Fever	2	F	2	0	0	0	1,690
Gray Forum	4	G	13	1	1	2	24,043
Gray Fox	2	C	1	0	0	0	0
Gray Glory	5	M	2	0	0	0	90
Gray Hawk	5	G	6	1	2	0	13,425
Gray Heat	3	G	3	1	0	1	7,975
Gray Is Great	3	G	10	3	2	1	36,960
Gray Is the Way	4	F	8	0	0	0	743
Gray Jag	3	G	2	0	1	0	4,600
Gray Line	6	G	22	0	4	0	10,229
Gray Me Not	3	F	1	0	0	0	0
Gray Millie	3	F	4	0	1	2	1,745
Gray Misty Dawn	5	M	8	0	0	2	2,140
Gray Morning	4	F	13	2	2	1	22,557
Gray Package	4	C	14	2	2	2	15,381
Gray Panther	4	F	8	1	2	0	5,545
Gray Rubiano	5	H	2	1	0	0	7,800
Gray Ryder	4	F	3	0	0	0	1,559
Gray Token	2	C	2	0	0	0	0
Grayboo	4	G	10	1	1	1	6,307
Graybull	2	C	9	0	1	0	3,955
Graydon Grey	2	G	4	0	1	1	17,740
Graydonna	3	F	7	2	1	1	21,048
Grayglen	3	C	16	1	3	5	39,937
Graypast	2	F	2	0	0	0	0
Grayquest	4	F	2	1	0	0	2,820
Grayross Gal	3	F	1	0	0	0	0
Gray's Classi Boy	2	C	2	0	0	0	210
Graysclassibabyboo	3	F	8	1	1	1	4,240
Grayson	4	C	3	0	0	1	780
Grayson Boy	3	C	1	0	0	0	0
Graystone Bobbie	3	C	4	0	1	0	506
Graysyoureyesonme	7	M	13	1	1	1	5,422
Graytful for You	2	C	2	0	0	0	516
Graze	6	G	7	2	1	1	62,730
Grazettes	4	F	6	0	0	3	23,564
Grazie Bocelli	4	G	6	0	1	0	4,550
Graziella	3	F	2	1	1	0	18,800
Grazing Grace	7	M	1	0	0	0	0
Greased Bullet	5	H	1	1	0	0	38,100
Greased Lightnin'	3	C	9	1	0	1	14,022
Greasy and Slick	8	H	12	0	1	0	1,258
Great Account	3	C	1	0	0	0	360
Great Advantage	4	C	21	3	4	3	20,920
Great Alarm	4	G	15	1	2	3	8,847
Great Alie	2	G	1	0	0	0	0
Great Ambassador (BRZ)	6	G	1	0	0	0	204
Great Aunt Alice	7	M	5	0	0	0	740
Great Auntee	3	F	9	2	0	2	83,106
Great Awakening	3	G	10	1	0	2	13,101
Great Baron	4	C	2	0	0	0	0
Great Bet	6	H	2	0	0	0	50
Great Big	3	C	4	0	0	0	1,385
Great Big Bag	6	H	3	0	1	0	3,358
Great Bloom	5	G	4	2	0	1	62,720
Great Charisma	2	C	2	0	0	0	0
Great Chinggis	2	C	3	0	0	0	358
Great Choice	3	F	2	1	0	0	9,600
Great Commander	3	G	14	5	2	2	70,573
Great Crossing	3	G	8	1	0	1	6,475
Great Dancer (CHI)	3	F	2	0	0	0	0
Great Debate	2	F	3	0	0	0	1,375
Great Defender	7	G	4	3	0	0	35,640
Great Dreamer	4	C	2	0	0	0	116
Great Eight	3	C	5	0	1	0	6,440
Great Executive	4	C	4	1	2	0	14,746
Great Finish	10	H	2	0	0	0	288
Great Flyer	3	C	10	2	2	1	10,820
Great Future	6	G	11	0	1	1	1,945
Great Game	2	F	6	1	1	0	19,110
Great Gentleman	4	G	12	0	2	2	8,340
Great Grandson	4	C	2	0	0	0	0
Great Honoree	3	G	17	1	7	2	33,260
Great Idol	6	H	4	0	0	1	1,085
Great Illusion	3	G	6	1	0	1	6,530
Great Interview	3	F	6	1	0	0	8,265
Great Kisser	3	F	11	1	2	2	7,471

Horse	Age	Sex	Sts	1st	2d	3d	Won
Great Lady Eleanor	4	F	3	1	1	0	8,220
Great Notion	3	C	8	1	4	0	150,000
Great One	4	G	6	0	0	0	440
Great Opportunity	6	H	12	0	0	1	444
Great Performer	5	H	2	0	0	0	0
Great Premise	5	M	6	0	0	0	531
Great Pride	8	G	8	2	2	1	22,324
Great Punch	4	F	3	0	0	0	210
Great Quest	4	G	12	2	3	1	11,941
Great Recording	3	G	2	0	0	0	169
Great Return	3	F	8	2	2	0	39,244
Great Rizzi	2	C	5	0	1	0	3,335
Great Romancer	2	G	4	0	0	0	1,260
Great Senaria	4	F	11	1	0	1	12,654
Great Sham	2	C	1	0	0	0	126
Great Stuff	3	G	9	1	1	2	8,636
Great Time	2	C	1	0	0	1	1,200
Great Trilogy	5	G	16	3	0	4	46,715
Great Warrior	5	G	7	1	0	0	9,231
Great Waters	3	G	12	1	0	6	31,594
Great White Father	5	G	4	1	1	1	16,720
Great White Shark	3	F	2	2	0	0	21,540
Great Wish	2	G	4	1	0	0	21,366
	11	H	9	0	0	0	806
Great Year	7	G	5	0	0	0	1,327
Greater Justice	7	G	12	3	2	2	14,159
Greatness	4	C	7	0	1	2	26,790
Greattobeloved	3	F	8	5	1	1	213,639
Grecian Court	4	C	2	0	0	0	315
Grecian Note	3	C	6	1	1	0	23,830
Gree Lee Dee	3	F	10	1	2	0	22,563
Greed	4	F	12	1	1	1	5,198
Greed'n'glory	3	G	5	1	0	0	12,600
Greedy Executive	2	C	4	1	0	0	31,225
Greedy Shyrlent	5	G	1	0	0	0	0
Greek Authority	7	F	7	1	1	3	35,595
Greek Ballet	4	F	9	1	3	1	7,945
Greek Echo	5	G	11	2	2	1	13,306
Greek Hero	10	G	7	3	2	0	48,600
Greek Legend	4	F	5	1	0	1	15,171
Greek Night	6	M	2	0	0	0	0
Greek Power	2	C	2	0	0	0	335
Greek Pride	4	G	1	0	0	0	0
Greek Speaker	3	F	4	1	0	0	3,312
Greek Spirit	3	G	6	0	1	1	3,072
Greek Stripes	4	F	6	0	0	0	1,230
Greek Sun	2	C	2	2	0	0	71,850
Greek Temper	2	G	6	1	1	2	7,395
Greeley Creek	4	F	4	1	0	1	14,160
Greeley's Bar	3	F	1	0	0	0	164
Greeley's Best	4	G	9	1	2	1	14,155
Greeley's Harbour	5	M	1	0	0	0	0
Greeley's Image	5	G	5	0	1	1	2,247
Greeleyschoice	2	F	8	0	1	0	3,740
Greeleytime	4	G	9	0	0	0	1,279
Greelite	3	G	3	1	1	1	5,346
Greely's Dream	4	F	11	1	1	2	20,595
Green Assets	7	G	3	0	0	0	114
Green Beer	2	G	1	0	0	0	145
Green Beret	7	G	18	5	1	2	51,533
Green Briar Rose	3	F	3	1	0	0	24,438
Green Canyon	3	F	2	0	0	0	0
Green Christmas	4	G	14	1	1	0	4,674
Green Cobra	3	F	8	0	0	4	8,244
Green Colony	3	C	5	0	1	0	9,430
Green Dancer Road	2	F	3	0	0	0	292
Green Dragon	7	M	8	1	0	1	13,747
Green Earrings	2	F	2	1	0	0	6,570
Green Fee	7	H	3	0	0	0	2,250
Green Fiddler	5	H	6	1	0	0	3,475
Green Gingham Girl	4	F	16	1	5	3	35,390
Green Holly	3	F	3	0	0	0	225
Green Jade	2	F	4	0	0	0	1,680
Green Jeans	4	F	5	3	0	1	91,220
Green Knight	4	G	2	0	0	0	262
Green Kuntry	4	G	7	1	0	0	4,040
Green Line (GB)	4	G	8	1	2	0	67,573
Green Links	6	H	7	0	0	0	895
Green Meadow	4	F	6	0	1	1	17,280
Green Music Stop	3	F	7	0	0	1	3,965
Green Power	4	G	11	3	3	2	32,250
Green Raskal	4	C	5	1	0	1	15,698
Green Riches	5	G	5	1	1	1	35,510
Green Ridge	2	F	9	1	1	2	10,900
Green Sedan	3	G	2	0	0	0	0
Green Speed	4	F	12	6	0	1	42,080
Green Station	5	G	4	2	1	0	18,300
Green Team	4	G	13	5	5	1	276,103
Green Thunder	4	C	1	0	0	0	340
Green Tomato	2	F	1	0	0	0	0
Green Valley	6	G	1	0	0	0	90
Greenback Gal	3	F	7	0	0	0	2,140
Greenberg	2	F	2	1	0	0	12,600
Greencielo	7	M	1	0	0	0	0
Greene County Lady	3	F	6	0	1	0	3,473
Greenhills (GB)	4	G	9	0	2	1	14,850
Greenlaw	3	F	5	0	0	0	210
Greenleaf Mountain	8	G	2	0	0	0	0
Greenlee	3	F	6	0	2	1	4,135
Greenlight Express	3	G	8	0	0	1	2,084
Greensbottom	5	G	7	1	0	1	2,656
Greenski	4	C	2	0	0	0	137
Greenstormacoming	4	F	3	0	0	1	5,855
Greenup	4	G	9	1	0	1	4,922
Greenway Diamond	3	G	7	0	1	0	4,095
Greeting Card	3	F	14	3	2	2	32,165
Greggie's Star	3	C	8	0	1	1	5,365
Gregg's Mistake	3	F	1	0	1	0	960
Gregnunn	3	C	4	0	1	0	2,100
Greg's Deck	3	C	15	1	0	2	14,915
Greg's Estrella	3	C	4	0	0	0	379
Greg's Reprized	2	C	5	0	0	0	1,285
Greg's Syrah	3	C	6	1	0	1	25,015
Greg's Turk	9	G	19	2	4	4	17,840
Gregson	2	C	1	0	0	0	0
Grendel	3	G	7	2	0	3	51,980
Grenfield	8	M	3	0	0	0	129
Greta's Joy	2	F	5	2	1	1	10,963
Gretchen	4	F	4	0	0	0	247
Gretchen's Boy	6	G	7	2	4	0	12,666
Gretchen's Star	8	G	7	2	2	0	124,275
Grettle	6	M	4	0	1	1	4,550
Grey Ballet	5	M	1	0	0	0	400
Grey Beard	4	C	7	0	0	0	8,402
Grey Bouquet	3	F	7	1	0	1	18,666
Grey Bullet	3	C	2	1	0	0	6,046
Grey Cart	5	G	6	0	0	1	3,608
Grey Charm	6	G	14	1	5	0	10,885
Grey Charmbracelet	2	F	5	0	0	0	708
Grey Comet	3	C	5	2	2	1	205,080
Grey Diamonds	2	F	2	0	0	0	2,204
Grey Gatita	4	F	4	1	0	0	3,462
Grey Memo	6	H	8	0	1	3	373,400
Grey Muse	2	G	1	0	0	0	515
Grey On Grey	3	C	9	0	1	1	3,312
Grey Pride	3	C	6	0	1	1	10,990
Grey Pu Ponchee	2	F	10	0	0	1	3,605
Grey Reagle	3	G	7	0	0	0	505
Grey Reef Bow	3	G	3	0	0	0	0
Grey River	3	F	3	0	0	1	996
Grey Ruby	3	F	14	4	2	3	84,910
Grey Rye	6	G	1	0	0	0	0
Grey Sea's Shining	6	M	13	0	1	4	4,785
Grey Velvet	8	G	10	2	2	1	31,810
Grey Wolf	11	G	2	0	0	0	200
Greybec	4	G	1	0	0	0	0
Greygoosegal	2	F	2	1	0	0	18,780
Greyhame	4	G	13	1	2	2	27,705
Greymon	2	C	1	1	0	0	31,225
Grey's Majesty	6	H	9	1	0	2	16,715
Greysum	5	G	3	1	1	0	4,343
Greyt Scott	4	G	11	1	1	1	7,685
Grid North	5	H	15	2	2	3	6,222
Griever Canyon	4	C	10	1	0	1	8,347
Griffinite	5	H	3	1	1	0	25,000
Griffin's Cow Girl	3	F	9	1	2	0	11,085
Griffin's Wake	2	G	3	2	0	0	22,731
Griffon Blue	4	G	2	0	0	0	0

Horse	Age	Sex	Sts	1st	2d	3d	Won	Horse	Age	Sex	Sts	1st	2d	3d	Won
Grifter	5	H	10	2	1	1	38,030	Ground Attack	4	G	12	0	3	2	2,488
Grigia	3	F	7	1	1	0	14,470	Ground Breaking	2	G	7	2	4	0	54,870
Grillberger	3	G	12	1	0	2	10,381	Ground Cat	3	F	10	1	1	1	11,310
Grilled Cheese	4	G	14	1	1	2	9,124	Ground Forces	4	G	4	0	0	0	883
Grillhouse	6	G	10	4	1	1	134,170	Ground Hero	3	C	1	0	0	0	2,800
Grimer	4	G	5	2	0	1	24,071	Ground Storm	7	H	5	0	2	2	51,627
Grimm	4	G	6	5	0	0	102,420	Ground Zero Hero	3	G	12	1	0	5	12,860
Grin and Frown	3	C	12	2	2	4	78,595	Group Estate	3	F	2	0	0	1	2,567
Grin and Picture	5	G	5	0	1	2	1,015	Grove Creek	4	F	5	3	0	1	20,230
Grin and Smile	3	F	10	1	1	3	28,295	Grovenor	7	M	3	0	0	1	1,716
Grinadine	4	F	18	2	1	3	13,007	Growing Gains	3	F	7	1	1	2	26,222
Grinamic	3	F	1	0	0	0	600	Growth Stock	5	M	9	0	3	2	28,530
Grinanbearit	7	G	2	0	1	0	2,310	Grrrgarious	4	C	10	1	2	1	34,540
Grinch	2	F	2	1	0	1	29,420	Grub for Gold	5	M	20	4	0	0	14,503
Grind	5	H	7	0	0	1	2,956	Grubby Soldier	3	G	1	0	0	0	0
Grind It Out	4	F	8	1	3	1	17,865	Grueling	2	C	7	0	1	0	2,511
Grind the Blues	3	G	8	2	1	3	29,619	Grumman	3	G	6	1	3	1	41,000
Grindavik	3	F	8	1	2	3	23,560	Grumpita	9	M	12	0	1	2	4,112
Grinding It Out	3	C	7	1	3	0	41,600	Grump's Wild Dream	2	G	1	0	0	0	0
Grindrock	7	G	9	0	0	0	3,440	Grumpy Sis	2	F	1	0	0	0	100
Grindstone Deputy	4	F	1	0	0	0	0	Grundlefoot Wood	3	G	2	0	0	0	129
Grindstone Gold	2	C	6	0	0	1	5,092	Grunt	5	H	5	0	1	0	3,045
Grindstone Lassie	5	M	2	0	1	0	1,600	Gruntled (GB)	4	C	4	1	0	0	39,858
Grindstone's Tina	4	F	11	1	1	1	6,476	Gruveebit	2	F	5	0	0	0	1,560
Grindtime	3	F	2	1	1	0	33,600	Gruvianna	3	F	14	2	2	1	17,230
Gringa Hug	3	F	11	2	4	1	15,875	Gryffindor	3	G	6	0	1	1	6,670
Gringo Joe	6	G	15	4	3	2	35,703	Gryphon Red	3	G	6	0	0	0	1,836
Gringo Legend	3	G	15	1	1	2	7,965	Guadalupes Tailor	5	G	9	1	1	1	5,927
Grininfromeartoear	3	G	5	0	0	0	490	Guaitil	3	G	14	2	4	3	33,039
Grinnin Bear	5	G	7	1	1	1	4,649	Guana (FR)	4	F	4	1	0	1	31,345
Grisaille	5	M	10	0	1	5	7,702	Guapazo (ARG)	5	H	10	0	5	2	41,820
Grit and Glory	3	F	17	0	2	2	4,677	Guarani's Daughter	2	F	4	0	0	0	2,550
Grit and Steel	2	F	2	0	0	1	1,180	Guaranteed	10	H	6	0	0	0	2,846
Grit Forever	7	G	4	0	0	0	340	Guaranteed Sweep	3	C	8	3	1	0	61,120
Grit Victory	4	C	1	0	0	0	91	Guaranteeddelivery	5	G	12	2	1	1	8,904
Gritty Kitty	2	F	7	1	2	1	12,560	Guard Cat	5	H	4	1	0	1	7,124
Gritty Madam	5	M	1	0	0	0	0	Guardian	3	C	8	2	2	2	80,900
Gritty Sandie	7	G	7	3	0	0	43,500	Guardian Angel	4	F	5	0	0	0	520
Gritty Smitty	4	G	9	3	0	0	17,820	Guardianofthegate	7	G	8	4	1	0	99,640
Grizz	7	H	6	0	2	0	3,406	Guardsman	6	G	9	1	1	1	7,649
Grizzley Queen	4	F	6	0	0	1	7,300	Guaritta	3	G	11	1	0	2	33,870
Grizzly Gulch	3	G	12	0	2	4	5,640	Guaymas Sky	3	C	15	2	0	2	9,432
Grog	6	G	5	0	1	1	3,484	Gubbio	7	G	11	0	0	1	1,531
Groom a Fire	5	H	13	2	2	2	11,098	Guerdon	6	G	7	2	0	1	36,953
Groom Me a Star	3	C	1	0	0	0	910	Guerrero	3	C	6	1	2	1	25,060
Groom On the Run	4	G	11	1	3	2	93,819	Guerrero Don (ARG)	5	H	3	0	0	0	600
Groomedforsuccess	2	G	3	0	1	1	5,070	Guess	5	M	1	0	0	0	0
Groomeroma	3	F	11	0	4	2	24,170	Guest Table	2	F	3	1	0	0	1,540
Grooms Derby	6	M	4	0	0	0	4,256	Guestbook	6	M	18	3	3	1	20,650
Groom's Kiss	3	F	15	1	3	4	42,010	Guestchance	5	H	3	0	0	0	301
Groom's Mia	4	F	17	1	1	1	4,090	Guestelaw	4	G	7	0	0	0	604
Grooms Pride	5	M	3	1	1	0	2,975	Guid	5	G	3	0	0	0	416
Grootka	4	G	5	0	1	1	2,050	Guidebook	3	F	7	2	1	1	38,440
Groove Girl	6	M	3	1	2	0	5,500	Guiding Angel	3	G	13	2	2	2	20,731
Grooved Swing	6	H	2	0	0	0	95	Guiding Force	6	G	3	1	1	0	18,400
Groover	7	H	7	0	0	0	0	Guido	2	G	1	0	0	0	380
Groovewiththebean	4	G	14	2	3	3	23,740	Guido's Thunder	4	G	3	1	0	1	4,270
Groovin Gary	3	C	5	0	2	1	5,040	Guilded Fantasy	7	G	15	3	1	4	5,584
Groovin Suzy	5	M	1	0	0	0	0	Guile	4	G	7	1	0	0	5,263
Groovin' Wind	8	H	4	0	0	0	0	Guillamou City (FR)	6	H	1	0	0	0	0
Groovy Add Vice	12	G	7	0	2	2	3,591	Guillotine	5	M	10	2	0	1	48,830
Groovy Bandit	2	C	2	0	0	0	180	Guilty Gal	7	M	9	1	1	1	8,530
Groovy Chief	3	G	9	2	2	0	25,010	Guilty Judgement	4	G	7	1	0	0	7,500
Groovy Duck	3	C	3	0	0	1	1,560	Guilty One	5	G	9	0	0	1	1,096
Groovy Fortune	2	C	9	2	1	1	21,950	Guiltyascaanbe	3	C	10	2	0	2	47,935
Groovy Hero	4	F	11	2	1	1	16,688	Guiltybysupiscion	5	M	9	5	1	2	25,988
Groovy Kat	3	G	8	1	0	1	7,665	Guineas Overload	4	G	3	0	0	0	564
Groovy Kinda Love	3	F	4	0	0	0	340	Guiness On Tap	8	G	13	3	3	1	21,292
Groovy Knight	3	C	8	1	3	0	8,183	Guitar	6	M	7	1	1	0	37,440
Groovy Minister	3	F	4	1	0	0	15,030	Gulch Approval	3	G	12	3	2	3	117,472
Groovy Rockette	3	F	6	0	0	0	812	Gulchie (GB)	5	H	9	0	4	2	57,860
Groovy Zone	3	G	14	1	4	1	25,569	Gulchrunssweet	3	G	7	1	2	0	99,812
Groovy's Rare Moon	3	F	8	0	0	2	2,780	Gulch's Echo	5	M	3	0	0	0	244
Groovy's Rose	2	F	3	0	0	0	340	Gulch's Sensation	5	H	9	1	0	0	18,751
Groovys Squall	9	G	3	0	1	0	10,500	Gulf Breeze	4	G	4	0	0	0	0
Gross Margin	3	C	5	0	1	1	13,920	Gulf Developer	9	G	11	4	1	1	23,742
Grossman	4	G	1	0	0	0	0	Gulf News	4	C	3	0	0	0	0
Grotto	5	M	8	2	3	2	35,200	Gulf of Gdansk	2	F	6	1	2	2	42,000
Ground Assault	5	G	9	1	1	3	13,730	Gulf of Mexico	2	C	2	1	0	0	34,400

Horse	Age	Sex	Sts	1st	2d	3d	Won	Horse	Age	Sex	Sts	1st	2d	3d	Won
Gulf Wind	4	G	9	1	1	1	10,453	Gypsy Peak	7	M	5	0	0	0	180
Gulfport	4	G	7	1	0	0	6,054	Gypsy Pole E Style	4	F	2	0	1	0	2,075
Gullen One	5	M	4	0	0	0	216	Gypsy Road	5	G	7	1	1	1	38,110
Gullible	7	G	2	0	0	0	750	Gypsy Romance	6	M	9	3	1	3	58,824
Gulliver Travels	3	C	4	0	1	0	2,916	Gypsy Sparkle	8	G	2	0	0	0	0
Gully Wash	4	F	8	0	3	1	3,057	Gypsy Tailwind	3	F	8	1	0	2	13,400
Gumbo Love	3	F	5	2	1	1	81,435	Gypsy Witch	3	F	8	2	1	0	13,495
Gumby Girl	4	F	13	4	4	1	32,184	Gypsygentelman	5	H	4	0	0	0	625
Gummies Symph	4	G	2	0	1	0	4,860	Gypsy's Fastness	3	F	2	0	0	0	425
Gummy Delight	6	M	16	0	3	2	5,906	Gypsy's Favour	2	F	2	0	0	0	145
Gump Can Run	3	G	11	1	0	0	2,669	Gypsy's Lad	4	C	7	0	0	0	1,088
Gumpy Toro	6	G	7	1	0	2	3,829	Gyrene	4	F	3	1	1	0	36,108
Gumshoe	6	G	9	2	2	3	34,943	Gyrfalcon (GB)	5	H	5	0	1	1	12,590
Gun Barrel	8	G	5	0	1	0	1,871	H and M's Prospect	3	G	9	1	3	0	8,059
Gun Barrel City	5	H	17	4	4	1	39,501	H B's Priscilla	5	M	7	0	0	1	3,040
Gun Boat	3	G	5	0	0	0	960	H C Express	2	C	1	0	1	0	4,340
Gun Deck	3	G	4	0	0	0	480	H C's Finale	3	C	2	0	0	0	110
Gun Hilda	5	M	8	1	1	3	14,290	H G's Jack	3	C	7	1	1	2	8,820
Gun Hill	7	G	8	1	2	1	18,490	H M S Pinafore	5	G	17	4	3	1	17,959
Gun Is Set	5	G	6	1	1	1	8,845	H M Slew	6	G	6	0	0	0	0
Gun Runner	6	G	5	0	0	1	1,150	H Potter	2	G	4	1	1	0	15,560
Gun Silencer	4	C	5	1	1	0	4,710	H Que	7	M	7	2	0	2	31,635
Gun Town	2	C	1	1	0	0	21,000	H. Hammer G.	8	G	11	0	0	1	4,194
Gunduwarrior	3	G	11	1	2	2	12,187	H. M. S. Hollywood	3	G	11	1	1	1	11,880
Gunitdownthewire	2	F	1	0	0	0	1,764	H. M. S. Jackson	6	G	10	1	0	4	24,470
Gunner	6	H	1	0	1	0	1,422	H. R. H. Doodle	3	F	6	1	0	0	17,540
Gunner Boy	3	G	4	0	0	1	1,414	H. V. A. C. Genius	7	M	1	0	0	0	0
Gunner Star Bopp	6	G	7	0	0	0	1,485	Ha Ha April Fools	6	M	19	0	3	4	5,411
Gunner Up	6	G	3	0	0	0	532	Ha Ha's Knight	4	C	8	1	1	2	6,245
Gunnerjack	4	G	7	0	0	1	1,401	Haam	2	G	1	0	0	0	0
Gunnery	4	G	16	3	2	2	26,309	Haande Cap Her	7	M	1	0	0	1	420
Gunning	8	G	9	1	1	0	12,260	Haasil (IRE)	5	H	7	2	0	1	28,380
Gunning For	2	G	2	1	1	0	8,360	Habaneros	4	C	2	1	0	0	30,000
Gunning for Eddie	4	C	5	0	1	1	1,800	Habano Daydreamer	4	C	1	0	0	0	0
Gunnison Mary	4	F	1	0	0	0	495	Habayeb	3	C	6	1	0	0	18,550
Guns a Blazen	4	G	14	3	6	1	11,505	Haberdasher	6	G	6	0	0	0	1,268
Guppie's Secret	4	G	5	0	0	0	1,480	Habibi	4	F	3	0	0	1	550
Gurnzi	2	F	1	0	0	0	115	Habitual Criminal	3	C	12	3	1	3	32,708
Gurza	2	G	5	0	0	1	4,720	Hacan (ARG)	5	H	9	1	3	1	12,895
Gus Again	6	H	7	1	1	2	11,474	Hacienda Del Mar	3	F	9	3	4	0	57,234
Gus D Dawn	6	G	4	0	0	0	273	Hackamans Dream	2	C	1	0	0	0	0
Gussie Guezano	4	F	2	0	0	0	250	Hackendiffy	3	C	8	2	1	0	122,200
Gussie Up	4	F	5	0	0	0	1,252	Hackle	7	G	1	0	0	0	0
Gussie's Secret	2	F	3	1	0	0	6,300	Hackleton's Cliff	3	C	9	4	0	1	72,916
Gusting Rain	4	C	4	0	0	1	420	Hackley	5	G	7	1	0	0	8,436
Gusto Forzado	8	G	1	0	0	0	184	Hacksaw Jane	4	F	11	1	0	1	8,251
Gustov's Mauler	7	H	1	0	0	0	0	Hacoda	5	G	14	2	2	3	34,315
Gusty Spirit	3	C	8	1	0	0	17,759	Had a Great Run	4	G	10	1	1	2	9,646
Gusty Wind	5	G	2	0	0	0	0	Had It All	7	G	3	0	0	0	169
Gut Wrench	2	G	2	0	0	0	0	Had to Be You	3	F	7	0	1	1	5,815
Gutcheck Gal	5	M	5	0	0	0	158	Hada Clue	4	G	1	0	0	0	0
Guten Tanzen	5	G	2	0	0	0	81	Hadalittle	7	H	11	0	3	0	3,002
Guts and Glory	3	G	10	1	4	1	30,240	Hadastar	5	M	1	0	0	0	456
Guv for a Day	4	G	1	0	0	0	0	Hadawitch	3	G	3	0	0	0	216
Guy Getaway	2	C	2	0	2	0	17,200	Hadenough	5	M	9	2	0	1	22,496
Guypowder Valley	4	C	1	0	0	0	0	Hades' Halo	5	M	10	2	1	1	8,757
Guysmarlene	9	M	2	0	0	0	3,062	Hadif Declares	2	G	5	1	3	0	12,900
Gwaihir (IRE)	2	C	7	2	2	2	110,268	Hadif Time Machine	4	C	5	2	1	1	23,198
Gwanaboa Vale	2	G	3	0	0	0	2,757	Hadifly	5	H	11	2	0	2	25,466
Gweniveve	4	F	11	3	0	2	25,065	Hadif's Allstar	3	F	1	0	0	0	0
Gwens Love	3	C	2	0	0	0	450	Hadif's Lover Boy	3	G	13	3	3	2	40,766
Gygistar	4	G	4	1	0	0	94,100	Hadifs Quality	3	F	2	0	0	0	0
Gym Kid	2	F	5	1	0	1	25,200	Hadifs Shoelace	4	C	7	0	3	0	6,195
Gymnastic Girl	2	F	5	0	0	0	0	Hadifson	3	C	9	2	3	1	20,560
Gymnist Jack	3	F	9	0	1	0	2,625	Hadigrant	10	G	11	1	4	2	4,352
Gypsen Moon	4	G	10	0	0	0	4,259	Hadivana	2	F	7	1	2	0	10,051
Gypsey Honey	5	M	13	3	3	1	10,942	Hadl	6	M	8	1	0	0	56,956
Gypsiesinthepalace	7	G	8	0	1	1	10,810	Hadley Hill	3	C	12	0	2	0	7,554
Gypsy Breeze	2	F	3	0	0	1	1,694	Hadley's Victory	3	C	12	2	3	1	31,240
Gypsy Chick	5	M	11	1	1	0	4,112	Hadtoomuch	3	G	17	0	2	1	8,925
Gypsy Dot	3	F	18	4	2	0	90,985	Hafez	5	G	16	0	4	2	6,446
Gypsy Jazz	3	G	6	1	0	0	12,679	Haflinger (CHI)	7	G	1	0	0	0	2,100
Gypsy Jet	3	F	3	0	0	0	225	Hafta Conquer	4	G	9	1	1	2	42,290
Gypsy John	7	G	6	0	2	2	10,509	Hagerstown	3	F	14	2	4	3	53,330
Gypsy Jubilee	11	G	4	0	0	0	227	Haggle	5	H	7	2	0	0	8,924
Gypsy Judge	4	F	1	0	0	0	119	Haggled Kiss	5	M	2	0	0	0	0
Gypsy June	6	M	10	1	3	1	5,035	Haggs Castle	5	G	9	0	1	1	52,198
Gypsy L	5	M	1	0	0	0	575	Hagy's Honey	4	F	4	0	0	0	190
Gypsy Music	5	M	16	0	1	3	3,347								

Horse	Age	Sex	Sts	1st	2d	3d	Won
Haiku	4	G	4	0	0	0	396
Hail Boppie	6	G	17	1	1	1	12,078
Hail for Buck	5	G	1	0	0	0	0
Hail Hillary	3	F	8	3	3	0	133,300
Hail Holy King (IRE)	2	G	5	0	0	1	792
Hail I'm Good	4	F	6	0	0	0	120
Hail Jeannie	4	F	5	0	0	1	756
Hail Lively One	7	G	6	0	1	1	3,643
Hail Luthier	4	C	1	0	0	0	0
Hail Mary Bishop	2	F	6	1	0	0	6,475
Hail Minister	6	H	1	0	1	0	1,800
Hail Patton	3	G	1	0	0	0	0
Hail She's Captain	3	F	10	0	3	1	7,105
Hail the Cat	5	G	6	0	0	2	1,706
Hail The Chief (GB)	6	H	3	0	0	0	460
Hail to Bag	4	G	2	0	0	0	2,100
Hail to Blue	5	H	4	1	0	0	1,470
Hail to Don	2	G	3	0	0	0	1,051
Hail to Love	2	C	1	0	0	0	1,263
Hail to Prospector	3	F	2	0	0	0	0
Hail to Smokester	2	C	6	1	0	1	22,390
Hail to the Lion	10	G	7	0	0	2	1,240
Hail to Wild Again	5	H	14	3	0	4	59,290
Hailey B	3	F	14	3	4	3	56,155
Haileys Bucks	4	C	1	0	0	0	0
Haillo	4	G	2	0	0	0	0
Haillye's A. T. M.	3	G	13	4	3	0	66,820
Haillye's Brother	2	C	9	0	1	2	6,445
Hailraiser	7	G	3	0	0	1	259
Hailtheliquidator	8	G	3	0	0	0	628
Haimish	7	G	6	0	0	1	720
Haint It Hot	2	G	1	1	0	0	5,225
Haint No Rose	3	F	3	0	1	0	1,060
Haint No Stopin Me	2	F	3	0	0	0	190
Haint You Grand	2	G	4	2	0	1	16,475
Hair Jordan	3	G	4	0	0	1	4,351
Hairy Stimets	5	H	1	0	0	0	0
Haiti Lady	2	F	3	0	1	1	6,690
Haitian Heat	5	M	3	0	0	0	453
Haitian Hit	4	G	12	2	0	1	16,442
Haitian Plantation	5	G	15	2	3	1	11,494
Haitian Princess	5	M	12	3	5	0	22,875
Haitianreiteration	4	F	15	2	3	3	37,029
Hajji Baba	4	G	14	0	1	1	9,877
Hajji Babe	3	F	7	1	2	1	42,315
Hajji's Bold Eagle	4	G	3	0	1	0	940
Hajji's Honor	2	C	7	2	2	0	71,305
Hakahana	3	C	2	0	0	0	0
Hale Ole	5	M	18	1	1	0	3,370
Hale the Bold	8	G	6	0	2	1	3,225
Haleakala Sunrise	2	F	3	0	1	2	19,960
Hales Blizzard	3	F	13	0	1	1	5,410
Haley Mac	2	F	3	0	0	0	275
Haley Makes Eight	3	F	4	0	0	0	385
Haley's Big Dream	6	M	6	0	0	0	1,122
Haley's Buddy	3	G	10	2	0	3	34,360
Haley's Classic	4	F	6	1	2	1	36,880
Half a Bag	3	C	4	1	1	0	7,700
Half a Case	3	G	6	1	0	0	6,600
Half a Dollar Maid	2	F	4	0	0	2	2,950
Half a Pat	3	F	1	0	0	0	0
Half Fare	4	F	2	0	0	0	2,625
Half Fast Passage	5	H	10	1	1	0	2,334
Half Hearted	3	F	5	0	1	2	4,330
Half Moon	4	F	11	0	3	1	13,211
Half Moon Hustler	8	G	7	0	0	0	820
Half Moon Romance	7	H	9	2	0	3	9,360
Half Off	4	F	16	1	3	4	8,029
Half Penny	3	F	4	1	0	0	2,760
Half Pint to Go	5	M	16	2	0	3	9,961
Half Steppin	4	F	4	0	0	1	1,350
Half Way Tree	5	H	1	0	0	0	0
Half Wild	4	G	3	1	1	0	8,700
Halfalert	4	G	4	0	0	0	0
Halfbaked	4	F	5	1	0	0	2,718
Halfbridled	2	F	4	4	0	0	849,400
Halford Road	9	H	6	0	0	2	1,575
Halfupy	4	F	3	0	0	1	312
Halfway Home	3	C	5	0	1	0	5,290
Halfway North	7	M	1	0	0	0	225
Halfway to Heaven	5	M	16	3	4	4	87,102
Halibear	5	G	9	1	0	1	3,572
Haliburton Honey	3	F	11	0	5	2	64,224
Haliburton Sky	3	C	1	0	0	0	0
Haliburton Storm	2	G	1	0	0	0	0
Haliburton Wild	3	G	15	0	1	4	19,803
Halic	7	M	3	0	0	0	700
Halissee's Son	3	G	5	0	2	1	6,261
Hall Lass	3	C	10	2	1	0	36,820
Hall of Angels	7	G	7	1	2	1	22,950
Hallandale Slew	4	C	3	1	0	0	3,720
Hallas	6	M	8	2	1	0	5,855
Halle	2	F	3	0	0	0	525
Hallelujahnpraise	2	F	5	1	0	0	4,140
Hallie Cat	4	F	15	1	1	2	20,428
Hallie Laredo	2	F	7	1	1	1	17,850
Hallie's Danzigjet	7	M	7	2	0	1	14,264
Hallo Bert	7	G	8	2	1	1	19,954
Hallowed	4	F	6	0	0	2	9,620
Halloween Fun	3	F	3	0	0	1	3,650
Hallshill Road	6	G	11	2	4	1	24,277
Halltheway	6	G	12	4	2	0	23,416
Hallucinogin	6	H	6	0	1	0	6,980
Halo and Roses	6	H	4	0	0	0	855
Halo Avenue	2	F	5	1	0	1	11,951
Halo Berlin	3	G	2	0	0	0	0
Halo Brite	4	G	9	3	2	2	28,612
Halo Can You Go	4	F	11	2	2	2	42,010
Halo Cat	5	G	7	2	3	0	128,650
Halo Colddeck	3	G	18	0	3	1	4,424
Halo Dancer	4	G	13	1	2	2	10,472
Halo Dare	5	G	7	1	1	3	15,041
Halo Dixie Land	3	F	3	0	0	0	660
Halo Dot Com	5	M	5	0	0	2	3,878
Halo Enclosed	7	G	9	3	2	0	34,058
Halo Flash	8	G	13	2	2	2	12,196
Halo Goodbye	2	C	3	0	0	2	3,595
Halo Halo Halo	3	F	6	2	2	0	68,184
Halo Halo Star	2	F	1	0	0	0	0
Halo Heaven	3	G	6	2	0	1	30,520
Halo Homewrecker	3	C	8	3	0	1	157,165
Halo Hunter (ARG)	5	H	5	0	0	0	2,370
Halo Kris	6	G	7	0	0	0	1,440
Halo Legend	3	G	2	0	0	0	135
Halo Light	3	F	12	1	4	3	11,746
Halo Malone	3	G	10	5	0	2	43,044
Halo Moon	4	F	12	3	2	2	49,810
Halo Nell	6	H	5	0	1	2	4,179
Halo of Hearts	4	G	10	1	3	0	15,938
Halo of Silver	3	F	10	0	1	2	8,846
Halo of Truth	5	M	10	2	1	1	36,810
Halo Point	4	G	3	0	0	0	600
Halo R. D.	4	G	12	0	0	3	6,900
Halo Romeo	7	G	15	2	1	5	10,556
Halo Rube	2	C	2	0	0	0	365
Halo Seeya	5	M	5	0	0	0	225
Halo Spirit	4	C	1	0	0	1	3,100
Halo Springs	5	M	12	2	2	2	9,975
Halo Sue	3	F	9	0	1	0	1,490
Halo Sun	2	F	1	0	0	0	0
Halo Sunny	2	F	2	0	0	0	0
Halo Tyra	4	F	6	0	3	1	31,150
Halo Virginia	6	G	10	1	0	2	7,140
Halo World	8	G	6	1	1	1	11,654
Halodramatic	2	F	1	0	0	1	2,860
Halodyne	4	G	3	0	0	0	156
Haloed	2	F	2	0	0	0	180
Halonator	2	F	2	0	0	1	3,094
Halophyte	6	G	1	0	0	0	365
Halory Clanton	2	F	3	0	0	0	1,030
Halory Hunted	2	C	1	0	1	0	1,860
Halory Leigh	3	F	11	4	2	1	178,238
Halory Lewis	2	F	2	0	1	0	1,500
Halory Too	3	F	2	0	0	0	792
Halory's Habit	2	F	3	0	1	1	7,530
Halory's Secret	3	F	12	2	1	3	17,090
Halo's Advantage	5	G	1	0	0	0	149
Halo's Alarm	3	G	11	0	1	1	3,737

Horse	Age	Sex	Sts	1st	2d	3d	Won
Halos and Stripes	4	F	2	1	0	0	5,606
Halo's Appeal	3	G	7	2	0	1	61,894
Halo's Bid	3	F	4	0	0	0	2,624
Halo's Bluff	3	G	5	1	0	0	6,100
Halo's Date	3	F	3	0	0	0	0
Halo's Defense	6	G	3	0	0	1	644
Halo's Echo	4	F	4	1	0	1	2,310
Halos for Hibiscus	3	C	13	3	0	1	33,400
Halo's Gem	3	F	14	3	5	2	40,338
Halo's Glow	4	F	9	2	1	2	22,216
Halo's Gold Mine	4	G	10	1	0	0	1,764
Halo's Hawk	3	C	1	0	0	0	0
Halo's Heartbreak	5	M	9	0	2	2	3,900
Halo's Honour	4	C	11	3	2	2	24,430
Halo's Investment	2	C	1	0	0	0	520
Halo's Match	3	F	6	1	1	1	10,480
Halo's Morpheus	2	C	5	0	0	0	3,038
Halo's Notebook	2	F	1	1	0	0	7,800
Halo's Pleasure	3	F	9	1	0	0	6,998
Halos Promise Land	3	F	3	1	1	1	14,900
Halo's Regent	3	G	14	1	1	4	22,064
Halo's Secret	5	G	12	1	1	1	13,021
Halo's Shadow	5	H	12	2	1	0	27,120
Halo's Song	3	F	14	4	4	2	33,384
Halo's Stride	5	H	3	1	0	0	25,581
Halo's Sugar	4	F	5	1	0	2	5,587
Halo's Tiger	4	G	13	2	5	3	87,926
Halos Tresses	2	F	2	0	0	0	0
Halo's Trial	4	C	4	0	1	0	2,092
Halo's Wildcat	2	F	5	1	0	1	12,175
Halo's Wish	4	F	7	1	0	0	4,019
Halosnglory	2	C	1	0	1	0	3,510
Halover	7	G	9	2	1	2	7,333
Halu Kour's Lady	3	F	8	2	1	1	16,101
Halve It All	3	C	5	0	0	1	3,540
Halvsies	4	F	8	1	0	1	1,634
Ham Sandwich	6	H	3	0	0	0	2,770
Hamaaly	3	G	4	1	0	1	14,460
Hamanjiz	4	G	16	2	4	2	27,328
Hama's	2	F	2	0	0	0	380
Hamburg Lady	5	M	3	0	0	0	753
Hamburger Chef	2	C	2	0	0	0	150
Hamdi	3	F	2	1	0	0	4,960
Hamering Heart	3	F	8	1	0	0	4,800
Hamilton Island	6	G	10	0	1	4	7,283
Haminahaminahamina	3	G	7	1	0	2	7,795
Hamlet	3	F	6	1	2	1	24,889
Hammer	4	C	14	2	3	2	13,034
Hammer Down	4	C	5	0	0	1	2,490
Hammer Down Hank	2	C	4	1	0	0	7,920
Hammerin	3	C	11	1	1	2	9,903
Hammerindown	4	C	3	0	0	0	1,540
Hammerlock Ridge	6	H	8	1	4	0	8,307
Hammersmith	3	G	2	0	0	0	1,492
Hampden	4	G	12	1	0	1	8,430
Hampon Baby (ARG)	5	H	5	2	0	0	22,260
Hamp's Champ	2	C	5	0	0	2	4,870
Hampshire Dancer	7	M	8	0	0	2	2,385
Hampton Bay	6	H	4	2	1	0	8,870
Hampton Express	3	F	6	0	0	0	592
Ham's Our Man	3	G	6	1	1	1	18,370
Hana Highway	5	G	5	3	1	1	85,765
Hananiah	4	C	8	2	2	1	11,591
Hand Maid Axe	4	F	3	0	0	0	0
Hand Signal	5	H	3	0	0	0	476
Handful of Heaven	5	M	10	1	0	3	12,126
Handful of Marbles	4	F	8	0	3	1	5,886
Handful of Stars	3	F	1	0	0	0	0
Handover d'Cash	3	G	13	0	1	1	3,291
Handpainted	3	F	2	0	1	0	59,600
Hands On	2	C	3	2	1	0	41,070
Hands to the Side	5	G	15	2	2	3	21,693
Handsome Darby	6	G	6	0	1	1	3,974
Handsome Face	3	G	19	1	5	4	28,538
Handsome Gent	4	C	8	5	1	0	112,580
Handsome George	4	G	4	0	0	2	9,250
Handsome Healer	4	G	2	0	0	0	122
Handsome Henry	4	G	7	1	0	1	4,470
Handsome Honoree	3	G	5	1	0	0	9,740

Horse	Age	Sex	Sts	1st	2d	3d	Won
Handsome Hunk	4	C	1	0	0	0	0
Handsome Jack	5	G	17	1	1	2	13,170
Handsome Jim	4	G	10	0	1	2	2,666
Handsome Jolly Jim	8	G	16	3	1	3	14,802
Handsome Man	5	H	5	0	0	1	464
Handsome Ransom	4	C	3	0	1	0	1,632
Handsome Smile	5	G	9	0	1	0	27,216
Handsome Tour	2	G	4	0	0	0	300
Handsome Twister	2	C	3	0	0	0	115
Handsome Will Do	5	G	10	1	2	0	8,073
Handsomest	5	H	4	0	0	0	330
Handy Andy	3	G	2	0	0	1	4,620
Handy Boy	3	C	8	1	3	1	6,846
Handy Cat	3	F	7	1	0	1	3,284
Handy Man Jeff	7	G	9	2	3	1	5,253
Handy N Bold	8	G	6	1	0	0	31,905
Handy Nutcracker	4	F	9	1	1	1	4,584
Handyman Bill	4	G	8	4	1	1	115,760
Handzz Up	3	G	15	0	6	0	11,302
Hang On Brenda	4	F	7	1	1	0	4,640
Hang Up Call	3	F	5	2	0	1	29,141
Hangin' by a Tread	4	F	15	1	2	0	6,480
Hangin Tuff	4	C	4	0	0	1	926
Hanging Jury	2	C	6	0	1	2	4,993
Hanging Sharp	5	G	5	0	1	1	1,627
Hanging Sparkles	3	C	1	0	0	0	0
Hangingontomyhalo	4	G	2	0	0	0	0
Hangmans Comin	2	G	5	0	0	0	1,300
Hangonslewpyhangon	7	G	4	0	0	0	4,363
Hangontight	4	G	1	0	0	1	2,040
Hangtime	3	G	12	3	2	1	51,666
Hangupthephone	4	F	6	0	1	0	1,426
Hangwiththehaves	2	F	3	1	1	0	18,380
Hank 'n Ace	4	G	2	0	0	0	1,320
Hankamer	9	G	8	0	0	1	3,976
Hank's Chance	3	G	12	2	2	3	59,814
Hank's Rib	4	G	5	3	1	0	24,740
Hanky	4	C	6	1	1	0	20,045
Hanlan	5	G	11	1	3	0	84,297
Hanna Rules	2	F	1	0	0	0	0
Hanna Senesch	4	F	4	0	0	0	2,595
Hannaboy	3	G	12	3	2	2	34,865
Hannah D	5	M	9	2	0	0	5,034
Hannah the Wrecker	4	F	13	1	4	2	31,540
Hannah's Baby	5	H	2	0	0	0	2,760
Hannah's Grace	3	F	1	1	0	0	16,800
Hannah's Royalrock	3	F	5	1	2	1	57,000
Hannah's Temper	4	F	13	2	1	0	43,572
Hanna's Flare	5	G	6	2	0	0	9,084
Hanna's Gamble	3	F	4	0	1	1	8,164
Hanna's K C	5	M	18	0	6	1	25,121
Hanna's Kat	3	C	11	1	2	1	16,640
Hanna's Luck	2	G	2	0	0	0	1,680
Hannia	2	F	4	2	1	0	15,045
Hannibal Kitten	2	F	7	0	0	1	4,910
Hannibal Lad (GB)	7	G	1	1	0	0	36,600
Hannie's Candy	4	F	6	0	1	1	14,820
Hanover Hollywood	6	G	7	0	0	1	7,740
Hanover Wharf	5	M	1	0	0	1	850
Hansbury	5	G	9	1	0	1	4,184
Hanselette	4	F	4	0	0	1	7,420
Hanselina	3	F	9	3	3	0	213,180
Hansel's Gretel	3	F	1	0	0	0	4,826
Hansom Lightnin	5	H	12	2	1	2	16,279
Hansome Jim	2	C	2	0	0	0	390
Hapes County Son	6	G	16	1	2	1	6,542
Hapes Jr.	5	H	11	1	2	1	4,566
Happee Kisser	5	G	12	1	3	1	9,847
Happily Unbridled	5	M	5	0	1	0	15,820
Happiness	4	C	11	0	3	2	40,123
Happony	4	F	9	1	1	2	12,892
Happy Acres	6	H	13	1	1	3	5,347
Happy Again	5	G	9	0	2	1	6,596
Happy and Glorious	5	G	4	0	0	0	261
Happy and Hasty	3	G	9	4	2	1	70,980
Happy Anna	3	F	3	0	1	1	4,510
Happy Apple	5	M	9	0	2	3	9,795
Happy Arc	5	G	8	2	3	0	31,550
Happy At Last	3	F	3	0	1	0	2,515

Horse	Age	Sex	Sts	1st	2d	3d	Won
Happy Cooking	7	G	14	0	0	1	1,072
Happy Coyote	6	G	23	2	0	1	10,523
Happy Cruiser	3	F	5	1	1	0	9,630
Happy Day	2	F	4	0	0	0	0
Happy Endings Too	2	F	4	2	1	0	36,486
Happy Face	4	F	9	2	4	0	75,100
Happy Flag	4	G	10	0	0	2	3,583
Happy Fleet	5	G	7	0	0	1	1,070
Happy Gigolo	3	C	3	0	0	1	4,680
Happy Go Glare	3	G	2	0	0	0	0
Happy Harper	5	G	2	0	0	0	126
Happy Hero	5	G	13	0	5	1	14,280
Happy Irishman	3	G	10	0	0	1	1,280
Happy Jackie	4	F	12	1	3	1	19,305
Happy Jazz	2	F	1	0	0	0	0
Happy Legionaire	10	G	6	0	0	1	973
Happy Legs	3	G	18	1	1	4	9,692
Happy Lil	4	F	8	0	0	1	1,102
Happy Maker	3	F	4	0	0	0	300
Happy Menocal	4	G	10	2	1	1	9,882
Happy Mermaid	6	M	6	1	1	0	4,735
Happy Native	4	C	7	0	0	0	509
Happy Numbers	3	F	2	1	1	0	31,080
Happy Pappy	9	G	2	0	0	0	244
Happy Pass	2	F	1	0	0	0	52
Happy Raphael	9	G	4	0	0	2	4,354
Happy Rivergo	4	G	12	0	0	3	3,385
Happy Roman	4	F	10	0	0	0	2,420
Happy Scamper	3	C	6	0	0	0	255
Happy Side	4	F	1	0	0	0	210
Happy Smile	7	G	1	0	0	0	509
Happy Sport	6	G	13	1	2	1	10,377
Happy Sweep	7	G	1	0	0	0	67
Happy Tapping	4	F	8	1	0	0	3,758
Happy to Smokem	3	G	8	0	1	3	6,050
Happy Tracks	4	F	5	0	1	1	5,620
Happy Trails	3	C	4	3	0	0	153,420
Happy Yodeler	2	C	14	1	7	2	63,276
Happybyalongshot	3	G	1	0	0	0	0
Happyeverafter	3	F	5	2	1	0	20,625
Happygolarky	3	F	1	0	0	0	42
Happyhazel	4	F	4	0	0	0	72
Happytalk	4	F	10	0	0	1	2,752
Hapsirishpub	3	C	7	0	0	0	881
Harbo	2	C	1	1	0	0	18,800
Harbor Blues	3	F	8	1	1	0	113,898
Harbor Chief	3	F	5	1	3	0	20,340
Harbor Court	3	F	10	3	0	4	53,299
Harbor Craft	2	C	3	0	0	0	3,360
Harbor Haven	4	C	10	0	0	1	8,820
Harbor Mist	5	G	20	2	3	3	13,970
Harbor Music	2	C	5	0	0	1	7,955
Harbor of Grace	7	G	3	1	0	0	17,632
Harbor Pass	4	G	14	4	0	1	51,170
Harbor Star	4	G	2	0	0	0	54,000
Harbor the Dream	4	G	9	0	3	1	9,880
Harbor the Gold	2	C	5	1	1	1	41,750
Harbor Wind	6	M	1	1	0	0	2,520
Harbor Worker	2	G	2	0	0	1	1,770
Harbord Grad	4	F	8	0	0	2	9,002
Harboringfugitives	2	C	3	0	0	1	1,485
Harbour Axe	2	C	3	0	0	0	348
Harbour Belle	2	F	10	1	7	1	57,790
Harbour Buoy	2	F	3	0	1	1	6,630
Harbour Crossing	6	G	12	4	4	0	60,145
Harbour Gate	2	G	1	0	0	1	2,340
Harbour Ice	5	G	10	0	3	1	16,962
Harbour Mountain	6	G	11	0	0	0	170
Harbro	5	G	12	0	5	2	7,930
Hard as Nails	3	F	6	1	2	1	55,620
Hard Bound	3	G	3	1	2	0	8,840
Hard Break Dancer	4	G	13	0	3	1	4,770
Hard Buck (BRZ)	4	C	4	3	0	0	203,636
Hard Candy	8	G	4	0	0	0	235
Hard Card	3	G	5	1	4	0	18,460
Hard Case	7	G	2	0	0	1	2,834
Hard Cider	4	F	6	0	0	0	506
Hard Coal	3	C	8	0	0	2	2,360
Hard Currency	7	H	6	0	0	0	5,340
Hard Dance	3	C	10	0	1	2	18,700
Hard Dancing Lady	4	F	11	1	0	0	3,946
Hard Delivery	8	H	5	1	0	1	29,630
Hard Drive	3	F	5	0	0	2	2,830
Hard Edge	4	G	10	3	2	2	175,562
Hard Gal B	3	F	13	1	3	3	42,620
Hard Head	2	C	5	3	1	1	55,150
Hard Headed Lover	3	C	4	0	0	0	0
Hard Held	7	G	11	0	1	0	5,676
Hard Hitter	5	G	6	2	0	2	3,991
Hard Knocks	2	G	1	0	0	0	0
Hard Luck Judge	3	F	13	0	2	1	4,051
Hard of Hearing	2	C	2	0	0	0	0
Hard Quality	3	C	1	0	0	0	0
Hard Runnin Hannah	3	F	4	1	0	0	5,100
Hard Times	4	G	4	1	0	0	8,710
Hard to Call	4	F	6	1	1	1	11,362
Hard to Come By	4	F	9	0	0	0	635
Hard to Stop	2	F	1	0	0	0	145
Harderthanpride	3	F	5	0	2	2	30,880
Hardhearted Hannah	2	F	1	0	0	0	0
Hardie's Ringer	3	G	3	0	1	0	797
Hardluck Hannah	3	F	4	0	0	1	320
Hardly a Lady	3	F	8	1	2	1	9,710
Hardridinheartache	3	G	16	2	2	1	42,399
Hardroadtohold	4	F	9	1	0	2	13,836
Hardtobethebest	2	C	7	1	1	0	30,514
Hardtolite	2	C	4	1	0	2	11,975
Hardwayman	4	G	17	2	0	1	6,941
Hardy Child	3	G	2	0	0	0	87
Hare Raising	11	G	3	2	0	0	3,360
Hares	6	G	5	2	0	0	16,088
Harford Ghost	3	F	3	1	1	0	31,440
Hark the Sound (GB)	4	F	3	1	0	0	9,000
Harlan Ash	6	M	5	0	0	1	4,720
Harlan Ave	4	C	7	1	0	0	4,733
Harlan Cat	4	F	3	0	0	0	3,960
Harlan Knight	6	H	1	0	0	0	0
Harlan Traveler	6	H	8	0	1	1	5,695
Harlan's Holiday	4	C	6	2	2	0	1,685,100
Harlanswitch	2	C	5	0	0	1	2,645
Harlee	4	F	3	2	0	0	8,832
Harleigh Babe	4	F	3	0	0	0	360
Harleigh David	4	G	15	3	2	1	15,425
Harlequina	5	M	4	0	0	0	523
Harley Country	3	F	15	1	3	2	16,420
Harley Garv	4	C	5	0	0	0	204
Harley Girl	3	F	8	2	2	1	17,970
Harley Queen	3	F	3	0	1	1	1,818
Harley Quinn	6	H	13	4	2	3	138,110
Harleys Gold	4	F	15	1	1	2	7,086
Harley's Star	3	F	4	0	0	0	0
Harlon's Gold	4	G	14	0	2	2	12,830
Harmonist	3	F	7	2	1	1	64,338
Harmony Bear	6	G	5	0	1	2	5,175
Harmony Hall	4	C	8	1	2	1	63,800
Harmony Holler	5	M	9	2	1	2	3,252
Harmony Light	2	F	5	0	1	2	10,060
Harmony Lodge	5	M	8	5	1	2	516,300
Harmony Park	3	G	5	0	0	3	8,424
Harmony Princess	4	F	9	2	2	1	6,542
Harmony's Prospect	2	C	1	0	0	0	319
Harold's Beginning	6	G	7	1	1	1	3,137
Harolds Memories	9	G	1	0	0	0	50
Harold's Nickel	8	G	13	0	2	0	2,678
Harper Valley	7	G	7	2	1	0	13,690
Harpers Crown	3	G	13	3	1	1	21,190
Harper's Ferry	6	H	5	0	0	0	0
Harperstown Wish	7	G	1	0	0	0	38
Harperstrack	3	G	2	0	0	0	0
Harpist	2	F	1	0	0	0	1,085
Harpoon	2	C	6	0	1	1	5,050
Harriet	6	M	14	0	0	1	1,540
Harriett Elaine	5	M	9	2	1	1	27,715
Harrikanna	6	M	8	0	1	0	7,354
Harrimans Image	9	G	8	0	2	0	3,970
Harrimans Question	5	H	1	0	0	0	0
Harri's Playmate	3	F	9	0	3	1	4,136
Harrisand (FR)	5	H	5	0	0	1	39,120

RECORDS OF HORSES

Horse	Age	Sex	Sts	1st	2d	3d	Won	Horse	Age	Sex	Sts	1st	2d	3d	Won
Harrison's Halo	2	G	4	0	2	0	10,200	Hatchets Last Wish	6	G	10	0	1	2	2,979
Harrogate Hills	4	F	7	1	3	2	24,125	Hate Mail	2	G	3	1	0	0	6,040
Harry Got Happy	3	G	10	1	1	2	16,451	Hatenot	6	M	6	2	1	1	47,326
Harry Jake (GB)	4	G	3	0	0	0	5,680	Hatheir	6	H	10	1	1	2	6,035
Harry Pietsch	4	G	9	1	2	0	16,379	Hatif (BRZ)	4	C	3	0	1	0	10,660
Harry the Barber	3	C	4	0	0	0	340	Hattab Be You	5	G	15	2	4	3	15,047
Harry the Prince	5	H	12	1	1	3	35,160	Hattie's Love	3	G	3	0	2	0	5,780
Harry the Rock	2	C	3	0	0	0	1,260	Hatton Cross	3	G	15	1	0	2	25,502
Harry the Taylors	5	H	2	0	0	0	0	Hatuey	3	G	5	0	0	0	920
Harry Trotter	3	C	3	0	0	0	690	Haughty Holly	2	F	3	0	0	0	0
Harry's Act	4	G	3	0	1	0	1,700	Haughty Lady	3	F	3	0	1	0	5,210
Harry's Deelite	4	C	1	0	0	0	0	Haunted Forrest	4	G	11	2	0	0	7,480
Harry's Holliday	5	M	9	0	0	0	598	Haunted Lass	4	F	9	1	2	2	95,371
Harrys Ina Hurry	3	G	4	0	0	0	560	Haunted River	4	F	8	1	3	1	17,130
Harry's Nimbus	2	G	2	0	0	0	1,085	Haunting Refrain	2	F	8	2	2	0	15,948
Harry's Rainbow	5	G	12	1	1	2	6,694	Haunting You	4	F	8	3	1	1	28,491
Harry's Tough	4	C	7	1	0	0	6,810	Hauntingly Wild	3	F	6	2	2	0	10,284
Harry's Whirl	3	G	6	0	0	0	500	Haute Move	3	G	10	2	1	2	23,640
Hart	5	M	4	1	1	0	7,800	Hava Court	3	C	2	0	0	0	0
Hartland Xpress	4	F	9	0	0	0	1,940	Hava Peer	7	M	12	1	2	2	36,482
Hartney Oak	4	F	10	2	2	1	13,363	Havan Fun Doll	5	M	3	0	0	0	170
Harts Gap	4	F	7	0	3	3	35,880	Havana	6	H	5	1	2	1	28,600
Harts Time	4	F	12	1	2	1	27,600	Havana Anna	2	F	11	0	1	4	11,235
Hartshorne	3	C	11	2	1	0	9,874	Havana Luke	7	G	5	0	0	0	412
Hartwell	7	G	9	0	2	3	9,240	Havana Perfecto	7	G	3	1	0	1	4,900
Harvard Avenue	2	G	6	2	3	0	61,706	Havaneclair	5	G	15	1	1	1	5,665
Harve de Grace	3	F	2	1	0	0	11,400	Havasu Canyon	5	H	3	0	0	0	1,020
Harvest Festival	3	G	13	1	4	3	53,310	Have a Great Day	4	F	5	1	0	1	8,550
Harvest Hoedown	6	M	9	1	0	2	4,832	Have a Herat	3	F	11	2	4	0	39,920
Harvest Singing	3	F	14	2	0	2	20,578	Have No Fear	4	C	6	0	2	2	15,223
Harvey Bengal	5	G	6	0	2	2	11,477	Have On Up	3	G	7	0	0	1	820
Harvey Girl	3	F	4	1	1	0	33,720	Haveitourway	5	G	9	0	1	0	1,536
Harvey's Delight	2	F	1	0	0	0	0	Haven Acres	2	C	3	0	0	1	4,500
Harveys Hammerback	2	G	3	0	0	0	434	Haven Heights	3	C	3	0	0	0	0
Harveys Rosebud	2	F	4	0	1	0	5,725	Haven's Rook	4	C	1	0	0	0	0
Harvey'sforharvey	5	H	1	0	0	0	50	Havespeedwiltravel	2	C	2	0	0	0	438
Harveyslittlething	3	F	9	2	3	1	23,164	Haveyouheard	4	F	6	1	2	1	25,480
Harvick	3	C	11	0	0	1	3,260	Havocry	5	G	12	0	5	5	9,598
Harwell	6	G	6	0	1	0	5,880	Havre Winds	5	G	14	3	3	0	20,145
Harwood	4	C	5	0	0	2	1,498	Hawa Mahal	2	F	4	1	1	0	34,640
Harwood Jr.	3	G	9	1	0	3	12,530	Hawaiian Lord (CHI)	8	G	18	2	4	2	30,538
Has Beauty	12	M	2	0	1	0	1,550	Hawaii Rose	4	F	1	0	0	0	0
Hasapiko	3	F	2	0	0	0	220	Hawaiian Attitude	6	M	12	4	1	1	23,516
Hashid	10	G	1	0	0	0	288	Hawaiian Boogie	4	G	8	1	1	2	12,480
Hasit	3	G	7	1	1	1	23,352	Hawaiian Honour	2	F	1	0	0	1	3,080
Haskin's Hope	2	C	2	0	0	0	500	Hawaiian Lullaby	4	F	12	2	1	1	10,932
Haslam	3	C	3	0	1	0	8,200	Hawaiian Lyon	3	G	7	3	0	0	16,495
Hasse	4	G	4	2	0	0	14,940	Hawaiian Nights	5	H	5	0	0	0	725
Hassledontheborder	4	G	11	5	2	2	53,120	Hawaiian Snickers	3	G	8	1	0	2	17,370
Hasslefree	2	C	7	2	2	2	108,869	Hawaiian Storm	4	G	8	1	0	0	7,418
Hasta La Vista	4	F	6	1	1	1	45,010	Hawaiian Symphony	4	G	11	4	1	2	16,624
Hasta Lavista Baby (BRZ)	4	G	2	0	0	0	500	Hawaiian Thunder	2	F	3	0	0	0	420
Hastego	2	G	2	0	0	1	1,770	Hawaiin Gold	2	C	1	0	0	0	0
Hastiannie	4	F	4	0	1	0	2,025	Hawg	5	G	4	0	0	1	2,438
Hastings Rocks	4	G	2	1	0	1	15,400	Hawk Chaser	3	C	3	0	0	1	1,810
Hastmakeswast	4	F	6	0	0	1	876	Hawk City Lord	3	C	7	0	1	0	4,730
Hastobegood	7	G	6	2	1	0	6,491	Hawk Cliff	6	M	4	0	2	1	4,354
Hasty	2	F	2	0	0	0	284	Hawk Hill Joe	4	G	9	1	1	0	6,840
Hasty Call	5	H	3	0	0	0	300	Hawk Royal	4	G	16	1	1	1	10,735
Hasty Cat	3	F	6	0	0	0	960	Hawkahontas	8	M	18	0	7	5	13,266
Hasty Deacon	9	G	3	0	0	0	0	Hawkaway	5	G	10	0	0	1	1,230
Hasty Decorated	6	G	13	1	1	2	13,395	Hawk'em	4	C	3	0	1	0	3,625
Hasty Dreams	4	F	13	3	3	2	34,707	Hawkes Bay	6	H	1	0	0	0	0
Hasty Fire	4	C	8	1	0	0	6,036	Hawkeye Pierce	3	C	2	0	0	0	280
Hasty Gus	3	G	8	3	0	0	59,845	Hawkins Little Guy	4	C	2	1	0	1	5,768
Hasty Hobo	7	G	14	0	2	1	6,384	Hawkish	2	G	2	2	0	0	12,900
Hasty Ide	4	G	5	0	0	0	774	Hawkless	4	G	1	0	0	0	0
Hasty Kiss	5	M	13	2	4	1	53,927	Hawkmoon	3	G	5	0	0	0	0
Hasty Kris	6	G	8	3	2	1	149,600	Hawks Easy Act	4	F	4	0	0	0	0
Hasty Lil Rascal	3	C	2	0	0	0	220	Hawk's Feather	7	G	13	2	3	1	23,624
Hasty Money	6	H	8	0	1	2	960	Hawks Pride	5	M	3	0	0	0	0
Hasty Satan	5	M	1	0	0	0	100	Hawks Slugger	8	G	5	2	1	1	4,928
Hasty Star	4	C	20	2	2	1	23,525	Hawks Street	9	G	5	0	0	0	1,306
Hasty's Devil	2	C	4	1	0	2	11,930	Hawk's Top Gun	4	C	13	1	0	3	16,041
Hastys Rose	6	M	1	0	0	0	71	Hawksters Champ	3	G	11	2	2	0	10,984
Hat Chequer	3	F	3	0	0	0	208	Hawksway	5	G	9	0	0	0	1,282
Hat Trick X Three	4	C	1	0	0	0	0	Hawkwatch	7	G	11	2	1	1	36,370
Hataab	6	H	3	0	0	1	16,080	Hawkworthy	11	G	4	0	0	1	504
Hatchet	4	C	8	0	1	1	926	Hawley Lake	4	F	12	1	2	3	29,953

Horse	Age	Sex	Sts	1st	2d	3d	Won	Horse	Age	Sex	Sts	1st	2d	3d	Won
Hawthorne Devil	3	G	2	0	1	1	6,262	Head for Home	3	F	5	1	1	0	59,778
Hay Allison	3	F	8	0	3	1	31,200	Head for the Hills	3	G	18	2	3	3	32,325
Hay Amy	2	F	2	0	0	0	0	Head In	6	G	11	0	3	0	13,349
Hay Ana	2	F	8	2	1	1	25,780	Head Majorette	5	M	8	1	1	2	6,140
Hay Bailey	2	C	1	0	0	0	780	Head of State	4	G	2	0	0	0	156
Hay Big Guy	6	H	14	3	2	3	25,740	Head of the Class	3	C	3	0	0	0	490
Hay Catch Me	5	M	10	1	2	2	7,797	Head of the Harbor	6	M	6	0	0	0	666
Hay Catie Phantom	5	M	14	0	0	2	2,383	Head of the House	2	C	2	1	0	1	31,680
Hay Cheryl	2	F	2	0	1	0	2,400	Head Office	4	G	9	3	1	1	39,564
Hay Costa	3	F	4	1	1	1	25,395	Head Over Heels	4	F	17	4	3	2	69,300
Hay Dave	2	C	3	0	0	0	720	Head Sweeper	6	H	12	0	1	0	5,985
Hay Dream Catcher	5	M	3	0	0	2	1,006	Head Tax	2	G	6	0	0	1	5,814
Hay Fat Mama	2	F	3	0	0	0	870	Head Turner	4	F	12	1	2	0	20,105
Hay Frolick	3	F	4	0	0	0	180	Headingforaruckus	7	G	10	0	2	2	3,063
Hay Getoutofmyway	4	G	10	1	0	2	41,220	Headline	3	G	8	0	4	1	15,265
Hay Hay Testamony	5	M	2	0	0	0	225	Heads I Win	2	G	1	0	0	0	240
Hay Jo	7	M	5	0	0	0	144	Heads Or Tails Hal	4	F	8	0	0	2	827
Hay Lauren	2	F	8	4	2	0	190,290	Healthy Addiction	2	F	1	0	1	0	7,200
Hay Low Halo	5	G	21	2	6	3	15,517	Heama Royal Ruckus	6	H	5	0	0	0	673
Hay Madison	3	F	3	0	0	1	4,370	Hear Come Peanut	3	G	7	0	1	0	5,105
Hay Matt	3	G	8	1	0	3	39,040	Hear Me Clearly	4	F	7	0	1	0	4,200
Hay Mr. Brassman	3	C	1	0	0	1	4,510	Hear Me Roar	5	M	10	1	2	0	15,009
Hay Princess	4	F	13	3	3	2	67,760	Hear No Evil	3	C	10	2	3	1	187,490
Hay Shea	3	F	16	2	1	1	18,118	Hear Now	3	G	8	0	0	1	967
Hay Whatsamaddau	4	F	1	0	0	0	0	Hear Regal Music	3	C	6	1	2	0	9,308
Haybug	2	G	2	0	0	0	411	Hear This	4	F	3	1	0	0	19,840
Haycountonme	3	F	10	2	1	1	21,690	Heard County	3	C	7	0	1	0	9,450
Hayden Storm	6	G	14	1	4	2	11,632	Heart Dancing	3	F	3	0	0	0	0
Haydens Belle	6	M	4	0	0	0	110	Heart Flash	7	G	13	1	0	2	5,599
Hayden's Law	4	C	9	1	1	1	7,625	Heart Flush	3	F	4	1	0	1	9,970
Hayes Road	3	G	14	2	1	1	33,182	Heart Head	3	C	8	0	0	0	110
Hayfield	2	C	4	0	0	0	520	Heart in Hand	6	M	7	0	0	0	1,575
Hayjimmy	6	H	10	0	0	0	0	Heart Lite Special	6	M	7	1	0	3	7,187
Haylee Moore	7	M	8	1	1	0	9,848	Heart Mender	9	G	3	0	0	0	157
Hayley Match Me Up	3	G	8	2	0	1	31,819	Heart N Soul	6	G	8	1	0	2	5,084
Hayley's Boom Boom	6	G	6	0	0	1	1,605	Heart of a Hero	2	G	6	2	2	0	34,590
Haylie's Dawn	4	F	4	0	1	0	4,800	Heart of a Leader	2	G	3	0	1	1	11,400
Haymaker's Lass	3	F	5	1	1	0	4,840	Heart of Jules	2	C	5	2	0	0	26,260
Haynow I'm Allstar	4	G	12	1	2	1	15,055	Heart of Kings	6	H	8	2	0	0	15,624
Haystack	3	G	11	0	0	1	2,310	Heart of Stone	6	H	13	1	0	1	10,950
Haytaxi	6	H	11	1	2	1	10,544	Heart of Texas	2	C	2	0	0	0	0
Haytown Hill	4	G	13	1	1	1	14,105	Heart of the Cat	3	F	9	3	2	1	81,200
Haz Majec	3	C	5	0	0	1	3,270	Heart Ofa Champion	3	F	4	0	1	0	17,760
Hazaamnaevus	2	G	4	0	0	1	2,185	Heart Ridge	4	F	8	2	0	3	3,718
Hazaam's Appeal	3	F	2	0	0	0	233	Heart Stormin On	5	M	8	1	1	1	4,780
Hazagrand	4	F	15	3	2	3	17,503	Heart to Burn	4	F	2	0	0	0	180
Hazel Dip	3	F	4	0	0	0	300	Heartbreak Express	6	G	1	0	0	0	0
Hazelhurst	2	F	2	0	0	0	240	Heartbreaker Heff	4	F	16	0	3	2	16,720
Hazen	5	M	14	5	2	1	127,850	Heartfelt Honor	3	G	11	1	1	2	21,454
Hazoom	3	C	11	2	1	0	10,308	Heartful of Storm	2	F	3	0	0	0	621
Hazor	3	F	10	0	0	0	817	Heartfullofcourage	5	M	2	0	0	1	220
Hazy Afternoon	4	G	15	1	1	2	5,322	Hearthrob Bob	5	G	1	0	0	0	70
Hazy Lady	3	F	9	1	0	2	5,841	Heartland Queen	2	F	4	0	0	0	400
Hazy Mirage	3	F	13	1	2	2	12,810	Heartless	6	G	15	3	4	3	21,949
Hazy Promise	5	M	1	0	0	0	100	Heartontheloose	11	M	14	2	0	0	8,845
He Be Irish	8	G	11	3	4	0	26,550	Heart's Cry	8	G	11	3	4	1	28,470
He Be Pretty	3	G	13	2	2	0	14,104	Heart's Girl	5	M	9	0	1	0	1,668
He Can Make It	3	G	3	0	0	0	262	Hearts in Motion	2	G	5	1	0	0	4,732
He Comes Quietly	8	G	2	0	0	0	120	Hearts of Jones	2	F	6	0	1	5	7,285
He Could Shock Us	5	H	10	1	1	0	28,669	Hearts too Da Wire	4	F	2	0	0	0	200
He Did It His Way	5	G	8	1	2	1	50,985	Hearts Up	3	F	4	0	0	1	925
He Flies	5	G	8	3	2	1	64,720	Heart'sonfire	8	H	4	0	0	0	1,010
He Ha	3	C	4	0	0	1	540	Heartstopper	3	G	5	1	1	0	5,097
He Has No Taste	9	G	5	0	0	3	2,146	Heat	3	G	10	1	2	2	12,560
He Is a Clown	4	G	17	0	2	3	6,135	Heat Bite	4	G	2	0	0	0	4,002
He Is a Hero	5	G	6	0	1	3	3,280	Heat Expectations	3	F	13	3	1	1	29,077
He Is Indeed	7	G	9	1	0	0	1,255	Heat Haze (GB)	4	F	7	4	1	1	1,101,460
He Loves Me	2	F	4	2	1	1	48,250	Heat of Dixie	6	G	5	1	0	1	17,369
He Might Tell	3	C	5	0	0	1	781	Heat of the Moment	3	F	14	8	1	1	156,257
He Rose Again	2	C	7	0	0	3	11,858	Heat of the Night	8	G	8	0	0	0	270
He Rules	2	C	2	1	0	0	21,894	Heat Seeker	5	G	12	1	1	0	23,701
He Shall Reign	3	F	10	0	3	0	12,557	Heatcus	3	C	1	0	0	0	0
He Sits He Sips	6	M	9	1	2	2	22,680	Heated Rivalry	3	C	10	3	0	0	10,216
He Told Coe	4	G	11	2	2	3	14,875	Heather Ann	6	M	15	4	3	0	70,616
He Won Laughin	4	C	15	1	3	0	17,938	Heather Fire Dance	4	G	13	1	3	3	3,970
Head Case	5	H	3	0	0	0	34	Heather Go Blue	6	G	6	0	0	0	367
Head Cat	3	G	2	0	0	0	74	Heather Hurry Up	4	F	13	2	0	1	11,445
Head Chief	5	G	20	1	0	3	29,380	Heather in Leather	5	M	3	0	0	0	202
Head Fake	6	G	10	3	1	0	7,480	Heather Light	6	M	9	2	3	2	65,510

RECORDS OF HORSES

Horse	Age	Sex	Sts	1st	2d	3d	Won	Horse	Age	Sex	Sts	1st	2d	3d	Won
Heather Louise	8	G	2	0	1	1	2,592	Heavy Cream	3	F	5	0	0	0	340
Heather On	8	M	18	1	1	3	5,692	Heavy Cruiser	2	C	2	0	0	0	225
Heather's Announce	2	F	4	0	0	0	696	Heavyweight Champ	4	C	3	0	1	1	12,400
Heather's Best	7	G	10	1	0	0	4,277	Heberts Impact	4	G	8	1	2	1	9,058
Heather's Blessing	5	G	1	0	0	0	0	Hecamefromaclaim	2	C	4	2	2	0	109,535
Heather's Boy	5	G	9	1	1	2	7,327	Hecandance	3	C	15	1	1	3	10,544
Heather's Fever	3	F	2	0	0	0	150	Hecandigit	4	C	6	1	0	1	40,320
Heather's Gate	5	H	6	1	0	1	10,100	Hecando	4	G	1	0	0	0	42
Heathers Key	2	F	2	0	0	0	396	Heck of a Boy	4	G	12	1	1	0	2,315
Heather's Lil' Boy	2	C	1	0	0	0	54	Heckle	2	C	4	2	0	0	103,045
Heather's Prized	3	G	8	0	1	1	9,310	Heckofacat	5	G	2	0	0	0	186
Heathers Warrior	2	G	8	1	1	1	12,145	Heckofanactofollow	3	C	12	2	3	3	54,970
Heathrow	2	C	1	0	0	0	0	Heckofapappy	7	G	6	1	0	0	7,492
Heath's Aletha	3	G	16	1	1	1	14,125	Hectic	3	G	15	2	1	5	15,989
Heath's Big Shot	7	G	7	2	2	0	3,436	Hector	7	H	1	0	0	0	0
Heath's Cookie	7	H	3	0	0	0	236	Hedgeapple	3	C	9	0	1	1	2,063
Heath's Go Blue	4	G	9	1	2	0	26,150	Hediditright	3	G	1	0	0	1	900
Heath's Hideaway	2	C	4	0	0	1	4,060	Hedley	3	F	2	0	0	0	0
Heath's Jet	4	C	10	3	1	0	52,727	Hedorunrun	7	G	7	0	0	1	1,066
Heath's Love	3	C	3	0	0	0	260	Hedsiwintailsulose	3	F	13	1	5	0	13,569
Heatmoney	3	C	6	0	0	1	4,881	Hedstartminer	4	C	8	1	2	1	9,445
Heatwaves Doll	4	F	7	0	0	0	495	Hedwig	4	F	5	0	0	0	540
Heave Ho	4	G	4	0	0	0	387	Heebie Jeebies	3	F	8	2	2	2	29,696
Heaven	6	G	12	4	1	2	16,030	Heel Dust	9	G	3	0	0	0	770
Heaven Blessed	4	F	6	0	0	0	0	Heels Street Blues	6	H	1	0	0	0	0
Heaven Connection	4	G	11	1	1	1	5,477	Heezatalknback	3	C	4	0	1	0	6,300
Heaven Only Knows	3	F	8	1	0	0	18,300	Heezelusive	4	G	6	0	0	0	892
Heavencountsonjt	3	C	3	0	0	0	228	Heezforshari	6	H	2	0	0	0	0
Heavenescent	3	F	6	0	0	1	2,451	Heff T. Attitude	5	G	6	0	0	0	0
Heavenleigh	3	F	1	0	0	0	0	Heffelfinger	4	C	12	1	2	0	16,577
Heavenly Account	2	F	2	0	0	0	420	Hefferius	8	G	5	1	1	0	5,225
Heavenly Arc	5	M	3	0	0	0	164	Hefner Road	9	G	10	1	2	0	3,896
Heavenly Cast	2	F	4	0	1	0	2,694	Hefty Taxes	5	M	9	0	4	0	10,218
Heavenly Chime	5	M	13	1	0	6	9,185	Hegira	5	M	6	0	2	0	9,880
Heavenly Dancer	4	F	6	0	0	0	1,954	Hego Looking	6	H	4	0	0	0	664
Heavenly Deputy	4	G	2	0	0	0	0	Hehaza Creta	3	C	1	0	0	0	130
Heavenly Funds	2	F	1	0	0	0	0	Heidi Cat	2	F	5	1	0	1	9,460
Heavenly Helper	2	F	4	1	0	1	5,520	Heidi Marie	3	F	13	3	1	2	26,413
Heavenly Hit	5	G	3	1	1	0	2,980	Heidi Sparkles	6	M	8	1	0	2	13,362
Heavenly Hope	6	M	7	0	3	2	11,579	Heidi's Affair	3	F	8	1	0	1	7,193
Heavenly Humor	2	F	2	1	1	0	21,000	Heidi's Nel	3	F	3	1	0	1	6,577
Heavenly Jet	3	F	6	4	1	0	55,620	Heidi's Rhythm	4	F	2	0	0	0	324
Heavenly Kevin	3	C	13	3	2	3	105,630	Heidi's Ruby	4	F	5	1	0	1	20,240
Heavenly Kisses	4	F	2	0	0	0	420	Heidi's Secret	3	F	7	0	2	1	53,580
Heavenly Leader	6	M	7	0	1	2	6,276	Height of Summer	2	G	4	0	1	2	9,000
Heavenly Lynn	3	F	6	1	0	0	5,520	Heightenedawarenes	7	G	13	4	1	2	16,286
Heavenly Meeting	3	F	1	0	0	0	700	Heightenedinterest	5	G	12	4	2	2	57,398
Heavenly Miss	3	F	13	2	2	0	69,830	Heir	7	G	6	0	0	0	400
Heavenly Monster	2	F	1	1	0	0	25,800	Heir D' Twine	4	G	10	2	2	0	37,830
Heavenly Performer	6	G	18	1	2	4	12,014	Heir to Spare	6	H	9	2	3	2	28,596
Heavenly Powder	2	F	11	2	2	1	26,630	Heir Two Debonair	8	G	8	1	0	1	4,140
Heavenly Prince	7	G	5	3	0	0	25,470	Heiresstothethrone	2	F	5	0	0	1	2,745
Heavenly Rose	4	F	14	1	2	3	30,905	Heirloom Diamond	3	F	3	0	0	1	4,400
Heavenly Scandal	2	F	4	1	1	0	17,960	Heisman	5	G	4	0	1	0	1,950
Heavenly Search	5	H	1	0	0	0	3,060	Heka	3	C	1	0	0	0	0
Heavenly Shades	3	F	2	0	1	0	1,824	Hela Prospect	4	G	4	0	0	0	1,038
Heavenly Shoes	5	G	4	2	0	0	9,099	Helabhai	7	G	4	1	0	0	750
Heavenly Trick	3	F	1	0	0	0	0	Helaine's Honour	3	F	4	2	0	0	15,210
Heavenly View	3	F	4	0	1	0	2,920	Held Accountable	3	F	10	1	2	1	16,770
Heavenlyoportunity	2	F	3	0	0	1	968	Heldatbay	3	F	11	3	1	3	23,990
Heavens Belle	3	F	14	5	2	0	82,070	Heldinhighesteem	3	F	11	4	2	0	30,854
Heaven's Border	2	F	3	0	0	2	2,500	Helen Anna	2	F	3	0	1	0	7,700
Heaven's Cat	2	G	1	0	0	1	2,280	Helen Darlin	3	F	5	1	0	1	11,000
Heaven's Deputy	3	G	1	0	0	0	0	Helen O	4	F	11	2	3	0	8,534
Heaven's Gain	3	F	5	1	0	0	7,824	Helenico (ARG)	6	H	1	0	0	0	700
Heaven's Hostage	3	G	10	0	4	1	11,613	Helen's Girl	4	F	22	0	4	6	7,253
Heavens Hunt	4	C	2	0	0	0	178	Helen's Legacy	3	F	6	1	0	0	11,960
Heaven's Joy	4	G	1	0	0	0	0	Helen's Mill	4	F	11	2	1	1	18,533
Heaven's Mirror	4	F	10	1	2	2	12,125	Helen's Shadow	5	M	10	0	2	1	6,247
Heaven's Mist	5	M	7	1	1	3	13,590	Helensinterrogator	3	G	19	2	1	2	12,484
Heaven's Notebook	2	F	10	2	0	2	37,875	Hell Cat	3	C	6	1	1	0	39,900
Heavens Passport	3	F	7	1	1	0	33,511	Hell to Pay	4	F	2	0	0	0	3,320
Heaven's Port	5	G	11	0	1	2	3,285	Hellacious Curve	3	F	10	0	0	2	3,750
Heaven's Prospect	7	M	16	0	0	2	6,092	Hellcat Pilot	5	G	13	1	2	2	14,357
Heaven's Sake	4	F	13	1	1	1	13,763	Heller	6	G	9	2	2	1	18,384
Heavens Throne	9	G	11	1	4	0	18,000	Hellish	3	F	11	2	2	1	22,748
Heaven's Thunder	2	F	2	2	0	0	11,220	Hello Callie	4	F	2	1	0	0	7,800
Heaven's Treat	5	G	6	2	0	0	29,460	Hello Carolyn	4	F	2	0	0	0	0
Heavy Chimes	5	G	9	0	2	0	3,219	Hello Charley	3	G	2	0	0	0	348

Horse	Age	Sex	Sts	1st	2d	3d	Won
Hello Crypto	6	M	9	0	2	1	4,140
Hello Dani	4	F	1	0	0	0	0
Hello Dear	2	F	1	0	0	1	910
Hello Dixie	3	F	11	4	3	1	71,880
Hello Fame	3	G	10	1	1	1	21,060
Hello Gitana	2	F	6	1	2	2	23,440
Hello Goodbye Cat	2	F	1	0	0	0	0
Hello Hatti	3	F	3	0	0	1	1,000
Hello I'm Me	6	M	5	0	0	0	55
Hello John	4	C	14	3	0	0	28,910
Hello Joker	3	C	11	2	0	1	4,903
Hello Judy	4	F	13	1	1	5	11,876
Hello Karakorum	3	F	5	1	1	2	42,440
Hello Kelli	3	G	5	0	0	0	218
Hello Lila	8	M	8	0	0	2	4,597
Hello Lilly	3	F	7	0	1	1	1,875
Hello Lonelyness	4	F	11	1	0	0	7,580
Hello Matilda	3	F	10	3	1	1	77,896
Hello McMinnville	5	M	7	0	1	3	4,664
Hello Miami	2	F	7	1	0	0	6,855
Hello My Friend	3	F	12	2	2	2	55,897
Hello Pepper	4	F	11	0	0	1	2,794
Hello Ruffie	4	F	5	1	2	0	52,880
Hello Saratoga	5	G	9	2	2	0	18,164
Hello Stranger	4	G	5	1	0	0	1,672
Hello Sunshine	2	F	2	0	1	0	2,740
Hello Trouble	2	G	5	1	2	1	16,394
Hello Val	3	F	7	0	3	0	7,025
Hello Victory	2	G	3	0	1	0	2,100
Hello Weggs	4	C	6	0	0	0	0
Hello Woodson	6	H	8	1	2	1	2,684
Hellsasmokin	4	G	5	0	0	0	1,272
Helltunerider	3	F	5	1	0	0	7,590
Helluvahullabaloo	4	C	3	0	1	0	3,090
Helms	3	C	7	0	0	0	0
Helms Deep (GB)	3	C	8	2	1	1	86,546
Helms the Man	4	C	9	5	0	0	24,253
Helmsman Star	4	C	10	0	1	3	10,668
Helmsman's Hellion	3	C	12	1	2	2	23,154
Help the Pilot	5	G	6	0	0	2	2,650
Helpful Hint	4	F	10	1	1	2	7,188
Helpisontheway	3	C	11	2	2	2	35,228
Helvetia	4	F	16	2	2	4	47,421
Hemakestherules	4	G	4	0	0	0	840
Heman Erickson	6	G	3	0	0	0	840
Hemandan	10	G	1	0	0	0	0
Hemet Thought	5	G	13	2	3	2	122,847
Hemisphere	2	C	4	0	0	0	340
Hemisphere Dancer	6	H	9	1	1	1	6,705
Hemlock	3	F	9	2	0	1	27,089
Hemlock Bay	3	C	5	1	0	1	5,325
Hemmingsway	6	H	2	0	0	1	897
Henbane Man	8	G	9	2	1	1	14,891
Henbane Speedster	6	H	1	0	0	0	61
Henbane's Cat	3	G	15	2	2	1	15,455
Henbanes Finale	3	C	2	1	0	1	7,455
Hence the Howl	4	C	6	1	0	0	4,812
Hendler	6	G	6	0	1	0	7,780
Heneresa	3	C	4	0	0	0	12,800
Heniu Island	6	G	12	0	0	1	1,945
Henko	3	C	2	0	0	0	150
Hennessy Bay	2	C	3	1	0	0	7,880
Hennessyalater	2	F	2	0	2	0	3,280
Hennessy's Best	4	G	10	0	0	2	6,841
Hennessy's Delight	3	F	4	0	0	0	265
Hennie's Song	3	F	5	5	0	0	226,800
Henora W	6	M	1	0	0	0	240
Henri Martin (GB)	3	G	5	0	0	0	1,715
Henry B.	4	G	1	0	0	0	0
Henry Hawk	4	C	2	0	0	0	339
Henry Higgins	3	G	12	1	3	1	14,328
Henry J	7	G	15	3	1	1	10,145
Henry Lee Moro	5	G	4	0	0	1	812
Henry Robinson	6	G	11	1	0	1	4,783
Henry's Pride	2	G	2	0	0	0	0
Hentastic	4	G	4	1	0	0	14,418
Hephzi Bah	2	G	4	1	0	0	5,050
Heptagone	5	G	11	4	1	2	52,373
Hepworth	2	C	3	0	0	1	5,790

Horse	Age	Sex	Sts	1st	2d	3d	Won
Her and Him	2	F	3	0	0	0	126
Her Badness	2	F	1	0	0	0	0
Her Brilliancy	4	F	5	3	0	0	6,886
Her Dashery	5	M	1	0	0	0	270
Her Emminence	3	F	5	0	0	2	11,340
Her Fling	3	F	20	1	1	1	13,995
Her Grayness	5	M	14	2	3	4	20,070
Her Great Affair	3	F	4	0	0	0	292
Her Highness	4	F	7	0	0	1	1,101
Her Honour	3	F	2	0	0	0	480
Her Majesty Sara	6	M	13	0	0	1	2,028
Her Name Was Maud	4	F	9	1	0	0	8,282
Her Own Terms	4	F	2	0	0	0	2,840
Her Place	3	F	12	3	3	1	35,890
Her Terms	3	F	1	0	0	0	0
Herald Harold	3	C	1	0	0	0	100
Heraldo (CHI)	9	G	9	0	2	1	7,737
Herati's Gold	2	F	7	0	1	3	3,316
Herb Avore	4	G	15	2	0	3	7,777
Herb E.	4	G	11	2	2	1	14,063
Herbal Avenue	2	F	1	0	0	0	0
Herbe Vert (BRZ)	7	G	11	3	5	2	22,505
Herb's Birthday	6	G	13	1	0	1	4,255
Herb's Folly	7	M	5	0	0	2	1,322
Herbs Spirit	4	C	4	0	1	0	13,574
Herculano	7	G	7	0	0	0	572
Herculated	3	G	5	3	0	1	56,814
Herdy's Charm	3	F	6	0	2	0	17,200
Here Comes Amos	3	G	1	0	0	0	0
Here Comes April	4	F	3	0	0	0	152
Here Comes Atitude	3	G	4	0	0	0	0
Here Comes Baby	4	G	2	1	0	0	7,700
Here Comes Bailey	2	G	3	0	1	0	1,505
Here Comes Big G	3	F	5	1	0	0	11,560
Here Comes Bill	4	G	12	2	2	2	19,035
Here Comes Billy	4	G	14	2	1	3	21,333
Here Comes Blaze	2	C	2	0	0	0	1,620
Here Comes Bullet	3	F	1	0	0	0	0
Here Comes Bully	2	G	4	0	0	2	2,579
Here Comes Cherry	5	M	14	0	2	4	17,360
Here Comes Country	6	G	13	0	3	1	20,275
Here Comes Deano	2	G	1	0	0	0	130
Here Comes Goldie	6	M	8	1	0	2	2,675
Here Comes Irish	3	C	1	0	0	0	100
Here Comes Jake	3	C	8	1	3	1	29,326
Here Comes Jewels	3	F	7	1	2	0	5,300
Here Comes Justice	3	F	16	6	0	0	60,910
Here Comes Kari	4	F	8	1	0	1	5,210
Here Comes Lucinda	4	F	3	0	0	0	1,085
Here Comes Magic	5	G	6	2	0	2	12,670
Here Comes Money	3	G	6	1	2	2	13,822
Here Comes Mr Gold	11	G	11	0	2	2	1,973
Here Comes Rebel	5	G	8	1	0	2	5,670
Here Comes Rootie	4	F	6	1	1	0	13,170
Here Comes Rusty	3	C	3	0	1	0	6,780
Here Comes Smarty	4	F	9	0	0	0	925
Here Comes Tee Pro	4	G	15	4	3	2	78,775
Here Comes Tiger	3	G	11	2	4	2	39,450
Here Comes Tridise	4	F	3	0	0	0	775
Here Comes Turner	5	G	10	2	0	2	45,260
Here Comes Zach	5	G	6	0	1	1	3,661
Here Fuji	4	F	2	0	0	0	1,350
Here He Goes	2	C	2	0	0	0	200
Here Is Lew	2	F	2	0	0	0	100
Here Me Out	5	G	8	0	0	0	1,215
Here 'n' Sassy	3	F	3	0	0	0	2,080
Here to Stay	4	C	4	0	0	0	329
Here Youcome Again	2	C	2	0	0	0	200
Hereafter	3	F	3	0	1	0	5,320
Herecomedacash	3	G	5	1	0	1	7,347
Herecomes Sunshine	2	F	2	0	0	0	150
Herecomes Unc	3	G	11	1	1	0	10,066
Herecomesacat	4	F	10	3	1	2	44,139
Herecomesashley	2	G	5	1	0	0	16,057
Herecomesawinner	3	C	14	2	2	1	16,775
Herecomesbrice	3	C	4	0	1	1	11,790
Herecomesdabossnow	4	G	13	2	0	0	9,109
Herecomesdafuzz	5	G	12	3	1	3	15,991
Herecomesrobin	5	M	11	0	1	1	5,893

RECORDS OF HORSES

Horse	Age	Sex	Sts	1st	2d	3d	Won	Horse	Age	Sex	Sts	1st	2d	3d	Won
Herecomesthebrat	6	G	16	3	4	2	19,042	He's a Fine Deal	5	G	14	3	3	1	25,689
Herecomesthelion	5	H	3	1	0	0	5,175	He's a Jones	2	C	4	0	0	1	1,105
Herecomesthemannow	3	G	17	4	2	3	75,957	He's a Knockout	5	G	3	0	0	0	1,080
Herecomesthewarden	4	G	4	0	0	0	650	He's a Lover	2	G	8	1	3	2	37,523
Herecomethegirls	6	M	7	0	0	2	6,864	He's a Mystery	3	C	10	1	1	2	27,340
Here's Allis	4	F	1	0	0	0	0	He's a Natural	4	G	8	3	1	1	41,820
Heres Awesome	6	G	5	0	1	1	769	He's a Performer	4	C	7	0	1	0	2,595
Here's Carrie	3	F	3	1	1	0	15,463	He's a Real Deal	4	C	2	0	1	0	2,900
Here's Hogan	2	F	8	0	0	2	3,780	He's a Ringer	5	G	10	3	0	0	14,750
Here's Hope	3	C	5	0	0	2	4,950	He's a She	2	F	1	0	0	0	0
Here's Houdini	9	G	3	0	0	0	204	He's a Slewpy	4	C	1	0	0	0	582
Here's Jessie	5	M	4	0	0	0	220	He's a Vandal	4	G	4	0	1	0	2,430
Heres Johnny	3	G	16	3	1	0	17,287	He's Agreeable	2	C	4	1	1	0	13,330
Here's My Heart	4	G	3	0	0	0	266	He's All Business	4	G	15	4	1	0	24,473
Here's Rosie	6	M	1	0	0	0	0	He's Awesome	3	C	1	0	0	0	1,500
Here's the Pitch	6	H	10	0	2	1	11,488	He's Back	4	C	1	0	0	0	0
Here's the Power	3	G	1	0	1	0	5,240	He's Bluffing	4	G	5	1	0	1	32,760
Here's to Andrew	3	G	6	1	0	3	37,013	He's Crafty	4	C	6	3	2	1	105,100
Here's Ya Mama	6	M	11	0	3	3	19,522	He's Dancing	9	G	11	0	1	0	987
Here's Ya Souvenir	2	C	4	0	0	1	4,630	He's Deeliteful	2	C	2	0	0	1	1,300
Here's Your Ticket	3	C	12	3	0	1	36,287	He's Devilish	4	C	2	0	0	0	0
Here's Zealous	6	H	6	0	3	2	70,340	He's Enchanted	2	C	1	0	0	0	0
Hereslookingatyou	3	C	5	1	2	0	28,633	He's Expensive	5	G	2	0	0	0	150
Heresyour Chickey	6	M	5	1	0	0	7,440	He's Fit	2	G	6	1	1	0	20,057
Herewego Champ	6	H	17	0	0	3	6,031	He's Game	4	G	5	0	0	0	1,540
Herewegoagain	7	G	1	1	0	0	5,100	He's Gone	5	G	4	0	0	0	1,140
Hergesheimer	6	G	13	1	0	0	12,205	He's Good to Go	2	G	3	0	0	0	1,580
Heritiere (AUS)	5	M	6	1	1	1	37,280	He's Got Charm	2	C	3	0	0	0	335
Herman On a Stroll	6	G	1	0	0	0	0	He's Got the Goods	5	G	6	1	0	1	9,989
Hermana	3	F	4	3	0	0	63,240	He's Grand	4	G	3	0	0	0	184
Hermanita	3	F	15	1	2	1	6,095	He's Hammered	3	C	3	1	1	0	23,804
Hermans Honor	4	F	12	3	0	1	94,297	He's Handsome	4	C	4	1	1	2	20,170
Hermin the Vermin	5	G	6	0	0	0	298	He's Live	5	H	9	0	2	1	4,624
Hermione's Magic	2	F	5	1	1	1	81,120	He's Mine Tooo	6	H	3	1	0	1	3,040
Hermosa Point	3	F	4	0	3	1	5,550	He's My Buckaroo	7	G	15	3	2	0	37,327
Hermosilla	11	G	7	0	2	1	2,642	He's My Idol	3	C	6	1	0	2	24,100
Hero Number Zero	2	G	2	1	0	1	9,195	He's My Man	2	C	2	0	1	1	5,890
Hero Through Time	4	C	7	2	1	0	8,694	He's No Saint	3	C	2	1	0	0	36,000
Hero Wood	4	C	6	0	1	1	2,648	He's Not Bluffin	3	G	14	1	2	2	12,240
Heroic Act	4	C	5	1	1	1	18,260	He's On His Toes	3	C	6	1	0	0	10,455
Heroic Deed	2	G	1	0	0	1	1,390	He's So Good	3	G	6	1	0	1	4,666
Heroic Firefighter	3	G	12	1	2	2	21,440	He's So Handsome	4	C	13	1	1	1	16,030
Heroic Flight	3	F	7	1	2	2	31,385	He's Souper	2	C	5	0	0	1	3,820
Heroic Moment	2	C	7	0	0	2	15,670	He's the Last	2	C	6	1	0	1	8,200
Heroic Peace	6	H	8	1	0	1	7,985	He's the Master	4	G	11	2	2	0	15,230
Heroic Sight	5	G	17	1	4	7	44,840	He's the Rage	2	C	3	1	0	1	80,040
Heroina	3	F	8	1	0	1	17,982	He's Tricky	2	G	3	0	0	1	825
Heron's Franklin	7	G	5	1	0	1	11,015	He's Truckin	4	G	5	1	0	0	6,300
Heroofthegame	7	G	15	6	0	6	145,160	Hesa Angel	3	C	2	1	0	0	10,355
Heros Among Us	2	C	1	0	0	0	0	Hesa Bad Cat	3	C	10	3	6	1	134,497
Hero's Emblem	5	H	9	2	1	0	9,320	Hesa Blumin Affair	2	C	6	0	2	3	5,196
Hero's Glow	4	G	9	2	1	2	61,544	Hesa Cadillac	7	H	1	0	0	0	0
Hero's Hour	2	G	2	0	0	1	1,364	Hesa Devin	3	C	9	1	2	2	18,360
Hero's Pleasure	3	C	12	4	2	1	111,195	Hesa Jeb	3	G	10	1	1	1	5,397
Hero's Siren	4	F	6	0	1	1	3,935	He'sa Littleturkey	4	C	15	2	2	2	10,153
Hero's Taps	3	F	1	0	0	0	0	Hesa Rebel Man	5	H	13	0	0	1	1,388
Hero's Tribute	5	H	6	2	1	0	307,660	Hesa Regal	3	G	3	1	1	0	8,765
Herosloveofthesea	6	M	4	2	0	0	9,405	Hesabullet	3	G	16	4	5	0	36,828
Herpotofgold	3	F	14	2	0	2	34,994	He'sachicmagnet	4	G	15	4	4	0	15,716
Herr Apparant	2	C	2	0	0	0	600	Hesacorkerto	5	H	6	0	0	0	210
Herr Ruby	4	F	11	1	0	2	9,570	Hesalittlerunaway	3	G	3	0	1	0	5,713
Herreid Special	4	G	5	0	0	0	620	He'sanoactor	3	G	11	5	2	1	83,035
Herrera's Gown	2	F	7	1	2	0	29,670	Hesapatriotstar	3	C	2	0	0	0	140
Herroyalcraziness	3	F	9	1	1	2	15,050	He'sapleasantdream	3	G	4	0	2	0	2,340
Hers Funny	5	M	11	0	1	3	4,129	He'sarocknringer	5	G	3	0	0	0	53
Hershea Bard	5	G	5	0	0	1	955	Hesarunaway	3	G	10	0	2	1	3,804
Hertemptingthought	5	M	6	0	1	1	1,735	Hesasurgeon	3	G	16	3	3	0	15,635
Herve	3	G	14	4	1	2	90,025	Hesatexashand	6	H	5	2	0	0	4,530
Hervy	7	H	1	0	0	0	225	Hesaves	2	C	6	0	3	1	10,696
Herwayorthehighway	2	F	4	1	0	0	4,583	Hesbullievable	4	G	8	1	1	1	17,180
Herzilein	4	F	1	0	0	0	0	Hesgotattitude	2	G	1	0	1	0	4,600
He's a Bandit	8	G	14	0	0	2	4,330	Hesgottabeadandy	3	G	15	2	1	4	11,533
He's a Boat	7	G	10	0	2	2	2,727	Heshimu	5	G	7	1	1	0	16,283
He's a Brat	4	G	6	0	0	0	10,425	Heshootshescores	3	C	2	0	0	0	40
He's a Charm	8	G	3	0	0	0	414	Hesitating Chester	10	G	2	0	0	0	40
He's a Copper King	6	G	4	1	0	0	3,030	He'snogamble	2	C	2	1	0	0	1,020
He's a Dancing On	4	C	9	0	0	1	998	Hesperus	2	F	2	0	0	1	1,650
He's a Doozie	4	G	14	1	1	0	2,697	He'ssuchabadboy	2	C	1	0	0	0	1,302
He's a Dreamer	5	G	8	1	0	0	16,310	He'stherealthing	6	H	4	0	0	0	2,845

Horse	Age	Sex	Sts	1st	2d	3d	Won
Hesthetopps	5	G	16	3	1	0	40,020
Hestillmovesstones	3	C	1	0	0	0	0
Hestosmartforyou	5	G	13	1	2	1	6,345
Hexagon (IRE)	7	H	2	0	0	0	0
Hexagram	4	F	7	1	1	2	7,030
Hexham	3	F	6	0	0	0	1,244
Hey Baby Hey	3	F	13	0	1	2	5,879
Hey Bajagaloop	3	G	5	2	1	0	19,632
Hey Billy	8	H	8	1	2	1	2,860
Hey Boss	6	G	7	1	0	0	2,835
Hey Bro	5	H	1	0	0	0	0
Hey Brother	4	G	14	0	3	3	9,439
Hey Bub	4	G	13	0	1	2	5,024
Hey Bubbah	3	G	9	1	2	2	15,915
Hey Bud	8	G	5	1	1	0	2,044
Hey Budman	3	C	8	1	2	1	6,770
Hey Buster	3	C	16	2	4	1	18,630
Hey Cap	2	G	2	0	0	0	375
Hey Chub	3	C	3	1	1	1	22,290
Hey Diddle Diddle	5	H	13	2	1	1	8,876
Hey Fabulous	4	F	10	2	2	2	17,305
Hey Freddie	3	G	12	0	3	1	6,192
Hey Georgia	2	F	1	0	0	0	0
Hey Hey	7	M	10	0	3	1	3,390
Hey Hey Sunny	6	M	12	2	2	1	20,563
Hey Hey Vinny	6	G	10	0	2	4	10,747
Hey Holly	3	F	8	2	0	0	18,877
Hey Ink	2	F	1	0	0	0	0
Hey It's Richard	3	C	7	0	1	1	9,100
Hey Jay	7	H	1	0	0	0	0
Hey Judy	5	M	1	0	0	0	0
Hey Lady	4	F	6	1	0	2	6,256
Hey Little Girl	5	M	2	0	0	0	204
Hey Little Lady	5	M	14	1	1	1	6,735
Hey Louie	3	C	9	2	2	0	36,920
Hey Lynn	2	F	7	1	0	0	13,950
Hey Mikey	2	G	4	0	0	2	4,905
Hey Mister B	4	F	19	3	2	4	18,781
Hey Mom	3	F	3	0	0	0	300
Hey Mr. Banjo	3	C	12	3	2	1	20,083
Hey Nonny Nonny	5	M	11	2	0	3	12,804
Hey Popcorn	4	C	2	0	0	0	104
Hey Poquita	3	C	6	1	0	0	17,963
Hey Ricky	3	C	11	1	2	3	19,776
Hey Rita	3	F	15	2	1	3	67,256
Hey Robbie	2	F	3	0	1	0	2,366
Hey Rube	2	G	3	1	1	0	12,658
Hey Sailor	4	C	3	0	1	1	3,140
Hey Sport	3	G	2	0	0	0	0
Hey Stan	10	G	2	0	0	0	0
Hey Stick	5	G	3	0	0	0	558
Hey Stretch	4	G	20	3	0	2	21,628
Hey Wajadoin	2	C	1	0	0	0	150
Hey Whitey	7	M	2	0	0	1	1,980
Hey Winnie	4	F	8	1	1	0	38,740
Hey Ya Handsome	4	G	14	2	3	0	29,331
Heyahohowdy	4	F	7	2	1	0	161,995
Heybaby	3	F	3	0	0	0	495
Heyday Halo	6	H	4	1	0	1	8,250
Heyhowhatdoyouknow	5	M	8	3	0	0	84,567
Heyshe'satrader	4	F	5	2	0	1	9,132
Hez a Bear	3	G	9	1	1	0	6,820
Hez Comin Thru	5	H	8	1	1	0	8,595
Hez Scott	11	G	13	2	1	0	5,294
Hez too Sharp	6	G	8	0	0	1	1,111
Heza Blue Nitro	4	G	3	0	0	0	126
Heza Classic	8	G	5	0	0	2	2,603
Heza Dashin Devil	3	C	1	0	0	0	666
Heza Gladiator	3	G	14	4	1	1	24,274
Heza Good Guy	3	G	14	1	5	2	45,432
Heza Hottie	4	G	9	2	3	1	5,387
Heza Houston	4	G	1	0	0	0	0
Heza Mama's Boy	2	G	2	0	0	1	738
Heza Memory Maker	4	C	3	1	0	0	5,645
Heza Mountain Man	2	G	5	3	1	1	70,583
Heza Pappy Slew	5	G	9	3	1	1	31,970
Heza Riverman	4	G	2	1	0	0	20,020
Heza Roany	5	G	12	3	2	0	21,604
Heza Spazz	2	G	3	0	0	1	422
Heza Starr	5	G	11	1	1	3	5,964
Heza Tell a Tune	4	C	2	0	0	0	0
Heza Wild Guy	2	C	4	1	0	0	9,063
Hezacatseye	5	G	1	0	0	1	4,800
Hezacharmer	4	C	4	1	1	1	5,838
Hezafreedomtoo	3	C	11	1	0	2	9,680
Hezafreespirit	4	G	12	1	2	2	25,590
Hezajewel	3	C	13	2	1	2	22,075
Hezalittleshady	3	C	2	0	0	0	240
Hezallheart	2	G	6	1	0	1	3,577
Hezamerican	3	G	7	2	0	1	16,636
Hezaroyalguest	4	G	7	0	0	0	0
Hezasprite	4	C	1	0	0	0	65
Hezaware	2	C	1	0	0	0	0
Hezawonder	4	G	2	0	0	0	80
Heze Hummer	4	G	9	0	0	1	2,280
Hezgotanothergear	4	C	7	0	0	1	2,564
Hezslightlyshady	3	G	16	1	1	2	6,432
Hi Andre	3	G	10	1	1	1	8,122
Hi Applause	9	G	2	0	0	0	0
Hi Avie	2	F	1	0	0	0	180
Hi Boy	5	H	9	1	1	1	2,483
Hi Brite Star	5	M	9	0	0	1	629
Hi Carson	2	G	3	0	1	0	2,480
Hi de Ho Miss	6	M	4	1	1	0	19,702
Hi Desert	2	G	3	0	0	0	570
Hi Dixie	3	F	7	1	2	0	5,677
Hi Dollar Haul	6	M	6	0	0	1	1,686
Hi Dubai (GB)	3	F	5	1	1	1	185,300
Hi Ena	4	C	2	0	0	0	30
Hi Flo	2	F	2	0	0	1	1,507
Hi Flyin Lion	3	F	1	0	0	0	50
Hi Friend Kiss	3	F	18	3	4	3	31,072
Hi Ho Sky	7	H	5	0	0	0	340
Hi Mounts Diamond	4	F	16	1	1	1	8,063
Hi Pro Gal	7	M	4	0	0	2	557
Hi Reagan	4	F	5	0	0	1	577
Hi School Football	5	H	4	0	0	0	960
Hi Tech Holly	6	M	3	0	0	0	261
Hi Tech Honeycomb	4	F	6	1	0	2	68,750
Hi Teck Man	2	C	6	4	2	0	99,816
Hi Time Scott	3	G	16	2	1	2	19,966
Hi Trail	5	G	2	0	0	0	118
Hiawatha	4	F	1	0	0	0	0
Hiawatha Limited	5	H	6	0	0	2	541
Hiball Jack	4	G	5	0	0	0	291
Hibernate	2	G	3	0	0	0	900
Hibury Lane	4	C	8	0	1	1	1,984
Hic Cup	4	G	5	0	0	1	2,085
Hick Chick	3	F	17	2	1	2	12,780
Hickey Lane	10	G	10	0	1	1	4,895
Hickory Dick Doc	5	G	16	2	4	3	23,205
Hickory Doc	3	G	8	1	2	3	18,900
Hickory Hawk	2	G	2	0	0	0	2,040
Hickory Hills	2	G	2	0	0	0	0
Hickory Sauce	9	H	2	0	0	0	270
Hickory Victory	3	F	5	0	0	0	242
Hickorys Hooknanny	5	G	13	1	3	1	10,775
Hidalgo	2	C	1	0	0	0	0
Hidden	4	F	14	4	3	0	57,603
Hidden Account	4	G	4	1	0	1	26,206
Hidden Cash	4	G	6	0	0	1	2,224
Hidden Code	7	G	4	0	0	0	480
Hidden Color	2	F	4	0	0	0	485
Hidden Curves	2	F	1	0	0	0	2,460
Hidden Danger	3	C	9	2	1	1	41,080
Hidden Eight	3	G	4	2	0	0	2,045
Hidden Glory	7	G	9	0	0	0	550
Hidden Halo	5	M	11	3	1	2	44,903
Hidden Image	2	F	1	0	1	0	4,200
Hidden Key	3	C	4	2	0	2	40,000
Hidden Path	4	G	11	0	2	2	7,012
Hidden Penny	3	G	12	1	2	0	26,686
Hidden Pitch	5	H	6	2	0	2	29,430
Hidden Ransom	3	F	10	3	3	0	111,980
Hidden Target	3	C	5	1	0	0	6,902
Hidden Truth	3	C	9	3	2	1	123,562
Hidden Video	11	G	6	0	1	0	1,078
Hidden Zone	2	C	1	0	0	0	86

Horse	Age	Sex	Sts	1st	2d	3d	Won
Hide and Cheat	3	F	5	0	0	1	1,623
Hide and Peek	5	H	2	1	1	0	17,600
Hide Song	3	G	5	2	1	0	7,604
Hide the Chianti	5	M	7	1	2	0	17,425
Hide the Ransom	5	H	1	0	0	0	49
Hideaway Cafe	4	C	9	0	0	0	8,240
Hideaway Heroine (IRE)	4	F	1	1	0	0	20,400
Hiding Place	3	C	8	0	0	1	3,452
Hierarchy Rules	3	C	4	0	0	0	1,181
Hieratic	5	G	13	1	3	1	7,807
High Above	7	G	14	3	1	4	22,345
High Above It	3	C	5	0	0	0	350
High Alert	4	G	7	1	1	3	48,880
High and Low Vixen	5	H	1	0	0	1	6,000
High Approval	6	H	5	0	1	1	2,830
High as the Sky	5	G	8	1	1	0	14,705
High At Last	3	G	9	0	1	2	1,809
High Ball	8	G	4	0	0	0	115
High Bet	5	H	3	0	0	0	0
High Blitz	3	G	4	2	1	1	37,070
High Bluebook	4	G	1	0	0	0	0
High Bo	2	F	1	0	0	0	755
High Brite Glory	5	M	8	0	1	1	2,055
High Caliber	3	G	1	0	0	0	0
High Cascade	5	H	11	3	3	2	52,225
High Chaparral (IRE)	4	C	4	3	0	1	1,717,124
High Chieftain	6	G	15	1	2	1	12,607
High Class Trash	3	G	1	0	0	0	0
High Commissioner	5	H	4	0	0	1	5,822
High Con	4	G	3	1	0	0	3,990
High Counselor	5	G	5	0	1	1	6,440
High Court Justice	5	G	8	2	0	0	5,643
High Dangig	2	G	7	0	0	1	3,140
High Danzer	3	C	1	0	0	0	115
High Descent	3	C	6	2	2	0	47,600
High Dice	8	G	10	3	2	2	53,522
High Diva	4	F	12	2	2	1	26,462
High Dollar Dude	6	G	5	0	1	0	735
High Dollar Gal	4	F	7	0	0	2	5,610
High Firm	4	C	2	1	1	0	8,220
High Fiver	8	G	1	0	0	0	0
High Flying Bid	5	G	9	2	2	2	59,924
High Flying Honor	2	F	3	0	0	0	7,140
High Forest	3	C	2	1	0	0	15,600
High Grade Silver	2	G	4	0	0	0	1,818
High Gun Ryder	9	G	9	2	0	2	8,163
High Hearted	3	C	3	1	0	0	8,418
High Heel Boots	3	F	10	1	1	1	5,969
High Heeled Dot	5	M	7	1	0	3	4,088
High Honor	6	G	11	3	4	2	27,238
High Honouree	4	G	1	0	0	0	0
High Hopes Canyon	4	G	7	0	1	0	2,265
High Hopes Irish	6	M	8	2	0	0	28,343
High Hopes Star	3	C	15	3	2	2	57,820
High Humidity	4	F	15	5	1	4	136,919
High Ideal	5	G	4	3	0	1	76,205
High Jackpot	3	F	11	0	0	1	3,066
High Lance	7	G	7	0	0	0	397
High Liability	2	F	8	0	3	3	19,025
High Lift	4	C	10	1	0	2	4,172
High Marion	2	C	1	0	0	0	0
High Merit	4	C	4	1	0	0	8,540
High Minded	2	C	2	0	0	0	0
High Noon Meeting	7	G	1	0	1	0	1,800
High Octave	3	G	6	2	0	0	13,020
High On Life	3	F	3	1	0	0	9,474
High On Luck	2	F	12	3	1	4	40,765
High On Madison	4	G	14	0	2	0	19,790
High On the Roost	7	G	18	2	1	5	11,338
High On the Throne	4	G	10	0	1	2	20,916
High Peaks	2	F	7	1	3	1	58,460
High Post	5	M	6	0	2	0	14,308
High Potential	4	F	6	0	0	1	6,860
High Powered Mack	7	G	5	0	1	3	3,341
High Priced	3	G	13	1	4	1	80,650
High Princess	4	F	16	1	1	2	26,742
High Promise	6	M	2	1	1	0	11,592
High Purr	4	G	9	1	2	0	8,740
High Rank	3	G	10	2	1	0	15,645

Horse	Age	Sex	Sts	1st	2d	3d	Won
High Rate	3	C	1	0	0	0	174
High Resolution	4	C	1	0	0	0	525
High Rhode	5	M	9	0	1	5	3,919
High Riser	7	G	11	3	5	1	7,528
High Rolla	6	M	7	0	1	2	3,360
High Score Wins	5	G	3	0	1	0	705
High Seas	7	G	11	1	5	0	8,134
High Service Ave	4	G	13	1	2	0	17,866
High Sheriff	6	G	10	1	2	1	17,476
High Shoals	3	G	9	0	1	1	1,810
High Shooter	4	G	4	0	0	1	1,855
High Silver	2	F	9	1	1	3	34,320
High Six Figures	5	M	4	0	0	1	2,105
High Smoke	5	H	14	3	4	2	12,406
High Society (IRE)	4	F	3	0	0	1	7,320
High Speed Access	2	F	4	0	2	0	18,535
High Speed Pursuit	3	F	4	0	1	0	2,620
High Speed Travel	6	G	14	4	1	4	156,307
High Spirits	6	M	8	1	0	0	2,960
High Storada	5	G	14	3	1	0	8,046
High Street Market	3	F	5	0	1	0	2,760
High Strike Zone	3	G	7	0	5	1	26,460
High Supreme	4	G	12	1	3	0	48,335
High Sweep	3	C	11	2	2	2	21,560
High Taxes	13	G	2	0	1	1	586
High Tech Racing	3	G	11	3	1	1	27,472
High Terror	6	G	6	0	0	0	348
High Thunder	4	C	2	1	0	0	10,200
High Top Miss	9	M	3	0	0	0	106
High Tracks (BRZ)	6	G	4	1	0	0	14,200
High Volt Jolt	3	C	3	0	1	0	16,976
High Vote Count	3	F	11	2	2	3	20,645
High Watermark	3	G	13	2	2	4	85,404
High Wide N Handsome	4	C	1	0	0	0	275
High Wire	3	F	6	0	0	2	10,870
High Wire Act	7	G	2	0	0	0	1,100
High Wire Dancing	4	G	3	0	0	0	914
High Wire Glory	4	G	5	0	0	2	20,458
High Wire Man	6	G	2	0	0	0	0
Highblast	12	G	4	0	0	0	300
Highboom	2	C	1	0	1	0	1,280
Highcastle	2	C	2	0	0	0	0
Highcat	7	G	3	0	1	0	1,268
Highdown	3	C	6	1	0	2	15,400
Higher Desire	11	G	9	0	4	2	11,445
Higher Gear	4	F	9	1	2	0	11,269
Higher Honor	6	G	11	0	1	0	1,332
Higher Impact	8	G	2	0	0	0	300
Higher Plateau	10	G	8	0	0	1	1,855
Higher Standard	5	G	8	1	0	2	13,070
Higher Than You	5	M	7	2	1	0	4,428
Highest Appraisal	6	G	3	1	0	0	1,556
Highest Authority	3	F	4	0	2	0	4,466
Highest Honoree	2	F	7	2	1	1	40,200
Highest Offer	3	F	14	1	0	4	31,640
Highest Order	4	C	5	1	1	1	14,270
Highest Value	3	C	19	5	2	3	65,595
Highgain	6	G	2	0	0	0	288
Highgate Park	2	F	6	2	0	1	49,410
Highland Alibhai	2	G	2	1	0	0	8,586
Highland Angel	4	F	8	0	0	1	3,166
Highland Baron	5	H	5	0	0	0	378
Highland Call	5	H	2	0	0	0	0
Highland Facts	4	F	5	1	1	0	24,400
Highland Falcon	7	M	8	1	1	2	7,292
Highland Gardens	7	G	10	3	0	1	30,100
Highland Heart	4	F	6	2	3	0	5,095
Highland Honey	4	F	4	2	0	1	48,625
Highland Hope	3	F	6	0	0	1	8,130
Highland Jabo	4	F	18	3	3	1	19,021
Highland Leader	8	G	10	2	1	1	32,330
Highland Lode	6	M	10	0	1	3	4,986
Highland Ocean	4	G	12	1	3	1	22,243
Highland Presence	3	G	10	1	1	3	39,085
Highland Rachael	6	M	1	0	0	0	0
Highland Reel	7	M	6	0	0	0	716
Highland Rim	4	G	7	2	1	0	19,600
Highland Road	8	G	11	2	1	2	12,875
Highland Sail	3	F	3	0	0	0	0

Horse	Age	Sex	Sts	1st	2d	3d	Won	Horse	Age	Sex	Sts	1st	2d	3d	Won
Highland Skies	2	F	1	0	0	0	278	Hips and Haws	3	F	8	1	1	0	12,801
Highland Skirt	4	F	17	2	1	4	40,720	Hirapour (IRE)	7	G	10	7	1	1	128,167
Highland Spy	7	H	1	0	1	0	6,000	His Bride	3	F	2	0	0	0	94
Highland Thunder	4	G	10	1	2	1	15,890	His Class	3	C	1	0	0	0	130
Highland Turn	4	G	11	1	0	3	65,613	His Excellent Z.	6	H	10	2	3	2	4,148
Highland Way	3	F	12	3	1	1	24,947	His Honor	9	G	8	0	2	0	5,658
Highlander West	3	G	1	0	0	0	130	His Majesty's Gold	7	G	1	0	0	0	64
Highlandflowergirl	4	F	15	0	3	0	5,500	His Mama's Son	3	G	8	1	0	1	8,930
Highlited	3	C	7	0	0	0	500	His Money	3	C	9	2	2	0	19,925
Highly Amusing	4	F	9	0	2	1	7,207	His Regency	4	G	5	0	0	1	4,256
Highly Arrogant	2	F	2	1	0	1	12,900	His Reverence	4	G	3	0	1	0	3,850
Highly Justified	3	G	13	0	1	1	4,556	His Smoothness	2	C	5	1	0	0	64,848
Highly Rated	3	G	14	4	0	1	16,750	Hispaniola	2	F	1	0	1	0	7,600
Highly Salted	5	M	2	1	1	0	17,640	Hisrealchoice	3	F	3	1	0	0	3,989
Highly Suspect	4	G	11	1	1	0	22,980	Hiss	2	C	2	0	0	0	0
Highly Tempting	4	G	12	4	1	2	148,280	Hisses N Kisses	3	F	6	0	0	0	1,210
Highly Threatened	2	G	1	0	1	0	900	Histoire Sainte (FR)	7	M	3	0	1	1	24,290
Highmountain Devil	6	G	3	0	0	0	244	Historic Countess	2	G	1	0	0	0	0
Highnest	2	F	4	1	0	0	8,176	Historic District	3	F	9	1	0	1	8,390
Highpockets Crane	5	G	3	1	0	1	3,763	Historic Moment	3	C	11	2	2	1	24,700
Highpoint Princess	2	F	4	0	0	0	985	Historic Native	3	G	3	0	0	0	248
Highrunner	4	G	11	3	2	2	12,627	Historic Speech	4	G	5	2	1	0	15,750
Highsideofthebay	2	G	5	1	1	1	17,950	Historic Treasure	3	F	10	1	1	2	24,248
Hightouch	5	H	5	0	3	0	11,707	Historical Drive	3	F	2	0	0	0	320
Highwater Express	5	G	3	0	0	0	0	Hit and Run	4	C	2	0	0	1	900
Highway Hero	2	C	5	1	0	3	21,862	Hit Em Again	6	G	10	0	1	0	2,230
Highway Home	10	G	5	0	0	0	544	Hit Em Hard	3	F	7	0	0	2	2,692
Highway One O One	5	G	17	3	1	3	44,680	Hit Em Low	9	G	1	0	0	0	273
Highway Prospector	6	G	13	5	1	4	290,397	Hit It	4	F	4	2	2	0	18,900
Highway West	5	G	2	0	0	1	2,530	Hit It Big	4	G	2	0	0	0	86
Highwayman (IRE)	8	G	2	0	0	0	375	Hit It Hard	4	C	1	0	0	0	223
Highwood Pass	3	F	4	1	0	0	5,120	Hit It Here Cafe	2	F	2	0	0	0	0
Hija de Plata	6	M	12	1	3	2	21,805	Hit Me	2	G	4	0	0	2	2,072
Hijo de Sue	4	C	3	0	0	0	145	Hit Now	4	C	5	3	2	0	66,720
Hiker	2	G	1	0	0	0	190	Hit of Poison	4	G	3	0	0	0	216
Hilarious Verdict	3	G	3	0	0	0	110	Hit Record	4	C	5	0	2	2	27,135
Hilary Hunter	3	F	14	1	4	1	26,920	Hit the Brakes	2	F	6	0	1	2	5,565
Hilary's Kid	8	G	10	0	0	0	330	Hit the Hardwood	6	G	4	0	0	0	196
Hilda	3	F	2	0	0	0	2,625	Hit the Lights	4	G	14	0	6	4	74,527
Hilda Browne	4	F	11	1	4	2	15,395	Hit the Press	6	M	12	2	2	1	17,452
Hilda Colero	5	M	2	0	0	0	0	Hit the Road	4	F	4	0	0	0	568
Hilda's Prayers	5	G	7	0	0	2	10,050	Hit the Road Babe	5	M	10	2	3	2	26,386
Hildy's Struggle	2	F	3	0	0	3	2,794	Hit the Silk	7	H	5	0	1	1	7,520
Hilga	4	F	13	1	1	1	11,277	Hit the Throttle	5	G	7	1	0	4	57,965
Hiljo's Joe	2	C	8	0	2	0	9,394	Hitamitten	4	F	3	0	0	0	2,028
Hiljo's Rumbler	3	F	4	0	1	0	1,980	Hitaway Jay	6	G	5	0	0	0	175
Hill Cat	3	F	20	1	4	5	19,551	Hitch Hike	2	G	4	0	0	1	1,524
Hill Hero	6	G	17	5	3	2	25,798	Hitchcock's Best	3	G	17	6	2	1	41,232
Hill of a Time	2	C	2	0	1	0	3,700	Hitchin' Post	5	G	8	1	0	2	18,440
Hill Road Reality	2	F	3	0	2	0	9,331	Hitnmiss	4	F	5	0	1	0	658
Hill Top Man	3	G	3	2	0	0	27,086	Hitower's Pride	4	G	5	0	0	0	2,170
Hillary (GER)	6	M	5	1	0	0	8,835	Hitthebar	5	G	7	1	0	0	1,736
Hillary's Fantasy	4	F	9	1	1	0	9,512	Hitthegroundrunnin	2	C	4	2	0	2	34,590
Hillaryscircuspony	3	C	4	0	0	1	11,220	Hittherhode	2	G	1	0	0	1	440
Hillbilly Prince	6	G	6	2	0	2	16,330	Hitting Home	3	C	2	0	0	0	0
Hillbilly Princess	2	F	1	0	0	0	0	Hittinonallfour	4	G	4	0	0	0	2,000
Hillsboro Kid	5	G	5	0	1	1	3,359	Hiusilver	3	F	3	0	0	0	144
Hillsdale	2	F	2	1	0	0	5,400	Hiwaytwentyone	4	G	10	4	1	0	24,471
Hillside Pete	4	G	10	2	1	1	17,739	Hizzoner	4	C	9	1	1	2	33,131
Hillside Run	4	G	8	0	0	0	541	Hmbls Independence	5	M	2	0	0	0	100
Hillview Cat	2	F	3	1	0	0	7,786	Hoadly Road	7	H	6	0	0	1	587
Hil's Baldski	2	F	2	0	0	0	0	Hoagie	5	G	6	0	0	0	391
Hiltons Revenge	3	F	9	1	0	0	15,410	Hoagies Lil Angel	6	M	8	1	1	1	4,154
Hilty	4	G	15	0	2	3	17,580	Hoax (IRE)	4	G	4	0	1	0	9,800
Him	5	G	4	0	0	0	655	Hobar	7	G	4	0	1	0	5,080
Himalayan	3	F	13	0	2	4	81,875	Hobert	7	G	2	0	0	0	0
Himdidit	2	G	11	0	0	0	2,285	Hobie Hobson	3	F	3	0	0	0	570
Hindostan Falls	5	H	4	0	0	0	193	Hobkirk Hill	2	C	1	0	0	0	195
Hindsight	4	F	4	2	0	2	29,000	Hobo Traveler	6	G	18	3	4	3	12,642
Hindu's Dancer	2	C	5	1	2	0	13,300	Hoc Your Silver	3	F	5	1	0	1	12,480
Hingthem Bernie	4	G	4	0	0	0	165	Hochs in Socks	5	M	11	3	0	1	26,776
Hinoon	4	G	10	0	1	1	2,208	Hockadaisy Four	5	M	4	0	0	0	1,140
Hint of Glory	4	C	5	1	0	1	9,923	Hockey Jock	2	C	5	0	1	0	10,405
Hint of Scandal	4	F	16	2	1	4	18,515	Hockey Man	4	C	1	0	1	0	5,460
Hip Holster	4	G	12	5	2	0	32,763	Hockley	5	G	15	3	4	1	26,579
Hip Hop Gold	6	G	7	0	0	2	3,830	Hodaruki	3	G	11	1	2	1	6,559
Hipica Flash	3	G	4	1	2	1	4,315	Hode's Benthere	3	G	5	0	1	0	1,050
Hippocrates	2	C	2	0	0	0	980	Hofre's Treasure	3	F	1	0	0	0	58
Hippogator	3	F	8	2	0	3	63,825	Hog Heaven	6	G	11	1	5	3	19,703

RECORDS OF HORSES

Horse	Age	Sex	Sts	1st	2d	3d	Won
Hog Run Creek	3	C	5	0	3	1	6,655
Hogan's Hero	8	G	2	0	0	0	0
Hogan's Spirit	3	G	13	2	2	3	91,060
Hoh Buzzard (IRE)	3	F	10	4	1	2	214,178
Hoh Steamer (IRE)	7	G	6	1	0	1	6,215
Hoho Tow	2	C	2	0	1	0	1,455
Hoist Anchor	8	M	9	0	0	1	2,892
Hoist My Colors	2	F	2	0	0	0	0
Hoist the Gold	4	G	15	1	2	2	6,234
Hoity Toity	5	M	5	0	1	0	12,366
Hoke	6	G	17	4	4	1	44,329
Hola C Bright	3	C	11	3	2	2	23,939
Holbrook	5	H	2	0	0	0	76
Hold Down the Fort	6	G	7	1	0	1	11,374
Hold Hard	2	C	7	0	0	0	1,050
Hold Her Wager	5	M	6	2	2	0	13,245
Hold Me Together	9	G	14	2	3	3	18,483
Hold My Mail	2	C	3	1	0	0	11,940
Hold On a Sec	5	G	15	3	2	2	15,131
Hold On Sugar	3	F	8	3	2	0	46,686
Hold That Bull	2	G	6	2	2	0	31,870
Hold That Glitter	4	G	4	2	1	0	27,040
Hold That Smile	3	C	18	4	4	3	40,305
Hold That Tiger	3	C	5	0	1	0	242,746
Hold the Ace	5	M	17	4	2	1	27,954
Hold the Cash	4	C	16	1	3	0	12,485
Hold the Flight	6	G	4	1	1	0	3,320
Hold the Lime	4	F	1	0	0	0	320
Hold the Wire	4	F	11	3	1	1	12,613
Hold to Ransom	3	F	7	1	1	0	82,863
Hold Your Boots	3	C	8	0	1	0	2,629
Hold Your Britches	7	M	5	0	2	1	2,284
Hold Your Thought	3	G	14	3	0	0	24,369
Holdamearound	3	F	7	1	1	2	22,350
Holddedough	4	F	9	1	0	0	4,995
Holdemplayer	4	G	8	0	0	0	393
Holden On	3	C	7	0	0	1	897
Holden Prosper	3	G	4	0	0	0	0
Holdin all Cards	11	G	7	2	1	1	13,530
Holding Dinner	4	G	5	0	0	1	2,080
Holding the Dream	4	G	2	0	0	0	755
Holdingontoadream	5	G	3	0	1	0	1,181
Holdmedaddy	2	F	4	0	1	0	3,830
Holdontoyourhalo	3	F	9	0	0	2	1,775
Holdthehelm	4	G	3	0	0	0	2,760
Hole in the Glass	4	C	10	2	0	2	17,604
Hole Ponche	3	F	6	1	2	0	8,885
Holee's Comet	4	F	1	0	0	0	80
Holes in My Shoes	5	G	14	1	2	2	9,116
Holiday Account	2	C	4	0	0	0	1,099
Holiday Coins	3	G	4	0	0	0	902
Holiday Countdown	4	G	2	0	0	0	718
Holiday Craft	4	C	4	0	0	2	2,380
Holiday Doc	6	G	10	1	0	1	24,993
Holiday Doll	4	F	6	0	0	0	1,251
Holiday Flight	6	G	5	0	1	0	2,251
Holiday Hills	4	G	7	3	2	0	9,776
Holiday Lady	3	F	10	1	3	2	139,675
Holiday Music	8	G	5	0	2	0	14,490
Holiday Pal	4	G	6	0	1	0	1,565
Holiday Peak	3	C	2	0	0	0	2,625
Holiday Prospect	2	C	1	0	0	0	0
Holiday Runner	3	F	7	1	2	1	50,450
Holiday Slew	6	M	11	0	1	1	2,808
Holiest Punch	5	H	10	2	2	0	27,389
Holland Polland	3	F	7	1	2	3	40,494
Holley's Ticket	4	F	7	0	0	0	575
Hollister Slew	5	H	4	0	0	0	188
Hollor Back	3	G	13	1	4	2	48,030
Hollow Memories	4	C	2	1	0	0	6,930
Holly Arts	3	F	7	0	0	1	1,152
Holly Day Groom	4	G	26	1	1	5	11,484
Holly Day Trend	5	G	12	3	3	2	35,670
Holly Dolly	4	F	5	0	1	1	4,235
Holly High	5	M	8	0	1	4	11,325
Holly Hill Flirt	4	F	4	1	0	0	8,370
Holly Hollywood	7	M	7	1	1	0	5,880
Holly Holy I	2	F	2	1	0	0	8,123
Holly Park	3	F	4	0	0	0	2,150
Holly Rae	2	F	2	0	0	0	1,270
Hollybeach Peach	3	F	1	0	0	0	0
Holly's Champ	2	F	1	0	0	0	0
Holly's It	2	F	3	0	1	0	8,103
Holly's Last Try	3	G	11	0	0	1	1,128
Holly's Loot	5	G	11	1	0	1	5,310
Holly's Wager	4	F	4	1	0	0	7,398
Hollywood Actor	4	C	1	0	0	0	0
Hollywood and Wine	2	F	2	1	0	1	15,906
Hollywood Bull	6	G	2	0	1	1	5,000
Hollywood Buzz	5	G	4	0	0	0	122
Hollywood Chaos	2	F	2	0	0	1	2,005
Hollywood D. A.	2	G	3	0	0	0	928
Hollywood Danseur	3	F	1	0	0	0	216
Hollywood Ending	5	M	9	2	2	0	95,578
Hollywood Fever	2	F	1	0	0	0	1,100
Hollywood Guy	5	G	11	0	2	0	1,577
Hollywood Harlot	3	F	1	0	0	0	0
Hollywood Henry	5	G	6	0	0	1	560
Hollywood Honey	3	F	6	2	0	1	71,080
Hollywood Hustler	2	C	5	0	1	4	13,656
Hollywood Lawyer	6	H	10	0	0	2	821
Hollywood M. D.	6	H	5	0	0	1	2,400
Hollywood Paragon	3	F	1	0	0	0	200
Hollywood Pirate	5	G	3	0	0	0	0
Hollywood Princess	3	F	7	2	2	0	70,100
Hollywood Rebel	3	F	4	1	1	0	4,140
Hollywood Reversal	7	M	8	1	0	1	17,166
Hollywood Robber	2	G	7	0	2	1	7,223
Hollywood Shame	3	F	11	0	1	0	3,160
Hollywood Showman	6	G	2	0	0	0	47
Hollywood Story	2	F	5	1	2	1	356,500
Hollywood Sunset	4	C	4	1	0	0	7,308
Hollywood Tiger	4	C	2	0	0	1	1,731
Hollywood Warrior	4	G	12	2	2	3	11,906
Hollywood Wonder	2	F	5	0	2	0	19,260
Hollywood's Gift	3	F	11	1	0	1	4,911
Holmdel	7	G	9	4	0	1	21,043
Holster	3	C	12	1	1	1	11,913
Holts Creek	8	G	4	0	0	0	198
Holy Area	3	G	10	0	1	1	4,489
Holy Astra	2	F	4	0	1	1	7,130
Holy Beau	4	G	4	0	0	0	864
Holy Bird	4	F	9	0	2	1	6,684
Holy Bubbette	3	F	9	4	2	0	132,995
Holy Bully	2	G	7	1	1	2	23,360
Holy Burrito	4	G	11	2	2	1	63,776
Holy Choice	6	M	5	0	0	0	357
Holy Conflict	6	G	9	1	4	1	67,670
Holy Connection	6	G	6	0	0	1	2,740
Holy Decree	5	G	11	5	1	2	29,720
Holy Devil	7	M	5	0	0	1	1,186
Holy Dough	4	F	5	0	0	1	807
Holy Gate	4	C	8	1	1	0	9,450
Holy Gem	5	G	5	1	1	0	10,998
Holy Hands	4	G	8	1	4	0	6,365
Holy Hazel	3	F	2	0	1	0	9,420
Holy Hutch	6	G	11	0	1	3	7,410
Holy Innocents	6	G	9	2	1	0	27,898
Holy Jo	6	G	10	2	2	0	7,060
Holy Kate	2	F	4	0	1	0	6,400
Holy Liason	3	F	7	1	0	1	20,380
Holy Man	3	G	19	2	5	3	22,960
Holy Manda	4	F	5	1	1	1	14,460
Holy Moly Oley	3	F	11	2	2	3	17,555
Holy Panache	3	G	7	1	1	1	41,460
Holy Prize	6	G	17	2	1	0	8,145
Holy R. N.	2	F	2	0	0	1	2,550
Holy Rakeen	4	G	8	0	0	0	325
Holy Relic	2	G	2	1	0	0	10,000
Holy Request	4	F	5	0	0	1	3,160
Holy Roller	3	F	4	0	0	0	1,900
Holy Run	4	G	3	0	1	0	1,260
Holy Secret	2	F	2	0	0	0	2,645
Holy Slate (AUS)	6	G	7	0	0	0	214
Holy Spark	3	F	4	1	0	0	22,020
Holy Sudan	2	C	1	0	0	0	217
Holy Testamony	5	G	2	0	0	1	1,500
Holy Toro	3	C	4	1	0	1	8,028

Horse	Age	Sex	Sts	1st	2d	3d	Won
Holy Triumph	4	C	9	2	2	1	68,079
Holy Vision	3	F	4	0	0	0	0
Holy Vision R. N.	3	F	5	0	1	3	19,300
Holy Wars	7	G	16	1	4	0	10,079
Holy Way	4	F	2	0	0	1	2,750
Holyday	3	C	7	0	0	1	490
Holzmann	11	G	6	1	1	1	6,600
Homah Hansel	3	F	3	0	0	1	4,620
Hombre Rapido	6	G	3	2	0	0	160,500
Home a Winner	9	G	15	2	5	2	26,365
Home Account	3	G	13	0	0	0	1,737
Home Brew	6	H	7	0	0	0	575
Home Cookin	6	M	9	1	2	0	20,840
Home Court	2	F	1	1	0	0	27,000
Home Dance	2	F	3	0	0	0	414
Home Deed	5	M	22	2	7	5	35,310
Home Early	8	G	9	2	1	4	8,490
Home Hill	3	F	16	1	1	3	31,256
Home in the City	4	C	8	2	0	0	16,050
Home James	3	G	8	0	0	2	2,870
Home Made Soup	3	C	6	3	0	1	30,760
Home Made Wine	3	F	4	0	0	0	340
Home of Stars	3	C	4	0	1	1	24,640
Home of Steel	3	C	5	1	2	1	14,783
Home of the Free	3	C	5	0	1	0	4,940
Home Place	3	F	9	2	1	0	10,530
Home Run Hitter	3	F	11	4	2	0	111,540
Home Silver	6	H	8	3	3	0	58,442
Home Stead	5	G	9	0	0	2	2,882
Home Style Dinner	7	M	3	0	0	0	1,142
Home Tonight	4	F	7	0	1	1	1,860
Home Tour	2	F	5	1	0	1	13,240
Home Town Touch	5	G	11	2	0	1	14,173
Homecomingprincess	7	M	8	1	1	0	12,695
Homecooking Ruby	5	G	11	0	1	3	20,980
Homeland Defense	3	C	1	0	0	0	435
Homem Ra	5	H	7	1	0	2	22,695
Homemade Sin	3	C	3	0	0	0	1,010
Homemaker	2	F	7	2	3	2	85,743
Homeonthenet	3	C	1	1	0	0	5,100
Homer Boyer	7	G	8	0	0	0	467
Homer Lee	6	G	17	1	5	3	20,386
Homer's Hero	3	G	10	4	3	0	36,413
Homers Macnificent	4	C	6	1	2	0	2,134
Homers White Sox	4	F	7	1	1	2	3,406
Homeschooled	4	F	2	0	0	0	482
Homesick	5	G	16	2	3	0	49,470
Homeside	6	H	7	0	1	3	4,565
Hometown	4	C	17	2	2	0	13,386
Hometown Band	4	C	7	1	1	0	5,165
Hometown Charm	4	F	14	0	3	6	5,010
Hometown Secret	8	G	3	1	0	0	5,616
Homie	3	C	3	0	0	0	582
Hominy Hill	2	F	6	0	0	0	2,140
Homoginize	4	F	4	0	0	0	2,460
Honacode	4	C	4	0	0	0	498
Honcho Poncho	4	G	9	3	2	1	14,854
Hondo County	2	C	11	2	2	4	15,960
Hondo Creek	4	F	7	2	0	1	39,285
Hondo Lane	2	G	5	0	1	0	2,306
Hondo Ruler	3	C	12	1	1	2	3,745
Honeagle	3	G	8	1	0	1	33,283
Honece Hokte	2	F	6	1	0	1	7,645
Honest and Valid	6	H	2	0	0	0	0
Honest Answer	3	F	9	2	4	2	126,440
Honest Art	6	G	8	2	0	1	3,687
Honest Deceiver	4	F	2	1	0	0	31,300
Honest Flight	5	G	1	0	0	0	76
Honest Girl	3	F	12	2	0	2	23,259
Honest Grade	3	F	5	1	1	0	8,180
Honest Groom	6	G	7	2	1	1	3,286
Honest Ice Age	4	F	12	3	3	3	24,932
Honest Illusions	2	G	3	0	0	0	690
Honest Jill	3	F	4	0	0	0	1,500
Honest Joker	4	C	1	0	0	0	0
Honest Leader	5	H	3	0	0	0	167
Honest Miss Bates	4	F	16	3	0	4	24,020
Honest n' Fit	7	M	7	1	1	1	3,304
Honest Oaks	4	C	7	0	1	2	1,342
Honest Ricky	9	G	1	0	0	0	0
Honest Ridge	6	H	11	3	2	3	4,617
Honest Sparkler	5	G	12	2	2	2	18,044
Honest Speed	6	G	9	1	0	1	3,796
Honest to Ghazi	3	C	16	2	3	2	23,094
Honest Victor	2	C	1	1	0	0	11,700
Honest Wish	4	F	12	1	4	2	9,752
Honey and King	5	G	13	0	1	0	2,224
Honey Baby	3	F	4	1	0	0	7,080
Honey Boy	5	G	12	1	1	1	7,090
Honey Bye Bye	2	F	2	0	0	0	146
Honey Come Home	6	M	1	0	0	0	0
Honey Dew	7	M	11	2	1	2	8,516
Honey Do Too	3	F	6	0	0	0	473
Honey Don't Belate	6	M	5	1	1	1	7,120
Honey Fritters	2	F	1	0	0	0	0
Honey Green	3	F	13	3	3	2	176,522
Honey Hit	2	C	3	0	1	0	4,340
Honey Hunt	4	G	9	2	1	1	15,075
Honey Hunter	4	F	3	1	0	1	4,500
Honey Im Charging	7	G	6	0	1	1	2,304
Honey in the Rock	3	F	2	0	0	0	0
Honey Jak	4	C	11	1	1	3	5,001
Honey Jet	2	F	3	0	0	0	488
Honey Mill	3	F	10	0	1	0	1,368
Honey Mustard Girl	5	M	5	1	0	1	7,013
Honey Rascal	3	F	8	2	1	2	13,572
Honey Ryder	2	F	5	1	1	2	46,080
Honey Sisaroo	4	G	6	1	0	0	3,020
Honeydunkel	5	M	14	2	3	2	22,818
Honeymoon Babe (IRE)	3	F	5	0	0	2	13,260
Honeymoon Blues	3	F	2	0	1	0	6,000
Honeymoon Island	6	M	1	0	0	0	120
Honeymoon Stitch	5	M	2	0	0	0	48
Honeymooner	4	F	11	3	2	0	88,630
Honeyofascore	3	F	10	1	2	0	32,120
Honeypenny	4	F	8	2	0	2	71,240
Honey's Half	8	G	3	0	0	0	101
Honeys Honest	7	M	8	0	0	2	5,139
Honey's Money	5	M	2	1	0	0	7,800
Honey's Music	5	M	9	0	0	0	1,137
Honey's Sky	2	F	2	0	0	0	1,140
Honey's Son	5	G	15	3	2	1	15,056
Honeysbestchoice	3	G	2	0	0	0	0
Hong Kong Henry	8	G	4	0	0	0	831
Hongkong Charley	6	M	4	2	0	0	45,000
Honiara	4	G	5	0	0	0	0
Honker	5	G	9	1	4	2	17,665
Honkin Norm	4	G	4	0	0	2	1,110
Honky Tonk Dance	4	G	10	2	1	2	20,474
Honky Tonk Dancer	3	G	6	1	2	0	19,360
Honolulu Lad	2	G	2	0	0	0	295
Honor a Leader	4	F	5	0	0	1	1,157
Honor and Obey	2	C	1	0	0	0	45
Honor and Valor	2	G	7	1	0	0	3,265
Honor Be Thy Name	5	G	11	1	1	1	11,330
Honor Bestowed	3	F	2	1	0	0	19,200
Honor by the Bay	6	M	1	0	0	0	0
Honor Class	3	F	2	0	0	0	780
Honor Defend	6	H	2	0	0	0	780
Honor Game	2	F	3	0	1	1	7,040
Honor in Battle	5	H	13	1	1	1	10,953
Honor in War	4	C	9	4	1	1	616,723
Honor Issue	4	G	4	0	0	0	1,140
Honor Ma	2	C	3	0	0	0	0
Honor Maker	3	G	7	0	1	0	2,769
Honor Me	5	G	4	1	2	0	72,160
Honor Me Always	7	G	6	0	1	0	7,950
Honor Play	4	C	14	1	6	1	18,546
Honor Prayer	2	G	1	1	0	0	9,000
Honor Pursuit	3	G	7	2	1	0	22,820
Honor Ruhls	5	H	4	1	1	2	2,010
Honor Stripes	3	C	7	0	0	2	7,050
Honor Student	2	F	5	0	2	0	9,420
Honor the Bear	6	M	1	0	0	0	114
Honor the Chief	4	G	9	1	0	0	8,280
Honor the General	4	F	14	4	1	1	29,885
Honor the Prince	4	G	9	1	0	0	1,092
Honor This Coyote	2	C	1	0	0	0	650

Horse	Age	Sex	Sts	1st	2d	3d	Won
Honor Thy Mother	3	F	3	0	0	0	174
Honor Thy Spirit	4	F	10	2	0	1	12,840
Honorable Answer	4	G	1	0	0	0	0
Honorable Book	3	F	12	3	2	1	50,010
Honorable Buck	2	G	1	0	1	0	2,250
Honorable Cat	4	F	9	1	4	1	63,786
Honorable Code	3	F	8	3	0	0	42,098
Honorable Dancer	2	F	2	1	0	0	7,175
Honorable Decision	4	G	15	4	1	1	17,654
Honorable Eagle	3	C	10	1	0	0	5,701
Honorable Feelings	3	F	13	2	3	0	49,060
Honorable Gal	3	F	12	0	3	4	22,915
Honorable Gold	3	G	7	1	1	1	13,575
Honorable Halo	3	F	5	1	0	1	11,300
Honorable Intent	5	G	18	2	5	1	4,920
Honorable Jewel	3	F	12	0	1	0	7,960
Honorable Judge	4	F	8	1	1	1	14,773
Honorable King	3	G	16	5	1	2	50,220
Honorable Knight	3	G	4	2	1	0	13,500
Honorable Love	3	G	7	2	1	0	40,460
Honorable Mark	2	C	9	1	1	3	13,235
Honorable Peace	4	F	1	0	0	0	0
Honorable Pic	6	H	6	1	1	0	31,641
Honorable Prince	2	C	6	1	1	0	7,473
Honorable War	3	G	17	1	0	1	9,905
Honorable Wish	2	G	9	1	1	2	8,215
Honorable World	3	F	18	2	1	1	26,695
Honoramongthieves	3	C	5	1	1	0	17,820
Honorary Doctor	2	G	2	0	0	2	10,791
Honorary Man	3	C	7	1	3	2	63,380
Honorell	6	H	4	0	0	0	550
Honorifico (ARG)	9	H	6	0	0	1	5,880
Honorlee	3	F	8	2	2	1	24,394
Honornpride	3	G	7	0	0	3	3,529
Honor's Ice Man	4	C	1	0	0	0	0
Honorvan	4	C	11	0	1	3	5,581
Honorville	4	F	5	1	1	3	34,740
Honour	4	F	9	0	0	1	3,240
Honour and Courage	3	C	5	0	0	0	3,990
Honour and Fame	5	H	8	2	1	2	8,054
Honour Attendant	5	H	2	0	0	0	108
Honour Brett	3	G	3	2	0	0	27,656
Honour Honesty	3	G	5	2	0	2	10,210
Honour Scout	3	G	5	0	0	0	2,730
Honour Star	2	G	2	0	0	0	1,980
Honour the Game	4	G	4	1	0	1	16,650
Honour the Moment	4	F	9	1	1	1	7,520
Honourable Asset	2	F	2	0	1	0	9,815
Honourable John	7	G	7	0	1	0	1,924
Hoo Gets the Gold	3	G	3	0	0	0	1,540
Hoo Knows	6	G	9	0	2	0	5,208
Hooch	2	G	2	0	0	0	0
Hoochy Woman	3	F	5	0	0	1	594
Hoodoo Peak	5	G	6	0	1	3	5,680
Hoofin Rocket Ron	3	G	2	0	0	0	190
Hook	4	G	18	7	0	3	33,650
Hook and Ladder	6	H	3	0	0	1	6,160
Hook Call (BRZ)	8	G	12	4	3	0	83,630
Hook Shot	5	M	19	1	0	3	8,325
Hookahey	4	G	10	2	3	0	14,235
Hooked a West	5	H	12	2	2	2	21,310
Hooked On Expresso	6	G	2	0	0	0	602
Hooked On Mackee	4	C	2	0	0	0	0
Hooked On Niners	4	F	5	2	1	1	55,950
Hooking Thefeeling	5	G	12	2	3	2	17,161
Hookshank	2	C	5	0	2	1	27,020
Hoolie Blue	3	G	4	2	1	0	26,244
Hoolie Terror	2	C	1	0	0	0	0
Hoolie Unexpected	3	C	4	0	0	0	1,232
Hooliea	4	G	8	0	0	2	3,811
Hoolies Best	5	H	5	1	0	1	6,356
Hoolies Flyer	3	C	6	1	0	1	10,952
Hoolies Gunfire	3	G	3	0	0	0	0
Hoop It Up	9	G	3	0	0	0	100
Hoopers Open Forum	2	F	4	0	0	0	1,080
Hoopsworld	3	C	1	0	0	0	600
Hoorayforhollywood	5	G	14	3	1	1	17,300
Hoosier Dandy	6	G	5	0	0	0	294
Hoosier Dealer	2	G	3	0	0	0	264
Hoosier Hero	6	H	4	0	0	0	182
Hoosier Hotty	2	F	3	0	0	0	360
Hoosier Lover	5	M	1	0	0	0	90
Hoosier Paw	3	G	11	1	2	1	14,869
Hoosier Time	4	F	10	1	0	0	2,913
Hoosier Waterlily	2	F	5	0	0	1	1,985
Hoosier Wildcat	2	F	4	1	0	0	5,460
Hoosierhubble	3	C	9	0	0	0	221
Hoosiermulliganbob	5	H	1	0	0	0	0
Hoosierville	3	G	9	1	1	1	12,407
Hoosyateach	3	F	11	0	0	1	963
Hoosyer Kharma	2	F	2	1	0	0	7,800
Hoot N Dasher	2	F	2	1	0	0	16,476
Hoot N Homer	2	F	3	0	2	0	2,386
Hootend	5	H	24	1	4	7	20,460
Hooterville	8	H	1	0	0	0	24
Hootiehoot	3	G	13	1	6	1	17,440
Hooties Gamble	4	F	3	1	0	0	4,380
Hoots Harri	3	G	2	0	0	0	450
Hoovergetthekeys	5	G	7	0	1	0	8,100
Hop Hornbeam	5	G	11	0	0	0	738
Hop On It	2	F	13	2	3	1	39,265
Hop Queen	3	F	4	0	0	1	726
Hope and a Prayer	6	M	4	0	0	0	720
Hope Anew	3	F	7	1	0	0	7,332
Hope Chapel	7	G	1	0	0	0	0
Hope Faithncharity	3	F	9	0	0	2	2,925
Hope for a Buck	6	G	16	2	4	4	15,170
Hope for Love	3	F	8	1	2	1	56,860
Hope for Luck	7	G	10	3	2	2	32,265
Hope I'm Lucky	4	G	6	1	0	0	6,591
Hope in Hand	5	H	4	0	1	0	2,678
Hope Is Forever	3	G	4	0	0	0	590
Hope N Again	4	C	4	0	0	0	303
Hope of John	4	C	3	1	0	0	3,642
Hope Reigns	3	F	4	1	0	0	1,705
Hope Revival	6	M	4	1	1	0	9,600
Hope Rises	3	F	3	2	0	0	62,400
Hope Soon	4	F	6	1	0	1	8,274
Hope Springs Up	3	F	14	2	1	2	17,515
Hope to Prosper	5	G	12	1	0	0	5,496
Hope You Dance	4	F	15	5	3	2	18,125
Hopeforthecat	3	F	8	0	1	1	4,620
Hopefortheroses	2	C	6	2	0	1	39,268
Hopeful (NZ)	4	F	3	0	0	0	2,940
Hopeful Affair	3	G	8	1	0	1	22,383
Hopeful Coed	2	F	1	0	0	0	0
Hopeful Heart	3	F	4	0	0	0	1,735
Hopeful Season	3	F	13	1	1	1	28,000
Hopeful Sky	6	M	6	0	1	2	964
Hopefully Clever	4	F	3	0	0	0	187
Hopefullyarunner	3	G	7	0	1	0	1,848
Hopeisfleeting	4	F	10	2	0	1	23,362
Hopelessly Devoted	2	F	1	0	0	0	125
Hope's County	3	F	1	0	0	0	0
Hope's Diamond	3	F	3	0	0	2	8,710
Hopes Passion	4	F	1	0	0	0	0
Hope's Secret Port	3	F	5	0	0	0	0
Hopethevictorious	6	M	9	1	0	0	8,919
Hopetobeastar	3	G	13	0	0	0	732
Hopeton County	4	C	9	0	0	0	1,546
Hopewell Hall	8	M	4	0	0	1	654
Hopi Lane	4	C	13	1	1	2	20,009
Hoping for a Halo	3	F	2	0	2	0	3,150
Hopis Useful	3	G	1	0	0	0	0
Hopitu	5	G	3	0	0	0	193
Hoppin' John	2	G	5	0	0	0	2,900
Hoppy's Goldmine	9	G	12	3	1	1	13,559
Hopso (IRE)	4	G	11	1	4	3	16,930
Hoptuit Bud	9	G	5	0	0	0	4,942
Horah for Bailey	2	F	6	2	1	2	58,550
Horatius Lake	4	F	5	0	0	1	966
Horizon Affair	3	F	1	0	0	0	348
Horizon Coast	3	G	5	2	1	1	10,329
Horizon Weekend	2	C	3	1	1	0	6,006
Horizon's Gold	5	G	5	1	1	1	8,780
Hornblower	5	G	2	0	0	0	550
Hornby	3	G	12	2	0	2	21,860
Horned Warrior	4	C	2	0	0	0	0

Horse	Age	Sex	Sts	1st	2d	3d	Won
Hornet's Nest	8	G	3	0	0	0	0
Hornshope	2	C	4	0	2	1	24,000
Horrible Evening	5	G	9	1	2	3	59,010
Horrible Helen	4	F	6	0	0	0	865
Horrify	4	F	9	0	3	4	6,630
Horse Heaven	4	F	13	0	1	0	1,754
Horse Hill	3	C	3	0	0	0	1,620
Horse Nut	2	C	4	1	0	0	4,890
Horse Words	2	C	5	0	0	0	1,915
Horsefollowclosely	3	F	1	0	0	0	94
Horseshoe Tear	3	C	1	0	0	0	0
Horsethief Creek	6	M	7	0	1	1	2,730
Hosco	2	C	2	2	0	0	46,800
Hosea Kaz	7	G	17	0	1	1	3,348
Hosebeast	2	F	2	0	0	1	214
Hoss of Fire	3	C	17	1	3	2	9,702
Host	3	C	5	1	0	3	45,040
Host a Ghost	8	M	7	1	1	1	4,996
Host the Ghost	3	F	5	0	0	0	263
Hosta	3	F	2	0	0	0	0
Hostess Mine	4	F	4	1	0	0	6,890
Hostile Driver	5	G	8	1	0	3	9,640
Hostile Jet	6	G	5	2	2	1	11,940
Hostile Miss	4	F	5	0	4	0	12,380
Hostility	3	F	15	0	3	4	43,449
Hot	3	G	11	3	2	2	78,600
Hot Aloha Cat	3	C	1	0	0	0	0
Hot and Crazy	4	G	5	0	0	0	624
Hot and Muggy	3	F	4	1	0	0	3,300
Hot and Sinful	4	F	11	0	2	3	8,741
Hot as a Pistol	4	F	9	3	1	3	36,790
Hot as Lightning	6	M	12	1	1	2	5,010
Hot Body	3	F	3	0	0	0	838
Hot C N Broken G	3	C	6	0	1	2	2,820
Hot Chipotle	2	F	5	0	2	1	11,780
Hot Chocolate	3	G	9	2	1	2	12,636
Hot Chocolate Mr.	2	G	7	1	1	0	16,623
Hot Commodity	2	C	7	0	2	0	5,120
Hot Connections	4	F	11	0	0	0	553
Hot Conquest	3	G	4	1	0	1	17,826
Hot Cookie	3	G	10	0	1	2	15,252
Hot Cowboy	5	G	7	1	0	1	5,157
Hot Dancer	3	F	5	1	0	1	13,770
Hot Dixie	4	F	10	2	3	0	12,521
Hot Dog	2	C	3	1	0	0	4,596
Hot Dog Queen	3	F	10	2	2	0	13,866
Hot Doggee	3	G	10	3	2	1	27,170
Hot Expectations	3	F	7	2	0	1	32,570
Hot Fast N Loose	3	F	12	1	0	1	8,599
Hot Feu	5	G	1	0	0	0	0
Hot Finance	2	C	10	2	3	2	33,410
Hot for Love	5	M	13	1	0	4	25,120
Hot for You	3	C	18	1	0	4	28,305
Hot Fudge Bundy	2	C	3	0	0	0	300
Hot Golden Jet	3	F	12	4	3	2	186,620
Hot Grip	3	G	18	2	2	3	68,775
Hot Hand	3	C	16	2	1	5	90,088
Hot Head	5	H	11	2	2	2	31,570
Hot Honey	4	F	6	0	1	0	1,728
Hot House	3	F	6	0	0	1	2,810
Hot Hula Hula	5	M	12	1	3	1	10,040
Hot Jelly Jam	3	F	18	1	7	3	29,680
Hot Jive	2	F	1	0	0	0	0
Hot Josh	3	G	12	0	3	3	22,680
Hot Jungle Love	4	F	4	0	0	0	719
Hot Justice	3	G	1	0	0	0	0
Hot Knickers	5	M	1	0	0	0	42
Hot Line	2	F	2	0	0	0	650
Hot Little Majic	3	F	7	0	1	1	766
Hot Lookn Doll	2	F	2	1	0	0	5,530
Hot Mail	2	F	4	1	0	1	25,761
Hot Market	5	G	3	0	0	0	20,158
Hot Meatball Red	4	C	3	0	0	0	0
Hot Message	2	C	3	0	0	0	1,520
Hot n' Fiesty	4	F	5	0	1	0	982
Hot N Go	2	G	3	0	0	0	1,302
Hot Nuggets	3	C	5	1	1	0	13,233
Hot Off the Grill	5	G	8	1	2	1	22,167
Hot On Ice	5	H	2	0	0	0	111
Hot Package	6	G	11	1	2	0	7,912
Hot Pants	4	F	7	1	0	2	47,099
Hot Pepper Hill	7	G	10	2	0	3	110,425
Hot Potato	5	H	3	1	2	0	16,540
Hot Press	4	F	6	0	0	0	0
Hot Pressed	6	H	1	0	0	0	0
Hot Prospect	2	C	4	1	0	1	19,830
Hot Quaker	3	G	13	0	1	0	1,948
Hot Red Candi	4	F	11	0	0	1	5,850
Hot Red Halo	4	F	8	1	0	3	12,135
Hot Redhead	2	F	2	0	0	0	0
Hot Riff	5	G	8	1	0	2	17,370
Hot Rod Express	2	C	2	1	0	0	3,480
Hot Rod Joy	5	M	12	2	0	1	8,025
Hot Rod Lincoln	2	C	5	1	2	0	9,296
Hot Rodin	3	C	10	1	4	1	17,523
Hot Rum Toddy	6	G	4	0	0	0	545
Hot Rumor	4	F	3	0	0	0	89
Hot Sarah	3	F	10	0	0	0	1,680
Hot Sauce Moma	4	F	8	1	0	1	1,597
Hot Saucy	3	F	3	0	1	1	718
Hot Scramble	4	F	10	2	1	1	33,525
Hot Sea	3	F	4	0	0	2	3,400
Hot Shot Bob	3	G	13	1	1	2	8,258
Hot Shot Diamond	4	F	10	0	1	1	4,570
Hot Shot Hoolie	4	C	14	0	0	3	10,043
Hot Shot Spirit	2	G	6	1	0	1	11,300
Hot Singe	3	C	8	1	1	1	8,100
Hot Slot	4	C	10	2	2	1	30,918
Hot Song	3	G	18	2	6	2	37,315
Hot Soup	4	G	5	1	0	1	17,590
Hot Springs	2	C	3	0	0	0	360
Hot Steel	2	C	1	0	0	0	145
Hot Stop (ARG)	5	H	8	1	0	2	16,465
Hot Stuff	2	G	2	0	0	0	5,823
Hot Sync	4	F	1	0	0	0	420
Hot Talent	4	F	4	1	0	0	59,250
Hot Talk	2	G	1	0	1	0	3,888
Hot Tam	3	F	6	1	2	0	6,695
Hot Tea	6	M	6	0	2	1	3,494
Hot to Spot	3	C	3	0	2	0	9,460
Hot to Tango	4	F	7	0	1	1	9,400
Hot Trick	2	F	5	0	0	0	988
Hot Trotter (GB)	4	G	4	1	0	0	14,380
Hot Video	8	G	6	0	0	1	2,205
Hot War	4	C	2	0	0	0	700
Hot Warsaw Nights	6	G	5	1	3	0	8,160
Hot Weather	5	G	2	0	0	1	2,050
Hot Weekend	2	F	7	1	1	3	72,915
Hot Wheels	9	G	8	1	0	2	8,865
Hot Woman	4	F	11	1	1	2	17,380
Hot Ziggity	6	H	1	0	0	0	0
Hotcey Totcey	5	M	5	0	1	0	1,360
Hotdiggitydoggedly	4	G	10	0	1	2	4,021
Hotel Del	2	G	3	0	0	0	1,160
Hotel Hall (IRE)	5	G	9	0	3	1	44,620
Hotnightindixie	5	G	5	0	0	0	1,615
Hotnswift	5	H	1	0	0	0	0
Hotrod Jones	3	G	1	0	0	0	0
Hots Is Hot	3	C	10	0	2	5	17,810
Hotsea Galpin	4	F	2	0	0	0	40
Hotshot Dewey	5	G	9	0	1	1	5,796
Hotsie's Buckaroo	8	G	3	1	1	0	23,637
Hotspur	6	G	7	0	1	1	29,556
Hotstufanthensome	3	G	5	0	0	1	7,220
Hotsy Act	5	M	11	1	2	3	15,977
Hottentot	4	F	7	2	0	3	48,980
Hotter Than Hot	4	G	7	1	1	0	5,946
Hottest Trends	3	F	9	0	1	0	7,235
Hottie	3	F	4	1	0	0	12,430
Hottie Girl	3	F	5	0	0	0	420
Houdini's Trick	2	F	6	0	0	2	1,794
Hound Again	7	G	6	2	0	1	14,715
Hound Deer	7	H	8	2	3	0	15,413
Hound of Silence	3	G	10	0	2	1	8,252
Houndstooth	2	C	2	0	0	0	0
Hour Brass Belle	5	M	6	1	3	0	9,242
Hour Cee Dee	8	G	3	0	0	0	163
Hour Man Uncle Sam	9	G	10	1	1	1	5,907

RECORDS OF HORSES

Horse	Age	Sex	Sts	1st	2d	3d	Won	Horse	Age	Sex	Sts	1st	2d	3d	Won
Hour of Justice	3	F	4	2	2	0	166,195	Howyadoinhon	6	H	4	0	0	0	850
Hour Outlaw	2	C	2	0	0	2	8,760	Howyouknow	4	C	1	0	0	0	0
Hour Pocket Change	4	G	11	0	1	0	1,366	Howyoulikemenow Tc	4	F	15	3	0	1	32,208
Hourglass Figure	3	F	6	1	1	2	9,983	Hoyt	2	C	2	0	0	0	0
Hourhopefulchanges	4	F	2	0	0	0	0	Hrishi	5	M	5	1	0	1	20,144
Hourly Storm	5	H	11	2	0	1	33,380	Hristoforos	5	H	8	0	1	1	14,536
Hourmissremy	3	F	9	0	1	2	7,182	Hs Suave Dancer	4	F	13	0	3	1	5,039
Hourparentspride	5	G	6	0	0	0	1,920	Hub Cap	6	G	4	1	0	1	2,774
Hourytwokprospect	3	C	4	0	0	0	0	Hub City Al	3	G	19	1	3	1	7,111
House Band	3	G	4	0	0	0	804	Hubba Hubba Hubba	4	G	11	1	1	1	12,324
House Dance	4	G	14	2	3	1	39,890	Hubbardcity	5	H	2	0	0	0	0
House Hunting	4	F	10	3	1	1	10,243	Huber Woods	4	C	1	1	0	0	6,600
House Key	2	C	2	0	1	0	23,296	Huck Berry	3	C	5	1	1	0	8,658
House Money	4	C	7	2	0	3	28,983	Hucklebear	3	G	9	0	0	1	11,756
House Number	4	C	1	0	0	0	0	Huckleberry Prize	4	G	4	0	0	0	183
House of Cheer	5	M	13	1	1	2	11,689	Huckleberry Ridge	4	G	7	1	0	1	10,060
House of Fortune	2	F	5	3	0	1	195,944	Huckleberry's Gal	2	F	1	0	0	1	704
House of Sensation	2	G	5	0	0	1	3,140	Huck's Comet	3	G	7	0	0	0	1,092
House of Sport	3	C	9	1	1	1	11,410	Huckster's Girl	9	M	4	0	0	0	310
House On the Beach	7	G	4	1	0	1	7,170	Hudson Bay (IRE)	4	G	3	0	1	0	7,575
House Party	3	F	10	5	1	2	551,354	Hudson Street	4	G	11	1	1	1	22,030
House Wine	4	C	1	0	0	0	290	Huelee's Fuzzy Man	6	H	6	0	1	0	1,913
Housebird	4	F	5	0	0	1	638	Hue's Power Man	3	C	1	0	0	0	0
Housebusterman	4	C	12	0	0	2	3,730	Huey	4	C	6	0	0	0	1,284
Housewife	4	F	3	0	0	0	144	Huffle Shuffle	4	C	6	2	0	1	14,151
Houstacat	7	M	10	1	0	0	4,491	Huff's Gnome	4	G	9	0	0	0	0
Houston B Sweet	3	F	1	0	0	0	0	Huff's Lady	5	M	19	3	4	2	24,524
Houston Express	5	M	13	1	0	2	7,052	Huff's Queenie	4	F	2	0	0	0	0
Houston Hawk	11	G	2	0	0	0	0	Huffs Roan	5	M	9	1	1	2	7,842
Houston Hero	8	G	4	0	1	1	2,384	Hug Me Royal	2	F	1	0	0	0	57
Houston Hustler	5	M	16	2	2	3	23,913	Hugger	3	G	4	0	1	0	1,966
Houston Launch	4	F	9	3	0	2	14,373	Huggy Boy	5	G	6	0	0	0	3,014
Houston Lights Up	3	G	2	0	0	0	0	Hugh Betcha	3	G	6	0	0	0	57
Houston Pro	5	M	8	5	1	1	43,212	Hugh Boy	4	C	11	2	2	1	29,214
Houston Rodeo	6	G	3	0	0	1	240	Hugh Hefner	6	H	3	0	0	0	5,046
Houston Shuffle	2	G	4	3	0	0	19,290	Hugh Will Do	7	H	4	0	0	0	0
Houston Sun	4	G	3	0	0	0	0	Hughes	7	H	15	3	3	2	16,334
Houston Texas	6	G	14	3	2	1	10,397	Hugh's Choice	4	C	1	0	1	0	2,000
Houston to Marilyn	4	G	19	0	1	4	7,270	Hugh's Mansion	5	H	11	2	4	0	20,560
Houstonic	4	C	1	0	0	0	0	Hugs for Terry	4	F	13	3	0	2	21,422
Houston's Hope	4	G	4	2	0	0	1,893	Hugs Legacy	7	G	2	0	0	0	122
Houston's Prayer	3	G	9	3	2	2	93,390	Huka's Diamond	4	G	4	2	0	1	28,080
Houston's Silver	7	G	4	0	0	2	1,144	Hula Boola	4	F	2	0	1	0	1,800
Houston's Touch	4	C	2	0	0	0	0	Hula Girl	4	F	1	0	0	0	0
Hover	4	G	13	2	3	1	18,412	Hula Hottie	3	F	1	0	0	0	0
How About It	4	F	7	3	1	1	59,975	Hula Kat	3	F	5	0	0	0	4,608
How Bout Jose	6	H	7	2	0	2	51,935	Hula Medlei	4	F	8	1	2	1	16,830
How Clever Trevor	4	C	1	0	0	0	185	Hula Passion	5	G	1	0	0	0	0
How Do You Do	2	G	2	0	0	0	0	Hulagal	3	C	1	0	0	0	0
How Fancy	2	F	5	1	0	0	7,240	Huleo's Quest	10	G	14	2	3	1	11,404
How Goes	10	G	2	1	0	0	7,500	Hull City Tiger	6	G	9	0	0	0	614
How Good Is That	2	C	2	0	0	1	6,830	Hum	5	M	2	0	0	1	1,450
How Great Thou Art	7	G	7	0	1	0	960	Hum Dewey Slew	8	G	9	0	2	0	1,498
How Little We Know	3	C	8	0	0	1	4,230	Humanist	3	F	2	0	0	1	5,760
How Lou Doin'	2	G	2	0	1	0	3,800	Humbertito (CHI)	9	G	1	0	0	0	0
How Many	2	G	6	0	1	1	13,285	Humberto	7	G	13	2	3	1	22,155
How Now	8	G	15	3	2	4	18,726	Humble Billie	4	F	5	1	1	0	33,920
How Sweet	3	F	12	1	0	0	5,183	Humble Bob	3	G	13	1	3	3	17,450
How Sweet I Am	3	F	2	0	0	0	190	Humble Charlotte	4	F	2	0	0	0	0
How Sweet She Is	3	F	3	0	0	0	197	Humble Chris	2	G	2	0	0	0	390
How U Like Me Now	3	C	8	0	2	0	3,386	Humble Dot	4	F	1	0	0	1	1,100
How Ya Doing	3	F	4	1	0	0	11,200	Humble Fourteen	9	G	5	0	1	0	2,228
Howaboutthat	2	C	1	0	0	0	0	Humble Hero	3	G	8	2	0	0	31,704
Howamidoin	2	F	3	0	0	0	0	Humble Homage	4	F	12	1	1	2	11,060
Howard County	4	C	5	1	0	0	6,300	Humble Karleen	2	F	2	0	0	0	360
Howard Way	6	G	6	0	0	3	2,357	Humble Kathy	3	F	13	1	0	2	16,150
Howard's Calling	3	G	4	0	1	1	3,300	Humble Lane	2	F	7	1	2	0	20,540
Howdidhedoit	3	G	8	1	0	1	7,878	Humble Lightning	3	G	17	3	1	4	71,250
Howdoigettolagotee	4	G	9	0	4	1	4,492	Humble Madeline	2	F	3	1	0	0	5,700
Howdoulikemesofar	5	G	1	0	0	0	182	Humble Maggie	5	M	3	0	0	0	440
Howdoyouknow	3	G	11	1	1	0	3,097	Humble Roannie	4	F	4	1	2	0	21,432
Howdy Do	6	M	1	0	0	0	0	Humblest	3	C	3	1	0	1	17,000
Howdy N Rowdy	5	G	7	1	1	1	24,892	Humbolt Avenue	4	G	6	0	0	1	10,555
Howgoesthebattle	4	F	6	0	0	0	585	Humdalila	3	F	4	1	0	0	16,710
Howies Hungry	5	G	14	2	0	2	10,850	Humm a Tune	6	M	9	0	2	1	5,878
Howlin Wolf	9	G	3	0	1	0	2,420	Hummel	3	F	7	0	1	1	9,190
Howlinmaggie	7	M	5	0	0	0	906	Hummer's Echo	4	G	11	0	2	2	2,111
How's Raybob	4	G	9	0	1	5	20,830	Humming Breeze	2	F	1	0	0	0	0
Howtoo	4	G	9	1	0	0	7,575	Humming Cat	3	C	1	0	0	0	0

Horse	Age	Sex	Sts	1st	2d	3d	Won	Horse	Age	Sex	Sts	1st	2d	3d	Won
Humor the Rumor	4	G	7	2	0	0	6,780	Huntmaster	5	G	10	0	0	1	3,403
Humoresque	4	F	17	0	1	1	3,547	Hunts Landing	6	H	14	1	0	0	4,921
Humoristic	2	F	5	1	0	1	14,290	Huon Kid	2	G	1	0	0	0	237
Humorous Guy	2	G	1	0	1	0	3,800	Hup Two	2	G	3	0	0	0	985
Humorous Lady	3	F	2	0	0	1	36,750	Hurley	3	G	14	1	1	3	8,175
Humorous Leader	3	C	12	3	2	1	29,440	Hurri to the Line	7	M	4	0	0	0	0
Humorous Miss	2	F	4	0	0	0	2,400	Hurricane Alan	4	G	9	1	2	2	7,778
Humorously	2	C	1	0	0	0	875	Hurricane Ally	3	F	17	2	1	2	20,594
Humphreys	4	F	9	0	0	0	434	Hurricane Carter	6	G	10	1	1	0	9,285
Humptys Alibi	4	G	2	0	1	0	2,994	Hurricane Charlie	3	G	4	1	0	1	15,819
Humptys Horsepower	3	G	11	2	2	0	11,114	Hurricane Devin	3	C	9	1	0	0	26,400
Hunch Play	4	C	17	1	0	1	6,952	Hurricane Earl	5	G	1	0	0	0	38
Hunch Punch	3	F	2	0	0	0	180	Hurricane Fly	2	F	1	1	0	0	4,200
Hundley Bug	5	G	3	1	0	0	3,599	Hurricane Fool	3	G	16	1	1	4	16,377
Hundred Bagger	4	F	6	1	1	1	8,125	Hurricane Gilbert	4	F	11	1	1	1	8,190
Hunforgun	4	G	14	5	2	1	70,241	Hurricane Haley	4	F	4	0	0	0	0
Hungarian Beauty	5	M	9	2	1	0	9,754	Hurricane Hannah	2	F	4	1	3	0	49,600
Hungarian Dancer	7	H	8	0	0	1	1,430	Hurricane Harbour	4	F	1	0	0	0	0
Hungarian Princess	2	F	1	0	0	0	300	Hurricane Havoc	6	G	16	7	0	1	78,923
Hungarian Slew	2	G	1	0	0	0	0	Hurricane Hebe	3	F	1	0	0	0	0
Hungarians Ba Ba	3	F	2	0	0	0	370	Hurricane Hunter	2	C	7	1	3	1	43,760
Hungry Shane	3	G	9	0	0	0	2,005	Hurricane Julia	3	F	3	0	1	1	4,550
Hunka	4	F	4	1	0	0	3,947	Hurricane K.	5	M	3	0	0	0	225
Hunka Hunka Lori Z	5	M	7	0	1	1	21,210	Hurricane Lilly	3	F	10	3	0	2	10,596
Hunkahunkamango	4	G	9	1	2	1	7,745	Hurricane Megan	4	C	4	1	0	1	34,560
Hunky Hill	4	C	16	1	3	4	11,596	Hurricane Merle	6	G	14	5	2	1	91,460
Hunt Cup	4	C	1	0	0	0	116	Hurricane Mike	4	G	13	1	4	3	28,924
Hunt for Glory	2	G	4	1	0	2	3,772	Hurricane Queen	6	M	3	1	1	0	22,800
Hunt for Joy	3	F	11	2	0	2	14,150	Hurricane Rose	4	F	5	0	2	0	26,638
Hunt for Love	3	G	11	1	1	0	21,888	Hurricane Shockey	2	C	4	1	0	2	40,400
Hunt for Paws	2	F	2	0	0	0	0	Hurricane Shonda	4	F	10	0	1	1	6,713
Hunt Gold	5	H	3	0	0	0	0	Hurricane Smoke	4	G	9	2	1	3	106,590
Hunt the Dream	4	C	10	1	0	2	4,922	Hurricane Sue	6	M	9	0	4	1	9,560
Hunt the Front	4	C	3	0	2	1	2,845	Hurricane Ursi	3	G	4	1	0	0	5,940
Hunt the Rainbow	2	C	1	0	0	0	0	Hurrikane Kane	3	C	5	1	0	2	12,200
Hunted	3	F	1	0	0	0	0	Hurrikane Tracey	4	F	3	0	0	0	180
Hunter B.	5	H	12	2	1	0	66,381	Hurri's Moose	5	H	4	0	0	0	96
Hunter Cat	3	C	2	0	0	0	0	Hurry Home	3	F	6	2	0	0	27,480
Hunter Down	2	F	4	0	2	2	13,020	Hurry Home Don	4	C	2	0	0	0	32
Hunter in the Sky	4	C	8	1	1	1	7,895	Hurry Me Home	6	G	12	2	0	4	29,359
Hunter Jay	3	G	11	1	1	2	36,125	Hurry On Reality	6	H	6	1	0	0	4,180
Hunter Jo	3	C	9	2	1	1	21,783	Hurry to Finish	4	C	3	0	0	0	804
Hunter Jr.	2	C	1	0	0	0	95	Hurry Up Sunny	6	G	17	0	5	1	12,955
Hunter Lady	3	F	9	2	1	2	13,400	Hurry Up Victory	2	C	2	0	0	0	0
Hunter Royal	3	C	18	1	7	7	28,560	Hurtgen Forest	6	G	7	1	4	2	12,819
Hunters Event	3	C	21	1	2	1	9,841	Hush Dottie	6	M	5	0	3	0	5,375
Hunter's Faith	4	F	1	0	0	0	1,560	Hush Money	5	M	6	0	1	0	6,488
Hunter's Gal	4	F	2	0	0	0	348	Hush N the Holler	4	F	9	0	0	1	1,305
Hunters Halo	5	G	8	1	1	2	22,395	Hush Now	2	F	4	0	0	0	755
Hunter's Mark	3	F	6	1	0	0	12,730	Hush U Dreamer	3	F	7	2	0	1	23,855
Hunter's Pet	4	F	1	0	0	0	180	Hushaby Adam	7	G	4	0	0	0	0
Hunter's Pride	2	F	5	0	1	0	5,440	Hushaby Babe	3	F	5	0	0	0	2,726
Hunter's Prize	3	G	9	3	1	2	50,100	Hushlee	3	G	4	0	0	1	1,515
Hunters Rae	2	F	4	1	0	1	15,280	Hushnlisten	2	C	2	0	0	0	200
Hunters Saloon	3	F	5	2	0	0	15,060	Husker Fan	7	H	8	0	1	1	1,851
Hunter's Slew	4	F	1	0	0	0	350	Husker Valley	3	F	8	0	3	1	4,993
Hunter's Sunrise	4	F	1	1	0	0	5,070	Husky Country	5	G	8	0	0	1	1,301
Hunter's Tale	3	G	5	0	1	0	2,260	Husky Playgirl	4	F	3	0	0	0	0
Hunter's West	3	F	10	2	0	2	11,593	Huslin Harley	7	G	4	0	0	0	0
Huntertown	2	G	2	0	0	0	175	Hussar	3	C	5	1	0	0	12,546
Hunterwood Point	3	G	10	5	0	1	32,685	Hussle Home	5	G	10	1	0	1	5,503
Huntfortherun	7	G	5	0	0	0	336	Hussy	3	F	9	1	2	1	53,930
Huntin for Bear	2	G	2	0	0	0	320	Hustle Up	2	F	1	0	0	0	100
Hunting Around	3	F	7	1	1	3	8,965	Hut	3	G	5	0	1	0	4,001
Hunting Cat	8	G	3	0	0	0	134	Hut Maid	4	F	15	0	1	2	5,394
Hunting Course	7	G	8	0	1	0	2,069	Hutchinson Island	3	G	6	2	0	1	8,011
Hunting for Action	3	F	12	2	1	4	32,277	Hutchison Station	3	C	1	0	0	1	2,700
Hunting Freedom	3	F	6	0	0	0	581	Hutney	6	H	1	0	0	0	310
Hunting Gold	3	G	13	2	2	0	15,170	Huttutrefo	3	G	6	0	0	3	10,910
Hunting Hillbilly	2	C	12	1	2	1	28,050	Hutzelhawk	3	G	11	1	2	1	5,083
Hunting in Gerarda	2	C	2	0	0	0	290	Hux (GB)	4	G	5	0	1	2	7,940
Hunting Roses	3	F	6	0	0	0	1,848	Huxley Hero	3	G	3	1	0	0	40,020
Hunting the Gold	5	G	13	1	0	1	47,926	Hy Angel	3	F	6	0	0	0	720
Hunting Trip	3	F	5	0	2	0	3,250	Hy Karate	3	C	4	0	0	0	179
Hunting Wild	5	H	4	0	0	0	293	Hy Lucky Rita	3	F	4	1	1	0	3,100
Huntinghardforit	4	F	11	2	1	1	4,666	Hy Maureen	2	F	5	0	0	0	780
Huntingthetruth	3	F	11	2	5	0	56,212	Hy Nick	5	G	10	3	1	1	7,908
Huntington Hill	3	F	12	3	1	2	39,125	Hy Proud Buddy	6	H	1	0	0	0	0
Huntington Viking	6	G	18	0	2	3	5,830	Hy Way Nine	6	G	5	2	0	0	7,124

Horse	Age	Sex	Sts	1st	2d	3d	Won
Hyannis	2	F	1	0	0	0	360
Hybla Two	3	C	6	0	1	0	6,437
Hyde Ho	4	F	5	0	0	0	481
Hyder	6	G	6	1	2	1	32,820
Hydration	4	F	2	2	0	0	37,200
Hydro	7	M	4	0	1	2	3,202
Hydrogen	4	C	10	2	3	2	175,764
Hydrophobia	4	G	9	2	0	3	17,657
Hyjab	2	C	4	1	1	0	29,100
Hy'm the Danzigkid	2	G	2	0	0	0	546
Hymies Jet	8	G	10	1	1	0	10,965
Hymns of Glory	2	C	9	2	1	3	38,752
Hyper Dancer	2	F	2	0	0	0	0
Hyper Drive	5	G	7	0	0	1	1,079
Hyper Haitan	4	G	4	0	0	0	297
Hypercat	3	C	5	1	1	0	31,716
Hypersonic Boy	6	G	7	0	1	0	970
Hypnos	3	G	14	1	3	1	32,390
Hypnotique Rial	6	H	6	2	0	0	6,856
Hypnotist	3	C	8	1	0	1	61,400
Hyrah	7	G	1	0	0	0	0
Hysanslew	4	F	4	1	2	1	11,290
Hysteria	7	G	10	0	1	0	1,056
I Ain't Pokeyman	4	F	10	2	5	0	49,685
I Ain't Skeered	3	G	3	0	0	0	0
I Ain't Talkin	5	G	13	3	3	1	22,710
I Ain't Your Honey	5	M	3	0	0	0	462
I Am (NZ)	7	G	3	0	0	1	1,900
I Am a Don	2	G	1	0	0	0	0
I Am a Livermore	2	C	4	0	1	0	3,240
I Am a Rigging	3	F	4	0	0	0	245
I Am Big Enough	2	F	1	0	0	0	0
I Am Excessive	3	F	3	0	0	0	148
I Am Gorgeous	3	F	15	0	3	3	54,064
I Am Hi	3	C	1	0	0	1	420
I Am Kodack Moment	2	C	4	0	0	0	70
I Am Sam I Am	3	C	9	0	0	0	848
I Am Speechless	3	F	3	1	1	0	7,390
I Am Superman	4	C	4	0	0	0	168
I Am the Champion	3	G	11	1	1	1	16,125
I Am the Count	3	G	6	1	1	0	15,920
I Am the Mail Man	5	G	14	2	0	5	20,055
I Am the One	4	F	2	1	0	0	2,310
I Am the Phantom	6	G	7	0	0	0	180
I Am the Way	9	M	2	0	0	0	122
I Am This Guy	8	G	5	2	1	1	3,275
I and I	6	G	2	1	0	1	19,136
I B Awesome	3	G	8	1	0	0	3,660
I B Bad	3	G	2	2	0	0	49,120
I B Right Back	3	F	10	2	2	4	13,147
I Be a Q. T.	3	F	6	0	1	1	3,230
I Be Casual	7	H	6	1	0	1	8,303
I Be Stylish	5	M	3	0	0	0	0
I Believe	3	F	2	0	1	1	8,040
I Believeitsmyturn	2	F	4	0	0	0	285
I Belong	4	F	7	2	1	1	13,106
I Belong to Winloc	4	F	14	4	1	4	42,160
I C U Looking	4	C	5	0	0	2	3,501
I Call Front	3	G	7	0	0	0	374
I Came to Play	4	F	8	1	4	1	4,016
I Can Cook	3	G	2	1	0	0	15,300
I Can Fan Fan	4	F	11	1	0	1	39,379
I Can Still See U	4	G	18	0	2	2	5,733
I Can't Believe It	3	G	6	0	0	1	1,890
I Cant Refuse	2	C	3	1	1	1	11,030
I Captain	4	G	10	1	0	1	6,265
I D Queen	3	F	14	1	1	4	17,220
I Dalee	5	M	5	0	0	1	1,428
I Dancer	8	G	13	0	1	2	14,075
I Dare Billy	2	F	4	0	0	1	2,399
I Did It	3	F	3	0	0	0	2,950
I Did It Ordway	2	C	2	0	0	1	1,320
I Died Laughing	3	F	4	1	0	0	10,155
I Dig Dancin	6	M	2	0	0	0	137
I Dig U	3	F	10	2	3	1	21,121
I Don't Care	7	G	5	1	0	1	2,736
I Dr. Joe	6	G	10	2	1	2	29,038
I Feel Good	5	H	12	1	2	2	13,846
I Follow You	2	F	2	0	0	0	1,710

Horse	Age	Sex	Sts	1st	2d	3d	Won
I for You	4	G	7	1	0	1	5,447
I Found Sarah	7	M	11	0	2	1	2,640
I Got Silver	7	M	5	1	0	1	17,382
I Gotcha Covered	6	G	1	0	0	0	0
I Grow On You	6	M	9	1	4	0	11,461
I Had to Laugh	4	F	12	1	5	1	36,346
I Have No Manners	4	C	9	0	0	1	1,460
I Have Wings	3	F	6	0	1	0	2,300
I Hear a Synphony	2	F	1	0	0	0	130
I Hear That	4	F	14	3	1	3	29,177
I Hear Voices	3	F	3	0	0	0	150
I Heard You	5	G	15	1	1	3	10,681
I Hit the Jackpot	4	G	6	0	0	1	6,775
I Hope You Dance	4	F	4	0	0	0	375
I Is Eyre	4	G	7	0	2	0	7,718
I Just Met a Girl	4	F	2	0	0	0	460
I Know Broadway	5	G	7	0	0	0	1,130
I Know My Bodie	8	H	7	1	0	1	6,101
I Know You	4	F	14	1	1	1	9,834
I Know You Can	5	H	13	1	2	2	29,860
I Like Spike	6	G	11	2	0	3	7,557
I Like You Tooo	5	H	9	1	4	1	17,054
I Love Billy	3	F	10	0	0	1	2,584
I Love Chicago	7	H	4	0	1	0	2,740
I Love Chocolate	3	C	11	1	3	4	25,129
I Love Lisa	4	F	9	2	0	0	14,760
I Love New York	3	F	4	0	0	0	0
I Love Racing	3	G	2	1	0	1	7,420
I Love the Organ	2	F	2	0	0	1	6,710
I Love to Win	3	F	1	0	1	0	3,800
I Luv This Country	4	G	10	1	0	2	13,278
I M Aking	3	G	12	1	2	1	6,310
I M Polish Meck	5	H	4	0	0	0	1,117
I M Polish Pride	3	F	12	4	4	0	50,660
I M Rudy D	3	C	3	0	0	0	760
I Match Too	5	M	6	0	0	1	2,420
I Met Somebody	6	M	11	0	4	0	35,840
I Miss You	3	F	9	0	1	2	9,340
I Need a Hero	5	M	3	0	0	0	134
I Need to Run	2	G	2	0	1	0	2,415
I Never Look	5	H	12	0	0	0	1,006
I Ninty	4	F	3	1	0	0	1,595
I Not Slow	3	F	4	1	0	1	5,096
I P O Dude	5	G	12	6	1	2	23,292
I P O Pat	4	F	11	2	1	1	45,040
I Pay the Bills	3	C	7	1	0	0	11,320
I Prefer Ladies	3	G	8	0	1	0	2,080
I Present	4	F	2	0	0	0	186
I R S Memo	5	G	4	1	1	0	2,247
I Remember You	4	F	4	0	1	0	7,500
I Said I Could	3	C	4	0	0	0	177
I Said Ready	3	C	4	0	0	0	0
I See the Cat	2	G	4	0	0	0	305
I Shine	3	F	3	1	0	1	6,080
I Shot the Deputy	3	F	11	2	1	0	10,519
I Siyah Dancing	4	F	12	1	1	1	5,327
I Spy Brennie	7	M	1	0	0	0	0
I Still Don't No	4	F	7	0	0	0	0
I Swear (GB)	4	C	1	0	0	1	6,120
I Take the Cinco	4	F	7	1	0	1	4,200
I Tell You	7	H	6	1	0	1	9,674
I Ten West	3	F	13	1	3	0	10,985
I Testify	3	G	10	0	1	2	34,291
I the Messiah	4	G	3	1	0	0	1,194
I Thee Wed	3	G	7	1	3	2	91,415
I Think I Can Fly	7	H	5	3	0	0	10,560
I Think I Cannes	6	G	11	0	0	1	1,547
I Think I Know	2	G	5	1	0	0	5,330
I Thought I Could	4	G	1	0	0	0	188
I Thought U Knew	2	C	3	0	1	0	4,820
I Two Step Too	10	G	7	0	2	0	1,248
I Useto Have Money	2	F	1	0	0	0	0
I Wanna Dance	6	M	13	2	3	3	10,843
I Wanna Go Go	4	F	14	0	1	1	4,970
I Wanta Be Alone	4	G	13	1	1	0	3,922
I Will	2	G	2	0	0	0	270
I Will Survive	4	F	8	2	1	1	42,391
I Wish I Slew	4	G	6	0	0	0	2,470
I Wish I Was	3	F	3	0	0	1	900

Horse	Age	Sex	Sts	1st	2d	3d	Won
I Won't Apollogize	3	G	5	4	0	0	22,140
I Wood Be a Winner	8	G	13	5	3	2	29,290
I Yai Yai	6	M	3	0	0	0	135
I. B. D. Chief	3	G	9	2	0	0	17,698
I. B. Deone	6	G	14	4	2	0	23,358
I. B. Hansie	4	F	5	0	0	0	0
I. B. Quick	8	G	4	1	0	0	21,173
I. B.'s Halo	3	F	12	4	3	0	69,270
I. C. Secrets	4	F	5	0	0	0	1,710
I. C. Tony	4	C	12	1	3	1	33,888
I. C. Turbo	6	G	6	0	1	1	2,073
I. D. Minted	7	G	7	1	1	1	8,623
I. L. C. U. Later	3	G	4	0	2	0	11,250
I. M. Awonder	4	G	6	0	0	0	345
I. R. Fast	9	G	12	0	2	2	4,730
I. R. Wood	4	G	2	0	0	2	11,280
Iaco (ARG)	6	H	19	2	2	2	27,985
I'am a Kamper	10	M	11	0	5	2	5,215
I'am a Red Sox Fan	2	C	7	1	2	0	31,980
Iam Compliant	5	M	9	0	0	0	1,027
I'am Listening	3	G	14	1	0	5	15,915
Iam Nobodys Fool	4	F	7	3	0	2	14,925
Iam T. N. T.	6	M	8	0	0	0	3,921
Iam the Hitman	5	G	3	0	0	0	0
Iamalegacy	4	F	6	0	0	1	1,693
Iamatowertoo	2	C	3	0	0	0	0
Iamawildcat	3	F	7	0	0	1	1,727
Iams Bound	3	G	12	1	1	1	31,322
Ian English	4	C	2	0	0	0	0
Ian's Blessing	2	G	3	0	0	1	5,530
Ian's Rocket	5	G	16	3	4	5	87,150
Ian's Thunder	8	G	3	0	0	0	570
Iatan	6	G	1	0	0	0	0
Ibelieveinmiracles	4	F	21	0	2	1	3,287
Ibelieveitsours	4	F	2	0	0	0	0
Iberian	2	G	3	0	0	0	0
Ibero Grace (ARG)	4	C	7	0	1	1	20,150
Ibis's Heart	3	C	10	2	0	0	10,141
Ibred	2	F	1	1	0	0	2,880
Icanhaul	3	F	9	1	2	1	36,790
Icanhearyousmile	3	F	11	1	2	2	8,327
Icanpunch	3	F	7	1	1	1	8,800
Icanscat	3	G	8	0	1	2	3,533
Icanseeclearly	5	M	13	2	3	1	19,650
Icanseeclearlynow	4	G	9	2	3	1	32,980
Icanseetherain	5	G	1	0	0	0	110
Icanseethesky	4	F	21	2	3	3	13,711
Icansoiwill	5	M	11	5	0	2	21,584
Icantgoforthat	4	F	12	2	1	4	210,724
Icantmember	5	H	7	1	2	0	19,314
Icantpronounceit	4	C	4	0	0	1	358
Icarian	6	G	7	3	1	2	37,720
Icarus in Flight	5	G	14	2	2	1	36,687
Ice and Vice	5	M	5	2	0	1	15,675
Ice Angel	6	M	3	0	0	0	0
Ice Bound	4	F	12	0	1	2	5,639
Ice Bullet	10	G	6	0	1	1	9,150
Ice Carnival	4	F	7	1	2	2	20,944
Ice Cold Alley	3	F	5	0	0	0	1,575
Ice Cream Lady	4	F	8	2	0	2	12,986
Ice Cream Maiden	4	F	14	1	0	0	4,144
Ice Cream Social	5	M	9	1	0	1	5,657
Ice Diplomat	3	C	3	0	1	0	1,075
Ice Dreams	3	F	11	0	3	1	11,551
Ice Dude	4	G	2	0	0	0	0
Ice Fella	4	G	5	0	1	0	2,897
Ice Forest	4	F	9	0	2	2	23,519
Ice Girl	3	F	12	3	3	1	36,839
Ice Glider	5	M	13	2	1	3	19,525
Ice Goddess	5	M	13	0	1	0	3,693
Ice Gold Dancer	2	C	4	0	0	0	2,880
Ice Gypsy	2	F	2	0	0	1	1,367
Ice House Max	7	G	11	1	2	0	4,781
Ice in the House	3	G	11	2	1	2	33,695
Ice It Honey	2	F	3	0	3	0	11,800
Ice Jam	4	G	8	0	0	0	359
Ice Jamer	5	G	3	0	0	0	96
Ice King	4	G	10	0	2	0	5,785
Ice Kit	3	F	4	0	1	1	2,691
Ice Legend	2	G	4	1	1	1	39,820
Ice Lemon and Rum	2	C	2	0	0	0	0
Ice n' Gold	3	F	14	3	2	2	75,310
Ice of Course	7	G	8	1	0	1	6,157
Ice Out There	9	G	16	0	6	2	12,682
Ice Pellet	4	F	10	4	1	1	44,002
Ice Prince (GB)	5	G	12	1	4	0	51,290
Ice Queen	6	M	3	1	0	0	8,940
Ice the Dice	5	G	2	1	0	0	3,355
Ice Water	8	G	11	2	1	3	47,668
Ice Wynnd Fire	2	G	3	1	2	0	33,200
Iceanwater	3	C	10	2	2	2	80,350
Iceberg Wayne	4	C	3	0	0	0	280
Icebreaker	5	H	3	1	0	1	7,810
Iced Tea With Lime	6	H	10	1	2	2	9,626
Icee Cheaspeake	4	F	8	2	3	0	84,730
Icee Somore	3	C	2	0	0	0	0
Ice-Girl (ARG)	4	F	4	0	1	0	17,720
Iceirez	11	G	8	1	0	2	9,426
Icekimo	5	G	11	0	1	3	4,132
Icelander	3	F	9	0	0	2	3,211
Icelandic	3	C	7	0	0	0	193
Iceman Runneth	2	C	1	0	0	0	145
Icepic	7	G	8	1	2	0	9,724
Iceplosion	3	C	7	3	2	1	81,324
Iceshack	3	F	9	1	0	1	6,842
Iceskate	5	G	5	2	0	1	9,315
Icey Gambler	8	G	4	0	0	0	620
Ichabod's Run	4	G	4	0	0	0	210
Ichiban Duc	3	G	10	2	0	3	41,031
Ichigo	3	G	6	0	1	2	18,203
Ichiro Run	4	G	14	1	1	4	4,743
Ichoseyou	3	F	3	1	0	0	17,040
Icicle Angel	6	M	12	3	1	3	23,685
Icicle Charlie	2	C	5	0	2	0	18,060
Icomefromswayback	6	H	3	0	0	0	0
Icrossmyhart	3	F	14	3	0	1	27,520
Icy Atlantic	2	C	2	0	0	0	2,700
Icy Avenue	4	F	6	2	1	0	87,940
Icy Banker	2	C	7	0	0	0	1,840
Icy Calm	5	M	9	1	0	1	6,472
Icy Cat	2	F	3	1	1	0	12,120
Icy Choice	4	F	9	2	1	2	65,255
Icy Flirt	6	M	8	4	2	0	38,420
Icy Glare	6	H	2	0	0	0	375
Icy Hill	4	G	7	2	3	0	4,815
Icy Interlude	4	F	8	0	0	1	5,725
Icy Lane	2	F	1	1	0	0	13,800
Icy Patina	6	M	7	0	0	1	2,055
Icy Ryan	4	G	6	0	0	0	658
Icy Sparks	2	F	5	1	0	0	3,785
Icy Star	4	C	2	0	0	0	1,196
Icy Tobin	3	G	10	0	3	3	25,980
Icy Urchin	3	F	5	1	0	0	6,500
Icy Venom	3	G	8	0	0	0	2,422
Icy Victory	3	G	1	0	0	0	185
Icy Waquoit	5	G	10	1	3	1	12,805
Icy Witness	3	G	14	3	1	1	18,320
Icyroundtable	3	F	8	1	1	1	5,220
Id	2	C	3	0	0	0	3,920
I'd Be First	3	F	14	3	1	2	15,548
Ida Be Bud	5	G	7	0	0	0	340
Ida Belle	4	F	6	0	1	0	1,727
Ida Hadit	6	G	16	4	3	0	16,262
Ida Vlaka	4	C	13	1	2	0	6,062
Idadidit	4	F	10	2	1	0	61,043
Idahill Tootsie	5	M	15	0	3	4	6,468
Idaho Kid	4	C	3	0	1	1	535
Idahoss	5	G	1	0	0	0	0
Idalea Bailey	4	F	8	0	0	0	882
Idalou	4	F	10	0	1	0	2,122
Idapink	3	F	2	0	0	0	785
Idarado	7	H	9	1	1	0	9,475
Idareya	2	C	4	0	0	0	240
Ida's Boy	2	G	1	0	0	0	100
Ida's Girl	3	F	8	1	0	0	7,163
Ida's Heart	3	F	1	0	0	0	0
Ida's Lil Brother	3	G	4	0	0	1	1,375
Ide and Seek	4	G	15	1	3	1	9,971

Horse	Age	Sex	Sts	1st	2d	3d	Won
Ide B Blue	3	F	11	1	1	3	11,658
Ide Be a Lady	2	F	3	1	0	0	34,645
Ide Be Brave	2	G	4	1	0	0	6,339
Ide Be Downtown	4	G	8	2	2	0	16,025
Ide Be Gone	3	G	9	3	2	1	121,812
Ide Be O for Ten	4	G	15	0	0	2	4,001
Ide Be Proud	2	F	6	1	1	0	11,214
Ide Be Spencers	4	C	12	4	1	2	85,691
Ide Be Your Slew	3	F	4	0	0	0	0
Ide Bet It All	4	F	9	0	1	1	9,430
Ide Boogie	3	F	15	2	5	3	28,920
Ide Got Style	2	C	2	0	0	0	137
Ide Rather	4	G	7	3	0	1	53,570
Ide Rather Not	5	M	6	1	0	2	9,506
Ide Tyme	4	F	7	1	2	0	6,294
Idea Man	3	C	8	2	0	0	9,780
Ideal Cut	5	G	9	2	3	1	54,200
Ideal Image	5	M	5	0	0	1	6,070
Idealism	3	G	4	1	0	0	20,166
Idealist	7	M	13	2	1	2	25,420
Ideate	5	M	15	1	3	4	28,382
Idebewinner	4	G	7	1	1	0	23,505
Idel Zack	4	G	16	2	0	2	8,973
Idelikeatoy	5	M	14	2	1	1	27,623
Ident	7	G	19	4	4	3	48,734
Identic	4	C	7	1	1	0	13,570
Identical Slew	4	F	1	0	0	0	0
Identity Theft	2	C	1	0	0	0	75
Ideratherbegamblin	2	G	11	1	3	1	11,300
Ides of Melissa	4	F	7	1	0	1	3,851
Ides Pride	2	F	3	0	0	0	1,140
Ideveter	4	F	17	4	1	3	66,619
Ideway	4	G	10	2	2	0	21,380
Ididarod Trail	4	G	10	2	2	0	6,970
Idididdi (NZ)	5	G	3	1	1	0	18,600
Idjanoah	3	F	3	0	0	0	282
Idle Day	5	M	10	0	0	1	3,465
Idle Dreamer	2	C	4	0	0	1	1,560
Idle Ide	3	C	9	0	1	1	2,980
Idle Ire	3	F	2	1	0	0	13,336
Idle Joan	3	F	12	0	0	3	2,960
Idle Luck	5	M	8	1	0	1	4,150
Idle Salute	5	H	8	2	3	0	13,689
Idle Spur	5	M	8	2	0	2	10,434
Idle Storm	3	F	11	1	1	1	5,886
Idle Waves	5	G	10	1	0	0	5,281
Id'lly Divine	6	G	7	4	0	0	36,859
Idol Gina	3	G	9	5	1	0	52,730
Idontneedone	5	G	15	1	4	1	12,476
Idorunrun	13	G	2	1	0	0	2,310
Idratherbedancing	3	F	12	0	0	2	2,937
I'dratherbegolfing	3	C	9	1	0	2	6,205
Idyllic	5	M	8	0	0	0	1,998
If by Magic	4	F	3	0	1	0	12,080
If He Hollers	4	G	1	0	0	0	360
If I Had	4	F	13	4	3	2	42,690
If I Had It All	3	G	10	1	0	0	3,862
If I Had Wings	3	C	1	0	0	1	1,275
If I Were You	4	G	7	3	0	1	50,788
If Ida	5	G	16	3	4	1	21,230
If I'm Spared	2	C	4	0	1	0	4,809
If Nine Was Six	3	F	6	2	0	1	41,620
If Not Me Who	3	F	9	0	1	2	6,740
If Not Why Not	7	G	11	3	2	1	19,280
If Six Was Nine	3	F	14	2	1	2	20,945
If You Believe	3	F	16	0	5	4	15,604
If You Don't	3	F	4	1	1	0	11,966
If You Please	4	G	12	1	3	1	12,607
If You're Lucky	2	F	3	0	1	0	5,880
Ifeelmisty	4	F	16	2	1	3	14,606
Iffah (IRE)	5	M	8	2	0	0	21,420
Iffey's Majesty	8	M	3	0	0	0	174
Iffy	4	F	11	3	2	3	60,430
Iffy Account	6	G	7	0	1	0	3,608
Ifineedyaillcallya	7	G	11	1	0	2	26,513
Ifitstobeitsuptome	6	G	9	2	1	1	27,306
Iflookscouldkill	2	F	3	0	0	0	2,640
Ifufeelfroggyleap	3	F	4	0	1	0	3,288
Ifyouknowwhatimean	4	F	8	0	0	1	1,392
Ifyouprefersilver	4	F	4	1	0	1	99,960
Ifyouvegotthemoney	4	C	21	1	3	5	14,918
Iggy's Education	3	C	2	0	0	0	170
Iglo Alpir	4	F	10	1	1	2	17,575
Ignatius	3	C	1	0	0	0	360
Ignitable	3	C	7	1	1	1	20,203
Ignition	3	C	2	1	0	0	19,570
Ignition Switch	3	G	5	1	0	0	8,765
Ignitro	3	G	8	1	0	0	16,329
Igo Creek	3	G	2	0	0	0	54
Igot It Goinon	3	C	6	0	0	0	0
Igothips	3	F	3	1	0	0	5,780
Ihaveadate	2	F	4	1	1	0	36,580
Ihaveseenthelight	3	C	2	1	0	1	13,200
Ihavevision	3	C	1	0	0	0	35
Ihavewhatitakes	5	M	2	0	0	1	328
Ihearyah	2	F	2	0	0	0	328
Ihopetobeawinner	3	F	12	1	0	3	4,912
Ijustdontcare	3	F	8	1	0	0	5,125
Ikari Caroline	2	F	8	0	2	0	7,647
Ike and Fannie	4	F	24	1	1	0	7,221
Ike'n Dunk	6	G	3	0	0	0	150
Ike's Cat's Gone	7	G	2	0	0	0	835
Ike's Kool Cat	4	C	6	3	0	1	4,809
Ikes Rabbit	5	H	8	0	1	1	889
Ikkimaani Otoom	5	G	2	0	0	0	0
Iknewicould	3	G	2	1	0	0	4,095
Iknowhowtodance	5	M	6	0	0	1	2,862
Iknowtheprogram	2	C	6	2	0	1	16,475
Ikon	3	G	6	1	0	0	2,890
Il Barone (IRE)	3	C	4	0	0	0	1,680
Il Capitano (GB)	6	G	8	3	0	3	65,860
Il Capriccio	2	C	6	0	1	2	18,640
Il Est Renard	4	G	20	1	1	1	8,651
Il Fait Du Soleil	5	M	10	1	2	1	5,022
Il Meglio (BRZ)	3	G	3	0	0	0	2,280
Ile de Ciel	7	M	4	1	0	1	3,103
Ile de Dixie Inn	4	F	6	0	0	0	1,868
Ile de France	4	F	3	0	0	1	13,500
Ile de Linda	4	F	11	0	2	0	4,862
Ileana	7	M	12	1	0	3	6,999
Ile'd Irish Rose	2	F	3	0	0	0	0
Ilene's Dream	5	M	1	0	0	0	0
Ilha Azul	8	M	8	1	2	0	12,470
Ilha Grande	4	F	7	3	0	0	73,500
Iliad's Classic	5	M	19	0	0	0	1,840
Iliamna	5	H	4	0	0	0	255
I'll Be a Marine	3	F	3	0	0	0	0
Ill Buy Dinner	3	C	4	2	2	0	26,600
I'll Cry for You	7	M	3	0	0	0	0
I'll Deliver	7	M	12	2	1	5	29,056
I'll Lead	3	F	11	1	2	3	12,310
I'll Pay My Way	3	F	9	0	0	2	2,412
I'll Play High	6	G	2	0	0	0	0
I'll Say	3	C	7	1	0	1	18,883
I'll Say Nelson	4	G	15	0	0	0	1,913
I'll Shake the Law	5	G	6	0	0	0	446
I'll Sing to Emily	3	F	7	0	0	1	2,459
I'll Survive	2	F	9	0	0	0	1,090
I'll Take the Gray	4	F	3	1	1	0	3,912
I'llcallyouback	2	F	9	1	3	0	12,785
Illegal	3	G	7	2	0	0	30,900
Illegal Hunter	4	C	11	2	0	1	25,827
Illegal Smile	6	G	14	0	3	2	27,710
Illini Belle	2	F	1	0	0	0	70
Illini Boogy Queen	2	F	2	0	0	0	360
Illini Queen	3	F	15	3	2	1	49,460
Illinois Moonshine	4	C	13	3	2	0	61,096
I'llmakeyousmile	5	H	5	1	0	0	1,390
I'llruinya	4	G	8	0	0	1	7,656
Illucination	2	F	5	0	0	3	10,120
Illuminance	3	F	10	2	1	1	30,470
Illusion	4	F	3	0	0	0	328
Illusion Confusion	6	M	8	1	2	0	2,960
Illusion of You	5	G	2	0	0	0	0
Illusionary	5	H	8	0	1	0	21,828
Illusionary Magic	2	C	8	2	1	1	40,979
Illusive Cause	7	M	2	0	0	0	0

Horse	Age	Sex	Sts	1st	2d	3d	Won
Illusive Force	3	G	7	1	1	0	55,936
Illusive Guy	3	G	6	0	3	0	42,702
Illusive Play	4	F	2	0	0	0	102
Illusive Prospect	5	H	10	1	2	2	11,167
Illusive Trick	4	F	11	1	0	0	12,932
Illustrated Man	6	G	7	0	1	1	6,842
Illustrious Legacy	3	F	7	1	0	2	24,330
Illustrious Legend	6	G	4	2	0	0	5,005
Ilovegold	4	G	10	1	1	1	25,599
Ilya Balos	2	C	7	2	1	0	38,880
I'm a Babe	2	F	3	0	0	1	2,011
I'm a Brass Lady	4	F	3	1	0	1	5,331
Im a Brazen Gal	4	F	14	4	3	1	15,776
I'm a Cash Crop	4	F	5	0	0	0	362
I'm a City Boy	3	C	6	0	0	0	228
I'm a City Girl	5	M	7	3	2	1	41,877
I'm a Coin	6	G	6	0	0	0	1,590
I'm a Cool Bull	2	C	5	1	0	1	8,136
I'm a Crafty Gal	4	F	5	0	0	0	1,870
I'm a Cutie	3	F	3	0	0	1	1,650
I'm a Doll Fan	2	F	2	0	0	0	150
I'm a Dominator	5	G	1	0	0	0	105
I'm a Era	3	G	6	0	2	0	5,054
I'm a Fast Cat	3	F	1	0	0	0	0
I'm a Frijole Baby	6	M	10	0	1	2	1,907
I'm a Frisky Devil	2	F	1	1	0	0	5,560
I'm a Gem	3	G	11	1	1	2	12,828
I'm a Goer	3	G	11	1	2	3	59,300
I'm a Happy Gal	5	M	1	0	0	1	1,730
I'm a Kuduza Too	2	F	3	1	0	1	5,560
I'm a Lil Happy	7	G	4	0	0	0	458
I'm a Lil Princess	5	M	5	0	0	0	1,350
I'm a Lil Salty	3	F	5	0	0	1	672
Im a Little Dudett	4	F	3	0	0	0	189
I'm a Little Fool	8	G	1	0	0	0	58
I'm a Little Nasty	4	G	7	0	0	2	5,014
I'm a Lover	5	G	18	0	4	1	7,688
I'm a Lucky Gal	2	F	3	0	0	0	260
I'm a Majek Girl	2	F	2	2	0	0	42,420
I'm a Playboy	8	G	7	0	0	0	476
I'm a Player	4	C	6	0	0	1	3,280
I'm a Rocket Man	4	G	5	0	1	0	1,580
I'm a Royal Pain	2	F	1	0	1	0	2,700
I'm a Sassy Al	4	G	9	1	0	0	11,073
I'm a Shadee Lady	4	F	12	2	1	1	7,585
I'm a Smart Alyk	4	G	6	0	2	1	6,475
I'm a Smarty Pants	9	G	5	0	0	0	1,021
I'm a Soccer Boy	3	G	12	2	0	2	35,509
I'm a Son of a Gun	6	G	10	2	2	3	15,521
I'm a Stinker	7	M	9	0	1	4	4,350
I'm a Stuka	5	G	6	1	1	0	8,929
I'm a Swinging Gal	3	F	4	0	0	0	82
I'm a Thunder Cat	2	G	5	0	1	0	1,744
I'm a Treasure	3	F	9	1	1	1	11,287
I'm a Wild Angel	4	F	9	3	1	2	28,190
I'm Alarming	2	C	1	0	0	0	1,500
I'm All Gold	4	C	2	0	0	0	570
I'm All Gussied Up	2	F	1	0	0	0	105
I'm All Yours	6	G	1	1	0	0	16,200
I'm Already There	2	C	2	0	1	0	1,490
I'm an Awesome Cat	3	C	9	1	2	1	25,311
I'm Angela	3	F	13	3	3	4	54,230
I'm Awesome Again	2	G	6	0	1	2	27,158
I'm Behaving	6	H	7	0	0	0	833
I'm Beyond Belief	6	M	5	0	0	0	420
I'm Blue Too	7	M	9	0	0	1	1,730
I'm Blushing	4	F	4	0	0	0	148
Im Bobby Sox	7	G	20	1	6	3	18,391
I'm Canadian	3	G	11	1	0	2	7,140
I'm Catisfied	3	F	8	2	2	1	7,863
I'm Charismatic	2	G	1	0	0	0	0
I'm Classified	2	F	2	0	0	0	2,135
I'm Concerned	6	G	4	0	0	0	261
I'm Confederate	3	C	6	4	1	0	26,026
I'm Connected	3	F	2	0	0	1	2,320
Im Cooler Than You	6	G	8	2	1	0	8,790
Im Crafty	2	F	2	0	0	0	0
I'm D One	3	G	18	1	2	2	6,873
I'm Dancing	2	F	6	0	0	0	1,370
I'm Due	4	F	14	1	3	1	9,374
I'm Exclusive	2	F	1	0	0	0	700
I'm Fast Too	3	C	2	1	1	0	7,840
Im Five	6	H	14	1	3	0	20,640
I'm for Joey	7	G	10	3	1	0	16,802
I'm Free	5	G	7	0	0	1	10,221
I'm From Texas	4	F	7	0	0	1	1,255
I'm Gonna Tell	3	F	3	0	0	0	0
I'm Hit Sarge	5	G	10	1	1	2	16,400
I'm Home Wrecker	6	M	5	0	0	1	541
I'm Homebound	4	F	12	0	3	4	3,639
I'm Howlin	6	H	9	0	1	1	6,526
I'm in Orbit	3	F	8	1	0	0	5,139
Im in the Soup	2	G	1	0	0	0	237
I'm Indy Red	2	G	2	0	0	0	44
I'm Innocent	4	F	5	0	1	1	1,533
I'm John's Problem	3	G	4	1	0	1	18,570
I'm Just a Peach	6	M	11	2	2	2	36,701
Im Just a Rebel	5	G	2	0	0	0	0
I'm Late	2	G	7	0	1	1	3,400
I'm Leavin Laughin	6	H	1	0	0	0	220
I'm Listed	4	F	11	2	0	7	15,260
I'm Lookin	3	F	3	0	0	0	455
I'm Majestic	5	G	13	3	2	4	37,720
I'm Nelson Black	3	G	4	1	1	0	22,320
I'm No Genius	3	G	3	0	2	0	7,490
I'm No Louie	5	G	13	2	3	1	23,090
I'm No Preppy	3	C	6	0	2	2	16,900
I'm Not Acting	3	G	13	1	2	3	27,320
I'm Not Bluffin	5	G	3	0	1	0	6,138
I'm Not Crazy	5	M	11	1	0	1	6,520
I'm Not Easy	3	F	1	0	0	0	0
I'm Not Posty	4	G	13	0	3	4	12,475
I'm Not Rediculous	4	F	7	0	0	0	573
I'm Not Sure	6	M	8	1	2	3	10,415
I'm Oliver	2	G	1	0	0	0	725
Im On Stilts	4	G	4	0	0	0	418
I'm One Tuff Cat	3	G	11	3	5	0	36,575
Im Poppy's Girl	2	F	1	0	0	0	0
Im Pretty	4	F	3	0	0	0	351
I'm Queen	4	F	1	0	0	0	105
I'm Quicksilver	3	F	4	0	0	0	3,124
Im Ready to Rumble	5	H	6	0	0	0	818
I'm Real	3	G	11	0	1	2	4,289
I'm Registered	7	G	10	1	2	0	9,300
I'm Rockin'	4	C	5	0	0	0	160
I'm Royalty	7	M	7	1	1	2	2,644
I'm Sailing Bye	3	F	4	1	0	1	23,100
I'm Silver Due	6	G	8	0	1	0	7,750
Im Smart Too	7	M	8	0	0	2	4,862
I'm Smitten	3	F	2	0	0	0	0
I'm Smokin	7	G	3	1	0	0	1,300
I'm So Cool	5	H	5	2	2	0	16,220
I'm So Silly	4	G	15	2	1	2	17,034
I'm So Special	8	M	1	0	0	0	0
I'm So Theatrical	5	G	19	1	2	6	15,266
I'm Speechless	3	G	7	5	1	0	152,314
I'm Squirley	9	M	6	0	0	0	320
I'm Stonehearted	3	G	2	0	0	0	82
I'm Suave Two	3	G	14	0	0	0	1,160
I'm Tellin' Ya Now	4	F	7	0	0	1	3,460
I'm the Business (NZ)	6	M	10	1	3	1	66,120
I'm the Coach	2	G	3	0	0	0	1,416
Im the Game	2	G	1	1	0	0	10,584
I'm the Reason	4	G	5	1	0	2	8,230
I'm the Show	5	G	15	0	1	1	4,916
I'm the Tiger	3	G	6	3	2	1	145,591
Im the Voice	2	F	5	1	0	2	13,750
I'm Tommy	3	G	5	0	0	0	158
I'm Tryon	6	G	8	1	0	0	4,140
I'm Ugly But Fast	2	F	5	0	0	1	3,255
I'm Willing	3	G	14	3	1	3	22,780
I'm With Norman	5	M	10	1	0	4	21,328
I'm Your Man	6	G	13	0	0	2	2,810
I'ma a Fax	3	G	11	1	2	1	27,426
Ima Cartwheel	2	F	2	0	0	0	710
Ima Champ	3	F	1	0	0	0	60
Ima Charmer	3	G	2	0	0	0	0
Ima Chukker	2	G	3	1	0	0	8,400

RECORDS OF HORSES

Horse	Age	Sex	Sts	1st	2d	3d	Won
Im'a Consultant	2	C	1	0	0	0	0
Ima Day Trader	4	C	6	2	0	2	3,153
Ima Deer	4	F	3	2	1	0	11,375
Ima Dream Catcher	3	G	24	1	6	6	17,589
Ima Fla Gator	3	C	4	0	3	0	11,140
Ima Fugitive Too	3	C	3	0	0	0	598
Ima Gentleman	3	C	6	0	0	0	0
Ima Gold Nick	4	G	2	0	0	0	0
Ima Grand Gal	7	M	13	1	0	1	2,841
Im'a Grey Prospect	5	M	8	1	0	0	21,990
Ima Gun of a Son	2	G	7	1	1	0	2,640
Ima Halo	7	M	3	0	0	0	881
Ima Jazzy Two	4	G	9	0	0	1	3,150
I'ma Joy	3	F	3	1	0	0	7,200
I'ma Kanu	2	F	4	0	0	0	2,760
Ima Koukla	8	M	11	2	0	3	10,446
Ima Kris S.	4	G	13	1	1	1	4,329
Ima Little Miner	5	G	9	1	0	0	8,014
Ima Little Rose	2	F	5	0	0	0	0
Ima Liva	4	F	3	0	0	0	0
Ima Looker	2	F	1	0	0	0	0
Ima Mermaid Too	2	F	1	0	0	0	0
Ima Mile High Guy	4	G	21	3	0	4	24,193
I'ma Miracle	3	F	8	2	2	0	22,660
Ima Momma's Girl	3	F	8	0	0	1	3,137
Ima Personal Flag	9	H	8	1	4	2	9,415
Ima Reel Bimbo	2	F	4	1	0	1	4,100
I'ma Rose	4	F	4	1	1	2	22,994
Ima Royal Empire	4	C	1	0	0	0	0
I'ma Saint	6	G	3	0	0	0	0
Ima Sassy Lassy	5	M	7	0	0	1	1,920
I'ma Smart Monster	3	F	1	1	0	0	10,200
Ima Smarty Boy	3	G	9	1	4	0	33,274
Ima Snow Man	6	H	3	0	0	0	0
Ima Threat	3	G	4	0	0	0	732
Ima Tornado	4	G	1	0	0	0	0
Ima Valentine	8	M	6	0	2	2	2,807
Ima Zuit Suit Riot	5	G	21	1	6	2	13,601
Imablazinbeauty	3	F	13	6	0	1	73,480
I'mabletoo	6	G	13	2	3	0	12,274
Imabucklite	10	G	9	0	2	0	3,162
Imaburnindaylight	4	C	3	1	1	0	11,215
I'machickeytoo	2	F	3	0	0	0	240
Imaclassy Lassie	3	F	2	0	0	0	330
Imaclown	9	G	3	0	0	0	283
Imacountintime	5	G	14	3	3	1	23,270
I'macraftychoice	2	G	6	1	2	1	9,825
Imadeitmom	3	F	2	0	0	0	0
I'madrifter	5	H	7	2	0	2	132,287
Image	5	G	13	4	2	2	135,224
Image d'Or	4	F	1	0	1	0	1,360
Image Master	3	C	7	0	0	0	35
Image Nation	4	F	6	1	1	0	7,759
Image of a Cat	5	G	9	0	0	1	4,710
Image of a Halo	4	F	16	5	1	2	34,301
Image of Affirmed	10	G	14	3	4	0	26,704
Image of Approval	4	G	11	3	2	0	83,849
Image of War	7	H	2	0	0	0	0
Imagebylamplight	2	F	8	0	2	3	8,030
Imageofanangel	4	F	12	0	0	5	12,791
Imageofhope	4	G	15	1	0	2	16,179
Imagery	3	G	4	0	0	2	10,172
Imaghost	2	C	3	0	1	2	7,880
Imaginary Dream	5	M	6	0	0	0	2,819
Imaginary Image	2	F	2	0	2	0	14,800
Imaginary Man	3	C	4	1	1	0	6,000
Imaginary Sweep	4	C	4	0	0	0	238
Imagine Me	5	H	12	1	0	2	5,102
Imagine Me Now	2	F	2	0	0	0	520
Imagine What	3	G	15	0	1	1	4,845
Imagineering	3	C	5	0	0	0	575
Imagoldseeker	2	F	1	0	0	0	0
Imahoneytoo	2	F	4	1	1	1	13,316
I'mallrightjack	4	C	7	3	2	0	29,460
I'mallwilly	4	G	12	2	5	1	52,480
Imaminister	7	G	10	0	3	1	2,190
Imanasset	2	F	1	0	0	0	150
Imanativeamerican	6	M	6	0	0	0	0
I'maprettyjudge	3	F	6	0	0	1	1,308
Imaprime	4	F	5	1	0	0	3,120
Imarealfancydehere	3	C	9	2	0	2	53,974
Imarock	2	G	1	0	0	0	744
I'maseriviortoo	2	C	1	0	0	0	308
Imasgoodasu	2	G	4	0	1	1	5,560
Imaslewoftrouble	3	F	4	0	0	1	540
I'masmash	4	F	5	0	0	0	0
Imaspeedygirl	4	F	11	2	3	0	21,586
Imastorming	5	M	3	0	1	0	6,000
Imaswingertwo	5	M	3	0	0	0	80
I'mavikingprincess	2	F	1	1	0	0	15,720
Imawahoogirl	5	M	14	0	0	3	5,174
Imawarrior	3	C	2	0	0	0	0
Imawhistlindixie	6	G	4	0	0	0	0
I'mbackinaction	3	F	13	1	1	0	29,840
I'mbethtoo	2	F	2	2	0	0	20,890
Imbrachium	4	F	9	2	3	1	34,163
Imdabossau	2	G	3	1	0	0	3,650
Imezru	2	F	1	0	0	0	120
Imgunabeinpictures	4	F	15	1	2	1	12,945
Imitate	3	C	1	0	0	0	0
Imitation	3	C	3	1	0	1	33,800
Imma Callin	3	F	2	0	0	0	109
Imma Sara	3	F	14	2	1	1	12,011
I'mmeanonthegreen	2	C	1	0	0	0	140
Immediate Chance	5	M	13	2	2	1	15,951
Immediate Reaction	2	C	2	0	0	1	7,195
Immense	2	C	1	0	0	0	0
Immolation	3	C	6	1	0	1	1,240
Immortal Charm	3	F	21	5	0	7	57,675
Immortal Cowgirl	3	F	4	1	1	0	7,164
Immortal Lock	2	C	2	0	1	0	1,080
Immsowaat Naamoo	4	G	12	2	0	1	11,873
I'muchthebest	4	F	4	0	0	0	4,200
Immunity Idol	3	G	12	1	1	1	11,541
Imnojoehernandez	5	M	4	0	1	1	3,375
Imnxcelentdriveray	4	G	10	4	1	2	62,622
Imogene's Sisters	5	M	3	0	0	0	190
Impact Survivor	2	C	4	0	0	2	3,105
Impala	6	H	8	2	0	2	19,036
Impartial Player	4	C	8	0	1	1	2,373
Impassable Gal	7	M	11	1	0	3	27,575
Impatient Michael	6	H	11	0	0	0	431
Impavid	5	G	9	2	0	0	7,416
Impeachable Affair	6	M	2	0	0	0	1,215
Impeachthepro	6	G	9	1	3	2	77,865
Impecable Manners	5	M	3	0	0	0	154
Imperatriz Rafaela (BRZ)	5	M	5	1	1	0	20,620
Imperial Alydeed	2	G	8	2	0	1	86,243
Imperial Caste	4	G	2	0	0	0	174
Imperial Chariot (BRZ)	6	H	10	0	4	2	13,530
Imperial Classic	4	G	9	1	1	2	12,115
Imperial Commander	3	C	4	0	0	1	6,666
Imperial Flight	2	C	5	1	0	0	7,590
Imperial Gold (NZ)	6	G	4	1	0	0	30,000
Imperial Grace	3	F	3	0	0	0	579
Imperial Hunter	3	F	25	2	3	6	31,666
Imperial Ice	4	F	2	0	0	0	0
Imperial King	6	G	6	4	0	0	48,070
Imperial Knight	7	G	13	1	2	0	7,738
Imperial Lady	6	M	8	0	1	0	1,290
Imperial Mistress	5	M	8	1	0	0	5,772
Imperial Orphan	5	G	10	1	0	2	7,459
Imperial Quest	3	C	2	0	0	0	810
Imperial Roger	8	G	8	1	0	1	4,209
Imperial Ruler	2	C	3	0	0	0	0
Imperial Scout	3	G	13	0	1	3	3,281
Imperial Sunrise	3	G	13	1	0	1	6,063
Imperial Sunshine	3	F	1	0	0	0	0
Imperial Theatre (IRE)	4	C	11	1	0	6	43,740
Imperial Wager	5	M	14	0	1	1	4,965
Imperial Warfare	4	G	9	0	1	1	2,661
Imperial Wells	3	C	1	0	0	0	72
Imperial Wind	10	G	8	2	2	1	7,360
Imperialism	2	C	11	3	3	1	74,605
Imperio	3	C	4	1	0	1	23,341
Imperioso	7	G	5	0	1	0	3,960
Impertinent Music	6	M	1	0	0	0	66
Impetuous Bell	3	F	6	0	0	1	1,505

Horse	Age	Sex	Sts	1st	2d	3d	Won
Impetuous Cat	3	F	5	0	1	0	1,219
Impetuous Fling	3	F	13	2	1	0	71,914
Impetuous Leader	3	C	14	1	1	5	11,465
Impetuous Molly	3	F	8	2	1	0	58,700
Impetuous Sea	2	F	1	0	0	0	140
Impetus	3	F	6	1	1	0	38,930
Impishly Devine	3	F	7	0	1	1	2,394
Implication	6	H	2	0	0	0	116
Implicit	3	C	9	3	2	3	81,010
Implicit Advantage	4	C	1	0	0	0	0
Impolite	3	F	14	4	1	2	147,860
Imposing	6	G	12	0	1	2	4,734
Impossible Curfew	3	F	1	0	0	0	960
Impossible Dream	9	G	8	2	1	0	8,027
Imppy	8	M	10	1	2	1	3,807
Impractical	6	M	9	0	0	2	2,398
Impress	3	F	2	0	0	0	300
Impress Me	6	M	6	0	1	0	5,257
Impressionable One	3	F	13	1	4	3	11,245
Impressionist	5	G	5	0	1	0	7,290
Impressive Grades	7	G	3	0	0	1	9,480
Impressive Note	3	F	9	2	1	0	12,625
Impressive One	4	F	1	0	0	0	0
Impressive Soldier	3	C	14	1	4	3	35,510
Impressive Spirit	5	G	8	1	3	0	5,781
Impressive Star	3	F	4	0	2	0	4,795
Impressmebonnie	7	M	3	0	0	0	453
Imprints in Gold	5	G	14	4	4	0	79,765
Improbable Dream	2	G	9	1	0	1	12,440
Impropriety	2	C	4	1	1	0	28,114
Improving Time	4	G	11	1	0	3	11,681
Improvised	3	F	11	3	2	1	46,095
Improviser	4	C	12	3	4	1	38,263
Imp's Extension	7	H	3	0	0	0	300
Impudent	4	G	4	0	0	0	657
Impulsive Bachelor	8	G	11	2	1	1	6,990
Impulsive Gal	2	F	1	1	0	0	4,800
Impulsive Willy	4	F	2	0	0	0	950
Impulsive Russian	7	G	14	2	4	2	14,322
Impute	3	G	4	0	0	0	444
Imputed	5	G	7	0	0	0	284
I'mroyallymecke'd	2	C	2	0	0	0	370
Imski	2	F	4	1	2	0	35,630
Imtheblues	5	M	2	0	0	0	400
I'mthedeal	2	C	3	0	1	0	3,800
Imtheman	4	G	1	0	0	1	1,380
Imus	7	G	11	2	2	1	5,537
Imveryprivate	4	F	3	0	0	1	1,276
Imworthetime	9	G	3	0	1	0	1,260
In a Dither	4	G	7	0	1	3	3,287
In a Flash	5	G	18	2	2	3	9,482
In a Pigs Eye	6	M	4	0	0	2	1,122
In a Romp	3	F	3	0	0	0	0
In a Run	5	G	6	0	2	0	3,236
In a Spin	7	M	1	0	0	0	0
In a Zone	6	G	11	0	1	0	9,400
In Accord	5	M	7	1	0	0	20,510
In Addy Case	2	F	4	0	0	2	12,189
In Barb's Honor	5	G	13	2	1	2	11,945
In Before Dawn	2	F	3	0	0	0	0
In Blazing Time	3	G	8	1	1	0	5,735
In Bocca Al Lupo	2	C	4	0	0	0	125
In C C's Honor	9	G	9	0	1	2	16,070
In Case of Slots	2	C	1	0	0	0	0
In Case of Thunder	3	G	1	0	0	0	0
In Case of Wind	3	F	13	0	4	0	29,537
In Case You Forgot	3	C	4	0	0	0	0
In Case You Win	5	G	7	2	1	2	24,985
In Chamber	5	H	8	1	0	0	4,685
In Charm's Way	2	F	1	0	0	0	145
In Dancing Order	5	M	20	1	4	1	34,464
In Deed a Fashion	6	M	8	0	0	1	2,180
In Defiance	5	M	3	0	0	0	1,266
In Disguise	2	G	2	0	0	0	0
Im Dutch	5	G	4	0	0	0	499
In Every Port	4	G	13	2	1	4	30,860
In Excess Success	3	G	4	0	2	0	7,180
In First Space	2	C	1	0	0	0	0
In Flying Colors	4	F	18	3	5	3	19,415
In Focus	3	F	5	0	0	2	3,130
In Frank's Honor	7	H	7	1	0	2	46,857
In Front	3	F	8	0	2	1	7,102
In Front by Two	9	G	5	0	0	1	2,749
In Front Quality	3	C	4	1	0	0	16,140
In Full Bloom	4	F	6	0	0	0	6,925
In Gold We Trust	3	F	9	0	0	1	1,165
In Hand	3	C	8	2	0	2	85,682
In High Gear	4	C	4	2	0	1	54,970
In Hot Pursuit	4	G	15	3	3	1	48,565
In Kent's Memory	4	G	2	0	0	0	500
In Love	3	F	4	2	1	0	28,020
In Love Again	3	F	7	3	1	0	83,210
In Love With Loot	3	F	8	1	2	0	10,885
In Memoriam	6	G	8	1	0	0	11,465
In Millie's Honor	3	F	10	2	1	3	16,822
In My Dreams	2	F	2	0	0	0	0
In My Footprints	4	F	1	0	0	0	400
In My Prime	5	G	9	1	0	2	17,292
In My Time	3	F	6	1	0	0	24,678
In Need of Reign	4	C	4	0	0	0	300
In One Basket	4	F	7	0	0	1	1,209
In Position	2	F	2	0	0	0	132
In Reverse	4	F	7	0	0	0	0
In Rome	2	F	8	2	1	1	88,740
In Season	6	G	16	6	1	3	111,921
In Secure	3	F	4	3	0	0	92,040
In Shape	4	F	6	0	0	1	2,266
In Spector	5	G	14	1	1	4	7,376
In Spyt of My Ex	6	M	12	3	0	1	33,345
In Stitches	7	H	8	0	1	2	6,037
In the Air	6	H	3	1	0	0	8,700
In the Beat	6	M	7	2	0	0	9,822
In The Box (BRZ)	6	M	6	1	2	1	14,445
In the Clear	4	C	12	3	1	2	57,425
In the Clutch	3	G	2	0	0	1	5,280
In the Crease	2	F	3	0	0	0	450
In the Cups	4	G	7	2	1	1	62,658
In the Facts	4	F	5	3	1	0	10,000
In the Game	4	C	6	1	2	1	7,336
In the Ghetto	3	F	8	1	0	2	22,880
In the Glen	4	F	4	0	1	0	5,460
In the Gray	3	F	10	0	4	4	15,145
In the Lea	5	M	2	1	0	0	18,900
In the Navy	4	F	1	0	0	0	57
In the Park	2	F	1	0	0	0	750
In the Pocket	3	G	14	2	1	2	28,947
In the Shadows	3	F	5	0	0	0	393
In the Show	4	F	15	3	3	1	21,202
In the Teepee	5	G	8	2	1	1	11,932
In the Weeds	2	G	2	1	1	0	17,680
In This Corner	4	F	7	0	0	0	370
In To	4	G	1	0	0	0	0
In too Deep	4	F	8	1	1	2	41,566
In Tune	3	F	6	0	0	1	4,040
In Two Notes	3	F	1	0	0	0	0
In Vogue At Last	3	F	2	0	0	0	115
In Vys'eyes	3	F	13	1	4	3	19,821
In Washington	3	F	12	3	2	1	30,214
In Your Hands	4	F	11	3	0	1	21,832
In Your Thoughts	8	H	2	1	0	0	5,738
Ina Nic of Time	3	F	13	1	3	3	20,380
Inajamma	5	H	3	0	0	0	636
Inajamsam	2	C	4	0	0	2	1,362
Inaki	7	G	1	0	0	0	0
Inamorato	3	C	7	2	0	4	382,078
Inanna	3	F	2	0	0	0	195
Inapinch	3	F	5	1	0	0	7,260
Inarush	3	G	8	0	2	1	13,224
Ina's Gold	6	M	3	0	0	0	280
Inatux	7	H	3	0	0	0	462
Inaugural Address	4	C	2	1	0	0	7,474
Inaugural Warrior	3	G	10	0	0	0	1,000
Inca Colony	8	G	2	1	0	0	9,000
Inca Halo	4	G	11	1	2	1	9,835
Inca Queen	6	M	6	0	1	0	3,510
Inca Storm	2	F	3	0	0	1	5,005
Inca Tupac (ARG)	6	H	7	0	2	0	5,695
Incantation	5	M	2	0	0	0	133

RECORDS OF HORSES

Horse	Age	Sex	Sts	1st	2d	3d	Won
Incase Shebets	4	F	11	1	0	0	4,320
Incased in Gold	6	M	9	2	1	0	12,055
Incaseyouraminer	2	G	6	0	0	0	1,221
Incendio	5	G	8	1	1	3	8,094
Incitatus	7	G	3	0	0	1	1,120
Inciting Prince	5	H	7	0	1	1	3,450
Inclement Weather	3	G	3	1	0	0	2,960
Inclinator	7	G	8	3	0	1	36,300
Income Statement	6	G	14	0	2	4	5,671
Incomplete	2	G	2	0	0	0	0
Incontestable	2	F	1	0	0	0	1,400
Incorrigible	4	G	16	2	2	2	24,350
Incredible Act	3	F	11	2	3	2	20,272
Incredible Bulk	6	H	7	1	1	1	8,711
Incredible Carson	4	G	8	1	0	1	4,195
Incredible Notion	4	F	6	3	2	0	10,192
Incredible Speed	2	G	3	0	0	0	0
Incredible Story	3	F	1	0	0	0	0
Incredible Year	4	F	5	0	0	0	765
Incrediblee	2	G	1	0	0	0	170
Inda Country	5	H	11	0	0	0	1,510
Indecent	3	G	7	2	1	1	10,300
Indeed	4	G	11	4	0	3	31,445
Indeed I Do	6	M	3	1	0	0	7,820
Indefensible	2	F	6	2	0	1	30,120
Indelible Image	2	F	6	1	0	0	18,382
Independent Cuss	3	G	21	2	5	6	15,669
Independent Gal	3	F	6	0	1	1	3,690
Independent Yankee	3	C	1	0	0	0	0
Indi Bimbo	6	G	14	1	1	6	14,043
India Sun	2	C	2	0	0	0	1,350
Indiahoma	9	G	10	0	1	3	24,095
Indian Attack	2	F	3	1	0	0	11,000
Indian Avenue	5	G	10	0	3	1	6,339
Indian Bank	6	H	12	2	2	2	6,399
Indian Blanket	3	F	8	2	2	0	77,020
Indian Card	4	G	15	3	3	3	128,740
Indian Charmer	3	F	11	2	2	1	19,095
Indian City	4	C	2	0	0	0	106
Indian Crusader	3	C	7	1	2	0	11,220
Indian Dan	5	G	4	0	1	1	5,534
Indian Dreamer	3	F	14	2	2	2	34,985
Indian Express	3	C	3	0	1	0	154,842
Indian Fight	3	F	8	1	0	1	12,097
Indian Game	2	C	7	1	0	0	24,177
Indian George	4	C	8	0	1	3	2,776
Indian Ground	4	C	8	2	0	1	37,366
Indian Hemp	5	H	4	0	0	3	1,496
Indian Hula	5	M	6	0	0	2	1,431
Indian Jewel	2	F	4	1	0	1	21,520
Indian Jo	5	G	8	1	0	0	6,068
Indian Love Song	6	M	2	0	0	0	0
Indian Miss	4	F	7	0	1	2	6,920
Indian Money	4	C	6	0	0	0	690
Indian Moonlight	3	F	12	0	2	1	8,255
Indian Mound	6	G	10	0	0	1	2,534
Indian Music	4	F	15	0	1	3	7,051
Indian Outlaw	2	C	1	0	0	0	175
Indian Penny	3	F	2	0	1	1	8,246
Indian Plume (GB)	7	G	3	0	0	1	11,385
Indian Point	3	F	11	0	1	0	2,773
Indian Pony	5	M	3	0	0	0	100
Indian Prospector	2	C	6	0	1	1	9,625
Indian Renegade	3	C	7	0	0	1	2,300
Indian Rhythm	3	C	4	0	0	0	1,090
Indian Ruler	3	C	8	0	0	0	204
Indian Run	3	C	3	0	0	0	320
Indian Starlet	3	F	13	1	2	1	11,354
Indian Style	8	G	2	0	0	0	0
Indian Sully	3	C	1	0	0	0	340
Indian Tango	2	F	3	0	0	1	4,340
Indian Territory	5	H	7	2	1	2	25,030
Indian Trouble	7	G	11	1	2	2	40,959
Indian Village	2	C	3	0	0	0	0
Indian War Dance	2	C	5	1	0	0	15,780
Indian Wells	8	G	3	0	0	0	42
Indian Willow	3	F	3	0	1	0	4,830
Indian Woman	3	F	1	0	0	0	729
Indiana Affair	6	G	16	0	3	0	5,161
Indiana Bobby	4	F	5	0	0	0	153
Indiana Charlie	2	G	3	0	0	0	2,160
Indiana Classic	2	G	6	0	0	0	1,194
Indiana Dad	6	M	6	0	0	1	3,274
Indiana Express	3	C	6	1	1	0	19,256
Indiana Flyer	5	H	8	0	0	0	449
Indiana Knight	4	C	3	0	0	0	540
Indiana Pete	4	G	6	0	1	3	2,040
Indiana Royale	7	G	12	1	1	2	6,273
Indiana Susie	6	M	7	0	0	1	963
Indianazona	5	G	3	0	0	0	0
Indians Melody	2	F	2	0	0	0	390
Indian'sarecoming	3	F	4	0	1	0	4,623
Indiansong	2	F	1	0	0	1	2,145
Indiantown Jones	4	G	7	0	1	2	12,220
Indigo Flyer	2	G	1	0	0	0	130
Indigo Myth	6	G	11	2	1	1	26,439
Indio Memo	2	G	2	0	0	0	0
Indio Red	3	G	6	0	1	2	8,175
Indirect Kick	4	G	11	1	1	1	15,640
Indispensable	9	G	9	1	2	1	56,818
Indisputable	9	H	1	0	0	0	36
Individual Star	3	F	9	0	2	0	3,528
Indivisible	4	C	10	2	2	0	50,760
Indixie	5	G	9	2	2	1	15,165
Indochina	2	F	1	0	0	0	145
Indomable	11	G	13	1	3	2	5,680
Indoor Games	7	G	8	1	1	2	4,360
Indougherty'shonor	4	G	10	2	2	2	22,545
Induction Day	6	G	13	1	2	2	8,514
Indy	2	C	4	0	0	0	7,395
Indy Afterglow	2	F	6	1	0	0	8,010
Indy Aly Style	4	F	1	0	0	0	57
Indy Annie	6	M	4	1	0	2	3,148
Indy Blues	3	G	3	0	0	0	180
Indy Buff	2	F	1	0	0	0	0
Indy Charmer	2	F	4	0	1	1	15,640
Indy Dancer	3	C	5	1	0	1	121,900
Indy Energy	4	G	12	1	2	2	37,496
Indy Fire	3	F	8	1	1	1	32,300
Indy Five Hundred	3	F	7	2	1	0	206,400
Indy Flag	3	C	2	0	0	1	5,980
Indy Glory	5	M	2	1	1	0	45,600
Indy Lady	5	M	7	0	0	0	546
Indy Lead	5	H	10	1	2	1	95,163
Indy Love	3	G	14	3	0	3	53,790
Indy Magic	5	M	11	2	6	3	44,730
Indy Man	6	G	2	0	0	0	120
Indy Outlaw	3	G	7	0	0	0	517
Indy Red	3	G	8	2	0	0	16,212
Indy Rhythm	2	F	2	0	0	0	95
Indy Rock	3	G	5	0	0	0	361
Indy Snow (GB)	2	C	2	0	0	0	0
Indy Stars	5	M	11	0	1	1	3,967
Indy Stormy	3	F	2	0	0	0	300
Indy Thunder	3	C	1	0	1	0	5,000
Indy Zone	3	C	3	0	0	0	60
Indydar's Race Car	2	F	4	0	0	1	1,160
Indydar's Sassy	5	M	1	0	0	0	0
Indygo	3	F	12	2	0	2	13,117
Indygo Shiner	5	H	1	0	0	0	420
Indy's Anna	4	F	8	0	0	0	4,110
Indy's Treasure	3	C	5	0	0	0	2,050
Inebriated	5	G	5	0	0	0	505
Inesperado (FR)	4	C	3	0	2	0	46,295
Inevitable Impact	4	C	7	1	2	2	22,035
Inexcessive Play	3	F	6	1	0	3	90,412
Inexhaustible	5	M	2	0	0	0	0
Inez's Delight	5	M	6	2	0	0	10,205
Infant Mystic	7	H	3	0	0	0	0
Infantry Liz	6	M	9	0	2	0	8,503
Infantry Man	4	C	5	1	0	0	7,070
Infernal McGoon	4	F	8	3	0	4	120,060
Infiltrator	6	H	8	3	1	0	81,080
Infinate Star	3	G	10	3	1	1	22,257
Infinite (ARG)	6	G	4	0	0	1	1,430
Infinite Faith	5	G	8	1	2	2	63,980
Infinite Freedom	3	F	2	0	0	0	233
Infinite Glory	2	C	7	2	0	1	34,890

Horse	Age	Sex	Sts	1st	2d	3d	Won
Infinite Justice	3	G	5	1	0	0	39,870
Infinite Miracle	3	C	1	0	0	0	0
Infinite North	3	C	8	1	1	0	6,808
Infinite Series	5	M	7	1	0	2	2,149
Infinitely Greedy	3	F	6	1	0	1	21,130
Inflammatory	2	F	1	0	0	0	150
Influenza	7	H	2	0	0	0	300
Inforaprettypenny	7	M	1	0	1	0	1,927
Inform	2	C	6	1	1	1	25,480
Informacion	4	F	5	1	0	0	8,876
Informality	3	F	9	0	2	1	2,840
Ing Ing (FR)	5	M	3	0	0	1	7,450
Ingenious (IRE)	7	G	14	1	2	4	12,989
Ingenius	8	G	17	2	3	4	38,030
Ingenuity	2	G	4	0	1	1	3,565
Ingenuous	3	F	10	1	1	4	12,178
Ingles	3	C	9	2	0	1	4,606
Ingredients	5	M	1	0	0	0	40
Inherent Gem	4	F	13	0	0	4	9,382
Inherimage	3	F	13	0	0	1	9,007
Inherit the Brass	3	F	4	0	2	1	4,821
Inherit the Torch	3	F	1	0	0	0	0
Inis	4	F	14	1	3	3	37,677
Inish Glora	5	M	6	3	1	1	359,667
Initial Approach	2	F	1	1	0	0	18,840
Initjustforfun	3	C	9	0	0	0	371
Injunear	3	C	4	0	1	0	5,090
Injustice	2	F	3	1	1	0	9,800
Ink Grimsley	2	C	2	0	0	0	235
Ink Jet	5	G	9	1	2	3	22,629
Ink Power	4	C	8	0	0	1	1,615
Inky Lawson	5	G	9	2	1	0	19,820
Inky Racer	7	G	13	0	0	3	3,914
Inlet	2	F	2	0	0	0	1,850
Inlineatthebank	4	F	4	0	0	0	0
Inlovewiththesport	11	G	5	0	1	2	1,161
Inmate	2	C	4	0	1	0	2,100
Innate	7	G	3	0	0	0	0
Inner Command	4	C	2	0	0	0	180
Inner Drive	3	F	4	0	0	0	0
Inner Glow	3	F	1	0	0	0	160
Inner Harbour	6	H	6	2	1	0	54,318
Inner Sanctum	2	C	1	0	1	0	6,000
Inner Spirit	3	F	2	0	0	0	0
Inner Thoughts	3	F	4	1	0	0	10,800
Innisfree Margaret	5	M	4	0	0	0	1,956
Innisfree Petite	4	F	1	0	0	0	0
Innit (IRE)	5	M	6	0	0	0	0
Innocent Gent	4	G	15	4	0	1	24,200
Innocent Kiss (BRZ)	5	M	3	0	0	0	875
Innocent Man	3	C	3	0	1	0	5,040
Innocent Remark	5	M	7	0	2	1	13,285
Innocent Within	4	C	9	1	0	0	3,351
Innovation	3	C	10	0	0	1	7,044
Innseattle	2	F	2	0	0	0	2,624
Inod	4	G	6	2	1	2	16,370
Inojay	3	G	3	0	0	0	0
Inox (ARG)	5	M	6	2	1	1	49,886
Inpassabull	3	F	5	0	1	1	916
Inpirer	6	H	2	0	0	0	0
Inquiring Picture	2	F	3	0	0	0	0
Inquisitive Flirt	2	F	4	1	0	0	13,300
Insane	3	G	13	5	3	2	21,778
Insanity Defense	3	C	9	0	3	0	18,000
Insatiable Sis	5	M	14	1	1	0	6,542
Inscribed	3	G	2	1	0	0	30,180
Inside America	5	H	1	0	0	0	0
Inside Pitch	3	G	8	3	1	1	53,055
Inside Tip	3	G	10	0	0	1	3,839
Inside Trader	4	G	12	0	1	0	2,113
Insidious Lass	4	F	7	2	1	0	37,147
Insinger	7	H	8	2	2	1	28,535
Insouciant	3	F	3	0	0	0	120
Inspector Tennison	4	F	1	0	0	0	76
Inspirational Kris	3	F	17	0	5	2	30,405
Inspire	3	F	3	0	0	0	300
Inspired Angel	2	F	1	0	0	0	0
Inspired Buck	5	H	1	0	0	0	91
Inspired Call	7	G	1	0	0	0	0
Inspired Delight	4	F	14	1	0	3	7,927
Inspired Magic	2	F	4	1	0	0	36,976
Inspired Purpose	3	G	9	2	1	0	40,417
Inspired Verse Won	4	F	10	0	2	1	3,230
Inspiring Alf	2	G	8	1	2	2	14,024
Inspiring Miss	2	F	4	2	0	2	28,755
Inspiring Year	7	G	1	0	0	0	700
Inspiteofitall	5	G	8	0	0	0	3,662
Instant Equity	4	G	1	0	0	0	0
Instant Glow	2	G	2	1	0	0	14,868
Instant Heat	4	G	3	0	0	0	207
Instant Integrity	4	F	3	0	0	1	1,148
Instant Karma	5	H	12	4	3	1	31,489
Instant Message	5	G	9	2	1	3	9,247
Instant Miracle	5	M	3	0	1	0	2,289
Instant Mocha	4	G	14	1	3	3	29,813
Instant Punch	5	H	7	0	0	1	1,170
Instant Reward	7	M	11	3	1	3	30,108
Instantly	3	G	8	2	2	1	17,282
Instead of Red	2	G	1	0	0	0	0
Instigator One	3	G	11	1	0	2	6,632
Instinctif (ARG)	3	C	4	0	0	0	0
Instructor	3	F	4	2	0	0	23,760
Instrument Flight	2	F	3	0	0	0	651
Insufficient Funds	3	F	4	0	1	0	3,180
Insumiso	2	C	1	0	0	0	0
Insurance Scam	7	M	10	2	1	2	5,235
Intact	4	G	9	1	0	3	12,726
Integer	3	C	6	0	0	1	5,790
Integral	3	G	13	1	2	4	34,450
Integrity	6	G	13	2	2	2	11,140
Intelligence	3	C	4	0	1	1	6,970
Intelligent Male	3	G	8	0	4	0	36,995
Intemperate	3	C	5	1	0	0	13,360
Intemporal (ARG)	5	H	1	0	0	0	1,000
Intense Moment	2	C	2	0	1	0	8,580
Intense Motion	2	G	5	0	0	1	1,300
Intense Paces	4	F	8	2	2	0	17,080
Intense Strike	6	H	8	1	0	1	5,245
Intense Thunder	3	F	4	0	1	0	3,040
Intensive Dancer	3	C	10	1	0	1	16,225
Intensive Invader	4	G	9	1	1	2	13,123
Intentional Winner	9	G	20	2	4	3	11,592
Inter Galactic	2	F	1	0	0	0	0
Inter Inter (ARG)	7	G	5	0	0	0	950
Interbell (ARG)	5	H	5	0	0	0	1,667
Intercosproblem	6	G	3	2	0	0	9,730
Interdigital	5	G	20	1	2	3	23,026
Interest Free	3	G	6	0	0	0	950
Interest Only	5	M	1	0	0	0	0
Interesting Man	2	C	5	0	0	0	0
Interesting Talk	3	F	3	0	0	0	200
Interior Decorator	5	M	9	0	0	0	803
Interlink	3	F	3	0	1	1	9,120
Interloper	3	C	3	0	0	0	1,520
Interlude	4	F	4	0	1	0	3,220
Intern	7	H	7	1	2	1	52,338
Internal Force	6	H	1	0	0	0	0
Internal Revenue	4	G	20	2	0	4	15,835
International City	4	F	13	1	3	3	37,896
Internet Boy (ARG)	4	C	2	1	0	0	10,170
Internet Bubble	3	G	11	1	0	3	9,542
Interpelador (ARG)	5	G	5	0	0	1	3,850
Intersection	2	G	4	1	0	0	3,141
Interspace	3	G	2	0	0	0	75
Intertwining	5	G	19	3	0	6	23,836
Intervene	3	C	13	5	2	2	47,588
Interway	4	G	3	0	0	0	781
Interwoven	3	C	2	0	0	2	9,080
Intheblack	8	G	4	0	0	0	0
Intheeventofafire	6	H	2	0	0	1	1,418
Inthefastlanejerod	4	C	13	0	2	3	17,946
Inthejailhousenow	3	F	1	0	0	0	750
Inthemeantime	5	M	4	1	1	1	8,308
Intheslickoftime	4	G	12	2	3	0	26,704
Inthetwilightzone	4	F	4	0	0	0	250
Inthreequartertime	2	C	1	0	0	0	105
Inti Raymi	5	G	13	2	4	2	21,160
Inticing Dancer	6	M	14	1	2	5	13,744

RECORDS OF HORSES

Horse	Age	Sex	Sts	1st	2d	3d	Won
Intimate Affair	4	F	3	0	0	0	0
Intimate Deelite	4	F	2	0	0	0	0
Intimate Encounter	6	M	8	0	0	0	840
Intimate Music	5	M	12	3	2	2	40,394
Intimate Terms	2	G	5	0	0	0	0
Intimately	2	F	1	0	0	0	720
Into Blue	6	M	1	0	0	0	0
Into the Dawn	3	G	10	0	2	0	24,805
Into the Mystic	3	F	6	1	2	0	12,874
Intore	4	G	11	2	2	1	26,509
Intothefuture	6	G	12	0	1	0	1,728
Intoxicant	8	M	2	0	0	0	170
Intoxicatedwildcat	3	G	11	0	1	1	2,483
Intoxication	3	F	4	0	0	0	370
Intoyourblues	5	M	7	0	2	1	36,960
Intractabie	3	F	14	2	3	1	43,879
Intrepid Gem	3	F	6	1	0	0	6,550
Intrepid Glory (BRZ)	6	H	1	0	0	0	0
Intrepid Jimmy	5	G	4	0	0	1	793
Intrepid John	2	C	5	0	1	0	7,760
Intricate	4	F	3	1	0	0	39,000
Intriguing Picture	4	F	5	1	1	0	4,812
Intrinsic Danielle	3	C	8	0	1	1	9,443
Intrinsic Worth	2	C	5	1	0	3	31,900
Introduce a Winner	3	F	9	1	1	2	11,355
Introducer	5	M	8	3	1	1	52,260
Introspect	3	C	8	3	0	3	94,885
Intuit	3	G	7	0	3	0	19,440
Intuitional	2	F	5	2	1	2	63,100
Intuitive Miss	4	F	2	1	0	0	3,598
Intuitive Storm	3	F	13	0	0	0	2,660
Inty Binty	6	M	8	0	0	3	14,160
Inuksuk	3	G	9	0	0	0	4,112
Invaded	5	G	15	0	3	1	5,438
Invader	3	F	9	2	1	2	52,990
Invaderfromtheeast	3	G	11	2	1	0	27,383
Invadersirishdream	8	M	3	0	0	0	132
Invalidate	2	F	4	0	1	0	3,895
Invent	4	C	12	2	2	3	65,780
Invergordon (GB)	8	G	7	0	1	1	2,935
Invest the Money	3	F	2	0	1	0	1,900
Invest West	8	G	1	0	0	0	0
Investinthefuture	5	M	10	1	0	0	6,020
Investor's Dream (BRZ)	5	H	6	0	0	2	22,541
Invincible Flight	3	G	20	2	1	3	17,406
Invincible Native	7	M	11	0	1	0	2,080
Invincible Vince	4	C	7	0	1	4	7,206
Invisible Ghost	3	C	3	1	0	0	11,805
Invocador (ARG)	5	G	5	1	1	0	40,200
Invocation	3	G	9	0	0	0	1,607
Invoice	8	M	7	0	1	0	3,109
Involvement	3	C	8	0	1	2	19,140
Inward Pike	7	H	12	1	5	0	6,830
Inwood	8	G	6	0	0	1	2,286
Inwood Home	3	G	13	2	0	2	27,150
Iny Belle	4	F	6	2	0	0	14,400
Inyourface	8	G	3	0	1	1	1,350
Iobelle	3	F	2	0	0	0	0
Iodized	3	C	2	0	0	0	120
Ionia	3	F	5	1	0	1	34,430
Ionix	5	M	12	2	3	1	8,125
Ionize	3	G	2	0	0	0	355
Ionizer	6	M	2	0	1	1	2,200
Ionlyhaveyesforyou	6	H	11	0	0	1	2,171
Ionlytango	3	F	7	1	0	0	3,883
Ionosphere	3	G	10	2	1	2	16,500
Ioskeha	3	C	6	1	0	0	11,259
Iota	4	F	13	1	0	4	33,600
Iowa Rocks	2	G	2	0	0	0	0
Iowa's Image	4	F	5	1	0	0	12,970
Ioya Forever	4	F	7	1	0	1	33,020
Ipapa Itsit	4	C	7	0	1	0	7,500
Iphicles	3	G	5	0	0	0	360
Ipi Tombe (ZIM)	5	M	4	4	0	0	1,416,273
Ipi'ko	4	C	5	0	1	0	2,761
Ippodamia	4	F	9	3	3	0	34,045
Ireland's Eye	3	C	3	0	0	1	4,075
Irenes' Song	2	C	2	0	0	1	3,920
Irestmycase	3	G	9	1	1	4	18,800

Horse	Age	Sex	Sts	1st	2d	3d	Won
Ireta	3	F	5	1	0	1	4,644
Irgee	5	G	13	1	0	2	5,486
Irgunette	4	F	12	5	3	1	46,890
Irgunomic	5	G	3	0	0	0	1,380
Irgun's Trial	5	M	10	3	3	0	21,327
Iridium	6	G	4	0	0	0	2,900
Irie Justice	5	G	10	1	1	2	22,860
Irie Sensation	3	G	13	1	1	2	19,541
Irina	5	M	18	4	1	1	27,671
Iris Road	6	G	8	0	1	0	2,342
Irish Account	4	G	11	0	3	3	11,755
Irish Acres	2	F	5	1	1	1	9,030
Irish Actor	3	G	9	0	1	3	17,160
Irish All the Way	2	G	5	0	1	0	1,900
Irish Ann	4	F	6	1	1	2	29,260
Irish Apple	3	C	18	3	4	6	26,216
Irish Bacon	10	G	13	4	0	0	24,380
Irish Baroness	2	F	9	1	1	1	21,565
Irish Blazer	3	G	5	1	0	1	5,615
Irish Blue Star	3	C	4	0	0	0	248
Irish Blues Singer	3	F	3	0	0	0	222
Irish Bob	3	G	5	2	1	1	5,785
Irish Boots	5	G	1	0	0	0	62
Irish Boots	3	C	3	1	0	0	21,170
Irish Breakfast	4	F	7	2	0	2	16,599
Irish Breeze	2	C	2	1	0	0	6,630
Irish Buddy	5	G	5	0	0	1	998
Irish Colonial	4	C	5	2	0	0	96,960
Irish Colony	3	G	14	7	2	0	104,255
Irish Concept	2	F	3	0	0	0	240
Irish Cream Taffy	6	G	9	3	2	0	36,840
Irish Crystal	4	F	4	3	0	0	34,500
Irish Custom	3	G	4	1	0	0	1,085
Irish Dart	3	F	12	0	3	3	9,370
Irish Dave	2	C	3	1	0	0	19,268
Irish Dawn	6	G	9	0	1	0	1,479
Irish Day	3	F	8	1	2	2	13,580
Irish de Slew	2	G	7	1	2	1	15,600
Irish Decision	4	C	16	1	1	2	20,039
Irish Decor	7	H	6	1	1	2	13,795
Irish Dove	3	F	11	0	0	1	1,644
Irish Dowry	5	M	5	1	0	0	4,550
Irish Duke	3	C	4	0	0	0	0
Irish Eh	4	G	12	1	1	3	29,398
Irish Emblem	2	G	4	0	0	0	125
Irish Emily	3	F	6	0	1	0	1,749
Irish Femme	3	F	6	3	0	1	29,230
Irish Flash	3	F	13	0	3	1	4,320
Irish Flight	5	M	1	0	0	0	124
Irish Flyer	5	M	7	1	1	2	20,497
Irish Freckles	2	F	4	2	0	2	21,185
Irish Frolic	2	F	4	0	0	0	868
Irish Futures	4	G	7	0	0	0	0
Irish Gale	2	C	3	1	0	0	3,540
Irish Gambler	3	C	3	0	0	2	5,280
Irish Gato	2	G	3	1	1	0	9,717
Irish Ginger	5	M	12	2	3	0	17,854
Irish Glory	4	F	9	2	1	1	64,420
Irish Gulch	6	G	2	0	0	1	440
Irish Honor	2	G	1	1	0	0	8,350
Irish Horn	7	M	2	0	0	0	0
Irish Ides	2	F	2	2	0	0	38,500
Irish Imp	3	F	4	0	1	2	3,968
Irish Intrigue	4	F	8	2	3	0	21,929
Irish Jet	2	F	6	0	0	2	2,308
Irish Jinks	6	G	9	4	1	1	52,799
Irish Jules	5	M	5	0	0	0	2,940
Irish Katie	6	M	11	0	1	2	7,640
Irish King	4	G	15	1	2	3	8,689
Irish Laddie	2	G	9	0	2	3	22,900
Irish Lake	8	G	8	1	0	1	3,204
Irish Laughter	3	G	11	1	2	0	48,440
Irish Legacy	4	G	7	2	1	0	23,545
Irish Legend	8	G	13	2	3	1	12,273
Irish Line	4	F	13	0	0	1	13,576
Irish Love	9	G	11	1	1	3	9,085
Irish Madam	4	F	9	0	0	2	1,744
Irish Magic	4	F	14	0	0	4	7,857
Irish Mat	4	G	3	0	0	0	0

Horse	Age	Sex	Sts	1st	2d	3d	Won
Irish Mettle	5	H	14	4	3	2	34,105
Irish Mick	4	G	15	1	1	0	4,844
Irish Milligan	4	G	17	5	2	6	46,142
Irish Miner	3	G	5	0	2	1	9,980
Irish Mountain	3	G	8	0	1	0	3,577
Irish 'n Stride	3	C	2	1	1	0	19,060
Irish Nip	7	G	12	0	2	1	24,130
Irish of Dobbin	3	F	13	3	3	1	32,460
Irish Opinion	6	G	11	0	4	2	31,075
Irish Pagan	3	F	11	2	2	1	18,791
Irish Pal	5	G	2	0	0	1	450
Irish Pidgeon	6	G	17	3	1	1	17,938
Irish Playmate	4	F	12	2	5	0	12,305
Irish Pleasure	5	G	11	2	2	2	53,372
Irish Power	4	C	1	0	0	0	0
Irish Prediction	3	F	7	1	0	0	4,757
Irish Princess	4	F	5	0	1	2	25,401
Irish Punch	4	F	12	1	3	0	11,155
Irish Quality	2	C	2	0	0	0	2,580
Irish Rail	4	F	9	1	1	0	41,920
Irish Rain	3	F	1	0	0	0	0
Irish Reb	6	M	2	0	0	0	137
Irish Rebel	5	H	9	0	0	0	1,613
Irish Red	2	C	1	0	0	0	230
Irish Rican	3	C	3	0	0	1	832
Irish Road	5	C	5	3	1	0	93,600
Irish Rogue	5	G	12	1	2	1	18,160
Irish Rooster	3	G	12	1	0	1	4,931
Irish Rope	4	G	9	1	1	1	7,303
Irish Ruckus	2	C	1	0	0	0	0
Irish Shots	5	H	19	1	1	3	3,371
Irish Silence	9	G	9	1	2	3	22,136
Irish Slew	4	F	11	3	3	3	41,650
Irish Slice	3	F	4	0	0	0	901
Irish Sound	6	H	5	0	1	1	1,784
Irish Sovereign	3	F	2	1	0	0	9,772
Irish Special	5	M	3	0	0	0	202
Irish Spin	5	F	14	2	1	4	50,130
Irish Statesman	3	G	12	1	2	3	18,284
Irish Step	3	G	4	0	0	0	2,250
Irish Storm	4	G	17	4	1	0	31,906
Irish Sunset	5	M	3	0	0	1	1,922
Irish Sunshine	7	M	7	0	0	1	1,080
Irish Sweep	4	G	16	2	2	4	33,440
Irish Teddy	5	M	6	0	1	1	2,550
Irish Terror	8	G	4	0	0	0	110
Irish Terry	4	G	4	0	0	0	136
Irish Tournament	2	G	5	1	0	0	9,900
Irish Trail (IRE)	4	G	4	1	0	0	17,130
Irish Treasure	3	C	3	1	0	0	4,620
Irish Tribute	4	G	8	2	1	2	17,525
Irish Vale (GB)	4	G	16	0	2	0	8,260
Irish Victory	3	G	11	1	0	1	3,472
Irish Viking	4	G	13	2	4	1	11,739
Irish Vixen	7	M	2	0	0	1	425
Irish Wager	4	G	12	2	0	5	90,609
Irish Warning	3	G	8	4	0	0	40,710
Irish Warrior	5	H	10	2	3	4	500,300
Irish Ways (IRE)	6	H	2	0	0	0	257
Irish Will	3	G	6	0	0	0	176
Irish Wind	2	C	8	0	1	2	7,790
Irish Wit	4	F	1	0	0	0	0
Irish Zippin Zel	3	G	8	2	1	4	38,440
Irisheyesareflying	7	H	2	0	0	0	4,780
Irishman	4	G	7	1	1	2	7,978
Irishskysarsmiling	2	C	1	0	0	0	360
Iris's Pie	7	H	4	0	0	0	294
Irma La Douce	3	F	6	0	1	1	5,062
Irmadohomemra	4	F	2	0	0	0	4,140
Irmaran	6	G	2	0	0	0	1,116
Iroc Street Jive	3	G	12	0	3	0	2,360
Irockdasauce	2	G	7	2	0	1	34,055
Irocksilver	4	G	7	1	2	1	12,020
Iron Ace	2	C	2	0	0	1	930
Iron Action	4	G	9	2	0	3	28,244
Iron Bison	2	G	3	2	1	0	31,400
Iron Bruce	3	C	4	0	1	1	1,100
Iron Cap	4	C	9	0	1	0	3,603
Iron Chancellor	6	G	6	1	2	1	62,589
Iron Charlie	4	G	3	0	0	1	1,665
Iron Clad Proof	5	M	17	2	0	2	17,468
Iron Classic	3	F	2	0	0	0	88
Iron Cloud	5	G	19	2	2	4	17,583
Iron Cop	8	H	1	0	0	0	55
Iron County Xmas	9	G	8	1	1	2	30,350
Iron Deputy	4	C	5	2	0	1	238,620
Iron Dragon	2	G	8	1	2	0	17,960
Iron Eagle	5	H	11	0	1	1	1,065
Iron Expectations	2	C	7	2	2	0	59,500
Iron Fantasy	9	G	15	1	0	3	9,901
Iron General	3	G	6	1	1	0	10,522
Iron Halo (ARG)	4	C	2	0	0	0	1,160
Iron Head	5	G	4	0	0	0	1,298
Iron Hill	3	G	15	1	4	3	18,775
Iron Hold	2	G	5	0	0	0	0
Iron Jaw	3	G	4	0	0	0	110
Iron King	5	G	11	0	0	1	1,650
Iron Kitten	3	F	6	0	0	1	1,632
Iron Lad (IRE)	3	C	4	0	0	0	1,040
Iron Madonna	3	F	14	2	1	2	20,180
Iron Maiden Too	3	F	14	1	2	5	14,284
Iron Monkey	4	C	1	1	0	0	4,500
Iron Mountain	2	C	1	0	0	0	145
Iron Orebid	7	G	1	1	0	0	9,000
Iron Pepper	3	F	2	0	0	2	3,388
Iron Post	10	G	6	0	1	2	2,434
Iron Power	3	F	4	1	0	1	4,340
Iron Prince	7	G	7	1	0	0	6,090
Iron Prospect	9	H	13	0	1	1	6,335
Iron Pyrite	7	H	12	2	2	0	11,969
Iron Rae	2	G	1	1	0	0	9,300
Iron Reality	4	F	2	0	0	0	53
Iron Relic	4	C	8	0	0	1	952
Iron Rogue	2	C	4	1	1	2	44,275
Iron Sailor	7	H	2	0	0	0	0
Iron Tiger	3	C	1	0	0	0	11,400
Iron Top	4	G	10	1	2	0	38,605
Iron Woodman	7	H	2	0	0	0	0
Irona	4	F	16	0	2	2	5,051
Irongray	3	G	1	0	0	0	0
Ironic Twist	4	C	1	0	0	0	101
Ironman Dehere	5	H	6	0	1	0	8,530
Ironton	3	C	9	2	2	1	94,134
Irony	3	G	5	1	3	0	18,100
Irony of Fate	5	M	7	0	0	0	820
Irrawaddy	3	C	6	0	1	0	13,080
Irrepressible Joy	4	F	8	2	0	2	10,507
Irrepressiblespeed	2	F	2	0	0	0	3,250
Irresistable You	3	F	8	1	2	0	15,962
Irresistible	3	F	8	0	1	0	11,425
Irrestible Force	5	G	18	1	5	1	13,259
Irrevocable	2	F	1	0	0	0	0
Irule	3	G	13	1	2	3	16,378
Iruntheshow	9	G	6	0	0	0	664
Irvington (IRE)	5	H	13	2	2	3	19,146
I's a Fact	2	F	3	0	1	0	10,925
Is Faaaast	4	F	8	0	2	2	7,195
Is It Bold	7	G	12	3	2	3	24,665
Is It Gold	3	F	8	2	2	2	20,810
Is It Peggy Or Sue	4	F	11	1	2	0	21,750
Is It Soup Yet	3	G	9	1	2	2	26,840
Is It True Mex	7	G	10	0	2	3	34,620
Is Kylie Good	3	F	3	0	0	0	2,240
Is That So	6	G	3	0	0	0	237
Is That You	4	F	13	1	2	1	29,110
Is This Heaven	3	F	3	2	0	0	8,362
Isa Nuisance	7	M	2	0	0	1	998
Isabarry	9	G	1	0	0	0	0
Isabel Isabel	3	F	3	0	0	1	1,680
Isabelita Lass	7	M	1	0	0	0	0
Isabella On Line	3	F	1	0	0	0	140
Isabella Victoria	7	M	10	3	3	0	13,394
Isabel's Dance	2	F	1	0	0	0	0
Isabel's Pride	4	F	12	1	0	3	10,990
Isaiah	4	G	9	2	1	1	11,101
Isawthelight	4	F	12	1	7	1	19,202
Isbon	2	G	3	0	1	0	6,750
Iseeyoubaby	3	G	20	2	0	5	12,821

RECORDS OF HORSES

Horse	Age	Sex	Sts	1st	2d	3d	Won
Iseult	4	F	1	0	0	0	0
Ish Ar	5	H	1	0	0	0	0
Ishkoodah	3	G	10	0	4	0	7,200
Ishudbdone	2	C	1	0	0	0	0
Ishwar	5	G	7	1	0	0	13,096
Isis Aire	3	F	3	0	0	0	0
Isit Still Legal	3	F	6	0	2	2	46,458
Isitdustybackthere	2	C	2	1	0	0	5,700
Isitever	7	H	10	0	1	1	3,231
Iskendarian	6	G	12	1	0	2	1,521
Isla	3	F	7	1	0	2	9,105
Islamorada	3	F	2	0	0	0	160
Island Banking	13	G	7	0	0	1	1,023
Island Brite	2	F	6	1	2	0	7,462
Island Caper	10	G	8	1	1	1	6,470
Island Charm	2	C	3	0	0	1	7,000
Island Chief	2	G	3	0	0	0	1,580
Island City	5	H	2	0	0	1	432
Island Dancer	4	C	7	1	1	1	10,179
Island Dawn	5	M	12	0	2	1	3,429
Island Delight	4	F	7	0	0	0	1,500
Island Deva	3	F	9	0	1	1	2,510
Island Doll	3	F	8	0	0	0	2,325
Island Dynamo	4	G	8	2	1	3	17,684
Island Express	5	H	5	3	0	1	22,934
Island Fashion	3	F	10	4	1	0	1,112,970
Island Getaway	7	M	14	5	2	2	68,073
Island Greetings	2	F	2	0	0	1	10,780
Island Guide	5	G	6	0	0	0	1,039
Island Hope	5	H	4	0	1	0	1,942
Island King	5	G	8	1	1	0	16,028
Island Mac	2	G	2	0	1	0	2,340
Island Mango	4	C	1	1	0	0	4,950
Island Maze	3	F	4	0	0	1	3,860
Island Melody	3	F	17	3	4	3	81,820
Island Mist	5	H	5	0	0	0	500
Island Music	5	M	5	0	2	1	3,462
Island N Abreeze	5	G	6	0	3	1	8,754
Island Oak	4	G	10	1	0	0	7,444
Island of Dreams	6	G	12	0	0	1	1,850
Island Pleasure	6	M	1	0	0	0	138
Island Prince	3	C	2	0	0	0	200
Island Rebel	2	C	2	0	0	0	120
Island Saga	2	F	2	0	0	0	2,500
Island Sand	2	F	4	2	1	0	46,980
Island Skipper	4	C	7	0	1	1	16,560
Island Squeeze	3	G	1	0	0	0	0
Island Sunset	7	G	5	1	0	0	3,311
Island Sunshine	5	M	6	0	0	0	168
Island Time	6	M	6	0	1	0	2,798
Island Twist	3	G	13	1	3	2	18,860
Island Will	6	G	2	0	0	0	150
Island Wonder	3	G	4	0	0	1	880
Islander	8	H	9	4	2	1	133,340
Island's Buster	5	H	5	0	0	1	2,050
Islands Sucess	2	C	2	0	0	0	190
Isle Arrest You	4	G	1	0	0	0	0
Isle Be True	4	F	9	2	4	1	17,205
Isle Dream	3	F	8	1	2	1	4,253
Isle of Capri	3	F	3	1	1	0	8,530
Isle of Chios	2	G	6	0	1	2	25,751
Isle of Mirth	2	C	3	1	1	1	20,429
Isle of Tunes	4	F	11	2	5	0	44,207
Isle Run for You	3	C	5	0	0	0	405
Isle Scamum	10	M	2	0	0	0	161
Isledustyou	2	G	2	0	0	0	285
Isleemailyou	5	G	1	0	0	0	0
Islefaxitagain	4	G	2	0	0	0	0
Islemissyou	4	F	11	0	0	1	4,523
Islendingur	3	C	3	0	0	0	5,637
Isleplunder	8	G	7	0	1	1	4,750
Isletrickyou	2	G	1	0	0	0	0
Islington (IRE)	4	F	6	2	0	2	955,142
Isn't He Tricky	7	H	3	0	0	0	158
Isn't It True	3	F	10	2	3	1	18,233
Isn't She Great	5	M	3	2	0	0	15,530
Isn't True	3	G	10	4	1	1	51,885
Ispeakasiplease	5	G	11	1	0	0	4,062
Issaqueena	4	F	3	0	0	0	2,880
Isstat a Trump	5	M	11	0	0	2	1,472
Issues Falstaff	7	G	2	0	0	0	150
Issylost	3	G	3	0	0	0	0
Istana Nurul	2	F	2	0	0	0	165
Istanbelle	4	F	8	2	1	3	12,803
Istanbull	4	G	4	1	0	0	12,090
Isthatyrfinalansr	4	F	1	0	0	0	204
Isthisplayforreal	4	F	10	0	0	1	1,530
Istillloveya	5	M	11	0	2	2	5,421
It Happens	2	F	1	0	0	0	230
It Is	7	G	11	4	1	2	139,693
It Is a Razor	5	H	6	2	0	1	7,758
It Is Private	5	M	15	0	3	4	12,470
It Is True	2	C	5	0	0	1	4,991
It Is What It Is	5	G	5	1	0	1	14,090
It Isn't Gold	4	F	2	0	0	0	0
It Was Meant To Be (GB)	4	F	9	0	0	4	23,620
Itakanrun	4	G	16	0	0	1	1,592
Italian Accent	2	F	1	0	0	0	0
Italian Bar Road	4	G	11	0	1	2	23,670
Italian Dish	2	F	5	0	2	0	11,340
Italian Diva	4	F	6	0	3	1	5,832
Italian Dreams	3	F	7	3	1	0	43,000
Italian Law	2	F	2	0	0	1	5,388
Italian Number	4	C	4	0	0	0	200
Italian Pride	7	G	12	0	1	2	14,426
Italian Slew	5	M	6	0	0	1	2,468
Italian Stogie	4	G	16	2	0	1	12,343
Italian Wine	4	F	13	0	1	2	10,248
Italiana	3	F	8	0	1	0	4,340
Itallrestsonyou	3	G	7	0	1	1	5,440
Italydar	3	C	5	0	0	1	2,565
Itanium	4	G	4	0	1	0	1,462
Itawtisawaputtytat	2	F	2	1	1	0	18,800
Itchetucknee	3	C	5	0	0	0	3,070
Itchislew Park	8	G	6	1	0	1	3,504
Ithinkican Abraham	4	G	7	1	0	0	3,933
Ithinkigotsomethun	6	M	1	0	0	0	0
Ithoughiwasacowboy	3	C	2	0	0	0	0
Itron Junior	3	C	1	0	0	0	0
Itron's Girl	2	F	6	0	0	1	3,045
Its a Blumin Storm	2	C	1	0	0	0	126
It's a Boy	4	G	19	3	2	4	49,800
It's a Gala	2	G	1	0	0	0	0
Its a Homer	2	G	6	1	1	1	7,400
Its a Jet	3	F	10	1	2	3	12,688
It's a Keeper	4	F	6	0	1	2	2,914
Its a Ladys Game	3	F	5	2	0	0	8,077
It's a Lock	2	C	3	0	2	0	4,395
It's a Monster	4	G	4	3	0	0	112,620
It's a New Moon	5	G	13	2	1	2	9,571
It's a Problem	5	H	7	2	0	1	10,675
It's a Reality	8	G	11	1	0	3	5,117
Its a Ringer	5	G	2	0	0	0	123
It's a Rock	5	H	8	0	1	1	2,035
It's a Storm	5	M	12	0	3	2	20,975
It's a Sweep	7	G	14	2	1	0	7,899
Its a True China	4	G	3	0	0	0	43
It's a Waki Fact	6	G	8	0	2	2	10,740
It's a Winner	7	G	1	0	0	0	113
It's a Woman Thing	6	M	2	0	0	0	0
It's About Silver	4	F	12	1	1	4	65,001
It's all a Blurr	10	G	7	3	2	1	8,307
Its All About Gold	2	G	3	0	0	0	2,154
It's All About Me	4	F	13	2	2	4	16,113
It's All About You	3	F	6	0	3	1	9,894
It's All Attitude	3	C	8	1	6	0	49,980
Its All From Above	3	C	1	0	0	0	0
It's All Jake	3	G	1	0	0	0	150
It's All Lies	3	F	12	1	3	1	29,548
It's All Mandy	4	F	2	0	0	0	0
It's All Personal	6	G	8	0	2	1	4,260
It's Always Boldly	8	G	15	3	2	3	30,764
Its Always Busy	4	G	4	0	0	1	825
It's Always True	5	G	15	1	1	1	8,610
It's an Emerald	3	F	14	2	7	3	11,830
It's Approved	8	M	8	2	0	1	8,410
It's Awesome Baby	2	C	3	1	0	0	20,050
It's Boldly's Baby	7	G	4	0	0	0	360

Horse	Age	Sex	Sts	1st	2d	3d	Won	Horse	Age	Sex	Sts	1st	2d	3d	Won
It's Brite's Turn	4	C	11	2	1	1	25,264	Itsurturn	6	G	10	2	3	1	13,695
It's Bubbles	3	F	2	0	0	0	279	Itsyourbid	7	G	11	1	1	1	13,131
It's Chilly	3	F	8	2	2	0	26,345	Itty Bitty Bit	4	F	12	0	0	2	6,290
Its Ctmarie C	4	F	9	0	1	1	3,791	Itty Bitty Girl	4	F	7	0	0	2	685
It's Electric	4	G	5	2	0	1	32,930	Ittybittybeau	3	F	14	4	2	4	40,704
Its Foxy	5	G	12	3	1	1	15,065	Ittybittygritty	3	F	4	2	1	0	21,455
Its Gold	2	F	2	0	0	1	1,610	Itybittyboo	5	H	4	0	0	0	512
It's Gonna Be Me	4	F	2	0	0	1	660	Itzcocktailtime	6	M	3	1	0	1	8,060
It's Gonna Happen	3	F	2	0	2	0	5,500	Itzshowtime	5	M	9	0	0	0	1,287
It's Groovy	4	G	7	2	0	0	7,452	Iv in the Heather	4	F	14	2	0	2	8,634
It's Hamer Time	2	G	11	0	0	2	5,440	Ivan Jay Perry	7	H	11	3	1	3	141,435
It's Heidi's Dance	3	F	1	0	0	1	4,920	Ivan Motley	4	C	5	1	3	0	32,860
Its Her Class	8	M	11	0	0	0	520	Ivan Petrick	4	C	5	0	0	0	168
It's in Da Cards	3	G	4	1	0	0	7,332	Ivan Willy	4	C	1	0	0	0	100
Its Inevitable	3	F	6	1	3	1	12,830	Ivana B. Alone	4	F	5	0	0	0	225
Its Jim Not Jimmy	3	C	2	0	0	0	550	Ivanavinalot	3	F	10	1	2	1	223,000
It's Just a Game	3	G	10	2	1	1	40,625	Ivan's Dmitry	8	G	6	1	1	0	2,960
It's Kobe	3	G	7	0	3	1	11,001	Ivans in a Tiz	2	G	2	0	0	0	0
Its Lily's Charger	4	F	3	1	0	0	9,034	Ivan's Song	3	G	10	2	1	0	31,770
It's Link Time	5	H	12	0	1	0	4,966	Ivar	5	H	6	0	1	0	5,756
It's Lively	10	G	1	0	0	0	0	Ivars Big Peaceful	6	G	1	0	0	0	40
It's Lucky	2	C	2	1	0	0	11,000	Ivars Blues	4	G	4	0	1	0	11,220
It's Magic	5	M	10	1	1	0	6,995	Ivars Ciao Bello	3	C	3	1	0	0	13,470
It's Me Margaret	7	G	6	1	0	0	6,330	Ivars Hazaam Groom	4	G	8	1	2	3	18,010
It's Mello Time	4	F	9	0	0	1	2,280	Ivar's Mission	6	H	2	0	1	0	2,920
Its Michael	6	G	10	2	2	2	28,294	Ivars Ms Mayhem	3	F	3	1	0	1	11,050
It's My Duty	4	C	6	0	0	1	1,880	Ivars Silver Sweep	3	F	1	0	0	0	0
Its My Option	2	F	5	1	2	0	31,410	I've Been Bad	6	G	6	0	0	0	367
Its My Pleasure	4	F	9	2	2	2	34,171	I've Been Crowned	5	G	19	3	4	2	27,822
Its My Secret	5	M	12	2	1	1	16,797	I've Been Spared	3	F	1	0	0	1	4,100
Its My Tyme	3	G	4	0	1	0	2,400	Ive Been There	8	G	6	1	1	1	6,358
It's My Way	4	F	8	0	0	2	1,570	I've Decided	6	G	9	0	1	1	15,580
It's Not My Fault	3	F	6	0	0	0	279	I've Got a Dream	5	H	2	0	0	1	632
It's Ok	3	G	5	1	0	0	4,560	I've Got Rhythm	2	G	2	0	0	0	497
It's Our Time	3	F	2	0	0	0	0	I've Got the Power	3	F	5	1	1	0	7,150
It's Poppy's Girl	6	M	1	0	0	0	54	Ive Got the Rhythm	3	G	17	1	0	2	11,014
It's Pure Excess	5	H	7	1	0	1	4,541	I've Got the Time	4	C	8	1	1	0	8,040
It's Roo	5	G	12	2	3	1	50,880	I've Got to Win	2	F	4	2	1	0	13,225
It's Saratoga	5	M	10	1	1	1	5,953	I've Had It	8	G	3	1	1	0	1,424
It's Slew to You	5	G	4	0	0	0	584	I'vegothemusicinme	2	F	10	2	1	1	49,120
It's Snow Time	4	G	3	0	0	0	765	Iverson	4	C	15	7	2	4	71,280
It's So Easy	3	F	6	1	0	0	4,792	Ivorget	3	F	17	1	5	3	19,440
It's So Simple	5	H	5	0	0	1	10,920	Ivorgorian	11	G	3	0	0	0	375
It's Spooky	3	F	6	3	1	1	75,400	Ivor's Motel	4	G	18	2	3	5	11,284
It's Stevie's Time	4	F	6	1	0	0	8,745	Ivor's Secret	6	G	12	2	4	5	6,672
Its Sylviesbag	4	C	20	6	2	1	33,870	Ivory	3	G	17	0	2	3	12,580
It's the Custom	2	G	2	0	0	0	414	Ivory and Lace	4	F	2	0	1	0	2,100
It's Triple George	5	G	12	1	1	3	29,051	Ivory Ring	5	M	3	0	0	0	196
It's Witchcraft	5	M	3	0	0	2	1,520	Ivory Tempest	4	C	7	0	0	0	1,440
Itsa Rizzi	2	C	9	3	0	1	24,485	Ivory Tower (ARG)	5	M	4	0	0	0	5,100
Itsacolddayinmay	5	M	6	1	0	0	5,185	Ivy Lane	5	M	2	0	0	0	400
Itsacryingshame	7	H	5	1	1	1	42,190	Ivy Summer	2	F	3	0	0	0	190
Itsagalthing	2	F	6	0	0	1	3,580	Ivy's Boy	5	G	7	1	1	0	5,880
Itsagreekthing	2	G	2	1	0	0	1,200	Iwantabelovedbyyou	4	F	4	1	2	0	7,920
Itsahotcat	2	C	2	0	0	0	290	Iwantodoctor	3	C	15	2	1	1	14,861
It'sallaboutmebaby	2	F	2	0	0	0	145	Iwin	4	G	11	1	3	3	66,800
Itsallaboutyou J C	4	C	9	1	0	2	8,299	Iwo Hero	3	G	9	1	0	2	14,730
Itsalluptoyou	2	C	4	0	1	0	2,599	Iwontell	4	C	9	0	1	1	1,351
It'samazing	2	F	7	0	0	0	4,190	Iwoodificould	5	H	7	3	1	1	74,626
Itsanewday	2	G	4	0	1	0	2,455	Iwritethesongs	6	M	10	0	0	1	1,541
Itsaprospector	2	C	3	0	3	0	16,800	Iz a Hasty Belle	4	F	6	1	0	3	11,977
Itsarichthing	3	F	1	1	0	0	13,800	Iz a Hunter	4	G	6	0	1	1	1,520
Itsa's Ali	5	M	8	1	2	0	12,851	I'z a Tuffy	5	M	3	0	2	0	6,020
Itsasgoodasitgets	7	G	2	0	1	0	8,550	Iz Hoolio	4	G	7	1	1	1	10,287
Itsasimplething	4	G	4	0	0	1	681	Iz She a Secret	4	F	9	1	2	0	9,976
Itsasuperrunner	2	C	4	0	0	0	630	Iza Big Star	2	G	16	2	4	0	63,190
Itsawonderfulife	2	C	4	0	1	2	17,890	Iza Bullet	5	H	3	0	0	0	130
Itsawonderfulworld	3	G	8	1	0	1	12,285	Iza Chili Bean	4	G	9	1	1	1	11,572
Itsgointobeafight	8	G	5	0	1	1	1,926	Iza Doozy	4	C	3	1	0	0	5,232
Itshardtobehumble	5	G	1	0	0	0	80	Iza Lucky Guy	4	C	12	1	4	0	9,885
Itskit	6	M	12	3	2	1	26,134	Iza Redhead	9	G	9	1	1	3	17,798
It'slonelyatthetop	2	F	6	1	2	2	28,952	Iza Righteous Dude	3	G	7	1	1	2	9,079
Itsmybag	3	F	11	3	2	2	99,950	Iza Ruler	5	G	3	0	0	0	330
Itsmyfinalanswer	5	M	3	1	0	0	31,560	Iza Tornado	5	G	8	2	3	2	24,030
Itsnowonder	6	M	16	0	3	2	11,502	Iza Tumin	6	M	5	0	0	1	280
Itsourgirl	4	F	2	0	1	1	1,643	Iza Twister	7	G	15	1	2	5	3,733
Itspartofthegame	2	F	5	0	1	0	2,613	Izamal	4	F	3	0	0	1	620
It'ssohardtobegood	3	C	8	1	2	0	18,230	Iza's Turn to Star	2	F	3	1	0	0	7,458
Itsthe Realthing	5	H	16	2	0	3	16,278	Izona	5	M	4	0	0	0	1,140

Horse	Age	Sex	Sts	1st	2d	3d	Won
Izzy Zipper	4	G	12	2	4	1	16,422
J Aled Rudolph	5	G	5	0	0	0	219
J and B's Nu Image	7	M	8	0	3	2	23,814
J and J Ruler	4	F	12	3	2	0	11,032
J B Escalation	4	G	12	3	1	0	16,143
J B Zero	4	G	13	0	0	2	7,383
J B's Crown	4	G	13	1	4	2	13,454
J B's Foxy Doc	5	M	17	1	1	0	6,402
J B's Girl	3	F	8	1	1	1	16,100
J B's Jessica	3	F	6	0	1	0	1,700
J B's Melanie	2	F	3	0	0	1	2,884
J B's Money	3	F	9	0	2	3	14,485
J B's Star	4	C	7	2	0	2	12,070
J B's Victoria	2	F	1	0	0	1	2,170
J C Bruiser	5	G	10	1	4	1	11,205
J C Jake	5	H	2	0	0	0	80
J C Steel	4	G	13	3	2	2	19,127
J C's Classic Con	3	G	7	1	1	0	17,780
J C's Mystique	5	H	5	1	0	0	6,330
J C's Pic Jr	6	G	5	0	1	0	1,348
J D Brooks	5	H	1	0	0	0	0
J D Dreamer	6	G	3	0	0	1	1,583
J D Man	3	G	12	2	1	1	27,698
J D's Dasher	3	C	7	0	0	0	1,170
J D's Diamond	7	G	2	0	0	0	650
J H Cheyenne	3	G	7	2	1	1	23,600
J H Sovereign Hour	2	C	1	0	0	0	60
J J Mystique	4	G	9	0	1	2	10,611
J J R Prideandjoy	3	F	7	0	0	2	8,670
J J S Laddie	10	G	10	1	2	2	4,638
J J Silver Blush	5	M	13	2	2	2	19,836
J J Thedotcom Man	5	G	18	2	0	2	5,083
J J Wantsthefront	4	G	8	1	0	3	28,545
J J Wish	2	C	2	0	0	1	2,530
J J Zar	3	F	6	0	2	1	3,564
J J Jacqueline	2	F	2	0	0	0	1,031
J J's Game Hunter	3	C	5	0	0	0	0
J J's Golden Dream	3	C	13	1	1	0	10,235
J J's Link	2	C	3	0	0	0	0
J J's Pride	4	F	8	2	1	3	14,812
J J's Prospect	3	C	11	2	2	0	19,575
J J's Secret Fund	4	C	1	0	0	0	0
J J's Son	2	G	7	0	1	1	2,563
J Letter Man	3	G	2	0	1	1	1,650
J Lo On the Go	3	F	2	0	0	0	215
J Loves J	2	F	6	0	1	0	4,447
J Man's Deelite	2	F	2	0	0	0	1,560
J M's Mad Groom	4	G	11	1	0	3	9,057
J N B N Me	2	F	8	0	1	2	7,323
J N M's Trick	3	C	2	1	1	0	7,640
J P Honey	3	F	11	4	0	2	19,865
J P Norcatco	2	G	1	0	0	0	0
J P Peterson	3	C	17	1	0	3	13,450
J P's Flash	5	G	1	0	0	0	0
J P's Lucky Bid	8	M	13	1	1	2	4,501
J Ride	3	G	8	1	0	2	7,550
J Ro	3	F	1	0	0	0	0
J R's Hammerhead	3	C	4	0	0	0	0
J S Mosby	6	G	1	0	0	0	0
J Star	2	F	7	1	3	1	34,420
J T's Honey	4	G	4	0	0	1	1,603
J T's Lemoon	4	F	13	0	7	1	21,929
J V Bennett	10	G	12	3	2	1	44,228
J W Black	5	G	1	0	0	0	0
J W Dude	3	G	3	1	0	0	5,173
J W Purple	5	G	3	0	0	0	333
J Whiz	2	F	2	0	0	0	132
J W's Wish	5	G	3	0	0	0	266
J. Alfred Prufrock	3	G	7	0	0	0	0
J. B. Jr.	3	C	2	0	0	0	0
J. B. the Vet	3	G	17	1	5	2	22,970
J. B.'s Annie	4	F	6	0	1	0	13,880
J. B.'s Ghost	8	H	10	1	2	3	14,300
J. B.'s Isis	5	H	1	0	0	0	363
J. B.'s Six Pack	7	H	10	2	3	2	10,743
J. B's Game	4	F	1	0	0	0	45
J. C. Blue	3	F	14	1	3	1	10,050
J. C. Crown	8	G	10	1	1	0	5,596
J. C.'s Crossing	3	C	1	0	0	0	0
J. C.s Joy	5	M	6	1	0	1	5,988
J. C.'s Sideoats	7	M	7	0	1	2	3,845
J. Cash	6	G	6	0	1	0	3,907
J. D. Belle	2	C	2	0	0	0	2,330
J. D. Cat	2	C	6	2	2	0	42,760
J. D. for Shur	6	H	2	0	1	0	500
J. D. Foxx	5	G	4	0	1	0	3,455
J. D. 'n Coke	2	C	3	0	0	1	1,370
J. D. Tyler	4	C	4	1	0	0	5,652
J. D.'s Easter	5	H	7	0	0	1	753
J. D.'s Holdin' On	5	G	9	0	0	2	3,849
J. G.'s Jazz	2	C	5	1	0	0	28,840
J. Gordon	3	C	3	0	0	1	1,050
J. Harmon	6	H	5	0	0	1	4,390
J. J. Honey	13	G	7	0	0	0	1,039
J. J. Sam	10	G	2	0	0	0	0
J. J. Sun Shine	4	G	11	4	2	0	7,063
J. J.'s Dixie Gal	5	M	3	0	0	0	40
J. J.'s Joy	4	C	14	1	4	4	52,346
J. J.'s Weekend	2	G	5	0	2	2	10,212
J. Jay	4	F	14	2	1	3	23,757
J. K.'s Freedom	4	G	9	0	0	0	413
J. L. A. Slew	5	G	14	1	1	4	3,672
J. M. Judge	3	C	2	0	0	0	0
J. P. Jet	4	C	4	1	0	1	26,822
J. P. McCain	6	H	3	0	0	1	680
J. P. 's Barbie	3	F	4	0	0	0	0
J. P.'s Magic	3	G	2	1	0	0	3,150
J. Q. Adams	6	H	11	1	3	1	8,539
J. R. Belongs	3	G	10	1	1	1	19,370
J. R. Hatfield	6	M	14	2	7	2	31,837
J. R. Honor	5	G	9	2	0	1	6,662
J. R.'s Star	3	F	8	0	0	2	3,476
J. R.'s Town	6	G	18	4	4	2	24,281
J. S. Online	4	F	12	0	4	2	13,095
J. T.'s Song	6	G	15	0	7	1	38,472
J. W.'s Redemption	2	F	1	0	0	0	0
J. W.'s Stacato	4	G	7	1	0	0	3,020
J. W.'s Synplay	4	F	11	1	0	1	3,847
Ja Zey	8	G	4	1	0	0	2,520
Jaarett Decor	3	G	1	0	0	0	0
Jab	7	G	6	3	1	2	52,922
Jab Jab Pow	2	G	1	0	0	0	0
Jabalski Princess	3	F	12	3	2	2	34,695
Jabberinjo	4	G	9	1	3	2	7,952
Jabibti (PER)	4	F	3	1	1	0	37,150
Jablunkov Pass	2	G	3	1	0	0	7,906
Jaboo	7	G	11	1	2	2	10,031
Jac Four Girls	5	G	14	3	1	3	10,911
Jac Tee Ess	3	G	11	0	3	2	11,830
Jaciro	3	F	11	1	3	4	85,651
Jack	9	G	15	1	1	0	5,623
Jack Ace Queen	5	G	5	0	0	0	288
Jack and Emma	4	G	7	1	0	1	17,009
Jack At the Bank	9	G	9	0	2	0	4,234
Jack Black and Ice	3	C	8	3	0	0	35,498
Jack Coleman	7	G	11	0	0	0	780
Jack Diamondfield	5	G	7	0	0	1	2,248
Jack Dugan	6	H	12	5	4	3	10,442
Jack High	5	H	2	1	1	0	8,700
Jack in a Jug	2	G	4	1	0	1	8,644
Jack in the Black	3	G	11	1	5	3	11,804
Jack Knife Judy	2	F	6	1	2	0	17,200
Jack Moonwalker	6	H	10	2	2	1	13,850
Jack Moore	3	C	4	0	0	0	700
Jack N Gin	4	G	6	0	0	0	1,650
Jack Noon	6	G	3	0	0	0	355
Jack O'Diamonds	4	G	2	0	0	0	0
Jack of Clubs	2	C	1	0	0	0	1,230
Jack of Hearts	7	G	4	0	0	0	473
Jack of My Heart	3	C	19	1	5	6	70,880
Jack of Slades	5	G	14	3	2	3	26,646
Jack Pot Charlie	10	G	1	0	0	0	50
Jack Star	4	G	17	0	2	1	4,357
Jack Tar	4	G	9	1	0	0	10,955
Jack the Bear	5	G	9	1	0	1	5,664
Jack the Cat	3	G	7	0	0	0	0
Jack the Jackal	3	C	6	1	0	0	7,665
Jack the Tiger	3	C	2	0	0	0	29

Horse	Age	Sex	Sts	1st	2d	3d	Won	Horse	Age	Sex	Sts	1st	2d	3d	Won
Jack the Zipper	2	C	6	0	0	1	1,275	Jadada	8	H	4	1	0	0	21,630
Jack to a King	5	H	8	1	0	1	16,532	Jade Air	3	F	13	1	3	3	29,890
Jackashton	6	H	2	0	0	0	94	Jade Anniversary	4	F	4	0	1	0	2,038
Jackberun	3	G	12	3	1	2	51,263	Jade Arrow	3	G	3	0	1	0	3,210
Jackdaw	2	C	1	0	0	1	2,340	Jade At the Gate	5	M	1	0	0	0	270
Jackette	4	F	1	0	0	1	6,120	Jade Butterfly	4	F	4	0	0	0	292
Jackie Carlotta	5	M	2	0	0	0	238	Jade Dancer	2	F	2	0	0	0	0
Jackie Jan	3	F	7	3	2	0	82,099	Jade Digger	4	G	7	2	0	0	46,830
Jackie M.	2	F	2	0	1	0	940	Jade Dragon	2	F	3	0	0	0	2,550
Jackie O's Diamond	2	F	3	0	0	0	621	Jade East	4	F	3	1	0	1	8,289
Jackie Paper	6	M	2	0	0	0	124	Jade Express	4	F	7	2	0	0	5,051
Jackie Too	6	M	14	0	0	1	3,075	Jade Forest	3	C	1	0	0	0	2,280
Jackie's Bidawalk	4	F	14	3	4	1	86,992	Jade Fox	3	F	4	0	1	1	11,080
Jackies Fur R A	10	G	1	0	0	0	0	Jade Girl	3	F	2	0	0	0	0
Jackies Gunner	8	H	8	1	2	1	10,313	Jade Green	5	G	4	2	0	1	18,583
Jackie's Hope	3	F	3	1	0	0	4,765	Jade Halo	4	C	7	0	0	1	2,414
Jackie's Hostage	6	H	3	0	0	0	519	Jade Journey	4	C	2	0	0	0	0
Jackies Plaything	5	M	6	3	0	1	10,206	Jade Julia	5	M	12	1	1	7	40,182
Jackie's Rainbow	2	G	3	0	0	0	443	Jade Light Foot	7	G	3	0	1	0	702
Jacki's Lil Wacki	10	M	8	2	0	3	3,552	Jade Myth	2	F	1	1	0	0	6,200
Jacki's Tuition	4	F	10	1	0	1	5,881	Jade of the Nile	3	C	4	0	1	2	665
Jackman Road	5	G	10	2	0	1	9,568	Jade Palace	3	F	8	2	0	0	22,520
Jackoranda	2	F	1	0	0	0	0	Jade Peony	5	M	12	3	2	1	30,720
Jackpot	5	H	5	1	1	0	39,200	Jade Trader	5	H	14	1	1	1	6,258
Jackpot Jo	6	G	1	0	0	0	420	Jade Vixen	4	F	11	0	0	3	13,150
Jackpot Party	2	F	4	1	0	0	6,750	Jadebquick	3	F	10	2	1	2	33,344
Jackrabbit Slim	6	G	8	1	0	2	5,538	Jaded Actor	3	G	2	0	0	0	0
Jacks Bigwheel	3	C	4	0	1	0	2,516	Jaded Heat	3	C	7	2	1	1	30,825
Jack's Birthday	2	C	1	0	0	0	570	Jaded Impulse	2	F	2	0	0	0	0
Jacks Bitrun	5	M	10	0	0	0	776	Jaded Juliet	3	F	11	0	0	1	3,015
Jack's Black Label	6	G	5	0	1	1	1,259	Jaded Love	4	F	1	0	0	0	174
Jacks Cat	3	F	1	0	0	0	84	Jaded Miss	4	F	3	0	0	0	270
Jacks Chance	5	G	6	0	0	1	1,047	Jaded Money	8	G	9	5	1	0	38,575
Jack's Clever Lady	5	M	5	2	1	0	5,710	Jaded Runner	5	M	9	1	0	1	19,270
Jack's Concielo	4	G	3	0	0	1	1,080	Jaded Slew	8	G	7	0	1	1	3,937
Jack's Cruiser	4	F	4	0	0	0	754	Jadent	10	G	5	1	0	1	4,663
Jacks Fancyman	4	C	2	0	0	0	976	Jade's Ace	5	M	10	5	0	1	46,740
Jacks Legal Eagle	4	G	5	0	3	1	2,627	Jade's in Uproar	2	F	2	1	0	0	20,178
Jack's Magee	4	G	14	0	4	4	14,246	Jadester	3	F	13	1	0	5	37,470
Jack's Niece	6	M	5	0	0	0	502	Jadetown	6	G	2	1	0	0	8,800
Jack's Olympio	6	G	7	0	0	1	3,128	Jadore (NZ)	5	M	3	0	0	0	0
Jack's Own Time	4	G	5	2	1	1	88,145	Jaeger	4	G	6	0	0	1	2,445
Jacks Romeo	4	G	4	0	0	1	4,649	Jaelon's Joy	5	M	3	0	0	0	0
Jack's Silver	4	C	11	1	2	3	75,364	Jaffa	5	G	17	1	2	2	4,031
Jacks to Win	5	G	10	2	1	0	7,581	Jaftica	3	G	5	0	0	0	2,902
Jacks Trait	6	G	5	0	0	0	0	Jagged Ice	4	G	5	0	0	1	4,955
Jacks World	3	C	6	1	0	1	5,730	Jagger	7	H	8	0	0	1	1,320
Jackson Hole	6	G	8	2	0	0	4,514	Jagger Wine	6	G	1	0	0	1	470
Jackson Point	7	G	14	0	1	2	13,068	Jaglander	2	C	1	1	0	0	24,600
Jackson Red	5	H	5	0	0	1	560	Jaguar Cielo	3	F	3	0	0	0	1,560
Jackson Run	3	G	7	1	3	0	56,625	Jaguar City	3	F	4	2	1	0	43,598
Jackson Spur	6	G	10	2	1	1	7,948	Jaguar Farma	7	H	5	0	0	0	1,005
Jackson Square	3	C	3	0	0	0	850	Jaguar Friend	2	C	4	2	1	0	75,520
Jackyscraftychance	4	G	9	4	1	1	84,157	Jaguar Groom	4	C	4	0	0	0	0
Jaclini	4	G	20	2	2	3	32,980	Jaguar Hope	5	H	11	3	2	3	14,084
Jacob and Julian	3	C	2	0	1	0	7,560	Jaguar Jade	5	G	14	3	1	0	14,411
Jacob Cade	3	C	2	1	0	0	3,240	Jaguar Joe	3	G	12	3	2	1	47,261
Jacob the Great	2	G	2	0	0	0	343	Jaguar Key	7	H	9	1	0	1	3,811
Jacobina	4	F	2	0	0	0	2,580	Jaguar Lord	5	M	14	3	0	2	12,397
Jacob's Arch	2	C	1	0	0	1	3,630	Jaguar Prospect	9	H	13	2	2	3	16,871
Jacob's Moon	3	G	4	0	0	0	0	Jaguar X Cat	3	G	3	0	0	0	0
Jacob's Pride	6	G	12	1	2	2	7,178	Jagular	4	G	7	0	0	0	300
Jacob's Prospect	4	G	13	3	1	0	74,645	Jaha (FR)	4	G	1	0	0	0	0
Jacobs Smile	3	F	3	0	1	1	11,900	Jahaam	7	H	3	0	0	0	1,040
Jacob's Trust	5	G	19	1	0	3	6,793	Jahafaslass	8	M	2	0	0	1	650
Jacoby Ray	3	G	2	0	0	0	0	Jahamour (NZ)	5	H	4	1	0	0	11,250
Jacqanna	2	F	1	0	0	0	0	Jahar	2	G	1	0	0	0	0
Jacque Z.	8	H	6	1	1	0	3,512	Jahbless	5	G	11	1	1	2	11,545
Jacqueline K	3	F	16	2	1	3	26,805	Jahman	3	G	5	1	1	0	15,196
Jacquelyn Lacy	2	F	2	0	0	0	0	Jahuan	2	C	7	0	0	0	2,070
Jacquelyn T.	5	M	9	0	0	2	8,420	Jailbird Jonah	3	G	4	0	1	2	13,850
Jacques Boy	4	G	14	1	1	2	7,086	Jaime Be Good	3	F	7	0	0	1	4,110
Jacques Swinger	4	C	4	0	0	0	0	Jaime Jack	5	G	9	0	1	1	4,375
Jacque's Tree Frog	3	F	3	0	0	0	480	Jaime's Jewel	5	H	1	0	0	0	390
Jacquie Rose	4	F	11	1	0	2	15,580	Jaime's Joy	4	F	13	0	2	0	6,649
Jacquies Red Glow	5	M	11	0	0	2	2,310	Jak D	4	G	2	0	0	1	515
Jacqui's Promise	3	F	8	2	0	2	60,086	Jake	4	G	2	0	0	1	1,430
Jada Bug	4	F	1	0	0	0	35	Jake Davis	5	H	1	0	0	0	0
Jada Jing	2	F	6	0	1	4	8,640	Jake Gonna Win	5	H	5	1	2	1	4,016

Horse	Age	Sex	Sts	1st	2d	3d	Won
Jake Jacoby	4	C	14	2	3	1	17,462
Jake Leader	4	C	1	0	0	0	52
Jake Skate	3	C	4	0	2	1	18,360
Jake the Gamer	5	G	3	0	0	1	5,880
Jake W.	7	G	5	1	1	0	1,720
Jakeman	3	G	12	1	1	2	8,013
Jake's Cielo	6	G	8	0	1	0	1,704
Jakes Corner	5	G	14	3	6	2	16,248
Jake's Fever	2	C	4	1	1	1	23,880
Jakes Fire	7	G	7	0	1	1	4,344
Jake's Flash	3	F	10	1	0	2	7,477
Jake's Grandslam	4	G	2	0	0	0	180
Jake's Guy	6	G	3	1	0	0	5,974
Jakes Wildindian	4	G	9	1	0	2	13,585
Jakey D	5	H	9	1	1	1	26,680
Jakey Too	3	G	5	0	0	0	0
Jakeybabes	3	C	3	1	1	0	12,970
Jaki's Magic	5	G	5	0	0	1	8,910
Jaklin Wine	7	H	9	0	2	3	1,884
Jaklin's Last Kin	6	G	2	0	1	1	5,440
Jakob Teddy	2	G	6	0	0	2	2,795
Jak's Makin Music	5	G	1	0	0	0	0
Jalaab (IRE)	8	H	8	1	0	1	13,811
Jalapeno	5	H	2	0	0	0	175
Jalapeno Popper	7	G	12	0	2	0	3,748
Jalavah	6	M	2	1	0	0	10,290
Jalyn	2	F	11	2	2	2	32,130
Jam Feu	6	G	11	1	0	2	10,763
Jam for the Lamb	4	G	10	0	0	0	1,536
Jam Won	2	F	1	0	0	1	3,402
Jama Gold	4	F	6	2	0	1	7,687
Jamaari Girl	4	F	5	1	1	1	43,751
Jamac's Prospect	4	F	12	2	2	1	15,613
Jamaica Bet	5	H	2	1	0	0	6,016
Jamaica Joe	2	C	1	0	0	0	0
Jamaican Fun	3	G	7	1	1	0	4,735
Jamaican Jade	2	F	4	0	2	2	20,460
Jamaican Justice	4	G	12	1	0	0	6,660
Jamaican Me Nuts	4	G	15	3	2	1	44,370
Jamaican Ruckus	10	G	4	0	0	1	440
Jamaican Smoke	3	G	7	0	2	2	10,276
Jambalar	3	G	4	1	1	0	54,414
Jambeau	4	G	11	1	2	2	61,065
Jamboree	7	G	7	0	0	0	503
Jamelao (ARG)	7	H	2	0	1	0	11,920
James	3	G	20	8	6	2	136,290
James B.	3	G	1	0	1	0	2,520
James Clarence	7	G	9	1	0	2	4,318
James Creek	3	G	11	3	3	1	21,781
James Jr	2	G	3	0	0	0	90
James Logan	7	G	12	2	1	2	24,880
James Madison	4	C	8	1	1	1	17,930
James Riley	2	C	2	0	0	0	180
Jamesflightforbuck	6	H	2	1	0	0	2,440
Jameson Point	4	G	8	1	0	0	4,640
Jamesport	5	G	7	0	0	0	1,479
James's Highlander	4	C	8	3	1	1	11,110
Jamessonjimmyjames	4	G	7	0	0	0	967
Jami Lynne	8	M	15	0	2	1	4,837
Jami N Motion	2	F	2	0	0	0	240
Jami Pari	7	M	13	0	2	2	3,409
Jamian	2	C	6	1	2	1	41,310
Jamican Blue	3	G	4	3	1	0	46,730
Jamie Jamie	2	C	2	0	0	0	0
Jamie N Jill's Way	2	F	6	1	2	0	8,670
Jamie O	6	M	4	0	0	0	164
Jamie T. James	5	M	10	0	0	1	5,810
Jamie the Duke	7	G	4	0	0	1	1,254
Jamielittledream	5	M	3	0	0	2	4,070
Jamie's Bad Boy	4	G	15	1	1	1	11,078
Jamie's College	6	H	6	0	2	0	8,960
Jamie's Image	7	G	10	0	2	2	5,261
Jamie's Leader	12	G	3	0	1	0	1,638
Jamie's Melody	5	G	15	2	2	1	19,770
Jamie's Tuition	3	C	4	0	0	0	780
Jamilah	3	F	12	2	2	0	35,160
Jaming Jammer	3	G	10	2	0	1	6,780
Jaming the Blues	4	G	7	0	0	1	4,757
Jamirach	2	F	1	0	0	0	115
Jammer	4	G	13	2	0	0	9,847
Jammin' Adam	3	G	2	1	1	0	7,125
Jammin' Dan	3	G	12	1	4	0	11,180
Jammin Java	5	M	11	2	5	0	11,811
Jammin Jimmy	5	G	4	0	0	0	120
Jammin Syd	2	C	4	1	0	2	13,610
Jamocha	2	C	2	0	0	1	6,020
Jamoke	5	G	11	1	1	2	12,667
Jams Fanci Mac	11	H	1	0	0	0	0
Jamuga	4	G	12	2	0	1	10,799
Jamye's Mugabucks	9	G	18	4	0	2	16,421
Jan Can Kankan	11	M	7	0	1	0	968
Jan Luck	6	M	17	3	1	4	15,494
Jan Ten Above	2	F	3	0	0	0	0
Jana o' Gaill	6	M	12	1	4	1	7,679
Jana Rae	2	F	2	0	0	0	0
Jana Sue	5	M	2	0	0	1	645
Jancy Girl	4	F	14	2	1	1	10,495
Jandemar	2	C	1	0	0	0	0
Jandy's Dandy	3	F	5	0	0	0	760
Jane B. A.	3	F	12	3	1	1	80,288
Jane Daniels	5	M	7	0	0	1	5,700
Jane Jane Jane	3	F	5	0	0	0	1,920
Jane Sharp	4	F	6	0	0	0	420
Janea's Dbldiamond	7	M	10	1	0	2	5,408
Janeian (NZ)	5	M	13	4	3	3	183,870
Janelle Ann	6	M	3	0	0	0	338
Jane's Big Boot	3	G	19	5	3	3	42,398
Janes Gift	2	F	2	0	0	1	2,604
Jane's Halo	2	F	6	1	2	0	14,380
Jane's Secret	3	F	6	0	2	1	15,422
Jane's Speed	4	F	5	1	0	3	29,794
Janet's Cat	6	M	1	0	0	0	76
Janet's Dream	3	F	1	0	0	1	880
Janet's Ruff Cut	2	F	2	0	0	0	813
Janey Girl	7	M	18	2	4	4	36,200
Jangled	4	G	22	1	4	2	17,432
Janice's Victor	5	G	7	1	0	1	1,152
Janies Enjoyment	6	M	10	2	2	2	10,626
Janines Secret	8	M	8	0	0	0	300
Janis J.	4	F	9	1	1	1	9,220
Jankin	5	H	11	2	2	2	7,667
Jannan Jewel	5	M	12	1	1	1	8,781
Janna's Flier	3	C	1	0	0	0	165
Jannetta Peers	5	M	5	0	0	0	1,080
Janon	4	F	8	0	0	0	3,786
Jans Brother	3	G	15	1	0	1	8,000
Jans Swetheart	5	M	4	0	0	2	2,778
Jan's Texas Boy	4	G	9	0	1	0	3,030
Jantha	3	F	3	0	0	0	90
Jantz the Man	3	G	7	0	0	3	7,610
January	2	C	3	0	1	0	6,760
January's Dynasty	5	G	6	0	1	1	3,095
January's Girl	2	F	3	0	0	0	273
Janzig	3	G	10	1	1	1	4,005
Janzig Affair	3	C	6	1	1	1	9,515
Janzig Warrior	3	C	13	1	1	2	17,715
Japanese Whisper (UAE)	2	F	2	0	0	0	780
Jar of Buttons	6	M	11	1	5	4	12,223
Jaramar Rain	4	F	8	2	1	2	163,455
Jarawara (PER)	5	M	11	1	0	1	13,036
Jared's Atv	2	G	2	0	0	0	180
Jareds Hope	5	M	5	1	0	1	1,692
Jared's Pride	4	G	3	0	0	0	0
Jared's Prospect	5	G	9	1	2	2	15,446
Jared's Shaddow	4	G	13	1	3	3	14,802
Jared's Stray Star	6	G	8	1	0	0	3,477
Jared's Twilight	4	F	6	1	0	2	5,840
Jarett's Choice	2	F	6	0	0	2	2,525
Jarett's Devil	3	F	4	0	0	1	1,732
Jarf	7	G	10	3	0	1	101,976
Jarret's Odyssey	7	G	14	1	4	2	38,990
Jarrett	4	G	6	0	0	0	555
Jas Minister	3	F	5	0	1	1	3,133
Jasmine Jones (GB)	6	M	2	0	0	0	0
Jason Beaver	6	H	1	0	0	0	0
Jason O	4	G	5	0	0	0	552
Jason Raj	3	G	8	0	0	2	1,376
Jasons Classic	4	F	3	0	0	0	3,240

Horse	Age	Sex	Sts	1st	2d	3d	Won
Jason's Five K Run	2	C	1	0	0	0	230
Jason's Halo	5	H	6	0	0	0	960
Jason's Love	4	G	17	1	0	4	14,562
Jason's Miracle	5	G	6	0	0	1	4,215
Jasper	4	C	4	0	0	0	0
Jasper Flash	2	C	3	0	0	0	0
Jasper Park	4	G	7	1	1	0	16,198
Jasper Wildcat	3	F	2	0	0	1	1,910
Jasper's My Name	6	G	5	0	0	0	0
Jasper's Secret	2	C	3	0	0	0	612
Jaunty Day	3	F	10	1	1	1	21,000
Java (GB)	4	F	4	1	0	2	45,720
Java Cat	4	C	1	0	0	0	0
Java Jake	4	G	8	0	1	1	11,520
Java Jasmine	4	F	17	2	4	3	13,646
Java Soup	3	G	7	1	1	0	19,290
Java Time	9	G	6	1	0	1	9,356
Java to Go	9	G	6	0	1	0	3,650
Java Wit	4	F	7	1	0	2	14,247
Javagoldstar	3	F	7	1	0	0	8,993
Javelin	4	G	12	1	0	3	11,640
Javenger	6	G	13	2	2	0	11,825
Javens Prodigy	3	G	16	2	7	2	65,548
Jawannabe	5	H	4	0	1	0	1,600
Jawletto	3	G	7	0	0	0	567
Jaworski	5	G	16	5	3	1	45,170
Jax's Cadillac	5	M	4	0	0	1	343
Jay Ar Jay	3	G	11	0	0	1	4,893
Jay Black	3	G	15	4	3	1	79,110
Jay Tee's Gem	3	G	13	0	3	0	42,222
Jay Z	5	H	16	1	1	2	20,100
Jayar	3	C	7	3	1	0	69,400
Jaybo	3	C	6	1	2	0	30,900
Jaycat	2	C	3	1	0	1	9,990
Jaycejace	3	G	12	1	1	5	21,884
Jaycox	2	C	2	0	0	0	0
Jaygar Dancer	2	G	6	1	0	3	18,200
Jayhawk Janet	3	F	2	1	0	1	5,560
Jayhawker	3	G	5	1	1	0	4,358
Jaylo J G	3	F	14	1	1	0	6,883
Jayme Brook	7	M	1	0	0	0	0
Jay'n Jeff	3	G	14	2	2	3	31,225
Jay's Buddy Bob	4	G	7	2	1	2	40,405
Jay's Helln	5	G	8	0	0	1	1,099
Jay's Holly	3	F	2	0	0	0	0
Jays Little John	3	C	1	0	0	0	0
Jay's Nature	7	M	5	0	0	2	3,151
Jay's Performer	9	G	5	2	0	0	9,674
Jay's Shawklit	4	F	15	4	4	1	38,986
Jay's Turn	6	G	7	1	2	0	6,284
Jay's Wish	3	G	7	1	2	0	30,650
Jayua	3	C	11	1	1	3	24,420
Jazatar	5	M	21	1	1	3	8,908
Jazlyn Slew	4	F	1	0	0	0	0
Jazz Age	6	G	8	2	1	1	5,820
Jazz Beat	4	G	11	3	0	3	30,270
Jazz Combo	2	F	1	0	0	0	0
Jazz Concert	2	F	1	0	0	1	4,320
Jazz Drive	7	G	15	1	1	1	8,299
Jazz Fest Weekend	5	G	5	0	2	2	28,690
Jazz Flight	4	F	7	1	0	1	4,093
Jazz Jazz Jazz	4	F	11	2	2	3	11,382
Jazz Lady	3	F	1	1	0	0	12,000
Jazz Mania	4	F	7	0	0	0	1,680
Jazz Meeting	2	F	2	0	0	0	572
Jazz Music	3	F	7	1	2	0	6,980
Jazz Parade	6	G	14	3	6	2	40,683
Jazz Pro	6	G	12	1	1	2	17,299
Jazz Rainbow Flier	5	H	1	0	0	0	0
Jazz Tradition	3	F	8	1	3	1	55,610
Jazz Ya	3	F	6	1	0	2	43,740
Jazzabell	3	F	2	0	0	0	0
Jazzamatassle	2	F	2	0	0	0	900
Jazzaroo	6	G	3	1	0	0	1,008
Jazzbit	4	G	13	1	2	1	62,617
Jazzer Queen	6	M	12	4	1	2	36,874
Jazzfield	6	M	11	1	2	0	9,198
Jazzie Moon	3	F	2	0	0	0	88
Jazzin Bayou	2	G	3	0	1	0	1,680
Jazzin Jeff	3	C	6	1	2	0	6,875
Jazzin Julie	4	F	10	0	3	2	4,072
Jazzin With Jazzy	4	F	1	0	1	0	1,880
Jazzing Jack	4	C	7	4	2	1	14,775
Jazzing Ralph	3	G	5	0	0	0	0
Jazzitupgeorge	2	G	4	0	1	1	5,200
Jazzman Brian	8	G	13	1	4	1	7,025
Jazzman's Prospect	3	C	6	0	0	1	4,560
Jazzmobile	6	G	2	0	0	1	780
Jazzn	7	M	4	0	0	1	324
Jazzring	2	F	1	0	0	0	270
Jazz's Legacy	4	G	9	1	2	0	3,190
Jazzy Al	3	G	15	2	0	2	15,604
Jazzy Artist	2	G	4	2	0	0	8,885
Jazzy Color	6	H	3	0	0	1	210
Jazzy Diamond	3	G	8	1	0	0	3,709
Jazzy Double	3	F	2	0	0	0	201
Jazzy Executive	5	M	3	0	1	0	2,415
Jazzy Gem	2	F	3	0	1	2	11,028
Jazzy Ginger	5	M	3	0	0	0	2,250
Jazzy Hostess	5	M	6	0	0	0	578
Jazzy Image	5	G	4	1	0	1	3,683
Jazzy Jay	2	C	2	1	0	0	36,360
Jazzy Jeanne	4	F	5	1	1	2	11,850
Jazzy Jill	3	F	2	0	0	2	1,700
Jazzy Jizzy	4	F	5	0	0	0	824
Jazzy Josh	3	G	1	0	0	0	0
Jazzy Legs	5	G	5	0	1	2	3,456
Jazzy Mac	8	G	11	1	3	1	16,545
Jazzy Miss	3	F	6	1	0	0	7,021
Jazzy Place	4	C	7	0	2	0	2,475
Jazzy Princess	4	F	6	2	0	1	7,380
Jazzy River	8	G	9	0	1	0	1,306
Jazzy Times	3	F	2	0	0	0	825
Jazzy Will	3	G	1	0	0	0	0
Jazzy Yacht	5	G	11	3	1	3	61,978
Jazzy's Sister	4	F	8	0	0	1	1,406
Jd's Lookin Snappy	4	F	17	1	4	5	33,105
Jd's Marmel	3	G	11	3	1	1	27,434
Je Suis	3	F	5	0	0	0	500
Jealous Act	3	C	5	0	0	0	880
Jealous Lover	5	M	9	3	0	2	28,373
Jealous Mistress	7	M	5	1	1	1	9,100
Jean Brady	4	F	13	3	2	3	33,923
Jean Wayne	4	C	10	1	2	2	3,370
Jeanie Sue	4	F	13	2	1	3	51,078
Jeanie's Charge	2	F	6	0	0	1	1,662
Jeanie's Gold	3	F	14	2	1	6	37,575
Jeanies Pistol	4	F	7	1	3	0	12,100
Jeanies Rob	7	H	11	1	3	2	43,580
Jeanie's Tread	6	M	6	1	1	0	3,931
Jeanne's Jet	6	M	3	0	0	0	0
Jeanne's Prospect	3	F	4	1	0	0	4,898
Jeannie Light	7	M	9	2	2	0	6,864
Jean's Lucky One	5	M	13	2	1	1	7,562
Jeans Premier	3	F	5	0	0	1	4,510
Jean's Way	3	F	3	0	0	0	111
Jeblar's Jette	4	F	2	0	0	0	0
Jeblette	5	M	10	0	0	1	5,330
Jebs Angel	5	M	4	0	0	0	605
Jeb's Honor	7	H	6	2	1	0	20,260
Jeb's Pleasure	5	H	9	0	0	0	570
Jeb's Secret	4	F	5	0	0	1	790
Jeb's Song	3	F	18	5	6	3	33,549
Jeb's Strategy	5	G	11	0	1	2	12,512
Jeb's Wild	4	C	10	1	2	2	91,102
Jebson	6	H	8	0	2	0	4,080
Jebular	7	H	11	1	1	1	6,120
Jeddah Harbor	4	F	1	0	1	0	10,000
Jedi Warrior	3	C	1	0	0	0	140
Jeep Tour	3	G	8	1	0	0	4,983
Jeepis Missed	4	G	7	2	0	2	102,792
Jeeter	4	G	11	3	2	2	41,169
Jeet's Devise	4	G	10	1	1	1	10,283
Jeeves	5	G	8	0	1	0	12,530
Jefe	3	G	3	0	0	0	0
Jefe de Jefes	3	C	13	1	1	5	36,960
Jefesito	4	G	3	1	0	0	3,566

Horse	Age	Sex	Sts	1st	2d	3d	Won
Jeff Dancer	9	G	7	0	2	1	3,319
Jefferson (MEX)	6	G	2	0	0	0	51
Jefferson K.	2	C	2	0	0	0	210
Jeffery	3	C	7	1	2	2	21,892
Jeff's Cat	4	F	5	1	0	1	11,920
Jeffs Ile De	4	G	2	0	0	0	0
Jeff's Pick	8	G	14	2	3	2	16,035
Jeff's Rae Sue	3	G	14	1	1	2	2,641
Jeff's Woodman	3	G	4	0	1	0	2,300
Jekyll and Hyde	6	H	14	2	3	3	53,160
Jellaba's Song	5	M	16	0	1	2	7,435
Jelly and Me	3	F	4	1	0	1	7,922
Jelly Bean Diamond	5	H	6	0	0	0	1,092
Jelly Bean Gene	4	G	9	1	0	0	3,721
Jelly Fish	7	M	3	2	1	0	50,220
Jelly On Top	5	H	3	0	0	0	200
Jelly Roll Horton	4	G	16	1	3	2	16,287
Jelly Roll Journey	3	F	4	1	0	0	4,950
Jelly Roll Rock	5	H	12	1	2	1	20,967
Jelly Roll Romp	6	H	5	2	0	0	40,050
Jellyrool	5	M	8	0	2	2	4,138
Jemma	2	F	3	0	0	0	195
Jemsek	7	G	7	0	1	1	5,451
Jena's Hope	6	M	7	0	0	0	1,742
Jeni's Tough Night	5	M	10	1	1	1	5,615
Jenizara (CHI)	7	M	3	0	0	0	466
Jenkins' Ferry	3	C	9	0	0	0	10,255
Jenna Lea's Jewel	5	M	5	1	0	1	5,164
Jenna's Devil	2	F	4	0	0	0	1,043
Jenna's Dream News	3	F	10	2	2	3	28,472
Jenna's Joy	5	M	3	0	2	1	42,128
Jenna's Li'l Star	4	G	11	1	0	0	3,865
Jenna's Promise	4	C	14	5	3	1	54,618
Jennasietta	5	M	2	0	0	0	0
Jennalilprincess	4	F	19	3	4	3	54,277
Jennaslollipop	3	F	17	1	0	4	6,846
Jennasluckypenny	5	M	1	0	0	0	270
Jennifer's Baby	8	G	10	2	0	0	16,306
Jennifer's Crown	4	F	8	2	1	1	5,030
Jennifer's Hope	2	F	3	0	0	0	572
Jennifers Pub	6	M	3	0	0	0	470
Jennifer's Queen	6	M	12	0	0	2	2,190
Jennifer's Revival	4	F	7	2	1	1	19,977
Jennpenn	6	M	14	1	2	2	6,249
Jenn's Girl	2	F	1	0	0	0	0
Jenn's Jet	3	F	2	0	0	0	0
Jenny Bet Her Boot	3	F	6	2	1	0	20,310
Jenny O	2	F	3	1	0	2	21,760
Jennys Badboy	8	G	10	2	2	2	10,045
Jenny's Diamond	4	F	2	0	0	0	412
Jenny's Gold	5	G	17	3	2	6	24,829
Jenny's Habit	3	F	7	0	1	2	2,671
Jenny's Jag	3	F	6	0	3	1	3,445
Jenny's Princess	4	F	5	1	0	0	21,000
Jenny's Prospector	3	F	10	1	0	2	43,454
Jenny'sbluecookie	6	G	6	0	3	0	1,863
Jenora	3	F	5	1	1	1	7,277
Jen's Diamond Girl	6	M	11	1	0	2	6,774
Jen's Joy	2	F	1	0	0	0	0
Jen's Secret	4	F	3	0	0	0	520
Jen's Spell	3	F	1	0	0	0	0
Jentzen	5	G	8	0	1	1	15,940
Jeopardize	3	F	10	1	1	1	11,813
Je'pardo	9	G	12	0	1	2	3,022
Jer Bear	2	G	1	0	0	0	840
Jeremiah John	2	G	2	1	0	0	5,700
Jercod's Myriah	8	H	7	1	0	3	5,329
Jeremiah Gent	5	G	5	0	0	0	200
Jeremiahdabullfrog	8	G	7	0	0	0	393
Jeremiah's Judge	4	G	5	0	1	1	3,080
Jeremiah's Story	7	G	15	1	2	0	13,115
Jeremy Fleet Feet	3	G	7	0	0	0	0
Jeremy's Jet	4	C	4	0	0	0	111
Jeremy's Quest	5	M	7	0	1	1	6,360
Jeremy's Traveler	3	F	4	1	0	0	6,376
Jeri Ruckus	2	G	1	0	0	0	0
Jericho Jed	2	G	8	0	1	1	4,335
Jerimi Silver	5	M	4	0	0	0	811
Jerobuck	10	G	5	0	0	0	0
Jerome Park	5	H	1	0	0	0	178
Jerrad's Desire	6	G	10	2	3	0	17,126
Jerrannama	4	F	1	0	0	0	100
Jerri Lynn	2	F	7	2	3	1	41,820
Jerry Got Luck	4	G	11	1	3	0	17,850
Jerry Pat Hayes	4	C	4	0	0	1	790
Jerry T	2	G	5	0	0	1	3,405
Jerry Wayne	2	C	5	0	0	1	1,272
Jerrys Baby	2	F	2	0	0	0	1,500
Jerry's Call	6	G	2	0	0	0	0
Jerrys Millenium	6	G	13	5	2	1	20,610
Jerry's Way	5	G	4	0	2	0	3,280
Jersey Breeze	4	F	10	0	1	2	6,240
Jersey Gia	2	F	4	2	0	0	21,601
Jersey Giant	4	G	7	4	1	1	160,600
Jersey Jack	5	G	6	1	2	0	12,138
Jersey John	3	G	12	0	1	1	1,718
Jersey Muscle	3	C	2	0	0	0	540
Jersey Rebel	5	G	4	0	1	0	7,960
Jersey Reef	2	C	4	0	0	1	1,084
Jersey Storm	4	G	6	0	1	1	18,500
Jersey Tomato	5	M	10	0	4	1	24,144
Jersey Transit	6	G	13	1	2	0	7,502
Jerzy Red	4	G	5	0	0	0	310
Jess Do It	3	G	6	0	1	1	1,507
Jess M	8	G	14	1	4	4	17,840
Jessamine Jake	6	G	26	3	4	3	13,691
Jesse Gee	7	G	1	1	0	0	2,420
Jesse Jammin	5	G	11	0	3	1	16,141
Jesse Lee	7	G	4	0	0	0	203
Jesse Ruhls	5	G	6	0	1	1	2,098
Jesse Time	3	G	7	1	1	1	6,070
Jesse's Chance	6	H	3	0	0	0	0
Jesse's Gal	2	F	1	0	1	0	1,660
Jesse's Gone West	3	G	8	1	0	2	18,520
Jesses Scandel	7	H	15	2	5	4	25,394
Jesse's Trump	3	G	6	0	0	1	5,491
Jessi J	5	M	13	3	2	3	48,755
Jessi Lynn	3	F	4	0	0	0	0
Jessica	2	F	5	2	1	1	54,320
Jessica Slew	3	F	2	0	0	0	70
Jessica's Angel	2	F	5	0	0	0	5,040
Jessica's Best	3	G	12	2	2	2	30,779
Jessica's Pride	3	F	7	0	1	1	3,189
Jessica's Way	3	F	8	2	2	0	46,900
Jessie Blessing	4	C	4	0	0	0	855
Jessie C.	5	M	1	0	0	1	1,050
Jessie Did It	12	G	7	1	0	2	7,220
Jessie Guest	3	F	11	2	1	1	35,358
Jessie's Baby	2	C	2	0	0	0	200
Jessie's Jewel	4	F	16	2	1	2	9,799
Jessie's Jig	6	G	6	1	1	1	5,515
Jessie's Joy	2	F	7	0	0	4	7,400
Jessie's Prayer	3	F	16	3	1	2	17,263
Jessie's Victory	6	M	2	0	1	0	2,990
Jessieville	3	F	7	1	3	2	17,875
Jessika's Award	3	F	6	0	2	1	6,412
Jess's Girl	2	F	3	0	0	0	0
Jest a Bag	6	G	1	1	0	0	3,780
Jest a Jonquil	6	M	6	1	0	0	3,761
Jest a Zeal	2	F	3	0	0	0	0
Jest Unreal	2	F	2	0	0	1	4,576
Jestakick	8	G	14	1	3	1	19,279
Jestalover	4	F	4	1	0	0	1,671
Jester	5	M	13	1	1	1	54,824
Jester Rahab	4	F	1	0	1	0	9,000
Jester's Pet	5	G	2	0	0	0	258
Jestin in Control	6	G	9	1	0	0	7,663
Jestina	4	F	3	0	0	1	374
Jesy Joe	5	G	4	0	0	0	0
Jet Alert	3	C	4	1	1	1	60,300
Jet Appeal	2	C	5	0	1	0	2,782
Jet Away	5	H	4	0	0	0	86
Jet Black Cadi	3	G	12	1	1	3	59,275
Jet Black Jack	2	G	2	0	0	0	1,236
Jet Black Magic	2	F	2	0	0	0	0
Jet Blast	4	G	13	3	1	0	13,620
Jet Cadet	5	M	3	0	0	0	0
Jet Car	3	F	8	0	3	3	27,720

Horse	Age	Sex	Sts	1st	2d	3d	Won
Jet City Woman	3	F	4	0	0	1	577
Jet Fighter	3	G	12	0	3	3	6,968
Jet Flight	3	C	19	0	1	3	7,040
Jet G Pride	4	F	9	4	3	0	56,135
Jet G Star	2	C	2	0	0	0	205
Jet G Sun	2	C	3	1	0	0	6,615
Jet in Time	5	G	7	1	2	2	14,431
Jet La Rail	6	G	8	2	1	3	12,809
Jet Legacy	4	G	6	1	0	1	9,627
Jet Line	7	M	11	3	2	0	24,431
Jet Love	3	G	7	1	0	1	22,350
Jet n' Expectation	3	F	16	2	7	3	64,496
Jet Pass	3	G	5	0	0	0	118
Jet Phone	2	C	2	1	0	0	15,600
Jet Princess	3	F	10	0	0	0	2,396
Jet Prospector	2	C	2	0	2	0	16,400
Jet Quest	5	G	12	0	2	1	3,708
Jet Set American	7	G	4	0	0	0	226
Jet Set Honey	3	F	1	0	0	0	0
Jet Set Jazz	4	F	5	0	0	0	1,443
Jet Set Joey G	3	G	4	2	2	0	13,870
Jet Set Liona	2	F	2	0	0	0	0
Jet Set Vet	4	G	7	1	0	1	6,035
Jet Ski	8	G	11	1	4	0	7,591
Jet Splash	5	M	2	0	0	0	86
Jet Thrust	4	G	2	0	0	1	638
Jet to Hawaii	4	C	1	0	0	0	110
Jet to Party	5	M	1	0	0	1	680
Jet West	2	C	2	1	0	1	25,480
Jetabud	4	C	3	1	1	0	6,380
Jetalito	4	G	9	1	1	2	15,105
Jethro Blue	5	G	9	6	0	1	48,918
Jethro's Fling	6	G	8	2	2	1	13,344
Jetinto Houston	4	F	6	2	1	1	134,581
Jet'n Jeanie	2	F	2	0	0	0	145
Jet's Account	4	F	18	1	2	4	9,387
Jet's Bonus	2	F	1	0	0	0	0
Jets Fan	3	G	9	3	4	0	72,575
Jet's Historic	2	F	2	0	0	0	0
Jetset Saint	4	F	10	1	2	0	19,900
Jetsetnpatsie	3	F	1	0	0	0	0
Jetson	4	G	2	0	0	1	4,770
Jetster	2	F	1	1	0	0	18,800
Jett Blue	4	C	4	0	3	0	5,481
Jett Buie	4	F	6	0	0	0	0
Jett of the Nile	3	F	6	1	2	3	10,760
Jett Stream	5	G	8	2	1	1	11,227
Jetta Lee	3	F	4	0	0	0	464
Jettalyn	5	M	12	0	0	1	11,210
Jettapower	5	G	2	0	0	0	1,092
Jetta's Golden Boy	4	C	9	0	1	0	4,000
Jettias	7	G	15	0	0	0	1,046
Jetticus	2	C	1	0	0	0	0
Jettin Fever	2	F	4	1	0	0	4,831
Jettin Suzy	2	F	1	0	0	0	100
Jettin to Dinner	4	F	12	1	3	1	13,533
Jettin Zone	5	M	5	1	0	0	1,996
Jettin'for Roobels	3	F	8	0	0	1	3,646
Jetting	4	C	7	1	1	1	8,600
Jettish	3	F	1	0	0	0	120
Jetts Delight	5	G	6	0	1	0	3,250
Jewel Alarm	4	F	7	2	2	0	15,411
Jewel Beauty	3	C	7	0	2	0	5,763
Jewel Case	4	F	8	1	1	1	11,144
Jewel Creek	3	F	17	1	4	3	12,503
Jewel Hunter	2	F	4	1	0	0	7,440
Jewel in the Hills	5	M	14	1	0	1	6,920
Jewel Magic (NZ)	7	M	6	0	0	1	1,650
Jewel of a Gal	2	F	2	0	0	0	115
Jewel of Asia	5	M	5	1	1	0	6,950
Jewel of Nahuel	4	F	9	0	0	0	475
Jewel of the Cat	2	F	2	0	0	0	420
Jewel of the North	5	M	3	0	0	0	2,120
Jewel of Toronto	5	H	2	0	0	1	1,888
Jewel Queen	2	F	4	0	2	1	11,776
Jewel Stick	8	M	2	0	0	0	220
Jewel Thief Jimmy	6	G	7	0	0	1	2,870
Jewelette	2	F	4	1	0	0	3,870
Jewelia	4	F	13	1	1	5	30,817

Horse	Age	Sex	Sts	1st	2d	3d	Won
Jewelite	3	G	10	0	2	2	7,322
Jewels Again	4	F	11	2	1	3	20,799
Jewel's Dream	3	F	5	0	0	1	975
Jewels for a Lady	3	F	9	4	1	0	65,528
Jewel's Haven	5	M	13	0	2	2	4,001
Jewels N Gems	2	F	3	2	0	0	34,800
Jewels of Nepal	5	M	4	0	0	0	198
Jewel's Passing By	4	F	6	0	1	0	1,740
Jewels Pride	5	M	14	3	0	2	17,560
Jewels Rocket	3	G	2	0	1	0	5,310
Jewels Togo	8	G	5	1	0	1	1,644
Jezabel Cant Spell	5	M	10	1	0	2	16,899
Jezabel's Magic	9	M	4	0	1	0	1,312
Jezebella	4	F	9	1	0	0	7,300
Jhecho	4	G	1	0	0	0	348
Jibarita	2	F	2	0	0	1	1,170
Jibber Jabber	2	F	5	0	1	1	5,842
Jibberlump	3	G	3	0	0	0	225
Jiffy Lou	5	H	11	1	0	0	5,340
Jiffy Native	2	C	4	0	0	1	1,913
Jiffy Wish	6	M	11	3	2	1	54,970
Jiffyjimmygee	3	G	9	0	1	3	14,232
Jig o' Scotch	7	G	15	0	0	1	8,895
Jig Step	3	F	3	0	0	0	420
Jiggly Puff	4	F	2	1	0	0	5,400
Jiggy Man	5	G	11	2	2	1	12,114
Jiggy With It	7	M	11	1	3	2	9,610
Jigsaw	2	G	6	1	0	2	8,360
Jigtime Jones	3	F	6	0	0	0	116
Jigtime Term	4	G	6	0	0	0	420
Jila (IRE)	8	H	14	3	2	0	77,400
Jill McGill	4	F	9	2	0	1	45,840
Jill Rabbit	4	F	11	1	1	3	18,380
Jill Regs Winner	3	F	8	0	2	1	9,415
Jill the Shill	3	F	1	0	0	0	0
Jillian Grey	3	F	4	0	0	0	573
Jillings	6	G	1	0	0	0	0
Jillmissedapill	6	M	4	0	0	1	1,837
Jills Accent	2	F	8	1	3	1	17,685
Jill's Bill	3	G	4	0	0	0	47
Jill's Ego	3	F	7	0	3	1	15,001
Jill's Joy	2	F	2	0	0	1	1,270
Jill's Jumpshot	4	C	10	0	0	2	9,300
Jill's Last Hero	5	M	2	0	0	0	780
Jill's Layup	3	F	6	3	1	1	75,250
Jill's Polka	3	C	10	0	0	2	3,694
Jilly Billie	3	F	7	0	0	1	260
Jillybell	3	F	2	0	0	0	0
Jiltaluck	4	G	11	1	1	3	7,767
Jilted	4	F	1	0	0	0	1,110
Jilted Groom	6	G	5	2	0	1	8,675
Jilted Heart	2	C	8	2	3	0	29,778
Jilted Lass	3	F	2	0	0	0	1,200
Jilted Love	4	F	12	2	2	2	28,964
Jim Abel	2	C	4	0	0	0	0
Jim Cat	5	H	8	0	0	3	2,468
Jim Dunham	12	G	2	0	0	0	0
Jim Jams	9	G	10	1	3	0	11,629
Jim the Gent	2	C	6	1	0	1	8,910
Jim Thirds Bolero	4	G	6	1	2	2	41,890
Jimani	3	F	7	2	0	1	26,390
Jimbo Don	6	G	12	1	2	4	8,469
Jimbob's Star	4	G	8	1	0	1	4,572
Jimbodini	3	C	6	0	1	1	6,407
Jimdandytodaresqu	6	G	10	0	2	1	1,386
Jimenez	3	G	8	1	1	1	6,460
Jimie Son	6	H	13	3	1	4	30,084
Jimini C. Dues	12	G	16	2	2	2	10,826
Jimmie J	4	C	11	2	1	1	25,620
Jimmielee	4	G	9	0	0	0	2,370
Jimmie's Button	3	F	3	0	0	0	152
Jimmies Pleasures	5	H	12	0	0	0	1,182
Jimmies Ticket	6	G	8	1	1	1	12,091
Jimmy Cracked Corn	2	G	4	1	1	0	21,860
Jimmy Diesel	2	G	2	0	0	0	144
Jimmy Driftwood	5	G	18	1	2	5	9,285
Jimmy Dunne's Boy	2	G	5	0	0	0	4,660
Jimmy Dunnes World	4	C	3	0	0	0	820
Jimmy Easter	4	C	10	0	1	0	11,225

Horse	Age	Sex	Sts	1st	2d	3d	Won
Jimmy John	4	C	11	0	2	0	3,230
Jimmy Jones	6	G	9	0	3	0	14,521
Jimmy Lapa	4	C	16	0	4	2	7,997
Jimmy Mack	2	G	5	0	1	2	2,496
Jimmy Moon	2	C	4	2	0	1	25,850
Jimmy O	3	G	8	1	1	2	75,336
Jimmy of Paraqua	2	C	4	1	0	0	2,840
Jimmy One Punch	2	G	6	0	1	0	9,829
Jimmy the Wise	3	C	3	0	1	1	2,571
Jimmy Who	4	C	3	2	1	0	6,440
Jimmy Z	6	G	7	1	0	1	43,825
Jimmyboy	4	G	3	1	1	0	11,090
Jimmy's Account	3	G	12	3	0	3	15,928
Jimmy's Appeal	4	F	7	0	0	1	1,319
Jimmy's Best	5	G	13	0	1	0	2,814
Jimmy's Boy	3	C	7	2	2	1	54,020
Jimmy's Instinct	2	G	4	1	0	0	21,540
Jimmy's Move	3	F	14	2	1	0	11,218
Jimmy's Prize	5	G	11	1	1	1	39,820
Jimmy's Saber	3	G	11	4	1	0	97,960
Jim's Account	11	G	7	1	2	1	4,140
Jim's Basque	3	G	11	1	2	1	30,840
Jim's Conquista	3	F	14	2	2	2	12,554
Jim's Country King	3	G	13	0	1	0	3,244
Jims Dreams	3	G	4	0	0	0	1,090
Jim's Drive	3	C	3	1	1	0	29,800
Jim's Gold	6	M	11	1	2	2	9,020
Jims Lil Lady	2	F	1	0	0	0	0
Jim's Lisa Nor	6	M	10	0	0	0	1,138
Jims Luck	8	G	6	1	0	0	3,120
Jim's Nasty	5	G	11	1	1	2	6,277
Jim's Pal	2	C	1	0	0	0	43
Jim's Relaunch	6	G	14	1	1	3	15,192
Jim's Remember Me	5	H	15	2	2	0	6,314
Jim's Ruckus	6	G	11	0	0	1	390
Jim's Rusty Gem	3	G	6	0	1	0	3,676
Jim's Super Bonus	2	G	9	0	0	1	1,294
Jim's Top	3	G	3	0	0	0	0
Jingle Bell Boy	4	C	5	0	1	0	1,394
Jinglethatbell	3	G	6	0	0	0	441
Jingling Coins	10	M	2	0	0	0	76
Jini's Jet	5	G	4	0	2	2	18,400
Jink	3	G	11	0	0	3	11,360
Jink Williams	3	G	6	0	1	1	9,360
Jinks Gold	8	G	13	1	3	0	15,846
Jinny's Gold	2	F	5	1	2	0	33,590
Jinx's Boy	2	G	6	1	1	2	6,689
Jirah	10	G	11	1	2	0	4,639
Jiroga Lite	4	F	10	0	1	5	17,393
Jiroga Winds	2	G	3	1	0	0	7,596
Ji's Hawkie	4	G	3	0	0	0	114
Jit	4	G	9	3	0	2	26,026
Jitter	3	G	5	2	1	0	30,100
Jitterbug	3	G	10	2	1	2	7,300
Jitterbug Jan	4	F	11	3	2	3	57,270
Jitterbug Joy	2	F	4	0	0	1	2,784
Jittery Bug	6	G	9	0	0	1	3,129
Jiva Ridge	3	F	5	0	0	0	305
Jive At Five	5	G	6	2	2	1	45,100
Jive Cat	2	F	1	0	0	0	195
Jive E Z	4	C	2	0	0	0	325
Jive Queen	3	F	1	0	0	0	0
Jive Talking	5	G	12	3	2	3	19,544
Jizzan	3	G	9	0	0	3	1,860
Jj's Greypinstripe	6	H	6	1	0	0	7,360
Jk's Dreamer	2	F	4	0	0	0	509
Jo Ante	3	F	9	0	0	0	173
Jo de Lune	7	M	5	0	1	1	1,392
Jo Dee Who	2	C	3	0	2	0	16,603
Jo Di	4	F	11	3	1	2	10,409
Jo Dinah	4	F	17	2	3	2	35,190
Jo Jo	2	F	5	0	0	0	1,885
Jo Jo Bean	2	G	6	1	0	2	7,530
Jo Jo Dancer	4	C	8	1	4	1	36,768
Jo Jo's Boy	5	G	3	0	0	0	620
Jo Jo's Time	2	C	8	0	2	1	16,765
Jo Mary	4	F	2	0	0	1	1,880
Jo Me the Money	3	F	12	5	1	1	79,270
Jo Right Side	2	G	1	0	0	0	60
Jo the Boss	3	F	1	0	0	0	118
Jo Z D	5	M	10	1	0	1	4,396
Joa	4	C	8	2	1	1	39,780
Joan	3	F	4	0	0	1	2,940
Joan and Mary	2	F	3	0	1	0	2,200
Joan Joan Joan	2	F	1	0	0	0	130
Joan Paul Jones	4	F	2	0	0	0	152
Joanair	3	F	1	0	0	0	0
Joanie B Good	3	F	12	1	0	2	11,480
Joanie B.	4	F	19	2	6	2	17,995
Joanie Gal	3	F	6	0	0	0	315
Joanie So Lucky	4	G	5	0	0	1	1,174
Joanie T.	3	F	5	0	0	0	225
Joanie's Hero	4	F	12	2	2	1	12,734
Joanie's Hit	2	F	2	1	0	0	4,620
Joanie's Jett	5	M	8	2	1	1	37,431
Joanie's Miracle	4	F	4	0	0	0	418
Joanies No Phony	6	G	13	1	3	2	20,583
Joanie's Prissy	7	M	11	0	0	2	3,204
Joanie's Smile	3	F	1	0	0	0	360
Joanie's Sweet Pea	5	M	10	2	0	1	16,835
Joanie's Way	4	F	5	0	0	0	282
Joanna's Tuition	4	F	9	2	1	1	16,790
Joanne Apple	5	M	3	0	0	2	1,763
Joannesprincesscat	4	F	7	0	0	0	655
Joann's Joy	4	F	18	2	6	2	45,722
Joans Charm	4	F	8	0	0	0	1,050
Joan's Gray Beauty	3	F	5	0	2	2	11,780
Joan's Rig	10	G	13	0	0	0	975
Joan's Sense	5	M	4	0	0	0	272
Jobetta	7	M	2	0	0	0	0
Jocasta	2	F	7	1	0	0	6,120
Jockeys Limo	4	G	2	0	0	0	180
Jocko	4	C	4	1	1	0	22,800
Jockos Bid	7	G	4	0	0	0	263
Jockos Command	8	G	9	0	0	1	760
Jocy's Coyote	5	M	9	0	3	2	5,403
Jodawn	5	G	13	1	0	0	8,979
Jodi H	3	F	10	1	1	2	9,136
Jodi's Wings	5	M	16	4	5	4	63,350
Jody Jet	2	F	3	1	0	0	5,810
Jodys Deelite	3	F	9	2	1	0	54,647
Joe	4	G	4	0	0	0	1,750
Joe At Six	7	G	5	4	0	0	18,375
Joe Bear	5	G	7	0	0	1	1,533
Joe Bear (IRE)	3	C	5	1	1	1	111,326
Joe Can't Quit	4	C	16	3	2	2	18,132
Joe Cat.	4	C	15	1	2	4	28,086
Joe Dancer Too	3	G	9	2	1	0	22,245
Joe Favorite	6	G	4	0	1	0	1,752
Joe Fehr's Winner	3	G	1	0	0	0	116
Joe Fraser	3	C	1	0	0	0	744
Joe Holiday	5	G	4	1	0	2	3,930
Joe Holster	7	G	9	2	1	0	6,982
Joe I Know	4	C	15	0	1	3	4,399
Joe Java	5	G	16	2	0	5	12,092
Joe Kellys Tune	4	G	10	0	0	2	1,442
Joe Kool	5	H	3	0	0	0	195
Joe Leo	3	C	5	1	0	1	7,470
Joe Move	3	C	7	0	1	0	6,670
Joe Pag	3	C	5	1	2	1	20,110
Joe Pat	4	G	13	1	2	2	17,308
Joe Six Pack	2	G	4	3	0	0	127,800
Joe Snell	4	G	5	1	0	1	5,413
Joe T Bailey	5	G	14	0	2	4	10,599
Joe Tourist	3	G	16	4	3	0	29,600
Joe Two Lips	6	H	5	0	1	0	7,260
Joe What	3	G	5	1	0	0	5,215
Joelino	5	G	2	0	0	0	301
Joepa	7	G	7	0	1	1	3,728
Joequette	5	M	6	0	0	0	50
Joeronohmoe	3	F	7	3	1	1	41,836
Joe's a Smokin	3	C	3	0	0	0	300
Joe's Baby Ruth	4	F	1	0	0	0	0
Joes Bad Girl Ed	5	M	7	0	0	0	884
Joe's Big Boy	4	G	22	2	1	4	12,152
Joe's Big Gun	7	G	7	0	1	1	3,734
Joe's Boy Adam	5	G	5	0	0	0	1,948
Joe's Charm	6	H	3	0	0	0	

Horse	Age	Sex	Sts	1st	2d	3d	Won	Horse	Age	Sex	Sts	1st	2d	3d	Won
Joe's Command	3	G	15	1	0	5	25,670	Johnny Law	4	G	4	1	0	1	5,740
Joe's Garage	5	H	2	0	0	1	1,760	Johnny Loves Jazz	3	G	24	3	2	1	26,613
Joe's Last Dance	6	H	6	0	0	1	1,002	Johnny Magic	3	C	6	1	0	0	41,346
Joe's Lovin It	3	G	14	2	1	0	19,212	Johnny Ola	3	G	9	1	2	2	41,540
Joes Lucky Girl	3	F	2	0	0	0	137	Johnny One Note	5	G	7	2	1	2	21,562
Joes Lucky Nail	4	F	2	0	0	0	246	Johnny One Sock	3	C	9	1	2	0	15,996
Joes Native Star	6	H	3	1	1	1	1,588	Johnny Red Kerr	3	C	1	0	0	0	0
Joe's Our Santa	4	C	3	0	1	0	790	Johnny Regency	3	C	3	0	0	0	0
Joe's Son Joey	5	H	6	3	1	1	163,186	Johnny Ringo	6	G	5	0	0	1	1,300
Joe's Trick	4	C	1	0	0	0	0	Johnny Show	6	G	6	0	2	1	13,050
Joes Wicked Aly	6	G	7	1	0	0	3,600	Johnny Tornado	2	G	6	2	1	0	28,612
Joe'sdancing Angel	2	C	5	0	0	1	4,715	Johnny Turk Band	5	M	8	4	1	0	25,500
Joeski	6	G	5	0	1	1	3,345	Johnny Two Dot	3	G	11	2	0	1	12,733
Joethehorse	2	G	1	0	0	0	0	Johnny Two Fingers	4	G	13	1	3	1	24,578
Joey Blueeyes	3	C	12	4	2	1	55,310	Johnnybean'shoolie	2	G	4	0	0	0	436
Joey Bota Bing	3	G	7	0	1	2	4,479	Johnnynmotion	6	G	16	1	3	1	10,955
Joey Elwhiz	3	C	11	0	0	1	1,540	Johnnyou	2	C	4	1	1	0	10,320
Joey Franco	4	C	10	4	1	0	452,361	Johnny's Cache	3	G	6	0	0	1	4,617
Joey G	2	C	4	1	0	1	13,702	Johnny's Chance	3	F	6	0	0	0	630
Joey's Femme	5	M	6	0	0	0	562	Johnny's Lil Girl	3	F	3	0	0	0	0
Joey's Girl	2	F	5	0	0	1	2,850	Johnny's Nickle	6	M	9	0	0	1	1,537
Joeys Great Esteem	4	C	3	0	0	0	713	John's Castle	5	H	15	1	4	2	21,629
Joey's Haji	8	G	7	0	1	2	2,598	Johns Cowboy	4	G	1	0	0	0	100
Joey's Law	7	G	15	2	3	3	39,880	John's Ensign	3	C	21	0	2	3	5,845
Joey's Queen	4	F	1	0	0	0	107	Johns Hot Water	4	C	7	0	2	1	7,585
Jog Trot	5	G	3	0	0	0	410	John's Interview	2	C	1	0	0	0	164
Joggy Told	5	H	13	1	2	3	4,791	John's Jet	3	C	13	1	2	3	67,230
Jogo Antigo (BRZ)	6	G	8	2	0	2	12,315	John's Joy	3	G	6	2	3	0	78,900
Johar	4	C	5	2	1	1	912,281	John's Kinda Girl	2	F	2	1	0	1	24,480
Joharra	3	F	5	0	3	0	33,894	John's Marq	4	C	11	4	3	2	58,400
John Alan	5	G	15	2	3	1	23,290	John's Mecke	2	C	6	0	3	0	11,575
John Bobby	4	C	6	2	1	1	9,952	Johns Order	5	G	6	0	0	0	545
John Brazil	6	G	2	0	0	1	3,000	John's Prince	3	C	1	0	0	0	0
John Calvin	3	G	15	3	1	1	22,160	John's Princess	4	F	7	0	3	0	9,302
John Cody	9	G	2	0	0	0	0	John's Proof	4	G	11	0	0	2	2,018
John Crainer	4	G	9	5	0	1	30,780	John's Rockfleet	7	G	9	1	1	2	12,122
John David	2	C	9	0	0	2	4,460	John's Royal Treat	5	G	16	2	2	2	9,727
John Dool (BRZ)	6	G	5	1	0	0	5,402	John's Run	5	G	6	0	0	0	432
John Galt	4	C	6	1	1	1	6,174	Johns Rush	3	C	5	1	1	1	18,485
John Glen	3	G	10	1	0	3	11,644	Johns Tofasttopass	3	G	1	0	0	0	0
John Grove	3	G	1	0	0	0	0	John's Wise	5	H	5	0	0	2	4,750
John Lack Land	12	G	2	0	0	0	0	John'sbirthdaygirl	5	M	11	1	0	1	12,517
John Little	5	G	8	0	0	0	6,540	Johnson County	4	G	3	0	0	0	267
John Morgan	3	G	11	2	2	2	23,510	Johnthegoodhusband	4	G	11	1	2	2	6,916
John Paul	6	G	20	7	3	3	34,363	Johnyefayesbo	3	F	5	0	0	0	360
John Paul Too	6	H	2	1	0	0	25,200	Johny's Champion	9	G	17	0	2	2	5,288
John Q	3	C	1	0	0	0	0	Join	4	F	1	0	0	0	0
John R	3	C	3	2	0	0	17,400	Joint Custody	4	G	8	0	0	0	1,320
John Ross	6	G	18	0	0	2	2,471	Joint Decision	6	G	10	0	1	2	4,860
John So n' So	2	C	1	0	0	0	52	Joint Lake	5	G	11	0	2	3	9,774
John the Broker	6	G	13	7	3	0	27,610	Jointed Glances	3	C	7	1	1	1	9,207
John the Diceman	2	G	5	1	1	3	17,290	Jojo Dadogfacedboy	2	G	4	0	0	1	3,315
John Thomas	4	G	8	0	2	0	4,828	Jojo Marie	2	F	2	0	0	0	1,170
John Wells	3	G	2	0	0	0	0	Jojo's Beau	4	F	7	0	2	0	4,328
John Wood	3	G	1	0	0	0	52	Jojo's Midas Touch	3	G	5	0	0	0	569
Johnarose	3	F	1	0	0	0	101	Jojo's Reality	3	C	1	0	0	0	47
Johnathan	3	G	4	1	2	1	29,480	Jojo's Sword	2	C	5	0	0	0	0
Johnato	3	G	9	2	0	2	12,075	Jojustice	6	G	14	3	2	1	8,606
Johnduffswood	4	G	14	1	1	1	7,296	Jokeisover	4	F	14	2	1	4	14,185
Johnir's Chance	4	F	4	0	0	2	3,454	Joker's Big Gun	4	G	3	0	1	0	583
Johnna Ray	6	M	6	0	0	0	300	Jokers Brat	4	F	2	0	0	0	0
Johnnie Five O	2	G	5	0	2	2	6,552	Jokers Dance	5	M	5	1	0	1	2,558
Johnnie On the Run	3	G	10	0	2	2	10,599	Jokers Frangrance	8	G	1	0	0	0	0
Johnnie Thirty Six	4	F	3	0	0	0	2,307	Joker's Gold	5	H	4	0	0	0	380
Johnnie Twentyfive	5	M	2	0	0	0	508	Jokesonme	7	M	7	1	0	1	14,520
Johnnie Twentynine	5	H	1	0	0	0	0	Jokey	6	H	4	1	1	1	21,940
Johnnies Wagon	5	G	12	2	4	1	20,557	Joking Around	4	C	15	2	1	0	15,600
Johnny Avenger	4	C	10	2	3	1	5,489	Jok'n Victory	3	F	1	0	0	0	540
Johnny Be Good	5	G	4	0	0	0	210	Jol	3	G	14	1	2	1	59,000
Johnny Box	3	C	11	3	0	3	80,660	Jolaris	3	F	6	1	1	1	5,415
Johnny Boy	2	C	4	0	1	2	9,860	Jolene's Turn	3	F	7	1	0	6	7,975
Johnny Bright	6	G	10	1	4	1	11,396	Joleur	11	G	6	0	2	0	5,770
Johnny Buck	6	G	14	1	2	0	5,851	Joley's Honor	6	M	9	0	1	0	5,891
Johnny Cake Road	3	G	8	0	1	1	3,389	Jolie	4	F	2	0	1	1	13,770
Johnny Canuck	3	C	3	0	0	0	722	Jolie Badgett	3	F	4	1	1	1	17,600
Johnny Corvette	3	C	3	0	0	0	570	Jolie Girlie	4	F	3	1	0	1	4,620
Johnny Dollar	7	G	2	0	0	0	1,860	Jolie Good	3	F	13	2	0	4	25,734
Johnny Fitz	3	C	2	0	0	0	2,750	Jolie Jet	4	F	1	0	0	0	75
Johnny Hollywood	4	G	11	1	3	1	102,297	Jolie Louise	2	F	1	0	0	0	75

Horse	Age	Sex	Sts	1st	2d	3d	Won	Horse	Age	Sex	Sts	1st	2d	3d	Won
Jolie Miss Jolie	3	F	13	2	2	2	12,104	Jose Gaspar	4	C	9	2	0	3	41,818
Jolie On a Roll	3	G	7	2	1	1	10,885	Josefa Star (ARG)	3	F	4	0	0	3	3,131
Jolie Raja	5	G	7	0	3	0	6,315	Josefina Verde	3	F	6	0	0	0	0
Jolie's Dream	6	M	7	1	1	1	7,785	Joseph Anthony	3	C	2	0	1	0	3,200
Jolie's Gift	2	C	6	0	0	1	2,075	Joseph B	4	G	10	0	0	0	1,345
Jolie's Gold	3	F	2	0	0	0	680	Joseph George	6	H	10	3	2	2	4,468
Jolie's Julia	4	F	9	0	1	2	13,848	Joseph G's Gal	3	F	15	2	2	3	22,557
Jolie's Leader	3	F	8	2	4	0	29,638	Joseph Smokineagle	5	G	12	0	0	1	1,961
Jolie's Star	7	G	14	2	3	0	9,049	Josephita	5	M	2	0	0	0	270
Jolie's Storm	7	G	4	1	0	0	2,205	Joseph's Aarival	3	C	2	0	0	0	320
Jolie's Thunder	5	G	10	0	3	1	25,090	Jose's Top Gun	3	G	8	0	0	2	3,905
Jolie's Victory	2	G	2	0	1	0	2,700	Joses Wild Event	2	F	2	0	0	0	333
Jollie Prince	4	G	14	1	2	2	18,845	Josey Hawk	4	G	4	0	0	0	329
Jollies Fortune	2	G	7	0	1	0	3,393	Josey Hill	2	F	1	1	0	0	38,820
Jollie's Gold Wand	3	F	3	0	0	0	0	Josey's Trick	5	G	13	3	1	2	14,984
Jolly D	3	C	3	0	0	0	485	Josh Daniel	2	C	2	0	0	0	140
Jolly Fraser	6	M	6	1	2	2	13,892	Josh On a Roll	5	H	5	1	2	0	11,816
Jolly Friar	3	G	11	2	1	2	23,656	Joshie's Prospect	2	G	1	0	0	0	126
Jolly Good Fellow	4	G	11	2	1	0	9,327	Josh's Apple	6	G	6	2	2	0	51,900
Jolly Lady	4	F	7	0	0	0	1,460	Josh's Babe	6	M	1	0	0	0	0
Jolly Ol' Nick	2	G	3	0	0	1	989	Josh's Madelyn	2	F	5	0	1	1	9,030
Jolly 'oliday	6	G	20	0	0	0	956	Josh's Pool	3	F	4	1	0	0	7,800
Jolly One	3	F	1	0	0	1	1,485	Josh's Slick Angel	3	G	3	0	0	0	225
Jolly Optimist	5	M	4	0	0	0	1,761	Joshua Jude	2	C	1	0	1	0	1,900
Jolly Saint Jade	4	G	4	0	0	0	0	Joshua Lightheart	2	G	2	1	0	0	7,620
Jolly Sammy	8	G	4	1	1	0	6,836	Joshua Storm	3	G	12	1	2	2	10,134
Jolly Taxpayer	10	G	1	1	0	0	4,095	Joshua's Fit	2	C	2	1	0	0	13,430
Jolly's Music	4	F	14	1	2	5	15,413	Joshua's Game	3	G	5	1	2	0	7,240
Jolteon	4	F	7	0	1	1	2,857	Joshua's Jaybird	4	G	4	0	0	0	0
Joltin Joe	4	G	4	0	0	0	0	Joshua's Jet	5	H	6	0	0	0	5,400
Joltin Vince	3	G	8	2	4	1	20,700	Joshuas Rider	3	G	5	1	0	0	3,584
Joma	2	C	4	0	2	1	10,510	Joshuas Symphony	3	G	10	2	2	1	18,053
Jomarsmutchkin	3	C	12	1	2	5	5,557	Josie	5	M	1	0	0	0	0
Jomax	7	H	10	2	3	2	39,879	Josie Bells	2	F	1	0	0	0	0
Jon Boy	4	G	8	1	0	1	8,734	Josie G.	2	F	7	2	3	2	55,325
Jon Michael	7	H	5	2	0	1	5,235	Josies Impact	4	F	11	0	2	1	6,425
Jonah	3	G	9	0	1	2	8,138	Josie's Luckycharm	5	M	2	0	0	0	0
Jonah B. Quick	5	G	2	0	0	0	268	Josie's Peak	3	F	11	0	1	2	5,319
Jonahs Praise	6	G	10	0	1	0	2,626	Josie'slil'actress	3	F	13	1	0	1	6,975
Jonas (URU)	5	G	19	1	5	2	19,210	Josphen	2	F	3	0	0	0	360
Jonathan Junior	6	H	1	0	0	0	3,300	Jostlin Kate	4	F	12	3	4	0	27,309
Jonathons Gal	4	F	10	1	1	1	16,700	Journey	4	C	11	0	1	1	3,742
Jones Lake	3	F	1	1	0	0	5,830	Journey Fever	2	F	9	2	3	1	131,484
Jones Reserve	6	G	12	2	2	2	18,987	Journey Leader	4	G	8	0	1	0	4,428
Jones Tale	3	C	2	0	1	0	11,340	Joust	3	G	10	1	1	1	11,000
Joneta	4	F	12	4	1	3	37,370	Joven	2	G	1	0	0	0	0
Joni Girl	3	F	12	0	0	0	620	Joveona	2	F	1	0	0	0	0
Joni's Rose	3	F	4	0	0	0	2,460	Jove's Aubee	6	M	2	1	1	0	19,800
Jonker	10	G	5	0	0	4	4,560	Jovi Slew	2	C	2	0	0	0	600
Jonniejonjon	3	C	12	1	2	1	9,241	Jovial Belle	3	F	10	1	1	1	9,846
Jonnygetachex	2	C	8	3	2	1	90,726	Jovial Cat	3	F	2	0	0	1	2,860
Jonquiere	4	G	8	1	1	2	32,439	Jovial Forecast	7	G	13	4	2	1	24,990
Jon's Raindrop	5	G	3	0	0	0	215	Jovial Joshua	2	G	4	1	2	0	8,600
Jonsdremingagain	4	G	11	2	1	1	10,248	Jovial Lady	4	F	8	2	0	1	12,805
Jonstar (NZ)	5	G	8	1	2	0	23,510	Jovially	2	F	4	2	0	0	36,270
Jordan Pond	2	F	5	1	0	0	8,040	Jovialness	3	F	6	1	1	2	35,560
Jordana	3	F	7	1	0	3	11,440	Jovite Knight	5	H	4	0	0	0	226
Jordan's Big Rig	4	G	8	2	1	2	13,505	Jovite's Angel	2	F	2	0	0	0	0
Jordan's Double	3	F	1	0	0	0	100	Jovocop	4	G	13	1	3	4	15,608
Jordan's Hope	3	G	9	0	0	1	1,791	Joxer	4	G	13	2	1	2	31,790
Jordan's Party	3	G	2	0	0	0	330	Joy N Spirit	4	F	9	0	1	0	2,988
Jordan's Tractor	3	C	5	1	0	0	15,600	Joy of Brandy	5	M	6	2	0	0	7,138
Jordan's Victory	3	G	2	0	0	0	174	Joy of It All	8	F	13	1	3	1	36,971
Jordi Moi	5	G	8	0	1	0	7,170	Joy of Life	2	F	1	0	0	0	2,286
Jordin Foo Da Ya	5	M	1	0	0	0	0	Joy of Millbrook	4	F	6	0	2	0	18,706
Jordo	2	F	3	1	0	0	5,820	Joy of the Game	2	F	4	0	0	0	1,010
Jordy B	4	F	7	0	1	0	2,400	Joy Shannon	3	F	5	0	0	0	502
Jordyn Macoma	4	F	2	0	1	1	13,270	Joya	3	F	9	1	1	0	10,556
Jordyns Justice	3	F	2	0	0	0	217	Joya de Saros	7	G	10	1	2	2	7,722
Jordy's Pride	2	G	5	0	0	1	3,067	Joybelle	3	F	4	0	0	0	3,147
Jorge	3	G	8	0	0	0	789	Joyce Ann	4	F	14	3	3	2	85,530
Jorgie Stover	5	G	13	1	3	1	79,800	Joyce Dianne	10	M	6	0	0	2	1,648
Jorja's Suite	3	F	6	0	0	2	2,528	Joyce in the Pink	3	F	1	0	0	0	106
Joronimo's Smoke	3	C	15	1	6	2	17,700	Joyce Loves Me	2	F	1	0	0	0	0
Jo's Dancing Boy	3	G	1	0	0	0	0	Joyeux Niner	3	C	14	1	1	2	11,659
Jo's Eddie	5	G	9	2	0	1	24,437	Joyeux Noel	5	M	3	0	3	0	4,500
Jo's Prospector	7	G	14	2	1	3	10,854	Joyeux Occasion	3	C	19	2	0	4	19,958
Jose Caballero	5	H	1	0	0	0	0	Joyful Ballad	3	F	4	1	1	0	13,370
Jose Can You See	4	C	10	1	2	1	12,748	Joyful Energy	5	M	2	0	1	1	8,040

RECORDS OF HORSES

Horse	Age	Sex	Sts	1st	2d	3d	Won	Horse	Age	Sex	Sts	1st	2d	3d	Won
Joyful Kay	2	F	5	1	1	0	7,360	Judge Jordan	6	H	11	2	0	3	11,148
Joyful Meeting	4	F	4	2	1	0	41,860	Judge Judy	8	M	14	1	0	2	10,164
Joyful Tune	5	G	8	3	0	3	86,725	Judge Laurenas	6	M	7	2	2	0	19,212
Joyjet	2	G	7	1	2	2	43,392	Judge Marquesa	4	F	6	0	2	0	6,150
Joyous Appeal	3	F	9	3	0	2	40,120	Judge Me Ifyoucan	4	F	1	0	0	0	2,028
Joyous Bride	3	F	1	0	0	0	0	Judge Me Ladies	6	G	11	1	1	4	13,462
Joyously	3	F	2	0	0	0	1,650	Judge Me Pretty	3	F	6	1	0	0	4,377
Joyride	2	C	6	1	2	1	96,153	Judge Mimie	4	F	2	0	1	1	3,136
Joyrider	3	G	4	0	0	0	0	Judge Nancy	4	F	20	5	5	3	33,870
Joy's Little Toy	5	G	14	1	1	3	10,445	Judge of Character	4	C	2	0	0	0	0
Joy's Toy	6	M	10	3	3	0	9,063	Judge Perkins	2	G	1	1	0	0	38,820
Joys World	3	F	14	1	2	5	45,792	Judge Pritty	2	F	3	0	0	0	1,010
Jozabr	4	G	1	0	0	0	180	Judge Quickly	3	F	9	0	0	0	976
Jr Jazz	3	C	1	0	0	1	260	Judge Ray	4	C	16	2	0	3	17,479
Jr Madeitpossible	2	C	6	0	0	0	655	Judge Relic Kelic	6	M	9	2	0	4	29,911
Jr. Cat	3	C	2	0	0	0	0	Judge Rocks	5	H	11	1	2	1	12,971
Jr. Conquistador	5	G	13	2	1	1	12,960	Judge Roy	5	G	1	0	0	0	0
Jr.'s Wager	2	G	3	0	0	1	450	Judge Ruckus	3	G	10	1	2	2	25,316
Jr's Bonus	8	G	13	1	0	3	10,413	Judge Silver	5	G	3	0	0	0	1,170
Jr's Legacy	4	G	8	1	3	0	9,703	Judge Sophie	3	F	9	1	2	1	6,847
Jr's Scotty	2	C	5	1	0	1	7,200	Judge Spada	5	H	11	2	2	2	23,842
Jr's Shadow Dancer	4	G	6	1	0	0	9,205	Judge Stetson	5	G	17	1	1	3	15,110
Jrsoutofcontrol	5	G	5	0	1	1	9,920	Judge Sweetie	4	F	4	1	0	1	1,807
J's Crafty Cat	3	F	3	1	0	0	8,700	Judge Swiss	3	C	1	0	0	0	20,000
J's Happy Holiday	4	F	16	0	2	4	12,613	Judge This Star	4	F	1	0	0	0	38
J's Jule	3	F	1	0	0	1	2,600	Judge Tyme	7	H	5	0	0	2	314
J's Magic Jet	7	G	8	2	1	2	9,712	Judgemeister	3	G	4	0	1	0	2,610
J's Wild Slew	4	G	11	1	0	0	7,690	Judgemental	4	F	10	1	5	0	9,574
J'ski	5	M	6	0	0	1	1,584	Judgemental Day	6	H	4	0	0	1	975
Jst Befor Valntine	2	F	4	0	0	0	960	Judge's Appeal	3	F	15	3	6	1	68,647
Jtl's Thunder Road	3	C	11	4	0	2	81,224	Judge's Case	6	G	11	0	4	3	119,345
Ju Ju Bean	2	F	6	0	2	2	7,280	Judges Decision	3	G	8	1	0	0	13,230
Juan Dixon	3	G	10	1	1	2	19,685	Judge's Delight	4	F	14	1	1	4	5,956
Juan Jose (CHI)	4	G	1	0	1	0	5,523	Judge's Halo	4	G	12	1	2	1	9,192
Juan of La Mancha	8	G	1	0	0	1	885	Judge's Legacy	3	F	3	0	0	0	4,800
Juan to Dance	8	G	27	2	4	3	38,885	Judge's Pegasus	2	F	3	0	0	0	420
Juan Valdez	8	G	19	5	3	2	57,390	Judge's Treasure	3	G	8	3	1	2	47,152
Juana	3	F	9	0	0	0	188	Judges' View	7	G	9	2	0	2	29,389
Juanita	4	F	4	0	0	0	105	Judging Lady	3	F	13	2	2	0	40,712
Juanky	4	F	9	5	0	0	23,045	Judgmatic	3	C	13	0	2	2	17,320
Juan's Bouncer	3	G	13	0	1	2	5,471	Judith Ann	5	M	9	3	1	2	31,380
Juan's Ivana	4	F	1	0	0	0	45	Judith Come Home	6	G	8	0	2	1	11,043
Juan's Pepe	6	G	5	1	2	0	1,801	Judith's Car	6	G	5	0	1	1	1,523
Juan's Tortilla	3	G	14	1	0	1	7,115	Judith's Deed	3	C	6	1	1	0	11,285
Jubalani	5	G	16	3	1	1	32,573	Judith's Jester	5	G	11	3	0	3	36,890
Jube Jube	4	F	1	1	0	0	12,960	Judiths Minister	2	G	3	1	0	1	5,785
Jubilant Launch	5	M	8	1	0	0	5,446	Judith's Mission	3	G	13	2	3	1	17,923
Jubilation	3	G	12	3	2	1	22,370	Judith's Pirate	2	G	2	0	0	0	3,063
Jubilee Lady	5	M	1	0	0	0	180	Judith's Road	5	M	18	2	4	2	44,291
Jubilee Twist	5	G	7	2	2	0	7,157	Judiths Rumour	3	F	3	1	0	1	10,311
Jubilee's Jasmine	3	F	12	0	1	2	2,192	Judith's Slew	4	G	2	0	0	0	178
Jubileetwothousand	3	G	5	0	1	0	2,020	Judith's Valley	4	F	11	0	0	2	3,330
Juddy's Storm	2	G	4	1	0	0	8,776	Judiths Wild Rush	2	C	4	3	0	0	141,915
Jude's Venture	3	F	1	0	0	0	0	Judo	2	C	3	0	1	0	6,750
Judge Advocate	3	G	8	0	0	1	2,347	Judson Jr.	7	G	6	1	0	1	23,270
Judge Al Cretella	2	C	1	0	0	0	164	Judy in Disguise	4	F	12	1	4	0	19,218
Judge Amy	3	F	6	1	2	1	11,370	Judy Jetson	5	M	11	2	1	1	26,776
Judge B Bourg	6	G	10	1	0	0	9,225	Judy Soda	2	F	5	1	0	1	31,344
Judge B C	4	G	7	1	0	0	3,101	Judy Would	3	F	9	1	1	2	6,459
Judge Ballad	5	G	7	1	0	3	18,580	Judy's Choice	5	M	11	0	0	2	1,765
Judge Barbara	3	F	2	0	1	0	8,050	Judy's Fancy	5	M	4	0	1	0	600
Judge Beautiful	5	M	14	2	1	0	16,110	Judy's Hunter	5	M	8	2	0	0	13,562
Judge Becker	4	G	8	0	1	1	3,784	Judy's Tee Time	3	F	10	1	2	1	14,813
Judge Ben	3	C	7	0	1	2	3,228	Judy's Toy	4	G	10	2	4	0	24,970
Judge Brandy	3	F	6	0	2	0	6,533	Judy's Valentine	3	F	6	2	1	0	25,230
Judge Champs	7	H	14	1	0	1	7,705	Juene Mariee	3	F	2	0	1	0	4,230
Judge Chris	5	H	7	2	0	0	60,490	Jug Rock	6	G	1	0	0	0	0
Judge Cielo	3	G	14	3	5	0	43,200	Jugabug	2	F	4	0	0	0	134
Judge E. C.	2	G	2	0	0	0	217	Juggernaut	4	C	3	2	0	0	39,720
Judge G A	4	C	8	1	1	0	2,056	Juicy Fruits	3	F	1	0	0	0	570
Judge Garr	5	G	3	0	0	0	86	Juicy Plum	6	M	5	1	1	1	4,626
Judge Goldilocks	4	C	16	3	4	1	37,240	Jujuba	4	C	6	0	0	0	676
Judge Harper	3	C	16	2	4	2	56,070	Jule Bandit	4	G	16	2	4	1	47,930
Judge Him Not	4	C	1	0	0	0	0	Jules At Four	3	F	8	0	2	1	24,080
Judge J B	2	F	3	1	1	0	15,076	Jules for A. J.	2	F	8	3	1	1	54,844
Judge J. G.	5	H	7	0	1	1	2,182	Jules Gem	3	F	11	2	2	1	19,649
Judge Jason	3	G	14	1	0	1	28,850	Jules Halo	2	C	2	0	0	0	460
Judge Jerry	5	G	1	0	0	0	54	Jule's Jewel	4	G	9	1	1	4	10,750
Judge John	5	H	3	0	0	0	1,160	Jules Joy	5	M	6	2	0	2	7,450

RECORDS OF HORSES

Horse	Age	Sex	Sts	1st	2d	3d	Won	Horse	Age	Sex	Sts	1st	2d	3d	Won
Jules Peak	2	F	1	0	0	0	1,980	Junior Delaney	4	G	6	0	1	0	3,535
Jules Pride	4	G	12	1	2	0	7,710	Junior Deputy	5	G	3	0	0	0	820
Jule's Promise	4	G	6	2	0	1	29,700	Junior Fager	5	G	9	0	0	0	806
Jules Rules	3	F	13	2	1	0	51,370	Junior G Man	5	G	9	0	1	1	4,009
Jules the Man	4	G	11	1	0	2	8,160	Junior Prom	7	G	8	1	2	1	6,171
Julesburg	4	G	11	2	1	3	22,813	Junior Ruler	2	C	2	0	2	0	920
Juley's Account	5	H	1	0	0	0	135	Juniors Song	2	C	1	0	0	0	0
Julia Faith	2	F	6	0	0	1	1,315	Juniper Kris	3	G	2	1	0	0	18,000
Julia John	3	F	1	0	0	0	220	Juniper Springs	5	M	2	1	1	0	35,000
Julia Singing Bear	3	F	6	2	1	1	52,640	Junk Man	11	G	2	0	0	0	204
Julia Smyth	5	M	5	0	0	0	1,182	Junk Yard Jerry	8	G	8	0	0	0	821
Julian's Commander	2	C	2	0	1	0	6,600	Junkanoo	11	G	9	2	3	0	8,394
Julian's Special	5	H	3	1	0	0	10,124	Junket	7	G	10	6	2	0	47,723
Juliard	3	F	3	0	0	1	3,000	Junkinthetrunk	3	F	8	1	1	0	20,320
Julia's Diamond	2	F	1	0	0	0	0	Jupiter and Mars	2	G	1	0	0	0	0
Julias Gem	3	F	2	0	0	1	923	Jupiter Gentlemen	3	C	1	1	0	0	9,300
Julia's Javelin	4	C	1	0	0	0	642	Jupiter Hollow	4	F	5	1	1	0	13,350
Julia's Legacy	2	F	4	0	2	0	6,000	Juramento	4	C	19	4	0	3	52,876
Julia's Signal	2	C	2	0	0	0	2,800	Jurisprudent	9	G	5	0	0	0	0
Julie Ann Can	3	F	12	0	1	0	1,478	Juro	6	H	2	0	0	0	0
Julie Connectical	3	F	9	1	1	2	14,008	Juroar	3	F	2	0	0	0	1,860
Julie Girl	3	F	3	0	0	0	850	Jury	5	G	11	0	2	0	7,220
Julie Light	6	M	1	0	0	0	0	Jury Box	3	C	1	0	0	0	0
Julie Truly	2	F	2	0	0	0	0	Jus' Lookin'	3	F	6	0	1	0	1,298
Julies Bad Girl	7	M	8	0	0	0	165	Juscauz	3	F	2	0	0	1	530
Julie's Bronzie	3	F	4	1	1	2	12,130	Juskeeprollinalong	4	G	9	2	0	0	13,038
Julies Crown	3	F	2	0	0	0	166	Juslyn	6	M	14	1	2	1	16,237
Julie's Fast Cat	3	F	4	1	0	0	2,640	Jusred	3	F	9	2	3	1	10,104
Julies Flying Now	4	F	10	3	2	1	28,795	Jussila	3	F	9	1	0	3	3,130
Julie's Go Baby Go	3	F	5	0	1	0	8,580	Just a Babe	3	F	12	1	0	1	25,403
Julies Journey	3	F	5	3	1	0	32,000	Just a Bella	5	M	2	0	1	0	2,268
Julie's Luck	3	F	12	2	3	0	15,296	Just a Berry	5	M	13	3	3	1	12,805
Julie's Prize	3	F	9	4	1	1	202,095	Just a Big Hit	4	G	7	1	0	0	2,135
Julie's Turn	4	F	9	1	3	1	37,233	Just a Champion	3	G	3	0	0	0	420
Juliet Rose	3	F	10	0	5	2	9,685	Just a Chip	3	G	5	2	1	0	37,770
Julietas Bolger	7	H	5	2	2	0	9,315	Just a Dance	4	G	10	0	1	1	1,822
Julietta	2	F	1	0	0	0	180	Just a Dancer	3	F	3	0	0	1	1,166
Juli's Jacket	2	F	5	0	0	1	812	Just a Devil	8	G	4	0	0	1	850
Julius T	4	G	13	1	0	3	13,125	Just a Eclipse	9	G	1	0	0	0	333
Julviya	3	F	13	1	0	1	6,675	Just a Falcon	4	G	5	1	0	1	3,987
July Child	3	C	11	3	3	0	95,870	Just a Flash	4	G	2	0	0	0	160
Jumangi (CHI)	7	G	10	1	0	1	10,110	Just a Fool	4	G	6	1	0	1	8,409
Jumby Bay	3	F	2	0	0	0	0	Just a Jewel	5	M	2	0	0	0	480
Jumdunn	5	H	4	0	0	0	0	Just a Kitty	3	F	7	1	1	1	10,946
Jumeirah Jane	6	M	1	0	0	0	38	Just a Lady	4	F	9	1	0	2	8,117
Jumeron Lady	2	F	2	0	0	0	0	Just a Lil Royal	5	M	10	1	1	0	9,119
Jumie	5	M	7	0	2	1	1,999	Just a Little Jo	7	H	3	0	0	0	630
Jump and Shoot	8	G	4	0	1	1	3,815	Just a Patton	3	F	8	0	2	2	6,700
Jump Bail	5	H	8	0	0	3	31,160	Just a Pistol	3	F	14	1	3	1	14,195
Jump for Joyeux	3	G	4	1	1	0	20,680	Just a Priss	4	F	11	2	0	1	11,083
Jumpin Dumplin	5	M	7	0	0	0	266	Just a Raise	6	G	4	0	0	0	0
Jumpin Jazz Man	2	C	1	0	0	0	125	Just a Rumor	5	G	4	0	2	0	1,626
Jumpin Joe	2	C	9	1	1	0	7,210	Just a Runaway	4	G	9	1	0	1	3,406
Jumping Jasper	4	G	8	1	1	1	3,929	Just a Sheila	4	F	15	4	2	2	29,992
Jumpingjupiter	3	G	14	4	2	1	29,180	Just a Shoemaker	5	H	8	0	0	1	2,463
Jumpmaster	4	G	5	0	0	0	391	Just a Sip	3	F	2	0	0	0	200
Jumpscatrun	6	G	8	1	2	0	2,912	Just a Tad Nasty	4	G	2	0	1	0	2,350
Jumpstarter	3	C	11	2	3	0	42,190	Just a Timemachine	4	C	6	1	0	0	7,047
Jumpupanwin	4	F	1	0	0	0	0	Just a True Man	3	G	13	0	2	2	6,635
Junaluska	10	G	9	0	1	0	1,944	Just a Whim	2	C	4	0	0	0	225
June Bug Baby	3	F	5	1	1	0	13,815	Just About Summer	5	G	1	0	0	0	127
June Lady	5	M	13	1	0	3	11,174	Just Alike	2	G	4	0	1	2	4,022
June Lou	4	F	1	0	0	0	0	Just Allen	5	H	12	6	0	2	56,107
June Springs	5	M	12	3	2	2	22,275	Just an Act	5	G	16	5	0	2	40,752
June Year	4	C	7	0	1	0	1,693	Just Another Day	5	M	9	2	0	1	9,152
Junes Fair Decor	6	M	5	0	0	1	1,100	Just Another Fact	2	F	4	1	1	1	23,660
Jungfrau	2	F	1	0	0	0	2,808	Just Another Kim	4	F	6	0	1	1	2,694
Jungle Drums	5	M	10	0	0	0	1,237	Just Ask Me	3	F	6	0	0	1	793
Jungle Jim	5	G	11	0	2	2	3,197	Just At Night	3	F	3	0	0	0	0
Jungle Juice	6	H	7	0	0	1	1,499	Just Awesome	4	F	1	1	0	0	7,500
Jungle Karma	4	F	3	0	2	0	3,496	Just Bagin It	3	G	6	0	1	0	8,318
Jungle Majesty	4	G	15	3	2	2	6,679	Just Baubles Baby	4	F	2	0	1	0	2,266
Jungle Prince	2	G	5	1	2	0	32,000	Just Be Quick	2	C	4	0	0	0	210
Jungle Red	2	G	6	0	0	0	790	Just Beforemidnite	8	H	10	1	2	0	16,420
Jungle Space	4	G	1	0	0	0	40	Just Begone	2	F	4	0	1	0	2,037
Jungle Tigre	2	C	2	0	0	0	204	Just Bill	6	G	8	0	0	2	2,457
Junior B.	4	G	10	0	1	0	2,502	Just Bill Me	3	F	7	2	0	0	90,004
Junior Banker	5	H	9	1	1	1	5,119	Just Blaze	4	C	6	0	1	0	1,287
Junior Bunk	2	C	1	0	0	0	0	Just Bloomed	3	F	6	0	0	0	285

Horse	Age	Sex	Sts	1st	2d	3d	Won
Just Bring It On	3	G	5	0	0	0	263
Just by Chance	3	F	8	2	0	1	40,680
Just Calamity	2	F	2	1	0	0	6,365
Just Call Me Angel	3	F	4	0	1	0	7,155
Just Call Me Berty	5	M	9	2	1	2	31,200
Just Call Me Ed	3	G	5	0	1	2	5,320
Just Call Me Irish	5	M	6	0	1	2	2,246
Just Call Me King	3	C	4	0	0	0	0
Just Call Me Max	4	G	5	0	0	0	0
Just Call Me Mom	5	M	1	0	0	0	0
Just Call Me Roma	2	F	2	0	0	0	2,220
Just Call Me Sal	2	C	4	0	0	0	0
Just Camrod	4	C	8	0	0	1	1,986
Just Cash	2	C	1	0	0	0	100
Just Chip	4	G	2	0	0	0	50
Just Class	3	F	4	0	1	0	2,275
Just Cool	5	H	10	3	1	1	37,433
Just Dancer	4	G	7	0	0	0	420
Just Dancing	4	G	2	0	0	1	456
Just Ducky Too	2	C	3	0	0	0	760
Just Email Me	5	M	7	1	0	0	4,770
Just Emma	4	F	10	1	2	3	24,494
Just Fab Dad	5	M	5	1	2	1	1,543
Just Flight	4	C	1	0	0	0	0
Just Follow Me	6	G	8	0	1	1	6,042
Just for Al	6	G	9	0	0	2	2,204
Just for Dani	4	G	1	0	0	0	420
Just for Deb	2	G	10	3	1	1	59,080
Just for Dino	12	G	4	0	0	0	385
Just for Jean	3	F	6	1	0	1	50,965
Just for John	5	G	19	0	0	0	2,022
Just for Love	5	H	6	0	0	0	522
Just for Money	5	M	14	1	2	3	41,704
Just for Show	4	G	3	0	0	0	0
Just for Snow	4	F	4	0	0	0	6,122
Just Forget It	3	C	10	1	3	1	18,365
Just Forty Five	6	G	5	0	1	0	3,700
Just Four Austin	4	C	15	4	1	4	58,940
Just Fred	3	C	12	1	4	2	9,223
Just Free	7	G	11	5	1	1	37,940
Just Fun	4	F	7	1	1	0	31,253
Just Gabi	3	F	6	1	3	1	53,710
Just Glorious	3	F	4	0	0	0	350
Just Gold	6	M	16	2	3	2	9,798
Just Gomer	3	C	2	0	0	1	260
Just Gossip	4	G	11	3	1	1	66,540
Just in Case Jimmy	2	C	5	0	1	2	55,017
Just Irish	3	F	2	0	0	0	0
Just Jackie	4	F	11	2	1	2	50,365
Just Janeen	3	F	6	0	1	1	8,010
Just Jesy	4	G	10	2	3	1	8,157
Just Jettin Holme	3	G	16	0	2	3	17,239
Just Jill	2	F	5	0	1	1	11,780
Just Joey	10	G	5	1	0	1	3,000
Just Jonathan	4	C	13	0	0	0	1,848
Just Kickin It	5	M	7	2	1	1	9,474
Just Kiss Me Quick	4	F	4	1	0	1	10,490
Just Lark	5	M	7	0	0	2	2,935
Just Le Facts	4	C	6	1	0	0	65,890
Just Like Bobbyjoe	5	H	16	1	4	1	12,858
Just Like Bossy	8	M	7	2	0	0	9,220
Just Like Dan	3	G	7	0	1	1	3,570
Just Like Elise	2	F	3	0	0	1	7,369
Just Like Gold	5	M	6	0	0	1	1,520
Just Like Jimmy	6	G	1	1	0	0	20,400
Just Like Mike	3	G	1	0	0	0	0
Just Like Polly	4	F	5	1	1	2	9,050
Just Like Prime	7	G	6	0	0	0	2,296
Just Like Royalty	6	M	1	0	0	1	825
Just Like That (FR)	3	F	3	0	3	0	22,284
Just Like Toddy	6	G	9	1	2	1	9,225
Just Like You	4	F	10	1	1	0	14,723
Just Listen	7	G	6	0	1	1	51,000
Just Love	3	G	2	0	0	0	0
Just Maggie	5	M	1	0	0	0	0
Just Max	2	G	1	0	0	0	0
Just Maybe Baby	2	F	2	0	0	0	85
Just Me	2	G	10	2	1	1	32,086
Just Michel	3	F	14	5	5	2	137,243
Just Missed	4	G	3	0	0	0	600
Just Murphy (IRE)	5	G	9	2	1	2	24,868
Just My Bill	3	C	6	1	2	1	20,260
Just Name Me	3	C	5	0	0	0	885
Just On Looks	6	G	12	3	0	4	11,957
Just One	4	G	9	0	0	0	465
Just One Kiss	5	M	8	0	1	0	2,668
Just One Rose	5	M	14	0	3	4	26,909
Just Outrageous	4	G	10	2	2	1	21,395
Just Parkin	3	C	5	2	0	0	55,200
Just Persist	3	C	2	0	0	0	270
Just Plain Bill	3	C	5	1	0	0	14,116
Just Plain Jessie	2	F	1	0	0	1	2,387
Just Plain Joe	4	C	3	1	2	0	44,000
Just Plain Lucky	2	F	2	0	0	1	1,480
Just Plain Vanilla	2	F	3	1	1	0	30,800
Just Pretend	4	C	2	1	0	1	4,063
Just Proclaim	3	G	2	0	0	0	2,790
Just Push Play	3	F	13	0	3	1	3,932
Just Real	4	G	4	1	1	0	3,982
Just Remark	10	G	5	0	0	0	317
Just Robin	4	F	5	0	0	2	6,535
Just Ruler	8	H	4	0	0	0	1,280
Just Sampson	6	G	3	1	0	0	5,848
Just Satisfaction	3	F	6	1	0	1	2,953
Just Say Go	2	G	4	1	0	0	8,184
Just Say the Word	3	C	12	3	3	2	87,434
Just Scarlet	4	F	5	0	1	0	3,204
Just Scotty	3	C	5	1	0	1	1,940
Just Sing	3	G	2	0	0	0	0
Just So Ya No	2	F	4	0	1	1	842
Just Sow Wild	3	G	4	0	0	0	0
Just Speechy	4	F	3	0	0	0	152
Just Spoof N	6	G	7	1	1	0	22,600
Just Super	6	H	2	0	0	0	0
Just Swell	3	C	6	1	1	2	30,142
Just to Show You	2	F	2	1	0	1	15,750
Just too Salty	4	C	7	0	0	1	2,113
Just Too Too	3	F	5	5	0	0	201,240
Just Tricks	5	M	4	0	0	0	567
Just Triple	5	M	11	1	0	2	11,005
Just Tucker	2	C	6	1	1	1	7,555
Just Twice	8	G	7	0	0	0	324
Just Two of Us	5	G	3	0	0	0	341
Just Us Honey	2	G	4	1	0	0	6,329
Just Vinnie	3	C	2	0	1	0	9,920
Just Walter	4	C	6	0	0	0	424
Just Waltz	3	C	12	1	1	1	12,417
Just Watch	6	M	3	0	0	0	206
Just Watch Me	3	C	9	1	1	1	41,852
Just Wellturned	3	F	6	0	0	0	254
Just Western	5	G	11	3	2	3	56,986
Just Whistle	4	F	5	0	0	1	2,070
Just Won Mo	7	H	1	0	0	0	0
Just Wonder (GB)	3	C	6	3	0	0	190,330
Just Wyatt	8	G	15	5	3	4	11,656
Justa	5	M	8	1	4	0	9,665
Justa Bar Fly	4	F	6	0	0	0	776
Justa Bigboned Gal	3	F	2	0	1	0	2,735
Justa Classy Lady	3	F	7	0	1	0	7,590
Justa Duck Snort	4	G	7	0	1	0	4,237
Justa Good Old Boy	2	G	2	1	0	0	10,206
Justa Gray	4	G	12	3	0	0	26,444
Justa Jitterbug	4	F	2	0	0	0	390
Justa Little Star	2	F	1	0	0	0	376
Justa Native Girl	5	M	1	0	0	1	600
Justa Nose	3	C	2	0	0	0	0
Justa Quick Silver	6	H	12	5	3	0	60,570
Justa Right	4	C	4	1	2	0	1,559
Justa Skip Away	3	F	3	0	0	0	0
Justa Smirk	8	G	13	3	1	2	16,275
Justa Spirit	6	M	7	0	1	1	4,702
Justa Toad	2	F	1	0	0	1	480
Justa Vacation	6	M	9	1	0	0	4,174
Justa Valay Girl	3	F	15	1	1	3	21,892
Justa Valentine	4	F	1	0	0	0	330
Justa Wink	4	C	10	0	0	0	5,025
Justabigsissy	3	F	4	0	0	0	430
Justabud	3	C	2	0	0	0	652

RECORDS OF HORSES

Horse	Age	Sex	Sts	1st	2d	3d	Won	Horse	Age	Sex	Sts	1st	2d	3d	Won
Justabull	5	M	13	1	1	0	8,735	K K Avey	3	G	8	1	0	0	17,930
Justafavorcat	3	F	11	1	0	3	5,424	K K D's Limestone	6	H	10	1	0	1	7,740
Justagallop	5	G	5	2	0	2	39,245	K K Robert	3	C	1	0	0	0	0
Justalittle Crazy	4	C	17	0	1	2	5,226	K Linda	4	F	10	0	1	2	11,584
Justalittleaffair	5	M	1	0	0	0	61	K Mac	5	H	3	0	1	1	7,352
Justalittlemagic	3	G	10	2	2	1	62,515	K O Gorgeous	3	F	5	0	1	0	934
Justamoment	2	C	3	0	0	0	720	K O Love	3	C	1	1	0	0	15,400
Justanick	6	G	8	2	0	2	3,291	K O River Crossing	2	C	5	1	0	0	8,256
Justanotheractor	2	G	3	0	0	0	825	K Onda	3	F	3	0	0	1	14,173
Justanothercruiser	3	G	10	1	2	2	7,995	K Patrick	4	C	10	1	1	0	5,631
Justanotherflame	7	G	12	1	1	0	4,717	K P's Kandy	3	F	10	2	2	1	27,561
Justanothersemoron	3	C	1	0	0	0	94	K S Gambler	4	C	5	2	0	2	6,597
Justanothertoddy	6	G	10	1	1	2	7,445	K Squared	4	F	16	4	3	1	38,430
Justaold Frank	10	G	7	0	0	0	495	K T and the Dance	5	M	2	0	0	0	180
Justaperfectscore	4	G	7	0	0	2	3,998	K W Jay Jay	4	C	10	1	1	0	2,074
Justaptobe	3	G	12	1	1	0	7,022	K. C. Boss Lady	4	F	9	1	1	1	8,152
Justart	2	F	3	0	0	0	220	K. C. Genius	4	F	6	2	1	1	25,098
Justastorm	4	G	4	0	0	1	2,520	K. C.'s Boy	4	G	15	4	1	3	52,088
Justavalay	6	M	5	0	2	1	3,861	K. D. Tam	5	M	7	1	0	0	3,296
Justcallmeclifford	4	G	1	0	0	0	72	K. J.'s Gold	3	C	5	1	1	0	24,000
Justcallmeprecious	4	F	4	1	1	0	4,410	K. K.'s Kiss	3	F	4	0	1	1	6,580
Justcallmesassy	3	F	10	1	3	2	8,555	K. O. Boots	7	G	4	0	1	0	800
Justcallmewill	6	G	6	0	0	0	474	K. O. Bride	3	F	7	1	1	1	15,100
Justdont	3	F	8	1	1	0	4,553	K. O. Kid	4	C	5	0	0	1	735
Juste Smile	4	F	9	1	3	1	19,765	K. O. Peace	3	F	12	3	3	1	13,390
Justfollowmyshadow	5	M	4	0	0	0	868	K. O. Phyllis	2	F	3	0	1	1	7,395
Justforgetaboutit	7	G	7	0	0	0	874	K. O. Power	3	G	9	2	3	1	51,075
Justica			8	1	2	1	6,474	K. O. Stretch	2	C	4	0	0	1	2,573
Justice B	3	G	9	0	2	0	5,385	K. O.'s Crypto	7	H	5	0	1	0	6,540
Justice Be Done	3	G	3	0	0	0	161	K. P. Express	3	G	6	1	1	2	7,422
Justice Bites	5	G	13	4	1	3	62,911	K. R.'s Misty	3	F	7	0	1	0	4,480
Justice Due	3	G	11	1	3	1	17,055	Ka Blui	4	G	4	1	1	0	21,598
Justice for Auston	4	C	8	1	2	2	49,240	Kaaabang	3	G	2	0	0	0	0
Justice Mark	6	G	12	2	3	1	18,525	Kabars Stay	4	F	3	0	0	0	0
Justice Minister	6	H	6	0	3	0	33,520	Kabeeb	3	F	4	0	1	1	23,052
Justice Now	4	G	8	0	0	0	540	Kabili Star	4	F	1	0	0	1	924
Justice Paul	4	G	4	1	1	0	3,325	Kabul	3	F	12	2	6	1	255,152
Justifiable Cause	4	C	4	3	0	1	6,309	Kabylia (IRE)	5	M	5	1	0	0	23,246
Justifiable Xpense	2	G	3	1	0	0	4,524	Kaceys Dancer	7	H	6	2	1	1	9,190
Justification	6	H	13	2	2	4	143,527	Kaceysexpelled	2	F	2	0	0	0	0
Justified Attack	4	G	2	0	0	0	0	Kachamandi (CHI)	6	G	13	0	3	3	79,460
Justified Devil	3	F	8	0	1	5	15,565	Kachi	4	F	4	0	0	0	633
Justin Charge	5	G	14	1	1	1	14,860	Kachina Girl	2	F	2	1	0	0	5,852
Justin Itforfun	4	G	13	3	4	2	8,025	Kadancer	4	F	11	0	0	1	755
Justin Ray	4	G	9	0	2	1	7,661	Kadeya	5	M	7	0	2	0	3,721
Justin Time Joe	4	G	11	2	0	4	44,170	Kadhaaf	6	H	7	0	1	0	5,116
Justincasei'msilly	4	F	4	0	0	0	1,500	Kadiddlehopper	8	G	7	0	0	1	1,224
Justin's Big Boy	3	G	11	1	2	0	4,813	Kadie's Quest	4	F	2	0	0	0	0
Justin's Halo	5	G	14	0	1	2	1,549	Kadillac Kole	5	H	5	0	0	0	570
Justjake	5	H	3	0	0	1	200	Kady Bee	4	F	11	0	2	1	5,432
Justlikedawg	3	C	12	2	3	2	70,925	Kafwain	3	C	3	1	0	1	180,000
Justlikejessejames	3	C	4	1	0	0	14,820	Kagan's Corner	6	G	15	2	3	1	35,576
Justloadthewagon	5	G	7	0	1	0	1,310	Kagels Fleetman	3	C	3	0	0	0	0
Justlord	2	C	1	0	0	0	0	Kahala	4	F	8	0	0	0	1,208
Justly Royal	3	F	3	0	2	0	15,800	Kahless	5	G	4	2	0	1	19,142
Justmakrya	4	F	19	0	2	7	6,417	Kahlua Hummer	3	G	7	1	1	0	8,610
Justnowayofknowin'.	5	G	10	2	1	2	19,970	Kahoka	4	G	15	0	1	2	4,072
Justntime	4	C	5	0	0	2	2,670	Kahula	2	F	2	0	0	1	1,540
Justonemorething	5	H	3	0	0	0	183	Kaibo (GB)	7	H	6	1	1	0	21,140
Justoneofdaboyz	4	C	5	0	0	0	1,250	Kaieteur	4	C	6	0	1	2	235,449
Justslewme	5	G	13	0	4	2	3,725	Kaili's a Princess	2	F	6	1	1	0	9,365
Justwhatineeded	3	F	1	0	1	0	3,800	Kailua Whirl	3	G	2	1	0	0	5,520
Juvee	3	G	9	0	0	1	4,784	Kaily's Star	3	F	2	0	0	0	255
Juventus	2	C	2	1	0	1	36,327	Kain's Dancer	3	G	11	1	0	0	26,437
Jux	5	G	9	1	2	1	40,060	Kain's Deed	2	F	2	0	0	0	0
K B E S Delight	2	F	2	0	0	0	361	Kain's Nijinsky	6	G	19	0	3	4	7,571
K Bo Sam	4	G	8	1	0	0	6,300	Kaiser So Say	7	G	5	1	0	1	8,474
K Brown	5	F	10	2	3	0	52,420	Kait Can't Wait	3	F	10	3	0	3	20,165
K C Jazz	5	G	12	1	1	3	15,118	Kaitlin's Boy	3	G	9	1	3	2	19,426
K C R's Pipe Dream	5	G	1	0	0	0	225	Kaitlin's Nick	4	G	10	1	3	1	26,727
K C's Charm	3	F	2	1	0	0	7,398	Kaitlyn's Komet	3	F	3	1	0	0	4,095
K C's Sunshine Bay	3	G	10	2	1	2	49,300	Kaizoku	7	G	2	1	0	0	4,950
K D Implosion	3	F	6	1	1	0	5,880	Kajen Lojo	2	C	4	0	1	0	2,270
K D Magic	3	C	6	1	3	1	19,430	Kajin Kelsey	9	G	12	2	1	2	6,813
K D Power	4	F	8	0	0	1	1,915	Kakapo	2	C	1	0	0	0	137
K D's Big Boy	4	G	5	0	0	0	0	Kalamari Sunset	2	F	3	0	0	0	189
K Hawk	3	G	3	0	0	0	228	Kalamazoo	5	H	4	0	2	0	5,995
K J's Dance	7	M	16	5	1	2	15,653	Kale	5	M	11	2	1	2	9,545
K J's Rose	5	M	12	1	2	3	13,075	Kalen	3	F	10	1	0	3	40,710

Horse	Age	Sex	Sts	1st	2d	3d	Won	Horse	Age	Sex	Sts	1st	2d	3d	Won
Kalens Jet	3	G	7	0	1	2	5,915	Karakorum Wonder	4	G	13	2	1	2	10,373
Kalfaari	6	G	8	5	0	1	113,386	Karakorumblackjack	3	C	11	0	2	0	15,225
Kaliga	9	G	10	4	1	4	20,547	Karakorumkarakorum	5	G	3	1	0	0	3,290
Kalik	6	G	10	2	1	0	10,791	Karakorum's Appeal	4	G	7	0	1	3	25,420
Kalimas (GER)	6	H	3	0	0	1	1,808	Karakorums R Wild	4	G	11	4	1	1	21,363
Kalim's Klassic	7	G	12	0	3	0	1,865	Karakorumseashanty	3	F	14	3	0	0	16,978
Kalim's Song	6	M	12	1	2	1	4,756	Karama Trapp	4	C	9	1	0	0	4,020
Kali's Cat	4	G	9	0	0	2	5,745	Karamanduka	3	G	11	1	1	0	20,190
Kali's Groomstick	3	G	10	0	0	2	4,510	Karaoke Ave	3	F	1	0	0	0	0
Kali's Smile	6	M	4	1	0	1	3,110	Karaoke Dancer	7	M	5	2	2	0	42,630
Kalish	3	F	1	0	0	0	0	Kararun	4	F	16	3	2	2	42,983
Kalizar	3	G	4	0	0	0	143	Karas Pride	6	M	2	0	0	0	76
Kalki	5	G	5	1	0	1	1,440	Karas Time	8	M	2	0	0	0	0
Kalki's Pride	3	F	16	1	3	4	48,218	Karat Tales	3	F	8	1	2	0	9,433
Kallie Bird	5	M	10	1	1	2	10,955	Karate Chris	3	G	12	0	3	0	6,467
Kalolo	4	G	11	2	2	3	13,157	Kardiac Kid	4	G	5	3	0	0	30,150
Kalookan Lady	2	F	1	1	0	0	15,600	Karear	6	M	5	0	1	0	2,595
Kalookan Star	6	H	16	2	1	2	27,855	Karen J.	2	F	2	0	0	0	0
Kalowana Sunrise	6	M	9	1	0	2	6,737	Karenkeel	6	M	9	0	0	1	1,734
Kalsem	7	G	9	1	0	3	8,145	Karen's Lullaby	7	M	13	2	3	3	36,063
Kalt Cafe	3	F	3	1	0	0	7,324	Karen's Namesake	5	M	1	0	0	0	37
Kalua's Back	4	F	9	0	1	1	1,138	Karen's Red Rose	2	F	5	1	0	0	13,220
Kaluha Kai	3	G	3	0	0	0	0	Karen's Star	4	F	15	2	2	3	55,985
Kama'aina Girl	2	F	4	0	1	1	6,320	Karenz Toy	4	G	7	1	2	0	11,080
Kamalani	2	F	1	0	0	0	0	Karenz's Brother	4	G	10	0	0	1	2,185
Kamarla	3	F	6	3	0	1	13,670	Kari Kate	7	M	5	0	0	1	1,350
Kami Dee	2	F	3	0	0	0	0	Kari Lea	3	F	8	1	2	0	16,915
Kamikaze Coyote	4	C	12	0	3	0	5,376	Kari the Basket	2	F	6	1	1	0	4,675
Kamikaze Kat	4	C	2	0	0	1	730	Karilocco	3	G	8	0	1	2	3,520
Kaminski	5	H	8	1	1	0	8,838	Karin's Girl	2	F	5	0	1	0	3,795
Kami's Wish	3	F	2	0	0	0	120	Karis Makaw	2	F	1	0	0	0	343
Kamolia	4	C	2	0	0	0	0	Karison	3	G	8	0	1	0	6,075
Kamoya	3	G	5	1	0	0	4,800	Karitsas Punch	5	M	1	0	0	0	0
Kamsack	4	C	1	1	0	0	31,200	Kark's Ark	9	G	1	0	0	0	38
Kan Fly	5	M	10	2	2	2	8,673	Karlan's Buddy	2	C	1	0	0	0	390
Kan Kan Katy	3	F	8	2	0	0	7,000	Karley Bug	5	M	1	0	0	0	0
Kan Two	3	F	17	2	2	6	12,435	Karley's Melody	5	M	8	0	5	0	13,540
Kanafa	3	F	8	1	2	0	12,011	Karlique	3	F	5	1	0	0	10,465
Kananaskis	5	G	3	0	0	0	0	Karluk	5	G	7	1	1	2	15,909
Kanata Ridge	4	G	9	2	1	4	33,218	Karlyn's Coast	3	C	8	0	2	0	3,678
Kanati	3	G	9	0	3	3	16,100	Karma Charma	2	C	1	0	0	0	0
Kanawha	9	G	2	0	0	0	4,450	Karmetory	3	C	7	0	1	0	2,400
Kandaroo	4	G	16	1	2	0	5,215	Karms Echo	3	G	11	2	1	1	18,940
Kandoolie	3	F	19	1	1	3	9,828	Karol's Sweet Pea	5	M	3	0	0	0	0
Kangaroo Jack	2	C	2	1	0	0	5,340	Karosel Dancer	5	M	12	1	2	2	6,675
Kanha	4	G	5	0	0	0	240	Karphil	9	M	1	0	0	0	0
Kanilla	2	F	4	0	0	0	1,174	Karra Kul	8	G	4	1	2	0	22,540
Kano Doble	4	G	13	0	2	1	11,860	Karratha (MEX)	6	H	5	0	1	0	2,982
Kanoa One	4	F	5	0	2	0	4,820	Karroo	3	F	3	0	1	0	4,768
Kanonika	6	H	1	0	0	0	72	Karsavina	3	F	1	0	0	1	6,000
Kanpai	8	G	3	0	0	0	110	Karsavina (IRE)	5	M	2	0	1	0	11,050
Kanrun	10	M	5	0	0	0	266	Kasby	4	F	1	0	0	0	38
Kansai	4	G	10	1	3	3	16,650	Kaschmir	4	F	11	3	0	0	14,877
Kansas City Knight	7	G	11	1	2	1	2,170	Kasey Rae	5	M	5	0	0	0	0
Kansas Gentleman	3	C	3	0	0	0	446	Kash a Rule	8	M	4	0	0	0	250
Kansas Pioneer	4	C	11	2	1	1	11,952	Kash Ante	5	H	7	0	0	0	0
Kansas Sonata	3	F	5	1	1	0	6,440	Kash Koy	8	M	7	0	4	1	2,156
Kansi La	5	G	9	0	1	4	2,541	Kashagawigamog	5	M	13	2	2	1	30,870
Kant Dance	5	M	5	2	1	0	12,060	Kashatreya	9	G	1	0	0	0	0
Kanuceeit	2	F	3	0	0	1	3,551	Kashelon	4	F	6	1	1	0	16,731
Kanwiaco	2	C	4	0	0	0	906	Kashes	7	G	7	0	1	1	2,900
Kaough	6	H	10	1	1	0	13,196	Kashua	5	M	15	0	0	0	1,856
Kapoza	3	F	1	0	0	0	126	Kasino Dealer	3	F	12	1	0	2	13,822
Kappa King	6	H	2	0	2	0	26,040	Kasparov	4	C	6	1	1	0	42,110
Kara Jean	6	M	7	0	2	3	4,015	Kassie Scates	3	F	3	0	0	0	122
Karabez	7	G	10	2	3	1	17,198	Kassoula's Best	3	C	11	2	2	0	12,895
Karakorum Blues	5	G	17	1	1	2	8,523	Kastile	4	F	14	0	1	3	6,752
Karakorum Cat	4	C	11	4	1	0	30,617	Kat Can Dance	5	M	13	1	1	2	9,005
Karakorum Conquest	5	M	5	0	2	0	2,613	Kat Class	3	G	2	0	0	1	690
Karakorum Crusader	5	M	17	1	4	1	78,556	Kat County	4	C	10	1	2	1	7,370
Karakorum Dixie	3	G	13	3	1	2	51,090	Kat Dancer	5	G	5	0	3	0	8,949
Karakorum Gemstone	2	F	3	1	0	0	25,830	Kat Kool	2	G	2	0	1	0	2,800
Karakorum Keepsake	2	C	1	0	1	0	8,200	Kata Commanchero	3	G	1	0	0	0	0
Karakorum Kiss	3	F	16	1	0	3	48,360	Katablastic	3	C	4	0	0	0	1,500
Karakorum Munk	6	G	11	2	3	1	13,856	Katahaula Myst	3	G	3	0	0	0	0
Karakorum Patriot	3	C	4	0	0	0	1,260	Katallini	3	F	8	2	1	2	16,270
Karakorum Rules	4	G	4	2	0	1	10,060	Kataloo	5	M	5	0	0	0	0
Karakorum Signal	5	H	8	2	0	0	8,436	Katalystic	2	C	3	0	0	0	0
Karakorum Tsunami	2	F	4	0	1	0	1,340	Katana Girl	4	F	13	0	0	1	3,792

Horse	Age	Sex	Sts	1st	2d	3d	Won
Katash (GER)	3	C	8	1	0	1	5,682
Katawin	3	G	14	2	2	1	11,379
Katch Karen	4	F	3	0	0	1	620
Katcherintherye	3	G	12	1	0	1	6,526
Katdawk	3	F	5	0	0	0	1,450
Katdillac	3	F	14	4	1	3	34,962
Katdogawn (GB)	3	F	10	4	3	1	320,580
Kate Regal	5	M	18	1	4	2	31,698
Kate the Great	4	F	5	2	1	0	71,468
Katee Jean	3	F	14	1	1	2	13,110
Katee Kris	3	F	6	0	2	1	22,140
Kateek	5	M	2	0	0	0	0
Katelyn's Star	2	F	5	0	2	1	8,316
Kate'n Amy	5	M	14	3	1	4	47,562
Kateri	3	F	1	0	0	0	0
Kate's Cat	4	F	11	0	1	1	4,900
Kate's Friend	5	H	10	2	3	0	22,316
Kate's Genius	2	C	3	1	1	0	28,140
Kate's Halo	3	F	2	0	0	0	0
Kate's Interview	3	F	11	2	1	0	11,880
Kate's Law	4	F	10	2	1	0	17,977
Kate's Pistol	4	F	3	1	0	0	5,480
Kate's Rocket	3	G	3	0	0	0	0
Kate's Trick	3	F	3	0	0	0	171
Kate's Wish	8	G	16	0	5	1	7,911
Katespreciousred	4	F	1	0	0	0	0
Katestormedthebird	2	F	1	0	1	0	3,000
Katherine Bug	3	F	18	3	1	5	15,788
Katherine Seymour (GB)	5	M	6	2	0	0	32,160
Kathie's Sibiling	6	M	8	2	0	2	25,160
Kathir	6	H	4	1	2	0	51,540
Kathleen Mahveryan	4	F	8	0	2	3	19,112
Kathryn the Granny	4	F	14	3	2	3	16,399
Kathryn's Ego	8	G	11	2	0	3	6,713
Kathy Ann	3	F	5	1	0	0	6,411
Kathy Cool It	4	F	14	0	0	3	2,393
Kathy June	5	M	3	0	0	0	185
Kathy K D	4	F	3	0	1	0	19,155
Kathy Lee G	3	F	13	1	0	3	28,330
Kathy Lynn	2	F	6	1	1	1	8,796
Kathy Shoppinspree	8	G	21	2	5	0	10,161
Kathy's Kadillac	5	M	1	0	0	0	0
Kathys Vengeance	3	G	12	2	1	3	8,617
Kathyspersonalhope	3	F	14	2	0	1	8,176
Kathythetraina	4	M	4	0	0	1	4,290
Katie Bug	7	M	12	0	2	0	4,818
Katie Camille	4	F	3	0	1	1	8,215
Katie First	2	F	1	0	0	0	110
Katie Jo	2	F	5	0	1	1	3,322
Katie Kosmos	5	M	9	2	1	2	30,679
Katie Kreitz	4	F	13	1	1	1	38,060
Katie Lang	3	F	1	0	0	0	1,100
Katie Last	2	F	5	1	1	2	19,320
Katie Miss	3	F	10	2	0	0	14,400
Katie's Bag	5	G	3	0	0	0	0
Katie's Best	3	F	7	0	0	0	780
Katie's Choice	5	M	18	3	0	2	14,930
Katies Danza	3	F	12	1	3	2	61,137
Katie's Diamond	2	C	1	0	0	0	0
Katie's Grace	3	F	6	0	0	0	408
Katie's Kalling	3	F	8	2	4	0	58,600
Katie's Katowice	5	H	6	0	0	0	682
Katie's Magic	4	F	6	1	0	0	4,618
Katie's Miracle	3	F	8	2	0	2	26,880
Katie's Payday	5	M	7	0	0	0	423
Katies Request	4	F	9	0	0	0	240
Katie's Son	5	G	11	1	1	3	6,507
Katies Success	5	M	11	2	3	1	5,728
Katie's Town	2	F	3	0	0	0	308
Katiesboy	2	G	4	1	0	1	11,400
Katiewilldance	3	F	6	0	0	0	331
Kativo	2	F	4	0	0	1	2,892
Katja Cat	5	M	5	1	1	1	6,433
Katlin's Rocket	2	F	4	0	0	1	2,530
Kato's Garden	5	G	13	0	2	1	7,647
Kato's World	5	M	9	1	0	2	6,631
Katotrick	3	F	8	2	3	0	30,745
Katovilla	5	G	18	6	2	2	39,555
Katrina Lea	4	F	1	0	0	0	0
Katrina Nipper	3	F	10	0	0	0	2,124
Kat's Cadillac	3	F	3	0	0	0	0
Kat's Malagra Fool	2	F	7	1	0	1	10,592
Kat's Samurai	9	G	1	0	0	0	206
Kat'sinthebag	4	C	1	0	0	0	0
Katskan	2	C	3	0	0	0	2,340
Katsu	2	G	1	0	0	0	400
Kattalk	4	C	10	0	1	0	2,464
Katty Du	2	F	5	0	1	3	3,100
Katty Scat	2	F	7	0	0	0	882
Katuna Terms	6	M	2	0	0	0	0
Katy Kat	5	M	2	0	0	0	460
Katy Katers	3	F	5	1	2	0	35,120
Katya	10	G	2	0	0	2	1,320
Katy's Quick	2	F	2	0	0	0	460
Katys Turn to Star	4	F	3	0	0	0	895
Katz Got Rhythm	4	C	6	1	0	1	4,920
Katzanova	2	C	7	1	2	2	29,856
Katzen	4	F	6	1	1	3	65,871
Kaufman Tornado	5	G	3	0	0	0	654
Kaufy Mare	2	C	3	2	0	0	28,230
Kavita Nadira	2	F	4	0	1	0	4,525
Kavon's Gold	4	F	4	0	0	0	244
Kaw Liga Sioux	3	C	3	1	0	0	27,600
Kawajlain	6	M	2	0	0	0	0
Kawiki	6	M	7	1	0	1	3,262
Kay Colleen	5	M	15	1	1	1	5,047
Kay Elaines Champ	4	F	3	0	0	0	0
Kay Gee Bee	8	G	5	0	0	0	215
Kayak Point	4	C	1	0	0	0	0
Kayamanan	4	F	6	1	1	0	5,480
Kayandeesdream	4	C	3	0	0	0	132
Kaycee's Diamond	3	F	2	0	0	0	92
Kaye Bear	6	M	4	0	0	0	980
Kayjon	7	M	2	0	1	0	1,334
Kaylan's Rose	3	F	8	3	0	0	36,340
Kaylazoo	4	F	9	1	0	1	16,756
Kaylee Bailey	4	F	15	1	2	2	24,024
Kayleigh Karat	8	M	8	0	3	0	6,525
Kaylie Kay	4	F	12	0	1	1	1,893
Kaylind	3	F	1	0	0	0	0
Kaylynn's Memory	2	F	3	1	0	0	3,480
Kayo Kat	3	G	10	0	1	0	1,801
Kayo Too	3	F	14	2	1	2	10,689
Kayoed	5	G	1	0	1	0	880
Kayraque	5	G	17	1	2	1	14,662
Kayrawan's Girl	3	F	10	1	0	2	10,687
Kay's Daughter	3	F	6	1	0	0	27,110
Kays Way	3	F	8	0	1	0	2,789
Kaysome	2	F	1	0	0	1	1,800
Kazaa	3	F	2	0	0	0	0
Kazliv	7	H	9	0	0	0	897
Kazoo	5	H	7	1	1	2	67,590
Kazotti	4	C	3	0	0	0	1,071
Kcdrew	3	F	8	1	2	0	4,310
Ke Bound	7	G	8	0	0	0	534
Keaheys Woman	3	F	5	2	1	0	11,270
Keante Too	6	M	1	0	0	0	65
Keats	5	H	4	1	0	1	75,240
Keats and Yeats	9	G	4	0	0	2	4,380
Kebo Valley	7	H	8	3	0	4	21,300
Kedington	4	G	15	6	3	3	199,548
Kee Aldi	3	F	9	1	2	1	19,420
Kee On Go	8	G	5	0	0	1	543
Keekee Manzotti	4	G	17	1	2	1	10,589
Keeler	7	H	9	0	1	3	6,900
Keelhauled	2	G	6	0	1	0	3,166
Keelyn	6	M	13	1	3	3	6,992
Keen Cut	9	G	13	0	0	1	1,775
Keen Decision	6	G	11	0	0	3	4,299
Keen Hope	4	F	13	2	1	2	16,653
Keen Intelligence	3	G	11	1	2	2	30,765
Keen Lean n' Gray	3	F	3	0	0	0	579
Keen Perception	3	F	2	0	0	0	400
Keen Scent	4	F	7	1	1	2	29,408
Keenan	2	G	2	0	0	0	0
Keene Executive	5	G	5	0	0	0	470
Keene Lady	3	F	7	2	0	0	19,320
Keene Othello	5	G	17	5	1	1	20,826

Horse	Age	Sex	Sts	1st	2d	3d	Won
Keep Cool	3	G	2	1	0	0	14,450
Keep 'Em Honest	4	F	11	1	1	0	6,592
Keep 'Em Rolling	3	F	6	0	2	1	7,230
Keep Hope Alive	3	G	8	1	0	1	10,525
Keep It At Par	4	G	4	1	1	0	7,849
Keep It Comin	3	F	25	4	4	2	53,965
Keep It Country	3	F	7	0	0	4	5,948
Keep It Holy	6	G	4	0	0	0	858
Keep It Karakorum	4	G	10	0	1	1	2,869
Keep It Personal	2	C	1	0	0	1	910
Keep It Quiet	2	F	2	0	0	0	0
Keep It Simple Guy	3	G	7	0	2	1	27,249
Keep It Strait	9	G	10	1	0	1	12,648
Keep Moving	4	G	6	0	0	0	570
Keep Moving On	4	G	10	0	0	0	1,750
Keep On Ponching	2	F	9	2	1	1	15,100
Keep On Rockin	5	M	11	1	1	3	5,792
Keep On Turkin	2	G	4	1	0	0	2,030
Keep Roll'n	7	G	9	0	1	0	4,209
Keep Shining	4	F	16	3	3	1	62,620
Keep Smilin	3	F	3	0	0	0	3,690
Keep Sparkling	10	G	5	0	0	0	0
Keep the Dream	3	F	3	0	0	0	358
Keep the Ring	8	M	9	0	0	0	1,063
Keep The Silver (GB)	4	G	10	0	5	1	9,609
Keep Thgrey Going	5	M	19	3	4	4	21,983
Keep This Cat	2	F	5	1	2	1	40,050
Keeper Kat	3	F	5	0	0	1	3,180
Keeper of the Bell	4	C	5	1	1	0	6,700
Keeper Ofthe Purse	7	G	8	1	0	1	4,895
Keeper Pocket	3	F	8	0	1	2	3,310
Keepers Hill (IRE)	4	F	1	0	0	1	6,840
Keepin' Idol	5	G	10	0	0	1	1,615
Keepin It Friendly	3	F	3	0	1	0	3,200
Keepin It Real	5	G	15	2	2	1	21,770
Keeping Cool	3	F	3	0	1	0	3,000
Keeping the Gold	3	F	6	4	1	0	140,960
Keeping Watch (IRE)	2	F	2	0	0	0	2,340
Keepingthepeace	3	C	11	0	4	2	14,490
Keepitinthebag	3	G	11	1	3	2	35,750
Keepondealing	5	M	2	0	1	1	7,670
Keeponthesunniside	3	F	12	1	2	2	9,865
Keepscratching	11	G	1	1	0	0	2,820
Keepthename	4	F	2	0	2	0	6,200
Keepurmuninupocket	6	M	12	0	0	1	7,630
Keepyoureyeonme	4	F	1	0	0	0	89
Keepyourhandsdown	4	G	12	1	1	2	23,722
Keepyourkool	4	F	1	0	0	0	0
Keepyourwitsaboutu	2	F	7	2	2	1	49,030
Keet Brown	2	C	1	0	0	0	570
Keg Kicker	4	C	18	3	0	0	21,372
Keg Wine	6	H	5	0	0	0	266
K'ehleyr	2	F	5	0	1	1	16,140
Keiai Mahha	3	G	7	1	1	1	16,674
Keiai Sakura	3	F	12	4	2	1	149,170
Keikik	3	F	14	2	2	4	34,027
Keiko Sofia	5	M	3	0	0	0	165
Kei's Van	8	G	1	0	0	0	217
Kel Lex Edition	3	F	8	3	0	0	17,900
Kela	5	H	6	1	1	0	81,915
Kelchinko	5	G	9	2	1	3	9,058
Keleb Ridge	8	G	5	0	2	1	6,070
Keles	4	F	11	1	1	2	24,660
Kell	2	C	2	1	0	1	20,270
Kell Belle	2	F	4	0	2	0	3,930
Kellans Night	3	C	8	0	2	0	1,120
Kellera	2	F	2	0	0	1	780
Kellerin	2	F	4	0	0	1	6,940
Kelleys Island	4	G	15	2	0	2	9,083
Kelleys Star	4	F	6	2	0	0	9,210
Kelli Lee	3	F	6	1	1	0	30,960
Kelli Likes Soccer	3	F	9	0	0	1	3,585
Kellie's Ghost	5	G	13	2	5	1	12,163
Kelli's Brneyez	5	M	5	1	0	0	11,224
Kelli's Good Pick	8	M	1	0	0	0	0
Kelli's Got Power	5	H	1	0	0	0	0
Kelli's Law	2	F	9	0	3	1	7,530
Kelli's Mad Girl	4	F	10	1	3	2	8,479
Kelli's Song	4	F	4	0	2	1	28,320

Horse	Age	Sex	Sts	1st	2d	3d	Won
Kelly Bay	4	F	8	1	1	1	4,046
Kelly Bear	3	F	12	2	0	1	23,940
Kelly Is a Honey	3	F	10	0	1	0	1,380
Kelly Kris	5	M	10	3	1	1	12,242
Kellynette	3	F	1	0	0	0	75
Kelly's Ash	2	F	1	0	0	0	582
Kelly's Desire	6	M	18	0	1	4	21,294
Kelly's Fuego	5	G	10	0	1	1	2,806
Kellys Guest	2	F	1	0	1	0	2,472
Kelly's Guy	3	C	3	1	0	0	5,123
Kelly's Hat	3	F	13	2	3	1	20,178
Kelly's Hero	7	G	3	0	0	0	178
Kelly's Lake	2	F	1	0	0	0	0
Kelly's Loot	3	G	14	1	0	1	7,798
Kelly's Moon	3	G	4	0	1	0	1,468
Kelly's Question	4	F	6	1	1	0	24,130
Kelly's Shadow	5	M	1	0	0	0	0
Keloland	6	G	6	1	1	0	5,507
Kels Four Winds	3	G	3	0	3	0	3,700
Kels On the Attack	9	G	18	1	2	3	8,882
Kelsey Face	4	F	7	0	0	0	433
Kelsey Jo Lee	3	F	1	0	0	0	0
Kelsey Park	5	M	10	1	0	1	6,951
Kelsey Q.	5	M	6	0	0	1	687
Kelsie Dawn	5	M	8	1	1	0	15,124
Kelsie Nelson	6	M	17	2	1	0	8,910
Kelsies Way	4	F	4	0	0	0	900
Kelsy's Charm	5	M	4	0	0	0	1,642
Keltic Dancer	3	G	6	0	0	2	4,660
Kelt's J Boy	3	G	6	0	0	0	158
Kemeka's Teresa	5	M	8	0	1	1	1,887
Kemerton	5	G	10	1	1	0	19,835
Kemp	2	C	1	1	0	0	18,000
Kemp Road Cavalier	10	G	3	0	0	0	440
Ken	4	C	7	3	0	0	27,795
Ken Can	3	C	2	0	1	0	1,200
Ken Doll	7	H	2	0	1	1	10,140
Ken Kam Kod	3	F	1	0	0	0	0
Kenai River	4	C	8	0	1	1	8,700
Kenala	5	G	7	1	1	0	17,791
Kendall Point	6	G	7	0	0	0	4,872
Kendall's Love	4	G	1	0	0	0	0
Kendi Lou	4	F	11	3	5	2	76,147
Kendra Lee and Me	3	F	1	0	0	0	434
Kendrick	5	G	10	3	0	1	69,555
Kendrick Peak	4	F	4	1	1	1	10,394
Kenickie	3	C	2	0	1	0	620
Kenjay	6	G	7	1	2	1	3,997
Kenmarita (FR)	3	F	7	1	0	0	7,047
Kenna	5	G	7	1	1	1	6,052
Kennedy River	3	C	5	0	0	0	47
Kennedy Sun	4	C	9	1	3	1	8,441
Kennedy's First	9	G	3	0	0	0	0
Kennel Up	2	C	4	0	0	1	9,260
Kenneth	10	G	14	0	3	2	6,491
Kennett Pike	4	C	13	3	2	2	35,575
Kennewick	4	G	20	4	5	3	28,015
Kennileeanme	3	F	4	0	0	0	576
Kenny B Quick	2	G	7	1	1	0	12,605
Kenny C	4	G	1	0	0	0	185
Kenny Edwards	4	C	1	1	0	0	10,740
Kenny Hawk	4	C	4	1	0	0	24,440
Kenny K	5	H	19	4	4	2	40,835
Kenny Mais	5	G	5	1	2	1	23,200
Kenny N Billy	5	H	10	2	2	2	22,440
Kenny's Crossing	5	G	8	1	0	1	11,960
Kennys Secret	8	G	2	0	0	0	300
Kenok	8	G	5	2	1	0	13,184
Kenouche	4	C	15	2	1	0	11,288
Ken's Kid Kit	8	H	5	1	0	0	3,575
Kensey Ricochet	3	G	9	1	2	2	9,840
Kensington Park	6	G	17	5	4	1	30,531
Kent Hall	3	F	2	0	0	0	1,500
Kent Island	3	G	8	1	2	1	9,989
Kent Ridge	2	C	6	1	3	0	112,837
Kenta	4	F	12	0	1	1	4,625
Kents Account	3	C	7	1	0	1	14,350
Kentucky Bay	5	G	11	4	1	2	68,244
Kentucky Breakdown	3	G	5	0	1	2	5,317

Horse	Age	Sex	Sts	1st	2d	3d	Won	Horse	Age	Sex	Sts	1st	2d	3d	Won
Kentucky Cat	4	F	12	1	2	1	33,797	Key Oui Two	3	F	1	0	0	0	1,230
Kentucky Champ	2	C	6	0	1	1	8,199	Key Prosecutor	2	G	2	0	0	0	0
Kentucky Charm	9	G	7	1	0	2	3,771	Key Rate	3	F	6	1	1	0	10,043
Kentucky Gamble	2	F	6	0	0	2	3,970	Key Reality	6	M	17	2	4	4	22,260
Kentucky Joe	2	G	2	0	0	0	145	Key Rebel	7	H	6	0	0	0	617
Kentucky Kris	2	C	6	0	1	2	8,420	Key Runner	5	G	7	0	2	0	5,360
Kentucky Lake	8	G	11	0	0	1	882	Key Signal	5	M	11	0	1	0	3,392
Kentucky Pride	3	C	2	0	1	0	10,500	Key Solution	4	G	6	1	1	2	34,380
Kentucky Ruckus	4	F	6	2	0	1	21,065	Key Squall	2	F	2	0	0	0	434
Kentucky Squall	5	G	8	0	1	1	5,251	Key Storm	3	F	2	1	0	0	12,600
Kentucky Steel	6	G	7	1	0	2	3,886	Key Sunday	2	C	1	0	0	0	0
Kentucky Strike	7	M	8	2	1	1	6,701	Key Time	8	H	1	0	0	0	0
Kentucky Trust	4	G	13	2	5	4	24,097	Key to Broadway	6	M	14	1	1	2	7,452
Kentucky Wind	2	C	1	0	0	0	65	Key to Fame	7	G	3	0	0	0	190
Kentucky Woman	3	F	13	1	3	2	58,798	Key to Love	3	F	13	2	2	3	80,250
Kenya	3	C	8	1	0	0	11,239	Key to My Fantasy	3	G	8	1	0	1	4,275
Kenyan	3	F	4	1	0	1	4,542	Key to My Mercedes	6	M	9	1	2	3	4,110
Kenyawin	5	H	9	2	2	1	20,616	Key to Paris	4	G	4	1	1	1	20,676
Kenyetta Go	3	F	3	0	0	0	138	Key to Passion	3	F	1	0	0	0	0
Kenzie Girl	5	M	6	1	0	0	18,180	Key to Success	7	H	7	1	0	1	10,537
Keoki Native	9	G	21	8	2	1	9,571	Key to the Bomb	3	G	10	1	2	2	8,459
Keona	5	M	10	1	1	1	13,071	Key to the Cat	2	F	6	1	1	0	24,275
Keosnative	2	F	1	0	0	0	100	Key to the Champ	5	G	12	2	0	1	12,646
Keppoch	2	C	1	0	0	0	0	Key to the City	6	H	1	0	0	0	0
Kept the Ace	2	G	5	2	0	1	21,940	Key to the Glory	5	M	4	0	0	0	241
Kept the Salt	5	G	13	0	2	8	5,689	Key to the Point	3	G	7	1	0	1	6,504
Keptherhuntinghard	3	F	7	0	1	0	2,767	Key to the Punch	2	C	2	0	0	0	114
Ker Ching	4	G	5	0	0	1	606	Key to the Stars	2	C	2	0	0	1	4,620
Keratoid's Chubbs	6	M	7	0	1	0	5,880	Key to the Storm	3	F	4	2	0	0	7,680
Keratonic	6	G	14	3	1	6	16,265	Key Tribute	4	C	1	0	0	0	270
Kermit's Choice	8	G	4	0	1	0	1,295	Key Water (VEN)	5	M	16	1	5	2	14,498
Kern River	5	G	4	0	0	0	1,230	Key West Kid	6	H	7	2	1	1	23,025
Kernal K	6	G	18	4	4	2	125,630	Key Wi Miss	5	M	1	0	0	0	0
Kernitre (GB)	6	M	9	0	0	5	29,060	Keyano	9	G	6	0	0	0	1,687
Kernoff	4	G	4	1	1	1	32,080	Keybascan	10	G	1	0	0	0	0
Kerosene King	2	G	9	0	2	0	3,750	Keyboard	3	G	10	1	2	2	21,819
Kerosene Prospect	2	F	2	0	0	1	528	Keylargo Lady	4	F	2	0	0	1	3,099
Kerri Berri Red	2	F	1	0	0	0	295	Keymar Express	5	G	4	1	1	0	16,982
Kerri Is Scary	4	F	9	2	0	2	7,760	Keynote Speaker	3	C	15	1	4	1	10,139
Kerries a Lady	8	M	2	0	0	0	0	Keyron	5	G	8	0	2	0	10,070
Kerrimeeg	4	F	13	1	0	0	3,630	Keys a Don Juan	2	G	4	0	2	1	4,685
Kerriokayjo	2	F	1	0	0	0	0	Keys to Astro	3	C	7	2	0	1	43,285
Kerry Blue	5	M	7	1	1	0	35,560	Keys to the Heart	4	F	8	1	1	2	111,600
Kerry Light	4	F	6	1	0	0	6,960	Keysaflirt	3	G	3	0	0	1	690
Kerry Offaly	8	M	11	4	2	2	17,753	Keysister	4	G	10	3	2	0	57,770
Kerrygold (FR)	7	H	15	3	4	3	78,930	Keystone Flight	3	G	1	0	0	0	0
Kes Kat	7	H	7	1	0	0	3,498	Keystone Point	2	C	2	1	0	0	11,325
Kesia	2	F	2	0	0	1	1,400	Keystop	4	F	1	0	0	0	0
Kesslars Pet	2	C	1	0	0	0	0	Keyth's Karma	3	C	2	0	0	0	840
Ketch a Hello	3	F	5	3	0	1	63,828	Keytothepenthouse	6	G	17	2	1	2	31,410
Ketchikan Miss	3	F	8	1	1	1	10,533	Keytothepurse	6	M	3	0	0	0	190
Keteky Kemoky	3	F	4	1	0	1	5,950	Khachaturian	10	G	2	0	0	0	300
Kettal Creek	2	F	1	0	0	0	0	Khaki Lee	2	F	6	1	0	0	8,434
Kevie	9	G	6	0	0	1	602	Khalifa Gold	3	F	6	1	0	1	6,523
Kevins Cherokee	8	M	13	0	2	1	20,270	Kham Beau	5	M	3	0	0	0	1,675
Kevin's Decision	3	F	11	0	4	3	40,410	Khamotia	4	F	1	0	0	0	0
Kevins Hope	5	H	2	0	0	0	780	Khan	7	H	8	1	0	1	7,186
Kevins Nightmare	3	F	10	2	2	1	12,801	Kharadi	5	M	1	0	0	0	0
Kevin's Secret	3	C	4	1	1	0	5,395	Kharkov Lady	3	F	8	0	2	0	4,745
Kevin's Way	4	C	15	3	2	2	15,096	Khatef	5	H	5	2	0	0	21,560
Kevmava	4	F	5	0	0	0	942	Khazi	4	F	7	0	0	3	15,060
Kev's Cosmos	2	G	1	0	0	0	0	Khe Sanh	2	F	3	0	0	0	45
Kewanee	4	F	9	2	3	1	13,869	Kherson	4	G	6	1	0	0	2,920
Kewanee Secret	3	F	11	1	1	1	11,520	Khumbaba	3	G	6	0	1	1	8,200
Kewen	3	G	7	2	2	3	109,320	Khyber Kelly	2	C	4	0	0	0	1,825
Key Account	3	F	11	3	2	2	21,450	Ki Request	4	F	1	0	0	0	100
Key Approval	5	M	5	1	1	1	26,750	Kia Ora	3	F	1	0	0	0	100
Key Cat	8	G	3	0	0	0	196	Kiala	4	F	7	1	1	2	11,191
Key Connection	5	M	4	0	1	1	3,150	Kiana (PER)	4	F	1	0	0	0	0
Key Dance	2	C	2	0	0	0	186	Kiati	4	F	4	0	2	0	16,260
Key Decision	3	C	3	0	0	0	2,520	Kiawah	3	C	2	0	0	0	435
Key Definition	3	C	3	1	0	0	28,980	Kiblah	9	G	4	0	1	0	2,325
Key Deputy	3	C	3	2	0	1	60,370	Kick Boxer (FR)	6	G	5	0	0	0	1,200
Key Document	5	H	7	0	1	2	14,925	Kick It in Gear	9	G	7	2	0	1	10,039
Key Expectation	4	F	6	0	0	0	526	Kick N Punch	3	C	14	1	0	2	9,996
Key Grip	7	G	3	0	0	0	0	Kick Sand	6	G	15	0	3	1	10,729
Key Mark	6	M	2	0	0	1	3,300	Kickaboom	4	F	13	1	1	2	10,040
Key Moment	5	H	8	0	0	0	1,195	Kickapoo Kid	2	C	6	0	0	1	1,590
Key of Love	4	F	8	1	1	0	6,515	Kickback	8	G	7	2	0	0	13,796

Horse	Age	Sex	Sts	1st	2d	3d	Won	Horse	Age	Sex	Sts	1st	2d	3d	Won
Kickboard	2	C	4	0	0	1	10,159	Kikino	2	C	1	0	0	0	0
Kickem Dalton	4	G	9	2	1	2	16,365	Kiki's Slippers	4	F	4	0	0	1	2,340
Kicken Kris	3	C	9	4	3	1	593,540	Kilauea	7	G	5	1	1	1	9,738
Kicker	3	F	5	0	0	0	612	Kilcullen	3	G	4	0	0	0	675
Kickety Katy	7	M	11	0	0	3	3,985	Kildare Dancer	4	G	8	0	4	2	8,378
Kickin Free	4	F	12	1	0	2	5,413	Kildeer's Flyer	5	M	3	0	0	0	0
Kickin Kountry	3	G	9	0	1	2	16,610	Kiley Slew	2	F	5	1	1	1	10,090
Kickin Woman	5	M	6	1	2	2	4,219	Kilgarten	3	G	11	2	1	0	27,272
Kickingbird	2	C	4	0	0	0	410	Kilgorie	2	C	1	0	0	0	0
Kickinit	3	F	2	0	0	0	100	Kilgowan	2	C	2	1	0	1	19,600
Kickit Baboom	3	F	16	0	1	3	8,131	Kili	4	C	13	0	2	1	8,333
Kickitupanotch	4	C	13	2	4	3	24,255	Kilkea Castle	3	C	5	1	0	0	29,340
Kickn Chickn	3	F	7	3	0	0	12,950	Kill Devil Hill	2	C	1	0	0	0	174
Kick'n Kacie	3	F	4	1	0	0	5,070	Killarney Gold	3	G	5	1	0	0	8,006
Kick'n the Pants	5	G	1	0	0	0	190	Killarney Kutie	3	F	13	1	4	0	23,090
Kickserve	4	G	4	2	2	0	18,600	Killer Ale	5	M	9	1	0	2	5,948
Kid a Lot	7	H	4	1	0	0	4,890	Killer Angel	5	H	10	2	1	3	32,100
Kid Amour	3	G	5	1	0	0	3,696	Killer App	3	F	2	0	0	0	540
Kid Attitude	2	C	5	0	0	0	1,560	Killer Creek	5	G	1	0	0	0	0
Kid Carrots	3	F	7	0	2	2	17,710	Killer Kyle	5	H	11	1	1	2	7,230
Kid Chocolate	7	G	10	0	0	2	4,981	Killian's Chin	2	C	2	0	0	0	434
Kid Chrome	6	G	7	0	1	0	951	Killing Frost	2	F	2	0	0	0	480
Kid Condo	2	G	4	0	0	1	768	Killycally	5	M	2	0	1	0	4,480
Kid Copper	5	G	10	1	4	2	23,240	Kiln	5	G	15	0	1	2	6,881
Kid Corona	11	G	5	0	0	0	177	Kilo S S	3	C	7	1	0	1	6,690
Kid Courageous	6	G	15	2	1	1	12,417	Kilowait	10	G	4	0	0	0	0
Kid Cum Laude	2	G	2	0	0	0	0	Kilpedder Lad	7	G	17	1	0	0	5,039
Kid Diamond	3	C	15	3	1	5	77,960	Kilroywas Here	5	G	10	1	1	0	3,730
Kid Elijah	12	G	6	0	0	0	108	Kilt Lilt	3	F	5	0	0	2	14,685
Kid Fireman	4	G	3	1	1	0	2,936	Kiltee	5	M	2	0	0	0	225
Kid Friday	5	H	9	2	1	1	7,586	Kim	7	M	12	0	2	2	19,289
Kid Halo	3	C	5	0	0	1	1,525	Kim Has the Power	3	F	1	0	0	0	50
Kid Joshua	6	H	9	1	1	1	3,617	Kim Le	5	M	3	0	0	0	285
Kid Kaelin	3	G	15	5	0	3	85,389	Kim Loves Bucky	6	G	8	2	0	0	177,940
Kid Katowice	5	G	10	0	0	2	2,885	Kim N Kes	3	F	9	0	0	0	1,480
Kid Killarney	7	H	3	0	0	1	1,100	Kim the Brat	3	F	15	2	4	2	31,430
Kid Maverick	3	G	15	1	2	1	2,762	Kimandani	4	G	9	1	0	2	8,326
Kid Miraglia	6	G	6	0	0	0	385	Kimangelique	5	M	3	0	0	0	270
Kid Pistolero	7	G	7	0	0	1	1,522	Kimbell's Dish	3	F	5	0	1	1	2,039
Kid Quixote	2	G	5	0	1	1	3,685	Kimberley Regiment	3	G	5	0	1	0	3,640
Kid Rich	4	C	9	1	1	0	10,150	Kimberleywithaneeh	3	G	8	1	1	0	11,115
Kid Rigo	5	G	8	2	1	0	33,821	Kimberly'sprincess	3	F	1	0	0	0	0
Kid Rio	3	C	14	2	1	0	39,300	Kimbow Slew	4	F	8	2	0	0	6,118
Kid Rocket	3	G	4	0	0	0	945	Kimbralata	5	M	4	0	1	1	12,240
Kid Royal	2	C	1	0	0	0	0	Kimis Delight	3	F	7	0	1	1	2,534
Kid Ruckus	4	C	13	1	2	2	8,038	Kimme a Star	6	M	14	0	2	3	19,505
Kid Russell	3	G	10	3	1	1	37,678	Kimmy's Kid	2	F	2	0	0	0	1,540
Kid Semoran	3	C	7	0	0	1	4,430	Kimo	4	G	3	0	0	0	378
Kid Shuailaan	6	G	1	0	0	0	53	Kimon	3	G	15	3	1	1	43,980
Kid Sid	3	G	3	0	0	0	0	Kimry Moor	4	F	18	2	2	5	47,068
Kid Slew	6	G	7	2	0	2	4,617	Kim's Affair	5	G	2	0	0	0	110
Kid Stuff	6	G	2	0	0	0	0	Kim's Angel	2	C	1	0	0	0	2,700
Kid Sugar	6	G	15	0	1	0	1,900	Kim's Attitude	2	F	3	0	0	0	230
Kid Trump	5	H	3	0	0	1	516	Kim's Baby	4	F	1	0	0	0	0
Kid Try On	8	G	10	2	0	4	8,280	Kim's Gem	2	G	3	1	1	0	34,333
Kid Tuaca	2	C	7	1	0	1	27,210	Kims Grounded	3	F	7	1	0	1	3,946
Kid Twister	10	G	15	0	0	0	865	Kim's Jet Air	5	H	12	0	0	2	3,783
Kid Valentine	4	C	12	0	0	2	3,690	Kims Last Trick	5	M	9	0	0	1	926
Kidd in Concert	3	C	2	0	0	0	390	Kims Miss Ree	4	F	4	0	0	0	167
Kidd Play	3	C	3	1	1	1	14,180	Kimster	4	F	9	2	1	2	40,658
Kidder Cat	5	M	1	0	0	0	0	Kin Roar	2	G	3	0	0	1	2,860
Kiddle Mischief	3	G	13	1	2	3	20,255	Kina Blessed	5	M	8	3	0	1	12,532
Kiddle Miss	3	F	1	0	0	0	0	Kina Flashy	5	M	4	0	0	0	0
Kiddo	4	C	16	3	2	2	7,584	Kind Connection	4	F	15	2	2	4	25,169
Kiddville	9	G	8	3	2	0	26,880	Kind Happiness	5	M	9	1	0	1	2,358
Kidkillam	4	C	9	0	0	0	493	Kind Lena	2	F	5	1	2	1	65,330
Kidney Bean	3	G	10	0	0	0	823	Kind Sir	3	G	15	3	0	2	22,185
Kidontheblock	4	G	5	0	2	0	3,170	Kind Slew	4	G	9	2	0	1	10,235
Kid's Girl Slew	3	F	3	0	0	0	124	Kinda Fast	2	C	1	0	0	0	0
Kids 'n Cats	6	M	11	1	1	2	32,114	Kinda Foxy	4	G	8	0	1	3	3,860
Kids Ridge	3	G	9	0	2	0	37,829	Kinda Gotta Wanna	4	G	13	2	1	2	10,019
Kiebaly	4	F	4	0	0	0	0	Kinda Louche	4	F	4	0	0	0	0
Kiechlin	3	C	1	0	0	0	1,320	Kinda Proper	6	M	9	2	4	2	12,364
Kielbasa Cutea	4	F	4	0	1	0	1,727	Kindand Generous	5	G	8	1	1	0	3,040
Kierins Kute Kid	5	M	6	0	0	1	1,775	Kindara	3	F	6	0	0	0	242
Kiersten's Flash	4	F	3	0	0	0	156	Kindleydeed	3	G	9	1	0	0	6,668
Kifissos (GB)	4	C	3	0	0	0	3,420	Kindness	4	G	3	0	0	0	52
Kiki Riki	5	M	10	1	0	0	6,880	Kindofanact	3	G	6	2	0	1	10,903
Kikika's Gold	2	C	3	1	0	0	10,458	Kindon	4	F	9	3	1	1	14,668

Horse	Age	Sex	Sts	1st	2d	3d	Won	Horse	Age	Sex	Sts	1st	2d	3d	Won
Kindred Spirit	10	G	5	1	0	0	1,420	King of Nasty	6	G	14	2	2	3	35,106
Kindsey's Racer	4	F	6	0	0	0	720	King of Nubia	4	C	22	1	2	1	11,452
Kinematics	3	F	4	0	1	0	7,897	King of Peace	3	G	10	1	1	2	29,555
Kiner's Korner	4	G	12	0	3	1	14,095	King of Prussia	3	C	1	0	0	0	0
Kinesthesia	3	F	13	1	2	2	24,716	King of Rulers	3	G	7	3	1	0	36,955
Kinetic Bend	6	G	2	0	0	1	3,000	King of Siam	3	C	10	2	2	0	37,120
Kinetic Rush	4	G	13	1	1	1	38,599	King of Spain	6	G	12	0	3	1	8,050
King Abed	2	F	1	0	0	0	0	King of Speed	4	G	17	5	2	2	100,774
King Adam	2	C	2	0	0	0	0	King of Swing	9	H	10	0	2	3	12,485
King Aha	2	C	2	0	0	1	975	King of Tap	7	H	6	0	0	0	840
King Alexander	4	G	10	0	1	1	3,733	King of the Blues	4	C	8	2	0	2	15,623
King Among Queens	4	G	9	2	1	2	31,580	King of the Brass	3	G	10	1	0	3	11,593
King and Queen	3	G	8	0	0	0	710	King of the Cats	3	F	9	1	1	1	16,845
King and the Beger	3	G	8	1	0	0	3,924	King of the Mount	4	C	7	1	0	1	32,649
King Augustus	2	C	3	0	3	0	18,900	King of the Night	3	G	1	0	0	0	120
King Baba	3	C	1	0	0	0	0	King of the Slew	4	G	2	0	0	0	427
King Beano	3	C	3	0	3	0	15,860	King of the Stars	2	C	1	0	0	0	110
King Ben	4	G	4	0	0	0	544	King of the Valley	2	C	8	0	1	0	5,893
King Biscuit	3	C	5	0	0	2	4,992	King of the World	3	G	9	1	0	2	39,019
King Bishops Ruby	7	M	16	1	1	1	10,010	King of the Yukon	3	G	3	0	0	0	144
King Bridle	5	H	2	0	0	0	92	King of Thieves	7	G	5	0	0	2	5,434
King Caesar	5	G	14	2	1	0	5,701	King of Thunder	7	H	6	1	0	0	8,390
King Cake	6	H	3	0	0	0	2,010	King of War	6	G	9	2	0	0	10,105
King Carlos	2	C	4	1	2	0	28,710	King Offthestreet	4	C	7	1	3	0	17,820
King Carson	3	G	13	1	0	3	13,820	King Oro	7	G	12	1	2	1	6,667
King Cassia	3	G	9	1	0	2	36,150	King Quin	3	G	5	0	0	0	50
King Cephus	4	C	7	0	0	0	429	King Richard	5	H	8	2	0	2	53,050
King Cha Cha	2	C	1	0	0	0	195	King Robyn	3	G	11	8	1	0	436,990
King Cielo	5	H	9	2	4	0	70,930	King Royal	3	G	4	1	0	0	6,148
King City	8	G	7	1	0	1	10,100	King Royale	4	C	6	3	0	0	49,610
King City Lady	2	F	2	0	0	0	882	King Ruler	5	G	14	2	2	2	12,069
King Code	3	G	4	0	0	0	196	King Sadler	2	C	7	0	0	1	2,881
King Crafty	7	G	9	2	2	1	36,955	King Simpatia (BRZ)	3	C	2	0	0	0	1,275
King Dale	4	G	15	2	3	2	13,491	King Slayer (GB)	8	H	14	4	3	1	56,465
King Decor	5	H	7	0	1	1	15,807	King Smokey	5	G	5	0	0	0	900
King Diablo	9	G	11	2	1	0	5,560	King Snake	5	G	9	1	1	0	9,090
King Ed	3	G	6	1	0	1	7,295	King Steven	3	C	4	1	1	0	21,960
King Eider	5	G	3	0	0	1	1,000	King Sweep	4	C	12	3	0	1	27,750
King Fox	3	G	10	2	2	0	13,392	King Taras	5	G	12	2	6	0	44,020
King Geno	4	C	15	2	2	1	23,396	King Tiara	6	H	1	0	0	0	70
King George W.	3	G	13	0	1	1	27,728	King Tower	4	C	3	0	0	0	452
King Ghazi	5	G	2	0	0	0	0	King Tritan	3	C	4	1	1	1	5,580
King Grader	5	G	18	2	0	10	19,998	King Troy	3	G	9	1	1	2	8,775
King Hanna	8	G	2	0	0	0	110	King True	2	F	3	0	1	0	2,660
King Hope	4	G	15	1	3	0	6,763	King Tutta	3	C	3	0	0	0	125
King Jazzman	5	H	2	0	0	0	225	King Vic	5	G	16	1	5	5	15,067
King Jedi	2	C	5	0	0	1	1,681	King Walter	3	G	3	0	0	0	225
King Jeremy	6	G	10	1	2	2	32,205	King Willow	9	G	5	0	0	0	170
King Jerome	5	G	5	0	2	1	3,350	King Wonderful	4	G	6	1	1	1	22,620
King Justin	2	G	3	2	0	1	14,290	King Zonic	4	C	9	3	1	0	69,050
King Kandy	5	G	10	2	0	0	5,842	Kinga	3	G	8	0	0	1	2,767
King Karl	2	C	3	0	0	0	240	Kingidashi	3	C	8	0	1	1	3,515
King Kevin	6	G	12	0	3	2	8,244	Kingmaker	4	G	3	2	0	0	47,010
King Knocker	4	G	10	4	2	0	64,090	Kingmont	5	G	3	0	0	0	301
King Kohota	3	C	9	2	0	0	22,602	Kingofbrokenharts	6	G	12	0	0	3	7,734
King Kokand	6	H	3	0	0	0	780	Kingofthe Raptors	3	G	1	0	0	0	70
King Ky	3	G	2	1	0	0	23,580	Kingofthemountain	5	G	4	1	0	0	21,080
King Lear	3	G	5	0	0	0	1,480	Kingoftherawbar	5	H	1	0	0	1	1,300
King Lex	4	G	1	0	0	0	0	Kings and Quinns	3	G	8	2	2	0	79,636
King Magic	3	C	8	3	1	1	59,080	King's Bid	2	G	7	0	0	0	360
King Matthew	3	C	7	2	0	1	20,820	Kings Category	2	G	5	2	2	0	24,520
King Maxwell	3	C	14	1	3	0	5,618	King's Charmer	2	F	3	0	1	1	18,020
King Me	8	G	13	3	0	2	37,715	King's Cloak	7	G	3	0	1	2	5,880
King Miles	2	C	3	0	0	0	330	King's Conclusion	3	C	14	1	0	4	27,755
King Mio Royal	8	G	7	0	0	0	744	King's Connection	6	H	13	2	2	2	14,375
King Muloon	3	C	8	1	2	0	8,510	King's Coronation	2	C	3	0	1	0	5,310
King Newt	10	G	8	5	2	0	46,110	Kings Course	3	C	3	1	0	0	21,600
King O ' the Igloo	6	H	12	3	1	5	20,915	Kings Creek	3	F	5	0	0	0	0
King of Adventure	6	G	3	0	1	0	754	Kings Cross	4	G	7	0	2	1	4,044
King of Arms	3	C	2	0	0	0	0	King's Crossing	3	G	3	0	0	0	0
King of Carnival	4	G	15	0	4	4	7,626	Kings Currency	3	C	3	0	1	0	2,016
King of Cash	3	G	11	0	0	2	2,216	King's Decree	3	G	2	0	0	0	728
King of Chicago	3	C	10	2	1	3	50,142	King's Deputy	4	G	8	1	1	1	33,377
King of Diamonds	7	G	9	2	2	1	6,933	King's Design	7	H	5	0	0	1	4,600
King of Dust	2	C	2	0	0	0	630	King's Drama (IRE)	3	G	11	3	4	3	153,493
King of Fling	3	C	3	0	0	0	517	Kings Empress	3	F	17	4	6	3	162,070
King of Gold	3	C	6	1	1	0	33,516	Kings Exchequer	3	G	8	0	0	0	450
King of Knights	7	G	12	2	3	1	30,112	King's Fancy	3	F	8	0	1	1	8,235
King of Mardi Gras	2	C	5	2	0	0	28,915	Kings Friend	3	C	8	1	0	0	14,900

Horse	Age	Sex	Sts	1st	2d	3d	Won	Horse	Age	Sex	Sts	1st	2d	3d	Won
King's Gate	4	G	4	0	0	1	280	Kipski	8	G	18	1	7	3	12,187
King's Honor	7	G	2	0	1	1	993	Kir	6	H	4	0	0	0	0
King's Intentions	5	G	7	2	0	0	8,869	Kiralik (GB)	3	F	5	1	0	1	46,971
King's J C	6	H	3	0	0	0	105	Kirbo Turbo	5	M	11	3	2	1	46,890
King's Justice	9	G	3	0	0	0	0	Kirby's Brogue	3	G	10	1	0	2	10,212
King's Lassie	2	F	5	1	0	2	11,370	Kirby's Fuse	3	F	1	0	0	1	6,666
Kings Lil Star	4	C	1	0	0	0	372	Kiri Camp	2	C	5	0	1	0	5,630
Kings Merit	7	G	5	0	0	0	432	Kiri Kennissa	3	F	11	2	1	2	30,967
King's Messenger	6	H	7	1	1	1	23,970	Kiri Tekanawa	3	F	5	0	0	0	0
King's Mill	2	G	4	0	0	0	300	Kirianna	3	F	12	2	1	2	58,447
Kings Miner	5	G	9	1	4	0	16,940	Kiridashi's Crown	3	C	3	0	0	0	409
Kings of the Ring	3	G	14	1	1	2	47,190	Kiri's Amour	3	F	8	0	0	0	743
Kings Own	5	G	9	2	0	3	18,234	Kiri's Clone	5	G	1	0	0	0	380
King's Palace	3	C	3	0	0	0	361	Kiris Fee	2	C	2	0	0	1	1,320
Kings Plan	3	G	7	1	2	2	12,050	Kiri's Princess	4	F	8	0	0	0	1,260
Kings Pride	3	F	5	0	0	2	3,510	Kirison	4	C	21	1	1	2	6,817
King's Reality	4	C	16	0	0	3	3,483	Kirk Best	6	G	16	3	3	2	17,893
Kings Reception	5	G	5	0	0	0	3,229	Kirkland Jct	4	G	5	2	0	1	6,690
Kings Request	2	F	5	0	0	2	3,618	Kirksboy	6	G	17	3	1	0	13,624
Kings Risk	5	H	4	1	2	0	7,739	Kirlan	3	F	5	0	1	1	5,450
Kings Sequence	4	G	18	1	4	1	12,851	Kirra's Toy	3	C	11	3	0	1	46,353
King's Tale	4	G	11	3	2	0	48,762	Kirschwasser	4	G	4	0	1	0	6,620
King's Taxes	5	G	9	2	1	1	15,870	Kirtle (GB)	4	F	1	0	0	0	1,220
Kings Temper	3	C	11	2	0	3	18,057	Kirtons	6	H	12	2	2	2	26,937
King's Tune	3	C	9	0	1	2	3,880	Kisatche	3	C	4	0	0	1	4,840
Kings Up	8	R	5	1	0	1	5,028	Kishore	3	G	12	1	2	2	14,523
King's Verse	6	H	9	1	2	1	29,920	Kismet	2	F	1	0	0	0	350
Kingsbury	3	C	13	1	3	2	14,470	Kismetoo	4	F	17	1	4	1	12,349
Kingsfirstgirl	4	F	4	0	0	0	0	Kiss	3	G	6	1	0	0	12,430
Kingsford Grey	6	M	13	0	2	3	4,936	Kiss A' Jule	4	F	13	1	1	2	6,940
Kingsland	5	M	1	0	0	1	5,280	Kiss a Miss	5	M	8	0	1	3	44,456
Kingsley Club	3	C	2	0	0	0	2,040	Kiss a Native	6	G	9	2	1	0	44,320
Kingsport	5	H	10	2	4	0	19,168	Kiss Alert	4	F	2	0	0	0	157
Kingstown	3	F	2	0	0	0	180	Kiss an Angel	4	G	5	0	0	1	4,847
Kingstyle	7	G	4	2	1	1	15,050	Kiss an Optimist	2	G	9	1	1	2	54,467
Kingsview	9	G	8	1	1	1	2,161	Kiss And Fly (IRE)	3	F	3	0	0	0	6,800
Kinita	7	M	4	0	0	0	228	Kiss for Julie	3	F	12	4	0	1	39,632
Kinjet	3	G	11	0	2	0	16,243	Kiss Kiss	4	F	2	0	2	0	5,600
Kinkennie	8	G	12	1	2	1	9,839	Kiss Me Again	2	C	6	0	1	0	7,670
Kinky Cowgirl	4	F	9	2	1	2	13,427	Kiss Me Cat	3	F	3	0	0	0	2,100
Kinley	9	G	4	0	0	0	89	Kiss Me Goodbye	6	G	6	1	0	0	5,260
Kinnelon	4	F	9	2	0	0	14,420	Kiss Me Jerry	3	F	6	0	0	0	1,112
Kinnikinnick	3	F	3	1	0	0	5,828	Kiss Me Jim	4	G	15	6	1	1	63,226
Kinscem	4	F	8	1	2	0	12,488	Kiss Me Katie	3	F	7	1	2	2	40,450
Kinshebebold	3	F	5	0	0	0	0	Kiss Me Patrick	3	C	1	0	0	0	0
Kinship	3	C	2	0	0	0	2,880	Kiss Me Twice	4	F	11	2	0	1	53,670
Kinslo Pride	2	F	8	0	0	0	1,700	Kiss Mom	4	C	12	1	2	3	8,539
Kinsman Valor	3	C	10	2	0	1	41,517	Kiss My Judge	3	G	12	2	2	4	33,213
Kinston	5	G	16	1	4	5	29,838	Kiss 'n a Smile	2	F	7	0	1	1	3,412
Kintu	2	C	1	1	0	0	15,600	Kiss Nana Goodbye	4	F	6	0	0	0	270
Kinuseo Falls	3	F	3	0	0	2	15,821	Kiss of Artie	4	G	12	2	0	1	4,235
Kinworth	3	G	3	0	1	0	2,240	Kiss of Fury	6	H	11	5	1	1	21,646
Kinz	6	H	11	1	2	0	6,020	Kiss of Life	4	C	11	0	6	2	17,355
Kinzie Woo	3	F	3	1	1	1	46,000	Kiss of Lion (ARG)	8	H	7	0	1	1	14,025
Kiosk	3	F	7	1	3	1	26,934	Kiss of Shame	9	M	4	0	0	0	327
Kioti	5	G	4	1	0	1	1,684	Kiss of the Cat	3	G	5	1	0	1	4,924
Kiowa Chief	3	G	7	0	0	0	1,013	Kiss On the Cheek	2	F	1	0	0	0	135
Kiowa Kandy	3	F	1	0	0	0	217	Kiss Pudding	11	M	7	1	1	0	3,980
Kiowa King	5	H	4	0	1	0	1,355	Kiss Roam Me O	4	G	10	0	1	0	1,300
Kiowa Prince	2	C	3	1	0	1	12,240	Kiss the Blarney	3	G	8	1	1	2	5,636
Kip	2	G	2	0	0	2	4,400	Kiss the Devil	5	M	3	1	2	0	150,626
Kip Along Molly	4	F	7	0	0	0	861	Kiss the Editor	3	G	6	0	0	0	497
Kip to My Lu	3	F	11	2	0	1	10,782	Kiss the Groom	2	C	4	0	1	1	15,640
Kiplinger	6	G	8	0	0	1	2,120	Kiss the Justice	3	G	5	0	0	0	285
Kipper Aired	4	F	8	0	4	1	6,460	Kiss the Lips	2	F	1	0	0	1	4,400
Kipper Bay	3	C	13	0	4	3	12,161	Kissalyssa	3	F	6	0	2	0	21,600
Kipper Blue	4	F	9	2	2	0	20,269	Kissame	5	M	11	4	1	2	21,049
Kipper Boy	8	G	8	0	0	0	904	Kissane	10	H	7	2	1	1	29,975
Kipper Chemo	3	G	15	2	1	1	55,829	Kisscozzen	2	F	1	1	0	0	5,700
Kipper Edge	3	G	2	0	0	0	200	Kissed by a Prince	3	F	6	3	0	0	161,931
Kipper Girl	3	F	3	0	0	0	860	Kissed Goodbye	5	M	12	2	2	2	26,879
Kipper Kellyson	8	G	2	0	0	0	141	Kissen Capote	3	F	4	0	0	1	7,680
Kippered Rue	4	C	2	0	0	0	0	Kisser	5	M	11	0	2	1	10,968
Kipperella	7	M	8	3	0	1	13,147	Kisses	4	F	11	0	0	1	1,295
Kipper's an Angel	4	G	15	2	2	1	26,025	Kisses for Candace	2	F	3	0	0	0	305
Kipper's Kitten	7	M	5	1	0	0	12,600	Kisses for Kara	3	F	17	1	4	0	17,328
Kipper's Night	2	C	7	2	2	2	84,550	Kisses for Rachel	5	M	9	2	2	0	22,259
Kippertip	4	F	9	1	3	0	14,560	Kisses From Kate	4	F	9	1	1	0	7,160
Kippy's Nancy	6	M	3	0	0	0	310	Kisses Hertfield	3	F	9	1	0	2	12,245

RECORDS OF HORSES

Horse	Age	Sex	Sts	1st	2d	3d	Won
Kisses in Clover	4	F	11	0	3	1	10,970
Kissim All	3	G	8	0	1	0	4,370
Kissin Angie	3	F	16	0	0	0	1,831
Kissin Ashley	4	F	12	1	1	3	11,826
Kissin Beauty	4	F	15	2	1	4	31,780
Kissin Bold	3	C	4	0	1	0	5,613
Kissin by Em	4	F	13	1	2	1	10,515
Kissin Charm	4	F	6	1	0	0	11,970
Kissin Concern	4	F	10	0	1	2	7,803
Kissin Cowboy	2	G	2	0	0	0	665
Kissin Donna	3	F	3	0	0	0	255
Kissin Fresh	3	C	7	0	0	1	3,009
Kissin Game	4	F	8	0	0	0	487
Kissin in the Caar	2	G	3	0	0	0	555
Kissin It Away	5	M	5	3	1	1	20,400
Kissin' Jack	3	C	6	2	0	0	36,340
Kissin Kevin	3	G	2	0	0	0	0
Kissin Kuz	2	G	2	0	0	0	152
Kissin List	2	F	4	0	1	1	3,275
Kissin Miss	3	F	1	0	0	0	110
Kissin My Friends	2	F	5	2	0	0	6,425
Kissin N Huggin	5	G	5	0	1	1	5,175
Kissin Paster	3	G	15	0	2	1	19,838
Kissin Saint	3	C	7	3	0	1	160,620
Kissin Sharp	2	F	3	0	0	0	1,315
Kissin Summer	5	M	16	2	3	4	26,180
Kissin Ty	2	G	9	3	1	1	67,660
Kissin Zak	3	G	5	1	3	0	7,900
Kissing Cobra	5	M	1	0	0	0	50
Kissing Cowgirl	3	F	3	0	0	0	339
Kissing Girl (ARG)	6	M	11	2	4	1	96,575
Kissing King	3	C	5	0	0	0	800
Kissing Rock	4	G	1	0	0	0	0
Kissing Time	5	M	1	0	0	0	0
Kissininseattle	3	C	1	0	0	0	97
Kissinleaf	4	F	15	2	1	5	40,125
Kissmecrazy	2	F	6	1	0	1	15,074
Kissmekissmequick	2	F	2	0	0	0	700
Kissonthespot	3	F	8	2	1	1	18,312
Kisssastar	3	F	6	0	0	0	644
Kissthissky	5	G	13	4	1	0	29,713
Kissy Kat	3	F	3	1	0	1	16,200
Kist All Over	7	M	11	0	0	0	596
Kistler	4	F	1	0	0	0	0
Kit Kat Kayla	2	F	4	0	1	1	9,521
Kit Kat Kool	6	G	8	1	0	0	9,418
Kit Katter	2	F	1	0	0	0	0
Kita's Flyer	6	M	13	1	3	3	14,563
Kitchen Bouquet	6	M	7	0	0	1	780
Kitchen Rade	4	G	11	1	4	1	3,366
Kite With Wings	3	G	9	1	2	2	11,728
Kite Wizard	3	G	9	0	0	2	4,855
Kith	4	C	8	1	0	0	41,284
Kitimat	3	F	7	0	0	1	4,680
Kitling	3	F	3	0	0	0	0
Kit's Kid	5	H	5	0	0	0	428
Kitscoty Klipper	5	M	11	2	5	2	57,354
Kitten On the Keys	5	M	10	2	1	2	9,919
Kitten's Baby Boy	8	H	5	1	0	0	10,680
Kitten's Joy	2	C	4	2	1	0	80,115
Kittens Tiger	2	G	1	0	0	0	0
Kitti Glitter	4	F	9	1	3	2	23,161
Kitti Lake	2	F	2	0	0	0	130
Kittiwood	6	M	12	0	3	1	3,048
Kittle Camp Girl	3	F	3	0	0	0	330
Kittoman	4	G	20	1	1	2	14,760
Kitty B.	5	M	5	0	0	1	1,426
Kitty Carnes	3	F	11	2	1	2	16,204
Kitty Carson	4	F	6	2	0	1	35,730
Kitty Cat Creek	3	F	5	1	0	1	8,580
Kitty Cat Wins	4	F	2	0	0	0	190
Kitty Catcando	3	F	10	0	0	1	1,180
Kitty Coast	2	F	2	0	0	0	570
Kitty Comedy	6	M	11	1	4	3	37,010
Kitty Connection	2	C	2	0	0	0	2,460
Kitty Conveyor	3	F	10	2	2	0	17,452
Kitty Go Lucky	4	F	2	0	0	0	0
Kitty Kiernan	3	F	1	0	0	0	0
Kitty Knight	3	F	5	1	1	1	45,626
Kitty On the Track	6	M	4	0	0	1	23,284
Kitty Would	7	M	9	2	0	1	8,515
Kittybangbang	2	F	3	0	0	0	700
Kittyhawk Lane	4	F	6	1	1	0	4,162
Kitty's Gold	6	M	9	2	0	0	9,359
Kittys Katalist	2	G	2	0	0	0	1,385
Kitty's Legend	3	F	11	2	3	1	78,075
Kitty's Mission	4	F	15	3	1	1	65,826
Kitz	2	C	1	0	0	0	0
Kiuah	4	F	1	0	0	1	583
Kivi	3	F	8	1	2	2	35,150
Kiwi Gold	3	F	6	1	0	1	6,105
Kiwi Zone	5	M	1	0	0	0	1,040
Kiznitti	6	M	5	1	1	2	39,130
Kizzie's Princess	9	M	3	0	0	0	0
Kizzy Kazoo	4	F	10	2	0	4	45,138
Klamath	6	G	11	1	3	0	6,452
Klamath Falls	3	F	2	0	0	0	780
Klassic Kordell	5	G	9	2	3	2	23,670
Klassic Pride	8	G	2	0	0	0	0
Klassikbud	3	C	3	1	0	0	3,012
Klassy Flag	8	G	3	0	0	0	215
Klassy Katlyn	2	F	6	0	2	0	24,360
Klassy Kira	3	F	9	0	0	1	562
Klassy Kliff	11	H	6	0	0	0	641
Klassy Knight	5	G	8	1	0	0	10,770
Klassy Kruzer	2	C	3	0	0	1	4,262
Klassy Woman	3	F	1	0	0	0	130
Klem	4	G	5	0	0	2	317
Kleofus	6	G	7	0	1	0	1,180
Klondike Hobo	6	M	3	0	0	1	336
Klondike Trail	7	G	12	1	1	2	20,828
Klubber Lang	3	G	13	0	2	3	29,200
Klueless Keith	2	C	1	0	0	0	0
Knave	9	G	1	0	0	0	2,200
Knee Monia	4	G	8	0	1	0	1,253
Kneel	3	F	7	1	3	1	57,065
Knews	7	M	5	0	0	0	496
Knico	5	H	3	0	0	0	194
Knievel	3	C	10	2	1	1	61,400
Knight Affair	8	G	12	1	0	3	12,966
Knight and Day	4	C	1	0	0	0	0
Knight Bite	6	H	5	0	0	0	0
Knight Deb	2	F	2	0	0	0	460
Knight Eliminator	3	G	1	0	0	0	0
Knight Errant	4	C	3	0	0	0	0
Knight Fortune	5	M	9	0	2	1	1,665
Knight Game	4	C	5	1	0	1	5,741
Knight Glory	3	G	3	1	0	0	7,265
Knight in Silver	3	G	8	2	2	2	22,055
Knight Mistress	7	M	2	0	0	0	598
Knight of Cups	3	F	3	0	2	1	7,150
Knight of Darkness	2	C	7	0	2	2	25,242
Knight of the Mt.	3	C	1	0	1	0	6,000
Knight Player	12	G	4	1	1	0	1,635
Knight Raider	6	G	11	1	2	2	6,990
Knight Rounds	6	G	14	2	1	0	10,796
Knight Teaser	6	G	7	1	2	1	4,304
Knight Templar	5	H	3	1	0	0	4,215
Knight Tres	9	G	12	1	1	1	6,474
Knight Villain	8	G	12	2	3	1	15,709
Knight Weave	5	M	4	1	0	0	2,510
Knight Writer	5	M	1	0	0	0	0
Knight Zone	3	F	11	0	2	1	2,891
Knightatthecasino	3	G	5	0	0	0	289
Knighthyme Ability	7	G	9	1	0	3	13,848
Knightly Ease	3	C	2	0	0	0	1,764
Knightly Signal	4	F	3	0	0	0	2,050
Knightly Swinger	3	G	7	0	0	0	1,264
Knightnsilverarmor	2	G	7	1	0	0	12,194
Knight'n'the Woods	3	G	2	0	0	0	278
Knightress Gem	3	F	2	0	0	0	150
Knight's Agenda	4	G	4	0	0	1	1,213
Knight's Glitter	5	G	12	1	1	1	4,324
Knight's Gumbo	6	G	10	1	2	2	14,454
Knights 'n Dragons	3	G	2	0	0	0	0
Knights Sovereign	5	G	9	0	0	1	1,385
Knightsbridge Road	3	G	8	1	4	3	69,520
Knightsound	2	C	5	1	0	0	30,120

Horse	Age	Sex	Sts	1st	2d	3d	Won	Horse	Age	Sex	Sts	1st	2d	3d	Won
Knill Creek	6	H	3	0	0	0	136	Kompressor Jack	3	G	11	1	5	1	40,996
Knimper	4	G	8	0	0	3	2,359	Kon Tiki	3	C	4	1	1	1	35,860
Knines Dream	8	G	17	1	1	4	15,088	Kona Beau	4	G	8	0	3	4	11,538
Knish	4	G	10	0	1	2	12,340	Kona Breeze	4	F	12	2	5	0	43,070
Knob Hill	2	C	4	1	0	0	4,639	Kona Brick	4	G	19	1	2	2	5,861
Knobby N Mert	4	C	8	1	2	0	5,876	Kona Coast	7	G	11	1	2	3	9,595
Knock Again	6	G	9	0	4	2	33,440	Kona Gold	9	G	4	1	0	0	95,680
Knock It Off	4	F	11	2	1	3	14,658	Kona Kokand	4	C	2	0	1	0	5,220
Knock Out Chick	4	F	1	0	0	0	0	Kona Princess	4	F	3	1	1	0	4,880
Knock Out Prospect	4	F	14	2	3	3	33,300	Kona Queen	5	M	13	2	3	4	76,760
Knock Twice	4	F	3	0	0	2	4,620	Kona Run	2	G	5	1	1	0	10,825
Knockabout	9	G	12	2	0	1	5,691	Konas Kannon	5	G	8	1	1	1	4,591
Knock'em Dead	4	C	7	0	0	1	2,610	Kondoa Way	4	C	8	0	0	3	5,295
Knockemout John	7	G	14	0	0	1	837	Konyak	5	G	12	0	0	2	6,085
Knockin Boots	2	F	3	0	1	0	5,250	Konza	2	F	5	0	2	2	16,920
Knockknock Knockin	3	F	3	0	0	0	0	Koo Bear	3	G	5	2	1	0	35,430
Knockout Crown	4	F	8	3	1	2	63,690	Koobalotchee	6	G	7	0	0	0	1,470
Knockout Kid	6	G	2	0	0	0	510	Kooka Munga	3	F	11	2	2	2	59,520
Knockout Speed	4	F	7	2	0	0	13,290	Kookaburra	3	C	10	1	1	0	41,797
Knockout the Truth	6	G	15	2	2	1	13,905	Kookie Gambler	5	H	1	0	0	0	87
Knockwood	5	G	12	1	2	3	6,248	Kookie Krusher	2	F	6	0	1	2	10,023
Knoll Lake	5	M	11	5	5	0	154,920	Kookie's Trick	3	F	7	0	0	0	587
Knott On Tour	5	G	1	0	0	0	61	Kookiesraisin	2	F	2	0	0	0	0
Knotting Hill	4	F	14	2	1	1	10,978	Kool Blue Steel	6	H	4	1	1	0	1,476
Knotty Behaviour	3	G	10	1	1	0	76,128	Kool Body	4	C	14	0	5	0	10,776
Knotty Knows	5	M	6	3	1	0	32,237	Kool Carma	2	F	3	0	1	0	6,620
Knottybutnice	5	M	14	1	4	1	13,786	Kool Daddy D. J.	3	G	15	1	1	1	7,555
Know How	5	G	11	3	0	1	47,564	Kool Humor	3	G	11	4	1	3	211,800
Know Sumthin	6	H	5	1	0	2	10,325	Kool Jazkey	8	G	6	0	4	0	4,524
Knowmee	6	G	19	2	0	3	24,926	Kool K. J.	3	F	7	0	1	0	7,795
Known Glory	3	F	10	0	0	0	469	Kool Kaleb	3	C	2	0	1	0	1,310
Known Land	6	H	9	0	2	1	4,170	Kool Kat Karin	4	F	9	1	0	1	1,510
Known Prospect	4	F	9	1	3	1	59,912	Kool Kool	4	G	8	0	0	1	6,130
Known Rhythm	5	G	3	1	0	0	3,347	Kool Kounty	2	G	1	0	0	0	0
Known Tender	6	G	8	1	2	1	86,574	Kool Smoke	3	C	5	0	1	2	8,240
Known Touch	3	F	1	0	0	0	2,195	Koola	5	G	10	4	0	1	21,863
Known Wonder	3	F	11	0	1	1	5,675	Koolau Summer	2	F	2	0	0	0	110
Knows No Boundary	6	G	12	3	1	2	25,850	Koorachee	4	C	2	0	0	1	2,160
Knowwhentofoldthem	5	G	11	0	1	2	4,619	Kootenai	2	F	2	0	0	0	1,980
Knox	2	C	6	1	1	2	35,036	Kootsopothee	5	M	23	1	2	2	13,300
Knox City	9	G	7	0	1	0	9,796	Koovey	7	G	11	0	1	3	4,797
Knuckleball	4	G	8	2	1	0	9,460	Koral Star	3	G	6	1	1	1	8,589
Knucklehead	4	F	9	1	0	4	25,152	Koran	2	G	6	1	0	1	27,009
Kobari Time	5	M	8	0	0	0	793	Korbyn Gold	2	C	9	4	2	0	159,728
Kobella Bean	2	F	7	0	2	0	7,070	Koree 'n Chris	4	F	3	0	0	0	340
Kobemon	4	F	12	2	1	3	10,757	Koritsimas	3	F	2	0	0	0	848
Kodan	6	G	11	0	0	3	8,375	Korra Nation	4	F	3	0	0	0	304
Kodema	4	G	9	4	2	1	121,795	Korsakoff	2	C	3	1	0	0	34,531
Kodiak	5	G	9	2	0	1	25,891	Kosade	3	F	4	1	0	0	24,980
Kodon	3	G	10	0	1	1	2,486	Koslanin (ARG)	9	H	2	0	0	0	0
Kody Karumba	7	H	2	0	1	1	1,800	Kossu (IRE)	3	C	5	0	0	1	10,901
Kody's Alibi	9	G	4	0	0	0	128	Kostaki	4	G	1	0	0	0	0
Kody's Best Move	5	G	1	0	0	0	0	Kostroma Pass	3	F	8	1	1	2	13,850
Koennecker	11	G	1	0	0	0	44	Kotumaslep	3	G	9	0	2	0	5,414
Kofi	3	G	10	1	0	0	36,164	Kotuspeeding	5	H	8	0	1	2	13,916
Kohuna Grande	6	G	9	2	3	2	62,908	Kountry Grammer	2	G	2	0	1	1	6,430
Koka Kola Kween	4	F	9	1	0	0	5,710	Kouri Jill	3	F	15	6	2	4	65,065
Kokand Kid	3	G	2	0	0	0	0	Kours Essence	4	F	6	0	0	0	493
Kokand Rum	3	F	5	0	0	0	1,145	Kourtly Rose	5	M	3	0	0	1	638
Kokandahotdog	3	F	7	0	1	1	4,470	Kovale	2	F	6	1	0	1	15,110
Kokando	2	C	6	3	2	0	67,460	Kowboy J. J.	5	M	3	0	0	0	382
Kokeshi	3	F	2	0	1	0	4,774	Kowboy Ronda	6	M	3	0	0	1	458
Kokie Grand	5	M	9	2	2	0	21,827	Kozy Polly	2	F	1	0	0	0	384
Kokinaras	7	G	15	0	1	1	5,815	Krabbie	11	G	3	0	0	0	761
Kokkola	3	F	4	0	0	0	100	Krafty Kaper	2	F	2	0	0	0	1,000
Koko Chico	3	G	11	3	0	4	40,600	Krakowviak	3	F	6	1	0	1	7,920
Kokokand	5	M	12	1	3	2	23,551	Kranky Karol	2	F	2	1	1	0	11,320
Kokomo Jo	9	M	14	1	1	3	7,553	Krasnaya	3	F	6	2	1	0	50,800
Kokopelli Kid	3	C	2	1	1	0	6,150	Kraz	3	G	9	0	2	0	11,400
Kola	3	C	1	0	0	0	0	Krazy Leo in Plaid	4	G	3	0	1	1	2,230
Kolinor	6	G	16	2	3	3	61,772	Krazycajun	3	G	9	2	2	2	5,672
Kolob	6	G	6	1	0	0	11,540	Kreb's Princess	2	F	3	0	0	0	651
Koloft	3	G	2	0	0	0	0	Krebsie	3	G	11	1	2	2	44,860
Koloszar	2	G	1	0	0	0	0	Kreems View	4	F	6	1	1	1	28,000
Kolour Coded	6	M	3	0	1	0	1,482	Kremke	3	G	1	0	0	0	1,300
Koluctoo's Man	6	G	10	2	2	1	4,720	Kremlin Princess	4	F	6	0	2	1	5,296
Komax	5	G	4	1	1	1	30,740	Kremmling	4	G	2	0	0	1	1,425
Komba	8	G	18	2	5	3	30,776	Krewman	3	G	12	0	2	1	5,884
Komistar (GB)	8	G	5	2	2	0	59,050	Krews Star	3	F	3	0	0	0	160

Horse	Age	Sex	Sts	1st	2d	3d	Won
Kricketeer	4	F	4	0	0	0	0
Krieger	5	H	5	0	2	1	47,550
Krigeorj's Gold	10	G	5	1	0	1	6,746
Kris Havingfunnow	5	H	4	1	1	1	47,675
Kris Karen	3	F	1	0	0	0	0
Kris Miss Spirit	5	M	5	1	0	0	6,079
Kris R	2	C	5	0	0	0	555
Kris S Niece	6	M	4	0	0	1	537
Kris Star	3	F	6	2	3	0	68,955
Kris Taly	4	G	2	0	0	0	78
Kris Taylor	4	C	8	1	2	0	26,245
Kris Venetian	7	M	6	0	0	0	136
Krisacia	5	M	3	0	0	0	1,120
Krisana	4	F	7	1	0	1	16,135
Krisari	4	F	9	2	1	1	9,114
Krisbluebayou	2	F	4	0	0	1	3,943
Krisco Kid	5	G	16	1	0	1	5,965
Krisherra	2	C	2	1	0	0	15,780
Krismas	3	F	9	1	0	2	24,610
Krisonette	2	F	1	0	0	0	0
Kris's Call	3	G	5	1	0	1	9,198
Kris's Cloud	2	F	1	0	0	0	140
Kris's Currency	4	G	5	0	0	0	1,295
Kris's Dancer	4	G	9	4	0	1	73,332
Kris's Ghost	3	G	13	2	2	1	21,941
Kris's Image	6	M	1	0	0	0	150
Kriss Is School	3	G	13	1	1	4	16,100
Kris's Valentine	2	F	4	1	0	0	6,306
Kris'sbest	5	M	12	3	5	0	37,630
Krissy Blue Eyes	2	F	8	0	0	0	2,214
Kristas Comet	3	F	4	1	0	2	10,432
Krista's Night	3	F	10	1	0	2	6,623
Kristens Bullet	3	C	5	0	1	1	3,245
Kristens Superstar	6	M	2	0	0	0	570
Kristen's Way	3	F	7	0	0	1	1,851
Kristenshadenough	3	F	4	0	0	0	378
Kristie H	2	F	2	0	0	0	432
Kristina K	4	F	10	2	1	0	16,189
Kristina's B D Boy	2	G	1	0	0	0	0
Kristina's Star	5	M	7	1	1	0	9,087
Kristina's Wish	3	F	8	1	2	2	35,380
Kristine's King	4	C	14	3	1	3	62,608
Kristi's Pleasure	6	M	15	1	0	4	8,416
Kristof	3	G	6	0	0	1	1,205
Kristoferobyn	4	G	9	1	3	1	12,744
Kristofferson	3	C	3	1	0	1	16,935
Kristopher Kross	9	G	1	0	0	0	0
Kristopher Road	6	G	4	0	0	1	1,652
Kristy Dale	3	F	5	1	0	1	27,010
Kristy Naevus	4	F	4	0	0	0	165
Kristylynnsregency	2	C	2	0	0	0	0
Kristy's Act	3	F	9	0	0	0	0
Kristys Classic	4	F	4	0	1	0	1,210
Kristys Crown	5	H	9	0	1	0	1,503
Kristy's Day	4	G	1	0	0	0	0
Kristy's Dream	3	F	10	0	2	2	8,569
Kristys Excellent	6	M	16	1	3	5	43,575
Kristys Fuegos	4	G	5	0	0	0	141
Kristys Gold Star	3	F	11	1	2	1	22,475
Kristys Golden Boy	3	C	2	0	0	1	638
Kristys Goldengirl	2	F	3	1	0	0	3,480
Kristys Lovesignal	6	M	11	1	2	1	14,920
Kristys Majestic	4	F	12	1	2	1	10,142
Kristys Prospector	2	C	2	0	0	0	0
Kristys Sunny	3	G	18	1	2	4	13,289
Krown Me King	3	C	1	0	0	0	840
Krupa	2	C	1	0	0	0	160
Krusin Kristen	6	M	5	0	1	0	1,280
Krybaby K T	5	M	4	0	1	1	2,869
Krypto Cajun	3	F	4	0	0	0	0
Krysams	7	M	11	1	2	1	12,996
Kryskaly	3	F	4	2	2	0	21,390
Krystals Kipper	5	G	7	0	2	2	8,606
Krystina Can Dance	3	F	11	0	3	0	5,044
Krystina's Day	3	F	10	0	3	0	5,367
Krz Ruckus	6	G	8	1	2	1	152,836
Krz Time	2	F	3	0	0	1	10,645
K's Big Bird	4	G	5	0	0	1	1,080
K's Charismatic	2	C	9	0	2	1	11,438
K's Commando	6	G	3	0	1	0	2,736
K's Fine Gal	3	F	10	0	0	1	1,126
K's Gold	2	F	6	0	0	0	1,175
K's Party	2	G	4	0	0	0	504
Kuanyan	3	F	4	1	1	1	32,250
Kubala's Keepsake	3	F	14	0	3	1	10,430
Kuch	3	C	4	0	1	1	14,250
Kudos	6	G	5	1	1	3	530,000
Kufta (IRE)	4	C	9	0	1	1	4,134
Kukenhof	3	C	3	0	0	0	330
Kukicha	3	F	1	0	0	0	380
Kukku	2	F	2	1	0	0	3,990
Kuko	7	G	11	3	2	3	20,457
Kuko Baluco	5	G	13	1	1	3	14,593
Kulik	2	F	3	0	0	0	720
Kultur	5	H	7	1	2	1	6,980
Kuranda	5	G	4	0	1	0	1,504
Kurt's Flight	9	G	7	2	1	0	2,971
Kuselecto	5	M	1	0	0	0	0
Kushka Boy	5	H	5	0	0	0	1,150
Kutenai	2	C	1	0	0	0	0
Kutsa	7	H	2	0	0	0	90
Kuwaiti Storm	4	G	2	0	0	0	95
Kwaito	3	F	4	1	0	1	16,580
Kwame	2	G	7	1	0	3	26,960
Kwik Kash	4	F	4	2	1	1	64,265
Kwik Start	4	F	6	0	0	0	515
Ky Deputy	2	C	1	0	0	0	0
Kya Jo	2	F	4	1	1	1	7,920
Kyle Anne	2	F	1	0	0	0	52
Kyle Man	4	G	6	1	1	1	9,750
Kylemore Abbey	4	C	11	2	5	0	65,660
Kylers Midge	4	F	13	7	0	0	133,000
Kyle's Ace	13	G	4	0	1	1	495
Kyle's Bluebird	3	F	13	1	0	1	5,544
Kyle's Cruiser	6	M	1	0	0	0	0
Kyles Keeper	3	G	6	0	0	1	1,646
Kyle's Lil Boy	3	C	9	1	3	2	21,195
Kyle's My Dad	4	F	5	0	0	0	753
Kyle's Reprized	4	G	6	0	0	0	315
Kyle's Secret	3	C	11	3	3	0	24,726
Kyle's Squaw	4	F	11	1	1	1	5,266
Kyle's T. L. C.	3	F	9	1	3	2	8,963
Kyle's Treasure	2	F	1	0	0	0	0
Kylie's Art	4	F	1	0	0	0	0
Kylie's Brush	4	F	6	0	0	0	3,260
Kylie's Choice	3	F	3	1	1	0	7,740
Kylie's Legacy	4	F	3	0	0	0	0
Kylor Creek	5	M	20	2	1	2	17,521
Kyra's Kin	2	F	2	0	0	0	0
Kyrenia	4	F	13	3	4	2	73,890
Kyungbokung	4	C	6	0	1	0	9,660
L and K's Dream	4	G	12	1	1	1	4,475
L' Astre	3	F	5	0	0	2	2,100
L B J J Express	3	G	9	1	1	3	10,165
L Bs Cien	2	C	1	0	0	0	0
L B's Express	3	G	7	1	0	2	3,064
L B's Raising Star	2	C	1	0	0	0	0
L C Mystery	2	F	1	0	0	0	118
L C Wheelofortune	4	F	4	0	0	0	198
L Caitlin Eades	3	F	13	0	2	4	33,328
L C's Opportunity	6	G	4	0	1	0	1,414
L D Country Road	2	G	1	0	0	0	0
L Diamond	5	M	1	0	1	0	460
L D's Hello Mom	3	F	8	1	3	2	36,115
L G Sweeny	5	G	4	0	1	0	1,566
L G's Gold	3	F	7	2	0	2	13,990
L J S Express	2	C	6	0	1	0	1,620
L J's Anabell	3	F	2	0	0	0	140
L L Hazer	4	G	3	0	0	0	132
L M Curiser	3	F	10	2	0	5	19,130
L N B Intimidator	3	G	5	0	0	0	0
L P Ensign	7	M	8	2	2	0	17,310
L P's Best	11	G	6	1	1	1	6,309
L P's First Choice	3	G	5	1	0	0	5,895
L S Gypsyannio	2	F	2	0	0	0	411
L S Matt's Dusty	5	G	7	1	0	0	4,275
L S Piannomagic	3	G	12	1	0	0	12,231
L T's Chick	3	F	2	0	0	0	42

Horse	Age	Sex	Sts	1st	2d	3d	Won
L. A. Albert	6	G	1	0	0	0	380
L. A. Bull	6	H	6	0	1	0	3,540
L. A. Elizabeth	5	M	3	0	0	0	221
L. A. Fitz	6	G	8	1	2	4	17,888
L. A. Jade	5	M	10	1	3	1	13,589
L. A. Queen	7	M	8	0	0	0	413
L. A. Spider Legs	7	G	9	0	1	2	22,240
L. A. Tootie	2	F	2	0	0	0	1,260
L. B. Down	5	M	9	2	0	2	6,000
L. B. Hoofin It	3	G	2	0	0	0	0
L. B. Long Gone	9	G	7	0	0	2	1,370
L. B. Won Kenobi	3	G	7	0	1	1	2,216
L. B.'s Charmer	3	F	1	0	0	0	0
L. D. Crowe	5	G	15	3	2	3	37,895
L. E. Weber	3	G	4	0	0	0	1,133
L. I. B. Proper	3	C	6	0	0	0	252
L. J. Johnson	3	C	4	0	1	1	3,740
L. J.'s Money Man	3	G	1	0	0	0	0
L. John P.	6	H	9	0	2	0	3,060
L. L. Cat	5	G	9	2	0	1	7,810
L. L. S. Cat	2	F	1	0	0	0	540
L. Ratt	5	H	14	1	3	3	18,592
L. S. Desdumonde	4	F	10	0	0	1	2,557
L. S. Gotcha	4	G	10	0	1	0	4,104
La. Explosion	2	F	2	0	0	0	370
La Aspera (ARG)	3	F	1	0	0	0	975
La Bala de Plata	2	G	11	0	4	1	19,370
La Ballerine	4	F	13	1	3	3	60,069
La Bandera	6	G	12	2	3	0	22,222
La Baquera	2	F	4	0	1	1	1,470
La Bella	3	F	10	3	1	1	26,760
La Bella Donna	6	M	8	0	2	0	7,342
La Bella Reina	8	F	7	2	2	1	65,320
La Belle Diamante	8	M	1	0	0	0	0
La Belle Fleur	3	F	8	1	1	0	16,802
La Belle Frenchie	4	F	12	1	3	2	32,117
La Belle Simone (IRE)	4	F	3	0	1	1	15,310
La Blonda (ARG)	7	M	3	0	0	0	162
La Blue Goose	2	F	5	0	0	3	7,040
La Bombonera	6	G	3	1	0	1	5,180
La Bonte Creek	3	F	2	0	0	1	580
La Brie Quette	4	F	15	0	0	0	2,333
La Brieanna	2	F	2	0	0	1	1,597
La Britnay	6	M	6	0	0	0	1,041
La Cachette	4	F	6	0	1	1	9,831
La Campanella (IRE)	3	F	5	0	1	1	18,480
La Candida	3	F	10	2	0	3	13,645
La Canoa Ranchaa	5	G	14	1	2	1	11,060
La Carina	3	F	5	0	1	0	5,750
La Cat	5	M	3	0	0	1	4,110
La Cerca	2	F	2	1	1	0	22,230
La Cerise	3	F	5	0	0	0	252
La Chaiym	6	G	6	0	0	1	535
La Chapelle	4	F	1	0	1	0	1,495
La Cheetah	3	F	10	2	2	2	36,650
La Chunk	4	G	17	5	0	4	66,149
La Cibaena	3	F	1	0	0	0	0
La Cicale	5	M	10	1	0	0	7,314
La Cochinada	2	G	3	0	0	1	3,281
La Coconelle	2	M	2	0	0	0	200
La Coda Del Gatto	3	G	5	1	0	0	10,110
La Confidencial	4	G	12	1	3	1	14,254
La Court	4	F	2	1	0	0	6,600
La Croisette (CHI)	5	M	4	0	0	0	6,000
La Dame Amour	2	F	2	0	0	0	320
La de Di	2	F	3	0	0	0	284
La Defiance	4	F	2	0	0	0	0
La Duncan (ARG)	4	F	9	1	1	0	26,260
La Fast Action	7	G	1	0	0	1	208
La Fast Cat	3	G	1	0	0	0	130
La Femme Galante	3	F	1	1	0	0	27,320
La Fino Vino	2	F	1	0	0	0	90
La Fleet	3	F	8	1	0	3	5,280
La Fontaine	5	H	3	0	0	0	576
La Fontainiere (IRE)	5	M	3	0	0	0	0
La Galga	3	F	1	0	0	0	0
La Gata Loca	2	F	2	0	0	0	335
La Gato Mio	4	F	8	1	1	0	1,737
La Geri	3	F	9	0	0	2	5,186
La Gloire	4	F	6	0	1	1	2,375
La Goomba	4	F	14	1	4	3	26,423
La Grande Ballade (GB)	6	M	6	1	2	3	18,574
La Grande Banc	3	F	7	1	0	2	9,300
La Grande Erreur	3	F	1	0	0	0	0
La Grande Mamma	2	F	4	2	1	0	143,975
La Grande Milagro	3	G	4	0	0	0	868
La Grange	3	G	15	2	3	5	25,970
La Hermosa	5	M	10	3	0	2	19,569
La Irish Charm	3	F	3	0	0	0	0
La Jefa	2	F	2	0	0	0	3,280
La Joconde	3	F	1	0	0	0	0
La Jolie Madame	4	F	1	0	1	0	3,720
La Junta	8	G	1	0	0	0	100
La La's Passion	5	H	8	0	0	2	12,235
La Libellule	3	F	5	0	0	0	1,937
La Linz	3	F	7	0	0	1	2,535
La Luna de Oro	2	F	4	0	1	1	10,145
La Luz Del Sol	6	M	4	1	0	1	17,067
La Maquina	5	G	12	2	1	1	15,901
La Mariacristina	3	F	1	0	0	0	0
La Mariah	4	F	6	2	1	1	11,745
La Memo	2	F	1	0	0	0	380
La Migra	8	G	9	1	2	0	5,630
La Naturaleza	2	F	6	1	0	1	4,734
La Nina Dancer	5	M	8	2	1	0	34,451
La Nina Mona	4	F	10	0	0	2	1,598
La Pascale (GB)	4	F	4	0	1	1	6,300
La Perfecta (CHI)	4	F	9	0	1	2	25,320
La Petite Justice	3	F	6	1	0	2	50,885
La Petite Sheet	3	F	15	2	2	3	39,966
La Picara (CHI)	6	M	5	1	2	0	40,900
La Pichona	6	M	3	1	0	0	4,500
La Pique Dame	3	F	3	0	0	0	4,140
La Prada	4	F	11	1	2	0	14,465
La Prado	4	G	9	2	3	1	20,620
La Premier Etoile	4	F	8	0	0	1	652
La Princesse Jolie	5	M	10	0	2	2	50,548
La Pro	4	F	11	0	3	2	33,690
La Proper	5	G	3	0	0	0	140
La Pryor Star	4	F	2	0	0	0	0
La Reason	3	F	12	3	2	1	101,845
La Rein	2	F	3	0	0	0	3,636
La Reina	2	F	4	2	2	0	142,420
La Rielera	3	F	2	0	0	0	180
La Roverina	3	F	9	2	1	1	33,410
La Rubia	6	M	9	0	0	1	3,502
La Rubia Peligrosa	3	F	1	0	0	1	780
La Sabana	4	F	3	0	0	0	207
La Salle Glory	2	F	6	1	4	0	89,756
La Salsa	5	M	7	0	0	4	11,380
La Sanchita	2	F	4	0	2	1	9,460
La Shoruka	3	F	6	2	1	1	22,295
La Skipper	4	G	3	0	0	2	1,495
La Sorpresa (ARG)	6	M	9	2	3	0	57,100
La Star	4	F	3	0	0	0	70
La Storm	5	H	5	0	1	0	920
La Taj	12	G	7	0	0	2	2,973
La Te Migon	3	F	4	0	0	0	0
La Tina	3	F	7	2	0	1	60,240
La Tinker	3	F	7	1	0	1	8,365
La Tizona	5	M	6	1	1	0	24,740
La Tour (CHI)	4	F	1	1	0	0	28,800
La Trapp	3	F	3	0	0	0	0
La Traviesa	3	F	16	3	2	2	14,925
La Truffe	3	F	6	1	0	0	6,334
La Truffe Grise	4	F	9	3	1	1	17,318
La Tulipe	4	F	4	0	1	1	6,848
La Vedette	2	F	2	0	0	2	7,750
La Vegena	5	M	7	0	0	1	1,980
La Vie Cielo	4	C	18	4	2	3	29,742
La Violette	3	F	2	0	0	0	1,302
La Vista	4	F	11	0	3	3	31,310
La Vita E Bella (IRE)	5	M	1	0	1	0	12,200
La Vitesse	7	M	4	3	0	1	36,480
La Walk	4	G	8	2	1	0	12,905
La Wapa	2	F	6	0	0	1	2,213
La Zuli	4	F	3	1	1	1	21,280
Labba	2	G	4	0	1	0	2,020

RECORDS OF HORSES

Horse	Age	Sex	Sts	1st	2d	3d	Won
Labaca	2	F	3	1	1	0	6,940
Labamta Babe	4	G	5	1	0	0	44,700
Labash	4	F	3	0	0	0	810
Labeeby	2	F	2	0	0	0	45
Labellebuttons	5	M	7	1	1	1	19,870
Labellum	4	F	5	1	3	0	28,670
Labido	5	H	11	0	2	1	5,195
Labirinto	5	G	15	5	3	3	234,633
Laborcita	2	F	5	2	1	0	9,380
Labozza	3	G	5	1	2	0	5,300
Labyrinth	4	F	9	1	1	3	17,815
Lac a Rock	3	G	4	1	1	0	9,990
Lac Bonhomme	10	G	4	0	0	1	2,280
Lac de Mere	5	M	9	2	4	0	15,832
Lac de Time	4	F	20	0	7	2	23,280
Lac Fontaine	3	G	8	0	1	1	4,174
Lac Grand	6	G	4	2	0	1	41,975
Lac Indy	4	G	7	2	1	0	15,986
Lac La Meade	10	G	2	0	0	0	0
Lac Laronge	3	G	13	4	2	3	156,308
Lac of Mission	5	G	12	1	1	1	10,443
Lac Ouiloose	5	M	5	1	1	2	43,620
Lace and Lightning	5	M	8	0	1	1	8,082
Lace Castelli	2	F	5	1	2	1	18,380
Lace Knighty	2	F	6	1	0	1	6,585
Lace N Leather	7	M	4	0	0	0	251
Laced Up	4	F	9	2	1	2	26,135
Lacenter Flash	3	G	14	2	1	1	13,657
Lacer	4	G	6	1	1	0	31,208
Lacewood	2	F	8	1	3	0	3,945
Lacey A	4	F	9	3	1	0	24,960
Lacey Begone	3	F	7	1	2	1	7,035
Lacey Dawn	2	F	4	1	0	0	6,210
Lacey My Shoes	3	F	11	0	3	0	8,621
Lacey Oakley	3	F	15	5	3	2	29,651
Lachance	4	F	2	0	0	0	60
Lacharme	5	M	4	0	0	0	546
Lacia	4	F	2	1	0	0	7,643
Lacie Girl	4	F	11	4	6	0	227,990
Lacing Up	6	H	6	0	1	1	5,857
Lack of Money	7	M	5	1	1	2	11,512
Lackapasser	7	H	7	0	0	0	0
Lacrosse	3	G	5	1	1	1	12,500
Lacrystal Classic	4	F	11	3	3	1	82,075
Lacy by Design	2	F	6	0	0	0	1,640
Lacy Lady	4	F	7	2	0	1	18,575
Lacy Longlegs	4	F	2	0	0	0	1,100
Lacy Lou	5	M	9	2	3	0	32,300
Lacy Rose	3	F	5	0	0	0	455
Lacykate	6	M	8	1	1	1	5,958
Laddies Kidd	2	C	3	0	0	0	370
Laddy	4	G	15	3	1	4	31,384
Ladies Dance	2	F	6	1	1	0	10,415
Ladies Din	8	G	2	0	0	0	11,250
Ladies Meetings	3	F	2	0	0	2	4,800
Ladies Over Jacks	2	C	3	0	0	0	560
Ladies Precept	3	F	12	2	3	2	49,477
Ladies Spur	3	F	5	0	0	0	231
Ladif	5	M	9	1	1	0	6,690
Ladkey	7	G	6	0	1	0	2,578
Ladle	3	G	8	2	0	1	26,283
Ladoma	3	F	2	0	0	1	8,400
Lador Vador	4	C	5	0	0	0	600
Lado's Champ	5	G	7	1	0	1	3,185
Ladra	3	F	6	2	0	1	9,736
Lad's Don	3	G	2	0	0	0	0
Lads Sweet Run	2	C	1	0	0	0	85
Lady	4	F	8	1	0	3	10,696
Lady Abadabba Due	3	F	12	2	0	0	26,070
Lady Abby	2	F	8	1	0	1	17,258
Lady Adare	4	F	9	1	2	2	47,460
Lady Aflair	2	F	8	1	0	0	34,805
Lady Afleet	2	F	3	1	0	0	6,360
Lady Aly	3	F	2	0	0	0	132
Lady Anet	3	F	12	0	0	1	2,028
Lady Ann	2	F	1	0	1	0	3,000
Lady Anna J	2	F	5	1	1	1	8,800
Lady Annahalf	4	F	11	1	2	1	3,623
Lady Annaliese (NZ)	4	F	4	2	1	0	116,470
Lady Anthony	3	F	4	0	0	2	2,388
Lady Athena	2	F	2	0	0	1	5,268
Lady Aurora	3	F	3	0	0	0	0
Lady Bana	5	M	9	2	1	0	9,360
Lady Bank	2	F	4	0	1	0	2,687
Lady Bates	6	M	4	0	0	0	215
Lady Beaver	4	F	11	2	1	1	7,505
Lady Beelzebub	2	F	6	3	0	0	49,900
Lady Begone	2	F	5	1	0	1	10,665
Lady Belle	3	F	18	3	3	5	37,380
Lady Benchmark	3	F	8	2	0	0	13,526
Lady Benton	2	F	3	0	0	2	1,960
Lady Berkley	5	M	11	1	0	2	8,692
Lady Bet Good	2	F	2	0	0	0	295
Lady Bi Bi	4	F	13	4	2	1	196,300
Lady Bianconi	2	F	3	1	1	1	7,020
Lady Blessington	3	F	2	0	0	0	0
Lady Board Member	3	F	13	1	0	1	7,700
Lady Bonny	5	M	1	0	0	0	70
Lady Boots	5	M	8	1	0	1	14,135
Lady Brentwood	4	F	12	0	1	0	1,704
Lady Brunswick	3	F	3	0	1	0	1,080
Lady Buccaneer	4	F	16	5	1	1	28,880
Lady Builder	4	F	10	3	1	1	39,526
Lady Button Eyes	5	M	8	1	0	3	19,684
Lady by Habit	8	M	8	1	0	2	4,409
Lady Capay	5	M	1	0	0	0	0
Lady Cappuccino	5	M	3	0	0	0	0
Lady Captain	4	F	13	3	2	2	15,512
Lady Caren	6	M	13	0	4	2	19,404
Lady Carlina	3	F	5	2	0	0	27,640
Lady Cassandra	4	F	5	0	0	1	2,280
Lady Castle	3	F	8	0	0	1	2,435
Lady Chelsea	5	M	14	3	2	2	20,611
Lady Chequer	3	F	4	0	1	0	1,735
Lady Cherie	6	M	6	1	1	1	38,670
Lady Chestnut	2	F	1	0	0	0	0
Lady Christine	4	F	8	1	2	4	90,499
Lady Clue	10	M	2	0	0	0	0
Lady Commando	4	F	6	0	2	1	27,090
Lady Continental	4	F	7	1	1	0	4,348
Lady Conveyor	3	F	7	0	3	1	7,836
Lady Crafty Dancer	7	M	20	1	4	3	12,982
Lady Curious	3	F	1	0	0	0	0
Lady Daisy	6	M	10	1	1	2	8,325
Lady Dashmore	3	F	2	0	0	0	0
Lady Dealer	5	M	11	2	2	0	43,460
Lady Deals	7	M	3	0	1	0	2,210
Lady Deane	6	M	4	0	0	0	0
Lady Deathstrike	2	F	9	0	1	0	12,024
Lady Deed	3	F	1	0	1	0	1,400
Lady Delaney	3	F	6	0	0	0	0
Lady Della Rayne	3	F	9	0	1	3	4,455
Lady Delphinus	3	F	13	1	2	1	7,557
Lady Demidoff	7	M	10	0	1	1	2,666
Lady Dodger	7	M	10	1	0	1	5,188
Lady Doms Tiara	2	F	2	0	0	0	0
Lady Doodles	3	F	10	3	1	2	34,587
Lady d'Or	2	F	6	1	0	0	5,085
Lady Dove	7	M	2	0	0	0	0
Lady Drama	4	F	11	1	4	3	47,497
Lady Dumaani	2	F	3	0	1	0	1,990
Lady Dynamite	6	M	7	1	1	0	3,564
Lady Elagence	3	F	6	0	1	1	3,020
Lady Emerald	3	F	6	1	2	0	5,970
Lady Etain	3	F	5	0	0	0	513
Lady Eureka	3	F	10	1	4	1	15,633
Lady Evergreen	5	M	2	0	0	0	3,120
Lady Fabulous	3	F	13	0	2	1	9,170
Lady Fannie	3	F	17	2	5	1	24,561
Lady Fax	4	F	8	0	0	1	2,414
Lady Fenwick	4	F	15	2	4	3	61,184
Lady Francine	4	F	13	1	3	1	6,163
Lady From Cheyenne	4	F	1	0	0	0	0
Lady Frost	4	F	1	0	0	0	960
Lady Fury	6	M	6	0	1	0	2,301
Lady G Ridan	4	F	6	0	0	0	688
Lady Gelaine	3	F	9	1	1	2	23,644
Lady General	3	F	3	0	0	2	7,680

Horse	Age	Sex	Sts	1st	2d	3d	Won	Horse	Age	Sex	Sts	1st	2d	3d	Won
Lady George	4	F	2	0	0	0	2,048	Lady Navigator	5	M	2	0	0	0	150
Lady Gina Rosa	5	M	11	2	0	1	18,052	Lady Nelson	4	F	3	0	0	1	7,480
Lady Glacken	2	F	3	2	0	0	16,860	Lady Nichola	2	F	1	0	1	0	9,800
Lady Gourami	4	F	13	1	3	4	13,105	Lady Norma Jean	4	F	14	1	1	2	10,360
Lady Grace	5	M	5	2	0	1	36,167	Lady of Darkness	4	F	13	4	0	1	17,960
Lady Graybody	3	F	2	0	0	0	65	Lady of Ice	2	F	1	0	0	0	0
Lady Greystoke	3	F	7	1	3	0	13,771	Lady of Peace	6	M	1	0	0	0	2,340
Lady Groush	5	M	11	1	2	1	54,060	Lady of Praise	3	F	8	2	0	1	34,119
Lady Gwen	3	F	11	1	3	3	58,420	Lady of Prestige	5	M	3	1	0	1	11,350
Lady Harlow	4	F	13	1	1	1	15,521	Lady of Quality	3	F	11	2	1	0	32,042
Lady Hazaam	5	M	10	0	0	0	2,387	Lady of Red	4	F	1	0	0	0	126
Lady Heart Break	3	F	6	1	0	1	8,192	Lady of Reign	7	M	2	0	0	0	0
Lady Helma	3	F	9	4	2	1	82,740	Lady of Roses	3	F	3	0	0	1	1,178
Lady High Indy	2	F	5	0	0	1	1,900	Lady of Savoya	4	F	7	0	1	1	3,563
Lady Highroller	4	F	2	0	0	0	690	Lady of the Future	5	M	9	1	0	3	100,653
Lady Honcho	7	M	1	0	0	0	0	Lady of the Hunt	3	F	11	0	0	2	2,100
Lady Honoree	3	F	10	0	0	1	4,545	Lady of the Press	6	M	14	4	2	4	38,286
Lady Hurricane	7	M	15	1	1	0	5,797	Lady of the West	4	F	12	1	0	4	12,648
Lady Ide	3	F	3	0	0	0	1,683	Lady of the Woods	3	F	4	1	0	0	6,678
Lady in Denim	2	F	3	0	0	0	0	Lady of Valor	3	F	1	0	0	0	95
Lady in Tails	6	M	8	0	2	1	37,064	Lady Offense	2	F	3	1	0	1	6,500
Lady in the Sun	4	F	9	1	1	0	17,605	Lady On Go	4	F	1	1	0	0	4,500
Lady Ingrain	4	G	2	0	0	0	0	Lady On the Go	5	M	4	0	2	0	10,080
Lady Intimidator	4	F	4	1	0	0	3,481	Lady On the Prowl	4	F	3	0	3	0	11,970
Lady Irene	2	F	9	1	6	2	28,110	Lady On Top	8	M	16	2	3	3	32,731
Lady Is a Scamp	2	F	7	0	1	1	7,476	Lady Ordway	3	F	5	1	0	0	9,030
Lady Itron	2	F	1	0	0	0	0	Lady Outlaw	5	M	8	2	0	3	13,955
Lady J J	4	F	3	0	0	0	300	Lady Patriot	4	F	5	0	0	0	417
Lady Justine	4	F	12	1	4	2	21,586	Lady Patton	3	F	10	1	2	2	32,239
Lady Kabbalah	3	F	5	1	1	1	41,330	Lady Penelope	3	F	3	0	0	0	110
Lady Katie	5	M	7	0	0	1	3,930	Lady Pickpocket	8	M	1	0	0	0	0
Lady Katy Did	4	F	1	0	0	0	0	Lady Pilot	2	F	1	0	0	0	0
Lady Kilkeelan	2	F	4	0	0	0	1,525	Lady Pinebourne	4	F	1	0	0	0	1,230
Lady Krew	3	F	7	0	0	0	4,070	Lady Prantlack	3	F	5	2	0	0	45,839
Lady Kyoto	6	M	5	0	0	0	1,775	Lady President	4	F	12	1	0	0	8,404
Lady L J	3	F	3	0	0	0	720	Lady Pulpit	4	F	16	2	6	4	33,079
Lady La Rue	9	M	10	0	0	2	1,681	Lady Redd	5	M	2	0	0	0	105
Lady Lana	2	F	2	0	0	0	1,560	Lady Riss	2	F	6	3	1	1	65,649
Lady Lancelot	3	F	1	0	0	0	0	Lady Rose Winalot	5	M	8	0	0	1	1,746
Lady Lang	4	F	1	0	0	0	1,680	Lady Roxie	3	F	6	0	0	0	820
Lady Larae	4	F	14	0	0	0	333	Lady Royale	6	M	10	0	0	1	1,092
Lady Larrupin	2	F	1	0	0	0	0	Lady Ruhlmann	5	M	9	3	3	1	13,864
Lady Lassie	4	F	10	0	4	1	10,214	Lady Rundell	2	F	1	0	0	0	0
Lady Latifa	2	F	4	0	1	0	2,235	Lady Sabrina	3	F	10	2	0	1	51,375
Lady Lear	6	M	10	0	1	3	6,848	Lady Satin	2	F	3	1	0	0	8,280
Lady Leslie	2	F	3	0	0	0	0	Lady Sauvage	3	F	2	0	0	0	345
Lady Libby	3	F	10	3	2	2	111,930	Lady Saw	2	F	3	0	0	1	704
Lady Liberty	4	F	9	2	2	1	91,319	Lady Scruff	3	F	13	2	2	2	19,352
Lady Lightning	4	F	4	0	0	2	2,535	Lady Seaberry	3	F	13	2	2	0	18,710
Lady Lileah	4	F	11	2	2	1	19,159	Lady Shaheen	2	F	2	0	0	0	88
Lady Linda	5	M	10	2	2	2	115,490	Lady Shari	4	F	3	0	0	0	1,200
Lady Linkage	4	F	4	1	1	0	26,600	Lady Sharon	3	F	8	1	0	3	11,884
Lady Livey Bodgit	2	F	3	1	0	0	6,215	Lady Shelley	3	F	13	3	2	2	26,330
Lady Livingston	2	F	2	0	0	0	390	Lady Show Me	3	F	3	0	0	0	180
Lady Lombardia	2	F	2	0	0	0	0	Lady Showtime	6	M	13	1	6	1	14,430
Lady Longford	4	F	1	0	0	0	300	Lady Silver	2	F	1	0	0	0	0
Lady Loot	3	F	13	3	3	0	43,426	Lady Siobhan	2	F	4	0	1	0	2,800
Lady Lover	4	G	11	1	3	2	21,081	Lady Skip West	5	M	3	0	0	0	0
Lady Lovesalot	3	F	9	2	0	0	19,665	Lady Slew	7	M	7	0	0	0	173
Lady Lu	4	F	12	1	2	1	5,362	Lady Sonya	4	F	11	2	2	1	28,970
Lady Luckster	7	M	9	0	1	2	8,006	Lady Speaker	2	F	2	0	0	0	0
Lady Lucky Play	2	F	2	0	1	0	4,530	Lady Stalwood	6	M	10	1	5	0	10,954
Lady Ludicrous	3	F	12	0	0	1	1,556	Lady Star Lite	2	F	3	0	1	1	2,062
Lady Luluann	3	F	3	0	1	0	1,755	Lady Stars	3	F	7	0	1	0	10,182
Lady Lure	3	F	3	1	0	0	3,032	Lady Struck Gold	2	F	2	1	0	1	24,750
Lady Lust	5	M	5	2	0	1	15,163	Lady T	4	F	8	0	2	1	3,465
Lady Lydia	3	F	16	1	1	5	46,790	Lady T N T	3	F	3	0	0	0	0
Lady Lynx	3	F	2	1	0	1	13,850	Lady Taat	5	M	14	1	1	2	5,462
Lady Lyra Lee	6	M	15	2	2	1	34,355	Lady Tak	3	F	9	4	3	0	675,350
Lady Mallory	3	F	10	3	4	2	129,961	Lady Tech	3	F	6	3	0	0	23,088
Lady Manila	2	F	1	0	0	0	0	Lady Tethra	5	M	1	0	0	0	0
Lady Marilyn	5	M	2	0	0	1	3,110	Lady Thatcher (CHI)	4	F	1	0	0	1	4,800
Lady Matty	2	F	3	0	1	0	3,225	Lady Tour	3	F	3	0	1	1	2,490
Lady McKenna	3	F	2	0	0	0	0	Lady Tracy	3	F	4	0	0	0	312
Lady Miriam	2	F	1	0	0	0	0	Lady Two Socks	3	F	1	0	0	0	192
Lady Moneymaker	5	M	1	0	0	0	340	Lady Two Swirl	5	M	2	0	0	0	0
Lady Monica	2	F	1	0	0	0	0	Lady V Eight	2	F	1	0	0	0	0
Lady Monopoly	5	M	7	1	1	1	6,397	Lady Val	5	M	7	0	1	0	1,658
Lady Mountbatten	3	F	10	4	2	1	21,145	Lady Vamp	6	M	12	2	3	3	21,970

RECORDS OF HORSES

Horse	Age	Sex	Sts	1st	2d	3d	Won
Lady Veronica	3	F	16	1	5	3	23,870
Lady Victoria	3	F	17	3	1	6	40,301
Lady Viking	3	F	8	1	1	1	22,665
Lady Vilzak	4	F	1	0	0	0	63
Lady Vizard	4	F	5	0	0	2	1,724
Lady Vye	4	F	7	3	0	0	147,941
Lady Wallenda	4	F	11	4	2	1	47,018
Lady Wardley	2	F	1	0	1	0	2,000
Lady Weatherford	3	F	5	1	0	0	9,252
Lady Whimsy	6	M	12	1	2	4	8,360
Lady Whippet	2	F	1	0	1	0	8,200
Lady Wildcat	3	F	5	1	1	1	36,560
Lady Will Power	3	F	9	0	0	0	649
Lady Willow	2	F	2	0	0	0	0
Lady Windham	8	M	3	0	0	1	1,785
Lady Wings	4	F	7	0	0	0	585
Lady Wink	3	F	5	0	0	0	76
Lady With a Kick	2	F	2	0	0	0	840
Lady Zone	2	F	3	0	1	0	7,676
Lady Zoom Zoom	5	M	11	3	1	2	41,408
Ladye Langfuhr	3	F	9	1	2	2	14,840
Ladyecho	3	F	11	2	4	3	273,593
Ladyfeather	2	F	5	0	0	0	910
Ladyfromdixieland	5	M	12	4	3	1	26,871
Ladyinareddress	2	F	6	0	3	2	27,165
Ladyinastorm	2	F	2	0	0	1	3,500
Ladykenita	6	M	1	0	0	0	43
Ladylore	4	F	3	0	0	0	1,926
Ladyonthewire	6	M	3	0	0	0	220
Lady's Advantage	2	F	7	1	0	2	11,360
Lady's Best Dancer	5	H	10	1	3	2	11,862
Lady's Comin Home	4	F	8	0	1	0	1,953
Lady's Don't Tell	2	F	4	0	0	0	410
Lady's Event	2	C	1	0	0	0	195
Lady's Fame	3	F	4	0	0	0	910
Lady's Hat	4	F	5	0	0	0	1,089
Lady's Jewel	5	M	6	0	0	2	9,331
Lady's Kiss	3	F	1	0	0	0	320
Lady's Legal Ma Ja	6	M	15	0	2	1	6,391
Lady's Lil' Missy	2	F	5	0	0	0	0
Lady's Lil' Ringer	5	G	13	2	0	2	14,074
Lady's Mantle (IRE)	3	F	11	1	4	2	64,860
Lady's Mark	4	F	11	0	2	3	4,245
Lady's Punch	3	F	6	1	0	0	2,700
Lady's Room	2	F	4	1	0	1	24,779
Lady's Rose	3	F	3	0	1	0	1,690
Ladys Target	3	F	12	1	0	4	8,326
Lady's Wager	5	M	11	3	2	1	17,193
Lady'sgoldenmemory	3	F	7	0	4	3	9,996
Ladysgotthelooks	2	F	3	3	0	0	29,640
Ladyslewmood	4	F	4	0	0	0	188
Ladyspursesnatcher	4	F	2	0	0	0	140
Ladyvictoriaatto	2	F	1	0	0	0	0
Laertes	4	G	5	0	0	0	476
Laffit	4	C	8	0	1	1	6,957
Lafleur	4	C	4	2	2	0	5,860
Lafouche Magnum	6	H	3	0	0	0	0
Lago d'Amour	6	G	9	1	1	0	4,076
Lago Maggiore	2	C	8	1	2	1	27,200
Lagrandechartreuse	3	F	6	1	1	0	13,740
Lagunatic	3	F	12	1	1	2	13,112
Lagunero	2	C	1	0	0	0	5,280
Lahaina	2	F	10	0	4	0	5,120
Lahaway Creek	4	F	8	0	1	1	3,705
Lahinch	4	G	15	4	2	5	52,905
Lahooq (GB)	4	C	11	1	1	1	26,501
Laines Motel	3	G	6	0	1	2	2,522
Laird Angus	3	C	6	2	1	1	65,570
Laird's Honor	3	F	2	1	0	0	6,245
Laisea	7	M	9	3	1	1	25,826
Laitee Legs	4	F	11	1	1	1	6,607
La'joleur	3	C	2	0	0	0	0
Lake	3	G	2	0	0	0	219
Lake Abandon	4	F	9	1	2	1	4,131
Lake Arrowhead	5	G	2	0	0	0	3,120
Lake Boone	3	F	1	0	0	0	0
Lake Breeze	5	G	5	2	2	0	19,922
Lake Charles	5	M	1	1	0	0	12,000
Lake Chicot	9	G	8	0	0	0	329
Lake Classic	2	C	2	1	0	0	8,280
Lake Danzig	3	C	13	1	0	3	43,240
Lake Effects	9	G	2	0	0	0	122
Lake Garda	7	G	8	0	0	2	5,018
Lake Hamilton	7	G	7	3	0	0	7,135
Lake Kinneret	3	F	9	3	0	1	81,165
Lake Lady	4	F	1	0	0	0	0
Lake Livingston	7	G	12	2	1	0	7,249
Lake Lolly	4	F	5	0	2	2	12,160
Lake Lure	7	M	2	0	0	0	850
Lake Marion	6	G	21	0	0	1	13,062
Lake of Bays	4	G	7	0	0	0	4,797
Lake Patrol	5	H	3	0	0	0	640
Lake Point	4	C	6	1	0	0	28,120
Lake Ponche	2	G	2	0	0	0	215
Lake Powell	5	H	9	1	0	0	2,829
Lake Ray	3	G	8	2	0	0	52,560
Lake Shore Limited	4	F	2	0	0	0	340
Lake Silver	5	G	5	1	0	0	19,708
Lake Skimmer	3	G	1	1	0	0	10,260
Lake Storm	6	H	11	1	1	1	19,590
Lake Trail	2	F	6	1	0	1	5,985
Lake Twister	3	C	2	0	0	0	320
Lake Village	5	H	1	0	0	0	90
Lake Vista	3	C	2	0	0	0	520
Lake West	3	F	9	1	1	0	32,444
Lake William	7	H	3	1	1	0	36,000
Lakefield	4	G	2	0	0	0	0
Lakehurst	8	G	1	0	0	0	0
Lakenheath	5	M	10	1	2	3	132,790
Laker Cheerleader	3	F	10	2	3	0	35,430
Laker Girl	4	F	1	0	1	0	9,600
Laker Lass	5	M	12	0	1	0	1,500
Lakerette	3	F	1	0	0	0	0
Lake's Legacy	5	H	5	3	0	0	12,210
Lakeshore	2	F	6	1	0	1	12,125
Lakeshore Bliss	2	F	1	0	0	0	126
Lakeside Gentry	5	H	3	0	0	0	600
Lakeside Trail	4	G	13	1	1	6	36,980
Lakesville	3	F	7	1	1	1	9,684
Laketon	3	G	9	4	1	1	26,285
Lakeville	4	F	4	0	2	1	17,681
Lakevillestar	3	G	18	3	1	3	20,936
Lakota	4	G	3	0	0	0	0
Lakota Creek	4	G	10	1	1	0	12,407
Lakota Road	4	F	5	0	1	0	560
Lakota Spirit	3	F	8	4	1	2	60,717
Lakota Way	3	C	6	0	1	0	3,455
Lalapamata	5	M	10	0	2	1	8,248
Lalene	3	F	2	0	0	0	0
Lalogized	9	M	2	0	0	0	0
Lamarche's Majesty	9	G	3	0	0	0	0
Lamarche's Oro	3	G	10	0	0	1	3,229
Lamartinique	4	G	3	0	0	0	620
Lambeau Field	9	G	5	0	0	2	3,575
Lambere	3	G	3	0	0	0	0
Lambourne	8	G	13	0	4	2	9,919
Lamb's Idol	5	M	5	1	1	0	7,958
Lamerie (IRE)	7	G	8	2	2	1	15,207
Lametta Light	3	F	10	2	0	0	13,695
Laminavic	3	F	3	0	0	0	0
Lammy	4	F	1	0	0	0	0
Lamp Black	3	C	13	4	3	1	20,169
Lampsas County	7	M	10	0	0	0	1,230
Lana Mae	5	M	3	1	0	0	1,495
Lanahan	5	G	5	0	0	1	3,410
Lanatoo of Ascot	3	F	1	0	0	0	91
Lancelot Link	4	G	3	0	0	0	735
Lance's Turn	4	C	6	1	1	2	6,890
Lancette's Wager	5	M	14	0	0	2	9,960
L'Ancresse (IRE)	3	F	9	1	3	0	380,738
Land Grab	3	C	10	0	1	2	8,670
Land Lover	4	G	3	0	0	0	2,358
Land Lubber	5	H	5	0	1	0	452
Land O Gold	6	G	7	1	0	0	1,252
Land of Dreams	2	F	1	0	0	0	0
Land Tax	5	M	13	0	1	1	20,590
Land the Limit	3	F	17	2	6	2	31,090
Land Yachting	4	F	2	0	0	0	1,350

Horse	Age	Sex	Sts	1st	2d	3d	Won
Landana	3	C	5	1	0	0	17,346
Landiland	10	G	7	1	0	2	21,260
Landing	3	C	4	0	1	0	2,070
Landing Gear	2	F	3	0	1	0	1,640
Landino	4	C	4	2	0	2	8,145
Landler	4	G	11	7	3	0	95,945
Landlord	4	G	3	0	0	0	262
Landofmagic	5	M	3	3	0	0	52,560
Landofmilknhoney	6	G	13	2	2	1	8,144
Landon	4	G	10	2	0	1	40,376
Landon's Lane	2	G	1	0	0	0	75
Landry	3	G	4	1	1	1	12,305
Lanerunner	3	C	2	0	0	0	360
Lanes Love	6	M	6	0	1	0	2,870
Laney	8	M	4	0	0	1	420
Langano	5	M	10	2	0	3	99,494
Langburg	2	C	5	1	1	0	63,357
Langfuhr's Allure	3	G	14	2	0	0	10,257
Langfuhr's Magic	2	F	5	1	1	1	17,300
Langley Invader	4	G	4	0	0	1	840
Lang's Glory	4	F	1	0	0	0	107
Languissa	3	F	7	1	0	0	5,374
Lannie's Lad	4	G	18	1	2	1	7,648
Lansil Field	3	G	10	1	3	1	11,675
Lap	4	C	1	0	0	0	0
Laphead's Brother	4	G	11	1	0	0	3,337
Lapherslastlaugh	4	F	17	2	7	1	26,388
Lapidus	3	G	9	2	3	0	43,044
Lapis	3	F	12	2	0	0	61,456
Laquick	4	G	4	0	0	0	285
Lara's Love	2	F	3	0	0	0	0
Larcenist	4	G	5	0	0	0	352
Larceny N Tended	2	G	3	0	1	0	2,200
Laredo Lad	2	C	2	0	0	1	1,660
Laredo Lil	3	F	18	4	2	5	45,788
Larens Bid	3	F	4	1	1	1	4,400
Largeandincharge	7	H	12	2	1	2	24,775
Larger Than Life	3	F	6	1	3	1	62,900
Largus	4	G	2	0	0	0	0
Lark's Halo	3	F	7	0	2	1	2,700
Lark's Impression	5	M	5	0	0	0	2,080
Lark's Song	6	M	11	3	3	2	15,093
Larkwood	4	F	8	1	3	1	8,785
Larranaga	4	G	11	0	5	4	16,009
Larrie's Legend	4	F	2	0	0	0	780
Larron	6	G	6	0	3	1	1,988
Larrupin's Music	3	G	6	0	0	2	7,000
Larry and Pete	2	C	2	0	0	0	570
Larry B	3	G	4	0	0	1	7,230
Larry King	3	C	6	0	2	1	27,160
Larry M'love	3	G	2	0	0	0	100
Larry the Longshot	6	G	10	1	1	1	3,423
Larry the Prez	4	C	4	0	0	0	0
Larrygene	4	G	17	2	2	2	25,302
Larry's Blackhoney	3	F	6	1	0	0	11,810
Larry's Bouncer	4	F	8	1	1	0	14,364
Larry's Last Code	2	G	8	0	0	2	3,580
Larrys Sister Lari	8	M	19	2	2	1	5,208
Larry's Smile	2	F	3	1	0	1	22,666
Larrywayne	2	C	1	0	0	0	60
Larson E Whipsnade	3	C	5	0	0	1	6,420
Laruel Co Girl	5	M	3	1	1	0	6,670
Larun	2	F	1	1	0	0	6,000
Las Brisas Boy	4	C	19	3	4	2	29,186
Las Brisas Girl	3	F	17	3	2	2	29,883
Las Devious	4	G	11	2	3	2	50,533
Las Malvinas	5	M	2	0	0	0	1,080
Las Vegas Ernie	9	G	13	0	2	4	6,200
Laser Cat	1	F	1	0	0	0	0
Laser Con	5	G	14	4	3	0	82,990
Laser Gun	6	G	5	0	1	1	1,100
Laser Jet	2	G	1	0	0	0	130
Laser Lite	4	C	5	2	0	0	10,407
Laser Loop	9	G	7	0	0	1	1,303
Laser Sharp	4	F	10	0	0	0	859
Laser Tag	3	F	4	1	0	0	3,810
Laser Zone	4	C	5	1	0	0	14,550
Laserblast	5	G	14	3	1	0	19,035
Lashburn	3	C	4	0	1	0	4,340

Horse	Age	Sex	Sts	1st	2d	3d	Won
Lasik	2	F	4	1	0	1	32,290
Laskeek Bay	2	G	2	1	0	0	10,206
Lasmoke	3	G	16	1	3	1	12,735
Lass Dance	2	F	2	0	0	0	2,460
Lass of Aughrim	2	F	1	0	0	0	110
Lasserre	5	G	9	0	2	0	2,597
Lassie Mackee	3	F	10	0	4	1	6,406
Lassie's Star	4	G	5	0	1	1	3,465
Lassiter	7	H	3	0	0	1	710
Last Affirmed	2	C	3	0	1	0	2,120
Last Answer	3	G	9	2	1	0	108,951
Last Call for Love	4	F	10	2	3	1	32,219
Last Call Lover	10	G	10	2	1	2	7,585
Last Caper	3	C	7	1	1	1	3,363
Last Chance Dance	3	C	5	1	0	0	6,885
Last Chance Flame	3	G	14	0	3	2	4,568
Last Chancecharger	4	G	12	0	1	2	4,022
Last Day of Winter	5	M	14	1	0	3	8,606
Last Drum	4	G	16	0	0	5	6,686
Last Epoch	4	C	15	0	0	4	16,490
Last Expression	8	G	12	1	1	0	3,731
Last Frontier	2	C	2	0	0	1	2,750
Last Haven	4	G	7	1	1	0	7,906
Last Intention	4	G	10	3	3	0	96,569
Last Khal	4	C	6	0	1	1	4,340
Last Kiss	3	F	2	0	0	1	4,440
Last Landing	4	F	1	0	0	0	0
Last Letter	2	G	5	2	0	1	59,738
Last Little Slew	2	G	2	0	0	1	1,480
Last Minute	3	C	1	0	0	0	0
Last Minute Detail	2	C	1	1	0	0	21,600
Last O Locks	3	G	2	0	0	0	123
Last One Standing	6	H	8	2	1	2	5,604
Last One Up	5	G	9	2	0	1	7,906
Last Palace	4	C	4	0	1	1	14,300
Last Parade (ARG)	7	G	9	0	0	2	12,100
Last Pax	6	G	21	3	2	2	19,646
Last Peak	6	G	11	0	0	2	1,556
Last Penny	8	M	5	0	0	0	611
Last Place	2	C	1	0	0	0	0
Last President	3	C	7	1	3	2	17,650
Last Puff	4	F	11	0	1	5	32,930
Last Queen	4	F	10	2	1	2	9,995
Last Rebel	8	G	9	5	1	0	34,046
Last Recourse	3	C	11	2	1	0	9,398
Last Ruler	6	G	6	0	0	0	420
Last Second Shot	2	G	2	1	0	0	3,025
Last Serenade	4	F	10	2	2	2	12,704
Last Shoot Out	4	F	13	2	2	2	24,344
Last Slew	4	G	14	4	3	0	37,613
Last Song	2	F	4	1	1	0	38,930
Last Stand	4	G	14	4	4	1	102,058
Last Step	4	G	3	0	0	0	730
Last Supper	6	M	13	3	1	3	13,657
Last Tag	5	G	7	1	1	1	23,323
Last Tango (IRE)	5	M	10	4	1	3	136,360
Last Time in Town	2	G	3	1	0	0	16,100
Last Time Pilot	3	F	10	0	2	3	3,263
Last Train Home	2	C	4	0	2	0	7,050
Last Trap	3	C	3	1	0	0	3,252
Last Trick	7	G	7	0	0	2	4,904
Last Trust	3	C	12	4	1	1	31,375
Last Two Dollars	4	G	3	0	0	0	0
Last Verse	3	F	4	3	0	0	36,420
Last Waltz	2	F	5	2	2	0	54,155
Lastcallforparis	5	H	10	2	1	1	19,557
Lastcallforwhiskey	2	G	4	0	0	0	730
Lastchancetoanswer	3	F	7	1	0	1	6,140
Lasterday	3	F	6	2	0	0	8,593
Lasting Affair	3	F	7	1	2	1	7,961
Lasting Diablo	5	M	2	0	0	0	0
Lasting Image	3	G	10	1	1	1	25,740
Lasting Kiss	3	F	9	3	1	0	13,784
Lasting Light	5	M	3	0	0	0	0
Lasting Look	7	M	1	0	0	0	0
Lasting Pleasure	4	F	1	0	0	0	0
Lasting Punch	2	F	5	0	0	2	13,957
Lastkickatthekat	3	G	7	1	1	1	7,772
Lastlee Ridge	2	C	8	0	0	1	950

RECORDS OF HORSES

Horse	Age	Sex	Sts	1st	2d	3d	Won	Horse	Age	Sex	Sts	1st	2d	3d	Won
Lastoftheline	4	G	1	0	0	0	0	Laurasbag	4	F	2	0	0	0	0
Lastreak	5	G	5	1	0	0	3,764	Laura'sluckycharm	5	M	11	1	1	2	13,570
Lasttorun	3	G	7	1	0	1	8,736	Laurceilo	3	F	11	1	0	3	28,939
Latched On	3	G	3	2	0	0	14,724	Laurel Street	3	F	2	0	0	0	275
Late Action	3	F	5	0	0	0	405	Laurels Harlequin	3	G	1	0	0	0	0
Late Afternoon	3	C	9	1	1	2	10,585	Lauren Brianne	4	F	4	0	0	0	650
Late Again	8	G	7	0	0	1	4,670	Lauren Janine	3	F	3	0	0	0	816
Late Carson	7	G	4	0	1	0	13,500	Lauren Lynn	3	F	7	3	3	0	70,400
Late Charge	5	G	6	0	1	1	6,650	Lauren N Blaine	7	H	12	0	0	0	1,484
Late Expectations	2	C	7	1	0	2	16,725	Lauren Nicole	4	F	5	1	0	0	3,121
Late Hitter	4	C	7	1	3	2	11,520	Lauren Rose	2	F	4	0	0	0	780
Late Night Leader	2	C	6	2	1	0	42,450	Lauren Won	2	F	5	0	1	1	4,032
Late Night Out (GB)	8	G	15	3	1	3	34,332	Lauren's Approval	3	G	5	0	1	0	1,212
Late Nite Fan	4	F	3	0	0	0	2,080	Lauren's Baby	3	C	11	1	1	2	14,265
Late Not Lost	3	G	4	0	0	0	0	Lauren's Girl	4	F	4	0	0	0	410
Late Survivor	3	G	2	2	0	0	21,460	Lauren's Halo	3	F	11	0	2	1	9,730
Late to the Dance	4	G	3	0	0	0	475	Lauren's Hot Dance	7	M	8	2	2	2	53,610
Late Word	3	G	1	0	0	0	0	Laurens Lacotte	3	F	1	0	0	0	100
Latenight Frannie	5	M	12	2	0	2	13,814	Lauren's On Fire	2	F	1	0	0	0	651
Latenite Trick	3	C	7	2	2	1	51,010	Lauren's Tour	5	M	11	3	2	1	35,815
Latent Image	2	G	6	0	0	0	0	Laurica	6	M	10	0	0	3	36,152
Later Years	6	M	4	1	0	0	5,215	Laurie Hope	6	M	10	0	2	3	13,447
Lateral Twenty	4	F	7	1	0	3	2,231	Laurie's Girl	2	F	3	0	0	1	1,005
Latest Chapter	4	G	1	0	0	0	47	Laurie's Rainbow	6	M	2	0	0	2	912
Latest Technology	3	F	8	3	1	1	35,495	Lava Lil	4	F	14	1	0	5	19,620
Latexo	3	C	9	1	3	2	20,143	Lava Man	2	G	5	1	1	1	30,595
Lathe	6	H	5	0	0	0	427	Lavaca	5	G	11	4	1	4	54,490
Latiki	3	F	5	0	2	0	4,980	Laveen	4	F	15	3	2	4	22,046
Latin Beauty	5	M	6	1	0	0	6,284	Lavender Baby	4	F	6	3	2	1	33,270
Latin Devil	2	G	1	0	0	0	0	Lavender Bob	3	C	7	0	1	0	970
Latin Elegance	4	F	7	1	1	1	3,472	Lavender Girl	2	F	6	1	2	0	32,190
Latin Express	3	G	1	0	0	0	0	Lavender Lace	2	F	3	0	0	0	0
Latin Louisa	2	F	2	0	0	0	713	Lavender Lady	6	M	3	0	0	0	168
Latin Love Bug	8	G	1	0	0	0	110	Lavender Lass	3	F	8	0	1	2	25,750
Latin Storm	3	F	15	0	1	6	12,075	Lavender's Lad	5	H	8	0	1	2	47,681
Latin Technology	5	G	4	2	0	1	35,770	Laventille	3	G	2	0	0	0	146
Latin Whiz	6	M	4	0	0	0	204	Lavere	3	F	4	0	0	0	1,960
Latin's Star	7	G	12	1	0	1	5,370	Laville	2	F	4	0	0	1	3,800
Latkin	5	G	6	0	0	0	532	Lavish Mulan	4	F	5	1	0	0	6,768
Latour	5	M	1	0	0	0	380	Law Judge	7	G	8	0	0	0	582
Latronica	4	F	3	1	1	0	15,480	Law of Attraction	11	G	1	0	0	0	0
Latter Day Ace	7	H	8	2	3	0	16,238	Law Partners	4	G	12	0	2	3	2,508
Lau Mor's Glitter	2	F	11	0	3	4	24,890	Law Review	6	H	9	4	2	0	74,124
Laugh a Little	2	C	1	0	1	0	3,800	Law School	11	G	5	0	0	0	231
Laugh Again	2	C	1	0	0	0	750	Lawbook	3	G	11	0	4	3	37,691
Laugh in Your Face	5	M	3	1	0	0	1,260	Lawn Mower	4	C	14	1	2	1	16,763
Laugh Lines	3	F	1	0	0	0	0	Lawrenson	4	C	1	0	0	0	1,140
Laughing	3	F	2	0	0	0	0	Lawyer Lauren	3	F	9	2	3	2	55,096
Laughing Academy	3	G	12	3	1	1	26,130	Lay It On Me (GB)	2	C	5	0	0	1	1,880
Laughing Jack	2	G	5	0	0	0	1,022	Lay Odds	7	G	1	1	0	0	4,440
Laughing Luke	3	C	18	1	3	3	43,485	Layla's Love	4	F	8	1	1	2	22,440
Laughing Rose	6	M	13	0	0	0	975	Layn the Smackdown	3	G	14	2	4	1	38,859
Laughing Sunrise	3	F	7	0	2	0	7,540	Layover	4	F	1	0	0	0	0
Launch	2	F	2	0	0	0	1,865	Laytons Raindance	4	F	3	0	0	0	0
Launch a Deacon	3	G	8	1	0	1	8,758	Layton's Warbonnet	4	F	9	2	1	0	23,210
Launch Alert	2	F	1	1	0	0	10,000	Lazar	7	G	15	1	2	2	8,895
Launch Ready	3	C	3	1	0	1	5,320	Lazarous	3	C	3	0	0	0	1,020
Launch Spot	3	G	5	0	1	0	9,500	Lazer Hill	4	F	2	0	0	1	1,528
Launch Stone	5	G	8	0	0	2	1,820	Lazer Speed	4	C	14	3	0	1	31,115
Launch the Cat	5	M	1	0	0	0	480	Lazer Storm	5	M	2	0	0	0	320
Launch Your Dreams	5	G	11	3	2	2	38,581	Lazer Sword	4	G	5	0	0	0	255
Laundering Money	3	F	10	2	0	1	6,352	Lazer's Alymagic	6	M	13	0	2	0	7,895
Laura Is Super	8	M	4	0	0	0	160	Lazy Sahana	5	M	5	1	1	1	21,926
Laura Jane	4	F	11	2	0	2	14,135	Lazy Son	4	C	2	0	0	0	0
Laura Lynn	3	F	2	0	0	0	660	L'Brown One	8	H	16	0	1	2	2,909
Laurabobsteve	2	G	7	0	1	2	5,105	L'Bruiser	3	C	5	0	0	0	0
Lauraelise	4	F	7	0	0	1	2,207	Le Beau Lei	3	F	4	0	2	0	9,250
Lauraelises Sister	3	F	23	2	2	3	55,045	Le Beaucet	7	G	12	1	2	0	17,080
Laura's Aura	6	M	3	0	0	0	0	Le Boss	3	C	6	0	1	0	5,691
Laura's Code	7	G	7	0	2	0	4,575	Le Boulevard	7	G	18	4	1	2	22,420
Laura's Harley	4	C	2	0	0	0	120	Le Bourget	5	H	6	1	0	2	30,990
Laura's Minstrel	3	F	3	0	0	0	5,820	Le Cinquieme Essai	4	C	5	1	0	0	54,284
Laura's Moment	3	G	4	2	0	0	3,870	Le Cocq	5	G	2	1	0	0	700
Laura's Prospect	2	F	4	0	0	0	2,920	Le Cosaire	3	F	6	1	2	0	13,500
Laura's Quest	6	G	7	2	0	0	12,840	Le Dancer (GER)	7	G	10	3	2	1	24,444
Laura's Testamony	5	M	7	2	0	1	21,120	Le Deputy	4	C	14	1	3	1	37,305
Laura's Theme	3	F	4	1	1	0	12,250	Le Feuvre Road	3	G	9	1	1	1	9,722
Laura's Tree House	3	F	2	0	0	0	0	Le George	4	G	17	1	3	1	16,789
Laura's Win	5	M	6	0	1	2	2,123	Le Grand Fromage	7	G	11	1	1	0	6,657

Horse	Age	Sex	Sts	1st	2d	3d	Won
Le Jester	3	G	7	1	1	1	26,733
Le Mans	4	C	5	2	0	0	66,126
Le Matin	4	G	4	1	0	0	11,400
Le Monde	5	H	12	2	0	1	58,881
Le Nard	5	G	14	2	2	5	9,780
Le Notre	3	G	12	2	1	2	33,240
Le Numerous	5	G	8	2	1	0	58,076
Le Petit Tigre	6	H	10	1	1	3	8,332
Le Peu Roi	3	G	7	1	0	2	3,364
Le Renard Subtil	4	G	11	0	0	3	14,390
Le Reve	3	F	7	0	1	1	3,900
Le Rumor Mill	4	G	9	2	1	3	10,326
Le Sovereign	6	H	12	0	3	2	8,144
Le Twister	6	M	19	2	2	4	10,996
Le Vainqueur	5	H	9	3	0	0	82,067
Lead by Example	4	C	4	1	0	0	44,606
Lead Em Home	7	H	1	0	0	0	0
Lead Hound	3	C	10	3	2	2	24,160
Lead Story	4	F	11	3	1	1	449,062
Lead the Pack	6	G	2	0	0	1	440
Lead the Parade	3	F	7	3	2	1	34,490
Lead Wolf	2	C	5	0	0	1	4,150
Leader Go Go	9	G	8	3	2	0	13,915
Leader Out West	6	G	4	0	0	0	162
Leader's Choice	3	G	1	0	0	0	0
Leadfoot Linda	3	F	6	0	0	0	361
Leading Brave	3	G	5	0	0	0	2,965
Leading Colors	6	H	5	0	0	0	484
Leading Comment	6	G	1	0	0	0	105
Leading Genius	3	F	16	2	1	1	16,630
Leading Lady Lisa	4	F	1	0	0	0	88
Leading Lena	8	M	1	0	0	0	0
Leading Lioness	2	F	6	3	0	1	71,620
Leading Off	2	C	4	0	0	2	8,420
Leading Prospect	4	F	20	0	0	3	2,943
Leading Prospector	7	G	6	0	1	0	1,236
Leading Role	5	M	8	2	1	1	172,019
Leading Ruler	6	G	10	0	0	2	3,960
Leading Rumor	3	C	2	0	0	0	0
Leading Runner	5	G	9	1	3	0	22,950
Leading the Witnes	8	M	15	2	2	2	10,454
Leading Toad	3	G	1	0	0	0	0
Leadingalltheway	5	M	3	1	0	0	3,876
Leadingwithmyheart	6	M	2	0	0	0	111
Leadingwithmynose	6	H	7	0	0	2	1,388
Leaf Town Boy	2	C	5	3	0	2	26,325
Leafoutofyourbook	2	G	6	0	0	2	2,870
Leagueofhisown	3	C	3	0	1	1	9,880
Leah's Legend	2	F	4	0	2	0	2,464
Leah's Look	5	M	11	0	1	3	13,667
Lean On Pete	2	G	1	0	0	1	600
Leanne's Shadow	6	M	12	0	3	3	8,967
Leap	6	H	11	0	1	3	5,467
Leap for Joy	4	F	10	2	0	1	14,519
Leap of Hope	3	F	3	1	0	1	8,596
Leap the Creek	2	C	3	0	0	0	500
Leap Year Linda	3	F	1	0	1	0	1,800
Leapin Lover	5	G	1	0	0	0	0
Leaping Leroy	6	G	9	0	0	1	588
Leaping Lord	3	G	1	0	0	0	0
Leaping Plum	12	G	3	1	1	1	11,315
Leapshin	5	G	10	1	2	2	15,191
Lear	3	C	3	0	0	1	3,708
Lear Account	5	G	10	0	2	1	2,363
Lear Charm	4	G	8	0	0	0	7,500
Lear Skywalker	5	M	8	1	0	1	9,879
Lear Vision	3	F	7	1	0	0	9,589
Learctic	3	G	3	0	0	0	0
Learman	2	C	4	1	0	0	17,600
Learned	5	G	3	0	1	0	30,000
Learned Leap	5	M	4	1	0	1	4,594
Learnin Experience	4	F	13	2	3	4	14,165
Lea's Mag	4	F	4	1	0	0	9,000
Lea's Siebe	4	G	17	1	4	1	9,858
Lease the Legand	5	H	14	0	0	2	5,270
Leasea Katera	7	M	8	0	0	2	808
Leaseholders Dream	3	F	6	2	2	0	59,290
Leathal Sting	4	G	5	0	0	0	210
Leather Liver	3	G	2	0	0	0	0
Leather N Lace	3	G	7	2	2	0	37,015
Leather Tough	4	G	3	1	0	1	12,960
Leathertuskadero	3	F	1	0	0	0	1,085
Leatherwood	5	G	2	0	0	0	0
Leave a Mark	3	F	17	1	5	3	12,420
Leave It	4	G	2	1	1	0	13,280
Leave It Alone	2	F	7	1	2	2	7,046
Leave It to Beezer	10	G	11	2	0	3	21,580
Leave It to Betsy	5	M	5	0	1	0	10,867
Leave Laughing	3	G	16	0	5	1	7,936
Leave M Dancin	3	G	12	0	0	0	566
Leave No Trace	10	G	6	0	0	0	332
Leave Us Leap	7	G	10	1	1	1	38,420
Leaven	7	G	1	0	0	0	188
Leavenopapertrail	5	M	7	1	1	1	8,080
Leavin Indy	3	G	6	1	0	0	4,666
Leaving Texas	5	G	8	1	1	0	3,616
Leavingemwet	4	G	10	2	3	1	31,853
Leavingonajetplane	3	G	7	2	2	1	22,777
Leavn Ona Jetplane	3	F	7	1	0	2	25,710
Leavuwithasmile	3	G	4	2	0	2	36,164
Lebam	3	G	5	0	0	1	522
Lebontempsroulet	6	G	4	3	0	0	79,500
Lector	3	C	8	0	0	0	2,049
Lecture Hall	3	G	5	0	0	0	377
Lecturn	3	F	2	0	1	0	6,750
Led by the Light	3	G	9	1	0	2	9,947
Ledbury	6	G	8	3	2	1	45,019
Lederhosen	3	G	2	0	0	0	102
Ledet's Kitty Cat	3	F	3	0	0	0	0
Ledge	3	F	4	0	0	0	520
Lee Gage	3	F	7	1	2	0	13,145
Lee Lee Anna	3	F	5	0	1	0	650
Lee Prize	5	M	9	2	0	0	5,953
Lee Roy Boy	3	G	2	0	0	0	0
Leaferd	8	G	19	2	5	2	14,769
Leebearski	5	M	5	1	0	2	41,140
Leedle Dee	2	F	7	2	0	1	86,643
Leeds Creek	2	G	4	1	0	0	10,950
Leenmealone	7	G	2	0	0	0	318
Leeper	7	G	4	0	1	1	1,750
Lee's Dream	3	G	7	0	0	0	300
Lee's First	9	G	1	0	0	0	36
Lee's Prospector	4	F	12	1	1	1	20,952
Lee's Receivable	2	G	3	1	0	0	15,670
Lee's So Tricky	6	H	6	0	0	0	1,350
Lees'dancer	2	C	1	0	0	0	786
Leestown Code	2	C	3	1	1	0	8,315
Leetariat	3	C	2	0	0	0	280
Lefa Theda	6	M	5	0	2	0	2,648
Le'femme Agenda	4	F	1	0	0	0	0
L'Effaceur	6	G	6	2	0	1	21,550
Leffy's Launch	5	M	5	0	0	0	104
Lefors	2	C	2	0	0	0	1,350
Left Coast	3	G	5	1	0	0	3,825
Left Early	7	G	10	1	2	0	7,638
Left Hook	4	G	15	2	1	3	37,100
Left Lane Lorrain	5	M	5	0	0	1	1,499
Left Right Left	6	M	13	1	2	3	10,112
Lefty	4	G	13	3	5	0	23,357
Lefty Marciana	6	G	4	0	1	1	1,918
Lefty McSlew	9	G	6	0	3	0	1,140
Leftyloosey	2	F	1	0	0	0	0
Lefty's Lady	2	F	2	0	0	0	0
Leg Up	3	G	10	3	2	3	35,540
Legacy Fighter	3	G	12	1	3	3	29,935
Legacy Ghost	3	F	4	0	0	0	74
Legacy's Silver	3	F	6	1	2	0	26,600
Legacy's Star	3	G	14	1	0	2	11,767
Legal Asset	3	F	3	0	0	0	0
Legal Bender	6	G	2	0	0	0	100
Legal Bill	4	F	5	0	1	0	4,510
Legal Eagle Tom	3	C	8	1	0	0	31,545
Legal Edition	3	F	6	0	2	0	4,465
Legal Emigrant	3	F	3	0	0	1	1,710
L'Egal Ethics	3	F	2	0	0	0	75
Legal Games	3	G	3	0	0	1	2,120
Legal Jargon	4	G	9	2	3	0	11,894
Legal Jousting (IRE)	6	H	3	0	1	0	7,824

Horse	Age	Sex	Sts	1st	2d	3d	Won
Legal Legend	5	M	7	0	2	1	3,570
Legal Linda	3	F	21	1	2	2	10,778
Legal Logic	3	C	4	1	1	0	37,800
Legal Lover	3	C	6	0	0	2	9,090
Legal Meridian	7	G	8	0	0	1	1,052
Legal Ploy	3	G	5	1	0	0	9,770
Legal Process	3	C	10	0	0	0	1,530
Legal Question	2	G	1	0	0	0	1,380
Legal Starlet	4	F	15	2	1	6	34,414
Legal System	5	M	4	0	1	0	5,860
Legal Tactics	3	F	10	0	0	3	3,213
Legal Thief	6	H	1	1	0	0	2,200
Legal Trap	4	G	7	0	0	0	1,790
Legal Waiver	4	F	3	0	0	0	1,169
Legalize	3	C	3	0	1	1	8,200
Legalize It	3	F	3	0	0	0	0
Legally	3	F	7	1	1	0	35,150
Legally Blonde	3	F	12	1	3	3	11,419
Legally Gray	3	F	4	1	1	0	6,260
Legally Insane	3	F	2	0	1	0	2,500
Legalopinion	5	M	6	2	1	0	18,713
Legend Has It	5	H	10	5	1	1	17,640
Legend in Disguise	3	F	2	0	2	0	18,600
Legend Man	2	G	3	0	0	1	861
Legend of Gold	4	G	12	0	1	0	4,695
Legend of Killian	6	G	2	0	0	0	0
Legend of the West	2	F	4	0	0	1	2,981
Legend Whisper	4	F	1	0	0	0	42
Legendary Dream	5	M	11	0	1	1	2,548
Legendary Halo	3	F	6	1	0	1	3,737
Legendary Lad	3	G	2	0	0	0	895
Legendary Lady	5	M	4	0	0	0	4,260
Legendary Larry	5	G	9	2	0	3	49,175
Legendary Legs	4	G	7	0	3	1	5,786
Legendary Manner	7	G	6	0	0	0	8,617
Legendary Peach	5	M	10	2	3	0	38,855
Legendary Penny	7	G	2	0	0	0	274
Legendary Prince	3	G	13	2	4	1	28,790
Legendary Queen	2	F	1	0	0	0	651
Legendary Run	4	C	1	0	0	0	0
Legendary Star	2	G	4	1	0	0	5,781
Legendary Status	3	F	2	0	0	0	340
Legendary Traitors	2	G	4	0	1	0	5,080
Legendary Weave	5	H	14	3	4	1	145,675
Legendaryleah	2	F	1	0	0	0	85
Legendinthemakin	3	C	1	0	0	0	0
Legend's Bullet	3	G	14	2	2	2	31,242
Legends Grandslam	3	F	4	0	0	2	4,050
Legends Never Die	5	H	5	0	0	0	620
Legend's Silver	2	C	3	1	2	0	24,750
Legend's Song	3	G	2	0	0	1	1,560
Leggo My Echo	2	G	2	0	0	0	2,280
Legg's Harding	5	G	7	0	0	0	192
Legion Field	6	H	1	0	0	0	0
Legion of Cats	3	F	4	1	0	1	14,400
Legionaire's Buddy	8	G	10	0	1	0	5,595
Legislator	4	G	1	0	0	0	0
Legislature	4	G	2	1	0	0	9,090
Legitimada (ARG)	6	M	9	1	1	0	30,094
Legs and Lashes	5	M	11	1	0	2	9,731
Legs Like I Likem	3	F	3	0	0	0	0
Legs O'Neal	3	F	7	1	2	0	45,310
Legstosee	4	F	2	0	0	0	696
Leh She Run	3	F	3	0	0	0	0
Lehigh Grad	3	G	5	0	0	2	9,240
Leianne's Pet Peve	3	F	1	0	0	0	0
Leida Irene	3	F	9	2	0	0	10,290
Leigh Gold	7	M	13	0	2	1	6,417
Leigh Lake	4	F	3	0	1	0	6,570
Leisa B Ware	4	F	1	0	0	0	0
Leisurely Kin	4	F	4	0	2	1	6,188
Leitrim Lakes (IRE)	3	G	2	0	0	1	3,600
Lejos	2	C	5	0	1	1	4,874
Lela	6	M	2	0	0	0	0
Leloup	4	G	6	1	2	2	60,951
L'Emeraude (FR)	5	M	1	0	0	0	0
Lemme Be Nasty	4	F	4	0	0	0	496
Lemon Angel	5	G	15	2	3	2	5,839
Lemon Twist	4	F	3	1	0	0	14,674
Lemonaids Hot Jazz	2	F	2	0	0	0	0
Lemonator	5	M	2	0	0	0	0
Lenado Girl	2	F	2	0	0	0	0
Lenarose	3	F	10	4	1	1	18,270
Lenatareese	2	F	2	1	0	0	23,020
Lendell Ray	6	H	1	0	0	0	48
Lendy	7	G	14	1	1	1	9,346
Lenient Policy	5	G	11	3	2	1	37,644
Leniently	3	F	6	1	0	1	33,006
L'Enjoleurs Tremor	5	M	1	0	0	0	0
Lennon	4	G	10	1	1	0	7,400
Lennoxwood	2	C	5	0	1	1	15,465
Lenny From Dal Rae	2	C	4	1	0	0	19,320
Lenny the Lender	7	G	9	0	3	0	98,282
Lennyfromalibu	4	G	6	2	0	1	161,766
Lenny's Halo	4	F	9	2	1	2	17,300
Lens Last Astro	4	C	8	2	3	1	29,199
Lentil	4	F	9	1	2	1	38,640
Lento	3	G	15	3	1	3	26,771
Leo and Mike	5	G	5	0	0	1	1,040
Leo B Tuf	3	C	8	0	0	1	2,715
Leo Quinella	4	C	3	0	0	0	0
Leon County	2	C	4	0	1	0	1,705
Leon Sez Win	4	F	10	0	0	1	1,320
Leona May	3	F	2	0	0	0	189
Leonald	3	C	4	0	1	0	3,549
Leonardtown	3	G	12	2	6	1	26,650
Leona's Dr.	3	F	17	5	1	6	71,570
Leona's Lies	4	F	6	3	2	0	27,085
Leonodus G	2	C	3	0	0	0	650
Leon's Deed	3	F	8	1	2	1	27,850
Leons Hellraiser	5	G	3	0	0	0	0
Leopard Lady	3	F	15	1	2	3	30,676
Leo's Act	4	G	2	0	0	1	2,610
Leo's Blue Moon	4	G	1	0	0	0	810
Leo's Clever Trick	4	G	18	2	1	3	17,244
Leo's Devil	5	G	10	0	0	1	1,344
Leo's Ego	4	G	1	0	0	0	0
Leo's Golden Tap	3	F	9	1	0	1	17,250
Leo's Joke	3	C	1	0	0	0	192
Leo's Kayo	4	G	5	1	1	0	5,710
Leo's Last Girl	2	F	3	0	0	0	0
Leo's Last Hurrahy	3	G	9	1	1	3	51,120
Leo's Last Love	4	F	15	1	5	1	17,876
Leo's Legacy	2	C	3	0	2	0	6,000
Leo's Lolly	3	F	1	0	0	0	0
Leo's Memory	2	C	2	0	0	1	2,160
Leo's Native Ruler	3	G	3	0	0	0	402
Leo's Philly	2	F	2	0	0	0	390
Leo's Sassy Girl	3	F	11	2	1	1	10,116
Leo's Twister	3	C	7	0	0	0	2,429
Leo's Way	2	C	1	0	0	0	0
Leprechaun Kid	4	C	10	1	1	1	59,574
Leriaville	3	F	10	1	1	4	15,330
Lermontov	6	G	4	1	0	0	23,925
Leroy Brown	2	G	5	0	0	1	2,980
Leroy Spuds	4	C	13	3	1	3	34,653
Leru	4	C	1	0	0	0	0
Les Be Friends	3	F	6	2	0	0	20,640
Les Be Quick	3	C	11	0	0	0	1,171
Les Crime	3	G	14	2	6	1	11,797
Les Gentil Hommes	5	G	11	2	0	3	18,121
Les Yeux Mauves (FR)	5	M	7	0	0	2	9,720
Lesley Joy	6	M	11	0	2	1	2,529
Leslie Star	5	M	2	0	0	0	76
Leslie's Love	6	M	15	6	5	0	176,140
Leslie's Runner	2	G	2	0	0	0	0
Lessluckydancer	3	G	3	0	0	0	163
Lesson in Leavin'	6	G	2	0	0	0	50
Lessons Are Extra	3	C	7	1	0	1	15,440
Lessur	2	G	1	0	1	0	3,800
Lest We Forget	3	G	1	1	0	0	16,800
Lester	5	G	3	0	0	0	248
Lester Lanin	10	G	4	0	1	0	854
Lester N Earl	3	G	8	0	1	1	2,420
Let 'Em Go	2	C	3	0	0	1	4,900
Let George Do It	5	G	9	3	0	1	3,324
Let Her Rip	5	M	9	2	1	2	11,960
Let Him Rip	5	G	2	0	0	0	6,438

Horse	Age	Sex	Sts	1st	2d	3d	Won
Let It Grow	4	C	6	0	1	1	1,836
Let It Shine	3	F	8	0	2	1	15,350
Let It Slide	5	G	4	0	0	2	4,300
Let It Snow	3	F	4	0	0	0	681
Let It Thunder	4	G	7	1	1	1	24,470
Let Me Dream	8	G	2	0	0	0	249
Let Ourfreedomring	2	F	4	1	0	0	14,680
Let Salt Fly	4	F	1	0	0	1	840
Let the Day Begin	3	F	4	0	0	1	1,736
Let the Lady Pass	5	M	1	0	0	0	40
Let the Sun Shine	3	C	4	1	1	0	8,675
Letart Island	3	G	5	0	0	0	1,175
Let'er Whirl	3	F	3	0	0	0	0
Lethal	6	G	13	0	0	0	667
Lethal Agenda	5	H	15	0	3	1	5,943
Lethal Cecil	4	C	5	0	1	1	3,863
Lethal Grande	4	G	15	4	4	1	51,720
Lethal Instrument	7	H	5	1	1	0	28,875
Lethal Justice	5	G	2	0	0	0	0
Lethal Lesson	4	C	18	0	1	2	7,104
Lethal Lily	3	F	2	0	0	0	810
Lethal Litigator	2	C	1	0	0	1	4,320
Lethal Lover	4	F	11	2	1	1	19,137
Lethal Secret	4	G	8	1	0	0	6,630
Lethal Temper	4	F	5	1	0	1	19,910
Lethal Too	6	G	14	0	3	1	3,187
Lethal Weapon (ARG)	5	H	4	2	1	1	70,250
Lethegoodtimesroll	2	G	1	0	0	0	425
Lethimrun	4	G	16	2	3	4	36,994
Lethimthinkhesboss	2	C	5	0	0	3	15,850
Letithappencaptain	3	F	11	4	1	3	188,325
Letmewreckem	3	G	16	0	0	0	2,870
Letmikiedoit	5	G	10	1	1	3	8,667
Letrado (ARG)	6	G	10	0	2	1	13,145
Lets All Smoke	3	G	8	0	0	1	3,540
Let's Bail	6	G	6	0	1	0	3,384
Let's Behave	5	G	12	6	0	2	64,060
Lets Believe C F	7	G	16	1	0	2	7,674
Let's Belly Up	2	G	5	1	0	0	4,020
Lets Bookit	7	H	9	0	2	1	1,003
Let's Canoodle	7	M	4	0	1	2	9,364
Let's Contend	4	F	14	4	4	1	40,486
Lets Count	5	H	2	0	0	2	3,300
Let's Dance Nance	4	G	12	3	2	2	28,917
Let's Face It	4	G	1	0	0	0	220
Lets Get Cracken	6	G	11	1	0	2	5,660
Let's Get It On	4	F	4	1	0	0	14,621
Let's Get Lucky	4	G	14	4	0	1	30,780
Let's Get Personal	3	F	2	0	0	0	140
Let's Go Race	4	F	9	1	2	0	14,552
Let's Go Rusty	6	G	8	1	1	1	66,836
Let's Go to Dodge	9	G	9	0	2	0	4,423
Let's Hang Out	3	F	12	1	0	1	12,615
Lets Just Do It	3	F	10	1	2	2	38,208
Let's Make Life	6	G	11	3	2	2	23,660
Lets Make Music	7	M	3	0	0	0	945
Let's Mombo	3	F	3	1	1	0	54,108
Let's Party	4	G	10	1	0	2	15,905
Let's Party Honey	2	F	7	0	0	1	1,588
Lets Pay Cash	4	G	14	3	4	1	21,485
Let's Play	3	F	11	0	1	1	5,322
Lets Playit by Ear	4	G	11	2	2	3	57,144
Let's Rap	3	C	13	1	1	1	9,085
Lets Roll Angel	3	F	2	0	0	0	360
Let's Roll Guys	2	C	1	0	0	0	270
Let's Roll Lady	2	F	1	0	0	0	1,550
Let's Roll Tally	3	G	3	1	1	0	22,500
Let's Tour	3	F	14	3	2	1	69,620
Let's Twist	4	F	7	0	1	1	2,904
Let's Zoom	2	F	3	0	0	0	82
Let'sbeefriends	3	G	7	1	0	0	3,570
Letscallmecarl	6	H	7	0	1	2	1,235
Letsgostreaking	2	C	1	0	0	0	44
Let'shavefun	3	F	12	3	0	1	25,860
Letsimpress (IRE)	2	F	11	1	2	2	25,055
Letsmakeadeal	4	C	6	0	0	1	984
Letsmoveon	4	F	10	0	0	0	8,214
Letspartyhotstuf	3	F	3	1	1	0	14,315
Letsrollem	6	G	10	2	3	1	13,920
Letter From Hoolie	3	F	3	0	0	0	1,326
Letter of Credit	3	C	7	0	1	2	11,750
Letter Rip Rosie	7	M	3	0	0	0	0
Lettergo Cart	5	G	3	0	0	0	124
Letters	3	G	11	1	3	4	54,000
Letters Lady	8	M	15	0	1	3	4,272
Lettertotheeditor	3	F	7	2	1	0	26,990
Lettet Rumble	6	G	8	4	0	1	20,033
Letthecameraroll	6	G	2	0	0	0	0
Letthecowboydance	8	G	11	4	0	2	27,738
Letthefreedomroar	3	F	8	3	0	0	84,240
Letthefunbegin	4	G	6	0	1	0	7,810
Letthelittlegirlgo	4	F	6	0	1	1	4,459
Lettherebejustice	2	G	4	0	1	0	9,793
Letthetigerloose	4	G	4	0	1	0	1,820
Lettie Dream	3	F	7	1	1	0	10,311
Lettingo	5	M	6	0	0	1	1,460
Lettuce Besplendid	4	G	7	2	0	0	14,190
Lettuce Pray	3	C	12	4	0	1	27,285
Lettucerace	3	F	7	2	0	0	4,223
Levada	2	F	2	0	0	0	1,077
Levee Town	2	C	9	2	3	2	69,350
Levees Trick	9	G	1	0	0	0	0
Level Bid	4	F	11	0	1	1	9,305
Level Lady	3	F	3	0	1	0	1,700
Level Playingfield	2	C	3	1	1	1	50,190
Level Three	6	H	9	1	4	1	33,460
Levendis	4	G	12	2	1	2	81,926
Lever Action	3	C	1	0	0	0	0
Lever Trick	5	H	6	1	0	0	3,860
Levi Lexi	5	M	8	1	0	1	6,275
Lew S.	5	G	9	0	0	0	2,220
Lewis	4	C	2	0	0	0	140
Lewiston	3	F	10	1	1	1	7,832
Lewistown	11	G	3	2	0	0	6,840
Lewtrenchard	5	G	7	1	0	1	6,926
Lex	2	C	3	0	0	1	4,570
Lex Luthier	3	C	7	0	1	0	23,750
Lexatonic	2	F	2	0	0	0	164
Lexie Dawn	4	F	12	1	0	1	5,196
Lexie's Charm	5	M	11	2	1	1	7,065
Lexiesride	5	M	2	1	0	0	9,000
Lexiloush	4	F	12	1	3	1	73,010
Lexi's Habit	4	F	15	0	1	3	9,176
Lexi's Hoss	3	F	3	0	0	1	2,004
Lexi's Moon	3	F	16	4	5	2	40,335
Lex's Last Stand	7	M	3	0	0	0	216
Lexster	4	F	15	0	4	3	12,362
Lextown Caller	5	M	7	0	0	0	136
Lexus's Dream	3	F	6	0	0	0	735
Lexy May	3	F	3	1	0	1	21,300
Leyenda	6	M	12	1	4	2	13,355
Leys a Leader	2	F	1	0	0	0	0
Leyte	3	F	1	0	0	0	2,160
L'Grand Dancer	3	F	5	0	0	0	3,330
Lhiz (CHI)	5	M	1	0	0	0	100
Liam E.	3	G	10	1	0	1	6,688
Liam of Cashel	3	G	9	2	1	3	40,150
Liam's Gladiator	3	G	13	1	4	1	61,829
Liam's Syn	4	G	2	0	0	0	103
Liane's Miss	4	F	6	0	2	0	5,595
Libbie's Love	4	F	7	0	0	1	2,135
Libbus	6	M	2	0	0	0	180
Libby La Vita Loca	3	F	7	1	2	2	19,911
Libby's Big Cloud	2	C	11	0	0	0	1,970
Libby's Dreams	5	M	13	2	1	2	10,141
Libby's Halo	4	F	1	0	0	0	0
Libbyslittlelibber	5	M	3	0	0	0	273
Liberal Media	4	G	15	0	3	4	12,540
Liberated	2	C	4	0	0	0	2,580
Liberated Look See	4	F	8	1	0	2	16,699
Liberatedbyforce	2	C	6	0	2	1	44,479
Liberation	4	G	14	4	1	2	51,130
Libertie Larue	3	F	3	0	0	0	0
Liberty Blues	8	G	2	0	0	0	119
Liberty Cat	3	F	1	0	0	0	0
Liberty County	5	M	6	0	0	2	1,887
Liberty Creek	4	G	11	3	2	0	14,018
Liberty Force	2	G	8	1	1	2	9,320

Horse	Age	Sex	Sts	1st	2d	3d	Won	Horse	Age	Sex	Sts	1st	2d	3d	Won
Liberty Fraternity (IRE)	5	M	2	0	0	0	186	Light as a Cat	4	F	15	1	0	0	9,150
Liberty Girl	4	F	13	2	2	0	15,665	Light Buster	4	C	3	0	0	0	360
Liberty Hill	9	G	9	1	2	1	8,356	Light Classical	3	F	2	0	0	0	0
Liberty Lady	3	F	8	0	2	0	26,800	Light Craft	6	H	14	2	3	3	18,515
Liberty Lake	4	G	2	1	0	0	3,716	Light Dancer	5	M	10	0	2	2	17,283
Liberty Miss	3	F	6	0	0	0	8,670	Light Duty	4	G	6	0	1	1	8,750
Liberty Nation	3	G	16	3	2	2	23,147	Light Fingered (IRE)	7	H	2	0	0	0	0
Liberty Pike	4	C	18	2	1	2	23,235	Light Fling	5	M	14	2	3	6	73,879
Liberty Place	4	C	13	1	3	3	9,241	Light Given	2	F	1	0	1	0	1,800
Liberty Quest	3	G	12	2	3	1	32,108	Light Hearted Lass	3	F	9	0	0	2	5,224
Liberty Run	4	C	3	1	1	0	22,540	Light in Your Eyes	4	F	2	0	0	0	0
Liberty Son	3	C	2	0	0	1	4,730	Light It Up (BRZ)	6	H	4	1	0	1	13,720
Liberty Township	5	H	4	0	0	0	310	Light Jazz	5	M	1	0	0	0	0
Liberty's Torch	2	F	5	2	1	0	33,950	Light My World	3	F	3	0	0	0	0
Libertyville	3	G	9	0	4	1	22,494	Light Night	4	C	10	3	2	1	66,220
Libertywithjustice	2	F	1	0	0	1	6,666	Light of Evening	7	M	4	0	1	0	2,645
Libito Point	5	H	13	2	0	0	8,730	Light of Justice	5	H	1	1	0	0	5,340
Liblo the Mighty	4	F	10	1	2	3	20,860	Light of Life	3	G	3	2	1	0	35,940
Libor	3	G	5	1	0	0	18,540	Light of Sky	4	F	10	2	1	0	27,060
Libretto	5	M	2	0	0	0	28,000	Light of the Woods	6	H	3	0	1	0	1,152
Librisong	2	C	1	0	0	0	75	Light On Her Toes	2	F	4	0	0	1	1,175
Lica Devilwind	4	F	13	0	0	1	2,342	Light On Track	6	H	9	0	3	2	2,300
Licari	2	C	4	0	2	0	21,500	Light Reflections	4	F	5	0	1	1	7,356
License to Run	6	G	8	2	0	2	13,143	Light Sand	2	G	11	1	2	1	11,145
License to Soar	3	G	3	0	0	0	646	Light the Dawn	3	C	3	0	0	1	550
License to Speed	4	F	7	1	0	1	22,820	Light the Path	4	F	10	2	1	0	11,988
License to Tour	3	C	5	0	1	0	2,824	Light the River	6	M	2	0	0	0	297
Licenseapproved	3	F	2	1	0	0	5,974	Light the Star	2	C	1	0	0	0	180
Lickety Slick	2	F	6	1	0	0	11,758	Light Tones	2	F	5	0	1	2	4,485
Licorice Lad	5	G	8	1	0	1	1,972	Light Up My Dreams	6	H	4	1	2	0	5,200
Licorish Village	3	F	1	0	0	0	0	Light Up My Light	8	M	1	0	0	0	170
Lid	3	C	3	1	0	0	24,600	Light Up the Board	3	G	8	2	0	0	27,255
Lido (IRE)	8	G	10	0	1	0	4,444	Light Up the House	5	H	8	1	0	3	11,356
Lido Girl	7	M	6	0	0	1	2,429	Light Up the Phone	3	G	8	0	1	2	10,640
Lieing Lary	5	G	14	0	1	1	7,509	Light Up the Sky	7	G	4	0	1	0	9,200
Liepers Fork	2	C	5	1	3	0	34,476	Light Up the Tower	3	G	3	1	0	0	3,260
Lies	2	F	2	0	0	0	0	Light Up Your Life	3	F	4	0	0	1	4,520
Lies Be Gone	7	M	6	0	0	0	2,280	Light Vision	3	F	3	0	0	0	940
Liese	4	F	6	2	0	0	19,783	Light Wave	5	M	9	3	0	3	45,570
Lieutenant Arch	3	C	10	1	3	1	11,120	Lightening	3	F	5	1	3	1	25,400
Lieutenant Tilly	5	G	13	2	0	1	20,335	Lightening Ball	7	G	6	1	2	0	30,532
Life	4	G	3	0	0	0	0	Lightening Dehere	4	C	4	0	0	0	3,400
Life and Liberty	3	F	3	1	1	0	18,400	Lightening Limit	4	C	4	0	0	0	702
Life At Sea	5	G	4	0	0	2	11,760	Lighter Knot	3	G	2	0	1	0	24,500
Life Estate	4	F	11	1	1	2	13,780	Lightfoot Lane	4	F	1	0	0	1	4,940
Life Jacket	4	F	8	1	0	0	4,482	Lightfoot Sis	2	F	5	0	0	0	0
Life of Luxury	2	F	2	0	0	0	1,764	Lighthouse Lil	4	F	4	3	0	1	49,434
Life On the Bayou	5	G	7	0	0	1	2,122	Lightin' Storm	5	M	5	0	1	0	934
Life On Thefreeway	4	C	2	0	0	1	4,510	Lighting Bug	6	G	4	1	0	0	3,933
Life Promise	4	G	4	0	0	0	270	Lighting Jay	4	C	17	0	1	1	2,915
Life Savior	3	F	12	2	0	2	36,114	Lighting Kwik	4	C	2	0	0	0	70
Life Sayver	6	G	12	2	0	4	21,216	Lighting Say	5	G	5	0	0	0	179
Lifebythedrop	4	F	14	4	2	2	67,030	Lighting Wanda	5	M	2	0	0	0	0
Lifeinthebigciti	3	G	8	1	2	1	11,975	Lightlively	2	F	2	0	0	0	4,080
Life's Blessing	4	F	4	1	0	0	11,700	Lightly Maid	5	M	1	0	0	0	0
Lifes Crown	5	G	8	2	0	0	5,346	Lightmywayhome	3	F	4	0	0	0	0
Life's Destiny	4	C	1	0	0	0	0	Lightness	2	G	5	1	0	0	10,925
Lifes Expectations	4	C	4	0	1	0	14,160	Lightnin Mac	6	H	7	2	1	1	4,962
Life's Pleasures	3	F	5	1	0	1	40,400	Lightnin Mike	4	C	9	0	0	0	1,861
Lifewithoutyou	2	F	4	0	1	0	1,820	Lightnin N Thunder	2	C	4	1	1	1	68,510
Liffey Boy	5	G	9	1	1	1	9,851	Lightning At Sea	2	C	2	1	1	0	9,280
Lift Kit	4	G	1	0	0	0	0	Lightning Attitude	4	F	6	1	0	1	6,997
Lift Up	4	G	7	3	2	0	38,663	Lightning Aurium	3	G	8	2	1	1	10,931
Lifted Pride	2	F	4	0	0	0	514	Lightning Bay	3	F	15	2	3	2	12,193
Lifted Rose	2	F	2	0	0	0	230	Lightning Bound	3	C	11	1	0	0	4,440
Lifticet	3	G	6	0	1	1	8,897	Lightning Cat	3	G	4	1	1	0	7,878
Lifting Fog	4	G	12	2	1	2	27,040	Lightning Charger	3	C	8	1	0	0	6,588
Lifting the Veil	3	F	10	1	1	1	30,586	Lightning Draw	7	G	4	1	0	0	3,310
Ligan's Best	3	C	5	0	0	1	4,894	Lightning Echo	3	G	15	3	0	8	40,164
Ligan's Brat	4	F	10	0	0	0	1,127	Lightning Fox	4	F	4	0	0	0	345
Ligan's Cross	3	C	1	0	0	0	52	Lightning Hit	3	G	4	1	0	0	7,920
Ligan's Jet Stream	6	G	5	0	0	1	1,027	Lightning Lydia	2	F	1	0	0	0	1,500
Ligan's Lady	4	F	8	1	0	1	5,202	Lightning Lyla	2	F	8	1	1	1	40,800
Ligan's Star	4	C	9	0	0	1	2,225	Lightning Miss	4	F	2	0	0	0	0
Light a Candle	4	F	5	0	0	0	765	Lightning N Rain	7	H	6	0	0	1	988
Light a Fire	3	F	5	0	0	0	0	Lightning Pace	5	M	3	0	0	0	3,866
Light Agenda	2	F	12	0	0	3	7,355	Lightning Paces	6	G	9	0	1	0	15,640
Light and Shadows	5	G	15	2	5	1	12,568	Lightning Quick	6	H	10	0	0	3	2,639
Light Artillery	3	G	7	0	0	0	1,039	Lightning Speed	4	F	3	2	0	0	42,000

Horse	Age	Sex	Sts	1st	2d	3d	Won
Lightning Stripes	5	G	9	1	3	2	69,330
Lightning Stroke	4	G	10	0	1	0	4,370
Lightning Tab	3	C	7	0	0	1	1,645
Lightning Time	9	M	7	0	0	0	185
Lightning Weststar	4	G	7	0	0	1	1,542
Lightninginabottle	6	H	2	0	0	0	237
Lightningintheair	3	F	3	0	1	0	4,130
Lightning's Kiss	6	M	5	0	1	0	1,725
Lightningsbigboy	2	C	6	0	0	0	768
Lights Away	3	F	1	0	0	0	0
Lights of Home	5	H	15	1	0	2	9,356
Lights of Santa Fe	3	G	15	1	1	3	13,941
Lights On	4	F	9	2	3	0	122,710
Lights On Broadway	6	G	6	0	0	2	13,370
Lights Out	7	G	7	0	0	0	0
Lightsafire	5	G	7	0	0	0	1,117
Lightspeedtoendor	5	H	10	0	1	4	5,535
Lignite	3	C	6	0	0	0	424
Like a Brick	6	G	1	0	0	0	53
Like a Hero	4	G	6	1	0	0	55,800
Like a Rabbit	3	F	10	1	0	1	5,076
Like a Rock	2	G	2	0	0	0	0
Like Broadway	3	F	8	0	1	0	6,350
Like Flying	4	F	14	1	5	3	16,776
Like It Is Lil	4	F	3	0	1	1	2,550
Like Magic	4	F	3	1	0	0	43,905
Like the Wind	4	G	7	0	0	1	1,501
Like This	2	F	4	1	0	0	15,464
Like to Keep Busy	5	M	7	0	0	0	280
Likeable Irish	10	G	16	3	2	3	33,360
Likely Lass	4	F	3	0	0	1	1,155
Likely Prospect	3	F	3	0	0	0	840
Likely Suspect	2	F	4	0	0	0	815
Lil' Awesome Annie	4	F	1	0	0	0	120
Lil Badger	4	G	13	2	3	0	28,150
Lil Barhop	7	M	9	2	1	0	12,890
Lil Big Man	3	C	1	0	0	0	47
Lil Bit Bull	3	C	11	1	2	0	20,064
Lil Bit Devilish	4	F	1	0	0	0	2,142
Lil' Bit Gone	2	C	5	0	0	1	1,162
Lil Bit O Fastness	3	F	7	1	0	3	11,754
Lil Bit o' Magic	3	F	7	1	0	0	4,720
Lil Bit of Country	6	M	3	0	0	0	3,350
Lil' Bit of Pucker	3	F	4	0	0	1	1,580
Lil' Bit of Rouge	2	F	5	0	2	2	11,578
Lil Bit Spacey	5	M	12	1	0	1	8,066
Lil Blackey	6	H	6	0	0	0	439
Lil Bobarino	4	G	2	0	0	0	219
Lil Bonit	2	F	9	1	0	1	8,499
Lil Bow	2	C	3	1	0	1	6,790
Lil' Bro Eddie	2	G	12	2	4	1	68,770
Lil' Brother Jack	8	M	1	0	0	0	0
Lil Brother Slew	4	G	15	3	3	4	21,775
Lil' Bull	4	G	2	0	0	0	0
Lil' Casino	7	G	7	1	2	0	4,960
Lil' Cassie Slew	5	M	2	1	1	0	1,255
Lil Charlie Brown	4	C	7	0	0	0	513
Lil Charlie Too	7	G	5	0	4	0	28,188
Lil Chick	5	M	8	0	2	3	5,955
Lil Chuckie	2	C	3	0	0	0	378
Lil Danslet	3	F	1	0	0	0	0
Lil Deputy	4	C	10	3	0	0	19,255
Lil Dickens	3	F	6	0	0	0	1,254
Lil Du	9	M	7	0	0	0	519
Lil' Duck	2	C	1	0	0	0	120
Lil Easy	2	F	2	1	0	1	6,830
Lil Ec	2	F	1	0	0	0	0
Lil E's Express	2	G	2	0	0	0	0
Lil Eva	3	F	4	2	0	1	18,830
Lil Fanciface	3	F	9	0	0	2	3,269
Lil Forrest	3	G	5	1	0	0	6,031
Lil Fortune	2	F	2	1	0	0	13,410
Lil G Man	5	G	9	4	1	1	82,550
Lil Gary Too	2	C	2	1	0	0	15,600
Lil General	4	G	16	2	3	3	18,662
Lil Ginny	2	F	1	0	0	0	270
Lil Giz	4	G	2	0	0	0	0
Lil Irish Eyes	5	M	16	3	1	1	34,180
Lil J. C.	6	G	8	0	1	1	2,198
Lil Jerry	4	G	7	2	0	1	9,570
Lil' Joe	4	C	5	1	2	1	34,200
Lil Joe Hossrite	7	G	18	0	3	2	5,402
Lil Joes Luckycent	7	G	6	0	0	0	636
Lil Kitten	4	F	4	1	0	0	3,908
Li'l Larry B	4	G	8	1	1	2	14,181
Lil Leslie	4	F	1	0	0	0	405
Lil Linzer	4	F	6	0	1	1	17,600
Lil Lucia	5	M	6	2	0	1	11,264
Li'l Lulu	5	M	16	5	3	3	22,695
Lil Mack	4	C	6	1	1	0	6,214
Lil Man	2	C	3	0	0	0	0
Lil Marine	5	H	7	0	0	0	440
Lil Michael	5	G	4	0	0	0	670
Lil Mike	4	G	2	0	0	0	0
Lil Miss Best	3	F	2	0	0	0	0
Lil Miss Casey	2	F	2	0	0	0	2,200
Lil Miss Devi	5	M	9	1	1	3	13,195
Lil Miss Gabi	8	M	10	1	0	1	4,832
Lil Miss Georgie	3	F	4	0	0	0	543
Lil' Miss Jillian	3	F	4	0	1	0	2,990
Lil Miss Obnoxious	5	M	10	1	0	0	8,408
Lil Miss Okie	3	F	3	0	0	0	1,280
Lil Miss Sophie	5	M	8	1	1	1	12,515
Lil Miz Charmer	7	M	2	0	0	1	420
Lil Miz Hip Hop	3	F	6	0	0	1	2,770
Lil' Mo' Rhythm	3	F	5	1	1	2	29,074
Lil More Jazz	4	F	2	0	0	0	1,050
Lil Ms. K K D	3	F	9	4	0	2	17,726
Lil' Nancy Dickens	3	F	3	0	0	0	0
Lil Nash Rambler	3	G	10	0	3	1	11,375
Lil Native Wulf	2	G	3	0	0	0	0
Lil' Nickii	4	F	5	1	1	1	11,015
Lil Nightmare	2	F	1	0	0	0	139
Li'l Orphan Arnie	4	G	5	0	0	0	0
Lil Pac O Dynamite	4	C	1	0	0	0	0
Lil Personalitee	6	G	13	5	2	1	175,930
Lil Princess Tee	3	F	11	2	1	2	7,691
Lil Purple Willie	3	F	3	1	0	0	8,450
Lil Red Flyer	2	G	7	1	1	1	10,160
Lil Red Rendezvous	4	F	15	0	0	1	4,629
Lil Rhett's Vet	3	F	4	0	1	0	3,302
Lil Rosa	2	F	3	0	0	0	186
Lil Rosalie	4	F	7	0	0	0	531
Lil' Sassy Gal	5	M	1	0	0	0	0
Lil Scout	3	F	9	3	1	0	67,436
Lil Shy Dancer	4	F	6	1	0	1	2,842
Lil Sister	3	F	1	0	0	0	0
Lil Sister Stich	6	M	1	0	0	0	0
Lil Sister's Lad	5	H	7	2	2	1	4,684
Li'l Smile	7	M	1	0	0	0	0
Lil Spark	2	G	2	0	0	0	265
Lil Star	4	F	8	1	2	2	8,818
Lil Starvin Marvin	11	G	3	0	0	1	1,900
Lil Sugarman	4	C	14	4	1	2	16,066
Lil Sweet Tee	2	F	6	0	2	0	5,700
Lil Take Out	7	M	6	0	2	0	3,312
Lil Taste	2	F	5	1	0	0	5,177
Lil Thomas Too	5	H	8	1	0	0	13,230
Lil Town Blues	10	G	4	0	0	0	310
Lil Whooter	4	F	4	0	2	0	4,620
Lil' Yiper	2	G	9	0	4	1	15,180
Lila B	3	F	1	0	0	0	260
Lila Hope	2	F	1	0	0	0	0
Lila Kay's Rose	2	F	2	0	0	0	2,750
Lila Mae	2	F	4	0	0	0	1,420
Lila Paige	2	F	2	0	0	1	7,650
Lilac Queen (GER)	5	M	5	3	0	0	144,858
Lilacs Dream	3	F	6	0	1	3	4,808
Lilah	6	M	13	4	5	1	153,520
Lila's Dream	3	F	3	0	1	0	2,025
Li'lbito'fudge	2	C	4	0	0	0	0
Lilfreddyfastfeet	2	G	2	1	0	0	1,980
Lilia	5	M	10	0	0	2	4,755
Liliana L	3	F	8	2	3	1	44,427
Liliano	5	G	8	1	0	1	9,060
Lilias Trotter	3	F	7	3	0	0	37,906
Lilide	2	F	2	1	0	0	5,100
Lili's Encore	7	M	2	0	0	0	0

RECORDS OF HORSES

Horse	Age	Sex	Sts	1st	2d	3d	Won	Horse	Age	Sex	Sts	1st	2d	3d	Won
Lilith	8	M	7	0	0	0	836	Linda's Prince	2	G	2	0	1	0	7,000
Lilith's Slew	3	F	16	1	0	3	11,031	Linda's Vixen	3	F	10	5	2	0	20,406
Lilkilngirl	2	F	5	1	1	1	20,283	Lindasladyluck	3	F	15	0	0	2	15,654
Lill Affirmed Slew	3	F	2	0	0	0	226	Linden Hill	7	G	15	3	2	2	16,840
Lillian West	4	F	8	2	1	1	8,871	Linden T	3	G	12	0	1	1	2,996
Lillian's Valley	4	F	11	0	3	2	5,280	Linder Blue	6	H	8	2	3	0	12,364
Lillie's Star	6	M	3	1	0	0	2,880	Lindero	2	C	6	2	1	0	32,785
L'Illusion de l'Or	5	M	2	0	0	0	1,055	Lindholm	5	G	16	2	2	1	14,306
Lilly A	4	F	5	0	0	0	4,020	Lindsay Jean	5	M	7	3	1	2	182,125
Lilly and Ice	8	M	6	0	0	0	1,740	Lindsay's Quixote	4	F	1	0	0	0	75
Lilly Be Nice	3	F	8	1	0	3	7,556	Lindsey Lark	8	M	2	0	0	0	101
Lilly Bee Blue	4	F	17	0	2	1	4,098	Lindsey O	4	F	5	0	0	0	850
Lilly the Kid	2	F	4	1	0	0	5,600	Lindsey's Dove	3	F	10	1	1	1	19,225
Lillyatthehelm	3	F	6	0	1	0	1,660	Lindsey's Pride	4	F	4	1	0	2	9,440
Lillyflower	4	F	6	0	2	0	2,240	Lindt	5	H	11	0	1	2	8,378
Lilly'softhefield	2	F	5	0	0	0	1,380	Lindy Wells	3	F	2	0	0	1	3,520
Lilmisshonkytonk	2	F	2	1	0	0	6,102	Lindys Dancer	4	C	6	4	0	2	16,420
Lilnome	3	F	1	0	0	0		Lindy's Kid	4	F	6	1	1	0	3,310
Lil'redheadeddevil	4	F	3	1	0	1	2,974	Line Buster	2	F	5	2	1	1	88,596
Lil's a Real Lady	3	F	5	1	0	2	40,830	Line Dancer	5	H	4	0	0	1	1,850
Lil's Act	3	C	4	0	0	0		Line Distribution	7	G	7	1	0	1	4,520
Lil's Angel	3	F	3	1	1	0	8,290	Line Error	4	F	1	0	1	0	2,460
Lil's Date	3	F	9	0	0	0	1,110	Line It Up	7	M	14	1	0	1	10,683
Lil's Golden Boy	4	G	11	0	1	2	2,433	Line O Scrimmage	3	F	4	0	0	0	0
Lils Golden Gem	4	F	8	1	1	2	6,131	Line of Defense	6	G	11	3	0	5	149,010
Lil's Sunnie Girl	3	F	5	0	1	1	6,709	Line of Duty	5	M	7	1	2	0	19,920
Lilsisterlightning	6	M	8	1	5	0	41,400	Line of Fire	4	F	6	0	1	0	4,456
Lilt	4	C	11	1	1	2	31,332	Line of Scrimmage	2	C	4	0	1	0	2,820
Lily Bea Squash	2	F	5	0	0	0	660	Line Rider	4	C	7	0	0	1	9,980
Lily Langfuhr	2	F	2	0	0	0	420	Line Sweeper	4	F	3	0	2	0	5,200
Lily Lou Roo	5	M	5	0	0	0	150	Line Topper	6	H	2	0	0	0	221
Lily Martini	3	F	8	1	3	3	13,660	Linear Lane	6	M	3	0	0	0	165
Lily of the Valley	3	F	9	1	1	1	20,780	Linear Lights	3	G	8	2	1	0	17,553
Lily Red Honey	8	M	9	0	0	1	1,920	Lineation	4	C	4	0	0	0	315
Lily Vanilly	4	F	12	3	2	2	34,668	Lined in Gold	6	H	1	0	0	0	0
Lily Von Stupp	3	F	2	1	0	0	3,180	Linefighter	3	F	4	0	0	2	2,640
Lilyan D.	9	M	9	1	0	0	3,367	Lines of Love	3	F	3	0	0	0	875
Lily's Big Boy	7	H	9	0	0	3	1,175	Lineuponthelevee	3	F	7	0	0	2	6,025
Lily's Lad	6	G	6	0	1	1	36,434	Lingard Cat	6	G	5	0	1	2	8,185
Lily's Prospect	4	F	11	2	2	1	13,134	Lingard Diamond	4	F	21	3	1	1	16,140
Lily's Testamony	3	F	2	0	0	0	0	Lingerie	2	F	4	1	1	0	9,900
Limbo Time	7	H	4	1	0	1	4,992	Linii	4	G	13	0	0	2	3,749
Limehouse	2	C	6	3	0	2	260,435	Linilee	6	M	8	2	1	2	9,777
Limelight Dancer	2	F	5	1	0	1	11,786	Linjack's First	4	G	2	1	1	0	7,620
Limelighter	3	F	6	0	2	1	30,985	Linjack's Legacy	3	F	12	1	0	4	13,309
Limerick Lad	3	G	3	0	0	0	0	Link Teegather	3	G	12	1	2	2	14,945
Limerik	6	G	13	1	2	1	13,157	Link to Jimmy	7	G	3	0	1	0	5,380
Limero (ARG)	4	C	6	0	0	1	7,630	Link to Link	5	G	1	0	0	0	0
Limestone	7	G	10	4	4	0	69,400	Link to Ordway	3	G	13	2	3	1	48,490
Limestone Gap	4	C	2	0	0	0	0	Link to Tour	4	G	13	5	0	2	25,774
Limit Free	2	C	2	1	0	0	27,000	Link Up	4	C	19	2	4	4	15,725
Limit the Pain	6	M	7	1	2	1	2,220	Linkoman	6	G	16	1	3	5	40,940
Limit Up	7	G	8	0	2	0	3,890	Linnie Belle	2	F	2	0	0	0	0
Limited	6	H	4	0	0	1	680	Lino's Lady	3	F	3	1	0	0	7,460
Limited Access	2	C	6	1	1	0	13,761	Lin's Forty Niner	3	F	12	0	0	2	3,600
Limited Issue	3	C	2	0	0	0	35	Linus	6	G	13	2	3	0	23,876
Limited Lisa	3	F	1	0	0	0	0	Linwin	6	M	11	1	2	0	11,742
Limited Number	6	H	9	1	0	0	3,331	Lion Castle	5	M	4	0	2	0	5,851
Limited Speed	5	H	8	0	0	1	682	Lion From Zion	5	H	1	0	0	0	0
Limo and Lunch	5	M	19	3	4	2	21,260	Lion Heart	2	C	3	3	0	0	310,800
Limo Kat	6	H	2	0	0	0	272	Lion King's Roar	3	C	7	1	2	0	20,654
Limone Forte	3	C	9	2	3	1	87,870	Lion Lad	2	C	5	1	2	0	28,260
Lin Mi Lin	3	F	3	0	0	0	84	Lion Land	2	C	1	0	0	1	6,468
Linc	4	C	4	0	1	0	7,770	Lion Leader	2	C	5	0	0	1	10,425
Lincoln Abbey	7	M	12	1	1	0	8,429	Lion On the Siphon	2	F	1	0	0	0	0
Lincoln Center	4	G	15	3	2	1	25,444	Lion Prince	8	G	10	0	2	1	4,025
Lincoln Lodge	5	H	7	0	1	0	2,094	Lion Tamer	3	C	4	2	0	0	135,400
Lincoln Parish	4	G	8	0	2	1	4,385	Lionardo	2	C	1	0	0	0	45
Linda Belinda	2	F	2	0	0	1	7,980	Lionel	3	C	1	0	0	0	0
Linda D's Roomy	3	F	2	0	0	1	3,460	Lionel C. On Ice	3	C	2	0	0	0	0
Linda Eder	4	F	8	0	1	1	22,800	Lionels Image	3	F	12	1	1	3	40,623
Linda Norman	7	M	12	0	2	2	8,690	Lionel's Lucky Hat	3	F	5	0	1	2	9,600
Lindamademedoit	3	F	13	2	2	3	16,668	Lions Roar	3	G	1	0	0	0	0
Linda's Fashion	4	F	4	0	0	0	675	Lionstigersnbears	3	C	6	1	1	2	2,794
Linda's Future	2	F	1	0	0	0	0	Lip Vice	3	F	8	0	0	2	2,492
Linda's Gold	4	F	12	1	0	1	8,870	Lipa	4	F	5	1	0	1	8,122
Linda's Lad	5	G	7	0	4	1	11,970	Lipan	2	C	3	0	1	1	14,260
Linda's Lass	2	F	2	0	0	0	0	Liplock	4	F	7	1	0	0	5,100
Linda's Miracle	4	F	1	0	0	0	0	Lipstick Kiss	5	M	14	2	3	1	11,266

Horse	Age	Sex	Sts	1st	2d	3d	Won	Horse	Age	Sex	Sts	1st	2d	3d	Won
Lipstick Lies	3	F	10	2	0	3	25,904	Lithgows Haymaker	3	G	2	0	0	0	300
Lipstick Traces	7	M	11	1	0	0	8,431	Lithian's Legacy	4	F	1	0	0	0	160
Lipstickonmycollar	4	F	2	0	0	0	0	Lithium	3	C	8	1	0	3	12,535
Lipsy Lake	2	C	1	0	0	0	0	Lithuanian Dan	6	G	6	0	1	0	1,016
Liquid Asset	5	G	14	1	0	1	3,081	Litigant Cat	3	F	8	0	0	0	765
Liquid Charger	7	M	14	0	1	2	3,009	Litigasion	5	H	8	3	2	0	18,980
Liquid Courage	9	G	4	0	0	0	2,315	Litigator	4	F	7	3	2	0	63,353
Liquid Ice	6	H	9	0	0	0	690	Lit'l D	6	G	9	1	2	4	6,087
Liquid Icon	7	G	10	2	2	1	13,845	Lit'l Nancy's Girl	5	M	8	1	1	2	6,875
Liquid Lightning	3	G	6	1	0	0	8,151	Lit'l Red Corvette	3	C	13	2	3	1	21,000
Liquid Sunshine	9	G	7	1	0	0	2,946	Litlbity Dot	4	F	9	1	2	1	5,091
Liquor Cabinet (IRE)	2	C	1	0	0	0	118	Litlmisscantbwrong	3	F	3	0	0	0	441
Lira Lira	2	F	3	0	0	1	800	Litter the Glitter	3	F	5	2	0	1	16,485
Lis Pendens	4	F	3	0	0	0	0	Little Abby Ann	6	M	10	1	0	1	2,637
Lisa Slew	2	F	2	0	0	0	150	Little Abner	3	G	5	1	1	1	8,945
Lisa's Approval	5	M	6	1	2	1	23,670	Little Advantage	7	M	1	0	0	0	56
Lisa's Baby	5	M	5	1	0	0	3,858	Little Alma	4	F	3	0	0	0	252
Lisa's Deelites	4	F	4	0	0	0	1,440	Little Amante	2	G	3	0	0	0	1,290
Lisa's Friends	2	F	2	0	0	0	375	Little and Bold	3	F	3	0	0	0	303
Lisa's Rainbow	2	F	3	1	0	0	22,900	Little Andrea	2	F	4	2	0	1	74,985
Lisa's Royal Guy	4	G	16	2	3	1	55,200	Little Angel	5	M	1	0	0	0	0
Lisa's Secret	2	F	2	0	0	0	780	Little Anna	5	M	4	1	0	0	2,640
Lisa's Windmill	4	F	1	1	0	0	5,400	Little Anns Secret	2	F	2	0	0	0	0
Lisasfriendlylover	2	F	6	2	1	0	22,770	Little Anthony	3	C	4	2	1	0	14,360
Lisa'sgoldenangel	4	F	12	0	0	0	2,740	Little Barbara	6	M	1	0	0	0	0
Lisboa (MEX)	6	M	10	0	1	2	2,475	Little Beau Pip	2	C	3	0	0	0	1,910
Lisduff	4	F	3	2	0	0	8,625	Little Bee Cee	5	M	2	0	0	0	0
Liska (IRE)	3	F	4	1	1	1	26,314	Little Betty Girl	4	F	13	1	0	3	21,307
Liska's Lyric	3	F	5	0	1	1	2,160	Little Big Guy	3	G	4	0	0	0	241
Lismore Knight	3	C	6	2	0	2	208,800	Little Big Hoss	2	C	3	0	0	0	145
Lisroe Lynne	5	M	4	0	0	1	1,755	Little Big Pistol	3	G	5	0	0	0	1,519
Lissa's Lad	2	C	3	0	0	1	1,890	Little Big Tye	2	C	3	0	0	0	104
Lissau	2	C	5	2	2	0	83,551	Little Bird	5	M	5	0	0	0	4,475
Lissome	4	F	5	0	0	1	8,630	Little Bit Absent	2	C	5	0	0	0	1,460
Lissys Smile	2	F	2	0	0	0	0	Little Bit Catty	3	F	2	0	0	0	50
Listen Indy	3	C	5	0	0	1	9,680	Little Bit Naughty	4	F	7	1	1	0	4,796
Listenforthetruth	2	C	1	1	0	0	29,400	Little Bit of Fame	2	F	3	0	0	0	0
Listening Fr Wings	4	F	15	0	2	2	18,312	Little Bit Sandy	2	G	6	0	1	1	2,480
Listening Springs	2	F	1	0	0	0	400	Little Bit Stormy	2	G	4	0	0	1	3,276
Listo	2	F	4	0	0	0	6,435	Little Bit Trickie	2	F	2	0	0	0	200
Lisura's Gem	3	F	4	1	1	0	7,020	Little Bit Western	3	F	1	0	0	0	1,500
Liszy	3	F	2	0	0	0	680	Little Bitof Spice	6	M	3	0	0	1	440
Lit D' Or	5	M	7	1	0	0	7,153	Little Blazin Sis	3	F	5	1	0	0	4,950
Lit de Beurre	4	G	14	1	1	1	5,442	Little Blessing	2	F	1	0	0	0	0
Lit de Cam	4	F	1	0	0	0	0	Little Bo Leap	3	G	5	1	1	0	9,350
Lit de Danseur	5	G	12	2	1	1	14,876	Little Bold Anne	5	M	10	4	4	0	21,296
Lit de Jimmy	2	F	3	1	0	0	59,875	Little Bold Sweep	5	G	3	0	0	0	176
Lit de Lace	5	H	5	0	1	0	3,625	Little Bonnet	3	F	9	3	2	2	132,806
Lit de Matrix	2	C	2	1	1	0	7,800	Little Boy George	3	G	3	0	0	0	0
Lit Up	2	F	3	1	1	0	11,840	Little Boy Lost	4	G	11	1	2	0	17,685
Litany	4	F	5	1	0	1	40,910	Little Brick Lane	5	G	9	2	1	1	12,965
Lita's Gold	3	F	10	1	2	0	4,107	Little Brown Brick	7	M	12	1	1	1	11,359
Litchfield Lad	3	C	11	2	1	2	37,670	Little Burner	3	F	4	0	0	0	1,006
Lite and Misty	2	F	1	0	1	0	1,500	Little But Lovely	5	M	7	0	0	0	182
Lite Duty Judy	7	M	5	0	0	0	502	Little Buttercup	3	F	6	2	2	2	79,460
Lite Medley	5	M	9	1	1	1	11,996	Little Button	3	F	1	0	0	0	0
Lite N Rite	4	F	5	0	0	0	345	Little Carbon	7	M	11	2	1	1	13,280
Lite O My Life	2	F	5	0	1	1	8,463	Little Cat Feet	3	F	5	1	1	0	11,516
Lite On My Feet	4	F	8	2	0	0	19,140	Little Caveat	11	G	6	0	1	0	7,300
Lite Onthe Spirits	5	G	13	0	0	4	2,706	Little Celebrity	3	F	1	0	1	0	14,100
Lite Ridge	3	C	13	3	2	2	21,103	Little Charmer	3	F	11	2	1	1	13,680
Lite Ruckus	4	C	13	1	0	2	7,798	Little Cindy Lou	4	F	7	2	2	2	16,550
Lite Source	5	G	7	0	0	0	1,872	Little Clown	3	C	5	0	0	0	305
Lite the Point	2	C	6	1	0	1	23,450	Little Cobra	2	C	10	0	0	0	0
Lite Toast	5	G	12	2	2	2	17,218	Little Compassion	3	F	3	1	0	1	9,665
Lite Up	5	G	15	1	2	3	36,270	Little Compton	3	F	10	0	3	1	12,890
Lite Up the Knight	5	G	5	1	0	1	7,565	Little Cowboy	2	C	3	0	0	0	0
Litefingered Louie	2	G	4	0	0	0	708	Little Crafty	3	G	4	0	0	0	1,830
Litelucky	3	F	3	0	1	1	2,980	Little Cutie	2	F	1	1	0	0	5,400
Litenup	5	G	4	0	0	0	355	Little Dancer	3	F	5	0	0	0	130
Literal Joy	5	M	6	0	1	1	1,548	Little Dandy	4	G	3	0	0	0	0
Literally Private	5	G	4	0	0	0	116	Little Dewey Know	4	G	14	3	0	1	16,930
Literary	2	F	2	1	1	0	15,440	Little Ditty	2	F	3	1	1	0	33,160
Literary Light	4	F	10	3	2	1	136,583	Little Diva	3	F	4	1	0	0	18,300
Literary Row	4	C	5	1	1	1	43,780	Little Dix Bay	3	C	2	0	0	0	2,040
Literati Miss	11	M	1	0	0	0	70	Little Doc	7	H	5	0	0	1	1,403
Literossi	2	G	3	1	0	1	7,025	Little Doctor	5	H	7	0	0	1	1,427
Litesom	4	F	4	0	1	1	16,975	Little Dom	2	C	3	0	1	0	4,095
Liteupthetoteboard	2	F	1	0	0	0	0	Little E C T	5	M	5	1	0	0	3,308

Horse	Age	Sex	Sts	1st	2d	3d	Won
Little Ed	2	F	10	0	0	0	830
Little Elf	2	F	3	0	0	0	390
Little Emmy	2	F	2	0	0	0	145
Little Fager	6	M	5	0	1	1	1,531
Little Fig	5	G	8	0	0	0	598
Little Filomena	3	F	3	0	0	0	390
Little Fireman	7	H	10	3	3	2	9,044
Little Floss	3	G	17	1	3	3	17,691
Little Forest	4	F	9	1	2	0	9,207
Little Foxy Baby	2	F	3	2	0	0	43,715
Little Frankie R	4	G	14	3	2	4	17,392
Little G.	5	G	2	0	0	0	325
Little Gabby	4	F	6	1	1	0	23,340
Little Geezer	4	G	11	0	1	1	4,885
Little Ghazi	7	G	9	1	1	1	44,580
Little Girl Curran	6	M	5	0	1	1	2,040
Little Gold Devil	3	F	6	0	0	0	330
Little Gossip	2	F	4	0	0	0	450
Little Grapette	4	F	13	1	3	0	11,090
Little Gray Storm	4	G	10	1	1	2	6,419
Little Habibi	3	F	13	1	3	5	27,583
Little Hank	3	G	12	1	0	1	7,869
Little Happy	4	G	11	5	2	1	89,575
Little Hawk	5	G	4	0	0	3	3,942
Little Hawk Rock	3	G	12	0	2	2	25,865
Little Hero	6	M	4	0	3	0	9,770
Little Hi	3	C	14	2	1	1	10,599
Little Hoppy	10	G	4	0	2	0	1,520
Little Horn	6	G	10	0	0	2	1,614
Little Hotfoot	4	F	9	1	0	0	13,882
Little I	3	C	5	0	0	0	0
Little Indian Girl	3	F	4	1	0	0	15,240
Little Inn	3	F	5	0	0	1	1,420
Little Irish	2	F	2	0	0	0	142
Little Irish Girl	6	M	12	0	1	4	9,310
Little Italy	3	F	1	0	0	0	38
Little Jackie	3	G	6	1	2	1	5,231
Little Jackson	9	G	11	0	0	1	3,136
Little Jag	3	G	2	0	0	0	0
Little Jenkins	4	F	1	0	0	0	60
Little Jody	4	F	9	0	4	2	13,275
Little Joe Lewis	6	G	6	1	0	0	2,240
Little Joe Tubb	4	C	8	0	0	0	3,000
Little Josie	2	F	5	1	0	0	17,413
Little Julie	3	F	16	3	3	1	35,995
Little Kisatchie	3	G	1	0	0	0	0
Little Kostroma	3	F	1	0	0	0	0
Little Lady Lark	4	F	2	0	0	0	0
Little Lady T	3	F	8	1	0	1	16,275
Little Ladybug	3	F	6	2	0	1	13,266
Little Lake Wier	4	F	6	0	0	0	1,390
Little Laney	3	F	6	0	0	2	2,401
Little Lea	3	F	3	0	0	0	555
Little Lee	7	G	2	1	1	0	7,780
Little Less Talk	6	G	20	4	7	3	45,682
Little Lighty	7	M	8	1	3	1	20,274
Little Lil	7	M	7	0	0	0	3,347
Little Liz	7	M	4	0	0	0	172
Little Lolitta	5	M	4	0	2	0	16,055
Little Lonnie Lou	5	M	5	0	0	0	965
Little Lori Lu	5	M	1	0	0	0	0
Little Lost Girl	3	F	12	0	0	4	4,630
Little Lucy	6	M	9	0	0	0	1,092
Little Mac Evil	5	H	4	0	0	0	330
Little Mack Truck	3	C	15	1	4	1	45,030
Little Magnolia	3	F	4	0	0	1	825
Little Malvern (GB)	3	F	2	0	0	0	2,270
Little Man Leo	4	C	5	1	0	0	5,240
Little Manistee	5	H	5	0	0	1	1,028
Little Maricat	2	C	5	1	2	1	32,600
Little Marshall	4	C	8	0	3	1	10,124
Little Martha	7	F	6	0	0	1	8,240
Little Match Girl	5	M	10	3	2	0	12,468
Little Matth Man	2	C	8	2	0	1	63,130
Little Me	5	G	5	0	0	0	564
Little Me Too	5	H	12	1	0	4	33,015
Little Millie	2	F	1	0	0	0	0
Little Mis General	3	F	5	0	0	4	13,980
Little Miss Ally	2	F	2	0	0	0	352
Little Miss Catey	4	F	2	0	0	0	0
Little Miss Code	6	M	6	0	0	0	374
Little Miss Deb	3	F	5	1	0	0	13,086
Little Miss Freeze	6	M	7	0	1	0	1,559
Little Miss Hurry	7	M	3	0	0	0	365
Little Miss Leap	3	F	3	0	3	0	5,100
Little Miss Mary	3	F	3	1	0	1	7,107
Little Miss Meadow	4	F	13	2	2	2	18,577
Little Miss Nickel	10	M	13	0	1	1	3,179
Little Miss Pamela	3	F	5	1	1	0	47,490
Little Miss Plundr	6	M	1	0	0	0	0
Little Miss Rocket	6	M	8	1	1	0	5,500
Little Mo	8	M	10	1	2	1	12,705
Little Mo G	3	F	2	0	0	0	0
Little Moe's Baby	4	C	4	0	0	0	526
Little More	3	C	7	1	3	1	26,430
Little Muffin	4	F	10	2	2	2	14,750
Little Napoleon	7	G	2	0	0	1	1,300
Little Nat	5	M	9	1	1	0	4,910
Little Nell	2	F	3	0	0	0	200
Little Nooster	2	F	1	0	0	0	0
Little Oneal	4	G	10	1	3	0	8,350
Little Paces	7	G	15	2	0	1	17,390
Little Pistola	3	G	10	1	3	1	11,997
Little Polish Wolf	3	F	11	1	2	1	18,920
Little Poopsie	2	F	1	1	0	0	6,840
Little Profit	3	F	12	2	3	1	9,838
Little Pursuit	4	F	11	3	0	4	13,649
Little Q. Tee	4	F	1	0	0	0	380
Little Quill	5	M	11	1	1	0	4,367
Little Realfire	7	M	2	0	0	0	80
Little Rebel	3	G	8	0	1	0	1,535
Little Red Ahead	4	F	2	0	0	0	200
Little Red Crimson	4	F	12	1	0	3	7,852
Little Red Devil	5	G	4	2	0	0	8,967
Little Red Ferrari	3	F	1	0	0	0	0
Little Red Rascal	5	M	9	1	3	0	10,360
Little Red Rocket	2	G	6	1	2	2	29,866
Little Red Train	4	C	5	0	0	0	0
Little Ribs	3	G	2	0	0	0	0
Little Rich	5	G	3	0	0	1	680
Little Rich Girl	3	F	2	0	0	0	787
Little Rock Lover	4	F	9	0	0	4	5,079
Little Rocket	3	G	15	1	2	1	18,896
Little Rocky	7	G	7	2	1	2	11,075
Little Rosa Lynn	4	F	10	2	0	4	25,298
Little Rose Queen	5	M	10	0	3	2	5,599
Little Rut	3	G	7	2	0	1	39,050
Little Ruthie	6	M	13	3	3	2	30,873
Little Sandy	6	G	10	0	1	1	4,845
Little Scholar	3	F	2	0	0	0	112
Little Ship	5	H	9	1	2	0	10,254
Little Shon	4	F	8	1	0	1	8,830
Little Silent Star	2	F	3	0	0	0	0
Little Silverghost	2	F	4	0	0	1	1,535
Little Skater	3	G	5	1	0	0	5,670
Little Sky Tracer	7	G	13	1	2	1	5,410
Little Slam	3	F	4	0	0	0	365
Little Slew	2	G	2	0	0	0	380
Little Smarty	5	G	4	3	0	0	8,364
Little Smokey	2	G	7	1	1	1	9,161
Little Snorkie	3	F	7	0	1	2	6,180
Little Soldiergirl	2	F	2	0	0	0	6,000
Little Sophia	4	F	2	0	1	0	6,000
Little South	4	F	2	0	0	0	0
Little Sparrow	3	F	3	0	1	1	5,640
Little Squirt	3	G	6	0	0	0	257
Little Stormy	3	G	5	1	0	0	6,395
Little Sun	4	C	6	0	3	2	1,625
Little Surfer	6	M	14	1	2	2	10,629
Little Swimmer	3	C	9	0	1	0	8,500
Little Switz	2	F	2	0	1	0	7,160
Little Tara	3	F	2	1	0	1	11,200
Little Temptress	3	F	9	0	0	1	1,764
Little Tennessee	6	G	3	0	0	0	159
Little Time	4	F	8	1	0	1	27,800
Little Timmy Love	4	C	2	0	0	2	492
Little too Big	3	G	1	0	0	0	0
Little Toolight	5	G	10	2	0	0	12,993

Horse	Age Sex	Sts	1st	2d	3d	Won
Little Town	3 C	3	0	1	1	7,646
Little Town Girl	3 F	4	0	1	1	4,127
Little Treasure (FR)	4 F	5	0	3	0	82,065
Little Tucker	6 G	4	0	0	0	0
Little Tune	9 G	10	1	2	3	8,724
Little Ugly	3 F	7	0	0	1	1,785
Little Velvet	4 C	10	5	0	1	63,605
Little Vernon	2 G	1	0	0	0	750
Little Villain	10 G	12	0	0	1	3,595
Little Villainess	4 F	14	0	0	0	2,510
Little Vixen	4 F	15	1	3	0	21,371
Little War	4 G	5	0	0	0	0
Little Warrior	3 F	9	1	0	2	29,382
Little Wilder	4 F	7	0	0	1	1,339
Little Willard	9 G	9	1	0	0	3,597
Little Wing	5 M	3	0	0	0	1,380
Little Wink	3 G	3	0	0	0	103
Little Wolfie	2 F	2	0	0	0	140
Little Won	8 M	1	0	1	0	14,500
Little Yeoman	4 F	14	4	2	2	27,420
Littlebambam	4 F	4	0	0	0	600
Littlebigthing	4 F	3	0	1	1	10,500
Littlebit Onery	4 G	13	2	3	1	14,794
Littlebitakris	2 C	1	0	0	0	195
Littlebitofjam	5 M	2	0	0	0	0
Littlebitoflace	5 M	4	0	1	0	1,000
Littlebullsbullet	3 F	6	0	0	0	612
Littledancansing	4 C	5	0	2	1	4,265
Littledrummergirl	8 M	16	1	2	7	12,962
Littlefield	10 G	14	2	5	3	4,699
Littleladiesman	3 G	14	2	2	4	21,092
Littlemagbrother	2 G	2	0	0	0	531
Littleman Wonsong	2 C	3	0	0	0	0
Littlemiss Sparkle	3 F	5	1	2	0	61,567
Littlemorgusto	3 F	10	2	1	1	11,655
Littlemowine	4 F	2	0	0	0	440
Littleone Joe	5 G	14	3	0	2	9,072
Littlepieceofpie	3 F	5	0	0	1	1,720
Littlepork	3 C	3	0	0	0	160
Littleredprincess	4 F	2	0	0	0	0
Littleriverqueen	5 M	13	1	3	2	29,155
Litunga	7 G	1	0	0	0	153
Liturgy	3 C	5	1	0	0	13,320
Litvak	9 G	1	0	0	0	0
Liv	3 F	2	0	0	0	0
Livadora	2 F	3	0	0	0	400
Livae	4 F	14	0	3	2	15,245
Live and Learn	5 M	13	0	0	0	3,116
Live Backwards	4 F	9	2	1	0	28,259
Live Doppler	5 M	11	2	1	0	22,330
Live for Today	3 G	5	0	0	0	0
Live Free Or Die	4 F	7	2	1	0	64,274
Live Larrupin	2 C	2	0	0	0	0
Live Show	5 H	2	0	0	1	2,525
Live the Dream	5 H	11	2	1	0	13,179
Live the Life	2 G	2	0	0	0	700
Live to Die	2 F	1	0	0	0	930
Live Trap	4 F	4	0	0	0	0
Live Well	2 F	2	0	1	0	16,822
Live Wire Lil	6 M	3	1	0	1	13,470
Live Wire Lucy	2 F	12	1	1	2	28,560
Live Wire Sally	2 F	2	0	0	0	0
Liveforthemoment	3 F	5	0	0	0	0
Liveitupnow	4 F	11	1	1	1	18,176
Lively Art	4 F	1	0	0	0	675
Lively Classicals	3 C	2	0	0	1	7,845
Lively Dancer	6 M	9	2	1	2	3,541
Lively Frolic	2 C	9	0	0	0	685
Lively Heather	2 F	1	0	0	0	80
Lively Kisser	4 C	2	0	0	0	720
Lively Larry	6 G	7	1	0	1	2,836
Lively Lew	5 M	2	0	0	0	185
Lively Liz	5 M	7	0	1	0	1,570
Lively Man	3 C	18	1	2	1	12,844
Lively Minister	7 G	11	2	1	3	63,726
Lively Moment	3 F	9	3	1	1	33,340
Lively Number	2 F	2	0	0	0	240
Lively Pistol	3 C	15	0	1	1	2,255
Lively Prospect	6 G	8	4	1	0	36,010

Horse	Age Sex	Sts	1st	2d	3d	Won
Lively Trix	6 G	4	0	0	0	0
Livermore Dream	2 F	1	0	0	0	66
Livestock Auction	2 F	6	1	1	2	6,015
Livewire	10 G	4	0	0	1	566
Livin Legend	5 G	8	0	1	0	2,950
Livin' On the Edge	3 F	9	1	0	3	12,670
Livin Without Fear	2 G	4	0	0	0	0
Living a Dream	6 G	7	1	1	1	19,340
Living Bade	3 F	7	1	1	0	1,487
Living Faith	5 M	4	0	0	1	472
Living Fully	2 F	5	1	2	1	28,870
Living in Style	6 M	2	0	0	0	0
Living Lavida Lisa	3 F	6	2	2	0	47,410
Living On Margin	3 F	1	0	0	0	94
Living Single	3 G	8	1	0	0	25,860
Livingood	3 G	5	0	0	0	0
Livingston Bay	8 M	2	0	0	0	0
Livingwill	3 C	8	2	1	1	8,236
Liz On Polk Street	2 F	1	1	0	0	15,600
Lizard Lick	4 F	6	3	1	0	21,320
Lizawatha	3 F	1	0	0	0	0
Lizbeth's Desire	7 M	4	0	0	0	0
Liz's Bandit	2 C	17	1	1	8	20,380
Liz's Rib	4 F	6	2	1	0	16,290
Liz's Secret	5 M	9	0	0	1	793
Lizzie Ann	4 F	4	0	0	0	630
Lizzie P.	2 F	2	0	0	0	0
Lizzie's Case	4 F	1	0	0	0	0
Lizzy Cool	3 F	3	1	1	0	66,120
Lizzy's Angel	5 M	9	1	1	0	4,929
Lizzy's Flyer	3 F	3	0	0	0	780
Ll Fast Play	3 F	1	0	0	0	0
Llama Jet	3 G	2	0	0	0	0
Llanmihangel	3 F	1	0	0	1	1,500
Llaves	4 G	8	0	0	2	2,296
Llegaste a Mi	4 F	5	0	0	0	440
Lloyd T	4 G	15	1	2	1	6,686
Lloydminister	12 G	7	0	1	1	2,419
Lloydminster	2 G	6	0	2	0	16,919
Lloyd's Ego	3 G	7	1	0	5	10,802
Lloyds Lady	3 F	2	0	0	0	530
Lloydtown	4 G	8	1	1	0	31,336
Ll's Big Boy	4 G	7	0	0	0	713
L'Natural High	6 G	11	2	2	2	27,060
Lo Life Avenger	4 G	20	1	3	5	13,035
Load a Chronic	3 G	6	1	2	0	14,536
Loaded Brush	5 G	6	2	0	2	48,430
Loaded Mischief	4 F	12	3	1	3	21,873
Loaded Soda	2 G	6	0	1	0	9,820
Loaded Springs	4 G	11	1	0	1	5,675
Load'eminthedark	4 F	1	0	0	1	940
Loadofwyatt	2 F	1	0	0	0	100
Loadsoffun	5 M	5	0	0	1	805
Loaf	9 G	2	0	0	0	339
Loafer	3 C	6	1	1	0	6,600
Loan Me a Fen	4 G	5	1	0	0	11,403
Loan Me the Money	2 F	1	0	0	1	750
Loban	5 M	1	0	0	0	0
Lobato	3 C	5	0	2	0	3,477
Lobbyist	5 M	3	0	0	0	200
Lobsterathepalms	2 F	2	0	0	1	3,120
Local Bum	5 G	2	1	0	0	5,080
Local Calling	6 H	13	1	1	0	12,629
Local Case	3 G	4	0	1	1	2,440
Local Headlines	7 G	1	0	0	1	450
Local Knowledge	8 G	6	1	0	0	7,884
Local Law	3 F	1	0	1	0	3,480
Local Nobility	6 M	6	0	0	0	514
Local Praise	5 M	5	0	0	1	2,085
Local Stranger	4 G	6	0	1	1	2,880
Local Ties	6 G	14	2	1	2	21,813
Local Treasure	5 H	10	1	4	2	13,810
Local Yokel	2 C	1	0	0	0	168
Localvibes	7 G	9	0	2	1	4,845
Location	8 G	6	0	0	1	1,714
Lochnagar	10 H	3	0	0	0	1,300
Lock in the Money	6 G	6	0	0	1	1,101
Lock Tender	4 G	12	1	2	3	15,140
Lock the Trigger	3 C	4	1	1	0	21,813

Horse	Age	Sex	Sts	1st	2d	3d	Won
Lockdown	3	G	11	2	2	1	34,060
Locked On	7	H	4	0	1	1	6,220
Locker Room	9	G	6	0	0	0	750
Locket	3	F	3	0	0	1	1,820
Lockjaws Grandson	7	G	2	0	0	0	396
Lockon Venus	5	M	14	0	1	0	926
Lockpicker	3	G	12	1	0	5	55,147
Lockton Lass	4	F	6	0	1	1	4,387
Loco Gringo's Lark	4	G	15	0	0	1	1,046
Loco Lobo	3	G	13	2	0	2	27,938
Loco Sombrero	3	G	7	0	1	0	2,431
Loco Tavares	5	H	2	0	1	0	2,877
Locomotive Springs	2	F	1	0	0	0	170
Locomotor	4	C	11	1	1	1	12,270
Locust Moon	5	M	5	0	0	0	696
Lode a Trouble	3	C	6	1	0	0	3,600
Lode Amighty	3	G	4	1	0	0	2,658
Lode Barron	3	G	5	0	0	0	196
Lode of Gems	3	F	1	0	0	0	0
Lode of Lilacs	2	F	5	0	0	1	1,875
Loded and Rolling	4	F	6	1	0	0	1,452
Loded Arrow	11	G	7	0	0	1	1,045
Loden Speed	3	G	8	1	1	2	19,777
Lodes of Class	4	F	3	0	0	0	675
Lodesofmagic	3	G	17	2	1	5	11,659
Lodi Renagade	5	M	17	0	1	1	6,957
Lodovico	3	G	2	0	0	0	200
Loebau Store	6	M	12	3	2	4	15,629
Loftinflight	4	F	2	0	0	0	500
Lofty Call	3	C	2	0	0	0	1,260
Lofty Flare	4	F	12	2	2	5	11,840
Log On	3	G	7	1	2	1	30,520
Logan B.	2	F	4	0	0	0	0
Logan Field	4	C	1	0	1	0	2,100
Logan Rye	4	G	12	2	2	5	15,865
Logans Dancer	3	G	8	0	2	3	4,260
Logan's Girl	5	M	10	4	1	1	29,350
Logan's Tech	6	H	1	0	0	0	0
Logan's Way	4	G	2	0	0	0	123
Logger	4	C	2	1	0	0	5,770
Logger (ARG)	5	G	4	1	0	0	5,895
Logic Lane (IRE)	5	G	5	0	0	0	1,295
Logical Choice	6	G	10	1	1	2	13,644
Logically Speaking	4	G	11	1	2	2	28,690
Logician	3	C	7	1	0	2	61,680
Loglor	3	G	5	1	0	0	3,200
Logold	5	M	10	2	0	1	12,690
L'Ohio	7	M	7	0	0	1	988
Lojo	4	F	9	3	3	1	152,810
Lokari	3	G	6	0	0	1	1,690
Loki	9	G	15	2	2	2	6,996
Lokomemo	7	G	4	0	0	0	180
Lokoya	2	F	4	1	1	0	74,800
Lola Darling	4	F	5	1	1	2	64,990
Lola's Fortune	4	F	23	3	4	5	19,020
Lolita's Gold	4	F	4	0	0	0	0
Lollypop Kid	4	F	4	2	1	0	7,855
Lollypop Lady	5	M	9	1	0	1	10,446
Lollypop Louie	5	H	7	2	1	1	12,340
Loma Listo	3	G	3	0	0	0	390
Lonche	4	G	21	5	5	6	75,280
Londistanceromance	4	G	4	1	0	0	3,781
London Follies (IRE)	4	G	1	0	0	0	0
London Lord	5	G	11	1	4	1	30,697
London Times	6	H	2	0	0	0	1,360
Lone Affair	6	H	3	0	0	0	0
Lone Arrow	2	C	7	1	1	2	73,180
Lone Fan	4	G	9	0	2	0	6,946
Lone Mountain	14	G	3	0	1	1	2,325
Lone Naskra	5	G	6	0	0	3	1,482
Lone Ranger	5	H	15	2	2	5	32,417
Lone Spat	4	C	4	0	1	0	2,005
Lone Star Dave	3	G	11	1	1	1	9,960
Lone Star Deputy	3	C	7	2	0	0	78,680
Lone Star Dream	7	M	4	0	0	0	542
Lone Star Family	2	F	3	0	0	0	0
Lone Star Lear	5	H	3	0	0	0	0
Lone Star Miss	2	F	6	0	1	0	4,932
Lone Star Sky	3	C	8	0	2	1	166,760
Lone Storm	6	G	2	1	0	0	4,380
Lone Traveler	5	G	13	1	2	1	24,714
Lonely Angel	3	F	4	1	1	0	11,300
Lonely Concorde	3	C	4	1	1	0	25,600
Lonely Dream	4	F	12	0	1	3	3,974
Lonely Groom	3	C	10	2	0	1	46,580
Lonely Huntress	4	F	5	0	1	0	2,160
Lonely Island	3	F	2	1	0	0	3,279
Lonely Knights	3	F	6	0	0	0	435
Lonely Rabbit	4	G	1	1	0	0	3,000
Lonely Reality	3	G	2	0	0	0	112
Loner Special	4	G	9	1	0	4	10,567
Lonesome Bay	3	G	7	1	0	0	10,326
Lonesome Dakota	3	G	5	0	0	0	691
Lonesome Dude	8	H	1	0	0	0	0
Lonesome Knight	3	F	10	2	0	3	32,450
Lonesome Lad	6	H	7	1	1	1	8,588
Lonesome Lianna	3	F	1	1	0	0	4,944
Lonesome Prairie	5	M	5	0	0	0	0
Lonesome River	5	M	17	1	2	5	28,831
Lonesome Stoney	4	G	5	0	0	1	2,212
Lonesome Wind	3	F	7	0	0	1	1,730
Lonesomenumberone	2	G	1	0	0	0	120
Lonesomeprospector	2	C	4	0	1	1	3,320
Lonestar Lover	3	G	5	1	0	0	5,896
Long Bay Dancer	4	G	13	1	2	3	14,012
Long Chun	4	F	4	2	0	2	37,270
Long Creek	3	C	4	0	0	0	905
Long Division	3	C	6	0	0	1	3,210
Long For	3	F	4	1	0	0	5,083
Long for You	4	F	3	0	1	1	4,097
Long Gone Con	5	G	7	2	1	1	108,430
Long Gone Kitty	4	F	2	0	0	0	0
Long Gone Lady	5	M	2	0	0	0	0
Long Haul	5	M	2	0	0	0	1,225
Long Kesh	3	G	3	1	0	1	5,930
Long Lance	13	G	2	0	0	0	0
Long Leg Lou	5	M	10	2	1	0	72,560
Long Legged Lady	3	F	6	0	0	0	720
Long Legged Lucy	7	M	21	2	1	4	8,138
Long Legged Lydia	5	M	9	0	0	1	3,100
Long Legs	5	H	5	1	0	1	2,321
Long Live the King	2	G	1	0	0	0	0
Long May She Run	3	F	2	1	0	0	4,950
Long Note	3	F	7	2	0	1	13,170
Long On Pride	4	G	9	1	0	2	16,608
Long Point	8	G	14	5	2	1	32,047
Long Pond	2	C	2	0	1	0	15,756
Long Range	3	C	6	1	3	1	22,068
Long Rifle	4	G	9	2	3	1	7,620
Long Run Road	3	C	1	0	0	0	1,100
Long Star	4	C	9	1	0	2	10,715
Long Term Investor	6	G	10	1	5	1	6,575
Long Term Wish	3	F	4	1	0	0	77,500
Long Trail	5	M	17	1	4	2	12,371
Long Voyage	6	H	6	0	1	0	3,260
Longblackskidmark	5	G	1	0	0	0	0
Longbranch Saloon	2	G	1	0	0	1	1,000
Longfield Spud	3	C	7	2	2	1	77,270
Longford Arms	4	C	10	2	0	2	55,908
Longgonetrevorsean	2	C	4	1	0	1	30,077
Longhorn Blues	3	C	6	1	1	0	26,220
Longingtobeme	6	M	9	1	1	1	45,343
Longlivethestar	4	C	7	0	3	2	15,600
Longnecken	3	C	2	0	0	0	0
Longonot	5	G	11	3	0	3	36,475
Longship	3	G	1	0	1	0	4,340
Longshoreman	3	C	9	0	0	0	1,288
Longshot Ray	2	G	2	0	0	0	0
Longstone	5	H	5	0	0	2	762
Longstreet	4	G	16	1	3	1	9,246
Longtown	3	G	8	1	1	2	5,370
Longview Legend	8	G	20	2	0	6	10,101
Longwood Lady	3	F	14	2	2	3	27,657
Lonikens	3	G	10	0	1	3	3,795
Lonnie's Favorite	6	G	6	0	0	0	159
Lonnies Song	3	F	12	2	1	1	22,760
Lonso Star	4	C	11	0	0	3	4,829
Lonzo's Cash Flo	4	C	1	0	0	0	61

Horse	Age	Sex	Sts	1st	2d	3d	Won
Look a Blade	5	M	4	0	0	1	1,784
Look At Al	6	G	19	2	1	2	13,296
Look At the Board	5	G	9	2	2	2	37,075
Look At You	6	G	11	2	1	2	20,943
Look for Good	4	F	8	0	2	4	21,240
Look Into the Past	5	M	8	1	1	0	16,684
Look N See	4	F	13	2	1	0	7,146
Look of Royalty	3	F	8	1	2	2	12,112
Look of the Lynx	5	M	1	0	0	0	0
Look Out Evan	3	C	9	2	1	4	81,690
Look Out for Loopy	3	F	2	0	0	0	53
Look Out Joe	4	C	2	1	0	0	11,400
Look Out Now	4	F	8	0	0	0	1,147
Look Out Point	7	G	6	1	1	0	7,409
Look Quick	4	G	10	3	1	1	66,200
Look to Heaven	3	F	13	3	6	2	76,410
Look to Luke	5	G	5	0	1	2	4,090
Look to the Day	9	M	10	1	2	3	20,760
Look Who	3	F	3	0	0	0	697
Look Who's Here	7	G	2	0	0	0	405
Lookie There	3	G	3	0	0	0	0
Lookin' Brass	6	G	5	1	1	0	2,700
Lookin for Love	6	G	9	5	1	0	34,465
Lookin So Right	5	H	6	1	0	1	7,017
Lookin Suspicious	4	G	12	1	1	1	6,306
Looking Afar	5	M	7	1	0	2	28,785
Looking Around	4	G	10	0	4	1	43,490
Looking Beyond	5	M	11	1	0	0	4,224
Looking Cool	5	M	1	0	0	0	0
Looking for a Way	6	M	10	5	2	1	15,456
Looking Grand	3	C	7	3	0	2	85,030
Looking Peachy	4	F	3	2	0	0	18,660
Looking Time	4	G	5	1	1	0	9,141
Looking Wealthy	4	G	10	1	2	0	4,948
Lookingforpleasure	2	F	1	0	0	0	0
Lookn At the Wire	4	G	4	1	0	0	6,825
Lookn Boldn Brassy	2	F	2	0	0	1	4,640
Lookn Mighty Fine	6	M	10	0	1	2	19,116
Look'n Smile	3	F	7	0	0	0	1,728
Looknsexy	4	F	3	1	1	1	41,680
Lookout for Ruth	4	F	11	3	1	1	8,016
Lookout Fox	6	H	1	0	0	0	42
Lookout Heights	3	F	6	0	2	0	3,580
Lookout Sue	5	M	16	1	3	2	12,425
Lookout Yall	2	G	1	0	0	0	45
Looks Bold	5	H	12	3	2	2	73,656
Looks Expensive	4	G	16	4	4	1	143,119
Looks Good	2	C	3	0	0	0	0
Looks Guilty	3	F	2	0	0	0	146
Looks Lika Fish	3	G	7	1	2	0	18,300
Looks Like Awinner	2	F	5	0	0	2	2,975
Looks Like Tim	5	H	3	0	0	1	826
Looks Right	2	F	6	0	1	2	6,096
Looks That Kill	5	M	11	1	0	1	9,849
Looks to Run	5	M	4	0	0	0	220
Looksgoodonpaper	9	G	18	2	0	5	18,958
Lookwhosglaring	3	C	2	0	0	0	0
Loomis Trail	5	G	12	2	2	1	3,746
Looney	3	F	17	0	2	2	3,820
Looney Lionel	3	G	17	1	3	7	36,560
Loonie B. Good	6	H	3	0	0	0	176
Loony Chick	4	F	11	0	0	0	2,415
Loophole	5	G	13	1	2	0	6,532
Loosahatchie	3	C	9	1	0	1	14,500
Loose Cash	4	F	9	3	1	2	13,435
Loose Connection	4	F	3	0	0	0	0
Loose Diamonds	3	F	8	1	1	0	5,940
Loose Fun	3	F	1	0	0	0	0
Loose Horse Lisa	4	F	1	0	0	0	0
Loose Knight	9	G	10	2	0	3	15,998
Loose Leotard	8	M	2	0	0	0	0
Loose N Up	3	F	7	1	1	1	8,145
Loose Rhythm	4	C	13	0	0	2	4,133
Loose Wrappings	6	G	6	1	2	0	6,642
Loosecannonondeck	4	F	12	6	2	0	71,590
Looseonthegoose	3	C	3	0	0	0	0
Loosin Screws	3	G	11	1	0	1	37,137
Loot	3	G	1	0	0	1	1,970
Loot N Plunder	4	G	16	6	2	1	43,231
Looter	10	G	6	1	0	1	4,156
Lootshootandboogie	3	C	5	1	1	0	11,157
Loquacious	8	G	6	1	0	1	9,520
Lora's Dream (BRZ)	3	F	7	0	1	3	9,870
Lord Abounding	4	C	7	2	2	0	82,894
Lord Aferd	4	G	8	0	0	0	537
Lord Albert	2	G	3	0	0	2	3,640
Lord Ale	5	G	4	1	1	0	8,860
Lord Alexander	3	G	13	4	3	2	69,563
Lord Aragorn	2	C	1	0	0	0	110
Lord Argyle	5	G	5	0	0	1	420
Lord At Play	4	G	9	0	4	0	12,510
Lord Beckett	4	G	11	0	2	1	17,826
Lord Billy	2	F	7	1	2	1	50,240
Lord Bon (ARG)	5	H	7	1	0	1	16,010
Lord Bonnivard	4	C	2	1	0	0	14,580
Lord Buckley	6	H	10	4	0	3	33,435
Lord Burleigh	4	G	7	4	0	0	71,524
Lord Carmen	2	C	3	0	1	1	9,620
Lord Chivas	3	G	10	4	2	0	30,150
Lord Commando	3	G	5	0	0	1	5,880
Lord Cool	4	G	9	1	0	2	5,219
Lord Dasher	6	H	3	0	0	0	0
Lord de Niro	3	G	12	2	0	1	5,535
Lord de Ville	4	G	5	0	2	2	21,940
Lord Don	10	G	9	0	4	1	14,625
Lord Emulous	3	C	5	0	1	0	2,235
Lord Exitor	4	G	15	4	2	2	25,323
Lord Fhazio	4	G	6	0	1	1	15,260
Lord Foxcroft	3	G	3	0	1	0	4,400
Lord Gandolph	3	C	7	1	0	1	5,773
Lord General	3	G	3	0	1	2	6,300
Lord Gladwin Jazz	5	G	3	0	0	0	287
Lord Gold	5	H	15	3	2	1	15,852
Lord Hamish	5	H	1	0	0	0	63
Lord Hamlet	4	C	2	0	1	0	2,860
Lord Harmony	4	G	15	2	3	3	22,793
Lord Herby	3	G	3	0	0	0	272
Lord Imajones	4	F	9	1	3	1	76,682
Lord Irish Jig	3	C	5	1	0	0	3,648
Lord Jaguar	6	M	1	0	0	0	0
Lord Jersey	3	C	2	0	1	0	8,600
Lord Jim (ARG)	6	H	6	0	0	0	9,460
Lord Jones	3	G	15	2	3	4	89,302
Lord Justin	2	C	4	1	0	0	10,200
Lord Keller	2	G	1	0	0	0	0
Lord Kenmer	4	G	5	1	0	2	8,172
Lord Kenneth	8	H	4	3	1	0	57,000
Lord King	3	G	3	0	0	0	550
Lord Knows	7	G	4	1	0	1	1,915
Lord Kokopelli	3	G	8	1	2	1	19,380
Lord Langfuhr	3	C	5	1	0	1	33,540
Lord Leta	4	C	8	1	2	0	12,423
Lord Lindsay	4	G	5	0	0	0	300
Lord Lionel	3	C	11	1	2	1	32,600
Lord Livermore	5	G	6	3	2	0	28,517
Lord Lloyd Outlaw	5	G	6	2	1	1	19,676
Lord Louis	3	G	9	2	4	1	70,500
Lord Luck	2	G	1	0	0	0	0
Lord Mac Lean	9	H	7	0	0	0	4,941
Lord Malibu	6	G	14	0	0	0	1,064
Lord Mendelson	6	H	3	0	0	0	0
Lord Nelson	6	G	5	2	1	2	161,023
Lord North	3	C	7	1	1	0	31,562
Lord of Ewhurst	5	G	12	0	1	3	6,740
Lord of Hosts	4	G	5	0	0	0	0
Lord of Speed	7	G	11	0	0	1	4,289
Lord of the Cats	2	C	5	1	1	1	23,650
Lord of the Reins	3	C	1	0	0	0	62
Lord of the Storm	5	H	8	2	0	0	3,744
Lord of the Street	4	C	7	0	2	0	5,295
Lord of the Sun	3	G	6	0	0	1	1,800
Lord of the West	4	C	6	1	0	0	2,125
Lord Ofthe Thunder	4	C	7	2	1	2	99,803
Lord Owen	6	H	2	0	1	0	810
Lord Pacal (IRE)	6	G	3	0	0	0	2,400
Lord Pat	4	G	7	0	0	0	1,248
Lord Patton	5	G	10	0	1	0	2,645
Lord Rainman	5	H	11	0	0	2	853

RECORDS OF HORSES

Horse	Age	Sex	Sts	1st	2d	3d	Won	Horse	Age	Sex	Sts	1st	2d	3d	Won
Lord Rambo	3	C	3	0	0	1	5,620	Lost in the Rush	3	F	2	0	0	0	0
Lord Ravenal	7	G	7	1	1	2	8,804	Lost in the Weeds	4	F	2	0	0	0	0
Lord Roanoke	3	G	12	1	1	0	4,212	Lost in the Woods	4	G	12	1	2	2	59,310
Lord Samarai	2	C	5	3	0	0	112,406	Lost in Transit	2	G	2	1	0	0	6,000
Lord Sanford	6	H	6	0	1	1	13,531	Lost Kitty	3	F	3	0	0	0	60
Lord Shogun	4	G	5	0	2	0	14,160	Lost Lariat	5	G	9	1	0	2	5,941
Lord Six	3	C	9	1	1	4	33,250	Lost Liberty	5	G	11	3	3	2	15,579
Lord Stanton	3	C	4	0	0	1	231	Lost Lisa	6	M	1	0	0	0	72
Lord Stephano	9	G	7	0	0	2	2,230	Lost Maid	4	F	3	0	0	1	2,025
Lord Stonewood	3	G	4	1	0	0	17,500	Lost Market	3	C	6	0	2	1	9,330
Lord Sunday	4	G	13	1	0	2	9,243	Lost Message	5	M	1	0	0	0	0
Lord Thomas	4	C	11	0	0	0	174	Lost My Mojo	2	G	3	0	0	0	2,472
Lord Too	4	C	5	0	1	2	9,059	Lost My Thong	3	F	7	1	0	3	2,472
Lord Valentine	7	G	8	0	0	1	2,918	Lost Picture	2	G	3	0	0	0	0
Lord Vilzak	2	G	5	1	0	0	7,441	Lost Pirate	6	G	4	0	1	0	1,650
Lord Wimsey	2	C	3	0	0	0	465	Lost Pistol	6	G	1	0	0	0	58
Lord Zada	10	G	2	1	1	0	48,000	Lost Pride	4	F	3	0	0	0	660
Lord Zotti	5	H	10	1	0	2	6,950	Lost Rainbow	2	C	1	0	0	0	0
Lordlebo N Marylou	2	C	3	0	0	0	898	Lost Recital Iron	7	M	13	0	0	0	1,560
Lord's Delight	5	G	9	0	0	2	1,269	Lost Reservation	3	C	4	2	1	0	23,000
Lord's Idol	4	C	12	4	0	0	53,680	Lost Rivers Mojo	2	C	2	0	1	0	3,680
Lord's Katie	4	F	7	1	1	3	21,205	Lost Rivers Rocket	5	G	12	1	1	4	9,370
Lords Ransom	5	G	8	1	2	1	11,486	Lost Romance	3	F	8	0	0	3	11,887
Lord's Salida	5	M	11	1	4	1	10,390	Lost Time	3	F	15	4	2	1	24,285
Lords Table	3	C	1	0	0	0	420	Lost Wine	6	M	5	0	0	0	1,320
Lordy Lordy Lordy	3	G	8	3	1	2	63,678	Lostcor	4	C	2	0	0	0	0
Loredo Land	2	C	2	1	0	0	11,160	Lostinadream	3	F	1	0	0	0	140
Lorelei's Song	5	M	6	1	1	0	6,810	Lostintheshuffle	4	G	4	0	0	2	6,160
Lorelie's Legacy	4	F	12	1	2	3	4,063	Lostmymaid	3	F	5	0	0	0	1,379
Lorena Maria	3	F	6	0	2	0	8,840	Lostriversprospect	3	F	11	1	1	0	13,343
Lorenchik	2	G	2	0	1	0	1,560	Lot a Smoke	3	F	10	3	2	1	31,205
Loren's Bet	4	C	3	0	0	0	174	Lot Angel	4	C	16	4	3	2	19,193
Loreny Benny	5	M	5	0	0	0	1,950	Lot o' Attitude	5	G	4	0	0	0	474
Lorenzon	2	C	2	1	0	0	8,820	Lot o' Charmin	6	M	2	0	0	0	130
Loretta Lane	3	F	2	0	0	1	1,980	Lot o' Currency	6	M	3	0	0	1	498
Lori Blue Chip	3	F	11	1	1	4	10,970	Lot O Razzledazzle	5	G	7	0	1	2	6,168
Lori M'love	4	F	13	1	4	5	41,825	Lot o' Rim Fire	5	G	12	0	0	1	1,065
Lori N Lynn	3	F	13	2	3	0	25,720	Lot of Hope	4	F	9	4	2	0	14,055
Lori Sue	2	F	6	0	1	1	18,153	Lota Prince	3	G	13	3	0	2	36,555
Lorie's Warrior	9	G	5	0	0	0	350	Lota Spunk	4	G	10	2	1	1	8,358
Lorilyn Is a Lady	3	F	4	1	1	1	9,170	Lotanortherndancer	4	G	8	0	4	0	5,970
Lori's Glory	2	F	2	0	0	0	252	Lothar	4	G	11	0	4	4	46,420
Lori's Last Dance	5	M	2	0	0	1	4,960	Lots Due	3	F	1	0	0	0	0
Lori's Littletrick	2	C	2	0	0	0	240	Lots O Power	4	G	5	1	0	0	7,130
Loris Mine	5	G	6	1	1	0	6,826	Lots of Cash	6	G	12	2	1	2	8,275
Lorraine's Secret	5	G	20	6	3	5	64,843	Lots of Chrome	6	G	19	1	2	6	12,226
Lorrainesvalentine	5	M	7	0	0	1	1,313	Lots of Night	4	F	12	1	0	0	4,668
Los Altos	4	F	4	1	0	0	4,173	Lots of Revenue	3	G	1	0	0	0	0
Los Cabo	8	G	3	0	0	0	47	Lots of Sizzle	3	G	6	1	0	1	29,880
Los Olivos	4	F	15	3	5	0	22,930	Lots of Speed	5	G	4	0	0	1	886
Los Pinos	4	G	11	1	0	1	7,630	Lots of Style	3	F	2	0	0	0	96
Los Solano (GB)	6	G	6	1	0	1	48,240	Lots of Truth	5	G	1	0	0	1	4,320
Lost Again	9	G	5	0	2	1	3,592	Lotsa Class	3	F	2	0	0	0	1,100
Lost Agenda	5	G	8	4	2	0	71,700	Lotsa Grins	3	C	6	1	0	1	5,307
Lost All Control	5	M	11	3	1	0	26,804	Lotsa White	3	F	8	0	0	0	731
Lost and Bound	3	F	7	1	0	2	17,965	Lotsalivin	4	F	9	3	2	1	5,486
Lost and Found	4	F	2	0	1	0	1,360	Lott	4	C	4	2	0	0	52,800
Lost Appeal	5	M	13	6	3	1	161,145	Lotta Dust	6	G	14	3	3	1	14,676
Lost At Sea	4	F	4	0	0	2	21,500	Lotta Glitter	8	M	17	0	4	4	16,890
Lost Bride	2	F	3	1	0	0	12,780	Lotta Hot	4	G	1	0	0	0	0
Lost Brigade	2	C	1	0	0	1	1,560	Lotta Kim	2	F	3	1	2	0	86,485
Lost Caper	4	G	3	1	1	0	14,800	Lotta Laughter	4	F	4	0	0	0	50
Lost Cherokee	2	C	2	0	0	0	2,955	Lotta Lotta	5	M	8	1	0	2	6,137
Lost City	4	G	13	2	0	1	23,758	Lotta Miss	3	F	5	0	0	0	453
Lost Composer	3	F	4	1	0	0	3,843	Lotta Moxee	3	G	6	0	1	1	3,115
Lost Connection	3	G	11	2	2	1	13,226	Lotta Power	4	G	6	0	0	1	1,070
Lost Count	3	C	3	0	1	0	1,555	Lotta Rhythm	4	F	2	1	0	0	21,000
Lost Creek	2	F	4	0	0	1	5,125	Lotta Run	3	F	2	0	0	0	100
Lost Dance	3	F	14	4	2	0	33,530	Lotta Slew	7	G	16	3	3	4	11,535
Lost Dove	2	F	1	0	0	0	120	Lottaballado	7	G	8	0	1	1	1,815
Lost Fact	4	F	10	2	0	1	13,680	Lottanoise	4	G	6	1	2	0	6,115
Lost Faith	5	M	11	1	2	2	2,996	Lottery Luck	3	F	8	2	2	1	46,285
Lost Flamingo	2	F	9	1	1	2	23,970	Lottery Ticket	6	G	17	0	3	0	3,578
Lost Furlough	3	F	7	0	0	0	1,620	Lotto Chips	12	G	9	1	3	1	8,901
Lost Hank	6	H	7	1	1	0	4,527	Lotto Magic	4	G	3	1	0	1	7,350
Lost Her At Dawn	3	G	14	1	1	3	25,853	Lottsa Appeal	4	F	6	0	0	0	2,460
Lost Her Rank	4	F	10	0	0	1	7,030	Lottsa Karakorum	3	F	5	0	0	0	53
Lost in Love	6	G	4	1	0	2	4,153	Lotty Lanyaa	6	M	1	0	0	0	0
Lost in the Music	3	F	13	1	4	2	17,300	Lotus Land	2	F	3	0	1	1	21,424

Horse	Age	Sex	Sts	1st	2d	3d	Won
Lotzakrugerand	3	G	6	1	0	0	4,690
Lou Doc	3	F	10	2	1	1	7,626
Loucille's Risk	3	F	9	1	0	1	5,198
Loud and Silent	4	G	12	1	3	1	19,657
Loudest	2	G	1	0	0	0	900
Loudy	3	F	8	1	0	2	5,810
Lough Conn	7	G	2	0	0	0	550
Loughbeg Rambler (GB)	8	G	5	0	1	1	3,400
Loughmore Lass	4	F	9	1	0	2	15,287
Loughran	3	G	13	0	0	0	1,355
Louie	3	C	10	1	0	2	9,213
Louie Decor	6	H	11	0	0	0	849
Louie Downtown	2	G	8	2	1	0	43,356
Louie Gold	3	G	8	2	0	2	26,946
Louie La Dew	6	H	4	0	0	0	490
Louie Loual	4	C	1	0	0	0	70
Louie Picarello	3	G	4	0	0	0	230
Louie the Jet	5	G	8	0	0	0	1,262
Louie Tune	3	G	4	0	0	1	1,950
Louie's Lady	2	F	3	0	0	0	0
Louie's Lover	4	F	4	0	0	0	687
Louie's Wizard	2	F	1	0	0	0	100
Louis Arthur	6	H	5	3	2	0	17,860
Louis Que	2	G	9	0	4	0	14,091
Louis Quinze	4	G	7	1	1	1	10,612
Louise's Time	6	M	7	0	0	1	3,888
Louisiana Allen	7	G	1	0	0	0	280
Louisiana Brun	2	G	1	0	0	0	0
Louisiana Cotton	3	G	9	2	1	2	14,631
Louisiana Fox	7	G	14	0	2	1	1,221
Louisiana Heat	6	G	1	0	0	0	0
Louisiana Lynda	3	F	3	1	0	0	3,450
Louisiana Storm	6	G	9	0	1	0	2,820
Louisianadecision	3	C	2	0	0	0	0
Loumel Boy	3	G	8	1	1	0	5,150
Loup de Loup	3	G	5	0	1	2	17,600
Loup Longshanks	3	C	8	0	0	0	1,610
Loup Masque (FR)	4	C	7	0	0	0	11,833
Loupe de Mer	5	H	1	0	0	0	0
Loup's Lady Love	3	F	3	0	0	0	1,245
L'Ouragan	2	F	2	0	0	0	0
Lou's Bucks	9	G	3	0	0	0	2,298
Lou's Expectation	4	G	9	6	2	1	148,740
Lous Spirit	3	F	9	2	1	1	32,272
Lov in Excess	5	G	6	0	0	1	1,713
Lovable Kristy	2	F	3	0	0	1	3,720
Lovable Lois	9	M	4	0	1	0	366
Lovable Luther	7	G	1	0	0	0	0
Lovable Trouble	3	F	3	0	0	0	272
Love a Bull	5	M	10	1	0	2	7,215
Love a Lot	2	G	1	0	1	0	5,472
Love Aflair	4	F	2	1	0	0	4,500
Love Again	4	F	2	0	0	0	0
Love All the Way	8	G	4	1	0	2	5,130
Love and Honor	3	C	8	0	0	2	9,845
Love At Sea	5	G	5	1	0	1	14,628
Love Attack	2	C	1	0	0	0	75
Love Bandit	4	G	4	0	0	0	0
Love Chat	3	C	1	0	0	0	0
Love City	3	G	8	2	3	2	48,070
Love Come Quick	5	H	5	0	2	0	2,150
Love Dimaggio	4	G	1	0	0	0	750
Love Em N Leave Em	2	F	2	0	0	0	0
Love Emblem	3	F	4	0	0	1	6,000
Love Eun Sun	4	F	1	0	0	0	375
Love Evermore	4	F	11	4	1	0	20,810
Love Fan	5	M	9	0	0	0	1,007
Love Flight	6	G	4	0	0	0	736
Love for Ali	3	F	5	2	1	0	39,970
Love for Lucy	3	F	7	3	1	2	56,311
Love for Sue	6	H	11	1	0	2	9,085
Love Game	2	C	8	1	2	1	23,195
Love Happy	5	G	7	5	0	0	129,240
Love Hill Lady	2	F	3	0	0	0	0
Love I. D.	3	F	5	0	0	0	510
Love in a Storm	3	G	8	1	0	1	28,221
Love in the Mornin	3	F	3	0	0	0	1,440
Love in Your Eyes	3	F	1	0	1	0	3,200
Love Is Blind (IRE)	3	G	8	0	0	2	11,700
Love Is the Hub	5	G	14	1	2	4	14,957
Love Jasmin	5	M	8	0	3	2	4,928
Love Jet	3	F	15	1	2	4	8,029
Love Johnny	3	F	1	0	0	0	100
Love Kiss	5	M	3	1	0	1	28,812
Love Lane (IRE)	6	G	9	2	1	1	25,480
Love Less	5	G	15	5	3	3	148,035
Love Love	2	G	1	1	0	0	7,800
Love Match	3	F	4	1	0	0	17,770
Love Me Always	2	F	2	0	0	0	270
Love Me Leave Me	3	C	10	0	1	1	13,910
Love Me R Leave Me	4	G	8	1	0	0	4,661
Love Mountain	3	G	10	2	4	1	57,870
Love My Flag	3	F	3	0	0	0	186
Love My Mountain	4	C	9	2	2	1	60,770
Love My Way	3	C	2	0	1	0	6,080
Love n' Kiss S.	5	M	8	3	2	0	152,558
Love N On the Run	6	M	1	0	0	0	0
Love Not War	5	M	16	3	0	2	54,320
Love On Hold	5	M	1	1	0	0	25,800
Love On the Run	2	C	1	0	0	0	3,528
Love One Another	6	M	9	2	1	0	16,795
Love Or Money	2	F	1	0	0	0	990
Love Power	2	F	3	0	1	0	10,665
Love Reigns	3	F	8	1	1	0	4,540
Love Rush	3	F	4	1	1	0	13,007
Love Sam	3	C	12	4	0	1	93,530
Love Shuffle	8	G	6	0	0	1	4,680
Love Sting	3	F	11	4	3	0	172,010
Love Storm	3	F	10	1	3	3	29,550
Love Struck	3	F	10	1	1	1	9,021
Love Sue	2	F	1	0	0	0	0
Love Talkin	4	F	3	2	0	0	58,206
Love Tap	6	M	3	0	0	0	0
Love That Amber	4	F	12	1	1	1	11,452
Love That Duck	9	G	4	2	0	0	6,935
Love That Green	4	G	8	1	0	1	2,675
Love That Lion	5	G	12	3	5	2	93,341
Love That Man	4	G	10	1	0	2	25,290
Love That Moon	4	G	15	5	2	1	208,265
Love That Music	3	C	8	1	2	0	32,720
Love That Punch	4	G	11	1	2	1	13,160
Love That Silver	5	H	3	0	0	0	1,227
Love That Song	2	G	6	0	1	1	6,280
Love That Spice	6	M	8	0	1	1	2,623
Love the 'do	6	M	7	4	0	3	43,615
Love the Game	5	H	8	3	2	1	125,565
Love the Princess	3	F	12	0	4	2	19,140
Love Thing	3	F	3	0	0	0	0
Love Tinks	5	M	8	1	3	1	30,432
Love to Mel	5	M	10	0	3	2	6,162
Love to Play	4	C	1	0	0	0	0
Love to Tango	6	G	10	2	1	3	58,590
Love When You City	3	G	10	1	1	3	8,378
Love You Charlie	6	H	4	0	0	0	185
Love You Dolly	2	F	3	1	0	0	6,180
Love You Madly	3	F	8	2	1	2	48,040
Love You More	4	F	7	1	1	1	1,880
Love Your Mom	3	F	4	1	0	0	4,830
Love Your Whit	3	G	13	3	1	1	34,615
Loveable Mandy	6	M	9	2	1	1	14,793
Loveable Manner	6	M	6	1	0	1	10,882
Loveamericanstile	7	G	7	0	1	2	7,160
Lovehermadly	6	M	13	1	3	2	22,982
Loveland	2	F	3	0	2	0	6,810
Loveliest of All	3	F	7	1	0	2	21,210
Lovell	5	H	4	0	0	0	341
Lovely Afternoon	2	F	6	2	0	2	63,117
Lovely American	3	F	5	0	1	1	4,470
Lovely Bettina	4	F	5	0	0	0	216
Lovely Bonita	4	F	15	3	0	2	31,220
Lovely Breeze	3	F	13	2	4	0	49,490
Lovely Candles	3	F	5	0	0	1	3,165
Lovely Dawn	4	F	1	0	0	0	0
Lovely Diamond	4	F	9	2	1	2	25,100
Lovely Discovery	3	F	11	1	1	2	7,304
Lovely Fiona	3	F	8	5	0	3	146,805
Lovely Fortune	3	F	12	3	2	3	29,952
Lovely G	5	M	4	0	1	0	1,644

RECORDS OF HORSES

Horse	Age	Sex	Sts	1st	2d	3d	Won	Horse	Age	Sex	Sts	1st	2d	3d	Won
Lovely Irish Lady	2	F	5	0	0	1	1,043	Loyal Royal	2	C	5	0	0	0	4,950
Lovely Jessica	7	M	6	0	0	0	1,476	Loyal Spirit	11	G	2	0	0	0	750
Lovely Jolie	3	F	1	0	0	0	70	Loyal Warrior	4	G	5	1	0	0	6,540
Lovely Lauren	4	F	7	1	1	0	6,500	Ls Believeinmagic	2	F	3	0	0	0	1,260
Lovely Lola	2	F	5	0	0	0	1,800	Ls Storming Gypsy	3	G	6	1	0	0	6,675
Lovely Louisia	2	F	9	0	0	1	3,330	Lt Boone	5	G	3	0	0	0	226
Lovely Lu	4	F	8	1	0	2	6,034	Lt Dynalode	4	F	2	0	0	1	280
Lovely Moon	4	F	10	0	2	1	4,643	Lt. Austin	3	C	11	2	3	0	9,910
Lovely n' Elegant	4	F	4	0	0	0	225	Lt. Barbizon	5	G	7	0	0	0	570
Lovely Naski	4	F	8	0	2	0	1,804	Lt. Dolly	6	M	3	0	1	1	1,012
Lovely Navita	6	M	3	0	0	2	1,100	Lt. Lucky	3	G	4	0	0	1	1,718
Lovely Prince	3	G	10	0	2	4	26,021	Lt. Sampson	2	C	1	0	1	0	3,402
Lovely Punch	2	C	2	0	0	0	375	Ltn. Larry	2	G	9	0	1	1	5,760
Lovely Queen	4	F	11	0	1	2	18,741	Lu Lu Ra Ra	3	C	10	1	1	0	15,281
Lovely Rafaela	2	F	3	1	0	0	36,480	Lu Lu's Law	4	F	18	1	3	3	13,913
Lovely Sage	3	F	8	1	2	1	64,130	Lualy	4	G	8	2	0	0	15,000
Lovely Scent	2	F	2	0	0	0	125	Luanne's Gift	4	F	9	0	1	2	7,480
Lovely Secret	3	G	6	1	1	1	15,392	Luau	4	F	4	0	0	0	285
Lovely Slew	3	G	7	2	1	0	8,960	Luby Blue	2	F	3	1	1	1	13,823
Lovely Syn	6	M	4	1	0	1	1,440	Luby Do	7	G	1	0	0	0	0
Lovely Ticket	5	M	7	3	1	1	26,525	Luca Laabity	5	G	14	1	3	3	15,879
Lovely Verse	4	F	8	1	0	1	8,175	Luca Luca	3	C	3	1	0	0	13,500
Lovem and Leavem	2	F	2	0	0	0	1,590	Lucas Creek	6	G	17	0	1	1	3,020
Lovenia	3	F	6	1	2	1	7,304	Lucas Pond	2	F	1	0	1	0	3,600
Lover Boy George	3	G	3	0	0	0	450	Lucayan Chief (IRE)	5	H	3	0	1	0	12,600
Lover Come Back	3	F	1	0	0	0	2,880	Lucayan Indian (IRE)	8	G	9	1	3	2	27,600
Lover Iam	2	G	7	2	2	0	29,865	Lucayan Rodeo	2	F	3	0	1	0	6,930
Lover Jones	3	F	9	0	0	1	8,980	Lucera	2	F	1	0	0	0	0
Lover Man	3	C	27	1	2	1	20,970	Lucerita	2	F	2	0	0	0	2,340
Lover of Mine	2	C	1	0	0	0	0	Lucero de La Noche	4	F	5	0	0	0	61
Loverboy Rebel	5	G	12	0	1	1	1,705	Lucharjon	3	G	4	0	2	1	3,200
Lovergirl	4	F	10	1	0	1	3,133	Luci Fina	3	F	9	0	1	0	4,186
Loverineveryport	6	G	1	0	0	0	375	Lucid	5	M	7	0	2	1	12,200
Lover's Lady	6	M	11	2	0	1	10,455	Lucid Dreamer	3	F	4	0	0	0	290
Lover's Palace	9	G	1	0	0	0	61	Lucid Interval	4	G	2	0	0	0	159
Lover's Price	6	G	11	1	0	1	3,523	Lucie's Bay	2	F	1	0	1	0	4,600
Lovers Son	6	G	14	3	3	2	14,163	Lucie's Lady	3	F	6	1	1	2	18,270
Lover's Vendetta	4	F	6	0	0	0	919	Lucifer's Lady	3	F	8	2	1	1	22,621
Loves a Fight	6	M	11	1	1	1	14,067	Lucifer's Stone	2	F	4	1	1	1	48,844
Love's Journey	3	F	1	0	0	0	0	Lucinda Dancer	6	H	2	0	0	0	0
Loves Palace	4	F	5	0	1	2	4,425	Lucinda's Flight	5	M	11	0	0	0	600
Love's Ponche	4	F	1	0	0	0	84	Luck Arrives	7	H	8	1	3	1	22,690
Love's Princess	4	F	2	0	0	0	345	Luck Be the Lady	4	F	2	0	0	0	0
Love's Strong Hart	2	C	2	1	1	0	19,500	Luck Del Sol	4	G	16	1	3	4	15,515
Lovesmegold	3	F	12	3	2	2	83,159	Luck Liz	3	F	12	2	0	0	8,141
Loveswept Cat	2	F	1	0	0	0	0	Luck My Way	2	F	3	1	0	0	26,140
Lovethatchocolate	4	F	11	1	1	0	7,684	Luck of Jake	4	C	13	2	2	1	19,947
Lovethatlegend	2	F	5	3	1	0	97,372	Luck of the Royal	3	G	8	1	1	1	9,630
Lovetheprospect	2	F	3	0	0	0	870	Luck Out	4	G	8	3	1	0	16,248
Lovetospendabuck	7	G	2	0	0	0	0	Luckalong	2	C	2	0	0	0	210
Lovetotalk	6	G	9	0	0	1	1,532	Luckaplenty	3	C	12	2	0	1	16,140
Lovetrando	4	C	4	1	1	1	4,940	Luckbealadytonight	2	F	3	1	0	0	21,500
Lovetrip	2	F	4	0	0	2	8,220	Luckie Thirteenth	5	M	1	0	0	0	77
Loveuplaindealing	4	F	9	3	1	0	12,072	Luckiestofthelucky	11	G	14	1	2	3	5,778
Lovewillgetya	9	G	10	0	0	1	1,985	Luckman Park	7	G	10	1	1	2	13,126
Lovey Lovey Lovey	9	M	2	0	0	0	280	Luckoftheknight	6	H	14	0	2	1	5,392
Lovin Laurie	3	F	3	1	0	1	7,240	Lucks Lady	9	M	1	0	0	0	0
Lovin' Life	2	C	3	1	0	1	14,730	Luck's Wager	5	G	9	0	2	2	8,330
Lovin Pappa	7	G	14	1	5	3	20,636	Lucks With Me	5	H	9	1	2	2	8,537
Lovin the Sunshine	2	F	11	0	0	2	14,160	Lucky Acres	3	G	5	0	2	1	5,960
Loving (BRZ)	7	G	6	2	0	1	81,285	Lucky Al	6	G	10	0	1	3	3,956
Loving Feeling	3	F	6	2	2	1	40,102	Lucky Alexandra	4	F	6	3	1	1	42,900
Loving Kindness	3	F	2	0	0	0	6,000	Lucky All the Way	7	M	6	0	0	0	187
Loving Lucy	2	F	3	2	0	0	54,249	Lucky Amigo	3	G	3	0	1	0	2,920
Loving Tribute	3	C	1	0	0	0	95	Lucky Amy	10	M	4	0	0	0	84
Loving Type (ARG)	4	C	6	0	0	0	7,960	Lucky Ann	7	F	5	0	0	0	0
Lovingraina	5	M	15	1	6	1	14,965	Lucky At Dawn	3	G	5	1	0	0	24,105
Lov'nue	6	M	8	0	1	2	1,310	Lucky Attempt	5	M	8	0	0	1	4,800
Low Flyin' Jones	2	C	2	0	0	0	0	Lucky Autum	3	F	10	2	2	1	12,724
Low Key Affair	3	F	13	3	4	2	100,086	Lucky Baldwin	5	G	14	2	7	2	52,836
Low Priced	2	C	4	0	0	0	165	Lucky Baroness	6	M	2	0	0	0	990
Low Talker	3	F	7	0	1	2	5,633	Lucky Bartender	2	G	1	0	0	0	156
Lowdowndirtydog	5	H	7	3	1	1	37,063	Lucky Basket	4	F	6	0	4	1	2,640
Lowell's Legacy	2	C	5	0	1	0	6,020	Lucky Bluff	5	G	11	1	1	1	6,810
Lowflyinpidgeon	3	G	6	0	0	1	914	Lucky Bob	3	G	4	0	0	1	914
Lowflyzone	6	G	16	3	4	3	9,571	Lucky Bohemian	7	H	10	2	1	1	25,838
Loyal American	5	M	3	0	0	1	3,194	Lucky Boss	10	G	11	0	0	3	1,980
Loyal Buddy	4	G	3	1	0	0	5,420	Lucky Bounty	4	C	4	0	2	2	1,402
Loyal Deputy	3	C	6	0	0	0	3,920	Lucky Buckley	3	G	10	0	0	1	3,155

Horse	Age	Sex	Sts	1st	2d	3d	Won	Horse	Age	Sex	Sts	1st	2d	3d	Won
Lucky Bucky	6	H	7	0	0	0	550	Lucky Lynnsay	5	M	7	1	1	0	13,523
Lucky Call	5	H	11	0	0	1	1,703	Lucky M	4	F	7	2	4	0	48,700
Lucky Carley	4	F	5	1	0	1	10,200	Lucky Magus	3	G	11	4	0	2	59,090
Lucky Catch	3	C	5	0	0	0	249	Lucky Man Reality	7	H	3	0	0	0	246
Lucky Chap	3	C	2	1	1	0	21,140	Lucky Margaret	2	F	3	0	0	0	182
Lucky Charleen	3	F	8	1	2	1	22,190	Lucky Mariah	3	F	3	0	0	0	0
Lucky Charm's Jet	5	G	10	1	1	2	15,562	Lucky Mark	3	G	6	0	0	0	418
Lucky Chick	3	F	8	1	0	1	11,450	Lucky Melody	5	M	3	1	0	0	2,587
Lucky Chip	5	G	13	4	0	4	61,830	Lucky Millennium	3	F	7	2	0	1	28,815
Lucky Clone	6	H	4	1	1	0	6,680	Lucky Miss Lark	4	F	5	1	1	1	2,680
Lucky Clover	6	H	11	1	1	1	6,058	Lucky Mister K	5	H	13	0	1	0	2,664
Lucky Clue	3	G	2	0	0	1	4,980	Lucky Molar	8	G	7	1	0	1	36,090
Lucky Comstock	4	G	8	0	0	0	665	Lucky Mount	2	C	3	0	0	0	305
Lucky Creation	2	C	4	1	0	1	42,780	Lucky Mudd	5	G	8	2	0	2	20,715
Lucky Creek	5	G	10	2	0	0	9,856	Lucky n' Foxy	4	F	2	0	0	0	210
Lucky Currency	9	M	17	1	3	1	7,782	Lucky Niner	4	F	10	0	0	0	1,039
Lucky Date	6	M	12	2	2	3	42,415	Lucky Nora B	5	M	3	0	0	0	122
Lucky Dazzler	3	F	10	1	1	2	49,552	Lucky November	2	F	3	0	1	0	3,434
Lucky Devil	5	H	1	1	0	0	27,000	Lucky O'Kelly	2	C	1	0	0	0	100
Lucky Dice	4	G	8	2	3	1	26,530	Lucky Old Sun	5	G	3	0	0	2	16,862
Lucky Dunant	5	G	1	0	0	1	260	Lucky Ole'	5	M	15	1	1	1	5,805
Lucky Dynahoosier	6	G	13	2	2	2	13,587	Lucky Ole Roan	2	G	2	0	0	0	285
Lucky Eleven	3	F	7	1	2	1	17,070	Lucky Patriot	5	G	5	2	0	0	10,885
Lucky Ending	4	F	13	3	2	1	20,449	Lucky Paul	2	G	2	1	0	0	7,200
Lucky Expectations	2	C	2	1	1	0	37,000	Lucky Paws	8	M	8	0	1	0	10,060
Lucky Explosion	2	G	4	1	0	2	12,875	Lucky Pioneer	5	G	11	1	2	3	5,720
Lucky Fab	3	F	10	0	0	2	5,931	Lucky Pogo	6	G	6	0	0	1	951
Lucky Fern	2	F	3	1	0	0	40,481	Lucky Pollock	5	G	14	2	0	1	5,260
Lucky Fib	3	F	3	0	0	0	309	Lucky Prince	5	G	8	3	1	0	16,783
Lucky Flight	7	G	6	2	0	0	5,469	Lucky Prize	8	G	4	0	1	0	441
Lucky Folly	5	M	13	1	1	2	8,106	Lucky Pulpit	2	C	6	2	2	1	95,260
Lucky Fourteen	4	F	1	0	0	0	340	Lucky Punch	5	H	4	1	0	1	8,640
Lucky Gamble	2	C	5	0	0	3	9,260	Lucky Quinn	4	G	2	0	0	0	290
Lucky Gambler	2	F	2	0	0	0	780	Lucky Quixote	3	C	10	4	0	3	53,020
Lucky George	4	G	7	1	1	1	11,130	Lucky Remruck	5	G	13	0	1	0	5,800
Lucky Gift	3	C	1	0	0	0	0	Lucky Ride	5	H	3	0	0	0	880
Lucky Gracie	3	F	5	0	0	1	2,490	Lucky Roberta	2	F	4	0	0	2	10,105
Lucky Guy	2	C	9	0	3	0	14,360	Lucky Ruckus	3	F	6	2	0	0	11,117
Lucky Heidi	3	F	11	1	0	1	3,119	Lucky Ryan	2	C	2	0	0	0	0
Lucky Hold	4	G	1	0	0	0	0	Lucky Ryder	5	H	21	1	0	0	6,949
Lucky Hooch	4	C	4	1	1	1	5,645	Lucky Sabre	3	F	8	1	4	2	79,125
Lucky Hugh	5	G	13	1	2	3	10,746	Lucky Sam	5	H	18	4	3	1	41,332
Lucky in Love	4	F	10	2	1	3	90,600	Lucky Sand	4	G	13	1	1	2	8,681
Lucky in the Lead	2	F	4	0	1	1	4,245	Lucky Sand Dancer	3	C	9	0	2	0	5,945
Lucky Irish Jewell	5	M	9	1	0	2	4,376	Lucky Sandman	8	G	9	2	2	2	20,707
Lucky J J	6	H	10	2	4	1	43,512	Lucky Scarab	5	G	6	2	2	0	94,560
Lucky Jim R	4	G	13	2	1	1	19,800	Lucky Scribe	4	G	16	3	1	6	32,620
Lucky John T	2	C	3	0	0	0	0	Lucky Signal	4	F	10	1	3	0	55,440
Lucky June	4	F	11	2	1	1	13,191	Lucky Sixes	2	C	3	0	0	0	175
Lucky Kaye	3	F	7	3	0	1	14,870	Lucky Slam	2	C	2	0	1	1	9,050
Lucky Kelly	2	F	4	0	0	2	4,324	Lucky Son of a Gun	5	G	9	0	0	0	460
Lucky Koo	2	F	2	0	0	0	0	Lucky Spin	2	C	2	0	0	0	0
Lucky Krew's	3	C	5	1	1	1	2,698	Lucky Spirit	4	F	8	1	4	2	83,590
Lucky Lady Go	5	M	4	0	0	1	1,088	Lucky Star Baby	6	M	9	2	1	1	11,820
Lucky Lady Liz	3	F	16	2	3	1	28,110	Lucky Streak	3	F	10	0	0	0	2,645
Lucky Lady Slew	3	F	18	1	2	3	6,771	Lucky Strike King	3	G	5	0	1	0	3,225
Lucky Lake	5	H	1	0	0	0	0	Lucky Sucre	4	F	2	0	0	0	2,700
Lucky Laki	4	G	5	0	0	1	200	Lucky Sweep	7	G	1	0	0	0	128
Lucky Landis	3	C	14	0	4	2	7,963	Lucky Tec	5	G	10	3	2	1	87,454
Lucky Laredo	3	G	4	1	1	0	12,075	Lucky Tee	2	C	2	1	0	0	12,150
Lucky Larue	3	G	9	1	2	4	36,433	Lucky They Call Me	4	G	14	3	3	1	40,480
Lucky Last Magic	3	F	9	2	0	1	12,407	Lucky Thirty	5	M	4	0	0	1	1,098
Lucky Lefty	2	F	3	1	1	0	36,672	Lucky Ticket	3	G	12	2	1	3	37,330
Lucky Lemon	3	F	1	1	0	0	3,960	Lucky Tie	2	C	1	0	0	0	400
Lucky Leo	2	G	5	0	2	0	6,455	Lucky to Repeat	4	G	2	1	0	0	4,882
Lucky Lief	3	C	8	0	2	1	25,788	Lucky Tom	3	G	8	2	1	4	123,481
Lucky Lil Choice	5	G	3	0	0	0	122	Lucky Triple	2	F	1	0	0	0	0
Lucky Li'l Imp	3	F	13	3	2	1	21,816	Lucky Tunnel	2	F	10	2	3	2	33,570
Lucky Lily	3	F	6	1	1	1	18,556	Lucky Turk	3	F	15	1	2	3	37,820
Lucky Lisa	3	F	4	0	0	1	2,599	Lucky Twosome	4	G	2	0	0	0	204
Lucky Little Guy	6	H	1	0	0	0	136	Lucky Valid	4	F	13	2	1	2	57,325
Lucky Little Lady	7	M	2	0	0	0	330	Lucky Wille C	4	G	7	1	0	1	9,671
Lucky Lloyd	5	G	12	0	0	1	2,099	Lucky Winner	6	M	4	0	0	0	0
Lucky Locomotion	4	G	4	0	4	0	11,290	Lucky Wish	3	F	13	1	6	1	35,210
Lucky Lookalike	3	F	8	1	0	1	3,748	Lucky Z	4	C	8	0	0	2	1,550
Lucky Louise	3	F	17	2	5	2	30,428	Luckyd	4	G	6	2	1	2	16,184
Lucky Luciano	3	G	6	1	1	0	2,420	Luckyemilycharm	2	F	1	0	0	0	0
Lucky Lucky Me	3	G	4	0	0	0	970	Luckyetta	4	F	2	0	0	0	420
Lucky Lure	2	G	2	0	1	0	12,120	Luckylicious	2	F	1	0	0	0	75

RECORDS OF HORSES

Horse	Age	Sex	Sts	1st	2d	3d	Won	Horse	Age	Sex	Sts	1st	2d	3d	Won
Luckymata	3	C	4	1	1	0	9,920	Lunar Explosion	3	F	4	0	0	2	2,365
Luckynfast	3	C	8	1	1	0	7,022	Lunar Lad	2	G	4	1	0	1	8,115
Luckynquick	2	G	6	1	0	1	16,883	Lunar Mon	4	G	9	1	4	0	71,020
Luckyto Havepapers	2	F	1	0	0	0	0	Lunar Orbit	6	M	9	1	1	1	7,115
Luckyustoo	4	G	13	0	3	2	6,450	Lunar Perigee	3	G	6	0	0	0	3,750
Lucy Angelicus	3	F	11	2	0	1	54,870	Lunar Power	2	C	2	0	0	1	2,320
Lucy Belle	2	F	1	0	1	0	960	Lunar Prospect	4	G	6	2	0	0	15,240
Lucy Belle B B	3	F	4	0	0	2	4,091	Lunar Secret	5	G	9	1	2	1	43,250
Lucy Bliss	4	F	1	0	0	0	0	Lunar Sovereign	4	C	7	2	0	1	410,000
Lucy Can Matach	4	F	4	0	1	0	2,100	Lunar Star	6	M	4	0	0	0	2,450
Lucy Darling	4	F	7	1	0	2	22,070	Lunar Storms	2	F	2	0	0	0	390
Lucy Does the Hula	6	M	10	3	2	2	23,826	Lunar Surprise	7	M	9	0	0	4	17,760
Lucy Glen	4	F	9	2	1	1	41,562	Lunarco	3	G	9	3	2	1	84,390
Lucy I'm Home	3	G	7	0	2	1	35,574	Lunaskra	5	H	15	2	1	1	10,219
Lucy Lettuce	2	F	3	0	0	0	230	Lunatic Fringe	4	F	2	0	0	0	657
Lucy Lightning	6	M	3	1	0	0	3,150	Lunch At T's	2	G	5	1	0	1	16,800
Lucy Loup	2	F	2	0	1	0	3,800	Lunch Bunch	3	C	5	0	1	0	11,385
Lucy Lu Wee	3	F	4	0	1	1	5,074	Lunch Honey	6	M	6	0	0	1	1,738
Lucyoso	5	M	13	3	0	2	9,759	Lune d'Argent	4	F	8	0	1	0	2,825
Lucy's a Pleasure	5	M	18	1	1	3	7,788	Lunelle's Pride	4	F	10	2	1	2	11,678
Lucy's Cat	4	F	8	1	0	0	5,400	Lunes Grito	2	F	3	0	3	0	7,130
Lucy's Got Rocks	4	F	19	1	3	3	7,933	Luneta Drive	4	F	11	0	0	1	2,520
Lucy's Our Hero	4	F	2	0	0	0	488	Lunette	5	M	7	1	0	1	7,550
Lucy's Ride	3	F	11	2	1	4	13,584	L'Unica Halo	4	F	4	0	0	2	1,743
Ludicrous Speed	4	G	6	3	1	2	64,380	Lupa	4	F	14	4	1	5	20,059
Ludovicus	7	G	5	0	1	0	5,200	Luray Louise	10	M	12	2	2	2	24,057
Luft	5	G	11	4	1	0	42,810	Lure Cat	4	G	2	0	0	0	136
Luga	2	G	3	1	2	0	26,000	Lure of Gold	2	F	5	1	0	0	29,280
Luganis	3	C	11	3	2	1	66,267	Lure of the Links	3	G	4	0	0	0	1,350
Luger	4	C	18	2	2	1	41,510	Lure Till Dawn	6	M	6	1	0	0	3,334
Lugny (FR)	5	H	8	1	0	1	56,180	Lu's Reality Point	2	C	4	0	0	1	1,490
Lugu Lake	5	M	3	0	0	0	0	Lu's Signal	4	C	1	0	0	0	300
Luis Alfonzo	3	C	13	1	0	2	4,440	Lusby	3	F	3	0	2	0	14,340
Luisathebeachhouse	2	F	1	0	0	0	0	Lush	7	H	20	1	5	0	16,501
Lujean	8	H	4	0	0	0	795	Lush Soldier	4	F	2	0	0	0	17,500
Lukanela	4	F	13	4	1	2	27,815	Lusheba	2	C	1	0	0	0	0
Luke	3	C	15	3	1	0	40,824	Lusi Pond	2	F	4	1	1	0	34,030
Luke and Jake	5	G	17	3	2	4	35,590	Lust for Green	4	F	12	2	3	0	22,809
Luke At Me Now	3	F	2	0	0	0	272	Lustrous Runner	9	G	8	5	1	1	24,045
Luke Hill	4	C	3	0	0	0	1,170	Lusty American	6	G	12	0	1	1	2,913
Luke in My Pocket	3	G	3	1	1	0	50,895	Lusty Guy	3	C	1	0	0	0	0
Luke Is Cool	5	H	9	2	1	0	5,782	Lusty Kelly	2	F	6	2	0	1	36,100
Luke the Great	11	G	3	1	0	0	3,933	Lusty Latin	4	C	7	0	0	0	6,084
Luken Boss	3	G	10	1	2	2	7,994	Lutece	4	F	13	0	0	5	3,712
Lukers Nativetexan	7	M	1	0	0	0	0	Luther	3	G	6	0	0	0	5,500
Luke's Finest	2	F	2	0	2	0	6,800	Luther Jr	3	G	5	2	1	0	10,920
Lukes Rapid Dash	3	G	3	0	0	0	1,572	Luther Wayne	3	G	13	0	0	1	3,524
Luke's Way	8	G	15	4	1	2	30,240	Luttie's Devil	7	M	11	0	0	2	4,125
Lukfata Cowboy	3	C	3	0	2	0	11,400	Lutz Exchange	3	G	12	0	4	1	10,866
Lukfata Louis	3	C	5	1	0	0	18,600	Luv Dat Gal	3	F	9	1	1	0	11,126
Luksor	6	G	3	0	1	0	1,842	Luv George	2	C	1	0	0	0	126
Lulabell	3	F	8	1	0	2	11,302	Luv Jack N Coke	6	G	6	0	0	0	0
Lullaby League	4	F	4	1	1	1	28,870	Luv Machine	5	M	3	0	0	0	146
Lulu Lemon	2	F	1	0	0	0	0	Luv Saint Ballado	4	C	1	0	0	0	0
Lulu Rose	4	F	7	1	2	1	9,383	Luv U Lady	3	F	2	0	0	0	780
Lulu Tunes	3	F	1	0	0	0	550	Luv U Me	6	M	6	0	2	1	6,610
Lulua	2	F	2	0	0	0	0	Luv Ya Big	2	F	3	0	1	0	4,634
Lulu's Chance	3	F	1	0	0	0	103	Luvagoodjoke	3	G	12	1	1	1	14,439
Lulu's Dream	4	F	8	2	0	0	29,880	Luvah Girl (GB)	3	F	1	1	0	0	66,480
Lulu's Love	6	M	17	1	0	2	6,023	Luvbnme	3	C	8	0	2	0	7,817
Lulu's Luck	2	C	6	0	0	0	1,535	Luvgetsmeeverytime	6	M	3	0	2	1	26,190
Lulu's Way	7	M	11	1	0	1	4,305	Luvinbillyiseasy	6	G	14	5	3	1	50,015
Lum Dee Dee	4	F	6	0	1	1	6,248	Luvinheriseasi	4	F	11	0	0	4	12,692
Lumberjack	3	G	7	0	2	0	9,460	Luvnluk	3	G	13	2	0	2	40,050
Lumiere Sprout (ARG)	5	G	10	0	1	1	12,760	Luvole'	4	F	3	0	0	0	0
Luminance	3	F	4	0	2	1	22,440	Luv's Gold	3	F	7	1	1	0	8,310
Lumineuse	3	F	1	0	0	0	0	Luvthat' Jackie	2	F	1	0	0	0	350
Luminism	7	H	5	2	0	0	10,298	Luvthedance	3	F	9	1	1	1	8,192
Lumpy	4	C	4	0	0	0	56	Luvtowatchimgroove	3	G	2	0	0	0	678
Lumpy Rutherford	5	G	17	5	0	1	44,714	Luvyoudad	3	G	5	0	0	0	3,000
Luna Gail Echo	3	G	5	0	1	1	4,095	Luxana	4	F	11	2	1	0	12,862
Luna Joe	5	G	12	1	0	2	13,775	Luxor	4	G	7	2	1	1	27,244
Luna Lace	5	M	5	0	0	0	0	Luxulyan	5	H	7	2	1	0	17,920
Luna Mundial (ARG)	6	M	1	0	0	0	0	Luxuponus	5	G	8	0	0	1	1,514
Luna Rainbow	2	F	8	0	0	0	902	Luxurious Cat	3	F	3	0	1	0	2,450
Lunacy (IRE)	4	F	4	0	0	0	5,200	Luxury Flight	2	F	4	1	2	0	34,680
Lunar Attack	3	F	7	3	1	0	35,590	Luxury Leader	9	G	3	0	1	0	920
Lunar Bay	2	F	3	0	2	1	15,050	Luxury Line	3	G	10	0	0	2	1,694
Lunar Bounty	4	G	4	0	1	1	9,640								

Horse	Age	Sex	Sts	1st	2d	3d	Won
Luxury Madness	4	G	7	0	0	0	489
Luxury Suite	4	F	2	0	0	0	2,100
Luz de Esperanza	7	G	11	2	1	0	20,370
Luz Lane	4	G	6	1	1	2	41,170
Luzern	3	C	13	5	4	0	72,225
Lx Commander	3	C	10	5	0	1	92,094
Lycius Darlin	2	F	5	0	0	0	805
Lycius Two	2	G	5	1	0	1	10,810
Lycka	6	H	16	3	0	2	16,982
Lyda Match	4	C	4	0	0	0	375
Lyde Award	2	G	4	0	0	0	1,062
Lydgate	3	C	5	1	2	0	39,700
Lydia A	5	M	4	0	0	0	420
Lydia Rosa	3	F	4	0	0	0	0
Lydia's Legacy	3	G	17	4	6	3	23,786
Lydiaswild	3	F	11	2	2	2	15,819
Lyd's a Winnah	4	F	15	2	3	2	28,740
Lyin Goddess	2	F	1	1	0	0	23,750
Lyin Jim	7	G	4	0	1	1	4,250
Lying Blue Eyes	3	C	4	0	2	1	5,445
Lying Eyes	6	M	10	0	0	0	2,331
Lyka Speedy	2	C	2	0	1	0	2,520
Lyle Lovesit	5	G	5	1	0	0	16,410
Lylee's Gold	6	M	1	0	0	0	0
Lyles Station	4	G	3	0	0	0	148
Lylle	4	F	2	0	0	0	221
Lymical	7	G	7	1	0	2	17,080
Lyncola (CHI)	5	M	12	1	1	4	80,060
Lynda Dee	8	M	5	0	0	1	909
Lynda Lucky	3	F	2	0	0	0	0
Lynda's Lady	9	M	1	0	0	0	0
Lyndee Jo	3	F	6	1	0	1	6,202
Lynhurst	3	G	16	1	0	0	3,950
Lynn's Halo	3	G	9	0	0	1	5,055
Lynn's Song	2	F	6	1	1	2	13,445
Lynn's Tour	6	G	10	1	1	0	11,013
Lyns Kissing Star	6	M	1	0	0	0	0
Lyn's Trinity	4	F	14	2	1	0	17,400
Lyphard Cat	3	G	6	0	0	0	455
Lypheor's Pirate	8	G	5	0	3	1	2,388
Lyphiano	6	H	16	3	7	3	18,526
Lypin Rivers	3	G	4	0	0	0	123
Lyracist	7	H	9	3	1	1	91,630
Lyre	6	H	7	1	0	0	5,256
Lyre Friend	4	C	4	1	0	0	4,950
Lyre's Peak	4	C	9	0	1	0	2,505
Lyric	4	F	1	0	0	0	300
Lyrical Fantasy	4	F	13	0	1	0	2,447
Lyrical Prado	4	F	9	1	2	2	57,790
Lyrical Song	3	C	1	0	0	0	0
Lysander	9	G	1	0	0	0	100
Lytle Creek	6	G	12	5	4	3	98,200
M and M Special	8	G	3	0	0	0	177
M B Little John	2	G	1	0	0	0	90
M B Sea	4	C	12	2	2	1	197,386
M C Squared	7	G	9	2	1	1	39,235
M D Twenty Twenty	2	C	3	0	0	1	2,754
M D's Moondancer	4	G	15	2	1	4	19,479
M J in the Morning	4	F	10	3	0	2	19,425
M Js Shady Dawn	4	F	5	0	0	0	1,575
M K Victor	2	C	3	0	1	0	5,671
M' lady's Honour	7	M	4	0	0	0	190
M' Lord	8	G	8	0	0	1	2,501
M R Hugs	4	F	6	0	0	1	2,260
M R Kisses	4	F	11	1	1	2	9,125
M Town	2	G	2	2	0	0	26,820
M. C. Halo	2	F	2	0	0	0	0
M. C.'s Pride	5	M	10	2	1	0	10,531
M. G. Ransom	3	G	1	0	0	0	498
M. H. Spirit	3	G	9	1	0	1	4,737
M. Jay Hawk	2	G	4	0	1	1	3,590
M. O's Dance	5	H	2	0	0	0	170
M. P. Cat	2	C	1	0	0	0	0
M. R. Books	3	G	7	2	0	0	16,533
M. R. Quick	6	H	2	0	0	0	432
M. S. Balkhair	4	G	1	0	1	0	5,200
Ma B	5	G	4	0	0	0	55
Ma Come Pretendi	2	F	7	1	2	2	21,645
Ma Femme	5	M	7	2	0	0	90,360
Ma Ma Lois	4	F	3	0	0	0	0
Ma Moutski	3	F	5	0	0	0	902
Ma Noblesse (ARG)	4	F	1	0	0	0	3,060
Ma Paloma	3	F	1	0	0	0	0
Ma Peche	3	F	2	0	0	0	0
Ma Tuohey	5	M	21	1	0	1	5,812
Mabel Kent	5	M	7	0	3	2	47,320
Mabelino	3	F	6	2	3	0	46,710
Mabilis Lady	4	F	6	1	1	0	5,841
Mabrak	5	H	2	0	0	0	132
Mabrooka Haviva	2	F	2	0	1	0	3,200
Mac a Do	3	G	10	0	0	1	2,560
Mac Balu	7	M	10	1	1	0	5,546
Mac Daddy	2	G	3	0	1	0	5,635
Mac George	6	G	3	0	1	0	1,900
Mac Justice	5	G	9	0	1	1	9,819
Mac Lady	4	F	9	5	1	1	61,237
Mac Melody (IRE)	3	F	7	0	1	0	13,975
Mac the Twister	3	G	9	0	1	0	2,814
Macaneo (ARG)	6	G	1	0	0	0	660
Macann's Promise	2	F	3	0	0	2	7,386
Macaquerie	6	G	15	2	0	2	16,956
Macarita	3	F	2	0	1	1	638
Maca's Last	9	G	5	0	0	0	130
Macatawa Bay	4	C	12	2	0	3	47,030
Macauley Gold	3	G	7	0	3	1	15,620
Macaw (IRE)	4	G	9	0	4	1	496,500
Macbird	3	G	4	0	1	0	3,848
Macbrae	2	G	5	2	2	0	32,010
Macchiato (FR)	3	C	1	0	1	0	11,200
Maccool	8	G	4	0	0	1	520
Macdashi	3	F	7	1	1	1	80,998
Macdavid	5	G	12	0	1	1	2,882
Macduff	2	G	5	1	0	0	15,042
Macgillicuddy	4	C	13	2	0	1	24,170
Macgrath	3	C	1	0	0	0	600
Mach Myth	6	H	8	0	1	2	3,042
Mach Ones Girl	2	F	8	0	2	0	2,476
Mach Speed	2	C	3	1	1	0	44,121
Mach Two	4	C	10	3	0	2	42,964
Machaera	2	C	1	0	0	1	2,123
Machiavelli	6	H	6	0	0	0	398
Machine to Tower	7	G	10	1	3	3	30,535
Machinegunmoutandy	3	C	7	0	2	1	20,890
Macho Bean	4	G	9	0	1	0	5,036
Macho Boss	4	G	11	2	0	0	10,166
Macho Bronco	9	G	4	0	0	0	176
Macho Gato	2	C	5	0	3	0	6,705
Macho Image	3	C	7	2	0	1	41,400
Macho Mana	6	G	7	1	0	0	5,277
Macho Miller	2	C	4	0	2	2	11,077
Macho Moment	10	G	7	0	0	0	156
Macho Rullah	2	C	1	0	0	0	100
Mack Be Quick	5	G	3	0	1	0	1,384
Mackaroon	2	C	4	0	0	0	332
Mackay Man	4	C	4	1	0	2	5,626
Mackeemade	4	G	5	0	0	2	975
Mackee's Wish	4	G	8	3	2	0	19,733
Mackenzie Elaine	6	M	2	0	0	0	97
Mackenzie Mist	3	F	1	0	0	0	0
Mackenzie Ridge	3	F	1	0	0	0	56
Mackinaw Bay	3	C	1	0	0	0	0
Mackinaw City	3	G	3	0	0	0	0
Mackinaw Island	2	F	3	0	0	1	3,260
Mackintosh	3	C	3	0	0	0	500
Macklin	4	G	1	0	0	0	119
Macks Mardi Graw	3	C	1	0	0	0	0
Macks Pleasure	4	G	7	2	0	2	9,900
Mack's World	5	M	3	0	2	0	10,200
Mackscode	6	G	10	1	0	1	9,366
Maclamor	4	C	3	0	0	0	94
Macmania	2	F	1	0	0	0	2,460
Macon County	4	C	3	0	0	1	5,340
Macon Dale	3	F	12	1	0	1	8,830
Macon's Magic	3	G	8	0	0	3	4,080
Macrogold	5	M	10	1	2	2	7,336
Macrorie	3	F	3	0	0	0	809
Mac's Flier	3	C	10	1	1	1	10,570
Mac's Ghost	9	H	10	1	4	0	12,791

RECORDS OF HORSES

Horse	Age	Sex	Sts	1st	2d	3d	Won	Horse	Age	Sex	Sts	1st	2d	3d	Won
Mac's Gold Deposit	4	C	6	2	0	0	12,670	Maddy's Partner	3	F	16	2	2	2	17,267
Mac's Golden Lad	3	G	3	0	3	0	7,500	Made Cents	3	G	8	2	0	2	11,283
Mac's Hope	3	C	3	0	0	0	0	Made for Taylor	3	C	5	0	1	0	6,005
Mac's Last Bucko	4	G	22	1	2	1	9,159	Made in America	2	F	2	1	1	0	5,680
Mac's Mark	7	G	15	2	4	3	16,871	Made in Marakesh	4	F	5	0	0	0	69
Mactaquac	12	G	15	2	0	4	25,503	Made in Nebraska	3	F	1	0	0	0	0
Macward	7	G	15	1	5	3	111,327	Made Ja Look	4	F	6	0	1	0	3,060
Macy B.	4	F	11	1	0	1	14,498	Made Nice	3	C	9	0	1	1	10,171
Macy Ducey	5	M	2	1	0	0	4,310	Made the Basket	3	G	10	0	0	1	860
Macy's Boy	3	G	13	2	4	0	16,034	Madeira Mist (IRE)	4	F	7	2	3	1	198,950
Mad About Julie	4	F	6	1	0	0	15,232	Madeittothemoon	6	G	7	1	0	1	8,740
Mad Anthony	4	C	8	2	1	0	45,240	Madelaine	4	F	4	0	0	0	1,840
Mad Banshee	2	F	4	0	0	0	470	Madeleine's Charm	6	H	2	0	0	0	45
Mad Dash Manastash	2	C	2	0	0	0	320	Madeleine's Jade	6	G	14	2	5	1	37,527
Mad Dog	5	G	2	0	0	0	0	Madeline's Manor	2	F	9	1	1	3	35,017
Mad Donna	3	F	11	1	1	1	16,300	Madera Canyon	5	M	3	0	0	1	1,300
Mad Kipper	5	G	8	0	0	1	2,574	Madge's Prize	2	F	5	0	1	3	7,160
Mad Mac	4	G	14	5	0	2	48,594	Madiera	4	F	8	2	0	0	67,980
Mad Man Max	3	G	2	0	0	0	197	Madigan	4	G	12	2	2	1	6,823
Mad Money Maggie	3	F	1	0	0	0	80	Madilynreign	3	F	2	0	0	0	900
Mad Native	3	C	9	0	2	0	7,013	Madi's Magic	5	M	7	2	1	0	7,046
Mad River	7	G	3	0	3	0	4,950	Madisen Kay	3	F	1	0	0	0	0
Mad Salad	3	G	2	0	1	1	704	Madison Davis	5	M	13	2	1	5	51,700
Mad Season	6	G	12	1	1	2	13,156	Madison Muffin	7	M	4	0	0	0	250
Madaboutloot	3	F	8	2	0	0	8,986	Madison Pike	3	C	4	2	1	0	12,860
Madalee	2	C	2	0	0	0	0	Madison Ridge	3	F	1	0	0	0	0
Madam Bahri	2	F	8	2	0	2	37,670	Madison Wolf	3	G	3	0	0	0	325
Madam General	3	F	5	1	2	0	47,240	Madison's Big Step	5	M	13	0	2	1	5,900
Madam Hertfield	3	F	7	1	0	0	20,890	Madisons Coin	6	M	4	0	0	0	180
Madam Kipper	4	F	18	3	2	3	46,739	Madison's Deal	4	F	9	0	0	0	676
Madam Mariko	4	F	7	1	0	2	7,492	Madison's Music	2	F	1	0	0	0	145
Madam Mud	4	F	5	0	1	1	2,125	Madison's Pleasure	5	M	5	1	0	0	9,280
Madam Nightingale	3	F	9	2	1	1	69,396	Madison's Wish	2	F	1	0	0	0	2,700
Madam P.	3	F	6	1	2	2	25,850	Madlyn Elise	2	F	7	0	1	0	5,504
Madam Persuasive	6	M	11	1	1	3	17,112	Madman Jones	5	G	3	0	1	0	2,136
Madam Rochas	4	F	5	0	0	2	12,600	Madringa	3	F	10	1	2	2	56,680
Madam Speaker	3	F	5	3	0	0	64,683	Madrone	2	F	1	1	0	0	15,400
Madam Spy	4	F	5	0	0	0	413	Mae and Ree	3	F	5	1	0	0	17,160
Madam Toolighsboy	2	C	2	0	0	0	2,262	Mae Be Kate	4	F	5	1	0	0	7,650
Madam War	4	F	4	0	0	0	473	Mae Forces	3	F	2	0	0	0	86
Madam Whozit	4	F	10	0	0	0	805	Mae Hap	3	F	5	1	1	1	36,655
Madame Boulangere (GB)	4	F	4	0	0	1	12,180	Mae Rules	2	F	3	0	1	0	4,925
Madame Cerito	4	F	3	1	0	0	34,972	Maelo	2	C	7	0	0	0	580
Madame Chat	2	F	1	0	0	1	1,210	Mae's Choice	6	M	8	2	2	2	10,101
Madame Commish	4	F	2	1	0	0	2,825	Mae's Mon	4	F	9	0	1	3	8,900
Madame Currie	2	F	5	0	1	0	3,326	Maestro's Debut	6	G	4	1	1	0	13,415
Madame Express	4	F	8	1	1	1	6,981	Maevadi	5	M	6	0	1	1	16,940
Madame Galore	2	F	1	0	0	0	0	Maeve the Rave	4	F	3	1	0	1	12,450
Madame Glamour	4	F	9	3	1	0	50,030	Maeve's Summer Sun	6	M	2	0	0	0	428
Madame Janette	3	F	10	3	1	1	24,082	Mafia Wife	6	M	13	2	2	3	19,478
Madame Midway	6	M	10	1	1	2	7,036	Mag Star	6	M	9	2	1	2	18,000
Madame Milenium	3	F	6	0	2	0	11,610	Maga Secret	4	G	3	0	0	0	91
Madame Perfecta	10	M	5	0	1	1	4,065	Magalhaes Star	4	G	9	1	0	0	4,255
Madame Pietra	6	M	3	2	0	0	201,580	Magarita Midnight	5	M	5	0	2	0	24,800
Madame Queen	8	M	1	0	1	0	2,180	Magasie	4	G	4	0	0	0	620
Madame Rouge	2	F	2	0	0	0	2,597	Magazine	2	C	2	0	0	0	1,250
Madame Stein	4	F	7	0	1	1	5,050	Magcargo	3	G	9	2	3	1	40,273
Madame Thor	4	F	4	0	1	0	8,400	Magdelena May	2	G	4	2	0	0	13,900
Madame X Ski	4	F	4	0	2	0	19,200	Magee	4	C	8	3	1	1	49,435
Madamne Q	4	F	17	2	1	2	20,210	Magestic Power	4	C	2	0	0	0	0
Madam's Prospect	4	C	4	1	0	0	7,071	Maggie B B	4	F	11	1	2	1	16,760
Madam's Reply	5	M	10	1	1	0	11,562	Maggie Bell	4	F	1	0	0	0	55
Madd Maddi	2	F	3	0	0	0	576	Maggie Cat	3	F	2	0	0	0	87
Maddashfordinner	2	F	2	0	0	0	295	Maggie Dawn	4	F	1	0	0	0	0
Maddie H.	3	F	19	2	3	2	10,669	Maggie Hennessy	3	F	1	0	0	1	1,430
Maddie Hattie	5	M	13	0	0	1	1,430	Maggie Iam	3	F	15	1	4	0	16,076
Maddie Irgun	3	F	13	3	2	4	12,230	Maggie Jane	6	M	5	1	0	0	4,500
Maddie K	4	F	10	2	1	1	10,307	Maggie Marie	3	F	4	0	0	0	1,114
Maddie Miller	2	F	3	1	1	0	7,628	Maggie McGee	3	F	10	1	2	1	11,565
Maddie Rose	4	F	15	0	3	3	13,450	Maggie Mooster	4	F	16	1	2	2	60,467
Maddie Z.	4	F	6	0	0	0	513	Maggie My Love	2	F	2	0	1	1	3,325
Maddies Blues	3	G	7	2	1	0	24,684	Maggie My Memory	3	F	10	1	0	0	1,336
Maddie's Charm	3	F	2	0	0	0	4,000	Maggie O'Cat	4	F	2	0	0	0	84
Maddox Road	5	G	2	0	1	0	1,520	Maggie Splasher	5	M	3	0	0	0	214
Maddy Moo	3	F	9	2	2	1	7,818	Maggie's Co Ed	4	F	2	0	0	1	1,880
Maddy Q	3	F	2	0	0	0	0	Maggie's Dream	5	M	5	0	0	0	2,848
Maddycakes	3	F	8	1	0	1	4,273	Maggies Jeopardy	2	F	2	0	0	0	420
Maddy's Advantage	6	G	5	2	1	0	22,527	Maggie's Mischief	5	M	7	0	0	0	2,480
Maddy's Bobcat	2	C	1	0	0	1	2,860	Maggie's Pearle	3	F	1	0	0	0	180

Horse	Age	Sex	Sts	1st	2d	3d	Won
Maggies Pies	6	M	7	0	0	1	638
Maggie's Revenge	3	F	2	0	0	0	259
Maggie's Song	4	F	13	2	0	2	10,710
Maggies Storm	2	F	2	0	0	0	300
Maggie's Turn	5	M	7	1	2	1	29,080
Maggie's Word	2	F	5	0	0	0	330
Magi Island	4	F	9	1	0	3	7,122
Magibel	3	F	4	0	1	0	12,740
Magic	2	F	3	0	0	0	1,760
Magic Anna	5	M	6	0	0	0	334
Magic At Last	4	F	8	1	1	1	8,380
Magic At Midnight	4	F	10	0	4	2	20,292
Magic Bid	4	G	14	1	4	1	24,697
Magic Breeze	3	F	10	1	2	2	7,980
Magic Carbo	7	G	3	0	0	0	131
Magic Carpet	4	G	9	2	0	0	13,405
Magic Catillac	2	F	4	1	1	0	9,142
Magic City Lass	2	C	1	0	0	0	40
Magic Conqueror	2	G	1	0	0	0	650
Magic Copy	4	G	12	3	4	0	6,981
Magic Crystals	4	F	3	1	0	0	3,180
Magic Doe	8	G	6	0	1	0	15,671
Magic Echo	6	M	13	2	0	1	9,594
Magic Ending	5	G	10	0	0	2	3,668
Magic Feather (AUS)	7	G	5	0	1	0	9,770
Magic Feet	4	F	8	3	0	1	21,835
Magic Fighter	5	G	9	1	0	0	3,855
Magic Flare	6	M	13	0	3	3	7,073
Magic Forest	2	C	1	0	0	0	0
Magic Forum	4	G	10	2	3	3	42,795
Magic Ghost	3	C	11	0	0	1	4,135
Magic Hat	3	F	4	0	0	0	430
Magic Ink	3	F	7	1	0	0	10,410
Magic Jack	3	C	9	2	0	1	43,839
Magic Jake	3	G	7	1	3	0	26,140
Magic Jet	3	C	10	0	1	0	6,375
Magic Key	5	G	17	3	0	4	25,304
Magic Kipper	2	C	10	1	1	1	9,455
Magic Lantern	4	G	12	3	2	1	28,678
Magic Lights	3	F	1	0	0	0	0
Magic Line	2	F	8	1	1	1	19,460
Magic Link	3	G	4	0	0	0	0
Magic Love	3	F	8	2	1	0	19,985
Magic Madam	5	M	3	0	1	0	3,540
Magic Maddie	2	F	3	0	0	0	850
Magic Malady	4	F	6	0	2	0	2,056
Magic Marlin	3	F	2	0	0	0	0
Magic Marwish	3	C	4	0	0	0	303
Magic Mary	4	F	2	0	0	0	0
Magic Masque (NZ)	4	F	3	0	0	0	1,560
Magic Matty	4	F	6	1	0	2	20,030
Magic Mecke	3	C	9	3	3	0	120,090
Magic Meeting	8	G	2	0	0	0	250
Magic Michael	6	H	9	0	0	1	1,238
Magic Midas	5	M	7	1	1	1	8,927
Magic Miles	6	G	14	1	0	2	6,009
Magic Million	3	F	17	1	1	0	9,194
Magic Mirage	5	M	2	0	1	0	848
Magic Mirror	2	F	3	0	0	0	1,475
Magic Mission (GB)	5	M	8	1	2	1	190,980
Magic Mite	6	G	2	0	0	1	2,400
Magic Mora	4	F	3	0	0	0	0
Magic On Call	2	G	1	0	0	0	0
Magic On Ice	7	G	3	0	0	0	1,305
Magic Peak	4	F	9	2	1	1	65,359
Magic Prospector	3	G	12	1	2	1	23,256
Magic Rain Dance	3	F	18	2	4	4	17,677
Magic Ridge	5	H	6	0	0	0	180
Magic Rover	5	M	9	0	1	0	2,068
Magic Ruby	3	C	13	2	1	1	28,760
Magic Secret	3	F	10	2	2	3	20,845
Magic Seven	3	G	3	0	0	0	0
Magic Shot	8	G	4	1	2	0	3,610
Magic Smoke	3	F	3	0	0	1	4,320
Magic Squall	7	G	12	2	1	2	18,968
Magic Storm	4	F	1	0	0	0	380
Magic Strider	8	G	11	0	0	0	940
Magic Strike	3	F	7	3	0	1	15,066
Magic Summer	8	H	2	0	0	0	100
Magic Talk	3	F	7	1	0	0	26,060
Magic Tech	7	H	12	0	1	0	3,161
Magic Thursday	5	M	10	1	0	2	20,050
Magic Tiara	3	F	3	0	0	0	740
Magic Trap	3	F	11	0	0	2	2,522
Magic Trial	3	G	5	0	0	1	2,070
Magic Trooper	5	M	3	0	1	0	1,800
Magic Trump	4	F	5	0	2	0	3,600
Magic Valay	4	F	2	0	0	0	0
Magic Valley	2	C	5	0	1	0	4,910
Magic Victory	2	F	4	0	0	1	1,425
Magic Walk	5	H	6	0	0	0	5,356
Magic Weapon	4	F	11	3	2	1	44,690
Magic Weisner	4	G	1	0	0	0	720
Magic Wish	4	F	6	0	0	0	500
Magic World	7	G	3	0	0	0	245
Magical Card	5	H	1	0	0	0	0
Magical Cause	5	M	3	0	0	1	2,150
Magical Chimes	4	F	12	1	0	3	1,614
Magical Dust	2	C	4	1	0	0	13,080
Magical Encounter	4	C	10	0	3	0	5,041
Magical Flight	4	F	6	0	0	0	679
Magical Jeannie	5	M	10	0	1	0	2,175
Magical Lily	8	M	4	0	0	0	440
Magical Madness	6	G	8	1	0	1	26,350
Magical Marissa	2	F	2	0	0	0	59
Magical Melody	3	F	2	0	0	0	460
Magical Miss	4	F	8	0	0	2	10,838
Magical Moment	3	C	3	0	2	0	8,800
Magical Monday	4	F	12	1	3	5	8,719
Magical Moon	2	F	5	0	1	1	3,780
Magical Nature (IRE)	4	F	12	1	0	0	18,985
Magical Rascal	4	C	3	2	0	0	12,412
Magical Rush	3	G	1	0	0	0	146
Magical Times (GB)	9	G	4	0	0	0	460
Magical Valentine	2	G	9	0	1	3	5,847
Magicalparisbreeze	2	F	1	1	0	0	7,560
Magician	4	G	11	3	3	0	16,257
Magicleigh	4	F	11	1	2	2	16,156
Magic's Back	11	G	4	0	3	0	2,478
Magics in the Wind	4	C	1	1	0	0	4,455
Magi's Mira	10	G	9	1	3	1	5,486
Magistrate	3	C	8	1	4	0	17,212
Magmar	4	C	5	1	1	0	8,460
Magna Cum Laude	3	F	9	2	2	3	48,574
Magna Kat	5	H	7	1	2	0	12,560
Magnetar	3	F	10	2	2	0	22,724
Magnetic	4	F	10	3	3	2	56,790
Magnetic Hill (IRE)	5	G	6	0	1	0	4,660
Magnetic Image	4	G	12	0	4	0	9,681
Magnetic Mel	5	G	8	1	1	2	8,979
Magnetic Place	3	F	2	0	0	0	880
Magnetic Storm	3	C	3	0	0	1	4,140
Magnettic Affair	3	F	4	0	0	0	2,991
Magnificent	3	F	5	0	1	0	5,200
Magnificent Fly	6	H	8	0	0	1	2,141
Magnificent Maid	5	M	4	0	1	1	2,070
Magnificent Val	4	F	13	2	2	2	88,350
Magnolia Fields	2	F	5	0	0	0	165
Magnolia Gold	2	F	1	0	0	0	786
Magnolia Hall	5	M	10	1	0	0	5,175
Magnolia Lane	3	G	6	1	0	0	6,965
Magnolia Park	4	G	11	1	0	3	21,107
Magnolia Road	6	G	5	0	0	0	299
Magnum Blast	4	G	7	2	1	1	9,704
Magnum Express	4	G	4	0	0	0	555
Magnum Mac	7	G	8	1	0	1	2,291
Magoffin	5	G	17	0	3	4	27,585
Magpie	3	F	4	0	0	0	2,190
Magtown	5	M	12	3	1	0	10,238
Magtown Missile	2	C	3	0	1	0	3,000
Magus D' Or	5	G	10	3	1	1	62,190
Magwire	6	G	3	0	0	0	0
Magyismagic	5	M	4	0	0	0	181
Mah Big Lady	4	F	14	1	4	2	11,212
Mah Ritaz	7	M	3	0	0	1	1,291
Maha Rushey	4	C	3	0	0	0	427
Mahabarat	6	G	6	0	0	0	899
Mahagony Chip	2	C	2	0	0	0	0

Horse	Age	Sex	Sts	1st	2d	3d	Won
Mahal	5	G	15	0	1	4	28,774
Mahalay	4	F	5	0	1	0	3,570
Mahane Dan	6	G	1	0	0	0	378
Mahebo	3	F	15	0	1	2	6,075
Mahera's Angel	7	M	13	1	1	1	5,670
Mahi	5	H	8	1	1	2	10,912
Mahican	2	C	6	0	3	0	17,750
Mahie Gold	6	H	4	0	1	0	1,960
Mahiyah	3	F	9	1	0	2	9,775
Mahlique	5	M	4	0	0	0	327
Mahogany Cat	4	G	6	0	0	0	357
Mahogany Midnight	2	C	4	0	0	0	576
Mahogany Mink	5	M	27	1	1	5	9,613
Mahogany Ship	5	H	6	3	1	1	36,930
Mahogany Skyy	5	M	4	0	1	0	6,280
Mahone Bay	5	G	7	0	1	1	4,765
Mahoning King	2	C	5	1	1	1	20,294
Mahrally	12	G	8	0	1	2	1,932
Mahzouz	2	C	2	0	0	0	2,760
Mai Tai Guys	6	H	4	0	0	0	0
Mai Tai Princess	4	F	5	0	0	1	1,140
Maid in Monroe	2	F	6	0	0	0	1,399
Maid in the Moon	6	M	1	0	0	0	0
Maid of Honor	4	F	6	1	0	0	13,913
Maid of Money	3	F	7	1	2	2	34,953
Maid to Be a Pain	4	F	1	0	0	0	0
Maid to Run	4	F	5	0	0	0	873
Maiden Stone	4	F	13	0	2	5	16,830
Maiden Tour	2	F	6	1	1	2	18,780
Maiden Tower (GB)	3	F	6	3	2	0	316,824
Maidez	2	F	3	0	1	0	1,820
Maidintheshade	2	F	5	0	0	0	3,770
Maid's Folly	4	F	16	2	3	2	19,687
Mail Call	5	G	11	2	0	3	78,710
Mail Carrier	5	G	15	4	2	4	20,089
Mail Ryder	3	F	2	0	0	0	146
Mail Time	2	C	2	0	1	0	5,000
Mailthecheck	5	H	8	0	0	1	453
Maimara (ARG)	4	F	2	0	0	0	1,450
Maimiti's Chant	3	F	3	0	0	0	400
Main Contender	4	G	11	3	0	1	20,010
Main Day	5	G	15	2	1	0	9,503
Main Gunner	6	H	5	0	1	0	894
Main Player	4	G	3	1	0	0	4,965
Main Position	3	G	5	1	0	0	2,090
Main Reef	4	G	2	0	0	0	260
Main Stream	2	F	4	1	1	0	39,300
Maine Song	4	F	7	1	2	0	21,630
Mainly Henry	4	G	11	2	0	1	20,870
Mainly Irish	3	F	3	0	0	0	0
Mainstay	9	G	1	0	0	0	300
Maintenancemandan	3	G	16	1	2	1	3,522
Maipo	10	G	2	1	0	0	0
Maisie's Son	2	C	6	1	1	0	21,330
Maita (FR)	4	F	9	1	0	0	27,490
Maitake Gem	4	G	8	1	2	2	5,275
Majani	4	C	3	0	0	0	2,580
Majesterical	4	G	15	2	1	0	21,280
Majestic Alliance	3	F	8	0	0	1	3,118
Majestic Blaise	4	G	7	2	1	0	9,850
Majestic Cat	6	G	9	1	1	0	3,800
Majestic Catherine	3	F	10	2	2	2	28,832
Majestic Ceeson	3	F	1	0	0	0	0
Majestic Cherokee	2	C	2	0	0	0	0
Majestic Cloud	8	G	16	3	0	2	11,575
Majestic Colors	10	G	5	0	0	0	405
Majestic Commander	3	G	7	0	2	0	9,800
Majestic Count	6	G	5	0	0	0	0
Majestic Country	4	G	10	0	0	0	1,156
Majestic Dreamer	3	F	6	0	1	1	3,725
Majestic Falcon	6	M	5	1	1	0	5,044
Majestic Falls	5	M	9	2	0	2	7,996
Majestic Fan	5	G	22	1	3	3	8,852
Majestic Girl	4	F	4	0	0	0	3,720
Majestic Glitter	3	F	9	2	2	1	17,236
Majestic Hawk	4	G	12	1	1	1	11,732
Majestic Homebuilt	4	C	12	0	0	2	3,960
Majestic Irish	8	H	10	0	1	5	10,008
Majestic Kite	6	M	3	0	1	0	1,550

Horse	Age	Sex	Sts	1st	2d	3d	Won
Majestic Kris	3	C	4	0	1	0	10,660
Majestic Lady Shu	4	F	5	0	0	0	455
Majestic Legs	4	F	10	1	0	1	6,416
Majestic Lightning	4	G	1	0	0	0	140
Majestic Lord	5	H	7	1	1	2	22,756
Majestic Majesty	9	G	7	0	1	1	965
Majestic Mama	3	F	1	0	0	0	0
Majestic Mermaid	3	F	9	1	0	0	3,300
Majestic Midnight	4	F	10	0	1	1	2,356
Majestic Miesque	4	G	5	2	0	0	50,400
Majestic Mike	5	G	10	0	1	1	4,783
Majestic Mill	4	G	10	2	5	1	14,590
Majestic Mommy	3	F	7	0	0	1	4,265
Majestic Perks	10	G	3	0	0	0	110
Majestic Reef	5	G	16	1	3	2	9,503
Majestic Rose	4	F	4	1	0	0	12,960
Majestic Runner	6	G	9	1	0	0	3,792
Majestic Sir	4	G	15	3	0	2	19,125
Majestic Smoke	3	F	13	2	3	4	123,129
Majestic Song	4	G	9	1	1	0	18,687
Majestic Special	4	F	9	2	0	2	20,543
Majestic Standard	4	G	1	0	0	0	54
Majestic Sword	3	F	2	0	0	0	280
Majestic Thief	4	G	10	3	3	1	135,974
Majestic Tour	2	C	3	0	0	0	1,075
Majestic Tower	3	G	12	0	0	0	1,123
Majestic Trick	3	G	11	5	0	0	23,281
Majestic Tuffey	8	G	1	0	0	0	0
Majestic Warlock	5	G	3	0	0	0	6,084
Majestic Willie	4	G	10	1	1	2	6,120
Majestic Wisdom	3	C	3	1	0	0	97,360
Majestics Tricks	4	F	3	1	1	1	2,920
Majesty Bay	3	C	8	1	2	2	6,088
Majesty Hill	3	C	3	2	0	0	10,900
Majesty Mesa	2	G	4	0	1	1	3,255
Majesty Night	3	F	2	0	0	0	0
Majesty Warrior	3	G	6	1	0	0	6,640
Majesty's Dancer	3	F	3	0	0	0	182
Majesty's Fling	6	G	10	0	0	1	5,765
Majesty's Girl	4	F	15	1	0	2	4,252
Majesty's Gold	4	G	10	0	0	1	1,586
Majesty's Lass	5	M	7	2	2	0	30,200
Majesty's Muse	5	M	1	0	0	0	0
Majesty's Quest	2	G	1	0	0	0	810
Majesty's Rolls	5	M	1	0	0	0	83
Majesty's Runner	3	F	3	0	0	0	340
Majesty's Tale	4	G	8	1	0	1	4,758
Majesty's Word	2	F	3	0	0	0	0
Majic Deal	6	M	12	0	0	2	7,030
Majo	3	F	15	1	1	5	17,151
Majolica	4	F	2	0	0	0	0
Major Alliance	2	C	2	0	1	1	3,705
Major Bay	5	G	12	3	4	0	49,095
Major Blues	4	G	7	1	1	1	5,156
Major Bodgit	3	G	6	1	1	0	4,873
Major Brass	4	G	5	0	3	1	6,082
Major Brat Angela	5	M	5	1	1	2	5,582
Major Caleb	6	H	2	0	0	0	356
Major City	5	H	15	1	1	3	11,466
Major Concern	5	G	8	1	1	0	5,917
Major Conquest	6	H	8	1	0	3	11,510
Major Crisis	4	C	7	0	2	2	7,841
Major Damage	3	G	11	2	1	1	7,652
Major Decision	3	C	7	0	5	0	38,460
Major Dreams	6	M	3	0	0	0	179
Major Dundee	3	G	6	0	0	0	632
Major Factor	5	G	10	2	1	1	8,965
Major Fire	3	C	5	0	1	0	7,680
Major Fitpitcher	2	C	1	0	0	0	0
Major Focus	4	G	4	1	1	0	20,800
Major Forbes	7	H	8	2	0	2	13,795
Major Frank	4	G	2	1	0	0	18,600
Major Guide	4	F	9	0	1	2	5,219
Major Hero	7	G	7	1	1	0	13,450
Major Idea	3	F	5	2	0	0	105,600
Major Interval	6	G	12	1	2	0	10,976
Major Jonathan	2	C	2	0	0	0	1,380
Major Leaguer	3	C	3	1	0	1	33,360
Major Lightspeed	3	G	3	0	0	0	205

Horse	Age	Sex	Sts	1st	2d	3d	Won
Major Look	2	C	2	0	0	0	1,140
Major Lynch	3	G	1	0	0	0	0
Major Magua	9	G	3	0	0	0	1,100
Major Meadow	2	C	1	0	0	0	195
Major Mecke	4	G	18	1	7	3	60,140
Major Melissa	2	F	4	0	0	0	0
Major Mill	7	G	1	0	0	0	0
Major Oak	4	G	8	1	0	2	11,679
Major Omansky	7	H	6	0	0	0	690
Major Power	3	C	10	1	1	2	6,874
Major Price	2	G	2	0	0	0	500
Major Review	6	H	7	0	1	0	1,174
Major Rhythm	4	G	7	0	1	2	39,840
Major Storm	4	C	3	0	0	0	567
Major Success	2	C	2	1	0	0	25,440
Major T Rex	3	C	4	1	1	1	1,560
Major Tanner	2	C	6	1	0	0	13,910
Major Zee	10	G	7	5	0	1	52,052
Majorannouncement	3	F	5	1	0	0	6,135
Majorbigtimesheet	8	H	6	1	1	1	17,701
Majority	3	F	2	1	1	0	6,276
Majority Man	5	H	2	0	0	0	0
Majority Whip	5	M	5	0	3	1	47,755
Major's Daughter	4	F	4	0	0	0	858
Maka Me Super	3	G	10	1	1	1	10,210
Makaha	5	G	2	1	1	0	15,300
Makaido Bay	5	G	7	1	1	1	3,790
Makam (IRE)	3	F	10	1	3	0	56,235
Makarumba	3	G	8	2	3	0	55,350
Make a Fortune	5	G	7	1	1	1	7,713
Make Fast	3	F	7	0	0	1	1,920
Make Her Mark	4	F	6	1	2	0	7,340
Make It Cash	5	G	10	2	0	1	17,348
Make It Final	3	G	1	0	0	0	0
Make It So Cutie	3	F	7	0	2	0	3,714
Make It to Cash	11	G	1	0	0	0	0
Make Joe's Day	3	G	12	1	0	0	5,970
Make Lemonade	4	G	16	3	0	3	21,095
Make Love	5	M	10	0	0	0	3,160
Make Me a Champ	12	G	2	0	1	1	12,000
Make Me a Star	5	H	11	1	0	1	6,477
Make Mike's Day	5	H	19	0	2	2	21,760
Make Mine a Makers	3	F	10	3	1	1	15,370
Make Mine Rosy	6	M	3	1	0	0	8,112
Make Mischief	6	M	7	1	1	1	18,006
Make My Day Jur	3	G	6	3	0	0	78,420
Make My Millenium	5	G	19	0	4	2	25,030
Make Smart	7	G	5	0	0	0	0
Make the Bend	4	C	4	0	0	0	1,920
Make the Deal	4	G	12	3	2	0	18,440
Make the Deposit	4	F	10	1	2	3	16,881
Make Up Heart	5	G	12	1	1	0	2,522
Make Your Move	4	G	13	5	1	0	42,781
Make Your Own	5	G	5	0	0	0	2,600
Makeawager	3	C	6	1	0	0	8,729
Makeeba	3	F	5	0	0	0	1,530
Make'er Roll	2	F	3	0	0	2	1,661
Makem Hagar	8	G	7	0	0	0	4,200
Makemeanoffer	3	G	2	0	1	0	2,184
Makemeawish	3	F	2	0	0	0	360
Makememoneyhoney	3	F	8	4	0	1	31,290
Makemeorbreakme	4	C	5	0	0	0	308
Makemineagoldmine	2	G	5	0	4	0	8,466
Makeminenine	4	C	3	0	0	0	504
Makes a Fist	5	M	13	1	3	2	13,924
Makes More Sense	8	H	1	0	0	0	0
Makeup Artist	7	F	3	2	1	0	128,100
Makeup Girl	2	F	5	0	0	0	320
Makewayforbighoss	8	G	8	5	0	1	8,548
Makewayforwendy	3	F	9	2	2	2	45,433
Makin a Fortune	3	G	10	4	2	1	58,610
Makin' Angels	5	M	10	2	1	1	14,364
Makin Headlines	3	C	10	1	0	3	21,379
Makin Heat	3	F	4	0	1	0	7,680
Makin Mani	5	M	2	0	0	0	0
Makin One Wonder	4	F	1	0	0	0	0
Makin Trouble	3	C	7	0	1	0	1,208
Makinafast Fortune	7	G	21	1	2	4	6,494
Making Music	5	M	5	0	0	0	0

Horse	Age	Sex	Sts	1st	2d	3d	Won
Making My Move	5	G	4	1	2	0	19,715
Making Tracks	6	M	10	0	1	1	3,704
Making Waves	3	C	8	2	0	2	16,322
Makingthegrade	3	F	7	0	1	2	11,290
Maki's Pleasure	3	G	4	0	0	1	2,262
Mako Shark	2	G	3	0	0	0	0
Makoo	5	M	13	2	0	1	8,703
Makopuna	6	M	7	0	1	0	3,630
Makors Mark	6	H	5	0	0	1	15,480
Malachite	3	G	13	3	1	1	11,424
Maladyscat	4	F	16	1	2	6	12,832
Malagambo	2	C	1	0	0	0	786
Malagash	5	G	7	1	1	1	20,890
Malagot	6	G	8	1	0	2	5,649
Malagra's Encore	2	G	2	0	0	0	0
Malagra's Gem	3	C	5	0	0	0	2,033
Malagrasmillennium	5	H	2	0	0	0	0
Malaka Head	8	H	2	1	0	0	4,080
Malalco	4	C	9	3	1	0	9,718
Malang	5	M	5	1	2	1	5,595
Malante	4	C	2	0	0	0	0
Malarkeys Tapestry	4	F	1	0	0	0	0
Malawi Bay	2	F	3	0	0	0	424
Malayeen	3	C	3	0	0	0	0
Malcoha	11	G	7	3	0	0	36,446
Malcolm Miss	4	F	20	1	6	2	10,764
Malcolmsmile	3	G	1	0	0	0	130
Male Supremacy	3	G	6	0	2	0	4,166
Maleficio	2	C	5	0	0	1	1,255
Malena	6	M	1	1	0	0	4,080
Malesian Cat	3	F	3	0	0	0	140
Malfuncion Juncion	3	F	6	1	0	0	3,040
Malhoof	2	C	3	0	2	1	22,330
Malia	3	F	15	3	1	1	26,854
Malibu Al	2	C	2	1	1	0	12,820
Malibu Ebony	5	M	2	0	0	0	463
Malibu Hagley	6	M	3	0	0	0	0
Malibu Jack	5	G	6	2	1	2	16,724
Malibu Man	3	G	6	0	2	0	12,500
Malibu Miss	2	F	3	0	1	0	4,070
Malibu Momma	3	F	1	0	0	1	2,640
Malibu Stacey	4	F	2	0	0	0	0
Malibu Thunder	4	G	9	0	1	1	5,459
Maliciousintention	2	C	4	0	1	0	4,816
Malifino	2	C	1	0	0	0	0
Malign	2	F	6	0	0	3	3,359
Malik Silver	6	H	9	0	0	2	1,320
Malindi	2	F	10	1	1	3	27,936
Malinverno (ARG)	7	G	3	0	0	0	0
Maliziosa	4	F	9	0	1	3	64,005
Mallard	3	C	2	0	0	1	710
Mallory's Charger	6	M	1	0	0	0	336
Mallory's Star	5	M	9	4	1	0	34,932
Mallory's Surprize	3	F	1	0	0	0	350
Malmaison	4	C	8	0	0	1	11,920
Malmo's Tough Boy	3	G	9	1	1	1	8,136
Malo	4	F	7	2	1	0	28,745
Malo Halo	8	M	6	1	0	0	8,783
Malone	4	G	7	1	0	0	14,850
Maloya's Sun	4	G	7	1	0	0	2,215
Malpro	4	G	3	0	0	0	0
Mal'sschool Tears	2	C	2	0	0	0	190
Malvern Rose	6	M	6	2	1	0	65,600
Mam	3	F	2	0	0	0	0
Mama Josie	3	F	9	1	1	1	6,440
Mama Lov	4	F	3	0	0	2	3,567
Mama Main	4	F	8	0	0	1	1,244
Mama Tried	6	M	7	0	0	0	285
Mamacafe	4	F	8	0	1	0	4,620
Mamaison Star	3	G	8	0	1	1	6,920
Mamaiswar	3	F	10	1	0	1	11,570
Mamaleen	6	M	9	1	1	3	44,932
Mamalopez	5	M	9	2	0	0	5,110
Mama's Advice	3	F	4	0	0	1	3,563
Mama's Copy	2	F	4	1	0	0	4,950
Mama's Crown	5	G	3	0	0	0	1,760
Mama's Dinner	6	M	14	1	4	1	34,904
Mama's Gotta Go	4	F	3	1	1	0	6,250
Mama's Hungry Eyes	4	F	6	0	0	0	210

Horse	Age	Sex	Sts	1st	2d	3d	Won
Mama's Joy	3	G	11	1	2	1	14,500
Mamas Last Girl	3	F	3	0	0	0	0
Mama's Magic	2	F	4	0	1	0	2,800
Mamas Poundcake	4	F	2	0	0	0	145
Mama's Pride	4	G	16	2	0	2	9,761
Mama's Prospect	3	F	5	1	0	0	9,670
Mama'sgoldsong	5	M	12	2	0	2	6,266
Mamatuks	5	M	13	2	1	1	11,805
Mamba King	3	G	5	2	1	0	86,600
Mambo Dot Com	7	H	1	0	0	0	53
Mambo Encore	7	G	9	0	0	2	1,218
Mambo Mia	3	F	6	0	0	0	216
Mambo Music	2	F	3	1	0	0	4,715
Mambo Slew	2	F	3	2	0	0	88,350
Mambo Train	2	C	5	1	1	0	37,400
Mamboaire	3	C	4	0	0	1	5,400
Mambolero	6	H	4	1	1	0	7,904
Mambo's Delight	7	H	5	0	0	0	197
Mambo's Nephew	3	F	4	0	0	0	291
Mame	4	F	8	0	1	1	4,760
Mame Lovely Mame	4	F	4	0	0	0	248
Mamie Jamie	3	F	8	1	0	1	21,580
Mamie Mom	2	F	1	0	0	1	1,650
Mamiko	3	F	7	1	1	1	7,135
Mammy	2	F	5	0	0	0	760
Mamone	4	G	15	2	3	2	37,849
Mamosa	3	F	11	1	1	2	11,850
Man Among Men	3	C	3	1	0	0	48,600
Man From Artemus	4	G	7	1	1	1	21,290
Man From Wicklow	6	G	3	1	2	0	190,000
Man I Love Clare	5	M	3	0	1	1	5,010
Man in Blue	4	F	4	0	1	1	2,435
Man I'za Shadow	4	C	10	0	0	2	945
Man o' Rhythm	6	G	14	0	3	6	46,120
Man o' Roar	3	C	10	0	0	0	2,150
Man of Conquest	2	C	9	1	2	0	43,375
Man of Means	7	G	20	1	3	6	13,181
Man of Mystery	4	C	13	2	5	1	18,895
Man of the Sea	7	H	4	0	1	0	1,265
Man On the Go	8	G	6	0	0	1	4,800
Man On the Moon	7	G	3	0	0	0	66
Man Overboard	9	G	7	1	0	0	8,030
Man the Shipp	9	G	11	1	1	2	10,057
Man Well	3	G	2	0	0	0	285
Mana Bubba	3	C	4	0	0	0	0
Mana Dot Com	6	H	5	0	0	1	1,180
Mana Torpedoes	6	G	15	1	3	1	15,069
Manabozho (AUS)	5	G	4	0	0	1	7,980
Manalapan Academy	5	G	3	1	0	0	6,946
Mananan McLir	4	C	4	1	1	0	41,900
Manastash Nation	4	G	8	0	1	3	4,217
Manastash's Doll	6	M	12	4	2	4	31,457
Manaus	3	C	7	1	0	1	21,215
Manchac	6	G	9	1	1	0	15,002
Manchac Man	5	G	10	2	1	1	20,030
Mancheshot	4	F	1	0	0	0	0
Manchineel	3	G	7	0	0	0	1,945
Manchurian	3	C	2	1	0	0	29,460
Mandango	7	H	9	1	0	1	23,304
Mandarin Marsh	6	H	4	0	0	1	1,568
Manda's Apple	3	F	14	0	1	5	9,808
Mandela (GER)	3	F	7	2	0	2	74,067
Mandella	5	M	4	1	0	0	4,760
Manderin Magic	7	F	1	0	0	0	0
Mandisa	4	F	21	2	4	0	24,984
Mandy G	6	M	5	0	0	2	2,484
Mandylynn	4	F	2	0	0	0	0
Mandy's Gold	5	M	6	2	0	3	243,100
Mandy's Magic	2	F	5	0	0	0	150
Mane Explosion	7	G	6	1	0	1	1,142
Maneater	4	F	10	2	2	2	8,660
Manele	3	C	12	2	2	2	26,280
Maneuverable	3	C	4	0	1	0	11,920
Manfromcolorado	3	C	10	1	2	3	9,603
Mango Dancer	5	M	4	0	0	0	1,426
Mango Escapade	3	F	10	1	1	4	52,495
Mango Lassie	2	F	7	1	3	0	24,410
Mango Marquerita	5	G	3	0	0	0	2,100
Manhattan Alice	5	M	20	0	1	1	2,830

Horse	Age	Sex	Sts	1st	2d	3d	Won
Manhattan Days	3	C	7	0	0	0	450
Manhattan Express	3	C	11	2	2	2	89,145
Manhattan Man	4	G	3	0	0	0	103
Manhattan Miner	3	F	13	2	1	0	48,415
Manhattan Moment	3	F	3	0	2	0	2,870
Manhattan Nights	3	C	15	2	0	3	34,632
Manhattan Skyline	4	F	7	2	4	0	88,360
Manhunt	3	F	3	0	0	0	0
Manicomio Tom (ARG)	6	H	1	0	0	0	620
Manila Light	7	G	1	0	0	1	247
Manila Summer	5	G	12	0	0	0	2,000
Manila Vanilli	3	F	6	2	1	0	16,000
Manimint	4	F	6	0	1	0	2,543
Maninyalife	4	G	4	0	0	0	1,444
Maniqui	2	C	2	0	0	1	2,850
Mani's Flier	7	H	7	0	0	1	816
Manishua	9	G	9	0	4	0	5,440
Manitowish	6	H	9	1	3	1	66,596
Manitoy	2	C	5	1	0	2	22,168
Manjrekar	2	C	7	1	0	2	30,961
Manly Jack (NZ)	5	G	2	0	0	0	2,000
Manly Valentine	8	G	12	1	2	3	19,347
Manned	5	G	2	0	0	0	42
Mannered	11	G	12	0	0	0	315
Mannie's Mistake	5	G	10	3	2	1	36,813
Manning Avenue	6	G	2	0	0	0	1,470
Manny Manny	5	H	10	1	0	1	9,255
Manny's D Actor	6	H	3	0	0	0	179
Manny's Gold Maker	3	F	12	0	3	1	12,280
Manofglory	6	G	4	0	1	0	12,900
Manofthecloth	4	G	3	0	1	1	6,525
Manofthehour	2	C	1	0	0	1	4,320
Manonthemove	4	G	16	4	0	3	39,555
Manor Springs	5	M	11	1	1	0	6,116
Manosteel	2	C	2	0	0	0	2,125
Manowasso	3	C	5	1	1	0	10,600
Man's Candy	7	M	7	1	3	0	14,460
Man's Gold	3	F	5	0	0	1	528
Mansilver	4	G	5	1	0	2	18,460
Mansita	2	F	1	0	0	0	0
Manstone	5	M	12	3	0	4	18,272
Mantastic	4	G	5	0	0	0	634
Mantis	11	G	6	1	0	1	1,410
Mantra	4	F	1	0	0	0	1,800
Manulamu	3	G	18	2	1	1	18,570
Manumit	6	M	3	0	0	0	235
Manwhataqueen	3	F	3	1	0	0	3,260
Many a Penny	6	M	1	0	0	0	815
Many Many Bows	2	F	7	2	1	0	22,570
Many Many Sweets	3	F	9	1	1	0	7,345
Many Ministers	5	G	9	4	0	0	20,425
Many More	4	F	9	0	0	0	1,740
Many Pearls	3	F	6	0	0	0	80
Many Smiles	4	F	9	1	2	3	39,540
Many Threes	4	F	8	1	1	0	15,180
Many Times Over	9	M	8	1	1	1	11,410
Manzanillo	3	F	1	0	0	0	0
Manzanola	10	G	10	0	2	2	1,931
Manzee Blue	4	F	5	0	1	1	13,288
Manzil	4	C	1	0	0	0	0
Manzotti Queen	3	F	10	2	0	2	32,160
Manzotti's Guest	3	C	4	1	1	0	21,600
Manzotti's Love	3	F	5	0	0	1	550
Manzotti's Revenge	5	G	3	0	0	0	0
Mapeb	6	H	2	0	0	0	170
Maple	2	F	1	0	0	0	1,350
Maple Affair	4	G	1	0	0	0	0
Maple Creek Magic	3	F	6	1	2	0	7,375
Maple Hill	4	G	3	0	2	0	5,035
Maple Park Road	3	F	15	2	3	1	8,460
Maple Run	11	G	3	0	0	0	1,748
Maple Syrple	2	F	3	2	1	0	166,260
Maplewoods First	4	C	5	0	0	0	0
Mapp Hill	4	G	9	0	2	2	46,085
Maps Marketing	3	G	6	0	1	0	1,447
Mapuchita	4	F	5	0	0	2	7,309
Mar Cielo	2	F	8	1	1	0	14,140
Mar Rojo	4	C	17	3	4	1	19,115
Mara Queen	4	F	19	2	3	2	28,020

Horse	Age	Sex	Sts	1st	2d	3d	Won
Maracaibo	9	H	2	0	0	0	0
Marais Bouleye	6	G	15	1	3	3	43,870
Marais des Cygne	3	F	2	0	0	0	0
Maramour	2	F	1	0	0	0	0
Maranatha Spring	6	M	4	0	0	0	540
Maranella	3	F	12	3	2	0	13,919
Maranilla (IRE)	4	G	9	0	2	2	38,120
Marathon Man	3	C	4	0	0	0	500
Maravich	6	G	6	0	1	0	2,614
Marazdotz	7	M	9	0	2	0	5,211
Marble Falls	4	G	3	0	0	0	0
Marble Mountain	3	C	7	0	0	0	219
Marbles	4	F	5	0	0	1	2,270
Marbow	7	G	9	0	1	2	4,348
Marbury	3	G	11	2	1	6	44,595
Marc Road	5	H	10	1	1	1	7,032
Marceau	5	H	11	0	0	2	3,470
Marcelle	5	M	5	0	0	0	572
March Bloom	5	M	11	2	3	0	10,520
March Breeze	5	M	3	0	0	1	2,423
March Brown	4	C	4	1	0	0	7,659
March Hare	4	F	13	4	2	1	16,943
March Million	6	G	9	2	0	1	21,901
March of Ides	3	G	12	2	2	2	10,728
March of Kings	10	G	5	2	0	1	11,385
March On	4	C	2	0	0	1	445
March On Selma	7	G	7	0	1	0	1,785
March Snowflake	4	F	4	1	0	0	2,349
March to My Rhythm	4	F	1	0	0	0	0
March to Virginia	6	G	12	0	0	1	1,136
Marchand Volant (FR)	5	G	2	0	0	0	0
Marche de Paix (FR)	4	F	2	0	0	1	7,216
Marching	2	F	2	0	0	0	1,350
Marching Orders	4	G	6	2	1	1	33,320
Marching Rhythm	3	F	10	1	0	2	24,170
Marciann	6	M	3	0	0	0	1,500
Marcia's Wildcat	3	F	3	0	0	0	0
Marcies Choice Ice	4	G	17	2	2	5	23,620
Marci's Baby	5	M	18	1	0	1	3,952
Marci's Doctor	5	G	2	0	1	0	1,196
Marco Cat	3	F	6	3	0	0	15,436
Marco Gray	3	C	2	0	0	0	271
Marco Mac	4	G	10	0	1	1	6,169
Marco Mania	2	F	4	1	0	0	8,332
Marco Pleasure	3	G	4	1	2	0	7,860
Marco T	5	H	11	2	1	3	11,385
Marcola	3	G	5	0	0	1	2,295
Marco's Wish	5	G	1	0	0	0	149
Marco's Word	5	G	13	5	1	3	87,930
Marc's Candy	4	G	3	0	0	0	160
Marc's Rainbow	3	F	8	1	0	1	41,610
Marcus Laments	3	G	1	0	0	0	615
Marcys Emperor	6	H	13	1	0	4	9,240
Marcy's Hope	3	F	12	0	0	1	1,817
Marcy's Red	6	G	8	2	5	1	15,669
Mardi Gra Gal	4	F	8	0	1	2	3,167
Mardi Gras Cat	4	F	4	0	0	0	908
Mardi Gras Marie	5	M	1	0	0	0	71
Mardi Gras Sauce	5	G	5	3	0	0	34,500
Mardigrascolors	3	G	14	0	3	0	5,311
Mare Donna	3	F	5	1	1	0	17,290
Maresha	4	F	7	1	0	2	38,469
Marfalous Star	6	G	11	0	1	3	3,206
Marfa's Lady Rhome	4	F	10	4	1	1	15,528
Marfa's Pirate	7	G	2	0	0	0	469
Marfa's Prospect	3	G	9	2	1	0	25,580
Marfa's Ridge	3	C	2	0	0	1	2,882
Marfa's Taxes	6	M	10	2	4	0	53,030
Marfin Dancer	4	F	14	2	2	2	13,173
Margaret Anne	2	F	5	0	1	1	4,600
Margaret's Fancy (IRE)	3	F	4	0	0	0	5,040
Margaret's Love	6	M	1	0	0	0	547
Margarita Maggie	2	F	1	0	0	0	195
Margaritafill	3	F	9	1	2	2	3,989
Margarita's Garden	4	F	12	8	1	1	139,451
Marge P	8	M	8	0	0	0	564
Margeds Delight	3	F	3	1	0	0	4,950
Margeds Dream	3	F	4	1	0	0	4,950
Marge's Bid	3	F	19	1	5	0	17,039

Horse	Age	Sex	Sts	1st	2d	3d	Won
Marges Stage	2	F	5	0	1	1	6,720
Margie Golden	2	F	3	1	0	0	15,720
Margie Good	3	F	7	1	3	2	17,710
Margie's Echo	2	F	3	1	0	0	13,378
Margie's Top Papa	11	G	1	0	0	0	0
Margie's Way	2	F	3	1	0	0	4,300
Margiesgolddigger	5	M	1	0	0	0	159
Margin Call	2	G	2	0	1	0	1,350
Margin Drive	3	F	8	2	0	0	10,006
Margin of Error	3	G	21	1	3	3	14,650
Margold	2	F	5	0	0	1	1,478
Margos Rib	2	F	2	0	0	0	200
Maria	6	M	3	0	0	1	4,070
Maria Clarissa	2	F	1	0	0	0	0
Maria Elena's King	4	G	8	2	0	0	19,110
Maria Farina	3	F	13	1	2	2	15,825
Maria Ferrante	4	F	14	2	3	0	4,884
Maria Is Business	7	M	4	0	0	0	1,103
Maria Kay	4	F	4	0	1	0	1,280
Maria Pistola	2	F	1	1	0	0	2,880
Mariage Royale	5	G	3	0	0	0	2,340
Mariah Prince	3	G	16	2	2	2	12,264
Mariah's Bullet	2	F	5	1	1	1	22,390
Mariah's Miracle	3	G	5	1	1	0	4,112
Mariah's Thunder	4	F	6	0	0	1	1,036
Mariakel	3	F	13	4	1	0	89,535
Marian Francis	4	F	10	0	2	5	30,520
Marian's Muse	4	F	4	0	0	1	1,339
Maria's Best	2	F	2	0	0	0	800
Maria's Dream	3	F	3	0	0	0	360
Marias Eclipitcal	3	G	13	3	1	3	56,760
Maria's Face	3	F	1	0	0	0	0
Maria's Halo	3	F	7	0	3	2	9,520
Maria's Image	3	F	11	2	3	0	25,915
Maria's Lypheor	4	C	4	0	0	0	561
Maria's Magic	2	F	3	0	0	1	1,900
Maria's Mirage	4	F	7	3	1	0	120,323
Maria's Mojo	3	F	6	0	0	0	3,540
Maria's Sunshine	5	M	12	0	0	0	1,760
Mariatom	9	G	13	0	2	3	11,218
Mariaworth	5	M	10	3	1	0	66,111
Maribel	3	F	2	0	0	0	123
Maricot	3	F	6	1	0	1	6,570
Marie Louise	5	M	1	0	0	0	45
Mariensky	4	F	7	3	0	0	255,300
Maries Can of Gold	5	M	7	1	0	0	5,625
Marie's Fast Halo	4	F	7	1	0	2	8,990
Marie's Gal	6	M	1	0	0	0	171
Marie's Girl	4	F	15	0	4	4	6,503
Marie's Pal	4	C	1	0	0	0	0
Marietta Pike	4	F	4	0	0	0	0
Marietta's Charm	4	F	2	0	0	0	1,476
Mariflor	2	F	4	1	0	1	10,470
Marilina	4	F	8	2	0	1	8,636
Marilyn My Marilyn	5	M	11	1	2	2	12,985
Marina de Chavon	2	F	5	2	1	0	100,565
Marina Del Sol	6	M	6	1	2	0	15,993
Marina Minister	3	G	9	2	0	1	63,006
Marina Mon	3	G	8	1	2	0	12,845
Marinade	4	F	2	0	1	0	7,840
Marinara	3	C	3	0	0	0	1,193
Marine	7	G	7	1	0	1	25,830
Marine (GB)	5	G	8	0	1	1	23,400
Marine Drive	6	G	10	4	2	2	24,210
Marine Gunny	4	G	8	5	2	0	24,352
Marine Landing	5	G	12	2	1	2	27,659
Marine Odyssey	4	F	3	0	0	0	0
Marine Plt.	6	H	6	0	0	1	1,050
Marine Point	2	G	3	0	0	0	240
Marine Salute	4	C	11	2	3	0	14,941
Marine Sgt Major	4	G	15	4	1	1	20,606
Marineland	2	F	2	0	0	0	210
Marino Feliz (CHI)	5	G	6	0	2	3	14,830
Marino Marini	3	C	5	1	1	2	89,366
Mariola	4	F	7	0	1	1	8,094
Marion Co Cat	4	G	21	4	3	4	33,931
Marionette	4	F	4	2	2	0	69,900
Marion's Man	3	C	13	1	1	2	31,160
Mario's Magic	4	G	3	0	0	2	528

RECORDS OF HORSES

Horse	Age	Sex	Sts	1st	2d	3d	Won	Horse	Age	Sex	Sts	1st	2d	3d	Won
Mario's Mirage	3	F	15	2	6	2	45,052	Marktwentyfive	5	G	19	0	5	1	7,633
Mariquita's Secret	7	M	8	1	2	1	14,875	Markus Muffus	6	H	5	1	0	0	3,320
Mari's Danz	6	M	12	1	1	1	6,228	Markye Royal	3	C	6	0	2	1	5,367
Mari's Pride	3	F	3	0	0	0	213	Marky's Man	7	G	13	0	1	1	3,887
Marisa Go	6	M	9	0	1	1	36,247	Marla Gold	2	F	5	1	0	0	6,297
Marisleysis	3	F	3	1	1	0	5,460	Marla T	3	F	7	1	3	0	23,100
Marissa Dawn	3	F	2	0	0	0	0	Marland	4	C	15	0	5	2	11,509
Mariuma	3	F	5	1	0	1	5,150	Marlarky	5	G	9	1	0	2	5,836
Marius	2	C	1	0	0	0	0	Marlene's Machine	2	G	5	1	1	1	9,198
Marja	8	M	6	0	2	0	4,595	Marley Hart	3	F	10	2	0	0	29,370
Marjan	3	G	11	1	2	0	17,152	Marley's Dancer	3	F	9	0	0	3	10,315
Marjorie Daw	5	M	3	0	0	0	267	Marley's Revenge	2	C	2	1	1	0	18,400
Marjorie V.	2	F	2	0	1	0	2,590	Marleys Song	3	F	8	1	0	0	1,210
Marjories Girl	3	F	5	0	0	0	693	Marlig	2	C	1	0	0	0	0
Mark Aim Fire	3	F	6	0	2	0	9,590	Marlin Dance	3	F	7	1	2	1	25,925
Mark de Triomphe	6	G	20	2	5	2	36,185	Marlin Monroe	3	C	3	0	1	2	8,940
Mark Me Special	3	F	6	0	0	2	7,000	Marlin 'n Motion	3	G	8	1	1	0	9,330
Mark o' Bondage	5	G	3	0	0	0	312	Marlin's Ruler	5	G	5	1	2	0	8,178
Mark of a Warrior	6	G	4	1	0	3	26,880	Marlissee	4	F	6	0	1	0	3,515
Mark of Courage	3	G	1	0	1	0	3,400	Marliz	3	F	3	0	0	0	2,000
Mark of Diablo	2	C	3	1	0	1	16,573	Marllyn's Girl	2	F	2	0	0	0	0
Mark of Perfection	4	F	4	1	0	0	10,020	Marlon's Girl	4	F	12	1	0	2	9,648
Mark of Silver	6	G	6	0	0	1	2,426	Marlos Secretary	5	M	15	1	1	0	10,562
Mark of Texas	2	F	4	1	0	0	5,940	Marlouza's Spirit	2	F	2	0	0	0	1,260
Mark of the Dragon	3	G	19	1	3	2	17,790	Marlukin	5	H	10	1	4	1	22,855
Mark One	4	G	9	3	0	1	180,972	Marlwood	7	G	4	1	0	1	2,626
Mark Out Rythm	2	C	3	1	1	0	8,216	Marme	4	F	5	0	0	1	2,540
Mark Pepn G	3	G	12	2	3	3	29,650	Marnesia Light	3	F	12	1	3	3	46,930
Mark the Bearcat	3	G	7	0	0	1	728	Marnesia's Girl	5	M	9	0	0	0	676
Mark the Shade	4	G	5	1	1	1	14,104	Marnie's Heirloom	2	F	1	0	0	0	0
Mark the Shark	4	G	8	0	0	0	6,090	Marnie's Wish	4	F	10	0	0	0	4,800
Mark Twelve	4	G	17	4	3	5	57,200	Marnita	3	F	14	1	2	3	23,420
Mark U With Class	5	M	9	2	0	2	9,697	Maroon Creek	5	H	3	0	0	0	372
Markada	4	F	1	0	0	0	1,377	Marplatense	4	G	8	1	2	0	45,828
Marked Ace	6	G	3	2	0	0	13,726	Marq Tribute	4	C	3	0	0	1	1,210
Marked Affair	5	H	2	0	0	1	1,155	Marque	8	G	5	1	1	0	8,220
Marked Express	2	F	5	1	1	1	10,715	Marque Mark	6	G	15	1	1	1	8,090
Marked for Cash	3	C	1	0	0	0	0	Marquee	2	F	3	2	0	0	29,377
Marked for Gold	4	G	8	1	1	0	4,200	Marquee Affair	2	C	4	0	0	0	2,460
Marked for Promise	5	G	16	1	3	1	9,161	Marquee Dancer	3	F	6	1	0	0	5,880
Marked for Ransom	3	G	3	0	1	0	10,720	Marquee Kelly	4	F	10	3	2	2	80,109
Marked for Sucess	4	F	3	0	0	0	690	Marquee Lady	5	M	12	1	2	4	16,480
Marked Leader	3	F	3	0	1	1	1,770	Marquee Mark	4	G	10	2	0	2	18,020
Marked Native	6	G	16	2	3	1	16,081	Marquee's Starlett	2	F	7	1	0	0	6,169
Marked Outlaw	3	G	8	1	1	0	7,295	Marquet First	3	F	13	2	2	1	27,737
Marked Private	3	G	7	0	0	0	2,044	Marquet Gold	2	C	2	0	0	0	0
Marked Ryder	4	G	2	0	0	0	0	Marquet Legend	2	C	3	0	1	0	7,680
Marked Silver	5	M	8	1	1	2	12,180	Marquet Memory	4	G	6	0	1	0	2,455
Marked to Run	2	C	2	0	0	0	0	Marquet Niche	3	F	5	0	1	0	3,501
Marked to Win	3	G	5	0	0	0	576	Marquet Rate	3	F	8	1	1	1	20,851
Marked Wish	6	H	13	2	3	0	18,545	Marquet Rent	4	F	9	1	1	2	48,280
Markedwithattitude	2	F	1	0	0	0	126	Marquet Star	2	C	2	0	0	0	150
Markee Girl	4	F	6	0	0	0	424	Marquetarian	2	G	1	0	0	1	1,020
Markervilleexpress	3	G	15	1	3	1	15,653	Marquetheat	3	F	12	2	3	2	52,960
Market Bluff	4	G	10	1	0	3	9,415	Marquetry Ridge	6	G	10	0	0	2	3,627
Market Bottom	3	F	5	0	0	0	205	Marquetryinmotion	2	F	4	0	1	0	2,728
Market Cap	5	H	7	3	1	2	20,255	Marquette	7	H	11	0	0	0	10,755
Market Driven	3	F	4	1	1	0	3,750	Marquis Du Lac	3	G	3	0	0	0	315
Market Forecast	6	H	5	1	0	0	6,200	Marriage License	2	C	4	0	0	1	2,945
Market Garden	3	F	9	0	0	2	37,800	Marron Glace	4	C	4	0	0	0	5,400
Market Guru	3	F	6	1	1	1	40,040	Marrustan	7	M	1	0	0	0	0
Market Hill	3	F	3	0	0	0	257	Marry Me	5	M	5	2	0	0	14,795
Market Hunter	4	G	5	0	0	0	492	Marry Me Monece	3	C	4	1	0	1	17,900
Market Maid	4	F	2	0	0	0	510	Marsh	3	G	10	3	0	1	64,542
Market Master	9	G	5	3	0	1	11,120	Marsh Harbour	3	G	14	1	2	2	37,013
Market Maven	8	G	8	0	0	0	344	Marshal Dilom (ARG)	4	G	4	0	0	0	355
Market Meltdown	6	G	15	2	1	1	14,125	Marshall Greeley	6	G	5	1	2	1	27,990
Market Power	3	F	8	1	0	0	7,115	Marshall Rooster (GB)	4	G	6	1	1	1	55,760
Market Report	2	G	8	2	3	1	75,685	Marshall Storm	3	G	3	0	0	0	84
Market Secret	3	F	2	0	0	0	81	Marsha's Affair	5	M	7	1	2	0	13,004
Market's Best	4	F	14	3	1	3	62,489	Marshmallow Drops	5	M	1	0	0	0	61
Markintime	6	H	1	0	0	0	0	Marshman	6	G	11	4	1	1	35,919
Markofclass	3	F	2	1	1	0	8,270	Martel	6	G	6	1	0	1	15,960
Mark's Last Dance	7	H	13	1	5	2	7,311	Martha On the Rise	5	M	2	0	0	0	0
Mark's Mane Man	7	G	14	1	2	0	32,075	Martha Rose	5	M	7	1	3	0	3,700
Marks Mark	9	G	14	5	0	2	49,291	Martha Say	3	F	1	0	0	0	0
Mark's Miner	5	G	9	1	2	2	9,956	Marthamountainmama	3	F	15	1	1	5	32,594
Mark's Mission	5	M	7	0	3	0	7,905	Martha's Music	4	F	1	1	0	0	30,000
Marks Tree Two	4	G	4	0	0	0	427	Martial Jerry	5	G	13	1	1	0	6,439

Horse	Age	Sex	Sts	1st	2d	3d	Won	Horse	Age	Sex	Sts	1st	2d	3d	Won
Martin County	3	G	11	0	1	2	2,895	Ma's Last Fight	4	G	3	1	0	0	4,095
Martin L K	3	G	12	3	3	0	12,878	Masakado Kid	5	G	10	3	2	1	32,420
Martinblestme	3	C	8	2	0	2	92,074	Masara Key	3	F	4	0	0	0	360
Martini Bay	4	C	10	3	1	2	13,782	Masaya	4	C	2	0	0	0	165
Martini Classic	3	G	12	2	2	1	42,800	Masbut (CHI)	3	C	1	0	0	0	0
Martini Justice	3	G	4	1	0	1	37,285	Mascalzone	2	C	8	1	0	0	13,831
Martini Lunch	3	G	13	1	3	1	15,760	Mashiko	3	G	9	1	4	1	27,510
Martini M. D.	4	G	3	0	0	2	940	Mashonthegas	3	G	9	2	2	1	33,800
Martinis Atmidnite	5	M	5	0	1	3	6,720	Masjim	3	C	2	0	0	0	161
Martino's Gold	3	G	7	1	1	0	9,290	Mask of Mystery	7	G	4	0	0	0	894
Martinville	4	C	7	0	0	0	427	Maskaya (IRE)	4	F	2	0	0	1	3,300
Martrina	6	M	9	1	1	0	14,495	Masked Ball	2	F	2	0	0	0	0
Marty's Legend	3	C	10	1	1	1	4,790	Masked Miracle	5	H	12	0	0	2	2,090
Marty's Lucky Coin	4	F	1	0	0	0	0	Masked Rider	7	G	1	0	0	0	0
Marty's Zee	6	M	9	3	2	0	108,138	Masked Warrior	2	C	1	0	0	0	0
Maruka	3	F	2	1	0	0	16,200	Maskra's Hombre	5	G	1	0	0	0	192
Marva Jean	3	F	10	3	1	2	37,004	Mason County	4	G	15	2	4	5	17,024
Marvalini	3	C	4	0	0	2	9,830	Mason's Entry	3	C	7	0	0	1	4,330
Marvel	3	F	3	2	0	0	36,730	Maspesos	4	G	11	0	0	0	1,209
Marvelous Cat	2	F	4	1	0	0	11,610	Masque of Slew	2	G	4	0	0	1	1,845
Marvelous Monster	3	F	5	1	3	0	22,125	Masquerade Parade	2	F	2	0	0	0	0
Marvelous Mover	6	G	13	1	1	0	11,168	Masquerading	3	F	1	0	0	0	0
Marvelous Rhythm	3	F	3	0	0	0	0	Mass Attack	3	C	8	1	1	1	24,411
Marvin	3	G	3	1	0	0	22,200	Mass Media	2	C	3	2	0	0	28,800
Marvy's Gal	3	F	2	0	1	0	4,780	Massasuta	3	C	2	0	0	0	3,120
Marwood	3	F	2	1	0	0	15,400	Massiah Street	4	G	7	1	1	1	52,170
Marxie	2	F	6	1	1	3	37,310	Massive	3	C	4	1	0	2	61,100
Mary Alice	2	F	1	0	0	0	50	Massport	2	G	7	1	1	2	41,480
Mary and Joan	3	F	15	3	2	4	49,675	Mast Dancer	12	G	3	1	0	0	1,260
Mary Ann	4	F	11	2	1	4	29,892	Master and Win	5	G	5	0	1	0	4,030
Mary B Sharp	2	F	2	0	0	0	540	Master Belt (NZ)	5	G	8	0	3	1	42,229
Mary Bob	4	F	5	0	0	0	210	Master Ben	2	G	4	0	0	1	5,378
Mary Boyd	4	F	8	0	0	1	2,080	Master Boy	3	C	2	1	0	0	4,640
Mary Can Fly	5	M	5	1	0	0	2,881	Master Caine	3	G	6	0	1	0	1,924
Mary Carlisle	4	F	12	3	2	2	38,330	Master Carver	3	G	13	2	1	0	32,543
Mary Charged It	3	F	15	1	0	0	3,273	Master Chop	3	C	8	0	2	1	1,558
Mary Darlin	4	F	5	0	0	0	2,175	Master Concerto	3	C	7	1	0	0	14,120
Mary Donnelly	2	F	1	0	0	0	910	Master David	2	C	4	1	3	0	51,916
Mary Elma	4	F	4	0	0	0	425	Master Executive	7	G	7	1	1	2	8,690
Mary Goodnight	3	F	11	2	1	1	58,650	Master Flag (NZ)	5	G	1	0	0	0	1,000
Mary Joanne	4	F	8	0	0	1	4,401	Master Fly	2	C	2	0	0	1	3,900
Mary Joe	6	M	9	1	0	0	1,648	Master Harry	5	G	12	2	1	1	4,570
Mary Langfuhr	4	F	4	1	0	0	4,800	Master Heat	2	G	6	1	0	0	5,680
Mary Leta's Halo	3	F	2	0	0	0	0	Master Is Ready	3	G	15	4	1	1	36,580
Mary Murphy	3	F	5	1	1	0	22,714	Master Jobie	5	G	7	2	1	1	31,338
Mary My Mary	3	F	5	1	1	1	20,765	Master Jon	6	G	11	4	0	1	58,586
Mary Nation	6	M	3	0	0	0	340	Master Mechanic	6	G	12	1	2	2	14,367
Mary Ruth's Secret	2	F	2	0	0	0	0	Master O Foxhounds	8	G	4	1	0	0	7,095
Mary Scott	3	F	5	0	0	1	4,805	Master of the Sea	4	G	8	2	0	1	33,600
Mary Swan	2	F	2	0	1	0	12,080	Master of Thyme	3	C	13	1	4	2	11,675
Mary Swanson	2	F	2	1	0	0	12,000	Master Ofthe Manor	3	G	3	0	0	0	0
Mary the Belgium	2	F	3	0	0	0	0	Master Oliver	3	C	15	2	2	1	11,103
Mary the First	5	M	1	0	0	0	0	Master Painter	2	C	5	0	0	0	1,155
Mary Thomas	6	M	12	1	3	3	16,566	Master Peppe	8	G	2	0	0	0	378
Maryett	6	M	10	1	1	1	7,597	Master Perfect	3	G	15	4	2	1	89,200
Maryfield	2	F	1	0	0	0	3,528	Master Plumber	4	G	17	2	2	1	12,879
Maryland Mist	4	F	4	0	0	0	3,500	Master Poet	3	C	12	2	1	0	8,386
Marylebone	2	F	3	2	0	0	147,000	Master Pretty	4	F	12	1	1	2	26,993
Marylee	5	M	2	0	0	0	95	Master Princess	3	F	6	1	0	3	22,320
Maryneill	2	F	1	0	0	0	720	Master Prospect	3	F	15	1	1	3	39,694
Maryon's Angel	6	M	10	1	1	3	14,501	Master Rasper	5	G	8	2	3	0	16,800
Marys Avie	4	F	3	0	0	0	0	Master Report	3	G	10	0	0	2	5,430
Marys Cool Million	2	F	4	0	0	1	990	Master Salty	4	G	14	1	3	1	8,575
Mary's Empress	3	F	11	1	2	4	22,231	Master Sandfield	4	C	2	0	0	0	0
Mary's Glory	3	F	6	1	0	0	2,262	Master Sergeant	5	H	2	0	0	0	0
Mary's Got Magic	3	F	12	1	2	2	11,128	Master Sleet	3	G	6	0	1	0	1,608
Mary's Lord	4	G	10	1	1	0	12,095	Master Swinger	10	G	16	5	1	3	17,059
Mary's Magic	3	F	5	0	0	0	946	Master Technician	3	C	2	0	0	0	0
Marys Mon	4	G	11	2	2	1	11,634	Master the Game	3	G	2	0	0	0	217
Mary's Music	3	F	2	0	0	0	348	Master Trey	3	G	11	2	1	3	20,562
Mary's Nickle	5	M	9	0	1	4	35,558	Master William	2	C	3	1	0	0	151,500
Mary's Rose	2	F	4	1	1	2	8,985	Master Zack	4	C	2	0	0	0	140
Mary's Special Pen	6	M	7	1	2	1	9,814	Masterful Harry	3	C	7	1	3	0	53,670
Mary's Wild Flower	8	M	9	0	2	2	6,099	Masterful Lullaby	5	M	1	0	0	0	0
Maryshesaqueen	2	F	1	0	0	0	0	Masterfully's Game	3	C	1	0	0	0	0
Marywhataday	4	F	10	2	1	2	14,614	Mastersdoubleeagle	3	F	7	0	1	0	1,664
Marzi	4	F	17	1	2	5	15,436	Mastic	4	F	6	0	1	0	1,293
Marzipan	4	F	16	4	1	4	76,500	Mata Mata (BRZ)	7	H	5	0	0	1	850
Ma's Girl	3	F	9	0	2	0	4,105	Matanzas Creek	4	C	9	0	2	4	25,313

Horse	Age	Sex	Sts	1st	2d	3d	Won
Match a Memory	4	F	2	0	0	0	97
Match Break	4	G	10	1	0	1	4,295
Match Chic	5	M	15	3	1	4	17,484
Match Me	6	G	1	0	0	0	240
Match Point (VEN)	6	G	3	1	0	1	7,980
Match Up	4	C	1	0	0	1	1,080
Matchbaby	4	F	10	1	1	0	7,192
Matchbox Patti	3	F	7	1	1	0	7,744
Matched	4	C	13	4	4	3	38,910
Matched Prospect	4	C	7	0	2	2	6,636
Matching Bag	4	G	1	0	0	0	0
Matching Colors	5	G	10	3	2	1	20,689
Matching Sox	2	F	4	0	4	0	47,400
Matchless Hunter	7	G	9	0	1	1	5,355
Mateeghan	6	H	3	0	0	0	926
Materna	4	F	12	0	1	1	6,322
Materofcutness	5	G	2	0	1	0	1,360
Mathews Gold	2	C	2	0	0	0	4,900
Mathida	4	F	2	0	0	0	150
Matin de Soleil	4	C	6	0	0	2	1,925
Matinee Fling	3	F	8	1	1	2	11,985
Matinee Marvel	4	F	1	0	0	0	145
Matinicus Rock	2	C	5	2	1	0	39,320
Matlab	10	H	6	0	0	0	362
Matlock	4	C	7	1	3	0	9,746
Matlock (IRE)	5	G	14	5	2	0	30,545
Matos Gold	6	G	15	3	3	1	16,498
Matos Land	4	G	13	1	2	1	8,858
Matriculate	7	H	19	4	4	0	37,220
Mats Magic	4	C	2	0	1	0	1,560
Matsui	2	G	1	1	0	0	11,400
Matsuri	7	G	4	0	1	2	1,575
Matt Dylan	4	C	11	0	2	1	3,324
Matt E. Cat	4	F	6	0	0	1	2,900
Mattaponi	5	H	3	0	0	0	0
Mattei's Smokin'	4	F	6	1	0	0	5,933
Matter of Fax	3	C	6	0	0	0	754
Matter of Honour (NZ)	7	G	4	0	0	0	9,100
Matter of Justice	6	M	12	0	6	4	24,855
Matter of Love	6	G	8	0	0	1	3,387
Matter of Pride	5	H	6	0	0	0	509
Matter of Reality	3	F	9	1	2	1	10,646
Matters Not	9	G	12	0	0	1	1,288
Matters to Me	5	M	1	0	0	0	133
Matte's Girl	7	M	3	0	0	0	0
Matthew J	5	G	1	0	0	0	84
Matthew Lee	5	G	10	2	2	2	19,363
Matthew's Blessing	2	G	6	1	0	0	29,610
Matthew's Cookie	6	M	5	0	0	1	790
Matthew's Majesty	4	G	13	1	4	1	16,623
Matthew's Moon	6	M	6	0	0	0	318
Matthew's Prospect	5	G	17	3	5	2	33,116
Mattie Silks	3	F	5	2	0	1	25,590
Matties Baba	5	M	12	1	1	0	5,440
Mattie's Code	3	F	6	2	1	0	12,185
Mattie's Partyline	4	C	3	0	0	0	0
Mattie's Star	5	M	5	1	1	0	1,748
Matts Cool D J	6	G	6	0	3	1	2,034
Matts Deeds	3	G	8	0	2	2	10,620
Matt's Mount	4	C	6	0	0	0	96
Matt's Music	3	C	12	4	1	0	15,109
Matts On Broadway	5	G	10	1	0	0	3,884
Matts Pic	3	G	8	2	0	0	12,120
Matt's Star	2	C	1	0	0	0	58
Matt's Terms	2	G	6	0	1	2	2,404
Mattssutterrun	2	G	1	0	0	0	675
Mattview Boy	6	G	2	0	0	0	61
Matty D	7	G	1	0	0	0	435
Matty Fine	3	F	6	1	1	1	7,950
Matty Mic	3	C	8	1	0	0	6,420
Matty R G	3	C	8	1	1	3	21,850
Matty's Encore	3	C	14	4	1	1	15,007
Matty's Gem	3	G	10	0	1	3	3,965
Matty's Shady Lady	3	F	4	0	0	2	3,020
Matty's Song	2	G	1	1	0	0	5,600
Mattysontherun	4	G	2	0	0	0	186
Matza's Chili	3	G	1	0	0	0	0
Matzo Ball	2	F	5	0	0	1	2,100
Matzoh Toga	2	C	1	0	0	0	0
Matzsayo	4	G	13	1	3	2	22,025
Maud Gonne	4	F	5	1	0	1	32,310
Maudel	5	M	5	0	0	1	1,376
Maudie K	6	M	10	0	1	2	2,700
Maudy	3	F	2	0	0	0	225
Maui Believer	3	G	6	0	0	0	2,472
Maui Madness	4	F	12	0	3	2	6,805
Maui Money	5	M	6	1	1	2	9,356
Maui Wish	3	C	3	0	0	0	50
Mauk Eight	3	C	4	2	0	1	48,225
Mauk Four	3	C	11	2	1	0	82,800
Mauk Hawk	2	C	1	0	0	0	0
Mauk Me	2	G	5	1	0	0	4,754
Mauk Place	2	F	1	0	0	0	0
Mauk Six	3	C	4	1	0	1	10,910
Maukey	5	H	8	1	2	1	19,200
Maumee	6	G	1	0	0	0	0
Maumee (IRE)	5	H	5	1	0	0	21,520
Maureen's Music	4	F	7	0	1	2	2,532
Mauriann	2	F	3	0	0	1	2,026
Maurice	4	G	13	1	3	1	16,640
Maurice Champagne	4	C	2	0	0	0	500
Maurice Jolie	3	G	10	0	0	3	2,528
Mauritania	6	G	6	4	0	0	36,000
Maury's Rainbow	4	G	7	1	3	0	10,600
Mauvais' Dude	3	G	9	3	1	1	45,863
Mav Cat	3	C	3	0	1	0	6,400
Mavelous Marva	2	F	3	0	0	0	360
Maveriki	3	G	10	2	0	1	7,380
Maverise	3	F	5	0	0	0	1,442
Mavoreen	3	F	7	2	2	1	73,950
Maw Irish Hope	7	M	12	0	0	4	10,375
Mawasasport	6	M	6	1	1	0	5,146
Maw's Vacation	11	M	2	0	0	2	445
Max a Million	3	C	7	2	1	1	42,400
Max Brand	3	G	1	0	0	0	755
Max Factor	6	G	10	3	3	0	21,942
Max Fast Flight	4	G	7	0	4	1	2,680
Max Force	3	C	16	6	1	1	39,147
Max Forever	3	C	10	3	2	0	158,940
Max Jones	5	H	5	0	0	1	9,684
Max Mercury	3	G	10	1	1	2	17,109
Max O Max	6	H	9	0	0	1	6,074
Max Patch	5	H	13	3	1	2	52,000
Max Power (AUS)	6	G	2	0	1	1	12,760
Max West	3	C	7	1	2	1	21,660
Maxamax	3	C	6	0	0	0	2,340
Maxamizer	5	H	2	0	0	0	0
Maxi Faxxi	5	G	5	0	0	0	420
Maxi Picasso	5	G	4	1	1	1	3,027
Maxi Tune	8	G	8	0	3	3	12,700
Maxian	5	G	8	2	2	0	14,294
Maxidaisical	5	G	13	0	0	1	3,821
Maxim Gold	4	G	15	2	0	2	8,432
Maximiliano (BRZ)	7	G	4	0	1	1	5,630
Maximillions	5	G	8	1	2	2	5,675
Maximum Appeal	3	F	8	0	2	2	22,850
Maximum Bid	3	C	6	0	0	0	273
Maximum Degree	4	F	19	1	2	1	7,245
Maximum Exposure	3	G	4	0	0	0	288
Maximum Impact	5	G	24	3	6	2	26,496
Maximum Reward	4	G	18	2	2	4	15,716
Maximum Velocity	3	G	7	0	1	2	2,083
Maximum Voltage	3	G	10	0	1	1	2,590
Maximus	3	G	17	3	1	2	18,111
Maximus Cash	4	G	14	2	5	3	17,536
Maximus Decimus	4	G	6	1	0	0	6,340
Maximus Honor	4	C	4	0	0	0	750
Maxinkuckee	2	C	3	0	0	0	0
Maxmilians Specter	9	G	7	0	0	0	1,365
Max's Ace	4	G	4	1	0	1	6,960
Max's Baby	3	C	3	1	0	0	10,740
Max's Buddy	4	C	6	1	1	1	39,900
Max's Cat	3	C	4	0	0	0	1,950
Max's Friend	5	H	10	2	2	2	49,970
Maxs Girl	3	F	14	1	6	1	23,750
Max's Star	3	F	2	0	0	0	0
Max's Tale	3	G	16	2	1	2	23,695
Max's Wish	4	G	3	0	0	1	1,102

Horse	Age	Sex	Sts	1st	2d	3d	Won	Horse	Age	Sex	Sts	1st	2d	3d	Won
Maxwell	2	C	1	0	1	0	3,860	McAllister Creek	4	G	4	2	1	0	5,275
Maxwell Steel	4	G	12	0	0	0	1,048	McAlpin Road	9	G	4	0	1	0	2,600
Maxwell Turner	4	C	4	0	0	0	365	McArdle	10	G	12	1	0	0	3,674
Maxwelsilverhammer	3	G	13	1	2	1	17,960	McBeal	5	M	5	0	1	1	7,600
Maxxe Set	5	M	1	0	0	0	0	McCain	2	C	2	0	0	0	252
Maxxswell Mouse	2	G	3	0	0	0	950	McCann's Mojave	3	C	2	2	0	0	74,880
Maxzilla	6	G	1	0	1	0	460	McCordnskuba	7	G	4	0	0	0	3,172
May Be Mabel	3	F	2	0	0	0	180	McCourt	4	G	3	1	0	0	14,770
May Be True	3	G	12	0	0	0	1,740	McCreary	5	G	9	0	0	1	5,770
May Boy	3	C	7	0	0	0	2,310	McDab	6	G	3	1	0	1	48,540
May Day Lady	3	F	4	0	0	0	140	McDevitt	3	F	2	0	0	0	0
May Day May	4	F	4	2	0	1	2,363	McDrake's Elf	4	C	2	0	0	0	180
May Day Mischief	5	M	2	0	0	0	100	McDynamo	6	G	3	3	0	0	252,025
May Daze	5	M	3	0	0	0	105	McFadden Creek	4	G	9	0	1	0	1,900
May Expectations	4	G	13	2	0	1	55,085	McGeever	3	G	8	0	1	0	7,065
May Gator	4	F	12	2	6	0	146,964	McGruddy's Tap	6	H	7	0	1	3	2,917
May H Berry	2	F	1	0	0	0	0	McGuerty Creek	4	F	10	2	2	2	13,341
May I Might	5	M	3	0	0	0	0	McIntyre	4	G	9	0	0	1	5,515
May Nard	5	H	13	0	1	4	14,223	McIvor	3	G	5	0	0	0	976
May Paul	4	G	1	0	0	0	0	McKee's Gallery	3	G	11	2	5	1	70,400
May Snow	4	F	11	0	0	2	2,263	McKenna	3	F	8	1	1	1	6,268
May Twentyfifth	4	F	2	0	0	0	129	McKenna Beach	2	F	4	3	1	0	69,526
Maya	4	F	9	2	4	0	72,275	McKenna Falls	2	F	4	0	1	0	5,160
Mayakovsky	4	C	3	1	0	0	36,600	McKennas Gold	5	M	3	0	0	0	268
Maya's Note	4	F	1	0	0	0	750	McKinley Rhodes	6	G	5	0	0	0	272
Maybe Brandon	5	G	9	0	0	0	563	McKinna G	2	C	6	0	2	0	3,680
Maybe Cora	2	F	4	0	1	0	7,430	McKinney	5	M	12	2	1	4	89,679
Maybe Doc	5	G	18	3	2	3	17,096	McLinda Deree	2	F	3	0	0	0	475
Maybe Friday	3	G	11	4	1	1	35,477	McManus	4	G	13	0	2	1	44,340
Maybe Jack	10	G	10	4	3	0	58,850	McMaster	3	G	2	0	0	0	163
Maybe Lin	4	F	13	3	1	0	47,200	McMazel	2	G	4	0	0	1	1,770
Maybe Maybe Maybe	4	G	2	0	0	0	48	McMerry	3	F	8	1	1	0	6,980
Maybe Me	8	M	16	1	1	1	11,870	McNally	4	G	6	0	0	1	1,385
Maybe Midnight	3	G	2	1	0	0	35,160	McNasty	2	G	4	0	2	0	17,280
Maybe Nextime Beau	7	G	12	1	1	0	3,848	McNellis	5	G	11	0	1	1	12,880
Maybe Not	4	F	4	0	0	0	384	McQueen	8	M	5	0	0	0	210
Maybe Rocco	3	G	14	2	2	2	32,870	McTavish's Case	5	M	2	0	0	0	114
Maybe Special (GB)	7	G	14	1	1	2	6,399	McWest	4	F	16	3	0	4	7,405
Maybeforeal	5	M	7	0	4	0	13,732	Mdme Allbright	2	F	2	0	0	0	800
Maybird	2	F	2	0	0	0	0	Me a Green	4	F	8	0	0	1	2,199
Maybry's Boy	4	C	12	2	1	1	72,740	Me a Spirit Too	7	M	3	0	0	0	180
Maydeuce	2	F	3	0	1	0	2,000	Me and J J	3	G	12	0	0	4	2,447
Mayihavethisdance	4	F	9	1	5	1	16,750	Me and Marie	2	F	1	0	1	0	5,200
Maymont	2	F	2	0	0	0	0	Me and Mr. Z	5	G	14	2	4	1	63,270
Maynard G	2	G	5	0	1	0	1,100	Me and My Shadow	5	G	10	0	1	0	2,952
Mayne Attire	4	F	7	2	1	0	8,425	Me and Thee	5	H	7	2	0	0	23,340
Mayne Stating	3	F	10	2	1	2	8,605	Me Be Jammin	4	F	1	0	0	0	0
Mayneunderfire	5	G	9	4	3	2	58,450	Me Coordinated	5	M	7	0	1	1	2,178
Mayo Man	7	G	6	0	0	1	884	Me Darlin Marty	4	G	9	1	0	2	21,738
Mayo On the Side	4	F	9	3	1	3	163,240	Me Get It	3	F	7	1	0	1	6,082
Mayor Fraze	6	G	8	1	0	2	13,912	Me Gotta Go	5	M	14	2	3	3	58,463
Mayor Murphy	4	G	9	1	1	1	11,840	Me Gusta Bailar	2	C	2	0	0	0	0
Mayor Pro Tem	3	G	4	0	2	0	3,000	Me I'm Amelia	5	M	12	2	0	0	13,884
Mayor Steve	8	G	8	2	1	1	46,093	Me in Shades	3	F	1	0	0	0	2,195
Maypole Dance	6	M	5	0	0	2	10,170	Me Inc.	2	F	2	0	0	0	0
May's Pride	3	F	8	1	3	2	23,280	Me Jane	4	F	7	1	2	0	2,359
Maysville Slew	7	G	12	3	2	0	137,690	Me Me Anna	5	M	8	3	1	1	20,334
Maytown	2	C	4	0	1	0	12,700	Me Me Me Me	4	F	6	0	0	0	275
Maytown Misstree	7	M	2	0	2	0	4,840	Me Moe N Joe	2	G	2	0	0	0	182
Maywood's Brianna	2	F	2	0	1	0	3,528	Me My Mine	3	G	10	2	3	1	63,600
Maywood's Charlie	2	G	5	0	0	0	630	Me 'n Linda Marie	5	M	3	1	0	0	8,400
Maywood's Doc	2	G	6	0	1	1	6,533	Me No Toad	4	G	15	2	3	3	8,822
Maywood's Good Boy	5	G	7	0	0	1	2,262	Me Tricky	3	C	4	0	0	2	3,550
Maywood's Jack	3	G	8	0	0	0	1,176	Meadaaar	6	H	8	1	2	2	29,763
Maywood's Jill	3	F	6	1	3	0	34,462	Meadow Aire	4	G	5	2	1	0	3,200
Mazalea	3	F	3	0	0	0	193	Meadow Belle	3	F	12	0	1	3	31,150
Mazel Pic	2	F	2	0	0	1	3,220	Meadow Champ	5	H	5	0	0	0	285
Mazel Tov	2	F	1	0	0	0	1,250	Meadow Crafty	2	F	1	0	0	0	150
Mazel Trickxy	2	F	1	0	0	0	0	Meadow Dance	4	F	12	3	1	0	53,640
Mazella	2	F	7	1	1	2	43,940	Meadow Dee	4	G	8	0	0	0	870
Mazen La Dawn	5	M	9	0	0	0	444	Meadow Fox	2	F	5	1	3	1	49,080
Mazengah	3	C	8	3	3	0	133,332	Meadow Fun	2	G	4	1	0	1	17,884
Mazoolian Ghost	4	C	9	1	1	0	16,780	Meadow Ghost	4	C	3	0	0	0	0
Mc Act	4	F	5	0	0	0	450	Meadow Gold	3	F	4	0	0	0	0
Mc Dubious	5	G	4	0	0	0	327	Meadow Light	4	F	2	0	1	0	6,820
Mc Henry Co. Kid	5	G	9	1	3	1	21,529	Meadow Love	4	F	17	2	2	3	50,858
Mc Mahon	5	G	10	3	3	0	98,940	Meadow Made	4	F	7	0	0	2	1,219
Mc Meese	3	F	15	2	5	2	17,149	Meadow Minister	3	C	5	0	2	1	32,289
Mc Quix	4	G	12	2	2	1	14,972	Meadow Monarch	4	C	8	1	1	1	13,087

Horse	Age	Sex	Sts	1st	2d	3d	Won
Meadow Mountain	4	F	10	0	4	1	9,873
Meadow Queen	2	F	1	0	0	0	85
Meadow Robin	10	G	12	2	0	0	7,576
Meadow Rue	3	C	2	0	0	0	850
Meadow Slew	4	G	3	0	0	0	261
Meadow Snowbird	3	F	12	1	1	3	7,185
Meadow Soldier	2	C	6	1	0	1	22,180
Meadow Song	9	M	5	1	0	2	4,960
Meadowcrest Kid	5	G	14	1	0	4	7,131
Meadowfella	3	C	6	3	0	0	25,891
Meadowlake John	3	C	3	1	0	0	14,217
Meadowlake Lodge	2	C	5	0	0	2	6,580
Meadowman	8	H	3	0	0	0	70
Meadowminer	5	H	5	0	1	1	13,458
Meama	3	F	18	1	2	6	40,865
Mean and Lean	4	G	8	0	0	0	1,530
Mean and Nasty	3	G	4	3	0	0	41,820
Mean Answer	4	F	1	0	0	0	32
Mean Flyer	5	H	4	0	0	0	261
Mean G. I.	3	C	7	0	0	0	1,395
Mean Irene	2	F	8	0	1	1	5,560
Mean Jean Ipock	4	F	9	0	0	3	4,455
Mean Kisser	2	G	4	0	0	0	300
Mean Ma Peters	6	M	6	0	1	0	666
Mean Margaret	7	M	6	0	0	0	198
Mean of Queen	8	M	11	1	0	0	2,771
Mean On Tequila	3	F	9	1	0	0	6,025
Mean Streets	3	G	13	3	2	1	27,459
Mean U Gene	2	G	3	1	1	1	22,477
Meandmyloveman	6	H	3	0	1	0	9,392
Meaner Than Mama	4	F	2	0	0	0	105
Meanest Hombre	2	C	2	0	0	0	170
Meaningless	5	G	11	2	1	4	23,290
Meanwhile	3	C	3	1	0	0	8,400
Measured Moment	6	H	6	1	1	1	5,558
Meauxjo	3	G	8	2	0	0	28,110
Mecanico	4	G	5	0	0	0	1,800
Meccajelso	7	G	5	0	0	2	2,109
Mecca's Orphan	6	H	3	0	0	0	468
Mecca's Pal	5	G	14	1	1	3	7,981
Mecca'screation	5	M	5	0	1	0	2,496
Mech Runner	2	F	1	0	0	1	3,840
Mechanic Man	5	G	10	2	2	0	7,995
Mechlin	5	M	9	1	0	2	8,443
Meckanical	4	G	16	0	0	4	11,585
Meckarenda	5	M	9	1	0	0	13,218
Mecke Man	5	G	8	2	0	0	34,730
Mecke Mantle	5	G	12	2	0	3	10,310
Mecke Mex	3	F	9	1	0	0	5,999
Mecke Monster	5	G	10	3	1	1	50,819
Meckeme	5	G	9	1	4	0	38,425
Meckenized	4	G	13	4	1	0	40,470
Mecke's Dancer	4	G	17	3	1	3	27,660
Mecke's Money	4	G	11	2	1	0	11,182
Mecke's Presence	2	F	3	1	0	0	7,740
Mecke's Princess	4	F	9	0	2	6	30,310
Mecke's Song	4	F	3	0	0	1	1,044
Medaglia d'Oro	4	C	5	3	2	0	1,990,000
Medal of Freedom	2	F	1	0	1	0	6,000
Medal Play (ARG)	6	G	5	0	2	1	28,245
Medea	8	M	15	3	3	3	25,170
Medecis (GB)	4	C	4	0	1	0	56,660
Medellin (ARG)	5	G	3	0	0	1	2,750
Medevil Wine	2	G	2	0	0	0	0
Media Access	5	M	6	0	1	4	42,953
Media Mogul (GB)	5	G	1	0	0	0	0
Media Rare	4	C	5	1	0	0	3,000
Media Saint	2	C	3	0	0	1	3,220
Mediate	4	G	16	1	3	1	16,788
Mediator	3	C	3	2	0	0	33,550
Medical First	4	G	10	2	0	0	18,480
Medicine Eyes	2	C	1	1	0	0	6,000
Medicine Hawk	5	G	4	0	0	0	170
Medicine Line	8	G	11	1	2	0	14,158
Medicine Man	6	H	3	0	0	0	0
Medicine Moon	8	M	8	0	0	1	1,549
Medieval Agenda	2	F	2	0	0	0	140
Medieval Jazz	3	F	10	1	2	2	10,700
Medieval Legend	8	H	7	1	0	1	9,121
Medieval Mistress	3	F	12	2	3	0	16,510
Medieval Parade	2	G	3	0	0	0	490
Medieval Quinn	4	G	2	0	0	0	260
Medieval Salute	3	F	10	1	0	0	36,370
Medieval Touch	3	F	3	0	1	0	6,220
Medieval Trick	4	G	7	0	0	0	1,195
Medina Ridge	6	G	16	3	3	2	17,691
Medinaceli (IRE)	4	F	9	2	0	1	78,970
Medio Creek	7	G	15	2	3	0	12,251
Medioluna Mistress	3	F	2	0	2	0	5,600
Meditate	5	M	12	2	2	3	9,850
Medium Rare	7	G	5	1	2	0	38,315
Medjugorje Vision	5	M	2	0	0	0	76
Medlin Road	4	G	9	3	1	1	48,743
Medly	5	M	3	1	0	0	6,300
Meega	3	F	2	0	1	0	2,310
Meercat	2	F	2	0	0	0	170
Meerkahn	3	C	7	2	0	0	5,979
Meet in Miami	5	M	11	1	3	2	26,335
Meet in Seattle	7	M	6	0	1	0	1,578
Meet Me At Midnite	3	F	13	3	2	2	103,430
Meet the Challange	7	G	18	1	2	4	9,461
Meet the Slew	3	G	1	0	0	0	0
Meeting of Minds	5	M	5	1	0	0	7,025
Meetmeatthegate	3	F	10	0	1	1	4,877
Meetmeatthegrill	2	C	2	0	0	0	4,312
Meetmeontime	3	F	2	1	0	0	8,100
Meetyouathebrig	5	G	1	0	0	0	832
Meetyouatthetop	4	F	3	0	0	1	7,136
Mefistofele	5	G	3	0	0	0	0
Mefoxytoo	6	M	4	0	0	0	187
Meg Pie Baby	6	M	2	0	0	1	421
Mega Breeze	9	G	1	0	1	0	3,547
Mega Gift	6	G	12	4	2	2	94,610
Mega Hit	3	C	5	0	1	1	13,000
Mega Max	4	C	3	1	0	0	5,329
Mega Mill	3	C	13	2	0	0	17,609
Megacles	6	H	9	1	3	2	29,895
Megaddim	2	C	2	0	0	1	1,887
Megahertz (GB)	4	F	7	2	1	3	534,480
Megaluno	4	C	3	1	0	0	5,815
Megan Capote	2	F	4	0	0	0	753
Megan Popz	2	F	6	0	0	0	5,530
Megann's Fame	3	F	4	0	0	0	1,375
Megan's Appeal	2	F	3	1	1	0	110,850
Megan's Cracker	5	M	14	1	1	1	21,709
Megan's Field	7	H	17	1	2	3	7,109
Megan's Fizzle	4	G	4	0	0	1	1,410
Megan's Halo	3	F	12	5	0	2	81,297
Megan's Man	3	C	4	0	1	0	2,858
Megan's Misty Morn	3	C	3	0	0	0	1,000
Megans Molly	3	F	12	1	1	1	11,657
Megan's Prospect	3	C	12	0	2	4	6,127
Megans Rainbow	3	F	1	0	0	0	0
Megan's Star	4	F	6	0	0	3	3,750
Megan's Storm	5	M	3	1	1	0	5,121
Megan's Way	2	F	4	2	1	0	9,816
Megantic	5	H	6	1	0	2	30,960
Megara	3	F	8	1	5	0	26,710
Megga Gee	3	G	6	1	0	2	21,320
Megmeister	2	F	3	0	0	0	390
Megoman	3	C	12	5	3	0	171,400
Megoodytwoshoes	5	G	9	1	0	0	5,952
Meg's Operator	2	F	1	0	0	0	0
Meguial (ARG)	4	F	10	1	0	3	61,980
Mehrizi	5	H	1	0	0	0	0
Mei Sing Star	3	G	6	2	0	0	23,900
Meigs	7	H	1	0	0	0	0
Meimgeorgeoustoo	3	F	5	0	0	0	0
Mejestic Creek	3	G	9	1	0	2	5,167
Mejor	7	M	18	1	2	2	25,495
Mekena South	5	G	15	2	2	1	34,715
Mekko Hokte	3	F	9	1	2	2	41,700
Mel Marie Ann	5	M	18	1	2	1	14,327
Meladrie	4	F	8	2	0	1	17,665
Melancholy	3	F	6	0	0	1	4,480
Melanie's Smile	3	G	16	3	1	1	17,825
Melanyhasthepapers	2	C	2	0	0	1	5,440
Melba Jewel	2	F	4	1	2	1	33,758

Horse	Age	Sex	Sts	1st	2d	3d	Won	Horse	Age	Sex	Sts	1st	2d	3d	Won
Melcapwalker	4	G	9	4	2	0	31,820	Menacing Dennis	4	G	5	1	1	3	99,912
Mele Kalikimaka	3	C	4	1	0	0	6,000	Menasha	2	C	3	0	0	0	2,370
Meleium	4	F	13	3	3	1	35,835	Mendacity	4	F	1	0	0	0	1,450
Melfi	3	C	7	0	2	0	6,430	Mendham	5	H	7	0	1	1	9,369
Melika Music	2	F	2	0	0	0	1,050	Menemsha	3	F	1	0	0	0	0
Melind's Adam	5	M	8	0	0	0	1,845	Menifeeque	2	F	8	2	1	1	35,870
Melisma's Valley	5	M	7	1	1	0	56,468	Meninano	2	C	1	0	0	0	0
Melissa Christine	4	F	13	1	4	0	11,632	Meno Fool	4	F	1	0	0	0	0
Melissa Lee	4	F	14	0	3	1	19,290	Menomaestro	3	C	1	1	0	0	10,920
Melissa's Glitter	3	F	5	0	1	2	2,034	Menorquin	2	G	2	0	0	0	150
Melissa's Luv Song	2	F	1	0	0	0	50	Menowyoulater	4	F	3	0	0	0	0
Melissa's Moment	6	M	4	0	0	0	698	Men's Exclusive	10	G	5	1	1	1	115,100
Melissa's Pancho	3	G	2	0	0	0	0	Mensa	5	M	11	3	2	1	10,973
Melissa's Success	6	M	3	0	0	0	1,072	Mensa Frenchie	4	F	14	1	1	3	10,557
Melissasfamousbaby	3	F	1	0	0	0	0	Mensa Madam	5	M	8	1	2	3	23,212
Mellaluka	3	F	7	1	1	1	10,200	Mensa Mom	2	F	3	1	0	0	13,050
Mellow Cielo	2	C	1	0	0	0	0	Ment to Be Clever	3	F	9	0	0	0	348
Mellow Fellow	8	G	3	0	1	0	48,528	Mental Floss	3	F	3	1	0	0	11,520
Mellow Marci	5	M	6	2	3	0	20,178	Mentir Pas	4	F	10	1	1	1	4,935
Mellow Mind	3	F	14	0	2	5	10,315	Mentos Double	7	M	1	0	0	0	46
Mellowes	5	H	8	1	0	2	31,750	Mentow	2	F	2	0	1	0	6,460
Melly	5	M	5	0	1	0	2,346	Menuhin (GB)	3	G	7	1	0	1	26,932
Melodar	3	F	5	0	0	0	2,280	Meow Meow	2	F	1	0	0	0	137
Melodioso	3	F	2	1	0	0	15,600	Mer Belle	3	F	8	0	2	0	10,438
Melodious Gem	4	F	6	0	0	0	0	Mer de Corail (IRE)	4	F	5	2	0	1	184,177
Melody Blue (FR)	4	F	7	1	0	2	54,040	Mercato Nero	4	C	1	1	0	0	2,773
Melody Light	2	F	2	0	0	0	425	Merce Honey	4	F	8	2	1	1	14,625
Melody of Colors	4	F	9	3	3	0	94,320	Merce Merle	4	G	9	0	2	1	3,318
Melody Prospector	2	F	1	0	0	1	2,700	Mercedees Red	3	F	4	2	0	0	38,545
Melody Ruth	3	F	3	0	2	0	1,935	Mercedes Ace	4	F	5	0	0	0	0
Melodyformorgan	4	F	1	0	0	0	69	Mercedes Dancer	2	F	2	1	0	0	15,000
Melody's Slasher	2	F	5	1	0	1	7,885	Mercedes Dream	2	G	3	0	0	1	3,765
Melora	2	F	3	0	1	0	2,028	Mercedes High	2	C	5	1	0	1	3,918
Melrose Falls	4	G	3	1	0	0	12,294	Mercedes Son	9	G	3	0	0	1	4,946
Melrose Miss	3	F	2	0	0	0	310	Mercenary	5	H	8	1	1	1	50,927
Melrose Nanny	4	F	10	1	1	3	32,749	Mercer	5	M	17	3	1	4	34,405
Melrose Orphan	4	G	8	0	2	0	2,466	Mercerized	3	C	6	0	1	1	11,180
Melrose Play Boy	3	G	8	0	0	0	800	Mercer's Cool Cat	3	G	13	0	2	1	13,112
Melrose Traveler	3	F	2	0	0	1	1,485	Mercer's Launch	4	F	7	1	1	2	17,395
Mel's Choice	4	C	4	0	0	1	1,226	Mercer's Millie	4	F	3	0	0	0	664
Mel's Marque	6	H	14	2	4	3	21,558	Mercers Run	3	F	1	0	0	0	615
Melt Away	5	M	4	0	0	1	792	Merchandise	2	C	4	0	1	0	8,100
Melt the Witch	4	F	6	1	2	3	9,675	Merci Melody	5	M	14	2	2	0	8,883
Melting	10	G	5	0	2	2	5,325	Merciless	3	F	10	2	1	1	10,939
Melting Point	3	F	13	1	3	3	93,080	Merc's Comet	7	M	1	0	0	0	0
Melvin Toaster	3	G	12	2	2	3	26,180	Merc's Melissa	3	F	7	0	0	0	1,590
Mema's Money	2	F	2	0	0	0	570	Merc's Miracle	4	F	10	0	3	3	10,983
Member of the Club	4	C	1	0	0	0	320	Mercuryontheroad	6	G	3	0	0	0	300
Memberwhen	3	F	6	1	0	1	10,797	Mercy Matters	2	F	2	0	0	2	7,260
Meme's Gaelic Act	7	G	3	0	0	0	325	Mercy Missile	4	F	12	1	1	0	4,064
Memmy O.	4	F	2	0	0	0	0	Mercy Ridge	6	G	15	3	1	1	19,474
Memo	3	C	8	1	2	0	47,280	Mercywhataleader	7	G	13	2	0	3	7,351
Memo House	3	G	2	0	0	0	340	Mere Legend	10	G	7	0	1	2	2,910
Memo Image	4	G	4	0	0	0	340	Mere Magic	2	F	2	1	1	0	12,588
Memo Queen	3	F	8	1	1	0	7,960	Mere Sheba	4	F	1	0	0	0	100
Memo to Cameron	3	G	3	0	0	0	225	Meregold	4	F	6	1	0	2	6,263
Memo to Dixie	6	G	15	2	1	1	41,547	Merely Art	5	G	7	0	1	2	3,695
Memo to Eve	6	M	9	0	0	1	2,115	Merely Money	8	M	12	0	0	1	1,983
Memo to Id	2	F	1	0	0	1	1,900	Merenguero	6	G	6	1	1	0	9,800
Memo to Lange	5	M	3	0	1	0	950	Meri Robyn	7	M	7	1	0	0	9,928
Memo to Me	4	G	10	0	1	1	8,844	Meriden Mist (GB)	5	M	3	0	0	1	825
Memo to Mike	4	G	7	0	1	2	9,400	Meridian Champ	3	G	2	0	0	0	132
Memo to Russ	3	G	8	2	1	0	36,680	Meridian Doc	3	G	8	0	1	3	1,976
Memoferu	4	C	2	0	1	0	2,575	Meridian Madness	4	F	11	3	0	1	13,075
Memofromjessica	2	G	1	0	0	0	1,260	Meridian Thriller	4	F	1	0	0	0	180
Memofromthelady	4	G	14	4	1	8	40,980	Meridiana (GER)	3	F	5	2	0	0	303,478
Memogram	3	F	6	2	0	0	31,880	Meriray Dawn	5	M	2	0	0	0	103
Memonte	4	G	10	0	4	0	5,604	Merisa G	5	H	4	0	0	0	346
Memorable Gent	4	G	1	0	0	0	0	Merits Centennial	5	H	5	0	1	0	1,127
Memoree	7	M	1	0	0	0	0	Merits Dublin	5	H	11	1	2	3	7,087
Memori	4	G	3	0	0	0	0	Merits Ruler	6	G	9	0	1	1	2,140
Memorial Daze	3	F	8	0	0	0	1,532	Merkaban	7	G	7	1	1	1	14,911
Memorolph	2	G	2	0	0	0	1,275	Merlin's Moon	5	G	6	1	1	1	77,350
Memory Hill	7	G	14	0	2	3	7,242	Merlins Odyssey	5	G	7	0	0	3	3,173
Memory Lane	3	G	7	0	0	0	3,038	Merlot High	6	H	3	0	0	1	341
Memory Tap	7	H	1	0	0	0	460	Merlot Moment	4	F	8	0	1	2	12,360
Memphis	5	G	13	4	1	2	38,980	Mermaid's Tavern	4	F	3	0	0	0	186
Memphis Kat	3	F	8	1	1	2	8,995	Merrian's Girl	6	M	8	0	0	0	776
Memphis Lady	3	F	10	1	2	2	9,775	Merrie Woode	6	M	5	0	0	0	1,203

RECORDS OF HORSES

Horse	Age	Sex	Sts	1st	2d	3d	Won
Merrigoldround	3	F	10	1	2	1	4,525
Merrimack Cat	3	C	4	0	0	0	79
Merrimack Sean Tog	6	G	2	0	0	1	620
Merry Grey	4	F	6	1	1	1	23,730
Merry Joyce	3	F	1	0	0	1	3,740
Merry Kippy	4	G	17	1	2	4	13,249
Merry Mary	2	F	8	2	0	5	88,059
Merry Mary K	3	F	7	1	0	1	13,676
Merry Minster	3	F	14	1	4	1	15,862
Merry Mist	3	F	3	0	0	0	3,233
Merry Sizzle	2	G	7	1	1	0	14,170
Merryhadalilwolf	8	G	20	4	1	1	13,395
Merryland Missy	3	F	10	3	1	3	79,270
Mertiggy	4	G	5	2	0	0	12,195
Merton	8	G	3	0	0	0	0
Mertz's Lil Nelson	3	F	11	0	1	0	3,663
Merychippus	3	F	1	0	0	0	0
Merzouga Night	3	C	2	0	0	0	0
Mesa Beauty	3	F	6	3	0	1	36,180
Meseta	4	F	4	0	0	0	0
Mesmerizing	3	F	3	1	0	1	47,514
Mesne Process	5	H	5	0	0	0	1,265
Mesohippus	3	C	4	2	0	0	8,961
Mesolithic	4	C	17	2	3	1	33,868
Mesotrouble	4	C	4	0	0	0	295
Mesquite Flat	4	C	7	3	0	0	17,780
Mesquite M	2	F	3	0	0	1	1,275
Message Red	4	F	8	4	3	0	158,475
Messageinabottle	3	G	14	3	1	2	11,676
Messaline	3	C	12	2	2	1	12,578
Messenger Springs	3	G	13	1	3	1	10,986
Messerschmitt	2	G	2	0	0	0	0
Messinger	4	F	3	0	2	0	14,800
Messinroundwithjd	2	G	3	0	1	0	1,100
Messomania	4	C	18	1	3	1	9,058
Messy Business	3	C	1	0	0	1	825
Mestiza's Rebel	6	G	6	0	1	0	1,050
Mestizio	5	G	5	0	0	0	520
Met At Dinner	2	G	6	1	0	1	12,305
Met City	2	C	1	0	0	0	75
Met'a Flew Z	4	G	4	1	2	0	13,650
Metal Master	4	G	15	3	0	4	40,750
Metal Vendor	4	G	13	0	0	2	5,910
Metalian	2	F	3	0	0	0	1,965
Metallica Two	3	F	2	0	0	0	0
Metaphysics	4	G	11	1	2	4	31,680
Metatron	4	G	9	1	0	2	48,290
Meteor Dream	4	F	2	0	1	0	3,610
Meteor Game	5	M	8	0	0	1	9,380
Meteor Impact	3	G	1	0	1	0	15,000
Meteor Light	5	M	6	1	0	0	14,400
Meteor Miracle	4	F	8	2	3	2	119,045
Meteor Star	4	F	1	0	0	0	510
Meteor Storm (GB)	4	C	4	2	1	1	80,120
Meteoric Rise	7	G	7	2	0	2	12,219
Meteoroid	3	C	1	0	0	0	0
Meter's Legend	2	G	2	0	0	0	651
Metfield Jr	6	H	9	0	1	1	3,848
Metfield Runner	3	G	2	1	0	0	5,065
Metfleet	6	G	11	0	1	2	2,790
Method Actor	3	G	8	1	0	2	12,745
Method Man	4	C	4	0	0	0	2,850
Methodist (IRE)	6	G	4	0	0	0	1,860
Metoometoo	2	G	5	0	0	0	1,511
Metro Tango	5	G	15	3	3	0	33,788
Metro Time	5	G	9	1	0	4	16,315
Metronome	3	G	3	0	0	0	310
Metrotown	4	F	15	5	2	5	18,430
Metsieh	3	F	8	0	1	2	4,645
Mettie's Way	6	M	4	0	0	0	0
Mettler	2	G	4	1	2	0	10,475
Mettlesome	3	F	5	0	0	0	173
Metts Reward	2	G	5	1	0	2	10,206
Metzo Soprano	3	F	2	0	0	0	528
Mewannaplay	2	F	4	1	0	0	4,920
Mexican Brass	3	C	7	0	1	0	1,444
Mexican Connection	6	M	16	6	0	2	38,380
Mexican Hey Day	7	G	3	0	0	0	0
Mexican Meazles	6	H	2	0	0	0	55
Mexican Moonlight	3	F	16	3	5	1	116,618
Mexican Riviera	3	F	3	0	0	0	0
Mexican Sunset	2	F	4	0	1	1	2,184
Meyer Katz	5	H	7	0	2	0	16,290
Mezamee	3	F	8	0	2	1	7,085
Mezcal	4	C	5	0	1	1	2,050
Mezmer Eyes	3	F	16	0	2	3	9,056
Mezzaluna	4	F	3	0	0	0	371
Mezzanine Money	4	F	2	0	0	2	9,900
Mezzanotte	4	F	5	0	0	0	621
Mezzo Soprano	3	F	8	3	1	2	401,920
Mhalik (CHI)	5	G	8	0	0	0	675
Mi Aloha	3	F	7	1	0	2	4,388
Mi Amante	2	G	3	0	1	0	15,288
Mi Amigo	2	C	5	1	2	0	19,470
Mi Angelica	7	M	5	0	0	1	761
Mi Bienvenida	4	F	20	2	3	1	19,563
Mi Brujo	4	C	15	2	2	3	45,243
Mi Camila	5	M	2	0	0	1	563
Mi Caramelo	2	F	2	0	0	0	380
Mi' Deserai	4	F	5	0	0	0	423
Mi d'Or	4	F	6	2	2	0	37,640
Mi J	4	G	10	2	1	0	26,240
Mi Jillian	3	F	12	0	1	3	6,630
Mi Karmee	3	F	6	0	4	0	26,764
Mi Life	4	F	2	0	0	0	320
Mi Loco Amante	2	G	4	0	0	2	2,250
Mi Lu	6	M	3	0	0	0	330
Mi Maria	4	F	9	3	2	0	37,978
Mi Miracle	3	F	2	1	0	0	13,520
Mi Mister D	5	G	16	1	1	1	8,295
Mi Narrow	9	G	5	0	0	0	550
Mi Pais	3	G	15	2	5	1	27,675
Mi Pequeno Amigo	5	H	11	0	0	1	792
Mi Quick	6	G	8	4	2	0	44,728
Mi Rio	3	G	18	1	1	4	14,695
Mi Serenade	6	G	16	4	2	2	18,584
Mi Tough	2	G	1	0	0	0	126
Mia Cat	3	F	1	0	0	0	140
Mia Dawn	4	F	6	2	0	0	14,306
Mia Editor	3	C	9	1	1	1	9,195
Mia Frilly Tudor	8	G	4	1	0	0	6,484
Mia Justice	3	C	13	2	3	0	17,186
Mia Marfa	3	F	6	0	0	1	1,027
Mia Mucho	5	H	14	1	0	1	7,654
Mia Rebecca	3	F	11	1	0	1	15,553
Mia Trapp Mountain	4	C	2	0	0	0	0
Mia Trick	3	F	5	0	0	0	900
Mia Valentina	4	F	5	1	0	1	4,292
Mia Villa	4	F	17	1	2	2	7,565
Miami Blue	2	F	1	0	0	0	195
Miami Gear	4	G	6	5	0	0	39,246
Miami Magic	4	C	3	0	0	0	546
Miami Mike	2	G	7	1	1	1	16,300
Miami Miracle	2	C	1	0	0	0	100
Miami Star	2	C	2	0	0	0	195
Mi'an Mar	3	F	1	0	0	0	0
Mia's Heartsnroses	6	M	3	0	0	1	3,585
Mia's John D.	5	H	14	3	2	4	48,364
Mia's Lil Rapture	4	C	6	0	2	1	4,941
Mia's Moment	4	F	9	1	1	1	4,648
Mia's Pal	7	M	1	0	0	0	55
Mic Cup	5	H	13	1	0	0	1,647
Mic Mac	4	G	11	3	4	1	34,415
Mic N Ali	4	F	11	1	2	2	7,370
Micado	5	G	4	0	0	0	70
Micah Doolittle	4	F	12	0	2	0	2,104
Micapeakmoonshine	3	G	1	0	0	1	220
Micayla's Peach	5	M	17	3	2	3	24,604
Miccosukee	3	F	14	2	2	1	17,205
Michael	6	G	7	1	2	0	17,040
Michael Again	4	G	10	1	0	1	6,625
Michael O	6	G	9	1	1	2	10,522
Michael On Sunday	10	G	6	0	0	0	1,392
Michael With Wings	3	G	7	0	1	1	3,815
Michaelmyboy	3	C	9	0	0	1	506
Michael's Crossing	5	M	3	0	0	0	0
Michael's Lead	7	G	3	0	0	0	165
Michael's Pine	8	G	16	1	2	2	8,582

Horse	Age	Sex	Sts	1st	2d	3d	Won	Horse	Age	Sex	Sts	1st	2d	3d	Won
Michael's Pride	6	H	8	2	2	0	87,190	Midnight Manner	4	C	2	0	0	0	66
Michael's Prospect	3	G	3	0	0	0	174	Midnight Marauder	2	C	4	0	0	0	427
Michael's Queen	5	M	2	0	0	0	460	Midnight Miner	7	G	12	2	4	1	15,540
Michael's Temper	4	C	7	2	3	1	34,300	Midnight Music	5	M	3	0	1	0	7,560
Michael's Will	3	C	11	1	0	1	6,948	Midnight Orders	9	G	17	2	0	0	5,370
Michael's Wolf	5	G	6	2	0	0	14,255	Midnight Red	8	G	4	0	0	0	275
Michals Chickadee	6	M	2	0	0	0	0	Midnight Rhapsody	3	F	14	1	4	2	56,472
Michel With One L	4	F	7	2	0	0	10,859	Midnight Rich	5	H	3	0	0	0	146
Michele Marieschi (GB)	6	G	2	2	0	0	27,000	Midnight Rider	10	G	8	1	3	2	2,292
Michele Mel	4	F	12	0	0	1	12,936	Midnight Run	3	F	1	0	0	0	0
Michelle Willpass	4	F	4	0	0	1	5,150	Midnight Sam	3	G	6	1	1	0	9,585
Michelle's Cap	5	M	13	3	5	1	22,106	Midnight Secret	6	G	11	2	0	3	14,325
Michelle's Diamond	3	F	11	2	0	2	19,005	Midnight Show	2	F	1	0	0	0	124
Michelles First	2	F	5	0	0	0	840	Midnight Silk	8	M	12	0	0	2	1,922
Michelle's Girls	4	F	1	0	0	0	0	Midnight Sky	3	F	5	0	0	0	0
Michelle's Gold	6	M	3	1	0	2	20,220	Midnight Special	5	M	6	1	1	1	23,475
Michelle's Soup	2	F	3	0	1	0	8,135	Midnight Stage	4	G	10	1	2	1	6,518
Michener	7	G	15	4	4	3	69,526	Midnight Starter	3	G	4	0	0	0	122
Michigano	3	C	8	0	1	1	3,178	Midnight Summer	4	F	1	0	0	0	0
Mich's Cure	5	M	7	0	0	0	2,041	Midnight Summit	3	G	8	0	0	2	10,390
Micjorgan	4	F	7	2	0	2	9,465	Midnight Velvet	2	F	8	1	5	0	44,900
Mick	3	G	8	2	1	2	52,699	Midnight Venture (GB)	5	G	5	0	2	2	8,400
Mick and Bubba	2	G	5	0	1	1	2,890	Midnight View	9	G	1	0	0	0	158
Mick Mick	5	M	4	2	1	0	17,530	Midnightresolution	2	F	5	0	0	1	4,795
Mick Mouse	3	C	5	0	2	0	9,765	Midnightvictory	3	F	8	1	2	0	20,400
Mickala	4	F	9	3	1	0	21,520	Midnite Black	4	F	3	0	0	0	39
Mickee	6	M	7	0	0	0	1,352	Midnite Coach	4	G	13	0	0	1	2,957
Mickey Dee	6	G	19	1	2	3	8,872	Midnite Deelite	4	F	6	0	0	1	1,890
Mickey M	4	C	7	0	0	0	220	Midnite Edition	6	M	12	1	0	1	5,971
Mickey Nicky D	5	M	6	0	0	0	1,041	Midnite Jo Boy	4	G	10	1	2	1	7,620
Mickey the Groom	5	G	14	0	1	0	7,374	Midnite Madness	6	M	3	0	0	0	3,060
Mickey's Bankroll	6	G	5	0	0	0	264	Midnite Meeting	5	M	5	0	0	1	15,528
Mickey's Hot Stuff	8	M	6	0	0	1	2,074	Midnite Orchid	5	M	10	0	0	0	1,504
Mickey's Magic	3	G	11	4	2	0	35,670	Midnite Rendezvous	6	G	4	0	0	0	467
Mickey's Malarkey	5	G	7	1	0	2	28,564	Midnite Rumble	4	G	12	0	5	2	23,239
Mickey's Mirage	2	C	2	0	2	0	18,000	Midnite Temptor	5	H	7	1	1	1	3,143
Mickey's Queenmary	2	F	3	0	0	0	95	Midnite Worri	9	M	6	0	0	0	0
Mickey's Reality	6	H	6	1	0	2	8,570	Midsummer Sun	3	F	3	1	0	1	6,500
Mickey's Spark	4	G	2	0	0	0	0	Midterm	5	H	10	2	0	2	16,559
Mickeys Wish	3	F	11	1	1	0	8,138	Midterm Habit	3	F	2	0	0	0	460
Micki Michelle	2	F	3	0	0	1	5,000	Midwatch	4	G	12	2	2	0	30,991
Micmaceuse	4	F	10	3	0	0	61,840	Midway Cat	3	C	3	1	0	1	42,400
Micman	7	G	3	0	0	1	809	Midway Girl	4	F	4	2	1	0	24,763
Microbodgit	2	F	2	0	0	0	195	Midway Road	3	C	5	1	1	2	270,146
Micropunch	3	F	6	2	1	3	14,220	Midwest Mania	2	F	1	0	0	0	70
Mid River	3	G	6	0	1	2	9,929	Midwife	2	F	4	1	0	0	5,865
Midafternoon	3	G	3	2	1	0	60,180	Miercoles Noche	2	G	3	0	0	0	355
Midas Eyes	3	C	6	2	2	1	333,788	Miesque Youtoo	3	C	2	2	0	0	4,235
Middaugh Road	3	C	1	0	0	0	1,500	Miesqued Man	3	C	2	1	0	0	6,225
Midday Madness	4	G	6	0	0	0	510	Miesque's Abrojo	5	M	16	2	2	3	19,810
Midday Son (NZ)	8	G	16	1	1	1	12,401	Miesque's Approval	4	C	4	0	3	0	116,630
Middle East	4	F	3	0	2	0	4,710	Miesque's Daughter	4	F	3	1	1	1	21,200
Middleweight	3	C	9	2	4	0	99,600	Miesque's Prospect	5	G	10	1	3	3	11,263
Middleworth Bay	7	G	2	0	0	0	680	Miesque's Royale	2	G	2	0	0	0	0
Midknight Flight	5	G	4	1	1	0	4,565	Miesques Testimony	4	F	11	1	3	1	48,180
Midknight Minister	3	G	2	0	0	0	0	Miffed	2	C	1	0	0	0	1,230
Midknightmass	6	G	19	3	2	5	8,378	Mig Twenty One	6	G	6	1	0	0	2,828
Midlothian	4	G	9	1	1	1	5,828	Mighbabe	8	M	6	0	0	0	1,425
Midnight Angel (GER)	4	F	3	1	1	0	39,112	Might E Man	2	C	5	1	1	1	9,014
Midnight Assassin	4	C	3	0	0	0	0	Might Pass	4	G	9	1	0	1	4,900
Midnight Charlie	3	C	9	3	0	0	97,041	Might Shape Up	5	M	14	0	1	0	4,089
Midnight Charmer	4	F	11	1	6	2	49,600	Might Tonight	3	F	14	0	1	0	4,089
Midnight Cognac	5	H	10	1	3	1	32,455	Mightbeachamp	4	F	14	0	0	0	555
Midnight Coyote	8	H	3	0	1	0	3,621	Mightiest Titan	3	G	5	1	0	0	10,950
Midnight Cruiser	5	G	16	2	3	3	8,140	Mighty Amanda	4	F	11	2	0	2	11,964
Midnight Cry	3	F	2	1	0	1	85,000	Mighty Aphrodite	4	F	6	0	0	0	435
Midnight Delight	3	F	15	2	1	2	51,940	Mighty Awesome	2	G	11	1	1	4	51,001
Midnight Delivery	6	M	3	0	0	0	240	Mighty Bad News	3	F	6	1	0	0	11,820
Midnight Echo	2	C	3	0	0	0	748	Mighty Beau	4	G	8	2	3	0	84,845
Midnight Explosion	2	C	1	0	0	1	2,170	Mighty Berto	2	G	2	0	0	0	720
Midnight Express	2	C	6	1	1	1	47,437	Mighty Cannon	4	C	10	1	0	2	8,060
Midnight Frolic	3	C	15	2	4	4	34,045	Mighty Cinderella	5	M	6	2	0	1	14,384
Midnight Gift	6	G	7	0	2	1	4,358	Mighty Confide	3	G	5	0	2	0	3,280
Midnight Habit	3	C	5	0	0	0	0	Mighty David	4	G	11	0	2	2	27,404
Midnight Interview	3	C	16	1	2	0	16,745	Mighty Dawn	5	M	9	2	1	1	9,355
Midnight Jet	5	M	1	0	0	0	60	Mighty Deelite	3	F	8	0	1	0	9,159
Midnight Judge	4	F	13	1	4	2	51,319	Mighty Diamond	4	C	4	0	1	0	3,840
Midnight Lightning	4	F	2	1	0	0	9,300	Mighty Dixie	6	M	3	0	0	1	7,091
Midnight Mango	6	M	8	0	2	2	19,920	Mighty Duckling	3	F	7	0	0	0	0

RECORDS OF HORSES

Horse	Age	Sex	Sts	1st	2d	3d	Won
Mighty Elusive	3	C	3	2	0	0	12,900
Mighty Fine Mike	5	G	8	2	3	2	27,850
Mighty Fortress	3	C	4	0	0	1	8,960
Mighty Forum	3	F	5	0	2	1	5,375
Mighty Friskie	4	F	4	0	0	0	925
Mighty G.	3	C	16	2	4	5	58,800
Mighty Good Friday	3	F	5	0	0	0	421
Mighty Gulch	4	C	13	2	6	2	104,870
Mighty Haggard	2	G	3	1	2	0	9,800
Mighty Jazz	6	G	5	1	0	0	8,345
Mighty Joe Young	8	G	14	0	0	3	3,547
Mighty Match	4	G	22	2	3	1	15,885
Mighty Matt	4	G	4	0	0	0	0
Mighty Max	4	G	1	1	0	0	17,820
Mighty Maxwell	9	G	2	0	0	0	0
Mighty Merlin	3	G	6	1	0	1	31,715
Mighty Military	2	C	2	0	0	0	1,125
Mighty Minoru	6	M	2	0	1	0	560
Mighty Mint	5	H	1	0	0	0	0
Mighty Monty	5	H	1	0	0	0	400
Mighty Morgan	2	G	1	0	0	0	0
Mighty Motion	4	C	18	3	2	0	26,049
Mighty Mr. T	5	G	3	0	0	0	315
Mighty Mud Bug	6	H	6	0	1	3	10,735
Mighty Mute	5	G	9	3	2	2	22,956
Mighty Mutt	5	M	6	1	0	1	4,860
Mighty Native	3	C	6	0	1	0	1,899
Mighty Nice Bet	7	G	4	0	0	1	1,826
Mighty Oak	3	C	8	4	1	0	115,405
Mighty Ohara	5	G	14	2	3	2	15,282
Mighty Patient	2	C	1	0	0	0	2,100
Mighty Patriot	5	M	7	2	1	1	17,600
Mighty Picture Too	4	F	6	1	2	0	26,740
Mighty Pointed	4	F	7	0	2	0	2,597
Mighty Proud	4	C	8	0	1	0	4,982
Mighty Raft	4	F	7	1	0	2	4,510
Mighty Rick	5	H	3	0	0	0	466
Mighty Roar	2	C	6	1	0	3	34,650
Mighty Sarah	4	F	15	1	3	0	8,008
Mighty Saviour	4	C	7	0	0	0	510
Mighty Sedona	2	C	4	0	0	0	145
Mighty Silent	3	F	7	0	1	1	959
Mighty Surprized	4	G	7	1	2	1	9,765
Mighty Tricky	7	H	5	0	1	0	4,475
Mighty Try	5	M	1	0	1	0	3,640
Mighty Warrior	3	C	7	1	2	2	5,840
Mighty Wind	8	G	12	1	3	1	7,552
Mightyouious	2	G	4	0	0	0	0
Migrating	4	G	8	0	1	2	5,910
Migrating Son	4	G	2	0	0	1	1,900
Migrating South	4	C	7	0	0	0	1,233
Migrating Zeal	3	F	8	2	1	1	17,126
Migration	5	M	1	0	0	0	46
Migwaki	7	G	6	3	0	0	15,370
Mija Flor	3	F	4	0	1	0	1,253
Mikango	3	G	6	1	0	2	59,957
Mikarenee	2	F	3	0	0	0	300
Mikayla's Prospect	4	F	2	0	0	0	870
Mike and Leo	5	G	6	3	0	1	26,183
Mike Ashley	5	G	11	0	1	1	5,075
Mike B's Bird	2	F	2	0	0	1	2,225
Mike Ken Bar	3	G	17	4	4	2	14,574
Mike Likes It Fast	3	G	5	0	0	0	840
Mike Milligan	4	G	9	1	2	1	7,450
Mike 'n Doc	3	G	11	3	1	1	81,525
Mike Pollio	3	G	14	2	1	2	23,836
Mike Reggie Jr	6	G	4	0	1	0	1,635
Mike Regs Winner	7	G	4	0	0	0	516
Mike Shannon	4	C	15	3	2	1	29,781
Mike the Mudder	3	G	6	1	0	0	16,020
Mike the Tiger	4	G	5	1	0	0	4,801
Mikelmagillicutty	4	G	11	1	5	2	9,916
Mikerto	6	G	12	2	1	2	6,772
Mike's Bay	4	G	15	3	3	3	27,776
Mike's Choice	6	G	2	2	0	0	10,200
Mike's Classic	4	G	12	5	3	2	183,520
Mike's Greenfields	2	G	5	1	1	0	6,250
Mikes Jessie Girl	4	F	1	0	0	0	370
Mike's Last Chance	4	F	10	1	1	3	21,432
Mike's Malagra	5	G	7	0	0	0	345
Mikes Mom Pat	2	F	1	0	0	0	0
Mike's Pappy	6	H	11	1	0	1	4,549
Mike's Pastry	7	G	7	0	2	0	8,060
Mikes Roy	3	G	2	0	0	1	630
Mike's Sister	5	M	1	0	0	0	2,490
Mikes Suite Buck	10	G	4	0	0	1	540
Mike's Thunder	6	G	8	3	1	1	79,900
Mike's Warrior	5	G	15	3	0	1	11,761
Mikesbrotherbuck	4	G	6	1	0	0	5,942
Mikesmrmeaness	2	C	1	0	0	0	0
Mikethespike	3	G	9	1	1	1	10,768
Mikey	5	M	7	1	0	1	6,410
Mikey Fever	3	F	5	2	0	0	17,580
Mikey Likes It	3	G	9	1	2	0	24,456
Mikeymon	3	C	2	1	0	0	25,380
Miki Mouse	4	G	1	0	0	0	0
Milady Can Fly	6	M	2	0	0	0	51
Milady Dee	4	F	12	1	1	4	7,998
Milady Larkspur	4	F	13	1	4	0	9,062
Milady Linda	3	F	9	1	1	1	9,048
Milady Tudor	3	F	4	0	0	0	1,520
Miladys a Prospect	6	M	5	1	2	0	10,215
Milady's Angel	3	C	2	0	0	1	7,000
Milady's Honor	5	M	17	5	5	5	23,735
Milagra	5	M	5	0	0	0	4,166
Milagro Del Paso	4	G	7	0	4	1	11,066
Milam County	2	C	7	0	1	0	2,480
Milan Taizen	6	H	5	2	0	2	22,910
Mila's Gold	4	F	12	1	1	0	6,506
Mild Expense	4	G	4	0	0	1	601
Mild Maggie	4	F	9	1	4	2	48,030
Mild Manor Bill	4	C	9	1	1	3	9,775
Mild Ride	3	C	1	0	0	0	43
Mile	5	G	9	2	2	0	84,546
Mile High Lover	3	F	1	0	0	1	820
Mile of Sunshine	3	F	7	0	0	0	433
Mile Zero	3	G	1	0	0	0	0
Mileage	5	H	5	0	0	0	0
Milenarian	5	G	6	1	0	0	7,670
Miles Ahead	6	G	8	1	1	2	40,060
Miles for Mickey	4	G	11	1	3	0	8,956
Miles of Glory	5	M	13	2	1	2	49,295
Miles River	6	G	11	2	1	0	7,576
Milesimo	4	C	15	1	3	2	3,902
Milestone	7	G	8	3	0	0	36,362
Milestone Victory	2	C	3	1	0	1	36,678
Miliblade	3	F	3	0	0	1	2,042
Militant	3	F	9	0	0	1	882
Military Academy	4	G	3	0	0	1	2,640
Military Affair	2	F	1	0	0	0	85
Military Band	4	C	6	0	0	0	700
Military Lass	2	F	4	0	0	1	3,560
Military Man	4	C	12	3	2	1	78,120
Military Mandate	2	C	3	1	0	2	59,400
Military Mission	2	F	11	2	1	3	33,174
Military Mystery	2	F	1	0	0	0	0
Military Presence	2	C	5	0	0	1	5,768
Military Road	2	G	2	0	0	0	305
Military Singer	2	G	4	0	0	2	19,107
Military Zone	2	G	4	1	2	0	29,210
Milk Man	4	C	6	0	0	2	2,942
Milk Money	8	G	13	1	3	3	8,668
Milk N Cookies	7	M	2	0	0	0	78
Milk River Ridge	4	G	2	1	1	0	3,040
Milk Thief	3	G	3	2	0	0	13,740
Milk Wood (GB)	8	G	8	0	3	5	29,560
Milky Bar (CHI)	7	G	9	2	3	1	49,475
Milky Way Guy	5	G	9	2	2	0	52,110
Mill Grief	3	G	3	0	0	1	3,300
Mill Haven Exit	9	G	5	0	0	0	0
Mill Kapp	3	C	7	0	0	2	5,264
Mill On the Vlas	7	M	2	0	1	1	3,930
Mill Rade	4	F	1	0	0	0	0
Mill Reef Affair	6	H	1	0	0	0	0
Mill Storm	4	G	5	0	0	0	368
Mill Street Blues	3	G	7	1	1	0	8,106
Millay	3	F	3	1	0	1	6,120
Mille Feville	4	F	9	2	3	1	159,329

Horse	Age	Sex	Sts	1st	2d	3d	Won
Millenimax	5	H	1	0	0	0	0
Millenium Beauty	2	F	1	0	0	0	100
Millenium Magic	3	F	2	0	0	0	48
Millenium Maiden	3	F	2	0	0	0	0
Millenium Meridian	4	G	9	1	2	1	3,602
Millenium Moe	3	G	1	0	0	0	0
Millenium Nugget	2	G	3	2	0	1	28,200
Millenium Princess (IRE)	5	M	2	0	0	0	675
Millenium Sis	3	F	3	0	0	0	1,020
Millenium Star	5	G	15	1	2	2	13,277
Millennia Miss	5	M	2	1	0	0	1,595
Millennial Meeting	4	F	5	1	0	0	3,360
Millennialdominion	5	G	6	1	0	0	2,005
Millennium Cat	4	G	7	1	0	2	7,274
Millennium Dragon (GB)	4	C	8	2	1	2	112,990
Millennium Dream (CHI)	3	G	9	0	3	0	19,778
Millennium Ghost	3	C	10	0	2	4	45,140
Millennium Glory	4	C	10	1	2	3	13,588
Millennium Manner	6	G	2	0	0	0	122
Millennium Moment	4	G	3	1	0	0	14,400
Millennium Moon	3	G	3	0	0	0	265
Millennium Morning	4	G	5	0	0	0	0
Millennium Music	3	F	11	0	1	1	3,900
Millennium Mystery	2	C	4	0	0	2	6,790
Millennium Rose	3	F	6	1	1	1	21,830
Millennium Song	5	H	7	2	0	3	19,625
Millennium Storm	3	G	14	0	1	1	37,078
Millennium Sun	4	F	15	1	1	2	10,906
Millennium Two	5	G	16	1	2	2	17,420
Millenniummillions	3	C	10	2	0	5	36,700
Miller Tyme	6	M	5	1	1	0	4,679
Miller's Legend	5	G	1	1	0	0	1,500
Millers Tavern	4	C	8	0	2	1	6,945
Millfleet	2	G	1	0	0	0	0
Millhopper	4	G	1	0	0	0	222
Millie Time	6	M	6	1	1	0	7,022
Milliedale	3	F	6	1	2	0	22,640
Milliemillie	4	F	6	0	2	0	6,200
Millie's Cat	4	F	4	0	0	0	669
Milligram	4	F	10	3	1	2	72,680
Millington Road	5	G	8	0	0	2	2,826
Million Coins	3	F	7	0	0	0	1,650
Millionaire's Row	6	H	6	1	0	1	4,647
Milliondollarlady	3	F	7	0	2	2	6,614
Millionheiress	5	M	1	0	0	0	63
Millonaria	2	F	9	1	0	0	2,267
Millstadt Express	5	H	3	0	0	0	122
Millwood	4	G	13	1	1	2	23,902
Millys Ghost	3	F	3	0	0	0	116
Milo	6	G	11	1	2	1	7,888
Milo Man	4	G	7	1	2	0	9,142
Milsean	3	F	10	1	0	1	7,424
Milton's Krugerand	4	F	5	0	0	0	3,180
Milwaukee Brew	6	H	4	2	1	0	743,000
Milyphesdream	5	G	3	0	1	0	1,840
Mima	4	F	2	0	0	0	0
Mimi Fontaine	5	M	13	1	3	2	13,110
Mimis Classic	3	F	3	0	0	0	1,007
Mimi's Deputy	4	F	5	3	0	0	10,756
Mimi's Mojo	2	F	1	0	0	1	860
Mimi's Song	4	C	3	0	0	0	0
Mimi's Swinghit	3	F	1	0	0	1	690
Mimi's Tizzy	6	M	3	0	0	0	460
Mim's Cat	4	G	14	3	1	1	4,331
Mim's Mime	5	M	3	0	1	1	3,273
Mimsy's Music	3	F	7	0	0	1	2,710
Min Royal	4	F	1	0	0	0	327
Minamala (IRE)	4	F	6	1	2	1	54,720
Minarri	2	C	3	0	0	1	4,940
Minaville	4	G	20	1	5	4	57,480
Minco Missle	3	G	4	0	0	0	340
Mind Body Soul	3	C	8	1	0	2	32,571
Mind Deals	3	C	18	1	6	2	22,320
Mind of Gold	4	G	5	0	1	0	4,220
Mind Reader	4	F	9	1	1	0	37,580
Mind Your Business	3	G	10	1	0	2	10,985
Minden Mist	3	F	4	0	0	0	567
Mindful	3	F	1	0	0	0	216
Mindful Music	3	F	4	0	0	0	539
Mindful Tactician	3	C	2	0	0	1	2,380
Mindsweeper	2	G	2	1	0	1	19,305
Mindyourownbidness	6	G	6	0	0	0	504
Mindy's Connection	3	C	13	2	2	4	37,450
Mindys Deputy	2	G	3	0	0	0	235
Mindy's Smile	6	G	2	0	0	1	1,001
Mindy's Token	4	F	4	0	1	0	2,890
Mine and Yours	6	M	1	0	0	0	0
Mine Glow	5	G	4	0	0	0	1,020
Mine Sweep	3	F	6	1	2	1	32,060
Mine the Gold	3	G	9	1	0	3	18,495
Mine Valentine	2	F	3	0	0	0	498
Mineisthehunter	4	G	18	1	1	3	6,344
Miner Distraction	3	F	3	1	0	0	26,655
Miner Moss	3	G	11	1	1	1	35,005
Miner Note	4	G	17	2	3	4	12,313
Miner Prospect	3	F	4	1	1	0	14,100
Miner Quatorze	3	C	2	0	0	0	690
Mineral Gist	6	M	15	0	1	3	3,094
Mineral Point	2	C	1	0	0	0	0
Miners Americanson	3	C	17	2	2	3	16,001
Miner's Chon	3	G	3	0	0	0	50
Miner's Clementine	7	M	16	1	2	4	34,687
Miner's Crown	5	M	12	0	1	0	1,922
Miner's Dance	5	G	4	0	0	0	780
Miner's Double	3	F	7	0	0	1	1,380
Miners Gamble	7	G	9	1	1	1	37,503
Miner's Marquessa	4	F	15	1	3	0	11,492
Miners Mate	3	F	3	1	0	0	14,770
Miner's Mint	3	F	8	1	3	3	36,080
Miners Patch	3	F	1	0	0	0	372
Miner's Prize	6	G	5	1	0	0	40,873
Miners Relief	4	G	6	2	0	1	19,275
Miner's Road	3	G	8	1	1	0	5,280
Miners Sin	4	G	11	2	1	1	31,380
Miner's Song	7	M	11	3	1	0	12,344
Miner's Star	3	F	5	0	0	0	1,405
Miner's Surprise	3	G	6	0	2	1	2,955
Miner's Trick	7	G	14	4	3	3	25,870
Miner's Wish	7	G	4	1	1	1	4,376
Minerva High	3	F	8	0	0	0	873
Minerva Leader	5	M	4	0	0	0	1,211
Minerva Lights	3	F	12	3	2	2	20,065
Minerva Newsleader	2	G	4	0	1	0	3,768
Minerveeni	4	G	3	0	0	0	1,440
Mineshaft	4	C	9	7	2	0	2,209,686
Miney's Awesome	3	F	9	2	2	2	35,915
Ming Toy	8	G	5	1	0	0	3,024
Minge Cove	2	F	1	0	0	0	2,195
Mingo	3	G	10	1	0	1	7,717
Mingo Menace	4	F	2	0	0	0	0
Mingo Springs	4	C	2	0	0	0	0
Mingos Go Go Girl	4	F	4	0	0	1	1,178
Mini Affair	2	F	2	1	0	0	4,880
Mini Brush	3	F	7	2	2	0	28,600
Mini Delini	7	M	1	0	0	0	0
Mini Fuegos	6	M	2	0	0	0	100
Mini Marauder	4	C	16	1	4	0	20,990
Mini Me	4	F	4	1	2	0	2,020
Mini Mind	3	G	3	0	0	0	0
Mini Mink	3	F	6	0	0	0	363
Mini Minou	3	F	2	0	1	0	6,000
Minifever	2	F	2	0	0	1	3,055
Minii'pokaa	5	G	12	1	0	4	10,075
Minimalist	4	F	1	0	0	0	380
Minimona	5	M	10	0	2	1	4,481
Minimuffin	4	F	6	0	1	0	606
Mining Cash	4	C	2	0	0	0	137
Mining Diamonds	3	C	9	1	1	2	49,865
Mining for Fun	5	G	14	2	7	1	29,559
Mining Missharriet	7	M	3	0	0	0	778
Mining Plan	4	F	10	2	0	1	9,148
Mining Shaft	2	C	1	0	1	0	3,192
Mining Silver	3	F	7	1	0	2	17,440
Minister Blair	2	C	1	0	1	0	7,600
Minister Eric	2	C	5	1	2	1	387,920
Minister Lady	4	F	11	3	1	3	34,539
Minister Lake	5	M	11	1	1	2	14,100
Minister o' War	4	G	4	1	1	0	5,185

Horse	Age	Sex	Sts	1st	2d	3d	Won
Minister of Note	4	G	12	1	3	2	16,884
Minister of Speed	5	G	6	0	0	1	1,080
Minister Princess	3	F	4	1	0	1	6,900
Minister Ron	8	G	2	0	0	0	76
Minister Varnie	3	G	3	0	0	0	138
Ministercoordinate	4	C	7	1	0	1	2,868
Ministeroftrucks	3	F	8	2	3	1	23,060
Minister's Baby	5	M	6	0	3	1	46,100
Ministers Bullet	3	F	3	0	1	1	5,575
Minister's Sin	5	M	7	0	0	0	0
Ministers Wild Cat	3	C	6	2	2	0	134,400
Ministry of Love	2	C	2	0	1	0	2,050
Mink Man	6	M	5	1	1	1	6,029
Minks Toy	4	F	1	0	0	0	0
Minnamana	2	G	5	1	1	3	27,600
Minne Bandera	5	M	2	0	0	0	145
Minneapolis Babe	6	M	6	0	2	1	11,050
Minneapolis Man	4	G	15	4	1	2	18,882
Minnesota Mackee	5	H	2	1	1	0	3,980
Minnesota Pitch	4	C	14	4	1	1	45,930
Minnesota Prospect	4	F	2	0	0	0	370
Minnesota Shuffle	6	G	10	2	3	2	29,822
Minni Sangue	4	F	1	0	0	1	3,960
Minnie Con	2	F	2	0	0	0	150
Minnie Jinnie	3	F	6	3	0	1	18,482
Minnieprize	7	M	6	0	1	0	3,290
Minnies Adam Ant	5	H	14	0	2	1	17,968
Minnie's Mickey	3	F	15	0	1	2	18,315
Minnie's Premier	5	M	13	2	3	1	15,923
Minnow Bucket	4	F	6	1	1	0	6,669
Minny Monster	4	F	4	0	0	0	110
Minny's Niece	3	F	2	0	2	0	18,780
Minor Magic	5	M	8	1	2	1	6,133
Minor Sam	3	G	4	0	0	0	178
Minor Wisdom	7	G	2	0	0	1	2,090
Minor's Gold	5	M	10	3	0	0	42,955
Minoruego	4	F	7	0	0	3	4,730
Minotaur	4	G	16	2	6	3	27,985
Minstrel Beat	3	C	12	1	0	3	7,749
Minstrel Bud	4	C	4	0	0	0	1,962
Minstrel Got Gold	4	F	23	3	7	5	21,936
Minstrel's Melody	3	C	8	1	0	3	30,160
Mint Breaker	5	G	7	1	0	0	6,150
Mint Condition	2	F	2	0	0	0	390
Mint Money	4	G	12	0	0	1	2,541
Mint of Gray	5	G	5	0	0	2	910
Mint Report	6	M	5	0	0	1	1,400
Mint Royale	6	G	18	2	3	2	15,783
Mint Swirl	7	M	2	0	0	0	164
Mint to Be Charly	4	G	5	0	0	0	1,650
Mint to Kiss	4	F	6	1	2	0	33,240
Mintano	4	F	1	0	0	0	450
Minted Age	5	G	11	2	3	1	37,300
Mintess	4	F	2	0	0	0	280
Minuano	2	F	1	0	0	0	0
Minus Three	4	C	7	2	0	0	9,879
Minutes Ahead	4	F	20	2	2	2	29,572
Mio Milo	3	G	2	0	0	0	95
Miossens Fireball	6	M	2	0	0	0	0
Mira Mesa	3	F	2	0	0	0	1,000
Miracle Boy	2	C	14	1	1	2	18,207
Miracle Flight	4	G	15	1	1	1	14,598
Miracle Glow	4	C	16	1	0	1	9,535
Miracle Mets	6	G	3	1	0	1	3,500
Miracle R. N.	4	F	3	0	0	0	210
Miracle Ridge	3	C	5	0	0	0	0
Miracle Tap	2	F	2	0	0	0	1,059
Miracle Twist	4	C	7	1	0	0	7,240
Miracle Whirl	4	C	12	0	0	2	1,798
Miracles	5	M	3	0	0	0	494
Miracolo	3	F	5	0	0	0	904
Miracolo Won	3	C	6	0	0	0	395
Miraculous Journey	3	G	1	0	0	0	0
Miraculousmichel	5	M	15	2	4	4	17,481
Mirage's Gambo Bay	5	M	6	1	0	0	6,600
Miramar (FR)	8	G	11	1	2	1	8,285
Miramichi Magic	4	G	9	2	2	3	17,744
Miranda Made	3	F	2	0	0	0	296
Miranda's Among Us	4	F	4	0	1	0	8,320
Miranda's Moon	5	M	9	1	1	1	4,120
Miranda's Wine	5	G	7	1	0	0	7,634
Mirando City	2	C	3	0	2	0	2,860
Mire Poix	2	F	1	0	0	0	780
Mirek	4	G	6	0	2	0	4,425
Mirific (IRE)	4	G	17	2	5	3	76,430
Mirka	3	F	10	1	1	0	13,297
Mirobolant	4	F	16	1	4	1	8,481
Miron's Gentleman	12	G	4	0	0	0	720
Miroslava	7	M	4	0	1	0	5,076
Mirror	4	C	8	1	1	2	24,240
Mirta	4	F	4	0	0	1	3,960
Mirush	3	F	3	0	0	0	1,890
Mis L. S.	5	M	7	0	0	1	1,111
Mis Steeling	4	F	11	1	0	1	9,002
Miscataway	2	F	7	1	3	1	19,095
Mischeviousdevious	3	F	3	0	0	0	0
Mischief Boy	4	G	1	0	0	0	123
Mischief Rules	8	G	8	0	0	0	1,418
Mischiefs Finale	7	H	4	0	0	0	300
Mischieviously	3	F	8	3	1	0	86,480
Mischievous Joke	5	H	3	0	0	0	52
Mischievous Lover	3	G	3	0	1	0	7,808
Mischievous Merlin	3	G	8	2	2	0	18,138
Mischievousmariner	8	G	11	1	0	1	6,107
Misconception	6	G	8	5	0	1	23,410
Miscreant	3	F	2	0	0	1	2,387
Misdotwo	8	M	3	0	0	0	172
Misensor	4	C	11	2	2	0	3,333
Misguided Left	2	G	5	2	0	1	40,900
Mismeridia	3	F	2	0	0	0	750
Miss a Note	3	F	9	1	0	1	13,762
Miss Abbey Lee	6	M	5	0	0	0	0
Miss Abby	5	M	8	3	1	0	9,759
Miss Aberdeen	2	F	2	0	0	0	400
Miss Adams	2	F	2	0	0	0	0
Miss Addie Downs	3	F	1	0	0	0	0
Miss Adventurest	4	F	6	1	1	0	6,060
Miss Adversity	5	M	5	0	0	0	290
Miss Air Won	3	F	5	0	0	1	803
Miss Airline	3	F	3	0	0	0	0
Miss Alamo	4	F	11	1	3	2	9,660
Miss Alexa	2	F	2	0	0	0	246
Miss Alexis	4	F	7	2	1	1	63,530
Miss Alezzotti	3	F	9	0	1	1	2,821
Miss Alfalfa	4	F	1	0	0	0	0
Miss Alice's Boy	5	H	15	1	0	3	6,698
Miss Aliwood	5	M	6	0	0	2	1,234
Miss All That	2	F	2	0	0	1	2,280
Miss Allie Gator	8	M	2	0	0	1	2,363
Miss Ally Bali	4	F	8	0	0	0	397
Miss Alyetta	5	M	2	0	1	0	6,400
Miss Alyssa	2	F	1	0	0	0	0
Miss Angel Face	3	F	5	1	1	2	20,900
Miss Angel G	3	F	5	1	0	0	6,540
Miss Anna Banana	3	F	6	0	0	1	1,127
Miss Anna G.	4	F	11	1	1	0	11,947
Miss Anna Lucille	4	F	2	0	0	0	188
Miss Annie Bea	5	M	12	1	0	2	13,438
Miss Arctic Chill	5	M	6	0	0	0	753
Miss Area Code	5	M	12	0	2	3	7,039
Miss Ash	2	F	2	0	0	0	0
Miss Ashley	4	G	5	1	1	0	7,970
Miss Attack	2	F	1	0	0	0	230
Miss Atticus	4	F	6	0	0	2	11,915
Miss Avalanche	3	F	9	2	0	2	5,978
Miss Avenue	4	F	3	0	0	1	2,475
Miss Awana	3	F	6	1	1	1	9,040
Miss Awesome	3	F	2	0	0	0	2,000
Miss Baba	3	F	6	0	0	1	7,140
Miss Bag Lady	4	F	9	0	0	1	3,452
Miss Ballard	4	F	1	0	0	0	0
Miss Baloo	4	F	6	0	0	1	880
Miss Barbara Ray	3	F	11	3	2	0	42,027
Miss Barbie Slew	3	F	22	1	2	1	9,921
Miss Barner	5	M	12	3	2	4	31,583
Miss Basket	6	M	1	0	0	0	72
Miss Bates	6	M	15	1	3	2	7,128
Miss Battisti	3	F	5	0	1	2	12,040

Horse	Age	Sex	Sts	1st	2d	3d	Won
Miss Bea Haven	7	M	5	0	0	0	366
Miss Bearcat	4	F	6	0	0	1	442
Miss Beaujo	7	M	9	1	1	0	3,145
Miss Beaulieu	2	F	8	0	1	1	3,515
Miss Beauty	4	F	2	1	1	0	5,856
Miss Becca	5	M	4	0	0	0	262
Miss Becky	5	M	6	0	1	0	1,023
Miss Believe It	4	F	7	1	0	0	7,089
Miss Benton Creek	4	F	3	0	0	1	725
Miss Beraven	4	F	10	0	5	2	20,295
Miss Bergdorf	2	F	4	0	0	0	11,960
Miss Bev Hills	8	M	1	0	0	0	300
Miss Bid Believe	4	F	4	1	0	1	7,260
Miss Billie Dee	3	F	7	1	1	1	5,990
Miss Bingo Bettie	3	F	7	1	1	2	39,594
Miss Bleus Clues	2	F	3	1	0	0	18,106
Miss Bling Bling	2	F	2	0	0	0	1,746
Miss Blt	4	F	9	0	0	0	282
Miss Blue Bayou	5	M	6	0	1	1	9,700
Miss Bo Blush	6	M	10	0	0	1	6,060
Miss Bold Peach	2	F	2	0	0	0	0
Miss Bollington	3	F	10	0	1	2	2,445
Miss Bonn Bonn	3	F	3	1	0	0	17,350
Miss Bonnet	5	M	10	2	0	0	9,671
Miss Boomtown	4	F	11	0	1	3	22,090
Miss Boundary	3	F	4	1	0	2	18,766
Miss Bradford Co	2	F	3	0	1	0	2,300
Miss Brassy	3	F	4	1	0	0	7,055
Miss Braveheart	3	F	8	0	0	0	1,230
Miss Briartic	5	M	10	0	3	2	14,139
Miss Bridget Jones	3	F	5	2	0	0	121,032
Miss Bright Lights	2	F	1	0	0	0	0
Miss Briteness	2	F	3	1	0	0	6,875
Miss B's Lucky	2	C	5	0	1	1	3,980
Miss B's Rythum	2	F	1	0	0	0	105
Miss Buffie	6	M	2	0	0	0	0
Miss Bullet	4	F	9	1	0	3	7,385
Miss Buona Sera	4	F	9	2	1	2	16,915
Miss C. B.	3	F	12	1	2	0	29,617
Miss Cajyn	3	F	2	0	0	0	0
Miss Candi Road	5	M	3	0	0	0	533
Miss Candice	3	F	1	0	0	0	0
Miss Canuck	5	M	6	1	0	1	5,180
Miss Cap	4	F	4	0	1	2	21,680
Miss Carlye Ann	4	F	2	0	0	0	0
Miss Carrera	3	F	2	0	0	0	2,340
Miss Cash	3	F	6	2	0	0	26,840
Miss Cat Ballou	4	F	13	0	4	0	20,600
Miss Catalina	2	F	1	0	0	0	0
Miss Catillac	2	F	1	0	0	0	928
Miss Cecilia	2	F	9	1	0	2	4,065
Miss Celene	3	F	3	0	0	0	434
Miss Centerville	3	F	11	2	1	2	25,786
Miss Chacha Dancer	7	M	13	1	3	2	24,902
Miss Chaffee	4	F	11	1	2	1	12,255
Miss Chalice	2	F	6	1	0	2	12,600
Miss Chance	3	F	7	2	0	2	19,888
Miss Change	3	F	13	0	3	1	12,508
Miss Charismatic	2	F	1	0	0	0	0
Miss Charlie Mac	10	M	15	1	4	1	6,830
Miss Charm Avenger	6	M	8	0	0	2	5,103
Miss Chatty	2	F	8	0	4	1	19,787
Miss Chaucer	3	F	4	0	0	0	69
Miss Cheech	4	F	1	0	0	0	0
Miss Cheektowaga	2	F	2	0	0	0	364
Miss Cherokee Sue	3	F	8	1	1	1	20,080
Miss Chevious	5	M	17	2	2	1	10,532
Miss Chief Woody	6	M	18	3	4	4	34,566
Miss Chieftain	4	C	11	0	0	0	707
Miss Chimes Band	8	M	8	0	1	1	1,945
Miss Chris	6	M	6	4	0	1	15,028
Miss Circle	4	F	11	0	1	0	3,849
Miss City Halo	4	F	3	0	2	0	11,560
Miss Clara Belle	4	F	7	0	0	0	561
Miss Clara Tess	4	F	11	5	0	1	66,660
Miss Cody	6	M	13	3	4	1	30,035
Miss Combo	3	F	6	1	0	1	16,865
Miss Communipaw	3	F	3	1	0	1	6,390
Miss Comstock	3	F	13	1	0	1	5,093
Miss Con	5	M	6	1	1	0	5,788
Miss Concern	3	F	3	1	0	0	13,757
Miss Concerto	2	F	3	1	2	0	19,000
Miss Confusion	3	F	12	3	4	0	63,850
Miss Congeniality	5	M	9	1	1	2	4,250
Miss Connie Sue	2	F	4	2	0	0	19,860
Miss Continental	4	F	2	0	1	1	4,480
Miss Corey	6	M	7	1	2	0	4,045
Miss Coronado	2	F	1	0	0	1	4,920
Miss Corrine	3	F	3	1	0	0	12,600
Miss Cortina	2	F	2	1	1	0	25,800
Miss Costello	3	F	9	2	0	1	85,522
Miss Cotton Candy	6	M	7	1	0	0	12,658
Miss Cotton Tail	2	F	3	0	0	2	9,600
Miss Count	3	F	1	0	0	0	92
Miss Crafty	2	F	2	0	0	0	0
Miss Crafty Pal	2	F	2	1	0	1	21,850
Miss Crane	4	F	8	0	1	1	3,307
Miss Cree	4	F	11	1	1	1	11,709
Miss Crimson Pine	3	F	5	0	0	0	348
Miss Crissy	3	F	8	1	3	2	220,687
Miss Cuch a Lou	5	M	2	0	0	0	0
Miss Curley Sue	5	M	9	0	4	2	9,285
Miss Curtain Call	4	F	2	0	0	0	0
Miss Custom Pro	4	F	2	0	0	0	292
Miss Cyprus	3	F	8	0	0	0	2,000
Miss D Flawless	2	F	3	0	0	1	4,620
Miss D' Or	6	M	9	2	2	3	36,910
Miss D. Falcon	4	F	6	0	0	1	1,521
Miss Dakota	3	F	9	3	0	0	70,490
Miss Dan Pat	5	M	7	0	0	1	1,887
Miss Dancin Diablo	5	M	2	0	1	0	1,367
Miss Dark Star	3	F	6	1	1	0	10,785
Miss Dashy Dawn	3	F	1	0	0	0	0
Miss Dazzling	5	M	14	2	3	3	13,840
Miss December Rose	3	F	6	2	1	0	23,200
Miss Dee Sean	5	M	6	1	1	0	8,575
Miss Deed	2	F	1	0	0	0	0
Miss Delia	3	F	4	1	2	0	24,170
Miss Dennette	5	M	1	0	0	0	0
Miss Denouncer	2	F	2	1	0	0	25,740
Miss Denver Mint	4	F	12	1	1	0	6,744
Miss Denzil	7	M	2	0	0	0	135
Miss Deputy	6	M	9	0	0	1	1,652
Miss Derbyship	5	M	5	1	1	0	3,334
Miss Diablo's Cav	4	F	17	3	1	1	22,735
Miss Dixie Brass	7	M	8	1	0	1	3,438
Miss Dixie Dream	8	M	3	1	0	0	14,130
Miss Dixie Dreamer	3	F	7	2	2	0	43,714
Miss Dixie Star	3	F	6	1	1	0	4,437
Miss Dixie Wynner	2	F	3	0	0	0	0
Miss d'Mina	5	M	10	2	2	1	25,260
Miss Docscott	5	M	7	1	2	1	19,397
Miss Doggedly	4	F	6	1	0	2	11,510
Miss Doggone	4	F	4	0	0	0	393
Miss Domuch (IRE)	5	M	1	0	0	0	0
Miss Double Dots	3	F	9	1	3	0	28,360
Miss Dragon	3	F	3	0	0	0	600
Miss Duchess	5	M	6	0	2	3	5,950
Miss Ducketts	5	M	5	0	0	0	156
Miss Dumaine	3	F	12	1	3	3	30,694
Miss Dusty	6	M	5	1	2	0	4,155
Miss Eagle	8	M	13	0	0	1	1,748
Miss Easy	2	F	1	0	0	0	0
Miss Einstein	5	M	2	0	0	0	1,232
Miss Elegance	5	M	10	0	2	3	3,417
Miss Elegant	3	F	5	0	0	0	890
Miss Elena	5	M	9	0	0	0	6,360
Miss Eltish	4	F	5	1	0	0	12,696
Miss Emma S	3	F	4	0	1	0	1,940
Miss E's Report	4	F	13	1	4	0	9,891
Miss Eternal Orage	3	F	12	0	0	1	3,200
Miss Ethel Jet	3	F	1	0	0	0	0
Miss Event	2	F	2	0	0	1	1,680
Miss Excavator	3	F	8	1	1	3	6,245
Miss Excellent	4	F	3	1	0	0	9,000
Miss Exotic	7	M	2	0	0	1	160
Miss Expensive (ARG)	6	M	10	1	0	2	39,408
Miss Eyra	2	F	2	0	0	1	1,540

RECORDS OF HORSES

Horse	Age	Sex	Sts	1st	2d	3d	Won	Horse	Age	Sex	Sts	1st	2d	3d	Won
Miss F D N Y	3	F	1	0	0	0	345	Miss Indian	4	F	4	0	0	0	226
Miss Fairfield	2	F	1	0	0	0	0	Miss Infidelity	2	C	4	1	0	0	8,400
Miss Fancy Free	3	F	2	0	0	0	0	Miss Interpreted	3	F	4	0	0	0	1,450
Miss Fatih	4	F	19	2	2	4	9,137	Miss Intrepid	2	F	6	1	0	0	3,738
Miss Faxawin	4	F	5	1	1	0	8,685	Miss Issy	2	F	2	0	0	0	500
Miss Feather River	4	F	5	0	1	1	3,979	Miss Ivy Hilton	5	M	1	0	0	0	1,110
Miss Feature	6	M	11	5	1	1	23,957	Miss Ivy League	2	F	2	0	0	0	0
Miss Fighting Fit	7	M	9	1	1	1	3,141	Miss J J Road	3	F	2	0	0	0	200
Miss Filibuster	3	F	5	1	0	0	33,878	Miss Jangle	3	F	8	1	0	4	7,550
Miss Fiona	4	F	6	0	1	2	3,135	Miss Jazzy	5	M	12	3	4	2	37,690
Miss Fire Fox	5	M	4	1	2	0	11,700	Miss Jeanne Cat	4	F	1	0	0	0	0
Miss Fire Water	8	M	7	0	0	1	1,320	Miss Jeannie	4	F	2	0	0	0	260
Miss Fixed Income	3	F	11	7	1	0	58,160	Miss Jekyll	2	F	2	0	0	0	0
Miss Flagship	5	M	4	0	0	0	534	Miss Jet Note	3	F	13	0	4	0	3,838
Miss Fliss	4	F	10	1	2	1	2,087	Miss Jetset	3	F	11	1	1	0	10,315
Miss Flit N Flot	2	F	2	0	0	0	1,380	Miss Johnson	2	F	2	0	0	0	0
Miss Flor (FR)	3	F	2	0	0	0	2,760	Miss Joker	5	M	10	3	1	1	64,910
Miss Fortunate	3	F	9	3	2	0	104,830	Miss Jolie Ann	2	F	4	0	2	1	5,900
Miss Foxcroft	5	M	11	4	2	1	17,842	Miss Judged Me	2	F	1	0	0	0	85
Miss Foxly	4	F	9	1	0	0	4,529	Miss Julian	6	M	7	1	0	0	5,934
Miss Freedom	3	F	10	1	2	0	11,410	Miss Kalena	4	F	5	1	0	0	4,446
Miss French	4	F	13	3	5	1	71,271	Miss Kammie	3	F	8	1	0	1	14,700
Miss Frenchie	5	M	10	1	0	0	9,461	Miss Kandygram	4	F	1	0	0	0	0
Miss Friendly	3	F	9	1	2	0	13,344	Miss Karry Thenews	3	F	10	1	2	1	26,369
Miss Friendship	6	M	14	1	0	0	8,489	Miss Kate Rusby	3	F	2	0	0	0	0
Miss Fudge	6	M	7	0	0	3	4,340	Miss Kelsey	3	F	11	0	1	1	5,410
Miss Fuzzi Diamond	2	F	2	0	0	0	0	Miss Kenny Penny	4	F	5	0	0	0	0
Miss G Force	2	F	4	0	0	1	4,060	Miss Kentucky	4	F	11	4	1	0	25,490
Miss Garrett	3	F	11	1	0	1	4,072	Miss Key Lar Go	3	F	2	0	0	0	0
Miss Gazon (IRE)	5	M	7	0	0	0	2,550	Miss Kipper Kitty	5	M	6	1	1	2	12,220
Miss Georgia	2	F	1	0	0	0	0	Miss Kitty Hawk	4	F	11	3	4	3	115,991
Miss Georgianna	5	M	8	0	0	0	727	Miss Kitty Saloon	6	M	6	2	1	2	10,600
Miss Gettysburg	3	F	3	0	0	1	715	Miss Kitty Slew	3	F	3	1	0	0	6,300
Miss Gilder	3	F	9	1	1	0	9,010	Miss Klamath	4	F	12	1	1	5	21,310
Miss Ginalie	2	F	8	1	1	0	15,104	Miss Lacy Shea	4	F	14	3	2	3	42,276
Miss Gina's Bag	4	F	3	0	0	0	180	Miss Lady Di	3	F	3	1	1	0	20,580
Miss Glitterman	7	M	4	1	0	0	9,785	Miss Lady Randolph	4	F	10	1	2	1	5,318
Miss Gneiss	2	F	3	0	0	0	0	Miss Laurel Canyon	3	F	10	2	3	2	13,170
Miss Gold Dee	4	F	3	1	0	0	9,504	Miss Leatherwood	3	F	4	0	0	0	420
Miss Gold Diva	4	F	6	1	1	2	6,288	Miss Legal One	3	F	3	0	0	0	0
Miss Golden Darby	7	M	1	0	1	0	250	Miss Legend	3	F	6	0	4	1	25,380
Miss Golightly	4	F	8	0	0	2	2,261	Miss Lemon	6	M	5	1	0	1	11,150
Miss Good Grades	4	F	1	0	0	0	1,135	Miss Libby	6	M	2	0	0	0	103
Miss Goose Creek	6	M	6	0	0	0	264	Miss Lickity Split	3	F	1	0	0	0	0
Miss Goosebumps	4	F	16	2	4	2	77,679	Miss Lil'	3	F	8	2	1	1	22,390
Miss Got Rox	4	F	5	0	0	4	1,988	Miss Lily Bee	4	F	2	0	0	0	365
Miss Gracie	3	F	9	0	2	0	9,741	Miss Linda (ARG)	6	M	5	0	1	3	130,825
Miss Gray Goose	4	F	7	1	1	0	8,019	Miss Listo	3	F	6	0	1	1	12,230
Miss Gregory	3	F	7	0	0	0	1,093	Miss Lit de Justic	3	F	5	0	0	0	0
Miss Gretchen	4	F	4	0	1	1	756	Miss Livingston	7	M	2	0	0	0	0
Miss Grindstone	4	F	8	4	1	1	148,176	Miss Lizzie Tish	3	F	6	1	2	1	25,081
Miss Groom	4	F	8	0	1	2	2,734	Miss Lodi	4	F	10	2	2	1	172,204
Miss Guts	4	F	11	0	4	3	50,263	Miss Loganville	3	F	12	0	3	2	10,930
Miss Hadley	4	F	3	0	0	0	0	Miss Logical	3	F	3	0	0	0	0
Miss Hamma	4	F	7	2	0	1	33,629	Miss Lonestar	2	F	3	0	0	0	2,500
Miss Happy	2	F	4	1	0	2	13,690	Miss Longevity	6	M	18	1	2	3	9,069
Miss Happy Hour	3	F	8	3	1	1	18,742	Miss Low Cut	4	F	9	2	2	1	20,402
Miss Havana	3	F	4	0	0	0	1,110	Miss Lucia	4	F	3	0	1	0	2,440
Miss Have	4	F	2	0	0	0	0	Miss Lucky Strike	5	M	5	0	0	2	5,210
Miss Hawfield	2	F	1	0	1	0	4,560	Miss Luttie Huck	2	F	1	0	0	0	0
Miss Hellie	4	F	9	3	2	1	97,600	Miss M. J.	5	M	3	0	0	0	564
Miss Hennessy	4	F	10	3	1	0	23,203	Miss Machisma	2	F	2	0	0	0	0
Miss Hester	3	F	8	1	1	1	10,976	Miss Maddilynn	3	F	8	1	2	2	12,280
Miss High Calling	4	F	5	0	0	0	325	Miss Malaga	5	M	13	0	0	0	3,630
Miss Holly Lynn	6	M	4	0	0	0	369	Miss Malthus	2	F	1	0	0	0	0
Miss Holy Moly	2	F	4	0	0	0	2,623	Miss Manastash	11	M	3	0	0	0	180
Miss Holy Toledo	4	F	15	1	2	0	9,552	Miss Mandi	2	F	3	0	2	0	3,700
Miss Honey Money	3	F	3	1	0	1	12,033	Miss Marcia	4	F	7	0	1	2	20,925
Miss Honeybee	5	M	13	5	2	1	35,394	Miss Marcy	5	M	5	0	1	0	2,884
Miss Hotsy Totsy	6	M	12	1	5	3	11,958	Miss Maria	4	F	11	2	3	3	13,572
Miss Hottie	2	F	2	0	0	0	1,302	Miss Mariah	3	F	4	1	1	0	9,280
Miss Houdini	3	F	2	0	1	0	11,800	Miss Marigold	4	F	22	6	4	1	31,225
Miss I. Q.	4	F	9	2	0	0	9,240	Miss Marina	4	F	8	0	1	3	3,246
Miss Icicle	5	M	5	0	1	1	27,592	Miss Marker	4	F	20	1	2	2	8,845
Miss Ida Belle	5	M	7	0	0	1	3,954	Miss Marni	4	F	7	0	0	0	5,625
Miss Imagination	4	F	9	1	1	3	21,460	Miss Martha Bell	7	M	5	0	0	0	338
Miss Imagine That	2	F	4	0	0	0	394	Miss Marvic	2	F	2	0	0	0	665
Miss Impromptu	4	F	4	1	1	0	21,650	Miss Mary Apples	3	F	8	2	2	1	60,997
Miss Independent	3	F	10	0	0	1	4,911	Miss Mattie Mu Mu	5	M	13	2	0	0	14,699

Horse	Age	Sex	Sts	1st	2d	3d	Won	Horse	Age	Sex	Sts	1st	2d	3d	Won
Miss Maudette	4	F	7	1	2	0	12,990	Miss Prestissimo	4	F	14	2	0	5	13,597
Miss Meanie	2	F	1	0	0	0	75	Miss Priss's Route	4	F	1	0	0	0	0
Miss Mecke	4	F	19	3	1	1	15,805	Miss Pritty Britt	3	F	2	0	0	0	0
Miss Meister	2	F	5	1	0	1	21,250	Miss Proof	9	M	5	0	0	1	881
Miss Memories	6	M	9	1	1	2	10,935	Miss Proper Ice	3	F	3	0	0	0	170
Miss Mercy	3	F	5	0	0	0	1,032	Miss Proper Too	3	F	5	0	0	0	2,985
Miss Mescalero	5	M	8	0	0	0	461	Miss Proper West	3	F	9	2	1	2	15,119
Miss Metropolitan	2	F	1	0	0	0	0	Miss Ptarmigan	4	F	8	1	2	0	29,180
Miss Michelle	5	M	13	2	2	2	23,168	Miss Puchski	4	F	1	0	0	0	120
Miss Midas	2	F	1	0	0	0	118	Miss Purtenance	4	F	4	0	2	1	2,600
Miss Miesque	4	F	14	4	2	0	30,745	Miss Puzzle (AUS)	5	M	4	0	1	1	23,480
Miss Millie Boone	5	M	13	1	2	1	7,626	Miss Quackie Creek	3	F	9	0	0	0	158
Miss Miracle	3	F	5	0	0	0	330	Miss Quick City	3	F	14	1	4	4	37,256
Miss Mirage (IRE)	3	F	6	1	1	0	13,016	Miss Quinn	2	F	2	0	0	0	0
Miss Misbehavin'	8	M	21	0	4	6	19,157	Miss Rachel Marie	3	F	9	5	1	1	147,788
Miss Misfit	2	F	5	1	0	2	18,840	Miss Rainbow	4	F	1	0	0	0	76
Miss Mizzou	2	F	4	1	0	0	6,860	Miss Rancho Vista	2	F	5	0	2	0	3,440
Miss Mollie M	2	F	2	0	0	0	265	Miss Real Buddy	6	M	3	0	0	0	110
Miss Monty	3	F	8	1	0	1	8,857	Miss Reiko	2	F	4	0	0	0	3,060
Miss Moon	4	F	10	3	1	0	38,192	Miss Ricki Racer	2	F	4	1	0	0	5,225
Miss Moonraker	4	F	5	0	0	1	6,620	Miss Riddler	4	F	8	1	0	2	13,496
Miss Morgan Ray	3	F	5	0	0	0	3,120	Miss Riley	4	F	12	1	2	2	30,370
Miss Morning Line	2	F	1	0	0	0	0	Miss Rita	6	M	7	1	2	1	4,764
Miss Mudville	4	F	7	3	0	0	10,500	Miss Ritz	4	F	2	0	1	0	3,700
Miss Mulie	2	F	3	0	0	0	1,015	Miss Roberson	3	F	9	2	2	0	23,224
Miss Musical Coin	6	M	11	0	1	2	4,793	Miss Roberts	4	F	15	5	1	2	20,830
Miss Muzzy	5	M	2	0	0	0	100	Miss Rocket Jet	3	F	5	1	0	0	15,720
Miss My Cat	4	C	2	0	0	1	1,650	Miss Rodeo	3	F	2	1	0	1	29,110
Miss Mystical Mon	3	F	2	0	0	0	322	Miss Roman's Quick	6	M	6	0	0	0	0
Miss Naab	4	F	2	0	1	0	4,554	Miss Romeo	4	F	9	4	2	1	22,420
Miss Nancy	4	F	6	0	0	1	667	Miss Rose S	9	M	9	0	0	3	2,444
Miss Nasty Top	6	M	10	1	1	2	5,643	Miss Roxana	3	F	18	1	4	2	15,015
Miss Nebraska	4	F	2	0	0	0	124	Miss Royal Dancer	6	M	13	3	0	0	15,600
Miss Necole	3	F	12	0	2	3	7,399	Miss Royal Ibis	5	M	8	2	0	1	37,210
Miss Nelson	5	M	2	0	0	0	0	Miss Ruby Jo	3	F	2	0	0	0	0
Miss Nelson Bid	3	F	1	0	0	0	0	Miss Ruby R	4	F	4	0	0	2	3,225
Miss Nena	6	M	20	1	0	3	6,275	Miss Rudi	5	M	6	0	0	0	485
Miss New York	5	M	12	4	0	1	102,400	Miss Rue Du Lac	2	F	2	0	0	0	155
Miss Nickels	4	F	8	1	1	0	37,574	Miss Ruffles	2	F	7	1	1	2	16,750
Miss Nicolie	3	F	4	0	0	0	0	Miss Ruth	5	M	3	0	0	1	1,174
Miss Nine's Wild	5	M	9	1	0	0	9,517	Miss Saga	3	F	12	2	4	2	12,217
Miss Nite Gold	5	M	4	0	0	1	456	Miss Sanata	4	F	16	2	4	1	50,530
Miss Noire	4	F	8	2	1	0	37,250	Miss Sand Bar	2	F	9	3	4	0	88,847
Miss Norma Jean	2	F	2	1	0	0	9,600	Miss Sandy	4	F	13	2	0	0	15,672
Miss Notable Claim	5	M	11	3	1	3	34,658	Miss Sandy Dee	7	M	13	3	3	1	39,984
Miss Noteworthy	2	F	4	2	0	0	12,659	Miss Sandy Ray	3	F	3	0	0	0	413
Miss Obedient	3	F	7	1	0	0	1,464	Miss Santa Ana	5	M	1	0	1	0	3,000
Miss O'Brannigan	7	M	13	0	3	3	4,351	Miss Santa Anita	3	F	14	4	2	1	170,165
Miss Olymic	3	F	3	0	0	1	384	Miss Santa Claus	2	F	5	0	0	0	202
Miss Ondatop	4	F	14	3	0	1	6,103	Miss Sarah C	2	F	2	1	0	0	10,740
Miss Ooh La La	2	F	7	0	0	1	9,150	Miss Sassy	4	F	8	1	1	2	5,028
Miss Otsego	7	M	6	0	0	0	883	Miss Satterlee	8	M	2	0	0	1	1,210
Miss Outrageous	2	F	3	2	0	0	36,600	Miss Scalliwag	3	F	8	0	2	3	11,772
Miss P G A	3	F	6	1	0	0	5,352	Miss Secret Ryder	3	F	7	0	1	3	3,378
Miss P H F	7	M	1	0	0	0	80	Miss Semoran	2	F	9	0	2	0	2,923
Miss Pagan Glare	3	F	5	0	0	0	0	Miss Sentry	3	F	3	0	1	0	3,484
Miss Paranoid	2	F	1	0	0	0	810	Miss Seven Eleven	2	F	4	0	2	0	2,560
Miss Park Place	2	F	1	0	0	0	0	Miss Sexy Legs	3	F	1	0	0	0	0
Miss Partee	3	F	1	0	0	0	0	Miss Shady Brook	5	M	5	2	1	0	4,756
Miss Patsy Lee	2	F	1	0	0	0	0	Miss Shaffer	4	F	10	0	2	2	5,154
Miss Patti	2	F	2	0	1	0	2,072	Miss Shahmeka	3	F	10	2	1	1	13,746
Miss Payton	4	F	9	1	2	2	17,180	Miss Shania	3	F	3	0	1	0	4,390
Miss Peggy Sue	4	F	3	0	0	0	136	Miss Shares	5	M	16	3	0	1	9,666
Miss Pennie's Case	5	G	17	1	1	3	14,183	Miss Shimmer	2	F	3	0	0	0	0
Miss Penny Fortune	3	F	4	1	2	0	26,956	Miss Shower	5	M	11	0	0	2	6,094
Miss Peppermint	3	F	1	0	0	1	1,000	Miss Shrewsbury	3	F	2	0	0	0	0
Miss Perkinsville	3	F	8	0	1	2	6,280	Miss Sig	4	F	11	1	0	0	9,580
Miss Pharly	3	F	1	0	0	0	250	Miss Silver Jab	3	F	1	0	0	1	2,882
Miss Philpott	2	F	3	0	0	0	260	Miss Silvia	2	F	10	1	1	2	9,830
Miss Phone Chatter	3	F	3	0	0	0	1,560	Miss Slew	3	F	11	1	2	1	6,872
Miss Photo Copy	4	F	1	0	0	0	0	Miss Smart Alec	2	F	2	0	0	0	1,260
Miss Photogenic	5	M	9	3	1	0	63,500	Miss Socks	7	M	1	0	0	0	0
Miss Pitz (GB)	5	M	5	1	2	1	52,960	Miss Song	3	F	8	1	0	1	5,863
Miss Pixie	6	M	11	1	0	3	24,475	Miss Spain	4	F	9	3	1	0	17,665
Miss Playbill	4	F	4	0	0	0	3,680	Miss Speed Dial	3	F	14	3	1	0	23,628
Miss Polly	5	M	8	1	0	5	22,000	Miss Spender	4	F	7	1	2	1	21,070
Miss Pompei	3	F	6	0	0	2	2,653	Miss Spicer's Best	4	C	2	1	0	0	7,800
Miss Powder Rhodes	6	M	5	2	1	0	3,356	Miss Splash	5	M	7	2	0	1	66,157
Miss Precocity	2	F	3	0	0	0	2,970	Miss Sport Trac	4	F	5	0	1	1	1,721

Horse	Age	Sex	Sts	1st	2d	3d	Won
Miss Spragg	4	F	11	3	0	2	74,113
Miss Steppin On	4	F	9	0	0	0	895
Miss Storm Song	5	M	14	4	2	2	59,385
Miss Stormy Pick	2	F	3	0	0	0	0
Miss Stovall	3	F	5	0	0	0	263
Miss Sturgeon	4	F	13	0	0	3	2,712
Miss Sugar	4	F	14	5	0	1	29,810
Miss Sugar Booger	3	F	7	1	0	0	6,254
Miss Summer	4	F	9	2	0	0	16,317
Miss Sun Dog	4	F	3	0	0	0	197
Miss Sunsation	4	F	6	0	0	2	8,615
Miss Supertime	5	M	14	0	0	0	1,932
Miss Susan	3	F	7	1	1	1	5,168
Miss Susan Lynne	4	F	2	0	0	0	0
Miss Susie Roo	5	M	8	1	0	1	10,875
Miss Suwanna	6	M	3	0	1	0	1,299
Miss Swain	2	F	2	1	0	0	15,600
Miss Sweep	4	F	8	1	1	3	86,868
Miss Sweet Time	3	F	6	1	0	3	25,500
Miss Swiss Appeal	5	M	8	1	1	1	8,770
Miss T K O	3	F	23	1	5	2	28,174
Miss T S's Rib	4	F	1	0	0	0	44
Miss T. V. G.	2	F	6	0	4	1	11,620
Miss Taat	4	F	7	0	0	1	1,285
Miss Tacky Trump	4	F	16	2	3	2	28,046
Miss Tact	3	F	12	1	3	3	22,440
Miss Tall Hammer	2	F	1	0	0	0	1,080
Miss Tamster	2	F	2	0	0	0	217
Miss Tarzan	2	F	3	0	0	1	983
Miss Tasha	5	M	1	0	0	0	0
Miss Tassy	3	F	8	1	2	2	66,060
Miss Tay Tay	3	F	9	2	1	1	14,624
Miss Taylor's Deer	4	F	5	1	0	0	3,210
Miss Tempest	5	M	1	0	0	0	360
Miss Temptor	3	F	1	0	0	0	456
Miss Temptress	2	F	4	1	0	0	7,875
Miss Terasita	6	M	11	0	1	2	19,345
Miss Terrible (ARG)	4	F	2	0	0	0	20,340
Miss Tester	4	F	11	1	3	1	8,728
Miss the Kiss	3	F	10	1	2	2	17,061
Miss Theatre Sap	4	G	2	0	0	0	0
Miss Thirtyfour D	3	F	3	0	0	0	4,468
Miss Tiki Regent	4	F	11	2	1	1	11,781
Miss Tilghman	6	M	8	2	2	0	16,450
Miss Tilley	5	M	8	0	1	0	2,420
Miss Timberlake	3	F	2	0	0	0	0
Miss Time	5	M	13	2	0	3	9,842
Miss Time Art	6	M	2	0	0	2	1,101
Miss Time Bank Two	4	F	1	0	0	0	0
Miss Tina	4	F	4	0	0	0	273
Miss Top Believe	4	F	4	0	1	1	9,120
Miss Top Hat	5	M	6	0	0	0	705
Miss Toronaga	6	M	1	0	0	0	66
Miss Towaoc	2	F	1	0	0	0	0
Miss Tralee	8	M	5	0	1	1	5,962
Miss Trapp	6	M	7	1	0	0	6,647
Miss Triple Turn	3	F	13	0	2	3	11,472
Miss Trixie	3	F	6	0	1	2	36,431
Miss Tropics	4	F	7	2	0	0	36,385
Miss Trouble	2	F	8	1	3	0	39,260
Miss Trueheart	5	M	7	0	0	0	315
Miss Twelve	3	F	6	1	0	1	11,580
Miss Two Bagger	7	M	15	1	4	3	6,437
Miss Uppity	3	F	9	2	1	2	8,371
Miss Uptown	3	F	10	1	2	0	6,986
Miss Valedictorian	5	M	10	0	0	4	11,220
Miss Valid Joann	2	F	2	1	1	0	6,715
Miss Vice Regent	3	F	15	0	4	3	15,867
Miss Victory	4	F	13	6	2	2	37,557
Miss Victory Lady	3	F	3	2	0	0	17,955
Miss Wana B	4	F	1	0	0	0	0
Miss Way West	4	F	7	0	0	1	2,000
Miss Weiser	3	F	11	0	4	2	18,690
Miss Wellspring	2	F	7	0	3	1	18,370
Miss What a Day	3	F	1	0	0	0	1,680
Miss White Bird	5	M	7	0	1	1	1,735
Miss Whitney	4	F	10	0	0	1	4,136
Miss Willie	4	F	8	2	1	0	22,872
Miss Willow Class	3	F	6	1	0	1	8,120
Miss Winetime	2	F	2	0	1	0	1,793
Miss Winnetka	3	F	5	0	0	1	2,305
Miss Wiserequest	3	F	10	2	2	1	8,981
Miss With It	4	F	6	0	0	1	658
Miss Woo	3	F	6	1	0	0	6,549
Miss Woodruff	3	F	3	0	0	0	200
Miss Woodville	3	F	13	2	3	3	28,005
Miss World's Pride	4	F	2	0	0	0	0
Miss Ya Madly	3	F	10	2	0	1	19,374
Miss Yazmin	3	F	7	0	0	0	1,080
Miss Yo Mama	3	F	4	1	0	0	5,700
Miss You Dearly	4	F	15	2	3	4	33,927
Miss You Mimi	3	F	2	0	0	0	0
Miss Zavalla	9	M	10	2	0	1	7,939
Miss Zebulon	3	F	17	3	2	3	59,795
Miss Zelda	2	F	3	0	0	0	910
Miss Zippy	3	F	5	2	0	0	14,638
Miss Zooha	5	M	5	0	0	0	304
Missacity Luke	2	C	4	2	1	0	41,591
Missagility	4	F	10	2	0	2	14,007
Missbehaviour	6	M	9	1	2	2	38,477
Missbigmama	3	F	5	0	0	1	1,200
Missbinalong	3	F	7	0	0	0	1,198
Misschristmasvaley	6	M	16	2	1	2	3,780
Misscrackerbarrel	4	F	2	0	1	0	11,960
Missdavilynn	3	F	3	0	1	1	5,120
Missed	7	G	12	0	1	1	2,123
Missed Account	4	F	8	2	0	1	22,982
Missed Call	4	G	11	2	0	1	10,271
Missed Connection	2	F	1	0	0	0	2,820
Missed Signal	5	G	11	0	0	0	1,058
Missed the Derby	4	F	7	0	0	1	1,893
Missed Treasure	4	C	1	0	0	0	0
Missgoodietwoshoes	4	F	4	0	1	0	3,874
Missice	2	F	9	1	1	3	34,940
Missigoni (IRE)	9	G	4	1	0	1	8,525
Missileer	5	G	12	0	2	0	2,036
Missilery	2	G	3	0	2	0	4,326
Missin At Midnight	4	G	3	0	0	0	327
Missin' Sis	4	C	2	0	0	0	0
Missin Tomahawk	3	F	7	0	0	0	100
Missin You	3	C	2	0	0	0	0
Missing Assignment	3	C	6	2	0	0	19,510
Missing Jackie	2	F	4	0	3	0	12,840
Missing Miss	4	F	6	3	1	0	145,935
Missing Night	2	G	2	1	0	0	4,620
Missing Position	3	F	1	0	0	0	0
Missing Silks	3	G	5	0	3	0	7,340
Missing Tab	3	F	15	1	6	3	14,244
Missing Verse	4	F	9	0	0	0	580
Missing Woman	2	F	5	0	0	1	7,447
Missins	4	F	1	0	0	0	200
Missintense	3	F	5	0	1	0	3,400
Mission Apollo	4	G	11	1	1	3	6,442
Mission Boy	3	G	5	0	1	1	2,975
Mission Commander	3	G	5	0	0	0	613
Mission Control	6	G	2	0	0	0	1,350
Mission Creek	3	F	15	3	2	4	25,985
Mission North	6	M	8	1	0	1	2,520
Mission of Love	3	F	6	1	1	0	5,128
Mission Showers	4	F	8	3	1	1	17,281
Mission Slew	7	H	8	1	2	3	4,311
Missionacomplished	4	F	8	2	1	1	35,900
Missionary Groom	7	H	2	0	0	0	271
Missionary Lady	5	M	3	0	0	0	1,050
Missionary Monk	8	G	6	2	2	1	14,050
Missions Gazelle	9	G	2	0	0	0	135
Mississaugas Magic	3	F	14	3	6	1	21,060
Mississippi Mine	5	M	8	1	0	0	8,580
Mississippi Money	5	G	16	3	1	3	16,070
Mississippi River	3	G	13	1	3	4	32,736
Mississippi Sam	4	G	5	0	0	1	1,194
Mississippi Sound	5	G	1	1	0	0	8,400
Missjudging Amy	3	F	3	2	0	1	33,400
Missle Do	3	F	2	1	1	0	7,825
Missle Long	7	H	12	1	0	1	3,582
Missluckywilldance	2	F	1	0	0	0	100
Missme	4	G	9	1	1	0	55,100
Missmelodramatic	5	M	4	0	0	0	0

Horse	Age	Sex	Sts	1st	2d	3d	Won
Missnifique	5	M	3	0	0	0	176
Missoni	2	F	5	0	0	0	250
Missouri Haze	5	G	3	0	0	0	323
Missouri Sunrise	3	G	1	0	0	0	0
Missparfectcherry	4	F	4	0	0	0	185
Misspent	6	M	3	0	0	0	570
Misspersimmon Hill	4	F	11	0	1	2	2,246
Missprincessashley	4	F	10	1	1	1	10,813
Missstormyatlantic	3	F	9	2	0	2	25,510
Missteasious	3	F	5	0	0	1	1,615
Missthewire	4	F	11	1	3	4	37,040
Misstincup	2	F	1	0	0	0	60
Missus Coop	3	F	5	1	0	0	14,544
Missus Reality's	3	F	12	1	0	0	3,587
Missvalley	2	F	5	1	0	0	7,395
Missy Can Do	3	F	9	3	5	0	32,109
Missy Dee	2	F	5	0	1	1	2,423
Missy Girl	3	F	1	0	0	0	82
Missy Kiri	4	F	2	0	0	0	0
Missy Krissy	4	F	7	1	1	0	12,180
Missy One Forum	3	F	4	0	0	1	1,000
Missy Turtle	5	M	4	1	2	0	21,740
Missy Won	2	F	1	0	0	0	0
Missy's Joy	3	F	10	1	0	1	35,370
Missys Last	3	F	2	0	0	0	140
Missy's Pal Morris	6	H	7	0	0	0	808
Missy's Shadow	3	F	7	1	2	0	21,275
Missyshy	5	M	11	0	0	0	3,210
Missywilldo	4	F	3	1	1	1	7,820
Mist Me	3	F	12	0	1	1	2,193
Mist N Rain	6	M	10	1	3	0	8,865
Mist of Honour	3	F	4	0	0	2	7,920
Mist of the Empire	3	F	14	1	4	1	33,386
Mist On Moon Hill	3	F	5	1	0	0	26,880
Mist Onthe Heather	5	H	4	0	0	0	399
Mist Walker	3	G	5	0	1	0	1,821
Mist Ya	4	F	3	0	0	1	7,220
Mista Mayberry	3	F	5	0	1	2	11,150
Mistakates Mystery	5	M	11	1	0	1	8,351
Mistakenly Special	7	G	9	2	1	0	19,899
Mistda	2	F	3	1	1	0	33,400
Mistee Meenor	5	M	7	0	2	0	2,300
Mister Acpen (CHI)	5	H	8	2	1	1	228,200
Mister Ajax	3	G	9	2	2	0	43,410
Mister Allen	4	G	8	1	1	0	11,460
Mister Approval	5	G	2	0	0	0	1,260
Mister Atlantic	2	C	3	2	0	0	28,200
Mister Banjo	5	G	7	2	0	0	3,795
Mister Blister	3	C	8	4	1	0	55,920
Mister Blues	6	H	2	0	0	1	5,280
Mister Bojangle	4	G	4	0	1	0	1,534
Mister Boots	5	H	5	0	1	1	2,605
Mister Boy	4	C	3	0	0	0	0
Mister Bravo	4	G	11	1	1	4	38,865
Mister Cisco	5	G	14	1	1	2	4,650
Mister Continental	7	G	9	1	1	1	12,341
Mister Coop	4	G	9	2	0	4	139,795
Mister Cosmi (GB)	4	G	8	0	0	0	3,063
Mister C's Song	3	C	1	1	0	0	25,690
Mister Cy	7	G	6	0	2	0	8,468
Mister Dance	4	C	1	0	0	0	0
Mister Deux	3	C	5	0	0	1	5,170
Mister Devil	4	C	5	1	0	1	5,550
Mister Diz	5	H	4	1	1	0	8,905
Mister Doeny	3	G	8	2	0	3	15,405
Mister Dv	2	C	1	0	0	0	0
Mister E. K.	2	C	3	0	1	1	7,170
Mister Eight	5	G	12	3	0	3	38,104
Mister Excess	4	C	4	0	0	0	6,322
Mister Fancy	6	H	6	0	1	0	2,175
Mister Fister	5	G	9	1	1	2	11,072
Mister Fizz	4	G	10	1	2	2	54,820
Mister Flowers	3	C	15	3	2	3	27,426
Mister Floyd	4	G	3	0	0	0	750
Mister Four	4	G	8	1	2	0	8,057
Mister Fox	3	G	12	4	4	0	90,240
Mister French	4	G	8	1	3	1	30,917
Mister Freud	7	G	14	4	3	3	22,059
Mister Goodie	4	G	16	0	5	0	7,192
Mister Hennessy	4	G	6	0	1	3	25,837
Mister Hollstep	4	G	6	0	2	2	5,296
Mister Ingapomppe	2	G	1	0	0	0	0
Mister Jerald	4	G	1	0	0	0	0
Mister Kick (IRE)	6	G	7	0	2	1	3,514
Mister Lucky	6	G	6	1	0	1	9,210
Mister M. E.	3	C	7	1	1	1	14,220
Mister Ma	4	C	2	0	0	0	182
Mister Mane Man	3	G	6	2	3	1	39,437
Mister Manx	3	C	8	1	0	1	18,270
Mister Matthew	7	G	11	1	1	2	4,903
Mister Meaner	3	C	6	1	0	0	11,250
Mister Melvin	2	G	1	0	0	0	45
Mister Michael	4	C	5	2	2	0	63,138
Mister Mighty Mac	9	G	9	4	3	1	18,545
Mister Misty	3	C	13	3	4	0	30,216
Mister Miyoshi	7	G	13	2	1	3	13,396
Mister Mud	6	G	11	0	2	0	3,236
Mister Party	4	G	12	2	1	1	17,414
Mister Riley	3	G	15	2	2	5	27,760
Mister Ripley	4	G	12	2	1	2	4,516
Mister Royal	5	H	2	0	0	0	0
Mister Silence	4	C	6	0	2	0	4,700
Mister Slew	3	G	4	0	0	0	3,360
Mister Slick	4	G	10	1	4	1	13,475
Mister Slinky	4	G	7	0	0	0	2,383
Mister Slippery	3	C	4	0	1	0	10,000
Mister Society	6	H	4	0	0	0	276
Mister Sordo	2	C	4	0	0	0	1,230
Mister Speckles	4	C	1	0	0	0	160
Mister Stip	3	G	12	2	2	4	41,920
Mister Sultry	2	G	4	1	0	0	14,440
Mister Syn	4	G	10	0	0	2	1,739
Mister Tricky (GB)	8	G	6	1	0	0	5,175
Mister Velocity	4	G	12	2	4	1	27,161
Mister Vine	5	G	6	3	3	0	35,692
Mister Vinson	5	G	5	1	1	0	4,702
Mister Volare	6	H	8	0	0	0	4,080
Mister Weinke	3	G	10	1	2	2	9,940
Mister Wilson	3	C	12	0	0	2	2,139
Mister Ye	10	G	4	0	0	0	344
Mistergoldmeridian	4	F	13	2	2	2	12,301
Misterioso	6	H	2	0	0	0	450
Misterrific	4	F	2	0	0	0	273
Mister's Sister	2	F	2	0	0	0	500
Misti Light	3	F	12	2	0	3	16,945
Misti Stephi	4	F	10	1	1	2	10,403
Mistic Sun (GB)	5	M	2	1	0	0	36,420
Mistical Fastness	3	C	8	1	1	1	42,170
Mistical Jaz	4	F	15	2	0	4	29,220
Mistical Magic	4	F	1	0	0	0	0
Mistical Miracle	3	F	4	0	1	0	2,572
Mistiff	3	F	6	1	0	1	10,130
Misting	4	F	6	1	0	0	4,676
Mistletoad	3	F	11	0	4	2	2,671
Mistpelled	6	M	17	2	5	3	19,097
Mistress in Red	2	F	2	1	0	0	6,600
Mistress Page	4	F	5	2	1	1	7,230
Mistress Vermont	3	F	3	0	0	0	840
Mistrick	2	F	3	0	0	0	0
Misty Account	2	F	3	0	0	0	0
Misty Appeal	2	C	1	0	0	0	0
Misty Approval	3	G	4	0	0	0	0
Misty Autumn	4	F	2	0	0	0	141
Misty B	5	M	7	1	0	0	2,126
Misty Blue Gal	2	F	1	0	0	0	0
Misty County	2	C	4	1	0	0	12,490
Misty Diablo	5	M	11	0	3	2	8,145
Misty Echo	4	F	8	2	1	1	8,520
Misty Evening	4	F	1	0	0	0	37
Misty Expectation	4	F	8	2	3	2	136,292
Misty Forum	4	G	15	0	5	3	9,860
Misty Ghost	6	M	3	0	0	0	0
Misty Glo	2	F	2	0	0	0	411
Misty Hawaiian	9	M	4	0	0	0	650
Misty Jazz	5	M	7	0	0	1	1,385
Misty Jet	4	F	2	0	0	0	326
Misty Kilarny	6	H	12	3	2	2	23,688
Misty Lark	4	F	10	0	0	0	914

Horse	Age	Sex	Sts	1st	2d	3d	Won	Horse	Age	Sex	Sts	1st	2d	3d	Won
Misty Leader	3	F	9	2	0	3	8,474	Miz Moody Blues	2	F	8	1	0	2	14,120
Misty Linda	5	M	4	1	0	1	8,831	Miz Myrtis	4	F	1	0	0	0	0
Misty Mae Rose	2	F	6	1	1	0	9,190	Miz Revenge	3	F	14	1	1	2	6,216
Misty Maggie	2	F	3	0	0	0	340	Miz Roadway	2	F	3	0	0	1	3,540
Misty Malibu	2	F	2	0	0	1	1,587	Miz Smoke'um	2	F	1	0	0	0	0
Misty Maud	3	F	3	1	1	0	9,063	Mizimoon	4	F	2	0	0	0	142
Misty Mountain	6	M	4	0	0	1	1,141	Mizz Charlee	4	F	10	0	1	2	3,300
Misty North	3	F	2	0	0	0	160	Mizzen Lass	2	F	3	0	0	1	3,715
Misty Play	7	M	2	0	0	0	0	Mizzou	2	C	3	0	0	0	0
Misty Pleasure	3	F	8	0	0	0	180	M'Lady Doc	3	F	1	0	0	0	0
Misty Rapids	6	H	11	1	0	2	2,397	Mlle. Rumble	4	F	17	1	1	1	11,390
Misty Reign	2	F	2	0	0	0	242	Mm River	4	F	7	0	0	0	450
Misty Riches	5	H	13	1	5	2	21,835	Mme. Espionage	2	F	1	0	0	0	2,160
Misty River	3	F	8	2	0	1	18,330	Mme. Soleil	7	M	7	0	0	0	396
Misty Season	2	F	1	0	0	0	0	Mo Cash	3	F	9	0	0	1	3,434
Misty Segula	2	F	1	0	0	0	100	Mo Dixie	4	G	9	0	0	0	657
Misty Sixes	5	M	10	4	0	1	153,004	Mo Fun Forus	4	F	8	1	1	1	10,010
Misty Son	3	G	7	0	0	0	273	Mo Gater	3	G	1	1	0	0	3,900
Misty Summer	2	F	6	0	0	0	948	Mo Harrington	7	G	12	2	1	1	7,480
Misty Tokenoflove	3	F	6	0	0	0	860	Mo Luck	4	C	7	0	1	0	1,595
Misty Wager	4	G	11	2	2	2	27,046	Mo Mon	5	H	1	0	0	1	2,820
Misty Walker	9	M	6	0	0	0	240	Mo Moscow	4	G	2	1	0	1	3,300
Misty Water	3	F	1	0	0	0	0	Mo Moses	2	G	2	1	0	0	5,250
Misty Way	5	M	1	0	0	0	35	Mo Steely	3	G	15	3	1	4	35,565
Misty Wonder	2	C	3	1	0	2	13,960	Mo' Supremo	5	H	9	1	1	0	5,096
Mistyandsuave	3	G	11	0	3	3	5,639	Mo Town Brown	2	C	4	0	0	0	900
Misty's Chance	3	C	1	0	0	0	0	Mo Town Gold	3	G	10	1	2	2	18,366
Mistys Dark Angel	3	F	6	0	0	1	1,128	Moab	2	G	3	3	0	0	28,024
Mistys Lady	4	F	2	0	0	0	0	Mob Enforcer	5	H	3	0	0	0	172
Misty's Legend	3	F	3	0	0	0	0	Mobeka	4	F	16	1	2	2	14,270
Misty's Princess	6	M	1	0	0	0	136	Mobettadancer	3	G	1	0	0	0	35
Misty'sgoldentouch	2	C	2	1	0	0	8,100	Mobil	3	C	9	5	2	1	753,405
Miswaki Babe	2	F	5	1	0	0	10,940	Mobil One (BRZ)	5	H	5	1	0	0	7,620
Miswaki Lady	2	F	3	0	0	0	1,575	Moby	4	G	17	1	2	2	7,654
Miswaki Mac	3	G	6	1	1	0	4,981	Moccasin Meadows	4	F	5	0	2	1	1,078
Miswaki Tex	7	G	4	0	0	1	484	Moccason Creek	4	G	10	1	3	1	7,379
Miswatal	7	H	1	0	0	0	120	Mocefis	8	G	7	0	0	0	2,130
Misyodl	3	F	5	2	0	0	4,950	Mocha Ice	3	C	14	1	2	1	17,088
Mitchaman	6	H	13	3	2	2	26,077	Mocha Jet	5	G	8	0	1	0	5,069
Mitchell County Hi	7	H	8	4	3	0	11,908	Mocha Queen	2	F	6	1	1	0	29,676
Mitchell Lee	5	H	3	0	0	0	257	Mocha's Ego	2	C	2	0	1	0	2,500
Mitchell's Delight	2	C	6	0	2	1	4,925	Mochatee	6	G	8	1	0	0	3,680
Mitchells Folly	2	F	4	0	2	1	7,090	Mockaskin	5	G	1	0	0	0	116
Mitchell's Mambo	4	G	4	1	0	2	8,640	Mode of the World	4	F	9	0	1	0	2,330
Mitchel's Reprized	3	G	9	1	1	2	10,205	Model Home	3	G	12	4	2	0	80,755
Mitey Nice	6	M	13	2	3	2	12,603	Model Tea	5	M	13	2	0	4	14,818
Mitey Star	6	G	13	1	2	2	12,645	Model Z Ford	7	G	10	1	2	2	4,188
Mith America	3	F	15	2	5	2	21,900	Modeling	2	C	1	0	0	0	0
Mithaal	2	C	3	0	0	0	4,080	Modeling Margot	5	M	11	1	1	0	4,086
Mitigate	10	G	7	0	0	0	517	Modem Down	2	F	3	1	0	0	7,506
Mito Way	9	G	1	0	0	0	0	Moderation	2	F	3	1	0	0	6,230
Mitota	3	G	4	1	0	0	2,893	Modern Art	6	M	5	1	0	0	9,848
Mitote Maya	3	F	5	0	0	0	3,015	Modern Day Mayhem	3	C	3	0	1	0	1,500
Mittens	3	F	8	2	1	0	18,555	Modern Design	3	F	1	0	0	0	0
Mittens Mambo	3	F	1	0	0	0	195	Modern Marvel	3	F	8	1	2	0	14,684
Mitty's Brite Girl	4	F	13	1	1	4	8,432	Modern World	4	G	5	1	0	0	9,964
Mitty's Main Man	4	G	4	1	0	0	1,710	Moderngirl Santa	3	F	6	1	1	1	12,200
Mitzies Lil Fun	2	G	7	1	2	2	17,850	Modest Lover	4	G	14	1	1	3	28,810
Mitzi's Oates	6	M	6	0	1	0	5,300	Modest Man	5	G	4	0	0	0	40
Miu Miu	4	F	9	0	2	2	16,416	Modest Mo	3	C	6	0	0	0	2,906
Miu Miu (AUS)	8	G	2	1	0	0	11,020	Modesto	8	G	2	0	0	0	541
Mix It Up	3	C	5	2	1	0	20,040	Modified	6	H	9	0	1	1	2,928
Mixed Dreams	4	F	4	1	0	1	6,400	Modigliani	5	H	2	0	0	0	800
Mixed Signals	3	F	2	0	0	0	140	Modoc Corvette	3	G	12	0	0	0	1,031
Mixed Truce	8	M	6	1	0	0	5,027	Modoc Star	4	G	8	2	0	2	4,242
Mixed Up	4	G	6	1	0	1	24,200	Modred	4	C	11	2	0	0	8,136
Mixer	3	G	9	1	0	0	12,998	Modus Viblairski	5	M	9	4	0	2	22,163
Mixie's Hoolie	4	F	5	0	3	1	13,809	Moe B Dick	6	G	7	2	2	1	36,156
Miya Kiya	3	F	14	1	1	5	12,346	Moe Boots	5	G	21	3	2	3	9,625
Miz Audacious	3	F	6	0	2	0	30,682	Moe Dickstein	4	G	14	2	3	1	25,036
Miz Bluestone	4	F	6	0	1	1	5,949	Moe Greene	6	G	15	7	1	2	45,820
Miz Cajun Decor	4	F	3	0	1	0	1,050	Moejoejane	5	M	14	1	1	1	2,888
Miz Catskatoon	2	F	1	0	0	0	0	Moel	3	F	11	0	2	2	21,830
Miz Flashy Power	4	F	7	1	2	1	10,040	Moe's Hoedown	4	F	11	4	2	2	45,397
Miz Heather	5	M	6	0	1	1	6,190	Moe's Mon	4	G	5	0	0	1	5,330
Miz Kool	5	M	3	0	2	0	9,600	Moette	4	F	10	2	2	2	7,547
Miz Landy	4	F	14	1	2	3	43,715	Mofus	4	F	15	3	4	2	38,310
Miz Lynne Kelly	4	F	12	3	1	1	32,820	Mogador	3	C	2	1	0	1	30,140
Miz Mitzie	2	F	1	1	0	0	6,120	Mohawk Marty	5	G	2	1	0	0	3,541

Horse	Age	Sex	Sts	1st	2d	3d	Won
Mohawkeye	6	G	8	0	0	2	1,683
Mohegan Warrior	2	G	3	0	1	1	5,630
Moher	5	G	9	0	2	2	10,770
Mohican Road	3	C	7	0	0	0	910
Mohigan Hill	3	G	13	2	0	1	30,335
Moi Ciel	7	H	9	4	2	0	16,065
Moi's Boy	6	H	4	2	0	0	6,406
Moisuisatoi	5	H	3	0	1	0	9,625
Mojita	2	F	1	0	0	0	0
Mojo Bag	3	G	1	0	0	0	0
Mojo Black Cat	4	C	4	0	0	0	0
Mojo Gal	5	M	6	1	0	0	29,610
Mojo Risin	5	G	9	3	2	2	10,734
Mojo Workin	3	G	5	0	2	2	11,480
Mojoe	7	G	12	1	1	3	13,808
Mojohn	4	G	6	1	0	0	20,216
Mojoman	6	G	7	0	0	1	600
Mokhieba's Bet	5	M	6	1	2	1	10,002
Molinaro Deer	3	F	1	0	0	0	0
Molinaro First Las	3	F	6	1	1	2	49,452
Molinaro Irish	3	G	3	0	0	1	2,887
Molinaro Melody	3	F	3	1	0	0	25,485
Molinaro's Missie	3	F	2	0	0	0	0
Molino Rojo	4	G	17	3	1	0	14,257
Molino Rosso (CHI)	5	G	5	0	0	1	8,330
Mollie B.	4	F	4	0	0	0	147
Mollie Malone	4	F	1	1	0	0	5,700
Mollie McLash	5	M	7	2	3	1	38,620
Molly and Me	5	M	7	1	0	0	2,630
Molly Beddard	4	F	11	1	2	2	11,627
Molly Blue Eyes	3	F	1	0	0	0	0
Molly M	4	F	12	1	1	2	15,165
Molly O'Grady	7	M	9	2	3	2	6,520
Molly Or Me	6	M	1	0	0	0	0
Molly Rochelle	3	F	17	1	3	3	10,314
Molly's Gem	2	F	6	0	2	3	13,630
Molly's Gone	2	F	6	0	1	3	42,156
Molly's Song	3	F	2	0	0	0	1,050
Molly's Wisdom	4	C	7	0	1	0	16,941
Moloch	4	G	14	2	2	4	13,821
Molodets	5	G	3	0	0	0	0
Molokai Connection	5	G	9	4	1	1	21,615
Molokai Express	4	C	5	2	2	1	7,192
Moloko	4	F	12	3	1	2	82,805
Molotov	3	G	2	0	0	0	340
Molto Bene	4	G	16	3	2	4	42,702
Molto Veloce	2	F	4	1	0	0	10,850
Molto Vita	3	F	11	4	1	0	136,680
Mom	3	F	3	0	0	1	650
Mom Liked You Best	3	F	9	0	1	2	8,320
Mom Mom's Boy	7	H	1	0	0	0	0
Mom N Donna	5	M	3	0	0	0	700
Momaless	5	M	14	2	1	1	19,795
Momalukas	4	F	13	0	1	2	3,300
Mombay	4	F	7	1	0	0	3,530
Mombita Loca	4	F	11	2	0	0	10,767
Mombo	5	G	8	0	1	2	2,894
Mombo Loco	3	C	10	4	1	0	60,660
Mombo Star	4	G	10	3	2	1	29,690
Moment of Attack	5	G	5	0	0	0	290
Moment of Ecstacy	7	G	9	0	0	1	1,405
Moment of Peace	2	F	1	1	0	0	35,280
Moment of Song	2	C	9	1	2	4	35,395
Moment of the Dice	6	G	8	0	0	0	498
Momentous Appeal	5	G	2	0	0	0	0
Momentous Drive	9	G	9	2	1	1	9,654
Moment's Champ	3	G	1	0	0	0	0
Moments Divine	6	M	1	0	0	0	58
Moments From Glory	4	F	3	0	1	1	3,809
Momma Jean	4	F	8	1	1	0	5,110
Momma's Girl	2	F	3	0	0	0	1,380
Momma's Image	2	F	1	0	0	0	350
Mommas Last Dollar	3	F	11	0	0	4	5,796
Momoney Moe	4	C	7	4	1	1	46,171
Mom's an Angel	3	G	9	0	3	3	16,300
Mom's Angel	4	G	6	0	0	0	472
Mom's Appeal	5	M	10	0	3	2	24,230
Mom's Bright Star	3	F	11	2	1	1	34,361
Mom's Deer	4	F	5	2	0	1	9,930

Horse	Age	Sex	Sts	1st	2d	3d	Won
Mom's Dream	5	M	7	1	0	1	30,665
Mom's Little Guy	9	H	9	3	0	0	21,829
Mom's Recruit	5	G	9	2	0	3	4,875
Mom's Reflection	3	C	11	2	1	1	21,090
Mom's Vow	6	M	2	0	0	0	0
Momskitchen	3	G	8	1	0	1	8,764
Momsmercedes	8	G	13	0	1	4	8,230
Momsnibblingcoyote	3	C	5	0	1	1	4,446
Mon Ami Amy	4	F	5	0	0	3	22,362
Mon Ange	5	M	2	1	0	0	36,910
Mon Avie Amour	4	F	15	1	4	3	11,545
Mon Bebe	3	F	3	1	0	1	12,120
Mon Cabo	3	F	16	2	3	3	25,345
Mon Cher	4	C	3	0	0	2	5,900
Mon Dieux	2	C	2	0	0	0	460
Mon General (FR)	5	H	6	0	0	3	7,280
Mon Ile	4	G	18	2	3	3	21,470
Mon Ouimet	4	G	4	0	0	1	5,204
Mon Petite	6	M	2	0	0	1	2,600
Mon Sang	3	C	3	0	0	0	1,000
Mon Sherri Amour	4	F	4	0	0	1	2,125
Mon Spirit	2	F	1	1	0	0	5,700
Mon Sweet's Crypto	3	F	15	1	2	2	6,291
Mon T. Hauls	4	G	6	2	2	1	4,940
Mon Treego Bay	3	G	4	0	0	0	450
Mon Tresor	3	F	11	2	0	2	11,699
Mona Corrine	4	F	10	1	3	1	7,505
Mona Lady	3	F	7	2	0	1	12,999
Mona Lisa	3	F	3	0	0	0	635
Mona Lisa Lady	4	F	6	2	1	0	20,996
Mona Rose	3	F	6	1	2	0	72,665
Mona the Snake	4	F	7	1	3	1	30,680
Monahans	4	G	8	0	0	0	709
Monahan's News	3	C	4	1	1	0	4,678
Monalina	4	F	6	0	0	1	1,880
Monanore	4	G	12	1	1	0	5,630
Monarch Bay	4	C	1	0	0	1	1,100
Monarch Brass	4	G	9	3	1	0	50,209
Monarch Hunter	2	C	1	0	0	0	510
Monarchoftheglen	4	G	3	1	0	0	21,600
Monarch's Gold	4	G	12	1	3	2	8,385
Monarch's Mon	4	G	13	2	1	1	9,126
Monarchski	9	G	4	0	0	0	178
Monarda	3	F	5	0	2	1	5,215
Monaree	3	F	7	0	0	2	9,139
Monarquica	4	F	15	7	1	1	75,140
Mona's Code	4	F	1	0	0	0	49
Monaube	2	C	2	0	0	0	0
Mondamin	8	G	11	0	1	3	7,960
Monday Nite Mac	7	G	11	1	3	1	17,534
Monet	8	H	6	3	1	0	49,380
Monetary Dancer	2	G	4	1	1	0	14,302
Monetary Justice	7	H	4	0	0	0	225
Monetary Lady	5	M	8	0	1	0	2,634
Monetary Star	3	C	8	3	2	1	135,110
Monetarymigration	6	G	10	1	1	3	18,548
Money Baby	8	M	12	2	1	2	23,773
Money Box	3	F	3	0	0	0	0
Money Buck	3	G	17	1	1	3	19,655
Money Call	2	G	8	0	0	2	4,850
Money Comin	10	H	1	0	0	0	38
Money Eater	3	C	1	0	0	0	0
Money Flies	3	F	4	1	0	0	3,480
Money in the Bank	3	F	3	0	0	0	1,260
Money Inthe Basket	3	G	8	2	0	1	7,420
Money Is Boss	3	G	5	1	1	0	8,225
Money Is Due	7	G	7	2	0	1	15,514
Money Is Power	4	F	9	2	1	0	10,128
Money Is the Key	2	C	2	0	0	0	1,302
Money Magnet	6	H	13	2	3	1	33,085
Money Management	5	G	10	2	0	0	2,828
Money Market Power	4	C	2	0	0	0	0
Money Marquet	3	G	2	0	0	0	840
Money Mover	3	F	7	0	0	0	715
Money River	5	M	6	1	0	0	20,585
Money Set	4	G	8	3	0	1	20,630
Money Shot	5	G	14	4	2	2	40,270
Money Spender	2	C	3	1	0	0	7,320
Money Stretcher	5	M	8	0	0	0	1,860

Horse	Age	Sex	Sts	1st	2d	3d	Won	Horse	Age	Sex	Sts	1st	2d	3d	Won
Money Trick	5	G	20	1	1	0	6,387	Montefiore	3	F	8	1	1	3	42,840
Money Trust	2	F	3	0	0	0	1,260	Montego Light	5	M	11	0	1	0	1,922
Moneycat	3	G	14	2	3	0	9,550	Montemiro (FR)	9	H	4	1	1	0	22,175
Moneyed	3	G	6	3	0	0	21,820	Montenapoleone	4	C	15	3	0	6	68,610
Moneyindesbank	4	F	9	1	1	2	12,805	Monterey Bay (NZ)	5	M	1	0	0	1	7,320
Moneymakinmamma	4	F	4	0	0	0	0	Monterey Bound	8	H	3	0	0	0	0
Moneyrun Up	2	C	1	0	0	0	285	Montessa	2	F	2	0	0	0	0
Money's Gift	4	F	5	0	0	0	1,280	Montezuma's Gold	7	G	5	0	0	0	23,817
Money's Star	5	H	4	0	0	0	600	Monthir	4	C	4	0	3	0	28,380
Moneytrain (GER)	4	G	4	1	0	0	28,828	Monthster Man	4	G	10	3	1	2	5,289
Moneywaster	4	G	4	1	0	1	10,150	Monticello	2	F	9	1	2	2	13,300
Mongeon's Thief	5	M	9	1	0	1	5,700	Montikarla	3	F	5	0	0	0	150
Mongol Sky	3	G	9	2	0	0	7,583	Montmorenci	4	G	9	1	2	1	21,100
Monica La Win	6	M	8	1	1	0	8,348	Montoro	5	G	9	1	2	0	6,203
Monica Stout	4	F	8	1	0	2	11,779	Montreal Princess	3	F	10	2	1	1	13,730
Monica Sue	4	F	9	0	2	2	12,400	Montreal Tootie	2	F	2	0	0	0	180
Monica's Halo	3	F	10	0	0	5	3,971	Montreal's Best	5	M	11	0	4	0	20,160
Monica's Song	5	M	1	0	0	0	136	Montrosecountyline	4	C	1	0	0	0	29
Monique	4	F	1	0	0	0	80	Montsmoke	2	F	6	1	1	0	9,890
Monique's Gold	4	F	7	0	1	1	3,800	Monty Man	3	C	8	1	0	1	30,730
Monique's Miracle	4	F	9	0	1	0	2,574	Monument	5	H	8	0	0	0	2,530
Moniquette	8	M	14	1	1	1	4,822	Monument Valley	6	M	12	4	1	2	46,216
Monivea	7	G	11	2	1	0	7,868	Monumental Factor	2	G	1	0	0	0	145
Monkey Junior	3	C	10	2	1	2	57,660	Monumental Upset	4	F	1	0	0	0	1,005
Monkey Puzzle	7	G	8	2	1	1	55,540	Monumental Vending	4	G	6	0	0	0	110
Monkey's Age	7	M	3	0	0	0	0	Moochie Magnum	2	F	3	0	0	0	2,460
Monkeys Uncle	4	G	1	0	0	0	150	Moochie Too	4	F	13	1	1	1	25,305
Monks Baby Sister	5	M	6	0	0	0	486	Mood Swinger	4	C	3	0	0	0	1,220
Monkton Miss	3	F	3	0	0	0	3,000	Moody Broad	2	F	1	0	0	0	0
Mono Ridge	2	G	7	1	1	2	37,102	Moody Bu	2	F	1	0	0	0	0
Monocacy Crossing	3	G	4	1	0	0	7,530	Moody Klair	3	F	6	1	0	0	14,266
Monocerus	4	F	3	0	0	0	386	Moody Mae	4	F	6	0	0	1	770
Monocle	4	F	4	0	0	0	2,750	Moody Mama	2	F	2	0	0	0	1,080
Monologue	6	H	15	3	2	1	15,184	Moody Slew	3	G	8	2	0	0	49,713
Monopoly	5	M	1	1	0	0	6,780	Moody Tune	2	G	7	0	2	2	5,679
Monopoly Money	2	C	5	1	0	0	28,350	Moogedy	4	F	13	4	4	1	76,291
Monroe Doctrine (IRE)	6	G	18	3	1	3	22,901	Mooji Moo	4	F	10	5	1	1	188,810
Monroe's Corner	6	G	6	0	1	1	6,874	Moomtazz	5	H	2	1	1	0	38,600
Monrow	7	M	2	0	0	0	0	Moon Ballad (IRE)	4	C	6	2	0	0	3,719,798
Monsajem	8	H	6	0	0	1	2,085	Moon Bay Dancer	2	F	3	0	0	0	9,657
Monsieur	4	G	11	0	0	2	2,050	Moon Bee	4	G	2	0	0	0	70
Monsieur Boulanger (GB)	3	C	10	4	1	0	119,320	Moon Bird	5	M	15	1	2	1	22,600
Monsieur Montreal	3	C	1	0	0	0	53	Moon Dancing	4	F	12	0	0	2	1,869
Monsignor	4	G	18	1	2	1	9,615	Moon Dove	2	F	1	0	0	0	0
Monsignor Paul	5	G	10	1	0	1	8,189	Moon Echo	5	M	2	0	1	0	1,321
Monsoon Sky	2	C	4	0	0	0	145	Moon Face	3	F	5	0	0	1	1,755
Monster Ballad	3	C	15	1	0	2	12,720	Moon Feather	2	F	2	0	0	0	1,350
Monster Be Gone	4	G	3	0	0	1	1,560	Moon in the Night	3	F	6	0	3	1	4,953
Monster Binge	3	F	8	0	1	0	5,337	Moon Light Win'd	4	G	9	0	0	1	1,297
Monster Ice	6	H	8	1	0	1	4,406	Moon Maiden	5	M	5	0	0	0	726
Monster Jack	3	C	10	2	2	3	61,640	Moon Minister	4	F	3	0	0	0	2,660
Monster Mac	2	G	4	0	0	1	790	Moon Mission	3	G	12	1	1	1	19,520
Monster McKilts	4	G	11	2	3	0	50,866	Moon Missle	3	C	5	0	0	1	1,674
Monster Mon	4	G	6	0	0	0	136	Moon Mullins	3	G	7	4	0	1	31,915
Monster Move	3	G	3	1	1	0	11,560	Moon Over Marilyn	6	M	1	0	0	0	35
Monsterous Mitch	5	H	8	0	2	1	7,310	Moon Over Miannie	7	M	9	0	0	0	783
Mont Devil	2	C	2	0	0	0	4,050	Moon Over My Angie	4	F	12	1	1	1	4,687
Mont Eagle	9	G	4	0	0	0	701	Moon Queen (IRE)	5	M	1	0	0	0	0
Mont Saint Michel (CHI)	5	G	7	2	1	1	97,435	Moon Rise Darling	3	F	7	4	2	1	16,854
Montana	6	G	10	2	1	0	7,675	Moon River	9	M	2	0	0	0	193
Montana Banana	3	F	5	1	1	1	28,588	Moon Shine Time	3	F	10	2	4	1	50,526
Montana Breeze	4	G	3	0	0	0	870	Moon Snow	3	G	1	0	1	0	400
Montana Carmella	4	F	12	1	3	2	33,835	Moon Speech	2	F	1	0	0	0	0
Montana Cat	5	M	2	1	0	0	29,010	Moon Spinner	3	G	9	1	0	0	30,360
Montana Cowboy	3	G	11	2	0	1	8,859	Moon Sprit	3	F	9	0	0	1	2,830
Montana Dreamin'	8	H	4	1	0	1	6,445	Moon Stories	4	F	5	0	0	0	221
Montana Hall	3	G	8	0	0	0	522	Moon Symph	4	G	4	0	1	1	2,220
Montana Moon	2	G	6	1	1	0	8,770	Moon Tap	3	F	5	0	0	0	2,200
Montana Rush	4	G	8	2	2	1	31,160	Moon Tip	4	G	9	0	0	0	8,942
Montana Skipper	2	C	4	0	0	0	1,000	Moon Walk	4	C	7	1	1	3	12,430
Montana Snow	7	G	4	0	0	0	696	Moon Warrior	2	C	8	1	0	2	38,210
Montanaro	5	G	4	0	1	1	6,030	Moon Witch	2	F	2	0	1	0	945
Montanasadixichick	3	F	2	0	1	0	2,550	Moonblaze	10	G	9	1	2	0	9,947
Montaraz	3	F	1	0	0	0	0	Moonchief	5	H	2	0	0	0	0
Montariat	4	G	3	1	0	0	3,841	Moondance	3	C	7	0	0	1	1,515
Montbretia	3	C	4	1	3	0	57,000	Moondog	3	G	4	0	0	0	380
Montbrooke Belle	3	F	15	1	2	1	6,543	Moonfest	6	M	1	0	0	0	0
Monte Vista	5	G	11	0	1	2	5,500	Moonlady (GER)	6	M	2	0	0	0	0
Montecastillo (IRE)	6	G	3	1	1	0	11,398	Moonlet Minister	4	F	12	2	2	3	75,270

Horse	Age	Sex	Sts	1st	2d	3d	Won
Moonlight	2	F	2	0	0	0	1,380
Moonlight and Lace	4	F	10	5	1	2	23,419
Moonlight Charmer	4	C	8	0	0	1	7,310
Moonlight Cocktail	2	F	3	0	0	1	3,600
Moonlight Crest	2	F	3	0	0	0	118
Moonlight Duel	2	G	2	0	0	0	3,882
Moonlight Flyer	9	M	8	0	2	0	1,915
Moonlight Gardens	4	F	1	1	0	0	18,386
Moonlight Magic	4	F	1	0	0	0	0
Moonlight Martini	2	F	1	0	0	0	50
Moonlight Meeting	8	G	3	0	1	1	34,688
Moonlight Melody	2	F	8	0	1	1	3,085
Moonlight Milagro	3	C	3	1	1	0	6,655
Moonlight Mood	8	M	2	0	0	0	0
Moonlight Rose	5	M	1	0	0	0	0
Moonlight Sonata	3	F	4	0	1	0	14,740
Moonlight Spy	8	H	1	0	0	0	0
Moonlight Storm	3	G	6	1	1	3	11,253
Moonlight Supreme	6	H	6	0	0	0	265
Moonlightandbeauty	4	F	12	3	3	2	129,073
Moonlightmargarita	2	F	3	0	0	0	115
Moonlit Cloud	4	G	4	0	0	0	222
Moonlit Maddie	5	M	6	1	2	1	41,780
Moonlit Moment	6	G	5	1	1	0	14,680
Moonlit Romance	3	F	6	1	1	1	12,886
Moonlite and Wine	2	F	1	0	0	0	0
Moonlite Deelite	4	F	1	0	0	1	450
Moonlite Escapade	5	G	10	3	0	1	37,687
Moonlite Walk	3	F	12	2	2	2	118,180
Moonluck	4	C	3	1	0	0	14,580
Moonmaster	5	G	11	0	1	4	6,152
Moonmon	4	G	12	4	0	1	25,190
Moonover Imacomin	4	G	1	0	0	0	0
Moonray	8	G	10	0	2	4	6,330
Moonridge Bay	3	C	12	1	4	0	11,338
Moonroper	3	G	10	2	1	3	28,393
Moonrush	3	G	4	0	0	0	0
Moon's Best Light	5	M	4	0	0	0	314
Moon's So Friendly	6	M	6	0	0	2	1,200
Moonshadow Gold	4	G	9	2	0	3	67,721
Moonshine Hall	3	C	9	3	2	1	168,001
Moonshine Mary	4	F	9	2	0	1	17,721
Moonshine Ridge	5	G	9	0	1	0	10,281
Moonshine Runner	4	G	5	0	0	0	0
Moonsight	9	G	9	0	0	0	573
Moonstone Bay	3	F	3	0	0	0	6,200
Moonstruck	5	H	8	1	1	1	8,035
Moonstruck Agenda	2	G	1	0	0	0	0
Moonthefield	5	M	9	0	1	0	1,987
Moony Cat	5	H	1	0	0	0	0
Moorebella	2	F	1	0	1	0	6,600
Moorestown	5	M	2	0	0	0	1,560
Mooring Sand	4	G	7	1	0	0	6,150
Moorish Prince	7	H	14	2	3	0	80,760
Moose Tracks	6	H	2	0	0	0	390
Moosehead Jr	3	C	4	0	0	1	864
Mooshoe	5	M	3	0	0	0	408
Moosup Valley	3	G	13	1	2	1	22,260
Mop Up	6	H	3	1	0	0	3,300
Mopbuckmolly	3	F	9	1	1	1	3,723
Moppy Jane	3	F	1	0	0	0	0
Moradeno	2	C	4	0	0	0	1,620
Moraluna	3	F	6	1	2	1	37,380
Moray Firth	3	F	4	0	0	0	161
Mordedor	6	G	10	4	2	0	34,685
More Bands	3	G	8	1	0	3	19,985
More Bragg	6	G	8	1	0	1	3,944
More Brass Mpg	5	H	11	1	1	3	3,406
More Cold Drinks	4	G	1	0	0	0	0
More Courage	6	M	2	0	0	0	0
More Crafty	5	H	10	2	3	1	87,950
More Daylight	3	G	11	1	2	1	40,545
More Heart	3	G	11	1	0	2	12,232
More Heck	3	C	6	2	0	1	58,460
More Hot Fudge	3	F	7	0	0	1	3,900
More Hot Gossip	4	F	7	2	3	1	34,618
More Influence	5	G	10	2	2	1	27,120
More Modern	5	H	2	0	1	0	12,520
More No	5	M	13	1	3	1	13,254

Horse	Age	Sex	Sts	1st	2d	3d	Won
More of This	3	F	2	0	0	0	0
More Red	4	G	7	2	0	0	11,432
More Ribbons	4	F	9	2	1	1	50,496
More Shenanigans	2	F	2	0	0	0	0
More Specific (GB)	4	C	8	1	1	1	7,950
More Speed	4	G	11	1	3	1	18,458
More Stars	7	H	2	0	0	0	0
More Suspect	6	H	1	0	0	0	0
More Tell	7	G	4	1	0	0	6,728
More Terms	7	H	1	0	0	0	0
More Than a Game	3	F	2	1	0	0	2,155
More Than Golden	4	F	7	1	0	1	8,930
More Than Honor	2	F	1	0	0	0	0
More Than One	5	H	1	0	0	0	0
More Tricks	3	F	1	0	0	0	75
Morelias Star	4	F	6	0	0	0	1,697
Morena Park (GB)	5	M	6	1	1	0	40,130
Morerunawaybride	3	F	3	0	0	0	200
Morethanastar	4	G	16	6	1	2	70,709
Morethanrisque	4	G	16	4	2	4	29,758
Moreto	2	C	3	0	1	0	5,602
Morfar	7	G	4	0	0	0	1,050
Morg	3	G	4	1	2	1	3,600
Morgan Canyon	4	G	2	1	0	0	4,775
Morgan Divy	3	F	2	0	0	1	1,364
Morgan Dollar	4	C	1	0	0	0	0
Morgan Looker	3	C	17	1	0	2	9,476
Morgan Made	4	F	8	1	0	4	7,748
Morgan Ridge	2	F	3	1	0	0	5,834
Morgane Ray	4	F	5	1	0	0	6,620
Morganite	6	H	2	0	0	0	750
Morgannes Hun	2	G	2	0	0	0	0
Morgans Creek	4	C	3	0	0	0	3,135
Morgan's Lad	4	G	6	0	3	0	5,680
Morgan's Peaches	3	F	1	0	0	0	0
Morgan's Renegade	2	F	2	0	0	0	179
Morganza	3	F	2	0	0	0	125
Morgnec Voodoo	5	H	10	0	1	0	1,016
Morine's Victory	2	C	3	0	1	0	12,375
Morisqueta	6	M	6	1	1	2	6,715
Morluc	7	H	3	0	1	0	23,060
Morn n' Mist	7	M	15	2	3	0	16,067
Morna's Girl (FR)	3	F	2	1	0	0	25,800
Morning Beauty	3	F	9	1	2	1	15,991
Morning Breeze	5	M	11	1	1	3	7,600
Morning Cat	3	G	14	1	1	2	7,401
Morning Domingo	3	F	11	1	1	1	8,560
Morning Edition	5	M	7	0	0	2	3,775
Morning Escapade	2	F	4	1	0	2	34,646
Morning Escar	3	C	2	0	0	0	210
Morning Express	6	H	11	1	1	2	13,676
Morning Fever	3	G	3	0	0	0	0
Morning Launch	6	M	1	0	0	0	105
Morning Light	4	F	2	0	0	0	0
Morning Line	6	H	8	0	0	0	850
Morning Love	5	M	11	0	0	4	2,988
Morning Maneuver	3	G	8	1	0	0	9,140
Morning Mass	10	G	1	0	0	0	0
Morning Merry	3	G	15	6	2	3	145,050
Morning Minstrel	6	G	1	0	0	0	0
Morning Play	4	C	16	0	0	1	10,565
Morning Prospector	3	C	10	0	0	2	2,490
Morning Riser	3	F	6	2	0	0	20,550
Morning Sky	3	F	4	1	0	2	31,260
Morning Special	10	G	1	0	0	0	0
Morning Surf	5	M	11	0	2	3	2,464
Morning Tune	2	C	1	0	0	0	220
Morning Walk	4	F	7	0	0	0	0
Morning Watch	3	G	7	1	1	0	38,530
Morning Wine	5	G	7	2	0	0	8,413
Morning's Image	4	G	5	1	1	1	19,140
Mornings Minion (GB)	6	G	7	0	3	3	18,130
Moro Grande	8	G	9	2	1	2	111,967
Moro Platino	3	C	3	0	0	0	300
Morocco	6	H	2	0	0	0	3,900
Moro's Lovely	3	F	5	2	0	1	26,856
Moro's Princess	3	F	9	1	1	0	15,808
Moro's Sugar	3	G	12	1	2	0	10,168
Morosino	7	H	1	0	0	0	0

RECORDS OF HORSES

Horse	Age	Sex	Sts	1st	2d	3d	Won	Horse	Age	Sex	Sts	1st	2d	3d	Won
Morrow	6	G	9	2	2	1	10,427	Mount Tora Bora	3	C	1	0	0	0	0
Mort	7	G	6	0	1	0	6,618	Mount Vesuvio	5	G	2	0	0	0	0
Mortgage Man	4	G	13	2	0	2	68,238	Mount Williams	6	G	9	0	2	0	6,327
Mortonsville	2	C	1	0	0	0	0	Mountain Ballad	7	H	3	0	1	0	1,400
Mortrump	2	C	1	0	1	0	1,125	Mountain Beacon	4	G	1	0	0	0	0
Morts Pleasure	3	F	2	0	0	0	215	Mountain Biker	5	G	5	0	0	0	767
Morty	4	C	1	0	0	0	200	Mountain Burgundy	4	G	6	0	1	0	1,410
Morty's Legacy	3	F	11	0	1	3	18,226	Mountain Chief	4	G	4	0	0	0	796
Mos Eisley	6	H	2	0	0	0	35	Mountain Creek	3	C	10	2	1	0	57,990
Mosayter	5	H	4	0	0	0	4,290	Mountain Dancer	6	G	12	1	4	1	14,315
Moscola	8	G	12	1	2	0	5,172	Mountain Dawn	3	F	11	1	2	1	109,593
Mosconi (IRE)	9	G	4	0	1	1	1,073	Mountain Destiny	6	M	3	0	0	0	0
Moscow Burning	3	F	9	6	1	0	179,565	Mountain Dispute	5	M	1	0	0	0	0
Moscow Caper	3	C	13	3	2	0	66,890	Mountain Eagle	5	G	12	3	1	3	38,005
Moscow Flite	4	G	15	2	1	0	10,624	Mountain Falls	5	G	12	0	2	2	3,705
Moscow Kitty	3	F	4	0	0	1	2,025	Mountain Forum	4	C	11	1	1	1	27,200
Moscow Mac	5	G	10	1	1	4	14,200	Mountain Fox	3	C	5	0	1	1	12,000
Moscow Song	3	F	1	0	0	0	0	Mountain Fury	3	G	9	1	0	2	12,781
Moscow Spy	2	F	2	0	0	2	930	Mountain General	5	G	6	2	3	0	212,580
Moscow Tech	3	F	9	1	1	1	7,003	Mountain Halo	3	G	7	0	0	0	2,122
Moscow Theatre	4	G	14	1	0	5	6,458	Mountain Hearted	3	G	4	0	0	0	218
Moscow Time	5	M	9	1	0	3	5,901	Mountain Jam	3	G	5	0	0	0	360
Moscows Quick Trip	5	G	12	0	1	4	3,497	Mountain Jamboree	5	G	16	3	1	2	30,316
Moses Jerome	3	G	18	2	2	4	65,105	Mountain Lake	5	H	14	0	3	5	19,998
Mosh Pit	3	G	8	0	3	1	5,010	Mountain Loba	5	M	6	1	0	1	3,114
Moss Agate	4	F	1	0	0	0	0	Mountain Maggie	5	M	4	0	0	0	325
Moss Boss	4	G	6	0	0	0	315	Mountain Memories	8	G	3	0	0	0	198
Mossant	2	G	4	0	1	1	8,500	Mountain Minister	3	G	10	1	1	0	12,250
Most	3	F	18	3	3	2	28,400	Mountain Miss	3	F	14	2	4	1	28,726
Most Admired	3	F	1	0	0	1	6,000	Mountain Music	3	F	16	4	1	1	49,690
Most Awesome	3	F	4	0	0	1	4,681	Mountain of Faith	3	G	12	2	2	2	19,591
Most Charismatic	2	F	1	0	0	0	145	Mountain of Glory	4	F	11	1	1	2	7,985
Most Charming	2	F	7	1	4	0	21,890	Mountain of Light	3	F	10	1	1	2	4,875
Most Dangerous	4	G	7	1	0	0	9,390	Mountain Orchid	4	F	2	0	1	0	14,440
Most Feared	3	G	5	0	2	0	104,749	Mountain Pride	4	C	16	2	1	3	31,805
Most Impressive	4	F	3	0	0	0	255	Mountain Pullet	3	F	1	0	0	0	0
Most Innovative	8	H	6	1	0	1	9,636	Mountain Rage	4	C	4	0	0	2	15,840
Mostly Ghostly	2	G	4	1	2	1	41,287	Mountain Ridge	2	C	5	0	0	0	2,825
Mostly Glory	4	F	12	2	3	1	8,726	Mountain Ruler	4	G	8	0	0	1	1,446
Mostly Red	4	C	19	3	6	2	52,207	Mountain Search	2	C	4	1	0	0	6,995
Mostly Sunny	2	F	1	0	0	0	0	Mountain Shadows	4	G	4	0	0	0	182
Mostly Tizzy	6	G	11	1	1	1	5,252	Mountain Slewpy	2	G	3	1	1	0	10,000
Motel Affair	3	G	5	1	0	0	15,300	Mountain Storm	6	G	4	0	0	0	212
Motel Cookie	3	F	5	0	0	1	710	Mountain Top	8	G	10	2	1	4	45,235
Motel Gossip	3	F	6	1	1	0	9,450	Mountain Village	2	G	1	0	0	0	1,140
Motel Love	3	F	15	4	1	1	63,714	Mountain Wave	2	F	5	0	0	1	1,421
Motel Mischef	6	M	3	1	1	0	4,600	Mountain Wild Cat	3	F	5	0	0	0	535
Motel Mystery	4	C	1	0	0	0	40	Mountainsofthemoon	3	C	1	0	0	0	85
Motel Notel	7	G	7	1	1	0	5,060	Mount's Moneymaker	5	H	7	0	0	0	349
Motel Shot	7	M	23	1	3	4	9,578	Mounty Python	2	C	1	0	0	0	204
Motel Staff	6	G	7	3	2	1	37,990	Mournful Defense	6	G	14	1	2	1	23,576
Motel Tricks	2	F	1	0	0	0	0	Mousse Glacee (CHI)	4	F	2	1	0	0	33,600
Mother Bates	2	F	1	0	0	0	0	Moussica	4	F	1	0	0	0	0
Mother Jones	10	G	6	0	0	0	329	Mouthadasouth	4	G	5	1	0	1	8,237
Mother Molly Boo	3	F	5	0	1	0	3,917	Movant	2	F	4	2	1	0	52,405
Mother's Dayruckus	5	H	8	1	1	3	20,487	Move On Slew	3	F	6	1	1	0	2,050
Mother's Dream	6	M	10	1	0	0	6,358	Move Outa My Way	3	F	3	0	0	0	665
Mother's Finest	6	M	3	0	0	0	0	Move Those Chains	4	C	8	4	1	2	136,020
Mother's Halo	4	G	5	1	0	1	15,420	Move to Strike	2	C	4	1	1	0	24,030
Mothers Message	8	M	1	0	0	0	50	Move to the Music	2	F	8	1	1	3	13,752
Mother's Sacrifice	2	F	2	2	0	0	141,503	Movealittlecloser	4	F	12	0	0	2	1,963
Motion Study	4	G	10	2	0	2	11,272	Moveinday	3	G	5	2	1	1	32,730
Motion to Suppress	11	G	16	0	3	2	3,984	Movesoupaige	5	M	12	1	0	3	4,293
Motives	4	C	2	1	1	0	34,440	Movewiththemaestro	4	G	5	0	0	0	866
Motivus	2	C	5	1	1	0	10,675	Movie Man	6	G	8	1	0	1	14,620
Motley Slew	3	C	8	1	0	0	9,396	Movie Review	6	H	3	0	0	0	306
Motocilla	4	F	1	0	0	0	0	Movin In	5	M	12	2	2	1	13,797
Motor City Slew	4	G	9	3	1	2	25,945	Movin N Crusin	2	G	7	2	0	3	13,060
Motorin	3	F	3	0	0	0	0	Movin South	3	F	2	0	0	0	705
Motto	8	H	7	1	3	1	60,460	Movin the Gold	4	F	7	1	0	0	1,575
Moujoudh (IRE)	3	C	6	0	0	4	23,880	Movin to the Music	6	G	10	3	1	2	27,477
Mount Alto	3	C	9	3	1	1	42,352	Movinanagroovin	10	G	7	0	1	0	1,319
Mount Angel	3	F	4	0	0	0	285	Moving Danzig	3	G	16	2	4	4	22,830
Mount Everest	5	G	16	1	1	1	14,955	Moving Experience (IRE)	6	M	8	0	1	1	17,020
Mount Gay	3	F	5	1	0	0	9,497	Moving Fever	3	F	7	3	1	0	24,710
Mount Gay Run	2	G	3	0	0	0	285	Moving Money	4	F	4	1	0	2	3,896
Mount Intrepid	6	G	4	0	1	0	12,727	Moving Mountains	5	G	2	1	0	0	6,554
Mount Rose	8	M	2	0	0	0	128	Movingmichael	3	C	12	2	2	1	17,135
Mount Suribachi	3	C	7	0	0	1	1,696	Moving's Gold	8	G	12	4	0	1	66,060

Horse	Age	Sex	Sts	1st	2d	3d	Won
Movinlikawinner	2	F	3	0	0	1	1,540
Mowata	6	H	3	0	0	0	190
Moxey Gulch	5	M	1	0	0	0	40
Moxie Man	8	G	12	1	2	2	7,062
Moxie Mollie	5	M	1	0	0	0	0
Moyamba	12	G	8	2	0	4	3,503
Moyie's Wildchild	3	F	8	0	2	0	4,252
Moyo Simba	4	G	13	1	3	2	16,310
Mozo Alegre (CHI)	7	H	1	0	0	0	450
Mozotti	4	F	5	0	0	0	2,100
Mr Ammo	8	G	6	1	2	0	12,214
Mr Atlantic (ARG)	4	C	2	0	0	0	0
Mr B Boss	3	C	7	1	1	0	6,150
Mr Bassett	4	G	6	0	1	3	23,490
Mr Big Stuff	5	G	2	0	0	0	122
Mr Big Time	4	C	8	1	2	1	15,272
Mr Bishop	3	C	1	0	0	0	0
Mr Blumin	5	G	12	2	1	2	19,059
Mr Bombastic (GER)	4	G	4	1	1	1	7,276
Mr Boom Bostic	3	G	10	2	1	1	15,470
Mr Bulldog	7	G	3	0	0	0	540
Mr Cartwheel	6	G	10	5	2	2	21,828
Mr Clearwater	4	G	5	0	2	0	5,075
Mr Clever	3	C	3	0	0	0	491
Mr Clever Socks	5	G	16	2	0	5	11,646
Mr Dandie	4	G	5	0	0	2	650
Mr Divine	8	G	10	1	1	1	5,324
Mr Don	3	C	8	1	1	0	14,525
Mr Double D Ana B.	3	C	1	0	0	1	600
Mr Dovic	3	G	1	0	0	0	0
Mr Elite	4	G	8	0	0	0	660
Mr Fiji	4	G	3	0	0	0	293
Mr Freckles	5	G	12	1	2	4	36,160
Mr Fuddy Duddy	8	G	7	0	0	1	2,552
Mr G	8	G	8	0	1	3	4,939
Mr Gator	5	H	2	0	0	0	0
Mr Gemeni Cricket	6	G	4	0	0	0	280
Mr Gil	2	C	7	2	0	2	24,503
Mr Gold Maker	9	H	4	1	1	1	2,134
Mr Graydon	4	G	12	1	2	2	22,329
Mr Hay	3	C	9	0	0	1	4,314
Mr Hayes	2	G	1	0	0	0	0
Mr Henderson	4	C	5	0	0	0	175
Mr Higgs	3	C	3	0	0	0	0
Mr Hilarious	5	H	13	1	2	0	50,540
Mr Huckster	5	H	4	0	0	2	1,260
Mr Humvee	8	G	11	1	0	3	8,808
Mr Illogical	3	G	13	3	2	0	12,412
Mr J. R.	4	G	16	1	0	2	9,520
Mr Jetset	5	H	17	3	1	6	69,465
Mr Joe B	3	C	4	1	1	0	24,520
Mr Juan Sock	10	G	9	1	1	0	2,180
Mr Kanga Roo	6	H	5	0	0	0	680
Mr Lanigon	4	C	4	0	0	0	0
Mr Lion	4	G	2	1	0	0	6,675
Mr Mac to You	5	G	4	0	0	0	250
Mr Mag	4	G	14	2	4	0	27,250
Mr Major	7	G	11	1	1	1	19,310
Mr McClelland	8	G	3	0	0	2	3,252
Mr Mico	4	C	1	0	0	0	58
Mr Mississippi	3	G	7	2	3	0	65,040
Mr Miswaki	3	C	10	0	1	1	5,950
Mr Mombo	3	G	8	2	3	0	20,135
Mr Motion	4	G	5	1	1	0	17,100
Mr Mt Vernon	7	G	10	1	3	4	2,608
Mr Nineball	5	G	9	0	0	1	8,870
Mr Notebook	5	G	11	3	2	2	49,350
Mr O'Brien (IRE)	4	G	7	2	3	1	73,740
Mr Oliver	3	G	18	1	1	4	6,445
Mr One Ring	9	G	3	0	1	1	761
Mr Patsy Kelly	5	H	10	2	1	1	24,875
Mr Perkolater	5	G	6	0	1	1	26,265
Mr Phoenician	4	C	15	1	2	3	6,517
Mr Pioneer	2	C	2	0	0	0	0
Mr Pop's Andreas	4	G	7	1	0	1	6,542
Mr Quick Quack	5	H	1	0	0	0	0
Mr Request	6	G	2	0	0	0	99
Mr Rhythm	4	G	6	0	0	0	1,340
Mr Rocket	3	C	9	3	2	3	95,035
Mr Rokeby	9	G	6	1	3	0	16,800
Mr Ross	8	G	2	0	0	0	2,280
Mr Salty	3	C	14	2	1	0	15,065
Mr Salty Jones	3	C	10	1	1	2	7,990
Mr Shaanshu	3	C	14	1	3	2	20,663
Mr Short Cut	6	G	17	2	4	2	18,635
Mr Silly	2	C	1	0	0	0	0
Mr Siphon	4	G	6	1	0	3	28,770
Mr Slewpy	7	H	1	0	0	1	940
Mr Smeadleysmearch	2	G	4	1	1	0	14,300
Mr Song and Dance	4	G	6	1	1	1	17,950
Mr Spark	6	G	9	0	0	3	3,133
Mr Sparkles Gem	4	C	11	2	1	1	15,235
Mr Sparrow Tan	4	C	12	0	1	0	917
Mr Steed	4	G	16	0	1	3	4,141
Mr Superior	3	G	16	1	0	3	5,635
Mr Superior Knight	8	G	11	3	0	1	6,220
Mr Tap Star	3	C	6	2	1	2	16,148
Mr Term	3	C	1	0	1	0	1,820
Mr Tickety Boo	3	G	13	3	2	0	79,204
Mr Toad (IRE)	4	G	9	0	2	1	23,480
Mr Toolighttoquit	4	C	3	1	1	0	13,980
Mr Tour	3	C	4	0	0	0	177
Mr Trey	4	C	4	0	1	0	1,596
Mr Twist	9	G	9	1	0	1	3,535
Mr Twix	3	C	5	1	1	0	6,855
Mr Victory	2	C	11	0	1	0	4,154
Mr Weiss	3	C	1	0	0	0	0
Mr W's Daughter	2	F	4	0	2	1	9,260
Mr Zanetti	3	C	1	0	0	0	54
Mr Zipper	5	G	11	1	1	1	5,383
Mr Zooha	6	H	12	2	4	0	17,799
Mr Z's	5	G	7	1	3	1	17,820
Mr. Acavano	6	G	7	0	1	0	2,850
Mr. Ace	4	G	8	0	1	2	18,868
Mr. Alchemy	5	G	14	1	3	1	5,161
Mr. Alybro	3	G	2	1	0	0	7,269
Mr. Amano	3	G	9	2	0	2	50,235
Mr. America	6	G	7	0	1	1	2,104
Mr. Ararat	5	G	9	2	2	2	58,855
Mr. Archibald	4	C	4	2	0	1	43,440
Mr. Authority	4	G	14	3	3	1	25,618
Mr. B Lucky	8	G	4	1	2	1	9,740
Mr. Bad Deal	3	G	10	1	1	0	5,705
Mr. Bad News	5	G	14	1	3	1	11,428
Mr. Bailey	6	H	2	0	0	0	56
Mr. Barricade	3	G	16	1	0	1	3,660
Mr. Bartlett	4	G	14	2	3	0	12,651
Mr. Baskets	5	H	10	1	1	2	41,140
Mr. Beecher	5	H	2	0	0	0	0
Mr. Believable	3	C	12	0	1	2	32,489
Mr. Belle Citi	8	G	12	0	1	3	3,450
Mr. Ben	3	G	3	0	0	0	193
Mr. Benton	4	G	3	0	0	1	1,440
Mr. Bertman	4	G	3	0	0	0	125
Mr. Bigbird	4	C	9	1	0	2	8,190
Mr. Bigglesworth	6	G	9	1	1	2	19,168
Mr. Billie P.	5	G	2	0	0	0	294
Mr. Bird	3	G	6	2	2	0	15,316
Mr. Bo Ally Ray	4	G	13	2	0	0	4,770
Mr. Bo Jo	4	G	16	2	2	2	13,853
Mr. Boaster	9	G	4	0	1	1	851
Mr. Bocephus	4	C	10	1	3	0	6,717
Mr. Bold Storm	6	H	3	0	0	0	270
Mr. Bones	2	C	9	1	2	1	19,710
Mr. Bosco	4	G	9	2	1	2	13,169
Mr. Brad	7	G	8	0	0	0	847
Mr. Brave Heart	2	C	1	0	0	0	909
Mr. Breeze	2	C	1	0	0	0	0
Mr. Brook	7	G	7	1	0	2	3,029
Mr. Bubbly	3	C	14	3	1	0	32,530
Mr. Bubby	3	C	1	0	0	0	750
Mr. Buffum	8	G	11	2	2	0	26,660
Mr. Burns	7	G	1	0	0	0	0
Mr. Butterscotch	11	G	15	1	1	2	7,068
Mr. C Note	2	C	1	1	0	0	15,600
Mr. Campbell Sir	4	C	9	1	0	0	5,898
Mr. Capote	2	C	1	0	0	1	6,468
Mr. Cara	3	G	6	2	0	0	10,920

RECORDS OF HORSES

Horse	Age	Sex	Sts	1st	2d	3d	Won
Mr. Carlos	6	H	2	0	0	0	148
Mr. Carpe Diem	2	C	3	0	0	0	100
Mr. Cash City	4	G	12	1	2	3	17,900
Mr. Cat	3	G	10	1	1	2	15,820
Mr. Cee's Tizzy	5	G	1	0	0	0	170
Mr. Center Storm	2	C	2	1	0	1	16,784
Mr. Charming	2	G	1	0	0	0	0
Mr. Chatter Box	5	G	1	1	0	0	15,840
Mr. Chicken Man	5	G	16	2	0	2	8,528
Mr. Chinaball	6	G	12	0	2	0	3,494
Mr. Chipping	5	G	5	0	1	1	3,689
Mr. Chisum	3	G	4	1	0	0	7,650
Mr. Chris Gibbs	4	G	10	2	1	2	13,587
Mr. Chris Kringle	3	G	8	0	0	0	872
Mr. Chubbs	6	H	16	0	2	1	4,323
Mr. Classy	6	G	1	0	0	0	2,755
Mr. Colin P.	3	G	12	3	0	1	34,579
Mr. Concerto	3	G	8	1	0	1	6,730
Mr. Court	5	H	8	1	0	2	22,719
Mr. Crimson	4	G	12	1	4	2	32,636
Mr. Crowe	4	G	1	0	0	0	0
Mr. Cub	3	C	10	3	0	0	10,566
Mr. Cuicchi	4	G	1	0	0	0	0
Mr. Damille	5	H	12	0	1	1	2,092
Mr. Dash	4	G	9	0	1	2	3,186
Mr. de Falls	7	H	18	2	2	1	13,002
Mr. Debeck	5	H	5	1	1	0	5,700
Mr. Decatur	3	C	3	2	0	0	106,580
Mr. Deelite	3	G	5	0	0	0	132
Mr. Deep Pockets	3	C	1	0	0	0	225
Mr. Delicious	5	G	3	0	1	0	640
Mr. Delma	4	G	6	0	0	0	0
Mr. Denim	5	G	3	0	0	0	140
Mr. Deputy	2	C	2	0	0	0	0
Mr. Determined	4	C	11	0	1	1	65,214
Mr. Digger	2	C	3	0	0	1	4,066
Mr. Dillon	5	G	4	2	1	0	21,050
Mr. Diplomat	4	G	8	3	1	1	29,554
Mr. Dutton	5	G	8	1	3	1	6,193
Mr. E Cat	3	C	6	1	0	1	4,610
Mr. Eddie R	2	C	3	0	1	0	3,120
Mr. Eldorado	3	G	2	0	0	0	390
Mr. Elegance	8	H	12	3	1	1	16,784
Mr. Eltish	3	C	4	0	0	0	583
Mr. Elusive	3	C	12	4	0	0	46,405
Mr. Elway	6	H	2	0	0	0	308
Mr. Endeavour	4	G	15	1	1	4	10,960
Mr. Energy	4	G	1	0	0	0	101
Mr. Epperson	8	G	11	2	4	2	160,079
Mr. Exchequer	10	G	2	0	0	0	0
Mr. Excitement	7	G	8	0	1	1	7,503
Mr. Expectations	2	G	7	0	1	2	5,195
Mr. Fancy Dancer	6	H	1	0	0	0	0
Mr. Fasty	6	H	3	1	0	2	9,286
Mr. Fater	6	G	3	0	0	1	4,500
Mr. Fine Fine	6	H	8	1	1	2	2,642
Mr. Fix	4	G	14	4	1	2	8,903
Mr. Fixed Income	2	C	6	1	1	1	24,261
Mr. Flakes	2	G	1	0	0	0	120
Mr. Fleet Feet	4	C	4	0	1	0	4,233
Mr. Foolish	7	H	2	0	0	0	0
Mr. Fools Gold	7	G	8	2	2	0	9,191
Mr. Fran Man	3	C	7	0	2	0	8,030
Mr. Francesco	3	G	3	0	0	0	0
Mr. Friday	3	G	12	0	0	1	1,430
Mr. Frog	4	G	9	0	2	2	13,210
Mr. Frost	5	G	10	1	4	0	23,250
Mr. Garry C.	6	G	8	1	1	2	4,628
Mr. Gehrig	3	C	4	1	0	0	29,120
Mr. Genoa	3	G	1	0	1	0	8,580
Mr. Gentle Ben	3	C	4	0	0	0	390
Mr. Gladiator	3	G	14	1	2	4	18,555
Mr. Glassware	7	H	9	0	0	2	1,915
Mr. Gleason	2	C	1	0	0	0	0
Mr. Glendale	3	C	1	0	1	0	3,800
Mr. Glenn	3	C	18	1	2	3	14,135
Mr. Gold Flight	4	G	12	1	1	1	6,645
Mr. Greedy	4	G	16	1	1	4	13,233
Mr. Gung Ho	7	G	10	1	2	1	10,708
Mr. Guyana	7	G	12	2	0	4	32,043
Mr. Hadley	5	G	6	0	0	1	1,140
Mr. Happy Hour	4	G	8	0	3	2	7,811
Mr. Headliner	3	G	2	0	0	0	0
Mr. Hemmingway	3	G	13	1	2	1	5,596
Mr. Hobo Joe	6	G	13	1	2	3	23,814
Mr. Hockey	3	G	18	3	3	1	20,666
Mr. Hooch	2	G	1	0	0	1	1,680
Mr. I R S	11	G	8	0	0	2	2,373
Mr. Insanity	8	G	10	1	0	1	5,419
Mr. Irish Love	2	C	2	0	0	1	1,390
Mr. Ivan	3	G	7	1	3	0	10,171
Mr. J. D.	3	G	7	0	2	2	15,546
Mr. J. T. L.	2	C	2	0	0	0	3,528
Mr. Jazz Man	3	C	2	0	0	1	1,400
Mr. Jerome	2	C	1	0	1	0	2,755
Mr. Jess	4	G	10	1	0	4	11,320
Mr. Jester	2	C	6	4	2	0	730,800
Mr. Jimmy Gimmie	3	G	8	2	1	1	18,757
Mr. Joe C	5	G	13	0	3	3	94,079
Mr. Joe Lee	2	G	1	0	0	0	115
Mr. John	5	H	5	0	0	2	32,665
Mr. Kenny H	2	C	1	0	0	0	0
Mr. Kimbo	3	G	12	1	3	2	33,844
Mr. King Pin	4	G	13	2	3	2	21,655
Mr. King Rex	3	G	3	0	0	0	960
Mr. Kipp	4	C	15	0	0	1	8,085
Mr. Kleven	3	G	3	0	1	0	3,350
Mr. Know It All	2	C	2	0	0	0	100
Mr. Kody	7	G	8	3	1	2	11,432
Mr. Krisley	5	G	8	1	1	0	52,398
Mr. Kuck	6	G	15	0	5	1	21,037
Mr. L.	3	C	7	2	2	0	72,265
Mr. L. D.	4	G	8	0	0	1	936
Mr. Lee	2	C	6	0	1	0	3,326
Mr. Lefty James	6	H	8	1	1	0	3,667
Mr. Leggs	5	H	3	0	0	0	0
Mr. Lewis	8	H	1	0	0	0	95
Mr. Lewis (PER)	3	C	4	0	0	0	819
Mr. Light (ARG)	4	C	2	0	0	1	7,990
Mr. Lincoln	2	C	1	0	0	0	330
Mr. Lion King	2	C	4	0	2	0	6,540
Mr. Livingston	6	H	10	2	0	2	68,030
Mr. Lover	5	G	14	3	3	0	25,677
Mr. Lucky Numbers	7	G	12	3	3	2	22,357
Mr. Lump	7	G	14	3	1	1	26,992
Mr. M. G.	3	G	8	1	0	2	1,651
Mr. Machine	3	G	5	0	1	0	2,250
Mr. Macphisto	4	G	6	0	0	2	2,958
Mr. Maggie	2	G	1	0	0	0	130
Mr. Makah	3	G	4	0	1	1	5,265
Mr. Marbelous	3	G	9	1	2	2	24,346
Mr. Marcellus	7	G	9	0	0	0	774
Mr. Marfa	7	G	2	0	0	0	0
Mr. Masquerade	4	G	8	0	3	1	11,487
Mr. Match	5	G	17	1	3	2	13,845
Mr. Matrix	4	G	4	0	0	0	219
Mr. Mauk	2	C	3	0	0	0	195
Mr. McCabe	5	H	14	1	2	3	32,190
Mr. McZu	2	C	1	0	0	0	78
Mr. Meanie	6	G	3	0	0	0	382
Mr. Megan	3	C	12	1	3	1	58,590
Mr. Melcap	4	G	11	2	0	2	4,912
Mr. Merrick	3	G	4	1	1	0	5,868
Mr. Merry	2	G	3	0	0	0	500
Mr. Meso	3	C	11	3	2	1	59,060
Mr. Mezo	4	G	11	2	0	1	6,845
Mr. Miesque	5	H	1	1	0	0	18,000
Mr. Mighty Coyote	5	H	4	0	0	0	302
Mr. Mingo	3	G	10	2	1	0	44,270
Mr. Mini	2	G	5	0	1	0	2,297
Mr. Mink	3	G	6	4	2	0	90,510
Mr. Missionary	6	G	14	0	3	0	4,345
Mr. Mister	7	H	2	0	0	0	83
Mr. Mobo	3	G	2	0	0	0	244
Mr. Monsoon	2	C	3	0	0	0	450
Mr. Monster	3	G	7	0	0	0	225
Mr. Moody Blue	5	G	18	2	1	1	9,196
Mr. Moses	3	G	12	2	2	1	10,520

Horse	Age	Sex	Sts	1st	2d	3d	Won
Mr. Moze	11	G	8	1	0	0	3,065
Mr. Mulgrew	2	C	3	1	0	0	3,450
Mr. Music Man	2	G	3	0	0	0	0
Mr. Newb	6	G	10	1	0	0	4,792
Mr. Nifty	5	G	9	0	0	0	205
Mr. October	3	G	7	1	1	1	27,980
Mr. O'Kaye	8	G	3	1	0	0	3,300
Mr. One Way	4	G	7	0	1	1	2,311
Mr. Otis	4	G	7	1	0	2	8,420
Mr. Outside	3	G	4	1	0	1	12,282
Mr. P T	5	G	14	0	1	0	5,387
Mr. Parks	3	C	4	0	0	0	0
Mr. Pat	4	C	3	0	0	2	7,700
Mr. Patience	2	G	5	1	3	0	12,070
Mr. Patrick B	4	G	21	2	0	2	8,256
Mr. Payt	3	C	9	0	0	0	822
Mr. Peacemaker	4	C	11	1	1	2	22,499
Mr. Peanut	5	G	12	1	1	3	5,621
Mr. Pentel	6	H	14	3	0	5	27,835
Mr. Peppers	3	G	14	2	1	2	15,235
Mr. Perpetuity	6	G	4	0	0	1	7,075
Mr. Persistency	3	G	14	3	2	2	49,628
Mr. Piano Man	2	C	5	2	0	0	24,410
Mr. Pickled Gap	9	G	16	1	4	2	23,077
Mr. Pistols	7	G	9	0	0	0	372
Mr. Pleasentfar (BRZ)	6	H	8	1	0	0	31,320
Mr. Plum	4	G	12	0	1	7	7,993
Mr. Popeye	4	G	10	1	1	4	8,605
Mr. Postmaster	7	G	11	2	1	2	8,118
Mr. Potter	4	G	6	1	1	0	16,549
Mr. Power Ball	2	G	2	0	0	1	720
Mr. Powerful	4	G	8	0	1	1	4,500
Mr. Presley	3	C	7	0	0	3	13,984
Mr. Punkindo	4	C	5	0	0	0	800
Mr. Quasar	2	C	2	0	0	0	196
Mr. Quick	3	G	8	0	0	0	306
Mr. Quickly	4	G	8	1	1	0	14,088
Mr. Quist	11	G	1	0	0	0	40
Mr. Quizzical	11	G	5	1	0	0	2,280
Mr. Raft	11	G	8	0	0	1	2,076
Mr. Rajiv	4	G	16	1	1	3	17,900
Mr. Rambler	5	G	12	0	1	0	2,805
Mr. Ranger	9	G	6	0	0	0	118
Mr. Reasoning	5	H	4	0	0	0	200
Mr. Red	4	C	14	3	1	2	19,782
Mr. Reed	7	G	13	0	2	1	6,685
Mr. Reins	3	G	8	1	0	0	13,620
Mr. Review	4	C	7	0	0	0	498
Mr. Riddler	7	G	10	1	3	1	19,084
Mr. Ridge	3	C	13	1	5	0	7,100
Mr. Roadway	3	G	15	2	2	1	52,600
Mr. Rob	3	C	2	0	0	0	105
Mr. Rock N Roll	8	G	11	2	2	2	2,322
Mr. Rocket Man	4	G	12	2	4	2	41,475
Mr. Rocky T	3	G	6	0	0	0	1,324
Mr. Romeo	3	C	6	1	2	1	29,880
Mr. Ron	3	C	9	1	1	2	16,530
Mr. Routine	9	G	3	0	0	0	675
Mr. Royal Twist	4	G	14	2	3	1	16,232
Mr. Rubicon	3	C	3	0	0	0	3,300
Mr. Rumson	4	G	12	3	1	0	43,074
Mr. Ruska	3	G	3	0	0	0	1,260
Mr. Sadler's Gulch	6	G	5	1	0	0	4,913
Mr. Sam	2	G	3	1	0	0	8,367
Mr. Samson	3	G	2	0	1	0	3,850
Mr. San Miguel	4	G	7	1	1	2	5,866
Mr. Sandstorm	5	G	19	3	3	3	47,750
Mr. Saratoga	4	C	2	0	2	0	3,600
Mr. Sass	3	G	15	4	0	2	31,730
Mr. Scott Man	5	G	11	0	1	1	4,469
Mr. Seafarer	7	G	5	4	1	0	29,820
Mr. Secret	5	H	2	0	1	1	370
Mr. Seldon	3	C	6	1	1	0	5,673
Mr. Sezwho	9	H	10	0	2	0	8,810
Mr. Shoplifter	4	C	2	1	1	0	27,240
Mr. Silencer	6	G	2	0	0	0	0
Mr. Simon to You	3	G	15	1	1	3	16,479
Mr. Sing	3	G	6	0	0	0	0
Mr. Sirenity	3	C	6	0	0	2	4,620
Mr. Slew's Valor	9	G	13	1	0	0	7,987
Mr. Smiley	2	C	2	0	0	1	2,750
Mr. Smoke	3	G	6	0	1	0	3,795
Mr. Speaks	5	G	13	1	4	2	14,230
Mr. Spectacular	3	G	11	1	0	1	4,600
Mr. Spock	2	C	3	1	0	1	17,990
Mr. Steadfast	3	G	4	1	0	0	2,800
Mr. Steve	7	G	5	0	1	0	10,780
Mr. Stone	3	C	8	1	2	0	50,140
Mr. Storm Dancer	4	C	7	0	0	1	1,265
Mr. Stress	5	G	17	5	4	3	68,120
Mr. Sulu	5	G	7	2	1	2	115,678
Mr. Sun	3	G	15	3	3	2	42,635
Mr. Sundancer	8	G	10	2	3	1	23,096
Mr. T D F	7	G	5	0	0	0	682
Mr. T. K.	6	G	9	1	1	1	8,474
Mr. Talisman	7	H	13	1	2	3	4,475
Mr. Tammany	6	H	14	3	2	4	14,942
Mr. Technique	3	C	5	1	1	0	81,275
Mr. Tipsy	5	H	14	4	4	2	86,446
Mr. Tobin	3	G	8	0	0	0	362
Mr. Trash Talk	2	C	1	0	0	0	123
Mr. Trieste	2	C	2	1	1	0	35,260
Mr. Trouble	4	G	15	5	2	2	71,708
Mr. Troublemaker	3	G	5	0	1	0	1,685
Mr. Truthful	3	G	18	2	2	4	37,530
Mr. United States	7	H	6	1	1	3	9,050
Mr. V.	4	C	6	0	3	0	30,790
Mr. V. I. P.	2	C	3	0	0	0	0
Mr. Value	4	G	3	1	1	0	18,520
Mr. Vic	8	G	5	0	2	1	6,114
Mr. Wakette	7	G	8	0	0	0	2,235
Mr. Whippet	4	G	1	0	0	0	50
Mr. Whitestone	3	C	14	3	4	2	117,484
Mr. Will	4	G	3	1	0	0	4,950
Mr. Williamson	4	C	10	2	0	2	11,996
Mr. Willie Joe	2	C	7	1	3	0	26,910
Mr. Williston	3	C	15	0	0	2	4,704
Mr. Willy B.	4	G	5	0	0	0	120
Mr. Windfall	2	C	1	0	0	0	148
Mr. Windy	4	G	12	0	0	2	4,889
Mr. Wonderful Man	8	G	18	4	2	8	21,832
Mr. Woods	8	H	10	1	1	0	4,955
Mr. Wooly	5	H	7	0	2	0	9,215
Mr. Word	2	G	6	0	2	1	4,782
Mr. Yano	3	G	12	2	1	2	29,730
Mr. Yatooma	3	G	5	2	1	1	30,645
Mr. Zach Man	3	C	11	2	3	4	47,576
Mralwaysatisfied	2	G	2	0	0	1	4,250
Mramerica	3	C	2	0	0	0	200
Mrs Beasley	4	F	1	0	0	0	60
Mrs Bigshot	4	F	10	1	2	1	25,160
Mr's Little Sister	5	M	12	2	1	1	4,513
Mrs Miniver	9	M	1	0	0	0	0
Mrs Sprinkle	3	F	7	0	0	1	1,117
Mrs. Bassett	2	F	2	0	0	0	440
Mrs. Beerman	2	F	6	0	3	0	12,595
Mrs. Bejany	3	F	6	0	0	0	450
Mrs. Brown Angel	2	F	3	0	0	0	192
Mrs. Burns	5	M	12	1	2	4	23,788
Mrs. Charles	2	F	3	0	0	0	831
Mrs. Clay	3	F	11	1	2	1	6,970
Mrs. Cook	3	F	11	1	0	1	4,356
Mrs. Coolidge	3	F	7	0	1	0	6,740
Mrs. Corley	5	M	1	0	0	0	0
Mrs. Costanza	3	F	3	0	1	0	1,040
Mrs. Dish	4	F	5	0	2	0	10,875
Mrs. Doyle	3	F	2	1	1	0	14,010
Mrs. Frosty	5	M	14	3	3	2	16,278
Mrs. Karakorum	3	F	5	0	0	0	0
Mrs. M	4	F	11	4	6	0	69,250
Mrs. Mac	6	M	10	1	1	1	16,660
Mrs. Mackey	2	F	2	0	0	0	1,470
Mrs. Mistofelees	2	F	5	0	2	0	47,720
Mrs. Motte	4	F	5	0	0	0	435
Mrs. Navarone	3	G	9	1	3	1	10,740
Mrs. Norvell Cat	4	F	3	0	0	0	0
Mrs. Obvious	3	F	15	4	4	3	30,100
Mrs. Piggle Wiggle	8	M	9	0	0	3	5,204

RECORDS OF HORSES

Horse	Age	Sex	Sts	1st	2d	3d	Won
Mrs. Robinson	2	F	2	0	0	0	105
Mrs. Rosalie C.	4	F	8	0	0	1	2,520
Mrs. Smooth Moves	3	F	6	0	0	0	0
Mrs. Soprano	4	F	8	0	0	2	3,972
Mrs. Strauss	2	F	1	0	0	0	185
Mrs. Witchworth	5	M	8	1	0	0	2,686
Mrscoppolaskitchen	4	F	19	2	3	4	58,555
Ms Afterglow	4	F	8	1	0	0	4,206
Ms Akins Outlaw	5	M	7	0	0	0	203
Ms Alex D.	5	M	10	1	0	0	3,669
Ms Alinna K	5	M	9	0	1	2	4,600
Ms Allen Oops	3	F	10	3	1	0	18,540
Ms Alleygirl	3	F	1	0	0	0	0
Ms Ally Allen	3	F	2	0	0	1	1,050
Ms Blue Speedy	4	F	4	0	1	1	2,725
Ms Bodgit	4	F	8	2	2	0	35,182
Ms Brookski	4	F	8	0	0	0	2,250
Ms Carissa	5	M	12	2	1	2	3,839
Ms Crazy Lady	2	F	1	0	0	0	100
Ms Crimson Star	3	F	5	0	0	0	0
Ms Deanor	4	F	10	2	3	1	29,428
Ms Erica	6	M	10	0	2	3	45,356
Ms Freddie Bright	3	F	7	1	0	1	15,120
Ms Gia's Wager	4	F	5	1	1	0	8,132
Ms Glamour Girl	2	F	2	1	0	0	3,300
Ms Global Warming	3	F	2	0	0	0	3,780
Ms Goda	5	M	15	2	3	3	15,223
Ms Good	4	F	13	3	2	2	30,910
Ms Grand Ole Opry	4	F	4	0	0	0	165
Ms Hayseed	5	M	9	2	1	3	14,690
Ms Holly	2	F	2	0	0	0	31
Ms Ida Dealer	5	M	10	1	0	1	10,292
Ms Infinity Slew	7	M	8	1	1	0	5,304
Ms Iroc	4	F	1	0	0	0	0
Ms Isadorable	4	F	10	1	2	0	36,020
Ms Jacqui	3	F	4	0	0	0	400
Ms Jessi	4	F	8	1	2	1	20,356
Ms Kitty Bag	3	F	4	0	1	0	645
Ms Knight Lane	4	F	5	0	0	0	3,038
Ms Lady Palace	2	F	6	1	1	1	8,539
Ms Louisett	4	F	2	0	0	0	0
Ms Ly Beau	8	M	2	0	0	0	0
Ms Maggie Sue	4	F	14	2	0	2	13,960
Ms Majestic Lady	3	F	12	4	2	0	13,091
Ms Maryann N	2	F	2	0	0	1	3,630
Ms Media	6	M	12	0	1	1	8,166
Ms Medill	6	M	8	0	0	0	275
Ms Mintons Excess	2	G	1	0	0	0	720
Ms Moonlite Dancer	2	F	2	1	0	0	7,650
Ms Moves	3	F	5	0	1	0	9,144
Ms Nancy S	2	F	4	1	1	0	7,720
Ms Piggie	4	F	6	0	0	0	320
Ms Powful	3	F	8	1	1	2	22,390
Ms Prime Minister	3	F	11	1	1	1	10,969
Ms Rainbow Cat	4	F	1	0	0	0	0
Ms Rainbow to You	2	F	7	0	1	0	2,928
Ms Reen	4	F	14	3	2	4	24,472
Ms Regina	1		1	0	0	0	6,600
Ms Runner Jones	2	F	2	0	1	0	2,600
Ms Shawcolat	4	F	6	2	1	1	13,450
Ms Southern Beauty	3	F	6	0	0	0	272
Ms Special Syn	4	F	3	0	0	0	288
Ms Technology	3	F	14	2	1	2	20,648
Ms Tish	4	F	18	1	2	1	14,210
Ms Tom Cat	3	F	2	0	0	0	563
Ms Well	4	F	6	0	1	0	4,210
Ms Zoom Zoom	2	F	2	0	0	0	173
Ms. Amours	4	F	8	2	0	0	14,940
Ms. Annie Oakley	3	F	3	0	0	0	0
Ms. April Foolish	4	F	3	1	0	0	2,300
Ms. Avis	2	F	6	0	2	2	9,200
Ms. Bag	4	F	8	1	0	3	21,835
Ms. Banker	2	F	5	2	1	1	25,180
Ms. Bella	6	M	11	0	1	3	2,863
Ms. Bluebird	3	F	4	1	0	1	20,000
Ms. Bonita	4	F	12	0	3	1	6,692
Ms. Brow	5	M	1	0	0	0	0
Ms. C D Player	6	M	9	0	1	2	12,120
Ms. Carpetbagger	2	F	7	1	0	1	3,540
Ms. Cougar Slew	3	F	1	0	0	0	0
Ms. Daisie's Pie	3	F	5	0	0	0	0
Ms. Dottie J	2	F	5	0	0	0	1,310
Ms. Dowden	4	F	13	1	5	3	48,490
Ms. Elenie	3	F	3	1	0	0	3,270
Ms. Era	4	F	10	1	1	0	5,163
Ms. Executive City	2	F	1	0	0	1	930
Ms. Foolish Dancer	4	F	4	0	1	0	4,097
Ms. Foxy Roxy	3	F	4	0	0	1	2,145
Ms. Guilderland	7	M	2	0	0	0	165
Ms. Inez	3	F	5	0	0	0	150
Ms. Inxs	2	F	3	0	0	0	0
Ms. Irish	3	F	7	1	0	0	3,643
Ms. Jodi	2	F	2	0	0	0	200
Ms. Jubilee	6	M	2	0	0	0	103
Ms. Justice	4	F	9	2	3	1	18,505
Ms. K. L. Cat	3	F	7	0	0	1	4,685
Ms. Kinsey	3	F	3	1	1	0	25,920
Ms. Kitti Carson	3	F	4	1	0	0	5,400
Ms. Lady Rose	5	M	7	1	0	3	12,350
Ms. Marlyn	4	F	3	0	0	0	0
Ms. Mary H	4	F	10	2	1	0	16,975
Ms. Mary Marie	4	F	8	2	1	0	21,982
Ms. Monroe	6	M	6	0	0	2	2,675
Ms. Pie	4	F	10	3	0	2	16,279
Ms. Prenup	5	M	9	0	1	1	2,475
Ms. Rapunzel	5	M	9	0	1	2	13,440
Ms. Rubirosa	3	F	12	1	1	1	14,565
Ms. Russian Cat	3	F	19	2	4	5	25,005
Ms. Sadira	6	M	7	2	3	1	60,240
Ms. Saskatoon	3	F	5	1	0	0	1,408
Ms. Sassy Lady	2	F	3	0	0	0	796
Ms. Sharoan	2	F	4	0	0	0	237
Ms. Speedo	3	F	5	0	1	2	5,990
Ms. Tahoe Ridge	2	F	5	0	0	2	2,555
Ms. Thunderpuddles	3	F	2	0	0	0	0
Ms. Top Pay	3	F	14	3	3	2	23,270
Ms. Tophamhat	3	F	3	0	1	0	1,352
Ms. Trick Or Treat	2	F	6	2	1	0	42,030
Ms. Via's Citation	7	M	8	1	1	2	7,037
Ms. Whiz	4	F	11	1	2	1	7,190
Ms. Will a Way	3	F	3	0	2	0	16,400
Ms. Winfrey	4	F	2	0	0	1	693
Ms. Wolf	4	F	14	1	2	1	22,525
Ms. Zipoy	6	M	8	0	0	2	2,498
Msaferd	4	F	9	2	0	2	10,211
Msaudrey'slegs	5	M	1	0	0	0	0
Msbaileyscream	5	M	6	0	1	2	35,536
Mshartlandwildagan	6	M	4	0	0	0	437
Mt Dylan	4	G	1	0	0	0	0
Mt Katahdin	2	F	5	2	0	0	14,400
Mt Pro	3	C	10	1	5	1	61,400
Mt Super	2	C	1	0	0	1	2,760
Mt Townsend	4	G	3	0	0	0	0
Mt Waverly	4	C	15	4	3	0	74,560
Mt. Blake	5	G	11	2	1	2	17,470
Mt. Carson	3	C	4	2	1	1	109,500
Mt. Corcovado	3	C	7	1	0	0	6,075
Mt. Crusade	5	G	1	0	0	0	0
Mt. Erebus	4	G	1	1	0	0	6,300
Mt. Gilead	6	G	2	0	0	0	944
Mt. Imagination	3	C	7	1	0	1	15,050
Mt. Irgun	5	G	2	0	0	0	105
Mt. Kenya	4	G	10	0	1	5	10,174
Mt. Kilimanjaro	3	G	4	0	0	0	3,600
Mt. Kobla	3	F	6	2	1	1	107,220
Mt. Logan	3	C	14	3	1	1	31,159
Mt. Margaret	4	F	10	2	2	1	36,354
Mt. Moran	4	G	7	1	0	1	20,240
Mt. Oliver	6	H	4	0	0	1	1,150
Mt. Ouray	6	G	9	1	1	1	11,649
Mt. Pauliano	5	G	5	0	1	1	2,745
Mt. Peek	7	G	2	0	0	0	300
Mt. Pilatus	3	G	2	0	0	0	0
Mt. Rainer	5	G	7	1	1	1	10,286
Mt. Rebel	5	H	2	0	0	0	0
Mt. Redbank	9	G	2	0	0	0	450
Mt. Silver	2	C	3	0	1	0	5,380
Mt. St. Patty	3	F	5	1	0	1	13,050

Horse	Age	Sex	Sts	1st	2d	3d	Won
Mt. Swoosh	3	F	5	0	0	0	445
Mt. Tallac	3	G	6	3	0	1	20,166
Mt. Triumph	2	G	4	0	0	0	651
Mt. Troodos	3	C	7	2	0	1	16,509
Mt. Vaughan	3	C	1	1	0	0	19,200
Mt. Vernon News	5	G	12	1	1	0	3,471
Mt. Vista	4	G	13	4	2	0	27,015
Mt. Washington	2	C	4	0	0	2	6,430
Mtn of Expectation	2	C	1	0	0	0	0
Mucciacciaro	3	F	12	2	0	2	12,309
Mucci's Market	4	G	15	5	6	0	47,667
Much	2	F	3	0	0	0	1,440
Much Respect	3	C	14	1	1	3	32,270
Mucha Muchachita	5	M	1	0	0	0	0
Muchacho Fino	9	H	8	1	3	2	11,675
Muchcat	3	G	6	0	0	0	495
Muchmusic	2	F	2	0	0	1	2,320
Mucho Bold	3	G	9	2	1	2	45,550
Mucho Borracho	4	G	2	1	0	0	6,300
Mucho Bravada	2	C	7	1	1	2	10,993
Mucho Daniero	7	G	14	4	0	2	15,797
Mucho Falstaff	3	F	14	0	0	0	682
Mucho Gusto Man	3	G	11	0	0	3	14,084
Mucho Mite	3	C	1	0	1	0	1,000
Mucho Rapido	4	C	14	1	3	1	51,640
Mucho Salt	2	C	3	0	0	0	1,340
Muchtael	7	G	11	0	2	1	3,463
Muckatuck	5	M	4	0	1	1	2,620
Mud Axe Trouble	3	G	2	0	0	0	0
Mud Man	2	C	3	0	0	1	1,780
Mud Puppie	3	G	6	0	0	0	328
Mud Shark	3	C	6	1	3	0	51,360
Mud Slingin' Cat	4	F	8	0	0	0	430
Mud Warrior	9	G	16	1	1	1	6,668
Mudalloverme	3	F	1	0	0	0	145
Muddy Banks	4	F	9	0	1	2	3,283
Muddy Creek	5	H	3	0	0	1	556
Muddy Sneakers	3	C	3	0	0	0	0
Mudslide	2	C	2	0	0	0	0
Mudslide Slim	6	H	8	3	1	1	81,140
Mufasa's Legacy	3	G	13	3	1	1	27,790
Mug of Love	3	C	11	1	0	2	34,190
Mugee	2	C	4	0	1	1	3,284
Muggles	5	M	9	0	1	1	17,432
Muggy	3	C	1	0	0	0	0
Mugli	6	H	3	0	0	0	0
Muguet	2	F	1	1	0	0	27,600
Muhtabid	5	H	15	5	2	1	50,710
Muir Beach	2	F	3	0	3	0	8,020
Muir Eireann	6	M	10	3	1	1	31,153
Mujado (IRE)	5	M	1	0	0	0	2,417
Mukaabed	6	H	12	3	4	2	66,309
Mukhtaser	3	C	5	1	0	2	37,280
Mukilteo Smoke	5	M	6	1	0	0	4,510
Mulahen (GB)	8	G	8	2	0	3	78,828
Mulans Magic	5	M	3	0	0	1	2,921
Mulberrywine	2	F	2	0	0	0	0
Mulhockaway	2	G	1	0	0	0	0
Mullen	5	G	9	3	1	1	24,788
Mulligan Man	2	C	3	0	0	0	210
Mulligan the Great	4	G	8	4	1	3	322,396
Mulligan's Rose	4	F	11	1	1	1	6,032
Mulrainy	4	F	6	0	0	0	11,334
Multi Deed	2	C	3	0	0	2	7,183
Multiple Choice	5	G	4	0	0	2	39,121
Multiple Metal	9	G	6	0	0	1	3,630
Multiple Wins	4	F	15	3	3	2	134,925
Multiplicity	5	M	7	0	0	1	7,360
Muma Shaina	7	G	1	0	0	0	0
Mumble Jumble	3	C	2	0	0	0	0
Mumbles	2	C	4	0	0	2	8,710
Mum's Gold	4	F	11	7	1	1	158,630
Munaadel	4	C	3	0	0	0	0
Munchies	5	M	24	1	0	4	9,740
Muncy	2	C	6	0	0	1	2,074
Mundo of Sea	5	M	4	0	0	0	0
Mundo's Fortune	5	H	13	0	0	3	9,493
Mundos Magic	4	F	11	0	2	1	4,729
Munjiz (IRE)	7	G	9	1	2	0	10,225
Muntej (GB)	6	H	8	0	0	1	22,902
Murachi	3	G	15	1	4	0	26,529
Murano	4	C	4	0	0	1	9,160
Murdock	6	G	8	1	0	1	10,855
Murmadon	3	C	7	0	1	1	3,265
Murmansk	4	G	6	2	1	0	5,922
Murmuring Sea	5	G	9	0	1	0	1,595
Murohce	3	F	2	0	0	1	1,430
Murph's Encore	6	G	14	1	0	4	18,407
Murph's Star	10	M	2	0	0	1	1,607
Murphy	5	G	11	1	0	3	9,055
Murphy's Road	3	G	5	2	0	0	9,150
Murphy's Star	4	C	7	0	0	0	485
Murray's D. J	4	C	14	0	0	0	2,111
Murray's Dream	3	G	6	1	2	0	15,407
Murray's Marauder	6	G	15	1	3	2	11,670
Murray's Mazal	3	C	8	1	1	0	12,647
Murrough	3	G	13	2	3	1	47,744
Musaa Ed	4	C	11	3	4	1	86,780
Musaranho (BRZ)	5	G	9	2	0	0	10,710
Musashi	6	G	19	2	3	4	22,630
Muschi	8	M	8	0	0	3	11,570
Muscle Beach	2	G	3	1	0	0	7,220
Muscle Up	5	M	13	1	2	1	22,088
Muscles Abound	3	F	6	0	1	0	1,070
Muscovy	6	G	12	3	3	2	15,680
Musetta (ARG)	5	M	1	0	0	0	1,900
Musetta's Waltz	2	F	4	2	0	1	26,600
Musgrove Mill	4	G	13	1	2	2	15,611
Mush Un Onions	8	G	8	0	1	1	1,022
Mushroom Countess (IRE)	4	F	2	0	0	0	1,120
Music Bythe Sea	4	C	13	2	1	0	55,987
Music City Miracle	3	G	3	0	1	0	1,800
Music Connection	7	M	8	1	0	3	5,695
Music Daze	7	G	9	0	2	1	6,395
Music in the Air	5	M	12	4	1	2	11,919
Music Land	2	G	2	0	1	0	640
Music Lesson	4	G	12	0	1	1	9,545
Music Lover	6	M	3	1	2	0	30,331
Music Muse	4	F	12	1	1	0	6,447
Music Ringing	5	M	2	0	0	0	0
Music Thunder	3	G	7	2	0	2	4,358
Music to My Heart	4	F	7	2	1	0	16,080
Music to Your Ears	4	G	8	1	2	1	11,700
Music Way	3	F	4	1	2	1	50,660
Musical Affair	10	G	2	0	0	0	110
Musical Axe	4	G	7	2	1	0	15,192
Musical Beauty	4	F	12	1	5	1	19,050
Musical Chairs	5	H	9	2	0	1	21,660
Musical Charmer	5	M	3	0	0	0	82
Musical Chimes	3	F	8	2	2	1	513,103
Musical Ending	6	H	3	1	0	0	3,912
Musical Groom	2	G	1	1	0	0	9,350
Musical Hill (ARG)	10	G	10	1	1	2	5,551
Musical Lady	4	F	3	1	0	0	4,600
Musical Link	4	F	7	1	2	0	10,821
Musical Lionel	2	G	5	0	1	2	20,225
Musical Magic	4	G	10	3	0	2	25,111
Musical Miracle	6	H	3	0	1	1	1,915
Musical Native	2	G	1	1	0	0	9,600
Musical Night	8	G	2	0	0	0	0
Musical Pirouette	3	F	3	0	0	0	550
Musical Pro	3	F	15	0	4	6	13,587
Musical Rebel	3	F	1	0	0	0	651
Musical Review	4	F	7	2	1	0	35,040
Musical Spin	3	F	8	0	1	0	2,945
Musical Tip	6	M	3	0	0	0	280
Musical Vision	2	C	5	1	1	2	44,120
Musical Voyage	3	G	5	0	0	0	743
Musical Wisdom	3	G	8	1	0	1	22,135
Musically	2	F	3	0	0	0	0
Musically Inclined	6	H	5	0	0	0	0
Musician's Pride	2	C	3	2	1	0	26,520
Music's Edge	2	C	2	0	0	0	333
Music's Storm	4	C	9	2	3	1	201,554
Musique Toujours	3	G	12	2	5	1	75,780
Muskatello	3	C	2	0	0	0	3,636
Musket Drill	4	G	5	0	0	0	225
Muskiki	3	G	6	1	0	0	4,200

Horse	Age	Sex	Sts	1st	2d	3d	Won	Horse	Age	Sex	Sts	1st	2d	3d	Won
Muskogee	4	G	7	1	2	0	10,108	My Boston Gal	3	F	4	1	1	0	216,714
Muskoka	2	G	2	0	1	0	6,060	My Boy Billy	5	H	11	1	2	3	8,411
Muskoka Love	4	F	1	0	0	0	420	My Boy Danny	3	C	3	0	0	0	420
Muskrat Ramble	5	H	10	1	2	0	8,673	My Boy George	4	G	5	0	0	0	698
Mussarana	4	G	10	2	2	1	16,346	My Boy Kyle	3	G	9	1	0	1	30,210
Must Approve	3	F	4	0	0	1	1,160	My Boy Lefty	6	H	1	0	0	0	0
Must Be Da Money	4	G	10	2	1	2	18,267	My Boy Leroy	3	G	8	1	0	2	9,122
Must Be St. Nick	7	G	10	0	0	0	1,080	My Boy Reno	5	H	8	0	0	1	1,090
Must Be True	5	M	8	0	0	1	1,530	My Boy Roy	2	G	3	1	0	0	16,950
Must Rush	5	M	1	0	0	0	0	My Broker	2	F	4	1	0	0	8,706
Must See T. V.	4	G	8	3	0	1	9,110	My Brother	3	C	10	3	0	0	25,572
Must Win Soon	2	C	2	1	1	0	26,400	My Brother Bill	3	G	10	2	0	2	12,575
Musta Been Dreamin	5	M	4	0	3	0	1,921	My Brother Joey	3	G	1	0	1	0	1,040
Mustafa	4	C	1	0	0	0	53	My Brothers Pals	7	G	16	1	0	0	5,457
Mustanfar	2	C	3	1	0	0	28,980	My Brown Eyed Girl	5	M	4	0	0	1	1,270
Mustang Jock	3	C	11	1	2	1	41,870	My Buba Boy	5	G	19	4	2	3	28,447
Mustard	6	H	7	2	0	1	3,360	My Buddy Badger	9	G	11	2	2	2	7,140
Mustbinthefrontrow	3	C	16	3	3	2	54,858	My Buddy Clyde	3	G	3	0	0	0	212
Mutachi	2	G	3	1	0	0	16,735	My Buddy Duddie	3	C	1	1	0	0	24,600
Mutamayyaz	7	H	11	1	2	2	53,657	My Buddy Harold	2	G	8	1	2	2	56,557
Mutawaged	4	C	5	1	0	0	14,040	My Buddy My Pal	2	C	2	0	0	0	2,700
Mutawwaj (IRE)	8	H	5	0	0	1	3,080	My Buddy Rob	6	H	14	3	5	4	16,968
Mutch Bigger Boots	4	G	7	1	2	0	5,790	My Buddy Sid	3	C	12	3	0	0	25,180
Mute Gingrich	5	G	5	0	0	1	1,188	My Calabrese	8	C	8	2	3	1	60,898
Muted	6	H	15	3	2	2	50,935	My Candi's Gold	3	G	3	0	0	0	0
Mutesa Blitz	3	F	2	0	0	0	0	My Canonero	5	H	8	0	2	4	13,273
Mutt Cats Winner	4	G	3	1	0	1	4,182	My Captain	4	G	11	5	4	2	173,450
Muttface Alison	4	F	5	2	0	1	22,398	My Carlsbad Cousin	3	C	2	0	0	0	78
Muttface Brad	3	G	5	0	0	1	1,565	My Carol Grand	5	G	11	0	2	2	5,432
Muttface Emily	4	F	2	1	0	0	4,290	My Carol June	4	F	4	0	1	0	2,509
Muttface Seamus	3	G	1	0	0	0	636	My Cash Time	2	G	1	0	0	1	1,944
Mutual Affair	2	F	5	0	2	1	33,175	My Cat's Meow	2	F	3	0	1	0	5,775
Mutual Consent	3	F	10	1	5	2	18,493	My Cat's Seeking	3	F	5	0	1	1	3,355
Mutual Guy	5	G	13	0	4	3	10,560	My Champ	4	C	10	3	2	0	12,000
Mutual Selection	9	G	4	0	0	0	203	My Chance to Dance	4	F	5	0	0	0	982
Muy Bien Chris	6	G	11	0	4	0	3,251	My Chanel	4	F	6	1	2	0	24,589
Muy Pronto	3	C	14	2	4	1	13,121	My Charlie Brown	2	C	5	2	1	1	28,201
Muzzleload	7	H	3	0	0	0	1,150	My Cher	2	F	1	0	0	0	270
My Account	4	G	15	3	1	1	14,013	My City Girl	5	M	11	1	0	1	14,157
My Adam Apple	5	M	6	0	1	1	6,978	My Classy Miss	5	M	2	0	0	0	130
My Advantage	4	G	3	0	0	0	0	My Commander	3	G	6	0	1	1	7,177
My Aeneas	2	C	1	0	0	0	112	My Constant Star	8	G	4	0	1	0	3,590
My Alexis	5	M	5	0	0	1	1,746	My Countess (ARG)	4	F	6	1	1	1	20,750
My All	3	F	3	1	0	0	25,200	My Cousin Harri	6	G	2	0	0	0	1,072
My Allegiance	2	F	4	0	1	0	16,155	My Cousin Matt	4	G	6	1	1	1	297,500
My Alley Cat	3	F	2	0	0	0	1,340	My Cousin Tom	4	G	10	1	0	0	4,110
My Alternate	4	F	8	0	0	0	521	My Cowboy	3	G	9	1	2	0	39,265
My Amandari	2	F	3	1	0	0	33,600	My Creed	2	G	2	0	0	0	2,100
My American Man	8	G	15	0	0	4	4,132	My Cupid	2	G	9	2	1	2	21,119
My Amore	3	F	11	2	1	1	8,702	My Cuz Al	7	G	10	3	1	0	6,042
My Amy My Amy	4	F	1	0	0	0	0	My Dad's Bad	7	G	9	1	1	0	8,238
My Angela	5	M	19	4	1	3	29,878	My Dance Is Up	7	H	1	0	0	0	186
My Angelina	5	M	3	0	0	1	882	My Dancin Girl	5	M	14	0	4	3	37,995
My Antonia	4	F	8	3	0	0	35,110	My Dancing Gun	2	C	7	1	2	2	26,332
My Antonino	8	G	3	0	0	0	180	My Danita	3	F	3	0	0	0	600
My Argentina	3	C	7	1	1	0	6,510	My Darling Brocco	5	M	6	1	1	0	7,008
My Athanasia	7	M	1	0	0	0	0	My Date	3	F	12	1	1	3	9,648
My Authority	3	G	19	3	2	1	27,200	My Dear Donna	4	F	4	1	1	1	2,972
My Baby Claire	4	F	10	1	0	1	9,565	My Dear Jazz	3	C	2	0	0	1	6,035
My Baby Girl	7	M	21	3	1	3	16,525	My Dear Lisa	5	M	11	1	2	1	7,626
My Baby Irma Bee	3	F	1	0	0	0	450	My Dear Michael	4	C	8	2	1	0	8,680
My Babycakes	4	F	5	1	0	0	12,120	My Dear Rose	3	F	10	0	2	5	27,671
My Barbie	4	F	4	0	0	0	222	My Deer Marti	3	F	13	1	5	0	32,220
My Beau Forever	3	C	9	0	0	0	1,036	My Devious Lady	4	F	13	3	4	2	12,226
My Beau Genius	10	G	9	1	0	0	6,462	My Diamond Lady	6	M	7	1	0	0	5,375
My Beau Mister Joe	3	G	6	2	2	0	88,280	My Diane	4	F	5	1	0	1	5,390
My Best Diamond	4	G	11	3	0	2	19,684	My Did It	4	F	4	0	0	0	347
My Best Prospect	2	C	2	0	0	1	5,280	My Dr Anne T L C	3	F	5	0	1	0	2,671
My Best Wish	2	F	9	0	0	0	5,436	My Dream	3	G	11	3	2	2	48,610
My Big Dream	3	F	4	0	0	0	185	My Dream Cat	5	G	17	1	4	1	11,310
My Big Girl	7	M	6	0	0	0	0	My Dreamer	4	G	9	1	1	0	8,690
My Birthday Boy	4	G	9	3	0	0	31,096	My Duty	3	G	3	0	0	0	0
My Blaze Son	3	G	14	1	0	1	6,703	My Easy Charm	2	F	5	0	0	3	13,217
My Blonde Honey	5	M	12	3	2	0	13,919	My Elegant Lady	7	M	2	0	0	0	840
My Bloody Lady	2	F	8	0	2	1	5,365	My Eloquent Miss	5	M	3	0	0	0	4,170
My Blue Catillac	3	C	1	0	0	0	116	My Eugenia	5	M	2	0	0	0	144
My Blue Moon	3	F	7	1	1	1	2,613	My Ex Wifes Ashes	4	F	4	1	1	0	4,242
My Blue Scooter	3	F	7	3	0	1	10,503	My Excavate	2	C	3	0	0	0	0
My Bluey	6	G	5	0	1	0	5,020	My Explosive Star	5	G	14	3	2	1	15,421

Horse	Age	Sex	Sts	1st	2d	3d	Won
My Extolled	6	H	6	1	0	1	2,077
My Extolled Honor	5	G	7	3	1	1	75,220
My Fair Angel	4	F	6	1	2	1	5,413
My Fashion	5	M	10	0	2	1	2,704
My Favorite Girl	3	F	14	2	3	0	28,260
My Favorite Lady	2	F	5	0	0	0	240
My Favorite Lord	3	C	10	2	1	0	42,166
My Favorite Rose	3	F	2	0	0	1	1,785
My Favorite Story	9	G	6	0	0	1	3,375
My Feather	4	C	5	1	0	0	2,334
My First Affair	7	M	6	0	0	1	1,250
My First Book	5	G	6	1	1	0	10,990
My First Lady	6	M	2	2	0	0	34,650
My First Roan	6	G	14	1	1	0	10,400
My First Wife	3	F	8	1	0	2	15,270
My Forbidden Past	4	F	14	5	0	0	33,295
My Fortune	3	G	3	0	1	0	2,185
My Forum	4	G	12	2	2	2	14,786
My Freedom	3	F	7	0	1	2	2,760
My Fresh Prospect	5	H	10	0	1	0	4,980
My Friend Artie	5	G	9	1	0	1	5,696
My Friend Ben	5	G	8	0	0	1	2,742
My Friend Bill	6	G	1	0	0	0	0
My Friend Bruce	2	C	3	1	0	1	22,000
My Friend Dave	3	G	4	1	1	0	3,635
My Friend Don	4	G	9	0	1	1	7,532
My Friend Forever	2	G	8	0	1	0	4,050
My Friend Frank	3	C	8	1	2	1	13,518
My Friend Fred	4	G	1	0	0	0	0
My Friend Henry	4	G	19	3	3	3	10,042
My Friend Lalo	6	M	5	0	0	2	5,259
My Friend Lumpy	6	G	5	0	0	0	3,270
My Friend Tuff	2	C	2	0	0	0	1,530
My Fuzz	6	M	8	0	3	1	11,698
My Gabrielle	4	F	7	1	1	3	50,963
My Gal Arissa	4	F	1	0	0	0	0
My Gal Friday	2	F	5	0	1	1	2,500
My Gal Jeanie	2	F	2	0	0	0	1,080
My Gamblin Lady	4	F	9	2	1	2	11,017
My Gamblin Man	4	C	8	0	1	0	4,458
My Ganesh	3	C	3	1	0	1	7,810
My Giddy Aunt (IRE)	3	F	7	0	0	2	3,970
My Gift of Joy	4	G	14	3	3	0	13,630
My Girl Lisa	5	M	5	0	1	0	7,400
My Girl Melissa	2	F	5	0	1	0	6,670
My Girl Natalie	4	F	12	1	0	2	42,287
My Girl Nessa	4	F	7	2	0	0	8,637
My Girl Nichole	6	M	1	0	0	0	0
My Girl Quigly	8	M	12	1	3	2	28,318
My Girl Shirl	6	M	4	0	0	0	624
My Goal	2	F	1	1	0	0	4,200
My Golden Karot	3	F	4	0	0	1	870
My Golden Tripp	2	F	3	1	0	1	10,210
My Good Trick	4	G	9	2	1	3	51,120
My Greatest Love	5	H	7	1	0	0	3,300
My Green Machine	5	M	18	1	1	1	14,203
My Happy Dream	3	G	3	0	1	0	3,300
My Heart Throb	3	G	1	0	0	0	430
My Hearts Desire	4	G	7	2	0	0	80,214
My Heat	2	C	3	0	0	0	125
My Hidden Storm	2	F	1	0	0	0	975
My Honey Bunny	3	F	7	1	1	1	37,884
My Hot Tea	6	G	5	0	0	0	290
My Husband	2	G	4	0	0	1	3,928
My Id Your Ego	4	F	2	0	0	0	124
My Imperial Jet	2	F	8	1	3	0	36,845
My Inspiration	3	F	1	0	0	1	182
My Intrigue	4	F	8	0	0	0	6,360
My Irish Dawn	3	F	8	0	3	0	4,536
My Irish Doll	2	F	9	1	1	1	5,623
My Irish Halo	5	M	11	1	0	0	5,928
My Ish Kee	2	F	2	0	0	0	410
My J J Rose	4	F	10	1	2	3	14,600
My Jeff's Mombo	9	G	8	3	4	0	37,100
My Jewel	3	F	6	1	1	0	4,303
My Kai	3	F	3	0	1	2	36,852
My Karlin Leigh	6	M	1	0	0	0	47
My Keepsake	3	F	11	3	2	1	25,676
My Khan	4	G	5	1	0	0	14,640
My Kimberlee Anne	4	F	5	0	2	1	9,040
My Kind of Day	5	G	7	4	0	0	41,984
My Kind of Gal	2	F	5	0	0	1	5,290
My Kind of Girl	7	M	9	0	5	1	9,285
My Kind of Heniu	6	G	1	0	0	0	69
My Kind of Town	5	G	13	4	3	2	95,660
My Kinda Gold	8	G	7	2	0	1	21,679
My Kinda Town	2	C	4	0	1	1	15,310
My Lady Cruella	3	F	8	1	1	0	8,862
My Lady Roanne	4	F	4	0	1	1	16,280
My Lady's Denaskra	3	F	1	0	0	0	1,750
My Laura Dear	6	M	10	0	1	1	3,075
My Lawyer John	2	G	3	2	0	0	24,747
My Le Roi	5	G	9	2	1	0	15,710
My Lee Lee	5	M	17	2	4	3	28,412
My Legal Alien	4	C	12	1	5	0	74,900
My Leos Lad	2	C	1	1	0	0	9,000
My Lil Cheyenne	5	G	4	0	0	0	515
My Lil Cup o' Tee	8	G	2	0	0	0	0
My Lil Lu	2	F	3	0	0	0	286
My Limit	2	F	3	0	1	0	8,730
My Little Angle	3	F	13	0	0	0	3,187
My Little Charm	2	F	3	0	1	0	5,590
My Little Genius	5	M	1	0	0	0	0
My Little Heiress	3	G	8	0	1	2	7,685
My Little Luxury	4	F	4	1	0	0	5,846
My Little Munchkin	3	F	5	0	0	0	0
My Little One	4	F	2	0	0	1	652
My Little Runaway	6	M	2	0	0	0	54
My Little Silver	4	F	5	0	0	1	1,180
My Little Val	5	M	8	1	2	1	4,333
My Littleman Kan	4	C	2	0	0	0	300
My Lord	4	G	12	1	3	2	43,500
My Lord's Majesty	4	G	15	1	3	3	24,020
My Lordship	2	F	2	2	0	0	75,960
My Lost Button	5	M	9	0	1	0	1,888
My Louise	6	M	3	0	0	0	40
My Love Marty Wood	5	M	8	2	1	1	9,932
My Lovely Louise	2	F	4	0	0	0	0
My Lucky American	2	F	3	0	0	0	200
My Lucky Ensign	3	F	6	0	0	0	1,870
My Lucky Mercury	2	C	3	1	0	1	17,500
My Lucky Number	4	F	6	1	1	0	7,670
My Lucky Strike	4	G	12	3	1	5	191,036
My Lunatic Dancer	4	C	6	1	1	2	8,615
My Lyndsey Joy	3	F	1	0	0	0	0
My Lyre	3	C	1	0	0	0	0
My Mad Money	5	M	6	1	1	0	4,020
My Magic Indian	5	G	18	0	2	1	4,051
My Magic King	3	G	9	1	2	2	28,507
My Man	6	H	10	1	0	2	8,169
My Man Alex	3	C	1	0	0	0	0
My Man Galloper	2	G	1	0	0	0	100
My Man George	3	G	5	2	0	0	19,020
My Man Gus	4	G	7	0	0	1	2,437
My Man Joe	9	G	3	0	0	2	840
My Man Maybe	6	G	13	0	3	1	4,845
My Man Nick	3	C	14	1	2	1	10,850
My Man Ryan	4	C	7	0	0	2	21,119
My Man Vincent	8	G	2	0	0	1	222
My Maseratti	4	F	7	2	0	2	12,365
My Master (ARG)	4	C	1	0	0	0	1,920
My Master Max	9	G	5	0	0	0	0
My Mega Man	2	C	4	1	0	1	9,152
My Meow	5	M	11	6	1	1	125,380
My Militia	5	G	8	1	0	0	3,654
My Mille M	4	F	11	0	1	2	3,866
My Miracle Man	4	G	8	2	1	0	14,630
My Mirage	3	F	3	0	1	0	5,760
My Misdemeanor	2	F	1	0	0	0	390
My Miss Emily	3	F	3	0	0	1	6,094
My Misty Princess	3	F	12	1	3	3	28,756
My Mon	5	G	8	1	1	0	3,600
My Monad	6	H	5	0	0	0	545
My Money Man	4	C	3	0	0	0	0
My Money Monster	3	G	4	1	0	1	8,604
My Moo	8	G	9	1	0	3	3,325
My More Love	5	M	2	0	0	1	660
My Mother's Name	3	F	4	0	0	1	1,606

RECORDS OF HORSES

Horse	Age	Sex	Sts	1st	2d	3d	Won
My Mother's Silver	3	F	3	0	0	0	130
My Mug Shot	4	F	6	0	1	2	5,810
My Musical	5	M	10	1	2	1	5,210
My My Secret	5	M	12	2	3	2	14,905
My Name Be Mrs.	7	M	17	2	3	3	16,468
My Name Is Al	3	G	6	0	0	2	4,200
My Name Is Francis	6	G	10	1	2	2	22,331
My Name Is Royal	6	M	18	1	5	5	11,118
My Name's Jamie	5	G	18	3	0	1	15,487
My Names Nicole	2	F	2	0	0	0	0
My Native Prince	2	C	1	0	0	0	70
My Navy	5	G	12	5	1	4	71,780
My New Account	4	F	2	0	0	0	119
My New Car	4	F	12	0	0	1	2,493
My New Love	5	G	10	2	1	1	29,618
My New Nickel	6	M	8	2	1	2	6,874
My Nickel	4	G	1	0	0	0	0
My Nin	3	F	9	3	2	0	41,910
My Niner	3	C	4	0	0	1	660
My Nona	3	F	3	0	0	0	0
My Numbers	5	M	18	1	3	2	10,809
My Obvious Choice	3	G	3	0	0	0	0
My Only Angel	4	F	9	1	0	1	6,450
My Outlet	2	F	2	0	0	0	0
My Oval Office	3	F	8	1	3	2	15,562
My Own Terms	10	G	8	0	0	1	839
My Pa Bob	4	G	4	0	0	0	269
My Pal Al	6	G	12	0	1	2	25,256
My Pal Candi	4	C	2	0	0	0	163
My Pal Joly	3	F	8	2	1	1	19,039
My Pal Lana	3	F	10	3	2	3	207,224
My Pal Ryan	8	G	15	1	2	0	11,658
My Pal William	2	C	1	0	1	0	11,760
My Papa	10	G	6	1	0	3	1,928
My Party	6	G	8	0	1	1	1,500
My Patriot Lady	2	F	3	0	0	1	3,640
My Peanut	2	F	7	0	0	1	3,180
My Petticoat	3	F	1	0	0	0	0
My Phone	3	C	4	0	2	0	9,740
My Pick to Klick	3	C	2	0	0	0	0
My Picture	2	F	1	0	1	0	5,208
My Pistol	4	F	10	1	2	2	8,008
My Place Tonight	2	F	5	1	0	1	25,320
My Plan	3	G	4	1	0	0	8,438
My Pleasant	2	G	1	0	0	0	0
My Pods Steve	3	G	14	1	3	1	10,227
My Poker Player	3	G	7	1	2	0	46,280
My Poppy Bert	6	G	5	0	0	1	664
My Portfolio	4	C	7	1	0	0	4,260
My Precious Indian	2	F	4	0	0	1	6,410
My Pretty Woman	4	F	9	2	2	3	67,728
My Prince	7	H	19	1	3	2	6,426
My Princess Hailey	3	F	9	2	2	2	90,747
My Private Model	8	G	1	0	0	0	47
My Problem	7	G	17	3	0	5	33,565
My Proximo	2	G	4	0	0	0	817
My Queen Burns	6	M	10	0	5	1	13,600
My Queenie	5	M	7	2	2	2	15,040
My Rahy	2	C	1	0	0	0	0
My Ranger	4	G	14	0	4	1	33,680
My Rare Prince	4	C	2	0	0	0	0
My Real Quiet Lady	5	M	10	2	3	1	153,084
My Red Cadillac	8	G	2	0	0	0	0
My Redneck	3	G	14	0	2	5	10,812
My Regal Solution	6	M	8	1	1	1	28,356
My Request	6	G	8	1	2	3	76,000
My Requiem	4	F	1	0	0	0	92
My Ro	3	F	2	2	0	0	54,910
My Roarer	3	C	2	0	0	0	0
My Romanella	4	F	6	1	0	0	6,375
My Romeo	3	C	15	3	1	2	69,950
My Royal Irish Pal	6	G	9	0	0	1	834
My Ruby Charm (NZ)	7	M	9	3	2	2	49,075
My Salute to You	3	G	15	2	3	2	26,680
My Sand Dollar	4	F	2	0	0	0	0
My Satin Doll	4	F	1	0	0	0	100
My Scarlet Lady	2	F	2	0	0	0	2,630
My Secret Brush	4	G	11	1	0	2	9,685
My Secret Fantasy	2	C	3	1	0	0	10,599
My Secret Spot	3	G	7	2	2	1	17,960
My Secretary	3	F	17	1	5	1	15,782
My Shahzada	5	G	7	1	0	0	3,075
My Shara de Gold	6	M	7	0	2	0	1,520
My Signals Busy	4	G	9	2	0	3	18,079
My Silver Dollar	5	G	9	1	0	1	4,067
My Sir Rah	5	G	6	2	0	1	8,331
My Sixtythreevett	4	C	7	0	0	0	2,625
My Sky	3	F	9	1	3	0	31,395
My Slews Princess	3	F	11	1	3	1	5,613
My Smokey Mike	4	C	15	3	3	1	14,185
My Snookie's Boy	2	C	3	0	1	0	7,580
My Snuggle Bunnie	4	F	3	0	0	0	560
My Son Jordan	2	C	5	0	1	0	6,100
My Southern Belle	4	F	9	1	1	0	23,128
My Special Dart	6	H	5	0	0	0	0
My Special Gift	3	F	3	0	0	0	942
My Spitfire	2	C	2	0	0	0	0
My Spot	4	F	14	0	1	3	8,875
My Star Edition	4	F	2	0	0	0	0
My Stars	4	F	10	2	3	1	18,138
My Statue	3	F	6	0	0	0	3,040
My Step	3	G	10	0	0	0	2,014
My Storm	3	G	13	2	1	0	8,579
My Stray Cat	5	M	9	1	3	0	17,180
My Sunny Deelite	2	F	5	1	0	1	5,857
My Sunny Halo	4	C	16	1	2	1	6,574
My Sunshine	9	M	3	0	0	0	1,245
My Superstar	8	H	4	0	0	0	271
My Supreme Vixen	4	F	5	2	0	0	23,760
My Sweet Elizabeth	2	F	6	1	2	1	14,370
My Sweet Heart	3	F	6	2	0	1	41,134
My Sweet Lucy	5	M	10	2	1	1	24,360
My Sweet Sandy	6	M	8	0	1	0	1,780
My Sweet Sug	3	F	3	2	0	0	15,550
My Sweet Tooch	3	F	7	2	0	3	138,214
My Sweet Twister	3	F	2	0	0	0	780
My Sweetcon	2	F	2	1	0	0	7,560
My T Sharp	3	C	7	0	0	1	2,019
My Target	5	M	3	0	1	2	1,708
My Texas Tim	2	C	2	0	1	0	3,400
My Tickety Bue	3	F	6	1	0	1	5,229
My Time Machine	5	G	11	0	1	0	4,846
My Time Now	2	F	1	0	0	1	4,270
My Tina	2	F	1	0	0	0	880
My Tony Boy	8	G	12	0	0	3	3,804
My Trusty Cat	3	F	8	1	0	1	94,153
My Turbeau Cat	2	F	1	0	0	0	0
My Turf Hero	4	C	11	1	3	2	14,185
My Turn to Burn	5	M	3	0	0	0	0
My Twilight	2	F	2	0	0	0	0
My Two Kings	3	G	1	0	0	0	0
My Two Sons	5	G	4	0	0	0	837
My Ty Tanya	5	M	5	0	2	0	1,056
My Unbridled	2	C	1	0	0	0	145
My Uncle Dave	3	C	11	1	1	3	11,870
My Vengeance	3	F	11	1	1	1	36,934
My Very Own Muggle	3	F	2	0	0	0	1,050
My Vintage Port	2	F	6	3	2	1	351,051
My Way All the Way	3	C	2	0	0	0	183
My Whole Enchilada	7	M	10	0	3	5	5,552
My Wild Rhoda	3	F	12	2	4	0	91,502
My Wingman	2	C	2	0	0	1	4,100
My Wonderful	4	G	10	1	0	1	7,506
My World	3	C	2	0	0	0	104
Myamar	3	C	9	1	0	0	11,770
Mybabypicture	4	F	5	0	0	0	160
Mybigfatluv	2	G	6	0	1	2	2,756
Mybingo	4	F	11	0	1	2	3,070
Myboybruno	2	C	6	1	1	0	20,290
Mybrinajill	6	M	12	1	0	4	18,850
Mycareer	3	C	1	0	0	0	110
Mychampion	3	C	14	2	2	0	70,526
Myclementine	3	F	8	0	2	1	4,080
Mycoco	2	F	9	0	0	0	484
Mydak	4	C	11	1	3	3	24,192
Mydogdreamer	3	G	6	0	0	0	464
Myella	6	M	10	0	1	4	11,294
Myer's Alina	3	F	2	0	0	0	0

Horse	Age	Sex	Sts	1st	2d	3d	Won	Horse	Age	Sex	Sts	1st	2d	3d	Won
Myfavorite Star	5	G	13	3	2	3	62,930	Mystic Man (ARG)	5	G	7	1	0	0	8,870
Myfavoritehigh	7	M	13	3	2	3	12,044	Mystic Markita	2	F	1	0	0	0	378
Myfavoritepassion	2	F	2	0	0	0	0	Mystic Melissa	4	F	21	2	3	5	45,756
Myfirst	2	C	6	0	0	0	499	Mystic Night	5	H	8	3	3	1	53,250
Myfriendlaurie	4	F	9	0	3	2	9,455	Mystic Notion	5	M	5	1	2	0	37,900
Myfriendlilly	3	F	11	2	1	0	26,181	Mystic Performer	4	F	2	0	0	0	90
Mygalsal	2	F	4	0	0	0	855	Mystic Pine	3	F	10	3	1	1	23,390
Myheartsinaruckus	4	F	4	0	0	0	200	Mystic Places	4	G	1	0	0	0	0
Myladyeve	2	F	4	0	0	1	2,504	Mystic Pointe	6	M	5	0	0	1	3,425
Mylilfellow	3	G	7	0	1	1	3,426	Mystic River	7	H	13	1	4	1	13,301
Mylinkum	5	M	4	0	0	1	462	Mystic Salse (GB)	4	C	8	1	1	0	28,740
Mylittleponyrose	4	F	13	2	1	1	12,061	Mystic Secret	4	G	7	1	0	0	4,482
Mymich	3	F	9	2	2	0	87,574	Mystic Spy	6	G	7	0	0	1	1,440
Mymomisaprincess	8	G	8	0	1	2	2,076	Mystic Storm	4	G	6	1	1	1	26,270
Mynamefit	3	G	3	0	0	0	302	Mystic Sword	4	C	9	1	0	0	5,110
Mynameischase	4	C	19	3	0	1	44,500	Mystic Too	4	F	3	1	0	0	5,900
Mynard Road	4	G	7	1	0	1	6,366	Mystic Valley	3	F	4	0	0	0	320
Mynavigator	2	G	6	2	1	0	101,286	Mystical Allure	4	F	12	3	1	4	32,258
Mynchasa	4	F	7	1	0	0	4,625	Mystical Beauty	3	F	15	2	2	6	69,755
Mynewfoundfriend	4	F	4	0	0	0	0	Mystical Blues	5	M	6	1	0	0	6,888
Myofficewife	3	F	10	0	3	2	37,220	Mystical Charge	4	G	3	0	0	0	2,784
Myownworld	3	F	7	0	0	1	4,010	Mystical Court	8	G	9	2	0	1	2,303
Mypleasantreality	5	M	12	0	0	2	3,342	Mystical Delite	2	F	3	1	1	0	26,295
Myra Gulch	3	F	9	0	2	2	7,946	Mystical Empire	6	H	7	0	1	0	2,158
Myra Jane	4	F	4	0	0	0	570	Mystical Ghazi	4	F	4	0	0	1	1,236
Myrack	4	F	2	1	1	0	5,720	Mystical Marlin	4	F	6	0	0	0	357
Myroan	6	H	8	1	2	2	7,052	Mystical Michael	3	G	11	1	1	1	9,683
Myrtle Grove	3	C	1	0	0	0	100	Mystical Moment	4	F	6	1	0	0	2,590
Myrtle's Brat	3	F	3	1	0	0	6,958	Mystical Ridge	3	F	7	1	1	3	6,535
Myrtle's Ex Ray	5	G	11	3	1	1	13,510	Mystical Sea	2	F	2	0	0	0	1,230
Myshareoflaughter	2	F	2	1	0	0	4,645	Mystical Susan	3	F	3	0	0	0	0
Mysia Jo	5	M	5	0	1	1	25,540	Mystical Wonder	6	M	8	0	1	0	2,199
Mysia Sue	3	F	2	0	0	0	2,520	Mysticize	5	H	1	0	0	0	500
Mysterfire	3	C	2	0	0	0	750	Mystics Blue Rose	6	M	3	1	0	0	10,800
Mysteria	3	F	1	0	0	0	0	Mystic's Fortune	5	G	13	3	2	2	46,800
Mysterieuse Etoile	3	F	9	0	2	3	30,330	Mystic's Karma	5	G	11	3	2	2	17,089
Mysterious Affair	6	M	12	1	3	4	214,926	Mystified	2	F	4	0	0	4	19,800
Mysterious Fame	2	G	1	0	0	0	0	Mystified Mitty	7	G	7	1	0	1	6,154
Mysterious Gal	2	F	2	0	0	0	217	Mystique Flight	9	M	21	1	5	4	25,580
Mysterious Girl	2	F	2	0	0	0	200	Mysweethearts Gone	2	C	2	1	0	0	6,780
Mysterious Man	4	G	13	4	0	2	50,750	Mysweetjoy	6	M	12	1	2	2	11,456
Mysterious Mist	10	G	18	4	4	2	15,283	Mythic Hero	3	C	3	1	1	1	11,865
Mysterious Peace	2	F	2	0	0	0	460	Mythical	2	F	2	0	0	0	900
Mysterious Seasons	3	C	7	1	3	0	10,355	Mythical Brownie	4	F	18	5	3	6	101,990
Mysterious Sword	3	G	17	4	2	0	27,050	Mythical Flyer	6	G	8	0	1	1	7,320
Mysterious Woody	3	C	5	1	0	2	34,440	Mythical Mirage	7	M	1	0	0	0	0
Mystery Blues	3	F	4	0	1	0	2,563	Mythical Mountain	5	H	7	0	0	2	1,210
Mystery Coast	3	F	4	0	1	1	1,041	Mythical Rebel	3	G	11	2	2	1	16,425
Mystery Dancer	10	G	15	1	2	2	5,600	Mythical Road	2	G	7	2	1	3	20,562
Mystery Deputy	7	H	1	0	0	0	0	Mythical Time	2	F	1	0	0	0	1,350
Mystery Dreams	4	G	7	0	2	2	13,749	Mythical Trick	3	F	14	1	4	4	21,988
Mystery Express	4	F	10	0	3	2	10,165	Mythique	4	G	4	1	1	1	10,048
Mystery Giver	5	G	10	2	2	1	256,260	Mytic Out	3	F	4	0	0	0	1,180
Mystery Grey	6	G	4	0	1	0	800	Myturntopick	6	G	11	0	1	1	9,960
Mystery Hit	4	F	6	2	0	0	14,050	Mytyboy	3	G	4	0	0	0	200
Mystery Itself	3	F	7	1	2	1	49,200	Myway Home	5	M	3	0	1	0	2,285
Mystery Lady	3	F	5	0	0	0	120	Myway West	5	M	7	1	1	0	44,622
Mystery Maiden	3	F	9	1	1	3	49,025	Mywayforever	6	H	14	4	3	3	24,629
Mystery Nickle	6	M	6	0	0	0	1,035	Mywifetheshrink	2	F	4	1	0	1	29,323
Mystery Rama	6	G	13	3	0	2	13,217	Mz Nanc B	4	F	9	1	3	1	23,832
Mystery Runner	4	F	4	1	0	0	3,445	N' Bearaly	3	C	7	0	0	0	748
Mystery Ship	3	C	8	1	0	2	8,018	N Etyme Gal	4	F	1	0	0	0	0
Mystery Squall	4	F	6	0	1	1	10,500	N H Returntosender	3	F	4	0	0	0	323
Mystery Tax	5	M	16	1	2	0	9,817	N H Steel Springs	4	G	11	1	1	2	4,891
Mystery Train	3	C	16	2	2	2	27,323	N J Devil	4	G	5	1	3	0	57,380
Mystery Vert	2	G	3	0	0	0	525	N Lou of Roses	4	G	10	2	1	2	11,050
Mystery Years	5	H	5	0	0	1	1,313	N Rawlens Honor	3	G	15	0	0	1	1,372
Mystery's Jules	2	F	10	3	2	1	56,260	N Square	3	F	9	1	1	0	22,420
Mystic Appeal	4	G	14	6	0	1	46,275	N Twalamea	4	F	1	0	0	0	0
Mystic Beat	5	M	5	0	1	1	2,448	N Y Remembered	3	G	2	1	0	1	18,360
Mystic Buck	3	G	6	0	0	0	3,294	N Y Rodeo	2	F	2	0	0	0	0
Mystic Cat	5	M	4	0	0	1	752	N. J. Norquestor	4	C	12	2	5	2	89,705
Mystic Crown	4	F	9	0	2	2	2,890	N. L.'s Dream	6	G	12	2	1	2	17,215
Mystic Dash	3	G	12	2	1	1	94,215	N. Y. Senorita	3	F	8	1	2	0	11,220
Mystic Gal	4	F	14	0	2	1	5,782	N. Y. Sharpy	7	G	12	2	0	2	5,185
Mystic Hawk	3	C	8	2	2	0	43,658	Na Devil	4	C	8	1	1	1	25,524
Mystic Jazz	3	F	1	1	0	0	6,000	Na Hila	3	C	9	1	3	1	30,070
Mystic Jet	4	G	10	0	1	0	4,612	Naab a Chance	5	M	4	0	0	0	150
Mystic Lady	5	M	2	0	0	0	3,460	Naab the Magic	5	M	3	1	1	0	1,388

RECORDS OF HORSES

Horse	Age	Sex	Sts	1st	2d	3d	Won	Horse	Age	Sex	Sts	1st	2d	3d	Won
Naab the Rose	3	F	10	2	2	1	25,318	Nancy Jo	4	F	7	0	2	3	6,698
Naaba Trip	2	G	6	0	3	0	7,317	Nancy McWin	3	F	2	0	0	0	428
Naaman (IRE)	8	G	2	1	0	0	6,000	Nancy N Waco	3	F	8	1	2	0	13,416
Nabatean	4	G	15	0	1	1	6,808	Nancybee	5	M	2	0	0	0	200
Nabber	7	G	13	0	3	0	2,520	Nancys Blazen Lady	5	M	8	1	3	3	7,806
Nabethian	5	M	9	0	4	1	34,248	Nancy's Corner	3	F	2	0	0	0	0
Nabisco Cat	5	G	5	0	0	0	431	Nancy's Delight	4	C	1	0	0	0	103
Nacheezmo	3	C	6	3	1	0	126,600	Nancys Golden Star	3	F	2	0	0	0	35
Nachen	3	F	6	3	0	2	23,680	Nancy's Joker	5	G	6	1	0	3	16,722
Nacious Gold	7	H	18	2	0	4	10,410	Nancy's Lilly	2	F	1	0	0	0	145
Nacona	4	C	18	3	6	1	19,569	Nancys Magic Brush	3	F	6	2	2	0	42,660
Nada Mais	3	F	8	3	1	1	20,086	Nancy's Slave	4	C	5	1	0	0	14,992
Nadias Cat	3	F	10	0	3	1	19,494	Nancy's Spirit	4	F	17	1	5	1	15,410
Nadine	4	F	2	0	0	0	200	Nancysgoldennugget	5	M	8	0	2	1	1,930
Nadine's Cape	3	F	8	1	2	2	8,586	Nanden	4	F	4	0	0	1	4,480
Nadira	3	F	6	1	1	2	20,820	Nandina	4	F	9	0	0	0	404
Nae Only	2	F	1	0	0	1	2,882	Nandu	2	F	1	1	0	0	21,600
Naev	3	C	7	0	0	0	624	Nandy	4	G	2	0	0	0	47
Naevus Rising Star	5	G	5	1	0	0	1,126	Nanie's Dinner	6	M	1	0	0	1	3,740
Naevus' Ritual	4	G	15	0	2	4	7,215	Nanjing	3	F	7	1	0	2	4,595
Nafka's Chance	6	M	12	5	2	2	15,438	Nankoweap	5	M	5	0	0	2	2,380
Nagem Nagem Nagem	2	F	7	2	0	3	46,082	Nannie's Fanny	4	F	3	1	0	0	4,700
Nah Nah Nah	3	G	14	2	2	2	34,086	Nannie's Sword	4	F	10	3	3	2	92,290
Nahaab	5	G	11	2	3	0	8,259	Nanny Lover	3	F	14	2	2	2	17,348
Nahane (IRE)	2	C	6	0	2	1	6,785	Nannycam	3	F	4	3	0	1	94,900
Nahanni Butte	3	F	5	0	0	0	776	Nanny's Dotcom	4	G	6	1	3	0	9,780
Nahant	3	F	4	1	0	0	5,400	Nanocity	4	F	14	2	0	2	10,230
Nahar	6	M	7	0	0	1	771	Nanogram	6	M	6	0	2	2	38,860
Nahdu's Tune	3	F	5	0	0	2	4,390	Nano's Groovy	3	G	3	0	0	1	1,856
Nahulaki	4	F	4	0	0	0	0	Nan's Lil Poopsie	4	F	10	2	0	1	35,663
Naif	3	C	1	0	0	0	77	Nan's Rose	5	M	11	3	2	1	18,155
Naikan	3	G	13	1	1	1	5,635	Nantucketeer	5	H	10	1	2	1	35,682
Nailbird	8	G	13	0	3	3	6,334	Nap for Sycamore	5	G	10	3	1	1	25,162
Najd	7	G	5	0	1	1	1,662	Napa Spring	7	G	15	2	2	2	3,784
Najibes Acre	2	F	2	1	1	0	18,905	Napa's Quest	5	G	6	0	0	0	203
Najjm	6	G	9	0	3	2	28,550	Naperville	6	M	15	2	1	3	20,552
Najran	4	C	7	2	1	1	305,700	Napoleon Solo	3	C	8	2	0	0	55,920
Nakai	7	M	3	0	0	0	960	Napster	3	C	4	0	0	0	0
Nakayama Kun	3	C	3	0	1	0	8,670	Napzak	2	G	8	0	1	3	8,036
Naked Ambition	8	M	2	0	0	0	0	Naraingang (BRZ)	5	H	6	1	0	1	33,130
Naked Fame	3	C	2	0	0	0	180	Narayan	3	G	17	1	2	2	16,314
Naked Lies	3	F	5	0	0	2	5,940	Narcissistic Girl	3	F	1	0	0	0	786
Naked Native	3	F	9	0	0	1	1,824	Narrow River	12	G	2	1	0	0	20,600
Nakeeb	3	C	3	1	0	1	23,600	Nasdaq Jack	4	C	18	3	2	2	24,204
Nakerra Choice	4	F	4	0	0	0	0	Nasdek Mayhem	4	G	2	0	0	0	1,320
Nakiewah	2	F	2	0	0	1	1,286	Naseer Spirit	4	C	3	0	0	0	171
Nakoda	5	M	6	0	1	0	8,421	Nashau's Ghost	4	C	5	0	0	0	317
Nale	6	G	8	0	0	0	522	Nasheba Dancer	8	M	10	2	3	1	14,648
Nalee's Classic	9	G	7	0	0	0	0	Nashinda	2	F	2	2	0	0	148,635
Nalees Girl	2	F	1	0	0	0	0	Nashly's Groom	3	G	7	1	1	1	26,690
Nalee's Ice Man	4	C	1	0	0	0	0	Nashman	6	H	6	1	0	1	5,195
Nalescavate	5	G	9	0	0	0	203	Nash's Prospect	5	M	8	3	1	0	61,170
Naletha Gray	3	F	10	1	1	1	11,265	Nashua's Asset	5	G	5	1	1	2	6,020
Nalgas de Acero	4	F	2	1	0	0	6,540	Nashua's Launch	3	C	8	1	0	2	16,770
N'all That Jazz	6	G	12	0	1	3	3,560	Nashville	8	G	4	1	2	0	10,805
Namaste	4	F	1	0	0	0	0	Nashville Native	3	F	3	0	1	1	1,575
Name Caller	3	C	4	0	0	0	555	Naskra Nick	3	G	4	0	0	0	700
Name for Norm	9	H	7	1	0	3	8,393	Naskramoon	6	G	5	0	0	0	3,060
Name Tag	4	F	9	1	1	1	9,940	Nasribot	3	G	1	0	0	0	0
Name the Prince	3	G	6	0	0	1	3,286	Nassau Rose	3	F	5	0	0	0	416
Nameless	7	M	1	0	0	0	110	Nasser	4	C	2	0	0	0	0
Nameless Lady	5	M	3	0	0	0	625	Nassuas Ruler	3	G	16	1	1	2	4,135
Nameless Soldier	2	C	2	0	0	1	1,858	Nastifir	13	G	8	1	1	0	5,143
Namememoney	6	M	3	0	0	0	310	Nasty	4	C	8	0	0	0	300
Namequest	7	H	4	2	0	1	54,670	Nasty and Brave	9	M	4	0	0	2	2,533
Nami	6	H	7	1	2	0	3,270	Nasty and Crafty	5	M	19	1	1	2	12,379
Nana Barb	2	F	3	0	0	0	2,202	Nasty Bird	5	G	8	1	1	0	10,864
Nana Lou's Boy	4	G	3	0	0	0	0	Nasty Bob	10	G	16	3	3	3	15,199
Nanacandypride	4	C	4	1	0	0	6,312	Nasty Business	4	G	13	1	1	3	27,530
Nanaletpride	4	F	9	1	2	2	12,681	Nasty Butch	2	G	1	0	0	0	2,400
Nanarae	2	F	6	1	0	0	18,820	Nasty Girl	6	M	1	0	0	0	42
Nana's Boy	5	G	20	3	4	4	43,023	Nasty Ice	5	M	11	1	0	3	9,615
Nana's House	4	F	3	0	0	1	2,370	Nasty Jab	2	G	1	0	0	1	480
Nana's Sparkle	8	M	1	0	0	0	0	Nasty Knight	6	G	7	0	1	0	2,420
Nanasalooker	4	F	1	0	0	0	0	Nasty Money	3	G	10	0	3	0	6,393
Nancibegood	2	F	2	0	0	0	0	Nasty Parrot	6	H	8	1	0	0	4,212
Nanci's Zoomstick	4	F	16	1	1	2	6,533	Nasty Pocket	10	M	4	0	0	0	105
Nancy Baybee	5	M	6	1	1	0	4,504	Nasty Rose	3	F	2	0	0	0	0
Nancy Get'n Sassy	4	F	4	0	0	0	98	Nasty Ross	8	G	5	0	0	2	920

Horse	Age	Sex	Sts	1st	2d	3d	Won
Nasty Sabrina	4	F	9	1	0	4	29,415
Nasty Saint	3	G	1	0	0	0	0
Nasty Secret	4	F	10	0	0	4	2,424
Nasty Storm	5	M	1	0	0	0	0
Nasty Won	4	C	7	1	0	1	6,576
Nasty's Progeny	5	G	10	1	1	1	10,170
Nat and Julie	4	F	12	6	3	1	109,925
Nat D Z	3	F	1	0	0	0	0
Nat Plays No Trump	5	G	6	1	1	1	9,090
Nataani	5	M	2	0	0	0	320
Natagar	3	C	7	0	0	2	2,720
Natalia	3	F	11	1	1	0	16,020
Natalies Commander	2	F	2	0	0	0	
Natalie's Gift	3	F	2	0	0	0	1,800
Natalies Interview	4	C	3	1	0	1	5,725
Natalie's Moment	5	M	3	1	0	0	9,034
Natasha Pumpkin	5	M	9	1	0	1	9,100
Natasha's Reno	4	F	11	1	0	3	13,310
Natboo	5	M	10	0	4	0	11,250
Natchez	3	C	10	1	4	4	24,400
Natchez Trace	5	G	12	0	2	1	14,320
Nate Jr	10	G	10	1	3	2	4,310
Nate's Castle	2	F	4	0	0	0	189
Nates Colony	6	G	12	1	1	3	68,045
Nate's Rib	4	G	9	3	2	2	47,755
Nathans Candy	3	G	8	1	0	1	3,250
Nathan's Way	4	G	7	2	3	0	11,720
Nation Wide News	3	C	3	1	1	0	45,760
National Alert	3	F	4	1	1	1	15,425
National Anthem (GB)	7	H	6	0	0	1	31,610
National City	7	G	7	1	2	1	6,152
National Courier	5	G	6	0	0	0	350
National Hunter	4	G	2	0	0	0	767
National Legend	2	C	2	0	0	0	2,050
National Park (GB)	4	G	5	0	1	0	4,706
National Pastime	3	F	7	1	0	1	42,359
National Pride (GB)	3	C	4	2	2	0	42,798
National Saint	7	H	2	0	0	1	12,000
Nationalistic (IRE)	3	G	3	0	0	0	1,440
Nationoflitigation	6	M	11	1	1	2	21,037
Nati's Cat	3	G	16	1	2	4	8,048
Native Air	5	M	1	0	0	0	452
Native Annie	2	F	2	2	0	0	83,400
Native Approval	2	C	7	0	2	2	32,180
Native as Well	3	G	3	0	0	0	0
Native Badger	7	G	4	0	0	0	338
Native Beauty	4	F	9	0	0	0	582
Native Brick	3	F	7	1	1	1	32,905
Native Cart	3	C	7	1	0	1	8,476
Native Cat Dancer	3	C	1	0	0	0	0
Native Clipit	5	G	11	1	1	0	4,269
Native Coast	8	G	12	2	3	3	35,333
Native Colony	6	G	1	0	0	0	225
Native Dance	4	G	7	2	1	1	9,975
Native Desert	10	G	8	0	1	3	74,266
Native Desire	3	C	1	0	0	0	87
Native Diablo	6	G	1	0	0	0	0
Native Dispersal	6	M	5	0	0	0	131
Native Drum Fire	5	G	1	0	0	0	70
Native Energy	5	G	6	0	0	0	615
Native Flag	3	C	1	0	0	0	47
Native Flagship	10	G	10	0	0	0	927
Native Gambler	5	G	12	1	4	3	9,770
Native Genius	3	C	12	1	1	4	38,440
Native Glide	6	G	9	0	0	0	450
Native Hadif	4	C	6	1	0	0	6,726
Native Hawk	3	G	7	2	1	2	28,095
Native Heartbeat	3	F	11	3	5	1	73,925
Native Heather	5	M	6	1	0	1	7,026
Native Heir	5	G	10	4	3	1	200,280
Native Hero	7	G	6	1	0	0	3,300
Native Ice	5	G	8	2	0	1	20,752
Native Image	6	G	7	0	2	0	9,007
Native in Kind	3	G	2	0	0	0	0
Native Jaja Ruler	8	G	8	1	0	0	3,480
Native Jay	8	H	9	0	0	0	470
Native Judge	3	G	11	2	1	2	44,205
Native King	2	C	2	0	1	0	2,760
Native Love	5	H	12	1	3	4	8,608
Native Mark	4	C	6	0	0	0	3,692
Native Midnight	4	F	2	0	0	0	115
Native Mint	2	C	1	0	0	0	214
Native New Yorker	4	C	5	0	1	2	5,155
Native of Paris	3	F	13	4	0	2	29,430
Native of Zignew	3	F	1	0	0	0	82
Native Plum	2	F	1	0	0	0	150
Native Prairie	5	G	10	1	0	4	14,100
Native Precipience	4	F	7	1	1	1	10,600
Native Princess	4	F	3	1	0	0	8,585
Native Reality	6	M	3	0	0	0	150
Native Red Fox	3	G	14	1	2	1	5,335
Native Rhythm	5	H	7	2	2	0	73,740
Native Ruck	5	G	11	1	4	2	12,384
Native Runaway	4	C	5	0	1	1	2,170
Native Savy	3	F	3	0	0	0	0
Native Seattle	3	G	5	1	1	0	7,071
Native Shot	5	M	16	0	0	0	2,378
Native Soldier	2	C	4	0	0	0	920
Native Spirit	3	F	5	0	0	0	776
Native Stone	3	C	9	0	0	3	22,729
Native Susieque	3	F	5	0	0	0	552
Native Tale	5	M	6	0	0	0	0
Native Texan	3	G	7	1	1	0	30,275
Native to Byram	5	H	11	1	4	2	10,292
Native Tourist	3	G	11	0	0	0	1,130
Native Tribe	11	G	5	0	0	1	1,860
Native Trinket	4	F	9	3	2	3	74,580
Native Two Stepper	7	G	10	2	4	1	61,780
Native Valor	2	G	1	0	0	0	75
Native Vitality	4	G	2	2	0	0	30,000
Native Wager	5	M	12	2	1	2	42,822
Native Waimea	4	F	6	0	0	0	1,020
Native War Dancer	8	G	3	0	0	0	388
Native Warrior	6	G	1	1	0	0	1,080
Native Will	5	M	14	0	4	2	8,528
Native Wonder	5	H	2	0	0	0	45
Native Zeal	2	F	8	0	0	0	5,382
Nativette	8	M	1	0	0	0	113
Nato	3	G	11	0	2	1	3,588
Natomas Baby	3	F	1	1	0	0	1,560
Natrona	4	F	8	0	2	1	14,452
Nat's Big Buckle	4	C	1	1	0	0	5,400
Nat's Flash	4	F	5	1	1	1	3,610
Nat's Fox	3	G	17	2	0	4	16,842
Nat's My Gold	3	F	6	1	0	2	8,180
Nattandyahoo	2	G	3	1	0	1	11,820
Natti Devil	4	F	7	0	0	1	2,384
Nattitude	3	F	3	1	0	1	29,485
Natty Boh	6	G	4	1	0	0	11,000
Natty Dreadlock	2	F	6	0	1	1	3,245
Natural	7	G	9	2	1	3	11,826
Natural Actress	3	F	13	1	1	0	27,020
Natural Affect	6	H	2	0	0	0	55
Natural Attraction	4	C	1	0	0	0	0
Natural Balance	3	C	2	0	0	0	0
Natural Born Lover	6	M	11	2	0	0	3,838
Natural Cat	3	C	5	0	1	1	2,541
Natural Enemy	4	C	15	3	5	2	53,512
Natural Glory	2	F	1	0	0	0	0
Natural High	5	H	8	2	2	2	19,419
Natural Image	3	F	4	2	0	0	32,400
Natural Nine	3	F	9	2	0	2	19,350
Natural Ridge	9	G	12	2	0	1	8,493
Natural Shade	9	M	15	1	1	3	16,012
Natural Star Speed	4	G	7	2	0	1	7,150
Natural Stone	4	G	6	1	1	0	7,412
Natural Style	6	H	9	3	3	1	35,068
Natural Touch	2	G	4	0	0	0	10,860
Natural Treasure	3	F	9	5	1	1	98,870
Natural View	3	G	6	0	0	0	588
Natural Wonder	5	G	5	1	0	0	6,445
Naturally Wild	6	M	9	2	2	3	90,350
Naturalreesehorse	5	M	3	0	0	0	518
Nature	6	H	10	0	0	3	14,711
Nature Boy Wonder	3	G	1	0	0	0	76
Nature Chant	6	M	6	0	0	0	450
Nature Coast	5	M	8	1	1	1	9,571
Nature Star	3	F	9	2	2	2	24,740

Horse	Age	Sex	Sts	1st	2d	3d	Won
Naturelle's Way	2	F	1	0	0	0	105
Natures Candy	4	G	12	2	2	1	22,393
Nature's Gold	2	F	4	0	0	0	808
Nature's Pick	5	H	16	1	1	0	5,014
Nature's Power	7	G	8	2	0	1	16,027
Nature's Realm	6	M	3	0	0	0	120
Naugatuck Sweetie	6	M	23	0	5	6	11,861
Naugatuckian	6	H	5	0	0	0	466
Naughte' Tom T	6	G	10	1	1	1	5,643
Naughtier	5	M	3	1	1	0	5,835
Naughty and Daring	3	F	3	0	0	0	0
Naughty Butterfly	4	F	2	0	0	0	70
Naughty Dreadlocks	4	F	9	2	0	1	11,488
Naughty E.	5	H	4	2	0	0	14,400
Naughty Kiss	2	G	5	1	1	1	12,600
Naughty Lady L	5	M	1	0	1	0	760
Naughty Laura	2	F	5	2	0	0	6,832
Naughty Lover	5	G	8	0	1	0	3,394
Naughty Mambo	5	M	1	0	0	0	0
Naughty Nacho	6	G	11	2	0	1	18,934
Naughty Nae	2	F	3	0	0	1	7,650
Naughty Nightie	3	F	1	0	0	0	150
Naughty Prince	4	G	7	2	1	1	57,116
Naughty Princess	2	F	2	0	0	0	1,230
Naughty So and So	2	F	1	0	0	0	100
Naughty T.	4	F	3	0	1	1	2,880
Nauiti Nine	3	F	6	0	0	3	6,280
Nault	3	F	12	2	3	1	69,900
Naushon	5	G	8	1	2	2	26,700
Naut	2	G	1	0	0	0	0
Nautical Allegro	6	G	11	2	2	2	42,774
Nautical But Nice	3	F	14	2	5	2	74,500
Nautical Miss	4	F	13	0	2	0	2,792
Nautical Noah	4	G	15	2	0	2	15,874
Nautical Prince	6	G	16	2	3	2	13,589
Nautico (ARG)	6	H	4	1	0	0	14,300
Nautilus	5	H	10	1	2	4	28,208
Nautique	3	C	8	0	0	0	1,310
Navagatior	5	G	4	0	0	0	487
Navajo Angel	4	F	2	0	1	0	280
Navajo Breeze	2	F	2	0	0	0	264
Navajo Code	5	G	14	1	3	4	24,595
Navajo Dan	6	G	6	1	0	0	3,663
Navajo Girl	4	F	7	2	0	3	20,780
Navajo Red	3	G	13	2	2	1	32,749
Navajo Talker	3	G	9	1	0	0	3,340
Navajoe	7	G	8	0	0	2	2,396
Navarena	4	F	9	0	1	1	12,360
Navastar	4	F	2	0	0	0	0
Navco Moon	4	G	3	0	0	0	0
Navegante's Seven	6	G	8	1	1	0	1,174
Navel (BRZ)	6	H	8	0	1	1	15,605
Nave's Prime Time	5	H	3	2	0	0	2,220
Navesink	5	H	2	1	0	0	39,480
Navesink River	2	C	1	0	0	0	1,350
Navesink Tide	3	C	6	2	2	0	20,360
Navesink View	4	C	3	1	0	0	6,000
Navigatrix	6	M	6	1	0	0	3,602
Navihawk	4	G	6	1	0	1	4,222
Navona	3	F	9	2	1	1	35,476
Navy Bird	3	C	1	0	0	0	2,500
Navy Blazer	4	G	11	0	1	3	6,840
Navy Brat	2	F	1	0	0	0	0
Navy Class	5	G	3	1	0	1	6,830
Navy Clipper	2	F	3	0	0	0	60
Navy Cross	4	G	5	0	0	0	186
Navy Girl	2	F	3	0	0	0	0
Navy Hymn	2	C	5	0	0	0	274
Navy J	3	G	12	2	3	3	11,459
Navy Recruit	11	G	6	0	1	2	1,715
Navy Seal	9	G	10	2	1	1	10,656
Nazareen	4	F	7	1	1	2	37,660
Nazirali (IRE)	6	G	8	1	1	1	92,540
Nazone	3	C	9	0	3	0	22,360
Neal's Rodeo	4	G	6	0	0	2	29,872
Nealville	6	H	7	1	0	0	8,850
Near and Dear	4	F	5	1	0	0	27,600
Near to You	3	F	6	0	0	1	3,925
Near Victory	2	C	1	0	0	0	66
Nearandfar	4	G	11	1	1	2	3,435
Nearco's Prince	5	G	8	0	0	0	707
Nearctica	2	F	1	0	0	0	3,528
Neardistracted	6	G	3	0	0	0	660
Nearly a Rascal	3	G	6	1	0	0	2,253
Nearly Forever	2	F	2	1	0	0	4,175
Nearly Lucky	3	G	12	1	2	1	7,163
Nearlymissthealarm	6	M	9	1	1	0	10,088
Neartic Ice	6	H	14	0	3	3	46,744
Neat and Sweet	5	M	11	4	2	1	19,422
Neat Cat	4	G	11	1	1	1	10,550
Neat Question	4	F	7	0	0	1	2,801
Neat Society	10	G	21	1	2	7	8,893
Neatbanker	5	G	2	2	0	0	9,000
Neblina	3	F	3	1	0	1	43,736
Nebraska Moon	2	C	1	0	1	0	2,200
Nebuchadnezzar	3	C	4	1	0	1	28,140
Necessaire	3	C	6	0	0	0	5,301
Necessary Evil	5	M	6	0	1	0	1,602
Nechisar	3	G	9	1	3	0	40,063
Nectarian	2	F	1	0	0	1	4,320
Ned Pepper	2	G	4	0	0	0	394
Neda Wina	3	G	16	3	5	4	19,944
Nedra	7	M	6	0	0	0	4,690
Nedra's Girl	4	F	3	1	0	0	3,972
Need a Light	2	F	5	1	0	0	5,321
Need a Rade	4	F	7	1	0	2	17,288
Need a Shot	4	C	12	1	1	1	5,562
Need to Diggin	3	F	1	0	0	0	80
Needadate	4	F	3	0	0	1	1,305
Needarunner	2	G	4	1	0	0	14,000
Needham's Point	5	G	13	4	1	2	52,961
Needwood Blade (GB)	5	H	8	2	0	0	87,201
Neeka	4	F	7	0	2	0	4,890
Neelam	3	F	5	0	0	1	6,414
Neemrana	4	F	3	0	0	0	244
Neenamusha	3	G	6	2	2	0	16,794
Neent	3	F	12	3	4	2	24,562
Neequoia	2	F	3	0	0	0	0
Neera	3	F	5	1	0	0	4,935
Neeshanha	4	F	1	0	0	0	0
Nefertiri	4	F	5	0	0	0	262
Negative Hope	8	M	5	0	0	0	912
Negative Love	8	G	3	1	0	0	6,000
Negativette	3	F	9	1	0	2	8,205
Negev Class	5	G	8	2	2	0	7,487
Negev Lady	7	M	7	0	0	1	1,074
Negev Wind	6	G	12	1	0	2	8,455
Negotiation	3	C	9	2	1	1	57,230
Negueva (FR)	4	F	4	0	0	0	1,320
Neighbora	4	F	1	0	0	0	2,640
Neighborhood Bully	6	G	9	3	1	1	7,937
Neil's Advice	3	C	13	6	2	2	17,279
Neil's Poor Boy	3	G	7	0	2	0	2,985
Neiman	4	C	4	0	3	0	6,100
Neither One	5	H	1	0	0	0	0
Neither We Do	8	G	5	5	0	0	5,820
Nelda Ann	6	M	1	0	0	0	47
Nelda Crypto	2	F	5	0	0	0	1,278
Nella Fantasia	2	F	1	0	0	0	110
Nellaluna	3	F	13	2	2	2	17,148
Nellie L	3	F	5	1	2	0	15,160
Nellie Magee	3	F	6	1	0	1	28,910
Nellie Road	3	F	4	2	0	0	42,000
Nellies Hero	10	G	1	0	0	0	0
Nellies Meadow	3	F	8	2	2	1	16,250
Nell's Angel	4	F	10	2	1	1	8,965
Nell's Miner	3	F	5	0	0	0	158
Nell's Niner	4	F	4	0	0	1	6,790
Nelly's Reef	3	F	10	1	1	1	8,895
Nelson Street	5	G	5	0	0	0	2,908
Nelson's Fling	4	F	8	0	0	1	2,655
Nelson's Foxy Lady	4	F	11	0	2	2	6,845
Nelson's Girl	3	F	6	0	0	1	1,373
Nelsons Gold	4	G	5	0	0	0	285
Nelson's Hawk	4	G	7	0	0	1	1,835
Nelson's Magic	6	G	15	5	6	1	78,110
Nelson's Pride	3	F	5	0	0	1	1,934
Nelsonstreetnancy	3	F	7	0	0	0	578

Horse	Age	Sex	Sts	1st	2d	3d	Won
Nelva's Nightmare	4	F	1	0	0	1	2,700
Nelzon	3	G	3	0	0	0	0
Nem Nem Shoa	2	F	5	1	0	0	4,875
Nenantena	3	F	5	1	0	2	25,620
Neo Brae	2	F	1	0	0	0	500
Neon Magic	3	C	3	0	0	2	12,220
Neon Playboy	3	G	3	0	0	0	0
Neon Queen	5	M	6	1	1	1	32,255
Neon Rainbow	3	C	11	2	1	3	62,920
Neon Shadow	9	G	3	1	1	0	31,720
Neons and Nylons	2	F	5	2	0	2	23,800
Nepal's Wickedwind	5	M	17	2	2	0	16,130
Nephrite's Best	4	C	2	0	0	0	0
Nerissa	4	F	1	0	0	0	0
Neruda	11	G	4	0	1	0	2,200
Nerv E Go	5	G	15	1	1	4	6,770
Nerve Ending	2	C	1	0	0	0	180
Nerveinthecurve	4	C	11	2	3	1	16,596
Nervous Naevus	5	M	17	0	2	2	4,305
Nervous Nelli	5	M	2	0	0	0	102
Neshama	3	F	1	0	0	0	0
Nestle Is Quick	2	C	1	0	0	0	0
Nestorius	3	G	11	1	2	0	23,058
Net Force	3	G	7	0	0	1	4,822
Net Threat	2	C	7	2	0	2	13,168
Netcong	4	C	10	1	2	3	66,586
Nettap	6	G	13	2	0	1	10,670
Netta's Poetry	5	M	10	5	3	1	26,008
Nettie R	3	F	4	0	3	1	5,872
Nettie's Rose	4	F	5	0	0	0	660
Nettleton	5	G	13	2	2	0	12,928
Nettso	5	M	8	0	0	0	1,842
Nettys Drum	5	G	13	1	3	2	8,614
Networking	5	G	1	0	1	0	5,260
Neucha Tel (ARG)	6	M	2	0	0	0	500
Neuf de Carreau	3	C	5	1	0	2	26,760
Neuf de Coeur	3	C	10	1	1	2	16,980
Neuf La Banque (PER)	5	M	6	0	0	1	2,940
Neumanns Cat	2	F	2	1	1	0	20,256
Neurotic	2	F	3	0	0	0	330
Neurotic Star	5	M	7	0	0	1	1,949
Neutral Bruce	2	G	9	1	0	2	12,660
Neutral Corner	3	F	15	2	1	4	28,579
Neutron	2	C	4	2	0	0	30,268
Neva Cloudy	3	C	5	0	1	0	3,766
Neva Fay	5	M	6	0	0	1	912
Neva Paranoide	6	G	3	0	0	0	465
Nevada Miss	3	F	10	1	3	4	76,710
Nevada Smith	10	G	2	0	0	0	163
Nevada Strip	6	H	12	3	2	2	64,090
Nevaeh	2	F	2	2	0	0	51,000
Nevano	3	F	2	0	0	0	0
Nevasayneva	5	H	2	0	2	0	3,280
Nevasca	3	F	1	0	0	0	320
Never Be Another	4	C	3	0	0	0	374
Never Been Caught	4	F	4	2	1	1	3,584
Never Better Baby	4	C	4	0	0	0	225
Never Blink	3	G	4	0	0	0	175
Never Blue	4	F	8	1	2	1	69,066
Never Close	8	M	9	2	2	1	7,212
Never Delay	4	F	2	0	0	0	1,165
Never Din	2	F	1	0	0	0	0
Never Ending	2	F	2	1	0	0	11,520
Never Ending Lunch	3	G	7	0	0	1	2,260
Never Fail	3	F	9	2	2	1	60,520
Never Forever	4	C	2	0	0	0	0
Never High	5	M	10	0	2	0	774
Never Late	4	G	5	1	3	0	10,350
Never Left	2	F	9	2	0	1	42,820
Never Look Back	2	F	1	0	0	0	4,087
Never Lookin' Back	6	G	3	0	0	1	268
Never Never	3	G	12	1	0	1	4,889
Never On Time	5	H	11	1	1	0	15,398
Never Out of Roses	5	M	4	0	0	0	445
Never Over	4	F	17	2	0	1	13,517
Never Pass a Kiss	8	M	1	1	0	0	6,420
Never Pete	3	G	8	1	0	1	10,630
Never Phoney	4	G	8	1	0	0	1,580
Never Plan Ahead	4	G	13	1	2	2	3,725
Never Rest	3	G	14	2	1	2	24,592
Never Satisfied	3	F	8	2	0	0	15,546
Never Stop	5	H	5	0	0	0	0
Never Surrender	2	G	2	1	0	0	3,715
Never Take Risk	3	C	5	3	1	0	14,802
Never Tap Twice	2	C	1	0	0	0	59
Never Under	3	F	5	1	1	0	8,160
Neverbroke	3	G	11	2	0	0	15,166
Neverdid	2	F	1	0	0	0	0
Neverenough Jewels	3	F	17	1	3	0	7,859
Neverhadadinner	2	G	2	0	0	0	0
Neverlostforwords	3	F	9	1	1	2	8,185
Nevermore	3	F	3	0	1	0	10,580
Neverrush	3	F	6	0	0	0	0
Nevers Trump Card	8	M	8	1	0	0	2,415
Neversaynevermind	4	C	2	0	0	0	120
Nevets	6	G	10	2	0	0	2,747
Nevetsderf	3	C	4	0	2	1	9,610
Neville	3	G	14	0	1	2	2,230
Neville's Gold	2	G	1	0	0	0	145
Nevoso	4	G	12	1	3	1	16,693
Nevva Betta	4	F	10	1	0	2	7,361
New Advantage	6	H	12	1	6	0	57,825
New Age Goddess	2	F	7	0	0	6	7,206
New Alpha	3	F	4	0	0	0	0
New Becky	3	F	4	0	0	0	220
New Brunswick	6	G	7	0	1	1	2,321
New Castle Lady	2	F	3	0	0	2	10,740
New Course	2	G	4	1	0	0	10,640
New Delight	4	G	10	0	1	0	2,230
New Diligence	3	F	12	2	3	2	120,779
New Doc Silver	5	M	2	1	0	0	2,525
New Economy	5	M	6	1	0	1	111,681
New Element	2	C	1	0	0	0	60
New Evidence	4	G	10	2	1	0	14,997
New Freedom	5	M	5	1	0	0	4,897
New Hampshire	4	C	1	0	0	0	0
New Hey	2	C	2	0	0	0	0
New Jag	5	G	6	0	0	1	7,160
New Jersey Phil	2	C	2	0	0	0	880
New Journey	10	G	9	2	3	2	9,606
New Judge	5	G	9	1	1	0	2,684
New Kid in Town	3	C	11	4	1	2	72,564
New Kinda Walk	2	F	3	0	0	0	139
New King	5	G	2	0	0	0	780
New Kirks Trick	2	G	1	0	0	0	0
New Lebanon	4	F	14	2	2	3	11,697
New Madrid	5	G	5	0	0	0	173
New Meaning	3	F	2	0	0	0	430
New Media	3	G	9	0	0	1	10,740
New Miracle	7	M	11	0	1	1	2,827
New Moon Rising	2	F	8	0	2	1	3,951
New Music	6	M	11	5	0	3	57,950
New Opposition	2	F	1	0	0	0	1,302
New Paradigm	5	G	14	2	2	0	38,300
New Passage	6	G	1	0	0	0	360
New Pembroke	3	G	4	0	0	1	1,531
New Prince	3	G	3	0	0	0	0
New Program	5	G	9	1	3	2	15,045
New Release	3	F	5	0	2	0	5,986
New River Star	3	F	5	0	0	0	911
New Sheriff N Town	4	C	13	3	0	3	14,871
New Shoes	3	C	5	1	0	0	14,220
New Spirits	3	C	2	0	0	0	360
New Storm	2	F	3	1	0	2	22,950
New Trieste	4	C	1	0	0	0	1,500
New Value	3	F	4	1	0	0	4,950
New Water	3	F	6	1	1	1	47,900
New Years Eve Gala	4	F	6	1	1	1	32,070
New Year's Frolic	3	F	1	0	0	0	155
New York Attitude	7	M	3	0	0	0	0
New York Cat	2	C	4	0	0	0	4,950
New York Fay	6	M	6	0	1	2	2,823
New York Gold	3	F	13	2	4	0	18,820
New York Harbor	2	G	5	2	0	0	69,470
New York Hero	3	C	14	4	3	0	465,860
New York Jessica	3	F	9	1	0	2	8,430
New York Joe	4	G	3	0	0	0	375
New York Minute	4	G	3	0	0	0	650

Horse	Age	Sex	Sts	1st	2d	3d	Won	Horse	Age	Sex	Sts	1st	2d	3d	Won
New York P D	3	G	3	1	0	0	9,725	N'ice Tea	8	G	5	0	0	0	612
New York Prospect	3	C	2	0	0	0	0	Nice Thag	3	F	6	0	0	0	573
New York Ryder	4	C	4	0	0	0	132	Nice Twice	3	G	2	1	0	0	6,475
New York's Picc	5	H	6	0	0	1	959	Nicebutnaughty	2	F	6	1	1	0	10,660
New York's Rudy	3	G	10	2	0	3	69,570	Nicelittlepackage	2	F	10	1	3	1	17,670
Newark	3	G	13	3	6	2	74,377	Nicely Accepted	3	F	5	2	1	0	12,250
Newer Technology	6	G	11	0	3	4	12,252	Nicely Nasty	4	F	5	1	3	0	84,068
Newfoundland	3	C	9	4	0	1	137,234	Nicely Toasted	3	G	7	2	0	1	11,510
Newgate	8	H	12	2	3	2	11,286	Nicholas Cal	3	G	6	1	0	1	15,620
Newhouse	2	G	3	0	0	0	285	Nicholas D	4	G	8	0	2	0	8,290
Newmanintown	4	C	6	1	1	2	4,808	Nicholas Love	6	H	4	0	0	0	186
Newport Nikki	3	F	2	0	1	0	5,450	Nicholas Rocco M	3	G	7	0	0	1	1,843
News Report	2	G	15	6	0	4	95,770	Nichole's Delight	4	F	7	2	1	1	13,023
News Reporter	2	G	2	0	0	0	300	Nicholle's Devil	4	G	9	0	5	1	56,841
News to Me	3	F	7	1	1	0	28,612	Nicholls	9	G	4	0	0	0	634
Newsboy	3	G	11	2	3	1	18,505	Nici's Gold	2	F	3	0	0	0	288
Newsbreak	8	G	8	0	0	4	14,350	Nick (CHI)	6	H	1	0	0	0	0
Newsman	3	G	14	0	2	3	15,218	Nick Berryman	8	G	14	4	3	2	19,652
Newsqueen	3	F	13	0	3	1	5,967	Nick Bollettieri	4	G	10	1	1	1	14,680
Newswoman	4	F	6	0	0	1	1,990	Nick Missed	2	G	5	1	1	2	17,159
Newt	7	H	5	1	2	0	1,000	Nick Mitchell	4	C	10	2	0	0	37,750
Newt Bunyard	5	M	7	1	0	2	5,599	Nick N Court	4	G	10	1	0	2	8,401
Newtown Pike	2	C	1	0	0	0	252	Nick Nak	6	H	11	0	0	3	2,783
Newtown Road	6	H	5	0	0	0	42	Nick of Gold	9	G	10	0	1	1	1,022
Newtrial	5	G	7	0	0	0	450	Nick of Grace	4	F	9	1	0	0	5,672
Newt's Big Boy	8	G	15	2	6	5	21,124	Nick of Time	5	G	6	2	0	2	9,224
Newyearresolution	2	F	2	0	0	1	2,063	Nick Oz	4	C	8	0	0	0	146
Newyorkssweetheart	4	F	7	0	0	0	1,490	Nick P	2	C	3	0	0	0	235
Nex Onecomin	2	F	3	0	0	0	0	Nick the Vest	3	C	8	0	0	3	23,300
Next Account	2	C	3	1	1	0	11,800	Nickabod	5	M	7	0	0	1	1,190
Next Bandit	2	C	7	3	1	1	157,838	Nicked	3	F	13	1	1	1	9,348
Next Best Thing	3	C	2	0	0	0	0	Nickel	6	G	11	1	2	0	4,490
Next Dove Hunt	2	F	8	1	3	0	13,555	Nickel Ice	3	F	6	0	0	0	177
Next Millennium	6	H	4	0	0	1	2,310	Nickel Lou	5	G	3	0	0	0	514
Next News	3	G	13	3	2	1	22,645	Nickie's Affair	4	G	6	0	1	1	11,900
Next September	4	G	12	1	0	0	11,623	Nicklas T.	5	G	14	0	1	0	2,297
Next Step	2	C	1	0	1	0	10,000	Nickle a Kiss	3	F	7	1	3	0	13,017
Next Summer	6	G	14	1	1	1	14,183	Nickle Oakie	6	G	6	2	0	0	20,065
Next to Bat	3	G	1	0	0	0	0	Nickle Seats	4	G	8	1	1	1	11,105
Next to Heaven	4	F	6	1	1	0	8,870	Nickname	2	F	6	0	1	0	3,560
Nextiger	3	C	2	0	0	0	428	Nickneye	3	F	2	0	0	0	1,250
Nextofkin	2	F	2	0	0	0	0	Nick's Delight	4	G	7	2	2	1	44,132
Nextquestionplease	4	G	9	0	3	2	10,790	Nick's Fancy	3	F	9	1	0	0	4,268
Nextquestor	3	G	10	1	1	3	41,825	Nick's Gladiator	2	G	3	1	1	1	3,080
Nextthirtyyears	5	G	10	0	0	0	464	Nick's Ligan	4	G	12	1	1	4	17,854
Nezzarina	2	F	5	1	0	1	12,120	Nicks Moment	4	F	9	1	1	0	7,285
Ni Jinxed	4	G	13	0	2	3	4,702	Nick's Noactor	5	G	7	2	0	0	20,213
Niall's Mozart	4	F	3	0	0	0	227	Nicky Jolene	3	F	13	2	1	4	22,306
Nibbles and Noble	4	G	4	0	0	0	410	Nickylane	4	G	3	0	0	0	475
Niblett	4	G	11	2	0	0	13,800	Nicky's World	3	C	1	0	0	0	82
Niblick	4	F	10	1	3	0	48,310	Niclie	3	F	10	2	1	2	57,430
Nicasio	5	G	2	2	0	0	10,375	Nicmick	7	G	1	0	0	0	0
Nicatnite	5	G	10	0	0	0	786	Nicobar (GB)	6	H	5	0	1	0	41,900
Nicca Tac Man	6	G	6	0	0	0	0	Nicol n' Dime Me	6	G	7	3	0	0	19,572
Nicco Nicco	3	G	5	0	0	0	0	Nicole	6	M	17	1	0	1	5,083
Niccola	4	G	11	1	1	3	5,432	Nicole and Ben	2	F	6	1	2	1	70,710
Nice and Frosty	6	H	4	1	0	0	5,205	Nicole Kathryn	3	F	13	2	4	3	106,110
Nice and Ready	4	G	13	0	0	2	10,634	Nicole M	4	F	13	3	2	1	20,350
Nice Baby	6	M	10	1	0	1	9,178	Nicole's Apollo	4	C	22	6	1	5	73,360
Nice Bet Mindy	3	C	3	0	0	0	255	Nicole's Dream	3	F	17	9	2	1	176,040
Nice Boy	4	C	8	1	0	0	23,690	Nicole's Pursuit	4	F	3	0	0	0	39,568
Nice Calves	4	F	9	0	2	0	3,156	Nicoleslilbaby	4	F	13	1	0	0	9,270
Nice Canter	3	F	8	0	1	2	25,940	Nicolo Pace	5	G	18	2	4	2	17,343
Nice Cat	3	G	4	1	0	0	3,881	Nicolov (FR)	3	G	4	0	0	0	280
Nice Choice	3	G	11	1	3	0	15,012	Nicoma Springs	3	F	7	1	0	0	5,304
Nice Fish	5	M	13	2	3	1	35,205	Nicosia	3	C	14	0	1	2	14,250
Nice Fit	3	G	11	1	2	2	18,715	Nicoyana	5	M	9	0	0	0	2,309
Nice Going	3	C	10	0	0	0	150	Nics Eclipse	6	G	6	0	0	0	980
Nice Ice Rush	2	C	1	0	0	0	3,200	Nidari	7	M	2	0	0	0	566
Nice Kipper	3	F	12	1	3	3	42,960	Nidol (CHI)	8	H	1	0	0	0	110
Nice Legs Nahla	4	F	11	3	1	1	16,995	Nieges Que Te Amo	3	C	16	0	1	5	6,965
Nice Little Girl	4	F	10	1	2	3	17,680	Niello	4	C	4	1	1	0	25,810
Nice N Crafty	2	F	2	0	1	0	700	Niesen	4	F	14	1	2	3	11,139
Nice N Nasty	4	G	8	2	2	0	29,514	Nieta	2	F	3	0	0	0	0
Nice N Quiet	6	H	9	1	1	2	11,470	Nietzsche	3	G	2	0	1	0	6,460
Nice n' Salty	9	G	7	1	2	1	20,530	Nifty Affair	3	F	3	0	0	0	450
Nice 'n Spicey	7	M	9	0	1	1	628	Nifty Lady	2	F	2	0	0	0	3,760
Nice Navajo	3	C	1	0	0	0	0	Nifty One	2	G	4	1	0	1	4,857
Nice Ride	8	G	3	0	1	0	1,105	Nifty Susie	4	F	6	0	1	0	5,874

Horse	Age	Sex	Sts	1st	2d	3d	Won
Nigel	3	G	9	1	0	2	9,410
Nighque Star	5	M	18	3	4	4	13,178
Night Accomplice	3	F	1	0	0	0	0
Night Ballet	5	M	10	2	2	2	18,141
Night Before	7	H	11	1	1	2	4,375
Night Caller	7	H	13	3	1	2	72,141
Night Charger	2	G	3	1	0	0	19,085
Night Drums	12	G	16	0	0	0	1,953
Night Edition	5	M	9	0	2	0	41,410
Night Flash	3	F	8	1	0	3	4,845
Night for Bells	4	F	11	1	1	3	3,431
Night Games (GB)	3	F	3	0	1	2	21,440
Night Gracie	3	F	2	0	0	0	0
Night Heat	3	C	5	1	1	0	6,540
Night Howl	5	G	10	0	1	3	3,803
Night Jasmine	4	F	6	0	0	0	450
Night Launch	3	F	2	0	0	0	0
Night Life (FR)	6	H	6	0	1	1	52,030
Night Music	3	F	4	0	0	0	1,000
Night of Delight	7	M	9	0	4	0	33,869
Night of Gold	5	M	9	1	1	1	7,380
Night On Broadway	4	C	15	1	3	1	9,610
Night Paige	4	F	5	0	0	0	67
Night Passion (GB)	4	G	4	0	0	0	1,090
Night Patrol	7	G	5	1	0	0	85,580
Night Plan	5	M	12	0	1	1	3,289
Night Predator	3	G	1	0	0	0	900
Night Preferred	4	F	10	0	0	0	298
Night Rhythms	4	G	6	0	0	0	246
Night River	3	G	11	1	0	0	4,035
Night Run	6	G	15	1	3	0	10,875
Night Sky	2	G	2	2	0	0	98,880
Night Speed (IRE)	3	G	7	0	0	0	276
Night Time Dixie	6	M	8	0	1	3	3,449
Night Verse	7	G	5	0	0	0	0
Nightair	6	M	3	0	0	0	565
Nightattheoscars	4	C	8	0	0	2	2,028
Nighthunter	3	G	6	1	0	0	28,892
Nighthunter Two	2	F	3	1	1	0	26,950
Nightingale	4	F	9	2	1	0	11,258
Nightingale Mill	2	C	3	0	1	0	1,675
Nightlifeatbigblue	2	C	2	1	0	0	17,730
Nightly Appeal	6	G	7	2	0	2	59,599
Nightly Delusions	3	G	5	2	1	0	6,055
Nightmare Affair	2	C	3	1	0	1	17,800
Nightsnwhitesatin	3	C	3	0	0	0	0
Nighttimeinthecity	2	F	2	0	0	0	700
Nighty	4	F	11	1	1	1	16,930
Nihilator	2	C	9	2	3	2	57,459
Niigon	2	C	3	0	1	2	50,504
Nijinsky Surprise	4	F	6	0	1	0	1,665
Nijinsky's Deed	4	F	2	1	0	0	6,447
Nijinsky's Lass	4	F	8	1	1	1	4,280
Nijinsky's Pride	4	G	6	0	2	0	5,343
Nijinsky's Pride (NZ)	9	G	3	0	0	1	5,750
Nik Gaylord	4	G	6	1	0	1	13,290
Nik the Stick	3	G	14	2	2	3	12,310
Nikama	7	H	6	1	1	0	9,677
Nikarosa	8	M	12	5	3	2	11,727
Nikawa	9	G	13	1	4	1	19,164
Nike's Friend	2	F	2	0	0	0	0
Nike's Woman	3	F	3	0	0	0	1,326
Nikie Your Honor	5	G	11	2	3	0	52,408
Nikita	8	M	3	0	0	0	810
Nikken Won	4	F	3	0	0	1	577
Nikki's Angel	7	M	2	0	1	0	6,012
Nikki's Growl	3	F	9	5	1	1	53,670
Nikki'sfirstformal	4	G	5	1	0	0	7,429
Niknar Esperanza	5	M	14	0	1	1	4,586
Niknardia	6	M	5	0	0	0	1,222
Nikobe	4	C	11	1	1	1	15,588
Nile Pyramids	2	C	1	0	0	0	0
Niles	3	C	1	0	0	0	137
Nilini	2	F	6	0	1	0	3,906
Nilly Style	2	F	3	1	0	1	6,154
Nimble	11	G	10	2	1	1	7,424
Nimble Good Fella	3	G	3	0	0	0	0
Nimble Princesse	3	F	10	3	1	2	18,120
Nimble Shank	2	F	4	0	1	1	7,860
Nimbus Twothousand	4	F	3	0	0	0	660
Nimmer	3	F	11	4	2	1	69,937
Nin Tproofprospect	3	F	4	0	0	0	510
Nina Del Diablo	6	M	1	0	0	0	0
Nina Especial	3	F	1	0	0	0	0
Nina Lyn	3	F	12	0	1	2	8,748
Nina Marie	4	F	11	3	3	0	20,258
Ninamite	3	F	5	0	1	2	3,936
Nina's Girl	4	F	1	0	0	0	0
Nina's Limelight	2	F	2	0	0	0	0
Nina's Taxing	4	F	10	4	1	2	24,657
Nindawayma	5	M	11	3	5	0	22,134
Nine Bucks	2	F	7	1	1	1	10,045
Nine Carats	2	F	2	0	0	0	3,636
Nine Chimes	3	G	6	1	2	1	35,490
Nine Factors	6	H	11	0	4	1	6,286
Nine for Nine	2	C	1	0	0	0	0
Nine Iron	11	G	11	1	2	2	10,661
Nine Meadows	3	F	2	0	0	0	0
Nine Moons	8	G	24	3	1	2	12,827
Nine Notes	4	G	13	4	2	3	46,477
Nine of Cups	6	M	7	2	0	0	5,387
Nine Pents	5	H	1	1	0	0	2,280
Nine Pines	3	F	4	2	0	1	29,970
Nine Shamrocks	5	H	1	0	0	0	0
Nine Tu Tu's	4	F	6	0	2	0	5,438
Nineandfourfifths	4	F	1	0	0	0	0
Ninebanks	5	G	9	3	2	1	310,400
Nineleventurbo	5	G	8	3	1	2	48,359
Nineninefine	3	F	2	0	0	2	2,775
Nineo'clockhigh	3	C	2	0	0	0	460
Nineofus	3	G	5	0	0	1	2,470
Niner River	5	G	2	0	0	1	1,870
Niner's Echo	5	G	10	1	0	1	30,529
Niners Gold Money	4	F	13	2	3	5	28,337
Nine's Appealagain	5	G	15	0	0	3	5,356
Nineteen Candles	5	M	7	1	0	1	8,157
Ninetenthsofthelaw	4	G	15	3	3	3	31,995
Ninety Day Note	3	C	5	1	1	1	9,940
Ninety Day Wonder	3	G	15	1	2	3	22,419
Ninety Mile Island	4	F	9	0	0	1	708
Ninety Nine Jack	4	G	2	0	0	1	6,554
Ninety Nine Mack	4	G	7	0	2	0	23,220
Ninety Second Fuse	4	C	1	0	0	0	900
Ninety West	5	G	2	0	1	0	4,300
Nino Alegre	4	C	2	2	0	0	30,360
Nino Dorado	5	G	10	1	3	1	14,575
Ninock	9	G	2	0	0	0	0
Nintyfiver	8	G	10	2	1	2	10,410
Nip and Run	4	F	1	0	0	0	0
Nip'n'tuck	9	G	8	0	0	1	612
Nippa Way	10	G	8	3	0	2	16,300
Nipper Nelly	3	F	8	3	1	2	24,024
Nippert	3	C	5	1	0	1	8,105
Nippy Ruckus	7	G	11	0	0	2	2,405
Nipstick	3	C	17	1	1	4	16,525
Nirav	3	C	7	1	2	2	31,700
Nirvana Blue	8	M	7	1	1	1	3,145
Nisga'a Treaty	5	G	2	0	0	1	1,383
Nishani	2	F	1	0	0	0	0
Nishapur	3	C	6	0	1	0	4,165
Nishe's Shadow	2	F	3	1	1	0	11,610
Nishnabotna	4	F	3	0	0	1	792
Nismat	2	F	1	0	0	0	0
Nister Bere (FR)	2	C	11	1	2	7	46,200
Nita Moon Up	3	F	15	4	0	3	35,680
Nita Wins Too	3	F	9	2	0	0	8,725
Nita's Notebook	6	G	9	2	1	3	9,070
Nita'sgotitgoinon	2	F	1	1	0	0	5,700
Nite At the Oscars	4	C	6	0	1	0	7,072
Nite Deelites	5	G	5	1	0	1	5,201
Nite Gaze	7	M	14	0	2	2	13,575
Nite of the Prom	4	G	13	1	0	1	5,178
Nite Out Woman	5	M	5	0	0	0	0
Nite Owl Nick	2	C	2	0	0	0	713
Nite Prowler	5	H	6	0	1	0	1,970
Nite Tower	4	G	13	1	0	4	6,746
Nitranna	8	M	7	1	0	0	4,260
Nitro Attorney	2	G	1	0	0	0	0

RECORDS OF HORSES

Horse	Age	Sex	Sts	1st	2d	3d	Won
Nitro Chip	2	G	5	4	1	0	103,220
Nitroisnick	4	G	9	1	2	2	6,446
Nitrous	3	G	4	0	0	2	2,835
Nitsa D	4	F	8	1	0	0	6,560
Nitschke	5	G	26	0	0	1	3,255
Nitty	6	G	8	0	0	0	672
Niunpasoatras	2	C	4	0	1	2	5,840
Nix of Time	7	G	12	2	0	0	10,290
Nizy Luck	7	G	5	0	0	0	1,071
Nlotsabutter	3	F	20	2	4	5	35,030
No Agenda	4	G	7	1	3	0	8,590
No Alibis	5	H	4	0	1	1	2,068
No Anchovies	7	M	11	1	0	1	3,249
No Appeal	7	M	2	0	0	0	132
No Approval	5	M	1	0	0	0	0
No Approval Needed	3	C	1	0	0	0	210
No Armistice	6	H	3	0	0	1	14,622
No Bad Habits	9	H	8	0	2	3	18,260
No Bare Feet	5	G	16	4	5	3	28,970
No Beans	2	F	4	2	1	1	128,821
No Betta Cat	3	F	9	2	2	1	10,125
No Bettor Love	6	M	4	0	2	0	14,040
No Bias	3	F	7	1	1	1	23,640
No Big Points	2	F	1	0	0	0	0
No Boots	3	G	4	1	0	0	12,105
No Brainer	2	G	3	0	0	0	375
No Britches	5	G	12	0	0	1	3,274
No Cal Bread	7	G	8	1	0	1	24,790
No Cal Bread Bro	6	H	18	3	0	4	34,880
No Chance to Ski	3	C	7	0	1	1	6,200
No Cheating	6	M	10	5	2	0	143,334
No City Limits	9	G	8	0	1	0	1,821
No Clue	5	G	11	0	1	1	4,268
No Coasting	4	G	3	0	0	0	0
No Coin to Toss	5	M	3	0	0	0	0
No Communication	2	F	1	1	0	0	15,400
No Comparison	3	F	13	1	3	2	8,196
No Complaints	8	G	8	2	0	0	7,976
No Comprende	5	G	10	2	3	1	298,700
No Cover Charge	5	G	10	0	0	0	1,242
No Coward	3	F	9	3	2	2	26,296
No Credit	5	H	3	1	0	1	9,420
No Crime Committed	3	C	3	1	0	0	17,280
No Curfew	6	G	17	2	4	1	15,530
No Day But Today	2	C	1	0	0	0	120
No Deadline	5	M	2	0	1	0	2,708
No Deposit	4	C	12	2	5	0	47,280
No Dice	7	H	3	0	0	2	1,670
No Dinero	3	C	9	0	0	0	354
No Dispute	3	F	6	1	1	1	11,730
No Down Time	6	G	6	2	0	2	3,408
No Dress Code	3	F	1	0	0	0	1,560
No Dumb Jokes	3	G	13	1	1	2	5,042
No Easy Answer	4	F	3	0	0	0	0
No Evil	5	G	2	0	1	0	2,180
No Excuse Needed (GB)	5	H	3	0	0	0	3,783
No Execution	6	M	6	1	0	3	11,783
No Explanation	11	G	1	0	0	0	190
No Fable	2	F	2	1	0	0	9,513
No Factor	2	G	3	0	0	0	280
No Fast Moves	5	G	5	1	2	0	14,700
No Fear	2	C	4	1	0	0	8,080
No Fears No Tears	3	F	10	1	1	1	38,180
No Free Lunch	3	G	12	1	2	2	7,216
No Garden Variety	3	F	10	0	0	1	9,346
No Gimme	4	C	2	0	0	0	0
No Givin Up	4	G	3	0	0	1	5,489
No Gray On Me	3	F	1	0	1	0	1,540
No Guts No Glory	4	G	7	2	1	2	9,798
No Halos Here	4	F	11	2	4	2	65,320
No Happy Love	2	C	6	1	2	1	11,580
No Hastle Mon	4	F	12	1	1	2	9,757
No Hold On Me	6	M	8	1	1	1	7,092
No Homework	3	G	12	2	2	2	16,800
No Honey	4	F	4	1	0	0	6,490
No Huddle	3	G	17	2	5	1	23,897
No I Can't	5	G	12	1	1	3	10,783
No Ice for Me	8	G	1	0	0	0	0
No Inclusions	6	M	6	2	0	1	8,145
No Issues	3	G	9	5	0	1	63,750
No Its False	2	F	3	0	0	0	280
No Its Not	5	G	9	4	2	0	161,210
No Jacket Required	6	G	12	4	2	0	130,454
No Jazz	3	F	15	0	0	1	2,810
No Joe No	5	G	5	0	1	2	2,740
No Kelp Weed	4	F	11	3	4	0	26,358
No Kid	5	G	1	0	0	0	160
No Kings	3	F	11	1	1	1	72,325
No Kowtowing	3	F	13	3	2	1	13,544
No Lak of Heart	3	F	3	1	0	0	6,500
No Laugh n' Kathy	9	G	4	0	2	0	5,730
No Law Breaker	5	G	10	0	1	0	2,138
No Lo Creo	2	F	3	0	0	0	265
No Looking Back	4	G	10	3	1	1	13,616
No Love Song	3	F	2	0	0	0	4,563
No Luck in Reno	9	G	3	0	0	0	0
No Magic	9	G	3	0	0	1	638
No Mama's Boy	5	H	2	0	0	0	116
No Manners Nelson	2	G	1	0	0	0	651
No Man's Island	7	M	15	0	0	1	3,297
No Markers	5	M	10	0	0	0	895
No Matches	3	G	1	0	1	0	2,340
No Matter Who	4	G	7	1	1	2	30,490
No Matt's My Kid	3	F	6	1	0	1	8,632
No Minimum	2	F	4	0	0	0	3,560
No Moon	4	G	10	0	0	3	1,949
No Mor Dough	5	G	6	0	0	1	632
No More Alibis	3	F	5	1	0	1	3,732
No More Chads	4	G	1	0	0	0	126
No More Choke	2	F	4	0	0	0	362
No More Gray	4	F	5	1	0	0	6,129
No More Two Call	3	F	11	0	0	0	456
No Music	4	G	12	3	1	0	39,204
No Mystery Here	4	F	22	4	6	2	44,997
No Name Setter	3	F	2	0	0	0	60
No Nap Time	2	F	3	0	0	0	300
No Net Needed	4	G	14	1	0	1	17,520
No Nice	3	C	3	1	1	0	21,600
No Night (GB)	7	G	10	0	2	1	22,763
No Nines	4	G	12	1	0	3	6,335
No No Angel	4	F	9	1	0	1	19,120
No No Cielo	2	F	5	0	0	0	3,689
No No Don't Shoot	5	H	1	0	0	0	0
No No Nicotine	2	F	2	0	0	0	154
No No Rene	3	F	12	2	2	2	32,758
No No Romeo	4	G	12	3	3	2	24,475
No Numbers	3	C	13	2	2	2	60,260
No Ones Fool	4	G	17	1	4	2	13,177
No Ordinary Stone	3	F	3	0	0	2	2,600
No Other Like You	3	F	5	1	1	2	29,360
No Other Lover	3	F	1	0	0	0	0
No Paige	4	F	18	3	4	1	16,615
No Pajamas	2	G	2	0	0	0	1,110
No Pardon	3	F	12	3	0	2	15,121
No Parole	4	C	10	0	0	2	36,893
No Pass Port	3	F	3	0	0	0	128
No Peso No Dance	4	F	10	6	2	1	95,442
No Phone Swabbe	6	G	15	1	1	0	6,916
No Picnic	4	G	7	0	0	1	2,779
No Place Like It	2	C	3	0	1	1	4,285
No Pressure	4	G	2	0	0	0	0
No Pretense	3	G	4	0	0	0	152
No Problem	3	C	8	1	2	2	8,297
No Que No	2	F	2	0	1	0	2,600
No Regular Cat	2	G	2	0	1	0	1,012
No Reservations	3	F	8	1	1	3	19,590
No Response	2	G	1	0	0	0	375
No Restraint	4	G	11	2	1	4	33,050
No Retreat	5	G	2	0	0	0	188
No Risk	3	F	3	0	0	0	263
No Rules	4	F	8	0	2	1	8,265
No Secrets Here	3	F	17	6	3	1	97,914
No Shades	3	G	17	2	1	0	24,601
No Small Wonder	4	F	10	1	3	1	17,250
No Smoochin	5	M	5	0	0	0	720
No Socks Doc	5	H	5	1	0	0	37,500
No Solution	2	C	4	2	0	1	14,470

Horse	Age	Sex	Sts	1st	2d	3d	Won
No Spin	3	F	12	1	0	1	6,247
No Spin Zone	4	C	11	2	1	1	9,486
No Stop in Me	4	G	21	3	1	1	9,721
No Stopping	3	F	3	0	0	0	680
No Storms	3	C	1	0	1	0	2,600
No Strings	3	G	7	2	2	2	45,460
No Stroke	7	G	1	0	0	0	0
No Surgeon	3	G	7	1	1	0	9,653
No Surprises	3	C	10	0	0	1	1,034
No Sweat Kristine	5	M	8	2	3	1	16,097
No Sweets	3	G	4	0	0	0	1,340
No Tan Lines	5	M	9	0	0	0	809
No Tax	2	C	1	0	0	0	0
No Thanks	4	G	1	0	0	0	0
No Tick	2	C	1	0	0	0	0
No Time Flat	4	G	3	0	0	0	2,200
No Time for Games	2	C	1	0	0	0	0
No Time Out	3	F	2	0	0	0	0
No Time Soon	4	C	4	0	0	0	260
No Time to Ponder	3	G	4	0	0	1	2,110
No Time to Weave	4	F	1	0	0	0	200
No Tolerance	2	G	5	0	2	1	11,110
No Toro	4	C	5	1	0	0	19,950
No Traitor	3	G	9	0	0	1	2,149
No Trespass	4	F	3	2	0	1	5,075
No Trouble	4	C	9	1	0	0	7,425
No Truer Words	3	C	2	0	0	0	0
No Turbulence	4	F	7	2	1	1	45,329
No Turk	3	G	6	2	0	0	22,371
No Vacancy	6	H	9	1	0	0	26,680
No Wager	6	G	6	0	1	0	3,585
No War and Tea	3	F	11	1	0	3	16,958
No Way a Lady	2	F	2	0	0	0	65
No Way Johnny Ray	4	G	8	0	0	0	630
No Whistle	3	F	7	0	0	0	2,028
No White Flags	5	G	7	1	1	2	44,500
No White Markings	8	G	2	0	0	0	0
No You Don't	3	F	5	0	0	0	122
Noadiah	3	G	18	1	1	5	15,511
Noah Jake	2	C	3	0	0	0	0
Noah's Catch	3	G	11	0	0	0	2,055
Noah's Chance	4	G	12	1	1	3	9,993
Noah's Secret	4	G	12	1	1	1	8,576
Noa's Toy	3	F	18	3	2	3	26,890
Noazzin	4	G	8	0	2	0	12,475
Nobel Mitterand	3	F	8	0	4	0	43,900
Nobella Prize	8	G	4	0	1	0	1,204
Nobilissime (GB)	4	F	1	0	0	0	0
Noble Ack	5	G	10	1	2	1	5,218
Noble Adversary	5	H	9	3	1	0	41,171
Noble and Just	4	G	13	2	2	2	11,842
Noble Ann	5	M	13	0	1	6	7,157
Noble Arkie	9	G	1	0	0	0	0
Noble Ballet	2	F	4	0	2	0	9,430
Noble Calling	4	G	13	0	1	0	3,040
Noble Carr	3	C	6	2	1	1	29,290
Noble Crown	6	G	22	3	2	5	16,951
Noble Decision	4	C	5	1	3	0	30,272
Noble Delight	3	F	10	2	1	1	23,493
Noble Deputy	2	G	3	0	0	0	349
Noble Destiny	7	G	5	0	0	0	398
Noble Dreamer	7	G	5	0	0	0	420
Noble Endeavor	3	F	8	1	3	2	6,865
Noble Fellow	6	H	6	0	0	0	182
Noble Fighter	2	C	2	0	0	0	0
Noble Gent	4	G	12	1	1	3	5,181
Noble Gray	8	G	7	0	1	1	2,100
Noble Halo	2	C	2	2	0	0	27,548
Noble Heir	3	G	1	0	0	0	0
Noble Honor	3	G	10	0	0	1	2,270
Noble Invitation	4	C	5	2	1	0	8,920
Noble Kinsman	5	G	5	0	0	0	3,000
Noble Kitten	4	F	6	0	0	0	396
Noble Masterpiece	4	C	5	0	0	0	5,075
Noble Minister	3	C	5	2	0	1	29,670
Noble Monarch	3	G	7	0	1	1	13,540
Noble Moor	5	H	5	0	0	0	54
Noble Place	3	F	6	1	2	0	22,640
Noble Proposal	3	C	2	0	0	0	174
Noble Ruler	6	G	7	1	2	0	27,345
Noble Scarlet	5	M	9	1	0	0	3,522
Noble Season	4	G	14	0	1	3	4,905
Noble Silence	3	C	2	0	1	0	11,604
Noble Spread	5	M	4	2	0	0	15,300
Noble Steed	2	C	1	0	0	0	95
Noble Strike	5	M	6	1	0	0	24,183
Noble Tigress	5	M	10	1	0	0	1,458
Noble Trend	5	G	4	0	0	0	285
Noble Warrior	6	H	6	2	2	0	7,442
Noble Wish	5	M	10	1	0	2	26,530
Noble Wizard	7	G	1	1	0	0	5,640
Noble Words	3	G	4	0	0	0	770
Noblest	4	G	8	1	2	1	50,000
Nobody Home	5	M	3	0	1	0	1,800
Nobody Knows	7	G	8	1	1	1	5,056
Nobody Picked Five	7	G	12	3	2	0	24,416
Nobody Say Nobody	7	G	14	2	2	1	12,895
Nobodyknowsbut Ed	5	H	11	0	4	3	19,480
Nobodys Listening	5	H	14	0	2	1	25,470
Nobu Special	2	G	2	0	0	1	1,920
Nobucksfortuck	3	G	4	0	0	0	3,330
Noches De Rosa (CHI)	5	M	5	2	1	1	192,860
Nocturnal Vision	4	C	6	0	1	1	3,063
Nocturnal Visitor	6	H	20	1	5	2	17,595
Nodaway Star	4	G	9	0	0	0	500
Nodoubtadude	7	G	19	2	4	4	13,691
Noeasyjob	7	G	10	3	3	1	35,732
Noexuse	2	C	2	0	0	0	230
Nofair Warning	3	F	13	2	2	1	11,008
Nogotahalo	4	G	5	1	2	1	26,780
Noi'manangel	4	F	12	1	2	1	6,676
Noinbetweeners	5	G	7	1	0	1	26,460
Noir Et Rouge	3	C	4	0	1	0	11,240
Noise Maker	2	C	5	0	0	1	2,180
Noisette	3	F	7	3	0	2	95,030
Noite	3	F	6	1	0	2	56,225
Nojokeownersbroke	5	H	1	0	0	0	0
Nokoma	4	G	11	2	2	1	31,360
Nolad	3	G	13	1	1	0	9,697
Nolan S	3	G	4	0	0	0	490
Noles	4	C	6	0	1	0	3,625
Nolichucky Jack	3	G	2	0	0	0	45
Nolimitbutthesky	3	C	2	0	0	0	109
Nolimosforyou	3	C	15	3	2	1	48,390
Nolovefortrucks	4	G	16	2	3	3	39,570
Nomadic Actor	3	G	12	1	3	1	23,870
Nominee	3	G	6	2	0	1	7,740
Nomissen Target	3	G	8	1	1	2	13,957
Nomisstaken Kris	4	G	10	1	1	2	13,873
Nomistakeaboutit	2	F	1	0	0	0	0
Nomo Questions	7	M	13	0	0	1	1,832
Nomobankers	6	H	13	0	2	0	1,605
Nomonynomonynomony	2	C	4	1	1	1	23,400
Nomorebills	3	C	1	0	1	0	1,425
Nomoredepazit	2	C	1	0	0	0	0
Nomoreseconds	6	H	5	0	0	0	400
Nomoreskoal	6	G	11	4	1	1	11,293
Non Descript	6	H	5	1	1	0	4,065
Non Sibi	3	F	6	1	3	1	26,300
Non Stop Action	3	G	2	0	0	0	120
Non Stop Country	3	C	1	0	0	0	315
Non Stop Scott	5	H	6	0	2	1	3,865
Nona Nona	3	F	16	0	1	1	2,910
Nonameit	4	C	10	0	1	3	4,175
Nonami	3	C	3	0	0	0	200
None But the Brave	2	C	2	0	0	0	0
Nonnegotiable	4	C	8	0	0	1	6,490
Nonno Guido	4	G	12	0	0	0	3,060
Nonothillary	2	F	3	0	0	0	250
Nonour	3	F	12	2	0	1	40,604
Nonrecourse	6	M	7	2	1	1	17,504
Nonstop Jesse	4	G	2	0	0	0	73
Nonsuch Bay	4	F	9	2	1	4	188,616
Noo Noo	4	F	14	1	2	1	14,280
Noodles	4	G	6	1	0	1	5,193
Noodlette	3	F	11	1	4	1	26,700
Nooligan	2	C	1	0	0	0	118
Noon Affair	6	G	12	1	4	0	56,200

Horse	Age	Sex	Sts	1st	2d	3d	Won
Noon Doll Three	2	F	1	0	1	0	5,240
Noon Meeting	4	F	4	2	1	0	22,025
Noon Time Dancer	3	F	8	3	1	0	47,200
Noonday Sun	11	G	1	0	0	0	40
Nooney Cake	6	M	4	0	1	1	4,680
Noordinarylove	3	F	2	0	1	1	4,800
Noorooma	5	M	4	0	0	0	450
Nopaynenogain	4	G	19	2	2	1	3,527
Nor Do Well	4	G	8	0	1	0	1,203
Nora Dooley	3	F	11	1	3	3	15,335
Nora Ellen	4	F	4	1	1	0	7,475
Nordan's Image	5	G	14	1	2	3	14,875
Nordansa	2	F	2	0	0	1	1,298
Nordic Cat	3	F	1	0	0	0	38
Nordic Hope	5	M	3	0	1	1	2,168
Nordic Lass	3	F	19	4	1	4	42,231
Nordic Native	3	C	6	0	0	0	493
Nordic Trapper	5	H	13	1	0	0	4,970
Nordique	3	F	1	0	0	0	0
Noreena the Great	6	M	11	0	0	1	5,560
Norfolk Knight	4	G	14	5	3	0	245,939
Norjet	4	C	13	6	1	2	59,967
Norlina	4	C	6	0	0	0	1,397
Norlos	8	G	19	3	2	4	34,540
Normally	3	F	13	2	3	2	10,444
Norman Creek	4	G	8	0	0	1	3,015
Norman One	4	G	10	2	1	2	11,797
Norman Vincent	4	G	1	0	0	0	545
Normandy Beach	7	G	12	3	0	4	61,260
Normandy Gold	5	G	9	2	2	0	27,540
Norman's Boy	6	H	10	0	0	3	2,151
Normans Speshul	8	G	17	0	1	0	1,046
Norms Destiny	5	G	4	2	0	2	9,470
Norm's Fire Light	4	G	4	0	0	2	1,680
Norm's Mistake	2	F	3	0	0	1	1,093
Noromeo	4	F	8	1	1	1	15,754
Norqueen	5	M	2	0	0	0	168
Norris Cut	6	G	4	0	1	0	2,790
Nors' Proud Birdie	3	G	15	0	1	3	8,510
Norte	3	G	4	1	1	1	4,770
North	4	C	17	2	1	2	22,799
North and South	7	G	15	3	6	1	17,487
North Broad	3	C	11	2	2	1	59,170
North Broadway	5	G	13	1	1	2	11,093
North Brooklyn	4	C	12	0	2	2	31,592
North by Six	3	F	2	2	0	0	33,550
North by West	5	G	2	0	0	0	0
North Cascade	6	G	5	0	0	2	672
North Coast Gold	4	C	6	0	0	0	348
North Decoder	3	F	8	1	1	0	11,575
North Duck	7	H	12	2	0	2	9,867
North East Academy	10	G	4	0	0	0	0
North East Bay	2	F	1	0	0	0	0
North East Belle	4	F	8	1	0	2	13,009
North East Bound	7	G	6	0	1	0	10,440
North East Star	3	F	4	0	0	0	1,270
North Flare	6	G	7	0	3	0	3,516
North for Her	6	M	1	0	0	0	0
North Freedom	8	G	12	0	2	2	3,368
North Hills	6	G	19	1	2	2	20,561
North Jersey Girl	3	F	3	0	0	1	950
North Man	4	G	7	0	0	1	4,212
North Mill	3	G	8	4	0	1	37,652
North of Dixie	4	G	10	2	1	3	18,600
North of Normal	5	G	12	2	0	0	17,756
North of Paris	5	G	6	1	0	3	8,100
North of Rio	3	F	11	3	1	1	19,890
North of Six	4	C	9	2	2	2	61,460
North Place	2	C	1	0	0	0	60
North Ponche	4	G	9	2	0	0	10,423
North Power	7	H	8	2	1	0	10,510
North Salem	9	H	13	2	1	1	25,834
North Star Love	3	G	7	1	0	2	3,503
North Texas	5	G	1	0	0	0	0
North Tide	6	G	8	1	0	0	6,087
North to Alaska	6	G	15	0	3	0	4,277
North View	8	M	3	0	0	0	0
North West Bay	2	F	4	0	0	1	2,596
North West Jazz	3	F	2	0	0	0	0
North Win	4	G	3	0	0	0	179
Northbound Sally	7	M	10	1	2	3	16,131
Northdrop	3	C	13	3	1	0	23,460
Northeast Winds	5	M	7	0	2	0	10,017
Northeaster	5	M	7	0	0	0	1,105
Northend	5	G	13	0	1	1	10,220
Northend of Boston	5	G	16	2	3	1	19,418
Northern Ace	5	G	12	2	2	2	21,865
Northern Acre	4	F	15	3	2	1	23,480
Northern Affair	3	C	8	4	0	1	62,980
Northern Air	3	C	10	4	2	0	135,020
Northern Alert	4	G	15	0	1	3	18,920
Northern Anziyan	3	C	1	0	0	0	0
Northern Apple	4	G	9	1	0	1	14,000
Northern Arrow	5	M	3	2	0	1	3,750
Northern Art	6	H	7	0	0	0	700
Northern Autumn	10	G	13	2	3	3	3,173
Northern Baby Bag	4	C	3	0	0	0	900
Northern Ballad	2	C	3	0	0	0	3,960
Northern Baquero	2	G	7	0	1	1	1,440
Northern Baucis	6	G	24	1	6	2	9,790
Northern Bishop	4	F	12	0	0	5	10,717
Northern Blaze	6	M	8	1	1	1	2,272
Northern Boots	3	G	4	0	0	0	0
Northern Brass	4	F	2	0	0	0	130
Northern Brave	4	G	3	1	0	0	11,572
Northern Broadway	15	G	7	1	0	0	2,620
Northern Buck	2	C	2	1	0	0	3,906
Northern Castle	5	H	5	0	1	0	1,500
Northern Catch	4	G	12	2	2	2	39,860
Northern Charger	6	G	8	0	1	0	1,417
Northern Cheyenne	5	H	6	1	1	2	3,288
Northern Colony	5	G	8	3	1	1	12,324
Northern Commander	3	C	5	0	0	0	486
Northern Computur	5	M	2	0	0	0	0
Northern Cowboy	5	G	3	0	0	0	0
Northern Cross	6	M	12	0	1	1	5,929
Northern Crown (NZ)	8	G	8	1	1	0	17,766
Northern Damascus	5	G	9	1	2	1	4,200
Northern Dandy	2	C	3	0	1	0	3,191
Northern Darkness	4	C	12	0	1	1	4,363
Northern Deelite	2	G	1	0	0	0	75
Northern Deluxe	5	M	3	0	0	1	3,380
Northern Deposit	4	F	9	2	1	3	20,597
Northern Deputy	2	F	1	0	0	0	0
Northern Desert	4	G	2	0	0	0	0
Northern Discover	3	G	8	2	0	1	23,400
Northern Dove	2	F	2	0	0	0	195
Northern Du	6	G	2	0	0	0	0
Northern Duck	6	G	6	0	0	0	184
Northern Energy	5	M	6	2	0	1	40,860
Northern Executive	3	G	7	0	2	0	26,654
Northern Exposure	3	F	5	1	0	1	28,330
Northern Fantasy	7	H	2	0	0	0	1,560
Northern Frolic	2	F	2	0	0	0	0
Northern Game	3	G	8	2	0	1	25,925
Northern Gift	6	H	13	2	1	1	9,720
Northern Girl	5	M	2	0	0	0	0
Northern Glow	3	C	1	0	0	0	0
Northern Gold	5	G	11	1	0	0	9,940
Northern Groom	2	C	1	0	0	0	0
Northern Heat	2	C	4	1	0	0	4,170
Northern Heights	2	F	2	0	0	0	665
Northern Honey	3	F	9	1	0	1	3,081
Northern Indian	3	G	15	2	4	1	18,071
Northern Intruder	7	H	4	1	0	0	1,315
Northern Joe	2	C	1	0	0	1	4,444
Northern Johnny	7	G	10	1	0	1	8,503
Northern Knight	10	G	4	1	0	1	2,736
Northern Land	7	G	5	2	1	0	3,396
Northern Leopard	5	G	4	2	0	0	28,200
Northern Line	5	H	3	0	1	0	4,425
Northern Luck	10	G	10	0	0	2	2,198
Northern Master	3	C	5	2	1	0	2,875
Northern Mint	5	M	1	0	0	0	44
Northern Mission	2	F	7	0	1	1	3,650
Northern Morning	4	C	7	1	0	0	3,102
Northern Most Star	4	F	6	1	2	1	10,632
Northern Neechitoo	6	M	9	4	3	0	109,068

Horse	Age	Sex	Sts	1st	2d	3d	Won
Northern Nile	3	F	13	2	2	3	15,946
Northern Notebook	6	M	7	0	1	0	1,803
Northern Pastry	5	M	3	1	0	0	5,892
Northern Quest	3	F	11	0	1	0	4,530
Northern Rain	3	F	11	1	4	1	15,070
Northern Request	4	G	17	1	4	4	12,058
Northern Rex	9	G	6	0	1	2	1,942
Northern Ricky	7	G	5	1	2	0	2,807
Northern Riviera	6	M	8	0	1	1	1,572
Northern Rock (JPN)	5	G	10	3	2	0	162,256
Northern Root	9	G	12	2	1	2	5,522
Northern Rumor	6	G	10	0	0	1	1,434
Northern Run	4	G	1	0	1	0	5,250
Northern Sands	3	F	4	0	0	0	0
Northern Satan	4	G	17	4	1	1	14,444
Northern Scene	2	G	1	0	0	0	0
Northern Scout	2	G	7	0	0	0	3,905
Northern Sioux	8	G	16	2	2	3	23,047
Northern Sleet	6	G	9	1	1	0	4,150
Northern Son	6	G	9	1	3	1	12,235
Northern Spring (IRE)	7	H	1	0	0	0	0
Northern Stealth	2	C	3	1	0	1	7,490
Northern Stepper	5	G	9	0	0	2	1,235
Northern Streak	6	M	16	1	0	3	20,740
Northern Stride	2	G	3	1	0	0	1,400
Northern Sword	3	F	1	0	0	0	0
Northern Symbol	6	H	1	0	0	0	400
Northern Task	9	G	1	0	0	0	600
Northern Thinking	7	H	6	1	2	0	10,000
Northern Threat	3	F	3	0	1	1	3,255
Northern Thrill	3	G	6	0	0	0	636
Northern Thriller	3	G	3	0	0	0	560
Northern Tide	7	G	6	0	2	1	10,962
Northern Tune	6	H	5	0	0	0	1,290
Northern Turnstone	5	M	8	2	0	1	34,004
Northern Twinkle	6	M	2	0	0	0	228
Northern Tye	5	M	1	0	0	0	0
Northern Venture	5	M	9	0	0	2	1,930
Northern Vice	6	G	5	0	0	1	1,051
Northern Victor	2	G	3	0	0	0	450
Northern Wager	5	G	7	2	2	0	5,955
Northern Won	4	G	11	2	2	2	24,700
Northern Wood	5	M	1	0	0	0	750
Northern Woods	7	G	14	2	1	0	5,230
Northern Yukon	5	M	8	0	0	0	158
Northernbluesjett	5	H	3	0	0	0	177
Northernprospector	10	G	19	2	4	3	35,057
Northglen	5	M	5	1	2	1	14,780
Northlander	3	C	17	4	1	3	40,327
Northlands Fancy	2	F	4	1	0	1	6,378
Northland's Gift	5	G	10	1	2	1	16,775
North's Fortune	4	C	4	0	0	0	264
Northshore Road	2	C	2	0	0	0	252
Northside	5	G	5	0	1	1	3,885
Northwest Attitude	2	G	6	0	1	0	2,650
Northwest Hill	5	G	10	5	1	1	114,500
Northwest Wind	4	G	8	1	2	2	11,925
Northwestern	3	C	2	0	0	0	217
Norton	4	G	9	2	1	0	10,429
Norton Peak	2	F	2	0	0	1	1,487
Norton Street	6	G	5	2	0	0	8,790
Nortouch	4	G	8	0	2	2	10,590
Norway Hope	4	F	13	1	1	2	11,047
Nor'wester	2	F	1	0	0	0	2,280
Norwoods	3	F	2	0	0	0	103
Nosara	8	H	11	1	1	0	24,543
Nose The Trade (GB)	5	G	4	1	1	0	62,000
Nose to It	2	C	1	1	0	0	15,400
Nose to Nose	5	G	7	0	0	0	0
Nosetothe	5	H	9	1	0	1	8,340
Nosey Shirley	3	F	10	0	0	0	2,527
Nosho	12	G	11	1	2	3	2,454
Nosotros Dos	5	G	19	4	1	1	14,957
Nostalgiaonmymind	9	G	8	0	0	0	421
Nosupeforyou	5	G	15	4	5	2	79,058
Nosy Tanikely	2	F	3	2	0	0	35,540
Not a Bad Boy	2	C	5	0	1	0	7,540
Not a Dollar Off	4	G	8	0	0	2	1,396
Not a Frown	6	M	13	2	2	2	13,283
Not a Problem	4	F	8	1	0	1	12,495
Not a Question	3	G	9	1	1	0	3,962
Not a Rookie	3	F	5	0	0	0	547
Not Acceptable	5	H	11	0	0	0	910
Not Accountable	4	G	18	2	3	3	31,352
Not Again Dan	2	G	3	0	0	1	6,666
Not Again Jansen	7	G	5	0	0	0	330
Not an Illusion	4	F	6	0	0	1	1,889
Not an Ordinaryjoe	3	C	6	0	0	0	225
Not Any Man	3	G	6	0	0	2	3,970
Not Dasher	5	G	4	1	0	0	880
Not Exactly	2	C	2	0	0	0	0
Not for a Million	7	G	3	0	0	0	206
Not for Me	5	G	20	3	6	2	102,050
Not for Me (ARG)	6	G	1	0	0	0	7,500
Not for Nana	5	M	12	1	3	1	25,176
Not for Profit	3	G	11	0	0	0	6,870
Not for Sam	5	H	6	1	1	2	41,245
Not Happening	6	G	12	3	3	2	14,830
Not Him Me	6	H	1	0	0	0	0
Not Impossible	5	M	13	0	1	2	14,015
Not in Order	7	M	11	0	1	3	18,325
Not Much	4	G	9	2	2	0	23,894
Not My Style	4	F	8	0	0	0	2,078
Not Paid For	3	F	9	1	0	3	11,687
Not Phone (ARG)	5	H	3	1	0	1	41,300
Not So Friendly	2	G	8	2	2	0	16,310
Not So Quiet	3	G	6	0	0	1	1,765
Not So Rough R N	3	F	1	0	1	0	7,280
Not So Wicked	3	F	4	0	0	0	292
Not Talking	5	G	11	0	1	3	4,035
Not too Sweet	3	G	2	0	0	0	1,575
Not Yet a Lady	2	F	5	1	0	1	4,690
Not You Me	3	C	5	0	0	0	897
Notable Beaux	3	C	8	1	0	2	9,060
Notable Craft	7	M	8	0	3	1	20,240
Notable Editor	4	C	13	2	4	1	36,238
Notable Kindness	2	F	5	2	1	0	31,070
Notable Knight	3	C	3	1	0	0	6,515
Notable Max	3	C	1	0	0	0	0
Notable Okie	3	G	8	2	2	1	45,878
Notable Secrets	4	G	9	2	1	0	17,346
Notable Sweep	3	C	15	2	2	2	27,791
Notable Weave	5	G	11	1	1	1	4,998
Notably Classy	3	F	3	1	0	1	2,759
Notably Frosty	7	G	15	2	1	4	52,390
Notably Gold	4	F	2	0	0	0	114
Notably Mystic	3	F	4	1	1	1	11,720
Notably Rare	5	H	4	1	0	0	5,695
Notate	4	G	21	3	3	2	13,511
Notatear	4	F	5	0	0	0	0
Notatfirst	3	C	4	0	0	0	3,280
Notavaca	2	C	3	0	0	1	1,430
Note Appeal	2	C	4	0	1	1	4,495
Note d'Or	3	F	12	2	1	2	11,597
Note Him Well	4	C	6	1	0	0	6,460
Note Taker	4	F	5	2	1	0	51,800
Note the Power	4	F	6	1	0	0	5,984
Noteable	8	M	16	3	2	2	77,200
Notes and Quotes	5	M	11	3	2	1	34,393
Noteworthy	3	C	8	0	3	1	13,190
Notforloveormoney	6	G	3	0	0	0	1,150
Notgoodenough	4	F	6	0	0	0	355
Notherdayinpardise	5	M	13	4	1	2	33,894
Nothin But Time	4	G	8	0	0	0	942
Nothinbutagoodtime	3	F	1	0	0	1	1,030
Nothinbutbadnews	9	G	14	0	4	1	6,872
Nothing But	4	F	6	2	1	1	38,965
Nothing But Luck	5	G	2	0	0	1	1,800
Nothing But Speed	5	G	1	0	0	0	0
Nothing Fancy	2	F	3	1	0	0	5,400
Nothing Flat	4	G	12	1	2	1	80,391
Nothing Left	4	G	7	3	0	1	35,680
Nothing Less	2	F	4	0	1	0	4,660
Nothing to Lose	3	C	2	2	0	0	120,000
Nothing Trendy	5	H	16	3	1	4	18,889
Nothing Wasted	4	G	12	3	2	1	44,710
Nothinglefttogive	5	G	9	1	1	1	4,848
Nothinlac'n	2	G	8	0	0	1	3,140

Horse	Age	Sex	Sts	1st	2d	3d	Won
Notice the Magic	6	G	3	1	1	0	24,192
Noticion (ARG)	6	H	3	0	0	1	3,520
Notimetomyself	3	G	1	0	0	0	0
Notinthecontract	2	C	1	0	0	0	1,764
Notion	7	G	19	1	6	0	11,911
Notjustanothertune	4	G	3	0	0	0	389
Notloc	2	C	3	0	1	0	3,654
Notmyfault	3	F	7	1	3	1	55,122
Notonetoquit	2	C	2	1	1	0	11,400
Notorious Bandito	4	G	14	2	3	2	21,471
Notorious Native	5	H	2	0	0	0	414
Notorious Rogue	2	C	4	1	0	2	68,730
Notoriously Elite	5	G	3	2	1	0	8,466
Notquietforlong	2	C	1	0	0	0	695
Notreallykissable	2	F	2	0	0	0	180
Notrestraintable	3	F	5	1	2	0	28,940
Notsoclever	4	C	14	0	1	1	9,224
Notsosaintly	7	G	11	0	0	2	2,476
Notting Hill (BRZ)	4	F	3	0	0	0	18,660
Nottinghill Gate	6	G	12	3	1	1	17,358
Nottooshabby	5	H	10	0	2	2	3,503
Nottoworry	2	C	2	0	0	0	0
Nott's Gold	3	G	7	0	3	1	9,730
Notus	4	G	8	1	2	3	10,953
Notyetbrette	3	F	5	0	0	0	298
Nou Graha	6	H	2	0	0	0	310
Nouf	4	G	4	0	1	1	2,145
Nouveau Riche	5	G	11	4	3	2	32,779
Nouvelle	5	M	1	0	0	0	400
Nova Blanca	3	F	7	0	1	1	5,728
Nova Ice	2	G	2	0	0	0	214
Nova Princess	6	M	1	0	0	0	24
Nova Sin	7	G	8	0	1	0	4,824
Novantuno	3	C	9	1	2	4	93,118
Nova's Star	2	C	1	0	0	0	0
Novecientos	3	F	8	3	1	1	48,345
Novel Robin	5	M	13	1	0	2	5,129
Novel T Dreamer	3	G	12	4	2	2	73,599
Novelado (CHI)	5	G	7	0	1	1	8,430
Novelista	2	F	9	0	1	1	6,812
Novello	3	C	2	0	0	0	0
Novelty Sue	4	F	7	0	0	1	1,169
November	5	G	1	0	0	0	1,800
November Payne	5	G	20	4	2	1	19,381
November Rose	4	F	10	3	2	0	18,050
November's Fury	2	G	2	1	1	0	7,280
Novia	4	F	3	0	0	0	475
Novice	3	F	5	2	2	0	39,020
Novice Prince	6	G	8	0	2	2	5,822
Novus Scofus	8	G	11	0	1	2	6,503
Novwar	5	G	9	2	0	1	10,535
Now Appearing	5	H	5	0	0	0	100
Now Im Cookin	5	G	17	1	1	1	7,051
Now Navajo	7	G	8	0	0	1	1,319
Now Now	3	F	3	0	0	0	182
Now Playing	5	G	8	3	1	1	57,489
Now Rock Around	7	M	5	0	0	0	0
Now Voyager (NZ)	7	G	4	0	0	2	14,560
Nowinedon'tpanic	8	G	4	0	0	0	86
Nowinefornana	5	M	2	0	0	0	550
Nowrass (GB)	7	G	5	1	0	1	69,545
Nowucmenowudon't	4	G	9	1	2	2	8,161
Nowush	7	G	6	0	0	1	2,800
Nowyouseeit	4	G	11	1	3	1	71,499
Noyana	4	F	13	2	2	2	26,445
Nsynctoo	5	G	7	1	1	0	10,049
Ntombi	4	F	1	0	0	0	0
Nu Cat	4	G	10	2	3	0	40,281
Nu Inspector	4	C	1	0	0	0	43
Nuangola	5	H	11	1	3	0	14,250
Nuclear Debate	8	G	6	0	0	3	55,974
Nuclear War	2	G	1	1	0	0	18,000
Nudanseur	2	C	1	0	0	0	125
Nudgito	3	G	4	0	0	0	80
Nudubya	3	G	6	0	1	0	2,920
Nuevo	4	F	10	0	0	1	1,691
Nugget Point	2	F	2	0	0	0	1,500
Nugget'o Gold	4	F	11	1	3	2	17,476
Nugrayontheblock	4	G	8	1	2	2	26,025
Nuit	3	F	9	1	2	3	11,550
Nuit de Siam (FR)	6	M	5	2	1	0	42,520
Nulli Secundus	3	C	11	1	1	2	5,218
Numattic	3	G	6	1	1	0	15,865
Number	2	C	2	0	0	0	390
Number Juan	2	C	2	0	1	0	12,740
Number One Cat	4	F	6	3	2	0	126,180
Number One Hammer	5	G	15	1	0	3	22,391
Number One Pegasus	4	C	6	1	1	0	7,070
Number One Sheikh	6	G	15	3	5	5	59,604
Number One Son	5	H	5	0	1	1	2,516
Number Twentythree	4	C	2	0	0	0	0
Number Two	3	G	9	1	2	2	6,148
Numbered Gold	5	M	21	1	1	5	8,076
Numbers Plus	3	C	5	0	0	0	0
Numbers Runner	6	G	7	0	0	0	325
Numdiddy	6	H	10	1	0	2	4,055
Numerian	6	G	11	0	3	2	25,224
Numerically	2	F	3	1	0	1	9,810
Numero	5	G	13	2	3	2	29,685
Numero Um	3	C	1	0	0	0	125
Numerous Affairs	3	G	2	0	1	0	3,435
Numerous Attack	3	G	8	0	0	0	449
Numerous Coins	4	C	2	0	0	0	0
Numerous Content	2	C	2	0	0	0	0
Numerous Dancer	3	G	3	0	0	0	0
Numerous Kidz	4	F	20	2	4	5	44,770
Numerous Lady	3	F	6	0	0	1	7,727
Numerous Moves	2	F	4	1	0	1	8,540
Numerous Rages	2	G	9	0	1	2	5,991
Numerous Squares	2	G	5	1	2	1	10,675
Numerous Times	6	H	4	0	1	1	35,249
Numerousasthestars	3	F	8	1	3	0	50,476
Nun Left (IRE)	5	M	3	0	0	2	4,282
Nun On the Run	6	M	10	4	4	0	70,690
Nunatall (GB)	4	F	1	1	0	0	42,000
Nunavut Rose	6	M	9	0	0	1	360
Nunsense	3	F	1	0	0	0	0
Nunziata	4	F	18	3	2	2	40,207
Nureyev's Knight	5	G	1	0	0	0	0
Nureyev's Niad	5	M	5	0	1	1	2,053
Nurey's Thunder	5	G	7	3	0	1	71,350
Nurse Betty	2	F	2	0	0	0	0
Nurse Culkin	2	F	4	0	2	0	20,090
Nurse Dora	4	F	1	0	0	0	0
Nurse Laura	6	M	10	0	2	2	6,246
Nurse Margurita	6	M	11	1	2	1	30,035
Nurse Peyton	4	F	1	0	0	0	38
Nurse Robin	4	F	13	3	0	0	11,087
Nurse Sharon	5	M	8	0	4	1	18,623
Nurse Type	4	F	8	0	0	1	3,963
Nut Lovin	2	F	1	0	0	0	0
Nutbush	5	M	6	3	0	1	47,211
Nutcase	4	F	5	0	1	0	1,348
Nuthin But Kuntry	6	G	4	0	0	0	160
Nutn But the Truth	3	F	10	1	0	1	4,982
Nuts and Chews	8	G	2	0	0	0	80
Nutter Bold Ivor	9	G	8	1	0	0	2,211
Nuttin But Net	4	F	1	0	0	0	1,860
Nuttin Special	2	F	2	0	0	0	0
Nutty Cat	3	F	3	0	0	0	1,230
Nutty Rene'	9	M	1	0	0	0	300
Nuttyboom	3	G	8	3	1	2	21,690
Nuvem	3	F	6	1	1	1	42,760
Nycity	3	G	11	1	1	3	24,204
Nykee	2	F	1	0	0	0	0
Nylo	3	G	5	1	0	0	7,806
Nypuddles	4	F	9	1	1	0	26,187
Nystar	3	F	6	1	1	0	59,685
Nystateofmind	5	H	5	0	1	1	4,892
Nytone	4	C	7	1	0	1	4,243
Nyuk Nyuk Nyuk	2	G	1	1	0	0	35,280
O' Actor	3	G	9	1	0	3	9,604
O and A	3	F	5	1	0	0	14,222
O B Girl One	4	F	9	1	1	2	7,687
O C Storm	4	F	2	0	0	0	910
O' classic One	4	G	10	1	0	1	6,265
O Could I	3	F	7	2	0	4	20,040
O Darlin Boy	4	G	12	2	1	3	14,378

Horse	Age	Sex	Sts	1st	2d	3d	Won
O D's Accelerator	2	G	2	0	0	0	475
O Golly Gee	9	G	14	2	4	4	21,042
O Henry	3	C	3	0	0	0	0
O Howey Beatum	3	G	11	1	3	1	11,387
O Howrude	4	F	6	2	0	1	29,208
O K Caracey	4	F	16	3	1	4	29,330
O K With Me	6	H	16	3	3	1	50,514
O Kudsai	3	F	9	1	0	2	9,345
O Linda Lu	4	F	2	0	0	1	900
O Lo	6	M	4	1	0	0	16,800
O' Murphy	4	C	4	0	0	0	0
O My Maria	3	F	3	0	1	2	7,410
O Nectar	3	F	6	1	0	0	23,460
O' Ririn	5	M	19	2	3	3	13,441
O Sequoyah	4	G	10	1	1	0	5,895
O Sweet P.	6	M	1	0	0	0	0
O' till Dawn	3	F	6	2	0	0	12,420
O U Bet	4	F	10	2	5	2	67,053
O U Kid	4	F	6	0	1	0	2,603
O Whatever	5	G	5	0	1	0	572
O Zone Layer	2	C	1	1	0	0	35,280
O. B. Quiet	6	H	1	1	0	0	7,440
O. K. Carby	8	G	6	1	2	1	6,175
O. K. Corral	3	F	11	1	2	5	29,141
O. K. Mikie	2	G	5	3	0	1	50,700
Oak Hall	7	G	4	1	1	1	84,125
Oak Hill	3	C	4	1	0	1	46,350
Oak Run	6	M	12	0	0	0	5,577
Oakhurst	9	H	9	2	1	0	11,060
Oakies Little Star	3	F	6	1	1	1	3,385
Oakland Boy	4	C	3	0	0	0	0
Oaks	4	F	5	1	0	0	5,016
Oaks Day Lily	3	F	15	3	2	2	22,085
Oaks Secret	6	G	3	0	0	1	1,159
Oakton	3	F	1	0	0	0	0
Oarsman	4	C	3	0	0	0	366
Oasis Dream (GB)	3	C	5	2	1	0	524,836
Oath of Office	3	C	13	5	3	4	84,120
Oatka Apollos Gold	4	C	5	0	0	0	1,608
Oatka Idas Destiny	4	F	7	3	0	0	40,920
Oatka Justa Prince	4	G	6	0	0	0	5,220
Oatka Little Girl	5	M	7	0	1	1	1,943
Oatka Trail Faith	3	F	3	0	0	0	53
Oatka Trail Joy	3	F	4	0	0	0	106
Oatsville	2	F	7	0	0	0	910
Obeah Man	8	G	8	0	0	1	1,604
Oberlin Yankee	4	C	17	0	3	3	5,684
Obermeister	3	G	12	4	3	1	113,025
Obermutten	2	G	3	0	0	1	2,580
Oberwald	3	G	18	1	4	0	62,280
Obey the Queen	3	F	6	0	0	2	2,123
Obeya	5	M	7	1	1	0	5,817
O'Biffs Bad	4	G	9	1	0	0	3,288
Obill	6	G	11	1	2	2	21,514
Object of Virtue	3	F	7	0	0	3	8,236
O'Blaney	3	F	12	0	1	1	13,290
Oblat	2	C	3	1	0	0	14,436
Obligate	2	F	2	0	0	0	0
Obligation North	4	F	7	1	1	0	14,310
Obligatory	3	F	7	1	0	0	18,225
Obliquity	3	G	4	1	0	0	32,274
Obliterate	3	C	1	0	0	0	0
Oblivious	2	F	4	0	0	2	35,000
Oblivious Alberto	9	G	2	0	0	0	0
Oblong	4	G	5	1	0	1	12,555
O'Bradovich	3	C	11	0	1	2	17,520
Obrien	3	F	6	0	0	0	120
O'Bryan's Luck	5	G	11	1	1	2	14,609
Ob'sbaby B	3	G	3	0	1	0	967
Obsesion Jig	5	G	3	0	0	0	188
Obsessedtoimpress	4	C	6	2	0	1	14,196
Obsidian Glass	5	H	3	0	0	0	0
Obstacle	4	C	1	0	0	0	500
Obstinate	3	F	13	2	1	5	22,968
Obtained	5	G	5	0	1	0	3,180
Obvious Advantage	5	G	3	0	0	0	258
Obvious Outlaw	7	G	5	0	0	0	255
Ocala Bandit	2	G	7	0	3	1	14,400
Ocala Brass	6	G	3	1	0	0	8,100
Ocala Cat	2	C	2	0	0	1	1,400
Ocala Eagle	7	H	7	3	2	0	8,568
Ocala Frost	4	C	5	1	0	1	14,486
Ocala Outlaw	2	C	1	0	0	0	0
Ocala Quaker	2	F	10	1	1	2	12,165
Ocala Signature	5	M	6	0	0	0	391
Ocala Story	5	G	8	0	2	1	9,555
Ocala True	4	F	9	1	1	3	17,003
Ocala's Appeal	4	G	12	2	0	1	12,372
Ocalasecret	4	G	8	2	2	2	11,495
O'Calaway	3	G	13	1	1	2	9,445
Ocali Flash	6	G	18	2	2	2	42,965
O'Cariline Babe	5	M	4	0	0	0	1,640
O'Cat	3	F	8	1	0	4	51,260
O'Cationally Windy	5	H	13	1	5	2	9,464
Occasional Demon	5	M	10	0	3	2	5,087
Occatilla	6	M	12	1	1	0	13,897
Occidental Tourist	4	C	8	2	1	0	33,530
Occult	3	C	9	1	0	0	15,375
Occupied	3	G	18	1	7	1	11,660
Ocean Affair	3	G	3	1	0	0	13,446
Ocean Bun	3	C	1	0	0	0	420
Ocean City	2	C	6	0	0	0	3,500
Ocean Commotion	4	G	8	2	0	0	8,477
Ocean Cove	3	G	6	1	0	2	6,900
Ocean Crossing	3	F	11	2	1	0	20,694
Ocean Drive	3	F	6	2	1	0	159,356
Ocean Effect	3	F	7	3	1	1	34,820
Ocean Fox	3	F	4	3	0	0	11,850
Ocean Front	6	G	6	1	0	0	68,775
Ocean Gate	5	M	8	0	0	1	1,420
Ocean Intrigue	4	G	12	1	1	4	17,238
Ocean Jet	5	M	6	0	0	0	170
Ocean Liner	10	H	3	0	0	0	0
Ocean Locater	8	G	9	0	1	2	5,095
Ocean Miss	4	F	6	2	0	0	7,446
Ocean Park	3	C	14	2	3	2	61,920
Ocean Quest	4	G	9	1	4	1	14,905
Ocean Ranger	3	C	11	1	0	0	9,980
Ocean Silk	3	F	8	2	3	1	228,430
Ocean Symphony	2	C	1	1	0	0	7,080
Ocean Terrace	3	C	4	2	0	0	141,200
Ocean Wild	6	M	5	0	0	1	5,489
Oceana Flyer	7	M	3	0	0	0	0
Oceana Miss	2	F	5	1	0	1	9,905
Oceania	2	F	5	0	1	1	5,080
Oceanic	3	G	16	1	5	3	28,570
Oceans Fair	4	C	3	0	0	0	192
Oceans of Love	4	F	11	1	2	4	17,929
Oceans Seven	3	G	5	2	0	1	25,455
Ocean's Spray	3	F	2	0	0	0	1,650
Ocean's Top Gun	4	G	3	0	0	0	387
Ocelot	3	F	14	3	1	2	27,030
Ochoco Kitten	5	M	1	0	0	0	50
Ocnus (ARG)	5	H	7	3	0	0	29,040
Oconomowoc	4	G	10	0	0	1	1,011
Oconto	10	G	3	0	0	0	0
Ocoonita	2	F	6	1	1	1	13,480
Octagon	3	F	8	2	2	1	49,920
Octibbeha	3	F	5	0	0	2	2,968
October Blues	4	G	9	4	1	1	14,443
October Dawn	4	F	2	0	0	0	0
October Dreamer	5	M	7	0	0	2	2,636
October Glory (IRE)	2	F	1	0	0	0	195
October Ice	4	F	4	1	0	0	4,095
October Optimist	5	M	7	1	0	1	19,815
October Storm	3	G	6	1	1	0	6,235
Octothorpe	3	F	3	0	0	0	330
Oda Mar	4	G	3	1	0	0	2,750
Odaat Cat	3	C	4	1	0	1	5,195
Odabella	3	F	2	0	0	0	35
Odacious	4	G	3	0	0	0	0
O'Danceagain	4	F	2	0	0	0	227
O'Dassuny	5	G	5	1	0	2	14,208
Odbeaslewpy	7	G	5	1	1	0	3,070
Odd Number	3	F	5	1	1	0	17,610
Odd Ree Jay	2	F	1	0	0	0	0
Odd Testamony	4	G	8	1	3	1	16,865
Odds Against	6	H	3	0	0	0	244

RECORDS OF HORSES

Horse	Age	Sex	Sts	1st	2d	3d	Won	Horse	Age	Sex	Sts	1st	2d	3d	Won
Odds On	2	C	3	1	1	0	39,200	Oh My Harlan	3	G	13	3	1	4	31,707
Oddsonjack	8	G	7	0	1	0	4,804	Oh My Heck	2	F	2	0	0	0	224
Ode to Joe	3	G	10	1	1	3	13,950	Oh My Honor	3	F	2	0	1	0	2,925
Ode to New York	3	G	1	0	0	0	500	Oh My How Fabulous	3	G	4	0	0	0	130
Odelien	5	G	9	3	1	3	40,390	Oh My Lordie	5	M	7	0	3	1	8,075
Odell	4	G	2	0	0	0	123	Oh My Love	5	M	8	1	0	2	14,540
O'Desadorable	4	F	6	0	1	1	12,360	Oh My Pretty Halo	6	M	2	0	0	0	252
Odie One	4	C	3	0	0	0	0	Oh My Sheerie	3	F	3	0	0	0	312
Odimas	9	G	7	0	0	4	9,220	Oh No Apolo	3	G	4	0	1	0	12,640
Odin the Viking	5	H	4	0	1	0	3,137	Oh Oleg	2	G	5	1	1	2	25,056
Odin's Warrior	6	G	8	0	3	0	1,860	Oh Personality	4	F	8	0	1	0	1,787
Odintsova	4	F	3	0	0	0	120	Oh Pine	3	F	2	0	0	0	2,640
Odyle a Genius	3	G	8	0	0	0	855	Oh Please Louise	4	F	3	0	0	0	0
Oedy's Riches	5	M	10	1	2	3	30,531	Oh Sable	4	F	9	2	1	1	43,980
O'Ell	3	F	12	1	3	0	7,401	Oh Savanna	5	M	2	0	1	1	3,184
Of All Times	2	C	1	0	0	0	0	Oh Say Glory	4	G	19	3	2	2	17,402
Of Legal Age	3	F	7	3	0	1	47,860	Oh Say Vicki	6	M	9	2	3	0	77,990
Ofcenterditchdiggr	2	F	2	0	0	0	278	Oh Say's Pleasure	3	F	6	1	1	2	7,372
Off N Annie	3	F	1	0	0	0	0	Oh So Easy	3	F	12	5	1	2	134,964
Off Shore Prospect	4	C	10	2	2	1	22,108	Oh So Fabulous	11	G	1	0	0	0	186
Off the Glass	4	G	13	3	4	1	47,580	Oh So Ruidoso	6	M	2	0	0	0	0
Off the Island	3	F	11	1	1	0	14,807	Oh So Sultry	3	G	3	0	1	0	4,000
Off the Screen	5	G	9	1	2	1	9,239	Oh Take (BRZ)	5	H	4	0	1	0	14,300
Off to the Opera	4	F	4	0	1	0	10,875	Oh Thank Evans	3	C	5	0	1	0	460
Off Track Firstcat	3	F	8	0	0	0	270	Oh Travis	5	G	2	1	0	0	3,180
Offensive	7	G	5	0	0	0	620	Oh Tri Avalli	2	C	1	0	0	0	60
Offensively	2	F	1	0	0	0	0	Oh What a Cat	3	G	13	1	1	1	4,556
Offhand	4	C	8	0	0	0	829	Oh What a Classic	4	C	3	0	0	0	0
Office At Night	2	F	2	0	0	0	0	Oh What a Doll	5	M	9	2	4	2	33,027
Office Ghost	3	C	13	4	3	2	64,460	Oh Wow	2	G	3	0	1	0	4,740
Office Mail	4	G	8	3	0	0	9,045	Oh Yah D J	5	G	7	0	0	2	1,023
Officer Loan	4	F	1	0	1	0	1,640	Ohbedawn	3	F	3	0	0	0	0
Officer Nasty	3	G	7	1	1	1	9,244	Ohforcraftsakes	4	F	4	0	1	0	11,780
Officer's Sword	5	G	12	6	1	2	93,120	Ohio Ann	4	F	1	0	0	0	0
Official Account	2	F	2	0	0	0	0	Ohio Bob	3	G	2	0	0	0	756
Offlee Wild	3	C	7	1	0	2	152,400	Ohio Don	2	G	1	0	0	0	85
Offshore Storm	8	G	2	0	0	0	0	Ohio Prospect	3	F	2	0	0	0	360
Offspring	5	G	13	0	2	0	7,063	Ohio Rose	2	F	6	1	2	0	11,400
Offtheoldblock	3	F	5	1	1	0	19,250	Ohiyesa	2	G	3	0	0	0	470
O'Fire Holler	7	G	12	1	3	1	6,272	Ohmychief	3	F	4	0	0	0	177
O'Fred	6	H	2	1	0	0	5,400	Ohmyfuzzy	3	G	9	1	0	0	7,458
Ofusca Who	5	H	9	1	0	1	1,352	Ohni	3	G	19	0	5	2	15,780
Ogee	3	F	15	1	1	0	9,470	Ohpoos	4	F	14	3	1	1	17,137
Ogeechee	2	F	2	0	0	0	0	Ohsoamerican	5	M	13	2	1	0	10,135
Oggi	3	F	12	2	3	3	66,510	Ohtobe	4	G	16	1	4	5	5,476
Ogilia (GB)	6	M	3	0	0	0	283	Ohtobeonbroadway	4	G	2	0	0	0	0
Oglala	4	F	3	0	0	0	160	Ohwhataparade	2	G	10	2	0	2	38,290
Oglala Sue	5	M	6	1	3	1	63,142	Oil Driller	7	G	9	0	0	0	627
Ogle	5	M	10	1	2	0	13,758	Oil Man	9	G	16	0	4	3	3,808
O'Greedy	2	G	8	0	2	3	10,110	Oil Strike	6	G	11	0	3	3	4,000
Ogygian's Rose	2	F	3	2	0	0	4,930	Oiltemp	6	H	7	1	2	1	7,388
Ogyjames	3	G	2	0	0	0	48	Oisin	5	H	1	0	0	0	2,034
Ogymadi	3	F	3	1	0	0	5,085	Ojeta	5	M	7	0	0	1	1,936
Oh Adam	4	C	8	1	1	1	6,349	Ojibway	2	G	1	0	0	0	1,350
Oh Banner Waive	5	M	4	0	0	0	720	Ojo del Diablo	3	G	3	0	0	0	150
Oh Blue	3	C	2	0	0	0	0	Ok Express	3	F	4	1	0	0	2,946
Oh Boy	4	C	9	2	1	0	7,138	Ok Gotta Go	3	F	5	0	0	0	0
Oh Boy Oh Boy	3	G	1	0	0	0	325	Ok Kiely	4	F	7	1	1	0	4,320
Oh Captain	3	G	3	0	0	0	309	Ok Let's Roll	3	G	3	0	0	2	8,920
Oh Carolina	3	F	10	0	0	2	24,587	Ok Monsoon	2	C	4	0	0	0	0
Oh Chez	4	C	11	2	2	1	28,334	Ok My Way	4	G	7	2	0	0	8,721
Oh Derek	3	C	8	2	0	2	11,248	Ok Thunderbird	3	F	20	0	0	1	4,336
Oh for Joanie	3	F	4	0	0	0	80	Ok Wager	5	M	4	2	0	1	6,768
Oh for Sure	3	C	2	0	0	0	0	Okahumpka (GB)	2	C	1	0	0	0	0
Oh Fudge	3	F	5	0	0	2	12,865	Okanogan Anna	2	F	1	0	0	1	700
Oh Gordon Look	3	G	15	3	3	1	18,317	Okawango	5	H	3	0	0	0	25,000
Oh Gracie	8	H	5	1	1	0	9,435	Okay Olay	4	G	11	1	3	1	4,635
Oh Holy Me	4	F	5	1	0	0	7,398	Okeechobee Lady	3	F	13	2	0	2	11,787
Oh Jazzy Day	7	G	12	2	3	2	4,093	Okeefe Creek	4	G	3	0	2	1	2,362
Oh Jolly	7	G	5	1	1	1	9,155	O'Kelly	5	G	15	3	1	4	19,207
Oh Kay Girl	3	F	2	0	0	0	1,531	Okey Dokey Doc	3	F	7	0	1	1	5,131
Oh Keanna	2	F	11	0	1	1	2,964	Okie Cat	3	G	3	0	0	0	0
Oh Leona	5	M	11	0	3	4	12,024	Okie City Cowgirl	3	F	1	0	0	0	500
Oh Livia D.	4	F	4	0	0	0	11,814	Okie Commotion	3	G	6	0	1	1	8,250
Oh Lucky Me	4	G	4	0	1	1	8,740	Okie Dokie Kookie	2	F	2	1	0	0	12,600
Oh Mar	7	H	11	0	4	3	21,938	Okie Dokie Smokie	4	G	7	0	3	1	11,598
Oh Molly	9	M	1	0	0	0	0	Okie Forbes	9	M	6	1	0	1	3,520
Oh My Ghazi	5	M	5	0	0	0	255	Okie I Am	7	G	16	3	1	1	24,950
Oh My Goodness	3	F	13	1	0	3	5,621	Okie Quit Drinkin'	4	G	11	0	0	0	1,287

Horse	Age	Sex	Sts	1st	2d	3d	Won
Okie Style	2	G	5	3	1	0	81,650
Okiedokiedon	3	C	2	0	0	0	0
Okiefest	5	G	1	0	0	0	0
Okiegolucky	2	G	1	0	0	0	720
Okii Arashi	4	G	9	1	1	1	23,160
Oklahoma	4	G	14	4	1	2	6,059
Oklahoma by Storm	2	F	2	0	0	1	1,085
Oklahoma Dandy	4	F	3	0	0	1	352
Oklahoma Natural	2	C	1	0	0	0	100
Oklahoma Option	6	G	4	0	1	0	2,490
Oklahoma Outlaw	3	C	14	0	0	0	817
Oklahoma Rose	3	F	10	1	0	2	8,487
Oklahoma Spirit	5	G	9	0	0	1	1,169
Oklahoma Star	4	F	7	2	0	1	12,815
Oklahoma Tornado	4	C	9	0	0	0	1,415
Oklahoma Way	7	G	13	0	2	2	3,933
Ol Buddy	3	C	5	1	0	0	2,048
Ol Charlie Boy	5	H	6	0	2	0	4,236
Ol Fifty	2	G	6	1	3	0	30,163
Ol Mike	4	G	12	0	1	2	3,345
Ola Amor	4	F	11	1	1	3	7,685
Ola Flake	2	F	6	1	1	1	6,490
Olan's Boy	5	H	10	1	0	2	8,591
Old Black Coyote	6	G	17	3	2	2	18,042
Old Blue	4	C	1	0	0	0	0
Old Chenin	3	C	2	0	0	0	1,280
Old Chief's Emblem	2	C	1	0	0	0	0
Old Chinese Copy	2	F	2	1	0	0	12,600
Old Court's Cat	4	F	4	0	0	0	1,800
Old Crow	3	G	5	1	1	0	34,860
Old Diesel	8	G	4	0	0	0	136
Old Dixie Home	3	F	15	2	4	2	53,040
Old Duke Puffer	6	G	10	2	4	1	22,810
Old Economy	2	F	2	0	0	0	0
Old Fashion	4	F	5	0	0	0	1,915
Old Fashion Girl	2	F	4	0	3	0	20,600
Old Forest	5	G	7	1	0	1	4,794
Old Forester	2	C	1	0	0	1	4,730
Old Gigalo	6	G	9	2	0	1	17,025
Old Happy	6	G	6	1	1	0	13,800
Old Hit	4	C	8	0	1	0	480
Old Indian Sign	9	G	12	2	5	0	9,507
Old Ironsides	2	C	4	1	0	2	17,120
Old Joe E	3	G	4	2	0	0	12,482
Old Kent Road	2	C	2	1	1	0	20,800
Old Lee	2	G	4	1	1	0	14,400
Old Lodge	7	H	8	0	1	1	2,750
Old Man's Delite	7	H	15	6	2	1	27,952
Old Mizzou	6	G	5	1	0	2	25,575
Old Monarch	5	G	1	1	0	0	3,240
Old Money (AUS)	6	M	2	0	0	0	0
Old Mother Goose	3	F	6	0	2	3	22,010
Old Oak Tree	4	G	4	0	0	0	300
Old Paddy Regan	3	C	4	0	0	0	238
Old Richmond	5	G	6	0	0	0	115
Old Salt	4	C	1	0	0	1	600
Old School	3	C	10	3	2	0	35,600
Old Scotch	4	G	11	2	0	2	18,674
Old Shanachie	9	G	7	1	0	0	8,104
Old Snively	6	G	13	1	2	2	7,569
Old Sparky	7	G	5	0	0	0	316
Old Sport	2	C	1	0	0	1	700
Old Style	2	C	5	0	0	1	1,900
Old Suede	3	C	14	0	0	1	2,411
Old Sugar Shoes	2	C	1	1	0	0	15,400
Old Tavern	5	H	5	1	0	0	9,797
Old Time High	3	G	4	0	0	0	0
Old Time Stories	4	F	9	1	0	2	4,880
Old Tin Lizey	4	F	3	0	0	0	760
Old Tuck	9	G	2	0	0	0	240
Old Twisted Coyote	2	C	2	0	0	0	130
Old Warrior	3	G	6	1	1	1	12,620
Old White Eyes	4	G	4	0	0	0	275
Olden Times (GB)	5	H	5	1	0	1	141,742
Older Whiskey	3	G	5	1	0	0	8,940
Oldfields	7	G	9	1	2	1	24,749
Oldsmar	6	M	3	0	0	0	295
Ole Bad Man	8	G	14	2	0	1	11,343
Ole Blue Boy	4	G	12	2	2	2	29,850
Ole Bull	4	G	2	0	0	0	0
Ole Cheryl	3	F	10	2	3	1	23,670
Ole Dixie	2	C	2	0	0	0	434
Ole Don	3	G	5	0	3	0	6,200
Ole Faunty	4	G	6	2	2	1	87,820
Ole Miss Twist	3	F	8	1	0	1	17,600
Ole Moses	8	G	12	4	1	3	24,981
Ole Pebble	5	M	5	0	0	0	450
Ole Rebel	4	C	6	1	3	0	43,580
Ole Rivers	4	C	3	1	0	0	935
Ole' Rose	2	F	1	0	0	0	0
Ole' Takeover	4	G	2	0	0	0	100
Olechunkofcoal	9	G	8	0	1	1	2,860
Ole'elena	3	F	8	2	2	1	32,940
O'Lee's Story	3	F	9	4	0	1	66,870
O'Lees Wish	4	F	11	2	1	2	13,837
Olen	2	C	2	0	0	0	0
Oleo Med Girl	2	F	6	0	2	0	3,490
Ole's Lightening	2	G	5	0	0	0	1,825
Olga S	2	F	3	0	0	0	1,386
Olguina	3	F	3	0	1	1	13,850
Oligarca	2	C	4	1	0	0	12,956
Olio Olia	7	M	4	0	0	1	1,086
Olive Drab	5	M	7	2	0	1	13,542
Olive Gold	3	F	7	1	2	1	8,008
Oliver Mellors	5	G	15	1	1	2	17,600
Oliver Owl	8	G	2	0	0	0	375
Oliver Street	2	C	1	0	0	0	430
Olivers Success	2	C	8	0	1	3	9,450
Olivette	4	F	5	0	0	0	553
Olivia Anne	4	F	8	1	1	2	8,430
Olivia Grace	3	F	6	1	1	1	22,920
Olivia Jo	4	F	13	0	5	2	20,880
Olivia Leigh	8	M	7	0	0	0	316
Olivia Loves Jesus	5	M	2	0	0	0	399
Olivia's Amour	3	F	7	1	2	0	13,790
Olivia's Notebook	3	F	8	0	3	1	9,410
Olivia's Present	3	F	7	0	1	1	2,282
Olivia's Way	5	H	5	2	1	1	19,900
Olmita	3	F	7	1	1	1	6,550
Olmodavor	4	C	4	1	2	0	241,080
Olmos Creek	3	C	6	1	3	0	15,060
Olofin's Girl	4	F	2	0	0	0	0
O'Lookit	3	G	8	1	0	2	6,554
Olustee Chic	4	F	2	0	0	0	0
Olympia Prince	4	C	8	3	2	2	17,792
Olympian	6	G	8	1	1	0	57,896
Olympian Speed	7	H	1	0	0	0	320
Olympic Advice	3	F	14	5	3	1	123,093
Olympic Bid	7	G	3	0	0	0	174
Olympic Bluff	3	C	1	0	0	0	0
Olympic Bon	3	C	10	1	0	0	6,675
Olympic Contender	3	C	10	1	0	1	36,843
Olympic Emblem	2	F	1	0	1	0	2,700
Olympic Gal	2	F	3	1	1	0	18,020
Olympic Games	3	G	10	0	0	0	790
Olympic Honor	6	G	3	0	0	0	281
Olympic Hope	3	F	7	1	1	1	6,337
Olympic Image	2	F	4	1	0	0	3,650
Olympic Junction	3	G	8	1	0	3	9,316
Olympic Knight	6	H	15	1	2	5	9,241
Olympic Light	5	G	1	0	0	0	0
Olympic Mettle	6	M	4	1	0	1	9,111
Olympic Miracle	4	G	12	0	0	3	4,095
Olympic Moment	3	G	4	1	0	0	6,060
Olympic Night	4	F	13	0	5	1	31,895
Olympic Prospect	3	C	3	0	0	1	270
Olympic Rule	7	H	7	0	0	2	1,608
Olympic Scandal	3	G	1	0	0	0	100
Olympic Skier	3	F	6	1	0	1	6,045
Olympic Success	6	G	5	0	1	1	6,820
Olympic Task	5	G	13	3	0	2	11,901
Olympio Barb	4	F	3	0	0	1	825
Olympio's Dream	3	F	5	1	0	0	4,600
Olympus Glory	2	F	1	0	0	0	456
Oly's Cowgirl	3	F	1	0	0	0	0
Olyzeus	7	G	2	0	0	0	0
Omaha Envy	3	F	11	0	1	4	5,231
Omaline	6	M	4	0	0	0	220

Horse	Age	Sex	Sts	1st	2d	3d	Won
Omali's Action	3	F	14	2	0	0	13,570
Omali's Player	2	G	6	0	0	0	252
O'Malley	4	G	12	3	2	1	46,530
O'Mariah	5	M	6	1	1	0	17,630
Omega Code	3	C	5	1	2	0	87,810
Omen Way	8	G	3	0	1	1	3,520
O'Mighty Roolah	3	G	6	0	0	0	606
O'Mike's Gotcha	8	G	6	1	0	1	2,984
Ominous	3	C	13	2	1	5	80,565
Omit the Dividend	5	G	5	0	1	2	12,880
Ommadon	5	H	2	0	0	0	1,680
Omshanti	4	F	8	1	1	0	45,246
On a Curve	3	G	10	0	0	1	4,070
On a Dark Knight	3	G	9	1	0	0	7,078
On a Dream	2	F	1	0	0	0	95
On a Jag	3	G	10	0	3	1	29,345
On a Rise	2	G	2	1	0	0	6,879
On a Whim	5	G	10	0	0	3	5,750
On American Ground	2	F	3	0	0	0	1,122
On and On	3	F	3	0	0	0	1,380
On and On and On	4	F	6	0	0	0	402
On April's Dawn	3	F	7	0	1	0	1,774
On Command	3	F	7	0	1	1	2,582
On Course	4	G	17	1	4	3	9,267
On Easy Street	5	G	18	5	2	1	23,245
On El Bon	5	G	8	1	0	1	3,113
On Exhibit	3	G	14	2	6	3	35,450
On Freedom	4	G	3	0	0	1	1,072
On Going Girl	2	F	2	0	0	0	156
On His Terms	7	G	19	0	3	2	5,102
On Home Ground	6	M	7	1	0	0	3,472
On Liberty	9	G	8	0	2	1	4,335
On Location	2	F	1	0	0	0	0
On My Birthday	3	G	11	0	3	1	8,229
On My Case	3	C	16	2	3	0	21,181
On My Honour	5	G	3	0	0	0	1,120
On My Wall	3	F	7	0	0	1	3,790
On Nike's Wings	2	F	3	0	0	0	300
On Our Own	4	F	4	0	0	0	248
On Parole	4	C	10	0	1	0	1,190
On Point	6	G	2	0	0	0	0
On Probation	7	G	6	0	2	0	2,444
On Ready	5	G	8	2	0	0	13,312
On Retainer	3	G	12	2	2	0	28,315
On Rush	3	F	12	2	1	1	8,362
On Rye	5	H	5	0	0	1	6,336
On Silver Wings	3	F	12	1	2	2	18,920
On the Alert	5	M	6	0	0	1	1,596
On the Bay	5	G	14	1	2	2	16,141
On the Bill Daily	3	C	6	3	0	1	4,387
On the Border	3	C	9	3	1	1	71,420
On the Bus	3	F	4	1	1	1	37,720
On the Deck	4	F	18	1	1	1	18,275
On the Fan	6	G	10	2	2	1	21,285
On the Fritz	5	M	9	1	4	2	108,711
On the Game	5	H	6	1	0	2	85,596
On the Henley	3	F	8	1	2	0	30,462
On the Main Line	3	C	7	2	2	0	19,178
On the Mend	4	G	15	1	6	2	22,520
On the Other Line	4	G	6	0	0	0	953
On the Q Tea	3	F	10	0	1	5	34,040
On the Right Side	2	C	2	1	0	0	12,250
On the Severn	3	G	19	2	0	0	11,724
On the Tee	7	G	15	5	2	1	58,190
On the Tour	8	G	1	0	0	0	0
On to Richmond	5	G	8	3	2	1	81,635
On to Victory	3	G	13	1	0	3	7,059
On View	4	F	1	0	0	0	125
On Your Honor	2	F	2	0	0	0	103
On Your Mark	6	H	8	0	2	1	12,945
Ona	6	M	1	0	0	0	0
Ona Nasza	4	F	5	0	0	0	630
Ona Rampage	2	F	5	2	1	0	23,408
Onaccountofyou	6	M	2	0	1	0	8,220
O'Naevus	4	G	3	1	1	0	5,600
Onasilverplatter	5	H	4	1	0	0	8,487
Onastar	4	G	8	1	1	0	5,395
Onawingandaprayer	6	G	14	0	2	1	11,532
Once Around	4	F	4	0	0	0	4,410
Once It Happens	6	G	7	1	2	0	7,387
Once Rich	5	G	14	2	2	2	23,185
Onceanangel	6	M	2	0	0	1	1,210
Oncearoundtwice	2	C	6	2	2	1	74,660
Onceinafullmoon	7	G	12	1	1	1	1,988
Onceinamillion	3	C	1	0	0	0	0
Oncore	5	H	13	1	0	0	8,310
Onda Ray	3	F	5	1	0	0	26,235
Ondif	3	F	8	0	0	1	1,687
Ondro	8	G	19	1	0	3	5,031
One Act	4	F	5	1	1	2	30,940
One Act Play	3	C	2	0	0	0	0
One and Done	3	G	7	1	2	0	25,970
One and Only	2	F	2	0	0	0	600
One and Only You	3	F	8	1	2	0	27,240
One and Twenty	3	F	6	0	0	0	2,880
One Bad Coyote	3	F	5	0	0	0	417
One Bad Dude	6	G	12	3	1	1	67,430
One Bad Sister	2	F	3	0	0	0	690
One Bad Storm	3	G	5	0	0	3	10,080
One Bell	5	G	2	0	0	0	0
One Bell Boy	4	G	8	1	2	2	14,925
One Below Zero	3	G	10	1	0	1	7,432
One Bid Max	3	C	3	1	0	1	1,540
One Blue Tech	3	F	4	0	1	2	3,609
One Brick Shy	8	G	4	0	0	0	0
One by Design	3	G	4	2	0	1	38,073
One Call Close	6	G	12	4	1	2	23,060
One Chance Fancy	2	F	6	0	1	1	3,505
One Charming Devil	2	F	1	0	0	1	4,390
One Classy Key	5	G	13	0	0	2	2,223
One Cold Witch	5	M	6	1	0	0	1,760
One Colony	3	C	3	0	1	0	7,450
One Cool Jewel	3	F	6	0	0	0	0
One Crazy Lady	2	F	3	1	0	0	8,460
One Creek	4	C	4	0	2	0	1,360
One Dangerous Lady	4	F	4	0	0	0	237
One Diablo	4	F	3	1	0	1	8,750
One Eye	2	C	3	0	0	0	169
One Eyed Bandit	3	F	19	2	1	4	25,940
One Eyed Cobra	3	G	3	0	0	1	7,200
One Eyed Jackie	4	F	11	1	2	1	26,318
One Eyed Joker	5	G	10	2	3	0	82,140
One Eyed Mike	6	G	7	0	1	0	1,427
One Eyed Peak	3	G	5	0	0	0	292
One Eyed Vern	5	G	5	0	0	1	2,553
One Eyed Willing	3	C	15	1	2	1	42,814
One Fast Girl	5	M	2	1	0	0	7,200
One Fiftyfour I Q	2	C	3	1	0	0	11,105
One Fine Asset	4	F	2	0	0	1	675
One Fine Family	8	G	2	0	0	0	280
One Fine Lover	3	F	13	3	3	1	43,508
One Fine Shweetie	4	F	9	2	2	4	91,912
One Flew Over	3	F	8	1	0	1	10,900
One for Katie	3	F	8	2	2	0	58,708
One for My Baby	5	G	5	1	1	1	25,450
One for Rose	4	F	10	6	2	0	476,377
One for Seattle	4	G	8	1	3	0	16,748
One for the Angels	5	M	6	2	0	2	39,597
One for Wanda	4	F	9	0	2	4	12,880
One for You	2	F	2	0	0	0	380
One Forty Four	4	C	6	0	1	1	4,867
One Foxy Lady	7	M	3	0	0	2	7,315
One Genius	2	F	4	0	0	0	960
One Giant Leap	3	G	12	3	0	0	8,641
One Goldengirl	4	F	3	0	0	0	0
One Green Peach	2	F	4	1	0	1	8,830
One Handsome Dude	2	C	1	0	0	0	230
One Happy Guy	3	C	1	0	0	1	2,860
One Heckova Deal	4	F	4	0	0	0	414
One Honest Heart	5	G	13	1	2	1	7,197
One Honest Man	5	H	5	1	0	0	2,100
One Hot Actress	3	F	1	0	0	0	84
One Hot Girl	3	F	8	2	0	4	45,350
One Hot Knight	9	G	1	0	0	0	0
One Hot Number	5	M	11	2	3	1	10,473
One Hot Pilot	4	G	8	1	1	1	6,256
One Hundred Slews	8	H	1	0	0	0	0
One in the Middle	3	C	6	1	2	0	11,420

Horse	Age	Sex	Sts	1st	2d	3d	Won	Horse	Age	Sex	Sts	1st	2d	3d	Won
One Iron	3	G	1	0	0	0	0	One Tough Dude	2	C	5	1	2	2	53,780
One Jazzy Lover	3	C	5	1	0	2	6,900	One Tough Eskimo	4	F	5	2	0	0	27,090
One Judge Trend	5	G	13	3	3	2	87,380	One Tough Note	4	C	12	2	3	2	37,935
One Knight	4	G	14	1	3	1	11,430	One Tough Raiser	3	C	2	1	1	0	25,900
One Kool Babe	3	F	10	1	1	1	6,531	One Tough Somethin	6	G	12	5	0	2	23,899
One Last Chance	3	G	4	0	2	1	20,910	One Trick Ata Time	4	G	8	1	2	2	19,486
One Last Trick	7	G	15	1	5	2	25,335	One Trick Pony	2	F	2	0	0	0	480
One Little Word	8	G	16	1	2	0	7,547	One Tricky Boy	5	G	6	2	0	1	8,060
One Look	3	F	14	3	0	4	15,129	One Troy Ounce	5	G	10	2	3	0	15,965
One Lucky Day	6	M	6	0	2	0	4,227	One Tuff Chick	2	F	2	0	0	0	600
One Lucky One	5	M	9	5	1	2	39,974	One Tuff Fox	4	C	4	1	0	1	38,950
One Lucky Storm	2	F	4	1	0	1	11,745	One Tuff Oak	4	C	3	0	1	1	488
One Lucky Strike	9	G	16	0	0	1	1,132	One Twist	7	M	11	3	2	1	64,516
One Mad Husband	2	G	3	0	1	0	6,015	One Two Ponche	5	M	12	1	0	1	5,663
One Manz Fortune	6	G	8	1	0	3	15,370	One Two Punch	3	F	9	1	1	2	23,020
One Mile Limit	6	M	17	2	3	2	28,655	One Up	6	M	7	0	1	0	4,012
One Missy Gal	2	F	2	0	0	0	0	One Up On Dad	3	F	2	0	0	0	0
One Momento	3	C	9	1	1	0	34,686	One Upman	6	G	7	2	2	0	29,390
One More Bragg	3	G	15	1	1	0	5,921	One Wild Angel	3	F	11	0	1	2	3,563
One More Brian	4	G	8	1	1	3	14,265	One Wild Cat	3	G	8	0	0	1	1,950
One More Cat	3	C	4	0	0	0	2,232	One Wild Lad	9	G	4	0	0	1	1,010
One More Cookie	3	F	11	1	3	1	14,867	Oneatmanale's	2	F	2	0	0	0	375
One More Judge	7	G	10	0	0	0	960	Onebadshark	3	C	3	1	1	0	29,750
One More Mecke	4	G	3	0	0	0	320	Onebigbag	3	G	7	1	0	2	44,520
One More Moondance	3	F	13	2	2	1	22,430	Onedancewithslew	3	F	1	0	0	0	675
One More Once	9	G	4	0	0	0	186	Onedrinkandnomore	7	H	2	0	0	0	0
One More Run	3	C	3	0	0	0	75	Oneexcessivenite	3	F	14	4	2	0	142,577
One More Secret	6	M	2	0	0	0	912	Oneforthegriffer	6	G	1	0	0	0	110
One More Storm	4	C	10	2	1	1	28,346	Onefortriss	4	G	10	1	2	0	6,719
One More Whirl	3	G	14	5	1	4	46,544	Onefourtwentyfour	6	G	11	0	3	2	10,713
One More Win	2	G	2	0	0	0	300	Oneguiltymoon	2	F	1	0	0	0	0
One N Three	4	C	4	1	1	1	86,530	Oneheckofaruckus	3	C	6	1	2	0	19,890
One Naughty Fool	6	M	5	0	0	0	270	Onehorsyoutside	7	H	2	0	0	0	0
One Neat Trick	2	F	1	0	1	0	3,000	Onehundredproofwin	3	F	7	1	2	0	11,130
One Nice Cat	3	C	5	1	0	1	32,725	Oneida	4	F	2	0	0	0	384
One Objective	4	G	17	0	1	2	4,708	Onekissisplenty	2	C	1	0	0	0	160
One of My Secrets	3	F	11	2	1	1	9,286	Onella	3	F	8	1	0	1	16,290
One of the Lonely	4	G	8	0	0	1	5,436	Oneluckygirl	2	F	3	0	0	0	585
One Only Fever	4	F	5	0	0	0	300	Onemore Missile	3	C	1	0	0	0	420
One Only Knows	3	F	11	4	1	2	225,349	Onemorefashion	3	F	17	2	3	3	78,590
One Out	5	M	7	0	0	1	3,745	Onemorewithclass	2	C	2	0	0	0	0
One Pacific Tower	3	F	1	0	0	0	1,031	Oneofacat	2	F	4	1	1	0	37,950
One Perfect Fit	3	F	10	0	0	1	9,624	Oneofthebirdboys	3	C	12	0	1	2	13,906
One Perfect Sailor	2	F	1	0	0	0	0	Oneofthegirls	4	F	18	3	3	2	21,444
One Pit Wonder	2	C	1	0	0	0	0	Oneofus	4	F	16	3	2	1	21,290
One Red Hot Mama	2	F	1	0	0	0	0	Onerous	6	G	6	0	0	0	407
One River Dolly	2	F	5	0	0	0	189	Onery Fella	3	G	4	0	0	0	0
One Sea	3	G	9	0	1	0	8,121	One's All You Need	4	C	7	1	1	2	11,653
One Shady Lady	4	F	6	0	0	0	389	Onesassyluckylady	3	F	7	1	0	1	13,060
One Sharp Friday	5	G	3	0	1	0	810	Onesorryladd	7	H	3	0	1	0	870
One Sharp Sword	3	G	17	2	4	2	24,090	Onestep	4	F	1	1	0	0	3,045
One Silent Love	2	F	2	0	0	0	2,300	Onestrikenoballs	7	H	10	0	2	0	2,409
One Silent Wonder	6	G	12	1	2	4	12,851	Onesweep	5	G	1	0	0	0	0
One Silver Lady	5	M	13	0	0	2	3,849	Onethindime	2	F	7	1	1	0	6,545
One Sixty	2	F	4	0	2	0	17,874	Onetrickphoney	4	G	2	0	0	0	0
One Slick Hot Dog	3	F	3	0	1	1	1,820	Onetwomanyfavors	2	F	2	0	1	0	4,860
One Smart Bet	5	H	4	0	0	0	960	Onewaytoheaven	2	F	7	1	1	2	13,166
One Smart Cat	4	G	4	1	1	0	22,930	Onewitha'lilguilt	3	G	4	0	0	0	158
One Smart Chick	4	F	9	2	1	0	21,984	Onewiththestars	2	C	4	2	1	0	24,110
One Smart Lady	2	F	4	1	2	0	34,650	Ongoing Melody	10	M	3	0	0	0	283
One Special Bob	4	G	14	3	3	2	16,387	Ongoing Star	2	F	3	1	1	0	12,672
One Special Judge	5	G	12	3	2	3	20,643	Ongoing Storm	5	H	7	0	1	2	6,755
One Stall	3	F	4	0	1	0	2,501	Onhighalert	3	F	12	2	2	0	34,279
One Star	5	G	6	0	0	2	1,433	Onion Powder	4	C	5	0	1	0	3,215
One Star General	2	G	7	0	1	3	4,392	Onion Soup	3	C	4	1	0	1	13,490
One Step Away	3	G	8	1	2	2	11,340	Online Class	3	G	7	0	0	0	294
One Stormy Lady	2	F	2	0	0	0	237	Online Intime	7	G	14	4	3	3	49,266
One Stormy Night	3	C	9	0	0	0	1,520	Only a Prince	5	G	9	0	1	0	1,877
One Superkiss	4	F	1	0	0	0	0	Only At Night	4	F	8	3	1	2	81,866
One Sweet Dash	3	F	9	1	2	1	15,800	Only Diamonds	10	G	5	0	0	0	450
One Sweet Day	2	F	6	1	1	0	11,871	Only Dixie	2	F	1	0	1	0	3,800
One Sweet Song	6	M	5	0	0	0	150	Only Fools Rush In	3	G	10	1	1	2	65,557
One Talented Pro	3	C	1	0	1	0	8,600	Only for Love	4	F	7	2	2	0	23,100
One Tall King	3	G	11	0	2	1	3,828	Only for Money	5	M	3	0	0	0	1,140
One Taraway	4	G	7	0	0	1	698	Only in America	4	F	18	2	3	1	11,583
One to Celebrate	2	C	3	0	1	1	18,228	Only in Dreams	3	C	8	2	1	1	21,979
One to Load	6	H	4	0	0	0	0	Only Irish	5	M	9	3	2	2	26,445
One to Want	2	F	5	0	0	0	2,000	Only Joe	4	G	6	1	0	1	7,675
One too Many	5	G	14	0	2	1	5,357	Only Kings	3	G	3	1	0	0	4,800

Horse	Age	Sex	Sts	1st	2d	3d	Won	Horse	Age	Sex	Sts	1st	2d	3d	Won
Only Love	4	F	7	1	3	1	35,840	Open Lock	2	C	5	1	1	2	61,080
Only Money	2	G	1	0	0	0	130	Open Manner	3	F	6	0	0	2	1,109
Only On	3	G	11	1	1	1	7,146	Open Minded	5	M	3	0	0	0	2,550
Only On Broadway	4	F	13	3	0	3	13,120	Open Now	2	C	3	1	0	0	5,820
Only One King	3	C	14	2	6	2	38,919	Open Promise	4	F	14	5	3	0	64,940
Only One Regal	2	F	1	0	0	0	1,085	Open Ribbon	2	F	1	0	0	0	660
Only Selina	6	M	1	0	0	0	0	Open Rocket	2	C	8	0	2	2	7,923
Only Seventeen	2	F	6	1	0	2	6,920	Open Runway	3	C	13	1	1	2	7,137
Only the Best	3	G	10	2	2	1	110,960	Open Scent	4	F	10	1	2	1	6,930
Only the Facts	3	F	15	1	1	6	7,691	Open Session	4	F	12	2	1	2	35,814
Only Thrill	3	F	7	2	2	0	28,936	Open the Bridge	3	F	5	0	0	0	348
Only Time	4	G	12	2	2	2	24,430	Open Ticket	3	C	2	0	0	0	5,060
Only Way	3	F	4	0	0	1	2,230	Open Vault	3	G	5	1	2	1	31,020
Only Wings	4	F	4	1	0	0	4,743	Open Water	3	G	2	0	0	0	0
Only Yesterday	3	F	4	0	0	0	732	Openforjoy	3	F	13	1	1	1	12,577
Only You	5	G	11	1	2	1	38,188	Opening Account	3	F	14	1	2	1	11,095
Only You and I	3	F	9	0	1	0	5,810	Opening Move	8	G	13	1	0	1	5,380
Onlycook Half Ofit	4	G	8	2	0	1	54,280	Opening Pace	3	C	9	1	4	1	35,280
Onlyfoolsfallinluv	5	H	9	0	1	1	2,377	Opening Soon	4	F	9	1	4	0	15,365
Onlynurimagination	4	G	4	0	0	1	4,405	Opening Word	8	G	14	3	2	4	23,310
Onlysplendidson	4	G	3	0	0	0	107	Openly	2	F	7	0	0	2	6,820
Onlytheshadowknows	4	F	6	0	1	1	4,024	Opennshutcase	3	C	22	2	3	3	27,661
Onmywaytoheaven	3	F	13	2	1	2	24,491	Opeongo	3	C	5	0	0	0	1,244
Onrichardsaccount	4	G	13	0	1	3	4,092	Opera Aida (IRE)	4	F	1	0	0	0	0
Onry Wonway	3	F	6	0	2	1	15,270	Operatic	3	G	5	2	2	1	51,500
Onside Kick	6	H	3	0	0	0	364	Operation Gloria	3	F	8	0	2	0	4,360
Onslaught	6	M	4	0	2	0	33,000	Opie	5	G	14	2	4	1	22,825
Ontario	3	C	6	0	0	0	2,500	Opie's Bonus	3	G	5	0	0	0	158
Ontario Road	3	G	7	1	0	1	17,952	Opie's Secret	2	C	1	0	0	1	120
Onthebrightcide	3	F	4	0	0	1	911	Opiethechimeman	4	G	1	0	0	0	40
Onthedeanslist	4	C	6	1	1	1	54,540	Opine	8	G	5	0	0	0	1,880
Onthemarquet	4	G	14	1	1	2	5,867	Opportune	7	H	4	0	0	0	336
Ontheqt	2	F	4	2	2	0	156,944	Opportunity Bay	3	F	14	1	3	0	7,219
Onthewingsofadove	3	F	7	1	0	0	5,432	Opposing Force	4	C	14	3	1	0	21,529
Onward Christian	4	C	14	1	2	1	17,527	Opprtunity Blue's	6	M	10	4	0	2	7,693
Onya	4	F	4	0	0	1	1,010	Ops Run	3	F	14	3	1	2	43,398
Onyx King	3	C	4	0	0	0	1,314	Opsail	3	C	5	0	0	0	0
Onyxntrue	6	H	9	4	1	0	13,722	Opt	6	M	20	2	4	6	11,754
Oobitwa	3	G	11	1	0	2	13,710	Optic Diversion	4	G	6	1	1	2	10,985
Ooby Dooby	3	G	2	0	0	0	170	Opticrectosis	8	G	5	0	0	0	253
Oodles	6	G	5	0	0	0	897	Optimistic Math	3	G	6	1	0	3	15,360
Ooh Man	3	G	7	0	1	1	5,390	Optimity	6	G	14	0	1	3	3,810
Ooh Sammy	3	G	6	0	0	0	530	Optimize	3	F	7	1	0	1	22,320
Oola Boola	5	M	13	0	1	1	3,052	Optimo	2	G	3	0	1	0	4,900
Oolamah	5	G	9	0	2	0	7,581	Optional	5	H	2	0	0	0	0
Ooma	4	F	4	0	0	0	475	Opus Creek	8	G	14	1	3	2	17,915
Oonagh	3	F	2	0	1	0	3,850	Opus Won	6	H	12	5	2	3	49,785
Oop Oopy Do	3	F	15	1	4	0	13,996	Or Holiday	5	H	1	0	0	0	0
Oop's the Red	3	G	14	1	2	1	33,827	Or O' Rosheen	4	F	8	1	1	0	7,915
Oopstheregoes	3	C	2	1	1	0	39,400	Ora	5	M	11	4	2	2	56,574
Oorali	5	G	5	0	0	0	490	O'Raaaily	3	F	5	0	0	0	0
Ootah	4	G	9	2	2	0	12,657	Oracle From Heaven	5	M	2	0	0	0	0
Opacity	5	G	1	0	0	0	282	Orage d'Hiver	9	M	7	0	0	1	5,880
Opalene	3	F	7	0	1	1	4,010	Oraibi Dancer	4	C	5	0	0	3	300
Opaline	3	F	5	1	0	0	8,910	Oraibi Sioux	4	F	2	0	0	0	0
Opal's Ghost	5	M	7	1	0	1	6,970	Oral King	4	G	10	1	0	0	6,960
Opal's Song	5	M	8	1	4	1	7,480	Orange Crusher	4	F	8	0	0	1	2,000
O'Pearcigan	3	F	1	0	0	0	0	Orange 'Em	4	G	12	4	1	2	60,860
Open Agenda	7	H	2	0	0	0	99	Orange Starburst	3	C	9	0	0	5	4,811
Open and Shut	3	F	10	1	0	1	31,360	Orange U Tricky	8	G	8	1	1	1	5,139
Open Box	3	C	1	0	1	0	3,640	Orangeberry	3	F	8	2	1	1	66,062
Open Call	5	M	11	1	0	2	14,799	Orangeman	6	H	5	0	0	0	1,500
Open Cat	3	F	10	1	0	1	6,685	Orangeville Rise	2	C	1	0	0	0	50
Open Chronicle	4	G	12	1	3	4	84,534	Oration	6	H	7	1	0	1	16,920
Open Concert	4	G	12	3	6	0	264,801	Oratorical	2	G	1	0	0	0	280
Open Dance	9	G	12	0	1	2	2,320	Orbea	3	G	7	3	1	1	26,550
Open Deeds	4	G	13	2	2	1	45,186	Orbited	4	F	8	2	2	0	40,550
Open Fairway	2	F	1	0	0	0	0	Orbiting	4	F	5	1	1	1	15,700
Open Flirt	2	F	2	0	1	0	9,460	Orbit's Dancer	5	G	9	1	3	3	19,440
Open for Business	8	H	2	0	0	0	100	Orbit's Holliday	7	M	9	0	1	1	3,640
Open for Love	5	H	10	0	1	1	1,386	Orbit'slastdance	5	G	3	0	0	0	210
Open Hearted	4	F	7	0	0	0	1,950	Orchard Park	4	C	3	0	0	0	905
Open Hunt	2	G	2	0	0	0	140	Orchard Street	5	G	9	1	1	0	16,185
Open Invitation	4	G	2	0	0	0	35	Orchestral	2	F	2	1	0	0	5,828
Open Jet	4	C	5	1	2	1	6,912	Orchestrated (AUS)	7	G	8	1	1	0	25,651
Open Kisses	3	F	8	0	1	2	5,045	Orchid Island	2	F	1	0	0	0	0
Open Late	3	G	12	2	2	2	25,906	Orchid Thief	2	C	5	1	0	0	16,030
Open Letter	4	F	7	1	1	0	3,923	Orchid's Son	5	G	12	3	1	1	41,618
Open Line's Dream	2	C	2	0	0	0	3,528	Orchid's Song	3	F	2	1	0	0	13,085

Horse	Age	Sex	Sts	1st	2d	3d	Won	Horse	Age	Sex	Sts	1st	2d	3d	Won
Orchids Spirit	3	C	11	3	1	1	39,818	Orphan Tinka	3	F	8	0	0	3	2,992
Ordained Magic	3	F	2	0	1	0	12,680	Orphaned	8	G	2	0	0	0	142
Order Chief	5	G	17	1	2	5	10,860	Orphaned Annie	4	F	5	0	0	0	136
Order Del Dia	4	G	2	0	0	0	0	Orphan's Wager	4	F	11	1	0	0	9,420
Order Me First	2	C	2	0	0	0	84	Orphie	4	C	2	0	1	0	882
Ordinary Hero	3	G	12	2	0	2	16,270	Orrs Station	5	G	10	2	0	0	8,888
Ordinary Luck	3	C	4	2	1	0	7,452	Ortiz	2	G	3	0	0	0	560
Ordinary Miracle	3	F	9	1	1	2	5,925	Orvald	7	H	7	1	0	1	9,498
Ordinary Paula	3	F	9	0	2	0	24,184	Orville Forest	3	C	3	1	0	0	21,940
Ordvou	3	G	11	0	1	2	2,573	Orwick	3	G	11	2	1	1	34,484
Ordwell	2	G	2	0	0	0	3,636	Osage Indian	8	G	2	0	0	0	450
Ore Mine	5	G	9	1	3	5	26,010	Osage Rosa Hoots	3	F	4	0	0	1	328
Ore 'n Hatch	4	G	3	1	0	0	3,102	Oscars Illusion	3	C	20	1	0	0	8,040
Ore Rush	3	G	7	1	0	0	7,170	Osceola	6	M	18	2	4	1	17,159
Oregon	3	C	8	1	0	0	4,552	Osceola Warrior	2	C	4	0	0	0	0
Oregon Gus	4	G	5	0	0	0	0	Oscoda	4	G	11	1	0	2	4,984
Oregon Native Sun	4	G	8	1	1	2	2,393	Oseaya	3	F	10	1	3	3	11,781
Oreo Hunter	4	G	17	2	1	2	11,908	O'Shay's Wolf	5	H	6	1	1	0	13,435
Orestes	3	G	10	1	0	2	8,775	Osikan	4	G	6	0	0	0	435
Orf	4	G	6	0	0	1	3,558	Oskar	4	G	6	1	1	0	9,267
Orfino (ARG)	8	G	7	1	0	1	17,250	Osmanbek	8	G	17	3	4	2	54,600
Orfun Ann E.	4	F	9	2	3	0	12,600	Oso Bravo	5	G	5	0	0	0	220
Organ Grinder	2	C	3	1	2	0	118,660	Oso Gothic	3	F	8	1	1	2	10,280
Organic	9	G	18	2	4	5	15,295	Oso Naughty	4	F	1	0	0	0	0
Organized	7	H	14	0	1	1	4,373	Ososmart	8	G	3	0	0	0	0
Organizing Chaos	2	C	10	0	3	2	34,745	Osprey	6	G	18	2	1	4	10,143
Oriana's Magic	4	F	3	0	1	1	19,380	Ossabaw	3	F	12	2	0	2	12,034
Orieal	2	F	2	0	0	1	2,380	Osskani	4	F	1	0	0	1	1,045
Orient Beach	4	C	8	4	0	2	65,819	Oswayo	4	G	13	1	2	5	56,426
Orienta	8	M	2	0	0	0	300	Otan	3	G	10	2	0	3	33,585
Oriental Bug Boy	3	G	9	0	0	1	4,480	Other Brother	3	G	5	0	1	0	5,660
Oriental Doll	2	F	7	0	0	1	21,531	Other Days	4	F	4	1	0	0	15,598
Orientalspringhope	7	M	7	1	1	1	47,530	Otherpeoplesmoney	5	G	5	0	0	1	1,315
Original Cast	6	H	2	1	0	1	16,500	Otherwise Engaged	4	F	14	1	0	3	12,065
Original Gold	3	F	6	1	3	1	43,677	Otisshoulderroll	4	G	6	0	0	2	1,776
Original One	7	G	12	2	1	1	41,011	Otro Mambo	10	G	3	0	1	0	3,750
Original Prospect	7	H	6	1	1	1	8,570	Ott	4	F	8	3	0	1	13,325
Original Score	3	F	2	0	0	0	150	Ottawa Chief	2	C	4	2	1	1	49,700
Original Song	3	F	3	0	1	0	14,121	Otter	2	C	4	0	0	0	1,900
Orimack	2	C	2	0	0	0	280	Otter Bay	3	G	10	1	0	3	7,266
Oriminer	3	F	6	2	1	0	28,615	Otter Be Running	2	F	7	0	6	0	12,100
Orinoco	5	H	3	0	0	0	150	Otter Do	6	G	3	0	0	0	476
Orion Red	3	G	11	2	4	1	21,191	Ottis P Coaltrain	4	G	7	2	0	0	7,404
Orion's Jade	4	C	8	1	3	1	22,800	Otto Be Lee	6	G	7	1	1	1	6,225
Orion's Light	5	M	10	0	0	1	3,617	Ouagadougou	3	G	7	2	1	2	42,950
Ori's Approval	2	F	4	1	1	1	15,180	Ouest Banque	4	F	2	0	1	1	6,740
Oriska	3	F	4	0	0	0	1,386	Ought a Bring Cash	4	G	2	0	0	0	0
Oritani	2	C	1	0	0	0	164	Oughta Ben Brown	3	G	5	0	0	0	210
O'Rival	5	M	5	1	1	0	6,485	Oui Mademoiselle	4	F	10	1	1	0	5,060
Orka	4	C	12	3	1	3	100,600	Oui Nelson Oui	3	F	5	0	3	1	18,080
Orkan	3	F	5	2	0	1	57,840	Oui Oui Cherokee	3	F	6	0	0	2	8,600
Orlando's Dream	4	G	15	3	1	3	19,538	Oui Oui Mon Amie	3	C	8	1	0	2	36,085
Orlik	2	C	1	0	0	0	195	Our Afternoon Boy	5	H	7	1	0	0	8,142
Orlinda	2	F	4	0	0	0	125	Our Ann	4	F	3	0	0	0	680
Orllijeta	6	M	4	0	0	0	0	Our Approval	3	G	1	1	0	0	7,800
Ormond Beach	3	F	4	0	0	0	217	Our Award	6	M	15	2	5	3	15,996
Ormonte K.	6	M	5	1	1	1	5,004	Our Bandit	5	H	2	0	0	0	210
Ormontes Baby	5	M	4	0	0	0	0	Our Basket	3	C	1	0	0	0	306
Ormsbys Treasure	3	F	5	1	0	0	35,220	Our Best Man	6	G	18	2	3	2	58,040
Ornery B. J.	4	C	16	2	0	0	12,972	Our Best Woods	3	C	1	0	0	0	42
Ornery Rascal	8	H	2	0	0	0	351	Our Blazing Belle	5	M	2	0	0	2	3,360
Oro Bandito	9	H	6	1	1	0	4,020	Our Bobby V.	3	G	5	0	1	0	42,000
Oro Caliente	3	F	5	0	1	2	7,188	Our Boy Champ	8	G	4	0	1	0	4,550
Oro de Oro	3	C	3	0	0	1	6,960	Our Breadwinner	4	F	9	1	2	0	39,875
Oro de Tejano	6	G	3	1	1	0	18,765	Our Buck	4	C	20	4	4	1	39,836
Oro Desert	3	G	11	5	1	1	83,255	Our Buckeye Star	4	F	10	0	0	1	3,135
Oro Grand	2	G	3	0	1	0	6,000	Our Buddy	6	G	5	0	1	0	856
Oro Horizonte	5	G	4	0	2	2	2,515	Our Caribbeanqueen	5	M	9	1	2	0	7,289
Oro Mountain	3	C	10	1	1	0	8,040	Our Carol	4	F	7	3	1	0	56,087
Oro Negra	6	H	3	0	0	1	1,250	Our Charlotte	4	F	8	0	1	1	2,124
Orofino Prize	2	F	4	0	0	1	975	Our Chef	8	H	8	0	1	1	4,290
Oros	7	H	4	0	0	0	379	Our Chequer Flag	4	F	9	1	2	3	22,679
Oro's Sugar	2	F	3	1	1	0	16,930	Our Cherokee	3	G	8	1	0	0	3,376
O'Rose	5	M	11	1	4	0	5,690	Our Cielo	5	G	4	0	0	0	0
Orphan Brigade	2	C	6	2	0	1	42,468	Our College Belle	3	F	1	0	0	0	0
Orphan Cartwright	6	G	11	3	3	1	70,682	Our Colors	5	G	10	2	0	1	10,279
Orphan Child	3	C	15	2	4	2	41,310	Our Columbine	4	F	7	0	1	1	2,969
Orphan Emmali	8	M	11	0	2	4	17,350	Our Country Gal	4	F	2	0	0	0	150
Orphan Lover	4	F	11	2	1	3	63,150	Our Country Girl	3	F	12	1	0	4	22,474

RECORDS OF HORSES

Horse	Age	Sex	Sts	1st	2d	3d	Won
Our Cousin Rex	3	C	10	1	2	2	42,481
Our Creole Lady	4	F	4	0	1	0	1,910
Our Cyclone	3	C	12	0	2	1	5,327
Our Daily Bread	4	G	6	1	0	1	11,230
Our Dalila	5	M	2	0	0	0	285
Our Danzig	3	G	2	0	0	0	726
Our Dear Jade	4	F	12	1	2	1	12,670
Our Decision	3	C	1	1	0	0	7,800
Our Diamond	4	G	1	0	0	0	0
Our Diamond Girl	2	F	4	0	2	0	7,730
Our Dreamcatcher	9	G	14	0	1	1	1,744
Our El Nino	5	H	2	0	0	0	206
Our Eleanor	7	F	6	0	0	1	2,450
Our Emerald	3	F	19	1	1	3	24,915
Our Exploit	2	F	3	1	1	0	28,350
Our Ferrari	3	G	4	0	0	1	1,140
Our Final Answer	4	F	1	0	0	0	1,080
Our Finale	3	C	1	0	1	0	6,480
Our First Furrari	5	G	4	0	0	0	525
Our Fling (NZ)	5	M	1	0	0	0	920
Our Forest Delight	4	G	10	1	2	5	8,060
Our Forum	3	F	2	0	0	0	340
Our Freya	3	F	9	0	2	2	24,185
Our Friend Perk	3	C	2	0	0	0	180
Our Gal Fatale	4	F	10	3	3	1	23,102
Our Gal Friday	5	M	1	0	0	0	103
Our Gal Irish	3	F	12	2	1	1	16,890
Our Game Plan	3	F	7	0	2	2	17,520
Our Gang	2	G	6	2	0	1	39,374
Our Gilty Call	4	F	7	0	2	1	1,317
Our Girl Shade	5	M	8	1	1	0	5,270
Our Girl Sue	3	F	1	0	0	0	0
Our Golden Boy	3	G	7	1	0	2	5,562
Our Golden Years	5	G	8	0	1	1	4,026
Our Guy	4	G	12	2	0	4	15,192
Our Here Tiz	6	M	14	1	2	2	53,880
Our Holy Venture	4	C	8	0	0	0	610
Our Houdini	3	C	14	0	4	3	43,900
Our Intention	3	F	7	2	0	2	40,033
Our Jock Julio	4	G	15	3	1	2	15,916
Our Josephina	3	F	4	0	1	0	11,170
Our Joy	2	F	2	0	0	0	1,140
Our Judy R	3	F	6	1	2	1	18,745
Our Kathrine	2	F	2	1	0	0	16,800
Our Kerri	9	M	8	0	0	0	400
Our Knockout	4	F	2	0	0	0	0
Our La Sheba	7	H	11	2	1	2	13,664
Our Lady Katie	4	F	1	0	0	0	180
Our Lady Megan	3	F	9	3	1	1	21,060
Our Lady Peace	3	F	1	0	0	0	45
Our Lady's Man	3	G	1	0	0	0	100
Our Last Novel	4	C	5	1	0	0	31,449
Our Laura Bell	2	F	3	0	0	0	300
Our Leader	6	G	7	2	1	1	27,300
Our Legal Eagle	13	G	14	0	1	0	2,128
Our Legend	5	M	10	0	1	3	6,461
Our Lil Affair	5	H	15	0	0	3	5,757
Our Lil Moe Joe	4	G	1	0	0	0	80
Our Lilly	3	F	4	1	0	0	16,378
Our Little Lucy	3	F	10	1	2	4	26,410
Our Little Runaway	3	C	4	1	0	2	4,040
Our Louie	4	G	10	3	3	0	36,770
Our Lov Bug	4	G	1	0	0	0	0
Our Love	3	F	4	1	1	0	18,056
Our Luc	3	C	5	1	1	0	30,420
Our Luck Will Turn	4	F	16	1	3	1	7,631
Our Lucky Bonnie	8	M	4	0	1	2	820
Our Lucky Kiss	3	F	8	1	0	0	3,290
Our Lucky Number	5	G	14	1	1	1	4,799
Our Lucky Pleasure	6	M	6	0	0	0	111
Our Luther	6	H	13	0	0	2	9,289
Our Magistrate	5	G	7	2	0	0	25,636
Our Majestic Cat	5	M	8	0	1	2	24,090
Our Man	5	H	5	0	0	1	1,910
Our Man Joe	2	C	4	0	0	0	360
Our Mango	4	F	8	1	2	0	45,237
Our March Hare	3	C	8	1	3	0	34,920
Our Mariah	3	F	11	3	0	0	61,090
Our Megabucks	4	G	7	0	1	0	2,966
Our Memento	2	C	5	1	3	0	33,300
Our Millennia	3	F	1	0	0	0	0
Our Mimi	4	F	12	2	1	1	70,890
Our Miss Emily	3	F	4	0	1	0	952
Our Miss Huff	4	F	13	1	2	4	12,135
Our Miss Janet	5	M	5	0	0	0	217
Our Miss M	3	F	7	0	0	1	1,925
Our Moment	3	C	17	2	4	3	39,945
Our Monstarr	2	F	5	1	0	2	14,418
Our Mud Pie	8	G	17	0	0	3	2,814
Our Nancy Lee	3	F	1	0	0	0	2,580
Our New Recruit	4	C	5	1	3	0	76,800
Our Niner	3	G	6	1	0	1	28,470
Our Olivia	2	F	1	0	0	0	217
Our Only Legacy	4	C	2	0	0	0	123
Our Only Option	3	C	2	0	0	0	0
Our Only Sunshine	6	M	3	0	0	0	150
Our Party Man	4	C	9	0	0	3	1,784
Our Pee Jay	4	F	7	1	0	0	3,225
Our Penny	3	F	8	2	2	0	9,548
Our Pet Julliette	4	F	1	0	0	1	1,019
Our Peteski	4	C	1	0	1	0	1,800
Our Pocketbook	7	H	2	0	0	0	273
Our Point to Point	3	G	5	0	2	0	8,670
Our Pop	4	C	13	3	0	3	26,070
Our Preciousmoment	5	M	15	5	2	1	61,042
Our Problem	3	G	11	1	1	0	11,470
Our Prospect	4	F	4	1	1	0	3,260
Our Queen Kathryn	3	F	4	0	0	0	0
Our Queen Rules	2	F	6	1	0	0	9,552
Our R. N.	5	M	9	3	2	0	12,372
Our Ramblin' Rose	3	F	5	0	0	1	1,286
Our Resolution	4	G	2	0	0	1	1,650
Our Revival	3	F	7	0	1	1	11,094
Our Rite of Spring	2	F	1	0	0	1	4,950
Our Ross	4	G	2	0	0	0	162
Our Royal Dancer	3	F	8	0	0	2	15,270
Our Ruby	2	C	6	1	1	1	8,685
Our Saint Ed	3	G	11	1	0	0	11,630
Our Senorita	2	F	1	0	0	0	0
Our Sharky	4	G	8	0	0	1	5,965
Our She Devil	4	F	11	1	0	0	4,440
Our Shining Star	4	F	20	2	0	2	9,913
Our Sister Gina	6	M	17	3	4	2	21,213
Our Slavic	3	F	4	0	1	1	2,890
Our Sleep Robber	5	G	13	2	4	2	9,290
Our Smilin Star	4	G	5	0	0	0	1,476
Our Soles to You	7	G	5	0	0	1	1,530
Our Song	4	C	6	0	0	1	6,000
Our Sophia	3	F	4	1	1	1	41,885
Our South	3	F	5	0	0	0	72
Our Southern Pearl	2	F	1	0	0	1	2,640
Our Sparkie	2	F	4	0	0	0	217
Our Steffi	3	F	8	0	0	0	558
Our Summer Storm	4	C	7	1	5	1	76,930
Our Sweet Emotion	5	M	3	0	0	0	402
Our Sweet Nadine	6	M	8	0	0	0	355
Our Swiss Account	3	F	4	0	0	0	0
Our Tanner Girl	4	F	13	1	5	1	8,174
Our Thomas	9	G	3	0	0	0	110
Our Three O Seven	3	G	4	0	1	0	1,165
Our Thunderbolt (NZ)	9	G	3	1	2	0	12,300
Our Top Gun	4	G	5	2	1	0	41,820
Our Town	8	G	1	0	0	0	1,290
Our Tune	3	F	14	4	3	1	123,706
Our Turn	4	G	4	0	0	0	244
Our Vision	3	G	8	0	1	2	3,182
Our Wildcat	4	C	8	2	1	2	65,000
Our Winston	9	G	5	0	1	1	1,483
Our Wizard	3	G	18	2	1	2	5,441
Our Year	4	F	2	0	0	0	72
Ourbobbygirl	5	M	2	0	0	0	126
Ourboymatt	3	C	2	0	0	0	0
Ourbronze Jet	3	G	5	1	0	0	7,510
Ourconsolation	10	G	15	3	2	3	12,442
Ourenay	6	G	8	1	0	2	8,325
Ourfirstattraction	4	F	1	0	0	0	188
Ourfirstbabyfund	2	F	5	0	0	1	1,045
Ourlittlemary	11	M	1	0	0	0	0

Horse	Age	Sex	Sts	1st	2d	3d	Won
Ourlove for Nikki	3	F	5	0	0	1	722
Ourninelives	2	C	1	0	0	0	651
Ourpennyfromheaven	3	C	1	1	0	0	4,980
Oursecondbuck	6	M	3	0	1	0	3,280
Oursweetpee	5	M	3	0	0	0	1,100
Ourwhistlebritches	3	F	16	0	1	5	42,520
Out At Home	3	F	10	2	1	2	63,157
Out Control (CHI)	5	G	19	3	3	4	29,314
Out for Gold	13	G	6	0	0	0	360
Out in Time	5	M	2	0	0	0	156
Out Late	3	G	7	0	2	0	2,963
Out of a Dream	7	M	3	1	0	0	10,760
Out of Bounds	3	C	4	0	1	2	28,024
Out of Champagne	6	H	14	3	3	2	25,205
Out of Clues	3	F	2	0	0	0	150
Out of Coal	2	G	2	0	0	1	4,600
Out of Darkness	3	F	3	0	0	0	990
Out of Dough	5	M	8	1	2	0	22,681
Out of Dreams	3	F	15	1	1	1	6,667
Out of Fashion	7	G	4	0	0	1	13,960
Out of Hand	5	G	10	4	0	1	33,221
Out of Hearts	2	F	1	0	0	0	124
Out of Here	4	G	4	1	0	0	4,140
Out of Jacks	3	C	11	2	3	3	38,743
Out of Jail	2	C	3	1	0	0	15,600
Out of Kilter	2	C	7	1	0	1	8,436
Out of Kindness	3	C	1	0	0	0	112
Out of M and M's	3	G	12	1	1	0	4,205
Out of Milk	3	F	1	0	0	0	0
Out of Mind	4	G	8	0	0	0	479
Out of Mind (BRZ)	8	H	10	1	2	3	57,240
Out of My Way	6	G	9	4	1	0	182,430
Out of Options	7	M	1	0	0	0	0
Out of Pocket	3	F	3	0	0	2	4,180
Out of Pride	4	F	8	2	2	3	19,735
Out of Questions	2	F	4	1	0	0	11,817
Out of Rules	5	M	7	0	3	1	4,433
Out of Sort's	3	F	2	1	0	1	29,110
Out of Spec	5	M	4	0	0	0	824
Out of the Bag	4	F	15	3	2	6	59,850
Out of the Gloom	4	G	14	1	2	5	10,211
Out of the Will	3	F	6	4	1	0	123,880
Out of the Woods	3	C	6	0	0	2	3,081
Out of Touch	7	G	15	1	0	0	5,730
Out of Tune	2	F	1	0	0	0	0
Out On Bail	4	G	15	2	0	1	9,482
Out Shinin'	2	F	11	0	0	0	1,100
Out There	3	C	5	0	2	1	15,600
Out to Get Ya	4	G	17	0	1	1	2,426
Out to Lunch	5	H	9	1	2	3	7,894
Out to Sea	4	G	2	0	0	0	300
Out Well	5	M	13	2	0	2	59,192
Out With It	6	M	7	0	1	2	7,465
Outa Me Bloominway	7	M	13	0	0	1	2,637
Outa My Way	4	G	6	0	0	0	1,115
Outa Space	4	G	16	3	5	2	17,143
Outathechute	4	C	7	3	1	1	98,328
Outatime	8	G	12	0	3	1	9,834
Outback Annie	3	F	2	0	1	0	5,750
Outcashem	2	C	1	1	0	0	14,250
Outcast	4	C	15	0	2	2	5,022
Outdo	9	G	9	1	1	5	13,466
Outdone	4	F	7	0	0	3	9,260
Outeniqua	3	F	2	1	0	0	8,205
Outer Bounds	3	C	10	2	0	3	38,040
Outer Marker	2	C	1	0	0	0	0
Outer Reef	2	C	1	0	0	0	0
Outer Zone	3	G	4	1	0	0	36,360
Outfield Shift	4	G	4	1	0	0	31,285
Outfielder	2	C	1	0	0	0	1,620
Outflankem	3	G	7	0	0	0	1,321
Outflanker's Star	4	F	4	0	0	0	577
Outflankerslass	2	F	1	0	0	0	0
Outing	4	C	3	0	0	1	4,450
Outlandishlady	4	F	10	0	0	1	2,308
Outlaw Bag	5	G	10	1	0	2	12,566
Outlaw Gulch	4	G	15	1	5	1	10,430
Outlaw On the Run	4	G	4	0	0	0	445
Outlaw Quick	3	G	8	1	1	2	3,665
Outlet	3	F	1	0	0	0	0
Outlook Express	3	F	2	0	0	0	0
Outofmoneyhoney	4	F	7	0	1	1	7,071
Outofnowhere	5	M	9	2	2	0	28,014
Outofthe Blue Slew	3	G	1	0	0	0	0
Outofthebank	3	G	13	1	3	3	13,840
Outoftheordinary	2	F	3	0	0	2	4,125
Outofthisworld	4	G	12	1	2	3	4,986
Outonthesly	3	G	12	1	1	1	19,550
Outrageous Oyster	2	F	3	1	0	1	40,385
Outrageous Queen	2	F	13	1	0	4	22,125
Outrider	5	H	8	1	2	1	3,275
Outright Buck	2	F	3	0	0	0	2,760
Outright Forum	4	G	12	0	1	2	5,843
Outright Stormy	3	C	13	1	1	5	43,942
Outright Wager	5	M	12	3	3	1	37,654
Outside Flanker	2	C	2	0	0	0	0
Outskirts	3	F	3	0	0	0	487
Outsmart	3	C	7	0	1	0	5,965
Outstander	4	C	5	1	1	0	37,560
Outstanding Hero	7	H	1	0	0	0	0
Outstanding Info	5	M	4	0	0	1	15,953
Outstanding Lady	2	F	11	4	1	1	120,753
Outta Here	3	C	7	0	1	1	154,912
Outta Luck	4	F	8	3	1	0	32,680
Outta Montreal	5	H	5	0	0	0	952
Outta Nowhere	3	C	4	0	0	0	164
Outta Print	5	H	5	1	0	0	4,212
Outta the Blue	3	G	11	3	2	1	40,465
Outta the Park	3	F	2	1	0	0	20,740
Outta the Way	2	F	5	1	2	0	10,418
Outtabeerouttahere	2	C	4	0	0	0	2,400
Outwit	3	G	9	2	2	3	24,205
Ovation	4	C	12	3	6	1	34,055
Over a Barrel	3	C	1	0	0	0	0
Over Alert	7	M	1	0	0	0	0
Over Budget	5	G	8	2	0	1	12,942
Over Concerned	4	F	4	0	1	0	3,630
Over Dere	5	M	2	0	0	0	418
Over Fan	7	G	13	2	1	1	9,858
Over Protected	8	G	3	0	0	0	0
Over Spicy	7	G	12	1	1	4	4,128
Over Sunset	4	G	15	0	0	0	1,209
Over the Creek	8	G	5	0	0	0	336
Over the Ranger	3	C	1	0	0	0	0
Over the Summit	3	G	18	0	5	2	22,326
Over the Transom	3	F	3	1	0	1	31,910
Over There	4	G	16	4	0	0	25,107
Over to You	9	G	6	0	1	1	9,090
Overact	2	F	4	2	2	0	47,840
Overbite	7	H	5	1	0	1	2,556
Overcame	4	F	8	0	1	1	4,965
Overclocked	3	G	7	0	0	0	2,994
Overcome Adversity	3	F	4	1	0	0	1,457
Overcrowded	4	F	5	0	1	0	9,560
Overdone	6	H	7	0	1	1	6,760
Overdue Lassie	3	F	2	0	0	0	0
Overflight	3	C	3	2	0	0	49,420
Overjoyed	6	M	7	1	1	2	4,344
Overkill	2	C	2	0	0	1	5,928
Overland Road	2	G	4	1	0	0	7,198
Overload	4	F	2	0	0	0	360
Overload Warning	4	C	9	1	0	0	5,850
Overly	4	G	9	2	2	0	20,706
Overnight Angel	5	M	12	3	2	2	17,319
Overnight Delivery	4	F	14	6	1	1	50,768
Overnight News	3	G	13	1	0	2	16,258
Overnight Storm	4	G	9	0	0	2	804
Overnite Case	4	F	7	0	0	2	1,889
Over'nout	10	G	10	1	0	1	4,994
Overpass	3	C	10	0	3	2	28,210
Overprint	6	H	10	1	1	3	4,496
Overreaction	2	F	4	0	0	1	10,950
Override	5	M	14	4	1	2	28,778
Override Battle	8	H	4	0	1	0	5,065
Overseas Account	3	F	6	4	2	0	49,200
Overt Action	4	G	9	1	0	3	10,602
Overtime Ali	5	G	13	2	0	1	10,092
Overtime Leeann	5	M	6	0	0	0	2,341

Horse	Age	Sex	Sts	1st	2d	3d	Won	Horse	Age	Sex	Sts	1st	2d	3d	Won
Overtone	5	G	9	1	1	3	6,604	Pacewaster	10	G	19	1	2	3	6,538
Overwhelming Cher	5	M	5	1	0	0	6,712	Pachara (GB)	4	G	13	3	2	3	83,980
Overzealous Judith	6	H	1	0	0	0	70	Pachaug	2	C	7	2	1	1	14,325
Ovo	3	C	13	2	2	1	21,380	Pache's Forum	4	C	11	1	1	5	31,114
Owego	3	F	13	1	1	2	9,104	Pacific Armada	3	G	9	1	2	0	23,084
Owens County	4	G	11	1	1	1	12,316	Pacific Colony	4	C	7	0	1	2	27,700
Owen's Way	8	G	14	0	1	3	12,589	Pacific Crest	3	G	13	0	2	0	2,934
Owensboro	5	G	6	1	0	0	3,267	Pacific Echo	8	M	4	0	1	0	1,240
Owl Le Oops	4	G	1	0	0	0	0	Pacific Island	2	F	5	2	1	0	48,050
Owned Exclusively	6	G	2	0	0	1	1,775	Pacific Jewel	3	F	6	1	0	0	17,030
Owsley	5	M	5	1	1	0	141,744	Pacific Journey	3	F	3	1	1	0	12,860
Owyee	5	M	14	2	3	0	10,797	Pacific Ocean	6	G	4	0	0	0	310
Ox Bow	9	G	7	2	0	3	12,457	Pacific Palisades	5	H	15	1	1	0	16,330
Oxalis	3	F	4	1	0	1	10,010	Pacific Plate	7	G	4	2	2	0	12,850
Oxana Mae	3	F	1	0	0	0	0	Pacific Pride	6	G	8	1	0	1	10,380
Oxford Grad	3	F	8	1	1	0	4,400	Pacific Reign	5	M	5	0	1	0	8,107
Oxford Tea Party	6	G	10	2	0	0	70,953	Pacific Spell	4	F	5	1	1	0	8,970
Oxsana Royale	3	F	5	1	2	0	7,080	Pacific Sunset	3	F	8	3	2	2	74,240
Oxymoron	3	C	10	1	0	1	8,668	Pacifico	3	G	15	1	1	4	27,001
Oyagi	4	C	4	0	2	0	3,680	Pacify	5	M	16	2	4	0	19,314
Oye Yoye Yoye	5	G	13	2	4	3	42,675	Pacify Me	3	G	7	1	1	1	10,002
Oyster Bay	3	F	2	0	0	1	3,540	Pacilla	10	M	3	0	0	1	1,059
Oyster Cove	4	G	5	1	1	1	28,140	Pacing the Cage	5	G	13	3	2	2	53,090
Oysterville	4	F	5	3	0	0	4,600	Pack and Drift	8	G	14	3	2	1	36,246
Oz	2	C	1	1	0	0	24,600	Pack of Six	11	G	5	0	0	0	192
Oza	5	H	9	3	0	1	78,140	Pack the Tack	3	G	5	0	1	0	9,274
Ozark	5	G	14	1	1	3	4,880	Package Store	5	H	4	2	0	2	135,984
Ozark Academy	4	C	9	3	1	1	34,093	Packin Glacken	3	C	16	2	0	4	46,652
Ozark Princess	3	F	2	0	0	0	1,080	Packing a Pistol	5	H	2	0	0	0	130
Ozark Surprise	5	M	6	1	1	0	3,395	Paco El Prado	6	G	8	0	3	0	12,284
Ozette Legend	2	F	5	0	1	0	2,889	Paco's Friend	9	G	2	0	0	0	0
Ozilda's Gale	7	M	1	0	0	0	56	Pad the Wallet	2	F	2	0	0	0	660
Ozilda's Karen	5	M	12	1	3	3	60,939	Paddington	2	C	5	2	1	0	109,620
Ozilda's Nancy Lee	3	F	11	2	3	1	66,618	Paddle's Big Boy	3	G	10	1	1	0	7,140
Ozilda's Ronny	4	C	2	1	0	0	12,050	Paddle's Big Girl	2	F	2	0	0	1	1,190
Ozone Al	5	G	12	0	1	1	1,472	Paddock Dancer	3	F	7	1	1	0	7,113
Ozoned	2	G	5	1	0	1	4,020	Paddy Drew	5	M	12	2	4	3	33,691
Ozzie Cat	3	C	10	0	1	1	32,770	Paddy Gorie	6	G	11	1	3	1	9,135
Ozzie Mozzie	3	C	3	0	0	0	323	Paddy Swazzie	3	G	2	0	0	0	0
Ozzie's J J	2	G	5	1	0	2	16,786	Paddyhannon	7	G	8	0	0	0	415
P Day	8	G	5	3	0	0	141,000	Paddy's Dasher	3	F	7	0	0	0	1,307
P F Don D	2	C	4	0	0	1	1,540	Paddy's Peace	6	H	1	0	0	0	0
P F Midnight	4	F	4	1	0	2	3,260	Paddy's Spy	8	G	12	3	0	2	87,457
P J Prado	3	F	1	0	0	0	0	Paden	3	G	2	0	0	0	0
P J's Choice	4	F	7	0	1	1	1,012	Paderewski	3	G	4	0	0	0	1,434
P J's Drummer	4	F	12	1	1	2	4,663	Padgett	3	G	6	1	3	2	15,506
P J's Kid	5	M	17	3	4	2	17,528	Padirac	5	G	9	1	1	1	11,199
P R Star	7	M	8	3	0	0	28,970	Padlock	4	G	9	1	0	2	35,160
P Ridge	4	C	5	0	0	0	0	Padmore	3	F	6	1	1	1	31,240
P Ridge's Keivyn	3	G	4	0	1	0	2,460	Padre	3	G	10	0	1	0	2,482
P T Papa	2	G	5	0	0	0	670	Padre Murphy	6	G	5	2	1	1	7,279
P Town John	2	G	7	3	1	0	89,580	Padre Pete	7	G	14	1	3	0	10,242
P Y Twenty	3	G	1	0	0	0	0	Padrone	4	G	5	0	0	1	693
P. A. Pistol	3	C	9	1	0	0	7,920	Padua's Pride (IRE)	6	H	7	1	1	0	31,165
P. A.'s Candy	4	F	10	3	2	0	6,515	Paducah	5	G	4	1	1	0	6,240
P. A.'s Iron Man	10	G	5	0	1	0	3,379	Paesano	3	G	15	1	0	2	6,790
P. B. and J.	7	M	1	0	0	0	38	Paesano's Pirate	5	G	3	0	0	0	550
P. C. Bad Girl	8	M	6	0	3	1	6,428	Paga (ARG)	6	M	4	0	0	3	26,522
P. C. Plod	7	G	3	0	1	1	5,750	Pagagar	12	G	8	1	1	2	17,817
P. C.'s Gift	8	H	4	0	0	0	0	Pagan Place	5	H	9	3	0	2	43,335
P. D. Bucky	2	C	1	0	0	0	195	Page Hunting	5	G	16	0	6	5	22,137
P. D. Quick	7	M	4	0	0	0	0	Page Me Later	3	F	12	2	1	1	42,755
P. G.'s Star	5	H	11	0	2	1	2,660	Page the Way	2	F	2	0	0	0	252
P. J. Brown	6	H	5	1	1	1	6,496	Page Two	9	G	11	3	0	1	30,835
P. J.'s Eskimo	3	F	11	3	0	1	41,513	Pageant Baby	5	M	4	0	0	0	2,656
P. J.'s Paulie Boy	5	H	9	2	1	1	96,572	Pager	4	C	10	3	0	2	42,942
P. Kerney	2	C	2	1	0	0	21,600	Paggy	9	M	12	0	2	5	6,111
P. Kris	6	H	2	0	0	0	150	Paging	5	G	13	2	0	4	97,010
P. M.'s Snacks	5	G	15	3	2	1	15,387	Paging Dr Kelsie	5	M	7	0	0	2	2,842
P. S. Saros	4	F	6	3	0	2	18,605	Paging Dr. Gober	3	G	9	0	1	2	6,947
P. T. Linnelli	3	F	4	0	0	0	1,080	Paging Joi	3	F	6	0	1	1	2,816
Pa Pa Da	2	G	5	1	2	1	67,150	Paging Maggie	4	F	11	0	1	4	6,567
Paavo's Princess	6	M	2	0	0	0	110	Pagliacci (GB)	5	G	12	3	1	0	36,220
Pablito Special	3	C	4	0	2	0	7,300	Pah	4	G	16	2	3	2	51,650
Pablo	3	C	8	0	0	0	510	Pahokee	6	M	10	1	3	0	20,220
Pablo Diablo	2	G	5	0	1	0	2,645	Pahsimeroi Smoke	4	C	9	1	1	2	5,232
Pac N Iron	3	C	7	1	0	0	7,134	Paid My Dues	4	C	5	0	1	1	2,370
Pacer	4	C	4	1	2	1	35,979	Paigaroo	3	F	8	0	0	0	2,115
Pacesetter	2	C	6	0	1	1	7,600	Paige	3	F	2	0	0	0	0

Horse	Age	Sex	Sts	1st	2d	3d	Won
Paige Kevin Kahuna	4	C	1	0	0	0	0
Paige Moro	3	F	12	3	0	0	37,727
Paige the Doc	2	G	4	1	0	1	11,251
Paiges Aly Birdie	2	F	4	0	0	1	1,600
Paige's Boo	6	M	9	0	1	2	30,398
Paige's Goal	9	M	3	0	0	0	0
Paiges Pebble	3	F	12	1	6	1	34,245
Paige's Recital	3	F	7	0	0	1	1,262
Paige's Sister	7	M	3	0	0	0	1,102
Paillette	4	F	4	1	0	1	11,592
Painless	2	F	7	1	0	3	10,695
Paint Ballado	2	G	3	0	1	0	7,260
Paint Her Silver	3	F	1	0	0	0	66
Paint It Black	3	F	7	1	1	2	41,010
Paint Me Quick	3	F	7	4	0	0	40,800
Paint the Wind	8	M	13	0	2	0	2,775
Paintball	3	F	5	1	0	1	27,730
Painted Avenue	5	G	7	0	1	1	2,910
Painted Bridle	3	G	12	0	0	0	828
Painted Dancer	3	G	3	0	0	0	1,430
Painted La Riva	4	F	11	1	1	2	4,701
Painted Lady	4	F	1	0	0	0	0
Painted Pistol	6	G	12	3	1	2	27,390
Painter's Creek	2	C	2	0	1	0	4,780
Painter's Sword	2	G	5	1	0	0	20,416
Pair a Aces	4	C	6	0	0	1	4,922
Pair o' Nines	5	G	8	0	1	1	2,160
Pair of Dice	4	F	5	1	2	0	29,400
Pair of Wings	3	F	9	2	2	3	54,818
Paisano Piccolo	8	G	2	0	0	1	806
Paisley Braes	6	M	7	2	2	1	20,895
Paisley Park	3	F	13	3	2	3	90,580
Pajaro	4	G	10	2	0	1	12,665
Pakenham	4	G	10	2	2	0	7,943
Pal Danny	6	G	1	0	0	0	73
Pal Joey	8	G	10	1	0	4	27,260
Pal McCartney	4	G	13	3	1	1	17,431
Pal Woodley	6	G	2	0	0	0	0
Pala Cielo	5	M	14	2	3	0	12,795
Palace Blues	7	H	10	0	0	2	2,106
Palace Blush	4	F	4	0	0	0	790
Palace de Lady	2	F	1	0	0	0	93
Palace Dove	3	F	2	0	0	0	165
Palace Heroine	7	M	12	1	4	1	18,891
Palace of Dreams	5	M	8	0	1	0	6,981
Palace Royale (IRE)	7	M	6	1	0	2	28,910
Palace Uprising	3	F	10	0	2	3	52,022
Palacity Star	5	M	6	1	2	1	6,964
Paladdie	5	G	7	1	2	2	24,427
Paladin Power	5	G	10	1	2	3	25,346
Palapeine	4	G	5	0	0	0	892
Palatine	3	G	11	4	2	1	28,975
Palazzo One	2	G	4	0	0	0	1,080
Pale Sky	4	C	3	1	0	0	5,828
Palenki	3	F	6	1	4	0	16,800
Palermo (MEX)	6	M	5	0	1	0	1,352
Paley Jr	7	H	4	0	0	2	487
Palguin (CHI)	8	H	4	0	0	0	355
Pali Princess	4	F	5	2	0	0	49,850
Palique (URU)	4	C	3	0	0	0	27,600
Palm Beach Bud	2	C	1	0	0	1	3,080
Palm Beach Shelly	3	F	6	2	1	0	12,046
Palm Bearer	7	H	10	1	1	0	4,624
Palm Canyon	5	M	4	0	1	0	881
Palmarola (ARG)	6	M	2	0	0	0	2,136
Palmeiro	5	G	7	2	1	0	75,170
Palmerston	2	C	2	0	0	0	1,680
Palmerton	4	G	6	1	1	0	11,708
Palmetto Dunes	3	F	1	0	0	0	40
Palmetto Girl	5	M	3	0	0	0	162
Palo Dura	3	F	3	0	0	0	156
Paloma Parilla	4	G	13	0	1	2	10,860
Palooka	2	C	4	0	0	1	2,025
Palouse Bruce	3	G	10	2	1	2	11,080
Palpen	2	C	2	1	1	0	32,350
Pal's Last Memory	5	M	13	1	1	2	15,258
Pal's Partner	4	G	5	0	1	1	6,714
Pals Pride	4	G	9	0	0	0	4,778
Pam and Gayla	3	F	3	0	0	0	0
Pam in the Gym	3	F	2	1	0	0	18,720
Pamela Wamela	4	F	8	0	1	1	1,689
Pammy n' Cami	7	M	9	4	3	0	56,480
Pammy's Grand	4	F	13	2	3	2	17,299
Pampered	3	F	8	3	0	1	62,057
Pampered Princess	3	F	7	3	0	3	72,370
Pampy Fit	8	M	2	0	0	0	125
Pam's Gale	2	F	1	0	0	0	370
Pam's Girl	3	F	3	1	1	0	14,675
Pam's Pearl	4	F	3	1	0	0	4,286
Pam's Ruckus	2	F	1	0	1	0	4,400
Pam's Wildcat	2	C	1	0	0	0	0
Pam'ssummerwind	3	F	1	0	0	0	0
Pan Adam	5	G	17	1	0	2	14,695
Pan de Vida	5	H	12	1	0	0	8,640
Pan Out	3	F	11	0	0	1	4,497
Panama Mon	4	F	2	1	0	0	8,760
Panasofskee	4	F	1	0	0	0	0
Panchie	5	M	2	0	0	0	0
Panchita Villa	5	M	13	6	2	0	32,855
Pancho Mac	6	G	1	0	0	0	0
Pancho Mirada	5	G	7	0	2	1	4,455
Pancho Norte	11	G	3	0	0	0	150
Pancho Pete	8	G	12	2	0	1	22,789
Pancho's Affair	4	F	8	1	0	0	9,052
Pancho's Alibi	4	G	9	1	1	3	9,983
Pancho's Gold	2	G	2	0	0	1	605
Pancho's Karma	3	C	12	4	0	2	31,362
Panchos Pleasure	4	G	9	0	0	2	1,990
Pancho's Pride	3	F	7	1	0	2	19,810
Pancho's Temptress	2	F	3	0	0	0	225
Panchromatic	5	G	4	0	1	0	270
Panda Bear	4	F	3	0	0	0	140
Pandora Petit	2	F	6	0	0	1	1,880
Pandora's Current	3	G	2	0	0	0	75
Pandorasconnection	3	F	8	1	0	2	20,296
Panfi	3	G	4	0	0	0	0
Pangloss	6	G	1	0	0	1	3,240
Pangress	6	M	6	0	2	1	2,726
Panhandle Prince	4	G	1	0	0	0	0
Panhandle Ryder	3	G	5	0	0	0	895
Panic Zone	3	F	3	0	0	0	0
Paniemoniam	2	F	7	1	1	0	56,547
Paniolo Gold	6	H	7	3	2	1	18,690
Paniolo Road	5	G	3	0	0	0	180
Panner	6	H	3	0	2	0	16,880
Pannier de Amour	3	F	10	1	2	2	7,361
Panning	3	G	12	0	0	3	10,370
Panning for News	4	F	6	1	0	1	1,576
Panning Gold	4	C	2	1	0	0	4,226
Panny O'Cake	10	G	5	1	0	0	6,836
Panola County	4	G	11	0	1	0	3,255
Panoplia	3	F	1	0	0	0	0
Panorama Ama	4	F	2	1	0	0	10,780
Panorama Drive	7	H	10	2	3	0	6,888
Panorama Village	3	F	7	1	2	0	5,440
Panoramic	3	C	4	0	1	1	14,620
Pan's Forum	4	G	4	0	0	1	5,421
Pansy Garden	4	F	9	2	1	0	13,173
Panta Ellinas	6	G	8	2	0	0	17,967
Pantages	3	G	8	1	0	0	6,665
Pantandroar	5	M	4	0	0	0	255
Pantar (IRE)	8	G	6	0	1	0	6,720
Panther Creek	4	C	10	1	2	1	6,140
Panther Pond	5	G	13	3	1	4	44,517
Panther Quick	4	G	4	0	3	0	6,300
Panther Street	3	G	2	0	0	0	0
Pantherilla	6	M	12	1	2	2	10,986
Pantry School	4	F	10	1	0	0	2,978
Pants N Kisses	3	G	10	2	1	3	148,117
Panzon	8	G	7	0	0	1	1,544
Paoli	4	G	8	0	1	1	9,185
Paolini (GER)	6	H	4	0	2	1	742,300
Papa Dan	6	G	5	1	1	0	8,200
Papa Ho Ho	10	G	5	1	0	1	25,200
Papa Luke	6	H	5	1	1	0	6,426
Papa M and M	5	H	10	2	1	5	42,830
Papa Sids Girl	2	F	2	1	0	1	36,225
Papa to Kinzie	2	F	1	1	0	0	23,400

Horse	Age	Sex	Sts	1st	2d	3d	Won	Horse	Age	Sex	Sts	1st	2d	3d	Won
Papago	7	G	5	0	0	1	1,619	Paraswap	4	G	16	2	1	1	13,488
Papalito	3	G	2	0	0	1	1,798	Paravaunt	2	F	2	0	0	0	100
Paparazzi	4	G	13	3	5	4	66,045	Parco Ducale	4	G	2	0	0	0	320
Paparazzi Miss	2	F	4	0	1	0	3,010	Pard E	2	G	5	1	1	0	9,900
Papa's Got Gin	6	G	10	2	1	1	15,054	Pardas	4	C	2	0	1	1	10,880
Papa's Lil' Darlin	3	F	11	0	4	2	10,785	Pardner	5	G	8	1	1	2	25,236
Papa's Pickpocket	2	F	6	0	4	1	24,185	Pardners Mountain	3	F	1	0	0	0	0
Papa's Preston	3	G	4	0	0	0	0	Pardon Him	3	F	13	2	1	2	8,211
Papa's Pumpkin	5	M	9	1	0	0	16,620	Parducci Ridge	4	G	11	4	2	2	9,005
Papa's Refund	5	M	5	1	1	0	4,053	Pareepassoo	4	F	6	0	0	1	6,306
Papas Texas Red	8	G	5	0	0	0	206	Parents' Reward	5	H	1	0	0	0	250
Papa's Wave	4	G	4	0	1	2	2,745	Perfect Dancer	3	G	9	1	2	0	24,068
Papas Yeehaw	2	F	2	0	0	0	600	Parfumeur (FR)	3	C	7	0	0	0	6,532
Papawin	4	G	5	0	0	0	930	Parfy's Legacy	4	C	4	0	0	0	3,610
Pape	4	C	11	3	2	1	55,561	Pargie	5	M	1	0	0	0	0
Papeete	2	F	6	0	0	1	1,190	Parham's Music	6	H	10	1	3	2	34,276
Paper Bag	3	F	10	2	1	1	12,355	Parhelion (GER)	3	C	7	1	1	0	16,688
Paper Clip	3	F	10	3	3	1	16,450	Pariente Barbara	10	M	1	0	0	0	61
Paper Copy	3	G	4	1	0	1	6,850	Parigi	3	G	7	0	0	0	1,635
Paper Cut	3	F	3	1	0	1	10,650	Parimac (NZ)	9	G	3	0	1	0	421
Paper Kite	3	C	2	0	0	0	0	Paris Academy	7	G	11	0	1	2	5,039
Paper Man	2	C	5	1	0	1	21,404	Paris Adventure	3	G	10	2	1	2	88,290
Paper Mountain	3	F	5	1	1	0	29,790	Paris Angel	3	F	2	0	0	0	40
Paper Storm	3	G	3	0	0	0	0	Paris Blue Grass	4	F	1	0	0	0	237
Paper Wings	4	F	8	1	1	0	4,177	Paris Bound	6	H	2	0	0	2	3,433
Papi Macho Man	3	G	1	0	0	0	0	Paris Caper	3	C	14	3	5	0	126,953
Papier Mache	5	M	16	2	3	3	51,855	Paris Dandy	4	G	9	0	1	1	2,932
Papiillon	3	F	5	0	0	1	2,120	Paris Gold	2	C	3	0	2	0	10,428
Papillon Dreams	4	F	8	0	0	0	4,353	Paris Legend	3	F	9	1	1	1	19,732
Papi's Pest	5	M	7	0	2	1	4,598	Paris Past	3	F	6	2	0	0	34,860
Pappa Carlos	4	G	8	0	0	0	1,065	Paris Sunrise	3	C	4	1	2	1	52,220
Pappa Joe's Gal	7	M	6	2	0	2	3,014	Parisall	5	M	11	1	2	1	8,578
Pappa Sureshot	4	C	12	0	0	0	3,055	Parish Princess	2	F	1	0	0	0	411
Papparizi	8	G	3	0	1	1	2,522	Parisian	2	G	4	1	0	0	25,012
Pappa's Dennis	5	G	17	0	0	4	2,854	Parisian Deputy	3	F	7	2	0	0	55,810
Pappa's Luck	5	H	16	1	1	2	14,065	Parisian Heart	4	F	1	0	0	0	0
Pappaw's Big Boy	3	G	7	0	1	1	3,510	Parisian Lord	5	G	10	0	2	2	22,176
Pappolino	5	G	3	0	0	2	1,447	Parisian Trip	5	M	11	4	2	1	79,200
Pappys Legacy	3	C	1	0	0	0	100	Parisienne	2	F	9	1	0	0	23,356
Pappy's Native	7	H	10	2	2	3	8,124	Parisino (ARG)	6	G	13	2	0	3	25,680
Papua	4	C	8	3	2	0	167,365	Parisky	6	G	8	0	0	1	3,428
Par a Mutual	3	G	4	0	0	1	1,827	Park City Playboy	5	G	11	3	2	1	20,940
Par Avon	6	M	8	0	2	2	1,430	Park City Red	4	G	8	0	0	0	2,101
Par de Deux	3	F	6	2	0	4	55,720	Park Falls	3	G	4	0	1	1	4,400
Par Golfer	5	M	11	2	2	3	34,992	Park Jet	4	G	1	0	0	0	0
Par Rules	3	C	15	2	1	2	24,985	Park Model	3	F	4	0	0	0	0
Par Say Doll	5	M	2	0	0	0	553	Park Place	4	F	2	0	0	0	220
Par Shooter	2	G	1	0	0	0	100	Park the Car	3	G	9	2	1	0	48,030
Para Alquilar	5	G	8	1	0	2	16,970	Park West	3	C	8	0	0	1	3,250
Para Belle	3	F	6	1	1	1	8,888	Parker P	4	G	18	0	1	0	7,138
Para Sixes	3	G	16	0	3	0	4,949	Parker Rounds	3	F	4	1	0	1	10,050
Para Usted	5	G	17	1	2	3	31,080	Parkers Chapel	5	H	9	3	0	1	19,200
Parachute	2	C	1	0	0	0	0	Parkers Mill	2	C	1	0	0	1	4,100
Paraclete	5	M	2	0	0	0	818	Parkers Peace	2	C	2	0	0	0	510
Parade Band	2	G	2	0	0	0	1,710	Parker's Pet	3	G	8	2	3	0	21,015
Parade Dancer	2	C	1	0	0	1	1,540	Parker's Prospect	5	M	1	0	0	0	180
Parade King	2	G	8	0	2	0	9,100	Parker's Storm Cat	3	C	3	1	1	0	40,800
Parade of Lights	3	F	6	1	1	3	7,514	Parkers Way	4	C	3	0	0	0	0
Parade of Music	4	G	15	4	2	0	61,215	Parker's Way West	3	C	8	2	2	2	66,500
Parade On By	5	M	10	2	0	2	3,194	Parkland	3	C	2	0	1	0	5,034
Parading Tomisue	2	F	1	0	0	0	0	Parklane Best	3	F	5	0	0	0	438
Paradise Dancer	3	C	3	3	0	0	36,900	Parklane Bite Over	4	F	3	0	1	1	1,465
Paradise Girl	3	F	8	0	0	0	180	Parklane Cargo	2	F	3	0	0	0	275
Paradise Heights	3	C	2	0	0	0	0	Parklane Patty	2	F	3	0	0	0	227
Paradise Patty	4	F	12	4	3	2	81,594	Parklane Thriller	2	F	4	0	0	0	675
Paradise's Boss	3	C	10	3	2	1	45,520	Parklane Toccata	3	F	4	1	0	1	4,111
Parado	4	G	9	0	2	3	7,410	Parksville	3	G	9	0	0	2	2,721
Parador	2	F	3	0	0	0	0	Parkway Express	5	G	8	0	0	1	1,574
Paradox Valley	2	C	2	0	0	0	280	Parlay Guy	4	G	10	0	4	2	10,547
Paragon John	3	G	15	2	1	3	10,100	Parlay Pride	3	G	4	2	0	0	14,096
Paragraph	2	C	5	1	1	0	8,840	Parlay the Bet	3	G	3	0	0	0	340
Paralegal	6	M	6	0	0	1	2,070	Parlay Your Talent	2	F	2	0	0	0	385
Paralink	6	M	13	2	6	1	27,781	Parlay's Charm	4	F	5	2	0	0	9,223
Parallax	3	G	5	1	3	0	43,760	Parlay's Princess	3	F	4	0	0	1	650
Parallel Pal	6	G	1	1	0	0	14,640	Parlay's Prospect	3	G	13	3	5	2	47,682
Paramount Spruce	9	G	4	0	0	0	84	Parlez	4	F	8	2	2	0	43,990
Paranoide Paul	4	G	4	2	0	1	9,468	Parliament Hill	6	G	12	2	2	2	12,834
Parasail	3	G	5	2	0	0	97,764	Parnell Square	3	C	6	1	0	0	29,720
Parasevens	4	G	5	0	0	0	1,752	Parose	9	G	9	3	1	2	250,177

Horse	Age	Sex	Sts	1st	2d	3d	Won
Parrott Bay	6	G	7	0	3	1	63,350
Pars Stellae	3	F	2	1	0	0	6,840
Parsaver	3	F	5	1	1	1	6,581
Parsippany	4	F	17	4	2	3	81,315
Parsnips	4	F	2	0	0	0	0
Parson Slough Two	3	G	7	0	0	0	0
Parson's Pleasure	5	M	9	1	1	1	23,680
Parsons Prospect	4	C	8	0	0	0	2,700
Part for Joe	10	G	9	0	2	0	3,661
Part Magic	4	F	12	2	2	2	16,980
Part of a Bet	6	G	12	3	1	1	13,427
Part of the Plan	3	F	5	0	0	2	6,560
Partager Valay	4	C	6	0	1	3	2,384
Parterre	6	G	12	2	1	1	24,540
Parthenon	2	C	3	1	1	0	37,210
Parthenope	2	F	4	1	0	0	8,734
Partigas	9	H	6	0	0	0	1,795
Parting	3	F	2	0	1	1	10,400
Parting for Home	3	F	11	0	2	1	4,492
Partner's Bite	3	C	14	2	2	1	24,780
Partners Choice	5	H	2	1	0	0	32,160
Partner's Gold	3	G	9	0	0	0	510
Party Airs	4	G	8	2	0	1	72,657
Party Asset	4	F	3	0	0	0	150
Party At Shu's	3	C	2	0	0	0	53
Party At the Bar	7	G	3	0	1	2	811
Party Believer	6	G	7	2	1	2	47,585
Party Boy	4	G	10	0	1	1	3,842
Party by Pyrite	5	M	6	0	4	1	2,958
Party Case	2	F	5	0	0	0	765
Party Chief	6	G	10	1	1	1	8,925
Party Date	3	F	7	1	0	0	17,385
Party Deeds	4	G	5	0	0	2	2,989
Party Diamonds	3	F	4	0	0	0	266
Party Down	3	F	9	1	2	0	26,380
Party Finale	4	F	14	2	1	2	16,394
Party Games	2	F	3	1	0	1	7,338
Party Girl Jo	3	F	4	1	0	0	6,630
Party Hearty	4	G	5	0	0	2	3,057
Party Hostess	2	F	3	0	0	0	415
Party House	3	C	1	0	0	0	0
Party in the Park	3	F	10	1	1	4	8,651
Party Island	5	M	11	2	1	1	7,100
Party Kiss	4	C	2	0	0	0	0
Party Lass	6	M	7	1	2	0	9,047
Party Miss	3	F	9	0	0	4	6,046
Party Mode	3	F	3	0	1	0	3,422
Party of Six	2	F	1	0	0	0	0
Party On	3	G	10	2	3	3	63,584
Party Pirate	7	M	8	0	0	1	20,898
Party Plans	3	C	7	0	3	2	16,900
Party Queen	4	F	5	1	0	0	22,800
Party Shu	5	M	10	1	2	1	16,010
Party Speech	3	G	11	0	2	0	4,186
Party Stripes	4	F	1	0	0	0	270
Party to Party	4	F	8	1	1	1	24,470
Party Town	5	G	13	1	4	3	10,196
Partybag	7	G	10	0	0	1	3,408
Partying	4	F	4	0	3	0	15,800
Partyongarth	3	F	1	0	0	0	500
Partytime (IRE)	7	G	5	1	0	0	5,325
Partywithavengence	3	G	16	1	1	0	14,265
Parytime	7	G	12	1	3	1	19,290
Pas de Fantasy	2	F	3	0	0	1	1,395
Pas de Memoires (IRE)	8	G	9	1	1	0	9,765
Pa's Princess Mi.	2	F	8	1	0	3	26,786
Pas Seui's Promise	4	F	5	0	0	0	405
Pascagoula	6	G	11	1	1	3	4,944
Pasco Fiasco	4	C	14	2	2	1	18,836
Paseana's Girl (ARG)	3	F	1	0	0	0	2,160
Pashabelle	2	F	2	0	0	0	150
Pashmina Princess	5	M	10	0	1	2	4,867
Pasing Monique	3	F	1	0	0	0	0
Pasketty	3	C	3	0	0	0	4,510
Paso Del Norte	7	H	5	0	0	0	674
Paso Pandy	11	M	1	0	0	0	35
Pasomonte Paul	6	G	12	3	1	0	25,270
Pasotex	9	G	4	0	1	0	1,891
Pasport	6	G	17	2	5	1	33,252
Pasquale	7	G	2	0	0	0	0
Pasqualino	6	H	1	0	0	0	0
Pass a Star	3	G	10	0	0	3	3,536
Pass Bye	5	M	11	5	1	2	59,046
Pass Go Collect	3	C	17	2	1	3	15,324
Pass Interference	2	F	5	0	0	1	2,080
Pass Me the Salt	2	F	1	0	0	0	0
Pass Muster	2	C	5	0	1	1	4,950
Pass Play	2	G	5	1	1	1	25,338
Pass Rush	4	C	9	1	3	1	261,865
Pass the Dice	8	G	2	0	0	0	0
Pass the Hat	4	G	12	1	2	2	48,908
Pass the Jewell	5	G	2	0	0	0	0
Pass the Luck	4	F	10	2	3	1	10,051
Pass the Pepper	4	F	4	3	0	0	66,600
Pass the Phone	6	H	7	0	1	0	3,040
Pass the Prospect	3	C	3	0	0	1	4,250
Pass the Puck	2	C	4	1	0	0	11,655
Pass the Reality	6	G	3	0	0	0	395
Pass the Sun	7	G	12	2	2	0	7,047
Pass the Test	3	F	2	0	0	0	1,350
Pass the Virtue	4	F	8	1	3	2	65,335
Passage	5	G	4	0	0	0	1,015
Passage Road	2	F	2	1	0	0	21,840
Passage to Ararat	6	G	7	0	0	0	6,530
Passaic	2	F	2	2	0	0	22,230
Passanova	3	C	6	3	0	2	29,135
Passante	4	G	2	0	0	0	0
Passcapade	4	F	3	1	0	0	4,284
Passe Approval	3	F	3	0	0	0	410
Passem All	7	M	14	1	4	0	6,591
Passen Time	4	F	1	0	0	0	0
Passerine	2	F	3	2	1	0	69,140
Passinetti	7	G	4	2	0	1	289,320
Passing Approval	2	C	2	0	0	0	0
Passing Flight	7	M	14	0	4	4	7,700
Passing Hero	5	G	9	1	2	0	6,566
Passing Proudly	4	F	3	0	0	0	0
Passing Ships	5	G	10	0	4	2	36,977
Passing Shot	4	F	10	3	2	2	362,637
Passing South	2	F	1	0	0	0	0
Passing Storm	3	G	14	3	2	4	25,686
Passing Way	2	F	7	0	0	0	1,973
Passing Willie	4	F	4	1	1	1	4,841
Passinville	5	M	10	0	0	0	3,241
Passion Cat	2	F	3	0	0	0	713
Passion for Purple	4	F	4	0	2	0	7,900
Passion for Words	2	F	1	0	0	0	0
Passion Maid	3	F	2	0	0	0	0
Passion Wheel	3	C	6	0	0	1	2,295
Passionate Bird	4	F	14	4	3	1	98,410
Passionate Bride	4	F	5	2	0	0	10,440
Passionate Caper	4	F	9	1	1	1	20,200
Passionate Flight	2	F	4	0	1	0	1,227
Passionate John	3	G	1	0	0	0	0
Passionate Lad	5	G	12	3	1	3	58,990
Passionate Lady	5	M	11	2	3	1	18,724
Passionate Pride	4	F	9	2	2	1	19,448
Passionate Soldier	4	G	10	3	1	1	49,500
Passionate Talk	4	F	7	1	0	0	6,063
Passionate Trick	6	M	13	2	2	3	18,975
Passionforall	3	G	11	2	1	0	59,056
Passionforanna	3	F	11	2	1	2	12,604
Passionforcashin	5	G	11	3	0	3	61,520
Passionforluck	2	F	1	0	0	0	0
Passion's Destiny	2	F	1	0	1	0	13,107
Passions Roar	2	F	4	1	0	2	16,460
Passive	4	G	7	2	2	1	27,140
Passmore	4	C	8	0	2	3	6,918
Pass'n the Test	2	F	6	0	0	0	1,185
Passum Once	5	M	3	0	0	0	0
Past Due Account	6	H	12	2	3	1	18,046
Past Time	6	G	12	2	2	4	26,003
Pasta	2	C	6	0	4	1	17,180
Pasta Due	3	F	6	1	1	0	37,560
Pasta Fazool	3	F	4	0	1	1	4,390
Pasta's Dream	2	F	2	0	0	0	1,050

Horse	Age	Sex		Sts				Won	Horse	Age	Sex	Sts	1st	2d	3d	Won
Paster's Baby	4 G	7	0	0	1			12,065	Patsy's Picture	3 F	2	0	0	0	0
Paster's Dutchess	4 F	6	0	1	1			5,660	Patsy's Prospector	7 H	3	0	0	0	1,133
Pasteur (IRE)	5 G	1	0	0	0			0	Patsy's Shadow	2 G	3	0	0	0	0
Pasture	4 F	5	0	1	0			1,085	Patter On	3 C	1	1	0	0	23,580
Pasture Boy	3 G	14	1	1	1			13,693	Patti Ching	3 F	5	0	2	2	24,960
Pat	4 F	8	0	1	3			12,810	Patti Peach	5 M	6	0	1	0	3,902
Pat a Stake	8 H	18	0	3	2			11,907	Patti Poole	4 F	9	0	0	2	1,580
Pat Com	3 G	3	0	0	0			0	Patti Three Socks	3 F	3	0	0	0	0
Pat 'n Matt	8 G	2	0	1	0			1,278	Pattiano	3 F	11	2	3	2	97,600
Pat of Air	3 F	2	0	0	0			136	Patti's Clown	2 F	5	1	2	0	19,852
Pat Speedy	2 F	5	1	3	0			15,255	Patti's Pro	5 G	10	1	3	3	14,717
Pat That Flower	5 G	5	0	0	0			265	Patti's Storm	4 F	10	0	1	0	1,098
Pat the Cat	2 G	2	1	0	0			7,080	Patti'sinparis	3 F	7	1	3	2	21,010
Pat the Gas	7 G	2	0	0	0			0	Pattison	7 G	9	1	1	2	6,352
Pat the Winner	3 G	6	1	0	2			11,490	Patton Leather	3 F	3	0	0	1	1,000
Patacon	3 C	4	0	1	2			16,100	Patton of Gold	5 H	9	1	0	0	40,827
Patapsco	2 G	3	0	0	0			900	Patton On Speed	2 G	3	0	1	0	2,270
Patch Conway	4 G	15	3	3	1			17,585	Patton Pending	5 G	10	1	0	3	14,436
Patchy Valentine	7 M	9	1	4	1			12,961	Patton Poser	5 G	12	2	1	0	7,919
Patent	6 H	7	0	1	2			14,120	Pattons Charge	4 C	14	2	3	2	65,520
Path	3 C	6	2	1	1			43,800	Patton's Comment	3 F	14	1	4	0	10,810
Path of Thunder	2 F	2	0	0	2			10,010	Pattons Girl	3 F	1	0	0	0	0
Patience and Hope	3 F	2	0	2	0			4,515	Patton's Prince	5 G	10	2	1	3	9,537
Patience Is Mine	5 M	9	1	1	1			3,305	Pattons Success	3 F	4	0	0	0	103
Patient Patty	3 F	1	0	0	0			0	Patton's Victory	5 G	13	6	0	2	223,501
Patient Pete	4 G	3	0	0	0			0	Patton's War	3 G	11	0	0	0	340
Patino's Diamond	3 G	3	0	0	0			100	Pattons Warrior	3 G	10	1	1	0	4,860
Patio Boy	5 G	11	5	1	2			23,247	Pattonthebreeze	3 F	5	0	0	0	0
Patito Feo	4 C	8	0	0	3			4,235	Patty Cakes	5 M	17	2	5	1	36,460
Patonia	5 G	8	0	0	0			922	Patty Go Easy	4 F	4	0	0	0	98
Patrician Power	10 G	2	0	0	0			600	Patty Perfect	3 F	4	0	0	0	0
Patricia's Delight	4 F	1	0	0	0			0	Patty Quake	4 C	8	1	1	2	8,057
Patricia's Song	2 F	1	0	0	0			0	Patty Sue	6 M	3	0	0	0	190
Patricio	6 H	1	0	0	0			115	Patty Takesthecake	4 F	9	1	0	0	9,277
Patrick McCourt	3 G	5	1	0	1			1,650	Patty Wack	2 F	1	0	0	0	0
Patrick's Echo	7 G	8	2	0	2			10,140	Patty's an Angel	5 M	5	0	0	2	1,319
Patrick's Exit	7 G	5	0	1	0			1,463	Patty's Picnic	4 G	7	1	0	0	9,279
Patrick's Promise	2 C	1	0	0	0			0	Patuxent Citi	3 F	8	1	2	2	13,210
Patrick's Talent	4 G	11	1	2	1			49,322	Patuxent River	6 G	9	1	2	0	7,028
Patrinos	4 G	11	0	2	1			3,672	Patuxent Ruby	4 F	6	1	1	1	7,300
Patriot American	5 H	1	0	0	0			79	Patuxent Valley	3 F	2	0	0	0	0
Patriot Dream	2 C	4	1	0	0			12,600	Paugus Bay	5 M	16	1	4	2	64,760
Patriot Noise	3 C	12	1	3	3			52,495	Paul H.	3 G	1	0	0	0	343
Patriot One	3 G	8	1	0	2			18,490	Paul the Speierman	2 G	2	0	0	0	0
Patriot Runner	2 C	4	0	0	1			3,470	Paula	5 M	14	2	1	3	19,245
Patriot Spirit	3 C	4	0	0	0			1,380	Paula Mae Fly	4 F	4	0	0	0	104
Patriot Station	2 C	6	1	0	2			20,279	Paula O	2 F	5	1	2	0	27,720
Patriot Sun	3 G	6	0	1	1			3,632	Paula Smith	4 F	4	0	1	0	9,600
Patriota	2 C	4	0	0	0			270	Paula's Approval	3 F	5	0	1	0	4,760
Patriotforpeace	3 F	3	0	0	0			0	Paula's Fireball	10 G	2	0	0	0	0
Patriotic Duty	3 C	4	0	1	0			1,881	Paula's Pride	3 C	7	2	0	1	33,316
Patriotic Emblem	2 C	3	0	0	0			0	Paulas Victory	6 M	12	2	1	0	12,619
Patriotic Fever	2 F	7	1	0	1			8,545	Pauley	4 G	6	0	0	2	1,162
Patriotic Flame	3 C	11	2	1	1			73,700	Paul's Accolades	3 F	6	0	3	1	23,300
Patriotic Legend	3 C	11	1	0	2			39,045	Paul's Dream	5 M	13	2	3	2	68,135
Patriotic Wac	3 F	1	0	0	0			130	Paul's Girl	2 F	1	0	0	0	0
Patriots Image	2 F	5	1	2	0			32,020	Paul's Part	3 G	8	0	1	2	5,929
Patriot's Legacy	4 F	1	0	0	0			0	Paul's Past	4 C	11	1	2	1	10,413
Patriot's Path	3 C	3	0	0	0			0	Paul's Paula	3 F	6	0	2	0	5,876
Patriots Peak	3 C	5	0	0	0			2,750	Paul's Princess	3 F	8	0	1	0	1,985
Patriot's Pride	3 C	6	1	0	0			10,414	Paul's Tazz	5 G	1	0	0	0	0
Patriot's Quest	2 G	2	0	1	0			5,120	Paulshomemadewine	5 H	12	2	0	4	40,192
Patriot's Song	4 C	7	1	2	2			60,006	Pauper's Pocket	2 G	5	0	0	0	2,710
Patrol	4 C	5	2	0	1			220,930	Pave the Road	6 H	4	0	0	0	282
Patron Silver	3 F	5	1	0	1			12,670	Pavillon	6 H	16	2	0	1	5,976
Pat's Approval	5 G	12	1	0	0			17,385	Pavlosk	6 M	1	0	0	0	0
Pat's Blast O.	5 G	12	1	0	1			13,441	Pavlovsk	4 G	12	2	1	2	62,770
Pat's Cowgirl	5 M	6	1	2	0			7,690	Paw Paw's Pride	6 G	9	1	1	2	26,565
Pat's Creek	4 C	11	0	0	1			1,777	Paw Paw's Primo	2 C	2	0	0	0	0
Pat's Expectation	4 C	10	4	2	1			208,041	Pawhuska	9 G	8	3	0	0	12,110
Pat's Girl	4 F	4	0	1	1			3,639	Pawley's Island	4 C	11	5	2	3	57,505
Pats Picture	5 H	8	0	2	1			5,121	Pawling	4 G	13	2	6	2	15,231
Pat's Possibility	4 F	10	1	4	0			41,680	Pawn Brat	11 G	16	1	0	3	7,892
Pat's Silver Queen	5 M	4	0	0	0			223	Pawn Shop Pistol	4 C	7	0	0	0	380
Pat's Style	4 F	8	0	1	3			3,475	Pawne Nights	7 G	11	0	0	2	1,109
Pats Wild Star	5 M	6	0	0	0			679	Pawnee Pass	6 M	9	1	1	0	9,810
Patsy Won't Tell	5 M	9	0	1	2			3,001	Pawnking	5 G	5	1	0	0	4,406
Patsys Act	2 F	1	0	0	0			473	Pawsie's Princess	3 F	3	0	0	1	1,068
Patsys Cookin'	2 C	1	0	0	0			42	Paxil	7 H	13	2	2	3	8,900

Horse	Age	Sex	Sts	1st	2d	3d	Won
Paxton	7	G	8	1	0	0	4,792
Pay an Take It	3	F	12	3	2	1	14,044
Pay Any Price	5	M	13	3	3	1	27,510
Pay Attention	2	C	5	1	0	1	33,510
Pay Back Time	4	C	6	1	0	0	5,230
Pay Daze	3	G	8	1	1	0	20,635
Pay Per Win	5	G	4	2	1	0	63,000
Pay Phone	2	C	1	0	0	0	0
Pay Raise	5	G	15	0	1	2	2,541
Pay Ransom	6	G	8	0	0	0	3,660
Pay Season	5	M	6	0	0	0	2,845
Pay the Dancer	3	F	3	0	0	0	0
Pay the Deputy	6	M	1	0	0	0	114
Pay the Devil	2	C	2	0	0	0	145
Pay the Fiddler	4	G	5	0	1	0	1,938
Pay the Lady	3	F	11	1	0	1	3,802
Pay the Mon	4	C	4	0	0	0	356
Pay the Preacher	5	G	3	0	0	0	9,190
Pay the Ransom	3	G	11	2	4	1	30,392
Pay the Secretary	4	F	3	0	0	0	510
Pay Up T C	4	G	16	2	2	5	13,064
Pay Ya Later	2	F	2	0	0	0	248
Payasito	4	G	5	0	1	0	5,100
Payback Period	2	F	2	0	0	0	214
Payetta's Flight	5	G	4	0	0	0	448
Payment in Full	4	C	12	1	1	0	10,436
Payne Manor	3	C	5	0	0	0	35
Paynes Bay	5	H	4	0	0	1	5,650
Paynes Station	5	G	7	1	1	0	2,461
Payroll Clerk	3	F	4	1	1	0	7,414
Payroll Deposit	7	H	1	0	0	0	0
Paythedevilatdawn	3	C	4	0	0	0	710
Payton's Pride	3	F	10	4	2	2	78,292
Pazhalsta	5	G	10	3	4	3	32,335
P'burg	7	G	13	2	0	2	4,250
Peabody Jo	2	F	2	0	0	0	205
Peabodys Coaltrain	2	G	3	0	2	1	15,312
Peace	3	F	6	0	0	0	967
Peace Above	6	M	13	0	0	4	4,516
Peace and Joy	4	G	14	3	1	3	65,591
Peace Bro	7	G	12	1	0	2	9,430
Peace Calling	3	F	2	1	0	0	420
Peace Flag	3	F	9	1	2	0	12,818
Peace for Gold	5	M	1	0	0	0	0
Peace Now	8	G	4	0	0	1	510
Peace of Power	3	C	2	0	0	0	225
Peace Pledge	3	F	4	1	0	1	15,650
Peace River Lady	4	F	2	0	0	0	3,210
Peace Rock	3	G	8	1	0	2	28,214
Peace Rules	3	C	7	3	1	1	1,850,000
Peace Symbol	7	F	7	1	2	0	47,813
Peacefally (IRE)	4	F	7	1	1	2	67,323
Peaceful Chimes	3	C	2	0	0	0	0
Peaceful City	3	F	6	1	2	0	12,170
Peaceful Morn	2	F	2	1	0	0	11,220
Peaceful Place	4	F	7	1	1	1	28,970
Peaceful Prince	2	G	2	0	0	0	0
Peaceful Queen	2	F	4	0	1	0	4,744
Peaceful Time	3	F	2	0	0	0	0
Peaceful Wager	5	M	12	1	3	2	12,688
Peacefully Accept	4	F	1	0	0	0	2,400
Peach Valley	3	F	5	0	2	1	7,825
Peaches a Flying	2	F	1	0	0	0	0
Peaches N Schemes	3	F	13	1	1	3	8,490
Peach's Adventure	6	M	3	1	0	0	1,506
Peachy Miss	5	M	12	1	1	2	15,403
Peacock Beach	2	F	8	0	3	0	18,840
Peacock Sally	2	F	6	0	1	1	12,810
Peacomb Hen	8	M	11	1	1	1	22,009
Peak a Boo Mt.	2	F	1	0	0	0	0
Peak Above	3	F	7	1	1	0	10,700
Peak Dancer	6	H	5	1	0	0	10,335
Peak Interest	8	G	11	1	4	2	14,537
Peak of Luck	2	C	1	0	0	0	0
Peak Time	3	F	5	1	1	0	17,470
Peakabbu Boy	4	C	10	2	1	1	28,540
Peakaboo Peak	3	F	13	2	2	2	86,051
Peaked Out	3	F	7	0	0	2	1,316
Peaking Diablo	4	F	10	2	0	1	18,187
Peaks	5	G	14	4	2	0	26,724
Peaks Jewell	3	F	12	1	2	1	13,665
Peaks Or Valleys	5	M	11	2	1	3	95,051
Peal Out	4	F	8	1	0	0	8,021
Peanut Buddy	3	G	10	2	1	2	11,509
Peanut Butter Kid	4	G	11	2	1	2	14,351
Peanut Butter Man	5	G	11	2	3	0	15,880
Peanut for Landry	3	F	7	0	2	0	5,810
Peanut Gallery	6	M	6	0	3	0	33,910
Peanut Parfait	4	F	1	0	0	0	192
Peanutbutter Blitz	3	G	10	2	0	1	10,380
Peanuts Banjo	3	C	1	0	0	0	49
Peanut's Ride	4	F	5	0	0	0	152
Peanutsinacoke	6	G	2	1	1	0	8,000
Pearcy Road	4	G	11	1	2	2	6,042
Pearl d'Azur	10	G	6	0	0	0	1,027
Pearl District	2	F	2	0	1	0	800
Pearl E.	3	F	6	0	0	1	2,444
Pearl Hunt	4	F	14	1	6	4	34,910
Pearl Romance	5	M	7	0	0	0	1,084
Pearls for Dixie	3	F	7	0	0	0	476
Pearl's Hickey	4	F	10	3	2	0	23,100
Pearls N Platinum	4	F	2	0	0	0	103
Pearls'n Wine	6	M	1	0	0	0	0
Pearly Starnet	5	M	11	0	3	1	19,202
Peasynq's	3	G	8	2	2	1	15,670
Peatterly	8	G	8	1	0	1	4,169
Peaty	4	C	5	0	0	0	762
Peavys Time	3	G	3	0	0	0	356
Pebbett	3	F	4	0	1	1	3,780
Pebble Springs	7	M	3	0	0	0	485
Pecabo Thunder	8	M	1	0	0	0	55
Peccadillo	2	F	2	0	0	0	1,500
Pecks Bad Girl	3	F	9	1	1	2	7,595
Pecos Duster	6	G	4	0	0	0	192
Pecos River Drink	5	G	1	0	0	0	61
Pedal Me Pretty	5	M	4	0	0	0	190
Pedaltothemetal	5	G	1	0	0	0	0
Pedernales King	2	G	2	1	0	0	5,040
Pedernales River	4	G	5	1	0	0	3,024
Pedro	5	G	16	0	2	2	8,726
Pee Wee Bee	5	H	12	2	2	2	7,557
Pee Wee Duncan	4	C	7	0	1	0	1,040
Pee Wees Kris S.	3	C	1	0	0	0	0
Peef	3	G	10	1	2	1	118,472
Peeglander	4	F	1	0	0	0	0
Peek a Blue Kiss	3	F	6	0	0	0	1,212
Peek a Boo Sara	5	M	9	1	0	0	44,337
Peek a Boo Who	6	M	12	1	0	0	3,100
Peek Account	4	C	9	2	0	0	18,761
Peek N Tell	2	F	3	0	0	0	252
Peekaboo Cash	5	M	12	0	5	3	6,679
Peekaboo Cat	2	F	1	0	0	0	145
Peekaboo Chad	3	C	3	0	0	0	1,120
Peekaboo Sez	2	F	6	1	2	0	22,401
Peekachoo	4	C	5	1	0	1	1,634
Peekskill	4	G	10	2	1	1	70,865
Peelapear	7	M	3	1	1	1	8,680
Peeler Gap	5	G	4	2	0	0	9,380
Peeping Tom	6	G	14	3	4	3	428,733
Peeps	2	F	2	1	0	0	6,861
Peepsight	4	G	9	2	2	0	10,547
Peering Over	7	M	11	1	2	2	13,875
Peerless Note	2	F	4	0	1	1	3,220
Peerless Price	3	G	2	0	0	1	1,110
Peerless Ryan	4	G	15	1	3	1	6,384
Peetie Pistol	2	C	1	0	0	0	0
Pegalee	4	F	7	1	3	0	18,848
Pegasu	3	F	6	0	1	1	3,030
Pegasus Belle	4	F	3	0	1	0	1,813
Pegasus Superstar	4	G	15	0	2	1	4,281
Pegasusdixiedancer	4	F	3	0	0	0	77
Pegasuseternldancr	4	F	9	2	1	2	38,390
Pegasusluckydancer	4	F	8	1	1	1	5,180
Pegasusnorthrnbabe	4	F	3	0	0	0	0
Peggy Jo's Pride	3	C	4	0	1	2	1,320
Peggy's Aly	3	F	7	0	0	0	898
Peggy's Approval	2	F	5	1	1	1	14,188
Peggy's Beau	7	G	16	3	4	1	21,207

Horse	Age	Sex	Sts	1st	2d	3d	Won
Peggy's Dream Boy	4	G	6	0	0	1	991
Peggys Falstaff	3	G	4	0	0	0	0
Peggys' Girl	2	F	5	0	2	1	2,747
Peggys Gold	2	F	2	0	0	0	114
Peggy's Hall Mark	7	H	8	0	0	1	1,309
Peggy's Lady	2	F	2	0	0	0	0
Peggys Mukora	4	G	14	4	2	1	41,060
Peggys Orchid	4	F	10	0	0	0	0
Peggy's Promise	2	G	1	0	0	0	1,680
Peggy's Secret	5	M	10	1	0	0	6,345
Peggys Winner	4	F	2	0	0	1	308
Pegs Halo	5	G	8	1	0	1	20,674
Peg's Pride	5	M	1	0	0	0	0
Peg's Princess	4	F	10	0	4	3	7,488
Pegylation	5	G	6	0	1	3	15,030
Peking Picnic	5	H	5	0	1	2	9,500
Pelagos (FR)	8	H	6	1	2	2	117,400
Pelican Beach	5	G	10	6	2	1	136,780
Pelican Island	3	F	5	1	0	0	14,510
Pelican Lane	5	G	20	5	2	3	64,812
Pelican Pete	2	C	13	1	1	2	27,255
Pelican State	5	G	2	0	1	0	806
Pelicano	5	H	6	0	0	0	491
Peligroso	5	H	2	1	0	1	13,610
Pelirrojo	4	G	7	0	0	1	10,380
Pell Mell	5	G	13	4	1	2	40,925
Pelli	3	G	4	0	1	0	1,368
Pem Bro	3	C	8	2	1	0	11,814
Pemaquid Point	4	G	3	0	0	0	823
Pember	3	F	7	1	0	0	30,720
Pembroke Dancer	6	G	18	0	2	1	5,457
Pembroke Hall	6	G	6	6	0	0	55,420
Pembroke Lass	5	M	2	0	0	0	274
Pembroke Palace	5	M	1	0	0	0	0
Pembroke Rd.	6	G	17	1	1	5	6,386
Pem's Hostess	3	F	3	1	2	0	22,800
Pen 'n Ink	2	C	2	0	1	0	1,970
Pen Prospect	7	G	3	0	0	0	0
Pen Up Lady	4	F	2	0	0	2	9,150
Penalty Declined	3	G	12	2	1	0	12,505
Penalty Peat	3	C	1	0	0	0	0
Penance Hall	6	M	14	2	2	2	15,357
Penaty Flag	6	G	13	1	0	0	3,533
Pender's Alarm	5	G	7	2	1	0	7,602
Pending Prospect	9	G	10	0	0	0	330
Pendolino	5	G	8	2	2	1	7,677
Pendoreille	4	F	5	0	0	0	62
Pendulum Swing	2	G	2	0	0	0	426
Penfold Place Boy	4	G	16	1	0	6	6,466
Peniforyourthought	4	F	4	1	0	0	2,820
Peninsula Player	2	F	2	0	0	1	900
Penitent	3	G	6	0	0	2	3,762
Pennant Dreams	3	F	1	0	0	0	1,290
Pennant Punch	8	H	4	0	0	1	891
Penne Ala Capaese	3	F	7	1	0	2	29,726
Penne Dancer (IRE)	4	G	10	1	0	0	8,530
Pennington Creek	4	C	4	0	0	0	0
Pennington Gap	3	F	9	3	0	0	31,420
Pennita	4	F	1	0	0	0	0
Penny Bright	4	F	4	1	1	1	12,640
Penny Dream	3	F	4	0	0	1	9,180
Penny Drive	3	F	10	1	0	1	3,298
Penny Express	4	F	4	0	0	1	1,815
Penny On the Post	3	C	15	1	0	2	29,135
Penny Pit	4	F	1	0	0	0	0
Penny Sixpence	2	F	1	0	0	0	0
Penny Special	4	F	2	0	0	0	175
Penny Wager	5	G	6	0	1	1	5,076
Penny's Best Shot	2	G	5	0	0	0	2,072
Penny's Boy Canrun	6	G	4	1	0	1	3,960
Penny's Flyer	6	M	11	2	3	2	15,518
Penny's Fortune	2	F	1	0	0	0	21,285
Penny's Halo	5	M	15	3	2	6	51,985
Penny's Odyssey	5	G	20	2	6	4	33,507
Penny's Quiet Guy	6	G	3	2	0	0	16,235
Penny's Turn	2	F	2	0	0	0	2,580
Penny's Voyager	4	G	6	2	1	0	9,008
Pennysvalentineact	4	F	4	0	0	0	270
Penobscot Bay	3	C	7	0	2	2	64,949
Penruth	5	M	1	0	0	0	42
Penryn Ghost	4	F	4	0	2	1	2,778
Pense	2	F	3	0	0	0	1,143
Pensglitter	6	H	17	4	3	2	34,357
Penshiel	6	G	12	1	1	1	8,743
Pension Plan	3	C	1	0	0	0	0
Pensive Mood	5	G	5	1	2	1	11,150
Pent Up Fantasy	4	F	8	4	0	4	39,513
Pent Up Speed	3	C	8	1	0	0	7,490
Pentakato	9	G	9	0	0	3	4,763
Pentathlon	4	G	20	1	4	5	21,222
Pentavirate	3	C	8	1	0	2	7,715
Penteliano	5	G	4	0	1	0	2,730
Pentelicus Gold	3	F	6	0	0	0	1,232
Pentelipiano	6	G	13	5	0	3	42,776
Pentelly Lil	5	M	2	0	0	0	280
Pentera	3	F	12	1	0	5	21,606
Penthium	5	G	11	1	2	2	16,516
Penthouse Prince	3	G	11	1	2	3	78,428
Penthouse Promise	3	C	13	1	2	3	43,230
Pentimento	4	C	10	0	2	2	28,170
Pentiumblues	4	F	2	0	0	0	0
Pentmandy	5	G	12	2	2	1	24,586
Pents Bride	2	F	3	0	0	0	1,280
Peoria Pearl	3	F	5	0	0	0	323
Pepcee	3	G	1	0	0	0	0
Pepe Le Moco	2	G	3	0	1	0	3,060
Pepesqueez	4	F	14	2	1	2	18,555
Pepi Explodent	6	M	16	2	2	1	8,770
Pepino Di Juno	4	G	15	0	0	1	2,229
Pepper Blues	5	H	8	4	0	1	31,532
Pepper Cove	2	C	1	0	0	0	0
Pepper Pack	3	C	13	1	2	2	13,090
Pepper Red	4	C	16	1	1	6	9,055
Pepper Rossi	3	F	3	0	1	0	2,750
Pepper Step	5	G	9	0	0	1	1,309
Pepper Taffy	7	M	15	3	3	3	17,282
Pepper Trail	2	C	2	1	0	0	14,400
Pepperbox	4	G	7	0	0	0	0
Peppered Cat	3	C	3	1	0	0	7,500
Peppermint Bay	8	M	12	2	3	1	23,022
Peppermint Flash	2	F	1	0	0	0	280
Peppermint Gift	2	F	3	0	0	1	1,290
Peppermint Love	3	C	6	0	0	0	3,840
Peppermint Road	5	M	8	3	0	1	11,675
Peppermint Rose	2	F	3	0	0	0	180
Peppermint Speedy	3	G	5	0	1	1	8,284
Peppermint's Quest	4	C	7	0	0	2	2,040
Pepper's Legacy	4	C	9	1	1	2	2,608
Pepper's Reality	4	G	6	1	0	1	1,721
Peppersandnoodles	4	F	4	1	1	0	3,440
Peppy	3	F	3	0	0	1	1,915
Peppy Candy	2	F	8	0	0	0	3,520
Peppy Mint	4	C	12	1	1	3	9,191
Peppy Mis	6	M	7	0	0	2	1,856
Peppy Priscilla	6	M	10	1	2	1	19,150
Peppy Shaker	3	F	9	2	1	1	30,480
Peppy's Present	7	G	1	0	0	0	672
Peptide	6	G	18	2	4	4	6,981
Pequannock	4	C	14	0	0	1	2,478
Per Diem	4	F	16	3	2	3	29,356
Perazzi	4	C	1	0	0	0	0
Perch	2	F	2	0	1	0	6,950
Perched High	6	M	12	3	1	1	33,220
Percipitate	3	G	10	0	2	0	5,515
Percy	4	G	7	0	0	1	2,765
Perdaro	3	G	9	1	1	2	14,140
Perdition'sredwing	3	C	2	0	0	0	81
Peregrine Falcon	2	G	6	0	0	1	6,654
Perennial Favorite	2	F	1	0	1	0	2,800
Perfect Again	2	G	7	1	1	0	17,346
Perfect and Regal	3	C	9	0	3	1	26,115
Perfect Angel	5	M	3	0	0	1	140
Perfect Attitude	3	F	7	2	0	0	27,695
Perfect Beau	3	G	8	2	0	0	16,665
Perfect Bet	2	G	3	0	0	0	690
Perfect Blue	3	F	6	2	0	0	65,415
Perfect Boy Chris	4	G	8	0	0	1	830
Perfect Brass	4	F	3	0	0	1	360

Horse	Age	Sex	Sts	1st	2d	3d	Won
Perfect Business	4	F	7	0	1	1	9,215
Perfect Call	2	G	4	2	0	1	28,789
Perfect Camber	4	F	5	1	1	0	17,380
Perfect Case	4	G	8	1	0	0	4,182
Perfect Commander	4	C	17	2	1	2	3,070
Perfect Cut	3	C	9	3	2	1	111,148
Perfect Darling	2	F	8	2	1	0	25,434
Perfect Dear	3	F	7	1	2	1	36,000
Perfect Decision	9	G	5	0	0	0	0
Perfect Design	4	F	1	0	0	0	1,410
Perfect Diamond	6	M	1	0	0	0	84
Perfect Double	2	F	2	0	0	0	200
Perfect Drift	4	G	8	5	0	0	1,505,388
Perfect Energy	4	F	6	1	1	1	68,770
Perfect Fantasy	4	G	12	3	2	0	20,235
Perfect Fit	3	G	7	1	1	3	5,940
Perfect Friend	3	C	14	2	2	1	35,725
Perfect Game	3	G	17	1	4	2	10,048
Perfect Guest	2	C	2	0	0	0	0
Perfect High	2	G	3	0	0	0	0
Perfect Home	3	F	6	1	0	0	3,990
Perfect Ice	4	C	12	1	1	3	5,762
Perfect Illusion	2	F	4	1	3	0	38,388
Perfect Judgment	4	G	12	5	2	1	62,825
Perfect Justice	2	G	8	2	0	1	13,070
Perfect Lady	3	F	7	1	2	0	43,510
Perfect Light	3	F	7	0	0	0	470
Perfect Lil	4	F	3	0	0	0	0
Perfect Man	4	C	1	0	0	0	56
Perfect Mark	5	G	9	0	1	1	1,755
Perfect Miss	3	F	11	3	1	3	41,305
Perfect Moment	3	F	6	3	0	0	91,883
Perfect Moon	2	G	10	3	1	3	353,870
Perfect Mystery	4	G	12	1	0	0	7,740
Perfect One	5	M	11	1	1	2	9,135
Perfect Paradise	3	F	4	0	0	2	4,870
Perfect Parfait	7	G	9	5	1	2	36,465
Perfect Partner	3	F	1	0	0	0	75
Perfect Party (ARG)	4	C	10	2	4	3	53,370
Perfect Pass	3	F	1	0	0	0	0
Perfect Patrick L	6	H	2	0	1	0	1,360
Perfect Performer	5	G	3	1	0	1	11,138
Perfect Plan	4	F	9	2	1	0	19,810
Perfect Policy	6	H	3	0	0	1	260
Perfect Present	3	F	7	1	0	0	11,762
Perfect Pretense	4	G	10	0	1	4	4,661
Perfect Prose	3	F	4	0	0	1	2,013
Perfect Ride	4	C	11	2	4	1	49,089
Perfect Risk	2	C	2	1	1	0	4,880
Perfect Run	6	H	1	0	0	0	240
Perfect Score	7	H	6	1	1	0	6,916
Perfect Script	3	F	1	0	1	0	5,250
Perfect Silver	4	F	19	0	1	5	5,495
Perfect Sleeper	6	G	15	3	3	2	14,327
Perfect Soul (IRE)	5	H	8	3	2	1	856,195
Perfect Speed	4	G	4	0	0	0	800
Perfect Storm B B	4	G	1	0	0	0	0
Perfect Story	3	F	4	2	0	0	52,200
Perfect Stranger	5	H	3	0	0	0	4,540
Perfect Stride	3	G	5	1	1	0	6,090
Perfect Summer	4	F	6	1	2	0	4,790
Perfect Sunset	4	F	8	1	0	0	3,914
Perfect Surprise	5	M	6	0	0	1	1,884
Perfect Sweeper	4	C	5	2	0	1	48,525
Perfect Ten	5	M	10	0	5	1	16,132
Perfect Truth	3	C	10	1	0	0	5,100
Perfect Wave	3	F	2	0	0	0	6,000
Perfect Whit	2	C	5	0	0	0	300
Perfect Wisdom	4	C	18	0	2	2	5,801
Perfect Woman	4	F	6	2	1	0	17,689
Perfect World	3	F	1	1	0	0	27,000
Perfectcombination	2	F	2	0	0	0	165
Perfectineveryway	3	F	10	2	1	1	9,656
Perfectly Agitated	4	F	3	0	0	0	0
Perfectly Catty	3	F	11	3	3	1	18,640
Perfectly Charming	2	F	2	1	0	0	5,896
Perfectly Chilled	4	F	4	1	0	2	16,605
Perfectly Cool	5	M	14	1	0	3	7,655
Perfectly Free	4	F	12	0	3	4	9,925
Perfectly Noble	4	F	7	0	0	0	382
Perfectly Penny	4	F	6	0	0	0	0
Perfectly Regal	3	F	8	0	0	0	976
Perfectly Right	4	F	4	2	0	1	32,150
Perfectly Stunning	4	F	6	2	1	0	62,275
Perfectly Theresa	2	F	6	0	1	1	6,150
Perfecto Westo	3	G	8	3	0	0	37,948
Perfectpurrfection	3	G	5	1	0	0	5,530
Perfectstormtoo	2	C	3	1	0	0	6,000
Perfellia	4	F	6	1	1	0	14,070
Performance Critic	7	G	6	0	0	0	150
Performance Report	3	G	11	1	2	2	11,255
Performer Inflight	2	F	2	0	0	1	2,138
Perfume and Honey	4	F	2	0	1	0	3,600
Perhaps Magic	3	F	9	1	2	1	25,151
Pericles	2	C	3	1	1	0	40,900
Perignon (CHI)	5	G	7	2	0	0	53,340
Perilad	5	G	13	1	0	2	6,173
Perilous Night	2	F	5	1	2	0	28,800
Perimeter	3	C	6	0	4	1	28,460
Periscope	5	G	2	0	1	1	5,235
Perissos	4	G	6	0	0	1	1,800
Perjury	6	G	6	1	1	1	6,090
Perkins Echo	5	G	10	1	1	1	5,790
Perkins Punch	3	C	1	0	0	0	0
Perks First Knight	3	G	8	0	0	0	72
Perky Peaks	4	F	10	1	2	2	31,118
Perky Pirate	5	G	15	3	3	1	15,495
Perkymon	4	G	5	1	1	0	1,300
Perla Ermosa	3	F	4	1	0	1	14,180
Perlong	8	G	5	1	1	2	40,278
Permiso	3	C	8	2	0	2	72,954
Permission Granted	4	F	3	0	0	0	640
Permission Slip	5	G	2	0	0	0	420
Permissiontopass	3	G	19	3	2	1	16,790
Permit Denied	4	F	2	0	0	1	1,980
Pero Dinero	8	H	9	2	2	1	3,376
Perocity	4	F	10	2	0	1	9,929
Perogi Pete	5	G	1	0	0	0	128
Peroni	5	G	6	0	0	1	1,769
Peronist	3	C	5	3	1	0	3,977
Peroxide Lady	7	M	2	0	0	0	218
Perpetual Motion	2	F	1	0	0	0	0
Perpetual Partner	5	G	3	0	0	0	126
Perpetual Peace	2	C	3	1	0	1	58,730
Perpetual Spirit	3	G	5	1	0	0	17,050
Perplexity	4	F	2	0	0	0	0
Perr Sabin	5	G	11	1	2	1	30,069
Perristyle	7	H	2	0	0	0	0
Perry Road Joy	2	F	2	0	0	0	447
Perry T.	6	G	11	0	1	2	2,413
Persee Joe	4	G	12	5	1	0	33,443
Perseid	4	F	6	1	1	1	6,715
Persevere Joe	4	G	8	0	0	1	968
Persevering	3	F	14	3	1	0	24,203
Persh	6	G	15	2	3	4	15,165
Pershing County	5	H	5	1	0	2	2,537
Persian Beauty	5	M	3	0	0	0	720
Persian Harmony	7	H	3	1	0	1	3,345
Persian Reign	4	G	9	1	3	0	9,020
Persian Silver	5	M	5	0	0	0	184
Persian Tower	3	F	4	0	0	0	311
Persianality	8	M	1	0	0	0	40
Persimmon Ridge	4	F	10	3	1	1	82,718
Persistance Pays	3	F	5	2	1	0	9,484
Persistence	8	H	2	0	0	0	0
Persistent Heart	4	C	10	0	2	1	1,640
Persky (ARG)	6	M	5	0	0	0	1,620
Persnickety Cat	4	G	7	1	0	0	3,090
Persnickity Gal	3	F	12	1	2	1	53,704
Persona Non Grata	2	G	1	0	0	0	0
Personable Pete	5	G	8	0	2	1	26,357
Personal Achiever	6	G	3	0	0	0	133
Personal Allure	4	F	8	2	1	0	36,617
Personal Amour	5	G	2	0	0	0	53
Personal Bag	3	G	14	1	1	2	7,467
Personal Banner	9	H	3	0	0	0	159
Personal Beau	7	G	8	4	1	3	94,860
Personal Best	6	H	1	0	0	0	450

Horse	Age	Sex	Sts	1st	2d	3d	Won	Horse	Age	Sex	Sts	1st	2d	3d	Won
Personal Best (NZ)	6	G	1	0	0	0	0	Peter the Pilot	8	G	2	0	0	0	75
Personal Case	3	G	1	0	0	0	0	Peter the Rock	2	C	3	1	0	2	24,080
Personal Clearance	4	C	10	3	1	1	74,400	Peterbilt Imp	5	M	7	0	0	1	388
Personal Deputy	3	C	4	1	0	0	7,150	Peter's Ballad	7	G	12	1	2	1	11,575
Personal Dream	5	M	15	0	3	4	10,485	Peters Dream	5	H	7	0	0	0	765
Personal Emblem	5	M	1	0	0	0	0	Peter's Jewel	4	F	7	2	1	1	10,020
Personal Flair	6	M	7	1	1	0	27,360	Peter's Pleasure	3	G	11	1	0	2	5,538
Personal Flyer	2	C	4	0	0	0	0	Peter's Posada	2	G	4	1	0	1	13,500
Personal Gain	4	G	16	4	1	2	13,260	Peters Punkin	4	F	11	2	1	2	28,690
Personal Half Mast	3	F	5	1	0	1	5,162	Peter's Quest	8	G	2	0	0	0	0
Personal Halo	3	F	3	0	0	0	397	Petersburg Knight	2	G	1	0	0	0	540
Personal Jewel	5	M	5	0	0	0	199	Petes Braggin	4	C	2	0	0	0	0
Personal Journey	6	H	6	1	0	1	16,790	Pete's Duke	7	G	9	0	1	2	1,487
Personal Legend	3	F	9	2	3	1	183,010	Pete's Flair	7	M	13	1	1	1	7,931
Personal Magic	4	G	10	1	3	0	10,047	Pete's Hairtrigger	2	G	5	0	1	0	12,040
Personal Memories	4	F	13	6	2	2	39,461	Petes Hick Chick	2	F	5	3	1	1	89,083
Personal Moon	8	G	6	0	0	0	575	Pete's Lady	3	F	14	2	0	2	6,820
Personal Opinion	4	G	1	0	0	0	0	Pete's Legacy	3	G	7	1	1	1	2,640
Personal Plan	3	G	9	2	2	1	21,318	Pete's Nina	4	G	15	3	1	1	12,757
Personal Prince	3	C	7	1	1	2	45,243	Pete's Panacea	6	G	14	0	1	1	3,524
Personal Prize	8	G	1	0	0	0	0	Pete's Prospect	4	G	4	0	0	0	0
Personal Revenge	2	C	2	0	0	0	170	Pete's Revenge	7	G	6	0	0	2	1,624
Personal Reward	4	C	15	2	4	3	32,357	Pete's Skianno	7	G	6	0	1	1	5,888
Personal Secret	6	G	5	0	0	0	3,814	Pete's Surprise	3	F	9	2	3	1	61,646
Personal Stash	5	G	16	1	5	1	26,283	Petes Tomboy	6	M	5	2	1	0	17,528
Personal Sweep	7	G	8	2	0	0	10,708	Pete's Trust	6	H	7	0	0	1	1,344
Personal Thunder	3	G	1	0	0	0	0	Petesamassbred	2	C	3	0	0	1	4,150
Personal Touch	3	C	13	4	0	1	98,970	Petesicle	3	C	1	0	0	0	0
Personal Tower	3	F	7	1	1	1	7,230	Peteski's Charm	6	H	7	0	0	1	12,350
Personal Trick	7	H	15	2	1	1	18,368	Peteski's Play	5	G	8	0	0	1	2,336
Personal Vendetta	6	G	10	4	2	0	50,080	Peteski's Rosita	3	F	1	0	0	0	217
Personal Wish	6	G	18	0	2	2	3,577	Petey Foster	2	C	2	0	0	1	1,025
Personally Au Some	6	G	1	0	0	0	0	Petie Boy	3	G	7	1	1	0	24,570
Personify	4	F	1	0	0	0	220	Petie J.	3	G	3	0	0	0	319
Perspective	6	G	15	1	3	5	22,465	Petion Pat	3	G	9	1	0	2	40,339
Perspicacious (ARG)	4	C	2	0	0	0	1,440	Petionville Indeed	3	F	8	2	0	1	91,950
Persuade	3	F	13	3	1	1	33,070	Petit Louis	3	C	6	0	0	0	863
Persuading Gold	3	F	8	1	0	1	8,176	Petit Marquis (FR)	6	G	3	1	0	0	17,610
Persuaggle	2	C	6	2	2	0	70,635	Petite Daphnee	4	F	5	0	1	1	5,774
Persuasive Lady	3	F	4	2	0	0	27,372	Petite Delight	3	F	6	0	0	0	486
Persue	5	M	13	4	1	2	59,271	Petite Diablo	5	M	11	1	3	1	33,118
Pert Reply	3	G	16	2	2	0	74,840	Petite Magon Rouge	2	F	1	0	0	0	0
Pertain	3	F	1	0	0	0	0	Petite Mermaid	3	F	14	2	1	3	55,179
Pertie Girl	3	F	11	2	0	3	10,412	Petite Motion	2	F	4	1	0	0	6,781
Pertiest	3	F	3	0	0	1	900	Petite n' Classy	4	F	14	5	4	1	76,812
Pertuisane (GB)	4	F	4	2	1	1	172,800	Petite Silver	5	M	12	1	1	1	6,026
Perty Gerty	3	F	9	2	2	2	26,747	Petite Zinger	4	F	8	1	1	3	29,454
Perty Late	3	F	2	0	0	0	80	Petites Direct Hit	4	F	2	0	0	0	0
Perty Number	5	M	13	7	6	0	65,404	Petrakos	5	H	2	0	0	0	105
Peruvian Summer	4	C	8	1	1	0	7,956	Petrina Above	8	M	11	4	4	0	159,302
Pesci	2	F	2	2	0	0	57,000	Petro Pete	5	G	11	2	2	1	12,361
Pesky	7	H	8	1	3	2	8,580	Petrolia	5	H	6	2	0	4	3,772
Pesky Pete	5	G	13	0	2	3	4,383	Petrov	5	H	1	0	0	0	0
Pesky Rascal	8	G	11	2	2	2	31,850	Petrus (MEX)	6	H	13	2	1	0	6,510
Peskybo	6	G	6	0	0	0	0	Petsy Deville	2	F	1	0	0	0	0
Peso Por Beso	2	C	3	1	1	1	34,630	Petticoat Girl	3	F	11	1	0	1	5,853
Pessoa's Pick	4	G	4	2	0	0	19,830	Petticoat Penny	2	F	4	0	0	1	2,520
Pestle	5	G	4	1	0	2	8,625	Pettit's Quest	7	G	2	0	0	0	0
Pesto	4	G	9	2	2	1	40,890	Petty Bandit	4	G	7	0	2	2	3,972
Pesto Perfetto	4	G	17	3	4	4	26,755	Petty County	2	G	2	0	0	0	0
Pet	3	F	2	0	0	0	0	Petty Giraffe	4	G	5	0	2	1	2,300
Pet Bob (ARG)	6	G	8	0	3	1	11,450	Petty's Way	4	G	16	3	2	2	9,241
Pet Bully	3	G	10	0	0	1	1,689	Pews Pond	4	F	10	1	0	3	7,288
Pet Wildcat	3	F	12	1	0	0	6,600	Pewter Princess	6	M	14	2	3	1	21,168
Pet Your Cat	3	F	5	1	0	1	7,377	Pewter Skies	5	G	11	1	1	2	10,505
Peta	5	M	8	0	0	0	6,030	Peycass	3	F	1	0	0	0	0
Petal (IRE)	7	M	3	0	1	0	4,563	Peytons Pleasure	5	M	14	0	5	2	15,462
Petalite	4	F	1	0	0	0	145	Peyvon	6	M	1	0	0	0	900
Petals	2	F	1	0	0	0	125	Pfenning	5	M	14	2	2	1	18,479
Petard	4	C	2	0	0	1	907	Pfilerup	3	F	7	1	0	0	9,440
Pete Attraction	6	H	1	0	0	0	0	Phabulous Love	6	M	2	0	0	1	3,040
Pete On the Fiddle	2	G	2	1	1	0	7,768	Phaedra	4	F	12	2	3	0	37,849
Pete Power	3	G	5	0	0	0	0	Phancy That Coyote	5	G	8	0	0	0	709
Pete Shure	5	G	9	2	3	1	12,527	Phantastic Secret	2	C	4	1	0	1	13,550
Peter Habit	6	G	4	1	0	2	2,366	Phantom Caller	6	H	2	0	0	0	346
Peter Pan's Shadow	2	C	6	0	0	1	2,190	Phantom Cat	2	G	2	0	0	0	810
Peter Peter Peter	3	G	4	0	1	0	2,120	Phantom Chief	3	C	3	0	0	0	1,600
Peter Punkin Eater	5	G	16	3	3	0	14,079	Phantom Fox	4	G	12	1	2	2	30,395
Peter Spats	4	G	10	2	3	1	6,336	Phantom Light	4	C	6	3	0	0	299,610

Horse	Age	Sex	Sts	1st	2d	3d	Won
Phantom of the Sea	6	G	14	0	0	1	1,704
Phantom Phair	6	M	4	0	0	0	662
Phantom Raider	3	G	7	0	1	1	8,064
Phantom Ranch	4	F	8	2	1	1	9,055
Phantom Rider	4	C	9	1	2	1	6,785
Phantom Song	4	F	1	0	0	0	360
Phantom Stampede	2	C	5	1	0	2	24,930
Phantom Storm	4	F	14	4	2	3	33,977
Phantom's Magic	3	F	4	0	0	0	318
Phar From Blonde	2	F	3	0	0	0	475
Phar Into Orbit	6	G	5	0	0	0	0
Phararah	5	G	12	0	2	1	5,277
Pharaoh's Cat	4	C	7	1	0	0	12,160
Pharaway Wedding	2	F	7	0	0	3	7,680
Pharisien Dancer	4	F	2	0	0	0	215
Pharly's Wars	4	F	4	1	1	0	10,066
Pharonic	4	G	9	2	1	3	11,707
Pharos Legacy	3	G	9	1	0	1	6,508
Phat	5	M	9	2	0	2	15,615
Phat Chance	3	C	1	0	0	0	0
Phat City Kitty	3	F	10	0	0	2	3,148
Phat Daddy	4	G	11	3	2	0	15,351
Phat Girl	6	M	13	1	0	1	4,589
Pheasant Run	4	F	2	1	0	0	2,200
Pheiffer	5	M	6	1	2	1	63,100
Pheisty Phoebe	3	F	9	1	0	2	28,185
Phenomenal Knight	6	G	3	0	0	0	150
Pheonia	3	F	5	0	0	1	3,300
Phi Beta Doc	7	G	1	0	0	0	153
Phighter	4	G	6	0	0	0	315
Phil a Glass	3	G	2	0	0	0	84
Phil the Bank	3	G	9	1	1	0	6,660
Phil the Gold	3	G	3	0	0	0	348
Philadelphia Jim	3	C	6	2	1	0	66,420
Philadelphiensis	5	M	2	0	0	0	80
Philantha	6	M	8	0	1	3	12,880
Philarro	3	C	3	1	0	0	3,058
Philbert	2	C	2	0	0	0	0
Philhippic Phrank	2	C	1	0	0	0	0
Philip Lacy	6	G	6	0	0	0	592
Philip's Ferrari	5	H	6	0	0	0	600
Philis D.	2	F	1	0	0	0	70
Philistine	8	G	10	3	1	0	3,880
Phillie City	3	F	18	2	0	4	18,452
Phillies Dream	4	F	7	3	1	0	26,660
Phillip El Guapo	6	H	9	0	1	0	1,330
Philly Girl	4	F	1	0	0	0	76
Philmo	4	F	13	2	1	1	15,326
Philon	4	C	13	0	2	1	16,350
Philosophers Stone	4	F	1	0	0	0	0
Phil's Cookie	3	F	7	0	1	2	6,458
Phils Mistake	6	G	18	2	2	2	14,152
Phil's Revenge	6	M	1	0	0	0	0
Phish	4	C	4	1	0	0	29,638
Phlying Phyly	5	M	2	0	0	0	314
Phoebe Phone Tag	4	F	3	0	0	0	405
Phoenicia	3	F	4	0	1	1	3,500
Phoenix Bird	3	F	8	0	0	0	0
Phoenix Blues	4	G	1	0	1	0	1,500
Phoenix Reach (IRE)	3	C	4	3	0	1	1,035,526
Phoenix River	5	G	6	0	0	0	80
Phoenix Song	5	M	2	0	0	0	800
Phoenixledo	3	F	6	0	0	2	3,735
Phonaghost	2	C	2	0	0	0	180
Phone a Friend	4	F	2	0	0	0	144
Phone Ahead	3	G	1	0	1	0	1,075
Phone Alone	6	H	7	2	1	0	8,096
Phone Change	4	F	3	0	0	0	5,988
Phone Dunc	2	C	5	0	0	1	992
Phone Fighter	3	G	4	1	0	0	4,215
Phone First	5	G	12	1	0	3	12,841
Phone Flash	4	C	11	1	2	2	10,575
Phone Good News	3	G	7	1	1	2	9,936
Phone Joan	2	F	4	1	0	2	6,755
Phone Me a Favor	4	F	10	0	4	2	42,800
Phone Prospector	7	G	13	6	3	1	50,261
Phone Ruler	5	H	1	0	1	0	7,200
Phone Scrambler	4	G	7	0	0	1	1,510
Phone Set	3	C	3	0	0	0	29
Phone Sport	8	G	5	0	1	2	4,780
Phone Tech	3	G	7	0	0	3	2,893
Phone the Diva	3	F	10	2	1	2	17,140
Phone the Nurse	5	M	13	0	0	3	4,155
Phone the Wizard	4	G	7	1	0	0	3,060
Phonecall Freddie	3	G	12	2	3	2	12,428
Phoneforchampagne	4	C	10	1	2	1	41,450
Phonetastic	2	F	2	0	0	0	900
Phoney Aura	2	F	1	0	0	0	195
Phoney Gold	4	C	13	2	1	2	10,438
Photo	5	G	1	0	0	0	0
Photo Baba	3	G	5	1	1'	1	4,749
Photo Delay	3	F	3	1	0	0	2,660
Photo Flash	3	C	2	0	0	2	7,700
Photo for Show	3	F	18	0	6	3	17,012
Photo Shop	3	C	2	0	0	0	164
Photo Star	4	C	9	0	1	2	1,756
Photo Store	5	G	1	0	0	0	0
Photographic	2	F	1	0	0	1	2,970
Phrase's Wildcat	3	C	5	0	0	0	885
Phuri Dai	4	F	7	1	0	3	6,873
Phylly's Boy	4	G	1	0	0	0	0
Phylogeny	5	H	2	0	0	1	616
Phyls Irish Lad	4	G	1	0	0	0	840
Phyls Runaway Cat	3	G	12	0	1	0	3,072
Phyl's Storm Cloud	3	G	14	4	1	2	19,858
Phylupthecup	3	F	1	0	0	0	430
Phyne	8	G	1	0	0	0	0
Phyne Chyna	6	M	2	0	0	0	156
Physical	5	G	13	2	2	0	11,407
Physical Force	4	G	4	1	0	1	8,475
Physiology	6	G	16	2	1	2	7,595
Phyxius	4	F	12	0	4	3	64,106
Pia Gold	4	G	3	1	0	0	11,660
Piana Anna	2	F	2	0	0	0	252
Piano Chimes	4	F	7	1	0	1	19,110
Piano Money	3	G	15	2	2	3	11,619
Piano Tunner	2	F	4	1	1	1	26,352
Pianopiano	3	G	5	1	0	0	9,711
Pia's Courage	4	F	9	1	1	1	7,745
Pia's Wager	4	F	3	0	0	0	0
Piazzola (NZ)	4	G	5	0	0	0	0
Pic Em Hof	3	F	2	1	0	0	6,460
Pic of the Week	2	F	2	1	1	0	8,225
Pic Pocket	5	G	12	3	1	2	25,197
Picabo Streak	5	M	16	0	2	2	6,619
Picadilly Bay	2	C	3	0	2	0	25,060
Picalook	8	M	3	0	0	0	88
Picante Falstaff	7	G	1	0	0	0	0
Piccolo Honey	4	F	16	9	3	2	124,920
Piccolo Player (GB)	5	G	2	1	0	0	4,950
Pichi Richi	3	F	3	0	0	1	640
Pick a Fight	3	G	10	0	1	3	6,275
Pick a Number	3	F	1	0	0	0	420
Pick a Penny	4	F	4	1	0	1	3,100
Pick a Winner Max	3	C	2	0	0	0	0
Pick Me Buzz	4	G	14	2	3	1	16,345
Pick of the Day	5	M	8	2	0	5	12,699
Pick of the Pack	2	F	5	2	0	0	36,820
Pick Pocket Buck	2	G	2	0	0	0	0
Pick the Best	8	G	14	3	2	2	13,267
Pick Your Passion	6	H	6	0	0	0	977
Picked Clean	3	F	12	0	3	1	17,696
Pick'em	3	C	6	3	2	0	126,500
Pickett's Charge	5	G	1	0	0	0	38
Pickety Witch	3	F	14	3	0	2	23,715
Picki	3	F	4	0	0	0	2,130
Pickin the Pace	6	M	14	1	0	1	8,758
Pickinupthedayroll	4	C	9	1	0	0	2,090
Pickled Bay	4	G	6	1	0	2	14,040
Pickled Pepper	3	C	6	0	0	0	0
Pickles	6	M	4	1	1	1	12,896
Pickpocket Express	2	G	4	1	0	0	25,428
Picks Image	5	H	3	0	0	0	444
Pick's Prospect	9	G	11	1	1	3	33,378
Pick's Top	4	C	4	0	2	0	7,825
Pickthekey	3	C	11	0	1	0	1,400
Pickup the Marbles	5	G	9	0	2	1	5,456
Pickupspeed	6	G	7	1	1	0	92,740

RECORDS OF HORSES

Horse	Age	Sex	Sts	1st	2d	3d	Won	Horse	Age	Sex	Sts	1st	2d	3d	Won
Picky Picky Picky	4	G	14	1	0	2	5,596	Pilsner	6	G	10	2	0	0	9,900
Picnic and Roses	3	F	4	0	0	0	1,050	Pilu Russu	3	F	4	1	0	0	6,536
Picnic Point P S	2	G	3	0	0	1	1,425	Pilum	4	G	9	4	0	1	39,266
Picnic Spread	7	M	5	0	0	0	1,355	Pilya	3	F	2	0	0	1	5,000
Picnic Theme	5	M	7	2	0	0	51,260	Pim Pim	4	G	4	0	0	0	171
Pico D J Alex	3	C	9	1	1	1	47,864	Pima Colada	4	F	6	1	1	0	8,170
Pico D. J. Nick	3	C	2	0	0	0	100	Pimento	6	M	10	2	2	3	31,971
Pico Duarte	4	G	6	0	0	0	-515	Pimpernick	2	C	3	0	0	2	7,280
Piconeach (NZ)	5	M	4	1	1	1	26,300	Pin and Peck	5	M	6	1	1	3	8,090
Pico's Fame	2	C	1	0	0	0	0	Pin Curl Peg	3	F	10	3	0	0	31,300
Pic's Legend	6	G	6	2	1	1	17,220	Pin Emerald	4	F	3	0	0	1	470
Pic's Paradise	5	H	1	0	0	0	59	Pin Jig	2	G	6	0	0	2	8,280
Pic's Rate	5	H	2	0	0	0	408	Pin Okie O	5	G	8	1	1	1	6,795
Picts	8	G	5	1	1	1	3,720	Pin Setter	4	G	9	3	1	0	18,909
Picture Book	6	H	11	1	1	2	6,096	Pin Up Pat	4	F	11	2	0	2	5,231
Picture Gallery	5	M	9	3	1	0	46,810	Pina Colada (GB)	4	F	4	0	0	0	7,166
Picture Isle	4	F	8	0	2	0	2,051	Pinacious	4	F	4	0	0	0	2,340
Picture Palace	5	M	4	1	1	0	64,117	Pinball	3	G	4	0	0	0	477
Picture Perfect	3	F	3	0	0	0	0	Pincay	2	C	2	0	0	1	7,820
Picture the Answer	3	F	7	1	4	1	7,890	Pinch Hill	5	M	11	1	0	2	6,042
Picture This	5	M	12	1	2	3	15,301	Pinch Hitter	4	C	9	3	1	1	92,890
Picture This Hour	4	G	10	2	0	1	9,994	Pinch of Reality	8	M	4	0	1	0	6,115
Picture This Ms.	3	F	6	0	0	0	0	Pinchme	3	G	4	0	0	1	3,090
Picture This Star	3	G	5	1	0	1	13,560	Pine Bend	3	G	4	1	1	0	14,040
Picture This Tux	4	F	11	2	1	2	15,860	Pine Breeze	3	C	2	0	0	1	1,900
Picturesofmemories	6	M	13	3	1	2	48,575	Pine Brook	3	C	11	2	0	3	15,042
Pidgeon's Angel	3	F	7	1	0	0	8,490	Pine Brook Road	4	F	7	0	1	1	6,560
Pie Corner	3	C	8	2	1	0	92,942	Pine Creek	3	C	8	0	0	1	1,830
Pie N Burger	5	G	7	5	0	0	373,800	Pine for Java	3	C	14	3	2	1	85,280
Piece Lane	4	F	2	0	0	0	600	Pine for Tate	3	G	13	2	2	3	27,305
Piece of Art	5	M	2	0	0	0	47	Pine Gulch	3	F	4	0	0	1	1,255
Piece of Change	2	C	2	0	0	0	0	Pine Love	2	C	1	0	0	0	0
Pieceofperfection	4	F	14	4	5	3	42,966	Pine Meadows	5	G	6	0	0	0	320
Pieces of April	4	F	7	2	2	1	11,020	Pine Penny	4	F	4	0	0	0	510
Pieces of My Life	3	G	13	0	1	3	4,882	Pine Rob	3	F	1	0	0	0	82
Piedmont Dan	4	G	11	1	2	1	5,113	Pine Thymeprincess	5	M	14	3	4	1	56,800
Piedmont Express	3	F	15	4	1	4	56,874	Pine Valley	5	M	14	4	1	1	40,060
Piedra de Rayo	4	G	3	0	0	1	2,620	Pineapple	3	G	10	1	0	1	6,272
Piedra Peak Lad	6	G	6	1	1	0	16,202	Pinecall	2	F	7	0	2	1	4,370
Pieman	3	C	15	1	2	3	11,511	Pinedale Star	4	C	14	1	1	5	55,357
Piensa Sonando (CHI)	5	H	9	1	2	1	206,773	Pineingmyheartaway	5	M	8	0	0	0	1,785
Pier Four	3	G	2	1	0	0	10,460	Piney Creek Duck	5	H	4	1	0	0	9,900
Pierced Navel	3	F	18	0	2	5	11,697	Piney Princess	3	F	4	0	1	1	2,325
Pierhead	3	C	4	0	0	2	8,646	Pinfeather	8	G	16	2	5	3	14,514
Pierhead Jump	8	G	8	0	1	1	888	Pinga	4	F	5	0	0	0	697
Pieria	4	F	6	3	1	1	100,483	Piniante	4	F	18	4	4	3	61,345
Pierian Spring	2	F	2	1	0	0	24,600	Pining for You	3	C	1	0	0	0	0
Pierre	3	C	9	2	0	2	11,868	Pink Camellia	3	F	9	2	1	0	14,700
Pierre Legrand	2	C	1	0	0	0	0	Pink Carnation	3	F	8	0	0	1	865
Pierre Sag Go	5	G	3	0	0	1	737	Pink Cat	5	H	1	0	0	0	0
Pierre's Wish	2	C	1	0	0	0	0	Pink Champagne	2	F	2	2	0	0	132,000
Piersixer	3	F	10	2	1	3	107,439	Pink Chips	5	G	5	0	0	1	5,100
Pie's Lil Brother	4	G	11	3	3	0	91,870	Pink Duck	5	H	13	0	0	4	36,585
Pies Prospect	2	C	1	1	0	0	27,000	Pink Dusty	2	F	3	0	2	0	4,490
Pietra's Girl	5	M	20	4	3	3	20,934	Pink Jade	4	F	9	2	1	0	67,672
Pigalle	2	C	2	0	0	1	1,190	Pink Meow	3	F	5	0	4	1	7,860
Piggle Stix	7	M	9	0	2	2	7,065	Pink Note	3	F	17	0	2	3	13,175
Piggy Bank	4	F	9	0	0	2	1,782	Pink Parfait	3	F	12	4	2	1	23,871
Pikachew	2	C	2	0	0	0	540	Pink Power	2	G	6	0	0	0	1,590
Pikake	4	F	9	2	1	0	12,890	Pink Sandals	3	F	7	1	0	0	7,800
Pike Place Gold	3	C	7	1	2	0	48,020	Pink Vice	4	F	2	0	0	0	0
Pikecity Baileys	3	C	3	0	0	0	0	Pinkerton	5	G	11	1	1	0	10,930
Pike's Beelzebub	3	H	1	0	0	0	0	Pinkies Valentine	2	F	1	0	0	0	1,380
Pikester	4	G	11	2	0	2	18,268	Pink'ster	2	F	5	0	0	0	1,940
Pikeville	5	G	13	2	3	0	16,445	Pinky Floyd	4	G	13	6	2	1	56,133
Pila	4	F	2	0	0	1	1,284	Pinky Pizwaanski	5	G	6	0	1	0	17,706
Pile of Gold	4	F	3	0	0	0	0	Pino Doll	5	M	5	1	1	1	10,526
Pilfer	2	F	2	1	1	0	16,860	Pinson	3	G	4	0	1	0	2,415
Pilgrim County	2	C	5	0	2	2	9,650	Pint o' Stout	6	G	13	2	2	3	10,016
Pilgrim Miss	6	M	9	4	1	2	43,690	Pintail	3	F	7	1	3	0	14,800
Pilgrim Road	6	G	9	1	1	1	14,036	Pinup	6	M	7	0	0	0	304
Pillar to Post	4	G	15	2	3	5	24,044	Pinwheel	3	F	3	0	0	0	0
Pillars of Fire	4	C	1	0	0	0	48	Pinwinee Whiskey	3	F	3	1	1	1	49,916
Pillar's Starbuck	4	C	9	0	0	2	2,227	Pioneer Boy	5	G	11	5	2	2	189,340
Pillow Talk	4	F	8	0	0	2	13,550	Pioneer Inn	5	M	8	3	0	1	54,794
Pillowtop	2	F	4	0	0	0	774	Pioneer Limited	5	H	6	0	0	1	322
Pilot View	3	G	8	0	0	0	807	Pioneer Pass	5	G	12	1	0	1	2,581
Pilot's Gone	2	C	2	0	0	0	0	Pioneer Pete	4	G	7	2	0	1	15,278
Pilots Last Flight	2	F	5	1	0	2	14,074	Pioneer Ruler	5	H	2	0	0	0	103

Horse	Age	Sex	Sts	1st	2d	3d	Won
Pioneerman	2	G	5	1	1	0	41,200
Pioneer's Gold	2	C	1	0	0	0	372
Pionera	4	F	10	2	2	2	15,637
Piority	3	F	4	0	0	1	1,430
Piotrus' Baby	3	C	9	1	0	0	11,205
Pip N Pop	3	F	3	0	0	0	340
Pipe Bomb	4	G	8	2	0	2	27,280
Pipeline	6	G	4	0	0	1	5,890
Piper Anne	2	F	3	0	0	0	0
Piper Two	2	F	1	0	0	0	0
Piper's Dream	3	F	3	0	0	0	53
Piper's Revenge	3	F	2	0	0	0	0
Pipers Trick	3	F	6	1	1	1	62,424
Pipila	3	G	9	1	0	1	3,344
Piping Hot	3	F	1	0	0	0	0
Pipo's	3	C	4	0	0	0	360
Pippa Squeaka	5	M	9	0	1	2	2,791
Pippinella	3	F	4	1	1	1	6,154
Pippy Dance	3	G	12	1	0	2	7,368
Pip's Angel	5	M	10	4	1	1	28,520
Pip's My Boy	4	G	6	0	0	2	1,820
Piranha	9	H	9	1	3	2	5,515
Piranhurst	8	H	6	1	0	1	11,124
Pirate Afleet	2	G	2	1	0	0	8,100
Pirate Expectation	4	G	14	2	2	3	20,897
Pirate Liason	2	C	5	1	1	1	12,903
Pirate Prince	4	C	5	1	1	1	1,675
Pirate Ship	3	C	6	1	1	1	13,750
Pirates Band	4	G	10	0	5	1	7,790
Pirate's Fleet	6	G	4	0	1	0	4,560
Pirate's Gem	7	M	5	0	0	0	960
Pirate's Gold	5	H	5	1	0	2	9,970
Pirate's Hostage	10	G	17	1	0	1	4,835
Pirate's Prize	3	G	10	0	0	2	1,898
Pirates Seed	6	H	3	0	0	1	345
Pirate's Slew	6	G	1	0	0	0	0
Pirate's Stash	7	G	14	0	3	3	4,606
Pirate's Swan Song	4	F	2	0	0	0	0
Pirate's Sword	5	H	8	3	0	0	24,180
Pirate's Wench	5	H	3	0	0	1	618
Piri the Champ	6	M	4	0	0	1	565
Pirkey	7	M	10	2	4	3	10,966
Pisca	5	M	4	0	0	0	951
Pisces	6	H	3	0	0	0	400
Piscolo	3	G	13	0	0	0	1,760
Pisgah	2	C	3	0	1	1	13,650
Pistareen	5	G	12	1	2	1	11,056
Pistol Avenue	3	G	12	2	1	4	58,440
Pistol Chief	6	H	2	0	0	0	210
Pistol Nui	4	C	6	1	2	1	2,375
Pistol Place	3	G	11	1	2	1	22,240
Pistol Polly	3	F	4	0	0	0	0
Pistol Power	7	M	8	0	0	3	3,705
Pistol Rose	7	M	1	0	0	0	55
Pistoldoone	4	C	18	2	0	2	11,457
Pistolero de Plata	4	G	11	0	1	0	4,556
Pistolina	7	M	5	0	0	0	655
Pistols and Music	7	G	11	0	0	1	1,590
Pistol's Baby Doll	4	F	16	0	1	0	2,289
Pistols Last Stand	2	F	2	0	0	1	1,525
Pistol's Missile	4	F	1	0	0	0	100
Pistols N Arrows	7	M	1	0	0	0	0
Pistols Prospect	6	H	2	0	0	0	0
Pistols's Wildcard	2	C	1	0	0	0	195
Piston	4	C	7	0	1	1	7,630
Piston Broke	3	G	11	1	0	3	6,054
Pit Drip	4	F	10	1	2	0	6,171
Pitati (BRZ)	5	M	14	3	6	1	23,015
Pitch a Penny	3	F	2	0	0	0	570
Pitchacurve	2	F	4	1	0	1	21,926
Pitchin' Kalim	6	H	6	0	0	1	440
Pito	4	C	5	1	0	0	7,692
Pit's Zagor	4	F	3	0	0	0	103
Pittsburgh Kid	5	G	5	0	0	0	3,185
Pittsburgh Star	6	G	6	4	1	0	59,290
Pitufa	3	F	9	1	3	1	11,460
Piute	6	G	11	2	1	0	83,227
Pivotal Moment	5	M	1	0	0	0	0
Pivotal Pete	2	C	2	1	0	0	7,800
Pixel	3	F	6	1	0	0	8,000
Pixie Emerald	5	H	3	0	0	0	175
Pixie Luv	7	M	4	0	0	0	1,145
Pixies Moon	3	G	2	0	0	0	0
Pizza Boy	3	G	10	1	2	2	15,660
Pizza Port	3	F	16	1	0	0	7,170
Pizzy	6	G	8	0	0	0	336
Pj's Halo	5	M	7	1	0	3	40,492
Pj'salarm	6	G	13	4	3	2	13,533
Pk's Gal	3	F	9	2	1	2	47,776
Placable	3	F	9	1	0	1	8,460
Place All Bets	3	G	7	1	1	0	55,167
Place Card	5	M	2	0	0	0	129
Place Kicker	5	M	5	1	2	0	12,146
Place My Star	8	G	4	0	0	0	240
Place to Hide	3	F	4	1	0	1	23,980
Placer Creek	2	F	1	0	0	1	1,800
Placer Gold	3	F	1	0	0	0	729
Placid River	3	C	2	0	0	0	2,220
Placid Star	2	F	1	1	0	0	7,500
Placido	3	C	8	3	0	1	55,280
Plaefare Lad	7	G	3	0	1	1	3,005
Plaid	2	F	4	0	1	0	9,000
Plaid Patches	6	M	2	0	0	0	146
Plain Brown Suit	7	H	7	1	3	2	14,630
Plain Clothes	4	G	5	1	0	1	27,044
Plain Ego	7	M	4	0	1	1	2,085
Plain Honey	8	M	11	0	2	1	4,022
Plain Jack	3	G	7	0	2	2	11,023
Plain Luscious	6	M	2	0	0	0	0
Plain Majestic	8	H	3	0	0	0	0
Plain Ole John	3	C	13	3	1	2	18,241
Plain O'Pete	3	C	1	0	0	0	0
Plainoleabe	4	G	11	2	5	1	25,377
Plainsong	4	F	1	0	0	0	0
Plait	3	F	4	1	1	0	34,480
Plamor Princess	2	F	2	0	0	1	3,234
Planca's Secret	4	G	11	1	1	1	5,404
Plancnorth	6	M	1	1	0	0	1,067
Planet Fitness	2	F	3	1	0	0	9,000
Planet Kind	2	F	2	0	0	0	746
Planet Ruler	5	G	10	1	0	1	7,052
Planets Aligned	2	C	4	0	0	0	5,520
Planoncometbebopin	5	M	10	1	1	0	31,100
Plans to Travel	3	F	6	1	0	2	7,430
Plant the Seed	3	G	14	2	4	2	25,395
Plantation Acres	2	C	6	0	1	2	7,340
Plantation Girl	8	M	17	4	2	0	34,126
Plantation Rose	3	F	15	3	2	5	21,931
Plaster de Lane	3	F	3	0	1	0	2,103
Plastic Payoff	6	M	10	1	1	3	22,333
Plate Boundary	5	M	4	1	0	0	9,280
Plate Tectonics	4	G	3	0	0	1	1,840
Platinum Account	4	C	5	0	0	0	900
Platinum Ballet	2	F	3	1	1	0	15,980
Platinum Bullet	4	G	7	0	1	1	2,045
Platinum Case	2	C	1	0	0	0	118
Platinum Coyote	3	F	10	0	2	0	2,726
Platinum Duke (GB)	4	G	6	1	0	2	30,800
Platinum Edition	3	G	1	1	0	0	26,705
Platinum Finish	3	F	1	0	0	0	0
Platinum Halo	7	G	15	1	3	0	9,697
Platinum Hawk	4	F	7	0	0	2	25,027
Platinum Hope	3	F	10	1	1	1	16,137
Platinum Priced	2	G	7	1	3	0	22,320
Platinum Prince	2	G	5	1	0	0	7,429
Platinum Princess	2	F	3	1	1	1	33,036
Platinum Rose	4	F	8	2	4	0	10,549
Platinum Rush	2	F	8	1	1	2	19,427
Platinum Score	3	G	9	1	1	2	49,826
Platinum Setting	7	G	10	1	1	3	54,340
Platinum Shoes	4	F	3	0	0	0	0
Platinum Ticket	6	G	8	2	1	1	43,710
Platinum Upgrade	2	C	2	0	0	1	1,430
Platinum Wildcard	2	F	3	0	0	0	225
Platitude	3	C	1	0	0	0	2,160
Plato	6	H	2	0	0	0	252
Platonia	4	G	11	1	1	1	5,686
Platonic Poker	5	H	2	0	0	0	0

RECORDS OF HORSES

Horse	Age	Sex	Sts	1st	2d	3d	Won
Platonic Zagor	4	C	1	0	0	0	0
Platte County	2	C	5	0	1	1	3,261
Platte Vally Girl	2	F	2	0	1	0	1,434
Plausible	4	G	15	3	3	4	78,380
Play	4	G	4	0	1	0	2,917
Play Action	5	G	2	1	1	0	8,214
Play All Night	2	C	1	1	0	0	25,200
Play Annie Play	3	F	4	0	0	0	0
Play Approval	5	G	6	0	0	0	1,888
Play Around	4	G	3	0	0	0	0
Play Around Sam	2	G	8	0	1	3	6,180
Play At Wrigley	2	C	3	0	0	0	0
Play Bingo	2	C	1	0	0	0	1,500
Play Fan	5	G	3	0	1	0	1,330
Play for Dixie	4	F	7	1	1	2	4,773
Play for Saratoga	4	C	13	3	1	4	18,303
Play Good (ARG)	7	H	4	2	0	0	7,356
Play Hookie	2	F	2	0	1	0	2,400
Play in the Sand	3	F	5	0	0	0	137
Play It Kerry	5	M	11	0	1	0	2,460
Play It Out	4	G	13	0	3	0	41,150
Play It Softly	2	G	3	0	0	0	0
Play Me a Tune	3	F	10	2	2	5	55,890
Play Me Dixie	5	H	3	1	0	0	7,020
Play My Music	4	F	5	0	0	0	627
Play N Fare	4	F	10	2	2	1	19,094
Play of the Game	2	G	5	0	1	0	4,130
Play Pad	6	G	16	0	1	2	3,565
Play Taps	7	H	2	0	0	0	450
Play the Devil	4	F	9	2	0	1	16,357
Play the Numbers	5	M	5	0	0	0	424
Play the Part	6	H	10	0	0	0	1,806
Play the Queen	3	F	2	0	0	0	0
Play the Tiger	6	G	3	0	0	1	650
Play the Trap	8	G	11	1	4	1	2,196
Play Well T C	6	G	1	0	0	0	0
Play Your Bluff	3	G	5	1	0	0	6,208
Play Zone	3	C	5	0	0	0	730
Playa Azul	4	G	14	0	2	1	8,706
Playa Maya	3	F	3	1	1	1	35,980
Playasultrytune	6	G	6	1	0	2	4,565
Playback	5	G	1	0	0	0	0
Playboy Hope	5	M	7	0	0	0	357
Playboy Jai	5	G	6	2	0	0	11,586
Playboy Pete	4	G	4	1	2	0	17,425
Playboy Slew	3	C	3	0	0	0	3,250
Playcodered	4	G	15	2	1	2	13,885
Playero	10	H	16	1	1	2	4,502
Player's Hillary	7	M	6	0	0	0	869
Player's Lastdance	7	G	3	0	0	0	114
Playersfirstchoice	4	F	8	1	1	1	5,810
Playfool	5	H	18	1	3	1	5,553
Playforme	3	F	1	0	0	0	76
Playful	4	F	3	0	0	0	2,160
Playful Billy Bob	3	C	4	0	0	0	1,452
Playful Cat	2	C	5	1	0	0	11,050
Playful Dancer	4	F	4	0	0	1	1,250
Playful Grin	4	F	11	0	1	3	1,040
Playful Prince	3	G	8	0	2	0	2,830
Playful Sara	5	M	12	0	0	5	5,770
Playful Squaw	7	M	14	4	1	0	17,383
Playgirl	3	F	6	0	0	2	13,200
Playgirls Beau	3	C	5	0	0	0	315
Playground Legend	3	G	8	3	0	0	27,595
Playhurt	2	G	5	1	1	0	22,360
Playin' All Day	3	G	1	0	0	1	1,900
Playin' With Magic	3	C	3	2	1	0	3,380
Playing Footsie	3	F	7	1	2	0	72,756
Playing for Keeps	7	H	3	0	0	0	160
Playing It Cool	4	G	12	4	0	3	50,626
Playing Lit	4	G	9	2	4	1	17,945
Playing Now	4	G	4	0	1	1	1,440
Playing the Game	4	C	8	1	0	1	9,960
Playing With Fire	5	G	4	1	2	0	45,080
Playitagain Leo	4	F	9	2	1	2	53,100
Playitagainforme	2	F	2	1	0	1	6,310
Playmera	6	M	9	1	2	1	30,834
Playmoney	7	M	2	0	0	0	0
Playoftheday	3	G	10	1	2	1	5,963
Playwithyourmoney	3	G	11	1	1	0	10,875
Plaza South	2	F	5	0	1	0	9,805
Plaza Suite	4	F	8	2	0	0	20,540
Plazas Lil Pistol	7	G	9	3	1	0	33,791
Plazas Lil Waki	5	G	3	0	1	0	2,500
Plea Be a Winner	3	F	5	1	1	0	2,558
Pleas Deal	3	F	10	2	2	0	36,240
Pleasant Addition	6	H	2	0	1	0	806
Pleasant Amigo	5	H	16	1	3	5	9,509
Pleasant Angel	7	M	18	2	2	5	13,578
Pleasant Bend	3	G	4	0	3	0	13,357
Pleasant Breeze	8	G	1	0	0	0	0
Pleasant Challenge	3	G	7	0	0	1	2,040
Pleasant Chap	3	G	1	0	0	0	0
Pleasant Chorus	5	M	3	0	0	0	0
Pleasant Cloud	5	M	13	7	1	1	27,059
Pleasant Company	4	G	14	6	2	1	90,805
Pleasant Crossing	2	F	3	1	1	0	8,275
Pleasant Divorce	5	G	3	0	0	0	1,740
Pleasant Ed	5	G	1	0	0	0	200
Pleasant Feeling	9	G	9	3	1	2	15,538
Pleasant Ghost	3	F	4	0	3	0	28,150
Pleasant Gulch	3	F	3	0	0	0	1,260
Pleasant Hall	4	G	2	0	1	1	11,180
Pleasant Honor	2	G	6	3	1	0	55,860
Pleasant Hope	4	F	7	0	1	0	4,610
Pleasant Hunt	5	G	14	0	0	1	2,036
Pleasant Italian	7	G	16	2	2	1	33,090
Pleasant Kaye	3	F	9	0	1	1	7,195
Pleasant Lady	4	F	1	0	0	0	0
Pleasant Living	4	F	6	0	0	4	9,815
Pleasant Lucy	4	F	1	0	0	0	0
Pleasant Magic	2	C	1	0	0	1	1,980
Pleasant Mood	5	G	8	0	0	2	1,349
Pleasant Noise	6	H	12	0	0	2	3,564
Pleasant Note	5	M	10	2	0	2	47,220
Pleasant Parcel	7	H	4	1	0	1	13,500
Pleasant Pastures	4	F	8	2	0	2	49,940
Pleasant Pick	4	G	8	1	0	0	11,965
Pleasant Point	3	F	4	0	2	0	16,230
Pleasant Ruler	3	C	1	0	0	0	0
Pleasant Sands	3	F	5	1	1	0	24,840
Pleasant Signal	4	C	1	0	0	0	1,050
Pleasant Skip	2	F	1	0	0	0	125
Pleasant Star	9	G	3	0	1	0	1,604
Pleasant State	8	M	14	1	1	2	37,036
Pleasant Success	5	G	16	1	1	2	8,175
Pleasant Tapper	3	F	11	1	1	3	11,095
Pleasant Trick	3	G	18	3	4	1	68,380
Pleasant Villa	3	F	7	2	2	0	41,430
Pleasant Wind	4	G	4	0	0	0	180
Pleasant Yukon	3	C	6	2	1	1	15,490
Pleasantdotcom	6	G	13	0	1	3	2,952
Pleasantly Perfect	5	H	4	2	0	1	2,470,000
Pleasantly Rich	6	H	4	1	1	0	8,100
Pleasanton	4	F	14	3	0	0	16,595
Please Be Seated	6	M	3	1	1	0	9,300
Please Believeit	3	F	3	1	0	0	5,400
Please Bill	3	G	17	1	4	2	14,894
Please Call Home	2	F	4	1	0	0	12,000
Please Dear Please	3	F	8	1	1	3	34,490
Please Follow Me	4	F	4	0	0	0	486
Please Louie	2	G	3	1	0	0	9,966
Please Pay Artax	2	C	5	0	0	1	2,916
Plazas Release Me	3	G	14	1	2	3	9,857
Please Repete	5	G	10	2	1	1	13,463
Please Run	6	G	3	1	0	0	6,500
Please Smile	2	G	3	1	0	0	5,859
Please Take Me Out	3	F	7	2	1	1	99,190
Please the Mind	3	C	5	1	0	1	7,845
Please U Me	5	M	1	0	0	0	0
Pleaser	7	M	5	0	0	0	3,370
Pleasing Dreams	7	M	1	0	0	0	0
Pleasing Louise	3	F	8	0	2	1	9,485
Pleasing Punch	3	F	6	0	0	1	2,115
Pleasing Tango	4	C	5	1	0	0	14,100
Pleasingagentleman	3	F	6	2	0	0	22,838
Pleasure Beach	4	F	1	0	0	0	40
Pleasure Cruise	5	M	1	0	0	0	54

Horse	Age	Sex	Sts	1st	2d	3d	Won
Pleasure Fighter	3	F	5	2	0	1	12,340
Pleasure Honor	2	G	5	2	0	1	47,440
Pleasure Hunt	2	F	3	0	0	0	460
Pleasure Is Racing	3	M	3	0	0	0	44
Pleasure J	9	M	8	1	0	5	1,832
Pleasure Mill	6	G	8	0	1	1	3,179
Pleasure Pit	4	C	5	0	0	0	8,100
Pleasure Pro	3	F	11	0	0	1	1,819
Pleasure Rocket	3	G	11	2	2	1	12,450
Pleasure Tree	3	G	9	0	2	0	4,385
Pleasurefight	3	F	3	0	0	0	0
Pleasureinnumbers	5	G	10	1	2	4	14,520
Pleasures all Mine	9	G	7	0	1	2	2,358
Plebe	7	H	1	0	1	0	3,960
Pledge of Peace	3	F	6	0	1	2	7,890
Pleezdontpunishme	3	F	5	1	0	0	5,150
Plenilunio	2	G	1	0	0	0	130
Plenty Easy	3	F	9	2	2	1	29,133
Plenty Keen	5	M	3	0	0	0	135
Plenty Lucky	4	C	11	4	4	0	45,025
Plenty O'Devil	3	C	3	1	0	0	8,035
Plenty of Heat	2	C	6	0	0	1	10,880
Plenty of Jacks	3	G	17	2	6	3	18,631
Plenty of Luck	7	M	10	0	0	3	4,645
Plenty of Pie	9	G	8	0	0	2	3,150
Plenty of Punch	3	F	9	1	1	2	22,569
Plenty of Sass	3	G	5	1	0	3	2,077
Plenty of Sweets	4	C	7	1	1	0	8,060
Plenty of Talk	4	F	6	1	2	1	3,612
Plenty of Time	7	G	14	1	0	0	6,325
Plenty Potentate	3	C	5	1	0	0	10,065
Plenty Story	3	F	12	3	3	0	8,203
Plinking	3	F	15	4	1	1	40,125
Plino	7	G	11	2	0	1	16,345
Plisky Steel	4	F	13	1	2	1	5,450
Plot Plan	6	G	1	0	0	0	0
Pluck's Doggie	5	G	11	0	1	2	3,737
Plucky Broad	4	F	13	3	2	1	58,784
Plucky Discovery	7	M	7	0	0	3	3,056
Plug	4	G	7	2	1	1	30,355
Pluie's Stock	6	H	2	0	0	0	130
Plum Branch	3	F	1	0	0	1	4,510
Plum Good Day	5	H	14	3	0	1	60,860
Plum Jules	4	C	1	0	0	0	0
Plum Puzzled	3	G	4	0	0	1	2,470
Plum Red	2	G	3	1	0	0	5,940
Plum Sober	2	G	3	2	1	0	71,888
Plum Wonder	2	F	9	2	0	2	15,355
Plumb	5	G	13	1	5	2	10,588
Plumb Salty	2	G	2	0	0	0	0
Plume	3	F	18	2	3	3	31,182
Plume Rouge (GB)	3	F	8	1	2	1	81,395
Plummersgoldmine	3	C	3	0	0	0	0
Plumnellie	4	F	6	1	0	0	5,982
Plunge	7	G	19	1	0	2	6,316
Pluperfect	5	H	2	0	1	1	2,300
Plus Iron	3	F	11	1	1	0	5,714
Plus Tax	2	F	1	0	0	1	1,425
Plus Three	3	F	12	1	2	3	64,830
Plush	5	M	8	1	2	2	19,745
Pnutbutterandjolie	4	F	8	1	1	0	7,070
Poached	5	M	11	2	2	1	26,110
Poaching	5	G	6	0	0	0	279
Pocahaba	4	F	6	0	2	0	19,484
Pocantico	5	G	4	1	1	0	8,550
Pocket Fullof Hope	6	G	5	0	0	1	1,363
Pocket Phones Baby	6	M	7	1	0	1	6,320
Pocket Treys	2	G	3	0	0	0	0
Pocket Wish	3	F	4	1	1	0	7,070
Pocketbrook	3	F	14	1	3	2	13,240
Pocketful O Mach Z	3	F	9	0	0	0	1,255
Pocketful of Magic	3	F	2	1	0	0	7,530
Pocketfullofpesos	3	F	4	1	0	0	43,826
Pocketfulofspirit	14	G	1	0	0	0	0
Pockets	5	G	17	6	2	2	69,961
Pocketsfulloftime	6	M	12	1	0	3	2,352
Poco	4	G	18	4	2	0	28,584
Poco Dinero	2	F	6	0	1	0	2,300
Poco Doc	3	F	5	1	0	2	7,826
Poco Judy	4	F	11	0	1	1	3,870
Poco Rey	5	G	10	0	2	1	7,714
Poco Rojo	7	H	4	0	0	0	142
Poco Senorita	4	F	3	0	0	0	219
Poco Stampede	5	G	6	1	1	0	6,540
Poco Star	5	G	6	0	1	0	901
Pocus Hocus	5	M	11	2	4	3	176,802
Poe Lighten	3	G	2	0	0	0	0
Poetic Honor	2	F	5	0	0	1	1,820
Poetic Romance	3	F	5	3	0	0	46,670
Poets and Angels	2	F	6	1	0	0	20,526
Poet's Lady	6	M	4	0	0	2	1,231
Poet's Pen	3	F	5	2	0	0	7,973
Poet's Studio	2	F	6	0	2	1	33,050
Pogolotti Hill	5	G	5	1	2	0	57,180
Pogowin	2	F	1	0	0	1	950
Pohatan Princess	7	M	3	0	0	0	1,160
Pohave	5	G	12	1	4	0	64,320
Point	7	G	1	0	0	0	135
Point and Shoot	3	G	15	1	0	1	4,641
Point Blank	5	G	15	1	1	2	25,225
Point Clear	3	F	4	1	0	1	39,072
Point Click	4	G	20	4	5	2	31,902
Point Dume	2	G	6	2	0	1	41,800
Point Fear	2	C	3	0	0	0	255
Point Five	8	G	12	2	2	3	36,358
Point Grey	3	C	11	1	3	1	11,146
Point Hidden	2	C	1	0	0	0	0
Point High	4	G	14	1	3	1	10,523
Point Info	3	F	9	0	1	1	9,940
Point Lily	3	F	10	3	1	1	32,875
Point of America	6	G	7	1	1	0	19,480
Point of Flight	2	C	2	0	0	1	7,020
Point of Light	3	G	6	0	1	0	3,422
Point Prince	4	G	5	1	0	1	94,500
Point South	2	G	5	0	0	0	876
Point Storm	7	G	20	2	6	4	26,125
Point Sunshine	3	F	4	2	0	0	20,960
Point Taken	3	G	7	0	0	1	5,498
Pointe Birds	3	G	6	2	1	0	37,220
Pointe Milou	3	F	2	1	0	0	14,250
Pointed	9	G	15	1	4	1	5,512
Pointed Stone	3	C	1	0	0	0	0
Pointin West	2	C	4	1	0	0	23,190
Pointmetothewire	3	F	3	0	1	0	1,767
Pointofive	3	G	3	0	0	0	400
Points On	3	F	6	3	0	0	38,460
Points West	3	F	6	1	2	0	45,540
Poise	4	F	4	2	0	1	19,726
Poison Ivah	4	F	6	0	0	1	633
Poison Ivy (FR)	4	F	12	3	1	2	94,600
Poison Letters	3	F	4	0	0	0	0
Poison Man Jack	2	C	5	1	0	1	9,182
Poison Oak	2	C	6	0	0	2	3,587
Poison Oak Camp	4	F	15	0	2	2	5,920
Pok Korn	3	C	2	0	0	0	0
Poka Dot Princess	3	F	10	4	0	1	70,780
Pokeemom	3	F	12	2	0	1	10,752
Pokemon Jo	3	G	13	0	2	1	7,132
Poker Brad	5	G	11	2	2	2	147,830
Poker Call	3	G	9	0	0	2	2,074
Poker Creek	6	G	1	0	0	0	0
Poker Dice	4	G	16	2	2	3	28,570
Poker Game	2	C	2	0	1	0	6,950
Poker Hand	4	F	7	0	2	0	5,150
Poker Little Devil	3	G	3	0	0	0	0
Poker Little Sugar	7	M	10	1	1	0	5,490
Pokerfaced	3	F	11	0	2	2	22,690
Poker's Charm	4	G	15	1	4	3	8,561
Pokey Aaron	3	G	6	0	0	2	6,971
Pokey Hontas	5	M	13	0	0	2	2,227
Pokey's Dream	3	F	9	0	0	0	1,365
Poks Destiny	3	F	8	0	1	1	2,694
Polaire (IRE)	7	M	1	0	0	0	4,866
Polar Baby	6	M	7	0	1	1	4,461
Polar Barron	7	G	8	2	1	1	20,255
Polar Bear	3	F	8	0	4	1	17,710
Polar Diamond	3	C	2	0	0	0	137
Polar Express	4	C	5	0	0	0	186

RECORDS OF HORSES

Horse	Age	Sex	Sts	1st	2d	3d	Won	Horse	Age	Sex	Sts	1st	2d	3d	Won
Polar Miss	4	F	3	0	1	2	3,822	Political Pull	4	G	10	1	2	2	20,394
Polar Pay Phone	4	F	7	0	0	0	419	Political Rhetoric	4	G	8	2	2	1	57,900
Polar Phlox	2	F	4	0	1	0	2,460	Political Risk	3	C	3	2	1	0	57,372
Polar Prospector	5	M	11	1	2	5	24,344	Political Savvy	2	F	1	0	0	0	0
Polar Ray	5	H	3	0	0	2	2,130	Political Storm	5	G	13	4	4	0	34,375
Polar Snow	3	F	1	0	0	0	2,520	Political Triumph	4	G	13	2	2	0	13,957
Polaris	2	G	4	2	0	0	43,084	Political Weapon	2	C	1	0	0	0	0
Polarmetry	5	M	17	0	1	3	19,770	Politicallycorrect	3	C	3	0	0	0	152
Pole to Pole	3	C	2	1	0	0	19,860	Politicalplayboy	5	G	11	1	0	1	14,164
Pole's Dancer	4	G	12	2	5	1	18,338	Politico	4	G	2	0	0	0	0
Pole's Fancy	3	F	1	0	0	0	455	Polka Coyote	9	G	12	3	4	1	17,865
Policy Cat	1	F	1	0	0	0	115	Polka Lady	4	F	14	2	3	6	12,936
Policy Decision	4	F	1	0	0	0	0	Polka With Me	3	F	9	2	2	2	15,810
Polish	4	C	7	0	0	0	2,050	Pollard's Vision	2	C	6	1	1	2	53,291
Polish Account	3	F	5	1	1	1	24,330	Pollica	9	M	9	0	2	1	4,881
Polish Broad	3	F	8	2	1	1	41,380	Pollinate	7	G	7	2	0	1	16,048
Polish Cargo	5	G	3	1	1	0	8,250	Pollock	4	G	1	0	0	0	2,280
Polish Choice	6	M	8	0	1	2	8,344	Pollock'smelody	4	F	5	1	0	0	3,303
Polish Crown	2	F	2	0	1	0	11,950	Polly B.	4	F	9	2	1	1	10,327
Polish Dancing	7	H	1	0	0	0	150	Polly Everafter	3	F	7	0	1	1	9,066
Polish Dee	5	M	14	0	0	0	1,403	Polly Moon	5	M	14	1	2	4	9,885
Polish Desire	3	C	6	1	1	0	5,262	Polly Peabody	2	F	2	0	1	0	2,600
Polish Dream	3	C	5	1	0	0	3,669	Polly Rout	3	F	1	0	0	0	0
Polish Flower	2	F	1	0	0	0	0	Polly T.	6	M	4	0	1	0	1,761
Polish Gentleman	7	H	1	0	0	0	0	Polly Tics	6	M	13	0	1	2	2,388
Polish Gift	3	C	3	0	0	0	2,640	Pollys Accelerator	2	F	5	0	0	1	5,290
Polish Ham	3	G	7	0	0	0	1,200	Polly's Choice	4	F	6	0	0	0	1,710
Polish Honey	5	M	10	1	4	1	7,650	Polly's Comet	6	H	1	1	0	0	2,280
Polish Influence	2	C	3	0	0	0	405	Polly's Folly	3	F	5	1	0	0	14,150
Polish Jewel	3	C	13	3	4	2	126,980	Polly's Persuasion	3	F	9	1	1	0	21,645
Polish Lady	3	F	4	0	0	1	650	Polly's Pistol	2	C	4	0	0	0	1,519
Polish Magic	5	G	9	1	3	1	22,655	Polo Grounds	2	C	1	0	1	0	4,400
Polish Mary	2	F	6	0	1	0	4,900	Polo Pro	9	G	5	0	1	1	1,815
Polish Memory	4	C	8	1	0	0	7,025	Polo Ridge	3	F	4	3	0	0	39,550
Polish Millennium	5	G	8	0	0	0	1,125	Polonia	3	F	3	0	1	1	12,828
Polish Missile	6	G	6	0	0	0	477	Poltical Party	2	C	6	1	0	1	13,295
Polish Moe	7	G	5	2	0	1	8,639	Polulu	5	G	14	0	3	1	2,828
Polish Music	6	G	4	1	0	0	16,060	Poly Is	3	C	2	0	0	1	2,193
Polish Nana	3	F	2	0	1	1	13,110	Poly Ole	4	F	4	0	1	0	4,200
Polish Navigator	2	C	8	1	0	0	6,600	Poly Pop a Top	3	F	11	1	1	0	14,980
Polish Outlaw	5	H	4	1	1	0	6,420	Poly Powered	5	G	6	1	2	0	4,513
Polish Pianist	7	G	4	0	1	0	2,087	Polyanna	2	F	1	0	0	0	192
Polish Pistol	4	G	9	1	0	4	14,080	Polygreen (FR)	4	F	4	2	1	0	90,860
Polish Police	6	G	14	3	0	2	20,510	Polymnia	3	F	1	0	0	0	248
Polish Poppa	8	G	12	2	1	6	9,864	Polympics	4	C	7	1	3	1	51,060
Polish Posh	3	C	6	0	0	2	6,700	Polynesian Friends	4	F	3	0	0	0	0
Polish Pride	5	H	6	1	2	1	45,920	Poly's Loose	5	H	8	0	0	1	940
Polish Reality	6	G	4	1	1	0	21,894	Pomeroy	2	C	4	2	1	1	88,000
Polish Remover	7	M	9	1	1	0	4,781	Pomme de Terre	3	G	16	1	1	2	10,730
Polish Rifle	2	C	4	2	2	0	95,850	Pomona Lisa	6	M	17	0	5	2	6,377
Polish Rogue	3	G	9	0	1	1	3,283	Pompamento	3	F	4	2	0	0	33,750
Polish Ruby	5	M	1	0	0	0	121	Pompano Beach	5	G	10	2	3	1	22,252
Polish Silk	4	F	6	1	1	0	32,670	Pompeii the Great	4	G	7	1	2	2	8,175
Polish Slip	2	C	4	0	0	1	2,130	Pomposity	7	G	9	0	2	2	9,040
Polish Snoop	5	M	14	1	1	3	5,395	Ponche Ahumin	2	G	2	0	0	0	175
Polish Summer (GB)	6	H	7	1	3	0	661,904	Ponche de Leona	4	F	4	0	0	0	2,650
Polish Times	6	G	13	4	2	3	131,960	Ponche Line	2	C	2	0	1	0	2,895
Polish Toy	6	G	12	0	3	1	5,089	Poncheaux Breaux	6	H	13	0	0	1	981
Polish Unity	4	C	11	0	2	0	9,285	Ponches Glory	3	G	9	1	1	0	4,687
Polish Valentine	4	F	2	0	1	0	2,180	Ponche's Image	5	G	14	1	2	4	17,113
Polish Virtues	3	F	12	0	4	3	30,750	Poncho Duck	9	G	11	1	1	0	10,399
Polish Vision	10	G	3	0	0	1	5,500	Ponder the Path	4	C	1	0	0	0	47
Polish Wish	5	H	3	0	1	0	1,700	Ponderos Dancer	5	M	4	0	0	0	357
Polished Brass	8	H	1	0	0	0	0	Ponderosa	4	F	12	1	3	3	10,834
Polished Deputy	3	F	2	0	0	0	900	Ponderosa Kid	3	G	5	1	1	0	6,509
Polished Halo	6	H	5	0	0	0	1,200	Poney Up	3	G	7	1	0	0	9,469
Polished Penny	3	F	9	1	0	1	3,150	Poni Lee	3	F	5	0	0	0	210
Polished Steel	4	G	14	1	3	2	11,564	Ponoka	2	G	5	1	3	0	21,493
Polished Stone	4	F	8	1	1	1	7,012	Ponopaan	4	C	12	3	2	1	67,237
Polishoffthebrandy	4	F	4	1	0	1	7,370	Ponsonby	9	G	1	0	0	0	0
Politarium	5	G	2	0	0	0	300	Pont Aven (VEN)	6	G	6	0	0	1	640
Polite Angel	9	G	7	1	0	0	6,335	Pontchartrain	7	G	12	1	0	1	6,319
Polites Beauty	3	F	5	1	0	0	25,038	Ponte Vedra	2	G	2	0	0	0	125
Political Attack	4	G	7	3	0	1	202,688	Ponti Victoria	4	F	5	0	0	0	976
Political Choice	2	C	2	0	1	1	2,728	Ponticiello (CHI)	5	H	7	0	2	0	4,796
Political Favor	5	M	7	0	2	0	2,815	Pony Pal	3	F	3	0	0	0	0
Political Freedom	3	G	14	0	3	2	8,645	Poochie Lou	4	F	4	0	0	0	192
Political Gun	7	H	2	0	0	1	1,000	Poofadini	4	G	10	0	1	2	13,360
Political Prize	2	F	7	0	2	2	12,540	Poohger	2	C	1	0	0	0	0

Horse	Age	Sex	Sts	1st	2d	3d	Won
Pool Music (GB)	8	G	13	3	2	0	25,430
Poolhall	2	G	9	1	2	0	12,855
Poolman	8	H	12	2	2	1	13,705
Poons	5	M	10	1	1	2	20,588
Poor for Now	3	F	2	1	0	1	5,180
Poor Man's Battle	3	G	3	0	2	0	20,000
Poor Pilgrim	7	G	1	0	0	0	0
Poor Pitiful Pearl	2	F	2	0	0	0	95
Poormanstealin	2	G	2	0	0	0	300
Poorpoor Pitafulme	7	G	1	0	0	0	43
Pop	7	H	8	1	1	0	4,890
Pop a Top Again	4	G	7	2	1	4	38,350
Pop Carn	8	G	1	0	0	0	0
Pop Dileo	5	G	8	0	0	1	1,744
Pop n' Tap	7	G	10	0	0	0	600
Pop On Top	2	C	1	0	0	0	0
Pop Pop's Fuse	3	C	4	1	1	0	12,960
Pop Pop's Hope	2	F	5	2	1	2	40,690
Pop Princess	3	F	2	1	1	0	50,520
Pop Rocks	6	G	14	1	6	2	122,669
Pop Star	3	G	12	1	1	0	7,631
Pop the Cork	5	H	12	2	1	1	11,038
Pop the Latch	2	F	2	0	0	0	0
Pop Up Joe	3	G	7	0	1	1	3,450
Popacap	3	G	3	0	0	1	3,302
Popcorn	3	G	7	1	1	0	18,670
Popcorn Deelites	5	G	14	3	2	3	18,433
Popcorn Lady	2	F	5	0	0	0	2,501
Popcorn Shaker	3	F	7	1	2	1	19,660
Popescu (BRZ)	6	G	8	0	1	1	1,035
Popgun	4	C	3	0	0	1	2,047
Poplar Lady	2	F	4	1	1	1	19,846
Popoki	2	C	1	0	0	0	2,160
Popozinha	2	F	1	0	0	0	840
Poppa Canihave Him	7	G	14	0	1	3	4,366
Poppa Corky	6	G	10	4	0	1	38,693
Poppa Paez	3	G	8	1	1	1	6,237
Poppa's Favorites	8	G	2	0	0	1	812
Poppa's Misty	4	F	2	0	0	0	0
Poppa's Plug	3	C	5	1	0	0	10,280
Popped Corn	7	G	10	1	2	1	19,772
Poppie's Plan	5	G	15	1	2	0	10,040
Poppins Popper	4	F	9	3	2	2	44,188
Poppi's Matthew	6	G	4	0	0	0	1,324
Poppo's Song	2	F	4	0	0	1	3,058
Poppy Hills	3	F	2	0	0	0	0
Poppy M	6	G	18	2	5	5	20,499
Poppy Seed	3	F	3	0	0	0	1,050
Poppy's Courage	4	G	16	4	2	3	78,259
Poppys Grey Cat	3	F	6	0	0	0	662
Poppy's Image	3	G	14	1	3	3	73,260
Pop's Angel	3	F	11	1	2	2	9,152
Pops' Bo Boy	10	G	8	3	1	1	24,840
Pops Pleasure	3	C	1	0	0	0	0
Pop's Tribute	3	C	4	0	0	0	97
Popsicle Pete	7	G	10	1	2	0	18,485
Popsy	5	M	4	1	0	0	11,475
Popular	4	C	7	0	0	3	29,865
Popular Blues	4	F	19	0	3	2	15,589
Popular Gigalo	9	G	3	0	0	0	2,500
Popular Groom	3	C	3	1	0	0	29,100
Popular Host	9	G	9	1	2	2	10,220
Popular Kat	6	H	11	1	3	2	12,071
Popular Number	4	F	2	0	0	0	660
Popular Patriot	4	F	7	0	0	2	2,350
Popularafterschool	3	F	6	0	1	2	5,625
Popularize	3	C	4	1	0	1	35,380
Poquito Amore	3	F	4	0	0	2	2,640
Poquito Blanco	3	F	3	0	0	0	1,746
Poquito Blue	3	C	5	1	0	0	7,560
Por Layo	3	G	24	1	2	4	16,990
Por Lucky	5	G	6	0	1	2	3,759
Por Maracaibo	4	F	13	2	2	1	9,969
Por Que No	5	M	8	5	0	1	18,964
Poras	3	F	1	0	0	0	0
Porcelain Theatre	2	F	5	0	0	3	2,412
Porches	3	F	11	1	1	3	17,865
Porey Spring	5	G	5	2	0	0	89,520
Porfirio Cadena	3	G	12	2	2	1	28,105
Porky	4	G	5	0	0	1	1,579
Port A	4	F	4	1	1	0	11,000
Port Au Prince	4	G	4	2	0	0	49,200
Port d'Enfer	8	M	4	0	0	0	928
Port Elgin	3	C	1	0	0	0	91
Port Gibson	2	C	3	0	0	2	2,363
Port Henry	5	G	4	0	1	0	5,570
Port Hueneme	3	G	1	0	0	1	1,560
Port Lockroy	6	H	6	0	1	1	2,860
Port n' A' Storm	3	G	5	0	1	1	2,385
Port Perry	10	G	11	0	0	0	903
Port Quippa	3	G	1	0	0	0	0
Port Royal Ciel	6	H	3	0	0	1	1,350
Port Sandringham	5	G	8	2	1	2	31,924
Port Vila (FR)	6	H	4	1	0	1	7,586
Porta Brera	3	F	1	0	0	0	0
Porta Nuova (CHI)	6	M	4	0	0	0	300
Portable Power	3	C	7	0	0	0	1,230
Portan	4	G	13	1	0	2	5,614
Portcullis	4	G	6	1	0	0	94,500
Portentosa (VEN)	4	F	12	0	2	1	9,510
Porters Pride	4	F	1	0	0	0	113
Portia Belmont	3	F	5	1	0	0	2,853
Portlandate	3	G	4	0	1	1	6,555
Portly Princess	3	F	15	1	2	2	25,710
Portobello Belle	4	F	3	1	0	1	9,560
Portofino Creek	3	C	1	0	0	0	91
Portrait of Choice	7	G	4	0	0	0	369
Portraitofcamelot	3	G	6	0	0	0	1,118
Portside	5	H	9	0	0	1	2,175
Portuguese Summer	4	F	1	0	0	0	170
Portwood	6	G	13	0	1	1	3,469
Posadas	5	M	1	0	0	1	1,600
Poseidon's Regret	6	G	7	0	0	0	166
Posh	4	G	10	1	1	1	8,842
Positive (IRE)	4	G	8	1	0	3	11,895
Positive Climb	3	F	13	1	0	2	14,770
Positive John	5	G	5	0	0	0	210
Positive Pete	6	G	4	0	0	0	358
Positive Spirit	4	F	12	2	2	2	21,754
Positively	7	H	13	0	3	1	10,098
Positively Gold	7	H	1	0	0	0	0
Positively Wild	3	F	9	1	2	2	52,340
Posse	3	C	11	5	1	1	478,426
Possess (GB)	2	C	2	1	0	0	16,800
Possession	2	F	2	1	1	0	35,000
Possibility	3	F	2	1	0	0	28,350
Possible Punch	3	F	2	0	0	0	0
Possuletta Sue	4	F	10	1	1	1	18,030
Post Chaplain	6	G	17	3	2	1	15,397
Post Hostess	7	M	4	0	0	0	586
Post Hotel	4	F	9	0	1	2	3,055
Post Its Awesome	3	G	5	1	1	0	8,635
Post Op	2	F	5	0	0	2	8,510
Post Pattern	3	G	8	2	0	1	43,315
Post Road	5	H	11	1	4	2	9,735
Post the Bail	3	C	3	0	0	0	4,165
Post This Memo	3	G	5	0	0	0	670
Post Toasty	4	F	15	1	2	3	13,783
Poster Boy	3	G	18	1	0	1	8,855
Postnuptial	2	C	6	0	0	1	4,910
Postulant	2	F	2	0	0	0	1,080
Posture	3	G	9	1	1	2	24,314
Pot Limit	4	G	6	1	1	1	14,902
Pot Luck	7	M	5	1	0	0	4,860
Potato Lad	4	G	13	3	2	2	135,458
Potent	3	G	14	2	2	0	8,898
Potentially	2	C	2	1	0	0	8,220
Potion	2	F	6	1	0	1	26,490
Potnia	2	F	3	0	2	0	13,200
Potomac Chase	2	C	7	2	0	1	33,900
Potomac City	5	H	12	2	1	1	17,837
Potomac Falls	3	G	9	2	2	1	47,510
Potomac Punch	8	G	1	0	0	0	0
Potomac Way	6	H	13	2	2	2	7,356
Potra Bid (ARG)	4	F	3	0	0	0	0
Potri Burn (ARG)	6	H	5	0	0	1	4,260
Potri Cacho (ARG)	5	G	9	1	1	2	17,455
Potri Mambo	3	F	2	0	0	0	2,760

RECORDS OF HORSES

Horse	Age	Sex	Sts	1st	2d	3d	Won
Potri Marshal (ARG)	4	G	4	0	0	0	0
Potri Star (ARG)	5	M	4	0	0	1	5,880
Potrilord (ARG)	6	H	4	1	1	0	26,620
Potrisunrise (ARG)	6	H	10	2	2	1	55,390
Potrithreat (ARG)	6	M	9	2	1	1	15,278
Potro Sol (ARG)	5	G	3	0	1	0	2,250
Potroast and Gravy	2	G	1	0	0	0	380
Pots and Pans	5	H	9	2	0	2	17,590
Potter	4	C	5	0	0	0	174
Potter's Field	2	G	4	0	0	0	265
Pottersville	4	G	15	0	2	6	19,980
Potus	5	G	8	0	1	2	7,710
Pouncer	2	F	2	0	0	0	0
Poundcake	3	G	14	1	1	2	17,995
Pounding	6	G	15	2	4	0	42,220
Pour It On	2	F	5	2	2	0	78,090
Pour Lil Devil	4	G	12	0	3	2	9,880
Pour Yourheart Out	3	F	1	0	0	0	960
Pouring Rain	5	M	13	3	1	0	36,018
Pout	2	F	2	0	0	0	0
Pow Wow Louise	3	F	11	2	1	1	68,911
Powder Keg	4	G	14	2	3	1	30,392
Powder Punch	4	F	4	1	1	0	22,400
Powder Your Nose	5	M	5	0	0	0	792
Powderet	3	F	1	0	1	0	700
Powderjay	5	M	3	2	0	0	60,090
Powders Wish	3	F	7	1	0	1	13,762
Powell Creek	3	C	17	1	7	3	42,120
Power and Achase	5	G	15	1	1	3	7,674
Power and Panache	7	G	11	0	1	0	5,900
Power and Peace	8	H	10	5	2	0	22,425
Power Appeal	6	G	4	0	1	0	874
Power Back	5	G	4	0	0	0	368
Power Boost	5	G	5	0	0	0	180
Power Boy	3	G	11	1	3	1	31,200
Power Buck	2	C	4	0	0	0	475
Power by Jules	2	C	1	0	0	0	195
Power Connection	4	C	12	2	0	3	11,861
Power Curtain	4	F	9	1	3	1	3,165
Power Dot	3	F	16	0	1	1	3,965
Power Du Jour	3	F	6	0	0	0	2,340
Power Dust	6	G	8	1	0	1	4,748
Power Failure	5	H	7	2	3	0	16,525
Power Flame	9	G	6	1	0	3	9,175
Power for Trey	3	G	16	2	3	4	18,048
Power Gem	3	F	11	4	2	2	172,878
Power Glide	5	G	9	2	2	1	26,310
Power Happy	3	G	4	1	1	0	3,513
Power Hawk	3	C	3	1	0	0	3,480
Power Jr.	4	C	6	3	0	0	16,717
Power Knock	2	C	2	0	0	0	0
Power Launch	2	C	1	0	0	0	330
Power Lion	3	C	4	1	0	0	18,086
Power Music	6	G	17	5	3	1	33,510
Power N Control	3	G	7	0	0	1	4,512
Power N Motion	3	G	1	0	0	1	450
Power Nap	4	C	10	2	0	2	12,993
Power of Dreams	3	F	6	2	1	0	12,213
Power of Elprado	6	G	9	2	0	2	21,640
Power of Faith	4	F	8	1	0	0	13,663
Power of Glory	4	F	11	1	2	3	13,187
Power of Hope	4	F	11	3	1	0	40,044
Power of Jane	4	F	9	1	0	2	9,541
Power of Lady	3	F	9	0	1	0	3,465
Power of Lite	2	C	3	0	0	2	4,600
Power of Pride	3	F	5	1	2	2	21,166
Power of Surprise	7	C	7	2	1	1	27,345
Power of the Pad	4	F	8	0	3	1	18,990
Power of Three	4	C	3	0	0	0	1,296
Power Phan	6	M	5	0	1	0	8,021
Power Pic	4	G	16	0	5	6	21,011
Power Potion	3	C	3	0	0	1	1,755
Power Power	8	H	16	3	0	0	48,279
Power Promise	3	F	6	0	1	2	3,035
Power Regent	2	G	2	0	0	0	0
Power River	4	G	9	0	0	3	1,759
Power Sander	2	C	9	0	0	1	2,660
Power Serge	5	M	11	4	1	0	26,742
Power Shower	2	F	4	1	1	0	30,484
Power Slew	3	G	9	1	2	1	14,850
Power Strategy	7	G	7	1	1	0	7,275
Power Strokin	2	G	6	0	1	1	3,460
Power Supply	3	C	12	2	0	1	11,148
Power Talk	2	F	2	0	0	0	217
Power Teapot	4	C	3	0	0	0	135
Power to Burn	6	M	8	1	2	2	66,303
Power to Fly	2	F	4	0	0	0	0
Power to Pass	9	G	1	0	0	0	0
Power Tripper	2	C	1	0	0	1	5,560
Power Wheels	4	G	6	2	0	0	7,207
Power Wing	9	G	14	4	3	1	60,436
Powerandauthority	8	G	6	0	1	0	3,630
Powerchess	6	H	7	1	0	0	12,900
Powered High	3	G	5	0	0	1	2,310
Powerful Appeal	6	H	9	2	2	1	60,830
Powerful Fleet	5	H	5	1	1	0	5,004
Powerful Katrinka	3	F	5	0	0	0	459
Powerful Magic	3	C	2	0	0	0	700
Powerful Mind	3	C	2	0	1	0	2,100
Powerful Potion	4	F	6	1	0	2	14,573
Powerful Prospect	5	M	9	0	2	0	2,070
Powerful Runner	2	C	1	0	0	0	75
Powerful Silver	3	C	12	1	2	2	15,730
Powerful Start	3	F	2	0	0	0	200
Powerful Touch	3	G	1	0	1	0	20,000
Powerfulallegation	3	F	2	0	0	1	1,085
Powerfulsubstitute	3	G	12	0	1	4	18,715
Powerofataka	4	F	5	1	1	1	4,099
Poweroyal	3	G	2	0	0	1	5,280
Powerpoint	5	M	2	0	0	0	0
Powers Prospect	3	F	8	3	1	1	85,990
Powey Bear	4	F	2	0	0	0	98
Poydras	3	F	6	1	2	0	50,140
Practical Paul	5	G	4	0	0	0	0
Practical Stan	4	G	16	0	4	3	32,006
Practicality	3	G	8	1	0	0	12,840
Prada Shoes	3	F	1	0	0	0	0
Prado Lady	3	F	3	1	0	1	14,700
Prado Maximus	3	C	1	0	0	0	780
Prado Power	6	G	14	4	3	2	56,195
Prado Queen	4	F	3	0	0	0	438
Prado Wells	8	G	15	2	1	5	25,345
Prado's Lass	3	F	8	1	1	0	23,458
Prado's Picture	3	F	9	1	0	2	8,839
Prag	3	F	17	3	3	2	20,797
Pragmatic Pursuit	4	G	6	0	0	1	2,055
Pragmatist	4	G	1	0	0	0	106
Praire Katydid	2	F	2	0	1	0	7,900
Prairie Blaze	3	C	4	1	0	1	2,244
Prairie Boogie	4	F	10	0	1	1	1,895
Prairie Butterbean	4	C	3	0	0	0	334
Prairie Chief	3	C	7	0	1	0	4,140
Prairie Connection	3	F	4	2	1	0	10,910
Prairie d'Ane	2	C	2	0	0	0	0
Prairie Doctor	4	F	3	2	1	0	3,920
Prairie Flame	3	F	1	0	0	0	0
Prairie Jane	3	F	1	0	0	0	0
Prairie King	2	C	4	2	0	1	42,374
Prairie Lady	5	M	11	3	0	0	8,530
Prairie Predator	4	G	6	0	1	0	9,075
Prairie Runner	5	H	2	0	0	0	0
Prairie Slam	3	C	6	2	1	1	45,780
Prairie Socialite	2	F	4	0	0	0	1,560
Prairie Swinger	6	G	10	1	3	1	7,223
Prairie View	4	F	7	0	2	2	4,225
Prairie Wolf	5	H	4	0	0	0	1,191
Prairie Zephyr	11	G	3	1	0	0	1,615
Praise From Dixie	7	G	10	2	3	0	111,308
Praise of Smoke	5	M	10	0	1	1	6,513
Praise the Prince (NZ)	8	G	5	1	2	2	124,002
Praiseyethelord	3	C	1	0	0	0	76
Prank Caller	3	C	2	0	0	0	87
Pranna	3	C	19	1	3	3	22,305
Pratti	4	C	6	1	1	1	11,039
Pray At Dawn	4	G	6	0	0	0	384
Prayer Bell	2	G	2	0	0	2	3,000
Prayer Card	4	G	11	2	3	1	28,008
Prayer Chain	3	F	6	1	0	0	9,395

Horse	Age	Sex	Sts	1st	2d	3d	Won	Horse	Age	Sex	Sts	1st	2d	3d	Won
Prayer Meeting	5	H	10	1	0	0	11,941	Prelim Tim	3	F	4	0	0	0	0
Prayer Warrior	3	C	1	0	1	0	2,400	Prelude to Puddles	2	F	1	0	0	0	980
Pre Game Show	4	C	2	1	0	0	10,985	Prember	3	C	11	1	2	1	17,542
Pre Haint	3	G	7	0	0	0	1,020	Premeditation	4	C	3	1	0	1	43,330
Pre World	4	F	2	0	0	0	0	Premier Clue	3	G	7	0	2	1	13,094
Preach It	2	F	1	0	0	0	0	Premier Cru	6	M	2	0	0	0	176
Preach the Blues	2	C	1	0	0	1	1,950	Premier Girl	2	F	2	1	0	0	5,700
Preacher Bob	3	G	10	2	4	0	39,960	Premier Gold	2	C	3	0	0	0	2,645
Preacher Don	8	G	1	0	0	0	0	Premier Hunting	2	C	4	0	0	0	680
Preacher George	3	C	1	0	0	0	0	Premier Kisser	3	F	1	0	0	0	0
Preacher Jim	6	G	7	0	0	0	1,207	Premier Liner	5	M	6	2	1	0	9,385
Preacher Joyce	3	F	2	0	0	0	0	Premier Performer	4	C	5	1	2	0	47,820
Preacher's Knee (AUS)	6	G	2	0	0	0	0	Premier Player	7	G	5	0	0	0	0
Preacher's Passion	3	F	1	0	0	0	420	Premier Princess	4	F	18	2	7	1	34,198
Preachinatthebar	2	C	4	1	0	1	32,820	Premier Promise	7	M	14	3	0	2	18,044
Preaching	3	F	3	0	0	1	9,080	Premier Report	5	G	9	0	2	1	26,390
Preamble	6	G	2	1	0	1	11,200	Premier Rocket	3	C	10	1	2	2	43,010
Preapproved	3	G	12	1	0	3	10,269	Premier Run	3	G	11	2	2	1	14,199
Precept	8	G	4	0	0	0	420	Premier Shot	6	H	5	0	1	0	3,411
Precioso Viva	2	C	6	1	2	1	19,420	Premier Style	10	M	3	0	0	0	197
Precious and Few	4	F	10	0	1	1	2,393	Premier Tea	2	F	1	0	0	0	0
Precious Art	5	M	2	0	0	0	763	Premier This	6	M	4	0	0	0	556
Precious Bag	2	F	1	0	0	1	4,320	Premier Token	3	G	15	3	3	1	19,849
Precious Currency	3	F	9	0	1	0	2,205	Premiere Dancer	7	G	10	1	2	1	8,782
Precious Encore	3	G	7	0	0	0	935	Premieress	6	M	1	0	0	0	47
Precious Erica	2	F	5	1	2	1	20,000	Premierily	4	G	7	0	0	0	420
Precious Erin	3	F	2	0	0	0	87	Premiering	4	F	7	4	1	0	31,624
Precious Heights	3	F	8	0	2	2	3,528	Premier's Turn	9	G	17	3	2	3	20,251
Precious Image	7	M	1	0	0	0	63	Preminission	3	G	3	1	0	1	2,612
Precious Karly	5	M	3	1	0	0	4,725	Premium Blend	4	G	11	0	4	1	13,300
Precious Leah	5	M	6	0	0	1	1,405	Premium Bragg	3	F	12	0	0	1	1,658
Precious Light	2	F	2	1	0	0	11,580	Premium Brew	6	G	7	0	2	1	11,407
Precious Luck	3	C	7	4	0	2	22,459	Premium Point	3	C	3	0	0	0	1,230
Precious Maid	3	F	13	1	1	1	7,311	Premium Port	2	G	1	0	0	0	182
Precious Mistress	3	F	3	0	0	0	0	Premium Position	4	F	5	2	0	0	25,800
Precious Morn	4	F	7	0	0	1	1,315	Premium Saltine	4	G	8	3	3	0	81,300
Precious Pidgeon	6	M	12	0	1	0	2,612	Premium Wish	6	H	3	0	1	0	1,184
Precious Plunder	5	M	6	0	1	1	1,130	Premo Copy	4	F	12	2	3	1	49,891
Precious Prado	4	F	15	1	0	3	11,811	Prem's Lord Lady	7	M	3	0	0	0	70
Precious Sands	2	G	1	0	0	1	1,045	Prendimi Cuore	7	F	4	0	0	0	115
Precious Sea	5	M	14	2	2	1	8,496	Preneer	3	G	8	1	1	1	13,096
Precious Testamony	7	G	4	0	0	0	252	Prenup's Drift	4	F	11	2	1	0	10,874
Precious Touch	5	M	6	0	0	0	3,460	Prenuptial Plans	4	F	5	0	1	2	10,200
Precipitory's Bid	2	F	2	0	1	0	7,180	Prenuptual Deal	7	G	3	0	0	2	8,520
Precise Victor	4	G	14	1	3	1	9,397	Preoccupied	5	H	9	0	1	1	3,565
Precise Victory	3	F	3	0	0	0	180	Prep School	2	G	2	0	0	0	840
Precision Cut	6	G	7	1	0	2	8,896	Prepare for Rain	3	F	7	0	1	1	24,459
Precision Hunter	5	G	7	0	0	0	332	Preppy Cat	2	F	3	0	0	0	300
Precocious Builder	2	C	3	1	1	0	23,300	Preppy Genius	3	F	2	0	0	0	0
Precocious Bunny	2	F	1	0	0	0	0	Preppy Music	4	F	8	3	3	1	17,822
Precocious Kat	2	F	2	1	0	0	12,000	Prep's Peak	3	F	12	1	4	1	22,051
Precocious Monster	2	G	2	0	0	0	200	Prepster	2	C	3	0	0	0	1,080
Precocious Notion	4	F	12	1	1	2	5,148	Prepstress	2	F	1	0	0	0	0
Precocity Princess	2	F	2	0	0	1	1,130	Prerequisite	3	G	11	1	2	1	33,834
Precosious Willy	2	F	1	0	0	0	182	Prescision Winner	5	G	21	1	1	2	12,028
Predadancer	5	H	8	0	0	0	531	Prescott Lad	3	C	6	1	0	2	5,870
Predatory Pidgeon	4	C	15	1	0	0	8,342	Presence	3	C	4	1	1	0	34,800
Predawn Raid	4	G	6	2	1	1	83,250	Present Image	2	C	2	0	0	0	0
Predict This Storm	5	G	1	0	0	0	131	Presentation	3	F	3	0	0	0	270
Predictable Dancer	2	F	7	0	0	0	721	Presenter	3	G	19	0	4	4	30,560
Predif	3	F	9	0	0	2	2,609	Presently Gone	3	G	12	1	1	2	16,309
Predjudice	3	G	1	0	0	0	0	Preservation Hall	2	F	2	0	0	0	0
Predominater	4	G	13	4	2	3	38,874	President Butler	4	C	5	0	0	3	12,450
Preemptive Strike	5	G	6	1	2	1	58,186	President Mac	3	G	7	1	1	2	64,998
Preface	3	C	2	1	1	0	17,586	President Shrub	3	G	3	0	0	0	261
Prefect	6	H	5	0	0	0	1,015	President Willie	8	G	2	1	0	0	3,800
Prefer	5	H	5	0	0	0	1,140	Presidential Lady	4	F	13	2	1	1	9,493
Prefer Blondes	3	F	3	0	0	1	3,545	Presidential Perk	2	F	2	1	0	0	8,359
Prefered Native	7	G	9	1	1	2	6,645	Presidential Rose	3	F	5	0	0	1	2,055
Preference's Gold	6	H	7	0	1	0	1,265	Presidentialaffair	4	G	9	5	1	1	188,140
Preferred	6	G	9	2	2	0	25,540	President's Decree	9	G	12	1	3	5	28,874
Preferred County	3	F	5	0	3	0	9,717	Presidents Do Tell	4	G	6	1	0	1	5,477
Preferred Guest	5	G	8	1	1	0	13,020	President's Lady	2	F	7	1	0	0	13,774
Preferred Lady	3	F	4	0	1	1	4,663	Presidio County	3	G	9	1	2	1	6,550
Preferred Option	4	F	4	0	0	1	20,460	Presidio Heights	5	G	7	3	0	0	88,300
Preflight	2	G	2	0	0	1	1,698	Presque Isle	3	C	1	0	0	0	0
Prejm	5	M	10	2	0	4	36,524	Press All Bets	3	G	11	0	0	0	2,547
Prejohn	4	G	9	0	1	0	3,055	Press Badge	4	C	7	1	2	0	9,040
Prejuzgada (ARG)	5	M	12	0	0	1	1,910	Press Beyond	5	M	11	1	0	2	16,212

Horse	Age	Sex	Sts	1st	2d	3d	Won	Horse	Age	Sex	Sts	1st	2d	3d	Won
Press Box	6	G	14	1	2	3	11,336	Pretty Precious	5	M	5	1	0	0	15,290
Press Cardinal	3	F	5	0	0	0	0	Pretty Princess	3	F	15	1	2	1	9,641
Press Doll	6	M	1	0	0	0	290	Pretty Pro	3	F	4	1	0	0	25,890
Press for a Change	6	H	7	3	0	0	21,559	Pretty Prospect	4	F	13	0	2	0	4,127
Press Go	4	F	13	0	3	2	9,585	Pretty Quiet Run	2	C	1	1	0	0	19,860
Press Kit	4	F	2	0	0	1	1,050	Pretty Rocky	5	M	16	1	3	3	47,295
Press Power	4	F	4	0	0	0	2,559	Pretty Shanks	7	M	8	0	1	0	1,856
Press the Bet	3	F	4	0	0	0	909	Pretty Sly	4	G	13	0	2	4	23,645
Press View	7	M	5	1	0	0	7,728	Pretty Sneaky	3	G	12	0	1	0	4,302
Press You	5	M	2	0	1	0	6,510	Pretty Soon Now	5	M	5	2	1	0	2,260
Press Your Luck	4	C	13	2	0	1	11,690	Pretty Spooky	4	F	3	0	0	0	128
Presscard Karma	4	G	8	1	0	2	8,670	Pretty Storm	5	M	7	1	2	1	12,040
Pressed Wood	2	C	2	0	0	0	117	Pretty Swanky	3	G	4	0	0	1	14,304
Pressin' Your Luck	6	G	8	2	1	2	22,193	Pretty Texas Aggie	2	F	5	1	0	0	16,860
Pressmenow	6	H	6	0	0	1	3,260	Pretty Toni	3	F	13	1	3	2	13,440
Pressure King	6	G	7	2	0	1	48,450	Pretty Wild	3	C	4	1	0	2	53,140
Pressure Seeker	5	M	2	0	0	0	34	Pretty Wild Again	2	C	4	1	0	0	32,412
Pressure Tester	6	G	11	3	2	4	30,018	Pretty Willie	5	G	12	3	0	1	12,440
Prestigious Image	6	H	4	0	0	1	860	Pretty You	5	G	9	1	2	0	23,366
Prestigious Xavier	3	G	8	1	2	1	14,145	Prettyboypatton	3	C	3	2	0	0	14,222
Presto Cavallo	3	C	10	1	2	3	33,987	Prettydarnspecial	5	M	9	1	0	1	6,904
Presto Fast	4	G	10	0	1	2	4,228	Prettymamma	5	M	5	2	1	0	12,570
Presto Jr	3	G	1	0	0	0	35	Prettypinkshoelace	2	F	2	0	0	0	0
Presto Ridge	4	G	9	0	2	0	3,868	Pretty's Last Aria	2	F	2	0	0	0	240
Preston Royal	7	G	9	3	2	0	9,336	Pretty's Zagor	5	H	12	2	1	2	31,340
Preston T	3	G	6	0	0	0	485	Prevalent	2	F	2	2	0	0	33,580
Presumed Innocent	6	M	5	1	0	0	33,150	Prever	4	C	12	2	1	0	13,653
Presumption	2	C	8	1	0	2	36,498	Previous Balance	3	F	4	0	0	0	295
Pretencia's Legacy	3	F	8	1	1	0	6,651	Previous Selection	2	F	1	0	0	0	1,230
Pretenciosa	3	F	3	0	0	0	560	Prey of the Cat	2	F	2	0	0	0	214
Pretentions	5	G	18	1	3	4	42,146	Price Discovery	3	F	2	0	0	0	100
Pretentious	5	M	8	1	0	3	18,805	Price Gesser	2	G	1	0	0	0	343
Pretext	5	M	7	1	1	3	4,720	Price of Champagne	6	G	12	1	1	1	24,310
Pretoius	3	G	13	2	3	2	4,308	Price of Honour	3	G	13	7	3	2	191,327
Pretolay	4	G	3	0	1	1	4,692	Price of Passion	3	F	3	0	1	0	3,676
Pretti Woman	4	F	1	0	0	0	0	Priced Smartly	2	F	3	0	0	1	12,114
Pretty Ambitious	5	M	8	3	1	2	37,154	Priced to Go	4	G	9	0	4	2	13,962
Pretty as Ashley	4	F	2	0	0	1	4,320	Pricedale Kid	5	G	5	0	2	0	3,295
Pretty Bad Boy	4	G	12	0	1	5	32,798	Priceless Darlin	4	F	4	0	1	1	5,846
Pretty Belle	4	F	13	1	0	2	10,387	Priceless Details	3	G	3	0	0	0	0
Pretty Bonnie	2	F	1	1	0	0	8,400	Priceless Fact	3	C	12	1	2	1	33,200
Pretty Boy Dalton	2	C	2	0	0	0	165	Priceless Jet	3	F	13	3	1	1	34,721
Pretty Boy Pete	8	G	19	5	3	3	25,117	Priceless Legend	3	G	10	1	2	3	72,480
Pretty Brassy	3	F	3	0	0	1	4,840	Priceless Storm	4	F	1	0	0	0	3,000
Pretty Briches	5	G	7	1	2	0	5,100	Pricey Gem	5	G	7	0	0	1	966
Pretty Caddy Slew	3	F	15	2	6	2	7,725	Pricey Tab	4	F	7	0	3	0	12,545
Pretty Cagey	3	G	11	2	4	0	61,720	Prickly Pirate	3	G	2	0	0	0	296
Pretty Castle	3	F	1	0	0	0	240	Prickly Pocket	3	F	7	2	2	0	27,142
Pretty Cat	2	F	4	1	0	0	3,758	Pride and Promise	4	G	15	2	2	2	16,650
Pretty Charmeleon	3	F	3	0	0	0	35	Pride City	3	F	2	1	0	0	7,330
Pretty Classy	3	F	4	1	0	0	17,260	Pride of Cats	5	G	7	1	1	1	8,620
Pretty Coed	6	M	18	0	1	2	4,322	Pride of Defense	3	C	9	2	1	2	26,360
Pretty Cozzene	4	F	9	1	1	4	23,750	Pride of Ownership	5	G	10	4	2	0	24,954
Pretty Dawn	8	M	10	0	3	1	4,639	Pride of the Fox	6	G	14	1	1	2	22,051
Pretty Deeliteful	4	F	4	0	1	0	5,778	Pride of the Group	6	G	15	2	4	4	17,404
Pretty Deputy	2	F	6	1	1	2	20,605	Prideful	7	M	14	0	1	0	6,672
Pretty Determined	5	M	8	1	3	1	12,957	Prideofthecoombe	6	G	9	0	0	2	15,208
Pretty Ditty	4	F	6	0	0	1	4,650	Prideov Fappiano	5	G	12	3	1	2	42,181
Pretty Elegant	3	F	1	0	0	0	125	Pride's Reward	4	G	1	0	0	0	0
Pretty Exciting To	4	F	11	1	2	1	6,421	Prieska	2	F	1	0	0	0	1,764
Pretty Fast Groom	3	F	3	0	0	1	1,430	Priest River	2	G	9	0	2	1	6,400
Pretty Fine Call	3	G	10	2	0	0	7,240	Prim Sunshine	5	G	2	0	0	0	455
Pretty Fur	3	F	4	0	0	0	1,400	Prima Bella	4	F	2	0	0	0	74
Pretty Gale	5	M	1	0	0	0	4,500	Prima Creatura (IRE)	4	F	8	1	0	1	37,600
Pretty Galore	3	F	11	3	3	2	40,692	Prima Dama	3	F	2	0	0	0	402
Pretty Girl Slew	2	F	2	1	1	0	8,490	Prima Green	4	F	10	3	1	1	93,968
Pretty Gritty	3	F	6	0	0	0	630	Prima Princess	3	F	7	0	3	2	9,643
Pretty Halo	3	F	6	0	3	0	12,180	Primacy	5	M	1	0	0	0	113
Pretty Honoree	2	F	7	1	0	2	7,315	Primadonna Poppy	5	M	7	2	0	1	7,767
Pretty Imposing	3	F	11	1	4	1	67,850	Primal Effort	3	C	5	1	2	0	15,874
Pretty Ironic	5	M	10	3	4	0	3,723	Primal Mist	5	H	24	3	5	6	23,043
Pretty Kitty Kelly	5	M	1	0	0	0	0	Primal Passion	4	F	11	2	1	3	17,115
Pretty Kool Dude	4	C	9	1	1	1	2,845	Primal Wizard	2	C	4	0	2	0	15,146
Pretty Littleangel	4	F	13	1	0	6	16,266	Primary Colors	4	F	7	0	0	4	21,333
Pretty Majestic	4	F	11	1	2	2	7,636	Primary Deed	6	H	4	1	1	0	4,960
Pretty Meadow	3	F	9	3	1	0	42,246	Prima's Gold	3	F	4	0	0	2	3,110
Pretty Miah	3	F	7	0	0	0	682	Primative Nature	4	F	4	2	0	1	12,525
Pretty Mille	4	F	10	1	2	1	2,316	Prime Advantage	3	F	11	2	1	2	30,090
Pretty Money	3	F	1	0	0	0	0	Prime Agenda	3	G	4	0	0	0	0

Horse	Age	Sex	Sts	1st	2d	3d	Won
Prime Angel	7	G	13	0	0	3	2,002
Prime Asset	6	M	4	0	0	1	720
Prime Candidate	6	G	4	0	0	0	340
Prime Commander	5	M	10	1	0	2	10,833
Prime Concept	5	H	8	1	1	0	4,864
Prime Cut	5	M	4	0	2	0	2,860
Prime Deposit	3	G	6	0	1	2	16,380
Prime Event	2	C	1	0	0	0	0
Prime Explodent	3	C	10	0	0	1	2,428
Prime Gypsy	4	F	7	0	0	2	2,546
Prime Hustle	3	C	3	0	0	0	140
Prime Jewel	4	F	12	2	2	1	35,590
Prime Juice	6	M	6	0	0	0	2,230
Prime Motive	3	G	9	2	0	0	9,900
Prime Mover	3	C	7	1	0	2	1,572
Prime Option	4	G	7	0	0	0	348
Prime Pine	6	H	3	0	1	0	6,800
Prime Quality	3	G	10	0	3	1	5,943
Prime Queen	5	M	9	2	1	1	58,998
Prime Sector	4	F	2	0	0	0	0
Prime Shine	4	G	3	0	0	0	636
Prime Step	5	M	10	6	0	2	75,210
Prime the Pump	3	G	8	0	1	3	7,234
Prime Time Billy	4	G	24	3	0	2	23,497
Prime Time Event	4	C	4	1	0	0	25,420
Prime Time King	4	G	4	0	0	0	345
Prime Time Man	6	G	16	3	0	1	15,743
Prime Time Phil	3	G	3	1	0	0	22,860
Prime Time Player	3	C	3	0	0	0	0
Prime Time Suzi	3	F	1	0	0	0	0
Prime Vintage	7	G	1	0	0	0	54
Prime Wisdom	4	F	2	0	0	0	0
Primecat	2	C	2	2	0	0	5,160
Primer Coat	5	G	15	0	0	2	2,387
Primer Cord	5	H	4	0	0	1	2,563
Primer Plano (CHI)	9	G	2	0	1	0	722
Primerica	5	G	7	2	3	2	147,640
Primetime Gigolo	3	G	7	1	1	0	3,651
Primetime Girl	4	F	15	2	2	2	19,362
Primetime Pirate	12	G	7	0	1	1	1,400
Primetimevalentine	4	F	9	3	1	0	101,220
Primitivestirrings	8	G	5	0	0	1	760
Primm	2	C	5	0	1	1	8,960
Primo Camino	5	H	10	2	0	2	17,434
Primo Cat	3	F	2	0	0	0	473
Primo Figlio	3	G	12	1	3	1	8,087
Primo Nova	3	C	2	0	2	0	14,130
Primo Primo	3	C	1	0	0	0	0
Primoliniator	6	G	11	0	5	0	3,024
Primordial Prince	6	G	9	1	3	1	27,093
Primos	4	G	9	3	1	2	16,259
Prince Alexander	6	G	9	5	2	0	21,662
Prince Allmouth	4	C	13	1	3	0	5,619
Prince Alphie	3	C	3	1	0	0	54,000
Prince Alueta	4	G	4	0	0	0	0
Prince Ante	5	G	14	0	1	6	20,604
Prince Appeal	3	C	8	0	0	2	6,540
Prince Arch	2	C	4	1	1	0	13,240
Prince Ashby	4	G	18	2	1	7	15,617
Prince Ballet	2	C	1	0	0	0	93
Prince Benjamin	3	C	8	3	1	3	93,280
Prince Cash	4	G	6	1	0	0	3,817
Prince Consort	4	C	11	3	2	2	83,320
Prince Dauntless	4	C	1	0	0	0	0
Prince de Reve (ARG)	7	H	8	1	1	1	15,010
Prince Decor	4	G	10	0	0	1	1,159
Prince Di	3	C	5	1	1	2	3,585
Prince Dixie	3	G	11	1	1	1	8,362
Prince Dumaani	4	G	1	0	0	0	0
Prince Excalibur	5	G	8	0	2	2	7,096
Prince Falkor	4	G	16	1	1	0	6,160
Prince Fashion (ARG)	6	H	3	0	0	0	0
Prince Forever	4	G	4	0	0	2	3,870
Prince Georgi	3	C	8	2	1	2	34,965
Prince Hadif	5	H	9	3	1	1	25,104
Prince Halo	2	C	2	0	1	0	5,400
Prince Harold	2	C	2	0	1	0	6,750
Prince Harper	10	G	2	0	0	0	78
Prince Harry L	3	G	1	0	0	0	264
Prince Hennessy	5	H	10	1	2	3	11,150
Prince in Command	3	C	2	0	0	0	360
Prince Joe (ARG)	10	H	13	2	3	3	16,959
Prince Joseph	2	C	1	0	0	0	1,140
Prince Julep	6	G	8	1	0	2	7,109
Prince Kisty	4	G	5	0	0	0	448
Prince Know It All	3	G	14	1	6	1	16,982
Prince Kokand	4	G	17	1	3	1	5,133
Prince Livermore	2	G	2	0	0	1	2,882
Prince Machiavelli	9	H	1	0	0	0	0
Prince Malagra	3	G	16	1	4	1	19,090
Prince Manila	6	H	2	0	0	0	234
Prince Martin	4	G	5	1	0	2	19,215
Prince Marty	3	G	4	0	0	0	0
Prince Monty	7	G	5	3	1	1	108,874
Prince Noah	3	G	10	0	0	1	2,307
Prince Nuntea	2	C	2	0	0	0	0
Prince o' Dreams	3	C	13	1	3	0	8,738
Prince of a Deal	4	G	1	0	0	0	0
Prince of Destiny	4	G	15	1	1	2	11,280
Prince of Dreams	2	C	2	0	0	0	112
Prince of Experts	6	H	8	0	0	0	1,006
Prince of Joy	2	C	2	0	0	0	134
Prince of Paradise	4	C	5	0	0	2	2,881
Prince of Rhodes	3	C	6	1	1	0	10,639
Prince of the Sea	2	G	5	0	0	0	868
Prince of Valor	7	H	6	0	1	0	2,300
Prince Ofthe World	4	C	4	1	0	0	13,836
Prince Paster	2	C	2	0	0	0	0
Prince Peter B B	3	G	3	0	0	0	0
Prince Prado	3	C	11	1	5	3	63,895
Prince Quiet	2	G	10	0	0	1	10,787
Prince Raykour	5	G	2	0	0	0	104
Prince Reed	3	G	10	2	1	2	10,491
Prince Rio	5	H	8	3	0	1	40,490
Prince Silverrod	2	C	3	1	0	2	17,230
Prince Skif	10	G	7	0	1	3	3,433
Prince Slavic	4	G	10	2	3	2	28,695
Prince Slew	5	G	7	1	1	1	130,000
Prince Sparkles	7	G	13	1	1	2	7,411
Prince Stately	3	G	10	3	1	0	6,625
Prince Tab	6	G	13	3	1	4	28,640
Prince to Be	2	G	1	0	0	0	0
Prince Ty	3	C	3	0	0	0	0
Prince Tyree	5	G	11	0	2	2	5,278
Prince Uppity	4	C	4	0	0	0	158
Prince Versailles	3	G	1	0	0	0	0
Prince Vitality	4	C	9	1	0	0	3,105
Prince War Cloud	6	H	6	1	1	0	10,144
Prince Warrior	6	G	6	0	0	0	0
Prince Wells	2	G	6	0	1	0	1,840
Prince Will	2	C	5	0	0	0	1,440
Prince Willie	4	G	4	0	0	1	758
Prince Wolfie	3	G	14	1	1	3	6,378
Prince Wynn	4	G	19	3	2	2	39,470
Prince Zignew	3	G	12	2	2	1	26,355
Princeapecia	4	F	7	1	1	1	12,308
Princely Affair	8	G	1	0	0	0	70
Princely Flag	9	G	13	1	1	4	10,697
Princely Heat	6	G	14	3	2	0	20,573
Princely Soldier	2	C	4	0	0	1	1,660
Princely Tour	2	C	3	0	0	0	0
Princeofthenorth	8	G	5	0	0	0	375
Princeps	5	H	1	0	0	0	0
Princes of Maine	4	C	14	0	1	1	2,915
Princes Terlingua	4	F	8	1	0	0	6,032
Princess A. P.	3	F	11	0	1	2	20,910
Princess Aire	4	F	7	0	1	2	9,153
Princess Alecia	3	F	1	0	0	0	140
Princess Alert	4	F	4	0	0	0	510
Princess Alex	2	F	2	0	2	0	7,345
Princess Alueta	5	M	14	2	3	3	10,322
Princess Aly B	3	F	3	0	0	0	231
Princess Appleby	2	F	7	1	0	0	21,013
Princess Ariana	3	F	2	0	0	0	700
Princess Atta	4	F	11	5	0	2	95,890
Princess Attitude	3	F	8	3	2	2	49,900
Princess Avalon	3	F	4	1	0	0	42,361
Princess B	3	F	3	1	0	1	19,240

RECORDS OF HORSES

Horse	Age	Sex	Sts	1st	2d	3d	Won	Horse	Age	Sex	Sts	1st	2d	3d	Won
Princess Bagheria	7	M	11	0	0	1	1,740	Princess Pater	7	M	13	4	3	2	21,561
Princess Bandiera	7	M	7	0	0	0	3,032	Princess Payton	4	F	11	1	1	0	5,968
Princess Barrow	2	F	1	0	0	0	0	Princess Peak	6	M	14	3	1	2	32,527
Princess Basque	3	F	5	0	0	0	410	Princess Pelona	3	F	4	2	1	0	56,172
Princess Birdeye	3	F	8	1	1	3	30,400	Princess Petrizzo	4	F	11	1	0	3	41,273
Princess Brenda	3	F	6	0	0	0	263	Princess Pookey	6	M	3	0	0	0	317
Princess Briartic	6	M	9	2	0	1	8,878	Princess Prospect	4	F	6	0	0	0	685
Princess Britt	6	M	4	2	0	0	21,201	Princess Pump Iron	3	F	15	2	3	2	21,785
Princess Cara	2	F	2	0	0	0	0	Princess Quista	7	M	1	0	0	0	61
Princess Carson	5	M	8	0	1	2	2,362	Princess Razyana	3	F	7	1	1	2	19,580
Princess Catie	5	M	8	1	2	1	14,890	Princess Red Bird	8	M	18	2	1	2	9,957
Princess Condo	5	M	6	0	1	0	5,427	Princess Rene	6	M	3	0	1	1	865
Princess Conquista	8	M	15	0	0	1	1,918	Princess Ride	3	F	2	0	0	0	81
Princess Del Sol	5	M	3	0	0	0	0	Princess Roney	4	F	14	4	1	2	25,152
Princess Dixie	4	F	6	2	1	2	181,946	Princess Ruby	5	M	16	0	3	0	7,487
Princess Dixton	4	F	2	0	0	0	696	Princess Sasnbrass	3	F	1	0	0	0	0
Princess Doodlebug	3	F	8	1	2	2	13,014	Princess Savannah	4	F	11	2	1	1	15,129
Princess Dream	3	F	16	2	0	3	36,155	Princess Serena	4	F	4	1	1	0	10,960
Princess E.	4	F	2	1	0	0	10,800	Princess Sheila	2	F	2	0	0	1	2,375
Princess Edwina	3	F	3	1	0	1	46,722	Princess Sheri	7	M	6	0	2	0	2,652
Princess El	5	M	11	2	0	1	18,313	Princess Slew	4	F	4	0	1	1	5,100
Princess Estella	3	F	5	0	1	0	1,685	Princess Sumi	5	M	4	1	0	0	8,052
Princess Fairy	4	F	8	2	0	2	21,320	Princess T	8	M	6	1	0	0	4,577
Princess Forever	4	F	8	1	1	0	21,139	Princess Terlingua	5	M	12	3	3	1	27,272
Princess Frances	9	M	1	0	0	0	0	Princess Tia	4	F	9	1	0	1	8,055
Princess Gina	6	M	2	0	0	1	620	Princess Tiara	4	F	5	0	3	0	4,650
Princess Ginny	2	F	2	0	0	0	246	Princess Tiffany	3	F	18	5	4	0	70,120
Princess Goneril	3	F	3	0	0	0	1,150	Princess Tish	2	F	4	0	1	1	19,867
Princess Grand	3	F	3	1	0	1	16,600	Princess Tonya	4	F	9	2	1	2	9,083
Princess Ha Ha	6	M	8	0	1	2	7,366	Princess Tooka	3	F	1	0	0	0	123
Princess Hanna	5	M	12	0	1	4	5,096	Princess Tune	4	F	5	3	1	0	26,420
Princess Heather	4	F	2	0	0	0	0	Princess V.	3	F	7	2	1	2	136,259
Princess Heidi	5	M	14	3	3	1	30,251	Princess Vice	4	F	1	0	0	0	0
Princess Helma	3	F	17	2	4	2	37,140	Princess Waki	4	F	4	1	1	0	4,553
Princess Iris	4	F	7	1	0	2	24,815	Princess Zaboo	3	F	8	1	0	0	11,400
Princess Is a Lady	4	F	9	1	1	2	8,466	Princessa Cielo	3	F	4	0	0	0	150
Princess Isabella	2	F	1	0	0	0	144	Princessaconcuervo	5	M	6	2	2	0	52,825
Princess Itron	2	F	6	0	1	2	5,445	Princessca	2	F	2	1	0	0	5,520
Princess Jade	4	F	2	0	0	0	0	Princesscassandra	3	F	7	2	0	0	34,247
Princess Jan Jan	2	F	3	1	0	1	19,066	Princesscopy	4	F	13	0	0	0	1,413
Princess Jeb	3	F	2	0	0	0	135	Princessdi's Folly	6	H	16	2	3	0	59,000
Princess Jen	6	M	11	1	3	0	52,100	Princessgonewest	7	M	7	1	1	0	13,979
Princess Jess	3	F	1	0	0	0	180	Princessgwenivere	5	M	8	0	1	2	5,570
Princess Joy	2	F	2	0	0	1	710	Princessinwaiting	2	F	6	0	3	0	7,170
Princess K.	3	F	5	0	0	0	390	Princessofkalithea	4	F	7	2	0	1	8,631
Princess K K	3	F	5	0	0	1	3,965	Princessofthebayou	4	F	6	1	0	0	9,240
Princess Kaiulani	5	M	14	4	6	0	26,890	Princessonthebayou	3	F	1	0	0	0	786
Princess Katrina	4	F	9	3	0	1	13,983	Princess's Bay	2	F	7	1	3	1	72,342
Princess Kaylee	4	F	6	0	2	0	3,718	Princeton Affair	5	G	18	4	3	1	32,286
Princess Kolo	6	M	5	1	0	0	1,320	Princeton Avenue	4	C	10	1	0	3	8,465
Princess Krista	6	M	1	0	0	0	0	Princeton Star	4	G	13	0	2	1	5,195
Princess Lanique	3	F	10	1	4	2	73,730	Princetonian	4	G	6	0	0	0	624
Princess Leal	7	M	17	0	3	3	10,549	Princhipesa (PER)	4	F	14	0	1	0	1,800
Princess Legacy	4	F	1	0	0	1	1,350	Principal Interest	7	M	4	0	0	0	1,010
Princess Liberty	3	F	17	0	2	3	5,585	Principal Ray	5	G	9	0	0	0	593
Princess Liza	9	M	1	0	0	0	0	Prindello	5	M	10	0	2	0	1,067
Princess Logan	3	F	6	1	0	4	10,421	Prineville	6	G	4	1	2	1	6,649
Princess Looney	3	F	5	1	0	1	13,340	Print in Black	2	G	3	1	1	0	9,100
Princess Lorna	3	F	21	0	2	4	11,797	Print Out	3	C	16	2	2	3	13,667
Princess Love	3	F	6	2	3	1	34,130	Printed Tongue	3	F	4	0	0	0	256
Princess Madmyr	5	M	3	0	0	0	231	Printemps (CHI)	6	M	7	1	1	1	170,800
Princess Majesty	4	F	6	1	0	0	992	Printers Comet	6	M	8	0	0	0	224
Princess Malice	2	F	1	0	0	0	1,260	Printer's Princess	4	F	9	2	1	1	21,717
Princess Marlin	3	F	1	0	0	0	195	Printer's Son	2	G	4	0	0	0	3,330
Princess Mikayla	3	F	15	2	4	1	24,891	Prior Lake Lady	2	F	5	1	0	2	17,752
Princess Minute	7	M	9	1	1	2	3,711	Pri's Premier	3	G	9	0	0	0	165
Princess Modiste	4	F	7	0	1	1	7,260	Priscilla's Chance	5	M	21	1	7	1	15,386
Princess Ms. Fit	3	F	7	0	0	0	1,380	Priscilla's Flag	2	F	7	0	1	2	21,840
Princess Muldoon	3	F	12	3	1	0	36,460	Priscilla's Way	5	M	3	0	0	0	1,350
Princess Nicolette	3	F	18	1	1	5	35,875	Prismatic	4	F	1	0	0	0	0
Princess Nonna	6	M	5	0	0	0	2,160	Prismatic Time	4	F	6	2	1	0	12,425
Princess of Ghosts	2	F	2	0	0	0	145	Prism's Sweetie	6	M	9	3	4	1	19,550
Princess of Holme	4	F	8	2	2	1	27,124	Prison Boy	5	G	9	3	2	1	114,731
Princess of York	6	M	15	0	2	3	7,997	Prison of Love	2	F	4	0	1	0	5,975
Princess Oonah	6	M	3	0	0	0	0	Prisoner of War	4	G	1	0	0	0	0
Princess Paleface	5	M	9	2	2	1	61,499	Prissy	6	M	12	2	2	1	12,076
Princess Pamela	4	F	6	1	1	0	11,360	Prissy Adagio	3	F	3	0	0	0	0
Princess Pancho	4	F	16	4	2	2	30,075	Prissy Britches	2	F	1	0	0	1	4,680
Princess Paster	3	F	12	3	2	1	71,514	Prissy Linda	5	M	1	0	0	0	118

Horse	Age	Sex	Sts	1st	2d	3d	Won
Prissy Pants	3	F	13	4	0	1	25,805
Prissy Scene	6	M	10	3	2	0	16,659
Prissy's Prince	3	G	1	0	0	0	600
Privacy Act	2	C	3	0	1	0	2,955
Privano's First	7	G	13	2	4	1	58,485
Privat Gold (ARG)	6	H	17	2	2	1	47,025
Private	5	G	2	0	0	0	115
Private Allay	5	M	1	0	0	0	270
Private Ambition	3	G	12	2	0	1	21,262
Private American	2	C	3	0	0	2	4,060
Private Attack	4	C	4	0	0	0	400
Private Aviator	4	G	9	3	2	1	65,705
Private Bail	6	G	9	1	1	2	12,422
Private Balcony	2	F	1	1	0	0	10,584
Private Bean	4	G	8	1	1	0	12,540
Private Bet	11	G	3	0	0	0	407
Private Boot	2	F	6	2	1	1	13,790
Private Bound	6	G	4	2	1	0	22,490
Private Buck	5	H	13	0	1	2	3,635
Private Canyon	4	C	11	0	0	0	5,520
Private Cat	5	G	18	4	3	5	45,682
Private Change	6	G	16	3	0	6	17,721
Private Chef	3	G	3	2	0	0	99,633
Private Christmas	5	F	5	1	1	3	44,230
Private City	3	C	15	4	4	2	168,530
Private Club	4	G	5	1	0	0	4,225
Private Coin	2	G	2	0	0	1	825
Private Connection	2	G	6	0	0	1	5,510
Private Council	4	G	3	0	0	0	174
Private Courage	3	F	7	0	0	0	488
Private Creek	6	M	13	1	0	1	4,057
Private Divinail	4	G	16	1	0	0	7,050
Private Doctor	2	C	12	0	1	0	3,980
Private Emblem	4	C	8	1	0	3	82,863
Private Enterprise	6	G	3	0	1	0	11,240
Private Equity	4	F	11	1	2	2	12,476
Private Estate	7	M	1	0	0	0	0
Private Extension	6	M	8	1	1	2	54,386
Private Feeling	4	F	2	0	0	0	465
Private Gamble	2	F	5	0	0	1	4,203
Private Gayla	2	F	3	2	0	0	39,420
Private Gold	3	C	4	1	0	1	75,272
Private Ground	2	G	6	1	0	3	13,200
Private Gump	9	G	8	1	3	1	6,868
Private Harbor	2	G	1	0	0	0	12,060
Private Henbane	5	G	9	1	1	1	12,640
Private Horde	4	C	9	6	2	0	411,582
Private Indeed	2	F	2	0	2	0	10,500
Private Inferno	6	M	9	0	1	6	3,422
Private Issue	2	G	7	0	4	2	17,932
Private J D	2	G	3	0	1	0	2,300
Private Jet	3	C	6	0	1	0	1,003
Private Joke	2	F	1	0	0	0	180
Private Justin	4	G	1	0	0	0	0
Private Lap	4	C	12	6	1	0	346,640
Private Lass	3	F	11	1	2	0	9,630
Private Luck	4	F	3	0	0	0	219
Private Lynn	4	C	10	3	3	1	18,132
Private Melody	4	F	1	0	0	0	0
Private Memoir	5	M	3	0	0	0	0
Private Memory	4	F	2	0	0	0	180
Private Michael	7	G	8	1	0	0	4,371
Private Mike	4	C	11	0	0	0	0
Private Mo	2	C	1	1	0	0	6,450
Private n' Preppy	4	G	7	0	0	0	446
Private Navy	3	F	7	0	1	0	3,119
Private Netizen	7	H	18	3	2	0	31,075
Private Oasis	5	G	8	2	2	1	85,525
Private Opening	4	G	5	0	0	0	7,950
Private Operator	2	F	4	0	0	0	450
Private Paradise	11	G	10	3	0	2	11,893
Private Pass	5	H	4	2	0	0	25,920
Private Petetion	4	C	12	1	0	1	7,943
Private Pilot	9	G	2	0	0	0	0
Private Placement	1	F	1	0	0	0	0
Private Pleasure	3	G	12	0	1	1	6,992
Private Port	4	F	8	3	0	1	66,800
Private Practice	4	C	14	5	2	1	89,120
Private Prescott	3	G	7	1	2	0	8,070
Private Promise	2	C	7	0	5	0	21,285
Private Prospect	6	G	13	1	0	3	3,881
Private Punch	4	G	4	0	0	1	8,170
Private Ransom	4	G	1	0	0	0	0
Private Rebel	6	G	3	0	1	1	1,782
Private Reflection	5	G	4	0	0	0	241
Private Reigns	3	F	15	1	1	1	12,196
Private Retreat	3	G	10	4	1	0	49,150
Private Ryan	6	G	8	0	0	2	9,775
Private Scandal	3	C	13	1	4	4	88,522
Private Signal	4	G	3	0	0	0	154
Private Skier	2	C	3	1	0	1	16,840
Private Skif	10	G	1	0	0	0	61
Private Slip	9	G	6	1	1	2	34,450
Private Son	5	H	10	1	1	1	36,950
Private Spector	3	C	7	0	0	0	460
Private Street	4	F	7	0	0	1	1,360
Private Summer	2	C	4	1	1	1	10,230
Private Tommy	6	G	3	0	0	0	235
Private Tribute	7	G	14	1	1	1	7,584
Private Union	1	C	1	0	0	0	0
Private War	3	C	6	2	3	0	47,108
Private Wild Gal	3	F	1	0	0	0	0
Privateer (ARG)	7	H	7	3	0	1	15,183
Privileged	6	G	1	0	0	0	0
Privy	4	F	13	2	2	3	28,046
Prize and Honor	3	F	1	0	0	0	0
Prize d'Or	2	F	2	0	1	0	1,280
Prize Editor	4	C	15	2	1	5	39,275
Prize Giving (GB)	10	G	12	0	2	0	12,695
Prize of Texas	5	H	4	0	1	1	1,750
Prize Performer	9	M	4	1	1	0	7,340
Prize Robber	3	G	6	1	0	1	4,527
Prize Rose	3	F	2	1	0	0	11,940
Prize Runner	2	F	5	1	0	2	17,810
Prize Statue	3	G	12	1	2	3	16,030
Prize Story	3	G	14	1	3	2	20,462
Prize Strudel	8	M	4	0	0	0	675
Prize Weaver	3	G	8	1	2	2	10,413
Prized Amberpro	6	M	9	2	2	3	143,210
Prized Art	3	G	10	2	0	0	7,745
Prized Bean	3	M	3	0	0	0	140
Prized Diamond	6	M	1	0	0	0	52
Prized Friend	7	G	4	1	1	0	47,560
Prized Gal	3	F	13	1	2	0	9,100
Prized Gem	5	G	3	0	2	1	26,000
Prized Halo	2	C	6	0	1	1	5,790
Prized Hoopster	5	H	1	0	0	0	0
Prized Kaelyn	3	F	2	0	1	0	2,790
Prized King	4	G	10	0	1	2	4,209
Prized Match	7	G	12	2	4	2	22,998
Prized Max	8	G	16	1	2	0	10,595
Prized Pistol	4	G	6	2	1	0	9,175
Prized Porsche	4	F	3	0	0	0	123
Prized Possession	2	C	3	1	0	0	6,840
Pro Band	2	C	1	0	0	0	2,700
Pro Fighter	7	H	7	2	2	0	9,430
Pro Forty	5	G	15	2	0	3	8,824
Pro Gamble	4	F	2	0	0	0	0
Pro Impact	4	G	4	1	0	0	2,118
Pro Love Ruhls	3	F	11	3	2	2	25,600
Pro Motion Days	7	M	14	3	1	3	62,420
Pro Occident	2	F	3	2	0	1	54,910
Pro On the Run	5	H	14	2	2	2	19,221
Pro Prado	2	C	3	2	0	0	53,784
Pro Prospect	3	C	5	0	0	0	0
Pro Punch	5	H	1	0	0	0	0
Pro Rated	3	F	1	0	0	0	64
Pro Scout	4	G	2	0	0	1	3,470
Pro Shopper	4	G	10	0	2	2	16,798
Pro Time	2	G	2	0	0	0	340
Pro Zackory	8	G	4	0	0	0	0
Proactive	3	F	12	1	0	4	21,618
Probability	5	G	4	1	1	0	14,000
Probably a Blitz	5	G	6	3	1	1	11,584
Probably for Real	5	H	3	0	0	0	282
Probably N Cahoots	6	G	6	3	0	1	11,887
Probably's Devil	6	G	3	0	0	0	2,051
Probatim	5	G	10	3	4	1	20,902

Horse	Age	Sex	Sts	1st	2d	3d	Won
Probation	4	G	2	0	0	0	0
Probition	4	C	10	1	2	1	23,886
Problem Solver	4	C	2	1	0	0	4,920
Proceed	5	G	3	0	0	2	672
Proceed With Care (GB)	5	G	11	3	0	0	71,500
Prochonic	2	F	3	1	0	0	8,250
Proclaimer	3	G	10	1	2	3	11,670
Procreate	5	G	12	2	3	1	32,309
Proctors Last Time	4	G	4	0	0	0	159
Procyon	4	F	6	1	1	0	18,650
Prodice Kid	5	G	5	1	1	1	2,095
Prodigal Stan	2	C	2	0	0	0	0
Prodigious	6	G	4	0	1	0	7,108
Prodigus (BRZ)	4	C	4	0	0	2	15,000
Producer	5	H	4	0	0	2	4,300
Produckson	6	G	6	1	2	1	5,600
Prof. McGonagall	3	F	4	1	1	0	27,230
Professional	3	F	3	0	0	0	2,250
Professor Biggs	2	G	7	2	1	1	29,572
Professor Higgins	4	G	6	2	3	0	36,050
Professor Jones	3	C	6	1	1	0	12,782
Professor Maxwell	4	C	2	0	0	0	1,140
Proficient	3	G	10	1	1	0	6,426
Profigliano	9	G	22	5	7	3	55,236
Profit Taking	5	M	2	0	0	0	70
Profitable Bet	7	H	5	0	0	0	236
Profit's Reward	3	C	4	0	0	0	311
Profound	2	C	5	0	1	1	12,660
Profumo Romano	3	C	5	0	0	0	1,920
Profuse	2	G	2	1	1	0	31,000
Programmed Appeal	6	G	1	0	1	0	1,580
Programmer	3	C	1	0	0	0	210
Prohibido Olvidar	2	F	9	2	0	3	95,748
Prohibitionist	2	C	2	0	0	0	0
Prohibitive	5	G	6	0	0	0	425
Project Hope	5	H	3	0	0	1	652
Projectile One	3	C	1	0	0	0	180
Prolon	8	G	17	1	3	1	6,112
Prom Date	7	F	8	2	0	3	52,420
Prom King	3	C	1	0	0	0	1,680
Prom Kiss	2	F	6	0	2	1	8,690
Promenade Again	3	F	2	0	0	0	750
Promenade Lane	4	F	3	1	1	0	7,020
Promenade On In	4	F	7	1	0	2	26,930
Promenade Road	3	F	6	1	2	2	75,703
Prominenta	8	M	5	0	0	0	321
Promisary	5	M	6	0	1	1	9,310
Promise Her Damoon	2	C	5	0	0	0	930
Promise Her Jules	3	F	12	2	0	2	17,670
Promise Me a Hero	4	G	8	0	0	1	1,313
Promise Money	5	H	9	0	2	0	6,096
Promise Mountain	5	G	15	0	6	1	54,840
Promise of War	7	G	8	2	0	1	35,290
Promise to Capote	4	F	2	0	0	0	270
Promised Call	3	F	6	2	0	1	16,001
Promises	5	G	4	1	0	1	34,080
Promising King (IRE)	3	C	5	1	1	0	8,965
Promising Light	3	F	6	1	0	0	10,980
Promising Reality	4	C	5	1	0	0	1,754
Promising Theatre	2	F	4	0	0	1	1,008
Promisor	5	G	8	0	0	0	1,815
Promontory Point	3	G	1	0	0	0	0
Promote Business	2	F	3	0	1	0	6,000
Promptly	3	F	5	1	0	0	4,882
Pronounced	2	G	7	1	1	0	20,604
Pronouncement	2	F	3	0	0	0	510
Pronto Dinero	8	G	7	0	2	1	1,988
Pronto One	3	G	4	0	0	1	4,255
Pronto Paco	2	C	5	1	0	1	9,075
Pronto Pancho	5	H	2	0	0	0	390
Proof Capede	5	G	16	1	2	1	8,830
Proofisinthepuddin	4	C	4	0	0	1	1,005
Proper Acacian	3	F	6	0	1	1	1,998
Proper and Sweet	4	F	6	0	0	1	498
Proper Beau	8	G	4	0	0	0	0
Proper Boy	2	C	2	0	0	0	0
Proper Card	4	G	9	1	0	3	27,940
Proper Conquest	6	G	9	3	2	0	38,938
Proper Dancer	2	F	8	1	0	1	9,780
Proper Direction	3	G	7	1	0	1	6,660
Proper Etiquette	5	M	8	2	1	0	10,536
Proper Fantasy	5	G	12	1	1	0	3,955
Proper Gun	4	F	9	2	0	0	8,935
Proper Joe	5	G	16	1	3	2	17,560
Proper John	4	G	2	0	0	0	1,100
Proper Lady	4	F	1	0	0	0	150
Proper Man	6	H	6	0	2	1	11,260
Proper Manners	2	F	6	0	0	3	31,669
Proper Mariner	4	G	3	0	0	0	480
Proper Moonshine	7	G	5	1	0	1	5,160
Proper Motion	5	G	1	1	0	0	4,950
Proper Music	4	F	1	0	0	0	0
Proper Name	5	M	6	1	1	1	6,030
Proper Oyl	3	G	10	1	1	2	10,510
Proper Paradise	6	M	8	0	1	1	3,543
Proper Plum	9	G	15	1	0	2	4,246
Proper Prado	2	C	9	2	1	3	100,571
Proper Prescision	6	M	2	0	0	0	255
Proper Prince	2	C	3	1	0	0	3,954
Proper Prospect	4	C	4	1	0	1	10,825
Proper Prospector	2	F	8	1	3	1	13,250
Proper Pudding	7	M	6	0	1	2	8,390
Proper Sandi	5	M	2	0	0	0	80
Proper Sunday	5	G	11	0	0	1	16,532
Proper Toffee	2	G	6	1	1	0	4,052
Proper Top	3	F	11	2	3	3	34,543
Properandsmelly	4	F	9	0	2	1	980
Properly Claimed	5	H	4	0	0	1	284
Properly Prim	4	F	4	1	2	1	2,672
Proper's Peak	8	G	6	0	1	1	557
Prophetic Call	3	G	8	1	1	1	9,222
Prophet's Reward	4	C	2	0	0	0	0
Prophet's Town	2	C	2	0	0	0	0
Propitious	4	G	15	4	3	1	28,413
Proprietor	4	G	4	0	0	0	188
Propriety	3	F	7	1	1	2	30,007
Propulsion Power	5	G	3	1	1	0	2,815
Prory	11	G	5	0	1	1	3,361
Prose	3	F	17	1	2	3	20,115
Prosecuter	3	G	14	1	3	1	8,292
Prosecution Rests	3	G	6	1	2	0	9,479
Prospect Crossing	3	G	12	0	0	1	2,160
Prospect Duchess	3	G	6	0	0	0	0
Prospect Ends Well	3	F	8	3	0	0	27,580
Prospect for J R	5	G	8	2	0	1	6,242
Prospect Gold	3	G	4	0	0	1	12,409
Prospect Green	5	G	7	0	0	2	11,520
Prospect Heights	7	G	14	0	0	3	1,937
Prospect Kid	5	G	7	1	2	2	30,240
Prospect Lane	5	G	2	0	1	0	1,824
Prospect Mark	5	G	2	0	0	0	1,680
Prospect Valley	4	G	17	2	2	1	24,893
Prospect Weaver	3	C	6	1	1	0	27,410
Prospect Won	4	C	9	0	0	2	9,835
Prospectforme	4	F	7	1	1	0	4,664
Prospectinforgold	2	G	1	0	0	0	130
Prospecting Dixie	4	F	8	2	4	1	31,020
Prospecting Guy	4	G	9	0	0	0	560
Prospecting Silver	2	F	3	0	0	0	405
Prospective Gal	6	M	16	3	2	2	113,559
Prospective Glow	4	F	1	0	0	0	1,080
Prospective Hit	3	G	11	4	1	0	45,637
Prospective Income	5	M	9	0	0	1	2,422
Prospective Kiss	2	G	2	0	0	0	3,600
Prospective Miss	2	F	4	0	0	3	7,445
Prospective Saint	2	F	2	1	0	1	19,080
Prospective Slew	3	F	6	1	0	1	14,795
Prospective Stutz	3	G	3	0	0	0	193
Prospective Titan	3	C	15	1	3	1	27,477
Prospective Wish	5	H	12	1	2	0	8,794
Prospector Cat	3	G	5	1	0	1	10,172
Prospector Jewel	4	C	17	2	2	4	22,605
Prospector Nick	9	G	6	0	2	1	9,443
Prospector Nugget	5	G	8	1	0	2	14,152
Prospector Running	6	M	6	0	1	1	5,383
Prospector Who	4	G	12	2	3	0	27,088
Prospectors Career	3	C	4	0	0	0	106
Prospector's Creek	7	M	2	0	0	0	630

Horse	Age	Sex	Sts	1st	2d	3d	Won
Prospector's Crown	7	M	1	0	0	0	400
Prospector's Dream	3	G	1	0	0	0	0
Prospector's Green	6	G	12	0	3	2	4,813
Prospectors Legacy	2	C	1	0	0	0	170
Prospectors Link	4	G	11	1	1	4	8,667
Prospectors Penny	2	C	5	0	0	1	912
Prospector's Road	2	C	5	0	2	1	18,490
Prospectors Shadow	2	C	4	1	2	0	16,159
Prospectors Silver	3	C	12	1	2	1	12,845
Prospector's Smile	3	G	11	1	0	0	6,940
Prospector's Son	2	C	2	0	0	0	0
Prospectors Strike	4	G	7	1	1	1	21,886
Prospector's Trick	3	C	5	0	3	1	20,800
Prospector's Way	3	C	5	1	2	2	12,360
Prospectors Wealth	2	F	2	0	0	1	2,482
Prospect's Delight	5	M	3	0	1	0	1,735
Prospect's Destiny	3	C	3	0	0	0	1,140
Prospects Gold	5	M	12	0	0	3	4,455
Prospect's Good	5	G	1	0	0	0	98
Prospect's Legacy	4	G	20	1	3	3	10,743
Prospects of War	3	G	3	0	0	0	100
Prospect's Pearl	4	F	12	0	1	0	5,320
Prospects Pleasure	4	F	9	0	1	1	3,030
Prospect's Prize	6	H	7	0	0	0	381
Prospect's Thunder	3	G	10	5	3	0	96,840
Prosper Quickly	4	G	14	2	2	1	12,055
Prosperity River	6	M	9	0	0	1	1,302
Prosperity Rose	4	F	11	2	1	2	7,146
Prosperous Light	3	G	10	0	1	1	4,002
Prosperous Night	10	G	3	1	1	0	2,025
Prosperous Way	3	C	8	0	1	1	4,773
Prospice	4	C	5	2	1	0	47,680
Pro'sprodigy	3	G	3	1	1	0	6,910
Prosser	3	C	8	0	1	3	7,913
Prostar	6	M	16	2	3	1	30,874
Protect	6	G	13	4	1	0	12,887
Protect Her Herman	3	G	8	0	0	0	4,520
Protect the Child	4	F	9	0	0	1	1,124
Protectorate	4	G	15	3	1	2	19,027
Protege's Lover	3	C	1	0	0	0	750
Protist	6	G	9	4	0	4	29,975
Proud Abby	2	F	1	0	0	1	1,650
Proud Advantage	4	G	2	1	1	0	8,140
Proud Alvin	4	G	13	0	0	0	2,710
Proud American	3	F	7	0	1	1	12,657
Proud and Bold	3	C	9	2	3	2	57,660
Proud and Fast	6	M	2	0	0	0	222
Proud and Free	5	M	2	0	1	0	10,000
Proud and Graceful	4	F	2	0	0	0	0
Proud and Lucky	4	F	5	1	0	0	3,224
Proud and Royal	3	G	8	2	0	0	11,175
Proud and Steady	4	C	14	0	4	4	19,805
Proud Andrew	6	G	13	2	2	0	22,500
Proud Arctic	3	F	5	1	0	0	7,240
Proud Beauty (IRE)	3	F	5	2	2	1	87,760
Proud Bounty	4	C	2	0	0	1	238
Proud Brook	2	F	3	0	0	0	510
Proud Carmela	3	F	12	3	2	3	67,660
Proud Citizen	4	C	7	1	0	0	76,705
Proud Creation	8	G	5	1	0	0	9,292
Proud Decision	2	C	3	0	0	1	3,235
Proud Deputy	3	G	4	0	0	0	990
Proud Dinero	3	F	13	1	0	0	6,689
Proud Edition	4	C	21	2	8	3	24,141
Proud Era	4	G	6	1	0	0	4,649
Proud Falstaff	7	G	4	0	0	0	696
Proud Friendly	5	G	2	0	0	0	1,160
Proud Gal	3	F	13	2	2	3	57,502
Proud Hart	6	M	9	0	0	2	1,566
Proud Hero	3	F	4	0	0	0	720
Proud Irma	2	F	8	0	0	1	1,680
Proud John	3	G	1	0	0	0	1,980
Proud Jolie	3	C	9	0	0	0	1,140
Proud Lady	3	F	10	0	2	0	25,458
Proud Lion	2	C	2	1	0	0	19,050
Proud Louie	7	G	14	5	4	2	22,060
Proud Man	5	H	7	2	3	1	203,142
Proud Mary Turnen	4	F	1	0	0	0	294
Proud Megan	4	F	15	2	3	4	54,160
Proud Memories	3	G	12	3	1	0	11,826
Proud Michael	2	C	1	0	0	0	1,150
Proud Mombo	5	M	6	0	0	0	705
Proud Moment	11	G	9	1	0	3	7,661
Proud Moon	4	C	4	1	0	0	6,780
Proud Mutesa	4	G	6	0	0	0	646
Proud N Perfect	3	F	4	0	1	0	3,935
Proud Native	5	G	2	0	0	0	0
Proud Nicole	3	F	12	1	1	4	58,700
Proud Night	3	C	11	2	0	2	23,258
Proud of It	6	H	7	1	1	1	9,710
Proud of Mamma	4	C	5	2	0	1	7,441
Proud of Pyrite	4	G	17	3	3	1	19,214
Proud One	4	G	5	0	0	0	150
Proud Partner	4	G	9	2	1	3	70,270
Proud Patrolman	5	G	11	1	4	2	20,925
Proud Peacock	6	G	10	0	3	2	12,978
Proud Phantom	4	F	10	1	0	1	11,058
Proud Phil	2	G	4	0	0	0	1,020
Proud Pia	6	M	7	1	0	2	1,475
Proud Pioneer	5	M	20	2	0	1	9,131
Proud Pixie	3	F	8	1	1	0	6,992
Proud Polina	4	F	7	1	0	2	12,450
Proud Premier	7	G	3	0	0	0	0
Proud Prince	4	G	10	1	1	1	8,294
Proud Princely	3	C	2	0	1	1	1,188
Proud Prize	7	G	2	0	0	0	792
Proud Punch	4	G	10	0	7	2	25,970
Proud Queen	4	F	1	0	0	0	84
Proud Rebel	6	G	11	1	1	1	4,204
Proud Son	2	C	7	3	1	0	108,076
Proud Statesman	2	C	4	1	1	1	9,420
Proud Suave	2	C	6	1	0	1	10,295
Proud Sunrise	3	G	7	0	1	1	1,798
Proud Tammie	6	M	4	0	0	1	3,620
Proud Tears	3	F	11	4	1	1	40,647
Proud Thunder	3	C	4	0	0	1	2,335
Proud to Be Bold	5	G	10	2	1	1	23,772
Proud to Be True	2	C	2	0	0	1	1,935
Proud to Reign	4	F	4	1	0	1	2,760
Proud Token	2	F	4	0	1	1	3,050
Proud West	4	F	1	0	0	1	4,730
Proud Yvett	4	F	2	0	0	1	1,350
Proudest Beauty	4	F	1	0	0	0	80
Proudest Queen	2	F	1	1	0	0	15,200
Proudest Sam	4	C	10	0	0	0	683
Proudest Woman	5	M	9	4	0	1	24,552
Proudly We Hailed	3	G	21	2	2	7	25,770
Proudsoldier	3	G	14	1	1	2	15,496
Proudtobeahalfterm	6	G	4	1	0	0	4,400
Proudtobecanadian	3	C	6	1	0	0	23,736
Proudtobecountry	4	C	3	0	0	0	159
Provable	4	G	12	2	3	1	21,895
Prove It Wright	4	F	2	0	1	0	3,719
Proved Them Wrong	3	F	14	2	1	2	21,885
Proven Brand	3	C	15	1	1	2	9,362
Proven Cat	2	F	3	0	2	0	12,480
Proven Cure	9	G	12	3	2	1	94,537
Proven Form	3	F	10	2	1	3	84,163
Proven Giltey	4	G	11	1	0	0	3,484
Proven Honor	3	F	16	8	1	1	57,930
Proven Promise	3	F	4	0	0	0	1,236
Proven Seattle	5	H	1	0	0	0	60
Provenance	6	G	10	2	0	1	10,020
Providence	3	F	4	1	1	0	21,100
Provincetown	3	C	3	1	0	0	27,780
Provisional	4	G	2	0	0	0	1,020
Provisionist	4	G	5	0	0	1	586
Provobay	3	F	4	0	0	1	4,200
Provocateur	3	G	16	5	2	2	49,467
Provoleta	3	F	5	2	1	0	17,550
Provost Marshall	6	H	2	0	0	2	2,860
Prowling	4	C	4	0	0	0	0
Proximos	4	C	11	1	2	0	67,304
Proxy Fight	2	C	3	0	1	0	5,124
Proxy Statement	4	F	2	0	0	0	1,500
Pru	5	G	18	1	0	1	4,378
Prudencia	2	F	7	2	1	0	44,650
Prudhoe Bay	3	C	7	3	3	0	30,951

RECORDS OF HORSES

Horse	Age	Sex	Sts	1st	2d	3d	Won	Horse	Age	Sex	Sts	1st	2d	3d	Won
Pruner's Speed	3	G	7	1	2	0	15,870	Punch Buggie	4	F	1	0	0	0	0
Prune's Hope	4	F	3	0	1	1	3,536	Punch D Lites Out	3	C	2	1	0	0	14,250
Prune's Interest	3	F	2	0	0	0	0	Punch Drunk	4	G	16	2	3	2	13,530
Pruney	4	G	17	1	2	2	12,754	Punch Em Out	4	F	8	1	0	1	8,665
Przedrzymirski	3	G	4	0	0	0	1,179	Punch Taylor	3	F	8	0	3	2	8,860
Psota	3	C	3	1	0	0	3,400	Punch the Moon	2	G	7	1	0	1	11,160
Psych	2	F	1	1	0	0	21,700	Punched	3	C	5	0	0	0	635
Psychedelia	2	F	2	0	0	0	0	Puncheon Run	5	G	14	2	1	1	20,273
Psychic Hotline	3	G	2	1	0	0	16,800	Puncher	7	G	16	4	2	0	43,484
Psychlotropic	2	F	1	0	0	0	0	Punches Treat	2	F	3	0	0	0	590
Psycho Mama	5	M	9	1	2	1	5,812	Punchess	5	M	5	1	1	1	12,925
Psychogallantry	7	M	10	0	3	1	4,997	Punchin' Gal	3	F	6	1	1	1	15,600
Psychotic	4	F	4	0	1	0	770	Punching	4	F	2	1	0	0	21,570
Psyco Gator	2	F	8	2	2	1	24,635	Punchino	5	H	2	0	0	1	1,000
Pt. Pleasant	2	F	2	0	0	0	0	Punchstorm	3	C	5	0	2	0	6,000
Ptah	3	G	10	4	1	0	78,650	Punchullah	3	G	5	1	0	0	35,600
Ptichka	3	F	11	1	2	1	19,420	Punchum	5	M	13	2	0	1	15,590
Pt's Grey Eagle	2	G	2	1	1	0	21,200	Punchy Princess	4	F	6	1	0	1	15,833
Pt's Mostnotorious	2	C	5	1	0	1	16,888	Punchy Victory	3	C	7	0	2	0	6,400
Pubelo Run	5	G	8	2	3	2	30,720	Punctuate	3	G	11	0	0	3	2,819
Public Address	4	C	10	1	1	5	33,137	Pungent	8	G	10	1	0	2	5,700
Public Official	3	C	2	1	0	1	25,680	Punitive	2	C	1	0	0	0	651
Public Support	5	G	13	0	2	2	4,349	Punjaboo	3	C	2	0	0	0	118
Publication	4	G	4	1	2	1	143,515	Punk	6	G	11	0	4	3	13,564
Publicly Known	3	F	2	0	0	0	450	Punkin	4	F	3	0	0	1	1,575
Publisher's Phil	3	G	2	0	0	1	2,640	Punkin Head	5	H	3	1	0	0	26,660
Pucci	3	G	4	0	0	0	0	Punkineer	4	C	1	0	0	0	0
Puchungo (PER)	7	G	16	4	4	2	44,780	Punny Guy	3	G	14	1	3	1	17,785
Pucker	3	F	2	1	1	0	41,900	Punta Mita	4	F	1	0	0	0	0
Pucker Power	4	F	6	0	1	1	8,010	Punxsutawney	3	F	1	0	0	0	325
Pucker Up Baby	7	H	2	0	0	0	0	Puny	7	M	8	1	1	0	22,894
Puckerupbuttercup	3	F	8	2	0	0	8,869	Pupil	4	F	3	1	1	1	66,080
Puckerupnkissme	5	M	3	0	0	0	275	Puppet Princess	6	M	3	0	0	0	132
Pud	3	G	12	2	3	1	49,380	Puppy Love	5	M	7	0	0	1	4,170
Puddin Tame	3	G	7	0	0	0	1,210	Purdee Purdee	3	F	11	1	2	2	5,018
Puddle Time	6	H	18	1	2	2	21,420	Purdy Baby	4	F	2	0	0	0	100
Puddles Pleasure	4	F	3	0	0	0	140	Purdy Tricky	5	G	15	4	0	3	21,295
Pueblo Peak	7	G	5	0	0	0	280	Purdy Zippy	5	M	12	2	0	3	9,318
Puerto Banus	4	C	8	3	2	0	183,560	Pure	2	C	4	0	1	0	10,220
Puerto Romeral (CHI)	6	G	2	0	0	0	2,700	Pure Amazement	4	C	11	3	1	0	48,844
Puff the Magic	4	F	1	0	0	0	920	Pure American	2	G	3	1	2	0	27,200
Puffer	4	G	10	3	5	2	207,654	Pure and Clear	5	G	10	0	0	0	677
Puffin Point	3	F	11	1	3	2	22,260	Pure Blue	4	C	6	0	0	0	370
Puffy Shirt	3	F	2	1	0	1	27,875	Pure Bull	7	M	4	0	0	0	270
Puget Sound	3	C	2	0	0	0	0	Pure Class	6	H	8	3	2	2	14,825
Puggy's Last Love	3	C	13	3	1	1	50,652	Pure Cyn	7	M	3	1	0	2	1,980
Pug's Pistol	6	H	11	1	2	3	9,545	Pure D' Dash	2	C	2	0	0	0	475
Pug's Pride	6	H	8	2	1	0	6,139	Pure Energy	2	F	3	1	0	0	7,200
Pugsly	4	F	11	2	1	1	12,066	Pure Finess	4	F	9	0	3	1	6,790
Pukka (NZ)	6	G	2	0	0	0	750	Pure Fun	3	C	7	1	1	0	8,197
Pulchritude	2	F	3	1	0	0	16,360	Pure Gossip	3	F	4	0	0	0	794
Pulitzer	5	H	7	1	1	0	8,612	Pure Harmony	6	H	12	1	1	0	26,334
Pull Me Out Poppy	2	F	1	0	0	0	0	Pure Heart	4	G	3	1	1	0	9,225
Pull My Chain	3	C	2	0	0	1	8,484	Pure Independence	4	F	8	1	1	1	3,894
Pull Over Please	4	C	7	4	0	1	25,570	Pure Poetry	5	M	3	0	0	0	0
Pull the Handle	8	G	9	2	2	1	10,871	Pure Pride	2	C	1	0	0	0	0
Pull the Lever	3	F	8	0	0	1	4,174	Pure Sweep	3	F	2	0	0	0	223
Pulled Together	4	F	3	0	0	0	0	Pure Talent	2	F	5	0	1	3	6,412
Pulling Pints	3	G	3	0	1	0	1,910	Pure Tranquility	4	F	5	0	0	1	1,757
Pulling Strings	7	G	2	0	0	1	1,500	Pure Wild	4	F	14	1	0	1	20,114
Pulpit Affair	3	F	12	1	3	2	17,206	Purely	4	F	9	1	1	1	23,110
Pulpit Harbor	6	M	8	0	1	0	3,092	Purely Classic	3	C	7	1	3	0	56,850
Pulpit Talk	3	G	4	1	1	1	35,840	Purely Devious	3	C	3	1	0	1	6,665
Pulpit's Edge	2	C	1	0	0	0	0	Purely Elegant	3	F	1	0	0	0	0
Pulteney's Thunder	5	M	2	0	0	0	136	Purely Fabulous	3	F	10	1	3	1	32,800
Pulverizingassault	7	M	8	0	1	0	2,709	Purely Judith	3	F	9	3	2	1	49,606
Puma	6	H	13	2	4	0	29,355	Purely Special	2	G	4	1	0	0	7,325
Puma (IRE)	3	G	6	1	0	1	33,300	Purge	2	C	1	0	0	0	27,000
Puma's Pride	3	F	13	2	2	4	90,160	Purifier	5	G	3	0	1	1	2,350
Pummel	3	G	17	2	2	1	14,197	Purify	2	C	2	0	0	0	0
Pump Slew	5	M	2	0	0	0	3,320	Purist	3	C	11	1	0	3	17,426
Pumpkin Pie to Go	9	M	9	0	1	1	2,524	Purloin	4	F	8	0	1	2	20,240
Pumpkin Ridge	3	G	2	0	1	0	2,575	Purple Bunny	3	F	2	0	1	0	1,700
Pumpkin Roll	3	F	9	2	2	1	16,300	Purple Cop	3	C	5	1	1	2	53,580
Pumpkin Soup	3	F	6	1	0	0	29,415	Purple Emblem	2	F	6	0	0	0	2,310
Pumpkin's Glow	3	F	1	0	0	0	118	Purple Fox	6	M	7	0	2	0	1,910
Pumpkin's Pride	3	F	14	3	2	0	49,166	Purple Hills	4	F	9	1	0	2	27,440
Punch	4	G	13	2	2	1	63,982	Purple J	5	M	6	0	1	2	3,264
Punch Bag	2	G	5	1	0	3	23,540	Purple Madame	4	F	11	0	0	0	958

Horse	Age	Sex	Sts	1st	2d	3d	Won
Purple Martin	5	G	1	0	0	0	0
Purple Mountain	3	C	6	0	0	0	220
Purple Pleasure	4	C	4	0	1	0	5,938
Purple Punch	5	M	1	0	1	0	1,890
Purple Sand	6	G	8	2	1	1	61,372
Purple Slippers	5	M	2	0	0	0	0
Purple Squall	7	G	9	0	1	0	2,966
Purple Thistle	2	F	2	0	0	1	4,250
Purple Toi	2	F	5	0	1	2	10,000
Purple Violets	6	M	13	0	2	2	4,935
Purple Wand	3	C	10	2	1	4	11,153
Purple Wonder	4	F	13	1	5	1	14,540
Purpleshade Jewel	5	M	5	0	1	0	2,575
Purplest	5	H	1	0	0	1	3,740
Purr Purr Purr	3	F	2	0	0	0	630
Purrcat	3	G	14	3	2	1	15,243
Purring Along	6	G	11	1	1	2	16,055
Purrowler	4	F	2	0	0	0	0
Purse Loot	5	G	6	1	0	0	2,760
Purse Raider	2	C	3	1	1	0	10,680
Purse Stealer	6	M	3	0	0	1	1,430
Pursecatcher	4	F	12	2	1	0	12,350
Pursenatcher	2	F	5	0	0	2	7,690
Push My Buttons	3	F	3	2	1	0	24,620
Push My Luck	3	F	6	0	0	0	3,990
Push Play	3	G	6	1	1	1	7,825
Push Push Push	2	C	3	0	0	0	125
Pusharata	6	M	4	0	0	0	315
Pushed	3	G	14	5	2	3	89,987
Put It On	7	M	5	1	0	0	14,610
Put It Out	3	G	13	1	2	3	16,401
Put Me In	3	F	8	3	1	3	95,408
Put the Heat On	2	F	1	0	0	0	180
Put Up Your Dukes	2	G	3	0	0	0	1,590
Putt Putt Dan	6	G	12	1	1	1	9,188
Puttinonthedog	8	G	1	1	0	0	1,675
Puxa Saco	3	F	4	0	2	0	47,400
Puzzle Girl	3	F	4	1	0	0	7,442
Puzzle Maker	4	F	8	0	2	1	18,862
Puzzle Palace	4	F	3	1	1	0	6,000
Puzzlement	4	C	11	2	2	3	470,450
Pyaar's King	5	G	5	0	0	1	4,370
Pyramid Girl	2	F	2	0	1	0	5,830
Pyramid Passage	2	F	10	0	2	2	3,705
Pyramid Performer	2	C	7	1	3	0	25,250
Pyramid Scheme	3	F	8	0	2	1	6,185
Pyrite Alena	2	F	5	1	1	1	9,125
Pyrite Alone	2	F	5	0	0	0	662
Pyrite Angel	6	G	11	0	5	0	12,907
Pyrite Dance	3	F	9	3	2	1	32,243
Pyrite Dash	3	G	7	0	0	0	2,505
Pyrite Forest	7	M	14	1	2	4	17,425
Pyrite Gun	2	F	6	1	3	1	20,000
Pyrite in Flight	9	G	17	6	3	2	39,527
Pyrite Jet	4	F	3	0	0	0	307
Pyrite Lady	4	F	13	0	4	6	24,239
Pyrite Mac	5	G	12	0	5	3	30,060
Pyrite Menu	4	F	15	2	2	2	34,071
Pyrite Monarch	3	F	8	2	0	3	11,242
Pyrite Or Bust	4	F	8	3	1	1	32,599
Pyrite Pansy	2	F	7	1	1	2	18,955
Pyrite Picnic	7	G	7	0	1	1	1,896
Pyrite Rain	2	F	4	0	1	0	4,165
Pyrite Romance	3	F	10	1	2	2	12,364
Pyrite Run	3	G	10	3	4	0	37,015
Pyrite Search	3	C	6	1	1	2	27,740
Pyrite Select	3	F	10	1	2	0	8,754
Pyrite Soup	3	F	4	0	0	1	1,578
Pyrite Vain	3	F	6	1	0	0	4,551
Pyrite Valentine	2	G	10	1	0	0	7,650
Pyrite Who	3	F	7	1	1	0	18,520
Pyrite's Passion	9	G	8	2	0	3	5,544
Pyritical	4	F	3	0	0	0	0
Pyro Tec	7	G	3	0	0	0	0
Pythagorus	7	H	4	0	0	0	1,078
Pyx	4	F	1	0	0	0	0
Q Commercial Jette	6	H	6	0	2	1	7,693
Q One	2	C	1	0	0	0	1,350
Q One for Two	7	G	9	2	3	1	34,808
Q Risk	3	G	10	0	0	3	4,007
Q Tricky Will	4	G	5	2	1	0	19,045
Q Will	4	C	1	0	0	0	0
Q. T. Quixote	7	M	16	0	0	0	800
Q. V. C. Karma	2	F	1	0	0	0	600
Qais	3	C	4	3	0	1	71,093
Qruiz Knight	3	C	4	0	0	0	306
Quacked Bag	3	F	4	2	0	1	33,415
Quadratic Equation	4	F	11	1	0	3	7,079
Quaffalino	3	F	12	0	0	0	823
Quail's Gate	5	M	12	2	3	1	19,812
Quake	8	G	6	1	0	2	23,445
Quakers Surprise	2	C	3	1	1	0	13,608
Qualify	3	F	2	0	0	0	0
Quality	6	M	9	2	1	2	18,990
Quality Affirmed	9	G	7	0	1	3	6,224
Quality Hero	3	C	9	0	2	0	3,102
Quality Kat	3	C	2	0	2	0	3,078
Qualitynotquantity	6	G	4	0	0	1	2,800
Qualls Road	4	G	5	0	1	3	2,190
Quanaco	2	C	8	2	3	0	38,530
Quanah County	2	F	5	1	3	1	75,639
Quanah's Angel	3	F	11	1	0	1	1,386
Quanjai	5	G	9	0	0	1	1,303
Quannapowitt	3	C	11	2	5	0	62,510
Quantico Joe	2	G	1	0	1	0	5,250
Quantify	3	F	7	0	0	0	726
Quantis	4	G	2	1	1	0	20,000
Quantum Link	5	H	15	2	3	1	14,059
Quantum Merit	4	G	8	3	1	2	176,180
Quapaw Charlie	2	C	2	0	0	2	8,330
Quarry Contender	4	F	6	3	1	0	11,585
Quarryville	3	G	13	1	5	0	9,727
Quarter Pounder	3	C	13	0	3	2	27,090
Quarter Slot	11	G	5	0	0	1	857
Quarter Time	3	C	6	1	1	0	25,580
Quarter to Nine	4	F	5	0	1	0	5,080
Quarter Ton of Fun	4	C	2	0	0	0	3,750
Quarterback Draw	4	C	14	3	0	3	14,928
Quarterelven	3	F	5	0	0	0	2,010
Quartermoonlanding	3	F	2	0	0	0	0
Quartez	2	G	4	0	1	0	10,260
Quartz Movement	2	G	10	0	2	3	10,423
Quassapaug	4	C	2	1	0	0	26,720
Quatre Dix Neuf	4	G	10	1	1	0	40,400
Quattro Latro	3	C	5	1	0	2	21,320
Quddam	4	G	1	0	0	0	0
Que Bonita	4	F	6	0	1	2	13,536
Que Borges (ARG)	4	C	3	0	0	0	0
Que Candy (ARG)	5	H	15	2	2	2	58,500
Que Cherie	2	F	6	0	0	1	1,465
Que Diablito	3	C	4	0	1	0	2,640
Que Facil Corazon	5	M	14	6	3	2	134,970
Que Feo	4	C	11	0	1	1	2,970
Que Guapo	3	G	8	1	0	0	3,908
Que Leo	2	C	1	0	0	0	0
Que Lindo	3	G	2	0	0	0	0
Que Polo	4	C	1	0	0	1	1,500
Que Tormenta	4	F	6	1	1	3	2,165
Quebelick	3	F	1	0	0	0	0
Quechee Gorge	5	M	12	0	3	4	9,152
Quecreek	3	F	3	1	0	1	13,520
Queen Alexis	3	F	11	0	3	1	3,772
Queen an E	3	F	5	1	1	2	12,520
Queen Anns Revenge	2	F	3	0	1	0	3,600
Queen At Heart	4	F	16	4	3	3	33,422
Queen Awad	3	F	4	1	0	0	14,620
Queen Chelsey	4	F	15	1	3	4	10,246
Queen Cheris	5	M	6	0	0	1	2,290
Queen Clever	4	F	4	0	0	0	694
Queen Corine	8	M	9	0	0	1	999
Queen Cornelia	4	F	2	0	0	0	270
Queen Creek	6	M	7	3	2	1	37,992
Queen Daisy	4	F	9	1	1	2	12,795
Queen De	5	M	18	2	4	1	11,241
Queen Ding	5	M	20	3	2	2	31,860
Queen Diva	3	F	2	0	0	0	150
Queen Evelyn	3	F	1	0	0	0	0

Horse	Age	Sex	Sts	1st	2d	3d	Won	Horse	Age	Sex	Sts	1st	2d	3d	Won
Queen Felice	3	F	8	3	1	1	22,520	Queen's Glare	4	F	1	0	0	0	0
Queen for Cats	4	F	2	0	0	0	315	Queens High	3	F	6	0	0	0	505
Queen Geraldine	2	F	5	1	0	0	21,056	Queen's Jeans	4	F	8	0	0	0	158
Queen Gloria	2	F	2	0	0	0	180	Queen's Jubilee	2	F	3	1	0	1	19,290
Queen Guinevere	4	F	9	1	1	1	8,651	Queen's Jungle Bee	5	G	7	0	0	1	2,508
Queen Halo	3	F	11	0	2	1	11,125	Queen's Kiss	4	F	15	4	1	4	73,076
Queen Irish	2	F	6	1	1	0	8,985	Queen's Last Hart	4	G	9	1	2	4	11,754
Queen Isabel	3	F	14	4	1	3	104,640	Queens Money	5	M	7	0	0	1	1,160
Queen Jennie	6	M	1	0	0	0	0	Queen's Secret	4	F	6	0	0	0	1,400
Queen Jimmy	5	M	16	3	5	1	54,428	Queen's Son	4	G	14	1	4	3	24,835
Queen K	4	F	8	2	1	0	14,871	Queen's Treasure	3	F	5	1	0	0	3,690
Queen Kelly	3	F	10	1	1	0	11,644	Queen's Tribute	2	F	2	0	0	0	630
Queen Lu Lu	5	M	2	1	0	1	7,524	Queen's Triomphe	4	F	8	5	1	0	135,865
Queen Maeve	4	F	6	0	0	0	336	Queen's Wager	4	F	16	3	1	9	33,522
Queen Marin	3	F	4	0	0	1	1,226	Queenscliff	4	F	8	2	0	1	6,075
Queen Mary J.	5	M	3	0	0	0	111	Queensorbetter	5	M	5	0	0	0	925
Queen Mary Jean	3	F	6	0	0	0	1,185	Queenstown	3	F	7	3	2	2	33,940
Queen Maya	3	F	1	0	0	0	0	Queensway Quay (GB)	3	C	2	0	0	0	0
Queen Mindy	3	F	5	2	0	0	63,660	Queentiye	2	F	7	0	0	0	838
Queen Morgan	4	F	5	0	0	1	894	Quel Senor (FR)	8	G	2	0	0	0	2,500
Queen Nel	3	F	4	0	0	0	372	Quemado	3	G	2	1	0	0	8,250
Queen Nova	4	F	9	1	3	3	17,800	Quench Wench	2	F	1	0	0	1	1,425
Queen of Cash	4	F	8	0	1	1	3,106	Quero Quero	3	F	6	2	2	1	192,420
Queen of Clubs	10	M	4	0	0	0	0	Queso Grande	5	H	5	0	0	0	529
Queen of Deals	3	F	1	0	0	0	960	Quest	4	C	11	2	4	3	637,860
Queen of Denial	3	F	2	1	1	0	3,970	Quest a Day	4	G	18	1	2	4	21,325
Queen of Dunollie	3	F	7	1	1	1	7,780	Quest Dancer	6	M	8	0	1	1	10,420
Queen of Esparanza	2	F	2	0	0	0	290	Quest for a Buck	3	G	3	0	0	0	78
Queen of Humor	3	F	8	1	1	2	7,005	Quest for Approval	11	G	6	0	0	1	1,982
Queen of Karakorum	4	F	7	3	0	1	10,330	Quest for Fun	6	M	15	1	1	1	31,810
Queen of Keno	2	F	2	0	0	0	0	Quest for Power	4	G	13	3	3	2	24,324
Queen of Mecca	6	M	10	2	2	2	27,465	Quest for Rain	5	G	5	0	1	1	8,500
Queen of My Castle	3	F	16	3	3	1	19,869	Quest for Silver	7	G	13	2	4	3	28,848
Queen of Nostalgia	6	M	2	0	0	0	0	Quest for Speed	5	H	4	0	0	1	675
Queen of Paris	4	F	11	2	0	0	14,745	Quest for Truth	3	F	12	7	1	1	125,712
Queen of Queens	3	F	7	1	1	0	53,360	Quest La Due	4	F	2	0	0	0	0
Queen of Runners	4	F	7	1	3	1	13,551	Quest Master	8	G	3	1	0	1	2,655
Queen of Saratoga	4	F	10	2	2	2	64,980	Quest of Fate	5	H	6	2	1	1	61,460
Queen of Slew	3	F	1	0	0	0	0	Quest Star	4	C	10	3	3	0	298,380
Queen of Slots	2	F	5	2	2	1	53,092	Questa Gold	3	C	6	0	0	0	0
Queen of Swain	3	F	7	1	0	3	7,052	Questador	4	G	4	0	0	0	621
Queen of the Isle	4	F	4	0	0	1	729	Questanado	2	C	2	0	0	1	2,880
Queen of the Road	4	F	8	2	1	0	12,020	Questfor Reverence	4	F	1	0	0	0	360
Queen of the Sky	4	F	2	0	0	0	426	Questforcamelot	5	M	5	0	1	1	4,396
Queen of the Zone	4	F	1	0	0	0	0	Questforredemption	3	G	7	1	1	0	2,080
Queen of Wands	3	F	4	3	1	0	21,850	Questfortheroses	3	C	3	0	0	0	0
Queen of Wheat	5	M	1	0	0	0	120	Questing Knight	4	G	10	1	1	2	28,063
Queen On Tour	6	M	9	0	2	1	4,870	Question Authority	3	G	4	0	0	0	0
Queen Sandy	3	C	13	0	4	0	13,240	Question of Gold	9	G	8	0	0	0	648
Queen Sheba	3	F	2	0	1	1	6,720	Questionable Miss	5	M	13	1	0	1	2,240
Queen Slew	3	F	3	0	0	0	0	Questionable Past	2	F	6	4	1	0	96,200
Queen Speech	4	F	6	0	3	1	52,591	Questionable Road	3	G	12	1	5	2	10,988
Queen Supreme	2	F	1	1	0	0	14,250	Queue	6	M	3	0	0	0	6,000
Queen Tango	4	F	2	0	1	0	471	Queue Up	4	G	3	0	0	0	1,230
Queen Teen	5	M	8	1	0	2	12,595	Quibbling Queeny	2	F	2	2	0	0	19,800
Queen Trigger	2	F	7	1	1	0	25,646	Quick Action	2	C	2	1	0	0	30,030
Queen Triton	2	F	5	1	0	1	12,883	Quick American	3	C	13	2	2	2	37,570
Queen Twilla	2	F	3	0	0	0	0	Quick Apalachee	7	G	8	0	2	0	2,680
Queen Twining	4	F	7	0	0	1	2,175	Quick as Pleasure	5	G	2	0	0	0	0
Queen Valentine	4	F	2	0	0	0	166	Quick Ball Run	4	G	13	3	1	3	39,314
Queen Valid	4	F	3	1	0	1	7,390	Quick Blue	5	M	6	0	1	1	31,020
Queena Corrina	4	F	4	2	0	0	37,320	Quick Charge	3	F	1	0	0	0	0
Queenhanna's Home	2	F	2	1	0	0	13,800	Quick Chill	3	C	8	1	2	1	14,126
Queenielaureenie	3	F	3	0	1	0	2,615	Quick Claim	4	G	12	2	3	1	46,580
Queenies Girl	5	M	8	0	0	3	5,404	Quick Corsage	4	F	21	4	6	0	32,696
Queenly Image	2	F	7	0	0	0	1,340	Quick Counter	3	G	3	1	0	0	6,646
Queenofluv	2	F	8	1	3	1	32,040	Quick Country	6	G	3	0	0	0	132
Queenofmountain	4	F	7	0	2	1	18,406	Quick Cover	2	F	2	0	0	1	2,160
Queen's Account	4	G	10	2	1	0	13,508	Quick Dash	3	C	6	0	0	2	1,954
Queen's Advantage	2	F	11	0	0	1	4,444	Quick Decision	3	F	5	1	0	1	3,775
Queens Are Wild	2	F	5	2	0	0	24,754	Quick Deed	3	G	1	0	1	0	0
Queen's Bouquet	3	F	10	1	2	1	32,445	Quick Divide	2	G	4	0	1	0	9,240
Queen's Caper	4	F	12	0	5	1	5,465	Quick Draw	3	C	6	2	2	0	57,420
Queens Carousel	4	F	2	1	0	0	27,960	Quick Draw Annie	3	F	11	1	2	2	15,347
Queen's Colony	10	C	13	2	2	5	9,906	Quick Draw Makah	4	C	4	0	0	3	4,200
Queen's Counsel	2	C	2	1	0	0	14,594	Quick Dude	2	C	3	0	1	0	14,370
Queen's Fancy	5	H	3	0	0	0	405	Quick Frost	3	F	10	1	1	1	2,731
Queen's Flag	7	M	2	0	0	0	290	Quick Fuse	4	F	3	0	1	0	3,470
Queens Fort	2	F	2	0	0	0	344	Quick Gainer	3	F	3	0	0	0	505

Horse	Age	Sex	Sts	1st	2d	3d	Won
Quick Grand	4	G	4	0	0	0	190
Quick Interview	5	M	14	1	2	0	19,495
Quick Kissin	5	M	4	1	0	0	4,047
Quick Lady	4	F	7	0	0	0	210
Quick Lighting	4	G	2	0	0	0	108
Quick Line	7	G	3	0	0	0	471
Quick Look	2	G	8	1	1	0	10,642
Quick Marie	5	M	2	0	0	0	975
Quick Mason	2	C	3	0	1	1	4,140
Quick Mick	2	F	5	1	0	1	10,330
Quick Mix	5	M	5	0	0	0	0
Quick Moment	4	C	1	0	0	0	0
Quick Mustard	3	F	6	1	1	0	5,680
Quick N Fancy	3	F	13	2	1	3	38,420
Quick N Quite	3	F	6	0	0	0	249
Quick N Red	5	M	4	2	0	1	5,724
Quick N Sweet	4	F	17	3	3	3	18,723
Quick Nip	4	F	6	3	0	1	58,380
Quick Print	5	H	6	0	2	0	10,855
Quick Proposal	4	G	10	0	1	2	5,120
Quick Punch	7	G	12	1	2	2	52,940
Quick Quack Cognac	10	G	2	0	0	0	90
Quick Quick	4	C	14	3	0	2	24,981
Quick Quiz	3	F	10	1	1	4	6,355
Quick Rate	3	C	5	0	0	0	267
Quick Release	3	G	12	1	2	2	11,268
Quick Rib	5	H	2	1	0	0	16,461
Quick Sand	4	G	2	0	0	0	150
Quick Save	5	M	16	0	0	2	2,488
Quick Sez Me	5	H	3	0	0	0	498
Quick Shot Annie	2	F	1	0	0	0	126
Quick Silver Miss	3	F	12	2	2	0	24,611
Quick Smoke	3	F	12	4	1	3	62,570
Quick Solution	2	C	8	2	2	0	34,655
Quick Start	2	F	3	1	0	0	32,365
Quick Storm	3	C	6	1	3	1	34,030
Quick Struggle	2	G	4	0	0	0	855
Quick Switch	4	G	8	1	0	3	4,398
Quick Take	5	M	10	0	0	0	1,203
Quick Talker	4	C	16	3	3	3	46,880
Quick Temper	2	F	2	1	0	1	32,455
Quick Thunder	3	G	6	0	0	1	848
Quick Tick	3	F	11	2	2	1	12,615
Quick Ticket	2	G	2	0	0	0	2,170
Quick Tip	5	M	11	2	3	1	221,582
Quick to Blush	2	F	2	0	0	0	270
Quick to Fight	2	C	5	1	0	0	17,280
Quick to Sin	6	G	6	1	3	0	2,790
Quick Trend	2	G	5	0	0	1	3,187
Quick Tune	4	G	12	2	3	0	26,902
Quick Volley	4	F	25	2	7	4	19,610
Quick Wings	2	F	3	0	0	0	0
Quick Wink	4	F	1	0	0	0	0
Quickandcutetoboot	3	F	4	2	0	0	14,400
Quickasalark	8	M	10	0	0	0	0
Quickdancin' Roger	3	C	6	0	3	0	11,092
Quicker Kelly	5	M	9	3	0	2	27,627
Quickest Way	3	F	15	0	1	1	3,910
Quickly Now	3	F	12	2	1	5	66,081
Quickrunningriver	6	G	7	0	0	1	1,215
Quick's Affair	6	H	8	1	5	1	8,700
Quicksideup	5	M	10	3	5	0	19,120
Quicksilverexpress	4	G	12	2	3	1	44,216
Quicktect	4	C	2	0	0	0	0
Quickwitch	4	F	4	0	0	0	185
Quickzotti	5	G	2	0	1	0	1,973
Quidditch Player	3	G	5	0	2	0	7,063
Quidditch Star	2	G	7	1	0	0	10,340
Quien Pregunto	4	G	16	2	1	2	7,403
Quiero Saber de Ti	3	C	6	0	0	0	1,305
Quiet Broad	4	F	2	1	0	0	7,500
Quiet Cash	2	C	6	1	2	0	69,000
Quiet Casper	4	G	11	1	2	1	7,630
Quiet Celerity	2	F	2	0	0	0	1,500
Quiet Challenge	3	G	8	1	3	1	55,410
Quiet Charm	4	F	15	6	1	1	55,972
Quiet Colony	4	G	7	1	0	0	47,730
Quiet Companion	4	F	1	0	1	0	2,800
Quiet Comradery	6	M	5	2	0	1	16,240

Horse	Age	Sex	Sts	1st	2d	3d	Won
Quiet Confidence	2	G	1	0	1	0	2,430
Quiet Dare	3	G	5	0	1	0	36,206
Quiet Deed	2	F	4	2	0	0	16,800
Quiet Delight	4	F	3	0	2	0	22,700
Quiet Desperation	4	C	4	0	1	1	15,988
Quiet Dinner	4	F	16	2	3	2	15,557
Quiet Down	2	F	8	1	2	2	51,710
Quiet Edition	2	F	2	0	0	1	4,100
Quiet Ghost	2	F	1	0	0	1	1,020
Quiet Gratitude	7	G	12	2	1	3	69,485
Quiet Hero	2	C	2	0	0	0	1,140
Quiet Journey	2	C	2	0	0	1	7,860
Quiet Joy	10	M	9	2	0	1	3,520
Quiet Julia	3	F	9	1	3	1	25,740
Quiet Knoll	5	M	3	0	0	0	330
Quiet Man	6	G	2	0	0	2	1,970
Quiet Master (CHI)	6	G	10	0	0	0	1,739
Quiet Menace	4	F	2	0	0	0	672
Quiet Mike	6	G	12	3	5	2	89,910
Quiet Minister	3	F	12	0	0	4	31,720
Quiet Motion	6	H	7	1	3	1	6,811
Quiet One	7	H	11	0	1	4	27,310
Quiet Qudible	6	H	3	0	0	1	1,108
Quiet R. N.	4	F	6	3	0	0	17,270
Quiet Rain	4	F	2	1	0	0	6,675
Quiet Reflection	6	G	12	2	3	2	19,696
Quiet Reward	3	F	2	0	0	0	0
Quiet Rhapsody	6	H	2	2	0	0	12,064
Quiet Rose	3	F	1	0	0	0	0
Quiet Ruler	5	G	11	1	1	0	103,809
Quiet Run	5	H	2	0	0	0	0
Quiet Runja	4	G	1	0	0	0	70
Quiet Shot	3	G	10	0	1	2	5,312
Quiet Soul	3	G	16	3	4	2	26,963
Quiet Spark	5	G	6	2	1	0	7,512
Quiet Sting	2	F	3	1	0	0	10,920
Quiet Strategy	7	G	9	0	3	1	9,358
Quiet Stripe	3	C	2	1	0	0	6,300
Quiet Syns	7	H	9	6	3	0	29,420
Quiet Tipper	3	G	2	0	0	0	510
Quiet Winner	2	G	3	1	0	0	6,235
Quiet Winter Sky	2	F	4	0	0	0	360
Quiet Woodman	7	G	3	0	0	0	453
Quiet Word	3	F	3	0	0	0	500
Quietamericanforce	4	C	4	1	0	0	10,983
Quietly Dreaming	6	H	5	1	0	1	7,238
Quietly Elegant	4	F	8	0	0	0	5,910
Quietly Quick	3	G	4	0	0	0	1,860
Quietly Rated	6	H	12	1	1	2	4,163
Quietus	3	C	11	1	3	0	21,235
Quigley	3	C	2	1	0	1	19,620
Quilceda	2	F	4	0	0	0	370
Quilimanque (CHI)	5	G	3	1	0	0	15,000
Quill Play	3	F	3	0	0	0	360
Quilled Bid	7	G	4	3	1	0	64,410
Quillo's Prince	3	G	8	1	0	0	9,366
Quillota	2	C	2	0	0	0	0
Quinary	5	G	10	2	1	3	18,650
Quincy Kid	5	H	3	0	0	0	485
Quincy Light	3	F	7	1	0	4	15,060
Quincy Market	4	F	4	0	0	0	0
Quincy's Quest	6	G	4	0	0	0	1,458
Quincy's Quiz	3	F	5	0	0	1	582
Quinessential	6	G	16	4	1	3	23,929
Quinlan's Lesnjake	6	G	16	1	1	1	6,620
Quins Return	7	M	3	0	0	0	675
Quintara	2	F	2	0	1	0	3,300
Quintina	7	M	7	1	0	3	4,490
Quintmor	5	G	12	3	1	3	11,145
Quinton's Gold	6	H	7	0	1	4	34,840
Quintons Gold Rush	2	C	1	0	1	0	7,600
Quinton's Quest	4	G	7	2	1	0	9,306
Quinton's Quick	7	G	2	0	0	0	136
Qui's Rush In	4	F	3	1	0	1	22,360
Quistadora	3	F	1	0	0	0	0
Quisty	2	F	1	0	0	0	0
Quit Dodging	6	H	4	0	0	0	483
Quit Smoking	3	G	8	1	1	0	7,175
Quitclaim	3	C	29	1	1	3	15,217

RECORDS OF HORSES

Horse	Age	Sex	Sts	1st	2d	3d	Won
Quite a Dancer	3	F	5	0	1	0	5,520
Quite a Lot a Go	7	M	11	1	1	0	6,681
Quite a Storm	4	C	2	1	0	0	7,907
Quite an Angel	3	F	13	1	0	1	13,937
Quite an Evening	5	M	7	0	3	0	25,372
Quite Bold	4	C	13	3	2	2	39,010
Quite by Chance	4	F	10	1	1	2	18,094
Quite Careless	5	G	6	1	0	0	29,480
Quite Exclusive	5	M	16	4	1	2	18,926
Quite Revealing	8	M	6	0	3	1	12,040
Quite Rightly	5	G	17	0	4	1	32,030
Quite Spender	5	M	2	0	1	0	3,550
Quite Tricky	5	H	1	0	0	0	100
Quiteaguy	2	C	10	0	1	2	10,324
Quiver Forever	3	F	9	1	2	1	11,434
Quiver Ridge	2	C	1	0	0	1	1,045
Quivering Delight	5	M	7	0	0	0	925
Quixote Jane	4	F	6	2	0	1	15,553
Quixote's Hope	7	M	8	3	4	1	39,790
Quixote's Prince	6	G	17	4	5	2	68,596
Quixote's Prospect	4	F	16	1	1	2	6,049
Quixote's Store	3	F	15	2	2	2	12,971
Quixotes's Best	3	C	3	0	0	0	0
Quixstar	5	H	2	0	0	0	0
Quiz the Maid	2	F	7	2	1	2	11,680
Quiz the Wizard	3	G	7	1	0	0	2,058
Quizzle	3	F	5	0	2	0	13,200
Quoit a Gala	3	F	5	1	3	0	13,280
Quoit a Lite	3	F	5	0	0	0	990
Quoit a Smile	4	G	4	1	1	2	9,000
Quoit Alarming	5	M	7	0	2	1	15,624
Quoit Amber	2	F	4	0	1	0	3,410
Quoit Jordan	2	C	1	0	0	0	0
Quoit Quick	4	F	9	1	3	0	37,335
Quonochontaug	8	M	11	2	1	2	11,795
Quorn	10	G	1	0	0	0	0
Quote Me Later	3	G	9	2	0	1	37,501
Quote This	3	C	2	0	1	0	8,446
Quotidian	2	G	6	1	3	0	21,190
Quppy	5	M	12	4	1	3	107,350
R a Wynn R	3	C	1	0	0	0	100
R Aly	7	H	4	0	0	0	107
R and R Dream Girl	7	M	5	0	1	1	2,356
R B J's Blaze	3	G	3	1	0	0	9,300
R B Women	2	F	7	1	0	0	8,854
R Bills Alibhai	3	C	12	0	0	0	1,232
R Blue Chip	4	C	2	0	0	1	470
R Bone Crusher	5	H	8	0	0	2	706
R Bonnie Cat	8	H	8	0	0	0	2,069
R B's Boy	4	C	16	3	2	3	62,601
R Bull	3	C	6	0	0	0	1,530
R C Brinker	7	G	9	2	0	1	16,002
R C Executioner	2	C	3	0	0	1	1,920
R C Gangster	4	F	11	3	0	2	43,516
R C Pretty Sunny	2	F	3	0	0	0	315
R C Stacz Miss Bar	4	F	7	2	0	0	3,509
R Choni Star	4	F	5	0	1	1	1,458
R Coastocoast	4	C	3	0	0	1	4,340
R Crafty Dancer	3	C	2	0	0	0	56
R Cs Slew	5	H	6	1	1	2	13,762
R C's Star Power	5	H	5	1	0	0	1,755
R D Lite	6	G	5	1	0	2	1,194
R Double Diamond	3	G	19	2	4	3	20,984
R Easy Money	4	C	4	2	0	1	2,832
R Einstien	7	G	5	0	0	0	600
R Elway	4	G	9	1	1	0	9,105
R Fallsheba	6	G	3	0	0	0	64
R Flashlight	4	F	3	0	0	0	0
R Grand Mohawk	4	G	9	0	0	0	845
R J Solo Flight	7	M	2	0	0	0	665
R J's Game	6	G	10	0	0	2	5,906
R Keeper	3	C	3	1	0	0	14,632
R L Ruby	3	G	13	0	1	3	3,963
R L Star	3	F	2	0	0	0	0
R Last Norquestor	5	M	3	0	0	0	0
R Little Lewie	5	H	14	1	3	1	23,634
R Lucero	4	C	6	0	0	0	825
R Maestro	2	C	3	1	0	0	20,300
R McLennen	5	G	3	0	0	1	6,750

Horse	Age	Sex	Sts	1st	2d	3d	Won
R Meadow Luck	5	H	4	0	0	1	7,488
R Muffin	2	F	1	0	0	0	0
R Nanee	4	F	9	1	2	1	5,201
R Noble Alaric	7	G	2	0	0	0	294
R Nurse C	4	F	6	1	0	1	11,702
R Obsession	2	F	4	0	2	0	9,890
R Pirate	5	H	1	0	0	0	35
R Pocketsfull	3	G	5	2	0	1	44,558
R P's Lady	4	F	11	0	1	1	2,803
R Raggedy Ann	3	F	3	0	0	0	0
R Rocket Man	4	G	8	1	1	1	4,973
R Ruby Rae	7	M	16	2	1	4	7,824
R S Express	4	G	6	0	1	0	2,499
R Sassy Lady	10	M	24	0	2	6	15,010
R Scooter	4	G	6	3	1	1	19,220
R Soc O Choc Quah	4	F	6	0	1	0	3,425
R Sunday	3	C	8	0	1	2	6,971
R Super Chief	3	G	4	0	0	2	4,240
R Team	4	G	8	2	0	0	12,454
'R Testadura	8	G	13	1	0	1	5,632
R Three	4	G	4	0	0	0	326
R T's Magic	4	G	1	0	0	1	1,980
R Two D Two	3	G	9	1	0	1	6,900
R U Joshin Me	2	C	1	0	1	0	2,250
R U Mad Or Fappy	3	F	2	0	0	0	782
R U Ready Carmen	4	F	6	3	0	1	4,398
R V Reina	3	F	1	0	0	0	95
R Valid Girl	3	F	5	0	0	0	1,410
R Zippee's Dream	2	G	2	0	0	0	0
R. A. F. Captain	5	G	7	2	0	3	17,851
R. Associate	3	C	5	2	0	1	35,880
R. B Spirit	7	G	11	0	2	4	23,460
R. Baggio	5	G	10	4	0	0	114,840
R. Bob	3	C	1	0	0	1	2,740
R. C. Slocum	2	C	2	0	1	0	12,350
R. C.'s Crisis	3	G	7	0	0	1	928
R. C.'s Dandy	3	C	10	3	1	3	11,218
R. Cash Back	3	G	4	0	0	0	1,200
R. Corizon de Leon	3	C	12	2	1	1	29,581
R. D.'s Girl	4	F	14	4	0	1	41,070
R. Dixie Chick	5	M	6	1	0	0	4,925
R. Double Click	6	M	13	1	1	1	13,070
R. E. Prince	4	G	7	0	0	0	2,280
R. Encounter	9	H	5	2	0	0	24,000
R. F. Burton	5	G	2	0	0	0	700
R. Faithful	4	G	19	1	6	2	16,192
R. G. Campbell	2	G	5	0	0	1	2,045
R. G. Georgeanne	4	F	11	1	0	0	5,078
R. Isabella	6	M	3	0	0	0	200
R. J.'s Quest	2	C	3	1	1	0	14,000
R. Kodiak	8	G	4	0	1	1	2,874
R. Lady Luck	4	F	7	0	0	0	657
R. Little Redhead	6	G	10	2	2	0	48,091
R. M.'s Lina	2	F	1	0	0	0	0
R. P. Quicken	4	G	10	1	0	1	5,117
R. Paychek	3	F	2	0	0	0	152
R. Popball	4	G	25	1	1	2	8,925
R. S. Bucks	5	G	12	1	1	2	6,272
R. T. Gulch	5	G	7	0	2	2	12,280
R. Uniphase	5	H	8	0	2	0	3,140
Ra Der Dean	3	C	5	0	0	1	3,320
Ra Devil	3	G	14	0	1	3	5,364
Ra Ha Re	3	F	12	2	1	1	12,867
Ra Ra Ricky	7	G	5	0	0	0	0
Raah	5	M	2	0	0	0	120
Rabbit Ears	4	G	1	0	0	0	240
Rabbit Punch	5	G	4	0	0	0	160
Raboso	6	M	3	0	1	0	6,060
Race for Glory	5	G	5	2	0	0	71,010
Race for Stace	4	G	5	1	2	0	2,838
Race for the Green	2	G	5	0	1	0	1,329
Race On Green	5	H	3	0	0	0	620
Race the Dawn	6	G	15	1	1	0	8,128
Race to the Moon	2	C	3	1	0	0	7,782
Race With a Plum	4	G	12	1	2	1	23,940
Racer Babe	3	G	8	1	0	3	5,384
Racer's Secret	5	G	4	0	0	0	0
Racer's Stew	3	G	1	0	0	0	0
Racetrack Charlie	6	H	11	1	2	0	12,386

Horse	Age	Sex	Sts	1st	2d	3d	Won
Racetrack Ruler	4	C	10	0	2	2	6,980
Racetrack Ryanne	3	F	2	0	0	0	1,800
Racey Casey	2	F	7	2	1	1	16,655
Racey Dreamer	4	G	4	2	0	0	23,400
Racey Leo	4	G	12	1	3	4	14,962
Racey Renee	3	F	1	0	0	0	280
Racey Stacey	8	M	10	3	2	2	9,879
Rach Three	5	G	12	1	2	0	34,970
Rachel B	3	F	2	0	0	0	0
Rachel Two Socks	5	M	5	0	0	0	282
Rachelle's Numbers	3	F	10	3	1	1	64,440
Rachel's Boots	2	F	5	1	0	0	6,844
Rachel's Choice	2	F	5	0	0	0	1,736
Rachels Diamonds	3	F	5	2	1	0	21,764
Rachel's Gold	6	M	9	2	2	0	8,290
Rachel's Mission	4	F	5	0	1	1	4,398
Rachel's Mt. Star	5	G	10	2	1	0	6,210
Raciandeed	4	G	13	2	1	1	7,227
Racie Jaycie	3	F	8	2	3	2	23,310
Racie's Runaway	3	F	9	2	2	1	39,087
Racin Jason	5	G	10	1	2	0	13,250
Racine Bandito	9	M	7	0	0	0	190
Racing Deelite	3	C	3	0	0	1	660
Racing Fit	3	F	6	0	0	3	2,494
Racing for Riches	6	M	11	3	2	0	57,444
Racing Free	5	G	11	1	2	1	13,660
Racing Luck	2	F	10	0	3	1	22,305
Racing Nut	4	G	8	1	2	1	20,070
Racing Ruby	4	F	9	0	2	2	15,988
Racing Sundown	4	F	8	0	2	5	17,778
Racino	5	G	2	0	0	0	0
Rack Em Up	5	G	12	0	3	3	16,525
Rackliff Island	4	F	1	0	0	0	96
Racquet Man	4	C	13	3	0	1	27,980
Racy Rachel	3	F	4	0	0	0	0
Radar Contact	7	G	8	0	1	5	78,550
Radar Trap	7	H	17	3	4	2	27,124
Radcliffe Yard	4	F	9	1	1	2	42,093
Radiance (VEN)	8	M	11	1	4	1	56,320
Radiant Cat	2	C	1	0	1	0	8,540
Radiant Lilly	4	F	1	0	0	0	0
Radiant Nancy	5	M	10	2	0	2	25,086
Radiant Rocket	3	F	1	0	1	0	1,908
Radiant Rose	5	M	3	0	0	0	534
Radiant Runaway	5	G	5	2	0	0	6,480
Radiant Smile (GB)	4	F	6	3	1	0	45,750
Radiantly	3	F	13	3	2	3	89,320
Radiata	6	G	6	0	1	0	33,780
Radiatin' Sunshine	4	F	10	1	4	1	10,000
Radical Activist	5	G	6	0	1	1	11,720
Radical Bubba	5	G	4	0	0	1	1,400
Radical Rage	5	H	8	2	2	1	7,564
Radical Reality	5	G	14	2	2	2	9,655
Radical Runaway	6	G	7	0	0	0	874
Radical Secret	3	F	1	0	0	0	430
Radio Caroline	2	F	2	0	0	0	343
Radio Frequency	5	G	1	0	0	0	47
Radio One	4	G	9	3	0	0	10,685
Radioactive Power	2	G	2	0	0	1	1,327
Rado Kid	3	F	8	1	0	0	6,814
Radon	4	F	17	2	3	4	59,420
Radyla	5	M	7	1	0	2	9,792
Raejean Star	3	F	3	0	0	1	1,710
Raelynn's Colony	4	F	5	1	0	0	10,175
Raes Irish Queen	5	M	12	1	1	0	4,083
Rae'salittlecain	5	H	15	3	2	3	16,423
Raewanda	3	F	13	2	1	1	39,822
Rafa	3	F	7	1	0	0	14,100
Raff	3	G	3	0	1	0	1,280
Raffie's Dream	3	F	12	2	3	1	98,850
Raffie's Passion	3	F	1	0	0	0	64
Raffie's Storm	3	F	10	2	2	2	61,455
Raffit	3	C	2	1	1	0	55,200
Raffle Ticket	4	G	19	2	4	1	18,981
Rafgaar	3	G	14	2	3	0	26,068
Rafid	6	H	1	0	0	0	0
Rafinesque	5	G	13	3	0	0	10,589
Raf's Society Girl	2	F	1	0	0	0	0
Rafter Cat	2	F	6	0	0	0	980
Rafter Man	5	G	6	1	1	0	6,899
Rafts to Riches	4	C	4	0	0	0	1,025
Rafty Don	5	M	1	0	0	0	315
Rag King	6	G	12	6	0	1	37,978
Rag Time Dancer	2	G	6	1	1	1	12,220
Rag Time Dolly	5	M	6	0	0	3	4,252
Raga Raja	4	C	7	0	0	0	565
Ragazzo	5	H	4	0	0	0	898
Rage in Warrior	3	G	3	0	0	0	0
Rageously	3	C	17	3	3	3	59,950
Raggamuffin	6	G	7	0	1	1	4,298
Ragin' Raja	7	G	12	1	0	1	4,080
Ragin' Raven	8	G	12	2	2	4	23,595
Ragin Reggie	7	G	9	0	1	1	6,563
Ragin T Rex	4	F	5	0	1	0	13,040
Raging Anna	6	M	6	0	1	2	2,856
Raging Bird	5	H	5	0	0	0	620
Raging Blade	9	G	17	5	1	2	36,227
Raging Dancer	2	F	6	1	0	0	8,470
Raging Fever	5	M	7	1	2	1	176,333
Raging Flag	4	G	9	0	0	0	1,283
Raging Jennie	4	F	3	0	2	1	7,680
Raging Passion	2	G	5	0	0	0	767
Raging Redhead	3	F	13	1	3	3	42,790
Raging Riley	3	G	4	0	1	1	15,360
Raging River	6	G	4	1	0	1	8,942
Raging Roman	6	G	8	2	0	2	7,038
Raging Ruby	2	F	2	0	0	0	1,394
Raging Springs	5	H	6	2	2	0	10,632
Raging Zack	4	G	3	0	0	0	368
Raglan Road	3	G	2	0	0	0	0
Ragna	4	F	7	1	0	3	3,732
Ragroid	3	F	15	2	4	3	33,330
Ragtime Fun	3	G	11	1	1	0	15,490
Ragtime Gunner	5	G	13	2	1	2	10,300
Ragtime Miss	5	M	8	3	0	1	28,020
Ragtime Ruthie	6	M	21	3	2	1	11,210
Ragtime Tale	3	G	8	1	0	1	16,895
Ragtime Tune	5	M	4	0	0	0	645
Ragul	4	G	15	2	2	4	27,892
Rah Rah Party	5	H	3	0	0	0	594
Rahab	5	M	6	1	2	0	15,267
Rahrah Bertie	2	F	4	0	0	0	120
Rahy Cat	5	G	6	2	0	1	24,060
Rahy Dolly	2	F	2	1	1	0	92,700
Rahy Pavo	3	G	10	1	1	1	17,600
Rahy Rhythm	6	H	8	1	0	0	14,722
Rahy Time	3	F	6	0	0	0	1,120
Rahy Vision	3	C	3	0	1	1	16,060
Rahyinsky	4	C	20	2	4	1	24,070
Rahy's Chance	3	G	3	1	0	2	15,984
Rahy's Darlin	3	F	3	0	0	0	360
Rahy's Gold	3	C	2	0	1	0	4,560
Rahy's Rambler	7	H	8	0	0	1	2,371
Rahy's Secret	5	H	6	1	1	2	42,090
Rahy's Song	3	F	2	0	0	0	0
Raichu	4	F	6	0	0	0	1,110
Raider Nation	3	G	5	1	0	0	11,950
Raidpilagenplunder	4	G	5	0	0	0	0
Rail Back	5	H	15	1	4	0	8,560
Rail Chot	4	C	8	2	1	1	12,882
Rail Hunter	4	G	10	4	1	1	25,792
Rail Me	3	F	8	1	2	0	5,841
Rail Rose	3	C	13	3	1	0	65,888
Rail to Seattle	5	M	3	0	2	1	12,820
Railed	5	G	8	1	2	0	5,007
Railroad Man Jim	2	G	1	0	0	1	2,170
Railroad Mills	4	G	2	0	0	0	182
Railroad Red	2	C	1	0	0	1	2,390
Railroader (GB)	6	G	11	1	3	3	15,460
Railway	5	G	22	1	0	4	8,056
Railway Avenue	4	C	3	0	0	0	0
Rain Boots	6	M	2	0	0	0	0
Rain Cat	4	F	10	3	1	1	16,112
Rain Dancer (NZ)	7	M	2	0	0	0	0
Rain Drummer	3	C	1	1	0	0	8,550
Rain Minister	6	G	1	0	0	0	0
Rain Slicker	5	G	3	0	0	0	50
Rain Taps	2	F	2	0	0	0	1,290

Horse	Age	Sex	Sts	1st	2d	3d	Won	Horse	Age	Sex	Sts	1st	2d	3d	Won
Rainbow Acorn	4	F	4	1	0	0	11,145	Raise Your Ante	7	G	2	1	1	0	3,960
Rainbow Blues	4	G	11	1	1	0	13,144	Raisearunningbill	5	G	4	0	0	0	720
Rainbow Bold	3	G	3	0	0	0	135	Raised Eyebrows	4	F	9	0	3	1	25,490
Rainbow County	6	M	13	0	1	3	2,693	Raised My Hand	7	M	3	0	1	0	1,000
Rainbow Flyer	3	G	2	0	0	0	195	Raised On Cue	4	C	5	1	0	0	3,498
Rainbow Knight	4	G	9	1	0	0	11,767	Raised Southern	4	F	12	1	0	4	13,567
Rainbow Lady	9	M	4	0	2	0	2,208	Raisedinthesouth	4	G	7	1	1	1	9,427
Rainbow Lake	4	C	10	1	1	3	15,017	Raisedonchampagne	2	F	2	0	0	1	1,425
Rainbow of Music	2	F	4	0	1	2	5,650	Raiser'n Class	5	M	9	2	1	2	26,180
Rainbow Palace	7	M	2	0	0	0	354	Raisetheslew	4	G	2	0	0	0	450
Rainbow Parcel	6	G	8	1	4	0	25,136	Raisin Dust	4	F	11	1	3	4	4,945
Rainbow Request	3	F	2	0	0	0	326	Raisin Slew	5	G	13	2	2	1	17,758
Rainbow Rider	2	C	2	1	1	0	36,000	Raisin Toast	7	M	3	0	0	0	140
Rainbow Robber	3	G	14	2	3	2	11,132	Raising Kane	4	G	8	2	0	2	21,337
Rainbow Room	6	H	3	0	0	1	1,097	Raising O. S.	5	G	8	2	0	0	23,760
Rainbow Rose	3	F	6	1	0	0	6,812	Raising Ransom	5	G	5	1	0	0	1,645
Rainbow Roy	5	H	2	1	0	0	3,072	Raising Salem	5	M	7	1	0	0	8,506
Rainbow Runner	2	F	3	0	0	0	684	Raising the Banner	5	G	6	1	4	0	33,378
Rainbow Sand	2	F	6	2	0	1	21,840	Rais'n Rampage	5	G	10	1	0	1	4,066
Rainbow Smile	4	F	5	0	0	1	7,285	Raizata	3	F	6	0	0	0	383
Rainbow Style (IRE)	6	G	5	0	1	2	10,076	Raizer Light	3	C	3	0	0	1	2,123
Rainbow Trail	4	F	11	4	2	0	15,322	Raj Road	11	G	3	0	0	0	0
Rainbow Valley	5	G	12	1	0	2	5,123	Raja Choice	6	H	1	0	0	0	185
Rainbowman	3	G	2	0	0	0	0	Raja Hindustan	3	C	1	0	0	0	126
Rainbows and Roses	7	M	3	1	1	1	11,440	Rajab's Dancer	7	G	5	0	0	0	567
Rainbows Bid	3	F	12	0	2	1	6,139	Raja's Connection	9	M	2	0	0	0	0
Rainbow's End	3	F	3	0	0	0	1,106	Raja's Gold Egg	4	G	4	0	0	0	214
Rainbows For All (IRE)	3	F	4	0	0	0	0	Raja's Jet	4	G	8	4	1	1	34,915
Rainbows for Luck	2	G	2	0	1	1	20,057	Raja's Omega	10	G	6	0	0	1	1,497
Rainbows Forever	3	F	17	1	3	1	35,954	Raja's Pearl	4	F	4	0	0	0	100
Rainbow's Glo	3	F	11	1	2	1	11,270	Raja's Rhythm	7	M	7	0	1	0	7,653
Rainbowsgold	8	M	11	2	3	0	5,315	Rajas Seattle Song	3	F	3	0	0	0	264
Raine Passer	3	G	7	0	0	1	1,460	Raja's Silk	12	G	1	0	0	0	110
Rainier Express	3	G	7	1	2	2	20,680	Rajing Bull	7	G	17	3	1	1	21,990
Raining Flame	2	F	7	1	1	0	6,170	Rakan Prospect	4	G	1	0	0	0	0
Rainman's Request	4	G	2	0	0	1	3,960	Rakeen Lake	5	M	9	2	1	1	38,650
Rainy Bengal	3	C	14	1	3	1	8,757	Rakeen Verdict	4	F	3	0	0	1	3,585
Rainy Day Blues	6	G	11	1	1	2	6,243	Rakeen's Reward	4	C	9	2	0	0	13,803
Rainy Day Jay	6	G	5	0	2	0	6,300	Rakhmones	4	G	8	0	0	0	569
Rainy Day Lady	3	F	4	1	0	0	4,465	Rakien	4	C	8	1	3	0	12,550
Rainy Day Romance	3	F	13	1	6	1	16,335	Raking in the Gold	2	F	6	0	0	0	2,707
Rainy Day Rules	3	F	6	2	0	0	22,380	Rakish Ryan	5	H	12	2	2	0	44,390
Rainy Parade	4	G	14	5	2	3	89,628	Rakoon	5	G	7	1	2	1	32,485
Raire Standard	7	H	1	0	0	0	865	Raku	4	G	12	2	4	1	13,792
Raise a Booger	4	G	1	0	1	0	2,835	Ralla	2	F	2	1	0	0	36,360
Raise a Brow	7	M	4	0	0	0	0	Rally Cry	5	G	1	0	0	0	0
Raise a Cozzene	7	H	3	0	0	0	0	Rally Hill	3	C	3	1	0	0	4,900
Raise a Dan	5	M	5	0	0	0	719	Rally Mode	4	G	12	0	2	3	18,122
Raise a Daughter	5	M	6	3	0	1	4,876	Rally 'round	3	G	8	2	0	0	31,067
Raise a Demon	4	C	3	0	0	0	0	Rally Time	4	C	1	0	0	0	0
Raise a Looker	9	G	3	0	0	0	199	Ralph's Rocket	2	C	3	0	0	1	1,600
Raise a Miesque	3	G	8	0	1	0	6,980	Rama Lassie	2	F	6	2	1	1	36,234
Raise a Nature	4	F	8	2	2	0	15,644	Ramadan Moon	4	F	1	0	0	0	0
Raise a Roar	4	F	3	0	0	1	3,607	Rambler	4	G	18	1	5	3	13,107
Raise a Royal	3	C	4	0	0	0	0	Ramblette	4	F	7	1	0	3	3,013
Raise a Ruckus	6	G	7	0	0	0	575	Ramblin Amber	4	F	5	1	1	0	3,921
Raise a Screen	4	C	4	1	1	0	5,925	Ramblin' Blue	4	F	15	1	3	2	16,923
Raise a Slipper	8	G	13	3	1	1	10,832	Ramblin Gypsy	4	F	12	4	1	1	31,185
Raise a Storm	8	G	11	0	1	1	2,527	Ramblin Hope	4	F	10	0	1	0	760
Raise A Storm (IRE)	6	G	8	3	2	1	76,742	Ramblin Rog	4	C	11	2	3	0	12,898
Raise a Trick	3	C	6	0	0	1	1,921	Rambling Along	3	F	9	3	1	1	24,036
Raise Afleet	2	F	3	0	0	0	0	Rambling Caveat	9	G	2	0	0	0	0
Raise an Emblem	3	C	11	1	0	2	38,970	Rambling Native	5	G	11	1	0	1	4,423
Raise Devil	4	F	9	1	1	3	63,850	Rambling Rasberry	4	C	1	0	0	0	0
Raise Expectations	4	G	14	4	4	0	116,785	Rambling Rod	6	G	13	3	1	1	4,720
Raise Her Flag	4	F	10	1	2	3	23,680	Rambling Ryan	8	G	8	0	1	1	1,000
Raise Irish Lady	4	F	6	0	0	1	1,282	Rambo Missile	4	G	18	1	1	2	6,817
Raise Some Bucks	3	F	8	0	2	0	3,134	Rambolina	3	F	4	0	1	0	2,684
Raise Tempo	4	F	11	2	0	3	6,714	Rambo's Gold	5	G	15	1	2	4	6,320
Raise the Beam	4	F	6	0	0	1	2,287	Rambunctious Lad	6	H	4	0	0	0	855
Raise the Capital	4	G	4	1	1	0	7,102	Rambunctious One	5	G	6	0	0	0	857
Raise the Heat	3	G	9	1	2	2	48,057	Rambunctious Reg	3	G	9	2	0	2	11,830
Raise the Level	3	F	8	2	1	1	39,930	Rambunctious Ryan	2	G	1	0	0	0	120
Raise the Max	5	M	3	1	0	0	6,883	Ramekin	4	F	7	1	0	1	8,015
Raise the Rafters	4	C	1	0	0	0	6,225	Rameses	4	C	17	1	0	1	6,225
Raise the Stakes	5	G	10	0	4	1	12,800	Ramiano	5	H	13	0	0	7	17,121
Raise the Stripes	3	C	12	4	1	1	76,890	Ramillus	3	G	6	2	0	1	60,480
Raise You One	4	F	1	0	0	0	0	Ramiro	4	G	12	2	2	2	22,325
Raise You Six	6	H	15	1	3	3	17,439	Ramito	10	G	9	2	0	0	12,970

Horse	Age	Sex	Sts	1st	2d	3d	Won
Rammers Best	2	F	4	1	2	1	16,238
Rammin Ralph	4	C	4	0	0	2	1,952
Rammstein	4	G	12	0	0	0	0
Ramon	6	G	6	1	0	1	4,432
Ramona C	2	F	1	0	0	0	195
Ramona Girl	5	M	4	1	0	0	19,965
Ramona's Way	3	F	9	1	0	0	4,848
Ramp Up	3	F	1	0	0	0	360
Rampaging Irish	5	M	3	0	0	0	1,626
Rampant Control	4	G	5	0	0	1	1,198
Rampant Roll	4	C	7	1	2	1	11,395
Rampoldi	4	G	10	2	3	2	34,700
Ramsey	3	C	1	0	0	0	50
Ran a Ground	8	G	11	3	3	2	13,289
Ran Chars Miner	7	M	1	0	0	0	180
Ran D Scott	5	G	2	0	0	0	1,320
Ran for the Dough	3	F	6	1	0	0	34,950
Ran South	4	C	11	1	3	1	49,751
Ranahan	6	G	4	1	1	0	7,800
Ranata's Gold	3	G	11	1	0	1	7,831
Ranch Hand	4	G	1	0	0	0	0
Ranch House Ruckus	2	G	6	0	1	2	4,324
Ranch Socks Betty	4	F	11	0	1	0	1,734
Ranchipur	3	F	12	1	3	1	13,308
Rancid Billy	5	G	16	1	3	7	8,151
Rancocas Mist	6	M	3	0	0	0	220
Rancour	6	G	7	1	1	2	30,475
Randaroo	3	F	10	4	4	0	401,500
Randell G	3	G	11	0	1	1	3,968
Randi	5	M	11	0	1	2	6,989
Randi Brandy	2	F	2	0	0	1	1,260
Randi's Man	11	G	6	2	1	2	10,795
Randi's Song	5	G	10	1	0	1	8,374
Randolph Attheloop	6	G	12	2	3	1	25,281
Random Chance	2	F	2	1	0	1	18,900
Random Illusions	3	F	4	1	2	0	10,750
Random Madness	7	G	8	2	1	2	12,319
Random Memo	2	G	5	2	0	1	19,717
Random Passage	2	F	4	0	2	0	7,213
Random Thoughts	3	F	13	6	1	1	42,378
Randwick	3	C	4	1	0	0	10,805
Randy Andy	9	G	14	0	3	1	13,867
Randy's Ex	5	G	17	1	0	1	4,352
Randy's Ruler	2	G	9	1	1	0	7,704
Randy's Trouble	3	F	4	0	0	0	365
Raneem	5	G	8	1	1	0	28,575
Ranelagh	3	C	12	1	3	0	30,860
Rang My Bell	5	M	1	0	0	0	54
Rang the Devil	4	F	3	0	1	0	2,889
Range Some	3	C	2	0	0	0	0
Rangeley Rebel	5	H	10	1	1	1	9,207
Rangeley Skier	7	M	5	0	0	0	1,050
Ranger Annie	4	F	13	1	0	4	6,765
Ranger B.	2	C	6	1	1	0	11,768
Ranger Chance	3	G	6	0	0	2	7,320
Ranger Girl	4	F	1	0	0	0	60
Ranger Gord	3	C	8	2	0	1	19,314
Ranger's G Man	2	G	1	1	0	0	5,896
Rangers Gone West	3	F	1	0	0	0	45
Ranglen Jack	3	G	11	0	2	1	5,918
Rani Ran	2	F	1	0	1	0	2,660
Raniata	4	F	11	2	3	2	12,644
Raniraj	6	G	1	0	0	0	0
Rani's Diablo	6	H	3	0	0	0	177
Ransom Bride	2	F	3	0	0	1	6,126
Ransom Cove	6	G	1	0	0	0	0
Ransom Demand	9	G	1	0	0	0	0
Ransom Kid	4	C	2	0	0	1	910
Ransom Love	5	G	2	0	0	1	872
Ransom Song	4	F	1	0	0	0	376
Ransom the Krooner	3	G	9	1	0	5	27,730
Ransom the Redhead	2	F	1	0	0	0	1,140
Ransom the Royalty	4	G	8	0	1	0	5,255
Ransome Money	3	G	3	1	1	0	10,170
Ransome Road	4	G	17	3	2	4	21,493
Ransomed Lady	5	M	3	0	0	0	450
Ransom's Fire	5	H	12	2	4	1	14,224
Rantnrave	5	M	15	0	2	3	11,099
Rao Man	4	G	10	1	0	2	5,529
Rap	4	C	6	2	0	1	18,822
Rap a Newe	3	F	6	0	0	0	370
Rap Jet	3	F	3	0	0	0	130
Rapadash (IRE)	4	G	5	0	0	0	900
Rapid	6	M	7	2	0	2	8,017
Rapid Audition	5	M	4	1	0	0	6,485
Rapid Baby	3	C	3	0	2	0	2,869
Rapid Bob	3	G	3	1	1	0	11,986
Rapid Charger	6	M	3	0	0	0	300
Rapid Grace	2	F	5	0	0	2	2,035
Rapid Hanna	6	M	11	0	0	0	2,171
Rapid Jett	4	C	9	0	0	0	0
Rapid Lady	2	F	1	0	0	0	50
Rapid Lee	3	G	8	0	0	2	3,476
Rapid Number	4	C	11	0	1	1	7,033
Rapid Proof	3	G	8	0	2	1	69,520
Rapid Punch	3	G	1	0	0	0	0
Rapid Raj	4	G	2	1	0	0	9,840
Rapid Red	3	G	8	0	3	3	9,052
Rapid Regal	5	G	9	3	2	2	22,544
Rapid Revalation	2	F	3	1	0	0	13,020
Rapid Rickey	2	C	1	0	0	0	118
Rapid Ripples	4	F	3	1	0	0	5,115
Rapid Rob	2	C	5	0	3	1	31,282
Rapid Roger	9	G	6	1	1	0	13,591
Rapid Rose	4	F	2	0	0	0	0
Rapid Rotation	4	C	6	0	1	1	2,938
Rapid Run	2	C	7	0	1	1	9,095
Rapid Rye	5	M	1	0	0	0	0
Rapid Slew	4	C	6	2	1	1	2,060
Rapid Vali	5	G	15	0	2	2	6,903
Rapid Wolf	3	G	4	0	0	0	620
Rapide	4	G	13	1	2	4	19,192
Rapido Caballo	4	G	6	1	0	2	6,230
Rapido Comandante	3	C	11	1	2	2	4,061
Rapido Too	3	F	4	0	0	0	0
Rapidough	8	G	4	0	0	1	10,908
Rapidrunstheriver	6	M	12	1	0	1	21,422
Rapier	10	G	1	0	1	0	2,540
Rapier Dance	3	C	5	1	1	0	42,877
Rappahannock	3	C	12	2	2	2	35,070
Rappatap	2	C	5	0	0	0	740
Rappel	3	C	3	1	0	0	19,920
Raptor Speed	2	F	1	1	0	0	21,540
Rapture's Report	4	F	12	2	1	2	17,959
Raquel	4	F	4	0	0	2	3,830
Raquette Lake	4	F	10	3	0	1	19,836
Rare Affair	6	M	16	2	5	2	16,009
Rare and Sixy	3	F	5	0	0	0	630
Rare Antique	4	F	10	1	0	1	17,386
Rare Approach	3	F	9	1	1	0	18,864
Rare Avenger	5	H	15	0	2	3	4,616
Rare Bush	3	C	6	1	1	1	27,840
Rare Call	2	C	2	0	0	0	684
Rare Catch	9	G	12	0	4	2	5,093
Rare Charm	3	F	6	0	0	0	1,072
Rare Creek	4	C	2	0	0	0	1,000
Rare Cure	5	G	14	2	1	2	105,730
Rare Deputy	4	C	7	1	0	1	10,190
Rare Dreams	3	G	6	0	5	1	23,590
Rare Echo	5	G	6	1	0	0	1,825
Rare Edition	7	M	8	1	0	2	1,985
Rare Elle	5	M	5	0	0	0	900
Rare Endeavour	5	G	11	1	0	1	12,520
Rare Fool	2	C	1	0	0	0	285
Rare Friends	4	G	4	2	0	0	123,165
Rare Fuse	4	C	6	0	2	0	11,200
Rare Gift	2	F	1	1	0	0	27,000
Rare Glitter	2	F	8	2	3	1	31,570
Rare Glorious	5	G	9	1	1	0	3,984
Rare Gold	3	F	1	0	1	0	4,780
Rare Henna	4	F	6	0	3	1	4,500
Rare Honor	3	F	12	4	0	0	35,790
Rare Jade	4	F	4	0	0	0	0
Rare Jewel	6	G	10	2	2	3	37,257
Rare Joy	2	F	7	1	3	2	20,560
Rare Kiss	2	F	1	0	0	0	0
Rare Little Lady	8	M	2	0	0	1	1,066
Rare Loom	6	G	7	1	0	0	6,154

Horse	Age	Sex	Sts	1st	2d	3d	Won
Rare Mark	5	G	2	0	0	0	35
Rare Master	5	M	14	1	0	1	7,157
Rare Miswaki	2	F	3	0	0	1	1,920
Rare N Pretty	2	F	2	0	0	0	0
Rare n' to Syn	4	F	4	1	1	0	1,660
Rare Native	7	G	11	0	1	0	5,867
Rare Note	6	G	8	1	0	0	4,328
Rare Paradigm	7	G	8	3	0	2	23,128
Rare Pass	4	F	2	0	1	1	3,000
Rare Phone	5	G	4	0	0	0	366
Rare Racer	4	G	19	2	3	2	12,339
Rare Rachel	4	F	12	1	4	1	16,339
Rare Remark	2	G	3	0	0	1	2,380
Rare Rum	6	M	5	1	1	0	3,352
Rare Sortof Devil	7	G	13	0	2	6	6,846
Rare Stone	4	C	6	1	2	0	8,885
Rare Sweetheart	3	F	1	1	0	0	8,100
Rare Time Machine	4	F	12	1	1	3	13,759
Rare Tower	3	G	6	1	0	0	7,451
Rare Twist	7	M	11	2	2	2	11,014
Rare Will	3	G	9	2	0	3	50,111
Rare Wisdome	6	G	11	0	3	1	8,465
Rarely Caught	2	F	2	0	0	1	1,639
Rarest Love	4	C	6	1	1	1	13,720
Rarified	3	C	10	1	3	0	28,270
Rarin Tearin Erin	3	F	1	0	0	0	0
Raring to Go	5	M	3	1	1	1	8,100
Rasberry Halo	6	G	8	1	0	2	10,792
Rasberry Road	3	F	3	0	0	0	0
Rasby	8	G	13	4	3	3	62,125
Rascal Russ	9	G	4	0	2	1	6,130
Rascallion	6	H	3	1	0	0	6,394
Rascal's Lynnie	4	F	11	1	2	3	36,620
Rase a Fraser	5	M	3	0	0	0	0
Rash Power	5	G	6	0	0	1	570
Rasha	7	G	10	0	4	2	4,846
Rashard Lamar	3	C	3	1	1	0	17,120
Rasor D	7	G	19	1	5	3	41,365
Rasputins Son	7	C	0	0	0	0	783
Rasty	4	G	11	0	3	1	14,215
Rat Like Cunning	2	C	1	0	0	0	220
Ratafee	2	F	6	1	1	1	2,880
Rate Above	4	G	4	0	0	0	861
Rate Base	7	G	9	0	0	1	13,890
Rated R	7	M	2	0	1	0	770
Rated Up Blue	3	F	15	2	1	1	6,421
Rateeki	5	H	10	0	0	1	651
Rathdrum	4	G	14	1	2	3	7,094
Rather B Pennyless	2	C	1	0	1	0	2,480
Rather Be	7	G	7	1	2	1	21,610
Rather Be Rare	3	F	14	2	0	3	11,007
Rather Be Wild	4	F	3	0	0	1	8,175
Rather Risky	3	F	12	4	2	1	19,740
Rather Russian	6	G	5	0	0	2	6,190
Rathleen	3	F	8	3	1	2	88,007
Rating Agency	2	C	3	0	2	0	15,000
Rational Logic	7	G	5	0	0	0	873
Rattata	3	G	16	1	1	2	5,346
Rattle	5	M	2	0	0	0	123
Rattle and Hum	4	G	1	0	0	0	0
Rattle and Roll	2	C	4	0	1	0	5,969
Rattle Dem Bones	5	G	1	1	0	0	40,560
Rattle On Son	4	G	11	2	2	0	20,450
Rattled	3	F	4	0	0	1	1,575
Rattlesnake John	3	C	2	0	0	0	0
Rattlesnake Ridge	6	G	14	2	3	4	14,024
Rattletrap Moment	4	G	8	1	1	1	2,936
Rattling Count	7	H	22	2	5	5	21,745
Raucous Ruckus	5	G	4	1	0	1	4,575
Raunchy	6	H	1	0	0	0	0
Raunchy Cat	3	F	3	0	0	0	630
Ravadon	2	C	6	2	1	0	60,344
Ravalli Girl	3	F	14	3	3	2	54,287
Ravaro (BRZ)	8	G	6	2	1	0	53,640
Rave a Pok	4	F	4	0	0	0	300
Rave Up	3	C	14	2	3	1	15,766
Raven Cliff Falls	2	C	1	0	0	0	0
Raven Halo	3	F	11	1	2	1	9,415
Raven Hill	5	G	2	0	0	0	60
Raven King	5	G	1	0	0	0	0
Raven Power	4	G	2	0	0	0	0
Raven Riot	7	M	4	0	0	0	265
Raven Ruhl	5	G	10	0	1	1	1,785
Ravenhawk	6	G	2	0	0	0	70
Raven's Baguette	3	F	4	0	0	0	93
Raven's End	2	F	5	0	0	1	6,385
Ravens Rock	4	C	1	0	0	0	0
Raviching's Boy	4	C	6	0	0	0	216
Ravidashinal	2	F	3	0	0	0	0
Ravine Rose	3	F	2	1	0	1	17,110
Raving	4	F	3	2	0	0	29,630
Raving Willie	4	C	2	1	0	0	7,800
Ravinia Girl	4	F	7	0	1	0	3,914
Ravish Me	5	M	12	3	0	2	100,835
Ravishly	2	F	3	1	0	1	24,750
Raw Energy	2	C	3	0	0	1	3,760
Raw General	2	C	5	2	0	0	48,120
Raw Imagination	7	G	8	0	1	1	4,106
Raw Power	3	C	6	1	0	1	54,708
Raw Roy	3	C	16	4	3	2	22,415
Raw Speed	4	C	3	0	0	0	119
Raw Talent	5	H	10	4	3	0	12,200
Rawlpindi Express	3	G	9	0	0	1	2,266
Rawson's Racer	3	G	8	0	2	1	3,570
Rawston	4	G	15	4	2	3	13,818
Ray Boy	5	G	8	0	0	0	532
Ray of Fire	11	G	3	0	0	0	0
Ray Smiley	4	G	17	2	3	1	18,699
Rayco Steel	3	F	16	2	1	4	8,384
Rayday	3	F	1	0	1	0	1,420
Raylene	3	F	10	6	2	0	339,687
Raylo	3	C	4	0	0	0	0
Raymond Springs	4	G	6	1	1	0	6,699
Raymond's Dream	5	M	6	2	2	1	69,300
Raymon's Revenge	3	G	8	0	0	0	1,553
Raymur City	5	G	3	0	1	0	1,367
Rayo de Plata	5	G	16	3	6	3	63,156
Rayo Island	4	G	4	0	0	0	264
Rayon	3	C	7	1	0	2	29,380
Raypour (IRE)	6	G	2	0	0	0	0
Rays a Ruler	6	G	14	0	3	2	11,508
Ray's Above	3	G	10	1	0	0	3,721
Ray's Ego	4	C	3	1	1	1	6,132
Ray's Future	7	G	8	0	0	1	2,620
Ray's Gray Gear	3	F	5	2	0	0	10,530
Rays Lucky Guy	7	M	1	0	0	0	110
Ray's Treasure	5	G	4	0	1	1	6,372
Ray's Two Grand	3	G	3	0	0	0	158
Raysin Thunder	8	G	3	0	0	0	2,726
Rayswest	4	C	3	0	0	1	462
Rayvo's Beau	2	C	10	2	1	1	41,688
Ray'z of Gold	7	H	2	1	0	0	5,213
Rayzi Zu	6	H	2	0	0	0	492
Razacat	3	F	5	0	0	1	1,430
Razarra	3	C	7	1	0	0	2,953
Razen Hazen	2	G	5	2	1	0	56,110
Razik	8	G	7	1	1	2	14,680
Razodiazo	5	G	9	0	2	2	4,869
Razoo Eighty Two	4	F	10	1	1	1	7,242
Razor Barb	3	F	10	2	2	0	30,453
Razor Blade	3	C	2	0	0	0	0
Razor Stubble	4	F	12	4	1	2	91,310
Razyana's Avenu	3	F	10	1	1	1	4,330
Razz	5	G	3	1	0	1	2,045
Razz Beret	5	G	9	1	1	2	9,392
Razzaam	4	F	4	0	0	0	630
Razzact	5	G	7	1	0	0	3,258
Razzle Dazzle Gal	2	F	5	0	0	0	605
Razzle Dazzle Guy	2	G	6	0	0	0	840
Rbrotherinthebooth	4	G	6	1	2	1	17,354
Rb's Glitter	2	C	7	2	0	2	110,907
Rchrystlsapistol	4	F	16	3	3	0	17,091
Re a Fax	6	M	15	2	1	1	20,950
Re Book	5	G	7	1	2	2	26,800
Re Lyd	6	M	7	0	1	1	12,200
Re Quest Approval	3	F	2	0	0	0	0
Reach for Ameri	7	G	13	1	1	1	4,592
Reach for the Top	4	F	5	0	0	1	1,581

Horse	Age	Sex	Sts	1st	2d	3d	Won
Reach On Scooter	11	G	11	0	0	1	911
Reaching Up	3	F	3	1	1	0	35,660
Reactionary	4	G	11	2	2	0	12,783
Read Me My Rights	4	F	5	3	1	0	85,320
Read the Cards	6	M	8	1	0	3	5,942
Read the Footnotes	2	C	5	4	0	0	240,660
Readers Eskimo	6	G	11	0	4	1	8,507
Readersbestbuilder	2	G	5	0	1	0	7,280
Reading Girl	4	F	7	0	0	0	158
Ready and Tough	2	F	4	2	2	0	75,430
Ready At Noon	3	F	6	1	0	0	5,703
Ready Falls	4	F	8	3	4	1	50,643
Ready Fire Aim	3	F	9	1	1	1	22,157
Ready for Change	5	G	2	0	0	0	164
Ready for Glory	3	G	8	3	0	2	24,462
Ready for Island	7	H	5	0	1	2	4,302
Ready for Love	4	G	14	2	1	2	22,935
Ready for More	5	G	10	0	0	0	1,254
Ready for Takeoff	2	C	2	0	0	0	396
Ready Girl	5	M	4	0	0	0	385
Ready Gold	2	C	1	0	0	0	528
Ready Hike	6	G	9	0	1	1	8,496
Ready Money	4	G	11	0	2	0	6,957
Ready 'n Gone	4	G	5	0	2	0	9,380
Ready Prospect	2	G	4	0	1	1	4,645
Ready Roy	2	C	1	0	0	0	120
Ready This Time	3	F	10	2	0	4	15,600
Ready to Flirt	2	C	1	0	0	0	1,260
Ready to Rage	2	C	3	0	0	0	0
Ready to Roll (IRE)	8	G	4	1	1	1	8,050
Ready to Ruckus	2	F	2	1	0	0	7,786
Ready to Strike	6	H	2	0	0	0	164
Reagally Light	3	F	10	1	2	1	28,969
Reagan Ct.	3	C	1	0	0	0	58
Real Actress	5	M	3	0	0	0	183
Real Addiction	4	G	17	2	0	2	21,905
Real American	5	H	4	0	0	0	715
Real Assets	4	F	18	1	2	3	14,689
Real Attitude	3	F	7	1	1	2	8,073
Real Bashful	3	G	6	1	2	1	2,850
Real Bear	3	F	9	2	5	0	75,615
Real Beauty	3	F	8	1	0	3	60,875
Real Big Rita	3	F	5	1	0	1	4,765
Real Big Spender	2	C	5	0	0	2	6,800
Real Boy (AUS)	7	G	7	0	1	2	3,255
Real Cause	4	F	6	1	0	1	9,714
Real Country	5	G	4	0	1	1	1,668
Real Creek	4	G	20	5	5	1	26,281
Real Dancer	12	G	16	1	3	1	3,009
Real Desire	3	F	4	0	0	1	1,510
Real Devious	4	G	10	1	1	0	3,668
Real Dignity	3	G	3	0	0	0	360
Real Doll	4	F	5	1	0	1	52,198
Real Encounter	6	G	15	2	4	2	13,309
Real Endurance	2	F	6	1	0	2	16,861
Real Excessive	2	F	1	0	0	1	1,300
Real Fappi	5	H	5	2	1	0	52,100
Real Forum	4	G	5	1	0	0	10,767
Real Frosty	5	G	16	2	2	1	17,736
Real Gallant	5	G	8	1	0	1	3,004
Real George	3	C	12	1	0	0	3,810
Real Golden	4	G	3	0	0	0	0
Real Good	2	G	2	0	0	0	0
Real Good Deal	2	F	2	0	1	0	4,550
Real Hot	3	G	13	0	0	5	13,205
Real Intrusion	7	M	9	3	0	2	32,494
Real Irish	2	C	1	0	0	0	0
Real Justice	4	G	4	0	0	0	225
Real Kassy	5	G	3	1	1	0	3,093
Real Kayla Dan	3	G	10	1	1	2	15,571
Real Kyle	8	H	2	0	0	0	0
Real Lady's Man	3	G	17	2	0	1	11,707
Real Leader	3	G	16	2	4	0	12,724
Real Life	4	G	14	1	2	4	46,431
Real Loud	5	G	4	0	0	0	497
Real Paranoide	5	M	10	1	3	1	85,094
Real Peachy	3	F	5	1	0	3	5,305
Real Pro	2	G	1	0	0	0	0
Real Queen	2	F	1	0	0	0	135
Real Quest	6	H	8	0	1	4	8,739
Real Quiet Heath	2	G	4	0	0	0	1,320
Real Red	2	G	5	1	3	0	30,117
Real Rhythm	4	G	6	1	0	0	9,450
Real Ringer	8	G	11	1	1	1	2,172
Real Risque	4	F	4	0	0	0	0
Real Salty	3	G	9	1	0	1	8,316
Real Saucy	3	G	12	2	4	0	26,057
Real Secret	7	M	5	0	0	1	555
Real Shock	4	C	8	2	1	0	15,635
Real Skippy	3	C	3	0	0	0	0
Real Slick Zeal	3	C	2	0	0	0	485
Real Special	6	G	6	1	1	0	19,738
Real Sterling	3	F	10	3	1	0	19,192
Real Style	4	F	8	0	0	1	390
Real Swell	2	C	1	0	0	0	95
Real Swiss Trick	5	M	2	0	0	0	101
Real Tears	4	G	16	3	4	2	30,165
Real Terms	6	G	12	2	1	3	11,737
Real Tomcat	3	C	9	2	0	2	9,482
Real Town Guy	2	C	6	1	0	0	6,000
Real True Spirit	5	G	18	2	4	2	7,300
Real War	8	G	1	0	0	0	0
Real War Dancer	10	G	1	0	0	0	0
Real Whisper	5	G	11	3	3	1	28,930
Real Wildcat	3	G	13	3	0	1	23,450
Real Women	7	M	2	0	0	0	0
Real Wonder	5	H	11	2	2	0	14,926
Real Zealot	3	F	1	0	0	0	330
Realacarr	4	C	18	0	0	5	10,341
Realignment	4	G	13	3	1	0	10,410
Realist	4	G	1	0	0	0	0
Realistically	3	C	1	0	0	0	0
Realities Runamuck	3	C	3	1	0	0	1,272
Realitize	4	F	3	0	2	0	7,200
Reality Affirmed	2	F	2	0	0	0	0
Reality Check	5	G	9	3	0	2	33,960
Reality Happens	3	F	6	1	1	1	10,525
Reality Lady	6	M	11	2	0	2	9,120
Reality Mine	2	G	1	0	0	0	0
Reality Mountain	2	G	1	1	0	0	6,450
Reality Pill	6	M	14	2	0	5	19,410
Reality Prevails	6	G	5	0	1	0	1,446
Reality Step	2	F	3	0	2	1	6,000
Reality Ticket	2	C	2	0	0	0	0
Realityiscountry	3	F	7	2	2	0	9,280
Reality's Affair	5	M	15	2	4	1	37,465
Reality's Gem	8	G	18	2	1	4	11,683
Reality's Pine	8	H	6	0	1	1	3,000
Realization	5	M	6	0	1	2	3,196
Really a Captain	3	C	4	0	0	0	324
Really American	2	F	6	2	0	0	37,170
Really Bad News	3	C	8	1	3	1	31,280
Really Big	5	G	4	1	0	1	12,285
Really Crafty	10	G	8	2	1	0	10,857
Really Flashy	5	G	2	0	0	0	305
Really Free	5	G	15	5	1	2	17,902
Really Frosted	10	G	1	0	0	0	0
Really Good Whisky	4	C	5	0	0	0	458
Really Groovy	5	M	10	1	2	2	14,152
Really Irish	6	G	7	1	0	1	10,400
Really Keen	5	M	11	1	3	2	41,420
Really Ladylike	3	F	7	2	1	1	9,147
Really No Saint	5	H	9	1	4	1	9,666
Really Orr Not	8	G	3	0	0	1	379
Really Perky	2	F	2	0	0	0	0
Really Radical	8	M	10	0	1	1	2,610
Really Ready	8	G	9	3	0	1	9,932
Really Regal	7	G	3	0	0	0	600
Really Royal	4	F	14	5	1	3	65,544
Really Rugged	2	C	4	0	2	0	16,270
Really Sharp	3	C	5	1	1	0	15,200
Really Shocking	5	M	2	0	0	0	180
Really Silver	4	F	9	2	1	0	6,879
Really Something	4	F	10	2	1	2	12,602
Really Sumptin	5	G	4	0	0	1	790
Really Suspect	3	G	1	0	0	0	840
Really Tough	3	C	14	4	4	2	81,870
Really Traveling	6	G	8	1	2	0	14,075

RECORDS OF HORSES

Horse	Age	Sex	Sts	1st	2d	3d	Won	Horse	Age	Sex	Sts	1st	2d	3d	Won
Really Tricky	2	G	1	0	0	0	0	Rebridled Secret	2	F	1	0	0	0	0
Really Unique	2	G	1	0	0	0	0	Rebroke	4	G	14	0	3	1	7,731
Really Who	3	C	10	2	1	3	29,733	Rebs Agenda	2	F	5	0	2	0	5,600
Reallyahotnumber	4	G	1	0	0	0	380	Reb's Drummer	3	G	8	3	0	3	61,738
Reallybelieveit	3	F	7	0	0	0	563	Rebs Fortyniner	3	C	4	0	0	0	231
Realriskybusiness	3	C	4	0	0	0	3,960	Reb's Gold	10	G	10	0	2	0	6,820
Realsharp	6	H	10	2	2	0	10,565	Rebuffed	8	G	7	3	1	0	29,124
Reanna's Pride	4	F	9	1	1	1	4,380	Recall	8	H	4	0	1	0	570
Reap the Wind	3	G	6	1	1	0	15,500	Recanting	9	H	1	0	0	1	1,000
Reaping Tirade	4	G	6	1	0	0	3,150	Received Your Fax	2	G	4	1	0	0	16,609
Rearadmiral Patton	3	G	12	3	1	1	30,583	Receivership	3	F	8	5	0	0	112,950
Reason for Justice	4	F	12	2	0	3	28,811	Recency	5	G	16	1	3	2	9,623
Reason Prevails	12	G	14	2	0	1	7,901	Recent Ruckus	5	M	9	0	0	0	320
Reason This	3	G	3	0	0	0	610	Recess in Heaven	5	M	11	2	0	2	17,161
Reason to Be Astar	9	M	11	1	0	0	7,375	Reche Diamant	4	F	8	2	1	3	46,958
Reason to Buck	3	F	6	0	2	0	3,030	Recherche	3	F	6	0	3	1	24,080
Reason to Change	5	G	12	0	0	0	618	Reciever General	6	G	11	0	0	3	3,417
Reason to Hail	6	G	9	2	1	4	82,130	Reciprocate	3	C	10	0	0	2	5,220
Reason to Jett	3	G	9	1	1	0	11,610	Recite	4	G	4	0	1	0	21,576
Reason to Please	4	G	2	0	0	0	0	Reckless Abandon	7	M	12	0	2	0	4,732
Reason to Ransom	3	F	10	1	1	0	7,978	Reckless Affair	4	G	6	0	0	1	1,780
Reason to Squall	6	G	4	0	1	1	5,550	Reckless Babe	3	F	4	0	0	0	700
Reason to Storm	3	C	4	1	0	0	3,864	Reckless Fox	5	G	16	1	1	3	16,195
Reason to Talk	4	F	12	4	2	0	194,384	Reckless Genie	4	F	4	0	1	0	2,885
Reason to Win	5	G	8	2	1	1	30,555	Reckless Ghost	3	G	10	1	2	1	32,578
Reason Unknown	4	G	5	0	0	0	405	Reckless Hero	2	C	1	0	0	0	0
Reasonable Avenue	2	F	2	0	0	0	280	Reckless Ruler	7	G	2	0	0	0	210
Reasonable Cat	3	G	14	1	1	2	9,890	Recky	3	F	1	0	1	0	2,200
Reasonable Code	3	F	8	1	2	2	19,165	Recognize	9	G	5	0	1	0	3,180
Reasonable Diane	5	M	3	1	0	0	6,544	Recognize Her	3	F	2	0	0	2	2,153
Reasonable Rita	6	M	13	1	0	1	5,102	Recognize Me	7	M	20	2	5	0	14,823
Reasonable Rumor	9	H	5	0	1	0	3,302	Recollection	3	C	9	1	2	1	47,020
Reasonforrejection	5	M	12	3	4	1	23,526	Recommence	7	M	3	0	0	1	900
Reason's Best	2	F	2	0	0	0	0	Recon Marine	4	C	2	1	0	0	9,600
Reasontofly	4	F	11	1	3	1	37,114	Reconnaissance	5	G	5	1	0	1	7,732
Reassess	4	C	14	7	3	2	48,210	Record Assembly	3	G	17	4	6	2	88,960
Reatta Pass	4	F	10	4	0	1	58,590	Record Avenger	2	F	5	0	0	0	348
Reaushambeaux	4	G	13	3	4	2	20,616	Record Charger	4	C	3	0	0	0	0
Reba	5	M	2	0	0	0	120	Record Deal	4	G	3	0	0	0	260
Reba's Gold	6	H	5	1	1	2	183,000	Record Level	11	G	12	3	0	2	19,861
Reba's Rebel	4	G	11	2	4	1	9,071	Record Pick	9	G	4	0	0	0	0
Rebbeca Gold	3	F	2	0	0	0	94	Record Smashed	2	C	2	0	0	1	4,900
Rebecca Dewinter	5	M	11	2	0	2	8,682	Record Tide	3	C	9	2	1	0	52,670
Rebecca G Dianne	3	F	2	0	0	0	1,090	Recordado (ARG)	4	C	1	0	0	0	0
Rebecca Larue	5	M	5	0	0	1	1,060	Recorded Time	3	F	8	2	2	1	26,399
Rebecca's Charm	4	F	12	3	3	1	110,740	Recount	4	G	5	2	0	1	19,216
Rebecca's Storm	10	G	8	0	0	0	360	Recount Slew	3	G	5	0	0	1	634
Rebel	3	F	2	0	0	0	300	Recreation	5	H	2	0	0	0	0
Rebel Band	4	G	3	0	0	0	0	Recycle Mike	2	G	1	0	0	0	1,144
Rebel Gal	2	F	2	0	0	1	3,630	Red a Raunchy	2	F	5	0	0	0	390
Rebel Genes	4	G	3	0	0	0	130	Red Ace	7	H	12	1	3	3	11,968
Rebel Grey	4	G	9	1	2	0	7,970	Red All Over	5	M	1	0	0	0	0
Rebel Johnny	3	C	7	1	0	1	7,350	Red and Ahead	4	F	5	1	0	2	8,126
Rebel Kid	8	M	3	0	0	0	0	Red and Free	3	F	13	0	1	2	8,839
Rebel King	5	G	11	1	1	1	17,567	Red and Rare	4	C	2	0	0	0	0
Rebel Lil	2	F	4	1	1	0	23,600	Red and Royal	2	G	4	0	0	0	380
Rebel Love	4	C	4	0	1	0	2,420	Red and White	4	F	5	0	1	1	2,275
Rebel Proud	3	G	4	1	0	0	5,190	Red Antics	5	G	10	1	2	3	50,170
Rebel Rage	4	G	5	0	1	0	6,860	Red Apache	3	C	2	0	0	0	0
Rebel Rex	7	G	12	4	1	1	16,542	Red Arc	5	G	4	0	0	0	200
Rebel Roots	3	G	4	0	3	1	2,880	Red At Morn	3	G	13	0	0	2	3,185
Rebel Rose	2	F	7	1	2	0	16,700	Red At the Helm	3	F	13	3	1	2	33,468
Rebel Roxy	3	F	3	0	0	0	0	Red At the Wire	6	G	15	1	1	2	2,990
Rebel Song	3	C	3	0	0	0	137	Red Azalea	3	F	13	2	0	1	22,555
Rebel Winner	3	C	3	0	0	0	50	Red Badge	7	G	11	0	4	2	6,829
Rebelano	4	F	8	1	1	1	20,973	Red Bails	5	G	16	2	0	2	8,704
Rebelcat	2	C	5	0	1	0	8,693	Red Bandit	4	G	4	0	0	0	0
Rebelette	3	F	8	3	0	1	18,487	Red Blur	6	M	4	0	0	0	1,234
Rebelious Peace	4	G	23	1	5	3	21,096	Red Book	7	H	3	0	0	0	178
Rebelous Zone	5	H	15	0	2	3	13,502	Red Booom	3	F	10	2	1	0	26,310
Rebel's Mission	4	G	17	4	3	2	63,110	Red Boots	2	F	3	0	0	1	1,980
Rebel's Revenge	3	C	4	0	0	2	5,382	Red Box	5	G	11	1	2	2	12,670
Rebmec Express	4	G	2	0	0	1	462	Red Briar	2	G	1	0	1	0	5,240
Rebob	4	G	2	0	0	0	70	Red Briar (IRE)	4	G	13	1	1	1	29,700
Rebolero	4	F	14	1	2	4	6,081	Red Brick Avenue	4	F	21	3	1	1	17,552
Rebonah	3	F	3	0	0	1	2,860	Red Card Carla	4	F	4	0	1	2	3,285
Rebound Boy	11	G	5	0	0	1	530	Red Carpet	5	H	5	0	0	2	4,980
Rebridled	9	G	10	2	0	0	42,120	Red Cause	4	F	7	1	0	0	14,655
Rebridled Dreams	3	F	8	3	0	1	100,856	Red Cell	3	F	4	0	0	1	6,038

Horse	Age	Sex	Sts	1st	2d	3d	Won
Red Cielo	5	G	16	2	1	5	21,375
Red Clay Coins	9	G	8	1	2	0	5,662
Red Copy	2	C	3	1	0	0	11,160
Red Corsair	4	C	9	0	0	0	2,300
Red Creek	2	C	2	0	0	0	0
Red Crusader	2	C	2	0	0	0	1,000
Red Detonator	3	F	3	0	0	0	207
Red Dice	3	F	9	2	3	0	29,089
Red Dirt Darlin	3	F	4	1	0	0	2,941
Red Dirt Roughneck	8	G	22	0	5	3	7,038
Red Donnit	8	M	3	0	0	0	174
Red Down South	3	C	3	0	2	0	19,320
Red Dragon	8	G	10	2	3	1	50,908
Red Duchess	3	F	6	2	1	0	35,320
Red Dynamo	4	G	15	2	0	1	15,775
Red Eagle	5	G	16	2	1	5	12,222
Red Earthquake	2	C	1	0	0	0	1,800
Red Emerald	3	F	8	1	3	1	16,602
Red Exit	6	G	8	0	2	1	11,116
Red Explosion	7	G	2	0	0	0	0
Red Eye	7	G	11	4	0	0	23,662
Red Eye Bishop	4	G	6	0	1	1	3,004
Red Eye Gravy	4	F	11	3	3	2	27,805
Red Eye West	5	M	5	3	0	0	20,661
Red Eyed Dolly	5	M	6	0	2	1	3,070
Red Film (GB)	4	F	7	0	1	0	3,870
Red Flag Ahead	5	M	8	2	1	3	27,192
Red Flush	7	G	10	0	0	0	577
Red Fox Fire	3	F	7	0	1	1	2,875
Red Fox Tail	6	H	9	0	0	6	3,097
Red Fred	6	G	10	1	2	0	4,600
Red Fred in Bed	4	C	3	0	1	0	1,734
Red G	5	H	11	1	0	2	14,199
Red Gem	7	G	8	1	0	0	19,280
Red Ginger	4	C	11	2	0	0	17,044
Red Glare	5	M	3	0	0	0	0
Red Hair Lady	2	F	2	0	0	1	2,400
Red Hawkeye	4	G	15	5	3	0	77,470
Red Headed Romeo	4	G	13	0	1	1	4,542
Red Heads Bay	5	G	16	0	3	4	4,404
Red Hot Affair	2	F	3	0	0	0	870
Red Hot Angel	6	M	10	2	2	2	6,999
Red Hot Bertie	3	F	5	1	1	0	26,520
Red Hot Chiquita	4	F	2	0	1	0	1,800
Red Hot Dollar	3	F	11	0	1	3	6,461
Red Hot Flyer	7	G	16	2	0	1	8,976
Red Hot Fox	4	C	9	2	2	1	8,412
Red Hot Gal	4	F	6	0	0	2	18,676
Red Hot Helen	3	F	10	4	2	1	37,482
Red Hot Honey	4	F	2	0	0	0	930
Red Hot Kitty	3	F	6	1	2	2	26,619
Red Hot Luke	7	G	13	1	1	1	1,906
Red Hot Pistol	5	G	9	2	2	0	12,244
Red Hot Prospect	3	G	22	4	2	5	19,034
Red Hot Rocket	5	G	17	6	2	2	28,101
Red Hot Secret	3	G	9	2	2	1	40,155
Red Hot Spot	4	G	4	2	1	0	34,830
Red Hot Star	3	F	7	3	0	0	31,220
Red Hot Sword	4	F	13	0	1	3	4,501
Red Hot Tequila	2	F	1	1	0	0	9,000
Red Hot Texan	3	R	3	0	0	0	0
Red Hot to Handle	2	F	1	0	0	0	135
Red Hot Wish	4	G	11	2	1	0	40,240
Red Hurricane	3	G	6	1	0	0	3,363
Red Ide	3	F	8	0	0	3	1,848
Red in the Morning	4	F	15	2	2	0	21,025
Red Jared	5	G	5	0	0	0	186
Red Jenny	3	F	2	0	0	0	167
Red Label	4	G	5	1	0	1	2,994
Red Lake Romance	2	F	2	0	0	0	97
Red Lava	2	C	1	0	0	0	450
Red Leave Rose	3	F	13	3	1	2	38,476
Red Licorice	4	F	2	0	0	0	0
Red Lifesaver	2	F	1	0	0	0	980
Red Light Ticket	6	M	2	0	0	0	0
Red Lightning	5	G	6	0	0	0	6,240
Red Line Seven	3	C	10	0	2	2	14,310
Red Link	3	G	23	2	4	3	27,600
Red Logan	5	H	4	0	0	0	242
Red M and M	2	C	1	0	1	0	4,400
Red Man Reaction	4	G	9	0	3	0	4,392
Red Man Walking	3	C	2	0	0	0	165
Red Marie	7	M	16	5	0	5	84,924
Red Meena	4	C	3	0	0	0	0
Red Mercedes	4	F	3	1	0	0	11,358
Red Miah	5	G	12	2	0	1	9,859
Red Mimi	5	M	5	2	1	0	40,800
Red Mints	3	G	3	0	0	1	2,810
Red Moment	3	G	2	0	1	0	1,980
Red Moon Rising	3	F	6	0	0	2	8,900
Red Mountain	6	G	15	1	4	2	103,730
Red Mountain Garth	8	G	9	2	2	1	6,418
Red Neck Girl	3	F	6	0	0	0	0
Red Neck Lady	3	F	4	0	1	0	3,940
Red n'Gold	5	M	7	1	1	1	84,765
Red Ninety Seven	6	M	4	0	0	1	1,015
Red Opal (IRE)	4	F	4	1	2	0	53,460
Red Orbit	4	G	1	0	0	0	56
Red Packet	4	G	3	3	0	0	49,500
Red Panda	7	H	2	1	0	1	7,500
Red Parka Mary	5	M	7	2	0	0	23,772
Red Pepper Martini	2	C	4	1	2	0	14,380
Red Phenomon	3	G	8	0	1	0	1,355
Red Plaid	5	M	9	1	0	0	6,074
Red Point	2	G	3	0	0	1	1,210
Red Pop	3	F	8	1	3	1	16,676
Red Press	7	G	1	0	0	0	0
Red Quest	4	C	7	0	0	3	4,860
Red Rage	3	F	8	2	0	1	16,745
Red Rapala	4	G	1	0	0	0	500
Red Raptor	6	H	1	0	0	0	0
Red Reaction	3	F	6	1	1	2	7,305
Red Regent	2	G	2	0	0	0	220
Red Reigning	4	G	11	3	1	0	22,133
Red Rhino	4	G	8	0	2	1	3,680
Red Ribbons	3	G	1	0	0	0	0
Red Rioja (IRE)	4	F	3	1	1	0	60,800
Red Ripper	3	G	1	0	0	0	75
Red River Aggie	3	C	15	4	3	0	72,900
Red River Annie	4	F	4	0	0	0	65
Red River Dave	3	C	9	5	1	1	61,900
Red River Gambler	6	H	2	0	0	0	0
Red River Girl	2	F	2	0	0	0	3,430
Red River Quest	9	G	5	0	0	2	480
Red River Rally	5	G	3	0	0	0	0
Red River Rapids	5	G	1	0	0	0	56
Red River Red	5	G	4	0	1	0	2,156
Red River Ridge	6	H	11	0	0	1	1,010
Red River Rock	7	G	7	0	0	0	228
Red River Rose	4	F	9	0	0	1	709
Red River Storm	3	G	2	0	0	1	1,430
Red River Valley	8	G	18	1	2	2	14,310
Red River Wine	5	G	10	1	0	0	3,036
Red Roan Dancer	4	G	7	2	1	0	16,471
Red Rock Creek	2	C	8	1	3	0	19,900
Red Rock Ridge	10	G	9	2	1	0	8,811
Red Rock Road	2	C	2	0	1	0	2,357
Red Rock Rosy	4	F	7	0	2	2	1,525
Red Rodeo	5	M	3	0	0	1	320
Red Rompin Rascal	6	G	9	0	0	2	1,280
Red Rosalyn	5	M	22	2	1	0	14,430
Red Rose Jake	3	G	14	1	1	2	20,657
Red Roses	7	M	1	0	0	0	0
Red Rouge	2	G	5	0	0	2	7,419
Red Rumpus	3	C	2	1	0	1	9,470
Red Ryder Band	8	H	11	1	0	2	4,325
Red Said	7	G	7	2	0	0	2,718
Red Sea (GB)	7	G	11	1	0	3	87,232
Red Seattle	7	G	7	2	2	1	9,424
Red Sherry	4	F	9	3	0	2	30,564
Red Shift	6	G	15	2	3	1	16,817
Red Silk	6	M	1	0	0	0	282
Red Siren	10	G	13	1	1	2	4,343
Red Sky At Morning	3	C	2	0	0	0	150
Red Sky Guy	4	G	8	1	2	1	7,874
Red Sky's	7	H	9	0	0	2	25,320
Red Snoony	2	F	3	0	0	0	0
Red Soldier	3	G	9	2	1	2	15,702

Horse	Age	Sex	Sts	1st	2d	3d	Won
Red Soxs	6	M	4	0	0	0	330
Red Spark	3	G	15	1	6	4	19,407
Red Spice	3	F	1	0	0	0	300
Red Sprinkles	3	F	19	3	3	4	33,883
Red Square	2	C	2	0	0	0	239
Red Strawberry	8	G	13	1	1	1	6,545
Red Streak	2	G	6	0	1	0	2,250
Red Street Mike	6	H	5	0	0	0	0
Red Strider	6	G	11	0	2	1	8,166
Red Sunday Racer	3	G	2	0	0	0	103
Red Sundown	6	G	16	5	2	3	35,059
Red T K's Star	2	C	2	0	0	1	3,950
Red Tag Clearance	3	F	1	0	0	0	75
Red Tag Special	3	G	4	0	0	2	1,222
Red Tail Angel	5	M	9	0	0	0	1,005
Red Tees	11	M	1	0	0	0	0
Red Threat	5	G	5	2	1	1	20,061
Red Tie Lady	2	F	2	0	0	0	0
Red Token	2	C	4	0	0	1	2,364
Red Torrent	3	F	3	0	0	0	872
Red Trackbarron	9	G	11	0	0	0	108
Red Tribute	8	M	13	1	2	1	8,235
Red Truck	2	C	2	0	0	1	1,650
Red Two	8	M	13	0	0	2	2,030
Red Valhalla	4	G	9	1	1	2	25,165
Red Velvet Cake	2	G	5	2	1	0	58,730
Red Veneer	5	G	2	0	0	0	0
Red Vil Do	5	M	9	0	2	4	5,320
Red Vintage (GB)	4	G	4	1	0	0	36,580
Red Wader	4	C	9	1	1	1	5,516
Red Wajir	2	C	1	0	0	0	75
Red Wand	3	C	11	1	0	1	14,485
Red Warrior	3	C	8	2	1	1	88,740
Red White and True	2	C	2	0	0	0	75
Red Wildcat	5	M	8	2	0	1	50,580
Red Will Win	2	F	1	0	0	0	110
Red Willy	3	G	5	0	0	1	1,254
Red Wing Evan	4	C	6	2	1	1	49,060
Red Wing Son	3	C	4	0	0	0	545
Red Wolf	9	G	13	1	1	1	8,232
Red Work	5	G	7	0	0	2	4,386
Red Wrecker	2	C	3	0	0	0	780
Red Zac	4	G	5	3	1	0	86,060
Red Zeppelin	5	H	5	0	0	0	120
Red Zinger	3	F	9	0	0	3	21,345
Redanddee	4	F	3	0	0	1	180
Redas Skydancer	6	G	12	2	1	2	31,137
Redattore (BRZ)	8	H	8	5	0	2	864,147
Redbird	3	F	6	2	0	0	12,885
Redbone	4	C	3	0	1	0	1,200
Redcarpettreatment	4	F	12	2	2	2	87,594
Redcliff Bay	7	M	8	2	2	1	16,355
Redcuda	3	C	5	1	0	1	13,610
Redd N Hot	4	C	11	0	0	4	4,541
Reddi Hope	3	F	2	0	0	0	100
Reddick	8	G	19	3	6	3	24,915
Redding Woods	5	G	19	5	4	4	58,500
Reddy Be a Groom	3	G	1	0	0	0	120
Redeye Girl	5	M	11	0	4	1	5,767
Redeyed Charmer	2	F	1	0	0	0	103
Redeyed Prospector	10	G	1	0	0	0	70
Redeyemidniteflite	3	F	2	0	0	0	86
Redfish	4	G	2	0	0	0	229
Redflex	3	G	10	1	0	2	5,311
Redford	2	C	4	0	0	0	360
Redhanded	8	G	6	0	0	0	172
Redhawk One	2	G	6	1	0	1	6,485
Redhead Riot	4	F	6	0	1	2	34,796
Redheaded Rue	3	C	10	1	0	1	6,003
Redheadeded	5	G	4	0	0	0	405
Redhook	3	C	4	0	0	0	1,515
Redhot Dy No Mite	3	F	11	0	2	1	4,623
Redhot Hadif	4	G	13	1	1	2	11,994
Redi Hot	4	G	15	1	1	0	9,866
Redinal	3	G	10	2	2	2	20,405
Redlick Chick	8	M	1	0	0	0	122
Redly	5	G	13	3	1	0	20,140
Redmarina	2	F	4	1	0	0	18,750
Redmond	4	F	4	0	1	2	18,375
Redneck Etiquette	6	G	9	0	0	2	2,560
Redneck Tune	2	F	1	0	0	0	0
Redon	3	C	2	0	0	1	2,270
Redoubled Miss	4	F	9	2	4	2	210,545
Redoys Move	6	G	16	1	5	0	3,600
Redraw	4	C	15	1	3	0	39,080
Redriverrendezvous	6	H	8	0	0	0	315
Redrock Theatre	3	C	2	0	0	0	169
Red's Account	2	G	4	0	0	0	280
Red's Bokay	3	F	7	0	1	0	1,868
Reds Glory	4	G	14	1	5	4	12,020
Reds Gone	4	C	5	0	0	0	733
Red's Honor	5	H	7	1	1	0	40,780
Reds Pal	3	C	1	0	0	0	195
Red's Place	5	G	8	1	2	1	33,870
Red's Rainbow	3	F	4	0	1	0	4,220
Reds Ready	4	C	8	0	1	0	3,800
Red's Red	4	G	11	1	2	1	22,331
Red's Rollin	4	G	12	2	3	3	8,836
Red's St. Pat	2	F	1	0	0	0	75
Red's the Range	3	G	13	3	1	1	31,058
Red's Top Gun	4	C	9	1	1	1	27,904
Redskin Warrior	2	C	3	2	0	1	60,150
Redstar Dancer	4	C	8	0	3	0	8,560
Redtailer	5	G	9	0	0	0	250
Reduced Sentence	3	F	2	0	0	0	1,135
Reduit (GB)	5	H	4	1	1	1	52,000
Redwalker	4	G	2	0	0	0	0
Redwinesipper	3	C	4	1	1	0	13,100
Redwood Knot	6	M	5	1	0	0	10,694
Redwood Star	3	C	6	0	0	0	224
Redyornothereicom	2	C	3	1	0	1	7,220
Redz Passion	3	C	4	0	0	0	75
Ree Rees Boy	5	H	8	0	0	1	1,310
Reeanita	6	M	13	1	2	4	3,206
Reece's Rocket	5	M	7	1	0	4	30,100
Reed Paige Won	3	F	1	0	0	0	0
Reedastraffer	2	C	1	0	0	0	0
Reed's Fund	5	G	5	0	1	2	2,384
Reeds Rich	2	G	2	0	0	0	0
Reef	3	F	2	1	0	0	24,875
Reef Alert	3	G	4	0	0	0	66
Reef Chief	6	G	5	1	0	1	32,240
Reef Diver (GB)	5	G	5	1	0	0	38,960
Reefs Sis (GB)	4	F	7	1	3	0	71,638
Reel Conviction	3	F	19	0	0	1	4,670
Reel Deco	2	F	1	0	1	0	1,800
Reel 'Em In	5	G	6	2	2	0	95,480
Reel Fast Marco	3	G	6	1	1	1	46,432
Reel Lass	4	F	18	1	5	2	24,535
Reel Pepi	6	M	14	0	2	2	4,841
Reel Shiney Chrome	2	F	1	0	0	0	126
Reel Slam	3	G	5	1	1	0	17,220
Reel Spiffy	8	M	6	0	0	0	1,313
Reel Trade	3	C	2	0	0	0	0
Reely Jamin	6	M	16	1	2	2	6,857
Reem	4	G	10	1	1	0	11,020
Reenergize	3	F	1	0	0	0	80
Reesa's Reack	4	F	3	0	0	0	0
Reese's Millennium	6	M	7	1	1	2	2,699
Reese's Preferance	4	G	1	0	0	0	65
Reeves Relic	6	G	17	0	0	0	1,825
Reeyre	4	F	5	1	0	1	5,105
Ref	6	H	4	0	0	0	0
Refapiano's Rage	5	M	4	0	0	0	313
Refax	3	F	17	3	5	0	56,035
Reference Mark	3	F	3	0	1	0	2,060
Referral	5	G	11	0	0	3	6,513
Refine	8	G	15	2	1	3	7,343
Refined'n'smart	3	F	7	1	4	0	17,910
Refiners Challenge	10	G	7	0	0	2	2,665
Refiners Fire	3	F	3	0	0	0	0
Refiners North	3	C	3	0	0	1	1,495
Reflect Royalty	4	G	8	1	0	0	7,601
Reflected Image	5	M	3	1	0	0	3,962
Reflecting Colors	5	G	5	1	1	2	36,433
Reflection Bay	6	M	13	1	1	4	14,046
Reflective Halo	2	C	1	0	0	1	1,260
Reflector	3	G	4	1	1	0	29,640

Horse	Age	Sex	Sts	1st	2d	3d	Won
Refocus	3	G	6	0	1	0	2,800
Reforest	2	F	2	1	1	0	19,590
Reformer	2	G	3	0	0	0	3,360
Refreshing Caron	2	F	3	0	0	0	220
Refunded	4	G	6	0	1	0	1,750
Refuse To Bend (IRE)	3	C	6	3	0	0	383,998
Refusilo Sur (ARG)	8	H	4	0	0	0	156
Regal Ability	4	G	4	3	0	0	109,270
Regal Again	5	G	9	6	0	0	48,450
Regal Amy	5	M	6	0	2	1	5,672
Regal and Cool	2	F	9	1	2	0	43,975
Regal Annie	5	M	3	0	0	1	547
Regal Anthem	4	C	6	1	1	0	7,485
Regal Appeal	7	G	7	1	0	0	16,208
Regal At Last	4	F	10	2	0	1	10,584
Regal Attitude	3	F	4	0	0	0	277
Regal Bear	3	C	7	1	0	2	37,329
Regal Beauty	2	F	5	0	0	0	1,680
Regal Beginning	4	G	14	1	1	3	9,533
Regal Ben	2	G	2	0	0	0	0
Regal Bev	4	F	3	0	0	0	394
Regal Blues	4	F	14	1	0	1	26,033
Regal Bounty	4	F	11	1	5	3	9,272
Regal Boy	4	C	2	0	0	0	0
Regal Buck	2	G	6	1	0	3	8,105
Regal by Design	8	G	8	0	1	1	2,992
Regal C Note	2	G	3	2	0	0	23,814
Regal Candy	3	F	6	1	0	0	10,560
Regal Case	2	F	1	0	0	0	1,195
Regal Champ	2	G	2	1	0	0	11,866
Regal Chance	2	F	2	0	0	0	0
Regal Choice	6	M	2	0	0	0	29
Regal Colours	3	G	14	2	2	2	8,307
Regal Commitment	3	C	1	0	0	0	0
Regal Council	5	G	8	1	1	2	6,196
Regal Cruiser	3	G	4	0	1	1	13,040
Regal D Lish	7	M	4	0	1	0	1,611
Regal Dancer	3	F	13	1	3	3	11,288
Regal Dandy	7	G	1	0	0	0	221
Regal Dinner	3	C	15	4	2	2	35,510
Regal Disclosure	4	G	13	1	2	1	45,187
Regal Dixie	3	G	7	0	0	0	204
Regal Dom	7	G	14	4	1	1	33,058
Regal Dove	4	C	2	1	0	0	3,296
Regal Dr. Stuart	4	G	9	0	0	1	2,994
Regal Drive	6	G	16	2	1	2	16,760
Regal Dynasty	7	G	1	0	0	1	6,545
Regal Edition	5	G	1	1	0	0	7,680
Regal Emblem	4	F	12	1	3	1	8,088
Regal Endorsement	3	F	1	0	0	0	0
Regal Explosion	6	G	12	0	2	3	14,915
Regal Fan	3	G	1	0	0	0	0
Regal Finesse	4	F	5	2	0	0	2,677
Regal Flip	8	M	11	1	1	3	6,914
Regal Getaway	5	G	6	0	0	3	1,708
Regal Ghazi	3	C	4	0	0	0	70
Regal Grace	2	F	6	2	1	0	54,794
Regal Heir	4	F	7	1	5	0	37,478
Regal Highlander	5	G	4	0	0	0	450
Regal Hit	3	G	13	0	3	1	7,303
Regal Honey	3	F	4	0	0	0	689
Regal Illusion	7	M	3	0	0	0	13,244
Regal Jackie	3	F	6	1	0	1	8,150
Regal Julie	4	F	7	1	2	1	14,280
Regal Justice	6	H	15	1	2	1	26,774
Regal Kawana	2	C	1	0	0	0	0
Regal Knight	5	G	6	3	1	0	19,435
Regal Laddie	2	G	3	0	1	0	2,366
Regal Lancer	4	C	8	1	2	1	5,630
Regal Legacy	4	G	10	1	1	4	19,012
Regal Lexie	4	F	9	4	2	1	47,165
Regal Louie	5	G	3	0	0	0	200
Regal Lullaby	3	F	11	1	0	0	5,356
Regal Lyric	8	H	7	0	0	0	822
Regal Ma	3	F	1	0	0	0	0
Regal Maria	5	M	1	0	0	0	38
Regal Maxim	2	C	1	0	0	0	506
Regal Meg	3	F	9	1	2	0	11,300
Regal Miracle	4	F	12	1	3	2	17,040
Regal Miss	2	F	1	0	0	0	195
Regal Mister	5	G	7	0	0	0	0
Regal Model	2	C	6	0	0	0	1,268
Regal Moment	3	C	10	0	0	0	1,970
Regal 'n Bold	3	F	6	3	0	1	130,689
Regal n' Classy	5	M	9	0	1	1	23,188
Regal 'n Clever	2	F	2	0	0	0	2,757
Regal 'n Valiant	2	G	4	1	0	0	5,825
Regal Orphan	7	G	2	0	0	1	1,320
Regal Perrot	4	G	13	0	0	4	2,468
Regal Plan	8	G	1	0	0	0	0
Regal Pro	3	G	6	0	0	0	3,690
Regal Punch	3	G	3	0	0	0	268
Regal Queen	3	F	6	1	1	0	6,890
Regal Rae Rae	4	F	9	1	1	2	16,377
Regal Randy	4	G	3	0	2	1	8,430
Regal Rebel	4	G	5	2	0	0	60,300
Regal Red	2	F	2	1	1	0	16,068
Regal Reproach	4	G	10	0	2	1	24,634
Regal Revolt	5	H	1	0	0	0	0
Regal Road	4	C	10	2	2	1	15,879
Regal Rock	4	G	1	0	0	0	0
Regal Rocket	3	G	7	1	0	2	44,935
Regal Romeo	5	H	13	2	5	3	14,409
Regal Roots	3	F	13	0	4	4	23,092
Regal Roulette	2	F	5	0	0	0	390
Regal Russ	9	G	9	2	0	0	13,183
Regal Sahib	8	G	10	2	1	1	84,950
Regal Sanction	4	C	8	2	1	1	92,151
Regal Sarah	6	M	13	3	1	1	13,964
Regal Sen	3	F	7	1	1	2	28,443
Regal Shivers	5	H	11	1	0	1	16,980
Regal Sierra	3	F	6	2	0	2	14,400
Regal Siphon	3	G	10	2	2	0	20,783
Regal Sky	7	H	1	0	0	0	390
Regal Slam	3	C	5	3	0	2	17,120
Regal Sport	6	H	3	0	0	0	240
Regal Step	7	M	7	0	0	0	1,010
Regal Sum	2	F	2	0	1	1	3,108
Regal Sunrise	2	F	8	1	1	2	28,689
Regal Sweets	5	G	6	1	0	2	30,280
Regal Sword	7	H	1	0	0	0	0
Regal Tour	5	G	8	1	0	2	6,785
Regal Treasure	6	G	18	2	3	0	12,656
Regal Turn	6	H	11	0	2	1	5,104
Regal Valley	2	C	3	0	2	0	43,706
Regal Vicky	2	F	1	0	0	0	182
Regal Victoria	7	M	13	1	0	3	16,658
Regal Victory	4	G	11	0	1	5	20,376
Regal Vision	2	C	1	0	0	0	0
Regal Watch	3	C	3	1	0	0	14,920
Regal Wings	3	F	12	2	2	1	64,063
Regalcy	6	M	3	0	0	1	1,440
Regale	3	F	8	0	2	2	12,760
Regalian	4	F	3	0	0	0	1,152
Regaligan	9	G	1	0	0	0	0
Regalism	5	M	3	0	0	1	3,467
Regallino Storm	3	F	6	0	0	0	225
Regally Expressed	3	F	4	0	0	0	151
Regally Real	4	C	4	2	0	1	15,791
Regal's Flirt	2	F	8	0	1	1	11,871
Regaltoni	3	C	2	0	0	0	285
Regan County	3	F	2	0	0	0	173
Regency Bay	3	G	10	3	0	2	46,722
Regency Park	4	C	3	1	1	0	33,340
Regency's Honor	4	C	12	2	0	2	24,403
Regent Commander	3	C	5	0	0	1	2,100
Regent Deputy	5	G	4	0	0	0	413
Regent Regent	2	G	5	0	4	0	7,488
Regent Ryan	3	C	3	0	0	0	265
Regent Times	3	G	10	2	0	1	11,780
Regently Bold	3	F	7	1	2	0	43,882
Regent's Hope	3	C	2	0	0	0	3,480
Reggae	5	M	5	0	0	2	5,060
Reggae Beat	3	F	3	1	0	0	12,365
Reggae Citi	3	F	5	0	1	1	6,650
Reggae Rhythm	3	G	10	1	2	1	8,930
Reggie Wins Big	3	G	6	2	0	0	18,019
Reggie's Magic	3	C	5	1	2	0	12,625

Horse	Age	Sex	Sts	1st	2d	3d	Won	Horse	Age	Sex	Sts	1st	2d	3d	Won
Reggie's Valentine	3	F	3	1	0	0	2,192	Remarkable Affair	4	C	7	1	0	1	1,540
Reggie's Winner	5	G	9	3	2	1	36,540	Remarkable Appeal	4	F	3	1	0	0	982
Regime Change	2	C	1	0	0	0	0	Remarkable Kat	3	G	7	1	2	0	5,110
Regimental	7	G	10	2	0	3	51,045	Remarkable Silver	4	G	10	1	1	0	19,394
Regimental Flag	7	G	11	1	1	0	11,588	Remarqable Tale	2	F	1	0	0	0	0
Regina Reason	3	G	9	1	0	1	8,016	Remarqable You	3	F	7	1	0	1	14,893
Regina's Mon	2	C	1	0	0	0	75	Remaster	4	G	13	1	0	3	20,815
Region of Merit	3	C	6	3	0	0	229,986	Rembo's Victoriana	4	F	11	0	2	4	13,794
Regular Babe	3	F	1	0	0	0	0	Remeber	9	H	3	0	0	0	0
Rehabilitated	4	G	13	2	1	1	20,916	Remediate	6	M	2	0	0	0	6,000
Rehear	3	F	3	0	0	0	0	Remember Brian	4	F	10	0	2	2	9,788
Rehearsal Hall	4	C	1	0	0	0	340	Remember Cecile	4	F	7	1	0	1	4,263
Rehny Skies	6	H	10	0	1	1	3,038	Remember Doc	3	C	4	1	2	0	8,520
Rehocracy	3	F	9	2	0	1	44,770	Remember Dorothy	5	M	11	2	3	1	43,391
Reid's Mess	2	C	3	0	1	0	2,040	Remember J. R.	4	G	7	0	0	0	231
Reign Down Fire	4	F	3	0	0	0	235	Remember Poppins	3	F	6	1	0	0	6,075
Reign Fire	3	C	3	0	0	0	0	Remember the Groom	3	C	4	1	0	1	8,186
Reign Girl	7	M	10	1	0	1	12,751	Remember the Mane	5	M	6	1	0	0	7,587
Reign of Class	9	M	6	0	2	1	2,196	Remember the Party	4	C	4	0	0	0	1,260
Reign of Tara	3	F	8	0	1	2	37,376	Rememberin Eleanor	2	F	1	0	0	0	220
Reign On Me	4	F	5	1	0	2	34,440	Remembering Beau	3	G	11	2	0	0	18,482
Reign Rose	8	M	8	0	1	1	5,440	Rememberthecowgirl	3	F	6	2	2	0	12,100
Reign Sox	6	G	8	1	1	0	3,985	Remembertheransom	4	G	1	0	0	1	2,340
Reigning Aly	4	F	6	1	1	1	9,420	Rememberthesecret	4	F	1	0	0	0	46
Reigning Bear	3	F	7	0	0	0	553	Rememberthetime	5	H	3	0	0	0	338
Reigning Justice	3	G	10	1	2	2	6,401	Remembrances	2	F	5	2	1	0	63,300
Reigning Witch	7	M	1	0	0	0	78	Remi Larue	3	F	4	0	1	0	1,261
Reignmaker	4	G	2	0	0	0	0	Remies	4	F	2	0	0	0	61
Reignsofire	2	F	1	0	0	1	540	Remiewaterbluz	4	F	13	5	0	4	84,460
Reima Rose	5	M	11	1	2	2	35,900	Remind	3	C	8	3	4	0	251,420
Rein Dancer	6	H	3	0	0	0	63	Remington Katrina	3	F	2	0	0	0	150
Rein Man	5	H	12	1	4	2	3,352	Remington Rock	9	G	1	0	0	0	960
Rein of Fire	2	F	3	0	2	0	0	Remi's Rocket	3	F	6	1	1	0	11,250
Rein On Me	5	G	15	2	2	3	14,191	Remission	6	M	4	0	1	0	4,859
Reina Blanca (GB)	5	M	2	0	0	0	4,764	Remix	2	C	1	0	0	0	920
Reina Glory	4	F	2	0	0	0	0	Remmed in Gold	5	G	7	1	0	0	3,598
Reine de Chateau	4	F	6	0	1	1	20,964	Remo	3	C	4	0	2	0	16,080
Reine des Neiges	4	F	9	5	0	1	77,160	Remonte	3	G	4	1	0	0	14,240
Reinforced	3	G	11	2	1	0	17,185	Remote Control	2	G	2	0	0	0	100
Reining Hearts	2	F	4	1	0	0	5,810	Rena Jean	3	F	7	0	3	0	2,309
Reinvigorate	3	C	2	0	0	0	660	Renaca	3	G	10	1	1	4	12,360
Reito Peito	2	F	1	0	0	0	0	Renade	3	F	6	0	0	0	330
Rejected	6	G	13	0	4	5	10,575	Renaissance Fair	5	M	1	0	0	1	3,740
Rejected Video	3	G	16	2	6	3	11,705	Renaissance Lady	2	F	9	1	4	0	111,850
Rejection	4	G	5	1	0	0	3,375	Renaissance Woman	4	F	2	0	0	0	3,360
Rejoice by Choice	7	G	11	0	1	0	2,091	Renard Bleu	2	C	2	0	0	1	2,535
Rejuvenator	3	F	4	1	0	0	9,135	Renato	8	G	11	0	1	1	1,429
Relapse	4	G	4	0	0	1	2,215	Renature	3	F	6	1	0	0	10,514
Relate	2	C	3	0	0	0	0	Rendezvous Man	8	G	9	1	0	0	4,148
Related Issues	3	F	1	0	1	0	3,150	Renee's Approval	4	F	8	0	1	1	5,790
Related Trump	7	G	8	1	2	3	24,184	Renee's Cat	2	F	3	0	0	0	1,250
Relativa (ARG)	5	M	1	0	0	0	960	Renees Dancer	5	M	4	0	0	0	245
Relato Del Gato	2	C	3	0	0	1	5,400	Renegade Force	6	G	10	2	0	1	2,746
Relaunch a Leader	7	G	9	0	1	2	1,320	Renegade Rogue	5	G	8	1	3	2	17,690
Relaunch Gal	6	M	13	0	1	0	9,100	Renege	4	C	3	0	1	0	6,355
Relaunch Star	5	G	9	2	0	1	95,024	Rene's Kickig Boot	3	F	4	0	0	0	252
Relaunch the Fever	3	F	1	0	0	1	1,128	Rene's Last	3	G	4	1	0	0	1,937
Relaxed Gesture (IRE)	2	C	4	1	1	1	45,821	Rene's Prime Time	3	F	5	2	0	0	8,456
Relaxing Green	3	F	11	1	3	1	42,480	Rene's Soldier	2	C	1	1	0	0	10,000
Relay Runner	3	F	9	1	0	1	8,638	Renewed Passion	3	F	1	0	0	0	100
Release Me	7	G	14	0	2	3	5,280	Reniesmanychances	2	F	4	0	0	0	915
Release the Power	4	C	2	0	0	0	182	Renig	2	C	5	0	1	1	4,857
Relentless Flight	4	C	9	1	1	1	11,150	Rennae N Nicole	6	M	8	2	1	0	6,413
Relentless Fury	2	C	3	0	0	0	1,800	Rennaissance Man	4	G	6	1	3	1	17,509
Relentless Red	2	C	4	1	0	1	32,520	Reno Bound	6	G	9	2	1	3	15,031
Relentless Seller	4	G	2	1	0	0	14,760	Reno City Jackpot	5	H	1	0	0	0	0
Relevant One	7	M	10	0	1	0	2,785	Reno Haines	2	C	1	0	0	0	0
Reliable Source	3	C	3	1	0	1	23,920	Reno Hill	3	C	6	1	0	0	3,730
Relicon	3	F	5	1	1	1	24,100	Reno Rumble	9	G	2	0	0	1	5,585
Religious	3	F	10	3	1	1	33,981	Renoir Red	7	G	12	3	2	2	18,869
Relish (IRE)	4	F	3	0	0	0	960	Renounce Reality	6	H	1	0	0	0	63
Reluctant Clown	4	G	6	0	0	1	2,955	Renovation	3	F	3	0	0	0	120
Reluctant Groom	5	H	7	0	0	1	6,527	Renton Benny	3	G	9	1	0	2	4,685
Reluctant Hero	4	G	1	0	1	0	5,400	Rentway	4	C	8	0	1	3	7,925
Reluctant Lady	3	F	2	0	0	0	315	Reoccurring Dream	10	G	4	0	1	0	2,583
Reluctant Leona	3	F	7	0	0	0	189	Reore	7	H	9	2	0	0	8,683
Reluctant Princess	4	F	3	0	0	0	0	Reo's Line	7	H	2	0	0	0	330
Rely On Me	2	F	10	0	1	1	6,540	Repartment	3	C	10	1	4	0	22,270
Remagen Bridge	5	G	16	0	4	1	12,080	Repayma (NZ)	8	M	4	1	0	1	10,850

Horse	Age	Sex	Sts	1st	2d	3d	Won
Repeat After Me	4	F	6	0	0	1	1,033
Repeated Blues	4	C	3	0	0	1	238
Repeatedly	4	F	7	1	0	0	4,092
Repeater Trooper	2	G	1	0	0	0	0
Repecci	4	G	19	3	1	2	13,355
Repent Again	2	G	1	0	0	0	0
Repete	4	G	5	0	0	0	990
Repido's Rascal	2	F	1	0	0	0	100
Replay	4	F	3	0	0	1	918
Repleted Prince	3	G	4	0	1	0	1,740
Repletions Victory	3	F	6	1	3	0	6,683
Replication	3	C	4	2	0	1	27,400
Replinka	7	M	13	3	1	4	26,729
Reply N Aces	3	F	4	1	1	0	5,740
Report	3	F	2	0	0	0	560
Report Dun	5	M	6	0	4	1	7,935
Report for Don	7	H	3	0	0	0	595
Report On Time	3	F	6	0	0	1	1,930
Report Stage	5	G	10	0	1	0	12,990
Report to All	4	G	13	2	1	1	46,760
Reporter	8	G	7	1	2	2	26,502
Reportorial	6	H	17	2	1	3	11,632
Repository	5	M	10	2	1	0	121,958
Reprehensible	5	G	4	0	0	0	136
Repriced Fame	6	M	9	0	0	2	7,726
Reprieve	5	G	11	0	0	0	114
Reprimand	3	C	6	0	3	2	26,310
Reprise	6	G	4	0	1	0	1,325
Reprized Angel	2	F	6	1	1	2	14,970
Reprized Doctor	4	G	8	0	1	2	4,930
Reprized Rebel	6	H	15	2	1	2	12,541
Reprized Romeo	5	H	5	0	0	0	437
Reprizedrullah	4	G	9	1	2	3	44,670
Reproof	7	G	10	3	1	1	14,060
Reptile	5	M	22	2	4	5	16,682
Republican Hawk	2	C	1	0	0	0	0
Republican Lady	3	F	3	0	1	0	5,208
Republicat	2	C	5	2	1	1	29,347
Repulse Bay	2	C	2	0	0	1	5,040
Repunzel's Knight	5	H	1	0	0	0	450
Reputable Norman	3	G	5	0	0	0	586
Reputare Two Win	3	G	9	0	0	0	545
Request	5	G	14	1	3	2	13,720
Request a Dance	3	C	12	0	0	1	5,280
Request a Star	12	G	6	0	1	0	2,660
Request All	3	F	2	0	0	0	0
Request Denied	2	F	5	1	1	1	13,340
Request for Parole	4	C	12	2	2	1	103,270
Request Granted	4	G	12	0	0	0	1,201
Request the Glory	3	G	7	0	1	4	4,505
Request the Magic	4	F	5	0	0	0	352
Requesto	4	C	9	2	2	0	73,205
Requestor	4	G	2	0	0	1	825
Requete (GB)	4	C	6	2	2	0	294,300
Requite	3	C	6	1	1	1	21,640
Reride	3	C	10	1	3	1	59,200
Rerun	4	G	13	1	1	0	11,017
Res Nullius	7	G	10	1	1	2	7,018
Resash	2	C	6	0	0	0	510
Rescue Five	3	F	7	1	2	0	34,720
Rescue One	3	C	9	2	0	1	13,025
Researched (IRE)	4	G	7	2	2	0	103,328
Reservations Only	4	C	7	1	1	1	28,061
Reserve Colonel	2	G	3	0	0	0	640
Reserve Fund	5	G	6	0	0	0	190
Reside and Abide	6	G	10	0	1	1	2,709
Resident Rogue	4	C	8	1	0	1	25,860
Residual	3	F	6	1	1	0	6,345
Residual Value	7	H	1	0	0	0	0
Resignation	6	G	11	1	1	1	8,227
Resistance	4	F	2	0	0	0	183
Resistant	5	G	9	0	0	1	4,813
Resisting	3	G	12	2	2	1	16,241
Resolve	5	G	3	1	1	0	50,800
Resolved	3	F	9	2	0	1	11,652
Resonant	3	F	3	0	0	0	5,278
Resounding Echo	4	G	8	2	0	1	14,607
Respect the Game	6	G	8	0	0	0	1,845
Respectabeau	2	C	10	0	1	1	11,300
Respectable Gal	3	F	17	1	4	3	31,590
Respectable Man	9	G	6	0	1	0	2,964
Respectful Tutu	5	M	5	1	0	2	3,480
Respectmyauthorita	4	F	12	4	3	1	54,862
Resplendence	3	G	6	0	2	2	14,345
Resplendency	2	F	3	1	1	0	37,520
Response Time	2	G	5	0	2	2	8,116
Repository	5	M	11	1	0	2	4,246
Restage	4	G	2	1	1	0	27,720
Restigouche	2	C	5	0	0	1	10,400
Resting Easy	8	M	10	1	1	2	14,076
Restitution	4	C	11	1	2	1	10,019
Restive	3	G	7	0	0	1	805
Restless Fever	4	F	13	3	2	1	18,046
Restless Flyer	4	C	3	0	0	0	261
Restless Halo	3	F	3	0	0	0	0
Restless Image	5	H	4	0	0	0	374
Restless Joshua	5	G	4	0	0	0	0
Restless Kind	5	M	12	0	3	4	12,294
Restless Luck	4	F	11	1	0	2	10,002
Restless Ruckus	6	M	1	0	0	0	0
Restless Slavic	3	C	5	0	1	0	2,520
Restless Sound	5	G	9	1	1	1	16,644
Restless Sunny	5	M	8	0	1	2	5,158
Restless Warrior	4	G	8	2	0	0	5,093
Restock	2	F	5	1	0	2	14,260
Restored Again	5	H	5	0	0	1	1,161
Restricted Access	5	M	9	1	0	3	5,756
Restrictions Apply	3	C	7	3	2	0	52,638
Resurgence	6	G	5	0	1	0	5,940
Resurrect	3	C	11	3	1	0	28,593
Resuscitate	5	H	2	0	0	0	0
Retail Sales	8	M	15	4	3	1	28,235
Retainer	5	G	9	2	0	3	10,039
Retaliation	6	G	9	1	1	2	24,512
Retaliator	4	G	8	1	2	2	6,472
Retam	3	G	9	2	1	0	69,460
Retardataire	3	C	2	0	0	0	2,520
Reta's Boy	3	G	5	0	0	0	61
Retention Bonus	2	C	5	0	0	0	200
Retinaculum	2	C	1	0	0	0	176
Retired Habit	6	G	1	1	0	0	40,560
Retirees Three	3	G	10	2	4	0	52,627
Retirement Gift	4	G	11	1	1	4	11,275
Retirement Plan	2	C	2	0	0	0	0
Retrial	3	F	6	1	0	0	10,710
Retrieve the Gold	3	F	17	1	4	1	25,929
Retro Fever	6	G	11	0	1	3	4,513
Retro Red	7	G	13	4	3	1	26,440
Retroactive	3	F	7	3	0	2	107,250
Retrogressive	6	M	11	3	2	0	12,955
Retsina Year	6	G	11	1	3	1	22,780
Return Daily	4	F	5	1	2	0	1,693
Return Flight	3	F	3	0	0	0	637
Return of the Mac	2	C	8	0	1	3	8,960
Return To	4	G	15	0	4	1	11,462
Reuben	6	H	9	1	2	1	29,536
Reuben's Rocket	6	G	8	0	1	1	9,948
Reunion Star	3	F	7	0	1	2	9,889
Reunite	5	G	8	0	0	0	1,136
Revalee	4	G	9	0	1	1	9,440
Revancha	3	F	16	3	2	1	26,925
Reva's Prince	3	G	3	1	0	0	7,499
Revcan	3	F	5	0	0	0	455
Reve D' Amazon	4	F	12	2	6	2	23,784
Reve d'Enfance	3	C	3	0	0	0	2,195
Reve Ryder	4	C	10	0	1	1	6,397
Reveal the Star	4	G	16	1	3	3	17,977
Revealing Blush	2	F	6	1	2	1	19,220
Revealing Slew	3	F	1	0	0	1	1,280
Revello	5	G	7	1	1	2	60,325
Revenal	2	G	3	1	0	0	3,440
Revenant	8	H	5	0	0	1	816
Revenante	4	F	2	0	1	0	16,200
Revenescent	5	H	3	0	1	0	11,200
Revenged	5	G	15	5	1	2	11,642
Revenue	8	G	16	6	2	3	10,339
Reverberation	2	F	4	0	0	0	205
Revered Judge	4	G	15	2	1	1	16,030

Horse	Age	Sex	Sts	1st	2d	3d	Won
Revered Scholar	3	C	5	0	0	1	6,650
Revered Soldier	4	C	3	0	0	0	1,500
Reverence	3	F	8	0	1	1	16,370
Reverend Jim	5	G	4	0	1	1	700
Reverend Rob	4	G	1	0	0	0	0
Reverend Swede	9	G	2	0	0	0	0
Reverend Woodard	4	C	3	0	0	0	191
Reverent American	3	G	10	1	3	2	21,000
Reverse Acquittal	4	G	10	0	0	2	4,470
Reverse Psychology	4	G	7	3	1	0	68,835
Reveur Belle	2	F	1	0	0	0	180
Review the List	2	C	1	0	0	0	0
Revillew Slew	7	M	5	1	0	0	17,540
Revington	5	G	7	3	0	2	19,390
Revised Note	4	C	2	0	0	0	0
Revision	4	F	17	1	1	0	10,890
Rev'n Evan	3	C	1	0	0	0	0
Revo (IRE)	4	C	1	0	0	0	0
Revolution Boy	3	G	14	0	0	1	2,150
Revolutionary	6	M	5	1	0	0	2,580
Revolutionize	3	C	3	0	0	0	0
Revolver	4	C	4	0	0	0	944
Revolver Six	2	C	1	0	0	0	0
Revolver Two	3	C	9	0	0	0	3,000
Revved Up	5	G	5	1	2	0	119,816
Rewire	4	G	15	2	2	1	11,070
Rexsonhopeprospect	2	G	7	0	0	0	1,215
Rey Sol	3	C	12	1	1	2	21,210
Reynoldsrap	3	C	9	1	1	1	18,854
Rez Runner	2	C	4	1	1	0	4,015
Rhapsody Red	2	F	2	0	1	0	1,400
Rheaxthus	5	G	8	1	0	2	19,282
Rhenium (IRE)	6	H	2	0	0	1	16,978
Rhetoric Express	4	G	11	4	1	0	94,290
Rhetorical	7	G	3	0	1	0	2,700
Rhett Henry	4	C	8	2	0	2	11,580
Rhiana	6	M	10	0	3	1	108,642
Rhiannon's Wish	3	F	5	1	2	1	36,772
Rhinestone Falls	3	G	2	0	0	0	0
Rhinestone Rita	4	F	9	1	0	3	5,123
Rhino Chaser	2	C	5	1	1	2	22,700
Rhodesian Storm	5	G	8	0	1	2	26,314
Rhodezone	11	G	8	1	0	1	2,406
Rhodif	2	C	2	1	0	0	9,720
Rhodilite Gold	3	C	1	0	0	0	0
Rhonda Del Cielo	3	F	10	1	1	0	8,829
Rhonda's Number	2	F	1	0	0	0	2,460
Rhonda's Rollin'	3	F	6	0	1	0	8,935
Rhonesquarterswish	8	G	3	2	0	1	46,420
Rhumb Line	3	F	7	3	0	1	96,074
Rhumjar	3	G	4	1	0	2	38,840
Rhydon	4	C	7	2	1	1	29,520
Rhyeliz	5	M	11	0	0	0	1,142
Rhyme	7	G	11	2	1	1	6,374
Rhyme Time	2	F	7	1	1	0	5,730
Rhyolite	4	G	13	0	1	0	4,280
Rhythm and Bloom	5	M	12	0	2	0	6,946
Rhythm Down Below	4	F	13	1	8	2	28,735
Rhythm in Shoes	3	F	8	2	1	1	38,431
Rhythm n' Roses	3	F	3	0	0	0	0
Rhythm of Life (GB)	4	F	6	2	0	0	71,560
Rhythmair	5	H	7	0	3	2	5,884
Rhythmic River	5	M	6	0	2	1	3,537
Rhythm'n Gold	4	F	3	1	0	1	12,176
Rhythmn Magic	4	F	13	2	0	3	25,125
Rhythm's Answer	3	C	1	0	0	0	0
Rhythm's Love	4	F	10	1	2	1	26,030
Riabs Radar	3	G	1	0	0	1	100
Rial Jersey	4	G	12	1	3	1	12,776
Rial Sea	6	G	14	1	3	0	2,276
Ria's Little Angel	5	M	10	0	1	1	5,563
Riata Goldrush	6	G	14	0	4	0	10,829
Riband	7	M	10	4	2	0	48,131
Ribbon Cane	4	F	5	3	1	0	97,808
Ribbon of Darkness	2	C	4	1	0	0	11,314
Ribockys Falstaff	6	G	7	0	0	1	896
Ribomoon	2	G	1	0	0	0	0
Ribot Line	6	G	9	0	2	2	11,449
Rican	3	G	7	1	1	1	7,525
Ricardo A	4	C	12	4	3	1	67,315
Ricardo Sioux	3	C	2	1	1	0	11,000
Ricco Cat	2	G	5	1	0	0	7,538
Rice and Beans	6	G	7	1	0	1	3,370
Rich and Happy	5	M	7	0	1	4	3,742
Rich and Lucky	6	M	16	3	4	3	25,440
Rich and Sassy	2	F	5	1	1	0	8,215
Rich as Croesus	3	C	2	0	2	0	7,215
Rich Assertion	4	F	4	1	0	2	60,762
Rich Bid	4	C	1	0	0	0	0
Rich Bon Bon	6	H	2	0	0	0	0
Rich Celebration	6	G	15	2	5	0	27,365
Rich City Girl	3	F	3	2	1	0	40,000
Rich Coins	5	H	17	1	4	4	38,335
Rich Dancer	3	C	9	0	0	0	720
Rich Deeds	5	H	16	0	0	5	12,428
Rich Desire	4	G	21	2	3	2	20,533
Rich Dixie	2	F	3	0	1	0	1,570
Rich Domino	5	M	4	0	0	0	2,025
Rich Dude	7	G	2	0	0	0	110
Rich Expression	4	F	9	3	0	1	22,594
Rich Fidler	3	G	10	1	2	0	10,992
Rich Find	2	F	3	1	0	0	16,005
Rich Flight	5	G	4	0	0	0	815
Rich Guarani	2	G	5	0	0	2	7,860
Rich Happiness	4	F	12	0	2	2	14,755
Rich in Dallas	8	G	10	1	1	3	6,511
Rich in Discretion	2	C	4	0	1	0	1,180
Rich in Love	4	F	7	0	4	0	17,430
Rich K M	3	C	3	0	0	0	60
Rich Kidd	7	G	3	0	0	0	384
Rich Lad	9	G	8	1	0	4	5,810
Rich Lady Anne	2	F	2	1	0	0	16,314
Rich Lode	4	F	7	1	2	2	5,326
Rich Machine	6	G	12	1	1	1	4,692
Rich March	5	G	13	0	1	2	11,850
Rich Max	3	C	3	0	1	0	7,160
Rich Mist	6	M	10	0	2	4	62,074
Rich Mover	3	C	6	0	0	0	1,245
Rich Musique	4	F	7	3	0	2	93,830
Rich Mystic	6	G	8	0	0	0	506
Rich Pal	3	C	5	1	0	0	3,792
Rich Peace	5	M	9	0	0	2	8,340
Rich Scent	5	M	10	0	2	0	3,442
Rich Search	5	M	7	4	0	0	45,665
Rich Secret	5	H	17	3	1	3	22,423
Rich Silver Swan	4	G	17	1	1	1	8,835
Rich Tone	3	C	7	3	0	1	20,237
Rich Tradition	3	C	10	2	1	1	10,410
Rich Vein (IRE)	6	H	2	0	0	0	0
Rich World	2	G	1	0	0	0	75
Richard the First	3	G	4	1	0	0	15,600
Richard's Boy	3	G	10	1	0	3	17,153
Richard's Delight	9	G	10	0	0	0	518
Richard's Dream	5	G	2	0	0	0	225
Richard's Love	7	M	3	0	0	0	90
Richardsawesomstar	4	F	11	2	2	1	10,879
Richesse's Lady	4	F	1	0	0	0	0
Richest Half	4	C	2	1	0	0	20,400
Richetta	2	F	6	4	0	1	168,110
Richierichierich	4	C	8	2	1	1	33,940
Richie's Cat	2	F	5	0	0	1	6,410
Richie's Reward	4	G	5	0	1	0	1,584
Richillini	5	G	13	0	3	2	10,547
Richjohnguy	3	G	4	0	0	0	0
Richland Holme	6	H	7	3	0	0	29,702
Richland Rebel	4	C	8	0	0	3	2,946
Richly Inflated	6	M	10	1	0	0	10,482
Richmond Rowdy	7	G	14	2	4	1	5,165
Rich'n Restless	5	M	7	0	1	0	4,465
Richochet	2	C	1	0	0	0	2,700
Rich's Breanna	6	M	5	0	0	0	0
Rich's Glory	4	G	9	0	1	0	1,972
Richter's Emblem	4	F	11	4	0	0	60,138
Richtsmeier	8	G	2	0	0	0	150
Richwood Girl	4	F	2	0	0	0	82
Richwood Rebel	6	G	10	2	1	2	31,725
Richwood Royal	2	F	1	0	0	0	0
Rickenbacker	2	G	2	0	1	1	4,350

Horse	Age	Sex	Sts	1st	2d	3d	Won
Rickety's Revenge	5	M	10	0	0	0	1,210
Ricki Power	7	M	1	0	0	0	0
Rick's Gold	5	H	2	0	0	0	368
Rick's Kick	5	H	4	0	1	0	1,210
Rick's Lad	2	G	1	0	0	0	204
Ricks Little Music	6	M	14	3	0	3	14,455
Ricks Mistress	2	F	3	0	0	0	264
Ricks Rascal	6	G	6	1	3	1	13,065
Rick's Reason	5	M	1	0	0	0	53
Ricky Gold	7	H	9	1	1	1	5,781
Ricky N Chip	4	G	7	1	1	1	12,914
Ricky Roma	2	C	1	0	0	0	0
Rico Ends Well	5	M	16	1	2	4	46,383
Rico Fighter (BRZ)	8	G	8	2	3	2	21,853
Rico Suave	9	G	6	0	0	2	1,073
Ricoboy	3	G	5	0	1	3	4,312
Ridacin	4	C	1	0	0	0	0
Ridan South	3	F	5	1	1	1	8,975
Ridan's Mon	4	F	6	2	2	0	56,460
Riddell's Creek	7	G	15	0	3	1	28,593
Riddle	2	C	3	0	1	0	9,200
Riddlesdown (IRE)	6	H	3	1	0	0	66,000
Riddling	3	F	5	0	0	1	810
Ride and Shine	6	G	18	1	3	3	143,669
Ride 'Em Rags	7	G	13	2	6	4	63,680
Ride Her Out	2	F	5	2	2	0	126,550
Ride Now	2	F	2	1	0	0	8,790
Ride of Your Dream	4	F	1	0	0	0	100
Ride On	3	G	5	0	2	0	8,540
Ride On J T	4	G	9	2	1	0	8,794
Ride the Light	6	G	12	3	2	0	50,256
Ride the Tiger	4	G	5	1	0	0	6,435
Ride the Wild Wind	2	F	2	0	0	1	1,980
Ride to Riches	2	C	1	0	1	0	1,900
Ride With Rythym	4	G	14	1	2	0	45,443
Rideintothenight	7	G	10	0	2	2	5,036
Riderwood	4	G	11	1	2	4	12,270
Ridge Above	3	C	9	1	1	3	6,204
Ridge Court Lady	4	F	10	2	1	4	20,260
Ridge Jumper	3	G	6	0	0	0	2,781
Ridge Racer	6	G	1	0	0	0	0
Ridge Runner (GB)	5	G	7	1	0	1	13,915
Ridgecrest	3	F	2	1	1	0	4,160
Ridged Appeal	7	M	8	0	0	0	507
Ridgefinder	5	M	4	0	1	1	3,658
Ridge's Boy	3	C	1	0	0	0	95
Ridgevalley	2	G	2	0	0	0	3,528
Ridgeway Circle	4	G	3	0	1	0	1,320
Ridgeway Dancer	5	H	14	0	1	2	7,452
Ridgeways Attitude	4	F	2	0	0	0	182
Ridgeways Charmer	4	C	9	0	0	1	3,267
Ridin the Blues	4	C	8	1	0	1	8,280
Riding	3	F	15	1	1	0	10,719
Riding the Waves	5	M	3	0	0	0	344
Ridingtherapids	3	G	9	1	2	1	11,535
Riel	4	F	1	0	0	0	0
Rienzi	3	C	3	1	0	1	6,255
Rifle Woman	4	F	10	1	3	4	16,360
Rigel	3	C	11	2	0	2	11,141
Riggin Lady	6	M	6	1	0	2	4,641
Riggo	5	G	16	2	3	3	35,610
Right Angle	4	G	4	0	0	0	720
Right Answer	3	F	1	0	0	0	0
Right At Home	4	F	15	2	4	3	18,450
Right Back Atcha	3	F	6	0	0	1	3,115
Right Decision	5	H	5	0	1	1	1,800
Right Direction	3	F	12	2	3	1	36,025
Right Girls Star	7	G	23	2	0	4	13,932
Right Here (IRE)	4	F	2	0	0	1	4,340
Right Hero	3	C	13	1	2	0	9,680
Right Lane	4	F	14	1	4	2	22,633
Right Moves	5	G	3	0	0	0	179
Right Nice	2	C	1	0	0	0	993
Right On Jeeves	4	G	9	1	0	1	5,301
Right On Lil	4	F	6	0	0	0	990
Right On Target	5	H	14	1	1	1	4,502
Right On the Hour	3	F	11	2	3	0	29,718
Right On the Line	3	C	11	2	0	5	19,700
Right On the Mark	9	G	6	1	1	1	10,575

Horse	Age	Sex	Sts	1st	2d	3d	Won
Right Opportunity	4	G	14	1	1	3	7,900
Right Out Ro	3	F	9	0	1	3	27,880
Right Proof	3	G	9	2	1	2	89,240
Right Return	5	G	11	2	3	3	19,075
Right Revved	9	G	9	4	1	0	29,755
Right Stop	5	G	9	2	2	2	67,796
Right to Run	2	G	3	0	0	0	1,050
Right too Refuse	4	C	15	4	4	1	101,410
Right Uppercut	3	G	12	0	4	1	19,720
Right You Are	3	G	10	1	2	1	14,900
Rightbyu	4	F	13	6	3	1	45,315
Righteous Desire	5	G	13	2	2	0	3,397
Righteous Struggle	4	C	12	2	3	0	36,030
Righteous Witness	2	C	1	0	0	0	370
Rightly Served	7	H	6	0	0	1	870
Rights Reserved	3	G	8	0	1	1	22,810
Rightside	3	C	11	0	0	1	3,020
Rigid Spur	6	H	7	1	0	0	6,450
Rigney	5	G	11	2	1	3	19,351
Riker	8	G	7	0	3	1	5,105
Rikers Island	4	G	14	2	1	0	11,429
Riki Ricardo	3	G	7	1	1	0	10,768
Riley City	4	G	11	0	1	0	2,610
Riley Irish	4	C	15	1	1	3	6,672
Riley J.	3	C	1	0	0	0	0
Riley James	5	G	14	2	5	3	9,958
Riley P. Moran	5	G	4	0	0	0	1,815
Riley Run	3	G	4	0	2	1	6,175
Riley World	3	C	13	3	1	2	10,408
Rileys Knight	2	G	5	0	2	1	3,348
Rileys Orbit	2	G	1	0	0	0	700
Rileys Ransom	3	C	8	0	0	0	2,240
Rileys Silver	3	F	7	1	2	1	7,381
Rileys Stuff	3	C	4	0	1	0	369
Rileys Turn	2	G	1	0	0	0	0
Rim Dancer	8	G	10	1	0	1	18,311
Rimfire's Thunder	5	G	7	2	1	0	20,700
Rimsky Korsakov	9	G	5	1	1	1	27,550
Rindanica	3	C	10	4	1	4	135,678
Rines Lil Attitude	5	M	7	0	0	0	1,260
Ring Bearer	3	G	8	1	1	1	38,050
Ring Fast	4	G	4	0	0	1	1,146
Ring of Friendship	3	G	2	0	1	0	4,200
Ring of Gold	2	F	4	1	0	0	5,700
Ring of Power	3	C	9	0	2	2	14,950
Ring of Reality	4	C	7	0	0	1	1,345
Ring of Stars	2	F	5	0	1	1	5,900
Ring of Thunder	4	F	13	1	2	3	19,950
Ring Ring	4	F	7	1	0	0	3,120
Ring the Witness	2	G	3	0	0	0	913
Ring Toss	5	G	4	1	1	1	11,052
Ringading	3	F	2	0	0	1	3,000
Ringadingding	4	G	5	0	0	0	1,220
Ringaling	4	F	14	1	2	0	20,890
Ringaring a Rosie	2	F	6	0	1	2	11,670
Ringaroundarosie	3	F	8	1	2	4	26,320
Ringgold Gap	4	C	10	2	2	3	15,892
Ringing Echo	4	F	10	1	4	2	32,220
Ringing Rock	3	C	5	0	1	0	4,455
Ringold	2	C	2	1	1	0	17,820
Ringo's Star	5	G	5	0	0	0	275
Rings and Things	2	F	3	1	1	0	40,590
Rings Ov Jade	2	G	4	0	0	1	1,853
Ringside Dream	4	G	3	0	0	1	435
Ringside Rhythm	5	G	3	0	0	1	720
Ringside Rumor	4	G	4	0	1	0	1,871
Ringthatbellagain	4	F	5	1	1	0	22,242
Rinka Bell	4	F	12	1	2	1	9,889
Rinka Dazzle	5	M	5	0	0	0	260
Rinka Jayne	2	F	4	0	1	0	3,060
Rinka Myth	3	G	14	1	1	4	11,614
Rinkatink	4	C	5	0	1	0	7,046
Rinkette	4	F	6	0	0	1	425
Rinky Dinky Do	4	C	5	0	0	2	5,389
Rio Cheep	4	G	19	2	0	2	3,320
Rio de Esperanza	5	G	15	1	4	1	24,295
Rio de Oro	4	F	1	0	0	0	0
Rio Dee Grande	6	G	8	1	1	4	25,756
Rio Diazo	6	H	2	0	0	0	0

Horse	Age	Sex	Sts	1st	2d	3d	Won
Rio Dorado	3	C	1	0	0	0	0
Rio Frio	4	C	4	0	0	1	750
Rio Gaza Montado	2	F	1	0	0	1	936
Rio Gold	5	H	6	1	0	0	8,811
Rio Grande Scandal	3	G	7	1	2	0	13,090
Rio Handfull	4	G	16	0	0	0	812
Rio Listo	3	G	6	1	0	0	5,838
Rio Man	2	G	3	0	0	0	74
Rio Neata	6	M	13	4	3	2	7,082
Rio Precious	5	M	4	0	0	0	200
Rio Reyes	3	G	9	2	2	1	41,600
Rio Rhythm	3	F	1	0	1	0	2,400
Rio River Rose	6	M	13	0	0	0	1,260
Rio Rocket	5	G	5	0	0	0	422
Rio Rosa	3	F	3	0	1	0	2,475
Rio Ruckus	2	G	1	0	0	0	0
Rio Sage	4	G	15	1	1	2	7,153
Rio Yelcho	5	M	11	1	1	1	4,731
Riomaimah	2	F	1	0	0	0	0
Rio's Chase	4	G	5	0	0	1	8,250
Rio's Rocket Man	4	G	7	0	0	0	214
Rio's World	4	F	2	0	0	0	140
Riot Gear	6	H	2	0	0	0	150
Riotous Miss	8	M	10	1	2	0	25,190
Riotous Red	3	G	14	1	1	1	6,771
Riot's Rebel	2	G	6	1	0	2	10,045
Rip an Zip Blaze	3	G	5	0	0	0	316
Rip N Out	2	C	1	0	0	0	126
Rip n' Roar	3	C	1	0	0	0	95
Rip N Snort	3	C	2	0	0	0	181
Rip Roaring Rhythm	5	M	3	0	0	0	186
Rip Roar'n Rita	6	M	10	2	2	2	14,493
Rip the Halo	3	F	3	0	0	0	0
Ripley	3	G	8	1	0	4	20,326
Rippen Away	6	G	2	0	0	0	0
Rippin N Roarin	4	C	2	0	0	1	4,200
Rippled Effect	3	F	1	0	0	0	0
Rippling Return	5	M	3	0	0	0	1,820
Riproaring Ride	4	C	8	1	0	2	11,260
Ripsaw	4	G	15	3	3	0	28,262
Rischio	4	C	6	0	0	1	2,920
Rise and Conquer	3	C	8	2	1	2	21,090
Rise and Fall	3	F	1	1	0	0	9,600
Rise and Smile	2	G	7	0	0	0	760
Rise Ball	5	G	7	1	0	0	3,707
Rise to Glory	8	G	17	0	4	2	6,985
Rise to Roar	3	F	9	1	0	2	10,020
Risen Creek	2	G	2	0	0	0	390
Risen Dancer	7	G	2	0	0	0	0
Risen Majesty	4	F	1	0	0	0	0
Risen Ruckus	5	G	7	0	0	1	1,311
Risen Ruler	5	G	4	1	0	0	6,651
Risen Warrior	7	G	11	1	2	2	27,950
Riserbee	4	C	1	0	0	0	100
Rising Account	5	M	7	1	1	0	5,779
Rising Agenda	4	F	8	1	1	0	3,496
Rising Artax	2	C	2	0	0	0	120
Rising Buck	4	C	3	0	0	0	0
Rising Gold Mine	3	C	1	0	0	0	28
Rising Promise	5	M	8	1	0	0	3,636
Rising Queen	4	F	11	3	1	4	42,705
Rising Rhythm	5	M	10	1	3	2	18,600
Rising Speed	4	G	9	2	1	0	18,350
Rising Tide	2	F	2	1	0	0	22,290
Risk and Return	3	C	1	0	0	1	4,620
Risk and Reward	4	C	10	4	0	2	57,902
Risk de Carr	2	F	1	0	0	0	80
Risk Free Rate	4	C	13	1	2	1	5,096
Risk It	4	F	16	2	4	1	9,478
Risk of Flight	2	C	4	0	2	2	12,420
Risk Reward	3	G	13	1	3	2	43,600
Risk Seeker	5	G	2	1	0	0	1,625
Riskaverse	4	F	8	2	1	2	336,324
Riskey Scheme	4	F	12	0	5	1	5,113
Risky Affair	2	C	3	0	0	1	1,130
Risky Bet	4	G	12	0	2	3	8,545
Risky Bid	6	H	11	0	1	3	5,529
Risky Bluff	2	G	4	0	0	1	4,728
Risky Cat	3	C	8	0	0	1	15,050

Horse	Age	Sex	Sts	1st	2d	3d	Won
Risky Darlene	3	F	8	0	0	0	1,877
Risky Doc	4	G	21	3	2	3	11,794
Risky Endeavor	3	F	6	1	1	0	17,840
Risky Fox	5	M	3	0	0	0	0
Risky Kitten	3	F	8	1	0	0	18,374
Risky Looking	2	F	2	0	0	0	757
Risky Mover	3	C	16	1	3	0	8,485
Risky Notion	4	F	7	1	0	2	22,330
Risky Occupation	5	G	3	0	0	0	642
Risky Pam	4	F	9	0	1	0	3,390
Risky Rascal	4	G	8	0	0	0	2,430
Risky Ruth	3	F	4	0	0	1	2,390
Risky Sham	6	G	16	0	0	6	5,570
Risky Starlett	5	M	3	0	0	0	0
Risky Stretch	5	M	6	1	2	0	8,363
Risky Trick	2	C	3	1	1	0	32,800
Risky Voyage	6	M	1	0	0	0	150
Risky Weather	2	C	4	0	0	0	3,300
Risotto	4	F	6	2	2	1	44,900
Risque Centerfold	2	F	8	1	1	0	20,720
Risque Copy	4	F	8	0	1	0	2,085
Risque Number	3	F	1	0	0	0	500
Risque'betty	4	F	14	3	2	0	27,805
Ristra	4	F	2	0	0	0	0
Rita's Cargo	5	M	2	0	0	0	0
Rita's Dancer	2	F	2	0	0	0	204
Rita's Defense	5	G	4	0	0	1	1,084
Rita's Ensignette	5	M	5	0	0	1	1,010
Rita's Grace	3	F	5	1	0	0	10,825
Rita's Partner	5	H	4	1	0	0	3,930
Rita's Picc	5	H	17	1	1	3	19,535
Rita's Royale	2	G	1	1	0	0	880
Rita's Ruthie	7	M	10	1	2	1	10,894
Rita's the One	3	F	17	3	4	2	56,400
Riteonkey	4	G	6	1	1	1	2,890
Ritz of Natal	7	M	4	0	0	0	0
Ritzy Dame	3	F	13	3	4	1	62,606
Ritzy Revue	2	C	7	1	1	1	6,034
Ritzy Teaser	8	G	5	1	0	1	1,325
Riv Orphelin	4	F	8	1	1	0	16,207
Riva Tango	3	F	9	1	2	0	13,230
Riva Way	5	G	8	4	0	1	28,505
Rivalry	9	G	13	1	2	2	7,610
Rivas	3	G	4	1	0	1	4,275
Riva's Affair	5	M	10	1	3	0	8,618
Riva's Image	2	C	3	0	0	0	360
Riva's River Rat	2	C	1	0	0	0	0
Riva's Tribute	4	G	6	0	1	1	23,093
Rivaz's Tour	4	F	2	0	0	0	108
River Adventure (BRZ)	3	G	8	1	0	0	18,720
River Angel	4	F	10	0	0	1	1,707
River Baron	3	C	5	1	3	0	6,680
River Bed	6	G	8	3	3	0	40,560
River Boat	10	G	6	1	0	1	18,625
River Bottom	4	G	16	1	1	0	7,097
River Bridge (FR)	8	M	8	2	2	1	73,200
River Cha Ching	2	G	4	3	0	0	21,600
River City Bert	3	G	8	2	1	0	25,110
River City Lady	4	F	7	1	0	0	4,197
River Course	5	G	4	0	0	0	193
River Cruise	3	F	8	3	3	0	139,160
River Cry	8	M	9	1	0	0	2,335
River Dandy	8	G	5	0	1	1	4,142
River Date	5	M	8	0	1	0	2,273
River Delights	7	G	7	0	0	1	6,270
River Diamond	3	F	3	0	0	0	225
River Eagle	3	C	2	0	0	0	1,660
River Ella	3	F	15	0	7	3	50,672
River Flower	5	M	6	2	3	0	67,090
River Freeze	10	G	3	0	0	0	206
River Getaway	3	G	5	1	0	2	7,630
River Girl's Boy	6	G	9	2	1	1	6,757
River God	5	H	3	2	0	0	79,020
River Hills Cat	4	F	12	1	1	3	5,481
River House	3	F	5	1	0	1	4,648
River Image	10	H	4	0	0	0	555
River Kwai	2	F	2	0	0	0	1,045
River Landing	8	H	13	0	1	1	2,771
River Legend	2	C	6	0	0	0	2,490

Horse	Age	Sex	Sts	1st	2d	3d	Won
River Lights	2	C	2	0	0	0	2,800
River Mine	7	H	8	0	0	0	757
River Miss	4	F	3	0	0	0	0
River Mo	5	G	8	0	0	0	450
River Monster	4	C	12	1	1	3	35,785
River Mount	4	G	6	0	1	0	5,760
River Mountain Rd	3	C	4	2	1	0	43,200
River of Daylite	4	F	4	0	0	0	345
River of Time	3	C	7	0	0	0	0
River Otter	5	G	14	2	5	0	27,725
River Power	5	H	11	1	4	2	65,968
River Raft	2	F	2	0	1	1	3,360
River Rammer	3	C	17	8	0	2	58,385
River Raven (GB)	5	G	16	4	2	4	34,484
River Reed	4	G	11	1	0	1	10,743
River Rennen	4	G	11	2	4	1	19,077
River Retreat	2	C	2	0	1	0	2,800
River Rhapsody	4	G	12	0	1	2	4,002
River Road Gal	4	F	5	0	0	0	228
River Run	4	G	9	1	2	3	24,438
River Salt	5	M	2	0	0	1	4,730
River Sass	8	H	2	0	1	0	4,300
River Side Drive	6	H	3	0	0	0	476
River Singer	3	G	7	1	0	0	5,700
River Smile	2	G	1	0	0	0	495
River Spirit	5	G	8	0	3	0	16,080
River Styx	5	H	10	0	1	2	3,290
River Surprise	6	M	3	0	0	0	88
River to Heaven	6	H	3	0	0	0	150
River Valley Lass	5	M	3	0	0	0	440
River Walk Bob	3	G	11	3	2	1	49,538
River Walker	2	C	7	1	1	1	35,370
River West	3	G	7	1	0	2	10,452
River Wild	9	G	11	2	0	3	28,049
River Zuppardo	9	M	18	3	2	4	36,322
Riverblack	11	G	8	0	0	0	0
Riverboat Casino	3	F	1	1	0	0	28,800
Riverboat Dan	10	G	1	0	0	0	66
Riverboat Party	5	G	11	0	0	1	1,061
Riverboat Surprize	3	G	9	0	1	1	2,014
Riverby Britishboy	4	G	6	1	1	0	7,355
Riverby Remenising	4	C	12	1	0	1	2,700
Riverbye Girl	3	F	13	1	0	0	6,247
Riverbye's Frosty	6	M	6	1	1	0	2,985
Rivercard	3	C	11	2	2	0	33,250
Riverdance Tour	4	G	19	3	1	4	43,003
Riverdancing	6	G	3	1	0	1	4,118
Riverdock Road	3	C	10	2	0	2	4,043
Rivergirls Runaway	2	F	2	1	1	0	10,080
Rivergirlspartyboy	3	G	2	0	0	0	0
Riveriarose	5	G	7	0	0	0	559
Riverman Dancer	2	G	1	0	0	0	0
Riverman's Tea	6	M	3	0	0	1	2,819
Rivermaster	2	G	6	1	0	3	37,160
Riverplay	4	C	1	0	0	0	0
Rivers Flagman	4	C	11	0	1	0	1,685
River's Solution	4	F	3	0	0	0	0
Rivershade	9	H	12	1	1	3	5,224
Riverside	8	H	6	1	1	0	6,522
Riverside Flight	3	C	11	1	2	1	6,764
Riverside Magic	2	F	8	0	1	0	1,730
Riverside Mystro	7	G	8	1	1	1	5,580
Riverside Rebel	3	G	1	0	0	0	150
Riverstar	3	G	7	1	0	0	7,830
Riveter	9	H	2	0	0	0	0
Rivets	6	H	12	4	2	3	27,638
Riviera	2	C	2	1	1	0	25,050
Riviera Dance	3	C	9	1	1	0	9,910
Riviera Kate	5	M	4	2	0	1	8,350
Rivulet	3	F	4	0	0	0	337
Rize	7	G	2	0	0	0	530
Rizen	4	F	11	0	1	3	8,987
Rizzado	2	G	3	0	0	0	305
Rizzaletta	3	F	4	1	0	0	12,450
Rizzen to Victory	2	G	5	1	1	2	15,850
Rizzi Bea	2	F	3	0	0	0	365
Rizzi Dancer	2	F	1	0	0	0	120
Rizzi Girl	5	M	15	3	3	2	46,511
Rizzi Lee	2	C	9	2	2	1	38,940
Rizzi This	2	C	9	1	1	1	15,280
Rizzis Brass Band	2	C	5	0	0	0	0
Rizzizzi	3	G	8	3	2	0	31,350
Rkatiwantsafastone	3	F	5	0	0	1	669
Ro Day Scious	2	C	9	1	2	1	48,410
Ro Ro	2	F	1	0	0	0	0
Road Afleet	5	G	12	1	2	3	46,390
Road Builder	2	C	5	0	1	1	10,470
Road Closed	5	M	13	2	0	0	20,760
Road Express	3	G	16	2	0	2	19,670
Road Flare	4	G	7	1	2	3	6,200
Road Games	6	M	15	2	4	0	4,905
Road Goesonforever	4	G	4	0	0	1	928
Road Grader	4	G	7	0	0	2	3,362
Road Hazard	3	G	4	0	0	0	1,500
Road Queen	5	M	10	1	0	2	7,895
Road Race	2	C	1	0	1	0	2,340
Road Ruhler	4	G	9	3	2	0	20,190
Road Runner Jr.	3	G	4	1	1	1	2,560
Road Test	4	G	12	0	3	1	6,971
Road to Honor	2	F	2	0	0	1	1,345
Road To Justice (GB)	4	G	12	3	0	3	23,345
Road to Kisses	5	M	13	1	0	2	8,844
Road to Mandalay	2	F	3	1	0	0	35,280
Road to Mortlock	3	C	4	0	1	0	6,200
Road to Power	3	C	13	1	1	1	12,325
Road to Recovery	2	G	2	0	0	0	1,130
Road to Slew	8	G	2	1	0	1	73,020
Road to the Castle	2	G	7	0	2	1	8,020
Road Town	3	G	3	0	0	0	840
Roada Ghost	3	F	6	2	0	1	6,275
Roadaway	7	G	8	1	0	0	2,220
Roadhouse Rose	3	F	2	0	0	0	450
Roadhouse Rosie	2	F	2	0	0	0	185
Roadrageous	4	G	3	0	0	0	476
Roads West	3	G	2	0	0	1	2,925
Roadside	11	G	1	0	0	0	138
Roadsideattraction	2	F	4	1	0	1	12,155
Roadsider	2	F	4	0	0	0	0
Roaming Back	4	F	11	1	1	2	12,515
Roan	3	F	13	1	2	2	9,466
Roan Chala Two	4	F	5	1	0	1	4,260
Roan Havoc	3	F	4	1	2	0	4,770
Roan Mountain	3	C	3	0	0	0	0
Roan Remark	6	G	3	0	0	0	130
Roan to Run	4	F	5	0	0	0	805
Roanoke Ridge	3	C	9	2	1	0	22,267
Roanoke River Rain	6	H	8	1	1	1	17,100
Roanoke Snap	4	F	7	1	0	1	5,043
Roar and Reign	7	G	18	1	2	2	14,257
Roar Ashore	2	F	2	1	0	0	6,000
Roar Away	2	G	3	0	0	1	2,580
Roar Emotion	3	F	3	1	1	0	150,660
Roar in the Night	6	H	4	0	0	0	88
Roar Madness	3	F	13	3	3	2	34,137
Roar of Africa	2	F	2	0	0	0	2,100
Roar of the Lion	2	G	1	0	0	0	0
Roar of the Tiger	4	C	1	1	0	0	19,200
Roar On Tour	3	G	14	5	0	3	56,336
Roar to Score	4	G	12	1	3	5	16,497
Roarin Brittney	2	F	2	1	0	0	7,200
Roarin' Gently	3	C	2	0	0	0	150
Roaring Along	2	C	3	2	0	0	24,570
Roaring Beauty	2	F	3	0	1	0	4,600
Roaring Dori	3	G	10	0	2	4	7,442
Roaring Fever	3	C	6	2	1	1	75,040
Roaring Icon	3	F	9	2	1	0	8,134
Roaring Jade	5	M	7	1	3	0	14,326
Roaring Mike	6	G	2	0	0	0	93
Roaring Power	2	F	1	0	0	0	375
Roaring Rage	5	M	14	3	0	2	29,794
Roaring Rapids	3	G	11	1	0	1	16,240
Roaring Springs	2	G	2	0	1	0	3,400
Roark	4	G	11	2	1	2	40,922
Roarofvictory	2	C	4	0	0	0	0
Roaronthunder	4	G	6	0	0	0	447
Roarzak	4	G	14	3	2	2	32,153
Roast Beef	5	M	2	0	0	0	274
Rob Bob	7	G	14	1	4	0	6,639

Horse	Age	Sex	Sts	1st	2d	3d	Won	Horse	Age	Sex	Sts	1st	2d	3d	Won
Rob Cat	4	C	2	0	1	0	5,800	Robyn's Request	2	F	1	0	1	0	3,888
Rob Rac	5	G	7	0	1	0	1,540	Robyns Trial	10	G	2	0	0	0	110
Rob the Gold	7	G	14	1	1	1	7,023	Robynthegold	3	G	6	3	3	0	44,655
Rob the Streaker	3	G	13	1	1	1	41,936	Roby's Shadow	2	F	2	0	0	0	0
Robahush	7	G	8	3	2	0	11,642	Roc King	3	G	13	0	1	3	8,190
Robber	4	F	16	1	2	0	4,543	Roca Jack	7	G	4	1	0	1	5,430
Robber Baron	3	C	2	0	0	0	0	Rocaco	6	H	6	4	0	2	48,000
Robber Rhodes	4	G	5	1	0	1	8,257	Rocajul	5	M	15	3	3	5	51,639
Robber's Roost	3	G	2	0	0	0	0	Rocamana Castle	2	F	2	0	0	1	4,070
Robbery	2	C	2	0	0	0	135	Rocchetto	9	G	12	0	0	1	1,230
Robbie	5	G	7	0	3	2	1,415	Rocco n' Rhino	6	H	6	0	0	2	1,210
Robbie's Prince	6	G	2	0	1	1	4,903	Roche Rock	12	G	7	1	0	2	12,188
Robbie's Rockin	4	C	8	1	0	2	56,725	Rochelle	4	F	13	3	1	1	30,300
Robbin Lynn	4	F	10	0	3	1	21,460	Rochells Boy	6	H	3	0	0	0	92
Robboo	6	G	3	0	0	0	177	Rocher's Approval	3	G	9	4	0	1	22,185
Robby D	7	G	11	1	1	1	4,021	Rochester	7	G	8	1	2	1	164,757
Robby's M and M	5	M	9	0	0	1	2,625	Rocinante	5	H	2	0	0	0	510
Robe Bayou	4	C	5	1	2	0	13,500	Rock a by Abby	3	F	7	2	0	1	7,434
Robert E	3	C	3	0	0	0	0	Rock a Lot	4	F	8	1	1	2	18,175
Robert R	3	G	1	0	0	0	0	Rock Again	3	C	5	2	2	1	211,320
Robert the Bruce	7	G	3	0	0	0	2,541	Rock Away Doeny	5	G	8	1	1	0	5,415
Roberta Alwumar	4	F	12	3	2	0	23,765	Rock Buster	3	C	7	2	0	1	47,750
Roberta Empress	6	M	8	1	0	0	3,268	Rock Canyon	6	G	4	0	0	0	294
Roberta's Mango	4	F	9	4	1	0	198,053	Rock City Falls	4	F	1	0	0	0	0
Roberta's Matt	3	G	2	0	0	0	2,550	Rock Climb	3	C	3	0	0	0	2,575
Roberta's Star	5	M	4	0	0	0	232	Rock Cod Johnny	4	C	11	3	1	2	43,260
Roberto Royale	6	G	10	4	4	1	31,080	Rock County	3	G	6	1	0	0	23,989
Roberto's Boy	4	G	3	0	0	2	359	Rock de Stars	5	G	17	2	2	2	16,140
Roberto's Honor	3	G	9	1	0	3	7,025	Rock Falls	3	C	11	0	1	2	6,967
Roberto's Minister	6	G	14	1	4	4	9,400	Rock Fever	5	M	3	2	1	0	20,700
Roberto's Pride	9	G	11	1	2	3	29,680	Rock Gap	4	G	1	0	0	0	77
Roberto's Show	4	G	9	0	3	2	48,920	Rock Island Rocket	5	G	13	2	4	0	13,486
Roberto's Victory	5	M	10	1	2	4	11,190	Rock Island Salami	3	C	5	1	0	0	11,400
Roberto's Viz	6	G	7	0	0	1	1,995	Rock Jock	5	G	11	2	0	0	7,098
Robert's Legacy	3	C	4	0	1	0	1,950	Rock Layer	5	H	14	2	3	1	30,670
Roberts Princess	4	F	3	0	0	0	0	Rock M.	6	G	1	0	0	0	0
Roberts Reprized	3	C	1	0	0	0	300	Rock Me Amadeus	7	G	1	0	0	0	0
Robert's the Boss	4	G	8	0	0	1	900	Rock Me Home	6	M	3	1	0	0	2,753
Robert's Tribute	4	G	3	1	0	1	39,720	Rock Me Honey	3	G	7	0	0	0	374
Robin de Nest	6	H	4	1	0	0	11,040	Rock Me Right	3	F	2	0	0	1	577
Robin des Tune	3	F	11	3	0	1	30,075	Rock N Merle	7	G	1	0	0	0	153
Robin of Sherwood	5	G	18	2	3	0	21,066	Rock 'n Red Pop	2	F	2	1	0	0	7,800
Robin of Trinidad	3	G	11	3	1	0	74,300	Rock N Role Dancer	2	F	1	0	0	0	0
Robin the Purses	2	F	3	0	0	2	3,276	Rock N Roll Baby	3	F	5	2	0	1	16,170
Robin Zee	4	G	3	1	1	0	27,200	Rock n' Romance	2	F	3	0	0	1	1,541
Robinera	4	F	4	1	0	1	5,210	Rock N Rosh	3	G	9	2	2	1	84,320
Robins Beauty	4	C	16	2	2	3	48,965	Rock of Gold	6	H	2	0	0	1	1,460
Robin's Fling	4	F	14	4	3	1	26,701	Rock On Harriet	4	F	2	0	0	0	756
Robin's Juel	4	F	16	1	0	2	4,834	Rock On Pro	3	C	1	0	0	0	107
Robin's Ridge	6	G	7	0	2	2	3,192	Rock On Red Robyn	6	M	10	2	1	3	22,320
Robins Shower	4	C	12	2	2	1	13,480	Rock Opera	4	G	2	0	0	0	2,880
Robin's Snow	3	F	12	5	1	1	26,400	Rock Queen	5	M	1	1	0	0	27,000
Robins Wish	3	F	11	1	1	0	14,732	Rock Seasons	3	G	9	0	2	2	3,870
Robinson Crossing	10	M	6	1	0	1	2,623	Rock Sez Win	3	C	11	1	0	1	23,480
Robinthestorm	3	F	4	0	0	0	1,050	Rock Slide	5	H	7	2	1	0	169,390
Robledo	3	C	2	1	0	0	60,000	Rock Steady Dan	2	G	5	0	0	0	1,530
Robnroy	7	G	9	1	0	1	20,074	Rock Tavern	3	C	13	1	4	0	16,904
Robot	6	G	13	1	2	2	29,233	Rock the Bank	5	G	8	1	0	3	13,505
Robotica	3	F	3	0	0	0	1,116	Rock the Comet	7	M	13	0	0	0	1,065
Rob's Bull	6	G	9	0	3	1	3,690	Rock the Nation	3	C	11	2	1	0	17,510
Rob's Charger	4	C	1	0	0	0	95	Rock the Point	6	M	3	0	0	0	0
Robs Coin	2	G	3	1	1	0	4,548	Rock the Stone	4	G	8	2	2	1	39,120
Rob's Frosty	2	F	1	0	0	0	0	Rockabye Music	6	G	8	1	0	2	9,820
Rob's Little Boy	4	C	9	2	0	1	15,616	Rockatowa	6	G	19	3	3	3	25,106
Rob's Pegasus	5	G	2	0	0	0	410	Rockbank	5	G	10	1	1	0	5,500
Rob's Quest	5	H	7	0	0	3	4,070	Rockchalk Jayhawk	5	G	11	2	2	3	68,987
Robthevet	5	G	10	1	2	1	14,482	Rockcliffe	3	G	7	1	1	1	58,782
Robust Ruby	3	F	1	0	0	0	110	Rock'd Em All	2	F	3	1	0	0	4,650
Robustinnier	5	G	9	5	1	0	38,420	Rockdale	7	G	5	0	0	1	1,375
Roby	8	M	6	2	1	2	22,100	Rockem Sockem	2	G	7	3	3	0	139,158
Robyn Ralph	5	H	5	0	0	0	748	Rockenelle	3	F	8	1	1	2	3,840
Robyn Regal	3	C	1	0	0	0	480	Rocker	4	G	12	1	2	2	18,934
Robyn Sings	3	F	11	2	3	0	24,016	Rocket Alert	4	F	15	2	3	0	11,741
Robyn the Till	2	C	8	1	1	2	13,645	Rocket Charge	3	C	8	0	1	1	2,752
Robyn's Cove	3	C	2	0	0	0	0	Rocket Doctor	3	C	7	1	0	4	17,100
Robyn's Diamond	6	M	2	0	0	0	237	Rocket Flight	4	G	8	3	1	0	29,608
Robyns Gold Charm	5	G	2	0	0	0	0	Rocket Hombre	4	G	10	3	3	1	25,672
Robyn's Pal	2	F	3	0	1	0	4,590	Rocket Island	4	G	3	0	0	0	0
Robyn's Pleasure	5	G	4	0	0	0	780	Rocket Junior	2	C	2	0	0	0	1,985

Horse	Age	Sex	Sts	1st	2d	3d	Won
Rocket Lady	3	F	7	0	0	0	0
Rocket Power	4	F	14	1	5	0	17,180
Rocket Rhonda	4	F	4	0	0	0	0
Rocket Ricky	4	G	9	0	1	1	2,980
Rocket Royale	3	F	4	2	1	0	29,100
Rocket Ryan	5	H	9	0	2	2	8,060
Rocket Star	3	G	9	0	1	0	5,970
Rocket Thruster	4	G	14	2	4	1	21,538
Rocket Wager	4	G	4	2	0	0	11,675
Rocket Whirl	2	G	5	0	1	1	3,000
Rocketdoubleoseven	4	G	8	1	0	0	2,946
Rocketeering	3	C	1	0	1	0	4,780
Rocketful	3	G	2	0	0	0	225
Rocket's Glow	5	M	13	2	1	3	21,365
Rocket's Jet	3	G	13	3	1	3	24,285
Rocket's Legacy	3	C	11	1	2	2	28,650
Rockets Red	5	M	1	0	0	0	288
Rocket's Revenge	3	G	10	0	0	1	2,605
Rockette Rankin	6	M	1	0	0	0	0
Rockette Road	3	G	6	0	0	0	1,530
Rockettorussia	2	C	6	0	1	1	1,770
Rockfield	3	C	4	1	1	1	64,028
Rockford	3	G	11	1	1	2	15,123
Rockhead	4	C	7	0	0	0	688
Rockhewn	2	C	1	1	0	0	11,400
Rockhills Jet Set	2	F	5	0	1	0	7,845
Rockhurst	4	C	18	2	4	2	61,300
Rockies	4	G	8	2	2	2	47,186
Rockim Gorge	4	C	8	0	1	2	2,633
Rockin' Again	2	C	3	0	0	2	5,040
Rockin Bankroll	5	G	9	0	0	0	1,453
Rockin' Bobby	3	G	11	1	5	2	31,655
Rockin Boy Rod	4	C	1	0	0	0	0
Rockin Early	4	C	11	1	0	1	5,090
Rockin' Johnny	4	G	12	0	0	1	860
Rockin On	2	F	3	2	0	1	35,119
Rockin On By	4	F	10	0	0	1	1,596
Rockin On Ice	4	F	13	4	1	1	101,268
Rockin On Ready	3	C	14	3	1	4	121,223
Rockin Rachel Anne	3	F	11	0	0	2	19,730
Rockin Rhythm	3	F	1	0	0	0	0
Rockin Rooster	4	C	10	1	2	1	20,817
Rockin Roy	6	M	12	2	1	3	38,250
Rockin' Shamrock	3	C	3	0	1	0	1,584
Rockin the Ship	2	C	1	1	0	0	22,800
Rockin Therockies	3	G	2	0	0	0	380
Rocking Bird	3	G	2	0	0	0	1,818
Rocking Chair Ride	5	G	7	1	3	2	5,640
Rocking in and Out	3	F	4	0	0	0	127
Rocking Trick (ARG)	6	H	11	2	1	2	49,960
Rockinmebaby	3	F	5	0	0	0	225
Rockland Harbor	3	F	5	1	1	0	10,580
Rockland Road	2	C	1	0	0	0	0
Rockmania	4	G	9	0	1	1	3,461
Rockmeister	7	H	6	0	1	0	1,392
Rockmill Two	9	G	16	0	3	0	10,416
Rock'n Metallika	5	M	7	3	2	1	19,755
Rockn' Roca	3	G	11	1	3	1	6,221
Rockonbambam	3	G	5	0	1	2	7,490
Rockport Gal	2	F	3	0	0	0	290
Rockport Road	3	G	11	1	0	1	7,140
Rockrupertrose	5	G	13	0	1	1	4,893
Rock's El Dorado	4	F	19	5	2	1	39,240
Rocks in the Mouth	5	M	5	1	0	0	9,675
Rockscissorsfoil	4	G	6	1	1	1	10,375
Rockshaan	5	M	10	1	1	2	2,425
Rock'spride	4	G	10	1	0	0	4,902
Rocky Bar	5	H	4	0	0	1	16,500
Rocky D' Or	6	G	12	2	1	1	7,038
Rocky Flight	3	C	7	0	0	2	4,260
Rocky Gulch	2	G	5	4	1	0	163,909
Rocky Harbor	5	H	2	0	0	0	0
Rocky Horatius	4	C	3	0	0	0	0
Rocky Jo Loney	4	C	10	0	0	0	1,110
Rocky Lane	3	G	12	1	2	1	13,973
Rocky Memories	3	F	5	0	1	0	1,014
Rocky Moment	5	G	14	2	1	2	4,452
Rocky My Boy	5	G	13	1	1	2	7,177
Rocky North	6	M	5	1	0	0	5,600
Rocky Plains	2	C	5	0	0	1	5,000
Rocky Power	3	G	1	0	0	0	0
Rocky Reality	9	G	5	1	0	0	3,669
Rocky Rhodes	2	G	4	0	0	0	662
Rocky Roan	3	F	13	0	2	1	14,120
Rocky Robyn	8	H	8	2	0	0	22,710
Rocky Royal	2	G	3	1	0	2	8,390
Rocky Shore	4	C	4	0	0	0	570
Rocky Treasure	6	G	4	1	0	0	2,100
Rocky Two	5	G	4	0	1	1	4,725
Rocky Won	5	G	8	2	1	1	14,499
Rocky's Crew	5	G	6	3	2	0	17,750
Rocky's Dilemma	3	C	6	0	0	1	2,994
Rockzan	4	F	8	0	0	2	5,267
Rod	5	H	15	7	2	1	122,166
Ro'dannigan	5	G	2	0	0	0	369
Rodayo Dancer	3	C	1	1	0	0	6,000
Rode Dancer	7	G	15	0	1	2	2,237
Rode to Resolve	4	F	1	0	0	0	140
Rodeo Champ	3	G	7	1	1	1	10,497
Rodeo Dad	2	C	5	0	1	0	4,984
Rodeo Drive (IRE)	3	F	5	0	0	0	3,150
Rodeo Fun	2	C	7	2	2	2	99,324
Rodeo Joe Wells	4	C	2	0	0	0	400
Rodeo Licious	2	F	4	2	2	0	90,500
Rodeo Pistol	3	C	1	0	0	0	0
Rodeo Red	3	G	1	0	0	1	288
Rodeo Ropey	2	F	2	0	0	0	450
Rodeo Sass	3	F	9	0	1	1	17,630
Rodeo Shopper	2	G	1	0	0	0	0
Rodeo Spirit	3	G	7	2	0	0	55,740
Rodeo Springs	5	M	7	0	2	2	17,600
Rodeo's Lady	2	F	1	0	0	0	230
Rodion (ARG)	5	H	3	0	0	0	3,300
Rodney Bay	2	C	3	1	2	0	41,000
Rodney Deal	8	G	7	0	0	0	150
Rodney's Pi	2	C	2	0	0	0	1,194
Rod's Vindicator	5	H	2	0	0	0	0
Roena	7	M	4	1	0	1	18,000
Roesch Jacky	6	H	5	1	0	0	5,962
Rogan Slew	5	G	8	2	2	1	3,655
Roger E	4	G	8	2	2	1	89,960
Roger P	5	G	2	0	0	0	320
Roger Roger	8	G	7	0	0	1	3,170
Roger Wilco	2	C	1	0	0	0	0
Rogers Aggravation	5	G	2	0	0	0	0
Rogers Gold Strike	5	G	1	0	0	0	172
Rogers Legacy	5	G	7	1	1	2	9,430
Rogue Agent	4	G	11	4	2	0	137,440
Rogue Rullah	7	G	7	0	0	0	758
Rogue Storm	3	G	11	1	1	1	16,310
Roguish Eye	12	G	14	1	0	1	3,860
Rohita	6	M	1	0	0	0	340
Roho	8	G	9	0	1	0	2,537
Roi Charmant	2	C	5	1	0	2	34,980
Roi Edward	6	G	6	0	0	0	342
Roi Roi	4	F	10	1	2	0	10,564
Rojo Lady	4	F	8	1	1	2	9,150
Rojo Rogue	2	G	4	1	0	2	4,850
Rojo Toro	3	C	2	1	0	0	121,614
Rokeby's Wish	6	M	13	5	1	0	14,359
Roker	2	G	5	0	3	0	11,200
Rola Sara	3	F	1	0	0	0	0
Rolando Furioso	5	H	15	2	1	3	17,932
Rolen to Jasper	6	G	13	3	0	2	11,982
Rolf's Black Gold	4	G	5	0	1	0	4,115
Rolfs Royce	3	F	1	0	0	0	1,140
Roll All Night	6	G	19	3	3	2	15,798
Roll Call	4	G	18	3	5	3	32,315
Roll Crystal Roll	4	F	5	0	0	0	0
Roll Hennessy Roll	3	C	5	0	1	0	25,111
Roll of the Dice	5	G	4	1	2	1	70,089
Roll On	3	F	4	1	0	0	4,309
Roll On Albion	9	G	8	0	0	2	57,208
Roll On Big Ball	4	G	15	1	1	2	5,126
Roll On Buddy	6	H	3	0	0	0	285
Roll On Henry	6	G	16	1	0	1	10,630
Roll On Partner	2	G	2	0	0	0	0
Roll Over Roy	2	C	2	1	0	0	29,640

RECORDS OF HORSES

Horse	Age	Sex	Sts	1st	2d	3d	Won	Horse	Age	Sex	Sts	1st	2d	3d	Won
Roll the Gold	3	C	5	0	0	1	1,980	Romantic Bull	5	H	5	0	0	1	2,886
Roll the Stage	8	G	5	1	0	1	3,178	Romantic Comedy	3	F	6	1	0	3	36,190
Roll West	7	G	13	0	0	1	1,956	Romantic Numbers	2	F	1	0	0	0	0
Roll Your Own	2	C	4	0	3	1	18,460	Romantic Rendezvoo	2	F	2	0	0	0	0
Rolla	2	F	1	0	0	0	100	Romantic Romeo	3	G	9	2	1	1	11,784
Rolled Stocking	7	G	7	3	0	1	64,990	Romantic Trick	4	F	8	0	3	1	10,260
Roller Derby Queen	7	M	16	1	4	0	18,348	Romantic Twist	3	F	2	0	0	0	0
Roller Girl	2	F	4	2	0	0	20,300	Romantic Victory	3	F	6	1	1	0	8,594
Roller King	9	G	11	2	0	1	7,244	Romantic Virginian	5	G	7	0	0	1	5,200
Rollette	7	M	8	0	2	2	26,125	Romantic Won	5	M	17	4	2	2	16,660
Rollicking Caller	2	C	4	1	1	1	9,750	Romanticizing	4	F	6	0	0	1	1,188
Rollicking Oddrock	4	G	8	2	1	3	18,918	Romanticon	2	C	5	1	0	0	19,095
Rollicking Times	3	F	14	2	3	3	24,739	Romantique Man	6	G	8	1	0	1	5,418
Rollin Lite	5	M	5	0	1	1	2,269	Romanus	5	G	3	0	0	0	0
Rollin Me Out	6	G	11	4	0	2	48,370	Romatwil	2	F	1	0	0	0	0
Rollin Nelson	4	G	12	0	3	2	9,055	Romazzino	2	C	2	0	0	0	2,340
Rollin' Rat	2	C	3	1	1	0	5,760	Romeo Tango	3	G	14	2	3	2	34,675
Rollin Store	6	H	3	0	0	0	46	Romeo's Key	4	F	11	1	4	1	9,681
Rollin Trial	4	G	8	3	0	0	10,708	Romeo's Pistol	3	C	1	0	0	0	0
Rolling Benz	3	G	5	0	0	2	13,805	Romeos Wilson	5	H	1	0	0	0	194
Rolling Blackout	3	G	2	0	0	0	0	Romin Ridge	3	G	8	2	1	1	15,552
Rolling Fork	4	F	7	1	0	0	16,272	Rommel's River	4	C	12	0	3	1	1,494
Rolling Gold	5	H	4	0	0	0	136	Romney Marsh	2	G	8	0	1	1	7,195
Rolling Home	4	F	12	2	1	3	19,544	Romo Cade	3	C	1	0	0	0	31
Rolling Hope	3	C	1	0	0	0	0	Romolo's Brush	4	G	17	3	3	5	35,253
Rolling Into Town	3	F	8	0	0	0	1,119	Romos Chocolate	6	M	4	0	0	1	550
Rollofthunder	2	G	9	3	1	0	36,600	Rompe Bolas	5	G	11	2	0	1	10,130
Rolls Joyce	5	M	13	1	2	2	7,099	Rompin Nelda G.	2	F	4	0	1	0	2,765
Rollthenumbers	3	C	12	1	3	0	3,001	Romping Rosie	3	F	13	2	1	4	14,467
Rollthesevens	3	G	12	1	0	2	6,933	Ron	2	C	2	0	0	0	0
Rollthepresses	6	M	14	1	4	0	8,608	Ron Bot Wat	3	G	3	0	0	0	130
Rolphs Way	4	F	4	0	0	1	1,208	Ron Cherry	5	G	19	0	9	4	27,082
Rolyph	4	G	12	0	0	2	4,349	Ronalda	8	H	11	4	2	1	21,305
Roma Gold	3	F	13	1	2	1	12,100	Roncoco	5	M	7	1	3	0	10,500
Roma Royale	2	F	3	0	1	2	9,520	Rondeau	3	F	5	1	0	2	10,320
Romaillian	2	F	4	0	0	0	285	Rondelet	8	G	9	0	2	1	2,149
Roman Buck	4	F	1	0	0	0	130	Rongus Hayman	12	H	3	0	1	0	2,700
Roman Centurion	3	C	2	0	0	0	2,245	Roni Rose	3	F	16	1	3	3	24,751
Roman Coin	4	G	1	0	0	0	0	Ronnet	4	F	15	1	2	1	26,612
Roman Countess	5	M	3	0	0	0	136	Ronnie B	4	G	7	0	1	0	2,060
Roman d'Amour	5	M	12	0	3	1	7,506	Ronnie Charmer	4	G	15	0	0	1	2,489
Roman Dancer	4	C	3	0	0	0	1,380	Ronnie Ray	10	H	1	0	0	0	163
Roman Empire	4	G	3	1	0	0	6,250	Ronnie's a Star	2	F	9	0	2	1	3,900
Roman Field	5	M	2	0	0	0	110	Ronnie's Boy	4	C	6	3	0	1	8,930
Roman Gladiator	3	G	18	2	1	1	15,996	Ron's Boast	6	H	12	1	1	0	3,601
Roman in the Hills	4	F	7	1	1	0	14,045	Ron's Gal	7	M	6	0	1	0	886
Roman Intellect	9	M	1	0	0	0	40	Ron's Lad	5	G	15	1	1	2	14,313
Roman Leader	2	C	2	0	0	0	250	Ron's Prince	4	G	22	1	5	2	42,760
Roman Market	3	C	7	1	0	1	5,730	Ron's Reason	4	C	12	1	3	2	7,999
Roman N Royal	4	C	1	0	0	0	650	Ron's Temptor	3	G	4	0	0	0	114
Roman Peace	4	G	8	1	1	1	64,584	Ron's Tornado	6	G	9	1	0	2	10,815
Roman Rambler	6	H	3	0	0	0	265	Rontu	2	C	1	0	0	0	0
Roman Reality	9	M	5	1	0	1	1,393	Roo Art's Flight	7	G	6	0	0	0	462
Roman Reckoning	7	G	3	0	0	0	146	Roo Ban	5	H	1	0	0	0	0
Roman Relic	3	C	1	0	0	0	0	Roo Royale	2	C	1	0	0	0	0
Roman Ripples	2	F	5	0	1	0	2,696	Roofus	4	F	2	0	0	1	1,216
Roman Romance	5	M	13	2	2	1	160,725	Rook'd	2	G	2	0	0	0	152
Roman Sea	7	G	8	4	0	1	35,997	Roolynn	7	M	2	0	0	0	76
Roman Slipper	3	F	2	0	0	0	0	Roomtwothirtyeight	4	G	11	1	1	1	3,610
Roman Star	5	H	8	0	0	0	600	Roop Karna	5	G	7	1	2	0	17,760
Roman Summit	10	G	2	0	0	0	0	Roo's Master Piece	5	M	7	1	2	1	4,330
Roman Sword	5	H	1	0	0	0	0	Roosevelt Run	3	F	4	0	0	0	570
Roman Tango	2	F	1	0	0	0	0	Rooska Warrior	3	G	3	0	0	0	0
Roman Thunder	7	G	9	3	2	1	15,281	Roosker	4	F	4	1	0	0	2,632
Roman Twist	4	G	16	3	3	1	61,961	Roostas Rastus	3	G	13	2	1	3	13,098
Romance Inthe Hall	5	G	5	0	0	0	0	Rooster Red	2	C	3	0	0	0	1,140
Romance Tunnel	5	M	3	0	0	0	320	Rooster Rock	5	G	10	2	1	1	5,696
Romanceishope	5	G	1	0	0	1	9,672	Rooster Time	4	G	7	0	3	0	2,525
Romancer	5	G	16	0	2	4	9,390	Rooster's Deputy	3	C	4	0	1	0	6,000
Romancera	4	F	1	0	0	0	330	Roostin Houston	8	G	2	0	0	1	390
Romancin Dixie	4	F	5	1	0	1	32,810	Roostin 'n Royalty	4	G	5	0	0	0	222
Romancin Lady	5	F	13	3	2	0	39,188	Root and Scoot	5	G	4	0	0	0	160
Romancin the Judge	6	M	3	0	0	0	0	Root Beer Float	5	G	8	2	3	1	21,600
Romancing	3	F	9	2	1	1	17,384	Root Boy's Revenge	3	G	4	0	0	0	432
Romancing the Jade	5	G	3	0	0	0	0	Root Boy's Wonder	5	M	5	0	0	0	815
Romandream	4	C	1	0	0	0	61	Root for Duke	6	H	4	0	0	2	1,040
Romanesque	3	F	13	3	3	0	66,560	Root for Shannan	6	M	2	0	0	0	0
Romaninahurry	2	C	7	2	1	0	27,770	Root With Style	4	G	5	0	0	0	3,660
Romantic Age (ARG)	5	M	8	2	1	2	23,635	Rootfurme	4	G	1	0	0	0	225

Horse	Age	Sex	Sts	1st	2d	3d	Won
Rootintootinjohn	3	G	3	0	0	0	0
Rootytoottoot	4	F	9	0	0	2	2,228
Rope a Rich One	5	M	11	1	1	2	7,302
Rope All Day	3	C	4	0	0	0	550
Roper Doper	4	C	1	1	0	0	5,415
Ropers	3	G	13	1	2	0	6,810
Roring Fork	3	F	3	0	0	0	180
Rorschach	3	C	1	0	0	0	0
Rosa de Lima (PER)	4	F	4	0	1	1	4,925
Rosa Dos Ventas	5	M	10	4	1	1	14,957
Rosa Mundi	2	F	2	0	0	0	3,528
Rosa Parks (GB)	4	F	3	0	1	0	11,580
Rosa Vanozza	3	F	4	0	1	0	3,400
Rosalino	4	F	14	1	2	3	6,040
Rosalita	4	F	16	1	3	2	12,287
Rosaloona	4	F	1	0	0	0	0
Rosanda	5	M	4	0	1	1	19,940
Rosanja	4	F	4	0	1	0	2,632
Rosarita Beach	3	F	5	2	3	0	38,200
Rosa's Cove	7	M	7	2	0	1	5,472
Rosa's Fella	3	G	12	0	0	0	1,873
Rosberg	2	C	2	1	0	0	26,180
Rosbrian (IRE)	8	G	6	1	0	3	23,400
Roscoe Pito	3	G	9	6	1	2	424,566
Roscoe the Rascal	8	G	11	0	0	0	1,253
Rosco'sgal	4	F	5	0	1	0	3,724
Rose	6	M	6	1	0	1	5,460
Rose City Special	6	G	14	2	6	2	10,751
Rose Country Man	2	C	5	1	0	0	9,015
Rose Creek	6	G	9	4	2	1	28,232
Rose Darling	7	M	14	2	1	3	27,583
Rose Dawson	6	M	5	0	0	1	476
Rose Du Roi	2	G	2	0	0	0	950
Rose Esther	7	M	8	2	2	0	60,376
Rose Frances	5	M	1	0	0	0	380
Rose Hunter	2	F	7	0	3	0	41,085
Rose Leaves	4	F	7	1	1	2	8,335
Rose Meadow Lane	4	F	1	1	0	0	2,200
Rose N Angelina	5	M	9	3	0	1	41,562
Rose Nessence	3	F	6	0	0	0	352
Rose of Boerne	6	M	3	0	0	0	349
Rose of Edmore	3	F	7	1	1	1	21,570
Rose of Galway	4	F	1	0	0	0	840
Rose of Hadif	2	F	2	0	0	0	795
Rose of Pembroke	2	F	6	0	0	3	9,495
Rose of Roxton	6	M	9	0	4	2	23,497
Rose of Savannah	4	F	10	1	3	1	48,060
Rose of Semoran	3	F	3	0	0	1	1,910
Rose of Sophia	2	F	4	2	2	0	86,673
Rose Punch	3	F	8	0	0	1	1,586
Rose Trick	6	M	8	2	3	0	24,540
Rose Troienne	6	M	6	0	0	2	4,364
Rose Wars	3	G	13	4	5	2	20,265
Rosebloom	3	F	3	1	0	0	10,800
Roseboom	4	F	2	0	0	0	0
Rosebudslilpistol	3	G	11	0	1	2	2,995
Rosecat	7	M	8	1	3	0	18,801
Rosecoloredglasses	4	G	1	0	0	1	3,575
Roseie's D. J. Cat	3	C	1	0	0	0	220
Rosella	3	F	9	3	1	1	33,075
Roseme	5	G	4	0	0	1	322
Rosemont Hope	3	F	16	1	3	3	30,008
Rosenball	6	G	17	2	2	5	10,653
Rosencrans	2	C	1	1	0	0	18,000
Rosenstein	3	F	7	0	0	0	2,850
Roserunner	3	F	7	0	0	0	124
Roses and Roses	4	F	11	2	2	0	9,984
Rose's Buddy	4	F	11	1	0	1	6,184
Roses Debut	4	F	5	0	0	0	236
Rose's Echo	3	F	11	4	1	1	19,020
Roses for Concorde	3	F	2	0	0	0	0
Roses for Lydia	4	F	14	2	2	5	12,117
Roses for Maria	2	F	7	0	1	0	4,190
Roses for Marti	3	F	17	3	2	3	37,030
Roses for Ruby	4	F	11	1	1	1	35,740
Roses for Sonja	3	F	4	0	0	1	4,320
Roses From David	4	F	12	0	2	1	11,852
Roses From Dora	5	M	10	1	3	1	20,567
Rose's Head Games	4	F	5	0	0	0	465
Roses in May	3	C	5	2	2	0	71,910
Roses N Bows	2	F	6	1	1	2	38,896
Roses Roses Roses	6	M	12	1	1	2	10,755
Rosesarefred	4	F	1	0	0	0	0
Rose'shoneybun	4	F	8	1	1	1	12,750
Rosesnpearls	2	F	2	0	0	0	0
Rosetide	5	H	9	1	2	4	53,625
Rosey Flyer	7	M	3	0	0	0	525
Rosey Glow	5	M	5	0	1	0	2,850
Rosey Lass	3	F	11	0	0	4	3,351
Rosey Teresa	3	G	13	3	3	2	11,342
Rosey's Rocket	4	G	11	3	4	1	18,316
Roshan	4	G	8	1	1	1	11,077
Rosharon	4	F	10	1	3	1	70,060
Roshneti	3	F	15	2	9	4	59,450
Rosiclare	4	F	1	0	0	0	70
Rosie Arcaro	4	F	1	0	0	0	0
Rosie Beau	3	F	5	0	0	0	0
Rosie Cotton	3	F	2	0	1	0	2,756
Rosie d'On	3	F	11	2	1	2	15,152
Rosie in the Sky	4	F	16	3	3	3	48,694
Rosie Is a Leader	3	F	8	1	1	1	30,530
Rosie Lee City	2	F	2	0	0	0	1,572
Rosie Lilac	4	F	5	1	1	0	8,822
Rosie My Buddie	5	M	5	1	0	1	3,826
Rosie o' Dawn	6	M	12	1	2	4	16,598
Rosie o' Mali	4	F	8	0	0	1	6,072
Rosie O'Neal	4	F	2	0	0	0	0
Rosie Position	3	F	5	1	0	0	13,631
Rosie Prospect	5	M	8	1	2	0	4,551
Rosie Times	5	M	3	0	1	0	1,122
Rosieposie	3	F	2	0	1	0	4,000
Rosie's Big Boy	3	C	12	1	1	4	60,950
Rosie's Boy	4	G	8	1	2	2	8,143
Rosie's Coyote	6	H	4	0	0	0	110
Rosies Dhabi Dude	4	G	10	1	3	1	19,963
Rosie's Gold	3	F	6	0	2	0	2,920
Rosie's Ransom	3	F	6	1	0	1	20,630
Rosie's Risk	4	F	8	0	0	1	2,315
Rosie's Shamrock	5	H	15	2	1	2	23,459
Rosie's Sister	4	F	4	0	0	1	4,840
Rosies Wild Lips	5	M	12	3	1	0	19,585
Rosie's Wish	2	F	1	0	1	0	4,340
Rosieville	2	F	3	2	0	0	13,440
Rosina Boy (NZ)	6	G	3	0	0	0	500
Rosita's Imp	3	F	8	0	1	0	1,142
Rosita's Power	4	F	4	0	0	0	207
Rosko	8	G	10	0	0	1	3,197
Rosmerta	4	F	13	2	2	2	34,411
Ross Is a Hoss	2	C	1	0	0	0	0
Ross n' Bens Girl	7	M	9	3	1	0	9,250
Ross Valay	3	F	1	0	1	0	5,250
Ross Verba	6	G	6	0	1	2	1,739
Rossard Star	4	C	5	0	0	0	1,941
Rossman	7	G	11	1	2	1	4,966
Rosso Toscano	11	G	3	0	0	0	0
Ross's Comedy	5	H	4	0	0	0	70
Rostral	3	G	4	0	0	0	0
Rosy M	3	F	9	0	3	1	5,123
Rosy Pete	4	F	9	2	4	1	6,978
Rosy Ran	5	M	7	3	3	0	12,451
Rosy's Babe	3	F	3	0	0	0	278
Rosy's Legacy	5	G	3	0	0	0	200
Rothko	5	G	9	2	0	3	17,434
Rotoga	3	F	9	0	1	0	8,883
Rototiller	3	F	6	0	0	1	4,755
Rotsa Ruckus	5	G	4	1	0	0	8,222
Rotten Ralph	4	G	3	0	0	0	0
Rotunda Beauty	4	F	13	2	2	1	10,674
Rouen (FR)	7	G	12	4	1	2	42,325
Rouge County	2	C	4	1	0	1	8,825
Rouge d'Or	4	F	8	0	1	1	3,433
Rouge Noir	3	F	3	1	0	0	6,670
Rouge Royale	8	G	9	1	2	3	4,880
Rouge Sensation	3	G	3	1	0	0	6,384
Rouge Stone	2	F	6	0	0	1	12,489
Rough	8	G	8	1	1	2	1,793
Rough Al	4	G	14	3	1	2	20,202
Rough and Robust	2	F	1	0	0	0	90

RECORDS OF HORSES

Horse	Age	Sex	Sts	1st	2d	3d	Won	Horse	Age	Sex	Sts	1st	2d	3d	Won
Rough Clouds	5	G	12	2	3	2	12,535	Royal Aggravation	3	G	5	0	0	0	360
Rough Copy	3	G	2	0	0	0	0	Royal Alba	5	M	12	2	2	2	31,520
Rough Day	3	G	3	0	0	0	1,818	Royal Alchemist	3	F	4	0	0	1	1,643
Rough Doctor	5	H	5	1	1	0	3,300	Royal Ambassador	3	C	12	2	2	1	22,580
Rough Draft	6	G	5	1	2	0	10,470	Royal American	5	G	14	0	2	2	5,878
Rough Energy	7	G	1	0	0	0	390	Royal Arts	7	M	9	0	0	0	285
Rough Fun	7	H	7	0	0	0	270	Royal Ascot	5	M	11	2	1	0	74,625
Rough House Ruby	3	F	7	0	0	0	2,040	Royal Ashley	3	G	7	0	0	0	415
Rough Life	5	G	9	1	1	0	13,856	Royal Attitude	3	F	5	0	0	1	1,660
Rough R. N.	4	F	3	1	2	0	50,980	Royal Attraction	3	F	3	0	1	0	12,142
Rough Storm	5	M	10	0	0	1	1,662	Royal Ballerina	6	M	2	0	1	1	3,300
Rough Trick	3	C	7	0	0	1	4,053	Royal Banquet	6	M	15	1	3	2	29,155
Roughjette	8	G	11	2	2	0	12,128	Royal Baron	3	C	11	3	0	0	32,780
Rough'n It	2	C	1	0	1	0	3,800	Royal Barter	5	G	2	0	0	0	105
Rougon	6	G	6	1	0	1	13,380	Royal Beau	2	G	5	0	0	0	626
Roulliana	3	F	1	0	0	0	0	Royal Bengal Tiger	3	C	8	2	2	3	31,220
Rounce	9	G	7	0	1	2	2,350	Royal Birth	3	G	4	0	0	0	0
Round and Flyin	6	M	2	0	0	0	0	Royal Bon Bon	4	F	14	4	3	3	29,430
Round Den	8	M	1	0	0	0	0	Royal Bonus	4	C	6	1	0	1	44,388
Round Girl	3	F	3	1	0	0	12,500	Royal Boots	5	H	1	0	0	0	0
Round Native Miss	4	F	8	1	2	1	13,627	Royal Brew	4	G	15	4	1	1	7,062
Round Rock	5	G	3	0	0	0	238	Royal Brittany	4	F	4	0	0	1	956
Round Tree	3	C	14	1	0	1	13,530	Royal Case	2	F	2	0	0	0	434
Roundabout Again	3	F	9	1	3	1	23,200	Royal Celebrity	3	F	5	0	0	1	1,050
Roundabout Jones	2	G	5	3	1	1	125,153	Royal Ceremony	5	M	11	1	3	2	23,591
Roundtree (IRE)	4	F	6	1	1	3	55,900	Royal Chalice	3	C	7	1	4	1	22,580
Roundtripper	2	C	10	0	0	2	3,875	Royal Champ	4	G	7	0	1	0	6,010
Rouquine	3	F	3	0	0	1	5,360	Royal Choice	2	F	3	0	0	0	2,203
Rouse Mountain	6	H	4	0	0	0	544	Royal City	2	C	1	0	0	0	123
Roused	2	F	2	1	0	0	27,455	Royal Colony	4	G	1	0	0	0	0
Rousing Again	3	F	9	3	2	1	60,320	Royal Conquest	4	F	7	0	0	0	1,710
Rousing Past	5	G	15	3	0	2	21,786	Royal Contessa	4	F	7	0	1	0	4,820
Roussanne	7	M	4	0	0	0	150	Royal Counselor	3	G	6	0	1	1	4,730
Rout N Dixie	3	C	8	1	1	0	1,990	Royal Cousin	4	F	13	2	1	2	40,236
Route Nine P	5	M	4	2	0	0	14,822	Royal Craft	3	F	2	0	0	0	205
Route Three	4	C	6	1	0	0	4,320	Royal Creek	4	C	16	1	1	3	11,440
Routine Panic	3	F	14	2	1	2	28,720	Royal Crystal	4	C	1	0	0	0	200
Rouvres (FR)	4	C	7	1	3	1	274,020	Royal Cup	2	F	6	1	1	1	17,394
Rouwaki	4	F	1	0	0	0	3,000	Royal D	3	G	2	0	0	2	13,585
Roux Then Gumbo	4	G	2	0	0	1	280	Royal Dalliance	6	M	13	3	3	2	252,064
Rouxbee	2	F	1	0	0	0	840	Royal Damsel	3	F	8	1	1	0	25,818
Rovanna	3	F	6	0	0	0	2,588	Royal Dauphin	3	C	1	0	0	0	0
Rover Ridge	4	C	9	0	1	0	4,666	Royal de Hope	4	C	3	0	1	0	7,118
Roving Marg	4	F	3	0	0	1	1,240	Royal Deal	4	G	6	0	0	0	892
Roving Singer	4	C	7	1	0	1	32,945	Royal Defiance	9	G	7	0	0	0	600
Row Row Man	4	G	8	2	1	2	9,881	Royal Dilemma	2	F	1	0	0	0	1,179
Rowan Express (GB)	3	F	7	0	1	0	11,900	Royal Distraction	4	F	9	3	0	0	95,748
Rowan Inish	2	G	4	0	1	0	2,640	Royal Doll	4	F	9	1	1	0	9,600
Rowans Park	3	C	8	2	2	2	131,735	Royal Dove	3	F	6	1	1	0	27,110
Rowdy Bear	3	G	6	0	1	1	2,315	Royal Drums	4	G	7	0	0	0	452
Rowdy Begone	3	G	4	0	0	1	2,052	Royal Duke	3	C	3	0	2	0	6,175
Rowdy Dinner	2	G	4	0	0	0	230	Royal Edict	13	G	3	0	0	1	850
Rowdy Girl	4	F	3	0	0	0	127	Royal Ego	6	G	16	2	2	5	21,208
Rowdy Lad	5	G	5	0	1	0	2,801	Royal Eltish	3	G	5	0	1	0	6,271
Rowdy Rae	4	F	18	3	3	2	25,749	Royal Emerald	3	G	9	3	0	0	28,745
Rowdy Rose	3	F	9	2	0	2	13,625	Royal Empress	3	F	5	1	1	3	11,340
Rowdy So n' So	3	C	7	2	0	0	6,163	Royal Escapade	4	C	17	1	4	5	12,659
Rowdy Sofia	3	F	3	1	0	0	3,775	Royal Event	7	M	5	1	0	0	1,492
Rowdy's Last	5	G	9	0	0	3	2,840	Royal Exile	3	F	7	1	0	0	3,364
Rowdys Move	3	G	2	0	0	1	976	Royal Fan	3	C	5	1	0	1	38,620
Rowsfashion Girl	5	M	1	0	0	0	345	Royal Feast	3	C	8	2	1	1	31,050
Roxade	7	G	18	0	2	4	6,615	Royal Folly	3	F	2	0	0	0	0
Roxaedit	4	F	9	2	1	1	76,708	Royal Footage	4	G	9	2	2	0	50,820
Roxbury Lady	5	M	1	0	0	0	0	Royal for Sure	7	M	7	1	2	0	9,137
Roxelana	6	M	1	1	0	0	22,200	Royal Force	2	G	5	1	0	0	27,320
Roxie Hart	3	F	6	0	0	0	348	Royal Forum	3	F	1	0	0	1	1,100
Roxie Lou	3	F	14	0	3	1	4,298	Royal Friend	7	H	1	0	0	0	0
Roxinho (BRZ)	5	H	6	0	2	1	37,700	Royal Fun	5	M	7	0	0	0	2,477
Roxstar	4	C	9	0	0	2	3,065	Royal Galaxy	3	F	1	0	0	0	400
Roxy Diamond	3	F	3	0	1	0	2,490	Royal Gambler	3	G	2	0	0	1	1,425
Roxy Roller	5	M	5	0	0	2	3,946	Royal Gate	6	M	9	1	0	1	12,551
Roy Boy	4	G	2	0	0	0	315	Royal Gem	4	C	4	0	0	2	29,560
Roy Rodjers	4	C	2	1	0	0	5,700	Royal General	2	G	3	0	0	1	1,507
Royal Act	3	C	1	0	0	0	220	Royal Groove	4	G	12	0	4	0	4,529
Royal Admirer	5	G	8	3	0	1	9,017	Royal Group	6	G	14	3	1	2	30,075
Royal Advantage	4	F	1	0	0	0	75	Royal Guard	4	C	2	0	0	0	0
Royal Affirmation	4	F	2	0	0	0	95	Royal Harvey	2	C	5	1	1	0	43,028
Royal Affirmed	5	H	11	3	2	2	101,040	Royal Highlander (IRE)	6	H	4	0	0	0	180
Royal Again	3	F	5	2	0	0	31,885	Royal Hint	3	F	6	2	3	0	44,400

Horse	Age	Sex	Sts	1st	2d	3d	Won
Royal Honey	4	G	6	0	0	1	1,630
Royal Hussy	3	F	12	2	4	0	16,208
Royal Illusion	2	F	5	1	1	0	21,300
Royal Impact	4	F	11	4	1	0	29,046
Royal Infantry	3	G	3	0	0	1	978
Royal Inspiration	3	F	4	0	0	0	125
Royal Intent	4	G	8	2	1	0	12,855
Royal Invader	4	G	9	1	1	0	11,653
Royal Irish	6	G	9	0	1	1	6,195
Royal Jeta	3	F	2	0	0	0	80
Royal Justin	3	G	5	0	0	2	1,451
Royal Kiss	2	F	6	0	1	2	3,515
Royal Kleven	3	F	1	1	0	0	4,950
Royal Lace	2	F	3	0	1	1	7,360
Royal Lady	3	F	4	0	1	0	7,665
Royal Lainie	2	F	2	0	0	0	0
Royal Lake	5	G	8	1	1	2	10,676
Royal Lee Ann	4	F	1	0	0	0	55
Royal Lullaby	4	F	4	0	0	0	949
Royal Magician	2	F	5	2	1	0	48,589
Royal Mambo	3	G	9	0	0	3	6,087
Royal Manor Way	5	M	1	0	0	0	0
Royal Marge	2	F	7	1	1	0	12,970
Royal Marquet	4	C	4	0	2	0	9,530
Royal Master	2	G	4	0	0	0	2,145
Royal Mecke	3	F	13	2	2	1	42,410
Royal Medal	4	C	4	1	1	0	15,009
Royal Messenger	4	C	11	2	3	1	48,940
Royal Millennium	3	G	5	0	1	0	7,840
Royal Miner	3	F	6	0	0	1	1,155
Royal Miracle	3	C	3	0	0	0	0
Royal Moonshine	3	F	2	0	0	0	90
Royal Moro	4	G	6	1	2	0	56,220
Royal Night Out	5	G	11	0	2	1	1,697
Royal No Trump	6	M	5	1	3	1	17,070
Royal n'Sweet	3	F	10	1	1	3	12,225
Royal Obsession	3	F	2	0	0	0	2,340
Royal On the Run	4	G	4	1	1	0	7,500
Royal Pac Man	7	H	2	0	0	0	0
Royal Palm Way	3	G	1	0	0	0	160
Royal Parade	2	F	2	0	0	1	2,340
Royal Payback	2	G	5	0	1	2	4,920
Royal Pet	2	F	7	3	2	1	72,283
Royal Peteski	5	H	16	5	3	2	68,190
Royal Photographer	2	G	6	2	0	0	28,740
Royal Place	3	C	14	3	2	1	147,432
Royal Powder	3	G	5	0	2	0	4,654
Royal Prairie	4	F	9	1	0	3	17,955
Royal Price (GER)	3	C	8	1	3	2	110,201
Royal Prize	3	F	12	2	0	1	29,360
Royal Prophet	3	G	1	0	0	1	2,390
Royal Providence	3	C	2	0	0	0	205
Royal Quack	5	H	10	1	1	0	4,516
Royal Rapids	5	G	7	1	0	0	12,700
Royal Raven	9	M	14	1	1	5	20,520
Royal Ray	2	C	8	1	0	0	11,768
Royal Rebecca	3	F	4	1	1	0	11,570
Royal Reception	3	F	10	1	0	1	24,540
Royal Recovery	4	F	1	0	0	0	0
Royal Regalia	5	G	9	4	2	0	102,252
Royal Regardes	4	F	3	0	0	0	140
Royal Return	5	H	3	0	0	0	441
Royal Revy	2	C	1	0	0	0	0
Royal Reward	3	F	3	0	0	0	50
Royal Rhythm	5	M	8	1	2	0	6,137
Royal Ridges	8	G	5	0	0	0	325
Royal Robe (IRE)	3	G	11	2	3	1	62,511
Royal Robey	2	C	6	0	0	0	2,285
Royal Roman	3	G	10	0	0	0	173
Royal Ruby	7	G	14	1	2	3	28,771
Royal Ruddy	2	F	1	0	0	0	0
Royal Rush	2	C	5	1	3	0	17,808
Royal Sabre	3	C	15	1	2	2	15,640
Royal Sailor	3	G	11	1	0	2	11,670
Royal Seas	5	M	2	0	0	0	258
Royal Sensation	2	C	1	1	0	0	11,200
Royal Serenity	4	G	4	0	0	0	126
Royal Severance	2	C	7	1	2	0	19,460
Royal Signe	5	M	5	0	2	1	5,810
Royal Silk	4	F	1	0	0	0	345
Royal Silver	11	G	8	1	1	1	5,544
Royal Siphon	3	G	5	0	0	0	3,720
Royal Sky	4	F	3	1	0	0	19,800
Royal Slewor	4	C	14	1	0	1	4,458
Royal Smoke	4	G	12	4	2	2	23,241
Royal Southerner	5	G	10	2	0	1	9,095
Royal Speech	3	F	17	0	2	0	6,630
Royal Speed	5	G	13	3	2	3	11,257
Royal Spirit	6	G	9	0	1	2	7,821
Royal Splash	3	C	6	0	0	0	0
Royal Spot	4	F	2	0	1	1	2,697
Royal Spy	5	H	3	2	0	0	169,000
Royal Squaw	2	F	2	0	1	0	5,880
Royal Status	4	G	5	0	1	2	14,140
Royal Sting	5	M	2	0	0	0	2,618
Royal Stroke	3	C	2	1	0	0	9,000
Royal Sue	2	F	2	0	0	1	649
Royal Sun	4	G	12	2	1	1	11,238
Royal T. K. O.	3	G	8	1	1	0	11,063
Royal Teresa	3	F	17	2	7	0	66,220
Royal Tiff	6	M	15	5	2	1	8,881
Royal Tour	2	G	8	1	2	2	9,990
Royal Tramp	10	H	3	0	0	0	1,148
Royal Tromp'e	2	F	5	0	2	0	17,580
Royal Tuneup	9	G	2	0	0	0	0
Royal Turmoil	3	F	2	0	0	0	0
Royal Twister	3	F	20	0	1	4	6,087
Royal Vixen	3	F	2	1	0	1	10,380
Royal War	4	F	12	1	2	2	30,500
Royal Watch	5	G	7	2	1	0	13,187
Royal Ways	4	C	8	0	0	0	0
Royal Wheaton	2	F	1	0	0	0	0
Royal Who	3	C	2	0	1	1	4,900
Royal Win	4	G	6	2	1	1	45,315
Royal Woodman	2	F	5	1	0	0	18,200
Royal Wulff	6	H	12	4	0	1	25,197
Royal Zar	3	C	2	0	0	0	0
Royale Rounder	4	G	9	1	4	1	10,700
Royale Show	5	H	9	0	0	3	1,873
Royalist	2	C	9	2	2	2	16,670
Royaljinski	4	G	1	0	0	0	0
Royally Blue	5	H	16	1	1	0	3,995
Royally Chosen	5	M	5	1	2	0	134,832
Royally Graced	4	F	11	1	0	1	6,422
Royally Minted	4	F	3	0	0	0	1,050
Royally Yours	2	F	6	0	2	1	8,460
Royalmissglitter	5	M	6	1	1	0	7,137
Royals Dream Baron	9	G	3	0	0	1	700
Royal's Quest	7	H	3	0	0	1	1,000
Royal's Way	5	H	6	0	0	0	302
Royalsaly	5	M	10	1	1	2	7,900
Royaltea Bey	7	G	2	0	0	0	114
Royalton	4	C	7	0	0	0	5,520
Royaltry	3	G	16	1	5	3	15,572
Royalty	9	G	7	4	0	1	22,495
Royalty Boy	2	C	4	1	2	0	37,571
Royalty Heights	2	G	2	0	0	0	200
Royalty of Iowa	3	C	5	0	0	0	3,860
Royalty Prospect	3	G	12	1	2	1	10,705
Royalty Rose	2	F	1	0	0	0	1,140
Roy's Boy's	10	G	12	1	0	1	6,805
Roy's Choice	4	C	2	0	1	0	3,510
Roys Hot Sauce	4	F	3	0	0	0	238
Roy's Jet	6	G	12	3	1	1	61,128
Roy's Joy	7	G	18	0	2	2	6,053
Roy's Raise	3	G	1	0	0	0	0
Roy's Remedy	3	G	1	0	0	0	0
Roy's Ruckus	8	G	10	1	3	2	55,734
Roy's Ruler	5	H	4	0	0	0	103
Roy's Secret	4	G	12	2	0	0	8,858
Roy's Trigger	3	C	8	1	0	0	22,320
Royster	3	G	14	0	7	2	70,441
Roythelittleone	11	G	5	1	1	1	7,850
Rozadante	3	G	6	1	0	1	8,450
Rozella Kay	3	F	11	0	0	1	3,310
Rozelle	3	F	1	1	0	0	4,920
Rozina	4	F	9	2	0	0	15,315
Rozys Account	4	F	11	2	1	2	82,291

Horse	Age	Sex	Sts	1st	2d	3d	Won
Ru Ready to Rumble	5	G	2	0	0	0	280
Ruanwar	4	F	14	3	5	0	4,398
Rua's Touch	4	F	3	0	0	0	250
Rub	8	G	6	0	0	3	7,845
Rub a Dubbs	5	M	11	0	4	4	12,237
Rub Don't Blot	7	H	3	0	0	0	174
Rub Down	6	G	7	0	0	1	2,552
Rub N Tug	3	F	2	0	0	0	96
Rub the Ring	4	G	8	0	0	0	232
Rubalamp	5	G	18	2	2	0	11,580
Rubber Band Man	6	G	15	0	0	1	2,595
Rubber Neck	3	C	8	1	0	0	4,246
Rubber Side Down	2	G	5	1	0	1	19,282
Rubbin' Noses	4	G	3	0	0	0	0
Rubelite	4	F	11	1	1	2	14,520
Ruben John	4	G	2	0	0	0	300
Ruben's Posada	3	G	4	1	0	0	9,600
Rubi Chunt	4	F	11	1	2	2	19,632
Rubi Echo	2	C	3	1	0	1	32,380
Rubi Elyse	4	F	1	0	0	0	101
Rubi Prince	2	G	3	1	0	0	8,400
Rubian Ridge	6	G	5	1	1	0	22,825
Rubiano Casey	4	F	6	0	1	3	5,695
Rubiano Kat	4	G	7	0	0	2	2,700
Rubiano Lad	2	C	5	1	1	0	15,965
Rubiano Star	3	G	17	0	1	3	6,809
Rubiano's Crown	5	G	6	0	1	1	1,829
Rubiano's Flag	3	G	15	3	3	0	28,099
Rubianos Image	3	C	12	4	3	3	102,152
Rubiano's Revenue	2	F	2	0	0	0	140
Rubiano's Touch	6	G	8	0	2	0	5,098
Rubiano's Wish	2	C	8	0	1	3	34,758
Rubies and Jade	5	M	16	2	1	2	13,022
Rubies N Roses	3	F	8	1	2	0	56,028
Rubies N Wine	3	F	9	0	0	1	1,009
Rubiesandstars	6	M	7	0	1	1	3,662
Rubietta	5	M	13	2	2	2	27,930
Rubikisses	5	M	10	1	2	1	34,140
Rubino	4	C	9	2	0	0	23,720
Rubin's Girl	6	M	15	2	3	0	29,087
Rubin's Pride	9	G	1	0	0	1	1,350
Rubin's Rose	4	F	11	1	5	3	54,160
Rubioso	5	G	5	0	0	1	1,894
Ruby Ballet	2	F	1	0	0	0	0
Ruby Brad	6	H	8	0	2	2	8,975
Ruby Choise	3	F	6	1	1	1	18,890
Ruby Dawn	3	F	9	2	2	0	19,757
Ruby Day	6	M	1	0	0	0	50
Ruby Essence	3	F	16	1	0	2	41,520
Ruby Falls	3	C	2	0	0	0	660
Ruby Fields	4	F	13	4	3	0	28,605
Ruby Franco	3	F	5	0	0	0	3,580
Ruby Glitter	3	F	12	2	3	1	44,140
Ruby J	3	F	4	0	0	0	900
Ruby Janes Girl	2	F	3	2	1	0	26,200
Ruby Lover	8	G	7	1	2	1	6,895
Ruby Mist	3	F	7	0	3	1	49,522
Ruby Montani	4	F	3	0	0	1	2,100
Ruby Moon	6	M	4	0	1	1	2,185
Ruby of Royalty	4	F	2	0	0	0	0
Ruby Princess	5	M	10	1	3	0	9,465
Ruby Prospector	6	G	9	0	0	3	3,088
Ruby Red	3	G	6	0	0	0	454
Ruby Red Slippers	4	F	13	1	2	1	27,802
Ruby Red Vette	3	F	4	0	0	0	403
Ruby River	4	F	9	0	3	3	14,788
Ruby Slew	2	F	4	2	0	1	8,245
Ruby Summer	2	F	1	0	0	1	4,320
Ruby Tango	5	M	12	1	1	2	43,535
Ruby Tutor	8	G	8	1	0	1	3,420
Ruby Valley Lady	2	F	2	1	0	0	3,240
Ruby Victoria	4	F	8	1	1	2	12,546
Rubyana	4	F	10	2	2	1	79,850
Rubys and Lace	5	M	3	0	0	0	216
Rubys Dove	3	F	4	0	0	2	2,856
Ruby's Orchid	3	F	7	2	1	1	31,854
Ruby's Princess	3	F	2	0	0	0	60
Ruby's Pro	3	C	7	2	2	1	74,170
Ruby's Reception	3	F	7	1	1	1	147,750
Ruby's Rocket	3	F	15	5	2	3	46,448
Ruby's Ruby	2	F	4	0	0	1	1,774
Ruby'sdream	4	F	6	0	0	1	929
Rubywood	3	F	7	2	1	0	59,400
Rucked	4	C	1	0	1	0	4,740
Rucker	2	C	4	1	0	0	20,718
Ruckiss Love	4	C	9	1	0	1	13,648
Ruck's Rapture	4	F	6	0	0	0	402
Ruckus All Night	7	M	2	0	0	0	0
Ruckus Dancer	2	G	7	0	1	1	3,050
Ruckus in Court	2	F	1	1	0	0	24,240
Ruckuslady	5	M	16	1	6	2	13,211
Rude Cat	5	G	4	0	0	0	972
Rude Coyote	7	M	4	0	0	0	3,960
Rude Dancer	3	G	3	0	0	0	0
Rude Ransom	5	G	8	0	2	0	4,820
Rudemood	3	G	16	1	4	2	27,917
Rudi J.	4	C	1	0	0	0	0
Rudirudy	8	G	10	0	1	1	24,180
Rudi's Leslie	2	F	3	0	1	1	6,240
Rudnick Bear	3	G	14	3	4	0	78,218
Rudolph	9	G	8	0	2	1	2,242
Rudster	4	G	17	1	2	5	13,213
Rudy Layne	5	G	2	0	0	0	97
Rudy Pooh Sue	3	F	5	0	0	0	1,495
Rudy Run	4	G	6	1	0	2	5,925
Rudy S	3	G	8	0	0	0	120
Rudy Tuesday	3	F	10	0	0	1	660
Rudy's Finest	3	C	2	1	0	0	6,240
Rudy's Last Reward	4	C	10	0	1	2	2,964
Rudys Mint	4	G	7	0	0	0	564
Rue de Bellechasse	4	F	1	0	0	0	0
Rue des Reves	4	F	6	2	1	0	16,090
Rue the Limit	3	C	6	1	1	1	9,850
Rue's Rebel	8	G	13	2	1	1	31,041
Rue's Rocket	4	C	1	0	0	0	0
Ruettiger	5	G	7	1	2	0	7,225
Ruff and Roady	3	G	1	0	0	0	0
Ruff Arrival	5	M	7	0	1	2	21,949
Ruff Flight	4	G	9	0	1	0	9,265
Ruff Halo	8	G	10	0	0	0	1,566
Ruff N Restless	6	G	7	3	0	1	37,580
Ruff N Ruckus	5	H	1	0	0	0	0
Ruff N Stormy	4	G	13	3	1	2	19,577
Ruff Ruff	3	F	4	0	0	0	1,061
Ruff Tuff Stuff	5	G	7	1	1	0	16,339
Ruffaire	5	M	10	2	2	0	25,944
Ruffena	5	M	5	0	1	2	13,404
Ruffino Gold	3	G	2	1	1	0	13,200
Ruftime	7	M	9	1	2	1	16,128
Rufus the Glider	3	G	10	3	0	1	55,240
Rufus the Red	2	G	3	0	0	1	1,862
Rufustheroadrunner	3	G	7	1	1	2	18,580
Rug (GB)	11	G	2	0	0	0	110
Rugala	3	F	1	0	0	1	1,350
Rugged Appeal	3	C	12	1	3	1	8,003
Rugged Cliff	5	G	9	1	0	0	8,034
Rugged Romantic	6	G	5	0	2	2	16,250
Rugged Russel	3	C	8	1	2	1	4,076
Rugged Zeal	7	G	10	1	3	2	18,846
Rugger	7	G	13	2	1	1	17,475
Ruggles Road	3	C	10	0	1	1	7,435
Ruhl With Approval	2	F	5	1	0	0	3,900
Ruhla	5	M	6	0	0	2	957
Ruhland	2	G	4	0	0	1	5,020
Ruhletta	3	F	17	2	4	3	23,108
Ruhlmoon	5	G	4	1	0	0	6,435
Ruissec	4	F	4	0	1	1	6,110
Ruji	4	G	17	0	1	5	10,913
Rule by Heart	3	G	8	0	1	2	4,170
Rule Change	6	G	5	1	0	0	7,483
Rule the Court	7	G	8	0	0	2	8,090
Rulebook	4	G	15	1	0	0	7,912
Ruler of the Seas	4	G	12	0	1	2	2,856
Ruler Red	6	G	10	1	1	3	5,502
Ruler Ruler	4	C	4	2	1	0	12,800
Ruler's Court	2	C	4	2	0	1	197,700
Rules of the Game	3	C	7	1	2	2	6,592

Horse	Age	Sex	Sts	1st	2d	3d	Won
Ruling House	2	F	9	1	0	1	24,307
Ruling Miner	4	G	2	0	0	0	0
Ruling Monarch	4	G	6	1	0	0	6,419
Ruling Star	4	C	6	0	4	0	25,400
Rullah's Bag	3	C	1	0	0	0	0
Rum Bird	5	M	6	1	1	1	18,620
Rum Candi	4	F	12	4	3	1	56,357
Rum Jungle	4	F	12	2	1	0	9,770
Rum N Raisin	5	M	1	0	0	0	430
Rum Rasin	6	M	2	1	0	0	7,444
Rum Reason	3	F	1	0	0	0	0
Rum Royal	7	M	7	0	0	1	908
Rum Shooter	4	G	5	1	0	1	5,325
Rum Splasher	4	G	9	1	0	4	15,515
Rum Talk	3	C	11	1	1	3	24,969
Rumarico's Lord	5	H	2	0	0	1	1,800
Rumba Jazz	5	M	1	0	0	0	90
Rumba Numba	2	F	3	0	2	0	16,400
Rumba Que Tumba	2	F	1	0	1	0	2,240
Rumbante (ARG)	6	M	7	0	0	0	1,424
Rumble	2	G	4	1	0	2	20,100
Rumble and Flash	5	G	3	0	0	0	0
Rumblefromabove	7	G	5	0	0	0	550
Rumbleinthejungle	3	G	2	0	0	0	0
Rumbletown	4	G	15	1	0	0	6,855
Rumbling Disco	3	C	3	1	0	1	6,875
Rumbo's Starlet	5	M	13	3	3	1	11,610
Rumbustious	5	M	2	0	0	0	1,120
Rumcake	4	F	1	0	0	0	140
Rumor Denide	4	G	13	1	0	0	3,902
Rumor Had It	4	F	4	0	0	0	116
Rumored Attack	7	G	3	0	0	0	0
Rumors Fly	5	G	6	1	0	0	2,927
Rumpus Kat	4	F	3	1	1	0	11,748
Rumway	2	G	4	0	0	1	1,714
Run Alexis Run	7	M	8	0	0	0	1,907
Run Along	3	F	8	0	0	0	1,355
Run Along Sonny	3	C	1	0	1	0	8,200
Run Aly Run	3	G	4	0	0	0	431
Run Amiss	4	C	2	0	0	1	3,333
Run Around Sue	8	M	9	2	2	0	24,945
Run At Night	3	C	4	2	0	0	13,572
Run Away Artie	4	G	18	3	1	4	39,450
Run Away Mama	2	F	2	0	0	0	400
Run Away Man	5	G	12	2	0	1	6,122
Run Away Mel	5	H	3	0	0	0	0
Run Becky Run	4	F	1	0	0	0	0
Run Big	3	F	11	1	2	1	12,370
Run Bootie Run	3	G	9	1	4	2	8,740
Run Boss Run	4	C	2	0	0	0	64
Run Bullseye Run	3	C	4	0	0	0	228
Run Cat Run	2	F	3	1	0	1	18,250
Run Chic Run	5	M	1	0	0	0	0
Run Com	5	G	3	0	0	1	1,236
Run Dancer Run	5	M	17	3	0	2	13,854
Run Devil Run	4	F	3	0	1	0	3,575
Run Doeny Run	3	F	2	0	0	0	0
Run Don't Dance	4	G	10	0	1	0	1,810
Run for Charity	9	M	5	0	0	0	290
Run for Daisys	4	F	4	1	1	0	1,288
Run for Dessert	2	F	1	0	0	1	5,880
Run for Fun	3	G	2	0	1	0	4,580
Run for Jerry	2	F	1	0	0	0	0
Run for Joy	7	M	11	3	1	3	74,161
Run for Lillie	2	F	3	0	0	0	305
Run for Little Bit	5	M	4	0	1	1	18,957
Run for Love	4	G	12	5	2	0	24,410
Run for Marc	5	M	9	5	1	0	27,780
Run for Masie	3	F	2	0	0	0	214
Run for Reda	5	H	3	0	0	0	0
Run for Slew	3	G	8	0	0	0	1,575
Run for the Money	2	C	4	0	0	0	0
Run for the Refund	9	M	1	0	0	0	65
Run for Trey	3	G	14	0	0	3	4,575
Run for You	3	C	12	0	3	1	10,222
Run Forus	6	G	1	0	0	0	73
Run Freddie Run	3	C	8	0	2	1	11,550
Run Free	3	F	14	4	4	2	27,073
Run Fun Sundial	4	G	9	3	1	0	12,850
Run Honey	3	F	3	0	0	0	225
Run in the Park	5	H	6	1	0	2	9,300
Run Irene Run	2	F	5	0	1	1	4,089
Run Irish Cream	4	F	12	2	2	0	10,372
Run Jesse Run	4	G	17	0	7	2	14,240
Run Judge Run	6	G	13	1	0	4	6,046
Run Kaitlyn Run	2	F	5	2	0	1	20,125
Run Kaya Run	3	C	11	1	0	0	8,620
Run Kiva Run	4	F	7	0	2	2	8,165
Run Kush Run	5	G	10	2	4	1	69,350
Run Like Hunter	3	G	5	0	0	0	522
Run Like Yamama	2	F	1	1	0	0	15,720
Run Lil Tooch	7	G	6	0	0	2	4,663
Run Little Richie	7	G	9	1	1	1	26,741
Run Little Sister	2	F	4	0	0	0	248
Run Looker Run	2	F	3	0	2	1	13,488
Run Lori Run	4	F	3	1	0	0	810
Run Lucile	3	F	5	1	0	3	42,760
Run Lucky Vera	3	F	4	0	1	0	1,385
Run Matty Run	4	G	10	2	2	0	16,345
Run Maurice Run	5	G	21	2	2	1	13,040
Run Max Run	3	G	6	1	0	0	14,715
Run Me Down	3	F	2	0	1	1	7,970
Run Me Out	4	G	8	0	0	1	3,882
Run Mickey Run	3	G	6	1	1	0	7,950
Run Mikey Run	2	C	5	1	0	0	12,400
Run More Pecos	5	M	2	0	0	0	47
Run N Coke	2	C	10	1	1	3	15,960
Run N Honey	6	M	4	1	0	1	1,580
Run N Love	2	F	6	1	0	1	13,655
Run of the Mill	2	C	4	0	0	0	618
Run Rate	5	M	4	0	1	0	3,750
Run Rayma Run	3	F	7	0	0	0	3,622
Run Rebecca Run	3	F	8	2	3	1	89,280
Run Retsina Girl	3	F	4	0	0	0	739
Run Ricky Run	2	C	4	1	2	1	34,030
Run Rita	4	F	4	0	0	0	565
Run Robin	6	M	3	1	0	0	4,441
Run Roger Run	5	H	6	0	1	0	2,943
Run Sarah Run	3	F	13	3	2	5	85,460
Run Shannon Run	4	C	6	0	0	0	340
Run Some	3	C	3	0	0	0	0
Run Sweetie	3	F	12	1	4	1	6,705
Run the Good Race	2	F	1	0	0	1	1,200
Run the Light	2	G	3	1	0	0	18,260
Run to Glory	3	C	11	0	2	1	26,425
Run to the Border	4	G	7	2	0	1	26,290
Run to Victory	4	C	9	3	1	3	114,456
Run Up the Flag	4	C	2	0	0	0	170
Run Willa Run	4	F	5	1	1	2	30,460
Run Wish	4	F	2	0	0	0	240
Run With Winds	6	H	13	0	0	2	1,884
Run You So n' So	4	G	13	0	3	1	5,407
Run Z Road	6	M	8	0	0	2	2,552
Run Zeal Run	5	G	11	5	2	2	63,935
Runagate	6	M	9	4	0	1	52,410
Runamucca	3	F	7	0	0	0	1,237
Runaround	2	C	1	0	0	0	0
Runaround Jazz	3	G	5	1	0	1	11,371
Runaway Angela	8	M	4	0	0	0	0
Runaway Beach	3	F	2	0	0	0	370
Runaway Bebe	3	C	3	0	0	0	420
Runaway Blaine	3	G	13	1	0	1	8,600
Runaway Briartic	2	G	2	2	0	0	7,480
Runaway Capade	7	H	17	1	1	6	13,200
Runaway Champ	4	F	3	0	1	0	2,828
Runaway Chanel	3	F	6	0	1	0	11,660
Runaway Child	4	G	15	1	3	2	9,392
Runaway Choice	4	G	5	0	0	3	20,900
Runaway Chris	2	C	2	0	0	0	332
Runaway Clara	3	F	1	0	0	0	0
Runaway Dancer	4	G	7	3	0	0	172,170
Runaway Dave	6	G	7	0	0	0	0
Runaway Doctor	6	G	4	0	0	0	796
Runaway Don	6	G	13	1	2	2	20,207
Runaway Driver	3	F	9	1	1	1	8,194
Runaway Eleanor	2	F	1	0	0	1	4,100
Runaway Fox	3	F	3	0	0	0	225
Runaway Frolic	2	F	7	2	0	2	13,410

Horse	Age	Sex	Sts	1st	2d	3d	Won
Runaway Froze	6	M	10	2	1	1	19,313
Runaway Heiress	5	M	4	0	1	0	1,612
Runaway Helen	4	F	16	0	5	1	6,858
Runaway Jet	6	G	9	1	0	2	12,585
Runaway Julie	2	F	5	0	1	0	3,914
Runaway Kate	5	M	21	0	2	6	14,711
Runaway Kidd	8	G	3	0	0	0	1,300
Runaway Lark	4	G	6	1	2	1	6,480
Runaway Lil	5	M	10	4	2	3	69,936
Runaway Limit	4	F	7	3	1	0	13,490
Runaway Love	6	G	1	0	0	1	5,874
Runaway Luck	5	M	4	0	0	0	573
Runaway Martha	5	M	1	0	0	0	1,440
Runaway Mate	8	G	9	1	0	0	1,370
Runaway Mike	6	G	4	0	0	0	333
Runaway Mist	5	M	1	0	0	0	36
Runaway Mother	3	F	5	1	0	0	25,510
Runaway Nancy	4	F	3	0	0	0	690
Runaway Peggy	3	F	12	0	1	3	6,080
Runaway Pro	4	F	5	2	1	1	85,600
Runaway Reality	5	M	12	0	1	2	5,665
Runaway Rich	5	H	4	0	0	0	180
Runaway Ride	6	G	13	2	1	1	10,269
Runaway Rizzi	2	F	6	1	1	3	95,500
Runaway Road	3	F	13	0	3	0	8,640
Runaway Rose	5	M	3	0	0	0	876
Runaway Rossi	3	G	5	1	2	0	14,025
Runaway Rubi	3	F	12	3	3	2	44,470
Runaway Rudolph	4	C	8	1	0	1	4,502
Runaway Ruffian	4	H	10	0	0	0	1,518
Runaway Runaway	3	G	12	2	2	3	32,483
Runaway Russy	3	G	9	2	3	1	62,220
Runaway Soon	3	G	5	1	0	0	8,820
Runaway Sreva	2	F	6	1	0	0	19,410
Runaway Steel	3	C	10	1	1	2	20,590
Runaway Storm	3	C	3	1	0	0	12,890
Runaway Stream	3	G	5	1	1	0	5,946
Runaway Style	3	G	13	1	3	2	28,060
Runaway Success	5	H	2	0	0	0	0
Runaway Thoughts	4	G	4	0	3	1	5,409
Runaway Tiger	5	M	8	3	3	1	74,388
Runaway Train	3	R	7	0	0	0	3,155
Runaway Turk	3	G	7	1	1	0	4,198
Runaway Twins	4	C	13	3	1	1	47,675
Runaway Valentino	4	C	3	0	0	0	0
Runaway Victor	7	G	14	0	2	1	26,238
Runaway Warrior	3	C	4	0	2	0	4,060
Runawayfun	5	M	13	6	1	1	91,956
Runawayskye	3	F	4	0	1	0	5,620
Runbayou	8	G	13	2	3	0	13,383
Runbeforethewind	3	F	5	1	1	0	10,410
Runco	4	F	9	0	0	1	4,552
Runder Thumble	6	M	10	2	2	1	10,660
Runderdancer	5	M	4	0	0	0	565
Rundle	4	G	12	2	2	1	54,313
Runemoutslew	3	F	3	0	0	0	154
Runinforacheck	2	F	2	0	0	0	0
Runingforpresident	2	C	2	0	1	0	10,660
Runingtothelimit	5	M	3	0	1	1	2,618
Runinthesun	3	G	13	2	2	0	9,832
Runmore Mema	6	H	4	0	0	3	23,310
Runner Up	2	C	3	1	0	0	7,590
Runners Name	3	G	1	0	0	0	0
Runnin Aarons	3	F	6	1	1	1	5,635
Runnin Cameron	4	G	2	0	0	0	0
Runnin Inthe Rain	6	H	6	0	0	0	312
Runnin N the Wind	3	F	10	2	1	1	11,138
Runnin On Brave	4	G	15	0	3	6	11,728
Runnin On Class	2	C	1	0	0	0	160
Runnin' On Nitro	3	G	6	1	0	1	35,640
Runnin Pollock	4	F	14	1	1	2	8,527
Runnin Rehaan	3	G	3	0	0	0	320
Runnin Rena	6	M	2	0	0	0	0
Runnin Renee	3	F	1	0	0	0	0
Runnin Stuff	3	F	5	0	0	0	539
Runnin Tella Fib	3	G	5	0	0	0	140
Runnin' the River	3	G	6	1	1	1	7,615
Runnin Ute	2	F	9	1	1	1	28,280
Runnin West	5	G	7	1	2	1	35,278
Runnin Wonder	4	F	2	0	0	1	4,030
Running Away	2	C	7	0	2	1	13,886
Running Bay	5	G	12	3	1	1	16,798
Running Brave	2	C	11	0	1	1	11,465
Running Charlie	3	C	5	1	0	0	16,500
Running Copelan	8	H	4	0	0	0	225
Running Count	5	G	15	3	1	4	50,388
Running Debate	3	F	8	1	0	2	88,699
Running Eleven	8	H	4	0	0	0	900
Running Footman	5	G	10	1	0	0	7,593
Running for John	3	C	13	1	1	1	7,720
Running Furiously	3	C	8	2	2	1	43,450
Running Gun	4	G	13	4	1	2	29,795
Running Hard	4	C	12	0	1	1	2,177
Running Hawk	3	C	9	0	0	1	549
Running Heel	3	F	8	0	0	1	2,811
Running in Style	5	H	7	0	0	1	1,750
Running Light	9	H	1	0	0	0	0
Running Mistress	7	M	8	3	1	0	18,197
Running Nelson	3	F	10	1	1	0	13,360
Running On End	6	H	4	0	0	0	3,810
Running Outta Time	4	F	4	0	0	0	180
Running Piper	3	C	1	0	0	0	0
Running Rahy	5	G	8	0	1	1	1,298
Running Rewana	3	G	5	0	0	0	226
Running Rhythm	2	C	4	0	0	1	4,160
Running Rooney	3	G	7	1	2	1	21,800
Running Ryan	9	G	3	0	0	1	3,170
Running Saint	2	F	5	0	1	1	20,724
Running Smooth	4	C	3	0	0	0	786
Running Tide	4	C	3	0	0	0	5,040
Running Today	5	H	4	1	0	1	12,240
Running Water	5	G	7	0	0	1	1,381
Running Zarb	5	G	17	1	2	2	10,161
Runningfordiapers	7	H	9	1	0	0	2,165
Runningwithfire	2	C	2	0	0	0	0
Runningwiththewind	5	G	7	1	0	2	5,810
Runnintothealter	2	C	3	0	1	2	13,500
Runninwithscissors	4	G	5	0	0	0	348
Runnymede Bride	4	F	1	0	0	0	0
Runoverumbaby	4	C	5	0	0	0	0
Runs All Knight	2	G	6	1	0	0	7,978
Runs Like a Benz	4	F	11	4	2	3	53,610
Runs Naked	3	F	13	2	1	1	12,150
Runs With Scissors	2	G	2	0	0	0	0
Runsoncruz	3	F	10	0	1	1	3,787
Runspastum	6	H	6	1	0	2	83,779
Runstohislooks	3	G	4	1	0	1	9,860
Runsumforme	3	G	6	0	2	2	5,609
Runtherapids	2	F	7	1	2	3	22,470
Runto the Mountain	8	H	2	0	0	0	234
Runup	4	F	1	0	0	0	0
Runway	4	C	10	1	2	1	33,410
Runway Dancer	3	F	7	0	0	0	0
Runway Heading	3	G	6	1	1	0	17,770
Runway Lollipop (ARG)	4	F	11	1	2	2	72,140
Rupert Haint	3	C	18	2	1	1	10,903
Rupert Herd	6	G	9	2	0	0	19,864
Rupert's Approval	6	M	4	0	0	1	908
Rupert's Fire	5	M	14	2	3	1	52,380
Rupert's Hard Fire	4	G	20	1	1	0	5,843
Rupert's Rose Morn	4	G	6	1	0	1	2,921
Rupert's Sun	5	G	6	0	1	2	3,346
Rupert's Win M All	3	G	6	1	1	2	11,811
Rural Queen	6	M	10	0	1	1	5,748
Rural Road	3	G	11	2	2	1	25,717
Rural Vision	5	M	11	1	0	2	4,326
Rurd	4	G	16	3	2	3	19,645
Ruready	2	F	1	0	0	0	0
Rush Around	3	C	9	1	3	1	51,040
Rush Buy	7	M	4	0	0	0	204
Rush C C	3	G	3	1	0	0	4,087
Rush Creek	3	F	8	1	1	1	29,320
Rush Haint Darla	3	F	11	0	0	4	3,880
Rush Into Heaven	2	C	7	2	0	0	74,063
Rush 'n Amigo	3	G	10	1	2	0	7,335
Rush Note	2	F	4	1	0	2	12,100
Rush of Wind	3	G	4	1	2	0	4,820
Rush Queen	7	M	8	2	1	2	3,008

Horse	Age	Sex	Sts	1st	2d	3d	Won
Rush Straight Thru	6	H	4	1	0	1	4,760
Rush Street	3	G	2	0	0	1	1,760
Rush Street Miss	2	F	9	0	0	1	3,290
Rush to Defend	3	C	4	0	0	0	1,230
Rush to the Wire	5	M	10	0	2	1	4,450
Rushalong Slew	6	M	2	0	0	0	0
Rushaway Native	2	F	1	0	0	0	0
Rushcliffe	3	G	13	1	2	1	20,660
Rushin' to Altar	4	C	6	1	1	1	90,538
Rushing	2	G	5	0	0	0	325
Rushing Force	3	F	9	0	0	1	9,800
Rushing Road	7	H	6	0	0	2	1,242
Rushing Sands	5	M	15	1	0	5	12,743
Rushing Stream (JPN)	3	C	2	0	0	0	300
Rushing Water	3	C	9	0	2	2	23,930
Rushmo	4	G	9	0	0	1	5,845
Ruskin	10	G	11	2	2	5	33,095
Ruskin Drive	3	C	11	0	0	1	3,516
Ruslanova	2	F	5	0	1	1	6,890
Russell Cave	7	G	15	4	3	0	53,215
Russell Earl	6	H	7	0	0	1	569
Russell Springs	4	G	9	1	1	0	5,696
Russellette	3	F	9	0	0	2	5,741
Russell's Devil	3	G	16	0	3	1	7,483
Russia	3	C	3	0	0	0	740
Russian Bear	3	G	4	0	0	1	820
Russian Bonus	3	F	6	2	1	0	23,872
Russian Dancer	4	G	9	1	1	0	1,309
Russian Emperor (IRE)	10	G	9	0	2	0	1,013
Russian Hand	4	G	10	3	0	0	22,609
Russian Inn	4	G	8	1	0	3	5,058
Russian Kat	5	G	7	0	0	3	2,130
Russian Momma	4	C	13	2	1	5	38,100
Russian Mystery	5	H	7	1	1	0	6,556
Russian News	3	G	4	2	0	1	27,430
Russian Package	7	G	7	0	1	1	7,954
Russian Palace	5	G	1	0	0	0	40
Russian Raj	5	G	1	0	0	0	83
Russian Roline	5	M	4	1	0	1	4,163
Russian Royalty	5	G	8	3	0	1	25,663
Russian Ruler	9	G	8	1	1	1	6,255
Russian Sweetiepie	6	M	12	2	2	3	77,736
Russian the Gold	5	G	6	1	1	1	4,852
Russian Tigress	5	M	1	0	0	1	1,500
Russian Tsar	6	H	5	0	0	3	24,533
Russian Wind	4	F	12	4	1	0	21,275
Russing	5	G	9	0	0	1	2,253
Rustic	4	F	8	1	5	0	27,560
Rustic Kitten	3	F	9	2	1	2	44,220
Rustic Revelation	2	G	5	0	1	1	3,968
Rustica	2	F	2	0	0	0	185
Ruston	3	C	2	0	0	0	0
Ruston Bearcat	5	G	5	0	1	0	2,480
Ruston Drive In	2	C	2	0	0	0	210
Ruston Rambler	6	G	1	0	0	0	0
Ruston Rifle	6	G	15	1	4	3	14,345
Rustridge Brix	7	G	19	7	1	3	34,455
Rustridge Zin	6	H	2	0	0	0	0
Rustrum	3	G	3	0	0	0	3,528
Rusty Amber	3	C	6	1	3	0	12,527
Rusty Angle	3	G	17	2	1	3	24,152
Rusty Boy	4	G	11	2	1	3	5,098
Rusty Gold	7	G	2	0	0	0	450
Rusty Gun	3	C	13	1	2	1	8,658
Rusty Man	4	G	14	3	4	2	17,810
Rusty Neil	5	G	1	0	0	0	100
Rusty Niki	6	H	9	0	0	0	1,635
Rusty Rocket	4	C	7	0	2	0	3,026
Rusty Spur	5	H	5	1	1	1	26,292
Rutabaga	4	G	10	1	1	3	10,842
Ruth Sage	2	F	1	0	0	0	164
Ruthie the Rocket	2	F	2	0	1	1	8,980
Ruthies Boy	2	G	4	0	0	0	0
Ruthie's Dance	2	F	3	0	1	0	3,738
Ruthie's Double	6	H	4	1	3	0	4,076
Ruthless Lady	5	M	19	3	0	0	16,320
Ruthless River	4	F	7	0	0	1	1,212
Ruth's Full Shadow	4	C	5	1	1	1	10,237
Ruth's Grey Girl	6	M	15	0	4	3	12,765
Ruth's Match Trick	3	F	2	0	0	1	2,520
Ruth's Route	3	F	4	1	1	0	7,875
Ruth's Sisu	3	F	8	0	0	3	3,577
Ruthy Red	3	F	9	3	1	2	41,751
Rutledge Dancer	4	F	2	0	1	1	8,760
Rutledge Gold	4	G	10	1	1	2	22,087
Rutledge Man	3	C	3	0	0	0	1,560
Rutledge Protocol	2	G	5	0	2	2	12,630
Rutledge Rebel	3	G	12	1	5	1	20,104
Rutledge Slew	4	G	9	2	1	1	25,280
Rutters Renegade (IRE)	3	F	3	0	1	0	24,946
Rven Hi	4	F	1	0	0	0	0
Ryan D	4	G	14	1	1	3	12,351
Ryan Is Flying	3	C	6	1	0	0	25,376
Ryan On Broadway	5	G	9	0	1	2	3,055
Ryan S	7	G	2	0	0	0	240
Ryan the Great	4	C	7	0	1	0	2,572
Ryan's Buddy	3	C	5	1	0	3	16,035
Ryan's Cookin	5	H	5	0	0	0	274
Ryan's Dancer	3	G	1	0	0	0	0
Ryan's Express	5	G	20	2	2	5	23,382
Ryan's Irish Slew	8	M	1	0	0	0	114
Ryan's Lad	4	G	10	2	1	4	10,325
Ryan's Nanny	7	M	3	0	0	0	0
Ryan's Partner	5	H	15	0	2	1	16,221
Ryan's Special	3	G	4	1	0	0	4,644
Ryans Super Star	3	G	4	2	1	0	28,470
Ryansdeputy	3	G	6	1	0	0	3,955
Ryanwood	6	G	5	0	0	0	481
Rydell	2	C	1	0	0	0	0
Ryding Newyork	5	M	6	0	1	1	6,886
Ryding Poupon	6	H	6	2	0	0	12,317
Rye	3	C	3	0	0	0	290
Rye Hill Miss	4	F	2	0	0	0	0
Ryjilla	3	C	5	0	1	0	540
Ryld	4	G	12	0	5	2	9,346
Rylee Boy	3	G	4	0	0	0	0
Rylee C T	2	C	5	1	1	0	8,625
Ryson	8	G	1	1	0	0	4,882
Rythem n' Blues	2	F	2	0	0	0	260
S Ball	4	F	3	0	0	1	220
S Lupe	3	G	15	1	1	2	5,421
S N J's Desire	3	F	12	1	2	2	47,705
S N R's Defense	2	F	3	0	0	0	318
S S C Moonfleet	4	G	15	1	2	3	20,408
S S Enterprize	2	G	3	0	0	1	2,895
S S Game	2	G	2	0	0	0	209
S S Scribble	3	F	12	1	0	4	39,506
S S Sheba	3	F	8	0	2	0	3,571
S Table Dancer	3	F	22	2	5	4	20,834
S Train	7	G	9	0	0	1	1,205
S W Flyer	3	G	8	0	0	2	5,130
S W Funny Money	5	M	1	0	0	0	0
S W Legion	7	H	2	0	0	0	52
S W Nina	4	F	2	1	0	0	4,536
S W Pocket Money	4	G	17	3	2	2	20,496
S W Stephie	5	M	13	2	1	1	11,420
S W Terry	4	C	3	0	0	1	858
S. A. River Walk	3	F	4	2	1	1	8,450
S. K. Boy	6	G	9	0	0	0	540
S. L. Charmer	4	F	12	1	2	6	48,708
S. L. Gamine	3	F	12	5	2	1	36,374
S. S. Bounty	3	G	14	2	4	0	52,429
S. S. Finesse	7	M	14	3	2	1	27,990
S. S. Hawkeye	7	G	13	0	3	0	11,450
S. S. Shadow	3	C	9	1	0	1	5,076
S. S. Spitfire	6	H	4	1	0	0	2,820
S. S.'s Gold Halo	6	M	14	2	1	2	21,506
S. W. Silver Sky	6	M	16	1	6	1	14,048
Sa Ad	6	H	12	5	2	1	73,528
Sa Boogie Dancer	4	F	5	0	1	1	4,200
Sa Moken	3	F	8	0	2	1	11,760
Sa Passem	2	G	2	0	0	0	0
Saami	4	G	17	2	1	3	16,012
Saanich Sam	3	G	6	2	0	0	9,243
Saarland	4	C	8	2	2	1	263,040
Sabaku	4	G	5	0	1	0	2,022
Sabalucious	3	G	13	5	0	1	91,920
Sabbatical	2	C	1	0	0	0	120

RECORDS OF HORSES

Horse	Age	Sex	Sts	1st	2d	3d	Won
Sabeena	3	F	5	0	0	0	328
Sabermetrics	2	G	7	0	3	0	4,850
Sabertooth	5	G	6	0	1	0	14,500
Sabiango (GER)	5	H	6	1	0	1	218,563
Sabina's Joy	4	F	3	1	0	0	12,891
Sable Cape	2	F	2	1	0	0	11,800
Sable Chase	4	F	3	0	1	1	5,300
Sablene	4	F	4	1	1	0	11,428
Sabogal	6	G	14	2	3	2	12,845
Sabotai	3	C	1	0	0	0	0
Saboya	6	M	13	2	3	2	28,448
Sabre Baby	2	C	5	1	1	1	21,210
Sabre Light	5	H	2	0	0	0	0
Sabre of Silver	5	M	16	2	0	2	95,100
Sabre Rattling	2	G	2	1	1	0	7,960
Sabre Tooth Tiger	5	G	1	0	0	1	2,040
Sabrina Slew	4	F	1	0	0	0	271
Sabrina Taryn	6	H	2	1	1	0	6,160
Sabrina's Quest	3	F	5	1	0	2	13,433
Sabrinas Spirit	5	M	2	0	0	0	0
Sacagawea's Spirit	3	F	4	1	0	1	26,688
Sacatricks	3	F	3	0	0	0	1,230
Saccharine	3	F	2	0	0	0	1,302
Sachem	6	H	14	2	2	1	33,284
Sachet	3	F	1	0	0	0	0
Sackville Parade	5	M	3	1	0	1	5,430
Sacre Bleu	2	F	6	0	0	0	541
Sacred Affair	4	G	10	3	2	0	49,568
Sacred Cat	2	F	4	1	1	1	43,788
Sacred Gem	4	F	10	1	2	1	17,955
Sacred Jewel	4	F	3	0	0	0	3,480
Sacred Lyric	3	C	3	0	0	0	0
Sacred Spirit	7	G	6	2	1	0	6,120
Sacred Vow	3	C	7	1	1	0	9,620
Sacred Winds	2	G	4	1	0	0	13,057
Sacrifice	2	C	3	0	0	0	1,460
Sacrifice Bid	8	M	11	1	4	1	18,464
Sacsahuaman (CHI)	5	G	3	1	0	0	13,770
Saddle a Dream	3	G	11	1	1	2	11,222
Saddle Oxfords	5	H	5	1	0	0	7,500
Saddle Up	6	M	1	0	0	0	89
Saddle Up Janet K	4	F	4	0	2	0	2,980
Saddlesong	2	F	2	0	0	2	4,950
Saddlespur	5	G	2	1	0	0	3,040
Sadie Bo	4	F	5	0	0	1	920
Sadie Mae	3	G	8	2	1	0	31,310
Sadie Ray	10	M	1	0	0	0	0
Sadie S.	7	M	9	0	0	0	1,101
Sadlers Pride	4	G	14	4	2	1	77,060
Sadler's Sarah	5	M	1	0	0	0	720
Sadler's Spirit	7	M	9	0	0	0	0
Saf Link	5	G	12	0	2	5	42,864
Safara	3	F	6	1	1	0	7,700
Safari	3	C	8	1	2	3	57,320
Safari Barbie	2	F	2	0	0	0	0
Safari Run	3	F	5	0	0	1	2,230
Safarid (FR)	9	G	15	0	3	3	4,456
Safe Expectation	4	C	13	3	1	1	22,045
Safe in the U S A	4	C	4	2	0	0	59,830
Safe Passage	6	M	5	0	1	1	4,800
Safe Signal	2	C	3	0	1	1	12,850
Safe Today	2	G	1	0	0	0	190
Safe Try	6	M	11	2	0	2	7,349
Safe Viewing	8	H	1	0	0	0	0
Safely At Home	3	F	9	1	0	2	40,592
Safely Guarded		C	1	0	0	0	140
Safety Lord	3	G	13	1	2	1	25,000
Safley's Social	2	F	9	2	0	1	15,100
Saga Boy	2	C	5	0	0	0	1,000
Sagacious	3	G	5	1	0	0	24,714
Sage Fire	6	M	5	0	0	2	1,485
Sage Road	4	G	20	6	3	4	31,194
Sage Valentine	3	G	7	1	0	1	4,637
Sage's Fifty Six	2	F	7	1	2	0	51,433
Sageworth	3	F	2	1	0	0	6,679
Sagi'sdream	4	C	2	0	0	0	0
Sagle	6	M	4	0	1	1	5,425
Sago	2	F	5	4	0	0	132,150
Sagreeno	9	G	10	1	1	1	5,730

Horse	Age	Sex	Sts	1st	2d	3d	Won
Sah Woosh	3	F	8	1	0	2	9,982
Sahab	2	C	3	1	0	0	12,423
Sahara Desert	3	G	15	1	3	4	13,861
Sahara Knight	3	F	9	1	4	0	5,282
Sahara Mist	3	F	5	1	0	0	7,027
Sahara Sands	6	M	1	0	0	0	0
Sahmkindawonderful	2	F	3	1	1	0	21,580
Sahoma Secret	3	C	9	1	2	1	6,640
Sahrano	3	G	3	0	0	0	100
Said Enough	8	G	13	4	0	1	12,112
Said So	4	G	13	1	3	1	17,050
Saigon Lieutenant	8	G	6	0	0	0	2,803
Sail Miss Gracie	4	F	10	2	2	2	25,743
Sail My Vessel	6	G	6	0	1	1	3,950
Sailaway	3	C	2	0	1	1	9,500
Sailborrun	2	C	2	0	1	1	5,220
Saildust	6	G	16	2	3	0	9,459
Sailing Images	3	F	4	1	0	0	6,716
Sailing Sal	3	F	12	0	2	0	3,545
Sailing Sioux	6	M	9	1	0	1	2,326
Sailing Skipper	4	G	9	0	1	0	2,559
Sailingforpennies	4	F	1	0	0	0	270
Sailinwithcaptain	3	C	5	1	1	2	36,696
Sailit	4	F	2	0	0	0	0
Sailmaker	3	F	8	0	0	2	10,790
Sailor Girl	7	M	12	3	0	1	28,672
Sailor's Dream	3	F	6	1	0	2	9,150
Sailor's Gold	2	F	1	0	0	0	975
Sailor's Lil' Lady	4	F	1	0	0	0	0
Sailor's Reward	8	M	3	0	0	0	390
Sailor's Wave	3	F	12	1	2	1	25,047
Sails Are Up	5	M	9	1	0	1	6,357
Saint Afleet	2	C	4	2	0	0	53,720
Saint Appeal	4	C	4	1	0	0	28,440
Saint Bernadette	4	F	2	1	0	1	46,284
Saint Brook	3	F	2	1	0	0	9,600
Saint Buddy	3	C	5	1	1	1	51,480
Saint D. M.	3	G	8	2	0	0	11,895
Saint Damien	5	G	7	0	1	1	15,410
Saint d'Or	2	F	4	1	0	0	13,900
Saint Dysmas	3	C	1	0	0	0	0
Saint Ernie	5	H	7	1	0	2	3,842
Saint Felix	4	G	3	0	1	1	689
Saint Golddigger	4	G	13	1	1	5	25,889
Saint Greer	3	F	1	0	0	0	0
Saint He Can't	3	G	6	1	1	1	9,910
Saint Joseph	6	H	2	0	0	0	1,620
Saint Julien	5	G	17	2	4	1	19,147
Saint Kilian	4	G	9	1	2	1	19,765
Saint Labradro	8	G	12	1	1	1	3,837
Saint Liam	3	C	9	3	3	0	141,275
Saint Lorenzo	3	C	11	4	2	1	88,880
Saint Louisa	3	F	1	0	0	0	0
Saint Marden	4	C	1	0	0	0	0
Saint Martin	2	G	3	0	0	0	0
Saint Mercedes	3	C	3	0	0	0	111
Saint Nick's Magic	2	G	4	0	0	0	675
Saint Nor Sinner	4	C	9	1	0	1	3,076
Saint of the City	3	G	1	0	0	1	5,880
Saint Olivia	2	F	2	0	0	0	180
Saint Or Sinner	2	F	1	0	0	0	1,080
Saint Pete	3	G	19	1	1	4	22,763
Saint Prairie	4	F	17	1	1	4	15,375
Saint Rocio	3	F	9	0	1	0	4,331
Saint Ronald	8	G	3	0	0	0	0
Saint Sabates	3	C	10	2	2	1	34,304
Saint Seminole	2	F	1	0	0	1	6,666
Saint Stephen	3	C	7	1	3	2	72,340
Saint Stormin'	3	C	3	0	2	0	3,500
Saint Verre	5	H	7	1	2	2	140,282
Saint Waki	3	C	12	3	3	3	124,580
Sainted Colony	3	C	5	0	1	3	25,480
Saintemerald	3	G	6	2	0	0	8,885
Saintly Act	5	G	8	1	0	2	28,840
Saintly Action	4	F	4	2	0	0	54,540
Saintly Cause	4	F	3	0	0	0	47
Saintly Corp.	3	G	7	0	0	2	5,677
Saintly Look	3	C	4	1	1	0	90,220
Saintly Native	5	G	3	0	1	1	3,530

Horse	Age	Sex	Sts	1st	2d	3d	Won
Saintly Persuasion	3	F	4	2	1	0	70,200
Saintly Slumber	4	F	1	0	0	0	0
Saintly Wish	5	M	8	1	0	1	10,753
Saints a Plenty	3	F	4	0	1	1	9,500
Saints and Sages	4	F	15	1	5	4	43,702
Saints Cup	6	H	6	2	0	1	19,540
Saint's Express	4	C	1	0	0	0	144
Saints Go Marching	4	C	4	1	1	0	23,130
Saints n' Sinners	3	C	3	0	0	3	14,960
Saints Never Waver	4	C	2	1	0	0	3,410
Sainttwok	5	M	3	0	0	0	4,020
Saison d'Or	6	M	15	1	2	2	29,117
Saitensohn (GER)	5	G	5	1	0	0	12,605
Sajjan	2	C	2	1	1	0	17,596
Sajon	5	G	20	1	4	3	29,700
Sajuriana (ARG)	5	M	16	3	5	3	46,860
Sako Oki'kaa	5	G	6	2	2	1	11,897
Sakrov	2	G	2	0	0	0	425
Sala de Oro	2	F	7	3	1	1	66,826
Salad Days	4	F	2	0	0	0	450
Salamaat	3	C	6	1	1	0	23,047
Salari's Dream	9	G	5	0	0	0	1,310
Salaverry	7	G	5	0	0	1	2,340
Salcanta	5	M	3	0	0	0	383
Sale the Atlantic	3	G	6	1	2	0	26,250
Salem Avenue	4	F	12	5	2	3	58,950
Salem County	4	F	10	0	1	0	3,102
Salem Times	4	G	8	2	0	2	12,780
Salem Too	3	F	4	0	0	0	0
Salem Willow	4	F	3	0	0	0	1,500
Salem Witch	3	F	8	0	0	1	1,182
Salems Drama	4	G	5	0	0	1	930
Salient Angel	5	M	1	0	0	0	525
Salient Sin	5	M	9	0	2	3	8,603
Salient Spring	5	M	5	0	0	0	140
Salim's Tip (AUS)	7	G	7	0	0	1	2,700
Salina's Boy S.	4	G	1	0	0	0	0
Salina's Gift	7	M	8	1	2	1	44,510
Salinas Regal Luck	4	F	7	1	1	2	8,884
Salinas Star	4	F	10	3	2	2	47,302
Saline	5	M	6	1	0	1	3,427
Salisbury Slew	3	F	8	1	1	0	12,830
Salish Basket	6	G	3	0	0	1	500
Salish Bull	9	G	6	0	0	1	1,280
Salish Legacy	3	F	7	1	0	1	3,495
Salish Miracle	5	M	4	0	0	1	5,160
Salish Prince	10	G	13	3	5	0	35,955
Salish Secret	3	F	5	0	1	1	2,664
Salitrosa	5	M	15	2	1	4	29,147
Sallie Dee	6	M	1	0	0	0	0
Sallie Mae	4	F	6	0	1	1	4,928
Sally Beth	5	M	6	0	0	0	479
Sally Dear	3	F	3	0	1	0	5,560
Sally Galore	3	F	5	0	0	0	392
Sally Got the Boot	4	F	8	0	0	1	3,225
Sally Q	7	M	1	0	0	0	190
Sally T	7	M	7	1	1	2	8,900
Sallylitefoot	3	G	3	0	0	1	922
Sally's Comet	6	M	5	0	1	1	5,144
Sallys Fashion	7	M	11	1	1	3	7,176
Sally's Jewel	7	M	13	1	1	1	5,968
Sally's My Gal	4	F	2	0	0	0	110
Sally's Sweep	4	F	5	1	0	0	6,408
Salmo	7	H	7	1	1	1	18,010
Salomon Swagger	6	G	9	4	0	0	33,200
Saloon Number Ten	2	C	3	1	1	0	6,934
Salooty	3	G	5	0	1	0	5,610
Sal's Gal	8	M	11	0	0	1	2,355
Sal's Prospector	4	F	2	0	0	0	82
Salsa Brava	3	F	6	1	1	1	7,915
Salsa Real	3	F	10	4	0	2	72,318
Salsa Sunny	6	G	6	0	0	0	330
Salsbury's Gate	5	G	11	1	3	0	14,445
Salsebelle	3	F	4	0	0	0	0
Salt Breeze	5	M	15	2	6	3	15,248
Salt Cave	4	C	4	0	1	1	25,460
Salt Chaser	3	F	9	1	1	1	7,289
Salt Coates	5	G	11	1	1	2	7,761
Salt Creek	6	M	16	3	1	4	18,053
Salt Flat	3	F	2	0	0	0	300
Salt Flat Kid	2	C	3	0	1	1	9,010
Salt Grinder	4	G	6	0	1	1	14,944
Salt Gulch	4	C	8	3	2	0	21,650
Salt in My Soup	2	G	3	1	0	1	10,200
Salt It Again	5	M	6	1	1	0	15,410
Salt It Away	3	C	5	0	1	0	2,100
Salt Lake Express	5	H	10	1	2	1	9,682
Salt Lake Gold	6	H	7	0	1	1	3,302
Salt N Water	7	G	10	1	1	0	5,784
Salt Please	8	G	14	2	1	1	20,090
Salt Raker	3	G	4	1	1	0	17,520
Salt Run	5	G	18	2	1	4	11,359
Salt Water Cowboy	4	G	7	1	1	0	46,280
Salt Wells	3	G	4	0	2	0	22,000
Salt Whistle Bay	4	C	7	1	2	1	11,460
Saltaire Slew	5	G	13	1	3	1	5,783
Saltant	2	F	1	0	0	0	100
Saltarina Lake (ARG)	3	F	1	0	0	0	1,980
Salted	3	G	4	0	0	0	865
Salteree	6	M	8	0	0	0	645
Saltiness	9	G	4	0	0	0	265
Saltire	2	C	5	1	0	1	29,470
Saltshaker	5	G	12	1	2	1	5,051
Saltster	2	F	6	3	0	1	38,910
Saltwater Runner	2	F	2	2	0	0	44,640
Salty Affair	5	G	15	3	4	2	54,290
Salty Boy	5	H	10	3	2	0	11,564
Salty Character	2	C	4	2	1	0	70,735
Salty Dog Destiny	2	C	1	0	0	0	300
Salty Expression	5	H	5	2	1	0	7,876
Salty Farma	5	M	12	2	4	0	164,020
Salty Genius	3	G	12	2	4	3	89,325
Salty Jak	5	M	5	0	0	0	611
Salty Langfuhn	2	G	2	1	0	0	23,526
Salty Looker	7	M	12	1	0	1	2,557
Salty M.	6	H	6	1	1	0	14,890
Salty M. D.	3	G	1	0	0	1	1,650
Salty n' Foxy	4	F	6	3	0	3	58,440
Salty N Sassy	2	F	2	0	0	0	0
Salty O'Rourke	6	G	12	6	1	1	83,071
Salty Pleasure	5	M	2	0	0	0	90
Salty Prince	5	G	13	2	0	1	37,530
Salty Punch	2	C	3	1	1	0	22,020
Salty Rocket	3	F	5	1	2	1	35,110
Salty Romance	2	F	3	2	0	1	178,440
Salty Sailor	3	C	4	0	2	0	13,720
Salty Senorita	6	M	2	0	0	2	1,200
Salty Siphon	2	F	3	0	1	0	1,450
Salty Sir	4	G	6	0	1	1	4,960
Salty Soup	3	G	3	0	0	0	440
Salty Spender	5	G	9	4	1	0	50,300
Salty Suzy	6	M	2	0	0	1	660
Salty Talk	4	F	6	0	1	0	2,987
Salty Train	6	H	11	1	4	2	14,544
Salty Treasure	6	G	14	3	2	4	17,286
Salty Win	7	H	5	0	2	1	2,275
Salty's Double	3	G	6	0	1	2	5,275
Salty's Home	5	G	11	0	4	2	23,260
Saluda	2	C	3	0	0	0	3,636
Salut Belek	4	G	4	0	1	0	4,000
Salutatorian	6	H	3	1	0	0	1,495
Salute America	2	C	5	1	0	1	9,560
Salute Her	3	F	5	1	0	0	27,420
Salute Him	5	G	12	1	5	2	136,838
Salute the Count	3	C	1	0	0	0	0
Salute Them	2	C	6	0	0	0	958
Salute This	3	G	17	0	5	4	8,420
Salute to Paulie	2	F	6	0	0	1	16,205
Salute Y'all	4	F	11	1	0	1	4,080
Salutee	5	G	6	1	0	2	8,677
Salvage This	4	C	4	0	0	0	340
Salvaje	5	H	7	0	0	0	1,733
Salvaje Memo	4	C	8	1	1	0	36,280
Salvaje Raton	6	M	4	0	1	0	432
Salvester	2	F	15	5	0	1	34,670
Salvino	4	C	2	0	1	0	6,000
Salzurita (ARG)	5	M	9	3	0	0	122,791
Sam Allen	4	G	12	0	0	0	2,070

RECORDS OF HORSES

Horse	Age	Sex	Sts	1st	2d	3d	Won
Sam Boo	3	C	8	0	5	0	45,140
Sam Burr	3	G	11	1	4	1	8,289
Sam Eye Am	4	F	8	1	1	1	40,700
Sam George Hill	9	H	7	2	1	2	7,811
Sam Hill	10	G	10	1	1	1	2,984
Sam I Am a Circus	3	F	6	2	0	0	15,779
Sam Lord's Castle	5	H	1	1	0	0	38,150
Sam McGee	5	G	16	2	1	2	9,309
Sam R.	6	H	1	0	0	0	0
Sam San	8	G	17	2	3	2	5,357
Sam Steele	5	G	14	0	0	2	2,261
Sam Sullivan	10	G	5	1	2	0	33,300
Sam Supreme	5	H	3	0	0	1	1,491
Sam the Sham	2	C	3	0	0	0	0
Samahan	4	F	16	2	2	1	9,811
Samand	5	H	3	0	1	0	1,400
Samanth Lake	7	M	7	0	0	0	415
Samantha B.	3	F	16	2	2	5	83,574
Samantha Cat	3	F	8	1	2	1	11,965
Samantha Slew	5	M	1	0	0	0	532
Samantha the Great	7	M	12	0	1	2	12,825
Samantha's Dream	3	F	8	0	1	0	1,350
Samaria	6	M	4	0	0	0	450
Samarid's Star	6	M	9	1	2	1	7,382
Samba in Rio	5	H	6	0	0	3	3,400
Same Day Blues	3	F	13	2	0	1	9,568
Same Dice	5	G	3	0	0	0	472
Same Old Song	7	G	2	0	0	0	100
Same Old Trouble	4	G	11	0	2	5	20,785
Same Tune	4	F	2	0	1	0	4,774
Samee Brass	7	M	13	1	5	2	22,534
Sami Ro	4	F	4	0	0	0	283
Samilark	4	C	5	1	0	0	1,785
Samir	2	C	1	0	0	0	195
Sami's Girl	2	F	6	2	0	0	40,350
Sami's Majic	2	C	4	0	1	3	8,020
Sami's Spirit	4	F	5	2	2	0	11,935
Sami's Tango	7	G	15	2	2	1	11,669
Samjack	3	G	4	0	1	0	1,170
Samlot	6	G	4	0	0	0	2,340
Sammi Gia	3	F	4	0	0	0	225
Sammi Sou Lin	4	F	5	0	0	1	1,634
Sammie	3	C	3	0	0	0	0
Sammieso Sah	3	G	10	1	0	2	24,621
Sammimur	3	G	10	0	2	1	13,542
Sammy Boy	3	G	1	0	0	0	100
Sammy Moonammy	3	F	15	5	2	1	63,544
Sammy Sweet	3	G	13	2	3	0	9,960
Sammy the Cat	3	G	3	0	0	0	2,500
Sammy the Champ	8	G	1	0	0	1	1,600
Sammybdancing	5	M	3	0	0	1	2,800
Sammys Lil Kister	3	C	12	1	2	0	17,196
Sam'n Sarah's Star	3	C	4	1	2	0	27,842
Samoan	4	C	2	0	0	0	350
Samoan Dream	2	F	6	0	0	0	1,208
Samoan Queen	3	F	4	1	2	0	35,050
Sampash	7	H	5	2	1	2	7,864
Sample Copy	7	H	14	1	2	3	7,057
Sampo's Fool	2	F	6	2	0	0	25,868
Sampson's Son	2	C	4	0	2	2	15,520
Sam's a Flying	5	H	4	0	0	0	441
Sam's All American	4	C	5	0	0	0	418
Sam's Boy	4	C	7	0	0	2	10,400
Sam's Concorde	6	G	2	1	1	0	25,400
Sam's Country Blue	5	G	3	0	0	0	290
Sam's Dream	4	G	1	0	0	0	110
Sam's Dusty	4	G	14	1	1	3	5,866
Sams Evening Girl	2	F	1	0	0	0	0
Sam's Farit	6	M	5	1	1	0	7,080
Sam's Fountain	5	M	2	0	0	0	131
Sams Halo	5	M	17	2	1	7	13,619
Sam's Honor	4	C	16	3	1	2	27,712
Sam's Last Call	2	G	3	0	0	0	270
Sam's Long Drive	5	G	1	0	0	0	0
Sams Market	10	H	1	0	0	0	0
Sam's Miki	6	G	8	0	0	1	2,276
Sam's Prince Who	5	H	3	0	0	0	935
Sam's Secret	4	G	8	1	2	2	14,703
Sams Sham Sheree	3	F	2	0	0	0	115
Sam's Sixteenth	2	F	2	0	0	2	2,394
Sam's Valentine	2	G	4	0	0	0	259
Sam's Weekend	2	F	4	0	0	0	0
Samstheman	3	G	13	2	2	1	7,769
Samsville	3	G	12	1	1	3	10,145
Samtheshoeinman	7	G	20	1	1	1	3,209
Samurai Nanao	2	C	4	2	1	0	16,317
Samuri	6	G	3	1	1	0	5,480
San Antonio Slew	3	F	4	0	1	1	2,232
San Antonio Star	4	F	10	0	2	1	2,920
San Bon Way	7	M	9	0	2	3	18,312
San Darbo	4	F	13	4	3	1	24,628
San Dare	5	M	10	2	1	2	190,939
San Diego Blowout	2	C	4	2	0	0	125,358
San Diego Pete	8	G	5	2	1	1	25,238
San Diego Stint	6	M	10	1	1	4	6,788
San Diego Sue	4	F	2	1	0	0	18,900
San Felipe's King	9	G	3	2	0	0	23,184
San Gabriel Spirit	4	F	2	0	0	0	0
San Martin	7	G	5	0	0	0	360
San Mont Andreas	5	H	2	0	0	0	608
San Nicolas	5	H	7	1	0	1	38,795
San Pedro	5	H	7	1	3	2	81,730
San Quentin	4	C	4	1	1	0	6,140
San Telmo	4	G	7	1	3	1	57,920
Sanadel	3	F	4	1	0	1	18,820
Sanctified	3	F	8	1	1	1	46,756
Sanctity	6	G	11	0	2	2	9,140
Sanctuary's Bid	4	G	4	0	0	0	255
Sanctuary's Omooni	3	C	2	1	0	0	15,900
Sand and Fight	3	F	14	2	3	1	9,606
Sand and Silver	2	C	9	1	2	3	41,316
Sand and Stars	9	H	1	0	0	0	0
Sand and Water	7	G	9	3	0	0	43,020
Sand Ballade	4	G	12	1	2	5	22,463
Sand Bird	4	G	9	1	1	1	17,860
Sand Blaster	2	G	3	0	0	0	225
Sand Burner	3	C	9	1	2	0	54,120
Sand Cat	4	G	9	1	2	1	8,845
Sand Cloud	4	F	6	2	0	0	15,000
Sand Commander	4	G	4	1	0	0	1,775
Sand Demon	6	H	5	0	1	0	3,304
Sand Digger	5	G	19	2	1	0	6,533
Sand Key	3	F	11	2	1	1	39,071
Sand King	2	C	8	1	2	3	14,065
Sand Lake	3	G	4	0	0	0	495
Sand Ridge	8	H	9	1	2	4	75,880
Sand Road	3	C	1	0	0	1	960
Sand Rush	3	G	9	2	1	1	28,821
Sand Save	2	C	1	0	0	0	0
Sand Script	2	G	3	0	0	0	557
Sand Slider	2	C	1	0	0	0	180
Sand Slough	3	C	3	1	0	0	6,960
Sand Snipe	10	G	7	1	3	0	23,448
Sand Spector	4	G	2	0	0	0	0
Sand Springs	3	F	7	4	1	0	451,390
Sand Star	4	F	4	0	1	0	2,024
Sand Stormer	2	F	1	0	0	0	95
Sand Town	3	G	8	1	1	1	4,724
Sand Trapper	3	C	5	1	0	1	5,742
Sand Trip	5	M	3	0	1	2	2,870
Sand Wolf	3	C	5	1	0	0	9,420
Sandalias	3	F	4	1	1	0	5,812
Sandals of Gold	3	C	6	1	2	0	8,212
Sandarac	6	M	3	0	1	0	924
Sandbag	2	C	3	0	0	0	420
Sandbagger Jones	2	C	1	0	0	0	0
Sandbar Sally	2	F	1	0	0	0	0
Sandblast	4	F	2	0	1	0	1,925
Sandburr	4	G	12	3	2	1	39,120
Sandcastles	7	M	6	0	1	2	2,730
Sandcette	4	F	2	0	0	0	265
Sanddoones	5	M	11	0	2	1	6,225
Sandee's Dynastee	5	M	9	0	0	0	960
Sandel Wood Fleet	5	G	18	0	2	3	8,902
Sanderling	3	F	10	2	2	0	46,713
Sandestin	2	C	3	0	0	1	1,320
Sandflea	3	F	8	1	1	0	10,878
Sandia Shadows	2	G	1	1	0	0	4,920

Horse	Age	Sex	Sts	1st	2d	3d	Won
Sandia's Flicka	2	F	2	0	1	0	3,800
Sandina	2	F	4	0	0	0	1,941
Sandinmyeye	3	F	9	0	0	2	2,575
Sandline Star	3	C	5	0	0	0	630
Sandlot Sue	2	F	6	0	2	0	6,170
Sandmandu	2	G	3	0	0	0	1,020
Sandmannli	3	G	5	0	0	1	5,872
Sandman's Dream	3	G	7	0	1	0	4,799
Sandmound	4	G	9	1	2	2	9,868
Sandoro	3	F	6	1	0	1	5,386
Sandpit Dancer	6	M	5	1	1	0	6,978
Sandpit's Delight	4	F	11	0	0	0	2,689
Sandra Therese	4	F	11	1	1	2	28,560
Sandra's Pride	6	G	3	0	0	1	1,090
Sandra's Song	5	M	2	0	0	1	4,400
Sandra's Star	4	F	5	0	0	0	0
Sandras Sweetie	5	M	8	2	2	1	12,015
Sandringham	4	F	13	3	2	3	27,409
Sandrover	2	C	3	1	0	0	5,360
Sands Fury	4	F	8	2	0	0	19,252
Sands of Time	4	G	17	4	3	2	45,960
Sands Thru Time	3	C	4	0	0	0	305
Sandshrew	4	F	9	3	2	0	17,910
Sandspit	4	C	10	1	0	3	37,835
Sandusky	5	H	6	1	0	1	12,159
Sandwoven (GB)	3	F	16	4	0	2	31,255
Sandy Country	4	F	7	1	0	0	12,330
Sandy Drawers	3	F	9	2	0	1	23,858
Sandy Hook	5	M	1	0	0	0	540
Sandy Mountain	3	G	1	0	0	0	5,880
Sandy Pandy	4	F	10	1	2	1	8,529
Sandy Princess	4	F	15	2	0	0	9,392
Sandy Rhythm	4	C	14	1	3	4	11,359
Sandy Ridge	3	F	2	0	0	0	0
Sandy Sifter	4	F	4	1	1	1	5,985
Sandy Sneakers	4	F	4	0	0	0	3,360
Sandy Time	7	G	6	0	0	0	336
Sandybrook	3	F	4	0	0	0	465
Sandye's Halo	6	M	5	0	0	1	2,440
Sandye's Love Not	5	H	9	1	2	3	8,623
Sandyford	2	C	1	0	0	0	0
Sandyfourthofjuly	3	F	10	1	0	0	10,504
Sandyland	5	G	11	2	1	3	18,656
Sandys Dandy	6	G	16	4	2	1	25,099
Sandy's Heritage	4	F	7	0	2	0	6,640
Sandy's Lil Devil	3	G	1	0	0	0	0
Sanford Sam	8	G	3	0	0	0	285
Sanfranciscoharbor	4	G	7	0	0	1	5,544
Sanger	4	G	8	3	2	1	68,445
Sangiovese	4	F	2	0	0	0	45
Sangue too Loud	3	F	20	1	2	3	62,150
Sangue's Crown	3	F	8	1	0	0	9,741
Sani Pass	2	C	1	0	0	0	0
Sanibel Anne	4	F	10	1	2	0	8,297
Sanibel Sam	4	C	9	1	1	3	19,474
Sanibel Sunset	3	F	9	2	1	3	58,510
Sankarang (GB)	9	H	6	0	0	0	657
Sankofa Two	3	F	6	0	0	1	1,602
Sanky Panky	3	C	9	3	1	3	67,396
Sanquinten Quail	4	F	5	0	0	0	490
Sans Foix	4	C	6	0	0	0	465
Sans Sauce	3	F	9	2	1	1	19,220
Sans Win	2	G	2	1	0	1	14,150
Sansa	3	F	6	0	0	2	13,455
Sanshu	6	G	1	0	0	0	40
Sanskrit	10	G	5	0	3	1	5,318
Santa Catarina	3	F	5	2	1	1	342,680
Santa Croce	3	F	5	1	3	0	54,000
Santa Fe Autumn	3	F	1	0	0	1	2,860
Santa Fe Chief	6	H	3	0	0	0	136
Santa Fe Slew	3	C	2	0	1	1	16,000
Santa Fe Slewpy	12	G	9	1	0	2	3,507
Santa Fe Strip	3	F	2	1	0	0	26,700
Santa Jovita	3	F	2	0	0	0	382
Santa Maria Jones	2	F	4	0	0	0	330
Santa Rosa Island	5	M	4	0	1	0	14,800
Santa Rosalia	2	F	4	0	0	1	7,650
Santano	6	G	2	1	1	0	21,000
Santa's Elf	4	F	2	0	0	0	0
Santa's Playboy	5	G	11	2	2	1	51,317
Santero	10	G	3	0	1	0	550
Santerra	3	F	6	0	1	1	95,678
Santia	4	F	5	1	0	0	5,187
Santiago Friend	3	G	4	0	0	0	220
Santiago Mist	4	F	4	0	0	0	1,505
Santiago Rojo	4	F	16	2	3	1	23,290
Santiam Storm Cat	6	G	7	1	2	1	1,814
Santiam Top Jazz	2	G	2	0	0	0	100
Santina's Gold	8	H	5	0	0	0	0
Santita Rosita	5	M	12	4	1	0	19,298
Santo Tomas	7	H	15	0	2	1	2,886
Santoni	7	H	1	0	0	1	840
Santor	3	C	13	1	4	0	15,165
Santos	2	C	3	0	0	2	2,145
Sanzibar	2	C	3	0	0	0	0
Saone River	7	M	5	0	0	1	992
Saphatic	2	F	1	0	0	0	100
Saphir Indien (GB)	4	G	3	0	0	0	1,975
Saphiria	3	F	2	0	0	0	680
Sapien's Sunrise	3	G	7	0	0	0	346
Sapna	2	F	5	0	0	0	2,580
Sapodilla	3	F	7	1	2	2	31,260
Sapore Di Mare (ARG)	4	C	5	0	0	0	5,880
Sapphire Blues	4	C	1	1	0	0	4,560
Sapphire Hill	5	M	9	3	1	1	53,080
Sapphire Lady	2	F	3	0	0	0	0
Sapphire Martini	3	F	6	0	1	0	1,766
Sapphireontherocks	4	C	5	2	2	0	16,706
Sapphirestruckgold	4	F	6	1	3	0	5,880
Sappy Lil Tune	6	G	13	1	3	2	19,077
Saquache	6	H	11	0	2	1	33,400
Sara Castelli	4	F	12	0	2	2	6,095
Sara G	3	F	6	1	2	1	7,262
Sara Is Peeking	3	F	5	0	0	0	1,343
Sara Katherine	2	F	1	0	0	0	264
Sara Lynn	4	F	1	0	1	0	460
Sara Margaret	3	F	2	1	0	0	7,620
Sara Say	4	F	15	2	3	5	13,491
Sara Sweet	6	M	4	0	0	1	1,760
Saradara	4	F	17	0	2	1	2,673
Sarafan	6	G	6	2	1	1	145,299
Sarah Beaner	4	F	7	3	0	2	34,655
Sarah Creek	4	F	6	0	2	3	11,762
Sarah Elmire	3	F	3	1	0	0	16,800
Sarah Honey	5	M	2	0	0	0	210
Sarah Jade	4	F	10	2	2	1	57,626
Sarah M.	5	M	5	0	0	0	474
Sarah Oteka	4	F	6	1	2	1	5,968
Sarah Says Go	6	M	1	0	0	0	0
Sarah Sits South	5	M	11	2	4	1	16,835
Sarah Something	4	F	2	0	0	0	504
Sarah the Terra	3	F	9	1	2	1	17,853
Sarahkee	5	M	7	0	0	0	5,400
Sarah's Beau	4	G	9	2	0	2	8,546
Sarah's Bid	5	G	13	2	0	2	16,755
Sarah's Caper	2	F	1	0	0	0	0
Sarah's Christina	3	F	6	1	0	1	9,307
Sarah's Code	3	F	4	0	0	0	384
Sarah's Goldengirl	5	M	9	1	3	0	13,826
Sarah's Goldie	6	M	6	0	2	2	19,870
Sarah's Script	5	M	4	1	0	1	22,721
Sarah's Solace	3	F	10	2	3	0	35,703
Sarahsdreamcatcher	2	F	4	1	0	0	11,466
Sarah's'zona	3	F	1	0	0	0	84
Sarahy	10	G	9	1	1	1	10,560
Saranac Lake	4	F	6	2	0	0	64,292
Saranoia	3	C	5	0	1	1	11,800
Sara's Crusader	4	G	8	1	1	3	8,037
Sara's Dove	4	G	14	3	0	0	11,163
Sara's Dream	4	F	5	0	1	0	2,720
Sara's Route	3	F	2	0	0	0	0
Sara's Sara Lee	4	F	12	1	3	1	18,372
Sara's Shadow	4	F	17	3	1	2	12,449
Sara's Silence	4	F	9	1	0	1	11,585
Sara's Sister	3	F	3	0	0	0	159
Sara's Success	5	M	6	1	2	0	86,080
Saras True Love	3	F	1	0	0	0	0
Sara's Tune	2	F	7	2	1	0	34,900

Horse	Age	Sex	Sts	1st	2d	3d	Won
Sara's Yankee Girl	3	F	8	1	2	1	28,004
Sarasabear	4	F	2	0	0	0	702
Sarasota Sunset	2	F	3	0	0	1	2,487
Sarastorm	5	M	8	2	0	1	43,820
Saraswatie	2	F	5	1	1	0	15,246
Saratoga Advantage	4	G	18	2	0	3	10,470
Saratoga Apple	2	F	1	0	1	0	1,860
Saratoga Bill	4	C	3	0	0	0	0
Saratoga Blues	4	C	16	6	0	2	65,810
Saratoga Bound	5	M	2	0	0	0	0
Saratoga Broadway	5	H	1	0	0	0	0
Saratoga Carnival	3	C	9	1	1	0	13,545
Saratoga Cat	4	F	7	1	1	2	76,139
Saratoga City	3	F	4	0	0	1	1,630
Saratoga Clipper	3	G	6	0	2	1	14,525
Saratoga County	2	C	2	1	1	0	29,200
Saratoga Episode	2	C	5	1	1	1	46,135
Saratoga Games	5	H	10	1	4	1	43,855
Saratoga Gent	2	C	8	0	0	2	3,670
Saratoga Gloria	4	F	7	0	2	0	7,101
Saratoga Hassle	4	F	5	0	0	0	275
Saratoga Heath	4	G	6	1	0	0	6,299
Saratoga Heights	3	G	8	3	0	1	26,983
Saratoga Humor	3	F	8	3	0	2	96,120
Saratoga Jules	2	C	3	1	0	0	13,500
Saratoga King	5	G	9	0	1	1	1,544
Saratoga Lake	4	G	12	0	1	3	7,659
Saratoga Law	3	G	1	0	0	1	2,310
Saratoga Master	5	H	2	0	0	0	600
Saratoga Rapture	6	G	15	0	0	1	3,756
Saratoga River	4	G	8	0	1	2	10,043
Saratoga Set	4	F	7	0	1	0	3,254
Saratoga Siro	2	G	2	0	0	0	0
Saratoga Slew	4	F	9	1	1	3	5,369
Saratoga Snowpuff	5	M	10	3	1	0	22,455
Saratoga Soft Shoe	4	F	10	2	1	3	16,590
Saratoga Song	4	F	15	1	2	4	16,685
Saratoga Souvenir	3	F	5	1	0	0	11,046
Saratoga Spar	3	F	9	1	1	3	12,065
Saratoga Sport	10	G	9	1	0	3	5,744
Saratoga Spring	2	F	4	0	0	0	780
Saratoga Way	4	C	4	1	0	0	4,697
Saratogarmanaleg	3	F	6	0	0	0	480
Saratoga's Mark	4	F	9	1	2	1	40,775
Sarava	4	C	1	0	0	0	0
Sarcastic	3	F	16	0	4	0	9,510
Sarcee Annie	4	F	15	1	4	4	13,211
Sardar	5	H	7	0	0	2	2,935
Sardaukar (GB)	7	G	9	0	1	2	61,600
Sardis	4	F	10	1	2	1	29,265
Saree (GB)	3	F	3	1	1	0	42,488
Sarellies Knight	7	M	7	1	0	0	3,570
Sarepta Sauce	7	G	12	2	0	1	26,362
Sargari (IRE)	7	G	7	1	0	1	18,580
Sargeant	4	G	9	1	3	3	10,581
Sargeants Village	5	G	3	0	0	2	4,866
Sargent Major	1	G	1	0	0	0	110
Sargent Olson	4	G	11	2	0	4	22,230
Sargentchilipepper	2	G	1	0	0	0	2,460
Sariano	2	F	4	1	1	1	22,063
Saribinda	4	G	5	0	0	1	1,315
Sarie Marais	3	F	6	1	1	0	28,361
Sarigor (IRE)	8	G	1	0	0	0	0
Sarina's Princess	2	F	2	0	0	0	540
Sari's Son	9	G	12	0	1	1	2,657
Sarmentose	5	M	6	2	0	1	17,140
Sarmentum	4	F	9	2	0	0	16,245
Saron's Time	4	F	12	1	0	0	11,245
Saros Princess	3	F	3	0	1	0	920
Saros Vamp	4	F	11	1	1	0	3,841
Sartorial Splendor	10	G	9	0	3	2	6,000
Sasafras	2	F	3	0	0	0	0
Sash	3	F	12	0	3	3	8,915
Sash of Glory	5	H	6	0	1	0	1,702
Sash of Silver	5	H	10	0	0	3	14,850
Sasha Rama Dew	4	F	1	0	0	0	44
Sashaun	3	F	1	0	0	0	0
Sashaying Slew	3	F	3	0	0	1	8,640
Saskatchewan	3	F	13	2	0	0	18,350

Horse	Age	Sex	Sts	1st	2d	3d	Won
Saskya	5	M	4	1	0	0	40,993
Sass Back	3	F	8	1	2	0	4,437
Sass Me Back Kate	3	F	11	1	0	2	9,394
Sass n' Class	6	M	3	0	0	0	1,120
Sass Valay	4	F	17	3	2	0	25,191
Sassilou	4	F	6	0	2	1	1,214
Sassiness	5	M	14	1	1	1	11,375
Sassy Again	2	F	4	0	0	1	1,183
Sassy and Blue	3	F	4	1	0	0	11,466
Sassy and Brash	3	F	3	1	1	1	8,059
Sassy and Classy	4	F	6	0	0	0	417
Sassy Angel	7	M	10	0	0	0	40
Sassy April	7	M	11	3	0	0	50,628
Sassy Bayou Belle	3	F	2	0	0	0	0
Sassy Bear	5	M	6	1	1	1	29,840
Sassy Becky	2	F	7	0	1	0	1,940
Sassy Belle	3	F	13	1	2	4	40,015
Sassy Bridget	3	F	1	0	0	0	130
Sassy Cat Diamond	5	M	5	0	0	0	1,398
Sassy Centerfold	3	F	6	0	0	1	1,014
Sassy Chequer	3	F	2	0	0	0	0
Sassy Conduction	6	M	2	0	0	0	542
Sassy Dancer	5	M	2	0	0	0	0
Sassy Decision	3	F	3	1	0	0	8,280
Sassy Edith	7	M	7	1	0	1	3,138
Sassy Egyption	3	G	4	0	0	1	1,171
Sassy Evie	3	F	6	0	0	0	4,035
Sassy Five	2	F	1	0	0	0	0
Sassy Haz Am	5	M	4	0	2	0	4,800
Sassy Hound	6	G	11	1	3	3	89,420
Sassy Kansan	3	C	6	1	1	1	8,481
Sassy Latell	4	F	3	0	0	0	0
Sassy Linda	4	F	11	2	0	1	14,859
Sassy Little Sarah	3	F	9	2	2	3	18,550
Sassy Lynn	5	M	5	0	0	0	124
Sassy M	3	F	3	0	0	0	425
Sassy Mary	4	F	11	0	1	4	5,236
Sassy Moment	4	F	8	0	0	2	3,941
Sassy N Slew	3	F	9	1	1	0	4,549
Sassy Nickle	6	M	3	0	1	1	7,412
Sassy Nicole	6	M	2	0	0	0	60
Sassy Nurse	8	M	2	0	0	0	690
Sassy Rebel	6	M	3	0	0	1	1,870
Sassy Romance	2	F	1	0	0	0	0
Sassy Sabrina	6	M	2	0	0	0	0
Sassy Safari	4	F	1	0	0	0	0
Sassy Sam	5	G	12	2	0	1	8,361
Sassy Scarlet	5	M	4	0	0	0	690
Sassy Shadeed	4	F	2	0	0	0	0
Sassy Shonda	4	F	11	0	4	1	8,692
Sassy Sissy	5	M	7	0	0	1	873
Sassy Six	4	F	16	1	3	0	13,251
Sassy Songster	2	F	3	0	0	0	635
Sassy Stephie	4	F	8	1	0	2	7,320
Sassy Tap	2	F	3	0	0	0	280
Sassy Tempo	7	M	10	4	2	2	48,150
Sassy Till Dawn	3	F	12	0	0	3	4,241
Sassy Tribute	3	F	3	0	1	1	2,730
Sassy Trisha	2	F	5	0	1	0	1,819
Sassy Vic	3	F	13	0	3	0	7,094
Sassy Won	4	F	8	4	0	1	27,450
Sassyclassygirl	2	F	2	0	0	0	780
Sassy's Money	5	G	11	0	0	0	158
Sassy's Rail	3	F	8	0	2	0	5,935
Sataniste	7	G	13	4	2	1	53,113
Satanonthdocothbay	4	C	4	0	0	0	840
Satan's Account	3	C	3	0	0	0	0
Satans All Around	3	G	3	1	0	1	1,163
Satan's Code	5	H	3	0	1	0	1,880
Satan's Prince	7	H	8	1	2	1	6,081
Satan's Song	3	F	9	3	1	1	34,500
Satan's Treasure	4	F	2	0	0	0	159
Satan's Valentine	5	M	5	1	0	1	6,300
Satansalittlerusty	5	G	2	0	0	0	0
Satantia	3	G	13	1	3	5	12,100
Satarra (GB)	6	H	5	1	0	0	2,573
Satchmo	9	G	1	0	0	0	0
Sateen	2	F	3	0	0	0	525
Satellite Dancer	6	G	7	1	0	0	2,513

Horse	Age	Sex	Sts	1st	2d	3d	Won	Horse	Age	Sex	Sts	1st	2d	3d	Won
Satellite Heart	10	M	13	4	0	2	17,498	Savannah Crest	5	M	11	1	2	0	10,131
Satellite Problem	2	C	1	0	0	0	125	Savannah Hanna	5	M	13	1	2	3	38,560
Satellite Skinner	2	C	1	0	0	0	186	Savannah Harbor	6	H	6	0	1	0	4,504
Sather Tower	3	G	7	0	0	0	1,203	Savannah Knight	5	G	1	1	0	0	4,950
Satiate	3	F	11	1	3	3	60,360	Savannah Light	2	F	5	0	1	0	4,170
Satin Black	3	F	12	0	5	5	7,146	Savannah Mist	3	F	8	1	2	2	10,384
Satin Boxer	9	G	16	1	2	4	11,418	Savannah Road	3	G	7	0	4	1	33,590
Satin Concern	3	C	4	1	0	0	8,661	Savannah Rules	3	F	6	1	0	0	6,000
Satin Creek	6	G	14	4	3	2	18,477	Savannah Thumper	3	G	8	2	1	1	15,175
Satin Dolly	4	F	24	2	1	6	39,565	Savannah Way	3	F	7	0	1	0	3,802
Satin Dress	2	F	3	0	0	0	0	Savannah's Gold	2	F	2	0	0	1	1,650
Satin Lady	3	F	6	0	0	2	1,649	Savannah's Prize	5	M	16	1	2	3	16,953
Satin Mist	3	F	17	0	2	4	8,880	Savannah's Wish	2	G	5	0	0	1	1,970
Satin Sage	5	M	6	0	0	1	1,479	Savanna's Folley	4	F	5	1	0	1	2,065
Satin Sami	3	F	2	0	0	0	260	Save a Nickel	7	H	6	2	0	1	2,499
Satin Song	2	F	2	0	0	0	2,250	Save Ground	3	G	15	3	2	1	27,872
Satin Spike	4	F	5	1	0	0	3,140	Save My Assets	3	F	5	0	0	1	1,586
Satin Storm	3	F	10	1	0	2	16,774	Save the Coins	2	F	2	0	0	1	1,080
Satina	4	F	13	2	1	0	11,475	Save the Deputy	3	F	4	0	0	1	2,463
Satine	2	F	4	1	1	1	18,542	Save the Forests	6	G	11	1	1	1	19,102
Satine Rouge	3	F	5	1	0	0	16,220	Save the Green	4	F	3	0	0	0	1,065
Satisfying Wager	5	H	2	0	0	1	1,045	Save the Moment	3	F	19	5	3	3	34,206
Satohina	2	F	3	0	3	0	30,140	Save the Profit	2	C	1	0	0	0	0
Satrap	4	C	6	0	2	1	6,250	Save the Queen	3	G	1	0	0	0	0
Sattolight	4	C	2	0	0	0	252	Save This Dance	3	G	2	0	0	1	3,234
Saturday	6	G	4	0	1	2	5,338	Savealife	4	C	1	0	0	0	0
Saturday Deelites	2	C	3	1	0	2	36,425	Saved	2	F	8	1	0	1	10,890
Saturday Detention	3	F	11	1	2	2	24,550	Saved by the Sword	5	H	10	2	0	3	38,280
Saturday Hero	4	G	8	1	1	1	7,875	Saved On Sunday	4	F	3	2	0	0	2,200
Saturday Nite Baby	5	M	3	0	0	1	470	Savedbythelight	3	F	7	2	0	4	229,080
Saturday Sin	3	G	11	3	1	0	22,312	Savior	6	G	12	3	1	1	36,770
Saturday's Warrior	3	G	2	1	0	0	4,200	Savonarola (GB)	3	C	2	1	0	0	7,488
Saturn Nine	3	F	2	0	0	0	0	Savorthetime	4	F	6	4	0	1	101,926
Saturn's Saint	3	F	4	1	0	0	5,469	Savory	2	F	2	0	1	0	7,540
Sauce	4	G	4	0	0	0	760	Savoy Special	3	C	8	3	3	2	122,513
Sauce of Sauces	4	C	3	0	0	0	455	Savoya On Ice	4	G	3	1	0	0	9,901
Sauce Pecan	5	G	12	2	4	3	23,206	Savoy's Prince	6	H	13	1	2	1	25,200
Saucemakesmeflirt	3	F	12	1	3	1	15,107	Savurtabs	4	G	10	2	1	0	8,018
Sauceonside	2	F	2	0	1	0	1,960	Savvy Connection	9	G	3	0	0	1	1,428
Sauceyrubin	2	F	1	1	0	0	6,000	Savvy Girl	3	F	16	3	5	1	27,993
Saucon Creek	3	C	5	0	1	1	13,670	Savvy Lad	4	C	12	1	1	2	9,526
Saucy Alliance	6	H	1	0	0	0	0	Savy Miss	5	M	15	4	2	1	21,159
Saucy Bid	2	F	8	2	2	2	55,012	Savy Siss	4	F	4	1	0	0	3,470
Saucy Cat	6	G	10	1	0	0	19,354	Saw Blade	2	C	2	0	0	0	0
Saucy City	4	F	1	0	0	0	342	Saw Grass Sabre	2	G	2	1	0	1	6,830
Saucy Devil	4	F	4	2	0	0	4,886	Saw See	4	F	4	0	0	0	0
Saucy Light	4	F	3	0	0	1	1,293	Sawdust	3	G	12	1	2	5	49,718
Saucy Performance	5	H	4	2	0	0	28,200	Sawdust Doll	4	F	9	1	1	1	4,350
Saucy Pick	2	F	2	0	0	0	322	Sawgrass	3	C	2	0	0	0	0
Saucy Tapanga	4	F	18	1	1	3	5,625	Sawko to It	3	G	3	0	0	0	993
Saucy Taste	3	G	10	0	0	0	757	Sawmill Dancer	4	G	1	0	0	0	0
Saucy Viv	3	F	6	0	0	1	5,482	Sawston Hall	3	G	7	2	0	1	29,430
Saucy Viva	4	F	10	1	2	2	13,458	Saxman Prospect	9	M	8	0	0	1	1,031
Saucy Vixen	4	F	9	0	1	1	5,868	Saxmeamemo	5	G	10	3	0	3	3,946
Saucy Ways	4	F	5	0	0	0	720	Saxony	4	F	5	1	1	2	48,640
Saucy's Fury	4	F	4	0	1	0	1,095	Sax's Tune	3	F	7	1	1	0	4,766
Saul	4	C	6	0	0	0	378	Saxton's Engine	3	C	13	1	3	4	46,370
Saumee Secret	6	H	12	0	1	1	2,255	Say Bee	5	G	1	0	0	0	0
Saups	10	G	9	0	0	1	2,595	Say Cousin Lenny	4	G	8	0	1	0	13,310
Sausage Link	4	C	2	0	0	0	0	Say Deniro	4	F	12	2	2	0	14,640
Sauvage Riviere	4	C	8	0	0	0	480	Say First Bid	6	G	15	0	3	2	23,766
Sauvignon	5	M	8	1	1	2	28,501	Say Florida Sandy	9	H	6	2	0	1	96,602
Savage (BRZ)	6	H	1	0	0	0	0	Say Goodnight	9	H	4	0	0	0	297
Savage Garden	6	G	17	1	0	0	3,486	Say Grace	3	F	3	0	0	0	98
Savage Glory	6	M	1	0	0	0	0	Say Grace First Jo	7	M	12	4	2	2	17,813
Savage Lass	3	F	8	1	0	2	5,314	Say Hay Mokay	6	G	4	0	0	0	254
Savage Sage	4	F	19	1	3	3	12,235	Say Hey Charlie	3	C	14	3	1	3	21,260
Savage Style	6	M	4	0	0	0	0	Say Hi as I Go By	5	H	6	0	0	0	519
Savage Sue	2	F	2	0	1	0	2,712	Say Hi to Joe	7	M	2	0	0	0	162
Savage Wit	5	G	6	1	0	1	7,147	Say It Ain't True	3	F	11	0	2	0	11,550
Savage Wolf	3	G	1	0	0	0	0	Say It and Smile	2	F	1	0	0	0	0
Savana D	8	M	7	0	0	1	785	Say It Both Ways	7	G	7	2	1	0	35,714
Savanah Go	3	F	6	1	1	0	5,212	Say It in Code	3	F	3	0	0	2	4,620
Savanalamar	3	F	15	0	2	1	5,911	Say La Via	5	G	6	0	1	1	1,651
Savanna Blue Jeans	2	F	2	1	1	0	11,187	Say Mystic	5	M	8	0	0	0	1,260
Savanna Moon	5	M	4	1	0	0	1,613	Say No Justin	4	G	5	1	0	1	7,736
Savanna Sam	5	G	6	0	1	0	619	Say No Maw	4	C	7	0	1	0	9,170
Savannah Bluff	6	M	12	3	2	2	14,932	Say Now	11	G	2	0	0	0	300
Savannah Creek	4	F	3	0	0	0	252	Say Ole	3	G	13	0	0	2	1,782

RECORDS OF HORSES

Horse	Age	Sex	Sts	1st	2d	3d	Won	Horse	Age	Sex	Sts	1st	2d	3d	Won
Say Somethin Funny	3	F	5	2	1	1	38,122	Scat Won	3	C	1	0	0	0	0
Say That Again	4	F	1	0	0	0	0	Scataway	2	F	10	0	1	1	2,534
Say The Word (IRE)	6	G	5	1	0	2	9,000	Scatcat's Dream	2	F	6	0	1	0	2,505
Say What You Think	3	C	1	0	0	0	900	Scatina	3	F	7	1	0	1	4,783
Say When	8	G	8	0	0	0	196	Scatincat	2	F	4	0	0	0	462
Say Yes	3	G	9	1	1	3	9,705	Scat's Mine	2	F	6	1	0	0	4,590
Say You Will	3	F	6	2	2	0	12,368	Scatter Creek	4	C	7	2	0	3	7,772
Say Your Mind	4	F	4	1	1	1	8,874	Scatter My Stars	3	F	7	1	0	2	8,429
Saya Little Prayer	4	F	1	0	0	0	101	Scatter Roads	7	G	4	0	0	0	244
Sayabec	4	F	12	2	0	2	24,790	Scatter' Um	8	G	9	1	0	1	4,914
Sayaprayerforme	3	C	5	0	0	0	0	Scatterbrain	2	F	4	0	0	0	335
Saygoodnightgrace	5	M	2	1	0	0	5,820	Scattered	3	G	3	0	0	0	1,320
Saying Grace	6	M	3	0	0	0	4,400	Scattering	4	F	8	0	0	5	10,265
Sayitain'tso Joe	3	G	11	1	2	4	52,734	Scattering Breezes	4	C	5	2	0	1	42,220
Sayitlikeumeanit	3	C	1	0	0	0	0	Scattermattic	4	G	4	0	0	0	0
Sayitwithdiamonds	4	F	4	0	0	0	0	Scatterthediamonds	4	F	2	0	0	1	1,441
Saylor Two	4	F	4	0	0	0	200	Scattin Mo Jo	2	C	1	0	0	0	0
Sayonara Told	3	C	12	3	3	1	52,177	Scattle Bud	3	C	10	0	5	2	32,850
Saysenor	3	C	5	0	2	1	5,710	Scenaroid	4	G	5	0	0	0	411
Sayucan Kid	5	H	12	0	2	1	4,794	Scene Maker	2	F	3	0	0	0	2,340
Sc Dazzle Me	4	F	6	0	0	2	1,076	Scenic Won	6	M	9	0	5	2	32,678
Scadadel	3	F	3	0	0	0	450	Scenic Wonder	3	C	4	1	1	2	36,760
Scaffold Man Two	7	G	14	4	2	1	16,025	Scenic's Easter	4	F	10	0	0	0	711
Scaffolds Legacy	5	G	14	2	5	3	11,161	Scenicsfinalanswer	3	G	10	0	0	1	2,649
Scagnelli	8	G	5	2	1	2	47,700	Scent a Grade	11	G	4	1	0	0	3,300
Scags	3	G	7	0	0	0	3,868	Scent of a Lady	3	F	16	1	0	1	10,244
Scales Springs	4	F	12	1	1	5	16,060	Scent of Gold	6	G	1	0	0	0	0
Scalia	4	G	14	1	4	1	21,984	Scent of Heather	6	M	11	2	0	3	5,175
Scalped Ticket	4	F	8	1	2	1	9,236	Scepter'd Isle	8	G	12	2	5	0	18,868
Scamp Along	4	F	3	0	0	0	990	Sceptical	6	M	10	1	1	0	35,568
Scamp Cz	4	G	11	1	4	0	9,920	Sceptical Diamonds	6	H	3	0	0	1	570
Scandalously	6	M	5	0	0	1	1,651	Schadow	7	M	12	3	1	2	14,423
Scandia	4	G	19	3	5	3	13,807	Schaller Haller	4	F	5	1	0	0	4,562
Scanno	4	G	6	1	0	0	6,150	Scharada	2	G	1	0	0	0	0
Scapade	3	F	9	3	2	3	218,440	Scharoot	3	F	16	3	2	3	40,588
Scare Air	3	G	6	0	2	2	7,750	Schatz Katze	3	F	2	0	0	1	1,540
Scaredcat	2	G	4	0	1	0	3,080	Schatzie Dreams	2	C	1	0	0	0	0
Scarengille	8	H	8	1	1	0	1,735	Schedule (GB)	2	F	2	1	0	0	27,840
Scarface Sal	7	M	13	2	1	1	7,809	Scheduled Event	3	C	14	2	1	2	40,847
Scarlet Appeal	3	F	5	0	1	2	3,250	Scheduled Flight	4	F	10	0	5	2	9,704
Scarlet Billows	3	F	4	0	0	0	1,020	Schemba's Tune	4	G	5	0	2	1	2,763
Scarlet Child	2	F	1	0	0	0	0	Schemer	2	F	6	1	2	1	59,770
Scarlet Classic	3	G	3	0	0	0	1,818	Schemes and Dreams	2	F	2	0	0	0	0
Scarlet Crown	2	F	2	1	1	0	9,600	Scheraboca's Tune	5	H	12	0	4	0	3,581
Scarlet Dress	3	F	1	0	0	0	0	Schex's Rail	5	H	1	0	0	1	1,067
Scarlet Express	5	M	3	0	0	0	0	Schlegel	3	C	8	1	1	1	19,640
Scarlet Gilia	5	M	10	1	1	3	36,600	Schmoopy Hang On	2	G	1	0	0	0	120
Scarlet Girl	4	F	1	0	0	0	48	Schnappsberg	4	C	7	0	0	1	2,507
Scarlet Glory	6	M	5	0	0	1	8,127	Schnarker	5	H	2	0	0	0	116
Scarlet Lad	5	G	14	3	3	1	29,264	Schnauser	4	G	9	1	2	2	7,885
Scarlet Lady Slew	4	F	8	1	1	2	2,795	Schneider	3	G	10	0	2	2	55,610
Scarlet Miss	4	F	13	0	1	0	3,340	Schnitzel (IRE)	7	M	2	0	0	0	1,200
Scarlet Moon	2	F	1	0	0	0	0	Scholar Warrior	9	G	1	0	0	0	0
Scarlet O'Claire	3	F	10	0	0	2	6,074	Scholarly	4	F	2	0	0	0	525
Scarlet O'Hara	4	F	2	1	0	0	12,330	Scholastica	3	F	9	3	2	1	67,040
Scarlet Peppers	3	C	11	2	2	2	19,227	School Bell	5	M	14	1	5	1	10,142
Scarlet Pimpernel	3	C	2	0	0	0	122	School Boy	6	H	5	1	0	1	6,300
Scarlet Rascal	7	G	7	1	0	1	7,308	School Fashion	6	M	10	1	5	0	11,227
Scarlet Rose	6	M	1	0	0	0	0	School for Scandal	4	F	7	3	1	0	61,800
Scarlet Splash	2	F	6	0	0	0	882	School of Thought	3	C	6	2	1	1	33,100
Scarlet Storm	2	C	2	0	0	0	0	School Town	4	F	3	0	0	0	0
Scarlet Tempest	3	F	4	0	1	0	3,255	Schooling	6	G	8	1	1	0	5,863
Scarlet Thorn	7	F	7	0	1	0	8,490	Schoolmaster	3	G	15	1	3	1	19,329
Scarlet Treasure	3	F	16	1	0	0	4,714	Schools Out	6	G	17	2	2	3	15,954
Scarlet's Magick	6	M	8	0	1	1	5,033	Schooner	4	G	15	2	0	2	14,230
Scarlet's Tara	3	F	7	3	0	0	55,495	Schoonertown Lass	2	F	2	0	0	0	0
Scarlett Memories	2	F	5	1	1	0	15,610	Schroeder	3	G	7	0	0	0	1,116
Scarlett Point	2	C	3	1	0	0	15,048	Schu Nine to Five	7	M	10	2	2	1	3,508
Scarlett Reef	5	M	5	1	0	1	8,708	Schwartzenegger	3	C	1	0	0	1	880
Scarlett Story	2	F	4	1	0	0	6,505	Schwarzwald	2	C	7	0	1	0	7,800
Scarlett's Ghost	2	C	2	0	0	1	860	Schwylerette	4	F	3	0	0	0	118
Scarlett'sprospect	5	M	11	1	1	4	5,810	Schymm Tyme	8	M	8	0	0	1	499
Scary Bob	2	C	4	3	1	0	95,760	Sci Fi	3	C	3	1	1	0	38,560
Scary Tim	5	G	12	1	3	1	15,388	Sci Fi Kin	4	F	2	1	1	0	15,600
Scarzane	4	F	9	3	1	3	84,183	Scifi Flick	4	F	2	0	0	0	1,258
Scat Bird	6	H	10	1	1	0	6,825	Scintilla	3	F	6	2	0	0	22,084
Scat Cat Jamey	3	C	6	1	0	1	19,105	Scintillating	5	M	10	2	2	1	81,552
Scat Sam Man	2	C	3	2	0	0	45,215	Scintillating Gal	7	M	8	1	3	1	12,235
Scat Singer	9	M	4	0	0	0	144	Scioto Bootski	5	M	6	2	3	0	51,116

Horse	Age	Sex	Sts	1st	2d	3d	Won	Horse	Age	Sex	Sts	1st	2d	3d	Won
Scioto Jo	5	M	7	0	0	0	440	Scratched	4	F	7	1	0	0	2,456
Scioto Seacat	2	F	4	0	0	0	1,235	Scraven	3	F	1	0	0	0	130
Scituate Harbor	3	C	2	0	0	0	0	Scream Machine	5	G	6	0	0	0	0
Sco Phone	2	F	5	0	1	2	9,000	Screamin Demon	5	H	2	0	0	0	2,058
Scobey	8	H	11	1	4	0	10,120	Screamin Passion	4	G	2	0	1	0	1,640
Scofflaw	5	G	9	1	3	2	5,582	Screamin Stacey	4	F	7	1	1	1	4,857
Scooby Drew and Me	4	G	5	2	0	1	15,672	Screaming	6	H	2	0	0	0	0
Scooby Who	3	G	11	2	0	1	7,295	Screaming Prince	6	G	4	0	0	1	725
Scoop of Ice	9	G	6	2	1	1	27,600	Screaming Willy	5	G	16	2	1	0	6,985
Scoot Mary Scoot	2	F	2	0	1	0	3,200	Screen Happy	5	M	9	1	1	2	38,701
Scoot Scoot N Go	2	C	8	0	3	1	5,608	Screen Kiss	4	C	1	0	0	0	0
Scoota Begga	3	G	7	1	0	0	2,202	Screen Latch	6	H	5	0	2	0	4,050
Scootch	7	G	10	1	2	2	11,509	Screen Legend	5	H	6	1	2	0	8,610
Scooter Boots	3	F	5	2	1	1	16,234	Screen Machine	3	F	1	0	0	0	201
Scooter Roach	4	G	10	1	2	1	94,256	Screen Pass	3	G	8	1	3	0	18,992
Scooters Knight	5	G	10	1	2	4	4,505	Screen Proof	3	F	9	1	1	0	32,040
Scooter's Sunman	5	G	11	2	3	1	25,325	Screen Runner	2	C	3	0	0	0	150
Scootin by Delmer	6	G	14	0	0	0	680	Screen Start	3	C	5	0	0	0	76
Scootin' Girl	5	M	9	0	2	0	24,799	Screen Test	4	G	13	3	1	0	22,667
Scootin N Bootin	6	M	3	0	1	0	1,612	Screenplay	6	G	13	4	0	1	78,440
Scootinaflash	3	F	8	2	1	0	33,577	Screw Loose Bruce	4	G	13	1	4	0	22,743
Scootintohollywood	3	G	1	0	0	0	0	Scrimshaw	3	C	8	1	0	2	352,479
Scorched Earth	4	G	9	2	1	0	11,128	Script Girl	4	F	1	0	0	0	0
Scorcher	6	H	3	1	0	0	1,465	Scriptoclearance	3	F	1	0	0	0	0
Scorching	4	F	9	1	0	3	19,431	Scrofa	2	F	8	1	1	1	25,840
Score Card	3	G	2	0	1	1	659	Scrubby	6	H	17	3	1	1	21,608
Score High	2	C	3	1	0	0	13,680	Scrublist	3	C	3	0	0	0	375
Score King	2	G	13	0	0	1	4,964	Scrubs	3	C	14	3	2	1	61,667
Score Six	3	F	8	0	2	3	41,020	Scrum	4	G	3	0	0	0	1,960
Score's Edition	5	G	4	0	0	0	0	Scuba Steve	3	G	5	1	0	1	16,880
Scoring Machine	5	H	2	0	0	0	186	Scuffler	10	G	3	0	1	0	1,148
Scoring Slew	6	G	11	1	1	2	14,849	Sculptor	4	G	8	2	1	1	14,050
Scorpio Scorpio	3	G	1	0	0	0	89	Scunnered	8	G	2	0	0	0	180
Scorpion Missile	3	F	15	5	1	1	58,740	Scuppernong	3	G	6	2	1	1	30,809
Scotch	4	G	11	1	5	0	12,162	Scurry Z	4	F	8	1	1	3	7,481
Scotch and Candy	6	M	3	0	0	0	546	Scusi	3	F	13	1	2	3	16,463
Scotch and Rum	3	F	2	0	1	0	7,280	Scuti Patuti	3	F	3	0	0	1	1,575
Scotch Cap	5	G	7	1	2	2	21,005	Scutterbotch	3	F	14	2	2	4	77,928
Scotch Dancer	5	M	7	1	0	0	14,727	Scuttlebuttin	3	C	14	3	0	1	47,450
Scotland Place	2	F	2	0	0	0	115	Se Me Acabo (CHI)	5	M	6	0	0	0	18,566
Scotlyns Mary	3	F	10	0	0	1	1,235	Se Poy Reggal	4	F	6	0	0	0	964
Scotman	6	G	3	0	0	0	1,827	Se Vera (CHI)	5	M	3	0	0	0	12,311
Scott	3	C	11	1	1	2	51,620	Sea Angel	4	F	10	1	3	2	32,741
Scott County Jim	3	G	3	0	0	0	0	Sea Bag	4	F	5	0	0	0	795
Scott Ross	3	F	5	1	2	2	9,000	Sea Beau	3	C	5	0	0	0	3,033
Scottago	3	C	10	3	0	3	116,390	Sea Bloom	3	F	5	1	1	0	25,800
Scottie	3	G	6	2	2	0	37,740	Sea Carrgot	5	G	6	2	1	1	28,874
Scotties Abity	2	G	1	0	0	0	1,050	Sea Chatter	3	F	3	0	0	0	830
Scotties Lasey	4	F	15	1	0	4	8,684	Sea Classic	4	F	12	1	1	6	38,634
Scottish Bubbly	5	M	9	3	3	0	73,160	Sea Clip	2	G	11	1	2	0	37,275
Scottish Heir	3	F	5	0	0	0	505	Sea Clipper	2	C	1	0	0	0	450
Scottish Heritage	3	F	10	2	0	3	63,229	Sea Cloud	4	G	9	2	1	2	73,310
Scottish Lisky	3	G	1	0	0	0	0	Sea Colony	6	G	7	4	1	2	27,140
Scottish Mist	2	F	8	1	0	0	18,514	Sea Daisy	8	M	6	0	0	0	693
Scottish Warrior	4	G	18	6	5	4	104,632	Sea Devil	4	G	3	0	0	0	2,385
Scottislittle Boy	6	G	7	0	1	0	1,326	Sea Doctor	2	C	5	1	0	0	18,065
Scott's Gold	4	G	7	0	0	0	1,750	Sea Dog	6	G	2	0	0	0	0
Scotts Noble Crown	4	F	9	0	2	1	2,501	Sea D's Salute	4	F	16	3	1	3	29,228
Scottsezso	2	G	2	0	0	1	900	Sea Dub	4	G	12	1	3	3	67,823
Scottston Style	6	G	14	0	0	2	2,961	Sea Dusty	3	C	14	0	0	3	4,215
Scotty Scotty	4	C	4	0	1	1	1,216	Sea Echo	4	F	16	3	4	3	18,730
Scotty Wotty	5	G	2	0	0	1	3,300	Sea Femma	5	M	2	0	0	0	500
Scottyhere	4	C	2	0	0	0	0	Sea Flasher	4	G	10	0	0	2	5,606
Scotty's Big Nite	4	C	10	2	0	4	24,968	Sea Force	4	G	17	2	0	1	18,440
Scotty's Bus	3	C	4	0	0	2	4,982	Sea Grouch	3	F	4	0	0	0	3,087
Scotty's Girl (GB)	5	M	3	1	1	0	21,840	Sea Gulch Sally	4	F	3	0	0	0	560
Scout Me	6	G	9	0	2	4	38,275	Sea Harbor	3	G	11	0	1	3	28,900
Scouts Emblem	3	C	10	2	3	3	74,855	Sea Island	4	F	5	0	0	0	347
Scouts Heartbreak	3	C	6	0	0	0	517	Sea Isle City	3	G	10	0	0	1	2,414
Scouts Honor	4	G	1	0	0	0	0	Sea Jewel	3	F	3	1	1	0	46,980
Scr Top Player	4	G	7	1	0	0	4,428	Sea Lady	3	F	11	2	2	1	10,975
Scrambling	2	F	4	0	0	0	0	Sea Leon	5	H	12	6	2	0	91,030
Scramjet	3	F	1	0	0	1	1,019	Sea Life	3	F	6	1	3	0	36,060
Scrap Man	2	G	2	0	0	0	0	Sea Light	4	G	16	3	2	1	9,590
Scrapping the West	5	G	5	1	1	0	5,642	Sea McLee	7	G	8	1	1	0	4,775
Scrappy	5	H	3	1	0	0	3,360	Sea Merge	2	F	4	0	1	0	4,280
Scratch Back	5	H	18	1	3	4	13,425	Sea Mission	5	M	3	0	0	0	70
Scratch N Dent	5	M	5	0	0	0	52	Sea Mist	5	M	6	0	2	1	27,430
Scratch This	4	G	3	0	0	0	599	Sea Mistress	3	F	8	2	0	1	57,760

Horse	Age	Sex	Sts	1st	2d	3d	Won
Sea My Darling	3	F	3	0	0	0	1,514
Sea My Style	4	F	4	1	1	0	7,760
Sea 'n Catch	5	G	8	0	1	2	1,597
Sea Native	4	C	3	0	0	0	790
Sea Navigator	5	H	13	1	6	0	15,068
Sea of Fire	3	F	14	0	4	1	14,235
Sea of Green	5	H	10	3	0	2	149,335
Sea of Hope	4	F	16	3	1	4	54,550
Sea of Intrigue	2	C	5	1	0	0	6,371
Sea of Joy	5	M	16	0	1	1	2,273
Sea of Lace	3	F	10	2	1	3	35,966
Sea of Love	6	M	12	0	2	2	6,579
Sea of Promises	2	F	5	2	3	0	64,250
Sea of Red	3	C	1	0	0	0	0
Sea of Showers	4	F	3	2	0	0	106,846
Sea of Silver	2	C	3	1	0	0	34,420
Sea of Sweets	2	F	4	0	1	0	4,630
Sea of Tranquility	7	H	9	1	1	1	48,407
Sea Pleasure	3	C	12	2	0	2	113,680
Sea Power	3	G	5	1	1	0	37,650
Sea Prairie	3	F	5	0	0	0	945
Sea Preacher	3	C	4	1	0	1	30,300
Sea Raider	6	H	1	0	0	0	140
Sea Ready	5	M	5	0	0	2	2,019
Sea Reel	5	M	2	0	0	0	6,070
Sea Robin	7	M	6	2	2	1	20,475
Sea Rock	3	G	3	1	0	0	10,920
Sea Run	6	H	7	0	0	0	1,765
Sea Scout	3	C	7	3	1	1	58,726
Sea Sense	2	G	5	0	0	1	3,470
Sea Span	4	F	7	2	1	2	62,909
Sea Squirrel	5	G	7	2	0	2	65,560
Sea Storm	6	G	8	0	1	0	3,344
Sea Strike	5	H	5	0	0	1	884
Sea Surf	4	F	2	0	0	0	200
Sea Tac Jet	4	G	13	2	2	1	12,502
Sea Tactical	3	F	4	0	0	0	3,495
Sea Tech	2	F	1	0	0	1	2,990
Sea to See	5	G	12	1	2	3	166,325
Sea to Sky	2	G	2	0	0	0	0
Sea Tow	2	F	11	0	1	3	5,625
Sea Trade	3	C	8	2	2	1	76,290
Sea Trek	2	C	1	0	0	0	0
Sea Victory	5	G	9	1	0	0	4,634
Sea Walker	3	G	5	0	0	2	37,499
Sea Warrior	5	G	7	0	0	0	668
Sea Way Lady	5	M	8	4	1	0	45,260
Sea Ya Mate	5	M	11	2	0	4	26,511
Seaana Gal	5	M	1	0	0	0	45
Seabuck Express	4	G	8	2	0	2	10,167
Seacliff Dusty	2	F	3	1	1	0	11,870
Seacliffbythedoor	3	F	5	1	1	1	6,825
Seacliff's Return	2	C	8	2	1	2	28,875
Seafarer	5	G	14	1	2	1	14,918
Seafaring Man	4	G	6	1	3	1	30,650
Seagull Beach	4	F	10	1	1	3	7,130
Seahorse Surprise	5	G	6	0	0	1	1,150
Seainsky	4	G	11	2	2	1	93,790
Seajebscharm	4	F	10	0	0	1	1,128
Seakeen	4	F	14	4	0	3	35,053
Seal Bay	3	F	7	2	3	0	92,805
Seal the Deal	3	C	6	0	1	1	6,650
Sealed Orders	8	G	1	0	0	0	0
Sealed With a Kiss	4	G	8	2	1	0	30,760
Seamaid	3	F	6	2	1	1	15,511
Seamster	3	C	11	5	0	1	61,950
Sean Sean	5	H	2	0	0	0	0
Seaninety	5	M	1	0	0	0	0
Seanmore Greek	4	C	2	0	0	0	730
Sean's Baby	2	F	1	0	0	0	0
Sean's Baby Boy	4	C	1	0	0	0	3,200
Seans Beauty	3	F	1	0	0	0	0
Sean's Pride	3	C	11	1	1	1	12,240
Seanster	3	G	12	1	2	1	1,981
Seaoflights	4	F	13	0	2	0	4,450
Seaquarius	3	G	5	1	0	2	38,510
Seaquay Ninty Nine	4	F	8	2	1	0	31,934
Searatic	3	C	9	1	1	0	8,928
Search and Rescue	3	C	6	2	1	0	13,855
Search Engine	8	G	19	2	2	5	14,459
Search for a Buyer	3	G	9	0	0	1	1,692
Search for a Cure	3	F	8	3	1	1	78,700
Search for Blue	5	M	6	0	0	0	2,347
Search for Luv	7	G	8	3	4	0	22,380
Search for Mindy	3	F	9	2	1	0	6,987
Search for Steve	7	G	4	0	0	0	217
Search Me	8	H	2	1	0	0	4,860
Search No More	7	M	17	1	2	1	9,144
Search the Church	2	F	1	0	1	0	7,860
Search the Facts	3	F	11	1	1	0	15,921
Search the Sky	2	F	6	0	1	2	7,150
Searchfor Diamonds	4	F	6	1	1	2	10,375
Searchforasecret	3	F	7	1	0	0	19,260
Searchforthebest	2	C	1	0	0	0	2,050
Searchfortreasure	6	M	6	0	3	0	10,840
Searchin South	3	F	5	1	0	0	30,012
Searchinfodacrown	2	F	13	1	2	2	11,515
Searchon	5	M	5	0	2	2	4,525
Seashore Paspalum	2	G	5	0	1	2	5,880
Seaside Dream	3	F	2	1	0	0	26,400
Seaside Hero	6	G	13	2	1	3	10,699
Seaside Tony	3	C	10	1	0	0	8,270
Seas'n Finale	4	C	3	0	0	0	0
Season for Glory	3	F	2	0	0	0	280
Season of Love	2	F	5	0	0	1	5,890
Season Series	8	M	2	0	0	0	130
Season to Win	4	F	4	0	0	0	165
Seasonal Change	5	M	5	0	0	0	700
Seasonal King	2	C	1	0	0	0	420
Seasoned Pro	4	F	9	4	1	0	19,220
Seasons Come	5	H	9	0	1	1	1,706
Seasons Promise	3	F	12	2	1	1	24,420
Seaswept	5	G	17	0	2	0	2,822
Seatac's in Charge	2	G	3	0	0	0	1,775
Seatovictory	5	H	5	0	0	1	1,128
Seatriscuit	2	F	5	1	0	1	14,846
Seattle Appeal	7	M	9	0	0	1	3,886
Seattle Ash	4	F	11	2	1	0	34,020
Seattle Band	4	G	2	0	0	1	4,420
Seattle Borders	2	C	5	1	2	0	34,740
Seattle Cue	6	G	5	1	0	0	7,326
Seattle Current	3	G	2	0	0	1	1,645
Seattle Doc	4	G	10	0	0	2	3,555
Seattle Emblem	3	F	13	1	2	2	22,280
Seattle Fitz (ARG)	4	C	12	2	2	2	170,636
Seattle Fling	4	F	5	0	0	0	431
Seattle Ghost	7	G	16	2	4	4	29,848
Seattle Glory	4	C	5	2	1	1	66,300
Seattle Groove	5	G	8	2	3	2	59,280
Seattle Hit	4	G	12	1	3	4	6,793
Seattle Hoofer	3	C	2	1	0	0	18,000
Seattle Hostage	4	F	4	0	0	0	372
Seattle Jolie	4	G	1	0	0	0	40
Seattle Katie	2	F	1	0	0	0	700
Seattle Kelly	3	F	6	0	0	2	1,900
Seattle Key	4	F	14	1	1	0	7,800
Seattle Lake	4	F	10	1	1	0	30,766
Seattle Lottery	2	F	3	0	0	0	750
Seattle Lou	5	G	7	0	0	0	299
Seattle Mailman	5	G	14	1	2	0	10,963
Seattle Majesty	4	F	12	2	1	5	15,749
Seattle Marker	5	G	5	0	0	3	2,420
Seattle Me Up	3	C	2	0	0	0	450
Seattle Minister	2	F	5	0	0	0	1,740
Seattle Native	4	G	18	1	1	0	2,857
Seattle Night	5	H	1	0	0	0	0
Seattle Oak	3	F	3	0	0	0	0
Seattle P D	2	F	2	0	1	1	2,294
Seattle Play Boy	5	H	9	1	0	2	2,670
Seattle Prospector	5	M	8	1	0	3	17,057
Seattle Quake	3	F	15	3	0	5	17,103
Seattle Queen	3	F	3	0	0	0	4,920
Seattle Qui	3	F	2	0	0	0	1,750
Seattle Reign	5	G	9	2	0	2	3,845
Seattle Rocks	8	H	1	0	0	0	0
Seattle Rookie	7	G	11	0	2	3	4,439
Seattle Santa	4	C	9	1	1	0	15,070
Seattle Savitar	5	G	8	1	0	3	8,320

Horse	Age	Sex	Sts	1st	2d	3d	Won
Seattle Shamus	4	C	8	3	2	0	123,640
Seattle Sheikh	6	G	10	0	0	0	458
Seattle Slammer	5	H	6	0	0	0	340
Seattle Slewis	3	C	7	1	2	3	20,780
Seattle Sloop	2	F	5	0	0	2	5,820
Seattle Smoke	3	C	5	2	1	0	19,430
Seattle Socialite	5	M	12	2	2	4	63,090
Seattle South	10	G	8	0	0	1	912
Seattle Spike	6	G	4	1	1	2	2,092
Seattle Summits	3	G	1	0	0	0	50
Seattle Sunshine	5	G	18	3	5	2	54,485
Seattle Surprise	3	C	11	3	0	0	69,150
Seattle Tac	3	F	3	1	1	0	43,252
Seattle the Great	4	C	2	0	1	0	6,480
Seattle Water	4	G	4	0	0	0	0
Seattle Weekend	2	F	4	0	0	0	5,455
Seattle Willy	2	C	4	0	1	2	19,680
Seattle Woodja	5	H	3	0	0	0	1,786
Seattlecity	7	G	16	5	1	3	23,020
Seattle's Fortune	5	G	15	4	1	3	53,326
Seattle's Witch	3	F	1	0	0	0	135
Seattlescatch	2	C	2	0	0	0	0
Seattlespectacular	3	C	5	1	2	1	61,120
Seavenger	3	G	1	0	0	0	420
Seaventure	3	F	4	0	0	1	1,580
Seaver	2	C	2	1	0	0	14,250
Seaway Salute	3	F	6	0	0	0	885
Seba Go Go	4	F	12	0	1	2	3,553
Sebastian	5	H	4	0	1	1	3,668
Sebastian Light	4	G	13	0	2	2	33,149
Sec C Cowgirl	6	M	17	1	3	4	11,084
Second Avenue	6	H	4	0	0	0	1,677
Second Collection	4	G	7	0	1	0	15,770
Second in Command	3	C	9	1	2	2	83,090
Second Lining	6	M	15	0	2	0	6,645
Second Manassas	6	H	6	0	0	0	800
Second of June	2	C	5	3	1	0	114,800
Second Opinion	4	F	2	0	0	0	91
Second Performance	2	C	1	0	0	0	2,760
Second Shift	3	F	15	3	1	0	11,020
Second Star	5	M	11	1	4	2	12,428
Second Storm	3	G	7	0	0	0	309
Second Tam Around	2	F	3	1	1	1	8,800
Second Tuesday	4	C	9	2	0	2	49,760
Second Wind	2	F	1	0	0	0	350
Secondary School	4	F	10	2	2	1	100,892
Secondvowsintheraw	4	F	2	0	0	0	260
Secret Ace	6	G	15	3	1	4	33,556
Secret Again	2	G	3	1	0	2	9,694
Secret Agent Man	4	C	4	0	0	1	2,028
Secret Agent Tom	3	G	12	1	5	4	21,309
Secret Ambition	4	C	1	0	0	0	0
Secret Approval	4	F	2	0	0	0	880
Secret Asset	6	M	1	0	0	0	82
Secret Banker	4	C	12	2	3	4	19,009
Secret Bayou	4	G	7	0	1	0	2,670
Secret Bluff	3	F	8	0	0	0	378
Secret Boundary	5	G	13	0	1	1	4,331
Secret Brand	2	C	1	0	0	0	350
Secret Brick	6	M	9	0	0	1	5,510
Secret Bullet	5	M	5	2	1	0	44,682
Secret Bundle	3	F	1	0	0	0	0
Secret Caller	5	G	14	2	0	2	8,884
Secret Caper	3	F	9	3	1	1	67,240
Secret Case	4	G	10	0	2	2	8,269
Secret Cat	4	C	8	1	0	1	7,650
Secret Chief	7	H	8	1	2	2	13,180
Secret Command	4	G	5	1	0	0	6,390
Secret Compliance	4	F	8	2	1	0	7,790
Secret Corsage	2	F	6	2	2	0	60,125
Secret Cousin	3	G	12	0	4	0	17,877
Secret Dash	4	G	19	0	0	1	4,567
Secret Data	3	F	1	0	0	0	135
Secret Delight	2	F	8	0	1	0	4,078
Secret Deposit	3	G	6	1	0	1	4,630
Secret Deputy	12	G	8	1	0	0	6,172
Secret Dispersal	6	H	5	0	0	0	477
Secret Dot Com	6	G	7	1	1	0	9,270
Secret Encore	3	F	4	1	0	0	4,363
Secret Escape	3	G	13	0	3	0	18,143
Secret Exchange	3	G	4	0	0	0	0
Secret Expectation	4	F	14	4	1	3	34,342
Secret Fire	3	F	2	0	0	0	182
Secret Formula	3	C	19	5	3	1	67,680
Secret Forum	4	F	11	2	2	1	29,840
Secret Garden (IRE)	4	F	2	1	0	0	36,600
Secret Glow	2	F	6	2	0	1	50,387
Secret Gold	4	F	5	0	0	0	225
Secret Guarantee	4	F	9	0	2	1	4,816
Secret Honey	3	F	2	0	0	0	0
Secret Impression	8	H	3	2	1	0	22,500
Secret in Paris	3	F	1	0	0	0	0
Secret Isout	5	H	5	0	0	0	857
Secret John	2	G	3	0	0	0	117
Secret Journey	3	F	15	3	7	2	29,098
Secret Lake	4	C	4	0	0	1	758
Secret Lane	4	F	3	0	0	0	80
Secret Liaison	5	M	4	2	0	0	136,719
Secret Life	5	M	1	0	0	0	80
Secret Look	3	C	5	0	3	0	11,460
Secret Lottery	5	M	1	0	0	0	36
Secret Luck	2	G	5	0	0	1	2,143
Secret Maneuvers	3	F	6	3	1	1	34,740
Secret Message	5	M	1	0	0	0	100
Secret Minister	4	G	1	0	0	0	0
Secret Motive	2	F	2	1	0	0	9,700
Secret Mover	4	F	6	1	0	2	8,583
Secret Moves	3	F	2	0	0	0	661
Secret Mystery	2	F	1	0	0	0	360
Secret Mystique	5	M	6	1	0	0	11,524
Secret Naevy	5	M	19	1	2	1	6,270
Secret of Fappiano	2	F	1	0	0	0	0
Secret of Front	6	M	5	1	1	0	12,470
Secret of Kentucky	10	G	3	1	0	1	2,430
Secret of Mecca	5	M	5	0	1	2	33,630
Secret of Success	3	G	5	1	0	1	12,377
Secret One	4	G	10	0	2	2	4,832
Secret Package	2	F	5	1	3	0	13,749
Secret Paradise	3	F	1	0	0	0	0
Secret Patriot	2	F	2	1	0	0	26,350
Secret Pine	3	F	11	1	3	3	14,335
Secret Pockets	6	M	4	0	0	0	135
Secret Pride	4	F	9	0	4	3	14,930
Secret Pro	5	G	4	1	0	1	5,250
Secret Purr	3	F	5	0	0	2	1,800
Secret Request	3	F	12	3	0	4	103,782
Secret Reward	7	M	3	0	0	0	300
Secret Rhythm	6	H	2	0	0	1	580
Secret Rite	7	M	1	1	0	0	5,040
Secret Romance	2	F	7	1	1	0	37,715
Secret Romeo	5	H	11	2	6	0	127,360
Secret Roses	3	F	2	0	0	0	0
Secret Rumor	2	C	1	0	0	0	0
Secret Run	3	C	14	4	2	1	100,300
Secret Runner	3	G	18	2	4	1	21,392
Secret Rush	4	F	9	1	1	1	61,770
Secret Saratoga	3	F	9	1	1	2	8,414
Secret Sea	3	F	9	0	0	0	1,953
Secret Secret Star	5	G	8	4	1	0	62,952
Secret Session	5	G	4	0	0	0	1,506
Secret Silence	2	F	4	0	0	0	615
Secret Slider	7	M	13	0	0	0	866
Secret Smoker	4	F	6	1	1	1	9,489
Secret Society	2	F	10	1	1	0	7,356
Secret Song	4	G	13	0	3	2	17,145
Secret Sounds	6	M	17	0	0	2	5,694
Secret Sparkle	3	F	1	0	0	0	0
Secret Speed	3	C	3	0	0	0	180
Secret Spender	7	M	6	2	0	0	36,800
Secret Splendor	3	C	1	0	0	0	189
Secret Spot	4	G	2	0	0	1	1,860
Secret Spy	3	G	4	0	1	0	1,590
Secret Squall	8	G	8	0	0	1	2,438
Secret Stash	4	F	1	0	0	0	350
Secret Sweep	5	M	2	0	0	1	2,268
Secret Sword	3	C	5	0	1	1	2,763
Secret Tales	4	F	7	1	2	1	12,870
Secret Tantrum	3	C	2	0	0	0	0

Horse	Age	Sex	Sts	1st	2d	3d	Won	Horse	Age	Sex	Sts	1st	2d	3d	Won
Secret Tea	3	C	3	0	0	0	0	Seeking the Money	4	G	8	1	2	2	55,360
Secret Tour	3	C	6	0	0	0	0	Seeking the Ring	3	F	7	3	2	0	314,515
Secret Trait	4	G	18	1	0	5	7,460	Seeking the Show	5	G	11	1	1	3	30,855
Secret Union	4	G	22	4	7	2	31,518	Seeking the Silver	3	F	10	2	4	0	57,160
Secret Waters	4	F	2	0	0	0	0	Seeking to Attaq	2	F	2	0	0	0	781
Secret Weapon	2	C	1	0	0	0	0	Seelessofmary	6	G	10	0	1	0	3,350
Secret Wedge	4	C	12	1	2	2	20,940	Seemeloadandfire	3	G	5	1	1	1	18,702
Secret Wildcat	4	F	1	0	0	0	1,000	Seemore Seemore	3	C	2	0	0	0	0
Secret Word	4	F	9	0	2	0	2,102	Seemslikeyesterday	5	H	17	1	0	5	9,128
Secret Zeal	2	C	1	0	0	0	0	Seeya in Dakota	3	C	4	0	0	0	224
Secretariats Fancy	3	F	2	0	0	0	270	Seeya Siyah	4	C	3	0	0	0	47
Secretariats Hope	4	F	8	0	1	2	2,790	Seeya Trouble	3	G	9	2	1	1	41,711
Secretaries Joy	6	G	3	0	0	0	107	Seeyaat Redtracton	4	G	11	0	0	1	3,205
Secretary Hit	2	G	2	0	0	0	86	Seeyahoney	3	F	5	1	0	0	8,700
Secretary Tracker	2	G	4	1	1	0	12,760	Seeyainseattle	7	G	11	1	2	1	8,034
Secretaryharriet	5	M	3	0	0	0	0	Seeyou in Camelot	3	F	6	0	0	0	507
Secretarys Booboo	7	G	6	0	1	0	5,590	Seeyouattheevent	2	C	7	1	4	1	46,620
Secretive	5	M	6	0	1	2	2,651	Seeyouinseptember	6	M	5	0	2	0	9,595
Secretively	3	F	16	3	3	1	68,820	Sefapianos Miss	3	F	15	3	4	3	59,692
Secretless	3	F	8	0	3	1	14,060	Sefapianos Way	3	C	14	0	3	1	11,063
Secreto's Ghost	3	G	4	0	1	0	2,070	Sefas Rebel	3	G	2	0	0	0	111
Secretssafe Withme	3	F	3	2	0	1	33,029	Sefas Rose	6	M	6	3	2	0	126,211
Secretstoforget	3	G	4	1	0	0	4,800	Segi Point	3	G	7	1	1	0	2,069
Security Comet	2	C	8	1	2	2	22,916	Segovia	3	F	8	1	0	2	32,680
Sedgewick	3	G	6	2	0	0	13,200	Segreto	4	F	16	3	4	0	27,205
Sedition	5	H	7	1	3	1	30,065	Seiche	4	F	1	0	0	0	0
Sedona Run	3	F	5	0	0	0	588	Seinne (CHI)	6	H	3	1	0	0	94,000
Sedona Sunrise	5	M	15	1	0	3	20,390	Seis Meses	5	G	4	0	0	0	684
Seductive	3	F	10	2	3	1	17,626	Seismic Cat	3	C	4	1	0	0	4,850
Seductive Lady	2	F	7	2	1	1	36,020	Seismic Wave	5	G	2	0	0	0	900
Seductress	4	F	13	3	3	2	19,186	Seize the Glory	4	F	11	1	1	0	10,200
See Ashleigh Run	2	F	1	0	0	0	500	Sejeana	6	M	15	1	2	1	5,451
See Clearly	3	C	1	0	0	0	0	Sejm Boogie	6	H	12	4	0	2	52,440
See Foolish Girl	5	M	1	0	0	0	348	Sejm's Madness	7	G	11	1	0	3	22,750
See How She Runs	4	F	7	3	2	1	169,900	Sekari's Fun	3	F	12	1	0	1	6,715
See Latham	2	C	5	0	1	1	19,300	Seldom Free	3	G	9	2	1	1	31,670
See Me Salute	3	G	10	2	1	1	11,699	Seldom Silent	3	F	12	1	5	1	13,049
See Me Strut	6	M	9	0	0	1	5,783	Select Decor	7	G	19	4	2	2	26,945
See Me Through	2	F	1	0	0	1	2,123	Select Few (GB)	10	G	9	0	0	1	1,798
See My Dust	2	G	1	0	0	0	300	Select Party	5	G	1	0	0	0	0
See Red Run	5	H	4	0	1	1	2,611	Select Step	5	M	8	0	0	0	0
See Sea Lady	6	M	7	1	2	1	2,196	Selective Security	8	M	6	0	0	1	723
See the Angel	4	F	5	0	1	1	2,673	Selective Wisdom	4	G	13	1	2	1	70,715
See the Stars	4	F	12	3	2	0	59,412	Selena Rose	4	F	2	1	0	0	15,810
See Tom Rowe	6	G	19	2	0	3	18,524	Self Employed	3	G	1	0	0	0	0
See U At My Window	6	M	2	0	0	0	164	Self Esteem	5	G	13	1	1	4	24,770
See Ya Cat	8	G	9	0	3	0	19,838	Self Rising	4	F	7	0	0	2	23,770
See Ya in Indy	2	F	3	0	0	0	300	Selfish	7	M	10	1	0	4	9,069
See Ya Rich	3	C	6	2	1	1	18,400	Selim Road	3	F	1	1	0	0	7,260
See Ya Zia	3	F	8	0	0	0	1,550	Selina Aurora	4	F	7	2	0	0	3,345
See You At Siro's	5	G	5	2	0	0	41,920	Selina Delight	2	F	2	0	0	0	744
See You in America	5	M	11	0	0	0	1,555	Selina's Buttercup	4	F	7	1	0	0	10,442
See You Real Soon	2	C	3	0	1	1	8,600	Selina's Starlet	4	F	5	0	1	0	1,835
See You Tricky	4	F	21	1	4	0	11,884	Selita's Dream	2	F	3	0	0	1	1,391
Seedoubleyoubee	2	C	1	0	0	0	0	Sell 'm Short	3	G	10	0	2	3	8,510
Seeds of Peace	2	F	9	0	0	1	6,939	Sell the Farm	9	H	7	0	2	0	3,400
Seeing Signs	3	G	26	0	0	2	7,204	Sell the Rallies	2	F	2	0	1	0	8,600
Seeitobelieveit	3	G	4	0	0	0	3,240	Sell to Survive	3	C	8	1	2	2	34,195
Seek	3	F	6	0	0	0	825	Selma Ala	7	G	7	0	0	0	710
Seek (GB)	7	G	3	0	0	1	3,100	Selva Mia	4	F	20	0	1	4	6,298
Seek Gold	3	C	4	0	0	0	2,653	Sem City	2	C	1	0	0	0	780
Seek the Dream	4	C	6	1	1	0	4,220	Semana Nautica	5	G	14	1	1	1	5,092
Seek the Gold	5	M	9	3	2	1	16,028	Semblance	2	C	1	0	0	0	909
Seek Up	5	H	5	0	0	0	1,480	Semi Annual	6	H	18	1	0	5	3,292
Seeker	3	G	8	2	0	0	18,910	Semi Broke	3	F	7	0	2	1	4,883
Seeker's Glory	5	M	3	0	0	0	113	Semi Sweet Dr	4	G	6	1	1	0	8,902
Seekin Treasure	6	G	1	0	0	0	113	Semifinal	3	F	13	3	1	1	70,605
Seeking Amusement	5	M	7	1	0	2	1,989	Seminary	2	C	4	1	0	2	11,755
Seeking Approval	4	G	14	1	1	2	14,286	Seminole Bid	2	C	6	1	0	3	13,740
Seeking Diamonds	3	C	12	2	2	2	54,850	Seminole Chief	8	G	3	0	0	0	0
Seeking Greatness	4	C	1	0	0	0	0	Seminole Dancer	7	M	9	0	1	1	1,713
Seeking Love	7	M	11	3	3	2	8,207	Seminole Gal	5	M	8	1	1	1	13,485
Seeking Red	3	G	9	1	0	3	9,188	Seminole Gale	2	F	1	0	0	0	130
Seeking Royalty	3	G	16	1	1	2	6,403	Seminole Kid	4	G	17	0	1	1	3,563
Seeking Seattle	5	G	5	1	1	1	26,480	Seminole Renegade	3	G	9	0	1	1	2,950
Seeking Snowdrops	3	F	7	0	0	0	743	Seminole Shoe	5	M	14	0	1	3	3,502
Seeking the Carat	2	C	3	0	1	0	17,052	Seminole Springs	4	G	8	1	0	0	4,554
Seeking the Cat	4	C	3	0	0	0	1,020	Seminole Squaw	5	M	2	1	0	0	19,200
Seeking the Glory	3	C	3	1	1	0	35,380	Semoran Royalty	2	F	7	1	0	0	7,145

Horse	Age	Sex	Sts	1st	2d	3d	Won
Semoran Street	3	G	11	1	0	3	4,901
Semoran's Decision	3	G	5	2	0	1	47,573
Sempai	5	G	7	1	4	1	51,275
Semper Tap	4	G	1	0	0	0	0
Sempre Blumin	4	G	12	1	4	1	25,010
Semtex Sally	3	F	11	0	1	0	2,775
Sen Yourita Oro	2	F	2	0	0	0	225
Senate Caucus	4	F	4	0	0	1	1,415
Senate Trial	5	G	12	2	0	3	14,723
Senatepage	5	G	7	0	0	1	1,536
Senator Bennett	4	C	5	0	0	1	2,130
Senator Dandy	3	G	2	0	0	0	0
Senator Dick	3	C	5	0	1	0	3,790
Senator J	2	G	4	1	0	0	12,480
Senator Jim	10	G	7	2	0	1	35,398
Senator Joe P.	3	C	3	1	0	0	9,800
Senator Martha	3	F	1	0	0	0	900
Senator Rock	4	G	10	1	0	4	5,254
Senator Ruby	5	G	21	3	2	0	15,069
Send a Pro	5	G	6	0	0	0	459
Send a Shell	7	M	2	0	0	0	229
Send 'Em Pakin	2	F	8	1	0	2	79,170
Send for an Angel	2	F	2	0	0	0	875
Send in the Clown	3	F	6	0	1	0	1,703
Send Loot	4	C	6	0	0	0	396
Send Me a Beau	3	G	7	0	1	0	1,421
Send My Pal	2	G	4	0	0	1	4,965
Send the Package	5	M	3	0	0	0	780
Senda	4	F	12	0	2	1	14,525
Sendamemo	5	M	3	1	1	0	2,227
Sendero de Oro	2	C	4	0	2	0	2,998
Sendmomoney	4	C	5	1	1	1	12,685
Sendtheprospector	8	G	7	3	1	2	11,732
Sendy's Fortune	5	H	6	0	0	2	3,215
Senearose	3	F	8	0	0	0	485
Seneca Bunny	2	F	3	1	2	0	13,600
Seneca Dolly	3	F	18	3	2	4	20,375
Seneca Falls	5	M	14	4	4	3	55,654
Seneca Lad	4	C	6	0	2	1	3,744
Seneca Lizzy	4	F	7	1	1	1	4,359
Seneca Point	2	G	1	0	0	0	940
Seneca Prowler	3	G	2	0	0	1	2,110
Seneca Rock	3	C	6	0	2	3	32,107
Seneca Song	2	F	7	1	0	2	10,440
Seneca Summer	2	C	5	3	0	0	96,300
Senfully Easy	4	F	6	1	1	1	22,050
Senior Lender	2	F	4	0	0	1	1,485
Senior Macho	4	C	2	0	0	0	246
Senisha	4	F	7	1	2	1	7,552
Senja	3	F	4	2	1	0	18,310
Senoir Zoren	4	C	5	0	0	0	498
Senor Amigo	3	C	2	2	0	0	54,165
Senor Arugas	3	C	10	0	1	0	1,950
Senor B R	4	G	3	1	0	0	3,180
Senor Badgett	5	G	8	0	1	0	2,501
Senor Baileys	3	C	8	1	1	0	9,860
Senor Bay	4	G	8	3	1	2	30,175
Senor Billy	6	G	1	0	0	0	0
Senor Billy Bob	4	C	3	0	0	0	187
Senor Bull	9	G	14	1	5	3	19,019
Senor Carlos	6	G	3	0	1	0	1,330
Senor Chapo	6	H	8	1	1	3	1,955
Senor Charismatic	4	G	10	2	1	2	52,572
Senor Cholo	5	H	4	0	0	0	319
Senor Chop Chop	8	H	4	0	0	0	780
Senor Cielo	4	C	6	1	0	0	2,960
Senor Cielo Two	3	G	9	2	3	3	62,940
Senor Coqui	4	G	7	2	1	0	10,300
Senor Corona	2	C	5	0	0	0	0
Senor de Sol	4	G	14	3	5	0	38,960
Senor Eddie	4	G	5	1	0	2	5,965
Senor Experience	4	G	13	1	5	1	22,365
Senor Francisco	4	G	6	0	0	1	408
Senor Gator	2	C	7	0	0	0	1,030
Senor Gran	8	G	9	1	0	3	21,239
Senor Gran Day	2	C	2	0	0	0	0
Senor Ladd	2	G	4	1	1	1	19,460
Senor Mac	4	G	7	0	2	1	25,890
Senor Markos	6	G	9	2	2	1	4,407
Senor Mas	7	G	7	2	1	1	5,952
Senor Melchor	4	G	4	3	0	0	36,000
Senor Moonlight	3	C	4	0	0	0	237
Senor Prado	6	G	16	1	0	4	8,693
Senor Que Sea	3	C	7	0	0	0	180
Senor Realidad	3	C	10	2	1	1	12,491
Senor Sal	5	G	3	0	0	0	0
Senor Sancho	3	C	15	1	2	1	12,215
Senor Shine	5	G	17	4	5	0	24,043
Senor Sterling	6	G	7	0	0	0	2,065
Senor Swinger	3	C	11	3	0	2	361,290
Senor Valdez	5	G	11	0	0	0	833
Senor Will	6	G	12	4	2	1	24,025
Senora Del Lago	3	F	13	3	4	2	32,490
Senora Poppy	5	M	4	0	0	0	3,120
Senorita American	3	F	7	2	2	0	34,785
Senorita Anita	3	F	6	2	0	0	56,400
Senorita Bear	2	F	1	0	0	0	70
Senorita Delores	4	F	16	0	0	1	1,420
Senorita Echo	4	F	12	2	1	3	14,874
Senorita Jazzy	2	F	2	0	0	0	0
Senorita Million	4	F	7	1	0	0	11,136
Senorita Sirianni	4	F	5	0	0	0	1,053
Senorita Valentina	4	F	3	0	0	0	238
Senorita Ziggy	5	M	8	2	0	1	37,780
Sensational Again	3	F	1	0	1	0	12,120
Sensational Bid	4	C	14	4	3	1	51,423
Sensational Cat	4	F	4	2	0	0	8,049
Sensational Charm	4	F	9	2	4	1	29,050
Sensational Jake	4	C	3	2	0	0	7,313
Sensational Memory	2	F	2	0	0	0	400
Sensationalplace	3	G	15	3	0	2	28,995
Sensationalshooter	3	F	4	0	2	0	4,200
Sensationalsonny	3	G	2	0	0	1	735
Sense of Reality	2	G	2	0	0	0	990
Sensible	3	F	1	0	0	0	340
Sensibly Chic	3	F	5	2	0	1	57,750
Sensitive Issue	9	G	1	0	0	0	0
Sensitive Penguin	3	F	3	0	0	0	0
Sensitive Woman	4	F	8	1	1	1	17,117
Senso	3	G	2	0	0	0	270
Sensorious Kiss	2	F	3	0	0	0	720
Sensual	5	M	5	0	2	0	6,062
Sensuous Cinnamon	3	F	13	3	1	2	65,200
Sensuous Silk	2	F	4	0	0	1	5,607
Sent	6	G	9	0	1	1	4,958
Sent Home	4	F	8	0	1	1	4,585
Sentenced	4	F	14	2	2	2	24,670
Sentimental Lad	4	G	1	0	0	0	230
Sentimental Miss	4	F	8	0	1	3	12,580
Sentimental Value	4	F	5	0	0	1	19,299
Sentimentalreign	8	M	1	0	0	0	0
Sentimentalromance	7	M	13	3	4	3	81,310
Sentinel Rock	5	M	6	1	1	1	1,970
Sentosa	12	G	5	0	2	1	4,149
Sentsure	4	C	15	0	0	2	5,115
Seoul Wild	2	F	1	0	1	0	2,000
Separato	2	C	1	1	0	0	12,000
Seppuku	5	G	21	2	4	0	13,381
September Dawn	2	F	4	1	0	0	11,749
September Eleventh	3	F	6	1	1	0	7,125
September Hero	3	C	6	0	0	1	5,880
September Remember	2	F	1	0	0	0	0
September Secret	4	F	3	1	0	1	61,163
September Storm	3	F	8	2	2	1	20,593
Septennial	5	G	9	3	1	2	5,841
Sequel Cat	3	G	13	3	2	1	14,416
Sequential's Boy	5	G	8	0	0	2	1,060
Sequoia Foya	3	F	1	1	0	1	3,884
Sequoia Man	6	G	7	1	0	1	4,000
Sequoia Rose	4	F	13	1	1	3	10,133
Sequoian	4	G	9	3	2	2	83,420
Sera Slew	4	F	6	0	0	2	1,500
Serafic Gold	3	F	10	1	0	0	7,088
Serafina Pekkala	3	F	7	1	0	0	27,550
Serai	4	F	11	3	2	0	68,200
Seranoide	4	G	10	1	2	1	6,572
Seraph	3	F	5	1	2	1	12,335
Seraphic Storm	5	M	9	0	0	1	2,579

Horse	Age	Sex	Sts	1st	2d	3d	Won
Seraphic Too	3	F	9	1	0	1	34,176
Seraphim	3	F	13	1	1	1	14,492
Serazzo	7	H	5	2	0	0	22,870
Serbia	5	M	11	1	1	0	11,852
Serco	3	G	4	0	0	0	465
Seream	5	M	6	1	0	3	5,424
Serena's Lady	4	F	5	1	0	1	57,267
Serena's Run	3	F	3	0	1	0	4,530
Serena's Storm	3	F	1	0	0	0	0
Serendipity Bull	3	G	12	1	2	1	18,003
Serene in Seattle	5	M	6	0	1	0	53,196
Serene Joy	2	F	4	0	0	0	0
Serene Lady	4	F	16	3	5	2	16,851
Serene Place	2	F	1	0	0	0	0
Serene Valor	4	F	4	0	0	1	3,765
Serene Wolf	3	G	10	0	1	1	2,477
Serenity	4	F	5	2	0	0	13,530
Serenityisavirtue	3	F	9	1	1	3	28,410
Serenity's Smile	4	F	6	1	1	2	48,008
Sergeant Lefty	2	C	3	0	0	0	0
Sergeant Mimi	6	M	13	2	2	1	20,044
Serial Bride	6	G	4	0	0	0	240
Serious Alert	3	G	10	2	2	2	38,251
Serious Bull	3	C	6	0	1	0	3,320
Serious Business (IRE)	4	C	3	0	0	1	2,975
Serious Sam	5	G	12	1	0	0	9,305
Serious Sister	6	M	13	1	2	3	10,231
Serious Smoke	3	G	13	1	4	0	17,904
Serious Susan	5	M	10	2	0	1	19,440
Seriousasicanbe	6	G	4	1	1	0	6,668
Seriously Funny	3	C	2	0	2	0	13,850
Serleena	3	F	6	1	1	1	13,650
Sermon	4	F	6	0	0	1	5,950
Sermon On the Run	4	F	8	2	2	1	10,702
Serpiente	5	G	2	0	0	0	0
Serpina (IRE)	4	F	1	0	0	0	0
Serra Retreat	6	G	7	2	1	1	50,727
Serrano Slew	3	F	1	0	0	0	0
Servant King	4	C	11	1	1	1	8,048
Servant of All	3	F	8	1	0	0	7,985
Serve Again	2	F	4	1	2	0	10,609
Serve It Up	3	G	4	0	0	1	9,155
Served	3	G	12	2	2	2	15,638
Serves Em Bud	8	G	2	0	0	0	160
Service	5	H	12	0	4	1	18,794
Service Charge	2	C	4	0	0	0	1,415
Service Medal	2	F	3	0	0	0	350
Service Miss	3	F	10	0	2	1	10,521
Serving Ma Man	6	M	4	1	1	0	9,042
Set Down	9	G	18	1	4	1	11,280
Set for Life	3	C	4	0	0	0	426
Set For More (GB)	6	G	9	3	1	0	33,713
Set Me Free	5	H	9	1	1	2	5,086
Set On Go	2	F	2	0	0	0	175
Set Over Set	5	H	2	0	0	1	806
Set Sail	7	H	2	0	0	0	0
Set to Music	4	F	5	0	1	2	2,781
Set to Sparkle	3	F	14	2	4	5	59,480
Setacourseforhome	3	F	5	0	3	0	8,000
Setanta	2	F	5	1	1	0	26,480
Setapiece	2	F	3	1	0	0	8,358
Setemup Joe	3	G	16	3	0	1	37,885
Seth a Roo	6	G	1	0	0	0	40
Setthehook	4	G	13	5	1	2	48,000
Settin Fancy Free	4	F	9	2	1	2	4,954
Setting Bull	5	H	2	0	0	0	0
Setting the Scene	2	F	4	1	0	1	29,751
Settle Down	2	C	4	1	1	0	15,800
Settle in Seattle	2	F	5	2	0	1	31,139
Settle Up	3	C	6	0	2	1	28,860
Settlethescore	6	M	8	0	0	1	1,173
Settling Mist	4	F	6	1	1	0	33,600
Setup Man	3	G	5	1	0	0	6,729
Seul Avenger	7	G	3	0	0	0	0
Seul Flight	5	M	3	0	1	0	1,916
Sevasmoke	3	F	4	0	0	1	2,350
Seven Brides	4	F	7	2	3	1	117,235
Seven Caged Tigers	7	H	2	0	0	1	390
Seven Card	6	G	5	1	0	0	5,628

Horse	Age	Sex	Sts	1st	2d	3d	Won
Seven Card Draw	4	C	7	1	1	0	8,367
Seven Charms	4	G	8	0	2	2	18,275
Seven Cities	2	F	2	0	0	1	2,640
Seven Come Eleven	2	C	2	0	0	1	5,770
Seven Counties	5	M	5	1	1	1	12,905
Seven December	3	F	5	0	0	0	774
Seven Four Seven	5	M	9	4	0	1	156,933
Seven Friends	7	G	3	0	0	0	1,255
Seven Gold Gems	4	F	16	2	1	4	40,500
Seven Grand	3	F	8	2	2	1	53,360
Seven Hearts	4	C	14	1	3	5	17,729
Seven Heaven	4	F	5	0	2	0	3,315
Seven Is the Charm	3	F	2	0	0	1	3,140
Seven Jillion	6	G	11	1	1	3	31,040
Seven Mag	8	G	7	1	0	2	4,644
Seven Moons (JPN)	3	F	3	0	1	0	10,960
Seven No Tremp	6	G	8	1	1	0	5,901
Seven O	5	G	14	1	1	0	5,635
Seven of Niner	4	F	5	0	2	0	2,860
Seven On Friday	4	G	2	0	0	0	0
Seven Peaks	3	C	1	0	1	0	1,900
Seven Pines	4	F	14	1	3	1	6,803
Seven Rings	4	C	5	0	0	0	716
Seven Sands	3	C	2	0	0	0	0
Seven Seven Adam	3	C	5	0	0	0	1,260
Seven Talents	3	G	8	1	1	1	14,990
Seven Times	4	G	9	2	1	2	10,238
Seven Way Shake	2	C	3	0	0	1	3,200
Seven Year Wonder	2	F	4	0	0	0	767
Seveneightone East	3	G	1	0	1	0	1,080
Sevenext	4	C	3	0	0	0	224
Sevenforbish	3	G	11	2	3	2	74,702
Sevenmiss	5	M	12	2	5	4	23,580
Sevens Rule	4	G	9	1	0	1	3,256
Sevens' Star	3	F	6	0	0	1	1,774
Sevens Wild	4	F	12	3	1	1	23,860
Seventeen Candles	6	H	5	0	0	1	2,636
Seventh Choice	4	F	3	0	0	0	4,056
Seventh House	2	F	2	0	0	0	0
Seventh Inning	3	G	8	3	0	1	78,315
Seventh Morn	4	G	14	2	0	2	15,585
Seventh N Laurel	4	G	6	1	0	1	12,775
Seventh Wish	6	M	2	0	0	0	0
Seventyfivesouth	5	G	16	5	5	1	48,850
Severado (BRZ)	7	G	7	1	1	1	33,070
Severo	4	G	5	0	0	0	216
Severus	5	M	11	2	1	0	36,400
Seve's Honour	2	C	1	0	0	0	145
Sevier River	3	F	14	0	2	2	4,164
Sevillano	3	G	7	0	0	0	569
Seville's Ace	7	M	2	0	1	0	833
Seville's Joker	7	H	11	0	0	1	1,576
Seville's Minister	2	C	2	0	0	0	0
Seville's Prince	4	C	8	1	0	0	3,244
Seville's Runaway	6	H	7	0	1	1	1,911
Seville's Trump	5	M	6	1	0	1	4,305
Sevnfordeesevn	2	C	4	0	0	0	464
Sew Gone	3	G	14	1	0	2	6,326
Sew Neva Ask	2	F	1	0	0	0	0
Sew Sangue Slew	4	F	2	0	0	0	240
Sew Slow	4	F	11	1	1	0	16,883
Sewing Bag	3	C	5	0	1	1	11,540
Sex Machine (AUS)	6	G	2	0	0	0	0
Sexcetera	4	C	8	1	0	0	6,570
Sexiano	4	F	10	2	0	0	14,479
Sextet	2	C	1	0	0	1	6,468
Sexual Harrasment	6	M	3	0	1	0	6,800
Sexy Appeal	4	F	8	0	1	1	4,620
Sexy Boots	3	F	8	4	1	2	78,068
Sexy Ex	3	F	13	1	0	1	9,713
Sexy Girl	6	M	2	0	0	0	0
Sexy Helmsman	2	F	4	0	0	2	8,400
Sexy Hooligan	7	M	6	0	0	0	0
Sexy Kid	11	G	5	0	0	0	108
Sexy Lexie	7	M	1	1	0	0	3,360
Sexy March	4	F	1	0	0	0	0
Sexy Mark	3	F	14	1	0	0	4,494
Sexy Mon	3	G	1	0	0	0	0
Sexy Rose	3	F	1	1	0	0	3,600

Horse	Age	Sex	Sts	1st	2d	3d	Won	Horse	Age	Sex	Sts	1st	2d	3d	Won
Sexy Secrets	3	F	5	0	1	0	4,447	Shadowy	2	F	1	0	0	0	0
Sexy Splasher	2	F	1	0	0	1	1,425	Shady Classic	3	F	4	2	0	0	56,040
Sexy Stockings	3	F	7	2	2	1	42,420	Shady Dancer	4	F	2	0	0	0	0
Sexy Sunrise	4	G	9	2	0	0	15,204	Shady Deal	3	C	8	0	1	1	15,020
Seyalateralligator	2	C	5	0	0	0	3,840	Shady Gal	3	F	7	0	0	1	780
Seyani	2	F	1	0	0	0	0	Shady Hill	4	C	7	1	1	3	10,068
Seymour Moves	3	F	16	6	0	2	41,297	Shady Inspiration	6	M	16	2	1	1	22,516
Seymoura Me	4	G	9	0	2	1	4,285	Shady Justice	3	G	11	2	2	1	22,480
Sez Who's Gold	4	F	11	3	2	3	97,238	Shady Kan Do	3	F	1	0	0	0	0
Sforza (FR)	4	C	12	3	2	2	117,067	Shady Lady Jane	4	F	8	1	1	0	6,154
Sgt. Dundee	3	G	16	0	0	2	3,010	Shady Lane	2	F	1	0	0	0	0
Sgt. Newman	6	G	1	0	0	0	0	Shady Light	2	G	5	0	1	0	3,142
Sgt. Shelley	3	G	10	1	2	0	8,175	Shady N Single	3	F	5	1	0	2	16,057
Sgt. Slew	3	C	1	0	0	1	1,740	Shady Remark	8	G	14	1	2	3	17,305
Shaack	8	G	11	2	3	0	11,481	Shady Report	3	F	19	1	1	2	5,164
Shaanmer (IRE)	4	C	3	0	1	0	9,600	Shady Romance	3	F	10	0	1	3	6,932
Shabang Shabang	3	G	17	1	2	4	10,634	Shady Stan Avedon	6	H	5	1	1	0	2,175
Shabango	3	F	10	0	3	3	20,560	Shady Strike	4	G	7	2	0	1	38,643
Shabanu's Jet	2	F	1	0	0	0	0	Shady Tree	3	F	1	0	0	0	0
Shabi Dabi	2	C	3	0	0	0	450	Shady Valley	4	C	9	1	2	2	26,972
Shablam	6	G	11	4	2	3	43,390	Shadyrest	3	F	8	0	0	1	3,255
Shaboom Shaboom	6	H	5	1	0	0	1,029	Shadyside	5	M	10	1	0	0	5,523
Shabozz	4	C	1	0	0	0	60	Shafeera	4	F	11	1	1	1	7,741
Shack a Tee	2	G	1	0	0	0	120	Shaffle	3	G	6	1	3	0	9,440
Shack Martin	3	G	5	0	0	0	1,122	Shaggar Rhaughton	4	F	5	1	0	0	8,800
Shackelford	7	G	6	1	1	1	5,186	Shaggin Girl	5	M	4	0	0	0	630
Shaconage	3	F	6	2	0	0	113,822	Shagging	4	C	6	1	2	2	13,200
Shadar	3	C	5	0	0	1	2,415	Shagkin	7	M	6	0	0	0	1,982
Shaddai's Crusader	4	C	16	0	6	1	16,514	Shagsville	5	M	6	1	0	0	5,200
Shade of Black	3	F	1	0	0	0	0	Shagtime Pauly	3	G	19	5	2	1	27,406
Shade of Damascus	4	F	8	1	0	1	3,023	Shagwell	4	G	14	4	2	3	16,862
Shade the Cat	3	C	2	0	0	1	4,060	Shagwong	6	G	12	0	0	2	16,020
Shade Tree Lady	6	M	6	1	0	0	6,938	Shah Imran	5	H	12	0	0	0	819
Shadeed's Image	6	G	3	0	0	0	491	Shah Jehan	4	C	13	2	2	0	95,981
Shades Creek	6	G	11	1	3	2	20,425	Shah of Shahs	3	C	3	0	0	0	540
Shades of Autumn	3	F	5	1	0	0	22,584	Shahalie Lake	3	F	10	2	0	0	30,375
Shades of Halo	4	F	6	1	0	1	5,190	Shaheen Shaheen	3	C	5	1	1	2	21,290
Shades of Light	2	F	2	1	0	0	38,976	Shahnana's West	6	G	13	0	3	1	21,863
Shades of Pale	4	F	7	0	0	0	0	Shahrahere	8	G	3	0	0	0	5,550
Shades of Reality	3	C	1	0	0	0	0	Shaka's Warrior	4	G	18	1	1	2	7,744
Shades of Royal	6	G	8	1	0	3	6,229	Shake a Jar	2	G	2	0	1	0	2,520
Shades of Sunny	5	G	12	3	3	3	100,385	Shake a Leg	3	F	13	1	1	3	20,029
Shades of Time	2	F	1	0	0	1	837	Shake It High	5	M	12	2	2	2	7,720
Shadesofaffection	5	M	8	2	2	0	6,790	Shake Me Wake Me	7	G	6	0	1	1	2,846
Shadey Mike	4	C	3	0	1	0	5,320	Shake Off	2	F	2	1	0	0	24,600
Shadi Sand	4	C	7	0	1	3	5,895	Shake Salt	5	H	5	0	1	0	10,220
Shadoc	3	C	3	1	0	0	8,760	Shake the Bank	3	C	8	1	1	1	44,080
Shadow and Lace	3	F	1	0	0	0	0	Shake the Dice	5	G	15	4	3	2	135,667
Shadow Book	5	G	13	1	3	4	7,254	Shake the Dust	5	M	13	1	2	2	8,639
Shadow Boots	6	M	14	0	4	5	4,250	Shake Thechampagne	2	F	2	0	0	1	1,350
Shadow Boxing	4	C	7	0	0	1	2,732	Shake Those Hands	6	G	10	1	1	3	6,965
Shadow Cast	2	F	2	1	0	1	30,005	Shake Up	3	F	4	0	0	0	161
Shadow Chaser	5	M	5	1	0	1	4,323	Shake You Down	5	G	13	7	2	2	829,160
Shadow Danceblaze	2	F	8	1	1	2	9,368	Shake You Up	2	C	4	0	0	1	3,630
Shadow Government	3	F	8	0	0	2	2,963	Shake'em On Down	4	F	9	0	0	1	5,515
Shadow Hawk	4	C	4	1	1	1	30,192	Shakeit Tothemoon	5	M	19	2	1	1	11,793
Shadow Hour	4	F	10	2	3	1	9,858	Shaker Made	4	F	14	1	4	3	38,325
Shadow Locket	4	F	4	0	0	0	380	Shakespeare Critic	3	F	14	2	0	4	23,501
Shadow Monster	4	G	11	2	3	1	32,778	Shakesperean Story	2	C	2	1	1	0	11,200
Shadow Mountain	9	G	16	5	2	4	47,485	Shakethemhatersoff	3	G	5	2	0	0	11,910
Shadow of Illinois	3	G	9	2	1	2	74,792	Shakey	2	G	2	0	0	0	70
Shadow of Mine	2	F	6	1	0	0	48,280	Shaky Town	3	G	7	3	2	0	100,160
Shadow of the Wire	6	M	6	0	0	1	706	Shaky Your Capote	2	G	3	0	0	0	0
Shadow On the Rail	6	G	12	0	0	2	1,339	Shal Tour	5	H	7	0	1	1	3,030
Shadow Play	3	F	4	0	1	1	15,580	Shalimar Sue	6	M	4	0	0	0	169
Shadow Raider	3	G	12	2	1	1	57,128	Shalini	4	F	9	3	1	1	230,159
Shadow Rider	3	G	13	1	2	1	13,360	Shalmarie	3	F	9	2	2	0	19,260
Shadow Shake	6	M	5	1	0	0	6,570	Sham Aciss	5	G	3	1	1	0	19,500
Shadow Steele	5	M	13	0	2	0	3,405	Shaman	5	G	8	1	0	0	4,734
Shadow Thief	3	G	6	1	0	2	21,360	Shaman Chocolate	8	G	10	0	0	0	1,200
Shadow Wave	2	C	3	0	0	0	690	Shaman Spirit	6	G	4	0	0	0	555
Shadowblade	3	G	2	0	0	1	1,570	Shaman's Drum	8	H	1	0	0	0	500
Shadowland	2	C	2	2	0	0	21,850	Shamarea	3	F	9	0	2	2	3,980
Shadow's Angel	4	F	5	1	0	0	9,388	Shambala	7	M	15	1	0	1	12,558
Shadows Dancing	3	F	7	2	1	1	36,560	Shame On Damascan	3	C	5	1	0	0	4,373
Shadow's Hope	2	F	2	0	0	0	575	Shame On the Moon	4	C	2	0	1	1	3,450
Shadow's Image	4	G	16	1	3	1	19,278	Shameful	4	F	3	1	1	0	97,190
Shadows Unexpected	5	M	7	1	0	1	6,870	Shamelessly	3	F	9	1	0	1	10,708
Shadowsoncanvas	2	G	4	1	0	2	9,250								

RECORDS OF HORSES

Horse	Age	Sex	Sts	1st	2d	3d	Won
Shamenda	2	F	5	0	0	0	45
Shamett	4	F	2	0	0	0	135
Shamless	3	F	7	1	2	1	8,333
Shamma	5	M	13	0	2	1	3,817
Shammy	7	G	1	0	0	0	0
Shamoiselle	2	F	9	1	3	0	52,978
Shampel	2	G	1	0	0	0	0
Shampelicus	3	F	8	1	0	1	18,700
Shampine Forbes	6	H	1	0	0	0	35
Shampoo Cape	6	M	3	0	0	0	200
Shamrock Affair	6	G	14	2	3	1	24,340
Shamrock Blues	5	M	11	2	2	3	67,110
Shamrock Cat	3	G	2	0	0	0	2,460
Shamrock Greene	2	G	7	0	0	0	612
Shamrock Isle	8	G	2	1	1	0	58,733
Shamrock n' Roll	3	F	5	1	2	0	17,365
Shamrock Peak	2	F	1	0	1	0	3,000
Shamrock Princess	3	F	8	0	0	0	393
Shamrock Secret	3	F	5	2	0	0	9,300
Shamrock Star	7	M	1	0	0	0	150
Shamrocker	3	G	5	0	0	0	406
Shamrock's Appeal	3	F	2	0	0	1	792
Shamrocks Fibber	8	G	16	1	3	2	17,765
Sham's the Man	3	G	14	0	0	3	6,274
Shamus Shea	6	G	5	0	0	5	21,700
Shamuuu	2	C	4	0	0	0	1,560
Shamyl	6	G	16	0	5	3	16,913
Shana Red	6	G	9	0	2	1	5,935
Shananie's Finale	10	G	2	0	0	0	0
Shandy	3	G	9	3	1	0	76,380
Shaneedmo'money	4	F	8	0	1	2	5,857
Shanes Light	2	G	1	0	0	1	1,360
Shane's Secret	4	F	3	0	0	0	0
Shanes Treasure	4	G	13	2	4	4	20,459
Shanghai Lady	3	F	4	1	0	1	21,932
Shanghied	2	C	3	0	0	0	1,290
Shania Moon	3	F	1	0	0	0	118
Shania's Shadow	3	F	9	2	1	1	8,247
Shaniko	2	C	2	0	1	0	11,940
Shanna's Viper	4	G	16	0	1	5	11,575
Shannochi	3	G	5	1	1	0	3,967
Shannon Arms	2	G	1	0	0	0	0
Shannon Kay	3	F	9	1	1	2	22,420
Shannon Lee	3	F	7	2	1	1	14,748
Shannon Miracle	4	C	9	0	1	1	21,296
Shannon Run	2	C	2	0	0	0	1,000
Shannon Select	6	M	8	0	1	1	6,271
Shannon Slew	4	G	11	0	2	1	4,965
Shannon the Cannon	5	G	14	0	2	0	17,554
Shannon's Ace	5	H	8	0	0	0	610
Shannon's Boy	7	H	9	1	0	1	6,843
Shannon's Delight	4	F	18	1	3	3	17,525
Shannons Secret	5	H	4	0	0	0	0
Shannons Valentine	3	F	9	2	1	3	30,870
Shanon's Sparkle	3	G	7	0	0	0	0
Shans Terror	3	G	9	0	1	1	2,997
Shante's Halo	6	M	2	0	0	0	114
Shantina	2	F	2	1	0	0	6,116
Shanty Lace	5	M	10	1	0	2	4,838
Shanty Town	3	G	2	0	0	1	1,405
Shanya	4	F	1	0	0	0	47
Shapes and Shadows	3	F	7	0	0	2	58,638
Shapiro's Hero	4	G	8	2	0	2	14,125
Sharacco's Revival	4	F	1	0	0	0	40
Sharbayan (IRE)	5	G	5	4	0	0	162,601
Sharday's Legacy	5	M	8	1	1	1	10,638
Shards of Silver	7	G	15	2	0	4	28,760
Share 'n Rainbows	3	F	16	0	3	3	10,273
Share the Court	7	G	1	0	0	0	0
Share the Magic	3	G	3	0	0	1	5,888
Share the Spirit	3	F	10	2	0	1	13,015
Shared View	5	H	7	0	0	0	985
Shareholder	3	C	3	0	1	0	6,350
Shareshten	2	F	2	0	0	0	204
Sharethetime	5	H	10	2	1	4	76,336
Shari Bank	5	M	8	0	3	0	9,244
Sharide	4	F	8	1	1	1	52,015
Shari's Gold Sole	3	F	1	0	1	0	5,600
Sharis High Cotton	3	F	12	1	1	0	10,624
Shari's Love	7	M	1	0	0	0	0
Shariya (GER)	4	F	4	2	1	0	38,600
Shark Attack	5	M	8	1	0	1	13,514
Shark Bite	2	C	4	1	0	1	16,100
Shark Eye	4	C	5	0	1	2	23,992
Shark Fin Soup	3	C	1	0	0	0	0
Sharkey's Gold	2	F	2	0	0	0	0
Sharkey's Iris	3	F	9	0	0	1	3,468
Sharkey's Treasure	2	F	1	0	0	1	2,520
Sharks and Lawyers	3	F	4	0	0	1	1,155
Sharky Bono	7	M	11	1	0	0	13,624
Sharky Brown	3	C	1	0	0	0	0
Sharky's Review	5	M	10	4	1	2	186,627
Sharne	3	F	3	0	0	0	77
Sharon Marie	9	M	5	1	0	0	1,260
Sharons Art	5	M	3	0	0	0	73
Sharon's Beau	5	H	2	0	2	0	6,400
Sharon's Gold	2	C	1	0	0	0	0
Sharon's Liberty	2	F	2	0	0	0	380
Sharon's Riches	4	F	12	2	1	1	11,591
Sharons Scoundral	3	C	2	1	0	0	4,950
Sharon's Victory	4	G	16	0	1	0	2,974
Sharp Account	2	C	1	0	0	0	0
Sharp Agenda	4	F	3	1	1	0	9,260
Sharp and Sassy	5	M	3	0	0	0	0
Sharp as a Fox	2	F	1	0	0	0	400
Sharp Boi	6	G	12	2	0	3	104,448
Sharp Chance	3	G	6	1	2	1	16,875
Sharp Command	4	G	10	1	2	0	6,730
Sharp Corner	7	M	1	0	0	0	0
Sharp Critic	6	G	5	0	2	1	10,327
Sharp Date	5	H	1	0	0	0	0
Sharp Deputy	4	G	5	0	1	0	2,285
Sharp Fling	6	G	9	0	0	2	1,762
Sharp Forty Niner	5	G	6	1	1	0	12,651
Sharp Halo	3	F	15	5	3	2	51,325
Sharp Image	2	F	1	0	0	0	0
Sharp Impact	3	C	8	2	0	2	141,768
Sharp Kelli	4	F	3	0	0	0	0
Sharp Lad	3	C	16	2	2	3	19,509
Sharp Lil Wildcard	5	M	10	3	2	0	10,259
Sharp Little Boy	4	C	11	2	0	3	43,270
Sharp Looking Dude	6	G	8	1	1	1	31,145
Sharp Looking Man	4	G	7	1	0	2	9,160
Sharp Miss	3	F	13	6	0	1	123,572
Sharp N Dazzling	5	H	7	2	0	1	6,328
Sharp Note	4	G	3	0	0	0	103
Sharp Park	4	C	4	0	0	0	190
Sharp Remark	3	G	4	0	2	0	2,925
Sharp Response	2	C	2	0	0	0	0
Sharp Roblar	3	G	1	0	0	0	0
Sharp Sailor	4	G	15	2	2	5	15,097
Sharp Shadeau	3	F	1	0	0	0	89
Sharp Smoocher	4	C	6	1	1	1	3,471
Sharp Spot	2	F	2	0	0	0	822
Sharp Star	3	C	7	0	0	1	2,630
Sharp Tax Lady	4	F	6	1	2	0	4,093
Sharp Ways	3	F	9	0	1	1	6,480
Sharpbill (GB)	3	F	6	1	1	2	75,654
Sharpen	2	F	10	1	1	2	10,150
Sharpened Copy	2	F	1	0	0	0	1,200
Sharpenupjoe	4	G	17	1	4	3	18,035
Sharper Reality	6	G	7	0	2	0	898
Sharpeshifter	2	C	4	0	0	1	2,080
Sharps 'n Flats	4	G	2	2	0	0	18,444
Sharpster	4	G	6	1	3	0	45,900
Shasta Cat	3	F	3	0	0	1	1,160
Shasta Joe	5	G	9	0	0	0	542
Shasta Lake	4	F	1	0	0	0	0
Shasta Ray	3	G	3	0	2	0	3,600
Shasta Storm	2	F	1	0	0	0	0
Shasta Willy	9	G	4	0	0	1	641
Shattered Crystal	5	M	7	3	0	0	36,486
Shattering	4	F	8	0	0	1	1,623
Shatterproof	6	M	9	1	0	0	7,959
Shattuck Street	3	G	1	0	0	0	130
Shaun Bashaun	5	M	5	0	2	0	2,698
Shauna's Song	3	F	14	1	2	4	10,534
Shauquillo	8	G	3	0	0	0	0

Horse	Age	Sex	Sts	1st	2d	3d	Won
Shaved Ice	3	F	6	1	1	2	13,040
Shawanet	2	F	1	0	0	0	0
Shawayback	3	C	6	0	0	1	789
Shawhaam	3	C	5	0	0	0	1,111
Shawkapello	4	C	3	0	0	0	1,050
Shawklit Cookie	3	F	9	1	2	1	16,350
Shawklit Liner	4	F	7	1	2	1	7,537
Shawklit Man	3	C	3	1	1	1	54,649
Shawklit Mint	4	F	11	4	1	0	232,725
Shawklit N Cream	4	G	4	0	1	0	1,265
Shawklit Premiere	2	F	4	2	1	0	10,875
Shawklit the Hawk	4	G	5	1	0	0	3,450
Shawklit's Gold	2	C	1	0	1	0	5,240
Shawklit's Pride	2	G	3	0	1	0	1,500
Shawlit's Flora	4	G	10	1	1	3	11,545
Shawnaroba	2	G	2	0	0	0	252
Shawnee Miss	3	F	12	1	2	1	14,395
Shawnee Sunrise	5	M	7	2	1	2	62,430
Shawnee Switch	4	C	4	0	2	1	4,017
Shawnee Vali	8	M	9	1	1	1	13,800
Shawniki	4	G	6	1	1	0	2,610
Shawo Mountain	7	G	8	1	1	2	4,170
Shaws Creek	4	C	1	0	1	0	32,940
Shawshank Shaun	2	G	3	0	1	0	1,835
Shawteesh	3	G	13	1	2	3	37,132
Shaxi Treasure	10	G	6	0	0	0	225
Shaye Alone	2	F	5	1	1	0	24,490
Shayna's Angel	6	M	6	0	0	0	166
Shazap	4	F	10	1	0	1	3,266
She Ain't No Saint	2	F	1	0	0	0	0
She B Cool	2	F	2	0	0	0	165
She Be Brewin	4	F	3	0	0	0	293
She Be Devil	3	F	3	1	0	0	2,760
She Be Fapiano	3	F	6	1	3	2	13,800
She Be Ready	11	M	1	0	0	0	0
She Belongs	4	F	5	1	1	0	17,820
She Canget	3	F	10	1	1	1	10,336
She Dance So So	5	M	10	2	1	1	7,389
She Did It Her Way	5	M	8	1	1	1	16,470
She Floor'd Me	2	F	2	0	0	1	600
She Go Flying	3	F	3	1	0	2	15,680
She Goes West	5	M	12	0	4	1	14,535
She Got the Edge	2	F	3	1	0	0	14,250
She Has Rhythm	3	F	14	1	0	2	6,214
She Is a Pistol	5	M	8	0	0	2	5,638
She Is a Ruler	4	F	8	0	1	0	4,125
She Is a Wild One	3	F	16	0	1	4	33,153
She Is in Orbit	6	M	4	1	1	1	2,010
She Is Raging	3	F	12	5	2	1	106,190
She Is the Secret	3	F	20	0	1	3	3,401
She Named Me Sammy	4	F	1	1	0	0	4,400
She Nuit All	4	F	6	0	2	2	42,822
She of Lawton	8	M	9	0	0	0	1,844
She Packs Apunch	2	F	2	0	0	0	0
She Rocks (IRE)	5	M	10	1	3	2	32,675
She Rules	6	M	7	0	0	0	2,070
She Runs Away	6	M	10	1	0	2	6,535
She Said Yes	3	F	7	0	1	0	1,900
She Salute	3	F	2	0	0	0	0
She Sizzles	6	M	6	2	1	0	7,386
She Surprises	3	F	2	0	0	0	132
She Wears Gold	5	M	12	1	1	4	6,726
She Went Cataway	2	F	2	0	0	0	127
She Went to Paris	3	F	3	0	0	0	0
She Who Dances	2	F	4	0	0	0	420
Shealli'vegot	5	M	4	0	0	1	1,259
Sheappealstome	3	F	11	3	1	1	21,015
Shear Attitude	2	F	4	0	0	0	1,650
Shearer	3	C	3	0	0	0	211
Shebakayskittycat	8	M	5	1	0	0	11,731
Shebang	5	M	12	1	0	1	8,990
Sheba's Secret	4	C	5	1	1	0	6,410
Shebas Stride	9	G	2	0	0	0	0
Shebatim's Morrow	3	F	2	0	0	0	237
Shecandoit	4	F	7	1	4	0	6,993
Shecanrun	3	F	7	2	1	1	51,924
Sheck	4	C	6	0	0	0	657
Shecks Account	2	C	2	0	0	0	115
Shecky Allusion	6	M	8	0	0	1	1,965
Shecky's Cowboy	5	G	5	0	1	0	1,141
Sheckys Preference	5	H	5	1	0	0	1,374
Shed Some Light	11	G	14	2	5	3	29,396
Shedancesforallen	2	F	2	0	0	0	1,200
Shedina's Jade	6	M	10	1	1	3	4,734
Shedoz Tricks	3	F	7	0	1	1	4,137
Sheen	8	G	24	0	2	2	7,467
Sheep Canyon	5	G	11	1	2	1	22,563
Sheer Enchantment	2	F	7	0	0	3	53,409
Sheer Intent	3	F	5	0	0	0	243
Sheer Luck	2	F	6	2	1	2	79,280
Sheer Numbers	2	F	3	0	0	1	2,715
Sheer Power	5	H	8	0	0	2	5,210
Sheer Sweetness	4	F	10	0	1	1	5,188
Sheer Tarra	2	F	6	0	0	1	1,645
Sheer Trouble	3	C	3	0	0	0	279
Sheersox	4	G	14	0	5	4	7,393
Sheet Lightning	5	G	12	1	2	2	6,960
Sheets Don't Lie	3	F	2	1	0	0	4,950
Sheezaccountedfor	4	F	6	0	0	0	103
Sheezforcourting	3	F	1	0	0	0	190
Shefa	6	M	4	0	0	2	641
Shegar Savage	3	C	3	1	0	0	8,400
Shegardi (GB)	8	G	9	1	0	1	7,489
Shegivesmefever	5	M	2	0	0	0	0
Shehasaeyeforyou	4	F	4	0	1	0	1,074
Shehaz Pazzaz	8	M	6	2	0	0	13,140
Shehazzit	5	M	7	0	1	0	2,757
Sheikh Albequick	6	H	4	0	1	0	1,973
Sheikh and Awe	2	F	3	1	2	0	21,860
Sheikh Dancer	4	G	10	1	1	4	6,157
Sheikh Fever	4	G	1	0	1	0	4,400
Sheikh Twenty	7	G	5	0	0	0	847
Sheikh'nnotstirred	6	M	12	4	3	3	24,128
Sheikhyabbadabbado	6	G	9	0	1	2	2,887
Sheik's Princess	3	F	7	1	1	1	14,070
Sheila	7	M	5	0	0	0	231
Sheila's Angel	3	F	2	0	0	0	480
Sheila's Catman	3	G	6	1	0	0	5,230
Sheilas Desire	3	F	5	1	1	0	15,050
Sheila's Prospect	5	M	6	0	1	1	42,344
Sheila's Wildcat	4	G	6	0	0	1	1,575
Sheisreal	6	M	7	1	1	2	19,760
Sheiswildncageytoo	2	F	1	0	0	0	1,110
Shek O Prospect	4	G	16	1	2	1	10,055
Shekotiche	6	M	9	1	2	0	14,199
Shelbar	6	G	3	1	1	0	8,870
Shelbe the One	4	F	1	0	0	0	58
Shelbi's Girl	6	M	4	0	0	0	506
Shelbi's Star	4	F	6	0	1	0	1,600
Shelby Blue	4	F	7	0	0	1	5,060
Shelby County	3	F	7	1	0	0	3,801
Shelby Lane	6	H	12	1	3	1	37,760
Shelby Madison	4	F	7	3	0	2	122,781
Shelby Slew	3	F	1	0	0	0	40
Shelbylyn	4	F	3	0	0	0	126
Shelby's Ace	5	M	3	0	0	0	103
Shelby's Angel	3	F	15	0	1	0	2,093
Shelby's Dancer	4	C	11	2	1	2	23,070
Shelby's Glory	5	M	2	0	0	0	82
Shelby's Halo	4	F	1	0	0	0	0
Shelby's Request	4	F	12	1	3	3	26,454
Shelby's Song	4	F	4	0	0	0	310
Shelbys Storm	4	G	16	4	2	2	23,740
Shelby's too Smart	3	F	12	2	2	1	18,717
Shelby's Turn	8	G	5	0	0	0	456
Sheldon's Case	3	G	13	0	0	0	2,703
Sheldon's Devil	3	F	11	2	1	1	20,777
Sheldon's Mountain	3	C	3	0	0	0	1,420
Sheldon's Success	3	G	13	1	1	0	11,162
Sheldrake	3	C	3	0	0	0	1,000
Shell Bell	5	M	3	0	0	0	240
She'll Sho Go	4	F	6	0	1	0	2,806
Shell Shock	5	G	10	0	0	1	1,414
Shellby Duxster	4	F	1	0	0	0	0
Shellimo	3	F	2	0	0	0	140
Shelly	2	C	2	0	0	0	0
Shelly Ha Ha	4	F	5	0	1	0	1,590
Shelly's Lady Jane	3	F	6	0	1	1	1,700

RECORDS OF HORSES

Horse	Age	Sex	Sts	1st	2d	3d	Won	Horse	Age	Sex	Sts	1st	2d	3d	Won
Shelly's Pride	3	F	7	3	1	1	22,330	She's a Mugs	2	F	1	0	0	0	66
Shellys Terms	3	F	9	2	1	0	41,720	She's a Native	4	F	2	0	1	0	891
Shelovesmeatballs	3	F	7	0	0	1	2,186	She's a Nice Color	4	F	8	1	1	2	6,264
Shelter Cove	8	H	3	0	1	1	13,040	She's a Olympian	2	F	2	1	0	0	12,000
Shelter Me Earl	5	M	12	2	3	1	14,701	She's a Punter	3	F	7	1	2	0	7,961
Shelter Rain	5	G	8	0	2	0	11,310	She's a Rebel Too	2	F	2	1	0	1	17,000
Shelter's No Fool	5	H	8	1	1	1	15,549	She's a Rich Girl	3	F	2	0	0	0	0
Shemakesmesmile	2	F	1	0	0	0	65	She's a Saint	4	F	3	0	2	0	9,040
Shemaydance	3	F	13	1	0	1	3,600	She's a Surprise	9	M	10	0	1	0	2,542
Shemoveslikeaghost	3	F	6	3	2	0	224,510	She's a Sweet Deal	4	F	3	0	0	0	2,100
Shenandoah King	2	C	5	0	0	0	442	Shes a Sweet Mertz	3	F	1	0	0	1	1,364
Shenandoah Rain	4	F	3	0	0	1	3,699	She's a Sweetheart	3	F	6	1	1	0	33,200
Shenandoah Smile	5	M	13	3	3	2	45,740	She's a Toy	3	F	4	0	0	0	209
Shenanigan Cat	2	F	1	0	0	0	330	She's a Tycoon Too	3	F	5	0	0	0	450
Shenogood	4	F	3	0	0	0	198	She's a Wild Deer	4	F	3	0	0	0	265
Shenuit	5	M	3	1	1	0	3,600	She's Actin Single	5	M	4	0	0	0	544
Shep	3	C	4	0	0	0	0	She's All American	3	F	2	0	0	0	100
Shepherd's Star	3	F	11	0	2	1	45,394	She's All Fired Up	3	F	12	2	3	4	33,210
Sheppard's Watch (GB)	5	M	6	1	1	0	72,463	She's an Angel	5	M	5	1	0	0	6,900
Sher Choice	4	F	6	2	0	0	2,904	She's Booked	2	F	7	0	1	1	11,320
Sher Class	5	G	6	1	1	1	5,712	She's Classy Two	3	F	6	1	1	0	6,200
Sher Crafty	5	G	14	5	3	0	43,245	She's Cooking Now	3	F	20	3	4	2	48,550
Sher Light	3	F	5	0	0	0	0	She's Cosmic	3	F	3	0	0	0	154
Sher Linka	3	F	1	0	0	0	204	Shes Dixies Eskimo	2	F	2	0	0	2	5,962
Sher Long	2	C	3	0	0	1	950	She's Enough	2	F	1	0	0	0	1,050
Sher Ridge	3	G	10	0	1	0	1,507	She's Exposed	2	F	2	0	0	0	144
Sher Time	2	C	3	1	1	0	2,812	She's Fantastic	3	F	10	2	3	0	96,857
Sher Veil	2	G	3	1	0	1	6,288	She's Finding Time	4	F	9	5	1	2	60,046
Shera	4	F	3	0	0	0	147	She's Flying High	3	F	2	0	0	0	145
Sherando's Star	4	G	14	1	2	1	10,920	She's Going Gray	3	F	2	0	0	0	105
Shergot Attitude	3	G	3	0	0	0	762	She's Got a Way	3	F	12	1	1	1	20,799
Sheridan Lake	4	G	7	1	0	2	20,850	She's Got Issues	3	F	9	2	1	2	11,531
Sheridan's Secret	4	F	10	0	2	3	7,525	She's Got It	4	F	13	0	2	1	6,216
Sheriff Dillon	2	C	1	0	0	0	0	She's Got Rhythm	4	F	5	1	0	0	6,353
Sheriff Reprice	6	G	13	1	2	1	15,540	She's Got the Beat	4	F	12	4	5	1	294,556
Sheriff Sale	4	C	1	0	0	0	0	She's Gottogetaway	2	F	4	2	0	1	99,066
Sheriff Sid Again	4	G	2	0	0	0	0	She's Home Alone	5	M	7	1	2	1	3,436
Sheriff's Posse	3	F	9	2	0	1	40,221	She's in Control	3	F	2	0	0	0	321
Sheringham Lady	5	M	15	0	2	2	15,831	Shes in Front	2	F	2	0	0	0	187
Sherippedherpants	2	F	6	0	0	0	2,370	She's Insane	2	F	4	1	0	2	6,375
Sherizod	3	F	12	2	1	1	11,704	Shes Kiddin Around	3	F	3	1	1	0	13,880
Sherman Road	3	F	1	0	0	0	560	She's Mine Forever	4	F	8	0	0	0	7,010
Sherpa Guide	5	G	5	0	0	2	30,821	Shes Mischief	3	F	7	0	0	0	2,220
Sherri Lisa	4	F	5	1	1	1	5,430	She's Misty	3	F	5	0	0	0	1,020
Sherri's Dream	3	F	14	0	1	0	2,265	She's Movin On	2	F	7	1	1	0	23,880
Sherroyal	5	G	3	0	1	0	780	Shes My Angel	8	M	1	0	0	0	120
Sherry Ann's Doc	5	G	1	0	0	0	35	She's My Bull	2	F	1	1	0	0	4,320
Sherry N Ice	4	F	6	0	0	0	180	She's My Darling	5	M	6	0	1	3	7,890
Sherry Spinner (GB)	5	M	1	1	0	0	13,200	She's My Girl	3	F	3	0	0	0	119
Sherrysredsilkslip	3	F	16	1	3	0	6,706	She's My Idol	3	F	2	0	0	0	34,200
Sherwood Forest	3	F	8	2	1	2	54,290	She's Nifty	3	F	7	3	1	2	15,160
Sherwood Oak	6	G	10	3	1	0	5,355	She's No Bo	4	F	19	5	2	3	33,520
Sheryar Special	5	H	7	2	1	1	73,100	She's No Copy	2	F	4	0	0	1	5,486
Sheryl Kay	3	F	5	0	0	1	3,640	She's No Sham	3	F	13	0	2	1	20,693
She's a Biscuit	4	F	7	0	3	1	6,570	She's Not a Bull	4	F	3	0	0	0	40
Shes a Bit Shady	2	F	4	0	0	1	1,800	Shes Not Idol	4	F	7	1	0	1	9,390
She's a Bombshell	2	F	3	1	0	1	69,548	She's Oakie Dokie	3	F	4	0	0	0	315
She's a Candice	6	M	21	3	2	1	31,574	She's On Her Toes	4	F	11	1	0	4	9,542
Shes a Catty Kitty	2	F	1	0	0	0	240	She's Our Cutie	3	F	2	0	0	0	285
She's a Charge	5	M	4	0	0	0	390	She's Our Demon	3	F	6	1	1	1	17,025
She's a Charm	3	F	4	1	1	0	7,750	She's Our Favorite	2	F	4	1	1	0	10,385
She's a Classic	4	F	8	1	1	3	8,225	Shes Out West	3	F	10	1	0	0	3,287
She's a Cool Cat	3	F	6	0	1	1	2,724	Shes Outa Bull	2	F	7	3	1	1	24,335
She's a Crook	3	F	15	1	0	1	5,235	She's Rapid	4	F	7	0	2	0	3,665
She's a Dandy	3	F	1	0	0	0	35	Shes Ready Buster	4	F	3	1	0	0	6,600
She's a Deputy	3	F	9	2	1	1	13,443	She's Really Cool	3	F	5	0	1	0	5,900
She's a Deputy Too	2	F	7	1	1	1	33,690	She's Risky	5	M	16	1	2	3	6,254
Shes a Disco Joyce	3	F	1	0	0	0	0	She's Rosalie Jane	3	F	11	2	2	1	64,650
She's a Dixieland	3	F	7	0	0	1	349	She's Royal Too	2	F	4	0	0	0	420
She's a Eight	3	F	5	0	0	0	0	She's Scrumpy	3	F	8	3	2	0	91,015
She's a Flashdance	3	F	2	1	0	0	8,400	She's Shameless	6	M	8	0	1	5	6,670
Shes a Freebie	4	F	9	3	1	1	20,387	She's So Cute	3	F	3	3	0	0	13,860
She's a Goer	4	F	14	4	1	2	17,043	She's So Mean	4	F	19	0	1	1	14,893
She's a Keeper Too	3	F	1	0	0	0	0	She's So Pretty	3	F	2	0	0	0	378
She's a Lady	3	F	1	0	0	0	0	She's So Rebel	2	F	1	0	0	0	786
She's a Marlin	3	F	1	0	0	0	100	She's So Witty	3	F	17	2	2	2	18,565
Shes a Matchlite	3	F	11	1	0	2	8,767	She's Some Fox	4	F	13	0	1	3	12,845
She's a Mayday	2	F	1	0	0	0	75	Shes Sopersonal	3	F	4	0	0	0	1,230
Shes a Melody	6	M	11	3	0	1	24,373	She's Sophia	6	M	16	0	0	0	2,765

Horse	Age	Sex	Sts	1st	2d	3d	Won
She's Sterling	2	F	1	0	0	0	0
Shes Stone Country	3	F	2	0	0	0	190
She's Striking	3	F	6	0	0	0	0
She's Suspicious	3	F	1	0	0	0	0
She's Taboo	5	M	7	0	1	2	10,728
She's Taken	3	F	8	1	0	0	5,247
She's the Answer	3	F	16	2	3	4	19,795
She's the Fashion	3	F	9	1	0	1	12,540
She's the Future	4	F	11	2	1	1	28,765
She's the General	2	F	3	0	1	0	11,798
She's the Ticket	3	F	15	2	0	6	22,851
She's too Much	3	F	2	0	0	0	450
Shes Toxic	5	M	4	0	0	0	70
She's Valid	3	F	12	1	3	1	14,510
She's Vested	4	F	11	1	3	0	51,699
Shes Wicked Wicked	6	M	3	0	0	0	343
She's Zealous	3	F	7	3	1	0	98,640
Shesa Axe Too	3	F	6	2	1	0	17,370
Shesa Nasty Girl	3	F	14	0	2	1	5,445
Shesa Spellbinder	3	F	11	3	1	0	10,216
Shesa Strodes Lady	3	F	10	0	1	1	3,890
Shes'a Whip	3	F	9	1	0	1	3,826
Shesabrick	4	F	7	0	0	0	605
Shesabrickhouse	3	F	3	1	0	1	7,020
Shesabullybabe	2	F	1	0	0	0	0
Shesafoxybay	3	F	6	0	0	0	975
Shesagamer	7	M	3	0	0	0	570
Shesagoldmine	3	F	7	1	2	1	12,802
She'saholyterror	3	F	1	0	0	0	0
Shesaidshe'scute	3	F	3	0	0	0	82
She'salark Two	4	F	1	0	0	0	0
Shesamoneyburner	2	F	1	0	0	0	0
Shesanactress	4	F	2	0	0	1	440
Shesanaturalactor	5	M	6	0	0	0	605
Shesanoactor	6	M	4	2	1	0	9,198
Shesanothergrump	4	F	9	2	3	1	81,949
Shesapartnerncrime	3	F	5	0	0	1	2,935
Shesarider	5	M	14	0	2	2	11,315
Shesasassiedancer	3	F	6	0	1	0	3,960
Shesasauceyturk	3	F	3	0	0	0	540
Shesasmokin	3	F	3	0	0	0	2,580
Shesasoprano	3	F	5	0	0	0	1,394
Shesaspaspecial	6	M	8	0	0	0	517
She'sasteadycat	3	F	5	0	0	0	490
Shesasureshot	3	F	2	0	0	0	320
Shesatotalwreck	4	F	4	0	0	0	213
Shesatreasure	5	M	12	0	1	0	7,190
She'saxaviermuskie	2	F	5	0	1	1	3,537
She'sbubba'sdelite	2	F	4	1	1	0	24,200
Shescape	5	M	10	1	0	0	3,757
Shescominundone	4	F	2	0	1	1	2,800
Shescute Asa Buton	4	F	11	2	0	0	16,959
Shesfastbutnoteasy	3	F	2	0	0	1	2,335
Shesfastnfurious	2	F	3	0	0	0	895
Shesfoxy	3	F	5	1	2	0	8,130
She'sfullofhope	4	F	16	1	1	3	14,230
Shesgonnabeastar	2	F	3	1	1	0	14,131
She'sgotgoldfever	2	F	2	0	0	1	5,280
Sheshe Bold	3	F	9	1	0	1	6,934
Sheshe Moran	4	F	7	1	1	2	21,030
Sheshe's Hawk	5	M	14	1	3	0	8,572
Sheshotthesheriff	3	F	4	0	0	1	1,684
Sheso	2	F	3	2	0	1	18,480
Shesomethinspecial	4	F	14	1	3	5	15,378
She'sonthemove	3	F	4	0	0	0	504
Shesprecocious	2	F	3	0	1	1	6,660
She'stohottohandle	2	F	2	0	1	0	4,100
Shewin	5	M	16	3	1	1	24,715
Shez a Dreamqueen	4	F	14	2	2	2	17,296
Shez a Falcon	2	F	4	0	0	0	300
Shez R Code	4	F	3	0	1	0	1,658
Shez Undeniable	2	F	4	0	0	1	2,079
Sheza a Nine Plus	5	M	3	0	0	0	867
Sheza Awesomecat	2	F	1	0	0	0	0
Sheza Barn Burner	4	F	13	1	5	0	46,863
Sheza Dream Chaser	5	M	6	0	3	1	19,997
Sheza Fast Machine	5	M	1	0	0	0	49
Sheza Fling	3	F	9	1	1	1	4,183
Sheza Gladiator	4	F	9	2	2	1	16,384
Sheza Kelly	4	F	14	3	0	5	13,263
Sheza Lee Gal	2	F	1	0	0	0	0
Sheza Love Bird	3	F	8	1	0	0	17,295
Sheza Lucky Son'so	3	F	7	1	1	1	13,840
Sheza Nasty Lady	4	F	3	0	0	0	1,680
Sheza Naughty Girl	3	F	5	0	0	0	73
Sheza Niner	5	M	1	0	1	0	2,000
Sheza Pretty Gal	3	F	8	1	2	2	21,822
Sheza Princess	4	F	4	0	0	1	1,730
Sheza Royal Dandy	4	F	9	0	3	3	2,683
Sheza Scamper	3	F	2	1	0	0	4,167
Sheza Sharkey	2	F	3	0	1	0	5,200
Sheza Slick Chick	4	F	1	0	0	0	262
Sheza Tomboy	4	F	9	0	2	2	3,548
Sheza Whiz	8	M	11	1	2	3	24,246
Sheza Wild Child	4	F	7	0	1	0	870
Sheza Wolf	7	M	2	0	0	0	110
Shezadiamond	7	M	15	2	1	4	13,655
Shezagatorgettor	8	M	17	0	1	3	3,147
Shezarealpeach	5	M	15	5	1	3	26,200
Shezaroner	3	F	5	1	1	3	19,010
Shezaseaheroine	3	F	2	0	0	1	2,520
Shezasummerbreeze	4	F	2	1	0	0	28,800
Shezsofoxy	4	F	7	0	0	1	10,810
Shezsospiritual	3	F	13	3	3	3	102,668
Shhh Please	2	G	6	1	0	1	31,140
Shi Kai	2	F	2	0	0	0	93
Shi Shi Doll	2	F	1	0	0	0	420
Shibui	4	F	2	0	0	0	1,680
Shidoobee	2	G	1	1	0	0	5,400
Shiek'n Shake It	4	G	2	0	0	0	120
Shiesh Kabeeb	3	C	1	0	0	0	120
Shift Key	4	G	13	1	4	0	13,565
Shift Leader	6	H	1	0	0	0	40
Shift Quick	7	G	2	0	0	0	168
Shift Right	5	H	14	0	3	2	16,288
Shift Shape	8	M	7	3	1	2	18,062
Shifter B	3	G	5	0	0	0	360
Shifti Terms	3	G	3	1	0	0	4,505
Shifting Sea	3	F	7	1	0	0	14,992
Shifting Storm	3	F	9	1	2	1	12,692
Shifting Trends	4	G	10	1	0	3	10,475
Shifty	4	F	10	1	0	2	10,740
Shifty Dae	2	C	9	1	1	1	16,520
Shifty Gear	4	C	17	1	1	2	12,360
Shifty Slew	7	G	2	0	0	0	50
Shifty's Delight	4	C	1	0	0	0	50
Shifty's Favorite	4	G	3	1	0	1	5,162
Shikari	2	F	3	0	0	0	750
Shilew	6	M	12	3	1	3	14,559
Shillelagh	3	F	1	0	0	0	123
Shiloh Billy	5	G	14	5	1	0	32,675
Shiloh Bound	2	G	2	2	0	0	31,640
Shiloh Dawn	3	F	7	1	1	2	12,250
Shiloh Gold	2	C	1	0	0	1	2,700
Shiloh Lane	5	M	6	1	0	0	13,845
Shilow	4	G	1	0	0	0	0
Shilukwa	4	C	16	4	3	4	27,405
Shimino Git	3	C	8	1	1	1	11,160
Shimmer Shimmer	10	G	1	0	0	1	2,000
Shimmering Bronze	8	G	3	0	0	0	960
Shimmering Brook	3	F	6	1	1	2	16,830
Shimmering Condido	4	G	15	4	4	3	18,759
Shimmering Sand	6	M	15	2	1	4	35,701
Shimmering Sea	4	F	9	0	2	1	7,480
Shimmon	3	C	7	0	2	0	5,740
Shimmy Doll	4	F	15	2	3	3	35,750
Shimmy Shake	2	F	4	1	1	0	19,240
Shimmy's Prospect	5	M	1	0	1	0	4,000
Shimokin	9	G	3	0	0	0	163
Shimshai	5	H	8	0	1	0	1,688
Shin Kan Sen	3	G	8	0	0	0	541
Shindigit	3	G	4	0	0	1	2,040
Shine	6	H	14	1	1	3	6,620
Shine Again	6	M	7	2	5	0	275,620
Shine Along	3	F	5	1	1	0	7,055
Shine Baby Shine	5	M	1	0	0	0	0
Shine For	4	F	11	1	1	2	6,604
Shine for a Reason	3	F	6	1	0	0	6,000

Horse	Age	Sex	Sts	1st	2d	3d	Won
Shine Forth	4	F	3	0	1	0	10,300
Shine Your Shoes	7	M	7	0	1	0	4,686
Shinegold	4	G	11	0	2	1	9,390
Shineing Arrow	3	F	4	0	0	0	1,918
Shineup the Silver	4	F	10	1	2	2	2,674
Shiney Jet	7	M	3	0	0	1	550
Shiney Souvenir	3	G	6	1	0	0	5,185
Shingen Deputy	4	C	2	0	0	0	216
Shingen Knight	9	G	11	0	2	1	5,055
Shingen Storm	6	H	6	1	0	0	12,936
Shingen Thunder	4	G	10	1	1	1	7,568
Shingen Victor	3	G	2	0	0	0	0
Shinijinsky	3	F	2	0	0	0	154
Shining Angel	2	F	7	1	0	0	14,101
Shining Bandit	2	G	2	1	0	0	2,880
Shining Beacon	3	F	5	0	2	1	14,000
Shining Blade	4	C	2	0	0	0	300
Shining Britely	5	M	15	6	6	0	112,886
Shining Career	4	G	12	1	2	2	34,080
Shining Forever	4	F	16	0	0	2	3,340
Shining Gem	5	M	7	1	1	1	20,550
Shining Glory	6	G	13	0	0	0	962
Shining Hawk	2	C	4	1	1	0	35,960
Shining Honor	3	F	9	1	2	1	12,269
Shining Jewel	3	F	7	3	0	0	82,230
Shining Marjorie	3	F	1	0	0	0	0
Shining Nuggets	5	G	14	2	3	0	20,733
Shining Rock	3	G	6	2	1	1	34,320
Shining Slippers	3	F	10	1	0	1	6,115
Shining Storm	7	G	8	0	0	2	1,953
Shining Strike	4	F	6	2	0	1	61,140
Shining Tap	3	F	3	0	1	0	2,100
Shining Tower	2	F	5	1	0	2	16,520
Shining Town	3	F	13	0	2	2	9,390
Shining Victory	2	F	1	0	0	0	0
Shiningofthesun	2	C	4	0	1	1	8,750
Shinoak	3	G	1	0	0	0	500
Shiny	5	M	1	0	0	0	226
Shiny Gray Comet	2	F	1	0	0	0	472
Shiny Meadow	3	C	18	5	2	4	78,027
Shiny Prize	3	F	3	1	1	0	11,520
Shiny Sheet	5	M	10	3	2	3	229,870
Shinystone	4	F	8	0	1	3	9,615
Ship Ahoy	4	G	4	2	1	0	15,016
Ship Ahoy Mate	6	H	3	1	0	1	3,490
Ship Alert	3	C	9	2	1	3	35,160
Ship of the Line	4	C	5	2	0	0	27,798
Ship Shape	5	H	15	3	3	0	35,487
Shipman	3	C	9	1	1	4	104,635
Shipping Dixie	4	F	9	2	0	0	11,521
Ship's Captain	2	C	4	0	0	0	125
Ship's Silver	6	G	7	2	1	2	12,015
Shirano	10	M	12	0	0	1	1,485
Shirazberry	4	F	15	2	1	2	26,587
Shire	3	C	7	1	2	1	29,340
Shirley Belle	3	F	5	0	0	0	348
Shirley D Feather	4	F	9	1	0	1	3,858
Shirley McLeggs	4	F	8	1	0	0	3,330
Shirley Patch	2	F	8	1	1	3	9,535
Shirley Valentine	11	M	12	0	0	0	1,737
Shirleygee	5	M	3	2	0	0	10,560
Shirleygettheloot	5	M	15	3	4	2	47,340
Shirley's Call	7	G	14	3	1	2	37,407
Shirley's Star	3	G	6	0	1	0	1,050
Shirley's Sweep	4	F	1	0	0	0	0
Shirttail	3	G	3	1	1	0	7,005
Shishkbob Hay	3	F	15	2	0	1	20,910
Shivermetimber	7	G	11	2	1	0	31,032
Shluke	3	C	12	2	0	3	15,186
Sho Me the Diamond	5	M	6	1	0	1	4,427
Shoal Water	3	G	7	2	1	2	325,690
Shoalihs Tale	3	C	15	1	4	2	76,630
Shock and All	2	F	2	0	0	0	120
Shock Treatment	2	G	1	0	0	0	0
Shocker's Beauty	4	F	12	0	0	2	5,193
Shocking Dancer	3	G	6	0	2	1	6,216
Shocking Maggie	3	F	3	0	0	0	71
Shocking Number	4	F	6	1	1	4	7,670
Shocking Speed	3	G	6	2	1	1	32,972
Shockittoem	4	C	15	0	1	0	5,980
Shocktics	3	F	11	2	2	2	43,640
Shoe n' Sandy	2	F	6	0	0	0	0
Shoe Queen	5	M	12	1	4	2	13,207
Shoeco City	3	G	14	3	2	1	31,751
Shoes n' Nails	4	F	5	0	0	0	254
Shoestring Bay	4	C	4	0	0	0	294
Shomrim's Guard	10	G	20	1	2	5	11,289
Shondel	3	F	7	0	0	2	1,720
Shonetonian	2	F	1	0	0	0	0
Shoo Brush	3	C	8	0	1	2	13,580
Shoo Fly Willie	7	G	14	5	2	2	36,914
Shoo Shoo Baby	4	F	3	1	0	1	1,020
Shoo Storm	4	C	6	0	0	1	848
Shoobie	5	G	8	1	0	0	4,824
Shooster	7	G	4	0	0	0	375
Shoot Dem Bees	5	H	5	0	1	0	2,494
Shoot for the Loot	4	F	12	3	0	1	23,691
Shoot From the Hip	3	C	1	0	0	1	2,390
Shoot It	4	G	13	7	2	1	54,290
Shoot the Loot	4	G	2	1	0	0	1,988
Shoot the Wad	3	F	9	1	0	0	9,491
Shoot Yeah	2	C	2	0	0	0	0
Shootandcharge	2	F	1	1	0	0	15,600
Shootin for Gold	3	F	8	2	1	2	18,714
Shooting First	5	G	6	1	1	0	5,850
Shooting Party	5	M	1	0	0	0	0
Shooting Range	3	F	4	0	0	0	0
Shooting Star	3	C	3	1	0	0	12,115
Shoot'nloot	2	G	2	1	1	0	10,080
Shootski	4	G	12	1	1	2	25,596
Shop Hill	3	C	6	0	3	1	39,837
Shop the Block	3	F	3	0	0	0	190
Shop Till You Drop	4	F	7	0	2	1	30,296
Shopper	3	G	4	0	0	0	1,080
Shoppers Shuttle	4	F	5	2	0	2	12,060
Shopping Around	4	F	5	1	1	1	6,030
Shopping Mary	3	F	2	0	0	0	2,640
Shoptaw	9	G	5	0	0	0	390
Shoptoyoudrop	7	M	4	0	0	0	323
Shore Breaker	3	G	14	2	3	3	42,185
Shore Breeze	5	H	6	0	1	1	9,720
Shore Girl	3	F	1	0	0	0	0
Shore Lover	4	F	15	0	5	5	26,010
Shore Weave	3	F	10	2	1	0	8,433
Shoreman	6	G	3	1	0	0	21,534
Shorewalk Drive	2	F	4	1	0	0	17,055
Shorhouse	2	F	1	1	0	0	24,600
Short a Boot	2	F	2	0	0	0	190
Short Fat Fanny	2	F	4	1	0	0	11,860
Short Fuse	5	G	13	1	1	0	18,985
Short Hair	4	C	6	1	1	0	44,240
Short Leach	3	F	3	1	1	0	8,085
Short Luck	4	C	5	0	2	0	3,132
Short Nite	5	H	4	0	0	0	310
Short Note	4	F	4	1	0	0	31,230
Short Notice	4	G	3	2	0	0	3,200
Short Odds	7	G	10	2	0	2	20,709
Short On Change	3	F	3	0	0	0	602
Short Putt	2	F	1	0	1	0	3,800
Short Shadow	3	F	12	0	3	2	48,753
Short Spark Louie	5	G	7	1	0	0	3,480
Short Squeeze	4	G	14	1	4	0	77,950
Short Stick	4	G	1	0	0	0	0
Short Term	3	G	6	0	0	0	1,098
Short to First	2	G	3	0	1	0	4,158
Short Trip Home	2	F	1	0	0	0	0
Short War	7	G	10	2	3	0	16,567
Short Wrappers	4	G	6	1	2	1	7,130
Shortbranch	2	F	1	0	0	1	1,166
Shortbrush	3	C	12	1	0	1	10,301
Shortstop Sal	3	F	3	0	0	2	8,665
Shorty Balero	5	G	20	1	2	2	7,062
Shortys Brightstar	3	G	15	0	1	2	8,909
Shorty's Dream	6	G	9	3	1	1	19,908
Shot Blocker	6	M	3	0	0	0	720
Shot for Shot	5	G	8	1	0	2	16,158
Shot From the Sky	4	C	10	3	0	0	27,213
Shot Gun Carolyn	4	F	10	2	2	1	37,840

Horse	Age	Sex	Sts	1st	2d	3d	Won
Shot Gun Catty	2	F	1	0	0	0	300
Shot Gun Favorite	3	F	9	4	0	2	160,230
Shot Gun Norman	3	G	8	0	2	0	4,450
Shot Gun Terry	2	C	7	1	1	0	10,770
Shot Gun Treasure	4	G	11	2	2	1	8,158
Shot Gun Uss Hoga	3	F	8	1	0	1	21,896
Shot Maker	4	G	4	1	0	0	4,529
Shot of Gin	3	C	8	0	0	2	4,419
Shot of Light	2	F	1	0	0	0	0
Shot On the Rocks	3	C	4	0	0	2	884
Shot Sea	2	F	1	0	0	0	126
Shot Silk	3	C	6	0	0	3	2,620
Shotafirewater	6	G	16	2	3	1	6,165
Shotgun	4	G	16	1	1	2	7,673
Shotgun Fire	5	H	8	1	2	2	55,442
Shotgun Gus	3	G	5	1	0	1	4,014
Shotgun Kato	6	G	1	0	0	0	0
Shotgun Man	8	G	12	2	3	0	23,100
Shotgun Proposal	3	G	7	1	0	1	6,735
Shotgun Star	2	G	3	1	0	0	9,439
Shotgunannie	3	F	9	1	2	1	8,175
Shotiche'star B B	5	G	2	0	0	0	0
Shotmo	6	H	13	3	2	2	6,292
Shots	2	C	4	0	2	1	23,850
Shots Dot	4	F	8	0	0	1	2,200
Shotsfired	6	G	23	2	2	0	4,594
Shoulda Been Me	2	G	5	1	0	0	17,940
Shouldabeenjoebob	2	F	1	0	0	0	100
Shouldbegold	7	G	4	0	0	0	660
Shouldbevictory	2	C	8	2	1	1	31,950
Shouldn't We All	5	M	7	0	0	1	5,180
Shout	2	F	9	1	2	1	36,180
Shout to the Lord	3	C	2	0	0	0	180
Shove Ha'penny (IRE)	4	C	4	0	1	0	3,200
Show Biz	5	M	4	0	0	1	2,000
Show Bug	3	F	6	2	1	1	69,055
Show Director	3	G	1	0	0	0	0
Show Hero	2	F	3	0	1	0	6,600
Show Killer	3	G	5	0	1	1	2,875
Show Me Gone	3	G	1	0	0	1	1,595
Show Me Mercy	4	F	3	0	0	0	256
Show Me Tazz	6	G	7	2	1	1	13,928
Show Me the Fox	6	M	3	0	0	0	165
Show Me the Glory	4	G	17	1	7	3	20,340
Show Me the Light	2	F	1	1	0	0	6,000
Show Me the Monte	7	G	7	2	0	0	7,960
Show Me the Moolah	6	G	11	2	1	2	50,680
Show Me the Stash	3	C	3	0	0	1	1,950
Show Me Your World	6	H	6	0	0	0	3,141
Show of Force	3	G	14	1	4	3	34,320
Show Pleasure	6	M	1	0	0	0	0
Show Ready	2	F	1	0	0	0	137
Show the Judge	3	G	10	0	0	2	6,619
Show Us the Check	2	F	8	0	1	1	6,765
Show Your Temper	7	G	13	0	0	0	2,727
Showboat Willy	2	G	2	0	1	0	5,200
Showcased	4	G	8	1	0	0	4,407
Showdown	3	C	8	2	1	1	63,935
Shower Lady	3	F	2	0	0	0	90
Shower Scene	3	F	9	1	3	1	36,310
Showhof	5	G	16	2	2	4	14,890
Showing the Flag	2	G	3	0	0	0	190
Showmeitall	4	G	7	1	3	0	38,595
Showmesomelove	2	F	3	0	1	0	13,680
Showmethebook	3	G	4	0	0	1	3,420
Showmetothevilla	3	F	9	2	1	1	31,660
Showmewhatyougot	2	C	1	0	0	0	770
Showmeyourtwist	4	C	8	0	1	0	9,063
Showpiece	3	F	13	2	3	2	56,140
Showtime	4	G	16	3	3	2	31,952
Showtime Dancer	2	F	1	0	0	0	150
Showtime Express	4	F	2	0	0	0	0
Showtime Girl	4	F	19	1	1	6	12,960
Showyourclass	5	G	8	1	0	1	4,698
Shoxy	2	G	4	1	0	0	4,140
Shred the Excess	5	M	12	2	3	1	46,920
Shrewd Deputy	2	C	2	0	0	0	2,978
Shrewd Money	5	M	14	3	2	4	13,617
Shrewd Stipulation	3	C	1	0	1	0	10,000

Horse	Age	Sex	Sts	1st	2d	3d	Won
Shrike One	2	G	2	0	0	0	1,050
Shril Bay	2	F	1	0	0	0	0
Shrill	6	G	2	0	0	0	550
Shrimp Cocktail	3	G	2	0	0	0	1,260
Shrimp Tempura	4	F	20	0	2	5	36,785
Shrimpee	2	F	4	0	0	2	4,670
Shu Fly Fly	5	M	1	0	0	0	0
Shuailaan Jennings	6	G	11	0	2	0	11,600
Shubby	9	M	5	0	0	0	646
Shudaben Franca	3	F	5	0	0	0	1,530
Shudabinajumper	5	M	11	3	3	3	49,178
Shudahbenastar	4	F	2	0	0	0	201
Shudahben'sbuoy	6	G	3	0	0	0	605
Shudasold	5	G	13	3	2	3	16,519
Shuffle Board	3	G	9	2	2	0	40,540
Shuffle Game	3	G	6	0	1	0	6,410
Shuffle N Deal	3	F	13	2	2	2	13,970
Shuffle Shot	6	H	6	0	0	0	186
Shuffle Up Front	6	H	5	1	0	0	4,810
Shuga Shaq	6	G	19	1	0	1	3,797
Shuga's Real Rush	5	M	5	0	2	0	6,445
Shujune	3	F	4	0	0	0	450
Shulana	3	F	3	0	0	1	704
Shulas Legend	6	G	5	0	0	1	718
Shultz	3	G	5	0	2	1	2,599
Shuperman	5	G	11	0	1	0	4,291
Shuperman Two	2	G	2	0	0	0	0
Shur Town	4	F	2	0	0	0	0
Shure	5	H	8	2	3	1	28,742
Shureamsweet	3	F	12	1	0	2	7,183
Shush Shush	9	M	4	0	0	0	780
Shut Out Time	7	G	17	7	3	2	79,335
Shut Up	4	G	12	3	2	0	24,400
Shutter Speed	6	G	10	1	0	1	7,522
Shuttle Lane	4	F	2	0	0	0	186
Shuttle Sam	5	G	15	2	1	4	15,972
Shuttlin	3	G	6	0	0	0	1,660
Shutupndeal	5	H	5	0	0	1	860
Shuya	2	C	2	0	0	0	0
Shwaling Along	4	F	1	0	0	0	430
Shwoodifshecould	5	M	15	2	4	3	19,200
Shy Alexandra	3	F	6	0	0	2	5,710
Shy Boots	11	G	4	0	0	1	450
Shy Dory (ARG)	6	M	8	0	0	4	21,348
Shy Lady	3	F	2	0	0	0	4,200
Shy Lil	2	F	4	0	0	1	4,620
Shy Patada (ARG)	6	M	12	1	5	1	65,360
Shy Phylly	3	F	20	2	0	5	10,296
Shy Rutilante (ARG)	5	M	4	0	0	1	5,690
Shybynature	7	G	8	0	0	0	5,790
Shyla's Diamond	9	M	2	0	0	0	788
Shypatriot	6	M	14	2	3	2	15,247
Shyrlents Dream	6	M	10	0	2	2	5,235
Si' Bon	5	M	9	1	3	1	6,956
Si Lo Tengo	3	F	7	0	1	0	2,100
Si Madre	9	G	2	0	0	0	0
Si' Si' Miranda	2	F	2	0	0	0	164
Si Si My Love	3	F	1	0	0	0	101
Si Tigre Lil	7	M	16	0	0	2	7,475
Si Ya Contenta	4	F	6	1	1	0	9,708
Siber Runner	3	F	4	0	0	1	2,643
Sibercrasher	7	H	14	1	6	4	30,695
Siberian Eagle	4	G	6	0	0	0	520
Siberian Falstaff	3	F	3	2	1	0	8,640
Siberian Fantasy	3	F	7	0	2	1	2,860
Siberian Flash	2	C	1	0	0	0	0
Siberian General	2	G	2	0	0	0	200
Siberian Katy	3	F	2	0	0	0	3,300
Siberian Knight	3	C	10	1	2	1	5,899
Siberian Paradox	4	F	11	3	2	3	16,315
Siberian Ridge	3	F	3	0	0	0	225
Siberian Seduction	3	G	11	1	0	0	14,195
Siberian Select	3	G	7	2	0	0	16,888
Siberian Shamrock	2	F	3	1	1	0	35,620
Siberian Snow	4	F	8	3	1	1	11,516
Siberian Style	4	G	8	0	2	1	13,765
Siberian Warrior	6	G	11	1	0	1	3,033
Siberian Wind	2	G	3	0	1	1	3,700
Siberianette	4	F	2	0	0	0	288

Horse	Age	Sex	Sts	1st	2d	3d	Won
Siberiano	6	G	11	1	4	3	17,883
Siberland	3	G	3	1	1	0	41,000
Siberschool	2	F	1	0	0	0	0
Sicilian Angel	2	F	2	0	0	0	165
Sicilian Boy	2	C	6	0	1	1	18,920
Sicilian Princess	3	F	9	2	1	3	73,660
Sicily Don	4	G	6	0	0	0	575
Sickling Greek	3	C	3	0	1	1	6,077
Sicnee	7	G	12	0	0	1	4,837
Sid	4	G	12	3	0	2	16,280
Sid Dithers	2	G	2	0	1	0	7,620
Side	5	H	12	2	2	3	14,325
Side Arm Sister	5	M	3	0	0	0	680
Side Bet	3	G	5	1	0	0	3,240
Side Pocket Tim	2	C	2	0	0	0	720
Sideburn (IRE)	6	G	7	2	2	0	3,324
Sidekick	6	G	14	4	2	4	40,165
Sideline Duchess	7	M	7	0	2	3	12,735
Sideofhappy	2	G	3	1	1	1	8,190
Sidepocketplayer	6	G	14	0	4	1	8,253
Sidereal	3	G	6	1	0	0	19,030
Sideshow Caper	3	F	7	1	0	1	5,706
Sideshow Mel	4	G	9	0	0	0	3,485
Sidestepping	3	F	2	0	0	1	6,370
Sidetracked	5	G	6	0	0	0	150
Sideways	4	F	8	0	1	1	12,375
Sidler	3	C	6	0	0	0	900
Sidney Stephen	11	G	2	1	0	0	3,224
Sidoslew	5	G	12	1	1	1	11,068
Siebetime	2	F	2	0	0	0	0
Sienago	5	M	14	2	0	1	15,128
Sienna Belle	3	F	4	0	0	1	200
Sienna Lady	3	F	1	0	0	0	0
Sienna's Honor	2	F	5	1	0	1	11,300
Sierra Kitty	3	F	13	1	0	2	37,764
Sierra Lady	4	F	9	1	0	0	43,904
Sierra Page	2	F	3	1	0	1	9,520
Sierra Red	3	F	4	0	0	0	55
Sierra Silver	7	G	10	1	1	2	9,461
Sierra Sky	5	M	6	0	0	0	157
Sierra's Sweedie	3	F	5	0	2	2	5,760
Sierra's Victory	2	F	5	1	0	1	10,480
Sierre Nevada	5	M	14	4	3	3	24,145
Siesmic Rhythm	4	F	13	2	3	3	19,188
Siesmic Sensation	2	G	3	0	0	0	2,580
Siesta Key	4	C	9	1	1	4	10,895
Siete Slew	4	G	2	0	0	0	1,140
Siffounas	2	C	5	0	0	2	5,280
Sifter Sister	3	F	3	0	0	0	258
Sifting Sand	3	C	8	3	0	2	5,976
Sigalaspam	4	C	4	0	0	1	660
Sigana	5	M	2	0	0	0	720
Siggie	3	G	7	2	0	0	9,200
Siggys Crystal	2	F	2	0	2	0	4,240
Sigh Lite	6	M	2	0	0	0	0
Sigh of Relief	4	F	6	1	1	1	40,890
Sighting	4	F	1	0	0	1	2,340
Sightseek	4	F	8	4	3	0	1,171,888
Sigint	3	C	13	3	3	0	119,700
Sigmud (CHI)	6	G	7	0	0	1	935
Sign	3	G	3	1	1	0	6,790
Sign a Prenup	4	G	9	1	3	1	16,270
Sign of a Bird	8	H	9	0	0	2	2,074
Sign of Greatness	4	C	8	0	1	1	12,590
Sign of Love	3	G	3	0	0	0	1,980
Sign of the Cat	3	F	9	0	0	0	514
Sign of the Chimes	2	G	1	0	0	0	100
Sign of The Wolf (GB)	3	C	8	3	0	0	74,586
Signe the Ticket	4	G	4	0	1	0	3,580
Signal Crossing	4	C	8	0	1	1	3,703
Signal Man	3	C	9	4	2	0	26,753
Signal Pat	4	F	17	1	1	2	4,981
Signal Red	4	F	4	0	0	1	2,780
Signal Service	5	G	3	1	1	0	2,175
Signal Spring	4	F	1	0	0	0	0
Signal Starlit	4	F	11	2	0	5	37,410
Signal Tower	5	G	5	0	0	0	706
Signal Won	3	G	3	0	0	1	3,610
Signals Diamond	4	G	11	0	2	2	10,993
Signalsncrossings	3	C	2	0	0	0	90
Signature Sunday (AUS)	3	C	3	0	0	2	9,480
Signature Sweep (AUS)	3	G	2	0	0	1	5,880
Signboard	3	G	5	1	0	0	15,930
Signed Secret	2	F	5	0	0	0	525
Significant One	2	C	1	1	0	0	6,552
Significant Risk	3	F	6	0	2	0	15,680
Significantly	2	C	3	0	0	0	860
Signkite	11	G	1	0	0	0	172
Signore William	2	C	1	0	0	0	0
Sik	5	H	3	0	0	0	1,184
Silas	5	G	13	1	3	5	14,546
Silber	2	F	2	0	0	1	6,260
Silent Academy	4	F	5	1	0	2	17,928
Silent Alarm	4	F	7	0	3	0	26,400
Silent Annie	3	F	2	0	0	0	2,460
Silent Bet	2	F	3	1	1	0	21,117
Silent Buck	4	G	14	0	0	1	1,805
Silent Charge	5	H	7	4	1	0	91,520
Silent Clearance	5	H	15	0	3	2	6,894
Silent Comand	4	C	1	0	0	0	0
Silent Counter	6	M	9	2	1	0	10,677
Silent Crystal	4	F	5	1	0	1	44,050
Silent Delight	6	G	7	0	1	1	4,120
Silent Demon	3	G	8	0	2	1	1,348
Silent Desert	4	G	5	1	0	0	5,418
Silent Diplomacy	7	G	7	0	1	0	940
Silent Dust	3	G	11	1	2	4	20,600
Silent Ego	4	G	6	1	0	1	9,697
Silent Embrace	3	F	8	1	2	0	19,440
Silent Flick	4	G	1	0	0	0	0
Silent Fred	4	G	9	0	5	2	57,636
Silent Gambler	3	C	3	0	0	0	0
Silent Glory	5	M	4	0	0	0	646
Silent Gold	2	C	2	1	0	0	17,500
Silent Goodbye	4	C	4	0	0	0	1,890
Silent Hawk	6	G	1	0	0	0	38
Silent Hayley	2	F	2	0	0	0	0
Silent Hero	3	C	6	0	0	0	0
Silent Ide	5	M	7	0	2	1	2,490
Silent Kingdom	2	F	4	0	1	0	6,560
Silent Lane	4	G	3	2	1	0	2,895
Silent Launch	7	G	4	2	0	1	3,865
Silent Manor	5	H	4	0	0	0	270
Silent Misty	4	F	22	1	7	4	19,287
Silent Monarch	3	F	5	2	1	0	23,814
Silent Mountain	4	G	8	0	0	1	723
Silent Number	4	F	8	1	1	3	13,788
Silent Oath	3	F	3	0	1	1	9,870
Silent Olimpian	4	F	6	1	3	1	21,710
Silent Picture	2	C	1	0	0	0	0
Silent Predator	5	H	7	0	1	2	6,910
Silent Prey	6	H	18	1	4	6	17,025
Silent Prospect	3	F	1	0	0	0	0
Silent Queen	3	F	3	1	0	0	15,440
Silent Rapids	4	F	5	1	1	0	7,760
Silent Reason	4	F	12	0	3	2	23,637
Silent Regent	5	G	6	0	0	1	1,913
Silent Revenge	3	C	2	0	0	0	0
Silent Reward	4	G	9	0	0	0	729
Silent Riflier	4	F	1	0	0	0	0
Silent Ruckus	4	F	10	3	0	1	15,113
Silent Run	4	G	1	0	0	0	35
Silent Sack	3	C	1	0	0	0	0
Silent Sam	6	H	13	2	2	1	31,830
Silent Sam Sparkls	6	M	1	0	0	0	0
Silent Samurai	2	G	3	0	1	0	1,200
Silent Scamper	5	G	2	0	0	1	955
Silent Scream	4	F	12	1	2	0	13,365
Silent Sea	3	F	5	0	0	0	786
Silent Secreto	6	G	4	0	0	0	126
Silent Service	4	G	5	2	1	0	8,840
Silent Sheikh	6	G	13	0	0	1	1,355
Silent Shoes	4	G	11	1	1	3	11,272
Silent Sighs	2	F	3	2	1	0	125,200
Silent Sins	4	F	10	4	0	1	15,062
Silent Sir	3	C	2	0	0	0	0
Silent Siren	2	F	1	0	0	0	0
Silent Snow	2	C	2	1	0	0	1,560

Horse	Age	Sex	Sts	1st	2d	3d	Won	Horse	Age	Sex	Sts	1st	2d	3d	Won
Silent Splender	2	F	3	1	1	0	9,360	Silver Bid	5	H	14	2	5	3	147,098
Silent Storm	2	F	5	0	0	0	8,100	Silver Bird	2	F	5	3	1	0	235,445
Silent Streaker	7	G	19	4	3	5	36,945	Silver Blessing	3	G	2	0	0	0	525
Silent Stream	6	M	4	3	0	0	109,655	Silver Bouquet	4	F	3	0	1	0	2,200
Silent Text	4	G	9	1	2	1	9,150	Silver Bow	5	G	2	0	0	0	131
Silent Thunder	7	H	8	2	0	1	18,177	Silver Box	4	F	6	1	0	2	20,750
Silent Treatment	4	F	5	2	1	1	23,400	Silver Brite	4	G	12	3	1	3	13,078
Silent Type	4	C	8	1	0	0	6,690	Silver Brother	4	C	7	0	2	1	3,968
Silent Verse	3	G	1	0	0	0	225	Silver Bullet Bee	4	G	9	0	3	1	2,814
Silent Whisper	6	M	3	0	0	0	0	Silver Buttons	5	M	11	2	2	1	31,311
Silent Wineo	3	C	3	0	0	0	0	Silver Calling	2	F	4	1	0	0	9,634
Silent Wishes	4	F	8	0	2	1	3,635	Silver Cavalier	3	G	6	1	2	1	11,720
Silent Zipata	6	G	9	0	1	1	5,700	Silver Celebration	5	G	3	0	0	1	2,365
Silentbutdeliteful	8	M	3	0	0	1	577	Silver Chad	3	G	14	2	1	1	9,269
Silently	4	F	7	0	2	2	9,025	Silver Chadra	7	G	13	2	1	4	19,240
Silentscreen Actor	2	C	3	0	1	0	2,613	Silver Challange	5	H	13	2	2	0	14,740
Silenus	4	G	7	0	0	1	2,071	Silver Champ	4	F	13	0	4	1	68,229
Silet	4	F	9	2	1	5	49,080	Silver Chaser	2	F	2	0	0	0	135
Silhouetta	4	F	3	1	0	0	6,628	Silver Chip	5	M	8	1	2	1	11,617
Silica	3	F	3	1	0	0	8,940	Silver Clipper	4	F	5	1	1	1	44,620
Silicon Alley	4	G	14	0	5	3	20,240	Silver Code	4	G	5	0	0	0	740
Silicon City	3	C	4	0	0	1	10,680	Silver Commander	3	G	8	0	2	4	21,460
Silicon Doll	2	F	2	0	0	0	510	Silver Country	6	G	4	0	0	0	206
Silk	3	F	8	0	0	0	5,158	Silver Crest	9	G	16	1	0	4	15,683
Silk Bandit	4	C	2	0	0	0	0	Silver Crown	2	F	4	2	0	0	49,634
Silk Ceremony	3	C	6	0	2	1	5,230	Silver Cup	5	G	8	2	0	2	7,239
Silk Concorde	5	M	8	2	0	2	74,032	Silver Daddy	2	C	1	0	1	0	3,800
Silk N Diamonds	3	F	12	1	4	1	32,820	Silver Debutante	4	F	8	3	0	1	28,665
Silk Road	5	G	1	1	0	0	6,322	Silver Design	4	F	8	1	0	1	7,965
Silk Safari	4	F	1	0	0	0	56	Silver Diablo	3	C	1	0	0	0	360
Silk Wine	4	F	1	0	0	0	0	Silver Dollar Day	3	G	13	2	0	1	20,555
Silkamean	4	G	5	3	0	0	18,559	Silver Dollar Girl	3	F	15	2	1	3	56,460
Silken Elegance	3	F	14	5	3	3	141,472	Silver Dollar Lady	4	F	3	1	0	0	7,200
Silken Purse	3	F	9	2	1	1	37,126	Silver Donn	4	C	8	1	1	1	39,691
Silken Smooth	6	M	4	0	0	2	1,526	Silver Dreamer	5	H	3	0	0	0	330
Silken's Eminence	6	G	10	2	1	2	8,908	Silver Drummer	5	H	14	1	0	4	19,934
Silken's Trick	8	M	11	0	0	1	3,210	Silver Ducats	3	F	6	1	1	0	5,720
Silkie's Diz	3	F	4	0	1	0	2,392	Silver Due	3	F	9	0	1	2	4,210
Silkiest	3	C	13	2	2	0	16,354	Silver Dynasty	4	G	7	0	0	2	4,225
Silks N Roses	5	M	13	0	0	4	8,012	Silver Eights	4	F	6	0	0	1	799
Silks Or Scarlet	9	G	2	0	0	0	189	Silver Endeavor	4	C	2	0	0	1	698
Silkworth	3	F	3	1	0	2	33,840	Silver Fact	3	F	1	0	0	0	0
Silky Bill	8	G	9	1	2	4	3,721	Silver Fax	8	G	2	0	0	0	340
Silky Black	2	F	3	0	0	1	4,704	Silver Flag	8	G	7	0	0	0	498
Silky Cat	3	F	6	0	0	2	3,755	Silver Fortune	2	F	1	0	1	0	3,000
Silky Flyer	2	F	5	1	0	0	6,060	Silver Gate	6	H	4	0	0	0	258
Silky Goose	5	M	5	0	2	1	3,292	Silver Gem	6	G	8	1	1	2	9,082
Silky Kiss	2	C	1	0	0	0	0	Silver Ghazi Girl	4	F	10	1	1	2	4,644
Silky Longlegs	2	F	1	0	0	0	0	Silver Girl	3	F	7	1	0	0	5,225
Silky Sauce	4	F	2	0	0	0	780	Silver Glen Lucy	3	F	4	1	0	0	7,470
Silky Secret	6	M	6	1	1	2	17,155	Silver Glide	4	G	2	0	0	0	525
Silky Summer	3	F	8	1	2	2	43,560	Silver Gloss	2	F	2	0	0	0	0
Silky Voice	2	G	7	1	0	1	10,290	Silver Goldnrobert	4	G	14	0	1	2	5,675
Silky Zarb	6	G	14	4	4	2	149,427	Silver Goose	7	G	18	0	1	2	2,930
Silkyence	2	F	5	1	0	0	14,280	Silver Graded	4	F	17	1	4	3	15,981
Silkys Magic	4	F	1	0	0	0	0	Silver Greek	4	G	8	1	1	1	32,920
Silla	5	M	1	0	0	0	930	Silver Gun	3	G	2	0	0	0	1,818
Sillio Season	5	G	10	1	0	3	5,940	Silver Gypsy	5	M	6	1	3	0	26,337
Silly Boy	4	C	5	0	1	0	890	Silver Halo	2	G	1	0	0	0	0
Silly Cec	3	F	2	0	0	1	456	Silver Hawk Lady	2	F	8	0	0	2	16,020
Silly Ghost	4	C	2	0	1	0	2,460	Silver Hero	6	M	9	3	0	2	12,586
Silly Girl	5	M	13	2	5	3	29,920	Silver Hound	5	G	2	0	0	0	82
Silmaril	2	F	2	1	1	0	19,500	Silver Ikon	4	C	15	1	3	2	10,348
Silo	3	F	17	1	3	3	13,861	Silver Illusion	4	C	18	3	1	1	26,260
Silt	3	F	10	0	0	1	2,970	Silver Indy	2	C	2	1	0	0	17,580
Silvanos	6	G	3	0	0	0	366	Silver Influence	4	G	7	0	3	1	22,829
Silver Airess	4	C	7	1	0	1	12,344	Silver Invitation	7	M	9	2	0	1	36,106
Silver Alarm	8	G	10	3	0	2	18,205	Silver Jet	6	G	18	2	1	2	29,442
Silver Albertson	3	G	8	0	2	1	31,568	Silver Jingle	6	M	5	0	0	0	144
Silver Ali	6	M	3	0	0	0	171	Silver Justus	3	F	5	0	0	0	285
Silver and Green	5	G	8	1	1	2	6,510	Silver Kestrel	3	F	4	1	1	0	29,730
Silver Artistry	4	C	11	2	3	1	13,888	Silver Lace	3	F	5	2	1	1	39,964
Silver Astro	3	C	3	0	1	0	2,470	Silver Lade	3	G	12	1	1	1	22,360
Silver Attack	5	G	20	1	0	3	6,040	Silver Lightning	3	C	5	1	0	1	4,763
Silver Award	5	H	10	1	4	1	15,808	Silver Lou	7	G	3	1	0	0	1,185
Silver Axe	6	G	8	0	2	1	29,344	Silver Lure	2	F	6	1	1	0	20,250
Silver B. Cash	3	G	9	1	1	1	7,760	Silver Maestro	5	H	3	0	0	0	0
Silver Banshee	5	M	12	0	2	4	14,295	Silver Magic	6	M	15	2	0	2	34,157
Silver Beauty	4	F	11	1	3	2	8,360	Silver Magpie	5	M	6	1	1	2	21,175

RECORDS OF HORSES

Horse	Age	Sex	Sts	1st	2d	3d	Won	Horse	Age	Sex	Sts	1st	2d	3d	Won
Silver Mark	3	C	8	0	0	1	3,600	Silver Sunset	5	G	11	0	2	2	10,976
Silver Matt	5	G	8	1	1	1	14,933	Silver Superior	4	G	3	0	0	0	53
Silver Meadow	3	F	3	1	1	0	21,960	Silver Swing	3	F	6	1	1	0	3,445
Silver Mesh	4	F	7	0	1	0	2,634	Silver Swinger	8	G	3	2	0	0	17,980
Silver Mica	3	G	3	1	0	0	861	Silver Ta Gold	7	G	7	2	0	1	7,492
Silver Midnight	11	G	5	0	1	1	5,060	Silver Talon	3	G	1	0	0	0	130
Silver Mine Ranch	3	C	2	0	1	0	2,700	Silver Tap	4	F	4	0	1	0	2,640
Silver Minister	2	G	3	1	2	0	31,890	Silver Things	2	F	4	0	0	0	0
Silver Mint	3	F	3	0	0	0	1,143	Silver Ticket	2	G	3	1	1	0	90,020
Silver Money	3	G	6	0	2	2	5,797	Silver Tie Lady	5	M	11	1	2	0	22,478
Silver n' Irish	4	G	14	2	0	0	7,881	Silver Toes	3	F	15	4	1	3	29,123
Silver Niner	3	F	1	0	0	0	195	Silver Top	5	M	14	1	2	1	10,645
Silver Nithi	4	F	4	0	1	2	43,161	Silver Touch	4	F	15	0	0	3	4,417
Silver Nitric	3	G	17	1	1	3	12,914	Silver Town	4	G	19	1	5	3	11,945
Silver Notebook	5	G	3	0	1	0	2,340	Silver Tree	3	C	6	3	0	1	390,660
Silver Owl	6	M	12	1	4	0	30,335	Silver Tricon	4	F	14	3	0	1	24,725
Silver Pact	6	G	10	0	0	0	2,404	Silver Trinket	5	M	7	2	2	0	17,313
Silver Patriarch	5	G	5	2	0	0	37,017	Silver Trooper	8	G	8	1	2	0	7,036
Silver Peagus	3	C	12	1	2	3	23,879	Silver Trophy	6	H	7	1	2	1	10,630
Silver Pen	3	F	12	1	3	2	18,750	Silver Tsunami	3	C	6	1	2	1	32,450
Silver Performer	3	C	6	0	0	1	2,225	Silver Valay	5	G	14	3	1	2	36,500
Silver Phone	4	G	7	1	2	1	35,400	Silver Vee	3	G	8	2	0	1	8,531
Silver Pines	4	C	12	2	3	0	16,018	Silver Wagon	2	C	4	2	1	1	162,140
Silver Pit	3	C	11	0	0	1	6,140	Silver Warrant	2	C	2	0	0	0	1,050
Silver Plated	2	F	3	0	0	1	3,270	Silver Wharf	5	G	6	0	0	0	196
Silver Prospect	5	H	2	0	0	0	0	Silver Wheat	2	C	5	0	0	1	2,471
Silver Rail	6	M	7	0	0	2	19,270	Silver Yen	4	F	9	2	1	0	83,375
Silver Rain	5	M	3	0	0	0	327	Silver Yukon	4	G	7	0	1	0	3,420
Silver Rapt	2	G	7	1	1	1	22,977	Silver Zipper	6	H	7	2	1	3	61,990
Silver Relic	3	G	3	0	0	0	123	Silverado Ridge	5	G	9	0	1	0	4,058
Silver Request	4	F	13	0	3	1	5,651	Silverado Streaker	5	H	5	0	0	0	456
Silver Review	4	F	5	1	0	1	11,040	Silverboy	5	G	7	0	1	1	3,850
Silver Rhythm	5	G	2	0	0	0	640	Silvercity Lady	2	F	6	1	1	1	32,050
Silver Richards	5	G	9	1	2	0	5,124	Silverella Charm	8	M	10	4	4	1	19,387
Silver Riddle	4	F	17	0	2	1	7,870	Silverette	4	F	6	0	0	0	554
Silver Rings	10	G	7	3	0	0	10,992	Silverfeet	3	F	3	0	0	0	648
Silver Rock	6	G	8	1	0	1	4,262	Silverfish	3	F	1	0	0	0	120
Silver Rolls	5	H	12	1	0	2	5,325	Silverfoot	3	G	1	1	0	0	11,470
Silver Rose	3	F	2	0	0	0	120	Silverio Time	6	H	3	0	0	0	450
Silver Ruckus	4	F	12	0	1	5	11,160	Silverlake Special	2	G	1	0	0	0	105
Silver Rush	2	F	1	1	0	0	18,800	Silvermin	3	G	14	0	1	1	5,810
Silver Sail	6	H	15	1	1	1	4,127	Silversandsoftime	2	C	4	0	0	2	3,950
Silver Sails	4	C	2	1	0	0	5,005	Silverspeed	5	M	10	2	0	2	24,314
Silver Saint	7	H	9	1	1	0	14,591	Silversplash	3	F	7	0	1	1	4,802
Silver Scamp	5	G	14	1	1	2	7,392	Silvertail Road	5	G	7	2	1	1	3,700
Silver Schmoozer	2	C	2	0	0	0	216	Silvertipkiller	2	C	3	0	1	1	11,580
Silver Scholar	2	F	7	0	3	1	13,425	Silverton Bay	4	F	13	4	3	2	60,350
Silver Scooter	2	G	2	0	0	0	134	Silvertongue Fox	5	G	3	2	0	1	11,600
Silver Screen Girl	5	M	7	2	2	2	55,805	Silverturfcloud	2	G	1	0	0	0	0
Silver Sequins	5	M	6	0	0	2	7,434	Silverwilldo	2	F	3	1	0	0	22,500
Silver Set	5	G	9	2	0	0	8,878	Silverwood	3	G	12	1	2	1	18,316
Silver Shaft	6	M	4	0	0	0	166	Silvery	4	F	1	0	0	0	0
Silver Shield	3	C	1	0	0	0	0	Silvery Crown	2	F	4	0	1	0	6,080
Silver Shine	4	F	5	1	0	2	14,040	Silvery Mamoon	3	F	1	0	0	0	206
Silver Shot	3	F	3	0	0	0	572	Silvery Pet	3	F	6	0	1	0	11,950
Silver Signature	3	G	1	0	0	0	0	Silvey's Muchacha	9	M	1	0	0	0	120
Silver Silence	5	M	9	3	2	2	36,660	Silvie's War	5	H	8	2	1	1	14,340
Silver Silk	3	F	3	0	0	0	0	Sim Sam	3	F	1	1	0	0	6,000
Silver Singer	3	F	1	0	0	0	1,980	Simacher	3	F	11	1	1	1	11,897
Silver Sir	7	G	6	0	1	0	660	Simbad	3	C	9	1	2	1	19,285
Silver Skater	3	G	3	0	0	0	501	Simbah	4	C	1	0	0	0	0
Silver Skip	3	F	4	1	0	1	5,620	Simcha	4	F	14	1	1	1	11,170
Silver Sky	5	G	11	3	2	3	43,703	Similar Power	8	M	3	0	0	0	540
Silver Slinkee	3	F	3	1	0	0	8,060	Similkameen Maan	3	G	11	1	2	2	10,720
Silver Sliver	8	M	8	1	1	0	12,352	Simmer	7	G	8	1	1	1	37,887
Silver Snow	3	F	18	2	0	3	18,342	Simmer Down Slew	3	G	6	0	0	0	80
Silver Sock	2	F	1	0	0	0	1,800	Simmerdown Now	3	F	8	1	1	0	4,530
Silver Song	5	M	15	0	0	2	2,322	Simon Slew	4	F	5	0	0	2	6,502
Silver Sonnet	4	F	6	1	1	4	35,140	Simone Symphony	4	F	17	3	3	4	22,073
Silver Soul	2	C	1	1	0	0	8,100	Simone's Show	4	F	1	0	0	0	0
Silver Spear	5	H	8	0	1	0	23,056	Simon's Birch	4	G	10	1	1	0	28,870
Silver Spoon Pete	4	C	1	0	0	0	0	Simony	6	G	16	0	2	4	35,102
Silver Sprout	3	F	5	1	0	1	13,260	Simpatico	3	G	2	0	0	0	364
Silver Squire	3	C	1	0	0	1	11,000	Simple Affair	2	F	7	2	1	1	39,310
Silver Step Lass	2	F	3	0	0	0	632	Simple Forest	5	G	12	1	0	0	2,595
Silver Storm	4	G	4	0	0	1	1,925	Simple Gift	3	F	1	0	0	0	84
Silver Strategy	3	G	5	0	0	1	1,220	Simple Pic	5	H	18	1	3	3	13,655
Silver Strip	2	G	1	0	1	0	2,340	Simple Search	3	G	9	2	0	2	15,840
Silver Sunlight	8	G	3	0	0	0	136	Simple Touch	4	G	13	1	0	1	4,686

Horse	Age	Sex	Sts	1st	2d	3d	Won
Simply a Jet	4	F	14	3	0	2	9,824
Simply a Storm	5	G	4	0	0	0	756
Simply Aly	4	G	19	3	1	1	25,360
Simply Buddy	3	G	4	0	0	0	272
Simply Caldo	11	G	8	1	2	0	6,018
Simply Class	3	F	10	0	1	2	6,690
Simply Fancy	2	F	2	0	0	1	2,000
Simply Golden	3	G	11	1	0	2	3,946
Simply Gorgeous	5	M	3	1	0	0	15,000
Simply Great	6	M	11	1	1	3	11,754
Simply Jolie	2	F	4	3	0	0	41,550
Simply Magical	4	F	7	0	0	1	3,030
Simply Nate	8	H	8	0	4	0	20,310
Simply Perfect	2	F	4	0	1	0	4,895
Simply Precious	4	F	11	2	1	1	68,425
Simply Rich	2	C	3	0	1	1	10,560
Simply Santa Fe	3	F	4	0	0	0	1,560
Simply Senseless	3	F	3	1	0	1	17,220
Simply Siber	3	F	3	0	1	0	7,000
Simply Simon	2	C	2	0	0	0	505
Simply Sir	5	G	10	2	2	1	23,080
Simply Splashing	7	M	7	2	1	0	18,410
Simply Superior	2	F	2	0	0	1	1,200
Simply Swiss	3	F	6	2	1	1	15,280
Simply Tricky	3	F	8	1	1	0	10,944
Simply Victorious	2	F	3	1	0	0	8,900
Simply Wahoo	9	G	1	0	0	0	0
Simplysammy	5	G	16	0	6	4	17,246
Simplysoreel	3	F	3	0	0	0	0
Simplytruth	4	F	13	2	4	2	56,247
Simsimmer	5	M	13	1	1	1	8,415
Sin Killer	3	G	11	1	0	0	4,427
Sin 'n Grin	5	G	16	2	1	2	26,055
Sin Wagon	3	G	5	1	0	1	6,940
Sinaloa	3	C	5	2	0	0	9,556
Sinca	3	F	5	0	1	0	4,820
Sinceifoundmycandy	3	F	7	0	0	0	276
Sincey's Girl	3	F	5	0	0	0	576
Sindbad	2	G	4	0	0	1	8,320
Sindbad the Sailor	5	G	10	7	2	0	44,980
Sindical	6	G	2	0	0	0	230
Sindi's Success	2	F	2	0	0	1	2,747
Sine Die	4	G	12	3	0	3	25,785
Sinful Lady	3	F	5	1	1	0	2,280
Sinful Miner	5	M	4	1	0	1	13,088
Sinful Pleasures	6	M	5	1	2	0	21,911
Sinful Storms	4	G	17	2	4	1	30,945
Sinful Success	5	H	1	1	0	0	3,480
Sinfulindulgence	3	F	6	1	0	3	22,520
Sing a Few Bars	5	H	6	0	1	1	3,116
Sing A'cord	5	M	18	1	3	2	11,064
Sing Aly Sing	3	G	2	0	0	0	0
Sing Because	10	G	4	1	0	1	15,060
Sing High Sing Low	3	F	17	1	4	6	28,765
Sing Me a Song	4	F	1	0	0	0	0
Sing Me Back Home	5	G	5	1	1	1	100,500
Sing My Song	5	M	5	1	0	2	6,148
Sing N Zing	4	G	14	1	0	3	11,486
Sing On Stage	5	M	7	1	0	0	2,368
Sing Out	3	G	18	0	4	6	10,202
Sing Softly	4	F	6	1	0	1	9,038
Sing Song	5	M	2	1	0	0	6,350
Singaballad	2	F	2	0	0	0	375
Singapore Charley	5	M	10	2	1	1	29,802
Singapore Deputy	3	C	6	1	0	3	26,340
Singasongforme	3	G	14	3	2	1	100,855
Singh Again	6	G	13	1	0	2	7,555
Singin N D Shower	8	G	2	0	1	0	3,030
Singing Deelight	7	M	2	0	0	0	0
Singing Dixie	4	F	8	2	0	0	17,795
Singing Flower	2	F	3	0	0	0	420
Singing Girl	2	F	4	1	0	0	7,760
Singing Hills	6	G	16	2	1	0	4,397
Singing King	3	C	4	0	0	0	259
Singing Laur	2	F	6	2	2	0	44,120
Singing Lines	4	G	10	1	0	0	4,000
Singing Man	6	G	3	0	0	0	360
Singing Sam	6	G	9	0	0	0	3,187
Singing Soldier	3	C	7	0	0	1	6,420
Singing Swiss	3	F	9	0	0	1	2,219
Singing Sword	4	F	10	2	1	2	49,500
Singinginthewoods	2	C	6	1	0	1	14,890
Singit	2	F	3	0	0	0	840
Single All All	3	C	8	3	0	2	33,360
Single Charm	4	F	4	0	2	0	4,400
Single Don	10	G	7	0	0	0	458
Single Edge	3	G	7	1	2	0	11,446
Single Factor	2	F	3	0	0	0	145
Single Feather	3	F	4	0	0	0	70
Single File	2	G	6	0	1	1	2,730
Single in Seattle	9	M	2	0	0	0	464
Single Prospect	4	F	8	1	0	1	8,305
Single Rainbow	4	C	2	0	0	1	3,145
Single Spur	5	M	1	0	0	0	0
Single Storm	5	F	1	0	0	0	0
Single Stroke	4	G	11	1	0	2	31,096
Single Track	5	G	15	3	2	3	13,969
Single Woman	2	F	1	0	0	1	6,468
Singles Last Kiss	3	G	11	1	0	0	12,972
Singles Legend	3	F	2	0	0	0	0
Singletary	3	C	8	2	2	1	206,352
Singleton	5	G	1	0	0	0	0
Singsweetgil	4	C	9	3	3	0	12,758
Sinhouse	5	M	10	4	1	0	170,302
Sinibion	5	M	9	1	1	0	13,028
Sinister Appeal	7	G	1	0	0	0	60
Sinister Crane	3	G	3	0	0	1	940
Sinister G	2	C	3	1	1	1	41,550
Sinjar	8	G	5	0	1	1	1,320
Sink the Bismark	5	G	10	0	0	1	1,148
Sinking Feeling	3	F	8	2	0	3	24,540
Sinless Sister	7	M	3	0	0	0	150
Sinn Free	4	F	6	1	1	0	20,640
Sinner Take All	5	M	3	0	0	0	328
Sinners Accepted	2	F	1	0	0	0	252
Sinners N Saints	2	C	1	0	0	0	420
Sins and Riches	5	G	10	4	2	0	63,612
Sins of My Youth	7	G	19	1	5	1	17,946
Sion Hill	3	C	1	0	0	0	130
Sione	2	F	2	0	0	0	660
Sionna	2	F	6	0	0	2	4,400
Siora	3	F	3	0	0	1	517
Sioux	6	G	6	1	1	0	2,510
Sioux Beauty	2	F	3	0	0	2	9,000
Sioux City Sue	4	G	7	0	2	3	3,232
Sioux D' Or	6	H	9	2	1	0	9,440
Siouxperchic	5	M	6	0	0	0	1,375
Siouxpersunny	4	F	4	0	0	0	823
Sipas	3	F	7	0	0	0	1,111
Siphia	4	F	2	0	0	0	112
Siphina	4	F	2	0	0	0	970
Siphon Honey	4	F	6	1	1	2	54,920
Siphonette	2	F	5	0	2	2	28,480
Siphonizer	2	C	5	2	0	0	197,400
Siphonophora	2	F	1	0	0	0	0
Siphon's Glory	3	G	3	0	0	1	3,130
Siphon's Tiera	3	F	9	1	2	0	6,702
Sip'n	4	C	8	1	3	2	18,200
Sippin' Devil	3	F	5	1	0	0	7,804
Sippin' Jack	4	C	4	0	0	0	300
Sippin T	5	M	4	0	0	0	1,089
Siptitz Heights (IRE)	5	M	8	0	1	1	6,114
Sir Alfred	5	H	5	0	1	0	7,160
Sir Allen	2	C	3	0	0	0	0
Sir Aly	4	G	10	2	2	1	20,412
Sir Anthony	4	G	5	1	0	1	3,070
Sir Antrim	4	C	2	0	0	0	0
Sir Apwith Pride	2	G	3	1	0	1	7,971
Sir Arthur	3	C	3	0	0	0	0
Sir Augustus	2	G	3	2	1	0	22,345
Sir Austin	4	G	16	1	2	2	18,965
Sir Bay Sky	4	C	10	0	1	1	1,256
Sir Bear	10	G	1	0	0	0	0
Sir Bedivere	4	C	6	1	0	1	10,170
Sir Blitz	4	G	8	2	3	1	130,122
Sir Bob a Lou	7	G	3	0	0	0	0
Sir Bodgit	4	G	3	0	0	0	0
Sir Bovary	5	G	6	1	0	3	2,119

RECORDS OF HORSES

Horse	Age	Sex	Sts	1st	2d	3d	Won	Horse	Age	Sex	Sts	1st	2d	3d	Won
Sir Brian's Sword	5	G	8	1	2	1	91,742	Sir Robbi	4	C	9	1	0	1	5,213
Sir Buffington	3	C	2	0	0	1	472	Sir Rocky	2	C	3	0	0	0	360
Sir Butch	5	H	3	0	0	0	225	Sir Rocky Slew	6	G	12	2	1	2	4,584
Sir Cassanova	4	G	7	0	0	1	1,407	Sir Royale	3	C	7	1	3	1	17,330
Sir Ceasar	3	G	5	0	1	0	1,157	Sir Rubi	3	G	12	2	2	2	16,987
Sir Chancellor	6	G	15	1	0	3	6,222	Sir Runsalot	2	C	2	0	0	0	205
Sir Charleston	9	G	3	1	0	1	11,500	Sir Sailor	4	G	10	1	0	1	2,130
Sir Cherokee	3	C	5	3	0	0	365,535	Sir Sashay	3	G	10	1	2	2	82,764
Sir Cheval	6	H	2	0	0	0	133	Sir Sauceboat	3	C	9	1	3	0	8,032
Sir Claude	3	C	9	1	0	2	8,246	Sir Secret	6	H	8	0	3	1	3,640
Sir Creek	2	G	2	0	0	0	2,358	Sir Seibert	6	G	9	2	1	2	17,784
Sir Crypto	3	C	3	0	0	0	435	Sir Shimmy	8	G	14	6	1	3	78,910
Sir Dane	5	H	6	1	0	1	5,206	Sir Sigmund	3	G	8	0	0	0	599
Sir Dayjur	3	G	15	2	3	2	24,747	Sir Siphon	2	C	4	0	1	2	13,880
Sir Debon Aire	6	G	8	1	2	1	14,332	Sir Slew	6	H	3	0	0	0	295
Sir Dorset	8	G	9	4	3	1	77,580	Sir Smart Lee	2	C	2	0	0	1	3,080
Sir E F	6	G	1	0	0	1	470	Sir Socrates	3	C	8	1	0	2	23,640
Sir Ebony Knight	10	G	14	0	2	2	8,326	Sir Spicy	5	G	8	0	0	0	437
Sir Echo	12	G	2	1	0	0	12,424	Sir Spunky	6	G	13	1	1	1	8,741
Sir Elite	3	C	7	1	1	1	21,600	Sir Sunny	3	C	7	1	0	1	4,057
Sir Emblem	3	C	4	2	0	1	28,683	Sir Theo Express	5	H	2	0	0	0	108
Sir Enchantment	8	G	8	1	1	1	5,869	Sir Tiff	8	G	3	0	0	0	576
Sir Excavator	2	G	2	0	0	0	0	Sir Tificate	5	G	19	1	3	4	27,152
Sir Fidgity	2	G	5	3	1	0	121,785	Sir Top	3	G	4	1	1	1	9,104
Sir Forest	2	C	2	0	0	0	0	Sir Traver	3	G	10	2	2	1	42,100
Sir Gavin	3	G	3	0	1	0	3,039	Sir Tricky	2	C	3	1	0	1	14,940
Sir Gawain	3	G	7	0	0	0	990	Sir Twister Dale	5	H	1	0	0	1	750
Sir Ghost	6	G	6	0	2	0	5,840	Sir Tyler T	2	C	2	0	1	0	9,890
Sir Golden	2	C	1	0	0	0	180	Sir Vincent	2	G	4	0	0	0	295
Sir Grunt	4	G	12	1	1	3	12,615	Sir Wagga Wagga	3	G	11	1	1	4	11,870
Sir Gulch	2	C	5	0	1	0	10,930	Sir Wall Street	4	C	5	0	0	0	648
Sir Hadley	6	H	13	1	2	0	18,570	Sir Walsh	6	G	10	1	0	1	3,905
Sir Harold	4	G	11	1	0	0	7,161	Sir Walter Rahy	3	C	5	2	1	0	66,000
Sir Hillard Lewis	8	G	14	2	0	2	18,174	Sir Walter Scott	2	C	1	0	0	0	0
Sir Honey	6	H	10	0	2	4	5,280	Sir Warrickonbasil	3	G	7	1	2	1	15,770
Sir Howard	4	G	4	1	0	1	5,760	Sir Way	4	G	13	0	1	2	4,932
Sir Howard (AUS)	7	G	5	1	1	0	13,350	Sir West	5	H	15	3	1	3	48,040
Sir Howard James	3	G	4	0	0	0	900	Sir Whinesalot	4	G	10	0	1	2	8,715
Sir Hurricane	4	G	15	3	2	0	23,996	Sir William D.	2	C	4	0	0	0	308
Sir Instigator	2	G	3	0	0	0	0	Sir Willie	6	G	3	0	0	0	276
Sir Irish	4	G	5	1	0	0	9,180	Sira	4	F	10	1	2	3	48,705
Sir Isaac	4	C	2	0	0	0	0	Siracoque	3	F	9	1	2	2	26,860
Sir Ivar's Invader	3	F	3	1	1	0	6,205	Sircatour	3	C	4	3	1	0	80,800
Sir Ivor's Comet	7	G	16	0	0	1	4,340	Sircharlesschnabel	3	C	10	2	2	1	80,080
Sir Ivory	7	G	8	0	0	1	1,313	Siren Chaser	9	H	3	0	0	0	0
Sir James Cognac	4	G	13	1	2	1	25,702	Siren Song	6	M	3	1	0	0	6,600
Sir Jay	4	G	8	2	1	1	12,920	Siren Star	4	F	6	1	1	2	12,715
Sir Joe Kelly	5	H	16	4	5	1	88,440	Sirena Sweet	7	M	11	1	1	2	5,556
Sir Kix Alot	5	G	3	0	1	2	930	Sirgun	3	C	3	0	0	1	1,997
Sir Lebold	2	C	4	0	1	0	2,567	Sirocco	5	M	19	0	5	2	13,110
Sir Leon's Dr.	4	C	8	1	0	0	3,525	Sirocos	6	G	14	4	5	2	29,585
Sir Libra	2	C	2	0	0	1	1,735	Sirona Gold	3	F	5	2	0	1	68,683
Sir Lochenlode	7	G	7	1	1	0	3,567	Sirpa	5	H	2	0	0	0	9,000
Sir Lochinvar	3	C	4	1	1	1	29,450	Sirrom Sirrom	6	M	14	0	2	3	7,286
Sir Louie	2	C	5	1	1	1	26,750	Sirtan Code	6	G	8	0	0	0	684
Sir Magic	5	H	7	0	0	0	1,792	Sirto	6	G	18	3	3	2	16,679
Sir Manfred	3	C	19	1	0	2	19,255	Sirvanna	4	G	5	1	1	1	3,186
Sir Marlin	2	C	4	1	0	1	12,608	Sirvictory	4	C	6	1	1	1	5,713
Sir Marvin	3	G	11	1	0	2	7,041	Sirwilliamwallace	3	G	6	0	1	0	6,108
Sir Maskalot	5	G	14	1	3	2	21,028	Sis Go Kid	4	F	5	1	0	1	18,370
Sir Miller	3	G	9	2	5	0	15,953	Sisbug	5	M	7	2	1	2	34,428
Sir Mombo	2	C	2	0	0	0	820	Sisco Sam	4	G	1	0	0	0	0
Sir Morgan	4	G	7	1	2	1	22,168	Siskins	6	M	9	1	0	2	6,942
Sir Nelson	4	G	9	0	1	1	2,584	Siskiyou	4	F	5	2	1	0	7,118
Sir Neptune	3	G	6	2	0	0	11,061	Sis's Girl	9	M	6	0	0	0	171
Sir Nigel's Lady	4	F	1	0	0	0	107	Sis's Honor	4	C	2	0	0	0	75
Sir Norman	4	C	3	1	0	0	1,770	Sis's Knight Out	5	M	13	2	3	2	4,254
Sir Oscar	2	C	6	6	0	0	528,800	Sissi Song (FR)	7	M	5	0	0	2	6,300
Sir Pentelicus	4	C	5	0	2	1	2,541	Sissta Suzzie	4	F	4	0	0	1	9,058
Sir Phil	4	G	1	0	0	0	0	Sissy Belle	4	F	6	0	0	1	5,586
Sir Prado	5	G	11	2	1	1	17,926	Sissy Goblin	3	F	3	0	0	0	95
Sir Proud	4	G	20	1	1	2	7,845	Sissy Jo	3	F	3	0	0	0	255
Sir Pucker	6	G	10	3	0	1	46,688	Sissy Seasons	3	F	4	0	0	0	184
Sir Purdue	6	G	17	0	1	1	5,002	Sissy's Devil	2	F	1	0	0	0	0
Sir Radar	6	G	1	0	0	1	1,110	Sissy's Gal	5	M	15	1	0	3	5,874
Sir Rascal	6	H	2	0	0	1	1,045	Sister Adiba	6	M	6	0	1	2	14,015
Sir Ray	3	C	15	5	2	2	135,560	Sister Bolton	3	F	3	0	0	0	1,129
Sir Retsina	10	G	1	0	0	0	35	Sister Brass	5	M	6	0	0	0	406
Sir Richardwinalot	6	G	1	0	0	0	750	Sister Breeze	4	F	10	2	2	2	20,455

Horse	Age	Sex	Sts	1st	2d	3d	Won	Horse	Age	Sex	Sts	1st	2d	3d	Won
Sister Carolina	2	F	5	0	0	1	6,380	Sixers Fan	2	F	4	0	2	0	12,160
Sister Cesira	5	M	11	1	0	3	5,594	Sixes Gone Wild	6	H	1	0	0	0	24
Sister Char	2	F	8	0	2	3	6,019	Sixkiller	5	G	14	0	0	1	4,959
Sister Dooley	4	F	19	1	3	2	13,994	Sixmoons	3	C	5	0	0	1	2,860
Sister Elsie	6	M	13	0	0	0	412	Sixpax	5	H	3	0	0	0	0
Sister Flag	2	F	3	2	0	1	10,540	Sixteen Colony	6	H	7	0	1	3	10,300
Sister G.	11	M	6	0	0	2	1,469	Sixteen Deputies	5	M	3	0	0	0	190
Sister Girl Blues	4	F	5	1	2	0	121,557	Sixteen Is Sweet	3	F	11	0	0	0	1,165
Sister Greeley	5	M	2	0	0	0	246	Sixteentwenty	3	G	2	1	0	0	7,800
Sister Halo	3	F	7	2	0	0	6,862	Sixth and Walnut	4	F	11	3	1	2	73,020
Sister Jean	3	F	12	2	3	1	50,691	Sixth Formal	4	G	9	0	2	0	10,521
Sister Kenna	4	F	3	0	0	0	0	Sixth Jeneration	2	C	3	0	0	0	780
Sister Mary Hugh	4	F	16	3	2	2	50,305	Sixthirtyjoe	5	G	9	3	3	1	114,456
Sister Patricia (AUS)	8	M	3	2	0	0	56,400	Sixto	4	G	13	1	0	0	5,516
Sister Ponche	4	F	10	1	4	1	18,000	Sixty Minute Man	5	G	11	4	0	1	30,180
Sister Rosie	4	F	9	1	4	0	22,590	Sixty Minutes	9	G	2	0	0	0	0
Sister Serenade	4	F	4	0	1	0	1,900	Sixty of North	4	G	12	0	3	1	6,642
Sister Sis	5	M	5	0	0	0	1,520	Sixty Percent	5	M	1	0	0	0	70
Sister Smoke	4	F	6	3	0	0	16,225	Sixty Seconds (NZ)	5	M	3	2	0	0	105,060
Sister Star	2	F	6	1	1	3	39,955	Sixty Sixty	2	C	1	0	0	1	2,860
Sister Strut	4	F	19	3	6	5	35,245	Sixty Stars	5	G	12	1	4	2	32,382
Sister Swank	2	F	3	2	1	0	36,800	Sixty Two Lincoln	4	G	8	0	1	0	8,125
Sister Vic	4	F	5	1	1	1	7,404	Sixtyone Margaux	4	F	4	1	0	1	31,050
Sister Vitalis	7	M	4	0	1	0	1,225	Siyah Bebo	4	G	10	0	1	0	3,165
Sister Whiz	2	F	7	0	0	1	4,739	Siyah's Lazer Beam	9	G	17	0	0	1	2,650
Sisterbull	8	M	15	1	3	0	13,483	Size Matters	4	G	8	2	0	2	61,634
Sisterlita	3	F	13	3	2	2	78,140	Sizzle'n' Sauce	3	F	10	0	0	0	2,210
Sisters Blackhawk	6	M	10	1	0	0	9,691	Sizzlin Cisco	5	G	10	2	0	2	4,378
Sisters Dream	5	M	3	1	0	0	5,798	Sizzlin Knickers	4	F	3	0	1	1	590
Sisters Wish	4	F	11	1	1	1	8,126	Sizzlin Mick	5	H	12	1	0	3	17,085
Sister's Word	5	G	12	0	0	1	1,126	Sizzling	5	G	4	0	0	1	1,750
Sistershag	3	F	2	0	0	0	67	Sizzling Dancer	2	C	2	0	0	0	185
Sisti's Pride	2	F	6	1	1	2	64,427	Sizzling Heat	5	H	9	1	1	1	12,435
Sisty Anne	4	F	7	2	1	0	36,587	Sizzling Kris	4	F	5	0	0	0	2,280
Sisu Ridge	5	M	7	0	0	1	844	Skagit	6	G	2	0	0	0	0
Sit Rep	3	G	1	0	0	0	500	Skaha Scooter	5	G	5	0	1	1	753
Sit Tight	3	F	11	1	2	1	11,298	Skake Em	5	G	10	0	1	0	10,896
Sita Ram	3	F	7	1	2	0	6,220	Skalite	4	G	11	0	0	5	6,331
Sitcom	3	C	4	1	1	0	29,160	Skally Wag	2	F	1	0	0	0	100
Site Alarm	2	G	8	0	2	1	6,965	Skamper	3	C	1	0	0	0	0
Sitkasam	3	G	4	0	0	0	980	Skandi Regent	5	G	1	0	0	0	0
Sittin On Ready	7	G	2	0	0	0	114	Skara Brae	3	F	1	0	0	0	0
Sittinonacloud	5	H	4	0	0	0	465	Skaramouche	7	G	2	0	0	0	570
Situation	3	F	3	0	0	0	402	Skary Karen	2	F	3	0	0	0	0
Sivam	4	F	8	2	1	2	22,210	Skate Away	4	G	15	2	5	1	170,890
Siward	5	G	13	8	2	2	34,768	Skater Dude	4	G	15	1	1	5	3,535
Six Am	5	H	8	2	1	1	12,063	Skattle	3	F	3	0	0	0	2,730
Six and a Half	8	H	4	0	0	0	868	Skava	4	F	6	0	0	1	1,139
Six Angry Men	6	H	7	0	0	1	981	Skaya	7	M	1	0	0	0	320
Six Away	3	F	2	1	0	0	5,100	Skeeder McGruder	8	G	2	0	0	0	119
Six Course Meal	7	G	3	0	0	0	2,530	Skeeman	5	G	20	6	4	3	45,892
Six Feathers	4	C	1	0	1	0	1,380	Skeemo	3	F	2	1	0	1	25,940
Six G's	4	G	5	1	0	0	11,840	Skeet	3	C	13	7	2	2	221,095
Six Halos	3	F	7	0	2	0	7,520	Skeet Shooter	7	G	2	0	1	0	1,800
Six Hitter	4	G	3	1	0	0	24,740	Skeeter Bite	5	G	5	0	0	0	0
Six Hour Wait	2	F	1	0	0	0	0	Skeeter Hawk Annie	4	F	8	1	1	3	12,195
Six Hundred	3	F	2	0	0	0	116	Skeeterbuzz	3	C	10	1	1	0	7,050
Six Inch Heels	5	M	8	1	0	0	2,123	Skeete's Bay	6	G	10	1	2	2	37,073
Six Jiggles	3	F	14	2	0	1	65,340	Skeptical Judge	4	C	3	0	0	0	137
Six Kings	3	G	8	1	0	0	7,183	Sketch	8	M	6	0	0	1	1,272
Six Months	3	G	1	0	0	0	0	Ski	4	G	2	0	0	0	134
Six Moon Dance	2	F	3	0	0	0	0	Ski Bowl	4	G	8	1	0	2	9,740
Six Numbers	3	C	12	1	3	1	76,820	Ski Breeze	3	F	5	0	1	1	3,560
Six Pac Aimee	7	M	8	0	0	0	0	Ski Bum	6	G	9	5	1	1	75,640
Six Pack Jack	10	G	8	0	0	0	436	Ski Hero	4	G	15	2	3	4	23,727
Six Pack Mike	5	H	15	0	0	2	1,871	Ski Lodge	2	C	3	1	1	0	15,600
Six Pack of Bud	3	C	12	3	0	1	14,313	Ski Song	3	F	1	0	0	0	520
Six Pack Sally	3	F	10	2	1	3	56,350	Ski the Bugaboos	4	G	14	3	2	1	19,375
Six Penny Lane	4	G	3	0	0	0	375	Ski Weather	5	H	1	0	0	0	53
Six Perfections (FR)	3	F	6	3	3	0	1,256,076	Ski Whiz	3	C	2	1	0	0	7,980
Six Point Eight	9	G	14	2	1	2	15,107	Skibabe	3	F	1	0	0	1	1,100
Six Red Rubys	5	M	13	1	1	1	6,730	Skid Boots	5	H	5	0	0	1	0
Six Sexy Sisters	2	F	2	2	0	0	140,218	Skid Row Express	3	C	8	1	1	0	8,030
Six Speed Grey	7	G	3	0	0	0	0	Skiddy	3	F	2	0	0	0	243
Six Straight Trics	6	M	9	0	2	1	10,480	Skide	3	F	1	0	0	0	220
Six Strings Down	4	F	8	2	4	0	7,175	Skiding	3	C	2	0	0	1	1,520
Six Tales	3	F	5	0	2	1	4,421	Skidipper	2	G	3	0	0	1	6,900
Six Thirty Wake Up	3	F	2	0	0	0	0	Skidoo	4	C	4	1	0	0	20,100
Six Trix	3	C	3	0	0	0	3,440	Skidsteer	6	M	6	0	1	1	1,872

Horse	Age	Sex	Sts	1st	2d	3d	Won	Horse	Age	Sex	Sts	1st	2d	3d	Won
Skier	3	C	11	0	0	0	1,420	Skipingo	6	H	1	0	0	0	0
Skier's Gift	3	G	3	1	1	0	42,480	Skipjack	5	G	2	0	0	0	0
Skifalett	10	M	6	0	2	1	15,612	Skipn Be Happy	9	M	5	0	0	0	1,670
Skiing Lamb	6	M	5	1	1	1	2,956	Skip'n Fool	3	F	3	1	0	0	13,515
Skill	5	G	14	4	1	2	25,240	Skip'n True	4	F	11	5	2	1	39,159
Skill Player	6	G	5	0	0	0	291	Skipper	2	G	4	1	2	0	11,700
Skill Prospect	4	G	7	1	0	0	4,692	Skipperess	2	F	5	0	0	0	1,755
Skillet	4	G	16	2	2	2	16,677	Skipper's Mate	3	F	4	0	0	0	2,790
Skillful Level	3	C	5	2	2	1	11,153	Skipper's Spirit	4	G	15	0	6	2	7,950
Skillful Royal Run	3	F	3	0	2	0	10,500	Skippers Wave	4	C	1	0	0	0	0
Skim Forever	4	F	10	0	0	1	4,256	Skipping North	3	F	9	1	3	1	21,400
Skimmer	3	F	3	0	0	2	960	Skipping School	2	F	4	0	1	0	2,050
Skin Deep	5	M	10	1	3	0	13,800	Skipping Stars	3	C	2	0	0	0	0
Skin Doctor	4	G	13	1	2	2	23,566	Skippingtomontana	3	F	15	0	1	3	41,000
Skinners Lane	2	G	3	0	1	0	2,545	Skippykeepswinning	2	C	3	0	0	0	305
Skinny Dipper	4	F	11	2	1	2	22,220	Skippy's Goldenboy	2	G	3	1	0	1	20,040
Skinnydippingtime	3	C	7	0	1	0	1,545	Skip's Best Girl	3	F	8	0	0	1	3,154
Skip a Dance	6	H	2	0	0	0	0	Skip's Fury	5	M	4	0	0	0	150
Skip a Dare	3	F	1	0	0	0	94	Skip's Last Quicky	3	F	10	2	0	1	7,723
Skip a Dee Doo Dah	2	C	2	0	0	0	2,970	Skip's Signal	3	C	4	0	0	0	2,638
Skip a Dream	9	H	4	1	0	1	3,008	Skip's Singer	5	M	8	2	2	0	22,482
Skip a Grade	6	G	8	0	0	4	22,620	Skip's Star	4	G	2	1	1	0	6,900
Skip a Nite	2	C	5	0	0	0	415	Skip's Trick	2	F	7	1	0	2	16,195
Skip a Page	5	G	10	1	2	3	32,610	Skipteaser	3	G	10	1	2	0	8,650
Skip a Payment	4	G	18	2	4	5	33,894	Skiptomloumydarlin	2	C	2	0	0	0	390
Skip Ahoy	5	H	6	0	0	1	1,950	Skiptothechase	3	F	8	0	0	0	760
Skip an Zip	3	C	3	0	0	0	0	Skiptothelou	3	F	4	0	1	1	1,875
Skip and Go	2	G	7	1	2	2	24,840	Skirl	7	H	10	0	1	1	1,934
Skip and Splash	4	F	1	0	0	0	0	Skirting the Issue	4	F	2	1	0	0	9,088
Skip Boldly	2	C	2	0	0	0	1,980	Skit	3	F	4	0	2	0	3,960
Skip Cat	3	C	8	0	2	2	5,910	Skokiaan	3	F	3	0	0	0	50
Skip Class	3	F	13	0	0	1	2,585	Skokie Dancer	4	F	7	1	0	0	4,429
Skip Command	2	F	4	0	0	1	2,140	Skol	11	G	10	2	2	0	12,071
Skip Court	2	C	7	2	3	1	43,020	Skooch	2	G	1	0	0	0	130
Skip Dessert	3	F	2	0	0	0	0	Skoogiedogood	4	F	3	1	0	0	6,125
Skip In	7	M	17	4	3	2	30,090	Skookum Pass	3	G	11	5	2	0	30,090
Skip Is Classy	2	C	1	0	0	0	0	Skoor	3	F	17	2	3	0	19,445
Skip It	2	C	1	0	0	0	195	Skooter's Drone	5	G	8	0	1	0	2,814
Skip N Bail	4	C	2	0	0	0	224	Skor Big	4	F	1	0	0	1	3,080
Skip n' Jump	2	C	3	0	2	0	4,820	Skorch	4	F	2	0	0	0	979
Skip On	6	G	9	1	0	1	7,720	Skorch Two	3	F	16	2	0	2	33,356
Skip On Ice	3	F	7	0	0	0	315	Skrate	3	F	6	1	1	0	24,350
Skip On Water	3	G	12	2	2	1	20,260	Sky Blew	5	M	5	1	0	1	5,695
Skip Over Clover	3	G	5	0	0	0	575	Sky Blue Bid	3	G	2	0	0	0	0
Skip Over Finish	4	G	7	1	0	1	10,712	Sky Calling	2	C	2	0	0	0	390
Skip Past	2	C	9	2	2	0	43,760	Sky Can Fly	5	M	2	0	0	0	0
Skip Poker	2	F	4	1	1	0	21,570	Sky Canyon	8	G	18	1	4	1	10,801
Skip Queen	3	F	5	1	1	0	39,200	Sky Chariot	7	G	1	0	0	0	8,734
Skip School	2	F	7	1	0	0	5,040	Sky Cover	5	M	8	1	3	0	66,360
Skip Skip	5	H	1	0	0	0	0	Sky Deputy	6	G	8	1	2	1	43,990
Skip Son	2	C	2	0	0	0	710	Sky Diamond	3	C	1	0	0	0	0
Skip Telbin	3	C	7	0	0	2	4,730	Sky Diver	6	G	8	4	2	0	82,463
Skip the Blues	2	F	5	0	1	1	4,070	Sky Dreams	2	F	1	0	0	0	1,780
Skip the Country	4	G	3	0	0	0	386	Sky Dweller	6	H	3	1	0	0	4,200
Skip the Dessert	5	H	1	0	0	0	110	Sky Encounter	4	C	7	1	2	0	6,200
Skip the Fuss	3	F	7	1	1	0	8,298	Sky Eyes	7	H	10	0	0	1	2,626
Skip the Party	8	G	8	0	1	0	2,147	Sky Forever	5	G	5	0	0	0	750
Skip the Print	5	M	5	2	2	0	83,860	Sky Gal	5	M	4	1	0	0	10,639
Skip the Promise	2	F	2	0	0	0	0	Sky Girl	5	M	19	0	0	0	2,160
Skip the Sale	4	F	13	3	1	3	24,256	Sky Hunter	5	G	6	0	2	0	22,058
Skip to Mizzou	2	C	4	0	0	0	0	Sky Jack	7	G	3	2	0	0	185,860
Skip to My Lucy	3	F	2	0	2	0	4,520	Sky Jiving	5	M	12	0	0	0	564
Skip to My Que	4	F	4	0	0	0	0	Sky Legacy	6	G	12	2	0	2	11,225
Skip to Savannah	5	M	12	2	3	5	45,828	Sky Lynn	3	F	5	0	0	0	734
Skip to the Beat	3	G	9	1	0	0	9,186	Sky Masterson	4	G	6	1	0	1	12,712
Skip to the Blues	5	G	9	1	1	2	13,023	Sky Mesa	3	C	3	0	1	1	216,500
Skip to the Stone	5	H	5	1	0	2	64,613	Sky Missile	2	C	9	0	1	5	16,245
Skip to Victory	2	F	1	0	0	0	0	Sky Mist	6	M	6	0	0	1	550
Skip Town	7	M	13	2	1	2	11,486	Sky of Gold	5	G	13	2	2	2	45,020
Skip Trial Miss	6	M	20	3	2	3	45,149	Sky Passport	2	F	1	0	0	0	373
Skip Vigorously	3	G	6	0	1	2	14,920	Sky Power	3	F	3	0	0	0	85
Skip With Julie	3	F	1	0	0	0	700	Sky Raise	6	G	5	1	0	0	6,478
Skip Wonder	4	C	2	0	0	0	144	Sky Ravenal	5	M	8	1	1	1	20,300
Skipage	3	G	5	2	0	1	14,578	Sky Reality	3	F	8	1	5	1	31,920
Skipamiss	3	F	7	1	1	0	36,485	Sky Ridge Dancer	4	F	15	1	1	1	3,847
Skipanote	3	F	2	0	0	0	1,000	Sky Search	4	G	13	0	0	0	704
Skipaslew	2	C	7	3	0	2	111,100	Sky Shadow	4	C	2	0	0	0	30
Skipats Star	8	M	11	1	0	1	8,680	Sky Soldier	3	C	5	3	0	0	84,000
Skiperoo	3	G	12	1	4	2	53,470	Sky Sprite	4	F	1	0	0	0	120

Horse	Age	Sex	Sts	1st	2d	3d	Won
Sky Strider	8	G	6	0	1	3	10,230
Sky Stutz	3	G	7	1	1	0	6,410
Sky Tern	6	H	1	0	0	0	0
Sky Terrace	4	C	2	0	0	0	1,515
Sky Tower	5	H	9	1	0	1	9,580
Sky Tracker	2	C	10	0	0	2	8,142
Sky Trick	7	G	13	1	1	0	10,035
Sky Valley Knight	8	M	1	0	0	0	0
Sky Wad	2	F	2	0	0	0	472
Sky Wars	5	G	7	1	0	1	4,043
Sky Wolf	2	C	2	0	0	0	230
Skybar	4	F	4	0	0	0	155
Skybound	9	G	10	0	2	1	6,662
Skyco	6	H	5	0	0	0	631
Skycrossing	3	C	4	2	1	0	44,070
Skydive	2	C	1	0	0	0	0
Skye Command	6	M	1	0	1	0	1,540
Skye's Lil Blazer	3	F	5	1	0	0	3,466
Skyey	3	G	1	0	0	0	100
Skykomish Slew	10	M	3	0	0	0	0
Skyladysky	2	F	1	1	0	0	11,400
Skyladywalker	4	F	7	1	2	0	23,806
Skylar May	7	M	10	1	1	2	13,208
Skylar's Daddy	2	C	3	1	0	0	5,285
Skyline	5	M	11	1	1	1	15,193
Skyline Band	4	G	12	2	4	1	40,385
Skylist	2	F	1	0	0	0	0
Skylord	4	C	13	0	0	2	1,954
Skymaster	4	G	9	2	1	1	49,060
Skyote	3	G	2	0	0	0	0
Skypirate	6	H	1	0	0	0	0
Skyrider	2	G	2	1	0	1	11,490
Skyridge Echo	7	M	4	0	0	0	950
Skyrocket	3	F	6	0	0	0	0
Skyrunner	6	H	6	1	0	0	7,485
Skys Bold Princess	4	F	8	2	2	2	15,162
Sky's Comet	4	F	14	3	1	0	23,968
Sky's the Tops	6	G	13	2	2	2	9,637
Skysail	4	F	2	0	0	0	480
Skysmoke	6	G	11	2	0	0	5,298
Skytech Missy	3	F	13	1	0	1	8,518
Skyview Scanner	4	F	1	1	0	0	4,380
Skywalker Red	3	G	11	0	5	3	71,320
Skywalking Babe	4	F	1	0	0	0	0
Skyward Rose	6	G	3	0	1	0	3,366
Slab Granite	3	G	8	1	1	0	10,940
Slabig	3	C	3	1	1	0	16,320
Slack Cat	2	C	2	0	0	0	205
Slade	2	C	5	0	1	2	13,570
Slade Runner	2	G	3	0	2	0	4,180
Slade's Bayou	4	F	13	3	2	2	25,754
Slade's Dancer	3	F	4	0	0	0	0
Sladybar	2	C	2	0	0	0	225
Slam Bam	3	C	4	1	1	1	28,500
Slam Dancing	2	F	2	0	0	0	780
Slam Inn	3	F	7	1	0	0	7,140
Slamat	5	G	21	2	4	4	15,388
Slamdancer	5	M	4	1	0	0	35,342
Slamma	3	F	4	1	0	0	7,140
Slammajamma	6	H	3	0	0	0	570
Slammeinthedust	8	M	7	0	0	1	2,778
Slammer	4	G	7	0	0	0	1,982
Slammers Last	2	C	2	0	0	0	521
Slammin' Lil	3	F	10	2	1	0	51,129
Slammin Sammy	7	G	4	0	0	2	3,488
Slammin' Slew	4	G	7	1	0	1	8,231
Slamminjamminjewel	3	F	4	0	0	1	825
Slang	4	C	4	0	0	0	308
Slapshot Dom	3	G	7	1	1	1	37,586
Slapshot Joey	5	G	2	0	0	0	204
Slash Dot Com	5	G	12	2	2	2	17,155
Slash N Bash	3	G	3	1	1	0	47,040
Slashback	2	C	6	1	0	0	10,080
Slatin N Lace	4	F	11	2	3	1	14,002
Slaughter and Run	6	M	14	1	1	1	8,586
Slave Driver	4	G	8	1	0	0	6,090
Slavic Turn	3	F	4	0	0	0	264
Slavic Wind	3	F	13	1	0	2	16,252
Slawn Cheh	3	F	6	1	2	0	23,410
Slay Ride	2	G	3	0	0	1	2,340
Slay the Bear	4	G	5	1	0	2	8,224
Sledge	4	C	8	2	1	1	45,698
Sledge Hammer	9	G	3	0	0	0	410
Sleek and Powerful	2	F	7	1	0	1	32,612
Sleek Dame	3	F	5	0	0	0	5,348
Sleep Away	3	F	16	2	6	2	42,730
Sleep It Off	3	F	4	0	0	0	0
Sleep Till Noon	7	G	6	0	0	0	326
Sleep Time	4	F	2	0	0	0	171
Sleeping Around	6	M	9	1	4	1	11,978
Sleeping Potion	4	G	5	1	1	0	31,560
Sleeping Tiger	6	G	12	1	1	1	5,619
Sleepover Bandit	3	G	3	0	2	1	30,906
Sleepy Dale	3	C	8	0	2	2	2,603
Sleepy Sky	3	G	6	0	0	1	3,395
Sleet Chief	3	C	6	0	0	0	0
Sleet Rod	2	G	4	0	0	1	2,805
Sleetwood Mac	6	G	5	1	2	0	17,069
Sleety	5	M	14	3	2	3	30,161
Sleeve Target	3	G	11	0	1	3	6,977
Sleezianna	3	F	9	0	0	0	767
Sleight	7	G	15	2	2	1	28,805
Sleight of Hand	3	F	5	0	1	1	7,360
Slentz's Prince	2	G	3	0	1	1	4,650
Slerps M and M	4	F	3	1	0	0	3,023
Slerpy Slew	3	C	9	0	1	1	740
Slerpy Water	3	G	9	2	3	1	15,694
Sleuthing	3	C	13	2	2	0	29,754
Slew Akoa	4	G	5	0	0	0	373
Slew Alta	2	F	1	0	0	0	515
Slew and a Half	3	G	7	0	1	0	1,586
Slew Angel	3	F	2	0	0	0	200
Slew Ann	6	M	11	6	1	0	71,172
Slew Brewed	6	G	5	0	0	2	1,431
Slew Buck	3	G	7	1	2	1	13,200
Slew Can Go	9	G	17	1	2	1	9,726
Slew Check	4	G	10	1	2	0	11,049
Slew City Charmer	5	H	8	1	2	1	11,120
Slew City Citadel	3	C	7	2	0	2	109,944
Slew City Dancer	3	F	4	1	1	0	13,120
Slew City Express	2	C	6	0	2	1	6,832
Slew City Jay	7	G	12	0	1	0	1,984
Slew City Knight	7	G	2	0	0	0	750
Slew City Lily	4	F	5	0	0	0	7,742
Slew City Mike	2	G	3	1	0	0	17,280
Slew City Miss	4	F	3	0	0	0	0
Slew City Scooter	3	F	3	0	0	0	0
Slew de Do	3	G	3	0	0	0	300
Slew Dejavu	3	F	3	0	0	0	0
Slew Deputy	3	F	2	0	0	1	4,270
Slew Design	7	G	5	1	2	0	2,794
Slew d'Or	3	F	4	2	0	1	20,360
Slew Drummer	5	M	14	1	0	6	4,321
Slew Falls	3	F	4	0	0	1	510
Slew Feliou	6	M	7	0	0	2	1,801
Slew Gulch	7	H	11	1	3	3	30,216
Slew Harpoon	4	C	3	0	0	1	220
Slew Has a Message	5	G	13	1	2	1	14,593
Slew Hunter	3	C	6	1	0	1	9,148
Slew In	2	C	5	1	1	1	10,920
Slew in the Face	7	G	15	2	4	2	12,473
Slew in Time	3	C	3	0	0	0	880
Slew Is King	3	G	10	3	0	3	38,791
Slew Leader	6	H	1	0	0	0	0
Slew Marshal (ARG)	5	H	14	2	5	3	78,360
Slew Meadow	2	F	1	0	0	0	0
Slew My Way	6	M	7	2	0	1	5,386
Slew o' Aces	7	G	4	0	0	0	288
Slew o' Asti	5	G	14	1	1	1	5,304
Slew o' Chances	3	F	1	0	0	0	0
Slew o' Rhythm	7	G	10	1	2	2	9,395
Slew of Grace	3	F	3	0	0	0	627
Slew of Jones	2	F	10	0	2	1	19,720
Slew of Lovers	2	F	2	0	0	0	70
Slew of Memories	3	C	8	1	0	4	21,130
Slew of the Night	4	G	3	1	1	0	55,000
Slew of the West	4	G	7	0	0	0	938
Slew of Tricks	5	M	3	0	0	0	293

RECORDS OF HORSES

Horse	Age	Sex	Sts	1st	2d	3d	Won
Slew On Fire	4	G	5	0	0	0	300
Slew On Slew	3	C	1	0	0	0	0
Slew Pointe	2	F	2	0	0	0	3,528
Slew Prized	7	M	15	1	6	2	16,564
Slew Reckoning	4	G	4	0	0	0	686
Slew Roots	7	G	18	2	3	3	9,924
Slew Rouge	3	G	8	1	1	1	11,830
Slew Royal	4	G	10	2	1	1	12,373
Slew Sally Slew	4	F	8	0	1	2	5,775
Slew Shaq	3	C	7	0	0	0	7,560
Slew Shine	2	C	5	1	0	0	19,518
Slew Six	5	H	7	2	3	0	6,011
Slew Slayer	2	C	2	0	1	1	3,090
Slew Stew	5	G	13	3	1	2	36,595
Slew Summer	6	M	8	1	3	0	24,760
Slew the Cat	4	F	10	0	2	0	1,837
Slew the City	4	G	15	4	1	2	13,892
Slew the Enemy	3	G	8	2	0	1	12,250
Slew the Fools	6	G	7	1	0	0	7,620
Slew the Monster	3	C	4	2	1	0	36,210
Slew the Nurse	4	F	11	1	2	1	6,848
Slew the Red	6	H	2	1	1	0	84,800
Slew Tin Tin	2	G	7	0	2	0	14,003
Slew to Siren	4	F	12	1	0	1	20,354
Slew to the Mint	4	G	2	0	0	0	938
Slew Valley	6	H	9	0	1	3	186,880
Slew Walker	4	G	7	1	2	0	2,446
Slewability	6	M	6	3	1	1	100,387
Slewacharms	3	F	4	0	0	0	0
Slewadora	4	F	7	1	1	2	9,793
Slewafun	3	G	5	0	0	0	0
Slewanna	5	M	8	1	1	1	29,076
Slewannavan	6	M	6	2	1	0	36,832
Slewanracey	3	F	8	0	0	1	2,570
Slewarama	6	M	6	2	0	1	9,848
Slewaway	2	G	9	2	0	3	13,560
Slewbacca	3	C	16	3	1	2	7,253
Slewby Do Be Do	3	F	6	1	0	0	2,920
Slewcidal	5	G	7	0	0	2	1,895
Slewd On Key	5	M	10	1	2	3	12,433
Slewdario	5	H	7	2	1	1	36,850
Slewdecides	6	M	9	0	1	0	1,794
Slewdiano	6	M	2	0	0	0	0
Slewdledude	3	G	2	0	0	1	2,590
Slewdle's Promise	3	F	14	1	3	3	27,562
Slewdorado	7	G	13	1	3	0	4,832
Slewds Sox	3	C	1	0	0	0	0
Slew'em and Run	3	G	12	1	0	1	19,406
Slewer Than You	10	G	2	0	0	0	130
Slewgiana	3	F	10	2	3	0	48,900
Slewgun	2	F	3	0	0	0	0
Slewicide Cruise	3	G	6	1	1	0	10,290
Slewinthespirit	5	M	13	0	0	1	1,257
Slewita	5	M	8	0	0	1	1,189
Slewium	3	F	1	0	0	0	0
Slewkowitz	5	H	1	0	0	0	33
Slewlee Ridge	5	M	11	2	0	0	6,941
Slewmagoo	6	G	6	0	0	1	728
Slewofhonor	3	F	8	1	3	2	28,525
Slewofintegrity	4	F	10	0	3	0	3,660
Slewp'a Doop	9	G	6	0	0	0	2,480
Slewper Sport	3	G	5	0	0	1	735
Slewpercat	3	G	6	0	0	2	4,144
Slewping	4	G	2	0	0	0	0
Slewplomacy	6	M	3	0	0	0	175
Slewpy B Fast	3	F	11	1	1	3	6,658
Slewpy Come Home	3	G	3	1	0	0	14,120
Slewpy Ruckus	3	G	6	1	1	0	22,512
Slewpy Time	4	F	8	1	0	0	13,829
Slewpy Time Gal	3	F	7	0	1	0	3,220
Slewpyana	4	F	2	1	0	1	15,600
Slewpy's Charm	4	F	7	1	3	0	10,990
Slewpy's Gold	6	G	4	0	2	0	5,426
Slewpy's Storm	2	F	2	1	0	0	13,640
Slewreen	7	M	7	1	0	0	6,238
Slewrue	3	F	15	2	0	1	25,412
Slew's Alibi	4	G	6	4	1	1	13,003
Slews Blitz	2	C	2	0	0	0	72
Slew's Bold Frank	4	G	7	1	0	2	4,652

Horse	Age	Sex	Sts	1st	2d	3d	Won
Slew's Bronze	4	G	7	1	0	0	5,687
Slew's Carousel	4	G	7	1	2	0	25,120
Slew's Cateringtoo	3	F	12	1	1	3	11,065
Slews Child	4	G	11	0	2	4	30,689
Slews Date	3	G	8	0	2	0	934
Slews Deputy Doll	6	M	4	0	0	0	305
Slew's Double Ego	6	G	19	1	2	3	5,075
Slews Final Answer	4	F	5	1	1	1	89,820
Slew's Fyre	5	H	1	0	0	0	0
Slews Gem	3	F	14	2	0	3	12,571
Slew's Ha Ha	3	G	12	1	3	0	18,283
Slews in Demand	2	F	2	0	1	0	1,900
Slews Inheritance	4	F	4	0	0	0	464
Slews Jackpot	6	G	3	0	1	0	685
Slew's Jewel	3	F	1	0	0	0	1,275
Slew's Lil Emerald	4	F	1	0	0	0	0
Slews Mistress	3	F	18	1	1	1	8,535
Slews Moment	3	F	5	1	1	0	8,450
Slew's Mystery	2	F	3	0	0	1	5,727
Slews' Mystic Echo	5	H	7	0	0	0	801
Slews On First	4	G	10	0	1	0	831
Slew's Pot of Gold	4	C	3	1	0	0	15,540
Slew's Prince	3	C	9	1	3	2	74,264
Slew's Prospector	4	G	2	0	0	0	1,080
Slew's Pyramid	3	F	8	1	0	0	2,530
Slews Resurrection	4	G	10	3	4	0	53,021
Slew's Right	8	G	11	2	1	4	4,746
Slew's Smile	6	G	11	1	0	0	19,971
Slew's Sparkle	3	F	4	0	0	0	1,420
Slew's Temper	3	G	5	0	0	0	910
Slews Thunder	4	G	6	0	0	0	473
Slew's Treasure	6	M	16	2	1	2	7,179
Slew's Warrior	5	H	4	0	0	0	0
Slewsgotthisdancer	5	G	8	0	1	0	1,639
Slewsilverbullet	3	F	6	1	1	1	20,327
Slewspree	7	M	14	0	0	0	1,138
Slewssurelucky	2	C	6	1	2	0	10,724
Slewston	5	G	3	0	0	0	7,200
Slewsydneyslew	3	F	10	2	4	1	15,997
Slewth Slayer	4	C	5	0	0	0	2,395
Slewtheboat	4	F	15	3	2	0	33,876
Slewz Q	4	F	12	3	0	2	34,455
Slewzo	4	G	6	1	0	0	3,191
Slewzuma Weave	3	F	2	0	0	0	0
Slewzy Floozy	4	F	20	6	1	2	63,412
Slice of Heaven	4	F	6	0	0	0	602
Slice of Light	9	G	4	0	0	0	310
Slice'er Dice'er	3	F	1	0	0	0	79
Sliceotrouble	6	M	16	1	2	0	15,269
Slick Advocator	5	G	10	0	1	2	4,306
Slick as Sleet	4	G	4	2	0	0	74,460
Slick as Slew	3	C	2	1	0	0	15,625
Slick Debbie	4	F	9	1	1	4	31,333
Slick Decision	7	G	10	1	1	4	6,471
Slick Kat Daddy	3	G	10	0	0	0	879
Slick Punch	3	F	6	2	0	2	46,960
Slick Sand	4	G	8	0	3	0	3,206
Slick Shadow	3	G	14	3	2	0	21,564
Slick Speed	6	H	1	0	0	0	0
Slick Vick	5	G	7	0	0	0	1,350
Slick Zap	9	G	9	0	0	0	0
Slicker Than Sleet	4	G	9	0	1	0	3,130
Slick's Lil Sister	4	F	7	3	1	1	51,756
Slicksonnylane	12	G	1	0	0	0	0
Slickster Nickster	5	G	10	3	2	2	16,376
Slide Red Slide	5	M	4	0	0	0	632
Slide to Glory	5	M	11	2	1	2	48,261
Slider	5	G	9	3	2	1	176,240
Sliding Home	2	C	2	0	0	1	6,330
Slight K. O's	4	F	15	1	0	0	7,404
Slightly Gold	4	F	10	1	3	0	7,214
Slightlymorelikely	2	F	4	2	1	0	112,730
Sligo Bay (IRE)	5	H	1	0	1	0	20,000
Sligo Creek	6	G	5	1	3	1	9,716
Sligo Jim	7	G	8	0	1	1	1,652
Slik Kris	2	G	3	0	0	0	1,392
Slim Dusty	4	G	12	2	0	0	80,578
Slimey Garfunkle	2	G	2	1	0	0	7,320
Slim's Secret	4	F	10	4	0	1	21,821

Horse	Age	Sex	Sts	1st	2d	3d	Won
Slims Song	5	M	8	2	2	1	11,914
Sling Shot	2	C	3	1	0	1	22,285
Slinger Woods	4	G	9	0	0	0	1,602
Slingo Man	5	G	19	1	3	1	14,525
Slinkin	2	F	1	0	0	0	350
Slip Me a Buck	5	G	2	0	0	0	326
Slip Me the Key	4	C	4	0	1	0	2,106
Slip N Dazzle	3	F	8	0	0	1	1,236
Slip On Back	5	G	2	0	0	0	0
Slip Side	3	C	1	0	0	0	0
Slipper Slew	5	M	10	0	0	0	6,209
Slippery Fool	3	G	14	2	2	1	16,533
Slippery Gator	4	C	7	0	2	0	11,246
Slippery When Bet	5	G	4	0	1	0	29,604
Slippin Sam	3	G	1	0	0	0	0
Slipping	6	M	3	0	0	0	5,320
Slipshoe	4	F	10	1	1	0	19,050
Slipstich	6	M	18	1	2	1	11,035
Slipthejab	4	F	12	1	2	3	24,839
Slitherin	2	C	2	0	1	0	3,280
Slo Gin Jack	4	C	1	0	0	0	340
Sloan	6	M	2	0	0	0	179
Sloansbelmontbreez	4	G	16	0	2	2	6,015
Slogan	4	G	11	2	1	0	16,900
Sloppy Joe	8	G	8	0	0	1	749
Slot Girl	4	F	6	1	1	0	23,407
Slot Happy	5	M	14	6	1	0	88,126
Slot Machine Jean	3	F	10	2	0	0	42,458
Slots Imp	6	M	3	0	0	0	260
Slotsarun	6	H	11	1	2	1	6,259
Slouisiana Lew	4	G	5	0	0	0	420
Slow and Steady	2	F	2	0	2	0	10,500
Slow Go	4	G	8	1	0	0	4,946
Slow Heat	6	G	9	0	2	2	2,555
Slow N Easy	2	G	1	0	0	0	0
Slow Signal	3	C	1	0	0	0	0
Slow Time	3	G	2	0	0	0	0
Slow Walkin' John	2	G	2	1	0	0	20,930
Slowboat to China	5	M	7	1	0	1	5,510
Slowfuses Bestboy	5	G	5	0	0	1	841
Slumber Party	3	F	3	0	0	1	4,477
Sly Buck	6	G	10	0	1	2	3,377
Sly Butterfly	4	F	8	2	2	0	72,972
Sly Chick	4	F	9	0	1	1	3,411
Sly Doc	3	G	1	0	0	0	0
Sly Grin	4	G	13	3	2	2	80,660
Sly Guy	3	G	16	1	0	1	6,604
Sly Guy's Up	4	G	7	0	2	0	7,853
Sly Irishman	3	G	7	0	0	1	1,773
Sly Lady	4	F	5	4	0	0	102,300
Sly Rascal	3	G	3	0	1	0	2,670
Sly Ruby	4	F	1	0	0	0	0
Sly Schemes	6	G	3	0	0	0	0
Sly Secrets	3	F	7	1	2	2	28,100
Sly Style	4	G	18	1	3	4	43,005
Sly Truth	4	G	9	1	2	2	15,945
Sly Wolf	4	G	4	0	0	0	2,104
Slyght Choice	4	G	2	0	0	0	558
Slypslydnaway	4	F	12	0	2	2	12,735
Slywalker	4	G	15	1	5	0	27,589
Smackincatz	4	G	12	2	1	1	12,036
Smackle	4	C	4	2	1	0	29,187
Small Bat Slew (ARG)	5	G	2	0	0	1	472
Small But Sweet	5	M	3	0	0	0	137
Small Call	7	G	9	0	2	0	3,246
Small Charger	3	G	8	0	0	1	1,430
Small Connection	2	F	1	0	0	0	0
Small Country	3	F	4	1	0	1	7,690
Small Promises	5	M	8	0	1	5	93,850
Small Town Girl	3	F	2	1	0	0	28,800
Small Town Gossip	4	C	3	0	0	0	173
Small Town Guy	2	C	3	0	1	0	1,924
Small Town Queen	3	F	8	1	1	0	1,564
Smalltown Slew	2	G	3	1	1	0	9,500
Smallville	2	C	1	0	0	0	0
Smart Admiral	7	G	1	0	0	0	240
Smart Again	3	C	6	1	1	2	51,820
Smart Agenda	4	C	3	0	0	0	0
Smart Albert	4	C	1	0	0	0	0
Smart Alert	7	H	7	0	0	1	5,221
Smart Alix	3	F	6	0	0	0	479
Smart Ana	4	F	1	0	0	0	1,050
Smart And Regal	12	G	1	0	0	0	0
Smart and Royal	6	H	4	1	0	0	7,580
Smart Angel	3	F	4	0	1	0	26,215
Smart Appeal	3	F	8	2	0	1	10,434
Smart Ascot	9	G	2	0	0	0	732
Smart Babe	2	F	1	0	0	0	690
Smart Baby	3	F	4	0	0	0	500
Smart Caller	2	F	11	2	5	1	42,110
Smart Choice	4	F	2	0	0	0	0
Smart Cid	6	G	9	2	0	4	16,375
Smart Confidence	2	G	15	2	1	4	26,625
Smart Coup	4	G	7	1	2	0	45,446
Smart Dare	5	M	13	0	2	2	5,217
Smart Date	2	G	2	0	0	0	360
Smart Devil	3	F	2	0	0	0	860
Smart Doc	5	H	5	0	2	0	5,560
Smart Doll	4	F	12	0	2	4	8,155
Smart Drive	4	C	6	0	0	0	879
Smart Figure	10	G	4	1	1	1	3,972
Smart Fire	2	C	1	0	0	0	100
Smart Gal's Halo	5	G	13	1	2	2	15,870
Smart Grace	4	F	11	1	1	0	31,950
Smart Graustark	13	H	9	0	2	0	4,160
Smart in Art	8	G	9	0	0	2	9,675
Smart Jenna	3	F	11	2	0	1	13,263
Smart Jet	4	F	9	1	1	0	3,306
Smart Juliet	3	F	8	3	2	0	69,564
Smart King	2	G	4	0	0	0	525
Smart Kitty	3	F	13	1	3	3	18,741
Smart Lacy	4	F	4	1	0	1	126,860
Smart Link	2	F	6	1	2	1	24,870
Smart Lovin'	2	F	2	0	0	1	2,880
Smart Mail	4	F	17	4	6	3	44,195
Smart Man	5	H	2	0	0	0	106
Smart n' Char	7	M	3	1	1	0	5,980
Smart N Classy	3	F	12	2	3	1	82,600
Smart 'n' Keen	4	C	1	0	0	0	0
Smart N Plasant	2	C	11	1	2	1	18,080
Smart N Polished	5	M	5	0	1	0	2,070
Smart N Sassy	4	F	3	0	0	1	2,963
Smart N Smooth	4	F	8	4	1	1	66,690
Smart October	4	G	5	2	2	0	41,400
Smart Ole Jackie	3	F	15	3	3	1	18,125
Smart Player	3	G	14	1	2	1	15,630
Smart Press	4	C	5	0	1	1	2,940
Smart Prospect	4	G	11	2	3	0	64,301
Smart Pursuit	5	M	7	2	0	0	21,077
Smart Regent	3	G	5	0	0	2	2,570
Smart Ring	7	G	11	0	3	4	18,260
Smart Score	4	C	5	2	0	0	38,377
Smart Serve	2	F	3	1	0	0	45,000
Smart Set	6	G	6	2	1	0	7,060
Smart Slew	3	G	5	1	0	2	6,110
Smart Sunny	10	G	3	0	1	2	9,895
Smart Swede	3	G	3	0	0	0	355
Smart Tale	3	G	10	1	3	2	16,486
Smart Tap	4	C	8	1	2	0	45,390
Smart too Late	6	G	7	1	0	2	10,870
Smart Wager	3	C	8	0	1	1	1,353
Smart Wiesen	3	G	1	0	0	0	0
Smartee	3	F	8	3	0	0	37,980
Smarten Up	10	H	4	0	0	1	790
Smarter Than Kris	4	C	5	0	0	1	1,540
Smarterthanallofya	3	F	2	0	0	0	810
Smartexcess	4	C	6	3	1	0	22,014
Smartie Britches	2	C	1	0	0	0	0
Smartlee Away	2	F	4	0	0	2	22,180
Smartly Suited	5	H	4	0	0	0	1,100
Smarts	3	F	15	2	4	2	14,703
Smarty Jones	2	C	2	2	0	0	49,620
Smarty's Money	3	F	14	1	3	4	24,153
Smash Hit	2	F	4	1	0	1	32,660
Smash Review	6	M	3	0	1	0	4,590
Smashed	4	F	10	1	3	0	12,293
Smashin Man	5	G	7	0	0	0	0
Smashing Beau	5	G	12	3	3	1	116,880

RECORDS OF HORSES

Horse	Age	Sex	Sts	1st	2d	3d	Won	Horse	Age	Sex	Sts	1st	2d	3d	Won
Smashing Brass	3	F	22	3	5	1	37,135	Smoken Shooter	3	C	8	3	2	0	69,340
Smashing Gail	3	F	1	0	0	0	0	Smoken Smoke	2	C	1	0	1	0	5,400
Smashing Pride	4	G	14	0	2	2	6,825	Smoken Winner	3	C	6	0	1	1	8,246
Smee	3	F	6	1	0	3	12,741	Smoker	3	G	5	1	0	1	19,680
Smell My Smoke	2	C	5	0	0	0	0	Smokers Delight	4	F	4	0	0	2	1,665
Smellinlikearose	4	F	7	1	1	1	10,860	Smoke's Bounty	4	G	2	1	0	0	11,075
Smell's a Winner	3	F	8	1	2	1	35,470	Smokester Horizon	2	F	6	0	1	0	3,226
Smells Girl	5	M	7	0	0	0	844	Smokester's Dance	5	G	15	2	2	3	16,571
Smelly Baby	3	F	2	0	0	0	0	Smokesters High	4	F	10	1	2	1	7,565
Smelly Mountain	3	C	17	1	5	2	15,047	Smokester's Knight	4	G	8	0	2	1	9,986
Smila Fawin	3	F	1	0	0	0	35	Smokesters O	3	G	7	2	2	2	12,955
Smile Again	8	H	5	0	0	0	1,170	Smokester's Pride	3	F	5	0	2	0	4,350
Smile as I Go By	6	H	7	0	2	0	3,851	Smokette	3	F	3	0	2	0	7,200
Smile Away	3	G	1	0	1	0	2,000	Smokeumifyougotem	4	F	8	0	2	1	23,590
Smile Dinners Here	2	C	3	0	0	1	3,220	Smokeville	6	G	14	2	6	1	39,565
Smile for a Buck	4	F	8	2	0	2	12,816	Smokey Blue	3	F	2	1	0	0	31,800
Smile for Love	3	F	5	1	0	1	25,940	Smokey Boy	3	C	9	1	0	1	13,545
Smile in Style	5	G	4	0	0	0	309	Smokey Busted	3	G	10	0	2	0	3,588
Smile Maker	2	F	1	0	0	0	0	Smokey Day	3	F	6	0	1	3	9,754
Smile My Lord	5	H	7	0	2	0	15,700	Smokey Diamond	3	F	9	1	1	1	37,395
Smile N Carson	2	C	4	1	0	0	9,530	Smokey Dreams	4	F	13	2	2	2	17,306
Smile n Wildcat	4	G	5	0	1	2	21,600	Smokey Glacken	2	F	4	3	0	1	140,820
Smile Pretty	3	F	14	2	2	1	16,380	Smokey John	7	H	7	0	0	0	398
Smile Smile Smile	4	C	1	0	0	0	0	Smokey On a Roll	5	G	7	0	0	0	543
Smileathebigdance	7	M	2	0	0	0	155	Smokey Session	4	G	10	0	1	3	11,727
Smiles Are Free	4	G	4	1	0	0	11,633	Smokey Springs	5	G	9	1	0	2	15,841
Smilesallaround	4	C	9	1	2	1	16,805	Smokey Way	11	G	6	1	2	0	2,525
Smilewithpleasure	3	C	2	0	0	0	330	Smokey's Jazz	2	C	1	0	0	0	750
Smiley Eh	5	G	16	1	3	5	13,583	Smokie	5	G	16	0	3	1	32,770
Smiley Face	3	F	9	2	0	3	26,775	Smokieisabandit	4	C	7	5	1	0	54,580
Smileyberg	7	G	17	2	0	2	20,055	Smokin Affair	5	M	8	1	1	2	3,875
Smileytime	5	G	12	1	3	2	25,600	Smokin Barkies	3	G	9	1	2	1	14,638
Smilin' Ali	4	F	14	3	4	3	24,164	Smokin' Blitz	3	C	3	0	0	0	0
Smilin' Baby	6	M	6	0	0	0	2,606	Smokin Brave	4	G	13	1	2	3	9,654
Smilin' Coyote	7	M	2	0	0	0	330	Smokin City Sue	3	F	9	0	1	1	3,367
Smilin' Kitten	5	M	1	0	0	0	0	Smokin Devil	4	G	16	1	2	1	12,780
Smilin' Minster	3	F	6	1	0	1	9,185	Smokin Dust	6	G	12	1	1	3	10,415
Smilin' Slew	7	G	15	1	5	4	81,514	Smokin Flo	7	M	6	0	0	0	225
Smilin Susan	3	F	12	1	4	1	31,795	Smokin' Forty Five	2	C	3	0	0	1	2,980
Smilin' Tom	3	C	5	1	1	2	12,684	Smokin' Forty Won	4	C	5	2	0	0	30,996
Smiling Betsy	2	F	5	0	1	0	3,060	Smokin' Freddy	4	G	4	1	0	1	2,506
Smiling Bob	6	G	1	0	0	0	115	Smokin Ghost	3	F	4	0	0	0	75
Smiling Eyes	3	F	1	0	1	0	9,600	Smokin in the Lane	2	F	5	1	0	0	10,085
Smiling Irish Eyes	5	G	14	1	4	0	10,008	Smokin Joe B.	3	G	4	0	0	0	1,980
Smiling Lord	6	G	8	1	1	1	10,624	Smokin' John	4	C	7	1	2	1	42,812
Smiling Skip	3	G	10	1	0	2	27,007	Smokin' Kelly	2	C	3	1	0	0	24,840
Smiling Sky	4	F	12	4	1	2	71,384	Smokin Like a Fire	6	M	1	0	0	0	58
Smiling Virginian	6	M	3	0	2	0	5,100	Smokin Nova	4	F	7	1	0	1	23,590
Smirk (GB)	5	H	5	0	1	1	40,020	Smokin' On	3	G	1	0	0	0	0
Smith Rock Road	7	G	3	0	0	1	663	Smokin Pirate	3	G	9	1	1	0	15,160
Smithtown Road	2	C	5	0	0	0	1,395	Smokin Pursuit	2	C	4	0	1	0	1,560
Smitten	2	C	1	0	0	0	110	Smokin Red	3	C	4	0	3	0	11,824
Smitten's Baby	5	M	13	0	1	2	7,486	Smokin' Sammy	3	C	4	0	1	0	8,340
Smoggy Doggy	3	F	4	0	0	1	3,490	Smokin' Six	4	G	12	1	0	3	9,885
Smoke and Fame	4	C	1	0	0	0	0	Smokin Tempo	3	F	5	0	1	1	10,670
Smoke and Ice	5	G	8	2	1	0	3,253	Smokincanofbeans	4	G	13	2	4	2	10,051
Smoke Bomb	4	F	10	0	1	3	36,010	Smokindowntheroad	4	G	7	2	1	0	29,700
Smoke Break	2	F	5	1	3	0	66,165	Smokinemall	3	F	13	3	1	2	43,550
Smoke Chaser	4	F	7	2	3	0	72,972	Smoking Attire	4	G	2	1	0	1	5,331
Smoke Dancer	4	G	4	0	0	0	746	Smoking Bear	3	F	2	0	0	1	1,510
Smoke Glack Attack	3	F	7	2	1	2	35,707	Smoking Hank	2	C	1	0	0	1	572
Smoke in Savoya	7	M	4	0	0	1	1,625	Smoking Hawk	4	G	14	3	4	0	18,830
Smoke N D C	3	G	2	0	0	0	38	Smoking Quality	2	F	2	0	0	1	3,676
Smoke N Vote	2	G	1	0	0	0	0	Smoking Rob	3	C	7	1	2	1	16,514
Smoke Quest	2	C	2	0	0	0	0	Smoking Signal	4	F	5	0	0	1	2,850
Smoke Stack Jack	4	G	12	4	4	2	62,974	Smoking Star	10	G	1	0	0	0	175
Smoke Till Dawn	4	G	18	7	2	0	56,170	Smoking Wine	3	F	11	4	2	0	89,146
Smoke Wagon	7	G	3	0	0	0	1,250	Smok'n Doc	3	G	3	0	0	0	94
Smokeater	3	G	4	0	1	0	1,627	Smok'n Frolic	4	F	11	3	3	1	776,856
Smoked Em	4	C	4	1	0	0	20,475	Smokum Joe	3	C	1	0	0	0	0
Smoke'em Gray Lady	5	M	7	1	1	0	7,422	Smokume	2	G	4	3	1	0	118,544
Smokegetenyoureyes	2	F	3	1	0	0	12,920	Smoky Jade	5	M	1	0	0	0	50
Smokegetsinmyeyes	2	F	6	1	0	0	3,360	Smoky Knight	3	C	5	0	1	0	4,230
Smokehouse	4	C	1	0	0	1	900	Smoldering Skies	3	F	2	0	0	0	0
Smokem Late	3	G	4	1	0	0	2,801	Smoochen Perner	3	C	2	0	0	1	1,937
Smoken Feathers	3	F	15	3	3	2	32,820	Smoocher	2	C	4	2	1	0	231,653
Smoke'n Jack	4	C	1	0	0	0	103	Smooching	3	F	2	0	0	1	1,016
Smoken Pass You	3	G	12	1	0	1	5,059	Smoot Mahootie	3	G	8	0	1	0	3,035
Smoken Rollin	3	C	4	0	0	1	3,910	Smooth	6	G	6	0	1	1	7,000

Horse	Age	Sex	Sts	1st	2d	3d	Won	Horse	Age	Sex	Sts	1st	2d	3d	Won
Smooth and Free	4	G	12	2	2	3	20,709	Snickerdoo	5	M	7	1	1	1	19,181
Smooth as Jazz	5	G	5	0	0	2	1,731	Snickers Storm	2	G	5	0	0	0	1,875
Smooth as Silver	3	G	12	2	3	3	46,188	Snickle Kiss	3	F	2	0	0	0	222
Smooth Beat	10	G	1	0	0	0	0	Sniffles	3	F	13	3	3	3	70,621
Smooth Blues	7	M	4	0	0	0	3,000	Snip Creek	2	F	2	0	0	1	4,356
Smooth Burglar	5	M	4	0	0	0	274	Sniper	4	G	4	0	0	0	4,094
Smooth Criminal	4	G	3	0	0	0	0	Snipp	4	G	3	0	0	0	325
Smooth Cruiser	4	G	7	1	2	1	30,541	Snipper	5	G	5	0	2	0	3,060
Smooth Cut	5	H	4	0	0	0	222	Snobby Princess	2	F	1	0	1	0	2,340
Smooth Italian	4	G	9	1	0	1	2,824	Snobby Secret	2	F	2	0	0	0	0
Smooth Jazz	4	C	2	1	0	0	175,725	Snogun	5	M	9	3	1	0	36,082
Smooth Lover	4	G	6	3	0	0	16,590	Snohomish Fantasy	2	F	2	0	0	0	0
Smooth Maneuvers	3	F	5	4	1	0	123,900	Snohomish Gemini	3	F	14	1	1	2	8,550
Smooth N Easy	4	F	4	1	0	1	12,995	Snohomish Loot	8	G	13	2	2	1	22,814
Smooth Passer	5	M	1	0	0	0	184	Snohomish Panther	3	G	8	1	2	1	10,260
Smooth Reality	4	G	5	0	0	0	365	Snohomish Princess	2	F	7	0	2	1	6,426
Smooth Rhythm	2	C	2	0	0	0	1,460	Snoopbformarriage	7	M	5	3	0	0	19,740
Smooth Roller	7	H	1	0	0	0	0	Snoopin for Gold	3	C	2	0	0	0	115
Smooth Satin	2	C	3	1	0	0	5,725	Snoopy Blues	4	G	14	1	2	2	30,650
Smooth Senorita	8	M	3	0	0	1	3,553	Snoopy Cat	4	G	9	3	1	0	64,292
Smooth Shannon	8	M	7	2	0	2	26,705	Snooze Alarm	4	F	3	2	0	0	36,876
Smooth Stone	3	G	11	2	1	0	11,612	Snooze Button	2	F	3	0	0	0	738
Smooth Talc	6	G	13	2	0	4	9,742	Snooze Zone	4	C	4	0	0	0	225
Smooth Talkin Jo	6	G	4	0	0	0	0	Snoqualmie Queen	3	F	4	0	0	0	410
Smooth Willie R.	4	G	2	0	0	0	0	Snoqualmie Ridge	3	F	9	3	1	1	28,178
Smoothmovinangel	2	F	3	1	1	0	18,800	Snoring Dan	2	G	2	0	0	0	0
Smoothsailinhoagie	12	G	9	1	1	1	3,709	Snorter	3	C	6	2	1	1	72,820
Smoothville	4	F	2	0	0	0	196	Snortin Norton	6	H	3	0	0	0	61
Smoozie	6	M	12	0	2	2	2,737	Snorty Cat	8	G	3	0	0	0	0
S'more Smoke	4	F	9	2	1	2	47,776	Snorzalot	3	G	6	1	0	0	7,830
Smorz	2	F	1	1	0	0	13,800	Snoshoe	3	F	13	3	2	1	46,780
Smuggle Me Home	2	F	1	0	0	0	0	Snow Blaster	3	C	2	0	0	0	1,302
Smuggler Moon	5	G	9	1	2	1	7,353	Snow Buck	7	G	13	3	3	2	13,652
Smugglers Basin	4	C	8	0	2	0	12,080	Snow Chic	3	F	1	0	1	0	440
Smugglers Cove	8	M	3	1	0	0	11,187	Snow Country Cat	3	C	1	0	0	0	0
Smuggler's Run	2	G	3	0	2	0	7,370	Snow Dance	5	M	8	1	1	2	220,510
Smuse	2	F	4	0	0	0	0	Snow Eagle	2	C	3	1	1	0	22,850
Smushy	2	G	2	0	0	0	780	Snow Fest	3	C	5	1	0	1	10,362
Snack Attack	3	G	9	1	1	1	9,630	Snow Flurry	4	C	1	0	0	0	0
Snackbasket	7	G	8	0	1	2	3,402	Snow Fortune	7	M	11	3	1	1	13,882
Snagged	7	G	9	2	0	1	7,729	Snow Leopard	3	C	3	1	0	0	5,400
Snake Fighter	6	H	6	0	0	1	958	Snow Luck	8	M	9	0	0	1	3,352
Snake in My Boot	2	G	3	0	1	0	8,638	Snow Mountain	3	F	5	0	0	1	2,288
Snake in the Grass	3	F	1	0	0	0	0	Snow Nose Cat	3	G	1	0	0	0	0
Snake Mountain	5	G	5	3	0	0	159,825	Snow On Cedars	3	G	8	2	1	0	8,233
Snake Oil's Glory	6	M	2	0	0	0	0	Snow Shot	3	C	4	1	1	0	23,205
Snake Pit	3	G	4	1	0	0	46,488	Snow Shower	9	G	11	3	0	2	24,025
Snakes B G	2	C	6	1	0	2	9,415	Snow Trump	3	F	1	0	0	0	0
Snakes P J	5	M	1	0	0	0	67	Snow Wonder M.d.	2	G	1	0	1	0	4,340
Snap Hook	4	C	15	5	2	3	46,706	Snowball Flannagan	8	H	4	1	1	0	29,000
Snap to It	3	F	4	0	0	1	3,000	Snowball King	4	G	14	1	0	0	9,561
Snapen Crackle	4	F	10	0	0	2	3,096	Snowballs Chance	3	G	2	0	1	0	1,306
Snapped Up	2	C	2	0	1	0	11,560	Snowbell	2	F	2	0	0	0	0
Snappin Good Girl	2	F	2	0	0	0	0	Snowbird	2	F	1	1	0	0	7,560
Snappy	3	F	2	0	0	0	400	Snowbound Bob	3	G	6	0	0	0	1,688
Snappy Drive	8	G	3	0	0	0	0	Snowbound Express	3	C	6	0	1	1	3,726
Snappy Little Cat	2	F	4	1	0	1	27,676	Snowbound Nan	2	F	5	1	1	1	14,250
Snappy Tale	3	F	8	1	0	3	26,740	Snowbound Native	3	F	12	6	3	2	25,038
Snappy Tim	3	G	8	0	2	0	30,787	Snowbound Oro	2	G	2	1	0	0	3,780
Snappy Tune	2	F	3	1	0	0	12,600	Snowbound Paul	3	C	8	0	2	0	2,984
Snaps Galore	8	G	12	1	2	2	2,857	Snowbound Star	3	F	9	0	1	3	2,306
Snatchit	3	G	14	1	2	5	20,525	Snowbound Writer	2	G	4	1	2	0	39,035
Sneakalilpeak	3	C	16	1	2	1	11,717	Snowbound Zulu	2	G	3	1	0	0	3,888
Sneaker Mike	4	G	8	1	0	4	23,232	Snowbound's Bonus	3	F	2	0	0	0	432
Sneakin Mac	7	G	11	0	1	2	1,875	Snowbound's Ghost	3	G	3	0	2	1	6,700
Sneaking Upp	3	G	6	1	0	1	15,300	Snowdance Kid	2	G	7	1	1	0	8,367
Sneaky	4	F	13	3	2	3	26,405	Snowdazzle	3	C	12	1	3	2	24,911
Sneaky Baby	7	M	2	0	0	0	0	Snowdrops (GB)	3	F	8	3	1	0	111,473
Sneaky First	3	F	12	0	1	1	3,722	Snowfire (GB)	4	F	1	0	1	0	10,400
Sneaky Kid	4	C	2	0	0	0	150	Snowflake (IRE)	5	M	3	0	1	0	16,220
Sneaky Partner	3	F	7	1	0	2	26,321	Snowflight	3	F	2	0	0	0	57
Sneaky Petey	7	G	11	2	1	0	18,280	Snowglory's Angel	3	F	6	0	0	0	0
Sneaky Sam	9	G	24	3	6	4	18,565	Snowman Hustle	6	G	7	2	2	1	28,900
Sneaky Secret	4	F	3	0	0	1	1,172	Snowrun	5	M	5	0	1	0	7,360
Sneek Gambler	4	G	9	3	2	3	51,296	Snowshoe Flyer	5	G	11	2	5	0	26,638
Sneezy Tab	4	C	9	1	0	0	2,443	Snowy Joe	4	G	6	2	0	0	6,350
Sneffels Street	3	C	5	1	0	0	3,738	Snowy King	4	C	7	1	1	1	8,858
Snertitude	3	C	7	4	0	0	16,431	Snowy Memo	2	C	2	0	0	0	1,020
Snickeez	5	M	13	1	0	0	19,740	Snowy Night	4	G	11	0	2	2	4,748

Horse	Age	Sex	Sts	1st	2d	3d	Won
Snoz	4	G	16	5	3	1	35,105
Snub the Devil	2	C	2	0	1	0	4,600
Snuce Queen	2	F	3	0	0	1	2,540
Snuffy	11	G	7	0	1	0	996
Snug by the Fire	3	F	3	0	0	1	715
Snuggle (NZ)	11	G	7	0	4	0	20,650
Snuggle an Cuddle	3	F	1	0	0	0	333
Snuggle Up	5	M	15	1	1	0	6,773
Snush	3	F	4	1	0	0	5,400
So Above Average	3	G	11	2	2	2	7,585
So Blue	2	F	2	0	0	0	0
So Catty	4	F	8	3	1	0	23,112
So Charmed	2	F	2	0	0	0	409
So Compelling	3	C	3	0	1	0	2,000
So Dapper	3	C	1	0	0	1	3,520
So Enticing	4	F	2	0	0	0	138
So Excited	4	F	11	1	0	4	33,570
So Grand	6	M	7	0	1	1	1,826
So Happy Together	2	F	1	0	0	0	0
So Hot	2	F	2	1	0	0	6,100
So Impetuous	7	H	3	0	0	0	0
So It Is	2	F	4	0	2	1	9,673
So Like Sarah	7	M	13	1	0	2	6,473
So Long Charlie	3	G	10	2	1	2	23,064
So Many Memories	5	M	5	2	0	1	8,920
So Miss Jeopardy	4	F	12	1	2	2	7,221
So Much Love	7	M	20	3	0	1	24,434
So Much More	4	F	9	2	3	2	174,295
So Nasty	4	G	14	2	2	3	27,598
So Nicely Done	4	F	2	0	0	0	0
So Pleased	8	G	13	0	0	0	1,497
So Proud	3	F	9	1	2	2	35,490
So Rakish	7	H	6	0	0	1	850
So Rare	3	F	6	0	0	2	4,870
So Run the Line	4	G	4	0	0	0	0
So Ruthless	3	C	2	0	0	0	5,520
So Saintly	5	M	3	0	0	0	245
So Shattered	4	G	22	4	4	6	32,720
So She Said	4	F	4	1	0	1	7,830
So Silent	2	F	2	1	0	0	11,400
So Silver	6	M	18	2	3	6	21,749
So Smart	3	G	2	0	0	0	104
So Smashing	4	F	1	0	0	0	0
So So Clever	4	G	9	2	1	0	5,745
So Social	5	M	15	5	2	0	97,645
So Soft Suzy	7	M	15	1	3	0	5,678
So Souix Me	6	M	1	0	0	0	50
So Stated	3	F	5	1	3	0	26,305
So Superior	4	G	2	0	0	0	318
So Sweet a Cat	2	F	6	2	3	1	158,278
So Synful	2	F	2	0	1	0	3,450
So Thrilled	4	F	2	0	0	0	0
So Tricky Mr. Ken	3	G	5	0	0	0	680
So Unique	3	G	3	0	0	1	4,050
So Urgent	5	H	2	1	0	0	40,300
So Welcome	4	F	16	3	2	1	52,040
So Wistfullee	7	M	2	0	0	0	1,622
So Wonderful	8	M	7	0	0	1	2,352
So You Say	4	C	11	1	3	2	38,480
Soaked	3	G	11	2	1	1	42,520
Soap	2	C	3	0	0	1	2,399
Soaring	2	F	5	0	0	1	2,220
Soaring an Action	7	G	10	3	2	1	20,444
Soaring Away	2	C	2	1	0	0	27,600
Soaring Baby	3	F	10	0	2	1	5,067
Soaring Breeze	5	G	2	0	0	0	120
Soaring Free	4	G	8	5	1	0	699,200
Soaring Games	6	H	12	2	1	4	23,496
Soaring Hawk	5	H	10	2	3	2	10,258
Soaring Leader	3	C	5	1	1	0	6,056
Soaring Magic	4	F	14	2	1	5	43,738
Soaring Miss	8	M	1	0	0	0	3,230
Soaring Sky	4	F	8	1	3	0	21,226
Soaring Wings	5	H	3	0	0	0	200
Soarlikaeagle	4	F	5	1	0	0	3,172
Sober	8	M	1	0	0	0	0
Sober Mac	7	G	10	0	0	0	669
Sober Moment	3	F	9	1	1	1	8,575
Sobers Lane	3	C	5	1	2	2	21,630
Sobriety	6	G	2	0	0	0	0
Sobriquet	2	F	1	0	0	0	720
Soccer Dan	2	G	4	0	0	2	4,410
Soccer George	7	G	11	1	3	1	23,370
Soccer King	7	G	6	1	0	1	1,417
Soccer Kylie	2	F	4	1	0	1	14,990
Soccory	6	M	7	0	1	1	24,076
Social Account	5	G	15	2	2	2	24,413
Social Bin Woodman	2	C	1	0	0	0	498
Social Delight	9	G	3	0	0	0	35
Social Expense	7	G	10	1	3	1	21,070
Social G Man	3	G	4	1	1	0	8,620
Social Graces	3	C	9	2	1	1	9,245
Social Jewel	9	M	1	0	0	0	0
Social Knight	5	M	7	0	1	1	7,924
Social Lies	4	G	7	0	2	1	8,170
Social Mix	4	G	8	1	0	1	15,921
Social Place	4	F	1	0	0	0	0
Social Sands	3	F	4	0	1	0	4,175
Social Savvy	4	F	1	0	0	0	0
Social Scene	3	F	2	0	0	0	2,500
Social Security	3	F	6	0	0	1	5,840
Social Top	5	M	14	3	3	2	62,788
Social Trends	6	G	5	1	0	1	8,170
Social Trouble	2	C	2	1	0	0	6,150
Socialize	3	G	5	0	1	0	2,060
Socially Brilliant	2	F	2	0	0	0	0
Socially Cleared	3	F	24	2	4	5	36,819
Sociano	8	H	3	0	0	0	0
Society Cat	2	F	5	0	4	0	14,779
Society Commander	3	F	4	0	1	0	5,400
Society Dame	4	F	6	0	1	1	7,920
Society Sal	3	G	8	1	1	2	20,140
Society Sam	2	C	3	1	0	0	21,780
Society Selection	2	F	3	2	0	0	327,000
Society Sis	6	M	1	0	0	0	194
Society's Child	2	F	1	0	0	0	118
Society's Desire	6	H	2	0	0	0	0
Sociology	3	F	7	0	0	0	270
Sock Hop	6	G	14	2	1	3	10,285
Sock Hop Sally	2	F	1	0	0	0	560
Socko	5	G	6	0	2	0	11,166
Socks Muldoon	3	G	4	1	0	1	6,603
Socorro County	2	F	1	1	0	0	13,085
Sod Hopper	6	H	6	0	0	1	893
Soda Pop Top	4	F	3	0	0	0	1,482
Sode'steddimou	4	C	1	0	0	0	140
Sodo Mojo	3	G	16	2	1	2	3,539
Soes Bandit	7	G	9	1	1	1	23,635
Soft as Velvet	3	F	7	0	0	0	312
Soft Coral	3	F	2	0	0	0	380
Soft Feeling	3	F	7	2	1	0	9,800
Soft Judge	4	C	19	3	3	4	26,621
Soft Lika Rock	3	G	12	0	1	1	5,120
Soft Machine	5	H	6	2	0	2	15,415
Soft n' Loud	3	F	13	0	1	0	2,761
Soft Rain	7	G	4	0	0	0	820
Soft Senor	5	H	11	2	1	2	18,240
Soft Twilight	2	F	1	0	0	0	0
Soft Weather	4	F	14	4	3	1	22,040
Softail Mark	3	C	3	0	0	0	204
Softie	3	F	2	0	0	0	500
Softly	5	M	2	0	0	1	22,000
Softly Blowing	3	G	3	1	1	0	5,350
Softly I Run	3	C	1	0	0	0	0
Softly Played	4	F	12	0	1	1	2,541
Softly Said	2	F	2	0	0	1	840
Softshoeshuffle	5	H	16	2	2	3	11,689
Software	3	F	15	3	2	2	22,050
Soggy Bottom Boy	3	C	4	0	0	0	238
Sohaib	4	C	5	2	0	0	64,560
Soiree Lady	6	M	8	0	1	0	3,230
Soitenly	3	G	12	1	2	1	61,428
Soixante Dix	5	M	5	0	0	0	649
Sol Tycoon	3	C	6	0	0	0	1,340
Sola Fide	3	G	5	0	1	0	3,855
Sola Topee (GB)	7	G	2	0	0	0	0
Solace	3	F	5	0	1	1	5,760
Solamente	3	F	9	1	3	0	9,467

Horse	Age	Sex	Sts	1st	2d	3d	Won
Solana Storm	5	M	26	1	2	6	17,295
Solar Cat	3	C	9	2	0	1	6,258
Solar Echo	3	F	4	3	1	0	155,400
Solar Express	4	G	3	0	1	0	2,750
Solar Fire	2	F	5	1	0	2	55,195
Solar Lea	3	G	2	0	0	0	0
Solar Man	3	G	6	1	0	1	34,460
Solar Panetella	5	G	14	0	1	2	2,311
Solar Power	5	H	8	0	1	0	1,583
Solar Sail	2	F	3	0	0	1	8,430
Solar Way	4	C	4	1	1	0	7,295
Sold Pending	9	G	4	0	0	0	0
Soldier Bear	4	G	19	1	5	3	20,935
Soldier in Action	4	G	13	0	0	4	21,300
Soldier McGee	3	G	6	1	1	1	8,382
Soldier of Fame	2	G	9	0	1	2	12,325
Soldier Song	4	C	10	1	0	0	31,984
Soldierofpleasure	4	C	8	2	0	2	78,494
Soldier's Angel	3	F	2	0	0	0	1,560
Soldier's Bid	3	C	4	0	0	0	0
Soldiers Fortune	6	G	8	3	1	0	34,840
Soldiers Quest	4	G	14	1	5	4	41,715
Soldotna	6	G	8	2	0	0	33,240
Sole Proprietor	7	H	4	0	2	1	7,790
Sole Prospect	6	H	12	0	2	2	4,750
Sole Request	2	C	1	0	0	0	195
Soleaido	4	F	5	0	0	1	1,502
Solicitor General	4	C	3	1	1	0	30,450
Solid Brick	3	F	3	0	1	0	2,455
Solid Mahogany	2	C	1	0	0	0	50
Solid Oak	9	G	1	0	1	0	314
Solid Red Rock	6	G	2	0	0	0	0
Solid Silver Star	3	G	2	2	0	0	36,370
Solid State	2	G	2	0	0	0	205
Solid Sterling	3	G	7	0	2	0	3,365
Solid Ten	4	F	8	2	0	0	11,680
Solid Wood	8	G	10	0	0	1	3,578
Solidarity House	3	F	2	0	0	0	147
Solidasarock	9	G	2	0	0	1	2,600
Solihull	3	C	5	2	0	0	96,960
Solina	3	F	2	1	1	0	47,040
Solingen	5	G	11	1	2	2	27,707
Solitario	5	G	4	0	1	2	21,600
Solitarius	2	F	1	0	0	0	450
Solitary	2	C	5	0	0	0	3,420
Solitary Code	3	G	4	0	0	0	0
Solitary Dancer	7	H	8	1	4	1	130,441
Solitary Emerald	2	F	5	0	1	3	16,370
Solitary Gold	2	F	2	0	0	0	0
Solitary Ritzi	2	C	1	0	0	0	700
Solitary Starr	4	G	11	1	0	2	9,664
Solitary Strife	4	F	5	1	0	2	12,305
Sollozo	3	G	11	2	2	0	6,226
Solmar	4	F	8	1	0	2	25,060
Solo Blitz	8	M	5	0	0	2	954
Solo Cat	3	G	8	1	2	1	33,769
Solo Number	4	G	6	0	0	0	496
Solo Player	3	G	9	2	0	0	8,184
Solo Reflection	3	G	3	0	0	0	0
Solo Singer	3	F	3	0	0	0	0
Solo Special	9	G	18	2	3	2	9,321
Solo Standard	4	G	6	1	1	1	2,184
Solo Strut	2	C	6	0	0	0	4,345
Solo Trumpet	4	F	10	0	0	0	500
Solocoexpress	6	G	15	1	5	1	12,825
Soloing	3	F	4	1	1	0	26,400
Soloist	4	F	7	2	3	0	20,737
Solomon's Decree	4	C	3	0	0	0	50
Solomon's Seal	5	H	5	0	1	0	4,704
Solongretsina	9	G	2	0	0	0	163
Solo's Hobo	4	F	8	1	1	0	15,090
Sol's Bag	3	G	8	2	1	1	18,810
Som of Time	12	G	3	0	0	0	162
Sombodyswatchnovme	4	G	10	6	2	0	120,700
Sombrero	2	G	5	1	1	0	11,469
Sombrio	4	G	9	1	0	2	56,056
Some Buttercup	3	F	1	0	0	0	0
Some Came Running	4	F	8	1	1	1	42,663
Some Chestnut	3	C	9	1	2	3	7,616
Some Curves	4	F	4	1	0	0	17,500
Some Ghost	2	C	2	0	1	1	3,070
Some Image	2	C	3	1	0	0	10,920
Some Irish Legend	7	M	8	0	2	0	29,150
Some Kind of Chic	6	M	2	0	0	0	150
Some Kind of Money	5	M	2	0	0	0	0
Some Kinda Class	3	G	8	2	0	2	19,400
Some Kinda Dancer	7	G	16	1	0	2	3,835
Some Kinda Guy	4	C	3	1	0	0	5,500
Some Kinda Miracle	4	F	1	0	0	0	0
Some Like Me Best	8	G	6	0	0	0	235
Some Little Miss	6	M	9	0	0	0	805
Some Lucky Star	8	G	8	0	2	1	2,750
Some More	6	M	2	0	0	0	152
Some One Free	5	G	2	0	0	0	0
Some Other Night	4	C	13	2	0	4	23,890
Some Party	2	C	1	0	0	0	1,980
Some Remark	4	G	12	1	5	0	12,360
Some Runaway	7	G	14	1	1	1	11,564
Some Sheik	6	G	9	0	0	1	2,389
Some Storm	3	F	2	0	0	0	0
Some Sweet Day	2	F	7	0	2	0	3,924
Someday's Queen	8	M	3	0	0	1	162
Somefine Groom	10	G	7	2	2	1	9,229
Somekinda Surprise	7	G	11	1	1	1	11,644
Somekindofire	5	G	11	2	2	3	23,805
Someones Coming	5	M	6	1	1	0	29,690
Someonestopme	3	F	1	0	0	0	0
Someplace Special	4	F	4	0	0	0	400
Somers Tour	3	F	15	0	2	2	19,344
Somerset House	4	G	14	3	3	0	59,100
Somerset Legend	2	G	2	0	0	1	1,997
Somerset's Husband	5	H	14	0	0	0	1,892
Somethin Brite	5	G	8	1	0	0	6,264
Somethinaboutmaggi	4	F	8	2	2	1	10,271
Something Bleu	4	C	8	1	0	1	5,022
Something Clever	3	G	12	1	4	0	20,482
Something Fierce	2	G	7	1	0	1	15,090
Something Gallant	4	G	1	0	0	0	0
Something Gorgeous	4	F	1	0	0	0	0
Something Magic	5	M	10	1	2	2	22,912
Something Majestic	3	C	2	1	0	0	14,120
Something Promised	2	F	2	0	0	0	127
Something Racy	3	F	4	0	0	0	120
Something Rushing	4	C	8	1	1	2	54,772
Something Silver	3	F	3	0	1	0	15,690
Something Sinful	2	F	2	0	0	0	0
Something Smith	3	C	8	5	2	0	171,100
Something Ventured	4	F	11	3	3	3	193,171
Something Wicked	6	M	10	2	0	0	46,380
Somethingbold	3	G	7	0	0	0	723
Somethingdangerous	5	G	9	2	0	1	45,700
Somethingnaabulous	3	G	11	1	2	0	3,421
Somethingquiet	2	F	3	0	0	0	360
Somethingsecret	3	F	10	1	1	1	2,265
Sometime Thing	3	F	9	1	2	2	11,668
Sometimesalvation	5	G	10	1	1	2	16,156
Somewhat Gray	3	F	9	0	0	0	1,390
Somfas Dancer	7	G	16	1	2	3	3,202
Sommelier	5	G	8	0	2	2	17,960
Somogyi	4	F	4	0	0	0	614
Son Also Rises	5	G	15	1	0	1	6,565
Son Chant	5	G	15	1	1	4	5,681
Son Et Lumiere	4	F	6	0	0	0	785
Son of a Fish	4	G	18	0	1	1	2,647
Son of a Lue	4	C	3	0	0	0	750
Son of Adrienne	2	C	3	0	0	0	471
Son of Fire	4	C	2	0	1	0	2,680
Son of Flame	3	C	1	0	0	0	0
Son of Jazz	3	G	3	0	0	1	2,025
Son of Man	4	C	1	0	0	0	570
Son of Mariah	5	H	3	2	0	0	5,568
Son of Pete	6	G	9	2	1	1	7,634
Son of Rehaan	5	G	7	1	1	0	9,417
Son of Rhea	3	G	10	1	5	1	30,760
Son of Syn	4	G	2	0	0	1	2,450
Son of Thunder	4	C	11	1	0	3	8,922
Son Ofa Factor	4	C	5	1	1	2	5,263
Son Ofa Prospector	2	C	6	1	0	0	6,222

RECORDS OF HORSES

Horse	Age	Sex	Sts	1st	2d	3d	Won	Horse	Age	Sex	Sts	1st	2d	3d	Won
Sonador	3	C	1	0	0	0	0	Soo Much	4	C	3	0	0	0	2,595
Sonadrum	7	G	5	0	0	0	524	Soobadd	2	C	2	0	0	0	500
Sonamack	6	H	6	0	3	0	1,338	Soobee Frost	2	G	2	0	0	1	1,323
Sonata Cosmos	5	M	8	0	2	0	29,640	Soon Be Gone	2	F	1	1	0	0	2,200
Sonata St	2	F	1	0	0	0	0	Soon Reality	6	G	2	0	0	0	0
Sonceore	3	G	4	3	0	0	30,542	Soon Soon	4	F	9	0	4	1	47,260
Sondeo	5	G	11	0	2	2	22,150	Soon to Be Family	2	F	3	0	0	0	213
Sondor's Queen	7	M	9	1	1	3	6,253	Soon to Be Single	5	M	5	3	0	0	115,080
Song Called	3	F	16	1	1	2	4,733	Sooner Defense	3	F	10	0	1	1	2,445
Song for Ashley	2	F	2	0	0	0	0	Sooner Gold	3	G	7	1	0	1	3,565
Song Forum	4	F	7	2	0	1	7,585	Sooner Land	5	G	4	0	1	0	880
Song Lyric	3	F	1	0	0	0	180	Sooner Shine	5	G	20	6	2	3	33,955
Song Minister (BRZ)	6	G	12	2	1	4	36,800	Sooner Than	3	F	3	3	0	0	22,638
Song of America	2	G	9	2	2	3	27,555	Sooner the Better	2	C	4	0	0	1	1,650
Song of Beauty	2	F	1	0	0	0	90	Soonersaige	3	F	3	0	2	0	1,805
Song of Hope	5	M	4	3	1	0	12,700	Soos Bells	3	F	6	0	1	0	2,700
Song of Nora	4	F	9	1	0	1	15,724	Soot	3	G	10	3	1	3	77,725
Song of Saba	6	M	4	0	0	0	216	Sootaa	4	F	8	2	0	1	30,145
Song of Saville	4	F	6	0	1	3	4,916	Soothe the Soul	4	G	15	3	1	2	10,806
Song of Shawky	3	G	15	0	2	1	3,638	Sooty Boy	4	G	5	1	1	1	1,546
Song of Stars	6	G	12	0	0	1	1,892	Sopheesawinner	5	M	6	0	2	1	4,865
Song of the Bull	2	G	2	0	0	0	413	Sophia Jones	2	F	2	1	0	1	21,550
Song of the Hawk	3	F	6	1	1	0	16,800	Sophia Ofthe Hills	3	F	2	0	0	0	0
Song of the Sea	3	F	2	0	0	0	162	Sophia Storm	2	F	2	1	0	1	8,080
Song of Tiger	2	F	4	0	0	0	560	Sophia's Gold	3	F	2	0	0	0	310
Song of Versailles	3	F	9	0	2	2	9,030	Sophias Humor	2	F	6	0	2	3	20,820
Song of Victory	2	C	3	1	0	0	19,195	Sophia's Prince	4	G	9	3	3	1	201,998
Song Or Psalm	5	M	15	2	2	2	25,789	Sophia's Secret	2	F	2	0	0	0	150
Song Sung Gold	2	F	2	0	0	0	1,130	Sophia's Twist	4	F	1	0	0	0	80
Song Track	2	F	2	0	1	0	7,735	Sophie	4	F	7	0	0	2	5,676
Songbrook Alice	3	F	13	1	0	1	8,762	Sophie and Al	2	F	4	0	0	1	2,660
Songcatcher	3	F	1	0	0	0	0	Sophie's Bold	6	H	11	0	1	2	18,006
Songinthedarkness	3	F	10	1	1	1	9,941	Sophie's Cat	3	F	5	1	0	1	7,609
Sonhouse	6	G	1	0	0	0	0	Sophie's Magic	2	F	7	0	0	0	2,130
Soni Deb	2	F	1	0	0	0	0	Sophisticated Babe	2	F	3	0	0	0	1,010
Sonia	4	F	2	0	0	0	58	Sophisticated Gold	4	F	1	0	0	0	220
Sonia (GER)	4	F	12	1	4	1	77,100	Sophisticated Man	8	H	8	1	1	0	36,400
Sonia's Sonata	3	F	13	1	2	2	21,434	Sophisticatedbluff	4	F	9	2	7	0	127,200
Sonia's Song	3	F	10	3	0	2	27,685	Sopi	3	F	1	0	0	0	340
Sonic Blum	4	G	3	0	0	0	829	Sopo Grande	7	H	3	0	0	0	1,072
Sonic Bonnet	4	F	14	1	2	2	8,734	Soppy (MEX)	8	M	4	0	0	1	750
Sonic Eagle	2	G	3	0	0	1	1,870	Sopwith Pup	4	G	6	1	2	0	10,520
Sonic Song	5	M	14	2	1	2	17,395	Sor De	4	G	7	0	1	0	2,778
Sonic West	4	G	9	4	2	1	200,970	Sorbet	3	F	3	0	1	1	7,480
Sonic Youth (GB)	3	C	3	0	0	0	56	Sordid Affair	3	F	8	2	2	2	24,070
Sonic's Golden Boy	5	G	20	4	5	4	25,621	Sorenstam	3	F	10	1	0	2	8,823
Sonique	4	F	9	4	1	0	11,978	Soriano Cat	2	G	10	3	2	2	36,650
Sonivere	3	C	2	1	0	0	35,280	Sorleigh	2	C	6	0	1	2	5,575
Sonn D' Oro	3	F	9	4	0	2	82,590	Sorority Gal	3	F	9	1	1	3	32,396
Sonny and Rose	2	C	3	1	0	0	17,040	Sorority Pledge	5	M	9	0	2	0	5,004
Sonny Boy Blue	6	G	14	3	1	2	15,391	Sorrel Cat	4	F	12	0	1	0	1,698
Sonny Boy G	3	G	2	1	0	0	2,200	Sorrentino (ARG)	4	C	2	0	0	0	160
Sonny Express	3	G	9	1	0	1	4,804	Sorrento Sara	4	F	2	0	1	1	2,250
Sonny Go West	3	G	13	4	2	0	29,320	Sorryforyourluck	3	F	2	0	0	0	199
Sonny Sal	6	G	6	2	1	0	18,220	Sorrytotellyou	3	F	7	2	2	0	33,340
Sonny the Sailor	6	G	6	1	0	0	30,330	Sorte	3	C	3	0	0	1	1,228
Sonny Vigors	6	G	11	0	0	4	3,700	Sorvel	2	C	2	0	0	0	650
Sonny's Double D D	3	F	5	0	1	3	2,075	Sosella	2	F	1	0	0	0	0
Sonny's Hammer	2	C	3	0	0	1	1,320	Soteras Queen	6	M	5	0	0	1	1,434
Sonny's Legacy	3	G	12	2	2	0	30,200	Sothypann	4	F	5	0	1	0	2,775
Sonny's Pride	5	G	6	1	2	0	2,730	Soto	3	C	3	2	1	0	473,200
Sonny's Warrior	3	C	9	1	1	1	1,093	Sotogrande	5	M	11	1	1	0	6,750
Sonny's Zone	5	H	7	1	0	3	4,069	Soud	5	H	7	3	2	0	122,000
Sonofa Gray Lady	5	G	3	1	0	0	6,300	Souffle Two Fly	8	G	1	0	0	0	0
Sonofablonde	3	C	2	0	0	1	260	Soul Comfort	2	F	1	0	0	0	980
Sonofawac	3	G	10	2	2	2	95,224	Soul Heaven	4	G	5	0	2	2	8,567
Sonofpreacherman	2	G	6	1	0	0	7,850	Soul Mate	3	F	6	0	2	1	15,680
Sonoita Sunset	4	F	6	1	2	0	26,225	Soul Obsession	5	H	1	0	0	0	0
Sonoma County	3	F	3	0	0	0	312	Soul of Diablo	7	M	12	2	0	2	9,961
Sonora Cisco	4	F	9	1	3	0	3,635	Soul of Kindness	4	F	3	0	1	0	8,190
Sonora Lady	6	M	2	0	0	0	72	Soul of Solitude	3	F	6	2	1	1	30,540
Sonora's Moon	3	F	20	0	2	8	22,585	Soul of the Cat	2	F	1	0	0	0	1,050
Sonorense	5	G	9	2	3	2	7,733	Soul of Wit	5	G	1	0	0	0	265
Sonori Silk	3	F	5	0	0	0	180	Soul Onarazorsedge	5	M	2	0	0	1	4,400
Sonorous (IRE)	4	F	3	0	0	0	1,160	Soul Searching	5	G	5	0	1	0	1,550
Sonriente	2	G	4	0	1	1	8,900	Soul Shaker	3	F	2	0	0	0	0
Sons Best Power	5	H	8	0	0	0	0	Soul Song	7	G	7	0	1	0	2,725
Sonya's Smile	2	F	3	1	1	1	13,800	Soulard Swirl	6	G	11	2	2	1	7,206
Soo	4	C	6	0	0	0	285								

Horse	Age	Sex	Sts	1st	2d	3d	Won
Soulmandance	6	G	15	3	2	3	17,448
Soulville	3	F	3	0	0	0	600
Sounce a Silence	2	F	5	1	0	2	18,970
Sound and Fury	3	G	13	2	3	2	30,115
Sound Force	4	C	1	0	0	0	1,140
Sound Logic	3	C	1	0	0	0	100
Sound of Colors	4	F	3	0	0	0	682
Sound of Gold	5	M	13	4	2	1	88,029
Sound of Power	4	F	13	2	4	4	6,060
Sound System	10	G	1	0	0	0	0
Sound Wave	6	M	11	2	1	2	36,848
Sounding Jewel	4	F	4	1	0	0	4,740
Sounds Fishy	4	F	11	0	2	0	19,360
Sounds Foolish	2	G	2	0	0	0	337
Sounds Great	4	G	11	1	2	2	14,589
Sounds Real	3	G	3	0	0	0	106
Sounds Sunny	8	G	1	0	0	0	324
Soundswiftprospect	4	F	5	0	0	1	1,855
Soundtrack	5	M	2	0	1	0	23,140
Soup	3	G	15	0	3	3	19,103
Soup Abc	3	F	5	1	0	0	13,796
Soup At Siros	3	F	2	0	0	0	0
Soup for Dinner	2	F	9	2	2	0	27,865
Soup for Lunch	3	F	11	3	3	2	104,042
Soup n' Crackers	4	F	10	2	0	3	37,370
Soup Spoon	3	C	16	2	1	3	83,994
Soup Time	3	C	3	0	0	0	1,080
Soupcon	3	F	3	1	0	0	8,780
Souper Denis	10	G	11	1	1	1	6,262
Soupolicious	2	C	1	0	0	0	0
Sour Grapes	3	C	1	0	0	0	0
Sour Mash Whiskey	8	G	3	0	0	0	214
Sour Note	3	C	2	0	0	0	160
Source	5	H	10	3	0	1	72,692
Source of Passion	2	G	2	0	0	0	0
Sources and Uses	2	C	1	0	0	0	168
Souris	3	F	10	2	4	0	169,896
South Africa	2	G	2	1	0	0	13,800
South Apple (ARG)	5	M	7	0	1	2	26,040
South Beach (CHI)	5	G	5	0	0	0	856
South Bound n Down	10	G	4	1	0	1	1,548
South by Gosh	5	G	12	0	1	2	10,170
South Christian	3	G	9	2	4	0	50,390
South City	7	G	4	0	1	2	7,213
South Country	2	G	6	0	3	1	5,966
South Girl	2	F	1	0	0	0	0
South Gone West	2	C	1	0	0	0	230
South Haven	6	G	9	0	1	1	6,390
South Lan Tour	2	F	1	0	0	0	110
South Magnolia	2	F	5	1	0	2	12,665
South of Dixie	4	C	1	0	0	0	0
South of Kandahar	3	F	3	0	0	1	770
South Side	9	G	8	2	0	0	9,753
South Slide	3	F	1	0	0	0	0
South Twentyseven	2	C	3	0	0	0	235
Southaintbad	3	F	15	0	0	6	8,224
Southbound Katie	2	F	1	0	0	1	1,107
Southeaster	3	F	6	2	0	1	24,814
Souther Division	2	F	8	0	2	1	12,650
Southerly Flow	5	M	13	4	5	2	34,212
Southern Alert	3	F	7	1	1	1	31,060
Southern Angel	4	F	2	0	0	0	123
Southern Assertion	6	M	6	2	1	0	24,372
Southern Barfly	2	F	1	0	0	0	110
Southern Bayou	3	F	4	0	0	0	0
Southern Beauty	5	M	9	1	2	1	4,750
Southern Blaze	4	G	15	0	5	1	9,616
Southern Boots	4	F	2	0	0	0	0
Southern Boy	7	G	11	2	2	1	33,450
Southern Broad	5	M	4	1	0	0	11,868
Southern Cartel	2	G	1	0	0	0	450
Southern Celebrity	3	C	3	0	0	0	4,323
Southern Chance	5	G	15	3	2	0	107,458
Southern Craft	9	G	1	0	0	0	0
Southern Cross Sky	5	H	7	0	0	0	114
Southern Cure	7	M	11	4	0	1	32,090
Southern Dance	4	F	3	0	0	0	136
Southern Diamond	3	F	13	2	3	0	29,906
Southern Dinner	6	H	17	2	1	1	25,282
Southern Dream	4	F	4	1	0	0	12,028
Southern Drive	2	C	3	0	0	0	1,942
Southern Duchess	3	F	2	1	0	0	10,520
Southern Elegance	3	F	4	1	2	0	27,600
Southern Eyes	2	F	1	0	0	0	1,350
Southern Fiction	5	M	6	2	0	0	74,193
Southern Fire	2	F	9	1	1	2	18,540
Southern Fleet	4	G	2	0	0	0	132
Southern Friend	3	F	12	0	1	2	18,200
Southern Frolic	3	G	11	0	0	0	1,775
Southern Gamble	2	C	3	1	0	0	7,540
Southern Genes	9	G	10	1	1	2	5,436
Southern Gentleman	6	H	6	0	1	0	2,205
Southern Heat	9	M	8	1	1	1	17,298
Southern Honoree	3	G	11	4	0	2	35,895
Southern Hope	3	F	9	1	1	0	10,270
Southern House (IRE)	7	M	1	0	0	0	0
Southern Ich	5	G	3	0	0	0	0
Southern Image	3	C	3	2	0	1	202,800
Southern Issue	3	F	2	0	0	0	0
Southern Jewel	3	F	12	0	2	3	12,648
Southern Kisses	5	M	5	0	1	0	980
Southern Legacy	3	C	9	0	2	1	10,680
Southern Livin	4	C	8	1	0	0	13,140
Southern Love	4	C	20	3	1	5	25,546
Southern Macho	4	G	2	0	1	0	560
Southern Militia	2	C	3	1	0	0	8,800
Southern Miss	3	F	2	0	0	1	3,640
Southern Nelle	4	F	6	2	2	0	12,185
Southern Oasis	5	M	8	3	1	0	131,400
Southern Okie	3	F	13	1	3	4	10,825
Southern Order	3	F	1	0	0	0	120
Southern Outlaw	2	C	1	0	0	0	3,822
Southern Pioneer	3	G	8	2	0	1	31,257
Southern Prime	4	C	11	2	1	0	15,525
Southern Promise	5	M	21	1	3	1	12,931
Southern Rage	3	G	8	0	0	2	3,175
Southern Rain	3	F	4	0	2	1	21,440
Southern Randy	3	G	5	0	1	0	2,050
Southern Revival	3	F	4	1	1	1	3,940
Southern Ridge	5	M	9	0	4	2	5,461
Southern Romp	3	F	6	0	0	0	5,390
Southern Royal	5	G	3	0	0	0	170
Southern Royalty	5	G	3	0	0	0	496
Southern Saint	5	G	15	0	2	2	4,895
Southern Salt	2	F	1	0	0	0	0
Southern Sanction	3	G	4	0	0	0	1,764
Southern Schemer	6	M	5	0	1	0	4,330
Southern Sensation	3	C	2	0	0	0	0
Southern Sentiment	7	G	1	0	0	0	0
Southern Shower	3	F	4	0	0	1	825
Southern Shuffle	8	G	6	0	1	0	1,270
Southern Smoke	3	F	7	2	3	0	65,796
Southern Snuggle	3	C	3	0	0	0	1,525
Southern Solstice	3	F	6	0	0	2	5,370
Southern Son	7	G	7	1	0	2	1,751
Southern Spring	2	F	2	0	0	1	900
Southern Spur	5	G	5	1	0	1	10,753
Southern Starr	4	G	2	0	0	0	100
Southern Stepper	3	F	11	3	1	2	33,420
Southern Storm	4	C	13	1	3	1	11,208
Southern Straight	3	F	4	0	0	3	3,950
Southern Surprise	4	F	9	3	0	0	92,775
Southern Survivor	4	C	13	2	3	2	20,160
Southern Sweet	5	M	5	1	0	3	23,121
Southern Sweets	5	G	2	0	0	0	975
Southern Tee	7	G	7	1	2	2	12,578
Southern Tour	5	M	9	2	4	1	98,000
Southern Treasure	4	F	6	0	1	0	5,400
Southern Trial	2	G	5	1	1	0	35,400
Southern Trick	2	G	4	0	0	1	1,375
Southern Twilight	2	G	3	0	1	0	1,720
Southern Viking	4	F	5	0	0	0	840
Southern Voice	3	F	19	2	2	4	31,675
Southern Whiskers	3	G	11	1	1	2	15,389
Southern Wild	6	H	5	0	0	0	100
Southern Wind	2	F	5	0	0	0	348
Southern Windsong	5	M	6	0	0	0	691
Southern Wolf	5	G	6	0	0	0	2,520

RECORDS OF HORSES

Horse	Age	Sex	Sts	1st	2d	3d	Won	Horse	Age	Sex	Sts	1st	2d	3d	Won
Southern Yam	4	F	8	0	1	0	1,240	Spanish Blush	4	F	6	1	0	0	2,792
Southernblue	3	G	6	0	1	0	6,820	Spanish Brandy	3	F	3	0	0	0	8,818
Southerndemolition	2	G	1	0	0	0	0	Spanish Castle	5	M	12	1	1	1	7,255
Southernsluckystar	3	F	2	1	0	0	5,100	Spanish Charm	4	C	10	0	0	0	2,700
Southernsturn	3	F	15	2	3	4	17,589	Spanish Curse	3	G	13	3	2	2	14,000
Southlake Drive	4	G	8	0	1	2	12,649	Spanish Decree	4	F	13	2	2	2	180,079
Southtown Slew	3	G	11	2	3	2	53,104	Spanish Empire	3	C	8	3	2	2	121,714
Southwell	5	M	13	0	0	1	2,118	Spanish Eyes	5	G	14	4	1	2	64,075
Southwest Shuttle	5	H	3	0	0	0	260	Spanish Fiesta	2	F	2	0	1	0	13,524
Souvenier Biz	3	C	5	2	2	1	107,996	Spanish Flyer	4	F	9	0	0	1	1,697
Souvenir Beads	5	M	9	0	0	0	316	Spanish Forks	3	G	9	0	2	1	1,850
Souvenir Doll	2	F	3	1	0	0	10,200	Spanish Fort	3	F	1	0	0	0	0
Souvenir Party	3	F	6	0	2	1	28,480	Spanish Groom	5	G	8	0	1	0	2,028
Souvenir Song	2	F	3	0	0	0	630	Spanish Guitar	5	M	3	0	0	1	6,832
Souvenir's Copied	3	C	4	0	0	0	0	Spanish Gypsy	4	F	10	6	3	0	24,785
Souvenir's Lad	3	C	5	1	1	0	30,025	Spanish Hall	7	H	1	0	0	0	0
Souvenir's of Old	3	G	7	2	1	0	36,550	Spanish Harlem	4	G	12	2	0	2	17,961
Sou'wester	6	G	11	0	5	0	8,280	Spanish High Rise	7	G	8	2	1	0	5,405
Souza	2	F	1	0	0	0	0	Spanish Highway	2	G	4	0	0	0	1,783
Sovereign Actor	3	C	8	1	3	0	32,140	Spanish Honor	3	G	10	3	1	3	21,889
Sovereign Attire	5	G	11	0	5	2	87,646	Spanish Johnny	4	G	12	2	2	2	39,954
Sovereign Creek	3	C	4	1	1	1	12,700	Spanish Lady	2	F	3	0	0	0	1,338
Sovereign Dreams	8	G	5	0	1	1	3,450	Spanish Lariat	4	C	6	0	0	0	219
Sovereign Episode	8	M	2	0	0	0	0	Spanish Lass	4	F	16	0	3	2	10,887
Sovereign Genius	5	M	3	0	0	0	0	Spanish Lover	5	H	3	0	0	0	164
Sovereign Gold	4	C	2	0	0	0	700	Spanish Mill	3	F	1	0	0	0	90
Sovereign Kit (ARG)	7	H	8	1	0	0	34,095	Spanish Miss	6	M	7	0	0	0	360
Sovereign Luck	5	G	15	0	2	1	5,685	Spanish Mist	6	G	9	1	1	0	11,840
Sovereign Miss	3	F	9	3	4	2	27,550	Spanish Nicole	5	M	2	0	0	0	160
Sovereign Power	4	C	11	1	2	5	23,335	Spanish Pearl	2	F	3	0	0	0	0
Sovereign Rip Torn	7	G	16	0	1	0	2,710	Spanish Rioja	2	C	4	1	0	0	3,855
Sovereign Salute	3	C	7	1	2	1	45,833	Spanish River	4	F	15	2	1	1	10,002
Sovereign Storm	9	H	1	0	0	1	5,000	Spanish Sage	3	F	10	0	2	0	14,300
Sovereign Sweep	4	C	10	2	1	0	74,260	Spanish Secrets	2	F	3	0	0	0	1,595
Sovereign Won	4	G	14	3	2	1	31,879	Spanish Slew	2	F	5	3	1	0	37,600
Sovereignadversary	7	H	7	0	2	0	2,389	Spanish Spur (GB)	5	G	6	2	1	2	76,392
Sovereignoftheseas	3	F	10	2	1	1	72,974	Spanish Tunnel	4	F	11	2	2	1	30,490
Sovereign's Prince	6	G	3	0	0	0	0	Spanish Valley	7	G	6	1	0	0	3,204
Soveriegn Time	3	C	6	2	0	0	9,075	Spanish Warrior	2	C	1	0	0	0	0
Soverign Honor	2	C	5	2	0	0	35,450	Spank	3	C	8	1	1	2	15,055
Soverign Sej	6	H	12	0	2	1	3,575	Spank Me Silly	3	F	6	1	0	1	14,980
Soverign Willy	3	G	6	0	1	0	2,663	Spanked	3	F	1	0	0	0	1,980
Soviet Colony	3	F	1	0	0	0	0	Spankintime	3	G	12	0	3	4	8,318
Soviet Flag	4	G	1	0	0	0	0	Spankstress	5	M	9	1	0	2	5,045
Soviet Gypsy	7	G	6	0	0	1	1,350	Spar	10	G	13	2	1	3	6,787
Soviet Ruhler	3	G	5	1	0	0	7,503	Spare Change	4	G	4	2	0	0	12,125
Sovran Ice	5	M	22	0	3	3	13,604	Spare Me	9	G	7	1	0	0	2,882
Sovrano	2	C	1	0	0	0	0	Spare No Expense	3	G	7	1	2	0	5,051
Sowhateverittakes	3	F	3	0	0	0	0	Spared	4	G	4	0	2	1	13,780
Sowhatsyourpoint	3	G	7	1	0	1	11,115	Spare's Memory	5	M	3	0	0	1	870
Sox for Millie	5	G	6	0	1	2	5,385	Spark Boulevard	8	G	7	0	0	0	0
Sox On Top	8	G	7	1	2	1	11,775	Spark Sept (FR)	4	F	6	0	1	1	23,616
Soy Chispita (ARG)	5	M	3	0	1	0	4,350	Spark Setter	7	G	11	3	0	0	25,960
Soy Desatanudos (ARG)	4	C	9	1	0	4	40,080	Spark the Nat	4	F	15	1	6	3	18,900
Soy Famoso	3	C	3	0	0	0	730	Sparkem	8	G	1	0	0	0	0
Soyabeanthere	3	G	7	1	1	0	11,109	Sparkle for Hailey	2	G	3	1	0	1	16,352
Soybeaner	6	G	6	0	0	0	634	Sparkle Free	8	M	15	1	5	1	7,999
Soyuz	7	G	14	3	2	4	28,424	Sparkle N Classic	3	G	9	0	0	3	5,788
Soze	3	G	12	1	3	2	33,633	Sparkle N Gold	2	F	1	0	0	0	990
Sozo	6	G	19	6	5	2	35,820	Sparkle Plentie	5	M	7	3	1	0	32,127
Spa City	4	F	2	0	0	0	387	Sparklead	3	G	14	0	3	2	5,170
Space Age	4	C	18	1	2	0	18,670	Sparkles Mattie	4	F	11	2	2	1	13,130
Space Cadet	3	F	4	2	0	0	8,016	Sparkles Prospect	7	M	11	1	0	1	8,560
Space Invader	3	C	2	0	1	1	10,880	Sparklesforrachael	4	F	3	0	0	0	540
Space Pirate	4	G	5	0	0	0	404	Sparklespeed	4	C	1	0	0	0	0
Space Probe	3	F	8	2	1	3	55,400	Sparklin Kat	3	F	3	0	0	0	916
Space Walker	5	M	12	3	1	0	23,282	Sparkling Ava	4	F	7	0	1	1	20,128
Spaceboy	7	G	12	1	2	3	11,269	Sparkling Blue	3	F	3	2	0	0	43,950
Spaced Out	3	G	13	3	2	2	40,350	Sparkling Borodin	5	M	1	0	0	0	38
Spacey Czarina	6	M	7	1	0	1	5,729	Sparkling Buck	4	C	10	1	2	1	6,980
Spacey Princess	2	F	5	0	1	0	1,930	Sparkling Catch	9	G	4	0	0	0	0
Spade	3	G	13	1	1	2	17,361	Sparkling Claim	3	F	7	1	0	0	8,498
Spade Royal Flush	5	H	9	1	3	1	8,683	Sparkling Glitter	8	M	4	0	1	0	1,431
Spainbird (IRE)	5	H	8	1	0	2	53,220	Sparkling Home	3	F	12	1	4	0	21,920
Span	5	G	14	2	0	1	23,329	Sparkling Hope	7	G	8	0	0	0	737
Spanish Aladosious	5	M	1	0	0	0	42	Sparkling Ice	3	G	3	0	0	0	140
Spanish Angel	7	H	5	0	0	0	470	Sparkling Jayne	2	F	2	0	0	0	60
Spanish Artist	3	G	14	0	2	1	16,750	Sparkling Kaye	4	F	6	1	1	1	7,490
Spanish Banks	6	G	12	2	3	2	25,479	Sparkling Pete	4	C	10	1	0	0	3,180

Horse	Age	Sex	Sts	1st	2d	3d	Won	Horse	Age	Sex	Sts	1st	2d	3d	Won
Sparkling Rozie	5	M	10	2	1	0	6,878	Special Jule	4	F	7	3	2	0	59,460
Sparkling Sabia	3	F	11	4	1	1	85,860	Special K. B.	3	F	11	3	1	1	20,290
Sparkling Sherry	3	F	6	1	0	1	7,235	Special Lady Jane	5	M	3	0	1	0	1,625
Sparkling Slew	2	F	7	0	0	0	625	Special Lessons	7	G	5	1	1	0	4,036
Sparkling Tyler	5	H	9	1	0	2	6,290	Special Lovin	2	F	4	0	0	0	0
Sparks a Flyin	3	C	3	0	0	0	52	Special Magnet	4	F	2	0	0	0	343
Sparks Hyati Fly	5	G	9	1	0	0	1,358	Special Marine	5	G	2	0	0	0	0
Sparks R Risen	5	G	4	0	0	1	1,433	Special Matter	5	G	9	1	2	1	169,660
Sparky Diamond	6	M	7	0	3	1	21,880	Special Meeting	4	G	4	0	0	0	499
Sparky Mon	4	G	2	0	0	0	0	Special Melody	6	M	2	0	0	0	60
Sparky Villa	9	H	6	1	0	0	3,726	Special Memo	3	G	7	0	0	1	1,430
Sparky's Mission	6	H	1	0	0	0	0	Special Menu	2	F	3	0	2	0	7,850
Sparky's Revenge	5	H	2	0	0	0	150	Special Motion	4	F	14	6	2	1	28,699
Sparky's Roll	4	F	6	0	0	0	0	Special Ops	2	G	2	0	0	0	135
Sparrow Hawk	2	G	6	0	1	0	920	Special Ops Force	3	F	1	0	0	1	1,870
Sparta	3	F	8	1	0	1	12,360	Special Orbit	4	C	2	0	0	0	0
Spartan Mission	8	H	7	0	2	2	4,889	Special Order	6	G	4	0	1	0	3,116
Spatial Luke	3	G	3	0	0	0	390	Special Payday	5	M	12	3	0	0	26,007
Spatso	2	C	3	0	0	1	7,030	Special Queen	4	F	8	0	1	1	4,508
Spatter	2	C	3	0	0	0	708	Special Rate	3	C	7	2	2	1	87,790
Spauce Creek	6	M	2	0	0	0	217	Special Report	2	F	1	1	0	0	15,200
Speak Compelling	6	M	4	0	0	0	1,020	Special Reserve	6	G	4	0	0	0	0
Speak Easy	2	F	2	0	2	0	11,200	Special Ring	6	G	5	1	2	0	383,000
Speak First	3	C	5	0	0	1	5,587	Special Royal Bell	3	F	5	0	0	1	517
Speak in Code	10	G	10	2	2	2	4,011	Special Saint	5	G	8	1	1	0	8,975
Speak in Passing	6	H	1	1	0	0	82,500	Special Sign	6	H	9	2	0	3	9,420
Speak of the Devil	3	F	10	2	2	1	23,002	Special Slew	8	H	12	1	3	1	6,311
Speak Out	3	F	12	1	0	0	64,819	Special Spender	5	H	2	0	0	0	225
Speak Out Loud	3	C	6	1	1	1	21,531	Special Spin	4	F	5	1	0	0	9,875
Speak the Language	2	F	3	1	1	0	39,235	Special Squall	6	G	12	1	0	0	4,804
Speakette	3	F	2	0	0	0	0	Special Status	3	C	4	1	0	0	13,908
Speakin French	4	F	4	0	0	0	1,950	Special Strike Out	5	H	6	0	1	0	693
Speaking Noty	2	G	4	0	0	0	1,096	Special Tactics	2	F	3	0	0	0	0
Speaking of Style	5	M	1	0	0	0	40	Special Terms	6	H	8	2	3	1	35,720
Speaks Volumes	4	F	10	1	0	2	15,104	Special Times	5	H	1	0	0	0	1,440
Speakster	3	G	7	3	2	0	25,255	Special too a T.	5	G	1	0	0	0	0
Spearsmill	4	G	5	1	0	0	16,835	Special Topics	2	C	4	0	3	0	8,000
Special	5	H	7	0	3	0	3,740	Special Tour	3	G	6	0	1	2	10,702
Special Allure	3	F	5	1	0	1	19,520	Special Trial	5	M	7	2	1	2	56,070
Special American	5	M	11	0	2	1	17,700	Special Variety	3	F	5	0	0	0	66
Special Answer	3	G	4	0	0	2	5,020	Special Version	2	F	3	0	0	0	275
Special Appeal	5	M	8	2	2	2	47,678	Special War	3	F	4	0	0	0	858
Special Assessment	3	F	3	0	0	0	226	Special Way	8	G	16	5	1	3	42,945
Special Ballad	4	F	3	0	1	0	7,700	Special Wayne	4	G	12	0	0	2	1,986
Special Beam	3	G	13	3	0	2	25,775	Special Weapon	3	G	3	0	0	0	1,260
Special Bet	3	G	4	0	0	0	0	Special Wife	5	M	4	0	1	0	9,660
Special Case	3	F	4	1	1	1	9,242	Special Willy	5	G	9	1	0	4	13,412
Special Cat	4	M	7	0	0	1	808	Special Yankee	3	C	5	0	0	0	502
Special Concern	3	G	7	0	2	0	8,870	Specialexpectation	4	G	23	2	2	5	17,151
Special Concerto	2	F	8	2	2	3	47,510	Speciality	3	F	12	2	1	3	32,920
Special County	5	M	6	1	4	0	58,600	Specialkindafan	8	M	14	2	4	0	8,980
Special D	3	F	3	0	1	0	2,205	Specious (IRE)	4	F	2	0	0	0	0
Special Dancer	7	G	13	0	2	5	14,742	Speck of Gold	5	M	9	1	3	4	47,608
Special Day	4	G	2	0	0	0	0	Speck of Money	3	G	16	2	5	3	26,414
Special Deed	2	F	8	2	0	1	28,495	Speck of Peace	3	F	13	1	6	5	42,750
Special Diamond	2	C	3	0	0	0	2,460	Speckled Spice	3	F	9	1	0	2	34,330
Special Dimension	5	G	3	0	0	0	180	Spectaculaireontap	5	M	8	0	3	1	23,330
Special Dolly	7	M	12	0	0	1	2,773	Spectacular Anzi	3	F	7	2	0	1	20,772
Special Dreams	3	G	2	1	0	0	6,030	Spectacular Baby	3	F	7	0	0	3	2,222
Special Eight	4	F	4	0	0	0	650	Spectacular Beamer	3	F	7	2	1	0	13,550
Special Emblem	4	G	1	0	1	0	1,440	Spectacular Caper	5	M	6	1	1	1	4,359
Special Engagement	3	F	11	2	2	1	11,605	Spectacular Cat	5	H	16	1	0	2	25,790
Special Era	2	F	1	0	1	0	2,184	Spectacular Chance	4	G	12	3	1	1	31,970
Special Express	6	G	9	0	1	2	4,619	Spectacular Chimes	3	F	5	0	0	1	1,105
Special Fact	4	C	8	2	0	1	7,177	Spectacular City	3	C	2	0	0	0	2,520
Special Forbes	3	F	3	0	0	0	0	Spectacular Crisis	3	G	8	0	3	1	10,365
Special Forces	4	G	11	2	1	3	21,400	Spectacular Dancer	6	G	9	2	4	0	8,914
Special Friend	4	F	1	0	0	0	960	Spectacular Dash	3	G	8	2	1	0	29,905
Special Gal	6	M	2	0	0	0	0	Spectacular Day	3	F	2	0	0	0	1,980
Special General	2	C	1	0	0	0	100	Spectacular Deal	6	G	5	0	1	0	5,980
Special Guest	3	F	7	0	1	1	7,044	Spectacular Dove	4	F	5	2	0	0	49,800
Special Home	5	G	21	0	1	4	6,303	Spectacular Editor	3	C	4	2	0	1	6,757
Special Insignia	5	M	15	2	5	2	42,705	Spectacular Eltish	3	G	14	2	2	3	19,283
Special Invader	7	G	3	0	2	0	1,300	Spectacular Factor	4	F	12	1	3	5	22,100
Special Invitation	2	G	5	0	1	1	3,909	Spectacular Fan	3	G	7	0	0	0	480
Special Jen	4	F	16	4	4	1	28,611	Spectacular Gray	5	M	3	0	0	0	510
Special Jet	3	C	1	0	0	0	1,230	Spectacular Greek	4	F	9	2	4	1	14,373
Special Journey	3	F	1	0	0	0	0	Spectacular Johnny	6	H	3	0	0	0	310
Special Judge	3	G	7	1	2	2	46,590	Spectacular Kim	6	G	1	0	0	0	810

RECORDS OF HORSES

Horse	Age	Sex	Sts	1st	2d	3d	Won	Horse	Age	Sex	Sts	1st	2d	3d	Won
Spectacular Light	6	G	9	0	1	3	23,112	Speedy Little Car	5	G	10	0	2	2	5,435
Spectacular Lisa	3	F	10	4	4	0	93,000	Speedy Mama	4	F	2	0	0	0	420
Spectacular Man	7	G	2	0	0	0	122	Speedy Matt	9	G	1	0	0	0	38
Spectacular Miss	3	F	4	0	0	0	540	Speedy Maverick	4	G	2	0	0	0	132
Spectacular Moon	2	F	5	4	0	1	139,190	Speedy Mohama	4	C	1	0	0	0	0
Spectacular Morn	4	F	16	3	2	2	11,107	Speedy Nessie	4	F	5	0	0	3	10,590
Spectacular Peaks	4	C	4	0	0	0	650	Speedy Nick	3	G	3	0	0	0	390
Spectacular Place	4	F	9	3	2	1	81,620	Speedy Petey	3	C	8	2	1	3	16,410
Spectacular Roy	3	C	3	0	0	0	0	Speedy Pick	5	G	7	1	1	1	30,470
Spectacular Rule	4	C	3	0	0	0	300	Speedy Pie	6	G	15	2	2	1	16,831
Spectacular Seven	3	C	3	0	0	0	105	Speedy Pieddy	3	G	7	0	0	0	1,530
Spectacular Slew	7	G	7	1	2	1	20,580	Speedy Ransom	4	G	14	2	1	1	16,350
Spectacular Spats	3	F	1	0	0	0	71	Speedy Reply	4	G	10	0	1	0	3,479
Spectaculareleganz	3	F	12	0	4	4	35,680	Speedy Rider	8	G	2	0	0	1	435
Spectacularly Pink	5	H	8	1	4	1	8,360	Speedy Rusher	2	G	4	1	0	1	8,470
Spectatular Bones	3	G	2	0	0	0	84	Speedy Sonata	2	F	7	2	1	2	53,306
Spectrin Seven	4	C	11	0	0	1	252	Speedy Spring	3	C	11	2	1	1	20,005
Speechless Diamond	5	H	5	0	0	0	150	Speedy Sweep	4	F	15	1	2	0	8,376
Speed Broker	3	G	8	0	2	0	4,920	Speedy Tiffany	2	F	2	0	1	1	3,600
Speed Demon	5	G	13	0	5	1	19,660	Speedy Tradition	5	M	12	1	2	2	16,652
Speed Dot Com	5	G	3	0	1	0	704	Speedy Treat	5	G	11	1	2	2	7,676
Speed Dreamer	6	G	3	0	1	1	1,000	Speedy Trial	6	G	5	0	0	0	212
Speed Echo	4	F	9	0	4	1	8,704	Speedy Willie	5	M	1	0	0	0	0
Speed Factor	2	C	3	1	0	0	3,610	Speedy Z.	6	H	3	0	0	0	0
Speed Fever	3	F	2	0	0	0	485	Speedys Invention	3	G	3	1	0	0	4,376
Speed Gun	5	G	5	0	0	0	835	Speedy's Links	4	C	4	0	0	0	0
Speed Home	5	G	1	0	0	0	100	Speedyslim Pickens	2	C	2	0	1	1	2,382
Speed Hunter	4	G	9	2	2	0	119,242	Speightstown	5	H	2	1	1	0	56,020
Speed in Motion	9	G	1	0	0	0	0	Spellbinder	2	C	5	1	0	1	41,260
Speed Is Priceless	3	F	6	0	0	0	354	Spellbook	3	G	16	3	0	3	32,385
Speed N Thru	5	G	3	0	0	0	203	Spellfire	2	F	3	0	0	1	1,588
Speed of Funny	5	M	9	2	2	0	22,146	Spelling	4	F	4	0	1	1	29,560
Speed of Hail	4	F	1	0	0	0	225	Spellmaker	3	F	6	0	1	3	20,580
Speed of Light (IRE)	5	G	7	2	1	2	69,340	Spencer Creek Miss	4	F	2	0	0	0	315
Speed Out Front	4	C	8	3	1	1	32,020	Spencer Falls	4	G	15	1	1	0	4,786
Speed Pocket	5	H	15	3	2	2	7,465	Spencer's Magic	2	C	1	0	0	0	1,680
Speed Producer	4	G	10	0	1	2	3,905	Spencers Storm	2	F	6	1	0	1	20,320
Speed Secret	9	G	5	0	0	0	405	Spend a Buck Baby	8	M	3	0	0	0	270
Speed Shot	3	F	8	0	1	0	1,119	Spend a Web	5	G	13	1	2	4	34,333
Speed Supreme	3	F	5	0	1	1	14,319	Spend and Hope	4	F	3	0	2	0	1,885
Speed to Speed	5	M	15	1	2	3	34,020	Spend Spend Spend	4	G	6	1	0	0	40,542
Speed Trial	6	G	9	1	1	2	3,063	Spend Your Raise	5	M	5	0	0	2	1,375
Speed Vike	6	H	13	4	4	1	21,475	Spenders Image	7	G	5	0	0	0	372
Speed Whiz	2	C	4	0	1	0	10,095	Spending Floozie	6	M	14	4	1	2	18,458
Speedball Tucker	5	G	11	0	1	1	4,885	Spending Jesy	3	F	1	0	1	0	5,600
Speeder	2	C	2	0	0	0	0	Spendn Spree	7	M	6	2	1	1	14,741
Speederhof	7	M	4	0	0	0	70	Spendthemoneyhoney	3	F	1	1	0	0	7,500
Speedfast	2	F	4	1	1	0	19,081	Spens Dawn	3	F	3	0	0	0	0
Speeding Fury	3	G	3	0	0	0	648	Spensive	3	C	6	0	2	1	164,070
Speeding Jim	5	H	4	0	1	0	7,050	Spice Is Nice	4	F	4	1	1	0	14,841
Speedjama	2	C	1	1	0	0	24,600	Spice Island	4	F	13	6	3	1	361,286
Speedman	5	G	7	0	0	0	384	Spice Rack	2	F	2	1	0	0	22,860
Speedmovesme	2	F	3	0	0	1	635	Spice the Price	4	F	7	2	1	0	8,764
Speedo the Gift	4	G	10	2	4	1	15,500	Spice Twice	7	M	18	1	1	5	8,380
Speeds the Key	3	F	12	4	0	2	24,454	Spiced	4	F	14	1	0	3	10,400
Speedster	7	G	10	0	0	2	1,166	Spiced Tea	4	F	10	2	0	1	16,140
Speedstruck Seeker	5	M	5	1	0	1	16,378	Spiced to Go	2	G	3	1	0	0	10,206
Speedwell Beau	2	C	1	0	0	1	2,090	Spiced Wine	3	G	7	2	2	0	26,074
Speedy and Bold	3	C	1	0	0	0	0	Spicey Game	4	F	13	4	2	4	18,660
Speedy Appeal	2	F	5	0	2	0	8,960	Spicey Savannah	5	M	6	0	0	0	2,310
Speedy Boy	2	C	2	0	0	0	0	Spicoli	2	C	2	0	0	0	0
Speedy Buster	7	M	12	1	3	1	7,472	Spicy Award	8	G	8	2	3	0	37,090
Speedy Comet	5	G	10	4	2	1	48,018	Spicy Cajun	2	F	10	1	1	1	16,462
Speedy Coyote	7	M	3	0	0	0	0	Spicy Devil	5	G	11	0	1	3	3,864
Speedy Dancer	3	F	2	0	2	0	4,200	Spicy Engagement	4	F	13	2	0	3	33,388
Speedy Dee	3	F	5	1	0	0	7,785	Spicy Light	2	F	3	0	0	0	570
Speedy Diplomat	4	G	6	1	0	0	6,510	Spicy Prospector	7	G	10	2	0	3	38,540
Speedy Doll	4	F	5	1	0	0	2,325	Spicy Soup	3	F	7	1	1	0	9,140
Speedy Escort	7	G	16	1	1	0	6,488	Spicy Stuff	6	H	10	1	4	0	74,120
Speedy Exit	4	G	7	1	0	0	4,016	Spider Annie	2	F	7	1	2	0	20,043
Speedy Falcon	2	F	5	4	0	0	56,467	Spider Canyon	2	C	6	1	1	0	87,188
Speedy Flight	4	G	19	1	2	2	12,941	Spider Dann	6	G	11	2	3	1	20,187
Speedy Gazelle	3	G	13	2	3	1	14,312	Spider Dash	3	C	6	0	0	1	3,187
Speedy Georgette	6	M	7	0	0	3	2,723	Spider Glide	3	C	5	0	0	0	610
Speedy Halo	2	G	5	1	0	0	5,795	Spider Spider	4	C	8	2	2	1	17,560
Speedy Hand Allen	4	C	11	1	0	2	8,391	Spider Time	2	C	7	0	2	0	8,005
Speedy Heels	6	G	15	0	0	1	1,473	Spider Wire	10	G	6	0	2	1	6,062
Speedy Lee	3	G	2	1	0	0	2,590	Spiders Dance	7	G	2	1	1	0	4,040
Speedy Lexi	4	F	7	0	2	1	2,915	Spiel	3	C	1	0	0	0	0

Horse	Age	Sex	Sts	1st	2d	3d	Won	Horse	Age	Sex	Sts	1st	2d	3d	Won
Spiel Meister	2	C	4	2	0	1	17,930	Spiritual Journey	4	G	13	1	1	0	5,626
Spiffee Gal	2	F	1	0	1	0	11,760	Spiritualist	2	C	4	0	0	0	7,720
Spike the Ball	3	G	5	1	0	0	5,625	Spirosandnicholis	4	G	6	2	0	0	26,480
Spike the Fever	2	C	2	0	2	0	15,000	Spit Shine	6	G	4	0	0	0	781
Spike Valay	4	C	12	1	1	1	11,341	Spite the Devil	3	G	14	1	3	3	217,924
Spiked Punch	4	F	7	1	0	1	22,410	Spiteful Love	3	F	4	1	1	2	38,140
Spilled Honey	4	G	14	4	5	0	63,610	Spitfire Ellie	2	F	5	0	0	0	465
Spillikin (GB)	4	C	11	0	0	2	11,715	Spitfire Man	4	G	4	3	1	0	134,680
Spin Breaker	7	H	9	0	0	0	239	Spit'n Nickles	8	G	8	1	1	1	2,033
Spin Citi	4	C	5	0	2	1	6,839	Spit'n Spat	3	F	2	0	0	0	0
Spin Control	3	F	6	3	0	2	79,310	Splash Dance	6	M	6	0	0	1	1,300
Spin for Cash	3	G	11	2	1	0	6,158	Splash Ensing	3	F	1	0	0	0	45
Spin Ghar	3	F	16	0	0	2	5,577	Splash o' Magic	4	F	11	1	3	3	10,432
Spin the Lover	2	F	5	1	1	0	17,800	Splash of Brat	7	M	4	0	0	0	630
Spin Time	6	G	7	0	1	0	4,140	Splash of Soda	3	G	8	1	2	3	8,138
Spin Zone	4	C	5	2	1	0	25,360	Splash of Winter	2	F	2	0	0	0	126
Spinal Tap	2	F	5	0	0	0	1,484	Splash Tour	3	F	8	2	1	1	10,358
Spinalong	4	F	8	2	1	1	26,100	Splasha	3	F	11	3	1	2	162,018
Spindini	2	C	1	1	0	0	16,416	Splashed	2	F	2	0	0	0	222
Spindrift (IRE)	8	H	1	1	0	0	5,640	Splashed Soup	3	F	5	0	0	0	795
Spinelessjellyfish	7	H	9	1	1	0	107,704	Splashin' Jack	3	G	7	1	0	0	26,217
Spinmeister	6	G	3	1	1	0	6,694	Splashing Jazz	6	M	16	4	2	3	30,405
Spinner Rules	3	F	11	0	0	0	740	Splashing Louis	3	C	6	0	2	0	9,800
Spinning Affair	6	G	5	1	2	0	11,759	Splashing Princess	3	F	9	0	4	1	27,340
Spinning At Dawn	3	F	7	3	1	0	48,000	Splashing Rose	7	M	10	0	0	2	7,730
Spinning Diamonds	4	F	1	0	0	0	0	Splashisagamelady	3	F	8	1	1	0	8,546
Spinning Heart	3	C	2	0	0	0	1,320	Splashy Jill	3	F	6	0	0	1	1,540
Spinning N Winning	4	F	2	0	0	0	96	Splashy Wolf	4	F	4	0	0	0	1,160
Spinning Tales	4	C	5	3	0	0	50,190	Splatter	6	M	14	3	1	2	13,502
Spinning Time	3	F	9	2	2	2	22,090	Splenderinthegrass	4	F	1	0	0	0	0
Spinning Wheel	3	C	3	0	0	1	1,200	Splendeur (FR)	4	F	6	1	1	0	45,800
Spinning Wind	3	F	2	1	0	0	20,400	Splendid Action	9	G	11	0	1	0	2,340
Spinozas Legacy	6	H	1	0	0	0	84	Splendid Devin	6	H	1	0	0	0	220
Spiral Dancer	3	F	9	1	1	1	8,823	Splendid Dilemma	3	F	9	1	1	3	19,900
Spires Bid	3	F	1	0	0	0	640	Splendid Fina City	4	F	14	2	1	4	17,198
Spirit Dance	10	G	4	0	0	0	447	Splendid Form	6	G	9	0	1	1	7,450
Spirit de Azure	4	F	8	3	0	2	70,934	Splendid George	5	G	9	1	0	0	4,252
Spirit Dreamer	8	G	14	1	2	1	17,434	Splendid Jaclyn	4	F	16	4	2	3	31,282
Spirit Gulch	2	G	4	0	0	2	3,014	Splendid Journey	4	G	17	3	0	3	10,986
Spirit in the Wind	8	G	10	2	2	0	11,719	Splendid Mover	3	G	8	1	1	1	19,100
Spirit Island	8	G	8	0	2	0	2,542	Splendid Nature	3	G	16	2	2	7	38,740
Spirit o' Diazo	3	C	4	0	0	0	0	Splendid Prospect	3	C	6	0	0	0	686
Spirit o' War	4	G	1	0	0	0	2,880	Splendid Splinter	9	G	5	1	1	0	6,070
Spirit of a Legend	3	G	10	3	1	0	31,170	Splendid Sunrise	7	M	8	3	0	1	23,189
Spirit of Chance	4	F	1	1	0	0	8,700	Splendid Times	4	G	7	0	0	0	2,780
Spirit of Flight	3	F	1	0	0	0	185	Splendid Torch	4	C	2	1	1	0	7,125
Spirit of Freedom	3	G	7	1	0	0	14,097	Splendid View	3	F	5	0	0	0	40
Spirit of Jack	4	C	3	0	1	1	7,250	Splendid Western	4	C	13	2	3	2	51,214
Spirit of Justice	4	F	3	0	0	0	0	Splinter	4	G	13	3	1	3	8,868
Spirit of Malagra	4	C	5	2	1	1	32,830	Splinter One	3	C	8	1	1	2	36,575
Spirit of Mike	5	H	2	0	0	0	720	Split Aces	3	C	9	1	2	1	13,820
Spirit of Montreal	2	C	3	0	0	0	1,191	Split Runs Angel	6	M	6	1	0	0	9,870
Spirit of Nature	3	F	1	0	1	0	8,800	Split the Sheets	4	F	11	2	2	1	2,948
Spirit of Pancho	3	C	3	0	1	0	6,615	Splitthedifference	2	F	2	0	0	1	3,949
Spirit of the Sea	5	G	6	0	0	0	362	Spodie	3	G	11	2	1	1	11,367
Spirit of Wailea	2	F	1	0	1	0	3,200	Spoiled	2	F	3	1	1	0	37,225
Spirit of Woody	4	G	8	1	0	1	11,273	Spoken Fur	3	F	10	5	1	3	670,630
Spirit One	5	M	6	0	0	3	2,700	Spoken Like a Pro	3	C	18	1	3	0	14,185
Spirit Run	3	F	3	1	0	0	36,744	Spoken Proposal	4	F	6	0	0	1	1,398
Spirit Star	2	C	2	0	1	0	1,280	Spontaneous Dino	4	G	5	0	0	0	865
Spirit Talker	4	G	3	0	0	0	0	Spontaneous Surge	4	F	8	0	1	1	1,964
Spiritaki	4	F	10	0	0	1	1,280	Spontaneous Wood	3	G	4	0	0	0	2,857
Spirited	2	F	6	1	1	0	19,900	Spoofin	6	G	5	3	0	0	41,311
Spirited Amanda	4	F	12	2	1	0	20,337	Spooky Mouse	5	M	11	1	0	2	4,676
Spirited Ghost	3	C	8	2	2	0	29,683	Spooky Mulder	5	G	15	6	3	1	101,912
Spirited Maiden	4	F	8	3	0	4	77,247	Spooky Tree	6	H	8	0	2	1	5,826
Spirited Market	4	F	17	3	2	3	37,343	Spoon Head	7	H	12	0	0	0	390
Spirited Moves	3	F	2	0	0	0	0	Spooners Hill	3	G	6	2	0	0	28,727
Spirited Niner	4	G	3	1	1	0	13,830	Spooning	7	G	11	1	0	0	17,427
Spirited Sis	3	F	10	2	1	3	27,942	Spoonman	4	G	10	1	2	2	24,400
Spirited Thunder	3	C	8	2	0	0	12,540	Sport Cafe	2	F	6	1	1	0	14,125
Spiritedtunetoo	2	F	1	0	0	0	0	Sport Coat	4	G	7	2	2	0	52,020
Spiritful King	4	G	14	2	0	0	5,444	Sport d'Hiver	11	G	8	0	1	2	6,753
Spiritofneworleans	4	C	7	2	0	1	14,881	Sport On Saturday	3	F	2	0	0	0	0
Spirit's Ace High	8	G	1	0	0	0	0	Sportin' Griff	10	G	14	2	0	1	9,703
Spirits Afar	8	G	3	0	0	0	485	Sportin Phil	4	G	14	3	2	2	21,802
Spirits Rock	3	F	2	1	0	0	3,624	Sportin'affair	4	F	16	2	1	0	20,504
Spiritual Drift	3	F	15	2	4	4	67,764	Sporting Lad	7	H	7	2	2	0	84,100
Spiritual Hand	2	F	1	0	1	0	3,800	Sportive Spirit	4	F	7	1	0	3	23,362

Horse	Age	Sex	Sts	1st	2d	3d	Won
Sports Bettor	2	C	1	0	0	0	1,300
Sports Channel	5	G	9	0	1	0	3,180
Sports Hero	4	C	2	2	0	0	26,890
Sports Mainia	4	G	9	0	0	0	0
Sports Maudle	5	H	2	0	1	0	1,744
Sports Medicine	3	C	9	1	1	0	10,640
Sports Queen	3	F	9	0	0	1	2,028
Sports Ridge	8	G	21	1	7	1	12,950
Sports Tour	3	G	6	0	0	1	1,115
Sportscaster	2	G	3	0	0	0	115
Sportscenter Hero	5	G	3	2	0	1	7,050
Sportsmen's Choice	6	M	2	0	0	0	425
Sportstarget	2	C	1	0	0	0	0
Sportstheone	4	C	4	0	0	0	435
Sporty	5	H	4	1	1	0	3,460
Sporty Heroine	3	F	8	0	0	0	2,160
Sposen	3	G	5	0	0	1	1,560
Spot Can Run	3	C	15	2	2	3	36,639
Spot Check	2	F	5	1	0	0	17,350
Spot Dot	3	G	14	3	1	4	44,517
Spot of Bay	4	F	7	1	1	0	10,577
Spot the Ferrara	2	G	6	1	0	0	8,536
Spotless	3	F	1	0	0	0	1,140
Spotlite Dancer	2	F	10	1	3	2	8,682
Spotlite On Macy	2	F	3	0	0	0	0
Spotted Flag	6	G	1	0	0	0	0
Spotted Owl	5	H	5	0	2	1	18,495
Spouse	3	F	14	6	4	0	72,610
Spray Lake	3	F	1	0	0	0	0
Spreadin Joy	2	F	5	0	0	2	2,030
Spreebee	4	C	2	0	0	0	270
Spright	4	F	5	1	1	1	7,225
Sprin Buck	8	G	4	1	0	0	4,080
Spring Act	2	G	2	1	0	1	7,450
Spring Affair	3	F	2	0	1	0	3,800
Spring Aire	4	F	9	0	1	4	20,204
Spring Amour	5	G	15	0	1	1	2,442
Spring Angel	4	F	5	1	0	1	16,000
Spring Barley	6	G	5	0	0	0	0
Spring Bold	5	G	14	1	4	5	10,400
Spring Breeze	3	R	5	0	0	0	272
Spring Cat	2	F	6	3	1	0	52,680
Spring Crystal	2	F	1	0	0	0	0
Spring Dip	3	G	6	0	1	0	4,755
Spring Dream	2	F	4	0	1	0	2,250
Spring Feather	5	M	6	0	0	0	1,894
Spring Feeling	3	F	7	1	0	0	11,280
Spring Festival	2	F	1	0	1	0	7,200
Spring Frolic	3	F	9	1	0	0	5,410
Spring Has Sprung	3	F	2	0	0	0	1,315
Spring Heroine	5	M	8	0	0	2	2,205
Spring Hill Miss	4	F	9	0	0	2	3,121
Spring in Paris	4	G	6	2	0	0	26,239
Spring Jet	6	H	14	0	0	2	6,520
Spring Kitten	4	F	4	1	0	0	17,880
Spring Meadow	4	F	10	3	0	3	204,002
Spring Mint	3	F	9	0	1	1	12,005
Spring Queen	2	F	2	0	0	0	333
Spring Rade	2	F	5	2	1	0	50,029
Spring Royal Pride	6	M	10	0	0	0	166
Spring Rush	3	F	7	1	0	0	25,320
Spring Scamper	3	F	2	0	0	1	1,210
Spring Season	4	F	8	1	4	2	56,270
Spring Sleet	3	C	5	1	0	1	8,235
Spring Spin	4	F	4	0	1	2	2,060
Spring Star (FR)	4	F	5	2	0	3	182,313
Spring Station	8	G	12	2	2	2	12,857
Spring Street	6	G	10	1	3	1	34,521
Spring Tonic	4	F	3	0	0	0	0
Spring Training	2	G	4	0	1	1	4,775
Spring Winds	4	C	9	0	3	0	3,679
Spring Zeal	4	F	12	2	4	1	23,840
Springbrakemistake	2	F	3	0	0	0	305
Springfield Boy	3	C	9	1	1	0	16,501
Springhill Dancer	4	F	2	0	0	0	252
Springhill Lucky	4	G	4	0	0	1	11,107
Springs Eternal	4	F	4	0	0	1	680
Springster	2	C	4	0	0	1	2,420
Springtime Flyer	3	F	11	0	2	3	12,795
Springtime Music	5	M	9	1	0	1	9,758
Springtime Special	7	G	1	0	0	0	0
Springtimeminster	3	C	9	1	1	3	7,745
Sprinklestothemoon	4	F	3	0	0	0	230
Sprint Dancer	5	M	9	0	3	3	2,088
Sprintaway	4	F	3	0	0	0	654
Spritely Walker	3	C	9	4	2	1	210,340
Spruce Belle	2	F	3	0	2	0	5,220
Spruce Hero	3	C	1	0	0	0	0
Spruce Hollow Babe	4	F	8	1	0	1	9,867
Spruce Lake	3	C	2	1	0	0	15,600
Spruce Meadows	2	G	3	0	0	0	0
Spruce Run	5	H	10	2	1	2	83,858
Spruce's Prince	2	G	4	0	1	1	5,670
Spry Street	3	G	8	0	1	0	3,215
Spud Man	4	C	10	3	5	2	6,504
Spudville	2	C	2	0	1	0	2,472
Spun Gold	3	F	2	0	0	0	0
Spunky Becky	2	F	3	0	0	0	177
Spunky Boy	5	G	22	2	2	4	13,007
Spunky Fun	3	F	1	0	0	0	100
Spunky Storm	4	F	8	0	0	0	708
Spunky Target	7	M	7	0	0	0	0
Spur Creek	4	F	12	4	1	0	71,180
Spur Man	4	C	2	0	0	0	0
Spuraway	3	G	11	2	3	3	22,154
Spurofthemorning	4	F	3	0	0	0	0
Spuron	4	C	7	0	0	1	1,047
Spurred On	4	G	11	1	1	2	21,800
Spurred On by Love	3	G	4	0	0	0	313
Spurs N Latigo	5	G	1	0	0	0	0
Spy Me Not (ARG)	6	G	11	2	5	2	65,875
Spy On Me	7	M	4	0	0	1	544
Spy Shark	7	G	6	0	0	0	338
Spy Trial	3	C	5	0	1	0	4,720
Spy Walker	8	G	1	0	0	0	40
Spyder Fyder	3	F	1	0	0	0	0
Spyman	6	G	6	0	0	2	1,455
Spyzotti	3	C	2	0	0	0	0
Squadron Commander	6	G	22	7	4	2	38,934
Squall	6	H	1	0	0	0	110
Squall Alert	4	C	12	2	2	0	11,057
Squan Rose	4	F	15	1	1	0	8,301
Square Bob	4	G	15	2	3	0	120,192
Square Cut Gem	2	G	5	1	0	0	14,080
Square Dance	5	M	6	0	1	2	29,580
Square Dancer	7	G	5	0	0	0	440
Square Expectation	4	C	6	1	1	0	9,983
Square Wheels	3	G	9	2	0	2	42,500
Squared Away	4	F	14	1	0	0	3,366
Squash	4	F	15	2	4	3	23,540
Squatti Again	3	C	3	0	3	0	5,616
Squaw Spirit	3	F	13	1	1	2	18,462
Squaw Valley	3	F	12	2	0	2	32,540
Squawk Box	5	M	4	0	0	0	682
Squaw's Tomahawk	6	H	7	1	0	0	3,501
Squeaky Boots	3	F	4	0	0	2	2,450
Squeaky Wind	5	G	8	1	1	1	9,614
Squeeky P.	2	F	3	0	2	0	8,700
Squeeze Me	3	F	6	1	0	1	5,725
Squeeze Me Darling	3	F	6	1	0	1	6,509
Squeeze Squeeze	3	F	2	0	0	0	53
Squeezin Season	4	G	6	1	2	2	22,470
Squib	3	G	8	1	1	1	16,267
Squillion	4	C	10	0	1	2	3,265
Squintz	2	C	5	0	0	1	3,870
Squire Boone	4	G	4	0	0	0	1,360
Squire West	12	G	8	2	2	1	3,625
Squirmin Dervish	4	C	2	0	0	0	100
Squirmlikeaworm	3	G	11	3	0	1	16,533
Squirrelnut Zipper	4	G	3	0	1	1	8,940
Squirt Monster	2	C	3	1	0	0	6,860
Sregor	4	G	1	0	0	0	100
Srijan	7	G	12	1	1	0	7,108
Ss Proven Reserves	6	H	2	0	0	0	100
Sssh It'sa Secret	2	C	1	0	0	0	0
St Averil	2	C	2	1	1	0	98,000
St Aye	4	F	2	1	0	0	16,800
St Johns Prospect	5	M	14	2	1	1	30,126

Horse	Age	Sex	Sts	1st	2d	3d	Won
St Louie Blu	2	C	5	0	0	1	2,739
St Pat	4	C	8	0	0	0	0
St Patti's Charm	5	M	10	2	3	3	9,518
St Soarbay	4	F	12	1	3	0	29,820
St. Amant Tsunami	2	C	1	0	0	0	0
St. Andrew's Star	4	C	7	1	0	0	1,605
St. Cajetan	3	G	2	0	0	0	0
St. Chad	3	G	2	0	0	0	450
St. Cielo	2	F	2	0	0	0	570
St. Crafty	5	M	1	0	0	0	0
St. Croix	7	H	7	0	0	1	525
St. Davids Road	4	G	14	2	2	2	28,711
St. Dehere	5	H	10	1	1	2	29,750
St. George	3	G	7	0	0	1	825
St. Hadif	6	G	2	0	0	0	121
St. Hilarion	4	G	8	2	0	0	10,365
St. Inigoes	3	G	9	1	2	2	15,555
St. Ives	2	C	4	0	0	0	0
St. Jude's Star	2	F	1	0	0	0	0
St. Louie Louie	2	C	1	0	1	0	8,540
St. Louie Red	3	C	3	0	0	0	200
St. Malachi	4	G	4	0	0	0	1,785
St. Martin's Cloak	6	G	11	1	5	1	18,305
St. Mary's County	3	G	3	0	0	1	850
St. o' Haint	3	G	12	0	1	3	5,090
St. Onge	4	G	3	0	0	0	0
St. Paddys' Star	3	F	1	0	0	0	80
St. Patty's Lass	4	F	1	0	0	0	0
St. Patty's Smile	3	G	21	4	3	6	24,900
St. Patty's Tour	5	G	11	1	2	0	18,214
St. Remy	6	G	1	0	0	1	1,800
St. Rett	3	C	4	0	0	0	770
St. Salt	5	G	13	3	5	0	24,172
St. Somewhere	3	G	7	1	0	0	4,881
St. Vidas Dance	2	F	5	0	1	2	8,891
Stability	2	C	3	1	0	0	12,020
Stable Secret	5	G	3	0	2	0	1,905
Stable Susie	5	M	4	0	0	0	763
Stable Unrest	3	C	3	0	0	0	0
Staceys Remark	4	F	9	0	1	1	3,182
Stach's Prospect	9	G	9	0	2	2	7,697
Stacie's Ballado	2	C	5	1	1	1	14,160
Stack Ana	4	F	4	0	0	1	2,910
Stack Bit	3	G	8	1	3	0	11,235
Stack Jet	3	G	3	0	0	2	4,980
Stack Lass	3	G	1	0	0	0	180
Stack Song	4	F	3	0	1	0	2,730
Stack Step	4	G	1	0	0	0	140
Stackal	4	F	8	2	1	1	36,701
Stackam	4	C	9	0	1	1	14,460
Stackanothertime	5	H	1	0	1	0	3,600
Stacked	3	F	14	2	1	5	16,722
Stacker	5	G	19	2	2	2	23,770
Stacy Brew	2	F	1	0	0	0	0
Stacy Brook	5	M	7	1	0	1	7,580
Stacy's Boy	7	G	4	0	1	0	1,725
Stacy's Choice	5	M	6	0	2	2	7,358
Stacys Crossing	4	F	1	0	0	0	0
Stacys Fan Club	2	F	7	1	0	0	4,845
Stacy's Favorite	3	F	9	1	1	4	30,315
Stacy's Squaw	3	F	8	3	1	1	85,180
Stacy's Tacoma	4	F	13	1	1	2	8,540
Stacys Toy	4	F	11	3	1	2	20,851
Staff Advantage	3	G	13	1	0	0	6,424
Stafina	5	M	4	0	0	1	2,590
Stag	6	G	11	2	2	0	12,473
Stag Party	4	G	6	0	0	1	2,525
Stage a Come On	3	C	5	0	0	0	2,610
Stage Boy	4	G	5	0	0	0	595
Stage Call	5	M	4	1	1	0	23,520
Stage Call (IRE)	4	C	2	1	0	0	30,000
Stage Classic	5	G	10	0	2	2	64,696
Stage Clearance	3	F	13	2	1	1	9,891
Stage Control	5	G	2	0	1	1	1,798
Stage Creek	4	G	8	2	1	0	7,450
Stage Dancer	6	M	14	0	0	5	17,464
Stage Deputy	5	M	8	1	1	3	9,545
Stage Doll	4	F	3	0	0	0	488
Stage Door Jade	8	G	16	2	0	4	31,804
Stage Down	4	F	13	4	1	2	61,758
Stage Drama	5	G	5	2	1	2	30,590
Stage Gal	3	F	14	1	4	2	21,614
Stage It	4	G	14	2	1	3	15,309
Stage Number	4	G	11	2	0	1	5,632
Stage One	4	F	3	0	0	0	158
Stage Player	4	G	10	1	3	0	41,480
Stage Radiance	10	G	3	0	0	0	3,750
Stage Run	7	G	18	0	3	1	5,579
Stage Runner	4	F	8	0	0	0	841
Stage Show	4	C	4	1	1	0	37,600
Stage Three	4	G	9	1	2	0	11,453
Stage West	5	H	1	0	0	0	0
Stage Whisper	2	G	5	2	0	1	13,722
Stagecoach Bandit	2	C	2	0	0	0	120
Staged Reality	8	G	6	3	1	0	6,338
Staging Post	5	H	3	0	0	0	5,000
Stagira	4	F	2	0	0	0	0
Stags Allen	4	C	10	1	0	0	4,449
Stagy	3	F	5	0	0	2	6,340
Stainless Steel	5	M	4	0	0	0	2,613
Stairway to Heaven	9	G	17	2	2	2	11,137
Stake	3	F	10	3	1	1	82,610
Stake Our Claim	4	C	1	0	0	0	61
Stakeholder	4	G	10	0	0	1	2,132
Stalburst	3	F	10	2	0	5	19,398
Stalisland	3	G	3	0	1	0	1,182
Stalk the Cat	6	H	5	0	0	0	515
Stalkerazzi	2	C	3	1	1	0	42,045
Stalking Tiger	2	G	3	2	1	0	96,730
Stall Hunter	5	G	6	1	0	1	9,080
Stall Swapper	5	G	8	1	0	0	10,022
Stallgirl Cindy	5	M	3	0	0	0	0
Stallvik	4	C	13	1	2	4	24,618
Stalwart Bull	4	G	8	2	0	1	27,660
Stalwart Member	10	G	9	1	2	3	25,110
Stalwart Memory	2	C	1	0	0	0	0
Stalwart Warrior	4	C	1	0	0	0	0
Stamford Bridge	3	F	11	2	3	1	20,108
Stamp n' Pirate	5	G	6	1	0	0	1,393
Stampede Dancer	4	F	11	2	2	1	13,972
Stamper	4	G	6	1	2	0	5,285
Stan Israelite	2	C	6	1	0	1	14,450
Stan the Cameraman	4	C	6	0	0	2	759
Stanbery Lane	2	F	3	1	0	1	8,180
Stanchip	5	M	3	0	0	0	224
Stand Alone	4	F	10	2	2	3	50,140
Stand and Fight	3	C	2	0	1	0	3,380
Stand Aside	4	C	4	0	0	1	2,370
Stand by Your Flag	3	C	6	1	0	1	38,560
Stand Down	3	G	10	2	0	1	61,899
Stand for Speed	3	C	5	0	0	3	4,950
Stand On Top	2	F	5	1	0	0	38,180
Stand United	3	G	9	2	0	2	12,655
Stand Up and Cheer	3	G	16	2	1	2	18,625
Standard Bearer	5	G	11	3	0	4	61,181
Standard Choice	4	G	12	3	2	1	35,010
Standard Setter	3	G	6	2	1	0	72,700
Standing Champ	2	F	2	0	0	0	0
Standing Ovation	9	G	5	0	0	0	501
Standing Regal	2	C	2	0	0	0	280
Standing Room Only	4	G	11	2	3	1	48,196
Standing Tall	3	G	5	1	2	2	33,460
Standing Wager	5	M	4	0	0	0	308
Standinsmall	4	F	2	0	0	1	1,500
Standoff	2	G	6	2	0	0	14,699
Standswithafist	2	F	8	1	2	1	50,010
Stang Thirtysix	2	F	2	0	0	1	3,080
Stanislas	4	G	6	1	0	1	28,398
Stanislavsky	3	C	5	1	2	2	74,400
Stanley Park	3	C	8	3	0	0	123,316
Stanley's Gift	3	C	10	1	3	1	32,735
Stanley's Light	4	F	13	1	2	0	10,086
Stanmore Crescent	3	C	1	0	0	0	0
Stans Dream	6	G	2	0	0	0	2,350
Stanton Street	4	G	7	2	0	1	27,524
Stanzaic (AUS)	8	G	12	2	0	1	43,400
Staples N Stitches	6	G	13	2	2	1	22,910
Star a Twinkling	3	C	12	0	1	1	4,580

Horse	Age	Sex	Sts	1st	2d	3d	Won
Star Adie	6	H	4	0	0	0	550
Star Advantage	7	H	12	2	4	0	13,702
Star Affair	5	G	8	0	0	1	1,563
Star Again	8	G	1	0	0	0	0
Star Anise	4	F	12	1	0	3	7,347
Star Armed	9	G	9	0	2	4	6,436
Star Beam	7	H	10	3	3	1	60,832
Star Believer	7	G	6	0	0	1	570
Star Blush	3	F	14	3	1	2	35,000
Star Brushed	6	H	1	0	0	0	47
Star Burst	2	F	1	0	0	0	140
Star Captain	4	G	11	1	3	0	36,105
Star Catcher	3	G	4	0	0	0	735
Star Celebrity	2	F	2	1	1	0	32,800
Star Change	2	F	1	0	1	0	640
Star Charger	5	M	11	0	0	1	4,982
Star Check	6	H	8	1	1	0	7,366
Star Chief	5	G	1	0	0	0	0
Star City Dancer	3	F	7	1	1	0	10,115
Star Class	5	G	2	0	0	0	588
Star Colony	7	H	13	1	1	1	5,549
Star Connection	9	G	2	0	1	0	6,109
Star Contender	4	G	10	2	2	1	37,801
Star Creek	5	M	1	0	0	0	250
Star Crest	2	F	4	0	2	1	9,415
Star Cross (ARG)	6	H	4	1	0	1	101,277
Star Cry	2	G	5	1	0	0	11,790
Star Dancing	5	M	9	0	1	2	1,144
Star de Bacchus	4	G	15	2	0	1	7,867
Star de Marfa	4	G	16	1	1	3	9,374
Star Diamond	2	F	7	0	0	2	5,585
Star El Gato	5	G	16	2	1	2	10,149
Star Escort	3	F	11	2	0	0	31,640
Star Express	3	F	1	0	0	0	82
Star From Heaven	6	M	7	0	0	2	1,816
Star Goldminer	4	C	8	1	0	0	36,320
Star Gone West	6	H	17	0	0	3	3,859
Star Hart	3	F	1	0	0	0	0
Star Honoree	2	C	1	0	1	0	2,800
Star Hurry	2	G	5	0	1	0	1,536
Star in a Hurry	4	F	8	1	2	1	2,681
Star in Reality	5	G	3	0	0	0	0
Star in Sugar	9	M	3	0	0	1	704
Star in the North	4	F	11	1	0	0	4,340
Star Invader	3	G	7	1	1	1	12,014
Star Island	7	G	10	0	1	0	1,920
Star Jessi	2	F	1	0	0	0	0
Star Junction	4	G	15	2	2	3	11,090
Star Kelly	6	G	10	1	3	4	12,135
Star Kitten	3	F	5	0	1	1	3,345
Star Lake Pete	8	G	8	3	0	3	11,220
Star Landing	4	F	1	0	0	1	2,860
Star Lashes	4	F	11	1	3	1	7,916
Star Launch	3	G	7	1	1	1	5,999
Star Leon	5	G	12	1	6	0	8,403
Star Light Bionic	5	M	4	0	0	0	724
Star Light Star	6	G	11	2	4	1	9,650
Star Lily	5	M	4	0	0	0	224
Star Lite Wish	4	F	1	0	0	0	0
Star Lover	5	G	12	2	0	2	9,825
Star Miswaki	4	G	3	0	1	1	1,860
Star Nebula	4	G	15	0	0	0	924
Star Odyssey Ann	3	F	3	0	0	0	380
Star of Anziyan	2	F	4	2	0	0	27,900
Star of Atticus	3	F	5	1	0	0	23,031
Star of Beauty	2	F	4	0	0	0	180
Star of Beijing	5	M	7	1	1	2	40,250
Star of Brian	4	F	15	1	1	2	10,653
Star of Caveat	5	G	13	0	3	3	28,570
Star of Christmas	6	G	12	4	3	2	21,951
Star of Colleen L.	5	M	10	1	2	1	21,100
Star of Elttaes	5	G	11	3	1	3	25,347
Star of Eria	4	G	5	0	0	0	1,110
Star of Florida	3	C	9	2	1	1	17,268
Star of Gdansk	4	F	1	1	0	0	17,710
Star of Ghazi	3	G	10	1	2	0	12,954
Star of Grace	3	G	5	2	1	0	34,040
Star of Humor	3	F	4	1	0	1	12,940
Star of Love	3	C	3	1	0	1	16,194
Star of Midnight	7	M	8	0	0	1	1,868
Star of Nite	3	F	4	0	0	0	1,389
Star of Press	4	G	10	0	0	1	1,705
Star of Prize	3	F	12	0	0	1	3,587
Star of Rapidanne	4	F	2	0	0	0	0
Star of Reality	4	F	16	2	5	4	34,066
Star of Rehaan	4	G	13	1	2	3	16,035
Star of Richard	7	G	21	1	5	3	13,216
Star of Rio	6	G	11	0	0	1	4,140
Star of Roanoke	3	C	14	1	0	0	11,520
Star of Rome	4	C	3	1	0	0	14,756
Star of Sahm	2	F	3	0	0	2	6,992
Star of Savannah	3	F	9	1	0	0	14,805
Star of Sheba	4	F	4	0	1	0	2,100
Star of Stage	4	G	10	2	2	1	12,565
Star of Synastry	5	M	3	0	0	0	98
Star of the Nile	4	F	6	0	2	1	5,869
Star of Unite	3	C	4	0	0	0	720
Star On the Water	3	F	12	1	0	1	5,770
Star On Tour	6	M	4	0	1	0	1,693
Star Over the Bay	5	G	7	1	1	0	32,800
Star Parade (ARG)	4	F	5	3	1	0	172,260
Star Pegasus	3	F	2	0	0	0	222
Star Prediction	8	M	3	0	0	0	341
Star Princess	3	F	1	0	0	0	0
Star Pyramid	2	F	5	0	0	0	750
Star Raider	3	C	6	1	1	0	13,410
Star Request	4	F	1	0	0	0	112
Star Review	5	M	3	0	0	0	1,089
Star Ring	4	G	6	1	1	0	1,890
Star Ring Jane	8	M	3	0	0	0	587
Star Rock	3	F	1	0	0	0	0
Star Rocker	5	H	4	0	0	0	234
Star Seeker	6	H	7	0	1	0	1,335
Star Seventyfive	2	G	2	0	0	0	200
Star Slugger	4	C	6	0	1	1	9,090
Star Smasher	4	C	7	3	2	1	117,299
Star Soldier	2	C	9	2	1	1	24,835
Star Spectacular	8	H	2	1	0	0	3,383
Star Splinter	5	M	8	0	1	0	5,830
Star Spy	4	C	10	2	1	4	11,254
Star Station	8	G	4	1	1	0	4,032
Star Stealer	5	G	9	2	2	1	18,910
Star Stretcher	3	F	5	0	0	1	1,610
Star Struck Latte	2	G	2	1	0	0	7,782
Star Survivor	6	G	5	0	1	0	3,600
Star Talk	5	H	3	1	1	0	1,760
Star Tap	4	G	6	0	0	0	2,520
Star Tier	3	G	10	2	3	1	40,830
Star to Star	3	F	16	1	2	2	13,383
Star Top	4	F	6	0	0	0	1,129
Star Traction	6	H	8	0	2	2	1,862
Star Treatment	2	F	5	1	2	1	23,550
Star Twister	8	M	14	2	0	1	8,606
Star Unlimited	4	G	6	1	0	1	17,500
Star Valay	3	F	2	0	0	0	110
Star Vega (GB)	3	F	7	1	1	0	115,670
Star Vision	2	G	2	0	0	0	0
Star Wager	5	M	8	0	0	0	523
Star Will Shine	2	G	4	0	2	0	4,390
Star Witness	5	H	2	0	0	1	1,345
Star Wizard	3	F	8	2	3	1	77,010
Star Wolf	2	F	1	0	0	0	0
Starbeau	5	H	4	0	0	0	1,315
Starbird Road	2	C	4	1	2	0	15,287
Starboard Stinger	5	M	1	0	0	0	143
Starbrow	4	F	3	0	0	1	1,725
Starbuck Thief	4	G	8	1	0	0	3,698
Starburst Queen	5	M	3	0	0	0	280
Starcheck Billy	7	G	11	1	1	4	7,604
Starcrossed Native	2	C	4	1	0	0	12,226
Stardan (IRE)	5	H	6	0	0	1	8,680
Stardelbar	3	G	11	1	3	1	17,393
Stardust Bertie	3	F	10	3	1	0	43,910
Stardust Special	3	F	13	2	2	3	34,317
Stare	2	F	4	1	0	0	9,300
Stareaux	5	M	4	0	0	1	2,050
Starella	4	F	11	0	0	0	1,783
Starez	6	G	4	0	0	0	1,236

Horse	Age	Sex	Sts	1st	2d	3d	Won
Stargaze	3	F	8	0	0	0	3,270
Stargazerslight	7	M	7	0	0	0	1,008
Stargazey	3	C	3	0	0	0	385
Stargazingal	3	F	10	0	1	1	3,135
Stargirl	3	F	10	1	1	2	34,000
Starglow	4	F	2	0	0	0	0
Stari	5	M	4	0	0	0	197
Starina's Stripes	3	F	8	2	1	2	14,039
Starindy (GB)	2	F	1	0	0	0	840
Staring Encore	3	G	2	0	0	0	0
Staring Harry	5	G	1	0	0	0	0
Staring Maura	5	M	13	1	4	1	10,514
Stark Bite	6	M	6	1	0	0	9,600
Stark Change	3	G	4	0	0	0	420
Stark Country	5	G	8	0	0	1	887
Stark Rullah	7	G	5	0	0	1	762
Stark Wish	7	G	5	0	0	0	114
Starks Folley	4	G	11	0	6	4	7,839
Starlet Anna	3	F	4	0	0	0	323
Starlet Approval	3	F	7	0	0	1	9,539
Starlet Cat	3	F	6	1	0	2	7,772
Starlet Music	4	F	5	1	0	1	5,555
Starlet Terms	4	F	6	2	1	0	34,910
Starletera	3	M	10	2	2	1	29,029
Starletraction	3	F	5	0	0	0	160
Starlight Dancer	5	G	9	1	1	3	14,368
Starlight Flyer	2	G	1	0	1	0	3,705
Starlight Wishes	3	F	3	0	0	0	0
Starlit Battle	4	F	1	0	0	0	0
Starlit Marque	4	G	11	1	2	0	7,260
Starlit Valley	4	F	10	1	1	1	13,561
Starlite Crown	8	G	12	0	0	1	954
Starlite Dreamer	6	G	8	2	4	1	8,912
Starlite Dust	4	F	7	1	0	1	6,390
Starlord	4	F	11	4	3	3	26,801
Starnas	5	G	24	4	3	3	21,711
Starobinets	3	G	13	0	5	2	7,430
Starofmynight	5	G	5	1	0	0	3,773
Staroftheship	3	F	1	0	0	0	1,800
Starofthevalley	3	C	2	0	0	0	303
Staronconcerto	5	H	6	0	0	0	186
Starp	6	G	10	2	1	1	9,770
Starr Just	6	G	3	0	0	0	0
Starr of Honor	5	M	16	0	0	0	1,110
Starrer	5	M	2	2	0	0	300,000
Starring Lady	3	F	11	1	0	0	5,294
Starring Maudlin	6	G	12	1	1	1	9,063
Starring Willy	5	G	1	0	0	0	1,120
Starr's Future	2	C	1	0	0	0	125
Starr's Image	6	M	2	1	0	0	3,900
Starr's Star	4	F	10	1	1	0	8,275
Starry De	5	M	5	1	0	1	24,260
Starry Halo	4	C	14	0	3	1	5,022
Starry Heaven	5	G	12	4	3	2	54,915
Starry Ide	4	G	10	1	0	0	6,725
Starry Mark	4	F	11	2	1	3	18,143
Starry Nugget	3	F	3	1	0	0	12,280
Starry Wager	5	G	11	3	1	0	14,463
Stars Aligned	3	G	18	2	2	7	104,200
Star's Copy Cat	4	F	8	0	0	0	1,392
Star's Forum	4	G	13	0	1	2	5,756
Star's Glitter	4	G	7	0	1	1	10,008
Stars Go Blue	3	F	8	0	1	4	15,250
Star's Gold	2	C	7	1	0	1	14,000
Stars in His Eyes	6	G	7	1	2	1	25,930
Star's Kandi Kane	2	F	6	2	0	3	30,270
Stars Last Chance	2	F	1	0	0	0	285
Stars Little Trick	5	M	3	0	0	0	135
Stars 'n Dreams	6	G	14	0	3	2	10,134
Stars N Sparks	6	G	3	0	0	2	1,319
Stars of Orange	2	F	5	0	0	2	2,278
Stars On the Water	2	F	2	0	0	0	0
Stars Royal	6	G	14	3	3	3	29,854
Star's Wild	8	G	6	1	2	1	4,913
Starship	7	G	11	5	1	0	11,928
Starship Admiral	5	H	6	1	1	1	10,568
Starship Bulletin	3	F	7	1	0	0	18,620
Starship Confetti	4	F	3	0	0	0	414
Starship Contessa	4	F	8	0	1	0	3,200
Starship Cowboy	2	G	4	0	0	1	1,330
Starship Cowgirl	3	F	4	0	0	0	505
Starship Dame	3	F	11	1	1	5	31,240
Starship Daydream	3	F	12	5	1	2	70,600
Starship Deputy	3	G	5	0	0	2	5,915
Starship Diligence	3	F	10	2	3	1	37,020
Starship Ensign	7	G	3	0	0	1	390
Starship Galaxy	2	C	1	0	0	0	300
Starship Garnet	4	F	8	1	3	1	13,510
Starship Glider	3	F	1	0	0	0	130
Starship Gold	4	F	13	2	1	1	22,465
Starship Kimberly	6	M	4	1	0	0	4,085
Starship Miss	6	M	9	1	0	0	24,611
Starship Missy	6	M	8	2	2	1	15,620
Starship Outlaw	2	C	2	0	1	0	2,395
Starship Rainbow	4	G	16	1	3	2	22,727
Starship Sandi	3	F	2	0	0	0	360
Starship Seminole (VEN)	7	H	4	1	0	0	3,840
Starship Smokester	3	F	12	3	4	0	60,370
Starship Splasher	4	G	8	1	3	1	20,486
Starship Stripper	2	F	2	0	0	0	2,280
Starship Sunrise	3	F	2	1	0	0	7,200
Starship Sunshine	4	F	12	0	2	2	5,224
Starship Wonder	4	F	3	0	0	1	2,235
Starshipenterprise	7	G	12	1	1	0	14,155
Starskeys Hunch	4	G	5	1	1	1	1,743
Starsoverparadise	2	C	1	1	0	0	12,000
Starspangled Sunny	3	F	2	0	1	0	1,248
Starsthelimit	3	F	2	0	0	0	0
Starsunday	4	G	7	1	0	0	6,962
Start Sooner	5	G	10	1	1	1	15,572
Start That Song	6	M	5	2	0	0	30,980
Start the Concert	4	F	1	0	0	0	150
Start the Fight	3	G	12	1	2	1	7,785
Start the Music	5	G	3	0	0	2	480
Start to Dream	3	F	2	0	0	0	0
Started Witha Kiss	2	F	1	1	0	0	31,225
Starthatshines	7	G	7	2	1	2	7,263
Startinover	8	G	4	0	0	0	496
Startle	7	G	3	0	0	1	600
Startthecommotion	2	F	3	0	0	0	575
Starvest	5	M	16	4	3	2	46,230
Starview's Rose	3	F	7	0	0	1	3,510
Stash the Boots	3	G	13	3	2	4	57,535
Stash's Lil Lady	5	M	1	0	0	0	0
Stat Cat	7	G	9	1	2	1	9,691
State City	4	C	8	2	0	1	1,292,469
State Deputy	2	C	1	0	0	0	137
State Executive	4	G	12	1	4	2	24,166
State Leader	4	G	5	0	1	2	9,882
State Mover	9	G	20	3	2	3	21,038
State of Reason	2	C	6	0	0	1	1,590
State of Shock	4	G	10	3	3	2	55,025
State of the World	2	G	5	1	0	0	5,347
State Ofthe Report	3	C	4	0	0	2	2,045
State Royality	8	G	1	0	0	0	0
State Shinto	7	H	8	1	1	0	315,701
State Street	3	C	11	2	2	0	27,600
State the Facts	7	H	9	1	0	1	5,056
State the Obvious	6	M	1	0	0	1	880
State Twice	3	G	11	0	0	1	3,255
Stately and Sassy	8	G	12	1	1	0	9,564
Stately Clock	2	C	3	1	1	0	47,040
Stately Deputy	3	C	4	1	0	0	28,530
Stately Jack Flash	3	C	9	1	2	1	12,366
Stately Key	4	G	15	1	3	3	5,265
Stately Manor	3	F	7	2	0	1	16,168
Stately Pal	3	C	4	1	0	0	7,230
Stately Sliver	3	F	2	0	0	0	0
Stately Whisper	6	M	4	2	0	1	5,225
Stately'n Nicer	3	G	9	1	4	1	24,347
Stately's Choice	4	F	13	5	3	0	29,259
Statement	5	H	8	3	0	0	103,512
Statement (IRE)	3	C	4	1	1	0	34,348
Statesville	6	G	9	2	0	1	24,967
Stateyourposition	9	G	2	0	1	1	548
Static	5	M	12	1	0	1	5,362
Static Rock	4	G	4	0	1	1	3,772
Statue of Liberty	3	C	5	0	1	0	101,323

RECORDS OF HORSES

Horse	Age	Sex	Sts	1st	2d	3d	Won	Horse	Age	Sex	Sts	1st	2d	3d	Won
Status	4	C	3	1	1	0	41,000	Steelaninch (GB)	3	C	2	1	1	0	106,220
Status Image	4	G	1	0	0	0	237	Steelbender	3	G	5	1	0	0	11,208
Staubach	3	G	7	1	2	1	38,062	Steele Creek	3	C	5	0	0	0	589
Stauch	5	H	9	2	2	1	64,680	Steeleon Season	4	G	13	1	2	5	38,250
Staunch Opponent	4	G	9	0	3	4	17,350	Steely Fox	3	F	5	0	0	0	457
Staunchy Rascal	4	C	14	1	1	1	4,212	Steely Look	3	F	12	1	5	1	16,259
Staunton	3	C	12	3	2	2	29,222	Steely Max	3	G	13	3	3	3	20,725
Stavanger Star	11	G	3	0	0	0	704	Steely Rose	3	F	6	1	0	1	3,530
Stavros	4	C	2	0	0	0	0	Steelyeyed	3	G	7	2	0	0	28,488
Stay	3	F	8	1	0	3	39,750	Steelyourluv	4	F	10	3	1	0	8,655
Stay for the Fun	2	F	1	0	0	0	120	Steep Climb	4	F	2	0	0	1	490
Stay Forever	6	M	3	1	0	0	198,500	Steep Sheet	7	G	6	3	0	0	30,546
Stay Forever Young	2	G	2	0	0	0	0	Steeple Hill	6	G	14	0	0	2	1,887
Stay Informed	6	M	5	0	2	0	3,060	Steersman	4	G	15	2	2	0	23,730
Stay Natural	2	G	5	0	0	1	3,333	Steev Skee	10	G	5	2	0	1	8,344
Stay Out Late	4	F	9	1	0	0	7,838	Steeveenix	3	F	2	0	0	0	0
Stay the Night	4	F	8	0	0	0	242	Stefandrew	7	M	4	1	1	1	16,640
Stay Tuned	2	F	3	0	0	0	800	Steffon	3	C	9	1	1	2	4,146
Stayofexecution	3	F	5	0	0	0	315	Steimaway	6	G	15	2	1	3	12,234
Stays Out Front	3	F	2	0	0	0	285	Stella Boreala	4	F	7	0	0	1	738
Stayton	6	G	9	3	2	2	9,410	Stella Come Back	2	F	4	0	0	0	0
Ste. Pecheresse	4	F	6	1	0	0	29,575	Stella Gold	3	F	1	0	0	0	0
Steadfast and True	4	C	7	1	1	1	46,720	Stella Marie	3	F	8	3	0	0	32,986
Steadiest	7	G	2	0	0	1	432	Stellacopter One	5	M	10	0	2	0	1,175
Steady Breeze	2	G	5	1	0	1	25,830	Stellar	3	F	6	2	0	1	95,820
Steady Course	2	F	5	1	3	0	57,405	Stellar Belle	3	F	4	0	0	0	730
Steady Glitter	3	G	10	2	4	0	32,490	Stellar Jayne	2	F	5	3	0	0	119,075
Steady Grind	3	C	2	0	0	0	480	Stellar Light	5	M	2	0	0	1	1,920
Steady Intention	4	G	1	0	0	0	140	Stellar Moment	2	F	6	0	1	1	8,375
Steady Ruckus	7	G	11	0	0	1	28,685	Stellar One	2	F	5	2	1	1	47,375
Steady Sammy	8	G	7	1	0	2	20,905	Stellar Prospect	5	M	8	1	2	1	9,936
Steady Smiler	3	G	11	3	2	4	142,726	Stellar Win	3	F	12	0	1	0	2,444
Steady Streak	4	G	9	0	1	2	26,845	Stellar Wisdom	2	F	1	0	0	0	0
Steady Stream	2	C	2	1	0	0	5,700	Stellas Command	3	F	2	0	0	0	240
Steady Won	5	G	7	0	1	2	3,552	Stella's Flare	3	F	2	0	0	0	0
Steakman	3	G	4	1	0	1	15,290	Stella's Legacy	6	G	5	0	0	0	289
Steal a Band	3	F	17	3	3	2	54,815	Stella's Storm	4	F	12	1	3	2	15,654
Steal a Mac	3	F	4	2	0	0	10,890	Stellaspeed	6	M	6	3	2	0	16,772
Steal Astaire	4	G	9	1	2	0	6,994	Stellianos	5	G	10	0	3	1	22,830
Steal My Kisses	2	F	5	1	0	0	40,840	Step and Go	3	F	10	1	1	2	19,690
Steal My Love	7	H	3	0	0	0	196	Step Aside Please	3	F	8	1	1	0	55,899
Steal the Claim	3	F	11	2	1	4	37,680	Step Close	9	G	1	0	0	0	32
Steal the Gold	2	F	6	2	0	0	10,465	Step in Time	3	F	1	0	0	0	0
Stealin' Gasoline	4	G	15	1	1	5	6,126	Step Into the Fire	4	F	17	2	2	1	12,396
Stealing Heaven	4	G	17	1	0	2	8,619	Step N Motion	8	H	5	0	1	0	2,600
Stealing Memories	3	F	10	3	2	0	51,570	Step Out Steven	3	C	9	0	1	1	3,262
Stealing Thunder	3	F	5	0	1	0	10,040	Step Twice	3	G	1	0	0	0	145
Stealth Commander	4	G	8	2	0	0	12,187	Step Up	3	F	4	0	3	0	16,250
Stealth Flier	2	C	3	0	0	0	1,800	Stepatatime	4	G	13	3	1	1	68,472
Stealthy Cat	6	M	8	0	2	1	13,570	Stephanie's Angel	4	F	14	2	2	3	11,440
Steam Ginny	2	F	2	0	0	0	250	Stephanie's Wager	5	M	9	0	0	1	7,568
Steam McQueen	3	C	8	0	0	0	2,290	Stephano	3	G	7	2	1	0	4,375
Steam Train	2	G	1	0	0	0	0	Stephan's Angel	2	F	3	3	0	0	61,440
Steamboat Road	8	G	10	1	0	2	10,473	Stephan's Prize	8	H	14	2	0	0	22,330
Steamboat Springs	2	C	1	0	0	0	0	Stephe Girl	7	M	14	2	3	3	31,795
Steamed	4	G	1	0	0	0	188	Stephen Hayes	4	G	14	1	4	1	17,175
Steamer Gold	4	G	5	0	0	2	2,600	Stephenes Baby	3	F	5	1	1	1	19,870
Steaming Home	4	F	6	0	0	1	6,542	Stephene's Cat	3	F	3	0	0	0	0
Steaminstacey	2	F	3	1	0	0	7,000	Stephen's Code	4	G	14	2	2	2	15,791
Steamroll Paradise	9	G	8	3	1	1	12,321	Stephen's Girl	6	M	2	0	0	0	270
Steamy Dancer	5	G	3	0	0	0	910	Stephen's Pride	4	F	10	2	0	2	7,860
Steamy Dreams	4	F	6	0	0	1	1,891	Stephentown	4	C	3	0	0	0	0
Steed	3	F	4	0	0	1	1,638	Stephie's Gold	6	M	5	0	0	0	315
Steel Butterfly	3	F	11	1	2	2	25,525	Stephie's Pistol	3	G	2	0	0	0	480
Steel Curtain	3	G	2	1	0	0	4,800	Steph's Meadowlake	2	F	2	1	0	0	11,700
Steel Dumaani	4	C	1	0	0	0	0	Steph's Smoke	3	F	7	2	0	0	5,210
Steel Lass	2	F	2	0	0	0	250	Steph's Tee	2	F	5	1	0	1	9,420
Steel Man	5	H	3	0	1	0	7,680	Steping Fast	4	F	7	4	2	0	24,280
Steel Nell	3	F	6	2	0	0	14,420	Stepit	3	F	7	0	0	1	3,750
Steel On Target	6	G	6	0	1	1	4,524	Steponit Bad Boy	7	G	9	2	1	2	29,635
Steel Petal	6	G	2	0	0	0	164	Stepp Ahead	5	M	2	0	0	0	117
Steel Power	2	C	1	0	0	0	750	Steppen Up	4	F	7	4	1	1	33,306
Steel Ray's	3	F	4	0	0	0	469	Steppers Gold	3	C	7	0	0	1	1,414
Steel Shot	5	M	1	0	0	0	0	Steppin	4	F	16	1	0	5	6,818
Steel Statement	4	C	4	0	0	0	924	Steppin Charlie	3	G	15	1	0	2	20,110
Steel the Roses	4	F	12	1	5	2	14,311	Steppin Hi	3	C	4	0	0	0	757
Steel Trap	7	H	1	0	0	0	0	Steppin Not Dragon	4	F	1	0	0	0	0
Steel Wheels	3	G	4	0	0	1	650	Steppin Reb	3	C	8	2	0	0	6,468
Steel Wool	3	G	13	1	1	1	12,378	Steppin Shoes	5	M	3	0	0	0	270

Horse	Age	Sex	Sts	1st	2d	3d	Won
Steppin Shoot	2	F	5	2	1	0	15,985
Steppin Steph	3	F	2	0	0	0	156
Stepping'sson	7	H	7	1	0	0	5,179
Step's Magical Hat	2	F	3	0	0	1	1,585
Step's Mischief	5	M	10	1	1	0	8,074
Sterling Ace	2	G	10	2	3	0	25,628
Sterling Dynasty	5	H	4	0	0	0	0
Sterling Gold	4	G	11	1	1	3	66,499
Sterling M P	6	G	24	1	2	2	4,848
Sterling Prospect	3	G	6	0	1	1	11,126
Sterling Slipper	2	F	3	0	1	1	5,943
Sterling Wisdom	4	G	7	0	1	0	7,100
Sterlings Jewel	4	C	5	1	1	0	9,000
Sterling's Lad	6	G	9	3	0	2	59,631
Stern Ties	4	G	10	2	0	3	10,481
Sterna	5	H	5	0	1	0	4,780
Sternman	3	C	14	4	2	2	33,485
Sterns Lad	5	G	9	1	1	1	12,895
Sterny	3	C	4	1	1	1	37,780
Sterrettania	5	M	1	0	0	0	54
Stetson Cat	4	G	13	4	2	0	26,125
Stetson R. L.	5	H	3	0	0	2	1,923
Stetter Jr	2	G	1	0	1	0	2,755
Steve K	4	C	4	1	0	0	10,145
Steve the Devil	5	H	2	0	0	0	0
Steve V Boy	4	G	3	0	0	0	75
Steve'e Gal	2	F	2	0	0	0	174
Steveneedsaposse	3	C	13	2	2	1	15,069
Stevens Day	3	G	9	0	0	0	1,684
Steven's Wish	6	H	5	0	0	0	652
Stevensbubba	5	M	9	0	1	1	4,963
Steves Eldorado	4	G	3	0	0	0	836
Steve's Escape	6	H	8	1	1	2	29,020
Steve's Memo	3	G	7	1	0	1	6,675
Steve's Rave	2	G	10	0	0	3	3,912
Steves Remark	3	C	1	1	0	0	15,400
Steves Sis	5	M	4	0	0	0	111
Steves Sunny Comet	4	C	13	2	0	1	49,560
Steve's Thunder	5	G	3	0	1	0	10,120
Steve's Turn	9	G	2	0	0	0	207
Stevia	5	M	1	0	0	0	825
Stevie Bubbles	6	G	10	2	2	0	11,576
Stevie Wonderful	3	G	1	0	0	0	71
Stevie's Flight	7	G	23	1	3	0	8,709
Stew N I	3	G	12	2	2	0	39,621
Stew Nada	4	G	11	1	1	0	7,093
Steward	3	C	8	0	1	1	3,890
Stewey	3	C	2	1	0	0	19,800
Stewing Hope	4	C	6	0	0	0	92
Stew's Embarcadero	3	G	2	0	0	0	0
Stew's Stone	2	C	8	1	3	0	15,440
Stick Baby	4	F	1	0	0	0	72
Stick N Stein	5	M	8	3	2	0	28,076
Stick to Roses	3	C	9	1	2	3	13,020
Sticker Shock	3	G	1	0	0	0	240
Stickers	4	G	2	0	0	0	0
Stickler	6	G	5	1	0	0	2,104
Sticky Gum	4	F	3	0	0	0	122
Sticky Note	4	F	4	0	0	1	3,740
Sticky Token	3	C	6	0	0	0	0
Stickyrope	9	G	4	0	0	0	53
Stickytrickydeputy	3	C	5	0	0	2	2,523
Stigler's Sorrel	3	G	14	1	3	2	30,451
Stilaferd	9	G	5	0	0	1	2,914
Still	4	G	3	0	0	0	219
Still a Bachelor	3	C	4	0	0	1	2,475
Still As Sweet (IRE)	6	M	8	1	2	1	32,370
Still Be Smokin'	4	C	12	0	2	1	27,650
Still Crazy	2	F	2	0	0	0	460
Still Dancing	2	G	2	0	0	0	1,260
Still Foolin Aroun	3	C	4	0	2	1	16,482
Still Water Creek	3	F	8	0	1	1	2,668
Stillwater Rose	2	F	5	1	1	1	14,370
Stilly Lucille	4	F	5	0	0	0	233
Stilly Vanilly	3	F	3	0	0	0	303
Stiltsville	7	H	16	0	1	3	7,595
Stiltzee	3	F	2	0	0	0	190
Sting King	3	C	9	1	2	1	20,100
Sting Lear	3	C	6	0	3	1	28,210

Horse	Age	Sex	Sts	1st	2d	3d	Won
Sting Man	3	C	11	1	2	1	72,234
Sting Ray	4	C	10	0	4	2	11,374
Stinger	4	F	1	0	0	0	0
Stinke Pant's	4	F	9	1	0	0	7,533
Stinky Secret	3	F	8	1	3	0	9,040
Stinky Twinkie	4	F	19	1	1	3	12,830
Stinson	5	H	8	1	3	0	8,624
Stir Fry	2	G	2	0	0	0	0
Stir N Things Up	8	M	2	0	0	0	220
Stir the Mix	3	G	11	0	3	2	6,335
Stirrin Up a Storm	3	F	2	0	0	1	1,760
Stirring the Stew	3	F	11	2	0	1	8,029
Stirring Up Magic	3	C	1	0	0	0	66
Stirum Up	6	G	1	0	0	0	0
Stitch n' Weave	7	G	3	0	0	0	114
Stitched Up	6	G	4	0	0	0	560
Stock Exchange	7	H	7	1	2	0	15,190
Stock Rocket	8	G	5	0	0	2	4,070
Stocked and Loded	3	F	5	1	2	0	7,260
Stockholder	3	C	6	4	1	0	126,700
Stockinbonds	4	G	6	0	0	0	1,470
Stockport	5	G	11	1	1	1	6,985
Stocks Are Rising	5	G	8	2	2	3	64,660
Stockton to Malone	4	F	7	0	0	0	1,096
Stogie Two	6	G	2	0	0	0	0
Stoic	2	F	7	2	1	2	81,684
Stoic Endeavour	3	G	4	1	0	0	13,443
Stoked (AUS)	5	G	5	0	0	0	750
Stoker	3	G	14	0	1	3	24,900
Stoker Bill	3	G	9	0	0	0	770
Stokin Coal	4	C	8	3	1	2	20,845
Stokosky	7	H	9	0	3	1	31,847
Stokowski	5	H	6	1	1	1	6,751
Stole	4	C	5	1	0	1	6,925
Stole My Heart	5	H	3	0	1	1	840
Stole One	2	F	3	1	0	1	15,803
Stolen Beethoven	2	C	5	0	0	0	840
Stolen Deal	5	G	10	0	0	1	3,615
Stolen Groom	5	G	1	0	0	0	305
Stolen Halo	3	F	13	1	3	2	42,131
Stolen Honor	5	G	13	3	3	1	20,466
Stolen Sham	3	F	1	0	0	0	188
Stolen Sheena	3	F	10	5	1	0	43,930
Stolen Time	2	C	4	2	1	1	99,440
Stolen Valor	4	G	5	1	0	0	5,891
Stolen View	5	H	2	0	0	1	1,700
Stolencon	3	G	1	0	0	0	66
Stolie's Stuka	4	F	7	2	3	0	18,278
Stompin Tom	6	G	7	1	1	2	7,621
Stomping	3	F	6	1	1	2	29,530
Stompum	4	F	1	0	0	0	55
Stone Age	5	H	2	0	0	1	2,970
Stone Brush	4	F	6	0	0	0	1,008
Stone Canyon	3	C	12	1	4	2	77,677
Stone Cat	3	C	6	2	0	1	102,530
Stone Cold	5	H	11	2	1	0	17,592
Stone Cold Kid	4	G	9	1	1	0	3,510
Stone Cold Rob	3	C	7	0	1	1	4,111
Stone Cold Truth	3	C	2	0	0	0	1,350
Stone Cool Cat	7	H	1	0	0	0	84
Stone Face	3	F	5	0	0	0	2,890
Stone Fleet	2	F	3	0	0	0	360
Stone King	3	C	8	1	1	0	14,720
Stone Ledge	4	G	5	1	0	1	7,059
Stone Legend	4	C	4	0	1	1	4,130
Stone Mill Maiden	6	M	18	2	3	6	39,660
Stone Pony	3	G	9	0	0	0	505
Stone Rain	2	G	5	3	1	0	52,620
Stone Striker	8	G	3	0	0	0	312
Stonebridge Lady	4	F	10	2	2	0	79,723
Stonecoldbroke	5	H	4	2	0	0	17,871
Stonecoldfox	3	F	2	0	0	0	12,500
Stonecreek	7	M	9	2	0	0	35,429
Stonefeather	3	F	4	0	0	0	103
Stoneman	6	G	14	1	2	2	8,680
Stonekiller	4	G	12	2	2	3	13,393
Stonemason	4	G	5	0	0	0	1,100
Stoneringer	3	C	14	1	2	2	6,498
Stones of Fire	4	C	10	0	1	1	3,325

RECORDS OF HORSES

Horse	Age	Sex	Sts	1st	2d	3d	Won
Stones R Rolling	4	F	1	0	0	0	0
Stonesoup	4	F	13	1	2	2	37,840
Stonewall Bob	9	G	1	0	0	0	0
Stonewall Harris	2	C	3	0	1	1	7,070
Stonewall Peach	2	F	1	0	0	0	43
Stonewater	5	G	4	0	0	0	1,307
Stoneway	2	F	4	2	0	1	35,110
Stonewood	2	C	5	1	0	1	13,900
Stoney Creek	4	G	7	2	1	1	17,397
Stoney One	5	M	7	1	0	0	2,718
Stoney Ridge	4	C	5	0	1	0	4,956
Stoney River	3	C	8	0	1	2	8,845
Stoneyeyes	4	C	2	0	0	0	175
Stonington	4	F	4	1	2	0	42,690
Stooge Lover	3	F	9	1	2	2	24,229
Stoogie Smoker	7	G	7	1	1	0	2,812
Stop and Sea	3	C	13	1	1	2	18,880
Stop Digging	5	M	4	0	0	1	638
Stop Dreaming	4	G	10	1	0	2	7,914
Stop in Paradise	7	G	4	1	1	0	6,032
Stop Like Bell	3	G	5	0	0	0	200
Stop Lollygagging	7	G	4	0	0	0	0
Stop Looking	3	F	3	0	2	1	47,140
Stop Loss	3	F	5	0	0	1	1,460
Stop Payment	5	H	2	0	0	0	1,000
Stop Seven	8	M	9	1	2	1	17,364
Stop Tapping	6	H	4	0	0	0	272
Stop That	4	G	7	0	0	0	1,110
Stop That Dancer	3	F	5	2	1	0	38,440
Stop That Music	7	G	1	0	0	0	0
Stop the Act	3	G	10	5	2	1	24,014
Stop the Bluffing	5	H	7	2	1	0	8,282
Stop the Meeting	4	F	5	1	0	0	5,120
Stop the Nonsense	3	F	15	1	1	3	11,310
Stop the Talking	6	M	7	0	1	2	29,236
Stop the Vice	7	M	11	2	3	1	23,584
Stop the Violins	4	G	6	3	0	0	8,252
Stop to Dance	4	C	9	1	1	2	16,120
Stop Twelve	4	G	13	1	0	1	9,942
Stopalong Cadillac	7	G	14	3	2	5	31,050
Stopline	6	H	4	0	0	0	0
Stopyourtwining	5	M	11	0	1	1	9,063
Stored	2	C	4	2	0	0	44,910
Storm Alarm	4	C	6	0	0	0	378
Storm At Sea	3	G	11	0	4	1	12,980
Storm Baby	2	F	5	1	1	0	4,916
Storm Bank	5	G	10	3	0	2	34,674
Storm Believer	4	F	2	0	0	0	1,818
Storm Bell	4	F	4	1	0	0	7,068
Storm Bite	3	C	8	2	1	0	3,750
Storm Booming	3	C	3	0	1	0	5,430
Storm Boot Gold	2	C	2	0	0	2	8,610
Storm Brat	3	G	6	0	0	0	699
Storm Breaking	3	F	2	1	0	1	21,100
Storm Brigade	4	C	12	1	1	1	6,535
Storm Bull	2	C	4	0	0	0	1,142
Storm Capsule	3	G	2	0	0	0	0
Storm Cat Larry	5	G	12	1	2	3	7,191
Storm Catcher	4	C	8	0	0	0	1,144
Storm Cat's Kitten	2	F	2	0	0	0	440
Storm Cave	4	C	8	4	0	2	51,992
Storm Chronicle	5	H	14	3	2	0	31,880
Storm City	4	C	9	1	1	1	6,036
Storm City Blues	2	F	1	0	1	0	5,250
Storm Clipper	3	F	4	1	0	0	12,740
Storm Clock	2	F	5	0	1	3	17,825
Storm Colors	3	C	1	0	0	0	0
Storm Commander	4	C	8	0	1	2	18,400
Storm Condition	3	C	6	0	0	1	2,003
Storm Count	4	F	5	0	0	0	458
Storm Country	2	F	1	0	1	0	4,200
Storm Craft	5	H	7	3	1	0	93,250
Storm Creek Cat	5	G	1	0	0	0	42
Storm Crest	9	G	7	0	0	0	630
Storm Crossing	2	C	2	0	0	1	4,130
Storm Cup	5	G	16	0	0	0	1,002
Storm Damage	3	G	7	1	0	0	9,266
Storm Dancer	4	F	12	0	1	2	15,071
Storm Dancing	5	G	13	2	1	1	22,223
Storm Devil	7	G	5	1	0	0	2,523
Storm Diamond	2	F	1	0	0	0	0
Storm Duck	3	C	7	1	0	0	12,320
Storm Envoy	5	G	11	0	1	0	11,686
Storm Express	3	G	4	0	0	1	5,425
Storm Fever	4	F	8	0	0	0	480
Storm Flag	3	F	6	2	3	0	118,285
Storm Flag Flying	3	F	2	0	1	0	21,580
Storm Flame	3	G	12	2	3	2	11,878
Storm Fleet	2	F	4	1	1	0	26,100
Storm Flite	3	F	1	0	0	0	500
Storm Forward	2	C	6	1	0	1	26,490
Storm Glory	3	F	5	2	0	0	17,676
Storm Guide	3	G	2	0	0	0	0
Storm Gulch	3	G	3	0	0	0	4,120
Storm Hen	3	F	7	1	4	0	34,170
Storm Hero	2	G	3	0	0	0	480
Storm in Philly	4	F	9	3	1	0	56,500
Storm in Session	3	G	8	1	2	1	6,198
Storm Kid	4	C	9	1	1	4	8,212
Storm Kisu	6	M	9	1	0	1	36,145
Storm Lad	4	C	5	1	0	0	12,700
Storm Lake	10	G	6	0	0	0	60
Storm Lamp	4	F	3	0	1	0	3,680
Storm Leaper	3	F	6	1	0	0	4,764
Storm Legacy	2	C	1	0	1	0	2,000
Storm Mill	2	C	1	0	0	0	822
Storm Minstrel	2	F	5	0	2	1	22,330
Storm Mistress	5	M	12	0	2	2	6,402
Storm Mont	3	G	3	0	1	0	1,760
Storm Mountain	4	G	2	0	0	2	1,300
Storm N Sunny	2	F	6	1	0	0	4,265
Storm 'n Z	2	G	6	1	1	0	14,640
Storm Nite	5	G	3	0	0	1	1,199
Storm Now	4	G	11	2	1	0	21,269
Storm of Liberty	2	G	7	0	0	1	1,185
Storm of the West	3	F	21	1	2	2	9,300
Storm On the Lake	3	F	10	5	0	2	95,300
Storm On the Way	2	C	3	0	0	0	2,760
Storm Out Front	10	H	14	0	1	1	3,221
Storm Page	3	F	5	0	0	0	311
Storm Passage	4	C	3	0	0	0	900
Storm Passer Bye	2	C	3	1	0	1	6,300
Storm Peace	5	G	1	0	0	0	672
Storm Petrel	2	C	1	0	0	0	0
Storm Power	6	G	9	0	2	0	7,539
Storm Prospect	3	F	15	2	2	4	46,340
Storm Punch	8	G	2	1	0	0	13,110
Storm Quest	3	G	13	3	1	3	38,480
Storm Reaction	2	F	1	0	0	0	0
Storm Reef	2	C	1	0	0	0	0
Storm Regent	10	G	13	2	3	2	12,921
Storm Ridge	4	C	5	0	0	0	186
Storm River Kelly	3	C	9	0	1	0	4,211
Storm Rose	9	G	5	2	0	0	4,956
Storm Ruckus	3	C	14	0	0	0	2,731
Storm Rush	2	F	2	0	1	0	13,524
Storm Saga	5	M	4	0	1	0	7,297
Storm Saint	3	F	5	0	1	0	3,210
Storm Shooter	4	C	7	2	0	0	16,605
Storm Signal	6	G	10	0	0	1	10,897
Storm Sizzle	2	G	2	0	1	1	9,870
Storm Stream	2	F	1	0	0	1	3,080
Storm Stuff	3	C	5	0	1	0	884
Storm Tale	3	G	9	3	3	0	50,860
Storm Talker	8	G	4	0	0	0	158
Storm Tap	3	G	2	0	0	0	0
Storm Tempest	4	F	20	2	2	2	11,931
Storm the Beach	2	C	2	0	0	0	0
Storm the Gate	6	G	12	0	1	3	27,620
Storm the Net	7	M	11	0	0	1	3,713
Storm Theatre	4	G	6	0	1	0	805
Storm This Picture	3	C	1	0	0	0	0
Storm to Glory	4	F	7	2	1	1	62,918
Storm to the Top	3	F	5	0	0	0	940
Storm Tone	2	F	1	0	0	0	0
Storm Touch	7	G	2	0	0	2	12,500
Storm Train	2	G	3	0	0	0	360
Storm Trial	2	F	5	0	1	0	1,740

Horse	Age	Sex	Sts	1st	2d	3d	Won	Horse	Age	Sex	Sts	1st	2d	3d	Won
Storm Twist	2	C	6	1	0	1	11,130	Stormn Robin	3	F	3	0	0	0	0
Storm Unbridled	3	C	6	2	1	1	34,050	Stormndownthelane	4	F	10	1	0	2	5,432
Storm Verse	5	G	11	0	3	0	26,135	Stormoffthecoast	3	G	4	0	0	2	2,006
Storm Watch	4	C	7	1	1	1	14,980	Stormofthecentury	5	G	10	0	0	0	333
Storm Wish	5	G	9	2	1	0	23,696	Storm's Cup	4	F	11	0	0	0	2,564
Storm Witch	4	F	5	0	0	1	5,165	Storm's Darling	2	F	2	1	1	0	22,190
Storm Witness	5	M	13	3	2	0	15,793	Storm's Finale	4	F	10	2	1	2	48,820
Storm Wreck	8	G	7	0	2	3	21,040	Storm's Lining	5	G	7	2	2	0	10,254
Stormalot	6	H	6	0	0	1	646	Storm's Muse	5	M	8	0	0	1	1,506
Stormcaster	4	C	6	2	2	0	65,690	Storm's Over	7	G	1	0	0	0	60
Stormcat's Atticus	2	F	3	0	0	0	838	Storm's Path	6	H	9	0	0	1	3,587
Stormcats Grandson	2	C	6	1	0	1	16,756	Storm's Roar	3	C	3	1	0	0	4,670
Stormcloudrising	2	F	2	0	0	0	460	Storm's Secret	5	M	18	2	3	1	21,232
Stormented	4	F	5	1	1	0	25,900	Stormscope	9	G	3	0	1	0	1,695
Stormhill	3	F	5	1	1	0	8,380	Stormthebarricade	2	C	4	2	1	0	149,055
Stormhouse	4	G	17	1	0	3	6,439	Stormy Act	2	C	2	0	0	0	365
Stormiano	5	H	2	0	0	0	570	Stormy American	3	G	13	2	0	1	13,689
Stormie Britches	7	G	14	2	3	2	13,370	Stormy Appeal	4	C	15	1	3	1	11,395
Stormie Normie	5	G	14	1	0	1	4,685	Stormy Black	3	G	7	1	1	1	3,874
Stormin	4	G	13	1	1	2	17,813	Stormy Blue Boy	4	C	9	1	2	0	2,683
Stormin Angel	3	G	10	1	1	0	9,598	Stormy Brew	4	G	10	2	0	1	21,798
Stormin Angie	3	F	4	0	0	0	330	Stormy Brie	4	F	3	2	0	1	43,460
Stormin Annie	4	F	5	0	0	1	2,145	Stormy Carol	3	F	7	1	1	0	7,785
Stormin Bayou	6	G	6	0	0	1	520	Stormy Child	2	F	1	0	0	0	0
Stormin' Betty	4	F	12	2	0	2	14,709	Stormy Colebrook	5	G	9	0	0	0	5,840
Stormin Bid	3	F	4	1	0	0	15,746	Stormy Conquest	4	F	9	2	0	1	29,280
Stormin Bill	3	G	5	0	0	0	678	Stormy Daisy	4	F	15	1	3	3	16,502
Stormin Bleasing	3	F	11	1	1	2	10,311	Stormy Danyelle	3	F	5	1	1	2	20,460
Stormin Cherokee	3	G	13	1	1	0	18,095	Stormy Davis	6	G	1	0	0	0	38
Stormin' Daina	2	F	5	0	0	2	4,670	Stormy Dawn	2	F	2	0	0	0	0
Stormin Dancer	2	F	2	1	0	0	6,550	Stormy Day	4	G	15	1	2	4	55,950
Stormin' Dee	4	G	5	0	2	0	2,090	Stormy Daze	5	G	6	0	0	0	415
Stormin Diva	7	M	9	0	0	1	1,004	Stormy Dear	2	F	2	0	0	0	0
Stormin' Dorothy	5	M	1	0	0	0	290	Stormy Deb	3	F	7	2	1	2	8,840
Stormin' Down	3	F	18	5	2	3	69,075	Stormy Debut	4	G	17	2	3	3	11,714
Stormin Fire	4	G	3	0	0	1	430	Stormy Do	10	G	11	2	1	2	20,620
Stormin Girl	2	F	2	0	0	1	2,080	Stormy Flight	4	G	3	0	0	0	460
Stormin Greek	2	C	5	1	2	0	27,950	Stormy Frolic	4	F	13	2	0	1	142,600
Stormin' Gun (AUS)	4	G	5	0	0	0	1,150	Stormy Future	3	F	2	0	1	0	6,240
Stormin' Heaven	5	H	5	1	0	1	43,060	Stormy Gambler	7	M	9	1	4	0	38,315
Stormin in Style	2	C	1	0	0	0	0	Stormy Gulch	4	G	6	0	0	1	2,175
Stormin Inthe West	3	F	8	1	0	2	8,613	Stormy Heroine	3	F	10	2	1	0	24,736
Stormin Jeannie	2	F	2	0	0	0	210	Stormy Hollow	3	G	4	0	0	0	550
Stormin Johnny	2	G	1	0	0	0	95	Stormy Honor	3	F	4	0	1	0	1,281
Stormin' Lad	5	G	5	2	2	1	32,500	Stormy Hostage	5	H	10	1	1	1	10,457
Stormin Lauren	2	F	6	0	2	2	11,870	Stormy Hour	5	M	5	1	2	0	21,200
Stormin' Lyon	2	C	2	1	0	0	17,875	Stormy Impact	4	C	11	0	2	5	52,508
Stormin Nikki	2	F	1	1	0	0	15,624	Stormy Isle	8	G	9	1	2	2	4,693
Stormin Oedy	6	H	11	0	1	4	37,800	Stormy Journey	3	G	4	0	0	0	150
Stormin' Oiseau	5	H	8	1	2	2	7,975	Stormy Kitty	2	F	1	0	0	0	195
Stormin Palm Beach	3	F	8	1	0	1	11,810	Stormy La Reine	3	F	10	0	1	0	7,435
Stormin Pat	2	F	1	0	0	0	195	Stormy Lane	3	C	9	0	3	1	47,241
Stormin Pattie	2	G	5	0	0	0	520	Stormy Looker	4	C	15	0	1	1	4,264
Stormin' Reprized	4	G	13	0	1	0	8,090	Stormy Lover	4	G	6	1	0	1	32,188
Stormin Sassy	4	F	11	2	3	0	44,439	Stormy Luvin	3	G	11	1	0	0	13,548
Stormin Sis	5	M	12	2	0	1	6,540	Stormy March	4	F	4	0	1	0	650
Stormin Tammy	4	F	6	1	0	0	4,746	Stormy Mary	4	F	8	2	1	0	9,984
Stormin Tia	3	F	14	3	1	0	18,615	Stormy Misty	2	F	3	0	0	1	907
Stormin Time	5	G	2	0	1	0	1,440	Stormy Music	2	F	1	0	0	0	537
Stormin to Victory	7	G	11	0	0	0	2,752	Stormy 'n Sly	3	F	8	3	2	1	34,736
Stormin Tony	4	G	12	0	3	3	27,349	Stormy Noche	2	F	1	0	0	0	0
Stormin Ty	3	G	7	0	0	1	820	Stormy North	3	G	5	0	2	2	6,183
Stormin Up Front	3	C	6	0	1	2	7,083	Stormy Numbers	2	F	2	0	0	0	420
Stormin Upthe Ave.	3	F	2	0	0	0	270	Stormy Outlook	3	F	3	0	0	0	1,260
Storminbayoubabe	3	F	9	2	2	0	16,860	Stormy Planet	3	G	6	1	2	0	11,810
Stormindisguise	2	C	4	0	1	0	3,420	Stormy Pleasure	5	H	14	0	1	3	13,391
Storming Ashley	3	F	6	0	3	2	7,135	Stormy Port	4	F	4	1	0	2	13,252
Storming Cajun	3	G	2	0	1	0	6,000	Stormy Pride	3	F	3	0	0	1	2,335
Storming Home (GB)	5	H	5	3	0	0	650,000	Stormy Raccoon	3	F	3	0	0	0	320
Storming Maria	2	F	7	1	1	1	15,875	Stormy Ray	4	G	12	2	2	2	58,670
Storming On By	2	C	2	0	0	1	1,740	Stormy Redman	3	C	1	0	0	0	35
Storming On Merit	4	F	12	10	0	0	108,643	Stormy Rockette	3	G	13	1	1	1	9,625
Storming Renee	5	M	10	1	0	7	9,446	Stormy Roman	4	G	6	1	1	0	117,225
Storming Way	2	F	4	1	0	1	22,030	Stormy Rosa	2	F	3	2	0	1	30,520
Storminoutahere	2	G	5	0	0	0	816	Stormy Seas	5	G	9	0	2	1	19,050
Storminthedesert	2	C	4	0	1	0	2,774	Stormy Season	2	F	4	0	1	0	5,380
Storminthevalley	2	C	1	0	0	0	0	Stormy Siege	2	C	5	2	0	1	46,050
Stormline	4	C	5	0	1	0	2,300	Stormy Sky	3	F	14	6	1	5	44,325
Storm'n J R	5	H	12	5	1	2	87,760	Stormy Society	5	M	7	2	2	1	52,518

RECORDS OF HORSES

Horse	Age	Sex	Sts	1st	2d	3d	Won	Horse	Age	Sex	Sts	1st	2d	3d	Won
Stormy Socks	3	G	11	0	0	0	300	Stratostar	3	C	4	0	0	0	460
Stormy Sonata	7	G	5	1	0	0	14,853	Stratton (IRE)	6	G	2	0	0	0	880
Stormy Sparks	2	C	3	0	0	0	137	Stratum	5	H	3	1	1	0	6,750
Stormy Spirit	5	M	8	2	2	1	62,840	Stratus (ARG)	5	H	6	1	2	0	59,100
Stormy Storm	2	C	1	0	0	0	0	Stratus (FR)	4	G	8	2	2	0	86,000
Stormy Sunset	4	G	14	0	1	1	4,218	Strausberg	3	G	11	4	0	2	47,528
Stormy Surprise	4	F	6	1	0	1	5,668	Straw Baby	4	F	1	0	0	0	40
Stormy Terms	2	F	4	1	0	1	17,310	Straw Boy	5	G	3	0	0	0	552
Stormy Thunder	2	C	3	0	0	0	440	Straw to Gold	4	C	6	0	0	0	605
Stormy Wars	6	M	7	0	0	2	3,087	Strawbailey	5	M	9	1	1	1	44,910
Stormy Waters	4	G	9	1	3	0	6,935	Strawberriesncream	2	F	5	2	1	0	29,790
Stormy Way	5	M	7	2	0	1	83,426	Strawberry Banks	3	F	12	1	2	2	13,620
Stormy Whitebrow	2	F	2	1	0	0	3,906	Strawberry Custard	2	F	5	1	1	1	14,870
Stormy Whitney	5	M	7	0	0	2	3,090	Strawberry Glaze	5	M	4	0	0	0	328
Stormy Zone	4	G	11	3	2	1	36,960	Strawberry Gone	3	F	8	0	0	1	3,349
Stormybdancing	3	F	9	2	2	2	51,780	Strawberry Halo	4	F	2	0	0	0	0
Stormyhill	3	G	9	0	3	1	4,385	Strawberry Ice	4	F	16	3	4	4	20,702
Stormy's Charm	4	F	1	0	0	0	35	Strawberry Jam	5	H	1	0	0	0	55
Stormys Treasure	2	G	3	0	1	0	5,000	Strawberry Kid	4	G	5	1	1	0	12,671
Stormy'sback	2	C	6	1	0	0	11,925	Strawberry Kwik	3	F	14	1	1	5	18,665
Story Book Love	4	F	8	0	1	0	4,516	Strawberry Line	2	F	3	2	1	0	23,820
Story Book Road	9	G	15	0	2	1	2,476	Strawberry Moon	6	M	16	1	0	2	6,594
Story Grinder	3	C	3	0	0	1	4,080	Strawberry Pop	8	G	9	1	2	2	7,088
Story of the Cat	2	F	1	0	0	0	0	Strawberry Sherie	4	F	8	1	0	1	2,515
Story Tails	3	G	5	0	0	2	826	Strawberry Soda	3	F	6	1	0	0	8,920
Storybook Ending	6	H	6	1	1	1	13,400	Strawberry Strut	2	F	3	0	0	0	745
Storybook Kid	5	G	12	4	1	3	152,050	Strawberry Sunset	2	F	2	0	0	0	190
Storybound	6	M	10	3	1	2	41,686	Strawberry Turn	7	M	11	1	1	1	4,524
Sto's Hole	2	C	1	0	0	0	64	Strawberry Twister	4	C	16	2	1	4	6,874
Stosky and Hutch	3	F	6	3	0	1	25,522	Strawberryfields	3	F	3	0	0	2	1,352
Stotz	3	C	8	1	1	2	11,304	Stray Bullet	4	F	10	4	0	2	46,388
Stowaway Kitten	2	F	6	1	2	2	10,045	Stray Cat Struter	4	C	2	0	0	0	0
Stowe	4	F	3	0	0	0	754	Streak a Roani	2	G	3	0	1	2	3,238
Stowe Creek	8	G	7	2	1	0	17,320	Streak Face J	5	G	6	0	1	0	800
Stower	3	C	8	2	1	0	37,960	Streak of Royalty	4	G	6	3	2	0	63,596
Straight	3	G	4	0	0	0	472	Streak of Smoke	2	C	6	2	2	0	72,104
Straight A	6	H	12	0	2	1	40,329	Streak Stroud	3	C	10	1	1	1	9,940
Straight Exchange	3	F	5	0	1	1	4,526	Streakednorth	3	F	6	1	1	2	20,380
Straight In	5	G	6	1	1	0	12,040	Streakin and Strip	2	G	3	0	0	1	3,620
Straight North	9	G	2	0	0	0	120	Streakin Baha	2	G	1	0	0	0	0
Straight Path	4	C	1	0	0	0	0	Streakin Bocario	4	C	7	1	0	1	6,465
Straight Putt	3	G	5	0	1	1	7,930	Streakin Devil	2	C	8	1	2	1	10,100
Straight Star	3	C	11	0	3	2	23,708	Streakin Gump	10	G	4	0	0	2	572
Straight Street	6	G	12	2	1	4	37,884	Streakin Monarch	3	C	10	3	1	0	21,945
Straight Tens	2	G	2	0	0	0	192	Streakin Rob	4	G	6	1	0	1	35,434
Straight Tequila	4	C	7	0	0	0	1,755	Streakin Zulu	4	G	7	0	0	0	402
Straight Vodka	3	G	2	0	0	0	0	Streaking Echo	4	F	9	2	0	3	46,646
Strains of Music	4	F	3	0	0	0	313	Streaking Rose	4	F	4	0	0	1	2,510
Strait From Texas	4	F	9	3	3	0	275,936	Streaking Woman	7	M	19	1	6	10	15,565
Strait Sparkle	6	G	3	0	0	0	0	Stream	4	F	2	0	1	0	1,820
Straitfrommyheart	5	M	18	4	2	1	33,194	Streambank	4	G	12	1	1	2	11,235
Strandhill	5	G	11	3	2	2	42,175	Streamline Gahl	3	F	1	0	0	0	300
Strange Candy	4	F	8	0	1	0	1,310	Strech Out Front	4	C	12	1	0	0	14,048
Strange Silhouette	3	F	2	0	0	0	382	Street Angel	5	M	9	0	0	2	1,786
Stranger	4	G	11	1	4	1	14,056	Street Band	4	F	8	6	0	0	52,260
Stranger Among Us	3	G	15	2	2	4	17,612	Street Chic	2	F	8	0	2	0	6,535
Strap	4	G	6	0	0	0	379	Street Con	10	G	3	0	0	0	225
Strap Notch	5	G	8	1	0	0	10,026	Street Dreamer	7	M	9	0	0	1	1,347
Straphanger	4	G	6	1	2	1	27,248	Street Dreams	3	F	6	1	0	0	8,955
Strapless Dancer	5	G	7	1	0	1	12,665	Street Life	4	G	10	1	4	3	70,650
Strappado	6	G	10	0	0	0	3,150	Street of Gold	3	G	7	1	0	0	2,390
Strapper Nick	3	G	9	0	1	2	2,563	Street Smart Sue	2	F	1	0	0	0	2,160
Strata Climber	2	C	2	0	0	0	1,590	Street Wheeling	4	F	10	2	3	3	76,294
Strate Excellence	3	C	3	0	0	0	1,400	Street Wild	3	F	1	0	0	0	0
Strategic	5	M	4	0	2	0	1,285	Streetfight	3	G	11	0	4	2	8,234
Strategic Intrigue	4	G	9	2	2	2	36,174	Streetmusic	4	G	5	2	0	0	22,500
Strategic Move	5	G	9	2	4	1	57,760	Streets of Fire	3	F	11	1	2	1	29,145
Strategic Partner	5	H	4	0	1	2	25,400	Streets of Laredo	9	G	17	1	2	1	13,738
Strategic Solution	3	F	2	0	0	0	1,680	Streets of Silver	5	M	13	1	4	0	15,979
Strategic Strike	3	G	14	1	1	2	70,052	Stregawood	7	G	7	2	2	1	5,137
Strategically	3	G	1	0	0	0	440	Stregone (IRE)	5	G	19	2	1	6	10,251
Stratego	4	G	8	1	1	0	5,453	Strength and Honor	4	G	5	5	1	0	46,115
Strategury	3	G	12	1	3	1	20,792	Strength of Will	9	G	19	0	0	0	1,069
Stratematic	4	C	12	1	5	2	64,580	Strength Within	3	G	11	2	4	3	119,010
Stratford Court	3	F	1	0	0	0	0	Stress Master	3	G	10	1	3	0	32,325
Stratford On Avon	3	G	3	0	0	1	3,080	Stretch for Home	3	C	1	0	0	0	0
Strathcona	4	G	11	0	3	2	6,640	Stretch Run	2	F	5	1	1	0	11,120
Stratify	3	C	4	0	0	0	1,615	Stretch Velvet	4	F	7	2	0	1	14,340
Stratoplan	3	G	5	3	1	0	78,380	Stretchin' North	3	C	10	1	2	2	49,860

Horse	Age	Sex	Sts	1st	2d	3d	Won
Stretching Out	6	G	1	0	0	0	0
Stretchyourfaith	4	C	15	4	2	0	30,560
Stretta	9	G	14	1	3	1	5,548
Strickly Business	8	G	14	0	0	0	3,437
Strict Forum	4	F	16	1	3	0	32,440
Strictly Business	3	G	6	2	1	2	20,800
Strictly High Brow	7	M	15	1	3	1	7,190
Strictly Legit	3	F	6	2	1	2	17,910
Strictly Personal	4	F	19	3	4	4	21,665
Strictly Physical	3	F	5	1	2	0	5,597
Stride On Over	7	G	2	0	0	0	480
Strider's Comet	6	G	6	1	2	1	16,472
Strider's Ormsby	2	G	2	1	0	0	7,950
Strider's Rocket	5	G	12	5	0	1	18,618
Strike a Match	4	G	10	1	0	2	7,837
Strike an Image	2	F	4	1	2	0	25,576
Strike and Run	2	F	2	0	0	0	0
Strike Bar None	4	C	8	0	0	0	424
Strike Breaker	3	C	2	1	0	0	6,000
Strike Commander	4	G	10	3	1	2	34,529
Strike de Ego	3	F	13	5	2	2	21,110
Strike Em Hard	2	G	7	2	0	1	78,516
Strike for Richard	7	G	13	2	2	0	23,558
Strike Force One	3	G	2	0	1	0	3,528
Strike Free	4	F	3	0	0	1	1,620
Strike Hound	3	G	7	0	2	0	5,720
Strike It Big	6	G	14	2	3	4	16,080
Strike M Red	6	G	1	0	1	0	2,440
Strike Mission	3	C	2	0	0	0	0
Strike 'n a Deal	2	G	4	1	1	1	28,932
Strike 'n Go	3	G	11	5	3	0	81,600
Strike n' Prospect	5	G	14	2	0	1	16,411
Strike Point	3	F	8	1	1	0	17,610
Strike Ranger	5	G	13	2	1	0	9,174
Strike Rate	3	F	7	0	1	2	20,885
Strike Reality	8	G	12	2	2	0	28,460
Strike Right	6	G	12	1	1	1	12,152
Strike Royalty	2	F	5	1	1	0	8,159
Strike the Brass	6	G	13	4	2	2	66,555
Strike the Chord	5	G	12	3	4	2	28,155
Strike the Harp	2	F	4	1	0	1	46,545
Strike the Lord	2	C	7	0	0	2	6,134
Strike the Moment	2	G	3	0	0	1	2,123
Strike Three	6	G	13	3	2	2	59,460
Strike to the Core	3	C	2	0	0	0	0
Strike Twice	5	G	8	2	1	0	13,230
Strike Up	3	C	4	1	0	0	24,776
Strike With Pasion	4	F	1	0	0	0	0
Strike Zone	10	G	6	1	1	0	29,700
Strikeapromise	4	F	9	0	0	0	3,293
Strikes Count	5	G	2	0	0	0	146
Strikes No Spares	4	F	5	1	1	1	46,760
Strikeski	8	G	5	0	0	0	170
Strikethegold Lass	7	M	14	3	2	1	23,409
Strikeupthemusic	4	F	3	0	0	0	476
Striking Audrey	2	F	3	0	1	0	3,780
Striking B	4	G	17	1	2	2	8,653
Striking Cobra	2	F	3	1	1	0	17,600
Striking Devil	6	H	3	0	0	0	0
Striking Flames	4	F	9	0	1	1	4,970
Striking Jaklin	3	F	1	0	0	0	0
Striking Ladd	7	H	3	0	0	1	575
Striking Michelle	6	M	12	2	6	4	37,500
Striking North	12	G	0	0	1	0	3,600
Striking Picture	5	M	5	1	3	1	19,880
Striking Poses	5	M	6	1	1	1	20,379
Striking Red Beth	3	F	8	0	0	1	897
Striking Silver	3	G	2	0	0	0	0
Striking Song	4	C	4	0	0	0	4,140
Striking Storm	5	H	10	1	1	1	17,048
Striking T	2	F	9	0	1	1	3,640
Strikingly	3	G	12	2	2	1	84,450
Strikingly Proud	7	G	14	2	0	1	7,761
String Quartet	2	F	2	0	0	1	1,650
Stringalongwithme	10	G	10	1	1	1	6,818
Stringtown Wonder	2	C	5	1	2	1	38,850
Strinnenia	4	F	3	1	0	0	5,586
Strip	6	G	6	0	0	4	5,555
Stripe Face	2	G	9	1	0	0	11,226
Striped Candy	3	C	5	0	0	0	459
Stripling Warrior	3	G	6	1	1	1	9,138
Striptease	4	F	18	2	5	1	14,809
Strive	4	C	8	0	3	1	104,500
Strizzi	3	C	8	1	2	0	113,914
Strodee	4	F	6	1	0	0	6,900
Strodes Commander	3	C	13	4	2	1	84,960
Strodes Lane	4	F	10	2	2	1	56,182
Strodes Station	8	G	2	0	0	0	0
Stroganof	3	F	5	1	0	0	4,140
Stroke	9	G	1	0	0	0	0
Stroke of Genius	8	M	14	0	3	2	4,040
Stroker	4	C	15	4	2	3	36,124
Stroker Jr.	9	G	4	0	2	1	1,988
Stroll	3	C	6	5	1	0	398,800
Stroll Fast	5	M	6	2	1	0	34,325
Stroll On	7	G	7	1	1	1	26,529
Strollin Slew	3	F	6	1	3	2	64,880
Strolling Kris	3	F	12	1	4	2	28,741
Strong as a Tree	4	G	7	0	0	0	876
Strong Cat	2	C	1	1	0	0	28,200
Strong Faith	2	F	1	1	0	0	7,563
Strong Girl	3	F	13	1	5	1	24,280
Strong Guy	9	G	3	0	1	1	1,550
Strong Hope	3	C	7	5	0	1	582,360
Strong Reader	6	G	6	0	0	0	617
Strong Stage	3	G	13	3	0	3	29,950
Strong Suit	7	G	2	1	1	0	3,000
Strongestsovereign	2	G	2	2	0	0	30,600
Strongwilled Stuka	3	F	9	1	0	0	12,845
Stroud	4	G	1	1	0	0	9,000
Stroud Bay	5	H	8	0	3	2	11,929
Struck by Luck	5	M	8	0	0	0	0
Structured	3	F	6	2	1	1	9,900
Strudel Lou	3	F	2	0	0	0	0
Struggler's Legend	2	C	1	0	0	0	0
Strugglingprisoner	4	F	15	1	0	0	162
Strumminwithrhythm	3	F	1	0	0	0	0
Strut	3	C	4	0	0	0	50
Strut Sharply	3	G	10	0	2	1	10,033
Strut the Stage	5	H	4	2	1	0	485,085
Struttin'	3	F	1	0	0	0	0
Strychnine	5	H	9	1	1	0	6,833
Stryker's Flight	4	G	9	1	0	1	5,803
Stuart Beau Gull	2	G	3	0	0	0	216
Stubborn	4	F	15	1	3	3	9,238
Stubborn Bull	7	G	11	0	0	1	935
Stubborn Charm	4	G	3	0	0	1	1,637
Stubbsville	2	G	3	0	0	0	0
Stubsy	5	G	10	1	1	1	12,454
Stuck in Canada	3	G	12	1	1	2	18,553
Stuck in Limbo	4	F	13	1	2	0	39,623
Stuck in Vegas	3	G	9	0	0	1	4,056
Stuck On Speed	7	G	11	1	2	3	13,910
Stuck On Stuka	3	F	13	1	1	2	7,606
Stuck Up	6	G	6	0	2	0	3,640
Stud Poker	4	G	1	0	0	0	0
Studio King	7	G	7	1	0	0	3,906
Studio Time	4	G	3	2	0	0	52,850
Stuff Enough	2	C	1	0	0	0	85
Stuff N Things	2	G	4	0	1	0	4,105
Stuff Shot	4	G	6	0	0	0	1,170
Stuka's Beauty	4	F	11	2	1	0	44,152
Stuka's Dancer	7	M	9	0	1	3	2,430
Stukcess	4	C	9	2	1	1	22,782
Stukkauppa	7	M	8	0	1	1	1,733
Stunning Image (IRE)	3	F	2	0	0	1	4,130
Stunning Stella	3	F	12	1	1	1	4,067
Stunt Double	3	C	6	1	0	1	9,618
Sturgeons General	4	G	8	0	0	0	420
Sturgeons Pal	4	C	8	0	0	2	744
Sturmovik	7	H	3	0	0	0	366
Stuttgart (NZ)	6	G	12	2	0	2	30,975
Stutz Dancer	3	G	8	0	1	1	3,430
Stutz Force	4	C	5	0	2	1	938
Stutz Passion	4	F	11	2	2	0	8,305
Stutz Power	6	M	19	0	3	5	19,740
Stutz's Star	5	M	4	0	0	0	940
Stydahar	4	C	9	2	1	2	71,972

Horse	Age	Sex	Sts	1st	2d	3d	Won
Style Champ	4	F	8	3	2	1	43,410
Style Maker	4	G	5	0	0	0	323
Styler	4	F	4	2	0	2	69,360
Stylin' Blues	3	F	3	1	0	0	1,650
Stylin Melody	5	M	6	0	1	1	1,860
Stylin' Music	4	C	2	0	1	0	1,500
Stylin' Okie	4	F	7	1	0	0	2,058
Stylish	5	M	6	3	0	1	270,955
Stylish Account	3	G	12	0	0	3	11,880
Stylish Beauty	4	F	7	2	1	1	28,154
Stylish Candy	2	C	3	0	0	0	0
Stylish Cat	3	G	11	1	1	2	5,578
Stylish Connection	6	M	4	0	0	0	342
Stylish Dancer	3	G	8	3	0	1	33,767
Stylish Dave	2	G	2	0	0	0	0
Stylish Design	3	F	6	0	1	0	3,940
Stylish Doug	3	C	5	1	0	2	2,128
Stylish Dreamer	3	C	8	0	0	2	2,472
Stylish Factor	2	F	1	1	0	0	5,700
Stylish Fire	4	F	9	2	1	1	12,518
Stylish Groove	4	G	5	0	0	1	2,039
Stylish in Red	4	G	6	0	0	1	5,440
Stylish Joe	3	G	8	1	0	2	13,961
Stylish Manner	3	F	3	0	1	0	5,900
Stylish Mission	6	M	8	1	0	1	15,915
Stylish Rita	4	F	7	0	0	0	1,448
Stylish Sensation	6	G	8	0	1	1	1,916
Stylish Stepper	7	M	4	0	0	0	0
Stylish Sultan	4	C	8	5	0	0	142,960
Stylish Times	4	F	6	0	0	0	464
Stylish Tour	2	F	1	0	0	0	0
Stylish Val	2	F	2	1	0	0	5,896
Stylishly	2	C	4	1	1	0	27,325
Styx Crossing	4	G	7	1	0	0	7,846
Su Tiempo	7	G	11	1	0	2	7,308
Su Tour	3	G	2	0	0	0	0
Suances (GB)	6	H	1	0	0	1	9,177
Suave	2	C	5	1	2	0	41,355
Suave Act	3	G	18	3	0	3	74,380
Suave and Pretty	3	F	16	1	1	4	15,036
Suave Appeal	3	C	7	1	2	1	9,520
Suave Charmer	3	G	14	2	0	3	15,127
Suave Colleen	2	F	2	1	0	0	10,725
Suave Darling	4	F	14	4	1	3	46,285
Suave Devil	4	C	17	0	4	1	32,993
Suave Gentleman	3	C	10	2	1	0	34,740
Suave Girl	2	F	3	0	1	1	4,785
Suave Guy	4	F	18	1	0	2	8,365
Suave Kat	7	H	8	0	0	1	787
Suave King	4	G	10	0	0	1	3,774
Suave Knight	3	G	14	3	3	3	54,389
Suave Lad	4	G	5	2	0	1	17,300
Suave Lass	3	F	22	1	3	3	22,285
Suave Man	4	C	15	0	3	4	15,328
Suave Meteorite	4	G	13	2	2	4	50,120
Suave Miss	4	F	10	1	1	2	24,320
Suave Nobleman	4	G	10	0	3	1	13,572
Suave Princess	4	F	16	1	4	4	23,815
Suave Queen	4	F	12	0	1	3	43,825
Suave Rhapsody	4	G	10	2	1	2	45,570
Suave Romancer	2	C	5	0	2	2	9,570
Suave Sentiment (IRE)	5	M	1	1	0	0	8,400
Suave Silhouette	3	F	4	0	1	0	4,442
Suave Squaw	3	F	9	3	3	2	54,850
Suave Star	3	F	5	0	0	0	440
Suaves Lightning	4	F	10	1	1	1	7,687
Sub Call	2	C	1	0	0	0	750
Sub Launch	3	F	3	1	1	1	15,877
Subject Matter	7	G	11	1	1	5	10,260
Subject to Fine	2	G	5	0	2	1	3,958
Sublet (FR)	4	G	5	0	0	0	6,720
Sublime Slew	3	F	4	0	0	1	2,760
Sublimity	2	F	4	0	0	1	1,834
Submarine	3	G	4	0	0	0	0
Submissive	4	F	2	0	0	0	0
Subordinate Sin	2	F	3	0	0	0	480
Subordinate's Lad	3	G	9	0	3	0	19,900
Subpoena	6	G	3	1	0	0	4,450
Subrogate	9	G	6	2	1	0	8,883
Subscription	7	H	1	0	0	0	46
Subsidy	3	G	12	1	3	1	43,730
Subtle Charm (GB)	3	F	2	0	0	0	780
Subtle Distinction	4	F	12	0	4	2	11,240
Subtle Glitz	3	C	9	0	1	0	16,080
Subtle Knight	3	G	5	0	0	1	2,420
Subtle Money	4	C	1	0	0	0	810
Subtle Remark	2	F	4	1	1	0	8,850
Subtle Saratoga	2	C	4	2	0	1	13,205
Subtle Style	3	F	16	4	1	3	15,072
Suburbanite	2	F	4	0	0	0	195
Subway Series	4	G	6	0	1	0	9,170
Succeedere	3	C	14	0	3	0	19,640
Success and Glory (IRE)	8	G	5	0	0	0	0
Success Rate	3	C	2	0	0	0	3,780
Success Trapp	2	C	1	0	0	0	0
Successful Cat	2	F	8	2	1	1	27,420
Successfull Mike	5	G	9	1	2	1	12,710
Successfully Lady	5	M	6	0	0	0	69
Succinctly	8	H	1	0	0	0	0
Such a Beezer	4	F	2	0	0	0	225
Such a Flirt	3	F	12	6	1	1	88,306
Such a Foxy Thing	3	F	9	2	1	1	12,428
Such a Lady	7	M	11	1	1	2	17,729
Such a Presence	8	G	8	0	0	1	1,106
Such Charisma	9	G	7	0	1	3	10,600
Such Gold	5	M	4	0	1	1	2,912
Sucha Dandy	4	F	8	1	1	1	2,824
Suchala	3	F	15	2	1	4	25,529
Suck Um Up Bro	3	G	5	0	1	0	2,250
Suckers Gold	3	F	4	0	0	1	3,780
Sudden Bluff	5	G	11	4	2	1	39,390
Sudden Fame	3	G	12	1	0	3	16,485
Sudden Fancy	3	F	8	0	0	0	2,689
Sudden Flight	3	G	8	0	2	3	18,330
Sudden Glory	5	H	11	1	2	1	20,359
Sudden Side	3	G	7	1	3	0	6,651
Sudden Streak	4	F	1	0	0	0	0
Sudden Sunny	7	M	2	0	0	0	0
Suddenly Alone	4	F	14	0	1	1	10,255
Suddenly Damascus	4	G	5	0	0	0	42
Suddenly Devilish	3	F	11	2	2	1	42,850
Suddenly Gone	6	M	7	1	1	0	17,170
Suddenly Sheila	4	F	8	1	1	2	4,540
Suddenly Sweet	3	C	2	0	0	0	0
Sudith	2	F	2	1	0	1	35,735
Sudjanas Finest	2	C	6	1	0	2	24,733
Sue Etta	2	F	5	0	0	2	2,095
Sue of Gold	2	F	3	0	0	0	891
Sue Ray	5	M	4	0	0	0	0
Sue Sues Asset	4	F	3	0	1	0	1,250
Suela West	3	F	3	0	0	0	266
Suelle Son	4	G	7	0	0	0	1,246
Suembul (NZ)	9	G	2	0	1	0	4,500
Suerte Proper	3	G	4	0	1	0	2,720
Sue's Adam Bomb	7	H	1	0	0	0	61
Sue's April Fool	9	G	5	0	2	1	5,540
Sue's Crew	5	H	3	0	0	0	360
Sue's Episode	5	G	7	0	3	3	18,179
Sue's Gold	3	F	7	0	0	0	629
Sue's Good News	3	F	8	5	0	0	160,800
Sues Hay	3	F	17	3	3	6	25,562
Sue's Legacy	3	F	6	0	2	0	4,930
Sue's Melody	2	F	2	0	0	0	348
Sue's Slew	7	G	11	1	0	1	11,916
Sue's the Boss	6	M	10	1	3	0	14,588
Suey Suey	4	F	5	0	1	1	3,541
Suezann Elizabeth	4	F	3	0	0	0	432
Suffire (ARG)	6	H	11	2	2	1	31,200
Sugah Sugah	4	F	10	1	1	2	26,520
Sugar Beat	4	F	3	0	0	0	159
Sugar Candy	3	F	4	0	0	0	1,700
Sugar Charm	3	G	4	1	1	1	2,104
Sugar Coating	8	G	7	0	0	0	804
Sugar Creek Girl	2	F	4	0	0	2	3,990
Sugar Daddys Man	3	G	4	1	0	0	5,445
Sugar Dipped	4	F	5	0	0	1	6,244
Sugar Dream	6	H	5	2	0	2	16,217
Sugar Free	5	M	6	1	1	1	43,500

Horse	Age	Sex	Sts	1st	2d	3d	Won
Sugar Gal	2	F	6	2	1	1	16,095
Sugar Glider	3	C	15	1	1	1	6,151
Sugar Hall	4	G	27	1	3	0	16,225
Sugar Hill	6	M	2	1	0	0	1,808
Sugar Kick	6	M	8	2	1	0	30,743
Sugar Lake Lass	3	F	11	1	1	0	7,014
Sugar Lips	3	F	6	0	0	0	686
Sugar Mags	6	G	11	3	2	0	33,868
Sugar Mama	3	F	17	0	0	3	4,112
Sugar Me	3	F	2	0	0	1	1,140
Sugar Plum Miss	5	M	4	0	0	0	1,067
Sugar Punch	2	F	1	0	1	0	8,200
Sugar Queen	4	F	15	1	3	3	17,387
Sugar Ray	6	M	3	1	0	1	11,718
Sugar Ray Gold	5	G	13	0	0	1	1,536
Sugar Ray Silver	5	G	10	2	0	0	14,394
Sugar Ride	3	F	4	0	2	0	11,150
Sugar 's Memory	2	F	3	0	0	0	700
Sugar Shack	7	M	6	0	2	1	9,612
Sugar Shaker	4	G	7	3	0	0	19,776
Sugar Six	5	G	1	0	0	0	0
Sugar Sleet	4	F	9	0	3	2	15,467
Sugarbaby Shirley	5	M	5	0	0	0	0
Sugarcreek Run	6	M	3	1	0	0	6,566
Sugarred	3	F	5	1	0	0	21,450
Sugar's Bullet	2	C	1	0	0	0	0
Sugar's Prince	5	G	8	0	1	2	3,265
Sugar'scube	9	G	9	0	0	0	315
Sugarslittleacorn	5	M	2	0	1	0	1,080
Sugarsway	3	G	12	2	0	2	31,665
Sugartoniteinmytea	4	F	11	0	1	2	10,785
Sugartown Rose	3	F	2	1	0	0	4,758
Sugarville	3	G	3	0	1	0	2,772
Sugg Walker	5	M	18	3	5	4	72,380
Sui Generis	8	G	6	0	2	2	7,864
Suicidal	6	G	8	0	0	1	1,546
Suicide Mission	3	G	2	0	0	0	875
Suit	2	F	5	1	0	0	11,020
Suitable Match	7	H	7	1	1	2	6,050
Suitable Suitor	3	C	14	4	0	2	51,642
Suitagold	5	M	5	0	0	0	826
Suits and Ties	5	H	3	0	0	0	594
Suits Her Well	4	F	1	0	0	0	0
Sukkot	6	M	7	2	1	1	12,844
Sula Mae	4	F	2	0	0	2	2,540
Sulamani (IRE)	4	C	6	3	1	0	2,603,842
Suleiman	3	G	6	1	0	1	15,255
Sulka	5	M	1	0	0	0	330
Sullana	6	M	9	1	0	1	23,630
Sullivanitis	5	G	10	2	0	0	14,880
Sullivan's Irish	4	F	3	0	0	0	186
Sullivans Travels	5	G	10	3	1	1	19,476
Sully's Girl	3	F	10	2	1	0	14,404
Sully's Silver	2	C	2	0	0	0	0
Sulmona	3	F	2	0	0	0	100
Sulphur Fork	6	G	5	1	0	0	6,030
Sultan Bey	2	C	1	0	0	0	0
Sultan of Spin	2	C	4	0	0	0	2,390
Sultan of Swat	5	G	17	2	1	2	10,465
Sultan's Gold	6	G	13	2	2	3	12,649
Sultan's Pride	7	G	15	2	1	2	9,998
Sulton's Glass	7	G	11	2	1	0	7,524
Sultress of Swing	5	M	9	1	1	1	22,970
Sultry Breeze	4	F	1	0	0	0	56
Sultry Cat	3	C	8	2	1	2	71,440
Sultry Danse	3	F	1	0	0	0	870
Sultry Eyes	2	F	4	1	2	0	24,700
Sultry Firm	2	C	1	0	0	0	150
Sultry Fluff	4	F	4	1	0	0	52,692
Sultry Interval	4	F	18	3	2	1	47,395
Sultry Mood	7	G	12	3	0	1	22,850
Sultry of Gold	4	G	2	0	0	0	44
Sultry Prospect	4	F	12	0	1	2	11,855
Sultry Rendevous	3	F	4	1	0	0	24,190
Sultry Sal	3	F	4	1	3	0	41,380
Sultry Sexy Susie	4	F	3	0	1	0	3,575
Sultry Silence	3	G	7	0	1	3	14,730
Sultry Siren	2	F	2	0	0	0	0
Sultry Sound	4	F	11	3	1	1	39,628
Sultry Sreva	4	F	8	1	1	2	31,560
Sultry Star	5	M	1	0	0	0	217
Sultry Style	6	M	8	1	1	1	11,155
Sultry Sunshine	3	F	9	1	0	5	12,020
Sultry Wonder	3	G	9	1	0	0	8,055
Sultryann	2	F	1	0	0	0	0
Sultry's Kazam	2	G	1	0	0	0	0
Sulzano	3	F	8	0	0	0	420
Sum Bad Lady	3	F	3	0	0	2	4,455
Sum Breeze	3	F	1	0	0	0	150
Sum Eagle	3	F	3	0	0	0	74
Sum Emblem	3	G	5	0	2	1	10,348
Sum Gun	5	G	4	3	0	0	9,005
Sum Heaven	5	G	1	0	0	0	0
Sum Lucky Ridge	7	H	3	0	0	0	0
Sum Marval	2	C	1	1	0	0	24,600
Sum Money Bag	2	F	3	0	0	0	3,864
Sum Reward	4	C	16	6	3	0	49,861
Sum Trick	3	C	4	0	1	1	54,760
Sumac Sue	5	M	9	1	2	2	11,106
Sumati (GB)	7	G	3	1	0	0	25,800
Sumcor	5	G	8	0	3	0	6,617
Sumerset	6	H	10	2	1	0	47,061
Suminister	7	M	8	1	0	1	7,532
Sumitas (GER)	7	H	6	0	1	1	34,940
Sumkindaglitter	8	M	5	0	0	0	0
Summarily	5	H	7	0	1	1	17,246
Summaryze	2	F	5	1	0	0	1,980
Summer Applause	3	G	7	3	1	1	21,960
Summer Blend	3	F	5	1	0	0	23,556
Summer Break	2	G	2	0	0	0	990
Summer Buy	7	G	14	1	0	1	3,607
Summer Camp	3	F	6	1	0	1	10,199
Summer Carnival	2	G	4	1	1	0	15,980
Summer Charm	4	F	10	0	1	1	5,985
Summer Citation	3	F	8	0	0	1	1,046
Summer Colony	5	M	5	1	1	0	256,500
Summer Crown	4	C	9	1	2	1	20,250
Summer Cure	4	F	16	2	0	2	9,407
Summer Dame	3	F	10	0	1	3	10,780
Summer Dance	3	F	1	0	0	0	0
Summer Delight	4	F	4	1	0	0	20,430
Summer Deposit	3	C	3	0	0	0	990
Summer Do Shine	2	F	3	0	2	0	6,240
Summer Doeny	5	M	1	0	0	0	0
Summer Dust	4	G	13	1	1	2	14,770
Summer Fashion	3	F	4	1	2	0	5,530
Summer Game	5	H	1	0	0	0	400
Summer Getaway	3	G	5	0	1	0	1,900
Summer Halo	3	F	6	1	0	0	9,282
Summer Hit	8	G	18	0	0	1	1,685
Summer Hound	3	F	11	0	0	1	2,501
Summer Imp	5	M	1	0	0	0	33
Summer in April	3	F	5	0	0	0	7,638
Summer Jam	2	F	10	0	0	2	11,695
Summer Joy	3	F	1	0	0	0	426
Summer Lass	3	F	14	4	3	4	117,330
Summer Lite	4	F	5	1	0	1	28,549
Summer Memories	3	F	1	0	0	0	0
Summer Mis	4	F	8	6	0	0	286,495
Summer Moment	2	F	4	0	0	0	0
Summer Note	6	G	2	0	1	0	7,600
Summer of Luck	3	C	1	0	0	0	61
Summer Prima	2	G	4	0	1	0	900
Summer Prince	8	G	10	3	1	2	8,900
Summer Pro	5	M	8	0	0	1	1,680
Summer Royalty	7	M	6	0	0	1	1,200
Summer Sails	3	F	4	1	0	1	19,563
Summer Savoya	4	F	1	0	0	0	100
Summer Scene	3	F	1	0	0	0	0
Summer Service	3	G	11	5	3	2	187,580
Summer Shenanigans	5	M	11	2	1	3	47,605
Summer Silk	2	F	5	0	1	0	1,960
Summer Sister	3	F	13	2	2	5	18,200
Summer Slew	3	C	9	2	1	2	74,935
Summer Sovereign	3	C	13	3	1	0	21,860
Summer Special	3	F	10	0	0	0	3,751
Summer Speed	4	F	1	0	0	0	0
Summer Spirit	5	M	4	1	0	1	19,197

Horse	Age	Sex	Sts	1st	2d	3d	Won	Horse	Age	Sex	Sts	1st	2d	3d	Won
Summer Sport	3	G	7	1	0	0	14,110	Sunco Chief	4	C	9	2	1	0	4,350
Summer Star	3	F	2	0	1	0	1,940	Sundae Passion	3	F	15	2	4	2	30,180
Summer Stone	3	F	12	3	0	2	45,040	Sundance Circle	2	G	4	3	1	0	50,133
Summer Surf	7	G	10	3	5	1	25,511	Sundance Fever	3	G	15	1	3	0	8,030
Summer Symphony	2	F	5	0	1	2	9,735	Sundance Square	4	C	14	3	0	4	29,913
Summer Tan	7	G	2	0	0	0	66	Sundar	4	G	6	0	1	2	15,336
Summer Tone	3	F	9	0	0	0	1,265	Sundari	5	M	2	0	0	1	668
Summer Torsion	4	F	11	1	3	3	8,822	Sunday Afternoon	2	F	2	0	0	0	375
Summer Trick	3	C	18	1	2	2	20,560	Sunday Break (JPN)	4	C	4	0	0	1	36,000
Summer Wind Dancer	3	F	6	0	3	1	92,692	Sunday Cash	4	G	10	0	2	1	6,682
Summer Wind Storm	3	F	2	1	0	1	17,200	Sunday Champ	3	C	9	1	1	1	8,230
Summerberry	2	F	4	1	0	0	21,840	Sunday Circus	4	F	10	0	1	4	5,248
Summerchance	2	F	5	0	1	1	3,650	Sunday Classic	4	C	1	0	0	0	75
Summerfield	4	F	6	0	0	0	2,720	Sunday Dinner	3	F	4	0	1	0	7,800
Summerhill Gal	7	M	6	1	0	0	24,852	Sunday Girl	3	F	5	0	1	2	1,865
Summer's Breeze	2	C	4	0	0	1	3,540	Sunday in Moscow	4	G	1	0	0	0	0
Summer's Chase	5	G	7	0	1	0	874	Sunday Knight	4	G	13	1	3	3	7,813
Summer's Comin	5	G	1	0	0	1	3,140	Sunday Linens	4	F	1	0	0	0	0
Summer's Cool	3	F	3	1	0	0	5,975	Sunday Magic	4	C	2	0	0	1	3,520
Summer's Signal	7	M	2	0	0	0	0	Sunday Myth	2	C	3	0	0	1	9,083
Summershadelimeade	4	F	3	0	0	0	0	Sunday Nap	3	G	2	0	0	0	0
Summerspark Delite	3	G	4	0	0	0	825	Sunday Quest	4	F	14	1	0	2	12,445
Summersville	5	H	7	1	0	1	35,155	Sunday River	4	G	11	1	1	0	12,132
Summertide	5	M	7	0	0	0	840	Sunday Roar	3	F	17	1	4	3	53,230
Summertime Alli	5	M	9	2	2	0	12,176	Sunday Robery	4	C	1	0	0	0	0
Summertime Fun	5	M	4	0	0	1	3,240	Sunday Sensation	3	F	6	1	4	1	38,110
Summertime Gold	6	M	1	0	1	0	2,660	Sunday Something	3	G	7	0	1	1	1,470
Summertime Mood	2	C	5	1	0	1	20,340	Sunday Song	4	F	10	2	2	3	25,096
Summertime Robin	2	F	4	0	0	1	1,038	Sunday Sport	4	F	12	1	1	2	10,922
Summerwood	4	F	1	0	0	0	0	Sunday Stroll	7	G	7	0	2	1	5,940
Summery Conflict	5	G	11	1	0	1	8,683	Sunday Style	4	F	4	0	0	0	180
Summery Wish	2	F	2	0	0	0	0	Sunday Sueanne	3	F	4	0	0	0	240
Summing Stars (IRE)	5	M	7	1	0	2	18,767	Sunday Supper	7	H	2	1	0	1	8,800
Summing Up Heaven	3	G	2	0	0	0	160	Sunday Synner	4	G	5	1	1	0	8,204
Summit Avenue	5	G	13	0	0	3	5,471	Sunday Thunder (JPN)	3	F	4	1	0	0	14,610
Summit Lite	3	F	2	0	0	0	2,060	Sunday Trigger	2	C	3	0	1	0	3,685
Summit Meeting	6	G	2	0	0	0	0	Sunday Wager	5	M	6	2	1	1	11,523
Summit Ridge	7	M	11	1	0	2	11,430	Sunday Whisper (AUS)	4	F	2	0	0	1	10,770
Summon Mi Cielo	4	F	8	0	2	1	3,536	Sundayblummer	3	F	11	4	2	2	38,719
Sumpter	4	G	7	1	0	3	21,120	Sunday's Miracle	5	M	9	0	0	2	3,804
Sumptus Lady	3	F	1	0	0	0	0	Sunder Bay	2	G	3	0	0	1	6,396
Sumter	5	H	6	0	0	0	63	Sundial Showboat	4	G	8	0	0	0	779
Sumthinbad	2	F	14	0	2	2	27,752	Sundown Doll	6	M	9	4	1	2	4,043
Sumthing for Alex	3	G	8	1	0	0	7,589	Sundown Meg	4	F	9	5	1	2	44,729
Sumtimsudont	4	F	5	1	1	2	28,080	Sundowncindy	7	M	4	2	1	0	2,550
Sumtin Bout Kat	3	C	5	0	0	1	1,285	Sundrenched	4	F	13	3	0	0	14,964
Sumu	6	G	6	0	1	0	1,248	Sune	3	F	7	0	1	2	9,380
Sun Again	6	G	12	0	0	1	1,100	Sungold Skippy	2	F	7	1	0	1	29,038
Sun and Sky	3	G	2	0	0	0	0	Sunk At Sea	9	H	5	0	0	1	1,533
Sun Block	3	F	7	3	1	1	44,870	Sunkosi	4	C	10	0	1	4	22,988
Sun Bonney	4	F	3	0	2	0	2,063	Sunlined	4	F	19	0	2	1	6,480
Sun Brightia	3	F	2	1	1	0	36,235	Sunlit Moon	3	F	7	1	3	1	24,450
Sun Cat	6	G	12	3	5	0	49,794	Sunlit Ridge	5	M	15	2	2	4	67,650
Sun City Bradley	3	C	4	2	0	2	64,440	Sunni Delite	6	M	1	0	0	0	58
Sun Commander	3	C	10	1	2	0	8,556	Sunnie Do It	9	M	1	0	0	0	1,168
Sun Country	4	G	23	3	0	5	51,456	Sunny Approval	7	G	8	1	1	0	26,390
Sun Fighter	7	H	5	3	0	1	48,270	Sunny Ballerina	3	F	1	0	0	0	0
Sun Kisses	4	F	12	3	1	2	21,823	Sunny Blossom	3	F	4	0	0	0	882
Sun N Ice	7	G	8	0	0	0	418	Sunny Bonhomme	8	G	3	0	0	1	480
Sun of a Blitzen	10	G	10	2	2	1	30,180	Sunny Brick	4	G	6	0	1	0	6,455
Sun of Mercer	3	G	9	0	1	0	3,583	Sunny Cameron	6	G	12	2	0	1	6,565
Sun On the Beach	4	G	1	0	0	0	0	Sunny Ciano	2	F	4	0	0	1	936
Sun Over the Pines	4	F	4	0	0	0	0	Sunny Ciegos	5	G	10	1	0	0	13,250
Sun Rise Express	5	G	9	1	1	1	10,235	Sunny Cielo	7	G	9	1	2	3	7,691
Sun Run Runner	4	F	7	0	0	2	3,643	Sunny Circus	4	G	10	2	4	1	23,111
Sun Ryder	8	G	11	0	0	2	1,796	Sunny Dawn	3	F	10	1	0	1	8,394
Sun Sapphire	2	F	4	2	2	0	29,640	Sunny Divine	3	F	16	2	4	1	18,410
Sun Seasons (IRE)	4	F	4	0	0	0	3,510	Sunny Extreme	4	G	6	1	2	0	10,300
Sun Shadow Marie	4	F	13	0	3	0	5,514	Sunny Fragrance	4	F	3	0	0	0	225
Sun Skier	2	F	9	1	3	2	89,413	Sunny Gal	2	F	2	1	1	0	14,800
Sun Spot Baby	3	F	12	3	0	0	25,265	Sunny Gold	3	G	11	2	1	2	15,010
Sun Stroke	2	G	6	0	2	2	7,435	Sunny in Kona	4	C	4	0	1	1	2,435
Sun Tzu	7	H	12	1	0	3	30,867	Sunny Isle	5	H	2	0	0	0	0
Sun Valley Anna	3	F	11	2	1	2	20,118	Sunny K Looker	2	C	1	0	0	0	42
Sunadir	2	F	4	0	0	1	8,420	Sunny Limbo	4	G	9	1	2	0	14,321
Sunatra	8	M	12	1	2	1	21,190	Sunny Loves Sallie	4	F	13	2	1	3	12,875
Sunbeam Music	2	F	1	0	0	1	2,500	Sunny Mulligan	3	G	9	1	1	2	13,870
Sunbelt	3	C	1	0	0	0	348	Sunny N Flashy	5	H	1	0	0	0	238
Sunchime	4	C	19	3	3	2	17,063	Sunny 'n' Glory	5	G	9	3	1	2	9,590

Horse	Age	Sex	Sts	1st	2d	3d	Won
Sunny Outcome	3	F	4	1	2	1	47,600
Sunny Rainbow	3	C	8	0	2	1	3,050
Sunny Report	4	G	1	0	1	0	2,340
Sunny Scarlett	4	F	5	0	0	2	15,972
Sunny Secretary	5	M	1	0	0	0	390
Sunny Serenata	2	F	1	0	0	0	0
Sunny Slope Gal	4	F	8	3	3	0	14,762
Sunny Snowbound	3	F	6	1	2	0	17,160
Sunny Stutz	8	G	8	0	0	1	4,560
Sunny Texan	4	G	15	0	3	4	8,910
Sunny Thoughts	3	C	10	3	0	2	15,039
Sunny Witch	6	M	3	0	0	0	636
Sunnydawn Miss	7	M	10	0	0	1	727
Sunnyridge Sam	3	C	6	3	2	0	42,200
Sunny's a Honey	4	C	8	0	2	1	13,040
Sunny's Angel	4	C	1	0	0	0	0
Sunny's Appleseed	2	C	1	0	0	0	0
Sunny's Bad Girl	4	F	3	0	1	0	2,040
Sunny's Bold Halo	4	G	10	1	0	2	11,627
Sunnys Buddy	5	G	14	1	3	4	24,245
Sunny's Classic	7	H	5	0	0	0	816
Sunnys Coed	3	F	3	1	1	0	4,368
Sunny's Colors	3	F	2	0	0	0	0
Sunnys Delight	3	G	2	0	0	0	0
Sunny's Kid	3	C	1	0	0	0	160
Sunnys Prancer	2	G	5	0	1	1	7,756
Sunny's Salty	4	G	1	0	0	0	0
Sunnys Siren	3	G	5	1	2	1	5,800
Sunny's Socialite	2	F	7	1	0	1	7,920
Sunny's Star	6	G	2	0	0	0	0
Sunnys Super Hero	4	G	15	3	3	1	7,583
Sunny's Thor	2	G	5	0	0	3	4,943
Sunny's Tychonic	3	G	11	1	3	3	11,835
Sunnyshook	3	G	11	3	1	2	22,081
Sunofacat	4	G	15	5	2	0	77,990
Sunofagun	5	G	5	0	0	0	250
Sunoke	8	G	8	2	0	0	14,167
Sunquero	2	F	5	0	0	0	0
Sunray Spirit	4	C	5	2	1	1	71,810
Sunrise Launch	2	G	4	1	0	1	12,180
Sunrise Miss	4	F	8	0	0	1	1,117
Sunrise Promise	3	C	7	0	0	0	676
Sunrise Royale	3	C	7	0	1	1	3,655
Sunrise Serenade	3	G	15	3	2	2	22,785
Sunrise Slew	3	F	2	0	0	0	350
Sunsational Julia	4	F	22	5	2	4	44,530
Sunscreen	6	M	1	0	0	0	380
Sunset Box	4	F	2	0	0	0	0
Sunset Boy	7	G	12	4	2	1	19,826
Sunset Cruise	6	H	7	3	2	0	9,468
Sunset Express	4	F	10	2	1	2	36,720
Sunset Hero	4	G	9	1	2	2	23,130
Sunset Kisses	3	F	8	2	2	2	53,500
Sunset Lane	5	M	18	3	1	1	22,909
Sunset Pass	4	F	5	1	1	0	27,674
Sunset Passion	3	F	12	1	1	1	18,890
Sunset Place	4	C	6	0	5	0	54,600
Sunset Rendezvous	7	M	4	0	0	0	0
Sunset Royale	3	C	1	0	0	0	0
Sunset Serenade	5	M	8	1	1	1	63,796
Sunset Side	4	G	7	1	1	1	6,057
Sunset Skies	5	M	12	1	1	0	16,869
Sunset Sue	6	M	11	0	0	0	773
Sunshine Adell	6	M	8	0	0	1	1,078
Sunshine Admiral	4	C	21	1	1	2	10,182
Sunshine Adrian	2	F	3	0	1	2	4,662
Sunshine Alan	2	G	4	0	1	2	7,814
Sunshine Allie	2	F	7	3	3	1	70,890
Sunshine America	4	F	7	0	1	0	17,260
Sunshine Ave	3	F	10	1	3	3	9,447
Sunshine Bear	4	G	12	1	2	4	13,773
Sunshine Belle	5	M	15	2	0	2	11,034
Sunshine Brian	3	C	14	3	4	1	86,150
Sunshine Bumblebee	5	G	4	0	1	1	740
Sunshine Classic	6	M	10	0	2	1	9,595
Sunshine Denise	3	F	16	4	2	3	30,006
Sunshine Dreamer	4	F	13	1	8	1	82,620
Sunshine Eric	4	G	10	2	0	0	6,192
Sunshine Glitter	2	F	3	0	0	0	635
Sunshine Gwen	6	M	3	0	0	1	1,265
Sunshine Jack	5	G	11	1	0	0	12,293
Sunshine Johanne	2	F	4	1	0	2	13,586
Sunshine Lake	2	C	2	0	0	0	600
Sunshine Marti	3	F	1	0	0	0	0
Sunshine Messenger (GB)	5	H	11	1	2	0	50,100
Sunshine Miss	5	M	6	0	0	0	1,682
Sunshine Nathan	3	G	10	1	2	0	11,352
Sunshine Papa	6	G	6	1	0	1	4,125
Sunshine Priscilla	2	F	5	0	0	0	636
Sunshine Red	5	H	2	0	0	0	0
Sunshine Rondevou	3	F	8	1	1	0	9,559
Sunshine Sandy	3	C	6	2	1	1	33,894
Sunshine Scott	6	H	10	2	2	2	9,981
Sunshine Service	2	F	1	1	0	0	8,100
Sunshine Star	3	F	4	0	0	1	1,365
Sunshine Summer	2	F	9	1	2	1	26,061
Sunshine Superstar	2	F	1	0	0	0	160
Sunshine Sylvia	5	M	13	1	0	1	8,408
Sunshine Useta	4	F	4	0	1	0	1,288
Sunshine Valentine	5	H	5	0	1	0	3,305
Sunshine Village	3	C	9	2	2	2	31,861
Sunshinenbeer	2	C	2	0	0	0	720
Sunshineonme	2	F	2	1	0	1	8,487
Sunshineorshadows	3	F	6	1	0	0	4,527
Sunshines	2	G	5	0	0	1	2,025
Sunshine's Hour	3	F	7	0	0	1	2,385
Sunsmanship	2	C	7	0	0	0	1,720
Sunspot	6	H	5	1	1	1	16,765
Sunstone (GB)	5	M	7	0	0	0	20,886
Sunsup	5	G	4	0	1	0	1,592
Suntan	4	F	2	0	0	0	412
Suntana	3	G	8	1	0	3	18,418
Sunup	3	F	7	2	1	0	45,660
Sunup Sundown	7	G	9	1	3	1	35,988
Survivor	3	C	3	0	0	0	105
Suora Notte (FR)	5	M	6	0	0	0	428
Sup a Looey	4	G	13	1	3	2	11,268
Supah Blitz	3	C	10	2	2	2	278,000
Supah Boots	2	F	5	0	0	1	2,060
Supah Brother	3	G	17	2	0	1	17,809
Supah Jackie	2	F	3	0	0	1	3,220
Supah Kelly	3	F	8	0	1	0	2,910
Supah Man	5	G	16	2	4	3	15,358
Supah Snowjob	2	F	1	1	0	0	18,800
Supah Sweet	4	F	12	0	3	2	11,360
Supah Sweetie	3	F	4	0	0	0	460
Supah View	3	C	5	4	0	1	35,280
Super	3	G	3	1	0	0	10,259
Super Anjo	2	C	3	0	0	0	348
Super Barbara	3	F	6	3	1	1	67,590
Super Be Buster	4	G	8	1	0	0	29,820
Super Blitz	6	G	14	1	3	3	25,949
Super Blue (CHI)	5	M	5	0	0	0	7,600
Super Bowl	6	G	9	1	2	3	13,250
Super Bowl Eddy	3	G	8	2	1	1	19,911
Super Boy	3	C	1	0	0	0	0
Super Case	3	C	2	2	0	0	72,240
Super Charge	4	C	13	1	0	1	14,714
Super Cherokee	2	C	4	1	0	2	21,400
Super Chief	4	G	6	0	0	2	7,468
Super Clearance	2	F	1	1	0	0	9,000
Super Coo	3	F	2	0	0	0	66
Super Cop	3	G	1	0	0	0	320
Super Coup	4	C	5	1	0	0	2,828
Super Coyote	2	C	1	0	0	0	0
Super Crown	5	G	14	1	1	4	22,893
Super Destiny	5	M	3	1	0	0	7,800
Super Don B	4	G	2	0	0	0	675
Super Donjuan	10	G	2	0	0	0	110
Super Dream	3	G	1	0	0	0	120
Super Dude	5	M	5	0	0	0	367
Super Duper Dude	4	G	8	1	1	3	6,466
Super Duper Kid	4	C	3	0	0	1	4,800
Super Duty	3	G	11	2	2	2	12,012
Super Editor	4	G	12	0	0	1	1,218
Super Fax	2	F	2	0	0	2	5,220
Super Flag	2	F	1	0	0	0	339
Super Frolic	3	C	6	1	0	1	42,960

RECORDS OF HORSES

Horse	Age	Sex	Sts	1st	2d	3d	Won
Super Fund	3	G	9	0	1	1	10,031
Super Furray	3	F	13	2	2	3	17,783
Super Fuse	3	G	11	1	5	2	130,320
Super Fuzzy	5	G	7	0	0	0	1,607
Super G I	2	F	1	1	0	0	15,200
Super Gal	4	F	2	0	0	0	0
Super Gold Miss	3	F	2	0	0	0	0
Super Grom	3	F	13	2	3	2	13,569
Super Gummi Girl	5	M	8	1	0	1	1,978
Super High	4	F	5	0	1	0	36,560
Super Highway (BRZ)	5	G	14	1	0	2	14,418
Super Innovation	3	F	6	0	1	2	2,195
Super Issue	9	G	9	2	5	1	7,600
Super Jam	4	C	14	2	1	1	8,915
Super Jules	4	F	2	1	0	0	9,910
Super Kitty	5	M	3	0	0	0	675
Super Kris	3	C	4	1	0	0	6,275
Super Moe	3	G	12	1	0	2	12,985
Super Mon	3	C	2	0	0	2	5,720
Super Mood	3	G	7	0	2	1	9,242
Super Mover	3	C	6	0	0	1	863
Super Natural	4	F	13	1	2	2	12,914
Super One	3	G	13	2	2	4	11,195
Super Patriot	3	F	5	1	1	1	18,260
Super Punch	4	F	10	0	1	2	7,460
Super Rain	4	C	1	0	0	0	0
Super Reviewer	3	G	19	2	5	6	51,360
Super Rival	4	G	4	0	0	1	3,140
Super Rorrie	4	F	10	1	2	3	9,519
Super Scout	2	C	6	0	0	2	5,257
Super Script	6	M	10	1	0	2	4,845
Super Seasons	3	C	12	1	0	1	6,850
Super Sensation	6	H	10	2	0	1	4,174
Super Shinkansen	4	G	10	1	0	0	8,190
Super Short Silver	6	G	8	0	0	0	1,523
Super Size	5	G	4	0	1	0	4,060
Super Skip	3	C	3	0	0	1	1,890
Super Sky	3	C	1	0	0	0	0
Super Slew	4	G	3	0	1	0	2,125
Super Smart Sam	8	G	11	4	0	1	31,334
Super Soup	3	C	14	1	2	1	40,945
Super Spin	4	G	1	0	0	0	0
Super Stalker	2	C	1	0	0	0	0
Super Step	5	G	7	0	0	0	1,290
Super Stinker	4	G	4	0	0	1	3,254
Super Streak	8	G	13	4	3	2	48,100
Super Striker	4	C	9	0	0	2	3,875
Super Stroke	2	G	10	1	0	2	15,436
Super Strut	3	G	1	0	0	0	460
Super Stutz	4	G	16	0	3	3	18,975
Super Suds	4	G	7	1	1	1	13,670
Super Sway	3	F	4	0	0	0	210
Super Swift	10	M	1	0	0	0	55
Super Tough	2	F	1	0	0	0	220
Super Trump	3	C	11	0	2	0	3,827
Super Valu	6	M	14	1	1	1	4,110
Super Vet	7	G	17	2	0	4	12,337
Super Wager	5	M	5	1	2	0	28,080
Super Will Power	2	C	3	0	0	0	1,351
Super Willy	5	G	10	2	4	1	28,167
Super Writer	8	G	11	3	1	0	6,092
Super Zim	2	G	2	0	0	0	781
Superb Position	4	F	8	2	1	0	3,300
Superbe Prince	4	C	8	1	1	1	8,135
Superbowl Sherry	4	F	11	0	1	3	7,827
Superchrome	3	C	5	0	0	1	2,236
Superconi	2	F	3	0	0	0	605
Superdumaan	3	F	4	0	0	1	7,200
Superfine Hayden	4	G	1	0	0	0	0
Superfines Luvey	5	M	3	0	0	0	840
Superfines Prado	5	G	14	1	1	2	30,571
Superfly T N T	5	G	7	0	2	2	12,697
Superget	7	M	7	0	0	1	2,288
Superific Season	4	F	1	0	0	0	50
Superior Decision	2	G	4	0	0	0	850
Superior Kris	5	M	14	3	2	0	14,390
Superiority	7	G	6	4	0	0	77,160
Superior's King	2	F	6	0	2	1	4,421
Superlang	3	C	14	0	1	3	26,300
Superlative Gain	4	F	7	0	2	1	8,020
Superlative Star	4	F	7	1	2	1	8,780
Superlooper Louie	4	G	11	0	2	4	3,910
Superlooper Sara	4	F	4	0	0	0	688
Superman Can	3	G	14	3	2	2	17,996
Supernal	7	M	1	0	0	0	0
Supernatural Storm	4	C	10	4	0	1	51,848
Superpointyoumade	2	F	3	0	0	0	225
Superpower (ARG)	6	H	6	0	1	0	7,962
Superson	6	G	5	0	0	0	308
Supersonic Mon	2	C	2	0	0	0	0
Supersonic Sun	3	G	7	0	1	1	12,810
Superstar Prospect	2	C	11	1	5	2	33,925
Superstitches	3	C	2	0	0	0	0
Supertramp	3	F	8	0	2	1	14,520
Supervelous	3	G	5	0	1	1	9,915
Supervisionist	5	M	2	0	0	0	699
Supervisor	3	C	12	1	0	1	102,624
Supplize	3	C	3	0	0	1	1,290
Supply Gal	3	F	3	0	0	0	536
Supply House	5	M	10	0	2	1	6,646
Supposedly	4	F	4	1	1	0	45,560
Supra	3	F	11	2	0	0	14,970
Suprduprbravisimo	5	M	4	0	0	0	372
Supreal	2	G	3	0	0	0	156
Suprem Devil	2	G	6	0	0	0	0
Suprem Dream	4	F	12	2	1	1	17,674
Supreme Bidness	3	F	7	0	0	0	493
Supreme Charm	3	G	4	1	0	0	3,406
Supreme Commander	7	H	16	2	3	2	13,621
Supreme D. C.	3	G	9	1	0	1	9,515
Supreme Discovery	4	F	6	3	0	0	64,740
Supreme Freedom	3	G	8	2	0	1	7,679
Supreme Jana	2	F	1	0	0	0	0
Supreme Judge	5	G	7	0	1	0	22,768
Supreme Law	6	H	1	0	0	0	32
Supreme M. D.	3	G	4	0	0	1	4,220
Supreme Pleasures	6	M	14	3	4	2	50,864
Supreme Plop	7	G	3	0	2	1	3,500
Supreme Power	5	M	9	2	3	2	7,596
Supreme Regime	3	C	7	1	1	1	44,663
Supreme Sam	2	C	1	0	0	0	0
Supreme Season	3	F	2	0	0	0	0
Supreme Silence	4	G	8	3	0	1	18,607
Supreme Song	5	M	6	1	0	0	8,499
Supreme Speed	5	H	2	0	0	0	109
Supreme Sun	3	G	14	3	0	3	16,332
Supreme Ward	6	G	10	2	1	3	11,050
Supremetta	3	G	14	0	2	1	4,571
Supremissima	3	F	13	1	5	1	24,487
Supremo Secret	4	C	9	0	3	2	8,930
Supremo's Baby	4	F	11	1	2	1	6,385
Supremo's Suprize	4	G	10	2	3	0	30,155
Suprise	6	M	6	0	0	0	1,320
Suprise Me Again	5	M	7	0	1	2	12,600
Suprise Package	7	G	16	0	3	2	8,911
Suprise Party	4	F	8	0	1	2	4,419
Suprisingly	6	M	9	1	2	2	3,025
Suprized	6	M	1	0	0	0	354
Sur Dixie	3	C	14	0	1	2	7,670
Sur Gem	7	H	10	0	1	0	4,105
Sur La Tete	5	G	8	3	2	0	93,020
Sur Sandpit	3	G	8	3	2	0	55,757
Sure a Gadabout	4	C	4	0	0	0	224
Sure as Shipp	6	G	13	2	1	4	24,130
Sure as Shootin	3	G	4	2	2	0	27,470
Sure Bet	3	F	8	0	1	0	5,439
Sure Caper	2	G	4	0	0	1	3,000
Sure Daylight	4	F	11	1	3	1	15,192
Sure Deposit	5	H	13	0	0	2	1,838
Sure Grit	7	H	1	0	0	0	46
Sure Hot	6	M	2	0	0	0	0
Sure I Will	4	G	2	0	2	0	6,840
Sure Is	4	G	10	4	0	2	16,243
Sure Is Exclusive	6	M	8	0	1	1	2,000
Sure Is Lucky	5	M	2	0	0	0	112
Sure It's True	4	G	1	0	0	0	45
Sure L C	2	F	3	0	1	0	1,410
Sure Nuff	7	M	3	0	0	0	699

Horse	Age	Sex	Sts	1st	2d	3d	Won
Sure Pleasure	5	H	2	0	0	0	160
Sure Prize	2	C	4	0	0	1	13,846
Sure Reply	4	C	4	0	0	0	293
Sure Shot Biscuit	7	G	5	0	2	2	17,461
Sure Shot Kelley	5	G	18	1	4	1	11,489
Sure Sonic	6	G	19	0	2	1	4,010
Sure Special	8	M	5	1	0	1	5,490
Sure Sure	5	M	6	0	0	0	565
Sure Uh Huh	8	G	7	0	0	2	1,161
Sure You Can	4	G	12	5	1	1	72,290
Surely a Lady	4	F	2	0	0	0	2,990
Surely a Treasure	3	F	3	0	0	0	0
Surely and Truely	3	C	7	3	1	0	16,980
Surely Mary	6	M	12	1	0	1	3,729
Surely Wood	6	M	2	0	0	0	0
Surenuff Sassy	6	M	2	0	0	0	142
Surescore	3	C	4	0	0	0	1,680
Sureshot Jennifer	3	F	4	0	1	1	2,080
Suretreat	3	C	1	0	0	0	0
Sureway	2	G	2	0	0	0	537
Sureyev	5	M	9	0	0	1	882
Surf Alert	4	F	8	2	2	1	27,443
Surf Fever	3	F	7	2	0	2	39,410
Surf Liner	3	G	2	0	1	0	2,262
Surf N Sand	4	F	5	5	0	0	165,125
Surface Strike	4	F	7	0	1	1	4,412
Surfer	3	F	3	0	0	1	957
Surfing Till Dawn	6	G	3	1	0	0	1,121
Surfwatch	4	G	3	0	1	0	2,600
Surgeon	5	M	4	0	0	0	432
Surging River	3	C	7	2	3	0	105,602
Suri	5	M	12	5	3	2	48,548
Surilla Slew	7	M	8	1	3	0	3,680
Surithani	3	C	1	0	0	0	60
Surly Sue	4	F	8	0	1	1	15,420
Surprise Affair	5	H	6	1	1	1	1,980
Surprise Arrival	3	F	4	0	0	0	172
Surprise Call	2	F	8	1	0	2	9,530
Surprise Halo	5	G	12	1	3	2	123,660
Surprise Punch	4	C	3	0	0	0	330
Surprise Splash	3	F	13	0	0	3	4,650
Surprise Tour	3	G	12	1	1	1	11,895
Surprise Visit	6	M	1	0	0	0	312
Surprise Walker	2	F	4	1	0	1	11,850
Surprised Humor	2	F	1	0	0	0	0
Surpriseloveaffair	4	F	4	1	1	0	15,260
Surpriseya	4	G	7	0	0	0	396
Surprisingly	4	F	7	3	1	1	98,578
Surprized	4	G	13	0	3	4	62,935
Surprizetome	9	G	6	0	2	1	9,292
Surreal Man	3	G	1	0	0	0	0
Surrender Intuit	4	F	2	0	0	0	0
Surrey	5	G	8	0	2	1	24,220
Surrey Down	2	F	2	0	0	0	0
Surrogate	2	G	5	0	0	0	562
Surrogate's Irish	8	G	14	1	2	2	14,615
Surround Sound	10	G	4	1	0	0	2,680
Surry's Prospect	8	M	11	0	1	3	2,292
Surtsey	4	F	7	2	1	2	8,770
Survik	3	C	4	0	1	1	5,655
Surville	7	G	8	2	0	0	19,010
Survita	2	F	1	0	0	0	145
Surviving Native	3	G	10	1	0	2	13,388
Surviving Princess	6	H	8	1	2	2	12,440
Surviving Speed	4	C	7	1	0	0	6,780
Survivor Kippy	4	G	5	2	1	0	39,000
Susan Astaire	6	M	3	0	0	0	672
Susan Bell	3	F	1	0	0	0	120
Susan Gracey	4	F	11	1	1	2	51,588
Susan Sea	2	F	2	0	0	0	145
Susanne (GB)	7	M	2	1	0	0	1,540
Susans Alarm	4	F	3	0	0	0	245
Susan's Angel	2	F	2	0	1	0	11,900
Susans Charmer	3	F	4	0	0	0	837
Susan's Classichik	3	F	18	5	0	1	18,596
Susan's Dreamer	10	M	9	0	0	1	3,298
Susan's Tower	3	F	3	0	0	0	0
Sushi	7	G	10	1	2	2	10,151
Sushi At Nobu's	3	F	9	1	1	2	7,193

Horse	Age	Sex	Sts	1st	2d	3d	Won
Sushi for Noah	5	M	14	2	2	2	12,112
Susie B. Good	6	M	5	0	2	0	12,760
Susie Blues	4	F	5	0	0	0	1,330
Susie Joe's	3	F	10	3	1	0	87,162
Susie Polly's Slew	6	G	17	0	0	0	2,955
Susie Savannah	5	M	1	0	0	0	42
Susie's Poker	4	G	7	0	1	3	13,960
Susie's Red Rolls	3	F	4	1	0	0	5,867
Susies Request	4	F	5	0	0	0	800
Susie's Way	3	F	11	0	0	2	1,389
Suspender	4	F	8	0	1	0	6,205
Suspicious	3	F	9	2	1	3	23,710
Suspicious Caper	3	F	9	2	0	1	36,540
Suspicious Cat	2	C	4	2	0	1	16,810
Suspicious Dogie	3	G	7	1	0	0	4,789
Suspicious Minds	6	G	4	1	0	1	11,900
Suspicious Red	2	C	1	0	0	0	1,368
Suspicious Town	2	F	1	0	0	0	0
Susquehannock	4	C	5	0	0	0	800
Sussieone	4	F	6	1	1	0	1,831
Sustainable	4	C	6	0	1	0	899
Sustainable Forest	5	G	7	1	1	0	8,628
Sustained	7	G	7	0	0	1	2,282
Susue Sue	7	M	3	0	0	0	510
Susy Rae	3	F	1	0	0	0	0
Susy's a Dealer	2	F	6	1	1	1	20,235
Sutro Tower	6	G	3	1	1	0	4,360
Sutter Butte	3	G	2	0	1	1	8,730
Sutter Hills	3	G	8	1	2	1	9,422
Sutter Street	3	G	7	0	1	4	18,140
Sutter's Galaxy	2	G	6	0	0	1	3,865
Sutter's Quest	5	H	6	1	1	0	18,980
Sutter's Ruckus	5	M	12	2	2	2	17,987
Sutter's Sparkle	6	M	2	0	0	0	0
Suwerte Dan	3	G	3	1	0	0	4,095
Suzanne's Flying	5	M	1	0	0	0	1,980
Suzans Love Report	2	F	4	0	2	0	17,325
Suzies Choo Choo	4	G	10	2	0	1	16,255
Suzie's Honor	3	F	13	3	2	0	26,255
Suzie's Monster	3	G	13	4	0	0	23,549
Suzy Creek Slew	4	F	4	0	2	0	6,840
Svea Dahl	6	M	1	0	0	0	59,840
Svengali	4	G	3	0	0	0	188
Svenson	3	G	3	0	0	0	2,940
Swadeshi	4	G	1	0	0	0	0
Swaggering	2	C	1	0	0	1	3,080
Swainbow	3	C	4	1	0	0	17,790
Swallowhawk (GB)	6	G	2	0	0	0	645
Swami Sez	4	G	7	1	0	0	4,875
Swamp Creek	3	G	2	0	0	0	1,230
Swamp Kitten	5	M	11	2	0	2	4,383
Swamp Lake	5	G	6	2	1	0	49,760
Swamp Monkey	4	F	15	1	3	3	26,852
Swamp Queen	5	M	5	0	1	1	7,164
Swamp Rat	5	H	17	3	1	5	45,293
Swamp Scare	3	F	7	2	1	0	49,406
Swamp Spirit	5	M	19	1	3	4	27,500
Swamp Wolf	6	G	11	0	5	0	14,416
Swampy	5	G	2	1	0	0	10,285
Swan	3	F	6	1	0	0	13,291
Swanky Song	6	H	9	2	1	2	16,355
Swans Star	2	F	3	0	0	0	85
Swap Bids	4	G	10	1	1	0	5,804
Swap One	10	G	5	0	1	0	344
Swaps Gift	5	G	3	0	0	0	145
Swasti	3	F	10	2	2	3	44,532
Swatagold	3	F	5	0	1	2	10,920
Swavy	4	G	8	0	0	1	1,413
Sway of Passion	3	C	3	1	0	0	25,800
Swayday	5	H	4	0	0	0	546
Swayer	7	G	4	0	0	0	232
Swaying Chevrons	4	G	3	0	0	0	169
Swayo	12	G	2	1	0	0	39,900
Swayzo	3	F	4	0	0	0	0
Sweap Clean	7	M	3	2	1	0	11,700
Swear by Luck	3	C	3	0	0	0	0
Sweat Equity	5	G	9	3	1	0	20,220
Sweat Lodge	4	C	7	1	3	1	8,730
Sweday	3	G	4	0	0	0	0

RECORDS OF HORSES

Horse	Age	Sex	Sts	1st	2d	3d	Won
Swede Flambe	4	G	15	1	6	2	31,245
Sweder Than Money	3	F	11	3	0	3	23,690
Swedish Sights	6	G	12	2	2	3	9,348
Swedish Son	5	G	10	0	1	1	4,453
Sweeney Astray	3	G	6	0	0	0	240
Sweep and Duck	6	G	8	2	0	2	6,770
Sweep and Go	4	G	2	0	0	0	579
Sweep Back	7	G	11	2	3	3	6,507
Sweep Dancer	4	G	10	1	2	1	32,993
Sweep Domino (CHI)	4	C	5	0	1	2	5,800
Sweep 'Em	5	G	6	1	1	1	28,005
Sweep in Philly	3	F	12	7	1	2	60,310
Sweep Katie	4	F	14	1	3	2	8,790
Sweep Left	3	G	5	0	1	0	1,950
Sweep N the Night	4	F	24	2	1	3	17,959
Sweep North	4	F	19	2	1	5	22,780
Sweep of Joy	3	F	1	0	0	0	1,240
Sweep Over First	5	G	11	1	0	1	5,380
Sweep Princess	4	F	8	0	2	4	57,190
Sweep Sweep	5	H	14	3	0	2	38,960
Sweep the Deck	4	F	1	0	0	0	0
Sweep the Shore	4	G	16	0	2	1	9,713
Sweep to My Lou	4	G	8	1	3	2	10,597
Sweep to Win	3	F	9	1	0	0	8,262
Sweep Up	3	F	6	2	1	1	43,880
Sweep Up the Gold	4	F	15	0	3	2	5,765
Sweepality	3	C	13	3	4	0	93,400
Sweepatatapi	3	F	16	4	2	1	25,876
Sweeper Four	5	G	16	2	1	2	12,407
Sweeping Analysis	6	H	5	1	0	2	24,490
Sweeping Beauty	6	M	4	0	0	0	1,354
Sweeping Cat	4	F	7	1	3	0	35,576
Sweeping Coyote	3	F	2	0	0	0	0
Sweeping Eight	4	F	8	0	0	0	2,087
Sweeping Eva	5	M	7	1	0	0	11,100
Sweeping Motion	7	G	14	3	0	2	14,263
Sweeping Odessa	7	M	8	1	1	1	17,404
Sweeping On Bye	3	F	9	1	1	2	21,530
Sweeping Prospect	4	F	14	0	0	2	5,497
Sweeping Respect	5	M	3	0	0	0	2,308
Sweeping Rita	5	M	13	0	0	3	3,742
Sweeping Smoke	5	G	9	1	3	1	40,590
Sweeping Warmth	5	G	14	2	3	1	14,647
Sweeping Way	5	G	14	1	2	2	10,909
Sweepingly	4	G	7	1	0	2	33,720
Sweepit	2	F	2	0	1	0	2,430
Sweep's Choice	3	F	16	1	4	4	17,700
Sweeps Week	5	G	4	1	0	1	27,524
Sweepthefinishline	5	M	6	0	0	0	372
Sweeptheway	3	F	4	0	0	0	2,860
Sweet Account	5	M	10	0	0	1	1,602
Sweet Addiction	2	F	2	0	1	0	2,003
Sweet Alaris	4	F	3	1	0	0	8,145
Sweet Alice	4	F	4	0	0	0	672
Sweet America	3	F	4	0	0	0	189
Sweet and Classi	3	F	2	0	0	0	217
Sweet and Dear	3	F	3	0	0	0	400
Sweet and Friendly	4	G	15	1	1	2	5,544
Sweet and Royal	3	F	8	1	1	1	10,310
Sweet and Spicey	3	F	7	0	0	0	620
Sweet and Wild	3	F	4	0	0	0	347
Sweet Anden	3	G	8	3	0	0	68,130
Sweet Angel Eyes	3	F	7	1	3	2	26,840
Sweet Announce	3	F	3	0	1	1	14,526
Sweet Annuity	6	M	9	2	2	2	102,300
Sweet Ante	5	M	18	4	3	2	33,103
Sweet Apple Annie	5	M	13	0	0	0	1,660
Sweet Apple Pie	4	F	10	1	0	4	13,835
Sweet as Candy	3	F	12	3	2	2	27,275
Sweet as Sarah	5	M	3	0	0	0	1,080
Sweet Attorney	2	F	1	0	0	0	0
Sweet Attraction	4	F	14	2	2	1	24,775
Sweet Baabaa	5	M	12	0	2	1	7,335
Sweet Baby	2	F	1	0	0	0	0
Sweet Baby Jake	3	C	9	1	0	3	25,845
Sweet Baby Jane	4	F	12	3	5	1	77,460
Sweet Baby Slew	2	F	1	0	0	0	185
Sweet Band	4	C	10	2	3	1	88,947
Sweet Bay	2	F	1	0	1	0	11,760
Sweet Beau	4	G	11	4	4	3	60,343
Sweet Bebe	6	G	2	0	0	0	134
Sweet Beginnings	4	F	6	1	0	1	8,540
Sweet Bernice	3	F	4	1	1	0	19,890
Sweet Bippy	3	C	4	0	0	0	496
Sweet Biscuit	4	C	14	0	1	0	3,865
Sweet Bitty Girl	4	F	2	0	0	0	219
Sweet Blessing	3	G	10	1	3	1	10,132
Sweet Bliss	4	F	8	1	0	2	27,120
Sweet Bold Nred	2	F	1	0	0	0	464
Sweet But Salty	3	F	4	1	0	0	8,750
Sweet Candy Red	4	F	9	1	1	2	8,207
Sweet Cane	3	F	14	0	1	1	9,939
Sweet Caper	2	F	1	0	0	0	195
Sweet Caprice	4	F	11	1	3	2	17,764
Sweet Carson	3	F	8	1	0	2	20,120
Sweet Cause	4	G	3	2	1	0	42,600
Sweet Chere	3	F	14	3	1	1	23,935
Sweet Cindy Lou	2	F	4	1	0	1	14,488
Sweet City Miss	3	F	7	2	1	0	21,860
Sweet Colony	6	H	2	0	0	0	0
Sweet Conquest	3	C	7	0	0	1	1,196
Sweet Country Girl	3	F	3	0	1	0	4,000
Sweet Creek	3	F	9	4	1	2	27,856
Sweet Davia	3	F	9	0	0	2	3,655
Sweet Debbie	3	F	6	1	1	1	6,690
Sweet Deimos (GB)	4	F	6	1	2	1	50,910
Sweet Destiny	4	F	7	0	1	0	2,139
Sweet Devil	3	C	1	0	0	0	0
Sweet Diazo	3	F	3	0	0	0	0
Sweet Divy	4	F	15	0	2	2	6,258
Sweet Donna Jean	2	F	6	1	0	0	7,643
Sweet Dream Rhody	2	G	5	0	1	0	2,670
Sweet Dreamin Suzy	4	F	2	0	0	0	0
Sweet Dreams Baby	4	F	4	2	1	0	20,250
Sweet Dreamy Syn	3	F	12	2	1	0	55,426
Sweet Drummer	4	G	12	2	0	2	37,825
Sweet Dunes	3	F	9	1	3	1	22,720
Sweet Dynamite	3	F	6	2	3	1	129,202
Sweet Fit	6	H	2	0	0	0	0
Sweet Fleet	7	M	1	0	0	0	89
Sweet Flute	4	F	5	0	0	0	150
Sweet Folly	3	F	3	0	0	0	120
Sweet Frippery	5	M	9	1	1	1	63,148
Sweet Gold Charm	4	F	1	0	0	0	75
Sweet Halt	4	F	4	0	0	1	1,730
Sweet Heat	2	F	2	1	0	0	13,860
Sweet Heather	5	M	2	0	0	0	392
Sweet Honeydoo	5	M	4	0	1	0	1,334
Sweet Jayana	3	F	1	1	0	0	19,200
Sweet Jessa	3	F	1	0	0	0	150
Sweet Jessie	3	F	3	0	0	1	955
Sweet Jo Jo	2	F	7	3	0	2	134,210
Sweet Jolie	4	F	18	3	2	1	21,482
Sweet Julie	2	F	7	1	0	1	6,870
Sweet Lad	6	H	9	1	0	2	5,620
Sweet Lady Brier	4	F	13	0	1	5	13,197
Sweet Latvia	5	M	11	0	1	1	2,717
Sweet Laural	2	F	8	1	3	1	11,050
Sweet Lauren	3	F	1	1	0	0	16,800
Sweet Like Honey	6	M	9	2	1	0	10,396
Sweet Little Avie	3	F	5	0	2	1	10,470
Sweet Little Buck	3	C	8	1	0	0	2,950
Sweet Little Irish	3	F	11	0	2	3	5,074
Sweet Loona	4	G	3	0	0	0	170
Sweet Loretta	2	F	3	0	0	0	284
Sweet Louis	4	C	6	1	0	0	2,547
Sweet Lucky Lady	3	F	10	3	1	1	46,780
Sweet Mama Maria	4	F	1	0	1	0	5,600
Sweet Maneuver	2	F	4	1	0	0	7,200
Sweet Maria	3	F	2	1	0	0	18,840
Sweet Mary Jo	3	F	2	0	0	0	0
Sweet Matriarch	6	M	1	0	0	0	225
Sweet Melody	2	F	1	0	0	0	0
Sweet Metal	3	G	12	1	1	1	11,692
Sweet Miracle	7	M	14	5	1	0	19,718
Sweet Miriam	4	F	7	1	3	0	6,748
Sweet Mt Music	4	F	3	0	1	1	2,550
Sweet Music	5	M	8	0	1	2	21,360

Horse	Age	Sex	Sts	1st	2d	3d	Won	Horse	Age	Sex	Sts	1st	2d	3d	Won
Sweet N Brassy	6	M	9	6	0	0	12,522	Sweet Willie G	2	C	6	0	0	0	80
Sweet N Crafty	4	F	5	0	0	2	1,004	Sweet Will's Joy	3	F	11	3	2	1	63,454
Sweet n' Deed	3	F	1	0	0	0	115	Sweet Women	3	F	6	2	2	0	75,696
Sweet 'n Fabulous	4	G	1	0	0	0	58	Sweet Word	3	G	13	0	0	3	5,914
Sweet 'n Fiesty	4	F	19	2	3	3	20,795	Sweetbriar Power	3	F	7	2	3	0	25,558
Sweet 'n Golden	5	M	10	0	1	2	5,430	Sweetbrook	5	M	5	0	0	0	1,216
Sweet N Tart	3	F	8	0	0	0	1,953	Sweetcakesanshakes	8	M	6	1	2	1	83,680
Sweet Nijinsky	3	F	7	1	0	0	8,607	Sweetcarolinagirl	2	F	1	0	0	0	0
Sweet Nine	2	F	8	1	1	1	32,632	Sweetdancingfolly	3	F	1	0	0	0	0
Sweet November	4	F	2	0	0	0	86	Sweeten Your Step	4	F	5	0	0	0	825
Sweet O'Dale	4	F	5	1	0	0	4,640	Sweetener	6	M	4	0	0	0	0
Sweet Ole Pat	2	C	3	0	0	0	1,110	Sweeter N Wine	4	F	3	0	0	0	55
Sweet Olympio	4	F	11	0	2	3	16,170	Sweetest of Sweets	3	F	13	2	2	4	13,893
Sweet On Me	3	F	6	0	1	2	4,985	Sweetest Star	5	M	3	1	0	2	6,400
Sweet On You Too	4	F	7	0	3	1	15,522	Sweetest Tour	4	F	13	2	1	1	15,429
Sweet One	3	F	2	0	0	0	290	Sweeteyedjessilou	3	F	8	1	1	0	7,600
Sweet Parcel	4	F	9	0	0	1	1,067	Sweetfingercharlie	3	C	13	1	1	0	8,055
Sweet Pea Mountain	4	F	8	1	0	2	6,916	Sweetgalintown	2	F	2	0	0	2	4,095
Sweet Pea to Me	4	F	4	0	0	0	476	Sweetgum	2	F	2	1	0	1	45,288
Sweet Peaches	3	F	15	4	3	1	30,663	Sweetheart Sami	3	F	10	1	0	4	32,740
Sweet Performance	6	M	10	1	0	1	8,117	Sweetheavenlycross	4	F	7	0	0	1	6,940
Sweet Potato Patch	5	M	6	1	0	0	4,533	Sweethrtofsigmachi	3	F	7	1	0	0	9,210
Sweet Potato Queen	3	F	5	0	0	0	3,750	Sweetie Baby	5	M	10	0	0	1	2,369
Sweet Prince	4	G	6	0	1	2	9,430	Sweetie Belle	4	F	12	0	0	5	4,300
Sweet Problem	2	F	5	2	1	1	86,852	Sweetie G	3	F	20	1	3	3	22,436
Sweet Promises	3	C	5	0	0	3	10,300	Sweetie Halo	3	F	10	2	1	1	10,663
Sweet Purrfume	2	F	3	0	2	0	11,600	Sweetiegunzallus	4	F	9	3	1	1	15,132
Sweet Rachael	5	M	6	0	1	1	1,702	Sweetjudyblueeyes	3	F	13	3	1	3	19,232
Sweet Rebecca N	7	M	19	4	5	3	26,097	Sweetly Bold	6	M	9	0	2	1	6,371
Sweet Red	2	F	5	0	0	0	240	Sweetly Defiant	2	F	2	0	0	0	150
Sweet Redemption	6	H	4	0	0	0	133	Sweetmilk Creek	4	F	10	1	1	3	47,155
Sweet Remiss	4	F	1	0	0	0	0	Sweetness 'nflight	6	H	9	0	1	1	4,362
Sweet Return (GB)	3	C	9	2	2	2	500,360	Sweetninnocent	5	M	6	1	2	1	16,370
Sweet Rhapsody	3	F	6	1	2	2	22,080	Sweetnquick	5	G	1	0	0	0	53
Sweet Rhythm	5	M	7	0	1	0	1,675	Sweets	3	F	6	0	1	1	3,225
Sweet Ride Laura	4	F	4	0	0	0	225	Sweetseattle	4	G	9	0	1	2	8,695
Sweet Road	4	G	6	0	1	1	2,586	Sweetsmellofsucces	2	F	2	0	0	0	1,050
Sweet Runner	7	M	7	0	2	0	3,722	Sweetsongofachoir	3	F	2	0	0	0	3,000
Sweet S Cookies	2	F	2	0	0	0	0	Sweetspot	4	F	2	1	0	0	5,375
Sweet Sailin	6	M	10	0	1	2	3,518	Sweettrickydancer	3	F	7	1	0	0	66,000
Sweet Samantha	3	F	2	1	0	0	27,700	Sweettwilitedancer	4	C	2	0	0	0	255
Sweet Sami Snit	6	M	4	0	0	0	0	Sweetwater Promise	4	F	12	1	1	3	56,170
Sweet Sammy	3	C	6	0	1	0	10,930	Sweety's Boy	6	G	5	0	0	0	563
Sweet Sandy	2	F	3	0	1	0	3,635	Swell Bell	5	G	6	0	0	0	366
Sweet Sarah	2	F	5	0	0	0	2,820	Swelter	3	G	9	1	0	0	16,820
Sweet Scottische	3	F	4	1	1	0	50,334	Swen	2	G	7	2	1	2	21,465
Sweet Screamer	3	F	4	1	0	1	32,490	Swept Clean	5	G	8	3	0	1	50,910
Sweet Serenade	2	F	6	1	0	1	22,710	Swept in Three	3	C	9	3	2	1	94,520
Sweet Share	3	F	4	0	0	0	1,500	Swerve	2	G	7	0	2	3	5,730
Sweet Siphon	4	F	3	0	0	0	0	Swift Admiral	4	G	6	0	1	2	5,100
Sweet Sir Galahad	2	C	1	0	0	0	0	Swift and Fit	4	G	8	0	1	0	4,891
Sweet Sister	3	F	9	1	0	1	8,462	Swift and Sultry	5	M	10	1	2	0	9,146
Sweet Slewellen	3	F	14	3	5	0	15,801	Swift Appeal	2	F	3	0	0	0	0
Sweet Sorrow	6	M	4	0	0	2	2,588	Swift Attack	3	C	10	2	0	2	38,140
Sweet Souvenir	2	F	2	0	0	0	942	Swift Attraction	2	C	1	0	0	0	675
Sweet Soviet	3	F	4	1	2	0	26,800	Swift Case	4	F	5	2	2	1	17,927
Sweet Stepper	4	C	11	4	2	1	140,760	Swift Decision	3	F	3	0	0	0	184
Sweet Storm Creek	3	F	7	2	0	1	112,366	Swift Defense	4	F	14	0	1	6	7,206
Sweet Sue	5	M	7	1	0	1	2,368	Swift Doeny	4	F	1	0	0	0	0
Sweet Sunday	5	H	6	1	0	3	7,025	Swift Enclose	8	G	2	0	0	0	48
Sweet Sweet Spell	5	M	13	3	0	2	15,430	Swift for Sure	5	G	9	2	1	1	26,225
Sweet Swinging Ms	2	F	1	0	0	0	265	Swift Hero	4	G	9	1	3	3	23,674
Sweet Taffy	3	F	17	1	4	2	16,530	Swift Illusion	4	C	1	0	0	0	0
Sweet Talk Me	3	C	1	0	0	0	0	Swift Intention	7	G	10	1	0	3	12,360
Sweet Talkin Babe	7	M	1	0	1	0	1,800	Swift Journey	4	G	1	0	0	0	0
Sweet Talkin Boy	2	C	1	0	0	0	100	Swift Lad	3	C	1	0	1	0	2,520
Sweet Talking Girl	2	F	3	0	0	0	1,409	Swift Merle	4	G	1	0	0	0	0
Sweet Talking Lue	5	M	2	1	0	0	4,500	Swift Mover	3	C	11	1	0	2	7,134
Sweet Teeth	2	F	1	0	0	0	0	Swift Moving Star	5	M	2	0	0	0	48
Sweet Tender Lover	4	F	5	0	0	1	1,097	Swift of Flight	3	F	3	1	0	0	36,360
Sweet Thing	3	F	3	1	0	1	3,850	Swift Oklahoman	4	C	2	0	0	0	0
Sweet Tiger Peach	4	F	11	0	1	1	2,432	Swift Place	6	M	12	1	2	1	5,806
Sweet Time	4	F	6	1	2	1	24,020	Swift Prospect	2	F	4	0	1	0	1,605
Sweet Tonka Dancer	4	F	3	0	1	0	1,323	Swift Replica	4	G	8	1	2	1	69,145
Sweet Trip	3	F	4	0	1	2	18,810	Swift Response	2	G	1	0	0	0	1,140
Sweet Triumph	2	F	1	0	0	0	425	Swift River	2	C	1	0	0	0	750
Sweet Vintage	3	F	7	0	0	0	797	Swift Sefa	2	F	1	0	1	0	1,900
Sweet Vision	2	F	4	1	2	0	48,730	Swift Sky	6	G	3	0	0	0	287
Sweet Water Canyon	4	F	2	1	0	1	11,800	Swift Terms	5	H	14	2	1	0	11,410

Horse	Age	Sex	Sts	1st	2d	3d	Won
Swift Thunder	3	G	17	3	2	1	44,305
Swift Trial	5	G	6	0	0	0	1,830
Swift Trick	2	F	4	1	0	0	16,010
Swift West	4	C	2	0	1	0	3,800
Swiftandsubtle	4	C	5	0	0	0	576
Swifterthaneagles	2	G	7	0	0	0	582
Swiftwatersweetpea	3	F	4	0	0	0	192
Swigerts Prince	3	G	3	0	0	0	212
Swim Boy	3	G	7	2	0	2	8,508
Swim Easy	3	C	5	1	2	1	20,979
Swimtime	3	G	9	0	3	1	12,779
Swindler	3	G	15	1	0	3	32,175
Swing and Shout	3	G	4	1	1	0	2,740
Swing Baby	3	G	3	0	0	1	1,380
Swing by the Bon	3	G	9	2	1	1	7,847
Swing in Satin	4	F	10	1	0	0	13,665
Swing Lord	5	H	8	1	0	3	19,400
Swing Master	5	G	6	0	1	1	3,390
Swing On	2	F	1	0	0	0	375
Swing Six	10	G	11	1	4	3	11,700
Swing Song	3	F	3	0	0	0	232
Swing Symbol	5	G	4	0	0	0	250
Swing the Belle	2	F	5	2	1	2	5,760
Swing the Cat (NZ)	3	F	2	0	0	1	4,926
Swing Wide	3	F	3	0	0	0	180
Swing Your Lady	5	G	10	0	0	1	3,990
Swingcat	6	H	6	3	1	0	28,632
Swingforthefences	2	C	2	1	0	1	31,950
Swingin Harry	5	G	8	1	2	2	11,594
Swingin Jason	4	G	2	0	0	0	510
Swingin Leroy	4	G	9	2	0	1	23,518
Swingin Sue	3	F	1	0	0	0	0
Swinging Breeze	3	F	4	1	2	0	20,940
Swinging Gate	4	F	4	0	0	0	960
Swinging Ghost	2	C	2	0	2	0	16,800
Swinging Guy	4	G	15	1	3	2	12,225
Swinging Janie Gal	6	M	5	0	2	1	10,905
Swinging Ridge	7	G	7	0	1	0	1,555
Swinging Romeo	3	G	2	0	0	0	0
Swinging Sammi	4	C	17	3	4	1	52,926
Swingingintherain	2	C	3	1	0	0	5,822
Swingin'ninetofive	3	F	4	0	0	0	680
Swingley Road	5	G	8	0	1	0	1,996
Swingn' Notes	2	F	8	2	3	2	67,494
Swinglisa	7	M	8	1	1	1	1,438
Swingsville	3	F	5	2	0	0	21,120
Swingtimes Appeal	3	F	4	1	1	0	9,360
Swirling	4	F	5	0	0	0	1,310
Swirling Sky	3	F	2	0	0	0	0
Swirly Boy	3	G	7	0	0	0	939
Swishingonastar	4	F	4	0	2	2	5,036
Swiss Attire	3	F	9	3	1	0	20,885
Swiss Banks Fraud	6	H	10	2	3	2	24,625
Swiss Bon Bon	6	M	8	0	1	0	875
Swiss Bounty	2	G	4	1	1	1	7,680
Swiss Cheese	2	F	6	0	0	1	1,485
Swiss Count	3	G	14	1	3	0	20,525
Swiss Dove	3	F	8	1	2	1	14,592
Swiss Fudge J. J.	5	M	10	0	1	1	3,800
Swiss Gambler	5	H	12	2	2	1	10,265
Swiss Guy	3	G	8	2	0	1	18,462
Swiss Key	3	C	4	0	0	0	180
Swiss Lake	4	F	4	0	2	0	31,825
Swiss Mocha	2	G	7	1	3	1	28,970
Swiss Sarah	5	M	11	1	1	4	6,774
Swiss Skeet	4	G	8	1	0	0	2,376
Swiss Skier	2	F	12	1	1	1	26,882
Swiss Strike	2	C	4	0	0	0	1,500
Swissarmyknife	5	H	11	1	1	2	6,790
Switch	6	H	6	0	0	4	9,270
Switch Lanes	4	F	12	4	2	4	90,081
Switch My Pic	6	M	8	1	0	1	5,984
Switched	2	C	1	0	0	0	195
Switcheroo	2	F	5	0	1	0	9,319
Switchgear	2	G	14	0	1	1	7,175
Switchin Gears	5	G	2	0	0	0	149
Swith	6	H	3	0	0	0	188
Swoon Me Baby	2	F	5	0	1	1	4,730
Swooner	3	F	9	1	1	0	5,923

Horse	Age	Sex	Sts	1st	2d	3d	Won
Swoon's Lady	4	F	14	3	1	2	42,609
Swoonseaster Comet	6	G	4	0	0	0	1,500
Swoony Girl	4	F	18	1	1	2	5,483
Swoop and Soar	6	G	10	0	3	3	17,830
Swooping	6	H	6	0	1	1	5,330
Swooshel	5	H	12	3	3	1	35,764
Swooshing	3	F	4	0	0	1	7,410
Sword and Stone	4	C	3	0	0	0	172
Sword Chief	5	H	20	1	2	5	19,195
Sword Fight	4	C	9	1	0	0	1,200
Sword of Iron	4	F	7	1	0	0	6,749
Sword of Lords	2	C	1	0	0	0	137
Sword of Lucky	5	G	9	2	1	0	19,242
Sword of the South	6	G	11	0	0	0	2,218
Sword of War	6	H	9	0	0	1	3,652
Sword Princess	6	M	1	0	0	0	143
Swordfish	5	G	4	1	1	1	67,550
Swordmaker	2	C	5	0	0	0	990
Sword's Flyer	2	C	8	1	4	1	16,140
Swordswiped	3	G	6	0	0	1	1,667
Sworn Princess	5	M	1	0	0	0	0
Swush	4	F	1	0	0	0	0
Syble Seattle	4	G	17	1	0	0	4,365
Sycamore Creek	5	G	14	2	2	2	47,848
Sycamore Springs	10	G	5	1	0	0	6,555
Sycamore Stu	5	G	5	1	0	2	3,154
Sydneyleigh	2	F	1	0	0	0	124
Sydney's Choice	2	F	3	0	0	0	822
Sydney's Dream	3	F	1	0	0	0	0
Sydney's Quincey	4	C	6	1	2	1	26,090
Sydney's Song	5	M	2	1	0	0	2,525
Syd's Pawpaw	2	C	1	0	0	0	0
Sygian	3	C	1	0	0	0	1,080
Sykes Alive	6	G	7	3	2	1	51,534
Syl's Aggravation	7	G	17	1	2	1	7,847
Sylvan Approval	3	G	5	1	0	0	9,692
Sylvester Questor	10	G	7	1	2	2	27,120
Sylviana	5	M	2	0	0	0	333
Sylvia's Charm	4	F	1	1	0	0	1,540
Sylvia's Dream	5	G	9	0	1	2	3,393
Sylvia's Hymn	7	H	4	1	1	0	8,948
Symbol of Freedom	3	F	10	1	1	1	6,883
Symbol of Love	4	F	4	0	0	1	1,200
Symbolic Times	3	C	9	1	4	2	93,288
Symmetron	3	C	2	1	0	0	36,960
Symmetry Slew	6	M	20	2	3	7	21,796
Sympathie	2	F	3	0	0	1	825
Symph	4	G	10	1	2	2	9,060
Symphonic Lady	6	M	3	0	0	1	3,738
Symphonic Melody	5	M	3	0	0	0	0
Symphony Bay	2	F	5	0	0	0	490
Symphony of Fire	2	G	2	0	0	0	0
Symphony of Gold	3	F	9	1	1	2	10,350
Symphony Sid	3	C	4	0	1	1	11,900
Syn Begone	4	G	26	2	2	6	24,632
Syn Can Do	4	F	7	0	0	1	1,602
Syn D Syn	4	F	11	2	2	1	10,968
Syn of a Gun	3	G	3	0	0	0	120
Synapse	6	G	8	2	1	1	6,589
Synaster Son	3	G	12	0	0	3	1,622
Synastry Rose	5	H	4	0	1	1	1,682
Synastry's Flight	5	M	2	0	0	0	175
Synchronistic	2	F	2	1	0	0	22,800
Synco Peach	3	F	3	1	0	1	18,460
Syncopated Slew	4	G	14	2	1	3	14,636
Syndication	6	M	3	0	0	3	7,360
Synergistic	4	F	6	1	1	0	44,693
Synergistic Effex	2	F	1	1	0	1	36,360
Synergize	4	G	8	0	0	1	3,275
Synful Cajun	4	G	3	2	0	1	49,140
Synful Cat	2	F	2	0	0	0	1,230
Synful Hour	5	G	5	0	0	0	1,218
Synfull Charmer	3	F	8	3	0	1	9,632
Synlimit	5	H	3	1	0	0	2,929
Synner Saint	8	G	9	0	0	2	3,990
Synonym	4	G	10	2	5	1	47,280
Syn's Baby Ruthe	6	M	15	1	1	4	7,127
Syns N Fantasies	4	G	7	1	1	1	4,598
Syphire Pine	5	G	17	1	0	0	5,718

Horse	Age	Sex	Sts	1st	2d	3d	Won
Syphon Says	2	C	2	1	0	0	27,600
Syrian Applause	4	F	8	0	0	0	504
Syrian Music	7	M	6	0	0	0	323
Syrian Sea	7	M	18	2	4	3	12,895
Syrian Silencer	5	G	2	0	0	0	118
Syringa's Bodgit	3	F	6	0	0	1	4,721
Sys Boy	3	C	6	1	1	0	9,339
Szczerbiak	6	G	1	0	0	0	0
Szep	5	H	6	0	0	1	9,520
T B Gumby	6	M	6	0	0	1	1,895
T Boy	5	G	13	1	0	0	5,809
T C Brooks	8	G	5	0	1	0	2,289
T C Ice	3	F	2	0	0	0	100
T C Kiss	5	M	10	1	0	3	46,279
T C Maiden	4	F	12	3	1	2	46,605
T C Rebel Rouzer	2	F	7	1	1	1	27,187
T C S Deacting	3	C	2	0	0	0	0
T C S Goldust Star	3	F	1	0	0	0	0
T C S Rebel	3	G	2	0	0	0	0
T C S Vichine	4	G	8	3	1	1	10,467
T C's Baby Bag	6	M	2	0	0	0	345
T C's Cherry Hill	5	M	9	0	1	1	4,989
T C's Connection	7	G	6	0	0	0	544
T C's Halo	5	M	3	0	0	0	221
T C's Lesia De	3	G	12	2	1	3	19,083
T Cs Orbiting Miss	5	M	8	1	4	2	7,134
T C's Revenge	3	G	7	0	0	0	3,827
T C's Roldaffair	3	F	12	2	1	2	11,828
T C's Supremo	4	G	5	0	1	0	1,650
T C's Swingshot	3	G	12	2	2	0	14,486
T D Defrere	2	G	7	1	1	2	16,060
T D Prospect	6	G	13	0	0	0	977
T D Silver	6	G	6	1	0	1	1,676
T D Tommy	4	G	2	0	0	0	455
T E Jones	3	F	2	0	0	0	2,140
T E Prospect Creek	3	C	3	0	0	0	0
T G's Prospect	2	C	1	0	0	0	0
T J Casey	4	F	15	2	0	2	8,049
T J Classy	2	F	1	1	0	0	7,560
T J Mac	10	G	5	0	0	0	715
T J My Man	4	G	7	1	2	1	11,272
T J Quigley	9	G	3	0	2	0	3,150
T J 's Moon Shadow	2	G	3	0	0	1	605
T Jay's Victory	5	G	9	1	0	0	5,070
T J's Dreamer	6	G	7	0	1	1	4,888
T J's Jackinthebox	3	C	11	1	2	1	17,810
T J's Lucky Moon	4	G	3	0	1	0	21,245
T J's Really Sharp	5	G	3	0	0	0	120
T J's Sweetie	3	F	1	0	0	0	0
T K's Blazin Code	5	G	16	0	3	2	8,329
T M Gray Ghost	4	G	9	1	0	0	5,700
T M T Insider	4	G	12	4	4	1	21,574
T M Warrior	5	G	6	0	0	0	420
T Man's Glitter	5	G	5	1	1	0	4,706
T M's Wildcard	3	C	2	0	0	0	0
T P Louie	5	G	17	3	2	1	45,150
T Rex Charlie	4	G	11	0	3	1	6,000
T Rex Sure	3	G	11	1	0	0	9,150
T S Eliot	3	C	4	1	2	0	32,800
T S Full Service	4	C	1	0	0	0	91
T Shirt	3	G	5	0	0	1	2,640
T Shirt King	10	G	8	0	0	0	586
T T Phares	5	G	11	0	0	0	987
T Tommie Too	6	H	2	0	0	0	0
T V Hunter	2	C	2	0	1	0	3,400
T V Tom	4	G	7	1	0	1	4,677
T. B. Track Star	7	G	4	1	0	0	5,958
T. B.'s Storm	5	G	6	1	0	1	6,225
T. C. Lu	5	G	9	1	1	2	16,067
T. C. Stingaree	6	G	6	1	1	1	7,958
T. C.'s Girl	3	F	4	0	0	0	250
T. D. Irish	6	G	12	1	0	4	8,928
T. D. the Dawg	3	G	8	0	0	0	315
T. G. and Jake	7	G	10	0	1	0	1,426
T. G. Power	4	G	11	1	1	0	9,155
T. G.'s Babe	2	F	4	0	1	0	5,440
T. H. Lear	5	G	2	0	0	1	9,828
T. J. Cruiser	4	G	10	4	1	1	7,831
T. J. Hunter	5	H	15	2	1	3	14,199

Horse	Age	Sex	Sts	1st	2d	3d	Won
T. J. Magic	7	M	7	2	1	2	10,182
T. J. 's Fred	4	C	2	0	0	0	860
T. J.'s Blackjack	3	C	6	0	0	0	1,535
T. J.'s Darling	6	M	3	0	0	0	700
T. J.'s Glory	3	G	11	2	2	1	18,264
T. J.'s Granny	5	M	3	0	0	0	460
T. J.'s Home Run	4	C	4	0	0	0	520
T. J.'s Ivy	5	M	13	4	4	1	60,419
T. J.'s Knicknack	5	G	7	4	1	1	117,370
T. J.'s Queen	5	M	6	0	0	0	412
T. K.'s Lou T	5	G	4	0	0	0	339
T. K.'s Turn	5	G	14	2	2	1	18,839
T. L. Three	3	G	3	0	1	1	3,487
T. L. Time	8	G	7	2	3	0	15,105
T. M. C.'s Hubble	3	G	11	0	2	5	6,700
T. M. Frank	3	G	3	0	2	0	17,630
T. McClain	2	C	4	0	0	0	885
T. R. Karat	7	H	13	1	0	1	6,660
T. R.'s Trouble	4	F	2	0	0	0	480
T. S. Dailey	2	F	2	0	0	0	1,450
T. V. Frost	4	G	16	2	5	1	11,803
T. V. Kiss	3	C	10	0	1	1	5,136
T. V. Secretary	5	M	16	1	3	3	22,685
T.j. Diamond	4	G	8	4	1	0	49,890
Ta Keel	3	C	5	1	2	1	5,791
Ta Ta Baby	4	C	17	1	2	7	21,410
Ta Ta for Now	2	G	1	0	0	0	100
Ta Ta Moro	6	M	3	0	0	0	116
Ta'am Clever	3	F	10	0	1	1	3,680
Tab	6	G	14	2	5	2	24,493
Tab Cat M. D.	3	G	4	1	2	0	28,425
Tab the Truce	4	G	5	0	2	1	3,020
Tab Wizard	3	G	6	0	0	0	0
Tabacchi	2	C	4	1	2	0	78,400
Tabacco Roots	3	G	1	0	0	0	96
Tabaco Y Ron	5	G	2	1	0	0	6,090
Tabanka Fella	2	C	4	0	1	0	3,995
Tabernacle	5	M	9	0	2	1	3,612
Tabiana	3	F	5	0	1	0	8,735
Tabiz	7	G	23	0	2	1	7,948
Table Bay	2	G	2	0	0	0	0
Table Creek	4	G	21	2	4	2	10,575
Table Hopper	4	G	15	2	1	2	10,130
Table Me N Saros	4	G	22	1	6	6	26,100
Table Mountain	3	C	4	1	0	1	11,595
Table Talk	5	G	16	1	1	4	34,215
Tabledancinpyrite	4	C	7	0	0	3	1,434
Tablet	3	G	10	0	1	1	5,885
Tabletop	2	F	5	0	0	0	2,905
Tabloid	2	F	2	0	0	0	127
Taboose Creek	3	F	2	0	0	0	960
Tabor City	3	G	4	0	0	0	4,920
Tabs Verdict	5	G	9	1	1	0	3,789
Tabulator	3	G	5	1	1	0	11,710
Tacaro's Heaven	4	G	6	0	4	0	22,005
Tacaro'slasthurrah	5	G	7	2	1	0	11,165
Tacful	6	G	1	0	0	0	0
Tacfull Tammi	5	M	2	0	0	0	0
Tach Magic	2	C	2	0	0	0	440
Tache	4	F	15	1	5	1	19,866
Tacirring	4	C	13	3	5	1	76,180
Tack Attack	3	G	7	0	3	0	35,660
Tack on the Magic	4	G	16	1	2	3	13,615
Tack Room	3	F	5	1	0	1	14,685
Tack Room Lady	4	F	13	6	0	1	57,580
Tackers Girl	4	F	4	0	2	0	7,848
Tackling Stress	3	C	3	1	0	0	46,899
Tacky	2	G	2	1	0	0	17,500
Tacky Affair	4	F	6	0	2	1	49,818
Tacky Town	4	F	10	3	1	2	16,837
Taco Boy	4	C	3	0	1	0	1,782
Taco Caliente	3	G	1	0	0	1	1,871
Taco Cat	5	G	13	0	0	1	1,426
Taco Man	5	H	2	0	0	0	122
Taco Tuesday	4	G	15	3	2	3	77,660
Taconic	3	C	3	0	0	0	1,320
Taconic Run	3	G	13	2	4	1	26,060
Tacony	3	F	7	1	0	1	12,760
Tact Reigns	5	M	13	2	1	3	14,200

Horse	Age	Sex	Sts	1st	2d	3d	Won	Horse	Age	Sex	Sts	1st	2d	3d	Won
Tactful Touch	4	G	8	0	3	0	4,487	Taint Saratoga	3	C	11	1	2	0	15,255
Tactfully	6	M	11	1	3	2	18,765	Taint True	3	F	1	0	0	0	240
Tactfully Ann	3	F	14	1	0	0	8,702	Tainted Chimes	5	G	6	1	0	1	6,539
Tactical Al	7	H	8	0	1	2	12,130	Tainted Facts	2	F	4	0	0	0	1,680
Tactical Allusion	5	G	8	1	1	2	20,600	Tainted Tripp	6	M	3	0	0	0	630
Tactical Blues	4	G	14	1	3	1	13,875	Tainwell (GB)	4	G	16	0	1	1	2,891
Tactical Chatter	2	C	2	0	0	0	230	Taipan	4	G	2	1	0	0	22,020
Tactical de Naskra	5	G	4	0	0	2	7,770	Taittinger Rose	2	F	5	1	2	1	64,100
Tactical Delight	3	C	4	2	0	2	54,940	Taiwan Charley	2	C	11	2	2	1	53,560
Tactical Friends	3	F	3	0	0	0	850	Taj	4	G	11	0	1	4	16,440
Tactical Gamble	2	F	3	0	0	0	1,380	Taj Ah Cailie	6	G	10	2	2	0	3,518
Tactical Gold	2	C	4	1	2	1	44,100	Taj and Turn	4	F	3	2	0	0	1,386
Tactical Guy	2	C	1	0	0	0	115	Taj Shotthe Deputy	7	G	2	0	0	0	290
Tactical Jet	4	G	7	1	1	1	7,248	Tajmarie	2	F	1	0	0	0	0
Tactical Juli	3	F	6	0	2	2	20,830	Tajranee Rose	3	F	6	0	1	1	1,800
Tactical Lady	5	M	16	0	2	1	4,582	Taka Time	4	F	13	0	1	0	6,245
Tactical Master	5	H	1	0	0	0	59	Take a Card	3	G	6	0	1	0	1,938
Tactical Miss	4	F	1	0	0	0	75	Take a Dip	9	G	7	0	0	0	496
Tactical Mission	5	H	10	0	0	1	2,720	Take a Gamble	5	H	11	0	0	1	1,650
Tactical Mover	3	F	15	1	0	3	11,477	Take a Left (GB)	10	G	1	0	0	0	380
Tactical Nova	7	H	3	0	0	0	428	Take a Long Look	2	F	4	0	0	2	4,560
Tactical Plan	5	H	4	0	0	0	890	Take a Look	5	M	9	5	1	0	56,425
Tactical Plus	3	F	10	2	4	1	105,200	Take a Taxi	3	F	4	1	0	0	12,090
Tactical Power	2	G	9	1	1	2	20,530	Take a Trick	6	G	16	1	1	3	13,525
Tactical Pride	5	H	13	1	4	3	16,645	Take Account	6	G	17	4	3	4	39,610
Tactical Prince	2	C	5	0	0	0	2,125	Take Achance On Me	5	G	15	2	9	2	167,200
Tactical Princess	3	F	8	3	1	1	65,167	Take Advantage	4	G	7	0	1	1	7,440
Tactical Punch	7	M	4	0	0	2	4,760	Take and Do	6	G	8	0	1	0	2,310
Tactical Pursuit	3	C	1	0	0	0	0	Take Another Bow	5	H	2	0	0	0	430
Tactical Rose	3	F	3	0	1	0	6,090	Take Back Cat	4	G	10	0	5	0	6,633
Tactical Scene	4	F	1	0	0	0	700	Take Charge Lady	4	F	7	2	3	0	720,026
Tactical Side	6	G	8	2	3	0	36,825	Take Courage	2	G	3	1	0	0	6,600
Tactical Stan	3	G	8	0	0	0	120	Take Down Johnny	6	G	7	0	0	1	1,017
Tactical Strike	3	C	5	0	1	1	9,250	Take Five	5	G	6	0	0	1	2,624
Tactical Tango	4	C	5	0	0	1	1,695	Take Her Out	2	F	6	0	1	0	11,480
Tactical Tina	3	F	14	0	2	5	19,020	Take Holy Out	4	G	13	4	1	1	18,097
Tactical Tracey	5	M	3	0	0	0	586	Take Into Account	4	F	12	2	1	2	23,435
Tactical Trick	6	M	1	0	0	0	0	Take Issue	4	F	11	2	3	0	8,544
Tactical Wings	4	F	5	0	3	0	10,778	Take It North	4	F	10	1	2	1	12,294
Tacticalfortyniner	4	G	2	1	0	0	12,240	Take It Off	6	M	1	0	0	0	720
Tacticmove	2	F	1	0	0	0	0	Take Me	4	F	1	0	0	0	510
Tacticts	6	M	6	3	0	1	12,467	Take Me Away	2	C	3	0	1	0	3,495
Taczar	6	H	15	0	2	0	6,246	Take Me Dancer	5	H	4	0	2	1	1,100
Tadda Ann	3	F	6	1	0	0	11,970	Take Me Down	3	G	3	2	0	0	18,240
Taddy	3	F	4	0	1	0	819	Take Me Home Lady	4	F	15	2	0	2	11,684
Tae Bo	3	F	4	0	1	0	11,000	Take Me On	3	F	4	1	0	1	9,620
Tafaseel	3	C	8	2	1	1	120,097	Take Me Out Back	3	G	12	2	0	0	37,590
Tafaul	2	C	1	0	0	0	1,350	Take Me Out Deputy	2	F	3	1	0	0	5,700
Taffeta	5	M	9	1	0	0	8,298	Take Me There	2	F	2	1	0	0	6,725
Taffy Pull	5	M	9	2	1	2	22,097	Take Me to Sealte	2	F	3	0	0	0	680
Tag Up	3	G	3	1	0	0	4,200	Take Me Up	5	G	6	3	1	0	142,355
Tagadance	3	G	7	0	1	2	10,392	Take My Heart	4	G	12	1	0	3	7,261
Tagged	6	G	9	1	1	2	10,831	Take No Bull	3	C	14	3	2	0	15,878
Taghkanic	3	F	5	2	0	1	57,524	Take One's Chance	4	G	8	1	0	1	8,605
Tagus	3	G	6	1	0	0	11,200	Take Out the Trash	4	F	10	5	1	1	105,679
Tahapo	10	G	6	0	1	0	2,707	Take Part	4	G	6	0	2	0	2,648
Tahiti Blues	4	F	6	0	3	1	8,080	Take the A Train	4	G	18	2	1	1	23,929
Tahitian Rain	4	F	10	1	2	1	40,170	Take the Back Road	3	G	1	0	0	0	91
Tahizztheman	2	G	3	1	0	0	1,760	Take the Bait	5	G	7	0	0	0	0
Tahoe Affair	6	G	8	1	2	0	21,014	Take the Blame	2	F	1	0	0	1	913
Tahoe Bay	3	F	15	2	0	4	14,941	Take the City	9	M	7	1	2	1	12,882
Tahoe Believer	3	G	8	0	1	1	9,351	Take the Jolt	3	C	13	1	1	1	8,105
Tahoe Honey	4	F	2	0	1	1	3,850	Take the Lady Out	6	M	20	1	4	4	23,583
Tahoe Ice	2	G	3	0	0	1	1,590	Take the Mickey	5	M	9	1	1	1	26,350
Tahoe Trip	2	G	6	1	3	1	8,395	Take the Plunge	2	G	5	4	0	0	120,053
Tahoe's Gem	2	F	2	2	0	0	8,250	Take the Prize	3	G	3	0	1	1	10,665
Tahquitz Pride	5	M	9	3	0	2	47,237	Take the Rate	2	F	2	0	0	1	5,740
Taiaslew	3	G	7	4	2	0	204,325	Take the Ship	2	F	4	0	2	0	4,660
Taiga Timber	3	F	3	0	1	1	2,850	Take the Stage	4	F	7	0	0	0	225
Taiga Two	5	H	7	1	1	0	43,300	Take the Van	3	C	8	0	0	0	504
Tail Gate	6	H	9	0	1	2	8,060	Take the Wheel	4	F	5	1	0	0	4,420
Tail Gunner	2	F	4	0	0	1	1,706	Take This	4	G	10	2	3	1	12,927
Tailfromthecrypt	5	H	7	3	1	0	83,016	Take Three	6	M	19	3	2	3	22,530
Tailgate Party	4	F	3	0	1	0	2,583	Take Two	6	H	11	1	1	0	2,373
Tailgator	4	F	17	5	4	0	70,303	Takealetter	4	F	8	2	2	1	20,120
Tails of the Crypt	4	G	8	0	1	1	26,530	Takealookatmenow	3	F	12	1	1	2	28,445
Tailsneverfails	3	F	8	1	0	0	5,121	Takeit Or Leave It	3	G	2	0	0	1	2,820
Taimazov (ARG)	7	H	1	0	0	0	0	Takeiteasyedye	5	M	7	1	1	1	38,925
Taint It the Truth	4	C	4	1	1	1	20,696	Takelit	7	G	13	2	2	3	10,732

Horse	Age	Sex	Sts	1st	2d	3d	Won	Horse	Age	Sex	Sts	1st	2d	3d	Won
Takem	4	G	10	3	0	2	22,502	Talking Leaves	4	G	9	1	0	0	8,580
Takem and Leavem	3	F	10	1	4	2	30,550	Talking Point	5	M	8	1	1	1	27,132
Takemebacktotexas	3	G	3	0	0	1	3,980	Talking Red	5	H	15	2	3	3	29,428
Takemeoutonthetown	3	F	3	0	0	0	0	Talking Rosie	2	F	6	0	3	1	7,280
Takemetofunkytown	4	F	11	3	1	2	13,826	Talkingaboutmygirl	7	M	8	1	1	1	5,055
Taken Back	4	F	7	1	0	1	2,820	Talkmeister	7	G	10	3	2	2	66,865
Takenbythesky	5	M	5	3	0	0	31,940	Talk'n Angel	4	F	11	1	3	0	10,425
Takenitallin	4	G	9	2	1	0	15,266	Talknoevil	2	C	3	0	0	1	4,920
Takeonefortheteam	3	C	3	0	1	1	12,200	Talknow	6	G	3	0	0	0	4,500
Taker' to the Bank	3	F	6	0	0	1	616	Talk's Cheap	7	H	11	0	2	1	12,548
Takes a Buddy	3	C	1	1	0	0	8,700	Tall American	7	G	2	0	0	0	0
Takethatwithyou	4	G	1	0	0	0	0	Tall Boy	3	G	10	1	0	0	3,218
Takethemoneyandrun	4	F	16	3	7	1	67,460	Tall in Seattle	3	F	4	0	0	0	0
Taketimetoshine	3	C	4	0	1	0	3,990	Tall Native	5	H	1	0	0	0	31
Takin Inventory	3	G	9	0	2	3	11,670	Tall Order	3	G	3	0	0	0	923
Takin' Up Space	3	G	5	0	0	0	230	Tall Wonder	7	H	10	2	2	3	21,115
Takincare Ofbiz	2	G	3	0	0	1	1,325	Talladega Sweep	2	C	1	0	0	0	0
Taking Advantage	9	H	4	0	0	1	4,000	Tallahaxie Blue	4	F	12	2	0	0	7,174
Taking Flight	3	F	7	2	2	1	56,300	Tallchief	3	C	5	0	1	0	1,205
Taking Sides	7	G	1	0	0	0	246	Tallchief Cove	5	G	5	0	1	0	3,900
Taking the Redeye	2	C	1	0	0	0	1,230	Tallest Mountain	5	G	1	0	0	0	0
Takki Tsunami	2	C	6	1	0	2	17,795	Tallest Timber	5	H	1	1	0	0	4,920
Talara	3	C	6	1	0	0	32,640	Tallgirl	3	F	2	1	0	1	4,970
Talaris	2	C	1	0	0	0	0	Tallie Light	4	F	5	1	1	0	11,360
Talavesa	3	F	11	2	4	0	13,545	Tallielane	3	F	3	0	0	0	40
Talbott Tavern	10	G	1	0	0	0	105	Tallon's Choice	3	G	6	1	1	0	8,202
Talc of Dreams	11	G	17	0	1	0	2,317	Tallonsy	2	F	4	0	0	1	3,380
Talc's Quick Cat	3	F	9	1	0	0	4,560	Tallow	7	G	2	0	0	0	0
Talculation	4	F	9	0	0	1	1,082	Tallow Creek	3	C	11	0	1	3	5,835
Tale of a Dream	3	F	4	0	1	0	19,875	Tally Belle	4	F	14	0	2	3	10,375
Tale of the Ticker	3	F	2	0	0	0	970	Tally Slew	3	F	12	0	1	1	7,099
Tale of Woe	2	C	2	1	1	0	36,720	Tally Toll	8	H	3	0	0	0	300
Tale Toppers	6	G	3	0	0	1	682	Taloberto	2	G	2	0	0	0	1,200
Tale Twister	8	G	13	0	1	1	3,110	Talon's Lark	5	H	6	1	1	0	8,099
Talega de Oro	2	F	3	1	0	1	12,720	Taltech	6	G	7	3	2	1	22,374
Talent of Morgan	2	F	4	0	0	0	617	Talullah Mae	4	F	11	2	2	1	41,071
Talented Runner	4	F	5	0	0	0	1,726	Tam Chief	4	C	2	1	0	0	914
Talented Won	7	G	9	1	1	0	7,052	Tam Win Tam	6	G	14	5	3	1	21,519
Taleofdistinction	3	C	1	0	0	0	350	Tama	4	G	2	0	1	0	7,360
Taleofthewampuscat	2	C	1	0	0	0	900	Tama Gold	3	C	12	2	2	3	17,206
Taleofthreeralphs	2	G	1	0	0	0	0	Tamaakajo	2	C	3	0	0	0	788
Tales of Glory	2	C	4	2	0	1	60,750	Tamadher	4	F	1	0	0	0	50
Tales of Tyler	5	G	1	0	0	0	100	Tamahka Princess	3	F	4	1	0	0	3,150
Talespin	5	M	14	3	0	3	21,873	Tamaki Lady	5	M	9	0	0	0	1,099
Taleur	5	M	13	1	3	2	18,610	Tamara	3	F	9	2	1	3	132,117
Talia	4	F	5	0	0	0	675	Tamara Princess (BRZ)	5	M	1	0	0	0	1,300
Taliano	3	G	8	1	0	1	15,260	Tamarack Bay	4	F	9	0	4	2	57,945
Talitha	4	F	8	1	0	3	4,732	Tamarack Creek	3	F	5	2	0	0	2,339
Talk	9	G	6	0	0	0	468	Tamarack Hills	4	G	11	3	0	2	43,465
Talk About Fast	2	F	1	0	0	0	0	Tamaram	4	C	9	0	0	0	1,904
Talk About Smart	3	F	3	0	0	0	5,823	Tamara's Babe	6	M	7	3	1	2	19,348
Talk Around Town	4	F	1	0	0	0	1,230	Tamaras Trend	7	M	12	1	2	4	10,533
Talk It Up	7	G	7	1	0	1	10,784	Tamarillo	10	G	6	0	1	1	4,626
Talk Me Again (ARG)	5	M	5	1	0	0	46,878	Tamarind Point	4	G	15	2	6	0	26,642
Talk of the Block	2	C	2	0	0	0	1,818	Tamasuk	3	G	4	0	0	0	1,850
Talk Sharply	4	G	24	1	4	1	9,587	Tamayaz Gal	3	F	10	0	0	3	3,630
Talk Show Tony	2	C	2	0	0	0	700	Tamayaz's Legend	4	G	1	0	0	1	3,600
Talk That Talk	3	C	1	0	0	1	1,160	Tamayno	4	C	4	1	1	0	6,330
Talk the Walk	2	C	1	0	1	0	4,800	Tamayo	4	F	6	0	1	2	14,260
Talk to Cathy	4	F	6	2	0	3	8,604	Tamble	3	F	4	0	0	0	179
Talk to Chrissy	4	F	16	3	2	3	25,590	Tamboorensnshampan	4	F	6	0	0	0	880
Talk to Me Baby	2	F	7	1	1	1	57,550	Tambourine Dancer	4	F	6	1	2	0	5,592
Talk to Me Jimmy	6	G	1	0	0	0	0	Tamburello	3	C	4	0	0	1	10,850
Talk Too	4	F	15	2	2	3	24,137	Tamburlaine (IRE)	5	H	1	1	0	0	21,600
Talka Lotta Bull	6	H	6	1	0	0	7,050	Tame	3	C	4	0	0	0	350
Talkabluestreak	3	C	5	1	1	0	5,148	Tamerice	6	H	6	0	1	0	750
Talkin George	4	C	15	3	5	3	29,345	Tamerlane Sham	3	G	6	0	0	0	1,025
Talkin' Kind	5	M	10	0	0	0	4,800	Tami Be Good	4	F	15	1	2	3	14,835
Talkin Lady	6	M	5	1	0	1	3,140	Tamingo	2	G	4	1	0	1	7,996
Talkin Money	3	F	5	2	0	0	34,220	Tami's Redemption	5	M	1	0	0	0	700
Talkin Rita	4	F	3	0	0	0	204	Tamisa	2	F	6	0	1	0	3,940
Talkin Saratoga	4	F	3	0	0	0	650	Tammany Dash	4	F	7	2	3	0	45,931
Talkin Song	4	F	3	0	0	0	122	Tammany Star	4	G	8	1	0	0	19,960
Talkin T J B	5	M	5	0	2	0	2,040	Tammaro	4	G	11	0	5	2	16,255
Talkin the Talk	2	F	6	0	2	1	7,715	Tammie's Tune	3	F	8	0	2	0	8,964
Talkin to an Angel	5	M	6	2	3	0	23,600	Tammy Star	4	F	8	1	0	1	17,509
Talkin Tough	2	C	7	0	2	1	23,450	Tammy's Carousel	3	F	3	0	0	1	1,350
Talking About	7	G	13	2	0	2	8,433	Tammy's Love	4	F	1	0	0	0	0
Talking Clues	3	F	4	0	0	0	502	Tammy's Surprise	3	F	8	1	0	1	3,925

RECORDS OF HORSES

Horse	Age	Sex	Sts	1st	2d	3d	Won	Horse	Age	Sex	Sts	1st	2d	3d	Won
Tammy's Tango	2	F	4	0	0	1	2,070	Tanya's Song	3	F	7	1	0	2	15,220
Tamono	2	F	2	0	0	0	300	Tanyaswindycaller	4	G	6	1	0	1	3,565
Tamorons Blade	4	F	9	3	2	2	35,639	Tanzer	3	C	3	1	1	0	11,700
Tampa	5	H	7	3	0	1	18,125	Taoiseach	4	G	8	0	2	0	4,210
Tamper	3	G	3	1	0	0	6,490	Taormina	5	G	5	0	1	1	5,480
Tams Big Pie	8	G	3	0	0	1	1,460	Tap an Sparks	3	F	5	1	1	0	7,825
Tam's Ice	10	G	10	1	1	1	4,910	Tap Dancer	2	C	7	2	2	1	148,735
Tam's Nitemare	6	G	3	0	2	0	2,940	Tap Dancing Kid	3	G	6	0	0	0	1,876
Tam's Rebel	7	G	12	1	0	1	2,080	Tap Dancing Mauk	2	C	3	1	0	1	19,080
Tam's Terms	5	G	6	4	0	0	125,520	Tap Day	2	C	5	2	0	0	48,407
Tam's Tune	3	G	3	0	0	0	820	Tap Into Fame	2	F	3	0	1	1	7,975
Tam's Yam	3	F	4	0	0	1	630	Tap Kid	5	M	9	2	0	2	6,809
Tamul (ARG)	5	G	8	0	0	1	1,830	Tap Machine	3	F	12	2	1	1	76,460
Tamusky	4	C	10	0	0	1	15,376	Tap N Go	2	C	2	0	0	0	189
Tan Campante (ARG)	4	F	14	7	2	1	67,768	Tap N Pack	4	G	1	1	0	0	3,300
Tan Czar	7	G	3	0	0	0	120	Tap Runner	4	C	3	0	0	0	307
Tan Goddess	5	M	2	0	0	0	136	Tap Tap	3	C	11	2	2	4	49,070
Tan Stack	5	G	23	0	1	0	2,771	Tap Tap Tap	3	F	13	3	0	2	22,740
Tan Tan Tillie	3	F	3	0	0	0	385	Tap the Admiral	5	H	6	2	0	1	265,046
Tanaja	2	F	1	1	0	0	5,460	Tap the Magic	2	F	1	0	0	0	0
Tanallover	5	M	11	2	0	0	24,094	Tap the Rockies	5	H	9	0	0	1	1,124
Tanantella	3	F	2	0	0	0	282	Tap the Sky	4	F	9	0	2	3	12,324
Tandy House	6	M	2	0	0	0	93	Tap Time	2	C	3	0	0	0	0
Tandy Lakes	2	C	1	0	0	0	525	Tap Trick	3	C	9	0	1	1	2,365
Taneum	4	G	4	0	2	0	4,000	Tap Twice	5	G	6	1	0	1	16,355
Tangara (NZ)	6	M	7	0	0	0	4,980	Tap West	3	G	7	0	1	2	2,897
Tangarae Tango	5	G	7	1	1	1	17,684	Tap Wood	3	C	1	0	0	0	200
Tangela	3	F	2	0	0	0	190	Tap Your Feet	5	M	1	0	0	0	0
Tanger	3	F	4	1	0	0	4,890	Tap Zappa	2	C	1	0	1	0	3,000
Tangerine	4	F	11	1	3	1	56,754	Tapantears	2	G	6	1	2	0	17,610
Tangi	4	F	9	1	0	1	11,452	Tapas	3	F	3	0	0	0	0
Tangier Sound	4	F	8	4	2	0	126,020	Tapatio	2	F	1	0	0	1	780
Tangle	4	C	8	1	0	1	13,260	Tapatio (ARG)	6	H	4	0	0	1	1,950
Tangle (IRE)	3	F	2	0	2	0	33,460	Tapaway	4	G	11	0	1	2	3,590
Tangled Creek	3	F	8	2	0	0	6,752	Tapdancinblues	2	F	1	0	1	0	425
Tangled Heart	2	F	1	0	0	1	4,100	Tapforaly	3	F	2	0	0	0	930
Tangled Mind	3	F	13	1	2	2	9,733	Tapit	2	C	2	2	0	0	79,800
Tangled Up In Blue (IRE)	3	C	3	1	1	0	43,320	Tap'n Tango	2	F	5	0	1	0	14,465
Tanglin Road	5	G	3	0	0	0	111	Tappat	8	G	6	0	0	0	4,148
Tango Devil	6	M	5	0	0	0	0	Tappedinto	2	F	2	0	0	1	1,000
Tango Fever	2	C	7	1	0	1	12,450	Tapper	5	M	17	2	4	5	38,716
Tango for Tips	2	F	2	0	0	0	2,700	Tappin' Tasha	2	F	2	0	0	0	0
Tango Gin	3	F	13	3	1	2	22,950	Tapping Tilly	9	M	3	0	0	0	174
Tango Princess	3	F	8	1	1	2	19,455	Tappy	4	F	10	1	4	4	75,575
Tango Shoes	2	F	1	0	1	0	2,200	Tapster	3	G	7	0	0	0	610
Tango Tales	2	C	1	0	1	0	8,540	Tapthewind	2	G	2	0	0	1	1,020
Tanja's Cat	4	G	11	0	3	1	11,012	Taptonite	3	G	17	0	3	2	10,591
Tank Commander	3	G	11	1	2	1	10,723	Tar Hill	3	C	6	0	1	0	1,680
Tank Force	2	C	2	0	0	0	1,920	Tar Pit	7	H	8	1	0	0	3,376
Tank Grrrl	5	M	6	2	0	2	46,079	Tara Arms	6	G	4	0	2	0	3,260
Tank Murdock	5	G	8	0	0	0	368	Tara Can Step	3	F	7	0	0	1	2,873
Tank Two	6	H	4	0	0	0	1,732	Tara Gold (IRE)	5	M	1	0	1	0	3,200
Tank Visit	2	G	2	0	0	0	0	Tara Ho	2	F	4	0	0	1	1,410
Tankit Or Leaveit	3	C	8	0	0	1	1,305	Tara Jean	4	F	3	1	0	0	13,800
Tankler	3	G	2	0	0	0	0	Tara On the Wire	3	F	8	1	0	0	7,770
Tank's City	4	F	6	0	0	0	1,303	Tara Run	4	F	9	1	3	3	7,209
Tank's Expectation	4	G	12	0	5	0	58,412	Tara Two	4	F	4	1	0	0	12,836
Tank's Lil Brother	4	G	12	2	3	0	39,951	Taradashi	3	F	10	0	1	0	5,707
Tanktown Drifter	4	C	11	2	2	3	36,203	Taraf	4	C	11	0	1	1	6,645
Tanky Boy	5	G	10	3	5	0	101,195	Taragon	5	M	7	1	3	0	16,430
Tanner Boy	4	G	1	0	0	0	35	Tarakan	4	G	8	1	1	1	46,280
Tanner Cole	4	C	2	0	0	0	0	Taramot	5	G	14	0	1	0	7,830
Tanner Danner	2	C	5	1	1	1	12,445	Taran T.	4	F	8	0	4	0	7,505
Tanner Fire	5	G	15	2	0	2	3,819	Tarantula Springs	3	C	3	1	1	0	5,600
Tanner Jon	5	H	8	1	1	2	2,722	Tarapoa	5	M	9	2	2	2	21,671
Tanner Sea	4	F	4	0	0	1	2,143	Taras Foxy Lady	4	F	5	0	2	0	5,284
Tannerman	6	G	4	0	0	0	217	Tara's Harp	6	G	11	0	2	2	7,657
Tanners Bullseye	3	G	11	1	1	1	17,878	Tarascon Diligence	2	C	5	1	0	0	11,425
Tanner's Isle	6	M	3	0	0	0	230	Tarasina	3	F	6	2	1	1	20,895
Tanoan	4	G	9	1	0	0	9,090	Taraval	3	C	5	1	1	1	48,472
Tanqueray (CHI)	5	H	1	0	0	0	88	Taraxacum	4	F	1	1	0	0	9,900
Tantalize	6	M	1	0	0	0	90	Tardy	4	F	5	0	0	0	90
Tantalizing Smile	6	H	9	2	0	0	15,144	Tarek	5	H	11	2	1	3	90,230
Tantallon	2	F	6	1	1	1	57,140	Tarfu	2	C	1	0	0	0	0
Tantalus	2	C	7	1	0	0	4,742	Targestina	2	F	4	2	0	1	13,252
Tantarella	5	M	1	0	0	0	40	Target Ahead	3	F	8	0	3	2	11,190
Tantoo	7	M	8	2	1	0	36,866	Target Lord	4	C	.7	0	0	2	3,601
Tanwi Spring	5	M	3	1	1	0	21,040	Target Miss	2	F	1	0	0	0	0
Tanya Tooker	5	M	6	0	0	0	336	Target Shoot	3	G	4	1	0	1	37,880

Horse	Age	Sex	Sts	1st	2d	3d	Won
Target Stripes	3	G	8	0	0	0	1,067
Target West	5	H	13	1	0	4	20,908
Targetry	2	F	1	0	0	0	0
Target's Away	6	G	3	1	1	1	13,020
Targets Gold	5	G	22	5	3	1	20,492
Tarheel Boy	4	G	9	1	1	2	9,294
Tarkio	3	G	8	0	0	1	3,010
Tarkovsky	3	G	6	0	2	1	24,040
Tarlow	2	F	3	1	1	0	79,400
Tarnation	5	H	15	1	3	1	6,436
Tarnished	3	C	7	1	0	0	2,936
Tarnished Halo	3	F	3	1	0	0	21,000
Tarnished Reality	10	G	1	0	0	0	0
Tarpon Bay	3	C	7	1	0	1	8,254
Tarrango	3	C	8	2	1	1	21,225
Tarrant County	3	G	2	1	0	0	3,660
Tarratine	7	G	11	3	1	4	23,956
Tartan Tutu	4	F	8	1	0	0	5,730
Taryn's Belief	2	F	3	0	0	0	708
Taryn's Favorite	3	F	1	0	0	0	0
Tarzan Cry (IRE)	5	H	4	1	0	0	23,740
Tarzan d'Monkeyman	8	G	4	0	1	2	5,085
Tarzen	4	G	2	0	0	0	0
Tarzette	7	M	9	2	1	1	12,530
Tasacion	4	F	3	1	0	0	16,620
Tasajara Road	5	G	6	0	0	0	136
Tash Dash	2	F	2	0	0	0	1,800
Tasha Legend	4	F	2	0	0	0	495
Tasha Sangue	3	F	6	1	0	0	13,920
Tasman Glacier	7	H	6	0	0	0	236
Tasmania Miss	3	F	14	1	1	0	13,626
Tasmanian Warrior	10	G	14	1	1	0	6,666
Tasso Run	4	F	13	1	1	3	36,264
Tassosflash	3	G	5	0	0	0	4,212
Tastamundo	6	G	12	3	1	1	11,586
Taste of Hadif	4	F	11	2	2	2	21,754
Taste of Life	5	M	1	0	0	0	44
Taste of Paradise	4	C	7	2	0	0	222,910
Taste Sweet	7	F	1	1	0	0	10,512
Tasting Champagne	2	C	6	0	2	1	26,210
Tasty Caberneigh	5	G	13	3	2	2	92,220
Tasty Chardoneigh	4	C	4	0	1	2	9,050
Tasty Lace	4	F	4	1	1	1	13,130
Tasunka Witko	5	H	1	0	0	0	0
Taswatha	3	F	1	0	0	0	140
Tata Pantoja	4	C	12	2	0	3	12,719
Tata Pelao (CHI)	5	G	12	0	1	1	4,525
Tate Express	11	G	24	3	8	1	19,926
Tate J	4	C	10	3	1	1	9,129
Tate Man	5	G	9	1	2	4	3,616
Tater Chip	5	H	15	4	0	0	14,176
Tater Tate	6	G	8	1	1	1	1,486
Tates Creek	5	M	5	3	1	0	704,067
Tate's Way	5	H	7	2	1	1	43,904
Tatiana B.	3	F	2	0	0	1	546
Tatie Dancer	3	F	1	0	0	0	195
Tatlock	5	G	9	1	0	0	12,046
Tattel Tale	4	F	16	3	2	2	6,491
Tattered Lace	3	F	9	0	0	0	803
Tattletail Charlie	3	G	10	1	1	1	14,850
Tattotail	3	G	7	2	2	0	70,378
Tatty's Tune	3	F	2	0	0	0	182
Tatum	3	C	8	0	2	3	7,025
Tatum Springs	2	C	7	1	1	0	20,699
Tatums Doll	5	M	12	0	1	0	2,240
Tau Ceti (GB)	4	C	4	0	0	0	10,659
Tauke	5	G	9	1	3	0	9,017
Taum Sauk Mountain	5	G	6	0	0	2	2,943
Taurus Gift	3	F	10	1	2	1	12,933
Tavacat	3	G	3	2	0	0	12,600
Tavasco	6	H	2	0	0	0	880
Tavern Time	3	G	3	0	0	0	460
Tavo	2	C	1	0	0	0	42
Tavolino	5	G	8	0	1	0	4,626
Tavy's Plan	3	F	8	2	1	2	52,846
Tawney Port	3	F	5	0	0	0	360
Tax Affair	6	M	2	1	1	0	28,800
Tax Court	6	G	4	0	0	0	304
Tax Dance	3	C	3	0	0	0	150

Horse	Age	Sex	Sts	1st	2d	3d	Won
Tax Day Dancer	4	F	1	0	0	0	70
Tax Deferred	4	C	9	1	2	0	53,665
Tax Evader	2	C	1	0	0	1	4,510
Tax Exempt	2	C	1	0	0	0	2,460
Tax Free	3	F	6	0	1	1	2,110
Tax Relief	8	M	1	0	0	0	0
Tax Write Off	3	G	12	0	0	2	1,558
Taxauditor	5	H	4	2	0	0	6,520
Taxed Out	3	G	18	1	2	1	10,235
Taxi Lady	3	F	2	0	0	0	210
Taxicat	3	C	9	1	4	1	53,700
Tay Laur	5	M	2	0	0	0	1,020
Tayla	2	F	2	0	1	0	2,410
Taylor Brat	4	G	9	1	0	0	3,064
Taylor Creek	8	M	4	1	2	0	2,100
Taylor Dean	4	G	8	0	0	0	1,112
Taylor Field	3	G	3	0	1	1	2,040
Taylor J	3	F	10	3	2	2	38,845
Taylor James	6	G	4	0	2	1	2,250
Taylor L.	4	F	9	1	1	1	6,167
Taylor Man	3	G	14	3	1	2	21,665
Taylorman (NZ)	8	G	12	2	2	1	10,922
Taylor's a Trip	3	F	8	1	2	3	7,673
Taylors Angel	6	M	7	0	1	0	1,361
Taylor's Blues	3	F	12	1	0	2	6,831
Taylor's Brook	2	F	4	0	0	0	590
Taylor's Cap	3	F	6	2	3	0	51,680
Taylor's Chief	2	F	2	0	0	0	0
Taylor's Choice	4	F	8	3	0	0	38,700
Taylor's Comedy	5	G	14	2	2	1	14,574
Taylor's Dancing	5	M	12	1	2	0	1,690
Taylor's Day	9	G	9	4	1	1	52,200
Taylor's Plan	3	F	7	2	0	2	42,260
Taylor's Pride	3	F	5	0	0	0	270
Taylor's Queen	4	F	5	0	0	2	9,090
Taylor's Ryde	5	M	2	0	0	0	0
Taylor's Series	2	F	1	0	0	1	2,400
Taylor's Spring	3	F	10	0	2	1	9,687
Taylor's Ticket	4	G	18	1	3	3	8,834
Taylor's View	3	C	3	0	0	0	828
Taylor's Way	3	F	1	0	0	0	1,260
Taylor's Zag	3	F	9	0	1	1	4,578
Taylortwofeathers	5	G	5	0	1	2	23,684
Taymadalex	3	F	2	0	0	0	330
Taz Diablo	3	C	6	0	0	0	1,134
Tazarr	4	G	8	0	2	1	6,635
Tazmanian Rebel	4	C	7	0	0	1	1,544
Tazotee	4	F	14	3	5	2	96,490
Taz's Treasure	9	G	10	1	4	0	10,101
Taztime	3	F	11	0	0	0	922
Tazzy Oka	2	F	2	0	0	0	0
Tcdinendash	5	G	2	0	0	0	0
Tchefuncte	3	G	11	0	0	2	3,102
Tchepone	4	C	12	1	2	3	10,215
Tchopitioulas	3	F	6	2	0	1	58,694
Tchotchke	4	F	13	2	0	0	7,940
Tchula Miss	4	F	7	2	1	2	78,146
Tcs Express Prince	5	G	12	2	0	2	17,637
Te Akau Five (NZ)	8	G	4	0	2	1	9,525
Te Conquistare	5	G	11	0	1	2	2,881
Te Cuira Mucho	2	F	1	0	0	0	2,730
Te Deum	5	G	2	0	0	0	357
Te Dusty Prospect	3	C	1	0	0	0	65
Te Jay Tejabo	4	C	17	2	1	6	39,309
Te Jw's Prospect	2	C	1	0	0	0	0
Te Quiero Champ (ARG)	6	G	9	2	0	1	36,810
Te Quiero Manana	3	F	10	0	1	0	4,147
Tea and Kippers	4	G	5	0	0	0	308
Tea Basket	4	F	9	2	0	1	5,413
Tea Dance	3	F	3	1	0	0	15,940
Tea Is Served	2	F	4	0	0	0	1,680
Tea Lady	3	F	2	1	0	0	12,040
Tea N Toddy	6	M	15	0	1	1	7,681
Tea Service	2	F	2	0	1	0	5,200
Tea Sipper	5	M	14	2	0	1	15,675
Tea Time Tom	4	C	6	0	0	1	1,051
Tea Time Tomorrow	2	F	3	0	0	0	640
Tea With Coco	4	F	9	0	0	2	2,350
Teachem Kelli	2	F	1	0	0	0	420

RECORDS OF HORSES

Horse	Age	Sex	Sts	1st	2d	3d	Won	Horse	Age	Sex	Sts	1st	2d	3d	Won
Teachers Nightmare	3	F	3	0	0	1	635	Tejabo's Charmer	4	F	2	0	0	0	713
Teaelo	4	G	3	0	0	0	264	Tejabo's Girl	7	M	11	0	0	0	1,725
Teague	4	G	11	2	0	2	24,193	Tejan	6	G	11	0	1	4	22,080
Teak Totem	3	F	6	2	0	0	36,820	Tejana Selena	7	M	2	0	0	1	825
Team Decision	2	F	1	0	0	0	910	Tejano Couture	9	H	19	5	2	3	30,616
Team Player	5	G	6	1	0	0	32,640	Tejano Dandy	2	C	3	0	1	1	4,340
Team Webster	4	F	7	0	0	0	646	Tejano Gal	3	F	11	0	2	3	6,732
Team Zachary	4	C	5	2	1	0	34,252	Tejano Honey	4	F	3	0	0	0	0
Teamaway	5	M	14	1	0	0	3,702	Tejano Rey	7	G	17	1	3	0	8,774
Teamster Joe	5	G	1	0	0	0	0	Tejano Ruler	7	H	8	2	0	3	14,610
Teamup	2	C	2	0	0	0	0	Tejano Tom	2	C	3	1	0	0	15,750
Teanaway Rose	4	F	12	3	3	3	21,713	Tejano Who	3	C	10	4	1	0	15,756
Teardownthatwall	2	F	1	0	1	0	9,800	Tejano's Echo	4	F	15	2	5	3	23,622
Tearful Comedy	4	F	5	2	2	0	17,370	Tejano's Sands	2	F	7	1	0	0	11,620
Tea's Mint Candi	4	F	3	0	0	0	0	Tejano's Son	4	C	10	0	0	1	4,186
Tease n' Delete	3	F	10	1	1	4	7,505	Tejanowoman	7	M	1	0	0	0	0
Teaseme	6	M	10	2	1	3	11,456	Tejas Lady	2	F	2	0	0	0	0
Teasing Arlena	4	F	12	1	0	2	4,718	Tejati	3	F	12	3	3	0	37,980
Teatros	4	G	2	0	0	0	300	Tejavu	4	F	5	0	0	1	1,222
Teazabull	3	F	15	3	6	0	18,195	Tekki	2	G	2	0	1	1	3,567
Teb's Bend	10	G	2	0	0	0	5,000	Teko	4	F	3	0	1	0	9,430
Teche Cowboy	2	G	2	0	0	0	1,572	Telaposa	3	F	2	0	0	0	0
Technical Analysis	2	F	2	0	1	1	11,400	Telefonista	3	F	3	0	0	0	2,325
Technical Question	6	M	13	0	3	3	8,940	Telegraph	7	H	10	2	0	3	7,529
Technickle	3	G	10	1	0	1	15,937	Telegraph Road	5	M	12	1	3	1	34,520
Techno Babble	3	F	10	2	0	0	11,703	Telegraph Trail	3	F	14	1	1	3	9,525
Techno Baby	6	G	11	1	3	0	10,898	Telemark	4	G	5	0	1	0	2,815
Techno Queen	4	F	1	0	0	0	110	Telemundo	3	C	5	1	0	1	14,200
Techno Vision	4	F	4	1	1	0	20,290	Telephone Call	3	F	2	0	0	0	0
Technoblaze	3	C	2	0	0	0	0	Telephone Talker	3	C	10	3	1	1	25,480
Technocat	8	H	1	0	0	0	0	Teleplay	4	C	7	2	3	0	27,075
Technologist	8	M	7	0	0	0	788	Telepsychic	2	F	1	0	0	0	45
Technology's Girl	3	F	1	0	0	0	0	Telescam	5	H	2	0	0	0	405
Ted	4	C	5	0	0	0	960	Tell a Calm	7	G	8	2	0	2	10,852
Ted Ted Ted	4	G	8	0	0	0	690	Tell All	2	F	7	0	0	1	2,890
Teddy Boy	8	H	2	1	0	0	4,400	Tell Belle	4	F	1	0	0	0	0
Teddy Light	6	H	7	3	2	0	10,299	Tell 'Em Off	3	G	8	0	3	2	16,190
Teddy Papa	5	G	10	0	0	2	4,847	Tell J	4	C	10	2	1	0	30,200
Teddykins	5	G	15	1	3	5	5,796	Tell Laura	4	F	10	1	1	2	39,468
Teddy's Girl	3	F	4	2	0	0	12,075	Tell Me Ellie	4	F	4	0	2	1	15,766
Teddy's Pick	5	G	13	2	1	0	18,913	Tell Me I'm Pritt	3	F	2	0	1	1	4,090
Teddy's Shamrock	5	M	2	0	0	0	0	Tell Me Jessie	5	H	4	0	0	0	555
Tedesco	2	C	2	0	1	0	6,000	Tell Me Mr G	3	G	6	1	0	1	4,985
Tee Believe It	3	F	4	0	0	0	0	Tell Me Sweetly	4	F	15	1	2	3	16,125
Tee Cat	5	G	5	1	2	0	68,130	Tell Me True	5	H	8	2	1	0	13,212
Tee El	2	C	1	0	0	0	0	Tell No Secrets	3	F	9	1	1	2	12,327
Tee Jay	3	F	16	1	1	4	17,921	Tell No Tales	3	F	16	5	4	2	52,905
Tee Lease	3	F	12	1	2	2	14,868	Tell One	3	F	4	0	1	1	3,417
Tee Love	3	G	1	0	0	0	0	Tell Tale	2	F	1	1	0	0	7,500
Tee Off Time	3	F	11	0	4	4	32,770	Tell Them Nothing	4	G	4	0	0	0	1,120
Tee Pee Tomahawk	2	F	1	0	0	0	0	Tell Will	3	C	5	0	0	0	0
Tee Phone Home	2	C	2	0	0	0	300	Tell You the Same	4	F	5	0	0	0	142
Tee Punch	3	F	4	0	0	0	503	Tella Soldier	2	C	7	1	0	0	22,040
Tee Times Two	2	F	5	2	2	1	23,423	Tellastory	3	F	2	0	0	0	0
Tee to Green	3	G	13	4	3	2	80,963	Tellek	3	G	11	2	0	3	20,118
Tee Tommy Slew	6	G	11	3	2	2	10,348	Teller Line	4	F	3	1	0	2	17,110
Teebar (AUS)	4	C	2	0	0	0	2,520	Tellheelikeitis	4	F	2	0	2	0	5,940
Teeboo	3	F	5	0	1	1	4,200	Telling Note	3	F	9	0	1	1	1,667
Teed Off	7	H	1	0	1	0	3,000	Tellme Truly	5	M	6	0	1	2	10,430
Teegeecee	5	G	2	0	0	0	213	Tellmeimyours	2	F	3	0	1	0	1,240
Teel Blue	4	F	6	0	0	0	170	Tellmewhatyawant	4	C	4	0	0	2	270
Teela	5	M	11	1	1	1	2,295	Tellyasay	4	F	6	1	2	0	2,588
Teeney Bubbles	2	F	7	0	3	1	16,760	Telmwillysgrlshere	3	F	3	0	0	0	194
Teenie Tally	3	F	4	0	1	0	2,600	Telomerase	4	F	5	0	0	0	337
Teen's Rachael	4	F	11	0	4	1	10,137	Telsi	5	M	10	1	0	3	2,623
Teepee Creeper	3	C	13	4	1	4	46,196	Temagami	5	M	1	0	0	0	0
Teequa	3	F	5	2	0	1	33,350	Tembra	8	M	8	0	0	0	335
Tee's Image	3	F	10	3	0	3	12,523	Temecula Wind	2	G	5	1	1	0	30,400
Tee's Lil Dancer	3	F	5	1	0	0	10,500	Temeritas (IRE)	3	G	5	1	0	1	29,420
Tee's Pearl	2	F	8	2	1	2	56,810	Temerity Plus	6	M	10	0	1	0	2,825
Tee's Tempter	2	C	1	0	0	0	40	Temescal Ridge	2	C	2	0	0	0	0
Teet Jr.	3	G	7	0	0	1	7,270	Temis (CHI)	7	M	10	1	2	1	48,766
Teetau Marie	2	F	1	0	0	0	135	Temperance Eagle	6	G	11	0	1	1	1,894
Teewee's Hope	3	F	9	3	1	2	143,751	Temperance Lake	3	F	9	2	2	2	114,612
Tef's Bashful	3	F	1	0	0	0	0	Temperance Legion	4	G	3	0	0	0	201
Tef's Moxie	4	F	12	0	1	2	7,358	Temperant Lady	7	M	1	0	0	0	0
Tef's Scarlett	3	F	3	2	0	0	15,784	Temperate Lady	4	F	6	0	0	0	229
Tejabelle	5	M	17	3	6	3	35,357	Tempered Appeal	6	H	11	2	1	2	142,546
Tejabo Blues	4	G	8	1	0	2	58,887	Tempered Steel	3	G	5	0	0	3	13,490

Horse	Age	Sex	Sts	1st	2d	3d	Won
Temperence Chief	7	G	4	0	0	0	420
Temperence Time	7	G	14	3	1	0	31,390
Tempers Rising	3	G	20	2	4	2	44,230
Tempest	2	F	1	0	0	0	75
Tempest (GB)	5	H	5	0	0	0	2,257
Tempest Fugit	6	G	4	1	1	2	89,200
Tempest Gladiator	4	F	12	1	3	0	12,329
Tempest Run	3	G	9	1	3	1	32,223
Tempest West	4	G	3	2	1	0	26,130
Tempestry	2	G	5	0	0	0	0
Tempestuous Lady	2	F	1	1	0	0	22,800
Tempestuous Wind	4	C	13	2	5	0	33,113
Templar	4	G	4	1	1	1	12,777
Templar Knight	5	G	9	0	0	3	23,860
Templar Park	6	G	14	0	1	2	2,766
Temple Hall	4	F	4	0	2	0	15,790
Tempo Fer Livin	4	G	4	0	0	0	467
Tempo Up T C	3	G	10	2	2	1	15,703
Temporary Madness	3	F	1	0	0	0	0
Temps Ghostly Star	2	C	1	0	0	0	0
Tempt Her	3	F	12	2	2	3	81,958
Temptable	2	F	2	0	0	0	210
Temptation Bound	7	G	8	0	0	1	1,933
Temptation Lady	2	F	1	0	0	0	145
Temptation Miss	4	F	5	0	2	0	3,450
Temptatious	3	F	7	0	3	2	13,913
Temptest	5	M	9	1	0	4	6,288
Tempting a Ruckus	4	G	5	1	1	1	4,075
Tempting Chance	3	C	1	0	0	0	0
Tempting Choice	4	F	11	2	1	5	57,755
Tempting Eyes	3	F	9	1	1	4	33,148
Tempting Fate	6	G	5	0	0	0	244
Tempting Heart	3	F	10	1	1	1	7,451
Tempting Note	2	F	5	2	1	1	42,570
Tempting Play	3	F	2	0	0	0	130
Tempting Smile	3	F	3	0	0	0	1,425
Temptinglittlemiss	4	F	7	0	1	0	1,645
Temptor Cielo	3	F	2	0	0	0	0
Temptor Man	2	G	1	1	0	0	17,010
Temptor Time	4	F	10	1	0	2	3,816
Temptors Alibi	2	G	4	0	0	0	1,144
Temptor's Darlin	3	F	8	0	0	0	455
Temptors Hit	3	G	12	1	2	2	8,959
Temptors Prodigy	4	G	9	1	0	0	15,052
Temptors Prospect	2	C	7	0	3	2	14,474
Temptors Temper	3	F	2	0	0	1	1,512
Tempura (ARG)	5	M	2	0	0	0	5,400
Tempus Fugit	3	F	8	2	1	0	69,345
Temtor's Pride	3	G	9	1	3	0	12,277
Ten Across	3	G	7	2	1	1	7,620
Ten Alarm Fire	4	G	7	2	1	1	35,068
Ten Carat Ruby	2	F	2	0	0	2	7,350
Ten Cents a Shine	3	C	6	1	0	0	14,040
Ten Connections	3	G	1	0	0	0	182
Ten Dreams	4	F	3	0	0	0	1,020
Ten Flat	5	H	3	0	0	0	7,040
Ten Foot Score	5	M	2	1	1	0	3,200
Ten Forty Easy	3	C	5	0	2	1	11,730
Ten Gallon Bonnet	2	F	3	1	0	1	4,300
Ten Hut	10	G	7	2	2	1	6,869
Ten Inches of Snow	3	C	5	1	0	0	6,360
Ten Kisses	3	F	4	1	1	1	22,080
Ten Mile Girl	4	F	15	2	5	4	20,342
Ten Mitchell	2	C	5	0	0	2	11,170
Ten Most Wanted	3	C	10	4	2	1	1,544,860
Ten o'Clock Watch	3	F	10	1	0	2	5,570
Ten Pound Bay	2	C	4	0	0	0	145
Ten Pound Test	7	G	14	4	2	3	47,471
Ten Queens	4	F	12	3	1	0	34,555
Ten Shades of Red	6	H	3	1	1	1	13,774
Ten Sharp	5	G	13	1	1	2	31,435
Ten Sleeps	6	H	3	0	0	0	225
Ten Something	4	F	11	0	1	2	6,035
Ten Speed	3	F	1	0	0	0	107
Ten Speedy	6	G	6	0	0	0	405
Ten Ten Twenty	4	F	1	1	0	0	5,700
Ten Times Better	2	G	6	2	2	1	79,335
Ten Times Nobility	10	G	9	0	0	1	4,100
Ten Treasures	2	F	2	0	0	0	4,050
Ten Wishes	2	F	1	0	0	0	515
Ten Years Gone	2	G	4	0	0	0	300
Tenace	2	G	4	1	1	0	18,425
Tenacious Affair	5	G	14	5	3	4	55,770
Tenacious Gal	5	M	2	0	1	1	5,360
Tenacious Kat	2	C	1	0	0	0	120
Tenacious Tart	3	F	3	0	1	0	1,880
Tenacious Tigress	3	F	3	0	0	0	0
Tenacious Tinker	3	C	3	0	1	0	372
Tenacious Tish	5	M	8	0	0	0	2,534
Tenacious Value	3	C	10	1	0	1	3,027
Tenafly	5	M	9	4	2	0	38,560
Tenaja Trail	4	G	2	0	0	0	0
Tenantry Road	3	F	8	1	3	1	27,207
Tenaway	4	G	3	0	0	0	208
Tencies Cat	2	G	2	0	0	1	2,970
Tend To	3	G	3	0	0	0	0
Tender Agreement	3	F	2	0	0	0	312
Tender Duet	6	M	6	1	0	1	28,390
Tender Feelings	5	M	8	0	1	2	4,400
Tender Lover	3	G	9	1	2	0	6,272
Tender Offer (IRE)	6	H	7	2	1	0	4,373
Tender Rosemary	5	M	9	0	0	1	1,246
Tender Ship	3	G	3	0	1	1	3,150
Tender Teen	3	F	4	2	1	0	66,800
Tender Toes	3	G	11	2	3	1	23,775
Tender Touch	5	M	10	2	0	1	36,299
Tender Trap	3	F	10	2	1	1	32,860
Tender Value	3	G	20	2	5	3	68,540
Tender Years	2	F	3	0	0	0	2,250
Tenderly (IRE)	4	F	2	0	0	0	0
Tendollaryo	3	G	10	3	2	2	18,892
Tenerumi	6	G	15	4	3	4	50,020
Tenet	2	F	1	0	0	0	0
Tenfortynine	5	H	17	1	6	3	38,447
Tenino	8	G	14	4	0	4	12,608
Tenkiller Tiger	2	G	1	0	0	0	52
Tenma	4	F	2	1	0	1	6,300
Tenmar	5	G	7	0	1	2	3,379
Tennessee Burbin	3	G	7	1	1	0	17,220
Tennessee Bid	3	C	4	1	0	0	6,225
Tennessee Dinner	3	F	12	0	0	2	6,845
Tennessee Tuxedo	5	G	12	2	1	0	17,665
Tennis C. Storm	2	F	3	0	2	0	4,300
Tenor Verse	3	C	10	0	0	0	2,875
Tenpins	5	H	5	2	2	0	512,760
Tensa Debut	2	F	3	1	0	0	10,080
Tensas Bodgit	2	F	5	0	1	0	1,950
Tensas Bolts	4	G	1	0	0	0	585
Tensas Bon Adeau	6	M	1	0	1	0	3,800
Tensas Canyon	6	G	18	3	2	3	13,668
Tensas Joe	5	G	4	0	0	1	1,690
Tensas Lake St Joe	4	G	10	0	2	1	6,515
Tensas Lightning	5	G	1	0	0	0	0
Tensas Sam	5	G	9	2	0	0	6,076
Tensas Sweetheart	3	F	15	1	1	1	24,550
Tensas Teejay	4	F	13	1	1	0	4,300
Tensas Zap	3	G	5	0	0	0	315
Tent City	6	H	1	0	0	0	0
Tententwotwenty	3	C	5	1	2	0	32,650
Tenth of a Cent	4	F	8	0	1	1	1,682
Tenthirteen	3	G	6	1	2	0	45,890
Teolawki	4	F	2	0	0	0	0
Tepid Lover	3	F	7	1	2	1	20,200
Tepu Sultan	4	G	7	0	2	0	36,746
Tequesta	5	C	5	1	0	0	33,120
Tequila Hombre	3	G	5	2	0	1	7,186
Tequila Line	2	F	5	0	1	1	2,685
Tequila Regal	3	G	3	0	0	0	0
Tequila Sunrise	4	F	3	1	2	0	12,244
Tequila Tina	3	F	13	1	1	1	5,722
Tequila Toast	5	G	8	2	0	0	8,558
Tequilacarmenlita	4	F	11	2	0	0	9,564
Tequilla Moon	3	G	16	4	1	3	33,090
Tequiza	4	F	8	2	0	0	7,256
Tera Kitty	7	M	11	2	0	1	15,702
Teralote	3	C	10	0	0	0	4,538
Teresa Ann	4	F	6	0	1	0	11,400
Teresa's Angel	4	F	9	0	4	1	28,120

Horse	Age	Sex	Sts	1st	2d	3d	Won	Horse	Age	Sex	Sts	1st	2d	3d	Won
Teresa's Pride	4	F	3	0	0	0	0	Tewkin	5	M	10	1	2	1	20,647
Teric Croy	3	G	6	1	1	1	19,034	Tewksbury	3	C	1	0	0	0	0
Teri's Wild	2	F	2	0	0	0	0	Tex Appeal	5	G	9	0	0	1	872
Teriyaki Twist	3	F	4	0	1	0	1,553	Tex Maring	3	G	8	2	1	0	16,635
Terlago Pete	5	G	8	0	4	1	2,558	Tex Taco	7	G	12	0	0	1	748
Term	5	G	13	3	2	1	14,095	Texan Storm	4	C	9	3	1	1	35,470
Term in Office	2	C	3	0	0	0	160	Texarkana	4	C	7	1	1	0	17,440
Term Sheet	5	G	7	2	0	1	65,168	Texas Agenda	3	G	9	0	1	2	3,228
Termagnet	5	H	7	1	2	0	13,572	Texas Best	3	C	2	1	0	1	10,980
Terminal	4	G	2	0	0	0	0	Texas Biscuit	2	C	2	0	0	0	0
Terminal Moraine	2	F	4	0	0	1	2,784	Texas Bob	2	G	2	0	0	0	0
Terminar	2	G	2	0	0	0	0	Texas Born	2	G	3	0	2	0	7,020
Termination	3	G	3	1	2	0	32,600	Texas Breakout	4	G	1	0	0	0	261
Termination Dust	4	C	19	1	3	3	46,710	Texas Chili	5	G	8	3	1	2	114,900
Terminator Won	6	G	5	0	2	0	9,313	Texas City Blast	2	F	3	0	0	0	0
Terminkator	3	F	9	0	1	0	4,785	Texas City Star	10	G	10	1	0	0	7,218
Term's Love	3	F	8	0	3	1	8,505	Texas Code	6	G	2	0	0	0	0
Terms of Glory	2	C	1	0	0	0	0	Texas Country	3	C	1	0	0	0	0
Ternespowertakeoff	4	C	1	0	0	1	360	Texas Deputy	2	C	7	2	1	2	61,048
Terr O Sonic	2	C	1	0	0	0	70	Texas Dewdrop	6	M	9	0	2	0	1,650
Terra Cynthus	7	M	5	0	1	0	9,570	Texas Diamond	2	G	2	0	0	0	210
Terra Kate	2	F	3	0	0	1	3,100	Texas Dude	2	G	3	0	0	0	348
Terra Maria	5	M	8	2	1	1	26,209	Texas Dumplin	5	M	12	0	3	1	4,320
Terracotta Cat	4	F	6	2	0	2	9,520	Texas Gold Digger	2	F	2	0	0	1	1,485
Terraforming	8	G	7	0	0	1	814	Texas Heat	5	M	13	2	4	1	40,565
Terra's Charm	4	F	7	2	0	2	11,234	Texas Hill	3	G	5	0	1	0	16,160
Terras Terry	3	G	8	2	1	1	14,130	Texas Holdem	3	G	11	0	1	1	6,118
Terrell	3	C	1	0	1	0	8,800	Texas Honey	3	F	6	1	0	2	9,970
Terre's Tree	6	M	2	0	1	0	344	Texas Ice	4	F	1	0	0	0	0
Terri Tom and A. J.	3	F	7	0	0	0	285	Texas Legend	4	G	6	0	2	1	2,461
Terrible Timmy	6	G	13	2	1	2	10,647	Texas Limit	6	G	14	1	2	2	5,785
Terrievil	3	F	4	0	0	0	545	Texas Lion	4	G	4	1	0	0	4,664
Terrific Beat	8	M	12	0	0	1	1,232	Texas Longneck	5	H	1	0	0	0	0
Terrific Shrimp	3	F	3	1	0	0	3,995	Texas Miss	6	M	8	0	1	0	1,940
Terrific Speed	4	F	6	1	1	1	9,135	Texas Moment	3	C	3	0	0	0	0
Terrified Ice	3	F	5	2	2	0	35,070	Texas Monarch	3	C	1	1	0	0	4,800
Terrifying (IRE)	4	C	1	0	0	0	0	Texas Oasis	4	F	12	3	3	1	39,934
Terris Misty	2	G	2	0	0	0	150	Texas Oil	9	G	4	1	0	1	1,484
Terri's Power	7	G	6	1	0	1	7,322	Texas Orbit	4	G	15	1	2	2	3,049
Terri's Toy	5	M	1	0	0	0	380	Texas Pete	3	G	13	2	4	3	68,455
Terrizing Jones	5	M	2	0	0	0	0	Texas Pioneer	4	G	12	1	3	2	31,095
Terroplane (FR)	2	C	5	2	0	1	33,126	Texas Prez	3	F	8	1	0	0	9,335
Terror Fabulous	2	C	1	0	0	0	0	Texas Princess	4	F	2	0	0	1	250
Terrors Hope	4	G	2	0	0	0	0	Texas Pro	2	C	2	1	0	0	24,600
Terry Dancer	2	C	6	1	1	0	6,150	Texas Prospector	2	F	9	1	1	1	5,305
Terry Kelly	5	G	13	2	2	2	31,430	Texas Queen	2	F	3	0	1	1	6,370
Tersiguels	5	G	5	1	2	1	22,910	Texas Rain	3	C	7	0	0	0	0
Tesla	3	F	6	2	0	1	13,130	Texas Rainbow	5	G	14	1	0	3	7,264
Tesni	4	F	3	0	0	2	2,240	Texas Red	2	C	5	0	2	2	10,080
Tesormo	6	G	5	0	0	0	304	Texas Sandman	6	G	4	0	0	0	166
Tesoro Told	3	F	3	0	0	1	857	Texas Secret	3	F	7	1	1	0	8,899
Tess Trueheart	4	F	7	0	0	0	260	Texas Sky	6	G	9	1	2	0	6,268
Tessarella	2	F	2	0	0	0	390	Texas Special	4	C	8	0	2	2	4,229
Tessa's Heart	4	F	3	0	0	0	264	Texas Style	6	G	16	5	2	2	77,878
Tesse Jo	4	F	8	0	0	1	1,479	Texas Thunder	4	C	7	0	1	2	5,165
Test Dance	3	F	2	0	0	1	1,025	Texas to a T	6	H	7	0	5	1	4,574
Test Drive	4	G	7	1	0	3	15,202	Texas Trail Boss	2	G	1	0	0	0	0
Test of Courage	3	F	10	0	1	0	8,547	Texas Tree	3	F	9	5	0	1	43,620
Test of Time	4	G	5	1	1	0	24,940	Texas Tumbleweed	4	G	6	0	0	0	251
Testa Lady's Event	3	F	4	0	0	0	0	Texasbluedif	2	F	3	0	0	0	1,080
Testame	6	G	10	1	3	2	17,841	Texasourtexas	6	G	9	2	0	2	16,346
Testamento	3	C	18	1	5	1	28,827	Texasquickstepper	5	M	6	1	0	1	4,876
Testhaven	6	G	2	0	1	0	745	Texastoothpick	8	G	10	0	1	1	1,785
Testify	6	G	10	2	2	2	139,975	Texastraveler	6	G	8	1	0	1	10,078
Testing Fate (IRE)	4	G	1	0	0	0	0	Texaway	3	G	18	2	2	2	8,727
Testing the Limit	4	G	8	0	2	2	15,000	Texiano	2	C	3	0	0	1	2,295
Testy Guy	4	G	14	4	2	4	51,579	Texmaman	10	H	3	0	0	0	105
Testy Mood	5	M	4	0	0	0	240	Texmckay	2	G	8	1	1	2	51,396
Testy Roo	7	G	6	1	0	0	1,903	Tex's Trick	5	H	14	1	1	1	13,125
Testy Two	6	M	9	0	3	1	4,121	Textbook	5	H	4	1	0	2	8,225
Tetaslew	7	M	3	0	0	0	212	Textbook Tillie	2	F	5	1	0	2	11,695
Tete's Giggle	2	F	2	0	0	0	1,077	Tez Tarak	6	G	12	1	2	2	10,583
Tetherette	3	F	4	1	1	1	53,816	Thady Quill	6	H	3	1	0	0	73,394
Tethra's Warrior	3	F	3	0	0	0	3,267	Thai's Lively One	8	G	1	0	0	1	300
Teton Echo	5	G	4	0	0	1	556	Thames	3	G	12	3	1	3	69,380
Teton Temptor	5	H	8	2	1	3	3,696	Thames Valley	4	F	7	0	1	0	1,853
Tetons Kaitlyn Jo	5	M	11	1	1	1	2,469	Thanasi	3	C	12	2	1	1	83,884
Tetons Rising Sun	5	H	7	2	3	1	3,121	Thank the Press	5	G	15	3	2	2	41,100
Tevya	3	G	12	2	3	1	9,710	Thank the Stars	4	G	13	0	0	3	2,658

Horse	Age	Sex	Sts	1st	2d	3d	Won
Thank You Dear	4	F	7	1	0	0	7,722
Thank You Mom	2	F	5	0	0	1	2,660
Thank You Montana	6	G	14	3	2	1	14,225
Thank You Sir	5	H	10	0	4	2	66,279
Thankless Child	2	F	4	0	1	0	4,284
Thankourluckystars	5	M	1	0	0	0	965
Thanks Al	2	G	2	0	0	0	240
Thanks Amy	9	M	15	2	1	6	23,625
Thanks Coach	6	H	1	0	0	0	0
Thanks Dr. G.	3	C	1	0	0	1	2,700
Thanks for Nothing	2	F	3	0	2	0	9,600
Thanks for Smokin	2	F	6	1	0	1	13,579
Thanks Franks	7	H	5	1	0	0	4,445
Thanks General	3	G	4	0	0	0	174
Thanks Hajji	3	C	3	0	0	2	13,750
Thankubellagio	2	G	2	1	0	0	8,550
That	3	G	9	1	1	0	8,941
That Allen Thing	3	G	1	0	0	0	1,260
That and This	5	M	13	2	3	1	17,658
That Being Said	5	H	4	0	0	0	272
That Big Tune	8	G	5	0	1	0	2,320
That Bum Charlie	9	G	8	0	3	1	4,922
That Cool Cat	5	G	13	1	2	4	52,270
That Darn Cat	3	G	3	1	0	0	9,925
That Final Answer	4	G	3	0	0	1	1,168
That Gift	6	H	10	1	1	2	16,950
That Girl Madison	4	F	14	1	2	2	11,641
That Hoarse	10	H	2	0	0	0	755
That Holme Man	10	G	13	1	3	1	8,800
That Is True	4	C	6	0	0	0	204
That Monetary	8	G	15	2	2	4	22,557
That Phat Cat	3	G	8	1	0	1	11,000
That Smith Girl	4	F	9	1	3	1	9,046
That Tat	5	G	9	5	2	1	201,700
That Wild Thing	3	F	6	0	0	0	574
Thatkrazzymissphit	6	G	1	0	0	0	105
That'll Work	8	G	7	2	1	1	9,790
That's a Cat	2	G	6	0	0	1	2,893
That's a Command	3	C	4	0	2	0	6,410
Thats a Foxy Lady	3	F	3	0	1	1	7,220
That's a Gimme	7	H	4	0	0	0	647
Thats a Match	3	F	8	1	0	0	6,067
That's a Nice Bet	12	G	10	0	1	3	2,287
That's American	3	F	6	1	1	0	15,585
That's an Outrage	2	C	8	1	0	2	83,880
That's Annie	2	F	1	0	0	0	0
Thats Another Song	2	F	3	0	2	0	3,371
That's Creative	5	G	10	1	1	0	9,653
Thats Cute	5	M	5	3	0	1	17,070
Thats Final	5	H	8	1	1	0	1,504
Thats How It Goes	4	F	9	2	0	1	23,261
That's Julia	6	M	5	0	0	0	690
That's Just Ducky	5	H	8	1	0	1	11,570
Thats Just George	10	G	2	0	0	0	156
That's Latin	7	G	3	0	0	0	295
That's Lucky	9	G	9	0	2	1	4,778
That's Me	4	G	17	1	4	3	20,184
That's Me Boy	2	F	4	0	2	1	7,580
That's My Babe	3	F	2	0	0	0	1,818
Thats My Buck	2	C	1	0	0	0	0
Thats My Daddy	5	H	11	2	2	3	53,115
That's My Line	2	G	6	0	0	1	1,255
That's My Luck	6	G	9	0	0	0	875
That's Nana's Boy	4	C	2	0	0	0	1,040
Thats No Bull	2	G	2	1	0	0	7,620
That's No Halo	4	G	5	1	1	0	3,345
That's Otis	4	G	7	0	1	0	3,404
That's Our Daisy	4	F	11	1	0	1	6,694
That's Our Gold	4	F	16	1	1	4	18,153
That's Our Jack	2	C	3	0	2	0	10,590
That's Our Pic	7	M	5	0	0	0	1,254
Thats Our Queen	4	F	5	0	0	1	1,956
That's Our Tricky	4	F	1	1	0	0	13,500
That's Outrageous	6	M	12	1	1	1	12,277
That's R Glory	3	F	2	0	0	0	325
Thats Some Baby	4	F	2	0	0	0	144
That's That Mister	3	G	14	2	3	0	28,450
That's the Berries	3	G	11	2	0	0	30,515
Thats the One	5	G	5	0	0	0	682

Horse	Age	Sex	Sts	1st	2d	3d	Won
Thats the Problem	4	G	6	3	1	0	133,346
That's the Story	3	F	3	0	0	0	370
That's Tricky	3	C	4	0	0	3	5,070
Thatsadoablething	4	G	9	0	0	0	152
That'sahandfull	3	C	4	1	1	0	3,140
Thatsallmon	4	C	17	1	1	4	28,797
Thatsitnthatsall	4	C	2	0	0	1	600
Thatsmygeorgiegirl	3	F	7	1	3	2	8,812
Thatsmyway	4	F	9	3	0	1	14,175
Thatsoneroyalchic	4	F	13	0	1	1	6,094
Thatspowerfulstuff	4	G	11	1	0	1	3,920
Thatsthe Fact Jack	2	C	5	0	0	1	3,055
Thatsthebottomline	5	G	2	0	0	0	166
Thatswhatshesaid	5	M	8	0	0	2	4,493
Thaw	5	G	3	0	2	0	2,430
Thawed	2	F	1	0	0	1	1,200
The Animas	4	G	5	0	1	4	5,260
The Annswer	4	F	8	0	2	1	3,681
The Answer Is No	3	G	1	0	0	0	387
The Band Plays On	2	F	4	1	0	0	8,580
The Barker	6	H	1	0	0	0	450
The Barking Shark	10	G	2	1	1	0	7,975
The Best Defense	8	M	1	0	0	0	105
The Best of Me	2	F	1	1	0	0	7,200
The Best of Times	4	C	2	0	0	0	700
The Best Sister	6	M	9	1	3	3	11,379
The Big Blond	6	M	15	1	5	3	8,464
The Big Cat	6	H	1	0	0	0	0
The Big Devil	3	C	7	0	0	0	902
The Big Edict	2	C	3	0	0	0	324
The Big L. T.	3	C	2	0	0	0	146
The Big Macaw	3	C	3	1	1	1	8,350
The Big Muddy	5	G	7	2	1	0	34,144
The Big O	5	G	12	1	3	4	16,071
The Big Ugly	3	F	9	2	1	1	10,213
The Bird Is Wired	3	G	8	0	1	0	2,888
The Black Monk	3	G	8	2	1	0	11,650
The Blank Vanman	4	C	6	3	0	1	45,150
The Blue Hole	2	F	1	0	0	0	0
The Boggie Man Can	3	G	9	0	4	1	22,453
The Bold Bruiser	7	H	12	2	0	1	19,036
The Boogie Man	3	G	11	1	0	4	9,298
The Boomer	4	G	3	0	0	0	0
The Borg Queen	3	F	12	4	3	0	91,980
The Boy's Babe	6	M	3	0	0	0	0
The Brass Peach	3	F	1	1	0	0	6,300
The Breeze	6	G	6	0	0	0	338
The Brew's a Flyin	4	G	2	0	0	1	640
The Bruce (NZ)	6	G	2	0	1	1	7,000
The Buggy Whip	4	G	5	0	2	0	4,460
The Buzz Express	2	C	2	0	0	0	0
The Call Stands	2	G	1	0	0	0	630
The Candi Kid	6	G	6	1	0	1	5,888
The Candi Queen	4	F	16	3	5	2	116,188
The Candy Queen	4	F	20	0	0	2	3,758
The Carrs Running	4	G	7	1	1	0	3,685
The Castle	3	F	8	1	1	3	35,360
The Cat and I	3	G	12	1	0	2	18,233
The Cat Steps Out	4	C	3	0	0	0	0
The Cats Back	6	G	22	4	1	5	9,288
The Cat's Out	6	M	6	0	1	1	3,380
The Cat's Tail	2	C	8	1	0	1	14,620
The Cat's Turn	4	F	8	0	4	0	3,642
The Chancer	5	G	7	0	0	1	1,967
The Chang	7	G	2	0	0	0	1,020
The Chosin Few	7	G	3	0	0	1	1,250
The Chubster	4	G	21	1	2	1	7,169
The Clarkster	3	F	7	0	0	1	1,439
The Cliff's Edge	2	C	5	3	1	0	255,258
The Clown	3	C	11	4	0	2	65,450
The Cluny Clipper	3	G	1	0	0	0	0
The Cobra Special	3	G	19	2	2	4	9,999
The Coffin	5	G	6	4	0	0	16,190
The Comissioner	2	C	2	0	0	0	0
The Comus Kid	3	G	3	0	0	0	0
The Cooksville Kid	4	G	11	3	1	0	42,310
The Cool Grape	6	H	2	0	0	0	750
The Count	5	H	11	2	1	1	24,620
The Craftsman	3	G	10	0	4	4	19,070

Horse	Age	Sex	Sts	1st	2d	3d	Won	Horse	Age	Sex	Sts	1st	2d	3d	Won
The Crag	3	C	8	0	1	0	2,814	The Indy Ripper	5	M	9	2	0	2	6,120
The Crystal Kid	4	G	5	1	1	1	1,839	The Invasion	8	G	12	3	2	1	12,517
The Cushite Woman	3	F	10	0	0	0	3,060	The Irish Nun	5	M	17	3	4	1	16,874
The Dallas Dancer	4	F	3	0	1	1	6,233	The Ironworker	4	G	11	2	2	2	55,200
The Dancer	7	H	13	2	3	1	13,050	The Issue Is Power	11	G	9	2	1	2	22,102
The Dark Night (FR)	3	G	6	0	2	1	24,880	The It Girl	2	F	1	0	0	0	0
The de Gray Flash	6	M	2	0	0	1	454	The Jeckle	4	F	1	0	1	0	3,200
The Dempsey Look	2	F	2	1	1	0	31,000	The Jet Wave	4	C	6	0	1	0	4,496
The Denver Dream	6	G	3	0	1	0	3,800	The Jeweler	4	G	5	1	1	0	1,762
The Deputy Is Home	5	H	5	1	1	1	44,520	The Judge Jose	4	G	4	1	0	0	9,660
The Devil 'n Honey	5	G	3	0	0	0	0	The Judge Sez Who	4	C	4	0	0	1	105,600
The Divas Judge	3	F	4	0	0	0	519	The K O Touch	2	F	2	0	0	1	4,950
The Docmeister	2	C	5	1	0	1	11,052	The Kandaly Kid	3	C	7	3	0	1	19,885
The Dr. Is a Lady	6	M	1	1	0	0	18,600	The Kaprikorn Kid	8	H	2	0	0	1	1,845
The Dream Is Alive	4	G	6	1	0	0	11,500	The Karakorum Rush	5	G	9	1	1	1	5,184
The Dream Lives	3	G	6	1	0	1	18,578	The Katy	4	F	5	0	0	0	816
The Duker	6	G	14	0	0	2	4,674	The Key to It All	3	G	2	0	0	0	300
The Dustman	6	H	3	0	0	0	1,680	The King Is Alive	3	G	17	0	0	0	3,858
The Editor's Son	4	G	6	1	0	1	11,900	The King N Rob	3	G	6	2	0	1	45,755
The Eighth Wonder	3	F	6	1	0	0	20,144	The Knife Speaks	7	G	3	1	0	0	7,750
The Emster	2	F	2	0	0	0	2,520	The Known Q	2	F	3	1	1	0	12,850
The Energizergirl	5	M	4	0	1	1	1,581	The Lady Excavate	5	M	11	1	3	2	43,077
The Evil One	3	G	2	0	0	0	0	The Lady Is a Fox	3	F	2	0	0	0	0
The Falcon	4	G	7	0	1	0	8,944	The Lady Is Red	4	F	2	1	1	0	10,800
The Fat Man	3	C	9	2	0	0	36,770	The Lady Roars	3	F	8	2	1	0	23,890
The Field General	4	G	14	1	0	2	5,357	The Lady's Groom	3	C	12	4	2	0	97,700
The Fifth Element	6	M	15	1	3	2	54,933	The Lamp Is Lit	2	F	1	0	1	0	8,200
The Fighting Chief	3	F	8	2	0	1	20,254	The Last Flower	7	H	5	0	0	1	3,014
The Final Toy	2	F	6	1	0	0	5,450	The Law of Seattle	3	C	17	2	0	2	21,525
The Finnish Cap	3	F	8	0	0	0	360	The Lawyer	3	G	3	0	1	0	4,200
The First Secret	5	H	1	0	0	0	0	The Lewster	3	C	6	0	2	2	6,905
The Flag Stands	3	F	14	1	1	5	6,068	The Lights Are On	5	G	7	0	1	0	5,035
The Flirt Is On	2	F	3	0	0	0	330	The Lion's Intern	4	F	4	0	1	0	1,570
The Flying Victory	3	F	9	3	1	1	23,467	The Little Boy	6	H	12	0	0	1	1,098
The Forham Flush	3	F	3	1	1	0	7,587	The Little Cat	3	G	11	2	1	3	9,718
The Fourth Ace	4	C	1	0	0	1	620	The Lizard Lady	4	F	3	0	0	1	580
The Fox Rocks	3	G	9	0	0	2	1,755	The Loop	4	G	4	0	0	0	649
The Friendly Ghost	3	G	10	2	2	1	39,846	The Looper	3	G	7	0	1	2	21,095
The Full Molly	4	F	4	0	0	0	0	The Lord Is Eager	5	G	10	2	1	2	4,473
The Fuse	5	M	2	0	0	0	2,880	The Lord's Club	3	G	9	1	0	2	10,105
The Fuse Is Lit	3	F	9	1	1	1	6,576	The Lovliest	5	M	4	0	0	1	1,223
The Fuzz	2	G	4	0	1	2	7,210	The Maccabee	7	G	7	1	1	0	33,270
The Garbage Man	5	G	14	7	1	3	51,743	The Mad Bear	4	C	9	2	0	2	21,106
The General's Bank	4	G	10	1	0	0	10,560	The Madison Man	6	G	13	2	3	2	25,747
The General's Lady	3	F	1	0	0	0	0	The Magic Lives On	7	M	7	0	0	1	1,502
The Generator	4	C	8	0	0	0	0	The Mailman	4	G	9	0	1	1	5,807
The Gin Game	3	F	3	1	0	1	16,700	The Man	3	C	7	1	1	1	23,990
The Gold Clove	2	C	1	0	0	0	0	The Man Himself	6	G	14	0	1	3	7,185
The Golden Floss	4	G	13	3	1	2	21,576	The Master's Word	4	G	2	0	0	0	0
The Golden Gent	8	G	8	0	2	0	3,005	The Menehounie	4	G	8	1	2	1	37,162
The Gooch	4	G	13	1	0	2	7,767	The Mercer Man	4	G	7	1	0	0	4,504
The Goodbye Girl	9	M	8	0	0	0	330	The Midnight Skier	2	G	4	1	0	0	5,040
The Grand High Ho	4	F	16	4	3	2	72,715	The Mighty King	4	G	8	0	2	1	17,100
The Gray Eagle	5	H	2	0	0	0	450	The Mill	5	M	9	0	1	0	9,160
The Gray Mile	3	G	1	0	1	0	5,240	The Minkster	3	G	3	1	0	0	12,022
The Gray Spur	5	M	15	1	2	0	9,102	The Mobile Man	4	C	3	0	0	1	9,360
The Great Aga	4	F	9	0	2	0	4,752	The Mold	2	G	1	0	0	0	120
The Great Buzzenie	2	C	1	0	0	0	0	The Morris Monroe	7	G	2	0	0	0	0
The Great Catsby	2	F	1	0	1	0	8,200	The Mosquito	5	G	8	1	1	0	7,265
The Great Dimaggio	5	G	16	0	3	2	5,252	The Mother Load	4	F	10	0	3	0	10,370
The Great Gilby	4	G	10	0	0	2	6,236	The Mutt	6	G	11	1	2	2	19,262
The Great Lar	4	G	2	0	0	0	0	The Name Was Gone	3	F	7	2	1	1	110,495
The Great Lover	4	C	2	0	0	0	141	The Name's Bond	3	C	9	5	1	0	201,850
The Great Mogul	3	G	4	0	2	0	8,690	The Name's Joshua	2	G	2	0	0	0	73
The Great Tony	4	C	8	0	2	0	1,384	The Names Kelsey	3	F	2	0	0	0	0
The Green Wave	7	M	2	0	0	0	258	The Names Niki	4	F	15	3	2	0	14,280
The Greene Man	3	G	11	2	0	0	20,340	The Name's Peanut	3	G	1	0	0	0	70
The Gregster	3	G	8	1	1	1	8,413	The Name'sdanzel	6	M	2	0	0	0	288
The Greyling	5	H	8	0	0	1	5,350	The Navy Man	3	C	1	0	0	0	0
The Griff	5	G	4	0	1	1	11,550	The Next Storm	4	F	6	0	0	1	2,955
The Hanging Judge	3	C	3	0	2	0	9,255	The Night Ridder	3	C	4	0	1	1	2,707
The Hard Way	5	G	7	2	2	1	11,520	The Niner Account	5	H	5	5	0	0	37,800
The Hat Is Back	7	M	15	0	1	1	3,191	The Novelist	8	G	9	2	1	2	13,635
The Heats On	9	G	8	2	1	1	5,234	The Nurse	6	M	1	0	0	0	118
The Heavy	6	H	8	1	1	1	6,989	The Ocala Flash	2	C	1	0	0	0	0
The Herc	2	C	7	3	2	0	118,435	The Odds I Love	2	C	3	0	0	0	422
The Hibb	4	C	9	0	1	0	1,508	The Old Ennui	5	G	8	1	0	0	3,258
The Hoedown Kid	6	H	15	2	3	1	16,627	The Old Hero	2	G	7	1	0	0	22,590
The Hot One	4	F	8	0	0	1	1,118	The One We Kept	2	F	1	0	0	1	1,100

Horse	Age	Sex	Sts	1st	2d	3d	Won
The Other Ghost	9	G	1	0	0	0	0
The Other Max	4	C	1	0	0	0	0
The Other Me	4	C	8	2	0	0	9,600
The Other One	6	G	17	2	1	1	9,917
The Parties Over	4	F	6	3	1	1	117,528
The Parting Glass	6	M	1	0	0	0	380
The Party Chairman	7	G	4	1	0	1	3,240
The Penny Drops	2	G	5	0	2	3	30,141
The Peoples Champ	3	G	7	0	0	0	92
The Percussionist	2	C	1	0	0	0	0
The Phantom Fuhrer	3	G	3	0	0	0	603
The Piper	6	G	1	0	0	0	0
The Plains	3	C	4	0	0	0	0
The Polski Prince	2	G	2	0	0	0	1,620
The Poseur	6	G	9	2	3	0	46,060
The Potters Hand	3	G	8	1	1	1	6,595
The Prez	4	G	15	0	3	5	12,196
The Pride of Dixie	2	G	2	0	0	0	600
The Prince of Fun	3	C	3	0	0	0	0
The Principal Man	4	G	7	1	1	2	11,735
The Punisher	5	G	8	0	0	1	946
The Purple Swarm	3	G	5	0	0	1	3,002
The Queen of Class	5	M	8	1	1	0	5,608
The Queen's Doc	2	G	7	0	4	0	10,010
The Quin Man	3	C	13	0	0	0	1,923
The Rain Is Gone	4	F	7	1	0	1	22,425
The Real Boss Man	3	G	8	2	1	1	16,210
The Real Jewel	5	M	15	5	1	2	52,990
The Real Odysseus	3	C	1	0	0	0	132
The Real Zeal Deal	4	C	13	0	1	1	2,216
The Red Danger	4	C	3	0	0	0	123
The Reign Review	7	H	8	1	0	0	2,593
The Reminator	8	G	19	1	1	4	6,246
The Right Call	5	G	5	0	0	1	704
The Right Fit	6	M	6	2	0	2	24,543
The Right Orbit	5	G	5	1	0	0	780
The Right Prize	4	G	13	1	0	1	5,728
The Riz Kid	4	C	2	0	0	0	730
The Road Boss	2	C	2	0	0	1	3,120
The Rodeo Express	3	F	5	1	2	1	45,633
The Rogue	5	H	21	2	0	4	38,523
The Roscoe Rumble	6	G	4	0	2	1	1,604
The Rum Runner	3	G	7	0	1	3	4,644
The Running Sioux	6	G	17	1	1	3	7,278
The Sarge	5	G	17	3	2	2	18,449
The Seahorse Two	3	G	12	5	1	0	38,915
The Seth Bomber	3	G	12	3	1	3	22,385
The Sewickley Kid	4	G	3	0	0	0	3,060
The Sherminator	3	G	10	1	0	1	41,695
The Silver Rod Kid	2	C	2	0	1	0	8,580
The Skelligs	3	G	11	3	1	3	21,430
The Smoothe Groove	4	F	7	2	1	0	37,780
The Soph	3	F	2	0	0	0	0
The Spirit Runner	3	F	4	0	0	0	528
The Springs	4	F	3	1	0	0	3,720
The Standard	3	G	5	1	1	1	39,950
The Star of Bohrer	3	C	7	0	0	0	1,582
The State	4	C	3	0	0	1	7,840
The Station	5	G	9	0	0	2	5,595
The Stigmata	3	F	13	3	2	1	25,132
The Storm Trackerr	4	G	22	1	5	4	14,342
The Strider	3	C	7	0	0	0	195
The Strodebrothers	3	G	13	1	2	1	14,261
The Strong One	3	G	5	0	1	0	580
The Student (ARG)	4	C	4	1	0	1	32,070
The Suave Commoner	2	G	4	1	0	0	10,939
The Time Is Now	2	G	1	0	0	0	75
The Tin Man	5	G	6	1	2	0	440,840
The Toast of Troy	3	F	7	0	0	0	3,700
The Toff	10	G	10	0	1	1	3,233
The Toolman	5	H	9	0	0	2	3,535
The Tricky Doctor	6	H	2	0	0	0	330
The Truth Hurts	5	H	2	0	0	0	0
The Usual	2	F	4	2	0	0	55,400
The Valiant Prior (IRE)	10	G	14	0	2	2	3,550
The Vids Kid	5	G	9	1	0	0	3,720
The Vilzak Kid	5	G	12	2	2	3	4,525
The Vincent Edward	3	C	4	0	0	0	750
The Voice (CHI)	5	M	1	0	0	0	0
The Warden's Prize	2	C	2	0	0	0	390
The Way Holme	7	G	13	2	2	2	23,726
The Weej	2	G	1	0	0	0	0
The Weez	8	G	12	0	3	0	4,347
The White Sun	5	G	8	3	1	0	50,280
The Wicked Fleet	4	G	1	1	0	0	3,120
The Wicked King	7	G	1	0	0	0	38
The Wicked Rose	4	F	1	0	0	0	0
The Wild Joker	7	G	2	1	0	0	1,815
The Wilder Side	4	F	3	0	0	0	507
The Wildest Rose	7	M	7	1	1	2	11,235
The Wine King	4	C	11	2	2	0	18,947
The Wiz Biz	5	G	13	2	1	1	17,552
The Woman in Black	5	M	4	0	1	0	14,208
The Wonder of You	4	G	10	2	4	1	22,058
The World Moved On	4	G	9	3	0	0	9,441
The Wrong Face	2	F	1	0	0	0	1,195
The Zach	4	C	1	0	0	0	0
The Zamp	5	H	2	0	0	0	0
The Zeal Deal	2	F	6	0	0	0	192
Theartfuldutchman	4	C	8	2	0	1	27,952
Theater R. N.	3	F	2	2	0	0	52,800
Theaterfest	8	G	14	0	2	1	1,928
Theatre Script	5	G	4	0	0	1	1,575
Theatre Thunder	4	G	4	1	0	1	1,218
Theatrical Affair	4	F	2	0	0	0	0
Theatrical Dancer	3	F	9	2	0	1	7,478
Theatrical Dawn	3	F	6	0	0	1	1,962
Theatrical Mark	4	F	8	0	0	0	540
Theatrikate	3	F	8	0	0	1	2,159
Thebannerflies	3	F	1	0	0	0	0
Thebigapple	4	G	6	1	2	0	56,556
Thebigbrushoff	3	G	10	0	0	5	12,080
Thecatbelongstome	4	F	11	3	0	1	22,328
Thecatinthespat	3	F	1	0	0	0	590
Theconfidenceman	2	C	4	1	0	1	29,880
Thecrazyminstrel	5	H	4	0	0	0	1,260
Thecrowdgoeswild	2	C	3	0	0	0	606
Thedevilinme	2	F	5	1	1	1	20,270
Thedominantfemale	3	F	4	0	0	0	2,001
Theflash	2	F	1	0	0	0	145
Thefull Circle	4	C	9	1	3	2	69,660
Thegirlsgotrhythm	5	M	11	2	3	0	15,870
Thegooddieyoung	5	G	6	0	1	2	13,060
Thegreatblissqueen	8	M	2	0	0	0	355
Thegreatschapiro	3	G	6	1	0	0	7,110
Thegrlfromyestrday	3	F	20	3	2	2	65,040
Thehighestbidder	7	H	9	0	1	0	2,085
Thehoneymoonsover	4	F	8	2	0	1	31,390
Theirelandexpress	3	F	2	0	0	0	176
Thekatsmeow	2	F	4	0	0	1	720
Thekingsqueen	3	F	5	0	0	2	11,933
Thekus	3	G	2	0	0	0	0
Theladyisholy	2	F	2	0	0	1	1,045
Thelady'saplayer	2	F	3	0	0	0	708
Thelast McKinty	7	H	5	0	1	0	1,287
Thelastword	2	C	6	0	0	1	1,687
Thelight Fantastic	4	F	5	1	1	0	9,135
Thelightsareon	2	G	6	0	1	0	1,970
Thelionshare	2	C	5	0	0	0	1,061
Thelittleirishman	2	G	1	0	0	0	0
Thelma's Beauty	2	F	7	1	0	1	11,120
Thelmas Sheikh	6	G	3	0	0	0	0
Them Thar Hills	4	F	8	2	2	2	17,551
Themanfromlincoln	2	G	1	0	0	0	413
Themanwiththebigcigr	7	G	5	2	0	0	9,395
Themoonshiner	4	G	20	3	4	1	26,198
Themus	3	F	9	0	1	1	10,670
Then She Laughs	2	F	5	1	0	2	34,060
Then Today Always	2	F	2	0	0	0	4,191
Thenameismolly	4	F	7	1	0	0	1,650
Thendara's Diamond	3	F	1	0	0	0	125
Theoakportduchess	4	F	3	0	0	0	187
Theodore's Devil	9	G	22	3	1	3	17,351
Theology	3	F	3	1	1	0	29,920
Theoriginalmrsimon	3	C	6	0	0	0	875
Theo's Saint	3	C	2	0	0	0	220
Thepostman	6	H	6	0	0	1	1,144
Theprideofoklahoma	3	G	2	0	0	0	115

Horse	Age	Sex	Sts	1st	2d	3d	Won
Theprinceofperu	5	H	10	2	0	0	9,943
Theprospectisababe	2	F	2	1	0	0	16,920
Therapy	5	H	10	1	0	1	8,448
Theratpackisback	3	C	5	0	0	1	638
There and Back	3	F	9	1	0	2	22,316
There Goes Nick	6	G	15	4	1	2	20,540
There Goes Rocket	2	C	6	4	1	1	199,500
There Runs Hattie	4	F	10	2	1	1	77,761
There You Go	8	G	13	0	0	4	4,213
Therecanbeonlyone	5	G	12	3	2	3	43,728
Thereisatigerahead	5	M	16	3	5	3	15,330
There's Hope Sir	4	C	12	2	1	1	24,140
Theres No Tomorrow	6	M	5	0	0	1	2,435
Theres Nohalo Onme	3	G	3	1	1	0	9,080
Theres Our Money	4	G	10	2	1	1	17,164
Theres Trouble	5	M	19	2	1	2	10,358
There's Waldo	4	G	3	0	0	0	345
There's Zealous	5	G	3	0	1	1	24,180
There'sa Catch	5	H	6	2	1	0	10,710
Theresa the Terror	3	F	10	0	0	1	1,329
Theresagirlnmysoup	4	F	1	0	0	0	120
Theresa's Memo	3	F	1	0	0	0	2,940
Theresa's Year	4	F	4	0	1	0	23,160
Theriverrunsgold	3	C	11	1	0	0	6,710
Therlo	6	G	11	3	2	2	10,504
Thermal Ablasion	4	F	11	3	2	2	126,241
Thermal Tay	3	F	14	1	2	1	9,471
Thermo Rocket	3	G	4	0	0	0	141
Thermopylae	5	H	14	3	4	2	73,569
Thermostat	2	C	3	0	0	0	150
Thermostatic	4	F	7	2	1	2	62,840
Thesecondwarrior	3	C	3	1	0	0	24,600
Thesis	5	H	2	1	0	0	3,720
Thesmellofhoney	2	F	4	1	1	1	22,010
Thesonofthesun	5	H	2	0	0	0	0
Thessaly	3	C	11	1	3	3	33,845
Thestormhascleared	3	F	17	2	2	3	46,843
Thesullivanfive	4	F	13	1	2	0	11,170
Thesyntaur	3	G	6	0	0	0	2,170
Thetactics Ofdance	2	F	1	1	0	0	21,540
Thetribehasspoken	2	G	8	0	1	4	4,615
Thewrightway	3	F	7	0	1	0	2,250
They Call Me Cody	5	G	7	3	2	1	97,835
Theycallmecolonel	6	H	18	7	3	1	15,326
Theyjustdontgetit	4	G	7	2	1	0	7,180
Th'girls Grand	3	F	3	0	0	0	47
Thick as Thieves	6	G	14	3	2	2	70,268
Thick Headed	3	F	3	0	0	0	960
Thickett's Ticket	4	C	8	1	2	0	5,510
Thief of Time	5	G	5	0	1	0	1,581
Thief River	4	C	8	0	1	1	1,025
Thiefs Hollow	4	G	1	0	0	0	50
Thieves Tactics	6	G	10	1	2	3	5,210
Thieving	3	F	11	4	1	1	51,740
Thimbleful of Gold	5	M	12	1	0	1	5,637
Thimble's Legacy	3	F	9	0	1	1	3,732
Thin Air	2	F	3	0	2	1	19,790
Thin Ice	4	G	6	1	0	1	6,437
Thin Man	3	G	6	0	1	2	2,244
Thing You Do	3	G	18	1	3	1	10,365
Think Big	2	G	3	0	0	0	380
Think Caper	3	G	14	1	2	2	14,290
Think Fast	4	F	9	1	2	2	24,123
Think Gold	3	F	1	0	0	1	1,375
Think Jazz	3	G	9	1	1	0	26,360
Think Mink	7	G	9	1	3	0	8,448
Think Pink	2	F	1	0	0	0	0
Thinkinabout Elvis	9	M	12	0	1	2	3,599
Thinking Irish	5	G	19	1	3	3	10,773
Thinkinofyoulou	4	C	6	2	0	0	13,530
Thinkinonit	7	G	9	0	1	1	2,340
Third Avie	5	G	6	1	0	1	1,280
Third Collection	3	F	9	2	1	2	73,920
Third Cousin	3	F	8	1	1	2	17,921
Third Crusade	5	H	6	0	1	1	4,925
Third Day	2	C	3	1	0	0	92,739
Third Gear	2	G	3	0	1	0	4,460
Third Half	3	G	7	1	3	2	66,220
Third Marine	4	C	3	0	1	0	875
Third Musketeer	3	C	3	1	0	0	4,775
Third Note	3	G	2	0	0	0	140
Third Prospect	4	F	3	0	0	1	2,480
Third Sacker	2	C	7	0	1	4	109,073
Third Shift	7	G	3	0	0	0	570
Third Shift Gal	2	F	1	0	0	0	70
Third Son	3	G	13	0	1	0	3,320
Third Time	4	C	5	1	1	0	5,168
Third Try	4	F	1	0	0	0	0
Third Wish	6	G	13	1	7	4	27,470
Thirdown Call	3	G	6	2	1	0	33,944
Thirsty Lulu	3	F	11	1	4	1	37,570
Thirty Eight Quest	8	G	14	0	3	0	6,964
Thirty Eight Tempo	6	H	1	0	0	0	0
Thirty Five Angels	3	G	2	0	1	0	4,600
Thirty One E.	8	G	5	0	1	0	843
Thirty One Jewels	2	F	2	0	0	0	115
Thirty One Jones	4	G	8	1	0	2	9,014
Thirty One Kisses	4	F	1	0	0	0	73
Thirty Six Hours	7	G	13	0	0	0	1,511
Thirty Six Reasons	4	C	8	0	0	1	749
Thirty Six Ten	4	C	7	1	0	0	4,478
Thirty Two Inside	7	M	1	0	0	0	40
Thirtyfivthirtyfor	3	C	10	1	2	2	13,354
Thirtythree O Nine	6	G	8	1	0	0	4,540
Thiruvengadam	2	G	4	1	0	1	14,510
This	3	G	5	0	1	0	1,160
This Books for You	3	G	8	1	1	1	12,000
This Brews Foryou	3	G	2	0	0	0	76
This Case Is Over	3	F	2	0	0	0	75
This Cat Can	5	M	8	1	1	2	30,008
This Cat Can Hunt	3	C	5	0	0	0	544
This Cat Can Run	2	C	2	1	0	1	5,250
This Cat Will Do	3	C	9	2	2	1	16,565
This Cats a Flying	7	G	13	0	3	0	9,850
This Cat's for You	3	C	13	7	3	1	158,581
This Cats Smokin	2	G	2	1	0	0	26,400
This Crime Pays	2	F	5	0	1	1	5,204
This Day Is Mine	4	F	9	1	2	0	12,600
This Fleet Is Due	5	H	4	0	0	1	9,410
This Guns for Hire	4	C	6	0	3	1	32,100
This Hicks Abeauty	4	G	7	2	1	2	14,271
This Is Bob	6	G	5	1	0	2	4,128
This Is Doc	3	G	6	1	1	1	12,192
This Is for Gran	2	F	4	0	0	0	993
This Is Fun Time	5	M	10	1	0	1	2,783
This I Know	4	C	5	2	2	1	20,080
This Is It	2	F	1	0	0	0	145
This Is My Account	4	C	5	0	0	0	444
This Is That	2	C	1	0	0	0	5,400
This Is Trouble	5	H	8	1	0	1	2,806
This Is Unreal	4	F	1	0	0	0	75
This Little Piggy	5	G	8	1	0	0	7,973
This Lord's a Lady	3	F	7	0	1	1	4,785
This Man's Darling	3	F	5	1	0	2	10,132
This N That	3	C	2	1	0	0	11,400
This One for Abbey	2	F	3	1	0	0	15,015
This One Won	3	G	10	0	2	3	4,976
This Slew Flew	3	F	11	1	1	0	38,338
This That N Other	5	G	6	1	0	0	4,638
This Train	8	M	11	0	3	2	3,952
This Tune Rocks	4	G	9	1	1	1	1,910
This Won	4	G	8	1	1	1	14,820
Thisaway	4	G	3	0	0	0	126
Thisbucksforyou	4	F	18	3	6	2	20,102
Thisbucksnoactor	7	M	9	0	1	1	10,721
Thiscannonsloaded	4	C	7	2	1	0	42,590
Thiscatskrafty	3	G	7	2	2	0	13,605
Thisdevilcanfly	4	C	16	3	2	1	8,695
Thisgigsover	3	C	4	1	0	0	10,120
Thisgirldontlaugh	2	F	1	0	0	0	1,195
Thisishowitis	7	M	8	0	2	3	3,301
Thisisit Adam	5	G	4	0	0	0	1,500
Thislilgirlcanrun	4	F	13	0	0	0	7,925
Thisoneisforujohn	5	G	8	0	0	1	816
Thisone'sfornernie	7	G	1	0	0	0	320
Thisonesforjerry	4	F	10	1	1	3	12,428
Thisonesforjoan	3	F	12	2	2	1	9,811
Thisonesformysis	2	G	6	0	0	1	3,280

Horse	Age	Sex	Sts	1st	2d	3d	Won
Thisracalsready	9	H	5	1	0	0	6,256
Thisrobyncanrock	4	F	2	0	0	0	498
Thisstrodesforyou	3	F	6	1	1	0	8,149
Thistles and Roses	3	G	4	0	0	0	493
Thomas B. Lucky	2	G	1	0	0	0	0
Thomas Crown	5	H	5	0	0	1	4,232
Thomas F	3	C	8	1	0	1	4,635
Thomas Has Promise	3	G	4	0	0	0	490
Thomas J	6	G	8	0	1	0	1,743
Thomas the Cat	3	G	7	2	0	1	15,285
Thomas's Ladybug	4	F	2	0	0	0	0
Thomenator	4	G	7	0	4	0	5,710
Thompson Gee	3	C	9	0	1	0	10,663
Thompson Rouge (IRE)	4	C	7	1	1	0	55,000
Thong	3	F	11	1	4	2	62,970
Thor Thors	12	G	3	0	0	0	2,750
Thorn Cat	6	H	1	0	0	0	360
Thorndale	7	G	12	1	3	1	16,244
Thorne in My Side	3	G	1	0	0	0	216
Thorne Road	3	C	3	0	0	0	223
Thornhill	2	F	7	2	0	0	49,975
Thornwood	2	C	5	0	1	0	6,350
Thoroughbabe	8	M	8	1	0	2	11,768
Thor's Fury	3	G	2	0	0	0	456
Thor's Revenge	4	G	4	0	0	1	1,965
Thought I Did	4	C	2	0	0	0	0
Thoughtful Girl	3	F	9	0	2	0	3,770
Thoughtful King	2	C	1	0	0	0	0
Thoughtfully	2	F	3	0	0	0	0
Thourougly Blue	3	G	7	0	0	0	1,025
Thousand and One	3	F	6	0	0	0	1,060
Thousand Secrets	8	M	7	0	2	1	4,185
Thread of Hope	2	G	6	0	0	0	480
Thread the Needle	7	M	7	1	1	0	12,294
Threat of Victory	4	G	13	4	6	0	70,620
Threaten	3	F	9	0	0	1	3,990
Three Amigos	6	G	4	0	0	0	300
Three B Bobbi	2	F	5	0	1	3	9,130
Three Bags Full	4	G	16	1	1	3	8,410
Three Banks	3	C	6	0	0	2	2,462
Three Carat	3	C	4	1	1	1	18,480
Three Cats	5	H	3	0	0	0	0
Three Chances	6	G	21	2	1	4	13,730
Three Charlie Two	7	H	4	0	0	0	616
Three Counties	4	G	10	1	0	1	12,857
Three C's	5	M	4	0	0	0	320
Three Day Bullet	4	F	8	2	2	1	10,899
Three Franks	2	G	6	2	1	0	16,320
Three Jack	4	C	12	0	3	1	25,900
Three Johns	6	G	2	0	0	0	0
Three Ladies Man	4	G	13	3	1	0	32,410
Three Little Words	7	M	12	4	3	1	14,680
Three Marks	2	G	2	0	0	0	0
Three Mile Creek	2	F	3	0	1	0	2,600
Three Mysteries	2	F	2	0	1	0	2,800
Three Oaks	4	C	1	0	0	0	0
Three Peaks	3	F	3	1	1	0	12,174
Three Penny Opera	4	F	2	0	0	0	900
Three Punch Louie	3	C	10	1	4	2	23,695
Three Rags Rappin	4	G	12	0	0	2	2,584
Three Ref's Girl	3	F	11	2	2	0	13,610
Three Rivers	3	G	5	0	0	0	343
Three Roses	3	F	4	1	0	1	34,239
Three R's	4	G	11	0	1	1	2,728
Three Sevens	9	G	15	3	1	1	16,100
Three Sheets	3	G	2	0	0	0	0
Three Sixes	5	G	10	0	0	0	1,228
Three Sixteen	4	C	2	0	0	0	113
Three Springs	4	C	8	0	1	2	5,175
Three Sticks	4	C	8	1	1	2	23,080
Three Strikes	4	G	11	2	2	1	26,250
Three Taps	2	G	3	0	1	0	15,642
Three Tee Three	3	F	1	0	0	0	700
Three Times	6	H	4	0	0	0	544
Three to Tango	4	G	6	1	1	0	10,129
Three Toms	6	G	8	1	3	0	1,962
Three Wonders	6	H	1	0	0	0	400
Threefingertony	4	C	10	0	0	2	4,399
Threeinone	2	C	2	0	0	0	0

Horse	Age	Sex	Sts	1st	2d	3d	Won
Threeninetytwo	3	F	1	0	0	0	780
Threepointer	7	G	9	0	0	3	5,355
Three's a Charm	7	M	9	0	2	1	4,854
Threewishesforme	5	G	14	6	2	3	55,836
Threewitt	3	G	15	2	6	1	23,525
Threshold	9	G	13	2	3	2	14,266
Threw It All	4	G	10	0	0	1	1,016
Thrift Plan	4	G	9	1	2	2	32,615
Thrifty Nickel	6	H	9	1	0	1	3,224
Thrill After Dark	3	F	4	2	0	0	26,338
Thrill of My Life	2	F	2	0	0	0	0
Thrill the Crowd	5	G	4	1	0	0	5,187
Thrillbound	9	M	1	0	0	0	150
Thrillin Discovery	8	G	9	1	1	0	12,180
Thrilling	3	F	2	0	0	1	1,320
Thrilling Request	4	F	6	1	1	1	5,230
Thrillisgone	3	F	11	2	2	1	17,162
Thrillogy	7	H	1	0	0	0	0
Thrilluponthrill	5	M	1	0	0	0	214
Thrive	6	H	7	1	0	1	16,435
Throbbin Robin	6	G	6	2	1	0	41,190
Throne	3	F	6	0	1	2	22,270
Trophy Wife	5	M	10	1	0	1	2,437
Through His Kid	2	C	4	0	0	0	882
Throw	7	H	9	2	1	3	9,935
Throw Her In	4	F	4	1	0	0	5,100
Throw Me Out	5	G	4	1	0	0	21,930
Throw Me Roses	4	F	5	1	2	0	55,420
Throwatizzylizzy	3	F	8	3	0	1	16,856
Throwin Heat	5	G	3	0	2	1	24,960
Thru the Mill	5	G	1	0	0	0	0
Thruitall	6	G	16	0	1	5	9,118
Thrust N Throttle	3	G	7	0	0	0	1,677
Thrym	4	C	4	0	1	0	7,700
Thug's Honey	2	F	1	0	0	0	230
Thumbsupfredrick	3	G	7	0	1	0	2,020
Thumper Bumper	2	F	4	0	0	1	1,664
Thumpers Gold	3	G	11	3	0	3	16,514
Thunder Alert	6	H	5	1	1	2	13,078
Thunder and Rain	4	F	7	1	0	2	35,735
Thunder Atsunrise	4	C	2	0	0	0	291
Thunder Babe	3	F	11	2	1	3	38,500
Thunder Bey	5	G	1	0	0	0	0
Thunder Bid	4	G	10	0	0	0	5,406
Thunder Blitz	5	H	8	2	3	1	143,720
Thunder Boot	4	G	11	5	0	0	86,610
Thunder Bull	5	G	11	3	0	3	86,339
Thunder Bullet	4	G	9	5	1	0	189,764
Thunder Buster	5	H	1	0	1	0	1,600
Thunder Chief	6	G	7	3	0	3	77,190
Thunder Dance	4	F	9	1	1	0	8,475
Thunder Days	4	G	3	0	0	1	3,970
Thunder Dragon (IRE)	7	G	13	0	0	1	5,637
Thunder Fire	5	G	11	2	0	2	18,320
Thunder Fish	6	G	1	0	0	0	0
Thunder Force	4	C	3	0	1	0	13,280
Thunder Ghost	5	G	8	1	2	0	16,495
Thunder Girl	3	F	2	0	0	0	0
Thunder Gold	4	C	3	0	1	0	4,844
Thunder Gulch Girl	2	F	3	0	1	0	6,540
Thunder Gus	4	G	2	0	0	0	1,050
Thunder Hawk	4	C	2	0	0	0	152
Thunder Jam	5	M	12	2	2	2	17,705
Thunder Jammin	3	C	14	1	0	0	8,850
Thunder Kat	5	M	1	0	0	0	0
Thunder Mac	4	C	15	3	2	2	10,642
Thunder Matt	7	G	9	1	0	0	9,914
Thunder N Bolts	2	G	4	0	0	1	9,487
Thunder Punch	8	G	14	2	3	2	13,622
Thunder Puppy	3	G	2	0	0	0	0
Thunder Quest	4	G	10	2	1	2	38,510
Thunder Rain	2	G	3	0	0	1	2,400
Thunder Reason	2	F	1	0	1	0	3,000
Thunder Rider	6	G	18	1	4	2	17,682
Thunder River	4	C	7	1	1	0	6,623
Thunder Rock	4	C	9	1	0	1	5,397
Thunder Rocket	5	G	8	1	2	0	61,039
Thunder Rollin	4	G	3	0	0	1	662
Thunder Run	3	G	10	0	0	0	1,128

Horse	Age	Sex	Sts	1st	2d	3d	Won	Horse	Age	Sex	Sts	1st	2d	3d	Won
Thunder Sands	5	M	7	0	1	1	12,435	Tidings	3	C	4	0	0	0	516
Thunder Score	3	C	4	0	0	0	819	Tidy Mack	2	G	1	0	0	0	596
Thunder Session	4	F	5	1	0	1	4,349	Tidy Sweet	5	M	1	0	0	0	65
Thunder Squall	3	C	7	1	0	1	23,920	Tidy's Mood Is War	2	F	1	0	0	0	120
Thunder Strikes	2	C	1	0	0	0	195	Tie Break	2	C	1	0	0	0	91
Thunder Twice	6	G	6	0	1	0	5,880	Tie de Sietes (PER)	5	M	2	0	0	0	110
Thunder Wave	4	C	2	0	0	0	100	Tie Pin	9	G	4	0	0	0	544
Thunder Zoot	5	G	14	2	4	3	12,810	Tieaknotnholdon	5	G	14	1	0	1	6,110
Thundercase	3	C	1	0	0	0	0	Tied in Knots	3	C	10	1	0	0	14,280
Thundering Herd	4	G	6	0	1	0	1,430	Tied to the Mast	3	C	3	0	0	0	680
Thundering Home	5	H	6	1	0	0	5,170	Tiedintwine	3	C	14	4	1	3	39,049
Thundering Paces	4	C	7	1	2	1	22,350	Tiempo Del Sol	4	G	9	0	1	1	4,856
Thundering Verzy	2	G	4	3	0	0	15,330	Tienneman Square	4	C	8	2	2	1	45,364
Thundering West	5	G	16	1	3	1	6,764	Tiercel	5	H	5	1	0	0	15,050
Thunderinthehills	6	G	6	0	0	2	4,916	Tiered	2	C	3	0	0	0	0
Thunderinthesky	4	C	6	1	1	0	1,936	Tierra Del Sol	5	M	8	0	0	1	1,159
Thundermann (AUS)	6	H	10	1	2	1	62,620	Tieta	4	F	9	3	1	0	46,496
Thunderoll	7	G	10	1	1	1	5,194	Tietjen	2	C	4	0	0	1	1,170
Thunderontherocks	4	F	3	1	0	0	3,798	Tiffa	5	M	9	1	1	2	7,607
Thunder's Echo	3	F	5	1	0	0	49,220	Tiffany Case	5	M	10	3	1	0	13,021
Thunder's Lit'nin	5	M	14	1	2	1	6,069	Tiffany Gold	5	G	12	3	1	2	13,084
Thunders Luck	6	G	4	0	0	0	450	Tiffany Ice Queen	5	M	9	0	2	0	2,540
Thunders On	6	H	5	1	1	0	3,870	Tiffany Jennifer	3	F	5	0	0	0	5,206
Thunder's Slew	4	G	2	0	0	0	1,260	Tiffany Ridge	3	F	6	0	1	2	4,504
Thundershower	4	G	18	1	3	2	12,062	Tiffany Rivers	3	F	1	0	0	0	0
Thunderstorm	4	C	10	1	0	2	16,720	Tiffany Tower	3	F	11	1	1	2	8,400
Thunzarr	6	G	8	0	0	2	5,240	Tiffany's Dancer	3	F	7	1	3	0	10,625
Thurber	3	G	4	0	0	0	166	Tiffany's Rodeo	2	F	3	0	0	0	0
Thurston	5	G	6	0	1	1	4,262	Tiffany's Talk	5	M	1	0	0	0	0
Thutmosis	3	G	1	0	0	0	217	Tiffany's Time	4	F	2	0	0	0	56
Thy Fare Lady	5	M	9	0	1	1	2,145	Tiffany's Wish	4	F	5	0	0	0	170
Thy Will Be Done	4	F	1	0	0	1	620	Tiff's Bonzai	4	F	11	2	2	3	27,875
Thyer's (BRZ)	7	H	2	0	0	0	1,796	Tiffy T	5	M	1	0	0	0	0
Thyme After Thyme	5	G	2	0	0	0	92	Tiffy's Pleasure	3	F	6	0	1	0	1,839
Ti Amo Mama	3	F	3	0	0	0	0	Tifice	5	M	7	0	3	0	2,748
Ti Neches	2	F	1	0	0	0	100	Tifonica (ARG)	5	M	9	2	1	4	91,123
Tia Maria	5	M	4	1	0	1	9,348	Tifton	5	M	10	3	0	3	20,020
Tia Marquetry	4	F	14	1	4	1	17,064	Tiger Babe	6	M	6	0	0	0	3,550
Tia Sesa	5	M	10	1	1	0	5,556	Tiger Bone	3	C	1	0	0	0	0
Tiajuana Tour	3	G	8	1	3	3	19,522	Tiger Brush	3	C	5	1	3	0	12,856
Tialinga	2	F	3	0	1	0	8,730	Tiger Catress	3	F	7	1	2	1	15,791
Tianna Road	5	M	2	0	0	0	320	Tiger Corner	8	H	7	0	2	2	5,524
Tiara Gin	2	F	2	0	0	0	124	Tiger Fan	3	F	2	0	0	0	335
Tiara Time	4	F	10	1	3	1	29,103	Tiger Flash	2	C	2	0	0	0	250
Tia's Miss	2	F	1	0	0	0	0	Tiger Grunk Again	2	G	4	0	0	0	170
Tia's Orphan Annie	8	M	20	2	0	2	12,830	Tiger Hawk	7	G	5	0	0	1	582
Tibado	9	G	11	1	1	2	10,595	Tiger Heart	2	C	2	1	1	0	36,705
Tibbs	5	G	20	1	3	2	14,611	Tiger Hunt	2	C	4	2	1	0	312,820
Tiber Tiger	4	C	9	2	0	1	20,415	Tiger Hunter	2	F	7	1	0	0	6,540
Tic N Tin	8	G	13	2	3	0	45,501	Tiger Mac	7	G	12	1	3	2	6,003
Tic Tac Man (AUS)	3	C	2	0	0	0	0	Tiger Mania	5	G	13	2	3	0	20,312
Tick Taat	4	G	9	1	0	3	16,003	Tiger Moon	7	H	12	1	0	1	7,806
Tick to the Wire	3	C	9	0	0	2	2,151	Tiger Run	4	C	7	1	3	1	2,816
Tickel Me War	5	M	6	0	0	0	0	Tiger Shrimp	3	G	8	1	0	2	45,112
Ticker Tape (GB)	2	F	8	2	3	1	108,351	Tiger Six	7	G	9	1	4	1	40,802
Tickers Diamonds	3	F	3	0	0	0	244	Tiger Slew	5	G	13	4	1	0	48,590
Ticket to Drive	3	C	3	0	0	0	137	Tiger Squad	5	H	11	0	0	0	2,728
Ticket to Freedom	6	G	11	0	1	1	22,560	Tiger Talent	2	C	1	0	0	0	0
Ticket to Fun	6	G	6	1	1	0	8,686	Tiger Tap	4	G	8	0	0	1	1,263
Ticket to Paris	4	C	4	0	1	0	9,682	Tiger Tiger Tiger	3	F	2	0	0	0	610
Ticket to Saratoga	3	G	12	1	2	1	6,897	Tiger Time	4	G	14	2	1	4	3,930
Ticketed	4	G	4	1	2	1	5,368	Tiger Tower	6	G	4	1	0	0	5,670
Tickin	4	F	1	0	0	0	0	Tiger Town	4	G	6	0	0	0	2,520
Ticking Red	3	C	6	0	0	0	862	Tiger Walk	8	G	1	0	0	0	0
Tickle Me Malmo	5	M	11	6	0	1	15,909	Tigerish	7	H	3	0	0	0	3,040
Tickle Me Red	7	G	20	1	8	6	30,070	Tigermite	4	F	13	1	2	1	19,910
Tickle Me Too	5	M	16	4	4	2	20,624	Tigermountain Road	5	H	2	0	0	0	65
Tickle the Ivories	4	G	14	1	0	6	12,384	Tiger's Edition	6	G	15	2	1	1	11,324
Tickled	5	M	2	0	0	0	237	Tiger's Fool	3	C	1	0	0	0	120
Tickled Purple	3	G	5	1	0	1	14,627	Tiger's Halfmoon	4	F	4	1	0	0	26,460
Tickles	4	F	8	1	0	1	31,830	Tiger's Paw	3	G	3	0	0	0	0
Tickles Prince	9	G	4	0	0	0	0	Tiger's Reign	5	M	9	0	0	1	8,770
Tickletime	4	G	5	1	1	0	11,330	Tiger's Silverlady	4	F	3	1	0	0	7,806
Ticklish One	4	F	16	1	2	1	9,040	Tigertail (FR)	4	F	8	0	2	1	535,164
Tickortwo	3	F	2	0	0	0	90	Tigerwood	3	C	3	0	0	0	0
Ticling Doc	4	C	9	0	0	1	577	Tigger Bay	2	G	5	3	0	1	89,461
Tidal Crest	5	M	3	0	0	0	0	Tight	3	G	4	0	0	0	420
Tidal Wave	3	C	12	4	2	4	90,340	Tight Chaps	6	H	10	0	1	1	1,480
Tidbits	5	G	10	3	2	0	31,075	Tight Rope	5	H	1	0	0	0	0

Horse	Age	Sex	Sts	1st	2d	3d	Won
Tight Security	3	F	8	1	0	2	10,970
Tight Wager	3	C	3	0	0	0	2,100
Tight Wire	5	M	6	1	1	0	6,510
Tightasamousesear	4	F	11	1	1	1	10,185
Tighten Up	6	G	14	2	3	3	15,511
Tighten Up Todd	6	G	12	0	0	1	1,671
Tigi	2	F	5	1	1	1	39,060
Tigress Bythetail	3	F	10	5	1	0	90,848
Tigress Six	3	F	3	0	0	0	0
Tigress Woods	4	F	11	1	0	0	27,298
Tigrina	5	M	5	2	0	0	7,072
Tijiyr (IRE)	7	H	5	0	1	0	11,580
Tijuana Brass	5	M	1	0	1	0	2,100
Tijur	3	C	3	0	0	1	1,650
Tika's Best	3	F	1	0	0	0	810
Tiki Tiki	2	C	2	1	0	0	11,160
Tikkun (IRE)	4	G	4	0	0	0	0
Tildafatladysings	2	F	4	1	0	0	17,849
Tillie Taylor	7	M	10	0	0	1	1,235
Tillie's Victor	7	G	4	0	3	1	8,000
Tilly Wagon	10	G	5	0	0	1	1,028
Tilt Luci's Odds	3	F	3	0	0	1	2,036
Tilt On Thejukebox	3	G	12	2	3	2	23,246
Tilt Time	2	F	1	0	0	0	0
Tilting Star	4	F	6	1	0	1	8,305
Timber Ack	10	G	7	1	2	2	7,420
Timber Baron	7	G	3	1	1	0	41,200
Timber Cowboy (JPN)	3	C	1	0	0	0	40
Timber Creek	2	G	4	1	1	0	14,220
Timber Cruiser	4	G	8	2	1	2	91,400
Timber Kitty	5	M	10	2	3	1	28,060
Timber Legend	4	C	5	1	0	1	25,440
Timber Roo	6	M	4	0	0	0	830
Timber Thunder	6	G	4	0	0	0	460
Timber Turn	4	F	3	0	1	0	6,000
Timbergreen	3	G	10	2	0	1	7,558
Timbers Two	4	G	7	2	2	0	28,965
Timberwolf Power	5	G	7	1	1	3	36,045
Timboruck	10	G	8	0	2	3	13,212
Timbos Dande	5	G	5	1	0	1	13,667
Time At the Line	5	G	8	1	0	1	7,380
Time Chief	5	G	10	2	0	2	10,383
Time Chopper	5	H	9	1	2	1	14,570
Time Counter	2	C	5	1	0	0	13,524
Time Digger	5	M	5	0	0	1	1,095
Time Eternal	4	C	7	1	0	2	6,440
Time Field	2	F	1	0	1	0	1,340
Time for a Blue	3	F	1	0	0	0	0
Time for a Heart	3	F	5	2	2	0	29,410
Time for a Prize	8	G	9	0	0	2	1,808
Time for a Tour	3	C	4	0	0	0	300
Time for a Win	4	F	2	0	0	0	120
Time for Ice	2	F	1	0	0	0	0
Time for Liberty	4	G	7	3	1	1	50,550
Time for Magic	2	F	5	1	0	0	6,250
Time for Minor	5	G	8	3	1	1	19,090
Time for Music	3	F	11	0	0	2	4,236
Time for Peaches	3	F	11	0	1	1	7,948
Time for Philip	3	G	12	2	0	1	4,632
Time for Ruby	6	M	6	1	1	1	4,387
Time for Scotty	3	G	9	1	0	1	10,018
Time for Smiles	4	F	6	1	0	1	1,795
Time for Tappy	3	G	14	1	0	5	13,070
Time for Victory	3	F	6	0	1	1	1,867
Time for Wine	10	G	15	2	4	2	36,098
Time Goes Fast	3	F	7	0	1	0	1,877
Time Gonnif	2	C	4	1	0	1	16,420
Time Honored	3	F	4	1	0	3	22,560
Time Is Fleeting	3	C	4	0	0	0	100
Time Is Gold	6	G	7	1	0	0	3,273
Time Is Money	5	M	13	2	4	0	51,335
Time Lea Season	4	F	3	0	1	0	1,010
Time Lock	3	F	12	2	1	2	19,950
Time Lord	9	H	1	0	0	0	80
Time of the Lepus	9	G	1	0	1	0	720
Time of Truth	4	G	12	1	0	2	21,865
Time of War	3	C	6	2	1	0	131,554
Time On the Run	5	G	13	1	2	1	9,247
Time Punch	4	G	5	0	0	1	6,970
Time Raider	3	G	2	0	0	0	1,519
Time Release	6	G	5	0	0	0	0
Time Simon	4	C	3	0	0	0	225
Time to Be Bold	4	F	6	1	1	1	3,885
Time to Be Sassy	4	G	6	1	0	0	7,047
Time to Blaze	2	F	1	0	0	0	0
Time to Call	2	C	6	0	0	0	320
Time to Di	6	M	13	1	1	1	8,850
Time to Dyne	4	C	7	1	1	2	20,330
Time to Enjoy	3	F	3	0	0	0	4,500
Time to Flare	6	H	21	4	7	2	28,125
Time to Frolic	3	F	8	1	1	1	5,073
Time to Jazz	4	F	5	1	0	0	7,920
Time to Jet	5	G	2	0	0	0	625
Time to Laugh	3	F	3	0	0	1	1,724
Time to Live	3	F	11	3	5	0	91,080
Time to Market	5	M	1	0	0	0	0
Time to Mine	3	G	12	0	1	2	3,505
Time to Please	3	G	12	1	1	0	18,650
Time to Rush	3	F	7	0	1	1	11,016
Time to Sail	6	G	3	0	0	0	1,056
Time to Start	3	C	3	0	0	0	133
Time to Strike	4	C	5	0	1	2	12,070
Time to Tell	5	G	1	0	0	0	0
Time to Weave	4	G	7	2	1	1	6,835
Time Two Come	4	F	1	1	0	0	1,525
Timeaday	5	G	14	2	1	5	13,710
Timeandahalf	2	G	1	1	0	0	8,800
Timeandtimeagain	3	C	3	0	0	0	106
Timebanks Baby	5	M	7	0	1	0	510
Timed	3	C	2	0	0	0	265
Timed to a T.	7	M	8	1	1	0	32,833
Timeforabud	5	G	7	0	0	0	1,560
Timeforamakeover	3	F	3	0	0	0	0
Timeforjewels	2	G	2	0	0	0	425
Timeform	3	G	9	1	2	3	44,439
Timeforyou	2	F	3	0	1	0	3,190
Timeframe	6	G	10	2	0	2	8,928
Timeinthecountry	8	G	4	0	1	0	2,690
Timeless	5	G	7	0	0	1	1,986
Timeless Charm	3	F	6	1	0	0	7,920
Timeless Deed	4	G	10	2	0	2	16,600
Timeless Dreamer	2	F	2	0	0	0	0
Timeless End	6	H	5	1	1	0	3,950
Timeless Glory	2	F	4	0	0	0	1,050
Timeless Love	4	F	11	2	2	0	91,055
Timeless Luv	3	G	18	1	5	1	29,394
Timeless Music	3	F	6	1	0	0	2,425
Timeless Note	5	H	3	0	1	1	2,982
Timeless Order	2	F	4	1	0	0	11,500
Timeless Poetry	2	F	2	1	0	0	7,229
Timeless Road	4	F	3	0	0	0	0
Timeless Search	4	F	8	1	5	1	13,090
Timeless Star	4	C	2	0	0	0	248
Timeless Sweep	4	C	4	0	0	0	112
Timeless Zeal	4	G	11	3	1	3	25,649
Timeliano	3	F	9	0	1	3	24,359
Timely	5	M	10	0	0	1	1,115
Timely Action	4	C	3	1	0	0	31,140
Timely Call	3	G	3	1	0	0	4,900
Timely Deed	3	G	1	0	0	0	0
Timely Devil	6	H	11	0	1	0	2,145
Timely Ending	5	G	18	5	2	0	59,380
Timely Factor	5	H	11	3	1	1	14,572
Timely Fortune	4	C	9	1	0	2	8,150
Timely Half	4	G	2	0	0	0	0
Timely Jeff	3	G	1	0	1	0	9,360
Timely Minister	6	H	9	0	2	1	8,744
Timely Oak	5	G	13	3	3	3	19,317
Timely Perfection	3	F	9	1	1	0	5,151
Timely Presence	5	M	3	0	0	0	0
Timely Reign	3	G	9	0	3	3	9,828
Timely Reminder	3	C	2	0	0	0	103
Timely Romance	3	C	3	2	0	0	10,113
Timely Ruckus	10	G	8	1	2	0	28,040
Timely Silver	5	M	7	1	1	3	7,419
Timely Stitch	10	G	11	2	0	1	5,982
Timely Toss	3	F	9	2	0	1	7,930
Timely Weave	6	G	10	5	1	0	30,137

RECORDS OF HORSES

Horse	Age	Sex	Sts	1st	2d	3d	Won	Horse	Age	Sex	Sts	1st	2d	3d	Won
Timely Whistle	3	G	3	0	0	1	1,195	Tiny Irish Dancer	5	M	10	0	1	1	2,424
Timely Writer	3	G	12	1	0	2	23,380	Tiny Katie	4	F	2	0	0	1	845
Timemaker	5	G	2	0	0	0	0	Tiny Lee	4	F	10	0	0	0	1,251
Timequake	6	G	4	0	0	0	280	Tiny Patrica	2	F	4	0	1	0	2,880
Times Change	5	G	10	1	0	2	8,715	Tiny Pink Pannies	6	M	10	1	2	1	11,987
Times Flight	5	M	5	0	0	1	1,346	Tiny Tilt	3	F	3	0	0	0	530
Times Like These	3	F	2	1	0	0	5,525	Tiny Tim	4	G	10	1	2	2	10,865
Times Square	3	F	4	0	0	0	733	Tiny Wonders	3	F	2	0	0	0	244
Times Thief	5	G	1	0	0	0	0	Tiny's Harper	2	G	3	0	0	0	2,170
Timesafleeting	6	G	12	1	3	1	9,403	Tiny's Warrior	3	C	2	0	0	0	0
Timesarollin	3	C	16	1	3	1	12,558	Tio Cavito (CHI)	6	G	14	2	4	4	67,034
Timescape	5	G	3	0	0	1	2,325	Tio Fidel	2	C	1	0	0	0	2,284
Timetime	2	F	2	1	0	0	6,660	Tio Lupe	4	C	11	3	2	0	77,540
Timeto Riot	6	G	4	1	1	0	1,300	Tio Titi (ARG)	7	H	7	0	0	1	2,643
Timetobwild	4	G	15	1	0	2	9,454	Tioga Lake	3	G	14	3	7	2	101,210
Timetoknowyou	4	G	9	2	3	1	17,075	Tip Away	2	G	4	0	0	0	0
Timetoprofit	7	G	4	1	1	0	3,160	Tip Included	2	C	3	0	0	0	165
Timetoshuffleoff	2	G	1	0	0	0	0	Tip My Cap	6	G	7	0	0	0	860
Timetotax	3	G	8	0	2	0	3,208	Tip the Man	5	M	1	0	0	0	0
Timetotrimthetree	4	G	10	0	1	0	2,095	Tip the Scale	6	M	3	0	0	0	2,850
Timing's the Key	5	G	15	2	0	2	6,222	Tipalou Honey	3	F	8	0	0	1	1,099
Timken	2	G	2	0	0	0	360	Tipaza	4	F	10	1	1	0	4,127
Timmeran	4	C	10	3	0	0	22,560	Tipfield	7	G	10	0	4	2	2,604
Timmy B.	4	C	7	0	0	0	0	Tipical Pipp	5	G	6	0	1	1	7,710
Timmy Boy	5	G	7	1	1	1	3,762	Tipie Time Slew	6	G	3	0	1	0	548
Timo	2	C	5	3	2	0	153,515	Tiplersville	2	F	1	0	0	1	700
Timoa Blossom	4	F	16	1	0	0	5,431	Tippa Tippa Tae	5	M	13	2	1	4	12,441
Timopocus	4	G	5	1	0	2	36,250	Tippecanoe	3	C	2	0	0	0	700
Timothy B.	3	C	1	0	0	0	0	Tipper Kelly M. D.	3	F	15	2	1	1	33,050
Timothy Mac	5	G	16	5	5	2	79,344	Tipping	2	F	2	1	1	0	10,500
Timpanogos	3	F	9	1	1	0	1,913	Tipping Lightly	4	F	12	1	3	2	13,965
Tim's Best	7	G	10	0	0	2	3,571	Tipping Point	4	G	6	3	2	1	16,478
Tim's Boy	5	H	2	0	0	0	0	Tipping the Hat	3	C	3	0	0	0	0
Tim's Hat Trick	3	C	4	1	2	0	15,600	Tippy Won	5	G	19	1	4	3	21,124
Tim's Talent	4	C	1	0	0	0	520	Tippyourhattojoe	3	F	10	0	0	3	5,474
Tim's Tuition	3	G	5	2	1	1	12,626	Tippytoebyme	3	C	3	1	1	0	6,474
Tin and Tonic	4	G	13	2	2	3	26,188	Tip's Red Rod	4	C	17	1	1	2	9,291
Tin Can Sailor	2	C	3	3	0	0	104,426	Tip's Secret	2	C	5	0	0	1	2,265
Tin Eye	3	G	2	0	0	0	754	Tipsey Tali	5	M	3	0	0	0	0
Tin Man Commin	3	G	7	2	2	0	29,675	Tipsy Indy	2	F	3	0	0	1	5,040
Tin Pan Man	3	C	15	1	3	6	10,816	Tipsy Lady	5	M	6	0	0	5	4,095
Tin Smithen	6	G	9	4	1	1	36,500	Tipsy Logic	4	C	5	0	1	0	7,134
Tin Star	5	H	10	1	1	2	9,217	Tipsy Scott	2	C	7	1	1	1	6,090
Tin Tin	3	F	12	2	3	1	14,896	Tiptoe In	8	H	8	1	0	2	19,210
Tin Type	5	G	4	0	0	2	3,344	Tiptoe With Me	3	C	16	0	0	5	3,760
Tina Bull	3	F	9	4	1	2	148,030	Tipton County	4	F	8	0	1	1	6,160
Tina Can Do	3	F	5	0	0	0	680	Tiptop Slew	7	M	16	0	0	0	6,947
Tina Sue	6	M	5	0	0	0	1,126	Tiptronic	5	G	1	0	0	0	0
Tina Tango	5	M	10	1	1	0	6,340	Tipyourbuddy	10	G	7	0	0	1	2,267
Tinagoldengirl	3	F	6	1	0	0	11,054	Tirade's Cure	4	F	10	0	2	2	2,650
Tinalee	4	G	11	1	2	3	10,260	Tirak	4	G	4	1	0	1	15,506
Tinandrose	5	M	1	0	0	0	0	Tire Biter	2	G	3	0	0	0	606
Tinarina	2	F	3	0	0	1	3,100	Tiryns	3	G	3	0	1	0	2,120
Tinas Angel	4	F	8	1	2	4	12,017	Tis	6	M	2	0	0	0	261
Tina's Love	2	F	1	0	0	1	4,920	Tis a Memoiry	2	F	1	0	0	0	0
Tina's Thunder	3	F	7	0	0	0	0	Tis a Star	3	C	3	0	0	0	1,620
Tincan	4	G	4	1	0	0	1,415	Tis Captain Jackie	3	F	1	0	0	0	360
Tincan Too	3	F	7	2	1	3	70,550	Tis Magical	4	C	10	0	3	0	22,920
Tincin	5	G	6	0	1	0	1,018	Tis Me	4	F	11	2	4	1	46,512
Tindell	6	G	12	1	2	2	20,120	Tis Nellie's Line	4	F	1	0	0	0	600
Tiney Girl	6	M	7	2	2	0	6,288	Tis Premixed	2	F	5	0	3	0	4,655
Tingwithasting	2	F	3	1	1	0	36,250	Tis Sharp	3	F	5	0	0	0	536
Tinievlas	3	C	8	1	4	0	23,295	Tis' Summer Wish	4	F	6	0	1	0	618
Tinker	4	C	11	1	0	1	18,740	Tis Yo	3	G	7	1	0	0	7,576
Tinker's Hope	4	F	11	1	1	1	5,738	Tis Your Country	6	M	5	0	2	1	13,070
Tinner So Slick	3	G	8	0	1	1	1,648	Tisawink	2	C	2	0	0	1	3,630
Tinners Belle	4	F	6	0	1	0	2,798	Tishaboo	4	F	7	1	0	0	6,144
Tinners Bucks	5	M	8	1	1	1	10,005	Tisofthee	5	G	9	0	0	1	2,444
Tinner's Storm	3	G	5	0	1	0	2,390	Tisontoo	4	G	10	1	1	0	4,705
Tinnian	2	G	3	1	0	0	4,500	Tisourturn	4	F	16	2	1	2	40,954
Tino Rossi	2	C	1	0	0	0	8,500	Tissington	9	G	10	3	4	2	9,749
Tino Terrace	2	F	4	0	0	2	4,764	Titan Steel	6	G	10	1	0	1	6,333
Tinsel Bits	5	M	10	2	0	0	37,263	Titanic Bea	2	F	4	0	1	0	2,941
Tinstack	2	G	4	1	0	0	6,555	Titanic Star	7	H	13	1	0	0	3,930
Tinta Negra	4	C	1	0	0	0	0	Titanica	2	F	1	0	0	0	0
Tinturn Abbey	4	F	7	0	1	0	9,429	Titanium Ghost	3	C	8	2	0	3	59,170
Tiny Bird	4	F	5	2	0	1	7,116	Titia	5	M	11	2	3	3	71,700
Tiny Comet	3	F	7	3	1	1	36,425	Titian	5	G	7	1	1	3	12,934
Tiny Facts	2	F	4	0	1	1	7,472	Titillation	7	M	3	0	0	0	544

Horse	Age	Sex	Sts	1st	2d	3d	Won
Title Contender	3	C	14	1	6	0	68,060
Title for Title	6	G	17	7	2	3	77,910
Title Force	6	G	9	0	0	1	665
Title Hope	3	F	7	1	2	0	11,960
Title Nine	4	F	4	1	0	0	23,790
Title Run	4	F	8	0	1	0	2,947
Title Shot	3	C	8	1	2	0	23,490
Titled Money	4	F	9	1	0	1	2,660
Tito	3	C	8	0	2	2	6,080
Tito's Beau	3	C	12	2	1	1	37,193
Tiva's Little Sis	3	F	11	3	5	1	132,343
Tivy's Beau	5	G	14	0	1	3	3,960
Tiz a Coup	3	C	10	2	0	2	89,889
Tiz a Windy Cee	2	F	3	1	1	0	18,480
Tiz Ago	4	C	3	0	1	0	3,918
Tiz Fleet	6	H	1	0	0	0	53
Tiz Lizzy	6	M	2	0	0	0	114
Tiz Royalty	3	F	5	2	0	0	48,270
Tiz Too	2	F	2	1	0	0	5,733
Tizaflyin	2	C	1	0	0	0	0
Tizagal	5	M	10	1	2	3	12,890
Tizamite	2	C	2	0	0	1	1,940
Tizawinner	4	G	9	2	2	2	112,483
Tizbud	4	C	3	1	0	1	179,292
Tizdubai	2	F	2	2	0	0	116,400
Tizfunnymagee	4	F	13	0	4	1	6,093
Tizimin	5	G	7	3	2	0	15,869
Tizmania	6	G	11	1	1	1	14,908
Tiznuf	2	C	1	0	0	0	0
Tizwar	2	G	7	1	1	0	22,540
Tizza Dude	3	G	12	1	1	3	13,006
Tizznizzel	4	F	5	2	0	1	10,805
Tizzy Boy	2	G	7	0	3	4	26,520
Tizzy Revenge	6	M	6	0	1	0	1,805
Tm's Private Line	4	F	3	2	0	0	10,200
Tnt Mill	3	F	9	0	0	3	5,064
Tnt Tower	3	G	8	2	1	1	22,793
To and Fro	4	F	3	0	0	0	619
To B Negotiated	4	G	2	0	0	0	150
To Be a Star	4	G	3	0	0	0	246
To Be Announced	3	C	8	1	1	0	8,740
To Be Or Not	2	G	1	0	0	1	2,550
To Be Springs	4	G	17	2	2	1	14,913
To Be Thrilled	5	G	5	0	1	1	1,722
To Bold to Blush	4	F	3	1	0	0	1,515
To Cute for You	2	F	1	0	0	0	0
To Cute to Dance	4	F	2	0	0	0	40
To Di for Again	5	H	11	4	2	0	52,600
To Do So	3	G	6	0	0	0	1,910
To Dream Again	3	F	10	4	3	1	52,647
To Fast Chica	3	F	7	0	0	0	1,490
To Go	3	C	8	2	1	1	69,234
To God's Ears	3	C	4	0	0	0	1,960
To Good to Love	5	M	3	1	0	0	1,330
To Little Justice	4	F	16	0	2	4	11,458
To Much Moonshine	3	G	5	2	0	0	8,250
To Much Woman	3	F	5	0	0	0	462
To Short to Punch	5	H	3	0	1	0	4,000
To Tall Dusty	2	C	3	0	0	0	840
To Tell the Truce	3	G	18	2	2	5	10,905
To the Alamo	2	F	4	1	0	0	13,230
To the Best	3	F	4	0	0	0	0
To the Chapel	3	F	7	1	0	1	37,455
To the Crowd	4	F	9	2	3	2	72,910
To the Gold	4	G	11	0	0	0	784
To the Moon	4	G	13	1	4	1	8,972
To the Point	4	C	1	0	0	0	0
To the Queen	4	F	3	1	0	1	44,955
To the Rescue	3	C	1	0	0	0	0
To the Test	4	F	5	0	0	1	1,908
To the Town	5	G	2	0	0	0	78
To the Victor	3	G	7	1	0	1	5,180
To the Whistle	2	G	6	1	1	1	20,320
To Wit	5	H	4	1	0	0	5,470
To Your Advantage	3	C	20	1	2	1	25,995
Toad You So	4	F	6	2	0	0	5,260
Toast for Mr. Expo	5	G	14	6	3	0	51,174
Toast My Catch	4	C	9	1	5	1	21,465
Toast of Hadif	2	C	1	0	0	0	0
Toast of the Year	4	F	5	0	2	0	10,220
Toast the Host	5	H	9	2	0	0	33,600
Toast the Queen	4	G	7	0	1	2	5,313
Toast to Stanley	9	G	5	0	0	0	0
Toast to Wesley	5	H	6	0	0	0	656
Toasttofriendship	2	F	4	0	0	0	3,659
Toatrickyend	5	M	1	0	0	0	0
Tobe Suave	2	C	5	2	0	0	59,226
Tobi Raj	2	F	3	0	0	0	532
Tobias	5	G	4	3	0	1	43,550
Tobicat	2	F	2	1	1	0	10,258
Tobie Lang	3	F	12	1	3	1	40,018
Tobin Miss	4	F	9	2	1	2	7,962
Tobin's Clue	5	H	1	0	0	0	153
Tobin's Gabby	4	F	8	1	1	3	20,030
Tobins' Irish Lady	3	F	3	0	0	0	0
Toby	5	G	6	1	1	2	5,065
Toby's Baby	4	F	11	1	0	1	2,643
Toby's Cookin	10	G	7	0	0	1	866
Toby's Success	3	G	2	1	0	1	19,330
Toca Araken	5	H	7	0	0	3	3,250
Toccet	3	C	7	1	1	1	92,180
Toco Drive	4	G	3	0	0	0	164
Tocool for Words	4	G	12	3	1	1	15,419
Toda Rouge	3	F	16	3	1	2	20,392
Todasha	5	M	5	0	0	0	100
Today Junior	4	G	2	0	0	0	0
Todays Kitten	3	F	3	0	1	1	5,160
Today's Tomorrow	7	G	8	1	2	0	20,500
Toddie C	6	M	9	0	1	0	2,991
Toddinator	6	G	12	1	1	3	4,882
Toddler	6	H	11	2	3	3	59,015
Todds Volcano	3	G	8	1	0	0	4,019
Toddteeontheteevee	3	G	4	0	0	0	0
Toddy'o	4	G	15	0	1	0	2,414
Todos Dicen (CHI)	5	H	6	0	0	0	165
Toe Dance	5	H	8	0	0	0	889
Toe Knee	6	M	1	0	0	0	0
Toe Knee Nose	5	M	6	1	1	0	4,730
Toe the Mark	4	F	10	1	2	1	9,663
Toga On	3	G	1	0	0	0	840
Toga Point	3	F	2	0	0	0	0
Toga Switch	4	G	7	2	1	1	24,088
Toga's Triumph	3	F	14	4	1	1	55,070
Togs	4	F	12	0	3	0	3,289
Toi Fund	4	G	2	0	0	1	3,204
Toi Sailor	2	G	3	0	0	0	1,265
Toin and Boin	2	C	4	2	0	0	44,455
Toke 'n Classics	5	G	8	3	0	0	34,535
Token of Honor	2	G	2	0	0	1	1,920
Token of Luck	4	F	8	1	1	2	6,200
Token Tonko	3	G	9	5	2	2	43,060
Token Treasure	3	G	1	0	0	0	0
Toketee	2	C	1	0	0	0	0
Tokin N Jokin	2	F	2	0	0	0	0
Toknowmeistoloveme	3	F	18	1	1	3	7,550
Tokyo Baby	2	F	6	1	0	0	14,904
Tokyo Gold (JPN)	5	G	15	1	1	2	5,462
Tokyo Spy	4	F	14	0	3	1	34,260
Toledo	4	G	16	1	2	3	12,757
Toledo King	2	C	5	0	3	1	6,140
Tolittletotalk	2	F	5	1	0	1	8,245
Toll Bandit	2	C	2	0	0	0	1,764
Toll Mighty	11	G	8	0	1	0	611
Toll Order	3	F	3	0	0	0	2,520
Tollgate's Account	2	C	1	0	0	0	0
Tollhouse Rita	3	F	3	0	0	0	240
Toluca Exit	2	F	1	1	0	0	3,120
Tom and Roses	3	G	2	0	0	0	130
Tom Brown	3	G	3	0	1	0	3,120
Tom Lane	3	G	18	2	4	4	49,540
Tom Maior (BRZ)	6	H	2	1	0	0	16,460
Tom the River Rat	5	G	5	1	1	0	14,970
Tom Tuppence	4	G	16	1	3	2	6,465
Tom Who	2	G	1	0	0	0	425
Tom Won	2	G	5	2	2	0	24,091
Tomadache	7	G	6	0	0	0	0
Tomahawk Lake	4	C	13	1	1	1	46,466
Tomahawk Walk	3	C	7	0	1	0	1,050

Horse	Age	Sex	Sts	1st	2d	3d	Won	Horse	Age	Sex	Sts	1st	2d	3d	Won
Tomarosa	3	F	7	1	3	0	3,040	Tonkawa	6	G	19	1	4	3	23,406
Tomars Last Birdie	5	G	18	1	1	3	9,872	Tonopah Joe	3	G	11	1	3	1	7,646
Tomas D	4	G	5	1	2	1	2,685	Tons	4	C	7	0	1	0	10,660
Tomas' Playmate	4	F	13	0	4	3	7,106	Tonshi	5	H	9	0	1	0	1,378
Tomata Buster	2	C	2	0	0	0	360	Tonto Bloomberg	3	G	17	2	1	3	21,530
Tomato Soup	2	C	4	0	0	0	1,560	Tonto Gusto	8	G	9	1	2	1	27,900
Tomb Raider	4	G	5	1	0	0	5,691	Tontoboychuk	6	G	2	0	0	1	1,536
Tomboy Lady	4	F	9	1	2	0	10,950	Tony and Shaye	6	H	4	0	1	0	2,709
Tomboy Mine	3	F	5	0	0	2	4,400	Tony Basich	7	G	16	1	3	6	27,587
Tombstone (ARG)	6	G	6	1	1	3	61,100	Tony Blue Blazes	3	G	3	0	0	0	1,077
Tomcolee	3	G	13	3	3	3	59,890	Tony Boy	4	C	1	0	0	0	135
Tomencino	4	F	2	0	0	1	373	Tony Curtis	3	C	4	1	0	0	7,245
Tommy Cat	4	G	6	0	1	1	10,710	Tony Drake	3	G	2	0	0	0	0
Tommy Crainer	4	G	7	4	0	0	15,893	Tony Island	2	C	1	0	0	0	0
Tommy Jeanne	7	G	10	1	3	0	11,990	Tony Soprano	3	C	8	1	0	0	16,310
Tommy Lees Shadow	6	G	4	1	1	0	13,288	Tony the Bear	7	G	11	2	1	1	7,198
Tommy O'Dea	3	G	10	1	4	3	21,840	Tonyanna	2	F	1	0	0	0	0
Tommy Rock	4	G	12	1	1	3	13,212	Tonya's Glory	4	F	2	0	0	0	228
Tommy T.	2	G	3	0	0	1	1,665	Tonyrony	5	G	12	3	3	4	42,300
Tommy the Gun	2	C	6	0	0	1	2,750	Tony's Birthday	2	C	1	0	0	0	115
Tommy Tough	5	H	3	1	0	1	1,535	Tony's Girl	3	F	8	2	0	1	43,010
Tommy Wells	3	G	6	1	1	0	17,540	Tony's Loc	5	G	10	1	0	0	14,698
Tommy's Lil Car	3	C	9	2	3	0	11,098	Tony's Melissa	7	M	2	0	0	0	138
Tommy's Ms America	5	H	9	0	0	1	882	Tony's Pal	2	F	3	0	0	0	5,343
Tommy's Prospect	4	G	5	0	1	0	1,689	Tony's Red Pony	4	G	9	0	0	0	563
Tomo	3	C	4	0	1	1	9,700	Tony's Rescue	4	F	21	1	3	1	7,488
Tomoka Bound	2	F	2	0	1	0	5,600	Tony's Royalty	5	G	1	0	0	1	6,825
Tomoka Joy	2	F	4	0	0	2	1,298	Tony's Tiger	3	G	13	2	0	2	18,390
Tomokas Outrageous	4	F	3	0	0	0	1,080	Tonys Touch	2	F	7	0	0	0	0
Tomorrow No More	3	C	7	1	3	0	49,810	Tonyspal Craig	4	C	6	0	1	2	17,440
Tomorrow's Affair	2	F	5	2	1	0	19,750	Tonz of Love	4	C	14	3	2	2	18,325
Tomorrows Banquet	3	G	5	0	2	2	31,780	Too Be a Gem	4	G	2	0	1	0	2,590
Tomorrows Beauty	2	F	3	0	0	0	1,230	Too Catty	2	F	1	0	0	0	0
Tomorrows Classic	3	C	9	1	1	3	24,239	Too Chilly to Tell	2	C	2	0	0	0	290
Tomorrow's Day	8	G	7	0	0	0	720	Too Clever	3	F	10	2	1	0	25,315
Tomorrows Destiny	3	F	2	1	0	1	25,240	Too Close to Call	4	C	6	1	1	1	2,267
Tomorrows Empress	3	F	2	0	0	0	1,230	Too Cute	3	F	5	0	2	1	7,630
Tomorrows Magic	2	C	2	1	0	0	24,600	Too Cute to Care	4	F	10	0	0	1	646
Tomorrow's Number	2	F	3	0	0	1	6,490	Too Darned Sweet	10	M	3	0	0	0	180
Tomorrows Peach	3	F	14	7	1	1	69,984	Too Fast for Last	5	H	4	0	0	1	1,026
Tomorrow's Star	3	F	3	0	0	0	2,490	Too Fast to Play	2	C	3	0	0	0	1,071
Tomorrow's Vision	3	F	7	0	0	0	1,158	Too Fast to Top	3	G	7	2	1	1	32,170
Tomorrows War Cry	3	G	3	0	1	0	9,550	Too Fine for You	4	F	11	1	2	0	5,941
Tomprado	4	C	10	3	1	1	26,860	Too Hot Girls	5	M	12	1	3	3	9,622
Tomregan	5	G	3	0	0	0	570	Too Hot to Trot	9	G	15	2	1	2	7,109
Tom's Angel	3	F	6	1	1	0	24,080	Too Irresistible	5	M	3	0	0	1	770
Tom's Boomer	3	G	14	0	0	5	6,971	Too Kool Jewel	5	M	15	1	2	1	7,297
Toms Choice	3	G	5	0	0	0	315	Too Late Now	3	F	7	4	0	1	566,110
Tom's Crozier	3	C	8	0	0	0	1,615	Too Many Bucks	5	H	3	0	0	0	4,031
Tom's Irish Lass	3	F	2	0	0	0	67	Too Many Choices	4	F	17	4	3	4	44,185
Tom's Memory	3	C	6	0	0	2	3,320	Too Many Knights	7	G	2	1	1	0	1,255
Toms Pickle	3	G	5	0	1	0	1,820	Too Many Mikes	2	C	3	0	1	0	1,280
Toms Retta	6	M	2	0	0	0	160	Too Much Class	2	F	5	0	0	2	8,270
Tom's Thunder	5	G	5	0	3	0	34,080	Too Much for T. V.	3	G	16	1	2	1	21,242
Tom's Treasure	4	F	2	0	0	0	290	Too Much Johnson	9	G	6	0	1	1	1,324
Toms Tuffanuff	2	C	2	0	0	0	240	Too Much Love	3	F	6	0	0	5	3,411
Tom'shreetees	2	F	1	0	0	1	2,750	Too Much Moxie	3	F	15	2	1	7	29,343
Tomtom Tommalice	6	G	5	0	1	0	7,742	Too Much Rouge	6	M	3	0	0	0	705
Tomufta	4	G	13	1	0	0	7,338	Too Much Swingin	5	G	2	0	0	0	90
Ton a Run	2	F	1	0	0	0	0	Too Much Time	6	M	1	0	0	0	86
Tonapah	5	G	10	2	2	3	17,752	Too Proud	3	G	5	0	1	0	3,255
Tonco	5	G	15	5	4	1	115,361	Too Real	5	G	6	1	0	0	5,348
Tone of Gold	6	G	7	0	3	1	16,890	Too Slew for You	6	G	5	1	0	1	1,700
Toneless	3	G	1	0	0	0	73	Too Suave	4	G	5	1	0	0	6,419
Tonelli's Legacy	4	F	3	0	0	1	6,120	Too Tall	5	M	17	4	3	2	41,002
Tonga Ridge	3	G	11	1	2	0	10,112	Too the Target	3	G	15	0	4	1	10,577
Toni Ann	6	M	2	0	0	0	400	Too Tough to Tame	3	F	2	0	0	1	2,046
Toni Michelle	3	F	12	0	1	3	5,072	Too Wet to Work	4	C	15	2	3	2	20,205
Toni T	3	G	13	5	0	1	167,621	Too Willing	3	G	15	1	2	2	14,453
Toni Zamora	3	F	7	1	0	0	2,220	Toobusytoocall	10	G	10	2	2	1	10,128
Tonic Nights	4	G	8	3	1	0	65,770	Toocloseto Comfort	3	F	4	0	0	0	360
Tonic Water	4	G	1	0	0	0	0	Toocutetoshoot	3	F	7	0	0	0	651
Tonight Rainbow	4	G	11	3	3	0	49,570	Toofastforyou	2	C	6	0	2	2	14,420
Tonights Prospect	2	F	1	0	0	0	100	Toogie too Shoes	3	F	6	1	0	2	21,310
Tonight's Wager	5	M	4	2	0	1	71,850	Toogoodforyou	3	G	13	0	1	4	7,856
Toni's Princess	4	F	4	0	0	0	212	Toogoodtobetrue	3	F	16	3	2	3	17,445
Toni's Target	3	C	7	0	0	1	3,051	Toogoolawa	5	G	3	0	1	0	843
Toni's Wildcard	5	G	1	0	0	0	89	Toohappy	3	F	3	0	0	0	300
Tonith	2	C	6	0	1	1	12,740	Tooitus	2	G	3	0	0	0	95

Horse	Age	Sex	Sts	1st	2d	3d	Won	Horse	Age	Sex	Sts	1st	2d	3d	Won
Took Out	4	F	6	1	1	2	57,550	Top of the News	5	G	14	2	3	2	53,375
Tookie	4	F	8	0	1	0	1,490	Top of the World	4	G	9	1	0	0	7,770
Tool Pusher	6	H	6	0	0	1	1,494	Top Ofthe Mountain	6	G	8	0	0	0	1,056
Toolate Kasey	2	C	3	1	0	0	6,150	Top Penny	3	F	9	2	3	1	64,230
Toolight Bracelet	3	F	11	1	1	3	20,003	Top Performance	4	G	1	0	0	0	0
Toolights' Music	4	G	7	1	1	1	6,653	Top Plum	2	C	7	1	0	4	16,155
Toolight's Notion	4	G	9	1	0	0	7,005	Top Pop	4	G	6	0	0	3	5,220
Toolighttonight	5	H	4	0	0	0	1,173	Top Prince	4	G	2	0	0	0	87
Toolighttoquittoo	5	H	7	0	1	0	3,666	Top Pumpkin	3	F	1	1	0	0	8,100
Toolin Around	7	H	17	0	0	1	860	Top Punch	6	G	7	1	1	3	15,450
Tooluckytoquit	3	F	4	0	1	0	2,650	Top Row	2	G	4	0	0	0	670
Toomanytomorrows	4	F	3	1	1	0	8,137	Top Sea Gal	2	F	1	0	0	0	0
Toomuch Chavez	4	G	14	2	3	3	60,205	Top Secret Affair	5	G	12	2	0	4	12,913
Toomuchinformation	5	G	20	1	1	4	20,726	Top Secret Code	2	C	2	0	0	0	118
Toomuchtrouble	3	G	19	1	3	6	24,675	Top Senor	7	G	7	1	1	0	8,257
Toons Tank	3	G	9	1	0	1	5,103	Top Shoter	4	G	7	3	0	1	59,290
Tooralooralooral	6	M	4	0	0	0	0	Top Shotta	4	G	3	0	0	0	165
Toosexyfor U	5	M	4	0	0	0	402	Top Snip	4	G	3	0	0	0	270
Toosie Town Snooks	3	F	8	0	0	0	605	Top Song	3	C	2	0	0	0	0
Toosixyformytoga	5	G	6	2	1	0	5,936	Top Spartan	5	H	1	0	0	0	55
Toot Your Horn	6	H	2	0	0	0	0	Top Spinner (NZ)	5	M	9	3	1	2	116,600
Tootalltofall	4	F	3	0	0	0	525	Top Stage Dancer	4	F	8	3	3	1	51,010
Tooth Doctor	4	C	13	5	2	0	24,400	Top Summer	7	G	9	2	2	1	12,910
Tootie Fruity	4	F	1	0	0	0	217	Top Target	2	C	5	1	2	0	12,294
Tooties Teddy	7	G	7	1	1	3	2,112	Top the Charts	5	G	9	0	0	0	1,283
Toot's Lil Chic	2	F	1	0	1	0	8,500	Top Tier	3	F	3	1	0	0	12,270
Tootsie Rapper	5	H	16	2	1	2	18,018	Top Treasure	3	F	10	0	2	0	3,810
Tootsie's Gal	4	F	2	0	0	0	0	Top Up	3	G	13	2	0	2	14,588
Toowildtodrive	9	M	14	4	2	1	8,543	Top Velocity	3	F	3	0	0	0	258
Top Account Queen	4	F	7	1	0	0	13,145	Top Victory	2	G	4	0	2	0	4,179
Top Arazi	5	G	6	0	0	0	718	Top Woman	3	F	12	2	2	0	11,389
Top Bananna	3	F	4	1	1	1	7,950	Top Zarb	6	G	5	1	0	1	16,104
Top Boot	3	G	5	1	0	1	10,560	Topango	2	F	4	3	0	0	84,000
Top Brass	5	H	17	3	4	3	29,536	Topaz Jewel	3	F	8	3	3	0	50,710
Top Buck	4	C	9	0	1	4	16,556	Topaz 'n Jazz	5	M	3	0	0	0	0
Top Bunk	6	G	5	0	0	1	11,314	Topdown	5	G	7	0	2	2	5,996
Top C Jim	7	G	2	0	0	0	180	Topeka	2	F	3	0	1	0	6,480
Top Call	5	G	11	1	0	0	5,140	Topflight Lady	3	F	1	0	0	0	0
Top Cappelletti	3	F	9	2	0	2	19,130	Topiary	2	F	1	0	0	0	0
Top Card	3	F	12	1	2	2	19,240	Topmost	4	C	3	1	0	0	25,150
Top Carte	3	G	16	3	2	5	40,649	Toppa the Hill	6	G	5	0	1	2	5,780
Top Case	3	G	9	2	2	0	11,864	Toppers Happy	5	M	1	0	0	0	0
Top Cash	3	G	10	2	0	1	10,455	Topping	3	G	10	1	4	0	47,015
Top Commander	3	C	3	0	0	0	2,000	Tops	4	F	1	0	0	0	0
Top Cut	3	G	5	1	1	0	12,860	Top's My Pop	4	F	7	0	2	2	2,545
Top Designer	3	G	7	0	2	2	15,090	Topsoil King	3	G	12	0	0	0	13,560
Top Drummer	4	C	3	0	0	0	291	Topsoil Lady	3	F	4	1	0	0	6,940
Top Elimator	4	G	13	2	4	3	18,774	Topspin Lob	4	F	16	1	1	0	10,735
Top Encounter	2	F	3	1	0	0	11,610	Topstitch	2	F	1	0	0	0	1,140
Top Event	6	G	6	1	1	0	29,949	Topwynson	4	G	14	2	2	3	49,328
Top Express	3	F	2	0	0	0	0	Tora Bora	3	G	7	1	0	2	4,786
Top Force Five	5	G	5	0	0	1	568	Toranado	2	C	1	0	0	0	0
Top Fox	3	F	4	0	0	1	2,796	Toratora	3	C	10	2	0	0	18,720
Top G Man	8	H	12	2	1	2	8,634	Torch It	3	G	4	1	0	1	6,878
Top Glory	2	G	5	0	1	3	16,020	Torch Relay	3	G	5	1	2	0	22,830
Top Groom	6	H	6	0	1	3	2,479	Torch the Halls	5	G	14	4	2	2	77,820
Top Gun Dancer	3	G	10	0	1	2	8,000	Tordue	3	F	8	2	1	0	35,086
Top Gun Penthouse	3	C	6	2	2	0	29,200	Toreo's Hurrah	6	G	9	0	1	1	1,037
Top Gun Princess (JPN)	3	F	9	2	0	0	5,544	Tori Cheyenne	7	M	3	0	0	0	0
Top Guy	6	H	9	0	0	0	450	Tori Dancer	8	M	2	0	0	0	83
Top Her	3	F	3	1	0	0	10,410	Toriano	7	H	7	1	2	1	5,734
Top Hit	5	H	4	0	1	0	10,350	Toriano Cat	2	G	6	1	0	0	14,550
Top Hombre	4	G	8	0	0	3	3,000	Tories Sweet Pea	3	F	2	0	0	0	112
Top Honours	5	G	5	0	0	0	11,480	Torioso	7	G	11	3	2	2	31,945
Top Ingredients	3	F	10	1	1	2	19,500	Tori's Portia	3	F	5	0	0	0	590
Top Interrogator	3	C	6	0	0	0	900	Tori's Scalawag	3	F	16	2	0	0	7,863
Top Lavenger	6	G	22	1	1	3	7,787	Tori's Thunder	4	G	7	1	0	0	34,512
Top Local	7	G	6	1	1	1	4,556	Torke	6	G	10	3	4	1	16,668
Top Machine	2	G	5	0	1	1	4,258	Torment	5	G	13	0	0	1	3,790
Top Man Up	5	H	2	0	1	0	1,740	Tormenta Del Gata	4	F	16	5	3	1	26,350
Top Mint	4	C	8	2	0	0	19,266	Tormentos	3	F	7	2	1	0	14,319
Top Mission	5	M	7	0	0	0	542	Tornadic	7	G	7	1	0	1	3,866
Top Move	4	F	2	0	0	0	240	Tornado Alley	4	C	1	0	0	0	204
Top O Morn	3	G	7	1	0	0	5,495	Tornado Bait	2	F	4	1	1	0	14,840
Top of Class	2	C	5	0	3	2	11,475	Tornado Ladd	4	G	8	0	0	1	1,338
Top of His Game	4	G	1	0	0	0	61	Tornado Warning	2	F	14	2	4	0	39,005
Top of Our Game	6	M	2	0	0	0	0	Tornados Jack	3	G	6	0	0	1	12,208
Top of the Bay	4	C	4	0	0	1	2,100	Torque Man	4	G	4	0	1	0	2,200
Top of the Hour	5	G	11	3	0	5	46,578	Torrantula	5	M	2	0	0	0	210

Horse	Age	Sex	Sts	1st	2d	3d	Won
Torre and Zim	3	C	4	0	0	0	9,820
Torre Dei Nolfi	9	G	11	3	1	2	27,000
Torrent of Song	2	F	5	0	0	0	2,452
Torrential Lady	2	F	7	0	1	0	2,190
Torrential Run	2	C	5	0	0	0	245
Torreon	7	M	10	3	1	3	4,379
Torrid Joe Al	5	G	14	1	0	2	9,586
Torrid Sand	7	H	8	1	0	1	7,994
Torrid Tryst	4	F	2	1	1	0	3,594
Torry	8	R	16	1	0	1	3,192
Torsionnaire (FR)	4	G	2	0	0	0	2,180
Tortoni	3	C	6	0	1	1	10,280
Tortuguero (IRE)	5	G	2	0	0	0	0
Torun	2	C	3	0	2	1	14,780
Torvellino	6	M	9	0	0	0	990
Tory's Tune	4	F	11	0	1	1	2,948
Tory's Victory	2	F	1	0	0	0	0
Tosayhowmuchicare	3	C	8	2	1	0	30,695
Toscani	3	G	8	2	3	2	54,540
Toscanini	2	C	1	0	0	0	180
Toscano	4	C	9	2	2	1	75,549
Toss Both Ways	2	C	8	1	2	1	28,920
Toss Me'the Money	5	G	10	1	0	0	1,363
Toss the Bag	7	G	2	0	0	0	645
Toss the Candi	5	M	3	0	0	0	0
Toss the Gold	4	F	7	1	1	1	6,993
Toss the Jockey	8	M	5	0	0	0	1,765
Tossed and Found	5	M	12	1	0	3	15,054
Tot	4	F	4	0	0	1	1,373
Total Advantage	3	G	2	0	0	1	7,080
Total Anilation	6	G	8	2	3	0	35,914
Total Anticipation	5	G	14	2	2	2	24,447
Total Arrogance	3	F	5	1	3	1	11,480
Total Blaze	4	H	4	0	0	0	0
Total Consent	4	C	13	1	0	1	3,540
Total Dominance	3	G	4	1	0	0	2,550
Total Gold	6	G	1	0	0	0	0
Total Impact (CHI)	5	H	6	2	1	0	163,400
Total Limit	4	C	7	1	1	1	51,810
Total Package	5	G	1	0	0	0	38
Total Reality	4	G	7	0	0	1	2,095
Totally Cosmic	4	F	1	1	0	0	26,400
Totally Crafty	4	F	5	0	0	0	2,570
Totally Gold	7	M	3	0	0	0	115
Totally Platinum	2	C	6	1	2	0	40,900
Totally Precious	4	F	8	1	2	3	41,290
Totally Private	6	M	4	0	1	1	4,530
Totally Terrific	4	F	1	0	0	0	0
Totalyseneca	8	G	8	1	1	1	4,132
Tote the Note	4	F	6	2	1	0	20,600
Totebook	3	F	5	0	0	1	3,790
Totem's Aly	3	C	4	1	1	0	2,900
Tothe Chase	6	G	14	1	1	2	7,924
Toto McKay	4	G	5	0	0	0	378
Totteridge	6	H	7	1	0	0	8,825
Tou Jake	4	G	4	1	0	0	19,200
Touch	5	M	3	0	0	0	496
Touch for Luck	2	C	3	0	0	0	5,700
Touch Jade	3	G	1	0	0	1	6,468
Touch Lightly	3	F	4	0	2	0	4,891
Touch Me Please	4	C	2	0	0	0	0
Touch 'n' Fly (IRE)	7	H	1	0	0	0	0
Touch of Fame	3	G	10	1	1	2	7,219
Touch of Ginger	4	F	7	2	3	0	133,936
Touch of Honey	10	G	2	0	0	0	880
Touch of l'Aiglon	3	F	5	0	0	0	380
Touch of Land (FR)	3	C	8	2	1	2	167,547
Touch of Mahogony	4	G	15	3	1	2	17,675
Touch of Platinum	4	C	2	0	1	0	4,775
Touch of Power	6	G	5	2	0	0	9,328
Touch of Quality	2	C	3	0	0	1	1,400
Touch of Spirit	2	F	4	0	1	1	5,290
Touch of the Blues (FR)	6	H	6	2	1	3	1,082,885
Touch of Victory	2	F	2	0	0	0	1,200
Touch Platinum	3	C	5	0	1	1	15,080
Touch Silver	7	G	14	2	7	1	34,740
Touch Softly	3	C	11	3	3	0	58,950
Touch the Wire	3	G	6	2	1	1	63,830
Touch This	5	G	4	0	0	0	0
Toucha Kansas	4	F	3	0	0	0	0
Touchabull	3	F	10	2	2	1	12,840
Touchdown Cat	2	C	4	0	0	0	1,386
Touchdown Ky	4	C	2	0	0	0	525
Touchdown Run	3	C	17	1	3	2	27,625
Touche Touche	7	M	1	0	0	0	0
Touched an Angel	4	F	3	2	0	0	4,840
Touched by Angel	2	F	1	0	0	0	0
Touched by N Angel	6	M	18	3	6	3	9,068
Touched by Whitney	4	G	4	0	0	2	1,540
Touching Gold	3	C	12	0	1	3	29,850
Touchmeifyoucan	3	F	1	0	0	0	0
Touchnow	2	F	1	0	0	0	0
Touchoville	8	M	14	1	2	3	11,811
Touchwood	3	F	5	1	0	1	15,925
Touchy	2	F	2	1	0	0	13,640
Touchy Remark	5	G	4	0	0	0	764
Touchy Situation	4	F	10	0	4	2	5,581
Touchy Trigger	3	F	5	1	1	0	16,495
Tough as Neatie	2	C	7	1	1	2	38,250
Tough Banker	3	G	5	1	1	0	8,655
Tough Buck	6	G	9	1	0	2	5,434
Tough City	4	G	7	0	0	1	805
Tough City Girl	2	F	9	0	2	2	33,180
Tough Cookie Baby	3	F	5	0	0	0	800
Tough Crowd	5	G	8	0	2	0	11,083
Tough Customer	4	G	6	2	2	0	20,304
Tough Dancer	5	M	4	0	2	0	2,103
Tough Devil	6	H	4	0	0	0	144
Tough Exercise	4	G	14	1	3	1	13,301
Tough Farm Boy	3	G	21	1	3	4	5,091
Tough Game	4	C	10	3	4	0	146,000
Tough Gus	6	G	9	1	3	0	17,692
Tough Hagerdorn	5	G	5	1	1	0	4,282
Tough Johnny G	3	C	7	1	2	0	16,060
Tough Little Man	3	G	3	0	0	0	177
Tough Mick	5	G	9	0	0	1	2,760
Tough Negotiator	2	C	2	0	0	0	19,600
Tough Rambler	6	M	8	2	1	1	16,865
Tough Sledding	5	G	5	0	0	0	1,349
Tough Speed	6	H	3	0	0	0	3,610
Tough Tike	8	M	2	0	0	0	0
Tough Tommy	4	G	9	0	0	1	2,895
Tough Turkey	8	G	3	0	0	0	150
Tougher Still	6	G	7	2	2	1	3,500
Toughkenamon	4	G	9	3	1	2	50,140
Toughman	4	G	3	1	0	0	2,190
Toughtalented	4	G	5	1	0	0	5,384
Toughonabankroll	3	F	3	0	0	0	1,085
Toujour Winning	4	F	7	0	1	2	13,680
Toujours	6	G	12	0	4	3	9,940
Toula	2	F	2	1	0	0	35,280
Tour Argentina	4	G	10	2	2	0	36,480
Tour D' Gold	2	G	1	0	1	0	12,120
Tour D' Triomphe	5	G	6	0	0	3	9,026
Tour d'Star	3	F	9	2	1	0	74,459
Tour Hostess	7	M	15	3	1	3	45,358
Tour in Style	3	F	4	1	0	0	9,685
Tour Japan	5	M	16	2	1	8	51,483
Tour Leader	3	F	4	0	1	2	10,170
Tour of the Cat	5	G	9	3	2	2	351,070
Tour of the Rose	6	M	21	6	3	2	61,308
Tour One	5	G	2	0	0	0	309
Tour Sez	6	M	16	4	3	2	43,060
Tour the Hive	6	G	8	3	0	4	132,071
Tour the Line	4	G	17	3	0	0	40,465
Tourdownmemoryjane	4	F	5	0	0	0	186
Touring England	4	C	3	0	0	1	3,020
Touring Star	4	F	5	1	2	0	22,322
Tourist	4	C	4	1	2	0	7,323
Tourist Trap	7	G	22	3	3	3	16,099
Tourmendous	3	G	4	0	0	0	620
Tournadoes	8	G	3	0	0	1	572
Tournament Play	6	H	3	0	0	0	1,440
Tour's Bluff	6	G	14	3	2	2	57,410
Tour's Energy	4	F	8	2	2	0	38,700
Tour's Quick Gal	4	F	3	0	0	0	200
Tour's Thunder	2	C	3	0	1	0	5,600
Tours Val	6	M	11	1	1	0	12,715

Horse	Age	Sex	Sts	1st	2d	3d	Won
Tovu Tiku Teivu	4	F	1	0	0	0	0
Tow Path	3	G	15	0	4	2	8,429
Towellwithit	5	M	4	0	0	0	556
Tower Battle	3	G	6	0	0	0	512
Tower Dream	3	C	3	0	0	0	640
Tower of Angels	8	M	8	1	0	2	9,505
Tower of Honour	4	F	10	1	1	3	57,185
Tower of Silence	4	C	3	0	0	1	916
Tower of Terror	3	C	6	0	0	0	2,080
Tower of the Winds	4	F	19	1	0	3	26,800
Tower Power	5	M	10	0	5	1	16,604
Towering Heart	3	C	2	0	0	0	0
Towering Pines	3	G	9	2	2	1	16,919
Towering Storm	9	H	16	4	3	2	40,575
Tower's Rebel	5	G	10	1	1	4	10,807
Tower's Turf	4	G	10	1	2	1	6,213
Towice Nice	6	M	5	0	0	0	728
Town Attire	2	F	1	0	0	0	380
Town Charmer	2	F	2	0	0	0	0
Town Gambler	6	G	10	1	1	1	5,515
Town Ghost	6	G	17	0	0	2	3,925
Town Hall	3	G	9	1	1	2	17,520
Town Lake	3	F	1	0	0	0	0
Town Luck	3	F	11	1	2	1	17,300
Town Meeting	3	C	13	1	1	4	11,628
Town Queen	5	M	3	0	2	0	20,000
Town Spirit	5	H	1	0	0	0	600
Town Without Pity	2	C	4	0	0	0	1,350
Townline	2	F	1	0	0	0	1,500
Towns Honor	5	M	3	0	0	1	1,214
Townsville	4	F	14	2	1	4	17,658
Toxic Country	4	C	3	0	0	0	70
Toxic Level	3	G	17	2	1	3	20,425
Toxic Substance	4	F	8	1	2	0	22,550
Toxic Tea	5	G	8	1	0	1	6,651
Toy for Roy	3	F	6	1	2	0	22,680
Toy Soldier (GER)	3	C	4	0	1	1	10,667
Toy Tiger Jr.	5	H	18	1	6	1	23,346
Toy Tigress	2	F	2	0	1	0	4,780
Toyland	7	G	8	2	1	0	2,436
Toysintheatticus	4	F	3	2	0	1	35,500
Trabajo Gold	2	C	1	0	0	0	120
Trace the Blush	4	F	18	1	1	3	8,308
Tracemark	4	G	14	0	3	2	113,565
Tracethe Call	5	G	15	5	1	1	45,760
Tracey's Babe	2	F	1	1	0	0	4,920
Tracey's Miner	3	F	3	0	0	0	841
Traci Girl	4	F	13	4	2	0	67,405
Traci's Wild	4	F	9	0	1	1	16,015
Track Bar	3	F	10	0	1	1	3,440
Track Boss	6	G	9	0	5	1	19,610
Track Cat	4	C	10	2	1	2	25,632
Track City Lad	8	G	5	1	0	0	3,681
Track Doc	10	G	18	3	2	1	14,295
Track Dynasty	3	C	3	0	0	0	636
Track Genius	3	G	7	0	0	0	438
Track Hoe Jo	3	G	1	0	0	1	2,882
Track Key	3	F	1	0	0	0	91
Track Lady	4	F	7	0	1	0	4,200
Track Light	7	G	2	0	0	0	0
Track Longer	3	G	9	2	1	0	6,902
Track Lover	5	G	3	1	1	0	6,580
Track Prince	4	G	9	2	1	2	13,033
Track Rumor	7	G	2	0	0	0	0
Track Terror	4	F	2	1	0	0	2,750
Track Thug	3	C	4	0	1	0	1,350
Track Tramp	2	F	3	0	0	0	237
Track Writer	2	G	2	0	0	0	252
Trackem 'n' Wackem	3	G	4	1	1	2	6,738
Tracker Bob	5	H	14	1	3	4	11,611
Tracking (GB)	8	H	4	0	1	0	2,175
Trackofthecat	5	M	4	0	1	1	21,420
Track's Dancingboy	9	G	6	0	0	0	175
Tracmac	3	F	7	1	0	1	8,460
Tract	2	C	3	0	2	0	6,100
Tractor Required	2	F	1	0	0	0	0
Tracy Lynn	5	M	7	1	2	0	3,994
Tracy's Act	8	G	3	0	0	0	50
Tracy's Reality	2	F	6	1	1	1	14,615

Horse	Age	Sex	Sts	1st	2d	3d	Won
Tracy's Reward	4	F	1	0	0	0	225
Tracy's Silver Cat	3	F	4	0	0	0	0
Tracy's Tonka Toy	3	G	8	1	1	3	73,600
Tracy's Tracton	3	F	9	1	2	1	42,200
Trade Beads	3	F	9	1	0	3	25,400
Trade Marker	3	C	11	2	0	2	34,020
Trade N Treasure	3	F	8	0	1	1	3,603
Trade Show	3	C	16	2	1	1	12,595
Trademark (SAF)	7	G	9	2	1	1	251,143
Trader Hill	7	M	9	2	1	1	12,885
Trader's Bluff	4	C	2	0	0	0	196
Tradesman	6	G	2	0	0	0	434
Trading Halt	2	C	2	1	0	1	8,200
Trading Hours	3	C	5	0	1	0	8,200
Tradition Rocks	4	G	4	3	0	0	104,880
Traditional	4	C	16	1	2	2	63,810
Trae Genius	5	G	3	1	0	0	7,304
Traffic Belle	3	F	6	0	0	1	3,653
Traffic Chief	3	C	6	4	1	0	262,890
Traffic School	4	F	2	0	0	0	1,560
Traffic Signal	4	C	1	0	0	0	1,020
Traffic Ticket	4	C	4	1	0	1	2,530
Traffic Update	2	C	2	0	0	0	820
Trafford Park	4	G	8	0	0	0	559
Tragic's Freedom	6	H	8	0	1	0	3,393
Trail	4	G	9	1	0	1	5,932
Trail Match	5	G	2	0	0	1	600
Trail Mix	2	C	4	0	0	3	19,788
Trail of Fortune	5	H	2	0	0	0	155
Trail of Honor	3	F	16	2	3	1	13,135
Trail of Tears	5	M	14	5	3	4	19,638
Trail Rider	3	F	5	2	0	1	17,480
Trail Ridge	5	G	9	2	2	2	24,577
Trail Striker	2	G	7	0	2	2	14,080
Trailer Man	6	G	10	1	3	1	7,588
Trailer Trash	4	F	4	2	0	0	9,330
Trailing the Comet	6	G	4	0	0	1	872
Traill County	4	C	5	1	0	1	3,390
Trailobrokenhearts	5	H	10	0	0	2	1,595
Trailode	2	C	3	0	0	0	252
Trails End	6	G	17	3	2	2	10,126
Trailthefox	5	H	1	0	0	0	2,520
Train in Vain	6	G	4	2	2	0	18,700
Trained Observer	7	G	1	0	0	0	149
Training Camp	3	C	2	0	0	0	174
Traitor de l'Amour	3	C	7	2	0	1	10,348
Tralee Gold	5	G	1	0	0	0	0
Trampus Too	6	G	9	2	2	0	28,764
Tranquility Base	4	F	18	1	2	3	27,300
Tranquility Bay	2	F	2	0	2	0	8,970
Trans Decor	6	G	6	0	0	0	0
Trans Electric	5	G	3	0	0	0	0
Transcendent	4	C	7	1	0	3	15,175
Transcontinental	3	G	11	1	0	3	11,540
Transient Voltage	2	G	4	0	0	0	0
Transin	3	C	3	0	1	0	920
Transition Time	4	F	1	0	0	0	0
Transmitter	2	C	2	1	0	0	36,360
Transparent	3	C	4	0	0	0	2,460
Transtar	10	G	10	0	0	1	1,500
Tranup	3	C	5	0	0	0	455
Tranzachion	7	G	11	1	0	0	7,680
Trap Seattle	5	M	13	1	2	2	8,641
Trap the Genius	4	C	3	0	0	1	320
Trap Thelast Tiger	6	M	2	0	0	0	120
Trapp Express	3	C	4	1	0	0	9,120
Trapp Rico	3	F	12	0	2	5	12,512
Trapp Trouble	4	G	7	2	1	0	16,782
Trapped Again	3	C	8	2	1	1	64,350
Trapped Echoes	6	H	11	0	0	0	660
Trapper	3	C	10	5	2	1	151,960
Trapper Meek	7	G	18	2	6	0	27,772
Trapper Peak	3	G	4	1	0	0	6,913
Trappings	3	F	7	0	0	0	4,130
Trash the Code	3	F	3	0	0	0	576
Trastevere	6	H	12	1	1	1	8,052
Traumatic	3	F	9	2	1	0	58,550
Trav a Long	4	G	15	0	0	1	2,295
Travel Advisory	5	M	2	0	0	0	306

RECORDS OF HORSES

Horse	Age	Sex	Sts	1st	2d	3d	Won
Travel Alarm	3	G	6	1	2	0	31,000
Travel Notes	5	H	5	0	0	0	427
Travel Wise	2	C	1	0	0	1	1,019
Travelator	3	F	12	6	3	1	248,071
Traveler	3	F	5	1	0	0	15,460
Traveler Two	4	G	5	0	1	0	2,205
Traveler's Son	4	G	7	0	0	0	784
Traveleze	3	G	7	2	3	0	38,028
Travelfourpay	4	C	12	3	1	2	15,660
Travelin Diamonds	2	F	2	0	1	0	1,240
Travelin Edgar	3	G	13	2	1	1	17,535
Traveling Connie	3	F	9	2	1	0	17,652
Traveling Derbygal	5	M	6	0	0	1	327
Travellin' Along	2	F	4	0	0	0	2,460
Travelling Free	4	F	4	1	2	0	2,080
Travelling Star	7	H	10	1	1	1	11,634
Travis Raymond	5	H	15	3	3	2	57,862
Travis Will	4	G	13	1	2	1	13,923
Travis Wish	3	F	3	0	0	0	0
Travlin Cat	4	F	9	0	0	1	2,933
Travlin' Polly	2	F	2	1	0	0	8,066
Treacherous Flight	6	M	5	0	0	0	302
Treacherous Quest	4	C	5	0	1	0	1,900
Treadstone	12	G	3	0	0	0	0
Treason	3	C	9	2	1	1	23,455
Treasure Beach	4	F	3	0	1	0	8,510
Treasure Coast Gem	4	F	4	0	2	1	12,740
Treasure Coaster	2	C	2	0	0	0	780
Treasure for All	4	F	2	0	2	0	2,720
Treasure Hunt	7	G	6	2	1	0	31,076
Treasure Run	4	C	9	2	1	1	17,214
Treasure Seeker	2	C	1	0	0	0	0
Treasure Taker	6	H	11	2	2	1	9,277
Treasure Won	5	G	14	3	1	1	19,075
Treasure Zone	4	G	12	1	0	2	23,830
Treasured Coin	6	M	15	0	2	2	4,588
Treasured Covenant	3	F	1	0	0	0	220
Treasured Freedom	3	F	7	1	0	1	11,370
Treasured Gift	6	H	5	0	1	1	12,460
Treasured Heart	2	F	4	0	0	0	2,220
Treasured Indian	4	G	10	0	1	0	4,047
Treasured Memory	4	F	4	0	0	0	420
Treasured Note	5	G	9	1	2	1	16,360
Treasure's Dream	4	F	15	4	1	2	71,010
Treatherlikealady	5	M	9	1	2	2	13,670
Treatwithkidgloves	6	M	6	1	1	0	4,428
Trebaw	3	G	13	1	2	3	12,924
Trebbiano	4	G	5	2	1	0	46,636
Trebia (CHI)	5	M	7	1	1	1	42,760
Trebizond (IRE)	7	G	8	2	0	1	147,488
Tree Bandit	5	M	15	3	2	1	16,545
Tree Foliage	6	G	7	3	0	1	7,830
Tree Legs	5	G	3	0	0	0	656
Tree Lover	2	F	10	2	3	0	23,020
Tree of Life	2	C	1	0	0	0	0
Treesome	3	F	5	2	1	0	13,000
Treetop Flier	6	G	2	0	1	0	560
Treetop Lover	4	G	9	1	1	2	5,415
Treetop's Glory	2	G	5	1	2	1	14,113
Trefinity	4	C	8	1	0	1	17,285
Treford	3	G	9	1	2	1	51,009
Treink	5	M	4	1	2	0	5,470
Trekking	4	F	4	1	1	0	93,340
Trembling Tyrant	6	G	3	0	0	0	372
Tremmor	5	G	6	0	1	1	10,060
Tremont Light	2	G	8	1	0	1	14,845
Tremp Star	4	G	9	0	0	0	1,260
Trempolino Trick	5	G	10	0	1	0	1,922
Tremp's Scholar	5	G	16	1	3	2	6,293
Trenchtown	3	G	1	0	0	0	1,350
Trendi Debut	3	F	5	0	0	0	300
Trendseeker	3	F	13	1	3	3	9,647
Trendy Native	2	F	5	1	0	0	9,720
Trentino	6	H	11	1	2	1	29,455
Trents Special	4	G	11	0	2	3	11,127
Tres Aimees's	2	G	1	0	0	0	0
Tres Diamantes	4	C	7	1	0	0	6,637
Tres Ladies	3	F	2	0	0	0	0
Tres Linda	2	F	11	2	4	1	45,000
Tres Lucy	2	F	3	0	0	0	241
Tres' Mauve	5	M	11	1	1	0	4,853
Tres Touche	6	G	7	1	3	2	94,703
Tresor Du Jour	2	F	1	0	0	0	237
Tresor l'Amour	2	F	2	0	0	0	0
Trevally (MEX)	6	H	7	2	1	1	8,480
Trevor Forever	3	G	12	2	2	0	28,351
Trevor's Lucky One	5	G	11	3	2	3	63,585
Trey Aero	5	G	8	0	0	0	1,595
Tri Chem	4	G	12	2	0	1	8,024
Tri Diplomacy	3	G	7	0	0	1	935
Tri for the Moon	2	F	1	0	0	0	195
Tri for the Stars	4	F	1	0	0	0	225
Tri M All	4	G	15	2	3	3	15,717
Tri n' Nickya	2	C	4	0	0	0	1,920
Tri Our Dan	3	C	10	1	0	0	9,102
Tri Out	4	G	2	0	0	1	280
Tri Paw	6	G	5	0	0	0	909
Tri Phailme	2	G	2	0	0	0	390
Tri Running	3	F	6	0	0	0	524
Tri So Sweet	2	G	5	1	1	1	10,920
Tri Some Irish	3	F	2	1	1	0	20,160
Tri the Waitress	5	G	5	0	0	0	250
Tri This Way	3	F	16	1	1	2	14,566
Tri to Be True	4	G	11	0	1	4	14,711
Tri Tong	2	G	3	0	0	0	201
Tri Tower's	10	G	5	0	0	0	146
Tri Wagering	6	G	13	2	5	0	19,058
Tria	4	F	10	0	0	0	1,532
Triactinglikealady	3	F	13	1	0	0	6,346
Triage	3	G	7	1	0	3	19,606
Trial and Error	5	H	10	1	0	1	4,323
Trial by Judge	3	F	4	0	1	2	3,845
Trial by Jury	4	C	10	4	2	1	158,960
Trial Dancer	4	F	6	2	0	0	15,390
Trial Prep	4	C	2	0	0	0	2,591
Tribal Advantage	3	F	4	0	0	1	2,262
Tribal Council	4	C	6	1	1	0	6,450
Tribal Gold	8	G	7	1	0	1	4,522
Tribal Impact	6	G	15	0	0	1	2,101
Tribal Leader	3	G	16	2	2	3	18,272
Tribal Prince	2	C	1	0	0	0	125
Tribal Quest	4	F	13	3	3	2	15,135
Tribal Rage	4	F	5	0	0	0	490
Tribal Trick	4	G	8	2	2	0	25,018
Tribal Warrior	7	G	3	0	0	0	1,020
Tribarge	3	G	9	0	5	0	7,720
Tribe	3	G	8	3	2	1	79,200
Tribeca Dancer	2	F	5	0	0	0	1,215
Tribellistic	3	F	8	1	0	0	6,345
Tribo Ka	3	F	2	0	0	0	50
Tribulator	3	C	14	3	1	3	49,720
Tribunal Run	2	F	2	0	0	0	1,180
Tribute Express	3	G	2	1	0	0	16,275
Tribute to America	3	C	2	0	2	0	12,580
Tribute to Heroes	3	C	7	0	2	2	31,390
Tributetojimnded	4	G	5	0	1	1	5,075
Tributetothatcher	3	F	6	2	0	1	33,385
Tricia	2	F	2	0	0	0	392
Tricia Anne	5	M	6	2	1	0	5,187
Tricia's Account	3	F	16	3	3	2	47,578
Trick a Toga	3	C	10	0	0	0	2,730
Trick Again	3	F	15	3	1	2	80,240
Trick Bag	6	G	18	0	6	6	38,110
Trick Ballet	2	C	5	1	0	0	7,200
Trick Card	4	G	5	0	1	1	4,155
Trick Conviction	5	G	4	0	0	1	480
Trick Game	3	F	1	0	0	0	0
Trick of the North	2	C	2	1	0	0	12,430
Trick of the Tale	2	G	2	0	0	0	0
Trick Or Trial	2	F	11	1	2	3	34,205
Trick Or Trixie	4	F	7	0	0	0	780
Trick Or Truth	4	F	5	0	0	1	770
Trick Shot Artist	2	C	3	1	2	0	8,200
Trick Shot Gal	2	F	7	0	2	0	4,739
Trick Show	3	G	12	1	1	2	5,530
Trick Taker	4	F	1	0	0	0	93
Trick Your Man	2	F	5	0	1	1	9,331
Tricked by Love	3	F	4	0	0	1	783

Horse	Age	Sex	Sts	1st	2d	3d	Won
Tricked Into Love	4	F	13	1	3	1	20,615
Tricked Twice	2	F	2	1	0	0	4,635
Trickey Crew	7	G	8	1	0	1	11,903
Trickey Jones	2	G	5	1	0	1	36,601
Trickey Mickey	3	G	12	0	2	0	6,025
Trickey Trevor	4	C	11	5	3	2	129,650
Trickinthepark	2	G	8	1	2	1	30,740
Trickmeister	6	G	4	0	1	3	13,616
Tricks and Grins	3	G	1	0	0	0	1,560
Tricks Are Great	4	G	9	0	1	2	4,407
Tricks for Tracy	7	M	10	1	0	0	3,805
Tricks Her	3	F	5	1	2	0	46,200
Trick's Lad	5	G	11	3	1	2	9,301
Tricks of Glory	2	C	2	2	0	0	32,700
Tricksand	4	F	9	1	0	1	5,108
Tricksey Miss	2	F	6	1	1	1	12,685
Trickster Trio	4	G	14	1	1	0	5,308
Tricksword	5	M	3	0	0	1	5,850
Tricky Account	7	M	6	2	1	0	25,360
Tricky Alex	3	C	9	1	4	0	20,119
Tricky Avenger	2	C	1	0	0	0	0
Tricky Booboo	3	C	1	0	0	0	100
Tricky Cal	2	G	3	0	0	0	670
Tricky Caller	5	M	8	3	2	0	15,580
Tricky Callie	2	F	5	0	0	0	500
Tricky City	2	F	1	0	0	0	120
Tricky Clearance	4	C	16	1	2	5	18,011
Tricky Crossing	5	H	2	0	0	0	0
Tricky Crystal	2	F	5	1	0	0	4,860
Tricky Dakota	4	G	14	2	2	3	15,652
Tricky Date	3	F	8	0	0	0	1,540
Tricky Deal	3	F	6	0	0	0	375
Tricky Dee	4	F	6	0	1	2	3,423
Tricky Details	8	M	12	2	3	2	37,220
Tricky Devil	2	C	2	0	0	0	0
Tricky Dreams	4	C	11	2	3	1	4,220
Tricky Ending	4	F	1	0	0	0	42
Tricky Flash Flood	2	C	15	1	2	1	50,281
Tricky Flyer	4	C	4	1	0	1	2,166
Tricky Gin	3	C	8	1	3	3	45,120
Tricky Greinette	2	F	3	0	0	0	110
Tricky Hawaiian	7	H	1	0	0	0	0
Tricky Hearts	6	G	5	3	0	0	44,460
Tricky Image	4	G	7	0	1	3	13,940
Tricky Inquiry	3	C	3	0	0	0	400
Tricky Jester	8	M	2	0	0	0	0
Tricky Katie	3	F	10	1	1	2	7,167
Tricky Kenny	7	G	11	0	3	0	3,870
Tricky Linklee	5	G	12	1	2	2	8,235
Tricky Logan	8	G	9	0	0	2	1,085
Tricky Luck	4	F	11	1	2	1	23,085
Tricky Machine	5	G	7	3	2	1	15,924
Tricky Mackee	5	M	9	1	0	1	9,242
Tricky Maddie	4	F	6	0	0	1	1,548
Tricky Maneuver	5	G	5	2	2	1	13,150
Tricky Mind	3	G	4	0	0	1	2,213
Tricky Mirage	4	F	5	1	0	0	24,826
Tricky Mistress	3	F	4	0	0	0	0
Tricky Mo Jo	4	F	9	1	1	0	12,006
Tricky Mocha	7	G	8	2	3	2	47,670
Tricky Now	6	G	13	3	4	1	16,515
Tricky Odie	4	C	4	1	3	0	10,735
Tricky On Ice	7	M	5	0	0	2	920
Tricky Pace	5	G	3	1	1	1	20,830
Tricky Phone	3	F	7	1	1	0	15,836
Tricky Pick Six	3	G	8	1	1	0	44,085
Tricky Prince	8	H	1	0	0	0	0
Tricky Princess	4	F	17	2	1	4	14,472
Tricky Purpose	3	C	13	1	2	2	15,380
Tricky Quicky	8	M	14	2	4	1	21,677
Tricky Ransom	3	C	8	1	2	0	11,150
Tricky Ray	2	F	3	0	0	1	990
Tricky Ray Source	8	G	15	2	1	4	7,233
Tricky Storm	4	C	9	4	0	2	105,890
Tricky Surf	3	F	5	1	1	0	45,300
Tricky Surprise	4	F	7	0	2	0	13,504
Tricky Taboo	2	C	1	0	0	0	725
Tricky Tami	5	M	9	1	0	1	9,855
Tricky Terms	2	F	1	0	0	0	0
Tricky Texas Lady	3	F	9	3	2	1	15,285
Tricky Time	7	G	11	0	2	0	3,845
Tricky Touch	2	C	5	0	1	1	15,760
Tricky Toy	3	G	12	1	3	2	20,675
Tricky Transaction	3	F	7	1	0	3	28,435
Tricky Travis	5	G	5	0	1	1	14,960
Tricky Trick	3	G	10	0	0	1	3,445
Tricky Truth	3	F	11	2	3	4	53,055
Tricky Twigs	6	G	8	2	1	4	34,675
Tricky Tyler	6	H	5	1	0	1	7,460
Tricky Wars	6	M	12	3	2	4	16,300
Tricky Work	2	F	1	0	0	0	0
Tricky's Gal	5	M	14	1	3	3	14,380
Tricky's Treat	2	F	1	0	0	0	0
Tricon Gold	2	C	4	0	0	0	300
Tricona	3	G	6	0	0	0	720
Trident House	3	C	9	1	1	0	22,100
Trieste	3	G	13	2	4	1	28,400
Trieste Cat	2	C	1	0	0	0	0
Trieste's Honor	2	C	4	0	0	1	8,100
Trifecta	2	C	5	0	0	2	6,665
Trigala	4	F	5	0	0	0	440
Trihighfive	2	G	4	0	0	0	682
Trijonia	3	F	13	7	0	0	81,273
Trillion Cazillion	4	F	4	0	1	1	3,741
Trillion Wing	3	F	4	0	1	0	5,980
Trillora Court	7	H	12	1	2	2	10,335
Trilogy (GB)	4	C	3	1	0	0	22,200
Trilok	2	G	1	0	0	0	230
Trim Image	4	G	17	1	4	0	17,135
Trimark Two	3	G	9	0	1	3	10,020
Trimont	5	G	9	1	2	1	8,512
Trimontium	4	G	4	0	1	1	8,740
Tri'n One	3	C	6	0	1	0	1,166
Trinas Other Son	8	G	12	0	1	4	11,119
Trinity Moon	3	F	4	2	1	0	37,420
Trinity River	6	G	11	2	2	3	36,450
Trinka	8	M	9	1	1	1	6,169
Triomphe Spitfire	3	G	2	0	0	0	217
Trion Georgia	5	H	5	2	1	0	69,082
Trip Charge	8	G	11	1	0	2	14,770
Trip Report	7	H	3	0	0	0	216
Tripat (IRE)	4	C	8	1	1	0	44,756
Tripcord	5	G	15	0	4	5	10,425
Triplane	5	G	12	1	1	2	8,956
Triplaymate	4	F	1	0	0	0	0
Triple a Society	5	G	11	1	3	3	7,018
Triple Ace	4	F	2	0	0	0	0
Triple Appeal	7	M	21	2	5	2	14,186
Triple Arts	5	M	4	0	0	0	236
Triple Aught	3	G	4	1	1	1	13,910
Triple Card	5	G	1	0	0	0	0
Triple Cash	4	G	13	1	0	2	6,995
Triple Chance	3	G	4	0	0	0	549
Triple Checker	5	G	4	0	0	0	52
Triple Deek	8	G	3	0	0	0	900
Triple Ears	3	G	1	0	0	0	0
Triple Fantasy	2	F	6	0	2	0	20,440
Triple Fax	4	G	17	2	3	3	33,580
Triple Gap	5	G	3	0	0	0	96
Triple Gold	4	F	6	0	1	0	8,250
Triple Great	9	G	4	2	1	0	3,540
Triple J	3	F	8	1	2	3	34,550
Triple Jacq	5	G	5	2	2	0	22,100
Triple Jim	8	G	12	4	2	1	18,352
Triple Man O	6	G	3	0	0	0	436
Triple Net	3	F	1	0	1	0	4,200
Triple Nickel Five	5	G	12	2	0	0	12,232
Triple Putt	5	G	13	0	0	0	1,336
Triple Slam	2	F	2	0	0	0	1,170
Triple Spin	5	M	12	2	2	1	16,531
Triple Steal	5	G	4	0	0	0	150
Triple Storm	3	C	10	0	0	2	1,459
Triple the Speed	3	F	2	0	0	0	0
Triple Threat	6	M	7	2	1	1	28,805
Triple Tiara	2	F	1	0	0	0	975
Triple Time	5	G	7	2	1	2	11,101
Triple Vice	8	G	2	0	0	0	244

RECORDS OF HORSES

Horse	Age	Sex	Sts	1st	2d	3d	Won
Triple Vixen	3	F	2	0	0	0	0
Triple Witching	5	H	13	3	1	2	45,739
Triple X.	2	C	1	0	0	0	750
Tripoleen	4	F	1	0	0	0	300
Tripp to Albadou	6	G	5	0	0	1	2,040
Tripp Wire	6	M	14	5	1	0	49,045
Triptips	3	C	10	2	2	1	10,418
Triptronic	5	H	4	0	0	0	225
Triptowin	3	G	8	1	1	2	18,280
Tri's Image	5	M	5	0	0	1	1,840
Tri's Moment	3	F	17	3	1	4	31,433
Tri's Passion	3	F	7	4	2	0	88,900
Trish	2	F	4	0	0	1	1,040
Trish Blusher	4	F	1	0	0	0	77
Trisher	5	M	16	2	1	0	6,595
Trish's Cajun	3	F	12	3	2	1	78,919
Trish's Diamond	2	C	7	1	2	2	62,795
Trisis	3	F	7	1	1	3	28,300
Triskaboo	8	M	7	0	0	1	980
Tristas Demon	3	G	9	2	0	3	8,265
Tristin's Race	4	G	12	0	2	1	10,980
Tristor Factor	8	G	1	0	0	1	1,730
Tristorm	5	M	11	0	0	0	1,200
Triton Missile	3	C	7	1	0	2	25,220
Trivial Amount	2	C	2	0	0	0	390
Triviality	5	M	15	3	1	2	22,960
Trix City	4	F	6	2	0	0	47,830
Trix for Love	3	G	1	0	0	0	360
Trixie C	3	F	5	1	0	1	6,505
Trixie Chick	3	F	10	0	0	1	11,220
Trixie Lady	2	F	6	1	2	0	19,800
Trixie Wac	4	F	2	0	0	0	405
Trixie's Chokem	4	G	8	3	0	2	55,692
Trodos	4	G	17	0	2	1	7,785
Trois Pesos	5	H	4	0	0	0	141
Trois Rivieres	3	F	7	1	2	0	12,263
Trois Villes	2	G	4	0	0	0	0
Troisieme Age (IRE)	3	F	5	0	1	0	2,390
Trojan Miss	3	F	14	1	1	1	10,615
Trojan Steele	2	C	1	0	0	0	2,335
Troll	3	G	8	1	0	1	22,560
Trollette	5	M	14	2	2	3	31,450
Tromador	3	F	13	1	1	4	14,575
Trombone Pete	3	G	4	0	0	1	1,210
Trompolino (CHI)	5	G	11	1	2	1	90,420
Tronare (CHI)	5	H	2	0	0	0	4,880
Troncom	7	G	12	0	0	1	3,232
Trone	3	C	14	2	1	3	35,241
Troody Booth	5	M	9	0	1	0	2,400
Trooper Lady	5	M	3	0	0	0	0
Trooper Red	7	G	7	1	1	1	22,800
Trophy Case	5	G	19	5	1	2	59,059
Trophy Edition Too	4	F	10	1	0	3	24,640
Trophy for Me	10	G	3	0	1	1	830
Trophy Gold	4	F	3	0	0	2	1,113
Trophy Lane	3	F	4	0	1	0	2,059
Tropical Blossom	5	M	9	3	1	3	197,616
Tropical Deputy	5	G	10	1	2	1	15,828
Tropical Exposure	4	F	4	0	0	0	360
Tropical Fever	4	G	1	1	0	0	4,500
Tropical Heatwave	3	G	9	2	2	1	29,392
Tropical Storm	3	C	1	0	0	0	2,135
Tropical Sun	7	H	6	0	2	2	12,000
Tropickid	3	G	9	1	0	1	4,500
Trouble At Dawn	3	F	11	1	1	0	5,748
Trouble D	10	G	8	0	0	1	450
Trouble Doubled	2	C	2	0	0	0	139
Trouble in Love	7	G	8	0	0	0	1,460
Trouble N Beantown	3	F	7	1	0	3	9,380
Trouble N Paradise	4	C	10	1	0	3	7,420
Trouble One	7	H	5	0	1	0	1,976
Trouble Spot	7	G	8	0	0	3	2,790
Trouble T.	6	G	2	0	0	0	120
Troubled Nation	6	G	3	0	0	0	0
Troubled Prospect	4	G	2	0	0	0	42
Troubled Son	6	H	3	0	0	0	0
Troubleinshangrila	3	F	5	0	0	1	4,820
Trouble'n'fortune	3	C	6	2	1	1	17,549
Troubles Gaylor	4	F	1	0	0	0	0
Troublesome	4	F	2	0	0	0	320
Troublesome Girl	3	F	1	0	0	0	130
Troublesomeaffair	3	F	3	1	0	0	990
Trounce	6	H	10	4	1	2	110,955
Troupe Disastor	6	H	8	1	2	1	2,385
Trove	3	F	9	1	2	1	24,260
Troy Ounce	2	C	1	0	0	0	0
Troyix	7	G	11	0	1	1	1,942
Troy's Honor	3	G	8	0	0	0	2,280
Troy's Peak	3	C	7	0	1	1	2,504
Troy's Tramp	3	F	1	1	0	0	15,960
Troy's Venture	7	G	2	0	0	0	250
Tru Aldi	2	F	4	0	0	2	7,200
Tru Bride	3	F	15	0	2	1	5,372
Tru Dazzler	4	F	13	1	1	3	14,097
Tru Flame	3	F	2	0	0	0	665
Tru Gal	3	F	5	0	0	0	1,311
Tru Piano	2	F	1	0	0	0	75
Tru Worthy	8	G	7	1	1	1	2,345
Truce N Hoedown	2	G	9	1	0	1	16,050
Truce Reigns	4	G	5	1	0	1	6,498
Truce Time	9	M	17	0	2	4	6,945
Truck	6	H	9	0	3	0	3,231
Truck Stop Trudy	4	F	2	0	0	0	92
Truckee Groom	2	C	2	0	0	1	3,310
Truckee Pal	2	C	3	0	0	0	0
Truckee River	3	G	3	1	0	2	31,255
Truckee Traveler	3	C	16	2	4	3	45,091
Truckee Tudor	2	G	5	0	0	0	636
Truckee Warrior	3	G	12	2	3	3	50,250
Trucker's Special	4	F	16	3	2	2	22,417
Truckin On	3	C	5	1	0	1	4,885
Truckin Baron	11	G	6	0	0	1	3,540
Truckle Feature	3	C	4	0	1	0	26,160
Truckstar	2	F	5	2	0	0	21,630
Truckstop Vicki	4	F	11	2	3	2	14,838
Truculent Pirate	4	C	3	0	0	0	0
Truculent Pow Wow	3	G	18	0	3	2	22,923
Trudge	5	M	4	0	0	0	879
Trudina	4	F	6	0	0	1	1,080
True Anticipation	2	G	2	0	0	0	0
True Appeal	3	F	1	0	0	0	0
True Aries	3	F	9	1	2	0	13,286
True Baloo	3	G	6	1	0	0	2,103
True Bet	2	G	3	0	0	0	451
True Blonde Beauty	2	F	2	0	0	1	3,760
True Blue Girl	4	F	9	2	1	1	17,560
True Blue Moon	4	G	9	0	1	0	6,430
True Blue Prospect	2	G	6	1	0	1	14,701
True Blue Rebel	3	G	7	2	1	1	19,120
True Bucks	5	G	11	2	1	0	7,570
True Charisma	2	C	8	0	0	1	3,000
True Cheers	5	G	6	1	0	1	7,299
True Concern	5	H	12	5	2	3	36,230
True Conquest	5	G	19	1	3	6	25,967
True Contender	2	G	3	1	0	0	28,566
True Crimson	3	C	3	0	0	0	410
True Cynara	6	M	2	1	0	0	5,400
True Dancer	3	G	6	1	1	0	21,890
True Dawn	4	F	9	1	0	1	8,588
True Direction	4	C	2	1	0	1	53,600
True Do	7	M	16	2	1	0	5,820
True Dreamer	3	C	5	0	0	1	2,730
True Dreams	5	H	4	0	0	0	111
True Enough	3	C	2	1	0	0	17,760
True Expectations	4	F	15	0	6	6	33,706
True Facts	4	F	4	1	1	0	14,400
True Fashion	5	M	15	0	0	1	6,914
True Gem	2	F	2	1	1	0	28,400
True Genius	4	G	14	5	1	2	103,028
True Gift	3	F	2	0	0	0	0
True Girl	3	F	1	0	0	0	0
True Glit	2	C	2	0	0	0	264
True Glitter	6	M	2	1	0	0	9,720
True Honor	3	G	13	2	1	1	21,680
True Hope	3	C	8	1	1	2	22,225
True Houston	4	F	3	0	0	0	150
True Identity	4	C	1	0	0	0	0
True Jest	4	F	12	0	3	1	8,923

Horse	Age	Sex	Sts	1st	2d	3d	Won
True Joy	4	F	7	0	0	0	1,190
True Kentucky	4	F	1	0	0	0	0
True Lord	7	G	19	4	2	2	31,430
True Love Is Gold	5	M	15	1	0	4	10,928
True Lover	8	G	8	2	0	3	8,466
True Love's Secret	6	G	10	3	0	0	63,460
True Luck	2	F	3	0	0	0	120
True Moments	2	F	5	1	1	0	18,450
True Monarch	4	C	9	2	1	1	15,609
True n' Distinct	7	G	1	0	0	0	0
True Nobility	4	F	2	0	0	0	145
True Pals	4	C	3	0	0	0	0
True Passion	5	G	12	2	3	2	67,910
True Patriot	3	C	5	1	0	2	34,880
True Phenomenon	4	G	6	1	1	0	15,210
True Play	3	F	9	1	0	1	9,330
True Prince	4	G	10	0	1	0	1,788
True Red	5	G	17	3	2	1	13,545
True Revenge	2	G	1	0	0	0	0
True Roledex	2	C	2	0	0	0	414
True Rose	5	M	8	0	2	0	21,660
True Ruby	6	M	11	1	1	4	37,111
True Runner	4	G	9	2	1	1	18,615
True Sailing	5	G	12	1	3	1	7,385
True Sensation	4	F	11	2	2	2	83,240
True Shrew	4	F	12	1	2	0	7,584
True Silver	8	G	7	1	1	1	8,276
True Solution	4	G	11	3	1	1	26,567
True Speed	3	F	14	2	3	2	21,824
True Statesman	2	G	2	0	0	0	185
True Storm	4	G	3	0	0	0	188
True Sunshine	5	G	2	0	0	0	0
True Survivor	8	H	11	2	0	0	7,791
True Tear Drops	4	F	5	0	0	0	1,695
True to Form	3	F	12	2	2	1	19,700
True to Slew	3	G	5	0	0	1	3,119
True Toyou	4	F	5	0	1	0	1,049
True Trick	3	C	10	1	3	4	38,480
True Tyrant	5	G	1	0	0	0	113
True Verse	2	F	1	0	0	0	0
True Wind	4	F	5	2	0	0	41,712
True Wisper	7	G	11	3	0	2	16,075
True Wonder	3	C	7	2	2	2	38,420
Trueamericanspirit	3	G	8	3	3	1	118,770
Truecat	2	F	1	0	0	0	0
Truelamar	6	G	1	0	0	0	0
Truely a Trooper	2	C	5	0	0	1	2,305
Truely Marked	2	G	9	0	0	1	1,815
Truely Perfection	3	G	1	0	1	0	1,900
Trueytoo	5	M	8	0	1	1	22,430
Truitte	4	G	4	0	0	0	0
Truking East	3	C	1	0	0	0	0
Trukndowntheavenue	3	F	19	2	4	4	48,935
Truly a Cherokee	5	G	1	0	0	0	0
Truly a Judge	5	G	10	1	3	3	135,063
Truly a Lady	5	M	2	0	0	0	150
Truly a Legend	4	F	9	1	0	0	33,900
Truly a Notebook	8	G	15	1	2	2	6,396
Truly a Runner	7	G	9	4	1	1	30,555
Truly Awesome	5	G	11	3	0	0	22,236
Truly Exclusive	5	M	11	0	0	2	2,102
Truly Fabulous	2	F	4	0	1	0	2,639
Truly Fantastic	6	G	12	0	3	0	9,748
Truly Fortunate	2	F	3	1	0	0	11,700
Truly Honored	2	G	7	0	3	1	15,761
Truly Obliging	5	H	15	3	0	2	14,439
Truly Orbit	4	F	3	0	0	0	0
Truly Our Secret	3	F	2	0	0	0	230
Truly Precious	2	F	3	0	1	2	5,660
Truly Relentless	5	H	12	2	1	1	40,724
Truly Special	3	F	8	0	2	1	22,650
Truly Spoken	3	F	11	4	2	1	36,836
Truly the Best	3	F	5	0	0	0	11,040
Trulyapirate	3	G	11	0	2	1	8,872
Trulyastarr	2	F	2	0	0	0	519
Truly's Teddy	5	G	4	0	0	1	445
Truman's Bad Girl	3	F	6	0	0	0	852
Truman's Raider	4	C	4	1	1	0	26,710
Trumbanick Charlie	5	H	13	0	0	4	3,152

Horse	Age	Sex	Sts	1st	2d	3d	Won
Trumbull	7	H	3	0	0	1	647
Trump Marina	4	C	1	1	0	0	23,400
Trumpeter Nine	6	H	2	1	0	0	272
Trumpeter Swan	3	G	1	1	0	0	24,600
Trumpeting Chelle	3	F	10	2	2	1	24,520
Trumpets Delight	3	C	6	1	1	1	14,386
Trumps Clown	9	G	13	8	4	0	54,170
Trumps Lil Kitty	3	F	4	1	1	0	11,050
Trumps Native Lady	5	M	11	2	0	3	24,070
Trumpster	6	H	5	0	0	0	1,500
Trumpty Dumpty	10	G	12	0	0	1	1,311
Trupon On	3	F	6	2	1	0	54,807
Tru's Last Ride	2	F	1	0	0	0	115
Trust	3	F	7	1	1	0	8,740
Trust a Buck	4	F	7	2	2	0	16,000
Trust Fund	4	F	1	0	0	0	222
Trust Her	3	F	5	2	0	1	90,414
Trust Me	2	C	7	1	1	2	32,035
Trust N Luck	3	C	4	1	1	1	344,684
Trustabull	3	F	7	0	0	0	570
Trusted Rumor	2	F	8	2	4	0	17,460
Trustee Man	3	C	11	1	2	4	70,150
Trustmenow	3	F	13	1	2	3	12,677
Trusty Hunter	3	C	10	0	0	0	3,149
Trusty Jett	4	C	9	1	1	1	11,585
Truth About Misty	5	M	7	3	1	1	15,310
Truth Be Known	6	G	10	0	1	3	3,096
Truth by Ruth	2	F	6	1	1	0	24,000
Truth Endures	2	G	8	1	1	1	7,420
Truth in Testamony	6	H	6	1	1	1	6,797
Truth Matters	4	G	12	1	3	4	35,822
Truth 'n Power	7	G	7	2	2	0	1,928
Truth of the Heart	6	G	10	2	0	0	6,779
Truth Or Dear	5	G	2	0	0	0	0
Truth Serum	2	C	6	1	2	1	67,491
Truthful Heart	2	C	3	0	0	0	530
Truthful Soldier	3	F	1	0	0	0	0
Truxton's Miracle	4	F	4	0	1	1	840
Try Again	6	G	13	3	3	1	36,780
Try Again Len	3	C	3	1	0	0	13,237
Try for Par	5	G	15	2	3	2	23,980
Try Hard Gal	2	F	1	0	0	0	95
Try Harder	3	F	3	1	0	0	26,400
Try My Tune	4	C	3	0	0	0	930
Try Season	5	H	3	0	0	0	0
Try Try Again	5	G	4	0	0	0	0
Tryityoullikeit	3	G	10	0	0	0	1,620
Try'nsteel	4	F	8	0	0	1	572
Tryon Tricks	6	M	2	0	0	0	115
Tryst At Sea	4	F	6	0	0	0	395
Tryst Twist	3	C	3	0	0	0	300
Tryst's Dancer	4	G	7	0	1	2	3,320
Trytobetricky	3	G	2	0	0	0	140
Trytocatchmary	6	M	1	0	0	0	0
T's Cafe	4	G	1	0	0	0	0
T's Halo	5	G	9	1	1	0	6,153
T's Mar Jon	3	G	4	0	0	0	1,094
Tsar Czar	6	H	5	0	1	1	12,340
Tslewnami	5	G	2	0	0	0	0
Tsu Tsu Oke	3	C	1	0	0	0	0
Tsu Tsu Ro	4	F	12	1	2	1	14,960
Tsu Tsu Won	10	M	10	2	2	2	41,764
Tsunami Surprise	3	F	8	2	1	0	7,278
Tsunami Wind	4	G	10	0	2	2	7,300
Tsunami's Majesty	6	M	7	0	0	1	1,370
Tsuniday	10	G	3	0	0	0	120
Tsuzomin	2	C	4	2	1	0	46,793
Tu La Pia	3	C	3	1	0	0	1,170
Tu l'Homme	3	G	4	0	0	0	0
Tu Pagaras	3	F	1	0	0	0	75
Tu Tea Attack	5	G	3	0	0	0	90
Tu Tone Brown	5	G	12	4	1	4	16,908
Tu Tone Corozon	5	H	12	1	1	0	9,858
Tu Tu Kool	3	F	1	0	0	0	217
Tu Z Potts	4	F	8	2	0	0	36,432
Tuacahn	3	G	4	1	0	0	5,900
Tualatin Honey	4	F	3	0	0	0	0
Tuamotu	6	G	11	2	2	1	3,053
Tub Tosser	5	G	6	1	0	1	10,502

Horse	Age	Sex	Sts	1st	2d	3d	Won
Tubacity	3	F	1	0	0	0	0
Tubbs	3	G	1	0	0	0	0
Tubby Cat	6	G	3	2	1	0	38,370
Tubby Clinton	7	H	5	0	0	0	158
Tubrok	6	H	6	1	2	0	21,780
Tucked Away	3	F	10	3	3	1	178,694
Tuckers Run	3	C	15	3	7	0	46,201
Tucknup	6	H	2	0	0	0	114
Tuck's Bag	4	C	4	0	0	0	0
Tucky Bound	3	G	10	3	3	2	15,002
Tucson City	3	G	15	1	3	1	15,765
Tudge	3	G	10	0	4	0	13,390
Tudi Cielo	4	F	7	1	1	1	17,655
Tudor Court	4	F	10	4	1	1	89,590
Tudor Knight	5	G	3	0	0	1	577
Tudor Ridge	5	G	2	1	0	0	1,320
Tudor Zie	5	M	3	1	0	0	3,100
Tudor's Baby	3	F	7	1	2	0	12,145
Tudor's Honor Roll	2	F	1	0	0	0	230
Tudy's Choice	3	G	9	1	0	0	43,479
Tudy's Rib	4	F	3	0	0	0	146
Tuesday Morning	5	M	12	0	1	0	4,310
Tuesday Prayer	2	F	2	0	0	0	0
Tuesday's Ghost	2	C	2	0	0	0	720
Tuesdays Heatwave	4	C	3	0	1	0	3,226
Tuesday's Lady	3	F	6	2	0	2	11,742
Tuff Ante	3	G	2	0	0	0	0
Tuff as Iron	4	G	13	2	4	3	47,855
Tuff Broo	4	F	4	1	1	0	26,540
Tuff Chick	5	M	8	1	1	0	80,940
Tuff Coach	3	G	4	0	0	0	530
Tuff Expectations	2	C	1	0	1	0	1,760
Tuff Hint	4	F	8	0	0	1	2,269
Tuff Man Dan	2	G	2	0	0	0	450
Tuff N Pugnacious	7	H	11	0	2	2	2,830
Tuff n Tenacious	10	G	5	0	0	0	354
Tuff Number	10	G	15	0	0	2	2,773
Tuff Old General	5	H	5	0	0	0	640
Tuff Racket	4	C	5	0	0	1	260
Tuff Ray	3	G	2	0	0	0	0
Tuff Tiger Joe	4	C	6	0	0	2	546
Tuff Tyler Man	2	C	7	1	2	1	6,633
Tuffy	3	C	5	0	1	2	2,176
Tuffy O'Brannigan	2	C	1	0	0	0	0
Tuffy's Halfsweep	3	F	2	0	0	0	550
Tufposition	5	G	8	5	1	2	8,650
Tuft of Flowers	4	F	3	0	0	0	384
Tufton Avenue	4	F	16	3	2	3	29,168
Tugboat Fanny	4	F	4	0	0	0	735
Tuk'n Sail	3	F	1	0	0	0	0
Tuktoyaktuk	5	M	8	2	3	1	40,158
Tukwilamina	5	M	8	0	2	0	5,825
Tulaji Taj	3	G	5	0	0	0	1,171
Tulalip Bay	3	G	7	2	1	1	11,088
Tulare Road	3	G	2	0	2	0	3,800
Tularosa Road	4	F	10	2	0	2	16,638
Tularosa Sands	4	F	7	0	0	1	688
Tuleyries	4	F	14	2	5	2	59,660
Tulips to Kiss	4	F	10	0	2	2	17,663
Tulira Castle	3	C	1	0	0	0	0
Tulisha	2	F	7	1	0	1	36,050
Tulla	3	F	1	0	1	0	2,700
Tullow	4	C	4	2	0	0	10,230
Tullynally	3	G	3	3	0	0	46,750
Tulogie	5	H	10	0	1	6	4,235
Tulsa	3	F	8	5	0	1	104,588
Tulsa Mambo	7	G	15	0	0	1	1,248
Tulsa Robery	2	C	2	0	0	1	800
Tulsa Slew	3	F	3	1	1	0	4,360
Tulsa Stride	5	M	2	0	0	0	0
Tulsa Sunrise	5	M	4	0	0	1	375
Tulsa Town	2	C	1	0	0	0	0
Tulsa World	5	M	7	0	2	2	6,183
Tulupai	3	F	5	0	0	2	17,660
Tumble Me Right (JPN)	3	F	3	0	3	0	21,120
Tumble 'n Nelson	4	G	2	0	0	0	378
Tumble Twice	4	G	2	0	0	0	364
Tumblebrutus	2	C	5	1	2	0	46,315
Tumbleweed Dancer	6	H	12	2	0	0	7,513
Tumbling Gold	5	M	2	0	0	0	75
Tumketa	3	C	15	3	2	2	25,385
Tuna Fish	3	F	8	0	1	1	3,560
Tunangannya	5	M	12	0	2	2	4,990
Tunder Ponche	2	G	5	1	0	2	19,025
Tundra Road	5	G	10	0	2	1	6,282
Tundras Token	2	C	5	0	1	1	1,968
Tune a Win for A B	6	M	21	3	4	4	27,051
Tune Lender	2	F	2	1	0	0	6,540
Tune of the Spirit	2	C	8	1	0	1	17,694
Tune the Harp	4	C	7	0	0	0	796
Tune Up the Band	3	F	7	1	0	0	12,620
Tuneable	3	G	3	0	0	0	0
Tuned Just Right	6	G	5	0	0	1	2,730
Tuned Out	7	H	2	0	0	0	0
Tuner River	6	M	4	2	1	1	36,106
Tune's Order	3	F	5	0	0	0	1,365
Tune's Tale	2	F	2	0	0	0	2,580
Tunesmith	6	G	4	0	0	0	354
Tunette	6	M	4	1	0	0	13,560
Tungo	9	G	14	1	3	1	7,293
Tunie's Secret	4	F	24	1	2	3	13,112
Tunintothebeat	4	F	5	1	0	1	10,509
Tunis	8	H	2	0	1	0	1,280
Tunk Ridge	5	M	4	0	0	0	670
Tunnel Fire	3	G	4	1	0	0	7,120
Tunnel Hill Lady	4	F	10	0	1	1	1,762
Tunnel Man	2	C	6	1	0	1	9,570
Tunnel Vision	2	C	8	1	0	0	9,630
Tunnell's Chapel	5	G	16	0	2	3	5,220
Tunon	4	G	8	3	0	0	19,078
Tupie's Parlay	4	C	14	1	3	1	16,454
Tupp Up	5	M	5	0	0	1	1,270
Tuppence	6	M	8	0	0	0	7,128
Turban	4	G	5	2	0	1	68,750
Turbine	3	F	2	0	0	1	1,440
Turbo Arrow	4	G	9	1	0	0	4,488
Turbo Bullet	5	M	4	0	0	0	0
Turbo Charger	8	G	11	1	1	3	25,704
Turbo Jet	7	G	11	2	0	3	10,032
Turbo Kat	6	H	6	0	1	0	2,225
Turbo Paddy	4	F	11	3	1	2	25,169
Turbo Robo	5	M	6	1	2	0	23,250
Turbo Thunder	3	C	2	0	1	0	2,060
Turbo Tiger	3	C	10	0	1	0	1,556
Turbo Tom	3	G	3	0	0	0	0
Turbotaxman	6	G	5	2	1	1	39,265
Turbulent Flight (NZ)	6	G	1	0	0	0	0
Turbulent Kiss	4	F	3	0	0	0	0
Turbulent Spirit	10	G	6	0	1	0	3,896
Turbulent Tigress	2	F	2	0	1	0	3,456
Turbulent Trick	2	F	1	0	0	0	0
Turbulento (MEX)	6	H	3	0	0	0	148
Turf Daddy	2	C	3	0	0	0	1,890
Turf Surfer	6	G	11	2	1	2	33,530
Turf Flyer	7	G	4	0	1	1	2,102
Turk Or Treat	8	H	1	0	0	0	0
Turkana's Treasure	3	F	1	0	0	0	0
Turketta	2	F	3	0	0	0	85
Turkey Creek	5	G	6	0	0	0	0
Turkey Joe	5	H	3	0	0	0	250
Turkish Corner	7	G	6	1	0	1	38,289
Turkish Echo	3	F	12	1	2	3	10,988
Turkish Intent	3	C	2	0	0	1	160
Turkish Lad	4	G	14	1	2	2	11,462
Turkish Princess	3	F	6	0	0	1	1,800
Turkish Prize	8	G	6	0	0	2	19,956
Turkish Red	3	C	4	1	0	0	3,551
Turkish Tart	2	F	2	0	0	0	525
Turkish Zaar	3	G	6	1	1	0	6,255
Turko Scene	5	H	4	1	0	0	3,600
Turkomanhattan	3	G	4	0	0	0	0
Turkothunder	2	F	2	0	0	0	834
Turkotreasure	4	F	4	0	0	0	2,346
Turk's Chum	3	G	2	0	0	0	428
Turks Galore	7	G	3	1	0	0	3,207
Turk's Luck	3	F	2	0	0	0	0
Turk's Magic	2	G	3	0	1	0	3,904
Turks Passage	2	C	1	0	0	0	258

Horse	Age	Sex	Sts	1st	2d	3d	Won	Horse	Age	Sex	Sts	1st	2d	3d	Won
Turks Pow Wow	5	M	3	0	0	0	216	Tweedside	5	M	2	1	1	0	140,000
Turk's Pride	3	F	4	0	0	1	1,182	Tweenthelines	4	G	6	2	2	0	12,308
Turk's Sparkler	6	G	13	2	5	0	15,484	Twelfth Honor	4	F	2	0	0	0	595
Turk's Traits	3	G	15	3	0	2	10,722	Twelve Bells	3	F	8	1	0	1	13,970
Turn a Profitt	4	F	4	1	0	1	19,242	Twelve Penny	4	G	5	0	0	2	1,353
Turn Alone	4	G	4	0	0	2	3,133	Twelve St. Andrews	4	G	8	0	1	1	3,848
Turn Back the Time	5	H	11	1	3	1	62,730	Twelve Twenty-One	4	C	7	0	3	1	8,130
Turn Card	4	C	2	0	0	0	360	Twelveyearslater	5	M	9	1	2	3	17,195
Turn North	6	G	3	0	0	0	440	Twenty Bubbles	4	F	10	0	0	0	1,565
Turn of the Tide	3	C	1	0	0	0	0	Twenty Carats	4	F	12	0	5	1	12,660
Turn On	2	C	3	0	0	1	4,070	Twenty Five Below	5	G	3	0	0	1	1,582
Turn Out the Light	7	H	9	0	0	1	1,196	Twenty Four Carrot	8	M	4	0	2	0	2,430
Turn Silver Togold	6	M	10	0	0	1	3,755	Twenty One Cats	4	G	11	1	2	1	22,400
Turn the Fire On	2	C	2	0	1	0	2,047	Twenty One Kisses	6	M	16	1	3	4	11,611
Turn the Lady	3	F	1	0	0	0	85	Twenty Puns	8	G	1	0	0	0	0
Turn to Angel	9	M	17	1	1	2	6,492	Twenty Won Nights	3	G	1	0	0	0	0
Turn to Avie	2	F	1	0	0	0	195	Twentyfrst Century	7	M	4	0	0	1	1,275
Turn to Classics	4	F	2	0	0	0	0	Twentyniner	6	G	7	0	3	0	4,145
Turn to Count	2	C	2	0	0	1	1,600	Twentyoneorbust	3	C	3	0	0	0	0
Turn to Lass	2	F	4	2	1	1	82,360	Twentonthenose	4	G	10	3	1	2	4,920
Turn to Silver	3	F	5	2	0	0	4,800	Twentysecond Str.	3	G	4	0	0	1	6,666
Turn to the Prince	3	C	4	1	2	0	14,800	Twentyseven	3	C	3	1	0	0	4,664
Turn to Victory	2	G	7	0	0	2	6,093	Twentythreejaybird	4	C	10	2	1	0	33,040
Turn to Zarb	5	G	17	1	5	0	22,076	Twentytwenty	7	H	4	0	1	1	1,370
Turn True	3	F	9	0	2	1	11,270	Twenyseventhstreet	4	G	4	1	0	0	6,560
Turnadieu	2	F	1	0	0	0	0	Twice a Barron	2	F	3	0	1	0	2,500
Turnapage	4	C	8	1	2	0	17,645	Twice a Deelite	2	F	3	0	2	0	9,200
Turnberry Condo	2	G	2	1	0	0	5,225	Twice Around	4	G	14	1	2	2	24,695
Turnbolt	2	C	1	0	0	0	780	Twice as Bad	2	C	12	2	3	1	106,280
Turncoat	3	G	12	1	0	1	8,506	Twice as Royal	3	C	5	1	0	0	21,234
Turncoat Jim	4	G	7	2	0	0	17,917	Twice as Sweet	5	M	6	1	1	0	38,277
Turned On	3	F	1	0	0	0	1,700	Twice Bid	4	G	9	0	1	1	21,170
Turner Flats	8	G	4	0	0	0	558	Twice Deceived	6	G	10	2	1	0	4,669
Turner's Hall	5	M	2	0	0	0	2,250	Twice for Money	4	G	13	1	3	0	13,670
Turning Colors	8	G	11	2	1	1	20,775	Twice Glory	3	F	4	0	0	0	660
Turnkey Job	3	C	1	0	0	0	0	Twice Is Nice	4	G	9	0	2	1	8,490
Turnoutthelites	5	G	6	0	0	0	122	Twice Mine	6	H	15	2	3	2	27,817
Turnpike Johnny	3	G	6	1	0	2	10,210	Twice Onabet	3	G	10	0	3	1	24,730
Turnpike Road	8	G	12	0	0	5	4,136	Twice Removed	2	F	3	1	0	0	8,380
Turnwestern	4	F	14	0	1	2	2,518	Twice Rhythm	4	C	14	1	5	3	16,237
Turquoise Bead	4	F	9	3	3	2	76,840	Twice Royal	7	H	18	1	2	1	29,465
Turret	3	F	3	0	1	0	3,950	Twice Southern	2	C	4	0	0	1	13,899
Turtle Beach	3	F	2	0	0	0	1,620	Twice Tempted	3	F	1	0	0	0	0
Turtle Bow (FR)	4	F	2	0	0	0	7,500	Twice the Energy	5	G	6	2	1	0	16,335
Turtle Drive	2	F	2	0	1	0	13,524	Twice the Fight	5	G	8	0	2	1	3,447
Turtle Member	6	H	4	0	0	0	0	Twice the Lady	4	F	3	0	0	0	645
Turtle Ridge	6	M	8	0	1	0	4,455	Twice the Mac	8	G	5	0	0	0	318
Turtle Soup	2	C	2	0	0	1	2,112	Twice the Ruckus	3	F	2	0	1	0	8,200
Tusayan	3	C	9	3	1	0	272,958	Twice the Syn	3	F	5	0	0	1	1,131
Tuscan Code	7	G	2	0	0	0	105	Twice Told	3	C	2	0	0	0	0
Tuscany (BRZ)	9	G	6	0	0	0	535	Twice Tricky	4	G	3	0	1	1	5,240
Tuscany Light	3	F	12	1	4	3	42,428	Twiceanangel	4	F	7	0	0	1	892
Tushar	7	H	9	1	1	2	17,966	Twiceasneat	2	G	6	0	0	0	0
Tusko Charlie	3	G	6	1	1	2	14,285	Twickin	3	F	2	1	0	0	21,600
Tustin	2	F	2	0	0	1	1,440	Twidle	3	F	14	1	0	0	5,369
Tustin Girl	3	F	5	1	2	1	28,438	Twiggams	7	M	8	0	1	1	9,538
Tutakdamoney	5	G	4	0	0	0	305	Twigs Dotcom	4	F	12	0	2	1	6,600
Tutta La Forza	2	F	6	0	0	1	2,295	Twiknight	5	G	11	1	0	1	4,672
Tutti Fratelli	3	F	9	2	2	2	36,591	Twilight Boogie	6	G	1	0	0	0	0
Tutto Finito	4	C	3	0	0	0	53	Twilight Career	7	G	11	2	1	1	6,502
Tutu's Barroom	4	F	4	2	1	0	14,200	Twilight Code	3	F	7	2	2	1	44,770
Tutu's Little Star	5	M	19	1	4	1	10,357	Twilight Devil	2	F	6	0	0	0	0
Tuvala	5	M	11	0	1	1	4,788	Twilight Diamond	3	G	10	1	0	2	8,386
Tux	6	G	7	0	1	1	5,188	Twilight Dreamer	3	C	5	0	0	0	158
Tux N Jeans	5	G	7	0	0	0	381	Twilight Fling	2	F	2	0	0	0	0
Tuxedo	6	H	9	0	0	1	3,051	Twilight Gallop	2	F	5	1	0	1	18,525
Tuxedo Cuff	7	G	7	0	0	0	597	Twilight Gleaming	3	F	7	1	0	3	16,710
Tuxedo Gold	5	G	13	1	2	3	29,970	Twilight Glow	4	F	7	1	1	1	42,750
Tuxedo Jr.	4	G	11	0	1	0	3,645	Twilight Hunter	2	G	5	1	1	0	9,713
Tuxedo Tie	5	G	24	1	1	2	5,412	Twilight Interview	5	H	7	0	0	0	2,431
Tuxson	3	C	15	4	1	1	42,825	Twilight Judge	5	G	7	0	1	0	2,200
Tuzigoot	4	C	3	0	0	0	0	Twilight Ladd	4	G	6	0	0	0	634
Tuzinama Run	8	G	5	0	0	0	1,620	Twilight Man	4	C	8	2	1	0	17,540
Tv Sports Director	5	G	15	0	0	3	19,501	Twilight Mirage	6	M	5	0	0	0	1,150
Twample	8	G	6	0	3	0	11,695	Twilight Morning	5	M	2	0	0	0	0
Twanpumall	2	G	1	0	0	0	0	Twilight Parade	3	F	4	0	0	0	5,020
Twas	3	F	8	0	0	0	1,555	Twilight Peak	4	F	11	2	1	1	16,402
Tweed	7	M	9	3	0	0	6,088	Twilight Prince	7	G	9	1	1	2	25,330
Tweedledeedledum	4	F	2	0	0	0	1,020	Twilight Racer	3	G	18	2	5	3	42,952

RECORDS OF HORSES

Horse	Age	Sex	Sts	1st	2d	3d	Won
Twilight Ride	4	F	1	0	0	0	1,320
Twilight Road	6	G	7	2	0	1	79,520
Twilight Time	6	H	12	3	1	4	68,190
Twilight Twilight	2	F	3	0	0	1	1,110
Twilight Vision	3	G	6	1	0	0	18,630
Twilight Vixen	5	G	11	0	0	0	1,543
Twilights Prayer	5	M	7	1	1	1	52,450
Twilite Testimoney	4	C	8	0	1	1	12,882
Twilite Tryst	5	M	1	0	0	0	0
Twin Cannons	3	G	4	0	0	0	1,170
Twin Cat	3	F	10	1	6	1	20,545
Twin Meteors	6	G	11	2	4	3	53,334
Twin Oaks A. L.	4	G	9	3	1	1	32,355
Twin Pines	6	G	5	0	0	0	544
Twin Shooter	5	G	8	1	1	1	26,580
Twin Stripes	4	F	17	4	7	0	43,055
Twin Talk	4	C	3	0	2	1	16,520
Twin Task	6	G	10	2	1	1	17,627
Twine Flies	4	F	11	1	4	3	26,680
Twine N Dine	5	G	9	1	0	0	4,607
Twine Power	4	G	16	4	1	1	19,517
Twine Traveler	3	F	13	3	1	4	47,246
Twining and Dining	3	F	9	1	3	1	58,770
Twining Dream	4	G	7	2	1	0	47,760
Twining Glow	5	M	7	1	0	1	13,250
Twining Moment	4	C	8	0	1	0	3,713
Twining Star	5	M	1	0	0	0	900
Twinkie Be Buggin	3	F	3	0	0	0	2,460
Twinkle and Shine	3	F	7	2	0	0	36,820
Twinkle Drive	6	M	8	0	2	0	5,151
Twinkle Twinkle	5	M	6	1	2	1	14,113
Twinkler	3	F	2	0	0	1	4,490
Twinkling Ofan Eye	2	F	2	0	0	0	250
Twinko	7	M	5	0	0	0	288
Twinwinwin	4	F	13	3	3	2	96,840
Twirlaway	2	F	6	0	1	0	12,720
Twirley	3	F	1	0	0	0	480
Twirling	3	G	1	0	0	0	0
Twist and Pop	4	F	6	1	0	2	17,070
Twist and Shoot	3	F	13	3	1	2	17,315
Twist My Switch	3	F	11	2	3	3	13,746
Twist N Stroll	4	F	8	0	0	1	1,022
Twist n' Turn	6	M	3	0	0	0	0
Twista Chu Chu	4	F	8	2	0	0	41,448
Twisted	5	G	15	1	1	3	13,548
Twisted Amour	3	F	7	2	0	1	20,530
Twisted Cord	6	M	8	2	2	0	26,551
Twisted Fate	4	G	1	0	0	0	0
Twisted Feather	2	F	3	0	0	2	2,600
Twisted Fortune	4	G	4	2	1	0	12,660
Twisted Humor	2	F	1	0	0	1	2,520
Twisted Kris	5	G	5	1	0	0	9,240
Twisted Mister	3	C	2	0	0	1	2,645
Twisted Truth	3	F	9	0	1	0	5,840
Twisted Tryst	7	G	7	0	0	1	2,350
Twisted Wit	2	G	5	3	0	0	234,855
Twistedervish	2	G	1	0	1	0	1,900
Twister Alley	2	F	3	0	0	1	2,680
Twister M	4	G	12	1	2	1	15,485
Twistin Bit	3	F	9	1	1	2	21,593
Twisting Coast	4	C	4	0	0	0	137
Twisting Sister	2	F	6	2	0	1	46,839
Twistingbythepool	6	G	14	1	2	1	14,832
Twisty	7	M	9	1	0	0	4,950
Twitch N Shout	3	F	2	0	1	1	4,774
Twitterpated	4	G	9	1	0	1	6,380
Twitty	4	F	3	0	0	0	270
Two Amigos	4	G	5	0	1	1	3,900
Two and Two	6	M	10	3	1	2	13,642
Two Bags Full	4	G	5	0	0	0	500
Two Bayou	2	F	5	2	0	1	25,900
Two Bit Betty	3	F	8	2	0	1	2,718
Two Bit Temptation	2	C	1	0	0	0	427
Two Bows	4	F	8	0	0	0	280
Two Centsworth	3	G	11	2	1	1	57,970
Two Chiefs	7	H	4	1	1	1	12,816
Two Coaches	4	G	2	0	0	0	310
Two Condos	3	F	10	0	1	2	4,119
Two Courts	12	M	1	0	0	0	0
Two Crows	3	C	1	0	0	0	0
Two Dot Slew	6	M	12	0	3	2	47,645
Two Double Shots	6	M	2	0	0	0	76
Two Down Automatic	2	G	4	2	1	0	45,000
Two Drink Date	3	F	9	1	1	0	11,120
Two Edge	3	F	9	1	0	1	13,280
Two Eyed Jackie	2	F	3	0	0	0	325
Two Feathers	5	G	4	0	0	0	205
Two Fer Marquetry	5	H	3	1	0	1	4,260
Two Fer Place	2	F	5	0	1	0	13,530
Two Fifty	4	C	3	0	0	0	72
Two for Hebe	8	M	6	0	2	0	1,000
Two Four	3	G	5	0	1	1	15,709
Two Four Dancer	6	M	13	3	3	2	70,162
Two Hand Dunk	4	G	12	0	0	0	2,632
Two Hope Diamonds	3	F	8	0	0	1	2,702
Two Hours to Go	5	M	2	0	0	1	1,375
Two Hurrahs	5	M	3	1	0	0	3,680
Two in the Basket	6	G	10	1	3	2	2,425
Two Inch Minus	2	G	1	0	0	0	0
Two Kisses	2	F	2	0	0	0	0
Two Knight's	5	H	6	1	1	1	35,732
Two Lanterns	5	G	13	1	4	1	16,838
Two Minute Warning	3	G	6	0	0	0	1,590
Two Night Stand	3	C	14	2	1	2	69,205
Two O Nine	6	G	17	4	2	3	18,530
Two Out of Three	3	G	7	1	0	0	6,010
Two Out Rally	5	G	3	0	1	1	6,800
Two Point Spread	5	H	5	0	0	0	0
Two Point Takedown	4	C	2	1	0	0	9,600
Two Prospectors	7	G	3	0	0	0	105
Two Punch Austie	3	C	14	0	1	2	2,903
Two Punch Gal	2	F	1	0	0	1	3,300
Two Punch Sonny	7	H	6	1	1	1	35,880
Two Queens	4	F	16	2	1	2	19,667
Two Raise Limit	5	H	4	0	1	0	6,200
Two Reasons	8	G	17	0	1	1	3,077
Two Rue	3	G	4	1	0	0	7,200
Two Sharky Betty	3	F	12	2	3	2	54,040
Two Shot Warren	3	C	4	0	0	0	47
Two Silver	5	G	2	0	0	0	732
Two Silver Dollars	5	M	5	0	0	0	0
Two Sleeve Zack	2	G	5	1	0	1	6,360
Two Snaps Back	7	M	2	1	0	0	2,745
Two Sparks	3	C	11	1	3	2	54,060
Two Spot Root	5	M	1	0	0	0	225
Two Stall	4	F	16	2	2	4	23,189
Two Star Story	3	C	9	1	3	3	26,897
Two Stars	3	F	11	0	0	0	1,663
Two Steppin Bert	3	G	2	0	0	0	1,260
Two Steppin Bob	5	G	8	2	0	3	6,280
Two Ta Load	5	M	3	0	0	0	734
Two Thirty Seven	3	G	13	3	1	1	46,255
Two Thousand Star	3	G	3	0	0	0	140
Two Thumbs Up	7	G	14	3	3	0	13,381
Two Times a Lady	4	F	8	0	0	1	9,660
Two Timin Goldie	3	F	2	0	0	0	70
Two Timin Lover	4	C	10	2	1	1	35,652
Two Timin' Talk	2	G	1	0	0	0	1,180
Two Timing Paul	4	G	9	0	0	2	313
Two Timing Tyler	4	F	9	3	1	0	14,196
Two Timing Waltzer	3	F	2	0	0	0	760
Two to Jig	4	F	8	0	2	0	6,295
Two Tops	3	G	11	3	2	2	24,178
Two Tour	6	G	12	3	0	1	21,841
Two Track	3	G	14	3	1	1	13,483
Two T's	2	G	6	1	0	1	9,240
Two Tsunami	5	H	9	1	2	1	7,607
Two Up	3	G	3	1	0	1	6,650
Two Ways to Toast	3	F	3	0	0	0	0
Two Ways to Win	9	G	2	0	0	0	84
Two Winner's Long	5	G	13	2	0	3	11,326
Two Wire	7	G	1	0	0	0	0
Two Wood	8	G	13	2	5	1	32,664
Two Year Waranty	3	F	8	0	0	1	7,616
Two Zip	6	M	6	0	1	0	1,875
Twoindytoo	4	F	11	1	2	4	19,369
Twolateinthegame	2	G	1	0	0	0	0
Two's a Jake	7	H	3	0	0	0	941

Horse	Age	Sex	Sts	1st	2d	3d	Won
Two's Fine	6	H	4	0	0	0	0
Twoshotsletsdance	3	C	2	0	0	0	273
Twosie Flyer	4	F	3	0	0	0	407
Twosisterslass	2	F	4	1	0	0	12,675
Twothousand Kisses	3	G	11	2	1	1	8,346
Twothousandegrees	6	G	9	0	1	2	3,732
Twotimes Terlingua	4	G	17	1	2	5	16,950
Twowayyo	5	G	7	0	0	0	428
Twylamite	4	F	4	0	0	0	210
Ty Coffee	3	F	3	0	0	0	640
Ty Jo	3	C	11	0	1	1	4,358
Ty Man	7	G	12	2	0	2	10,096
Ty the Score	2	G	6	0	0	1	1,835
Tyaskin	10	G	10	3	0	2	48,320
Tybee	3	G	4	1	1	0	8,000
Tychonic Lady	3	F	3	0	1	0	3,900
Tycho's Star	4	C	4	0	0	1	8,840
Tycode	4	G	2	0	0	0	152
Tycoon	3	C	8	1	2	0	21,790
Tycoon County	2	G	1	0	0	0	0
Tycoona	3	F	2	0	0	0	150
Tycoota Hane	7	H	3	0	0	0	450
Tyee	9	G	11	0	1	2	2,695
Tygemini	3	G	11	0	1	1	9,978
Tyger Mam	2	F	3	0	0	0	451
Tyger River	4	F	9	2	0	1	23,886
Tyger Smiles	5	G	5	2	0	0	12,681
Tygh	5	G	4	1	0	2	9,415
Tyke	5	M	2	0	0	1	3,080
Tyko Tycoon	6	G	6	2	1	0	44,902
Tyler County	5	G	12	2	1	2	29,189
Tyler Jay	6	H	14	2	3	3	18,473
Tyler Rain	5	M	6	0	0	2	1,956
Tyler Rex	5	G	11	3	1	1	65,442
Tyler Tack	2	C	2	0	0	0	0
Tyler W	2	C	6	0	4	1	8,400
Tyler's Dream	3	C	1	0	0	0	0
Tyler's Grandslam	5	G	3	0	0	0	503
Tyler's Jewel	3	C	2	1	0	0	18,000
Tyler's Miss	3	F	1	0	0	0	0
Tyler's Stash	2	G	1	0	0	0	1,416
Tym Beau	2	C	6	3	1	0	172,400
Tymatt	3	G	1	0	0	0	0
Tynan	2	C	4	1	0	0	30,076
Tyne	3	F	6	2	1	1	62,254
Typhoon Alex	3	C	2	0	0	1	7,940
Typhoon Island	2	F	1	1	0	0	9,350
Typhoon Taffy	8	M	3	0	0	1	794
Typical Bragg	6	M	1	0	0	0	40
Typical Situation	3	F	3	0	0	0	450
Typo	3	C	13	2	1	1	14,129
Tyrade's Best Bet	3	F	3	1	1	0	10,340
Tyrebby	2	F	1	0	0	0	0
Tyrone's Terms	4	G	11	3	1	3	30,284
Tyronia	3	F	3	0	1	0	2,899
Tyro's One Shot	3	F	2	0	0	0	0
Tyrus Creek	4	G	5	1	1	1	6,352
Ty's Kaos	4	C	1	0	0	0	178
Ty's Princess	2	F	1	0	0	0	0
Tyson's Squall	5	H	17	3	2	1	11,871
Tysun	8	H	7	0	0	0	1,400
Tyvara	3	F	8	1	3	0	45,310
Tyzbay	8	M	5	2	1	0	6,624
U B C N Me	4	F	17	1	2	4	8,132
U B Chief	5	G	3	0	0	1	1,442
U B the Judge	3	G	17	2	1	2	17,722
U Betcha Joe	2	G	2	0	0	0	190
U Betta Believe It	5	M	8	0	0	0	300
U Blue	3	C	7	1	2	1	8,166
U Da Gal	4	F	12	4	3	2	36,486
U F Appeal	3	F	4	1	2	0	15,400
U F P T Express	3	G	1	0	0	0	0
U Go Can	3	C	5	0	0	0	530
U Go Hugo	2	C	6	1	1	0	4,820
U Got the Touch	2	F	6	1	1	1	28,719
U Hear Me	5	M	2	0	1	0	3,000
U K Champ	2	C	5	2	0	1	14,900
U K Jane	6	M	10	1	2	1	12,390
U K Limey	5	G	2	0	0	0	0
U K Special	8	M	3	0	0	0	0
U K Trick	3	F	7	0	1	1	24,745
U Lover U	12	G	9	2	1	2	4,784
U Madea Fortune	3	C	13	0	5	2	16,055
U Otabe Wild	5	H	12	0	1	1	5,574
U R Earl	4	F	5	0	0	0	978
U R My Sunshine	3	G	6	0	0	1	998
U R Smart	8	G	11	2	1	1	6,363
U R Theweakestlink	3	F	1	0	0	0	0
U S Cotton	3	C	3	0	0	0	217
U S S Tinosa	4	G	3	0	0	0	900
U S West	3	G	1	0	0	0	0
U Silly Rabbit	4	G	11	1	2	3	8,866
U Snooze U Lose	3	C	9	2	3	1	104,088
U U Star	5	G	13	1	3	2	28,080
U Wonder Why	6	H	2	0	0	0	145
U. B. Quiet	4	G	3	1	1	0	7,746
U. K. Kat	4	C	12	1	0	1	8,454
U. R. My Hope	6	G	8	1	3	0	14,259
U. S. Gold	8	G	4	0	0	0	1,800
U. S. Indy	3	F	3	0	0	0	1,580
U. S. Jay	7	G	1	0	0	0	74
U. S. Jets	6	H	11	2	3	2	80,460
U. S. Patriot Day	2	G	2	0	0	0	713
U. S. Prospector	8	G	3	0	0	0	225
U. S. Spirit	2	G	5	0	0	1	1,430
U'All	9	H	15	2	3	4	28,156
Ubet	7	M	9	2	2	0	10,714
Ubetski	4	F	4	0	0	0	254
Ubi's General	3	G	12	1	2	1	15,026
Ucantpass Imtofast	4	F	14	3	3	2	29,170
Udancegirl	4	F	4	0	0	1	1,020
Udazzleme	6	M	7	1	2	1	11,370
Udeman	4	G	7	1	2	0	25,950
Ufology	4	G	3	2	0	0	10,450
Ugopepper	4	G	15	3	2	4	7,860
Ugotadowhatugotado	2	F	5	3	0	1	23,665
Ugotit	6	G	6	0	1	0	4,570
Ugottaseethisplace	4	C	13	2	4	2	31,810
Uhave Light	5	G	1	0	0	0	0
Uhohwhathappen	2	G	2	0	1	0	3,200
Ulcnutnbutmytalits	4	C	6	1	0	0	7,709
Ulees Ghost	4	G	6	1	0	0	3,780
Ulloa	3	G	16	2	5	2	66,080
Ulltimate Gold	2	G	2	0	1	0	3,360
Ullysses	4	C	3	1	0	0	4,508
Ulterior Motives (GB)	6	G	12	2	2	1	67,800
Ultimate Diva	3	F	4	0	3	1	6,882
Ultimate Ego	4	G	12	3	3	0	17,286
Ultimate Encore	5	G	10	2	1	0	11,887
Ultimate Hitman	4	G	6	1	3	0	32,210
Ultimate Karma	2	F	3	1	0	0	3,300
Ultimate Light	2	C	4	1	1	0	20,460
Ultimate Prize	4	F	15	0	2	3	7,083
Ultimate Warrior	6	G	5	1	0	0	32,082
Ultimato	3	G	3	1	1	0	27,300
Ultra Chic	2	F	2	0	0	0	0
Ultra Code	5	G	3	0	0	1	1,620
Ultra Cruise	3	C	7	0	1	4	7,460
Ultra Heat	3	F	7	0	2	2	23,402
Ultra Slew Fast	4	C	16	2	3	3	40,234
Ultravivid	4	F	12	1	1	5	16,420
Ultro	4	G	6	0	0	2	4,460
Uluvitnunoit	4	F	3	0	0	1	3,585
Umademyday	3	G	6	0	0	0	0
Umatilla Ridge	5	H	5	1	0	0	1,016
Umberto	5	H	7	0	1	0	6,020
Umbrella Girl	3	F	7	0	3	3	27,965
Umcane	3	G	20	2	2	1	15,767
Umiak	4	F	4	0	0	0	1,250
Ummummgood	4	F	10	1	1	1	23,297
Umpa	3	C	5	0	0	1	1,146
Umpateedle	4	F	12	4	1	1	89,730
Umpqua	5	G	7	1	0	1	5,077
Umpqua Echo	8	G	3	0	0	0	134
Un Fino Vino	6	G	12	3	2	1	64,850
Un Ochio	5	M	18	4	4	2	42,937
Unaccountably Fast	3	C	3	0	0	0	515
Unaccounted Affair	5	H	7	2	3	0	35,420

Horse	Age	Sex	Sts	1st	2d	3d	Won
Unacop	3	G	16	1	1	4	23,165
Unalienable Right	6	G	6	1	1	0	13,550
Unamedthegame	3	G	7	1	1	1	23,910
Unanimous Decision	4	G	11	1	1	1	29,830
Unannounced	2	F	4	2	0	0	17,780
Unanswered Prayer	3	F	16	1	2	2	9,565
Unbearable	5	H	14	0	0	2	8,095
Unbelekable	10	G	9	0	1	2	4,535
Unbelievable Run	5	M	7	3	1	0	34,589
Unbendablebaby	4	F	1	0	0	0	0
Unbendebell Cary	7	G	7	0	0	0	495
Unblessed	3	G	18	1	4	3	9,301
Unbounded Vision	5	M	2	0	0	0	0
Unbrakeable George	2	G	9	1	1	1	25,954
Unbridels King	3	C	9	1	1	0	40,590
Unbridled Affair	4	C	8	0	0	1	4,990
Unbridled America	3	C	6	2	0	1	41,280
Unbridled Approval	5	M	2	0	0	1	3,170
Unbridled Ashley	3	F	8	1	4	0	29,850
Unbridled Beauty	2	F	4	1	2	0	88,535
Unbridled Boy	2	G	1	0	1	0	2,400
Unbridled Colors	3	F	4	0	0	1	4,620
Unbridled Cyclone	3	F	7	1	2	0	22,800
Unbridled Devotion	4	G	13	0	1	4	6,482
Unbridled Dignity	5	H	4	0	0	0	3,750
Unbridled Drive	3	G	9	0	0	0	8,110
Unbridled Femme	3	F	7	1	1	1	80,672
Unbridled Freedom	3	C	1	0	0	0	0
Unbridled Fury	6	H	1	0	0	0	101
Unbridled Gamble	7	H	10	5	0	0	25,830
Unbridled Game	3	G	5	1	0	2	28,010
Unbridled Guy	3	G	9	1	0	0	6,605
Unbridled Honor	5	H	1	0	0	0	217
Unbridled J. J.	3	G	13	1	2	2	18,850
Unbridled Lad	3	C	10	1	2	1	12,285
Unbridled Mate	3	C	3	0	0	0	4,560
Unbridled Moon	3	F	5	0	0	0	630
Unbridled Passion	3	G	1	0	0	0	0
Unbridled Phantom	2	C	2	0	0	0	1,380
Unbridled Resolve	3	G	9	0	0	1	5,780
Unbridled Run	3	F	6	0	0	0	6,025
Unbridled Skip	2	F	3	0	0	0	655
Unbridled Soul	4	F	5	0	0	0	1,757
Unbridled Speed	4	C	6	2	0	1	6,068
Unbridled Spirit	3	F	1	0	0	0	0
Unbridled Sunn	2	F	2	0	0	0	753
Unbridled Trick	4	G	7	0	2	1	20,660
Unbridled Valor	3	F	6	1	1	0	26,600
Unbridled Vision	5	H	7	2	1	0	64,495
Unbridled Waters	6	M	1	0	0	0	460
Unbridled's Amour	3	F	4	2	0	0	12,840
Unbridled's Comet	3	C	2	0	0	0	1,780
Unbridled's Evie	2	F	8	0	1	1	6,640
Unbridled's Gal	3	F	1	0	0	0	315
Unbridled's Image	3	C	2	0	0	0	540
Unbridled's Lady	3	F	8	3	0	0	63,000
Unbridled's Pride	4	F	2	0	0	0	700
Unbridled's Storm	4	C	5	0	0	0	1,724
Unbroken Spirit	4	G	8	1	2	1	24,270
Unbuckle	2	C	7	1	1	2	43,169
Unbuttoned Blouse	3	F	3	0	0	0	288
Uncalculated	3	C	10	1	2	4	60,410
Uncanny	3	C	2	1	0	1	13,490
Uncanny Annie	3	F	3	0	0	0	72
Uncas Ruckus	7	M	1	0	1	0	3,912
Uncertain Wonder	4	G	8	2	1	1	10,382
Unchain My Soul	5	H	3	0	1	0	617
Unchain the Stars	5	M	2	0	1	1	8,640
Unchecked Melody	2	F	1	0	0	0	0
Uncivil	2	C	2	0	0	0	840
Uncle Ack	4	G	6	1	1	1	7,647
Uncle Arthur	2	C	1	0	0	0	0
Uncle Bert	2	G	2	0	0	0	1,920
Uncle Bill	3	G	22	1	1	3	17,660
Uncle Brother	3	G	12	2	2	1	15,895
Uncle Bruce	3	C	3	0	0	1	7,310
Uncle Bryce	7	G	10	3	1	1	19,078
Uncle Bud	4	G	9	0	0	1	1,738
Uncle Bus	6	G	13	0	1	1	7,037
Uncle Camie	3	C	7	3	0	2	102,960
Uncle Chris	8	H	4	0	0	0	0
Uncle Cook	5	G	13	1	1	2	6,800
Uncle Eugene	4	C	1	0	0	0	0
Uncle Freddie	6	G	10	1	1	4	6,528
Uncle George	2	G	4	0	1	0	3,780
Uncle Homer	4	G	7	0	0	0	318
Uncle Itchy	2	C	1	1	0	0	5,160
Uncle Jack	3	C	7	2	2	0	101,180
Uncle James	2	C	2	0	0	0	285
Uncle Jer	5	G	9	0	4	0	4,310
Uncle Joey	4	G	2	0	0	0	573
Uncle Johnny	4	C	2	0	0	0	0
Uncle Lee	3	G	5	0	2	1	5,844
Uncle Leo	3	G	9	3	3	1	26,046
Uncle Luis	3	G	24	1	0	2	9,102
Uncle Mike	2	C	1	0	0	0	0
Uncle Mose	4	C	4	0	0	1	3,445
Uncle Nealy Bug	3	G	1	0	0	0	0
Uncle Ock	3	G	12	0	0	5	13,287
Uncle Paul	2	C	2	0	0	0	730
Uncle Punk	5	H	9	0	2	2	16,632
Uncle Red	9	G	3	0	0	0	0
Uncle Rocco	6	H	6	0	0	0	1,489
Uncle Sonny	2	C	1	0	0	0	2,700
Uncle T	6	H	2	0	0	0	0
Uncle Vic	4	G	15	1	2	2	24,918
Uncle Walter	2	C	4	0	1	0	10,520
Uncle Wendell	4	G	4	0	1	0	1,053
Uncle Whiz	4	G	15	3	2	1	10,777
Uncle Zeff	4	G	8	0	1	0	6,001
Uncledannysbrother	3	C	3	0	0	0	3,160
Unclouded	2	F	1	0	0	0	125
Uncoil	2	G	3	0	0	2	4,930
Uncontested	3	G	2	0	0	0	3,420
Uncontrollable	2	F	3	1	1	0	28,560
Uncontrolled Burn	4	C	12	1	1	2	28,990
Uncopyable Bid	4	C	3	0	0	0	35
Uncork	3	F	2	0	0	0	680
Uncorked	3	G	2	0	1	1	8,000
Uncoupled	8	G	12	1	2	0	6,480
Uncross the Stars	2	C	1	0	0	0	0
Uncrowned	5	G	11	2	0	0	12,384
Uncut Diamond	4	F	2	0	0	0	346
Undaunting	2	C	1	0	0	0	270
Undecided Now	3	F	6	2	0	0	13,394
Undeclared	3	F	1	0	0	0	0
Undeniable Revenge	5	M	1	0	0	0	0
Under Arrest	4	C	10	1	1	1	9,116
Under Budget	3	G	1	0	0	0	42
Under Caution	2	C	3	1	0	0	18,300
Under Control	3	F	12	1	1	5	5,214
Under Desert Skies	2	F	4	0	0	1	898
Under Repair	3	G	9	0	0	0	722
Under the Desk	4	G	10	0	2	2	4,946
Under the Hill	4	F	7	1	0	0	6,526
Under the O	9	M	12	0	2	2	3,138
Under the Sun	2	C	1	0	0	0	0
Under Wraps	4	G	3	1	0	1	17,217
Undercover	4	F	4	3	0	1	103,610
Undercover Agent	3	G	2	0	0	0	0
Undercover Guy	4	G	15	0	2	1	5,741
Underneath It All	3	F	9	1	1	1	19,360
Underpinning	3	G	10	0	1	3	16,730
Understood	7	G	4	1	1	0	38,584
Undertheinfluence	2	G	5	0	1	0	4,770
Underwood	7	G	1	0	0	0	53
Undisclosed	2	C	5	1	0	2	33,660
Undisputed Terms	4	C	4	0	0	0	80
Undoubted	2	G	1	0	0	0	237
Undun	4	G	5	0	1	0	4,161
Unend	6	G	4	1	1	0	7,340
Unequal	4	F	1	0	0	0	61
Unexpected Cat	3	C	11	1	0	1	8,100
Unexpected Glory	5	G	18	1	2	1	6,445
Unexpected Heat	3	G	5	0	0	0	572
Unfaced	4	G	14	3	2	0	16,633
Unfair Currency	7	G	3	0	0	0	0
Unfaithful	3	C	9	0	0	0	185

Horse	Age	Sex	Sts	1st	2d	3d	Won
Unfathomable	5	M	7	1	1	0	9,582
Unfazed	5	M	3	0	0	1	946
Unflappable	7	G	3	2	0	0	17,400
Unforgetable Mabel	3	F	17	1	0	3	7,801
Unforgetable Song	3	F	1	0	0	0	0
Unforgetabull	5	M	3	1	2	0	28,480
Unforgettable Max	3	C	5	1	1	0	77,515
Unforgettable R N	4	F	12	1	2	3	18,285
Unforgettable Too	3	F	8	2	2	1	112,425
Unforgotten Speed	3	F	8	1	1	0	3,285
Unforgotten Spring	2	G	4	1	0	0	7,365
Unfundisi	5	G	14	0	1	3	11,930
Unfurl the Flag	3	G	6	1	1	2	59,148
Ungoverned	4	C	6	1	0	0	12,619
Ungreatful	2	G	6	0	1	1	3,741
Unheard Of	3	F	2	0	0	0	967
Unhinged Fager	5	G	17	1	1	0	5,226
Unhurried	3	F	17	2	3	2	41,770
Unificada (BRZ)	4	F	3	0	0	0	0
Unified Field	4	C	5	1	0	0	6,089
Unimagined	3	G	21	1	3	3	11,652
Uninhibited Song	2	F	1	0	1	0	5,600
Union Address	7	M	8	0	0	2	2,478
Union Alert	3	G	18	2	1	2	19,346
Union Assault	2	G	3	0	0	2	13,783
Union Builder	4	G	9	0	0	0	0
Union Bulldog	4	G	8	0	0	1	1,204
Union Dues	4	G	13	0	6	1	10,384
Union Mills	6	H	8	0	0	2	5,280
Union One	6	G	5	0	2	2	29,486
Union Park	3	G	7	0	0	0	546
Union Place	4	C	7	1	0	0	24,500
Union Smoke	3	G	4	2	0	0	12,313
Union Station	3	G	6	1	0	1	4,134
Union Street	3	C	6	1	1	0	4,666
Union Suit	3	G	8	0	2	1	5,050
Unionboss	3	G	4	1	0	0	18,735
Unique	3	F	2	0	0	0	103
Unique Dancer	5	M	5	0	0	0	1,247
Unique Devil	4	G	11	1	1	4	34,143
Unique Dream	3	G	5	0	0	0	430
Unique Mystique	8	M	7	0	0	1	1,242
Unique Opportunity	4	F	13	3	4	3	105,844
Unique Reality	4	C	5	0	0	0	288
Unique Ronique	2	C	2	0	0	0	460
Unique Savings	3	C	1	0	0	0	0
Unique Technique	7	M	7	2	0	1	31,744
Unique Way	3	F	4	0	0	1	2,310
Unique Weave	6	G	2	0	1	0	940
Uniquely Lucky	7	G	1	0	0	0	0
Uniqueness	2	F	2	0	0	0	460
United We Stand	3	C	1	0	0	0	0
Unite's Windstar	8	G	11	0	0	0	1,362
Universal Boy	4	C	4	0	1	0	2,100
Universal Form	2	C	4	1	0	0	10,000
Unkept Secret	2	F	1	0	0	0	45
Unknown Agenda	4	G	2	0	0	0	158
Unknown Fact	6	M	9	1	1	0	8,530
Unknown Galaxy	4	G	10	1	0	1	8,434
Unknown Jester	3	F	4	0	0	1	5,075
Unknown Prospector	3	C	4	1	2	0	8,569
Unknown Wind Chill	3	C	2	0	0	0	540
Unlace	4	F	11	2	3	0	34,872
Unlaced Waters	5	G	6	3	2	1	56,400
Unlawfulwrangler	3	C	4	0	0	0	3,270
Unleash the Law	3	G	7	1	0	0	4,650
Unleash the Power	3	G	5	0	0	0	3,880
Unlicensed	4	C	17	2	2	4	45,600
Unlimited	4	F	7	0	0	0	976
Unlimited Faith	3	F	4	0	0	1	8,880
Unlimited Honor	3	C	4	0	2	1	5,680
Unlisted Phone	8	G	10	0	0	1	1,564
Unlock My Heart	5	M	18	4	3	2	36,270
Unlock the Vault	3	G	14	3	2	3	83,009
Unmerciful	3	G	10	1	0	0	4,581
Unnamed Soldier	6	H	13	4	2	1	10,888
Uno Bruno	5	H	4	1	0	0	2,442
Uno Cuatro	2	G	6	1	1	2	16,900
Uno Fun	3	C	3	0	0	0	275

Horse	Age	Sex	Sts	1st	2d	3d	Won
Uno I'm Special	2	F	2	0	1	0	2,040
Uno Passer	3	G	14	2	5	1	33,480
Uno Sham	2	F	3	0	0	0	300
Uno Zana	5	M	8	1	0	2	3,895
Unodatsrite	2	C	5	0	0	1	5,610
Unoi'mawinner	3	G	3	0	0	0	0
Unokia Thunder	5	G	16	1	2	2	34,266
Unokie	3	C	3	0	0	0	1,290
Unome's Star	3	C	4	0	0	0	0
Unorthodox	4	F	4	0	1	2	4,360
Unovision	3	F	13	4	1	1	29,065
Unpeteable	6	G	15	7	3	2	85,709
Unplain Jane	5	M	5	0	0	0	0
Unpredict Prospect	2	C	2	1	1	0	14,800
Unpredictable B	6	H	12	2	0	0	2,848
Unpredictable K D	4	F	12	1	1	2	58,321
Unpromised	2	F	5	1	0	0	5,310
Unquenchable Seven	4	G	4	0	0	0	476
Unquestioned	6	H	10	2	2	2	18,056
Unquizzible	3	F	4	0	3	0	1,452
Unreal	4	G	8	1	0	1	6,366
Unreal Adventure	4	F	15	1	2	0	22,343
Unreal Dancer	6	G	2	0	0	1	1,830
Unreal Dream	4	F	13	0	1	0	2,773
Unreal Fantasy	4	F	10	0	1	1	9,710
Unreal Favorite	5	H	6	2	1	0	23,962
Unreal General	4	C	13	0	3	2	42,310
Unreal Illusion	4	G	4	1	0	0	9,428
Unreal Joey	4	C	3	0	0	0	0
Unreal Madness	8	G	3	0	0	2	7,110
Unreal Muffin	3	G	15	1	1	3	30,350
Unreal Optimist	3	G	2	0	0	0	0
Unreal Party	5	H	9	4	1	0	92,813
Unreal Rapids	4	C	12	0	1	0	6,155
Unreal Tune	4	C	7	1	0	2	5,143
Unreasonable Woman	10	M	5	0	1	0	1,444
Unrelenting Desire	6	G	10	0	1	3	7,105
Unrelenting Grit	5	G	1	0	0	1	1,800
Unrepentant	3	F	9	1	1	1	49,060
Unrullah Bull	6	G	6	1	1	1	24,730
Unruly Sun	5	G	11	0	1	3	3,333
Unruly Zeal	11	G	2	0	0	0	0
Unscripted	3	F	5	0	2	2	4,240
Unseen	4	F	11	2	2	2	28,936
Unseen Power	5	M	2	1	0	0	3,806
Unshackled	6	G	8	1	1	2	29,041
Unshuttered	2	F	4	0	1	1	16,360
Unsolved Mistress	3	F	1	0	0	0	0
Unspeakable	6	G	8	0	0	1	5,255
Unsprung	3	F	16	1	2	4	18,870
Unstable	3	G	11	1	0	0	6,974
Unsteelable	3	G	8	0	1	1	2,540
Unsurpassed	4	F	4	0	1	0	11,800
Unswept	3	C	5	2	0	1	70,506
Unswerving	4	F	13	5	2	3	43,421
Untamed	3	G	4	0	0	1	1,240
Untamed and Uncut	10	G	6	0	0	0	571
Untamed Heat	3	F	9	1	0	0	16,416
Untamed Passion	4	F	3	0	0	0	375
Untapped Resource	9	G	3	0	0	0	96
Untenable	8	G	4	0	0	0	100
Unthinkable	2	F	1	0	0	0	0
Until Now	4	F	14	1	1	3	20,073
Untimely Dancer	2	C	3	0	0	1	3,597
Untold Tale	3	C	12	0	5	0	26,545
Untouchable Aly	4	G	3	0	0	0	110
Untouchable Blade	4	G	5	0	1	0	4,230
Untwined	4	G	14	2	0	1	8,447
Unusual Glory	3	G	16	2	0	4	44,480
Unusual Mist	3	G	8	2	2	2	18,520
Unusual Sonata	3	F	9	1	1	1	8,087
Unusual Summer	2	C	4	0	0	1	4,700
Unusual Sunrise	2	C	2	0	0	1	3,000
Unusual Syndrome	2	F	3	1	1	0	14,000
Unusually Sweet	4	F	1	0	1	0	2,100
Unvested Value	4	F	3	0	1	0	1,281
Unwaquoited Love	5	M	18	4	2	3	31,297
Unwavering Honour	2	F	1	0	0	0	0
Unwearied	3	C	1	1	0	0	4,800

RECORDS OF HORSES

Horse	Age	Sex	Sts	1st	2d	3d	Won
Unyielding	3	G	7	5	0	0	74,892
Unzag	5	M	7	0	0	0	105
Up a Creek	2	G	5	0	1	0	11,590
Up a Notch	4	G	2	0	1	0	2,180
Up Anchor	2	C	6	2	1	2	61,575
Up At the Top (IRE)	8	M	4	0	0	0	2,740
Up Front	8	G	14	0	4	1	19,918
Up Front Now	3	F	2	0	0	0	660
Up Henshaw Hill	2	C	1	0	0	0	0
Up Hill Survivor	5	G	7	0	1	2	14,080
Up in Smoke	9	G	13	0	0	0	692
Up Jump the Devil	5	H	14	5	1	2	27,555
Up Mim's Aly	5	G	14	1	1	3	4,703
Up Noble's Alley	4	G	7	0	1	0	2,033
Up North	3	C	2	0	0	0	363
Up Periscope	3	C	5	1	1	2	43,360
Up the Volume	5	M	7	1	1	1	5,041
Up This Creek	3	G	6	2	0	0	8,760
Up to Dusty	5	G	11	0	0	2	1,426
Up to Glory	6	G	14	0	0	2	2,364
Up to Me	5	M	7	1	0	0	12,642
Up to the Stars	6	G	12	1	4	3	6,873
Up With the Flag	9	G	10	4	5	0	57,580
Upagainstthewall	3	C	5	0	1	0	5,432
Upgrade	6	G	12	0	0	0	1,082
Upheld (NZ)	7	G	7	1	1	0	11,800
Uphere	6	G	15	1	4	1	3,865
Uphill Skier	3	F	9	4	1	2	147,350
Upickedafinetime	3	F	15	2	1	1	12,789
Upindeed	3	G	4	0	1	0	5,460
Uplifting	3	F	6	0	2	0	14,570
Upnotdown	4	F	13	4	4	0	21,444
Uppatuppa's Charm	2	F	6	2	0	0	22,294
Upper Class	5	M	12	1	1	1	15,858
Upper Echelon	5	M	2	0	0	1	3,100
Uppity Daze	3	F	6	2	3	1	9,860
Uppity Kitty	2	F	4	2	1	1	78,780
Uproariously Vicky	5	M	9	0	1	1	4,404
Upsman	2	C	2	0	0	0	
Upstage	3	G	2	0	0	0	340
Upstage Them All	4	F	7	0	0	0	1,872
Upstate Do	6	M	3	0	0	2	4,466
Upsy Daisy	5	M	3	0	0	0	462
Uptake	10	G	5	1	0	1	1,892
Uptasnuff	4	G	10	2	1	5	16,650
Uptown Brown	9	G	14	0	3	2	3,665
Uptown Chatter	9	M	9	1	3	2	6,158
Uptown Groom	2	C	2	0	1	1	4,150
Uptown Gyrl	4	F	4	0	0	0	234
Uptown Lad	5	G	10	0	1	4	11,261
Uptown Parade	2	C	1	0	0	0	880
Uptown Sport	4	F	6	0	2	0	2,835
Uptown Tornado	4	F	3	1	0	1	7,560
Upturn	3	G	14	2	2	7	72,340
Urania	3	F	9	1	1	0	41,380
Uranito (CHI)	4	C	1	0	0	0	0
Urban Angel	5	M	7	3	0	2	40,670
Urban Dancer	5	M	2	0	0	0	2,160
Urban King (IRE)	3	C	7	0	2	4	111,460
Urban Space	3	G	9	1	1	2	28,911
Urban Warrior	2	C	2	2	0	0	44,250
Urbana Light	4	F	6	0	0	2	18,472
Urblockinme	3	G	3	1	0	0	4,100
Urge	3	F	7	1	3	0	14,600
Urgent Call	5	H	1	0	0	0	150
Urgent Man	4	G	1	0	0	0	0
Urgent Matter	6	G	15	3	1	1	18,219
Urgent Start	4	F	5	2	1	1	21,240
Urgent Valentine	4	F	6	1	1	1	8,165
Urgently	4	G	16	2	5	0	28,125
Uriah (GER)	4	F	1	0	0	0	3,000
Uriah's Begining	3	G	4	1	0	0	9,300
Urlacher	4	G	7	3	1	1	61,675
Urn and Ashes	4	F	8	1	0	2	8,372
Urnotdabossame	3	F	4	0	2	2	3,530
Ursula	5	M	14	0	3	5	7,161
Ursula Go	2	F	1	0	0	0	0
Ursula's Dreamer	5	G	10	2	1	2	14,293
Us	5	G	10	2	1	3	96,064
Us Better Hurry	2	F	5	0	0	1	1,260
Us Tonight	2	F	1	0	0	0	0
Useable	2	F	6	1	0	1	10,465
Useppa	3	F	9	2	0	1	20,589
Useyourimagination	5	M	15	3	6	1	43,751
Usher In	3	C	6	0	0	1	3,965
Ushudbeconcerned	2	G	5	0	0	0	489
Usual Manner	2	F	7	2	2	1	86,123
Utah Sky	2	C	3	1	0	0	17,025
Utellum	5	M	8	0	3	1	3,216
Utopian Splash	2	F	2	0	0	0	0
Uwana Prop	11	G	5	0	0	0	400
Uwinthegreen	7	G	1	0	0	0	50
Uzki Zu	4	C	2	0	0	1	697
Uzura San	4	F	3	0	2	0	1,880
V Eight Rocket	4	G	4	1	1	0	14,600
V F Private Flyer	3	C	16	2	2	2	32,663
V G's Catch	3	F	5	0	0	0	1,125
V J's Boy	3	G	2	0	0	0	645
V J's Rascal	5	H	6	0	0	0	450
V. I. P. Kipper	3	G	11	4	2	1	33,050
Vaalthazar (PER)	4	G	1	0	0	0	0
Vaca City Flyer	2	F	1	0	0	1	5,460
Vaca Flyer	3	F	11	1	2	1	12,574
Vacamonte (GB)	5	H	8	1	2	1	68,680
Vacancy	4	C	3	1	0	1	29,095
Vacarri	5	M	3	0	1	0	3,240
Vacation Day	4	G	2	0	0	0	450
Vacationland	3	C	3	0	2	0	2,520
Vaclav (ARG)	9	G	20	1	1	8	13,022
Vademecum	3	F	3	0	0	1	5,480
Vagabond Queen	3	F	4	0	0	0	488
Vagabond Saint	2	F	1	0	0	0	0
Vagabond Star	4	G	11	2	0	4	10,565
Vaganova	3	F	3	1	1	1	44,710
Vage	2	F	6	0	2	0	25,836
Vague Hint	4	C	4	1	1	1	16,800
Vague Memory	6	M	7	0	0	2	8,320
Vaguely Mambo	8	G	4	0	0	0	0
Vai Via	5	H	15	2	0	6	12,607
Vail Peak	5	G	6	0	1	1	4,925
Vaillante	2	F	2	1	0	0	14,460
Val de Dance	4	G	4	0	1	1	18,078
Val d'Isere	3	F	12	4	1	1	42,332
Val Rah	2	G	3	0	0	0	
Valamy	2	F	5	0	0	0	415
Valante	3	F	3	0	0	0	96
Valash	4	F	8	0	0	1	2,175
Valatie	3	G	8	0	0	1	4,510
Valay Moon	2	G	5	1	0	0	14,966
Valdancer's Gate	7	G	8	0	1	1	4,082
Valdasia	3	F	11	0	2	1	7,167
Valderstand	5	H	7	1	1	2	7,985
Valdez's Mon	5	G	5	1	0	0	3,637
Valdivia	3	F	1	0	0	0	1,818
Valdostana	5	M	6	0	0	2	1,311
Valdoura (FR)	3	F	8	2	0	0	59,084
Vale	5	M	1	0	0	0	40
Vale of Glamorgan	6	M	4	0	0	0	695
Vale of Tears	6	M	4	0	0	0	0
Vale of Wings (GB)	4	F	14	0	5	0	36,071
Valemes On Fire	5	G	15	0	0	0	835
Valentin Deldiablo	6	M	1	0	0	0	0
Valentina Rose	3	F	18	1	4	3	18,598
Valentine Dancer	3	F	14	5	3	2	312,846
Valentine Delivery	9	G	19	0	1	3	4,545
Valentine Fling	2	F	3	0	0	0	165
Valentine Girl	4	F	1	0	1	0	3,640
Valentine Jones	5	M	5	1	0	0	4,756
Valentine Lassie	6	M	14	0	1	1	2,924
Valentine Rose	4	F	1	1	0	0	10,790
Valentine Surprise	3	F	10	2	3	4	14,571
Valentine's Chime	4	F	12	0	2	3	12,391
Valentine's Moment	5	M	13	2	4	1	19,969
Valentini	3	F	1	0	0	0	0
Valentino Bob	6	H	20	0	4	2	9,423
Valenzo	3	G	12	2	4	1	82,080
Valera	3	F	1	0	0	0	350
Valerina	7	M	17	1	1	2	11,528

Horse	Age	Sex	Sts	1st	2d	3d	Won
Valero	4	F	4	0	1	0	1,023
Valesia	3	F	1	0	0	0	0
Valet Express	4	C	12	0	0	3	8,625
Valet Girl	4	F	9	1	0	3	6,166
Valexi	4	F	8	1	1	2	34,690
Valhol	7	G	2	1	0	0	60,000
Valiant Anna	3	F	7	4	0	0	88,200
Valiant Crusader	2	C	1	0	0	0	0
Valiant Dawn	2	C	1	0	0	1	1,020
Valiant Edge	3	C	2	1	0	0	29,400
Valiant Fighter	5	M	8	1	1	1	5,416
Valiant Gal	3	F	3	0	1	0	1,845
Valiant King	4	C	13	3	2	4	96,365
Valiant Knight	4	G	8	0	1	0	2,973
Valiant Leader	5	G	10	1	1	2	8,250
Valiant M. D.	4	G	4	0	0	0	654
Valiant Michael	3	G	9	1	1	2	22,810
Valiant Prince	6	H	6	0	0	1	2,600
Valiant Spirit	3	F	7	0	0	2	3,287
Valiant Splash	3	G	5	0	0	1	1,540
Valiant Storm	3	F	12	1	1	0	8,054
Valiant Style	6	H	10	0	1	1	10,770
Valiant Vera	4	F	11	2	5	1	13,929
Valiant Victory	5	G	5	2	1	0	17,465
Valiant Vision	6	G	1	1	0	0	7,150
Valiant We Stand	3	G	1	0	0	0	675
Valid	4	C	7	2	1	2	18,255
Valid Acquisition	2	F	5	0	0	0	3,426
Valid Action	4	G	6	1	1	0	7,705
Valid Afleet	2	C	4	0	0	0	358
Valid Again	2	C	2	0	1	1	5,655
Valid Anthem	6	M	9	0	0	0	8,358
Valid Assembly	7	G	11	2	2	0	15,508
Valid Cash	2	C	2	0	0	0	2,280
Valid Chad	3	C	2	0	0	0	175
Valid Company	8	G	18	5	3	3	46,606
Valid Dancer	2	G	7	1	0	0	14,635
Valid Desire	3	F	14	2	2	2	16,185
Valid Double	4	F	10	0	1	1	4,345
Valid Excuse	3	F	14	1	5	3	22,689
Valid Flight	5	H	9	3	1	0	58,695
Valid Forum	3	G	9	0	2	1	5,164
Valid Fund	4	G	4	0	0	0	436
Valid Fury	4	G	12	6	0	2	56,705
Valid Hero	3	G	9	1	0	2	11,210
Valid Jet	4	C	11	0	2	0	4,131
Valid Kiss	6	G	5	0	0	1	858
Valid Lass	4	F	9	1	0	0	2,188
Valid Lightning	7	H	6	0	0	1	3,480
Valid Magic	3	C	10	1	0	2	5,688
Valid Miss Chain	7	M	2	0	0	0	2,850
Valid Move	2	F	1	1	0	0	35,280
Valid N Bold	7	H	2	0	0	1	3,190
Valid Oaks	3	F	15	2	1	0	39,780
Valid Patriot	2	G	1	0	0	0	405
Valid Prime	6	H	14	0	3	2	35,040
Valid Pro	3	F	6	1	1	0	35,316
Valid Pulpit	3	F	5	2	0	0	55,845
Valid Purchase	2	F	2	0	0	1	2,275
Valid Queen	4	F	4	1	0	0	10,860
Valid Redress	5	G	5	2	0	0	13,300
Valid Respect	3	C	17	1	1	3	18,590
Valid Reward	3	F	5	0	2	0	11,220
Valid Rush	2	C	4	0	1	1	8,060
Valid Russian	4	C	20	1	3	1	9,009
Valid Shuffle	2	G	6	0	0	0	0
Valid Skip	2	F	8	1	2	0	16,595
Valid Sunrise	6	G	4	2	0	1	4,956
Valid Sunset	3	F	3	1	0	1	8,140
Valid Ticket	5	G	14	4	5	3	42,248
Valid Video	3	G	7	4	1	0	474,500
Valida	2	F	3	1	0	0	16,650
Validating	3	F	9	4	1	0	63,825
Validcardealer	8	H	11	2	2	1	21,161
Valid's Beauty	2	F	2	0	0	1	3,940
Valient Phenom	5	H	2	0	0	0	180
Valieo	2	F	5	2	0	0	26,210
Valintine Pebbles	7	M	11	1	2	1	7,628
Valintineforvickie	3	F	8	1	1	2	12,685
Valjean	11	G	6	1	0	0	4,479
Valjoy	5	G	8	1	0	1	4,167
Vallarta	5	G	9	4	1	0	93,275
Vallelunga	2	G	2	0	0	0	0
Vallenato	3	C	3	0	0	0	345
Valley Affair	5	M	7	2	0	0	21,623
Valley Doll	3	F	4	1	1	1	4,021
Valley High	4	F	8	2	0	1	14,145
Valley Home Rose	5	M	1	0	0	0	0
Valley Mist	4	C	20	2	3	1	17,825
Valley of Roses	3	F	1	0	0	0	160
Valley of the Gods	3	F	12	2	2	3	96,067
Valley of Violets	6	M	3	0	0	0	480
Valley Parking	5	M	10	2	1	2	53,270
Valley Queen	3	F	12	1	5	0	31,170
Valley Town	2	F	3	0	1	0	3,345
Valley True	7	G	3	0	0	0	120
Valleybrook Gal	3	F	5	0	1	2	3,223
Valleyman	3	C	16	2	5	4	103,716
Valley's Passion	3	G	7	1	2	0	24,910
Valmer	4	F	11	1	1	2	23,876
Valor Award	6	H	4	1	1	0	6,630
Valor Jaket	2	G	3	0	1	1	9,662
Valor Victory	4	C	1	0	0	0	80
Valorosa	4	F	14	2	6	2	31,720
Val's Expo	2	F	1	1	0	0	13,800
Val's Frankie Boy	4	C	4	0	0	0	462
Val's Girl	6	M	20	0	2	4	6,559
Valtry	3	C	11	0	1	3	6,617
Valuable Asset	3	F	5	1	1	2	34,450
Value Beyond	5	M	2	0	0	0	50
Value Oriented	3	F	3	0	0	0	1,020
Value Play	4	G	10	1	1	3	57,690
Value Plus	2	C	4	1	1	0	87,000
Value Taker	2	C	4	0	0	0	1,230
Valuebull	5	M	12	0	3	0	11,905
Values of the Hunt	3	C	5	2	0	2	45,568
Valyah	3	F	4	1	0	0	15,390
Vamonos	4	G	8	0	1	1	3,448
Vamos Nina (CHI)	6	M	13	0	5	1	55,990
Vamp Inthe Heather	5	M	8	0	2	2	3,402
Vampira	4	F	7	3	1	0	14,370
Van Every Way	4	F	9	2	1	1	12,925
Van Houghten	3	C	9	1	2	0	15,397
Van Minister	4	G	5	0	0	1	5,700
Van Patten	10	G	3	0	0	0	598
Van Rouge	4	C	7	1	0	2	54,120
Van Whoa	2	F	5	1	1	0	2,954
Vana Val C	5	M	3	0	0	0	0
Vanan	4	F	8	1	0	1	4,260
Vanastash	2	G	4	0	1	0	4,236
Vancouver	2	C	2	0	0	0	0
Vancouver Vice	8	G	10	0	2	0	4,490
Vanda Spector	5	H	7	1	1	1	2,600
Vandaniere	6	M	9	1	0	0	3,135
Vandiano	5	G	14	2	2	1	26,773
Vandistar	5	M	3	0	0	0	166
Vandulka	2	F	5	0	0	0	1,893
Vanessa's Gem	4	F	13	3	1	0	32,956
Vangelia	5	M	9	1	0	0	12,480
Vangelis	4	C	8	2	0	1	63,062
Vanilla Dancer	3	C	3	0	0	1	1,285
Vanilla Extract	6	M	14	1	2	1	8,190
Vanilla Sky	2	F	3	1	0	1	4,786
Vanilla Sky (IRE)	3	F	11	1	0	2	55,091
Vanilla Twist	2	F	1	0	1	0	6,620
Vanishing	4	F	3	0	0	1	911
Vanity Affair	3	G	9	0	2	0	25,610
Vanity Flair	3	F	9	1	2	1	41,315
Vanity's Forum	4	G	2	0	0	0	326
Vanna Whitesox	4	F	7	1	0	0	2,320
Vannacide	2	F	3	1	1	0	7,510
Vanna's Honeybear	2	C	2	0	0	1	2,721
Vannieloona	3	F	2	0	0	1	520
Vantage Star	2	F	4	0	0	0	850
Vany Expectations	3	F	7	0	0	1	4,060
Vany's Forum	4	G	8	2	2	0	90,336
Vaquera Bonita	4	F	1	0	0	0	239

Horse	Age	Sex	Sts	1st	2d	3d	Won
Var	4	C	11	4	0	1	99,955
Vara Lucky	4	F	6	0	2	0	1,692
Varadero	2	C	1	0	0	0	230
Varaka	3	F	5	0	0	1	4,840
Varda	3	F	11	1	4	3	14,106
Varian	6	G	9	1	1	0	5,949
Variety Act	3	C	8	1	1	0	14,230
Variety Gem	5	H	1	0	0	0	149
Variety Prince	4	C	2	0	0	0	184
Variety Show	4	G	2	1	0	0	13,200
Varina	5	M	3	0	1	0	1,183
Variversatile	4	G	13	1	4	3	17,865
Varmit	8	G	1	0	0	0	0
Varmits Way	4	F	5	0	0	0	2,382
Varner	3	G	3	0	0	0	158
Varnished	3	F	3	1	1	1	42,800
Varsity O	6	G	15	0	0	1	1,824
Varsity Player	4	C	14	1	2	2	8,629
Varykino	2	F	4	0	0	0	733
Va's Final Answer	3	C	5	0	0	0	1,373
Vasant	2	G	3	2	0	1	45,981
Vaskrissenya	7	M	13	0	2	3	13,383
Vassago	3	C	5	0	0	0	94
Vatic	3	F	1	0	0	0	0
Vatrena Raketa	5	M	12	2	3	1	37,065
Vaudeville Time	4	G	13	0	0	0	1,782
Vault	4	G	2	2	0	0	54,000
Vaulted Numbers	3	F	6	1	0	2	20,520
Vaux l'Taire	6	M	13	2	3	3	46,594
Vauxhall	5	M	1	0	0	0	380
Vaya Del Sol	3	G	5	0	0	1	3,080
Vayamos	4	C	1	0	0	0	320
Vazandar	2	C	2	1	0	1	12,588
Veazey	5	G	12	1	0	0	10,690
Vector	5	H	17	1	1	4	8,796
Vega Sicilia	2	G	3	0	0	0	0
Vegas Alarm	9	M	14	5	3	2	64,380
Vegas Folly	3	F	10	2	2	3	56,963
Vegas Showgirl	3	F	8	0	0	1	932
Vegas Venture	3	G	4	0	0	0	8,484
Veiled Danger	4	F	12	2	1	3	8,130
Veiled Threat	3	F	6	0	0	3	20,290
Veiled Token	4	F	5	1	0	0	3,654
Velis Et Remis	2	F	1	0	0	0	0
Velma Kelly	2	F	2	1	0	0	18,800
Velm's Riot	3	C	4	0	1	0	3,025
Veloce	6	G	10	0	1	2	2,280
Velourious	6	M	12	2	2	2	19,580
Velva	2	F	2	1	0	0	9,756
Velvet Beauty	5	M	1	0	0	0	0
Velvet Cup	3	F	10	0	1	1	5,625
Velvet Drive	7	M	4	0	0	0	678
Velvet Elvis	5	G	7	0	0	0	1,760
Velvet Gin	5	M	1	0	0	0	0
Velvet Naskra	2	F	4	0	0	0	0
Velvet Sunshine	5	M	1	0	0	1	252
Velvet Vest	3	C	6	0	0	1	930
Velveteez	6	M	9	1	0	2	1,781
Velvetry	2	F	7	1	1	0	6,705
Velvets and Silks	3	F	11	1	4	2	28,536
Velziegellaub	3	G	8	2	1	2	23,113
Venator (FR)	5	G	1	0	0	0	0
Vencedora Amiga	2	F	4	0	0	2	12,500
Vendavalada	10	M	2	1	0	0	4,450
Veneno	5	M	10	0	0	2	666
Venerable	4	C	7	1	0	2	7,474
Venerado (BRZ)	7	G	13	0	0	0	1,330
Venetian Glass	4	F	7	0	2	1	19,390
Venganza Dulce	3	G	9	0	0	4	11,460
Vengeful	3	F	1	0	0	0	45
Vengeful Baby	4	F	7	0	1	0	1,952
Vengeful Fire	3	F	5	1	0	1	5,631
Vengeful Sis	5	M	4	0	0	1	846
Venizia	2	C	5	1	1	2	28,917
Vennys Deal	6	H	2	0	0	0	0
Vennys Dollar	3	G	5	0	0	0	180
Ventada	5	M	3	0	0	0	0
Vente Mai	3	G	11	1	3	1	21,410
Venticello	3	G	6	0	0	0	0

Horse	Age	Sex	Sts	1st	2d	3d	Won
Ventura Hotel	3	F	6	1	0	0	4,284
Venture Cat	3	C	10	3	2	2	61,730
Venture Forever	5	M	8	1	4	0	12,315
Venture to Say	3	F	6	0	0	1	7,720
Venturesome Beau	7	G	17	3	1	3	31,230
Venturous	3	F	8	0	2	2	19,737
Venturous Lady	2	F	3	0	1	0	3,820
Venus Diablo	4	F	9	1	0	0	4,470
Venusian	7	M	3	1	0	0	8,700
Venusinorbit	6	M	5	1	0	0	7,722
Venys Problem	4	G	6	0	0	1	1,680
Vera B	5	M	8	1	0	0	4,652
Vera Claudine	2	F	3	0	0	0	450
Veracus	4	C	4	0	0	0	525
Vera's Joy	3	F	3	0	0	0	2,340
Vera's Luck	2	F	5	0	0	0	1,480
Verbal Inspiration	4	F	8	3	1	0	58,220
Verbal Warning	6	G	4	0	0	0	168
Verbalize	3	F	1	0	0	0	0
Verbatim's Chrome	4	G	12	2	5	0	11,796
Verbatinsintegrity	3	G	2	0	0	0	675
Verbeyor	5	G	1	0	0	0	70
Verdick	10	G	2	0	0	0	288
Verdict's Quest	4	G	9	1	2	2	9,295
Veredus	2	C	5	1	0	1	20,915
Vergennes	8	G	2	0	0	0	1,560
Veri Light	3	F	6	1	2	0	18,440
Verily	5	G	15	4	4	0	22,386
Verkade	3	C	5	1	1	1	18,760
Verle's Victory	2	C	3	0	0	0	204
Vermont Appeal	2	F	2	0	0	0	425
Vermont Breeze	3	F	9	1	1	0	9,480
Vermont Bunny	3	F	4	0	0	0	0
Vermont Gold	8	G	4	0	0	0	244
Vermont Miss	3	F	2	0	0	0	260
Vermont's Crown	6	G	16	1	3	1	11,350
Vermonts Harmoney	3	F	12	2	1	2	13,172
Vermonts Marie	3	F	8	1	1	0	13,017
Vermont's Pocket	4	G	7	2	1	1	12,187
Verna Kay	2	F	3	0	0	1	1,046
Vernon Invader	8	G	8	0	2	0	26,063
Vernon Lodge	4	G	5	1	1	0	7,360
Vernon's Spirit	4	G	2	0	0	0	0
Vernors	4	G	6	0	1	0	1,040
Vern's Boy	5	G	13	2	2	3	15,049
Vero Missy	2	F	3	1	1	0	5,440
Verolita	3	F	12	1	1	2	12,930
Verondigo	5	M	5	0	1	1	2,074
Veronica Charmer	8	M	1	0	0	0	40
Veronicas' Dreamer	4	F	21	0	4	4	8,993
Verry Cherry	3	F	7	1	0	2	5,523
Versaltile	5	M	19	3	0	0	15,370
Versatiles Secret	3	F	12	0	0	1	5,295
Versatility	5	G	6	1	1	1	11,034
Verse Nine	5	M	7	0	0	3	1,792
Version	2	C	1	0	0	0	120
Vertical	2	F	2	0	0	0	360
Vertigo	4	G	9	2	2	0	21,196
Very Caerleon (IRE)	8	H	2	0	0	0	2,010
Very Concerned	3	G	9	3	1	2	38,655
Very Decent	3	G	5	0	1	0	7,680
Very Eloquent	3	C	10	2	0	1	37,030
Very Femme	2	F	4	1	2	0	8,107
Very Formal M. D.	2	G	3	0	2	0	14,475
Very Geri	4	F	13	2	1	0	43,860
Very Gifted	3	F	3	2	0	0	15,840
Very Gold	3	C	1	0	0	0	50
Very Lucky	4	G	8	0	1	2	9,110
Very Presidential	3	G	5	0	1	1	7,900
Very Professional	5	G	14	1	1	3	66,684
Very Vegas	2	F	6	3	0	0	57,200
Very Very	4	F	11	2	1	4	43,710
Very Vicki	5	M	9	0	0	0	1,995
Verybrightnshiney	2	F	4	0	1	1	37,440
Verzene	3	F	2	1	0	1	18,240
Verzy Man	8	G	3	0	0	0	406
Verzy Power	8	G	11	1	3	2	6,200
Verzy Tune	5	M	12	4	4	1	16,545
Vespasian (GB)	3	G	5	0	0	0	1,720

Horse	Age	Sex	Sts	1st	2d	3d	Won	Horse	Age	Sex	Sts	1st	2d	3d	Won
Vespers	5	M	9	1	3	1	65,720	Victory Cigar	3	C	5	2	0	2	15,625
Vest	3	C	4	1	0	1	31,960	Victory City	3	C	1	0	0	0	200
Vesta	4	F	4	0	1	0	13,620	Victory Crossing	4	G	4	1	0	0	17,910
Vestry	2	C	1	0	0	0	0	Victory Cup	4	G	12	0	1	1	1,580
Vettriano (IRE)	3	G	2	0	0	0	4,500	Victory Dawn	4	C	5	1	0	2	20,770
Vexation	2	G	4	1	0	0	19,899	Victory Day	2	G	6	2	0	1	22,145
Via Amalfi	2	F	1	0	0	0	100	Victory Dinner	3	C	2	0	1	0	1,000
Via Columbo	3	G	10	2	1	2	101,352	Victory Empress	5	M	1	0	0	0	0
Via Con Clase	6	M	1	0	0	0	0	Victory Encounter	3	F	7	5	1	1	156,600
Via Condito	4	C	9	0	2	1	2,789	Victory for D J	3	F	13	2	2	0	26,035
Via Galactica	3	G	1	0	0	0	0	Victory for Judge	4	F	6	0	0	1	2,150
Via Sacra	2	F	3	1	0	1	22,000	Victory Girl	2	F	1	0	0	1	5,880
Via Ventriloquist	4	G	4	1	0	1	2,963	Victory Hotel	7	G	4	1	2	0	3,345
Viagra River	3	G	11	2	2	2	21,005	Victory in Valley	2	F	2	0	0	0	1,125
Vianne	3	F	1	0	0	0	0	Victory Is Sweet	3	C	5	0	0	0	1,125
Viansa Ossidiana	3	F	7	1	1	1	35,890	Victory Island	3	G	7	0	0	1	3,045
Viasec Son	6	G	4	2	0	0	15,276	Victory Jive	4	C	1	0	0	0	0
Vibes	4	F	7	0	1	0	11,176	Victory Lad	4	C	8	1	0	1	1,425
Vibod	4	C	15	3	2	2	14,093	Victory Light	2	C	4	1	1	1	89,960
Vibra	2	C	2	0	0	0	0	Victory Matters	4	C	2	0	0	0	136
Vibrado (URU)	6	G	12	0	1	3	4,779	Victory Mis	3	F	9	0	1	2	11,003
Vibs	3	F	6	1	0	0	32,845	Victory Moment	4	F	2	0	0	1	3,420
Vic Jr.	5	G	2	0	0	0	0	Victory Moondance	2	C	1	0	0	0	0
Vic Mason	2	G	10	1	0	4	27,869	Victory Parade	4	F	10	0	0	0	663
Vicarious Sara	7	M	3	1	0	1	16,500	Victory Peak	4	F	13	0	1	1	8,093
Vice Coolo	4	F	14	2	4	2	32,741	Victory Plus	5	G	10	0	0	1	1,426
Vice Squad	5	G	19	3	0	4	51,267	Victory Pose	6	H	8	6	1	0	52,100
Vicechairman	5	G	12	5	0	1	39,710	Victory Prospect	4	F	16	2	1	4	55,090
Vicesarenowhabits	4	F	7	0	2	0	3,840	Victory Prospector	3	C	3	1	1	0	9,810
Vicester	3	C	9	1	1	0	8,040	Victory Punch	2	F	7	2	3	1	54,666
Vichory Gold	4	G	4	0	0	0	241	Victory Red	4	G	15	2	1	2	8,255
Vicious Boy (CHI)	4	G	3	0	0	0	2,320	Victory Rising	5	H	16	1	6	1	11,213
Vicious Crook	3	F	15	2	2	0	13,160	Victory Rose	3	F	7	1	0	2	48,160
Vicki Darling	3	F	3	1	0	0	4,020	Victory Serenade	7	M	14	2	1	3	21,445
Vicki Vallencourt	4	F	11	3	2	1	163,390	Victory Smile	3	C	9	1	0	1	11,145
Vicki's Reward	3	F	16	0	8	3	16,475	Victory Snit	4	F	17	1	2	0	27,170
Vicki's Sister	2	F	3	0	0	1	915	Victory Song	3	C	3	0	1	0	9,000
Vicks Shuffler	5	M	2	0	0	0	0	Victory Spin (GB)	7	G	8	4	1	0	38,100
Vick's Trick	3	C	1	0	0	0	270	Victory Sweep	4	G	14	3	2	2	32,687
Vicky's Genius	4	F	13	3	3	2	22,936	Victory Tower	13	G	1	0	0	0	0
Vicky's Stage	3	F	11	1	2	1	21,915	Victory U. S. A.	2	F	6	2	1	2	350,370
Vicky's Verse	3	F	10	0	1	2	3,550	Victory Venture	3	G	4	1	1	0	6,105
Vic's Big Boy	3	C	1	0	1	0	1,800	Victory Waltz	3	F	8	2	1	1	8,968
Vic's Hope	4	G	17	4	1	2	23,847	Victory Won	4	C	7	0	2	1	7,115
Victor Lehman	6	G	15	2	0	3	3,844	Victory Zone	3	C	12	2	0	0	45,880
Victor o' Hara	4	G	16	4	2	1	20,979	Victoryhanna	4	F	15	2	1	0	9,619
Victor Slew	4	G	12	3	4	0	43,420	Victoryinovertime	2	C	6	1	0	3	17,477
Victor Watz	2	C	1	0	0	0	0	Victorys Call	4	F	13	0	0	0	2,150
Victoria Marie	4	F	5	1	0	0	20,160	Victory's Sister	3	F	7	0	3	1	17,320
Victoria Princess	3	F	7	2	2	0	96,480	Victorytonitehey	2	C	3	0	0	0	2,500
Victorian Bride	2	F	5	1	1	1	17,410	Vid Farewell	3	F	6	0	1	0	7,352
Victorian Damask	3	F	3	0	0	0	1,764	Vidalia Storm	3	F	3	0	0	0	213
Victorian Dancer	7	M	2	1	1	0	20,460	Video a Go Go	6	H	2	0	0	0	0
Victorian Park	4	F	3	0	0	0	400	Video Cat	6	G	8	2	1	2	15,070
Victoria's Garden	4	F	9	0	3	2	23,380	Video Magic	4	F	4	2	0	1	10,535
Victoria's Jewel	4	F	13	3	3	3	33,869	Video Man	2	C	2	0	1	0	4,600
Victoria's Redoy	8	M	7	0	1	1	4,150	Video Replay	9	G	1	0	0	0	0
Victoria's Slew	2	F	3	0	0	0	1,290	Video Secret	5	G	3	0	0	0	85
Victorias Surprise	3	F	5	0	1	1	3,619	Video's Account	4	G	8	0	2	1	3,836
Victoria's Wedding	4	F	2	0	0	0	300	Vidlocity	5	M	7	1	0	0	17,356
Victorioso	3	C	3	0	0	0	1,540	Vids Babie	5	M	2	0	0	0	533
Victorious Dancer	6	G	1	0	1	0	1,260	Vid's Ego	3	G	3	1	0	0	7,800
Victorious Kiss	2	F	1	0	0	0	0	Vids Last Chance	3	G	17	0	0	5	3,899
Victorious Recall	6	G	12	1	1	1	20,250	Vie for Fame	5	H	9	0	0	0	2,999
Victorious Sky	2	F	4	0	0	0	920	Viejo's Pleasure	3	C	4	0	0	0	358
Victorious Slam	2	C	1	0	0	0	137	Viennetta	4	F	5	3	0	1	22,672
Victorious Vicki	5	M	6	2	1	1	19,114	Viento	5	H	5	0	2	0	12,043
Victor's Gem	3	C	6	0	0	0	1,200	Viernes (BRZ)	6	M	1	0	0	0	0
Victor's Honor	5	G	1	0	0	0	0	View At Beaches	2	G	4	0	0	0	3,120
Victors Princess	3	F	3	1	0	0	5,175	View From the Top	4	F	9	1	0	3	54,260
Victor's Quest	6	G	11	1	1	4	3,053	View Halloo	2	F	3	0	0	0	1,900
Victor's Secret	4	F	9	4	2	0	75,422	Viewtoakill	8	G	1	0	0	0	0
Victor's Song	4	F	10	2	1	1	28,903	Vif	6	G	14	4	2	2	50,909
Victory At Sea	5	M	6	3	1	1	95,740	Vigilant Site	3	G	8	3	1	1	30,412
Victory Bay	3	C	9	0	1	3	5,565	Vigorous Attack	5	M	14	2	1	3	14,282
Victory Boat	2	F	1	0	0	0	126	Vigors Regard	10	G	7	1	1	2	5,620
Victory Capp	5	H	7	1	1	1	8,131	Vigrid	4	F	7	1	2	0	7,052
Victory Case	4	C	11	2	2	1	22,653	Vijeth	4	G	1	0	0	1	410
Victory Catch	3	C	2	0	0	0	480	Viking	4	C	5	1	0	1	1,229

RECORDS OF HORSES

Horse	Age	Sex	Sts	1st	2d	3d	Won
Viking Sky	4	C	4	0	1	0	1,560
Viking Walk	4	G	3	0	0	0	0
Vikings Bay (GB)	2	C	4	2	1	0	25,680
Vikingsholm Castle	4	G	18	2	6	4	15,967
Vikki Slew	6	M	11	1	2	2	40,800
Vilamoura (GB)	2	G	3	1	1	0	7,733
Vilar	6	G	19	2	4	4	23,020
Viljo	3	G	5	0	1	1	2,562
Vilkee	4	F	1	0	0	0	515
Villa D Marie	2	F	2	0	0	0	1,230
Villa Roja	3	C	12	1	1	1	9,895
Village Affair	3	F	6	0	2	1	12,120
Village Band	3	C	1	0	1	0	5,250
Village Circle	3	C	1	0	0	0	0
Villa's Man	3	G	3	1	0	1	4,415
Villas Rainier	7	H	1	0	0	0	0
Villvillumson	4	G	4	0	0	0	0
Vilma Bankey	3	F	2	0	0	0	0
Vilzak Dancer	7	G	1	0	0	0	0
Vilzak Sun	4	G	10	0	0	2	2,580
Vim N Vinegar	3	F	2	0	0	0	180
Vin Mann	3	G	7	0	0	0	400
Vinalhaven	5	G	14	2	3	2	16,606
Vince	6	G	3	0	0	1	768
Vince the Mayor	5	G	9	0	1	0	1,739
Vinceformom	5	G	12	2	1	3	19,490
Vincent De Paul	5	G	17	2	1	1	12,155
Vincenzo	6	G	4	0	0	1	1,731
Vince's Dream	8	G	6	0	0	0	138
Vindobona	2	F	1	0	0	0	125
Vine Grove	6	G	11	1	0	1	6,729
Vineci	12	G	14	0	5	2	3,017
Vinemeister	4	C	8	1	1	1	75,840
Vines and Wines	6	G	30	2	0	10	28,173
Vingt Sept	9	M	9	1	1	2	24,450
Vinnie Babe	4	G	11	0	0	1	1,887
Vino Classico	4	C	1	0	1	0	2,600
Vino Rossi	7	G	13	3	5	3	21,103
Vino Solo	5	G	2	0	1	0	10,560
Vino Tinto	2	F	4	2	0	0	37,800
Vin's Golden Voice	4	F	6	0	0	1	1,642
Vintage Champagne	3	F	1	0	0	0	0
Vintage Class	6	G	5	0	0	0	0
Vintage Trial	6	G	16	0	1	3	3,936
Vinters Reserve	4	G	14	0	0	3	2,814
Vinthea (IRE)	4	F	2	0	0	1	5,720
Vinton	2	G	4	0	2	1	9,070
Violanda	4	F	6	2	1	0	11,720
Viola's Reward	3	C	1	0	0	0	0
Violate	7	G	16	1	3	5	13,477
Violet Eyed Diva	3	F	8	2	0	3	48,210
Violet Hill	4	F	2	0	0	1	3,100
Violets for You	3	F	4	0	0	0	0
Violette Jolie	6	M	8	0	0	2	5,460
Violette Native	4	F	12	2	3	1	31,930
Violins	4	F	4	0	0	0	50
Vip Tourist	3	G	7	3	1	1	30,630
Viper Mad	3	F	2	0	0	0	0
Vipervapor	2	F	5	2	1	0	48,874
Virata	3	C	4	0	0	0	545
Virgie's Vikinette	4	F	1	0	0	0	0
Virgin Snow	5	M	15	1	4	1	10,144
Virgin Voyage	3	F	10	1	4	2	124,980
Virginia Accent	3	F	5	0	0	1	3,960
Virginia Bee	5	M	13	3	1	0	45,487
Virginia Clay	6	M	2	0	0	0	366
Virginia Dayre	3	F	11	3	2	2	23,943
Virginia Flash	4	C	13	0	1	3	16,165
Virginia Forum	4	F	11	0	1	1	5,499
Virginia Golfer	2	F	6	1	2	1	15,730
Virginia Lad	10	G	2	0	1	0	2,000
Virginia Miss	3	F	7	2	2	1	67,655
Virginia Native (IRE)	7	G	1	0	0	0	0
Virginia Pride	5	G	10	1	2	5	38,830
Virginia Sunset	2	F	1	0	0	0	0
Virginia Sunshine	4	F	2	0	0	0	76
Virginian Silver	4	F	9	1	1	2	11,826
Virginia's Jewel	4	F	7	0	0	1	1,255
Virginia's Pride	5	M	5	0	0	0	0
Virtual G	5	H	6	1	0	1	24,667
Virtual Love	6	M	2	1	0	0	3,544
Virtual Nightmare	6	G	8	1	0	0	11,817
Virtual Prophet	7	G	9	2	0	2	4,082
Virtual Storm	3	F	2	0	0	0	120
Virtual Warfare	3	C	4	3	0	0	25,860
Virtual Zone	4	G	7	1	0	3	50,020
Virtue Ohso	3	F	9	2	2	1	37,880
Virtueless Woman	6	M	3	0	0	1	6,170
Virtuosa	3	F	3	0	2	0	14,550
Virtuous Image (IRE)	4	F	12	2	2	1	19,908
Virtuous Victory	5	H	4	0	0	1	650
Vi's Opener	3	F	4	0	0	1	647
Visa Tour	3	C	8	2	2	0	8,391
Visceral	8	G	5	0	1	2	7,200
Visible Song	3	F	6	1	2	3	12,960
Visigoth	3	C	11	3	0	1	27,445
Visinand	2	C	3	0	0	0	570
Vision Boy	4	G	9	0	2	1	6,283
Vision in Flight	4	F	13	2	8	1	224,430
Vision of Division	4	F	7	2	0	0	11,160
Vision of Gold	6	M	8	0	0	0	642
Vision of Hope	5	M	5	2	1	1	14,990
Vision of Sue	2	F	6	1	3	1	35,696
Visions of Sunset	7	H	2	0	0	0	136
Visions of Victory	3	F	6	2	1	0	54,570
Visit the Circle	8	G	4	0	0	0	473
Viski	5	M	4	0	0	0	531
Visual Art	4	F	10	2	0	2	69,905
Visual Energy	8	G	1	0	0	0	0
Visual Poem	4	F	2	0	0	0	49
Vital Asset	4	F	5	0	0	0	3,540
Vitamin Bag	4	F	5	0	1	0	8,104
Vitamin C	4	G	12	1	1	2	16,806
Vitamin Fortified	4	G	6	0	0	1	1,199
Vite Vite Vite	8	G	12	2	1	1	8,988
Vitesse de Fusil	8	M	8	1	1	2	10,873
Viticus	3	G	10	3	0	1	18,049
Vito Corleone	4	G	9	1	2	2	33,878
Vito Dee Man	3	C	5	0	0	0	115
Vitrify	6	M	11	2	2	0	8,170
Viva Blanda	4	F	9	2	2	2	37,642
Viva Bourtai	3	F	14	4	2	2	20,253
Viva Colonia	3	F	3	0	0	0	1,334
Viva Concorde	5	M	15	1	4	2	10,373
Viva El Gato	3	G	4	0	0	0	2,520
Viva La France	4	F	4	0	0	0	260
Viva Lavilla	5	G	11	3	2	0	7,057
Viva Los Vegas	3	F	9	2	0	0	14,351
Viva Natasha	3	F	3	0	0	0	378
Viva Pentelicus	7	G	8	2	1	4	45,110
Viva Ruckus	8	M	10	2	0	3	37,796
Viva Vizcaya	4	C	11	0	5	2	13,755
Vivaki	4	F	10	1	0	2	10,205
Vivaladiva	4	F	4	1	1	1	23,297
Vivalariva	4	F	5	1	1	0	3,284
Vivara	9	G	20	3	5	2	22,061
Viva's Pride	3	F	17	2	1	3	25,555
Vivavista	4	F	8	2	3	0	15,279
Vive Bene	3	G	8	1	1	0	14,220
Vive Le Roi	5	G	1	0	0	0	95
Vivian	2	F	2	0	0	0	900
Vivian's Amour	2	F	8	0	0	1	2,215
Vivid Bridget	6	M	8	0	1	1	4,330
Vivid Diamond	3	C	2	0	0	1	2,390
Vivid Gold	4	F	8	1	1	0	5,065
Vivid Imprint	5	G	4	0	0	0	126
Vivid Lynne	6	M	4	0	0	0	70
Vivid Reality	4	F	18	0	5	2	11,720
Vivid Views	4	C	9	3	3	0	48,069
Vivious	7	H	9	0	0	0	150
Viv's Key	9	G	1	0	0	0	110
Vixen	5	M	9	0	1	0	4,782
Viza Verzy	8	M	2	0	0	1	777
Vobiscum	8	G	6	0	0	1	16,734
Vocally	3	F	6	1	0	0	14,778
Vodka	6	G	12	0	0	4	57,262
Vodka and Tonic	4	C	9	1	2	0	41,660
Vodka Martini	3	F	10	2	1	5	12,637

Horse	Age	Sex	Sts	1st	2d	3d	Won	Horse	Age	Sex	Sts	1st	2d	3d	Won
Vodka On the Rocks	5	M	3	0	0	0	1,140	Vying Vixen	3	F	14	2	1	6	12,110
Vogue Girl	2	F	3	3	0	0	100,200	W F First Try	4	G	5	0	0	0	186
Voice of Power	3	G	2	0	0	1	2,750	W F Rare Chance	5	M	6	0	0	1	1,097
Voice Port	7	H	7	2	0	0	6,491	W F Rushingly	3	C	2	1	0	1	10,860
Voir Dire	3	G	8	0	1	2	25,200	W G's Talkin to Me	6	G	3	0	0	1	1,650
Voladera	4	F	6	0	0	2	1,403	W R Funny Face	4	G	11	1	1	2	2,368
Voladero	2	G	10	1	4	1	72,625	W W Board	3	G	3	1	0	0	7,320
Volante Vision	5	M	4	0	0	0	290	W W Dot	7	M	5	0	0	0	132
Volcanic Hill	5	G	15	2	0	3	42,950	W W Robin de Hood	5	G	13	6	7	0	102,920
Volcano Cat	4	C	4	0	0	1	1,703	W Won	3	G	7	0	0	0	0
Volcano Mtn	3	C	13	2	2	0	40,680	W. Dee	3	G	12	1	1	1	13,514
Voldmort	4	G	10	3	1	0	9,848	W. L.'s Legend	6	G	3	0	1	1	3,600
Volga (IRE)	5	M	6	3	2	0	730,800	W. Sutton	2	C	1	0	0	0	45
Volhynia	3	F	8	2	3	0	44,245	W. W. Dixie	7	G	16	0	1	2	2,940
Volkonsky	4	C	5	0	1	0	16,800	Wa Dancer	5	H	3	0	0	0	3,010
Volley	5	G	8	1	0	1	14,234	Wa Ha Jones	5	G	4	0	0	0	283
Volleyball Bag	5	M	7	0	1	0	2,090	Wa Pete	5	H	10	1	1	2	4,328
Volnay	4	C	6	1	0	2	20,920	Wa Sarah	4	F	4	2	1	0	18,417
Volobee (FR)	3	F	2	0	0	0	195	Wa Tal	3	G	4	0	0	0	152
Volponi	5	H	8	0	5	2	438,256	Waac	5	M	15	0	1	3	6,755
Voltemort	3	C	11	1	2	0	11,010	Waakomim	4	G	22	1	2	1	9,851
Volterromo (ARG)	5	G	2	0	0	1	10,200	Waakootsa	4	G	5	0	0	2	2,667
Voluntas	7	G	6	0	0	1	1,690	Waapatohs	5	H	4	1	2	0	6,710
Volunteer Annie	3	F	11	1	1	3	22,425	Waapo'pi	4	C	2	0	0	0	0
Volunteer Soul	3	G	1	0	0	0	0	Wabaroani	6	H	8	2	1	1	9,328
Voluntown	2	F	1	0	0	0	0	Wac	3	F	4	0	0	0	350
Von Bellinghausen	6	G	9	3	4	0	19,820	Wackeyetoldyou	3	G	8	0	1	1	8,372
Von Braun	2	F	3	1	1	0	22,400	Wackie Mackie	5	M	2	0	0	0	213
Von Daun	4	G	11	0	0	1	920	Wackman	2	G	3	1	0	0	10,580
Von Stauffenberg	6	G	7	1	3	1	7,909	Wacko Jacko	10	G	9	2	1	1	11,367
Von Zella	5	M	16	2	0	4	47,341	Wacky for Love	3	C	8	3	1	3	83,270
Vonnalee	2	F	2	0	0	0	388	Wacky Patty	2	F	7	4	0	0	184,569
Voodo Kiss	5	H	16	2	3	2	64,680	Waco Ali	3	F	5	0	0	0	474
Voodoo	5	G	6	2	0	0	108,942	Waco Dynasty	3	F	7	0	1	0	1,038
Voodoo Aly	3	F	5	0	0	0	0	Waco Legend	5	G	7	0	1	0	2,088
Voodoo Chile	4	F	2	0	0	0	900	Waco Ruler	5	H	14	1	2	1	8,582
Voodoo Dancer	5	M	4	0	0	1	432,364	Wacona	5	M	11	0	2	2	5,395
Voodoo Hoodoo	2	C	6	0	0	0	298	Waconda Lake	2	G	4	1	0	1	7,950
Voodoo Lady	4	F	7	0	2	1	41,014	Wacos Prospector	4	G	3	0	0	0	243
Voodoo Tricks	4	G	16	0	2	3	5,605	Waco's Surprise	4	F	3	0	1	0	2,700
Voodoo Valentine	4	F	12	1	2	5	17,783	Wadadli	3	G	6	0	3	0	10,240
Voodoo's Sister	3	F	4	1	0	0	18,150	Waddle Me This	3	F	3	0	0	0	482
Vopo	3	F	3	0	0	0	820	Wade and Tay	2	G	3	0	0	0	310
Vorticity	6	G	4	0	1	0	4,720	Wading One Punch	5	H	8	0	0	4	3,890
Voryias	4	C	2	1	0	0	7,200	Wading Terms	4	F	11	1	5	1	14,395
Vosges	4	G	11	3	2	0	27,470	Wadjolino	3	C	1	0	0	0	0
Vote for Me	3	F	4	0	0	0	104	Wadsworth	4	G	14	2	1	1	36,572
Vote for Verway	4	C	9	2	1	1	14,000	Waecool Wally	9	G	1	0	0	0	47
Vote of Honesty	9	G	14	1	1	3	7,234	Wafer Me	3	C	6	1	0	2	4,845
Voteforhennessy	3	F	1	0	1	0	5,250	Waffle Head	4	G	2	0	0	0	0
Voto	3	F	9	2	1	0	16,342	Wag Alley	5	G	12	2	1	0	14,140
Voucher	9	G	1	0	0	0	95	Wage a Penny	2	F	6	3	2	0	84,320
Vouch's Son	3	G	6	2	1	1	14,510	Wager for Love	3	F	8	0	0	0	2,903
Vous	2	F	4	2	1	0	82,400	Wagering Angel	5	M	9	1	4	1	19,304
Vow	5	H	9	1	0	2	38,960	Wager's Joy	5	M	13	0	2	1	33,452
Vowel Play	4	G	14	3	1	6	73,520	Waggaman Road	4	G	14	2	1	1	9,638
Vowtovictory	8	G	11	1	0	2	5,294	Waggle It Red	4	F	14	1	2	1	8,040
Voyage of Reason	3	C	4	0	0	1	1,280	Wagon Road	2	C	3	0	0	1	2,670
Voz De Colegiala (CHI)	4	F	5	1	0	0	50,700	Wagon Train	4	G	9	1	2	0	23,786
Vrancon	7	G	11	2	2	2	7,923	Wagon Wheel	5	G	7	2	1	2	44,771
Vronsky	4	C	2	0	0	0	4,240	Wagoneer	4	G	9	0	1	2	8,160
Vroom Hilda	3	F	2	2	0	0	72,240	Wagonmaster	2	G	1	0	0	0	0
Vuelo Brass	9	H	4	0	0	0	0	Wagons Ho	4	F	15	1	2	4	11,861
Vuelo Libre	6	M	3	0	0	2	940	Wags	3	C	1	0	0	0	434
Vuitton	3	F	2	1	0	0	20,400	Wagul	6	G	8	0	1	0	2,245
Vulcan's Pulpit	2	C	1	0	0	0	0	Wahama High	5	G	18	1	2	2	13,578
Vulpine	6	M	1	0	0	0	0	Wahatoya	7	G	7	1	1	1	8,144
Vulpix	4	F	8	0	2	1	11,618	Wahiawa's Star	2	F	1	0	0	0	0
Vunerability	4	F	9	2	0	0	10,590	Wahine	3	F	2	0	0	0	360
V'ville Lady	3	F	10	2	1	2	14,694	Wahines Reality	12	G	9	1	1	0	2,128
Vyask	5	G	2	0	1	1	2,872	Wahoo Bobcat	3	F	7	0	0	3	3,875
Vye Me to the Moon	3	F	5	0	1	1	7,848	Wahoo Wa	3	C	1	0	0	1	2,280
Vying Dan	3	G	4	1	0	0	4,882	Wahoo's Chief	3	C	5	0	0	1	2,865
Vying for a Dream	8	M	3	0	0	3	380	Wahsa Se	6	H	6	0	0	2	4,286
Vying for Gold	6	G	11	0	1	1	5,517	Waif	4	G	4	0	0	0	480
Vying for Time	2	F	4	0	1	2	3,020	Waikoloa	2	F	5	3	0	0	41,837
Vying Princess	4	F	9	1	1	0	21,812	Wailea Warrior	3	G	9	2	0	1	14,383
Vying Road	6	G	8	0	2	1	13,725	Waingarth	5	G	6	0	2	1	54,370
Vying Rose	3	F	4	0	0	1	4,950	Waist Gunner John	5	H	7	2	1	0	38,285

RECORDS OF HORSES

Horse	Age	Sex	Sts	1st	2d	3d	Won
Wait Your Turn	3	C	3	0	1	0	4,230
Waited	9	G	4	0	1	1	6,724
Waitin for Pete	10	G	14	3	0	8	17,981
Waitinoutthestorm	2	G	2	0	0	0	0
Waitonme	4	F	17	1	3	3	11,367
Wait'tilotisseesus	4	F	8	1	2	0	38,830
Wake At Noon	6	H	10	3	1	1	303,671
Wake Me At Noon	13	G	8	0	4	2	3,857
Wake of the Storm	5	G	10	1	2	0	7,153
Wake Turbulence	8	H	7	1	5	0	8,120
Wake Up Edna	6	G	3	0	0	1	838
Wake Up Kiss	5	M	2	2	0	0	111,570
Wake Up Maggie B B	2	F	3	0	0	0	810
Wake Up Sugar	5	M	11	0	0	1	1,168
Waki Affair	2	F	2	1	0	0	25,972
Waki American	7	H	10	2	1	1	29,420
Waki Baby	3	F	2	1	1	0	18,800
Waki Bob's Babe	4	F	11	2	2	0	16,986
Waki Dame	3	F	9	1	1	1	6,840
Waki Dancer	9	H	7	1	2	3	15,340
Waki Daybreak	2	C	7	0	2	1	7,945
Waki General	4	C	16	4	2	3	41,250
Waki Jeannie	5	M	1	0	0	0	119
Waki King	2	C	1	0	0	0	0
Waki Lady	6	M	6	0	0	0	0
Waki Rocket	4	C	3	1	1	0	17,374
Waki Wac	3	F	1	0	0	0	320
Waki Wanda	4	F	7	0	1	3	10,597
Wakidevil	4	F	1	0	0	0	73
Wakiewakieglenie	8	G	3	0	0	0	0
Wakigrapes	5	M	4	0	0	0	757
Waky Matty	5	H	2	0	0	1	374
Wakya	4	C	1	1	0	0	6,300
Walapie	4	C	18	3	1	2	13,463
Waldo Pepper	10	G	11	0	2	1	4,106
Waldron	2	C	7	1	0	1	8,955
Walenjack's Dejavu	4	F	2	1	0	1	39,840
Walesa Miss C	3	F	2	0	1	0	1,535
Walesageorgia	5	G	3	0	1	0	900
Walevee	4	F	2	0	0	0	0
Wali Esquire	11	G	2	0	0	0	32
Walk About Creek	3	G	12	1	2	2	9,492
Walk in the Snow	4	G	4	1	2	1	36,750
Walk That Walk	7	H	1	0	0	0	3,480
Walk the Walk	3	G	14	0	1	4	11,436
Walk This Way	2	G	6	2	2	0	87,460
Walk Your Talk	4	F	4	1	1	0	6,513
Walkaroundtheclock	4	F	1	0	0	0	0
Walker Bay	4	G	9	2	1	1	31,568
Walker's Gal	3	F	2	0	0	0	0
Walkes Spring	4	F	5	0	1	0	10,380
Walkin' On By	2	F	1	0	0	0	1,150
Walking Around (FR)	5	G	5	0	0	0	1,860
Walking On Ice	4	F	1	0	0	0	0
Walking On Water	2	C	1	0	0	0	666
Walking Over	2	C	2	0	0	0	260
Walking Sassy	5	G	6	1	2	0	14,405
Walkington'orleans	4	C	1	0	1	0	2,050
Walkonthewildside	3	F	6	0	1	0	2,040
Walks Lik'n Angel	2	F	6	1	3	1	58,634
Walks On Water	7	G	9	2	1	1	6,861
Walkthruthevalley	6	H	4	0	0	0	240
Wall Magic	7	G	5	1	3	0	8,760
Wall Street Bull	6	G	2	0	0	0	108
Wall Street Madam	6	M	14	0	3	2	4,785
Wall Street Money	9	G	9	0	5	2	6,000
Wall Street Rally	6	M	11	1	0	0	9,200
Wall to Wall	6	G	12	2	2	2	8,904
Wallendiana Dancer	4	F	13	1	0	1	5,834
Waller	7	H	12	2	4	0	40,740
Waller Jr.	3	C	7	0	3	1	13,573
Wallet	2	F	2	0	0	0	0
Wallis	7	M	1	0	0	0	0
Wallop	3	F	7	2	0	4	28,190
Walls of Jericho	3	G	1	1	0	0	40,020
Wallstreet Analyst	4	G	14	2	2	0	12,789
Wallstreet Raider	5	H	16	1	1	3	5,127
Wally Ballou	5	G	5	2	0	0	16,365
Wally Bear	3	G	4	0	0	1	2,764
Wally Bengal	4	G	7	1	1	2	7,909
Wally Boy	2	C	3	1	1	0	9,483
Wally Wall Street	6	G	3	0	0	0	282
Wally Wally	7	G	12	2	0	2	27,280
Wally's Choice	2	G	5	2	0	2	29,029
Wally's Faygo	2	G	10	0	1	2	8,350
Walnut Slew	4	G	17	1	1	0	8,664
Walt	6	H	2	0	1	0	486
Walt M	5	H	4	1	2	0	8,435
Walter On My Mind	3	C	1	0	0	0	0
Walter Ringer	2	C	8	1	0	5	26,780
Walter Star	3	G	11	1	0	0	14,547
Walter William	5	G	9	0	0	2	5,562
Walterdontfalter	5	H	3	0	0	0	350
Walt's Heaven	3	F	1	0	0	0	0
Walts Wharf	5	M	5	1	0	0	35,120
Waltz King	5	G	5	0	1	1	14,360
Waltz Me Not	4	F	5	1	2	1	7,391
Waltzin' Storm	5	H	2	0	0	1	5,520
Waltzing Home	3	G	16	2	1	2	30,247
Waltz'n M. D.	10	G	6	0	1	0	689
Walzerkoenigin	4	F	5	1	1	1	312,320
Wam Bam Hazaam	3	G	4	0	0	0	665
Wamp	2	C	1	0	0	0	1,550
Wampum Wager	2	F	4	1	2	0	5,290
Wan too Free	2	F	4	0	1	2	6,063
Wana Warrior	10	G	10	0	0	0	673
Wanaka	2	C	7	1	3	3	51,030
Wananikki	3	F	6	0	0	1	1,998
Wanchuan	3	G	3	0	0	0	0
Wand	3	F	9	1	0	0	3,168
Wanda Warbucks	5	M	8	0	0	1	3,500
Wanda Woman	4	F	16	4	3	1	31,835
Wandaland's Turk	4	G	6	1	0	0	21,150
Wandassilverstreak	2	F	3	0	0	0	295
Wander Alley	8	H	4	0	1	1	748
Wander Mom	5	M	3	1	0	0	53,000
Wander Time	2	C	4	1	0	1	14,250
Wandering Rose	9	M	3	0	1	0	1,370
Wandi	2	F	1	0	0	0	137
Wando	3	C	8	5	1	1	2,017,323
Wandofwands	7	M	5	0	0	1	4,800
Wandsong	3	G	1	0	0	0	300
Wanessa	5	M	2	0	0	0	0
Wango Tango	4	F	11	0	2	0	1,565
Waniski	2	G	5	0	1	1	4,027
Wanna Be a Hero	3	G	12	1	0	3	17,279
Wanna Be Bad	3	F	6	0	0	1	650
Wanna Be Like Dad	3	C	12	2	3	1	27,969
Wanna Kat	5	M	7	1	1	1	6,386
Wanna Make It	3	C	8	1	1	1	8,339
Wannabe Faster	4	F	2	0	0	0	0
Wannabeflying	4	F	6	2	0	0	5,076
Wannabeslew	2	F	8	0	2	3	6,552
Wannabgood	3	F	9	0	1	0	4,638
Wannagoto Court	2	G	5	0	0	0	305
Wannaknowme	4	F	13	4	3	1	17,312
Want Love	5	M	4	0	0	0	0
Want Summore	5	H	14	3	4	1	15,031
Wantabe Perfect	4	C	6	0	0	1	1,432
Wantagh Wildcat	2	C	1	0	0	0	0
Wantanotherwon	5	G	4	1	0	0	36,870
Wantedtobeagray	2	G	7	1	2	1	29,640
Wanton Discovery	7	H	9	0	3	2	5,636
Wanton Woman	3	F	11	1	1	1	12,834
Wapato Gold	3	G	10	4	2	1	28,355
Wapella	2	C	2	0	0	0	0
Wapiti Creek	4	G	3	1	0	0	4,095
Wapsi	2	C	1	0	0	0	0
Waquoit's Tam	2	C	1	0	0	0	0
War Alliance	3	C	3	0	0	2	7,084
War Bandit	3	C	11	0	5	2	36,275
War Beau	3	F	11	1	4	3	85,881
War Buckaroo	6	G	7	0	0	0	1,316
War Chatter	3	C	6	0	0	1	2,455
War Chest	3	C	12	1	1	2	7,361
War Council	5	G	10	0	1	1	7,080
War County Road	5	G	8	0	4	0	10,145
War Crest Dancer	4	F	1	0	0	0	0

Horse	Age	Sex	Sts	1st	2d	3d	Won	Horse	Age	Sex	Sts	1st	2d	3d	Won
War Diamond	2	C	1	0	0	1	1,200	Warrantee	5	G	1	0	0	0	130
War Doctor	8	H	7	0	1	0	3,100	Warren Avenue	4	G	7	4	2	0	52,857
War Dog	2	G	4	0	0	1	2,340	Warren's Classic	3	C	9	1	3	0	39,287
War Eyes	3	F	3	0	0	0	0	Warren's Whistle	5	M	2	0	0	0	2,250
War Fellow	4	G	18	1	4	3	11,843	Warrior Fan	3	G	12	1	1	2	12,572
War Fever	2	C	3	1	0	0	28,800	Warrior Revenge	3	C	13	3	2	1	56,790
War Game	7	G	1	0	0	0	0	Warrior Woman	4	F	12	0	1	1	2,899
War General	4	G	13	3	0	1	54,850	Warrioress	3	F	3	0	0	0	349
War Hawk	3	C	8	0	0	2	9,020	Warriorprince	3	C	10	1	1	2	4,591
War Image	2	C	5	2	0	0	13,930	Warrior's Dance	3	G	9	1	2	0	10,565
War Judge	5	M	9	1	3	1	24,398	Wars Done	4	F	1	0	0	0	192
War Just Begun	6	G	11	1	1	4	4,562	War's Prospect	2	C	6	2	2	1	76,310
War Letters	3	G	5	0	0	1	1,600	Warsaw Girl (IRE)	4	F	2	1	0	1	18,680
War Link	4	G	5	1	2	1	2,222	Warsaw Phil	2	C	4	0	0	0	3,000
War Maji	4	F	2	0	0	0	540	Warshine	3	F	1	0	0	0	40
War Marshall	2	C	1	0	1	0	9,000	Warship	4	G	11	2	0	0	9,137
War Medal	4	G	5	0	1	0	8,530	Wart	6	H	7	1	0	2	21,147
War Minister	7	G	6	0	0	1	1,961	Warthawk Boy	8	G	5	0	0	3	4,422
War Mistress	2	F	7	0	0	1	4,501	Wartock	5	G	5	1	0	0	9,980
War Nose	6	M	12	1	2	0	13,766	Warwhatisitgoodfor	9	G	11	0	0	0	3,160
War Paint	3	C	8	4	1	0	100,540	Was a Poor Man	4	C	7	0	0	0	575
War Paint Dancer	5	G	4	0	0	0	605	Was a Zeal	9	G	17	3	3	4	17,973
War Pidgeon	3	C	16	0	2	2	17,872	Was My Case	3	C	3	2	0	0	26,250
War Pig	4	G	6	1	0	1	3,670	Wasabi Cat	2	C	5	1	2	0	44,515
War Prize	6	M	2	0	0	0	204	Waseem	7	G	8	1	0	1	4,559
War Reality	2	G	5	1	2	0	38,514	Washakie	9	G	14	2	2	4	14,803
War Room	2	F	2	0	0	0	500	Washington Apple	2	G	6	1	3	0	10,070
War Special	3	F	10	2	1	2	17,840	Washington Belle	2	F	1	0	0	0	411
War Struggler	4	C	4	0	0	0	480	Washington Boogidy	3	F	5	0	0	0	744
War Surgeon	5	G	8	0	1	3	6,485	Washington Fox	3	F	5	2	0	1	25,767
War Threat	5	G	16	2	3	1	19,819	Washington Moon	5	G	12	2	1	2	47,493
War Time Affair	3	C	6	0	0	2	2,990	Washington Spring	5	M	10	0	1	1	2,823
War Toad	4	C	7	1	3	0	3,668	Washingtonprincess	5	M	6	0	1	0	1,050
War Trace	2	C	1	0	0	0	118	Washita Countess	5	M	1	0	0	0	0
War Trick	3	F	14	2	6	1	14,235	Washita Jule	3	F	1	0	0	0	52
War Tunes	6	M	6	0	0	0	483	Wasioto	4	F	3	0	0	0	805
War Uprising	2	C	1	0	0	0	195	Waskom	6	H	3	0	0	1	900
War Valor	4	G	10	2	3	0	53,029	Waste of Money	3	F	11	2	1	2	15,713
War Woman	5	M	14	3	1	4	34,040	Wasted Money	2	F	3	0	0	0	0
War Zone	4	C	5	2	0	0	120,436	Wasted Wisdom	4	F	4	1	0	1	26,000
Waracle	3	G	3	0	0	0	0	Wata Sunrise	3	F	5	1	3	1	12,890
Warbib	4	C	5	2	0	1	41,405	Watafleet Miss	5	M	1	0	0	0	0
Warbond	2	F	1	0	0	0	278	Watasha	3	F	18	1	0	0	4,808
Wardship	4	G	16	1	3	0	13,720	Watch and Wager	5	G	7	2	1	0	22,804
Wardy	3	G	7	1	1	1	40,508	Watch Breaker	4	F	3	0	0	0	0
Warehouse Ed	5	G	4	3	0	0	20,588	Watch Captain (NZ)	9	G	3	0	0	0	500
Warehouseman	3	G	9	0	1	0	1,429	Watch Closely Now	3	F	3	0	0	0	132
Wares Wharf	6	H	5	1	1	0	10,700	Watch Commander	3	C	3	1	0	0	7,404
Warhead	7	G	3	0	0	2	3,950	Watch for Gold	2	C	1	0	0	0	0
Warhound	5	M	2	1	0	0	5,974	Watch for Smoke	4	G	3	0	1	0	1,800
Warlago	6	M	11	1	4	2	5,222	Watch Her Punch	4	F	13	1	2	3	17,025
Warleigh	5	H	8	5	1	0	217,545	Watch Me Dazzle	5	G	15	8	4	2	39,497
Warlike	3	F	8	2	0	0	8,021	Watch Me Fire	4	G	9	1	0	0	9,571
Warlock's Crypt	4	G	17	2	1	0	13,081	Watch Me Fly	4	C	7	3	2	1	34,477
Warm April	7	G	8	1	1	2	12,660	Watch Me Leave	3	F	10	1	0	2	10,117
Warm Breeze	2	F	1	1	0	0	4,500	Watch Me Momma	3	C	4	0	0	0	122
Warm Colors	6	G	1	0	0	0	0	Watch Me Shine	3	C	2	1	0	0	1,200
Warm Expectations	4	F	10	2	2	2	16,373	Watch Me Smoke	2	C	1	0	0	0	380
Warm Feelings	3	F	11	1	2	1	27,340	Watch Me Sweep	3	C	5	0	0	0	339
Warm Grace	3	C	5	2	2	0	27,340	Watch My Boy Run	3	G	6	0	2	1	6,869
Warm Regards	4	F	3	0	1	0	449	Watch My Dust	7	G	4	0	0	0	1,150
Warm Snow	2	F	4	0	0	0	480	Watch My Feet	3	C	1	0	0	0	0
Warm Up	3	F	18	2	2	3	20,874	Watch My Gold	7	G	6	1	2	0	12,792
Warm Welcome	3	C	2	0	0	0	880	Watch My Six	4	F	10	3	0	2	16,942
Warmnfuzzyfeelin	2	F	6	2	2	2	27,001	Watch Out Boys	3	F	2	1	0	0	20,460
Warn Me Again	5	G	6	3	0	0	46,252	Watch Out Forlefty	11	G	10	2	0	1	8,145
Warners Music	3	F	12	0	3	3	6,633	Watch Out World	3	F	6	0	2	1	34,550
Warning Crossing	4	G	11	2	1	2	13,730	Watch Over Me	2	G	2	0	1	1	24,360
Warning Light	6	M	13	1	4	3	11,350	Watch Primetime	3	G	4	0	0	0	636
Warning Note (IRE)	6	G	3	0	0	0	1,980	Watch the Lady	3	F	2	0	1	0	3,747
Warning Sign	3	C	6	2	3	1	38,175	Watch Your Pennies	6	G	11	2	0	2	42,250
Warning Signal	4	C	4	0	2	0	19,260	Watchem Smokey	3	G	7	5	0	0	144,200
Warningonthelake	2	G	2	0	0	0	3,560	Watch'er Dance	4	F	6	1	0	2	10,201
Warp	7	M	7	0	0	1	5,855	Watcherstrut	3	F	14	0	2	1	23,689
Warp Drive	6	G	6	1	1	2	5,735	Watching	5	H	1	0	0	0	380
Warp Speed Scottie	4	C	6	1	1	1	15,963	Watching You	3	F	3	0	2	1	69,885
Warpfactorten Brag	3	G	5	0	1	3	3,805	Watchman's Warning	8	G	14	1	4	2	66,279
Warplane	4	C	11	4	4	0	96,004	Watchmedothis	2	C	1	0	0	0	0
Warrant	9	G	3	0	0	0	780	Watchmemove	3	F	14	2	1	1	9,773

Horse	Age	Sex	Sts	1st	2d	3d	Won	Horse	Age	Sex	Sts	1st	2d	3d	Won
Watchsusanrun	2	F	5	0	1	2	3,825	Wavering Rhythm	5	M	2	0	0	0	1,460
Watchthisangelfly	3	F	1	0	0	0	185	Wavering Seasons	4	G	7	0	0	0	1,790
Watchthistrick	3	F	1	0	0	0	113	Wavering Thought	6	M	8	1	1	0	5,456
Water an Lighting	4	F	11	2	1	4	11,945	Wavering Truth	2	G	2	0	0	0	650
Water Bag	4	G	4	0	0	0	473	Wavering Warrior	10	G	9	0	1	2	3,196
Water Bug	2	F	1	0	0	0	0	Waverly Girl	2	F	3	1	0	0	5,070
Water Cannon	2	G	7	1	2	1	32,500	Waverly Gold	5	M	4	1	0	0	3,708
Water Czar	5	G	7	1	2	1	17,180	Waverly Naskra	6	G	3	0	0	0	0
Water Gap	3	F	15	4	1	4	31,795	Waves of Beauty	3	F	5	0	0	0	3,360
Water Hunter (GB)	6	G	3	1	1	0	22,000	Waves of Torrie	5	H	8	1	2	2	10,455
Water Issues	3	F	10	0	2	3	8,985	Wavey Davey	7	G	11	2	0	0	7,698
Water Quint	5	G	10	3	1	0	42,009	Waving Girl	4	F	7	1	0	1	7,240
Water Related	3	F	4	1	0	0	11,220	Waving Hart	3	C	2	0	0	0	0
Water Rights	4	F	2	0	0	0	1,230	Waving Monarch	2	G	6	0	1	0	4,290
Water Ski	3	F	11	3	3	1	60,860	Waving Past	6	H	3	1	0	0	4,039
Water Sports	4	G	8	0	2	0	5,210	Wavy	4	F	14	4	2	1	29,500
Water to Wine	6	M	1	0	0	0	0	Wawota	3	F	5	0	0	0	340
Water Tune	4	F	5	0	0	0	0	Wax	3	C	8	1	1	1	10,600
Waterbuck	6	M	6	0	0	1	1,619	Waxy's Choice	3	G	8	2	0	1	12,141
Watercolour	3	F	8	0	0	0	585	Way Beyond	3	F	9	3	1	0	16,460
Wateree	2	F	6	0	3	1	23,475	Way Brite	3	F	5	1	0	1	7,775
Waterloo Gin	4	G	6	0	0	0	1,221	Way Fast Beauty	4	F	10	1	3	0	18,315
Waterloo Run	2	G	4	0	0	0	690	Way Fleeter	3	F	11	2	3	2	26,309
Watermellon Run	6	G	12	2	1	1	12,702	Way Marie	4	F	5	0	0	0	441
Watermelon Wine	4	F	5	1	2	1	44,600	Way of the Knight	6	H	2	0	0	0	360
Watershed Event	2	C	2	0	0	0	0	Way of the Star	2	F	1	0	0	0	0
Watershed Park	5	M	4	1	0	0	19,025	Way Out Story	4	C	7	0	2	2	8,000
Waterundrthebridge	4	C	11	2	1	0	16,999	Way Out Verdict	2	F	2	0	0	0	290
Waterwheel	3	F	2	0	0	0	2,880	Way Out West	6	H	10	0	2	2	5,187
Watery Tart	4	F	4	0	0	0	588	Way Over Due	3	F	5	0	1	1	1,165
Watery Wager	4	C	4	0	1	0	3,236	Way Pretty	3	F	1	0	0	0	130
Watkindadealisthis	7	G	2	0	0	0	185	Way Sexy	2	C	1	0	0	0	300
Watkins Glen	9	G	6	0	0	0	513	Way Sharp	5	M	12	5	2	2	18,715
Watral Dixie Ridge	3	G	6	0	0	3	17,250	Way South	3	F	2	0	0	0	360
Watral Fool Michel	4	F	3	0	0	0	271	Way to Go Dad	4	G	6	0	3	0	11,860
Watral Lady Rider	4	F	12	2	1	2	9,389	Way to Go Liz	2	F	4	0	0	0	555
Watral Outer Space	5	G	4	0	0	0	2,580	Way to the Stars	4	G	1	0	0	0	0
Watral Swee Dixie	4	F	9	1	4	1	16,180	Way to the Top	5	G	12	4	2	2	187,800
Watrals Abiskipper	3	F	2	1	1	0	4,240	Way to Verify	7	H	3	1	0	0	9,000
Watrals Brass Hood	3	G	4	0	0	1	648	Way too Fun	3	F	7	1	0	1	11,985
Watrals Cloud Nine	5	H	11	2	1	0	9,155	Way too Salty	3	G	1	0	0	1	6,240
Watrals Daytripper	3	F	1	0	0	0	159	Way West Dolly	3	F	2	1	0	1	6,728
Watral's Doonsday	4	F	6	3	1	0	19,196	Waybil	5	G	2	0	0	0	1,320
Watrals Glory	5	G	7	2	0	0	7,618	Waycross City	7	G	4	1	0	1	8,630
Watrals Hula Girl	3	F	1	0	0	0	0	Wayinthebacktwo	3	F	6	0	0	1	3,307
Watrals Lady Hanne	4	F	6	0	2	1	24,970	Wayland	6	M	11	0	0	1	1,008
Watral's Nashua	3	F	9	0	1	2	3,982	Wayne Henry	2	C	1	0	0	0	1,140
Watrals Old Timer	4	G	10	2	0	2	13,745	Wayne Newton	5	G	1	0	0	0	0
Watrals Prom Dance	4	F	12	4	2	1	17,648	Wayne O	5	H	4	1	0	1	10,140
Watrals Rich Brass	7	G	13	3	2	3	25,375	Wayne's Boy	4	G	14	2	1	1	21,215
Watrals Rodeo Bob	7	G	12	0	4	4	22,402	Wayne's Choice	8	G	17	5	4	0	21,458
Watrals Sea Trip	12	G	6	0	0	1	4,600	Waynes Irish	7	G	10	1	1	1	8,362
Watral's Senor	2	C	2	0	0	0	2,460	Wayne's Mister C	8	G	14	5	3	1	23,374
Watrals Speed Zone	4	F	5	0	0	1	743	Wayne's Princess	4	F	14	5	2	2	56,880
Watrals Stephanie	6	M	10	0	0	2	5,534	Wayne's Star	2	F	2	0	0	0	0
Watrals Strike Go	4	F	15	4	2	3	38,232	Wayneschoclatebar	5	G	7	2	0	0	11,220
Watrals Twelvbelow	8	M	3	0	0	1	3,561	Waynestro	3	C	4	1	0	2	10,375
Watralsoutherncure	4	G	8	3	0	2	33,870	Wayoutview	4	F	4	1	0	0	3,559
Watshername	6	M	1	0	0	0	120	Ways to Win	2	F	6	0	0	2	2,760
Watt Ever	4	F	2	1	0	0	3,510	Waytocutewaytocool	6	M	12	2	1	3	9,600
Watterston	2	G	4	1	0	0	9,926	Waytoocoolcat	3	C	6	0	0	0	818
Wattle's Throttle	2	F	1	0	0	0	0	Waytopersonal	8	G	11	1	2	1	7,450
Watuga	2	G	7	1	1	0	11,339	Wayuphi	3	G	3	0	0	0	450
Wauchula Dancer	7	H	3	0	0	0	140	Wayward Lad	5	G	3	0	0	0	466
Waukee Taukee War	4	F	6	1	1	0	8,080	Wayward Liz	2	F	1	0	0	0	0
Waupaca	3	C	12	5	1	0	131,380	Wayward Vern	3	G	2	0	0	0	122
Wave	5	G	16	3	3	4	82,810	Waz the Devil	4	F	4	0	0	0	0
Wave Babe	2	F	2	0	0	0	906	Wazee Moto	2	G	6	0	0	1	3,665
Wave in Defiance	3	F	3	1	0	0	3,810	Wazza Cat	4	F	9	1	2	2	9,017
Wave On By	6	G	8	1	1	1	4,265	We	5	H	4	0	0	1	680
Wave That Flag	2	G	1	0	0	0	135	We All Love Aleyna	2	G	11	2	0	0	31,520
Wave the Blues	3	G	2	0	0	0	0	We Be Cuzzins	8	G	11	2	2	1	18,084
Wave the Sword	5	H	5	0	1	2	22,440	We Be Glenoaks	5	G	15	0	0	1	1,936
Waveband	5	M	11	4	2	3	97,019	We Be Movin	4	F	1	0	0	0	0
Wavemaster	3	G	6	1	0	1	6,780	We Be Smokin	4	G	10	0	1	1	2,903
Wavering Chief	4	G	13	3	4	2	30,030	We Be Spotless	12	G	8	2	0	0	5,420
Wavering Creek	2	C	5	0	0	0	390	We Both Walk	3	F	7	0	3	0	6,687
Wavering Lines	4	F	6	2	0	0	11,652	We Can Do	2	F	2	0	1	1	9,600
Wavering Marci	6	M	5	1	0	0	6,013	We Danced Anyway	3	F	8	1	2	1	17,477

Horse	Age	Sex	Sts	1st	2d	3d	Won
We Did It My Way	2	F	1	0	0	0	684
We Expect Mary	3	F	1	0	0	0	0
We Fly Delta	3	F	5	2	0	0	6,187
We Have a Problem	3	G	4	1	2	1	49,080
We Like Green	4	F	1	0	0	0	1,135
We Love It	4	G	12	0	2	3	7,750
We Met Once	8	G	9	0	3	0	5,850
We Miss You Son	2	G	1	0	0	0	0
We Sportin'	3	G	4	0	0	1	1,306
We Think So	5	G	14	1	0	1	16,924
We Will Prevail	3	G	8	2	2	0	15,200
Weakly Wages	5	H	5	0	0	0	0
Wealth of Gold	3	C	9	1	2	1	8,433
Wealthy Belongings	6	M	2	0	0	1	1,840
Wealthy Cat	3	G	5	0	0	0	156
Wealthy Rhythm	3	F	11	0	1	2	3,500
Wealthy Winner	4	F	6	0	1	1	2,380
Weapon of Choice	2	G	4	0	0	1	1,297
Wear	3	F	3	0	0	1	5,740
Wear It Well	6	M	3	0	0	0	234
Wearing Me Slick	5	G	13	2	5	0	9,774
Weary Blues	3	F	4	0	0	0	724
Weather Advisory	4	G	5	0	0	1	2,112
Weather Eye	3	G	2	0	0	0	0
Weather Ranger	10	G	10	0	0	1	960
Weatherbug	7	G	15	1	5	2	10,348
Weatheringthestorm	5	M	11	1	2	0	11,473
Weatherman	5	H	4	1	1	1	38,280
Weatherwise	2	F	3	0	0	1	3,125
Weave a Wager	2	F	5	1	0	2	9,914
Weave Dreamer	2	F	6	2	1	1	14,880
Weave It to Me	4	G	7	1	2	1	8,335
Weavemesomefreedom	4	G	8	1	1	0	1,653
Weaver	5	G	9	1	0	2	4,592
Weavin Millie	3	F	14	0	4	1	5,537
Web Caster	3	F	16	2	6	4	57,920
Web Waltzing	4	F	4	1	1	0	8,785
Web Watch Too	3	G	8	1	0	0	5,520
Webbles	5	G	9	0	3	1	2,929
Webee	3	F	3	0	1	0	5,000
Webejamminmon	2	C	6	0	1	0	10,980
Weber	4	C	6	0	1	2	4,308
Weberrunnin	9	G	1	0	0	0	0
Webster's Gold	4	C	11	1	1	3	52,480
Wed in Dixie	3	F	3	2	0	0	51,000
Wedad	3	F	14	0	0	2	4,481
Wedding Bells	4	F	8	1	2	1	9,947
Wedding Day Lover	3	F	7	1	1	0	8,425
Wedlock	5	G	2	0	0	0	0
Wedonit	3	G	10	5	3	0	59,862
Wedwood Wose	5	G	1	0	0	0	0
Wee Biscuit	3	C	5	0	0	0	237
Wee Bit Excitable	7	G	2	0	0	0	0
Wee Bit Lucky	2	F	4	0	0	0	216
Wee Bit Wild	3	F	8	1	0	1	4,506
Wee Burn	4	F	8	2	1	1	40,250
Wee Dance	2	F	2	0	0	0	0
Wee David	2	C	5	1	1	1	22,330
Wee Georgie Porgie	7	G	11	1	0	1	2,967
Wee Katie	4	F	3	0	0	0	900
Wee Okie	3	F	10	5	1	0	48,560
Wee Robin	5	M	12	1	1	5	6,562
Wee Sister	3	F	1	0	0	0	0
Wee Tell	3	C	7	0	0	0	220
Wee Wonder	5	G	12	1	4	1	5,633
Weed Runner	4	C	2	1	0	0	38,514
Weedle	3	C	7	1	2	1	26,560
Weedwacker	5	H	11	1	1	3	23,750
Weekend Baby	3	F	2	0	0	0	105
Weekend Binge	4	G	6	0	0	1	870
Weekend Ceilidh	2	F	2	0	0	0	324
Weekend Challenge	3	G	5	1	2	0	4,394
Weekend Escape	6	G	4	0	1	0	1,403
Weekend Hideaway	4	F	5	0	0	1	1,235
Weekend in Devon	4	F	14	2	2	2	16,839
Weekend in Vegas	4	G	3	0	1	0	1,782
Weekend Miracle	4	C	10	1	0	0	8,964
Weekend Pow Wow	3	G	4	0	0	0	98
Weekend Pro	3	G	12	1	3	2	14,362
Weekend Romance	4	F	10	1	0	0	4,367
Weekend Rules	2	G	7	1	2	1	22,821
Weekend Special	9	G	12	3	3	3	10,652
Weekend Willie	2	G	5	1	3	1	23,138
Weeks Bay	5	H	6	0	1	1	1,978
Weepecket	6	M	13	0	2	5	33,755
Weepinbell	3	G	6	1	0	2	19,558
Weeping Willow	2	C	1	0	0	0	0
Weez Jammin	3	G	25	2	3	1	35,765
Weezy	5	M	12	1	0	2	5,028
Wegota Cisco	2	G	3	1	1	1	3,100
Wegota Slewzy	6	M	8	5	1	0	20,056
Weho	3	F	11	1	0	3	25,840
Weigelia	2	C	5	2	1	0	32,920
Weigh the Coin	4	G	15	1	1	0	2,959
Weight's Bally	4	F	12	1	1	3	7,388
Weinerwatersoup	5	M	5	1	0	1	5,093
Weinhard	7	G	17	1	4	6	14,603
Wekiva	5	G	7	0	0	0	1,725
Wekiva Luck	4	G	16	1	3	1	12,105
Wekiva Mist	2	F	7	1	3	0	29,285
Wekiva Queen	3	F	5	0	2	0	2,394
Wekiva Storm	4	F	11	2	3	1	19,590
Wekiva Sun	2	C	2	0	0	0	920
Wekiva Woods	5	G	8	1	2	1	10,060
Wekiva's Awesome	4	F	17	2	4	3	38,455
Wekiva's Slew	2	G	4	0	0	0	2,340
Welch	4	G	6	2	1	2	8,842
Welcome Aboard	4	G	9	3	1	0	37,275
Welcome Matt	5	H	1	0	0	0	0
Welcome Millenium (FR)	3	F	5	0	0	2	40,302
Welcome Shower	5	M	6	0	1	0	2,056
Welcome Sign	4	G	7	1	1	0	10,056
Welder's Flash	4	G	9	3	1	2	15,956
Weldlock	7	G	14	2	2	3	24,555
Well	3	F	3	1	0	0	18,250
Well At the Top (IRE)	3	F	6	0	0	0	920
Well Briefed	5	M	4	0	0	0	328
Well Clipped	7	G	8	0	2	2	2,852
Well Done My Love (GER)	3	F	8	0	1	1	32,697
Well Dressed Man	2	G	2	0	0	0	0
Well Dun Ferdinand	6	G	12	1	0	0	4,978
Well Educated	4	G	13	2	5	0	28,010
Well Enough	4	G	2	0	0	0	700
Well Fancied	5	G	8	4	1	1	350,164
Well Frosted	2	F	6	0	3	0	9,040
Well Go Then	4	F	11	5	2	2	54,010
Well Heeled	6	G	9	0	0	1	570
Well Hello Clarice	3	G	8	1	1	2	9,240
Well Involved	2	F	1	0	0	1	2,880
Well Known Act	5	G	1	0	0	0	0
Well Maid Woman	3	F	3	0	0	0	895
Well Mam	3	F	4	1	1	1	10,340
Well Planned	7	G	6	0	2	2	11,715
Well Protected	9	M	1	0	0	0	100
Well Pulverized	4	C	11	2	3	1	13,480
We'll Sea Ya	5	M	9	0	0	1	8,793
Well Struck	4	C	1	0	0	0	2,640
Well Tested	7	G	1	0	0	0	0
Well Travelled	4	C	10	4	3	2	37,555
Well Versed	3	G	3	0	0	0	123
Well Water	3	F	3	0	0	1	1,590
Well Worth It	3	C	3	0	0	0	0
Wellesley Grad	4	F	10	0	1	3	7,088
Wellfleet	3	G	9	2	2	0	30,200
Wellgetem	3	C	9	1	1	1	9,405
Wellgiven	2	C	3	0	0	0	7,440
Wellpartnered	3	F	2	1	1	0	20,280
Wells Draw	7	H	7	0	0	3	2,910
We'llsee Gold	3	F	7	0	1	1	10,257
Well'sfargoexpress	3	G	9	0	1	3	8,633
Wellsona Road	2	G	5	1	1	0	4,068
Welo	7	G	6	0	0	2	1,428
Welsh Spirit	4	F	15	1	3	1	13,585
Welsh Witch	6	M	6	0	0	0	450
Wemisscam	3	F	5	1	0	0	4,565
Wendlar	3	C	6	1	1	1	20,704
Wendover	5	H	10	0	2	2	22,760
Wendy Darling	2	F	6	1	0	1	9,125

RECORDS OF HORSES

Horse	Age	Sex	Sts	1st	2d	3d	Won
Wendy Road	3	G	12	0	1	3	3,110
Wendys Choice	5	H	2	0	0	0	0
Wendy's Explosion	3	C	8	2	1	0	21,100
Wendy's Furl Sail	7	M	10	0	0	3	2,123
Wendy's On to Me	2	F	6	0	2	1	27,570
Wendy's Savior	3	F	6	0	1	1	4,541
Wendy'smaegadancer	2	F	1	0	0	0	500
Wenloch's Pleasure	8	M	4	0	0	1	929
Went South	7	M	4	0	0	0	210
Went West	6	H	5	1	0	0	7,320
Weoka	2	F	1	0	0	0	195
Werblin	4	C	2	0	0	1	6,840
We're Ok Now	5	M	5	2	0	1	8,075
Weregladyourcandy	3	C	4	0	2	0	7,605
Werehere	6	G	5	0	3	1	3,100
Werewolfer	3	G	5	0	0	0	0
Werewoofy	4	F	5	1	0	0	9,870
Wertz	7	H	11	0	3	0	30,350
Wes Side Story	3	G	10	1	1	1	16,695
Wescat	4	G	11	1	0	1	25,014
Weshes Pearl	3	F	14	2	2	0	18,571
Weshing for Gold	4	F	12	0	1	1	5,549
Weshudaknownbetter	5	G	14	2	6	1	36,940
Wesley David	10	G	8	0	0	0	0
Wesley H.	7	G	4	0	0	0	305
Wesley U.	3	G	10	0	2	2	5,940
Weslow	3	G	10	0	0	2	3,613
Wesman	3	C	9	1	0	0	23,980
Wessex (ARG)	4	C	1	0	0	0	0
Wesson Way	4	G	5	0	0	0	420
West Allis	3	F	16	2	2	2	9,783
West Baby	5	M	7	0	0	0	667
West Beware	4	F	10	1	3	1	62,485
West Boggs Park	4	G	9	1	1	2	7,139
West Bound Dream	2	F	2	0	0	0	0
West by Dixie	3	G	8	0	0	1	6,500
West Cat	3	C	3	0	0	0	0
West Coast Fun	3	F	5	2	2	0	21,120
West Coast Gee Gee	3	F	9	2	1	0	55,498
West Coast Philly	2	F	4	1	0	0	7,800
West Coast Talk	4	G	8	1	0	2	8,850
West Coast View	9	G	9	2	0	0	5,341
West Code	6	G	6	3	1	0	33,690
West Cork Tour	6	M	12	1	1	1	6,656
West Dallas	2	C	3	1	1	0	11,204
West East Rumble	3	C	3	1	1	0	12,450
West Edition	2	C	1	0	1	0	1,890
West End Lady	2	F	1	0	0	0	0
West Erie	3	C	5	0	0	0	787
West Flank	2	C	1	0	0	0	150
West for Gold	3	C	9	1	0	1	6,740
West Fort Knox	6	G	4	2	1	0	26,400
West Forty Six St.	3	G	9	0	2	4	25,475
West Is Best	3	C	1	0	0	0	1,290
West Jet	2	G	3	0	0	0	795
West Lakeshore	5	G	12	2	2	1	7,892
West Madisyn	4	F	6	0	0	3	29,151
West Meadow Majic	4	G	6	0	0	1	1,529
West Mountain	3	G	3	0	0	0	440
West of Houston	4	F	8	3	1	1	41,438
West of McGuire	4	G	13	2	1	0	12,774
West of the Brazos	10	G	9	0	0	1	646
West of the Citi	2	F	3	0	1	1	6,310
West of the Pecos	7	H	12	1	1	1	6,054
West of the Wind	4	C	8	1	0	0	7,227
West Philadelphia	4	F	7	2	2	0	18,600
West Point Gent	3	C	14	0	1	0	5,960
West Point Grad	6	H	7	1	1	0	5,170
West Renovado (ARG)	5	H	12	0	2	2	6,765
West Ridge	4	G	7	0	0	0	660
West Road	3	G	11	1	1	1	12,174
West Saratoga	3	G	13	2	2	2	58,237
West Seattle	9	G	10	0	0	0	1,225
West Seattle Boy	4	G	13	4	2	1	10,553
West Side Maria	5	M	12	0	1	3	11,593
West Slew	3	F	12	3	5	1	42,845
West Texas Wind	3	G	7	0	3	0	3,249
West to Coast	2	C	2	1	1	0	18,220
West Virginia	2	C	5	3	0	1	172,405
West Virginia Girl	6	M	6	0	0	2	2,622
Westaway	4	C	8	0	0	0	173
Westbound Actress	6	M	2	0	0	0	0
Westbound Buzz	3	C	7	1	1	1	7,281
Westbriar	2	G	1	0	0	0	0
Westcliffe	4	G	4	0	0	0	1,300
Westcoast Thunder	2	G	2	0	0	2	10,560
Westcoastwildcat	3	C	16	2	1	3	26,885
Westender	6	G	4	0	0	0	124
Westendvalues	3	G	10	0	0	2	5,185
Westerly	8	G	10	0	2	2	6,476
Westerly Breeze	3	F	9	0	2	3	47,631
Westerly Flow	5	M	11	2	3	1	38,140
Western Abbey	3	F	4	0	0	0	412
Western Admiral	2	G	4	0	1	1	6,277
Western Apache	3	C	4	0	0	0	450
Western Applause	4	G	2	0	0	0	0
Western Arrival	5	M	2	0	0	0	0
Western Artist	6	M	3	0	0	2	630
Western Beau	5	H	10	0	0	1	6,729
Western Blossom	2	F	5	0	1	0	6,950
Western Book	3	G	7	2	1	0	14,914
Western Boot	5	H	4	1	1	0	14,579
Western Camp	4	G	2	0	0	0	0
Western Cee	3	F	13	1	0	0	12,205
Western Chick	2	F	4	0	0	0	970
Western Circuit	2	F	2	0	0	0	460
Western Colony	6	G	8	0	0	2	2,058
Western Cooking	3	C	9	0	0	1	1,965
Western County	2	C	2	0	1	0	3,826
Western Cove	3	G	12	0	0	3	10,385
Western Cruzer	4	F	11	1	1	1	9,097
Western Dame	3	F	12	2	1	1	34,414
Western Deb	3	F	4	0	0	0	0
Western Devil	3	G	11	1	0	1	6,208
Western Doll	2	F	2	1	0	1	32,280
Western Dream	7	G	15	2	0	1	10,792
Western Drouilly	2	G	1	0	0	0	960
Western Drums	4	G	3	0	0	0	1,184
Western Duels	3	G	3	0	0	1	1,500
Western Dust	4	F	11	1	0	1	4,247
Western Edition	5	G	16	3	2	0	16,649
Western Elegance	4	C	3	0	0	1	480
Western Envoy	3	C	1	0	0	0	0
Western Fling	3	G	4	0	1	1	11,655
Western Fly Way	8	M	2	0	0	0	0
Western Fox	6	M	13	1	1	1	13,039
Western Future	3	F	7	0	0	0	0
Western Gale	3	G	5	1	0	1	12,127
Western Glamour	4	F	7	1	0	1	1,303
Western Glitter	4	F	17	0	1	2	4,206
Western Glo	3	F	1	0	0	0	0
Western Glory	6	G	12	2	2	2	6,774
Western Halo	7	H	8	1	2	0	30,800
Western Hawk	3	G	5	0	3	1	6,490
Western Heritage	5	G	12	2	2	3	9,929
Western Hills	4	C	2	0	0	0	0
Western Honoree	3	F	9	1	4	1	19,801
Western Honors	6	G	3	0	1	0	2,510
Western Hussy	2	F	6	0	1	1	6,899
Western Ivy	3	F	3	0	0	0	0
Western Jeff	2	C	1	0	0	0	0
Western King	4	G	5	1	0	0	13,480
Western Kiss	2	C	7	0	1	1	2,914
Western Legacy	4	G	13	1	1	3	33,499
Western Man	2	C	8	1	4	0	34,740
Western Marshall	4	G	10	1	1	0	7,426
Western Mindy	2	F	1	0	0	0	1,560
Western Miss	4	F	4	0	0	0	1,080
Western Novel	5	H	5	0	3	0	4,719
Western Outlaw	2	C	2	0	0	0	1,230
Western Pleasure	5	G	6	0	1	0	3,680
Western Premier	4	C	19	2	1	2	15,756
Western Pride	5	H	6	1	1	0	214,750
Western Punch	4	F	15	6	1	2	72,656
Western Quest	3	C	8	1	2	1	9,609
Western Quitz	11	G	7	1	2	0	6,300
Western Rampage	2	C	2	1	0	0	13,800
Western Ransom	2	F	2	0	1	1	7,430

Horse	Age	Sex	Sts	1st	2d	3d	Won
Western Reason	2	G	7	2	0	4	22,448
Western Resolve	4	F	14	1	3	2	14,251
Western Revenge	3	C	11	0	2	3	28,215
Western Ridge	2	G	6	3	0	1	32,012
Western Roar	2	G	2	0	1	0	7,735
Western Rodeo	2	G	4	2	1	0	35,260
Western Rosy	5	G	20	1	2	1	7,861
Western Royalty	2	C	3	0	1	0	10,220
Western Ruler	3	G	17	1	2	3	10,856
Western Runner	2	C	2	0	0	0	0
Western Rush	3	F	6	1	3	1	55,380
Western Sassy	5	M	6	3	1	0	5,600
Western Shore	5	G	1	0	0	0	136
Western Showdown	3	G	3	0	0	0	307
Western Siam	3	G	4	0	0	1	1,925
Western Silk	6	G	12	4	3	1	38,723
Western Solo	3	G	2	0	0	0	850
Western Special	5	G	13	0	2	0	7,343
Western Spirit	7	H	4	1	0	0	4,250
Western Spur	2	C	2	0	0	0	0
Western Squire	6	G	6	2	0	1	14,215
Western Stage	4	G	10	3	2	3	18,682
Western Stranger	4	G	11	2	1	1	14,177
Western Summer	6	H	4	1	1	0	9,360
Western Sun	4	G	6	0	0	1	1,331
Western Sunrise	3	F	6	0	0	0	5,454
Western Sunset	3	F	2	2	0	0	17,084
Western Tears	3	F	6	0	2	1	6,210
Western Temptation	3	G	3	0	0	0	390
Western Temptress	4	F	4	0	0	0	0
Western Territory	2	C	1	0	0	0	0
Western Tery	4	F	2	0	0	0	0
Western Thunder	6	H	24	0	1	1	6,264
Western Times	2	F	5	1	2	0	29,400
Western Tradition	4	G	4	1	0	1	2,264
Western Type	6	M	12	1	1	4	20,680
Western Variety	3	F	4	2	0	0	17,510
Western View	3	F	10	2	4	2	30,780
Western Voyager	4	F	1	0	0	0	76
Western Wave	5	G	6	2	0	0	5,465
Western Willie	2	G	7	0	1	0	3,640
Western Winner	4	G	1	0	0	0	0
Western Witch	4	F	13	3	4	1	15,956
Westernholme	8	M	6	0	1	0	962
Westernize	3	F	3	0	1	0	6,780
Westerntock	3	G	10	0	1	1	4,960
Westfield	6	G	3	0	0	0	833
Westgate Pub	6	H	5	1	1	0	6,170
Westhaven	3	F	4	1	1	0	5,272
Westmead Empress (GB)	4	F	5	1	0	1	16,500
Westmeadow Cowgirl	5	M	1	0	0	0	181
Westmoon	3	G	13	0	3	2	7,711
Westofdixie	5	G	4	0	2	0	5,085
Weston Electric	4	G	12	5	1	2	28,961
Weston Field	5	G	14	4	2	3	86,500
Weston Road	3	G	3	0	0	0	0
Westrika	5	M	11	2	2	0	8,160
Westside Rhythm	5	H	3	1	1	0	7,020
Westview	10	G	14	5	3	2	6,498
Westward Miss	2	F	6	1	1	0	11,028
Westward Mountain	3	C	8	2	0	0	27,420
Westward Star	3	G	18	2	6	3	65,858
Westward Way	3	G	3	0	0	0	794
Westwiththenight	4	F	3	0	0	1	840
Westwood Rhythm	5	G	12	5	1	4	31,437
Westwood Windy	6	M	7	0	2	1	11,634
Wesubaka	3	F	2	0	0	0	0
Wet Hen	5	M	3	1	0	2	9,130
Wet N Wild Money	2	F	3	1	1	0	14,832
We'vecomealongway	2	F	1	0	0	0	0
Wewantdagold	3	C	1	0	0	0	180
Weyauwega	2	F	3	1	1	0	7,280
Whadagal	5	M	1	0	0	0	56
Whadapurl	3	F	1	0	0	0	126
Whadathrill	3	F	2	0	0	0	40
Whamo	3	G	3	1	0	0	17,175
Wharf n' Lady	6	M	6	0	1	1	1,612
Wharped	3	F	7	1	1	1	24,126
Whassup World	2	G	3	1	0	0	3,025

Horse	Age	Sex	Sts	1st	2d	3d	Won
What a Bargain	6	H	9	3	1	1	25,320
What a Buck	5	H	2	0	0	0	0
What a Cat	3	F	5	0	0	1	1,751
What a Cook	2	F	2	0	0	0	90
What a Dr.	4	G	13	1	2	3	33,079
What a Falstaff	7	G	21	0	1	2	3,508
What a Filly Les	5	M	16	0	3	3	11,068
What a Form	2	F	7	1	1	1	39,770
What a Ghost	9	G	1	0	1	0	2,100
What a Jewel	3	F	1	0	0	0	0
What a Lark	5	M	3	0	0	0	0
What a Looker	4	C	4	0	0	0	209
What a Pose	3	F	7	0	1	1	3,528
What a Price	5	M	8	1	3	1	66,510
What a Queen	5	M	11	2	3	0	15,335
What a Racket	9	G	9	0	4	2	11,180
What a Rebel	3	G	13	1	1	2	14,681
What a Rumor	3	G	4	0	2	0	1,014
What a Sensation	4	F	15	4	0	2	35,905
What a Show	5	H	12	1	2	3	28,120
What a Smoke	3	F	16	2	0	7	33,390
What a Splash	3	F	13	3	0	0	20,025
What a Strike	7	G	10	3	1	1	36,666
What a Sweep	4	F	10	0	1	0	3,090
What a Touch	3	G	5	0	0	0	1,696
What A View (GB)	4	C	1	0	0	0	0
What About Bill	3	C	1	0	0	0	220
What About David	4	G	7	1	3	1	10,628
What About Now	6	M	22	0	1	1	3,675
What About Quin	3	C	3	0	0	0	1,594
What About Sue	3	F	1	0	0	0	55
What an Advantage	3	C	2	0	0	0	0
What Chew Say	4	G	2	0	0	0	1,680
What Comes After	3	F	9	0	2	3	7,910
What Do I Do	2	F	6	1	0	1	17,854
What Four	4	F	11	0	3	3	12,278
What Fuhr	3	C	6	2	0	1	10,275
What Her Name Is	3	F	12	2	5	0	77,560
What in the World	3	F	2	0	0	0	0
What Me	4	C	13	5	1	0	30,857
What Money	2	G	1	0	0	0	0
What Next Bert	2	G	3	1	1	0	14,580
What Say	4	G	4	0	0	0	200
What Say Lou	2	C	4	0	0	1	3,704
What Say You	7	G	1	0	0	0	0
What to Wear	2	F	1	0	0	0	625
What U No	6	G	17	1	2	5	6,423
What Wars	4	F	2	0	0	0	188
What You Looken At	4	F	2	0	0	0	129
Whata Bear	5	G	9	1	0	1	4,330
Whata Brainstorm	6	H	4	0	0	0	15,900
Whata Gem	4	F	3	1	0	0	27,600
Whata Kiss	6	G	9	1	2	1	27,677
Whata Knight I Had	5	M	10	0	2	2	2,389
Whata Lotta Fun	7	G	16	1	0	3	14,231
Whata Love	4	F	22	3	2	3	25,188
Whata Pretty Woman	2	F	2	0	0	0	0
Whata Skandal	4	C	5	0	0	0	897
Whata Smoothie	4	F	2	0	1	0	3,035
Whata Soldier	2	C	2	0	1	0	5,180
Whata Tan	3	F	10	1	0	1	8,590
Whata Trickster	2	C	3	0	0	1	1,675
Whatabeauty	2	F	2	0	0	0	460
Whataburger	10	G	1	0	0	0	0
Whatadish	6	M	3	1	1	0	2,175
Whataflirt	6	M	10	1	4	3	47,810
Whatagirl	4	F	1	0	0	0	70
Whatagoodboy	4	C	13	0	1	3	17,170
Whataluckypunch	2	C	2	0	0	0	295
Whataman Sam	4	C	9	1	1	0	9,410
Whataman Whataman	3	G	7	0	0	2	8,837
Whatamate	6	G	7	0	0	2	3,370
Whatanactress	4	F	11	2	4	1	21,822
Whatarocket	5	M	14	1	0	1	7,350
Whatasaint	4	C	12	4	0	0	70,840
Whatasassysong	2	F	1	0	0	0	50
Whatashamemaryjane	4	F	5	1	0	1	5,556
Whatasteel	4	F	13	1	1	2	12,880
Whatastitch	3	C	3	0	0	0	187

Horse	Age	Sex	Sts	1st	2d	3d	Won	Horse	Age	Sex	Sts	1st	2d	3d	Won
Whatasun	6	G	2	0	0	1	748	Where It's At	4	G	3	1	0	0	4,143
Whataweekend	3	F	10	2	4	2	63,983	Where Ja Go	2	F	3	0	0	0	144
Whatchamabodgit	3	F	3	1	0	0	14,026	Where Magic Lives	2	G	6	0	0	1	3,248
What'd I Say	4	F	5	1	0	2	4,080	Where There's Fire	4	C	2	0	0	0	2,400
Whatdidshesay	5	M	6	1	3	1	25,155	Where We Left Off (GB)	3	F	6	3	1	0	96,559
Whatdreamswillcome	6	H	9	0	1	1	2,924	Wheredshego	6	M	5	0	2	0	6,170
Whatever I Want	3	F	9	4	2	1	54,831	Whereisspringfield	6	G	13	3	3	1	35,315
Whatever Jim	3	G	11	1	0	2	13,940	Where's Ashlee	7	G	16	2	1	1	14,419
Whatever Will	2	F	5	0	0	1	1,075	Where's Bobby B	2	F	8	0	0	1	6,184
Whatever's Fair	7	M	8	0	1	0	2,385	Where's Charlie	4	G	12	2	5	1	22,179
Whatevershewants	5	M	13	2	4	3	41,090	Where's Geoffrey	3	C	6	0	0	2	7,482
Whateveruwantittob	3	F	12	1	0	1	6,034	Where's George	2	C	1	0	0	0	230
Whateveryouwant	4	G	14	2	6	1	30,824	Where's Jasper (IRE)	5	G	6	0	3	0	8,385
Whatisayisgold	4	F	5	3	0	0	12,885	Where's Mike	2	C	3	0	0	0	490
Whatnif	5	G	1	0	0	0	62	Where's Mindy	4	F	9	0	3	1	7,460
What's Available	4	G	3	0	0	0	413	Where's My Mama	2	C	1	0	0	0	0
Whats Gonna	8	G	5	2	2	0	8,831	Where's Ralph	5	H	14	2	1	0	19,812
Whats His Face	3	G	6	1	1	0	8,768	Where's Red	3	F	12	1	2	2	13,043
Whats in It for Me	3	G	20	3	1	4	16,573	Where's the Church	3	F	6	0	2	2	18,600
What's It's Name	3	C	2	0	0	0	2,880	Where's the Ring	4	C	8	5	1	0	125,050
What's Next	4	G	11	1	1	2	4,550	Where's the Wire	7	G	2	0	0	0	455
Whats Normal	3	C	4	1	2	0	12,410	Wheresheat	3	G	8	2	3	0	13,293
What's So Funny	6	M	8	0	0	1	2,678	Whetstone	2	C	1	0	0	0	0
What's That	2	F	9	0	1	0	4,920	Which Witch	2	F	3	0	0	0	3,233
Whats the Big Idea	6	G	4	0	0	0	0	Whichi Coax	4	C	6	3	0	0	52,350
What's the Buz Cuz	4	C	7	2	0	0	10,789	Whichway'sthemoney	3	G	8	1	0	0	7,352
Whats Up Doc	4	G	10	0	1	1	1,492	Whidbey	3	G	4	1	1	0	3,600
What's Up Dog	5	G	16	4	2	1	46,205	Whiffed	5	G	8	1	3	0	35,484
Whats Up Pussycat	3	F	10	1	2	2	33,369	While We're Here	4	G	12	1	1	5	10,242
Whats Up World	3	F	12	2	2	1	12,173	While Your Here	3	F	2	0	0	0	300
Whats What	3	G	12	3	2	1	101,930	Whileaway	5	G	9	1	3	1	8,730
Whats Your Angle	5	G	9	1	1	1	2,430	Whiletheiron'shot	4	F	5	1	0	1	71,625
What's Your Beef	3	G	10	0	1	0	2,152	Whimsical Day	3	F	7	1	0	1	18,392
Whatsername	5	M	18	3	3	4	62,510	Whimsical Tammy	3	F	15	0	1	2	11,320
Whatshisname	5	G	7	0	0	0	156	Whimsical Thoughts	3	F	13	2	1	3	42,100
Whatsinstore	5	M	10	1	3	3	10,318	Whimsical Ways	4	F	2	0	0	0	740
Whatsis	3	G	10	0	0	0	539	Whin Truth Knocks	4	F	14	1	3	1	15,310
Whatsitallabout	4	G	10	1	1	1	5,957	Whining	4	G	9	0	4	1	14,045
Whatsmineisyours	2	F	3	0	1	1	11,800	Whining Jacob	4	G	13	1	0	0	1,837
Whatson	3	G	13	1	1	5	11,096	Whip	5	H	11	1	2	3	29,875
Whatsthecode	4	F	11	2	0	2	20,175	Whip Away Girl	5	M	1	0	0	0	0
Whatstheline	3	F	7	1	1	0	13,842	Whip Creme Cookie	3	F	4	1	1	0	10,849
Whatsyourdrink	5	M	8	2	2	0	10,533	Whippee	3	G	4	0	0	1	9,220
Whatta Big Ruckus	4	G	9	2	1	2	44,798	Whipple Creek	3	G	8	0	1	1	4,463
Whatta Brave	8	G	12	0	1	4	3,298	Whip's Baby	5	M	10	0	3	2	5,024
Whatta Hunc	5	G	11	2	0	0	8,685	Whipstar	4	G	11	0	0	2	2,312
Whattacapote	4	F	3	0	0	0	1,240	Whirl Forever	4	C	13	3	0	0	10,864
Whatuc Iswhat Uget	5	G	16	0	3	1	10,390	Whirl On	5	G	4	0	0	0	0
Whazat	3	C	8	0	0	1	1,360	Whirlacat	7	G	7	0	0	0	669
Whazupsammy	3	G	12	1	1	1	5,564	Whirley	6	H	7	1	0	1	11,975
Wheat Queen	4	F	10	1	1	1	11,794	Whirling Ace	7	G	18	0	4	7	5,469
Wheater	4	G	4	0	0	0	1,165	Whirling Colors	5	G	16	3	2	3	13,118
Wheathill (GB)	4	F	8	0	1	0	3,846	Whirling Dervish	4	F	9	3	0	4	8,562
Wheaton One	4	G	9	1	3	2	17,760	Whirling Skys	2	C	1	0	0	0	195
Wheaton's Aly	4	C	6	0	4	2	26,230	Whirling Willie	5	G	11	3	0	1	15,164
Wheaton's Boy	5	H	14	2	4	1	16,745	Whirlonby	3	C	15	1	0	0	8,786
Wheaton's Chessie	3	F	1	0	0	0	69	Whirlwind Charlott	2	F	8	2	2	1	74,218
Wheaton's Joy	5	M	7	0	0	1	2,271	Whirlwind Trip	3	F	3	1	1	1	20,560
Wheaty	2	C	2	0	0	0	1,680	Whirlwind Wanda	6	M	20	5	5	5	35,430
Wheel a Mint	3	F	4	1	0	1	8,660	Whirlyburn	7	M	1	0	0	0	0
Wheel and Deal	4	C	7	1	1	0	13,780	Whirly Wind	4	G	2	0	0	0	0
Wheelchair Willie	4	C	13	4	2	2	41,288	Whisk	4	G	8	1	3	1	22,700
Wheel'ndeal'njohn	4	G	15	1	2	0	23,690	Whiskey Babe	4	F	4	1	1	0	10,055
Wheels N Wings	4	C	6	1	1	2	15,460	Whiskey Bill	4	G	2	1	0	0	5,379
When Doves Fly	2	F	2	0	0	0	100	Whiskey Business	3	G	12	1	0	0	6,295
When I Grow Up	4	F	4	0	0	0	2,180	Whiskey by the Bay	5	G	10	0	0	3	4,267
When in Rome	2	C	1	0	0	0	0	Whiskey Chaser	4	G	16	1	1	1	10,582
When It Rains	4	F	14	3	1	5	84,365	Whiskey City Jr	4	G	14	1	2	3	11,899
When It Was	4	G	13	3	2	4	44,575	Whiskey Dancer	4	G	7	0	0	2	1,529
When Pigs Fly	4	G	8	1	1	1	5,087	Whiskey Gal	4	F	3	0	0	0	150
When She Sings	4	F	4	0	0	1	7,047	Whiskey Grin	3	G	7	0	0	1	5,739
Whenever Wherever	4	G	7	0	1	1	5,910	Whiskey Knights	3	F	5	0	1	0	3,381
Whenmyshipcomesin	4	G	3	0	0	0	620	Whiskey Park	4	C	1	1	0	0	27,600
Whenthedoveflies	3	F	7	3	2	1	48,010	Whiskey Pete	3	G	10	0	1	2	4,325
Whenthesmokeclears	4	G	12	1	1	1	18,416	Whiskey Rhythm	3	G	2	0	0	0	0
Whenthewindblows	3	G	5	0	0	1	9,700	Whiskey Riverman	3	C	3	0	0	0	0
Where Are You	3	F	11	1	0	0	11,771	Whiskey Sez	3	G	6	2	1	1	71,163
Where Echo's End	3	G	6	0	1	1	8,090	Whiskey Sour	3	G	8	2	2	0	58,882
Where Is My Daddy	3	F	3	3	0	0	41,190	Whiskey Tango	4	F	3	1	1	1	18,900

Horse	Age	Sex	Sts	1st	2d	3d	Won
Whiskey Til Dawn	4	F	7	3	2	0	37,016
Whiskey Wizard	4	G	4	0	0	2	12,405
Whiskeygrunkagain	5	G	3	0	0	0	120
Whiskey's Girl	3	F	8	1	3	0	12,915
Whiskeywater	4	F	2	1	0	0	4,410
Whisky Wise	4	G	8	2	2	0	102,616
Whisper Bay	2	F	1	0	0	0	0
Whisper Brightly	3	G	3	0	0	1	1,120
Whisper for Gold	5	G	12	0	2	2	5,265
Whisper Handsome	4	C	4	0	0	0	431
Whisper Inthesand	4	F	5	1	0	0	4,222
Whisper Low	8	G	15	4	2	2	21,926
Whisper My Name	2	F	2	1	0	0	5,646
Whisper Papa	3	C	6	1	2	0	32,340
Whisper to Lou	2	C	1	0	1	0	1,620
Whisper Whiz	8	G	1	0	0	0	0
Whispered Affair	2	F	3	0	1	1	3,940
Whispered Call	4	F	4	0	1	0	3,880
Whispered Illusion	5	M	11	3	0	2	15,526
Whispered Ways	2	C	7	1	1	0	16,190
Whisperer	2	G	1	0	0	0	370
Whisperhof	3	F	1	0	0	0	0
Whisperin Girl	3	F	17	2	5	2	15,920
Whispering Angel	6	H	13	4	1	0	12,674
Whispering Bells	3	F	4	0	3	0	10,080
Whispering Chords	5	H	2	0	0	2	400
Whispering Fever	3	C	7	3	1	2	25,289
Whispering Hope	3	F	2	0	0	0	197
Whispering Merit	6	M	6	0	1	0	1,750
Whispering Miss	2	F	4	0	0	0	125
Whispering Sage	5	M	6	0	0	0	763
Whispering Storm	3	G	14	4	0	2	52,985
Whispersinthemine	3	G	6	0	1	1	3,865
Whispher Honey	3	F	3	1	0	0	6,480
Whister's Student	5	M	13	1	2	0	9,087
Whistle Blower	8	G	7	1	0	1	5,191
Whistle Dick	3	G	2	0	0	0	525
Whistle Tester	4	F	7	1	2	2	3,156
Whistler Run	8	G	7	1	1	2	12,715
Whistling By	3	G	5	0	0	1	1,400
Whistling Eskimo	7	G	16	2	3	0	15,904
Whistling Maid	4	F	8	0	2	2	50,608
Whistl'n Jack	3	G	12	0	1	1	3,540
White Angel Light	2	C	7	0	1	4	16,910
White Bean Soup	3	G	7	1	1	1	4,044
White Bronco	9	H	4	2	1	0	47,700
White Buck	3	G	14	2	1	3	129,923
White Cargo	3	C	10	1	1	0	19,445
White Cat	3	C	4	1	2	0	97,000
White Cloud	7	G	7	2	0	1	76,020
White Diplomacy	3	G	9	1	0	1	6,333
White Dutch Clover	3	F	12	3	2	3	23,120
White Dynacat	4	F	2	0	0	0	0
White Eagle Hall	3	C	20	4	2	1	69,068
White Empress	5	M	4	0	1	1	896
White Flag	5	G	11	2	1	1	16,167
White Flame	4	C	5	0	0	0	2,214
White Gold	2	F	3	0	0	2	7,130
White Hall Express	7	H	6	0	0	0	1,482
White Heat	2	C	1	0	0	0	0
White Hot (GB)	9	G	9	4	0	0	26,520
White Hot Rocket	3	F	12	3	5	1	39,846
White Ice	2	F	1	0	0	0	0
White Letter	4	C	4	0	0	1	850
White Mercedes	3	C	10	0	1	1	16,319
White Mocasin	4	G	3	0	0	0	0
White Mountain Boy	2	C	3	3	0	0	110,250
White Mtn. Breeze	5	M	9	1	1	1	9,910
White Mud	2	G	1	0	0	0	0
White O Morn	4	F	8	1	0	2	27,844
White Pass	3	C	1	0	0	0	0
White Rino	4	C	12	1	3	4	10,587
White River	4	C	5	1	0	1	7,740
White Rocket	5	G	8	0	0	2	2,316
White Sage	3	F	13	2	2	1	11,134
White Scarf	4	F	5	0	1	0	7,100
White Secret	3	G	3	0	1	0	1,160
White Sox Slew	4	C	6	1	1	1	2,714
White Star	6	G	14	4	1	2	118,875
White Tie Ole	4	G	8	2	1	0	32,782
White Tigress	3	F	2	0	0	1	880
White Wedding	2	F	3	1	1	0	34,030
Whiteglovesandcain	3	C	1	0	0	0	0
Whiteglovesandlace	5	M	8	0	0	1	3,206
Whitehorse Pass	7	H	2	0	0	0	287
Whitehorsecantjump	4	G	8	0	1	0	2,240
Whitehouse Gold	3	G	3	0	0	0	676
Whitehouse Grounds	2	C	1	0	0	0	123
Whitehouse Texas	2	C	2	0	0	0	0
Whitehousetryst	4	F	2	0	0	0	388
Whitelaunch	4	G	3	0	0	1	1,030
Whitewashed	4	F	5	0	0	0	1,398
Whitewater Wave	2	F	5	0	0	3	9,850
Whitewater Way	3	F	11	2	2	5	43,014
Whitewaterspritzer	6	G	13	2	1	2	77,691
Whitfield Valay	6	M	4	0	0	0	1,102
Whitmore's Conn	5	H	6	2	0	1	404,236
Whitney Flyer	3	G	3	0	0	0	302
Whitney High	3	F	8	1	0	0	7,155
Whitney Willie	3	G	5	1	0	1	16,452
Whitney's Agenda	3	G	5	1	0	1	11,657
Whitney's Legacy	8	H	2	0	0	0	300
Whitney's Merlot	3	F	9	1	1	0	10,825
Whitney's Wish	6	M	13	1	1	2	5,000
Whitney'srainmaker	3	G	2	0	0	0	250
Whitsonatthewire	2	C	2	0	0	0	504
Whitton Court (IRE)	5	G	7	0	0	0	0
Whitty Cait	3	G	3	0	0	0	137
Whiz Bang Boom	4	G	2	0	0	0	0
Whizbang	2	G	3	1	0	2	33,410
Whizbyou	8	G	7	1	3	2	15,494
Whiztar	4	F	13	0	1	4	5,672
Whizter King	2	C	2	0	1	0	2,700
Whizway Joey	7	G	5	0	0	0	0
Who Asked You	3	C	2	0	0	0	0
Who Can Tell	3	F	6	1	0	0	22,740
Who Cares Girl	6	M	15	3	1	2	38,058
Who Devil Who	5	G	13	1	3	0	18,649
Who Dis	5	M	11	2	1	0	6,612
Who Does	5	M	16	3	3	3	11,517
Who Ezze	7	G	2	0	0	0	450
Who Fired Who	4	F	12	1	5	0	14,406
Who Goes There	2	C	4	1	0	1	18,250
Who Is Chris G	2	C	3	1	0	1	32,241
Who Let the Katout	2	F	2	0	0	0	820
Who Loves Aleyna	4	F	2	0	0	0	3,120
Who Rah Minerva	7	M	6	1	1	1	6,439
Who Slew Osiris	3	G	8	0	0	0	720
Who Won	3	G	2	0	0	0	240
Who You Gonna Call	2	C	8	1	0	1	11,240
Whoa D	3	G	3	0	0	0	134
Whoa Joe	3	C	15	2	7	0	24,644
Whoboo	5	G	14	2	3	1	37,740
Who'd Believe It	7	G	7	0	1	1	1,942
Whodeguy	5	H	6	0	0	1	1,755
Whoisvendeladente	4	F	13	0	1	1	5,084
Whole Lotta Love	2	F	5	1	0	0	22,620
Wholehearted	2	C	3	0	0	0	2,100
Wholelotofimage	2	F	4	0	0	0	665
Wholesale	2	F	4	0	0	0	762
Wholetthebullout	3	F	7	2	2	1	55,950
Wholetthedogzout	3	G	4	0	0	0	255
Wholetthegirlout	2	F	1	0	0	0	0
Wholetthishorseout	3	G	15	2	2	0	24,176
Wholly John	3	C	1	0	0	0	3,000
Whoneedsafive	5	G	8	1	0	0	11,430
Whoo My Daddy	2	G	1	0	0	0	70
Whoop Dee Doo	4	C	18	3	3	1	21,377
Whoopddoo	5	M	1	0	0	0	12,000
Whoopi Cat	2	F	2	2	0	0	115,800
Whoop's Ah Daisy	4	F	7	2	1	0	61,280
Whoopsy Doopsy	2	F	3	0	0	0	420
Whoosh Cat	4	F	16	0	2	4	6,675
Whopaho	5	H	9	0	1	2	16,942
Who's Bluffing	3	G	12	3	1	1	68,830
Who's Bluffing Who	3	F	2	1	0	0	3,600
Who's Ciaran Dunne	5	G	7	1	1	1	6,992
Whos Crying Now	3	G	12	4	4	0	132,798

Horse	Age	Sex	Sts	1st	2d	3d	Won
Who's Dusty	4	C	8	2	0	2	18,136
Who's First	2	C	3	0	0	2	6,570
Who's for Doon	3	F	1	0	0	0	0
Who's Looking Now	4	C	5	2	0	0	54,160
Whos Mad	2	C	2	0	0	0	0
Who's Musique	4	F	1	0	0	0	0
Who's News	4	C	2	1	0	0	19,200
Who's On Stage	3	F	9	1	1	0	4,505
Who's Rumor	3	F	6	1	0	0	3,460
Who's Slewon Who	4	F	15	1	2	2	8,010
Who's Talking	8	G	8	2	3	1	10,810
Who's That Girl	3	F	10	0	2	2	7,865
Who's This	5	M	14	2	1	3	24,875
Whos Twining Who	4	C	7	1	2	2	23,694
Who's Who	9	G	2	0	0	0	0
Who's Ya Mama	5	M	12	4	2	1	86,523
Who's Yer Man	2	G	2	0	0	0	165
Who's Yo Papa	3	G	4	0	0	0	40
Whosgotthejohnnie	3	G	6	1	0	0	26,806
Whosis	4	F	14	1	0	0	4,336
Whosnicerthanme	4	F	1	1	0	0	2,220
Whosoeverbelieveth	4	F	14	2	2	0	28,527
Whosthatmaskedman	4	C	7	2	0	1	13,315
Whosthebetterhalf	4	F	12	2	2	1	18,750
Whosyourdaddyangus	2	G	2	0	1	1	3,060
Whowantstoknow	7	M	1	0	0	0	0
Whozoominwho	6	G	15	3	2	2	15,648
Why	3	F	6	1	0	1	6,334
Why Grampy	7	G	18	0	3	4	5,324
Why Have a Plan	2	F	1	1	0	0	5,225
Why Indeed	9	G	10	1	2	1	10,145
Why Not	6	H	8	0	0	1	973
Why Not Baby	3	G	3	0	0	0	0
Why Not Gold	2	C	7	0	1	1	22,590
Why Not Lucky	6	M	3	0	0	0	200
Why Not Smile	5	H	3	1	0	1	5,380
Why Not Whitney	3	F	9	1	0	1	23,720
Why Say Goodbye	4	F	1	0	0	0	0
Why So Quiet	7	H	2	0	1	0	1,240
Why So Wild	3	F	7	0	1	2	6,645
Why Why	2	C	2	0	0	0	126
Why Worry	3	G	14	3	0	0	49,954
Whyatch	2	G	2	0	0	0	0
Whynotthistrina	4	F	7	2	1	0	13,020
Whysettleforless	7	G	14	1	1	1	2,857
Whysoshy	3	F	7	1	0	0	5,663
Whyte Avenue	5	G	1	0	0	0	119
Whyte Dayse	4	F	7	4	1	1	91,520
Whytwocayman	4	F	7	0	1	1	5,934
Whywhywhy	3	C	4	0	0	1	30,955
Wibby	4	C	9	1	2	1	9,132
Wichita County	8	G	4	1	0	0	2,292
Wicked Britches	6	G	3	0	0	0	940
Wicked Charms	3	F	12	3	4	0	18,218
Wicked Cool	4	F	10	1	0	2	12,754
Wicked Falena	5	M	6	1	0	1	4,682
Wicked Fast	3	C	7	1	0	0	13,160
Wicked Game U Play	7	H	1	0	0	0	0
Wicked Lass	3	F	10	3	3	0	39,130
Wicked Mood	4	F	9	2	3	0	15,337
Wicked Mountain	7	G	7	0	0	0	0
Wicked Promise	4	F	5	0	1	0	3,410
Wicked Sami	3	G	8	1	0	0	11,400
Wicked Slick	2	C	3	0	0	0	180
Wicked Star	7	G	2	0	0	0	189
Wicked Tudor	6	G	1	0	0	0	50
Wicked Wahina	4	F	5	0	0	3	3,905
Wicked Weapon	5	G	9	1	2	3	15,258
Wicked Will	5	G	5	1	2	0	17,140
Wicked Willie	3	F	15	3	4	2	21,706
Wicked Zip	2	G	6	0	0	0	780
Wickedsisofthewest	3	F	15	2	0	2	18,981
Wicken Fen	7	G	7	1	0	1	12,805
Wicken Rede	2	F	4	0	0	1	3,333
Wickenburg	4	C	5	2	0	1	28,890
Wickette	6	M	3	0	0	1	1,175
Wicki Up	2	C	5	0	0	0	3,900
Wicki Wicki	3	G	10	0	0	0	669
Wickle Snickle	8	G	6	0	0	0	150

Horse	Age	Sex	Sts	1st	2d	3d	Won
Wicklow Devil	2	G	3	0	0	0	305
Wicklow Echo	4	F	18	1	0	3	5,563
Wicklow Gate	4	G	6	0	1	0	1,258
Wicklow Highlands	7	H	11	2	3	1	61,133
Wicklow Isle	5	G	12	2	0	1	8,990
Wicklow Miracle	4	F	11	2	1	1	18,978
Wicklow Sermon	3	G	3	0	0	0	225
Wicklow Spa	3	F	2	0	0	0	150
Wicklow Vamp	2	F	1	0	0	0	520
Wicklows Irishrose	3	F	1	0	0	0	120
Wicksy	3	G	5	2	0	0	61,782
Widows' Night Out	4	F	2	0	0	0	0
Wide Eye Bayou	6	G	7	3	1	0	41,540
Wide Eyed Warrior	3	G	7	1	0	0	25,560
Wide Out	4	G	16	0	1	1	11,290
Wide Release	9	G	4	1	0	0	33,770
Wider Smile	7	M	3	0	2	0	7,714
Widows Mite	6	M	4	0	0	1	1,540
Widow's Whirl	7	M	3	0	0	0	342
Wie Geht's	3	F	11	0	5	3	9,840
Wifely Duties	2	F	6	0	0	1	2,500
Wiggins	3	C	7	5	0	1	263,444
Wiggle Away	5	H	2	0	0	0	296
Wiggle Room	3	F	7	2	0	0	6,833
Wiki Wiki Magic	3	F	5	0	0	1	3,060
Wila West	3	F	11	1	3	3	46,555
Wilbur	8	G	15	0	2	2	8,800
Wild About Bertie	4	F	8	2	3	0	18,090
Wild About Debbie	3	F	6	0	0	0	3,340
Wild About Harry	2	C	4	1	1	0	11,820
Wild About Jackie	7	M	3	0	2	0	3,512
Wild About Maddie	3	F	9	2	1	0	32,450
Wild About Mari	3	F	2	0	0	0	170
Wild About Rachel	3	F	5	1	0	2	18,000
Wild About Ryan	3	G	4	0	0	0	0
Wild About Silver	4	G	15	1	1	1	4,690
Wild About U	11	G	4	1	2	0	11,400
Wild Adam	4	C	13	0	1	3	11,930
Wild After Dark	5	G	13	1	2	1	6,310
Wild Again Again	5	G	9	2	0	1	13,056
Wild Aly	2	F	6	0	1	1	12,064
Wild Amber	2	F	3	0	0	0	795
Wild American	5	G	9	0	0	3	3,665
Wild Amy	2	F	6	1	1	1	15,020
Wild and Dangerous	2	G	2	0	0	0	0
Wild and Icy	4	F	2	0	1	0	9,400
Wild and Lively	3	F	11	1	1	1	6,611
Wild and Lovely	3	F	1	0	0	0	145
Wild and Moody	5	M	9	0	0	2	1,670
Wild and Obsessive	5	M	7	0	0	2	1,880
Wild and Peppy	4	C	5	0	1	0	7,000
Wild and Rakshes	2	F	1	0	0	0	0
Wild and Risque	2	C	3	0	0	0	2,194
Wild and Stormy	4	G	11	1	1	1	11,152
Wild and Striking	7	G	3	0	0	0	0
Wild and Wicked	3	C	5	3	0	0	358,480
Wild and Wired	3	F	3	0	0	0	101
Wild and Wise	5	G	12	0	5	0	30,830
Wild and Witty	4	G	9	0	2	4	5,396
Wild Annie	3	F	1	0	0	0	0
Wild Arrival	3	C	1	0	0	0	400
Wild Arrow	3	G	10	2	2	0	78,286
Wild as Ever	2	F	1	0	0	0	0
Wild as the Wind	5	G	12	0	0	0	1,661
Wild Aspidistra	4	F	7	1	0	3	5,185
Wild At Times	3	F	6	0	0	0	1,170
Wild Attraction	2	F	3	0	0	1	7,117
Wild Axe	5	H	9	1	1	2	11,955
Wild Babe	2	C	5	1	1	1	46,120
Wild Bag	3	C	2	0	0	0	400
Wild Ballad	3	C	2	0	0	0	0
Wild Bandit	5	G	4	0	0	0	2,028
Wild Bargain	5	M	13	2	0	3	21,671
Wild Bea	2	F	7	1	2	2	35,855
Wild Bell	3	F	6	0	0	1	4,620
Wild Berry	2	F	6	2	0	0	59,787
Wild Bid	3	C	2	1	0	0	7,410
Wild Bill Hiccup	3	G	19	0	3	0	17,380
Wild Bill R.	5	G	9	1	1	1	19,162

Horse	Age Sex	Sts	1st	2d	3d	Won
Wild Blaze	5 M	13	1	5	3	30,224
Wild Blueberry	3 F	9	0	0	2	2,521
Wild Boar	6 G	11	0	3	3	10,950
Wild Bounty	3 G	1	0	0	0	0
Wild Bredan	6 G	8	0	2	0	6,205
Wild Buckaroo	2 C	5	1	3	0	26,600
Wild Buddy	4 G	10	3	1	1	76,120
Wild Bulette	5 M	6	0	1	2	771
Wild Bull Cody	3 G	3	0	1	1	1,107
Wild But Worth It	3 F	9	1	2	0	28,690
Wild by Nature	4 G	2	1	0	0	4,950
Wild Call	3 F	1	0	0	0	95
Wild Card Deck	3 C	9	2	4	1	54,940
Wild Card Wilda	2 F	1	0	0	0	0
Wild Caribe	2 G	6	1	1	1	26,497
Wild Cat Run	7 G	7	0	0	0	0
Wild Catseye	2 F	4	2	0	1	69,464
Wild Celebration	4 G	1	0	0	1	4,050
Wild Centurion	4 G	13	1	3	2	28,958
Wild Charger	3 G	10	0	2	3	6,712
Wild Charm	4 F	6	0	0	3	5,655
Wild Chatter	4 F	7	1	1	2	8,630
Wild Cherokee	3 F	5	1	3	0	26,670
Wild Child	2 F	5	0	2	2	5,945
Wild Chill	5 G	11	1	0	4	28,440
Wild Choice	7 H	5	1	2	1	12,000
Wild Cider	2 G	4	1	0	1	5,880
Wild Coast	6 H	2	0	0	0	152
Wild Colonial Boy	3 G	5	0	0	0	540
Wild Connection	4 G	13	1	3	1	75,106
Wild County	2 F	1	0	0	0	190
Wild Cowboy	5 H	5	0	2	0	1,990
Wild Cure	5 M	17	0	3	1	22,005
Wild Current	5 G	4	1	1	0	19,138
Wild Cut	3 G	9	2	1	0	21,401
Wild Cyrina	3 F	15	1	2	2	19,035
Wild D R	3 F	3	0	0	0	453
Wild Dan	8 H	11	2	2	1	39,404
Wild Dance	5 G	10	0	1	2	2,178
Wild Darby	6 G	4	0	0	0	228
Wild Dare	5 G	12	0	2	1	16,053
Wild Data	2 F	2	0	0	0	325
Wild Deal	3 C	8	1	1	1	5,991
Wild Dimension	2 C	2	0	0	0	420
Wild Dina	3 F	8	1	1	2	18,560
Wild Ditty	2 F	1	0	0	0	450
Wild Doctor	3 F	14	1	2	3	21,313
Wild Double Down	3 G	4	0	1	0	771
Wild Dream	10 G	10	3	1	1	36,161
Wild Dude	4 C	5	0	0	0	126
Wild Eagle	2 C	3	1	0	1	8,635
Wild Enjoyment	3 F	10	2	2	1	18,100
Wild Era	5 G	2	0	0	0	0
Wild Eskimo	3 G	19	2	0	2	9,350
Wild Evening	3 C	3	0	0	0	0
Wild Eventure	2 C	3	2	1	0	37,600
Wild Eye Bill	5 H	7	2	0	0	6,940
Wild Eye Willie	4 G	6	1	0	0	22,200
Wild Eyed Cat	4 C	6	0	1	1	7,950
Wild Eyed Wonderer	4 G	4	0	0	0	780
Wild Eyes	4 G	13	1	2	2	7,891
Wild Fever	2 C	7	1	1	0	8,320
Wild Fiesta	3 G	11	2	3	0	24,199
Wild Flo	3 F	6	1	0	0	8,100
Wild Flying Kite	5 M	4	0	1	0	3,978
Wild for Jeanne	2 F	6	2	1	0	29,360
Wild Force	3 C	2	1	1	0	19,600
Wild Friar	2 G	2	0	0	0	0
Wild Friends	4 F	5	0	1	0	1,000
Wild Fuss	2 G	1	0	0	0	0
Wild Gate	4 G	3	0	0	0	281
Wild Ghost	3 C	3	0	0	0	600
Wild Girl	3 F	8	2	1	1	53,597
Wild Gladiator	4 G	17	2	2	2	35,299
Wild Glory	2 F	5	1	0	1	57,122
Wild Goldie	5 M	3	0	0	1	1,318
Wild Goose	4 G	12	0	2	0	14,227
Wild Grades	4 F	3	0	2	0	2,668
Wild Horse Jones	5 G	6	0	1	1	5,830
Wild Horses	4 C	7	1	2	0	40,980
Wild Houston	3 C	1	0	0	0	150
Wild Icecapade	5 G	9	0	1	2	2,314
Wild Imagination	9 G	2	0	0	0	630
Wild Imp	2 F	1	0	0	0	0
Wild in the Lane	3 C	4	0	1	0	4,640
Wild Intentions	5 M	7	1	0	0	1,612
Wild Irish	5 M	12	2	2	2	21,120
Wild Irish Dancer	2 F	2	0	0	0	150
Wild Irish Dream	2 F	1	0	1	0	1,900
Wild J J	5 G	5	1	0	1	9,869
Wild Jake	3 C	15	5	3	2	64,505
Wild Jet	5 H	8	2	0	1	23,630
Wild Jezabel	3 F	4	0	0	3	3,100
Wild Jim	2 C	4	1	0	1	21,510
Wild Joe	7 G	2	0	0	0	340
Wild Kandace	4 F	1	0	0	0	2,700
Wild Keven	2 C	5	1	0	0	12,000
Wild Landing	4 F	11	1	1	3	11,199
Wild Legacy	3 F	2	0	0	0	0
Wild Lies	5 G	14	3	3	1	69,011
Wild Light	3 F	5	2	0	0	42,000
Wild Lillian	2 F	3	0	1	0	1,585
Wild Linear	4 F	6	2	0	1	13,840
Wild Liz	3 F	12	3	3	0	51,390
Wild Look	5 G	6	1	0	2	19,380
Wild Louise	3 F	7	0	1	2	3,265
Wild Maid	5 M	3	0	0	0	405
Wild Mak	3 C	8	0	0	0	800
Wild Maple	4 G	15	0	2	4	37,000
Wild Margaret	4 F	16	2	2	3	14,926
Wild Market	5 G	11	0	1	1	4,284
Wild Martha	5 M	12	0	1	1	10,130
Wild Meeting	2 F	2	0	0	1	5,820
Wild Meri	4 F	4	0	0	0	837
Wild Mistress	2 F	8	1	1	0	22,160
Wild Money Zone	3 C	10	2	0	3	18,209
Wild Mouse	6 G	5	0	0	0	497
Wild Move	3 F	12	1	2	2	6,313
Wild N Devious	4 F	1	1	0	0	4,800
Wild 'n Famous	3 G	14	1	0	3	5,562
Wild 'n Rare	4 F	3	0	0	0	558
Wild Native Lady	3 F	5	1	1	1	7,970
Wild On Rio	3 G	1	0	1	0	1,800
Wild On Salt	3 F	5	0	0	1	1,236
Wild Osceola	3 C	16	2	3	3	39,604
Wild Over Ian	6 G	3	0	0	0	1,350
Wild Ozone	3 C	11	0	2	2	14,739
Wild Past Times	2 C	1	0	0	0	0
Wild Patience	4 F	11	2	2	2	21,627
Wild Patrick	2 C	4	0	0	0	1,002
Wild Patton	3 F	8	0	0	0	0
Wild Percussionist	5 H	6	0	0	1	1,375
Wild Princes	5 H	6	0	2	1	3,599
Wild Pro	4 C	4	0	2	0	8,490
Wild Proposal	3 C	2	0	0	0	101
Wild Punch	4 F	6	1	0	2	40,090
Wild Quest	3 C	5	0	1	0	3,589
Wild Rascal	4 G	14	0	0	2	2,047
Wild Recall	2 F	1	0	0	0	380
Wild Red	3 G	10	0	1	1	2,065
Wild Red Bird	5 H	8	0	1	2	4,500
Wild Review	3 C	9	0	0	4	14,015
Wild Rezonution	2 F	7	2	2	1	36,730
Wild Rhett	5 G	19	0	1	3	6,805
Wild Rice	3 F	14	1	0	1	5,405
Wild Roar	5 G	9	0	1	1	6,439
Wild Rocket	5 G	6	0	2	0	5,980
Wild Romance	5 M	10	0	0	1	1,019
Wild Romeo	3 C	6	0	0	0	526
Wild Romp	3 F	2	0	0	0	0
Wild Rooster	3 C	3	0	0	0	380
Wild Ruler	3 C	10	0	2	1	20,660
Wild Run	6 G	4	0	0	0	0
Wild Runaway	5 G	13	1	0	3	6,644
Wild Rusty	3 G	5	0	0	0	418
Wild Ruthie	4 F	6	1	0	0	3,725
Wild Samba	3 F	3	1	0	1	18,885
Wild Scarlett	2 F	5	1	2	0	24,607

Horse	Age	Sex	Sts	1st	2d	3d	Won
Wild Search	3	F	2	0	0	0	200
Wild Season	5	M	2	0	0	0	0
Wild Senorita	2	F	2	1	0	0	19,380
Wild Shaman	2	C	3	0	1	0	8,200
Wild Shamir	3	G	13	1	5	0	27,250
Wild Sheriff	2	G	6	1	1	3	12,755
Wild Sign	3	G	13	2	0	4	27,412
Wild Silky	3	F	12	2	1	0	24,782
Wild Smile	3	C	19	2	0	3	11,257
Wild Snitch	3	F	4	1	0	1	33,000
Wild Some More	6	H	1	0	0	1	1,920
Wild Soul	2	G	3	0	0	1	5,364
Wild South	2	C	5	2	0	0	12,125
Wild Speed	2	F	3	2	1	0	29,150
Wild Spender	2	F	4	0	0	0	452
Wild Spirit	3	G	1	0	0	0	0
Wild Spirit (CHI)	4	F	4	3	1	0	830,000
Wild Squaw	5	M	3	0	0	1	6,740
Wild Steph	3	F	4	0	1	0	1,700
Wild Stories	4	G	12	0	1	3	8,370
Wild Strike	5	G	7	1	0	0	63,736
Wild Success	4	G	8	2	1	1	10,710
Wild Summer	5	H	5	0	0	1	8,180
Wild Suwannee	5	M	4	1	0	0	7,144
Wild Suza	3	F	10	0	1	0	2,540
Wild Tale	2	C	2	1	1	0	27,600
Wild Tears	2	F	2	0	0	0	1,275
Wild Term	3	C	6	0	0	0	140
Wild Texas	3	G	12	1	2	1	16,245
Wild Thang	3	F	9	3	3	2	23,035
Wild Thrill	3	G	4	0	2	1	4,955
Wild Thunder	4	C	10	1	4	0	18,704
Wild Tickle	5	M	7	0	1	3	53,733
Wild Tie	5	H	5	0	0	0	910
Wild Tiger	3	C	11	1	3	0	36,840
Wild Tijera	3	F	12	0	4	2	12,185
Wild Time	4	F	1	0	0	0	120
Wild Tip	5	M	13	4	3	0	37,285
Wild T'mater	2	C	3	0	0	0	4,050
Wild to Believe	3	F	4	0	0	0	860
Wild Toga Nites	3	F	12	2	2	1	22,420
Wild Tom	2	C	1	0	0	0	0
Wild Trip	4	C	12	3	2	3	28,385
Wild Trumpet	4	G	5	1	0	1	33,931
Wild Tune	3	F	13	2	2	2	22,344
Wild Twist	4	G	5	1	1	1	29,813
Wild U R	2	C	9	0	1	0	6,760
Wild Valay	3	G	6	0	0	0	200
Wild Valley	4	C	13	1	1	1	12,860
Wild Vessel	4	C	10	1	1	2	11,290
Wild View	5	H	7	0	1	1	4,870
Wild Wadi	2	C	1	0	1	0	8,800
Wild Wager	2	G	3	1	0	1	17,880
Wild Warrior Woman	5	M	15	3	2	4	16,858
Wild Wave	3	F	1	0	0	0	510
Wild Wavering	6	H	3	0	0	0	0
Wild West	4	C	8	1	0	1	26,000
Wild Whiskey	4	C	8	1	0	1	92,905
Wild Whitney	3	G	14	2	4	4	58,470
Wild Wild West	2	G	1	0	1	0	4,200
Wild Wildcat	2	C	1	1	0	0	21,000
Wild Will	3	C	6	0	1	0	2,108
Wild Willard	3	G	10	4	2	1	115,884
Wild Willow	4	C	19	4	3	2	34,957
Wild Willys Philly	2	F	8	0	1	0	3,025
Wild Winner	2	F	1	0	0	0	140
Wild Witch	2	F	5	0	0	0	1,768
Wild Won	6	M	5	0	0	1	1,745
Wild Years	5	H	4	0	0	1	5,640
Wild You	3	G	11	2	1	0	42,992
Wild Zampano	4	G	4	1	1	1	40,526
Wildandcrazyfellow	2	F	2	0	0	0	300
Wildarada	3	F	10	1	2	3	11,470
Wildastheycome	3	G	2	0	0	0	1,740
Wildatbest	3	G	1	0	1	0	2,340
Wildcard Cat	2	F	1	0	0	0	0
Wildcat Annie	3	F	4	0	0	0	2,300
Wildcat Brody	3	G	10	2	1	4	13,960
Wildcat Dancer	3	F	3	1	0	0	8,100
Wildcat Dee	3	F	2	0	0	0	0
Wildcat Heir	3	C	1	0	1	0	9,400
Wildcat Lady	2	F	4	0	1	1	6,309
Wildcat Queen	3	F	3	1	1	0	31,200
Wildcat Shoes	2	C	4	3	0	0	90,910
Wildcat Traitor	3	C	10	1	0	1	7,400
Wildcat Widow	3	F	4	0	0	0	2,440
Wildcat Willow	5	G	1	0	0	0	51
Wildcat's Babe	4	F	2	0	0	0	603
Wildchild Bragg	4	G	17	1	0	3	5,793
Wilde Whirlaway	4	G	8	1	1	2	12,880
Wilde Wilde Honey	4	G	13	0	0	2	7,534
Wilder Than Syn	4	C	2	0	1	1	2,800
Wilder Than Wild	2	G	2	0	0	1	540
Wilderness Call	2	F	2	0	1	0	3,450
Wilderness Lodge	3	G	5	1	1	0	6,624
Wildess	4	F	1	1	0	0	6,120
Wildest	5	G	14	1	4	1	41,368
Wildforyou	3	G	6	0	0	2	25,277
Wildinthepark	2	F	3	0	0	1	2,430
Wildisthewind	5	G	10	2	2	1	26,784
Wildleigh Lavish	3	F	4	1	0	0	13,369
Wildly	2	C	2	1	0	1	31,950
Wildly Excessive	5	G	4	0	0	1	11,760
Wildly Rewarding	5	M	3	0	0	0	218
Wildly Ruth	3	F	11	2	2	2	25,999
Wildly Simple	3	F	3	0	0	0	128
Wildman Joey	3	C	14	2	4	3	76,203
Wildmaninflight	4	G	5	1	0	0	3,995
Wildmanstan	5	G	3	1	0	1	2,840
Wildn'mischievious	4	F	10	0	1	1	2,308
Wildpayday	2	G	1	0	1	0	1,800
Wildski	3	G	3	0	1	0	3,200
Wildtat	4	G	3	0	0	0	150
Wildville	3	G	9	1	2	1	11,883
Wildwonderfulwoman	2	F	1	0	0	0	0
Wildwood Approved	5	M	2	0	0	0	160
Wildwood Crest	3	F	10	2	2	1	39,650
Wildwood Firewood	4	F	15	2	1	3	11,449
Wildwood Flower	2	F	3	3	0	0	67,100
Wildwood Gabe	6	G	12	0	1	1	2,638
Wildwood Ghost	6	M	5	2	1	2	16,221
Wildwood Jackie	5	G	13	0	0	1	1,068
Wildwood Mahogany	4	F	3	0	0	0	126
Wildwood Pip	4	C	7	0	2	0	1,068
Wildwood Robin	7	G	6	0	0	0	1,100
Wildwood Royal	3	F	13	5	1	0	152,150
Wildwood Sam I Am	2	C	3	0	0	1	4,420
Wildwood Skier	2	G	7	1	1	0	7,490
Wildwood Sparkles	5	M	15	4	3	0	19,072
Wildwood Sugarbear	3	C	5	0	0	0	630
Wildy Hot	3	C	5	1	1	0	15,456
Wile Victory	4	G	2	0	0	0	70
Wileaway Kelly	7	G	6	0	0	0	463
Wileaway's Baby	10	M	7	1	0	1	9,096
Wiley	2	G	2	0	0	1	2,031
Wiley Grey	4	G	14	0	1	2	4,358
Wiley Hunt	3	G	16	4	3	2	41,760
Wilgis	4	G	10	2	3	2	34,300
Wilhebeacrook	6	G	16	3	4	1	29,722
Wilkie	4	G	9	1	1	0	3,352
Will	2	G	2	0	0	0	1,320
Will B Bootscouten	8	M	7	1	2	1	6,996
Will Be a Bates	5	M	8	1	0	1	4,365
Will Be Rockin'	5	G	8	0	0	0	558
Will Be There	6	M	6	0	1	0	4,560
Will Be Wicked	4	F	4	0	0	0	312
Will Belong	4	C	13	1	2	0	7,997
Will Dance With Me	5	M	9	0	1	0	2,939
Will Dare It	10	G	18	3	1	0	12,230
Will He Crow	2	C	2	0	1	0	19,875
Will I Do	3	F	6	3	2	1	50,620
Will J	2	G	3	0	1	1	1,406
Will O Be Fast	5	H	8	1	3	0	7,500
Will Oblige	6	G	2	0	0	1	1,642
Will of the Woods	4	C	10	1	2	1	11,230
Will On Wheels	4	G	8	3	0	2	17,657
Will Prevail	10	G	2	0	0	1	1,500
Will Reason	4	G	10	0	1	1	1,684

Horse	Age	Sex	Sts	1st	2d	3d	Won	Horse	Age	Sex	Sts	1st	2d	3d	Won
Will Rullah	5	H	2	0	0	0	125	Willy B Tackett	2	C	2	1	0	1	11,375
Will Savell	9	G	12	0	2	1	2,434	Willy B. Silver	7	H	5	2	0	0	6,755
Will Spot Ya	3	C	3	0	0	0	190	Willy Be Gold	2	G	1	0	0	0	0
Will the Fool Run	4	G	10	0	0	1	1,080	Willy Bear	4	G	8	1	0	1	4,000
Will the Pill	6	H	3	0	1	1	2,960	Willy Nilly	4	G	10	1	2	1	24,995
Will the Thrill	4	G	3	0	0	0	506	Willy the Tuff	4	C	9	0	0	1	2,950
Will Willie Win	3	C	8	3	1	0	31,156	Willy Won't Gossip	4	G	4	1	0	1	3,575
Willa Beauty	4	F	12	3	3	2	62,085	Willys Royal Lady	3	F	2	0	0	0	0
Willa Broke	3	F	7	1	2	0	31,535	Willy's Way	4	G	6	0	0	0	890
Willa Cather	4	F	10	1	4	1	23,504	Wilmaglen	2	F	2	0	0	0	0
Willa On the Move	4	F	5	3	0	0	166,390	Wilma's Dollie	2	F	6	0	1	2	4,005
Willard K.	3	G	11	0	2	1	6,901	Wilshe Amaze	3	F	9	2	1	3	52,275
Willard Straight	3	C	8	4	0	0	115,590	Wilshewed	4	F	1	0	0	0	0
Willcox	4	G	11	0	1	1	2,894	Wilson's Connect	5	H	5	1	1	1	8,870
Willendya	6	G	1	0	0	0	0	Wilson's Rascal	3	G	12	3	3	1	14,270
Willful Devil	2	F	2	0	0	1	1,075	Wilson's Slew	3	C	6	0	0	0	0
Wilhanna	4	C	4	0	0	0	148	Wilsonsrumblinwind	3	F	3	0	0	0	0
Williams Creek	4	G	9	0	0	2	5,830	Wily Russian	3	F	10	3	2	1	16,480
Williams Grace	3	F	5	1	0	0	6,345	Wily Walter	3	G	13	1	1	3	25,950
Williams Hall	6	H	11	2	0	1	7,267	Wilya Love Me	3	F	4	0	0	1	3,650
William's Lad	4	G	10	2	1	3	24,065	Wilyacrossmyvalle	5	M	10	2	2	1	13,243
Williams News	8	G	5	0	0	1	27,585	Wilzada	4	F	5	2	0	0	79,525
William's Park	4	C	12	2	1	1	13,100	Wimauma Mama	5	M	16	3	2	2	28,661
William's Token	4	F	4	0	1	0	1,240	Wimberly's Bliss	2	G	4	0	0	0	1,264
Williamsburg Blue	3	F	2	0	0	0	810	Wimbledon	2	C	3	0	2	0	18,580
Williamstown Cat	3	G	15	3	1	5	23,140	Wimplestiltskin	2	G	2	0	1	0	9,800
Williamstown Hall	4	G	6	0	3	1	8,740	Win a Feu	6	M	1	0	0	0	159
Willie B Good	3	C	9	0	0	2	1,602	Win a Slew	4	G	8	2	0	2	5,660
Willie B. Furst	3	G	6	1	0	1	3,888	Win by Five	5	H	3	0	0	0	230
Willie B. Trouble	3	G	11	2	2	0	9,430	Win Cresent	2	G	2	1	0	0	5,833
Willie Blue	8	H	2	0	0	0	76	Win for Avie	3	F	6	3	1	0	30,548
Willie Call	4	G	1	0	0	0	60	Win for Destiny	2	F	4	0	1	0	3,900
Willie Cruise	4	G	16	2	3	0	26,588	Win for Nan	3	F	2	1	0	0	10,030
Willie Dunn	2	C	3	0	0	0	3,528	Win for Roberta	3	F	2	0	0	0	0
Willie Or Wontie	5	G	12	1	2	1	8,070	Win for Trey	4	G	5	0	0	0	893
Willie the Cat	4	G	1	0	0	0	0	Win Four Chory	5	M	3	0	0	0	300
Willie Waylon N Me	4	G	11	2	3	1	19,885	Win Free	4	G	3	0	0	1	957
Willie White Shoes	3	C	3	1	2	0	35,200	Win Island	2	F	2	0	1	0	2,023
Willie Wire Wheels	4	G	6	1	0	1	6,021	Win Jimmy Win	2	G	4	0	0	0	329
Willie's Luv	4	F	5	2	0	1	67,732	Win M All Merna	4	F	4	0	0	0	385
Willing Coalition	2	C	2	0	0	0	2,250	Win Mambo	7	G	13	0	0	0	340
Willing Consort	7	G	14	4	2	3	38,311	Win N Grin	4	G	4	1	1	1	15,877
Willing Maid	4	F	4	1	1	1	10,236	Win N Secretary	3	C	6	1	0	0	4,980
Willing Star	3	F	6	0	1	2	14,820	Win Need	3	F	14	0	2	1	3,450
Willing Trick	7	G	2	0	0	1	1,375	Win One for Erma	5	M	2	0	0	0	0
Willing Way	2	G	6	0	0	1	5,249	Win Only	5	G	19	1	2	2	10,975
Willing Wizzard	3	C	4	0	0	0	651	Win Randi Win	3	C	3	0	0	0	282
Willionaire	2	C	3	0	2	0	12,704	Win Ray	3	G	3	1	1	0	5,375
Willitstorm	3	F	1	0	0	0	45	Win Star	2	F	9	1	2	2	10,810
Willo' Sweep	4	C	16	3	2	0	10,693	Win Sucka Win	6	M	6	2	0	2	8,578
Willosbabe	4	C	6	0	0	0	392	Win the Crowd	4	C	11	4	1	1	40,256
Willow	5	M	9	1	1	3	8,144	Win the West	2	C	1	0	0	0	0
Willow Bend	4	F	14	2	2	1	14,245	Win to the End	4	G	15	4	2	2	14,531
Willow Bunch	3	F	5	4	0	0	288,483	Win Win	4	F	2	0	0	0	0
Willow Cove	2	F	5	1	2	1	37,660	Win With Beck	2	C	3	0	0	0	0
Willow Dancer	2	G	2	0	0	0	240	Win Won	5	M	9	3	1	2	100,085
Willow Island	8	M	9	1	1	1	6,010	Win Zone	3	F	3	0	0	0	217
Willow Lane	2	F	2	0	0	0	114	Winaferd	4	C	9	1	0	0	5,216
Willow Makes Bail	4	F	6	0	0	0	1,580	Winagain Mambo	2	C	3	0	0	1	3,160
Willow Oak Dancer	2	C	1	0	0	0	1,620	Winalo	4	F	3	0	0	0	183
Willow Ridge	6	G	8	0	1	2	1,632	Winalot Wanda	3	F	14	0	0	0	360
Willow Rush	2	F	6	0	2	1	27,680	Winalotagreen	8	M	1	0	0	0	54
Willow Springs	4	C	10	1	1	1	4,968	Winalta	6	M	2	0	0	0	0
Willow Wind	4	F	13	1	2	2	42,900	Winaprize	3	C	8	2	0	0	27,650
Willowbee's Girl	3	F	4	1	0	1	8,050	Winatbingo	2	F	2	0	0	1	758
Willowtree Diamond	4	F	4	0	0	0	180	Winazul	4	F	5	0	0	1	936
Will's a Player	2	C	1	0	0	0	0	Winburn	4	G	6	2	0	0	19,312
Will's Cannon	3	G	4	0	1	2	11,960	Winburnt	10	G	3	1	1	1	1,810
Will's Cat	3	G	13	2	4	3	51,915	Winchime	5	M	5	0	4	1	38,220
Wills Commander	3	G	1	0	0	0	135	Wind and Rain	5	H	6	1	0	1	13,800
Will's Gal	4	F	17	2	1	5	45,844	Wind At My Back	7	G	1	0	0	0	0
Will's Journey	3	C	2	1	1	0	32,800	Wind Chymes	4	F	1	0	0	0	0
Will's War	2	C	3	0	0	0	2,069	Wind Dance	4	F	8	0	3	2	4,640
Will's Wings	5	G	2	0	0	1	240	Wind Digger	6	G	2	0	0	0	123
Will's Wish	1	G	1	0	0	0	0	Wind Flow	2	F	5	3	0	0	122,495
Will's Woo Woo	2	G	4	0	0	1	3,478	Wind Glider	2	C	7	2	0	1	40,132
Willstep	4	G	12	2	2	1	48,900	Wind Hacker	2	G	3	0	0	0	0
Willy At Work	5	H	2	0	0	0	164	Wind in the Sky	5	H	11	2	2	3	9,560
Willy B Chic	7	G	15	0	1	2	7,489	Wind in Your Face	4	C	8	1	3	0	35,110

Horse	Age	Sex	Sts	1st	2d	3d	Won
Wind Kiss	3	C	12	2	0	1	22,257
Wind Knot	4	F	14	4	3	2	56,835
Wind N Sea	4	G	2	0	0	0	675
Wind Princess	3	F	2	0	0	0	41
Wind Riddle	3	G	6	1	0	1	8,835
Wind Sand n' Stars	3	C	5	0	0	1	1,912
Wind Seeker	10	G	1	0	0	0	0
Wind Spirit	2	F	1	0	0	0	195
Wind Surfing	8	G	5	0	2	0	3,060
Wind Talk	2	F	1	0	0	0	0
Wind Trail	6	M	11	3	1	1	6,852
Wind Treader	4	G	8	2	1	1	9,687
Wind Trick	4	F	9	0	1	0	1,847
Wind Warning	3	G	5	1	0	0	9,986
Windblown Star	4	F	9	0	0	0	1,209
Windemere Girl	5	M	6	1	0	0	1,453
Windham Chief	2	C	5	1	1	0	14,040
Windham Flash	3	G	5	3	0	0	42,190
Windie Willie	3	C	1	0	0	0	0
Windigo	2	C	1	0	0	0	2,500
Windimuss	4	F	5	0	0	0	570
Winding W C	4	F	13	1	1	0	11,962
Windinthevalley	3	F	12	2	1	4	73,567
Windjammin Lady	4	F	7	0	1	1	11,300
Windlass	3	F	1	0	0	0	0
Window B	5	H	1	0	1	0	2,200
Window to the Soul	5	M	1	0	0	0	810
Winds of Love	5	G	14	2	1	5	47,392
Windsatilting	4	F	11	1	0	0	16,275
Windscore	3	G	13	2	5	2	53,170
Windsor Boy	6	H	5	0	0	0	318
Windsor Castle	5	H	7	2	1	1	165,880
Windsor Court	5	G	3	0	1	0	1,736
Windsor Dickens	3	C	7	1	0	3	25,430
Windsor Lodge	3	G	5	0	0	0	5,460
Windsor One O One	3	F	4	0	0	1	6,640
Windstrike	9	H	4	0	0	0	350
Windswept Anji	3	F	8	0	1	1	2,191
Windswept Paddy	5	H	9	2	2	1	17,267
Windswept Way	3	G	12	1	2	1	12,099
Windumoni	3	F	6	1	1	1	7,150
Windward Bound	4	F	4	0	0	1	884
Windward Call	5	G	15	2	3	3	24,090
Windward Lady	8	M	10	1	1	0	3,233
Windward Passage	4	G	7	1	1	1	40,625
Windwashed	3	C	1	0	0	0	320
Windy Flapper	2	F	3	0	0	0	3,760
Windy Hills Pride	9	G	3	0	0	0	450
Windy in Seattle	5	M	9	0	1	0	1,504
Windy Lane	3	F	1	0	0	0	45
Windy Morning	2	F	5	0	0	0	1,026
Windy O'Neill	4	G	14	3	1	2	61,600
Windy Way	5	M	13	2	3	3	24,839
Windy Zeal	4	G	16	0	2	1	6,536
Windy's Escapade	4	F	1	0	0	0	145
Windy's Halo	11	G	13	3	2	3	20,218
Wine Card	6	G	12	0	1	2	4,040
Wine Express	4	F	1	0	0	0	0
Wine Goddess	3	F	2	0	1	1	8,260
Wine Maker	6	G	15	0	0	3	4,972
Wine N Silver Blue	3	F	7	0	0	1	1,252
Wine Spoken Here	2	C	1	1	0	0	5,225
Wine Spot	3	F	3	0	1	0	2,130
Wine Time	9	G	3	1	0	0	3,120
Wineglass	3	C	2	0	0	0	0
Wineglass Steel	8	G	8	0	1	2	2,180
Wineing and Dining	3	C	6	1	1	0	12,040
Winendynme	2	F	5	2	0	1	66,280
Winewomenandsong	3	G	1	0	0	0	760
Winforme	4	C	3	0	0	0	445
Wing Dancer	5	M	13	1	1	0	6,468
Wing On Shing	3	F	1	0	0	0	0
Wing Tips	3	G	12	3	1	0	43,748
Wingate	8	M	4	0	2	0	6,259
Wingbrook	3	C	5	1	0	0	16,835
Wingding	4	C	8	1	1	3	7,875
Winged Amonia	6	M	2	0	0	0	390
Winged Foot Willie	3	C	6	1	1	0	30,920
Winged Sumac	3	C	11	1	2	1	23,870

Horse	Age	Sex	Sts	1st	2d	3d	Won
Wingedlover	3	G	16	1	2	1	8,665
Wingley	4	F	5	0	0	0	488
Wingold	6	G	6	0	0	0	560
Wingover	5	M	2	0	0	0	400
Wings Alight	4	F	8	0	1	0	2,900
Wings Big Boy	8	G	8	0	1	1	6,851
Wings for Charlotte	7	G	7	0	0	1	162
Wings o' Change	3	F	8	3	1	1	14,551
Wings of Flight	2	G	3	0	0	0	3,528
Wings of Hope	3	G	8	1	0	2	4,150
Wings of Jones	7	G	17	4	1	4	35,390
Wings Of Love (DEN)	3	C	3	0	0	0	250
Wings of Oisin	5	G	9	1	2	2	14,650
Wings of Power	6	M	12	0	0	1	2,644
Wings of the Storm	5	M	9	2	1	0	21,660
Wings of Time	4	C	6	0	2	1	6,336
Wings On Springs	2	G	6	2	1	0	34,140
Wings Over Texas	6	M	3	0	0	0	856
Wings Play Tag	6	M	10	1	2	2	14,013
Wings True	4	F	10	3	1	1	46,423
Wingsforwish	3	C	8	1	0	0	3,038
Wingsong	6	M	4	1	0	1	2,789
Winitall	8	G	1	0	0	1	4,200
Winitformom	2	C	2	1	0	0	9,000
Winkey's Image	3	C	11	1	2	1	15,835
Winking	4	G	12	1	1	4	15,735
Winkle Free	3	G	14	1	1	2	9,057
Winky Bear	3	F	4	0	0	0	0
Winlocs Anzio	4	F	6	1	1	1	13,650
Winlocs Articchill	2	F	2	0	0	0	1,740
Winlocs Big Wonder	4	C	13	1	4	1	23,679
Winlocs Glory Days	2	F	3	0	2	0	17,800
Winlocs Grama Rose	6	M	5	0	0	1	6,126
Winloc's Gramie	6	M	2	0	0	1	1,845
Winloc's Lady Love	5	M	4	0	0	0	960
Winlocs Leap Year	7	M	5	0	0	0	800
Winloc's Majesty	2	F	9	1	2	1	16,510
Winloc's Mickey	8	M	23	4	3	2	27,297
Winloc's Nelson	5	H	3	0	0	0	0
Winloc's Pilgrim	6	M	5	0	0	1	3,431
Winlocs Saint Jude	2	G	3	0	0	0	168
Winloc's Sunshine	4	F	9	4	1	1	68,917
Winlocslastduchess	4	F	11	1	1	3	5,685
Winner From Mars	2	C	1	1	0	0	24,600
Winner Haven	3	F	7	0	0	0	1,778
Winner of the Day	7	G	9	1	3	0	13,743
Winner Season	5	M	12	2	2	0	8,102
Winner Squall	3	F	11	2	2	0	12,009
Winner Takes All	3	F	6	2	0	0	39,680
Winner Whirl	4	G	9	0	1	1	1,846
Winneratthewindow	2	C	9	2	1	2	14,980
Winner's Bid	7	M	3	0	1	0	4,195
Winner's Code	5	G	10	1	2	1	14,347
Winner's Lad	6	G	21	2	5	4	7,768
Winners Table	2	C	6	1	0	1	14,840
Winniedawhale	5	M	19	1	3	1	13,610
Winnie's Pooh Bear	5	G	3	2	0	1	20,498
Winnie's Tash	6	M	13	1	2	2	19,725
Winniewood	4	F	9	1	0	2	4,692
Winnin Coin	5	H	6	0	0	2	3,059
Winning Affair	6	H	12	2	1	2	19,160
Winning Approach	4	F	8	1	0	2	19,106
Winning Brief (AUS)	6	G	5	1	2	0	20,800
Winning Chance	4	F	8	3	4	0	317,435
Winning Chief	4	C	1	0	0	0	87
Winning Connection	7	G	11	2	1	1	72,115
Winning Current	3	C	1	0	0	0	118
Winning Date	2	F	4	0	1	0	2,800
Winning Edge	4	F	7	2	0	0	8,638
Winning Enemy	8	G	5	1	0	0	5,880
Winning Fans	3	C	6	0	1	1	19,400
Winning Fever	3	C	10	1	2	0	20,545
Winning Fever (AUS)	9	G	10	1	1	2	13,666
Winning Flag	3	F	5	1	1	0	6,181
Winning Flames	4	G	25	4	2	1	45,716
Winning for Me	10	M	9	0	1	3	6,842
Winning Gal	4	F	15	2	0	3	10,900
Winning Genes	6	M	9	1	2	1	5,415
Winning Glance	4	F	6	1	0	0	3,824

Horse	Age	Sex	Sts	1st	2d	3d	Won	Horse	Age	Sex	Sts	1st	2d	3d	Won
Winning Honor	3	G	8	2	2	0	19,815	Winter's Sequel	3	F	2	0	0	0	0
Winning Intentions	4	G	11	1	4	0	13,626	Winters Thunder	4	F	12	1	3	0	22,630
Winning Link	5	H	5	0	0	0	990	Winterstarr	5	G	11	2	1	0	10,756
Winning March	6	G	13	2	0	1	7,865	Winthrop Joe	6	G	13	0	2	3	15,990
Winning Memories	3	F	6	0	0	0	3,823	Wintrick	2	G	2	0	0	0	190
Winning Note	3	C	5	0	0	0	0	Wintry Twist	2	C	1	0	0	0	2,135
Winning Partners	7	H	8	0	2	1	5,321	Wintuition	2	F	5	2	1	0	17,360
Winning Pretty	3	F	5	0	1	2	4,206	Winturman	3	C	5	0	2	0	4,651
Winning Races	3	F	1	0	0	0	78	Winvovers Gal	3	F	3	0	0	1	1,245
Winning Request	9	G	12	2	3	0	18,681	Winwonsoon	5	H	9	2	0	0	3,692
Winning Run	2	C	5	1	0	0	10,075	Winyah Bay	3	G	1	0	0	0	0
Winning Shows	4	F	16	5	3	1	40,342	Wire Bound	2	G	3	2	0	0	39,030
Winning Song	8	M	5	0	0	1	665	Wire It Up Baby	3	F	11	2	0	4	17,168
Winning Stripes	3	C	12	2	3	0	123,346	Wire Lass	3	F	2	0	0	0	0
Winning Sweep	6	H	9	3	0	1	11,950	Wire Leader	6	G	12	5	0	0	22,806
Winning Sword	4	G	11	2	2	3	22,550	Wire Tap	6	G	2	0	0	0	104
Winning Talk	4	G	7	4	0	1	41,730	Wire to Wire Waltz	3	F	3	0	0	0	0
Winning Testamony	4	G	1	0	0	0	0	Wire Transfer	3	G	10	1	1	2	33,970
Winning Tunes	4	G	10	4	2	1	30,591	Wire Whip	4	G	8	0	4	2	35,495
Winning Wager	3	G	13	2	3	1	10,372	Wirebender	4	G	13	3	0	4	43,938
Winning Weave	2	F	6	1	2	1	12,052	Wired N Ready	3	F	6	3	0	0	64,650
Winning Witness	2	C	3	0	1	0	4,910	Wired Rose	3	C	2	0	0	0	0
Winning Won	3	G	3	0	0	0	480	Wired to Win	7	G	9	3	2	1	18,422
Winning Wonder	2	F	5	1	2	0	30,220	Wireless World	3	G	3	0	0	0	125
Winningseasy	6	G	2	0	0	0	0	Wisdom Maker	2	G	1	0	0	0	0
Winology	5	G	6	0	0	1	1,745	Wisdom's Mark	3	G	12	1	0	1	11,381
Winona	5	M	10	0	0	1	1,693	Wisdom's Whisper	3	C	2	0	0	0	0
Winoxi	4	F	1	0	0	0	0	Wise Bid	5	G	3	0	0	0	328
Win's Fair Lady	4	F	10	3	2	0	114,185	Wise Child	4	F	12	2	2	2	22,902
Winslow Arizona	3	F	9	1	3	0	12,559	Wise Control	8	G	12	1	2	0	7,098
Winsome Dame	4	F	5	1	1	0	49,868	Wise Dancer	8	G	7	3	3	0	13,990
Winsome Merit	7	M	1	0	0	0	0	Wise Ending	6	M	14	4	4	2	74,295
Winsome Miss	3	F	11	1	0	3	6,214	Wise Fool	4	G	11	1	1	1	10,411
Winsome Prose	4	F	4	0	0	1	2,280	Wise Gift	2	F	4	0	0	0	3,783
Winsome Silverlady	3	F	5	1	0	0	4,735	Wise Guy	4	C	8	0	2	0	2,428
Winsome Wampum	4	F	2	1	0	0	8,820	Wise Indulgence	3	G	4	0	0	1	1,210
Winsome Weekend	3	F	8	1	2	1	20,414	Wise Kracker	5	G	10	1	2	0	5,473
Winsome Witch	3	F	9	1	2	1	24,930	Wise Money	2	F	5	1	0	0	15,550
Winspear	3	G	11	1	5	1	35,823	Wise N Valid	3	F	14	1	3	0	20,080
Winston Chapel	4	G	9	1	0	1	15,949	Wise Remark	3	G	8	2	1	1	11,076
Winston Chi	5	G	5	0	0	0	6,808	Wise Return	4	G	15	0	0	0	2,022
Winston Winsome	4	G	6	1	1	1	9,559	Wise Romance	8	M	8	2	0	1	6,347
Winsumgelt	10	G	6	0	0	0	664	Wise Sweep	7	G	5	4	0	1	64,270
Winsurance	13	G	8	3	1	0	2,667	Wise Talk	7	G	8	4	1	2	51,028
Wintaplay	3	F	8	0	1	1	2,319	Wise Tod	3	G	6	1	0	2	18,490
Winter Air	3	G	3	0	0	0	1,245	Wise Wish	3	G	2	0	0	0	2,046
Winter Award	2	C	2	0	0	1	1,067	Wiseguy's Out	4	C	5	0	1	0	3,150
Winter Cameo	3	F	1	0	0	0	0	Wiseman's Ferry	4	C	2	0	1	0	10,448
Winter Classic	4	F	8	1	0	3	14,600	Wisenheimer	3	G	6	1	1	2	12,815
Winter Clouds	3	F	7	1	3	0	12,630	Wiser'swisdom	3	G	13	1	0	3	8,838
Winter Escape	6	G	22	2	4	5	16,261	Wish and Try	4	C	6	1	1	1	23,860
Winter Games	3	G	7	0	1	1	4,572	Wish Boutique	2	F	3	0	1	0	2,430
Winter Garden	3	F	9	6	1	2	470,826	Wish Cashmere	4	F	1	0	0	0	240
Winter Glitter	6	H	1	0	0	0	130	Wish for Gold	2	F	6	1	1	1	37,066
Winter Gold	2	F	2	0	0	0	900	Wish From Heaven	3	C	6	0	0	0	595
Winter Harbor	3	F	10	0	1	3	12,780	Wish It Were	4	F	7	1	0	2	70,650
Winter Lady	8	M	7	0	1	2	1,955	Wish Mount	3	G	17	2	2	3	24,383
Winter Leaf	5	M	2	0	0	1	3,960	Wish 'n Wild	3	F	11	1	2	1	9,083
Winter Meeting	4	F	3	0	0	1	3,738	Wishes Gone West	4	C	5	0	0	1	1,081
Winter Moon	2	F	3	0	0	0	825	Wishful Cat	2	F	1	0	0	0	0
Winter News	5	G	11	0	2	0	3,537	Wishful Kris	5	H	2	0	1	0	6,510
Winter Olympic	3	C	2	1	0	0	13,336	Wishful Past	3	C	2	0	0	0	270
Winter Rules	3	C	8	0	1	0	10,830	Wishful Splendor	4	F	7	1	3	1	61,461
Winter Runner	2	F	1	0	1	0	5,600	Wishful Whitney	6	M	1	0	0	0	0
Winter Squall	2	C	6	1	2	1	57,777	Wishfull Thinking	3	F	1	1	0	0	1,460
Winter Storm Watch	5	G	14	1	3	2	4,189	Wishgirl	4	F	16	0	1	4	4,619
Winter Tide	2	F	2	0	0	1	8,232	Wishing Dixie	2	F	3	0	0	0	1,725
Winter Trick	3	G	6	2	1	0	31,983	Wishing Heart	4	G	8	0	2	0	3,458
Winter Whiskey	2	G	6	3	0	0	225,093	Wishing Lilly	3	F	14	0	2	2	12,578
Winter Win	5	G	12	2	1	3	8,940	Wishing Miss	2	F	6	0	0	1	3,152
Winter Wonder	5	M	2	0	0	0	0	Wishing to Win	3	F	5	1	0	1	6,150
Winter Wonderland	9	G	14	1	0	1	4,629	Wishing Zone	3	F	10	2	3	2	26,480
Winterfield	8	G	12	1	1	1	11,771	Wishingitwas	4	C	7	2	1	2	53,150
Winterhawk	6	G	11	0	1	0	3,800	Wishinonastar	5	G	10	1	0	2	8,062
Winterized Star	4	F	6	0	1	0	2,903	Wishi's Girl	3	F	7	2	0	0	8,180
Wintermix (FR)	4	F	4	0	0	1	4,950	Wishka (NZ)	8	M	8	0	0	2	1,279
Winter's Coin	3	G	14	1	3	3	49,828	Wishy Washy Colton	3	G	9	0	1	0	1,160
Winter's Quest	3	F	3	1	1	1	28,680	Wishy's Mark	5	M	16	1	2	3	12,592
Winters Rainbow	2	F	1	0	0	0	400	Wisman Road	3	G	5	0	0	0	0

Horse	Age	Sex	Sts	1st	2d	3d	Won
Wisperingwhitelies	3	F	11	2	0	3	17,216
Wispy Whiskers	3	G	7	0	1	0	2,196
Wisset	3	F	6	1	0	0	4,742
Wistla	3	F	2	0	0	0	3,528
Witch Approval	3	F	3	0	1	0	8,840
Witch Carafe	5	G	7	0	0	0	2,100
Witch Love	5	M	22	1	1	5	10,902
Witch On a Stick	5	M	2	0	0	0	0
Witch Revival	3	F	15	6	1	0	65,080
Witch Tradition	4	F	7	1	0	2	19,019
Witcher's Creek	8	G	6	0	1	0	3,727
Witches Above	6	M	7	0	0	1	2,032
Witches Match	2	F	3	0	0	0	430
Witches Rose	4	F	19	2	2	1	11,999
Witchesyn	3	F	9	2	1	2	13,235
Witchful Thought	5	M	1	0	0	0	520
Witchie Woman	8	M	4	0	0	0	660
Witchonabroomstick	3	F	10	2	0	0	11,010
With a Little Luck	4	F	13	3	3	2	26,955
With a Purpose	5	G	9	5	2	2	31,160
With a Rush	3	G	3	1	0	1	18,230
With a Song	3	F	6	0	0	1	4,695
With a Star	4	G	5	0	1	1	8,080
With a Whisper	2	G	6	2	0	0	13,480
With Ability	5	M	1	0	0	0	0
With Affection	2	F	1	0	0	0	750
With All My Heart	4	F	4	1	0	0	6,660
With Anticipation	8	G	3	0	0	0	13,359
With Assurance	3	C	2	0	0	0	0
With Certainty	3	F	5	2	1	0	52,400
With Charm	6	H	4	0	0	1	2,400
With Clearance	2	C	1	0	0	0	750
With Delight	3	F	10	0	0	1	2,314
With Diamonds	5	M	10	1	0	3	8,642
With Faith	4	F	4	1	1	0	13,845
With Fun	4	F	8	0	0	2	4,090
With Glory	3	C	7	2	0	2	10,518
With Hildy's Way	5	M	6	0	1	1	3,456
With His Authority	3	C	9	2	1	0	7,918
With Imagination	11	G	2	0	0	0	48
With Intent	6	M	4	1	0	1	8,110
With Iris	6	G	9	1	0	3	61,480
With Liberty	2	F	7	1	1	2	8,821
With Magic	5	H	6	0	2	0	6,932
With Malice	2	F	6	0	0	3	2,050
With My Approval	4	F	7	0	0	3	1,985
With My Blessings	3	F	7	0	0	1	4,315
With My Consent	3	F	13	0	1	1	4,232
With No Knickers	4	F	5	0	0	2	3,002
With Papers	8	G	2	0	0	0	220
With Patience	4	F	6	1	1	1	34,030
With Probability	2	C	1	0	0	0	1,290
With Roses	4	G	19	1	6	4	15,424
With Star Approval	7	G	4	0	0	0	324
With Sugar On Top	3	F	7	1	0	0	11,400
With the Works	4	F	6	0	2	0	11,720
With Zest	4	F	12	2	0	0	29,225
Withaclick	3	F	2	0	0	0	0
Withallmyrage	4	G	6	0	1	2	2,102
Withdrawn	2	F	3	1	1	0	13,200
Withe	5	M	4	0	0	1	583
Witherbee	7	H	2	0	1	0	1,092
Witherbee Hall	4	F	4	0	0	0	186
Withflagsaflyin'	3	F	4	0	0	0	186
Withholding Info	5	G	9	4	2	1	64,000
Within My Heart	3	F	3	0	0	0	140
Within Range	3	F	7	0	0	4	3,510
Withmom's Image	2	F	4	0	0	1	2,805
Withorwithoutyou	4	F	8	1	2	0	33,406
Without a Doubt	4	G	7	3	2	1	70,040
Without Bond	3	G	17	6	0	3	33,498
Without Concern	4	F	15	1	2	3	20,317
Without End	5	M	23	2	5	3	16,064
Without Objection	3	G	1	0	0	0	0
Without Regret	4	G	21	2	2	3	9,634
Without Reproach	5	G	2	0	0	0	156
Without Warning	3	G	2	0	0	0	690
Witness the Music	3	G	10	1	0	4	8,673
Witness the Queen	5	M	14	5	3	0	61,267

Horse	Age	Sex	Sts	1st	2d	3d	Won
Witness This	2	C	1	1	0	0	35,280
Witnessthesunrise	5	G	12	0	2	0	2,493
Wits End	4	G	7	4	0	1	71,520
Witt Ante	3	G	7	2	0	1	123,000
Wittenberg Time	3	G	2	0	0	1	2,940
Witty Bill	5	G	18	1	2	3	8,477
Witty Lady	2	F	1	0	0	0	0
Wixoe Express (IRE)	4	G	6	1	1	1	38,760
Wizard of Iron	5	G	17	1	0	0	4,458
Wizard of Odds	4	G	9	4	0	0	20,900
Wizardry	8	G	13	2	1	3	9,915
Wndy's Tan	3	F	8	0	2	0	3,400
Wnrwnrchickndnr	2	F	4	1	1	0	4,870
Wobinann	4	F	14	1	1	2	5,332
Wojo	7	G	2	0	0	0	150
Woke Up Dreamin	3	C	2	0	1	0	16,080
Woking	8	G	6	2	0	0	14,535
Wokokin Raven	4	C	8	2	0	0	14,040
Wolf (ARG)	5	H	3	1	0	0	13,680
Wolf and Hawk	7	H	11	1	0	0	4,386
Wolf Appeal	6	M	7	0	0	0	1,173
Wolf Bay	6	H	4	0	0	0	510
Wolf Class	2	C	2	0	0	0	420
Wolf Colony	3	C	6	1	0	0	6,300
Wolf Creek	2	C	3	0	1	0	1,540
Wolf Doctor	5	G	3	0	0	0	225
Wolf for Queenie	2	F	6	1	0	2	7,270
Wolf Gal's Print	2	G	1	0	0	0	0
Wolf Girl	4	F	14	3	1	1	15,300
Wolf Howl	4	G	9	1	2	1	68,441
Wolf Running	2	C	1	0	0	0	0
Wolf Trick	3	G	18	3	1	1	28,840
Wolf Wizard	3	C	7	0	0	1	1,383
Wolfmon	2	G	6	0	0	0	2,010
Wolfnbankersclothn	2	F	1	0	0	0	651
Wolfpak	5	G	2	0	0	0	0
Wolf's Honor	5	H	9	3	1	0	21,563
Wolf's Prospect	3	G	13	3	4	1	27,200
Wolfwithintegrity	6	G	5	1	1	1	43,160
Wolfzak	4	C	8	1	0	2	8,178
Wolkie the Editor	5	G	6	1	0	0	9,443
Wolley	6	H	9	1	2	1	5,460
Wolverine	4	C	4	0	1	2	28,685
Wolverton Mountain	4	G	7	1	2	1	15,155
Wolvspa	6	G	7	0	0	0	5,415
Woman Onfasttrack	3	F	13	5	1	0	157,780
Woman's Touch	4	F	13	2	3	3	25,276
Womble	6	H	6	1	0	0	5,361
Women Warrior	6	M	6	0	0	0	37
Womenwhiskeyngold	8	G	1	0	0	0	300
Won Arm Bandit	3	G	8	1	1	0	9,797
Won Better	4	G	9	1	2	2	20,227
Won Bright Nickle	2	F	4	0	0	0	717
Won C C	5	G	12	0	2	0	18,220
Won Dozen Roses	3	F	13	4	1	1	85,910
Won Fancy Dancer	7	H	9	3	2	2	10,629
Won for Chopper	4	C	12	3	1	2	20,939
Won Forceful Lady	6	M	13	4	2	2	47,285
Won Great Kiss	3	F	3	0	0	0	0
Won Handsome Devil	2	G	1	0	1	0	3,232
Won Jenelle	7	M	6	0	0	1	6,450
Won More Hill	3	G	5	1	1	1	8,014
Won More Song	5	M	4	1	0	1	12,195
Won Moro	6	M	5	1	1	1	22,690
Won Mugg	5	H	8	0	2	1	8,073
Won On the Run	2	C	1	0	0	0	126
Won the Derby	9	G	11	2	3	2	10,355
Won Ton Win	5	M	7	3	0	1	28,570
Wondancewilldo	3	G	12	1	0	1	20,202
Wonder Again	4	F	6	1	1	1	176,075
Wonder Bull	5	M	1	0	0	0	450
Wonder Lady	2	F	1	0	0	0	0
Wonder Weapon	6	G	9	1	1	0	17,760
Wonder Woman	4	F	1	1	0	0	28,800
Wonderboy	3	C	2	0	0	0	0
Wonderful Drummer	3	F	18	0	1	2	3,290
Wonderful H. O. A.	2	C	2	1	0	0	25,950
Wonderful Heather	2	F	7	0	1	2	9,480
Wonderful Larry	7	G	5	0	0	2	3,018

Horse	Age	Sex	Sts	1st	2d	3d	Won
Wonderful Miss	3	F	13	2	2	2	25,829
Wonderful News	2	F	1	0	0	1	4,510
Wonderful Prospect	5	H	16	3	2	2	110,730
Wonderful Victory	3	C	18	1	1	2	49,850
Wonderful World	4	C	5	0	0	0	2,905
Wonderous Woman	3	F	9	1	2	4	43,940
Wonderstreak	9	G	14	1	5	3	21,327
Wondrous Won	5	H	3	0	0	1	737
Wondrous Zeal	5	G	10	3	2	3	41,730
Wonforyoutwoforme	4	F	3	1	0	1	3,425
Wong Choy	3	C	11	2	0	0	14,195
Wonhoneyofaknight	3	G	4	0	0	0	0
Wonhorsepower	3	C	7	1	0	0	4,040
Won't Belong Now	4	C	2	0	0	0	520
Wont to Be Good	4	F	5	0	0	0	100
Wonwaygirl	4	F	14	3	2	0	30,856
Wood and Plenty	6	G	6	0	0	1	1,000
Wood Dixie Dance	2	F	13	2	2	2	39,150
Wood Kat	7	G	6	3	2	1	31,420
Wood Lily	6	M	20	3	2	5	48,722
Wood Not	2	F	6	0	2	0	12,040
Wood Polish	5	G	8	0	0	1	636
Wood Pound	7	G	4	1	1	0	12,450
Wood Ridge	4	G	7	1	0	1	5,967
Wood Whistle	9	G	3	0	3	0	22,500
Wood You Be Mine	6	H	6	2	0	2	21,441
Wood You Leave	4	F	2	1	0	0	18,000
Woodbegoodificould	4	G	3	0	0	0	0
Woodbend Lass	3	F	4	0	0	1	1,039
Woodbine Willie	3	C	12	1	0	2	9,992
Woodbuck	4	G	9	0	2	1	10,930
Woodburner	3	G	7	3	1	1	63,579
Woodbury	6	G	7	0	0	0	1,731
Wooden Phone	6	G	4	0	0	0	3,000
Wooden Ships	2	F	3	0	0	0	1,764
Wooden You	2	F	2	0	0	0	1,270
Woodend	3	F	5	0	0	1	3,536
Woodfield	4	G	11	1	4	1	26,508
Woodford Princess	5	M	5	0	0	0	1,250
Woodford Reserve	3	C	6	0	0	1	4,210
Woodhugh	5	G	7	2	0	0	18,445
Woodkhieba	6	H	3	0	0	0	600
Woodland Shadow	4	F	4	0	0	0	3,060
Woodlands House	6	H	4	0	0	0	853
Woodlass	3	F	6	2	0	2	60,331
Woodlyon	4	G	19	0	2	2	7,930
Woodmans Smile	2	F	6	1	0	0	7,610
Woodman's Star	2	C	4	0	1	0	5,208
Woodmaven	3	F	2	0	0	1	2,170
Woodmeister	2	C	11	2	0	1	22,250
Woodmont	3	G	9	1	0	0	5,539
Woodmoon	5	H	9	2	0	3	139,125
Woodnote	2	C	4	1	0	1	22,550
Woods	9	G	3	0	0	0	160
Wood's Belle	2	F	1	0	0	0	0
Woodsia	4	F	2	0	0	1	4,140
Woodside	5	H	6	0	2	1	3,100
Woodside Parkway	7	G	13	5	2	1	24,051
Woodsie's Smokin	4	G	10	0	1	0	1,128
Woodsnwaters	5	H	10	2	1	0	12,196
Woodtown Bob	5	G	2	1	1	0	16,600
Woodward Smiles	4	G	5	1	0	1	5,410
Woody Haze	5	G	10	3	1	1	94,665
Woody Jo Harriman	5	M	3	0	0	0	150
Woody Run	6	G	9	0	1	1	1,981
Woody's Ack	5	G	16	1	0	1	4,829
Woody's Dan D Pine	6	H	6	0	0	0	906
Woody's Dancer	3	G	13	2	4	3	43,928
Woody's Diamond	4	C	12	3	0	1	35,756
Woody's Jet	2	G	5	0	0	0	192
Woof	3	F	3	0	0	2	6,590
Wooglin	5	G	16	2	3	2	23,618
Woolfwoolfbaby	4	F	10	0	2	4	4,384
Woolski	4	G	7	0	0	0	217
Wooohoooyahoo	3	G	3	1	1	0	7,500
Woo's Prospect	5	H	16	3	2	1	37,304
Woostershear	6	H	14	1	2	2	44,470
Woota	6	H	2	1	0	0	6,660
Wooti Toot	4	C	13	1	2	3	8,723
Wootsie Dean	4	F	17	0	1	1	2,726
Word by Word	3	C	12	2	2	0	42,428
Word of Advice	6	G	12	0	3	2	4,371
Word of Gold	4	F	19	2	5	2	15,187
Word Puzzle	5	M	1	0	0	0	1,800
Wordless Monarch	5	H	4	0	0	0	594
Words Cant Explain	3	C	14	2	3	1	21,247
Words in Poetry	3	F	4	1	0	0	16,740
Words of Warning	2	C	6	0	1	0	4,931
Words of Wisdom	8	G	4	2	1	1	18,940
Work for Boots	3	G	3	0	0	0	5,308
Work Hard	5	G	11	0	2	1	4,290
Work Out Queen	4	F	2	1	0	0	6,000
Work Visa	6	G	6	1	2	1	35,579
Workaholic	6	G	9	2	0	1	16,801
Worker Man	3	C	8	1	1	1	29,160
Working Awesome	8	M	13	0	0	1	4,184
Working Class	2	G	7	0	3	1	10,999
Worksformoney	2	F	4	0	1	1	15,100
Workum	5	G	5	3	1	1	35,560
Worland	5	G	3	2	1	0	26,935
World Bank	8	G	11	2	3	1	9,803
World Best	4	G	17	2	2	2	17,582
World Champion	4	C	9	2	0	0	23,720
World Class	2	C	1	1	0	0	24,600
World Class Flyer	5	G	4	0	0	0	223
World Class Hoofer	3	G	10	1	2	1	18,012
World Class Smile	4	F	3	0	0	0	570
World Escapade	3	G	3	0	0	0	720
World Event	2	F	3	1	1	0	22,190
World Light	4	C	2	0	1	0	10,200
World Meeting	3	G	6	2	0	0	23,310
World of Charm	4	G	10	0	0	3	2,056
World of Gold	4	F	2	0	2	0	6,000
World of Reason	4	F	2	0	0	0	192
World of Wonder	5	G	9	1	2	0	68,440
World Premier	4	G	18	1	2	3	13,182
World Prince	4	G	1	0	0	0	130
World Ruler	3	G	2	0	0	0	0
World Shamp	6	H	7	0	0	0	696
World Stage Dance	3	C	10	2	1	2	30,152
World Tour	4	G	11	1	1	2	11,200
World Trade	4	C	7	0	0	1	3,720
World Vision	6	G	7	0	0	1	4,603
Worldlee Woman	2	F	3	0	0	0	0
Worldliness	2	F	2	1	1	0	15,955
Worldly Charm	4	G	8	0	3	0	8,581
Worldly Excess	5	M	7	0	3	1	27,240
Worldly Kiss	5	H	10	0	3	2	5,642
Worldly Navy	4	G	7	1	1	2	42,958
Worldly Pleasure	3	F	14	4	2	1	98,410
Worldly Treasure	6	G	10	1	0	0	11,004
Worldwidetestimony	4	C	7	1	0	1	8,035
Worldwind Romance	5	H	8	2	1	1	37,100
Worldy Image	3	F	11	3	0	2	13,829
Worldy Reason	3	G	7	0	4	2	19,180
Worrier	7	H	11	1	0	0	7,700
Worry Beads	3	F	10	3	1	1	38,945
Worry Free	2	G	6	0	4	1	18,580
Worth a Billion	5	M	5	0	0	0	0
Worth a Dime	5	M	5	0	0	0	0
Worth My While	3	C	9	1	3	2	12,344
Worth Springs	5	H	8	1	2	1	10,091
Worth the Kissin	5	M	4	0	0	1	1,177
Worth Watching	3	G	5	1	0	1	3,687
Worth Winning	3	F	8	2	1	2	36,015
Worthethegamble	6	M	6	2	0	1	23,876
Worththewait	6	G	10	3	0	2	17,745
Worthy Adversary	3	G	6	1	1	0	8,800
Worthy Find	8	G	9	0	0	0	1,555
Worthy Forum	4	C	8	0	1	0	6,160
Worthy Gift	2	C	4	0	0	0	713
Worthy Present	5	G	17	1	3	2	10,338
Worthy Soldier	4	G	10	3	1	2	41,905
Worthy You	5	M	18	2	5	4	41,878
Would You Be Mine	3	F	7	0	1	0	10,125
Wouldilietoyou	4	F	4	0	0	0	574
Wouldn't We All	9	H	3	1	1	0	6,900
Wouldyoutouchgold	3	F	2	0	0	0	795

RECORDS OF HORSES

Horse	Age	Sex	Sts	1st	2d	3d	Won	Horse	Age	Sex	Sts	1st	2d	3d	Won
Wovaka	6	G	9	0	2	0	6,709	Xcape	3	G	7	1	0	2	11,880
Woven Dream	2	F	2	1	1	0	13,300	Xcitable Field	3	F	4	0	0	0	133
Woven in Spirit	4	F	2	0	0	1	1,970	Xclusive Imp	9	G	6	0	0	0	407
Wow Man	6	G	6	1	1	0	8,125	Xedrun	7	H	4	1	0	0	2,948
Wow Thing	6	G	2	0	0	0	165	Xelena	5	M	4	0	0	0	248
Wrangler	5	G	2	0	0	0	3,090	Xelodonia	4	F	5	0	1	0	1,500
Wrangler Red	5	M	15	3	0	5	17,139	Xena Peach	3	F	14	2	2	1	28,744
Wrangling	4	F	2	0	0	0	0	Xenellen	4	F	6	0	0	0	540
Wrecking Crew	5	G	9	0	3	2	7,663	Xenodon	5	H	6	0	0	1	1,600
Wren	3	F	1	0	0	0	0	Xenos Salotos	3	G	1	0	0	0	0
Wrench It	3	G	1	0	0	0	1,260	Xi'an	6	M	4	1	2	0	34,430
Wrestler	5	G	1	0	0	0	0	Xilef	5	H	5	0	0	0	0
Wretched Excess	2	F	6	1	1	0	26,000	Xocolata (GB)	3	F	3	0	0	0	2,700
Wright Dream	4	F	1	0	0	0	150	Xordinary Love	3	F	10	0	2	1	15,825
Wright Wing	2	G	2	0	0	0	140	Xpedite	4	C	3	0	0	0	610
Wrinkle Free	7	G	10	2	0	1	4,843	Xpress Xcess	2	F	5	0	1	1	17,260
Write It Down	7	G	10	1	0	2	4,792	Xspeedious	4	G	14	5	0	1	27,854
Write Rare	7	H	2	0	0	1	680	Xtra Ace	2	C	2	1	1	0	8,500
Write the Check	2	F	4	0	0	1	1,140	Xtra Dancer	2	F	3	0	0	0	230
Write the News	3	F	8	4	0	1	15,597	Xtra Dash	3	F	4	0	1	0	5,600
Writehof	6	M	4	0	0	1	450	Xtra Emblem	3	F	2	1	1	0	10,480
Writers Detention	4	G	5	0	0	0	0	Xtra Heart	3	F	6	0	2	1	53,874
Writetobefree	9	G	9	0	1	1	1,430	Xtra Heat	5	M	2	2	0	0	150,000
Writtillion	5	G	9	1	0	2	24,078	Xtra Jack	2	C	6	2	1	0	4,185
Wrong Girl	8	M	2	0	0	0	0	Xtrasensory (GB)	4	F	8	1	2	1	59,020
Wrong Road	3	C	2	0	0	0	79	Xtreamotion	2	C	3	2	0	0	42,180
Wrong Spell	2	F	1	0	0	0	0	Xtreme Heat	2	F	2	0	1	0	3,600
Wrong Target	2	C	2	0	0	0	1,024	Xtreme Monique	4	G	13	3	1	3	71,827
Wrong Way David	4	F	2	0	0	0	0	Xtreme Rush	5	H	8	0	1	0	5,513
Wrong Way Rocky	3	C	2	1	1	0	20,160	Xtreme Success	4	G	17	1	4	3	15,172
Wry Humor	2	G	7	0	0	3	13,700	Xylocoe	8	G	5	0	0	0	370
Wrzeszcz	2	G	1	0	0	0	1,275	Y B Red	5	G	2	0	1	0	1,222
Wucky Ray Ray	2	G	5	0	1	2	4,545	Y Country	3	F	11	2	1	1	31,780
Wudacudashuda	3	F	4	1	1	0	30,109	Y Not Winter	3	F	12	3	1	1	23,322
Wudantunoit	5	G	11	3	1	3	87,157	Y Two J	4	G	13	2	1	2	72,300
Wulpe	2	C	2	1	0	0	14,550	Y Two K Compliant	5	M	6	1	1	0	8,139
Wunderbar	2	G	5	1	0	0	5,610	Y Two K United	4	G	9	1	1	0	8,580
Wundrcolthundrbolt	6	H	2	0	0	1	1,050	Y. V. Five	3	C	9	1	3	0	63,068
Wutcudposblygorong	4	F	4	0	0	3	792	Ya Lajwaad	3	C	5	2	0	0	41,286
Wuzzup Dunc	4	G	7	0	1	0	14,760	Ya Lateefah	4	F	11	1	1	0	16,528
Ww Conquistador	3	C	13	5	0	2	71,304	Ya Who	4	C	7	1	2	0	4,244
Ww Country Women	3	F	3	0	2	0	4,474	Ya Ya Dew	4	F	4	0	1	0	1,158
Wwwdotwindotcom	7	G	12	4	4	4	22,660	Yacht Club	3	F	2	1	0	0	10,030
Wyatt Act	2	G	2	0	0	0	60	Yacht to Pay For	4	F	7	1	0	1	18,860
Wyatts Fancy Flyer	2	G	2	0	0	0	172	Yada Boy	2	C	3	0	0	1	1,647
Wyatt's High Noon	2	F	6	1	2	0	18,590	Yada Yada Yada	3	G	3	0	1	0	840
Wyatt's Magic	5	G	12	0	1	0	8,008	Yaeger	5	G	10	3	2	2	65,310
Wyconda	7	G	6	1	1	2	11,150	Yaelforhadif	3	F	5	1	2	0	12,900
Wye River Rugrat	2	F	1	0	0	0	0	Yaffa	4	C	18	2	1	0	20,265
Wyndham Bay	8	G	12	3	1	0	2,975	Yagottaapprover	6	M	6	0	2	0	13,414
Wynhurst	7	G	5	1	0	1	6,075	Yagudin	3	C	8	1	2	1	44,874
Wynn Dot Comma	2	C	5	4	1	0	139,525	Yah Sure Olaf	5	G	1	0	0	0	61
Wynn Seeker	4	F	6	2	0	1	12,587	Yaheremenow	3	G	3	0	1	0	1,645
Wynn With Quinn	5	G	5	0	0	0	949	Yahoo	3	F	13	2	3	2	23,236
Wynning Rainbow	2	F	5	0	0	0	1,377	Yahuh	3	F	3	0	0	0	0
Wynnsrazamatamayaz	2	G	5	1	1	1	26,210	Yak	5	M	2	0	0	0	88
Wynsome Roses	5	G	5	0	0	0	728	Yakima Canutt	4	C	23	1	5	3	43,000
Wynter Sunshine	7	G	2	0	0	0	48	Yakima River	3	G	9	3	1	0	14,118
Wyoming Wish	4	F	11	2	1	2	11,015	Yakster	4	G	15	0	2	2	4,426
X Be Thy Name	2	G	3	0	0	0	1,160	Yale Camp	4	F	7	1	0	2	6,912
X Box	2	G	2	1	0	0	24,240	Y'All Can	9	G	2	0	0	0	348
X Country	5	G	6	1	2	0	66,191	Y'all So Pretty	5	M	9	0	2	1	7,153
X Deal	3	F	11	1	1	0	6,630	Yalta	4	F	4	1	1	1	32,200
X Games	3	F	1	0	0	0	150	Yamika	9	M	11	1	2	1	10,681
X Melrose Rascal	4	G	11	1	2	2	10,932	Yanaba	5	M	1	0	0	0	0
X Partner	2	G	5	1	0	1	35,420	Yanaguana	4	G	6	2	1	1	8,985
X Press Pass	5	M	7	0	0	0	1,593	Yancey Cravat	8	G	2	0	0	0	148
X Rated Fantasy	4	G	6	3	3	0	18,896	Yangtzee	5	H	11	0	0	0	1,022
X Rated Movie	3	G	5	1	1	2	4,928	Yank	10	G	2	0	0	0	100
X Slews Me	4	F	2	0	0	0	525	Yankee Captain	3	G	2	0	0	0	0
X Streme	3	G	5	1	1	0	10,896	Yankee Crossing	4	F	8	1	4	0	14,785
X to the Tee	2	F	10	1	1	2	17,004	Yankee Dan Dee	2	F	3	0	2	0	2,581
X Tra Brassy	3	F	2	0	0	0	0	Yankee Debonair	3	C	1	0	0	0	0
X Z Bit	3	G	2	0	0	0	185	Yankee Devil Matt	4	G	13	1	0	1	5,146
Xalt	9	G	5	1	1	0	3,268	Yankee Doodle	3	C	3	0	0	0	155
Xanamistique	5	M	8	0	0	1	1,432	Yankee Doodle Boy	5	H	4	0	0	3	25,900
Xander	6	G	13	2	4	1	14,076	Yankee Doodle Doll	3	F	2	0	0	0	105
Xanpit	3	G	6	1	1	2	8,055	Yankee Exchange	3	F	4	0	0	0	175
Xanthos	3	G	15	4	3	2	50,060	Yankee Fashion	2	F	5	0	1	0	6,000

Horse	Age	Sex	Sts	1st	2d	3d	Won
Yankee Flag	2	C	1	0	0	0	0
Yankee Fleet	3	G	1	0	0	0	130
Yankee Gentleman	4	C	4	2	0	0	129,247
Yankee Pirate	5	G	12	3	0	3	18,916
Yankee Prospect	4	F	2	0	0	0	0
Yankee Ruler	7	G	13	1	3	1	15,611
Yankee Run	5	H	11	0	2	2	4,180
Yankee Trader	4	C	14	1	3	0	6,174
Yankee Trial	3	G	14	1	2	2	9,326
Yankee Tribe	7	G	20	5	2	5	40,546
Yankee Wildcat	5	G	4	0	1	1	8,530
Yankele	3	C	5	0	3	1	7,460
Yaqui River	4	F	1	0	0	0	130
Yarak	9	M	3	0	0	1	770
Yard Sale Slew	5	M	3	0	0	0	463
Yardstick Forum	3	C	2	0	0	0	53
Yarico's Pond (IRE)	3	F	4	1	1	1	30,910
Yarnell	4	F	16	3	4	5	14,160
Yarnell Hill	6	M	13	1	2	2	15,545
Yarny's Star	12	G	10	0	3	1	3,683
Yaros Express	5	G	7	0	1	0	2,655
Yarra (MEX)	6	M	3	0	0	0	120
Yarray	3	F	1	0	1	0	5,250
Yarrow Dream	3	F	4	0	1	2	4,050
Yarrow's Chief	2	C	7	0	0	0	0
Yashari	4	C	10	1	5	0	20,820
Yasinister	3	G	5	0	0	0	2,340
Yasou Doc's Angels	3	F	9	2	1	1	25,390
Yasou Johnny B	3	G	9	0	1	1	6,540
Yasou Niko	5	G	10	0	1	0	8,650
Yasou Rob's Wife	3	F	1	0	0	0	255
Yasou Sister Jenny	3	F	9	1	1	1	7,731
Yasou Ted G	5	G	18	2	4	2	15,210
Yasow Kerri	2	F	4	1	2	0	19,400
Yavapai	7	G	11	1	0	1	18,633
Yawls Special	5	M	8	1	0	0	5,056
Yaz Am Smart	3	G	13	1	1	3	18,358
Yazalweed	3	F	5	0	0	0	0
Yazoo City	5	G	10	2	1	2	24,873
Yazor	3	F	4	2	2	0	36,520
Yazzero (ARG)	7	G	3	0	0	2	4,740
Ye of Little Faith	5	G	8	0	1	2	11,205
Ye Roo	5	M	3	0	0	0	96
Ye Songs Last	4	F	8	1	2	1	4,806
Year for Gold	4	C	1	0	0	0	0
Year of Savings	4	G	3	0	0	0	999
Year of the Fox	4	G	5	2	1	0	3,620
Year Two Thousand	5	G	1	0	0	0	0
Yearbook	5	G	4	0	0	2	628
Yearbrook	2	F	3	0	0	1	2,002
Yearly Copy	3	F	5	1	0	0	19,440
Yearly Report	2	F	2	1	1	0	48,400
Yearly Surprize	4	F	15	2	0	3	7,364
Yearn	2	G	4	0	0	0	105
Yell	3	F	9	3	1	1	408,527
Yellow Beauty	6	M	13	0	3	0	6,790
Yellowstone Kelly	3	G	4	0	0	0	345
Yellowstone Lady	4	F	3	0	1	0	12,250
Yelp	4	G	10	3	1	2	43,628
Yen	2	F	3	0	1	0	9,200
Yenom	3	F	4	0	0	0	285
Yeowzer	6	G	10	1	0	2	7,670
Yerevan Express	6	H	11	1	2	2	5,700
Yes	2	C	2	0	0	0	0
Yes He Is	2	C	3	1	0	1	4,085
Yes I Do	3	F	11	0	4	1	23,786
Yes I'm No Fool	10	G	4	0	0	0	63
Yes I'm Sweet	4	F	9	1	3	1	12,925
Yes Money Yes	3	F	4	0	0	2	3,105
Yes Shes O. K.	4	F	2	0	1	0	1,400
Yes Uconn	5	G	23	2	0	8	40,836
Yes We Can	2	C	5	0	1	0	4,320
Yes We Do	4	M	6	0	0	1	7,096
Yes You Will	4	F	13	2	1	1	23,802
Yessirgeneralsir	3	C	5	1	1	1	24,305
Yesss	5	G	12	5	1	3	32,980
Yester Morn	3	F	6	0	2	0	5,480
Yesterday (IRE)	3	F	7	1	3	1	689,791
Yesterday Is Gone	3	C	1	0	1	0	4,200
Yesterday's Luv	5	M	11	1	2	0	14,780
Yesterdays News	3	F	5	0	0	0	525
Yesterman	2	G	1	0	0	0	110
Yesyoudo	2	F	1	0	0	1	1,777
Yet Anothernatalie	4	F	1	0	0	0	0
Yetta	3	F	12	0	1	3	5,580
Yield to Habit	10	G	6	0	0	0	510
Yifter the Shifter	8	H	11	0	4	1	7,639
Yikes More Hikes	5	G	4	0	0	0	130
Yimmy	2	C	2	1	0	0	12,600
Yingyingying	2	F	5	0	3	0	27,050
Yippee	4	G	15	4	3	2	45,694
Yo	3	C	5	2	1	0	78,980
Yo Baby Yo	3	G	9	1	1	2	19,000
Yo Bets Wuz Up	3	C	2	0	0	0	0
Yo Billie Bateman	4	F	6	1	3	0	14,625
Yo Buddy	6	H	8	0	3	0	2,985
Yo Can Do	2	C	7	2	2	1	20,115
Yo Cuz	2	C	3	1	0	1	18,886
Yo Dan	4	G	4	2	0	1	4,700
Yo Jake Won	2	G	3	0	1	0	2,120
Yo Key	7	G	7	1	0	0	1,798
Yo Quiero Disco	5	H	3	0	0	0	0
Yo Yo Man	3	G	10	2	1	1	46,920
Yodelin Two	3	C	4	0	2	0	14,694
Yodeltilyourblue	2	G	8	1	4	2	22,800
Yoga	4	C	4	1	1	0	21,060
Yoga Girl	2	F	4	0	1	1	1,925
Yogi's	2	F	5	1	1	3	22,860
Yogi's Connection	2	F	6	0	1	0	2,330
Yogi's Polar Bear	2	F	3	1	2	0	70,345
Yoh Morty	4	C	7	2	0	1	12,705
Yoka's Knight	3	G	12	1	1	1	5,557
Yokazona	4	G	11	1	1	0	13,000
Yoke (FR)	8	G	5	0	0	1	1,500
Yokozuma	3	G	3	0	0	0	171
Yolanda a Token	2	F	5	0	3	1	32,898
Yonder	6	G	1	0	0	0	0
Yong Feathers	3	F	8	1	2	0	10,670
Yoren	3	F	2	0	0	0	0
York Air (ARG)	5	H	9	3	1	0	44,700
York County	5	G	5	1	1	0	6,631
York Encounter	9	G	5	0	0	1	884
York Harbor	8	G	13	1	2	3	9,851
York Hills	5	M	8	1	1	3	24,584
Yorkin	7	H	2	1	1	0	11,700
Yorkshire Lad	4	G	6	3	1	2	15,800
Yorkton	6	G	9	2	1	1	11,417
Yorktown	6	G	1	0	0	0	220
Yoruba	5	G	6	0	0	1	2,260
Yoscha Bosche	2	C	4	0	0	0	145
Yosemite Falls	3	F	6	0	0	1	2,212
Yoshida's Choice	4	C	5	0	0	0	0
Yost Road	5	G	14	1	0	0	7,264
Yoto Speakes	9	G	2	1	0	0	12,900
You	4	F	8	2	4	1	677,108
You a Cat	2	G	5	2	1	0	31,180
You and You Alone	6	H	3	1	1	0	7,638
You Are Mine	3	C	4	0	1	2	4,242
You Are Stormy	2	F	9	2	2	2	25,290
You Bet We Win	4	F	16	1	4	3	36,485
You Can Call Me Mr	5	G	12	3	1	0	9,159
You Can Too	6	M	7	3	0	0	11,129
You Can't Hide	2	F	2	1	0	0	6,145
You Choose	5	G	9	0	0	1	2,907
You Crack Me Up	3	G	14	2	4	2	50,130
You Da Ant	6	M	2	0	0	0	330
You Da Bomb	3	G	17	0	0	4	5,602
You Da Mon	5	G	3	0	2	0	1,800
You Do the Math	4	C	8	0	3	1	19,124
You Glitter Girl	3	F	9	5	1	0	109,434
You Go Roudy Wilma	4	F	4	0	0	0	200
You Got It Guy	7	G	9	0	0	1	2,796
You Know Who	5	H	1	0	0	0	0
You Leader	4	G	9	1	2	2	31,630

Horse	Age	Sex	Sts	1st	2d	3d	Won
You Left	4	F	1	0	0	0	85
You Left Me	2	F	1	0	0	0	0
You Look Good	7	H	6	0	1	1	3,400
You Lov Racey	4	F	11	1	1	1	7,515
You Lucky Devil	2	G	7	1	0	2	7,015
You Make Me Laugh	4	C	5	0	1	1	4,064
You Missed	3	F	20	1	3	2	16,523
You No Jack	3	G	9	0	1	1	10,467
You P. S.	4	F	15	2	2	3	17,603
You Pay the Bill	3	F	6	1	0	1	3,611
You Promised	2	F	1	0	0	0	0
You Rang	3	C	5	0	0	2	5,085
You Rule My World	3	G	6	0	0	2	1,511
You Say Grace	8	M	2	0	0	0	103
You Will Cry Devil	3	G	18	0	1	2	2,472
Youareaggravatin'	2	C	5	3	1	0	49,017
Youaresweet	2	F	3	1	0	1	17,928
Youbetshecan	4	F	3	0	0	1	6,300
Youcandpendonme	3	G	2	0	0	0	355
Youcan'ttakeme	3	F	9	5	0	0	138,665
Youdrivemewild	6	G	17	4	2	3	23,160
Yougonow	2	C	2	0	0	0	0
Yougottabuck	6	G	15	1	3	3	28,005
Yougottawanna	4	G	9	0	1	2	32,889
Youimpressme	2	F	2	0	0	0	200
You'll Be Happy	6	M	10	2	2	0	52,560
Youmakemethorbaby	5	M	1	1	0	0	13,200
Young	10	G	2	0	0	0	134
Young and Handsome	3	G	3	0	0	0	136
Young and Restless	2	F	1	0	0	1	4,070
Young Country Star	7	M	6	0	1	2	3,230
Young Dubliner (IRE)	14	G	6	3	0	0	37,200
Young Emotions	2	F	1	0	0	0	0
Young Jack	3	G	2	0	0	0	115
Young Ladies Day	3	F	2	0	0	1	6,370
Young Man's Fancy	5	M	4	0	0	0	260
Young Neil	4	C	1	0	0	0	50
Young Pioneer	3	G	3	0	2	0	21,320
Young Runaway	11	H	11	4	1	2	54,712
Young Sage	2	F	4	0	1	0	5,980
Young Star	4	F	9	3	1	2	94,006
Young Trev	6	G	11	3	0	1	27,533
Young Trooper	3	G	12	1	0	1	8,925
Young Whiz	4	G	3	0	0	0	10,101
Young Wolf	7	G	4	0	0	1	2,732
Youngs Neck Arod	5	H	1	0	0	0	0
Youngus	4	F	4	0	1	0	3,246
Youowemeone	3	F	5	0	0	0	1,215
Your Abc's	4	C	7	1	1	2	19,020
Your Add	3	G	15	3	4	2	30,275
Your Bluffing	3	G	11	4	1	0	85,390
Your Cat	3	F	4	1	1	1	21,820
Your First	8	G	7	0	0	2	2,650
Your Friend	3	C	4	0	0	1	2,656
Your Jules	4	G	6	0	0	0	5,580
Your Knightmare	2	F	2	0	0	0	0
Your Lion Eyes	2	G	1	0	0	0	760
Your Momma	5	M	7	0	0	0	409
Your Over	3	F	7	0	1	3	7,590
Your Private Stash	2	C	2	0	0	0	479
Your Prize Anytime	2	F	6	0	0	0	560
Your Regal	7	M	4	0	1	1	2,486
Your Selection	3	F	4	0	0	1	1,663
Your Serendipity	4	C	8	1	1	1	3,291
Your Song	6	M	1	0	0	0	1,150
Your Welcome	4	G	12	3	4	1	33,278
Your Wiggle	5	M	4	1	0	2	15,490
You're a Funny Guy	3	C	12	2	2	1	19,457
You're a Good Man	6	G	12	1	1	2	7,115
You're a Monkey	2	F	8	1	0	0	18,060
You're Blessed	2	F	3	0	0	1	8,484
You're Darn Tootin	3	G	12	5	1	1	60,217
You're Faded	3	F	14	2	3	2	19,883
You're In	3	C	1	1	0	0	14,250
You're On Your Own	4	F	5	0	0	0	1,128
You're So Lucky	4	F	11	0	2	2	5,945
You're Such a Deee	4	F	9	1	3	4	42,098
You're Up	2	F	1	0	0	0	2,180
You'redusty	4	G	14	1	3	2	13,457
Yourfinalanswer	4	F	6	0	1	0	5,340
Yourfunnyhoney	4	F	12	2	1	5	17,398
Yourgonnagogirl	2	F	5	0	0	2	2,240
Yourhonorspleasure	4	F	4	0	0	0	33
Yourloveisfadin	3	F	4	1	1	1	21,676
Yours At Six	2	F	4	0	0	0	5,553
Yours Forever	3	G	11	1	2	0	10,525
Yours Onli	2	C	3	0	0	0	3,240
Yoursmineours	2	F	5	2	0	1	18,790
Yourspot	5	G	3	0	0	0	439
Yourstocommand	3	G	10	2	2	1	76,984
Youthful Comment	2	C	2	0	2	0	12,650
You've Got Mitch	4	F	3	0	0	0	0
Youvegotmeflying	5	H	7	0	1	4	1,595
Youwantapieceame	3	G	10	4	0	0	24,295
Youwillaire	3	F	17	3	5	3	49,740
Yoyo Jabo	4	G	10	2	1	3	36,649
Yoyoyo	7	G	1	0	0	0	0
Yozo	3	C	6	0	1	2	15,780
Ys	4	G	4	0	0	1	3,500
Yu Gold	3	F	8	2	1	1	9,471
Yucca Road	6	H	14	4	1	1	31,444
Yucon Go	2	G	5	0	1	0	3,430
Yuge	4	G	2	0	1	0	3,039
Yukan B a Lady Too	7	M	4	0	0	1	1,602
Yuki No Princess	5	M	12	2	3	2	53,712
Yukon Amazon	8	M	2	0	0	0	120
Yukon Charley	5	G	17	1	3	4	15,728
Yukon Loot	3	G	16	3	4	0	21,245
Yukon Mac	6	G	20	1	3	5	6,347
Yukon Strike	7	G	4	0	0	0	432
Yukon Tour	3	G	11	0	0	2	3,487
Yukon's Angel	3	F	12	1	2	1	14,750
Yukon's Sugar	7	M	9	2	1	2	9,068
Yule Be Blue	5	H	12	1	4	1	5,531
Yulitemyfyr	4	F	6	1	0	0	2,960
Yuma	5	G	1	0	0	0	0
Yumeko	4	F	9	2	1	1	36,110
Yummy	3	F	12	2	2	0	10,504
Yummy Yummy	2	F	1	0	0	0	0
Yur Regressing	4	F	9	0	1	1	2,336
Yuriquest	3	G	6	2	0	0	18,035
Yvonne County	2	F	2	0	0	0	0
Yvonne Goes On	4	F	18	3	1	3	50,033
Yvonnesladydelite	3	F	4	0	0	0	0
Yyyyes	2	F	10	0	1	2	13,120
Yzerman	2	G	3	0	0	0	360
Z Account	3	C	10	0	0	0	1,350
Z Belle	6	M	4	0	1	0	3,107
Z B's Carson City	4	G	6	0	0	0	350
Z Cool	6	G	18	4	3	1	23,023
Z Cover Realestate	3	G	4	1	0	0	3,480
Z Cute One Two	3	F	7	1	0	0	6,581
Z Dolly	8	M	4	0	0	0	0
Z Goodtobetrue	10	G	2	0	0	0	240
Z Halo's Secret	3	C	11	2	1	1	7,981
Z Man	6	G	13	1	2	3	11,275
Z Mariachi	3	C	9	0	1	2	3,130
Z Me Zipp	3	F	19	1	2	1	16,135
Z Minion	4	C	1	0	0	1	560
Z Silver Cat	6	M	8	0	0	0	1,247
Z Smoking Roberto	3	G	3	0	0	0	0
Z Z Haze	4	C	3	0	0	0	180
Z Z Jaber Jaws	3	F	12	1	2	1	13,812
Z Z Peacock	3	F	13	1	3	2	10,305
Z Z Zoey	2	F	1	0	0	0	0
Z Z's Destiny	3	C	1	0	0	0	0
Z Z's Fantasy	3	G	18	4	1	2	24,163
Z. Frere	4	G	18	1	1	2	20,744
Za Zoomer	2	G	2	0	0	0	252
Zaby	3	C	1	0	0	0	430
Zaca	5	M	15	2	4	2	5,864
Zach Slim and Eddy	2	G	6	0	0	1	5,130
Zacharias	3	C	5	0	0	0	230
Zacharov	9	G	14	5	3	1	47,490

Horse	Age	Sex	Sts	1st	2d	3d	Won
Zachfiftyfour	5	G	18	4	2	3	21,846
Zach's Contender	3	G	5	1	0	0	12,939
Zachs Girl	4	F	4	0	0	1	1,040
Zachs World	4	F	14	2	1	4	21,852
Zack Attack	2	G	3	1	0	0	15,750
Zack Barron	4	G	2	0	0	0	0
Zackdar	2	G	3	0	0	2	2,483
Zadar	5	G	11	1	1	1	22,794
Zafari	3	C	3	0	0	0	86
Zafonic's Song (FR)	6	H	7	1	0	1	8,480
Zafrika	2	C	3	0	0	0	196
Zagor's Deco Due	8	G	18	2	2	2	8,393
Zagor's Genie	4	F	7	1	1	0	9,703
Zagor's Sierra	3	C	2	0	0	0	0
Zagor's Walter's H	5	M	6	0	0	0	945
Zagor's War	3	C	3	0	0	1	5,980
Zagros	4	G	3	0	0	0	200
Zahalee Red	2	G	2	0	0	0	2,740
Zairsaplan	3	F	9	1	1	3	15,627
Zakocity	2	C	9	1	1	2	101,003
Zakofalltrades	4	F	5	1	0	0	6,090
Zak's Precocious	2	F	4	2	1	0	64,170
Zakster	3	G	8	0	1	1	1,732
Zalema	3	C	9	1	1	1	36,347
Zales Champagne	4	F	9	1	2	0	6,570
Zal's Pal	2	G	5	1	1	1	6,326
Zam Lady	3	F	10	1	0	1	6,963
Zamanda	4	F	13	1	5	4	52,037
Zamaroo	3	G	7	0	2	0	13,980
Zambizi Adventure	2	C	2	0	0	0	390
Zambonus	7	M	2	0	0	0	67
Zamboon	2	F	8	1	1	1	6,954
Zamek	6	G	11	2	0	1	23,240
Zaminister	3	F	1	0	0	0	0
Zanakar (FR)	4	G	4	0	1	0	12,320
Zanda's Bonus	2	G	5	0	1	1	13,180
Zane's Way	5	G	7	0	0	1	808
Zanny's Dancer	6	M	10	0	2	1	2,639
Zanshin	4	G	18	3	2	3	22,383
Zantango	2	F	2	0	0	0	475
Zany Baby	8	M	17	0	5	2	6,040
Zany Girl	5	M	2	0	0	0	116
Zany Lady	7	M	6	2	0	1	11,867
Zapata	4	C	15	1	1	2	6,150
Zapped in Time	5	G	13	4	2	2	14,561
Zar Kissin	6	M	4	0	0	0	165
Zara's Place	4	C	9	2	3	2	12,400
Zarbo	4	G	2	0	0	0	0
Zarb's Cat Lady	4	F	5	0	0	0	2,160
Zarb's Crystal	6	G	7	0	0	0	323
Zarb's Cutie	3	F	10	0	1	0	1,208
Zarb's Dahar	3	G	4	0	1	0	6,380
Zarb's Dreamer	2	C	3	2	0	0	29,940
Zarb's Echo	8	G	8	1	0	2	12,030
Zarb's Halo	4	F	13	3	2	0	17,989
Zarb's Hoedown	2	G	1	0	0	0	1,080
Zarb's Love	5	M	10	2	3	1	38,390
Zarb's Luck	6	G	8	2	2	2	169,405
Zarb's Lucky Charm	6	G	7	2	0	1	16,260
Zarb's Magic	10	G	5	1	0	0	5,040
Zarb's Miss Belle	4	F	10	0	2	3	7,785
Zarb's Music	3	G	12	3	1	1	128,670
Zarb's Passion	3	F	8	0	1	1	7,077
Zarb's Pet	7	G	11	0	1	0	2,826
Zarbsflight	6	M	10	1	1	0	10,495
Zarbysteppes	7	M	6	0	2	1	9,355
Zardoz (CHI)	6	H	15	5	1	2	59,770
Zarlingo	8	G	8	1	1	0	4,022
Zarpa	5	G	6	1	1	0	5,385
Zarpen	2	F	2	1	0	1	11,570
Zarro	3	G	11	1	3	0	50,087
Zars Charger	5	H	3	0	0	0	495
Zarzuela	4	F	1	0	0	0	600
Zat Chew	10	G	6	0	0	2	3,307
Zat Darn Cat	4	F	9	1	3	0	55,653
Zatara	2	G	2	0	0	1	2,280
Zata's Secret	3	G	1	0	0	0	174

Horse	Age	Sex	Sts	1st	2d	3d	Won
Zathras	3	G	8	0	0	0	960
Zatoff (BRZ)	4	C	3	0	0	0	360
Zatso	3	F	4	0	0	0	583
Zatz Mr. Cool	8	G	2	1	0	0	1,440
Zavalla Dandy	6	G	14	3	3	1	52,262
Zavata	3	C	7	2	0	0	120,493
Zawadayougot	3	F	12	2	1	2	18,809
Zawzooth	4	F	5	1	0	1	59,160
Zaya (GB)	8	G	1	0	0	0	0
Zayed	3	G	4	2	0	0	40,950
Zayla's Fire	4	F	7	1	0	2	4,888
Zbone	5	G	19	1	3	2	9,877
Zcat Lady	3	F	6	0	0	1	2,062
Zdonsdream	4	G	5	0	0	0	366
Zdravo	4	F	7	2	1	0	14,860
Ze Fact	6	G	4	2	1	0	12,900
Zeal It Witha Kiss	3	G	14	1	1	0	18,105
Zeal Power	5	G	18	2	0	3	21,078
Zeal With a Kiss	6	H	2	0	1	1	4,340
Zealian	5	G	7	3	1	0	24,484
Zealous Baby	3	F	11	0	1	1	5,060
Zealous Capote	2	C	5	1	0	0	6,855
Zealous Flite	5	G	16	2	1	1	12,612
Zealous Glory	10	G	11	1	2	0	7,502
Zealous Kate	9	M	15	1	1	5	10,108
Zealous Love	5	G	2	0	0	0	116
Zealous Z	5	M	6	1	0	0	4,755
Zeal's Star	2	G	6	0	0	1	2,060
Zeanne	2	F	2	0	0	1	2,400
Zebadiah Eagle	8	G	12	0	0	1	2,088
Zebecca	4	F	4	0	0	0	186
Zebedee	4	G	1	0	0	0	350
Zebra	3	C	13	2	0	2	16,870
Zebulon	2	G	1	0	0	0	0
Zede's Copy	2	G	3	0	0	1	2,095
Zee Anna	5	M	8	1	0	1	6,897
Zee Best	4	F	11	2	1	1	24,420
Zee Chalupa	6	H	9	0	3	1	1,685
Zee Fox	4	G	13	0	2	3	8,992
Zee Lady's Man	2	C	1	0	0	0	0
Zee Oh Six	4	G	11	1	1	1	35,700
Zee Power	4	G	11	1	0	2	11,206
Zee Topper	3	F	12	0	3	4	21,280
Zeeba Lily	3	F	5	0	0	0	631
Zeebirdie	4	F	3	0	0	0	0
Zeeflaco	3	G	11	0	2	5	6,381
Zee's Top Ruler	5	H	1	0	0	0	0
Zeeville	2	G	4	1	0	0	5,400
Zeewitch	2	F	3	0	0	0	0
Zekim	8	G	3	0	0	0	122
Zelig	2	C	2	0	0	0	2,460
Zellie	3	F	1	1	0	0	11,470
Zelmira	3	F	1	0	0	0	0
Zelna J	3	F	4	1	0	0	4,650
Zeloma	3	F	9	1	0	1	5,515
Zen Diva	4	F	10	1	2	3	38,020
Zen Me a Runner	4	G	7	0	0	0	390
Zen Risen Star	5	G	3	1	0	0	4,602
Zencredable	6	G	14	2	1	2	17,120
Zend Gold	3	F	8	1	0	1	12,001
Zenda (GB)	4	F	1	1	0	0	30,000
Zenia Zeal	4	F	21	0	2	1	4,916
Zenion	4	C	1	0	0	0	0
Zenith Dancer	3	F	10	3	0	2	18,615
Zennamatic	7	H	5	0	0	1	3,944
Zen's a Zooming	3	G	6	0	1	0	2,429
Zen's Country	3	F	7	0	0	0	0
Zen's Secret	3	C	2	0	0	0	0
Zen's Silverbuck	5	H	2	0	0	0	385
Zentsov Street	6	H	3	0	1	0	12,200
Zeph's Future	3	F	7	0	0	1	986
Zephyr's Boy	2	C	4	2	0	0	25,852
Zeppo	2	G	1	0	0	0	0
Zero	3	C	1	0	0	0	654
Zero Absolute	2	G	2	0	0	0	50
Zero Degrees	3	C	6	1	1	0	12,890
Zero Financing	2	G	4	1	0	0	8,485

RECORDS OF HORSES

Horse	Age	Sex	Sts	1st	2d	3d	Won		Horse	Age	Sex	Sts	1st	2d	3d	Won
Zero In	4	G	11	1	2	4	24,337		Zoe in Red	3	F	6	0	0	0	1,020
Zero U	3	G	12	3	2	0	17,273		Zoe Roe	2	G	4	0	1	0	6,145
Zero Visibility	2	G	2	1	0	0	10,200		Zoe's Dream	4	F	5	0	1	0	2,369
Zerotosixty	3	C	9	2	2	0	25,936		Zoe's Trick	3	F	12	1	3	1	18,540
Zes Tee	2	F	4	0	1	0	4,145		Zoezeebear	3	F	11	2	1	1	13,090
Zesti Zu	6	G	5	1	0	0	1,687		Zohra's Web	3	F	3	2	0	1	27,465
Zesty Dance	3	F	4	0	0	0	360		Zolinda	2	G	3	0	0	0	1,110
Zesty Diablo	5	G	14	1	0	2	17,440		Zolishka	6	M	17	4	2	3	32,934
Zeuqram's Boo Boo	3	G	4	0	0	0	0		Zombie	3	C	2	1	0	1	6,910
Zeuqram's Dondi	6	G	8	0	0	0	2,436		Zonaki	4	G	3	0	0	0	0
Zeuqram'smichael L	7	G	9	0	0	0	1,268		Zona's Zipper	5	M	6	1	3	0	14,649
Zi Pep	9	G	9	2	1	2	21,635		Zone Defense	3	G	3	1	0	0	12,586
Ziada	4	F	9	3	0	0	36,520		Zone Girl	3	F	1	0	0	0	0
Ziarita	3	F	4	1	0	0	22,500		Zone It	2	C	5	1	1	0	12,150
Ziasquatrosocks	3	F	2	0	0	0	164		Zone Judge	5	H	1	0	0	0	8,595
Zig a Little	6	G	23	2	1	3	12,528		Zonely Money	3	C	1	0	0	0	0
Zig Zag Leigh	2	F	5	0	0	0	953		Zoneout	4	F	1	0	0	0	50
Zig Zag Sam	4	F	5	0	0	0	638		Zone's Ebony	3	G	8	0	1	0	2,555
Zigeuner	6	G	6	2	0	0	64,716		Zoning (GB)	6	H	8	2	1	2	79,051
Zigfire	6	H	12	0	1	1	11,548		Zonk	5	M	3	1	0	0	77,760
Ziggedy Bop	2	F	1	0	0	0	100		Zonker	8	H	5	0	0	0	1,125
Ziggie	5	G	6	3	0	0	26,919		Zooby Doo	4	F	4	0	0	0	396
Ziggy	4	F	2	0	0	0	0		Zooey	3	F	9	0	0	1	3,821
Ziggy Zaggy	3	G	17	2	4	2	27,372		Zoof	2	F	2	0	0	0	834
Ziggydarbona	8	M	5	0	2	1	6,555		Zookie	8	H	3	0	0	0	336
Ziggy's April Fool	2	F	2	0	0	0	200		Zoolu Nights	3	G	11	2	4	0	55,460
Ziggy's Haylo	4	G	15	3	3	3	27,270		Zoom Zoom	4	C	2	0	0	0	140
Zignal	4	G	5	1	1	0	19,020		Zoom Zoom Meri	3	F	4	0	0	3	1,879
Zignor	4	F	10	2	2	0	21,990		Zooma	2	F	3	0	0	0	0
Zig's Quiet Lady	5	M	5	0	2	1	12,600		Zoot	3	G	12	1	2	0	11,849
Zigzag Dan	3	C	5	0	0	0	1,275		Zoot Scootin Hurli	4	F	17	5	5	1	15,116
Zigzag Dancer	6	G	8	0	0	1	901		Zopic	4	F	2	0	0	0	450
Zilia	3	F	8	0	1	2	8,035		Zora's Vijay	3	G	2	0	0	0	0
Zillabreeze	3	F	11	1	2	5	10,810		Zorba El Griego (CHI)	7	H	6	1	2	1	6,249
Zimbabwe	3	G	2	0	0	0	0		Zores	4	C	10	1	2	0	28,182
Zimbali	2	C	9	1	0	2	8,750		Zorka	2	F	1	0	0	0	0
Zina Cause	3	G	7	3	0	0	64,215		Zorlak's Back	7	G	4	0	0	0	185
Zinash	5	G	6	2	1	1	16,890		Zorro n' Toro	6	G	8	1	1	0	5,649
Zinga Deebleuz	3	F	14	2	3	1	21,622		Zorubabel	6	G	12	2	2	0	7,130
Zinger Go	3	F	1	0	0	0	72		Zosia's Genius	2	F	4	2	1	0	38,850
Zinger Man	2	G	2	0	0	0	0		Zosima	2	F	5	3	1	0	135,440
Zinzee	3	F	12	2	3	0	16,421		Zottex	3	F	2	1	0	1	5,390
Zip by Zak	8	G	8	0	0	0	948		Zoucha Nutcracker	8	M	2	0	0	0	0
Zip Gun	3	C	10	3	1	1	31,145		Zowie	3	G	5	0	0	0	1,486
Zip It	3	F	7	1	0	1	3,819		Zowie Strikes	2	F	1	0	0	0	123
Zip N Buster	4	C	4	1	0	0	3,600		Z's Star	5	M	15	3	3	3	14,789
Zip N Go	3	C	6	1	0	1	11,258		Zucchini	7	M	5	0	0	2	2,527
Zip N Scoot	5	G	5	0	0	0	310		Zuckabarr	5	G	7	0	4	1	18,488
Zip Round	3	F	2	0	0	0	224		Zudora Jane	6	M	5	1	0	0	3,615
Zip the Bright	4	G	10	2	0	4	22,189		Zukinikiki	3	F	10	1	3	2	61,696
Zip to Moscow	2	C	2	0	0	0	0		Zula Bay	3	C	2	0	0	0	0
Zip Zap Zip	3	F	7	0	2	1	1,782		Zuley	5	M	7	0	0	0	2,090
Zip Zip Boom	2	F	6	0	0	0	275		Zulu	4	C	18	3	2	4	22,991
Zipaway	6	G	1	0	0	0	149		Zulu Bag	3	G	1	0	1	0	1,450
Zipcody	2	C	7	2	1	1	33,115		Zulu Lulu	3	F	7	1	0	0	4,403
Zipledo	6	G	13	2	3	1	20,450		Zumbafizz	2	C	5	0	0	0	1,030
Zipolator	7	G	17	1	3	5	16,223		Zumbi	7	H	10	3	1	2	13,231
Zipper Zipper De	2	C	9	2	0	2	39,220		Zumerous	5	H	1	0	0	0	150
Zipperfoot	5	M	22	4	7	1	38,496		Zuper	8	H	6	1	0	0	7,152
Zipper's Down	4	F	5	0	0	0	973		Zuppar Mistress	3	F	2	0	0	0	0
Zippin Zane	3	C	9	0	2	1	3,047		Zuppardon Bleu	4	C	5	0	0	0	840
Zippity Zak	7	G	4	1	0	0	8,121		Zuppardo's Doll	2	F	1	0	0	0	0
Zippity Zappin	4	F	7	0	0	0	0		Zuppardos Huzzy	3	F	4	0	0	0	0
Zippitydoodaaa	4	F	14	1	1	1	6,269		Zuppy	4	C	2	0	0	0	220
Zipporah	3	F	4	0	0	1	5,278		Zur Guten	7	G	17	3	2	3	12,691
Zippy Chippy	12	G	0	0	1	0	582		Zuryev	7	G	14	0	1	1	4,843
Zippy Intrigue	7	G	14	0	0	1	2,406		Zuzax	4	C	5	0	0	0	56
Zippy Longstocking	6	M	12	2	0	3	9,295		Zuzi Deer	4	F	7	1	0	0	3,874
Zippy Zo Zo	3	F	11	3	2	2	40,910		Zuzu's Petals	4	F	2	0	0	0	110
Zirconia	4	F	5	2	2	0	13,968		Zwena	2	F	5	0	1	0	1,650
Ziroq	3	G	12	0	4	3	23,940		Zydeco Affair	3	G	10	1	3	0	65,549
Ziskel	4	C	1	0	0	0	0		Zydeco Blue	5	G	6	1	1	0	5,228
Zitlaly	2	F	6	1	2	1	43,109		Zydeco Imp	3	F	2	0	0	0	0
Zloty	5	G	5	0	0	1	5,520		Zynastry	5	G	11	1	5	2	16,451
Zmoneygirl	4	F	5	0	0	1	944		Zyphyr Cove	2	G	7	0	1	1	1,540
Zodiamond	2	C	5	1	0	0	6,340		Zz Open	4	G	10	1	2	1	15,575
Zodiaque	6	M	8	2	1	1	21,024									

2003
RECORDS OF TRAINERS

The record of each trainer, who raced
thoroughbreds in the United States and Canada
during 2003, appears in this section,
showing the number of starts, firsts, seconds and thirds,
and the total purses earned by these horses.

Trainer	Sts	1st	2d	3d	Purses	Trainer	Sts	1st	2d	3d	Purses
Abbott, Frank	14	1	0	1	$7,372	Albulov, Jr., James M.	12	0	1	5	4,457
Abbruzzese, Eugenio	48	5	4	7	95,610	Alcoser, Jr., Erasmo C.	8	0	1	1	2,736
Abell, Joseph E.	35	3	0	4	47,675	Alcoverde, Ernesto	18	0	0	4	1,422
Aberhamson, Lynn	12	1	0	3	5,908	Aldavaz, Hermengildo G.	3	0	0	0	260
Ables, Milburn R	1	0	0	0	0	Alder, Zane G.	30	4	6	5	7,369
Abraham, Tim	5	1	3	0	3,652	Alderman, Emery	21	9	3	0	22,572
Abrahamson, Randy	7	0	2	1	1,069	Alderson, Anthony J.	25	2	1	4	49,342
Abrams, Barry	365	38	39	53	1,526,968	Alderson, Ian	62	6	4	8	116,913
Abrams, Ronald B.	30	4	3	1	35,345	Alecci, John V.	146	27	25	13	684,316
Accardi, John	62	15	14	6	116,483	Aleman, Juan G.	18	6	2	5	35,652
Acerno, John	1	0	0	0	420	Alessandrini, Donna	16	2	2	2	13,853
Achord, Clint E.	9	1	0	1	2,010	Alexander, Bruce F.	162	31	27	18	514,774
Ackel, Don	9	1	2	0	18,114	Alexander, Frank A.	147	20	22	21	1,033,210
Ackerman, D. Kelly	103	23	15	12	201,933	Alexander, L. C.	20	2	5	1	6,554
Ackerman, Thomas M.	4	0	1	0	1,292	Alexander, Landry Dale	7	0	0	0	0
Acorn, Danny J.	34	4	4	3	59,854	Alexander, Peter B.	45	7	6	7	173,955
Acosta, Charles	36	0	2	3	2,659	Alfano, Ronald A.	12	1	1	5	22,000
Acosta, Robert	17	1	0	5	2,488	Alfir, David Jeff	67	8	9	5	119,823
Acquilano, James S.	206	44	39	26	304,657	Alfonso, Adolfo	3	0	0	0	385
Acuna, Louisa	74	4	6	9	89,290	Alford, Claudie M.	17	1	0	1	7,050
Adair, George H.	5	0	0	0	0	Alford, Mac	2	0	0	0	0
Adamo, Anthony	132	15	15	14	231,050	Alford, Walter E.	2	0	0	0	0
Adams, Billy E.	91	17	16	13	133,905	Alfred, Jr., Carl F.	1	0	0	0	0
Adams, Darrel K.	98	4	11	10	44,449	Alfstad, Allene D.	28	1	1	2	36,411
Adams, Douglas S.	70	4	8	9	26,392	Algerio, Richard M.	37	0	1	2	8,529
Adams, Harlan C.	13	0	3	0	3,636	Ali, Alnaz	48	0	2	3	16,859
Adams, John B.	12	1	0	1	18,148	Ali, Androus	2	0	0	0	0
Adams, John K.	5	3	0	0	29,466	Alicea, Linda	3	0	1	0	3,206
Adams, Keith U.	8	0	0	0	0	Alire, Aniceto Mike	11	0	0	0	644
Adams, Krystal	45	5	2	7	13,904	Allain, Emile M.	59	3	7	9	416,019
Adams, Lynn A.	33	0	4	3	15,401	Allard, Edward T.	395	71	54	58	1,218,361
Adams, Michael T.	16	0	0	1	2,440	Alleman, Joseph	11	1	3	1	17,534
Adams, Norman	6	0	1	0	892	Allen, Ann	3	0	0	0	228
Adams, Robert J.	12	1	4	1	14,591	Allen, Cheryl C.	5	0	1	0	3,244
Adams, William A.	5	0	0	0	515	Allen, Daniel	43	3	7	3	52,240
Adams, William E.	41	3	4	7	17,539	Allen, Jack L.	12	2	2	1	30,714
Adams, Jr., John S.	29	2	0	0	24,983	Allen, Jeffery S.	115	8	7	16	110,947
Addicott, Ronald W.	1	0	0	0	36	Allen, Jo Ann	114	7	8	13	52,148
Addison, Elizabeth	2	0	0	0	0	Allen, Johnny	23	0	1	3	3,072
Adkins, Mary	21	3	2	2	24,201	Allen, Marlene C.	8	0	0	0	420
Adorno, Luis	5	0	0	0	570	Allen, Mickey	8	0	0	0	1,012
Adwell, David J.	6	0	0	0	840	Allen, Randy	394	58	49	59	835,398
Agilar, Anthony	59	6	2	7	60,423	Allen, Robert	21	0	2	1	3,364
Agosti, Thomas M.	319	66	49	47	1,068,801	Allen, Terry	2	0	0	0	250
Agrinsoni, Jose F.	99	8	15	14	94,745	Allen, Truman	60	3	3	8	35,885
Aguayo, Ramon Davilla	8	0	0	1	3,666	Allen, William E.	10	0	0	0	1,535
Aguayo, Vernon E.	36	2	0	3	17,126	Allen, III, A. Ferris	690	98	118	104	1,861,729
Aguilar, Joe	3	0	0	1	1,345	Allen, Sr., Ronald D.	269	39	35	27	396,529
Aguilar, Rodolfo	27	4	0	3	16,208	Alley, Jess S.	18	0	0	4	33,496
Aguilar, Rosario	114	10	8	18	113,344	Allinson, Vernon J.	16	3	0	4	37,810
Aguirre, Anthony	89	11	19	15	334,522	Allison, Melinda	42	1	6	4	20,534
Aguirre, Horacio	19	3	2	3	22,325	Allison, Norman E.	15	0	0	3	8,182
Aguirre, Juan Raul	24	2	1	6	28,383	Allred, Alexa	9	2	0	0	8,995
Aguirre, Paul G.	201	39	34	22	1,195,370	Allyn, William F.	16	1	0	1	4,272
Aguirre, Rey	43	2	9	4	87,777	Almond, Daniel	8	0	4	0	5,970
Ahalt, Ronald S.	80	8	9	8	121,137	Alonso, Enrique	246	43	22	28	824,300
Ahaus, Frank E.	36	3	2	3	22,838	Alonzo, Howard	82	14	14	14	285,797
Ahern, F. Michael	3	0	0	0	291	Alonzo, Isidoro	7	1	0	0	1,986
Aitchison, Lisa M.	18	2	1	4	24,410	Alpers, Jr., Curtis L.	8	0	1	0	2,937
Aker, Wiley	112	9	25	17	30,640	Altemeier, Mark	10	1	1	4	13,915
Akers, Stacey	12	0	1	1	4,260	Alter, Happy	72	9	4	8	213,468
Akin, Steven R.	5	0	0	0	0	Alvarado, Jose L.	2	1	0	0	1,825
Akoury, Jr., Michael	12	0	0	0	1,580	Alvarado, Juan	6	1	0	1	7,610
Alari, Luciano	3	0	0	0	519	Alvey, Darrell E.	126	14	15	18	92,553
Albers, Dick	53	2	5	5	15,163	Ambrogi, Leo J.	25	2	3	3	35,410
Albert, Linda L.	207	33	37	40	551,335	Ambrosia, Joseph E.	96	9	11	11	149,183
Albert, III, Talbot J.	27	2	1	4	42,280	Amescua, Rene	194	37	31	21	370,014
Albertrani, Louis	44	2	7	6	58,204	Amico, Lori	1	0	0	0	80
Albertrani, Thomas	41	7	6	5	405,794	Amico, Vincent	68	6	9	6	83,019
Alberts, Nancy H.	35	3	3	5	53,555	Amodie, Tracy	15	2	0	1	8,820
Albright, Amy	111	32	27	14	512,435	Amonte, Andrew	34	0	4	2	18,680
Albright, Dona M.	127	5	14	19	72,612	Amonte, Jr., Frank A.	33	3	3	2	109,588
Albright, George R.	197	17	23	23	150,752	Amonte, Sr., Frank A.	1	0	0	0	0
Albright, Phillip	13	2	0	1	6,469	Amoroso, Jr., Louis C.	39	1	1	1	15,345
Albright, Robert	27	3	2	4	39,693	Amoss, Thomas M.	445	118	84	52	3,217,121
Albu, Ken	85	11	10	13	171,850	Amparan, Alberto	9	0	0	2	4,677

Trainer	Sts	1st	2d	3d	Purses	Trainer	Sts	1st	2d	3d	Purses
Amshoff, Steven L.	102	20	16	9	215,083	Apodaca, Ramon	8	0	0	0	511
Amthor, K. Gordon	9	1	1	0	12,620	Apperloo, Joe	5	2	0	2	68,144
Ananas, Edwin	39	11	2	3	32,737	Applebee, David	23	0	1	0	5,806
Andelmo, Joseph J.	23	0	1	5	12,352	Applegate, David V.	4	0	0	1	1,184
Andersen, Ralph W.	56	8	5	4	49,510	Applegate, Elbert	30	3	3	2	8,078
Andersen, Ron L.	79	3	10	8	85,485	Applegate, Kevin	4	1	0	1	11,040
Anderson, Bill R.	28	4	3	0	26,234	Applegate, Ronald D.	15	1	0	2	5,292
Anderson, Bob D.	16	2	3	1	11,824	Aquilino, Joseph	195	10	16	33	463,266
Anderson, Brent R.	1	0	0	0	0	Aquino, Angela M.	16	5	4	2	32,115
Anderson, Bruce D.	269	35	45	46	286,660	Aragon, Lee	3	0	0	0	109
Anderson, Carl Norman	39	6	7	5	95,738	Araiza, Albert P.	4	0	0	0	1,447
Anderson, Carmela	37	3	6	5	152,715	Araiza, Arnulfo	33	4	6	9	21,088
Anderson, David C.	519	125	82	65	749,333	Araya, Rene A.	114	9	18	17	473,036
Anderson, Dawna Z.	25	0	3	8	18,463	Arboleda, Arturo	27	1	4	3	15,864
Anderson, Dee	45	3	7	5	54,584	Arboleda, Oscar	14	0	0	1	2,773
Anderson, Don	23	0	0	0	2,173	Arcaro, Louis	11	1	1	3	4,944
Anderson, Donald J.	6	0	0	3	2,700	Arceneaux, George	65	7	4	2	58,003
Anderson, Doug L.	58	8	10	10	137,605	Arceneaux, Victor	108	16	16	14	198,774
Anderson, Erin Lee	92	14	7	12	82,759	Arceneaux, Jr., Edward	43	1	2	9	14,586
Anderson, Frank L.	3	0	0	0	2,100	Archer, Roberta	2	0	0	0	93
Anderson, Gary L.	67	10	9	8	30,112	Archuleta, Mike	6	0	1	0	4,310
Anderson, George D.	22	1	3	4	20,859	Arens, John T.	36	2	0	5	16,321
Anderson, J. D.	11	0	0	2	1,995	Ares, Paul S.	2	0	1	0	1,636
Anderson, James E.	91	14	12	9	86,251	Arey, Anthony	1	0	0	0	255
Anderson, Jann P.	18	2	1	4	32,916	Argyle, Bert H.	12	0	0	0	1,456
Anderson, John E.	89	10	9	8	250,548	Aristone, Phillip T.	395	52	61	56	630,553
Anderson, Keith	20	1	2	3	7,199	Armata, Ross	174	24	19	18	893,805
Anderson, Kenneth Ellis	3	0	0	0	0	Armata, Vito	242	42	28	41	1,699,311
Anderson, Kenton	69	5	6	10	61,113	Armata, Jr., Ross	91	17	10	10	522,102
Anderson, Paul	33	2	5	6	18,171	Armor, Randy	5	0	0	0	0
Anderson, Perry W.	5	1	2	1	7,559	Armstrong, Barbara L.	31	0	0	4	8,686
Anderson, Pete D.	2	0	0	0	230	Armstrong, Bryan R.	139	16	16	19	110,887
Anderson, Rex C.	41	2	7	9	9,194	Armstrong, Busanda C.	17	5	4	2	45,608
Anderson, Robert J.	126	13	20	26	315,756	Armstrong, C. Robert	11	4	3	0	24,135
Anderson, Roger J.	139	9	14	5	123,541	Armstrong, Holly	6	1	4	0	12,300
Anderson, Rosann M.	7	0	3	0	9,769	Armstrong, Horace W.	46	2	7	4	48,820
Anderson, Susan L.	62	6	11	11	70,753	Armstrong, Jack J.	1	0	0	1	1,570
Anderson, Suzanne A.	26	0	3	6	26,756	Armstrong, Janet	24	5	4	4	70,785
Anderson, Tim L.	38	4	2	4	33,530	Armstrong, Johnny G.	6	0	0	1	766
Anderson, Vicki	18	5	3	2	9,697	Armstrong, Sharon	1	0	0	0	0
Anderson, Wendy	138	18	9	22	138,480	Armstrong, Sherry	5	0	2	1	7,516
Anderson, William D.	185	25	28	26	374,046	Armstrong, Tim H.	9	1	0	1	3,483
Anderson-Smith, Karen	18	0	2	1	7,893	Armstrong, Zachary	142	28	27	14	238,211
Andis, David L.	28	1	2	3	13,128	Arnaud, Gus O.	4	0	1	2	7,592
Andrade, Pablo	178	24	26	22	302,997	Arndt, Theodore	8	2	0	0	9,557
Andrade, Wayne	9	0	0	3	6,180	Arnett, Bob E.	171	24	18	24	275,541
Andreasen, Gillian	10	2	0	1	11,075	Arnett, Jon G.	407	75	70	59	776,172
Andrews, Tom	60	8	7	5	49,574	Arnold, Bart D.	11	0	1	0	3,110
Andros, Patricia	5	1	0	2	13,984	Arnold, John S.	30	1	2	1	11,926
Andrus, Susan	6	0	0	0	1,367	Arnold, Oscar	41	0	0	2	5,303
Andry, Doug	6	0	0	1	1,848	Arnold, Pamela A.	144	16	13	18	148,302
Ange, Cheryl E.	7	0	1	0	2,160	Arnold, Rise	11	0	0	1	3,310
Angelle, Christopher	88	6	6	6	79,038	Arnold, II, George R.	259	34	47	35	1,961,444
Angelle, Dale	380	73	79	49	950,202	Arnold, Jr., Ralph E.	101	14	13	10	96,845
Angelle, Grover J.	18	2	1	1	25,353	Arnold, Jr., Richard D.	118	11	12	16	193,677
Angelle, James R.	80	6	5	7	52,692	Arnold, Sr., George R.	30	4	6	8	38,026
Angelle, Joseph D.	180	16	19	15	127,203	Arnouville, James C.	2	0	0	0	1,680
Angelle, Keith J.	109	8	12	12	104,867	Aro, Charles	54	4	3	3	27,751
Angelle, Rene D.	19	2	0	3	27,035	Aro, Michael Charles	252	31	29	32	426,840
Angelopoulos, George K.	20	2	2	1	34,850	Arrigo, Dan W.	8	3	1	0	22,105
Angevine, Pamela J.	177	28	17	23	383,598	Arriola, Thomas	24	2	1	1	20,830
Anglin, L. D.	47	2	3	3	14,050	Arruda, Aaron D.	1	0	0	0	35
Anonychuk, Lawrence	3	0	1	0	2,395	Arterburn, Lonnie	107	16	16	18	266,051
Ansell, Laurie	8	1	2	1	4,240	Arthur, Floyd M.	149	30	25	34	485,644
Anson, Peggie	74	5	4	10	29,694	Arthur, Lyle	22	5	6	4	13,408
Anter, George	2	0	0	0	83	Artwohl, Shirley	2	0	0	0	443
Anthony, Priscilla J.	20	2	7	4	28,499	Artz, Deborrah J.	197	27	24	19	274,947
Anthony, Wilma	2	0	0	1	550	Arzola, Luis D.	131	13	13	8	111,507
Anthony, Sr., Alton	12	0	2	1	9,355	Asbury, David W.	204	29	24	21	233,010
Anton, William	195	12	23	25	164,934	Asbury, Lonnie	1	0	0	0	44
Antonucci, Peter G.	17	6	2	3	37,860	Ashabraner, Billy G.	74	9	7	8	125,424
Antoniuk, Jerry	18	3	3	0	33,412	Ashauer, Norman	47	2	3	5	24,367
Antrim, Arthur M.	26	7	2	1	122,284	Ashbaugh, Richard E.	26	1	0	1	11,468
Antus, Lawrence	42	3	6	2	62,264	Ashby, Charles	2	0	0	0	0
Antwine, Michael	19	1	1	4	13,464	Ashby, Lynn A.	13	1	1	4	29,320
Anuario, Thomas A.	27	5	6	4	125,140	Ashby, Lynnett A.	17	4	1	3	213,513

Trainer	Sts	1st	2d	3d	Purses	Trainer	Sts	1st	2d	3d	Purses
Asher, Kenneth E.	32	0	2	6	14,121	Bailey, Wayne M.	42	2	2	4	58,497
Asher, Paul	14	0	0	2	2,041	Bailey, Jr., David L.	8	0	1	3	3,955
Ashford, Jr., H. Ray	178	23	25	32	378,900	Baim, Greg	2	0	0	1	775
Ashlock, Zack	100	5	17	12	32,777	Bainum, Kelly	90	15	13	12	104,121
Ashor, Jacob	49	7	7	6	92,185	Bainum, Troy	127	44	22	20	261,843
Asmussen, Steven M.	1,949	452	352	301	11,725,782	Baird, Barbara A.	34	4	5	3	128,677
Assimakopoulos, Charles	185	32	26	23	499,190	Baird, Bart	152	7	8	9	112,206
Assimakopoulos, John	30	9	7	2	130,970	Baird, Dale	1,072	137	147	151	2,041,179
Assinesi, Paul D.	44	5	2	2	153,540	Baird, J. Michael	361	73	51	41	925,061
Assoon, Jennifer	23	3	3	4	25,105	Baird, John W.	383	53	49	40	844,800
Astling, Joseph F.	8	0	2	0	4,790	Baker, Bryan R.	79	5	0	9	52,835
Atala, Jose	72	16	8	11	115,525	Baker, Carl A.	22	2	4	1	20,145
Atencio, Bill	8	2	0	1	28,013	Baker, Charlton	293	79	47	38	778,301
Ater, Richard	28	1	2	5	10,033	Baker, D. Wayne	104	2	6	11	170,133
Ates, Cheramy	116	15	12	17	118,095	Baker, David F.	79	7	10	8	48,166
Ates, James	1	0	0	0	570	Baker, Dennis	5	1	1	0	3,380
Atkin, Jerry	297	46	43	38	231,126	Baker, Harold	16	1	2	1	3,162
Atkins, Michael G.	85	6	6	7	83,444	Baker, James E.	96	12	11	12	509,656
Atkinson, Gracie	15	0	1	1	5,485	Baker, James T.	13	1	0	1	7,064
Atkinson, James	1	0	0	0	95	Baker, Jeff	18	1	0	0	4,224
Atkinson, Leonard L.	21	3	5	3	35,989	Baker, Jerry R.	5	0	0	0	318
Attanasio, Robert T.	18	0	1	2	14,169	Baker, Ken	65	4	2	7	24,359
Attard, Kevin	84	14	7	12	453,451	Baker, Reade	191	48	34	28	2,687,183
Attard, Paul	87	11	12	10	363,761	Baker, Terri M.	12	1	2	1	5,292
Attard, Sid C.	278	54	45	26	2,894,519	Baker, Jr., Ceburn L.	10	0	0	0	360
Attard, Steve	147	20	28	13	867,768	Balcewicz, David M.	1	1	0	0	1,525
Attard, Tino	171	13	13	15	655,705	Balcom, Cliff	51	10	3	5	100,967
Attfield, Roger L.	330	32	44	50	2,993,896	Balcom, Sharon	72	11	15	10	36,079
Aubrey, J. Kevin	23	1	1	6	13,616	Balderas, Alfonso	94	6	6	8	60,684
Auger, Raymond J.	29	4	4	2	21,110	Balderas, Damon	48	5	0	2	39,348
Austin, Charles	3	0	0	0	760	Balding, Andrew	2	1	0	1	950,000
Auten, Vern E.	6	3	1	2	5,467	Baldwin, Alexander D.	15	0	3	2	8,846
Autrey, Cody	66	9	12	7	110,050	Baldwin, Douglas W.	12	0	0	1	3,517
Auwarter, Edward K.	104	7	7	12	117,974	Baldwin, James	57	10	12	7	78,885
Avalon, Jr., William A.	4	1	1	0	9,603	Baldwin, Lynette	3	0	1	1	2,562
Averett, Jr., Gerald	36	1	2	7	29,730	Baldwin, Patrick J.	4	0	0	0	348
Aversa, Albert P.	6	0	0	0	186	Balker, Edward G.	5	0	0	0	840
Avery, James T.	2	0	0	0	0	Ball, Brad	9	4	2	0	3,229
Avila, A. C.	143	19	14	14	462,095	Ball, Darla M.	61	1	2	5	21,171
Axmaker, Peter	193	21	20	21	133,646	Ball, Donald R.	32	2	5	1	28,615
Aylor, Jr., William L.	152	17	14	18	182,753	Ball, Glen	9	0	1	0	2,476
Aylor, Sr., William L.	14	0	0	2	3,590	Ball, Jerry	13	1	0	1	1,784
Ayres, Jr., Joseph W.	14	0	1	2	12,275	Ball, Katherine G.	30	2	5	3	97,321
Ayres, Sr., Joseph W.	64	2	3	10	40,635	Ballard, Frank	7	0	4	0	5,710
Azpurua, Manuel J.	229	25	19	32	921,348	Ballhagen, LaVerne J.	50	9	9	5	62,119
Azpurua, Jr., Eduardo	29	1	2	2	18,856	Ballou, Lloyd H.	6	1	0	0	7,335
Azpurua, Jr., Leo J.	32	1	5	2	39,950	Balmer, Bruce B.	15	1	1	0	11,996
Baare, John	11	0	0	0	894	Balo, Jerry L.	128	24	23	12	192,277
Babbington, Grace A.	10	0	0	0	1,120	Balsamo, Diane	56	3	4	7	149,162
Babbitt, Clifford	37	10	5	4	20,514	Baltas, Richard	14	4	2	0	41,565
Babcock, Edward J.	180	11	19	23	113,652	Balthazar, Jr., Andrew	73	4	2	6	52,356
Babin, Jed	13	2	2	1	15,382	Balut, Irene	16	1	1	5	17,346
Babineaux, Theo	24	1	3	6	25,889	Banach, Darwin D.	14	2	2	0	51,828
Baboolal, John H.	17	1	1	3	15,314	Bandel, Delmer W.	32	0	0	1	4,211
Bachman, George T.	5	0	0	0	510	Bandle, Thomasine L.	5	1	0	0	4,797
Bachmann, Charles A.	1	0	1	0	1,260	Banford, Sharon	36	4	5	5	39,288
Back, Richard	1	0	0	0	100	Bango, George A.	70	10	13	14	79,723
Backer, Jesse L.	21	1	1	3	11,640	Banks, David P.	113	14	18	12	300,247
Backhaus, Levi	6	0	0	0	290	Bankson, Gay	3	0	2	1	6,000
Backman, Larry	1	0	0	0	675	Bankston, Earl	41	5	4	8	51,246
Bacorn, Herbert L.	45	3	10	4	195,905	Bankuti, Alex	69	11	13	8	351,721
Baddeley, Charles W.	81	11	9	10	97,194	Banyots, Roger J.	12	0	0	0	1,870
Bader, Mark S.	91	11	8	14	304,970	Barana, Leo	18	1	3	3	12,996
Badgett, Jr., William	133	22	17	13	612,493	Barba, Alexis	32	2	5	5	75,428
Badilla, Sr., Jose G.	14	2	1	1	5,183	Barba, Robert	201	29	16	24	1,239,853
Baffert, Bob	674	127	119	80	9,442,281	Barbaran, Horacio	18	2	2	0	14,411
Bagby, Calvin E.	5	0	1	0	1,835	Barbarin, Laurent	1	0	0	0	94
Bagnell, Dale	40	7	7	8	25,252	Barbazon, Jr., Lester J.	3	0	0	0	480
Bailes, W. Robert	210	23	28	30	442,613	Barber, Donald C.	129	13	20	10	247,094
Bailey, Charles E.	43	0	5	4	24,883	Barber, James R.	32	1	1	4	27,334
Bailey, Clifford	15	1	0	0	5,070	Barber, Michael K.	143	19	23	16	222,337
Bailey, Gurvin	3	0	0	0	0	Barber, Stanley L.	21	3	1	3	26,116
Bailey, Hugh	4	0	0	0	60	Bard, G. Leon	31	2	3	2	31,553
Bailey, Isaac Leonard	50	3	7	8	69,915	Bardin, Arnold R.	107	7	7	3	59,743
Bailey, Kelly Lynn	63	10	12	9	196,375	Baresich, Stanley	41	4	3	8	182,234
Bailey, Robert H.	19	1	0	2	11,072	Barger, Charles	2	0	0	0	132

Trainer	Sts	1st	2d	3d	Purses	Trainer	Sts	1st	2d	3d	Purses
Barger, John D.	81	7	4	7	74,309	Bazdor, Joseph F.	20	3	1	1	13,839
Barker, Charles D	29	2	0	1	8,862	Baze, Robert	192	26	18	26	159,235
Barker, Edward R.	102	13	7	9	348,820	Bazeos, Peter	223	28	32	27	546,673
Barker, James R.	125	22	13	16	185,471	Bazley, Tom	12	2	3	2	12,274
Barkley, Jeff	23	5	3	2	82,463	Bazurto, Ramon B.	41	3	8	5	21,318
Barnard, R. Kenneth	12	0	0	1	9,544	Beaber, Jeri A.	107	7	9	16	79,227
Barndollar, Sheilagh	70	7	3	5	72,477	Beach, Anthony E.	53	8	8	8	110,206
Barnes, Bart A.	10	2	0	0	19,210	Beach, Betty J.	17	1	1	2	4,798
Barnes, Bill	1	1	0	0	3,120	Beach, Donnie	1	0	0	0	450
Barnes, Carnie	3	0	0	0	0	Beach, George	2	0	0	0	550
Barnes, Edward C.	3	1	0	0	7,380	Beach, Randall R.	17	0	3	0	2,859
Barnes, James A.	32	9	6	4	87,331	Beach, Richard D.	23	0	2	2	8,573
Barnes, Robert	28	2	2	4	7,611	Beach-Orr, Joanie	5	0	0	0	225
Barnes, S. William	4	1	0	0	5,892	Beagle, Barbara	10	0	0	0	2,559
Barnes, Tommy	1	0	0	0	120	Beakley, Daryl L.	92	15	8	6	144,165
Barnett, Bobby C.	350	45	36	36	1,143,246	Beall, Jr., John M.	23	6	2	1	49,228
Barnett, Robert Earl	82	4	8	9	343,402	Beam, Edward	31	2	1	7	64,804
Barney, Edward H.	41	1	0	9	31,707	Beamer, Bill	174	26	30	26	234,906
Barney, Jessie	5	0	1	1	2,987	Bean, Robert A.	67	4	5	6	90,052
Barnhart, William D.	17	1	3	2	13,462	Bearden, Wayne	55	7	10	8	62,239
Barnhill, J. Carroll	4	0	0	0	266	Beasley, Rebecca	38	2	2	3	35,976
Barnwell, Jerry	43	1	2	1	12,071	Beaton, Doug	2	0	0	0	300
Barocio, Librado	18	1	2	4	40,165	Beattie, Dennis M.	32	1	0	1	6,196
Barr, Bob	54	10	9	12	28,478	Beattie, Stephanie S.	113	20	22	14	234,566
Barr, Donald H.	98	18	13	9	346,596	Beattie, Thomas G.	78	13	11	6	113,488
Barr, George N.	3	0	0	2	6,480	Beattie, Todd M.	318	78	61	39	954,343
Barreira, Antone	6	0	0	0	210	Beaudoin, Thomas M.	3	0	0	1	2,104
Barrera, Emilio L.	27	4	2	4	28,845	Beaulieu, Norbert	11	1	2	5	2,158
Barrera, Guillermo S.	1	0	0	0	0	Beavers, Donald	33	5	3	3	20,853
Barrera, Larry S.	41	4	6	6	280,755	Becerra, Rafael	235	48	41	33	1,897,983
Barrera, Jr., Oscar S.	293	57	45	32	494,451	Becht, Elizabeth	65	2	7	6	41,895
Barrett, Eli E.	10	0	1	1	4,086	Beck, Edward L.	1	0	0	1	2,690
Barrier, Marguerite V.	38	0	4	2	16,542	Beck, Michael T.	13	1	1	2	12,335
Barrio, Sergio	40	8	5	7	29,968	Becker, Brian S.	1	0	0	0	0
Barroby, Frank E.	129	14	29	16	279,496	Becker, Nadine A.	217	19	20	19	246,770
Barroby, Harold J.	276	29	47	43	602,569	Becker, Wayne	11	0	0	2	4,500
Barron, Douglas R.	170	7	13	10	76,924	Beckner, Robert	129	16	18	17	42,274
Barron, Mary Anne	93	16	9	5	108,856	Bedard, Alan	95	9	17	6	203,353
Barrow, Harold	3	0	0	0	0	Beddo, Howard L.	9	0	1	2	14,465
Barrow, Paul W.	209	38	27	30	241,584	Bedford, Janet	32	4	2	6	232,424
Barrow, Thomas	12	0	2	2	7,680	Bedinotti, Peter	2	1	1	0	13,000
Barry, James	9	1	1	0	8,460	Bedrin, Tatiana	11	0	1	0	4,006
Barry, Thomas	29	0	0	0	2,783	Beebe, Crescent	25	5	2	4	23,857
Bartels, Werner J.	11	3	0	0	28,022	Beech, George S.	98	7	7	9	95,466
Barth, Charles J.	46	2	5	4	21,703	Beekman, Jon	46	3	1	8	13,174
Bartlett, Desiree	1	0	0	0	0	Begley, Melissa	3	0	0	1	3,710
Bartlett, William H.	115	7	7	18	69,595	Begley, Jr., Earl P.	176	32	21	22	442,345
Bartol, Tom W.	52	5	8	7	36,140	Begnaud, Charles	260	26	32	40	254,125
Barton, Dallas J.	21	3	5	2	45,874	Begnaud, Louis	65	6	8	4	49,794
Barton, Glenn A.	32	1	2	1	17,463	Behler, Frank	8	1	0	2	22,493
Bartoni, Wayne P.	1	0	1	0	1,380	Behling, Jason	24	0	1	3	5,857
Bartram, M. Bradley	1	0	0	0	35	Behrens, Ronald P.	200	14	29	23	189,442
Bartscher, Henry	1	0	0	0	0	Behrle, Bruce D.	27	2	3	2	15,994
Bartscher, Tony	37	2	1	4	8,902	Beidel, Aaron C.	18	1	0	1	6,963
Bary, Pascal F.	2	1	0	0	780,000	Belaire, Conrad A.	12	0	1	2	8,777
Basham, J. Ryan	21	0	4	1	4,114	Belden, Tiffany	70	4	12	10	47,430
Bass, Fred	9	2	0	1	6,765	Belgarde, Stuart	5	0	1	0	790
Bass, Randy	63	5	8	8	35,272	Belgarde, Wanda	1	0	0	1	336
Bass, Tomi E.	36	1	0	0	10,905	Belknap, David M.	23	1	3	3	13,530
Bast, Jr., Gerald D.	173	26	22	10	383,548	Bell, Charles R.	48	3	3	2	20,630
Bastida, Ladeana	47	6	8	4	63,888	Bell, David R.	298	38	36	46	2,358,956
Bastin, Mike	3	0	0	0	0	Bell, Donovan K.	13	1	1	3	15,924
Bates, C. Louis	38	7	5	6	85,111	Bell, Graham G.	2	0	0	0	590
Bates, Charles	11	0	0	0	948	Bell, Janet E.	3	1	0	0	4,960
Bates, Larry	180	12	13	21	191,014	Bell, Ken	40	5	1	4	32,417
Bathon, Scott L.	9	0	1	3	5,789	Bell, Lloyd	6	0	1	0	512
Battaglia, Anthony J.	17	1	0	5	7,795	Bell, Michael H.	15	2	0	2	75,208
Battaglini, Vicky	7	0	0	0	1,955	Bell, Wayne L.	15	2	2	4	3,737
Bauer, Diane E.	1	0	0	0	0	Bell, II, Thomas Ray	68	6	14	9	378,764
Bauer, Erich	52	7	4	4	286,932	Bell, IV, John A.	117	14	11	14	251,339
Bauerelen, Charlie	24	1	1	1	4,126	Belland, Ronald W.	18	1	4	4	10,254
Baumgartner, Maryanne	7	0	0	3	3,173	Bellard, Jerome G.	36	0	1	1	7,122
Bausch, Jim	341	28	36	36	282,171	Bellard, Larry	14	0	2	3	7,281
Bay, Betty	4	0	0	0	192	Bellard, Ronald	28	2	0	3	18,999
Bayley, Perry H.	95	12	8	20	85,952	Bellard, Ronald	54	6	5	8	56,482
Bayley, Randy	6	1	2	1	12,857	Bellasis, R. P.	6	0	0	0	0

Trainer	Sts	1st	2d	3d	Purses	Trainer	Sts	1st	2d	3d	Purses
Bellasis, Richard L.	1	1	0	0	2,200	Betancourt, Frank	5	0	0	1	4,650
Bellasis, Tim	184	9	13	25	146,594	Betancourt, Jr., Eli	110	4	16	15	118,883
Bellini, Gilberto	22	0	1	3	9,777	Bethke, Troy A.	92	6	9	10	67,296
Bellos, Tom	8	1	0	0	3,065	Bethke, William H.	61	4	3	10	43,396
Bellucci, Bruno M.	380	39	50	51	284,676	Bettis, Charles L.	168	25	28	22	619,230
Bellucci, Patricia D.	1	0	0	0	146	Betts, John V.	94	11	9	16	199,454
Belmonte, Rocco J.	2	0	0	0	0	Betts, Nancy	16	3	2	6	29,637
Belsoeur, Yvon	7	0	0	0	612	Bevelacqua, Leo J.	18	0	0	1	1,747
Beltran, Jesus G.	7	0	0	0	313	Biamonte, Ralph J.	162	42	27	22	1,142,839
Belvoir, Howard	406	46	71	61	590,530	Biancone, Patrick L.	135	26	15	21	1,711,726
Belvoir, Vann	152	17	25	23	168,494	Biddle, Glen	25	3	1	3	11,889
Bemiss, James H.	32	2	3	5	43,135	Bidleman, Darin L.	1	0	0	0	110
Bencivenga, Anthony J.	69	5	3	6	58,621	Biehler, Michael E.	176	34	21	22	514,485
Bends, James P.	36	4	1	5	21,976	Bienvenu, Russell	1	0	0	0	0
Bendzunas, Joseph	6	0	0	0	493	Big Hair, Gerald P.	1	0	0	1	554
Benjamin, Kelly	39	6	6	1	31,201	Bigelow, Carl E.	38	7	3	2	91,395
Benko, Ronald V.	30	0	1	1	11,116	Bigelow, Clayton	2	0	0	0	0
Bennett, Adele M.	23	1	1	1	6,563	Bignault, W. Paschal	73	7	10	9	124,225
Bennett, Dale	97	12	12	16	234,095	Billers, George	7	1	2	0	28,936
Bennett, David	235	22	24	36	190,668	Billingsly, Max L.	1	0	0	0	100
Bennett, Donald W.	2	0	0	0	50	bin Suroor, Saeed	16	2	4	5	1,290,330
Bennett, Gerald S.	551	103	98	68	1,350,507	Bindner, Chris	2	0	0	0	163
Bennett, Jerry T.	11	1	3	0	20,714	Bindner, Jr., Walter M.	120	16	28	12	826,546
Bennett, Keith	142	38	23	19	314,493	Bingham, Patrick	21	1	0	5	11,733
Bennett, Marvin	35	6	3	5	60,019	Bingham, Wesley A.	5	0	0	0	270
Bennett, Melinda A.	3	0	0	0	160	Binning, Michael J.	47	3	3	6	17,480
Bennett, Michael D.	6	0	0	0	696	Bir, Barbara J.	18	1	1	1	15,270
Bennett, Seymour	21	2	4	3	67,553	Bir, Robert A.	1	0	0	0	546
Bennett, William D.	3	0	1	0	2,878	Birch, Charles G.	49	3	5	8	18,843
Bensmiller, Twylla	18	3	0	1	24,583	Birch, David A.	9	0	1	1	10,200
Benson, David C.	29	3	3	1	15,973	Bird, Alan F.	25	4	5	4	63,211
Benson, Harry	98	26	13	11	716,257	Bird, Danny R.	252	22	33	30	201,582
Benson, Macdonald	120	13	19	9	1,156,115	Bird, Dennis	14	2	3	4	4,634
Bentler, Don	95	4	10	16	53,205	Bird, Richard J.	98	3	12	8	63,296
Bentley, Jack D.	28	0	5	3	11,381	Birdow, Oscar	3	0	0	0	132
Bentley, Thomas	1	0	0	0	132	Birdrattler, Evelyn	13	2	0	1	2,816
Benton, James C.	29	3	6	4	28,857	Birdrattler, Harlan	3	1	0	1	1,678
Benton, Raymond P.	13	0	1	2	22,258	Birdrattler, Joe	2	0	0	0	0
Benyak, David V.	8	0	0	0	1,529	Birdrattler, Shawn	4	0	1	2	625
Bera, Joseph	104	8	12	10	80,521	Bireta, Donna	133	22	20	17	332,488
Berdejo, Victor	25	0	2	5	8,549	Birtch, Daniel R.	11	0	0	1	2,771
Berg, Harvey Lowell	100	5	2	5	68,788	Bischoff, Eulia R.	131	14	21	17	66,807
Berg, Lorne E.	14	3	1	2	25,684	Bischoff, Thomas E.	44	6	8	3	63,710
Berg, Roger	9	1	0	0	3,347	Bish, Walter F.	48	1	5	5	28,420
Bergeron, John	1	0	0	0	0	Bishop, Findley G.	6	0	1	1	8,800
Bergeson, Clair	6	3	0	1	4,387	Bishop, Jimmy R.	6	0	0	0	195
Bergin, Tom	42	4	3	8	67,976	Bishop, Norman	22	0	0	1	3,342
Bergstrom, Mary Julianne	4	0	0	0	1,432	Biszantz, Ralph V.	11	1	0	3	37,050
Berkeley, Christine	55	1	2	7	27,161	Bjarnarson, Don	42	16	6	7	37,154
Berkelhammer, Barry	18	3	4	2	46,292	Black, Burl	3	0	0	0	844
Berkram, Mel	88	20	13	19	60,283	Black, Casey	7	0	1	0	1,960
Bernardini, Jay P.	147	17	18	21	244,468	Black, Donald G.	30	6	4	2	14,839
Berndt, Joel	144	15	23	16	327,372	Black, Joanne	2	0	0	0	0
Bernhart, Walter J.	52	2	2	3	25,003	Black, Mary Ann	34	1	1	2	5,444
Bernis, Glynn	262	27	29	26	427,008	Black, Maurice	9	0	1	0	1,490
Bernis, Kenward	166	12	16	26	104,007	Black, Ralph D.	14	2	1	3	15,740
Bernis, Tammy	1	0	0	0	126	Black, Jr., Ralph W.	195	21	21	16	244,125
Berns, Terry	13	1	0	0	7,700	Blackburn, Joseph Eugene	5	0	0	0	504
Bernstein, David	37	4	6	5	255,726	Blackburn, Joseph L.	1	0	0	0	119
Berntson, Brian	6	0	0	1	580	Blackwood, Jim	15	1	4	0	11,830
Berrett, Robert W.	39	4	3	2	24,332	Blain, Earl	37	2	4	1	16,885
Berringer, Peter	45	2	6	6	233,029	Blair, Greg	1	0	0	0	0
Berrios, Manuel	160	5	9	19	212,609	Blake, Albert Edward	17	5	1	0	53,551
Berry, David	3	0	0	0	177	Blake, Arlene	98	11	6	13	75,584
Berry, James F.	11	1	1	2	14,035	Blanchard, Abel J.	99	9	7	11	77,435
Berry, Michael J.	2	0	0	0	230	Blanchard, Harold E.	34	1	1	3	6,543
Berry, Rick	9	1	0	2	46,595	Blanchard, Patrick A.	11	0	0	0	441
Berry, Tom	12	2	1	2	6,477	Blanchard, Recaldo	1	0	0	0	83
Berry, William C.	38	4	3	3	56,570	Bland, Roy	32	3	1	3	11,364
Berry, Jr., William J.	41	1	1	2	9,346	Blankenship, Deborah K.	17	0	0	1	2,601
Berry, Jr., William S.	78	12	4	10	115,012	Blankenship, Donald E.	84	5	4	15	80,444
Berry, Sr., William R.	118	9	9	13	141,214	Blankenship, Hubert	42	3	5	7	12,108
Berryman, Michael	26	1	1	2	20,820	Blasi, Joel E.	35	5	4	4	43,041
Berthold, George C.	40	4	3	8	54,045	Blatchford, George	28	4	2	3	18,967
Bertrand, Jr., James Dale	3	1	0	1	3,727	Blatt, Barbara	28	1	2	1	7,411
Bertschy, Randy L.	26	2	0	3	6,335	Blaze, Arturo	19	0	0	3	10,212

Trainer	Sts	1st	2d	3d	Purses
Blea, III, Tony	1	0	0	0	166
Blea, Jr., Tony R.	11	0	0	1	4,135
Bleak, Travis D.	2	1	1	0	880
Blend, Zachary	9	0	0	2	8,020
Blengs, Vincent L.	185	26	19	19	629,401
Blevins, Billy C.	5	0	0	1	2,085
Blincoe, Thomas H.	48	4	5	8	138,793
Bliss, Darlene	15	1	2	2	3,820
Bliss, Richard Dean	67	3	8	4	19,180
Block, Chris M.	259	50	35	31	1,407,832
Blood, Susan	25	0	3	2	7,514
Bloomquist, Charles E.	2	0	0	0	150
Blouin, Marc A.	9	1	0	2	28,185
Bloy, Thomas H.	1	0	0	1	1,019
Blue, Don	32	5	6	7	14,498
Blue, Wayne	116	4	8	7	26,395
Blue, Jr., Harvey	11	1	2	0	6,020
Blume, Hans	2	0	0	0	0
Boak, Ingrid I.	18	0	0	0	2,093
Bobadilla, Jose F.	222	30	30	28	254,217
Bobier, Bob	24	0	1	1	2,123
Bodie, Dennis	30	2	8	3	11,886
Bodner, Deborah S.	91	5	3	8	145,756
Boe, Mark	5	0	0	0	612
Boegner, John	11	1	0	1	9,783
Boehm, Jim	80	10	14	9	95,506
Boehm, Walter	9	1	1	4	8,919
Bogart, Robert B.	27	1	0	1	6,604
Boggess, Lawrence E.	35	0	1	2	5,054
Boggs, Joanna	17	1	3	4	21,180
Bogue, David	7	0	1	0	8,588
Bogue, Jeff	7	0	0	0	1,074
Bogue, Mike	6	1	1	2	12,611
Bohl, Bradley	18	0	1	4	19,200
Bohlander, Steven	6	1	0	2	11,510
Bohner, Verle	2	0	0	0	0
Boillard, John A.	28	0	3	3	6,964
Bolden, William	3	0	0	0	318
Bolen, Bradley C.	27	2	2	0	23,998
Boles, Jennifer	4	0	0	1	669
Bolinger, Michael R.	26	1	1	2	14,280
Bolinger, Nancy	3	1	0	1	3,280
Bomback, Bob	7	0	0	0	630
Bona, Steven A.	5	0	1	1	1,718
Bonaventura, Paul	44	2	9	6	60,780
Bond, H. James	196	46	20	16	1,932,521
Bonde, Jeff	358	63	60	49	1,831,339
Bone, Curtis	2	0	0	0	136
Bone, Robert H.	58	3	8	8	31,205
Boniface, J. William	1	0	0	0	0
Boniface, Kevin C.	181	29	28	32	515,635
Boniface, Kim	25	0	2	3	33,401
Boniface, Jr., John W.	51	5	5	3	66,611
Bonilla, Raymond	112	3	14	15	103,803
Bonn, Craig	11	2	3	2	6,582
Bonn, Randy	4	2	1	0	3,920
Bonnett, Gerald	3	0	0	2	1,979
Bonno, Clyde	4	1	0	0	10,835
Booker, John A.	73	4	8	8	93,579
Bookman, Billy	1	0	0	0	0
Bookman, Clark A.	72	7	6	4	43,351
Boone, Earnest J.	10	3	2	2	41,600
Boone, Marion	1	1	0	0	1,500
Bordner, Benjamin E.	13	0	2	1	6,495
Bordonaro, John A.	33	1	2	8	24,369
Borel, Cecil P.	44	8	8	3	120,585
Boreland, Devon	3	0	0	0	2,477
Boreman, Roger D.	21	0	0	2	4,034
Borg, Joseph A.	23	1	3	4	26,588
Borges, Israel	6	0	0	0	144
Borhaven, Roger	5	1	1	2	2,225
Boris, Robert P.	107	3	5	11	34,163
Borosh, Allen	1	0	0	0	130
Borsk, David	25	2	2	10	104,364
Bosarge, Ronald	105	2	9	15	42,971
Bosley, Arthur M.	40	5	6	7	42,252

Trainer	Sts	1st	2d	3d	Purses
Bosley, John M.	9	0	2	1	13,700
Bosley, Patricia L.	113	15	9	16	178,658
Bosley, Paul V.	39	3	2	3	30,152
Bosma, Dawn M.	1	0	0	0	90
Bostock, Ken	3	0	0	1	260
Botello, Carlos	18	2	1	1	11,291
Botello, John	8	0	0	0	753
Botkins, Dan	64	4	10	8	64,447
Bott, Sharon	32	6	0	4	82,894
Bottazzi, Patrick L.	13	5	1	4	88,090
Botty, John T.	79	9	15	9	143,918
Bouchard, Leslye G.	68	4	2	6	38,260
Boucher, Lilith E.	41	2	4	2	42,453
Bouk, Terry A.	20	1	0	2	5,135
Boulet, Joey	1	0	0	0	0
Boulmetis, Tanya	76	6	10	10	120,490
Bourgeois, Keith L.	774	144	120	118	1,783,385
Bourke, W. John	140	19	18	19	316,062
Bourne, Elige	81	10	8	14	78,646
Bourne, Leonard	5	1	1	0	3,268
Bourne, Lori J.	186	12	24	22	241,370
Bourne, William T.	1	0	0	0	0
Bourque, Charles	14	1	0	0	7,328
Bourque, Kevin	2	0	0	0	390
Bourque, Ricky	46	7	11	4	59,637
Bourque, Scotty	72	4	4	9	79,594
Bourque, Wilbert	5	0	1	0	2,213
Bouslaugh, Connie	40	9	6	7	65,514
Boutte, Thomas	20	1	0	1	8,815
Bowden, Thomas R.	24	2	2	3	79,436
Bowers, Janet L.	36	4	2	7	115,218
Bowers, John K.	15	1	2	0	22,343
Bowers, Ray	4	0	1	1	3,780
Bowers, Robert	1	0	0	0	0
Bowersock, Gary	12	0	0	1	2,854
Bowles, Norman W.	65	5	1	5	102,988
Bowman, Carl	93	15	19	16	331,573
Bowman, Carl E.	18	0	1	0	2,025
Bowman, Elex D.	26	1	1	0	14,101
Bowman, Gregory H.	13	2	0	2	24,948
Bowman, Lavern A.	67	7	13	14	87,823
Bowman, Robert	56	13	12	3	79,787
Bowman, William	1	0	0	0	0
Box, Charles A.	1	0	0	0	0
Boxie, Jonathan	19	0	0	2	7,653
Boxie, Joseph Stanley	32	2	2	2	17,431
Boxie, Jr., Joseph Herman	1	0	0	0	0
Boyarsky, S. David	13	0	1	1	3,676
Boyce, Brian L.	4	0	0	1	1,780
Boyce, Joseph S.	16	1	1	0	16,109
Boyce, Michele	191	37	25	15	951,314
Boyd, Preston	12	4	2	3	10,322
Boyd, Renee M.	13	0	4	2	11,728
Boyd, Terry L.	70	14	14	7	168,216
Boyd, William R.	3	0	0	1	3,108
Boyer, Darryl L.	117	9	6	16	122,526
Boyer, Leroy W.	9	1	1	0	13,545
Boyer, Michael	37	3	3	9	18,222
Boyer, Timothy D.	2	0	0	0	0
Boyer, V. Brooke	14	0	0	2	3,350
Boyett, Bobby C.	14	0	0	3	2,623
Boyle, Jon	5	0	0	0	214
Bozell, Alan	64	8	3	7	44,811
Bozzo, Jerry	87	11	12	11	157,429
Bracciale, Jr., Vincent A.	18	3	0	0	43,884
Bracey, John	49	3	1	3	48,773
Bracken, James E.	89	18	10	13	297,835
Brackenrich, Monica	17	1	0	1	6,287
Brackett, Shawn D.	1	0	0	0	120
Braddy, J. David	270	43	40	41	737,465
Braden, Derral	26	2	1	1	4,082
Braden, Patty J.	13	2	1	2	8,933
Bradford, Carolyn	5	0	0	0	600
Bradford, Joyce	9	2	0	1	6,246
Bradish, Raymond A.	10	3	0	1	13,533
Bradley, William	185	16	18	17	434,614

Trainer	Sts	1st	2d	3d	Purses
Bradshaw, Gregg A.	52	2	3	4	12,344
Bradshaw, Linda	40	1	6	5	48,396
Bradvica, Louis A.	39	3	1	6	54,365
Brady, Amy	6	2	0	1	2,744
Brady, Brenda	40	6	9	2	131,800
Bragg, Patricia A.	73	15	7	11	60,392
Bragg, Willard J.	10	0	1	0	1,705
Brajczewski, Jr., Eugene F.	70	11	9	6	390,826
Bramante, Bernard	72	2	5	8	26,739
Bramble, Clyde D.	181	13	14	26	168,068
Branch, Teresa Gail	70	4	5	17	80,194
Brand, Elizabeth	11	1	0	2	5,195
Brandenburg, Ron L.	228	31	27	30	296,487
Brandenburg, Stephen	6	0	0	0	512
Brandt, Fred	7	0	0	0	1,831
Branger, David J.	6	0	1	3	3,320
Branton, Anita	15	2	2	1	4,854
Branton, Bill	7	1	3	0	3,220
Brashear, Jr., Earl	56	3	2	4	20,414
Brashears, Bill	298	55	48	48	305,084
Brasher, Harry L.	15	1	2	1	5,335
Brasher, Wayne	67	6	3	5	20,837
Brasseaux, John	22	1	1	4	6,232
Bratcher, Jason	9	0	0	0	1,436
Brathwaite, Richard	11	3	0	0	113,370
Bratton, Charles	22	2	5	3	6,594
Bratton, Clinton S.	20	2	1	3	30,660
Brau, Albert W.	7	0	1	0	1,741
Bravenec, Darrell W.	26	1	1	3	18,890
Bravo, Francisco	158	17	17	9	208,613
Bravo, George	2	0	0	0	0
Bray, Harold L.	5	1	0	0	4,125
Bray, Simon	84	7	8	10	330,974
Breaux, Samuel	382	68	48	50	982,876
Brecheisen, Dale	3	0	1	1	3,621
Brecheisen, Dale Lynn	79	5	2	5	25,985
Breckenridge, Kris	54	5	8	4	39,249
Breed, Debra A.	117	15	9	14	103,422
Breeden, Ernest L.	21	0	2	1	4,080
Breen, Kelly John	81	13	13	12	339,476
Brehm, Joel D.	2	2	0	0	12,600
Brehm, Kenneth L.	17	0	1	3	2,020
Bremer, Dean	31	6	8	1	17,995
Bremner, Brent	5	3	0	0	35,260
Bremner, Kathy	16	1	1	2	11,446
Brenchley, Alexandra	15	1	3	0	10,807
Brendemuehl, Danzel	11	1	1	2	6,643
Brenden, Jeanette	37	1	3	6	10,265
Brennan, Brian E.	34	2	8	2	77,920
Brennan, Niall J	9	2	0	1	66,328
Brennan, Rosalind	1	0	0	0	0
Brennan, Terry J.	98	16	14	8	172,245
Brennan, William	27	3	1	4	44,181
Breshears, Floyd Don	1	0	0	0	75
Breslin, Debi	8	0	0	0	580
Bretthorst, William F.	57	1	6	7	52,318
Brettin, Scott	3	0	0	1	956
Breuer, Denise E.	20	2	4	2	50,440
Brewer, James R.	8	0	2	2	6,720
Brewer, Jimmy L.	6	2	1	0	9,886
Brewster, Larry Joseph	33	3	1	6	29,599
Brian, E. Dean	7	0	0	2	494
Brice, Michael	145	14	21	28	557,988
Brida, Juliane	23	1	5	6	99,500
Bridge, Donald L.	54	2	4	8	15,975
Brigden, Ross	3	0	1	0	650
Brigden, W. R.	26	5	4	3	17,338
Briggs, Asa	63	5	6	6	41,926
Briggs, Don	8	0	0	0	1,407
Briggs, William E.	16	2	4	4	4,085
Briley, Lonnie	107	10	13	12	215,800
Briley, Ronald	1	0	0	0	0
Brinegar, Tanya P.	29	0	0	2	4,859
Bringhurst, J. Owen	22	3	4	2	31,507
Brinkerhoff, Dan B.	10	0	2	2	9,500
Brinkerhoff, Jere	5	0	1	2	981
Brinkley, Franklin	65	3	5	5	46,484
Brinkley, Melvin	40	8	2	6	43,423
Brinkman, Brett	8	0	2	1	8,177
Brinsfield, Brooken	108	10	8	4	95,993
Brinsfield, Farley	4	0	0	0	0
Brinson, Clay	68	10	11	10	60,512
Brito, Manuel J.	29	0	2	4	7,964
Brittingham, E. Earl	23	1	2	3	13,138
Brittle, III, Clay T.	10	0	0	2	4,470
Brittle, Jr., Clay T.	40	3	4	5	92,694
Britton, Irene	59	2	14	7	12,199
Brobst, Floyd D.	24	1	5	2	8,585
Brock, Jim N.	15	0	4	0	11,260
Brock, Kenneth	94	7	8	9	39,235
Brock, Randy	55	2	1	2	8,680
Brocka, Laurence	26	2	0	2	16,694
Brockert, Ron	9	0	0	0	225
Broers, John E.	15	1	1	1	13,895
Bronson, P.	1	0	0	0	60
Bronson, Ron	9	1	1	1	1,770
Bronson, Vern	5	2	1	1	3,340
Bronson, Virgil	4	0	1	0	660
Brook, Joseph	35	5	6	5	60,335
Brooke, Crystal	20	1	0	2	3,772
Brooker, Terry W.	10	1	1	0	17,224
Brookfield, James	31	5	3	4	69,946
Brookfield, Ward	1	0	0	0	0
Brooks, Christine	12	0	2	1	6,940
Brooks, Clifton D.	29	6	3	6	15,291
Brooks, Gerald E.	8	1	0	2	5,082
Brooks, Jim Dale	71	6	8	8	23,637
Brooks, Lanny G.	69	1	3	5	22,510
Brooks, Rex Dean	9	0	2	0	3,234
Brooks, Ronald R.	4	0	0	0	169
Broome, Edwin Thomas	200	37	34	36	888,510
Broomfield, Ian	27	2	4	3	64,966
Brophy, George E.	34	0	0	2	1,798
Brothers, Frank L.	167	22	33	19	725,550
Broussard, C. J.	14	1	2	2	11,641
Broussard, Joseph E.	153	20	18	20	593,301
Broussard, Kelly	43	8	6	7	131,658
Broussard, Kevin	5	0	0	1	1,870
Broussard, Mitchell	34	1	4	2	18,714
Broussard, Nathan	99	10	18	11	130,893
Broussard, Ricky John	2	0	1	0	3,600
Brown, Al P.	1	0	0	0	0
Brown, Allan	34	3	3	2	11,658
Brown, Andrew C.	10	0	0	1	1,805
Brown, Barbara Jean	68	2	11	10	72,275
Brown, Barry D.	87	10	13	8	167,697
Brown, Bert F.	4	0	0	0	545
Brown, Brenda Kay	1	0	0	0	60
Brown, C. Wesley	32	6	4	2	17,515
Brown, Carl W.	85	1	3	3	16,945
Brown, Christine M.	9	0	3	0	13,970
Brown, Dickie	80	4	10	7	19,840
Brown, Dwight	51	10	4	5	60,920
Brown, Francis J.	10	3	1	1	12,234
Brown, Frank	8	1	0	0	1,370
Brown, Gary W.	38	2	5	4	21,414
Brown, George F.	38	3	2	5	63,040
Brown, Glenroy	54	4	2	4	22,499
Brown, Herbert Lee	14	0	1	0	5,623
Brown, James E.	9	1	1	1	25,049
Brown, James H.	7	0	1	2	19,680
Brown, James I.	47	3	2	3	27,619
Brown, James L.	5	0	1	2	3,936
Brown, James R.	161	19	20	27	384,853
Brown, Jared	131	8	5	10	54,907
Brown, Jim H.	5	0	2	1	1,240
Brown, June M.	31	4	5	2	37,325
Brown, Keith A.	2	0	0	0	334
Brown, Ken S.	70	9	7	15	45,172
Brown, Kristina L.	4	1	1	0	4,794
Brown, Larry Ronald	12	0	2	5	18,000
Brown, Matthew	3	0	0	0	82

Trainer	Sts	1st	2d	3d	Purses
Brown, Mazie	68	2	2	5	36,571
Brown, Noble D.	6	0	0	0	1,173
Brown, Robert V.	2	0	0	0	43
Brown, Ronald G.	79	4	6	8	60,522
Brown, Ronney W.	770	142	93	95	1,373,599
Brown, Steven R.	93	13	11	14	190,193
Brown, Susan L.	63	6	4	8	59,905
Brown, Ted E.	41	7	3	5	37,395
Brown, William R.	18	0	0	1	1,675
Brown, Wilson L.	130	21	22	19	351,371
Brown, Jr., Charles H.	26	3	0	5	36,880
Brown, Jr., Lewis W.	60	6	7	9	92,653
Brown, Jr., Paul H.	20	1	2	2	29,871
Brownfield, III, Claude L.	139	7	15	17	149,377
Brownlee, David R.	122	14	17	19	482,736
Brownlee, William Earl	100	10	12	12	118,875
Bruce, Dennis R.	7	2	2	0	7,920
Brueggemann, Roger A.	174	14	14	19	311,554
Brumbaugh, Roland J.	50	4	4	3	11,255
Brumley, William S.	45	3	5	6	60,287
Brumlow, Glenn A.	37	2	3	1	38,303
Bruner, Jack A.	101	27	19	14	490,808
Brunton, Robert L.	8	2	1	0	18,240
Bryan, James A.	21	1	1	0	1,889
Bryant, George R.	5	0	0	0	1,650
Bryant, Jeff	20	2	3	2	10,441
Bryant, Jerry	6	0	1	1	557
Bryant, Larry W.	38	0	0	2	3,832
Bryant, Michael Dean	3	0	0	1	1,100
Bryant, Quincy L.	5	0	2	0	2,515
Bryant, Sherwood F.	2	0	0	1	2,388
Bryant, Steve	107	20	11	12	365,402
Buc, John R.	64	5	10	12	114,648
Buchanan, Allen Wayne	11	2	2	2	22,798
Buchanan, John S.	1	0	0	0	780
Buchholz, Ralph	5	3	1	0	27,673
Buchholz, Rick	5	0	2	2	6,424
Buchko, Joseph	47	2	5	2	33,015
Buck, Beverly	66	3	14	3	239,896
Buck, Larry Don	8	0	3	0	1,349
Buckingham, James B.	10	0	1	1	4,762
Buckler, Allison	74	8	10	10	79,925
Buckley, Jonathan M.	306	32	57	58	427,357
Buckley, Mark	26	5	4	4	9,633
Buckman, Gilbert L.	99	9	10	15	57,379
Buckmaster, Chad	9	0	2	1	4,526
Buckridge, Gloria	56	5	0	11	76,847
Budhoo, Steve	15	2	2	1	27,295
Budrewicz, Richard	15	2	2	1	5,040
Buechler, Simon J.	155	17	19	12	209,106
Buehler, Gordon R.	16	1	2	1	8,850
Buehrer, Mark W.	46	1	7	3	23,896
Buehrer, Wayne C.	38	2	3	6	33,601
Buentello, Michael	4	0	0	0	273
Buffalo, Blaine	40	3	6	4	20,004
Buffalo, Floyd	2	0	0	1	220
Buffalo, Marvin	38	3	4	2	22,928
Buhacevich, Rod M.	11	1	1	0	7,380
Buhrow, Jamie D.	42	1	1	2	12,501
Bukowiecki, Chris	47	9	4	5	133,670
Bulloch, Michael G.	14	1	1	1	13,299
Bullock, Steve L.	124	16	15	16	155,429
Bulmer, Valerie J.	1	0	0	0	640
Bumgardner, Jim	6	1	0	0	2,857
Bump, Susan	39	0	4	4	38,228
Bundy, Trevor	75	6	13	12	64,631
Bunting, Edward L.	21	2	0	1	14,139
Bunting, Kent	3	0	0	0	173
Bunting, Nelson	11	0	0	0	2,213
Bunyard, Lowell N.	88	28	13	14	41,401
Burbank, Nancy	13	3	5	2	7,030
Burbank, Rosa Lee	6	4	1	0	8,345
Burch, Audrey	5	1	0	0	5,528
Burch, Eldwin	40	1	1	3	18,609
Burch, Sandra E.	24	1	1	3	30,010
Burden, Gene L.	13	1	2	3	15,184
Burdick, Barbara E.	35	3	1	2	52,180
Burdick, Ed	5	0	0	0	2,270
Burelsmith, Jr., Emmitt B.	11	1	2	1	9,239
Burger, Burton B.	7	0	0	1	1,951
Burger, Wayne	13	0	0	2	1,261
Burgess, Daniel	21	1	2	1	14,379
Burgess, Dondra	4	1	1	0	6,140
Burgess, Mike	5	0	0	2	9,630
Burke, John G.	57	5	6	6	75,374
Burke, Ronald G.	29	2	1	5	87,374
Burke, II, Donald J.	16	0	2	1	40,062
Burkes, Sr., Bobby	17	1	1	0	13,861
Burkhardt, Alfred G.	11	0	0	3	1,320
Burlingame, Thomas	4	0	0	0	210
Burnam, Norma	20	0	1	3	2,667
Burneson, Jr., Charles	1	0	0	0	42
Burneson, Sr., Charles	6	0	0	2	1,451
Burnett, Glenn	53	3	8	13	31,027
Burnett, Laurie	7	2	0	0	8,138
Burnie, Jennifer L.	39	6	4	5	85,752
Burnison, E. G.	16	1	4	2	54,572
Burns, Dale	143	19	19	13	85,476
Burns, Daniel T.	1	0	0	0	110
Burns, Eugene	2	0	0	0	0
Burns, Gerald L.	37	2	6	2	39,115
Burns, John	17	3	1	2	5,156
Burns, Kenneth H.	9	0	0	2	2,775
Burns, Patty A.	116	15	9	17	315,546
Burrell, Andrew	5	0	0	0	0
Burrell, Ron P.	39	5	3	6	60,207
Burress, Debbie	1	0	0	0	0
Burress, Sr., Billy B.	4	0	0	0	260
Burrington, Wallace D.	6	1	1	1	4,838
Burt, David K.	7	1	2	1	1,814
Burt, James Arthur	19	2	4	0	18,362
Burton, D. K.	2	0	0	0	828
Burton, Rob	1	0	1	0	640
Burton, Roger E.	17	2	3	2	23,545
Burton, Roger Mack	1	0	0	0	0
Burwell, Kevin C.	12	0	0	0	2,700
Bush, George S.	29	3	3	0	16,694
Bush, Judith B.	2	1	0	0	3,782
Bush, Lynette A.	46	2	7	3	36,870
Bush, Thomas M.	90	14	11	9	647,171
Bushong, Delbert	94	8	14	11	73,538
Bushrod, Lawrence L.	83	5	3	10	57,862
Buskey, Michael L.	6	0	0	2	2,588
Buskey, Robert E.	28	1	1	3	16,705
Buskey, Jr., Robert Edward	15	2	2	2	24,170
Bustamante, J. Ray	9	1	0	0	4,935
Bustamante, Johnny G.	177	7	14	27	67,355
Bustamante, Justo	27	5	1	3	18,695
Bustos, Jesus	64	3	2	13	30,657
Butcher, Charles L.	22	5	0	1	29,623
Bute, Wayne Lee	11	0	1	0	809
Butkevic, Richard	15	3	2	2	25,600
Butler, Bobby J.	3	0	0	0	427
Butler, Doug	5	0	1	0	1,348
Butler, Gerald	98	12	7	15	74,567
Butler, Gerard A.	1	0	0	0	0
Butler, Larry Jack	4	1	0	0	8,150
Butler, Lonnie	4	0	1	1	3,330
Butler, Jr., Wilbur R.	25	4	5	4	36,679
Buttieri, Stephen A.	15	2	1	0	6,842
Buttigieg, Erin	2	0	1	0	874
Buttigieg, Kevin	23	5	0	5	75,123
Buttigieg, Pasquale J.	1	0	0	0	50
Buttigieg, Paul M.	135	11	17	17	690,001
Butts, David H.	5	0	0	1	3,490
Butts, Jr., Richard P.	85	6	5	8	64,717
Buxbaum, Edward	49	9	7	6	26,765
Buxton, Ken	5	2	3	0	16,243
Buzzard, Ralph	9	0	2	0	2,295
Byers, Larry	3	0	0	0	342
Byler, Andrew	6	0	0	0	0
Byrd, Suzanne	15	1	4	2	38,096

Trainer	Sts	1st	2d	3d	Purses	Trainer	Sts	1st	2d	3d	Purses
Byrd, William R.	3	1	0	0	2,508	Campos, Bernardo	7	0	0	0	1,560
Byrne, George	10	0	1	1	2,282	Campos, Orlando	3	0	0	0	0
Byrne, Hugh P.	12	1	2	0	5,447	Canady, Tony	6	0	0	1	420
Byrne, Patrick B.	119	25	27	14	1,396,421	Canani, Julio C.	165	35	22	26	1,896,774
Byrne, Stephen	9	1	1	0	8,420	Canani, Nick	253	43	40	35	1,522,828
Byrnes, Leah W.	2	0	0	0	1,394	Candelaria, Cosme G.	8	0	0	0	384
Caballero, Lloyd	58	6	2	5	63,075	Candies, Christopher	17	3	5	2	67,423
Cabello, III, Carlos	6	0	1	0	9,550	Candlin, John	227	10	10	9	385,240
Cable, Matt L.	1	0	0	0	52	Canet, Julian	101	13	10	15	142,505
Cabral, Dan	24	0	2	3	14,180	Cannedy, Eddy	7	1	0	1	4,783
Cabrera, Jose A.	141	7	9	10	82,353	Cano, Gerado	1	0	1	0	1,510
Cacchiotti, Mary	235	31	29	27	209,868	Cansler, Misty	1	0	0	0	0
Caddell, Teddy D.	4	1	1	0	4,760	Canterbury, Susan	2	0	0	0	50
Cadena, Emilio	2	0	0	0	0	Cantlon-Bubolz, Corleen	35	4	2	3	44,212
Cahanin, J. Terry	25	0	2	2	5,221	Cantrell, Margie	40	4	7	8	17,369
Cahill, Steven F.	127	17	12	15	197,416	Capacchione, Frank	28	6	5	1	40,426
Caillouet, Howard J.	26	0	4	2	10,820	Capasso, Frank	17	1	0	0	6,255
Cain, Carla	7	1	0	1	3,085	Capasso, Larry	60	5	5	7	31,890
Cain, Don E.	77	5	4	8	117,404	Capellini, John A.	38	1	6	6	40,554
Cain, Lewis B.	1	0	0	0	0	Capestro, Paula S.	204	46	36	28	594,573
Cain, S. Joseph	214	45	33	27	962,647	Capi, Louis M.	101	7	10	20	200,826
Caine, Robert E.	3	0	0	1	1,184	Caple, Gary R.	219	30	17	34	301,959
Calais, Ivory S.	2	0	0	0	0	Cappadona, Joseph F.	12	0	0	0	1,420
Calais, Joseph Lonzo	18	1	0	0	5,280	Cappellucci, Dick	89	27	10	17	476,037
Calais, Richard W.	61	5	10	6	62,332	Cappellucci, Robert A.	115	15	14	8	277,675
Calais, Sonny	12	0	0	1	2,735	Capps, Stacey	22	1	3	1	5,593
Calais, Jr., Phillip	21	3	0	3	48,824	Cappuccitti, Audre	274	22	32	35	1,201,140
Calais, Sr., Phillip	2	0	0	0	720	Capuano, Dale	778	164	151	95	2,775,536
Calas, Aldo	25	4	3	1	37,335	Capuano, Gary	208	40	38	29	989,710
Calascibetta, Joseph G.	218	29	33	22	636,739	Capuano, Louis J.	21	6	1	4	64,319
Calderon, Enrique A.	153	6	5	11	41,735	Capuano, Phillip L.	11	0	2	2	15,720
Caldwell, D. Jared	53	8	6	8	56,178	Caraker, Doug	34	7	2	5	23,449
Caldwell, Delmar R.	140	16	15	8	152,875	Caraman, Gerald E.	2	0	0	0	611
Caldwell, J. R.	9	0	1	0	1,368	Caraman, Michael	85	9	12	7	152,031
Caldwell, Roscoe	38	1	1	1	6,612	Caraman, Norman	83	7	3	16	50,573
Caldwell-Babb, Lillie	11	0	0	2	1,045	Caramori, Eduardo C.	69	8	5	9	147,415
Calfrobe, Noran	17	1	0	2	4,066	Carango, Anthony	88	10	10	16	166,719
Calhoun, John	43	4	4	9	182,601	Carava, Jack	361	61	51	57	1,624,102
Calhoun, Karl	22	2	4	6	25,158	Cardella, John	186	23	30	23	1,170,397
Calhoun, W. Bret	634	156	120	69	3,088,177	Carden, Kevin C.	2	2	0	0	29,100
Callahan, Thomas D.	42	2	1	4	11,838	Cardenas, Ruben	184	34	26	25	898,573
Callejas, Alfredo	69	4	6	10	208,980	Cardone, Steve	9	1	4	1	18,625
Calton, Kurt	50	9	15	7	117,147	Cardoza, Daniel	3	0	0	0	12,500
Calucag, Heather	1	0	0	0	0	Carey, Charles A.	26	2	6	3	45,676
Calvario, Manuel	87	7	10	17	117,605	Carey, Julia	19	2	0	2	85,054
Calvin, Jerry D.	87	12	10	13	233,015	Carle, Jeffery C.	46	4	2	5	87,855
Camardo, Joey M.	171	16	16	21	206,716	Carlesimo, Jr., Charles J.	104	8	13	12	187,683
Cambray, Everado	4	0	0	0	1,778	Carlisi, Frank	108	12	10	19	334,078
Cameron, Anne	99	7	6	9	144,293	Carlisle, John C.	18	7	2	1	83,294
Cameron, Brian	17	0	0	2	1,012	Carlisle, Jr., Raymond M.	32	3	1	1	28,422
Cameron, Dean	6	1	0	2	1,980	Carlson, Johnny D.	29	2	5	2	46,009
Cameron, Michael C.	18	4	2	1	31,383	Carlson, K. L.	6	0	1	0	544
Cameron, Raymond A.	14	0	0	2	18,756	Carlson, Tony	4	0	0	2	1,306
Cameron, Robert B.	2	0	1	0	5,400	Carlton, Anthony Daniel	4	0	0	0	2,520
Cameron-Liechty, Monique	18	3	1	1	67,005	Carlton, Laura S.	34	5	1	2	35,262
Camilo, Juan	98	6	12	13	93,880	Carlton III, O. S.	3	0	1	1	1,900
Campanile, David	39	6	2	4	100,650	Carlton, IV, O. S.	77	3	5	6	28,282
Campbell, Brian	3	0	1	0	6,060	Carlyon, Ron	14	0	0	2	2,095
Campbell, Charles J.	10	1	0	0	3,308	Carmello, Rhonda L.	10	1	1	1	4,777
Campbell, D. Mike	109	9	14	13	139,516	Carmichael, Jr., Ian L.	33	4	3	2	57,207
Campbell, Darice E.	10	0	1	0	2,961	Carneal, Kenneth R.	2	0	0	0	123
Campbell, Donald Edward	52	8	8	8	122,244	Carneal, Steve	1	0	0	0	53
Campbell, Donald J.	28	0	2	4	52,545	Carnes, Gregg R.	28	7	0	6	100,330
Campbell, Elizabeth	14	0	0	2	1,188	Carney, Hugh D.	2	0	1	0	1,137
Campbell, Gilbert N.	2	0	0	0	210	Carney, Hugh J.	33	4	5	5	23,432
Campbell, Jean	73	4	1	8	45,136	Carno, Louis R.	20	3	2	1	142,899
Campbell, Jim	2	0	0	0	0	Carolan, George P.	15	0	0	1	8,895
Campbell, Lawrence H.	20	2	0	1	14,972	Caroli, Donald	135	21	18	15	261,908
Campbell, Marshall T.	56	2	4	3	45,972	Carollo, Alphonse H.	33	2	2	5	21,372
Campbell, Michael B.	77	3	11	7	91,949	Caron, Darrell	57	9	14	6	31,448
Campbell, William A.	62	0	7	13	61,893	Caron, Luc	5	0	1	1	13,288
Campbell, William J.	2	0	0	0	0	Carone, Anthony	52	2	4	3	25,543
Campisano, Ronald	66	10	8	5	230,850	Carothers, Theresa	6	0	1	0	2,903
Campitelli, Francis P.	166	22	25	26	560,017	Carr, Brian	2	0	0	1	1,700
Campitelli, Jessica J.	1	0	0	0	240	Carr, Donald R.	31	1	5	5	27,282
Campo, Jr., John P.	147	8	10	10	186,423	Carr, Mairead	5	0	0	0	0

Trainer	Sts	1st	2d	3d	Purses	Trainer	Sts	1st	2d	3d	Purses
Carrasco, Jr., Abel	1	0	0	0	174	Cataldi, Tony	133	12	11	23	206,151
Carrelli, William	18	2	0	3	24,033	Catanese, III, Joseph C.	85	13	9	11	388,485
Carrete, Oscar V.	4	1	0	0	3,480	Catania, Michael T.	19	0	1	0	28,655
Carrier, Cheryl L.	18	0	0	0	2,685	Catanio, Paul A	11	1	0	0	5,120
Carriker, Ashley	9	1	1	2	27,420	Cathey, Bradley J.	58	6	7	8	125,294
Carrillo, Cheryl	75	6	2	10	30,546	Catrone, Patrick	5	1	0	1	8,050
Carrillo-Dominguez, Cheryl	28	4	0	7	17,755	Caudill, Donald	46	2	2	4	25,725
Carrillo-Dominguez, Gerardo	129	6	9	13	40,467	Caudill, Jesse E.	24	1	3	0	12,667
Carrizales, Edelmiro	2	0	0	0	0	Caughron, Christopher N.	38	8	2	3	28,845
Carroll, David M.	132	35	16	15	1,266,858	Cavanaugh, Edward J.	7	0	0	0	364
Carroll, Henry L.	94	11	17	19	338,132	Cave, Hubert L.	47	2	5	1	31,291
Carroll, Josie	273	47	39	36	2,496,163	Cazares, Frank P.	8	0	0	0	992
Carroll, Klobia S.	5	1	0	0	3,168	Cazaubon, Daniel F.	9	0	0	1	3,075
Carroll, II, Del W.	147	16	11	14	918,441	Cecil, Ben D. A.	77	7	12	9	743,174
Carson, Max W.	29	3	4	6	9,021	Cecil, Willis J.	34	3	1	3	33,809
Cart, Jerry D.	143	20	18	24	352,146	Ceciliano, Misael	21	0	4	1	19,552
Cartagena, Julio R.	191	32	34	34	515,390	Cefalo, Alfred E.	44	8	5	9	103,174
Carter, Allyson	7	0	1	0	2,462	Celestine, Charles Ray	6	0	0	0	495
Carter, Andrew B.	73	13	7	12	162,491	Celsie, Ernie A.	38	1	3	5	90,264
Carter, Cary	151	15	21	17	179,412	Cenicola, Lewis A.	91	12	10	9	320,685
Carter, Elmer	74	7	14	10	97,018	Cerin, Vladimir	268	49	37	44	1,997,149
Carter, George M.	20	2	1	3	73,866	Cermack, Larry	29	3	5	3	10,093
Carter, James R.	45	1	1	3	14,300	Cervantes, Juan M.	152	5	10	21	79,682
Carter, Marvin Ray	30	2	3	4	14,232	Cerveny, Steve	27	2	2	2	8,087
Carter, Robert Lewis	33	0	3	6	17,185	Cesare, William J.	242	26	28	32	701,916
Carter, Ronald P.	2	0	0	1	235	Cesarini, Diana L.	19	1	6	1	14,145
Carter, Susan C.	1	0	0	0	0	Cesarini, Joseph A.	202	11	28	23	132,948
Cartwright, Michael	84	7	5	11	104,477	Chabot, Rob	82	13	10	13	195,886
Cartwright, Ronald C.	79	14	11	9	276,250	Chadborn, Jr., Kenneth K.	132	11	11	13	139,575
Carty, Treville	10	0	0	0	5,530	Chadwick, Gordon	2	0	0	0	0
Caruso, Thomas	16	1	2	1	22,243	Chadwick, James	12	2	2	0	23,476
Carver, David	1	0	1	0	460	Chadwick, Morris	1	0	0	0	60
Casado, Luis	82	7	6	8	71,532	Chaffee, Gary W.	18	1	2	2	14,710
Cascio, C. W. Bubba	169	30	21	28	438,691	Chaffee, Pete	3	0	0	1	435
Case, Owen Clark	9	1	0	0	3,096	Chalich, Nick	66	8	3	5	18,657
Casella-Stark, Judy K.	3	0	0	0	0	Chalk, Ted W.	1	0	0	0	42
Casey, James M.	53	2	5	8	47,491	Chambers, Gary R.	3	0	1	1	840
Casey, James W.	220	20	22	28	475,839	Chambless, Anna M.	27	0	0	2	5,073
Casey, Joe D.	28	1	2	5	12,369	Champagne, Carroll	1	0	0	0	0
Casey, John A.	75	9	3	11	180,524	Champagne, Dana L.	5	0	0	0	0
Casey, Ronald B.	9	2	1	1	11,810	Champagne, Neal J.	3	0	1	0	8,360
Casey, Stephen E.	43	5	6	8	37,634	Champagne, Winona	18	2	0	3	11,011
Casey, Stephen M.	44	4	3	6	47,035	Champange, Randy	1	0	0	0	80
Cash, Edward C.	57	6	7	8	79,410	Champegnie, Stanford A.	65	1	4	5	39,414
Cash, Russell J.	63	3	6	8	123,441	Chan, Gary P.	21	0	1	2	22,446
Casse, Mark E.	465	59	61	68	3,466,964	Chance, Linda	20	3	2	3	19,166
Casselman, Gail	20	4	5	2	312,174	Chandler, J. M.	37	1	4	4	23,300
Cassidy, James M.	155	15	22	15	1,158,021	Chandler, Kevin	172	15	23	24	79,524
Cassidy, Joseph	2	0	0	0	0	Chapa, Joe	9	1	3	0	6,192
Cassil, Wayne V.	42	1	5	7	32,543	Chaparro, Dubis	19	2	0	3	34,385
Cast, Carol	26	4	3	3	20,248	Chaparro, Gayla	19	0	2	2	6,298
Castaneda, Kelly	18	0	0	1	3,748	Chapman, Bertha M.	44	0	4	5	15,080
Castaneda, Marco A.	6	0	0	0	417	Chapman, Dorothy Jean	5	0	0	0	625
Castellano, Mary	4	0	0	0	96	Chapman, Gary	1	0	1	0	420
Castellanos, Armando	3	1	0	0	808	Chapman, James K.	126	15	17	14	778,818
Castellanos, Jaime	170	23	24	28	170,615	Chapman, James R.	2	0	0	0	307
Caster, Boyd	146	10	15	15	118,821	Chapman, Jolaine	9	0	0	2	1,218
Castille, Carrol	50	6	9	3	135,277	Chapman, Kim	5	0	0	0	376
Castille, Lee	13	0	2	1	5,884	Chapman, Robert K.	11	2	1	2	12,655
Castille, Mark	36	1	4	2	35,172	Chappell, Allan	1	0	0	0	0
Castillo, Judy	6	0	0	0	504	Chappell, Ronald M.	124	9	6	11	44,675
Castle, Doyle E.	1	0	0	0	35	Charalambous, Elizabeth R.	8	0	0	1	3,332
Castle, Jr., Edward J.	15	0	0	2	3,023	Charalambous, John	97	13	14	15	564,355
Castleberry, Chris J.	26	1	1	4	6,995	Charette, Stacy S.	1	0	0	0	0
Castleberry, William J.	27	0	5	4	3,567	Charles, Freddie	16	1	1	1	8,415
Casto, Bill	24	2	5	2	21,706	Charles, George	1	0	0	0	0
Castor, Donald F.	11	1	1	1	10,251	Charlton, Brent W.	51	7	7	7	64,523
Castor, Gail A.	6	1	1	0	5,274	Charlton, Daryn	9	2	0	2	3,208
Castor, Shane	129	26	14	11	135,674	Charlton, V. Joan	38	4	11	4	77,179
Castro, Jorge	16	0	0	3	16,035	Charoo, Wellesley	45	2	4	3	32,975
Castro, Manuel S.	3	1	0	0	5,827	Chase, Timothy K.	124	14	20	14	155,207
Castro, Rafael	37	5	5	8	36,682	Chastain, Rick	40	0	6	7	59,600
Castro, Raquel A.	13	4	1	3	21,748	Chatlos, Jr., Donald	51	8	10	6	367,812
Caswell, Bradley S.	3	0	2	0	5,820	Chatters, Benard	34	4	7	7	41,469
Catalano, Wayne M.	356	106	53	42	1,917,636	Chatters, Maynard	24	10	7	2	129,935
Catalano, Jr., Michael L.	19	3	4	3	67,130	Chavers, Jr., Howie	7	0	0	0	432

Trainer	Sts	1st	2d	3d	Purses
Chavez, Alex L.	2	0	0	0	131
Chavez, Baldomero	1	0	0	0	35
Chavez, Christie	2	0	0	0	0
Chavez, Enrique	8	2	0	2	4,675
Chavez, Felix E.	128	21	18	21	289,972
Chavez, Francisco	54	5	5	4	21,212
Chavez, Jesus	91	5	12	14	159,681
Chavez, Joe R.	20	0	2	4	9,561
Chavez, Lori	54	1	4	8	34,530
Chavis, Rellis	1	0	0	1	1,067
Cheek, Crystal	5	0	1	1	5,287
Cheeks, Joseph	183	34	29	16	329,881
Cheeks, Kitty R.	14	4	1	3	48,767
Cheff, Chrissy	63	3	8	6	13,106
Cheff, Kenneth R.	14	2	1	2	4,085
Cheff, Michael E.	12	1	1	0	11,198
Cheff, William	14	0	1	0	3,932
Cheloha, Donald F.	30	4	4	2	37,227
Chesmore, Gayle	34	4	3	2	7,693
Chevis, Vincent A.	18	0	0	3	2,501
Chew, Matthew	78	9	7	11	205,240
Chiasson, Kenneth F.	17	0	1	2	2,764
Childers, James R.	44	5	3	4	70,775
Childress, Lucy	87	10	8	13	74,280
Chin, Peter A.	15	0	2	3	41,129
Ching, Edylyn	5	2	0	2	22,580
Chinn, Fred J.	40	0	1	1	3,410
Chleborad, Lynn	402	40	56	59	724,490
Cho, Alexander	63	7	15	14	51,500
Cho, Myung Kwon	17	1	2	1	43,598
Chong, Patrick	23	1	3	2	19,811
Christa, Jill	27	1	1	1	7,579
Christensen, Al	66	7	9	14	69,342
Christensen, Warren	9	0	1	3	4,061
Christenson, Jackie	36	3	3	3	96,174
Christian, Billy	23	3	6	4	10,550
Christian, Mike	2	0	0	0	0
Christiansen, Cathy L.	4	0	0	1	1,218
Christie, Clifton A.	15	0	3	0	5,500
Christman, Louis E.	6	1	2	2	13,822
Christmas, William G.	120	9	14	16	100,131
Christoffersen, Farrell	12	2	0	1	4,788
Christopherson, Pam	23	5	3	2	11,777
Chubb, Beverly	71	7	10	5	311,393
Chumney, Kevin K.	47	6	6	3	78,973
Chung, Victor	34	2	8	4	100,540
Churchill, Donald J.	5	0	0	0	300
Churchman, Jr., John E.	26	2	5	3	35,255
Chysyk, Morris	40	3	1	2	24,278
Ciaio, Charles A.	26	1	3	1	9,343
Ciardullo, Jr., Richard J.	406	69	62	42	1,196,596
Ciavaglia, Gilbert	116	14	7	16	141,347
Cibelli, Jane	118	12	20	12	199,973
Cicero, Salvatore J.	3	0	0	0	0
Cifarelli, Frank	20	0	0	2	10,258
Cilio, Gene A.	353	48	60	44	1,770,255
Cimini, Paul	55	2	9	4	50,969
Cimini, Peter	7	1	1	1	3,015
Cioffi, Antonio	61	5	6	5	58,190
Ciresa, Martin E.	119	22	19	21	424,916
Cirian, Phil	37	2	4	3	13,528
Cirillo, John	43	5	4	11	269,706
Cisman, Renee	13	1	0	1	6,746
Cizik, Tony	30	2	1	4	33,196
Claflin, Ruth	127	6	8	10	52,387
Clagett, Christine F.	6	0	0	1	6,480
Claridge, Jimmie D.	77	7	10	7	117,450
Clark, Clay W.	27	0	0	0	2,012
Clark, Dale T.	51	4	5	4	58,516
Clark, Derran Joseph	3	0	0	0	0
Clark, Dick R.	402	77	63	54	1,142,583
Clark, Edward T.	127	13	16	11	143,701
Clark, Justin	9	3	2	2	5,330
Clark, Keith	55	3	4	6	29,644
Clark, Kelly D.	5	0	1	0	2,774
Clark, Kevin G.	214	30	34	25	253,705
Clark, Kimberly	2	0	0	0	0
Clark, Kirt W.	2	0	0	0	250
Clark, Phillip	19	1	0	1	9,043
Clark, Sharon B.	8	2	0	0	19,140
Clark, Tammy	4	0	0	1	1,595
Clark, Thomas A.	80	11	5	8	69,398
Clark III, Henry S.	1	0	0	0	0
Clarke, Jamie	70	10	6	8	143,002
Clarke, Ronald A.	48	4	6	7	71,045
Clark-Loza, Beth A.	35	5	3	6	75,088
Clarkson, Steven	9	0	0	2	2,655
Clarkston, Fred	11	3	0	1	4,883
Clary, Donald	3	1	0	1	2,800
Class, Raymond E.	6	0	1	1	5,570
Clatterbuck, Ronald L.	1	0	0	0	633
Clauson, Connie	25	2	2	7	17,845
Clauson, Geoffrey	10	1	0	2	5,700
Clauss, Keith	2	0	0	0	173
Clay, Brent	9	0	0	0	548
Clay, Gerald	13	1	0	1	7,962
Clay, Royce G.	7	0	0	1	2,696
Clay, Jr., Raymond	10	0	1	2	8,695
Clay, Jr., Shirley W.	73	7	9	8	138,557
Clay, Sr., William E.	43	4	4	4	10,326
Clayton, W. L.	17	0	3	3	62,670
Clayton, William L.	5	1	0	1	13,567
Cleary, Bryan A.	27	1	5	5	59,359
Cleary, Kevin	1	0	0	0	35
Clelland, Odessa J.	10	0	3	4	6,986
Clemans, Mark A.	4	0	0	0	86
Clemens, Darryl J.	6	1	0	1	14,992
Clemens, James	24	2	2	1	12,619
Clement, Christophe	389	75	65	39	5,558,742
Clement, Linda M.	145	11	19	17	129,657
Clement, III, Roland P.	3	0	0	0	630
Clements, Alvin H.	49	3	4	6	27,764
Clements, Bob	7	0	2	1	2,913
Clements, Doug R.	51	3	8	11	64,238
Clements, John R.	19	1	2	1	7,716
Clemmer, Gregory P.	4	0	0	0	251
Clemmer, Phillip J.	6	2	1	2	4,914
Clemmons, Jim	1	1	0	0	11,400
Clemmons, John	1	0	0	1	650
Clemson, Elmer E.	11	1	1	0	7,292
Cleveland, Bev	16	2	4	3	10,054
Clevenger, Carl	8	1	0	0	4,197
Clevenger, David Lee	12	1	1	1	12,920
Clifton, Cheryl L.	14	0	1	1	6,701
Cline, Leon	75	6	7	15	68,658
Cline, Robert C.	92	9	10	10	66,570
Clinton, Butch	9	2	2	0	3,412
Clopton, Joe	1	0	0	0	465
Close, Lewis P.	154	5	13	11	107,514
Cloud, James	7	0	2	0	3,810
Cloud, L. D.	16	3	0	0	9,633
Clouston, Edward	189	24	32	24	278,923
Clouston, III, Burley	135	23	17	26	336,994
Cloutier, Richard	46	8	4	6	99,228
Cloutier Jacobson, Toni	60	14	10	12	302,711
Cloyd, Roy M.	3	1	0	0	7,232
Cluley, Denis	80	9	12	10	131,066
Clum, James	117	10	15	10	59,091
Clute, Robert	24	1	2	2	7,702
Clyde, Doug	9	1	0	1	10,714
Clyde, Terry	194	34	37	31	387,414
Coates, Lowell F.	35	2	5	3	16,520
Coatney, Betty C.	161	16	14	26	229,504
Coatney, Charles R.	53	4	2	2	22,979
Coatney, Gerald J.	1	0	0	0	285
Coatrieux, Eric	38	3	5	7	269,308
Cobb, Maurice W.	49	9	0	5	58,913
Coble, Kenneth	23	1	1	1	11,564
Cocciolone, Gus J.	11	0	0	0	720
Cocelli, Jr., Louis J.	13	1	2	1	31,475
Cochran, Henry S.	50	9	8	2	250,468
Cochran, Michael A.	1	0	0	0	0

Trainer	Sts	1st	2d	3d	Purses	Trainer	Sts	1st	2d	3d	Purses
Cockburn, Bay	6	0	0	0	2,150	Conley, Richard	7	0	1	0	1,512
Cockrell, John	3	0	0	0	725	Conley, Warren L.	3	0	0	0	135
Cockrill, Richard H.	59	4	4	4	67,138	Conlon, Bette	27	0	3	1	8,658
Cocks, Edwin Burling	9	0	0	0	360	Conlon, Melody	12	0	0	1	5,900
Cocks, William Brinton	5	1	1	0	26,310	Connelley, Richard L.	7	2	0	1	6,113
Coffelt, Cliff	6	0	0	0	166	Connelly, Ed	7	1	3	1	3,600
Coffey, Junior L.	50	9	10	7	98,286	Connelly, Robert B.	43	12	5	11	54,696
Coffey, Marialice	110	1	8	11	41,630	Connelly, Ronald Rex	36	1	6	4	45,834
Coffey, Jr., Chester	2	0	0	0	103	Connelly, Teresa	42	6	3	3	92,413
Coffman, Ray	3	0	0	1	474	Connelly, William R.	180	23	23	25	514,497
Cogburn, Orrin	21	4	6	3	15,412	Conner, Barbara Jean	36	0	4	3	15,031
Cohen, Michael	150	13	13	15	175,359	Conner, Bobby N.	30	3	1	2	32,616
Cohn, Alice G.	45	5	6	2	135,303	Conner, John D.	89	11	8	14	137,813
Colalillo, Dominic	4	0	0	2	3,659	Connolly, Michael	82	6	11	1	56,867
Colando, Sr., Andrew C.	4	1	0	0	9,190	Connor, III, James P.	80	6	7	7	113,857
Colbourne, Gordon C.	55	2	6	10	209,097	Conover, Roy T.	26	0	2	4	8,256
Cole, Bryan D.	31	2	4	7	24,630	Conrad, Paul	29	3	4	5	56,420
Cole, Eddie A.	97	9	15	12	171,300	Conrad, Wayne	8	0	2	0	7,674
Cole, Harvey	1	0	0	0	0	Constant, Chester	28	5	4	5	9,246
Cole, Jason L.	2	0	0	0	0	Constant, Tom	54	9	4	4	50,965
Cole, Jerry M.	76	7	6	10	45,174	Constantine, Carol	144	10	7	15	89,461
Cole, Keith	8	1	0	2	3,936	Contessa, Gary C.	528	59	58	64	2,235,357
Cole, Kim	63	3	5	6	21,887	Conto, Kevin	8	1	0	1	11,015
Cole, Ralph W.	11	2	0	1	3,672	Contreras, Javier	124	22	19	14	413,180
Cole, Scott	3	1	0	0	4,720	Contreras, Martin	10	1	2	1	13,175
Cole, Terry James	18	0	1	1	2,057	Conway, Michael A.	42	8	6	6	95,157
Cole, III, Philip J.	46	0	4	9	15,183	Conyers, William F.	80	15	7	7	56,981
Colee, Frank	30	7	4	3	43,706	Conza, Valerie A.	20	3	6	3	28,698
Colello, Sr., George	84	10	15	8	69,353	Cook, Brian	10	1	0	0	2,240
Coleman, James	19	0	1	0	3,206	Cook, Carol	25	2	0	1	11,012
Coleman, Thomas R.	63	8	6	7	56,804	Cook, Chad	64	6	8	4	30,957
Coletti, Jr., Edward J.	259	55	47	38	987,350	Cook, David D.	51	3	2	4	26,844
Colflesh, Craig M.	28	1	1	2	16,278	Cook, David K.	26	1	1	0	10,903
Colgan, Kelly A.	7	0	0	2	3,187	Cook, Deanna	52	2	7	6	35,649
Collazo, Henry	477	63	57	65	1,099,754	Cook, Don C.	3	0	0	0	0
Collazo, Victor O.	82	7	6	11	90,665	Cook, Jason G.	52	3	5	6	68,030
Collet, Robert J.	2	0	0	1	55,000	Cook, Joanie M.	33	1	0	4	10,893
Collet, Rodolphe	3	0	2	0	177,850	Cook, Joe R.	5	0	0	1	1,375
Collier, Jimmie C.	72	11	3	8	198,468	Cook, lyle	5	0	0	1	324
Collier, Rickey L.	5	0	0	0	0	Cook, Robert D.	63	3	4	9	32,177
Collier, Robert W.	68	2	2	11	19,858	Cook, Ruth A.	87	10	10	11	85,858
Collier, William M.	9	0	0	2	3,778	Cook, Thomas W.	9	2	3	1	17,370
Colligan, Ronald	64	4	9	5	71,047	Cooksey, Gene	10	0	0	0	1,310
Collins, Andrew	25	3	1	7	33,450	Coombs, Jack	81	8	11	12	47,047
Collins, Charles M.	1	0	0	0	217	Coombs, Leroy G.	9	1	1	2	2,659
Collins, Debbra	3	0	0	0	750	Cooney, Susan S.	176	9	13	9	255,728
Collins, Dick	41	1	2	5	8,774	Coonse, Tracy	34	5	3	2	39,766
Collins, Don	72	2	7	19	74,740	Cooper, Carl J.	60	1	5	5	30,239
Collins, Holly	23	0	2	4	16,346	Cooper, Franklin D.	30	3	3	4	24,067
Collins, J. C.	7	0	0	2	5,083	Cooper, Fred	1	0	0	0	0
Collins, John	2	0	0	0	292	Cooper, J. Curtis	18	1	0	1	5,618
Collins, Lee	5	0	0	1	1,315	Cooper, Jack	40	3	5	5	38,354
Collins, Michael G.	2	0	1	0	2,070	Cooper, John D.	12	1	2	2	6,803
Collins, Michael J.	299	25	37	35	214,005	Cooper, John L.	14	4	1	3	23,748
Collins, William G.	12	1	1	0	8,429	Cooper, Kay Penny	2	0	0	0	2,655
Comber, James	1	1	0	0	2,200	Cooper, Stacey	15	5	1	2	53,319
Combest, Reed M.	128	9	14	19	225,670	Cooper, Steve B.	31	4	4	2	69,140
Combs, Don J.	65	8	6	6	147,044	Copeland, Jimmy	73	13	5	4	156,740
Combs, Leonard R.	18	0	0	1	3,252	Coppola, Joseph M.	40	4	1	1	39,950
Comer, Earl Wayne	28	1	0	2	13,899	Copsey, John W.	26	0	2	4	17,314
Comer, II, Lon	4	0	0	0	390	Corbel, Emile	160	21	15	13	168,355
Comi, Ralph W.	41	5	8	7	61,206	Corbel, Keith	34	9	2	6	118,954
Comontofski, Sandy	37	3	3	4	25,520	Corbett, Brian	11	1	0	1	17,514
Compher, Clark	17	1	0	2	4,685	Corcoran, William J.	7	1	0	0	8,549
Compton, James R.	138	26	24	26	131,408	Cordero, Angel M.	5	0	0	0	275
Comstock, J. D.	19	2	3	4	14,597	Cordova, Armando	6	0	2	1	835
Conaway, Jr., Charles C.	2	0	1	1	4,512	Cordova, Joe G.	81	8	7	11	132,268
Concessi, Armand	118	13	18	16	294,728	Corley, Jr., William Hart	1	0	0	0	0
Condilenios, Dino K.	201	39	32	29	726,424	Cormier, Edward	50	7	5	4	58,219
Condon, Jean	10	1	0	0	1,962	Cormier, Houston	85	7	9	10	82,512
Condon, Leslie A.	49	2	7	3	53,678	Cormier, John E.	93	4	2	11	72,938
Condren, W. H.	18	0	5	2	12,589	Cormier, Jr., Donald	96	6	8	12	138,397
Cone, Rodney J.	128	11	11	19	194,040	Cormier, Sr., Donald J.	406	31	46	52	341,442
Conklin, Susan	23	1	0	1	12,695	Cornelius, Carl W.	71	2	0	4	27,843
Conley, Alice	4	0	0	0	0	Cornwell, Fred E.	3	0	0	1	2,190
Conley, Cathy	7	0	1	0	1,638	Cornwell, Jr., James L.	56	4	4	4	66,077

RECORDS OF TRAINERS

Trainer	Sts	1st	2d	3d	Purses
Coronado, J. Guadalupe	15	0	1	0	2,843
Corrado, Robert	55	5	5	3	96,323
Corrales, Jose	37	9	6	3	137,735
Correa, Alex A.	39	2	1	3	27,589
Correa, Jeff	49	2	2	4	75,840
Correa, Ray	58	1	9	7	19,283
Correas, IV, Ignacio	8	1	1	1	15,010
Corredor, Enrique	50	9	4	6	130,937
Correnti, Anthony	303	38	43	42	708,825
Correnti, Armand W.	12	3	0	1	24,310
Corrigan, Jimmy	46	4	8	4	52,085
Cortez, John E.	15	1	0	1	13,340
Cortolillo, Gary	45	2	7	7	75,448
Cory, William R.	27	2	1	1	8,210
Coryat, John A.	23	0	0	2	15,990
Cosme, Pablo	53	4	2	1	33,825
Costa, Frank	149	10	14	16	256,025
Costa, Fred	61	4	1	9	42,250
Costantino, Frank S.	1	0	0	1	1,560
Costew, John B.	40	8	4	4	126,680
Cote, Jr., Fred	2	1	0	0	806
Cote, Sr., Fred	1	0	0	0	70
Cotey, David	177	19	23	25	1,111,582
Cotrone, Denise	35	5	8	5	67,865
Cotrone, Jr., Frankie	13	1	0	1	13,550
Cotter, Mike	18	2	3	1	9,286
Cotto, Luis	31	2	1	1	12,951
Cotton, John M.	40	3	1	7	33,933
Couch, Terry N.	10	0	1	1	2,270
Couchenour, Lee	58	5	2	6	65,848
Coughlin, Daniel	81	11	12	16	55,037
Coughlin, Edward D.	34	1	1	5	6,205
County, Patrick	36	3	1	5	61,646
County, Jr., Patrick	65	6	8	11	141,906
County, Jr., Thomas J.	40	5	2	3	98,992
Coursey, Elmer D.	2	0	0	0	135
Courtemanche, Candy R.	5	0	0	0	414
Courville, Leroy	11	0	0	1	1,615
Couse, Maggie P.	39	8	4	5	88,621
Covello, Andrea A.	35	2	1	1	22,293
Covello, Frank W.	48	7	7	7	63,320
Cowan, Elmer C.	150	23	27	18	161,828
Cowan, Gary	48	6	4	8	52,742
Cowan, Jon M.	3	0	0	0	140
Cowan, Linda	2	0	0	0	0
Cowans, William D.	103	26	25	10	151,837
Cowden, James H.	6	0	1	0	920
Cowgar, Steve	26	3	5	5	21,040
Cowgill, Charles P.	5	0	0	1	846
Cox, Amalia B.	31	6	2	2	93,952
Cox, George	3	1	0	0	1,170
Cox, Greg D.	51	8	5	5	276,904
Cox, Jerry	23	2	3	4	4,442
Cox, Jimmy	47	2	1	4	6,384
Cox, John E.	102	15	9	17	93,816
Cox, John M.	81	10	7	10	37,434
Cox, Kenneth M.	174	25	34	20	394,247
Cox, Kyle M.	10	1	0	1	9,895
Cox, L. Craig	338	58	58	45	846,969
Cox, Loren G.	258	23	29	40	419,987
Cox, William B.	80	8	5	8	39,752
Cox, III, William T.	20	1	4	2	11,774
Coyle, George R.	22	1	0	2	27,899
Coyle, Vernon D.	147	10	13	17	83,267
Coyote, Jason J.	154	9	15	7	120,813
Crabtree, Bobby L.	11	3	1	1	73,605
Crabtree, Cecil	58	12	6	10	110,183
Crabtree, Larry W.	33	2	6	4	22,934
Crabtree, Lynn	11	4	2	1	30,569
Craddock, Kari	156	22	29	26	406,018
Craddock, Patrick J.	9	1	0	2	12,597
Craft, Micky F.	21	2	3	1	15,174
Crago, Alan P.	3	0	0	0	1,210
Crago, Holly	72	7	6	6	48,875
Crago, Terry J.	51	3	8	3	62,475
Cragun, Blake L.	9	4	3	0	5,831
Craig, Gary	26	0	2	2	3,863
Craig, James R.	16	5	2	3	7,562
Craig, Jr., Lewis E.	69	6	4	6	72,758
Craig, Sr., Lewis E.	15	1	0	1	14,932
Craigmyle, Scott J.	221	9	17	12	127,501
Crandall, Cynthia A.	6	0	0	0	1,068
Crandall, David E.	11	0	0	0	935
Cranfield, Ernest M.	82	9	8	12	116,697
Cranford, Britt G.	51	8	11	7	27,863
Cranwell, James E.	44	7	6	8	85,353
Cravens, III, Ronnie	46	1	1	3	11,620
Crawford, Clinton	16	3	1	2	6,068
Crawford, Frankie	30	0	0	4	6,492
Crawford, George	3	0	0	0	261
Crawford, Gerald Anthony	3	1	0	1	3,565
Crawford, John D.	30	2	3	5	11,292
Crawford, Ray	8	0	2	1	17,999
Crayne, Jeff A.	38	1	3	5	23,918
Creager, Tommie	32	2	3	3	38,581
Crean, Robert F.	39	3	2	4	182,582
Creath, Heather	29	1	4	6	79,487
Creaton, Scott	21	1	1	1	18,406
Credeur, A. J.	89	6	3	8	56,557
Creel, Rick	23	2	3	3	24,113
Crescini, Joseph D.	16	0	1	0	2,485
Crete, Pierre	8	1	2	2	17,399
Crichton, Sandy	6	0	0	0	415
Crider, Charlotte	64	4	11	6	59,097
Criollo, Manuel	204	11	15	20	185,755
Crippen, Albert	8	0	0	0	261
Cripps, Kenneth	56	4	1	1	44,311
Cristel, Mark J.	182	15	15	18	319,940
Crock, Michael W.	11	1	1	2	6,833
Crocker, Alan	250	56	32	35	287,125
Crofoot, Eric	1	0	0	0	0
Croft, Barry N.	139	18	11	17	321,455
Croll, William E.	74	7	10	15	149,505
Cronise-Santis, Heather E	25	0	0	2	5,306
Cronk, Samuel F.	204	18	19	19	240,655
Crook, W. Byron	85	9	6	6	122,301
Crooks, Jeffrey S.	174	18	28	14	249,767
Crosby, Jr., Donald	2	0	0	0	123
Cross, Cathy	26	0	1	1	3,850
Cross, Edward D.	11	0	0	1	1,008
Cross, Gary W.	271	52	51	44	849,264
Cross, Judy	24	3	3	4	40,883
Cross, Timothy W.	1	0	0	0	47
Cross, Sr., Kenneth G.	40	0	1	0	4,969
Crotts, Jim	22	4	3	3	15,728
Crouse, Drexel E.	75	4	7	7	79,032
Crouse, Jr., Leo H.	5	0	1	0	1,295
Crowder, Mike	63	8	1	6	111,693
Crowe, Chris M.	21	3	0	3	36,518
Crowe, Kenneth W.	15	3	3	2	39,620
Crowell, Duane E.	2	0	0	0	140
Crowell, Howard G.	1	0	0	0	65
Crowell, Robert V.	2	1	0	1	1,680
Crowell, Susan L.	52	3	6	5	37,617
Crowl, Danny	2	0	0	0	500
Crowley, Joseph J.	3	0	0	0	990
Crowley, Tom	12	0	0	1	2,916
Crozier, Jeff	8	0	1	0	1,900
Crozier, Thomas A.	71	7	11	6	40,786
Cruce, Tina	2	0	0	0	135
Crumley, Jevon	133	11	9	15	118,124
Cuadra, Victor	66	7	1	4	223,515
Cuadras, Jose	22	2	4	8	22,985
Cuccia, L. Jay	52	9	7	11	78,475
Cuccurullo, Pat	202	32	30	23	421,123
Cucinotta, Anthony	75	5	3	6	44,058
Cuevas, Dealus Wayne	4	1	0	1	4,627
Cullum, William H.	22	1	1	2	14,150
Culotta, Ray J.	25	3	4	5	44,250
Cumani, Luca M.	1	0	0	1	233,200
Cumberlidge, Theresa L.	5	0	0	1	760
Cumbie, Cora Lee	26	1	0	2	3,101

Trainer	Sts	1st	2d	3d	Purses
Cummings, David	46	2	5	3	29,988
Cummins, Cindy M.	8	2	1	3	9,009
Cummins, George	76	9	9	12	97,147
Cunard, Murray	15	4	2	3	14,298
Cundiff, Roy	11	2	1	0	6,297
Cunningham, Andrea L.	40	4	3	1	30,046
Cunningham, Anthony F.	3	0	0	1	658
Cunningham, Carl Anthony	4	0	0	0	0
Cunningham, Donna	17	1	1	0	8,251
Cunningham, Michael W.	22	0	1	5	7,685
Cunningham, Rita F.	2	0	0	0	258
Cuprill, Charles A.	119	12	18	11	225,875
Currin, William L.	56	4	6	16	251,628
Curry, Dee	158	19	21	24	316,332
Curtis, James F.	20	3	5	1	46,674
Curtis, Larry F.	36	3	6	4	55,754
Curtis, Mark	56	3	4	6	43,795
Curtsinger, Scott	1	0	0	0	0
Cuthbertson, Norm	6	0	0	0	977
Cuttino, Marion L.	52	6	4	11	85,325
Czerwonka, Richard	6	0	0	0	658
Czerwonka, Roger D.	8	0	0	1	1,680
Czyzewski, Joseph	18	1	1	1	5,090
Dagg, Larry	3	0	0	0	857
Daggett, Michael H.	73	2	10	7	177,405
Dagonel, Ari	2	0	0	0	0
Dahl, David	37	4	1	3	62,751
Dahle, Norm	51	9	9	1	56,780
Dahlke, Kyle	3	1	0	0	4,950
DAiello, George C.	3	0	0	0	5,100
Daigle, Ronnie J.	27	1	5	1	12,523
Daigle, Walter C.	15	1	1	1	9,229
Daigrepont, Vicki	32	1	4	3	18,373
Dailey, Jon	21	1	2	4	14,575
Dailey, Melissa L.	3	0	0	0	180
Dailey, Randy	6	2	1	1	13,853
Dailey, Ronald W.	90	6	6	9	52,444
Dailey-Karcher, Lisa Lynn	7	1	1	1	4,419
Dale, Jack W.	46	1	4	6	22,120
D'Alessandro, Ralph	272	36	36	25	448,652
Daley, Bruce	4	0	0	0	560
Dalke, Ray	5	0	1	1	1,386
D'Aloia, Carol	4	0	0	0	134
Dalrymple, Darcie C.	24	1	1	4	25,259
Dalton, Kenneth W.	14	1	1	0	12,592
Dalton, Tim	7	0	0	1	2,220
Daly, Patrick J.	72	10	11	10	395,681
Daly, Peter J.	4	0	0	0	1,230
D'Amario, Michael	216	28	30	31	459,436
Damm, Raymond C.	22	5	4	6	13,565
Damron, Gary	18	2	2	1	12,684
Damron, Jerry W.	17	1	1	2	8,828
Damron, Patricia	11	2	0	1	7,906
Danaher, James E.	75	8	7	9	163,890
Dancer, Marvin J.	28	2	5	3	74,607
Dandy, Ronald J.	601	104	96	74	1,070,833
Danelson, Gary	189	55	38	27	417,424
D'Angelo, Michael T.	40	3	4	6	95,551
D'Angelo, Jr., Anthony F.	29	1	1	3	27,880
Danger, Kevin	87	7	6	8	76,968
Daniel, Kellie	3	0	0	0	0
Daniels, Connie L.	82	4	7	8	65,761
Daniels, Hugh	8	0	1	3	3,366
Danielson, Del S.	18	1	1	4	9,990
Danks, Thomas	57	5	7	7	93,118
Danley, Dennis B.	17	1	1	1	24,090
Danley, Fred I.	252	32	42	37	828,191
Danley, John L.	50	1	3	4	21,215
Danner, Douglas W.	100	14	15	9	153,646
Danner, Mark	36	3	2	8	60,053
Danylchuk, Dave A.	3	1	0	1	1,415
Daria, Angelo J.	228	5	12	17	82,487
Darjean, Paul	61	5	5	7	124,588
Darling, Connie	1	0	0	0	0
Darnell, Cliff W.	25	2	2	2	14,035
Darrus, Thomas	8	0	0	1	1,155

Trainer	Sts	1st	2d	3d	Purses
Dartez, Lawrence	18	0	0	1	1,837
Daugherty, Allen	7	0	1	0	3,718
Dautreuil, Calvin D.	15	1	1	1	12,514
Davenport, Sr., Franklin R.	8	0	0	1	2,104
David, Paul	1	0	0	0	0
David, Ron	61	6	7	12	32,761
David, Jr., Sam B.	241	35	32	41	633,795
Davidovich, Andrew	101	5	6	8	106,401
Davidson, Bryan	1	0	0	0	350
Davidson, Doug	21	2	5	1	42,429
Davidson, Ernie	6	0	0	1	2,029
Davidson, Gordon J.	34	2	0	2	29,987
Davidson, Milo Brent	250	18	21	31	277,896
Davidson, Nan	25	1	1	1	18,885
Davidson, Robert J.	4	0	0	0	312
Davidson, Jr., Donald D.	10	1	4	2	4,208
Davies, Alberta	8	1	0	0	9,849
Davies, Alex S.	1	0	0	0	0
Davies, Deanne	53	9	6	4	151,507
Davies, Jerry A.	3	0	0	0	155
Davies, Norman S.	51	5	2	3	83,035
Davies, Ronald	7	1	0	1	4,339
Davies, Stewart G.	8	0	0	0	1,854
Davis, Charles F.	19	2	0	2	9,660
Davis, Charlie	30	2	2	3	44,212
Davis, Clarence L.	9	1	0	0	9,870
Davis, Debra	4	1	2	0	2,080
Davis, Donna M.	22	1	1	1	22,045
Davis, Duke	24	0	0	5	13,065
Davis, Frank	24	2	2	3	9,422
Davis, Gary K.	70	9	6	6	61,786
Davis, Gene	83	10	11	17	29,426
Davis, George	106	5	5	15	18,183
Davis, Henry S.	9	1	1	1	5,617
Davis, James A.	7	1	0	1	12,350
Davis, Jodi L.	56	0	4	8	21,262
Davis, Joe	38	4	4	7	61,873
Davis, Joseph D.	202	27	27	23	346,780
Davis, Keith	19	4	4	4	6,179
Davis, Liane P.	31	3	1	1	32,282
Davis, Marvin J.	22	1	1	1	42,348
Davis, Melvin W.	119	16	10	10	70,445
Davis, Nicole	22	2	3	4	19,388
Davis, Peter	19	3	4	5	11,413
Davis, Randy J.	4	0	0	0	150
Davis, Raymond A.	35	3	1	4	33,109
Davis, Rhonda B.	15	1	1	2	12,275
Davis, Ronald D.	6	0	0	1	840
Davis, Russell E.	130	11	19	21	217,418
Davis, Sammy	3	0	0	0	152
Davis, Samuel G.	23	1	8	3	30,893
Davis, Scooter	471	98	72	53	1,312,698
Davis, Shawn H.	37	6	9	5	51,580
Davis, Steve T.	2	0	0	0	200
Davis, Terry	7	0	1	1	1,014
Davis, Tom	2	0	0	0	198
Davis, Wayne E.	4	0	1	2	3,072
Davis-Parke, Kathy	7	0	2	1	7,804
Dawes, Gene	7	1	1	1	2,965
Day, Danny	10	0	1	5	1,285
Day, Diane M.	94	11	12	18	160,526
Day, James E.	104	14	5	11	1,139,974
Day, James M.	101	5	12	11	118,405
Day Phillips, Catherine	93	18	11	15	1,234,298
De Amelio, Gerald	26	2	4	4	26,705
De Angelis, Steven A.	1	0	0	0	0
de Brevedent, Bertrand	63	10	7	9	212,900
De Camillis, George E.	14	1	0	1	5,570
De La Cruz, Inez	26	0	1	3	3,263
De Marni, Caesar	86	11	17	19	157,350
de Roualle, Jean	1	0	0	0	12,000
De Santis, Anthony	32	2	0	3	18,945
De Seroux, Laura	111	14	13	11	1,965,242
De Stefano, Jr., John M.	128	10	15	23	406,701
Deacon, Charles E.	9	0	0	1	1,425
Dean, Dana D.	3	0	0	0	810

Trainer	Sts	1st	2d	3d	Purses	Trainer	Sts	1st	2d	3d	Purses
Dean, Kathy	6	0	0	1	635	Depew, Jim	36	5	10	7	24,936
Dean, William L.	4	0	0	1	730	Deroin, David B.	11	3	0	2	13,262
Dean, III, Victor	73	12	10	10	70,144	Deroin, Gene	131	26	22	11	112,552
Deane, Samuel C.	23	2	1	4	24,710	Deroin, Jamie	9	0	1	3	2,292
Dearinger, Beaman N.	1	1	0	0	2,400	DeRosa, Alexander	38	1	2	1	28,800
Dearringer, Darrell	28	2	2	3	18,308	DeRose, Frank	17	0	0	0	1,380
Dearth, Donald	17	2	1	2	24,460	Derouen, Kenneth	1	0	0	0	0
Deaton, William E.	27	1	3	1	11,409	DeRousselle, Peter P.	139	14	18	14	166,131
Deboise, Harry L.	1	0	0	0	0	DeSanctis, Jaclyn	33	1	2	2	12,605
Deboise, Howard	14	0	0	0	3,054	DeSanctis, Ralph V.	41	0	3	3	32,880
DeBruhl, Kevin B.	52	4	5	9	42,917	Desautel, Dave	9	4	2	1	6,027
deCesare, Barbara	26	1	2	3	52,473	Desensi, Robert L.	48	5	3	8	101,089
Decker, John B.	40	0	0	3	6,225	Deshotel, Justin Wayne	3	1	0	0	5,460
Decker, Kenneth	18	3	4	3	145,853	Desjarlais, Arnold	20	1	3	0	2,814
Decker, Steve	8	2	1	1	41,591	Desmarais, Wayne M.	2	0	0	0	0
Decker, Willette	52	6	6	1	85,928	Desormeaux, J. Keith	232	39	28	35	532,568
Decker, Jr., Cecil	16	0	1	0	2,012	Desoto, II, Donald G.	21	1	1	6	10,298
Decoteau, Blaine	2	0	0	0	130	DeSouza, Bancroft	18	2	4	2	19,889
Decoteau, Wally	1	1	0	0	1,250	DeSouza, Easton	28	2	3	2	27,510
Dee, Tony	71	8	3	11	128,052	DeSouza, Norman	124	30	17	21	734,225
Deibler, Tina L.	66	6	7	11	68,523	DeStasio, Richard A.	70	7	5	9	283,072
Deisley, Doug	2	0	0	0	0	Destefano, Mario R.	16	3	2	2	21,812
Deisley, Virgil L.	52	11	11	11	40,183	Deters, Celia J.	57	5	6	7	37,468
Dejarlais, Joe	3	0	0	0	108	Detiege, Clifton	8	0	1	0	935
DeJesus, Rebel	2	0	0	0	76	DeToro, Nickolas	117	15	10	9	464,835
Del Castillo, Janet	105	0	7	11	64,046	Dettwiller, Daniel	5	0	0	0	60
Delahoussaye, Darrel	106	13	10	10	157,535	Deuel, Jr., William	1	0	0	0	0
Delahoussaye, Glenn	183	17	13	18	232,043	Deutsch, Leo D.	46	2	1	6	12,575
Delahoussaye, Harold J.	62	5	1	5	24,043	Devargas, Julian S.	5	0	1	1	2,481
Delahoussaye, J. Huey	14	0	1	0	3,016	Deverell, Siobhan	26	3	0	3	83,896
Delahoussaye, Kenneth W.	9	2	0	0	12,345	Devereux, Joseph A.	40	6	4	7	223,360
Delahoussaye, Mickey	59	5	1	4	35,285	Devereux, Patrick B.	3	0	0	0	183
Delahoussaye, Minos	53	8	6	9	56,987	Devereux, Jr., Patrick	1	0	0	0	60
Delahoussaye, Tommy J.	75	3	2	7	28,782	Deville, Dwayne	11	0	1	1	1,958
Delaney, Jr., Ralph J.	11	0	1	2	8,220	Deville, Nicholas Lynn	5	0	0	0	100
Deleon, Pilar A.	4	0	0	0	333	DeVille, Carl J.	105	8	13	8	310,226
Delgado, Lucy	28	5	2	4	50,042	Devooght, Dennis	6	1	1	1	6,030
DelGiudice, Kris	97	10	16	7	148,445	Dewey, Homer	2	1	0	0	6,110
Delhomme, Jerry	35	4	4	3	23,916	Dewey, Tom	47	11	4	3	109,728
Delia, William	226	27	34	22	485,453	Deyotte, Ronald A.	26	3	3	6	28,318
D'Elia, Jenny	36	2	2	7	27,451	Di Marsico, Elaine	40	3	4	2	40,279
DeLima, Clifford	178	18	33	24	473,161	Diavolikis, Paul A.	2	1	0	0	9,600
DeLima, Jose E.	94	11	9	19	291,085	Diaz, Antonio L.	16	3	2	3	46,909
Delk, Danny	119	14	14	13	211,742	Diaz, Juvenal L.	9	0	0	1	4,589
Delnegro, Brian	10	2	0	1	4,067	Diaz, Martin	5	0	1	0	1,784
Delnegro, Michael	47	4	5	6	18,932	Diaz, Pablo F.	28	2	6	1	25,490
Delong, Gary	51	5	5	1	105,062	Diaz, Jr., Salvador	3	0	1	0	2,824
Delong, Sr., Robert E.	39	2	8	6	46,983	Dibbens, H. Kathleen	31	6	2	2	103,744
Delozier, Laura S.	1	0	0	0	0	Dibona, Robert S.	40	9	4	4	117,690
Delozier, III, Joseph W.	27	0	1	2	8,995	Dicato, Jr., Joseph A.	42	2	2	8	16,505
Delp, Grover G.	149	29	24	20	688,276	Dickey, Charles L.	87	14	26	7	233,663
Deluca, Louis J.	7	1	0	1	21,000	Dickey, Keith C.	102	12	12	12	196,775
Deluca, Shirley M.	5	0	0	1	2,280	Dickey, William E.	7	1	0	0	3,480
DeMario, Charles A.	111	7	13	12	56,819	Dickinson, Cecil D.	65	3	5	7	49,962
Demasi, Kathleen A.	535	63	62	63	1,100,301	Dickinson, Dennis	19	4	4	5	15,582
Demasi, Patricia	2	0	0	0	800	Dickinson, Michael W.	152	37	30	19	2,286,371
DeMatteis, Mike	31	7	2	4	18,232	Didio, Keith	38	2	5	8	60,048
Demczyk, Virginia	72	2	3	5	37,277	Diekema, Judy E.	2	0	0	0	180
Demeritte, Larry W.	61	4	7	8	105,751	Dieno, Arlen	19	5	2	1	8,592
DeMola, Richard	81	1	4	9	155,154	DiGiovanni, John	9	2	0	1	81,830
Demorest, Gary E.	88	26	19	11	313,919	Dileno, William E.	22	3	1	5	37,376
Dempsey, Robert S.	43	6	6	8	71,735	Dillion, Jimmy L.	46	5	5	11	90,522
Dempsey, Susanne	31	1	2	1	26,069	Dillon, Jacob L.	46	3	1	4	38,401
Demull, Vicki C.	4	0	0	0	250	Dillow, Daniel E.	108	12	11	15	216,313
Dennehy, Donna	7	1	2	0	8,160	Dillow, John H.	184	14	28	18	270,887
Dennis, Betty Lou	22	1	2	2	9,152	Dilodovico, Damon R.	87	10	15	19	155,057
Dennis, David H.	20	2	1	5	17,382	DiMarco, John	28	2	3	4	90,103
Dennis, John D.	17	1	0	0	3,835	Dimas, Robert E.	2	0	0	0	67
Dennis, Larry	29	3	5	1	19,627	DiMauro, Stephen L.	253	26	31	36	637,217
Dennison, Dan H.	176	19	22	18	207,137	Dimitriou, Harry E.	19	2	2	2	42,064
DeNoia, John A.	2	0	0	0	205	DiMuro, Anthony	29	0	2	0	4,384
Denzik, Jr., William J.	15	3	4	0	32,107	DiNatale, Judith Z.	35	3	4	3	46,385
Depalo, Thomas	3	1	0	0	7,910	Dini, Michael	189	13	20	20	368,623
Depalo, Vincent D.	97	11	7	15	305,221	Dinoto, Lori	59	4	3	7	48,002
DePaulo, Michael P.	182	17	23	18	1,065,288	Diodoro, Robertino	301	30	45	39	382,529
Deperrio, Frank	8	0	0	1	1,612	Dion, Andrew W.	16	0	1	2	5,321

Trainer	Sts	1st	2d	3d	Purses	Trainer	Sts	1st	2d	3d	Purses
DiPasquale, Peter	3	0	0	1	2,673	Douglass, Thomas D.	8	0	2	1	14,877
DiPasquale, Sam	48	6	9	7	222,845	Doutrich, David K.	55	6	5	8	120,698
Disanto, Glenn B.	41	1	2	2	59,215	Dovalina, Cristoval	4	0	0	0	330
Dittfach, Hugo	27	5	4	0	250,907	Dove, Stephanie	12	2	1	0	17,285
DiVito, James P.	137	26	17	24	595,509	Dowd, John F.	130	23	23	20	553,113
Divitto, Debra	30	2	2	4	24,872	Downer, Harold R.	7	0	1	0	9,915
Dixon, Linda	53	1	5	2	15,967	Downey, Francis L.	68	3	16	19	35,473
Dixon, Tim	3	0	0	0	70	Downey, Maureen	26	2	0	4	18,457
Dobbie, Edward R.	11	1	0	0	9,732	Downie, Lofflin	4	2	0	0	3,350
Dobbs, Jerry D.	113	21	9	18	156,932	Downing, Dwight	1	0	0	0	44
Dobbs, Phillip	4	0	0	0	0	Downing, William	49	9	4	9	65,193
Dobson, Kimberly A.	107	9	19	12	191,251	Downs, Lincoln	33	3	4	7	33,790
Dodd, Carl	1	0	0	0	0	Downs, Jr., Leonard J.	76	12	6	7	116,435
Dodds, Louis W.	22	2	0	5	52,926	Doyle, Casey	42	2	7	3	48,900
Dodds, Thomas A.	73	8	8	14	105,030	Doyle, Michael J.	262	17	37	45	1,278,554
Dodge, Albert	1	0	0	0	0	Dragoo, Larry L.	40	5	1	3	40,863
Dodgen, James A.	20	7	3	0	47,018	Drake, David	10	1	3	1	4,004
Dodson, Alice J.	3	0	0	0	1,140	Drake, Robert	1	0	0	0	80
Dodson, Cliff	15	2	1	2	15,689	Drake, Sherren A.	9	0	0	1	812
Dodson, Phillip	25	2	2	2	17,478	Drake, Suzanne M.	13	1	0	1	13,514
Dodwell, Ed	122	15	10	12	237,713	Draper, Carl W.	10	2	2	2	56,070
Doege, Glenn	70	7	9	8	56,625	Draper, Marlon	45	4	6	5	22,731
Doering, Mark	116	14	16	15	111,316	Draper, Otto	7	0	0	0	3,675
Doire, Ronald O.	2	0	0	1	1,600	Dresch, Heath D.	2	0	0	0	0
Dolan, John K.	68	6	6	17	229,650	Drexler, Martin	42	5	3	7	38,911
Dolan, Michael D.	11	0	0	0	1,108	Drexler, Steve	9	0	0	3	6,653
Dollase, Aimee	7	1	0	1	26,529	Driever, Doug	84	7	8	9	118,875
Dollase, Craig	142	32	22	20	2,366,273	Driever, Jr., Jack W.	1	0	0	0	0
Dollase, Wallace A.	95	24	14	17	3,168,828	Drinkard, Elbert L.	4	0	1	0	5,250
Dollinger-Stehr, Linda	63	2	8	5	59,789	Driskill, Jolly	8	1	2	0	4,894
Dolph, Darla	38	1	2	6	13,094	Driving Hawk, Jr., Ed	43	1	1	6	11,731
Dominguez, Caesar F.	151	19	17	15	661,945	Dronen, Sam	7	1	2	2	4,740
Dominguez, David	3	0	0	0	2,737	Dronet, James	27	6	6	2	47,951
Dominguez, Henry	442	108	75	62	1,413,493	Drozdowski, Mike	6	0	0	0	244
Dominguez, Jose Luis	8	2	1	1	21,949	Drummond, Robert	5	2	0	0	2,595
Dominguez, Luis R.	114	19	13	20	147,487	Drummond, S. Diana	36	4	5	2	53,789
Dominguez, Roberto	37	4	8	11	38,743	Drumwright, John	6	0	0	0	385
Domino, Carl J.	72	7	3	3	148,670	Drury, Jr., Thomas	82	18	11	16	114,804
Donaghey, Dianna	5	0	0	2	2,484	Drysdale, Neil D.	182	34	27	37	3,676,819
Donaghey, John R.	9	1	1	0	9,600	Dubois, Pete	31	5	3	5	15,036
Donaho, Anthony	5	0	0	1	1,403	Dubois, Todd	2	0	0	0	288
Donahue, Denise M.	12	0	0	3	6,530	Duby, Carol M.	20	8	4	2	34,522
Donald, Ira J.	97	10	12	9	101,425	Ducoing, Sturges J.	14	3	0	4	28,475
Donaldson, Billy M.	1	0	0	0	0	Dudley, Patricia A.	5	0	0	0	0
Donaleshen, Nick	17	0	1	3	1,672	Duffy, Joseph	56	3	2	2	39,709
Donathan, David B.	30	2	6	3	19,123	Duffy, Patricia L.	11	1	0	2	12,180
Donato, Robert A.	1	0	0	0	455	Duffy, Jr., Arthur A.	103	15	19	14	284,284
Donelan, Gary	10	0	1	3	2,468	Duffy, Sr., Arthur A.	4	0	1	1	2,486
Doner, Jill	1	0	0	0	0	Dufrene, Nicky	53	7	7	6	91,480
Donk, David G.	270	29	25	48	1,034,471	Duhon, James	102	7	13	8	93,172
Donley, Jim	49	3	3	5	23,252	Duhon, Joe	215	20	21	33	349,333
Donley, Robert	4	1	0	0	2,686	Duhon, R. Paul	206	27	28	13	381,440
Donlin, Larry D.	85	8	6	11	61,909	Duhon, Roland J.	70	3	15	8	59,015
Donlin, Jr., Larry D.	10	2	0	0	17,494	Duke, Caleb	9	3	0	0	60,086
Donmoyer, Steve J.	8	0	1	0	3,750	Duke, David L.	21	2	4	2	7,075
Donnelly, Michael	13	2	0	0	14,873	Duke, Gary	5	3	0	2	3,142
Donovan, Patrick R.	41	4	1	5	26,068	Duke, Karen E.	61	5	8	6	218,893
Dorchester, Dennis	23	2	5	3	11,334	Duke, Steven	29	0	2	1	5,658
Dore, Ralph J.	7	1	0	1	9,782	Dukes, Harris T.	104	5	4	7	73,202
Dorfman, Leonard	15	3	2	2	161,080	Dukes, Robert	144	4	11	14	48,318
Dorochenko, Gennadi	138	14	15	24	203,796	Dullea, Francis M.	196	13	17	16	209,655
Dorris, Chris	171	19	14	27	317,475	Dumas, Brian E.	5	1	0	1	3,475
Dorris, Thomas P.	10	4	1	3	27,504	Dumont, Marti L.	40	3	2	5	26,606
Dorris, Tom	344	43	43	44	883,985	Dunaway, Keith	15	1	3	1	20,848
Dorsch, Ramona	47	4	9	7	57,538	Dunbar, Julia	14	1	1	2	21,370
Dorsey, Sam A.	36	1	3	2	22,335	Dunbar, Larry	71	6	14	10	144,869
Dortch, David L.	17	0	1	3	4,594	Duncan, Bill D.	207	31	28	26	190,910
Doss, Carlos	3	0	0	0	655	Duncan, H. R.	16	0	0	0	1,783
Doth, Peter	22	0	0	2	2,960	Duncan, James A.	18	2	0	5	22,726
Dotolo, David	61	6	8	6	171,841	Duncan, Leonard M.	157	17	24	15	456,583
Dotson, Millard F.	104	5	4	10	71,802	Duncan, Steven L.	71	4	9	10	64,526
Doucet, Glen	94	15	13	13	117,614	Duncan, Susan A.	2	0	0	0	275
Doucet, James Roger	120	17	13	16	211,623	Dundon, James C.	3	0	1	0	5,880
Doucet, Terry	28	0	1	0	5,241	Dunford, Justin	10	0	1	2	1,347
Douglas, Andrew	6	1	1	1	7,469	Dunham, Bob G.	35	0	5	3	61,917
Douglas, Sue	2	0	0	0	0	Dunham, Daniel	73	4	8	10	96,285

Trainer	Sts	1st	2d	3d	Purses	Trainer	Sts	1st	2d	3d	Purses
Dunivan, Janice A.	97	9	9	9	135,337	Eickerman, Gary	5	0	0	0	658
Dunkelberger, Casey A.	77	13	7	10	141,383	Eikleberry, Clifford R.	13	0	0	1	860
Dunlavy, Terrence W.	66	4	11	12	106,470	Eikleberry, Donald	57	2	3	7	36,686
Dunlevy, Gary R.	4	0	0	1	1,300	Eikleberry, Kevin	178	21	22	25	301,876
Dunlop, Edward	1	0	0	0	8,370	Eilers, Larry J.	164	15	13	17	187,097
Dunlop, John L.	1	0	0	0	0	Einerson, Kerry	30	2	2	0	25,390
Dunn, Henry Ray	18	0	2	4	11,229	Einhorn, Raymond P.	47	3	7	5	55,605
Dunn, John J.	50	6	9	6	156,519	Ekins, Dennis	31	5	2	5	24,567
Dunn, Stephen D.	60	10	6	8	149,368	Ekins, Ronald W.	1	0	1	0	320
Duplechin, James H.	144	10	14	12	124,264	Elamri, Hassan	108	4	11	5	115,218
Duplichan, William R.	60	6	9	6	53,546	Eldridge, Carol L.	4	0	0	0	0
DuPont, Laurent E.	92	7	5	13	65,654	Eldridge, Patricia K.	4	0	0	0	634
Dupps, Kristina	30	5	6	6	242,158	Eliott, Roger	21	0	1	3	7,370
Dupre, Alain	1	0	0	0	0	Elison, Dennis	1	0	0	0	0
Dupuis, Jean-Pierre	47	8	9	8	319,953	Elison, Gary C.	16	2	6	4	18,203
Dupuis, Randel	4	0	0	0	0	Elison, Tawnja	33	14	8	2	48,707
Dupuy, Allen C.	48	2	8	5	41,506	Elison, Tim W.	60	13	13	8	74,234
Dupuy, Donna L.	58	2	3	11	84,778	Ellersick, Roger	5	0	0	0	386
Dupuy, Sonja	6	1	1	1	11,992	Elliot, Janet K.	78	7	3	5	147,566
Durbin, James R.	75	6	6	8	49,346	Elliott, Kermit R.	3	0	0	0	0
Durbin, William R.	11	0	1	0	4,638	Elliott, Teri	41	5	3	5	41,601
Duree, Dominic C.	42	6	6	6	57,382	Elliott, Tim	24	6	1	2	12,808
Durham, Corliss	5	1	1	0	11,111	Ellis, James W.	2	0	0	0	210
Durrett, Walter J.	115	16	13	14	251,358	Ellis, Kelly	3	0	0	0	100
Durso, Robert J.	104	12	5	16	324,415	Ellis, Larry	15	0	0	0	686
Duschka, Steve	168	25	25	28	74,735	Ellis, Leonard E.	166	13	13	17	110,324
Dussembaev, Talgat	23	1	3	1	14,834	Ellis, Randy J.	48	5	5	8	88,223
Dutrow, Anthony W.	297	89	65	39	2,448,827	Ellis, Robert J.	1	0	0	0	0
Dutrow, Sydney	27	7	4	3	68,510	Ellis, Ronald W.	115	16	21	19	836,445
Dutrow, Jr., Richard E.	531	132	90	85	4,917,280	Ellis, Sam H.	96	11	6	13	98,657
Dutton, Jerry	170	19	20	23	533,839	Elmegreen, David	73	9	10	7	136,226
Dwight II, Francis M.	10	2	1	2	14,480	Elordi, Donna R.	145	22	16	19	429,075
Dwoskin, Angel	1	0	0	0	684	Elrod, Richard L.	9	1	0	0	5,718
Dwoskin, Steven	168	31	27	24	527,076	Elsom, Laurie	3	0	0	1	923
Dwyer, Dave	33	11	5	3	428,978	Elston, Brent	45	6	1	2	27,257
Dye, Heather	64	5	11	9	19,461	Elsworth, David	1	0	0	0	0
Dye, Steven	4	0	0	0	417	Elter, Bradley J.	19	2	1	0	16,513
Dyer, Carl M.	222	27	31	35	427,507	Ely, Janice L.	84	4	17	5	209,625
Dyer, Debbie Holland	109	12	17	11	142,447	Embry, Gene	62	9	4	2	95,920
Dykeman, Pamela	34	2	7	4	18,942	Emery, Ronald W.	13	0	1	0	9,436
Eade, William J.	5	0	0	0	2,119	Emery, Velma	1	0	0	0	0
Eafford, James	58	7	3	8	42,941	Engebretson, Art C.	2	0	0	1	260
Eagan, Mark	37	2	4	1	18,157	Engel, Rick S.	115	25	20	10	283,137
Eanes, Charles	75	6	5	8	55,544	Engel, Roger F.	102	26	15	10	228,114
Earle, Bill K.	26	2	3	3	5,196	England, Clyde W.	47	2	4	8	11,623
Earlywine, Christopher	32	2	6	4	22,578	England, David P.	71	9	4	2	40,616
Easley, Pat	20	1	3	1	4,787	England, Deborah	54	5	7	7	174,966
Eason, Ralph	12	0	0	1	660	England, Phillip	70	9	3	3	357,627
Eastwood, Rae	14	1	0	2	4,181	England, Jr., G. Marion	12	0	0	0	4,153
Eaton, Charles K.	53	7	6	6	86,692	Engle, Kathleen	7	1	0	0	4,969
Eaton, Terri	149	3	12	12	121,556	Englehart, Chris J.	575	111	89	82	1,039,199
Ebardt, Janice	3	0	0	0	115	Englehart, Jeremiah C.	29	2	3	3	109,965
Ebardt, Tom L.	128	7	15	8	116,972	English, Edward T.	42	5	2	7	55,535
Ebert, Dennis W.	96	17	19	14	490,347	Enloe, Dennis	4	0	0	0	150
Eck, Jake	13	2	5	3	4,745	Enlow, John A.	24	0	3	2	7,699
Eckrosh, James J.	27	0	1	0	21,026	Enlow, Ray A.	3	0	1	0	667
Ecoffey, Gilbert L.	61	7	2	6	22,609	Enright, Angela	1	0	0	0	180
Eddings, Larry	22	2	0	3	10,255	Enriquez, Jesus J.	16	3	0	3	10,581
Edelman, Don	40	5	7	2	32,039	Ensom, Jim	9	1	1	1	14,722
Edelman, George	14	4	0	1	37,610	Entenmann, William J.	37	6	6	4	170,230
Edgar, Ernest E.	14	3	3	2	29,796	Eoff, Terry	31	3	3	2	15,976
Edgerly, Ken	2	0	0	0	0	Epley, Jr., Steve	78	8	6	9	130,700
Edwards, Angus L.	1	0	0	0	0	Eppler, Mary E.	154	17	15	26	485,474
Edwards, Daniel C.	52	1	3	5	39,729	Epsteen, Wayne	1	0	0	0	50
Edwards, Dennis Scott	28	7	6	3	93,564	Erb, Darrin	76	13	5	4	60,951
Edwards, F. Bart	24	2	8	4	32,120	Erb, Michael D.	2	1	0	0	6,704
Edwards, Michael L.	40	6	1	3	27,986	Erb, Peter F.	20	2	4	3	38,153
Edwards, Oliver	188	20	28	32	500,273	Erickson, Darrel L.	4	1	0	0	5,370
Edwards, Oliver S.	11	0	1	2	7,971	Erickson, Elwood C.	34	1	1	7	25,667
Edwards, Parke	42	5	6	9	12,644	Erickson, Kathy	4	1	1	1	2,796
Edwards, Shirley A.	21	3	0	2	27,256	Ericson, Tiffany	31	2	2	3	18,568
Edwards, Stephen	41	6	5	3	190,413	Erler, Jacqueline J.	43	1	2	4	21,161
Edwards, Toby D.	43	5	5	6	98,130	Ermineskin, Curtis	4	0	0	0	130
Edwards, Walter L.	10	1	1	0	10,559	Ersoff, Stanley M.	91	8	12	14	139,746
Eff, Joseph A.	58	4	8	8	92,843	Ervin, Jody	48	2	1	2	10,346
Ehret, Sandra	85	6	9	8	38,685	Ervin, Raymond E.	21	3	3	6	38,121

Trainer	Sts	1st	2d	3d	Purses	Trainer	Sts	1st	2d	3d	Purses
Ervin, Timothy	10	0	1	0	1,666	Farias, Adan	22	6	3	1	32,464
Ervin-Mezzacappa, Jody	2	0	0	0	0	Fariello, Vincent	18	1	4	0	12,208
Erwin, Dennis M.	48	4	4	4	112,035	Farkosh, George	14	1	1	2	12,199
Erwin, Ted	13	0	0	2	1,801	Farler, Larry	88	7	8	14	62,280
Eshelman, Bonnie	12	1	0	1	6,430	Farley, Burton	1	0	0	0	288
Esner, Tommy Lynn	15	2	2	2	13,530	Farley, James	31	3	4	5	45,888
Esparza, Osvaldo	56	1	2	7	15,077	Farmer, Murrell K.	10	2	0	0	9,856
Espinosa, Victor M.	37	2	1	3	28,634	Farnsworth, Deloy	19	2	3	1	15,670
Espinoza, Leonard A.	188	13	16	20	66,814	Farrell, Tom	34	3	3	6	7,949
Espinoza, Valentine	25	1	5	4	10,794	Farris, Kevin	5	0	0	1	1,174
Esposito, Michael F.	28	0	0	2	3,834	Farris, William L.	6	0	0	0	230
Espy, Jim	35	2	2	2	11,954	Farro, Patricia	486	69	59	68	1,063,345
Esquibel, Allen J.	2	0	0	0	150	Fauchald, Philip C.	8	1	2	1	19,836
Esquibel, Charlotte	5	0	0	0	340	Faul, Leo P.	5	0	0	0	0
Esquibel, Mark	76	10	2	14	65,088	Faulkner, Floyd	5	0	0	0	450
Esquibel, Mike	7	0	0	1	636	Faulkner, Jeffrey	38	5	12	5	22,057
Esquibel, Robert L.	8	0	0	0	783	Faulkner, Randy Joe	69	3	2	12	23,761
Esquibel, Sr., Richard Dean	67	2	1	8	11,120	Faulkner, Rodney C.	727	133	113	107	785,605
Essenpreis, Eddie M.	433	76	65	75	674,080	Fawcett, Russell	5	0	1	0	1,900
Essex, Charles	59	2	4	9	64,681	Fawkes, David	242	32	31	30	648,359
Estep, Gary D.	13	2	5	1	16,863	Fazekas, Frank E.	2	0	0	0	0
Estes, Michael R.	61	6	12	7	106,155	Feasel, Steve	1	0	0	0	40
Estevez, Edgar A.	2	0	1	0	1,500	Feathers-Murray, Amy	43	4	4	9	26,431
Estevez, Manuel A.	155	8	10	26	213,764	Fede, Pietro	100	2	4	14	47,640
Estilette, Earl	15	4	2	0	25,967	Federouch, Bernadine	2	0	0	0	1,050
Estrada, Sr., Salvador Z.	1	0	0	0	47	Fee, John J.	36	0	6	3	49,301
Estvanko, Richard	164	25	22	18	206,662	Feebeck, Thomas H.	67	3	8	10	30,854
Etheridge, Milton B.	23	0	0	2	4,767	Fehr, Alec	61	9	11	3	745,784
Eubank, Nadine	22	2	2	2	11,188	Feilner, II, Raymond F.	1	0	0	0	0
Eubanks, Annette M.	130	6	17	20	164,716	Feliciano, Benny R.	88	20	11	12	158,876
Eurton, Peter	115	16	22	16	592,575	Feliciano, Miguel A.	338	49	52	47	801,443
Evans, Bart B.	61	8	5	9	150,606	Feliciano, Trudy Veinot	16	0	5	4	15,604
Evans, Dan	39	3	7	4	30,588	Feliciano, Jr., Benjamin M.	294	66	46	46	1,310,170
Evans, Donald J.	4	0	0	0	800	Felipe, Dan	73	9	5	10	68,200
Evans, Holly	17	2	2	2	67,835	Fenack, Wayne	10	2	2	2	15,233
Evans, Jim	38	10	2	6	28,606	Fenack, Jr., Tony	10	1	1	2	14,701
Evans, Justin	340	60	53	50	374,013	Fendenheim, James R.	31	1	2	3	5,610
Evans, Roy	79	4	2	6	42,468	Fenimore, Elbert	40	1	1	1	14,785
Evans, Suzanne G.	118	15	12	15	252,086	Fenimore, Floyd E.	52	9	6	9	84,694
Evans, Timothy	5	1	1	0	27,674	Fennell, Ernest	38	2	1	5	10,310
Evans, William	66	6	5	2	27,370	Fennell, Kelly Kory	3	1	0	0	550
Evans, Jr., George A.	10	0	0	1	2,495	Fennessy, Michael	59	6	5	3	64,470
Everard, Elizabeth	7	1	0	2	9,243	Fenwick, Jr., Charles C.	4	1	0	0	0
Everett, Scott	90	8	5	18	273,701	Fergason, Jim	262	47	50	40	194,703
Everetts, Lester P.	4	0	0	0	0	Fergason, Rolland R.	158	18	19	19	128,088
Everman, Joseph	42	9	4	3	115,173	Fergason, Terry Lee	35	9	4	3	16,065
Ewell, Rodger	5	1	0	0	3,120	Fergason, Vernon A.	20	0	3	5	5,890
Ewing, Kim S.	154	12	19	28	156,854	Ferguson, Aileen D.	9	1	1	0	12,567
Exposito, Adolfo J.	29	6	0	4	48,683	Ferguson, Chad M.	113	12	20	11	141,508
Eyerman, Lee J.	29	3	5	4	17,479	Ferguson, Curt	49	8	6	7	49,065
Eyre, Brady	4	0	2	0	2,265	Ferguson, Darl W.	6	1	2	0	12,138
Ezekiel, Jr., Marshall	27	1	0	4	6,885	Ferguson, Deas	5	0	0	1	2,920
Ezra, Daryl	193	25	30	22	655,775	Ferguson, Debi	54	11	3	8	44,364
Fabre, Andre	2	0	1	0	122,500	Ferguson, Deborah A.	6	0	0	1	4,270
Fabre, Jamie	1	0	0	0	0	Ferguson, Jimmy	1	0	0	0	0
Fagan, Lawrence G.	8	0	0	0	657	Ferguson, Jolene	2	0	0	0	563
Fagan, Patricia L.	9	0	0	1	1,585	Ferguson, Ron W.	6	0	2	1	9,790
Fahy, Timothy J.	4	0	2	0	1,520	Ferguson, Shauna	12	1	2	2	32,697
Fair, James L.	91	4	5	4	80,997	Ferguson, Sr., John W.	13	1	1	0	14,090
Faircloth, Aveory	15	1	2	4	44,511	Fernandes, Vernon	37	2	7	7	53,859
Faircloth, Ronnie E.	48	0	2	0	10,495	Fernandez, Rafael A.	11	0	0	0	2,020
Fairfield, Don	4	0	0	0	120	Feron, Kathleen M.	27	1	2	3	76,720
Fairholm, Ronald D.	23	1	0	0	5,945	Ferraiola, Frank L.	9	1	1	0	7,956
Fairlie, Scott H.	338	84	55	55	2,816,357	Ferraioli, Joseph	19	0	1	1	15,020
Faist, Carolyn Y.	21	0	1	0	1,826	Ferraro, James W.	140	9	9	13	419,900
Falat, Stephen	8	0	2	0	2,652	Ferraro, Michael Anthony	408	97	66	53	874,216
Falk, George W.	5	0	0	1	1,045	Ferraro, Michael S.	304	73	47	30	510,423
Falkner, John	7	0	1	0	2,708	Ferraro, Robert G.	5	0	0	0	904
Falldorf, Fred J.	20	1	4	2	64,731	Ferreira, Fernando	93	4	7	13	47,079
Falls Down, Adlai	11	1	0	0	1,758	Ferrell, D. Lynn	2	0	1	0	840
Falzone, Victor	72	4	5	7	62,290	Ferrell, Jory	70	6	9	8	51,449
Fanara, James	21	0	2	1	17,040	Ferri, Elaine	54	4	2	13	82,315
Fanning, Jerry M.	89	4	7	10	153,232	Ferris, Jerrald M.	40	5	7	7	173,422
Fanning, Marvin E.	39	2	4	6	19,236	Festenese, Marla	1	0	0	0	0
Faraci-Walder, Francine	1	0	1	0	4,560	Fetherolf, John D.	16	0	0	3	2,022
Faragoza, Rene	43	4	1	3	23,567	Fett, Brandi Jo	5	0	0	0	0

Trainer	Sts	1st	2d	3d	Purses
Fetters, Michael C.	1	0	0	0	0
Fetty, James H.	3	0	0	0	657
Fewell, Danny	59	5	6	8	43,592
Fiddler, Richard	18	2	2	2	3,097
Fields, Harry C	21	0	3	2	8,930
Fields, James V.	34	2	2	4	6,704
Fields, Kevin L.	3	0	0	0	110
Fields, Lon E.	4	2	0	0	5,730
Fiesman, Robert	94	4	9	4	38,269
Figgins, Raymond R.	1	0	0	0	0
Figgins, Jr., Ollie L.	26	2	0	1	16,490
Figueroa, Carlos R.	166	20	12	21	109,315
Figueroa, Jimmy M.	9	2	3	1	27,826
Figueroa, Juan	6	0	0	1	721
Figueroa, Manny A.	56	6	10	8	14,985
Figueroa, Jr., Pablo E.	1	0	0	0	0
Figueroa, Sr., Pablo C.	33	5	6	6	17,310
Filbey, Richard L.	31	2	3	4	24,816
Filewich, Jerry N.	15	1	2	2	19,717
Filipelli, Jr., John	4	0	0	0	325
Filipowski, Denise L.	6	1	0	0	9,480
Finch, M. Shawn	109	8	7	11	64,758
Finch, Richard	3	0	1	0	1,980
Fincher, Leroy A.	48	8	4	5	86,810
Fincher, Todd W.	125	29	18	19	753,156
Findlay, Chuck	41	8	3	8	43,922
Fine, Larry	15	1	2	0	6,186
Fink, Jr., William J.	2	2	0	0	34,200
Finley, Bruce L.	25	1	0	0	9,123
Finn, John T.	9	0	0	0	2,480
Finn, Sherry	10	1	1	2	11,115
Finnell, Clay	14	0	4	0	2,831
Finucane, Richard	78	4	10	15	110,400
Fior, Dick	5	1	0	1	1,940
Fiore, Nicholas J.	5	0	0	0	576
Fires, William H.	176	22	17	23	477,342
Firestone, Kermit L.	25	0	4	0	8,222
Fischer, Mary Ann	52	1	4	8	20,792
Fischer, Robert L.	21	1	0	2	7,001
Fisher, Allen	5	0	0	0	915
Fisher, Bill	6	1	1	0	1,831
Fisher, Dan	2	0	1	0	440
Fisher, Jack	142	27	24	20	532,010
Fisher, John L.	20	0	1	0	8,695
Fisher, John R. S.	67	5	7	9	178,520
Fisher, Kerri L.	4	1	0	1	15,506
Fisher, Mark	2	0	0	0	0
Fisher, Robert A.	48	2	2	4	13,485
Fisher, Steve	13	0	1	3	6,582
Fisher, Susan	71	9	12	1	101,460
Fisher, Verna	4	0	0	0	185
Fisher, III, Janon	32	2	5	2	31,541
Fishman, Stanley	53	7	9	5	139,456
Fisichello, J. C.	15	2	0	2	6,590
Fister, John Kyle	37	4	3	1	96,266
Fite, Walter	19	2	1	2	24,163
Fittante, Ruth M.	28	2	1	3	17,312
Fitz, Ernie	1	0	0	0	51
Fitzgerald, Nancy P.	9	2	1	2	9,768
Fitzgerald, Shelley E.	34	3	4	4	193,072
Fitzpatrick, Joe	14	2	4	2	4,716
Fitzpatrick, Robert	58	10	9	8	65,439
Fix, Jr., Henry G.	19	3	2	2	71,541
Flagle, John	2	0	0	0	112
Flatland, Dean	2	0	0	0	129
Flegel, Arlene	37	5	6	7	17,116
Fleischman, Ronald W.	14	1	1	1	34,177
Fleming, Rhonda	2	0	0	0	0
Flemings, Joe	103	19	14	16	185,769
Flenner, Andreana	1	0	0	0	220
Flenner, Kenneth	23	0	4	4	30,212
Fletcher, Kevin	47	2	9	3	56,432
Flick, Amos	1	0	0	0	0
Flint, Bernard S.	634	128	81	71	2,566,975
Flint, Steven B.	116	22	19	9	692,788
Flom, Amber	14	2	3	2	4,776
Flores, Gilberto M.	47	3	2	8	28,592
Flores, Jose Antonio	7	0	0	0	690
Flores, Manuel	15	0	0	2	2,640
Flores, Moses	2	0	0	0	0
Flores, Rafael Q.	4	0	0	0	0
Flores, Ramon	62	10	8	9	101,041
Flores, Rigoberto	7	1	0	1	1,660
Flores, Sr., Luis A.	1	0	0	0	47
Florez, Carlos	7	0	1	0	3,061
Florie, Bryant Sterling	1	0	0	0	43
Floyd, Billie F.	80	9	11	2	170,549
Flud, Jr., Richard D.	12	1	1	0	6,200
Flugence, Freddie	19	0	0	2	3,299
Flugence, Wilson	27	1	4	3	21,124
Flynn, Ernie D.	68	4	3	4	31,336
Foggiano, Donna	28	7	4	5	50,141
Foglia, Anthony M.	1	0	0	0	125
Fojan, Emilie	116	19	16	12	462,145
Foley, Dravo G.	38	6	5	4	117,360
Foley, Gregory D.	230	50	28	40	1,196,620
Foley, Mark L.	12	2	0	1	10,510
Foley, Sean P.	98	9	14	14	79,889
Foley, Vickie L.	148	15	23	29	339,393
Foley, Jr., Robert B.	16	1	3	0	25,566
Follett, Norman C.	75	3	1	8	30,785
Folting, Christy V.	6	0	2	2	21,800
Fonnesbeck, Marc D.	4	0	0	1	396
Fontenot, Alfred Joseph	21	0	2	0	3,710
Fontenot, Allen	27	2	3	4	22,138
Fontenot, Jr., Larry L.	2	0	0	0	190
Fontes, Jr., Ramon	6	3	1	1	5,134
Foos, Lawrence E.	39	1	4	10	19,009
Fopp, Nikki	52	2	7	9	44,320
Forbes, John H.	132	10	22	16	280,673
Ford, Donald E.	13	3	0	2	9,716
Ford, James P.	8	2	0	1	6,347
Ford, Jesse	16	1	4	1	12,538
Ford, John	9	0	0	0	761
Ford, L. D.	7	0	1	2	3,825
Ford, William R.	81	8	15	13	109,600
Ford, Jr., Don H.	6	0	1	0	2,700
Ford, Jr., Stephen F.	113	14	18	15	167,416
Forehand, Jr., Charles	23	3	7	4	8,936
Foreman, Thomas R.	23	1	0	1	20,370
Forster, David	101	16	18	12	350,048
Forster, Grant T.	166	32	27	30	677,663
Forster, Richard C.	6	2	1	1	3,286
Forston, Roy A.	18	1	4	2	20,827
Forsyth, Robert	7	0	0	0	0
Fortner, William	2	0	0	2	1,460
Fosdick, Stephen V.	113	11	14	13	139,388
Foster, Angela	9	1	1	2	7,042
Foster, Brenda	8	0	0	0	0
Foster, Dale	96	11	7	13	33,992
Foster, Daniel H.	22	0	5	0	16,669
Foster, Everett	1	0	0	0	144
Foster, James R.	11	0	0	1	2,093
Foster, Joseph M.	114	7	7	8	68,181
Foster, Lawrence L.	8	0	2	0	4,360
Foster, Linda L.	66	9	6	10	44,055
Foster, Steven D.	4	0	0	0	70
Foster, Thomas P.	8	1	0	1	6,844
Foster, Jr., Val Ray	73	10	11	5	145,722
Fournier, Mark	24	6	0	3	66,635
Fout, Paul Douglas	77	9	11	9	247,329
Fout, Paul R.	15	2	2	2	41,820
Foutch, John	8	0	0	1	1,050
Foutz, A. Kneale	3	1	0	0	6,720
Fowler, Beverly A.	61	4	4	6	54,402
Fowler, Earl	15	3	3	2	8,479
Fowler, Joe	1	0	0	0	95
Fowles, Bryce A.	1	0	0	0	44
Fox, Fred E.	18	2	3	2	28,685
Fox, Jamie	31	1	6	3	92,386
Fox, Sondra	49	4	8	7	42,409
Fraley, James E.	27	0	3	3	11,140

Trainer	Sts	1st	2d	3d	Purses	Trainer	Sts	1st	2d	3d	Purses
Frame, Melvin	114	6	10	19	56,763	Furlong, Kenyon G.	19	1	4	1	37,940
Francis, Michelle	25	3	1	0	19,160	Furness, Ronald W.	34	2	6	9	23,676
Francisco, Dan C.	7	2	4	0	9,249	Furnish, John	1	0	0	1	750
Francy, Kate	69	4	7	11	102,255	Furr, Daniel R.	90	10	11	16	226,718
Frangella, Jr., James A.	3	0	0	0	3,180	Furr, Mike A.	45	5	5	5	45,371
Frank, Clement A.	35	1	4	4	17,384	Furr, Sr., Robert W.	8	0	3	0	8,901
Frank, Jeffrey	9	2	0	0	3,127	Fusco, Mark	298	59	50	41	890,069
Frankel, Robert J.	411	114	79	57	19,143,289	Gabbard, Andrea	13	1	1	2	17,909
Franklin, Denise	3	0	0	0	850	Gabbard, James	2	1	0	0	3,150
Franklin, Don W.	2	0	0	0	175	Gabbard, Ronald C.	154	7	21	18	121,694
Frasca, Steven J.	3	0	0	0	480	Gabriel, Bettye A.	73	11	6	9	151,400
Frasca, Thomas C.	8	1	0	2	9,310	Gabriel, Sondra	6	1	1	1	1,921
Frasson, Armand	6	0	1	1	6,031	Gabriel, Toni	29	5	2	3	89,519
Fratangeli, Salvatore	15	1	1	2	18,672	Gabriel, Jr., Leo G.	106	16	15	9	509,955
Frazee, Larry	129	9	14	14	122,405	Gabrielli, Gino	77	4	7	9	34,811
Frazier, F. C.	157	22	20	21	110,824	Gach, Richard	13	0	2	4	47,381
Frazier, Murray L.	63	7	7	11	78,015	Gaede, Milton M.	129	24	18	16	97,831
Frazier, Walter J.	2	0	0	0	100	Gaffka, Sean B.	10	1	0	4	7,960
Frederick, Edward Harrison	59	4	4	5	86,718	Gaffney, John P.	1	0	0	0	0
Frederick, Isaac A.	5	0	1	0	3,972	Gaffney, Ronald	34	3	5	2	64,225
Frederick, Raymond	47	5	10	1	87,813	Gafka, Gregory Wade	16	3	1	2	20,066
Fredo, Patricia A.	18	0	1	0	4,195	Gagliardi, Jill	26	2	3	2	30,207
Freel, Byron	9	1	0	0	3,766	Gainer, William B.	4	0	0	0	478
Freeman, Edward R.	67	8	8	5	173,760	Gaines, Carla	159	23	32	20	1,094,952
Freeman, Kenneth C.	25	0	3	2	5,113	Galayda, Keith A.	4	0	0	0	781
Freeman, Robert J.	17	0	0	0	1,784	Gale, Bryce	50	3	4	6	21,695
Freeman, Scott	48	10	7	9	68,464	Gall, David A.	149	24	16	13	115,648
Freeman, Todd	3	0	0	0	950	Gallagher, Alfred	12	2	0	2	11,225
Freeman, Willard C.	32	2	4	5	64,840	Gallagher, Dorothy	33	4	2	5	42,952
Freer, Karen M.	67	4	4	3	73,643	Gallagher, Liam	2	0	0	1	801
Fregara, John	16	1	0	0	24,055	Gallagher, Patrick	238	24	31	32	1,293,652
Freije, Claude F.	11	1	3	3	7,672	Gallant, Ernest J.	29	2	3	6	21,716
French, Calvin W.	8	0	0	0	590	Gallant, Jr., Ernest J.	1	0	0	1	1,320
French, Neil	64	13	13	13	612,993	Gallegos, Jose A.	125	21	26	23	317,184
French, Quinton A.	25	0	0	3	3,049	Gallegos, Rudy	2	0	0	0	245
French, Robert Mark	20	1	2	3	8,561	Gallegos, Teri L.	32	1	0	1	7,835
French, Wayne R.	18	1	4	3	17,195	Gallegos, Tony M.	1	0	0	0	156
Fresquez, James	1	0	0	0	0	Gallion, Shane	20	0	0	2	3,139
Frey, Carson	64	7	10	16	84,785	Gallo, Louis P.	99	12	8	5	194,083
Fridley, Steve	21	2	5	2	17,048	Galloway, Rod L.	3	0	0	0	40
Friedberg, Jean S.	6	0	0	0	2,168	Galluscio, Dominic G.	239	35	30	33	1,198,681
Friedman, John C.	30	0	6	3	47,195	Galvan, Jose Luis	16	2	2	1	30,900
Friedman, Lesley	38	1	4	3	12,855	Galvez, Emmanuel	1	0	0	0	0
Friedman, Mitchell E.	91	5	7	18	302,159	Galvin, Derek	2	0	0	0	1,545
Frierson, James	29	2	0	3	11,132	Gamber, Robert E.	49	2	3	2	35,993
Friesen, April	18	3	0	1	93,366	Gamble, Melvin	18	1	1	3	2,861
Friesen, Stan	4	0	0	0	220	Gambolati, Cam M.	109	20	12	10	496,375
Friley, Willis R.	23	2	0	4	23,395	Gamez, Gloria	6	0	0	1	720
Fritz, Mario	15	2	0	3	10,150	Gamez, Greg	15	3	3	3	4,250
Frock, Charles L.	174	14	21	15	185,521	Gamez, Ruben	1	0	0	0	81
Frodsham, Vincent	58	4	6	10	42,219	Gammon, Kimmy L.	83	0	4	5	15,156
Frost, Leslie J.	14	2	1	0	26,689	Gannaway, Rebecca	10	0	1	1	2,522
Frost, Stephanie	4	0	0	1	3,380	Gape, John H.	28	1	1	3	14,975
Frostad, Mark R.	206	44	34	31	3,918,142	Garcea, Eric	42	9	4	6	442,423
Frousiakis, George P.	57	4	13	7	41,283	Garcia, Amalio	6	2	2	0	42,380
Fruzzetti, Mary Ann	69	5	7	16	56,945	Garcia, Benny	7	1	1	1	4,130
Fruzzetti, Richard J.	96	8	10	10	73,834	Garcia, Carlos A.	186	25	21	28	511,873
Fry, Toni	2	0	0	0	107	Garcia, Efrain T.	156	19	22	20	235,294
Frye, Greg	48	12	6	7	84,589	Garcia, Enrique P.	46	0	6	3	31,080
Fryman, David R.	1	0	0	0	0	Garcia, Evelio	79	14	16	11	141,287
Fuchs, John W.	33	7	5	2	123,847	Garcia, Harold	14	0	1	0	4,274
Fuchs, Mark J.	25	1	2	3	21,709	Garcia, Juan J.	23	1	1	0	8,486
Fuchs, Thomas L.	12	1	1	3	9,697	Garcia, Juan Jose	264	27	36	30	911,021
Fuentes, Jaime Jose	27	2	8	3	33,010	Garcia, Kathren D.	2	0	0	1	550
Fugate, James F.	11	1	5	1	12,925	Garcia, Mario L.	31	0	2	4	17,582
Fulgham, Billy W.	8	1	0	2	5,840	Garcia, Mark	10	2	0	0	3,997
Fuller, Bonnie	69	1	1	2	12,292	Garcia, Monica	3	1	0	0	3,600
Fuller, William George	4	0	0	0	193	Garcia, Oscar L.	25	1	1	2	23,620
Fuller, Jr., Billy	32	0	1	1	6,646	Garcia, Phyllis D.	8	1	1	1	8,013
Fuller-Catalano, Abigail	45	6	7	9	97,670	Garcia, Rodolfo	196	22	21	22	586,365
Fulmer, Drew C.	142	13	26	18	110,517	Garcia, Ruben B.	10	0	2	2	3,486
Funk, Sidney J.	10	1	0	0	8,503	Garcia, Salvador	22	3	3	6	32,495
Funk, Stephanie	3	0	0	0	0	Garcia, Sr., Randy L.	7	1	2	2	17,497
Fuoco, Carlo	9	0	1	1	36,247	Gardenhire, Wiley D.	3	1	0	0	1,495
Furbee, William	4	0	0	2	1,500	Gardipy, Ken	17	2	2	3	4,944
Furer, Bobby C.	40	4	5	6	23,586	Gardipy, Russell	40	8	7	4	20,536

Trainer	Sts	1st	2d	3d	Purses	Trainer	Sts	1st	2d	3d	Purses
Gardipy, Jr., Tom	148	25	23	24	176,391	Gholson, Clyde J.	9	0	1	2	17,470
Gargasz, Donald W.	45	6	7	7	68,655	Gibbs, Jim	6	2	1	1	3,684
Garner, Tim D.	120	23	19	12	159,320	Gibbs, Randy	1	0	0	0	53
Garner, Tom F.	1	0	0	0	0	Gibbs, Terrill	55	8	13	9	33,025
Garner, William G.	3	0	0	0	255	Gibson, Bob E.	53	1	1	7	8,701
Garner, Sr., Louis M.	18	4	0	1	25,655	Gibson, Claude	76	13	13	12	78,322
Garofalo, Gregory P.	17	0	1	1	6,840	Gibson, Dewayne C.	19	3	1	2	30,860
Garoffalo, Jose	108	12	10	21	210,705	Gibson, Homer R.	49	5	4	4	23,480
Garrett, Alva L.	17	0	2	3	2,050	Gibson, Linda M.	15	2	0	1	24,303
Garrett, Billy R.	11	0	1	1	2,375	Gibson, Monte L.	3	0	1	1	760
Garrett, Dan	15	0	0	4	8,290	Gibson, Ralph E.	3	0	0	0	546
Garrett, James A.	1	0	1	0	400	Gibson, Richard D.	1	0	0	0	0
Garrett, Phil	4	0	1	1	3,466	Gibson, Rod	48	6	9	9	22,289
Garrett, Terry Wayne	15	1	0	1	6,247	Gibson, Ronald A.	25	2	5	3	32,637
Garrett, Ty J.	12	5	3	3	16,133	Gibson, Vince	88	11	10	10	53,061
Garrette, Merle K.	26	3	2	3	14,959	Gideon, Deborah	16	1	3	1	16,738
Garrick, Worrell A.	52	6	5	7	92,260	Giesbrecht, Brian	57	5	4	9	90,560
Garrido, Raul	113	10	9	15	140,406	Giesbrecht, Lance B.	89	15	20	10	229,789
Garrigan, Alfred	16	0	2	2	6,356	Giesse, Carl	81	9	14	12	212,569
Garrison, Diane	5	1	1	0	3,085	Giglio, Heather A.	49	7	10	5	213,964
Garrison, James O.	33	1	5	4	18,002	Gilbert, Bryon J.	59	17	13	7	379,187
Garrison, Mark	10	4	3	2	6,265	Gilbert, Darrel	3	0	0	0	111
Garroutte, James R.	63	7	10	5	90,602	Gilbert, Jack	11	0	2	1	6,133
Garroutte, John L.	17	6	0	1	15,186	Gilbert, Joseph A.	94	8	10	12	62,099
Garry, Thomas J.	9	2	0	0	16,946	Gilbert, Robert J.	28	1	4	4	19,016
Garvin, John Hart	77	9	7	10	25,563	Gilbert, Steven C.	11	0	1	3	5,611
Gary, Albert J.	3	0	1	0	2,705	Gilbert, Timothy R.	8	0	1	2	4,419
Gary, Marty	44	3	2	3	29,336	Gilbert, III, Riley Miles	104	5	4	5	47,095
Gary, Paul Brent	143	6	12	5	87,788	Gilchrist, Greg	200	34	37	39	769,411
Gary, Ray	3	0	0	0	315	Gilday-Retamoza, Glenda J.	17	0	0	0	1,330
Garza, Roberto R.	13	1	2	3	5,874	Giles, Lee A.	6	0	2	1	941
Gass, Mark E.	26	2	4	4	23,369	Giles, Wes	14	1	3	1	11,538
Gass, II, Michael A.	82	8	7	4	91,356	Gilgore, Carl	7	1	0	1	4,198
Gass, Sr., Michael A.	107	13	9	8	71,027	Giliforte, Jason	60	9	7	7	130,989
Gastal, Glenn C.	3	0	0	0	0	Giliforte, Layne S.	484	68	94	59	1,543,790
Gaston, Jim L.	275	37	39	40	499,338	Gilker, Robert	68	13	11	8	168,980
Gates, Allen L.	25	1	2	2	17,656	Gilkyson, Don	198	26	21	30	502,782
Gates, David N.	22	3	2	2	10,960	Gillam, Jeremy J.	28	4	4	4	80,820
Gates, Lawrence T.	12	0	1	1	2,338	Gillespie, Gary R.	2	0	0	0	924
Gatis, Christos	12	0	0	2	4,634	Gillett, Peter D.	13	1	0	2	5,480
Gatlin, Troy	6	0	0	0	88	Gillette, Kenneth D.	46	4	4	5	29,664
Gaucher, Robert	8	0	1	0	3,008	Gilliam, James D.	2	1	0	0	5,080
Gaudet, Edmond D.	284	39	48	39	899,145	Gillihan, Terry	239	49	38	25	505,058
Gautreaux, Allen	1	1	0	0	4,320	Gillions, Claudia J.	123	15	12	18	195,970
Gautreaux, Raymond	55	4	4	4	74,088	Gilmour, Sue M.	81	14	15	8	43,630
Gauvreau, Pat	1	0	0	0	206	Gino, Luigi	59	5	8	9	106,265
Gavin, Robert J.	2	0	0	0	173	Ginter, Jr., Raymond E.	18	5	2	2	91,306
Gayheart, Troy	38	6	2	5	51,596	Gioitta, Patrick	61	2	1	4	18,173
Geary, Kenneth E.	18	4	1	5	35,741	Girdley, Bernard L.	6	1	2	0	14,536
Gebler, Robert E.	9	0	1	1	8,190	Girdley, James R.	67	3	4	9	28,719
Geer, Roger	8	0	0	0	370	Girten, Shirley K.	1	0	0	0	92
Geier, Greg	8	0	0	0	5,790	Girten, Tim	171	33	34	11	432,269
Geist, David W.	425	85	56	54	710,652	Givens, Dennis	22	3	6	5	26,178
Gelner, John Charles	293	36	39	37	485,795	Gladd, Frank E.	18	2	9	1	23,901
Gelner, Scott	3	0	0	0	159	Gladd, Paul B.	18	1	2	4	4,289
Gendron, Ernest L.	1	0	0	0	51	Glatt, Mark	235	42	28	20	1,066,929
Generazio, Jr., Frank A.	206	23	30	30	866,708	Glazier, Leslie G.	91	3	22	11	166,200
Genovese, Richard L.	40	7	4	5	39,130	Glazier, Michael	57	10	5	9	72,165
Gensler, Harold K.	131	7	8	13	145,700	Gleason, Kenneth	263	43	48	26	481,228
Gentile, Victor	10	1	1	2	9,251	Gleason, Timothy Mark	383	61	41	55	763,194
Gentry, Craig W.	15	0	0	0	1,340	Gleason, Tyrone	56	4	4	6	25,742
George, Donald A.	21	2	1	1	10,023	Gleaves, Philip A.	93	13	7	8	342,255
George, Donald J.	8	1	2	2	3,560	Glenn, Dwaine A.	1	0	0	0	0
George, Ernest	49	11	5	4	162,048	Glenn, Jr., James W.	5	1	2	0	1,979
George, Gus	71	3	5	5	17,679	Glenney, John	86	6	6	10	427,615
George, Wayne F.	21	1	2	0	4,194	Glennon, Darren C.	52	2	4	4	87,872
George, Jr., Miles R.	34	0	2	4	8,531	Glessner, Gene F.	35	0	2	6	13,966
Gerace, Janis L.	261	13	15	22	359,833	Glidden, Darrell	9	0	0	0	1,289
Gerber, Norbert	57	7	8	7	65,948	Glorioso, Joe	26	1	2	2	9,885
Geremia, Jr., John	2	0	0	0	0	Glorioso, Ronald S.	96	18	16	11	249,986
Germany, Barry H.	86	9	8	5	307,038	Glossbrenner, Gloria L.	28	0	2	1	16,705
Gerteisen, Adam	31	5	5	4	85,784	Godeaux, Oscar	15	0	3	2	17,776
Gertz, Lisa	2	0	0	0	346	Godfrey, Brenda M.	46	1	2	13	41,805
Gervais, George	58	15	16	8	31,967	Godinez, Linda S.	2	0	0	0	100
Gervais, Shannon	29	1	2	6	13,739	Godsey, Claudie Marshall	42	3	8	8	45,529
Getto, Larry	15	0	0	0	130	Godshall, Joanne M.	13	1	2	3	18,330

Trainer	Sts	1st	2d	3d	Purses	Trainer	Sts	1st	2d	3d	Purses
Godwin, Albert	8	1	2	0	13,920	Gowan, William G.	19	3	1	3	21,434
Godwin, Carroll W.	56	8	8	3	84,749	Gowdy, Donna	13	3	0	1	29,362
Goeing, Donald L.	53	6	13	4	108,187	Goydich, George	7	1	0	1	15,812
Goff, Jr., William T.	13	1	4	0	19,086	Grace, Allan	28	7	2	8	14,632
Goforth, Richard	5	1	0	0	16,115	Grace, John R.	269	20	31	18	125,709
Gogas, Frances	71	10	10	12	136,694	Grace, Lori	42	7	7	4	60,934
Gogel, Donald Carl	3	0	1	1	2,310	Grace, Lynn	85	13	8	10	46,916
Gogel, Donnie Charles	40	4	12	8	90,878	Gracey, W. Phillip	89	6	11	9	364,825
Going, Lori	92	6	7	7	124,216	Graci, Kimberly A.	15	1	2	0	14,000
Goldbeck, Ernie	32	3	7	6	71,049	Graci, III, Joseph J.	58	6	3	2	60,015
Goldberg, Alan E.	222	39	33	24	1,265,895	Gracia, Humberto	79	6	4	6	122,620
Goldfine, Mickey A.	70	15	9	11	329,960	Gracida, Ruben	7	0	1	0	4,620
Goldman, Marilyn	16	1	1	2	11,160	Graham, Barbara C.	14	4	2	3	47,925
Goldstein, Morton	11	1	0	0	10,230	Graham, Edward L.	9	1	2	2	20,170
Gomena, Julie	3	0	0	1	1,000	Graham, George F.	32	4	6	2	25,853
Gomes, Monte M	89	0	3	6	30,945	Graham, Lynell S.	2	0	0	0	0
Gomez, Eduardo	6	0	0	0	1,140	Graham, Patrick J.	24	3	4	2	36,206
Gomez, Frank	229	27	32	35	684,788	Graham, Robin L.	45	7	7	3	254,880
Gomez, Pedro	13	2	1	2	5,997	Graham, II, Clifford P.	3	0	0	0	1,908
Gomez, Rafael	24	3	4	0	41,010	Grams, Timothy C.	106	20	17	11	542,471
Gonsalves, Robert	25	4	2	4	60,340	Granados, Oscar	9	0	1	2	3,130
Gonzales, Thomas	6	0	1	0	1,824	Grande, Joseph	113	16	26	16	190,885
Gonzales, Jr., Angel	25	0	2	3	11,785	Granger, Bobby	95	8	8	9	78,358
Gonzalez, Andrea	171	20	19	30	258,778	Granitz, Anthony J.	169	27	25	17	884,309
Gonzalez, Carlos	118	22	13	14	184,255	Grant, Jr., William E.	25	2	5	2	48,798
Gonzalez, Felix A.	76	11	13	9	103,468	Grantham, Glenn	2	0	0	0	142
Gonzalez, J. Paco	67	8	8	7	400,412	Gravelle, Colinda M.	23	1	5	6	37,854
Gonzalez, Jaime	17	2	2	3	15,567	Graves, Heather	28	1	5	5	5,830
Gonzalez, Jose A.	133	8	24	23	175,001	Graves, Russell B.	2	0	0	0	40
Gonzalez, Jose L.	76	9	6	11	70,777	Graves, William K.	3	0	0	0	252
Gonzalez, Jose M.	4	1	1	0	2,625	Graves, Jr., Ted	1	0	0	0	240
Gonzalez, Jose R.	54	6	0	7	50,586	Graves-Keckler, Heather	4	0	0	0	72
Gonzalez, Luis A.	11	1	0	1	4,654	Gray, Bill L.	13	0	1	1	6,781
Gonzalez, Nicholas	213	38	17	28	700,787	Gray, Blair A.	8	0	0	0	136
Gonzalez, Ramon Fuentes	1	0	0	0	450	Gray, Charles A.	4	0	0	0	577
Gonzalez, Ramon G.	60	2	4	5	44,166	Gray, Charles W.	13	0	0	1	3,567
Gonzalez, Ramon O.	353	45	45	44	702,930	Gray, Clayton	155	26	16	22	266,999
Gonzalez, Raul A.	74	13	13	11	62,821	Gray, Dennis	11	1	0	0	15,475
Gonzalez, Reina E.	78	6	5	11	78,283	Gray, Gary L.	33	6	2	2	29,529
Gonzalez, Richard C.	18	3	2	0	21,238	Gray, Karen	10	0	0	1	5,650
Gonzalez, Sal	63	11	8	5	60,710	Gray, Kenneth M.	16	3	1	4	48,142
Gonzalez, Silvano M.	53	5	4	4	87,948	Gray, Lorna M.	82	7	11	10	90,854
Gooch, Boyce K.	128	15	14	19	109,886	Gray, Robin A.	1	0	0	0	0
Good, Dennis F.	112	12	12	22	167,060	Gray, Ron	122	8	10	12	69,479
Goodale, Adam	21	5	3	3	52,734	Gray, Sid J.	40	6	5	8	72,884
Goodin, B. Mike	87	4	4	13	127,490	Grayson, Bobby Wayne	11	0	1	1	6,208
Goodlet, Mark D.	2	0	0	0	0	Greaves, William	24	4	2	3	108,370
Goodman, James A.	13	0	2	2	3,042	Grech, Tom	8	1	2	3	26,149
Goodman, Mary M.	92	7	8	7	83,690	Greco, Emanuel J.	21	0	0	0	1,320
Goodman, Randy J.	97	12	12	11	113,580	Greelish, Patricia M.	20	0	2	2	9,529
Goodnight, Bill R.	2	1	0	0	6,235	Greely, C. Beau	126	20	13	19	1,323,774
Goodridge, Ronald O.	301	26	35	34	603,383	Green, Clint	89	4	4	7	37,046
Goodwin, Duane	2	1	0	0	1,788	Green, Darlene	41	0	1	1	6,175
Gordon, Anthony K.	2	0	0	0	184	Green, Donna	24	5	4	2	60,930
Gordon, Cleveland G.	13	0	1	0	7,968	Green, Edith J.	9	2	1	2	8,965
Gordon, Dorna M.	30	0	1	2	13,370	Green, Ike	10	3	1	2	13,732
Gordon, George L.	24	2	0	2	14,948	Green, James D.	1	0	0	0	80
Gordon, Howard R.	15	2	0	1	12,771	Green, James T.	26	3	0	3	24,465
Gordon, Jim A.	24	3	3	4	11,614	Green, Jerry L.	5	0	0	0	171
Gordon, Rohn	26	0	1	2	3,147	Green, Lewis A.	30	1	4	3	22,003
Gordon-Watson, Alexander	16	1	0	1	7,147	Green, Martha C.	18	1	2	0	16,832
Gore, Catherine A.	9	0	2	0	6,946	Green, Marvin D.	13	2	2	0	13,260
Gore, Terrel	105	16	10	13	296,170	Green, N	23	4	2	1	184,195
Gorham, Michael E.	388	64	55	60	1,833,673	Green, Newcomb	8	1	2	2	52,200
Gorham, Robert M.	417	71	63	67	1,077,422	Green, Raymond A.	53	2	5	1	20,933
Gorham, Jr., Robert M.	41	12	4	4	94,600	Green, Richard D.	2	0	0	0	0
Goruk, Pat	7	3	1	2	18,791	Green, Shelly	9	2	1	1	25,301
Gosden, John H. M.	1	0	0	0	0	Green, Wilford H.	11	2	4	1	6,482
Goss, Richard T.	2	0	0	0	98	Greene, Shirley A.	8	3	0	0	110,298
Gothard, Akiko M.	104	23	22	9	392,540	Greene, Thomas M.	104	13	8	17	313,814
Gould, Ellen	12	0	1	1	2,193	Greenhill, Jeffrey L.	121	16	21	16	212,054
Gould, Steve K.	6	0	0	0	440	Greenman, Dean	58	5	12	7	267,599
Gourneau, Jason	5	0	0	2	500	Greenslate, Sam	21	0	0	2	5,859
Gourneau, Jerry	78	15	14	12	93,193	Greenway, Brad	2	0	0	0	0
Gourneau, Jr., Larry	50	7	9	9	34,314	Greenwell, Jerry Joe	46	3	6	5	46,436
Goutierrez, Jr., Ned	5	1	0	0	7,200	Greenwood, Claire B.	3	1	1	0	15,872

RECORDS OF TRAINERS

Trainer	Sts	1st	2d	3d	Purses	Trainer	Sts	1st	2d	3d	Purses
Greenwood, Dale	209	26	24	30	419,149	Guerrero, J. Guadalupe	96	19	6	12	259,182
Greer, Bernard	1	0	0	0	0	Guerrero, Juan Carlos	162	20	32	22	483,138
Gregg, Carol A.	15	1	1	0	7,185	Guerrieri, Dino	51	9	7	4	106,857
Gregg, Garry	1	0	0	0	109	Guessford, Walter Ben	3	0	1	0	5,700
Gregg, Patricia	1	0	0	0	0	Guettler, Robert R.	2	0	0	1	390
Gregg, Tony	39	5	6	4	35,857	Guidos, John	9	6	0	0	11,051
Grego, Donald R.	31	3	4	3	75,224	Guidry, Connie Mack	39	3	0	6	24,455
Gregoncza, Ben	4	0	0	0	160	Guidry, Susan	31	2	1	3	15,712
Gregory, George E.	4	0	0	0	210	Guilbeaux, Sr., Louis	3	0	0	1	1,275
Gregory, Peter	28	5	3	5	37,001	Guillory, James	14	0	0	2	3,380
Gregory, Ray W.	5	0	0	0	52	Guillory, Raymond	15	2	2	0	11,515
Gregory, Robert E.	1	0	0	0	182	Guillot, David M.	5	0	0	0	900
Gregory, Theodore C.	11	1	0	1	5,013	Guillot, Eric J.	88	6	3	6	71,979
Gregory, Sr., Kenneth	27	2	1	1	13,145	Guinn, M. Dooley	93	9	14	8	154,901
Greiner, Gary	59	6	2	12	28,685	Guitard, David J.	37	4	0	5	105,882
Griego, Fabian	4	0	0	1	852	Gulash, Rodger	2	0	0	0	0
Griem, Robert J.	15	1	2	1	55,444	Gulewich, Grace	20	0	0	1	2,764
Grieve, Larry	40	7	6	2	86,047	Gulick, James M.	84	10	13	8	193,467
Grieves, Kelly	66	9	5	10	120,047	Gullo, Gary P.	39	1	4	6	49,100
Grieves, Ron	253	48	44	32	695,001	Gumbel, Thomas O.	33	2	4	2	32,223
Griffin, Bill	4	0	0	0	287	Gundlach, Raymond	13	0	0	1	1,989
Griffin, Jacqueline	46	4	2	4	39,233	Gunter, Michael C.	34	5	2	1	22,971
Griffin, Roger	9	0	0	0	1,115	Gurney, Marilyn M.	29	1	1	2	10,407
Griffin, Timothy L.	19	0	7	0	9,424	Gurrola, George T.	2	0	0	0	260
Griffin, Sr., Frederick H.	1	0	1	0	5,460	Gurule, Saby B.	1	0	0	0	54
Griffin, Sr., John W.	3	0	0	0	384	Gustafson, Ricky J.	210	29	29	27	220,224
Griffith, Gregory A.	196	31	23	26	363,883	Gustafsson, Rolf	1	0	0	0	1,140
Griffith, Terry	18	0	0	0	2,385	Guste, Eddie R.	32	2	3	0	18,068
Griffiths, Eugene I.	6	0	0	0	249	Gutierrez, Angel	158	21	12	18	227,777
Griggs, Dana S.	12	0	1	2	2,659	Gutierrez, Jorge	72	9	9	11	470,487
Griggs, John K.	8	0	0	1	4,050	Gutierrez, Luis	171	13	17	17	146,629
Griggs, Kenneth F.	9	1	0	0	7,636	Gutierrez, Rosie	42	0	2	5	18,915
Griggs, Veronica	103	8	9	17	108,491	Guyah, Hopeton R.	8	0	1	0	1,023
Grigsby, Anthony K.	1	0	0	0	0	Guyton, Brad	3	0	1	1	2,206
Grijalva, Jose	23	1	7	4	12,582	Guzzetti, James R.	6	0	0	0	186
Grimaldo, Jose	17	1	2	4	10,535	Gwaltney, John	2	0	0	0	65
Grimes, David	132	21	19	18	86,933	Gwilliam, Harry	12	1	1	0	3,579
Grimes, Michael H. R.	9	0	2	0	3,908	Gwilliam, Robert	53	9	7	6	37,758
Grimm, Margaret E.	48	9	6	5	175,661	Gyarmati, Leah	164	20	21	17	582,214
Grimm, Jr., Philip I.	20	3	2	2	77,990	Haas, John	10	0	0	0	471
Grimsley, Cindy R	9	0	1	0	7,490	Haas, Phil	1	0	0	0	78
Grinolds, Douglas	19	4	1	3	40,047	Haasl, Ron	60	6	5	6	17,551
Grinolds, Rod	7	0	2	1	12,552	Habeeb, Donald J.	81	11	9	9	143,729
Grisham, Christie	6	1	1	1	3,385	Hackett, Gary	73	7	12	10	66,219
Grissom, Bobbie	102	10	18	11	99,955	Hacking, A. L.	23	1	3	3	9,690
Grissom, O. Dwain	2	0	0	0	1,160	Hackney, Karen L.	12	0	1	0	1,290
Grizzard, Render Lee	21	1	5	5	20,882	Hackney, William N.	104	11	7	11	136,064
Grobe, Nathan	3	0	0	1	1,430	Hackworth, Jr., Robert S.	21	2	1	2	42,348
Gross, George F.	123	7	16	14	226,449	Haden, Jr., J. B.	1	0	0	0	0
Gross, James A.	8	1	1	1	8,470	Hadfield, Bridget L.	26	1	2	2	9,271
Gross, John C.	40	1	4	4	30,410	Hadley, Sherman	2	0	0	0	40
Gross, Reid	611	48	52	58	337,166	Hadry, Charles H.	19	5	3	4	123,305
Grove, Christopher W.	374	41	47	43	941,024	Hadry, Charles J.	115	23	18	17	701,540
Groves, W. Fred	19	2	2	4	33,994	Haehn, Cindy Lee	98	9	15	15	94,281
Grubb, Harold	48	7	5	8	57,201	Haehn, Douglas G.	71	8	5	7	94,412
Grubbs, Jamie L.	74	14	11	12	159,222	Haehn, T. R.	226	8	17	15	71,817
Grudzien, Gerald	13	1	1	2	4,501	Haffelt, Mark W.	8	0	1	0	3,388
Grudziewski, Bob	15	2	1	1	14,722	Haffner, Randy	68	2	7	6	48,732
Gruenemeier, Michael	38	7	6	8	31,066	Hagenauer, Jim	17	1	3	2	9,626
Gruich, Philip P.	13	0	1	3	3,450	Hagge, Ron	9	1	1	0	5,618
Grusmark, Karl M.	280	37	41	48	445,052	Hagy, E. Elaine	4	1	0	0	10,200
Gruss, Janell	11	3	0	0	11,241	Hagy, Titus	249	15	24	32	292,311
Gruwell, Bessie S.	134	20	23	19	451,502	Hahn, Albert N.	19	1	2	0	11,440
Gryczewski, Jerry L.	94	13	19	13	304,056	Hahn, III, Harold L.	106	14	21	12	224,365
Gubanski, James H.	3	0	0	0	533	Haiber, Homer H.	14	0	1	4	6,879
Gubanski, Mary Margaret	22	1	6	3	26,360	Haignero, Robert	17	0	0	0	1,057
Guciardo, John	36	1	4	3	14,770	Hair, Lea M.	9	2	0	1	7,505
Guciardo, Kathleen A.	68	9	9	6	77,890	Hairfield, William E.	15	3	2	1	31,880
Guciardo, Robert	155	23	23	18	326,990	Halbak, Jay	10	1	3	4	4,945
Guerin, Andre	3	0	2	1	3,620	Halcomb, Denny R.	16	1	1	0	5,914
Guerin, David	7	1	2	3	14,240	Hale, Jimmie L.	81	5	8	9	43,077
Guerra, Jacque	35	10	8	5	45,762	Hale, Joseph T.	13	0	3	3	9,077
Guerra, Jr., Jimmy W.	4	1	0	0	3,858	Hale, Robert A.	193	31	30	23	543,241
Guerra, Sr., Jimmy	1	0	0	0	0	Hale, William G.	80	7	6	12	115,665
Guerrero, Angel	39	4	5	8	44,363	Hale, Willie B.	8	1	0	4	3,147
Guerrero, Helberth M.	77	2	2	9	24,196	Hale, Jr., Ronald T.	108	8	13	13	67,170

Trainer	Sts	1st	2d	3d	Purses	Trainer	Sts	1st	2d	3d	Purses
Halerewich, Wanda	3	0	0	0	130	Hansen, Dean	82	10	6	5	38,596
Haley, Gloria	44	3	4	6	90,401	Hansen, Gordon A.	176	17	16	16	76,639
Hall, Aimee D.	119	6	16	24	162,643	Hansen, Kevin	27	3	2	3	15,693
Hall, Bruce A.	11	0	3	1	9,592	Hansen, Roger W.	98	12	13	11	184,043
Hall, Calvin	38	3	7	2	23,887	Hansen, Scott	163	28	23	18	558,293
Hall, Carollyn J.	18	1	0	4	14,027	Hanson, Deborah M.	10	0	0	2	1,980
Hall, Carroll L.	19	3	1	2	4,704	Hanson, George H.	30	1	4	4	7,287
Hall, Charlotte M.	47	2	7	8	47,602	Hanson, Jim	41	10	4	10	21,354
Hall, Connie	2	0	0	0	100	Hanson, Victor	57	9	10	4	149,370
Hall, Craig	16	0	0	0	1,544	Hanson, Wayne	6	1	0	1	1,705
Hall, Darrel V.	72	11	5	13	61,344	Harasta, Steven P.	49	2	6	5	23,725
Hall, Dennis	72	16	9	6	158,801	Harbort, Willie R.	55	4	8	8	51,203
Hall, Dick	38	4	2	7	39,895	Hardcastle, Bill	14	0	1	0	2,220
Hall, Dru S.	144	31	22	20	224,368	Harder, Richard L.	34	1	5	2	9,792
Hall, Eldon	2	0	1	1	9,850	Harder, Tim	53	6	4	4	67,705
Hall, Gary B.	49	2	3	7	12,436	Hardie, Wade	58	4	8	12	19,128
Hall, Jay	6	0	1	0	1,810	Hardin, Angel	82	5	7	12	58,127
Hall, John L.	99	9	11	11	147,519	Hardin, Jerry K.	153	19	23	19	227,160
Hall, L. E.	45	5	7	4	20,730	Hardin, Ty	11	2	0	0	18,633
Hall, Larry R.	123	8	14	13	91,298	Hardy, Fred J.	42	2	5	1	25,396
Hall, Mark E.	47	11	8	7	84,967	Hardy, James Mort.	87	10	14	14	708,801
Hall, Peggy M.	25	0	5	4	29,149	Hardy, Rosamond	18	1	0	1	9,721
Hall, Rachel	3	1	1	0	8,440	Hare, Jearl Ace	73	5	10	12	50,829
Hall, Randall J	5	1	0	0	6,180	Hargens, Robert C.	16	0	1	3	9,225
Hall, Robert K.	4	1	0	0	4,430	Harigeorgiou, Konstantinos	107	5	6	4	40,008
Hall, Ronald D.	7	0	0	1	2,870	Harigeoriou, Gus	2	0	0	0	360
Hall, S.	1	0	0	0	230	Harknett, Alice T.	3	0	0	0	1,305
Hall, Sean	56	2	13	4	190,950	Harless, Gary E.	4	0	0	0	0
Hall, Steve L.	82	19	9	12	102,876	Harneck, Donald J.	5	0	0	1	1,274
Hall, W. Monk	57	6	4	6	47,365	Haroldson, Lowell	6	0	0	0	650
Hall, William E.	71	13	8	8	196,818	Harper, Charles W.	5	0	1	0	2,476
Hall, Jr., Oscar J.	6	1	1	0	5,798	Harper, Jackie L.	73	3	8	8	69,871
Hall, Sr., Oscar J.	39	3	5	4	30,155	Harper, Richard L.	112	16	15	18	105,803
Haller, Valerie K.	20	6	3	1	66,338	Harrell, Dan L.	31	5	1	5	33,155
Hallgren, Sven	22	2	4	2	21,111	Harrell, James D.	9	1	0	2	1,693
Halloran, John A.	58	10	8	5	132,386	Harrell, Linda Lee	27	2	1	1	17,098
Hall-Sabol, Tamara Joan	17	0	0	0	3,797	Harries, James E.	5	0	0	0	2,401
Halpern, Edward I.	2	0	0	0	1,500	Harrigan, William B.	8	1	3	2	53,200
Halter, James K.	31	3	6	4	65,858	Harrington, Glen	32	1	5	3	31,922
Ham, Doug	22	2	0	2	17,515	Harrington, Jack	24	2	1	0	9,276
Haman, Julius	2	0	0	0	160	Harrington, Maury	2	0	0	0	450
Hamblin, Leon H.	5	0	0	0	158	Harrington, Mike	235	24	33	27	965,653
Hamer, Sr., William E.	86	6	5	5	30,728	Harrington, Patricia	3	0	0	2	5,520
Hamill, Lisa	60	11	6	7	50,908	Harris, Alva S.	9	0	0	1	2,430
Hamilton, Beverly	38	3	5	4	19,573	Harris, Bob J.	35	0	3	6	16,558
Hamilton, Brenda S.	19	0	2	3	9,413	Harris, Chris Michael	135	5	9	7	33,569
Hamilton, Harry W.	63	2	6	8	36,705	Harris, Clifford V.	1	0	0	0	65
Hamilton, Jimmy D.	13	0	1	0	4,460	Harris, Clint	2	0	0	0	0
Hamilton, Walter C.	5	1	0	0	8,259	Harris, Dennis E.	9	0	2	0	5,600
Hamilton, William F.	2	0	0	0	510	Harris, Dennis J.	4	0	0	1	1,067
Hamm, Timothy E.	278	36	44	41	708,341	Harris, Everton Alex	64	4	9	9	78,780
Hammes, John D.	4	1	0	1	12,140	Harris, George R.	21	3	2	1	21,896
Hammett, Jody	33	1	7	3	44,591	Harris, Herbert W.	34	0	1	1	10,579
Hammond, Jack R.	26	1	0	2	4,943	Harris, Holly L.	39	4	2	2	43,587
Hammond, Jerry	269	19	34	25	175,605	Harris, John R.	10	0	1	4	2,364
Hammond, Joanne	9	0	1	1	8,440	Harris, John William	33	4	4	0	17,742
Hammond, John E.	3	0	0	0	45,000	Harris, Joyce A.	17	3	5	1	33,266
Hammond, Kim	503	93	79	64	608,524	Harris, Larry W.	9	0	0	0	0
Hammond, Robert J.	5	0	0	0	470	Harris, Lisa	2	0	1	0	1,835
Han, Moon S.	8	2	1	1	25,225	Harris, Lyndel	5	0	0	0	271
Hancock, David L.	106	7	10	12	45,743	Harris, Mike	1	0	0	0	0
Hancock, Jack L.	24	0	1	0	4,398	Harris, Nancy S.	1	0	0	0	135
Hancock, John A.	82	0	5	7	21,573	Harris, Phil	2	0	0	0	0
Hancock, Kerny B.	50	9	12	4	78,605	Harris, Rickey B.	16	0	0	1	7,930
Handy, George R.	190	36	31	27	632,420	Harris, Tyrone	165	18	12	11	229,530
Hanford, E. R.	9	2	0	0	14,275	Harris, Walter L.	20	3	3	2	22,686
Hanford, Gail M.	35	2	3	3	37,935	Harris, William S.	27	1	1	5	8,432
Hanford, Peggie	39	2	5	7	28,072	Harris, II, Doyle	8	0	2	0	934
Hanley, Larry	54	0	3	3	8,211	Harrisko, Dennis	29	0	3	6	10,606
Hanna, Clark	31	1	2	5	22,572	Harrison, Don K.	6	0	0	0	1,740
Hanna, Mark A.	14	1	6	2	21,115	Harrison, Glenn N.	72	1	3	6	28,792
Hanna, Patricia	16	0	5	4	35,990	Harrison, Jason	10	1	1	2	12,415
Hanna, Susan	9	0	0	0	3,325	Harrison, Joe	1	0	0	1	360
Hansen, Andrew M.	36	3	4	5	86,300	Hart, Floyd	10	1	0	2	1,951
Hansen, Betty	43	5	5	2	63,918	Hart, Quindie	3	0	0	0	90
Hansen, Dale A.	29	1	2	1	9,853	Hart-Burroughs, Lori	13	2	0	1	5,994

Trainer	Sts	1st	2d	3d	Purses	Trainer	Sts	1st	2d	3d	Purses
Harte, Michael G.	31	2	4	5	82,040	Heaps, Cornell M.	4	1	2	0	8,340
Hartlage, Gary G.	95	11	8	14	214,745	Heard, Jr., Thomas H.	111	9	24	18	241,321
Hartlage, Mark G.	23	1	2	4	17,590	Heath, George	44	5	5	6	89,348
Hartley, Darrell	76	9	19	16	89,104	Heath, Robert	1	0	0	0	100
Hartley, James E.	4	1	0	0	9,159	Hebb, Kurly	1	0	0	0	0
Hartman, Alex T.	50	14	6	8	127,319	Heberle, Arthur H.	170	12	25	18	135,004
Hartman, Chris A.	9	1	2	0	21,221	Hebert, Ackel	12	0	0	2	2,276
Hartman, Chris J.	42	7	5	4	70,926	Hebert, Chris	31	6	3	4	43,993
Hartman, Mary	129	18	13	19	404,505	Hebert, Doris	409	70	80	70	1,072,945
Hartman, Paul	10	1	2	1	14,360	Hebert, Ernest	11	1	1	0	4,996
Hartman, Stan	136	7	14	9	44,508	Hebert, Frank J.	9	0	1	2	5,469
Hartnett, Ronald W.	45	1	5	2	21,599	Hebert, J. Purvis	57	3	10	9	49,926
Hartsell, Duane L.	1	0	0	0	0	Hebert, Jeff A.	56	6	7	4	86,934
Hartsell, Jr., John J.	88	19	18	9	245,242	Hebert, Kitty A.	43	1	2	3	34,593
Harty, Eoin G.	110	30	21	9	1,257,859	Hebert, R. Pete	38	5	5	6	50,153
Harty, Nicholas A.	5	1	0	1	2,881	Hebert, Rodney	1	0	0	0	330
Hartz, Douglas S.	9	1	0	0	3,331	Hebert, Rylan	76	10	8	13	126,018
Harvatt, Charles R.	172	11	11	19	203,910	Hebert, Sylvie	5	0	0	0	379
Harvey, Edward J.	44	6	5	3	25,028	Hebert, Sr., Henry	8	0	0	1	605
Harwood, Doris	85	15	11	18	160,151	Hecker, Donald	109	7	7	18	118,557
Harwood, Ryland M.	25	3	5	3	10,522	Heckrotte, Beverly L.	28	1	0	2	28,050
Haskins, Steve	1	0	0	0	750	Hedary, Antoine Y.	27	2	2	0	13,014
Hasmatali, Daryl	14	1	0	1	44,706	Hedegaard, Randy	34	12	5	5	55,928
Hasmatali, Roger	22	0	2	3	14,116	Hedge, Rick	211	31	41	28	488,318
Hassenpflug, Chad	148	33	24	21	420,201	Hedges, Dianne E.	11	0	1	0	5,448
Hastings, W. Shannon	46	1	3	4	14,451	Hedges, Tony	12	1	0	3	22,534
Hatcher, Harry	1	0	0	0	0	Hedus, William C.	115	16	12	17	164,716
Hatcher, Linda	13	0	1	1	3,683	Heggie, Rod	119	16	26	12	246,414
Hatcher, Nathan D.	24	3	3	2	46,625	Hehn, Donald	64	2	2	3	20,782
Hatchett, James	264	42	45	32	1,051,662	Heidelberg, Bradley N.	5	0	1	0	3,455
Hatfield, Kevin	11	0	0	0	1,852	Heidelberg, Lee Roy	36	4	1	2	15,875
Hattori, Bruce	9	0	3	2	2,783	Heil, Nancy B.	63	1	7	6	76,890
Haubrich, Wendy	9	0	0	0	359	Heim, Richard	4	1	0	0	3,908
Haught, Dawn	92	7	7	12	46,222	Held, Dieter K.	40	3	3	1	60,385
Haughton, Donnovan	108	14	9	13	181,174	Heldt, Donald C.	16	0	2	3	9,679
Hause, Ronald D.	5	0	0	0	576	Heldt, Merle	49	5	4	7	70,268
Hauswald, M. James	104	13	5	10	109,681	Helfenstein, Alvina	20	0	1	2	7,398
Hauswald, Philip M.	74	9	10	7	283,560	Helfenstein, Dino	21	1	0	2	7,234
Havener, John T.	4	0	1	2	660	Hellman, Leroy	348	69	54	48	552,731
Haverkamp, Charles K.	38	3	8	10	84,510	Helmbrecht, Jo Dawn	4	1	0	1	5,324
Haverty, Karen	68	3	12	8	26,772	Helmbrecht, William M.	5	0	0	0	845
Hawkes, Darcy	181	17	16	18	152,808	Helmbrecht, William R.	85	6	4	5	104,652
Hawkes, Twyla	23	0	2	2	6,638	Helmetag, Robert W.	93	3	7	11	78,813
Hawkins, Charles R.	19	1	1	0	17,750	Hemba, Brad	24	2	0	6	14,055
Hawkins, Douglas	49	8	9	5	129,660	Hemby, Jack R.	21	3	3	1	57,877
Hawkins, Franklin C.	2	0	0	0	136	Hemmer, Terrell M.	21	4	1	4	35,541
Hawkins, Lizbeth	8	3	2	1	47,460	Hemmerick, Anthony J.	25	0	2	5	14,637
Hawkins, Tom	80	11	4	12	45,046	Hemmings, Glendon	48	3	4	5	21,911
Hawley, Reba M.	24	0	0	1	2,413	Hemsworth, Roy	7	1	0	2	2,233
Hawley, Sherri-Lee	10	1	1	4	39,741	Henderson, Eddy	13	0	1	1	4,930
Hawley, Wesley E.	174	37	27	23	714,625	Henderson, Frances	61	3	4	7	74,477
Haydel, Cliff	127	10	18	17	179,410	Henderson, Max	8	1	1	3	3,684
Hayden, Jean	57	6	5	7	14,224	Hendricks, Dan L.	176	28	21	28	1,413,975
Hayes, Breeda	2	0	0	0	1,818	Hendricks, Frank J.	11	1	1	2	8,227
Hayes, Frank Foster	12	2	2	2	20,918	Hendricks, Jalene	30	2	5	4	7,138
Hayes, Larry W.	71	4	4	17	58,580	Hendrickson, David L.	70	8	5	4	119,491
Hayes, Marvin	40	3	2	4	22,110	Hendrickson, Lori	69	12	11	10	136,626
Hayes, Michael S.	30	2	7	3	26,398	Hendricks, Elizabeth M.	60	9	6	11	142,330
Hayes, Robert D.	9	1	1	0	6,833	Hendriks, Richard J.	240	28	34	38	483,389
Hayford, Jennifer A.	118	5	10	10	254,171	Hendriks, Sanna N.	81	15	19	9	623,517
Haynes, Brady	29	1	2	3	4,362	Hendrix, Coy	85	17	10	14	238,745
Haynes, Bruce	20	4	2	3	48,017	Hendrix, Laurie	2	0	0	0	38
Haynes, Ernest M.	187	36	25	29	503,519	Heninger, Morgan	6	2	0	0	8,786
Haynes, Penny	5	1	1	1	2,082	Henington, Kevin	1	0	0	0	240
Haynes, Rodney	223	31	31	26	620,314	Heniser, Tim	2	0	0	0	259
Hays, Danton C.	32	5	0	4	43,779	Henley, Michael R.	37	4	3	2	41,149
Hays, George	1	0	0	0	162	Hennessy, Joseph	28	2	1	3	36,715
Hayworth, Dwayne	5	2	1	1	6,090	Hennig, John K.	99	13	10	15	413,120
Hazel, Robert A.	28	2	3	3	14,027	Hennig, Mark A.	503	73	85	74	3,954,020
Hazelton, Richard P.	253	40	33	40	1,102,397	Hennigh, Alan W.	15	0	2	0	3,375
Hazelton, Steve	20	3	3	2	71,199	Henry, Ignatius	37	1	2	3	25,080
Hazen, Jr., William E.	9	1	1	0	18,930	Henry, Larry O.	1	0	0	1	940
Headlee, J. W.	5	1	2	1	4,235	Henry, Neville	48	5	4	9	53,432
Headley, Bruce	138	29	17	26	1,806,298	Henson, Frank	1	0	0	0	0
Head-Maarek, Christiane	2	0	0	0	7,500	Henson, Joe	2	0	0	1	1,383
Heads, Barbara	150	26	20	18	434,117	Henson, Steve	70	7	9	12	164,227

Trainer	Sts	1st	2d	3d	Purses	Trainer	Sts	1st	2d	3d	Purses
Hepton, Fred	10	1	0	0	2,020	Hill, Jimmie E.	31	2	2	3	5,939
Herber, M. Paula	36	1	1	3	8,470	Hill, Joe	23	4	2	2	12,519
Herbert, Grant H.	17	2	2	2	16,550	Hill, John F.	3	0	0	0	178
Herbert, Mark	6	0	1	1	1,758	Hill, Rickey F.	1	0	0	0	95
Herbst, Preston L.	198	30	19	32	323,807	Hill-Cogswell, Roberta A.	3	0	0	1	728
Herdy, Fred J.	16	2	4	2	30,417	Hille, Jack	36	1	3	4	9,716
Herie, Edward	12	0	0	0	1,988	Hille, Jim	14	2	4	3	5,227
Herlinger, Victoria M.	24	2	0	3	20,460	Hille, Wayne	3	1	0	0	2,600
Herman, Dev	80	10	8	16	22,433	Hilling, James M.	42	0	9	5	52,748
Herman, Robert	2	0	0	1	270	Hills, Timothy A.	479	81	64	61	2,617,324
Herman, Sonja	36	1	6	3	20,256	Hillstead, Rick	1	0	0	0	95
Herman, Steve	2	0	0	1	320	Hillyard, Jim	5	1	1	1	4,079
Herman, Thomas	3	0	0	0	282	Hilton, Ann B.	19	1	3	2	34,434
Hernandez, Antonio B.	75	5	5	7	63,069	Hilts, Nancy	15	2	0	1	34,017
Hernandez, Felix	53	4	5	10	55,670	Hinckson, Martin	60	3	9	5	80,406
Hernandez, Gerald	8	1	0	2	6,312	Hindman, Ed	35	3	4	3	42,867
Hernandez, Gilberto J.	2	0	0	1	1,456	Hinds, Austin	18	1	1	3	38,093
Hernandez, Jose G.	48	4	2	6	22,754	Hinds, Lonnie	8	3	0	0	12,520
Hernandez, Obidio Otis	2	0	0	0	0	Hinds, Steven	18	1	1	3	14,183
Hernandez, Pedro	26	1	3	6	4,285	Hinerdeer, James	21	0	0	3	8,411
Hernandez, Ramon M.	106	12	13	9	644,044	Hines, Nicholas J.	181	25	26	21	590,480
Hernandez, Raul F.	24	3	1	1	15,408	Hinkle, Luther G.	31	1	2	4	12,907
Hernandez, Salvador	8	0	0	0	2,710	Hinojosa, Gerardo Jerry	21	0	2	0	3,977
Hernandez, Jr., Sandino R.	20	1	2	3	35,500	Hinojosa, Ricardo	5	0	0	1	550
Herndon, Paul H.	1	0	0	0	70	Hinshaw, Gary D.	12	3	2	0	31,333
Herndon, Terry	4	0	1	0	1,496	Hinsley, David H.	287	35	33	43	646,476
Herold, Russell J.	15	0	1	2	5,957	Hinton, Stacy	41	6	7	6	61,298
Herrell, Ron D.	2	1	0	0	7,330	Hinton, William H.	12	0	0	2	6,378
Herren, Gene	13	2	3	0	10,779	Hirst, Robert E.	43	4	6	6	42,320
Herrera, Albert	1	0	0	0	0	Hite, Dennis	40	2	1	7	25,060
Herrera, Arnold G.	11	2	1	1	7,378	Hixon, Fred	34	4	6	2	16,602
Herrera, Arturo F.	20	1	1	2	8,340	Hjelm, Lawrence	11	1	0	0	1,258
Herrick, Joe	22	2	2	1	59,660	Hobbs, Don	74	1	8	10	16,869
Herrin, Denise	2	0	0	0	225	Hobbs, Kyle A.	14	0	0	1	1,454
Herrington, Paul	48	3	6	7	74,951	Hobbs, Laura	4	1	0	0	3,139
Hershbell, Lynnett A.	13	1	1	0	16,980	Hobby, Steve	144	30	21	21	852,228
Hertler, John O.	178	18	16	24	935,337	Hobson, Don	3	1	0	0	5,102
Heskett, Theodore R.	18	0	0	1	6,032	Hobson, Doug	6	0	1	1	5,096
Hesler, Ed T.	9	0	0	0	998	Hobson, Larry	5	1	1	2	3,895
Heslop, Joanne M.	6	1	1	0	18,221	Hobson, Ronnie	6	0	0	0	255
Hess, Jacob G.	85	8	16	10	138,752	Hobson, Simon	32	1	4	7	25,035
Hess, Jr., Robert B.	215	26	25	24	1,091,267	Hoburg, Bill C.	2	0	0	0	128
Hess, Sr., Robert B.	153	19	22	28	292,300	Hoch, Jr., Frank B.	6	0	0	0	0
Hestekin, Lee	1	0	0	0	350	Hochsteiner, Gail	11	4	3	0	6,296
Hester, Leanne	2	0	0	0	575	Hodge, Mary E.	170	20	13	20	112,683
Hewitt, Michael	102	5	10	11	36,703	Hodges, James E.	74	15	8	8	257,276
Hext, Kim L.	3	0	0	0	278	Hodges, Jodie	57	5	5	4	57,195
Hiatt, Charles E.	80	6	7	9	29,739	Hodges, Lorena	6	0	0	0	842
Hiatt, Kathleen M.	36	0	1	0	2,160	Hodges, Sharon E.	40	0	1	3	6,634
Hibdon, Mark N.	137	7	10	13	59,557	Hodges, Walter N.	24	4	3	6	21,369
Hickam, William K.	168	26	19	25	158,553	Hodgin, R. E.	16	2	3	1	12,372
Hickey, P. Noel	298	37	40	25	824,044	Hodgson, Barry	15	3	3	3	10,883
Hicklin, Judi A.	210	24	33	25	362,855	Hodson, Kevin D.	2	0	0	0	88
Hickman, Charlie	2	0	0	0	79	Hoegerl, Cliff	30	3	2	1	10,494
Hickman, Kenneth G.	68	5	7	6	113,378	Hoetzendorfer, Johanna	47	2	3	9	90,492
Hicks, Cyril F.	37	5	4	4	107,230	Hof, Bill	37	4	4	8	8,663
Hicks, Denette L.	122	14	9	14	291,215	Hoff, Susan J.	7	1	0	0	9,440
Hicks, Harry	18	1	4	0	10,943	Hoffman, Harold	1	0	1	0	483
Hicks, Morris	15	2	2	1	10,372	Hoffman, James H.	35	2	4	4	6,916
Hicks, William H.	4	0	0	0	930	Hoffman, Kenneth E.	22	4	3	2	121,200
Hicks, William R.	48	1	2	5	20,970	Hoffman, Mark	8	3	1	0	33,362
Hieatt, Derek	10	2	0	0	10,779	Hoffman, Michael	2	0	0	0	228
Higgins, Dennis J.	13	0	0	0	702	Hoffman, Robert G.	1	0	0	0	0
Higgins, Hope M.	2	0	0	0	123	Hoffner, Jeannie L.	10	0	0	0	595
Higgins, Martha	9	0	0	2	434	Hoffpauir, Thaddeus	19	1	0	2	22,069
Higgins, III, John J.	6	0	0	2	1,835	Hoffrogge, Todd M.	114	7	18	17	177,453
Higgs, Ricky	1	0	0	0	1,100	Hofmans, David E.	113	17	10	18	1,655,369
Hightower, James	1	1	0	0	960	Hofmans, Grant	42	4	6	2	116,000
Hignite, James	24	3	1	4	11,044	Hogan, Sara L.	3	0	1	1	2,325
Hild, Glenn L.	57	0	4	3	24,583	Hogue, James L.	11	0	2	1	7,141
Hiles, Rick	98	13	15	13	463,313	Hohensee, Karl M.	8	0	0	0	1,449
Hill, Albert	5	0	1	1	862	Hohle, Nina	1	0	0	0	0
Hill, Bill F.	14	1	0	0	13,640	Hoksbergen, Allen D.	64	9	10	3	61,484
Hill, Brenda M.	129	22	21	16	392,622	Hoksbergen, Larry A	32	6	3	6	42,851
Hill, Floyd	108	9	10	14	99,316	Holas, Scott S.	41	0	1	3	11,180
Hill, Jim	113	29	26	12	216,484	Holden, Jay J.	63	0	4	7	14,992

Trainer	Sts	1st	2d	3d	Purses	Trainer	Sts	1st	2d	3d	Purses
Holden, Mark	21	3	0	5	24,432	Householder, Charles F.	20	3	2	0	21,250
Holder, Tedston	7	0	0	0	976	Householder, N. Eddie	264	24	25	33	376,613
Holifield, Jerry	31	3	7	3	9,139	Houston, James W.	2	0	1	0	2,868
Holland, Bobby G.	8	2	1	1	14,499	Houston, Mickey D.	3	0	1	1	3,650
Holland, Mary	5	0	0	0	610	Houston, Theodies B.	11	0	0	2	1,847
Holland, Troy S.	39	5	5	4	77,519	Houston, Wayne	34	3	1	0	21,835
Hollar, Donald B.	78	4	4	3	55,237	Hout, Darrel E.	3	0	0	1	1,390
Hollendorfer, Jerry	1,216	282	211	193	6,260,305	Houtchens, Raymond J.	4	0	0	0	0
Hollett, Richard	21	2	2	4	22,134	Hovezak, James F.	1	0	0	0	0
Hollingsworth, Dustin	4	0	0	0	96	Howard, Bart D.	8	0	0	1	654
Hollingsworth, Lloyd	14	0	1	2	2,696	Howard, Dar	1	0	0	0	120
Hollingsworth, Rick	1	0	0	0	35	Howard, Ian	21	3	4	1	188,095
Holloway, Ashley	3	0	0	0	0	Howard, Jack E.	47	2	5	6	29,124
Holm, Dalyce	41	3	10	8	15,057	Howard, James A.	6	0	0	0	2,150
Holman, Robert P.	45	6	8	3	64,046	Howard, L. Sam	47	3	1	3	9,417
Holmes, Barry	123	17	15	18	139,351	Howard, Leigh Ann	19	1	0	1	11,550
Holmes, J. R.	12	0	1	1	1,330	Howard, Neil J.	156	31	26	18	3,620,359
Holmes, Lloyd S.	62	7	11	11	22,689	Howard, Sam H.	6	0	0	0	509
Holsapple, Gary	3	0	0	0	210	Howard, Steve J.	53	0	5	6	27,874
Holson, Wesley H.	14	0	1	0	1,152	Howard, Thomas	6	0	2	1	5,425
Holst, Nicole	3	0	1	0	870	Howard, William M.	24	3	1	3	65,948
Holstein, Craig T.	29	3	4	2	20,477	Howarth, Sr., Albert L.	3	1	0	0	3,930
Holt, Burlin C.	1	0	0	0	180	Howell, Ronald E.	1	0	0	0	0
Holt, John T.	14	2	1	2	3,170	Howland, Edith	29	0	5	3	41,770
Holt, Larry W.	162	20	17	17	230,927	Hoy, Ramona	12	0	1	1	2,711
Holthus, Robert E.	312	53	44	51	1,595,737	Hrymak, Brent	24	3	1	2	17,281
Holtzinger, Cara	17	1	4	4	14,438	Huarte, Frank	64	9	5	8	343,231
Homan, Harold J.	9	0	2	1	4,881	Hubley, Mark	32	6	6	4	180,197
Homeister, Sr., Rosemary	126	10	21	20	158,911	Huckabay, Sid T.	22	1	2	3	13,124
Homer, A. Lynn	43	6	7	5	12,939	Huddleston, Richard W.	1	0	1	0	1,500
Homer, Jason	102	16	15	14	51,242	Hudepohl, John R.	5	0	0	0	598
Hone, Bart G.	256	54	46	35	611,980	Hudgens, Rodger	4	0	0	0	678
Honeyman, Bob	3	1	2	0	2,795	Hudman, John R.	10	0	0	1	1,270
Hoobler, Jimmy Dale	10	1	1	3	4,264	Hudnut, Steven L.	44	6	5	1	65,237
Hood, Jr., John R.	4	0	0	0	0	Hudson, Howard L.	8	0	0	2	2,750
Hooper, Jeff D.	76	10	11	5	159,125	Hudson, James C.	195	29	21	21	459,577
Hooper, Pamela	11	1	0	1	8,881	Hudson, Jeff D.	158	9	7	20	71,728
Hooper, Timothy	42	7	2	6	94,081	Hudson, Randy	31	3	6	3	18,613
Hoover, Anthony	8	3	1	0	6,256	Hudson, Robert	11	0	3	1	16,302
Hoover, Cindy	123	6	19	19	31,115	Huelsman, Ray	12	1	0	2	6,923
Hoover, Gregg	15	1	5	1	19,866	Huepenbecker, Loren	9	1	4	2	7,750
Hoover, Herbert	21	1	2	1	19,021	Huff, Darin	8	0	0	1	1,390
Hop, Michael D.	113	6	9	15	62,008	Huff, Kathleen A.	2	0	0	0	100
Hopf, Jerry L.	7	1	0	0	4,660	Huffman, David James	2	0	0	0	150
Hopkins, Brett	1	0	0	0	110	Huffman, Dean	12	0	1	0	770
Hopkins, Dennis	245	24	40	34	370,805	Huffman, Kenneth G.	82	3	3	10	58,890
Hopkins, Terry L.	87	8	9	10	51,145	Huffman, Larry G.	12	2	2	2	23,540
Hopmans, Jr., C. Cliff	171	23	23	19	1,418,810	Huffman, Neil C.	45	3	8	4	56,726
Hoppel, Darryl G.	3	0	0	0	684	Huffman, Patrick	45	5	2	5	38,398
Hopper, Carroll R.	5	1	0	1	7,567	Huffman, Roy L.	34	0	4	1	4,841
Horn, H. Ray	10	1	2	1	26,219	Huffman, William G.	114	14	16	19	538,658
Horn, James M.	4	0	0	0	875	Huffman, Jr., John H.	2	0	0	0	0
Horning, Jr., Lawrence E.	35	6	6	2	100,880	Hughes, Baden H.	41	5	3	6	81,440
Hornsby, William	3	0	0	0	860	Hughes, Bernard F.	74	5	4	5	53,253
Horrell, Donald G.	113	10	20	14	112,777	Hughes, Bev	5	0	0	0	1,190
Horrigan, John	52	0	0	9	12,839	Hughes, Byron G.	47	6	5	4	131,387
Horst, Scot	2	0	0	1	1,085	Hughes, Dennis P.	101	4	11	13	55,262
Horton, Jr., Curtis J.	113	5	9	17	71,679	Hughes, Donald W. O.	6	0	0	0	595
Horvath, Sandor	7	0	0	1	1,028	Hughes, Jeff	13	1	0	1	9,103
Hosang, Jr., Oliver P.	1	0	0	0	0	Hughes, Judy E.	39	3	5	5	58,012
Hosie, Pat	61	8	8	7	24,190	Hughes, Justine M.	4	0	0	0	585
Hoskins, Ken	53	4	10	5	40,121	Hughes, Lawrence D.	34	3	5	7	48,708
Hostler, Jr., Charles N.	130	7	9	8	99,719	Hughes, Mary J.	29	5	2	4	75,785
Hough, Stanley M.	289	50	55	37	2,107,589	Hughes, Raymond C.	7	3	0	1	11,981
Houghton, John W.	21	0	0	3	2,977	Hughes, Jr., Don E.	49	6	4	6	61,285
Houghton, Melvin M.	24	5	1	3	25,987	Hughes, Jr., Fred J.	2	0	1	0	4,990
Houghton, Ronald B.	165	15	24	30	316,252	Hughes, Jr., Richard E.	8	0	0	3	10,145
Houghton, Roy D.	129	11	10	12	150,942	Hughes, Sr., Donald E.	70	13	12	11	141,232
Houghton, Terry	29	0	3	2	31,388	Hukill, Charles P.	186	22	32	22	330,724
Houle, William	51	5	4	5	70,824	Hulobow, Larry	8	0	1	1	4,845
Houliston, Bill	1	0	0	0	96	Hummer, Jerry	66	2	2	6	30,887
Houliston, Milton	9	3	2	2	35,639	Humphrey, Shirley A.	12	2	2	2	21,549
Hounyovi, Didier G.	9	0	0	0	210	Humphries, Gene	8	1	1	4	1,974
House, Brian S.	74	10	9	10	102,771	Humphries, Thomas	1	0	0	0	204
House, Gary F.	23	1	2	2	16,035	Hundt, Robert L.	49	1	6	2	10,851
House, R. Wayne	13	0	0	0	1,004	Hunkapiller, Louis	31	0	3	3	12,121

Trainer	Sts	1st	2d	3d	Purses	Trainer	Sts	1st	2d	3d	Purses
Hunley, Jerry D.	11	1	2	0	1,822	Ishaq, Abdallah H.	32	1	5	7	34,315
Hunsaker, Danny J.	57	12	8	7	68,980	Issac, Randy	16	2	3	3	14,510
Hunt, Charley	1	0	0	0	300	Iverson, Mitchell L.	13	1	0	1	3,306
Hunt, Charlton	2	0	0	0	139	Ivie, Jimmy C.	17	0	0	1	3,535
Hunt, Donald F.	8	0	1	0	2,268	Ivory, John C.	21	1	2	3	25,180
Hunt, Gary	13	2	2	1	8,042	Iwan, Marilyn	26	3	2	4	14,678
Hunt, Glen E.	49	5	5	7	80,644	Iwersen, David K.	6	0	0	1	2,147
Hunt, J. Sue	21	2	3	3	11,344	Iwinski, Allen	598	148	117	81	4,053,035
Hunt, Richard	23	1	2	1	5,444	Jacavone, Jr., John J.	266	9	24	33	107,130
Hunt, Vannessa	73	13	14	8	32,266	Jack, Allan	48	12	7	5	128,832
Hunt, Sr., Larry E.	49	8	3	7	201,694	Jack, Crystal	3	0	0	0	172
Hunter, F. E.	15	1	1	0	15,956	Jacklin, Theodora S.	92	5	6	6	46,939
Hunter, Judy	38	6	8	7	16,286	Jackson, Bruce C.	128	22	23	16	397,271
Hunter, Karline J.	17	2	4	1	20,750	Jackson, Bruce L.	58	4	1	3	126,060
Hunter, Rick	3	0	0	1	374	Jackson, Christopher J.	16	0	0	3	6,515
Hunter, Thomas E.	60	11	7	10	28,178	Jackson, Dale L.	27	1	2	6	29,225
Hunter, Thomas W.	19	0	0	0	1,750	Jackson, Declan A.	7	0	0	0	1,680
Hunter, Jr., Allan	26	3	0	5	58,717	Jackson, Elizabeth R.	9	0	1	1	4,978
Huntington, Dougal A.	17	0	3	1	7,864	Jackson, Ellen	83	7	6	8	123,659
Hurdle, Joe A.	1	0	0	0	120	Jackson, Fred L.	8	1	0	0	6,777
Hurley, Dennis	133	7	11	15	29,102	Jackson, Harvey	40	2	3	7	15,132
Hurley, Jim Bob	7	3	2	1	6,017	Jackson, Helmut S.	15	0	2	1	4,499
Hurley, Kenneth L.	7	1	2	2	5,386	Jackson, James D.	18	0	0	0	676
Hurley, Mary L.	57	4	4	9	29,583	Jackson, James R.	242	24	23	24	521,834
Huron, Ray G.	1	0	0	0	0	Jackson, James W.	3	0	0	0	176
Hurt, Clayton C.	215	39	25	22	326,610	Jackson, Jeffrey D.	18	0	0	1	3,676
Hurtak, Daniel C.	304	39	47	42	583,330	Jackson, Leroy	15	0	0	1	4,151
Husak, Robert	12	3	2	0	22,814	Jackson, Richard D.	77	5	13	11	91,305
Husak, Jr., Robert J.	3	0	0	1	735	Jackson, Robert D.	9	0	0	0	0
Husbands, Anthony	10	1	1	2	15,463	Jackson, Ronald D.	9	4	3	2	27,313
Hushion, Michael E.	211	52	36	24	1,775,506	Jackson, Roy J.	5	0	1	2	1,000
Hussey, David	64	1	8	5	39,835	Jacobs, Daniel C.	11	1	2	2	6,916
Husson, Damie L.	8	0	0	1	2,347	Jacobs, Nita	6	0	0	2	1,076
Huston, Sharon T.	91	5	10	10	192,677	Jacobs, Stephen	22	2	2	5	17,710
Hutchison, David J.	29	2	0	3	21,510	Jacobs, Jr., John F.	11	0	1	0	5,877
Hutchison, James A.	17	3	1	1	53,337	Jacobsen, Harvey T.	9	0	1	0	2,468
Hutchison-Hand, Julie P.	15	0	0	2	14,884	Jacques, Dennis S.	165	14	18	18	109,957
Huth, Bill	15	1	0	1	14,783	Jacquot, Gene	32	4	6	3	48,230
Hutt, Danny	23	4	3	3	106,636	Jaggers, Donnie	22	0	0	2	2,544
Huval, Brian A.	109	10	9	13	82,169	Jahns, Debi	6	2	0	3	3,234
Huval, Robert Lee	95	14	15	10	88,490	James, Greg R.	152	19	22	16	235,946
Hyatt, Freddie	22	4	3	4	47,605	James, Lorenzo	5	1	0	0	1,094
Hyland, Angel	57	8	8	8	144,655	James, Melvin R.	7	0	1	0	2,958
Hysell-Berryhill, Robin E.	15	1	0	1	4,075	James, Robert E.	1	0	1	0	425
Iacone, Maryann	13	1	1	2	13,022	James, Roosevelt	22	0	0	5	3,776
Iacovacci, Cynthia L.	1	0	0	0	140	Jamison, O. D.	93	16	12	11	304,502
Iacovacci, George A.	105	12	13	13	77,703	Janes, Mark	27	2	6	0	23,852
Iams, Wendell	6	1	0	0	4,260	Janks, Christine K.	196	35	35	17	753,986
Iannotti, Robert	2	0	0	0	0	Jansen, Gail T.	37	2	2	5	34,540
Iannotti, IV, Thomas	3	0	0	0	0	January, Elmer	61	3	10	6	41,350
Ibarra, Jose	104	9	10	5	33,194	Jaquillard, Arthur J.	11	2	1	1	15,399
Iglar-Hughes, Joanna	24	3	5	4	275,445	Jaros, Ronald J.	45	2	2	2	24,257
Ilicin, Jr., Al	48	5	1	3	23,952	Jarvis, Kathy	100	13	18	6	163,245
Imperio, Joseph	151	17	19	16	502,340	Jarvis, Pat	20	6	1	2	36,164
Inabinett, Johnny	29	5	5	1	59,689	Jeannont, Dianne M.	145	7	23	22	188,698
Inda, Eduardo	63	4	6	8	358,294	Jeanotte, Bob	120	23	27	22	237,494
Ingebritson, Mark	5	1	0	0	5,950	Jean-Pierre, Albert	39	3	8	3	68,880
Ingels, Jerry	4	0	1	0	555	Jeansonne, Albin	57	5	9	6	30,751
Ingenito, Angela M.	24	2	3	1	25,100	Jeffries, Donald L.	17	1	0	0	4,549
Ingram, Kevin	82	9	7	18	51,542	Jeffries, Patrick	48	5	3	1	26,472
Ingram, Steve	20	0	1	2	8,314	Jeffries, Robert A.	20	2	2	3	24,553
Inman, Robert L.	67	4	6	8	58,535	Jencik, Barbara Jo	3	0	2	0	5,370
Inman, Ronald P.	41	3	1	4	21,553	Jenda, Charles J.	282	38	46	43	909,214
Inouye, Tak	26	3	5	1	68,627	Jenkins, Bobby A.	106	12	10	16	105,389
Iorfida, Lou	2	0	0	0	0	Jenkins, Brandon	13	1	4	1	9,820
Iorio, Jr., Sal	100	8	10	18	94,776	Jenkins, Norris William	61	6	7	5	110,216
Ireland, Marty R.	7	1	0	0	1,754	Jenkins, Reed L.	85	7	15	8	57,973
Irion, Sue	107	20	15	13	107,464	Jenkins, Rodney	263	56	46	33	1,284,474
Irish, Ray E.	6	0	1	0	812	Jenkins, Suzanne H.	95	3	4	11	51,260
Irlando, Steve R.	3	1	1	0	1,275	Jenkins, Wallace A.	37	7	1	3	87,180
Irwin, Alex T.	43	1	1	5	23,739	Jenkins, William E.	60	14	9	9	67,228
Irwin, Lawrence	1	0	0	0	0	Jenkins, Jr., Norman W.	4	1	0	1	7,650
Irwin, Ralph R.	108	21	18	12	259,630	Jenne, Bonnie	93	15	17	12	154,926
Irwin, Robert D.	100	8	12	15	228,591	Jennings, Dennis E.	23	3	2	1	9,196
Isbell, Jr., Ron	10	3	2	0	129,548	Jennings, Ronald A.	13	0	3	2	3,180
Isburg, Jr., William	100	5	18	7	35,074	Jensen, Eric	6	2	1	0	5,750

RECORDS OF TRAINERS

Trainer	Sts	1st	2d	3d	Purses	Trainer	Sts	1st	2d	3d	Purses
Jensen, Kent	39	4	8	5	54,449	Joles, Judith	7	1	1	1	12,693
Jensen, Mark	60	3	2	6	20,785	Jolley, James E.	1	0	0	0	0
Jensen, Megan	4	0	0	0	104	Jolley, Leroy S.	72	7	4	8	206,840
Jerkens, H. Allen	359	73	82	62	5,173,434	Jones, A. Mark	49	6	13	10	25,371
Jerkens, James A.	194	46	30	30	2,303,508	Jones, Brian K.	54	5	8	2	100,633
Jerkens, Steven T.	103	10	12	18	385,250	Jones, Carl C.	27	2	4	1	23,615
Jermain, Kathie C.	79	6	2	11	62,781	Jones, Carol L	21	0	1	3	10,113
Jerman, Jerry	93	4	15	8	90,924	Jones, Casey	35	1	5	5	11,707
Jiles, Eddie T.	1	0	0	0	119	Jones, Charles Franklin	23	1	6	3	12,440
Jimenez, Carlos	14	1	0	0	10,667	Jones, Dal	4	0	0	0	380
Jimenez, Lisa	32	4	7	3	140,395	Jones, Daniel T.	45	7	4	8	52,486
Jimenez, Sr., Guillermo	35	3	2	4	5,771	Jones, Daren K.	35	2	2	3	10,084
Jocson, Gwen	6	1	0	1	9,005	Jones, Donald L.	15	0	0	3	5,496
Johns, Justin	36	4	3	2	61,591	Jones, Duwayne	8	1	0	0	10,810
Johnson, Andrew H.	46	4	2	6	16,238	Jones, Erika U.	1	0	0	0	0
Johnson, Armand	30	3	5	3	8,198	Jones, Harold R.	14	1	3	1	4,772
Johnson, Brian S.	4	0	1	0	5,126	Jones, Harrison	5	0	0	1	1,095
Johnson, Bruce	21	2	3	1	13,468	Jones, J. Larry	146	33	21	16	806,085
Johnson, C. Allen	17	2	1	2	13,256	Jones, Jack Craig	27	2	1	4	29,806
Johnson, Calistine I.	12	0	1	0	4,310	Jones, Jack W.	17	1	1	1	21,760
Johnson, Carrie L.	10	0	0	1	911	Jones, James E.	92	14	12	12	149,483
Johnson, Cecil H.	34	3	5	5	35,683	Jones, James R.	50	7	3	5	112,498
Johnson, Claudia	6	0	0	1	1,650	Jones, Jann K.	19	2	0	4	13,342
Johnson, Danny Smith	34	1	7	6	45,579	Jones, Jeff S.	65	6	10	5	130,770
Johnson, David F.	12	1	2	0	16,988	Jones, Jeffrey Allen	6	2	1	1	9,678
Johnson, Doug	34	4	7	6	12,743	Jones, Juanita	26	4	3	1	7,721
Johnson, Douglas L.	157	13	15	10	228,608	Jones, Laurie	107	8	16	16	25,454
Johnson, Earnest	4	0	0	0	3,920	Jones, Lloyd Jackson	6	0	0	4	3,226
Johnson, Frank R.	15	0	2	1	9,058	Jones, Lynda	16	2	0	1	7,916
Johnson, Frazer	64	8	6	5	67,030	Jones, Mark W.	35	2	3	4	17,885
Johnson, Freddie R.	27	5	2	3	90,094	Jones, Martin F.	135	22	21	17	879,193
Johnson, Gail	8	0	0	0	1,108	Jones, Michael David	80	5	2	14	52,631
Johnson, Gary L.	658	87	77	78	835,709	Jones, Michael P.	22	0	0	2	5,137
Johnson, Gene A.	89	15	12	8	152,750	Jones, Paul C.	6	2	0	3	8,700
Johnson, Harry	24	1	0	1	8,705	Jones, Phillip L.	3	0	0	1	696
Johnson, Heather A.	25	3	3	3	19,749	Jones, Richard J.	26	1	2	3	12,613
Johnson, James R.	6	1	0	0	5,240	Jones, Roy C.	6	0	0	0	2,294
Johnson, Jennifer A.	35	1	7	4	45,650	Jones, Scott	2	0	0	0	0
Johnson, Jerry W.	1	0	0	0	450	Jones, Steve	29	4	4	2	34,325
Johnson, Jill	1	0	0	0	90	Jones, Ted	12	2	1	2	5,621
Johnson, John Michael	35	7	8	1	51,785	Jones, Tommy Lee	41	0	8	3	37,598
Johnson, Joseph E.	59	12	10	9	116,909	Jones, Tony Dean	9	0	1	0	2,042
Johnson, Joseph H.	59	14	10	7	432,949	Jones, Wilfred	48	7	3	13	140,693
Johnson, Keith M.	55	3	7	10	28,635	Jones, William I.	3	0	0	0	390
Johnson, Kenneth L.	3	0	1	0	3,675	Jones, Sr., Herbert W.	2	0	0	1	800
Johnson, Lee E.	5	0	0	0	122	Jordan, Mary C.	5	0	0	0	1,765
Johnson, Mark	2	0	0	0	0	Jordan, Michael B.	10	0	0	0	923
Johnson, Marvin A.	297	35	43	34	322,396	Jordan, Rick G.	78	4	7	2	109,079
Johnson, Murray W.	101	14	5	11	1,732,941	Jordan, Roland G.	40	4	4	10	40,553
Johnson, Norman A.	72	4	4	3	43,975	Jordan, Steven C.	26	2	2	5	38,928
Johnson, Paul E.	16	2	0	5	14,034	Jordan, Steven W.	25	2	2	4	19,909
Johnson, Perry E.	11	1	0	2	34,954	Jordan, Terry	72	13	15	7	193,922
Johnson, Philip G.	166	20	22	26	1,376,268	Jordan, Jr., Harold Z.	25	2	1	2	45,938
Johnson, Rae	52	3	8	7	78,247	Jordano, Salvatore	23	2	3	1	27,325
Johnson, Regina	26	1	1	2	9,998	Jory, Ian P. D.	220	16	26	20	961,370
Johnson, Richard G.	30	1	1	2	7,098	Joseph, Dalton	7	2	0	0	27,030
Johnson, Robert D.	14	0	2	1	2,490	Joseph, Judy	22	0	1	1	14,230
Johnson, Roscoe E.	49	3	6	5	28,380	Josephson, Jedd B.	236	34	36	33	560,258
Johnson, S. Eugene	2	0	0	1	468	Journet, Theo	87	8	9	9	86,690
Johnson, Sonny	54	3	5	3	25,228	Joy, Kevin J.	455	72	65	53	661,822
Johnson, Sterling	4	0	0	0	790	Joyner, Linda	1	0	0	0	0
Johnson, Tammy Kay	1	0	0	0	435	Juarez, Clare A.	11	0	0	1	2,967
Johnson, William D.	12	1	1	0	4,602	Juarez, Silvester	57	6	8	10	19,011
Johnson, Jr., Henry B.	109	9	13	15	111,545	Judge, Phillip G.	22	1	2	1	15,603
Johnston, Carlton R.	34	0	2	5	19,880	Judice, Shelby	20	2	0	1	8,348
Johnston, Edward J.	26	10	4	4	323,433	Jukosky, Richard H.	51	6	8	9	282,714
Johnston, George R.	8	0	2	3	2,856	Julian, Louis J.	5	0	2	1	6,555
Johnston, Johnny	9	2	1	1	30,290	Julian, William A.	45	3	2	4	66,682
Johnston, Lyle D.	1	0	0	0	0	Junker, Jr., Milton H.	44	3	5	2	29,404
Johnston, Marilyn T.	16	3	3	1	38,497	Jurado, Luis	1	0	0	0	50
Johnston, Marion	10	2	1	1	11,315	Justice, Patricia D.	8	0	0	0	955
Johnston, Patrick	57	4	6	6	84,610	Juvonen, Erik R.	54	7	7	11	214,475
Johnston, Jr., Dean	2	0	0	0	0	Kaelberer, Kelly	29	5	2	3	13,054
Johnstone, Bruce	44	1	3	3	64,887	Kaelin, Forrest	151	11	14	18	285,259
Johnstone, Frank W.	41	0	4	5	25,349	Kagee, Mary	19	0	3	2	2,938
Joiner, Michael W.	3	1	2	0	16,911	Kagee, Jr., William H.	99	14	8	15	33,938

Trainer	Sts	1st	2d	3d	Purses	Trainer	Sts	1st	2d	3d	Purses
Kagel, Thomas F.	16	0	2	0	2,661	Kendall, Vechel E.	17	1	2	0	21,415
Kaimimoku, Kalei	11	0	0	1	2,010	Kendrick, Melvin A.	40	3	3	5	47,408
Kaiser, Yvonne	1	0	0	0	0	Kenneally, Eddie	100	20	9	11	588,953
Kaiswatum, Joe	43	3	6	7	6,855	Kennedy, Bill E.	78	7	11	12	43,662
Kallenberger, Hans	13	1	1	0	3,950	Kennedy, John K.	24	1	2	1	25,469
Kamps, Rick	38	14	6	3	165,707	Kennedy, M. Brent	93	15	11	15	144,416
Kane, Mark D.	7	2	0	0	20,393	Kennedy, Richard W.	46	3	2	6	55,407
Kane, Stephen	33	0	6	1	6,521	Kenney, Daniel	86	9	12	10	72,465
Kanhai, Joseph	43	1	1	4	28,483	Kenney, Martin	205	18	23	26	352,966
Kaplan, William A.	76	6	8	17	207,200	Kent, Justine	16	0	2	1	1,758
Kappel, Petra	6	1	1	0	11,690	Kenway, Tom	1	0	1	0	440
Kappes, Steven W.	41	4	7	5	264,184	Kenyon, Charles D.	10	2	1	0	5,546
Karcher, Douglas W.	36	6	3	7	42,449	Keogh, Michael	97	17	7	8	3,262,209
Karcher, Lisa Lynn	22	1	3	3	7,920	Keplin, Kevin	15	2	5	4	9,076
Kargus, Kevin C.	28	4	2	2	18,984	Keplin, Steve	36	8	2	5	23,062
Karpon, Julie	1	0	0	0	500	Kerchner, Ann E.	2	0	1	0	1,794
Kasmerski, Len	96	15	11	15	154,093	Kereluk, Edward J.	26	0	2	4	6,656
Kasmir, Joycelyn	1	0	0	0	0	Kereluk, John	38	5	4	6	19,987
Kasparoff, James M.	10	4	0	0	40,080	Kereluk, William S.	21	2	0	2	8,108
Kasperski, Jr., Joseph E.	132	10	19	18	286,126	Kerins, Patrick J.	34	2	2	3	15,725
Kassen, Bonnie	24	4	1	3	50,325	Kern, David	5	0	0	0	199
Kassen, David C.	114	12	15	16	566,729	Kern, Jr., Berkley W.	50	2	6	5	48,999
Kassen, Scott	104	3	3	6	27,889	Kerns, Perry R.	17	0	1	3	6,459
Katryan, Abraham R.	301	57	34	48	2,612,005	Kerr, Jim	27	2	6	0	13,074
Kattell, James	1	0	0	0	250	Kerr, Wayne	52	10	10	10	99,470
Katz, Gary R.	10	0	0	0	3,190	Kerr, Jr., Robert W.	11	1	1	2	3,913
Kaufman, Neil	8	1	1	1	7,168	Kerrone, Don	50	2	8	5	24,936
Kaufman, Jr., Jack S.	45	4	2	4	61,095	Keshane, Alex	3	0	1	1	428
Kay, Gary A.	54	0	2	8	18,839	Keshane, Dan	8	3	2	1	5,860
Kay, Robert	9	3	0	1	42,950	Keshane, Dana	1	0	1	0	260
Kearl, Judd S.	11	3	0	1	9,698	Keshane, Elton	77	15	11	16	20,343
Kee, Willie J	31	2	3	2	20,790	Keshane, Henry	7	1	1	3	1,511
Keefe, Susan	5	0	0	0	315	Keshane, Leon	20	3	1	9	4,132
Keefe, Timothy L.	82	9	9	7	175,938	Keshane, Lindsey	30	6	4	3	9,001
Keegan, John	70	8	9	7	60,267	Keshane, Norbert	16	1	2	4	3,848
Keel, Michael W.	9	0	0	3	5,226	Keshane, William	5	1	2	1	1,330
Keelan, Oliver P.	19	1	0	2	13,390	Kessinger, Jerry	1	0	0	0	0
Keeler, Sandra	1	0	0	0	385	Kessinger, Jr., Burk	15	1	1	2	35,895
Keely,	4	0	1	0	3,210	Kestler, Larry A.	69	6	5	4	105,082
Keen, Dallas E.	195	23	22	21	478,951	Ketcher, Henry Lee	2	0	0	0	0
Keen, Jim	202	39	29	40	110,155	Ketchum, Billy	2	0	0	0	0
Keenan, Edward J.	24	2	5	0	33,913	Ketring, Brenda	65	10	4	2	84,602
Keener, Dee	6	0	1	2	2,731	Kettell, James	168	8	11	16	105,903
Kees, Barbara M.	59	11	10	7	115,614	Ketterman, Debra J.	109	15	13	11	195,865
Keeton, Toby	3	0	0	0	237	Keuer, Jan E.	25	4	5	3	22,631
Keiffer, Luann	91	10	8	7	152,290	Key, Tommy	15	1	0	3	5,702
Keil, Steven D.	18	2	1	2	16,323	Keyes, Joseph S.	22	1	1	1	6,228
Keiser, Deborah	10	0	0	0	554	Keyrouze, Samuel J.	383	52	44	37	313,194
Keller, Caryn	48	4	5	6	47,474	Khalsa, G Dharma	18	5	4	0	30,780
Keller, Christopher M.	48	0	1	2	8,670	Kidd, Lynda Ann	12	2	2	0	13,004
Keller, Ernie J.	172	21	30	26	359,504	Kidder, Keith	11	0	2	2	5,237
Keller, Franklin V.	29	3	4	5	41,360	Kielty, Donald E.	79	7	6	11	119,090
Keller, Robin M.	100	7	13	10	36,322	Kierans, Renee D.	5	1	1	1	20,530
Kelley, Arthur L.	6	1	0	0	4,043	Kieser, Charles H.	72	2	5	8	54,648
Kelley, Brent	92	7	11	4	115,554	Kilmister, Bob	1	0	0	0	0
Kelley, Gary L.	107	14	5	10	51,575	Kimmel, John C.	317	45	30	46	2,014,841
Kelley, Mark T.	1	0	0	0	228	Kinch, Bill	58	6	7	10	85,505
Kelley, Michael P.	1	0	0	0	0	Kinchen, Herman L.	123	13	14	11	191,543
Kelling, Charles B.	4	0	0	0	834	Kinder, David L.	20	3	3	1	12,101
Kellogg, Cory J.	37	5	3	4	24,090	Kindle, Jason	4	2	0	0	8,400
Kelly, Cody	8	0	1	0	3,690	King, Eric	45	3	3	4	23,634
Kelly, David	15	0	0	1	2,285	King, Gary M.	99	17	20	7	213,635
Kelly, Dennis D.	28	5	1	3	43,942	King, George A.	65	9	5	10	125,337
Kelly, Donna L.	5	0	2	0	3,520	King, Gorden	2	0	1	0	6,260
Kelly, Donnie	7	0	1	2	12,180	King, Hunter L.	6	0	0	1	1,520
Kelly, Mark A.	6	0	0	2	4,606	King, James W.	36	2	3	2	34,234
Kelly, Patrick J.	266	21	31	33	1,710,927	King, Kevin T.	6	0	1	1	1,860
Kelly, Robert M.	45	3	1	6	19,649	King, Paul M.	1	0	0	0	211
Kelly, Robert W.	31	2	5	4	41,918	King, Richard D.	1	0	0	0	0
Kelly, Suzanne F.	118	27	18	10	225,152	King, Robert Eric	9	1	0	0	4,825
Kelly, Timothy James	68	8	15	12	339,002	King, Stephen H.	4	0	0	0	150
Kelly, III, John J.	57	3	6	1	39,797	King, Tannis	1	0	0	0	0
Kelsey, Bob	1	0	0	0	147	King, Terry Pat	17	0	1	1	4,456
Kemling-Mohr, Laura	4	0	0	0	0	King, Warren L.	82	14	5	11	149,555
Kendall, Connie	3	0	0	0	424	King, Yolonda Y.	58	8	5	6	93,257
Kendall, Jason L.	4	1	1	0	2,480	King, IV, Hugh G.	8	0	0	1	1,528

Trainer	Sts	1st	2d	3d	Purses	Trainer	Sts	1st	2d	3d	Purses
King, Jr., Robert J.	35	3	6	3	149,738	Kohlheim, Edward C.	5	0	0	0	868
Kingery, Diana	7	2	2	1	9,100	Kohlheim, Mark A.	34	1	1	3	17,430
Kinghorne, George A.	38	2	3	8	52,685	Kohnhorst, Richard B.	125	18	17	14	264,110
Kingsland, Pamela	8	1	1	3	14,290	Kokoronis, Athanasios	31	4	4	1	68,478
Kingsley, Jr., Archibald J.	9	2	2	1	28,070	Kokoski, Gerald	32	4	3	2	37,836
Kingston, Robert C.	52	5	3	6	83,086	Kolarik, Jeanne M.	26	2	4	6	71,200
Kinmon, Ronald Keith	18	1	2	0	20,177	Kolb, Christopher L.	20	4	2	0	43,720
Kinnamon, Wendy	60	4	9	5	108,619	Kolb, Gary Lee	67	3	2	6	45,727
Kinney, Karen	15	0	1	0	3,839	Kolbrick, Cheryl R.	38	0	1	1	7,020
Kintz, S. Matthew	177	21	18	18	301,407	Koler, Dale	16	0	1	1	2,259
Kipling, Gerry	103	13	15	14	172,527	Koler, Steve	34	1	4	5	15,334
Kirby, Frank John	494	53	64	78	1,261,312	Koller, William C.	21	0	1	3	3,584
Kirby, James F.	7	2	0	2	26,705	Kolochuk, John	17	1	0	0	5,853
Kirby, Kenneth M.	60	2	9	6	58,841	Komardley, Evans	42	1	0	3	4,073
Kirby, Mike	26	5	3	3	62,514	Komlo, Edward C.	11	1	2	1	7,025
Kirby, Timothy	50	2	7	7	89,322	Komlo, John E.	22	2	1	2	12,769
Kirby, Violet	2	0	0	0	155	Komlo, William R.	53	7	5	5	90,585
Kirk, Sherry	5	0	1	0	740	Kong, Winston C.	5	0	0	1	3,965
Kirk, Jr., David	9	0	1	0	1,694	Konkoly, Andrew	340	42	38	50	507,462
Kirkpatrick, Alex	3	0	0	1	520	Konrath, Frank L.	18	0	0	1	2,425
Kirkpatrick, Sylvia	8	1	0	1	1,655	Konyk, Jr., William J.	11	0	0	2	3,322
Kirlin, Thomas	16	0	2	3	15,000	Koonce, Roland	23	0	1	1	5,594
Kirn, Margo	14	0	0	2	4,788	Kopaj, Paul	59	6	2	9	64,360
Kisielewski, Eric	20	0	1	4	4,086	Kopycinski, Larry	19	3	2	3	21,623
Kisielewski, George T.	38	4	6	4	18,746	Koriner, Brian J.	291	56	51	41	930,474
Kisielewski, Gina M.	27	0	0	0	2,175	Korrell, Elizabeth	10	0	2	3	9,215
Kissoon, Raphael B.	5	1	0	1	20,140	Koski, James	30	1	1	3	11,620
Kitchingman, Adam	42	12	1	9	288,021	Kosmas, Mike	2	0	0	0	0
Kite, Sandra M.	51	4	6	10	79,750	Kotenko, Robert	125	5	13	14	61,703
Kittson, Dorotha A.	24	1	0	2	2,667	Kotsos, Patricia	42	2	0	4	13,115
Klapatch, Nancy	27	6	5	6	15,456	Kott, Rose	12	0	0	1	2,820
Klecka, Donald W.	23	0	0	4	4,170	Kovach, Charles A.	65	5	6	2	62,206
Kleier, Michael	6	1	1	0	19,980	Kowalsky, Harley	61	1	5	2	19,754
Klein, Linda	4	1	0	0	6,000	Koza, Kristine M.	83	7	5	11	52,937
Klein, Sheila S.	1	0	0	0	126	Krafjack, Leonette	5	0	0	0	500
Klemme, Lem W.	36	6	3	6	30,501	Kramp, Jerri L.	33	0	4	5	11,883
Klenakis, Tony	169	23	15	23	111,533	Kranz, Mark A.	25	1	0	5	27,967
Klesaris, Peter	173	14	20	23	222,592	Krasner, Cindy	118	21	16	17	282,415
Klesaris, Robert P.	419	60	69	80	1,461,391	Kravets, Bruce M.	1,118	198	159	164	1,561,062
Klesaris, Steve B.	347	77	54	55	2,635,382	Kravets, Lori	5	0	0	1	1,908
Kline, Daulph A.	1	0	0	0	0	Krebs, Steven	222	45	35	34	675,047
Kline, Lynnelle M.	8	0	0	0	594	Kreiser, Gina M.	68	7	8	8	41,256
Kling, Barry	14	2	1	0	19,930	Kreiser, Timothy C.	208	43	39	28	549,409
Kling, Guy	50	5	3	4	70,377	Kreitzberg, Jennifer	12	0	3	0	3,408
Klinger, Gary	13	1	0	2	2,236	Krieger, Heinz	5	0	1	1	1,710
Klokstad, Bud	285	46	44	44	774,302	Kriple, Zvi	78	12	10	11	53,829
Klopp, Randy L.	128	6	6	11	57,386	Kriser, Roland D.	8	1	2	0	12,851
Kloth, David R.	28	3	2	1	18,855	Krohn, Pete	2	0	0	0	255
Klutts, Frank E.	1	0	0	0	275	Kromann, Lloyd N.	19	1	1	6	31,638
Knaggs, Robert	1	0	0	0	0	Krone, Bryan	44	13	7	6	23,670
Knapp, Neil	39	5	6	4	32,148	Kropius, Linda	62	3	12	10	25,797
Knapp, Steve	275	32	32	45	971,502	Krueger, Linda J.	3	1	0	0	11,680
Knechtel, Lianne	128	23	17	13	226,302	Kruger, Wendy J.	87	9	9	7	242,614
Knee, Lynda	110	10	16	16	201,280	Kruljac, J. Eric	311	74	52	41	1,037,384
Knepper, James M.	201	9	20	15	168,704	Krummen, Paul	6	0	0	1	2,121
Knepper, Julie	1	0	1	0	2,180	Kube, Harry	98	14	9	20	148,209
Knight, Mary	2	0	0	0	0	Kubovchik, Donald	31	3	2	5	26,193
Knight, Robert B.	13	0	0	2	2,580	Kudla, Edward T.	11	0	1	2	2,790
Knight, Terry	152	25	15	27	567,535	Kueffner, Dave	125	24	17	22	288,816
Knight, Thomas E.	20	2	2	0	16,002	Kuhn, Marvin H.	21	1	3	3	16,990
Knighton, Judy L	22	0	0	1	3,145	Kuhns, Sr., Ernest E.	113	11	8	13	55,524
Knipe, Duane	241	33	27	28	436,195	Kuiken, Randal	36	4	1	4	67,859
Knippenberg, Brian	1	0	0	0	45	Kumke, Myron D.	144	11	18	15	77,459
Knisley, Heather	40	3	1	6	67,165	Kunes, Karen M.	275	27	30	35	217,511
Knoblauch, Michelle	51	5	3	7	48,030	Kuns, Martin C.	1	0	0	0	0
Knowles, Lucinda C.	116	2	0	2	30,141	Kuti, Ann	16	1	2	2	49,078
Knowles, Robert A.	10	2	1	1	4,697	Kutt, C. Michael	37	7	5	6	59,679
Knox, Dennis	2	0	0	0	828	Kutz, Dean	3	1	0	2	2,472
Knudsen, Don	45	6	4	6	15,123	Kuwik, Gregory	21	0	2	1	7,890
Knudsen, Kevin	72	13	8	9	25,955	Kuykendall, Mary Ann	2	0	0	0	0
Kobza, Lee	46	2	9	6	18,753	La Croix, David	105	9	7	16	336,526
Koch, Neil A.	123	7	14	11	54,024	La Mew, Brian	57	4	6	7	36,051
Kocher, Robert	1	0	0	0	605	LaBoccetta, Frank	5	2	2	1	43,450
Kocijan, Boris	42	3	2	5	53,280	LaBoccetta, Jr., Frank	179	43	44	16	1,050,658
Koenenn, Yancey	12	1	0	0	4,444	Laborde, Amos	250	21	37	32	246,729
Koertgen, Timothy C.	26	2	1	0	21,940	LaBorde, Donald	61	5	6	6	40,442

Trainer	Sts	1st	2d	3d	Purses	Trainer	Sts	1st	2d	3d	Purses
Labrie, Marie L.	2	0	0	0	300	Larue, Bobby	22	4	3	1	47,949
Lacey, Jodie	19	2	1	4	4,168	Larue, C. Steve	110	4	8	8	32,756
Lackey, James E.	12	2	2	3	50,395	Lasky, Harvey	26	0	0	1	9,662
Lacy, James	12	1	2	0	5,248	Lason, James	5	0	1	0	486
Laczo, Brandt	54	10	7	10	47,228	Lathrop, David	133	13	21	23	109,402
Ladd, Don	75	10	6	13	50,466	Latimer, Samuel	21	2	1	7	13,878
Ladd, Perry R.	46	5	7	7	32,921	Latiolais, Benoit	3	0	0	0	0
Ladd, Ronald	43	4	2	6	23,930	LaTour, Theodore J.	81	12	9	12	153,745
Ladner, Bernie	19	1	2	4	24,054	Lattimer, Gail L.	57	8	5	5	132,275
Ladner, Edwin Lee	30	3	1	0	32,709	Lau, Kam Tak	4	0	0	0	1,584
Ladner, Patrick L.	63	6	9	16	156,582	Laudati, Kim	25	1	2	4	38,757
Ladner, Roger Joe	27	1	2	2	11,086	Lauer, Michael E.	173	26	20	19	429,773
Ladner, Terry	1	0	0	0	0	Laugherty, Joe	60	8	7	5	66,424
Ladner, Jr., Herman F.	7	0	0	1	8,255	Laurine, Frank	5	0	1	0	4,000
Ladouceur, Jr., Doug	38	4	5	2	30,799	Lausten, Carl	59	3	18	9	77,634
Laducer, Jack	1	0	0	0	50	Lautzenheiser, Sr., Robert	21	0	1	2	6,710
Lafavers, Laurie	48	2	7	8	176,026	Lavallee, Alphonse	56	10	8	10	22,032
Laffin, Bill	6	0	0	0	336	Lavallee, Gary J.	13	0	0	2	9,104
LaFlamme, Jr., Albert J.	4	1	0	0	2,275	Lavanway, Dayson	99	8	9	10	44,373
LaFleur, Girard E.	86	9	6	9	70,169	Lavanway, William	31	3	5	2	28,378
Lafontaine, Bernard	3	0	0	0	578	Lavell, Richard A.	14	1	1	0	6,830
Lage, Armando	801	141	145	117	2,407,056	Laviolette, Gerald	32	1	4	3	34,347
Lagorio, William G.	26	1	0	1	6,116	Laviolette, Harold J.	70	3	7	2	50,362
Lagrone, Selwyn	14	2	2	1	20,738	Lawrence, Coleman J.	11	0	1	1	4,563
Laibly, Charles N.	3	0	0	0	180	Lawrence, Donald L.	7	0	0	2	1,505
Laing, Sherry	3	0	1	1	396	Lawrence, Robert D.	112	19	15	13	133,342
Lake, Barry K.	18	2	1	1	8,335	Lawrence, Robert L.	79	18	13	8	44,663
Lake, Charles Michael	97	8	7	9	190,254	Lawrence, Robert M.	6	2	0	0	19,149
Lake, Donald D.	4	0	0	0	70	Lawrence, Wray I.	104	7	10	15	335,870
Lake, James Y.	41	5	2	3	92,547	Lawrence, II, James L.	148	10	20	16	259,296
Lake, Scott A.	2,009	454	345	280	9,152,959	Lawrence, Jr., Raymond S.	20	1	1	0	26,255
Lalman, Dennis	19	3	2	1	56,537	Laws, Arlene	7	0	1	0	2,460
Lam, Kwong C.	1	0	0	0	0	Lawson, Charles	149	21	24	22	112,825
Lamazor, Fredric P.	2	0	0	0	100	Lawson, Edward	25	1	1	2	9,807
Lamb, Jodie L.	33	1	3	1	7,780	Lawson, Peggy	7	1	1	0	6,819
Lamb, Pam	1	0	0	0	50	Lawson, Richard E.	6	0	0	0	825
Lamb, William F.	34	0	0	3	7,581	Lay, Jordan B.	2	0	0	0	208
Lambert, Jacques A.	9	1	2	0	6,994	Lay, Larry	89	16	8	9	95,308
Lambert, Joanna	84	9	5	13	43,417	Layman, Ernest L.	35	2	1	3	21,507
Lambert, Sr., Clifford C.	245	28	30	31	266,217	Layne, Bret H.	107	12	13	24	138,339
Lamm, Ludwig	112	14	23	12	140,454	Layton, Beth	1	0	0	0	45
Lamont, Warren D.	148	14	18	15	202,502	Layton, John W.	52	8	9	4	39,515
LaMonte, Joe	38	3	4	2	38,780	Layton, Paul H.	9	0	0	0	1,200
Lamparter, Larry C.	7	0	1	3	6,735	Lazenby, Jerry Wayne	18	1	3	3	9,492
Lance, James L.	18	0	0	0	764	Lazuka, William E.	76	6	5	3	70,790
Landers, Bill	50	4	2	5	53,669	Le Febre, Walleah C.	1	0	0	0	339
Landers, D. E.	53	0	1	2	5,980	Leach, Tony W.	29	1	3	1	18,533
Landers, Larry	8	0	2	1	4,390	Leach, William F.	113	12	13	11	375,380
Landicini, Jr., Chris	197	20	26	34	454,049	Leaf, Michael L.	31	3	2	1	17,538
Landis, Margaret A.	49	3	3	4	14,175	Leaf, Raymond P.	8	0	0	1	2,890
Landon, Donna J.	14	1	0	2	5,447	Leaf Jr, Robert	22	1	2	0	7,480
Landry, Ernest	49	3	6	6	67,433	Least, ll, Gary L.	72	10	5	6	58,859
Landry, Fred J.	105	5	14	6	45,599	Leatherbury, King T.	273	37	45	35	553,513
Landry, Joseph C.	48	2	2	3	14,404	Leatherman, Nina L.	56	3	6	7	23,418
Landry, Larry J.	96	8	5	7	116,410	Leavitt, Clifford N.	60	12	4	7	60,033
Landry, Jr., Maxful	53	7	5	3	172,807	Lebarron, Keith W.	120	21	18	19	271,576
Lane, Larry L.	3	0	0	0	0	Leblanc, Kirsten	2	0	0	0	0
Lane, Mitch T.	97	11	7	8	84,944	LeBlanc, Jeanne	33	1	0	3	10,040
Lane, S. Eugene	22	0	1	1	4,557	LeBlanc, Johnny	26	1	1	1	14,420
Lanerie, Gerald	40	4	4	0	30,830	LeBlanc, Melvin	36	1	3	2	9,726
Laneve, Anthony F.	7	0	1	1	6,697	LeBlanc, Milton	27	0	1	4	5,806
Lang, Danny B.	101	2	6	6	29,926	LeBlanc, Richard Paul	15	1	3	3	14,802
Langemeier, John L.	25	4	1	4	38,598	LeBlanc, Shelton J.	30	5	2	1	25,983
Langford, Richard A.	22	5	2	4	54,216	LeBlanc, Jr., John P.	82	12	8	8	589,887
Langley, Wilson C.	95	8	5	5	91,376	LeBlanc, Sr., Linton	14	1	0	0	9,420
Lankford, Billy	11	2	0	1	10,434	Leboeuf, Anthony L.	19	0	0	0	2,601
Lanning, C. L.	5	0	1	0	544	Lebret, Tracy	31	5	5	4	8,198
Lanning, Forrest H.	29	1	5	6	33,715	Lebsock, Manuel M.	16	1	0	4	15,683
Lantier, Jude G.	5	0	2	0	7,450	Lebsock, Jr., Paul	6	0	0	0	104
Larmon, Julie	53	8	10	13	54,090	Lecesse, Michael A.	378	75	64	58	660,640
Larsen, Shane F.	10	0	0	0	370	Leckey, Michael	71	7	7	3	45,912
Larsen, Stephen Jay	1	1	0	0	4,500	Ledet, Ernest J.	42	2	0	2	11,393
Larson, Bill	3	0	0	2	3,558	Ledezma, Sergio	318	38	47	42	617,084
Larson, Darlene	6	0	1	1	1,000	Ledgess, C Dale	145	11	15	16	209,268
Larson, Michael	55	8	7	8	106,782	Lee, Don	4	1	1	0	21,598
Larue, Benjie	63	5	12	7	84,275	Lee, Douglas L.	7	1	0	0	5,652

RECORDS OF TRAINERS

Trainer	Sts	1st	2d	3d	Purses	Trainer	Sts	1st	2d	3d	Purses
Lee, James M.	1	0	0	0	527	Leyva, Fernando	21	1	2	3	8,993
Lee, Louis A.	1	0	0	0	369	Li, James K.	71	5	3	6	52,113
Lee, Mark C.	54	5	7	5	185,547	Libolt, Richard	3	0	0	2	1,923
Lee, Oswald	82	2	8	8	46,225	Liebenow, Carl B.	5	0	0	0	0
Lee, Robert Enos	21	1	5	5	11,797	Liebeskind, Louis R.	10	0	0	0	1,840
Lee, Ron	17	0	1	1	8,007	Lies, Richard D.	6	0	0	1	1,680
Lee, Steven	68	7	5	4	135,713	Light, Frank D.	7	0	0	1	1,300
Lee, Suzie M.	20	1	3	1	12,420	Lightfoot, Butch	4	1	0	1	2,530
Leech, William H.	5	2	2	0	6,701	Lightfoot, Chester Lee	2	0	0	0	0
Leeson, John D.	10	1	0	1	8,189	Lightner, Michael	20	3	1	2	31,455
Leger, Jake E.	110	15	10	14	153,638	Lilly, James P.	33	0	3	5	17,726
Leggio, Frank	161	24	24	14	308,654	Lima, Rolando J.	70	2	5	4	47,610
Leggio, Jr., Andrew	128	22	19	9	1,075,581	Limbaugh, James M.	25	4	8	0	15,358
LeGrande, Cheryl A.	33	3	3	3	15,073	Linafelter, Paul	79	19	13	11	82,287
Lehman, Steven A.	11	3	2	0	8,125	Lind, Darlene	16	1	2	1	13,290
Lehman, Thomas D.	126	3	13	17	47,421	Lindemann, Lorita	100	3	10	11	41,098
Leifeld, Donald J.	28	2	4	3	101,480	Linder, Louis C.	18	3	2	3	25,570
Leis, Victor J.	8	1	2	3	10,953	Linder, Jr., Louis C.	50	2	7	5	29,320
Leith, Steve	4	1	0	0	1,550	Lindsay, Frederick	57	2	4	16	25,615
Lejeune, Callan	50	2	2	10	38,477	Lindsay, Ricky	135	11	9	14	180,105
Lelito, Timothy L.	50	7	6	11	56,122	Lindsay, Tanya	74	8	15	9	64,133
Lello, Tony P.	4	2	0	0	9,480	Lindsay, Sr., Wilbur P.	36	1	3	6	24,100
Lellouche, Elie	1	0	0	0	0	Lindsey, Chuck	6	0	1	1	941
Lemaire, Sr., Alvin	11	1	0	2	8,200	Lindsey, Jack E.	6	1	2	3	2,621
Lenz, Marillee	25	1	4	3	21,408	Linet, Lucy	6	0	0	0	275
Lenzini, Michael	429	64	53	39	550,312	Lingenfelter, Thomas H.	101	12	9	10	108,169
Leon, Priscilla	96	19	12	18	80,483	Lingo, Jr., Robert	1	0	0	0	3,300
Leonard, Bruce	32	3	0	2	21,505	Link, Linda L.	3	0	2	0	3,371
Leonard, Dorothy	4	0	0	0	660	Linn, Lauren	86	8	10	11	61,934
Leonard, Robert W.	23	3	3	0	74,617	Linsey, Arthur T.	61	7	5	6	35,373
Leonard, III, George	225	31	30	36	306,387	Lipowicz, Zenon	98	9	8	17	64,406
Leonardi, Hugo	174	15	26	28	141,690	Lippman, Ed	2	0	0	0	350
LePaine, Paul	4	0	0	0	146	Lissarrague, Christian M.	12	1	2	1	23,988
Lerille, Jr., Arthur J.	23	0	1	3	8,780	Listen, Robert L.	81	12	6	12	132,814
Lerman, Michael	6	1	0	0	32,640	Literal, Lee Ann	10	1	1	0	1,522
Lerman, Roy S.	58	9	9	4	253,106	Litfin, Nevada	65	8	5	10	35,376
Lesher, Karen	60	5	10	7	36,678	Litt, Joshua M.	53	4	8	11	127,630
Lesher, Michael D.	42	3	3	4	31,267	Little, Donna	1	0	0	0	0
Lesher, Robert E.	50	3	6	7	24,140	Little, James E.	16	1	1	3	6,153
Leslie, Sue	118	11	19	15	666,642	Little, James H.	18	1	0	2	40,733
Lester, Robert A.	9	2	3	1	30,973	Little, Jeffery	13	2	0	2	29,683
Lester, Troy L.	5	0	0	1	550	Little, Marilyn C.	16	2	0	5	19,188
Letarete, Tina	33	2	10	3	10,872	Little, Niel	1	0	0	0	0
LeTarte, Alejandrina	1	0	0	0	33	Little, Pamela A.	172	19	21	21	402,709
Letts, Jr., John D.	55	9	4	14	125,299	Littlelight, Curtis	15	1	0	1	1,792
Levendis, Peter	15	0	1	2	12,150	Liu, Raymond	59	6	7	10	74,356
Levine, Bruce N.	366	66	41	56	2,038,357	Livesay, Charles	148	17	22	22	530,493
Levine, Carol Lynn	42	7	2	2	120,504	Livingston, Conna	3	1	0	0	3,672
Levine, Earl	69	4	8	7	47,757	Livingston, Jerry C.	14	1	1	0	6,050
Levine, Peter	22	2	0	5	57,318	Llorens, Maribel	10	1	0	0	8,408
Levine, Robert L.	80	14	12	15	365,405	Lloyd, Charles W.	113	15	8	16	248,770
Levisay, Leo O.	1	0	0	0	0	Lloyd, Margo	18	0	4	2	7,443
Levitt, Jeff	3	0	0	0	0	Lloyd, Sandra	25	2	2	0	38,448
Lewellyn, Paul	120	9	16	9	222,881	Loatman, Glenn	1	0	0	0	0
Lewis, Craig Anthony	209	30	25	26	1,024,093	Lobo, Paulo H.	62	7	7	11	364,765
Lewis, Craig Chester	5	0	0	0	302	Lockard, Donna B.	10	1	0	2	18,220
Lewis, Dennis	27	0	1	0	3,640	Locke, John G.	384	40	56	47	681,242
Lewis, Gary J.	7	1	0	0	7,675	Locke, Royce	2	0	0	0	822
Lewis, Gary O.	106	4	7	11	63,702	Locke, Tony	107	3	4	8	57,603
Lewis, Jehu	10	1	0	1	4,330	Lockhart, Jeffrey L.	54	9	11	7	89,410
Lewis, Jerry D.	5	0	0	0	268	Lockhart, Lloyd W.	76	1	4	7	75,849
Lewis, Jim B.	8	1	3	1	3,958	Lockhart, Lori L.	274	26	17	29	367,250
Lewis, Joseph A.	27	1	2	3	10,781	Lockridge, Monica	33	5	5	4	48,342
Lewis, Katherine E.	1	0	0	0	0	Lockwood, George T.	40	6	1	10	67,276
Lewis, Kelly Maureen	7	1	1	0	5,438	Lockwood, Richard L.	30	3	5	2	17,844
Lewis, Kevin	270	58	41	34	730,996	Loescher, Paula	48	6	3	0	62,762
Lewis, Lisa L.	99	17	14	12	654,621	Loetscher, Clay	12	1	0	1	7,480
Lewis, Michael D.	3	0	0	0	0	Lofton, Hannis E.	5	0	0	0	0
Lewis, Richard I.	1	0	0	0	0	Loghry, John E.	63	5	4	9	25,364
Lewis, Roberta M.	6	1	0	1	2,105	Logsdon, G. K.	4	0	0	1	1,745
Lewis, Warren C.	1	0	0	0	100	Logue, Jr., F. M.	47	3	5	10	93,012
Lewis, Wilfred J.	26	5	5	0	102,900	Lombardi, Vincent	3	0	0	1	1,840
Lewis, Jr., William R.	22	1	0	0	6,694	Londono, Jr., Odin J.	126	13	17	29	134,015
Leyba, Bernie A.	48	2	0	3	13,411	Londono, Sr., Odin J.	103	18	9	7	197,020
Leyba, Percy J.	5	0	0	0	0	Loney, A. Radlie	24	7	2	1	278,884
Leyba, Ruben	4	0	0	0	0	Long, Edwin C.	22	0	0	5	12,849

Trainer	Sts	1st	2d	3d	Purses
Long, J. Scott	72	1	5	6	45,567
Long, Lewis	1	0	1	0	1,430
Long, Marty	170	13	14	21	96,215
Long, Raymond	1	0	0	0	0
Long, Vaughn	58	12	9	4	123,702
Longacre, Charles	8	2	1	1	10,000
Longan, Mary Ellen	4	0	0	0	2,623
Longie, Duane G.	3	0	0	1	245
Longstaff, Tom	79	18	13	6	483,625
Looman, Dennis M.	39	2	3	0	28,096
Looman, Donna	4	0	0	0	360
Lopes, William	4	0	0	0	2,820
Lopez, Angel L.	9	1	1	2	10,205
Lopez, Carlos Cruz	12	4	2	1	42,010
Lopez, Ceasar J.	40	4	10	2	13,977
Lopez, Daniel J.	86	17	13	7	202,539
Lopez, Harold	10	1	1	3	8,130
Lopez, Jodi	109	8	6	11	39,150
Lopez, Joe E.	16	1	2	0	5,583
Lopez, Jose A.	15	2	2	1	35,701
Lopez, Lisa L.	45	4	4	1	57,890
Lopez, Pedro	117	6	7	9	74,314
Lopez, Robert E.	293	34	34	39	232,171
Lopez, Tracy	74	8	10	7	65,413
Lopez, Jr., Braulio	28	0	2	4	18,165
Lopez, Jr., Frank	1	0	0	0	196
Lopresti, Charles	67	7	9	5	186,385
Lore, Steven	1	0	0	0	0
Lorimer, Suzanne	7	0	0	1	6,270
Lorito, Mario	6	0	0	0	880
Lorts, Terry	32	3	2	4	19,664
Loseth, James Peter	110	10	12	12	151,860
Lostritto, Joseph A.	101	4	11	7	257,736
Loter, Betty	70	7	5	10	52,447
Lothringer, Roy	48	7	3	5	58,208
Lotruglio, Edward	53	5	6	8	68,460
Lott, Jessie D.	1	0	0	0	0
Lott, Woodrow C.	17	1	3	3	19,920
Lotze, Larry E.	53	3	6	7	46,685
Loudermilk, Penny	7	1	2	3	6,200
Loudin-Smith, Lori	10	1	1	2	9,027
Lough, Thomas	14	1	0	0	21,395
Louviere, Kenneth J.	2	0	0	0	0
Love, Michael	87	2	10	6	68,804
Love, Sr., Alan	48	2	4	4	39,599
Loveland, Del	29	0	0	3	10,315
Lovell, Jack	42	2	0	4	12,007
Lovell, Michelle	7	0	1	1	3,055
Lovin, Randy	11	2	1	2	12,990
Lovin, Sammy	1	0	0	0	0
Lowder, John M.	55	1	6	4	19,961
Lowe, Nick	194	22	32	25	88,990
Lowe, Santiago	31	3	5	3	6,313
Lowery, F. A.	72	4	4	4	38,462
Lowry, Kathleen A.	13	2	1	0	7,549
Lowry, Sr., Autry	32	3	2	3	54,004
Lowry, Sr., Richard H.	35	0	6	1	16,946
Loy, F. Dewaine	258	14	29	29	205,927
Lozano, Adalberto	26	2	2	4	76,820
Lozano, Martin	100	22	27	10	191,093
Lozano, Mauro	1	0	0	1	1,240
Lozier, Kelly S.	84	7	6	7	83,096
Lozier, Michael	1	0	0	0	524
Luark, Monty	81	5	15	10	39,159
Lucarelli, Frank	286	40	43	40	409,615
Lucas, Angela	10	0	1	0	5,885
Lucas, Flo Ann	16	2	2	1	16,080
Lucas, Joe	186	19	28	23	235,048
Lucas, Robert J.	20	0	2	2	9,910
Lucas, Ted W.	10	0	1	0	1,927
Lucero, Lorence	52	13	7	6	231,809
Lucko, Gerry	28	0	1	7	11,055
Ludwig, James B.	44	3	3	3	30,027
Luellen, Roger D.	12	1	4	0	15,560
Luft, Kirsty-Anne	1	0	0	0	0
Lugovich, Richard J.	20	1	2	2	63,000

Trainer	Sts	1st	2d	3d	Purses
Lujan, Ramon	1	0	0	0	0
Lukas, D. Wayne	663	71	73	80	4,179,832
Lukenbill, Rick	4	1	1	0	5,370
Lumm, Roy	199	36	30	21	319,987
Lumpkin, Roy M.	61	5	9	4	63,307
Lumsden, John Rennie	13	2	1	3	9,117
Luna, Daniel G.	42	17	7	4	72,823
Lund, Valorie	145	24	29	27	223,028
Lunsford, Darrell A.	138	7	16	25	107,280
Lunsford, Kim	3	0	0	0	230
Lupo, David C.	7	0	0	0	435
Lusk, Travis	5	3	1	0	3,885
Luther, III, Andrew T.	21	2	2	3	15,482
Luzzi, Ray	18	3	2	1	24,510
Lybert, Randal J.	42	5	3	1	55,611
Lyman, Audrey	13	1	3	4	10,390
Lyman, Claude	29	5	1	2	9,400
Lyman, Jr., Arthur J.	14	2	1	3	5,306
Lynch, Brian A.	71	8	12	10	307,714
Lynch, Cathal A.	178	22	20	17	467,759
Lynch, Harry E.	8	0	1	0	1,100
Lynch, Martin	6	0	1	0	4,115
Lynde, John M.	67	14	8	6	52,434
Lynn, Jeffery C.	130	11	10	18	250,983
Lynn, Kevin	17	0	0	1	2,653
Lynn, Wilmer T.	15	1	2	1	23,550
Lyon, Hazel E.	11	2	1	1	31,380
Lyons, Arnold	61	1	4	2	26,806
Lyons, Christopher	3	0	0	0	1,950
Lyons, Henry D.	7	0	1	0	1,945
Ma, Francisco	20	1	3	3	15,170
Mabbott, Paul	23	3	7	3	59,228
Macari, Gail	4	0	0	0	246
MacDonald, Doug	75	14	5	9	98,697
MacDonald, Rita	32	4	5	5	19,050
MacDonald, Robert A.	62	3	7	9	40,829
Machovec, Joseph	12	3	1	2	21,823
Machowsky, Michael	185	28	33	23	1,298,638
Mack, Summie	13	0	0	1	1,140
Mackaben, Paul	5	0	0	0	680
Mackay, D. Verle	3	0	1	0	260
MacKenzie, Jason	46	5	2	8	31,270
MacKenzie, John P.	145	16	23	16	681,738
Mackert, Werner P.	36	4	5	2	55,080
Mackey, Wayne	52	10	7	3	188,879
MacKey, Jodi L.	5	0	0	1	976
Mackin, J. Lynn	6	0	0	2	2,335
Mackinnon, Bradley W.	19	1	3	2	35,630
MacKinnon, Scott A.	65	14	11	9	217,285
MacKinnon, William R.	20	0	1	0	8,178
MacLean, David L.	34	1	2	2	61,550
Macon, Kevin	33	8	4	2	23,527
MacPherson, Craig	48	6	4	4	120,543
MacRae, Donald C.	127	34	22	11	504,816
Madden, Eddie	46	4	4	2	20,362
Maddox, Cody	5	0	2	0	2,090
Maddox, Mark	116	6	4	11	76,603
Madison, Paul	10	2	2	2	2,943
Madrigal, Sr., Rodrigo	246	54	36	23	794,519
Madsen, Deborah	2	0	1	1	1,297
Madsen, Kjeld	62	8	7	6	56,777
Maelfeyt, Bruno	99	9	11	6	27,603
Maes, Cynthia A.	82	7	1	11	41,110
Magadini, Leigh S.	32	2	2	3	6,676
Magana, Hector	173	29	33	15	538,715
Magee, J. Noel	23	2	1	3	28,154
Magee, Paul	13	2	2	2	18,043
Magee, Sean C.	1	0	0	0	290
Magee, Walter B.	35	4	4	4	33,306
Magill, Patrick J.	16	2	0	2	17,440
Magnon, III, Cleve	24	3	2	4	36,464
Magnuson, Lyle	46	4	3	3	9,817
Magnusson, Glenn	111	6	11	15	288,616
Magrell, Jr., Jack	98	3	5	15	62,154
Magrell, Sr., Norman C.	31	6	3	5	59,302
Mahalik, Stephen L.	1	0	0	0	0

Trainer	Sts	1st	2d	3d	Purses	Trainer	Sts	1st	2d	3d	Purses
Mahan, Hugh W.	42	4	3	6	47,446	Marks, Deborah J.	87	3	5	12	63,930
Mahan, Joseph P.	122	14	11	16	186,989	Marks, Garry	93	11	18	11	108,139
Mahan, Kathy	79	8	8	10	61,436	Marks, Stan	91	30	13	15	101,052
Mahan, William H.	27	2	1	0	5,769	Marler, Jerry L.	8	1	0	0	26,400
Mahler, Janine	42	2	2	6	34,758	Marll, Lee	11	3	1	2	4,505
Mahn, John W.	63	5	7	11	32,043	Marlow, Mike	103	12	7	11	342,942
Mahoney, James G.	4	0	0	0	528	Maroun, Maureen Ann	21	2	2	0	10,726
Mahoney, Robert	23	3	3	4	19,624	Maroun, Jr., George C.	30	3	4	4	22,848
Mahoney, Thomas J.	5	0	1	0	1,550	Marquez, Alfredo	57	9	3	9	209,072
Mahorney, William	29	3	5	1	117,305	Marquez, George J.	11	0	0	0	477
Maier, Roger L.	29	2	6	2	22,993	Marquez, Jose Luis	65	7	3	3	29,448
Majette, Jennifer	7	3	0	1	126,385	Marquez, Juan	10	0	0	0	2,095
Majors, Sheridan	41	3	2	7	16,365	Marquez, Rey M.	47	1	3	1	18,274
Maker, Michael J.	114	14	17	7	288,921	Marr, Gerald E.	110	8	9	12	137,475
Maker, Rebecca	161	25	18	19	629,191	Marr, Joel H.	249	43	32	37	755,410
Malaterre, Blaine	7	2	1	1	3,290	Marrotta, Patrick	4	0	0	0	400
Malaterre, Jennifer	8	0	3	1	2,471	Marsh, Gordon E.	81	11	13	8	87,599
Malcolm, Blaine L.	10	0	1	2	902	Marshall, John Terry	239	39	33	35	600,874
Malcolm, Roger H.	15	5	0	2	18,043	Marshall, Kenneth W.	13	1	3	2	9,291
Maldonado, Edgar S.	11	0	1	1	4,902	Marshall, Larry C	14	0	1	2	4,392
Maldonado, Jesse	13	0	0	1	1,238	Marshall, Michael	8	1	0	2	5,253
Malek, Raja	18	1	1	0	33,814	Marshall, Robert W.	6	1	0	2	93,180
Malgarini-Mawing, Tina	59	5	11	11	84,507	Marshall, Roy	22	1	0	0	7,418
Mallory, Dale	23	0	1	2	6,096	Martens, Robbin	61	6	6	5	41,948
Malone, Thomas C.	3	1	1	0	11,800	Martin, Albert R.	3	0	0	0	1,260
Maloney, John D.	19	3	2	3	18,480	Martin, August R.	14	1	2	0	20,456
Mamakos, Jason	6	0	0	2	4,740	Martin, Cal E.	45	6	10	2	160,950
Mammen, Dennis	37	3	3	2	26,107	Martin, Carlos F.	144	16	20	19	690,731
Manahan, Patricia	41	1	0	4	12,220	Martin, Charles Lee	4	0	1	0	1,770
Manchio, Linda L.	14	0	0	3	2,766	Martin, Dean	39	1	6	6	10,298
Manchio, Robert S.	26	0	0	0	1,247	Martin, Dennis C.	9	2	1	0	22,680
Mandalfino, Paul R.	50	5	3	7	97,019	Martin, Eleanor	40	9	7	6	31,437
Mandella, Gary	86	12	17	6	607,160	Martin, Elmer L.	8	0	1	0	1,129
Mandella, Richard E.	253	51	40	38	9,869,548	Martin, Gregory F.	157	35	29	19	896,075
Mangum, Kim	8	1	0	1	1,972	Martin, Jack R.	49	2	2	6	16,165
Maniatis, Arthur T.	2	0	0	0	0	Martin, Jerry D.	9	2	1	0	15,225
Mankin, Stanley C.	19	4	5	3	21,549	Martin, John A.	7	1	0	2	6,365
Manley, Steve	379	60	56	50	491,600	Martin, John F.	335	103	60	41	1,222,893
Mann, Johnny P.	11	1	1	0	1,689	Martin, John W.	48	3	4	4	28,469
Mann, Michael Herbert	85	1	4	1	25,950	Martin, Joseph R.	424	43	48	53	555,137
Mann, P. Renia	69	9	3	6	52,849	Martin, Kevin D.	88	9	14	9	105,645
Manning, Dennis J.	155	21	10	24	1,494,773	Martin, Lynne K.	3	0	0	0	1,316
Manning, Don Louis	52	1	4	5	13,471	Martin, Marjorie A.	14	3	5	0	60,583
Manning, John F.	1	0	0	0	140	Martin, Ramon F.	165	13	10	21	188,160
Manning, Kathleen A.	9	0	0	0	1,452	Martin, Robert B.	42	2	6	5	153,206
Manning, Richard C.	72	2	5	5	22,856	Martin, Robert L.	203	21	24	35	367,576
Manning, Robert E.	97	3	5	7	46,799	Martin, Roxanne	5	0	1	0	8,610
Manocchia, Diane	2	0	0	0	0	Martin, Sidney	52	8	12	6	104,803
Mans, Astrid	6	0	0	0	1,490	Martin, Thomas P.	5	0	0	0	150
Mansell, Harrold Ray	9	2	1	2	10,286	Martin, Timothy E.	239	25	19	24	353,702
Mapel, Bert J.	3	0	0	0	378	Martin, Weston	32	7	2	3	72,438
Maragh, Collin	57	3	8	5	62,935	Martin, Jr., Charles E.	5	1	1	0	4,800
Maraspin, Lyno E.	6	0	0	0	2,580	Martin, Jr., Frank	39	3	3	9	41,966
Marble, James L.	53	6	5	9	68,586	Martin, Sr., Frank	70	2	7	5	92,150
March, Rhoda	34	0	4	5	25,794	Martinez, Alexander	72	10	10	6	100,384
Marcom, Jr., Roy L.	116	12	19	15	211,347	Martinez, Concepcion	61	7	3	6	68,949
Marcoux, Wayne J.	193	34	29	25	379,151	Martinez, Danny E.	11	2	0	1	14,812
Marechal, Merlin	63	11	9	10	154,852	Martinez, Fernando	3	0	0	0	764
Mareina, Michael	78	13	11	15	527,208	Martinez, Joey A.	286	31	34	47	212,750
Margolis, Stephen R.	94	16	16	16	1,089,523	Martinez, Jose A.	731	128	109	102	904,069
Maria, Sr., John J.	28	0	1	1	4,725	Martinez, Juan A.	10	0	2	0	3,738
Maricle, Essie	6	0	0	0	1,572	Martinez, Kelli	71	9	10	8	60,625
Marinay, Joe L.	29	0	4	5	34,148	Martinez, Leonard	10	3	2	0	25,902
Marini, Thomas	9	1	2	0	6,213	Martinez, Lorenzo A.	131	14	12	21	160,694
Marini, Jr., James V.	40	5	2	4	39,622	Martinez, Pedro	209	18	30	28	364,272
Marino, Gary	92	16	10	5	102,072	Martinez, Rafael A.	14	2	2	1	35,590
Marino, James G.	68	4	4	9	29,693	Martinez, Ralph	708	208	136	112	1,293,698
Marino, Joseph E.	63	7	12	13	77,427	Martinez, Roland J.	2	0	0	0	0
Marino, Marilyn L.	57	2	3	5	31,854	Martinez, Sal M.	2	0	0	0	162
Marino, Paul	66	6	7	5	40,036	Martinez, Jr., Eleuterio	60	6	11	6	87,093
Marino, Phillip J.	50	6	5	7	69,658	Martino, Phyllis	6	0	1	1	15,510
Marino, Thomas	121	13	8	17	265,900	Martino, Ronald D.	15	1	0	1	6,438
Markgraf, David	157	19	17	27	145,038	Marton, Joseph J.	31	1	1	7	8,713
Markham, Richard L.	87	2	1	1	39,910	Marzullo, Vincent	15	0	0	2	7,480
Markle, Dan L.	192	32	36	33	454,831	Mascari, James E.	7	0	0	0	425
Marks, Brandon	77	7	10	12	114,099	Masilowsky, Alfred E.	7	0	0	0	100

Trainer	Sts	1st	2d	3d	Purses
Mason, Larry A.	7	3	2	1	13,915
Mason, Lloyd C.	274	50	34	36	801,568
Mason, Sr., Ralph	24	0	3	2	5,281
Massaro, James	9	0	0	0	390
Massengale, Ronald	8	0	1	0	2,841
Massey, Charles M.	2	0	0	0	0
Master, Bobby Jack	3	0	2	0	5,188
Masters, Clay	24	1	3	3	9,157
Mastin, Bill	9	0	0	0	1,268
Mastin, Kathleen	64	5	6	6	50,167
Mathieson, Jr., R. Glen	29	2	2	3	22,870
Mathis, Andy	34	7	6	5	64,256
Matier, Bud	30	5	3	0	16,753
Matier, C. William	49	11	8	6	122,237
Matier, Sandra	1	1	0	0	5,733
Matlock, Vance A.	25	0	2	1	4,478
Matlow, Richard P.	53	8	13	5	305,230
Matos, Gil	243	28	38	30	479,729
Matranga, Roy J.	52	3	4	5	38,739
Matt, Wendell L.	46	7	5	10	44,920
Mattarelliano, Pasquale J.	2	0	0	0	0
Matte, Blane	16	2	2	1	10,175
Matthews, Doug	81	9	8	12	136,198
Matthews, Jay	48	5	8	6	54,405
Matthews, John V.	21	2	0	2	8,515
Matthews, Larry P.	26	5	2	8	30,265
Matthews, Pat	22	3	2	2	45,102
Matthews, Randy	46	5	2	8	52,836
Matthews, Richard	6	0	0	2	735
Matthews, Jr., Erwin H.	1	0	0	0	940
Matthieu, Ronald J.	110	6	14	13	65,505
Matties, Gregg M.	52	4	7	8	55,132
Mattine, Michael	95	11	9	14	568,803
Mattine, Tony	69	10	14	4	558,316
Mattingly, James E.	24	3	0	2	21,930
Mattingly, Tony G.	13	3	1	2	17,072
Mattis, Errol	3	0	1	0	3,000
Mattox, Charles W.	11	0	0	0	803
Maturin, Chad	57	4	3	8	36,022
Maturin, Ronald	12	2	0	2	10,852
Matz, Michael R.	187	25	33	19	1,694,615
Mauberret, Michael E.	4	0	0	1	2,360
Mauk, Fletcher	12	3	0	1	40,484
Maul, Fred	6	0	0	1	2,909
Maupin, Mike	41	15	9	4	42,635
Maver, Eduardo	83	12	11	8	142,255
Maxey, Carl L.	25	2	3	1	9,415
Maxey, Tamara L.	12	1	2	1	18,639
Maxey, Tim	59	3	4	7	19,987
Maxville, Rick	2	0	0	0	100
Maxwell, Curtis	45	2	6	5	22,734
Maxwell, Paul M.	33	5	7	7	213,560
May, Eddy Lenard	83	0	1	1	11,130
May, Jean	6	0	0	0	1,060
May, John T.	1	0	0	0	0
Mayberry, Summer	90	7	24	23	464,027
Maybin, Robert	65	7	7	13	177,109
Mayer, Karl	6	0	0	1	859
Mayfield, Jerry	72	7	6	8	111,076
Mayfield, Patrick	45	3	2	1	22,875
Mayfield, Randy	184	26	18	29	363,668
Maynard, Desmond	31	1	1	1	24,532
Mayo, Larry A.	73	10	9	6	114,899
Mayo, Paul	41	4	3	5	26,288
Mays, Sam C.	1	0	0	0	50
Mazur, Joseph W.	45	9	8	5	56,763
Mazza, John F.	24	1	2	0	41,870
Mazzacco, Joseph	14	1	0	0	17,249
Mazzarini, Louis M.	9	0	1	1	3,995
Mazzaro, Rebecca	2	1	0	0	3,300
McAlester, Garland	18	1	1	2	19,275
McAlister, Bobbie J.	29	0	7	5	19,769
McAlister, Joe	78	5	6	9	64,202
McAnally, Ronald L.	312	44	38	29	4,309,058
McArdle, Paul B.	19	0	1	1	14,194
McArthur, Donna	7	0	1	1	2,451
McArthur, F. James	27	5	4	0	66,901
McArthur, James J.	10	1	1	0	14,508
McArthur, Jerry	69	19	14	7	194,130
McBride, Barbara I.	328	68	48	36	437,982
McBride, Burl D.	63	7	4	4	64,704
McBride, Patrick M.	17	0	0	1	5,095
McBride, Susan	7	0	2	1	6,255
McCabe, Nancy	121	9	4	8	60,914
McCabe, Quinton	48	7	4	10	71,663
McCain, Doyle	2	0	0	0	0
McCall, Don	3	0	0	0	0
McCall, Lee Ann	16	1	1	1	13,985
McCall, Richard H.	34	4	6	5	28,250
McCaman, Sam	8	0	1	0	2,560
McCann, Sr., Elwood D.	61	6	9	4	122,621
McCanna, Tim	296	56	46	47	501,178
McCarron, Gregg	93	15	11	7	253,643
McCarthy, Brenda	172	17	10	22	209,831
McCarthy, Michael J.	98	14	16	10	363,784
McCarthy, Robert	1	0	0	0	0
McCarthy, Sean	40	2	3	6	77,285
McCarthy, Thomas R.	13	2	0	1	30,335
McCarthy, Timni S.	4	3	0	1	6,309
McCarthy, William E.	75	1	11	13	86,190
McCarty, George S.	34	1	3	2	36,809
McCaslin, John S.	366	100	71	51	1,332,327
McCaul, James H.	1	0	0	0	1,155
McClain, Stanley	38	7	4	7	27,854
McClanahan, Gilbert W.	14	2	1	3	11,956
McClarney, Jerry L.	79	6	3	8	71,898
McCleary, Karen Lee	31	1	3	3	16,489
McClelland, Paul G.	32	7	2	6	125,082
McClendon, Leon	8	0	0	0	307
McClure, Diana L.	21	1	0	0	9,080
McClure, Kenneth R.	112	10	9	6	49,692
McCollum, Daniel	12	1	0	2	20,360
McComb, Samuel A.	29	2	2	2	54,085
McConnell, Orland	8	2	2	2	39,404
McCooey, Jr., Thomas S.	125	13	16	8	271,455
McCord, Larry	1	0	0	0	40
McCord, II, John M.	17	0	2	1	6,023
McCormick, Earl H.	46	1	1	0	17,762
McCormick, John F.	1	0	0	0	0
McCormick, Merril L.	4	0	0	1	2,595
McCoy, James B.	332	27	27	25	544,654
McCoy, James E.	11	1	0	1	2,355
McCracken, Mark	4	0	0	0	0
McCracken, Memory	22	1	4	6	5,224
McCulloch, Scotty	61	5	4	5	249,473
McCullough, Donna	6	0	2	1	9,612
McCutchen, Jason	3	0	0	0	0
McCutchen, Robert B.	12	1	0	1	34,045
McCutcheon, James R.	16	0	0	0	1,542
McDaniel, Carlos W.	34	1	1	5	29,284
McDaniel, Ted	85	11	9	12	52,254
McDaniel, Wendell L.	37	1	0	2	19,601
McDevitt, John	84	9	11	14	31,948
McDonald, Brandi Rae	6	0	0	0	4,070
McDonald, Charles Butch	20	3	2	4	14,449
McDonald, Earl L.	26	4	2	5	84,668
McDonald, Ian	27	2	6	5	23,730
McDonald, James Scott	49	7	3	5	26,897
McDonald, Matthew K.	1	0	0	0	85
McDonald, Melanie W.	56	1	5	7	32,071
McDonald, Michael B.	12	1	0	0	8,015
McDonald, Michael K.	155	20	15	17	287,538
McDonald, William R.	40	3	3	3	40,249
McDonnell, Jim	33	4	2	5	6,660
McDonnell, Wayne	100	10	9	9	125,687
McDonough, Eric S.	59	1	6	5	29,181
McDonough, Francis J.	4	0	0	0	180
McDonough, Steven L.	74	4	3	6	63,710
McDougall, Pam	98	18	13	19	163,908
McDougall, Wilf	51	6	4	11	16,953
McDowell, Becky	12	1	0	2	8,541
McDowell, Dave	2	1	0	1	3,800

Trainer	Sts	1st	2d	3d	Purses
McDowell, Laurie A.	36	2	4	3	61,488
McDowell, R. James	1	0	0	1	450
McEachern, Michael	275	38	51	37	293,080
McElhannon, Rick	6	0	1	0	1,133
McElroy, Jr., Robert L.	5	1	1	0	7,183
McEwin, Cathy A.	11	0	0	0	3,094
McFadden, Jada K.	27	3	6	8	43,674
McFadden, Pamela A.	12	0	0	2	3,291
McFadden, Thomas Edward	126	4	8	4	34,706
McFadden, William C.	41	7	5	1	80,751
McFall, Robert E.	5	0	0	0	1,486
McFarlane, Dan L.	411	74	89	68	679,479
McGaffic, Sr., Robert T.	47	3	8	6	60,106
McGarry, John F.	7	0	2	1	4,619
McGaughey III, Claude R.	259	48	40	36	2,723,707
McGee, Gail J.	44	1	2	3	24,894
McGee, Paul J.	309	46	46	41	1,833,433
McGee, Rebecca K.	33	2	4	5	28,712
McGee, William E.	114	15	10	14	194,222
McGhee, Jr., Thomas	3	0	0	0	204
McGhie, James L.	4	1	0	0	2,272
McGill, Barry H.	4	0	0	0	0
McGill, Harold W.	14	0	0	0	691
McGill, Harry	29	5	1	2	34,251
McGill, Mary Welby	31	2	3	4	87,481
McGill, Sylvester	4	0	0	0	0
McGirr, Shelly	21	1	0	2	11,055
McGivern, Thomas P.	65	8	7	5	133,636
McGlasson, Galen W.	15	1	2	1	16,828
McGowan, Sean	25	2	1	0	15,645
McGrail, Linda	1	0	1	0	3,600
McGrath, Andrew	11	1	0	1	5,332
McGrath, Gerard D.	50	5	8	8	79,067
McGraw, Paul	31	0	1	2	5,044
McGreevy, James L.	56	4	2	6	60,120
McGreevy, John P.	2	0	0	0	106
McGregor, Rose Marie	2	0	0	0	0
McGrew, Robert L.	1	0	0	0	0
McGuire, Dr. William J.	41	2	3	3	4,920
McGuire, James D.	45	0	5	5	13,171
McHargue, Gladys	10	0	5	0	20,145
McIlvain, Vickie Lea	8	0	0	1	1,011
McIntosh, Henry A.	14	1	1	1	12,210
McIntosh, William A.	10	0	0	2	2,959
McIvor, George D.	18	3	1	2	18,662
McKanas, Leona	91	9	9	13	150,577
McKee, John D.	337	32	37	31	545,064
McKeen, John R.	46	4	3	5	24,340
McKeever, Andrew	57	3	7	5	83,031
McKeever, Jocelyn M.	7	0	3	0	8,170
McKeever, Jr., Billy C.	107	11	12	10	457,373
McKeever, Jr., Robert J.	41	4	5	2	63,885
McKellar, Joe	53	6	4	6	178,798
McKenney, Charles	10	0	0	0	420
McKenzie, Dan R.	24	2	4	4	6,002
McKenzie, Michael B.	24	2	3	2	11,646
McKenzie, Robert Alexander	98	7	7	17	75,869
McKenzie, Scott A.	38	2	6	4	28,772
McKeon, John P.	70	5	9	7	41,826
McKibben, Roger	5	0	0	1	3,765
McKinnell, Michael	34	1	3	1	35,685
McKinney, F. Lee	31	2	0	1	47,410
McKinney, Russ	10	0	1	0	1,439
McKinnon, Earl E.	15	2	6	3	12,034
McKinster, Leonard	16	1	2	1	16,147
McKnight, Norman	247	28	30	26	1,121,242
McKnight, Rennie	150	4	7	12	59,671
McLaughlin, Kiaran P.	186	46	26	20	3,157,180
McLean, Bill	200	13	26	19	274,384
McLean, Donald	14	1	4	1	4,702
McLean, Louise	1	0	0	0	0
McLeod, Kelly	3	0	0	0	1,300
McMahon, Richard	6	0	0	0	1,765
McMeans, Bill	93	12	7	9	78,633
McMeans, Bob	31	3	4	6	101,582
McMichael, Larry	2	0	0	0	330
McMillan, Donald	82	3	1	6	33,060
McMillen, Mike	71	3	14	10	45,443
McMinn, Nancy	5	1	0	1	16,378
McMullen, James R.	55	10	4	6	213,512
McMullen, Marilyn G.	84	2	8	6	92,092
McMullin, Stacy	44	1	4	9	58,953
McNally, Kathy	59	4	8	15	25,233
McNeil, Emmanuel	14	1	1	0	8,215
McNerney, Gerald R.	16	0	0	3	4,323
McPeek, Kenneth G.	400	61	61	57	3,647,975
McPherson, Alexander F.	173	33	24	19	1,217,381
McQuade, Kathy	3	0	0	0	919
McQuade, Owen	23	1	2	1	11,952
McQueen, Richard O.	29	7	3	3	59,942
McReynolds, Kenneth E.	80	12	10	14	57,090
McShane, David D.	251	45	33	31	827,307
McVay, A. M.	21	2	0	4	8,391
McWade, Barbara E.	22	1	1	2	21,150
McWaters, Alton D.	3	0	0	0	378
Meacham, Sheila	34	1	3	8	12,360
Meachum, Todd	32	4	3	4	33,772
Meade, Sherryl F.	51	1	3	5	19,677
Meadow, Patricia E.	9	0	0	3	14,170
Meadows, Bascum E.	6	0	0	1	2,042
Meairs, John M.	46	0	2	6	61,980
Meals, Lois	59	2	4	3	38,783
Meares, Francis A.	45	2	4	7	28,727
Meaux, Lisa Ann	9	1	1	0	6,153
Meaux, Michael	5	0	0	0	0
Meaux, Patrick G.	9	1	0	0	5,910
Meaux, William	74	18	9	7	211,112
Meche, Harold	3	0	0	0	645
Meche, Robert	2	0	0	0	0
Meckling, Susan	4	0	0	2	2,100
Medicine Horse, Jr., Cleo	20	2	3	2	4,826
Medina, Angel M.	107	9	9	8	138,290
Medina, Jose D.	15	3	2	2	37,910
Medina, Santiago	3	0	0	0	0
Medley, Joseph A.	23	0	2	1	10,342
Medrano, Marcos G.	30	2	7	5	40,948
Meehan, Brian	3	1	2	0	340,000
Meehan, Elizabeth E.	103	7	11	9	90,250
Meek, Leon	2	0	0	0	0
Meeking, Robert A.	38	5	8	3	33,705
Meeks, Karl W.	38	3	5	4	23,811
Meese, Michael T.	56	4	3	4	36,930
Mefford, Kenneth A.	1	0	0	0	0
Megariz, Alex L.	6	2	0	1	2,422
Megariz, Jr., Michael	9	3	0	0	10,043
Megerle, Richard	43	2	2	3	12,208
Mehok, William L.	89	10	3	10	41,566
Meier, Leland R.	17	0	1	3	4,489
Meineke, Jack	3	1	1	0	1,775
Meister, William S.	24	0	1	2	9,560
Meittinis, Louis N.	109	13	8	5	421,930
Melancon, Donald	24	2	1	2	25,283
Melancon, Jr., Antoine	6	0	0	0	536
Melancon, Jr., Francis	241	26	28	24	195,781
Melendy, Lisa	27	1	1	1	17,269
Meling, Jerry	5	0	0	0	210
Mello, Ernest	39	1	3	2	24,354
Melson, Benny	47	7	2	4	39,684
Melson, Glen	7	0	2	1	1,667
Melton, Christopher W.	6	2	0	0	11,435
Melton, John D.	14	2	0	3	18,910
Melton, Lin	3	0	0	0	150
Menard, Charlene	9	0	1	1	1,785
Menard, Dirk J.	20	0	1	0	4,301
Menard, Jr., Alton J.	11	1	0	3	9,280
Menarde, Frank J.	25	3	1	2	23,325
Mencio, Raymond E.	4	0	0	1	390
Mendenhall, M. Roberta	13	1	0	2	12,150
Mendez, Jose A.	128	17	12	18	218,684
Mendez, Manuel	4	0	0	1	1,050
Mendoza, Carmelo	273	27	27	34	309,183
Mendoza, Jesus	22	1	1	3	44,960

Trainer	Sts	1st	2d	3d	Purses	Trainer	Sts	1st	2d	3d	Purses
Menefee, Barry	5	0	0	2	4,221	Miller, Valerie J.	23	2	1	1	40,912
Mentuck, Herman Eric	2	0	1	0	250	Miller, William C.	5	1	0	0	16,835
Mercer, Thomas F.	15	2	3	1	31,012	Miller, III, Norman C.	32	4	2	3	151,183
Meredith, Derek	22	3	0	4	63,165	Miller, Jr., F. Bruce	44	3	4	5	80,275
Meredith, Jim	5	0	0	0	866	Miller, Jr., Henry D.	63	4	7	3	47,066
Merola, Vito	53	7	6	7	144,258	Miller, Jr., Henry M.	103	8	9	21	112,339
Merrick, Joe D.	28	3	3	2	22,727	Milligan, Allen	318	28	33	31	271,119
Merrill, Richard	7	0	0	0	1,129	Milligan, Sherry	13	1	0	0	5,160
Merritt, Clayton A.	10	1	0	2	6,110	Milligan, Jr., Eddie	1	0	0	0	0
Merritt, Lester	24	1	3	9	12,134	Milligan, Sr., Eddie R.	183	18	13	15	226,651
Merritt, Lisa L.	9	0	1	2	6,505	Millington, Brinnard	15	0	4	3	9,968
Merryman, Ann W.	134	12	10	15	240,743	Million, William N.	100	11	19	14	318,147
Merryman, Edwin W.	38	4	3	3	84,621	Milliron, John	3	0	0	0	570
Mersereau, Nanine L.	6	1	0	1	4,156	Millonas, Don	93	7	7	8	111,145
Mesenbrink, Jennie S.	3	0	0	1	5,530	Mills, Dale L.	57	9	7	3	72,965
Metcalf, Jr., Robert J.	11	1	1	0	13,289	Mills, Dennis R.	131	12	21	19	126,626
Metcalf, Jr., Tommy	18	0	1	1	5,090	Mills, Don J.	339	96	62	45	828,506
Metz, Jeffrey	43	2	3	4	32,327	Mills, Ernie	126	7	15	11	155,034
Meyaard, Jim	94	28	19	9	94,946	Mills, Philip W.	41	3	3	7	26,478
Meyer, Donald S.	3	0	1	0	2,727	Mills, Tommy Ray	3	0	0	0	750
Meyer, Jerome C.	45	7	5	2	272,707	Mills, Sr., Ray C.	6	0	0	1	3,777
Meyer, Paul R.	2	0	0	1	4,490	Milne, Janie	5	1	0	0	2,053
Meyers, Errol	2	0	0	0	372	Milner, Kerwin E.	5	0	0	0	0
Meyers, Robert W.	2	0	0	0	240	Milone, Patrick A.	3	0	0	1	869
Meza, Martin M.	2	0	0	0	0	Milton, Rowena A.	75	9	7	11	106,081
Miceli, Michael	159	23	17	14	793,338	Minard, Dick	57	5	3	7	57,889
Michael, Brian	43	4	6	3	49,099	Minnock, Wayne G.	176	24	27	27	255,176
Michael, James A.	57	8	3	4	142,479	Minogue, George	23	0	1	3	10,829
Michaels, Jr., Thomas H.	72	3	4	6	43,736	Minor, Suzanne	47	5	5	5	44,411
Michaelsen, Dick	3	0	0	0	205	Minshall, Barbara J.	132	16	15	16	992,019
Michelena, Jr., Charles	6	1	1	0	1,529	Miracle, Jr., Norman D.	39	8	3	2	68,954
Mick, Stephen R.	66	18	8	13	240,069	Miranda, Efrain	107	15	14	16	173,095
Mickey, Joseph C.	2	0	0	0	0	Mirza, Claudia	8	0	0	1	4,535
Middlebrooks, Don A.	3	0	0	0	0	Mita, Michael	6	0	0	1	1,313
Middleton, G Allen	20	0	1	3	9,850	Mitchell, Anne	33	4	4	5	76,121
Middleton, Sarah	5	0	0	4	14,273	Mitchell, Anthony	67	22	4	8	817,836
Miesse, Sr., David L.	120	8	18	13	117,221	Mitchell, Billy	3	0	0	0	405
Mikhalides, George	32	4	2	9	74,810	Mitchell, Mike R.	262	65	51	48	2,019,188
Mikkelson, Eric D.	44	5	8	6	39,704	Mitchell, Paraskevas G.	68	7	5	8	123,106
Milburn, Dave	87	10	6	18	100,642	Mitchell, Patrick S.	66	6	5	6	139,195
Milburn, Peter	7	0	0	1	2,208	Mitchell, Philip	2	0	1	1	102,000
Miles, Diane	7	1	2	0	32,970	Mitchell, Ralph H.	25	0	2	3	12,226
Milian, Michael	47	2	4	6	18,492	Mitchell, Sherman S.	32	2	6	4	62,193
Millar, Mac	102	14	10	9	195,008	Mitchell, Suzun	11	1	2	1	22,005
Miller, Allan R.	46	3	2	6	24,294	Mitchell, Thomas M.	18	3	5	2	69,990
Miller, Amy S.	5	0	2	0	5,280	Mitchell, William G.	15	0	0	1	2,610
Miller, Blair A.	82	12	9	7	89,425	Mitzner, Robert R.	12	2	0	3	3,359
Miller, Craig S.	41	2	1	0	9,994	Mix, Kenneth R.	11	1	5	2	10,167
Miller, Daniel Charles	4	0	0	0	362	Miyadi, Steven	51	17	8	10	155,014
Miller, Danny L.	104	3	7	13	109,520	Miyashiro, Leanne	18	3	4	0	11,097
Miller, Darrin	102	11	14	10	440,476	Mize, Raymond S.	89	5	8	6	39,760
Miller, Edward C.	18	4	1	1	50,533	Mobberley, Gretchen B.	104	6	15	10	122,675
Miller, Elizabeth A.	69	8	9	10	85,995	Mobley, Brook	25	1	3	2	6,417
Miller, Elmer J.	75	7	5	9	103,439	Mock, Thaddeus A.	14	3	1	2	22,723
Miller, F. Bruce	138	10	22	22	400,040	Moehlig, Albert	6	1	1	1	13,151
Miller, Gary M.	5	0	0	0	484	Moeller, John R.	1	0	0	0	270
Miller, Gregory D.	100	20	17	13	298,882	Moffitt, Charles F.	31	0	0	1	1,751
Miller, Herbert	57	4	6	4	43,702	Moga, Lucian V.	85	3	7	11	60,839
Miller, Irene	8	4	2	1	6,722	Moger, Jr., Ed	346	45	37	51	838,242
Miller, John Mark	22	2	1	2	7,697	Mogge, Wayne D.	185	31	21	21	385,138
Miller, Karen L.	4	1	0	0	1,100	Mohamed, Dr. James A.	23	2	1	1	26,392
Miller, Kenny	8	1	0	0	8,873	Mohar, Kenny	12	2	1	2	10,979
Miller, Larry A.	16	2	1	1	22,920	Mokry, Michael J.	18	1	0	1	11,809
Miller, Laurel M.	14	2	2	1	29,620	Molina, Mark S.	68	8	13	16	55,100
Miller, Melissa	24	1	2	3	14,678	Molinaro, Kent R.	50	20	4	5	260,358
Miller, Otis	6	0	0	0	0	Moloney, James J	3	0	0	0	4,719
Miller, Patrice	10	0	0	1	4,950	Monahan, II, Robert E.	83	2	6	8	42,914
Miller, Peggy	5	0	1	0	920	Monahas, Dimitrios	75	7	8	7	50,933
Miller, Quentin B.	69	4	6	6	78,553	Monbarren, Gary	1	0	0	0	52
Miller, Richard E.	14	0	2	0	5,528	Mondick, Wayne	3	0	0	0	300
Miller, Robert M.	196	30	26	38	358,640	Mondol, Eduardo	43	4	5	6	53,595
Miller, Rory C.	48	0	2	1	11,148	Mongeon, Kathy P.	65	3	3	4	65,171
Miller, Roy Lee	7	1	1	0	1,738	Monjes, Ruben A.	63	4	6	7	68,589
Miller, Sandy Jean	32	4	5	3	30,929	Monk, Elmer	25	1	1	1	7,436
Miller, Shirley T.	20	3	0	0	22,219	Monroe, Sherrie	88	6	18	12	159,077
Miller, Thomas R.	27	2	3	7	41,092	Monserrate, Felix O.	229	19	24	29	182,819

Trainer	Sts	1st	2d	3d	Purses	Trainer	Sts	1st	2d	3d	Purses
Monson, Micheal N.	1	0	0	0	60	Morris, Homer	2	0	0	1	1,105
Monson, Mylo C.	41	5	6	4	34,012	Morris, John	2	0	0	0	0
Montano, Vince B.	2	0	0	0	117	Morris, Michael L.	2	0	0	0	286
Montano, Sr., Angel O.	103	8	14	15	161,756	Morris, Ned	2	0	0	0	0
Montchal, Jr., Raymond	6	0	0	0	656	Morris, Neil R.	99	21	17	9	394,121
Monteleone, Frank A.	1	0	1	0	1,540	Morris, Robert	1	0	0	0	0
Monteleone, Frank J.	86	16	13	11	534,106	Morris, Valerie L.	17	0	0	0	215
Montes, Danny S.	3	0	0	1	1,350	Morrison, George E.	60	8	10	8	183,179
Montes, Jr., Johnny R.	76	15	7	9	186,805	Morrison, John	63	5	9	3	245,636
Montet, Ralph	82	1	11	8	40,588	Morrison, John D.	27	3	4	4	27,984
Montgomery, Danielle	9	1	0	0	7,300	Morrison, Mike J.	32	3	2	3	29,470
Montgomery, Darwin L.	45	3	5	5	59,838	Morrison, Scott D.	7	0	0	0	998
Montgomery, David P.	5	1	0	0	8,131	Morrow, Ann L.	47	2	1	8	41,275
Montgomery, Gary	24	4	1	7	95,715	Morrow, T. Gail	45	1	3	6	27,641
Montgomery, Lori Hill	11	2	1	0	43,389	Morse, David L.	33	10	5	4	94,134
Montgomery, Sandra	18	1	1	3	9,163	Morse, Randy L.	215	45	42	23	884,787
Montgomery, Timothy	149	17	23	12	101,479	Morse, Ronnie	3	1	1	1	25,800
Montgomery, William E.	2	0	0	0	570	Morse, Scott A.	19	5	1	3	25,553
Montgomery, Jr., Harry B.	31	4	3	0	23,784	Morsello, Joseph R.	21	2	1	2	11,112
Montoya, Marya K.	66	14	6	6	136,652	Mortensen, Dale	8	1	2	2	7,955
Mooney, Bill	35	0	1	2	4,385	Mortensen, Lyle	9	1	0	2	5,304
Moore, Adrienne	1	0	0	0	550	Mortensen, Ted C.	1	0	1	0	2,100
Moore, Billy R.	15	1	1	2	7,674	Morton, Blueford G.	9	1	2	0	5,500
Moore, David	2	0	0	1	1,320	Morton, Frank	9	0	2	4	10,812
Moore, Dennis T.	326	45	43	56	371,818	Morton, James	8	0	1	0	1,037
Moore, Dorris L.	13	1	1	1	18,229	Morton, Larry R.	11	0	0	2	2,708
Moore, Jerald E.	22	0	0	1	2,452	Morton, Sr., Frank	1	0	0	0	0
Moore, Lance R.	4	0	0	1	725	Moscarelli, Vincent W.	111	14	14	11	198,613
Moore, Merel E.	45	1	8	1	10,398	Moschonas, Gerasimos	68	4	4	3	73,998
Moore, Mike	4	0	0	0	130	Mosco, Robert	243	47	32	29	589,858
Moore, Nicky	6	0	0	0	84	Mosley, Tom	11	2	2	2	14,828
Moore, Peter	3	0	0	0	0	Mosley, Walleah L.	1	0	0	0	0
Moore, Richard L.	19	0	1	0	7,482	Moss, Albert C.	43	0	7	6	37,160
Moore, Sr., Chester	25	3	0	2	43,532	Moss, Buford A.	12	0	1	1	2,322
Moorhead, Clifford W.	11	2	1	0	5,620	Moss, G. Harold	2	0	0	0	215
Moosman, Ron	1	0	1	0	425	Moss, Joseph A.	73	6	7	17	107,396
Moquett, Ron	368	29	44	46	710,507	Moss, Ken T.	4	0	0	1	320
Mora, Myra	154	22	11	16	570,268	Moss, Thomas J.	68	11	6	15	121,004
Morales, Carlos J.	81	11	10	11	363,997	Motion, H. Graham	318	55	47	53	2,822,266
Morales, Mario	51	5	13	4	77,435	Mott, William I.	718	138	101	85	6,866,320
Morales, Nabu	92	8	8	12	161,314	Moulton, Michelle	11	0	0	0	2,170
Morales, Ricardo	81	6	3	9	98,616	Moulton, Susan	2	0	0	0	870
Moran, Betty L.	2	0	0	0	239	Mourar, Buck K.	16	2	5	4	33,710
Moran, Bill	54	6	9	6	94,452	Mourier, Frank	11	4	2	2	275,579
Moran, Michael J.	24	1	4	3	54,897	Mourning, Don L.	1	0	0	0	55
Moran, Sr., Donald W.	85	9	8	3	82,702	Mouton, Chadwick J.	20	0	0	2	2,654
Morano, Deborah	6	0	0	0	2,009	Mouton, Enis	36	6	4	2	71,867
Morden, Lyle	129	19	17	15	272,790	Mouton, Patrick	194	27	36	27	668,668
Moreno, Carlos	25	3	5	2	15,153	Mower, R. D.	36	4	4	3	17,675
Moreno, Henry	42	1	1	5	49,680	Moyer, Meredith	12	0	1	4	8,920
Moreno, Jaime	15	0	3	2	5,985	Moyer, Raymond	3	0	0	1	767
Moreno, Tito	225	25	21	24	364,520	Moyer, Steven L.	57	12	8	4	179,520
Moreno, Tomas D.	7	0	1	0	1,577	Muckey, Sally	91	4	7	9	25,590
Morey, William E.	401	100	70	68	1,554,868	Mueller, Russell	36	3	2	1	163,008
Morey, Jr., William J.	181	27	27	39	757,069	Muench, David L.	115	11	22	15	225,780
Morgan, Brian A.	48	5	5	4	172,455	Mulcahy, Geoff	27	2	3	4	20,708
Morgan, Carla L.	7	1	0	0	2,819	Mulhall, Kristin	105	15	20	9	1,062,473
Morgan, Clifton J.	15	0	1	1	6,895	Mullaney, Deryle	57	8	5	10	87,768
Morgan, Dan	126	21	19	20	247,427	Mullen, Blair W.	30	4	4	3	42,741
Morgan, Evan B.	4	1	0	1	1,221	Mullens, H. R. Pat	75	9	9	9	67,847
Morgan, James E.	209	34	32	25	448,116	Muller, Sr., Thomas J.	113	5	12	14	56,884
Morgan, Janet L.	37	0	5	5	45,700	Mullins, Buddy R.	14	3	0	0	14,752
Morgan, Julie	3	0	1	1	1,775	Mullins, Jeff	313	94	61	35	4,383,866
Morgan, Kenneth A.	181	16	11	16	77,605	Mullins, Leonard S.	3	0	0	1	110
Morgan, Phillip C.	3	0	0	0	0	Mullins, Michelle	36	6	5	3	59,677
Morgan, Robert V.	2	0	0	0	0	Mulvey, Arthur V.	11	5	1	1	39,291
Morgan, Tommie T.	368	54	62	45	807,199	Mumaw, Benjamin T.	107	8	18	15	101,288
Morin, Shaun	12	1	0	2	1,804	Munds, Sue	29	0	2	3	23,331
Morisak, Robert W.	6	0	0	0	300	Munger, Don L.	123	10	13	19	54,763
Morison, Don F.	51	4	7	2	65,214	Munoz, Jose Juan	11	0	0	0	535
Morreale, Jake V.	254	16	26	28	230,843	Murawski, Rachael	10	1	0	2	6,969
Morris, Andrea S.	12	1	0	0	7,065	Murdock, Cal	2	0	0	0	66
Morris, Brent	89	10	10	13	77,785	Murillo, Ricardo A.	41	5	3	7	70,823
Morris, David	136	12	14	19	127,890	Murnan, G. Scott	1	0	0	0	0
Morris, Donna	2	0	0	1	610	Murphy, Alicia	30	4	3	2	69,050
Morris, Gregg	3	0	0	0	252	Murphy, Don	160	8	13	28	34,383

Trainer	Sts	1st	2d	3d	Purses	Trainer	Sts	1st	2d	3d	Purses
Murphy, Earl C.	18	3	2	2	49,395	Needham, Jr., Bobby	97	4	13	6	62,400
Murphy, James W.	137	14	29	17	407,882	Neff, Myles I.	29	4	5	2	96,682
Murphy, Pat	6	4	0	1	6,076	Neff, Pamela J	6	3	1	1	15,914
Murphy, Patricia	22	2	4	2	26,482	Neff, Robert	5	1	0	0	6,220
Murphy, Paul H.	163	25	16	21	427,867	Neichter, Patrick	3	0	0	0	740
Murphy, Raymond T.	7	0	0	0	5,570	Neilson, Katherine	118	23	13	16	566,176
Murphy, Scott R.	131	14	23	17	195,093	Neilson, Wallace C.	88	9	6	7	126,778
Murphy, Steven H.	14	0	0	0	1,781	Neilson, III, Louis	13	4	0	0	23,025
Murphy, Susan E.	24	1	5	1	32,823	Neiman, Fred	1	0	1	0	6,480
Murphy, Susan S.	6	2	0	0	10,500	Nellessen, Leonard	46	0	3	4	8,487
Murphy, Timothy P.	166	19	21	24	168,254	Nelson, Barry R	4	0	0	0	446
Murphy, Tom G.	11	4	1	2	37,378	Nelson, Fred B.	19	2	1	3	13,830
Murphy, Wayne L.	138	6	21	19	145,189	Nelson, Harry N.	137	10	11	15	89,627
Murphy II, Thomas J.	11	1	0	1	13,305	Nelson, Kathleen S.	43	2	2	6	26,390
Murr, Bill	4	0	0	1	876	Nelson, Mary	39	4	2	3	30,939
Murray, Alex D.	37	5	9	5	76,269	Nelson, Michael C.	7	1	2	1	3,396
Murray, D. Milton	29	6	6	4	74,886	Nelson, Sam D.	7	0	0	0	396
Murray, Dave	24	7	4	1	87,551	Nelson, Stan	25	3	2	4	25,332
Murray, Donna	4	2	0	0	4,440	Nelson, Thelma	21	0	1	2	2,473
Murray, Douglas A.	1	0	0	0	38	Nemann, Fred A.	57	4	2	5	35,432
Murray, Jack	29	6	3	5	56,593	Nemann, Kris	106	8	12	15	94,706
Murray, Lawrence E.	129	22	17	13	1,025,526	Nemett, George S.	77	10	13	9	640,273
Murray, Michael E.	12	0	1	0	2,572	Nepple, Lloyd	65	5	6	3	44,250
Murray, Scott M.	15	2	4	1	6,076	Nesbitt, Kim	69	9	6	7	83,821
Murtough, Gary	4	1	0	0	2,190	Nesky, Kenneth A.	66	2	6	12	160,353
Murtough, Stephen B.	6	0	0	0	188	Ness, Jamie	182	30	19	33	241,752
Murty, Wayne	12	3	0	0	123,621	Ness, John	55	16	8	8	43,773
Musarro, Jamie	9	0	0	2	2,408	Nettles, Kenneth	20	1	3	1	21,130
Muse, Brian E.	23	1	2	2	21,391	Neubauer, Michaela	135	32	19	28	724,033
Musgrave, Shawn	153	22	30	21	377,050	Neubuhr, Sam L.	42	2	5	5	16,729
Mustard, J. Douglas	29	1	2	7	16,855	Neumann, Robert E.	16	2	0	0	73,284
Mustard, Wendell R.	2	0	0	0	328	Nevin, Michael	96	5	16	9	272,062
Mustoe, Cindy	52	10	3	3	141,202	Newbold, Jon W.	45	1	0	2	8,562
Myers, Daniel W.	5	0	2	0	3,553	Newbrough, Steven	18	1	0	1	9,192
Myers, John M.	6	0	3	0	9,470	Newell, Kenneth R.	3	0	0	1	3,120
Myers, Karl	74	9	13	14	87,017	Newell, Michael	471	52	64	53	571,159
Myers, Larry M.	124	4	14	17	129,767	Newland, George	9	1	1	2	27,964
Myers, Steven E.	18	1	3	1	50,974	Newlin, Jr., Albert	3	1	0	0	12,760
Myers, William A.	1	0	0	1	770	Newlun, Ronald Colver	2	0	0	0	110
Myers, William H.	5	1	0	0	14,287	Newman, Gabe	39	1	1	3	7,824
Mynster, Patrick M.	10	1	3	0	14,588	Newman, Gabriel G.	19	1	2	3	19,469
Nafzger, Carl A.	285	31	30	47	1,868,359	Newman, Tracy L.	43	2	3	3	21,352
Nafzger, Larry	4	0	0	0	256	Newport, Kim	53	3	6	7	19,033
Nagel, Clayton	19	4	1	1	11,964	Newsom, Jack E.	23	0	7	5	11,833
Nagy, George	38	0	7	8	42,976	Newsome, Clement	22	4	0	3	13,106
Nall, Johnnie L.	105	20	21	12	330,662	Newton, Charles R.	28	1	0	2	4,242
Nalley, Rhonda	52	5	5	7	97,692	Newton, Troy	50	2	9	3	35,583
Nance, Jonathan	236	43	37	37	185,465	Ney, Andrew T.	203	31	22	22	472,634
Nance, Michael W.	375	69	66	34	939,295	Nibarger, Larry	8	0	0	1	1,515
Nance, Scott	35	5	9	5	14,348	Nicholas, Sr., Robert Lee	33	3	1	3	23,769
Nanez, Danette E.	39	4	5	3	58,334	Nichols, Bessie Sue	4	0	0	0	120
Napier, William J.	59	6	9	2	124,686	Nichols, Bill	1	0	0	1	220
Napolitano, Sal	14	1	5	3	25,596	Nichols, Brent	8	0	1	0	1,896
Nasby, Dale R.	28	1	3	4	15,871	Nichols, Jessie	25	2	2	5	21,358
Nash, Christopher	30	2	1	4	32,253	Nichols, Pat	19	1	1	1	12,628
Natale, Michael	158	19	21	18	220,276	Nicholson, Craig P.	57	9	12	8	116,457
Natho, Randy Lee	21	2	9	1	13,478	Nicholson, David	106	11	19	17	185,608
Nations, Keith	29	6	2	1	37,136	Nicholson, Junior W.	37	6	3	2	55,055
Naughton, Anthony	11	0	0	1	2,400	Nicholson, Jr., James E.	48	0	1	0	6,040
Naugle, Kenneth W.	19	1	4	6	5,153	Nickels, Eddie	13	0	0	0	126
Nault, Michael	78	7	9	3	57,072	Nickerson, Victor J.	1	0	0	0	0
Navarre, Cindy	2	0	0	0	174	Nicks, Morris G.	156	28	12	27	507,907
Navarre, Jacqui	10	5	2	1	13,015	Nicol, James	4	3	1	0	73,164
Navarro, Jose	76	7	16	12	87,616	Nicolo, John	7	0	2	1	7,256
Navarro, Marcial	80	12	21	12	211,055	Niehaus, Jonathan	8	2	1	1	11,932
Nazareth, Jr., John	4	0	1	0	3,660	Nielsen, David B.	44	1	0	4	16,062
Nazareth, Sr., John Antonio	152	15	6	18	256,492	Nielsen, David D.	12	1	4	1	2,697
Meadow, Charles P.	6	0	0	0	620	Nielsen, Paul	22	4	4	2	170,595
Neal, Mike	1	0	0	0	0	Nielsen, Robert A.	5	0	0	0	200
Neatherlin, Mike R.	47	4	4	6	53,993	Nieminski, Richard S.	12	2	2	1	76,400
Neatherlin, Tommy	17	1	2	2	12,249	Nikiforuk, Raymond	66	1	4	6	20,839
Necaise, Christopher Ray	4	0	0	0	0	Nilsen, Victor W.	4	0	0	0	0
Necaise, Elliot C.	46	3	2	6	37,747	Nisser, Ernest	14	1	0	0	7,034
Necaise, Garrie	34	0	4	5	16,591	Nix, Allen	9	1	2	1	2,026
Necaise, Larry	17	0	1	0	1,366	Nix, C. L.	113	16	9	11	173,352
Nechamkin, II, Leo S.	45	8	7	6	313,900	Nix, Eugene H.	8	1	2	0	5,345

Trainer	Sts	1st	2d	3d	Purses	Trainer	Sts	1st	2d	3d	Purses
Nixon, Bobby Joe	2	0	0	0	189	Ocker, Robert	27	2	6	2	16,653
Nixon, David R.	20	2	0	1	18,843	O'Connell, Brian J.	20	2	0	2	25,677
Nixon, Justin J.	61	13	17	9	309,765	O'Connell, Kathleen	511	82	60	67	1,451,667
Nixon, Lawrence	32	2	1	7	14,083	O'Connor, John	4	0	0	0	305
Nixon, Stephanie B.	30	5	3	2	69,250	O'Connor, Kathleen E.	18	4	3	2	79,590
Noble, Allen	13	0	0	1	1,706	O'Connor, Ray L.	82	6	11	4	128,775
Noble, Edward L.	58	5	6	5	97,065	O'Connor, Stephen T.	149	35	26	19	283,719
Noble, James F.	13	1	2	0	5,786	O'Connor, II, Robert R.	52	7	5	5	121,585
Nobles, Reynaldo H.	87	9	12	15	322,450	O'Dea, Mike	9	0	1	0	2,763
Nocero, Rinzy	277	33	30	25	170,881	O'Dell, Christopher G.	42	7	6	6	101,547
Nocero, Roger	48	4	5	9	25,093	Odintz, Jeff	128	8	13	17	418,302
Nocero, Roggiero L.	19	2	1	1	12,345	Odom, David William	1	0	0	0	43
Noe, Albert W.	6	0	1	1	1,504	Odom, Robert L.	11	0	1	2	4,298
Noel, Bob J.	128	14	19	24	329,672	Odom, Sr., Raymond	9	2	2	2	21,060
Noel, Cody L.	5	0	1	1	4,487	Oest, Joshua	8	1	0	0	3,412
Noel, Wayne L.	99	8	4	9	90,929	Offield, Duane	136	8	17	21	211,727
Nolan, Donna M.	31	0	2	6	33,660	Offolter, Joe S.	391	66	51	42	554,371
Noland, Kamala J.	18	3	0	1	44,522	O'Gara, Kenneth J.	28	1	2	1	20,370
Nolen, Harold Whitey	33	2	2	3	24,008	Ogg, Raymond L.	33	2	6	1	12,896
Nolen, Kenneth	115	23	15	17	255,319	Ogilvie, Les	21	2	4	3	18,054
Nooner, John	7	0	0	0	695	Ogus, Daniel	86	8	5	7	95,540
Nor, Fabio	28	4	1	4	108,726	O'Harra, David C.	10	0	1	0	3,103
Norman, Cole	1,086	290	183	125	5,496,689	Ohlhauser, Robert F.	14	1	5	0	17,180
Normand, Dale	1	0	0	0	0	Okawaki, William N.	15	2	0	1	7,975
Norris, C. David	77	13	9	8	187,206	O'Keefe, Thomas	41	2	3	6	118,829
Norris, Kathleen	3	0	0	0	0	Olaivar, Benny D.	26	1	5	2	15,973
Norris, Mike	1	0	0	0	0	Old Horn, Dale	4	0	0	0	76
Norris, Tracy A.	14	0	0	0	888	Old Horn, Jack	2	0	0	0	62
Northam, Linda Bartels	54	5	6	5	37,583	Olesiak, Jesse	198	11	23	24	102,857
Northrop, Jr., George	172	15	19	22	117,443	Oliphant, Claude	16	2	1	3	12,298
Norton, Melissa J.	23	0	0	0	3,493	Olito, Verla	18	0	2	1	5,195
Norton, Norbert E.	106	22	20	22	88,735	Oliva, Jr., Louis M.	3	1	2	0	7,260
Noseda, Jeremy	1	0	0	0	18,000	Olivares, Frank	28	2	0	1	38,320
Noss, Jerry A.	14	1	1	0	5,490	Olivares, Luis	302	32	44	40	578,163
Nouwens, Preston	13	1	1	0	34,033	Olivarez, Manuel R.	4	0	0	0	150
Novak, Marshall L.	196	32	30	38	464,927	Olivarez, Mario	37	0	5	3	13,971
Nowak, Elizabeth	1	0	0	0	0	Olivas, Cesario G.	136	12	13	18	78,750
Ntonados, Gerasimos J.	42	0	1	1	4,235	Oliver, Barry E.	21	0	0	0	0
Nuckols, Gerald A.	11	1	1	5	8,793	Oliver, Doug	274	40	42	29	591,772
Nuesch, Patrick F.	98	13	12	10	210,533	Oliver, Patricia J.	5	0	0	0	954
Nunez, Jesus	356	37	38	42	254,927	Oliver, Philip J.	117	15	5	20	447,500
Nunez, Mauricio	24	4	3	2	31,374	Oliver, Vicki	82	14	7	9	385,282
Nunez, Osvaldo M.	22	0	1	3	11,780	Oliverre, Sylvester	18	2	0	2	10,905
Nunley, Randy	87	12	11	10	120,398	Olivier, Rogers	6	0	0	0	293
Nunley, Tracy L.	139	13	22	21	336,050	Olman, Ronald R.	4	0	0	0	713
Nunn, David	37	7	9	2	73,580	Olmos, Juan C.	125	13	12	19	147,961
Nunn, Douglas	113	14	11	11	152,945	Olsen, Ron	30	4	7	4	29,692
Nunnally, Chris	6	0	3	1	2,310	Olsen, William Edward	2	0	0	0	0
Nunnally, James	40	2	3	3	17,860	Olson, Daryl	12	2	1	1	4,424
Nydam, Michelle L.	64	9	8	9	130,050	Olson, Kenneth	25	2	2	4	5,944
Oaks, Finley	4	1	0	1	3,160	Olson, Lynn	18	0	3	2	10,682
O'Bannon, Cynthia E.	225	17	32	30	307,778	Olson, Selmer B.	12	1	3	1	25,330
Oberdorff, Barry E.	1	0	0	0	0	O'Neal, Bob	9	0	0	0	1,527
Obergfell, Sarina	92	9	11	12	97,419	O'Neill, Doug	760	133	119	109	6,438,799
Oberholtzer, Kevin	77	7	15	11	39,049	O'Neill, Robert B.	1	0	0	1	522
Oberlander, Randy	89	13	17	10	157,730	Ontiveros, Lalita	15	2	2	1	12,558
O'Bray, Todd	22	4	1	1	40,719	Opperman, Beach W.	21	0	0	1	1,256
O'Brien, Agnes	11	0	0	2	5,105	O'Quinn, Earl	47	7	4	8	87,559
O'Brien, Aidan P.	10	1	2	2	1,496,800	O'Quinn, Kristen Lee	23	3	2	2	18,343
O'Brien, Colum	70	6	11	5	265,693	Oran, John T.	29	3	4	2	34,428
O'Brien, Danny	10	1	0	1	3,067	Orellana, Oscar J.	30	1	3	4	25,910
O'Brien, Debbie	24	3	1	0	17,064	Orlando, Peter L.	14	3	2	2	34,590
O'Brien, Declan	10	1	0	2	7,353	Orm, Jerry	169	16	23	13	167,585
O'Brien, Elmer J.	35	3	4	4	42,051	Orm, Mike	11	0	0	0	351
O'Brien, Gerald L.	39	7	0	6	31,653	Orman, J. Michael	34	3	3	2	61,980
O'Brien, Gerard P.	56	5	3	10	112,296	Ormesher, Arthur	9	0	0	1	567
O'Brien, Keith	75	8	6	12	308,789	Ormesher, Sarah J.	1	0	0	0	100
O'Brien, Lawrence	4	0	1	1	5,891	Orona, Martin	9	1	1	1	6,383
O'Brien, Leo	135	9	15	10	417,113	Orozco, Salvador	24	5	2	2	44,790
O'Brien, Maura C.	45	10	9	3	139,045	Orr, James	53	7	8	8	51,479
O'Brien, Michael Scott	1	0	0	0	129	Orr, Thomas Stephen	71	5	6	9	19,767
O'Callaghan, Carl	25	1	1	2	41,026	Orseno, Joseph F.	385	42	64	44	1,395,614
O'Callaghan, Danny M.	91	11	9	9	435,167	Ortega, Jr., Art S.	16	0	0	1	824
O'Callaghan, Niall M.	243	25	20	41	1,406,322	Ortega, Sr., Jesus Fernando	9	4	1	1	5,950
O'Callaghan, Sarah	1	0	0	0	0	Ortenzi, Giovanni	9	0	0	0	324
Occhiuto, Richard	106	15	14	19	92,406	Ortiz, Arthur Curly	23	4	4	3	18,787

Trainer	Sts	1st	2d	3d	Purses	Trainer	Sts	1st	2d	3d	Purses
Ortiz, Jose M.	41	4	4	4	31,807	Papiska, Trever	13	0	0	1	2,494
Ortiz, Joseph	10	0	1	1	3,634	Pappada, Michael C.	195	39	29	28	618,450
Ortiz, Juan	61	2	4	2	95,197	Pappas, John	3	1	1	0	15,560
Ortiz, Paulino O.	46	6	2	4	151,530	Paquette, Chantal L.	42	2	4	2	215,781
Ortiz, Ralph	1	0	0	0	150	Paquette, Ida	216	14	16	13	194,730
Ortiz, Sr., Manuel	63	4	5	3	29,078	Paquette, Linda	23	1	1	1	14,406
Ory, Dennis	1	0	0	0	0	Paquette, III, Raymond J.	85	5	6	11	41,654
Ory, Melanie	11	0	1	0	5,521	Parada, Tom	1	0	1	0	1,520
Osborn, Jan	13	3	2	1	6,793	Paradise, Jerry P.	25	4	2	1	99,783
Osborn, O. J.	90	9	6	9	121,953	Parga, Joe	85	8	12	10	262,710
Osborne, Dara J.	49	5	10	8	29,513	Parisella, John	136	16	29	16	514,393
Osborne, Linda K.	60	4	14	9	69,238	Parisi, Horacio	7	1	0	0	5,791
Osborne, Michael R.	126	8	18	13	202,312	Parisi, Jr., Paul J.	64	11	12	7	297,805
Osment, Robbie J.	51	2	4	8	32,669	Parke, Kathy	10	0	1	3	9,683
Osorio, Osvaldo	16	0	0	1	1,921	Parker, Bob D.	70	3	8	9	37,320
Osuna, Alejandro	4	1	0	0	1,089	Parker, C. C.	10	0	0	1	200
O'Toole, James J.	13	2	4	1	15,584	Parker, Danny	1	0	0	0	0
Ott, Betty L.	44	0	1	3	8,454	Parker, F. Hill	27	3	0	4	22,719
Otteson, David L.	41	4	5	5	28,639	Parker, Horace M.	69	3	5	6	54,048
Otteson, Kenny	8	0	1	0	2,375	Parker, Joseph G.	12	1	0	0	11,460
Oughton, Julie E.	36	2	5	4	36,595	Parker, Kathleen	19	1	3	4	12,666
Oulton, Wes	5	2	2	0	4,550	Parker, Kevin	14	1	5	1	7,952
Overton, Taff F.	40	0	1	2	5,406	Parker, Mark	49	8	9	11	75,176
Overturf, Roger	1	0	0	0	80	Parker, Robert W.	149	12	14	19	61,968
Oviedo, Phillip S.	83	7	8	14	119,767	Parker, Jr., Elmer L.	5	1	0	0	14,645
Owen, Nate	13	2	4	2	13,186	Parkin, Gary W.	13	0	0	2	6,519
Owens, Alan D.	2	0	0	0	1,572	Parkinson, Ron	2	0	0	0	0
Owens, Martin D.	112	36	12	17	274,545	Parks, David S.	17	0	0	0	1,625
Owens, Mickey	17	1	1	2	10,149	Parks, Raymond G.	4	0	0	0	1,085
Owens, R. Kory	48	8	6	5	162,301	Parmlee, Judith	6	1	0	0	2,828
Owens, Steve	86	11	14	10	651,592	Parnell, William E.	16	6	1	2	19,717
Owens, III, Edward	13	0	2	3	9,340	Parody, Albert E.	3	0	0	0	681
Oxman, Carol	53	2	8	5	72,653	Parris, Jim L.	77	7	8	8	77,046
Oyster, Charles H.	3	0	0	0	300	Parrish, Steven G.	13	0	0	1	3,571
Paasch, Christopher S.	96	5	12	20	407,909	Parrish, Sr., George W.	68	4	6	8	65,455
Pabon, Heriberto	37	3	3	3	45,705	Parrott, Gary D.	10	1	0	2	3,087
Pace, Phillip Donato	32	1	0	0	6,466	Parsley, Ken B.	35	9	4	7	604,987
Pacheco, Elsie	3	0	0	0	165	Parsons, Dean	16	1	3	3	9,734
Pacheco, Leo J.	5	0	1	1	1,458	Partington, Jerome	6	0	1	2	4,305
Pacitti, Michael G.	25	2	3	3	26,832	Partridge, Robert E.	107	15	6	11	95,004
Padgett, Virginia	6	1	0	1	6,660	Parum, Brandon	2	1	1	0	3,960
Padilla, Leslie	1	0	0	0	0	Paschal, Richard	2	0	0	0	15
Padilla, Tim P.	279	26	34	37	202,208	Pascual, Maria Virginia	56	8	7	8	112,625
Padilla, Victor	2	0	0	0	368	Pascucci, Ambrose	91	7	18	10	113,445
Padilla, Willie C.	70	10	5	11	133,425	Passero, Gino S.	45	3	6	3	90,071
Paez, Carlos E.	106	19	12	18	430,389	Passero, Jr., Frank A.	18	0	1	2	8,860
Pafford, Jr., Walter C.	7	0	0	0	300	Passley, Mark	90	13	15	13	78,046
Page, Gary	130	26	20	19	137,634	Pastor, Jude	93	9	17	5	128,469
Page, Tommy	59	5	9	9	81,360	Paszkeicz, Alex	102	6	3	11	120,300
Paige, Guy	22	1	0	1	9,183	Patch, Sandra A.	64	4	3	3	48,916
Palacios, Luis Albert	339	65	60	50	893,833	Pate, David E.	83	10	6	11	274,804
Palagi, Kenneth C.	9	3	1	2	6,354	Pate, William D.	1	0	0	1	1,000
Palaniuk, Brian	84	7	13	7	327,915	Paterno, Robert T.	16	0	2	1	2,960
Palecki, Henry J.	7	0	1	1	27,592	Patout, Lloyd D.	3	0	0	0	0
Pallanes, Art	9	0	0	1	1,051	Patrick, R. Gary	418	48	43	49	454,838
Pallas, Ray J.	75	11	13	10	54,906	Patrick, Tom	24	4	0	5	17,278
Pallister, Kevin	19	1	1	0	14,188	Pattah, Shahab D.	94	5	9	7	42,981
Palman, Darrin	59	4	1	9	86,170	Pattershall, Mary A.	5	1	0	0	7,260
Palmer, Aaron	23	2	5	1	28,048	Patterson, Alan	16	0	3	1	7,210
Palmer, Charles C.	38	3	3	3	27,656	Patterson, Dennis M.	78	9	7	10	146,831
Palmer, Charles G.	6	0	0	0	277	Patterson, Jeanne B.	20	0	1	0	2,232
Palmer, Jay H.	52	5	6	3	52,577	Patterson, Loren	31	4	2	4	48,978
Palmer, Jim E.	1	0	0	0	0	Patterson, Jr., Thomas L.	68	9	9	10	203,125
Palmer, Lloyd L.	63	12	13	5	140,128	Patti, Gale A.	26	3	4	3	69,050
Palmer, Perry	6	4	1	0	15,488	Patton, Kathy	67	4	10	5	206,975
Palmisano, Gary	35	4	4	4	150,645	Patton, Robert E.	1	0	0	0	0
Palone, Eileen	92	3	12	16	42,772	Patykewich, Alexander P.	16	2	3	2	27,239
Pane, Pasquale J.	35	5	2	0	41,125	Paul, Ronda S.	22	1	1	1	5,392
Panico, Nello	1	0	0	0	0	Paul, Wayne J.	2	0	0	1	1,163
Pantaleo, Joseph	15	0	2	0	7,990	Pauley, Jr., James E.	20	1	3	3	22,436
Pantall, Henri-Alex	3	0	1	1	127,500	Paulson, Gary E.	21	1	0	1	6,373
Paone, John A.	14	0	0	1	2,970	Paulus, David E.	219	21	30	26	412,895
Papania, Robert A.	4	1	1	1	39,240	Paulus, Richard E.	45	6	2	6	102,599
Papaprodromou, Andreas	20	1	0	3	10,670	Pavlick, Thomas B.	295	22	19	38	320,710
Papaprodromou, George	13	1	1	3	31,120	Pawlitsky, Joan M.	15	0	4	3	10,413
Papillion, Merrick	46	2	2	3	15,152	Payne, Curtis Beale	35	3	1	4	50,682

Trainer	Sts	1st	2d	3d	Purses	Trainer	Sts	1st	2d	3d	Purses
Payne, Danny W.	10	1	0	1	6,400	Perry, Sr., Lyle	12	1	3	4	3,916
Payne, Helen	6	0	0	0	187	Persaud, Eddie	17	0	0	1	5,645
Payne, Jerry	20	2	8	3	14,290	Person, Kenneth A.	37	6	6	6	30,026
Payne, Linda S.	12	0	2	1	6,440	Pesina, Pablo	4	0	0	1	419
Payton, Recil L.	26	4	5	3	11,045	Pessin, Neil L.	15	1	3	2	15,925
Peacock, Shane	181	30	29	23	294,189	Petalino, Joseph	223	32	22	23	491,625
Peacock, Jr., Roy M.	30	0	0	3	10,551	Peters, Anthony G.	11	0	0	0	1,910
Pearce, Jerald W.	9	0	0	0	1,350	Peters, Dennis D.	13	1	2	2	4,693
Pearce, Ross R.	24	0	6	3	16,525	Peters, Gary	6	0	1	0	574
Pearce, William E.	51	5	2	3	182,509	Peters, Robert G.	54	11	11	4	83,151
Peardon, Josephine	10	0	0	0	540	Peters, Virginia	15	1	0	0	9,102
Pearson, Michael A.	39	3	2	1	33,097	Petersen, Dawn L.	23	0	1	2	20,459
Pearson, Michael R.	8	0	0	0	1,470	Peterson, Alan	1	0	0	0	0
Pearson, Molly J.	243	46	29	46	462,443	Peterson, Bob	21	1	0	2	12,531
Pearson, Paul M.	235	39	38	26	859,591	Peterson, Dana L.	11	1	2	0	4,079
Pearson, Randy	4	0	0	0	0	Peterson, Douglas R.	88	7	7	11	196,042
Pearson, Ronald N.	29	1	4	2	32,208	Peterson, Drew	1	0	0	0	223
Peck, D. Scott	43	2	6	7	71,110	Peterson, H. Zip	8	2	0	3	6,170
Peck, Tammy	10	1	0	4	4,758	Peterson, Linda	6	0	1	0	2,750
Pecoraro, Anthony	304	49	39	29	681,857	Peterson, Matt	4	0	0	0	100
Pecoraro, Matteo	1	0	0	0	145	Peterson, Raymond F.	2	0	0	1	1,570
Pedersen, Candy	3	0	1	1	3,480	Peterson, Sr., Michael J.	83	6	7	5	46,995
Pedersen, Jeff E.	38	0	1	2	13,780	Petro, Michael P.	208	30	43	35	918,835
Pedersen, Jennifer	320	30	41	36	1,754,511	Petrowski, Joan	314	37	44	39	484,681
Pederson, Dean	146	36	24	17	429,404	Petrozzo, Frank C.	31	3	2	5	40,335
Pedigo, Randy	36	6	1	7	47,956	Petten, David W.	14	0	3	2	7,499
Peery, Ann	29	4	6	1	10,348	Pettit, William A.	139	13	20	12	166,937
Peery, Chuck	233	46	45	32	950,490	Pew, Karl	24	7	4	4	27,613
Peery, Durk	6	1	1	1	1,864	Pezzarossi, Frank	13	0	0	2	9,289
Peery, Ken	5	0	0	0	0	Pfeifer, Randy	77	10	6	11	52,938
Peitz, Daniel C.	118	14	18	18	592,284	Phalin, Doug	5	0	0	0	1,030
Pellegrini, Frank	5	0	0	0	339	Pham, Van	13	0	0	0	1,395
Pellegrini, Ronald	71	7	5	6	128,106	Phar, Theresa	24	3	1	2	5,908
Peltier, Bonnie Lynne	1	0	0	0	0	Pharis, Ron	19	3	1	2	10,708
Peltier, Joseph	2	0	0	1	150	Phelan, Bruce Fred	30	5	8	2	78,204
Peltier, Walt	114	8	13	20	63,183	Phelps, George	19	1	0	0	4,371
Pena, Diego	18	1	0	2	22,995	Phelps, Jr., Charles W.	30	1	3	2	17,180
Pena, Juan	3	0	1	1	1,860	Phelps, Sr., Charles W.	2	0	0	0	456
Pencheff, Dimitar I.	42	5	3	4	38,185	Phillips, Arlene	17	0	5	1	10,520
Pencheff, Robert	7	0	0	0	1,290	Phillips, Christine Sonya	7	1	0	1	1,404
Pender, Jack	27	1	3	4	8,627	Phillips, Debbie	4	0	0	0	0
Pendergraft, Terry E.	7	0	0	0	322	Phillips, John L.	36	4	1	2	32,996
Penna, Jr., Angel J.	72	3	6	10	166,345	Phillips, Patrick D.	1	0	0	0	1,272
Pennella, Rhea M.	133	3	11	8	89,497	Phillips, Wayne	1	0	0	0	0
Penner, Larry	159	16	23	19	112,976	Philpott, Stephen	32	0	3	11	69,591
Penney, Jim	190	30	25	33	379,865	Phipps, Micky	10	2	1	1	12,491
Pennington, J. Benny	5	0	2	0	1,780	Piantes, John	10	3	1	1	3,244
Pennino, Joe	22	1	3	0	15,597	Piatt, Bob	11	1	1	1	10,230
Penrod, Steven C.	63	9	4	10	298,080	Picazo, Juan M.	4	1	1	0	9,260
Peone, Sam	8	0	3	2	1,507	Piches, John G.	7	0	0	0	2,297
Percival, Mimie D.	5	0	0	0	1,400	Pichette, Raymond	5	0	1	0	2,800
Perdomo, A. Pico	5	1	1	1	43,215	Pickard, Jim	64	6	8	11	43,215
Perdue, Edward C.	194	25	17	22	222,461	Pickard, Robert J.	71	3	11	10	40,059
Perez, Dagoberto L.	34	1	6	3	53,830	Pickerell, William D.	32	1	1	2	6,991
Perez, Felix	13	2	1	1	9,126	Picon, Juan	8	0	0	0	4,525
Perez, Joel	15	1	4	1	7,496	Picou, James E.	59	2	6	5	165,241
Perez, Jose	5	1	2	1	14,010	Pierce, Clayton	46	5	12	6	156,665
Perez, Lorenzo C.	11	2	1	1	12,568	Pierce, Malcolm	249	34	35	29	2,259,868
Perez, Mag	34	2	0	1	35,919	Pierce, Michael Lee	15	1	1	1	5,734
Perez, Nicolas	87	4	2	3	83,815	Pierce, Oliver D.	1	0	0	0	0
Perez, Pedro W.	18	0	2	2	5,828	Pierce, Raymond A.	55	0	5	4	18,279
Perez, Ramon	80	7	5	12	58,032	Pierce, Robert G.	10	2	2	1	6,325
Perez, Ricardo	55	3	5	6	62,777	Pierce, Thomas W.	13	0	3	0	6,359
Perkins, Diane L.	28	1	3	4	53,675	Pierce, Vickie	17	0	0	0	2,941
Perkins, Edward Ray	3	0	0	0	198	Pierce, Jr., Joseph H.	143	12	20	20	392,588
Perkins, Larry	18	0	0	0	490	Pierson, Richard A.	1	0	0	0	133
Perkins, Lorna M.	1	0	0	0	0	Pigeau, Christal	16	2	4	0	7,857
Perkins, Jr., Benjamin W.	190	36	22	19	1,227,899	Pigeau, Nellie Opal	32	0	7	4	8,737
Perrotta, Joseph M.	16	0	5	5	33,860	Pike, Alexis	14	1	1	3	3,685
Perry, Don R.	2	0	0	1	1,485	Pike, Stewart	8	1	0	1	1,374
Perry, Lisa C.	1	0	0	0	80	Piker, Robert E.	23	2	0	2	9,277
Perry, Rolf	9	0	1	0	4,495	Pilmer, Ted G.	11	1	2	1	31,220
Perry, Stephen J.	31	3	3	5	47,041	Pilon, Hubert	67	19	7	11	90,250
Perry, Susan K.	10	1	1	2	2,371	Pilotti, Larry	268	47	53	31	820,864
Perry, William W.	82	4	10	8	183,295	Pilotto, Linda	1	0	0	0	149
Perry, Jr., Lawrence E.	12	0	3	0	18,242	Pimental, Alfred J.	59	11	7	4	156,671

Trainer	Sts	1st	2d	3d	Purses	Trainer	Sts	1st	2d	3d	Purses
Pimental, John I.	37	3	4	4	35,386	Popp, Dana	264	37	33	39	291,813
Pinchin, Jose	108	13	17	18	328,355	Portell, Neal	8	0	1	2	2,180
Pincins, Robert J.	84	16	12	14	242,740	Porter, Bryan	57	13	10	8	150,429
Pincione, Vito	62	4	5	7	59,710	Porter, John E.	18	1	2	2	5,804
Pinelli, Laura	6	1	1	1	6,900	Porter, Kimberly	2	0	0	0	0
Pinero, Christian J.	6	0	0	0	478	Porter, Ron	17	2	1	3	80,700
Pino, Michael V.	422	127	77	62	2,111,952	Posada, Frank A.	6	0	0	2	1,647
Pinzon, Maria E.	177	19	23	24	249,550	Posada, Laura	250	29	25	28	478,593
Pion, Raymond	104	16	12	5	207,164	Poteet, Don R.	2	0	0	0	0
Pion, Robert A.	51	4	6	13	175,061	Potter, Douglas G.	138	11	10	9	219,133
Pion, Jr., Rene	14	0	1	0	6,783	Potter, Norman D.	31	2	2	5	20,770
Pirie, Barbara A.	51	5	4	6	108,771	Potts, Carl	22	0	0	1	7,635
Pish, Danny	656	123	95	73	1,450,581	Potts, Kevin	7	0	0	0	0
Pitnick, Brian J.	59	7	9	9	75,481	Potts, Jr., Ron G.	96	10	16	12	184,882
Pitrone, Christopher	12	3	2	1	46,530	Potts, Sr., Ron H.	5	0	0	0	87
Pittman, Donald M.	77	6	7	10	56,792	Poujol, Al	3	0	0	2	2,805
Pittman, Jodie Mack	35	0	0	1	5,329	Poulos, Dee	162	13	17	19	340,930
Pitts, Daniel C.	39	4	4	3	23,732	Poulos, Luke E.	22	2	3	1	35,724
Pitzer, Floyd D.	56	4	12	8	70,693	Powell, Billy H.	11	1	1	0	7,337
Pitzer, Jeffrey W.	65	7	11	6	122,290	Powell, Claude A.	53	1	1	7	11,562
Pixley, Carlis	17	1	1	1	2,491	Powell, Dick	16	0	1	0	4,560
Pizarro, Donna L.	19	1	2	4	39,566	Powell, Gina	16	0	1	4	25,903
Pizzitola, Julia E.	28	0	2	1	4,670	Powell, Joy A.	12	1	0	0	3,674
Pizzurro, Antonio N.	197	12	17	16	187,842	Powell, Leonard	1	0	0	0	0
Pizzurro, Jessica L.	16	1	0	1	10,082	Powell, Ron	375	48	40	34	304,068
Pizzurro, Peter	92	9	13	8	170,522	Powers, James M.	33	3	2	3	22,082
Plaisance, Doug	70	5	9	9	71,764	Powers, Jerry W.	25	1	3	3	12,837
Plato, Sandy	37	2	7	3	24,114	Powers, Kenneth	5	1	1	1	3,440
Platts, Fenton	5	0	1	0	11,078	Powers, Paul E.	67	2	4	11	39,792
Plaza, Alberto	21	5	2	5	57,020	Powers, Paul J.	50	3	2	6	46,695
Pledge, Robert M.	12	0	2	1	1,458	Powers, Robin	58	5	3	4	41,639
Plesa, Jr., Edward	437	76	62	60	2,520,681	Powley, Cam	85	5	9	8	69,515
Plesa, Sr., Edward	27	5	2	1	77,460	Poxon, Alfred J.	10	0	0	0	0
Pletcher, Todd A.	826	199	132	105	12,356,924	Poxon, Jr., Ernest	66	4	3	5	21,609
Pleterski, Don	46	7	5	3	315,367	Poyadou, Bruce E.	26	2	3	2	21,199
Plever, Jr., Oden D.	16	0	3	3	11,458	Pozzo, Jack	9	1	0	0	4,810
Plummer, Doug	1	0	0	0	0	Pradenas, Sergio H.	10	1	0	1	7,460
Poalucci, Frank J.	6	0	0	1	2,180	Prado, Alex	1	0	0	0	220
Podrapovic, Dragan	11	0	2	0	3,845	Prado, Jorge	31	2	3	4	37,572
Poe, Albert O.	16	1	0	1	9,246	Prainito, Frank	141	14	16	16	91,981
Poe, John	45	12	11	6	268,606	Prather, Jr., John Henry	4	0	0	1	2,645
Pogue, William R.	61	10	4	13	147,486	Pratt, Everett	25	0	3	3	18,451
Pointer, Norman R.	313	51	52	35	1,104,835	Pratt, James M.	1	0	0	0	0
Poirrier, Arthur	7	0	0	0	330	Pratt, Laurie	2	0	0	0	573
Poitra, Sylvester	26	5	3	4	30,390	Preciado, Guadalupe	487	73	69	80	1,478,601
Poitras, Dennis	18	5	4	2	9,384	Preciado, Ramon	133	22	20	19	300,736
Poitras, William Myles	27	5	4	4	11,318	Predium, Raymond	9	0	2	0	5,208
Polachek, Janet	30	2	1	2	18,740	Preger, Mitchell C.	28	3	5	2	111,905
Polanco, Marcelo	91	7	15	17	525,868	Pregman, Jr., John S.	87	11	10	9	592,636
Polese, Ralph	20	2	0	0	56,194	Prejean, Norris	30	2	0	3	16,643
Polichena, Anthony J.	156	18	13	12	234,161	Prejean, Raymond	35	2	2	4	18,046
Polichena, Russell	112	2	3	10	48,231	Premus, Ed	3	0	0	0	193
Polillio, Frank	6	0	0	1	3,360	Prendergast, Kevin	1	0	0	0	0
Politano, Ralph J.	66	6	12	8	66,551	Prescott, Calcy Lee	27	2	0	5	18,314
Polito, Nancy	84	13	14	8	54,786	Prescott, Calvin	79	6	10	4	93,717
Poliziani, Daniel J.	169	12	21	18	237,479	Prescott, Sir Mark	1	0	1	0	100,000
Polk, Charlie	2	0	1	0	344	Preston, Dwight	34	1	4	3	9,956
Pollara, Frank L.	143	14	19	17	240,898	Preston, Michelle	5	1	0	0	5,354
Pollard, Stephen N.	5	0	0	0	1,918	Preston, Patrick K.	8	0	1	0	1,564
Pollock, Bruce M.	37	6	3	10	345,725	Preston, Randy L.	9	0	2	2	9,002
Pollok, Leroy J.	7	0	0	0	0	Preston, Stephanie	5	0	0	1	1,851
Polsinelli, Dominic J.	41	3	5	2	90,848	Pretty Weasel, Leon S.	2	0	0	0	161
Polsinello, Anthony F.	7	0	1	2	7,160	Prewett, Miranda L.	2	0	1	0	1,730
Poluch, Jr., Patrick J.	25	5	3	1	48,823	Pribble, William J.	2	0	0	0	399
Pompay, Teresa M.	256	29	43	35	851,740	Price, Angela	12	2	1	1	27,012
Pomposelli, William R.	21	3	1	1	44,527	Price, Barry R.	10	0	0	0	229
Ponte, Heather	9	0	2	2	4,216	Price, Chuck	3	1	0	0	1,190
Ponthieux, Gary	20	1	1	1	10,115	Price, Faith A.	14	1	1	0	3,789
Poole, Jami C.	214	20	28	20	264,932	Price, Ira	14	1	0	3	3,442
Poole, Jeffrey A.	2	0	0	0	275	Price, Kathleen A.	10	1	2	1	26,369
Poole, Jr., Jack G.	65	6	8	10	96,113	Price, Paul	60	2	4	8	29,641
Poole, Sr., Jack G.	112	5	11	14	153,769	Price, Twilla K	27	1	0	1	9,376
Poore, Gene W.	2	0	0	0	0	Price, Valerie Lynn	17	0	0	0	579
Pope, Stuart	20	1	4	4	4,325	Price, Vic	1	0	0	0	0
Pope, Sr., Robert H.	4	0	2	0	1,983	Price, Jr., Harry W.	22	1	1	0	10,995
Poper, Donald E.	38	0	1	1	6,051	Prier, Connie	1	0	0	0	40

Trainer	Sts	1st	2d	3d	Purses	Trainer	Sts	1st	2d	3d	Purses
Primiano, Judy	1	0	1	0	8,500	Rak, Kevin	12	2	1	1	3,652
Primrose, Valerie	6	1	0	0	3,499	Rakers, Steffanie	76	10	11	8	85,227
Pringle, Edmund	51	1	5	4	55,870	Raley, R. Scott	34	6	10	7	16,120
Pringle, Ned Wilkerson	20	1	1	2	2,226	Raley, Ronald E.	22	5	1	3	8,382
Pritchard, Virgil C.	28	1	1	3	8,168	Ralph, Darcy	13	1	0	2	7,962
Procino, Gerald	124	16	15	12	297,502	Ramey, Bob	2	0	0	0	0
Proctor, Thomas F.	138	31	28	16	863,870	Ramirez, Alfonso R.	16	0	0	3	5,306
Progno, Christopher	46	5	3	8	60,590	Ramirez, Richard	97	8	5	11	18,656
Progno, John	258	43	25	31	595,849	Ramirez, Jr., Rudy R.	1	0	0	0	0
Progno, Michael I.	55	3	1	5	28,889	Ramos, Faustino F.	339	47	33	36	864,990
Progno, Michael S.	5	1	0	0	15,572	Ramos, Jose R.	3	1	0	0	8,495
Proteau, Gail A.	20	3	0	4	55,592	Ramos, Victor	2	0	0	0	1,848
Prout, George D.	6	0	0	0	495	Rampadarat, Roopishwar	38	7	3	5	122,754
Pruce, Ellis Y.	33	2	0	2	20,401	Rampellini, Ralph	6	1	1	1	3,925
Pruett, Connie	99	6	4	9	34,727	Randall, Casey	24	2	1	3	40,400
Pruett, Paul G.	75	3	6	10	49,526	Randall, David A.	9	0	2	0	23,120
Pruitt, Jody	74	8	6	5	46,437	Randall, Noel	20	1	4	0	55,818
Pruitt, Lise	45	15	13	6	115,336	Randazzo, Teddy C.	244	17	28	39	173,449
Pruitt, Peggy E.	79	3	5	8	58,790	Randazzo, Jr., Frank C.	223	27	30	37	163,187
Pryor, Sheri B.	9	0	1	0	1,210	Randle, Robert K.	21	2	4	2	31,880
Pryor, Thomas J.	90	6	11	12	108,962	Randolph, Amy	46	1	2	5	16,595
Puckett, Dwight E.	25	3	1	2	37,470	Randolph, Frank T	19	0	3	0	5,939
Puckett, Earl J.	2	1	0	0	24,875	Ranford, Kathryn	24	3	4	3	99,107
Puertas, Jerry F.	28	1	2	6	20,187	Rangel, George	11	1	1	1	9,014
Puett, Jr., Lloyd J.	45	2	3	7	27,912	Rankin, Doreen	70	7	5	11	85,342
Puett, Sr., Lloyd J.	1	1	0	0	4,125	Rankin, Ken	2	0	0	0	84
Pugh, David	2	0	0	1	2,890	Ranno, Sheryl A.	21	1	3	2	21,850
Pugh, Ellis	10	1	1	1	3,962	Ransibrahmanakul, Vachari	13	2	0	1	13,160
Pugh, Penelope	53	3	3	8	60,512	Rao, Larry	20	3	5	1	30,420
Pugh, Peter D.	27	1	0	3	39,790	Raper, Ron	14	4	3	2	12,960
Puhich, Michael	71	8	8	11	351,960	Rarick, Todd A.	193	24	14	31	131,819
Puhl, Kim A.	11	2	3	1	8,174	Rasmussen, Peter	14	0	4	1	13,376
Puhl, Ronald W.	110	16	11	12	209,671	Rasmussen, S. Candy	3	0	1	0	6,615
Pujol, Jean B.	27	2	7	5	33,717	Rasmussen, Stig T.	3	0	0	0	0
Pulliam, Curtis L.	32	2	0	2	15,238	Raszewski, Joseph R.	75	7	5	9	97,571
Pullins, Harold	20	0	0	0	1,260	Ratcliffe, William H.	7	2	1	0	7,602
Purcell, Vicki	6	1	0	0	3,150	Rathman, Elisha	88	7	14	8	122,425
Purdy, Simon	15	2	2	4	34,670	Rathman, Michael L.	32	7	7	4	74,093
Purdy, William R.	3	0	0	0	983	Ratliff, Marlene C.	21	1	0	1	5,327
Putzier, Marvin	7	1	2	0	2,289	Rauert, Kelley	11	1	1	0	3,160
Puype, Mike	62	9	8	4	306,981	Rauf, Naseem	30	0	0	4	9,577
Quaid, Eddie	8	0	0	0	265	Raver, Nick	94	6	8	8	32,555
Qualls, Bill	2	0	0	0	78	Rawlins, Jerry	57	2	7	5	24,745
Qualls, Wayne	1	0	0	0	0	Rawson, Fred	39	3	5	6	34,280
Quanbeck, Alton H.	1	0	0	0	0	Ray, Dale V.	68	6	9	12	53,488
Quaranta, Ralph S.	79	6	13	9	124,390	Ray, Jimmy V.	104	12	6	9	65,341
Quaranta, Samuel R.	67	9	10	10	183,629	Raymond, Larry	1	0	0	0	128
Quartier, Joseph A.	1	0	0	0	0	Raymond, Lyn L.	12	1	2	0	15,457
Query, Marysue	8	0	0	0	1,330	Raymond, Robert A.	318	48	40	45	498,295
Quesnelle, Cindy	15	1	1	3	9,763	Razo, Alfonso	1	0	0	0	0
Quick, Patrick J.	63	4	5	12	197,709	Razo, Eusebio	196	20	24	34	325,569
Quiles, John N.	47	1	3	1	51,833	Rea, Michael	65	7	9	7	70,483
Quinn, Alonzo	15	3	0	0	8,879	Read, Randall R.	5	0	0	0	200
Quinn, Jerry	43	2	6	3	57,550	Reading, John F.	182	18	25	25	143,272
Quintanilla, Jr., Armando	15	3	1	1	42,065	Reagan, Jeffrey W.	9	0	1	2	5,948
Quintanilla, Sr., Armando	10	1	0	0	10,404	Reagan, Norman G.	45	0	2	1	8,994
Quintero, Felipe A.	3	0	1	0	1,957	Reavis, Michael L.	475	100	73	69	1,675,106
Quirk, Paul E.	11	0	0	1	1,775	Redden, James	10	0	0	2	780
Quiroga, Alex	20	2	0	2	3,152	Redding, Robin L.	74	4	3	5	36,250
Quiroga, Jose E.	18	2	1	1	26,540	Rednour, Jr., John	13	0	0	4	5,670
Racanelli, Mark Joseph	70	4	3	8	47,920	Redwood, Michael	10	1	0	2	18,235
Racca, Curley	25	6	4	4	66,221	Reece, Joyce	7	0	0	0	1,260
Radcliff, Jr., Donald L.	55	5	7	5	44,175	Reed, Cynthia L.	29	3	2	5	41,080
Radford, Kathryn I.	46	4	4	6	27,408	Reed, David E.	11	0	0	2	4,012
Radis, Judy	8	0	0	1	1,581	Reed, Delores J.	25	0	6	3	11,047
Radosevich, Jake S.	447	66	72	59	520,967	Reed, Eric R.	138	27	22	21	472,253
Radosevich, Jeffrey A.	469	75	72	56	731,442	Reed, Gene A.	18	1	2	0	27,832
Radosevich, Joseph L.	54	8	7	6	122,519	Reed, Larry M.	2	0	0	0	0
Radosevich, Shelly R.	6	0	0	1	1,896	Reed, Larry R.	39	2	7	10	48,879
Radul, Jodie	32	0	3	2	7,366	Reed, Marvin	16	3	2	2	16,807
Radulski, Susan	51	5	9	8	36,053	Reed, Philip E.	60	2	3	4	15,338
Rafaeli, Uri	7	0	1	1	7,520	Reed, Ralph E.	5	0	0	0	840
Ragain, Russell B.	13	0	0	2	6,276	Reed, Rodney	2	0	0	0	73
Ragan, Billy H.	1	0	0	0	0	Reed, Tom	1	0	0	0	0
Rahaim, Michael J.	9	0	3	0	7,140	Reeder, Donald S.	433	79	69	52	1,047,158
Raia II, Francis	79	6	9	7	43,542	Reedy, Elizabeth M.	2	0	0	1	671

Trainer	Sts	1st	2d	3d	Purses	Trainer	Sts	1st	2d	3d	Purses
Reedy, Vincent W.	36	5	3	2	37,056	Richards, Jerry Lee	28	2	4	7	60,324
Reedy, III, Chester E.	15	1	2	2	12,067	Richards, Lorne	70	12	9	14	648,262
Reese, Cynthia G.	77	16	14	6	323,882	Richards, Rodney T.	3	0	0	0	75
Reese, Darlene E.	54	5	8	8	59,457	Richardson, Deborah D.	3	0	0	0	35
Reese, Walter C.	18	7	5	3	77,502	Richardson, Donald P.	29	1	5	5	35,234
Reeves, Lloyd F.	14	0	0	4	6,265	Richardson, Susan C.	1	0	0	0	85
Reeves, Tommy	5	0	1	0	900	Richardson, Susan G.	1	0	0	0	82
Reffner, Tara B.	21	2	1	1	8,231	Richardson, Temple Scott	1	0	0	0	0
Regalbuto, Delores M.	4	0	0	0	0	Richardson, Toni	7	2	1	0	2,216
Regalbuto, Jr., Anthony R.	28	3	2	2	52,594	Richey, Tony J.	28	0	4	0	50,445
Regan, David	12	0	1	0	4,700	Richmond, Linda L.	5	0	0	1	1,097
Regan, Timothy	28	2	3	2	138,177	Richter, Stephanie	37	4	5	4	44,523
Regensberg, Jacob L.	2	0	0	0	173	Rickly, Stephanie	4	0	0	0	360
Register, Alison	53	8	11	8	275,449	Ridder, Karel A.	58	6	4	7	98,677
Reid, David R.	58	3	9	6	79,656	Riddle, Jackie E.	11	3	1	1	44,804
Reid, Ruth Ann	42	5	2	6	32,920	Riddle, James E.	18	3	3	1	33,000
Reid, Sally M.	7	1	0	2	2,800	Ridgeway, Elvy	6	0	0	1	836
Reid, Sylvia	50	3	5	2	42,340	Ridgway, Marlon	1	0	0	0	55
Reid, Jr., Robert E.	53	7	4	4	94,910	Ridgway, Michelle J.	3	0	0	0	0
Reidhead, B. Odell	47	10	11	6	16,621	Riecken, Bruce L.	93	5	18	7	123,430
Reiff, Eugene	13	1	1	3	33,210	Riecken, Herb	165	14	21	24	162,656
Reightler, Sr., Jeffery C.	80	3	5	11	55,020	Riecken, Keith	20	1	1	3	6,515
Reihart, Gary D.	20	3	2	5	78,934	Riegler, Patricia	82	11	8	6	120,430
Reilly, Joseph	40	1	0	1	12,362	Riesenbeck, Robin	3	1	0	0	5,848
Reinacher, Jr., Robert J.	34	4	3	4	137,765	Rieser, Raymond	62	4	5	7	23,767
Reinholtz, Theodore	30	1	1	5	22,182	Rife, Philip	39	1	2	6	28,507
Reinstedler, Anthony L.	190	34	25	17	1,741,618	Riffle, Roberta N.	4	0	0	0	0
Reiste, Tim F.	11	2	2	0	18,074	Riffle, Ronald J.	39	1	6	0	27,572
Renfro, Ben A.	10	0	1	1	4,431	Rigattieri, John	305	47	48	31	552,606
Renfroe, Lillian	22	0	1	3	4,759	Rigby, Terrence	16	1	2	0	44,976
Rengstorf, Tony	111	7	11	13	109,261	Riggleman, Jr., Ray	29	2	5	3	53,071
Renken, Dale S.	1	0	0	0	165	Riggs, Conrad E.	1	0	0	0	50
Renn, Carol	18	2	4	2	40,845	Riggs, Ronnie L.	33	2	3	5	15,305
Rennekamp, Nick	32	2	5	8	32,612	Riggs, Jr., Clifford A.	34	1	2	6	19,251
Retamoza, Jr, Ernest P.	3	0	1	0	1,701	Rigney, Susan	1	0	0	1	840
Retamoza, Sr., Ernest P.	29	2	2	2	51,905	Rijos, Julio	4	0	2	1	6,070
Rettele, Carol	1	0	0	0	400	Riley, Barbara	69	6	7	9	64,568
Rettele, Richard R.	303	39	56	38	371,825	Riley, Marcia	37	1	3	3	7,580
Reuer, Sharlene	14	1	3	2	4,470	Rinaldo, Sal	23	3	0	6	14,120
Reveglia, Brenda	1	0	0	0	786	Rindahl, James Eric	6	1	1	0	1,539
Revell, James E.	1	0	0	0	185	Ring, Robert D.	33	4	2	9	19,162
Reyes, Raul	13	1	0	4	17,016	Ringfield, Arthur K.	2	0	0	0	211
Reyes, III, Aurelio	31	2	1	3	15,052	Ringhoff, Robert	116	14	14	18	133,335
Reyes-Frisby, Pedro	1	0	0	0	0	Rini, Anthony F.	166	27	24	23	241,954
Reynolds, Joan A	57	12	8	4	107,888	Rios, Juan	4	0	0	2	5,210
Reynolds, Kerry L.	10	0	0	2	666	Rippee, Tommy Gene	7	1	2	0	4,494
Reynolds, Kevin	1	0	0	0	0	Rising, Bob	92	5	6	6	29,204
Reynolds, Patrick L.	217	38	30	32	1,694,627	Rissi, Luiz	83	12	12	13	72,394
Reynolds, Rod	1	0	0	0	350	Ritchey, Timothy F.	405	79	60	72	2,388,246
Reynolds, Ryan	43	4	3	4	44,065	Ritchie, Kelly D.	44	6	11	3	94,185
Reynolds, Stephanni	2	0	0	0	92	Ritchie, Robert G.	29	1	3	3	22,085
Rheinford, Mark	22	3	1	1	23,620	Ritchie, Wanda	31	2	4	1	13,295
Rhine, Vannessia	2	0	0	0	0	Ritschard, Troy	23	0	1	3	7,580
Rhodes, Les	88	3	4	8	23,413	Ritter, Jack	41	1	0	0	3,740
Rhodes, Patrick	3	0	2	0	3,114	Ritter, Randy	7	0	0	0	66
Rhodes, Willys W.	61	6	7	8	64,732	Ritvo, Kathy P.	36	6	3	6	66,445
Rhone, Bernell B.	301	52	34	35	517,735	Ritvo, Timothy	533	71	72	64	1,329,337
Ribaudo, Robert	63	9	5	6	346,827	Rivas, Judith A.	4	0	0	0	730
Riccardi, John	9	3	1	0	24,960	Rivelli, Larry	238	49	31	26	692,808
Ricciardi, Archie	76	5	6	6	57,134	Rivera, Armando	3	0	0	0	2,902
Rice, Annette	3	0	0	0	340	Rivera, Gilberto R.	145	9	9	17	89,552
Rice, Anthony	13	2	2	2	34,065	Rivera, Gregorio P.	69	7	10	6	58,886
Rice, Carol A.	57	5	4	2	60,447	Rivera, Gregorio Q.	30	0	0	0	992
Rice, Clyde D.	1	1	0	0	8,060	Rivera, Juan R.	6	0	1	2	4,325
Rice, Craig	111	11	13	13	68,606	Rivera, Miguel A.	105	7	16	13	163,260
Rice, Don R.	241	43	44	31	640,577	Rivera, Osvaldo	11	2	0	1	8,560
Rice, Gregory A.	4	1	0	0	4,441	Rivera, Robert A.	45	4	0	3	31,183
Rice, Howard	43	5	10	5	83,135	Rivera, Susan	4	0	0	0	405
Rice, J. Timothy	1	0	0	0	248	Rivera, Tirso	9	0	0	2	4,382
Rice, Jeffrey B.	3	0	0	0	0	Rivers, Woodrow V.	9	1	0	1	16,315
Rice, Julia Ballard	15	2	1	1	34,712	Riviere, Ray	4	0	0	0	270
Rice, Linda	352	51	53	52	1,818,043	Riviezzo, Ralph R.	225	23	29	20	257,458
Richard, Earnest	31	4	5	9	54,318	Rizo, Juan P.	31	1	2	1	57,739
Richard, Russell C	4	0	0	0	720	Rizo, Tony	2	0	0	0	100
Richard, Terry L.	4	0	0	0	179	Rizzi, Joseph	1	0	0	0	560
Richards, Corale A.	298	34	31	34	735,361	Rizzo, Ella	28	4	3	2	36,106

RECORDS OF TRAINERS

Trainer	Sts	1st	2d	3d	Purses
Rizzo, Eve M.	3	0	1	0	2,120
Roadcap, Jerry E.	59	11	3	5	156,300
Roarty, Jim	13	1	1	2	12,509
Robb, John J.	430	72	71	53	1,686,593
Robb, Lawrence M	51	2	4	7	29,058
Robbins, Carlton	16	0	3	2	6,182
Robbins, Charles R.	66	6	11	6	106,269
Robbins, H. Ray	1	0	0	1	1,764
Robbins, Jay M.	62	3	8	10	264,134
Robbins, Mark A.	10	0	0	1	2,466
Robbins, Richard	6	3	2	0	25,255
Roberson, Denis W.	26	3	3	5	49,862
Roberson, Don	362	49	61	42	718,510
Roberson, Kevin K.	69	5	5	6	28,555
Robert, Maryanne	58	4	5	10	45,659
Roberts, Brian M.	188	33	31	27	199,916
Roberts, Craig	95	8	16	10	136,406
Roberts, Donald	5	0	1	0	7,260
Roberts, Garry	154	7	16	10	26,953
Roberts, Kenneth L.	1	0	0	0	252
Roberts, Leon	34	2	3	4	15,914
Roberts, Robert W.	94	14	17	11	65,592
Roberts, Roy	3	0	0	0	0
Roberts, Scott Lynn	43	0	2	3	5,579
Roberts, Sharon	68	0	2	4	21,041
Roberts, Stanley W.	640	90	82	85	1,489,610
Roberts, T. Mark	4	2	0	0	20,450
Roberts, Tom C.	22	3	6	2	40,238
Roberts, Wilbert	1	0	0	0	405
Roberts, Jr., J. Doyal	5	0	0	0	842
Roberts, Jr., Wilfred	14	1	2	2	9,665
Robertson, Craig W.	107	13	20	17	173,496
Robertson, David W.	23	0	4	2	11,111
Robertson, Elizabeth L.	2	1	0	0	20,600
Robertson, Hugh H.	412	81	64	55	1,645,507
Robertson, Jack	105	15	15	14	185,294
Robertson, Jerri R.	96	17	18	14	157,464
Robertson, Marie	9	1	2	0	9,146
Robertson, Robert M.	17	1	2	4	25,869
Robideaux, Jr., Larry	251	44	39	35	1,118,345
Robillard, Joshua	363	28	42	37	435,035
Robin, Manuel	42	3	5	13	42,288
Robinson, Catherine H.	81	19	16	9	245,780
Robinson, Gayle M.	13	0	0	1	2,154
Robinson, Gerald E.	44	8	4	4	15,783
Robinson, Kelly	2	0	0	0	810
Robinson, Michael R.	12	1	1	3	13,764
Robinson, Owen L.	5	2	1	0	22,884
Robinson, Richard L.	4	0	1	1	2,320
Robinson, Rick K.	7	0	2	0	3,367
Robles, Leonso	20	3	1	6	13,568
Robson, Christopher B.	9	0	0	0	8,160
Rocco, Annie M.	19	0	0	1	3,781
Rocha, Pedro	5	0	0	0	279
Roche, Cathy E.	2	0	0	0	0
Roche, John Mario	4	0	0	1	2,325
Rodak, Geraldine	263	20	24	33	127,030
Rodak, Ronald	2	0	0	1	425
Roden, Ralph	9	2	1	0	10,396
Rodgers, Cindy	42	12	6	4	53,832
Rodgers, Paula	39	4	8	5	36,162
Rodriguez, Angel L.	2	0	0	0	450
Rodriguez, Armando	16	0	0	2	2,001
Rodriguez, Franklin	12	1	3	1	8,104
Rodriguez, Jennifer	1	0	0	0	0
Rodriguez, John M.	214	21	31	29	296,252
Rodriguez, Mario R.	132	9	8	14	78,349
Rodriguez, Rudy G.	44	3	7	5	10,902
Rodriguez, Santiago C.	144	17	19	14	128,244
Roe, Larry	69	8	5	17	93,919
Roe, Loraine M.	8	0	0	0	998
Roe, Robert W.	57	9	11	8	41,509
Roesener, Thomas E.	2	1	0	0	3,240

Trainer	Sts	1st	2d	3d	Purses
Rofe, Jean L.	42	3	2	2	36,424
Rogers, Allen E.	49	6	6	5	70,643
Rogers, Arlin R.	24	0	0	0	2,164
Rogers, Elizabeth M.	48	1	4	6	48,754
Rogers, Gary	172	8	17	14	100,270
Rogers, J. Michael	210	21	27	32	573,460
Rogers, Jeff	14	0	0	3	2,581
Rogers, Maurice S.	25	1	0	2	17,782
Rogers, Ronald W.	23	1	2	2	12,467
Rogers, Jr., Ernest	23	4	0	2	41,286
Rohaut, Francois	2	0	0	0	9,000
Rohman, Robert	95	17	7	12	201,498
Rohner, James	147	20	15	23	234,443
Rohnke, Gustave C.	15	0	0	0	360
Rojero, Luis C.	11	2	0	2	32,828
Rolffs, Marianne L.	11	1	1	1	5,257
Rolffs, Mikhael	11	1	2	2	7,541
Rolla, Lawrence	29	2	6	1	64,770
Rolle, Elliston C.	25	1	2	0	15,625
Rollheiser, Don	3	0	0	0	0
Rollins, Bradley L.	17	2	3	2	13,914
Rollins, Lyman H.	67	10	12	9	99,117
Rollins, Nicole M.	30	3	3	3	15,555
Rolon, Ezequiel M.	62	10	8	11	119,995
Romano, Raymond	6	0	0	1	4,014
Romano, Richard J.	5	0	0	0	0
Romans, Dale L.	638	113	98	71	3,987,852
Rombis, Debra E.	184	12	32	20	423,244
Romeka, Steven	77	12	13	6	132,743
Romero, Adalberto G.	14	2	3	1	5,037
Romero, Blaine	22	1	2	0	33,740
Romero, Dub D.	3	0	0	0	550
Romero, Edward J.	4	0	0	0	263
Romero, Gerald J.	155	29	19	26	399,212
Romero, Harold Lee	15	2	2	2	18,993
Romero, Jorge E.	31	1	2	0	18,235
Romero, Joseph M.	96	13	11	2	136,374
Romero, Lloyd J.	73	11	5	8	184,242
Romero, Markel D.	77	7	6	7	65,713
Romero, Terry M.	255	20	27	21	246,240
Romero, Sr., John J.	31	2	1	1	42,120
Romero, Sr., Lynn J.	11	0	1	0	1,050
Romine, Jr., Robert	17	0	0	3	4,104
Romney, Bob	1	0	1	0	361
Roncone, Peter	31	3	5	4	41,785
Ronen, Assaf	13	0	3	1	37,130
Ronquillo, Ramon	23	2	1	2	39,927
Ronquillo, Roy V.	14	3	6	1	10,159
Rooney, Ronald G.	42	2	2	5	41,309
Roos, Barry D.	62	4	5	9	44,424
Root, Ben	92	17	17	4	73,856
Root, Heidi	32	0	2	0	10,465
Root, Margaret	56	11	11	6	53,276
Root, Richard R.	126	14	11	17	337,460
Ropar, Theresa	4	1	1	0	2,392
Ropp, Donald	23	5	1	3	34,184
Rorie, Joe D.	12	1	1	3	3,290
Rosado, Juan R.	104	11	22	10	97,471
Rosado, Vicki	33	3	3	4	40,700
Rosales, Richard	10	1	0	2	9,982
Rosas-Canessa, Walter	83	3	8	13	176,499
Rose, Barry R.	98	16	15	9	199,225
Rose, Billy	12	0	0	1	748
Rose, David J.	281	33	42	29	423,931
Rose, Donald E.	22	1	0	5	7,210
Rose, Harold J.	145	10	15	13	199,378
Rose, Michael	11	0	0	0	802
Rose, Paul K.	5	0	0	0	1,800
Rose, Ralph T.	12	1	0	0	10,524
Rose, Robert J.	12	1	1	0	16,882
Rosenbaum, Bruce	1	0	0	0	0
Rosenthal, Henry J.	49	2	3	3	19,998
Rosenwasser, Laurie	71	6	8	8	36,265

Trainer	Sts	1st	2d	3d	Purses
Roset, Olaf	15	2	2	1	40,498
Rosier, Charlie	33	0	4	2	21,899
Rosier, Laura	1	0	0	0	0
Rosier, Timothy	9	0	0	0	4,920
Ross, Jill	58	4	2	5	47,752
Ross, Jim	31	5	6	3	7,244
Ross, John A.	142	18	23	25	1,437,072
Ross, Larry D.	97	11	10	16	390,747
Ross, Pam R.	14	1	3	1	7,531
Ross, Patti	61	7	8	8	90,960
Ross, Sharon	233	36	40	30	360,180
Rossi, Albino A.	40	3	5	4	76,195
Rotella, Domenico	10	0	0	0	2,875
Roth, Jack	5	0	0	1	930
Rottweiler, Glen P.	53	5	10	6	49,558
Roubion, Steve	9	0	0	1	1,446
Rouck, Martin L.	43	4	5	2	84,057
Rougeau, Abrin	41	1	2	4	22,001
Roughton, Robert L.	68	13	8	5	51,655
Rounseville, Frenda D.	17	3	0	0	31,329
Rountree, Cathy	54	5	6	5	75,545
Rouse, Randolph D.	19	1	1	1	7,836
Roush, Chuck	50	4	2	5	26,722
Roussel, III, Louie J.	124	27	14	18	669,843
Rowan, Dana	2	0	0	0	202
Rowan, Steve E.	166	13	17	18	220,282
Rowda, Aldo G.	45	5	5	4	27,379
Rowe, Donn A.	108	26	14	19	271,134
Rowe, Edward E.	17	3	0	3	24,077
Rowe, Sarah L.	22	0	1	1	6,568
Rowland, Paul A.	6	1	2	1	58,186
Rowland, Tamela M.	123	24	24	13	188,447
Rowntree, Gil H.	30	3	3	3	172,535
Roybal, Gary	7	1	0	0	6,064
Royster, Jr., Archie	22	0	0	0	2,146
Rozanski, Cathleen	7	0	0	1	2,135
Rozell, Ron	15	0	0	0	819
Rubchinuk, Robert	77	6	8	7	55,336
Ruberto, Jr., Louis V.	69	10	12	10	186,911
Rubin, Donald	6	0	0	0	3,360
Rudibaugh, Terry	52	1	0	1	15,578
Rudis, Charles A.	80	7	3	10	46,984
Rudolph, Sherry K.	10	1	1	2	12,540
Ruehr, Jeff	39	2	3	1	22,237
Ruffu, Gail E.	2	0	0	0	225
Rugar, Joseph	13	1	3	1	15,860
Ruhsam, Joey	109	16	11	8	263,813
Ruiz, Edward R.	4	1	0	1	14,650
Ruiz, Manuel A.	3	0	0	0	165
Ruiz, Jr., Rudy G.	15	1	2	0	6,823
Rumsey, Jack	9	1	0	0	4,758
Runco, Jeff C.	649	118	112	90	1,585,486
Runyon, David P.	33	6	2	9	24,388
Rupert, John	244	21	32	38	178,726
Ruppelius, Lisa	20	1	2	2	45,450
Ruppert, Gerard	1	0	0	0	80
Rushton, Stacey	12	1	1	2	6,117
Rushton, Temple D.	294	20	32	33	164,898
Russek, Ann	1	0	0	0	0
Russell, James F.	5	0	0	0	300
Russell, Monica	4	0	0	1	936
Russell, Randall R.	380	63	46	47	449,401
Russell, Roy	28	2	6	3	73,126
Russo, Frank J.	46	2	4	4	22,529
Russo, Joseph F.	3	0	0	0	774
Russo, Robert Dello	31	1	0	0	20,341
Russo, Sal	82	7	9	13	282,451
Russo, Scott	146	27	25	17	198,562
Russo, Settimo	89	5	4	6	61,442
Rust, Blake	65	7	11	7	68,865
Rust, Terri	4	0	0	2	2,037
Ruther, Clarence E.	2	0	0	0	0
Rutherford, Eddie H.	16	1	1	0	1,907
Rutherford, Ella Mae	83	10	12	14	111,276
Rutherford, Lyndel G.	63	5	8	9	12,834
Rutland, Jeffrey T.	51	7	5	5	69,731
Ryan, Anthony J.	49	3	4	5	37,206
Ryan, Chris A.	43	1	5	3	37,265
Ryan, Derek S.	204	25	29	29	483,124
Ryan, Lawrence B.	28	0	2	3	4,951
Ryan, Patricia B.	16	3	4	1	23,700
Ryan, Thomas J.	14	0	1	0	2,673
Ryan, Thomas V.	1	0	0	0	66
Rycroft, Carla	12	1	5	2	12,075
Rycroft, Delbert	6	0	1	2	3,674
Rycroft, Kelly D.	32	3	5	2	32,631
Rycroft, Riley	60	11	9	8	203,032
Rycroft, Tom	34	5	4	11	15,140
Rydowski, Steven	33	2	2	8	51,345
Ryerson, James T.	201	36	25	23	827,871
Ryno, Robert N.	32	0	2	9	13,136
Saavedra, Anthony K.	41	4	2	5	116,452
Sabine, Michael T.	9	0	0	0	2,370
Saccardo, George A.	100	12	18	8	191,587
Sacco, Gregory D.	124	10	19	12	258,240
Sacco, Richard W.	14	1	1	2	15,630
Saccocia, Jr., Gary	2	0	0	0	496
Saccocia, Sr., Gary	1	0	0	0	186
Sackett, Betsi	30	2	1	7	14,862
Sadler, John W.	375	71	56	59	2,782,405
Sadler, Ronald H.	13	1	3	4	81,434
Saenz, Jr., Octavio	1	0	0	0	0
Saffel, John	79	4	5	6	56,571
Sahadi, Jenine	155	22	20	16	1,200,976
Sailor, Christian L.	14	0	1	6	4,399
Saip, Jack	8	0	0	0	6,200
Saitz, Garry	34	2	1	1	32,382
Saland, Richard	10	0	2	0	23,071
Salazar, Anthony	12	0	0	0	1,812
Salazar, Marco P.	49	3	12	2	96,840
Salcedo, Ramon	131	8	6	15	82,642
Saldana, Ricardo	19	2	2	3	4,173
Sale, Luigi	1	0	0	0	100
Salih, Ahmad	26	4	5	1	100,990
Salim, Adel D.	48	7	8	5	77,614
Salinas, Angel C.	335	52	52	39	898,313
Salinas, Jose	129	8	14	13	63,362
Salisbury, Duane	15	0	0	4	3,700
Salisbury, Joyce	25	4	6	2	40,424
Sally, Greg	17	2	3	3	30,906
Salmen, Jr., Peter W.	82	8	11	5	149,972
Salmon, Ron	1	0	0	0	57
Salter, Rick	27	0	2	5	16,343
Salvaggio, Jr., Michael W.	191	39	50	31	403,620
Salvato, John A.	71	7	13	7	65,232
Salvato, Larry	47	5	6	8	37,322
Salvino, Neal	17	2	2	2	34,895
Salvino, Roger J.	37	5	4	6	112,940
Salzman, Robert J.	16	0	1	3	14,362
Salzman, Timothy	1	1	0	0	7,125
Salzman, Sr., John E.	371	54	52	67	1,322,984
Sam, Thomas W.	154	19	19	21	314,087
Samaniego, Beatrice D.	11	0	1	5	12,919
Samaniego, Jose I.	13	3	1	4	55,092
Sammons, Ricky Dale	7	2	0	1	11,055
Sammut, Charles J.	99	5	12	18	152,022
Sampia, Gerald A.	7	0	0	0	1,230
Sams, William D.	41	2	5	4	34,873
Samulak, Julia A.	10	0	0	0	1,693
Sanchez, Adrian	57	5	7	5	58,424
Sanchez, Albert	2	0	0	0	570
Sanchez, Alejandro E.	3	1	0	0	2,385
Sanchez, Andy H.	36	0	2	2	11,010
Sanchez, Francisco	3	0	1	0	1,946
Sanchez, Osvaldo	33	1	2	5	24,828
Sanchez, Patrick L.	9	1	2	1	14,510

Trainer	Sts	1st	2d	3d	Purses
Sanchez, Raul	6	0	0	1	2,830
Sanchez-Pinero, Angel	23	1	0	2	7,950
Sandberg, Terry	5	0	0	0	70
Sander, Terri	2	0	0	0	106
Sanders, Brent	238	23	33	33	119,316
Sanders, Cindy	57	4	3	4	20,524
Sanders, Gregg A.	26	2	3	3	12,034
Sanders, Lewis L.	3	0	0	0	0
Sanders, M. Larry	71	12	5	8	104,695
Sanders, Marvin L.	13	2	1	1	25,572
Sanders, Melinda K.	65	2	4	5	36,469
Sanders, Nevin	16	0	2	3	6,335
Sanders, Richard A.	26	2	3	1	34,040
Sanderson, Garnet	29	6	7	5	12,239
Sanderson, Richard H.	5	0	1	1	8,607
Sanderson, Robert D.	69	2	5	6	31,831
Sanderson, Jr., Luther E.	25	1	1	1	9,453
Sandoval, Gaston D.	91	2	12	13	104,524
Sandoval, Jonna D.	5	1	0	0	4,979
Sandrowski, Gene J.	13	0	1	1	2,838
Sands, Barry E.	7	0	0	0	0
Sanelli, John A.	13	2	2	1	33,560
Sanner, Daniel E.	2	0	0	0	76
Sano, Merle	12	0	0	0	1,136
Santeramo, Thomas	3	0	0	0	250
Santillo, Thomas F.	37	1	2	3	24,872
Santmyer, Ron E.	96	14	16	11	173,696
Santucci, Gary F.	17	0	1	2	8,092
Sargent, Wayne E.	27	2	2	2	24,193
Sarmiento, Ernesto	47	5	4	4	74,093
Sarmiento, Hector	44	4	8	5	36,394
Sarson, Alisa Brooke	37	1	5	4	14,919
Saucedo, Rene	1	0	0	0	466
Sauer, Barbara J.	55	1	2	3	18,734
Saul, Beth	52	3	6	6	26,423
Saul, Heather	2	0	1	0	3,500
Saunders, Connie	4	0	2	0	2,292
Saunders, Dale L.	295	44	43	42	673,428
Saunders, Jerry	26	7	1	3	29,124
Saunders, Leslie	37	7	2	3	105,664
Sauque, Alex	23	2	1	1	42,595
Savary, David A.	24	2	2	2	10,556
Savell, Steve	10	0	0	0	1,345
Saville, Donald P.	36	4	5	6	80,451
Savina, James H.	25	0	2	3	9,925
Savoie, Sherman	77	9	12	12	175,355
Savoy, Aaron	32	1	5	6	24,568
Savoy, John David	32	4	6	0	49,457
Savoy, John M.	33	2	4	3	20,875
Savoy, Kevin	36	3	5	2	24,038
Sawyer, Donal	2	0	0	0	0
Saxer, Jr., Phil E.	10	0	2	0	9,800
Sayeed, Murad A.	1	0	0	0	0
Sayler, Ardell	230	38	34	28	320,031
Sayre, Michael R.	1	1	0	0	3,960
Sayre, Ronald D.	23	1	0	1	4,567
Scace, Lynne M.	156	27	21	13	240,546
Scanlan, John F.	120	14	17	27	437,594
Scarberry, Howard	143	13	23	25	373,922
Scarborough, Kenneth	49	5	4	5	87,600
Scarnati, Criste	2	0	0	0	0
Scarvace, Joseph	3	0	0	0	1,760
Scetta, Robert T.	44	0	1	2	8,633
Schaber, Debbie	72	2	3	10	40,422
Schaefers, Larry	57	4	6	10	24,810
Schaffrick, Dale	19	2	4	0	7,045
Scheff, Olan S.	2	0	0	0	0
Scheffer, Denis	27	4	3	5	180,073
Schembri, Albert	18	2	5	4	121,412
Schenk, Kathy	41	7	9	4	140,344
Schepis, Raymond J.	3	0	0	0	335
Scher, Carol	1	0	0	0	0
Scherbenske, Elery H.	25	2	0	1	21,244
Scherbenske, Percy E.	127	14	10	8	198,158
Scherer, Merrill R.	213	35	36	25	774,148
Scherer, Richard R.	272	31	44	35	742,063
Schettino, Dominick A.	146	11	23	20	434,328
Schexnider, Raymond	16	1	0	0	7,359
Schiano-Dicola, Raimondo	204	23	25	21	376,821
Schiemann, Shana A.	1	0	0	0	0
Schiergen, Peter	4	1	1	0	239,180
Schiesel, Leonard	29	2	5	3	8,040
Schiewe, Paul	31	2	4	3	33,170
Schindler, Jeff	54	5	7	7	24,022
Schlarbaum, Max	2	0	0	0	0
Schlender, Fred	15	2	1	2	7,166
Schlesinger, Renee A.	22	8	5	0	95,244
Schlich, Joseph P.	29	7	1	6	57,235
Schling, Brian L.	5	0	0	0	234
Schmidli, Ted M.	26	2	0	5	7,521
Schmidt, David S.	157	22	26	28	397,774
Schmidt, Denise	78	15	12	8	197,084
Schmidt, John R.	8	0	0	0	488
Schmidt, Robert D.	5	2	0	2	12,712
Schmidt, Stan	15	1	3	3	5,540
Schmitt, Bill C.	21	3	1	3	6,696
Schmitt, John H.	12	1	1	2	1,800
Schneider, Bill	1	0	0	0	0
Schneider, Charles M.	190	24	27	27	386,587
Schneider, Geoffrey L.	68	6	5	12	99,247
Schneider, Lisa	2	0	0	0	145
Schnell, Don	1	0	0	0	0
Schnitzler, Rita A.	88	5	6	13	317,866
Schoenborn, Everett F.	3	0	0	0	0
Schoeneman, Jared	91	9	8	7	57,437
Schoenthal, Phil	62	11	9	6	223,124
Schoepf, Janis D.	20	4	6	3	13,483
Scholes, Sherry	3	0	0	0	0
Schooler, Fred A.	18	4	3	0	18,749
Schooley, Harold	218	11	21	27	77,526
Schooley, J. D.	21	0	3	2	8,206
Schosberg, Richard E.	187	27	27	33	1,102,228
Schrage, Joseph S.	14	4	3	2	54,815
Schriock, Bob	5	0	1	0	1,227
Schroeder, Peggy	77	4	7	7	37,286
Schroeder, Robert L.	28	2	5	4	6,511
Schu, Sally Sue	63	7	2	5	127,959
Schuetta, Regina	24	1	1	2	14,038
Schuette, Sheryl	12	0	3	2	4,941
Schuh, Tim	32	9	8	3	147,863
Schulhofer, Randy	146	23	16	18	1,326,465
Schultz, Art	9	1	0	0	5,843
Schultz, Bill	6	0	0	1	525
Schultz, Harold F.	51	5	3	4	78,486
Schultz, John C.	16	0	1	1	7,885
Schultz, Robert D.	114	22	14	13	189,891
Schulz, Roland D.	34	2	3	5	16,046
Schunk, Byron	13	1	3	2	22,131
Schuster, Chris	13	1	0	1	4,909
Schvaneveldt, Blane	27	4	8	2	33,435
Schwab, Heinz	9	0	1	1	9,935
Schwan, Emmagene K.	93	11	11	13	176,105
Schwandt, Emile	73	10	8	7	71,529
Schwartz, Herbert T.	1	1	0	0	36,000
Schwartz, Jason E.	46	5	2	9	39,831
Schwartz, Richard F.	8	3	1	1	29,492
Schwartz, Scott M.	137	17	15	17	901,823
Schwing, Terry A.	16	0	0	2	2,161
Sciacca, Gary	376	18	25	39	1,077,920
Scicchitano, James V.	28	1	0	4	10,090
Sciro, Joseph M.	20	0	0	3	4,987
Scocca, Linda K.	43	4	5	1	27,868
Scolamieri, Sam J.	28	3	4	3	94,198
Score, Robert A.	82	9	4	12	91,115
Scott, Christine D.	76	4	6	5	27,350
Scott, Jack	3	0	0	0	415

Trainer	Sts	1st	2d	3d	Purses	Trainer	Sts	1st	2d	3d	Purses
Scott, Joan	43	9	8	5	433,151	Shane, Ken	4	0	1	0	697
Scott, Kelly Lynn	31	7	2	5	103,123	Shaneybrook, Sandra L.	27	1	1	2	16,016
Scott, Lloyd L.	81	25	8	2	268,302	Shank, Robin M.	17	3	1	2	21,973
Scott, Louis E.	11	0	0	0	3,105	Shankle, Sr., Ronald E.	35	3	2	7	34,844
Scott, Ronald	138	18	19	13	144,890	Shankleton, Dennis	52	5	4	7	37,089
Scott, Russell	22	0	3	2	4,514	Shanley, Gary William	118	14	9	13	85,505
Scott, Jr, Larry D.	2	0	1	0	920	Shannon, Frank P.	179	23	30	26	313,651
Scott, Jr., Alfred H.	86	6	5	8	95,940	Shanyfelt, Douglas E.	390	45	60	51	702,298
Scramstad, Harold	42	2	5	5	23,508	Shanyfelt, Sr., William	74	5	8	6	40,001
Scramstad, Kenton	9	1	0	2	7,990	Shapoff, Alan W.	33	6	3	3	130,342
Scrimshire, Shane G.	9	0	1	0	2,677	Sharp, Lanny Z.	35	6	5	1	34,006
Scudder, Mike	104	13	14	17	41,690	Sharp, Marc J.	58	3	5	6	36,131
Scudder, Richard J.	2	0	0	0	143	Sharp, Michelle S.	22	1	1	1	25,215
Scully, P.	2	0	0	1	1,448	Sharp, Rodger	4	0	0	0	244
Seagle, Stan	45	3	6	4	40,470	Sharpe, Gary	15	3	3	1	6,322
Sears, Leon B.	17	0	5	3	33,470	Shartle, Tom	2	0	0	1	1,388
Sears, Michael	1	0	0	0	2,275	Shauf, Walter J.	16	1	1	2	8,885
Seaton, Shad	63	2	7	4	27,205	Shavelson, Pam	190	25	24	26	307,403
Sebastien, James Roy	30	2	4	6	26,742	Shaw, John	11	2	2	0	15,027
Sebastien, Tim	14	2	0	3	17,532	Shaw, Timothy J.	49	3	1	0	36,045
Sebreth, Odalie A.	8	0	0	0	1,064	Shaw, Tyrone	1	0	0	0	105
Secor, John B.	28	1	1	1	11,836	Shaw, Sr., Gerald L.	35	0	1	2	4,181
Sedillo, Carlos	227	41	20	30	578,677	Shea, Timothy H.	85	10	10	10	100,241
Sedillo, Paul	19	2	4	2	24,531	Shears, Simon	8	1	1	3	20,078
Sedillo, Tony E.	54	3	3	6	61,437	Sheena, Kamal S.	52	6	3	7	86,215
Sedlacek, Michael C.	107	4	13	17	358,708	Sheets, Jeffrey	20	1	2	3	13,869
Sedlacek, Roy	38	2	3	5	80,720	Shehorn, Debbie	3	0	0	0	0
Seeger, Robert J.	343	36	30	40	563,434	Shelansky, Richard	4	1	0	1	1,553
Seesequasis, Elmer	27	2	3	3	5,668	Sheldon, Donald	185	25	25	31	341,007
Seewald, Alan S.	187	31	27	23	634,943	Shelley, Bill	30	1	2	2	15,173
Seglin, Luis E.	26	1	1	0	31,600	Shelley, Helen	13	0	2	2	3,605
Segura, Elton	2	0	0	0	0	Shelley, Warren	6	0	0	0	1,031
Segura, Kearney	326	45	36	34	447,324	Shelton, Dan	2	0	1	0	425
Segura, Roy	47	1	2	2	11,549	Shelton, Roy R.	11	1	0	0	2,850
Seifert, Janet	24	4	3	2	25,652	Shenofsky, Ronald L.	179	35	26	32	643,951
Seitz, Elizabeth C.	10	0	0	0	511	Shenski, Shawn	4	0	0	0	651
Sellers, Mark J.	2	1	1	0	6,150	Shepard, Carol	53	4	10	8	42,462
Seltrecht, Judy	103	10	12	11	101,608	Shepherd, Gus R.	1	0	0	0	0
Selyem, Louis	23	3	1	5	20,830	Shepherd, Roxann C.	21	1	4	5	35,793
Semer, John R.	324	40	42	30	579,097	Shepherd, Shannon M	45	2	7	4	50,880
Semer, Sr., Brian J.	18	0	0	0	3,092	Shepherd, Sherri L.	103	9	11	11	75,102
Semkin, Sam	6	0	0	0	2,886	Sheppard, Catherine	1	0	0	0	0
Semona, Ron	5	0	0	1	1,246	Sheppard, Jonathan E.	460	54	63	76	1,845,326
Senebald, Don	46	0	4	4	11,354	Sheppard, Kevin R.	56	4	3	10	42,376
Senegal, Clayton J.	22	1	0	1	5,113	Sheppard, Lynn W.	7	0	0	1	1,365
Senert, Richard W.	7	1	0	0	8,687	Sherer, Sandra L.	4	0	0	0	651
Sepich, Sr., Edward F.	20	2	0	2	7,384	Sherman, Art	501	113	86	76	2,129,897
Seremba, Francois J.	21	2	2	2	27,803	Sherman, Lauren	16	1	1	1	23,605
Serna, III, Julian	18	4	0	2	43,898	Sherman-Jimenez, Lauren	35	4	2	5	37,500
Serpe, Philip M.	203	21	31	24	996,232	Sherr, Michael B.	31	3	1	7	47,066
Serrano, Emileo	64	11	11	14	106,049	Sherron, Theresa	39	0	1	2	5,819
Serrano, Marcos A.	2	0	0	0	230	Sherwood, Colin G.	103	9	6	20	218,999
Servideo, Cindy	8	1	0	1	8,016	Sherwood, Dale E.	18	1	2	1	9,766
Servideo, Robert	44	4	1	4	24,834	Shetron, Phyllis	84	14	11	12	98,044
Servis, Jason	191	30	24	25	707,105	Shevy, Michael J.	8	0	0	2	10,390
Servis, John C.	325	62	58	43	1,670,665	Shidaker, Duff	12	0	0	0	1,136
Sessa, Melanie	14	1	0	1	7,350	Shields, Barbara A.	1	0	0	0	0
Settles, Holly	53	1	3	7	12,028	Shields, Thomas C.	10	1	0	2	4,303
Severin, Barbara K.	71	9	11	9	71,379	Shilling, J. Edwin	133	17	13	15	283,881
Severinsen, Allen	105	11	16	18	242,119	Shipley, C. Larry	12	1	3	2	17,261
Sevy, Brad	10	1	0	2	2,039	Shipp, Michael	6	1	1	1	4,852
Seward, Norma	1	0	1	0	2,200	Shipton, Jennifer	42	4	4	7	41,976
Seward, Richard	2	0	0	0	330	Shirk, Joann	48	5	5	10	24,013
Shabaga, Patrice	7	0	4	1	2,156	Shirley, Luthia	12	1	1	2	24,058
Shackelford, Deby J.	24	1	0	5	28,870	Shirley, Patricia K.	113	14	10	15	180,373
Shackelford, Lloyd	6	0	0	0	483	Shirota, Mitch	57	7	5	8	334,653
Shade, Dale W.	76	7	12	9	101,689	Shirreffs, John A.	163	33	18	25	2,237,892
Shade, Donald D.	4	0	0	0	1,536	Shockey, Dale E.	100	12	10	9	133,029
Shaffer, Charles E.	35	0	2	1	3,338	Shoemaker, Leonard	50	8	3	5	108,008
Shaffer, Jon T.	37	2	7	2	36,165	Shopf, Arthur G.	13	1	2	1	11,160
Shamsie, Paul	62	3	5	7	40,440	Shorkey, Patrick	51	1	1	3	4,200
Shamsie, Sr., Randy	1	0	0	0	372	Short, Billy	11	0	1	1	4,882
Shamtanis, Alex	7	0	1	0	3,630	Short, Ricky J.	91	11	17	11	129,631

Trainer	Sts	1st	2d	3d	Purses	Trainer	Sts	1st	2d	3d	Purses
Short, Tommy C.	255	22	17	34	292,821	Sipe, David L.	126	10	13	14	156,326
Shows, Kenneth	23	2	3	5	19,517	Sipes, Jerry W.	4	1	0	1	3,763
Shreve, Michael B.	2	0	0	0	0	Siravo, Florence Gemma	309	35	48	40	430,070
Shryock, John C.	56	9	13	6	70,582	Siravo, Jr., William	22	4	1	3	19,531
Shuchman, Allan	5	0	0	0	612	Sire, William M.	3	0	0	0	3,060
Shufelt, Joseph A.	13	1	2	3	10,231	Sirianni, Louis	21	1	1	1	7,251
Shuldberg, Boyd	83	10	6	7	72,064	Sirota, Keith	118	10	8	16	311,090
Shuler, Donald W.	2	0	0	0	1,380	Sirucek, David	4	0	0	1	1,420
Shulman, Sanford	93	12	13	15	628,380	Sise, Jr., Clifford W.	409	73	63	56	1,639,135
Shultz, John W.	7	0	0	0	516	Sisko, Lisa	11	0	3	2	2,300
Shumake, Ray	133	8	11	19	109,279	Sisterson, John	2	0	0	0	500
Shuman, Joseph P.	288	42	44	44	384,533	Sitsler, Virgil L.	4	0	1	0	1,637
Shuman, Mark	1,105	225	177	128	5,633,150	Skaggs, Clayton Z.	9	0	0	0	809
Shurtz, Larry	2	0	0	0	0	Skaggs, Dodson H.	50	5	4	6	62,500
Shuster, Patricia C.	25	5	5	2	55,224	Skaggs, Gregory	67	6	9	9	43,223
Sibille, Ronnie	1	0	0	0	0	Skaggs, Winston R.	22	1	1	0	7,146
Siciliano, Matthew J	11	0	2	4	3,665	Skeen, Mark V.	37	6	3	2	11,264
Siddall, Bobbi	1	0	0	0	0	Skelton, Chad T.	34	0	0	1	10,375
Sider, Alvin	89	7	16	9	175,037	Skelton, Thomas R.	7	1	0	1	7,921
Sides, Robert C.	79	3	8	9	149,577	Skiffington, Thomas J.	90	6	17	13	357,718
Sienkewicz, William M.	33	3	3	9	17,192	Skinner, Albert T.	18	6	2	1	36,113
Sierra, Cirilo M.	44	3	6	3	43,038	Skinner, Diana L.	26	5	3	5	45,541
Sigler, Ronald G.	7	2	1	1	27,244	Skinner, Elmer	1	0	0	0	112
Signore, Jr., Joseph L.	23	5	0	2	56,230	Skinner, Gary	4	0	0	1	526
Signore, Sr., Joseph L.	24	5	3	5	76,715	Skinner, Teresa M.	9	1	0	1	4,020
Signs, David	5	0	0	2	3,300	Skultin, Jeffrey M.	4	0	0	0	498
Signs, Nancy L.	32	3	6	2	28,335	Slack, James G.	11	2	0	1	7,510
Siler, Leroy	2	0	0	0	184	Slane, J. C.	1	1	0	0	1,200
Sillars, Belinda	1	0	0	1	1,000	Slang, J. R.	4	0	1	0	500
Silva, A. Clare	6	0	0	1	2,794	Slater, Ivan	23	2	4	0	10,820
Silva, Butch	4	0	0	0	840	Slater, John	2	0	1	1	896
Silva, Fernando	26	4	3	4	27,330	Slater, Lawrence	1	0	0	0	180
Silva, Juan Pablo	41	7	2	7	97,662	Sleeter, Kevin G.	101	19	11	12	566,933
Silva, Paul P.	56	8	5	5	32,145	Sliney, Patrick	7	0	1	0	1,407
Silvera, Arthur	74	4	6	14	245,330	Slisz, Daniel J.	209	20	18	24	131,043
Silvera, Laurie	147	23	23	15	1,217,366	Slivka, Sandra L.	62	5	10	9	141,410
Silvers, Darren	44	1	3	5	28,760	Sloan, Barbara	15	0	0	0	315
Simkins, Rosie	2	0	1	1	1,745	Sloan, Harry	19	0	0	4	9,172
Simmons, Charles E.	26	0	2	3	6,224	Sloan, Todd	3	0	0	0	160
Simmons, Jack R.	3	1	0	0	3,900	Slone, Charles E.	116	4	10	14	40,589
Simmons, Kasey B.	26	0	1	1	3,441	Slone, Mike	66	2	7	12	38,890
Simmons, Kory	6	2	0	0	21,668	Slot, Sonia	50	2	5	5	17,649
Simms, Charles W.	88	6	9	14	113,316	Sluder, Arlie K.	1	0	0	0	250
Simms, Debra M.	29	1	4	3	15,589	Slysz, Margaret A	7	1	1	0	9,080
Simms, Garry W.	64	6	11	7	149,737	Smalios, Margaret	6	0	0	0	2,341
Simms, John	264	43	26	38	862,904	Small, Richard W.	206	38	33	29	823,041
Simoff, Andrew L.	59	10	10	10	163,079	Smalley, Jr., Gerald	7	1	1	0	5,513
Simoff, Richard A.	14	1	2	3	11,898	Smallwood, William N.	4	0	0	2	3,050
Simoff, Stephen C.	23	1	1	1	8,370	Smart, Jonathan	13	0	1	1	7,750
Simon, Charles	194	23	21	27	843,757	Smart, Leonard	4	0	0	0	0
Simon, Ivory	5	0	0	0	270	Smellie, Vernon	21	0	2	2	11,653
Simon, Leroy	34	1	3	1	12,743	Smith, A. Pete	20	1	2	1	6,652
Simon, Linda	18	1	0	2	8,125	Smith, Andrew	16	2	1	2	55,996
Simon, Lynn M.	102	11	10	9	407,567	Smith, Angie D	18	1	3	1	21,736
Simon, Stuart C.	212	31	28	32	347,707	Smith, Antonio	2	0	0	0	165
Simone, Victor	55	4	9	3	42,045	Smith, Austin K.	118	29	15	14	487,552
Simons, Howard F.	32	3	4	4	38,657	Smith, Brent A.	11	0	0	0	1,250
Simpson, Charles	3	0	0	0	0	Smith, Candice	8	0	0	0	666
Simpson, Deborah M.	79	9	8	10	167,713	Smith, Charlene	11	1	1	0	21,582
Simpson, Gary	53	5	10	11	18,092	Smith, Charlie Joe	18	1	4	1	3,193
Simpson, Gene	16	0	0	2	4,310	Smith, Chester	15	0	0	2	3,971
Simpson, George E.	128	6	11	13	61,687	Smith, Clay M.	6	0	1	0	1,000
Simpson, Gerald R.	46	8	1	6	57,032	Smith, Clyde N.	5	0	0	0	55
Simpson, Pamela P.	81	9	11	10	127,254	Smith, Constance A.	17	0	0	0	1,400
Simpson, Patricia A.	135	6	11	12	119,950	Smith, Curvin D.	40	5	5	5	32,803
Simpson, Willoughby	41	4	3	6	78,643	Smith, Dana W.	2	0	0	1	895
Sims, Philip A.	100	12	15	12	270,922	Smith, Danny L.	93	12	10	7	47,321
Sinanovic, Richard R.	5	0	0	0	0	Smith, David S.	20	0	0	1	11,344
Sing, Antonio J.	20	3	1	1	24,850	Smith, Debbie	18	4	5	4	8,599
Singh, Satrohan N.	20	1	3	3	27,031	Smith, Dennis D.	6	1	0	0	2,567
Singletary, Robert	9	1	0	1	3,424	Smith, Don R.	91	16	6	9	48,529
Singleton, Larry A.	12	0	0	0	1,094	Smith, Donald F.	1	0	0	0	180
Sinn, Michelle M.	72	8	7	8	125,206	Smith, Donald W.	9	1	2	1	4,867

Trainer	Sts	1st	2d	3d	Purses	Trainer	Sts	1st	2d	3d	Purses
Smith, Doug R.	110	4	9	15	71,536	Smylie, Jon J.	106	10	15	16	142,359
Smith, Douglas D.	27	4	2	5	26,130	Smylie, Timothy J.	9	0	1	0	4,590
Smith, Earl D.	9	0	1	3	4,665	Snapp, Fred	24	3	2	3	11,592
Smith, Gary L.	7	0	0	0	386	Snarski, Francis P.	7	0	0	1	5,995
Smith, Hallet P.	32	6	5	1	34,793	Snatchko, Paul A.	39	1	1	5	21,743
Smith, Hamilton A.	490	73	64	81	1,528,726	Sneed, Dale	25	5	1	5	31,585
Smith, I. Henry	9	0	0	0	1,116	Snell, Billy Joe	2	0	0	0	0
Smith, James J.	78	10	9	7	614,766	Sniffen, Charles W.	11	1	1	2	7,891
Smith, Jaqueline	54	16	13	7	34,219	Snipes, Bruce	27	1	1	2	22,774
Smith, John C.	50	0	6	6	30,118	Snodgrass, John	9	0	0	0	900
Smith, John H.	12	0	3	2	5,834	Snow, Brian	44	5	10	4	72,814
Smith, John P.	27	1	0	2	8,381	Snow, Daryl	101	13	11	13	195,795
Smith, John S.	37	2	9	3	44,728	Snow, John	50	12	5	6	485,404
Smith, Joseph B.	22	2	2	2	19,565	Snow, Melvyn	148	20	20	17	264,870
Smith, Justin D.	60	2	7	3	18,665	Snyder, Floyd W.	73	8	15	6	128,520
Smith, Justine A.	22	1	2	1	12,150	Sobol, Alan	62	6	7	6	174,431
Smith, Kenneth	24	2	2	4	11,713	Socks, Terry W.	20	3	2	1	21,045
Smith, Kenneth J.	2	0	0	0	0	Soileau, Darrel	1	0	0	0	0
Smith, Kenneth R.	119	7	16	17	129,793	Soileau, Diana	49	6	4	5	90,975
Smith, Kenny P.	233	18	20	27	362,560	Soileau, J. Y.	19	2	0	1	26,572
Smith, Kimberly J.	3	0	0	0	225	Soileau, Samuel D.	25	3	2	2	114,874
Smith, Kimberly M.	37	0	4	1	27,742	Soileau, Sharon	47	0	1	3	7,769
Smith, Larry D.	83	6	4	11	62,731	Sola, Joseph L.	37	4	4	4	17,436
Smith, Larry E.	90	19	13	12	108,065	Solberg, Melanie Cornwell	12	2	2	1	5,367
Smith, Larry O.	20	3	5	2	13,750	Soliz, Jr., Carlos S.	46	5	3	5	42,811
Smith, Laurie	39	5	2	5	68,086	Solway, Melvin	3	0	0	0	228
Smith, Lavona	5	0	0	0	410	Somers, Conrad	2	0	0	0	300
Smith, Lawrence M.	55	2	4	5	28,670	Sones, Debra	33	4	3	8	122,115
Smith, Marirose	16	0	2	2	15,976	Sonnier, Gerald	39	5	8	6	59,647
Smith, Mark F.	63	1	1	10	27,981	Sonnier, James Bert	2	0	0	0	660
Smith, Mary C.	5	1	0	0	3,195	Soos, Herman	72	1	0	6	28,748
Smith, Michael R.	8	0	0	1	39,150	Sorensen, Mike	24	1	2	2	6,935
Smith, Norman H.	47	3	4	4	46,203	Sortino, Shannon	6	0	0	0	856
Smith, Paul A.	121	5	14	14	82,296	Sosa, Felipe J.	57	4	3	5	37,755
Smith, Peter G.	7	2	1	1	13,490	Sostre, Israel	93	5	9	12	52,247
Smith, Richard Louis	7	0	0	1	2,990	Soto, Antonio	141	5	12	15	84,360
Smith, Robert G.	25	1	4	3	27,673	Soto, Carlos	17	4	3	4	36,079
Smith, Robert H.	9	2	1	0	10,128	Soto, Ignacio R.	49	4	3	8	19,483
Smith, Ron K.	328	71	61	54	962,661	Soto, John	19	1	0	3	11,964
Smith, Sandy C.	7	1	1	0	12,680	Soto, Manuel	3	1	0	0	935
Smith, Sheila A	19	1	0	0	4,545	Soto, Rick G.	3	0	0	0	0
Smith, Sheryl D.	10	0	1	0	2,469	Soto, Jr., Herbert	64	5	7	12	71,903
Smith, Stanley G.	140	19	12	23	259,464	Souder, Donald E.	96	8	12	18	191,325
Smith, Steve C.	4	0	1	0	6,660	Sousares, Jr., James F.	1	0	0	0	0
Smith, Terrance	29	1	4	3	20,962	Souter, Paul	2	0	0	0	134
Smith, Thomas R.	5	1	1	0	7,776	Southard, Anne C.	67	5	3	12	60,488
Smith, Thomas Victor	81	7	11	12	378,730	Souto, Gerald A.	228	32	25	30	268,465
Smith, Tim R.	1	0	0	0	336	Sowers, Dennis T.	187	23	32	27	150,943
Smith, Tony	1	0	0	0	0	Sowers, Larry	7	0	0	1	1,265
Smith, Tracie L.	107	8	12	7	128,617	Sowle, Donald G.	2	1	0	0	5,213
Smith, Troy	45	4	4	4	27,892	Sowle, Scott	109	30	17	10	388,314
Smith, U. R.	2	0	2	0	774	Spady, Harold	39	3	11	4	53,650
Smith, Vertis E.	5	0	0	0	0	Spady, Lorne D.	15	1	4	2	7,200
Smith, Vince	1	0	0	0	315	Spagnola, Ida	64	2	12	5	87,840
Smith, W. Bret	59	11	6	3	151,370	Spanabel, Harriette	57	3	5	6	17,987
Smith, Wayne Harold	34	0	3	4	10,184	Spanu, Antonio	2	0	1	0	9,800
Smith, William J.	63	17	12	12	146,596	Sparks, Brad	45	9	3	6	79,181
Smith, William M.	2	0	0	1	2,035	Sparks, Dennis W.	3	0	0	1	9,840
Smith, William Raymond	5	0	0	0	0	Sparks, J. Clay	14	1	1	1	5,553
Smith, Jr., Alvin	3	0	0	0	0	Sparks, Jerry S.	220	32	43	38	525,016
Smith, Jr., Crompton	2	0	0	1	1,500	Sparks, Ken	5	1	2	0	2,990
Smith, Jr., Frank	48	3	2	9	43,021	Spathanas, William	11	0	1	1	7,910
Smith, Jr., Franklin G.	105	10	8	16	143,893	Spatz, Ronald B.	201	16	32	17	649,996
Smith, Jr., Jere R.	150	19	19	22	470,048	Spawr, William	297	65	47	25	1,715,806
Smith, Jr., Ralph R.	50	3	2	4	47,626	Spaziano, Joyce M.	41	3	0	4	26,407
Smith, Sr., Jere R.	279	38	36	36	731,360	Speaks, Dennis	15	0	0	1	1,518
Smither, Bruce R.	11	0	2	0	24,805	Spears, Louis T.	8	0	1	1	6,851
Smithwick, Daniel Michael	10	0	2	0	5,995	Spears, Stephen A.	107	7	16	7	111,882
Smithwick, Dorothy F.	29	1	3	1	15,225	Specht, Steven	199	33	23	29	663,272
Smithwick, Jr., Daniel Michael	83	4	7	10	120,078	Speck, Bobby C.	13	3	2	2	28,162
Smock, Lori A.	249	19	20	22	239,240	Speckert, Christopher	41	2	2	4	49,579
Smoot, James M.	3	0	0	0	0	Spence, Debbie	30	4	4	1	24,178
Smullen, Sean	31	8	3	2	260,251	Spence, James T.	88	5	8	4	122,571

Trainer	Sts	1st	2d	3d	Purses	Trainer	Sts	1st	2d	3d	Purses
Spencer, Clark	38	5	3	5	39,987	Stender, Karen E.	1	0	0	0	0
Spencer, Margaret A.	16	4	1	2	122,013	Stenslie, Chris	12	1	1	3	6,729
Spencer, Ray	62	3	6	2	34,429	Stephen, Peter	106	14	14	13	293,081
Spencer, Robin Lee	14	1	2	3	11,811	Stephens, David	17	0	1	2	7,851
Spencer, Sr., Rollen L.	4	1	0	0	1,968	Stephens, George A.	31	0	3	3	7,995
Spicer, James T.	48	2	4	3	38,109	Stephens, James A.	18	2	1	2	4,524
Spicknall, James I.	47	4	5	2	30,992	Stephens, John D.	1	0	0	0	106
Spiess, Roger D.	103	9	11	11	131,676	Stephens, Steve W.	30	2	2	1	32,675
Spiess, Shane M.	265	24	36	41	222,825	Stepp, Rochelle Lenee	2	0	0	0	130
Spieth, Nancy	2	0	0	1	600	Sterl, Kimberly	9	0	0	0	150
Spina, Chuck	84	6	10	4	144,310	Sterling, Larry J.	4	1	0	0	21,460
Spradling, Roy N.	3	0	0	0	750	Sterling, Michael E.	27	3	3	4	36,274
Spraggins, Kenneth R.	25	2	3	3	46,237	Steve, Chris	14	0	0	0	3,301
Sprague, John A.	15	3	1	1	7,970	Stevens, Frank	30	1	2	5	6,943
Spreen, Debbie	14	1	3	2	5,350	Stevens, Richard	13	1	2	0	12,800
Springer, Frank R.	114	27	11	12	660,684	Stevens, Ron	57	3	4	3	18,221
Springer, Hayden W.	1	0	0	0	456	Stevens, Wesley Royce	8	0	1	1	1,944
Springer, John	15	6	1	0	58,913	Stevens, Jr., Lowell T.	48	4	2	4	45,530
Springer, William F.	1	0	0	0	0	Stevenson, Daniel G.	21	2	3	3	79,784
Springman, Donald A.	10	0	1	1	1,976	Stevenson, Janet	2	0	1	0	7,846
Sprock, Sondra	10	0	1	0	1,300	Stevenson, Roger M.	117	18	27	13	67,848
Sprouse, Loretta	22	1	2	1	6,742	Stewart, Ann D.	7	5	1	0	98,400
Spurlock, John H.	14	0	0	1	1,977	Stewart, Cecil	83	3	10	12	133,851
Spurlock, Lee	27	3	3	3	24,023	Stewart, Chad J.	9	0	1	0	2,349
St. John, Thomas M.	26	0	0	5	3,712	Stewart, Dallas	308	49	41	38	1,855,344
St. Leon, Gene	2	0	0	0	1,930	Stewart, Daryl J.	25	1	1	3	12,951
St. Leon, Kate Francy	13	1	2	1	19,706	Stewart, Gene N.	22	1	2	0	7,534
St. Lewis, Uriah	285	11	28	23	284,452	Stewart, George	18	1	2	3	15,171
St. Louis, Clement J.	18	5	1	0	43,929	Stewart, James G.	14	1	1	2	7,443
Stabenfeldt, John	8	1	2	1	3,443	Stewart, John A.	1	0	0	0	0
Stabile, Anthony A.	7	1	1	0	43,640	Stewart, Perry B.	2	0	0	0	520
Stack, Tommy	1	0	0	1	19,250	Stewart, Thomas J.	82	2	6	7	97,261
Stackhouse, David	1	0	0	0	50	Stewart, William J.	79	3	11	16	239,460
Stackwood, Carol	6	0	0	1	1,896	Stewart, Sr., James R.	2	0	0	0	0
Stafford, Tamara	2	0	0	0	204	Sticka, Ron	49	5	7	8	120,992
Stahlin, John L.	218	23	25	24	306,679	Stickler, Jr., Lester J.	105	15	12	15	120,632
Stalhiem, Kim	16	1	0	1	7,688	Stickley, Mark	4	0	0	1	2,400
Stall, Jr., Albert M.	309	53	40	50	1,495,011	Stidham, James H.	50	2	4	5	34,472
Stamps, Dusty	12	1	1	0	2,129	Stidham, Michael	292	51	40	43	1,343,812
Standifer, H. E.	1	0	0	0	192	Stidham, Susan D.	29	1	5	1	25,471
Standridge, Steven W.	103	17	14	9	436,488	Stifano, Raymond E.	287	32	32	29	394,534
Stanford, Myrl	15	2	2	1	8,492	Stillwell, Maureen	16	0	0	0	1,380
Stanger, Kirt G.	3	0	0	0	84	Stinebaugh, John A.	21	1	0	1	10,063
Stanley, Oral	2	0	0	0	51	Stites, Flint W.	652	81	92	88	874,855
Staples, John	11	1	1	2	19,187	Stitzel, Marion	48	5	7	6	12,967
Stark, Jonathan S.	1	0	0	0	540	Stitzel, Patrick	11	0	2	1	1,650
Stark, Stacey A.	2	0	0	1	1,980	Stivers, Brian J.	18	1	2	5	11,159
Starkey, Billy F.	7	1	0	1	6,465	Stivers, Ryan	4	0	0	0	144
Starkey, Charles T.	2	0	0	0	519	Stober, David T.	38	4	3	5	24,538
Starkey, James H.	107	12	15	8	207,695	Stockwell, Buckey A.	3	1	0	0	2,259
Starks, Gilbert	6	0	0	0	1,700	Stodghill, Jonathan A.	143	8	11	10	125,850
Starks, Tecumseh	1	0	0	0	0	Stoehr, Helmut E.	12	0	2	0	16,541
Starlin, Gene	48	6	9	10	49,022	Stogner, James H.	48	1	4	4	12,587
Staroscik, Larry L.	96	7	11	12	41,106	Stohr, Lewis	8	1	2	0	5,760
Starritt, William D.	87	6	9	8	137,481	Stokalko, Carol	9	0	0	1	1,277
Statler, Valerie	6	2	0	1	15,926	Stokes, Lance	17	4	2	1	47,472
Stauffer, Sr., Arthur F.	152	9	17	18	251,667	Stokes, Lonnie	92	22	16	14	245,149
Steadman, Earl S.	40	1	1	1	14,958	Stokes, Rex	162	20	20	10	95,664
Steele, Karen E.	81	11	12	4	159,495	Stoklosa, Richard L.	75	5	6	4	216,745
Steele, Jr., Hal W.	13	1	1	1	15,678	Stolp, Roger	29	6	3	3	15,660
Steeves, Robert	7	0	0	4	6,502	Stone, Earl L.	9	0	1	0	4,831
Stehr, Hank A.	87	2	0	6	59,647	Stone, Edward H.	20	5	1	4	86,940
Stehr, Joseph P.	34	1	1	2	24,982	Stone, Jonnel	2	0	0	0	40
Stehr, Vicki L.	24	0	0	0	2,798	Stone, Jr., Charles L.	5	0	0	1	382
Stein, Roger M.	100	4	12	12	246,140	Stopherd, Edwin C	64	7	9	12	72,695
Steiner, Jack	3	0	0	1	2,317	Storlazzi, Elena A.	1	0	0	0	0
Steinmiller, Brad Jay	3	0	0	0	1,781	Storms, Phil B.	3	0	0	0	276
Steinmiller, Gordon	1	1	0	0	7,620	Storms, William	1	0	0	0	0
Stelly, Frank J.	13	1	0	1	6,862	Stortzum, Devin L.	139	7	13	13	53,130
Stelly, Jane	1	0	0	0	0	Story, Chad	23	1	2	3	4,697
Stelly, Levan	20	1	1	1	8,562	Story, Dennis B.	52	7	5	6	39,410
Stemmans, Don	44	5	5	6	81,811	Story, Kent	5	0	0	0	101
Stemmans, II, Don	17	1	0	0	4,568	Story, Shaun	4	2	0	1	1,670

Trainer	Sts	1st	2d	3d	Purses
Stotler, Gary L.	22	0	1	1	3,299
Stout, Michael R.	21	0	3	2	6,483
Stout, Robert Shane	37	2	4	2	21,717
Stoute, Sir Michael R.	2	1	0	0	553,985
Stovall, Terry W.	29	3	2	1	15,098
Stradling, Bruce	29	1	1	1	7,277
Straightnose, Calvin	25	3	5	4	25,768
Strain, Jerry	5	0	2	0	2,565
Strandquist, Calvin	7	0	2	1	2,661
Strandquist, Orville	2	0	1	0	1,155
Strange, William R.	148	15	19	15	98,489
Strawn, Ernest	4	0	0	0	70
Streeper, Doug G.	25	1	5	1	8,905
Streicher, Kenneth	41	2	7	12	184,640
Stricker, Willie	29	4	2	1	31,937
Strickland, Linnwood A.	16	0	0	0	1,792
Strickland, Marcus C.	4	0	0	0	392
Strickland, Ruddell	24	1	4	1	10,032
Striegel, Shannon	6	0	1	0	1,554
Strode, Donald D.	14	1	0	2	3,674
Strode, Ronald Eugene	3	0	0	0	410
Strong, Brian A.	10	0	0	0	4,690
Strong, Dennis E.	15	2	1	2	5,301
Stroope, Larry	18	0	1	5	16,131
Stroud, Brian	2	0	0	0	100
Stroud, Gene C.	27	0	2	5	11,539
Stroud, Richard W.	1	0	0	0	78
Strumecki, Albert	42	12	7	5	229,822
Stuart, Clinton C.	213	38	38	31	359,473
Stufflebean, Terry	11	2	0	2	20,550
Stump, Kathleen	2	0	0	0	32
Stumpf, Daniel P.	31	3	1	1	28,158
Sturgeon, Robert C.	80	3	3	14	36,354
Sturrock, Billy G.	48	8	3	2	62,131
Stute, Gary	101	14	18	13	454,570
Stute, Melvin F.	175	15	23	17	715,890
Stute, Warren	127	10	17	24	632,003
Stutts, Jr., Bennie F.	44	10	9	6	241,554
Suarez, David	3	0	0	0	595
Suarez, Jesus I.	10	1	2	1	9,788
Suarez, Sergio	7	1	2	0	16,240
Suckie, Henry	5	0	0	0	400
Suerland, Rolf	1	0	0	0	4,500
Suire, Lane P.	15	0	0	1	2,801
Sullivan, David E.	43	7	9	6	62,151
Sullivan, Donald	3	0	0	0	151
Sullivan, John	17	0	3	1	15,620
Sullivan, Les	29	2	0	0	4,619
Sullivan, Lynn	19	2	1	1	12,470
Sullivan, Mary	4	0	0	0	146
Sullivan, Michael	25	1	2	3	11,949
Sumja, Brent	235	44	40	33	779,332
Summers, Earl L.	57	0	1	2	12,918
Summers, Robert	4	1	0	0	4,161
Summers, William	8	0	0	1	1,315
Sun, Truth	30	0	1	1	2,798
Suppah, Joyce	1	0	0	0	100
Suter, Buddy L.	3	1	0	0	3,360
Suttle, Richard	2	0	0	0	0
Sutton, Philip Q.	61	9	6	5	165,451
Swan, Jean	3	0	1	1	2,172
Swan, Patrick E.	13	0	2	0	9,080
Swartz, Barry R.	36	4	4	4	60,990
Swartz, Jack	6	1	0	1	6,949
Swatuk, Barry E.	22	1	2	2	80,097
Swearingen, Thomas H.	147	16	22	23	304,749
Sweatt, Arthur T.	108	4	10	15	86,676
Sweazey, Scott	53	4	8	8	65,798
Sweeney, Ronald M.	13	3	2	1	27,869
Sweet, James	11	2	2	3	6,118
Sweitzer, Mark	2	1	0	0	2,520
Sweitzer, Randy	31	2	0	3	17,730
Swenson, Dennis	8	1	0	0	958
Swentkowski, Kimberly B.	105	10	13	15	150,474
Sweredoski, Chris	5	0	1	1	1,325
Swingley, Duane	39	2	3	5	29,222
Switzer, Daniel G.	31	6	6	1	99,325
Syed, Riaz N.	50	2	3	5	23,586
Sylvester, Suzanne	8	1	1	0	2,510
Synar, Cynthia	7	1	0	1	1,008
Synnefias, Dimitrios K.	149	26	21	8	438,815
Szafranski, Edward E.	14	0	0	0	1,320
Szeyller, Robert A.	66	11	15	11	142,047
Tabler, Greg A.	21	3	1	2	68,434
Tabor, Darold R.	6	0	2	1	18,490
Tabor, Johnny M.	51	6	5	7	44,097
Tackett, Hiram	11	1	0	0	7,675
Tackett, Samantha	10	2	2	1	4,015
Tagg, Barclay	166	16	23	24	3,542,297
Tagg, Taryn	30	1	2	0	25,625
Taglianetti, James P.	97	8	10	16	159,558
Takemori, Hugo	7	1	1	0	10,167
Talamo, Joseph	1	0	0	1	880
Talley, Jeff	21	4	2	2	61,079
Talsma, Al	14	3	0	0	18,087
Tamargo, Raymond	47	5	4	7	69,617
Tamberino, Steven M.	5	0	0	1	1,300
Tamburello, Joey	41	9	7	5	100,960
Tammaro, Michael A.	261	23	20	22	371,381
Tammaro, III, John J.	297	28	37	41	633,012
Tanner, Carolyn	47	2	3	9	38,970
Tanner, Lynda R.	218	16	34	31	112,715
Tanner, Robert	109	11	9	13	116,777
Tanory, Dan	50	9	10	6	30,350
Tanzell, Michael	7	0	0	0	910
Tapp, John Wayne	40	0	6	3	15,802
Tapscott, Carlyne	3	0	1	0	4,668
Tapscott, Jenile T.	23	1	1	2	14,887
Tarmon, Ronnie G.	15	3	1	2	27,147
Tarrant, Amy	39	1	2	6	53,455
Tassistro, Connie	30	6	6	2	107,714
Tatarniuk, Steve	32	2	1	4	5,296
Tate, Noral J.	27	2	2	5	174,577
Tate, Stephanie N.	39	6	2	6	36,281
Tatonetti, Charles A.	19	1	1	4	9,186
Tattersall, Peter D.	4	0	0	0	610
Taulbee, Mark	5	0	1	1	4,892
Taulton, Gary L.	3	0	0	0	0
Tauzin, Guy E.	90	8	13	14	116,701
Tauzin-Roe, Colleen	13	3	0	1	24,822
Taylor, Aaron	50	5	6	5	62,443
Taylor, Anthony	5	2	0	0	9,987
Taylor, Barbara	4	0	0	1	200
Taylor, Brant L.	90	17	10	9	185,663
Taylor, Brent	60	9	16	14	43,648
Taylor, Bryant R.	19	2	0	1	15,537
Taylor, D. R.	2	0	0	1	322
Taylor, Daniel A.	72	5	4	7	71,453
Taylor, David M.	37	3	8	3	28,867
Taylor, Donald	131	9	13	10	128,016
Taylor, Gene C.	29	2	2	0	22,197
Taylor, Gerald E.	5	1	2	0	12,130
Taylor, Herman R.	156	17	22	23	350,559
Taylor, Jed	4	0	0	0	104
Taylor, Jeff	6	0	0	1	1,388
Taylor, John Brookshire	12	0	0	1	884
Taylor, John F.	126	12	10	18	298,835
Taylor, Mark C.	12	2	0	0	8,928
Taylor, Mike D.	41	10	6	9	19,481
Taylor, Morris E.	17	3	3	3	35,005
Taylor, Pat	7	0	1	1	2,652
Taylor, Randall P.	61	2	6	4	31,931
Taylor, Rex	3	0	0	1	384
Taylor, Richard D.	2	0	0	0	55
Taylor, Robert J.	25	4	2	5	38,361
Taylor, Ronald E.	151	13	10	16	128,593

Trainer	Sts	1st	2d	3d	Purses	Trainer	Sts	1st	2d	3d	Purses
Taylor, Terry L.	4	0	0	0	230	Thompson, Arcott H.	17	0	0	0	1,350
Taylor, Troy	53	10	7	6	55,236	Thompson, Bill J.	11	1	2	3	40,770
Taylor, William Dewayne	38	5	4	3	33,332	Thompson, Brian	6	0	0	2	3,500
Taylor, William H.	177	13	19	21	64,529	Thompson, C. Edward	50	5	8	6	83,803
Taylor, William Michael	10	0	0	3	2,719	Thompson, Dabney S.	12	0	0	0	4,675
Taylor, Jr., C. Thomas	1	0	0	0	73	Thompson, Daniel	67	4	7	14	71,513
Taylor, Jr., Roy F.	1	0	1	0	1,240	Thompson, David Brian	14	0	1	1	6,207
Taylor, Jr., Roy Stanley	27	3	1	4	13,216	Thompson, Edward Joe	12	0	0	0	682
Teafoe, Jerry	27	2	3	7	19,622	Thompson, Glenn R.	81	8	8	6	213,958
Teal, J. L.	15	0	0	1	3,065	Thompson, Gordon	1	0	0	0	150
Teater, Louise M.	3	0	0	0	440	Thompson, J. Willard	273	16	38	41	581,378
Tebbutt, John	163	13	23	13	131,297	Thompson, James Emory	28	7	3	2	31,200
Teel, Mike R.	104	19	14	12	111,785	Thompson, Larry	3	0	1	1	2,015
Tekos, Jr., Angelo	34	4	6	8	61,467	Thompson, Mark E.	6	1	0	1	37,095
Tellez, Eddie	88	12	9	9	26,397	Thompson, Mark L.	38	4	5	3	126,365
Tenhundfeld, Ronnie G.	42	2	1	2	33,335	Thompson, Michael R.	86	12	10	12	168,095
Terpak, Evangela	7	0	1	0	8,200	Thompson, Ron	7	1	0	0	3,174
Terracciano, Neal	45	3	6	0	85,360	Thompson, Sharon	6	1	0	1	2,240
Terrace, Tara	3	0	2	0	5,103	Thompson, Steven	26	0	0	1	2,350
Terranova II, John P.	149	22	22	21	905,457	Thompson, Terri L.	40	3	3	4	60,370
Terrenzio, William	5	1	0	0	12,600	Thompson, Yvette	94	6	3	9	108,250
Terrien, Gary E.	12	2	0	3	13,032	Thompson, Jr., Harry F.	1,023	197	162	148	1,612,055
Terrill, Sr, Robert	6	3	1	0	59,780	Thomsen, Paula	12	0	0	1	1,813
Terry, Dennis L.	4	0	0	0	0	Thomson, Ronald	22	3	3	3	55,334
Terry, Rick	130	17	19	20	232,157	Thornbury, Jeffrey D.	124	18	18	15	388,568
Terry, Robert J.	38	5	5	10	27,056	Thorne, Joe	6	3	0	0	1,600
Tesher, Howard M.	102	3	10	14	251,025	Thornton, Chris	4	0	0	0	0
Tesoro, Vincent E.	15	1	3	1	57,262	Thornton, Eric	4	0	1	1	3,500
Testerman, Valora A.	215	18	16	28	403,101	Thornton, Nancy	129	6	7	12	61,452
Tetrault, Mark R.	44	6	1	2	48,759	Thorp, Michelle	8	0	0	2	1,379
Tetreault, Arthur	4	0	0	0	600	Thrasher, Amy	13	1	1	0	5,298
Tetreault, Scott	33	4	2	1	19,164	Three Irons, Gale	9	1	0	1	2,140
Thacker, Debbie	24	2	0	2	30,564	Three Irons, Melvin	26	3	3	1	6,821
Thacker, Elbert	31	3	4	2	27,647	Threewitt, Noble	22	1	2	5	69,740
Thacker, Harry G.	17	2	2	1	40,150	Thurston, Harold	65	4	3	10	33,418
Thacker, Howard L.	1	0	0	0	53	Thurston, Jerry A.	61	13	10	11	192,819
Thayer, Allan G.	1	0	0	0	0	Tiamfook, Steve C.	15	0	1	0	5,870
Theisen, Alice	69	4	5	11	81,699	Tibbitts, Bobby K.	46	4	4	0	84,721
Theriot, Harold J.	79	9	7	8	85,576	Tiller, Robert P.	254	73	41	37	4,090,391
Thibodeau, Pamela	110	16	17	20	113,969	Tillis, Jerry E	31	1	1	1	7,508
Thibodeaux, Kenneth J.	19	0	1	3	4,109	Tillotta, Nancy L.	107	10	10	19	152,465
Thibodeaux, Kenneth W.	12	0	2	0	6,590	Timm, Robert H.	31	5	1	5	32,420
Thoburn, William R.	42	0	4	4	20,673	Tinsley, John L.	3	0	0	0	132
Thomas, Alan R.	7	0	0	0	370	Tippett, Steve	27	4	3	1	28,803
Thomas, Charles M.	11	0	0	0	1,292	Tipton, Larry	6	0	0	0	400
Thomas, Charles W.	1	0	0	0	100	Tirella, Carl	2	0	0	0	80
Thomas, Ed	1	0	0	0	129	Tisbert, Louis	23	3	0	2	24,870
Thomas, Gary A.	85	9	9	9	228,046	Tobin, Edwin L	81	4	13	8	166,758
Thomas, James A.	1	0	0	0	50	Tobler, Robert	11	1	4	2	10,330
Thomas, Jamey R.	129	15	17	18	160,604	Todd, Jerry	22	2	1	2	11,642
Thomas, John E.	49	4	4	5	26,859	Tofte, Vicki	7	1	0	0	4,571
Thomas, Karen	89	12	13	9	65,388	Tohill, Val	20	0	0	2	5,000
Thomas, Mark E.	108	12	16	18	136,905	Tolbert, Ron	1	0	0	0	60
Thomas, Michael W.	3	0	0	0	190	Toledo, Herberto	25	5	3	2	74,631
Thomas, Mike D.	12	1	2	0	4,116	Tolle, Bonnie	2	0	0	0	0
Thomas, Monte R.	27	0	6	3	16,531	Tollett, Bill	119	22	11	8	137,861
Thomas, Ray	79	6	9	12	78,523	Tomaselli, Anthony S.	22	1	0	2	17,917
Thomas, Richard L.	17	4	0	1	45,638	Tomillo, Thomas F.	632	65	61	66	1,057,825
Thomas, Sandra L.	26	1	1	2	16,848	Tomlenovich, Anthony	12	1	0	0	7,624
Thomas, Susan C.	5	0	0	1	990	Tomlinson, Michael A.	97	14	15	10	628,980
Thomas, Terry Mike	9	1	2	1	15,780	Tomlinson, Norman	40	3	3	4	44,843
Thomas, Thomas J.	27	1	2	4	20,271	Tompkins, Dune C.	8	0	2	2	4,565
Thomas, Travis O.	48	1	1	7	27,407	Tompkins, Floyd	1	0	0	0	0
Thomas, W. Bret	154	13	21	13	272,274	Tompkins, Jimmie D.	7	1	0	0	3,168
Thomas, Jr., Norm	21	0	2	1	7,674	Toner, David	56	9	4	6	186,927
Thomas, Jr., Philip J.	11	1	4	2	57,800	Toner, James J.	102	13	12	10	742,071
Thomas, Sr., Joe Frederick	116	36	22	15	144,132	Toon, Kathy	58	3	6	6	39,485
Thomas, Sr., William Joseph	3	0	0	0	850	Torelli, Stacy	210	28	35	31	290,876
Thomaselli, Richard	3	1	0	0	6,667	Torevell, Chad	166	22	20	14	205,530
Thomason, Glen	75	3	9	9	42,412	Torres, Ben	9	1	2	2	27,156
Thomason, Sam L.	5	2	1	0	37,600	Torrez, Jerenesto	190	21	24	22	254,462
Thomasson, Marion L.	6	1	0	0	4,577	Tortora, Emanuel	438	66	64	58	1,894,152
Thompson, Alex	1	0	0	0	0	Toscano, Jr., John T.	93	7	11	14	306,765

Trainer	Sts	1st	2d	3d	Purses	Trainer	Sts	1st	2d	3d	Purses
Totland, Mike	9	0	0	3	2,549	Turner, Tom L.	6	1	0	0	1,461
Touchet, Glenn	61	5	5	9	45,217	Turner, Jr., William H.	140	15	10	20	637,411
Touchet, Joseph L.	5	1	1	1	19,151	Turpin, Richaleen	107	15	23	16	122,829
Touchet, Michael	33	1	0	7	22,328	Tuttle, Chris	504	65	72	58	1,009,239
Toups, Brent	102	7	16	7	79,832	Tuttle, Woodard F.	25	3	2	3	36,400
Tourangeau, Mike	69	10	13	6	15,537	Tveit, Dwaine	9	3	2	2	4,446
Tourangeau, Russell	34	2	3	4	9,523	Tweed, Perri	6	0	0	0	108
Towne, Steve	90	11	9	11	223,907	Twigg, Jim	7	0	1	0	1,088
Townsend, Richard	17	1	2	2	16,525	Twiggs, Leroy	69	6	12	12	24,792
Toye, Joe	274	31	39	36	232,921	Twileger, Gordon	8	1	4	1	7,480
Tracy, Greg	42	8	10	5	273,182	Twinn, James L.	5	0	0	0	675
Tracy, Jim	153	17	17	15	200,675	Twyman, W. Noel	10	1	1	2	9,299
Tracy, Jr., Ray E.	294	34	32	32	475,799	Tzortzakis, Emmanuel	64	7	5	7	79,853
Trahan, Jeff	1	0	1	0	1,000	Tzortzakis, Margarita	29	3	5	5	50,142
Trahan, Oran	51	6	2	5	43,189	Uballe, Daniel T.	1	0	0	0	0
Traitz, Angel	42	5	8	5	70,675	Ubbink, Stephen P.	62	12	8	11	95,418
Trapani, Jerry	3	0	0	1	2,240	Ubide, Max	4	0	0	1	902
Treadway, Diane M.	24	2	7	0	19,298	Uelmen, Larry R.	162	26	20	27	220,920
Treadway, Robert W.	4	1	1	0	4,124	Ugalde, Arsenio	4	1	0	0	4,380
Treasure, Paul	90	11	14	12	116,677	Uhacz, Wendy	2	0	0	0	156
Treece, Charles S.	298	44	34	30	317,983	Ulibarri, Travis B.	13	0	0	1	992
Trejo, Amalio R.	122	13	14	14	85,038	Ulmer, Cissy	1	0	0	0	0
Trela, Rosemary	25	3	4	6	32,136	Underdahl, Brice	10	0	1	2	1,875
Trent, Jr., Charles	44	6	1	3	53,880	Underwood, Sidney	57	5	4	8	107,944
Trevino, Stephen G.	123	23	14	16	173,875	Underwood, Terry L.	37	1	4	5	7,875
Tribert, C. Douglas	4	0	0	0	3,000	Ungles, Ken	18	0	4	0	4,254
Trimmer, Richard K.	49	3	6	6	94,393	Unwin, Bruce	13	4	1	1	81,783
Triola, Robert	22	1	1	1	45,966	Upham, Craig D.	13	2	1	2	23,640
Trione, Jr., Thomas E.	197	23	30	24	152,207	Uphaus, Jacque	31	3	6	3	27,492
Trivigno, Michael T.	94	16	15	4	208,701	Upton, Thomas M.	13	1	1	2	15,165
Troiani, Rico	39	3	3	3	16,445	Urdiales, Ray	38	3	5	9	28,322
Trombetta, Michael J.	150	33	25	14	786,158	Uriegas, Jr., Jose	2	0	0	1	660
Tronco, William L.	9	0	1	1	4,105	Urioste, Manuel D.	28	1	0	1	10,249
Trosclair, Jeff	63	6	12	11	289,280	Uselton, Roy Gene	2	0	0	0	180
Trotter, Jesse E.	31	0	2	3	7,082	Utley, Doug	217	24	36	31	434,971
Trottier, Burton	8	1	3	2	8,580	Utley, Sue	50	2	11	9	33,329
Trout, C. R.	87	16	9	12	418,654	Uyeyama, Spud	32	1	4	4	16,575
Trout, Joan	15	2	1	2	16,819	Vacca, Joseph	4	0	0	0	138
Trout, Robert G.	38	0	0	0	2,550	Vaders, Jayne	44	15	5	5	187,295
Troyer, Garnet H.	24	3	5	2	23,070	Valdes, Aurelio P.	38	3	4	0	37,795
Troyer, Mark	2	0	0	0	875	Valdez, Arnulfo R.	12	0	0	0	834
Trudel, Yves	105	18	10	18	199,334	Valdez, Jesse A.	1	0	0	0	0
True , Art	20	1	1	0	7,295	Valdez, Ralph J.	23	0	0	0	1,866
Truex, Randall D.	1	0	0	0	0	Valdivia, Samuel E.	5	1	1	0	2,168
Truitt, Pat	21	2	2	1	12,412	Valencia, Samantha Dyan	4	0	1	0	1,261
Trujillo, Michael F.	33	1	3	1	17,623	Valentine, Richard L.	31	8	2	3	122,984
Trujillo, Jr, Celio	21	2	1	3	25,604	Valenzuela, Jr., Martin	27	1	2	3	18,365
Truman, Eddie	85	8	8	12	232,283	Valerio, Raymond G.	7	0	0	1	2,493
Truocchio, Robert	4	1	0	0	3,372	Vales, Michael A.	10	0	1	0	6,552
Truppa, Gaetano A	4	0	0	0	970	Vallance, Paul	10	0	0	1	3,428
Tsagalakis, Mark D.	8	1	1	1	47,160	Vallejos, Salvador O.	1	0	0	0	188
Tschan, April E.	1	0	0	1	4,730	Vallejos, Tomas G.	47	4	4	4	37,525
Tschirgi, Brian	27	3	3	5	7,052	Van Arem, Brian	30	4	3	3	139,249
Tso, Sr., Justin	2	0	0	0	109	Van Bebber, Janet A.	1	0	0	0	0
Tubbs, Scott	98	9	9	15	140,106	Van Berg, Jack C.	144	7	12	13	196,483
Tucker, Robert R.	37	2	4	1	21,945	Van Berg, Thomas L.	196	37	26	15	578,208
Tulloch, Roger A.	32	0	1	1	7,736	Van Horn, Tracy L.	2	0	0	0	338
Tullock, Jr., Timothy J.	156	26	29	27	611,095	Van Horne, Debbie	98	16	17	14	127,924
Tuminelli, Joseph M.	38	4	4	7	60,083	Van Loon, John	98	15	15	12	99,202
Tunks, Fred G.	10	0	1	0	2,152	Van Overschot, Robert	195	30	28	31	666,024
Turant, Jr., John F.	28	0	0	4	3,132	Van Pelt, Charlotte M.	13	2	2	0	26,757
Turchi, Frank	31	4	5	2	45,835	Van Tassell, Glade W.	13	5	1	1	4,368
Turco, Chuck	114	10	16	12	119,540	Van Voorhis, Jan	18	0	1	2	11,240
Turetsky, Judy E.	33	5	6	3	36,300	Van Winkle, Brian	3	0	0	0	658
Turlington, Stuart	21	2	2	4	16,634	Van Winkle, David	303	43	45	47	509,904
Turner, Betty J.	2	1	0	0	1,210	Van Worp, Judson	9	1	0	0	11,329
Turner, Eric	10	1	3	1	2,867	Vanatta, Bert L.	2	0	0	0	0
Turner, Gus	48	6	12	8	42,626	Vanatta, James Bart	18	1	3	3	9,146
Turner, Jack H.	5	1	0	0	8,256	Vance, David R.	282	40	30	32	1,148,462
Turner, John W.	1	0	0	0	0	Vance, David W.	18	3	2	2	22,488
Turner, Kris	266	29	34	32	253,764	Vandane, Joseph	17	1	3	5	3,724
Turner, Michael A.	21	1	1	1	14,911	Vandernat, Reinier	2	0	0	0	0
Turner, Robert E.	1	0	0	0	160	Vandersalm, Suzanne J.	76	9	7	3	115,520

Trainer	Sts	1st	2d	3d	Purses
Vandervort, Bernice E.	16	1	1	0	2,747
Vandervort, G. R.	23	7	5	3	14,682
Vanier, Harvey L.	247	26	31	35	744,220
Vankeulen, Rebecca	4	0	0	0	254
Vannorsdel, Dana A.	5	0	1	1	866
Vanorio, Joe A.	8	0	1	0	6,438
Vardeman, Alfred	2	0	0	0	0
Vargas, Hector	10	0	0	3	3,022
Vargas, J. Buenaventura	76	5	4	7	83,878
Vargas, Nerio	25	4	3	3	94,896
Vargo, Irene	4	1	1	0	1,027
Vargo, Paul	9	0	0	1	3,526
Vargo, Virginia	9	1	2	2	1,549
Varner, Carrol	6	1	0	0	2,495
Varrelli, Joseph D.	38	2	4	3	31,201
Vasquez, Dario A.	97	11	13	6	165,399
Vasquez, Lona	10	0	2	1	4,863
Vasquez, Ramon	42	2	1	5	22,794
Vasquez, Reyes Orozco	3	1	0	0	3,828
Vaughn, Curt	13	0	1	2	4,285
Vaughn, Debra	57	7	4	6	75,881
Vaught, Marie E.	11	0	2	1	6,443
Vaught, Mary L.	2	0	0	0	188
Vazquez, Edwin	15	0	1	1	2,657
Vazquez, Gamaliel	283	46	34	42	820,156
Vega, Richard	318	38	40	39	544,670
Vegh, Leslie L.	60	7	6	10	43,571
Veiga, Frank D.	25	4	5	2	95,840
Veitch, John M.	43	2	1	2	73,265
Velarde, Tina Rena	4	0	1	0	884
Velasquez, Danny	50	3	5	8	112,640
Velasquez, Rigoberto	39	6	8	5	32,682
Velazquez, Alfredo	255	34	31	39	445,895
Velez, Javier	14	0	0	0	3,900
Velez, Roberto	40	3	6	3	41,370
Vella, Daniel J.	192	42	31	13	2,435,069
Venable, Ronald	45	4	8	7	49,145
Venable, Terry	10	0	1	0	3,450
Venham, Lyn Dee	16	2	2	1	40,409
Ver Mett, Chuck	8	1	2	2	3,319
Verderber, Greg	45	0	3	3	9,159
Verderosa, Lou	7	0	0	0	471
Verdesi, Alberto	13	0	3	4	23,525
Vest, Reeves R.	18	0	0	1	1,807
Vestal, Peter M.	71	10	9	14	649,789
Viator, Dwight J.	60	11	6	3	111,063
Vickers, Robert N.	9	1	0	3	13,815
Vickers, Traci	34	6	3	3	45,109
Vickers-Smith, Katharine L.	15	0	0	2	6,941
Vickery, Bret	3	1	1	0	1,746
Victoria, Patrick O.	15	0	0	1	2,730
Vidrine, Velton	38	3	4	6	37,230
Vienna, Darrell	303	51	52	34	2,393,598
Viera, Hector	8	0	3	2	19,500
Vigneault, Julie	3	1	1	0	17,445
Villafranco, Luis	3	0	1	0	1,410
Villalobos, Miguel A.	7	0	0	1	2,798
Villalobos, Sr., Rigoberto T.	15	0	3	1	13,572
Villanueva, Jesus	3	1	1	0	1,260
Villari, Barbara E.	30	1	2	4	36,490
Villarreal, Reynaldo C.	5	0	0	0	189
Villela, Jose Felix	36	1	3	0	11,495
Villyard, Aubrey	68	16	11	9	107,593
Vilunas, John	11	0	0	1	11,561
Vincent, Rodney B.	4	0	0	0	0
Vinci, Charles J.	290	37	39	27	699,438
Vineyard, Vance	5	0	1	1	3,462
Vineyard, Jr., John W.	9	0	0	2	3,486
Vinson, Lynn	8	2	0	0	49,743
Violette, Jr., Richard A.	178	28	19	35	1,656,468
Virts, Joseph F.	1	0	0	1	1,100
Vitale, Francis J.	7	2	1	1	42,400
Vitali, Marcus J.	138	21	13	20	191,348
Vititow, C. F.	4	0	0	0	0
Vittur, Wilson E.	48	5	6	8	88,692
Vivian, David A.	95	13	15	13	362,358
Vivian, Jr., David A.	80	6	10	7	134,975
Vizcaya, James S.	7	1	0	1	1,303
Vizena, Herman	8	0	0	0	582
Vojin, William J.	3	0	0	0	171
Volk, Scott J.	1	0	1	0	1,700
Von Hemel, Don	294	39	53	46	1,065,533
Von Hemel, Donnie K.	416	94	81	59	2,576,588
Von Hemel, Kelly R.	295	51	44	43	1,013,877
Von Wise, Kriston	25	1	2	2	28,620
Vondy, Terry	7	0	0	0	100
Vosler, Durward L.	40	2	3	2	9,135
Voss, Katherine M.	105	12	9	11	262,076
Voss, Thomas H.	168	23	22	23	643,788
Voss, III, Ronald L.	70	8	11	12	152,682
Vowell, Dwayne	16	0	0	1	2,603
Voyce, Robyn	28	1	4	3	36,071
Vucurevich, Robert G.	35	4	1	5	21,717
Vuyosevich, Jeanne L.	50	2	4	6	43,970
Wadams, Dwight J.	86	9	2	8	64,232
Waddle, Diane	6	2	2	0	4,510
Wade, Charles J.	34	4	1	7	37,685
Wade, Deanna	14	2	0	1	5,579
Wade, Garey	40	2	3	3	8,130
Wadsworth, Hal	14	0	0	0	1,573
Wafer, George	25	4	3	7	33,140
Wagner, John G.	14	2	0	2	27,408
Wagner, Karin	12	0	2	1	7,350
Wainscott, Richard	9	1	0	2	8,117
Wainwright, John C.	212	24	26	38	339,681
Waite, Del	130	16	16	21	177,113
Waite, Dennis L.	67	1	2	1	28,283
Wakefield, Michael	18	2	2	3	19,059
Walcott, Sr., Charles A.	89	17	10	13	241,630
Walden, W. Elliott	289	67	53	36	3,509,486
Walder, Peter R.	156	24	27	27	450,501
Waldie, Jack	158	21	16	20	210,370
Waldman, Leah	2	2	0	0	14,400
Waldron, Bill	21	3	2	2	35,301
Waldron, Dianne K.	3	1	0	0	9,890
Wales, Dale E.	21	3	2	5	5,560
Walgren, Scott T.	10	0	1	1	1,880
Walker, Brad	11	0	1	0	2,860
Walker, Charles A.	40	2	2	3	41,350
Walker, Charles R.	7	0	3	2	5,246
Walker, Devin D.	79	3	10	13	84,376
Walker, Donald E.	39	4	2	7	55,350
Walker, Earl	37	4	4	5	30,167
Walker, Elmo K.	7	1	0	1	4,258
Walker, Leland R.	3	0	0	0	0
Walker, Lloyd E.	16	1	2	2	15,120
Walker, Paul R.	2	0	0	0	525
Walker, Phillip	2	0	1	0	5,805
Walker, Roger D.	32	1	3	2	26,107
Walker, Sheldon E.	69	5	3	6	31,855
Walker, Terri D.	2	1	0	0	13,156
Walker, Terry A.	97	11	9	18	252,477
Walker, Jr., Charles C.	275	30	37	31	200,654
Wall, John	48	5	2	2	32,264
Wallace, Bradley W.	3	0	2	0	10,980
Wallace, Ronnie	17	4	1	1	36,575
Wallace, Roy L.	36	7	7	2	121,620
Wallace, Waldyn H.	5	0	0	1	5,065
Wallack, Patrick H.	42	2	1	3	39,155
Wallerstedt, Heather	2	0	0	0	0
Wallerstedt, Mark	6	0	0	0	162
Wallette, Terry	1	0	0	0	50
Wallis, Nathan	27	0	7	3	15,443
Walls, Joseph F.	51	4	5	8	224,281
Walmer, Dale	8	0	0	0	1,407
Walper, Deanna	80	12	13	10	111,138

Trainer	Sts	1st	2d	3d	Purses	Trainer	Sts	1st	2d	3d	Purses
Walsh, Edward	29	6	5	3	19,397	Watkins, William L.	32	4	4	5	34,533
Walsh, Eric	1	0	0	0	140	Watson, Jack R.	15	0	0	0	149
Walsh, Joseph	6	0	1	0	3,650	Watson, Janene M.	24	3	0	5	30,033
Walsh, Kathy	68	11	12	8	692,792	Watson, Kari	33	4	1	3	15,389
Walsh, Rachael L.	6	0	0	0	542	Watson, Kelly	4	0	0	0	390
Walsh, Richard A.	24	2	1	1	11,673	Watt, Randy	11	1	2	1	11,544
Walsh, Ryan D.	36	3	4	3	20,881	Waugh, Joseph R.	36	6	7	7	52,631
Walsh, Thomas M.	27	3	1	1	139,556	Waugh, Virginia	3	0	0	0	418
Walsh, Timothy	18	3	4	3	51,528	Waunsch, Joseph J.	106	11	16	12	252,024
Walsh, III, Michael G.	1	0	0	0	400	Waxman, Katherine	4	0	0	0	255
Walsh, Jr., James J.	49	5	4	6	54,359	Wayar, Manuel J.	59	8	7	6	181,805
Walsky, Michael S.	9	2	0	1	19,738	Weatherwax, Robert	27	6	3	3	21,539
Walston, Lawson	38	1	1	3	14,952	Weaver, David	14	0	0	1	1,591
Walt, Nicole L.	5	0	1	1	3,665	Weaver, George	224	33	30	24	1,177,404
Waltermire, Bruce	11	2	2	1	13,188	Weaver, Jerry	40	10	6	6	27,768
Walters, David	271	39	40	27	659,183	Weaver, Joe Reese	68	8	5	12	67,824
Walters, Fred E.	14	1	1	2	6,305	Webb, Delmer L.	128	27	7	16	132,864
Walters, Henry R.	56	10	9	11	199,180	Webb, Edward	68	8	6	6	74,678
Walters, Philip L.	8	1	0	1	18,340	Webb, Lucy B.	68	4	13	7	114,155
Walton, Madeline	8	0	2	1	1,276	Webb, Samuel	214	24	30	27	231,226
Walton, Tommy L.	23	2	6	0	14,763	Webb, Stan	10	2	0	2	3,978
Waltz, Brian	85	12	11	14	127,251	Webster, Alfred C.	15	3	3	2	18,892
Wames, John J.	26	3	3	2	26,920	Webster, Caroline	6	0	0	0	1,365
Wansborough, Martin	21	0	3	0	34,200	Weckerle, Kathy E.	7	0	1	2	29,236
Ward, Brian D.	5	0	1	0	3,790	Wedge, John	23	4	2	2	23,475
Ward, Dale T.	3	0	0	0	252	Wedge, Terry	13	3	5	2	28,420
Ward, Dean	5	1	0	1	16,500	Weeder, Tim	73	8	9	4	56,865
Ward, Glenn S.	83	8	9	9	146,628	Weekley, Jerry W.	5	0	0	0	438
Ward, John C.	41	5	2	4	40,178	Weeks, Thomas C.	150	27	16	20	359,991
Ward, Joseph D.	20	1	1	1	5,725	Weems, George	15	0	0	1	1,897
Ward, Kenneth J.	4	0	0	0	825	Weger, Bill R.	5	1	1	1	4,190
Ward, Lida J.	18	1	2	7	8,060	Wehrli, Gerald R.	61	10	11	8	24,914
Ward, Nicola J.	3	0	0	0	2,271	Weimer, Edward R.	45	7	6	5	34,551
Ward, Ronnie P.	247	21	35	25	208,623	Weimer, Jackie	9	0	2	2	3,385
Ward, Sonny	6	0	0	0	625	Weir, George L.	48	0	3	1	13,254
Ward, Wesley A.	508	93	99	79	2,102,262	Weir, Gregory H.	18	4	3	1	33,669
Ward, William L.	5	0	0	0	420	Weir, Kelly	59	13	7	2	87,770
Ward, Jr., John T.	90	17	9	13	1,551,218	Weiser, Sr., Stan	1	0	0	0	0
Ward, Jr., Roger D.	1	0	0	0	100	Weiss, Frank R.	6	0	0	0	2,815
Ware, Cody	4	0	0	0	0	Weissman, Michael F.	68	8	6	9	190,937
Warner, Alison	1	0	0	0	2,520	Welch, C. Eugene	24	3	4	1	18,603
Warner, Merrilee	4	0	0	1	951	Welch, Gary R.	1	0	0	0	37
Warner, Robert K.	9	0	0	0	1,265	Welch, J. Michael	86	9	10	11	112,086
Warnimont, Ralph B.	124	21	18	22	171,710	Welch, Needham W.	30	4	3	5	26,343
Warnke, Eugene E.	30	6	2	2	20,062	Welch, Scott	3	1	1	0	7,520
Warpool, Michael Shane	60	5	11	7	79,197	Welch, William L.	1	1	0	0	8,040
Warren, Donald	86	10	7	10	451,935	Weld, Dermot K.	8	3	1	0	1,108,000
Warren, Fred G.	327	23	29	47	477,010	Welden, Joyce	9	0	0	0	1,027
Warren, Ronnie G.	55	2	9	5	64,663	Wells, Darrell	17	1	0	2	6,379
Warren, Tom M.	4	0	0	1	6,630	Wells, David H.	10	1	3	0	12,605
Wartchow, John	7	1	0	0	6,358	Wells, Debra Ann	17	0	6	2	17,928
Wartchow, W. Lewis	19	2	2	3	23,598	Wells, Donald V.	33	6	11	5	51,251
Warvell, Jim	58	9	8	2	71,854	Wells, Gordon	25	5	7	2	43,089
Warwick, Candice	78	4	14	4	99,806	Wells, J. C.	1	0	0	0	87
Warwick, Mike	1	0	0	0	0	Wells, John Lee	15	3	1	2	25,902
Washer, David J.	15	0	1	1	3,565	Wells, John N.	3	0	0	0	325
Washington, Adrian	29	2	3	2	18,608	Wells, Larry	93	6	9	12	54,463
Washington, Richard G.	2	0	0	0	0	Wells, Tonya M.	21	1	1	2	8,634
Washington, Thomas H.	71	6	4	7	82,016	Welsh, Gary	133	9	18	19	205,635
Wasilewski, Christine	29	4	1	3	45,055	Welsh, Julie A.	2	0	0	0	0
Wasiluk, Jr., Peter	322	17	37	30	218,574	Welsh, Regina	5	0	2	0	6,300
Waskow, John E.	6	2	0	0	36,390	Wendel, Arthur	4	0	0	0	0
Wasserman, Richard A.	126	15	21	15	138,945	Wenderoth, Gloria M.	37	3	3	3	47,707
Wasson, Glen Stanley	143	5	11	12	69,411	Wendling, Ronald	25	3	4	2	53,454
Waterman, Jill F.	4	1	2	0	12,750	Wendt, Chris	3	0	0	0	288
Watermeier, Ann	69	8	4	14	208,728	Wenner, Robert F.	5	0	1	1	2,618
Waters, Dean	15	0	0	0	735	Wenzel, Tom	133	18	14	16	169,161
Waters, Faryn	58	5	6	4	55,470	Wermes, Margaret	38	3	3	7	22,584
Waters, Karl S.	91	10	13	13	81,617	Wern, George	135	19	16	19	108,757
Watkins, Edward J.	68	4	5	1	33,758	Werner, Robert Russell	112	11	8	5	72,965
Watkins, Harold F.	3	0	0	1	1,190	Werner, Ronny W.	247	55	49	33	1,528,906
Watkins, Robert L.	21	4	0	3	14,543	Werner, Russell F.	4	0	0	0	0
Watkins, Shannon	52	5	2	5	58,495	Werneth, Roger	54	4	4	5	103,201

RECORDS OF TRAINERS

Trainer	Sts	1st	2d	3d	Purses	Trainer	Sts	1st	2d	3d	Purses
Werneth, Jr., Hilton E.	3	0	0	1	1,066	Whitson, Robert	7	2	0	0	10,300
Wessels, Amy L.	5	0	0	0	347	Whitt, John H.	4	0	0	0	357
West, Benjamin F.	93	6	19	15	68,601	Whitte, Samanthe	2	0	2	0	1,160
West, David L.	43	5	5	6	21,132	Whittingham, Michael C.	29	3	0	4	161,648
West, Delmer G.	20	2	0	3	14,308	Whitton, Mark	81	3	3	10	37,003
West, Gareld F.	34	1	1	1	11,228	Whylie, Herold O.	118	8	8	10	83,877
West, James	1	0	0	0	317	Wicker, Cheryl	5	0	0	0	311
West, Jerry W.	8	2	0	0	9,180	Wicker, Lloyd C.	4	0	1	1	3,380
West, Marcella K.	5	0	0	0	0	Wideman, Jane	13	0	3	2	9,815
West, Martha J.	20	1	2	3	13,750	Widenmaier, Mel	5	0	0	0	424
West, Raymond P.	46	3	4	9	32,341	Widmer, Wayne	30	3	2	4	88,585
West, Steve W.	4	0	0	0	605	Wiebe, Christy	21	8	6	1	59,531
West, Ted H.	167	39	33	27	1,802,147	Wiest, Phil	43	9	10	5	33,062
West, Wayne	21	1	0	3	14,352	Wiest, Rick	1	1	0	0	2,145
West, Jr., Henry	16	0	0	1	1,746	Wig, Janet C.	86	14	14	11	176,063
West, Jr., Roy W.	54	5	6	7	38,016	Wiggins, David	7	1	0	1	10,910
Westergaard, Robert L.	18	1	2	5	23,798	Wiggins, Deborah A.	10	0	1	0	5,200
Westermann, Ronald L.	76	6	6	6	41,112	Wiggins, Hal R.	272	37	42	31	1,163,606
Weston, Charles	57	9	7	11	79,163	Wiggins, Lon	112	9	10	15	152,621
Weston, Susan	24	0	2	4	12,112	Wigginton, Jesse N.	74	11	14	11	307,953
Westwood, Terry	36	3	3	5	31,418	Wilborn, Beverly C.	5	1	0	1	8,750
Wetherington, Margaret	54	5	4	6	92,701	Wilborn, J. Kevin	119	15	19	17	140,580
Wethey, Floyd J.	14	1	2	0	3,739	Wilcox, Bruce W.	36	5	2	2	28,426
Wever, Cynthia S.	67	10	10	13	158,018	Wilcox, Ron	4	1	0	1	4,544
Wever, Jr., Alston A.	6	1	0	0	6,470	Wilcox, Warren	166	15	13	21	666,145
Weymouth, Eugene E.	117	26	9	7	246,281	Wilensky, Herman	110	13	20	9	291,635
Whalen, Betty W.	1	0	0	0	50	Wiley, Chuck W.	45	6	8	8	35,008
Whalen, Bill	1	0	0	0	64	Wiley, Don	5	0	0	0	536
Whalen, Henry	173	27	21	16	474,798	Wiley, Sue	8	0	0	2	2,240
Wharton, Cliff	13	0	0	1	1,168	Wiley, Jr., Leslie J.	102	20	16	6	117,555
Whatley, Archie E.	53	10	4	9	139,112	Wilhelm, David L.	64	4	3	6	70,439
Wheatley, Leo A.	32	0	1	4	4,033	Wilhelm, Jennie	32	1	3	4	21,545
Wheeler, Larry A.	94	4	7	8	37,396	Wilhelm, Larry	155	12	11	16	58,560
Wheeler, Tandi	131	6	10	20	119,745	Wilhelm, Jr, James R.	6	0	1	1	4,295
Wheeler, Wilmer E.	74	6	7	7	44,063	Wilhelm, Sr., James R.	93	4	1	9	47,993
Wheeler, Jr., Grover Cleveland	2	0	0	0	124	Wilhelm-Saldana, Jennie	15	0	0	4	5,695
Wherry, Bill	10	0	1	3	4,638	Wilhide, Jr., Arthur E.	6	0	0	0	204
Whipple, Tim	41	0	0	3	5,763	Wilke, Gordon	17	0	2	1	2,836
Whitaker, Clarke D.	130	18	9	11	156,866	Wilkerson, Tom	12	0	0	2	5,369
White, A. Ridgely	13	2	0	1	21,394	Wilkes, John T.	27	0	1	4	13,617
White, A. Timothy	53	1	6	8	63,419	Wilkins, F. Bryan	55	3	5	2	42,690
White, Alan D.	130	15	6	10	98,711	Wilkins, Joe L.	38	9	6	7	43,320
White, Alexandra	1	0	0	0	0	Wilkinson, James D.	113	13	10	8	187,674
White, Conover	7	0	0	3	8,090	Wilkinson, Sherman	29	1	1	1	11,485
White, Donald R.	85	4	3	2	61,249	Wilkinson, Winston	99	9	10	5	118,587
White, Gary B.	71	8	4	15	21,244	Wilkinson, III, Jack R.	40	6	2	7	95,292
White, J. V.	12	3	1	1	5,571	Williams, Andrew	4	2	0	0	27,500
White, Jacqueline M.	27	0	1	1	4,207	Williams, Bryan H.	15	0	0	1	2,445
White, Jimmy L.	2	0	0	0	0	Williams, Charlie J.	1	0	0	0	66
White, Keith	1	1	0	0	1,100	Williams, Cheryl	10	1	1	3	32,749
White, M. Victoria	2	0	0	0	249	Williams, David John	8	2	0	1	4,583
White, Mel	45	4	7	5	12,599	Williams, Edward L.	31	6	7	0	61,154
White, Mike	3	0	0	0	363	Williams, Ellen	4	1	1	0	5,158
White, Robert T.	4	0	0	0	260	Williams, Ernest R.	1	0	0	0	0
White, Robert W.	5	0	0	0	0	Williams, George	25	1	1	2	12,171
White, Ron E.	25	1	1	3	15,439	Williams, George E.	58	1	2	9	23,653
White, Tammy	70	7	9	5	36,198	Williams, George L.	17	3	0	5	67,525
White, Vincent	80	8	7	8	43,562	Williams, Gerald	5	0	2	1	1,100
White, William P.	386	74	41	54	1,642,373	Williams, Harold G.	16	3	2	0	111,670
White, Sr., Dale	2	0	0	0	360	Williams, Herbert B.	12	1	1	2	7,787
Whited, Danny W.	69	7	10	7	92,364	Williams, J. Alan	93	6	9	11	30,861
Whited, David L.	109	10	16	10	158,135	Williams, James L.	198	16	22	24	214,011
Whitehouse, Thomas W.	9	0	2	2	4,888	Williams, James Milton	66	9	16	13	60,114
Whitehouse, W. R.	108	8	11	13	82,341	Williams, Jeffrey M.	80	13	10	11	115,140
Whitekiller, Matt	4	0	0	0	170	Williams, Jesus	2	0	0	0	150
Whitelaw, Michael R.	34	4	3	5	35,659	Williams, L. C.	1	0	0	0	0
Whiteside, Charlene	9	1	1	1	2,192	Williams, Leroy	1	0	0	0	342
Whiteside, Sr., Jim	1	0	1	0	340	Williams, Robert H.	31	2	7	4	68,832
Whitford, Linda J.	7	0	0	0	466	Williams, Robert L.	28	2	1	0	13,670
Whiting, Lynn S.	155	21	23	24	727,956	Williams, Sandra E.	4	0	0	0	336
Whitlock, John R.	3	0	0	1	212	Williams, Sean	3	0	0	0	310
Whitner, IV, James H.	3	0	0	0	1,275	Williams, Thomas O.	10	1	0	3	6,831
Whitney, Pamela	25	1	2	0	7,521	Williams, Wendy	15	2	2	1	23,615

Trainer	Sts	1st	2d	3d	Purses
Williams, II, Roger L.	24	0	2	3	4,488
Williams, III, Robert	28	0	1	1	4,134
Williams, Jr., Gary L.	32	3	3	2	62,087
Williams, Jr., Robert C.	5	0	0	1	2,661
Williams, Sr., Edward E.	2	0	0	0	335
Williamson, Brian	207	17	25	26	564,936
Williamson, Joseph P.	32	0	2	6	28,160
Willick, Cathy G.	5	0	0	1	1,997
Willis, Bobby D.	2	0	1	0	540
Willis, Eddie D.	2	2	0	0	5,850
Willis, Frank	10	1	0	1	1,522
Willis, Joe Don	27	1	3	4	7,037
Willis, Mindy J.	171	8	23	29	140,040
Willis, Patricia Ann	36	2	3	5	35,826
Willis, Jr., Alfred	50	3	6	10	18,577
Willoughby, Mark	1	0	0	0	95
Willoughby, Scott L.	14	2	3	0	12,108
Wills, Daniel	65	9	7	12	175,413
Willsey, Duncan	25	1	2	1	5,480
Willson, Clint D.	41	6	6	7	151,160
Wilmot, William B.	12	3	0	1	51,754
Wilson, Alonzo	1	0	0	0	80
Wilson, Angelle	10	2	0	4	4,254
Wilson, Ariane B.	78	1	4	4	21,992
Wilson, Brad V.	30	4	2	3	22,046
Wilson, Brenda	79	2	8	9	93,527
Wilson, C. L.	22	2	1	0	36,989
Wilson, Campbell	105	15	10	7	192,686
Wilson, Carol A.	2	0	0	0	0
Wilson, Ed	6	0	0	0	0
Wilson, Elijah	9	0	0	0	5,840
Wilson, Frank R.	15	0	2	3	2,425
Wilson, Gene K.	103	23	17	13	37,300
Wilson, Gordon	10	2	1	1	13,746
Wilson, Gregory L.	61	4	4	9	72,145
Wilson, Irene N.	5	0	0	1	330
Wilson, Jack B.	7	3	2	1	20,165
Wilson, James G.	10	1	1	0	10,679
Wilson, John R.	96	11	16	14	239,558
Wilson, John S.	18	0	2	1	4,051
Wilson, John W.	4	0	0	0	124
Wilson, Larry L.	18	1	1	1	11,718
Wilson, Lorna S.	42	2	2	5	21,902
Wilson, Lynn	24	4	4	3	22,380
Wilson, Mark M.	2	0	0	1	426
Wilson, Nancy J.	2	0	0	0	326
Wilson, Peter	40	4	2	6	53,930
Wilson, R. Scott	20	5	2	2	28,730
Wilson, Raymond	42	3	5	10	11,217
Wilson, Ronald	10	1	1	0	3,085
Wilson, Russell	2	0	0	0	84
Wilson, Shane	236	23	24	31	418,553
Wilson, Stephen R.	10	0	1	0	2,978
Wilson, Tara	27	6	5	3	51,285
Wilson, Tony	17	3	1	1	26,664
Wilson, W. D.	5	1	0	0	2,912
Wilson, Wallace C.	13	1	0	1	3,922
Wilt, Ronald J.	134	2	8	9	66,252
Wimberley, Jessie	23	2	2	4	20,123
Wimberly, Tommy	1	0	0	0	0
Wimpfheimer, Donald C.	1	0	0	0	360
Wind, Charles M.	24	2	3	6	15,170
Windle, Richard L.	22	4	3	3	45,957
Winfree, Donald R.	80	9	14	7	635,051
Winfrey, Troy B.	4	0	0	0	385
Winick, Randy	1	0	0	0	4,920
Winkelmann, Erika	48	2	5	4	51,425
Winney, Melvin	3	0	2	0	16,400
Winstead, Robert D.	41	8	5	9	118,862
Winston, Fred D.	3	0	0	1	682
Winter, Robert M.	1	0	0	0	0
Winters, Michael R.	10	0	1	2	4,106
Wippert, Jori	3	0	0	0	0
Wippert, Jr., Harold	4	0	0	0	232
Wireman, Kelly	3	0	2	0	2,054
Wirth, Kenneth B.	71	14	12	8	133,341
Wirtzberger, Jodi L.	5	0	0	0	567
Wirtzberger, Paul	2	0	0	0	0
Wisdom, Lascelles	97	9	10	16	59,588
Wise, Anthony D.	18	2	0	1	24,446
Wise, Holly	6	1	1	0	24,076
Wise, Rick A.	47	5	6	9	71,818
Wise, Ron	19	3	4	2	13,955
Wiseman, Barry G.	24	3	8	4	69,306
Wiseman, Jason A.	14	1	1	1	20,362
Wiser, Jimmy L.	142	22	13	22	342,277
Wismer, Glenn S.	138	13	14	12	183,305
Wismer, Norman P.	84	6	4	9	53,301
Wisner, Tracey J.	256	33	44	38	277,265
Wisniewski-Johnson, Mary	23	1	2	4	44,251
Withee, Henry E.	90	5	9	9	82,706
Witherow, Sandra J.	30	1	1	3	17,824
Witte, Samantha	6	1	0	1	3,463
Witthauer, John K.	119	6	6	7	61,077
Wohler, Andreas	3	0	1	0	240,000
Wolbert, Tyler	19	2	0	2	13,362
Wolf, Joan	12	0	3	2	8,460
Wolf, Larry	96	18	15	15	142,005
Wolfe, Clement	10	1	1	1	10,166
Wolfe, Greg	11	1	0	4	7,625
Wolfe, John R.	66	6	5	8	27,667
Wolfe, Judith A.	19	0	1	2	6,193
Wolfe, Jr., Robert A.	115	7	9	17	116,313
Wolfendale, Howard E.	261	73	44	46	1,130,425
Wolfendale, Ross B.	238	31	31	26	704,019
Wolfendale, Sue A.	18	5	1	3	42,399
Wolfendale, III, William H.	173	13	28	17	207,068
Wolferseder, John M.	18	1	2	1	33,550
Wolff, Perry	51	5	6	5	52,474
Wolfson, Martin D.	184	36	39	21	1,926,533
Wolfson, Milton W.	131	19	21	21	524,395
Wollfarth, III, Charles	24	1	1	4	15,006
Womack, Hulon Leslie	59	4	5	3	21,701
Wonders, Jr., John	27	2	4	4	17,146
Wood, Darwin K.	12	1	2	4	11,293
Wood, Holly	1	0	0	0	0
Wood, Jerry S.	10	0	0	0	2,801
Wood, Robert C.	90	4	9	8	42,681
Wood, Sr., Glen R.	59	4	7	5	21,619
Woodard, Joe	397	73	62	45	790,108
Woodard, Walter H.	61	3	1	4	37,393
Woodger, Patricia	20	3	2	3	32,919
Woodhouse, Edward	2	0	0	1	505
Woodhouse, Martin	57	2	4	6	38,695
Woodington, Jamie	79	8	16	11	370,197
Woods, James W.	61	3	9	7	110,930
Woods, Ronald A.	6	0	0	1	10,454
Woods, Toni	1	1	0	0	5,040
Woodward, Norm	6	0	1	1	1,025
Woolfolk, Dan	7	0	0	1	2,437
Woolley, Tim	75	14	9	14	146,401
Woolley, Jr., Bennie L.	136	11	14	18	153,482
Woolsey, Dennis D.	4	0	0	0	44
Wooten, Donald W.	23	7	4	2	103,179

RECORDS OF TRAINERS

Trainer	Sts	1st	2d	3d	Purses
Wooten, Manuel	84	4	3	9	57,606
Worcester, III, Henry E.	205	38	32	29	420,923
Worsley, John E.	40	5	5	7	54,788
Wortman, Chris	8	0	0	0	597
Worton, Jack	5	0	0	1	1,827
Wren, Bobby C.	10	0	1	0	1,680
Wren, Steve	69	12	9	9	843,190
Wright, Charles D.	96	2	14	12	101,585
Wright, Clinton W.	7	0	0	0	313
Wright, Donnie	2	0	0	0	70
Wright, James T.	240	44	36	29	326,808
Wright, Jeremy	37	2	5	5	7,900
Wright, Kairle Rindfleisch	6	0	0	0	100
Wright, Keith	8	0	1	0	1,100
Wright, Michael W.	61	6	7	11	287,973
Wright, Richard D.	66	15	14	11	108,350
Wright, Sean	2	0	0	1	1,580
Wright, William E.	1	0	0	0	0
Wright, Jr., Michael	114	16	15	15	622,059
Wrigley, Robert	7	1	0	0	6,838
Wurster, Michelle C.	6	0	2	2	6,867
Wykoff, Michael	46	4	7	6	35,516
Wynn, George A.	20	2	1	1	11,554
Wyrick, Jeff	38	3	4	5	11,180
Xerri, Louis	18	0	0	2	24,888
Yaegel, James F.	2	0	1	0	2,785
Yaegel, Thomas	49	8	3	4	34,436
Yanez, Moises R.	462	37	53	52	903,933
Yaquinta, John	10	0	1	0	3,470
Yarberry, Gene M.	6	0	0	1	912
Yarberry, Laura Jan	1	0	0	0	43
Yarger, Jerry	59	4	9	6	41,908
Yates, Jim	62	4	9	6	86,079
Yates, Michael	5	0	0	0	2,590
Yates, Richard	14	2	2	3	20,375
Ybarra, Patricio G.	27	4	1	5	5,811
Ybarra, Rudy D.	15	0	2	0	1,371
Yeagley, William R.	77	2	3	10	24,040
Yearout, Judi	40	6	3	6	12,010
Yeigh, Raymond R.	19	1	1	1	9,134
Yellowmule, Mike	3	1	0	1	1,616
Yelvington, Mel	30	2	8	2	6,843
Yerke, Gordon	27	1	6	5	5,212
Yetsook, George G.	54	10	14	5	241,101
Ylioja, Ken	14	0	0	1	1,280
Yochum, Charles	1	0	0	0	72
Yon, Jeff C.	11	1	0	0	3,920
Yonker, Lyle A.	6	2	0	0	4,700
York, Gene	27	6	7	2	72,411
York, Jack William	140	9	10	13	69,664
York, Keith L.	6	0	0	1	3,274
York, Michael	98	2	4	4	21,133
Young, Brent	8	2	2	0	3,228
Young, Daniel J.	20	3	2	6	9,758
Young, David A.	4	0	1	0	5,920
Young, David P.	1	0	0	1	6,864
Young, Don A.	40	2	3	6	28,581
Young, Don D.	90	12	11	7	22,257
Young, Donald M.	4	0	0	0	0
Young, Eugene	79	7	13	6	66,697
Young, Jack	42	3	10	5	55,508
Young, Joe D.	8	0	4	2	8,921
Young, John W.	37	2	1	4	14,808
Young, Louise	8	1	0	0	2,220
Young, Mary	6	1	0	0	7,076
Young, Nicole	54	2	6	9	45,164
Young, Phebe D.	70	9	7	14	102,856
Young, Phillip	11	1	0	0	1,736
Young, Robert A.	178	25	32	24	338,160
Young, Steven W.	81	15	6	13	447,640
Young, Teresa L.	13	1	1	0	5,246
Young, Terry R.	38	0	4	1	24,535
Young, Troy	260	42	38	35	980,844
Youngs, Frank W.	85	9	4	9	99,956
Yourchisin, Joseph E.	134	26	19	17	334,763
Yourman, Ernest E.	49	3	3	7	57,244
Yousif, Edmond	11	1	4	2	25,579
Yovanovich, Donald	53	2	3	6	54,694
Yu, Danny	56	7	7	4	331,766
Yuelapwan, Kintai	33	3	3	3	82,700
Zacco, Mario T.	20	1	2	2	76,360
Zagin, Nancy Ann	62	7	8	6	48,059
Zahl, Robert	93	17	18	9	219,077
Zajaczkowski, Cezary	8	0	0	1	2,860
Zamora, Jamie	6	0	4	1	18,465
Zamora, Ricardo	48	2	3	3	49,912
Zanelli, Dante	84	6	7	11	148,404
Zanette, Peter P.	9	2	0	1	30,041
Zanini, Maribeth	2	1	0	0	7,218
Zanni, Domenic	5	0	0	0	540
Zavash, Kerry	56	5	5	8	119,052
Zavitsanos, James	87	11	11	8	85,952
Zawislak, Dale	3	1	0	1	956
Zawitz, Joel	20	2	0	3	35,660
Zazueta, Hector	21	3	1	1	42,850
Zdunick, Fern	48	10	6	14	73,252
Zeek, Jeffrey	51	2	2	5	42,451
Zegowitz, Raymond W.	69	7	8	9	99,893
Zehnder, Charles D.	8	1	1	0	10,159
Zehnder, Clarence F.	150	15	10	24	170,754
Zeigler, Larry E.	12	0	2	0	6,278
Zeis, Arthur J.	134	18	21	13	199,824
Zeis, Kevin J.	79	6	7	10	70,900
Zelasney, Emil A.	44	1	4	6	13,604
Zele, Mark	67	2	5	6	31,500
Zeltt, Scott M.	16	0	2	1	9,713
Zenon, Alvin	17	1	0	0	6,600
Zenon, Jr., Curley	102	3	8	8	45,232
Zeringue, Jr., Whitney J.	64	11	7	8	191,137
Ziadie, Kirk	62	14	14	8	285,203
Ziadie, Ralph	375	44	53	55	1,389,608
Ziccardi, Arnold W.	13	1	1	2	11,689
Ziegler, Peggy Sue	4	0	0	0	0
Zielinski, Greg	97	13	13	7	162,628
Zielinski, Richard	28	4	1	4	33,925
Zilber, Maurice	1	0	0	0	6,000
Zimmer, Mark	2	0	1	0	4,392
Zimmer, Thomas L.	19	1	0	0	5,553
Zimmerman, John Charles	553	132	101	69	1,654,261
Zimmerman, Jon Phil.	209	34	26	35	205,760
Zimmerman, Mary B.	46	3	5	8	98,082
Zimmerman, Sr., Reggie N.	11	0	0	3	3,505
Zingelmann, Michael S.	3	0	1	1	1,627
Zingelmann, Tiffany	3	0	1	0	1,910
Zissides, Gust	63	7	9	6	158,861
Zita, Danny	24	2	2	2	59,952
Zito, Nicholas P.	507	77	86	59	5,344,914
Zmyewski, Stephen A.	15	0	4	0	11,341
Zook, Donna S.	41	0	2	3	12,988
Zook, Jimmy	164	34	25	24	620,618
Zoppi, Joseph	31	5	1	3	68,730
Zucker, Howard L.	96	5	13	13	491,147
Zureick, Frank J.	14	0	0	0	2,451
Zuver, Shannon	10	1	2	2	11,280
Zwiesler, Michael	60	12	6	5	206,474

2003
RECORDS OF JOCKEYS

The record of each jockey, who rode
thoroughbreds in the United States and Canada
during 2003, appears in this section,
showing the year born, place of birth, number of starts,
firsts, seconds and thirds, and the total purses
earned by the horses ridden.

RECORDS OF JOCKEYS

Jockey	Sts	1st	2d	3d	Purses	Jockey	Sts	1st	2d	3d	Purses
Abbott, Emma Jane	105	16	15	13	$170,058	Baker, Christopher John	406	43	59	48	457,300
Abernathy, Becky	70	4	9	10	22,095	Baldillez, Orlando	2	0	0	0	1,560
Aceves, Eddie	1	0	0	0	50	Baldillez, Roy	3	0	1	0	1,612
Acosta, Edgar	3	0	0	0	265	Balls, Jim D.	160	9	21	14	45,500
Acosta, J. D.	1,193	152	152	134	2,360,396	Balsom, Lisa	11	2	0	4	4,030
Acridge, Jeremy	353	23	29	28	270,506	Barajas, Jose J.	56	3	5	4	34,513
Adam, Mathieu G.	678	59	70	70	523,438	Barber, Monica	174	26	25	24	69,023
Afanador, Benjamin	2	1	1	0	13,000	Barber, Ryan	86	7	10	6	113,460
Agnew, John	4	0	1	0	660	Barber, Shawna	169	21	15	16	111,760
Agrasal, Jorge	2	0	0	1	1,815	Bariain, Juan	1	0	0	0	330
Agro, Janet A.	2	0	0	1	213	Barnes, Elmo	41	1	1	3	13,691
Aguilar, Manuel	1,142	113	167	140	2,846,007	Baros, Russell Anthony	32	2	1	3	17,965
Aguirre, Eric	151	9	15	15	101,354	Barrio, Anna M.	233	14	21	33	49,128
Aguirre, Silverio	4	0	0	0	760	Barrow, Nate	12	0	1	1	1,573
Ahern, Eddie	1	0	0	0	0	Barton, Jake	617	88	100	67	2,228,485
Albanese, Harry	15	0	0	2	2,703	Bautista, Alex	166	49	25	35	265,163
Albarado, Robby	1,123	185	205	180	11,061,314	Bautista, Carlos A.	2	0	2	0	4,500
Albright, Amy R.	1	1	0	0	14,250	Baxter, Dennis E.	72	0	1	8	7,677
Alcala, Natividad	105	6	11	3	60,610	Bazan, Jesus	10	0	1	0	2,941
Alexander, Samuel H.	1	0	0	0	100	Baze, Gary	713	109	106	104	1,473,126
Alferez, Jose O.	217	18	24	36	349,412	Baze, Michael C.	633	86	94	94	1,689,908
Alfred, Jr., Ricky	29	0	0	2	2,603	Baze, Russell A.	1,359	410	289	192	6,917,685
Alicea, Manuel	23	1	2	4	23,829	Baze, Tyler	1,299	175	178	187	7,518,061
Allardyce, Ross A.	29	0	2	2	12,130	Beach, Everett Lee	123	5	8	16	51,572
Allen, Joel William	143	12	17	15	40,330	Bealby, Ashley	1	0	0	0	750
Allen, Mike	470	38	52	53	548,884	Beasley, Jeremy	997	201	133	127	2,567,947
Almeida, G. F.	447	40	55	51	1,620,798	Beauregard, Shannon	371	47	45	44	387,203
Alpander, Tamay B.	149	4	6	15	91,781	Beck, Daniel Lee	314	28	38	43	221,059
Alvarado, Frank T.	839	111	124	115	3,074,049	Beckner, Dale V.	522	66	45	53	1,584,120
Alvarado, Luis	18	0	0	1	4,410	Beckner, Twyla	397	79	59	65	261,854
Alvarado, Nazario	389	35	29	39	310,254	Beckon, Chad	49	3	1	6	138,534
Alvarado, Pedro V.	551	124	104	78	1,951,115	Beech, Clive T.	347	35	34	34	290,617
Alvarado, Jr., Roberto	910	193	154	131	4,026,410	Begley, Jr., Earl	2	1	0	0	4,490
Ambrosino, Gary	3	0	0	0	805	Beischer, Danielle	49	11	10	6	12,609
Amonte, Frank	11	1	0	3	4,391	Beitia, Alexis O.	8	0	0	1	5,314
Anderson, Brett W.	23	0	2	2	2,279	Bejarano, Rafael	1,440	260	202	190	4,912,559
Anderson, Dennis	4	0	0	0	260	Bell, Derek C.	563	105	80	72	1,230,614
Anderson, Devon	143	8	9	15	136,369	Bello, Jose M.	243	17	28	25	160,660
Anderson, Mark	538	57	65	52	296,441	Bellocq, Remi	1	0	0	0	1,020
Ando, Happy H.	16	0	0	1	4,048	Belmonte, Luis A.	903	120	130	109	875,121
Andrews, Maureen E.	402	32	30	30	577,017	Belmonte, Willie	584	62	51	53	416,087
Appleby, Jr., David L.	161	7	13	16	73,322	Benavides, Daniel	507	60	76	54	420,693
Aragon, Jorge	58	1	1	5	20,182	Benitez, Jose	88	3	3	5	50,307
Arango, Luis E.	314	33	37	42	631,187	Benitez, Pedro	107	4	4	8	48,889
Ardoin, Ronald D.	65	4	6	3	67,380	Benjamin, Chad	39	6	2	3	11,997
Arechiga, J. Efrain	24	1	2	0	9,657	Bennett, Tony Ray	20	1	3	3	4,441
Arguello, Jr., Fabio A.	551	42	42	50	630,325	Bentley, David	122	16	16	32	458,091
Arias, Juan Carlos	5	0	2	1	7,845	Bermudez, Jose E.	336	42	37	39	665,117
Arias, Juan Pablo	59	4	5	4	30,837	Bernal, Octavio	860	99	101	116	912,070
Arreola, Alberto Hernandez	32	4	3	3	24,647	Berrio, Omar A.	419	46	35	48	1,098,777
Arreola, Enrique H.	88	6	7	5	77,600	Berry, Lisa	6	0	1	0	7,700
Arriaga, Gregorio	1	0	0	0	190	Berry, Monte Clifton	1,057	199	175	146	2,114,269
Arriaga, Otto	204	7	16	4	145,992	Berryhill, Dale	46	6	2	8	23,558
Arroyo, E. Nelson	204	21	22	24	233,663	Berryhill, Dennis P.	19	6	4	1	16,980
Arroyo, Wilfredo	10	1	0	0	5,420	Betancourt, Headley	231	18	23	29	187,691
Arroyo, Jr., Norberto	475	48	47	52	2,146,662	Betancourt, Nick	1	0	0	0	0
Arruda, Tonja A.	376	54	35	37	330,220	Bethley, Stanley	40	0	2	2	16,049
Arteaga, Juan	1	0	0	0	0	Beverly, Ronald	228	27	25	32	72,598
Ashburn, Mark	3	0	0	0	0	Bickel, Richard	65	6	12	3	78,550
Atkinson, Paul	217	15	14	24	485,860	Biles, Stephen	2	0	0	0	115
Atkinson, Travis	15	1	0	5	2,800	Bilodeau, Ronald Joseph	86	25	19	14	45,820
Austin, Keith A.	115	5	5	9	49,566	Birzer, Alex	938	104	125	119	1,624,996
Avant, James E.	175	19	19	19	249,685	Birzer, Gary A.	1,202	142	164	136	2,250,055
Averill, Scott Alan	60	12	8	15	33,895	Bishop, Mike J.	127	9	11	14	27,080
Avila, Juan	59	1	1	4	20,965	Bisono, Alex	100	9	10	13	162,048
Bacchas, Gerry	7	0	0	0	620	Bisono, Caesar V.	156	17	15	13	222,932
Badamo, Joseph J.	332	74	57	43	588,799	Black, Anthony S.	705	131	127	103	3,466,248
Badilla, Jr., Joe	1	0	0	0	170	Blake, Janice	190	4	14	10	102,442
Bahen, Steven Ronald	604	61	56	59	2,915,223	Blanc, Brice	349	41	30	46	2,549,334
Bailey, Jerry D.	776	206	149	97	23,354,960	Blanco, Andry	2	0	0	0	160
Bain, Gary Wilbert	403	17	23	29	491,527	Blinston, Ron Darryl	505	61	48	54	601,168
Baird, E. T.	697	99	83	86	2,125,954	Boag, Daniel Raymond	512	56	68	63	316,633
Baird, Jerry	146	11	12	11	363,013						

Jockey	Sts	1st	2d	3d	Purses
Boag, Gary L.	260	31	33	43	244,478
Bocachica, Orlando	589	94	80	72	1,234,898
Bochinski, Brian Todd	587	80	59	71	1,764,119
Boeuf, Dominique	1	0	0	0	0
Boisgontier, Jean-Philippe	5	3	0	1	31,530
Bombek, John Joseph	2	0	0	0	300
Borel, Calvin H.	1,220	162	150	136	5,163,800
Bosley, John M.	5	0	0	1	4,000
Boucher, Richard	161	10	15	18	247,933
Boudreau, Daniel	381	42	37	47	747,260
Boulanger, Gary	1,254	183	150	181	4,656,376
Bourdieu, Jorge Martin	702	123	118	108	2,126,591
Bourque, Coby J.	299	24	29	25	260,204
Bourque, Curt C.	867	131	98	122	3,210,402
Bourque, Steven Joseph	1,026	159	145	165	2,659,284
Bowen, Chris	1	0	0	0	60
Boxie, Patrick	42	3	5	3	46,045
Boyce, Robert	111	10	16	16	74,698
Boyd, Josh S.	301	31	42	42	342,098
Bracaloni, Natasha D.	373	31	64	56	604,170
Bracetty, Jose A.	2	0	0	0	0
Bracho, Agustin P.	22	1	0	1	12,813
Bracho, Jesus A.	123	6	13	14	167,367
Bracho, Jorge G.	434	66	54	50	508,878
Bracho, Richard A.	626	71	81	74	1,699,812
Braden, Darlene	210	6	15	15	30,309
Bradley, John R.	21	0	0	1	589
Brady, Amy	1	0	0	0	69
Bramblett, Jennifer	101	3	8	10	127,615
Brasser, Jen	1	0	0	0	0
Bravo, Joe	590	128	97	84	4,928,660
Brennan, Mary Jo	59	6	5	7	141,581
Brewer, Kelvin	5	0	1	2	2,320
Brewster, Danielle	1	0	0	0	0
Bridges, Kelly	788	140	118	115	951,561
Bridgmohan, Shaun	1,166	154	118	147	6,765,343
Brimo, Julia	651	75	96	80	2,906,771
Brinkley, Darryl W.	424	21	29	33	365,489
Brinlee, Douglas Elton	8	1	0	1	1,605
Brock, Mary C.	9	0	3	3	41,816
Bronstad, Charlotte	141	6	14	13	61,453
Brooks, James Norman	1	0	0	0	132
Brooks, Jimmy Dean	1	0	0	0	294
Brooks, Melody	17	2	0	1	5,451
Brooks, Paul	6	1	0	0	1,100
Brown, Bobbie Jean	10	0	0	2	1,550
Brown, David Deforest	60	11	10	6	18,585
Brown, David Eugene	250	20	15	26	153,704
Brown, Gus M.	84	13	19	9	394,211
Brown, Ronald L.	59	1	1	3	25,650
Brown, Russell	161	13	12	10	97,446
Brown, Tracey M.	52	6	4	5	83,527
Bruin, James Edward	595	38	53	65	742,355
Brum, Nilo	4	0	0	0	200
Brutscher, Geoffrey	1	0	0	0	0
Bryan, Desmond	606	65	70	78	813,150
Bryan, Michael Wayne	81	6	6	10	76,502
Bryson, Danny	31	5	7	6	11,450
Buckland, Mark	87	4	8	5	56,583
Buckley, Parker R.	557	73	57	60	996,263
Bugeaud, Laurina	68	13	14	9	35,466
Bui, Quyet E.	157	17	18	23	189,158
Burch, Lucy	19	0	1	1	4,377
Burman, Jennifer L.	2	0	0	0	225
Burningham, Jeffery	666	35	51	78	596,899
Burns, James E.	33	0	2	3	19,535
Burress, Billy	125	6	6	14	55,873
Bush, Vernon	693	89	96	74	1,196,008
Bustamante, Ignacio	2	0	1	0	660
Butler, Beth S.	484	37	51	65	253,390
Butler, Dean P.	1,033	103	102	119	1,948,310
Butterfly, Roger	36	2	5	4	6,692
Byrne, David	2	0	1	0	2,350
Byrne, John	612	39	43	51	437,506
Cabassa, Jr., Abad	295	35	26	35	748,137
Cabrera, Francisco	1	0	0	0	140
Cabrera, Javier G.	196	18	13	22	119,144
Cabrera, Samuel	7	0	0	1	1,426
Cacha-Padilla, Benjamin	471	33	41	68	315,676
Cadman, Zoe	626	71	71	77	1,508,392
Cahanin, James Tucker	30	2	2	1	17,787
Calais, Joseph Alton	163	14	13	22	225,212
Calavia, Roberto Martinez	2	0	0	0	600
Calderon, Mario Romero	9	0	1	0	1,875
Callaghan, Slade	474	47	42	73	2,592,417
Calo, Jose Luis	1,043	119	110	116	687,424
Calucag, Caesar M.	163	7	8	12	86,592
Calva, Robert	68	3	5	8	10,033
Camacho, Fernando	171	16	30	18	66,623
Camejo, Jose M.	11	0	0	1	2,410
Camejo, Omar	453	28	37	48	638,002
Caminita, Tony	332	17	30	33	201,976
Campbell, Cameron	32	8	7	3	9,265
Campbell, Danny L.	14	0	0	2	1,559
Campbell, Danny R.	5	0	0	0	837
Campbell, David	4	0	0	0	300
Campbell, Floyd	1	0	0	0	210
Campbell, Jesse M.	790	83	93	87	1,806,903
Campbell, Joel	388	48	43	45	438,489
Campbell, Shannon	37	1	0	1	27,468
Campos, Marcial R.	4	0	0	0	378
Candanosa, Adalberto	19	0	0	2	3,089
Cano, Jr., Jack	5	1	0	1	2,804
Canon, Ricardo A.	138	4	17	19	78,362
Capanas, Steve	210	21	15	23	329,470
Capeles, Steve	666	58	76	73	423,681
Cappacetti, Gilbert	52	5	4	5	44,442
Caraballo, Jose C.	767	107	102	112	2,568,865
Cardenas, Daniel	2	0	0	0	179
Carkeek, Jerome	831	134	108	116	692,422
Carlos, Marino	258	16	25	30	230,552
Carmichael, Mikhail	2	0	0	0	0
Carmouche, Kendrick	1,081	147	180	145	2,304,251
Carmouche, III, Sylvester Joseph	75	4	7	4	47,524
Carmouche, Jr., Sylvester Joseph	570	34	52	58	512,270
Carr, Dennis	297	37	37	41	899,049
Carrasco, Ronald Lewis	46	1	5	6	12,376
Carreno, Jorge	483	64	55	49	537,645
Carrero, Victor	528	45	52	56	1,565,383
Carrizales, Santos	244	11	14	24	106,444
Carroll, James T.	1	0	0	1	2,000
Carstens, David	71	6	8	7	143,986
Carter, Peter D.	17	0	0	2	4,790
Carter, Phillip Gene	39	2	4	4	7,658
Carter, Tyrone	24	0	2	0	8,306
Carter, Jr., G. R.	88	15	19	8	141,524
Carwood, Gerry	31	3	4	3	50,150
Casebolt, Matthew	93	3	3	5	20,958
Casey, John	43	0	0	1	1,720
Castaneda, Bonnie	317	23	24	35	273,407
Castanon, Antonio Lopez	412	50	44	43	530,567
Castanon, Jesus Lopez	954	145	126	124	2,320,572
Castanon, Jose German	106	8	11	12	116,167
Castellano, Javier	1,235	182	202	177	9,558,978
Castellano, Jr., Abel	1,083	160	157	149	3,374,772
Castillo, Elaine	13	0	0	1	1,281
Castillo, Freddy A.	19	0	1	2	10,635
Castillo, Kendri	1	0	0	0	75
Castillo, Luis A.	472	38	47	54	1,428,458
Castillo, Oliver	894	103	123	126	2,794,258
Castillo, Pablo J.	18	0	0	3	5,176
Castillo, Pedro C.	302	22	38	46	301,922
Castillo, Jr., Heberto	537	37	46	40	2,052,260
Castro, Carlos L.	952	96	116	116	1,394,313
Castro, Eddie	1,256	242	257	174	3,931,877
Castro, Edwin	2	0	0	0	1,300

Jockey	Sts	1st	2d	3d	Purses
Castro, Joe M.	708	96	102	93	2,118,858
Cayo, Denis J.	18	0	1	3	13,700
Cazares, Jose	10	1	2	2	5,560
Cazares, Michael Alan	112	4	12	8	14,907
Ccamaque, Marco A.	916	138	111	93	787,850
Ceballos, Oscar	29	3	1	3	56,298
Cedeno, Amir	539	54	61	76	518,298
Cedeno, Lizetta M.	1	0	0	0	75
Cedeno, Osman	278	11	24	48	242,979
Centeno, Daniel	447	51	53	65	387,163
Cervantes, Edward Daniel	171	14	14	13	137,790
Chapa, Isaac	33	3	6	2	13,578
Chapa, Roman	871	148	129	107	2,745,909
Chaparro, Cayetano	260	28	21	31	368,293
Chapman, Kristi L.	73	4	9	11	58,461
Chappell, Sally	285	19	23	27	133,836
Chaves, Nathan J.	248	17	27	36	177,114
Chavez, Casey R.	552	50	57	59	442,179
Chavez, Hugo	17	0	2	1	6,397
Chavez, Jorge F.	1,064	154	176	126	6,736,591
Chavez, Luis D.	612	75	80	84	2,859,212
Chavez, Mark L.	3	2	0	0	8,580
Chavez, Santos Noe	25	2	1	2	27,735
Chen, Men B.	136	14	6	15	95,699
Chiappe, Ricardo	53	2	6	6	44,230
Chickeness, Sheldon	186	33	20	32	76,517
Chin Sue, Roger Terrance	213	11	12	17	111,996
Chirinos, Roimes	1	0	0	0	525
Christensen, Elisabeth	1	0	0	0	750
Chuzon, Romulo	16	0	0	0	1,329
Cisneros, Mario	8	1	1	1	7,555
Clair, Brian Thomas	24	2	1	1	19,188
Clark, Cory	319	38	37	41	759,882
Clark, David	662	104	85	70	5,677,197
Clark, Kerwin D.	1,012	155	137	119	1,753,187
Clark, Michael Dennis	390	46	63	51	735,439
Clark, Ronnie	15	0	0	0	4,455
Clark, Trevino	131	3	5	8	64,598
Clemente, Alfredo	620	57	60	73	454,545
Clemente, Alfredo V.	475	60	45	60	1,461,373
Clifton, Thomas	961	204	144	110	1,629,820
Cline, Vincent E.	696	30	47	66	606,953
Cloninger, Jr., Weldon T.	639	73	80	80	900,336
Coa, Daniel	543	74	60	59	1,399,934
Coa, Eibar	1,275	209	196	176	8,274,472
Coates, Jimmy Ray	489	51	45	55	804,897
Coburn, Lori A.	128	5	11	11	63,723
Cocks, Edwin Burling	4	0	0	0	0
Codilla, Alfredo	52	1	4	4	18,007
Coffee, Candice	3	0	0	0	0
Cogburn, Kevin Leon	969	118	131	152	1,538,569
Cohn, Gregory Eric	5	2	2	0	31,560
Collazo, Jr., Jorge E.	287	17	21	38	117,152
Collazo, Sr., Jorge E.	386	24	39	36	167,034
Colledge, Cameron	30	5	4	6	38,444
Collier, Jeremy	411	41	54	42	461,978
Collier, Tuffy	175	7	10	15	88,840
Collins, Dennis Michael	516	86	77	62	418,348
Collins, Harold	27	1	3	4	13,606
Collins, Rhonda M.	605	67	59	59	550,310
Colon, Jose A.	47	1	2	3	10,740
Colon, Oscar	1	0	0	0	0
Comfort, Martin	22	0	2	2	6,555
Compton, Perry	768	155	109	94	1,504,347
Concha, Gilbert	364	36	36	58	266,072
Condie, Kendall	22	0	1	1	3,477
Condie, Nathan R.	27	10	5	5	38,483
Conheeney, Jr., John	67	2	0	6	8,909
Conklin, Jay	152	37	32	13	138,180
Conn, Linda P.	22	1	2	0	18,759
Contreras, Baltazar	347	78	66	45	424,504
Contreras, Cruz	415	46	45	52	881,328
Conway, Christopher L.	120	11	10	17	74,642
Cooksey, Patricia J.	101	11	12	11	188,667
Cooney, Michael	24	1	0	2	12,300
Cooney, Patrick	12	0	1	2	14,250
Cora, David	1,265	244	176	172	1,688,801
Corbett, Glenn W.	939	168	155	135	2,285,784
Cordero, Luis	10	1	0	0	13,705
Cordrey, Nicholas	2	1	0	0	19,200
Cormier, Darren	16	0	0	1	893
Cormier, Logan H.	559	88	74	73	901,083
Cornwell, Richard Milton	496	62	54	59	879,568
Corrales, Max	91	4	10	4	125,349
Cortez, Alcibiades C.	606	55	64	69	956,690
Cosme, Emanuel	151	15	15	11	155,039
Costa, Antonio J.	129	4	6	9	70,987
Cotrone, Jr., Frankie	42	0	3	6	9,051
Cotto, Jr., Pedro Luis	499	39	54	48	1,274,333
Court, Jon Kenton	1,137	146	151	142	3,965,598
Coversup, Joey	29	1	2	1	3,066
Covington, Raina	327	25	23	26	227,689
Cox, Danny W.	375	38	43	37	362,924
Cox, Roger W.	19	2	0	1	11,666
Crandall, Amanda L.	118	8	11	4	66,912
Crane, Dirk	50	11	6	7	24,050
Crawford, Juan	326	55	41	42	455,249
Crispin, Joe A.	537	90	98	83	263,458
Crissup, Troy	2	0	0	0	70
Cromer, Leslie	167	10	7	13	116,843
Cruz, Anthony S.	270	12	22	19	144,392
Cruz, Antonio A.	2	0	0	1	713
Cruz, Carlos M.	355	40	45	46	1,272,164
Cruz, George Luis	101	7	9	15	56,451
Cruz, Hermes G.	2	0	0	0	107
Cruz, Joel V.	1	0	0	0	50
Cruz, Jorge B.	16	0	3	1	6,119
Cruz, Jose A.	110	18	18	18	112,988
Cruz, Manoel R.	1,579	262	241	228	5,353,375
Cuevas, Joseph	7	0	0	0	465
Cullum, Walter	109	3	13	9	93,026
Cunningham, Ferrell	1	0	0	0	0
Cunningham, Randy	94	4	15	14	33,581
Curry, Blake	2	0	0	0	1,000
Cushing, John L.	56	1	4	4	19,153
Cusson, Albert George	61	4	0	10	29,422
Cuthbertson, Alan	166	30	30	24	349,648
Dacosta, Roderick	38	3	3	2	82,592
Daigle, Eric Thomas	16	1	3	2	9,166
Dailey, Douglas Allen	7	0	0	0	1,073
Dailey, James Ray	137	8	15	15	66,567
Dale, Ashton	21	1	0	3	6,334
D'Amico, Anthony J.	466	51	44	59	1,153,896
D'Amico, Duane Lee	162	7	17	14	45,058
Dangerfield, Ty	129	21	24	23	46,973
Daniel, Clarence	110	0	4	8	41,031
Dapp, Holly	5	0	0	0	649
Darcy, Tony	23	0	1	3	11,650
Dasilva, Axel	146	14	14	13	180,943
Davenport, Christine Lynn	81	0	7	10	72,993
David, Daniel J.	320	70	43	35	1,204,246
Davies, Joe	2	0	0	0	900
Davila, Jose M.	428	41	52	55	417,670
Davila, Jr., John R.	720	141	115	89	1,164,666
Davila, Jr., Michael A.	456	54	59	47	466,617
Davis, Kenyatta	193	19	12	18	179,042
Davis, Terry	4	0	1	1	500
Davison, Adam	1	0	1	0	3,400
Day, Pat	985	215	175	110	13,378,292
De Jesus, Enecio	10	0	0	1	5,277
DeAlba, Cesar	95	16	9	9	270,960
Deaville, Kevin	756	63	66	81	560,397
DeCarlo, Christopher P.	459	47	51	56	1,553,865
Deegan, Joseph	207	19	15	23	309,243
Defreitas, Carl	21	0	0	1	5,322
Dehn, Michele	2	0	0	0	160

Jockey	Sts	1st	2d	3d	Purses
Dejesus, Esait	29	1	1	4	10,694
Del Valle, Angel	2	0	0	0	1,170
Deleon, Miguel	9	0	0	0	0
Delgado, Alberto	343	21	37	36	490,536
Delgado, Gilberto	2	1	0	0	6,360
Delgado, Gilberto Ramos	107	6	10	14	91,433
Delgado, Hector	71	6	6	9	33,738
Delgado, Jose H.	344	34	24	26	320,926
Delgado, Jose J.	665	61	50	72	796,460
Delgado, Juan F.	1	0	0	1	600
Delorme, Larren	241	34	35	36	231,891
Demesme, Elliott	58	6	2	2	41,066
Demuro, Mirco	1	0	0	0	0
Deno, Patrick	1	0	0	0	0
De'Oliveira, Wanderley G.	19	0	2	1	10,060
Deonauth, Kenneth P.	193	11	17	9	77,817
DeRidder, Karel A.	1	0	0	0	750
DesAutels, Jacques	353	38	55	47	393,553
Deschamp, Jarrod	1	0	0	0	0
Desormeaux, Kent J.	579	78	98	77	6,033,136
Dettori, Lanfranco	7	0	2	1	159,300
Deveaux, Sean R.	258	16	19	24	314,530
Deyan, Carlos	151	8	9	6	91,984
Diaz, Gadiel	1	0	0	0	1,500
Diaz, Luis Felipe	93	1	14	3	66,375
Diaz, Marcial	2	0	0	0	53
Diaz, Mario	2	0	0	0	200
Diaz, Renzo	195	13	16	20	202,390
Diaz, Sunday	540	60	66	63	807,277
Diaz, Victor M.	148	21	23	24	131,866
Diaz, Vladimir	1,029	146	150	182	1,288,382
Dickinson, Amber	41	4	2	5	10,052
Diego, Inosencio	625	61	54	60	596,628
Diego, Iram Vargas	484	45	46	54	436,674
Dieguez, Wilson Omar	908	119	108	134	987,066
Dieseth, Nils	1	0	0	0	0
Dionne, Monique J.	164	7	10	21	152,709
Doll-Carriere, Connie	113	4	6	14	22,955
Dominguez, Carlos Vicente	281	34	43	35	263,522
Dominguez, Ramon A.	1,627	453	316	252	11,359,767
Donaghey, Edgar C.	276	19	27	31	134,509
Donald, Mary	1	0	0	0	0
Doocy, Timothy T.	616	67	76	76	1,514,145
Dooley, Clifford D.	239	13	27	26	179,597
Dore, Jason	29	1	2	1	8,476
Dorr, Sandi	281	34	37	36	473,712
Dos Ramos, Richard Anthony	448	43	61	51	3,040,134
Doser, Mary Elizabeth	805	132	136	112	1,302,322
Douglas, Frank Giovanni	401	24	25	38	430,627
Douglas, Rene R.	1,075	201	170	160	6,482,949
Dow, Andrew H.	21	0	0	1	1,902
Doyle, Michael	95	2	9	8	109,877
Drexler, Hoogie	349	57	37	43	372,799
Duarte, Jr., Jorge C.	579	53	68	83	824,965
Dubois, Justin	3	0	0	1	120
Dunbar, Clay	90	9	18	19	30,949
Dunkelberger, Travis L.	1,105	219	193	131	3,283,544
Dupas, Gino	8	0	0	1	1,942
Dupuy, Allen C.	16	1	2	0	15,079
Duran, Francisco	1,153	144	165	153	2,883,409
Duran, Rodrigo Calvo	7	0	1	1	5,020
Durham, Micheal Bartlet	113	9	13	9	61,741
Durigon, Joseph L.	530	25	35	45	165,020
Durocher, Lawrence	48	11	7	9	12,156
Duys, Dodie Cartier	468	58	49	56	690,603
Dvorak-Collier, Kim	3	0	0	0	0
Dwyer, Martin	1	1	0	0	900,000
Eads, Jason R.	570	67	66	73	1,074,281
Edwards, Toby X.	1	0	0	1	1,000
Elliott, Stewart	1,314	249	205	175	3,539,826
Ellis, Philip	24	3	2	1	27,507
Ellis, Shane	124	6	12	13	361,350
Elsner, Drew	16	1	2	1	3,546
Elston, David C.	67	1	4	3	13,800
Elvira, Ignacio	3	0	0	0	0
Emerson, Liz	16	1	2	3	3,370
Emigh, Christopher A.	1,117	143	160	160	3,652,638
Endres, Jessica	680	37	34	51	261,209
Engblom, Henryk	4	0	0	1	1,755
Enriquez, Isaias D.	529	39	47	46	1,307,675
Epsteen, Joyce	92	5	8	4	13,642
Ernst, Bryan	127	12	12	16	42,654
Escobar, Edward	6	0	0	0	960
Escobar, Martin	886	113	127	87	1,166,117
Escobar, Victor	484	45	36	65	525,429
Espada, Jose E.	109	4	6	12	106,065
Espindola, Miguel Angel	79	5	4	9	84,911
Espinosa, Luis	543	76	59	67	569,019
Espinoza, Jose L.	536	31	49	46	1,975,306
Espinoza, Victor	1,325	206	182	203	10,004,495
Espitia, Jorge	2	0	0	0	262
Esposito, Anthony C.	158	6	6	9	75,208
Espy, Kym	94	8	10	12	37,713
Esquibel, Richard D.	257	5	17	17	81,441
Essman, David Wilder	501	36	30	45	449,196
Estevez, Rafael	11	0	1	1	4,935
Estrada, Alex	169	14	15	11	208,560
Estrada, Eberd	196	27	21	16	365,198
Estrada, Luis	1	0	0	0	700
Estrada, Jr., Salvador	63	6	4	5	71,649
Estrella, Rafael I.	335	15	21	38	264,559
Evans, Ann	3	0	0	0	312
Evans, Burton	116	7	26	18	36,736
Evans, Sean P.	294	36	32	33	364,997
Everingham, Keith	1	1	0	0	9,000
Faine, Craig Phillip	326	7	14	24	161,985
Fallon, Kieren	2	1	0	0	553,985
Farachio, Giordano	29	0	2	3	7,478
Farina, Tony	157	22	14	25	1,081,670
Farrar, Jimmy	43	2	3	7	6,698
Faul, Jeffrey Harvey	401	60	50	33	539,668
Faul, Ricky J.	217	16	20	23	343,849
Favero, Kirk	4	0	0	0	104
Feliciano, Daniel	20	1	3	1	9,554
Feliciano, Ricardo	666	92	100	89	1,212,892
Felix, Angel	266	14	8	24	95,500
Felix, Julio E.	881	137	105	117	1,618,096
Fennell, Herman	13	7	2	2	5,220
Fenwick, III, Charles Cuthbert	7	4	1	0	58,500
Fernandez, Rene	1	0	0	0	85
Ferrer, Felix O.	25	2	1	1	21,414
Ferrer, Jose C.	644	111	90	53	3,041,892
Ferris, Alex Stan	50	6	7	4	79,409
Fetters, Michal	43	1	2	4	27,075
Feurtado, Edmund	3	0	0	0	154
Fewster, Emily	1	0	0	0	0
Fiddler, Roy	18	1	2	4	2,489
Fields, Danny	2	0	0	1	600
Figueroa, Jose	339	28	33	53	262,460
Figueroa, Louie Araiza	30	2	1	5	4,931
Figueroa, Omar	416	48	49	70	924,645
Fires, Earlie	607	76	77	79	2,130,783
Fisher, Jack	3	1	0	0	16,450
Fisher, Shelia	8	3	0	4	21,300
Fitzpatrick, Ashton	169	12	8	14	176,030
Fletcher, Jr., Charles A.	105	2	5	6	20,173
Flett, Gary	4	0	0	1	712
Flores, David Romero	1,039	155	168	122	10,759,008
Flores, Emilio	1,261	184	159	158	1,487,158
Flores, Fredric R.	101	9	8	11	76,595
Flores, Isaac Meza	34	1	2	0	14,909
Flores, Jeremias	606	61	71	84	525,110
Flores, Jose Luis	1,115	205	171	144	2,747,252
Flores, Jose M.	152	6	4	15	83,039
Flores, Laureano	159	16	17	18	194,869
Flores, Oscar	1,044	183	150	127	2,486,401

RECORDS OF JOCKEYS

Jockey	Sts	1st	2d	3d	Purses
Flores, Pedro	4	1	0	2	8,020
Flores, Ramon	1	0	0	0	100
Flores, Vicente	772	67	81	73	478,001
Fogelsonger, Ryan	1,388	278	234	257	5,903,822
Foley, Tom	121	16	22	18	556,350
Fongsue, Garth W.	90	1	3	6	26,006
Fontanez, Jorge L.	176	21	16	28	59,764
Fontenot, Timothy J.	495	32	31	58	293,262
Forgar, Brian	3	0	0	0	360
Forgar, Eric	19	1	2	4	8,038
Forkhamer, Pauline	255	16	20	30	163,559
Forrest, Charles W.	797	72	89	80	1,138,554
Fortner, Joddie Lee	461	29	32	37	266,540
Fortuna, Jesus	9	0	0	0	186
Foster, Cody	45	11	8	8	20,012
Fox, Tammy Lee	49	8	5	6	145,936
Fragoso, Pablo	909	103	120	103	3,987,229
Fraser, Cory	29	4	4	1	106,815
Frates, Dean Joseph	428	38	34	56	302,648
Frazier, Don Lee	454	32	42	56	252,586
Frazier, Ricky	325	36	40	33	573,265
Frazzitta, Jr., Leonard J.	593	38	56	42	273,739
Freeman, Debbie A.	29	8	7	2	19,812
Freeman, Gregory	2	0	0	0	0
Freeman, Roger	6	1	1	0	4,574
French, Don Lee	142	12	13	19	31,137
Fritz, Julie	62	10	9	9	41,185
Fuarez, Guillermo	1	0	0	0	130
Fuentes, Adan	434	44	51	47	710,862
Fuentes, Alfonso S.	14	0	2	2	8,128
Fuentes, Edwin	156	6	9	14	79,977
Fuentes, Francisco Perez	435	59	58	63	1,032,798
Fuentes, Freddy	263	35	22	33	343,536
Fuentes, Mauricio E.	24	3	1	3	33,750
Fuentes, Miguel Sanchez	325	38	31	35	584,057
Fusilier, Casey	824	98	116	97	1,206,325
Gabriel, Ron E	270	27	29	43	226,826
Galarza, Neftali	14	1	2	2	11,366
Gale, Michael Allen	359	59	44	60	410,194
Gallo, Anthony	193	9	7	14	114,523
Galluccio, Joseph	1	0	0	0	0
Galvan, Mario A.	162	6	6	11	91,309
Gamez, Fernando Manuel	334	56	58	41	122,382
Gamez, Larry	98	4	5	6	91,007
Gann, Sandi Lee	490	84	69	62	640,999
Ganpath, Ray	94	15	15	10	847,600
Garcia, Alan	209	27	26	32	551,279
Garcia, Alejandro	115	15	10	13	88,679
Garcia, Carlos	382	43	34	29	501,573
Garcia, David	478	34	41	45	546,031
Garcia, Eddie V.	1	0	0	0	315
Garcia, Enrique	20	0	1	1	7,070
Garcia, Francisco	386	34	44	55	554,664
Garcia, Francisco F.	37	0	2	2	11,967
Garcia, Gilberto	11	0	0	0	680
Garcia, Jason	53	1	2	4	36,083
Garcia, Jesse Jimenez	18	0	2	2	9,047
Garcia, Jose A.	1	0	0	0	130
Garcia, Julio A.	536	105	84	64	2,790,993
Garcia, Luis	1,270	179	178	165	2,603,914
Garcia, Luis A.	447	40	28	43	520,939
Garcia, Manuel	3	0	1	0	840
Garcia, Matt S.	462	40	50	58	1,698,728
Garcia, Noe	10	0	1	3	4,620
Garcia, Pedro L.	11	0	0	1	995
Garcia, Jr., Ralph J.	20	8	4	4	13,532
Garcia, Jr., Randy L.	23	4	1	2	38,369
Gard, Terry Lee	164	15	21	21	44,158
Gardiner, Timothy N.	348	43	44	42	383,444
Garner, Cathleen J.	330	48	30	27	373,481
Garner, Charles Edward	6	0	0	0	495
Garnett, Garfield E.	5	0	0	0	230
Gates, Lee	44	5	4	3	19,885
Gelpi, Jr., Angel	65	3	7	9	33,838
George, Duane David	117	2	5	9	90,148
George, Harold	2	0	0	0	0
Geraghty, Barry	1	0	0	0	0
Gerardo, Ronald	2	0	0	0	0
Giacomelli, Tim	7	0	1	0	679
Gibson, Sarah	47	1	1	6	24,174
Giles, Chad	5	0	0	1	1,141
Gillam, Diana	15	1	3	2	48,307
Giraldo, Alfreado J.	16	0	0	0	3,839
Glasser, Todd	450	69	65	62	1,047,227
Goad, Jr., Kenneth Ray	55	4	6	5	25,725
Goberdhan, C. Paunchie	1	0	0	0	91
Goff, Jr., B. L.	41	0	3	2	7,103
Gold, Benjamin Kevin	39	1	1	4	6,329
Golibrzuch, Siggy	123	4	9	5	43,675
Gomez, Alvaro	5	0	0	1	2,000
Gomez, Alvaro	1	0	0	0	50
Gomez, Emilio R.	7	0	0	3	9,380
Gomez, Esteban Angel	1,171	195	166	160	1,333,625
Gomez, Luis Norbeto	5	1	0	0	2,480
Gomez, Octavio	6	1	1	1	1,820
Gomez, Oscar	121	3	2	0	102,743
Gomez, Roger	407	36	41	54	360,280
Gondron, Ted D.	636	93	68	70	1,081,215
Gonsalves, Frank Albert	533	81	79	67	774,390
Gonzales, II, James Julian	89	10	8	7	130,833
Gonzales, Alfredo	25	0	0	3	3,288
Gonzalez, Carlos	735	96	88	92	1,651,015
Gonzalez, Ivan R.	823	143	131	107	980,238
Gonzalez, Luis Antonio	933	157	122	108	1,666,350
Gonzalez, Omar D.	46	1	4	2	17,044
Gonzalez, Roberto M.	855	166	130	104	3,237,018
Gonzalez, Jr., Angel	15	1	2	1	18,590
Gonzalez, Jr., Sal	221	35	27	18	999,489
Goodgame, Rachel	4	0	1	1	2,195
Goodwin, Nik G.	586	43	69	57	1,002,504
Gordon, David Joseph	106	13	9	12	91,642
Gordon, Duncan S.	65	3	5	9	12,398
Gorman, David	1	0	0	0	0
Govia, David	5	0	0	0	510
Grabowski, John A.	553	128	88	85	1,037,942
Gracie, Chris	15	2	1	2	52,650
Grafton, Dwayne A.	151	18	16	12	212,135
Graham, James	419	20	43	47	434,454
Granda, Alejandro T.	589	61	63	68	349,314
Granda, Romel	9	0	0	0	1,606
Gray, Akili	277	6	10	16	67,646
Gray, Christina	271	11	19	24	138,107
Green, Brian D.	41	2	3	4	7,212
Green, Christopher	5	0	0	0	510
Green, Mandy	23	0	0	1	3,379
Greene, Casey	21	5	4	5	12,875
Greenway, Thomas Edward	5	0	0	1	2,200
Grenamyer, April J.	30	1	1	1	8,389
Griffin, Everett D.	18	1	2	7	8,060
Griffith, Christopher	610	77	89	96	1,617,098
Griffiths, Mark	47	1	4	3	42,450
Grove, Larry	1	0	0	0	0
Gryder, Aaron T.	756	78	94	94	3,797,879
Guajardo, Alonzo	497	47	55	50	267,834
Guce, Ramon	376	36	44	45	304,814
Guerra, Jorge A.	855	100	94	111	577,306
Guerra, Vince J.	698	81	94	94	540,348
Guevara, Tito	1	0	0	1	975
Guidry, Mark	868	117	95	109	4,763,739
Guillory, Susan	56	3	2	5	27,861
Gulas, Laurie L.	96	3	12	23	266,979
Gunn, Remi	73	3	5	9	41,751
Gutierrez, Guillermo R.	299	34	49	42	246,175
Gutierrez, Jose Arturo	384	36	33	52	301,400
Gutierrez, Juan M.	926	194	156	141	1,165,975
Gutierrez, Pedro	2	0	0	0	100

Jockey	Sts	1st	2d	3d	Purses
Guymon, Tony F.	98	9	5	6	54,555
Haden, Larry	16	0	1	1	1,124
Hadley, Russel	18	3	2	1	3,193
Haire, Timothy	6	0	0	1	2,040
Hall, Jesse	1	0	0	0	0
Hambleton, Anne	7	1	2	1	7,500
Hamel, Richard Harvey	649	82	88	85	1,197,401
Hamilton, Donald Bruce	54	4	8	4	14,839
Hamilton, Jennifer S.	1	0	0	0	
Hamilton, Quincy	82	7	7	7	64,181
Hamilton, Travis	47	6	15	7	26,037
Hammett, Lisa	111	13	12	12	218,052
Hampshire, Jr., Josiah Francis	833	168	135	89	1,924,804
Han, Amanda	60	4	10	3	34,247
Hanna, Weldon	1	0	0	0	210
Hannigan, Lyndon	901	82	115	104	683,946
Hansby, Antonio E.	3	0	0	0	0
Hanscom, Sherry	1	0	0	0	0
Hansen, Larry	1	0	0	1	252
Hansen, R. J.	8	0	1	2	560
Hanson, Joe	1	1	0	0	7,500
Harding, Tyrone	401	38	53	52	853,026
Harmon, Kim	12	0	0	1	1,697
Harris, B. Buck	568	44	40	63	424,712
Harvell, Mike W.	189	29	26	26	87,447
Harvey, Barrington	233	12	20	19	181,850
Hastie, Robert M.	201	9	9	19	84,110
Hawkins, Scott	11	0	0	0	1,290
Heard, Loring	3	0	0	1	2,250
Hebert, Amy	4	0	1	0	2,750
Hebert, Carl	207	32	32	32	106,118
Hecio, Ashley	6	0	0	1	1,000
Heiler, Stephan	576	91	80	89	1,137,043
Heim, Kenneth	21	1	0	1	2,530
Helton, Rita M.	307	19	38	19	190,950
Hemmings, Tara	611	46	46	76	400,887
Hemsley, Dale	346	32	25	34	449,319
Hendricks, Ken	199	19	31	29	267,526
Henry, Guy	3	0	0	0	700
Henry, Wesley	19	0	7	0	10,622
Henry, William T.	86	9	10	7	100,459
Henson, William	291	18	24	29	138,614
Herber, Jr., Donald D.	47	3	3	12	19,322
Herbert, Roman	4	0	0	0	346
Heredia, Julio J.	111	5	4	14	67,745
Hernandez, Adrian	463	45	41	52	518,013
Hernandez, Alexander A.	90	3	7	7	22,121
Hernandez, Alfredo B.	191	3	3	7	49,815
Hernandez, Brian Joseph	712	84	95	83	1,113,190
Hernandez, Carlos Alberto	229	17	26	29	471,829
Hernandez, David C.	184	8	7	14	67,364
Hernandez, Miguel Luis Gaeta	1,031	161	177	177	1,122,416
Hernandez, Noe A.	52	1	5	2	15,803
Hernandez, Ruben	18	0	1	1	4,161
Hernandez, Jr., Brian Joseph	68	12	16	3	168,249
Herrell, James Christopher	704	84	86	72	567,724
Herrera, Ramiro	6	0	1	2	7,396
Hershbell, Alison L.	127	9	11	18	199,484
Hicks, Shannon M.	1	0	0	0	0
Hightower, Travis Wayne	448	100	66	50	783,767
Higuera, Alberto R.	908	118	123	131	849,912
Hilburn, Wendell John	465	34	46	42	208,397
Hill, Channing	3	0	0	0	151
Hills, Claire	6	0	0	1	460
Hinojosa, Thomas	33	2	4	5	16,771
Ho, Sunny	78	2	1	6	32,200
Hodsdon, Danielle	56	8	5	4	132,378
Hogbin, Leigh	3	1	1	0	13,200
Holassie, Raynau K.	4	0	0	0	379
Hole, Taylor M.	770	122	115	105	1,358,068
Holland, Darryll	1	0	0	1	233,200
Hollick, William J.	294	17	27	22	303,840
Holmes, Mike	21	1	3	5	9,130
Holmes, Jr., Joe S.	24	1	1	1	3,194
Holmes, Sr., Joe	97	11	19	19	36,699
Homeister, Jr., Rosemary B.	996	107	127	120	2,717,392
Horner, Ellen	2	0	0	0	800
Houghton, Rick L.	139	19	15	15	130,019
Houghton, T. D.	63	9	6	9	99,484
House, Cody	33	4	2	1	8,223
Hoverson, Chad	98	8	9	9	75,963
Howard, William E.	11	1	1	2	4,793
Howarth, Jr., Albert L.	71	9	11	16	34,923
Huayas, Rafael	1	0	0	0	75
Hudson, Kehron	8	0	0	0	629
Hughes, Richard	2	0	0	0	3,180
Hundley, John D.	24	2	1	3	11,674
Hunt, Charleen	268	18	32	27	366,819
Hunt, Jimmie J.	12	0	0	0	691
Hunter, Michele L.	5	4	0	0	18,375
Husbands, Patrick	882	168	144	117	11,168,817
Husbands, Simon P.	419	38	33	43	2,075,204
Huston, Sharon T.	1	0	0	0	150
Hutton, Greg W.	272	22	19	24	636,657
Iammarino, Michael Phillip	478	52	40	60	472,262
Iniguez, Salvador	46	0	3	2	9,055
Iorg, Shawn	1	0	0	1	330
Irion, Heather	30	5	2	3	20,236
Irving, Mark Neil	55	1	2	7	22,794
Itschner, Christine	33	3	2	1	10,027
Jacinto, John	1,163	140	148	129	2,006,702
Jaen, Abdiel	57	5	3	1	66,521
Jaime, Ricardo	613	117	94	83	1,797,654
James, Lee	7	2	0	3	4,180
James, Michael C.	595	64	64	70	475,130
Jaramillo, Emisael	130	8	12	15	128,945
Jarvis, Jennifer	1	0	0	0	0
Jauregui, Luis H.	225	16	15	15	473,919
Jawny, Alvaro	378	42	56	37	639,601
Jean, Patra	5	0	1	0	2,130
Jellison, Jill Ann	390	54	47	54	633,286
Jenkins, David C.	249	21	27	24	325,166
Jensen, Cody	16	2	4	3	32,975
Jensen, Loren Dale	4	0	0	1	2,027
Jerman, Jeff B.	202	17	25	20	187,951
Jessup, Timothy V.	114	15	8	9	112,066
Jewell, Jerry William	125	9	13	12	64,446
Jimenez, Ada	1	0	0	0	205
Jimenez, Alex	433	22	35	37	358,693
Jimenez, Ender	163	7	11	19	153,425
Jimenez, Fabrizio M.	102	10	8	14	167,052
Jimenez, Rafael S.	22	1	3	1	12,620
Jimenez, Silvester R.	5	0	0	0	237
John, Kerwin	241	17	21	29	252,473
Johns, Thomas Cecil	113	6	5	11	73,505
Johnson, Bobby L.	210	33	27	19	312,858
Johnson, Del M.	2	0	0	0	144
Johnson, Joe M.	554	65	63	60	1,251,770
Johnson, Patrick A.	234	9	21	29	283,850
Johnson, Richard	323	24	28	33	298,178
Johnson, Robert W.	441	45	48	63	635,123
Johnson, Stephanie A.	15	0	1	1	3,996
Johnston, Jeff	915	123	109	105	1,634,848
Johnston, Mark T.	440	36	62	44	1,036,783
Jones, Clark E.	282	31	30	42	239,082
Jones, Doug A.	106	16	20	12	41,574
Jones, Jono C.	646	91	74	101	5,348,472
Jones, Robert A.	2	0	0	0	61
Jordan, Jimmy	22	1	0	2	5,523
Jouteau, Etienne	1	0	0	1	1,870
Juarez, Calixto	150	6	7	11	114,531
Juarez, Jr., Alfredo J.	538	43	59	56	1,179,167
Juarez, Sr., Alfredo V.	23	2	2	4	28,025
Judice, Joseph C.	1,221	276	191	155	2,563,372
Jurado, Enrique M.	406	53	47	45	1,111,905
Juvonen, Allison	6	1	1	2	16,255

Jockey	Sts	1st	2d	3d	Purses
Kabel, Todd	836	160	163	110	11,323,313
Kaenel, Jack Leroy	4	0	0	0	839
Kallse, Anita	1	1	0	0	7,800
Karamanos, Horacio	1,286	179	176	191	3,740,427
Karn, David A.	2	0	1	0	240
Karr, Dan	47	7	7	4	14,556
Karr, Stephen Michael	380	42	50	53	115,362
Kato, Akifumi	196	7	13	20	75,279
Kaufman, Casey	698	68	90	100	546,192
Keckler, Ron W.	475	44	62	76	209,711
Keefer-Muniz, Marge	25	3	0	1	26,114
Keiser, Justin	12	0	2	1	4,440
Kelsey, Zack	9	2	1	0	3,598
Kenny, Jocelyne	146	11	14	15	81,813
Kenny, Mike	18	1	0	0	11,807
Kenny-Martin, Jocelyne	150	16	17	16	106,596
Keshane, Norbert	16	0	3	1	1,773
Kewin, Steve	8	0	1	2	4,804
Kimes, Curtis	446	43	58	60	483,860
Kinane, Michael J.	4	1	0	1	899,800
King, Dallas	381	26	13	25	250,851
King, Diane Lynn	8	1	0	0	4,759
King, John	2	0	0	0	150
King, Jr., Edwin L.	688	65	87	104	1,946,284
Kingrey, Russell David	74	16	8	8	32,241
Kingsley, Jr., Archibald	27	9	2	5	114,960
Kinsey, Jill E.	110	11	7	13	133,706
Kirlew, Lenworth G.	177	9	17	21	156,718
Kirlin, Thomas	9	0	1	1	4,550
Kistler, Dan	14	0	4	2	2,807
Klinger, C. Omar	407	44	44	44	860,118
Knapp, Karen	258	40	32	40	156,126
Knight, Lester Cash	750	87	110	99	929,632
Knott, Rick L.	399	32	40	32	254,631
Kohlweiss, Irene	1	0	0	0	390
Korrell, Brian	6	0	2	2	5,325
Krasner, Samuel B.	240	45	37	33	887,925
Kravets, Justin	560	74	53	72	890,387
Kreidel, Kaymarie	250	20	25	24	388,232
Kretzer, Kerry D.	352	23	26	25	378,706
Kreutziger, Monalee	4	0	0	1	775
Krigger, Kevin	629	64	77	92	1,417,232
Krone, Julie A.	806	139	103	93	8,202,107
Kuntzweiler, Greta	592	51	52	50	1,078,370
Kurek, Gary	398	61	63	54	416,140
Kutz, Carl Mel	210	21	12	29	171,975
La Forge, Frank	50	6	8	11	10,417
La Sala, Jerry	266	31	32	37	566,569
Labonte, Arthur	2	0	0	0	168
Lacoursiere, Larry J.	394	43	52	49	665,105
Laducer, Cody	2	0	0	0	100
Lake, Anne-Marie	61	2	2	4	21,285
Lakeman, Andrew	12	0	1	0	8,510
Lambert, Casey T.	790	120	106	109	1,898,311
Lambeth, Denise	81	10	12	13	36,444
Lampton Jr., Mason	6	0	1	0	3,300
Lanci, Howard L.	108	7	11	12	34,117
Landaker, Terri	190	50	37	31	177,726
Landeros, Benny C.	147	9	15	18	83,095
Landry, Leo	1	0	0	0	0
Landry, Robert C.	451	53	61	70	4,243,567
Lanerie, Corey J.	1,341	231	225	215	6,187,084
Lang, C. T.	20	0	1	2	10,490
Lapensee, Michel	136	8	18	16	102,645
Larrosa, Gustavo	592	33	47	55	509,984
Larsen, Shaunda L.	52	7	8	6	16,000
Lasso, Yonis	276	17	38	28	163,014
Latchman, Rennie	212	55	44	33	164,209
Latham, Jeremy	54	8	10	7	21,907
Laurente, Godofredo	4	0	0	1	2,315
Lauzon, Jack M.	471	59	55	52	1,222,205
Lavergne, Danny J.	26	3	3	3	16,171
Laviolette, Shane	853	89	81	109	1,856,532
Lavoy, Rachel	201	15	20	17	400,160
Lawrence, II, James	2	0	0	0	1,045
Laws, Nicky M.	2	0	1	0	1,200
Lawson, Mark	217	16	21	37	258,477
Leacock, Jason	316	47	46	43	404,838
Leaf, Jr., Robert	2	0	0	0	0
LeBlanc, Don C.	229	1	9	8	45,580
LeBlanc, Kirk Paul	1,030	154	156	126	2,972,269
Leeds, Damon	587	67	63	45	997,376
Leggett, Tad W.	4	0	0	0	0
LeJeune, Ronald J.	1	0	0	0	0
LeJeune, Jr., Sidney P.	815	84	91	97	1,040,279
Leon, Filiberto	8	1	1	1	45,220
Leonard, Brian Leslie	71	1	5	5	16,522
Lester, Robert Neal	479	44	55	46	496,073
Lewis, Cedric Orlando	6	0	0	0	600
Lewis, Jr., William R.	4	0	0	0	651
Leyva, Juan C.	474	48	49	52	598,762
Lian-Reavey, Twei	3	0	0	0	100
Lidberg, David W.	2	0	0	0	0
Linares, Modesto	302	27	26	25	249,873
Lindsay, Eldridge K.	235	20	22	22	347,704
Lister, Mark	121	11	13	8	64,686
Lockett, Rochelle	2	0	1	0	1,300
Logan, Allison	1	0	0	0	0
Logan, Greg	8	0	0	0	267
Long, Brian	62	4	2	6	71,447
Long, Daron Kay	1	0	0	0	125
Long, James S.	30	0	5	4	16,480
Lopez, Adalberto Diaz	452	56	73	61	1,128,033
Lopez, Charles C.	995	141	146	148	4,610,902
Lopez, David G.	989	123	157	168	2,101,889
Lopez, James	565	60	80	55	1,566,172
Lopez, Jose E.	611	75	86	88	1,080,804
Lopez, Lorenzo Castane	658	82	86	79	572,035
Lopez, Uriel A.	658	43	74	69	1,040,268
Lopez, Jr., Carlos E.	25	1	0	2	35,785
Lordan, Wayne	30	4	1	2	27,022
Loseth, Chris	449	59	56	60	945,024
Lott, Robert	3	0	0	0	0
Louchart, Ronald Alan	22	1	2	4	8,840
Lovato, Anthony J.	241	24	24	37	586,554
Lovato, Jr., Frank	697	82	94	82	2,400,210
Love, Lisa	37	0	1	1	9,602
Lovelace, Austin K.	2	1	0	0	7,800
Lozano, Jr., Wilfredo L.	603	65	52	82	750,534
Luark, Mark	48	0	0	2	4,280
Lucero, Delano	58	1	3	4	18,957
Luciani, Dino	466	55	54	52	2,784,710
Ludlow, Megan	319	37	28	37	229,607
Lujan, Alfonso	1	0	0	0	0
Lumpkins, Jason P.	958	197	127	129	3,515,564
Luna, Alejandro	1	0	0	0	133
Luna, Ramon	653	70	68	71	425,281
Lundberg, Elizabeth L.	11	0	0	1	3,453
Luttrell, Michelle	14	2	1	4	28,625
Luzzi, Michael J.	1,248	165	157	198	7,772,168
Luzzi, Jr., John B.	394	31	35	45	492,496
Lydon, P. J.	80	5	5	10	123,498
Lynch, Fergal	2	0	1	0	8,200
Lyons, Christopher	2	0	0	0	1,950
Lyons, Gabe	1	0	0	0	0
Macias, Guadalupe	292	10	16	29	211,118
MacKay, Kelly A.	162	12	17	22	234,089
Maddock, Patrick	2	0	0	0	380
Maddrix, Tim	3	0	0	0	0
Madeira, Carlos D.	502	60	56	65	1,076,508
Madrid, Nicky A.	170	20	18	24	183,008
Madrid, Sebastian O.	225	26	29	19	472,265
Madrid, Jr., Art	79	5	5	9	109,620
Madrigal, Jr., Rodrigo	802	119	102	109	2,723,456
Magera, Clint	282	19	25	29	136,578
Magrell, Jane M.	543	37	61	59	444,621

Jockey	Sts	1st	2d	3d	Purses
Mailhot, Pierre	213	12	24	17	274,667
Maldonado, John I.	105	7	10	10	67,146
Maldonado-Alicea, Edwin	780	61	71	85	622,934
Maloney, Paul	407	26	42	40	242,568
Mancilla, Oscar G.	230	18	13	22	226,059
Mancuso, Andrea A.	48	1	3	2	16,887
Mangalee, Navin	239	14	26	41	175,036
Mangold, Kevin	522	28	30	46	440,558
Mangual, Samuel	148	2	5	14	73,334
Manickram, Macelin	307	29	39	43	231,077
Maragh, Allen	210	17	15	20	218,507
Maragh, Rajiv	1	0	0	0	80
Marcial, Alejandro	106	3	10	6	90,428
Marcial, Benjamin	546	36	52	45	645,939
Margrave, Loecca	1	0	0	1	288
Markham, Jr., Richard Leroy	490	30	31	31	435,230
Marks, Ronald J.	139	3	9	4	48,873
Marquez, Jr., Carlos H.	841	145	93	113	3,422,747
Marshall, Danny	19	1	3	2	2,716
Marshall, Melissa	9	1	0	2	2,168
Martin, Christopher	250	29	25	25	507,574
Martin, Clyde W.	353	32	53	48	766,928
Martin, Kenny	1	0	0	0	2,855
Martin, Jr., Eddie M.	1,175	203	179	162	4,846,092
Martinez, A. J.	1	0	0	0	0
Martinez, Armando	878	129	114	95	631,805
Martinez, Eddie	2	0	0	0	448
Martinez, Felipe F.	766	59	87	92	1,857,407
Martinez, Frank O.	3	0	0	0	345
Martinez, Frankie W.	5	1	0	0	8,424
Martinez, Freddie L.	53	6	5	0	44,473
Martinez, Jaime	102	8	11	8	29,979
Martinez, Joe A.	64	5	5	10	94,712
Martinez, Luis Angel	7	2	0	0	22,998
Martinez, Luis Jeronimo	510	85	72	86	865,781
Martinez, Manuel	73	2	8	5	87,675
Martinez, Orlando A.	760	81	113	84	551,312
Martinez, Pedro	1	0	0	0	60
Martinez, Roberto	2	0	1	0	5,664
Martinez, Seth B.	667	120	105	86	1,306,289
Martinez, Willie	840	82	97	86	2,328,580
Martinez, Jr., Jose R.	517	55	59	55	1,269,915
Martinez, Jr., Luis J.	501	46	47	47	619,586
Martinez, Jr., Severiano	37	2	3	2	29,129
Marzullo, Vincent	3	0	0	1	2,500
Mascarte, Magali	111	4	11	13	57,921
Mason, Ingrid	17	1	1	3	18,068
Massey, Robert	106	14	19	10	442,150
Mata, Federico	1,378	206	173	168	1,779,351
Matias, Mike	10	2	0	0	13,060
Matilda, Mike	17	1	2	1	3,040
Matos, Juan G.	40	2	4	4	35,201
Matteucci, Tony	387	34	26	38	266,395
Matutes, Leoncio	370	29	29	50	278,029
Matz, Nena	637	116	100	71	1,099,653
Mauldin, Jerry E.	17	0	1	0	1,163
Mavec, Kathleen	41	3	2	5	26,817
Mawing, Anthony	1,453	211	169	192	3,434,041
Mawing, Leslie	737	79	102	105	872,808
May, Robert Houston	271	28	25	29	391,991
Mayhew, Glenmore W.	132	4	12	6	60,908
Maysonett, Francisco Z.	357	29	32	37	492,262
Mayta, Jorge	6	0	0	0	61
McAleney, James	734	112	101	95	6,672,531
McAleney, Peter	138	35	22	23	114,091
McBean, Keith A.	12	1	0	2	9,650
McCarron, Matthew Otis	99	17	16	6	302,250
McCarthy, Christopher	1	0	0	0	300
McClaran, W. Bill	25	0	1	1	2,784
McClellan, Charles Lyn	191	12	14	14	44,401
McClurg, Leroy	1	0	0	0	160
McCormack, Calvin	28	3	3	3	64,425
McCormick, Mark L.	440	47	47	60	426,285
McDaniel, Tina	2	0	0	0	330
McDonogh, Declan	1	0	0	0	0
McFadden, Bridget	1	0	0	0	400
McFadden, David J.	870	132	125	97	2,204,616
McGee, Terrence	237	8	9	19	50,581
McGowan, Mathew Carroll	898	95	95	104	1,306,632
McIntosh, Edgar	26	0	0	1	3,705
McIntosh, Kimberly R.	191	5	17	22	185,885
McKann, Patrick	3	0	0	1	1,210
McKee, John	1,475	212	202	230	6,027,114
McKee, Kevin Richard	19	1	1	0	6,865
McKnight, James	292	51	40	45	2,516,379
McMahon, Charles Warren	29	0	4	1	17,353
McMahon, Cynthia Jean	95	17	13	9	321,724
McMillan, Kenneth McKay	169	18	12	17	213,391
McMullen, Michael Joseph	133	4	15	9	144,000
McNeece, Jerry Odell	60	4	4	5	17,417
McTurner, Teri	180	11	13	13	222,400
McWade, Richard	10	0	0	1	3,210
McWhorter, Robert S.	117	3	5	9	35,625
Meador, Michael V.	30	2	1	3	12,320
Means, Dennis M.	89	19	12	10	212,898
Meche, Donnie J.	208	26	21	19	830,620
Meche, Lonnie	1,026	162	156	131	3,725,447
Medellin, Alejandro	12	2	1	3	38,110
Medina, Cynthia M.	320	66	57	54	472,459
Medina, Nelson R.	50	4	11	5	33,550
Medina, Jr., Rafael	109	5	18	12	67,783
Meier, Randall A.	632	74	67	74	1,698,435
Meister, William	8	0	0	2	3,400
Mejia, Cesar	10	0	0	0	1,340
Melancon, Gerard	1,409	247	205	183	4,927,346
Melancon, Kevin Lee	86	3	4	4	31,261
Melancon, Larry	521	65	56	58	2,576,557
Melancon, Larry J.	639	61	72	63	624,305
Melancon, Paul	2	0	0	0	0
Melchor, Victor W.	20	0	0	2	5,921
Melenciano, Valentin	132	5	7	17	55,815
Mellish, Brooke	179	18	20	36	78,910
Mello, David	131	8	12	18	105,522
Memis, George	14	0	2	0	1,433
Mena, Manuel	1	0	0	1	900
Mena, Miguel	149	13	11	18	185,655
Mendez, Emmanuel	311	25	28	39	350,822
Mendez, Jose P.	181	15	19	27	108,660
Mendoza, Angel	12	0	0	1	1,338
Mentuck, Vince	5	1	0	0	1,140
Mera, Julio C.	19	0	1	0	3,035
Mercado, Pedro	248	33	26	28	365,161
Mercado, Victor V.	305	51	37	42	130,862
Mercieca, Marty J.	256	19	27	25	361,594
Messina, Robert	618	103	82	86	913,588
Meyers, Richard	4	0	0	0	433
Meyers, Tommy	171	21	23	13	257,445
Meza, Nicholas	207	8	19	14	155,354
Migliore, Richard	1,027	186	132	133	9,505,289
Milian, Jorge Luis	199	7	17	25	127,450
Millan, Sheila T.	16	0	0	1	1,046
Miller, Zach	12	0	0	3	4,070
Miller, Jr., F. Bruce	50	7	11	4	212,584
Minks, John	1	0	0	0	420
Mino, Oclides A.	55	2	1	5	21,195
Miranda, Alfredo	460	40	51	50	543,497
Miranda, Victor	299	30	25	36	326,251
Mitchell, Gallyn Vick	488	70	98	81	807,567
Mitchellhill, Sally	1	0	0	1	2,750
Miyashiro, Cliff James	134	17	24	14	83,682
Moccasin, Andrew	39	2	1	2	3,803
Moccasin, Tim	176	36	32	26	107,929
Mojica, Orlando	1,365	209	187	165	1,959,350
Mojica, Jr., Rafael	453	37	45	48	965,971
Molina, Tommy	662	71	92	65	1,686,372
Molina, Victor H.	612	75	72	69	1,223,413

Jockey	Sts	1st	2d	3d	Purses	Jockey	Sts	1st	2d	3d	Purses
Molinari, Edwin	284	43	38	39	552,786	Odom, Carl Mccannan	5	0	0	0	145
Mondragon, Sergio	8	0	0	0	532	O'Donnell, Kristin	156	21	16	24	59,895
Monette, Sidney	5	0	2	0	1,035	O'Farrill, Orlando	115	6	7	6	25,456
Montalvo, Carlos	596	53	58	64	1,180,555	Offutt, Leigh	77	2	4	7	50,870
Montano, Chris	125	12	12	12	136,992	O'Hara, Liam	16	0	1	3	10,050
Montehermoso, Edgar	189	15	19	26	46,324	Olesiak, Jake	4	0	1	1	1,703
Monterrey, Pedro	37	1	0	3	10,845	Olesiak, Jordan	318	18	22	27	110,232
Monterrey, Richard	1,164	172	187	143	2,869,556	Olguin, Ever Romero	202	24	18	21	242,609
Monterrey, Jr., Peter	5	0	0	1	3,435	Olguin, Gerry	433	49	44	42	2,362,545
Montoute, Schemlin	22	2	1	5	67,398	Olivares, Frank	100	8	12	9	198,846
Montoya, Daryl	390	48	49	41	736,990	Oliver, Rick	11	1	0	0	1,638
Montoya, Jose	1	0	0	0	132	Olivera, Juan Manuel	154	7	14	16	63,732
Montpellier, Constant	658	80	96	97	4,678,130	Olmo, Christian J.	115	6	8	10	101,712
Moore, Kathleen E.	25	5	0	6	7,063	Olmstead, Jason	21	0	3	3	6,102
Moore, Rory T.	37	2	2	4	22,038	Orantes, Faustino	1	0	0	0	110
Morales, Adolfo A.	1	0	0	0	65	Ore, Zarella	15	1	0	2	6,868
Morales, Christobal E.	172	11	5	18	87,520	Orm, Scott	25	1	0	2	7,715
Morales, Jose A.	23	1	2	1	9,166	Ortega, Aurelio	2	0	0	0	275
Morales, Luis D.	1	0	0	0	348	Ortega, Javier A.	50	3	8	1	20,066
Morales, Oscar	12	0	0	1	6,950	Ortega, Juan	1,038	101	123	127	1,635,569
Moran, Shelley Lee	537	43	46	55	275,908	Ortega, Oscar	1	0	0	0	920
Morgan, Luis	315	22	27	42	72,377	Ortiz, Felix L.	495	39	53	46	891,920
Morgan, Michael R.	533	56	61	58	770,759	Ortiz, Jr., Ivan	276	27	29	28	180,394
Morris, Liz	267	22	24	18	353,401	Ortiz, Jr., Manuel Figueroa	220	17	17	33	183,063
Morris, Ryan	490	29	58	54	537,815	Osorio, Jose David	216	17	17	17	110,967
Moss, Rick	35	2	4	3	26,106	Otero, William P.	808	117	122	100	945,395
Mower, Lavar	3	0	0	0	132	Ouzts, Perry Wayne	1,406	198	187	184	1,523,268
Mudd, James	2	0	0	0	0	Pabon, Jr., John C.	349	17	21	31	159,346
Mueller, Tiffany	9	2	2	2	31,200	Pacault, Anne-Sophie	1	0	0	0	780
Munar, Luis H.	476	45	60	60	679,342	Pacheco, Enrique	18	2	2	0	14,465
Munoz, O. Robert	281	27	24	37	195,061	Packer, Berkley R.	329	67	50	43	287,006
Murphy, Chad K.	965	156	132	125	2,794,719	Padilla, Juan	324	24	25	25	167,847
Murphy, Cyril	69	13	4	8	321,916	Pagan, Norberto	130	2	6	18	52,410
Murphy, Glen	458	55	57	56	890,734	Page, Mark	260	24	24	25	213,100
Murphy, Jeff	47	3	3	3	54,975	Pailhes, Patrick	2	0	1	0	3,000
Murray, Kelly Michael	588	57	61	55	618,961	Painter, Leanne M.	677	96	95	108	1,452,572
Murray, Kevin C.	398	35	31	33	223,958	Pakootas, Scott	4	0	0	3	730
Nagle, Valerie	41	2	4	2	52,034	Palmer, Lisa	1	0	0	0	55
Nakatani, Corey S.	922	124	131	149	8,518,363	Palmer, Roy Walter	53	4	5	4	70,783
Napravnik, Jazz	1	0	0	0	0	Panas, Deirdre A.	447	31	31	37	335,390
Naupac, Alejo	41	1	5	3	23,424	Panell, Dyn	688	99	106	97	1,278,089
Navarro, Dionicio	57	1	3	4	17,316	Pantall, Demelza	1	0	1	0	5,250
Navarro, Victor G.	275	18	26	36	249,671	Papineau, Cammie	85	13	19	10	36,373
Navedo, Edwin	216	12	19	24	131,768	Parenti, Jr., Jerry J.	111	8	13	11	108,958
Neal, Tim	1	0	0	0	132	Parish, Ramon	8	1	2	0	13,535
Ned, Hosea A.	54	1	2	1	21,107	Parker, Deshawn L.	1,497	236	200	184	3,561,933
Neilson, Katherine S.	1	0	0	0	375	Parra, Hernan	34	1	2	3	16,508
Nelson, Ashlie	1	0	1	0	960	Paschal, Vince	3	0	0	1	1,300
Nelson, Diane	113	11	16	18	421,280	Patrick, Marty	3	0	0	2	1,675
Nelson, Leroy	213	18	15	20	255,405	Patton, David Burton	486	56	60	54	581,609
Nelson, Tyler	6	0	0	0	110	Paucar, Edgar	251	32	26	22	187,229
Nguyen, Tho	598	64	72	72	1,055,902	Payne, Eric R.	497	45	53	58	463,912
Nichols, Jerri Elizabeth	708	71	65	79	913,443	Payne, Larry D.	62	18	11	13	127,010
Nicol, Jr., Paul Albert	644	110	94	76	1,259,019	Peck, Brian Dale	363	34	41	33	1,019,526
Nieto, Carlos	914	129	126	107	938,243	Peck, Donna	64	2	3	9	61,970
Ning, Stan	298	12	25	40	252,197	Pedroza, Eduardo	1	0	0	0	45,000
Nixon, Keith	5	0	0	0	529	Pedroza, Martin A.	946	144	132	126	3,983,182
Noel, Rory Garrell	79	3	5	11	27,229	Peery, Melissa	324	49	42	46	140,689
Noguez, Tony	394	43	47	38	439,978	Peltroche, Freddy	28	2	0	6	25,150
Nolan, Paul M.	779	96	94	102	816,496	Pena, Antonio	230	18	23	27	284,104
Noll, Cindy Sue	577	67	79	86	1,244,230	Penalba, Cecilio	507	53	46	51	863,222
Nollar, Flip John	679	67	79	88	248,679	Pennington, Frankie	247	28	23	31	195,502
Nomee, Shann	9	0	0	1	326	Perdomo, Teofilo A.	118	10	13	17	87,042
Norris, Michael J.	133	4	12	8	55,461	Pereira, Oswald M.	1,164	155	142	155	2,279,108
Norwood, Jake K.	2	0	0	0	543	Perez, Antonio	39	10	5	4	12,786
Nuesch, David C.	436	35	34	41	982,459	Perez, Bonifacio	40	3	7	5	57,199
Nunez, Eduardo O.	944	87	103	141	2,224,296	Perez, Eduardo E.	537	57	68	54	1,294,570
Nunez, Rafael A.	9	3	0	0	20,119	Perez, Edwin	640	89	82	78	614,853
Nunn, David G.	4	2	1	1	16,050	Perez, Luis E.	258	20	25	34	345,168
Nunn, Doug	1	0	0	0	150	Perez, Miguel A.	464	61	47	83	877,906
Nuttall, Todd J.	358	49	38	34	129,192	Perez, Nilo	474	36	44	39	678,590
Obed, Keturah E.	135	3	10	9	45,943	Perez, Roberto A.	1,014	95	97	111	1,640,171
O'Callaghan, Gina	2	0	0	0	2,000	Perez, Salvador	415	30	24	42	233,117

Jockey	Sts	1st	2d	3d	Purses
Perez, Jr., John A.	370	26	21	33	399,751
Perkinson, CC	41	3	1	4	22,882
Perret, Craig	90	16	13	14	1,061,940
Perrodin, Elvis Joseph	525	85	66	75	2,432,172
Persaud, Randi	31	1	1	1	25,890
Peslier, Olivier	2	0	0	1	26,970
Petro, Nicholas J.	192	30	41	30	887,415
Pettinger, Donald R.	448	71	70	55	2,113,937
Petty, Jody	91	11	12	12	263,685
Petty, Kristy	75	5	2	7	70,216
Pezua, Julio Molina	200	10	19	19	523,892
Pham, Van Dung	3	0	0	0	0
Phillips, Mark	764	107	114	102	1,179,954
Phillips, Michael D.	8	0	0	0	0
Phillips, Tony	18	0	0	1	5,371
Pierce, Brett Taylor	5	0	0	0	0
Piermarini, Tammi	650	65	86	81	888,999
Pimentel, Julian	670	107	97	98	3,326,817
Pimentel, Rui M.	236	33	22	28	832,094
Pincay, Jr., Laffit A.	229	49	34	31	1,967,131
Pindell, Michael Duane	605	66	60	88	1,039,919
Pineda, George	2	0	0	0	69
Pino, Mario G.	1,175	247	184	165	5,265,850
Piques, David A.	294	21	24	35	464,778
Pizarro, Juan	75	5	4	8	75,675
Pizarro, Ruben	13	0	0	0	1,298
Platts, Lisa	161	11	16	12	393,515
Poe, John	4	0	1	0	6,140
Poleo, Cesar	65	1	5	2	29,547
Polkey, Melissa	12	0	0	1	3,436
Pompell, Thomas L.	1,218	180	161	147	1,907,249
Portillo, Douglas A.	50	1	5	3	26,020
Potts, Clinton L.	675	116	99	89	2,535,014
Powell, Dean	1	0	0	1	758
Poznansky, Neil	559	87	62	77	1,608,504
Prado, Anibal	906	89	88	109	1,168,620
Prado, Edgar S.	1,478	259	235	207	18,475,582
Prather, Kris	155	16	11	14	183,451
Pratt, Robert	1	0	0	0	288
Prescott, Rodney A.	1,564	185	201	186	2,051,659
Price, Andro Lee	27	2	3	1	18,077
Privitera, Richard	19	4	3	6	49,265
Pruitt, Jerry	273	32	43	38	332,660
Puello, Nathaniel	33	1	1	1	7,906
Puglisi, Ignacio	497	46	65	36	2,026,425
Purdome, Johanna	94	6	5	11	24,229
Quewezance, Enoch	16	2	3	4	2,866
Quinn, Christopher A.	128	6	13	16	65,614
Quinones, Luis M.	438	26	38	31	440,918
Quinones, Jr., Esteban J.	18	1	1	0	9,778
Quinonez, Belen	432	24	31	38	375,774
Quinonez, Luis S.	1,018	154	131	133	2,993,293
Quong, Michael D.	264	10	27	27	269,777
Rabbitskin, Hector	104	6	15	12	15,961
Radke, Kevin	971	186	140	147	2,034,196
Raghunath, Raymond	36	2	1	3	57,511
Rambaran, Lester L.	18	0	2	0	4,177
Ramgeet, Andrew R.	582	76	81	73	1,385,754
Ramirez, Antonio	130	9	18	17	58,506
Ramirez, Esgar	5	0	0	0	708
Ramirez, Martin Ramos	928	153	125	109	2,596,851
Ramirez, Ricky	14	0	3	1	6,754
Ramirez, Roberto	181	7	21	28	171,148
Ramirez, Victor	200	7	13	11	124,341
Ramirez, Jr., Raul	1	0	0	0	50
Ramos, Adrian B.	718	55	71	83	598,825
Ramos, Hector A.	6	0	0	0	810
Ramos, Hector G.	505	88	62	69	1,024,110
Ramos, Ramon	42	1	1	1	17,203
Ramos, Jr., Walter W.	5	1	0	0	2,665
Ramsammy, Emile	838	127	104	99	7,203,924
Ramsammy, Mark	35	1	2	3	29,120
Ramsay, Robert	6	0	0	1	1,655
Randle, Stephen	106	12	10	7	27,850
Raney, Leon Anderson	61	3	1	5	39,210
Ranilla, Luis	619	79	91	87	419,760
Ransom, Bobby	2	0	0	0	0
Rasmussen, Judd	12	0	0	2	494
Razo, Jr., Eusebio	978	163	148	115	4,410,042
Read, Christopher	21	5	3	1	104,200
Rechy, Ramon	225	18	21	29	145,671
Reeves, Jr., Robert F.	228	9	20	24	128,597
Reid, Alphonso	13	0	0	1	2,760
Rennie, Chandra R.	388	35	32	39	753,364
Retana, Gabriel Compos	113	6	11	18	44,195
Reyes, Mario Jose	476	22	43	42	267,091
Reyes-Frisby, David	96	4	9	7	18,660
Reynolds, Larry C.	553	47	55	52	878,995
Reynolds, Lori E.	5	0	0	0	1,898
Rice, Alan	5	0	0	1	2,750
Rice, Bacarra Lynne	99	6	6	9	48,016
Rice, Jessica	35	2	3	0	29,411
Richards, Gary	284	17	16	20	282,276
Rini, Wade P.	517	43	67	66	600,815
Rios-Conde, Alexis	660	49	62	87	715,699
Riquelme, Jose	239	20	16	15	266,420
Riston, Joseph A.	50	3	7	2	14,915
Rivas, Carlos	227	24	26	16	281,351
Rivera, David M.	667	82	89	83	642,754
Rivera, Gilbert D.	8	0	2	1	2,160
Rivera, Gregorio A.	5	1	0	0	4,725
Rivera, Heriberto	14	0	0	0	1,874
Rivera, Hiram G.	720	97	78	97	1,111,529
Rivera, Jorge	268	25	28	26	285,375
Rivera, Jose M.	3	1	0	0	3,355
Rivera, Juan G.	480	41	58	58	394,881
Rivera, Luis Raul	1	0	0	1	1,265
Rivera, Marco A.	114	4	8	11	57,947
Rivera, Miguel L.	36	1	4	4	39,315
Rivera, II, Jose Alberto	543	47	54	66	964,231
Rivera, Jr., Jose L.	749	86	80	95	1,222,196
Rivera, Jr., Jose M.	228	22	26	28	82,391
Rivera, Jr., Luis Romero	497	53	40	55	949,844
Rivera, Sr., Luis D.	1	0	0	0	0
Robertson, Alexandra	2	1	0	0	20,600
Robinson, Edward Keith	459	27	39	56	644,684
Robinson, Kristopher	210	21	25	25	425,483
Robinson, Rick B.	3	0	0	1	425
Robletto, Luis	406	54	60	60	476,045
Rocco, Joseph	583	73	66	77	1,244,338
Rocco, Jr., Joseph	505	40	55	57	985,591
Rocha, Jorge O.	142	8	11	18	99,421
Rocha, Jose O.	21	0	0	0	405
Rochabrun, John	269	17	17	32	215,706
Roche, Jennie	39	4	8	8	33,861
Rocheleau, Serge R.	179	36	31	29	83,275
Rock, Damien	2	0	0	0	0
Rodriguez, Adolfo C.	77	3	4	9	46,068
Rodriguez, David	46	1	1	4	13,359
Rodriguez, Edilberto	129	5	14	10	127,145
Rodriguez, Eduardo E.	22	0	1	4	14,922
Rodriguez, Erick D.	1,060	128	155	144	2,132,617
Rodriguez, Filemon T.	164	6	9	18	66,722
Rodriguez, Gabriel A.	98	9	9	15	63,798
Rodriguez, Hector Q.	34	3	1	1	25,320
Rodriguez, Jesus G.	109	0	0	3	8,994
Rodriguez, Macario	461	43	54	66	595,399
Rodriguez, Marcelino	97	7	8	10	47,379
Rodriguez, Pedro A.	729	112	123	105	1,181,989
Rodriguez, Rudy R.	134	11	3	12	223,723
Rodriguez, Victor	4	0	0	1	896
Rogers, Jan	128	7	5	19	68,871
Rohena, Juan	58	4	1	5	23,084
Rohena, Manuel	510	79	80	81	718,753
Rohena, Jr., Rafael	231	27	33	19	194,784
Rojas, Christian	650	65	70	68	514,586

RECORDS OF JOCKEYS

Jockey	Sts	1st	2d	3d	Purses	Jockey	Sts	1st	2d	3d	Purses
Rojas, Eduardo E.	1	0	0	0	230	Scarlett, Andy	156	27	23	31	64,669
Rojas, Fernando S.	188	7	19	17	75,099	Schacht, Randy	237	31	29	21	299,021
Rojas, Johnny	140	10	17	15	98,693	Schaefer, Gregory Allen	591	54	67	64	725,012
Rojas, Raul I.	272	13	18	23	514,480	Scharfstein, Jillian	449	37	54	55	1,512,398
Rojas, Ruben	112	6	14	7	55,597	Schindler, Scot A.	173	25	23	24	155,068
Roll, Michael	149	14	12	10	145,523	Schmidt, Jennifer	127	4	12	6	52,447
Roller, Robert Edward	9	0	3	1	3,176	Scholes, Adrian	2	0	0	0	400
Rollins, Chance J.	1,054	168	171	155	3,044,796	Schooley, Chris	41	1	1	1	4,301
Romero, Arturo	84	5	7	11	55,925	Schvaneveldt, Chad Phillip	870	168	142	126	3,345,865
Romero, Hector R.	195	17	24	18	238,335	Schwartz, James Daniel	533	64	62	73	476,556
Romero, Josh M.	991	93	106	106	885,951	Scocca, Dante	28	5	1	4	77,315
Romero, Shane P.	318	24	26	19	294,983	Scott, Joy Marie	168	7	16	16	104,306
Roncin, Terry R.	154	15	12	9	96,907	Sealock, Regina	233	14	23	24	306,293
Rosado, Roberto J.	408	44	62	64	821,286	Searchwell, Gilbert Rodney	66	1	3	2	31,039
Rosales, Arturo Garcia	251	18	25	31	201,554	Seesequasis, Janice	157	13	21	31	47,246
Rosario, Yamil	337	27	37	28	344,081	Segundo, Manuel A.	8	0	0	0	1,286
Rosario, Jr., Hector L.	949	161	173	122	1,290,526	Sellers, Shane J.	971	163	159	124	6,556,788
Rose, Jeremy	1,008	154	170	148	4,516,749	Sensenbach, Lee	512	31	55	56	200,986
Rosendo, Irwin J.	505	72	67	84	560,488	Serna, Fernando	168	11	21	24	258,662
Rosenthal, Mark E.	764	97	84	68	1,628,197	Serrano, Angel	71	2	7	7	41,549
Rosier, Chris R.	197	7	13	15	109,113	Serrano, Robert	9	0	2	1	12,665
Roughley, Adam Wade	123	10	16	16	34,955	Sessions, Nick	7	0	0	0	1,165
Rowland, Michael Francis	923	155	152	102	1,554,297	Shamsie, Clayton P.	129	4	8	9	52,143
Rozas, Emeterio	3	0	0	0	0	Sharp, Joey	1	0	0	0	0
Rozman, Albert A.	202	6	9	10	59,516	Shaw, Aaron	3	0	0	0	263
Rubio, Carlos	1	0	0	0	320	Shaw, Rusty D.	5	1	0	1	11,620
Ruhe, Schad	4	0	0	0	1,093	Shaw, Wayne	1	0	0	0	0
Ruis, Mick	510	85	73	57	727,690	Shepherd, David R.	43	1	2	4	16,612
Russell, Ben	343	63	63	55	762,958	Shepherd, Justin	479	44	41	48	742,363
Russell, Chris	3	0	0	0	1,460	Shepler, David	17	2	2	3	27,145
Russell, Wazzeer B.	19	0	1	1	5,014	Sherbino, Shawnette L.	13	0	1	1	4,901
Ryan, Colvin G.	37	4	1	3	42,450	Sherman, Casey	20	2	6	3	6,799
Ryan, Jamie Scott	2	0	1	1	4,220	Shino, Ken A.	798	95	95	97	1,337,632
Sabourin, Raymond Brian	317	30	41	34	1,685,052	Sibille, Ray	231	21	23	26	618,359
Saint-Martin, Eric	72	7	11	10	290,575	Siddo, Augustus	151	2	10	12	118,538
Saito, Scott T.	591	95	84	96	846,173	Siebeneicher, Laura H.	64	0	5	4	14,015
Salazar, Hector	59	2	4	7	40,947	Sierra, Joseph A.	152	9	12	18	86,905
Saldanha, Alessander	4	0	0	0	1,410	Sillars, Belinda	1	0	0	1	1,000
Salguero, Salomon	54	0	2	2	14,757	Silva, Carlos H.	702	84	76	93	2,073,144
Salvaggio, Mark V.	207	32	36	28	308,808	Silva, Carlos Ignacio	39	4	2	7	41,413
Salvino, Duane Michael	311	25	36	22	137,470	Silva, Jose	37	4	3	5	94,623
Salvo, Paula Frances	5	0	0	2	4,409	Simard, Real E.	634	82	70	77	1,273,095
Sam, Connie	9	0	2	1	842	Simington, Donald Edward	976	123	142	118	1,770,847
Sampson, Kelly	9	0	1	0	4,555	Simpson, Gillespie	10	0	0	1	5,740
Samyn, Jean-Luc	373	36	35	50	2,377,998	Simpson, Mike	38	6	10	5	27,660
Sanches, Jose H.	10	1	1	1	19,676	Singh, Rohan R.	282	41	47	34	592,481
Sanchez, Andre	185	3	10	12	101,234	Singh, Sunny	235	25	26	25	789,063
Sanchez, Angel B.	12	3	2	1	20,935	Sit, Vincent	3	0	0	0	708
Sanchez, Carlos	221	13	14	14	102,166	Skaggs, Tad Wayne	204	22	26	29	70,950
Sanchez, Jesus	817	92	72	90	1,256,890	Skelly, Robert V.	356	32	46	49	590,919
Sanchez, Joseph	362	45	23	41	256,807	Skerrett, Jeffrey	806	108	83	94	1,196,232
Sanchez, Marcos	20	0	1	1	4,965	Skinner, Colin	652	77	73	75	613,706
Sanchez, Miguel A.	99	6	8	13	88,238	Slaughter, Dayton	199	7	9	25	158,462
Sanchez, Richard A.	305	26	30	29	126,616	Slaven, Mark	41	1	2	3	8,481
Sanchez, Jr., Jose A.	296	36	48	38	396,100	Smallwood, Vickie Yolanda	143	11	18	14	152,397
Sandoval, Donald	5	1	1	0	1,946	Smith, Ariel	443	30	27	40	847,756
Sanguinetti, Anne	4	0	0	0	1,095	Smith, Dewey Paul	3	0	0	1	385
Santagata, Nick	1,095	114	130	145	2,078,607	Smith, Earl	1	0	0	0	0
Santana, Daniel	207	25	20	28	258,091	Smith, Guy	1,179	181	161	152	2,735,124
Santana, Jozbin Z.	923	128	126	121	2,731,042	Smith, Hugh	5	0	0	1	747
Santiago, Cruz	38	2	1	4	18,750	Smith, Mike E.	939	162	115	99	8,401,045
Santiago, Felipe R.	4	0	0	0	0	Smith, Nate	13	0	1	1	2,155
Santiago, Joel	842	110	112	89	881,721	Smith, Rodger W.	76	8	7	7	35,929
Santiago, Miguel D.	1	0	0	0	0	Smith, Stormy	476	26	31	48	409,934
Santiago, Jr., Manuel A.	198	16	16	10	257,774	Smith, Tammy	13	0	0	1	1,846
Santos, Bernie P.	8	0	1	1	6,200	Smith, V. L.	383	18	34	33	319,115
Santos, David	1	0	0	0	800	Smith-Hebert, Jackie	111	11	16	20	49,133
Santos, Felipe J.	672	60	80	89	662,911	Smullen, Pat	7	1	0	0	172,000
Santos, Jose A.	1,157	176	183	162	11,472,287	Snatchko, Johnna	12	0	1	0	4,184
Santos, Romualdo	272	16	26	28	169,475	Solberg, Curt	30	2	2	3	8,151
Sarvis, Dean A.	150	11	20	17	191,144	Solis, Alex O.	1,115	203	170	175	16,304,252
Savastano, Mark	1	0	0	0	77	Solis, Ruben Dario	97	6	12	7	64,688
Scantling, Vernon	74	2	7	10	56,083	Solomon, Nathan	17	1	1	1	22,633

Jockey	Sts	1st	2d	3d	Purses
Somers, Conrad	2	0	0	0	300
Sommers, Jr., Leroy Allen	84	13	7	11	50,027
Somsanith, Na	368	42	45	45	1,814,145
Sone, Joel	235	22	24	26	157,844
Soodeen, Rodney	433	22	37	41	419,099
Soodoo, Kevin	2	0	0	0	0
Sorenson, Danny	89	4	7	13	220,773
Sorrells, Janna	316	13	12	18	95,862
Sorto, Domingo	68	4	2	4	46,899
Sosa, Jr., Peter	548	60	55	64	571,396
Soto, Daniel	19	1	1	5	10,299
Soto, Domingo	1	0	0	0	130
Soto, Jr., John A.	61	2	2	5	31,210
Soumillon, Christophe	1	0	0	0	0
Sowle, Scott A.	1	0	0	0	0
Spanabel, Kelly R.	125	10	10	10	51,949
Spence, Ian J.	346	13	21	36	139,785
Spencer, Jamie	2	0	0	1	210,000
Spieth, Rhonda G.	12	1	2	1	7,096
Spieth, Scott	475	32	47	57	385,497
St. Julien, Marlon	599	63	72	62	1,347,810
Stanley, Angel Ortega	378	40	46	36	349,849
Stanley, Monica Kay	167	5	12	12	60,614
Stanton, Terry A.	874	126	123	105	1,529,513
Staples, Craig	145	14	14	8	311,582
Stein, Gary Raymond	137	4	3	7	34,809
Stein, Robert	12	2	2	3	4,320
Steiner, Joseph J.	127	9	6	16	287,023
Stephen, Anthony	324	19	31	37	341,287
Sterling, Jr., Larry J.	766	130	104	119	2,909,942
Sterr, Scott	229	44	43	38	200,582
Stevens, Gary L.	345	58	62	50	5,829,570
Stevens, Scott A.	882	127	126	128	1,575,422
Steward, Keenan	93	4	8	9	41,895
Stianson, Janine	119	14	19	14	76,193
Stinn, Caroline	34	4	9	10	14,439
Stokes, Joseph	754	110	130	74	1,830,185
Stokes, Louis A.	544	42	50	59	456,315
Stokes, III, Rex A.	718	112	81	77	943,963
Stortz, Marcia	540	54	55	68	752,048
Straightnose, Les	1	0	0	1	120
Strongarm, Thomas	18	3	3	2	7,254
Stubblefield, David P.	102	20	17	21	42,271
Sturgeon, Roy	3	0	0	0	96
Sturgeon, Tyrone	24	1	5	3	11,790
Suarez, Gabriel	400	41	44	52	350,571
Suarez, Guillermo	1	0	0	0	50
Suborics, Andreas	2	0	1	0	185,000
Suckie, Marland C.	69	3	7	9	136,099
Sukie, Danush	387	63	55	55	502,863
Sullivan, Steve D.	104	7	8	14	39,038
Summerlan, Anthony	1	0	0	0	0
Summerlin, Thomas A.	5	0	1	0	1,975
Summers, Nancy Nichols	204	26	18	26	336,674
Sunseri, James Joseph	283	8	12	33	93,265
Surrency, R. Scott	162	14	15	20	116,953
Sutherland, Chantal	471	48	54	60	2,613,807
Sutton, Earl Boyd	97	10	10	8	42,450
Swan, Tomey Jean	1	0	0	0	0
Swatuk, Brian	10	2	1	0	30,575
Taber, Alex	3	0	1	0	2,700
Tabor, Jeremy L.	1	0	0	0	1,608
Talarico, Michael V.	14	0	0	1	6,328
Talbot, Crista R.	59	1	3	7	15,325
Talman, Katherine G.	320	27	41	44	128,676
Talser, Alex	1	0	0	0	690
Tatushiro, Ryuji	4	0	0	1	1,275
Taveras, Reino A.	168	20	14	27	59,492
Taylor, Kendra T.	5	0	0	0	567
Taylor, Larry	784	63	93	90	627,426
Teague, Rahede	341	13	23	34	175,870
Teator, Phillip A.	407	25	34	35	505,951
Tejera, Edward A.	26	0	3	2	16,075
Telg, Tram	8	3	0	0	9,381
Terleski, Marijo H.	241	23	32	29	101,298
Termini, Chip M.	20	0	0	0	1,724
Terry, Dominic M.	76	6	4	7	86,545
Tervort, Jason	674	73	51	70	702,831
Thacker, Nathan	312	14	21	30	120,541
Theriot, Brian James	431	52	58	40	499,499
Theriot, Jamie	1,105	213	161	121	3,959,033
Thibodeaux, Ronald L.	2	0	0	0	165
Thomas, Michael	467	29	37	34	211,597
Thomas, Todd	32	3	2	2	9,326
Thomason, William Thomas	67	6	5	9	17,288
Thompson, Junior A.	2	0	0	1	1,200
Thompson, Ted	11	0	0	0	4,450
Thompson, Terry J.	1,171	181	153	161	4,059,292
Thompson, Winston Albert	860	118	108	106	1,597,691
Thornton, Craig	7	4	1	0	288,725
Thornton, Timothy	417	49	53	47	1,158,983
Thorwarth, Otto	529	40	50	51	435,946
Tillman, Kathy	1	1	0	0	3,300
Tipa, Jorge	640	43	69	78	404,592
Todd, Jr., Frank	314	24	37	43	933,814
Tohill, Ken S.	548	93	98	90	1,431,125
Tolentino, Pablo	225	15	13	29	279,620
Topp, Valerie	6	0	0	0	1,422
Torbit, Renee	274	20	29	33	129,295
Toribio, Abdiel	345	37	41	50	1,352,281
Toribio, Jr., Aurelio	810	104	97	98	1,800,832
Toro, Melvin	140	8	12	13	171,230
Torres, Abdel	1	0	0	0	0
Torres, Cesar A.	1	0	0	0	0
Torres, Jose	202	11	12	19	99,590
Torres, Raymond	565	54	56	61	911,665
Torres, Robert Valesquez	100	4	6	10	34,256
Toscano, Paul R.	700	78	68	85	1,753,236
Tourangeau, Bernie	9	0	1	2	624
Trader, Rodney R.	366	30	35	33	556,805
Traurig, Michael	66	8	3	10	152,865
Trimble, Patricia	336	38	42	33	769,618
Troilo, William D.	795	86	89	103	1,594,440
Truitt, Myra Suzanne	117	7	7	9	69,818
Trujillo, Elvis	376	46	44	50	1,249,755
Turner, Tom G.	221	22	25	34	617,398
Umana, Juan	911	96	107	121	1,560,908
Unsihuay, Arnaldo	495	50	61	62	933,188
Unsihuay, Esteban E.	108	7	2	8	70,831
Urriola, Alexis	236	8	23	29	92,824
Uske, Shannon	227	24	39	25	1,087,016
Vaid, I. Josh	5	0	1	0	1,060
Vail, James S.	264	22	24	30	288,903
Valdes, Ricardo A.	448	60	51	56	1,148,924
Valdez, Felipe	647	91	95	94	1,657,853
Valdez, Martin	22	0	2	3	9,614
Valdivia, Jr., Jose	833	82	95	121	5,401,879
Valene, Kym I.	24	1	1	1	12,190
Valenzuela, Fernando H.	138	7	10	13	192,590
Valenzuela, John Raul	54	3	3	3	28,643
Valenzuela, Patrick A.	1,447	287	266	237	15,697,352
Valera, Jr., Juan R.	57	0	1	0	3,965
Vales, Daniel I	11	2	0	4	7,815
Valles, Eric S.	5	0	2	0	3,260
Van Der Ham, Loek	4	0	0	0	1,876
Van Hassel, Chip	49	4	4	13	59,522
Vanderwoude, Justin	183	13	16	19	30,605
VanderWoude, Matthew	3	0	1	1	2,325
Vanek, Helen Marie	483	35	45	53	584,558
Vannozzi, Lauren	353	40	43	41	361,381
Vargas, Jorge L.	174	14	18	21	223,999
Vasquez, Juan L.	1	0	0	0	0
Vasquez, Richard M.	196	29	19	31	182,586
Vasquez, Rolando	166	13	16	13	132,605
Vaz, Eriluis	6	0	0	0	2,218
Vazquez, Gilberto	18	0	1	2	6,890

RECORDS OF JOCKEYS

Jockey	Sts	1st	2d	3d	Purses	Jockey	Sts	1st	2d	3d	Purses
Vazquez, Jeovani	22	2	0	4	21,180	Whittaker, Dale	151	3	10	14	247,520
Vazquez, Julian J.	129	5	16	5	99,628	Whittle, Stoney D.	62	13	11	7	28,548
Vega, Antonio	13	0	2	0	5,540	Wiley, Henry William	1	1	0	0	3,300
Vega, Harry	565	100	78	86	1,614,471	Will, Julia	1	0	0	1	1,430
Vega, Jesse	1	0	0	0	95	Williams, Carl S.	26	0	2	1	8,593
Velasquez, Argelio	446	49	65	45	353,618	Williams, Dorothy	7	0	0	1	1,151
Velasquez, Baudelio	2	1	0	1	12,240	Williams, Douglas A.	230	8	7	15	137,108
Velasquez, Cornelio H.	1,696	273	249	235	10,577,461	Williams, Dustin W.	88	9	12	11	40,899
Velazquez, Daniel C.	383	24	33	47	282,982	Williams, Jimmy Donald	1	0	0	0	400
Velazquez, John R.	1,308	306	193	175	15,425,501	Williams, Justin B.	120	2	3	10	36,077
Velazquez, Lucino	7	0	1	2	4,440	Williams, Matt	226	31	25	36	146,784
Velazquez, Mario	246	9	23	24	176,109	Williams, Michael	1	0	0	0	0
Velez, Juan J.	110	6	4	6	61,515	Williams, Percy	89	8	5	5	84,207
Velez, Pedro J.	208	9	8	18	84,657	Williams, Raymond Allen	123	12	16	19	156,868
Velez, Roger I.	276	30	26	37	854,363	Williams, Robert Dean	882	112	113	117	1,457,246
Velez, Jr., Jose A.	588	80	92	86	3,038,413	Wilson, Billy M.	140	1	3	4	42,153
Ventura, Jr., Hector	43	4	3	5	29,935	Wilson, David	769	108	106	123	1,534,562
Verenzuela, Jose L.	84	7	8	13	167,648	Wilson, Janet Leah	183	5	13	9	51,321
Vergara, Daniel P.	58	4	8	11	51,013	Wilson, Melissa E.	48	1	5	5	16,540
Vergara, Octavio	117	3	13	11	169,147	Wilson, Melton	173	12	13	7	113,194
Verge, Mario E.	358	26	27	31	563,736	Wilson, Randy G.	157	1	4	4	25,763
Vicchrilli, Russell	240	35	41	16	335,665	Wilson, Randy R.	111	17	20	16	109,189
Vidal, Francisco A.	126	15	21	15	120,980	Wilson, Rick	680	127	114	102	3,122,717
Villa, Mark Anthony	422	48	39	46	633,297	Winants, Garet W.	12	1	1	1	20,050
Villafan, Roberto	55	2	4	5	60,374	Windt, Laurina	4	1	1	0	3,050
Villa-Gomez, Huber	1,012	208	160	138	1,453,253	Winkle, Curtis W.	33	6	1	9	11,421
Villeneuve, Francine	563	94	70	78	1,880,371	Winklepleck, Bobby	22	3	3	4	8,789
Villeseche, Anrella J.	167	12	16	11	136,846	Winters, Jerry L.	159	7	6	12	83,483
Villicana, Edward	14	0	0	0	1,656	Winters, Perry A.	672	88	96	87	1,375,987
Vitek, Justin J.	437	40	41	48	907,535	Wippert, Shannon	215	29	24	22	81,676
Von Rosen, Anne	88	8	12	3	74,794	Wirth, Keith F.	23	1	2	3	14,782
Wabash, Ross	1	0	0	0	0	Wloka, Jr., Ricardo A.	7	0	0	0	1,460
Wade, Gary	59	6	12	6	18,441	Womack, Wayne	5	3	0	1	6,848
Wahlen, Kelly J.	8	0	2	4	1,665	Wong, Peter K.	497	59	54	63	619,887
Walcott, Rickey	229	41	51	34	733,649	Wood, George	3	0	0	0	1,000
Wales, Dale	4	0	1	0	450	Woodley, Carl James	1,126	203	151	171	2,444,883
Wales, Travis	387	59	57	47	569,176	Woodley, John B.	144	29	26	14	237,770
Walker, Pedro L.	18	0	1	0	4,929	Woods, Jr., Charles R.	41	6	3	5	62,667
Walker, Jr., Bobby J.	664	96	99	78	1,563,326	Woolsey, Russell W.	789	137	105	109	1,421,536
Wall, Newil	242	12	19	25	108,644	Worst, Gary L.	37	3	2	7	10,717
Walsh, Michael P.	50	1	3	3	25,573	Wortman, Tim A.	31	1	1	0	5,394
Walsh, Peter B.	50	0	1	0	11,983	Wright, Jody	64	5	5	10	36,806
Walsh, Rachel	1	0	0	0	500	Wright, Larry	5	0	0	0	210
Walsh, Robert	67	4	7	2	117,650	Wright, Michael L.	939	58	110	116	573,154
Ward, Anderson	173	15	17	15	132,041	Wright, Nicola	518	103	88	63	1,573,058
Ward, Skeet	1	0	0	1	225	Wynter, Noel A.	20	0	1	1	9,125
Warhol, Vicki Lynn	253	20	22	33	167,250	Yaegel, Jr., Tommy	4	0	0	0	1,085
Warner, Terry Neal	102	5	11	8	108,110	Yang, Chin C.	990	121	139	129	1,248,572
Warren, Chad	25	3	3	2	5,776	Yaranga, Yuri	535	35	47	57	241,576
Warren, Jr., Ronald J.	962	171	150	141	3,823,529	Yetsook, Sylvia Maria	41	1	5	6	37,792
Waterman, Blair	35	6	13	5	174,218	Yoakum, Jerry Lee	1	0	1	0	840
Watson, Donald	1	0	0	0	0	Young, Paddy	28	7	3	2	105,100
Watson, Patrick James	202	22	23	24	292,983	Young, Scott Eugene	7	0	1	0	448
Weatherly, James T.	789	60	86	78	773,957	Young, Tracey J.	4	0	0	0	0
Webb, Harla Kay	66	3	9	5	52,895	Yount, Jr., Robert H.	56	0	5	3	8,321
Webb, Robert	588	116	113	91	386,292	Zamarron, Mario	2	0	0	0	116
Welch, Quincy	655	141	131	91	1,761,060	Zambrana, David A.	180	13	11	15	91,900
Wellington, Thomas	123	11	9	11	116,353	Zambrana, Eddie Joe	307	24	24	30	167,027
Wells, Lindell	129	5	6	11	61,032	Zamora, Christopher G.	115	13	20	10	266,318
Wethey, Luke E.	74	3	3	8	24,986	Zamora, Tomas A.	102	6	8	11	100,055
Wharton, Garet	1	0	0	0	0	Ziegler, Michael G.	937	142	124	121	1,323,996
Wharton, Michael	1	0	0	0	0	Ziesing, Scotty	108	4	7	7	123,298
Wheat, Jr., Jesse R.	130	25	18	14	142,287	Zimmerman, Ramsey	633	117	99	80	870,188
Whetstone, Perry S.	458	41	49	58	369,977	Zuniga, Eddie	781	58	81	76	943,387
Whitacre, Brandon	55	7	8	9	109,935	Zunino, Jose Luis	6	0	1	1	6,894
Whitacre, Gordon	402	31	33	41	193,087						
Whitaker, Jennifer	367	47	61	52	428,707						
White, Andrew	8	1	1	1	9,110						
White, Eddie H.	28	3	2	5	16,725						
White, James Bo	38	5	7	2	51,518						
Whiteside, Jim Bob	64	2	5	6	9,583						
Whitner, IV, James H.	6	0	1	0	2,925						
Whitney, Dana G.	903	147	102	124	2,263,859						

2003
RECORDS OF SIRES

The record of each sire
represented by at least one winning
thoroughbred or more who raced in
the United States or Canada in 2003,
showing his total performers, number
of winning performers, the number
of times they started and their
total placings and earnings.

Sire	Perf	Wnrs	Sts	1st	2d	3d	Purses
A Change for April	10	7	57	8	10	5	$55,281
A Corking Limerick	3	1	20	2	1	1	11,038
A Man of Class	4	1	13	1	1	2	11,276
A. M. Swinger	8	1	41	1	3	2	16,103
A. P Jet	112	56	721	98	112	84	2,177,411
A.P. Indy	162	86	744	153	116	78	8,827,360
Aaron's Concorde	30	13	189	20	35	14	341,040
Aaron's Gold	5	1	9	1	0	0	13,221
Abaginone	54	23	330	42	30	39	700,401
Abbadabbadubai	2	1	15	3	2	0	11,602
Abel Prospect	22	18	250	34	31	45	586,545
Abi Yo Yo	5	2	38	3	8	1	39,205
Above Normal	23	14	199	22	25	27	228,315
Abri Fiscal	3	1	17	1	0	2	2,883
Absent Russian	28	14	236	24	19	29	363,448
Abstract	30	16	177	30	18	22	226,342
Academy Award	40	16	252	25	24	23	402,590
Acallade	5	1	38	3	7	7	38,976
Acaroid	19	7	145	11	13	14	132,408
Acatenango (GER)	4	1	7	1	1	0	136,612
Accelerator	44	12	160	15	18	15	328,541
Acceptable	32	17	168	32	25	13	539,848
Accoustical	4	3	38	3	1	6	44,978
Ack Ack Heir	2	2	14	2	3	4	10,119
Acquitted	5	2	30	2	2	6	12,427
Across the Field	8	2	43	3	1	5	28,970
Act Smart	2	1	7	3	1	0	70,358
Activado (URU)	6	2	25	3	4	3	10,436
Active Wear	1	1	19	2	0	1	6,097
Activist	4	2	21	2	6	3	24,260
Adbass	7	4	76	8	9	12	27,332
Adhocracy	13	11	106	18	14	14	423,391
Adventure Road	17	10	105	14	13	15	143,700
Advocate Training	4	3	42	4	3	4	42,705
Aegean's Bolger	8	3	60	8	7	11	45,530
Aerial Display	6	2	53	2	6	6	33,876
Aferd	14	8	114	14	15	13	106,004
Affirmed	62	29	376	50	46	45	2,343,824
Afleet	10	4	59	9	9	3	98,434
Afleetknowsasecret	2	2	15	2	3	1	24,765
Afternoon Deelites	110	59	797	111	102	110	2,245,346
Aggie Southpaw	9	5	55	6	8	7	140,136
Aggressive Chief	14	6	97	14	12	14	260,976
Ago	15	10	73	16	10	9	211,776
Agressive Hawk	6	1	20	1	1	0	14,402
Air Forbes Won	68	35	523	75	80	69	1,217,226
Airdrie Apache	1	1	11	1	1	2	4,701
Al Mamoon	15	7	90	11	7	12	232,524
Al Sabin	20	12	147	17	10	16	204,132
Alamo Road	3	2	19	2	4	2	18,435
Alamocitos	5	3	19	5	1	6	184,520
Alan's Ace	1	1	2	1	0	0	19,200
Alannon (AUS)	1	1	5	1	1	0	13,350
Alaskan Frost	37	20	318	27	42	38	463,402
Alfaari	60	37	436	63	57	72	1,000,747
Algenib (ARG)	1	1	9	1	0	4	40,080
Alhaarth (IRE)	7	4	16	4	1	3	1,133,848
Ali Gaziba	12	3	77	4	6	2	45,809
Ali-Royal (IRE)	3	1	15	1	0	3	47,080
All Gone	64	35	485	61	63	65	1,031,771
All of a Sudden	6	1	46	2	5	5	59,888
All Thee Power	14	8	103	14	14	18	216,334
Alladin Rib	9	5	62	9	7	12	180,365
Alleged	5	2	21	2	0	2	61,336
Alleged Account	1	1	6	1	0	0	11,666
Alleged Stardom	4	1	22	1	1	1	10,320
Allen Charge	8	3	31	4	3	1	126,852
Allen's Prospect	192	94	1,312	173	144	143	3,357,625
Allied Forces	18	5	94	5	11	11	188,730
Ally Runner	1	1	14	3	3	1	25,226
Alnaab	42	18	304	32	36	26	245,482
Aloha Prospector	45	31	348	58	58	54	695,082
Aloma's Ruler	13	7	80	13	11	6	113,593
Alphabet Soup	137	83	896	132	111	113	4,796,799
Alster	4	2	23	2	0	1	13,535
Altazarr	7	4	61	8	8	9	116,171
Always a Classic	26	14	171	26	25	23	386,650
Always Fair	19	10	132	16	15	22	194,834
Always Run Lucky	2	1	20	1	3	3	10,099
Always Silver	9	1	76	3	8	6	52,685
Alwuhush	12	4	63	6	12	4	51,459
Aly Galore	2	1	17	1	1	1	7,662
Aly T	3	1	30	3	3	1	18,131
Alybel	4	1	20	1	0	3	8,291
Alybenbo	4	3	23	3	2	4	11,659
Alybro	23	12	132	18	21	16	255,598
Alydarmer	2	1	8	1	1	0	5,418
Alydeed	103	52	757	82	83	127	1,591,930
Alyfoe	19	7	173	15	13	17	158,248
Alyhuista	1	1	5	3	1	0	49,017
Alymagic	13	4	91	6	5	9	185,582
Alyone	6	4	61	5	10	6	74,443
Alyshadeed	3	1	25	1	2	1	29,967
Alysheba	44	15	300	30	45	28	299,429
Alyten	22	12	182	23	14	17	328,971
Alzao	10	5	47	9	7	2	225,441
Am all Charged Up	20	6	148	12	19	20	135,333
Amaruk	4	3	25	5	2	2	91,325
Ambassador in Love	1	1	8	1	3	1	20,274
Amber Colero	3	1	14	1	0	0	9,915
Amber Sioux	5	3	19	3	1	4	16,437
Ambessa	6	4	48	7	7	5	53,490
Ambivalent	5	3	38	8	7	5	44,497
Ameri Valay	46	28	377	48	49	47	707,991
American Champ	3	2	16	4	1	2	38,180
American Chance	101	53	705	97	106	88	2,148,378
American Day	15	6	67	10	10	8	166,734
American General	8	3	39	4	6	4	45,126
American Standard	27	11	201	18	15	22	959,582
American Wings	2	1	23	1	4	3	10,770
Amerigo	2	1	18	3	4	3	12,734
Amerrico Double	2	1	16	3	4	1	26,579
Amerrico's Bullet	5	3	55	4	7	7	104,502
Amigo Menor (IRE)	3	2	15	2	1	2	11,531
Amy's Intention	1	1	6	1	1	1	3,862
An Eldorado	2	1	34	1	1	0	6,799
Anabaa	7	5	29	5	5	3	439,465
Ancient Oaks	9	3	60	5	7	6	31,204
Andean Chasqui	2	2	18	3	5	2	32,280
Andover Man	4	2	21	3	3	1	8,819
Anet	55	27	338	41	53	35	613,507
Anita's Prince	1	1	4	1	0	0	3,008
Anjiz	49	27	416	51	44	50	951,336
Announce	82	29	434	45	28	60	833,421
Another Reef	12	4	110	6	18	18	113,087
Another Summer	1	1	9	2	2	1	12,910
Anshan (GB)	1	1	11	6	3	1	120,300
Anziyan	23	11	122	17	10	22	307,447
Apalachee	13	4	109	8	15	13	66,967
Apalachee Prince	1	1	14	2	6	2	18,822
Apollo	43	25	303	45	31	45	565,576
Appeal for Justice	3	1	12	2	1	1	15,898
Appealing Guy	11	3	76	4	7	9	87,480
Appealing Skier	69	44	463	68	57	59	1,216,233
April Axe	4	1	22	1	2	0	10,389
Arab Speaker	1	1	9	2	1	2	36,450
Arabian Sheik	2	2	12	2	1	2	5,965
Arabica	1	1	12	2	1	1	13,708
Araby Ace	7	1	43	1	3	5	6,460
Aras an Uachtarain (IRE)	3	1	12	2	1	1	32,107
Arazi	8	5	67	14	8	8	1,778,350
Arch	47	26	273	39	50	48	1,108,938
Archers Bay	22	7	66	7	9	12	513,021
Arctic Blitz	12	4	72	8	1	7	26,711
Ariosto (ARG)	1	1	9	2	0	0	10,710
Aristocratic Cross	5	2	18	2	0	1	8,779
Arkoma	1	1	15	3	0	0	15,600
Armed Truce	3	2	28	3	5	2	24,303
Arrived On Time	8	2	53	3	4	2	24,153
Arroyo	14	1	120	1	10	8	40,684
Art of Dawn	3	1	30	1	1	2	12,161
Art of Living	4	2	14	2	1	0	6,776
Artax	24	3	53	4	7	7	203,790
Artema (IRE)	4	2	26	3	3	4	20,759
Artic Tracker	1	1	4	1	1	0	12,760
Artichoke	1	1	11	1	1	0	17,495

RECORDS OF SIRES

Sire	Perf	Wnrs	Sts	1st	2d	3d	Purses
Artillerist Two	3	3	41	6	5	8	22,478
Ascension	4	2	30	4	8	6	19,186
Ascot Knight	60	25	385	41	53	42	1,263,576
Ashdown	12	6	73	11	14	8	109,684
Asimov	3	1	25	1	2	5	6,107
Ask a Nice	2	1	18	1	0	3	7,706
Askmewhy	4	1	16	1	0	0	4,239
Aspen Peak	1	1	12	1	0	2	11,600
Aspro	1	1	9	2	2	3	143,210
Assembly Dancer	4	1	32	2	7	6	48,823
Assertive Joe	3	2	19	2	1	4	27,857
Astro	13	5	88	12	13	10	264,592
Astudillo (IRE)	9	7	78	14	11	5	128,199
At Full Feather	6	4	30	4	2	1	24,209
At the Threshold	31	14	198	20	28	35	228,142
Ataka	12	7	98	10	7	8	65,476
Ataki	1	1	12	2	3	0	16,510
Atlantian	4	2	37	4	6	3	28,110
Atticus	56	26	283	36	40	37	930,002
Attribute	6	3	65	10	7	5	55,436
Au Point	6	2	39	3	5	4	48,231
Aurium	11	4	64	6	8	12	42,501
Autocracy	11	3	44	6	4	11	240,036
Autoroute	4	1	8	1	1	0	7,875
Avenger M.	6	1	33	1	3	5	14,025
Avenue of Flags	91	46	532	89	65	66	1,858,685
Avery	3	1	19	1	1	2	24,710
Avies Copy	18	8	146	9	8	14	78,592
Awad	44	16	218	19	17	27	346,076
Awesome Again	70	36	368	57	53	56	2,759,659
Awesome Blue	1	1	13	2	1	0	11,492
Awesome Cat	2	1	7	1	0	0	7,538
B. G.'s Drone	5	2	15	3	1	2	86,089
B. Hoedown	11	4	51	7	3	4	63,201
Baatish	2	1	22	1	0	4	16,367
Baby I Lied	3	1	10	1	3	4	3,365
Baby Slewy	10	2	49	2	8	11	23,743
Back Alley	2	1	8	1	0	2	2,068
Back When	4	1	33	1	0	4	13,710
Badger Land	16	6	100	12	16	14	159,347
Baederwood	11	2	56	4	10	3	71,044
Bag	123	52	703	77	65	85	1,093,470
Bagdad Road	14	7	123	10	12	17	103,785
Baha Butch	1	1	8	1	1	0	6,024
Bahhare	1	1	10	4	3	1	320,580
Bahri	18	6	88	10	9	12	235,933
Bailbucks	2	1	17	2	1	2	18,860
Bailjumper	2	1	12	2	1	1	2,742
Balboa Native	2	2	22	2	1	4	9,565
Baldy's Dream	1	1	5	1	0	1	8,257
Ball's Bluff	9	4	63	5	15	10	210,912
Ballindaggin	2	1	9	2	0	0	3,455
Ballistic Billy	10	5	68	12	9	8	158,441
Ballydoyle	5	1	52	1	9	8	14,273
Band Practice	10	9	90	18	8	14	150,690
Banjo	4	1	6	1	3	0	14,158
Bank of Sharacco	5	2	16	4	0	1	17,017
Bankbook	27	19	223	31	28	25	328,032
Banker's Gold	65	29	368	46	50	54	1,007,086
Banks Well	3	1	22	2	3	1	13,236
Banmyrh	5	2	25	4	3	3	62,393
Baquero	20	7	78	12	10	9	174,595
Bar	6	1	26	1	0	1	14,258
Barathea (IRE)	10	5	52	9	3	8	270,104
Barb's Relic	3	2	21	2	0	3	12,625
Barbaric Commander	1	1	4	1	0	0	1,775
Barbeau	39	24	314	53	41	31	1,198,796
Barberstown	19	6	104	8	8	15	151,138
Barcelona	14	7	104	10	14	7	77,799
Barkerville	44	24	301	38	22	42	1,166,025
Baron de Vaux	27	12	179	20	14	19	238,159
Baron O'Dublin	3	1	22	1	0	2	3,780
Barrera	16	8	71	10	8	5	33,529
Barrett's Bullet	5	2	16	3	1	0	30,214
Barricade	19	9	116	10	12	11	67,502
Bartok (IRE)	7	3	40	6	6	8	411,497
Bashful Cloud	8	3	39	3	0	6	14,437
Basic	4	2	17	2	1	3	19,969
Basic Rate	15	5	74	7	9	5	39,093
Basket Weave	78	43	490	64	76	60	584,952
Bastogne	7	6	58	9	5	8	78,840
Bates Motel	72	42	641	79	81	85	863,562
Batonnier	30	10	153	15	16	28	204,800
Batshoof (IRE)	3	3	21	6	3	2	71,277
Battle Creek	22	11	135	19	15	18	177,390
Battle Launch	10	4	76	6	14	9	86,132
Bay Street Star	19	7	125	7	22	19	94,803
Bayou Blurr	2	1	13	1	0	0	4,304
Bayou Hebert	23	9	181	14	17	23	227,897
Be a Prospect	1	1	5	4	0	0	22,258
Be My Chief	3	1	9	1	0	1	5,178
Be My Guest	1	1	4	1	0	1	1,226
Be Scenic	5	1	39	1	2	1	15,175
Bea Ray'z Gold	1	1	2	1	0	0	5,213
Bear Games	1	1	10	1	0	0	5,261
Beat Inflation	2	2	11	3	3	2	27,409
Beau Genius	127	69	939	133	139	117	2,612,636
Beau Monde (IRE)	3	2	26	5	6	4	26,103
Beau Sultan	1	1	11	2	3	3	106,520
Beau's Eagle	1	1	8	2	1	1	14,135
Beau's Leader	2	1	23	2	2	0	28,827
Beautiful Crown	13	7	77	10	14	10	256,784
Becker	5	3	54	9	5	8	220,708
Beefchopper	11	5	61	9	13	8	70,283
Belek	47	22	319	36	32	28	520,453
Believe It	51	16	264	20	26	34	310,955
Believe It Doctor	2	1	8	1	0	0	15,426
Believe the Knight	2	1	13	1	0	0	10,770
Belong to Me	152	87	959	136	116	133	3,537,419
Belted Earl	1	1	14	1	1	1	4,110
Benchmark	49	33	312	58	44	37	1,372,242
Bengal Bay	20	14	173	19	23	17	164,116
Benny Q.	2	1	17	3	2	3	52,442
Benny the Dip	34	15	193	23	18	21	426,585
Benton Creek	60	39	367	67	64	46	741,595
Beowulf	5	1	19	3	0	1	11,622
Bering (GB)	6	3	38	6	4	5	68,595
Bertrando	124	56	616	100	75	81	2,346,053
Best Jest	4	4	43	6	5	4	74,643
Best Man Out	2	2	23	3	4	6	61,603
Bet the Omen	1	1	5	2	0	2	4,885
Bet Twice	3	1	17	1	1	0	5,525
Better Believe Me	2	1	16	2	2	1	23,916
Better Guess	1	1	9	1	2	4	2,804
Beveled	1	1	8	4	1	0	38,100
Beyond His Years	1	1	8	1	4	1	7,480
Beyond the Mint	11	6	73	9	17	8	136,099
Bianconi	26	12	72	13	6	10	205,216
Bid Higher	2	1	14	1	1	0	9,978
Bidding Proud	6	2	37	3	5	6	66,081
Bien Bien	24	10	151	19	18	15	1,045,889
Big Chill	4	1	22	1	1	2	4,575
Big Jewel	14	8	94	14	10	11	156,494
Big Mukora	19	13	195	25	24	18	315,953
Big Pistol	38	17	271	34	31	32	347,725
Big Play	1	1	18	1	3	3	30,474
Big Sal	12	6	125	11	15	16	91,659
Big Shuffle	2	1	7	1	0	1	5,150
Big Sky Chester	1	1	4	2	1	0	16,317
Big Splash	19	5	120	10	12	11	157,988
Big Stanley	7	3	53	9	6	2	92,694
Big Sturgeon	5	2	40	2	1	6	19,670
Big Wig	1	1	9	2	1	2	44,798
Bigstone (IRE)	3	2	12	3	2	2	119,560
Billy Blue	5	2	34	4	8	2	31,498
Bin Ajwaad	4	2	20	4	2	1	58,362
Binalong	46	20	325	32	45	40	479,885
Bionic Light	9	5	49	7	6	3	83,150
Bionic Prospect	13	8	90	12	8	5	94,087
Birdies Dee Cee	3	1	18	1	0	2	7,774
Birdonthewire	71	35	431	63	62	52	1,303,848
Bishop Family	2	1	13	3	4	1	23,526
Bishop Northcraft	5	1	26	1	1	1	10,878
Bishop's Choice	2	1	7	3	1	0	55,900
Black Mackee	39	16	207	26	33	22	200,858
Black Moonshine	23	16	238	32	40	28	395,815

Sire	Perf	Wnrs	Sts	1st	2d	3d	Purses
Black Pretender	1	1	6	1	1	0	2,694
Black Prospector	1	1	9	1	1	2	6,645
Black Tie Affair (IRE)	60	30	511	51	73	64	1,134,514
Blair's Cove	4	3	36	5	1	2	23,892
Blare of Trumpets	13	8	113	13	10	17	131,759
Blazing Bart	4	1	12	1	0	1	2,046
Blazing Drums	2	1	18	2	1	2	3,780
Blazing Fire	17	8	85	10	10	13	90,654
Blind Man's Bluff	9	2	35	3	5	3	97,128
Blind Spot	3	1	16	2	4	4	8,735
Bloodstock	1	1	10	1	0	1	9,873
Blu Tusmani	1	1	8	1	0	1	5,022
Blue Buckaroo	10	6	101	10	8	6	97,846
Blue Ensign	35	13	278	21	27	27	250,000
Blue Grass Magic	6	2	51	2	12	6	56,925
Blue Jester	2	2	28	3	1	0	11,169
Blue Moonofalaska	3	2	31	2	3	5	8,167
Blue Ocean	1	1	7	1	1	0	115,670
Blue Orca (IRE)	5	3	41	3	5	7	47,024
Bluebird	5	2	31	4	6	4	582,347
Blues Traveller (IRE)	1	1	7	3	0	0	30,660
Blumin Affair	58	32	399	60	52	48	793,960
Blush Rambler	22	9	182	10	23	22	157,056
Blushing John	19	5	145	6	19	11	147,641
Blushing Stage	5	2	51	4	3	10	67,702
Blushing Star	4	3	17	3	4	2	62,867
Boanerges	9	2	55	2	6	8	42,530
Board Member	8	3	47	5	0	2	74,359
Bob's Dusty	3	2	36	6	5	6	32,668
Bob's Ticket	3	1	14	1	1	2	6,765
Bobby B Free	1	1	10	1	1	2	9,903
Bobby Ben	6	3	39	4	3	2	84,045
Bobrobbery	3	1	13	2	3	0	33,146
Boca Rio	9	5	79	11	12	13	125,911
Bojima	2	1	8	1	3	1	3,111
Bold and Greene	2	1	10	2	1	1	18,757
Bold and Vibrant	1	1	9	1	1	1	6,167
Bold Anthony	33	10	179	20	17	20	278,911
Bold Badgett	67	41	440	63	57	70	2,131,846
Bold Catch	1	1	14	1	2	1	12,762
Bold David	5	3	48	4	5	8	42,299
Bold Ego	8	4	56	6	6	11	37,826
Bold Executive	92	49	603	82	78	78	2,617,203
Bold Gusto	5	2	37	3	2	4	12,793
Bold Ivor	1	1	8	1	0	0	2,211
Bold Jag	1	1	6	1	0	3	7,025
Bold Josh	2	1	4	1	0	0	4,840
Bold Laddie	23	15	143	24	21	17	306,823
Bold n' Flashy	35	13	201	20	31	21	962,526
Bold Nix	4	2	36	3	0	4	27,821
Bold Pac Man	21	5	112	8	8	10	101,913
Bold Revenue	9	3	46	4	6	7	126,082
Bold Roberto	8	5	83	10	17	15	106,448
Bold Ruckus	18	8	141	16	17	19	530,289
Bold Run (FR)	5	2	36	4	3	4	99,814
Bold Smoocher	7	5	52	7	6	5	72,384
Bold Southerner	1	1	7	2	1	0	2,971
Bold Target	4	1	16	1	1	3	4,264
Bold Testimony	7	6	31	4	4	7	19,768
Bolger	4	3	35	6	6	5	27,170
Bolting Holme	2	1	14	1	1	1	10,202
Bombardier	9	3	60	4	5	10	69,990
Bon Point (GB)	22	9	121	13	10	12	269,670
Bonus Money (GB)	43	23	297	39	45	37	749,670
Bonus Time Cat	3	2	19	4	3	2	52,860
Boomerang	8	5	75	8	4	11	157,617
Boone's Mill	117	75	931	128	121	120	1,561,681
Bordagaray	5	3	49	4	2	2	27,719
Bordeaux Bob	3	2	19	3	5	5	64,715
Border Guard	3	1	21	2	1	5	32,303
Border Patrol	10	5	60	10	6	4	110,327
Born Wild	21	7	100	10	16	13	94,193
Borzoi	2	2	9	4	0	2	11,844
Boss Koss	2	1	12	1	2	1	20,564
Boston Harbor	105	56	551	92	59	65	2,475,884
Botanic	9	5	80	10	13	13	128,629
Both Guns Blazing	1	1	10	2	2	3	15,521
Boulder Dam	9	3	52	4	4	3	67,264
Bound by Honor	22	10	186	19	21	23	160,623
Boundary	95	59	640	101	105	82	2,500,681
Boundary Ridge	7	2	56	5	6	8	26,740
Bounding Basque	30	14	223	23	30	20	326,005
Boundlessly	4	2	29	5	4	1	103,339
Boutinierre	18	9	164	15	25	28	64,779
Bowler's Wharf	6	2	31	2	5	2	32,928
Bowmans Express	1	1	10	1	0	2	9,260
Boyish Charm	9	6	66	8	7	9	64,515
Boys Nite Out	2	1	10	1	2	0	7,150
Bramante (ARG)	2	1	12	1	3	2	4,310
Brandon's Slew	5	1	31	1	1	2	14,580
Brass Minister	58	32	405	57	51	57	648,453
Brave Romane	3	1	19	2	2	1	20,206
Bravoure	2	2	32	2	2	7	21,707
Breeders Bonus	5	4	59	7	6	14	82,910
Brenda's Ziggy	2	1	15	4	0	1	26,005
Brent's Danzig	12	3	64	6	4	8	67,475
Brents Colony	5	2	18	2	3	0	24,479
Brentwood Style	7	3	33	3	1	1	13,993
Brett's Lick	6	2	24	2	3	1	15,975
Brian's Time	1	1	2	1	0	0	27,840
Brick House	3	1	18	1	1	3	18,129
Brick's Image	2	1	16	1	1	2	12,219
Bridlewood	5	1	35	1	4	4	31,345
Brief Ruckus	48	22	395	33	46	52	554,594
Brief Truce	9	5	59	8	5	5	115,050
Bright Launch	38	23	271	42	30	37	766,591
Brilliant Leader	4	2	35	3	0	4	19,389
Brilliant Protege	1	1	6	2	0	1	18,822
Brilliant Sandy	11	4	94	4	8	14	77,092
Bring To Light	1	1	5	1	0	0	10,557
Brisk Affair	8	5	44	5	5	6	12,151
British Banker	1	1	4	1	0	0	9,900
Broad Brush	100	57	646	104	73	85	2,707,093
Broadway Bullet	5	3	37	3	3	8	39,080
Broadway Harry	1	1	8	2	1	1	118,114
Broadway's Top Gun	6	5	30	7	2	7	19,503
Brocco	27	13	183	24	13	19	312,357
Brodgar	2	1	12	1	0	1	17,341
Brogan	8	1	71	1	11	14	44,489
Brooklyn Nick	2	1	13	1	1	1	18,431
Brookover	2	1	10	1	1	1	11,758
Brown Arc	6	5	61	12	11	9	180,938
Bruces Son	10	6	53	7	4	8	35,201
Brunswick	55	33	501	70	71	62	1,164,443
Buchman	1	1	11	1	0	0	7,680
Buck Aly	6	2	24	2	3	2	29,139
Buck Forbes	1	1	17	7	2	2	33,689
Buck Strider	4	1	25	1	0	2	12,690
Buck's Last Dream	3	3	23	3	5	3	22,826
Buck'sinthebank	1	1	6	2	3	1	30,460
Buckaroo	12	6	90	10	15	8	152,851
Buckbean	13	8	96	12	11	10	268,175
Buckfinder	11	6	103	9	7	14	57,933
Buckhar	49	20	353	27	36	55	387,358
Buckley Boy	12	7	106	15	14	5	143,167
Bucksaw	1	1	9	2	1	2	4,784
Bucksplasher	33	13	236	23	33	23	432,313
Bucky Raj	12	6	86	8	10	10	48,911
Budd Believes	4	2	13	2	2	0	8,137
Buddy	11	4	70	8	5	14	69,177
Bugatti Reef (IRE)	5	1	11	1	1	2	11,424
Buie	12	6	71	9	12	10	135,123
Bull Inthe Heather	32	10	211	16	23	31	101,284
Bull Marquetry	1	1	13	2	1	0	12,127
Bull Shoals	2	2	19	2	3	1	52,929
Bull Sluice	2	1	17	1	3	1	11,800
Burn Annie	1	1	12	2	3	1	46,580
Burnt Hills	4	3	34	3	5	2	15,829
Burooj (GB)	3	1	20	3	7	1	31,585
Burts Star	1	1	11	2	3	2	28,091
Busterwaggley	8	5	42	8	4	5	60,092
Bustopher Jones	6	4	12	5	2	1	17,320
Buyimback	1	1	10	1	2	1	2,316
Buzz Saw	3	1	33	4	3	2	89,462
Byars	8	3	46	6	7	4	162,187
Bye Bye Curly	1	1	19	2	2	4	10,996

Sire	Perf	Wnrs	Sts	1st	2d	3d	Purses
C B Connection	2	1	7	1	1	2	10,758
C Spot Go	1	1	10	1	3	2	8,682
Cabrini Green	2	1	15	2	4	3	161,579
Cachuma	8	3	67	3	7	9	43,696
Cadeaux Genereux (GB)	8	4	54	6	8	10	1,224,079
Caerleon	12	6	53	9	10	5	1,066,849
Cafe Creme	1	1	12	1	4	3	9,770
Cagey Bidder	1	1	4	3	1	0	64,410
Cahaba Gold	1	1	7	1	2	1	19,397
Cahill Road	58	27	365	51	47	41	812,248
Cailuet	2	1	24	1	6	2	34,533
Cajun Cadet (GB)	1	1	8	1	0	1	54,797
Cajun Flagman	3	1	20	1	2	2	14,984
Cajun Jack	2	1	16	4	2	1	21,160
Caldiero	6	3	47	5	3	4	29,053
Caller I. D.	105	52	709	90	70	100	1,312,731
Calumar	7	2	40	2	8	5	57,558
Cam a Rhett	7	3	65	5	0	9	31,030
Camisite (GB)	2	1	22	1	3	1	14,710
Camp Izard	3	3	43	6	6	5	75,464
Can Can Sam	1	1	16	1	0	2	4,813
Can't Be Slew	33	15	210	23	36	20	104,851
Canadian Factor	2	1	12	3	3	0	22,421
Canaska Dancer (IRE)	10	2	51	2	3	7	23,832
Canaveral	39	17	223	26	23	21	336,014
Cancun	1	1	4	1	0	0	6,651
Candi's Gold	79	34	556	67	44	58	902,101
Candid Cameron	37	19	277	37	32	42	320,955
Candy Stripes	80	46	494	82	72	56	1,583,586
Candyman Bee	6	4	51	7	6	6	51,312
Cannon Royal	1	1	15	3	6	3	24,506
Cannon Zana	1	1	8	1	0	2	3,895
Cantcatchmickey	2	1	10	1	0	3	12,490
Canvas	8	4	51	6	2	7	39,365
Canyon Creek (IRE)	49	19	275	30	19	28	779,390
Canyon Run	2	1	3	1	1	0	21,580
Cape Lazaref	1	1	5	1	1	0	4,095
Cape Light	2	1	12	2	2	1	8,157
Cape Storm	14	5	83	8	7	12	73,824
Cape Town	63	36	289	49	29	33	2,046,576
Capitalimprovement	10	4	63	9	7	6	94,444
Capitol South	6	3	54	6	2	11	51,571
Capo Maximo (ARG)	1	1	2	1	0	0	20,290
Capote	120	61	752	98	95	104	3,267,146
Capote's Promise	5	2	29	9	6	1	187,648
Capote's Prospect	17	9	112	16	11	19	124,006
Cappuccio	12	8	84	9	8	10	96,418
Captain Arthur	2	1	18	2	1	3	24,334
Captain Bash	4	2	15	3	2	2	8,088
Captain Bodgit	111	59	681	98	94	85	1,970,672
Captain Codex	12	3	68	7	3	10	38,251
Captain James (IRE)	1	1	10	1	2	3	20,760
Capture the Gold	7	2	33	2	5	2	62,839
Car Dealer	8	5	47	6	2	5	51,660
Caracey	9	4	68	7	2	9	67,495
Carborundum	12	7	83	10	12	11	89,948
Careless Secretary	1	1	3	1	0	0	12,158
Carey's Boy	8	4	48	7	3	7	30,245
Cari Jill Hajji	10	5	81	11	12	15	184,382
Caribe	2	1	12	1	3	1	15,940
Carjack	1	1	12	2	1	1	11,704
Carnivalay	84	45	621	70	78	74	1,467,894
Carolina Kid	13	6	64	9	7	3	49,753
Carolingian (AUS)	1	1	7	1	1	0	11,800
Caros Love	11	6	105	8	8	13	52,307
Carotic	1	1	15	3	2	2	15,613
Carr de Naskra	55	28	389	46	58	55	581,249
Carry Over	3	2	34	3	4	6	36,439
Carson City	181	103	1,113	191	163	145	5,061,522
Cartwright	89	44	631	74	71	84	1,324,945
Casa Dante	4	4	38	5	6	8	37,178
Case the Joint	5	3	41	3	6	7	93,857
Casey On Deck	4	1	24	1	0	2	8,741
Casey's Lady	1	1	26	1	0	1	10,265
Castle Guard	14	7	124	11	13	16	145,951
Castle Howard	5	1	33	1	2	4	6,575
Cat Creek Slew	16	8	88	13	8	8	117,567
Cat Doctor	5	1	17	1	3	2	12,352
Cat in Town	7	2	43	2	3	2	25,140
Cat's Career	80	42	562	72	56	77	892,928
Cat's Spats	2	1	11	1	1	0	10,056
Catastrophic	16	6	91	14	14	12	107,108
Category Five	7	4	24	7	4	1	119,459
Cathedral Bells	11	4	72	4	14	10	40,965
Cathy's Regal Son	8	2	44	3	3	7	41,118
Catillac	9	2	31	2	7	7	57,979
Catonie Choke	3	2	23	3	2	6	37,893
Catrail	7	4	46	5	3	5	64,200
Cause for Pause	24	9	113	15	9	14	232,624
Cave Creek	4	2	34	3	8	5	19,869
Caveat	8	1	30	1	2	0	28,382
Cayeli	7	2	56	2	3	6	23,809
Cee's Tizzy	87	47	464	74	62	79	2,037,868
Cefis	10	5	64	5	5	4	67,711
Celtic Swing (GB)	1	1	1	1	0	0	780,000
Centaine (AUS)	1	1	3	2	0	0	105,060
Center Cut	4	2	19	2	3	1	7,493
Chad's by Geo.	7	2	51	3	7	4	29,131
Chaka	6	4	46	6	6	5	40,397
Champagneforashley	18	8	108	10	9	13	95,607
Chanate	10	3	27	3	4	4	49,873
Change Takes Time	14	4	80	6	12	6	109,491
Chapel Creek	32	14	209	22	25	30	209,078
Character (GB)	3	2	24	6	4	5	47,473
Charging Through	6	1	23	1	1	1	14,360
Charismatic	35	5	108	6	7	14	228,766
Charlie Barley	12	4	67	7	13	7	196,795
Charlie Cielo	2	2	6	2	1	0	4,165
Charlie's Orphan	1	1	9	2	1	1	6,382
Charmin' Merlin	4	1	33	1	1	2	15,839
Chas Conerly	1	1	5	1	0	1	2,881
Chateaubay	9	2	41	2	1	0	12,582
Chelsey Cat	6	4	35	5	3	8	94,140
Chenin Blanc	42	10	250	15	15	39	294,907
Cheque Froid	1	1	11	1	1	1	8,227
Chequer	61	28	455	51	59	65	681,138
Cherokee Colony	31	13	229	22	36	32	300,573
Cherokee Fellow	8	4	52	6	6	7	30,996
Cherokee Run	153	79	985	137	147	128	3,985,515
Chicago	2	2	22	4	1	3	56,237
Chidester	9	3	46	8	2	6	60,457
Chief Bandito	1	1	11	1	1	0	10,200
Chief Honcho	35	20	315	44	57	44	503,468
Chief Persuasion	2	1	15	1	0	0	22,004
Chief Prospect	12	4	83	5	6	5	64,760
Chief Protocol	4	1	33	1	7	4	34,553
Chief's Crown	16	11	173	20	17	21	206,421
Chief's Hope	1	1	9	1	4	1	10,482
Chief's Reward	13	7	76	16	13	10	101,933
Chilito	7	4	47	7	9	5	197,102
Chillon	2	1	16	2	1	0	7,468
Chimes Band	61	38	514	64	80	78	1,347,541
Chimineas	1	1	14	1	1	0	11,498
Chinati	8	2	45	4	2	4	22,040
Chisos	14	8	89	15	8	9	62,436
Chivalry	2	2	13	3	1	0	16,154
Choctaw Ridge	4	2	25	2	2	4	43,032
Chopin	12	8	82	8	8	12	70,840
Chromite	24	13	241	23	35	29	182,797
Chunkus T	3	3	21	5	2	2	22,973
Churl	2	2	16	2	1	1	11,560
Ciano Cat	17	7	57	10	4	6	145,865
Cien Fuegos	41	13	230	24	19	22	264,770
Cimarron Secret	7	3	17	3	0	0	20,026
Cipayo (ARG)	1	1	11	1	1	0	14,450
Circulating	23	14	162	23	24	22	251,782
Circus Surprise	11	5	79	12	5	11	134,188
Cisco Road	69	45	496	81	64	80	528,547
Citidancer	84	52	585	96	85	86	1,861,021
Clackson (BRZ)	2	1	9	1	2	1	45,470
Claim	11	9	111	19	21	18	112,726
Claramount	45	22	362	48	42	43	676,333
Clash of Steel	8	3	57	9	5	7	33,821
Class Hero	3	1	31	1	2	1	11,991
Classi Envoy	4	2	30	6	1	2	23,376
Classic Account	30	13	237	25	20	14	453,262

RECORDS OF SIRES

Sire	Perf	Wnrs	Sts	1st	2d	3d	Purses
Classic Go Go	2	1	11	3	2	0	13,915
Classified Facts	20	10	128	13	10	15	266,989
Classy Prospector	7	1	34	1	3	8	31,688
Claudius	1	1	6	4	2	0	99,816
Clear Course	13	7	117	11	10	11	220,607
Clever Allemont	1	1	6	1	0	3	1,928
Clever Champ	11	7	84	13	13	4	139,595
Clever Gold	4	2	30	3	3	3	34,717
Clever Leader	2	1	11	1	0	2	3,654
Clever Trick	105	53	736	89	98	75	1,287,634
Clever Wake	1	1	4	1	0	0	3,365
Cliff Flower (ARG)	2	1	18	2	2	4	10,934
Cliffs Place	3	1	15	1	1	0	4,819
Closing Fast	1	1	16	2	2	2	10,826
Cloud Cover	9	3	31	5	4	1	76,485
Coach George	1	1	9	2	2	0	24,945
Coach Rabbey	2	2	21	4	1	0	44,460
Coastal Voyage	8	6	63	13	14	7	198,268
Coax Me Chad	18	7	161	9	15	19	94,934
Cobra King	78	44	551	78	66	68	2,133,282
Cock O'Hoop	2	1	19	2	0	3	16,378
Cocobuddy	1	1	6	1	1	1	4,600
Codex's Reflection	6	2	63	2	1	3	14,367
Codified	10	6	84	10	6	6	96,574
Codys Key	5	1	15	1	0	0	13,442
Cognizant	14	5	87	5	8	9	60,778
Cohiba	9	7	71	10	12	6	99,880
Cojak	2	1	11	1	0	2	13,778
Col. Denning	2	1	19	1	0	1	8,749
Cold Bid	13	11	121	18	21	13	251,409
Cold Digger	5	2	24	2	2	4	46,553
Cold Hearted Man	12	6	109	10	14	9	133,483
Cold Hoist	1	1	4	1	0	1	996
Collegian	8	4	68	7	9	8	65,543
Collier	5	1	22	1	0	2	12,312
Colonel Gay	3	1	19	1	3	2	19,171
Colonel Stevens	5	1	21	1	2	3	30,619
Colonial Affair	68	35	460	73	65	56	1,488,091
Colony Light	68	34	461	46	55	60	973,318
Color Bearer	2	1	15	2	0	2	19,221
Colorful Crew	5	1	28	2	1	1	19,118
Colway Rally (GB)	2	1	5	1	0	0	2,090
Combat Ready	13	8	82	18	10	5	299,551
Combsway	2	1	13	1	0	1	13,146
Comet Kat	7	4	54	6	5	7	34,517
Comet Shine	66	31	568	52	56	73	778,064
Comic Strip	17	3	42	4	4	5	99,460
Commemorate	43	20	288	30	18	29	233,222
Commodore Spurwink	4	1	27	1	5	2	11,161
Common Grounds	7	3	35	4	6	1	107,550
Community Interest	2	1	13	1	0	5	22,925
Compadre	34	20	210	14	29	20	1,030,253
Compelling Sound	48	20	291	27	36	25	366,559
Compliance	39	20	355	33	52	40	679,527
Composer	12	6	82	8	9	7	96,007
Compton Place (GB)	1	1	10	4	1	0	119,320
Comstock Lode	46	18	291	27	26	25	266,389
Con Fool	1	1	1	1	0	0	3,000
Concern	70	39	490	71	54	73	1,252,978
Concerto	47	37	315	56	42	33	1,177,356
Concorde Prince	4	1	34	2	3	2	17,465
Concorde's Future	5	4	47	7	11	5	71,658
Concorde's Tune	71	45	539	81	68	65	1,717,410
Conduction	5	2	39	2	3	5	20,981
Confide	61	24	279	38	25	36	766,860
Connecticut	20	10	160	18	19	20	152,588
Conquer	7	4	46	7	5	6	43,253
Conquista Fager	6	3	47	4	3	4	27,419
Conquistador Cielo	109	52	712	101	85	89	2,512,730
Conquistador Oro	3	2	45	4	3	2	18,097
Conroe	1	1	5	1	1	0	4,916
Consigliere (GB)	35	15	168	22	21	24	177,719
Constant Demand	2	1	10	1	0	1	11,455
Conte Di Savoya	40	13	292	23	29	37	461,953
Contempt	2	1	9	1	2	0	4,692
Contested Bid	5	1	34	1	2	1	45,263
Contested Colors	19	7	136	9	22	24	192,952
Conveyor	55	28	445	48	54	44	652,077
Cool Fragrance	4	3	56	7	6	7	93,211
Cool Groom	13	4	61	6	14	9	132,002
Cool Halo	11	6	96	7	13	9	76,368
Cool Joe	3	1	14	2	1	2	208,347
Cool Victor	8	5	77	15	10	9	206,738
Cooleen Jack (IRE)	2	1	13	1	3	0	25,788
Coordinator	49	17	247	26	28	30	258,121
Copelan	6	1	35	3	5	3	48,182
Copper Man	7	3	57	4	4	7	71,374
Copper Mine	2	1	15	1	2	1	17,677
Cork (FR)	4	3	25	4	2	4	62,772
Cormorant	5	5	42	14	4	5	255,295
Cornish Hill	2	2	28	4	6	6	35,505
Coronado's Quest	58	19	225	31	30	28	1,278,475
Corporate Report	66	27	569	59	77	68	720,680
Corridor Key	31	12	173	22	19	19	293,648
Corslew	41	24	296	45	46	38	642,290
Corwyn	6	1	11	1	0	0	8,220
Corwyn Bay (IRE)	20	8	130	16	20	17	234,042
Cost Conscious	5	3	51	3	8	6	24,861
Cote d'Ivoire	1	1	7	1	0	0	9,400
Counsellors Image	1	1	14	1	1	1	11,816
Count Francescui	2	1	22	1	4	4	20,407
Count the Time	62	29	375	52	52	33	686,862
Count von Count	5	2	49	3	6	5	33,721
Counterfeit Money	1	1	7	1	1	1	6,397
Country Light	22	7	104	9	16	13	74,482
Country Manor	2	1	17	5	0	2	49,443
Country Pine	19	10	137	15	23	18	232,817
Country Store	27	9	193	13	17	24	100,443
Court Procedure	3	1	9	1	1	5	6,790
Court Trial	6	3	46	7	3	6	24,862
Coverallbases	13	6	87	9	10	10	111,818
Covered Wagon	12	5	86	6	11	11	59,818
Cowboy Posse	3	1	11	1	0	1	5,493
Cox's Ridge	22	9	168	17	24	24	263,223
Cox's Time	2	1	8	1	1	0	5,393
Cozy Drive	19	4	94	4	4	10	94,548
Cozzene	92	48	551	71	69	84	2,041,800
Crack Shot	1	1	13	2	1	1	11,024
Crafty	29	8	119	11	9	7	95,187
Crafty Dude	29	17	211	38	22	26	375,997
Crafty Friend	31	10	93	12	10	5	240,889
Crafty Harold	7	2	28	3	3	2	19,770
Crafty Mana	7	4	55	5	5	5	60,665
Crafty Prospector	135	88	949	152	158	123	3,567,141
Crafty Ridan	23	16	210	28	23	25	147,052
Crater (ARG)	3	1	27	1	6	2	22,895
Crawford Special	4	4	24	6	4	2	30,392
Creative Act	14	6	91	7	6	0	161,250
Cresta Powered	3	1	22	1	2	1	3,125
Cresting Water	11	4	59	9	7	6	99,690
Crimcino	10	7	86	8	6	13	75,223
Crimson Guard	14	4	69	7	6	9	88,570
Crimson Slew	13	5	88	11	11	9	94,247
Critical Mass	1	1	14	1	0	1	6,110
Cromwell	3	2	26	2	2	4	27,225
Crown Ambassador	35	24	242	39	36	27	818,055
Crown Attorney	10	1	24	1	1	3	49,785
Crown Pleasure	2	1	21	1	4	5	14,816
Crowning Decision	17	5	58	5	9	5	116,627
Crowning Season (GB)	36	19	268	31	45	43	188,772
Cruisin' Prince	1	1	8	2	1	2	26,526
Crusader Sword	63	30	435	47	46	42	767,311
Crypto Star	16	6	51	9	6	8	222,077
Cryptoclearance	223	103	1,653	191	189	203	3,739,880
Crystal Gazer	8	2	31	2	2	4	11,552
Crystal Run	2	1	11	1	1	1	1,909
Crystal Star	1	1	3	1	1	1	1,436
Crystal Tas	3	2	26	3	2	5	29,466
Cullendale	3	2	17	2	2	2	7,771
Cup Challenge	7	6	53	9	8	6	101,988
Cure the Blues	77	42	644	73	75	77	1,952,700
Current Pleasure	1	1	15	2	0	2	8,049
Custom Body	7	1	38	4	6	3	58,892
Cute n Common	3	1	13	1	0	0	3,324
Cutlass Fax	11	8	93	10	11	9	179,800
Cutlass Reality	31	20	185	28	24	32	409,817
Cuzzin Jeb	4	1	15	1	1	1	5,784
Cyberspace	17	4	110	12	10	10	306,630

Sire	Perf	Wnrs	Sts	1st	2d	3d	Purses
Cyrano	6	4	57	7	6	6	67,633
Cyrano de Bergerac	2	1	8	1	2	1	68,300
D'Accord	10	5	97	7	9	16	89,108
D'Hallevant	17	10	118	11	9	11	159,873
D. C. Tenacious	13	6	92	6	8	11	89,299
D. J. Cat	25	14	167	22	21	26	307,227
Daddy Bish	1	1	4	1	1	1	1,560
Daddy Watch	7	5	54	7	7	8	67,044
Daily Ballot	6	2	48	3	2	5	19,789
Daily Review	1	1	16	3	5	0	38,455
Dakota Pride	3	2	15	2	2	2	18,993
Dakotas Bold	1	1	13	4	4	1	21,475
Damascan	4	1	28	1	1	6	20,861
Damone	5	3	40	4	5	3	32,878
Dan's Diablo	1	1	15	1	0	0	9,133
Danasinga (AUS)	2	2	21	4	2	3	132,062
Dance Brightly	93	47	538	71	58	64	1,707,304
Dance Centre	20	12	159	29	33	20	159,515
Dance Floor	28	13	130	16	18	15	142,824
Dance in Time	6	3	37	3	3	1	31,563
Dance to the Wire	3	1	15	1	0	1	6,193
Dancebel (GB)	4	3	38	4	2	4	16,486
Dancer's Boots	2	1	13	1	4	2	23,523
Dancing Count	1	1	5	1	0	0	6,256
Dancing Crown	10	6	96	12	6	13	101,336
Dancing Glamour	5	1	33	1	4	0	27,831
Dancing Groom	1	1	6	1	0	0	16,152
Dancing Native	6	2	26	5	0	1	8,006
Dancing Pirate	6	2	33	3	1	3	8,232
Dancing Torch	2	1	10	1	1	1	3,723
Dancinwiththedevil	15	8	85	10	9	15	129,399
Danehill	28	8	107	12	12	13	864,749
Danehill Dancer (IRE)	2	1	13	3	0	3	23,345
Danjur	16	8	143	20	20	22	224,004
Danotable	7	1	40	1	3	4	20,101
Dansil	5	1	29	1	2	2	9,279
Danski	7	2	43	2	5	5	41,011
Danzatame	16	6	119	6	11	13	280,150
Danzatore	39	10	206	12	23	21	254,021
Danzig	41	20	172	31	20	13	1,614,085
Danzig Connection	10	5	71	8	7	12	84,249
Danzig Dancer	2	1	17	1	3	1	3,181
Dapper's Attache	2	1	14	1	2	0	7,167
Darby Creek Lance	12	2	71	6	7	9	66,417
Dare and Go	61	28	469	40	65	59	884,610
Dargai	5	2	33	3	2	3	16,281
Daring Damascus	3	3	19	5	0	2	32,983
Daring Groom	3	1	18	2	3	3	13,099
Dariyoun	7	2	49	5	4	8	36,833
Dark Hyacinth	5	4	45	6	1	7	36,486
Dark Mystery	7	3	67	6	5	9	82,342
Darn That Alarm	49	27	376	63	49	44	655,615
Dashing Blade	3	2	10	2	0	0	45,255
Dashing Lad	2	1	6	1	0	0	6,345
Dashing Writer	3	1	24	2	4	6	40,505
Daufuskie Pirate	4	2	23	3	2	1	52,333
Dave's Reality	8	4	49	4	6	3	23,604
David's Wolf	1	1	12	2	1	2	7,604
Dawn of Creation	2	2	14	3	0	1	22,357
Dawn Quixote	37	22	312	35	23	21	423,335
Daygata	8	2	45	4	5	8	112,876
Dayjur	50	28	329	51	44	32	732,917
Daytime Dancer	7	1	38	2	3	5	46,638
Dazzle Us	1	1	6	2	0	0	8,486
Dazzling Falls	26	17	215	37	33	32	468,629
De Braak	16	3	97	4	4	8	34,882
De Guerin	12	4	67	7	7	6	97,594
De Jeau	4	2	16	2	1	2	11,028
De Niro	42	22	335	33	45	34	404,400
De Sarmiento	9	4	47	5	0	8	66,276
Deamon's Pouch	5	1	21	2	1	0	11,708
Dean Dill	2	1	14	1	3	0	8,878
Dearborn	3	2	16	2	2	1	22,768
Dee Lance	12	5	76	6	9	13	61,906
Deerhound	101	45	659	69	92	66	1,376,999
Defense Verdict	2	1	15	2	3	5	4,972
Defense Witness	14	6	107	15	12	13	170,380
Defensive Play	43	17	274	30	29	31	362,212
Definite Article (GB)	4	1	11	1	2	2	38,150
Definite Signs	1	1	7	2	1	0	16,636
Definitive	1	1	11	1	0	1	5,090
Defrere	113	62	755	103	104	110	2,474,043
Dehere	115	63	712	97	129	85	3,672,157
Delineator	66	30	406	47	63	61	569,246
Delinsky	1	1	3	1	0	0	1,980
Delta Wolf	5	1	32	1	3	3	9,976
Demaloot Demashoot	85	51	742	97	91	87	1,350,968
Demidoff	72	31	489	44	62	72	833,914
Demons Begone	90	42	597	62	80	98	672,962
Denouncer	8	5	62	7	9	1	121,700
Departing Cloud	3	1	29	1	3	4	17,235
Departing Prints	1	1	10	1	2	1	35,682
Deploy (GB)	1	1	13	2	2	1	57,295
Deposit Ticket	76	34	527	59	73	64	973,722
Deputed Testamony	46	18	296	40	31	40	656,485
Deputy Bodman	28	16	202	33	16	24	261,529
Deputy Commander	88	36	489	54	68	64	3,483,253
Deputy Minister	121	54	626	83	91	71	3,475,392
Deputy Regent	8	2	48	3	10	4	37,231
Der Rosenkavalier	4	3	56	6	0	3	29,446
Derby Wish	16	7	111	12	15	9	209,968
Dervish Master	2	2	13	2	0	1	7,242
Desert Classic	37	14	244	23	17	38	393,533
Desert Glow	1	1	15	2	0	1	8,646
Desert God	15	8	92	13	10	11	137,007
Desert King (IRE)	10	5	63	6	10	11	394,053
Desert Prince (IRE)	2	1	6	2	0	0	73,500
Desert Rival	3	2	30	7	5	2	38,819
Desert Royalty	15	13	115	31	15	10	602,112
Desert Secret (IRE)	48	22	332	38	28	30	455,583
Desert Wine	28	9	131	11	11	11	113,171
Detox	11	4	46	9	4	3	105,810
Devil Begone	25	7	141	13	9	14	223,508
Devil Diamond	7	1	40	1	7	5	30,424
Devil His Due	171	102	1,330	186	185	166	3,438,838
Devil On Ice	49	25	290	47	43	27	519,591
Devil's Bag	89	45	505	73	57	52	1,734,065
Devil's Cry	32	7	214	12	13	24	167,610
Devil's Delight	7	3	63	4	1	7	31,737
Devil's Joy	6	1	47	1	0	8	19,479
Devil's Punch Bowl	3	1	9	1	0	0	3,009
Devil's Rock	8	4	62	5	10	11	99,280
Devil's Share	8	1	56	2	6	9	45,424
Devious Course	54	24	375	37	52	40	443,261
Devon Lane	51	24	276	35	42	36	800,523
Devongate	34	16	239	27	23	28	725,838
Dewdle's Dancer	4	1	23	1	1	3	20,157
Diablo	65	32	475	60	57	62	863,179
Diamond	20	6	55	7	11	4	175,555
Diamond Sword	18	6	90	12	7	3	93,372
Diazo	37	16	198	25	22	24	341,885
Dickerson's Gold	2	1	11	1	0	0	5,850
Diegos Dominator	1	1	9	1	2	4	6,087
Diesis (GB)	30	7	129	10	14	23	783,854
Dig Zig	1	1	13	1	5	2	10,588
Digamist	27	13	180	20	24	14	283,802
Digging In	11	2	53	2	6	10	27,041
Dignitas	32	11	232	20	27	36	287,476
Digression	12	2	75	5	8	7	81,468
Diligence	43	25	275	34	26	27	676,323
Dilum	2	2	15	4	2	0	57,608
Din's Dancer	24	11	193	24	18	15	207,866
Diogenes	5	1	29	1	1	3	7,005
Diplomatic Jet	24	10	146	20	20	10	193,788
Diplomatic Note	4	1	14	1	1	0	5,154
Direct Hit	11	6	33	7	4	3	81,080
Directed Energy	5	1	23	1	0	2	10,983
Discos My Name	3	1	14	1	0	3	17,269
Discover	19	5	104	9	14	17	178,200
Dismissed	3	1	13	1	1	3	8,375
Dispersal	17	7	117	16	13	15	239,617
Distant View	57	27	383	56	50	49	2,547,336
Distinct Reality	4	2	35	4	6	6	57,089
Distinctive Cat	80	36	452	54	61	65	646,240
Distinctive Pro	98	50	753	90	109	120	1,988,114
Distorted Humor	79	50	449	84	67	67	4,978,239
Dixie Brass	125	73	933	136	139	148	3,609,466
Dixie Jazz Band	5	2	37	3	5	3	28,621

RECORDS OF SIRES

Sire	Perf	Wnrs	Sts	1st	2d	3d	Purses
Dixie Power	29	11	177	17	18	26	313,006
Dixieland Band	129	63	738	98	88	96	2,551,284
Dixieland Brass	38	16	241	30	43	27	449,703
Dixieland Heat	46	26	275	43	38	30	761,370
Dmitri	7	3	50	8	4	3	57,959
Do It Again Dan	17	13	152	22	18	19	168,197
Doc's Leader	36	15	241	27	20	31	668,353
Doctor's Orders	2	2	12	2	0	2	7,315
Dodge City	1	1	8	1	1	1	5,442
Doggedly	11	2	71	2	3	10	31,450
Doinitthehardway	4	3	18	3	1	0	8,295
Dollar Away	2	1	16	1	2	1	4,970
Dolphin Street	2	2	21	3	9	2	210,355
Dom Dancer	3	1	13	1	3	4	40,462
Domasca Dan	24	14	169	26	22	11	1,093,027
Dome Mountain	6	4	39	5	1	2	28,205
Dominated	9	3	69	3	4	6	25,676
Dominated Debut	6	2	18	3	3	4	38,005
Don Gabriel (MEX)	2	1	9	2	2	1	9,796
Don's Choice	12	4	101	5	12	14	66,358
Don't Fool With Me	7	2	35	3	3	3	18,132
Don't Forget Me	1	1	9	1	1	0	9,765
Don't Hesitate	7	1	44	1	5	7	25,970
Don't Say Halo	1	1	7	2	0	1	12,730
Doneraile Court	37	16	154	24	25	18	768,687
Doonesbear	3	1	30	2	0	6	14,294
Doppler	2	2	17	7	1	6	50,625
Dot's Silver B.	3	1	21	1	1	3	8,864
Double Bed (FR)	1	1	7	2	2	0	39,985
Double Cash	1	1	4	1	0	1	10,070
Double D. Slew	5	3	20	3	4	1	22,252
Double Honor	85	58	586	112	77	62	1,651,091
Double Negative	18	13	178	23	26	37	351,638
Double Niner	13	6	92	13	11	15	240,671
Double o' Slew	1	1	19	1	2	3	5,075
Double Quick	4	1	28	2	1	4	14,651
Double Reach	1	1	10	1	2	3	8,577
Double Ready	8	3	58	3	7	9	29,457
Double Sonic	8	5	81	9	10	11	75,841
Double Spark	2	1	22	1	2	2	13,656
Doubledova	2	1	5	1	1	0	6,810
Doug's My Doc	5	5	43	7	7	10	65,045
Dove Hunt	99	57	739	92	83	74	1,709,822
Dover Ridge	25	10	173	19	24	20	346,526
Downing	3	2	25	2	5	2	14,833
Doyoun (IRE)	3	1	17	4	1	3	193,285
Dr Devious (IRE)	6	4	28	10	3	0	500,219
Dr Fong	1	1	3	1	1	1	27,400
Dr. Adagio	58	35	489	74	67	60	1,362,231
Dr. Blum	9	2	49	2	4	6	61,149
Dr. Caton	55	34	481	59	55	52	791,096
Dr. Dalton	10	4	76	9	5	8	38,292
Dr. Dan Eyes	9	3	68	3	3	9	41,048
Dr. Danzig	8	4	58	4	3	10	58,304
Dr. Dave	5	3	49	5	10	7	39,819
Dr. Geo. Adams	2	1	13	1	2	1	12,390
Dr. Giggles	4	2	19	2	2	1	17,380
Dr. Greenberg	2	1	11	1	0	1	3,298
Dr. Koch	5	3	41	4	5	11	52,796
Dr. McGuire	1	1	4	1	0	0	988
Dr. Messina	5	1	30	1	2	2	8,903
Dr. New	1	1	4	1	1	0	4,724
Dr. Nureyev	4	1	22	1	2	2	9,130
Dr. Reality	8	7	67	17	12	8	98,815
Dr. Schwartzman	3	2	32	5	2	1	34,988
Dream Trapp	2	2	11	2	0	4	7,619
Dream Valley	3	1	16	2	0	4	8,886
Drouilly (FR)	1	1	5	2	1	2	7,864
Drumalis (IRE)	10	3	48	5	5	5	104,693
Dry Gulch	5	4	49	7	8	8	322,220
Dubious Connection	3	1	28	1	4	0	25,591
Due to the King	3	1	16	2	3	2	19,537
Dumaani	53	22	295	28	35	38	700,828
Dunant (IRE)	4	2	26	3	3	5	8,202
Duplicity (IRE)	3	3	31	4	3	2	27,178
Dusty Sassafras	2	2	24	3	4	3	22,239
Dusty Screen	42	20	285	30	27	34	428,366
Duxster	3	2	21	2	3	4	15,179
Dynaformer	147	76	907	131	114	129	7,788,577
Eagle Eyed	19	11	155	20	19	20	804,381
Eagletar	1	1	7	2	0	3	1,973
Earth Star	8	5	67	9	9	5	77,343
Earth Station	2	1	11	1	0	2	8,541
Earthmover	6	2	32	2	4	8	31,366
Eastern Bazaar	1	1	13	2	2	2	7,356
Eastern Echo	93	51	664	88	70	82	1,885,557
Eastern Lord	1	1	6	1	0	2	9,261
Eastover Court	26	11	204	17	39	23	321,297
Easy N Dirty	5	1	25	2	1	2	7,370
Easy Riser	2	2	21	2	3	2	9,968
Easy Squeezy	3	1	12	1	0	1	7,031
Echelon's Ice Man	5	1	29	1	0	3	8,715
Eclipso	1	1	10	2	1	2	41,930
Ecliptical	9	6	65	10	2	10	115,704
Ecstatic Ride	8	2	28	2	0	2	9,017
Edgy Diplomat	2	1	12	6	1	1	222,850
Editor's Note	107	67	844	118	99	106	2,424,453
Efisio	6	2	33	5	3	6	53,120
Eight Letter Man	5	1	26	1	3	4	11,368
Eighty Below Zero	5	1	24	2	2	4	21,845
Einherjar	1	1	10	1	1	1	9,836
El Amante	17	5	59	8	10	6	137,843
El Gran Senor	16	7	79	8	6	7	781,400
El Mandingo	8	4	61	7	8	3	111,039
El Mayaguezano	15	7	91	15	8	4	261,007
El Meteoro (ARG)	1	1	9	1	1	2	14,434
El Prado (IRE)	192	106	1,331	200	175	172	7,758,497
El Raggaas	2	1	15	3	2	0	29,451
El Set	2	1	14	1	3	4	9,106
El Sultan (ARG)	1	1	5	2	0	0	22,260
El Torre	3	1	10	1	1	0	4,076
Elajjud	10	5	56	8	2	9	190,431
Electric Blue	9	2	45	2	4	3	21,130
Elegant Gold	4	1	16	1	2	0	5,842
Elegant Life	6	3	36	5	7	5	32,571
Elk's Uz	7	3	26	6	2	2	85,586
Elmaamul	1	1	9	2	2	2	500,360
Eltish	42	23	257	47	36	32	1,029,213
Elusive Quality	93	51	466	79	72	48	2,915,950
Emancipator	5	2	14	2	2	3	53,815
Embrace the Wind	2	1	15	2	1	1	9,893
Emerald Creme	4	2	31	3	4	3	42,342
Emerald Jig	22	8	143	16	14	21	310,935
Emigrant Peak	10	4	64	6	8	10	39,983
Eminency	5	2	28	3	1	3	17,774
Emmson (IRE)	1	1	8	1	0	0	31,320
Emperor Jones	5	2	17	2	0	1	31,404
Emphatic One	8	1	33	2	0	3	50,089
Empire Glory	4	3	47	5	9	4	47,824
En Tete	10	4	53	7	8	2	84,154
Encino	5	4	49	8	7	11	64,243
End Sweep	201	135	1,693	253	207	221	4,712,517
Endless Wonder	3	1	14	2	2	2	15,039
Ends Well	23	11	159	16	18	8	288,107
Endured	1	1	20	1	4	3	12,982
Enemy Number One	6	2	24	2	1	1	15,910
England	1	1	5	1	0	1	3,119
Enough Reality	4	3	34	3	3	2	27,075
Entertain	1	1	8	1	1	1	5,580
Entropy	8	2	40	3	4	4	81,977
Epic Honor	9	3	30	3	2	4	49,112
Equalize	9	6	61	11	3	12	282,264
Erland	2	1	7	1	0	1	8,874
Eshu Be Elegua	4	2	26	4	2	4	26,772
Eskimo	32	14	220	32	26	21	537,059
Esplanade Ridge	3	1	7	1	0	1	7,765
Esteem	5	3	16	4	5	1	98,864
Estes	2	1	25	1	3	3	13,941
Etbauer	4	1	6	1	0	0	6,960
Eteelya	2	1	16	3	2	1	20,582
Eternal Orage	9	5	93	11	9	12	162,919
Eulogize	4	2	39	3	3	9	19,523
Evansville Slew	55	39	459	70	66	60	1,260,750
Even Faster	6	2	47	3	3	6	14,609
Evening Kris	31	15	200	23	26	27	640,239
Event of the Year	12	3	36	3	11	7	144,651
Evzone	3	1	18	1	1	4	15,839
Exbourne	9	3	55	5	8	7	67,556

Sire	Perf	Wnrs	Sts	1st	2d	3d	Purses	Sire	Perf	Wnrs	Sts	1st	2d	3d	Purses
Excavate	94	35	601	54	84	73	970,743	Feather Ridge	4	1	36	1	2	4	16,148
Excellent Secret	17	8	110	11	14	7	114,555	Feel the Power	34	12	200	23	27	17	566,738
Exceller Vice	15	3	64	3	6	4	56,006	Feeling Gallant	5	2	31	2	1	1	7,730
Exclusive Darling	2	2	15	4	3	3	21,262	Fenter	20	10	132	13	13	14	101,586
Exclusive Encore	7	2	51	3	5	7	36,453	Ferdinand	3	2	25	3	7	3	29,553
Exclusive Energy	1	1	12	2	1	0	7,843	Ferdinandthegreat	1	1	12	1	0	0	4,978
Exclusive Enough	6	1	51	1	6	3	45,923	Ferrara	21	9	166	15	15	19	174,253
Exclusive Era	37	19	242	31	27	33	401,552	Fervently	1	1	3	1	0	0	16,800
Exclusive Praline	4	1	27	1	3	7	45,721	Festin (ARG)	14	7	96	15	14	14	164,356
Exclusive Ribot	5	2	27	2	4	5	121,631	Festive	12	4	92	9	13	10	223,044
Exclusive Zone	2	2	19	4	2	1	42,660	Feu d'Enfer	43	26	295	53	36	36	470,257
Exclusivengagement	5	2	32	2	4	4	36,646	Fey Tru	3	1	5	1	1	0	6,172
Executive Counsel	1	1	7	1	0	4	3,247	Fibak	1	1	10	2	1	0	8,018
Executive Order	17	6	105	7	6	11	120,267	Fierce Fighter	4	1	22	2	1	2	13,592
Exemplary Leader	17	10	133	11	10	18	275,217	Fiery Best	3	1	24	11	5	0	64,602
Exetera	14	2	59	2	4	10	43,981	Fiftysevenvette	6	1	26	1	1	1	14,678
Exile King	2	2	20	6	3	2	117,430	Fight Over	24	5	131	5	11	10	53,864
Exit to Nowhere	7	3	51	6	6	4	182,026	Fighter Joe	5	1	26	1	0	3	9,310
Exotic Eagle	12	6	78	11	6	11	51,831	Fighting Affair	6	2	19	2	0	3	16,887
Expanding Man	1	1	2	1	0	0	6,570	Fighting Fantasy	12	6	91	11	13	11	67,690
Expedition Moon	3	1	18	1	3	3	12,078	Fighting Fit	19	7	131	13	15	16	151,800
Expelled	18	7	70	9	10	9	228,050	Figure the Facts	6	4	39	5	3	2	22,156
Expense Account	17	10	112	16	19	13	227,855	Figure This	3	1	25	1	6	4	19,791
Expensive Decision	13	9	166	17	26	22	421,294	Filipino Boy (ARG)	3	1	23	1	3	3	12,582
Explodent	6	2	42	2	8	3	26,687	Final Act	3	2	20	5	3	3	33,991
Exploding Rainbow	8	4	31	6	3	5	30,570	Final Luck	2	1	19	1	1	2	4,810
Exploit	43	14	145	15	20	19	515,992	Financial Matter	10	7	85	11	6	11	96,558
Explosive Red	93	42	709	72	101	71	1,012,346	Fincher Branch	1	1	4	1	0	0	5,370
Expressman	11	4	57	4	4	5	45,449	Finest Hour	14	8	51	12	3	9	296,527
Exuberant	14	4	103	7	3	13	89,594	Finocchio	2	1	17	1	3	3	19,041
Ezzoud (IRE)	1	1	6	1	2	3	18,574	Fire Dancer	17	10	155	17	15	20	202,367
Fabulous Champ	53	23	287	47	53	37	492,329	Fire Maker	23	8	164	16	17	19	181,201
Fabulous Dancer	1	1	10	3	2	1	24,444	Firery Ensign	1	1	7	3	1	2	231,405
Fabulous Frolic	43	12	265	26	21	32	298,888	Firestar	2	1	7	1	0	1	13,435
Fact Book	2	1	5	2	1	0	12,900	Firmlin	7	1	21	1	2	0	3,552
Fair American	34	15	267	31	30	27	222,681	First Albert	3	1	25	1	4	2	8,841
Fair Decor	13	3	76	3	7	8	83,510	First and Only	27	14	193	27	29	26	355,622
Fair Skies	11	5	69	11	8	4	69,623	First Beginning	3	1	17	1	2	2	10,047
Fairly Affirmed	4	4	67	8	3	18	64,066	First Patriot	14	6	91	10	14	11	113,915
Fairway Topper	3	3	25	6	4	2	23,549	First Rate (IRE)	1	1	15	1	2	0	7,881
Fairy King	5	2	15	2	3	2	277,918	First Trump (GB)	2	1	5	2	0	0	55,910
Falkenham (GB)	5	2	29	3	0	5	32,540	Fit to Fight	130	74	1,004	125	138	117	2,018,651
Falstaff	46	23	336	43	30	48	599,305	Fitzcarraldo (ARG)	4	3	25	3	3	5	129,851
Faltaat	17	12	153	33	18	13	624,621	Flag Down	22	13	162	19	20	24	341,936
Family Calling	33	17	178	24	25	23	519,840	Flagman Ahead	12	6	107	13	20	14	171,597
Fanatic Boy (ARG)	8	3	59	6	5	2	32,510	Flame	5	1	20	3	2	3	8,784
Fancy Hoofer	1	1	11	5	2	2	54,010	Flare Dancer	30	15	202	21	17	34	166,113
Fantastic Fellow	23	11	116	13	7	19	177,679	Flashy Pocket	1	1	13	2	2	1	10,847
Fappavalley	1	1	6	1	3	1	23,950	Fleet Paul Allison	1	1	7	1	1	1	4,996
Fappiano	1	1	2	1	1	0	8,580	Fleet Sudan	8	3	60	6	8	11	56,352
Fappiano Road	3	1	16	1	0	1	9,575	Flight Forty Nine	34	13	246	22	27	37	244,215
Fappiano's Star	1	1	13	3	2	3	62,930	Flight of Time	1	1	9	1	2	1	16,128
Far North	7	3	53	5	6	6	40,668	Fly a Kite (IRE)	5	3	30	3	3	4	44,290
Far Out East	20	8	138	19	17	26	216,980	Fly Cry	8	3	64	7	10	7	125,690
Far Out Wadleigh	7	5	81	8	14	10	190,500	Fly Fly Fly	1	1	12	2	1	1	8,988
Faraway Island	1	1	11	1	0	1	6,107	Fly So Free	74	34	484	57	61	57	861,093
Farma Way	57	24	352	43	27	34	531,689	Fly Till Dawn	40	18	290	30	22	25	362,959
Farofino	1	1	11	1	4	1	8,289	Flying Chevron	43	20	293	38	37	39	860,768
Fashion Find	8	4	40	6	5	8	66,827	Flying Continental	136	71	1,044	120	135	131	2,151,137
Fashionable Enough	2	1	7	1	2	0	3,588	Flying Drone	4	3	32	3	4	3	28,708
Fashioned Gold	2	1	13	2	1	3	11,431	Flying Paster	1	1	16	1	0	1	4,496
Fasliyev	3	1	12	1	3	0	74,732	Flying Pidgeon	30	15	269	23	27	29	307,252
Fast 'n' Gold	8	4	61	8	5	7	92,858	Flying Spur (AUS)	2	2	15	2	2	2	108,551
Fast Account	21	13	124	22	14	12	228,080	Flying Victor	43	17	254	27	35	26	267,845
Fast Cure	5	3	26	4	1	0	18,587	Flying With Eagles	5	1	7	1	0	1	11,850
Fast Enough	1	1	12	1	0	1	6,805	Foligno	20	12	172	19	17	26	348,449
Fast Ferdie	3	3	22	3	3	3	47,568	Follow the Drum	1	1	15	1	1	3	16,012
Fast Five Six	2	1	9	1	0	0	7,440	Fool the Experts	17	10	132	16	16	14	120,214
Fast Forward	10	4	83	5	8	11	58,643	Foolish Flash	2	2	16	3	2	1	16,662
Fast Gold	7	3	44	5	6	6	89,541	Foolish MacDuff	4	4	59	6	9	6	38,571
Fast Passage	5	3	48	8	6	4	73,903	Foolish Pleasure	1	1	4	1	0	0	3,300
Fast Play	61	28	432	53	47	53	1,022,121	For Really	27	12	158	19	17	20	145,811
Faster Than Quick	3	1	21	4	2	2	27,162	For Sure	14	2	71	2	4	5	20,215
Fastness (IRE)	49	25	315	37	36	31	559,264	For Uncle Mike	2	2	20	3	2	3	36,444
Fatih	3	1	34	2	3	7	13,615	Forbidden Valley	1	1	11	2	1	3	33,955
Favorite Danzig	3	1	34	2	2	6	21,425	Force Play	1	1	3	1	0	0	1,170
Favorite Trick	63	34	434	54	59	70	1,285,063	Foreign Holding	17	9	119	13	12	10	105,228
Faygo	13	8	83	14	12	6	152,769	Foreign Legion	4	1	21	2	1	2	13,520
Fayruz	2	1	10	1	0	3	11,895	Foreign Survivor	14	4	111	5	11	14	270,214

RECORDS OF SIRES

Sire	Perf	Wnrs	Sts	1st	2d	3d	Purses
Forest Angel	2	1	32	2	3	3	15,926
Forest Gazelle	15	14	124	22	19	13	266,482
Forest Wildcat	158	80	877	129	89	101	3,096,878
Forestry	19	11	65	18	12	14	716,645
Forever Dancer	17	11	154	23	26	18	392,045
Forever Silver	21	7	180	10	17	24	131,576
Forever Whirl	13	5	85	8	14	11	166,910
Forli Winds	12	4	72	7	9	11	71,756
Formal Dinner	148	90	1,307	170	174	150	2,570,233
Formal Gold	79	49	472	77	67	45	1,811,473
Former	2	1	14	2	1	2	5,715
Fornell	1	1	13	1	1	1	4,022
Fort Chaffee	45	24	350	49	51	53	706,171
Fort Wayne	13	3	93	3	5	12	70,759
Fortunate Moment	1	1	5	1	0	0	2,280
Fortunate Prospect	128	69	1,051	138	133	127	1,979,103
Forty Niner	9	4	58	4	9	11	119,362
Forty Won	56	25	338	39	27	36	580,912
Forzando (GB)	2	1	14	3	2	0	26,190
Fountain of Gold	12	5	67	7	5	8	57,911
Four Seasons (GB)	41	16	281	23	27	39	239,441
Fourstars Allstar	2	1	9	1	1	2	41,767
Foxhound	76	47	644	84	68	81	1,142,548
Foxtrail	22	11	177	23	26	15	545,249
Franklin Me	2	1	7	1	1	2	13,415
Fraser River	47	24	342	41	37	47	493,040
Fred Astaire	33	14	204	23	21	28	338,380
Free and Equal	3	2	21	2	3	3	23,807
Free At Last	106	71	820	113	125	115	1,049,263
Free Colony	1	1	18	5	5	3	48,508
Free House	21	7	83	9	7	10	349,079
Freezing Rain	2	1	20	4	4	4	19,228
French Deputy	100	57	574	93	82	75	3,025,445
French Legionaire	49	20	405	28	30	43	275,800
French Magistrate	4	2	30	2	3	6	24,345
French Parliament	5	2	21	2	4	4	36,760
French Seventyfive	5	2	39	4	7	3	88,159
Friendly Ed	4	1	28	2	3	4	12,979
Friendly Lover	108	61	796	98	112	82	1,785,157
Frio River	3	2	24	2	2	2	21,660
Frisco View	4	2	28	5	2	5	68,142
Friscosilverdollar	4	1	18	1	3	0	5,411
Frisk Me Now	11	3	32	3	5	2	66,581
Fritz	1	1	14	1	0	2	14,418
Friul (ARG)	2	1	6	1	0	1	10,550
Frosty the Snowman	21	14	175	22	31	16	346,597
Fruition	20	7	113	12	17	10	252,161
Fugitive	2	1	8	1	0	0	4,207
Full Choke	15	7	108	15	16	15	263,470
Full Count	4	2	21	3	2	3	37,202
Full Honor	1	1	9	1	0	0	1,092
Full of Fight	2	1	6	2	1	1	13,416
Full of Tricks	17	5	121	8	12	17	82,614
Fulmar	1	1	12	2	1	2	5,522
Fumbo Jumbo	1	1	8	2	1	1	21,024
Funboy	2	1	9	1	1	0	10,871
Funontherun	10	4	42	6	10	2	84,730
Furiously	21	11	137	13	11	15	242,759
Future Storm	82	35	589	58	69	57	1,025,191
Fuzziano	20	7	139	12	21	18	175,222
Fuzzy	16	6	148	12	20	21	264,252
Gaelic Garden	1	1	9	3	1	0	3,105
Gain	1	1	5	1	0	1	3,620
Gala Array	1	1	12	4	2	2	24,545
Galaxy Road	2	1	14	1	3	1	15,138
Gallant Best	1	1	6	1	0	1	1,410
Gallant Prospector	7	3	68	8	6	9	247,023
Gallant Rake	2	1	18	1	2	2	21,170
Gallant Step	4	2	17	2	3	3	27,322
Gallapiat	15	2	78	4	2	10	39,707
Gambler's Debt	1	1	12	2	2	1	10,265
Game Plan	90	57	570	95	82	80	1,159,721
Ganday	2	2	20	3	3	1	25,621
Gardone	1	1	10	1	4	1	10,000
Garthorn	10	4	55	5	9	10	44,404
Gary Gumbo	2	1	12	2	1	1	9,124
Gas Guzzler	2	1	11	2	0	1	8,859
Gate Dancer	32	12	258	29	28	19	433,203
Gato Del Sur	3	2	42	3	2	4	66,157
Gee Ryder	9	3	54	7	4	4	76,576
Geiger Counter	35	21	301	41	51	44	637,042
Gem Master	3	1	21	1	4	1	55,159
Gemini Dreamer	11	3	67	7	7	8	67,920
General Meeting	110	50	607	68	85	77	2,034,114
General Royal	18	5	70	8	14	10	204,145
General Silver	6	2	42	5	1	4	38,282
Generous (IRE)	2	1	9	1	0	0	30,350
Gentleman Gene	4	2	33	3	8	7	77,117
Gentlemen (ARG)	57	19	241	23	22	26	669,551
Genuine Reward	14	8	117	12	16	11	134,665
Genuine Silver	2	2	32	4	5	6	63,948
Genuino	5	4	44	5	4	2	39,087
Georgeff	3	2	24	2	0	3	13,222
Georgia Two	4	2	31	3	0	1	20,016
Geri	60	34	366	48	43	39	912,455
Get Me Out	10	2	25	3	4	1	36,200
Gettin Over	4	2	18	3	1	3	26,193
Ghadeer (FR)	3	2	7	2	0	0	30,660
Ghaza	3	2	16	2	1	1	9,454
Ghazi	104	45	675	81	81	84	1,582,746
Ghost Power	23	10	122	11	14	12	104,659
Ghost Ranch	10	3	46	6	4	5	134,745
Ghostly Moves	19	8	92	15	20	9	623,180
Giant Asset	6	2	36	2	6	5	21,720
Gift of Gib	12	8	43	9	7	0	132,733
Gilded Rooster	3	1	25	1	4	1	19,871
Gilded Time	134	81	938	146	142	133	4,025,053
Giuseppe	17	5	123	9	10	13	131,194
Give Me Your Ear	6	3	62	3	4	6	30,736
Glaring	36	5	141	7	9	6	83,644
Glenview	10	8	105	11	23	20	111,457
Glide	11	6	103	9	13	7	164,381
Glitterman	147	93	1,084	174	153	123	4,156,373
Globe	1	1	3	1	0	0	3,480
Glomar	13	8	98	17	14	11	266,802
Glyer	2	1	13	2	2	1	38,453
Go and Go (IRE)	14	5	111	6	12	11	108,911
Go for Gin	70	34	484	54	69	63	1,266,698
Go Go Gold	1	1	18	2	4	2	16,449
Gogarty (IRE)	3	2	15	5	2	1	58,371
Gold Alert	62	34	550	64	52	73	995,824
Gold Angle	2	1	26	2	0	4	11,058
Gold Bazaar	3	1	15	1	2	3	6,849
Gold Case	107	63	637	106	85	79	2,885,508
Gold Crest	5	1	40	2	6	5	37,468
Gold Crest Express	3	2	19	2	4	1	15,281
Gold Decorum	3	1	10	1	1	1	5,148
Gold Fever	125	57	744	99	107	119	2,906,828
Gold Legend	66	34	470	65	62	69	1,163,390
Gold Market	3	1	18	1	2	2	17,138
Gold Meridian	50	24	303	36	27	34	239,799
Gold Pack	9	5	71	7	9	6	72,301
Gold Regent	17	7	53	8	9	7	165,418
Gold Ruler	37	21	232	37	45	32	351,170
Gold Saga	11	7	72	15	11	14	136,539
Gold Spring (ARG)	46	24	345	46	39	34	359,455
Gold Token	45	23	222	40	33	23	834,726
Gold Tribute	32	18	207	29	33	30	757,575
Golden Act	17	7	134	12	8	12	115,005
Golden Dodger	15	7	109	8	14	11	67,099
Golden Gear	67	35	468	56	58	53	1,007,596
Golden Legend	8	4	71	4	2	5	46,416
Golden Voyager	5	3	19	5	3	1	343,580
Golden Whirl	2	1	10	1	1	0	2,471
Goldlust	31	11	213	25	25	27	454,119
Goldmark (SAF)	1	1	4	2	1	0	233,240
Goldminers Gold	13	5	61	7	7	4	205,393
Goldwater	7	2	48	3	3	5	25,430
Goliard	24	8	207	15	17	30	226,533
Gone for Real	11	4	71	6	12	8	207,464
Gone West	92	38	448	57	52	55	2,955,826
Good and Tough	20	9	80	11	13	10	352,341
Goodbye Doeny	66	28	342	44	32	45	642,850
Goofalik	1	1	8	2	3	0	62,710
Gorky Park (FR)	5	3	43	5	2	3	80,022
Goshen Store	2	1	17	1	1	2	11,319
Gothic Revival	12	6	57	8	4	7	75,037
Gourami	13	5	99	7	11	12	73,342

Sire	Perf	Wnrs	Sts	1st	2d	3d	Purses
Grace of Darby	8	5	55	7	7	4	111,769
Gracious Ghost	6	2	38	4	2	4	23,555
Granacus	1	1	10	1	1	2	6,366
Grand Allegiance	3	1	11	1	0	0	11,185
Grand Circus Park	2	1	6	2	0	0	20,880
Grand Flotilla	13	7	94	10	13	8	141,398
Grand Jewel	12	6	66	12	9	8	136,756
Grand Lodge	8	4	37	6	6	8	402,183
Grand Slam	129	71	628	124	93	82	5,806,236
Grande Jette	5	2	34	5	7	1	45,516
Grant Approval	1	1	11	3	2	0	83,849
Gravitating	1	1	10	2	1	1	13,660
Gray Slewpy	17	7	77	9	8	8	61,727
Graydon Pool	18	12	152	18	10	16	206,391
Great Above	14	4	120	9	8	13	210,729
Great Allegiance	4	2	22	4	3	5	21,884
Great Gladiator	34	18	233	31	21	31	1,065,698
Great Prospector	5	4	45	5	4	6	38,903
Great Regent	5	1	21	2	0	1	68,370
Greek Costume	10	5	65	13	14	12	112,769
Green Alligator	11	8	111	19	14	11	364,149
Green Dancer	66	31	445	53	41	49	1,515,680
Green Desert	8	6	43	10	8	3	1,292,972
Green Street	3	1	18	1	1	1	7,725
Green Tune	3	1	8	2	3	0	134,860
Greensmith (GB)	2	1	15	1	3	2	70,610
Greggie's Wheel	5	1	32	2	3	4	31,145
Gremlin Grey	7	4	52	9	6	7	75,438
Grey Counter	3	3	22	3	3	2	63,589
Grey West	4	3	20	4	4	3	21,338
Grindstone	96	57	566	90	76	77	2,578,938
Gringo Pilot	4	2	32	3	5	3	23,840
Groom Dancer	3	1	11	2	2	1	216,470
Groom's Image	5	1	39	1	1	1	5,285
Groomstick	58	21	441	32	37	58	439,385
Groovy	33	19	253	32	23	27	366,579
Groovy Jett	9	5	69	7	8	6	93,005
Groshawk	2	2	11	3	3	1	17,142
Grub	8	5	59	10	9	6	73,051
Guadalupe Peak	5	5	48	7	7	4	63,426
Gulch	112	55	739	99	104	99	3,320,379
Gulf Star (BRZ)	1	1	6	1	0	1	33,130
Gumboy	21	11	135	18	12	20	129,088
Gunston Road	2	1	10	1	2	2	4,430
H. J. Baker	9	3	51	4	8	4	76,758
Habitonia	7	3	60	5	8	9	58,574
Habitony	11	2	61	3	2	2	26,157
Habitony's Ace	2	1	22	1	1	2	10,182
Hadif	110	62	727	98	95	92	1,159,973
Hagley's Reward	2	1	12	3	2	4	21,783
Hail the Ruckus	16	9	112	15	16	21	287,558
Hail the Truth	1	1	10	1	1	0	4,705
Hail Victorious	5	1	28	2	2	6	11,740
Haint	20	13	149	20	11	22	285,750
Half a Year	52	19	303	24	28	27	352,735
Half Term	73	34	440	55	63	46	841,356
Halissee	21	9	145	12	18	14	204,906
Halling	3	2	13	3	0	0	35,800
Halo	1	1	15	1	3	0	9,697
Halo Sunshine	3	1	11	2	1	0	48,500
Halo's Image	79	43	615	86	85	95	2,195,790
Halory Hunter	55	32	432	51	58	63	877,006
Halos and Horns	8	2	31	3	7	4	69,890
Hamas (IRE)	1	1	3	1	0	0	22,500
Handsome Halo (ARG)	1	1	10	1	2	1	64,620
Hannibal Cat	14	3	77	7	8	10	81,070
Hansel	41	12	221	27	20	29	784,655
Hapes Mill	4	3	37	3	4	5	15,506
Happy Bid	5	1	31	2	1	1	13,381
Happy Caro	1	1	15	1	6	1	21,484
Happy Escort	1	1	4	1	0	1	1,970
Happy Intentions	3	1	23	1	2	3	12,703
Happy Toss (ARG)	1	1	10	1	0	1	1,363
Happy Trap	16	9	111	13	14	13	141,295
Happyasalark Tomas	9	3	47	6	8	6	51,614
Hard Circle	8	3	104	5	8	9	53,444
Hard Rock Express	1	1	4	1	0	1	3,960
Harlan	32	16	238	28	24	34	1,100,346
Harmony Creek	1	1	3	1	0	1	3,345
Harperstown	17	8	90	15	12	10	136,565
Harriman	32	16	206	24	18	25	317,493
Harry	3	2	15	2	1	0	8,020
Harry the Hat	12	6	73	8	9	9	213,005
Harsh Facts	1	1	10	1	0	2	3,511
Hasten To Add	17	8	106	11	11	14	152,646
Hasty Groom	5	1	35	2	3	4	26,060
Hasty Spirit	5	1	38	3	2	4	80,678
Hatchet Man	8	2	48	4	2	9	67,084
Have Fun	12	4	70	6	11	8	83,905
Hawaiian Cat	1	1	2	1	0	0	3,279
Hawk Attack	16	9	140	14	15	14	333,900
Hay Halo	48	18	331	32	42	50	687,174
Haymaker	34	10	208	13	30	22	230,862
Haymarket (GB)	15	7	104	15	11	10	134,907
Hazaam	60	33	409	57	43	56	826,323
He's a Looker	25	6	150	10	10	12	170,126
He's Tops	32	13	174	22	21	19	407,773
Heather's Prospect	23	8	165	13	11	9	152,650
Heaven's Wish	8	2	57	2	8	9	60,807
Heavenly Legacy	3	3	29	5	2	5	47,111
Hedevar the Gold	2	1	9	1	1	2	2,999
Heff	18	9	153	15	23	20	210,726
Heir to Drawers	2	1	6	1	1	0	2,975
Heir to Nijinsky	3	2	17	2	2	2	18,910
Helmsman	70	40	519	75	80	63	1,501,782
Hemi Head	2	2	18	4	3	1	65,801
Henbane	23	9	171	14	23	26	193,300
Heniu	9	5	67	8	7	8	73,784
Hennessy	141	69	695	112	73	84	3,591,219
Herat	3	3	14	4	1	0	33,164
Here We Come	67	33	417	56	54	48	637,159
Hermes	7	5	57	7	7	10	60,099
Hermitage	19	5	124	7	9	12	121,789
Hernando (FR)	4	3	11	6	0	0	1,324,330
Heroicity (AUS)	1	1	8	1	2	0	23,510
Hesabull	18	14	120	21	18	10	230,985
Hesaluckycat	2	1	17	1	0	1	4,668
Hestheman	3	2	17	3	4	1	19,174
Hey Big Spender	1	1	8	1	1	0	38,740
Hey Rob	16	7	71	14	9	6	63,286
Heza Champion	4	1	37	1	0	4	14,109
Hezafastgold	6	1	33	2	0	2	19,794
Hi Plains Drifter	7	3	33	4	3	3	22,013
Hickman Creek	13	4	89	5	6	5	71,324
Hickory Ridge	13	7	93	12	9	6	81,876
Hidden Prize	4	1	21	6	2	3	188,418
Hidden Tomahawk	2	1	11	2	0	0	2,145
Hidden Vice	2	1	20	1	0	5	7,240
High Brite	131	73	983	140	124	130	2,250,658
High Comedy	10	4	82	6	16	6	47,674
High Counsel	1	1	7	1	0	3	4,088
High Energy	10	3	58	8	4	7	59,517
High Occupancy	1	1	3	3	0	0	41,190
Highest Honor (FR)	5	1	32	1	2	2	182,695
Highest Ody (FR)	1	1	8	3	2	1	68,445
Highland Blade	6	1	40	5	2	7	42,872
Highland Light	3	1	28	3	2	1	8,177
Highland Park	6	3	26	4	2	6	40,899
Highland Ruckus	52	24	346	35	38	56	566,872
Highly Praised	2	2	29	6	4	1	26,908
Hilal (IRE)	2	1	17	2	1	1	13,259
Hill Pass	4	1	48	5	4	7	35,136
His Excellence	16	5	110	7	11	9	69,109
His Majesty	6	2	60	6	4	11	198,707
Historic	11	2	37	2	3	3	52,059
Hoedown's Day	11	6	89	12	13	12	84,709
Hoist the Silver	1	1	10	4	4	1	19,387
Hold for Gold	34	17	175	23	25	18	510,212
Hold On Chris	5	2	33	3	4	3	41,271
Holding Court	9	3	32	6	3	1	35,596
Hollywood Brat	2	2	8	2	0	2	46,340
Hollywood Knight	3	1	20	1	4	5	6,266
Hollywood Reporter	26	9	150	10	15	27	105,412
Holme On Top	4	4	49	7	8	4	81,543
Holy Bull	147	91	979	159	119	113	3,570,267
Holy Mountain	33	15	201	27	23	23	358,890
Holzmeister	17	6	73	8	13	8	174,958
Home At Last	36	16	312	23	40	48	519,779

RECORDS OF SIRES

Sire	Perf	Wnrs	Sts	1st	2d	3d	Purses
Home Run Trot	7	6	46	8	10	5	20,817
Homebuilder	33	18	260	39	34	25	692,839
Homo Sapiens	2	1	16	1	0	0	3,604
Honest Bullet	3	2	36	3	4	2	17,226
Honest Ensign	13	6	85	11	6	9	131,556
Honeyland	19	9	130	15	12	14	139,560
Honeys Alibi Lad	2	1	16	4	1	1	31,590
Honkytonk Blaze	2	1	13	1	1	2	9,684
Honor Grades	121	51	746	90	96	85	3,010,960
Honorable Hero	3	2	20	2	1	1	34,809
Honour and Glory	141	73	857	131	119	116	2,587,268
Hooched	5	1	21	1	1	2	39,163
Hoolie	13	4	68	5	5	10	87,232
Hopedale O	1	1	11	1	2	1	7,628
Hopeful Word	3	1	29	2	5	5	17,487
Hopeville	1	1	13	2	3	3	24,839
Horatius	51	17	359	27	31	48	438,577
Horse Chestnut (SAF)	15	4	38	4	7	1	177,941
Hot and Smoggy	1	1	11	3	2	0	7,057
Hotoffthepress	3	1	101	1	0	1	19,533
Housebuster	59	33	476	68	64	58	1,211,227
Houston	45	19	288	39	21	33	514,970
Houston Sunrise	3	3	14	5	3	0	22,311
Hubble	15	5	115	8	12	18	105,153
Huckster	25	9	175	12	18	21	132,986
Huddle Up	6	4	47	9	10	6	332,375
Huff	16	8	136	14	20	23	236,034
Hula Blaze	3	1	20	2	2	0	12,871
Hulas Sun	1	1	20	2	4	3	14,404
Humble Eleven	7	4	33	4	7	4	66,662
Humble Story	1	1	8	1	2	1	6,081
Humpty's Hoedown	11	8	94	20	16	12	128,869
Hunter's Glory	1	1	4	1	0	2	3,772
Hunter's Phone	2	1	10	1	0	1	17,128
Hunting Hard	46	21	372	36	51	48	792,117
Hunting Horn	13	4	95	5	4	9	47,385
Hurlingham	4	1	21	1	4	3	12,569
Hurricane Ed	5	1	29	1	2	4	11,353
Hurricane Mars	2	1	9	1	0	0	4,290
Husband	25	8	156	15	9	14	361,876
Husk	2	1	10	1	0	1	3,273
Hussonet	12	5	44	8	6	2	1,256,344
Husyan	1	1	6	1	0	3	23,400
Hy Lucky Jay	3	3	19	3	4	4	21,387
I Am the Game	8	2	49	3	2	8	25,000
I Can Fly	1	1	3	1	0	0	5,280
I Can't Believe	48	24	341	37	45	23	965,655
I Enclose	10	4	81	10	12	7	121,932
I'll Be Good	1	1	15	1	1	2	2,990
I'll Raise You One	18	6	113	6	14	15	85,756
I'm a Lyre	4	1	20	1	1	0	7,455
I'm Glad (ARG)	1	1	14	1	2	4	18,555
I'ma Hell Raiser	46	20	273	30	37	33	417,809
I'mallears	1	1	7	1	0	1	8,190
Iam the Iceman	19	7	122	11	20	16	297,225
Ian's Affair	3	1	25	1	1	3	10,268
Ibero (ARG)	5	4	36	6	3	8	199,617
Ice Age	12	7	101	12	18	14	177,763
Ice Hole	6	3	33	4	0	5	64,155
Icy Glow	5	2	41	2	0	5	18,747
Icy Kevin	4	2	30	2	2	6	16,444
Idabel	35	21	280	36	33	40	430,012
Idaho's Majesty	2	2	23	5	1	3	32,827
Ide	110	72	885	127	109	113	2,541,136
Ideologico (ARG)	1	1	3	1	0	0	27,600
Idle Son	7	6	57	13	4	6	80,813
Ihtimam	23	15	172	28	25	13	195,927
Ikari	7	2	41	3	7	2	53,255
Ile de Jinsky	15	5	103	6	7	8	81,431
Illinois Storm	19	9	100	13	11	10	262,915
Ima Buck Too	3	1	15	1	1	0	8,080
Image	1	1	4	1	0	1	1,548
Imperial Ballet (IRE)	18	7	109	11	7	16	119,787
Imperial Falcon	29	11	181	17	17	19	183,250
Imperial Gold	5	2	33	3	4	5	31,756
Imperial Guard	1	1	20	1	2	5	11,289
Imperial Seal (GB)	1	1	4	1	0	0	30,000
Important Notice	1	1	9	3	3	1	114,456
Imtoocool	2	1	13	1	1	0	8,800
In a Walk	35	19	229	31	36	22	665,255
In Case	112	49	695	72	77	81	1,267,685
In Character (GB)	2	1	20	3	2	1	31,174
In Excess (IRE)	124	63	681	121	88	78	4,259,537
In Excessive Bull	31	17	144	25	19	12	472,993
In the Ruff	1	1	7	2	2	1	6,869
In the Slammer	9	2	55	4	12	7	46,262
In the Swing	10	5	63	7	13	8	89,898
In the Zone	14	5	101	8	14	14	82,791
Inca Chief	3	1	13	1	0	0	3,400
Inchinor (GB)	4	1	9	1	1	0	107,935
Incinerator	20	11	146	18	19	20	426,086
Incurable Optimist	7	3	31	3	3	4	153,472
Indian Charlie	80	43	411	78	59	58	2,326,849
Indian Detail	2	1	16	1	1	3	5,330
Indian Groom	6	3	39	3	7	3	131,191
Indian Ridge (IRE)	16	9	89	13	16	10	439,339
Individual Style	10	5	84	7	9	6	46,001
Individualist (GB)	1	1	14	1	1	6	14,043
Indy Mood	27	6	144	7	12	14	96,402
Inevitable Hour	1	1	5	1	2	0	21,200
Inherent Kal	11	1	76	1	1	8	22,532
Inishpour (IRE)	1	1	7	1	1	2	7,978
Insistent Beat	8	3	70	4	7	10	21,064
Inspired Prospect	27	15	205	23	23	22	461,091
Instant Pleasure	2	1	14	2	5	0	9,507
Instrument Landing	2	1	18	1	1	4	9,524
Intensity	6	1	11	1	0	0	25,230
Interco	9	5	65	8	5	6	115,318
Interprete (ARG)	10	3	47	5	3	2	187,753
Intimidation	1	1	10	3	3	2	9,044
Introductivo	1	1	7	1	0	0	4,260
Intrusion	5	3	47	5	3	5	47,230
Irgun	38	22	267	39	29	29	389,428
Irish Bear	4	2	21	4	4	1	46,753
Irish Dreamin	7	4	48	12	3	3	98,661
Irish Fighter	1	1	8	2	3	2	21,853
Irish Open	101	53	800	92	91	113	1,017,272
Irish River (FR)	38	18	219	26	29	28	1,076,709
Irish Scoundrel	1	1	8	1	0	2	8,232
Irish Sur	6	2	44	3	4	4	51,625
Irish Tower	15	11	155	20	17	21	138,298
Iron	6	3	41	4	6	6	82,568
Iron Cat	9	8	57	19	14	5	270,296
Iron Courage	4	1	29	1	7	7	26,646
Iroquois Park	16	8	130	16	17	17	167,223
Is It True	107	68	809	142	117	103	2,484,585
Is Sveikatas	1	1	12	2	0	1	9,976
Iskandar Elakbar	20	9	148	16	23	21	594,533
Island Born	2	1	7	1	1	1	4,130
Island Whirl	38	19	272	42	31	31	648,803
Islefaxyou	67	28	457	45	52	58	822,609
Isnad	6	1	31	1	2	2	9,424
It's Always You	7	4	70	8	12	9	101,360
It's Not My Job	4	1	16	3	3	1	36,072
Itajara	1	1	20	1	1	8	13,022
Itaka	34	10	249	17	16	26	305,656
Itsallinthegame	2	1	17	2	1	3	9,080
Ivan the Terrible	1	1	6	1	1	0	2,960
Ivor's Desert	2	1	17	2	4	5	7,648
Iz a Saros	13	9	99	11	16	16	190,757
J P Hamer	35	15	247	19	30	17	467,470
J. B. Magesty	2	2	12	3	3	0	20,021
J. C.'s Challenge	11	1	52	2	6	4	32,275
J. L. Sullivan	3	3	30	6	1	2	29,604
J. T. Hurst	2	2	31	3	1	1	7,047
Jack Livingston	23	10	181	13	20	13	325,743
Jack n Coke	2	1	18	1	3	1	19,305
Jack of Clubs	1	1	16	1	5	2	14,498
Jack Wilson	33	12	183	18	29	24	458,024
Jackson	2	1	19	3	2	2	14,925
Jackson's Gap	2	1	21	1	2	1	14,423
Jacksonport	17	10	138	16	17	21	235,175
Jacodra	27	11	194	16	24	16	175,671
Jacquelyn's Groom	21	11	118	15	13	11	209,559
Jade Hunter	112	46	703	79	72	62	2,507,628
Jaggery John	13	4	74	8	9	9	72,804
Jahafil (GB)	3	2	18	3	0	3	42,875
Jaklin Klugman	4	2	16	3	2	1	196,367

Sire	Perf	Wnrs	Sts	1st	2d	3d	Purses
Jalaajel	3	2	20	4	3	6	37,809
Jambalaya Jazz	18	7	96	12	10	7	329,255
Jamiano	16	9	132	14	12	18	167,551
Jan's Kinsman	1	1	11	2	2	2	7,667
Jarraar	1	1	6	2	1	0	53,640
Java Gold	10	6	79	14	8	6	211,995
Jawski	3	2	21	2	3	0	19,371
Jay Cee Slew	1	1	16	3	1	2	7,253
Jazzing Around	70	33	421	48	63	58	436,264
Jd's Determination	4	2	33	4	4	2	44,729
Jeblar	93	41	739	83	101	81	1,309,151
Jeep Shot	3	1	12	1	0	0	4,983
Jeff's Companion	8	5	80	12	11	11	46,605
Jelly Roll Blues	3	3	22	7	1	3	46,401
Jeloso	5	3	41	8	3	6	77,588
Jerrio	1	1	12	3	3	2	26,093
Jessie Jet	8	1	60	1	8	4	71,010
Jestic	15	6	83	7	8	12	70,313
Jett Sett Joe	6	6	56	10	10	8	86,775
Jetting Home	5	3	47	4	5	12	36,162
Jeune Homme	2	1	3	1	0	0	33,600
Jiltaloom	3	3	43	6	5	11	43,357
Jimmy Barnie (GB)	11	8	94	15	11	10	164,445
Jitterbug Chief	6	2	46	2	4	4	27,530
Jo's Eleven	2	1	14	2	0	1	7,916
Joanie's Chief	8	3	62	7	7	5	87,799
Jocko J.	1	1	8	1	0	5	1,832
Joe D	6	4	73	5	3	11	47,495
Joe K. Jr.	2	1	22	1	5	3	16,238
Joe Spatts	1	1	4	3	0	1	36,480
Joe the Dancer	2	1	31	1	6	4	23,817
Joey the Student	9	3	71	3	5	8	52,760
Jog My Memory	9	3	50	3	5	6	51,233
Johann Quatz (FR)	1	1	11	1	1	2	40,120
John Alden	4	2	36	4	1	7	19,822
John Quincy	3	1	24	1	3	3	10,635
John the Magician	4	3	23	4	0	2	105,617
John Willy	3	2	20	4	3	2	39,646
Johnny Blood	2	2	22	2	2	1	14,585
Johnny's Prospect	2	1	17	7	2	1	67,768
Joker	5	4	45	5	4	2	56,384
Jokester	6	2	34	2	2	1	33,260
Jolie's Halo	22	14	169	24	12	17	458,993
Jolies Appeal	3	2	17	2	3	0	31,553
Jolly Blade	4	2	11	3	1	1	11,957
Jonathan's Gold	2	2	8	2	1	1	9,742
Joseph Paul	1	1	9	1	0	0	7,037
Journey's End	1	1	15	4	2	2	14,531
Jovial Turn	1	1	13	4	2	1	24,990
Joy's Report	4	3	44	5	8	7	55,620
Joyeux Danseur	48	22	262	34	29	29	688,679
Jr. Prospect	16	5	111	6	10	13	49,487
Judge Smells	60	34	497	69	48	60	827,238
Judge T C	156	85	1,266	140	174	136	2,575,212
Judge Vonsteubon	2	1	8	2	1	0	18,240
Judy's King	3	2	18	2	0	3	49,417
Jules	94	56	616	113	71	74	4,228,948
Jump Over the Moon	1	1	8	2	0	0	5,420
Jumron (GB)	36	14	205	22	27	27	200,995
June's Blazer	1	1	13	1	4	1	31,709
Jungle Blade	5	1	13	1	0	2	5,036
Jungle Express	5	3	33	4	5	5	59,743
Just a Cat	42	23	281	39	17	37	492,051
Just a Dancer (NZ)	1	1	11	4	3	0	83,150
Just a Swangin	7	1	36	1	3	1	11,267
Just a Tab	8	4	66	7	7	10	71,507
Just a Tune	13	3	64	5	2	4	58,052
Just Like Jo	5	1	48	1	4	3	24,967
Just Like That	3	1	25	1	1	4	18,153
Justtofit	2	1	10	1	1	1	5,958
K. O. Punch	70	36	451	53	54	51	894,214
Kadial (IRE)	10	3	62	3	9	5	25,476
Kahili	2	1	23	2	2	2	10,097
Kahyasi	3	3	15	4	1	3	169,040
Kalim (IRE)	9	3	50	4	7	4	21,224
Kan d'Oro	14	6	80	8	9	3	67,722
Kandaly	8	5	61	9	5	7	78,886
Kansas City	6	2	33	2	3	4	6,597
Karate Kick	3	1	16	2	1	2	16,681
Kashgar	3	2	17	3	2	1	39,426
Katahaula County	66	42	498	64	79	67	1,116,897
Katowice	60	32	421	59	51	49	643,232
Kayrawan	25	13	204	24	38	27	597,816
Kazabaiyn	1	1	11	1	4	1	8,607
Keep Dreaming	25	10	180	24	21	22	274,266
Keep It Down	11	7	88	12	17	10	145,866
Kell's Sea Captain	4	1	22	1	2	1	10,617
Kellsapaul (IRE)	2	1	29	5	2	1	9,561
Kelly's Gold	5	1	34	2	5	4	22,995
Kenfair (NZ)	3	1	12	1	0	1	15,830
Kennedy Factor	13	5	75	6	10	4	42,739
Kentucky Cookin	4	1	38	1	0	3	12,876
Kentucky Jazz	22	15	163	28	21	20	325,142
Keos	9	1	35	1	1	4	20,402
Kept His Cool	3	2	29	5	1	4	59,476
Keratoid	7	3	62	8	5	8	52,934
Kerosene	12	5	94	10	7	13	135,838
Key Contender	50	33	457	69	61	59	1,093,455
Key Image	4	2	30	2	4	7	10,352
Key Recognition	9	3	70	4	8	5	47,548
Key to the Carr	18	7	100	12	13	13	65,207
Key to the Flag	5	2	33	2	2	4	20,898
Key to the Mint	2	1	14	3	2	1	44,228
Kicking Boot	11	2	53	2	5	3	26,356
Kid Blue	1	1	4	1	0	1	1,807
Killarney Road	5	1	46	2	6	2	31,821
Kilty	1	1	14	1	0	0	1,504
King Crypto	4	1	28	1	0	2	5,070
King Mutesa	7	2	44	4	6	1	30,851
King of Kings (IRE)	51	15	239	18	22	22	731,388
King of Storyland	5	2	49	2	7	5	23,366
King of the Heap	6	2	35	4	3	6	73,215
King Riviera	2	1	4	1	0	1	19,066
King's Canyon	4	3	44	3	10	3	32,861
King's Grant	8	4	35	4	2	3	60,066
King's Nest	29	18	223	25	25	23	276,257
King's Theatre (IRE)	3	1	14	1	4	3	127,360
King's Wailea	8	5	60	8	9	5	113,353
Kingdom Bay (NZ)	1	1	16	1	1	1	12,401
Kingdom City	3	1	16	1	2	2	16,318
Kingmambo	74	35	379	52	48	45	2,005,610
Kings Fiction	3	2	40	5	10	4	175,821
Kingsboro	11	1	67	2	2	6	36,320
Kinnett	1	1	9	1	1	0	12,260
Kipper Kelly	81	42	623	73	83	70	1,142,336
Kiri's Clown	25	4	154	4	4	13	114,046
Kiridashi	58	26	357	39	33	33	1,489,181
Kirov Danseur	1	1	11	2	0	0	8,534
Kissin Kris	136	59	893	106	94	103	2,458,136
Kissinsky	1	1	12	1	2	3	8,539
Kitwood	17	7	108	10	10	9	129,433
Kleven	10	5	53	10	8	14	225,420
Knick Press	1	1	7	4	1	1	117,370
Knight	5	4	62	6	8	9	41,362
Knight in Kentucky	1	1	3	1	0	1	2,430
Knight in Savannah	26	18	160	28	29	19	248,905
Knight of Old	1	1	12	1	1	1	6,474
Knight Skiing	11	6	62	10	12	11	53,252
Knighthyme Charmer	1	1	9	1	0	3	13,848
Knightly Rapport	2	1	6	1	3	0	3,635
Known Fact	66	34	427	48	58	55	1,283,522
Known for Style	2	1	19	1	1	3	2,758
Kodiack	10	3	63	3	5	7	29,067
Kokand	77	42	553	87	78	72	1,280,953
Komaite	1	1	5	2	2	0	59,050
Kracotowa	1	1	19	3	3	3	25,106
Kris (GB)	8	5	47	7	5	3	175,152
Kris S.	98	54	546	90	79	65	5,340,284
Kriskris (IRE)	6	2	22	4	2	3	8,666
Krona (NZ)	1	1	5	1	0	0	6,235
Kuetch	4	2	38	3	2	2	33,080
Kunjar	2	2	20	2	7	6	15,091
Kuwaiti Brass	4	1	11	1	0	2	6,275
Ky Alta	1	1	8	2	0	3	3,552
Kyle's Our Man	34	14	267	23	31	21	220,842
L'Eau Vivre	1	1	5	1	0	0	2,904
L'Enjoleur	18	6	133	10	17	14	112,879
L'Express (ARG)	1	1	8	1	2	1	11,368

RECORDS OF SIRES

Sire	Perf	Wnrs	Sts	1st	2d	3d	Purses
L. B. Jaklin	16	4	103	7	14	19	67,528
L. D. Bowers	2	1	12	2	2	5	14,881
L. J. Express	4	2	25	2	4	6	33,746
La Saboteur	22	11	127	19	15	17	198,299
Laabity	40	16	305	20	34	35	276,295
Labeeb (GB)	30	15	150	23	20	17	632,522
Lac Ouimet	88	46	579	79	67	63	1,319,247
Lacotte (IRE)	21	8	116	11	15	9	72,005
Lado Dancer	1	1	7	1	0	1	3,185
Lahib	3	2	33	5	3	6	54,773
Lahint	7	5	46	6	6	5	90,480
Lajara	6	4	41	4	6	4	14,848
Lake District	1	1	12	1	1	0	1,801
Lake George	35	16	238	28	25	41	398,046
Lammtarra	1	1	5	1	0	0	2,573
Land Speed Record (AUS)	1	1	9	2	1	0	76,631
Lando (GER)	5	2	18	3	3	0	195,308
Langfuhr	164	94	1,047	175	142	134	6,675,994
Larrupin'	46	25	325	43	38	38	595,804
Larry the Legend	18	6	76	7	12	8	113,519
Last Lion	10	5	54	9	5	6	133,252
Last Spy	1	1	10	4	1	4	20,547
Lasting Approval	24	10	113	12	14	17	373,188
Lasting Value	4	2	26	6	2	2	27,526
Late Nite Louie	2	2	11	2	1	0	9,090
Latin American	41	23	291	37	29	25	564,332
Latvia	7	3	70	4	7	10	63,517
Launch a Leader	21	12	156	17	12	18	157,933
Launching	1	1	12	2	2	2	17,705
Law Me	3	1	12	1	0	1	6,186
Law Society	1	1	5	3	0	0	144,858
Laxey Bay (IRE)	2	1	24	3	4	4	43,765
Lazaz	6	5	61	15	12	10	150,425
Le Ciel	10	5	74	7	10	8	103,401
Le Danseur	7	4	64	6	0	9	49,922
Le Merle Blanc	5	1	21	2	2	1	13,598
Leading Hour	3	2	19	3	1	2	16,196
Lear Fan	68	30	409	40	56	55	1,925,682
Leave Seattle	11	3	83	6	14	12	75,091
Lee n Otto	3	3	26	3	4	4	33,996
Lee's Badger	2	1	6	1	0	4	9,740
Leestown	30	12	117	15	15	17	326,942
Left Banker	11	4	68	7	16	6	119,634
Legal Prospector	7	5	40	8	5	5	46,708
Legatee	2	2	25	4	3	5	20,463
Lemhi Slew	1	1	15	2	1	0	11,390
Lenmars Express	1	1	8	1	3	2	8,580
Lens	8	2	49	2	1	7	19,634
Leo Castelli	88	42	582	63	80	63	939,456
Leonard's Lad	1	1	11	2	1	3	11,398
Leroy S.	3	1	21	1	0	0	7,121
Let Goodtimes Roll	1	1	2	1	0	0	32,100
Let's Go Blue	12	4	59	5	2	8	94,355
Level Sands	67	30	461	42	48	59	588,046
Liberalartsdiploma	3	1	19	4	2	2	23,746
Life Interest	7	1	28	1	2	3	10,783
Ligan's Gold	9	2	70	2	3	9	42,574
Light Idea	9	5	69	9	13	10	90,913
Light of Mine	5	1	17	6	2	3	428,329
Light of Morn	27	18	234	34	17	31	407,591
Light Pleasure	1	1	7	3	2	0	10,299
Lightning Leap	33	12	229	17	21	26	113,755
Liginsky	3	2	25	2	2	3	26,043
Like a Brother	3	1	21	1	0	4	9,555
Like a Soldier	8	4	59	10	5	4	106,247
Lil E. Tee	66	35	441	54	53	56	827,459
Lil Fappi	9	4	68	7	3	10	81,687
Lil Tyler	46	21	325	36	36	37	542,672
Lil's Lad	32	9	97	10	14	13	301,404
Limit Out	7	4	32	5	6	5	84,636
Lindsey's Roberto	10	3	59	4	8	4	91,341
Line Dance	2	1	6	1	1	0	1,947
Line In The Sand	142	61	1,135	96	127	129	1,494,447
Linear	2	1	5	1	1	1	9,314
Lines of Power	12	4	89	6	10	10	63,220
Linkage	20	10	190	20	33	25	279,783
Lion Cavern	12	6	51	15	6	8	492,686
Lion d'Or	4	2	34	4	3	5	35,695
Lit de Justice	112	73	836	133	125	92	3,188,818
Lite the Fuse	75	41	506	68	75	80	1,855,165
Literati	8	2	29	2	2	7	19,869
Little Current	2	1	20	4	0	1	30,295
Little Miracle	1	1	12	2	1	2	3,839
Little Missouri	36	14	315	21	36	39	347,098
Little Nureyev	6	4	38	6	6	7	99,482
Live At the Half	6	2	29	2	2	4	6,611
Lived It Up	7	5	32	8	5	1	75,756
Lively One	16	5	93	8	10	14	278,553
Llama Lover	12	3	75	4	8	9	65,351
Loach	10	5	88	7	13	11	78,114
Local Artist	12	3	83	6	8	11	55,098
Local Talent	7	6	54	10	5	6	96,489
Local Time	15	5	123	7	8	16	147,901
Lockjaw	5	2	38	3	3	0	21,448
Locochon (MEX)	2	1	13	1	3	2	11,810
Lode	14	3	79	5	8	7	189,524
Lone Star Bar	2	2	20	5	2	0	38,566
Look See	15	8	117	12	15	8	233,774
Lord At Law	12	5	95	7	16	11	181,834
Lord At War (ARG)	31	17	197	35	29	19	1,581,531
Lord Avie	102	44	612	76	73	79	1,648,916
Lord Ballina (AUS)	1	1	2	2	0	0	36,000
Lord Carlos	12	4	112	8	10	8	113,335
Lord Carson	103	64	745	129	89	93	2,303,117
Lord Charmer	8	2	42	5	7	8	57,480
Lord Florey	1	1	10	1	2	1	48,766
Lord Hailey	2	2	13	2	1	4	77,110
Lord John	5	1	29	1	3	3	16,787
Lord of All	4	3	28	5	2	6	22,239
Lord of the Apes	10	6	82	14	19	12	95,112
Lord of the Night	1	1	36	2	4	4	26,288
Lord of the Sea	1	1	5	1	1	2	5,582
Lord Parham	13	8	104	11	11	13	193,011
Lord Pleasant	8	5	58	11	10	11	141,340
Lord Rebeau	2	2	28	5	6	2	49,295
Lord Tiger	3	1	19	2	0	3	11,684
Lordhyexecutioner	9	5	53	5	6	9	139,773
Lost Code	114	53	779	98	110	87	1,557,714
Lost Opportunity	19	8	121	13	8	11	57,313
Lost Soldier	102	48	600	76	64	69	1,957,014
Lost World (IRE)	1	1	3	1	0	0	17,610
Lot o' Gold	12	4	86	7	11	13	98,936
Lot o' Rem	9	1	52	1	3	4	19,277
Loto	2	1	14	1	2	2	19,379
Lots to Avenge	3	1	18	1	0	0	5,004
Louis Le Grand	1	1	12	1	1	4	80,060
Louis Quatorze	92	45	496	66	60	57	1,560,179
Louisiana Slew	26	7	180	14	25	13	112,743
Loup Sauvage	31	7	170	14	19	17	270,624
Loustrous Bid	11	4	81	9	10	6	77,769
Love That Mac	13	2	89	3	9	10	33,490
Lover's Trust	4	1	29	1	6	4	33,065
Loverue	2	1	22	2	3	1	33,510
Loyal Double	14	7	87	11	12	8	67,036
Lucayan Prince	4	1	15	2	1	1	38,415
Luciano P.	4	2	26	4	1	1	25,219
Lucky Lionel	61	37	392	55	47	61	1,421,516
Lucky North	59	28	414	40	45	47	710,846
Lucky Point	1	1	13	3	3	2	26,955
Lucky Roberto	11	2	28	4	1	4	146,423
Lucky Sec	2	2	12	3	1	2	5,526
Lucky So n' So	23	11	157	20	16	26	266,409
Lucky South	12	6	96	11	12	9	69,543
Luhuk	7	4	51	6	4	6	323,341
Luthier Fever	16	7	133	14	17	18	198,581
Lycius	23	6	90	8	10	10	247,379
Lympstone	3	1	17	3	2	2	21,925
Lyphaness	10	7	47	8	6	7	122,086
Lytrump	41	15	315	27	26	33	228,604
M.D.'s Relampago	1	1	14	1	0	2	7,515
Mach One	3	1	22	1	2	0	12,511
Machiavellian	20	8	89	14	9	12	1,358,003
Madjaristan	1	1	14	2	4	4	67,034
Mag Power	2	1	17	1	2	1	5,402
Magabird	12	4	89	7	8	20	123,443
Magesterial	3	1	21	1	4	1	7,879
Magic Banner	2	1	24	1	5	3	22,367
Magic Level	13	7	45	13	10	4	43,530

Sire	Perf	Wnrs	Sts	1st	2d	3d	Purses
Magic North	2	1	4	1	0	0	3,280
Magic Prospect	38	13	258	23	27	25	363,328
Magic Rascal	4	2	40	4	3	1	40,965
Magic Ring (IRE)	4	1	20	1	2	0	19,081
Magical Mile	5	2	37	6	4	4	134,531
Magloire	18	11	172	17	21	29	233,166
Magnificent One	2	1	25	1	0	0	5,773
Maha Baba	1	1	12	1	1	0	5,440
Maheras	1	1	13	1	1	1	5,670
Mahogany Hall	45	26	375	46	41	42	783,649
Majesterian	42	26	344	48	56	43	425,780
Majestic Light	35	14	227	20	18	29	299,883
Majestic Shore	1	1	9	2	0	1	16,002
Majestic Style	5	3	43	5	12	3	59,081
Majestic Tweeleven	4	2	24	3	1	0	24,420
Majesty's Imp	26	9	198	18	28	22	193,565
Majesty's Prince	14	3	65	5	4	6	82,120
Majesty's Time	8	3	52	4	2	5	56,763
Major Current	4	2	25	5	0	4	76,015
Major Howey	2	1	16	1	1	5	16,485
Major Impact	35	15	229	25	25	28	416,523
Major Luck	2	1	17	1	2	3	6,410
Major Moran	3	2	17	2	2	3	17,327
Majority of One	5	2	30	3	2	1	14,753
Makaleha	21	7	133	15	19	23	236,664
Make Luck	3	1	19	2	3	0	35,055
Makhraj	19	6	113	7	14	9	56,213
Makin	13	5	73	12	14	5	358,112
Makin Money	2	1	16	1	1	0	20,800
Malagra	39	16	228	25	22	16	359,462
Malibu Moon	21	12	70	18	10	8	652,179
Malmo	16	7	111	15	14	15	105,846
Maltese Flag	2	1	12	1	1	1	4,661
Malthus	5	2	19	3	0	2	17,217
Mamaison	8	3	40	4	4	5	26,561
Mambo	19	6	126	9	11	15	77,404
Man From Eldorado	22	10	139	18	25	15	325,708
Man of Heart	2	2	32	5	4	2	43,688
Manastash Ridge	26	8	135	19	15	19	191,176
Mandamus	3	1	25	2	6	6	35,880
Mane Minister	15	6	122	9	18	15	187,443
Mangaki	6	2	38	3	1	4	13,467
Manila	10	5	72	11	6	4	197,762
Manitonga Soutana	7	3	39	3	1	8	11,401
Manlove	35	15	255	27	22	26	654,396
Manshood (GB)	1	1	1	1	0	0	101,928
Many a Wish	8	3	62	7	6	3	114,044
Manzotti	54	30	336	42	27	38	482,288
Marcellini	1	1	11	1	2	1	14,710
Marchand de Sable	5	1	19	1	2	3	93,416
Marco Bay	16	9	103	15	14	11	292,174
Marco Ricci	1	1	20	3	5	2	22,061
Marfa	31	13	231	28	32	34	388,769
Maria's Mon	131	70	760	115	89	107	2,586,346
Marinaio (FR)	1	1	11	3	1	2	25,169
Marine Brass	13	2	55	2	6	5	24,552
Marju (IRE)	5	2	33	2	7	3	133,625
Mark of a Dancer	2	1	16	1	5	2	7,311
Mark of Esteem (IRE)	1	1	7	2	1	2	112,990
Marked Tree	103	53	708	101	88	78	1,247,920
Marlin	70	22	532	30	42	30	934,911
Marquee Star	8	3	93	7	12	13	116,944
Marquetry	161	86	1,098	147	141	157	2,861,992
Marscay (AUS)	2	1	10	2	0	1	59,880
Martial Law	6	3	43	3	4	4	53,027
Masakado	3	2	18	4	4	1	41,055
Maskrullah	3	3	19	5	3	7	18,754
Master Bill	43	23	357	40	46	47	727,520
Master Christopher	1	1	10	2	3	0	17,126
Master Lode	4	2	32	2	4	6	25,660
Master Slew	5	2	25	3	7	0	11,567
Masterful Advocate	2	1	4	1	0	0	1,320
Masterfully	12	4	99	6	14	18	72,250
Match Trick	6	1	23	1	2	2	14,381
Matchlite	44	20	352	28	31	44	332,579
Maton	1	1	15	1	2	0	11,780
Matter of Honor	43	20	303	29	44	47	894,563
Matthews Keep	6	2	35	3	3	5	21,887
Mattress	1	1	9	1	1	2	6,352
Matty G	53	26	340	37	33	45	863,202
Maudlin	47	35	415	63	57	68	972,512
Maximilian (ARG)	1	1	9	2	1	1	12,570
Mayanesian	3	1	20	1	3	2	8,356
Mayano Top Gun (JPN)	1	1	9	2	0	0	5,544
Mazel Trick	42	13	119	14	9	12	514,053
McCallister's Risk	2	1	9	1	2	0	8,363
McGinty (NZ)	1	1	9	3	2	2	49,075
Meacham	3	1	10	1	0	0	9,361
Meadow Flight	40	20	357	38	36	52	751,195
Meadow Monster	39	30	270	53	34	39	1,034,173
Meadowlake	111	64	637	108	75	68	2,401,796
Mecke	88	49	676	87	97	88	2,033,996
Media Starguest (IRE)	2	1	17	1	1	1	11,166
Medieval	9	3	37	7	6	4	119,031
Medieval Man	3	3	24	3	4	1	22,257
Medieval Victory	2	2	21	3	3	1	21,394
Medifast	7	2	50	4	2	6	31,917
Medium Cool	10	1	79	1	6	2	46,764
Mehmet	1	1	10	1	1	0	1,815
Melodisk	13	2	69	2	3	8	59,993
Meloy	5	4	35	5	8	8	33,224
Memo (CHI)	74	33	434	65	55	61	1,580,689
Menifee	17	7	66	8	15	13	373,055
Mercedes Won	27	6	135	9	7	23	202,757
Mercer Mill	48	26	364	48	29	49	571,570
Meritable	9	3	65	4	7	7	18,351
Mertzon	10	3	45	7	4	4	48,332
Meshach	3	1	18	1	2	1	20,997
Mesopotamia	17	13	171	26	27	16	328,688
Metfield	48	23	383	40	41	39	639,244
Mexican Bandit	7	2	30	2	3	4	27,058
Mi Cielo	59	30	504	60	65	57	801,512
Mi Selecto	23	9	147	21	11	17	214,934
Mia's Boy	6	3	37	6	6	6	71,160
Mia's Indian Boy	2	2	18	2	1	1	6,813
Michael's Flyer	12	9	93	15	14	10	174,862
Mickey's Road	3	2	18	9	0	1	46,673
Midnight Drama	6	2	26	3	3	2	17,739
Midnight Tiger	2	1	9	1	0	0	5,402
Midyan	1	1	12	3	1	2	94,600
Miesque's Son	61	36	428	67	56	48	987,560
Mighty Adversary	1	1	9	4	1	1	52,200
Mighty Forum (GB)	2	1	14	1	0	2	8,985
Mighty Magee	17	7	128	10	23	12	141,091
Migrating Moon	46	24	343	46	31	53	998,438
Military	16	9	63	13	7	7	367,616
Militron	5	3	35	5	6	1	40,220
Mill Native	7	3	55	3	7	13	82,846
Mind Games (GB)	2	1	16	3	3	5	105,420
Miner	22	13	147	19	18	16	285,393
Miner's Mark	90	47	754	80	106	79	1,313,335
Mineral Ice	8	5	67	9	9	11	96,687
Mining	5	2	38	3	3	2	21,020
Minister's Mark	7	3	19	3	2	5	43,623
Ministry	1	1	12	1	0	1	8,413
Minneapple	7	2	46	3	5	3	30,934
Minor Saint	4	1	20	1	2	1	16,215
Minstrel Alley	17	4	101	8	8	4	88,071
Minstrel Dancer	17	12	171	29	20	20	276,108
Minstrel Glory	3	1	19	1	4	2	32,250
Minted Gold	2	1	14	1	1	2	6,833
Miracle Heights	15	3	81	4	10	10	53,975
Miroman	1	1	7	1	0	1	10,209
Missionary Ridge (GB)	30	11	224	21	31	22	354,371
Mister Baileys (GB)	63	35	449	58	41	53	1,380,417
Mister Frisky	3	1	29	3	1	3	15,183
Mister Jolie	77	50	610	90	91	94	1,287,302
Mister Modesty	1	1	12	3	3	2	20,865
Mister Slippers	16	4	85	4	6	7	78,284
Mister Wonderful (GB)	9	6	54	8	7	6	66,215
Misty Wind (IRE)	6	5	52	7	8	8	42,792
Miswaki	85	30	485	45	79	53	1,174,200
Miswaki Bandit	4	1	13	1	1	1	15,620
Miswaki Gold	11	2	60	5	11	6	41,907
Mitey Mad	1	1	13	1	2	2	12,645
Mocito Fogoso (CHI)	1	1	3	1	0	0	27,500
Mogambo	1	1	8	2	0	4	3,503
Mokhieba	7	3	41	4	6	1	114,359

RECORDS OF SIRES

Sire	Perf	Wnrs	Sts	1st	2d	3d	Purses	Sire	Perf	Wnrs	Sts	1st	2d	3d	Purses
Mombo Gambo	4	2	23	5	5	1	50,780	Mujadil	5	1	18	2	3	6	188,241
Mombo Jumbo	1	1	8	3	4	0	37,100	Mujtahid	3	2	27	6	2	3	88,549
Moment of Crisis	10	3	57	5	5	8	23,419	Mukaddamah	4	3	15	4	4	1	102,420
Moment of Hope	4	2	33	4	4	10	54,251	Muldoon	23	14	115	21	12	10	168,170
Mommu	1	1	12	1	3	1	8,087	Multiengine	1	1	18	2	4	2	30,538
Momsfurrari	6	2	39	6	6	2	64,720	Munch n' Nosh	11	4	113	6	3	10	67,066
Mon Capitan	3	1	17	1	1	1	8,004	Murrandana	1	1	8	1	1	0	5,270
Monde Bleu (GB)	2	2	23	3	6	2	17,355	Murrtheblurr	9	7	67	12	6	10	49,963
Monetary Gift	25	11	205	19	30	31	357,346	Music Master	5	2	19	2	7	4	59,427
Money by Orleans	2	1	21	1	4	1	39,786	Music Prince	5	4	44	5	4	7	43,524
Money Run	3	1	14	2	2	0	13,786	Music Prospector	2	1	24	4	3	3	51,830
Mongol Warrior	5	3	39	5	6	3	39,359	Musical Dreamer	5	2	45	3	5	7	44,861
Monsieur Champlain	1	1	14	1	1	1	4,822	Musical Fappi	9	5	66	10	11	8	87,146
Montbrook	112	60	704	107	98	79	3,916,782	Musique d'Enfer	5	3	30	4	9	3	119,505
Montreal Marty	2	1	11	1	1	3	34,252	Muskoka Music	2	1	11	1	1	1	7,850
Montreal Red	54	27	369	46	45	38	536,630	Mutah	6	2	41	7	2	6	62,374
Moon Prospector	5	1	38	2	1	4	14,856	Mutakddim	83	54	682	102	94	89	3,091,705
Moon Up T. C.	14	8	131	17	13	18	140,236	Mute Dancer	6	3	51	5	4	5	47,047
Moonlight Dancer	18	7	83	11	12	6	183,542	Muttering	1	1	8	1	0	0	3,065
More Pleasure	2	1	10	1	1	0	7,305	My Boy Adam	56	18	350	26	30	34	586,876
More Royal	4	2	18	2	3	0	43,205	My Favorite Grub	1	1	6	1	0	0	18,820
More Style	3	1	11	1	0	0	6,783	My G. P.	4	1	32	2	4	2	22,695
Mornin' My Lord	2	1	16	1	2	3	17,972	My Habitony	2	1	17	1	2	3	5,605
Morning Bob	3	1	35	1	1	3	6,187	My Imperial Slew	2	1	10	1	3	1	41,201
Moro	17	1	57	1	3	5	14,263	My Kentucky Home	2	1	24	2	5	6	23,307
Moro Oro	16	8	98	13	10	11	197,982	My King (GER)	8	2	64	3	5	9	41,092
Mortlock (FR)	10	3	49	7	9	2	57,926	My Liege	3	2	13	3	1	2	22,679
Moscow Ballet	61	35	393	55	72	64	895,598	My Memoirs (GB)	3	1	9	1	0	0	4,804
Moses Tablet	4	1	22	1	3	5	12,089	My Mike	18	12	156	24	23	16	241,166
Most Welcome (GB)	4	1	33	1	3	2	61,343	My Prince Charming	18	6	145	7	11	9	123,365
Moudix Bleu	1	1	14	2	3	1	21,622	Myrmidon	7	1	26	1	2	5	14,306
Mountain Cat	135	74	960	139	140	102	2,923,110	Mysterious Vice	1	1	12	1	3	4	214,926
Mountain of Laws	12	5	94	9	5	5	89,728	Mystery Storm	48	24	384	61	44	61	948,540
Mountdrago (ARG)	1	1	10	1	1	2	5,551	Mythical Ruler	1	1	7	1	2	1	76,115
Moving Shoulder	12	6	113	15	11	12	129,813	Mytimetodance	1	1	10	1	0	0	6,960
Mr Ballew	1	1	11	2	2	1	13,130	Naevus	89	45	720	86	88	85	983,094
Mr Peter P.	1	1	3	1	1	0	17,120	Naevus Star	6	3	26	3	1	2	29,601
Mr Purple	20	8	116	11	16	20	205,620	Nahuel	4	1	26	1	4	1	13,536
Mr. Badger	7	3	46	4	12	8	45,073	Nalees Man	1	1	17	3	2	1	25,153
Mr. Beasley	5	1	35	1	3	4	22,821	Namaqualand	3	2	29	3	3	6	52,481
Mr. Big L.	2	1	10	1	2	3	7,826	Nancy's Champion	7	2	44	2	10	8	16,957
Mr. Bolg	5	2	41	4	1	0	24,468	Napa Sonoma	3	1	20	3	1	1	26,595
Mr. Brilliant	14	6	98	9	10	8	110,717	Napa Valley	3	2	36	9	3	5	38,239
Mr. Button's	1	1	10	1	0	0	19,596	Naroctive	5	2	36	2	3	3	51,351
Mr. Dreamer	2	1	13	1	1	1	5,439	Nasgame	8	2	44	4	3	7	24,034
Mr. Easy Money	15	10	88	19	19	11	274,048	Nashwan	3	1	12	1	1	2	32,756
Mr. Exclusive	1	1	10	1	1	1	2,984	Nassau Square	3	1	22	1	1	2	4,135
Mr. Explosive	13	3	100	5	8	6	65,974	Nasty and Bold	34	15	248	23	23	29	274,210
Mr. Expo	15	8	97	21	18	11	154,991	Nasty Charger	1	1	5	1	1	4	5,681
Mr. Goldust	16	10	146	14	11	22	155,645	Nataraja	3	1	18	2	1	1	21,245
Mr. Greeley	183	93	1,127	154	138	140	3,726,374	Native Bidder	3	1	29	1	1	1	7,258
Mr. Integrity	25	15	186	23	29	21	245,334	Native Factor	34	18	223	29	26	20	221,704
Mr. J. C.'s Mons	2	2	17	3	1	2	22,649	Native Fir	7	3	65	4	5	7	36,367
Mr. Kasanova	1	1	3	1	1	0	3,093	Native of Seattle	4	1	35	1	3	7	23,295
Mr. Krugerand	4	2	29	3	3	1	26,445	Native Prospector	28	14	190	31	34	25	323,120
Mr. Leader	6	3	36	5	3	4	165,628	Native Regent	33	17	253	30	36	25	526,286
Mr. Listo	2	1	12	2	0	0	8,869	Native Slew	21	7	181	8	5	19	162,146
Mr. Nasty	10	7	104	10	8	13	109,384	Native Tactics	11	3	45	4	6	6	90,832
Mr. O. P.	18	6	64	9	10	4	32,350	Native Uproar	9	2	66	4	4	6	60,327
Mr. Odd Dancer	1	1	10	0	0	0	10,216	Natural Ability	3	1	12	1	2	0	5,876
Mr. Procrastinator	21	10	145	13	21	20	156,133	Naturally Nicer	3	1	19	1	5	3	29,724
Mr. Prospector	41	15	191	27	26	25	1,999,854	Naturals Grand	6	2	43	4	8	4	30,734
Mr. Redoy	9	6	88	9	17	10	93,710	Navarone	25	8	127	15	10	7	186,772
Mr. Roberts	4	2	32	8	5	5	44,570	Navegante (CHI)	5	4	38	6	4	3	19,873
Mr. Secretary	1	1	6	1	0	0	4,980	Navy Admiral	12	3	96	7	14	4	56,560
Mr. Shawklit	32	16	228	32	29	23	431,606	Near the Limit	4	2	25	2	3	1	32,212
Mr. Sparkles	39	18	300	29	28	38	316,874	Neff Lake	3	1	8	2	2	1	12,818
Mr. Sutter	11	7	51	9	11	5	208,368	Negative	7	4	42	5	3	6	34,448
Mr. Twice Worthy	2	2	33	6	4	2	31,517	Nelson	78	36	556	61	55	64	960,966
Mt. Livermore	135	70	881	123	126	93	2,603,783	Nepal	19	7	123	16	13	12	179,287
Mt. Magazine	28	15	187	23	26	16	240,097	Nephrite	5	1	32	1	1	3	8,256
Mt. Ruritania	2	1	13	1	0	2	9,874	Neptuno (ARG)	4	1	19	2	0	0	6,802
Mtoto	5	2	24	2	4	1	39,523	Net Asset	6	3	28	4	0	2	57,262
Mud Route	8	3	25	4	0	3	102,263	Never Wavering	24	11	145	17	13	14	201,046
Mufti	6	2	36	4	4	2	27,393	New Doc	2	2	15	3	4	3	21,299
Mughtanim	2	1	14	2	4	1	43,244	New Way	7	3	25	3	0	3	26,418
Muhayaa	5	4	26	5	3	0	57,719	Newton's Law (IRE)	13	5	58	8	9	6	127,402
Muhtafal	13	7	88	13	12	13	255,632	Nice and Easy	5	1	22	4	2	2	20,709
Muhtarram	3	1	17	1	3	1	94,540	Nice Krews	5	2	17	2	1	2	7,389

Sire	Perf	Wnrs	Sts	1st	2d	3d	Purses
Nicholas	34	18	281	25	27	31	371,720
Nickel Slot	13	8	114	14	9	17	58,761
Nicklelobe	3	2	17	3	1	1	5,016
Nicou Nicou	4	2	39	5	4	5	52,705
Night Above	19	11	150	18	17	16	128,705
Night Fright	1	1	11	2	1	1	12,874
Night Runner	9	5	75	6	9	7	48,709
Night Shift	10	3	45	3	9	6	222,094
Night Visitor	2	1	13	1	6	0	13,633
Nightofthegaelics	7	4	64	7	11	11	126,663
Nijinsky's Table	2	1	22	1	3	2	7,730
Nikos	1	1	7	1	1	1	27,140
Nineeleven	16	5	87	6	12	6	130,695
Niner Bush	5	2	27	4	5	2	18,388
Nines Wild	60	20	419	35	36	42	418,016
No Bondage	4	1	30	2	0	3	11,844
No Budget	3	1	26	1	2	4	13,459
No Malice	2	1	11	3	2	2	55,141
No Marker	1	1	9	3	4	1	19,550
No Points	5	1	44	1	3	5	29,507
No Tie Please	1	1	12	1	0	0	5,919
No Upper Limit	3	1	13	1	4	3	11,102
Noactor	68	39	503	64	61	46	907,581
Noble Assembly	5	3	28	6	3	4	152,165
Noble Bronze	1	1	3	1	0	1	1,020
Noble Cat	18	8	89	15	12	9	221,605
Noble Classicist	1	1	13	2	0	1	10,683
Noble Imperator	1	1	14	1	1	1	5,304
Noble Moment	2	1	11	1	0	0	3,687
Noble Novice	6	1	31	1	6	0	22,466
Noble Savage (IRE)	2	2	7	3	0	0	23,700
Noble Title	1	1	7	1	0	2	7,220
Noon Prospect	4	1	19	1	2	2	17,079
Nooo Problema	3	1	32	2	4	1	13,896
Nordic Legend	2	1	14	2	0	1	45,660
Norquestor	78	41	607	73	78	85	1,322,983
North Breeze	1	1	13	2	1	0	6,933
North of Eden	3	1	17	2	2	2	11,960
North Pole	4	3	43	7	5	5	66,719
North Prospect	33	17	247	29	24	21	259,883
North Woodsman	6	3	48	4	4	4	26,787
Northern Afleet	43	33	280	63	37	30	1,224,867
Northern Andy	2	2	7	2	1	0	5,415
Northern Baby	60	18	322	24	39	34	419,946
Northern Cut	3	1	14	2	1	0	15,392
Northern Flagship	17	8	108	13	6	14	101,736
Northern Hal (IRE)	2	1	6	1	0	1	22,721
Northern Horizon	5	4	42	8	8	7	44,684
Northern Idol	52	28	352	52	32	45	1,130,701
Northern Jay	3	1	13	1	2	1	3,640
Northern Magus	6	2	29	2	2	0	11,846
Northern Majesty	3	2	32	2	5	3	23,330
Northern No Trump	29	17	231	37	36	34	373,880
Northern Park	13	6	97	11	11	13	161,393
Northern Prospect	24	12	206	22	21	32	284,802
Northern Raja	7	1	31	1	4	2	30,583
Northern Spur (IRE)	31	13	189	25	26	17	774,312
Northern Strike	3	1	10	1	0	0	42,911
Northern Symphony	15	7	109	12	16	15	100,022
Northern Taste	1	1	6	2	0	0	122,040
Northern Trend	20	14	219	40	27	33	541,683
Northern Wolf	6	1	25	1	3	1	34,255
Northernhemisphere	3	3	39	4	9	7	63,185
Northrop	3	1	21	1	2	3	23,358
Norway Gray	3	1	21	1	4	2	20,467
Nostalgia's Star	2	2	23	4	4	6	22,270
Not Affordable	3	1	10	1	0	1	6,870
Not For Love	157	100	1,177	208	185	153	4,969,343
Not Tricky	3	2	21	3	1	2	44,133
Notable Cat	29	15	150	25	10	14	145,298
Notation	1	1	8	2	0	2	12,315
Notebook	137	76	1,039	143	150	140	3,377,149
Nova Scotia	4	1	29	1	1	5	26,264
Novel Nashua	5	3	44	4	6	4	38,956
Now Listen	11	4	88	8	12	4	76,981
Nowi'veseenitall	2	2	19	2	2	4	23,756
Nowork all Play	1	1	10	1	2	5	8,060
Nucay	8	6	43	7	6	3	88,312
Numerous	145	74	1,058	123	149	135	2,478,264
Nureyev	25	13	110	17	12	9	933,217
O'Brannigan	23	11	131	19	14	12	163,641
O'Reilly (NZ)	1	1	2	1	0	1	103,320
O. K. by You	2	1	17	1	2	0	12,185
Oakmont	4	4	22	5	1	0	50,760
Obligato	21	6	108	10	8	9	141,645
Obstructed	1	1	11	1	2	0	11,010
Ocala Angel	1	1	12	2	0	1	12,372
Ocala Slew	42	19	337	28	37	43	433,635
Ocean Crest	35	16	214	27	26	20	554,552
Ocean Splash	5	2	53	6	5	7	88,744
Octagonal (NZ)	1	1	3	1	0	0	7,501
Odyle	35	11	222	23	22	22	244,398
Ofuscador (BRZ)	1	1	9	1	0	1	1,352
Ogydoug	7	2	39	3	2	2	27,830
Ogygian	5	3	44	9	6	3	117,841
Oh Fabulous Day	2	1	13	2	2	3	13,217
Oh Say	38	18	231	28	30	23	575,594
Ojai	1	1	7	4	1	0	20,311
Oklahoma Express	1	1	6	1	0	1	3,520
Olaf	4	1	11	2	2	1	16,029
Old Chapel	1	1	5	1	1	0	9,236
Old Stories	38	21	318	40	42	40	213,185
Old Trieste	19	8	64	9	14	7	692,090
Ole'	54	26	450	49	68	50	553,012
Oliver's Twist	39	19	274	32	38	33	516,467
Olmos	6	3	36	3	8	1	33,805
Olympic Native	2	1	17	1	1	2	22,195
Olympic Win	1	1	2	1	0	1	5,768
Olympio	77	39	488	60	58	67	1,003,763
Omali's Buckaroo	4	2	35	3	1	2	26,932
On Report	5	3	68	5	5	5	69,215
On Target	83	44	529	73	62	67	923,242
On the Sauce	17	9	128	15	15	17	222,466
On to Glory	3	1	21	1	0	1	26,363
Once a Dancer	4	1	25	1	0	1	10,117
Once a Sailor	9	2	42	4	4	8	89,529
Once Wild	18	8	88	10	7	4	79,277
One Golf Sierra	2	1	9	1	3	1	22,600
One in a Mil	7	5	58	8	9	8	75,972
One Little Hustler	5	3	39	8	5	1	29,323
One to Envy	2	2	14	2	1	0	3,888
One Tuff Oop	1	1	15	1	4	0	13,996
Onefinesilverbuck	5	2	33	4	5	2	52,335
Ongoing Mister	2	1	5	2	0	0	23,202
Onion Juice	1	1	18	3	1	0	12,230
Onward	6	2	33	2	6	5	76,577
Open Forum	110	56	757	80	98	112	1,986,973
Opening Verse	55	29	412	43	59	50	676,947
Ops Smile	27	12	178	23	20	29	336,682
Oraibi	13	6	76	9	8	13	58,983
Orbit Dancer	27	12	182	16	20	19	115,821
Orbit's Revenge	7	2	22	3	2	1	23,311
Orbit's Scene	7	5	53	10	10	5	82,441
Orchid's Devil	11	6	59	9	11	11	177,700
Order	12	5	82	6	11	10	107,119
Ordway	44	23	277	46	40	33	638,827
Ore Grade	8	5	29	5	2	0	25,569
Organizers Cousin	7	2	35	3	3	5	63,480
Ormonte	10	6	83	8	13	10	43,926
Ormsby	40	14	229	28	18	21	674,090
Othello	22	6	153	8	20	14	242,383
Our Emblem	85	35	488	55	57	51	1,099,968
Our Gary	11	7	99	10	22	10	162,039
Our Lewis	1	1	12	3	1	3	14,559
Ourcurtaincall	8	1	34	1	6	4	15,732
Out of Place	143	80	1,083	145	158	133	2,730,120
Out of the Realm	6	3	33	4	4	1	35,694
Outflanker	42	21	279	42	40	37	875,313
Outlaw Image	1	1	8	2	0	3	13,955
Overpeer	7	6	74	12	9	11	126,819
Overskate	1	1	12	3	0	2	19,861
Owens Troupe	3	2	19	2	3	2	10,195
Owington (GB)	1	1	15	1	3	4	26,933
Oxalagu (GER)	1	1	3	1	0	1	36,507
P Fifty One	1	1	14	4	8	1	152,008
Pachinko	3	3	48	5	3	11	30,110
Pacific Waves	12	10	107	22	20	7	279,494
Pal's Memory	2	2	25	3	3	4	32,413

RECORDS OF SIRES

Sire	Perf	Wnrs	Sts	1st	2d	3d	Purses
Palance	3	3	20	8	2	0	96,638
Palmister	11	2	60	2	6	7	31,087
Pancho Press (ARG)	8	4	78	6	13	11	81,654
Pancho Villa	64	33	501	57	53	53	570,148
Pangbourne	5	1	31	1	2	4	20,760
Papa Banks	2	1	10	1	0	1	4,173
Papa Chan	1	1	10	2	2	2	57,350
Pappa Riccio	30	15	228	18	28	34	340,133
Parade Ground	20	4	61	5	4	9	124,635
Parade Marshal	10	5	72	10	11	8	382,980
Paramount Jet	6	1	22	1	0	1	9,274
Paranoide (ARG)	37	18	244	32	35	25	292,876
Parentheses	8	2	31	2	4	2	47,036
Parfaitement	18	4	87	6	11	6	100,349
Parlando	1	1	13	2	1	0	6,510
Parlay Me	10	6	63	13	11	10	384,414
Partner's Hero	64	32	398	55	53	58	1,639,645
Party Manners	47	20	338	33	46	49	542,123
Pas de Cheval	2	1	16	2	1	2	20,431
Pas Seul	7	1	41	1	2	3	13,675
Paskanell	6	4	36	4	4	8	14,131
Pass Fail	4	2	38	4	0	2	20,273
Pass the Line	9	4	45	5	5	5	85,618
Paster's Caper	6	3	55	6	10	8	98,696
Patchy Groundfog	2	2	18	5	7	1	122,029
Patriot Strike	7	3	35	6	5	1	58,406
Patriotically	3	2	18	3	0	1	20,525
Patton	128	75	1,012	134	104	108	2,025,282
Pauliano	14	4	76	4	13	12	219,194
Pax Nobiscum	2	1	27	3	2	3	36,380
Payant (ARG)	4	2	25	5	2	0	56,525
Peace Arch	1	1	8	2	1	2	17,525
Peace Prize (IRE)	2	1	14	2	2	1	9,846
Peaked	2	2	29	6	5	2	20,782
Peaks and Valleys	137	81	1,048	154	161	138	3,536,454
Pecos River	3	1	18	1	1	1	6,973
Pedigree Unknown	2	1	7	1	1	0	6,785
Peintre Celebre	5	2	18	3	1	3	177,893
Pembroke	120	65	974	134	137	125	2,045,784
Penalty Shot	2	2	26	3	1	1	19,535
Pendleton Ridge	7	3	35	3	4	3	12,688
Pennekamp	2	1	15	1	0	2	21,790
Pentelicus	160	92	1,259	172	175	182	2,605,459
Pep Up	5	2	37	3	8	6	18,900
Percival	9	3	63	3	11	6	85,408
Perfect	22	9	184	16	19	17	191,065
Perfect Mandate	5	3	16	4	4	2	193,730
Perfect Parade	3	1	14	2	4	3	53,870
Perfect Vision	22	10	126	16	12	11	308,642
Perfecting	21	9	165	12	19	17	253,607
Perforce	12	5	78	6	6	11	47,617
Perkin Warbeck	4	1	20	1	2	1	9,380
Personable Joe	49	28	297	47	37	38	339,150
Personage	2	1	9	1	2	1	2,196
Personal Five	2	1	13	1	1	1	5,756
Personal Flag	127	64	946	123	114	121	2,399,689
Personal Hope	34	17	286	32	30	31	374,294
Perugino	6	5	48	6	8	9	201,535
Peruvian	20	9	153	16	22	16	242,592
Pesty Axe	1	1	7	1	3	0	2,539
Petardia (GB)	4	2	45	3	3	2	55,604
Peterhof	56	30	397	53	54	61	352,630
Petersburg	55	36	427	72	61	62	726,099
Peteski	59	26	439	60	43	49	880,913
Petionville	93	54	692	104	91	90	3,301,287
Petorius	2	1	13	1	1	2	8,729
Petra Forbes	2	1	8	1	0	3	4,800
Petrel's Flight	7	2	40	4	1	6	24,157
Petroenergy	4	1	20	1	1	0	4,627
Peyrano (ARG)	11	5	50	9	14	5	127,282
Phantasma	5	2	38	2	2	1	9,187
Phantom Jet	11	5	86	8	6	14	108,618
Phardante	1	1	2	1	1	0	17,700
Pharisien (FR)	7	2	35	3	2	3	14,774
Philadream	10	3	58	3	1	6	32,263
Philosophical	1	1	15	1	3	2	54,933
Phoenician	5	3	45	4	6	4	23,570
Phone Fantasy	2	1	11	1	0	1	8,100
Phone Order	1	1	9	1	3	0	2,279
Phone Roberto	10	4	44	4	3	8	54,569
Phone Saga	12	3	63	5	11	9	79,937
Phone Trick	142	76	956	122	121	139	2,178,999
Photo Memory	7	2	15	2	1	1	7,785
Pic Iron	1	1	15	1	0	3	9,901
Piccolino	37	15	279	22	35	35	411,653
Piccolo	5	4	24	4	4	3	75,290
Pick Up the Phone	12	6	89	16	5	8	126,190
Pine Bluff	105	56	723	101	83	109	2,840,677
Pineing Patty	12	3	68	4	3	3	45,615
Pioneering	81	54	584	91	87	77	1,912,534
Pirate's Bounty	43	20	319	46	42	38	451,679
Pistol's Cowboy	2	1	10	1	3	2	13,895
Pistolet Bleu (IRE)	2	1	7	1	1	0	38,584
Pistols and Roses	36	9	229	16	15	9	166,207
Pitso Cassello	2	1	5	2	1	0	4,248
Pivotal (GB)	6	2	20	3	5	3	668,196
Placid Fund	20	8	95	14	9	13	241,338
Plain Dealing	35	16	267	33	30	17	279,710
Plain Spoken	1	1	5	1	1	0	7,038
Play Fellow	11	4	62	8	8	3	69,339
Play On	1	1	4	1	0	0	3,840
Play Safe	1	1	17	1	0	1	6,952
Play the Gold	1	1	3	1	1	0	37,150
Pleasant Colony	78	42	538	77	71	72	4,871,583
Pleasant Dancer	6	2	33	2	1	1	23,959
Pleasant Line	10	6	69	7	5	10	96,940
Pleasant Tap	104	41	644	67	74	93	1,605,609
Pleasant Variety	1	1	7	1	0	2	57,248
Pleasure Bent	5	5	41	12	2	11	79,727
Plenty Chilly	11	3	64	5	3	4	48,887
Plentyofit	4	2	20	5	5	1	47,680
Pocket Book	4	1	44	3	10	11	61,340
Pocket Park	1	1	12	1	0	0	1,285
Pocket Phone	3	2	20	2	2	4	17,349
Pocketful in Vail	2	1	11	2	2	0	12,071
Pok Ta Pok	24	12	159	21	18	19	250,580
Polar Falcon	4	2	30	2	7	4	77,690
Pole Position	32	19	226	43	34	26	522,892
Poles Apart	8	3	53	5	6	6	153,856
Poliglote (GB)	2	2	11	2	1	3	112,980
Polish Navy	13	3	36	4	3	5	90,318
Polish Numbers	142	74	805	121	115	102	2,826,367
Polish Precedent	5	1	10	1	1	1	50,195
Polish Pro	50	22	353	46	49	39	873,921
Political Ambition	12	7	75	15	13	8	306,354
Polka	11	4	87	8	15	11	92,792
Pollock's Luck	40	20	325	26	31	46	249,737
Polynesian Flyer	5	1	33	3	4	5	15,943
Ponche	50	25	392	42	66	67	1,010,525
Porto Foricos	3	1	15	3	2	2	372,582
Portoferraio (ARG)	1	1	9	1	3	1	12,895
Portroe	6	1	40	1	4	2	30,109
Positiveness	3	1	24	3	2	5	49,126
Post Up	1	1	7	1	2	0	6,302
Poster Monarch	3	2	37	3	4	2	59,568
Potentiate	2	2	27	3	3	3	20,648
Potrillazo	6	4	41	6	5	6	124,883
Powderityourself	7	5	52	11	12	4	68,158
Power Boat	3	1	23	1	3	6	8,012
Power of Mind	37	12	266	19	33	37	383,293
Powerful Venue	2	1	8	1	1	0	5,353
Powis Castle	3	1	23	2	0	1	12,374
Preacherman	15	5	99	6	6	14	87,273
Precisely Noble	2	1	17	1	0	0	2,669
Precocity	15	7	60	8	9	9	306,966
Predecessor	12	2	80	4	8	9	36,395
Preferences	8	2	41	3	1	7	25,804
Premier Ministre	4	2	24	5	6	2	35,082
Premiership	68	27	484	52	68	49	581,586
Premium Spirits	1	1	16	3	1	1	24,376
Prenup	49	30	355	49	39	29	805,783
Preponderant (FR)	2	1	18	2	2	2	14,160
Present Value	30	11	185	20	27	22	357,032
Presidential Order	32	19	244	27	36	37	469,118
Press Card	108	61	803	109	89	113	1,766,565
Presto Lad	10	2	53	2	4	6	16,019
Preston Road	4	1	33	3	4	2	14,548
Prete Khale	1	1	15	2	1	2	9,998

Sire	Perf	Wnrs	Sts	1st	2d	3d	Purses	Sire	Perf	Wnrs	Sts	1st	2d	3d	Purses
Primal Innocence	2	2	25	3	1	3	18,401	Raamz	2	1	4	1	0	0	5,314
Primo Dominie (GB)	3	2	27	4	1	2	38,439	Racing Rhinocerous	4	1	20	1	0	6	15,188
Prince Alydar	1	1	7	1	0	1	3,630	Racing Star	2	1	25	4	1	3	23,922
Prince Cox	4	2	36	6	2	2	86,812	Radical Change	2	1	10	1	0	4	10,592
Prince Don B.	4	2	19	2	3	0	11,435	Radio Daze	13	5	63	7	4	8	72,351
Prince Gala	1	1	5	1	0	0	1,317	Raffie's Majesty	14	7	77	11	10	11	483,419
Prince of Fame	24	13	210	16	23	24	186,353	Raft	16	3	89	3	4	17	57,674
Prince of Praise	1	1	5	1	2	2	124,002	Rage	11	5	71	8	9	12	160,185
Prince of the Mt.	14	8	80	11	12	12	163,842	Ragtime Rascal	2	1	11	5	1	2	60,471
Prince Spellbound	1	1	9	1	1	0	1,930	Rahy	92	41	484	67	67	51	2,812,767
Priolo	5	1	25	1	4	3	168,400	Raider	2	1	13	1	0	0	6,444
Privano	1	1	13	2	4	1	58,485	Rail	30	18	197	29	27	24	518,559
Private Account	4	2	21	4	2	3	35,116	Railway Cat	11	6	78	7	9	7	64,946
Private Admirer	9	5	53	7	4	5	48,709	Rainbow Blues (IRE)	4	1	17	2	2	1	30,081
Private Chieftain	9	2	59	3	4	10	61,192	Rainbow East	2	1	20	1	6	0	27,470
Private Express	1	1	8	1	0	0	4,371	Rainbow Prospect	8	3	43	6	7	3	141,333
Private Interview	44	21	339	33	30	39	674,074	Rainbow Quest	7	4	28	5	2	4	383,272
Private Key	28	9	182	13	20	11	189,329	Raise a Champion	16	9	98	14	8	8	118,470
Private School	24	12	179	19	14	29	169,095	Raise a Govenor	14	7	94	16	10	8	83,410
Private Talk	17	10	132	15	21	17	278,711	Raise a Man	8	1	69	2	7	10	53,666
Private Terms	102	50	695	103	80	87	2,052,259	Raise a Rascal	13	8	102	12	13	12	101,470
Private Thoughts	3	2	25	2	5	2	15,255	Raise a Stanza	1	1	8	2	0	1	43,400
Private Treasurer	8	3	45	6	6	2	63,134	Raise Caine	2	1	12	1	1	0	4,851
Private Venture	4	2	37	2	1	3	52,445	Raise the Price	2	1	8	2	1	0	8,948
Prized	89	41	616	59	71	88	1,162,925	Raised On Stage	2	1	17	1	0	2	5,603
Probable	8	2	38	6	2	3	27,397	Raising Hill	1	1	16	3	3	0	17,091
Proof	8	3	70	6	7	6	70,984	Raisor Smart	2	1	21	1	2	7	12,055
Proper Challenge	3	1	22	4	0	3	25,657	Raj Waki	9	5	45	11	5	6	860,446
Proper Reality	64	35	472	53	56	64	464,535	Raja Native	1	1	5	1	0	0	6,570
Prosetflanker	1	1	1	1	0	0	5,160	Raja's Best Boy	14	5	96	9	10	14	158,687
Prospect Bay	83	51	537	90	93	65	1,499,758	Raja's Revenge	10	2	67	3	4	7	120,021
Prospect Feature	17	3	99	8	6	2	50,128	Raji	6	4	33	4	4	6	112,621
Prospect North	12	4	85	5	6	8	28,113	Rakeen	43	25	322	42	39	37	688,223
Prospector Jones	54	23	336	37	43	42	882,680	Rambo Phil	5	2	37	3	5	8	81,586
Prospector's Halo	37	24	360	41	37	65	485,419	Ramplett	7	2	37	2	5	3	36,822
Prospector's Music	64	39	482	70	65	55	1,013,777	Ranger (FR)	13	4	52	4	6	3	23,369
Prospector's Pick	4	2	34	4	3	5	47,059	Rapacity	3	1	15	1	1	1	4,834
Prospectors Gamble	86	37	592	60	63	62	1,012,744	Rappin Rumor	4	2	27	2	1	4	21,836
Prosper Fager	36	15	256	24	26	28	744,577	Rare Brick	75	35	604	60	78	75	868,024
Prosperous	3	1	15	1	1	0	3,113	Rare Performer	4	2	33	4	6	4	30,787
Proud and True	45	20	318	42	41	36	646,507	Rare Red	9	6	93	14	5	19	91,596
Proud Birdie	11	7	97	11	14	9	124,983	Rattenburys Bank	1	1	3	1	0	1	2,045
Proud Cat	2	1	5	1	0	0	1,743	Ravenwood	9	3	59	4	7	7	78,408
Proud Dhabi	6	2	37	2	8	4	36,548	Ray's Word	20	10	156	16	13	19	148,996
Proud Irish	35	21	267	40	33	35	498,059	Raykour (IRE)	14	3	82	9	11	5	96,460
Proud Northern	5	3	35	7	5	8	77,093	Reach for More	7	3	61	4	5	3	26,503
Proud Truth	34	19	327	41	46	38	680,920	Reaffirming	4	1	18	1	1	2	9,621
Proudest Duke	10	2	65	5	4	6	47,237	Real Partner	7	2	38	3	3	2	40,947
Proudest Romeo	21	12	119	28	17	20	574,789	Real Quiet	30	8	102	12	9	10	329,331
Providential (IRE)	4	1	10	1	2	1	42,782	Real West	9	3	65	6	9	12	104,028
Prudent Manner (IRE)	9	4	49	4	1	7	64,216	Realitos	2	1	11	1	2	1	14,292
Prune	5	1	26	1	3	2	27,731	Reality Road	4	2	21	2	5	2	35,986
Puchi's Rambo	1	1	15	1	2	4	6,320	Reality's Conquest	2	1	13	1	0	0	3,647
Pug's Hart	9	4	70	5	14	15	47,745	Really Awesome	7	3	55	4	3	4	34,223
Pulpit	82	42	410	63	57	50	2,411,485	Really Golden	11	6	74	9	21	10	49,162
Pulverizing	6	2	48	3	8	7	38,228	Rebmec	13	7	101	13	17	16	152,483
Puntivo	4	2	35	4	2	6	20,449	Recital Hall	2	2	9	2	1	2	14,225
Purple Comet	16	7	95	9	8	8	144,802	Reclassify	3	1	27	1	3	2	12,269
Pursuit of Love	4	3	16	3	4	1	74,860	Recognized	7	4	28	4	2	1	64,140
Put Em Up	6	5	33	8	1	6	18,836	Record Catch	24	9	177	14	25	15	183,289
Pyramid Peak	21	8	102	10	18	12	250,282	Red	22	12	130	16	26	20	189,723
Pyrite	11	5	75	13	11	11	72,752	Red Attack	16	6	142	17	16	19	212,980
Quadratic	1	1	9	1	1	0	8,928	Red Bishop	28	10	189	17	17	26	378,037
Quaker Hill	10	5	49	5	5	5	66,469	Red Clay Country	3	2	17	2	2	0	9,778
Quaker Ridge	13	5	63	5	10	10	130,713	Red Lad	2	2	22	2	3	5	14,911
Queen's Gray Bee	13	3	86	5	10	11	62,036	Red Rang	2	1	11	1	0	0	2,633
Quest for Fame (GB)	27	12	181	20	22	19	280,183	Red Ransom	95	38	453	54	48	60	1,883,523
Qui Native	1	1	21	8	2	1	9,571	Red River Gorge	24	9	151	16	22	18	180,804
Quick Cut	25	8	107	9	11	7	136,192	Red Scamper	14	8	142	9	21	17	137,742
Quick Snap (GB)	2	1	19	1	3	2	5,156	Red Screen	5	2	42	3	5	4	31,798
Quick Speed	3	1	9	1	0	0	7,357	Red Wing Bold	9	1	40	3	7	5	39,069
Quiero Dinero	4	1	27	3	2	2	68,134	Red Wing Prince	1	1	2	1	0	0	3,300
Quiet American	158	68	936	122	122	131	3,248,609	Reel On Reel	15	7	106	9	11	15	125,470
Quiet Enjoyment	24	17	140	32	18	19	277,447	Regal Affair	13	3	63	3	6	7	41,472
Quintillion (IRE)	2	2	19	4	1	2	66,087	Regal Affirmation	6	3	31	4	6	5	35,769
Quinton	5	4	31	6	1	7	29,331	Regal and Royal	9	3	65	5	8	8	59,495
Quite Special	6	3	35	3	5	10	88,125	Regal Classic	159	83	1,234	145	151	145	3,652,402
R. Cooper	4	2	46	3	8	4	48,409	Regal Discovery	5	3	41	3	6	6	120,797
R. Payday	14	3	58	3	3	5	65,135	Regal Flier	3	1	24	1	3	6	6,876

RECORDS OF SIRES

Sire	Perf	Wnrs	Sts	1st	2d	3d	Purses	Sire	Perf	Wnrs	Sts	1st	2d	3d	Purses
Regal Groom	6	3	47	3	8	10	118,160	Rock City (IRE)	1	1	1	1	0	0	36,600
Regal Humor	22	7	166	14	14	18	163,363	Rock Hill	10	4	71	10	6	8	113,696
Regal Intention	71	40	473	69	61	66	1,045,312	Rock Point	9	1	47	1	3	1	44,378
Regal Remark	93	53	629	98	98	84	1,245,995	Rock Royalty	2	1	13	1	0	1	6,544
Regal Search	55	33	454	49	55	43	663,258	Rockamundo	14	8	99	13	8	9	141,774
Regal Song	1	1	11	3	0	1	24,373	Rocky Mountain	21	9	150	14	21	13	278,840
Regalberto	3	1	20	2	2	4	22,909	Rodayo	1	1	3	1	1	0	3,670
Regent Act	2	1	21	1	5	2	22,485	Rodeo	55	24	258	30	32	20	809,342
Rehaan	20	9	152	13	14	34	170,418	Rodeo Road	3	2	14	3	2	0	4,712
Reign Road	22	6	118	8	8	10	82,572	Roi Danzig	2	1	15	2	3	2	17,434
Reigning King	3	1	22	1	4	2	18,137	Roi Normand	7	1	31	5	1	6	875,957
Reincarnate	6	2	68	6	5	13	80,843	Rokeby (GB)	14	5	78	11	2	8	62,864
Relaunch	20	10	145	25	19	19	253,920	Roll Credits	5	3	24	3	3	1	15,315
Relaunch a Tune	10	7	84	13	14	14	64,741	Roll On Roberto	5	2	27	3	3	1	25,354
Relic Relic Relic	3	1	15	2	0	4	30,177	Rollin On Over	1	1	8	1	1	1	7,168
Remember Hope	2	2	20	4	3	2	29,615	Rolls Aly	9	6	73	9	8	11	89,710
Remington Slew	5	1	35	2	4	3	12,892	Roman Bend	1	1	11	1	1	2	12,515
Renegade Spirit	3	2	27	2	9	3	17,283	Roman Diplomat	7	2	38	4	6	3	37,272
Reno City	2	1	14	1	2	4	3,206	Roman Majesty	5	2	48	3	4	12	41,878
Renteria	5	2	22	2	3	2	56,805	Roman Mombo	3	1	28	2	1	0	17,174
Replant	1	1	8	1	1	2	1,793	Roman Reasoning	1	1	8	4	0	1	35,997
Repletion	13	7	77	9	14	10	192,625	Romanov (IRE)	23	6	136	9	15	12	200,641
Repriced	67	31	485	56	51	61	905,331	Romantic Prince (IRE)	2	1	8	1	1	1	1,675
Reprimand (GB)	2	1	7	1	0	2	30,800	Romo	2	1	13	2	1	2	16,420
Reprized	24	7	147	11	13	22	199,343	Roo Art	49	19	315	29	26	38	242,471
Reputed Testamony	5	3	35	6	2	5	49,349	Root Boy	18	9	119	18	10	13	236,332
Restless Con	10	7	78	18	12	7	415,701	Roscius	4	2	22	2	0	2	38,814
Retirement Account	2	1	12	1	1	3	9,566	Rosenose	1	1	4	1	0	1	1,915
Reuben's Grand	7	2	40	3	4	2	47,207	Rougemont	4	2	24	3	5	5	9,148
Reve Dore	1	1	6	1	2	1	14,445	Rough Pearl	2	1	12	1	1	0	3,570
Reve Du	7	2	47	5	9	6	57,422	Rouse the Louse	5	3	44	6	7	4	78,995
Revelrout	4	1	17	1	2	1	3,528	Rowdy Regal	4	1	26	2	2	2	8,929
Reverse Mulligan	6	3	44	3	5	3	22,371	Roxbury Park	13	3	88	8	10	11	65,116
Revoque (IRE)	2	1	12	1	4	3	16,930	Roy	97	57	663	107	71	94	2,723,175
Rewana	6	2	24	2	2	1	8,586	Royal Academy	99	47	499	76	61	57	2,364,725
Rhodes	25	13	189	21	15	27	248,154	Royal Applause (GB)	8	2	32	3	4	4	193,428
Rhythm	64	26	417	43	52	52	824,501	Royal Dixie	2	1	14	1	0	0	3,010
Rial (ARG)	15	8	132	16	19	9	108,196	Royal Egyptian	25	12	150	18	14	20	165,514
Ribot Land	1	1	6	1	0	1	7,295	Royal Empire	25	7	108	9	10	11	156,517
Rich Man's Gold	1	1	7	1	1	0	37,416	Royal Gardener	2	1	12	1	0	2	3,782
Richland Native	3	2	24	5	6	0	47,195	Royal Link	5	4	47	6	7	6	113,444
Richman	3	2	31	2	4	7	40,032	Royal Martial (ARG)	1	1	15	3	3	1	21,335
Ridan Clarion	5	2	25	2	3	1	15,727	Royal Merlot	1	1	5	1	1	0	43,028
Ridaway Jig Time	1	1	4	1	0	1	2,736	Royal Mews	2	2	20	2	0	3	4,229
Ride the Rails	9	3	59	7	5	7	807,785	Royal Monarchy	3	1	18	3	2	2	23,597
Ride the Storm	6	4	46	5	7	6	97,743	Royal Pennant	13	4	62	5	8	5	40,610
Ride to Win	2	1	16	1	1	1	3,816	Royal Quiz	12	7	79	8	18	19	49,560
Riflery	5	2	33	2	3	7	37,129	Royal Roberto	18	15	147	20	18	21	180,235
Right Con	2	1	16	1	2	3	12,452	Ruben's Dancer	1	1	11	1	0	3	5,457
Right Jab	9	4	58	5	7	9	91,478	Rubiano	139	87	1,117	161	136	159	3,525,061
Rine's Hope	7	1	48	1	6	2	21,044	Rubiyat	3	3	11	3	2	3	94,560
Ring Proud	5	2	32	2	5	4	8,573	Ruckus Hosner	8	3	68	10	9	7	87,317
Ringside	23	10	126	21	15	22	233,814	Rudy's Fantasy	1	1	17	2	2	1	47,025
Rinka Das	49	19	332	34	35	53	515,766	Ruhlmann	31	16	233	32	35	31	347,687
Rinoso	1	1	11	2	2	1	39,404	Rumbo	2	1	15	3	3	1	11,660
Rio Verde	10	7	70	10	8	10	204,584	Run a Native	1	1	12	1	1	0	3,848
Rio's Lark	21	8	145	12	4	17	85,607	Run On the Bank	8	4	45	6	3	8	40,608
Rip Entry	4	1	11	1	1	1	5,993	Run Paul Run	6	4	55	8	7	10	98,475
Risen Roman	3	1	22	1	0	0	17,227	Run Softly	49	21	307	34	38	41	473,446
Risen Star	28	14	203	20	21	25	198,308	Run Turn	7	4	38	7	5	1	83,578
River Flyer	19	7	104	12	13	7	142,380	Runaway Casting	3	1	11	1	0	1	12,534
River of Kings (IRE)	2	1	13	2	0	1	11,385	Runaway Groom	171	87	1,116	149	125	142	3,550,370
River Special	43	15	245	19	25	25	518,048	Runaway Macho	1	1	12	1	2	0	17,196
Rivergo	5	3	37	3	1	4	15,147	Running Memories	2	1	14	1	5	3	21,327
Riverman	6	3	67	6	6	8	90,931	Rush	3	1	16	2	1	2	3,212
Rizzi	83	42	566	74	75	69	1,369,941	Rushing Velex	1	1	7	1	1	1	3,145
Road Rush	3	1	17	2	0	1	13,504	Russellthemussell	4	2	24	2	3	2	20,581
Road to Seattle	1	1	9	2	1	2	34,466	Russian Connection	1	1	5	1	0	0	4,140
Roanoke	65	33	509	54	70	70	819,225	Russian Courage	11	6	67	9	7	7	190,640
Roar	132	73	850	137	112	109	3,439,069	Rustic Light	3	2	26	3	5	8	27,565
Roaring Camp	18	13	143	19	16	21	263,272	S. W. Wildcard	6	2	44	3	9	3	33,883
Rob an Plunder	15	7	108	17	14	17	67,921	Sabona	25	12	201	28	24	26	607,224
Rob's Freeze	13	5	84	10	12	7	156,611	Sadler's Wells	28	9	97	13	11	15	3,202,155
Robannier	14	7	89	16	15	13	414,037	Sadr	1	1	11	1	4	1	56,320
Robellino	8	3	43	4	6	4	181,186	Safawan	1	1	6	1	1	0	21,140
Roberto Grande	2	2	16	5	1	5	128,632	Safe Ground	6	1	22	3	3	2	16,419
Robin des Pins	48	36	446	62	52	49	779,839	Safe Prospect	16	8	170	20	16	20	263,734
Robyn Dancer	111	67	932	127	105	102	2,193,413	Safely's Mark	7	4	33	7	1	4	92,624
Rock Band	11	6	88	12	15	10	124,120	Sahm	14	3	46	4	3	6	101,094

Sire	Perf	Wnrs	Sts	1st	2d	3d	Purses
Sail Me Again	17	6	111	8	17	12	136,117
Saint Ballado	172	83	892	141	148	121	5,953,038
Saithor	4	3	49	5	9	6	91,291
Salem Drive	14	7	96	10	11	9	168,047
Salse	2	1	12	1	1	0	32,250
Salt Dome	10	4	67	8	12	6	67,877
Salt Lake	166	100	1,170	204	194	147	3,796,108
Salty Shoes	8	2	53	3	7	14	29,174
Salutely	6	2	35	3	3	6	51,125
Salydar	1	1	10	1	1	2	7,900
Sam M.	1	1	4	1	0	0	2,395
Sam's Sunny Hour	7	1	33	1	5	3	24,038
Samarid	1	1	9	1	2	1	7,382
Same Day Delivery	10	6	75	10	5	7	109,702
San Romano	3	3	32	8	5	4	200,768
San Simon	3	2	19	3	0	1	18,301
Sanctuary	15	5	97	10	6	9	107,315
Sand Tunnel	5	5	37	6	9	4	86,805
Sandia Slew	5	3	14	4	4	1	43,876
Sandpit (BRZ)	97	56	691	99	82	71	1,503,005
Sandrigo	5	4	52	4	6	11	51,162
Sandy's Honey	1	1	11	1	1	2	28,560
Sanglamore	2	1	14	2	2	1	73,857
Santana Sands	1	1	3	1	0	0	1,615
Santiago Peak	7	5	53	14	5	6	112,206
Saratoga Express	7	4	42	6	11	3	55,346
Saratoga Six	57	25	387	38	46	53	541,758
Saros (GB)	18	9	119	11	15	20	146,351
Satellite Signal	13	3	68	3	5	8	25,122
Saucy Token	15	4	114	8	6	10	84,919
Savings	11	2	51	5	3	2	56,371
Savona Tower	4	2	26	2	1	7	8,361
Saxton	5	1	28	1	7	8	61,715
Say Guv	6	2	56	2	7	8	48,463
Sayaret	2	1	11	1	2	0	62,190
Scarlet 'n Gray	10	3	74	8	6	7	183,266
Scarlet Ibis	34	19	268	29	34	30	423,050
Scatmandu	25	6	75	7	9	8	171,867
Scenic (IRE)	1	1	10	1	1	2	13,666
Schaufuss	1	1	3	1	1	0	1,125
Schembechler	14	3	71	3	8	12	53,198
Scherando	9	4	95	7	7	17	73,039
Schossberg	21	15	166	28	24	23	809,714
Score Quick	14	7	89	11	13	9	227,899
Scottsville	13	4	60	7	1	7	168,678
Screen Trend	5	1	31	1	2	1	15,855
Scroll	7	1	36	1	0	3	21,495
Sea Hero	113	71	911	129	112	125	2,767,674
Sea of Secrets	24	11	95	17	16	13	403,478
Sea Salute	62	34	495	77	60	47	1,383,584
Sea Wall	43	23	318	38	38	41	1,273,177
Seacliff	32	19	259	34	36	35	543,275
Seaport Mac	1	1	11	1	3	1	17,534
Search for Gold	1	1	22	4	6	2	16,924
Seattle Battle	5	2	28	3	1	6	23,081
Seattle Bound	25	8	161	12	17	17	137,975
Seattle General	8	1	34	2	1	4	12,674
Seattle Knight	3	1	28	1	4	2	11,894
Seattle Morn	14	9	137	14	12	22	154,889
Seattle Proud	10	2	53	8	5	6	213,557
Seattle Shuffle	1	1	5	1	0	0	4,810
Seattle Sleet	52	27	332	50	43	41	775,324
Seattle Slew	71	28	386	45	48	46	1,694,329
Seattle Song	4	2	22	2	5	7	49,896
Seattle Sun	8	4	65	5	10	5	104,676
Sebrof	8	6	47	9	8	5	46,522
Second Childhood	9	2	39	5	4	7	85,483
Secreniner	3	1	7	1	0	0	7,695
Secret Claim	33	14	188	26	30	17	240,076
Secret Ghost	2	2	9	2	2	0	13,580
Secret Hello	64	36	478	70	74	79	1,100,390
Secret Odds	23	15	189	21	13	30	245,944
Secret Prince	11	4	90	6	8	12	61,053
Secret Slew	1	1	12	3	2	1	12,517
Secretariats Ghost	2	1	22	3	5	3	59,590
Seeker's Journey	9	5	57	10	5	7	104,304
Seeker's Reward	1	1	3	1	0	0	13,770
Seeking the Gold	71	36	414	67	56	48	2,889,240
Sefapiano	66	39	464	66	74	63	1,024,547
Sejm	11	4	102	8	5	14	138,004
Sekari (GB)	7	4	55	6	6	4	61,164
Selkirk	4	2	20	3	3	2	125,640
Semoran	29	13	169	23	10	21	328,880
Seneca Jones	34	16	209	26	30	35	595,812
Senor Conquistador	10	5	64	8	9	6	145,270
Senor Foxfire	7	4	45	5	1	6	23,144
Senor Speedy	70	33	516	60	60	60	824,949
Sentinel Star	5	3	30	5	1	7	24,627
Sepoy (ARG)	9	4	80	4	8	7	67,802
Septieme Ciel	26	16	194	33	24	27	444,284
Serves Em Right	10	2	49	8	2	4	95,107
Service Stripe	29	20	217	35	38	32	870,673
Sestero (BRZ)	1	1	10	1	2	3	57,240
Set Free	6	1	50	1	2	8	10,995
Seven Rivers	13	6	67	8	4	6	47,551
Seven Zero	12	4	67	7	10	12	78,728
Sewickley	7	1	42	3	2	8	83,875
Shadeed	21	7	156	11	15	14	192,666
Shadow Launcher	3	2	24	3	4	2	48,000
Shaheen	6	3	24	4	5	1	46,374
Shakeel	16	10	121	19	14	11	135,497
Sham	2	1	14	1	2	2	6,407
Shamrock Ridge	11	6	91	7	16	13	115,709
Shamtastic	4	1	20	1	2	2	5,755
Shanekite	14	5	113	9	12	19	91,619
Shaquin	6	4	33	5	2	2	39,752
Sharkey	21	7	154	11	11	15	327,017
Sharp Frosty	44	19	348	35	40	49	376,082
Sharp Victor	39	14	269	29	36	27	677,311
Sharper One	7	4	45	5	10	10	30,107
Shawklit Player	2	1	6	2	2	1	14,142
Shawklit Won	3	3	37	4	6	8	42,151
Shawlneck	2	2	25	3	6	2	26,121
Sheikh Adel	2	1	12	2	3	1	23,598
Sheikh Albadou (GB)	30	13	214	27	22	37	427,540
Shelter Half	14	6	118	9	11	11	122,251
Shergar's Best (IRE)	21	11	128	22	19	14	123,242
Sheryar	5	3	28	5	5	2	107,795
Shifty Sheik	5	1	16	1	1	1	7,160
Shining Steel (GB)	1	1	7	1	0	0	35,460
Shipmate Sam	3	1	10	1	1	5	4,523
Shirttail Flying	7	4	39	4	7	5	55,676
Shoal Creek	5	2	35	2	2	5	17,559
Shoot Again	3	1	16	1	0	0	9,795
Shortys Moovr	2	1	11	1	0	1	3,102
Shot Block	6	2	32	4	4	1	64,833
Shot Evening	2	1	16	1	1	4	16,965
Shot Gun Scott	3	2	26	4	4	0	24,036
Shotiche	23	10	157	12	16	14	163,738
Shots Are Ringing	4	2	26	2	4	3	8,201
Show Dancer	2	1	25	1	2	2	10,995
Show'em Slew	4	3	38	4	4	1	26,735
Shuailaan	38	20	222	37	23	24	717,645
Shudanz	2	1	5	1	0	1	13,720
Shuttleman	12	4	89	5	4	9	58,827
Shuvinski	2	1	12	1	1	1	6,097
Shy Tom	6	2	38	2	5	6	102,497
Siberian Express	6	2	59	2	15	11	54,330
Siberian Pine	16	6	97	8	10	11	66,649
Siberian Summer	72	30	466	72	57	52	1,235,659
Siberian Tiger	1	1	5	1	0	0	8,820
Sicilian Law	2	1	16	2	3	3	39,880
Side Note (GB)	1	1	5	1	0	0	3,240
Siebe	11	5	85	7	11	8	59,993
Sifounas	3	1	44	2	2	8	27,778
Signal	10	5	69	7	3	14	143,352
Signal Tap	88	38	624	61	64	61	1,923,787
Signoir Valery	2	1	13	4	2	0	21,538
Signoretto (FR)	3	1	20	1	0	0	12,618
Sijjaal	1	1	17	1	1	4	8,796
Silent Fox	2	1	11	2	3	4	11,576
Silent Generation	6	2	46	3	7	5	34,029
Silent King	20	9	152	16	19	18	179,278
Silent Link	2	2	23	2	2	3	31,001
Silent Tempest	4	3	25	5	1	0	46,565
Silken Reality	8	3	62	4	7	11	25,233
Sillery	1	1	4	1	0	1	31,345
Silver Badge	1	1	8	1	1	1	5,544

Sire	Perf	Wnrs	Sts	1st	2d	3d	Purses
Silver Buck	54	30	462	50	41	66	747,415
Silver Charm	30	15	101	16	12	12	573,638
Silver Deputy	153	86	986	161	123	121	5,606,973
Silver Element	4	1	34	2	3	5	19,291
Silver Finder	1	1	16	3	5	3	46,860
Silver Florin	1	1	12	2	2	2	24,057
Silver Fox	18	6	127	12	15	19	160,813
Silver Ghost	119	59	775	104	98	99	2,155,020
Silver Hawk	20	8	96	11	12	11	453,810
Silver Minstrel	4	3	29	3	1	3	27,808
Silver Music	19	9	110	10	8	14	236,802
Silver of Silver	20	7	104	8	10	11	118,041
Silver Ray	3	1	28	1	2	2	7,228
Silver Ring (FR)	3	2	20	2	2	4	14,277
Silver Surfer	2	1	5	1	0	0	1,252
Simi Dancer	9	1	34	1	4	1	15,945
Simon Lord Lovat	1	1	9	1	0	0	12,998
Simply Majestic	20	5	100	5	16	7	72,218
Sinceilostmybaby	9	2	52	4	3	6	29,635
Sing Sing	1	1	7	1	0	1	32,945
Single Solo	3	1	18	4	3	0	12,475
Single Time	2	1	16	1	0	0	13,524
Singspiel (IRE)	3	1	4	1	0	1	66,648
Siphon (BRZ)	109	42	502	57	69	72	1,726,394
Sir Ap	20	7	147	8	17	22	159,155
Sir Cat	101	66	665	123	110	80	2,622,760
Sir Eric	26	10	197	12	14	22	180,986
Sir Fir	6	3	18	3	6	2	46,640
Sir Francis Fru	2	2	17	2	2	3	9,918
Sir Harry Lewis	1	1	14	2	0	2	18,174
Sir Jinsky	2	1	22	1	2	2	17,006
Sir Keys	1	1	6	1	1	1	3,385
Sir Leon	24	13	200	30	17	22	467,281
Sir Naskra	2	1	17	2	2	4	23,595
Sir Reed O	5	2	24	3	2	6	18,981
Sir Richard Lewis	16	10	142	22	16	18	273,598
Sir Riddle	4	1	34	1	3	2	22,859
Sir Spellbinder	5	3	29	6	2	0	39,406
Sitting Appeal	1	1	6	1	0	1	1,280
Six Fast Nickles	4	3	37	7	5	5	32,548
Six Speed	14	5	84	9	8	5	117,319
Siyah Kalem	28	13	195	19	19	27	235,825
Skeet Shoot	2	1	11	2	1	0	10,940
Ski Champ	3	2	15	3	2	1	74,210
Skip Away	95	36	511	51	67	67	1,546,413
Skip Out Front	3	2	37	4	4	6	58,463
Skip Trial	87	44	601	69	75	77	2,241,963
Sky Chase (NZ)	2	1	4	1	2	0	12,300
Sky Classic	133	51	736	74	109	96	2,727,998
Sky Command	2	1	4	1	2	0	2,830
Sky Harbour	4	2	27	2	6	3	12,359
Sky Tracer	5	2	38	2	3	1	12,540
Sky White	18	10	117	25	13	14	267,090
Skywalker	86	37	565	73	75	54	1,691,212
Slavic	33	10	179	12	29	25	335,397
Slerp	4	3	19	4	3	1	24,130
Slew Baby	3	2	24	3	4	4	32,793
Slew City Slew	121	62	728	112	86	65	2,041,332
Slew Express	3	2	18	3	2	2	13,183
Slew Gin Fizz	1	1	9	2	3	0	57,100
Slew Mood	13	7	93	9	8	9	98,051
Slew o' Gold	30	13	184	19	18	18	846,627
Slew of Angels	16	9	119	15	20	16	208,184
Slew Pilot	2	1	24	1	2	9	7,584
Slew Sangue	21	13	190	17	21	25	305,398
Slew the Bride	9	6	67	8	5	6	65,438
Slew the Coup	37	19	259	32	23	29	222,095
Slew the Knight	20	9	138	13	9	15	172,261
Slew the Slewor	42	21	322	33	26	20	278,470
Slew the Surgeon	12	5	86	8	14	6	64,713
Slew's Royalty	28	17	184	26	22	24	524,302
Slew's Verdict	2	1	17	2	0	1	16,171
Slewabration	1	1	10	2	0	0	10,631
Slewacide	78	35	481	51	47	55	647,717
Slewdledo	128	66	710	109	87	93	1,467,244
Slewdonza	4	2	11	3	1	0	8,735
Slewly Yours	2	1	17	1	0	4	8,684
Slewpy	33	17	210	20	32	28	390,878
Slews Gold	8	2	49	3	2	5	30,519
Slewship	1	1	10	5	1	0	48,560
Slewvescent	9	6	90	8	15	13	208,305
Slice of Reality	17	8	142	13	17	24	151,874
Slick	6	4	48	4	3	9	52,061
Sligh Jet	8	3	84	6	15	10	94,014
Smart Alec	4	2	46	4	7	4	31,031
Smart Magician	10	3	48	4	3	4	24,011
Smart Stevie	1	1	7	1	0	0	3,102
Smart Strike	118	68	730	121	106	110	5,489,374
Smarten	19	9	132	14	24	19	188,989
Smelly	9	3	51	3	5	4	59,543
Smile	5	1	23	3	1	2	16,760
Smilin Singin Sam	10	3	57	8	8	11	112,100
Smoke Glacken	122	75	879	157	132	124	4,587,386
Smoke Jumper	3	2	15	2	1	3	7,858
Smokester	139	78	927	145	137	100	2,507,258
Smokey Oso	2	1	10	2	1	1	14,184
Smooth Performance	1	1	12	4	2	0	86,050
Snake Doctor	7	2	34	2	2	6	26,245
Snake Oil Stevie	2	1	25	1	3	0	8,709
Snow 'em	10	6	85	10	14	13	65,910
Snow Chief	11	3	29	3	2	4	24,764
Snowbound	32	16	156	26	26	20	292,112
So Ever Clever	8	3	38	6	5	3	27,106
So Factual	1	1	2	1	0	1	36,960
So La Me	3	2	29	4	1	5	27,380
So Private	4	2	25	2	2	3	20,536
Soaking Smoking	5	3	51	6	4	13	109,718
Social Diamond	5	4	30	5	2	2	45,183
Society Max	46	28	340	44	50	54	482,090
Society Road	3	2	28	2	2	2	27,353
Soft Gold (BRZ)	16	6	104	8	18	20	266,595
Solar Launch	1	1	6	1	1	1	5,635
Soldier Boy	6	2	30	4	1	1	41,686
Solo Guy	2	2	23	3	4	3	13,666
Something Lucky	8	4	62	6	12	14	122,767
Son of a Roman	2	1	13	1	1	2	16,990
Son of Briartic	77	43	565	75	82	54	748,537
Song's Son	2	1	10	1	0	1	5,863
Songhay	1	1	16	1	1	2	4,733
Sonny's Solo Halo	4	1	15	1	0	0	2,728
Soon a King	1	1	16	2	0	0	7,863
Sounds Fabulous	11	5	55	5	8	7	37,054
South Boy (JPN)	4	1	19	1	3	1	7,695
South Pass	7	1	14	1	3	1	6,219
Southern Fire	14	8	113	13	17	17	120,863
Southern Halo	160	73	1,000	120	136	119	3,031,599
Southern Rhythm	22	12	165	18	19	22	210,066
Southern Sign	12	6	79	8	11	16	50,656
Souvenir Copy	104	57	529	86	73	72	2,212,419
Sovereign Dancer	3	1	25	4	3	5	66,030
Sovereign Romance	5	3	34	4	1	6	22,365
Sovereignall	3	3	44	5	5	8	31,338
Space Mountain	2	1	18	4	4	1	27,619
Space Rider	2	2	25	4	1	0	33,739
Space Station	3	1	16	1	1	0	1,519
Spanish Dancer (IRE)	1	1	7	2	1	0	16,471
Spanish Drummer	25	9	182	14	15	19	180,004
Spanish Drums	24	10	188	13	19	22	123,714
Sparkling Blade	4	1	22	1	3	4	30,609
Sparkling Jay	2	1	11	1	1	1	3,677
Spartan Victory	12	6	59	11	10	7	178,700
Speak	20	9	100	11	11	9	97,541
Speakerphone	2	2	13	2	1	3	46,796
Spearhead	2	1	13	1	0	2	4,945
Special Advice	5	1	24	2	1	2	12,123
Special Invention	4	1	13	1	3	2	7,316
Special Lineage	4	1	18	1	0	2	7,880
Spectacular Bid	30	12	159	19	14	15	275,781
Spectacular Love	1	1	4	1	1	1	26,300
Spectacular Prince	3	1	15	2	2	1	9,952
Spectacular Round	4	2	24	2	3	5	27,475
Spectacular Sound	1	1	5	1	2	0	1,000
Spectaculardynasty	5	3	39	5	2	3	39,028
Spectacularphantom	1	1	10	1	3	1	66,120
Spectrum (IRE)	10	6	64	8	6	7	238,870
Speeding Light (ARG)	2	1	17	3	2	2	15,973
Speeding Moment	6	1	22	1	2	0	25,438
Speedy Cure	10	4	59	5	9	4	55,029

Sire	Perf	Wnrs	Sts	1st	2d	3d	Purses	Sire	Perf	Wnrs	Sts	1st	2d	3d	Purses
Speedy Nijinsky	16	8	83	8	11	10	98,938	Storm Broker	48	23	288	34	34	33	582,929
Spellbound	8	5	57	6	4	14	58,710	Storm Cat	105	43	410	66	53	44	3,193,360
Spend a Buck	65	25	403	49	61	52	768,614	Storm Center	20	9	118	13	11	10	195,833
Spend a Franc	2	1	8	1	1	4	3,292	Storm Creek	140	63	995	116	109	129	2,324,822
Spicy Monarch	1	1	13	2	2	2	13,283	Storm of Angels	60	25	383	40	26	37	399,641
Spinning World	43	26	257	49	34	29	1,477,669	Storm of the Night	2	1	3	1	0	0	4,206
Spinoza	4	2	25	2	1	1	8,244	Storm Time	7	2	39	4	3	5	21,505
Spirit Voices	6	3	53	3	3	7	33,775	Stormin Fever	35	16	124	17	15	19	529,054
Splendid Son	2	1	11	2	0	0	14,190	Stormy Atlantic	72	33	372	63	45	67	1,984,441
Split Run	2	1	7	1	0	0	9,870	Stosky	2	1	13	3	1	2	30,653
Sport Royal	5	1	24	3	3	0	25,452	Straight Polarity	1	1	9	1	0	0	6,074
Sportful	3	2	15	2	2	1	23,615	Stravinsky	20	8	68	9	4	15	314,798
Sportin' Life	4	2	42	4	1	1	30,207	Strawberry Road (AUS)	8	6	70	9	15	9	140,397
Sports View	6	3	47	3	7	2	24,240	Strelka	4	3	44	3	3	5	59,402
Spotter Bay	7	3	49	3	8	5	45,679	Strike Gold	43	22	242	43	31	35	408,319
Spreadthealarm	4	1	18	1	2	1	10,084	Strike the Anvil	12	3	78	3	3	9	30,829
Sprizzo	9	3	40	4	3	1	45,235	Strike the Gold	58	27	444	48	45	42	616,744
Spruce Bouquet	5	3	31	5	6	3	93,515	Strodes Creek	58	39	429	74	63	47	1,100,559
Spunky Rascal	9	6	75	10	6	4	59,586	Strolling Along	3	2	29	4	3	7	59,009
Spy Signal	22	6	132	11	14	20	210,437	Strong Gale	1	1	6	3	0	0	37,200
Squadron Leader	23	8	149	14	16	15	242,801	Strong Minded	4	1	12	2	0	0	2,637
Squan Lake	13	2	85	2	6	6	38,990	Strong Performance	7	3	50	3	6	6	26,806
Sri Pekan	5	3	22	4	4	3	337,779	Strug	1	1	15	1	1	4	7,127
St. Forbes	6	1	53	2	0	2	12,355	Struggler (GB)	30	12	238	22	36	29	504,008
St. Jovite	33	17	235	26	27	23	340,098	Stuka	51	27	388	59	40	43	1,015,290
St. Valentine	6	1	47	2	4	4	19,281	Stutz Blackhawk	56	31	477	47	50	50	452,526
Stack	52	20	370	27	44	40	787,113	Stutz Keys	3	1	30	1	3	3	8,654
Stacked Pack	3	1	13	1	1	1	39,872	Suave Prospect	79	49	655	96	79	94	1,928,234
Staff Riot	6	5	30	7	3	2	36,514	Subordination	41	19	208	30	23	23	545,405
Stage Colony	57	25	420	45	41	42	471,066	Sudden Flare	2	2	10	3	0	0	15,954
Stagecraft (GB)	6	4	54	9	5	8	287,940	Suggest	6	2	30	3	3	6	110,984
Stake a Claim	4	2	24	3	0	1	16,899	Sultry Song	103	51	616	84	71	75	2,019,262
Stalwars	54	29	435	49	82	74	603,037	Summer of Storms	3	2	34	6	5	6	154,813
Stalwart	42	23	301	35	37	43	319,044	Summer Squall	75	47	531	84	50	69	2,226,196
Stalwart Boy	2	1	9	1	2	0	6,284	Summing	11	4	62	6	4	6	33,565
Standing On Edge	7	2	33	2	2	4	73,500	Sumsing Sweetly	8	4	66	12	14	11	155,245
Stanstead	1	1	4	2	2	0	12,850	Sun Catcher	4	3	33	4	3	1	19,485
Star Choice	6	2	23	3	7	3	28,905	Sun Czar	1	1	11	1	2	0	4,639
Star de Naskra	65	37	455	60	64	52	939,910	Sun Man	2	2	19	3	3	4	43,743
Star Gallant	20	12	223	17	26	21	386,447	Sun Master	9	6	72	8	6	6	71,121
Star of Halo	5	3	30	3	1	2	18,298	Sun War Dancer	4	3	54	5	10	7	80,900
Star Of Luskin (AUS)	1	1	8	1	1	0	17,766	Sundance Ridge	6	4	61	11	9	9	327,990
Star of the Crop	29	13	192	26	20	26	310,309	Sunday Minister	23	15	139	21	11	10	240,572
Star of Valor	8	3	33	3	4	7	71,907	Sundial	8	2	46	4	5	2	36,371
Starbank	1	1	3	1	0	0	4,524	Sunny Clime	1	1	8	1	0	1	4,224
Starbird Glacier	2	1	13	1	1	4	6,655	Sunny Feet	24	14	145	24	21	16	134,525
Stark Ridge	5	4	28	5	8	4	66,284	Sunny's Halo	104	42	644	70	69	73	749,254
Stars n' Stripes	4	1	24	3	3	3	80,586	Sunrise Shower	36	19	243	32	41	29	272,871
State Craft	14	5	64	6	2	8	45,887	Sunset Ridge	6	1	47	2	2	2	16,363
State Dinner	10	3	64	6	7	5	47,955	Sunshine Forever	9	3	66	8	9	9	121,305
State Performer	20	10	142	15	18	17	253,985	Sunshine Money	2	1	19	1	0	4	8,691
Stately Cielo	19	11	158	16	12	12	231,208	Sunshine Today	1	1	7	1	5	0	8,120
Stately Slew	4	4	41	7	3	6	68,693	Super Code	5	3	32	3	0	5	25,746
Stately Wager	11	8	100	19	20	9	101,242	Super Gun	7	1	29	1	3	2	30,122
Statesmanship	9	3	41	3	1	5	30,122	Super May	6	2	22	2	3	0	9,084
Stauder	8	3	63	4	12	15	49,836	Super Native (IRE)	15	3	63	5	6	9	120,357
Stay the Course	1	1	7	3	2	0	48,600	Super Seven	7	5	48	7	6	7	23,814
Steady Effort	3	2	19	2	2	2	11,955	Super Squall	1	1	4	1	0	0	7,920
Steady Naskra	2	1	28	2	4	7	17,619	Superbity	4	2	22	3	7	2	19,476
Steel Robbing	14	9	117	11	14	18	87,884	Superior Success	4	2	42	5	7	3	30,387
Steinlen (GB)	8	3	49	5	4	4	45,526	Superoyale	4	2	22	2	8	3	74,140
Stephanotis	8	4	22	5	7	0	116,940	Supposition	2	2	20	3	2	2	11,625
Stephen Ray	1	1	2	1	0	0	3,224	Supremo	80	44	674	70	71	66	1,020,345
Stephene Mon Amour	8	2	25	2	3	2	27,032	Surachai	2	1	5	1	0	0	12,780
Stewing Sid	3	1	34	2	5	3	38,526	Sure Swift	2	1	15	1	0	1	4,633
Sticks and Bricks	9	4	56	6	6	10	61,472	Survival	3	2	22	5	2	3	8,899
Stolen Gold	7	6	44	13	5	6	108,303	Sutter's Prospect	30	15	199	26	25	20	359,146
Stolen Script	1	1	4	1	0	0	2,118	Swain (IRE)	18	12	76	17	6	11	1,352,277
Stone Harbor Mate	3	1	18	1	1	1	12,825	Swamp King	12	4	85	7	10	10	138,265
Stop the Fighting (IRE)	6	4	50	4	4	5	24,008	Swear by Dixie	18	6	112	11	20	14	266,331
Stop the Music	33	13	238	16	36	23	225,917	Swedaus	11	4	98	11	22	11	104,304
Stop the Stage	13	9	79	21	15	11	135,458	Swelegant	5	3	46	10	10	4	85,013
Storada	3	1	25	3	2	0	9,574	Swing and Miss	25	12	128	17	15	23	117,939
Storm a Head	5	2	35	2	1	2	13,723	Swing Shift (GB)	9	3	44	4	2	5	32,741
Storm Ashore	4	1	15	2	0	0	8,369	Swing Till Dawn	3	2	10	2	1	0	22,305
Storm Bird	14	7	98	10	11	14	224,258	Swingin Sway	5	2	31	2	5	3	20,699
Storm Blast	22	12	164	22	14	15	150,988	Swiss Native	2	1	22	4	4	3	47,720
Storm Boot	181	101	1,053	173	128	107	2,966,974	Swiss Trick	21	5	130	7	13	18	77,259
Storm Brewing	12	6	72	8	0	9	67,587	Swiss Yodeler	54	35	358	55	61	40	1,391,389

RECORDS OF SIRES

Sire	Perf	Wnrs	Sts	1st	2d	3d	Purses
Swoon	3	1	24	3	1	2	44,788
Sword Dance (IRE)	144	82	1,095	136	133	142	2,398,148
Sword Devil	1	1	10	1	0	2	8,100
Synastry	75	40	484	63	59	52	584,780
T. H. Bend	4	2	35	4	4	7	23,244
T. H. Fappiano	14	1	35	1	3	3	22,311
T. U. Slew	11	5	59	7	5	5	79,224
Tabasco Cat	134	85	939	146	137	117	4,118,417
Tabib	11	3	49	3	7	7	29,845
Taconic Road	8	4	66	10	13	6	118,007
Tactical Advantage	173	87	1,238	138	145	181	2,587,942
Tactical Cat	24	10	78	12	14	8	491,972
Tagish	12	5	76	6	8	11	94,648
Tahoe City	22	11	133	19	19	17	217,975
Tail Toss	1	1	10	2	2	1	11,822
Taj Alriyadh	16	6	97	12	6	8	47,700
Tajawa	15	7	119	15	10	18	112,991
Take Me Out	107	53	709	100	71	88	1,958,424
Take Risks	2	1	7	2	1	0	43,280
Take That Step	10	4	94	9	10	16	188,030
Takur	3	2	12	2	1	2	23,555
Tale of the Cat	134	70	634	98	106	90	4,053,160
Talinum	4	2	23	3	4	3	30,147
Talk Nice	6	2	52	6	6	7	108,850
Talkin Man	34	17	174	33	12	18	638,987
Tall Ships	3	2	14	4	1	1	57,949
Tamarisk (IRE)	1	1	5	1	0	1	29,420
Tamayaz	81	35	555	48	59	65	900,181
Tammany	12	7	97	11	13	11	151,734
Tamourad	1	1	4	2	2	0	5,860
Tank	5	3	34	5	4	9	97,477
Tank's Number	11	6	81	21	18	10	192,294
Tank's Prospect	3	3	16	6	1	1	49,738
Taos Tewa Dancer	2	1	17	3	0	2	15,738
Tarakam	12	1	44	1	6	2	25,485
Tarr Road	4	1	29	2	3	7	16,419
Tarsal	8	5	37	6	6	4	51,821
Tasso	4	1	40	3	1	4	20,296
Tasting	2	1	15	2	0	4	10,085
Tatibah (IRE)	1	1	7	2	1	1	12,340
Tatum Canyon	7	3	37	5	5	3	53,743
Tax Collection	22	6	188	12	19	25	98,330
Taylor	1	1	5	1	0	1	1,393
Taylor Road	1	1	15	1	1	2	14,313
Taylor's Special	7	2	35	2	6	7	23,218
Technology	62	31	460	62	52	47	748,627
Tejabo	55	24	474	44	60	62	1,572,103
Tejano	23	13	214	27	26	34	275,039
Tejano Run	48	25	361	50	54	46	1,319,507
Tel Quel (FR)	2	1	17	3	4	3	81,430
Telemarket	2	1	33	5	3	6	40,907
Tella Fib	7	4	39	7	4	5	21,926
Temper Time	3	2	30	2	5	1	25,890
Temperence Hill	28	14	255	28	37	28	415,957
Temperence Two	5	2	36	2	2	3	31,882
Tempolake	2	1	9	1	1	3	52,339
Temptor	41	22	262	29	29	34	373,872
Ten Gold Pots	7	2	63	6	1	6	80,583
Ten Keys	7	3	43	4	3	6	53,519
Ten Sins	2	2	18	5	0	3	28,558
Tenoch	1	1	16	1	0	1	3,865
Tepee Creek	2	2	25	2	10	6	61,803
Terry's Image	2	1	16	3	2	1	24,853
Tethra	60	35	409	62	60	43	2,041,074
Tex R. Rabbit	9	5	101	6	8	14	86,285
Texas City	31	21	244	32	23	40	295,676
Texas Road Runner	1	1	4	1	1	1	2,560
Thank the Bank	3	1	19	3	2	2	22,417
That's a Nice	7	3	57	5	7	7	116,644
Thats Our Buck	30	12	230	24	25	30	406,491
The Cool Virginian	5	2	36	3	4	3	33,198
The Deep (IRE)	2	1	9	1	1	2	41,746
The Gifted One	1	1	12	1	1	0	3,731
The Great Shark	4	3	28	5	7	2	133,095
The Jogger	1	1	13	4	3	3	183,870
The Mad Doctor	1	1	6	1	1	2	2,338
The Miller (FR)	1	1	17	2	3	2	5,357
The Name's Jimmy	51	20	373	36	35	30	519,778
The Pilot	4	3	31	5	2	7	74,625
The Prime Minister	54	19	286	27	24	24	284,294
The Red Rolls	1	1	4	1	0	0	5,867
The Silver Move	3	1	13	1	0	1	9,740
The Vid	31	9	217	13	18	28	203,746
The Wicked North	31	10	162	14	20	20	255,661
Theatre Critic (IRE)	25	8	181	12	9	16	143,805
Theatrical (IRE)	66	21	286	29	31	32	1,356,134
Then Again (IRE)	1	1	14	1	1	2	6,399
Third and Lex	2	1	8	1	0	1	4,200
Thirty Eight Paces	11	6	69	9	8	5	110,352
Thirty Six Red	5	2	54	6	3	3	70,921
This Bulls for You	1	1	5	1	0	0	10,543
This Picture	28	11	183	15	19	21	197,591
Thisjudgeisaprinc	3	2	38	5	4	7	31,571
Thisnearlywasmine	9	6	65	14	12	9	117,762
Thorn Dance	18	8	106	15	10	15	95,846
Three Martinis	3	2	25	2	2	3	36,791
Three Torsions	7	1	50	1	4	9	19,803
Thunder Gulch	87	41	502	56	63	67	1,826,050
Thunder Puddles	19	9	124	13	14	14	200,181
Thunder Rumble	32	12	216	22	25	14	314,452
Thunder Runner	2	1	28	3	5	2	26,232
Thunder Within	1	1	9	2	1	0	10,128
Thundering Force	1	1	6	2	0	1	81,285
Tibrack	5	1	24	1	1	2	26,951
Tiffany Ice	17	4	87	6	4	5	45,025
Tiger Lure	1	1	15	2	1	1	11,324
Tiger Star	5	1	33	3	5	5	16,886
Tiger Tiger	6	4	42	7	6	4	69,570
Tilt the Odds	23	10	130	18	16	15	306,739
Tilt the Stars	2	1	20	2	3	0	15,648
Tilt Up	4	1	22	1	1	6	24,622
Time Bandit	10	5	46	8	8	14	328,928
Time for a Change	9	5	68	10	11	13	126,667
Time to Explode	5	2	28	3	4	1	18,737
Timebank	22	8	136	11	16	19	81,574
Timeless Endeavor	1	1	11	1	1	0	7,337
Timeless Native	8	2	40	3	4	2	21,628
Timely One	1	1	3	1	0	0	11,187
Tinners Way	55	26	389	40	43	53	462,242
Tinterosse (FR)	1	1	2	1	0	0	11,020
Tip On Slew	11	5	77	13	12	9	47,029
Tirade	18	10	107	12	16	14	190,988
Titus Livius (FR)	1	1	3	1	0	0	12,730
To a Wild Kris	1	1	11	3	4	1	25,466
To Freedom	17	7	102	10	13	21	160,913
To the Quick	10	2	65	4	13	7	42,010
Toddy T.	4	2	37	2	4	3	19,210
Tom Cobbley	14	4	93	9	9	10	167,240
Tom Cruiser	5	1	20	2	2	6	25,492
Tomorrows Cat	74	26	314	39	44	38	1,336,519
Tong Po	2	1	20	1	6	3	22,695
Toolighttoquit	30	13	175	17	14	25	323,510
Toooverprime (IRE)	4	2	38	5	6	3	19,742
Toot'n Tudor	1	1	4	1	0	0	6,484
Top Account	62	28	424	48	42	67	755,983
Top Gear	2	1	9	2	2	0	14,996
Top Secret Formula	5	1	20	2	2	3	49,328
Torcher	5	4	37	7	2	4	42,986
Torey Ridge	15	8	76	11	5	13	70,044
Torontonian	11	5	44	7	1	4	22,713
Torrential	57	25	402	35	40	58	650,069
Tory Hole	5	1	32	2	4	2	26,069
Tossofthecoin	64	30	428	46	37	45	996,514
Totem and Taboo	8	2	46	3	5	6	23,172
Touch Gold	85	33	373	48	51	43	2,259,048
Tough Call	7	2	34	4	2	1	49,237
Tough Knight	40	21	246	27	39	39	186,808
Tour d'Or	118	73	982	158	125	118	2,993,015
Tower of Power	9	4	52	6	6	7	50,097
Town Caper	18	11	117	19	11	14	358,938
Track Barron	25	11	161	18	15	16	123,486
Track Dance	1	1	18	3	2	1	14,295
Track Rebel	21	8	151	13	26	17	166,174
Traffic Zack	4	2	40	4	3	5	51,226
Trail City	7	2	25	2	3	8	68,768
Trail Class	2	1	17	3	3	2	21,695
Traitor	37	14	241	21	23	21	389,146
Tralos	3	1	28	3	2	4	36,538

Sire	Perf	Wnrs	Sts	1st	2d	3d	Purses
Trancus	4	1	22	2	0	2	16,474
Trapeze Dancer	14	7	107	11	17	18	113,157
Trapp Mountain	31	14	238	20	21	37	204,177
Treasure Kay	1	1	4	1	0	1	8,525
Treasured One	1	1	5	1	0	0	1,805
Tree	5	2	24	2	5	1	63,385
Treetopper	2	1	16	3	1	3	8,868
Trempolino	48	21	371	31	36	27	529,544
Tri for the Gold	18	12	171	28	12	14	389,094
Tri Line	6	3	35	3	2	2	30,217
Trick Me	14	3	72	7	9	6	85,242
Trick Question	3	3	37	7	3	8	18,564
Tricky Creek	91	49	721	85	92	73	1,278,733
Tricky Fun	36	21	225	32	32	33	309,499
Tricky Six	16	8	99	12	13	12	119,143
Tricky Tab	2	1	15	1	3	2	56,950
Tricon	18	5	112	7	7	15	96,867
Tricuit	4	1	31	2	10	3	26,895
Tridessus	5	2	35	3	1	3	12,366
Triple Sec	5	4	58	9	7	9	55,572
Trouble Onthe Line	3	2	26	3	3	0	15,543
Truce Maker	15	7	138	14	19	24	127,118
Truckee	19	7	139	13	22	21	270,173
Truculent Schular	21	6	115	8	14	10	120,289
Trulo	1	1	7	1	1	1	2,345
Truly Met	5	3	41	7	3	11	80,069
Truman's Tiffany	10	3	62	4	5	9	70,545
Trump an Ace	2	1	8	1	1	0	11,050
Tsunami Slew	19	6	110	6	8	7	97,009
Tuckerstown	2	1	23	5	3	4	48,685
Tuesday's Special	5	2	27	4	0	2	31,997
Tunerup	6	2	56	5	3	8	40,193
Tunnel of Love	3	2	14	2	0	2	10,943
Turbulant World	2	1	16	4	1	2	34,666
Turbulent Dancer	1	1	17	3	2	0	34,120
Turbulent Kris	41	15	221	20	22	24	301,555
Turkoman	83	41	624	71	90	79	1,080,175
Turkonoir	7	2	23	3	4	0	45,119
Turn Out	1	1	5	1	1	0	8,720
Turn West	4	1	25	1	6	4	47,177
Turnberry	3	1	27	1	4	3	9,578
Twanger	1	1	14	1	3	0	20,640
Twice Burned	4	2	49	2	4	6	23,218
Twilight Agenda	67	24	408	37	43	37	516,814
Twin Bridges	2	1	9	1	0	0	17,759
Twin Spires	23	9	110	15	20	16	256,148
Twining	130	76	1,100	150	145	144	2,831,454
Two Bagger	3	3	33	3	5	7	27,327
Two Davids	18	9	155	17	20	19	190,440
Two Punch	157	84	929	142	106	139	2,808,808
Two Smart	1	1	6	1	0	1	17,854
Two's a Plenty	12	4	97	7	5	8	73,968
Tychonic (GB)	27	10	140	13	23	16	193,443
U. S. Flag	13	6	104	13	9	11	138,158
Ulan	3	1	12	1	0	2	4,020
Ulises	9	4	53	9	7	3	202,929
Ultrasonido (ARG)	1	1	8	1	1	1	15,010
Umrigar	4	2	23	3	4	2	106,666
Unaccounted For	96	56	731	105	105	81	2,222,355
Unbridled	121	53	637	93	85	78	5,626,637
Unbridled Success	6	2	46	2	3	3	33,428
Unbridled's Risk	18	5	130	7	11	18	108,281
Unbridled's Song	130	71	649	104	78	84	3,825,586
Uncas Chief	8	2	59	4	9	10	70,631
Undeniable	8	2	39	3	1	5	19,292
Under David's Wing	13	5	60	7	12	4	78,630
Under Orders	2	2	20	3	0	1	8,108
Unfinished Symph	5	2	29	2	5	5	21,761
Unite	29	9	214	17	23	18	191,733
Uno Elite	3	1	8	2	0	1	1,919
Unome	9	2	23	2	2	0	11,010
Unpredictable	9	3	74	7	10	9	41,807
Unreal Currency	5	1	43	1	2	6	17,682
Unreal Zeal	105	68	917	134	98	117	1,742,414
Unsecured	2	1	19	1	6	3	26,717
Unusual Heat	40	22	304	48	39	45	1,535,387
Unusual Performer	3	1	18	2	0	4	45,548
Unzipped	22	9	167	23	29	21	403,142
Up Sharpen	1	1	8	1	0	3	11,826
Up With Your Dukes	1	1	8	1	4	0	39,970
Upmost	6	3	48	10	6	7	51,824
Upping the Ante	28	11	189	17	15	26	396,487
Uprising	1	1	11	3	5	1	7,528
Urgent Request (IRE)	37	15	248	21	30	34	519,599
Urigo	3	2	17	2	3	1	50,476
Val d'Arno	2	1	14	2	3	1	15,422
Valanour (IRE)	2	1	5	1	0	1	44,954
Valdali (IRE)	13	6	109	8	18	17	77,175
Valedero	1	1	10	1	0	1	12,230
Valiant Lark	3	2	30	11	6	2	150,343
Valiant Nature	48	24	330	45	35	45	823,031
Valid Appeal	26	15	232	36	37	28	772,297
Valid Expectations	115	72	896	145	156	118	3,728,127
Valid Trefaire	3	2	21	3	2	5	51,636
Valid Vengeance	9	9	90	12	15	6	194,844
Valid Wager	90	55	707	102	89	99	2,350,593
Valley Crossing	80	39	574	71	70	74	1,535,022
Valoric	3	1	31	1	6	2	46,360
Valorous Prospect	2	2	19	3	2	3	24,562
Van Go	8	3	33	3	2	3	60,871
Varennes	6	2	37	3	3	5	20,622
Variety Road	13	5	61	6	12	9	89,960
Vaudeville	32	15	144	17	15	9	177,186
Vendor	3	1	12	1	0	0	10,310
Ventriloquist	15	2	77	2	7	9	37,112
Verge	1	1	14	1	2	2	14,615
Verification	6	3	39	4	3	5	69,601
Vermont	28	16	213	27	31	20	459,315
Veronica's Sir	2	1	10	2	0	2	21,453
Vert Amande	3	1	13	3	5	2	22,805
Verzy	56	30	412	53	62	51	536,480
Vettori (IRE)	2	1	11	1	1	5	65,644
Via Lombardia (IRE)	3	1	8	1	1	0	21,560
Vice Regent	5	2	42	3	6	2	23,460
Vicksburg	13	4	115	16	12	6	320,441
Victor's Gent	6	2	27	2	1	5	11,821
Victorian General	1	1	5	1	0	1	8,122
Victorian Line	3	1	25	1	2	4	14,560
Victorious	11	6	108	9	8	17	94,597
Victory Gallop	40	11	107	14	16	14	914,179
Victory Speech	76	41	594	86	63	53	1,311,379
Video Ranger	20	10	170	16	15	21	137,551
Vigors	4	2	21	2	2	4	16,582
Vilzak	42	18	261	25	26	42	236,793
Vindictive Silence	3	1	16	1	3	1	8,345
Virginia Rapids	40	29	382	48	53	40	913,859
Vittorioso	1	1	11	3	2	2	31,945
Viva Deputy	11	10	110	18	19	13	185,330
Vivid	4	1	44	3	8	6	80,470
Vixens Native	5	2	24	2	3	1	11,671
Vizard	6	4	45	5	4	10	26,749
Vote Them Out	2	1	13	1	1	3	5,665
Vouch for Me	5	3	42	6	5	6	72,928
Vying Victor	103	54	755	108	100	105	2,123,434
W. D. Jacks	2	1	20	1	1	2	13,515
Wa Bert	9	6	70	9	8	8	76,058
Wabasha	3	1	16	2	1	2	9,930
Waco Connection	9	5	64	6	11	7	52,821
Wagon Limit	10	5	40	7	6	8	318,950
Wait Till Monday (IRE)	2	1	14	1	1	0	5,397
Wajir	10	5	49	7	2	5	76,866
Wake Up Alarm	11	4	93	11	16	7	94,992
Waki Bob	16	4	64	7	8	10	128,780
Waki Warrior	19	10	145	13	12	13	128,745
Walesa	13	4	61	7	9	2	53,818
Wall Street Dancer	21	12	180	22	27	19	246,830
Wallenda	38	17	318	30	38	42	401,612
Walsingham	1	1	6	2	0	2	8,160
Walter Willy (IRE)	48	22	324	34	42	38	527,287
Waltzing Along	4	3	30	3	3	7	34,904
Wander Kind	4	3	32	3	5	4	30,952
Wanpum	11	3	74	5	5	4	18,236
Waquoit	93	47	654	98	102	78	1,826,931
War	11	5	84	5	3	6	50,780
War Deputy	56	29	427	55	52	50	1,738,196
War Machine	3	2	30	3	1	2	35,503
War Secretary	3	2	32	5	3	3	70,002
Wardrobe Test	4	3	28	3	2	5	38,590

RECORDS OF SIRES

Sire	Perf	Wnrs	Sts	1st	2d	3d	Purses
Warfield	9	5	67	9	17	12	39,095
Warlaunch	3	2	15	2	1	0	7,697
Warner Jones	2	1	20	1	3	3	9,667
Warning (GB)	5	3	29	6	4	3	168,718
Warrantor	2	1	20	1	3	1	13,740
Wasa	3	2	31	4	3	5	20,488
Washita County	2	1	19	1	2	1	7,648
Watch Me Mom	1	1	10	3	4	0	36,234
Water Bank	24	10	131	14	14	12	95,154
Water Gate	3	2	50	3	7	5	28,097
Wave to Seattle	1	1	10	2	2	0	52,560
Wavering Amigo	5	1	27	1	0	2	14,438
Wavering Monarch	59	30	441	55	50	37	704,920
Way West (FR)	76	39	553	65	68	59	1,364,935
Way Wild	6	2	46	2	3	4	20,815
Wayne County (IRE)	66	35	431	60	54	49	1,117,955
Wayne's Crane	52	31	413	68	41	49	631,658
Wee Thunder	7	2	25	4	1	5	50,932
Weekend Guest	51	28	324	39	42	53	511,196
Weekend Truce	2	1	14	1	0	2	8,460
Weiss Rennen	4	2	26	4	5	2	35,881
Wekiva Springs	126	64	838	103	112	102	1,776,811
Weldnaas	1	1	9	4	0	0	26,520
Well Decorated	63	36	514	60	68	58	628,500
Well Selected	5	2	32	2	3	5	65,181
Wertaloona	10	4	40	6	5	8	112,408
Weshaam	51	20	400	29	54	44	715,842
West Acre	21	14	131	21	17	19	564,382
West Buoyant	12	4	81	4	6	6	59,955
West by West	171	104	1,399	183	162	179	2,975,350
Western Borders	10	3	35	3	4	6	72,260
Western Cat	31	19	299	31	29	28	435,711
Western City	2	1	21	1	5	6	16,180
Western Echo	28	9	182	14	18	30	229,379
Western Fame	37	21	196	33	22	27	635,961
Western Gentleman	20	10	123	21	15	13	258,045
Western Jove	5	2	29	3	2	4	14,686
Western Miner	19	4	124	8	4	13	114,113
Western Playboy	25	13	193	20	23	23	327,892
Western Regent	1	1	7	1	2	0	6,300
Western Trick	44	22	320	30	26	46	327,181
Westminster	13	9	71	11	9	7	91,213
Westway	2	1	9	2	2	1	3,725
Whadjathink	6	4	24	7	2	1	64,560
Wharf	3	1	14	1	1	1	39,282
What a Copelan	1	1	15	4	0	2	35,905
What a Gent	3	1	18	1	1	3	5,781
What a Shock	8	4	46	6	5	7	52,750
What a Spell	10	6	61	12	9	7	173,048
Whatever For	8	3	45	7	4	5	93,039
Wheatly Hall	9	3	66	6	6	3	77,793
Wheaton	61	36	472	61	77	57	949,352
Whiskey Wisdom	65	32	378	44	51	46	2,035,214
White Mischief	2	1	13	1	2	3	30,200
White Rammer	2	1	6	1	2	1	16,413
White Tie Tryst	6	5	49	7	3	10	91,079
Whitebrush	10	5	58	6	7	6	110,520
Whitney Tower	89	41	603	63	63	74	982,708
Whiz Along	9	5	109	10	11	10	123,366
Who's John Galt	3	1	8	2	1	0	32,395
Whodam	4	1	19	1	0	0	3,150
Whosinfront	3	1	13	1	1	1	6,328
Wild Again	125	69	851	116	118	128	4,744,488
Wild Deputy	34	11	204	19	28	25	438,558
Wild Escapade	47	30	332	54	47	38	932,005
Wild Event	22	11	96	14	5	9	258,723
Wild Gale	11	5	79	10	5	10	175,616
Wild Gold	39	24	244	36	29	33	532,339
Wild Harmony	2	2	18	3	3	0	78,234
Wild Invader	18	8	112	13	12	6	140,926
Wild Kiss	9	5	110	11	14	11	141,708
Wild Phantom	8	4	42	5	6	4	33,799
Wild Rush	86	49	494	91	82	57	2,548,056
Wild Syn	17	5	88	10	10	10	118,076
Wild Too	2	1	20	1	0	1	3,000
Wild Wonder	21	8	66	9	6	12	197,015
Wild Zone	111	57	719	93	81	92	1,684,562
Wilde Rufo (GB)	4	1	42	1	6	6	42,774
Will Be Dancing	11	6	80	11	13	11	76,881
Will Win	1	1	8	3	1	0	2,667
Will's Way	52	33	357	62	53	47	1,189,099
Willard Scott	4	2	23	2	1	1	23,600
Williamstown	79	40	584	68	70	80	1,312,269
Willing Worker	5	1	22	1	0	2	13,928
Willowy Ambassador	4	3	24	4	3	0	142,916
Win M All	8	4	72	6	5	8	101,790
Wind and Wuthering	2	1	16	1	5	2	10,448
Wind Chill	2	2	14	4	1	3	44,520
Wind Flyer	4	4	36	7	8	5	66,207
Windsor Blaze	4	2	30	2	7	4	24,011
Windy'slittleman	1	1	3	1	0	0	3,260
Wing Commander	5	2	29	2	1	0	10,578
Winsum Bucks	1	1	4	1	0	1	5,126
Winter Halo	25	12	145	15	10	24	160,020
Winthrop	9	3	20	3	4	2	28,571
Wise Times	1	1	8	2	0	1	6,347
With Approval	155	74	1,080	126	127	111	2,539,789
With It	14	8	106	12	16	13	75,758
Wolf Power (SAF)	92	33	563	60	58	69	834,263
Wolf Touch	14	8	72	11	13	3	104,177
Wolfire	3	1	15	2	1	4	5,684
Wollaston	3	1	12	4	0	0	21,500
Won Song	8	3	69	7	11	8	111,849
Wood	2	1	11	2	1	1	9,932
Wood Reply	2	2	17	4	2	2	15,498
Woodman	133	65	823	106	68	93	2,669,346
Woody Win	5	1	31	1	0	1	5,906
World Appeal	27	7	198	11	19	14	94,102
World Order	2	2	17	2	1	0	9,004
World Stage (IRE)	59	21	400	33	38	45	386,966
Worldly	8	3	35	5	3	3	18,142
Worldwide (IRE)	1	1	10	1	1	0	5,556
Worthingtonhills	2	1	6	1	0	1	6,800
Xray	14	4	75	6	9	10	88,951
Yankee Fan	32	12	203	21	21	22	136,839
Yarrow Brae	37	14	236	25	38	32	697,519
Yellow Creek	1	1	26	3	4	3	13,691
Yesterdays Hero	4	2	32	3	1	5	17,303
Yeti	4	4	43	4	9	7	53,169
Yoh May Kenta	2	1	8	2	0	1	14,205
Yoonevano	17	5	73	9	8	11	264,311
York Shire (ARG)	1	1	9	3	1	0	44,700
You and I	98	60	711	106	105	89	2,523,314
You're No Bargain	2	1	19	2	2	1	9,230
Youmadeyourpoint	17	11	143	12	23	27	273,570
Young Devil	7	5	44	10	4	6	113,555
Young Ralph	6	4	63	5	4	10	84,398
Young Turk	9	2	28	3	1	4	35,430
Your Majestic	3	1	24	1	1	2	23,613
Yukon	6	2	34	4	3	2	29,682
Yukon Son	2	1	13	2	1	5	5,529
Z Z Cat	35	15	248	25	29	26	346,414
Zafarrancho (ARG)	12	4	111	7	9	17	109,849
Zafonic	12	3	69	3	12	12	294,924
Zagor	10	3	64	5	4	5	57,199
Zalipour	3	1	13	1	1	3	14,055
Zamboni	7	2	39	3	8	8	39,104
Zamindar	2	2	5	3	1	1	202,800
Zapped	9	6	81	9	12	9	42,450
Zarbyev	58	32	443	48	58	51	1,044,727
Zealot	1	1	7	1	0	0	4,613
Zeeruler	14	3	99	8	12	17	70,640
Zen	6	3	41	6	2	7	166,356
Zero for Conduct	1	1	12	2	2	2	23,029
Ziad	2	1	15	1	2	2	7,850
Zie World	3	2	20	3	3	2	16,161
Zieten	6	3	50	5	5	8	168,780
Ziggy's Boy	4	2	38	4	5	5	46,110
Zigiante	2	1	21	1	2	5	36,503
Zignew	13	5	75	8	8	5	103,510
Zocor	3	1	10	1	0	0	7,900
Zuppardo's Crown	5	1	23	1	2	2	12,185
Zuppardo's Future	12	4	75	6	8	11	92,975
Zuppardo's Love	4	2	20	2	0	4	26,406
Zuppardo's Prince	63	22	379	29	50	42	509,332

2003
RECORDS OF
JUVENILE SIRES

The record of each juvenile sire
represented by at least one winning
thoroughbred or more who raced in
the United States or Canada in 2003,
showing his total performers, number
of winning performers, the number
of times they started and their
total placings and earnings.

RECORDS OF JUVENILE SIRES

Juvenile Sire	Perf	Wnrs	Sts	1st	2d	3d	Purses
A Man of Class	3	1	9	1	0	1	$9,296
A. P Jet	21	3	43	3	5	4	76,407
A.P. Indy	44	18	125	23	22	10	1,114,966
Abaginone	10	2	35	2	2	5	36,008
Absent Russian	3	1	16	1	2	1	16,115
Abstract	5	2	14	2	1	2	10,610
Accelerator	44	12	160	15	18	15	328,541
Acceptable	17	8	66	9	5	7	163,518
Act Smart	2	1	7	3	1	0	70,358
Activist	3	1	10	1	2	0	10,154
Adhocracy	1	1	7	1	2	1	12,328
Afternoon Deelites	20	9	83	12	17	13	366,280
Aggie Southpaw	4	2	14	2	2	1	29,683
Ago	7	3	26	3	7	3	65,948
Alamocitos	5	3	19	5	1	6	184,520
Alfaari	6	2	18	2	3	4	30,300
All Gone	12	4	50	6	4	9	110,799
Alleged Account	1	1	4	1	0	0	11,500
Allen Charge	5	2	11	2	0	0	28,530
Allen's Prospect	24	6	65	6	7	7	168,147
Allied Forces	8	2	23	2	5	3	126,214
Alnaab	4	1	10	1	3	0	12,567
Aloha Prospector	4	3	21	4	3	4	72,275
Alphabet Soup	26	6	86	7	5	9	144,554
Always Fair	3	1	8	1	1	0	9,100
Alybro	3	1	20	3	3	1	66,219
Alydeed	14	2	49	4	2	8	169,827
Alyhuista	1	1	5	3	1	0	49,017
Amaruk	1	1	5	1	1	0	8,159
Ameri Valay	3	3	18	4	2	4	98,672
American Champ	3	2	16	4	1	2	38,180
American Chance	29	11	88	17	13	7	457,090
American Standard	3	1	5	1	0	1	9,681
Amigo Menor (IRE)	2	1	8	1	1	0	5,932
Andean Chasqui	1	1	5	1	1	0	11,120
Anet	14	5	45	7	4	5	165,777
Announce	23	5	76	6	6	8	110,524
Anziyan	6	3	19	4	0	3	48,283
Apollo	2	1	6	1	1	2	14,042
Appealing Skier	24	16	97	17	15	10	327,824
Arch	22	7	67	7	11	10	207,842
Archers Bay	22	7	66	7	9	12	513,021
Artax	24	3	53	4	7	7	203,790
Artema (IRE)	1	1	4	1	1	1	9,645
Artic Tracker	1	1	4	1	1	0	12,760
Ascot Knight	8	1	14	1	1	2	43,292
Atticus	13	1	24	1	2	2	33,333
Avenue of Flags	12	3	37	6	4	6	206,807
Awad	11	2	27	2	0	2	23,678
Awesome Again	18	6	49	8	5	7	316,989
Awesome Cat	2	1	7	1	0	0	7,538
B. G.'s Drone	2	1	5	1	0	0	14,130
Bag	9	2	29	4	7	1	128,951
Bahri	3	2	14	3	2	2	46,270
Ball's Bluff	2	1	6	1	2	2	27,335
Banjo	4	1	6	1	3	0	14,158
Banker's Gold	26	8	91	11	12	10	184,374
Baquero	20	7	78	12	10	9	174,595
Barkerville	11	1	27	1	1	4	74,059
Barricade	5	2	16	2	3	2	12,864
Bartok (IRE)	5	1	26	1	4	7	149,197
Basket Weave	18	12	70	14	9	9	107,354
Beau Genius	24	7	99	9	11	13	238,943
Beefchopper	5	2	13	2	4	1	18,142
Belek	4	3	23	4	4	0	54,167
Believe It	9	1	26	1	0	1	22,945
Belong to Me	24	10	71	11	11	7	405,627
Benchmark	15	9	57	17	9	4	563,129
Benny the Dip	6	2	11	3	2	2	70,207
Benton Creek	19	7	57	7	5	6	61,333
Bertrando	22	8	61	9	12	12	377,898
Bianconi	26	12	72	13	6	10	205,216

Juvenile Sire	Perf	Wnrs	Sts	1st	2d	3d	Purses
Big Jewel	4	3	26	6	1	4	58,786
Big Pistol	4	1	12	1	0	1	24,284
Big Sky Chester	1	1	4	2	1	0	16,317
Binalong	4	2	18	3	5	1	53,710
Bionic Prospect	1	1	5	1	1	1	14,370
Birdonthewire	9	3	25	4	4	1	91,377
Black Mackee	5	1	14	1	3	0	22,421
Blazing Fire	6	2	13	2	0	3	17,756
Blumin Affair	14	5	43	9	8	8	205,209
Blushing Star	1	1	3	1	1	0	13,895
Bobby B Free	1	1	10	1	1	2	9,903
Bold Anthony	14	1	37	3	3	2	68,627
Bold Badgett	7	3	40	7	5	7	191,259
Bold Executive	16	8	69	11	11	12	639,798
Bold n' Flashy	10	2	26	2	1	2	82,107
Bon Point (GB)	8	2	28	2	3	1	81,320
Bonus Money (GB)	13	4	68	5	6	8	100,021
Bonus Time Cat	3	2	19	4	3	2	52,860
Boone's Mill	4	1	24	1	4	2	26,675
Born Wild	7	2	25	3	1	5	26,214
Boston Harbor	34	18	125	24	12	15	667,301
Bound by Honor	2	1	7	1	0	0	6,139
Boundary	15	8	46	13	7	5	386,078
Brass Minister	5	4	20	4	2	2	33,281
Brian's Time	1	1	2	1	0	0	27,840
Brick House	2	1	8	1	1	3	16,328
Bright Launch	6	4	21	5	3	3	137,767
Broad Brush	11	5	33	7	2	3	245,563
Brunswick	5	1	12	1	1	2	31,595
Buck Strider	4	1	25	1	0	2	12,690
Bucky Raj	3	1	10	1	0	0	8,029
Bugatti Reef (IRE)	5	1	11	1	1	2	11,424
Bull Inthe Heather	3	1	8	2	0	0	5,683
Bustopher Jones	6	4	12	5	2	1	17,320
Byars	5	2	18	2	1	1	14,700
C Spot Go	1	1	10	1	3	2	8,682
Cahill Road	15	5	53	7	8	6	126,980
Caller I. D.	22	7	80	8	15	10	190,052
Canaveral	12	1	32	1	3	4	26,184
Candi's Gold	11	2	35	3	2	4	52,807
Candid Cameron	2	1	6	1	0	2	8,754
Candy Stripes	8	4	34	5	3	2	96,737
Canvas	2	1	5	1	0	2	9,345
Canyon Creek (IRE)	12	4	33	4	0	2	107,495
Canyon Run	2	1	3	1	1	0	21,580
Cape Town	26	9	69	15	9	6	554,002
Capote	22	6	69	10	6	5	399,654
Capote's Prospect	9	4	32	4	2	2	38,647
Cappuccio	4	1	16	1	0	3	13,866
Captain Bash	2	1	5	2	0	1	4,914
Captain Bodgit	25	10	80	14	11	10	403,757
Capture the Gold	3	1	11	1	0	0	23,482
Car Dealer	2	1	6	1	0	0	8,255
Carnivalay	8	5	40	5	5	5	115,077
Carolina Kid	4	2	12	2	0	1	18,844
Carr de Naskra	4	1	9	2	1	0	30,541
Carson City	28	13	92	19	13	13	803,926
Cartwright	18	5	84	5	9	8	131,450
Cat Doctor	5	1	17	1	3	2	12,352
Cat's Career	19	7	78	14	5	5	165,595
Catastrophic	4	1	11	1	3	2	16,690
Category Five	7	4	24	7	4	1	119,459
Catillac	6	2	17	2	4	1	41,496
Cee's Tizzy	15	5	35	6	3	5	213,226
Chanate	10	3	27	3	4	4	49,873
Chapel Creek	5	1	15	1	1	0	16,696
Charismatic	35	5	108	6	7	14	228,766
Chelsey Cat	6	4	35	5	3	8	94,140
Cherokee Run	35	13	127	17	13	13	664,678
Chopin	6	3	22	3	2	3	30,145
Ciano Cat	17	7	57	10	4	6	145,865
Cien Fuegos	9	2	33	2	4	2	33,112

Juvenile Sire	Perf	Wnrs	Sts	1st	2d	3d	Purses
Cimarron Secret	7	3	17	3	0	0	20,026
Circus Surprise	1	1	4	1	0	1	11,850
Cisco Road	4	2	15	3	2	5	24,852
Citidancer	9	3	21	4	0	2	58,230
Claramount	2	1	6	1	2	1	14,460
Classified Facts	2	1	5	1	0	0	17,160
Classy Prospector	7	1	34	1	3	8	31,688
Claudius	1	1	6	4	2	0	99,816
Clear Course	4	1	26	1	2	0	34,344
Clever Trick	14	3	44	3	5	4	69,956
Cloud Cover	9	3	31	5	4	1	76,485
Cobra King	14	4	34	4	6	2	80,630
Codys Key	2	1	5	1	0	0	12,894
Cold Bid	4	3	25	4	3	5	78,772
Colony Light	16	8	84	10	9	10	180,894
Combat Ready	5	2	13	2	1	3	25,471
Comet Shine	8	1	37	1	4	2	34,252
Comic Strip	17	3	42	4	4	5	99,460
Commemorate	9	2	25	2	2	3	44,333
Compadre	6	2	22	3	1	3	191,426
Composer	4	1	20	1	2	2	17,325
Comstock Lode	11	1	34	1	2	4	37,970
Concern	12	4	54	4	7	5	152,116
Concerto	19	12	70	14	8	9	301,499
Concorde's Tune	7	3	39	3	6	6	65,544
Confide	28	7	95	9	11	13	341,474
Connecticut	1	1	2	1	0	0	7,560
Conquistador Cielo	25	4	82	6	8	13	259,582
Conroe	1	1	5	1	1	0	4,916
Consigliere (GB)	9	3	22	3	4	2	35,233
Constant Demand	2	1	10	1	0	1	11,455
Conveyor	1	1	8	2	1	1	23,295
Cool Halo	3	2	10	2	0	2	15,252
Copper Man	1	1	4	1	0	0	1,820
Coronado's Quest	29	5	67	7	5	8	536,328
Corslew	6	2	19	2	1	1	20,357
Corwyn	6	1	11	1	0	0	8,220
Count the Time	21	10	85	13	10	6	289,380
Covered Wagon	3	1	14	1	2	1	8,585
Cozzene	14	1	46	1	5	10	141,577
Crafty	7	1	17	1	1	0	4,795
Crafty Dude	4	3	35	3	5	4	34,610
Crafty Friend	31	10	93	12	10	5	240,889
Crafty Prospector	23	12	73	13	18	9	394,808
Creative Act	2	1	4	1	0	0	14,009
Crimcino	2	2	7	2	1	3	22,400
Crown Ambassador	8	4	24	4	3	2	71,036
Crown Attorney	10	1	24	1	1	3	49,785
Crown Pleasure	1	1	13	1	2	2	11,515
Crusader Sword	4	2	11	2	0	0	12,470
Crypto Star	16	6	51	9	6	8	222,077
Cryptoclearance	38	10	134	13	14	12	346,186
Cutlass Reality	4	4	12	4	3	0	36,225
Cyberspace	5	1	27	1	3	2	35,850
D. C. Tenacious	5	2	13	2	0	1	16,577
D. J. Cat	8	4	20	5	1	3	68,564
Dance Brightly	36	17	147	19	13	16	360,657
Dance Floor	9	5	35	5	5	6	64,033
Dancinwiththedevil	1	1	1	1	0	0	14,250
Danzatore	12	3	46	4	7	4	89,407
Danzig	5	2	10	3	2	0	91,905
Dariyoun	2	1	6	1	1	1	11,399
Darn That Alarm	7	2	27	2	2	2	24,925
Dawn Quixote	3	1	10	1	2	1	17,560
Dayjur	7	3	19	4	1	2	50,379
De Guerin	3	1	10	1	2	0	22,913
De Niro	6	1	19	2	4	1	62,804
Deerhound	7	3	20	3	2	3	40,348
Defensive Play	6	2	33	2	3	5	36,324
Defrere	26	11	75	13	9	11	235,919
Delineator	9	5	38	5	7	8	62,333
Demaloot Demashoot	9	3	27	4	6	0	44,179

Sire	Perf	Wnrs	Sts	1st	2d	3d	Purses
Demidoff	28	10	94	12	7	13	206,943
Demons Begone	15	5	38	5	2	8	68,292
Denouncer	3	1	8	1	2	1	37,510
Deposit Ticket	6	1	16	1	6	1	47,930
Deputy Commander	26	5	86	7	10	9	224,188
Deputy Minister	23	4	52	4	8	5	191,379
Desert Classic	3	1	12	1	0	2	19,562
Desert God	1	1	5	1	1	1	17,950
Desert Royalty	4	4	24	7	5	1	135,269
Desert Wine	7	2	20	2	2	4	17,465
Detox	2	1	5	1	1	0	11,610
Devil Begone	8	2	21	2	2	3	27,644
Devil His Due	20	6	60	11	6	7	198,403
Devil On Ice	5	1	18	1	2	1	14,060
Devil's Bag	14	4	42	4	6	4	116,203
Devious Course	8	2	27	2	5	2	29,305
Devon Lane	17	8	47	10	11	3	171,734
Diamond	20	6	55	7	11	4	175,555
Diamond Sword	6	1	10	1	1	0	9,133
Diesis (GB)	5	1	15	1	2	4	46,912
Diligence	16	7	64	8	5	1	153,584
Din's Dancer	3	1	10	1	1	1	11,385
Diplomatic Jet	5	2	17	2	4	1	34,600
Direct Hit	6	2	10	2	1	1	28,810
Dismissed	1	1	3	1	0	0	5,775
Distant View	11	4	33	6	3	1	136,756
Distinctive Cat	26	10	91	10	13	19	249,993
Distinctive Pro	10	2	30	3	4	5	156,803
Distorted Humor	29	13	76	16	6	12	660,199
Dixie Brass	6	1	15	2	0	3	157,036
Dixieland Band	21	7	59	11	7	5	338,097
Dixieland Brass	9	2	26	2	6	4	117,706
Dixieland Heat	9	3	26	6	2	3	102,993
Doc's Leader	7	3	19	5	1	2	133,952
Doneraile Court	37	16	154	24	25	18	768,687
Doppler	1	1	3	1	0	1	6,300
Double D. Slew	1	1	5	1	1	0	8,507
Double Honor	40	23	172	31	26	21	576,513
Double Niner	7	2	33	2	5	6	55,564
Dove Hunt	22	10	105	12	14	11	268,667
Dr Fong	1	1	3	1	1	1	27,400
Dr. Adagio	7	3	36	4	8	1	112,588
Dr. Caton	13	5	51	7	6	5	135,041
Dr. Giggles	3	1	12	1	1	0	5,090
Dry Gulch	2	2	14	5	3	2	198,085
Dubious Connection	1	1	4	1	2	0	16,159
Dumaani	9	4	46	5	8	3	121,461
Dusty Screen	6	1	23	1	6	3	56,787
Dynaformer	12	7	47	9	6	10	318,778
Eastern Echo	13	6	58	8	5	2	132,735
Editor's Note	19	10	79	13	8	8	252,368
El Amante	17	5	59	8	10	6	137,843
El Prado (IRE)	28	11	88	19	8	11	761,232
Elegant Life	1	1	7	1	0	0	4,845
Eltish	13	6	33	8	6	5	202,194
Elusive Quality	36	10	91	11	9	12	429,167
Emancipator	5	2	14	2	2	3	53,815
Emerald Creme	4	2	31	3	4	3	42,342
Epic Honor	9	3	30	3	2	4	49,112
Erland	2	1	7	1	0	1	8,874
Esteem	5	3	16	4	5	1	98,864
Etbauer	4	1	6	1	0	0	6,960
Evansville Slew	7	5	30	8	3	5	138,632
Evening Kris	4	2	12	2	3	4	97,980
Event of the Year	12	3	36	3	11	7	144,651
Excavate	14	1	31	1	3	1	31,503
Exclusive Enough	2	1	10	1	2	1	10,496
Exclusive Era	7	2	20	2	1	5	22,388
Executive Order	1	1	6	1	0	0	29,610
Expanding Man	1	1	2	1	0	0	6,570
Expelled	18	7	70	9	10	9	228,050
Exploding Rainbow	2	1	7	1	2	1	10,720

Sire	Perf	Wnrs	Sts	1st	2d	3d	Purses
Exploit	43	14	145	15	20	19	515,992
Explosive Red	23	5	76	5	15	7	180,587
Fabulous Champ	14	3	50	3	7	4	113,479
Fabulous Frolic	13	1	42	2	3	6	30,814
Falkenham (GB)	4	1	19	2	0	2	25,940
Family Calling	33	17	178	24	25	23	519,840
Fantastic Fellow	7	3	20	3	2	3	30,257
Fashion Find	4	1	22	2	3	6	37,917
Fasliyev	3	1	12	1	3	0	74,732
Fast Account	3	2	10	2	1	0	17,755
Fast Play	13	5	40	7	4	2	140,151
Favorite Trick	17	9	65	11	10	9	204,539
Faygo	5	2	18	2	1	2	32,650
Feel the Power	2	2	10	2	1	0	26,649
Ferrara	4	2	21	2	0	3	17,753
Feu d'Enfer	4	2	17	2	3	3	29,856
Fincher Branch	1	1	4	1	0	0	5,370
Finest Hour	14	8	51	12	3	9	296,527
First and Only	5	2	15	2	1	1	20,630
First Patriot	1	1	5	1	2	0	32,020
Fit to Fight	18	6	58	6	6	8	107,448
Fly a Kite (IRE)	1	1	1	1	0	0	5,820
Fly So Free	11	4	34	4	2	5	58,539
Flying Continental	9	3	37	4	9	1	201,563
Flying Victor	7	3	29	3	5	2	60,847
Flying With Eagles	5	1	7	1	0	1	11,850
Foreign Holding	1	1	5	2	0	0	28,215
Forest Gazelle	4	4	21	5	2	4	65,247
Forest Wildcat	42	23	136	27	19	14	837,625
Forestry	19	11	65	18	12	14	716,645
Forli Winds	1	1	3	1	0	0	7,596
Formal Dinner	30	12	152	18	25	18	462,161
Formal Gold	21	10	62	10	3	7	204,449
Fortunate Prospect	23	14	125	19	20	12	293,580
Forty Won	11	2	30	3	1	3	58,207
Foxtrail	1	1	4	2	1	1	162,170
Free At Last	11	3	48	3	9	8	44,351
Free House	21	7	83	9	7	10	349,079
French Deputy	17	8	52	9	5	5	226,721
French Legionaire	1	1	6	1	0	0	8,434
French Parliament	5	2	21	2	4	4	36,760
Friendly Lover	21	10	103	13	17	9	259,250
Frisk Me Now	11	3	32	3	5	2	66,581
Fruition	4	1	13	1	3	1	32,860
Funboy	2	1	9	1	1	0	10,871
Furiously	4	2	9	2	0	0	18,450
Future Storm	8	3	37	3	3	3	50,531
Gallant Step	3	1	9	1	3	1	16,020
Game Plan	22	8	75	9	11	15	151,471
General Meeting	15	5	42	6	7	7	245,840
General Royal	18	5	70	8	14	10	204,145
Gentlemen (ARG)	19	4	63	4	4	10	96,142
Get Me Out	4	2	9	3	2	1	32,729
Gettin Over	1	1	4	2	0	0	21,557
Ghazi	22	4	79	6	10	11	247,033
Ghost Ranch	3	1	10	1	0	1	11,924
Ghostly Moves	8	2	24	2	5	8	98,007
Gilded Time	18	6	67	7	8	10	178,478
Glaring	6	1	8	1	0	0	8,202
Glitterman	18	9	69	13	15	11	392,611
Gogarty (IRE)	1	1	4	2	0	1	40,800
Gold Alert	2	1	3	1	0	0	10,225
Gold Case	32	11	104	16	17	18	664,913
Gold Fever	40	8	121	12	18	14	650,260
Gold Legend	15	6	52	9	5	11	199,844
Gold Market	3	1	18	1	2	2	17,138
Gold Meridian	9	1	18	1	0	3	11,725
Gold Regent	17	7	53	8	9	7	165,418
Gold Ruler	6	2	19	2	2	6	30,493
Gold Token	25	7	66	7	11	9	249,331
Golden Gear	18	7	71	10	12	4	201,050
Goldminers Gold	1	1	2	1	0	0	17,820

Juvenile Sire	Perf	Wnrs	Sts	1st	2d	3d	Purses
Gone for Real	3	1	4	1	0	1	8,870
Gone West	12	1	29	1	1	7	67,123
Good and Tough	20	9	80	11	13	10	352,341
Goodbye Doeny	18	2	52	2	5	11	71,469
Gothic Revival	5	2	21	2	0	2	21,675
Grand Slam	42	14	115	23	20	22	1,369,174
Graydon Pool	1	1	3	1	0	0	12,192
Great Gladiator	4	1	12	1	1	1	37,014
Grey Counter	1	1	5	1	1	1	30,502
Grey West	1	1	2	1	0	0	6,861
Grindstone	18	8	58	12	11	4	659,176
Groomstick	5	1	11	1	0	1	34,415
Groovy	3	2	17	2	2	2	32,014
Gulch	10	4	32	7	8	2	539,019
Gumboy	1	1	5	1	0	1	4,690
Hadif	25	14	121	15	16	11	245,166
Haint	4	3	13	5	1	1	39,990
Half Term	13	4	38	4	5	4	133,058
Halissee	1	1	7	1	1	1	17,850
Halo's Image	23	9	109	18	11	19	892,481
Halory Hunter	19	5	70	6	8	8	123,422
Halos and Horns	8	2	31	3	7	4	69,890
Hay Halo	11	3	41	7	7	3	248,571
Hazaam	14	9	75	12	9	13	226,942
He's a Looker	5	1	10	1	1	0	10,322
He's Tops	14	4	49	5	9	7	71,312
Heaven's Wish	1	1	4	1	0	0	8,080
Helmsman	10	2	32	2	12	6	128,827
Hennessy	30	12	83	19	6	2	601,014
Here We Come	9	3	21	4	1	1	32,490
Hesabull	5	3	12	4	2	0	57,600
Hey Rob	6	1	12	1	2	0	7,247
Hickory Ridge	3	1	15	1	1	2	10,780
High Brite	13	5	47	5	12	5	94,860
Highland Ruckus	9	5	19	5	2	2	43,289
Historic	6	1	13	1	1	1	22,233
Hoedown's Day	1	1	9	1	0	1	16,050
Hold for Gold	9	3	27	3	8	4	75,982
Hold On Chris	3	1	16	1	0	1	12,525
Hollywood Reporter	4	1	18	1	4	5	35,938
Holy Bull	17	2	49	2	6	7	81,740
Holy Mountain	11	2	27	4	2	3	93,836
Holzmeister	17	6	73	8	13	8	174,958
Home At Last	4	1	13	1	1	1	29,079
Homebuilder	4	2	15	2	1	1	41,202
Honest Ensign	3	1	7	1	0	0	11,820
Honkytonk Blaze	1	1	8	1	1	2	9,368
Honor Grades	22	9	78	12	10	8	270,040
Honorable Hero	2	1	10	1	1	1	29,108
Honour and Glory	36	10	101	15	16	18	487,049
Horse Chestnut (SAF)	15	4	38	4	7	1	177,941
Houston	3	1	12	3	1	1	25,003
Houston Sunrise	1	1	1	1	0	0	6,489
Hubble	2	1	6	1	0	1	9,409
Humble Eleven	2	2	10	2	2	0	26,240
Hunter's Glory	1	1	4	1	0	2	3,772
Hunter's Phone	1	1	4	1	0	1	15,280
Hunting Hard	4	1	13	1	2	0	34,369
Hurlingham	2	1	8	1	1	1	5,110
I Can't Believe	14	6	53	8	4	5	283,356
I'ma Hell Raiser	6	1	10	1	1	0	21,924
Iam the Iceman	4	1	16	1	4	4	50,280
Idabel	6	1	11	1	0	1	26,390
Ide	11	7	51	7	6	2	116,228
Ihtimam	2	2	6	2	0	0	7,761
Imperial Falcon	4	1	17	1	2	3	26,752
In a Walk	3	1	14	2	3	0	91,790
In Case	17	5	56	5	6	9	108,785
In Excess (IRE)	17	4	49	4	7	6	129,484
In Excessive Bull	17	9	56	16	5	9	270,906
Incurable Optimist	7	3	31	3	3	4	153,472
Indian Charlie	21	7	79	11	11	18	420,710

Juvenile Sire	Perf	Wnrs	Sts	1st	2d	3d	Purses	Sire	Perf	Wnrs	Sts	1st	2d	3d	Purses
Indy Mood	8	1	19	1	0	0	9,114	Lite the Fuse	21	9	75	10	8	17	268,648
Inspired Prospect	3	1	8	1	0	0	37,886	Literati	2	1	5	1	0	2	11,900
Intensity	6	1	11	1	0	0	25,230	Lived It Up	2	1	5	1	0	0	7,786
Irish Open	12	4	64	4	7	8	41,896	Lord At Law	3	1	19	2	2	2	58,629
Irish River (FR)	2	1	6	1	0	0	33,256	Lord Avie	13	2	26	4	2	0	147,952
Is It True	16	6	68	7	8	10	268,829	Lord Carson	18	9	78	14	14	7	441,296
Island Whirl	3	1	8	1	3	0	21,810	Lost Code	12	5	50	5	7	8	107,032
Islefaxyou	13	2	41	4	3	6	79,213	Lost Soldier	28	11	104	14	12	13	640,364
Itaka	4	1	14	1	0	1	17,405	Louis Quatorze	29	8	87	11	11	6	355,078
Iz a Saros	2	1	24	2	4	0	64,890	Louisiana Slew	1	1	4	1	1	0	16,500
J P Hamer	3	1	26	1	2	6	17,939	Lucayan Prince	4	1	15	2	1	1	38,415
Jack Wilson	4	2	17	2	2	4	28,789	Lucky Lionel	28	12	94	14	11	10	427,958
Jade Hunter	15	2	38	2	10	1	109,672	Lucky North	10	2	31	3	2	6	44,618
Jaggery John	1	1	6	1	1	1	14,088	Lucky Roberto	11	2	28	4	1	4	146,423
Jazzing Around	6	2	17	5	1	1	35,446	Lucky So n' So	4	2	13	2	2	4	31,251
Jeblar	13	3	58	6	4	6	124,699	Lucky South	1	1	1	1	0	0	5,880
Jestic	2	2	5	2	0	0	8,120	Lycius	22	5	82	7	10	8	181,839
Jolies Appeal	2	1	13	1	1	0	16,153	Majestic Light	2	1	4	1	1	0	10,900
Joyeux Danseur	21	5	61	7	8	7	170,891	Major Impact	8	1	21	1	0	2	19,510
Judge T C	9	1	26	1	4	4	56,537	Malagra	11	5	35	6	5	3	147,553
Jules	20	10	83	21	5	4	424,378	Malibu Moon	21	12	70	18	10	8	652,179
Jumron (GB)	7	2	19	2	1	3	16,566	Mambo	2	1	6	1	0	1	7,875
Just a Cat	4	1	8	1	1	0	9,073	Manlove	3	1	8	1	0	1	13,800
K. O. Punch	18	5	61	6	5	11	189,408	Manzotti	5	2	15	3	1	0	92,135
Katahaula County	17	9	58	14	10	6	352,094	Marco Bay	4	2	16	2	3	1	81,565
Katowice	7	3	28	5	2	3	69,644	Marfa	2	1	4	2	0	1	68,127
Keep It Down	2	1	8	2	1	1	46,009	Maria's Mon	33	7	100	7	12	14	342,610
Kell's Sea Captain	2	1	7	1	1	0	7,685	Marked Tree	10	5	27	5	3	5	75,730
Kennedy Factor	3	1	8	1	0	0	4,037	Marlin	12	3	25	3	2	3	35,003
Keos	9	1	35	1	1	4	20,402	Marquee Star	1	1	7	1	0	0	6,169
Key Contender	4	2	11	4	0	2	62,984	Marquetry	30	8	95	11	10	12	243,510
King of Kings (IRE)	21	3	61	4	7	5	266,473	Master Bill	10	3	44	4	3	5	86,577
King of the Heap	6	2	35	4	3	6	73,215	Matchlite	3	1	13	1	0	2	13,800
King Riviera	2	1	4	1	0	1	19,066	Matter of Honor	4	1	15	2	1	7	80,071
King's Grant	4	2	21	2	1	3	27,915	Matty G	11	4	38	5	5	6	143,991
King's Nest	4	3	19	3	2	3	38,491	Mazel Trick	42	13	119	14	9	12	514,053
Kingmambo	16	3	49	4	3	8	213,410	Meadow Monster	5	3	15	3	2	1	78,752
Kipper Kelly	18	10	82	14	8	13	273,202	Meadowlake	22	9	78	13	6	9	311,360
Kiridashi	12	4	33	6	3	4	394,382	Mecke	22	4	76	4	12	7	135,998
Kissin Kris	36	7	138	11	16	11	449,583	Memo (CHI)	12	3	29	4	2	2	48,657
Knight in Savannah	2	1	6	1	1	2	12,448	Menifee	17	7	66	8	15	13	373,055
Known Fact	5	3	22	3	3	2	82,574	Mercedes Won	8	1	21	1	1	5	17,744
Kokand	10	4	38	8	5	5	190,483	Mercer Mill	6	4	30	4	2	6	50,087
Kris S.	9	4	20	6	4	0	1,177,260	Metfield	9	2	34	2	1	0	23,500
Kuwaiti Brass	1	1	5	1	0	2	5,442	Michael's Flyer	2	1	6	3	0	2	56,160
Laabity	5	1	12	1	0	0	6,336	Miesque's Son	8	1	26	1	0	6	54,349
Labeeb (GB)	11	3	33	3	3	2	34,356	Migrating Moon	9	4	40	8	4	10	249,528
Lac Ouimet	15	4	58	4	3	11	87,107	Military	16	9	63	13	7	7	367,616
Langfuhr	41	18	147	26	20	22	825,193	Miner	1	1	3	1	0	0	8,400
Larrupin'	13	3	65	4	9	5	108,432	Minister's Mark	7	3	19	3	2	5	43,623
Larry the Legend	6	1	17	1	3	1	16,125	Mister Baileys (GB)	3	2	23	4	3	3	280,694
Lasting Approval	7	2	24	2	2	2	59,900	Mister Jolie	15	5	59	11	10	17	256,943
Latin American	13	3	41	3	6	4	99,493	Miswaki	10	2	35	2	6	4	61,789
Latvia	1	1	4	1	1	1	13,316	Miswaki Bandit	4	1	13	1	1	1	15,620
Le Ciel	1	1	4	1	0	0	5,462	Montbrook	27	8	98	11	12	11	732,590
Lear Fan	9	4	39	5	1	4	136,058	Montreal Red	16	1	65	1	6	3	48,524
Lee's Badger	2	1	6	1	0	1	9,740	Moonlight Dancer	7	2	15	2	3	0	24,996
Leestown	30	12	117	15	15	17	326,942	Moro Oro	6	2	20	2	3	3	50,950
Leo Castelli	7	2	16	2	2	1	29,072	Mortlock (FR)	4	1	18	2	3	1	23,555
Let Goodtimes Roll	1	1	2	1	0	0	32,100	Moving Shoulder	3	1	11	2	0	3	13,390
Level Sands	18	5	64	5	8	9	150,364	Mr Purple	4	1	13	1	1	2	28,576
Light Idea	2	1	3	1	0	0	8,783	Mr. Greeley	11	3	38	4	5	6	147,300
Light of Morn	2	1	5	1	0	0	8,922	Mr. Procrastinator	4	1	11	1	1	0	11,978
Lightning Leap	1	1	6	1	1	1	6,490	Mr. Shawklit	5	1	12	1	2	0	15,260
Like a Soldier	2	1	7	1	0	1	10,990	Mr. Sparkles	3	1	6	1	0	1	18,956
Lil E. Tee	19	9	73	11	8	12	181,528	Mt. Livermore	18	4	48	6	5	5	185,192
Lil's Lad	32	9	97	10	14	13	301,404	Mt. Magazine	2	2	6	2	0	2	19,320
Limit Out	7	4	32	5	6	5	84,636	Mud Route	8	3	25	4	0	3	102,263
Line In The Sand	41	9	184	9	21	24	196,670	Muldoon	6	2	22	2	2	1	23,747
Linear	2	1	5	1	1	1	9,314	Mutakddim	12	5	37	7	2	6	179,055
Lion Cavern	7	2	23	5	4	4	169,250	My Favorite Grub	1	1	6	1	0	0	18,820
Lit de Justice	21	11	86	14	15	11	534,872	My Imperial Slew	2	1	10	1	3	1	41,201

RECORDS OF JUVENILE SIRES

Sire	Perf	Wnrs	Sts	1st	2d	3d	Purses	Juvenile Sire	Perf	Wnrs	Sts	1st	2d	3d	Purses
My Liege	1	1	9	2	1	2	21,119	Pleasant Tap	22	5	54	7	7	6	190,030
Mystery Storm	9	3	29	4	3	5	87,642	Pole Position	5	1	21	1	6	6	52,260
Naevus	4	2	22	2	3	5	26,602	Polish Navy	13	3	36	4	3	5	90,318
Native Factor	3	1	9	1	2	1	16,182	Polish Numbers	19	4	60	9	5	9	414,140
Native Prospector	3	2	8	3	1	0	41,052	Polish Pro	4	1	9	1	3	1	51,670
Native Regent	11	4	32	5	5	0	77,498	Pollock's Luck	9	3	45	4	4	7	40,021
Native Slew	4	1	22	1	0	4	21,676	Ponche	10	3	53	6	7	4	99,620
Nelson	4	1	10	1	1	1	12,498	Porto Foricos	3	1	15	3	2	2	372,582
Net Asset	3	2	9	3	0	2	49,696	Precocity	15	7	60	8	9	9	306,966
Never Wavering	2	1	17	1	1	6	18,505	Premiership	15	1	42	2	7	3	55,782
New Way	7	3	25	3	0	3	26,418	Prenup	1	1	1	1	0	0	16,416
Nicholas	3	1	12	1	3	1	24,981	Present Value	6	1	14	1	1	3	13,211
Nineeleven	4	2	23	3	6	2	104,602	Presidential Order	8	2	22	5	3	3	129,129
Nines Wild	6	2	24	3	3	0	48,524	Press Card	4	1	9	1	1	0	10,630
Noactor	9	2	28	2	1	3	30,808	Prince Don B.	1	1	1	1	0	0	5,225
Noble Cat	7	4	29	8	5	2	142,873	Prince of Fame	4	3	25	3	1	1	25,973
Noble Novice	1	1	8	1	5	0	19,250	Prince of the Mt.	5	3	20	3	2	3	43,321
North Prospect	4	1	11	1	1	1	15,939	Private Interview	5	1	19	1	2	1	57,562
Northern Afleet	14	8	47	11	8	4	229,825	Private School	4	1	15	1	0	5	15,846
Northern Andy	2	2	7	2	1	0	5,415	Private Talk	5	2	35	3	10	5	116,098
Northern No Trump	3	1	9	1	2	0	11,148	Private Terms	15	1	40	1	1	5	29,797
Northern Strike	2	1	7	1	0	0	42,911	Prized	8	4	43	4	4	8	69,318
Not For Love	17	8	53	9	14	10	342,238	Proper Reality	3	2	8	2	0	1	11,894
Not Tricky	1	1	4	2	0	0	24,900	Prosetflanker	1	1	1	1	0	0	5,160
Notebook	15	6	56	8	7	5	139,329	Prospect Bay	14	5	34	7	3	2	91,750
Numerous	20	7	80	7	10	9	150,840	Prospector Jones	11	1	35	1	0	3	14,508
O'Brannigan	6	2	19	2	5	3	68,793	Prospector's Music	5	3	18	4	5	1	132,153
Old Chapel	1	1	5	1	1	0	9,236	Prospectors Gamble	13	2	49	2	3	6	59,392
Old Trieste	19	8	64	9	14	7	692,090	Prosper Fager	7	1	23	2	2	3	33,670
Oliver's Twist	5	2	18	2	2	4	38,046	Proud and True	18	2	54	2	5	8	70,372
Olympio	11	5	28	5	2	3	71,311	Proud Irish	4	2	11	3	0	2	61,465
On Target	19	7	54	8	6	4	152,891	Proudest Romeo	6	3	14	3	2	2	47,526
On the Sauce	2	1	11	2	0	1	34,670	Pulpit	26	10	64	12	8	12	423,658
One Golf Sierra	2	1	9	1	3	1	22,600	Pyramid Peak	15	4	50	4	8	5	72,434
Ongoing Mister	2	1	5	2	0	0	23,202	Quaker Hill	6	3	24	3	3	1	46,914
Open Forum	26	8	79	8	7	12	231,849	Quaker Ridge	13	5	63	5	10	10	130,713
Ops Smile	8	2	25	2	3	1	23,320	Quick Cut	13	3	39	4	3	4	69,109
Orchid's Devil	4	1	9	1	3	2	33,702	Quiet American	37	11	122	14	15	15	499,637
Order	1	1	9	1	4	1	41,840	Quiet Enjoyment	2	1	6	1	2	1	38,490
Ordway	13	5	41	7	8	8	137,505	Radio Daze	2	1	5	1	1	1	13,920
Ore Grade	2	1	3	1	0	0	5,828	Raffie's Majesty	7	1	23	1	2	2	18,456
Ormsby	3	1	9	1	1	1	14,993	Rage	5	1	15	1	1	3	12,424
Out of Place	28	8	92	8	15	6	248,125	Rahy	14	2	33	2	3	4	153,140
Outflanker	14	5	62	8	13	8	195,210	Rail	5	1	9	1	0	0	5,555
Pacific Waves	3	2	9	3	2	0	37,443	Railway Cat	3	2	15	2	1	2	24,864
Pancho Villa	6	1	15	1	0	5	7,825	Rainbow Blues (IRE)	4	1	17	2	2	1	30,081
Parade Ground	20	4	61	5	4	9	124,635	Raji	1	1	7	1	0	1	4,466
Paranoide (ARG)	4	1	13	1	1	4	14,313	Ranger (FR)	7	2	19	2	4	2	18,965
Partner's Hero	17	3	49	4	6	7	125,697	Rare Brick	6	1	20	1	4	3	25,234
Party Manners	7	2	29	2	3	5	49,071	Real Quiet	30	8	102	12	9	10	329,331
Pass the Line	4	1	14	1	1	3	35,135	Reality Road	4	2	21	2	5	2	35,986
Patriot Strike	1	1	4	1	2	0	25,576	Record Catch	3	1	11	1	0	1	5,066
Patton	14	4	44	4	3	6	63,225	Red	11	7	34	8	5	4	84,229
Pauliano	6	2	27	2	1	6	110,250	Red Ransom	12	3	33	3	3	7	88,660
Peaks and Valleys	17	5	75	7	11	8	358,776	Red River Gorge	1	1	4	1	1	1	9,610
Pedigree Unknown	1	1	4	1	1	0	6,050	Reel On Reel	4	2	12	2	1	2	10,566
Peintre Celebre	2	1	2	1	0	0	60,000	Regal Classic	20	4	69	4	5	6	116,857
Pembroke	9	2	26	2	0	5	39,513	Regal Intention	16	7	50	9	4	5	188,836
Pentelicus	26	9	114	9	12	15	199,188	Regal Remark	13	4	34	5	3	9	110,584
Perfect	1	1	7	1	1	0	17,346	Regent Act	2	1	21	1	5	2	22,485
Perfect Mandate	5	3	16	4	4	2	193,730	Relaunch a Tune	1	1	3	1	0	0	5,760
Perfect Vision	15	8	71	14	8	6	285,247	Renteria	5	2	22	2	3	2	56,805
Perforce	2	1	11	1	1	2	10,150	Repriced	10	2	30	2	0	3	39,004
Personal Flag	14	3	42	3	2	5	103,771	Reprized	9	4	51	7	6	8	107,225
Peruvian	6	1	24	1	2	0	19,378	Ringside	4	1	13	1	1	3	13,791
Peterhof	4	1	17	1	3	1	11,928	Rinka Das	8	3	34	3	4	5	47,660
Petersburg	5	3	14	5	3	0	34,285	Rio Verde	5	4	23	5	3	5	159,950
Petionville	19	5	56	9	4	4	211,982	Rio's Lark	1	1	5	2	0	1	20,125
Phone Trick	22	8	73	8	10	7	202,105	Rizzi	34	12	146	18	15	16	434,609
Pioneering	23	11	93	11	15	10	310,661	Roanoke	10	3	36	3	3	6	61,631
Pistol's Cowboy	2	1	10	1	3	2	13,895	Roar	32	15	96	17	17	13	538,247
Placid Fund	6	3	22	5	1	2	66,071	Rob's Freeze	4	1	11	1	3	1	28,840

Juvenile Sire	Perf	Wnrs	Sts	1st	2d	3d	Purses
Robannier	3	1	11	1	2	1	31,010
Robyn Dancer	14	6	74	7	6	7	110,747
Rodeo	20	8	54	10	10	3	343,521
Rokeby (GB)	2	1	6	1	0	2	12,913
Roll Credits	1	1	2	1	0	0	3,809
Roy	7	5	23	5	4	2	131,307
Royal Academy	14	4	42	4	7	5	155,290
Royal Empire	4	1	6	1	0	0	21,364
Royal Merlot	1	1	5	1	1	0	43,028
Royal Pennant	2	1	2	1	0	0	937
Royal Roberto	1	1	4	1	0	0	6,860
Rubiano	11	5	44	7	3	9	137,581
Rubiyat	3	3	11	3	2	3	94,560
Ruhlmann	1	1	5	1	0	0	3,900
Run Softly	6	2	13	2	1	0	36,200
Runaway Groom	38	6	119	7	15	16	246,501
Russellthemussell	2	1	7	1	0	0	8,215
Russian Courage	2	1	13	1	3	3	75,815
Safely's Mark	7	4	33	7	1	4	92,624
Sahm	14	3	46	4	3	6	101,094
Saint Ballado	31	11	97	16	19	14	1,255,985
Salt Lake	30	13	90	22	9	13	679,760
Sand Tunnel	5	5	37	6	9	4	86,805
Sandia Slew	5	3	14	4	4	1	43,876
Sandpit (BRZ)	13	2	30	2	2	1	23,495
Saratoga Six	8	2	29	3	8	5	53,769
Scarlet Ibis	2	1	8	1	0	2	10,385
Scatmandu	25	6	75	7	9	8	171,867
Schembechler	4	1	16	1	3	3	17,950
Score Quick	3	1	13	1	2	2	25,600
Scottsville	3	1	6	1	0	1	18,256
Sea of Secrets	24	11	95	17	16	13	403,478
Sea Salute	6	2	17	2	2	1	47,968
Sea Wall	4	2	12	2	1	1	83,058
Seacliff	6	4	26	5	3	3	66,145
Seattle Sleet	9	4	30	9	1	6	121,649
Secreniner	3	1	7	1	0	0	7,695
Secret Ghost	1	1	3	1	2	0	9,800
Secret Hello	6	3	24	4	2	6	102,616
Seeker's Journey	1	1	9	2	3	2	57,459
Seeking the Gold	6	2	15	2	3	2	92,100
Sefapiano	21	7	78	7	15	7	141,955
Semoran	11	2	45	3	4	4	51,372
Seneca Jones	14	8	65	12	13	15	435,394
Senor Conquistador	2	1	11	1	1	1	20,490
Service Stripe	3	2	14	2	1	2	39,941
Shaheen	6	3	24	4	5	1	46,374
Shamrock Ridge	1	1	1	1	0	0	18,800
Shaquin	1	1	3	2	0	0	19,200
Sharp Frosty	4	1	10	1	1	0	10,954
Shawklit Player	2	1	6	2	2	1	14,142
Shergar's Best (IRE)	7	3	22	3	4	4	28,849
Shirttail Flying	3	2	17	2	1	1	27,321
Shotiche	4	1	18	1	1	1	29,889
Shuailaan	5	2	26	2	2	4	38,059
Siberian Summer	13	1	48	1	4	2	45,638
Signal Tap	13	4	50	4	3	3	90,519
Silent Generation	1	1	2	1	0	0	1,560
Silver Charm	30	15	101	16	12	12	573,638
Silver Deputy	23	11	68	17	11	3	1,331,908
Silver Fox	6	1	21	2	6	2	41,455
Silver Ghost	26	4	78	6	10	8	256,854
Silver Hawk	2	1	5	1	1	0	35,960
Silver Music	1	1	4	1	0	0	8,580
Siphon (BRZ)	37	6	106	8	13	19	455,534
Sir Ap	5	2	17	3	3	3	62,014
Sir Cat	27	13	96	16	16	9	389,844
Sir Fir	6	3	18	3	6	2	46,640
Sir Leon	6	1	33	1	3	1	16,335
Sir Spellbinder	1	1	2	1	0	0	7,860
Skip Away	37	12	138	15	14	18	452,071
Skip Trial	18	6	68	8	12	8	217,470

Sire	Perf	Wnrs	Sts	1st	2d	3d	Purses
Sky Classic	20	4	43	5	4	3	174,442
Sky White	6	1	20	1	1	3	17,823
Slew City Slew	38	14	113	15	12	7	231,003
Slewacide	6	3	15	3	3	1	41,348
Slewdledo	23	12	77	16	7	15	241,073
Smart Magician	2	1	7	1	0	1	5,296
Smart Strike	17	5	49	6	4	5	202,241
Smoke Glacken	29	17	112	29	19	13	1,094,563
Smokester	32	13	102	16	13	10	360,416
Snake Doctor	1	1	6	1	0	2	9,415
Snowbound	6	6	25	6	5	3	93,690
Social Diamond	1	1	2	1	0	0	6,150
Soft Gold (BRZ)	2	1	4	1	0	1	80,082
Son of Briartic	13	5	51	6	6	3	51,356
Sounds Fabulous	2	1	8	1	1	0	10,004
Southern Halo	32	7	125	9	22	16	354,265
Souvenir Copy	37	15	124	17	16	18	550,100
Spanish Drummer	6	1	15	1	1	0	26,768
Spartan Victory	2	1	9	2	3	1	54,666
Speak	3	1	8	1	2	2	15,254
Speedy Nijinsky	3	2	9	2	1	0	14,639
Spruce Bouquet	3	1	10	1	3	1	15,390
Stacked Pack	1	1	7	1	1	1	39,680
Staff Riot	1	1	2	1	0	0	3,480
Standing On Edge	7	2	33	2	2	4	73,500
Star of Valor	8	3	33	3	4	7	71,907
Starbank	1	1	3	1	0	0	4,524
Stark Ridge	1	1	4	1	0	0	7,760
State Craft	1	1	1	1	0	0	4,800
State Performer	3	1	9	2	1	3	65,238
Stately Cielo	1	1	8	1	1	0	14,140
Stately Wager	3	1	10	1	2	0	5,605
Statesmanship	9	3	41	3	1	5	30,122
Stephanotis	8	4	22	5	7	0	116,940
Sticks and Bricks	3	1	9	2	0	1	23,385
Stolen Gold	3	3	18	5	2	1	43,880
Stop the Stage	5	2	15	4	1	3	26,330
Storm Boot	47	17	141	24	12	22	471,166
Storm Brewing	2	2	7	2	0	0	11,050
Storm Broker	10	4	24	5	2	2	57,602
Storm Cat	20	5	45	5	6	4	235,793
Storm Center	6	2	18	2	0	1	35,732
Storm Creek	31	5	94	5	5	6	110,903
Storm of Angels	10	1	35	1	4	3	26,998
Storm of the Night	2	1	3	1	0	0	4,206
Stormin Fever	35	16	124	17	15	19	529,054
Stormy Atlantic	38	13	117	18	16	25	524,799
Stravinsky	20	8	68	9	4	15	314,798
Strong Performance	1	1	7	1	2	1	6,633
Struggler (GB)	12	3	51	8	6	7	230,642
Suave Prospect	24	14	96	18	10	14	270,083
Subordination	15	6	51	6	3	7	115,879
Suggest	5	1	22	1	0	5	33,974
Sultry Song	16	5	42	6	4	5	114,473
Summer Squall	15	4	53	4	4	10	150,190
Sundance Ridge	1	1	2	2	0	0	30,600
Sunday Minister	3	1	6	1	0	0	7,234
Sunny's Halo	15	3	34	3	1	2	22,958
Super Code	2	2	7	2	0	2	18,160
Super Gun	1	1	7	1	2	2	26,332
Super Squall	1	1	4	1	0	0	7,920
Surachai	2	1	5	1	0	0	12,780
Sutter's Prospect	7	1	17	1	2	1	15,615
Swain (IRE)	6	2	19	2	1	2	61,179
Swing and Miss	8	5	33	6	6	5	42,339
Swing Shift (GB)	4	1	9	1	0	1	14,334
Swiss Yodeler	25	14	129	17	24	18	558,892
Sword Dance (IRE)	27	11	114	13	14	13	365,755
Synastry	11	6	49	7	11	2	110,380
T. U. Slew	2	2	7	4	0	0	34,805
Tabasco Cat	11	6	36	9	6	0	309,660
Tabib	2	1	6	1	2	0	10,594

Sire	Perf	Wnrs	Sts	1st	2d	3d	Purses
Tactical Advantage	25	11	104	11	12	17	223,047
Tactical Cat	24	10	78	12	14	8	491,972
Tahoe City	11	7	53	9	8	10	123,259
Take Me Out	21	7	77	8	9	4	289,390
Takur	1	1	2	1	1	0	17,596
Tale of the Cat	57	24	162	34	26	21	1,918,383
Talkin Man	4	2	15	5	0	1	86,406
Tamayaz	14	4	39	4	4	2	70,847
Tank's Number	3	1	3	1	0	0	9,150
Tarsal	1	1	3	1	1	1	22,477
Tejano Run	9	3	18	3	2	1	41,695
Temptor	4	1	13	1	3	2	33,055
Tethra	11	4	32	4	7	2	218,984
Texas City	8	4	29	4	2	5	71,631
Thats Our Buck	10	2	35	2	4	8	60,531
The Name's Jimmy	5	1	14	1	1	1	23,492
The Pilot	1	1	5	1	0	2	14,074
The Prime Minister	5	1	20	1	5	1	16,260
The Silver Move	3	1	13	1	0	1	9,740
Theatre Critic (IRE)	3	1	15	1	1	4	9,643
This Bulls for You	1	1	5	1	0	0	10,543
Thisnearlywasmine	3	2	8	2	0	2	18,630
Thorn Dance	1	1	2	1	0	0	3,906
Thunder Gulch	20	3	55	3	8	8	147,417
Tilt the Odds	5	2	28	5	6	2	125,227
Time Bandit	10	5	46	8	8	14	328,928
Tirade	4	2	10	3	3	0	89,602
Tomorrows Cat	45	16	142	20	18	13	765,059
Toolighttoquit	7	3	21	3	2	4	35,466
Top Account	4	2	20	2	1	4	30,342
Torey Ridge	4	3	17	3	0	5	19,731
Torrential	14	2	58	3	7	3	78,213
Tossofthecoin	14	4	48	4	4	4	76,052
Touch Gold	28	7	66	9	4	8	263,178
Tough Knight	4	2	18	2	3	3	12,813
Tour d'Or	14	6	68	7	10	7	135,104
Track Barron	4	1	13	1	3	2	11,166
Trail City	7	2	25	2	3	8	68,768
Traitor	11	3	40	3	8	6	61,221
Tri for the Gold	2	1	11	1	0	1	15,920
Tricky Creek	13	4	49	5	3	2	128,634
Tricky Fun	8	3	26	3	4	3	34,824
Tricon	4	1	13	1	1	2	14,937
Truculent Schular	8	2	24	2	0	1	27,348
Turbulent Kris	7	1	19	1	2	3	18,430
Turkoman	11	2	26	2	0	1	18,120
Twin Spires	11	3	39	5	8	6	170,665
Two Punch	18	8	56	9	5	8	164,684
Two Smart	1	1	6	1	0	1	17,854
Tychonic (GB)	9	2	27	2	1	4	27,775
Ulises	7	2	29	4	4	1	166,955
Unaccounted For	17	6	51	7	8	4	157,296
Unbridled	14	3	35	6	4	4	1,024,658
Unbridled's Song	35	16	100	18	18	12	1,071,880
Under David's Wing	5	1	13	1	2	0	11,540
Unreal Zeal	19	9	66	14	6	10	352,710
Unusual Heat	10	4	35	5	3	5	123,105
Valiant Nature	11	3	43	4	2	6	72,891
Valid Expectations	38	17	131	26	18	20	814,703
Valid Trefaire	3	2	21	3	2	5	51,636
Valid Vengeance	1	1	3	1	0	0	5,285
Valid Wager	11	3	36	5	3	4	128,731
Valley Crossing	7	3	28	3	3	7	49,201
Vaudeville	10	3	27	3	3	1	22,433
Verzy	5	1	11	3	1	2	21,083
Via Lombardia (IRE)	3	1	8	1	1	0	21,560
Victory Gallop	40	11	107	14	16	14	914,135
Victory Speech	12	4	44	5	2	5	67,405
Vilzak	7	2	27	2	5	6	35,263
Viva Deputy	3	3	23	3	7	2	47,207
Vizard	1	1	5	1	0	0	3,537
Vying Victor	10	3	30	3	4	1	55,305

Juvenile Sire	Perf	Wnrs	Sts	1st	2d	3d	Purses
Waco Connection	1	1	7	1	1	2	10,993
Wagon Limit	10	5	40	7	6	8	318,950
Wajir	5	2	15	2	1	2	48,795
Walesa	3	1	10	1	2	1	16,057
Walter Willy (IRE)	2	1	13	1	1	6	34,300
Waquoit	5	1	17	1	3	2	38,080
Water Bank	5	1	24	1	0	3	10,504
Wavering Monarch	7	1	26	1	1	0	15,429
Way West (FR)	15	6	47	6	7	5	93,480
Wayne County (IRE)	6	3	23	4	4	5	55,785
Wayne's Crane	7	3	29	3	3	5	75,227
Weekend Guest	16	7	48	7	12	9	103,835
Wekiva Springs	31	7	104	10	14	10	217,300
Well Decorated	5	3	24	3	8	2	42,485
Wertaloona	3	1	10	2	2	0	75,530
Weshaam	6	1	26	4	4	0	153,622
West Acre	9	5	28	5	5	2	106,091
West by West	19	6	73	8	13	9	149,620
Western Borders	10	3	35	3	4	6	72,260
Western Fame	10	4	25	5	2	3	95,282
Western Playboy	5	2	25	2	3	3	64,653
Western Trick	11	5	49	6	6	11	110,653
Westminster	6	4	18	5	3	0	39,420
Wheaton	16	8	69	10	11	5	173,611
Whiskey Wisdom	11	3	42	5	6	7	490,037
White Rammer	1	1	4	1	2	1	16,238
Whitney Tower	3	2	8	2	0	2	28,060
Wild Again	14	5	39	5	7	1	184,837
Wild Deputy	4	1	10	1	1	3	13,135
Wild Escapade	14	6	38	7	2	3	123,101
Wild Event	22	11	96	14	5	9	258,723
Wild Gold	9	6	25	9	3	1	163,572
Wild Kiss	1	1	3	1	0	0	8,100
Wild Phantom	1	1	3	1	0	0	3,480
Wild Rush	28	11	86	17	19	11	997,759
Wild Wonder	21	8	66	9	6	12	197,015
Wild Zone	31	12	114	17	16	13	313,959
Will's Way	7	1	33	1	6	3	61,993
Williamstown	11	4	37	5	3	4	133,914
Willowy Ambassador	2	2	7	2	1	0	17,991
Wind Chill	1	1	5	1	0	2	26,775
Winthrop	9	3	20	3	4	2	28,571
With Approval	16	3	47	3	6	4	85,945
Wolf Power (SAF)	20	2	48	2	5	5	80,464
Woodman	15	8	65	9	5	8	247,775
Worldly	1	1	3	1	0	0	3,025
Worthingtonhills	1	1	3	1	0	1	6,410
Xray	3	1	16	2	1	3	22,535
Yarrow Brae	13	3	49	5	9	5	102,830
Yoonevano	8	1	18	3	0	3	121,503
You and I	10	5	38	7	9	4	202,467
Youmadeyourpoint	3	2	12	2	1	0	34,118
Young Devil	3	3	11	3	0	2	30,341
Z Z Cat	10	4	41	4	8	5	108,303
Zalipour	3	1	13	1	1	3	14,055
Zamboni	1	1	8	1	1	1	6,954
Zarbyev	10	3	23	4	0	3	58,769
Zeeruler	3	1	9	2	1	0	9,380
Zocor	2	1	8	1	0	0	7,450
Zuppardo's Prince	7	2	19	2	0	1	28,715

2003
RECORDS OF
BROODMARE SIRES

The record of each broodmare sire
represented by at least one winning
thoroughbred or more who raced in
the United States or Canada in 2003,
showing his total performers, number
of winning performers, the number
of times they started and their
total placings and earnings.

Broodmare Sire	Perf	Wnrs	Sts	1st	2d	3d	Purses
A Gypsy Says	3	1	23	1	1	2	$19,444
A Native Danzig	8	6	44	11	5	2	1,171,787
A Run	2	1	10	1	0	1	20,333
A Sure Hit	1	1	10	2	2	1	36,354
A Title	7	1	50	1	4	9	21,866
A Toast to Junius	7	3	69	5	10	6	58,255
A-Okay	1	1	15	2	4	2	36,098
A. M. Swinger	3	2	23	5	4	2	45,775
A.P. Indy	40	22	191	32	27	23	1,108,370
Abahazy	1	1	9	2	1	0	9,754
Abebe Bikila	1	1	14	1	3	2	12,632
Abel Prospect	4	1	10	1	0	1	8,695
Absalom	3	1	18	1	1	3	14,291
Absent Russian	1	1	19	2	4	5	25,005
Academy Award	31	12	179	20	21	22	447,244
Acallade	8	2	37	3	4	6	47,374
Acaroid	30	11	194	24	28	20	329,867
Accipiter	25	12	193	20	19	22	289,914
Accomplished Lover	3	2	29	3	2	2	31,786
Accoustical	4	1	23	3	1	4	82,215
Accused	12	2	56	2	3	4	40,837
Ace II	4	3	30	3	3	1	21,110
Ace of Aces	7	4	54	11	10	7	111,680
Achieved (IRE)	5	4	41	6	2	5	45,377
Ack Ack	86	39	554	75	68	52	1,179,785
Ack Kerala	8	4	49	5	8	6	116,567
Acque	2	1	28	1	5	2	18,087
Adam Blue	1	1	1	1	0	0	3,000
Addy Boy	4	4	74	5	10	9	60,325
Adios (GB)	2	1	11	1	0	1	4,572
Admiral's Flag	3	2	17	2	3	1	19,721
Admiral's Shield	7	1	47	4	5	6	35,064
Advance Guard	4	3	40	5	5	7	63,318
Advance Man	2	2	10	2	3	4	15,520
Advertent	8	3	45	5	9	5	42,624
Advocator	36	18	289	26	33	38	435,597
Advocatum	4	1	13	1	1	1	10,045
Aegean's Bolger	2	1	3	1	0	0	9,735
Aerial Dancer	1	1	12	2	4	1	21,359
Aeronaut	1	1	4	1	0	0	6,660
Aferd	27	13	175	18	16	21	244,528
Affiliate	5	2	25	2	2	3	50,935
Affirmed	215	122	1,515	206	190	185	7,440,542
Afleet	141	76	940	136	131	138	3,543,800
Aforethought	1	1	16	2	6	0	17,380
African Sky (GB)	12	6	95	11	11	10	152,289
Africanus	1	1	15	1	1	0	8,128
After Eight	2	2	28	5	6	2	33,986
Age Quod Agis	1	1	4	1	1	0	25,600
Aggravatin'	7	3	30	7	2	1	188,845
Agile Shoebill	1	1	6	1	0	0	2,005
Agitate	41	17	271	34	25	30	612,351
Ahdeek	1	1	6	1	0	0	4,180
Ahira	3	1	31	2	2	4	12,620
Ahmad (ARG)	13	5	94	6	14	6	251,318
Ahonoora (GB)	9	4	43	9	5	3	989,453
Air Cover	4	2	27	4	7	1	73,308
Air Forbes Won	144	79	1,100	159	155	141	3,326,490
Air Rights	1	1	16	3	0	3	21,095
Ajdal	5	4	32	5	2	4	87,476
Akarad	8	3	52	5	11	7	183,622
Akureyri	28	14	184	24	22	20	453,907
Al Hareb	2	1	9	1	1	1	7,177
Al Hattab	34	20	241	28	33	27	571,959
Al Mamoon	41	19	311	28	41	39	629,106
Al Mufti	1	1	11	2	0	1	5,632
Al Nasr (FR)	55	24	361	47	33	56	1,046,272
Alaskan Frost	9	2	60	5	6	6	84,110
Albert Rocks	6	3	49	10	7	16	105,103
Alberta Green	3	2	26	2	4	7	13,444
Alcimedes (GB)	1	1	7	1	1	0	11,800
Alhambra	1	1	9	1	3	2	15,045
Ali Oop	17	8	141	15	17	20	154,624
Alias Smith	6	4	36	5	6	5	90,258
Alien	1	1	11	1	4	1	56,320
All Glory (NZ)	5	2	35	3	3	7	76,040
All Hope (FR)	2	2	20	2	0	1	8,862
All of a Sudden	3	2	26	3	1	3	71,203
Alla Breva	10	4	83	5	5	8	61,647
Alleged	170	78	1,120	137	144	132	4,792,122
Allen's Prospect	143	75	979	139	110	132	2,259,101
Alley Fighter	1	1	21	1	2	3	4,916
Allgrit	1	1	4	1	0	0	11,250
Alligator Reef	1	1	8	2	1	2	12,218
Alnaab	6	2	39	3	6	5	25,991
Aloha Mood	2	1	10	1	0	1	15,544
Aloha Prospector	12	7	77	14	7	14	318,318
Aloma's Ruler	30	16	204	24	24	32	445,215
Alomado	3	1	31	2	2	2	26,770
Alphabatim	20	6	134	14	5	11	158,736
Alvin Jack	2	1	14	1	0	1	20,345
Alwasmi	28	13	184	22	16	26	396,509
Always a Cinch	2	1	18	2	2	3	58,166
Always Gallant	5	1	35	2	3	1	15,325
Always Run Lucky	7	2	38	2	3	8	52,596
Alwuhush	74	31	434	47	46	58	941,953
Aly North	5	1	22	1	0	2	22,807
Alybrave	9	5	54	8	10	10	75,215
Alycotta	2	1	32	1	8	2	47,801
Alydar	193	103	1,198	171	160	168	3,921,744
Alydar's Prophecy	1	1	7	2	1	0	37,147
Alydart	3	1	30	1	0	3	4,627
Alydeed	29	13	134	16	31	19	454,789
Alyone	2	2	14	2	0	0	11,580
Alysheba	107	54	723	103	100	101	3,439,854
Alzao	17	8	56	10	7	3	471,880
Amasport	8	5	42	9	5	5	59,397
Amazing Prospect	9	4	58	6	8	7	90,228
Ambehaving	2	2	25	3	2	6	59,363
Amber Eagle	2	1	35	3	6	6	37,875
Amber Morn	2	1	11	1	2	3	20,821
Amber Pass	26	12	194	20	23	19	221,873
Amber Sioux	1	1	7	1	0	0	3,102
Amberbee	4	2	26	4	3	1	32,752
Ambernash	13	8	128	13	10	13	277,365
American Chance	2	1	10	1	1	2	28,220
American History	3	1	37	1	4	4	25,930
American Legion	11	4	79	5	12	14	88,031
American Standard	46	24	324	42	38	39	773,675
Amerrico	15	9	102	13	12	8	227,957
Amino	2	2	17	4	1	4	17,585
An Act	7	5	52	7	8	2	109,822
An Eldorado	6	2	48	2	2	7	17,750
Ancestral (IRE)	20	13	155	18	28	19	221,815
Anfield	2	1	17	3	2	2	113,559
Angle Light	17	8	120	16	10	8	168,925
Ankara	11	4	52	5	8	5	48,909
Annihilate 'em	11	8	96	12	12	11	138,000
Another Practice	3	1	21	2	1	3	25,805
Another Reef	5	1	54	3	11	12	115,087
Anshan (GB)	1	1	9	2	0	2	83,106
Antheus	2	1	5	1	0	0	11,480
Anticipating	21	11	128	14	14	16	357,169
Antidiluvian	3	1	20	1	0	1	6,193
Apalachee	189	89	1,246	163	142	159	2,809,311
Apollo	2	1	8	1	0	1	3,540
Apostolic	3	1	24	1	2	3	9,404
April Fool	1	1	5	2	1	2	7,864
Arabacus	6	3	39	10	6	8	71,041
Arabian Law	3	2	17	4	3	1	26,620
Arabian Sheik	2	2	29	2	4	6	15,512
Araby Ace	4	3	27	6	1	3	44,444
Arachnoid	2	1	9	1	1	2	9,429
Aragon	1	1	11	4	2	1	28,975
Aras an Uachtarain (IRE)	9	1	31	1	2	3	25,213
Arazi	6	3	29	3	3	7	30,366
Archie Who	1	1	6	3	1	0	19,435
Architect	23	12	179	17	23	27	234,761
Arctic Ace	1	1	8	2	1	2	26,526
Arctic Action	4	4	36	7	6	4	24,697
Arctic Blitz	6	2	38	3	5	2	24,570
Arctic Groom	4	1	38	1	4	6	30,639
Arctic Tern	62	23	382	42	55	50	855,869
Are You Foolin' Me	3	1	9	2	1	1	18,577
Argument (FR)	2	1	10	3	2	1	168,321
Ariva	1	1	11	1	2	1	7,630

Broodmare Sire	Perf	Wnrs	Sts	1st	2d	3d	Purses	Sire	Perf	Wnrs	Sts	1st	2d	3d	Purses
Armor	4	2	53	3	6	8	49,686	Bancinto	2	1	10	2	0	0	12,634
Arms and the Man	2	1	12	2	1	1	12,348	Band Practice	18	10	134	20	24	20	371,059
Arrogant Boy	4	2	32	4	2	4	35,928	Banderilla	17	9	127	14	11	22	313,509
Artaius	2	2	29	4	2	6	45,028	Bandwagon	2	1	26	1	7	6	67,170
Artichoke	14	6	109	10	9	15	145,615	Bang Boom	3	1	13	2	2	1	12,347
Artie Baby	1	1	7	1	0	4	16,155	Banner Bob	10	6	86	11	15	12	124,907
Artistry (SAF)	3	1	18	3	1	4	50,117	Banner Sport	10	6	83	21	16	8	150,813
Arts and Letters	46	16	306	25	28	21	391,683	Banners Image	1	1	10	2	3	1	6,336
As Alleged	2	2	16	8	2	1	15,035	Banquet Table	32	11	217	21	27	21	207,287
Ascot Knight	58	31	395	44	50	54	1,388,667	Bar Dexter	2	1	9	1	1	1	12,105
Ashabit (GB)	1	1	16	1	1	1	12,401	Barachois	38	15	256	22	25	30	341,268
Ashdown	1	1	9	1	2	1	20,250	Barathea (IRE)	1	1	5	2	0	2	15,625
Ashmore	2	2	21	4	2	3	22,880	Barbaric Spirit	19	10	108	19	12	19	76,599
Ask Me	9	6	96	11	8	18	111,354	Barberstown	15	7	90	13	9	9	195,941
Ask Muhammad	10	4	51	4	5	5	22,850	Barbizon	5	1	34	1	4	2	14,198
Ask Us	3	3	25	3	1	4	21,142	Barbizon Streak	2	1	15	4	0	2	33,887
Aspro	10	4	64	9	8	7	185,801	Barboon	5	2	29	4	5	3	33,118
Assagai	11	2	52	2	2	3	17,970	Barcelona	8	6	70	13	8	6	173,989
Assagai Jr.	4	1	26	1	4	1	15,465	Bargain Day	25	11	151	17	12	22	224,152
Assault Landing	16	6	102	9	11	17	219,651	Barjo's Bay	2	1	14	2	2	1	27,124
Assert (IRE)	59	31	402	51	53	53	1,572,239	Baron O'Dublin	9	3	59	6	7	14	54,536
Astray	2	2	18	3	5	3	26,276	Baronius (BRZ)	1	1	4	1	0	1	43,551
Astro	2	2	7	3	0	1	54,100	Barrera	42	17	250	24	26	36	368,578
At Full Feather	8	2	54	2	4	2	21,754	Barrydown	2	2	9	2	1	0	29,319
At the Threshold	48	27	340	48	53	52	1,275,756	Bart's Bounty	1	1	12	1	1	0	18,650
Ataviado (ARG)	1	1	9	2	1	1	12,570	Bartizan	1	1	15	2	0	4	28,760
Atmosphere	2	1	18	2	2	3	5,367	Bask	8	4	76	6	6	10	69,989
Atta Boy II	1	1	5	1	2	0	7,150	Basket Weave	10	6	75	8	11	7	114,125
Attengur	5	1	17	1	1	0	11,360	Bataan (AUS)	1	1	5	2	2	0	153,397
Au Point	17	10	91	14	7	13	86,137	Bates Motel	136	69	894	122	133	101	2,124,650
Auction Ring	8	4	45	6	7	3	72,297	Batonnier	37	17	214	28	25	29	435,556
August Agent	3	2	22	4	3	0	29,150	Battle Call	5	2	39	3	5	4	27,567
Aurelius II	4	2	25	5	1	1	31,949	Battle Launch	16	3	76	6	7	4	95,179
Aurium	8	3	54	5	9	6	65,562	Bawld Hornet	1	1	5	1	1	1	3,980
Authenticity	5	1	26	1	3	5	13,866	Bay Express	2	1	8	1	2	2	60,584
Autumn Double	1	1	13	2	3	3	3,173	Bayou Black	9	4	77	13	5	12	226,165
Avant	1	1	9	1	0	1	5,851	Bayou Hebert	34	13	191	23	25	32	751,254
Avatar	79	39	554	65	58	58	1,015,617	Be a Native	19	6	122	10	17	15	391,530
Avenger M.	7	2	51	5	9	10	114,079	Be a Prospect	32	14	147	18	16	14	211,686
Avenue of Flags	27	16	168	33	26	20	529,617	Be a Rullah	15	3	102	6	10	13	76,825
Averof	1	1	5	1	0	1	33,612	Be My Guest	42	13	222	19	17	20	485,368
Avies Copy	14	6	81	9	6	8	168,463	Bear Hunt	6	5	43	10	6	2	349,095
Avodire	13	6	98	10	15	19	133,295	Bearer Bond	3	2	26	2	3	2	39,418
Awd Rock	1	1	8	1	0	1	5,354	Beat Inflation	21	13	149	24	22	14	223,402
Ax the Fax	3	1	23	1	5	1	26,835	Beau Genius	65	36	457	69	59	42	1,585,037
Axe T. V.	6	2	35	2	1	5	17,357	Beau Groton	21	5	115	6	12	11	114,386
Aye's Turn	20	6	146	6	19	14	184,669	Beau Sovereign (NZ)	1	1	9	2	1	0	76,631
Ayman	6	1	35	1	5	3	25,431	Beau's Eagle	54	20	335	39	46	33	862,924
Aythorpe (IRE)	1	1	8	1	1	0	17,766	Beaudelaire	39	19	328	32	39	25	469,474
Azirae	2	1	16	3	1	3	40,151	Beautiful Music	7	3	66	6	9	9	43,390
Baalbek (CHI)	1	1	12	4	2	0	86,050	Bedford	15	6	133	9	14	13	97,848
Baba's Blessing	3	3	24	8	6	1	36,878	Bee Gold	4	3	32	3	3	3	18,952
Babur	2	2	18	2	1	4	11,019	Bee's Prospector	2	1	16	1	3	2	18,100
Baby Chile	2	1	9	1	0	1	5,693	Beechcraft (NZ)	1	1	9	3	2	2	49,075
Baby King	3	1	23	2	2	1	22,877	Beforehand	2	1	7	1	0	2	1,980
Baby Slewy	6	3	31	3	1	3	10,027	Bejilla	12	5	76	5	6	10	49,580
Back Alley	4	3	29	3	4	3	67,962	Bel Baraka (FR)	1	1	6	1	1	1	5,415
Back Bay Barrister	7	4	49	7	9	8	81,163	Bel Bolide	48	22	334	40	36	44	562,862
Back'n Time	3	2	25	3	4	2	32,846	Bel Sorel (GB)	2	1	11	1	1	0	2,821
Backbencher	5	2	50	3	6	6	29,394	Belek	5	3	23	5	1	2	27,513
Badger Land	46	28	342	56	41	38	1,018,256	Believe a Little	3	2	31	3	7	5	31,671
Baederwood	57	28	396	50	52	55	1,148,400	Believe It	145	65	873	103	106	81	1,513,974
Baffle	1	1	3	1	2	0	6,200	Believe the Queen	22	12	166	20	23	22	294,473
Bag	6	3	28	5	3	4	62,084	Bellman	2	2	11	3	2	0	12,276
Bagdad	8	3	57	6	3	6	79,452	Bellvoy	6	4	25	6	2	2	45,122
Bagfull	2	1	12	3	0	3	16,514	Bellypha (IRE)	5	1	21	1	0	0	10,930
Bahri	1	1	5	1	2	1	89,875	Belmez	2	1	16	1	5	2	106,760
Bailjumper	52	26	365	54	43	45	2,777,488	Belmont	2	1	11	2	0	2	10,086
Baillamont	6	2	21	2	3	5	58,367	Belong to Me	10	2	39	4	4	2	68,882
Balconaje	6	3	32	3	5	3	22,093	Belted Earl	9	4	71	5	10	10	68,570
Balcones	1	1	10	2	2	1	58,820	Ben Adhem	3	1	32	1	7	7	31,137
Balderson	2	1	17	1	2	1	4,209	Ben Fab	13	5	83	6	7	12	105,552
Baldski	138	69	985	136	106	119	3,027,716	Bends Me Mind	8	4	71	6	13	6	51,878
Ballacashtal	3	2	21	2	4	4	68,494	Benedictor	2	2	15	2	1	1	54,758
Ballad Rock	6	3	35	4	1	3	37,008	Benefactor	3	2	22	4	3	6	35,779
Ballindaggin	1	1	3	1	0	0	1,474	Benefice	10	4	63	5	4	10	142,015
Ballydoyle	24	9	144	18	14	16	148,027	Bengal Tiger	4	1	30	1	5	6	10,526
Balzac	30	12	207	13	22	27	351,974	Benny Bob	9	6	54	9	8	3	142,225

RECORDS OF BROODMARE SIRES

Sire	Perf	Wnrs	Sts	1st	2d	3d	Purses
Benny Q.	2	1	23	1	2	2	14,753
Beque	2	1	7	1	0	0	4,798
Bereber (ARG)	1	1	13	2	0	3	11,461
Bering (GB)	27	10	130	15	20	9	837,216
Bert B. Don	3	2	30	4	6	4	151,354
Bertrando	18	9	81	14	14	6	276,908
Best Award	3	1	24	4	5	3	30,292
Best Native	2	2	15	2	1	1	12,863
Best of Both	4	1	21	1	2	3	20,467
Best of It	5	2	49	3	10	4	67,496
Best Piece of All	2	1	10	1	3	1	22,135
Best Turn	31	13	200	18	18	27	289,040
Bestofive	1	1	7	1	0	0	1,736
Bet Big	51	28	436	46	55	67	761,071
Bet on the Blurr	2	1	20	2	1	1	9,204
Bet Twice	54	24	333	36	33	38	464,429
Better Arbitor	27	16	226	33	20	26	734,163
Beveled	3	2	19	2	8	4	119,406
Beyond the Mint	10	4	61	5	4	7	60,643
Bicker	8	3	72	3	6	6	68,895
Bien Bien	2	1	18	1	0	5	15,401
Big Bluffer	7	3	46	5	6	6	92,824
Big Bold Sefa	14	6	109	9	16	10	147,863
Big Burn	24	13	205	29	38	17	319,554
Big Current	1	1	4	1	0	0	5,190
Big Doug	2	1	3	1	0	0	6,600
Big Event	2	1	18	1	1	4	10,646
Big Jess	5	2	32	4	5	1	79,461
Big John Taylor	4	2	49	2	11	11	48,564
Big Kohinoor	6	1	20	1	2	2	15,953
Big Leaguer	4	1	33	1	2	3	8,920
Big Mukora	9	4	67	16	8	11	223,424
Big Pistol	18	10	123	17	16	10	192,804
Big Presentation	7	2	33	2	5	1	27,738
Big Raff	1	1	7	1	4	0	6,993
Big Sal	4	3	28	4	5	3	74,807
Big Sam	2	1	14	1	1	2	9,461
Big Spruce	98	46	674	82	79	75	1,695,139
Big Stanley	4	1	21	1	4	4	65,970
Billboard	1	1	4	1	0	0	4,784
Billy Blue	1	1	5	1	1	0	9,350
Bimini Captain	1	1	10	2	2	1	10,085
Binalong	1	1	7	1	3	2	26,840
Bionic Light	30	14	183	24	13	22	395,466
Bionic Prospect	3	1	16	1	2	1	16,652
Bishop's Choice	2	2	14	3	1	2	16,190
Black Is Beautiful	3	3	21	4	2	1	16,733
Black Mackee	31	20	203	30	23	24	253,527
Black Mountain	4	2	32	4	3	4	14,525
Black Reason	2	2	21	4	1	5	24,636
Black Tie Affair (IRE)	116	55	717	83	104	99	1,855,890
Blade	62	26	417	50	46	48	1,030,144
Blair's Cove	2	1	14	1	4	0	13,732
Blakeney (GB)	5	1	49	1	7	5	33,204
Blare of Trumpets	1	1	8	1	2	1	10,100
Blazing Bart	3	1	11	1	0	0	10,721
Blazing Ryder	4	2	21	4	0	1	13,314
Bless Saggy	2	1	18	1	0	0	6,417
Bletchencore (AUS)	1	1	11	2	1	4	13,584
Bletchingly (AUS)	5	2	20	2	6	2	35,729
Blind Spot	4	1	14	1	2	3	25,442
Blini	1	1	8	1	1	1	5,869
Blood Royal	13	5	105	10	22	10	208,943
Blue Buckaroo	11	6	78	6	9	11	97,068
Blue Cashmere	3	1	18	1	3	2	12,440
Blue Ensign	91	49	599	82	57	68	1,266,151
Blue Eyed Davy	4	2	28	9	5	4	41,885
Blue Grass Magic	6	2	43	3	3	7	34,835
Blue Jester	5	5	33	7	1	5	154,211
Blue Quadrant	6	3	53	8	3	3	73,214
Blue Serenade	2	1	15	2	2	2	53,975
Blue Times	4	3	31	5	6	4	59,817
Bluebird	4	1	47	3	2	4	109,677
Blues Parade	4	3	40	7	11	8	147,015
Blushing Groom (FR)	93	50	530	84	85	58	1,852,933
Blushing John	90	50	645	83	84	83	1,548,351
Bo Jinsky	7	3	41	8	3	2	77,763
Board Marker	3	1	27	1	5	3	16,703

Broodmare Sire	Perf	Wnrs	Sts	1st	2d	3d	Purses
Bob Mathias	1	1	14	2	6	2	38,919
Bob's Dusty	51	26	421	47	48	48	1,436,778
Bobby Ben	14	3	62	4	7	7	52,424
Boca Rio	14	8	92	15	11	15	173,548
Boitron (FR)	8	5	61	6	3	8	149,574
Bojima	3	2	20	2	0	3	7,588
Bold 'n Impressive	1	1	11	1	1	0	6,256
Bold Agent	8	4	63	4	7	4	87,713
Bold Arian	7	3	40	3	5	6	111,467
Bold as Blade	4	3	34	4	6	5	64,269
Bold Badgett	13	7	77	14	16	10	267,480
Bold Bidder	18	8	112	15	18	12	272,071
Bold Commander	4	2	38	3	5	2	130,871
Bold Conquest	2	2	18	2	0	3	17,210
Bold Destroyer	2	2	18	3	4	5	8,000
Bold Dun-Cee	7	3	59	5	5	5	65,924
Bold Ego	68	26	424	46	59	52	583,701
Bold Executive	30	16	166	27	25	22	1,112,795
Bold Favorite	2	1	15	1	4	2	42,506
Bold Forbes	101	58	748	110	97	92	1,238,896
Bold Forli	4	3	36	8	4	7	217,128
Bold Gun	3	2	20	6	3	2	40,451
Bold Gusto	2	1	13	3	2	4	20,852
Bold Hitter	6	3	34	7	4	3	89,024
Bold Hour	24	14	184	26	23	25	368,556
Bold Josh	15	8	102	11	14	11	193,143
Bold Kabota	3	1	14	1	0	2	13,131
Bold L. B.	12	1	77	1	9	11	66,337
Bold Laddie	47	28	321	40	34	48	510,942
Bold Legend	2	1	28	4	1	4	59,688
Bold Monarch	3	1	16	1	1	0	8,804
Bold n Bizarre	14	8	92	12	13	9	138,063
Bold Navy	7	4	66	8	3	3	61,367
Bold Nix	5	3	51	7	8	6	44,614
Bold Nuisance	3	1	14	2	1	3	28,919
Bold Owl	1	1	14	1	1	1	5,092
Bold Pac Man	4	1	19	1	3	7	28,899
Bold Preference	1	1	6	2	0	1	2,422
Bold Rapport	4	1	13	2	1	2	10,423
Bold Reason	19	6	135	9	14	11	95,005
Bold Relic	2	1	8	1	1	2	11,700
Bold Revenue	13	8	98	16	12	14	240,287
Bold Ruckus	221	135	1,409	256	198	191	6,719,445
Bold Run (FR)	4	1	34	1	5	4	28,226
Bold Second	1	1	8	1	1	1	15,010
Bold Show	1	1	17	3	1	0	14,257
Bold Skipper	1	1	8	2	2	2	77,220
Bold Sphere	1	1	14	1	1	4	5,956
Bold Tactics	1	1	10	2	0	3	37,796
Bold Tropic (SAF)	16	6	86	6	6	10	135,012
Bold Vantage	2	1	10	1	0	2	2,919
Bold Victor	3	1	18	2	2	0	7,177
Bold Vigil	2	1	6	1	1	0	2,295
Bold Wizard	2	1	11	1	0	2	24,661
Boldacious	1	1	4	1	0	0	2,520
Bolder Tactics	1	1	11	2	3	0	12,898
Bolductive	2	2	18	2	2	1	24,898
Bolger	52	24	310	38	31	30	506,000
Bolting Holme	1	1	2	1	1	0	9,600
Bombay Duck	9	3	47	3	5	4	68,343
Bonne Noel	1	1	1	1	0	0	5,640
Bonnie Tim	5	2	34	3	1	2	23,701
Bonsoir	2	2	13	3	1	2	65,896
Boogie Woogy	1	1	16	2	3	1	18,173
Boots n' Slippers	1	1	18	2	1	7	15,617
Borzoi	9	2	46	4	4	5	73,899
Boss Hoss	2	1	13	3	3	1	12,652
Boss Koss	3	1	13	2	1	4	47,726
Botchery	4	2	33	3	3	4	39,442
Boulder Dam	5	1	41	1	5	2	18,794
Boundary	10	4	49	4	5	8	129,637
Bounding Basque	63	34	463	59	63	46	1,146,790
Bowmans Express	7	1	40	3	8	8	56,082
Boys Nite Out	8	5	51	8	7	2	90,447
Bramante (ARG)	1	1	11	2	1	2	10,952
Brambles	3	2	19	4	3	0	34,950
Brandied Sunset	1	1	3	1	0	1	5,162
Brass Minister	7	6	57	9	7	9	90,645

Broodmare Sire	Perf	Wnrs	Sts	1st	2d	3d	Purses
Brave Bidder	2	2	18	2	3	4	16,720
Brave Flyer	1	1	10	2	0	0	8,600
Brave Lad	13	4	87	4	9	7	200,640
Brave Reason	1	1	6	2	2	0	7,880
Brave Regent	8	1	68	1	5	7	56,951
Brave Rider	2	2	15	2	3	4	8,592
Brave Scout	2	1	14	2	0	0	20,335
Brave Shot (GB)	40	20	336	38	44	40	1,180,763
Bravest Roman	4	1	19	2	0	3	20,740
Bravissamo	1	1	3	1	1	0	17,374
Bravo	4	2	32	2	4	3	24,146
Brazen Brother	15	5	89	11	11	4	99,013
Break Up the Game	1	1	4	1	1	1	8,308
Breeders Bonus	6	3	53	8	5	10	135,674
Breezing On	6	3	39	6	3	5	100,649
Brent's Prince	40	14	277	26	49	28	391,574
Briar Bend	6	4	50	7	3	7	79,277
Briartic	77	30	519	50	54	62	1,087,829
Brigadier Gerard (GB)	2	1	11	1	0	0	9,601
Brilliant Leader	5	2	34	2	0	2	8,310
Brilliant Protege	27	9	146	12	19	9	190,787
Brilliant Sandy	23	10	144	13	18	17	171,354
Broad Brush	165	93	1,053	162	168	106	3,680,598
Broadway Forli	20	14	165	28	18	23	426,923
Broadway's Top Gun	2	1	5	1	2	0	4,869
Brocco	7	2	24	2	4	1	59,250
Brogan	9	4	58	5	4	9	105,289
Brookover	3	2	31	4	4	5	29,919
Brother Liam	2	2	27	2	3	4	30,429
Brother Machree	1	1	10	1	2	4	16,103
Brothers Three	3	3	43	6	11	5	117,563
Brown Arc	3	1	21	4	3	1	76,250
Bruni (GB)	2	1	12	1	2	2	17,402
Buck 'n Bronc	5	1	31	1	1	4	31,497
Buck Forbes	1	1	7	1	1	0	10,504
Buck Private	8	6	59	7	4	8	54,994
Buck Wood	2	1	5	1	0	0	2,640
Buck's Club	6	1	16	1	3	2	13,544
Buckaroo	120	67	888	115	99	95	1,897,332
Buckboard	2	1	24	1	3	7	25,253
Buckfinder	83	47	581	87	88	82	1,357,908
Buckley Boy	25	12	174	22	24	24	718,085
Buckpasser	8	2	48	3	9	5	71,961
Buckpoint (FR)	5	4	34	7	5	6	140,607
Bucksaw	4	1	33	1	1	4	9,646
Bucksplasher	102	50	764	102	80	72	1,873,091
Bucktail	1	1	9	1	0	2	8,789
Bucky Raj	3	2	25	4	3	2	15,622
Buddha King	1	1	7	1	1	1	3,143
Buddy	4	2	27	3	2	3	119,227
Buen Jefe	1	1	8	1	4	1	7,480
Buffalo Lark	7	3	41	4	2	4	56,333
Bugle Note	3	1	24	6	3	3	12,089
Bulldar	3	1	21	3	4	2	20,687
Bumpy Landing	3	1	13	1	2	2	15,825
Bupers	11	7	86	15	11	11	145,814
Burd Alane	3	1	28	1	5	5	18,278
Burning On	3	3	32	5	3	3	35,921
Bushido	6	1	39	2	3	4	16,858
Busted (GB)	5	3	34	5	4	3	52,542
Bustino (GB)	7	3	40	5	2	1	81,766
Busy Chief	3	2	14	4	1	0	15,040
By the North	1	1	4	1	1	0	16,982
Bypasser	4	1	16	1	0	0	5,899
Cabildo	6	4	56	9	8	6	118,035
Cabin	3	2	21	3	2	1	18,625
Cabrini Green	26	10	157	14	19	12	273,903
Cabriole	7	2	40	3	5	4	41,342
Cactus Road	6	3	43	6	7	5	41,837
Cadoudal (FR)	1	1	7	1	1	1	27,140
Caerleon	37	18	181	32	20	19	1,790,810
Caesar's Dream	2	1	9	1	2	0	6,457
Cahaba Gold	4	2	28	3	3	3	16,200
Cahasa	3	1	33	2	1	1	20,560
Cahill Road	37	22	255	35	33	24	611,949
Cajun Prince	16	8	98	12	12	20	147,259
Calender Stack	2	1	7	2	1	0	19,523
Caller I. D.	28	18	173	30	24	21	584,087

Sire	Perf	Wnrs	Sts	1st	2d	3d	Purses
Caltech	9	4	76	8	14	10	204,749
Calumar	7	6	52	8	3	5	115,402
Cambiar la Suerte	1	1	7	1	0	0	4,040
Canadian Bound	7	1	54	1	4	11	26,890
Canadian Gil	12	3	60	8	7	9	82,756
Candi's Gold	30	16	188	27	31	21	475,033
Candle Stand	3	3	33	5	2	6	83,059
Candy Command	1	1	14	1	2	1	8,040
Candy Stripes	5	3	23	5	1	3	772,307
Cane Field	3	1	14	1	0	0	5,626
Cannon Dancer	4	3	41	6	8	3	78,345
Cannon Shell	13	6	72	8	8	9	76,632
Cannonade	49	23	369	45	49	49	529,318
Cantatore	1	1	9	1	0	1	1,803
Canyonland	4	2	52	4	6	8	27,607
Capacitator	2	1	12	1	0	1	2,660
Capital Idea	7	5	61	11	7	10	132,255
Capital Punishment	1	1	7	2	1	2	9,510
Capitol South	14	4	68	4	6	11	56,511
Capote	153	85	982	147	121	125	3,449,163
Capote's Promise	2	1	8	3	1	1	24,335
Capt. Don	10	3	56	5	9	5	66,549
Captain Cee Jay	3	2	30	2	7	2	9,913
Captain Codex	2	1	7	1	1	0	6,940
Captain Courageous	27	13	166	18	33	20	149,956
Captain Dare	1	1	5	1	1	0	4,095
Captain James (IRE)	3	2	14	2	1	1	16,857
Captain My Captain	2	1	15	1	0	2	6,848
Captain Nash	1	1	5	1	0	0	7,722
Captain Nick (GB)	4	3	30	5	7	4	161,990
Captain Valid	2	2	21	3	1	5	110,306
Caracolero	10	2	54	4	5	6	70,097
Carborundum	9	4	55	7	1	4	36,825
Cari County	3	3	27	4	3	6	76,788
Caribbean Line	1	1	8	2	0	1	9,857
Caribe	1	1	19	2	1	2	12,484
Cariellor (FR)	3	2	25	6	4	3	70,193
Carload	10	2	43	2	0	7	25,482
Carmelite House	2	1	18	4	1	4	33,843
Carnivalay	75	29	502	39	48	56	611,325
Caro (IRE)	76	39	527	76	66	47	1,759,155
Caro Bambino (IRE)	1	1	8	1	0	2	38,645
Carodanz	4	2	33	2	5	3	72,243
Caros Love	8	5	48	7	4	9	90,512
Carr de Naskra	93	40	558	77	65	72	1,572,958
Carry Sabers	1	1	8	1	0	1	2,406
Carson City	110	57	650	108	105	103	3,065,777
Cartesian	15	3	65	3	4	3	15,835
Cartwright	4	1	12	1	0	1	14,194
Casa Dante	9	7	76	13	11	13	133,236
Case the Joint	1	1	8	1	0	3	26,786
Cash the Ticket	1	1	10	3	1	1	38,133
Cassaleria	44	22	292	33	19	33	398,959
Castle Guard	23	14	211	23	15	17	328,405
Castle Howard	3	3	25	8	5	3	102,196
Catalpa Lane	1	1	2	1	0	0	10,614
Catane	4	1	22	1	2	3	40,891
Cathedral Bells	3	1	17	1	2	1	15,047
Cathies' Goal	1	1	7	1	0	3	9,077
Cathy's Reject	15	8	132	14	10	9	154,281
Caucasus	42	18	257	30	37	28	447,421
Cause Celebre	12	6	84	9	10	13	88,075
Cause for Pause	8	3	32	4	5	3	64,160
Cautious Prince	1	1	8	1	0	0	3,654
Cavalry	3	2	14	3	1	1	54,801
Cavanagh Special	2	1	22	1	3	1	13,559
Caveat	148	74	995	137	131	118	2,829,672
Cavo Doro (IRE)	1	1	13	2	2	3	19,146
Cee's Tizzy	20	7	60	10	7	4	255,494
Cefis	1	1	11	1	2	2	9,897
Celebrated	1	1	12	2	2	1	12,173
Centaine (AUS)	11	7	67	12	8	6	288,393
Center Cut	8	3	52	3	4	4	46,772
Centrust	4	2	17	4	2	3	25,780
Century Prince	7	2	47	2	11	4	49,596
Certain Times	3	2	18	6	2	3	55,751
Chalk Hill	4	1	20	1	0	1	6,333
Champagne Charlie	8	5	86	9	13	11	85,255

RECORDS OF BROODMARE SIRES

Sire	Perf	Wnrs	Sts	1st	2d	3d	Purses
Champagne Supper	5	2	31	3	4	3	30,122
Chanago	7	3	38	5	7	4	90,567
Chapel Creek	9	6	67	12	10	11	182,163
Chapman's Charge	2	1	12	1	1	1	8,465
Charging Falls	15	9	105	20	14	10	282,791
Charging Prince	1	1	8	2	2	1	17,970
Charging Through	1	1	4	1	1	0	6,770
Charlie Barley	7	4	48	7	6	11	196,897
Charlie Cielo	1	1	11	1	1	3	5,001
Charlie's Laundry	2	2	16	4	1	4	13,868
Charlie's Star	3	1	8	1	2	1	4,532
Charming Turn	14	6	116	11	11	19	153,468
Chas Conerly	13	6	58	7	9	9	202,041
Cheer On	3	2	29	4	5	2	32,095
Cheque Froid	4	2	31	4	2	5	24,450
Cherokee Colony	56	22	292	32	31	42	644,568
Cherokee Fellow	44	24	380	50	59	52	1,087,852
Cherokee Run	1	1	3	1	0	1	10,210
Cherry Pop	7	5	40	5	8	4	155,409
Chewy Slew	3	2	45	2	6	2	21,750
Chic Boutique	1	1	17	2	6	1	19,625
Chicago	7	2	40	4	4	6	138,282
Chicago Bound	1	1	12	1	2	1	6,897
Chicanery Slew	1	1	16	4	3	3	33,422
Chichester	1	1	13	1	2	7	26,584
Chidester	8	5	59	10	7	10	93,183
Chief Honcho	3	2	16	2	2	1	53,757
Chief of Dixieland	3	1	12	1	1	2	12,277
Chief Seabird	8	2	51	2	6	5	58,479
Chief Singer	8	5	52	12	6	5	439,791
Chief's Crown	104	58	702	101	89	79	2,164,346
Chief's Reward	2	1	6	1	0	0	1,775
Chieftain	30	14	205	21	26	25	287,524
Chilicote	5	3	27	4	3	1	26,142
Chillon	1	1	12	2	1	2	11,828
Chimes Band	1	1	8	1	0	5	26,780
Chimineas	5	2	34	3	6	3	137,415
Chip o' Lark	6	2	40	2	3	5	17,372
Chip's Ahoy	6	1	36	1	1	2	9,707
Chiromancy	2	1	11	1	1	4	8,922
Chisos	24	6	86	11	10	16	115,194
Choreographer	7	2	28	3	0	1	12,608
Christopher R.	18	6	140	8	12	14	135,504
Chromite	32	11	197	16	21	17	283,038
Chumming	12	2	62	2	2	6	38,233
Chumwar (GB)	2	1	16	3	4	2	55,600
Cigar City	1	1	8	1	0	0	11,952
Cinco Grande	3	2	20	2	2	3	30,067
Cinteelo	3	1	24	2	3	2	41,130
Cipayo (ARG)	13	6	84	10	7	15	295,470
Cipol (ARG)	2	2	13	2	1	3	16,340
Circle	7	3	26	3	6	3	57,772
Circle Home	17	9	134	12	13	17	200,192
Circle of Steel	2	1	9	1	1	0	7,128
Circus Prince	3	1	15	2	0	1	21,675
Cisco Road	1	1	5	1	1	1	3,200
Citidancer	31	20	214	36	43	32	853,325
Clackson (BRZ)	1	1	12	2	1	4	36,800
Claim	40	19	255	32	35	22	515,884
Class Chief	1	1	19	1	1	4	6,246
Classic	4	3	37	6	5	1	84,747
Classic Account	14	8	98	10	13	8	255,632
Classic Fame	2	1	22	1	1	0	13,973
Classic Go Go	48	25	310	43	44	44	808,751
Classic Music	1	1	8	1	2	0	40,730
Classic Secret	1	1	12	1	0	0	18,985
Classical Ballet	4	2	23	2	4	1	29,740
Claude Monet	1	1	9	2	2	2	500,360
Clear Choice	1	1	5	1	2	0	20,800
Clear Course	1	1	5	2	1	0	37,655
Clear Iron	1	1	5	1	0	0	10,825
Clear Sun	1	1	16	2	2	3	11,702
Clem	1	1	11	2	0	2	7,349
Clev Er Tell	11	6	72	9	7	16	200,177
Clever Allemont	7	2	31	5	4	5	18,879
Clever Champ	36	22	279	32	24	40	478,065
Clever Secret	12	7	124	11	14	18	83,823
Clever Trace	1	1	5	1	0	0	3,584

Broodmare Sire	Perf	Wnrs	Sts	1st	2d	3d	Purses
Clever Trick	277	143	1,753	232	224	230	4,509,542
Cliff Flower (ARG)	2	1	19	2	5	3	18,100
Clint Maroon	5	4	37	9	4	5	123,086
Cloudy Dawn	14	9	116	13	11	20	112,229
Coastal	85	37	560	58	66	70	942,909
Coastal Voyage	1	1	5	1	1	2	36,696
Coax Me Chad	11	7	87	9	8	13	90,425
Code of Honor	1	1	4	1	1	1	2,104
Code Word R.	1	1	15	1	3	4	13,861
Codex	12	7	96	18	14	12	159,275
Cogency	8	2	62	4	8	8	33,158
Cognizant	6	1	35	1	3	2	25,598
Cojak	43	16	259	27	34	37	431,762
Cold Reality	2	1	18	1	2	1	9,766
Cold Reception	14	8	99	12	13	16	166,719
Collectible	3	2	35	4	6	9	43,295
Collier	26	8	169	15	22	18	175,116
Colonel Power	15	4	105	9	10	16	87,277
Colonel Stevens	9	3	74	4	8	12	23,638
Colonial Affair	4	1	15	1	0	0	11,172
Colony Light	7	3	59	5	4	9	117,228
Color Bearer	7	4	40	7	3	3	55,552
Colorful Leader	1	1	8	3	2	0	13,915
Combat Ready	3	2	21	5	2	4	163,643
Combatant	2	1	16	1	2	3	7,786
Combe (ARG)	2	1	11	2	3	2	22,213
Come Rain Or Shine	4	2	36	2	2	5	27,488
Comeram	1	1	13	1	0	1	3,922
Comet Kat	10	7	94	10	6	10	103,479
Comical Clown	4	2	28	5	3	3	53,481
Commadore C.	11	6	81	8	8	13	196,101
Commanche Run (GB)	2	1	8	1	1	1	9,308
Command Control	7	2	63	6	5	12	67,684
Command Module	1	1	3	1	0	1	6,650
Command Performer	2	1	11	1	2	2	12,408
Commanding Lead	2	2	12	2	2	1	34,595
Commanding View	5	2	29	3	4	2	34,914
Commemorate	44	24	282	47	31	25	924,480
Commissioner	9	5	85	11	11	12	96,729
Common Grounds	8	5	51	9	4	4	186,911
Compelling Sound	5	2	33	5	6	3	82,503
Competitiveness	1	1	9	1	0	2	3,152
Compliance	35	17	248	26	29	34	386,899
Con Man	2	1	10	1	0	1	9,468
Concertino	1	1	12	1	3	1	13,127
Concierge	1	1	8	1	1	1	12,145
Concorde Bound	24	12	184	21	30	24	725,653
Concorde's Tune	5	1	8	1	0	1	22,690
Condorcet	1	1	12	3	0	2	59,603
Confederate	1	1	9	1	1	1	5,927
Confidant	9	5	69	12	7	9	82,392
Connaught	1	1	6	1	0	1	48,240
Conquistador Cielo	242	136	1,638	235	237	187	5,297,591
Conquistador Oro	2	2	20	2	5	4	27,601
Consigliere (GB)	3	1	13	1	4	1	26,553
Consultant's Bid	1	1	5	1	0	0	43,028
Contador (ARG)	1	1	7	4	2	0	5,969
Contare	14	9	106	11	10	11	143,902
Conte Di Savoya	3	2	17	2	3	0	35,299
Conte Grande (FR)	2	1	14	3	2	3	100,650
Contested Colors	3	1	28	1	1	1	12,583
Contorsionist	7	3	55	6	2	7	81,610
Convincingly	4	1	19	4	2	1	73,415
Convoy Scout	1	1	5	1	1	1	2,095
Cool Frenchy	1	1	12	1	0	2	4,414
Cool Groom	4	2	28	2	4	3	36,197
Cool Halo	15	7	88	17	7	12	112,796
Cool Joe	1	1	5	3	0	1	10,420
Cool Moon	2	1	15	1	1	3	6,402
Cool Northerner	2	1	11	1	2	1	9,192
Cool Victor	19	9	124	15	13	22	626,095
Coolfin (IRE)	1	1	15	2	3	3	29,428
Copelan	159	80	1,059	138	131	129	2,922,240
Coppabella	2	1	22	1	5	2	19,740
Copper Mel	1	1	5	2	0	0	10,440
Cormorant	117	72	837	119	103	96	2,620,373
Cornish Cup	2	1	17	1	3	5	11,711
Cornish Music	1	1	17	3	3	6	25,562

Broodmare Sire	Perf	Wnrs	Sts	1st	2d	3d	Purses
Cornish Prince	36	17	218	26	29	24	360,201
Corporate Report	56	34	359	58	51	39	1,646,496
Corridor Key	25	11	200	22	18	27	486,935
Cortan	4	2	19	2	2	2	53,894
Corwyn Bay (IRE)	15	9	101	13	11	12	251,490
Cosmic Voyager	1	1	6	1	0	0	3,752
Cost Conscious	9	3	41	3	3	4	44,561
Cougar II	51	24	407	45	48	55	704,746
Cougar's Crown	6	4	49	5	7	6	79,765
Council Rock	4	1	20	2	2	3	33,304
Count Brook	7	4	32	4	4	4	45,081
Count Eric	6	3	64	6	9	11	109,014
Count Francescui	6	3	41	5	3	2	63,752
Count Giacomo	2	1	15	1	1	2	7,667
Count Me Gelt	2	1	8	2	0	2	13,150
Count My Love	3	2	26	4	3	3	22,662
Counterfeit Money	4	1	24	1	0	3	6,950
Country Boy Jim	3	2	26	7	4	2	102,347
Country Doctor	2	1	12	1	1	2	14,434
Country Light	27	10	179	17	25	21	256,601
Country Pine	57	41	445	76	55	59	1,012,650
Coup de Kas	8	5	51	7	13	11	146,691
Courageous Sailor	3	1	16	1	0	1	2,220
Court Open	2	2	21	2	3	4	31,623
Court Ruling	13	6	89	10	11	12	67,557
Court Trial	29	16	237	23	32	29	422,035
Couvreur (IRE)	2	1	23	1	2	4	16,964
Cox's Ridge	268	144	1,892	221	244	255	5,133,980
Cozzene	137	67	879	114	123	102	2,740,716
Crafty Drone	16	8	95	20	16	9	415,709
Crafty Khale	5	3	44	4	3	3	38,731
Crafty Native	13	6	102	9	14	19	142,186
Crafty Prospector	261	146	1,742	256	240	218	6,079,316
Crawford Special	4	2	28	3	7	2	20,275
Creag-an-Sgor	2	1	8	2	0	1	41,922
Creme dela Creme	7	2	35	4	1	1	21,603
Creole Dancer	11	7	69	11	13	6	95,096
Cresta Rider	25	8	126	15	7	12	167,554
Crested Wave	2	1	8	1	0	1	10,606
Cresting Water	3	1	12	1	0	0	3,300
Crewman	5	3	45	3	0	2	29,225
Cricket Drummer	1	1	7	1	2	2	26,332
Criminal Type	56	31	414	59	62	39	2,608,774
Crimson Battle	12	4	71	4	7	9	78,117
Crimson Falcon	16	6	115	10	12	10	74,666
Crimson Satan	25	6	149	10	12	13	157,745
Crimson Slew	3	1	16	2	0	3	24,173
Crimsons Thrill	2	1	17	3	3	1	20,085
Critique	7	4	40	7	5	6	102,035
Crocation	2	2	21	4	6	2	16,846
Crow (FR)	13	6	89	8	11	13	207,794
Crown Gift	1	1	2	2	0	0	20,890
Crowned Jewel	8	5	52	7	3	8	84,677
Crowning Honors	8	4	55	4	6	6	32,701
Crozier	18	6	104	9	14	13	102,555
Cruise On In	2	2	38	4	4	7	47,154
Crusader Sword	52	23	351	36	50	37	681,347
Crusoe	2	1	20	1	0	8	5,896
Crying to Run	1	1	6	2	1	0	53,640
Cryptoclearance	127	61	795	93	104	95	2,882,609
Crystal Glitters	8	2	40	4	7	7	126,453
Crystal Palace	4	2	33	5	2	5	129,872
Crystal Water	26	12	113	18	12	16	322,333
Cuchillo	2	1	18	1	1	1	9,787
Cullendale	4	2	29	3	2	8	24,346
Cup Race	1	1	8	1	0	0	7,418
Cure the Blues	209	104	1,334	178	173	164	4,711,825
Current Blade	1	1	9	1	0	0	3,595
Current Concept	3	1	16	1	2	1	20,282
Current Hope	8	7	64	9	5	7	155,066
Currock	2	1	5	1	0	0	3,300
Curtain King	8	3	76	3	14	15	57,886
Cut Throat (GB)	19	6	107	14	3	9	145,193
Cutlass	124	66	874	102	106	114	2,283,405
Cutlass Reality	30	20	163	31	21	18	420,690
Cyane	26	16	197	30	27	23	598,741
Czar Alexander	5	2	37	4	3	6	30,224
Czar Nijinsky	2	1	15	3	2	1	22,326

Sire	Perf	Wnrs	Sts	1st	2d	3d	Purses
Czaravich	53	26	386	45	45	41	715,053
D'Accord	110	48	800	94	92	113	2,037,492
Da' White Judge	4	2	26	4	2	3	46,829
Dactylographer	23	13	179	25	27	17	346,972
Dahar	56	30	429	61	37	52	1,528,852
Dalry (GB)	1	1	5	2	0	0	22,260
Dalsaan	1	1	12	1	1	3	7,388
Damascus	123	57	823	104	114	103	2,794,271
Damascus Silver	1	1	7	1	1	1	42,760
Damister	4	2	18	4	2	2	40,580
Damitrius	1	1	12	2	1	2	10,330
Dan Black	2	1	11	1	0	1	13,842
Dan Kano	1	1	5	1	1	0	40,200
Dance Bid	33	22	267	36	39	27	453,827
Dance Centre	4	3	23	7	7	0	164,704
Dance Furlough	3	3	36	3	4	3	19,893
Dance God	1	1	4	1	1	1	3,027
Dance in Time	21	12	123	15	15	15	232,484
Dance of Life	8	2	34	2	2	4	45,475
Dance Spell	8	2	45	3	2	4	29,422
Dance With Dan	2	1	8	3	1	1	14,398
Dancer's Bo Jin	1	1	8	2	0	0	18,877
Dancer's Image	1	1	11	4	1	1	31,840
Dancing Again	7	4	30	5	4	6	104,532
Dancing Brave	14	5	75	10	10	4	323,637
Dancing Champ	11	4	86	6	14	5	202,551
Dancing Count	58	22	339	38	31	31	776,044
Dancing Crown	10	2	55	5	7	6	39,761
Dancing Czar	19	6	116	6	7	17	148,695
Dancing Dervish	10	1	76	3	9	6	33,819
Dancing Dissident	1	1	3	1	1	0	7,200
Dancing Moss	3	1	30	2	3	4	24,001
Dandy Binge	6	4	59	9	7	8	69,019
Danebo	4	1	23	1	2	1	7,375
Danehill	13	7	75	9	5	8	178,748
Daniel Boone	7	3	36	5	2	2	131,421
Daniri (FR)	3	1	14	2	0	5	142,877
Danny's Keys	5	4	28	4	5	3	54,037
Danotable	6	4	56	8	7	6	50,228
Danski	10	5	64	9	9	5	171,224
Dansons	16	5	145	10	19	14	161,092
Danzatore	66	31	475	49	48	65	746,337
Danzig	187	96	1,125	170	145	131	5,662,881
Danzig Connection	115	62	863	109	92	128	1,660,112
Danzig Dancer	2	1	4	1	1	1	7,925
Daranstone	5	3	32	7	3	2	29,211
Darby Creek Road	62	25	417	40	37	43	529,564
Dare to Command	4	3	39	4	8	4	117,477
Daring Groom	8	4	57	7	8	9	75,079
Daring Jim	4	3	30	6	5	2	52,910
Daring March	3	3	26	3	3	5	58,430
Dark Brown (BRZ)	2	1	4	1	0	0	10,145
Dark Illusion	1	1	14	2	3	1	22,152
Darly	1	1	6	1	2	0	10,537
Darn That Alarm	50	27	371	60	49	40	1,012,408
Darshaan (GB)	21	9	129	16	19	20	1,870,150
Daryl's Joy	2	1	16	3	2	1	16,529
Dash It Off	1	1	11	1	1	3	7,020
Dash n' Raja	1	1	6	1	0	0	4,690
Dauphin Fabuleux	23	13	162	20	17	23	373,383
Dauphiny	2	1	5	1	0	0	1,350
Dave's Reality	4	2	37	2	5	4	33,743
Dawn of Creation	10	4	44	6	3	5	70,957
Dawn Quixote	13	10	108	19	15	17	412,016
Dawn Revival	1	1	13	2	2	4	17,916
Dayjur	50	29	307	53	38	38	1,670,982
De Braak	10	2	24	2	2	1	15,480
De Jeau	10	7	93	15	7	13	145,988
Dead Ahead	2	1	10	2	0	2	12,912
Dean Dill	3	1	21	1	3	1	9,535
Dearest Doctor	12	4	65	7	3	6	115,664
Deba's First	1	1	14	1	0	0	3,379
Debonair Roger	25	14	160	22	22	11	399,398
Debut	2	1	15	1	2	5	14,410
Decidedly	11	3	93	4	11	8	45,165
Decies II	3	2	30	3	3	6	36,871
Decimator	4	3	53	3	9	7	23,104
Deck Hand	15	7	140	12	26	15	105,709

Sire	Perf	Wnrs	Sts	1st	2d	3d	Purses
Dedicated to Peace	2	1	24	2	0	2	10,216
Dee Lance	9	5	47	9	5	4	71,731
Deerhound	14	5	72	8	7	6	187,611
Defense Verdict	17	10	123	19	17	23	229,657
Defensive Play	7	2	23	2	2	2	29,560
Defiance	16	7	116	9	5	12	102,152
Degenerate Jon	4	3	46	4	4	8	113,165
Dehere	10	5	61	8	12	9	203,760
Delaware Chief	9	4	55	5	10	6	63,409
Delegant	1	1	10	2	2	4	13,147
Delinsky	6	3	42	4	3	7	33,324
Delta Ban	3	1	28	6	5	1	78,568
Delta Flag	10	5	65	8	12	6	77,517
Delta Judge	3	1	18	1	2	2	14,248
Delta Oil	9	4	67	5	8	9	80,028
Delta Way	4	1	19	1	0	4	12,325
Demons Begone	34	18	213	32	26	26	410,165
Dendron	1	1	7	2	1	1	16,210
Deposit Ticket	18	8	87	9	8	15	165,408
Deputed Testamony	57	32	404	60	56	42	1,576,702
Deputy Governor	2	1	17	1	1	4	3,672
Deputy Minister	316	184	2,036	311	273	266	11,645,931
Deputy Regent	3	1	20	1	1	1	4,690
Derby Wish	16	8	106	16	16	9	337,402
Desert Classic	2	1	12	1	2	1	19,531
Desert Wine	91	41	572	76	70	70	1,688,424
Destroyer (SAF)	4	2	35	3	6	6	37,066
Determinant	4	2	19	2	1	3	10,992
Determined Cosmic	9	6	57	8	3	4	94,517
Determined King	3	3	25	5	2	2	32,112
Determined Man	1	1	3	1	1	0	22,900
Devil On Ice	2	1	6	1	1	1	14,483
Devil's Bag	195	85	1,167	138	141	148	3,722,080
Dewan	33	14	252	28	27	28	553,241
Dewan Keys	23	8	130	11	19	10	237,791
Dewdle's Dancer	2	2	18	4	6	1	34,186
Diablo	25	11	136	15	17	15	374,177
Diabolo	14	4	79	5	8	9	56,032
Diamond Prospect	45	21	324	26	32	43	391,773
Diamond Shoal (GB)	16	10	116	14	19	17	241,744
Diamond Sword	6	3	37	6	4	5	86,530
Diamonds Are Trump	3	2	18	2	3	0	15,069
Diazo	1	1	6	1	1	1	7,555
Dickens Hill (IRE)	11	4	90	4	6	8	58,891
Dickerson	1	1	9	1	0	1	7,312
Diesis (GB)	68	38	387	54	48	45	2,055,049
Digamist	3	1	15	1	1	2	21,144
Digression	6	2	18	2	3	2	22,668
Dike	11	4	118	8	17	17	88,498
Dimaggio	34	12	205	12	16	25	205,305
Din's Dancer	7	1	34	1	0	1	20,305
Ding Dong Daddy	1	1	5	1	0	0	3,498
Diplomat Way	30	10	180	15	16	21	235,598
Diplomatic	3	2	21	4	1	1	25,220
Diplomatic Note	14	7	94	9	16	9	85,315
Direct Descent	3	1	25	2	3	5	29,997
Dirham	1	1	6	1	0	3	8,100
Discovered	1	1	8	1	0	0	11,768
Discretion (FR)	1	1	9	2	2	1	16,300
Dispersal	9	5	54	8	11	8	237,181
Distant Day	5	2	37	5	1	4	60,336
Distant Heart	1	1	9	2	2	3	4,071
Distant Land	6	2	47	3	4	8	41,788
Distant Relative (IRE)	3	2	12	2	2	1	71,591
Distant Ryder	12	6	80	10	8	8	52,336
Distinctive	36	28	314	54	35	41	666,376
Distinctive Pro	123	69	945	114	131	136	2,320,130
Distinctly North	3	3	19	6	1	3	116,015
Distinctpartner	2	1	22	2	4	1	13,403
Divine Royalty	3	1	20	2	2	0	19,900
Dixie Brass	20	10	105	16	13	13	315,312
Dixieland Band	298	165	2,090	309	263	280	7,437,808
Dixieland Brass	33	18	251	39	37	34	607,024
Dmitri	7	2	38	3	6	4	91,869
Do It Again Dan	7	4	49	8	8	7	54,818
Do Lishus	6	3	38	6	3	7	81,749
Do Tell George	2	1	9	1	1	2	5,473
Doc Laragh	1	1	15	1	1	2	2,990

Broodmare Sire	Perf	Wnrs	Sts	1st	2d	3d	Purses
Doc Van	4	3	52	6	6	7	95,367
Doc's Leader	6	3	36	6	4	3	106,640
Docile Boy	6	5	46	7	5	6	79,664
Dock Robbery	2	1	19	2	1	2	12,943
Dock Side	3	2	21	4	3	2	27,811
Doctor Stat	41	22	321	32	42	37	233,658
Doctor's Orders	7	4	48	7	8	3	72,421
Dodge	6	3	38	5	7	3	66,360
Dogwood Passport	19	10	125	19	24	13	172,002
Dolly's Prince	2	1	2	1	1	0	8,020
Dom Alaric (FR)	52	20	398	34	54	51	545,580
Dom Dancer	3	1	23	3	3	3	97,827
Dom Pasquini (FR)	1	1	10	1	1	2	23,681
Domasca Dan	8	1	33	1	4	5	72,172
Dominant	1	1	7	1	0	0	3,530
Dominant Star	6	1	32	1	4	1	8,702
Dominated	4	3	41	6	4	4	73,233
Domineau	4	2	26	7	1	4	266,574
Domineering	1	1	8	2	3	1	3,527
Dominion (GB)	10	4	76	12	10	11	354,885
Don B.	37	12	231	21	30	25	219,244
Don Rickles	5	3	33	3	7	2	28,705
Don Roberto	4	3	34	4	3	3	98,110
Don Sebastian	3	2	17	2	3	3	30,482
Don's Choice	7	4	56	6	5	5	53,975
Don's Joke	2	1	9	1	1	0	20,742
Don't Be Late Jim	2	1	20	2	3	4	15,900
Don't Forget Me	1	1	11	1	0	1	12,115
Don't Hesitate	10	4	38	5	5	2	72,199
Donut King	2	2	16	4	2	2	53,537
Doonesbear	3	1	28	2	5	2	26,412
Doonesbury	34	22	245	38	37	36	558,317
Dot Ed's Bluesky	1	1	15	1	4	0	16,076
Double Avenger	2	1	11	1	1	2	3,831
Double Bed (FR)	2	1	10	1	0	0	8,433
Double Edge Sword	4	2	25	3	2	2	38,285
Double Hitch	5	2	22	3	2	3	47,395
Double Leader	7	2	42	6	3	5	76,038
Double Line	4	2	23	3	1	1	23,989
Double Negative	19	4	79	5	11	9	287,323
Double Quick	2	1	6	1	0	0	3,426
Double Ready	4	2	21	5	6	3	72,979
Double Schwartz (IRE)	1	1	9	1	3	2	27,600
Double Sonic	15	4	67	8	6	8	123,955
Double Zeus	26	18	216	34	31	26	744,316
Dover Ridge	6	2	35	2	9	4	40,900
Downtown Davey	1	1	7	2	1	2	24,985
Doyoun (IRE)	5	2	31	2	4	3	32,983
Dr. Adagio	5	3	15	4	0	2	44,728
Dr. Blum	88	36	498	56	64	64	1,210,223
Dr. Carter	61	33	448	72	57	43	1,326,522
Dr. Dalton	4	1	9	1	1	0	4,940
Dr. Danzig	5	1	26	2	1	2	25,891
Dr. Do Much	7	4	48	5	8	4	73,378
Dr. Fager	5	2	27	2	3	0	46,975
Dr. Geo. Adams	10	7	61	8	10	3	112,918
Dr. Jarrell	8	1	40	1	1	5	12,122
Dr. Koch	5	2	54	6	3	6	74,948
Dr. McGuire	15	2	78	2	7	10	55,677
Dr. Reality	3	3	15	3	2	1	41,790
Dr. Schwartzman	14	4	98	7	10	9	334,701
Dr. Valeri	4	2	22	4	5	3	22,169
Draconic	7	5	49	9	14	9	234,387
Drapier (ARG)	1	1	9	1	0	0	2,165
Dreadnought	4	3	33	4	5	3	119,168
Dream 'n Be Lucky	1	1	4	1	1	0	1,635
Droll Role	8	3	57	5	6	8	32,022
Drom	2	1	13	3	3	3	21,783
Drone	88	40	587	76	85	85	1,661,504
Drone's Reward	2	1	13	2	0	3	41,031
Drop Your Drawers	2	1	29	1	1	0	8,564
Drouilly (FR)	39	21	255	34	34	36	403,657
Drouilly's Boy	3	2	23	2	0	6	17,331
Drum Fire	25	15	182	35	23	27	273,562
Drumalis (IRE)	2	2	23	3	2	6	29,393
Drums of Time	2	2	13	2	3	1	47,960
Dual Honor	5	1	27	2	1	0	14,273
Dublin the Green	2	2	17	2	2	3	20,239

Broodmare Sire	Perf	Wnrs	Sts	1st	2d	3d	Purses
Duck Dance	16	8	135	18	16	19	169,456
Duero	1	1	13	2	1	0	6,510
Duke Mitchell	2	1	12	1	0	0	5,266
Duke Tom	3	2	30	4	5	2	35,274
Duluth	6	2	25	2	3	2	26,978
Dunant (IRE)	4	1	26	1	3	3	7,246
Dundee Marmalade	3	1	12	1	0	0	19,118
Dunfee	1	1	5	2	1	1	26,345
Dunham's Gift	19	7	100	9	9	7	118,060
Duns Scotus	14	6	105	12	20	13	196,153
Durban Deep	1	1	11	1	0	1	5,090
Dust Commander	64	27	443	38	47	60	461,271
Dusty Canyon	2	1	15	1	3	1	12,247
Dynaformer	102	55	680	92	99	84	3,087,376
Dynastic	6	3	46	5	6	4	48,499
Dyno Stat	4	3	34	4	0	4	20,666
Eager Eagle	6	4	54	4	7	5	20,111
Eager Native	6	4	50	5	6	4	57,541
Easter Sun	1	1	10	3	2	3	41,730
Eastern Bazaar	5	2	32	2	5	4	33,986
Eastern Echo	56	33	410	60	64	48	1,548,558
Eastern Lord	11	5	62	12	9	7	60,349
Eastern Music	3	1	17	1	1	5	38,034
Easy Goer	41	21	257	38	38	34	1,079,933
Ecliptical	10	4	77	7	5	5	107,672
Effervescing	21	13	143	30	22	16	329,127
Efisio	5	3	38	4	9	7	150,251
Egg Toss	7	2	45	5	3	5	68,922
Eighty Below Zero	2	1	12	1	1	3	24,884
El Asesor (ARG)	7	3	50	4	3	5	117,701
El Baba	49	26	386	49	32	45	532,080
El Barril (CHI)	5	3	33	3	5	2	51,843
El Corazon	2	2	22	4	5	5	62,392
El Dorado Bob (GB)	6	3	42	8	5	2	47,978
El Dude Grande	1	1	10	1	0	3	2,623
El Gran Capitan (ARG)	10	6	54	14	6	5	164,243
El Gran Senor	71	35	392	59	49	47	3,797,049
El Lagarto	5	1	18	1	1	4	3,849
El Mandingo	4	1	32	1	7	1	19,826
El Pitirre	8	1	49	1	2	6	20,890
El Prado (IRE)	19	12	114	20	15	9	635,094
El Raggaas	29	15	258	28	30	24	486,226
El Rastro (IRE)	6	3	36	5	3	5	68,500
El Rosillo	3	2	17	2	0	1	10,321
El Senor	4	3	30	4	2	3	40,512
El Terresto	2	1	6	1	0	1	4,070
El Tiron	5	4	36	7	3	4	115,211
El Toro	1	1	9	2	3	0	8,394
El Virtuoso (ARG)	1	1	8	2	1	2	23,635
El Vistobueno (ARG)	2	1	20	1	6	5	17,281
Ela-Mana-Mou (IRE)	10	5	53	5	8	5	201,343
Elbow Grease	3	1	25	1	1	2	19,336
Eldag's Boy	1	1	13	1	2	2	25,511
Eldorado Kid	3	1	15	1	1	2	12,340
Electric Blue	6	4	25	6	2	3	49,764
Elegant Life	4	2	19	2	3	1	8,925
Elevation	1	1	9	2	1	2	111,967
Eleven Stitches	7	1	32	1	2	2	23,249
Elk's Uz	1	1	14	2	3	1	21,622
Elkadi	1	1	3	1	0	0	27,600
Elliodor (FR)	1	1	4	2	1	0	233,240
Elmaamul	9	5	63	7	12	7	151,980
Elocutionist	69	32	414	48	45	49	872,984
Elva's King	2	1	14	1	0	1	12,760
Embassy	2	1	17	1	4	0	7,352
Embezzler	2	1	27	1	4	2	13,426
Embrace the Wind	8	5	54	10	3	4	52,136
Eminency	12	5	85	9	6	8	102,877
Emmons Corner	12	5	64	6	9	7	48,316
Empery	16	7	101	9	13	9	341,498
Empire Glory	14	5	88	14	12	15	221,821
Enchanted Hemp	3	2	22	4	3	1	14,231
Encino	40	25	315	54	36	41	872,975
Encourager	7	5	56	13	11	12	121,049
Endow	6	4	56	11	11	9	88,404
Ends Well	41	17	263	26	23	41	463,013
Enemy Number One	1	1	7	1	2	0	20,654
English Master	2	1	15	1	3	1	20,406
Enhance	2	2	13	3	0	1	22,294
Entitled To	1	1	10	3	0	3	62,160
Entropy	34	17	195	29	26	23	391,759
Envoy	4	1	21	2	2	0	13,719
Epic Journey	8	4	48	7	4	5	78,323
Epicurean Delight	1	1	10	2	0	0	8,888
Equalize	4	3	39	6	7	4	134,251
Erimo Ciboulette	4	2	25	2	1	6	42,969
Erin's Tiger	1	1	6	1	2	2	13,822
Erins Isle (IRE)	22	11	140	23	15	20	360,131
Escaped	2	1	13	3	0	1	72,075
Eskimo	55	34	451	68	48	54	914,418
Esops Foibles	4	4	20	5	6	3	49,517
Esprit Du Nord	1	1	8	2	2	0	86,000
Estoril	8	3	54	4	3	10	35,494
Eteelya	3	2	15	2	1	1	16,151
Eternal Prince	19	7	127	13	17	21	202,875
Eternal Table	1	1	8	3	2	0	19,733
Euclidean	2	1	10	1	0	0	4,206
Even Stephen	2	1	13	1	3	4	18,922
Ever On	1	1	17	2	1	1	40,972
Evzone	4	3	27	3	3	4	88,445
Exactly Sharp	2	1	16	1	1	7	41,342
Exalted Rullah	4	2	39	5	5	3	34,237
Exbourne	6	1	27	1	4	4	64,730
Exceller	60	22	339	35	33	37	615,651
Exclusive Bidder	3	1	17	2	1	2	27,638
Exclusive Darling	9	4	50	5	6	9	46,959
Exclusive Encore	5	1	34	1	4	6	29,848
Exclusive Enough	15	6	82	12	7	7	98,305
Exclusive Era	48	21	319	39	45	41	646,455
Exclusive Gem	4	4	66	7	7	3	181,627
Exclusive Lad	3	1	18	1	3	0	6,437
Exclusive Native	44	21	274	38	28	23	525,461
Exclusive One	10	3	55	4	5	5	52,349
Exclusive Ribot	9	2	77	5	18	5	69,892
Executioner	7	1	41	3	9	5	47,647
Executive Intent	7	2	24	5	0	7	65,208
Executive Officer	2	1	13	1	3	1	4,635
Executive Order	41	22	295	41	35	27	405,436
Executive Pride (IRE)	14	8	90	13	7	12	268,422
Exile King	10	3	57	7	3	5	34,943
Exit to Nowhere	4	1	18	2	2	3	37,164
Expense Account	2	1	18	5	1	2	20,995
Expensive Decision	7	3	59	4	8	6	106,249
Experteeser	1	1	5	1	0	1	1,325
Explode II	3	2	21	4	4	4	54,849
Exploded	2	2	17	5	0	5	171,078
Exploding	171	91	1,172	147	136	139	2,606,173
Exploding Prospect	1	1	4	1	1	1	26,300
Explosive Bid	52	33	441	60	44	42	787,186
Explosive Wagon	21	13	128	17	11	16	178,537
Expressman	17	8	109	14	5	10	183,969
Extra Man	1	1	12	3	1	3	14,559
Extra Turn	3	1	19	1	5	3	22,600
Exuberant	85	36	635	63	79	62	1,102,242
Eye of the Morn	2	2	10	2	0	5	9,937
Ezzoud (IRE)	1	1	4	1	0	1	5,522
Fabled Monarch	21	14	174	25	32	22	266,456
Fabuleux Dancer	11	6	82	9	7	9	395,895
Fabulous Dancer	7	5	50	11	7	8	451,261
Fabulous Pleasure	3	1	21	1	0	2	17,730
Fabulous Reason	5	4	41	6	1	7	40,292
Face the Moment	1	1	6	1	2	0	2,134
Fair Skies	2	2	15	4	1	3	31,125
Fair Test	2	1	7	1	2	0	5,917
Fairway Fortune	10	6	72	8	5	11	78,890
Fairway Phantom	20	7	102	8	10	12	96,365
Fairy King	9	4	52	7	9	6	126,738
Falamoun (FR)	3	1	20	1	4	2	33,128
Faliraki (IRE)	10	6	62	8	8	7	97,747
False Prophet	2	1	20	4	0	0	25,668
Falstaff	37	20	198	31	32	19	1,361,267
Fame and Power	4	2	31	4	4	2	69,763
Fame International	2	1	16	1	1	3	9,202
Family Crest	1	1	4	1	0	0	2,395
Family Doctor	28	12	198	25	25	20	376,468
Family Physician	1	1	5	3	1	0	8,695

RECORDS OF BROODMARE SIRES

Broodmare Sire	Perf	Wnrs	Sts	1st	2d	3d	Purses
Famous	1	1	5	1	0	1	16,960
Famous Star (GB)	3	2	7	2	0	0	60,780
Fancy Tammy	1	1	9	1	1	1	8,136
Faneuil Boy	2	1	17	2	2	1	9,935
Fantasy 'n Reality	5	2	27	3	3	1	46,903
Fappiano	172	89	1,136	169	149	127	4,243,864
Far East Sun	3	2	36	5	4	7	74,808
Far North	126	52	749	78	79	78	1,471,857
Far Out East	118	53	821	84	98	118	1,550,824
Faraway Son	27	16	210	21	30	26	365,030
Farewell Party	1	1	10	4	1	1	14,957
Farley (ARG)	2	2	24	2	3	2	20,895
Farma Way	65	39	490	61	58	60	1,125,838
Farnesio (ARG)	11	5	64	11	6	12	295,937
Fast	17	7	89	10	14	12	136,948
Fast 'n' Gold	5	3	32	10	3	2	128,536
Fast Account	11	3	58	7	8	8	173,041
Fast Consent	1	1	13	3	3	0	19,040
Fast Fellow	3	1	22	2	2	2	27,588
Fast Forward	7	3	45	3	4	2	27,873
Fast Gold	62	27	393	42	57	44	707,536
Fast Hilarious	6	1	34	1	3	2	24,104
Fast Passer	8	2	30	3	1	4	42,109
Fast Play	85	56	577	91	73	62	1,610,263
Fast Prospect	3	2	23	4	7	2	40,350
Fasten	2	1	13	2	1	0	17,215
Faster Than Sound	5	2	32	2	3	4	37,641
Father Elmer	1	1	9	1	1	1	6,518
Father Hogan	4	2	29	2	3	2	27,702
Fatih	14	7	94	8	11	8	78,971
Favorecidian	3	1	11	1	1	3	28,995
Fearless Knight	4	1	18	2	5	1	13,115
Feather Dollar	1	1	14	2	0	0	5,444
Feather Ridge	3	1	23	1	1	4	18,156
Featherfoot	2	1	8	1	1	0	6,509
Feel the Power	29	12	217	21	34	25	521,518
Feisal	2	1	17	1	0	0	2,098
Felonious	1	1	3	1	0	0	3,150
Felter On the Quay	2	1	10	1	0	0	6,445
Fenter	4	1	21	1	1	6	23,203
Ferdinand	61	22	380	36	51	60	639,503
Festin (ARG)	6	3	43	4	3	5	73,776
Festive	14	7	116	10	11	5	196,845
Festive Lad	4	1	17	2	1	4	38,440
Feu d'Enfer	10	3	64	4	5	6	49,712
Fiasco	2	1	16	1	1	3	10,745
Fichte	8	2	43	2	4	5	50,735
Fiddle Dancer Boy	5	3	34	3	1	4	37,871
Fiery Best	2	1	30	1	3	5	27,263
Fiery Sea	1	1	4	3	0	1	6,309
Fiestero (CHI)	2	1	16	1	1	0	17,993
Fiesty Fouts	8	3	39	5	4	3	20,476
Fifth Marine	24	11	132	17	11	10	239,822
Fifty Six Ina Row	3	1	33	4	3	3	53,662
Fight Over	47	21	287	35	34	21	702,163
Fighting Bill	2	2	19	3	4	3	28,408
Fighting Fit	54	30	373	48	38	41	690,056
Figonero	3	1	13	1	0	0	3,528
Fijar Tango (FR)	1	1	11	1	1	2	40,120
Filiberto	11	4	71	9	7	4	129,036
Final K.	4	2	29	3	4	7	31,829
Final Straw (GB)	2	1	14	3	0	2	9,759
Finisterre	1	1	9	1	0	1	9,758
Fioravanti	3	2	18	2	1	3	57,763
Fire Dancer	98	49	870	96	105	84	1,329,537
Fire Maker	2	1	17	3	1	5	74,228
First Albert	19	7	145	10	22	15	258,933
First Ambassador	2	1	10	1	1	0	4,180
First and Goal	4	2	35	2	3	6	43,173
First Dawn	5	1	30	1	2	3	14,746
First Draft Choice	6	4	59	5	9	12	72,912
First Landing	9	1	46	2	9	2	97,441
First Norman	1	1	11	1	0	1	3,996
First One Up	1	1	5	1	0	1	6,940
First Patriot	2	1	20	3	0	5	19,197
Fit to Fight	172	86	1,181	136	155	164	2,453,370
Fitzcarraldo (ARG)	9	4	45	7	3	11	520,031
Five Star Flight	19	13	149	19	19	21	357,619
Five Star's Peace	1	1	11	1	0	2	7,369
Fix North	1	1	10	1	2	1	12,294
Flag Officer	13	5	95	6	10	12	81,922
Flag Raiser	6	3	20	3	3	5	25,714
Flagman Ahead	1	1	12	1	0	1	9,585
Flare Dancer	3	1	21	1	0	3	5,707
Flaring Dancer	11	5	72	8	6	9	162,632
Flashy Image	7	3	35	3	6	5	29,393
Flashy Mac	2	1	25	1	6	6	17,631
Fleet Algonquin	2	1	24	2	3	3	21,433
Fleet Elite	3	1	16	2	0	1	4,155
Fleet Excuse	2	2	19	3	2	3	15,858
Fleet Mel	2	2	19	3	2	2	35,240
Fleet Nasrullah	7	1	59	2	5	6	34,248
Fleet Rhythm	1	1	13	2	3	3	19,188
Fleet Sudan	4	1	14	1	2	2	15,909
Fleet Swaps	12	6	82	8	10	11	58,035
Fleet Twist	20	11	180	18	29	27	292,300
Fleet Velvet	3	2	21	2	7	3	34,523
Flip Sal	11	6	76	8	6	6	81,050
Flitcraft	2	1	14	1	2	4	18,534
Floating Reserve	4	1	30	2	3	4	24,628
Floriano	6	3	38	5	2	5	91,437
Florida Sunshine	11	5	87	12	13	10	129,889
Flout	2	1	11	3	3	2	52,551
Flow Swiftly	6	1	57	2	10	12	38,922
Fluorescent Light	32	14	211	24	23	25	451,631
Fly a Kite (IRE)	3	1	22	1	3	1	12,388
Fly Johnny Fly	1	1	8	1	2	0	22,520
Fly So Free	21	9	99	18	7	12	513,423
Fly Till Dawn	7	4	49	13	8	4	150,611
Flying Ace	1	1	12	2	3	4	19,009
Flying Brick	1	1	9	1	1	2	6,352
Flying Continental	2	2	10	2	5	0	39,010
Flying Granville	5	3	23	6	5	1	166,554
Flying Lark	9	5	69	7	6	5	46,105
Flying Paster	172	83	1,179	148	156	149	4,096,306
Flying Pidgeon	22	8	125	12	11	14	282,695
Flying Target	3	1	6	1	0	0	5,085
Flying Victor	12	5	54	9	7	6	278,280
Fobby Forbes	8	2	63	3	11	10	83,125
Fol's Native	3	2	15	3	4	1	31,876
Foligno	6	3	35	3	9	3	48,177
Folk's Pride	5	3	50	5	4	6	34,303
Follow the Drum	14	9	94	19	4	14	209,059
Fool the Experts	19	7	87	8	16	19	193,795
Foolish Pleasure	104	44	722	84	80	93	1,573,609
Fools Dance	13	8	104	15	11	17	379,041
Fools Turn	2	1	14	2	1	2	18,156
For Love and Glory	2	2	18	6	3	2	231,160
For Really	3	2	30	4	3	3	680,423
For Sure	2	1	18	1	2	3	17,290
For The Moment	29	14	215	20	23	21	311,023
Forbidden Pleasure	5	2	20	3	1	0	37,934
Forceful Intent	1	1	4	1	0	1	8,652
Forceten	18	7	112	13	16	15	170,669
Foreign Comet	5	2	21	2	1	1	13,011
Foreign Legion	1	1	7	4	0	0	16,431
Foreign Power	7	1	27	4	0	1	26,002
Foreign Survivor	11	4	89	6	6	9	65,896
Forest Fire	1	1	10	2	2	2	15,637
Forest Of Dean (GB)	1	1	5	1	1	1	10,815
Forever Casting	17	11	125	17	13	10	180,678
Forever Dancer	2	1	13	1	1	0	10,320
Forever Silver	14	4	110	8	8	14	132,195
Forever Sparkle	19	8	140	11	15	14	425,160
Forget the Showers	4	2	25	2	1	3	24,626
Forlaurels	1	1	4	1	1	1	17,600
Forli	55	30	398	46	56	44	632,679
Forli Winds	13	7	97	11	13	9	102,903
Forlion	6	3	30	3	2	1	25,580
Forlitano (ARG)	2	1	8	2	1	2	87,990
Formal Dinner	6	2	32	2	2	6	57,598
Formidable	3	1	19	5	1	0	125,350
Formula One	4	3	39	6	2	4	32,618
Forsythe Boy	12	6	93	12	12	12	111,769
Fort Calgary	12	7	88	16	8	12	269,524
Fort Prevel	16	7	118	15	14	14	126,966

Broodmare Sire	Perf	Wnrs	Sts	1st	2d	3d	Purses
Forthetwo Ofus	1	1	5	1	1	1	2,107
Fortunate Dancer	2	1	9	1	1	1	7,021
Fortunate Moment	6	5	36	7	2	4	103,016
Fortunate Prospect	121	66	934	99	124	122	1,841,813
Forty Niner	143	84	890	149	129	100	4,018,963
Forum	1	1	13	1	0	2	11,575
Forzando (GB)	5	4	29	7	5	2	194,875
Fountain of Gold	39	20	265	35	47	34	620,900
Four Fingers	3	1	18	5	3	4	59,790
Four Ten	5	2	41	3	4	3	53,763
Foyt	19	8	118	9	10	17	92,863
Fratello Ed	2	1	14	1	0	2	9,436
Fred Astaire	74	39	484	63	57	57	1,071,607
Free At Last	7	3	38	6	4	4	47,842
Free Barb	1	1	10	1	2	4	4,505
Free Space	3	1	25	1	3	5	11,048
Free State	2	2	16	5	3	1	65,633
Free Up	3	2	19	2	0	2	8,758
Free Valley	1	1	2	1	0	0	5,213
Free Water	1	1	4	1	0	2	3,896
Freetex	2	2	18	2	1	1	20,413
Freezing Rain	9	4	62	4	8	9	49,629
French Colonial	8	5	41	5	3	9	46,239
French Cut	3	1	26	1	5	2	10,122
French Legionaire	11	5	87	8	11	10	123,108
French Regency	1	1	13	2	1	1	12,150
French Sassafras (GB)	5	1	34	2	3	7	17,087
Friend's Choice	23	8	148	16	18	17	246,907
Friendly Blue	4	1	17	1	1	0	8,958
Friendly Sword	2	2	22	2	0	2	8,699
Friscosilverdollar	2	1	9	2	0	0	14,137
Friul (ARG)	1	1	3	1	0	1	6,390
Frosty the Snowman	19	8	118	17	14	12	217,705
Frosty's Luck	1	1	16	4	4	2	44,780
Fuego Seguro	7	3	53	3	5	11	50,547
Full Choke	31	8	153	19	20	18	530,865
Full Circle	1	1	9	2	1	1	17,849
Full Director	1	1	5	1	0	0	6,079
Full Intent	10	5	76	12	15	7	164,078
Full of Drive	2	1	16	2	2	1	15,541
Full of Promise	4	1	33	4	4	2	17,899
Full Out	56	26	385	46	51	39	810,388
Full Partner	20	11	134	17	22	20	162,486
Full Pocket	79	46	562	76	68	65	1,049,600
Fulmar	11	7	85	14	16	7	173,090
Funny Fellow	2	1	17	2	2	0	22,331
Future Hope	7	1	32	1	2	2	22,022
Future Storm	11	6	76	11	10	7	97,318
Fuzzbuster	16	8	125	11	17	21	177,833
Fuzziano	6	3	22	5	2	3	67,527
Fuzzy	13	5	76	5	10	11	82,110
Ga Hai	4	3	41	4	4	5	59,160
Gaelic Christian	6	4	39	4	7	5	35,584
Gaelic Dancer	6	2	37	9	7	2	26,469
Gala Array	5	2	33	3	1	2	32,535
Gala Double	8	3	42	3	7	6	37,081
Gala Harry	8	3	29	5	2	3	131,510
Gala Skipper	8	2	33	4	4	4	72,104
Galaxy Libra (IRE)	17	8	135	14	12	16	208,212
Galaxy Road	6	2	40	2	5	5	30,277
Gallant Best	20	9	130	14	16	15	85,742
Gallant Knave	8	5	61	10	8	6	126,766
Gallant Lt.	1	1	16	3	4	1	21,207
Gallant Man	8	3	23	4	1	4	77,277
Gallant Prospector	1	1	5	1	2	0	5,300
Gallant Rake	2	1	13	1	0	2	5,570
Gallant Romeo	34	15	210	29	27	20	449,808
Gallant Serenade	1	1	10	2	2	2	12,704
Gallantsky	5	3	24	4	3	1	204,967
Gallapiat	31	12	246	17	26	26	331,000
Garibi	2	1	16	1	3	2	11,431
Garthorn	29	10	169	18	19	12	460,504
Gas Energy	6	4	50	8	3	10	119,481
Gate Dancer	123	64	829	121	75	110	1,854,189
Gato Del Sol	16	4	98	6	7	8	42,113
Gattor	2	1	7	1	2	1	10,660
Gay Fandango	1	1	10	2	4	3	53,370
Gay Mecene	10	6	80	10	13	7	191,754
Geiger Counter	107	54	716	95	65	102	2,253,602
Gemini Dreamer	4	2	17	2	3	2	51,759
General (FR)	1	1	10	2	1	1	12,373
General Assembly	89	44	590	69	70	69	1,538,893
General Holme	20	13	179	26	23	18	545,885
General Meeting	26	11	129	15	17	19	303,477
General Pleasure	6	2	36	2	6	3	37,113
Generous (IRE)	7	5	56	7	12	10	157,933
Gentle Bluffer	2	1	14	1	0	1	13,262
Gentle King	23	12	175	20	18	24	240,457
Gentleman Gene	11	7	95	15	12	7	276,984
Gentleman's Word	1	1	16	1	5	2	14,498
Genuine Silver	2	2	14	5	2	2	85,847
George Lewis	1	1	6	1	1	0	5,880
George Navonod	7	2	40	3	5	4	37,191
George Royal	2	1	10	1	1	2	12,892
Georgeandthedragon	6	2	44	2	1	8	55,708
Georgeff	5	3	27	4	5	0	31,123
Get to the Point	1	1	15	1	0	1	5,235
Getit	2	1	13	3	1	2	32,149
Ghadeer (FR)	8	1	38	1	1	8	95,165
Ghazi	3	3	25	4	2	5	102,454
Giboulee	32	23	288	37	34	36	486,220
Gifted Dancer	6	3	32	4	3	4	26,844
Gilded Age	16	7	87	10	4	7	239,188
Gilded Time	25	11	138	15	20	14	320,084
Gin Tour	1	1	10	6	2	0	47,723
Ginistrelli	18	13	151	28	16	17	346,926
Girl's Castle	5	2	31	2	6	4	36,662
Giuseppe	8	1	36	4	3	4	29,222
Give It a Chance	5	2	24	4	1	5	37,056
Give Me Strength	7	3	33	4	4	5	37,048
Glamor Kid	1	1	17	4	4	1	44,329
Glaros (FR)	3	2	21	2	4	2	248,815
Gleaming	3	3	26	3	4	5	16,019
Glenstal	2	1	18	2	3	5	92,529
Glint of Gold	2	1	6	2	2	0	59,050
Glitterman	45	24	275	40	31	32	437,725
Globe	8	4	56	4	5	7	54,524
Glorious Flag	4	2	19	4	3	3	46,213
Glorious Light	1	1	12	2	0	1	12,372
Gnome's Gold	6	5	41	15	4	6	312,488
Go and Go (IRE)	4	1	15	1	3	2	17,967
Go Exclusive Go	2	1	16	2	0	1	16,695
Go for Gin	1	1	3	1	0	0	22,062
Go for It Matt	2	2	14	2	1	1	10,814
Go Go Roger	3	1	12	1	1	4	22,723
Go Knobs	2	1	11	1	2	0	8,768
Go Marching	1	1	16	1	1	2	4,502
Go Step	35	12	210	16	17	20	183,260
Go to the Bank	3	1	24	1	1	4	14,673
Goal Line Stand	3	1	17	3	1	2	39,452
Godswalk	4	3	42	7	6	5	48,930
Going Straight	10	4	80	4	5	12	36,635
Gold Alert	48	18	343	35	43	36	756,023
Gold and Myrrh	17	5	118	7	11	11	277,648
Gold Angle	2	1	11	1	2	0	8,881
Gold Blend	3	2	23	2	4	3	19,112
Gold Crest	50	24	359	36	43	47	487,199
Gold Crest Express	1	1	12	1	2	1	1,981
Gold Exchanged	3	1	25	6	3	3	61,872
Gold Legend	5	3	35	6	6	6	117,155
Gold Medalist	1	1	12	1	0	0	3,587
Gold Meridian	45	21	310	38	29	48	529,493
Gold On Green	1	1	6	1	3	1	17,509
Gold Prince	3	2	26	3	6	3	24,373
Gold Ruler	3	2	26	2	2	3	15,141
Gold Seam	6	2	37	3	0	1	40,130
Gold Spring (ARG)	1	1	3	1	0	0	4,900
Gold Stage	61	28	437	48	49	41	681,328
Golden Act	73	41	609	65	83	76	1,069,316
Golden Derby	7	3	35	4	5	1	55,919
Golden Eagle II	40	20	311	37	43	30	777,040
Golden Fleece	5	3	39	12	6	4	247,972
Golden Hill	1	1	12	1	3	1	13,533
Golden Pal II	1	1	13	2	3	2	26,955
Golden Peak	7	1	44	1	5	3	37,583
Golden Reserve	46	28	302	46	43	38	706,207

A-590   RECORDS OF BROODMARE SIRES

Broodmare Sire	Perf	Wnrs	Sts	1st	2d	3d	Purses
Golden Ruler	1	1	12	4	3	3	24,128
Golden Souvenir	1	1	7	2	2	1	9,658
Goldlust	16	6	87	16	8	7	273,609
Goldwater	5	2	26	2	2	1	26,435
Goliard	2	2	29	3	5	2	18,764
Gone Digging	2	1	4	1	1	0	12,110
Gone West	121	58	650	90	92	77	2,492,754
Gonzales	18	8	157	10	19	17	95,252
Gonzo's Mistake	1	1	13	1	3	2	8,614
Good Behaving	16	9	122	15	18	14	555,001
Good Counsel	12	3	73	6	5	11	163,599
Good Doctor	4	2	13	3	1	1	13,625
Good Manners	5	2	25	2	0	3	23,799
Good Old Mort	2	2	22	4	0	5	65,340
Good Tensions	1	1	9	1	0	0	5,952
Good Time	1	1	14	1	0	2	14,418
Good Times	1	1	9	2	1	1	31,568
Goshen Store	1	1	13	3	3	1	22,710
Gothic Revival	10	5	78	11	4	4	104,533
Gotzum	1	1	8	1	2	2	4,430
Gourami	3	1	15	3	3	2	37,101
Government Program	6	4	58	9	8	5	73,211
Gran Secreto	2	1	12	3	2	0	36,291
Gran Zar (MEX)	20	11	141	19	20	20	310,442
Granacus	2	1	14	1	1	2	25,733
Grand Allegiance	2	1	20	3	2	2	11,047
Grand Alliance	6	4	39	7	8	1	72,431
Grand Central	4	2	33	4	2	5	26,556
Grand Encore	2	1	22	2	2	4	41,170
Grand Mogol (FR)	1	1	16	2	0	3	9,961
Grand Premiere	3	1	14	2	1	1	8,757
Grand Revival	23	9	119	11	16	17	130,419
Grand Rivulet	2	1	14	1	0	1	6,909
Grand Ruler	2	1	11	2	0	2	4,363
Grande Jette	1	1	14	1	3	0	7,219
Grannys Boy	1	1	10	1	1	1	5,907
Gratification	4	3	49	6	5	6	62,625
Graustark	70	27	416	37	49	66	931,332
Graustark Bolero	1	1	21	2	2	7	25,770
Gray Dandy	1	1	5	1	1	0	7,055
Gray Slewpy	8	3	52	7	8	7	80,110
Gray's Exclusive	9	5	46	9	5	5	37,250
Great Above	156	83	1,013	128	113	118	2,795,155
Great Charmer	3	1	19	3	4	5	63,425
Great Deal	6	1	29	2	4	1	60,645
Great Gladiator	49	28	338	51	51	30	1,246,414
Great Mystery	5	2	50	3	9	6	58,172
Great Neck	13	7	100	18	12	9	209,251
Great Nephew (GB)	4	3	24	3	2	3	166,420
Great Prospector	13	7	66	11	13	8	104,936
Great Substence	4	1	19	1	1	1	5,681
Great Sun	4	1	13	1	2	2	12,508
Greatest Roman	4	3	37	5	5	5	50,630
Greek Answer	13	6	88	13	16	11	230,524
Greek Sky	6	2	47	2	9	3	26,185
Green Dancer	205	101	1,308	163	161	171	5,192,910
Green Desert	12	7	71	14	7	8	478,056
Green Forest	97	55	713	86	89	90	1,718,824
Green Shoon	1	1	6	1	0	3	23,400
Green Ticket	1	1	12	1	1	0	3,848
Greenough	8	2	34	5	8	5	76,184
Gregorian	27	12	203	21	23	23	351,184
Greinton (GB)	72	40	451	71	39	55	1,256,828
Grenfall	16	5	95	7	3	14	63,427
Grey Dawn II	132	53	921	81	125	114	1,615,251
Grey Judgement	4	4	48	10	5	7	158,504
Grey Legion	3	1	21	3	1	0	3,285
Grey Parlor	7	5	73	6	6	3	54,227
Grits and Gravy	1	1	10	3	1	0	5,355
Groom Dancer	9	3	51	4	7	9	458,520
Groomstick	6	5	62	6	5	12	64,801
Groovy	81	44	547	84	76	52	1,212,989
Groshawk	13	5	56	5	4	7	102,960
Grosvenor (NZ)	1	1	4	2	1	1	116,470
Groton	21	7	145	10	7	13	105,687
Groton High	7	3	24	5	3	3	27,606
Ground Breaker	2	1	21	2	1	2	42,454
Grub	10	5	61	10	5	6	149,680
Grundy (IRE)	2	1	15	2	1	0	16,110
Guadalupe Peak	2	1	12	1	1	1	12,274
Guards	3	1	30	2	4	2	15,638
Guillaume Tell	5	1	19	2	0	3	20,969
Guilty Conscience	14	4	81	12	5	11	126,308
Gulch	95	45	652	96	100	76	1,764,808
Gum Tree Danny	2	1	13	1	0	0	2,940
Gumboy	29	20	181	31	26	15	327,565
Gummo	31	18	234	37	24	38	563,718
Gun Bow	1	1	12	4	1	0	26,906
Gunner B (GB)	2	1	16	1	0	8	10,292
Gustoso	8	3	58	9	5	2	54,425
H. D. Orphan	2	2	15	3	5	3	23,057
Habitat	13	3	76	4	8	12	118,655
Habitonia	11	8	94	18	17	11	303,130
Habitony	62	31	411	54	49	45	662,477
Habitual Violator	1	1	6	1	0	0	6,888
Hadif	17	4	98	9	15	13	146,302
Hagley	89	46	602	76	91	87	1,552,751
Hagley's Nest	4	3	20	3	2	3	14,563
Hagley's Reward	2	1	6	1	0	1	7,740
Hail and Farewell	1	1	9	1	0	0	2,544
Hail Bold King	20	4	101	6	4	12	46,114
Hail Emperor	16	10	135	15	17	24	279,978
Hail the Pirates	29	10	175	17	24	17	272,317
Hail the Prince	1	1	10	1	0	0	4,673
Hail the Ruckus	10	3	66	7	5	13	125,218
Hail to Reason	5	3	41	6	4	4	63,357
Hajji's Treasure	2	1	28	2	6	6	25,047
Half a Year	48	25	264	42	35	35	1,018,924
Half High	4	2	25	6	2	5	84,428
Half Iced	2	1	4	1	1	0	15,520
Half Magic	2	2	20	4	3	2	13,114
Hall of Reason	10	3	53	3	6	3	22,067
Halo	286	130	1,922	229	255	221	5,022,274
Halyard	9	5	63	6	7	13	72,515
Hamza	7	2	33	3	0	3	28,568
Hang Ten	1	1	7	1	1	1	33,070
Hansel	22	12	128	20	19	18	617,616
Hapgood	10	5	90	11	11	11	66,329
Happy Bid	3	1	28	1	4	6	12,359
Happy Cake	2	1	10	1	0	1	1,890
Happy Delegate	2	2	11	2	1	0	5,059
Happy Escort	4	1	20	2	1	6	17,513
Happy Gaelic	1	1	5	1	0	0	7,510
Happy Hooligan	4	2	23	2	1	1	16,600
Harbor Prince	2	1	7	1	1	1	44,610
Harbour Bridge	1	1	8	1	0	2	6,034
Hard Crush	3	1	33	3	5	4	41,133
Hard Work	24	13	171	16	23	15	176,099
Hardy Hawk	5	1	22	3	2	0	52,044
Harlan	1	1	7	1	2	1	22,821
Harmony Creek	1	1	6	2	1	0	7,278
Harperstown	3	1	19	3	3	5	110,027
Harriman	4	1	22	3	4	4	108,134
Harry 'n Bill	3	1	24	4	3	5	148,177
Harry the Great	2	1	9	1	1	2	30,008
Harry's Cary	3	1	17	1	2	2	8,768
Harry's Secret Joy	4	1	27	2	7	5	31,343
Harsh Facts	1	1	9	2	1	0	10,128
Harvard Man	16	10	129	21	10	15	326,714
Harvest Boy	1	1	17	1	0	2	4,339
Hasty Flyer	16	5	103	10	16	13	107,884
Hasty Groom	1	1	17	2	2	2	11,220
Hasty Judge	1	1	11	2	2	2	11,625
Hasty Runner	1	1	14	1	5	4	12,020
Hasty Spring	9	3	73	7	3	7	66,580
Hasty Tam	3	3	28	5	4	5	33,472
Hasty Tudor	1	1	18	1	2	1	6,445
Hasty Turfstar	1	1	7	3	1	4	4,908
Hatchet Man	91	43	613	75	70	66	1,533,690
Hatim	1	1	1	1	0	0	900,000
Havanace	3	2	29	6	4	3	91,410
Hawaii	82	42	547	71	64	60	1,181,260
Hawaiian Sound	4	1	28	1	1	1	11,044
Hawkin's Special	54	27	337	41	49	40	566,089
Hawkster	41	16	264	26	27	34	446,671
Hay Halo	14	5	95	5	7	19	152,484

Broodmare Sire	Perf	Wnrs	Sts	1st	2d	3d	Purses
Haymarket (GB)	1	1	6	1	1	0	9,190
Hazaam	2	1	5	3	0	0	43,100
He Loves Me	3	2	27	4	1	7	103,759
He's a Looker	5	2	35	7	7	5	98,726
He's Bad	3	2	20	3	5	1	100,195
He's Our Native	8	6	55	7	5	10	263,146
Heart of Steel	3	1	19	2	2	5	18,620
Hearts of Lettuce	2	1	19	2	1	3	5,896
Heathen (GB)	1	1	9	2	0	0	10,710
Heavenly Plain (IRE)	5	2	46	7	6	7	46,225
Hechizado (ARG)	8	6	59	11	10	8	109,615
Hedevar the Gold	2	1	14	1	2	3	9,965
Heff	6	2	37	3	3	3	41,808
Heir to the Legacy	2	2	20	4	2	5	18,665
Heir to the Line	5	2	31	3	4	5	19,633
Heisanative	2	1	20	1	3	3	17,164
Heliologist	1	1	4	1	0	0	7,200
Hello Gorgeous	24	15	209	23	26	30	374,565
Henbane	22	12	172	22	20	21	331,771
Herat	60	32	421	65	48	63	1,371,436
Herb Water	3	1	27	1	0	2	7,737
Herbalist	5	3	36	3	5	5	47,297
Herculean	12	5	89	7	11	16	128,148
Here We Come	15	7	83	13	12	4	184,194
Hermitage	17	5	123	9	11	14	173,445
Hero's Honor	58	34	428	65	64	53	1,098,225
Hey Rob	6	3	28	4	4	6	40,722
Hi Pi	2	1	12	3	3	0	49,670
Hickman Creek	5	1	20	1	5	2	26,345
Hickory Ridge	2	1	8	1	1	0	1,831
Hidden Capital	1	1	4	2	0	2	40,000
High Brite	76	35	518	57	67	70	820,966
High Comedy	10	5	75	6	6	12	65,591
High Counsel	16	6	77	9	6	12	120,862
High Echelon	16	9	127	15	9	13	177,228
High Energy	2	2	13	4	5	1	103,579
High Estate (IRE)	4	1	9	1	1	1	33,870
High Gold	6	2	54	3	4	7	49,499
High Honors	10	5	53	6	7	5	87,035
High Roll	1	1	10	1	0	1	8,947
High Steel	5	2	17	2	2	2	31,208
High Street	3	1	12	1	0	0	6,699
High Top	2	1	18	4	4	1	66,265
High Tribute	10	2	45	4	5	3	49,286
Highest Honor (FR)	3	2	23	2	3	0	54,036
Highland Blade	73	43	618	78	79	77	1,443,930
Highland Drummer	7	3	42	3	4	6	71,710
Highland Park	51	27	355	40	44	38	572,584
Highland Ruckus	16	7	81	7	10	6	126,638
Highly Praised	3	1	23	1	1	0	12,845
Hiromi the Great	1	1	12	1	2	3	12,300
His B.	2	1	23	1	2	2	15,321
His Majesty	170	78	1,242	159	156	159	2,792,926
Hit in Haste	6	2	24	2	0	0	14,674
Hittite Glory (GB)	2	1	12	1	2	1	17,185
Hoedown's Day	23	9	153	17	18	25	374,952
Hoist the Flag	19	10	128	17	22	16	341,583
Hoist the Silver	37	21	298	27	40	39	552,020
Hold That Fool	2	1	9	1	0	1	6,056
Hold Your Peace	119	66	919	118	120	128	4,038,897
Hold Your Tricks	9	5	77	10	3	10	104,685
Hollywood Brat	3	1	35	2	0	11	28,813
Hollywood Reporter	3	2	11	2	2	0	19,311
Holme On Top	6	2	61	6	5	8	76,901
Holme Tonite	1	1	10	1	0	1	4,602
Holy Bull	16	5	84	9	11	17	156,787
Holy War	20	11	134	15	12	18	100,619
Homasassa	3	2	6	2	0	0	27,000
Home At Last	9	5	52	10	1	13	159,608
Home Guard	2	2	14	3	2	3	46,310
Homebuilder	33	21	252	32	38	34	1,139,908
Homeways	3	3	31	6	5	3	73,253
Honest Bullet	5	3	51	3	3	4	27,355
Honest Moment	15	6	95	15	12	12	236,274
Honest Pleasure	74	32	546	54	54	54	577,737
Honey Jay	79	43	546	74	67	56	825,359
Honeyland	14	5	91	7	17	10	198,960
Honor Grades	18	8	102	18	14	14	792,514
Hooched	66	34	541	60	71	76	1,120,510
Hookano (JPN)	5	2	31	4	5	4	88,805
Hopeful Venture	3	1	13	1	2	2	12,266
Hopeful Word	20	13	179	25	26	23	378,610
Hopeville	4	2	27	2	2	2	27,783
Horatius	93	43	581	91	88	82	1,757,005
Horse Flash (FR)	3	1	19	1	2	3	41,540
Hostage	47	22	299	34	28	34	493,660
Hot Oil	13	5	103	11	10	13	217,515
Hot Words	1	1	8	1	1	1	3,818
Hotfoot	2	1	13	1	0	1	6,686
Housebuster	60	32	328	47	46	44	1,136,684
Houston	89	42	604	73	72	74	1,200,215
How Curious	5	1	38	2	5	6	33,403
Hubbup	2	1	8	1	1	1	6,704
Huckster	36	18	268	33	39	25	505,313
Huddle Up	7	3	56	6	5	3	34,105
Huge Success	1	1	16	2	3	0	9,459
Hula Blaze	12	4	67	5	7	8	67,333
Hula Chief	10	3	64	5	5	8	35,308
Humbaba	3	2	8	2	1	0	4,880
Hunters Creek	1	1	10	2	2	1	11,615
Hunting Cap	1	1	8	1	1	2	5,028
Hunting Horn	7	4	49	8	9	2	109,854
Hurlingham	5	1	29	2	5	3	54,763
Hurok	13	4	66	9	7	6	74,847
Hurontario	7	1	22	1	3	1	20,636
Hurricane Ed	14	2	98	2	8	16	38,038
Hurry to Market	6	3	28	6	8	1	27,799
Hurry Up Blue	10	3	67	4	11	8	70,543
Husband	1	1	5	3	1	1	70,583
Hush Hush Flash	3	2	23	3	1	2	24,521
Husvik	1	1	8	2	2	0	11,835
Hy Lucky Jay	3	2	24	3	4	2	26,306
Hyannis Port	8	6	69	10	7	11	142,843
Hyperborean	26	10	189	20	24	19	207,281
I Am the Game	15	6	110	12	16	11	188,561
I Enclose	16	5	79	7	15	9	151,754
I Find Gold	1	1	8	2	1	1	61,372
I Really Will	4	2	27	4	7	5	30,530
I'm a Banker	2	2	6	3	0	0	90,085
I'm a Lyre	5	3	37	5	7	8	163,739
I'm Daring	1	1	8	2	1	0	25,434
I'm For More	13	7	95	12	10	10	129,627
I'm Glad (ARG)	15	3	122	3	9	13	80,806
I'm No Sissy	2	2	17	2	0	3	13,524
I'm Superman	3	1	18	1	1	3	11,152
I'ma Hell Raiser	49	19	298	27	27	34	493,239
Iades (FR)	8	5	58	9	8	2	172,754
Ibacache (CHI)	1	1	11	1	0	2	6,774
Ice Age	20	12	146	25	21	20	400,260
Icecapade	111	52	763	94	96	104	1,576,373
Icehot	1	1	16	4	2	3	38,484
Icon	2	1	10	1	0	0	4,652
Idabel	10	7	61	8	5	4	90,637
Idaho's Majesty	4	3	22	5	2	5	27,619
Idyll	3	1	5	1	1	0	9,260
If This Be So	12	4	85	4	13	8	124,623
Ile de Bourbon	4	2	23	2	6	1	111,714
Illiopolis	5	3	35	4	4	8	59,002
Illuminate	11	8	113	17	15	16	179,713
Illustrious	10	8	60	14	7	6	209,594
Im Maheras	3	2	16	2	2	4	23,231
Imacornishprince	2	1	21	1	5	4	10,940
Image of Greatness	26	11	195	14	19	20	241,527
Imasmartee	3	2	18	3	1	6	54,960
Imp Society	63	30	398	48	47	48	591,095
Imperial Dilemma	3	2	17	2	1	1	18,173
Imperial Falcon	67	31	569	66	56	50	1,262,703
Imperial Fling	10	5	101	7	11	12	118,937
Imperial Guard	10	2	55	2	2	8	21,612
Imperial Guard (GB)	1	1	6	1	0	0	11,540
Imperial Native	7	4	54	7	8	5	102,661
Imperial Prince (IRE)	3	2	22	3	5	3	56,362
Implore	1	1	4	1	1	0	3,100
Impressability	3	2	22	3	4	2	25,807
Impressive	20	10	165	16	27	20	156,566
In a Trance	4	1	26	1	2	3	16,011

Broodmare Sire	Perf	Wnrs	Sts	1st	2d	3d	Purses
In Excess (IRE)	16	6	65	9	7	5	175,572
In Fijar	7	3	65	4	3	9	54,439
In From Dixie	6	3	50	5	2	11	44,486
In Good Tune	6	2	23	3	1	2	17,496
In One Era	1	1	6	1	3	0	9,780
In Reality	96	52	663	91	98	78	1,801,968
In the Slammer	1	1	7	2	2	2	16,550
In the Swing	5	2	36	3	5	2	63,935
In the Woodpile	6	3	57	7	8	7	29,635
In Tissar	11	3	72	4	7	9	46,425
In Totality	3	1	17	1	1	2	6,592
In Zeal	2	1	11	1	5	3	4,168
Incinerator	26	13	164	22	21	18	294,560
Income Tax	3	1	15	1	2	0	17,682
Incredible Ease	5	2	20	4	2	3	70,380
Indefatigable	1	1	11	1	1	1	4,998
Indian Chief II	1	1	2	1	0	0	3,300
Indian Courage	3	1	27	1	3	5	13,599
Indian Detail	4	2	32	4	1	2	37,072
Indian Groom	7	3	27	4	5	3	73,700
Indian King	3	2	14	3	2	0	165,149
Indian Ridge (IRE)	4	1	17	1	0	1	130,609
Indian River	1	1	13	1	0	3	12,272
Induit	1	1	11	1	4	1	8,289
Indulge	4	1	25	1	2	2	10,373
Industry Standard	4	3	25	3	2	1	9,206
Infantry (GB)	2	2	18	4	0	0	80,890
Info	8	2	63	2	4	9	46,305
Ingot's Ruler	2	1	17	2	5	0	17,840
Inherent Star	8	5	53	7	11	7	131,353
Inland Voyager	6	5	42	7	3	8	93,126
Instant Profit	3	1	14	1	3	1	14,551
Instant Ruler	1	1	8	1	5	0	19,250
Instead of Roses	1	1	11	4	2	2	9,005
Instrument Landing	10	4	66	10	13	3	261,376
Insubordination	6	2	34	3	0	7	22,328
Interco	40	17	234	31	24	24	391,680
Interdicto	18	11	125	17	19	15	211,042
Interestelar S. (MEX)	3	1	13	2	0	1	13,266
Interprete (ARG)	3	2	19	2	2	0	33,142
Intimidation	12	5	72	7	8	8	38,078
Intrepid Hero	3	2	12	2	0	0	8,905
Intrepid Hitter	2	2	13	2	3	1	41,340
Introienne	2	1	17	1	3	3	30,679
Intrusion	5	3	37	6	5	5	33,119
Inventive	1	1	8	2	2	1	18,570
Inverness Drive	55	20	319	34	37	30	401,738
Invincible Dooley	2	2	19	3	4	4	129,670
Irepeat	1	1	8	1	5	0	41,400
Irish Bard (IRE)	1	1	10	1	0	1	2,783
Irish Bear	2	1	11	1	0	2	1,605
Irish Caper	1	1	5	1	1	1	2,600
Irish Castle	27	13	226	23	28	27	226,325
Irish Conn	6	2	48	4	3	6	36,884
Irish Escapade	8	1	40	1	3	4	39,355
Irish Faberge	2	1	12	1	0	1	3,847
Irish Open	30	14	188	20	22	22	377,891
Irish River (FR)	121	56	706	97	75	91	1,945,282
Irish Ruler	20	6	130	14	18	14	323,492
Irish Stronghold	10	4	68	9	10	7	252,561
Irish Sur	5	3	48	6	5	1	83,402
Irish Tower	152	83	1,107	132	126	171	2,375,550
Iron	33	21	253	35	24	32	501,900
Iron Constitution	33	18	261	28	29	22	493,871
Iron Courage	14	4	103	4	14	10	202,992
Iron Duke	5	2	29	3	1	4	250,107
Iron Glove	1	1	19	4	2	4	68,741
Iron Ruler	31	14	235	23	31	23	280,403
Iron Warrior	17	7	119	9	12	10	174,816
Iroquois Park	2	2	15	3	2	4	106,967
Is It True	3	2	15	2	3	1	31,124
Isella	3	3	22	4	1	6	29,977
Isgala	4	1	22	2	5	3	34,378
Island Agent	5	1	23	2	4	4	15,744
Island Fling	6	3	62	4	10	6	68,621
Island Kingdom	2	1	14	1	0	1	3,339
Island Sultan	4	1	37	2	4	6	17,039
Island Sun	5	3	29	3	4	1	17,005
Island Whirl	84	34	519	64	46	59	798,492
Isle Charge	4	3	42	6	4	5	109,679
Isle of Crete	1	1	6	2	1	0	18,800
Isopach	2	2	15	2	1	1	39,944
Isopropyl	1	1	10	1	1	1	7,958
It's Freezing	149	74	1,034	128	135	122	2,427,735
It's Not My Job	1	1	3	1	1	0	1,275
It's the One	11	3	66	4	5	8	104,405
It's True	11	6	98	10	15	12	153,735
Itajara	4	1	9	1	2	1	39,799
Its Acedemic	2	2	28	5	4	5	75,927
Ivan Lendl	9	4	49	6	7	6	138,664
Ivan Phillips	8	2	54	4	7	5	65,122
Iverson	4	1	20	1	0	3	16,771
Ivy's Prince	5	2	38	4	3	5	79,544
J. B. Tipton	1	1	4	1	2	1	2,672
J. Burns	5	3	43	4	10	6	56,344
J. O. Tobin	53	24	429	39	49	58	376,844
J. P. Brother	2	1	15	1	0	2	6,585
J. R.'s Pet	5	3	25	3	2	3	20,000
J. T. Hurst	1	1	6	1	1	0	2,420
Ja Aglo	1	1	7	1	0	2	7,691
Jac's Song	3	1	7	1	0	2	14,963
Jacango	10	6	79	9	14	6	35,930
Jace	1	1	7	1	0	1	2,592
Jacinto	9	2	34	2	3	3	27,745
Jacinton	2	1	13	3	3	2	12,561
Jack Frost	2	1	27	3	2	0	14,384
Jack Hylton (IRE)	5	2	51	5	2	4	18,696
Jack Slade	7	2	51	6	5	5	57,544
Jack Wilson	5	1	33	1	3	7	29,492
Jack's Charger	1	1	8	1	1	1	8,263
Jacques Who	16	9	117	17	17	11	387,201
Jade Hunter	107	63	793	109	90	103	2,393,713
Jahan	3	1	18	2	0	4	25,701
Jaklin Klugman	21	6	136	12	25	13	251,734
Jammed Gold	3	3	28	4	3	5	114,380
Jan's Kinsman	1	1	14	1	3	1	23,634
Janus (ARG)	1	1	10	1	2	3	57,240
Jatski	2	2	24	6	3	2	16,996
Java Gold	80	41	479	54	56	67	1,258,797
Jay's Double	1	1	10	1	0	1	6,625
Jayan	1	1	3	1	0	0	15,000
Jaycean	1	1	21	4	2	2	44,982
Jazz Singer	6	3	57	5	8	7	41,157
Jazzing Around	31	17	196	25	31	28	310,768
Jeblar	57	27	428	43	49	45	807,275
Jeff D.	1	1	18	7	0	3	33,650
Jeff's Companion	5	2	30	3	3	2	14,032
Jeloso	7	3	59	4	8	7	51,347
Jeopardy	2	2	24	7	6	1	56,707
Jerimi Johnson	13	8	86	11	14	10	161,648
Jerry Crow	2	2	25	6	10	3	50,999
Jersey Pleasure	3	1	19	1	2	1	5,335
Jester's Run (IRE)	1	1	7	1	0	0	5,179
Jesterson	4	1	27	1	1	4	16,847
Jet Diplomacy	6	2	33	4	2	4	40,689
Jet Sail	1	1	7	2	3	0	45,027
Jet to Damascus	2	2	33	7	8	4	41,837
Jetting Pleasure	2	1	16	4	2	1	21,160
Jig Away	2	2	16	2	1	3	22,846
Jig Dancer	1	1	11	1	2	1	7,574
Jig Time	27	13	223	25	21	25	445,750
Jihad	5	2	17	3	1	0	13,231
Jim J.	8	3	47	7	3	6	43,529
Jimmy Plains	7	4	44	7	1	7	126,528
Jitterbug Chief	7	2	32	2	3	5	33,190
Jiwani	1	1	8	1	0	3	11,826
Jo Moses	1	1	9	2	1	1	21,783
Joachim	3	1	16	2	1	1	18,838
Joanie's Chief	24	13	168	24	19	16	280,947
Joduke	2	2	19	2	5	0	29,140
Joe K.'s Lester	1	1	4	1	0	0	4,595
Joey Bob	8	4	67	11	7	6	102,516
John Alden	62	33	467	61	49	53	1,501,546
John Casey	12	6	64	10	9	10	51,758
John John John	2	1	8	1	1	2	2,764
John M.	1	1	7	2	0	2	19,888

Broodmare Sire	Perf	Wnrs	Sts	1st	2d	3d	Purses
John Riggins	2	2	20	2	3	5	17,020
John's Choice	5	3	33	5	2	5	78,855
John's Gold	20	8	141	15	17	11	179,470
Johnlee n' Harold	3	2	15	2	1	1	5,544
Johnny Appleseed	4	1	18	1	6	2	29,168
Johnny Pro	3	1	12	3	0	1	43,349
Johnny's Prospect	2	2	18	5	3	4	103,665
Johns Treasure	2	1	13	2	0	1	31,201
Jokester	4	2	41	4	3	10	59,123
Jolie Jo	17	12	146	20	18	21	338,542
Jolie's Halo	36	24	228	40	41	26	935,879
Jolly Johu	11	5	85	9	6	12	122,317
Jon George (GB)	1	1	8	1	2	0	23,510
Jontilla	3	2	18	3	4	4	23,009
Jordana's Count	2	1	12	1	0	3	9,300
Jose Binn	5	1	28	3	5	2	55,151
Journey At Sea	17	8	112	12	10	11	101,720
Jovial Judge	2	1	13	2	0	2	8,798
Jovial Turn	2	1	13	3	1	4	80,390
Juddken	1	1	10	1	3	1	3,837
Judgable	10	2	65	2	3	6	29,645
Judge Kilday	3	2	21	3	1	2	31,365
Judge Lex	5	2	43	9	5	2	165,520
Judge Smells	72	37	512	68	71	50	823,329
Judger	23	9	151	14	10	19	299,511
Judy'sotherbrother	1	1	8	1	1	1	16,100
Jugah	1	1	5	2	0	0	52,440
Julio Mariner	5	1	36	5	5	8	74,694
Jump Over the Moon	10	4	65	5	7	7	33,704
Jumping Hill	4	1	26	2	1	7	17,397
Junction	9	5	58	9	8	7	99,017
June's Blazer	10	2	64	3	7	8	49,415
Jungle Blade	18	7	121	10	15	16	282,950
Jungle Boy (GB)	2	1	9	1	1	1	39,465
Jungle Express	1	1	8	1	2	2	21,822
Jungle Pocket	8	3	58	5	9	5	63,532
Jungle Savage	16	9	84	15	6	13	331,929
Just a Tab	9	5	53	6	5	2	76,479
Just a Tune	2	1	17	2	3	0	33,311
Just Plain Tuff	1	1	15	2	3	5	6,474
Just Right Mike	10	5	72	8	5	10	68,344
Just the Time	61	32	356	55	58	40	475,251
Kadampa	1	1	7	2	1	1	3,700
Kahuna Kai	1	1	13	3	5	1	71,271
Kahyasi	3	2	17	8	3	1	1,280,601
Kaintuck	1	1	16	4	5	0	36,828
Kajun Native	3	1	20	1	0	3	7,328
Kalaglow	8	3	36	3	4	3	92,970
Kalim (IRE)	6	2	27	2	5	5	77,681
Kamehameha	3	1	12	1	2	2	11,520
Kan Reason	2	1	12	1	1	1	4,333
Kansas City	4	2	36	4	4	3	12,097
Kaoru Star (AUS)	1	1	3	2	0	0	56,400
Karol	1	1	5	1	0	0	6,235
Kaskaskia	4	3	27	4	2	3	30,410
Kasteel (FR)	8	3	52	3	2	13	152,787
Katowice	12	5	63	9	10	8	93,205
Kay's Exchange	1	1	5	1	0	0	6,900
Keats	1	1	7	1	0	1	17,250
Kebrimo (IRE)	8	4	30	5	3	7	23,835
Keel	2	1	7	1	1	0	4,856
Keep It Down	3	2	30	5	3	5	69,422
Kelly's Aura (IRE)	1	1	15	2	2	5	40,889
Kelly's Might	4	2	31	4	2	3	30,124
Kendor (FR)	3	1	8	1	1	0	7,825
Kenmare (FR)	6	1	40	2	4	3	84,970
Kennedy Road	101	52	636	104	57	64	1,580,680
Kentuckian	8	7	70	11	10	8	189,417
Kentucky Cookin	5	1	25	2	4	4	35,477
Kentucky Gold	11	6	77	7	7	7	66,482
Kentucky Jazz	8	4	54	4	9	3	57,262
Kerosene	4	3	26	7	5	4	395,091
Kerriby	4	2	25	2	1	1	18,462
Kew Gardens (BRZ)	1	1	5	1	0	0	7,620
Key to Content	15	3	94	4	10	11	84,795
Key to the Carr	1	1	6	1	1	1	2,890
Key to the Derby	1	1	3	2	0	0	2,220
Key to the Flag	1	1	8	1	1	0	6,808

Broodmare Sire	Perf	Wnrs	Sts	1st	2d	3d	Purses
Key to the Gun	2	1	12	1	0	0	3,737
Key to the Kingdom	57	22	398	44	36	31	590,490
Key to the Mint	160	77	947	106	112	100	3,190,715
Key to the Moon	14	6	102	10	10	11	212,556
Key to the Sea	3	1	10	1	0	2	5,193
Kfar Tov	2	1	20	4	2	1	16,391
Khartoum	3	2	35	5	5	3	31,097
Khatango	5	3	28	4	2	4	69,574
Khyber King	3	2	15	2	0	0	7,745
Kibe	5	1	37	1	5	6	31,621
Kick	6	2	43	2	4	6	44,260
Kid Colin	1	1	4	1	0	2	10,432
Kid Kas	2	2	25	6	1	6	41,189
Kigrandi (BRZ)	2	1	9	2	0	1	81,285
Killany River (IRE)	4	1	23	3	2	3	41,515
Kind of Hush	3	1	27	3	5	5	53,224
King Alphonse	8	3	40	6	5	4	38,517
King Cane	1	1	12	2	1	1	31,984
King Celebrity	8	3	42	4	3	2	68,151
King Concorde	3	1	10	1	0	2	4,224
King Emperor	12	6	72	14	7	7	133,479
King Jody	12	5	72	6	7	7	107,815
King Lyph	2	2	18	3	4	2	59,920
King Nerraw	2	2	23	5	2	2	47,366
King of Clubs (GB)	1	1	9	1	2	1	17,853
King of Kings	10	7	45	15	7	2	241,672
King of Macedon	3	2	21	4	1	3	74,936
King of the North	8	4	65	6	10	5	93,971
King of the Sea	2	1	10	1	2	1	2,846
King Pellinore	43	16	302	31	37	19	569,494
King's Bishop	16	5	86	7	10	6	124,710
King's Canyon	1	1	15	1	2	1	6,697
King's Hussar	1	1	11	1	2	1	6,259
King's Nest	7	3	60	5	5	7	83,218
Kingdom Bay (NZ)	3	3	32	4	6	5	60,720
Kingdom Keep	2	1	9	2	2	0	8,831
Kingmambo	13	6	58	9	5	8	237,392
Kings Lake	11	3	64	4	10	8	148,091
Kinsman Hope	4	2	21	3	0	5	13,342
Kipper Kelly	16	5	96	9	8	6	78,626
Kirby Lane	4	3	42	6	4	2	57,911
Kirrary	1	1	6	2	0	0	36,190
Kirtling (IRE)	6	3	30	3	2	3	44,569
Klassy Flight	2	2	22	4	6	4	46,469
Kleven	8	2	19	2	5	4	67,238
Knight	25	12	151	24	30	26	535,643
Knight Counter	3	1	25	2	1	1	11,022
Knight in Savannah	3	2	14	4	1	1	56,670
Knight of Honor	1	1	12	1	1	1	6,474
Knight Skiing	5	4	34	6	3	4	36,324
Knightly Dawn	5	1	22	4	3	4	214,127
Knightly Rapport	1	1	5	2	1	0	6,055
Knightly Sport	4	3	49	5	5	10	90,502
Knights Choice	123	66	829	117	113	103	1,281,543
Know Your Aces	7	2	39	2	4	3	19,188
Known Fact	119	68	752	108	82	100	2,174,549
Kodiack	6	4	32	5	9	4	60,530
Kohoutek	5	3	46	4	4	6	42,592
Kokand	11	6	67	15	10	8	199,749
Koluctoo Bay	17	10	144	15	16	17	266,999
Kona Tenor	4	1	9	1	1	1	1,487
Kreisler	2	1	9	2	2	2	18,708
Kris (GB)	24	10	125	15	12	11	303,704
Kris S.	194	97	1,157	169	148	149	4,114,120
Kunjar	4	1	26	1	6	3	10,472
Kuryakin	2	1	16	3	4	2	15,814
Ky Alta	2	2	18	2	3	3	21,879
Kyle's Our Man	11	3	39	3	4	3	41,313
L'Aiglon	6	1	53	3	5	6	23,865
L'Amour Rullah	5	4	43	6	2	11	116,826
L'Chicle	1	1	4	1	0	0	4,428
L'Emigrant	40	17	280	31	34	44	914,217
L'Enjoleur	123	65	1,002	106	135	156	1,806,560
L'Heureux	8	5	52	7	9	10	155,988
L'Natural	53	26	370	42	47	56	589,220
L. B. Commander	2	1	20	3	0	1	9,762
L. B. Jaklin	5	1	17	1	0	4	23,515
La Cima	3	1	20	4	2	2	21,136

Broodmare Sire	Perf	Wnrs	Sts	1st	2d	3d	Purses
La Saboteur	12	6	59	13	5	6	158,757
Lac des Cygnes (FR)	1	1	5	1	0	0	1,672
Lac Ouimet	27	11	204	16	19	32	307,827
Ladnesian	5	2	35	3	4	7	23,228
Lahib	2	1	10	2	2	1	71,700
Lanburg	2	1	25	1	5	3	21,730
Lancastrian (IRE)	3	2	19	2	3	3	69,134
Land of Eire	5	2	34	4	3	4	45,282
Landscaper	3	1	25	1	3	7	11,965
Lanvin	1	1	10	1	0	1	16,225
Lanyon	9	5	54	7	4	2	46,350
Laomedonte	26	8	140	11	15	15	187,288
Laramie Trail	4	1	16	2	0	3	142,546
Large as Life	2	1	19	1	1	2	16,709
Lark Thor	1	1	8	2	0	3	19,927
Lascaux	1	1	11	2	3	3	106,520
Laser Light	1	1	10	1	3	1	19,680
Last Dance	4	1	39	3	8	2	66,400
Last Raise	3	2	19	3	2	0	23,210
Last Tycoon (IRE)	20	13	119	26	11	17	930,914
Lasting Value	14	7	67	12	4	10	61,624
Late Act	12	6	72	13	14	6	209,410
Latin American	4	1	18	4	4	0	47,345
Laughing Boy	2	1	11	1	1	1	42,963
Launch a Leader	2	1	9	1	1	2	19,126
Launch a Pegasus	4	1	11	1	0	2	16,127
Law Society	8	2	41	4	5	5	315,209
Lawmaker	16	4	130	8	14	13	104,438
Lazaz	1	1	2	1	0	1	15,600
Le Braconnier	1	1	4	1	3	0	38,388
Le Cou Cou	2	1	17	1	1	3	5,592
Le Danseur	8	3	52	6	7	4	156,920
Le Fabuleux	30	17	180	24	17	22	417,787
Le Gosse	6	3	48	7	5	7	47,167
Le Gros Lot	4	1	28	3	0	3	13,948
Lead Astray	5	1	27	3	3	2	29,700
Lead On Time	3	2	11	2	1	0	35,689
Leanant	1	1	12	3	1	1	16,784
Lear Fan	115	51	695	84	100	72	3,541,348
Leather Lyon	1	1	9	1	0	3	18,495
Leematt	9	5	77	6	7	8	79,161
Lefty	4	1	16	2	1	1	31,165
Legal Bid	5	1	21	1	1	4	38,544
Legal Prospector	16	9	91	14	11	18	102,516
Legarde (IRE)	2	1	12	1	1	1	6,290
Legatee	5	2	20	2	0	1	17,392
Legend in My Time	1	1	11	2	1	1	7,198
Lejoli	10	2	64	3	2	6	35,888
Lemhi Gold	29	10	171	14	11	17	173,320
Lend Lease	3	2	16	2	3	1	12,344
Leo Castelli	42	17	233	29	27	34	478,453
Leonardo Da Vinci (FR)	3	1	20	1	0	3	6,630
Leonato	5	2	34	2	5	5	34,576
Leprechauns Wish	5	2	46	3	4	6	33,719
Leroy S.	10	4	68	6	8	15	44,796
Les Aspres (FR)	10	7	60	10	10	12	75,813
Letsboogietonight	2	1	7	1	0	1	8,100
Levee Dancer	3	2	34	5	3	3	40,527
Liberty Hall	3	1	29	1	1	1	25,762
Liberty Lane	5	4	42	8	5	4	101,704
Libra's Rib	1	1	9	1	0	1	9,515
License to Steal	1	1	8	2	0	2	13,143
Lieutenant Corley	6	2	31	2	3	3	25,077
Lieutenant's Lark	2	2	15	2	0	1	54,979
Light Idea	15	8	96	14	7	11	336,232
Light of Morn	3	3	31	5	5	5	92,497
Light Olympia	1	1	8	1	0	2	6,916
Lightfeet	5	4	26	6	4	2	33,731
Lightning (FR)	1	1	9	1	0	0	27,490
Lightning Leap	12	7	71	13	9	10	198,990
Lil E. Tee	13	4	45	4	6	4	112,664
Lil Fappi	6	3	35	4	8	8	118,314
Lil Tyler	8	4	67	5	12	13	116,362
Liloy (FR)	39	16	212	20	18	23	343,118
Limbo	2	1	14	1	3	0	8,068
Limbo Dancer	3	2	32	3	8	1	86,338
Limit to Reason	14	4	85	5	13	7	78,840
Lin D. Charger	12	6	77	6	2	7	61,246
Linamix (FR)	2	1	8	1	2	0	326,850
Line In The Sand	5	2	30	2	0	5	32,261
Lines of Power	60	26	329	37	38	32	459,681
Lingot d'Or	5	1	32	2	5	2	13,411
Linkage	76	45	590	77	66	73	1,024,696
Linnleur	2	1	14	1	1	0	4,401
Lion Cavern	5	1	18	1	4	1	42,940
Lion d'Or	21	8	142	13	12	14	169,538
Lion of the Desert	2	1	12	2	1	0	5,859
List	21	7	113	9	7	20	78,611
Lite Line	3	2	25	4	1	4	83,962
Literati	5	2	46	2	8	9	21,216
Litigator	2	1	18	3	4	3	42,830
Little Current	61	19	332	28	24	31	557,773
Little Missouri	44	21	296	32	32	43	546,150
Little Nureyev	2	1	15	4	4	1	35,155
Little Secreto	6	1	20	1	2	0	10,455
Lively One	42	19	256	26	25	27	320,473
Living Proof	1	1	7	1	3	2	9,086
Lizard Point	1	1	10	2	1	5	5,385
Lobbit (GB)	1	1	6	1	0	1	13,290
Lobsang (IRE)	3	2	25	5	3	0	48,433
Local Suitor	2	1	4	1	1	0	21,840
Local Talent	20	13	142	20	21	15	247,274
Lockjaw	11	3	59	3	6	9	92,312
Locust Bayou	2	1	16	1	0	0	9,167
Lode	13	6	65	9	8	8	143,739
Lodz	1	1	16	3	2	1	26,925
Loft	15	6	101	10	9	17	123,135
Logan Elm	2	2	12	3	2	0	30,750
Logical	12	8	78	14	6	8	495,628
Lomax	7	4	53	5	6	4	38,375
Lombardi	22	11	197	19	16	18	178,294
Lomond	55	28	359	41	63	39	1,018,230
London Bells	16	8	99	11	18	15	184,873
London Company	20	7	139	11	18	25	164,650
Longleat	3	2	16	6	2	1	183,360
Look See	3	2	17	4	3	0	32,945
Loom	9	6	71	11	6	6	105,910
Loose Cannon	9	2	69	5	7	8	70,384
Lord At War (ARG)	91	46	484	75	58	51	1,430,721
Lord Avie	143	76	920	113	131	131	2,280,717
Lord Carlos	9	4	86	6	12	8	84,956
Lord Date	1	1	7	1	0	0	17,385
Lord Double Gate	1	1	9	2	2	3	67,728
Lord Durham	9	2	52	2	2	2	88,935
Lord Gaylord	90	38	567	65	78	80	1,857,345
Lord Ligonier	9	4	64	6	5	7	78,311
Lord of All	16	8	118	13	17	9	72,353
Lord of the Apes	4	2	20	4	1	0	25,568
Lord of the Night	9	4	62	7	3	6	73,960
Lord of the Sea	12	4	87	9	9	7	124,791
Lord of Trillora	3	1	17	1	1	0	5,280
Lord Parham	3	2	18	3	2	1	112,082
Lord Protector	1	1	8	1	0	0	4,734
Lord Rebeau	34	12	210	22	22	28	363,165
Lord Triad	2	2	19	2	2	4	30,436
Lord Vancouver	4	2	27	3	3	4	114,329
Lordedaw (IRE)	2	2	9	4	1	0	79,340
Lordly Love	4	3	42	7	7	7	140,749
Lords	2	2	29	2	3	7	22,120
Lorenzaccio	3	2	20	2	5	1	58,041
Lost Atlantis	12	3	36	3	2	2	17,538
Lost Code	171	78	987	154	128	119	3,243,714
Lost Mountain	7	2	37	6	3	2	79,206
Lost Opportunity	12	5	66	6	8	7	151,522
Lot o' Gold	32	15	215	22	23	21	234,513
Lothario	6	2	47	3	2	4	53,751
Loud and Clear	2	1	5	1	0	2	11,345
Louis Le Grand	3	2	26	2	2	4	18,158
Louisiana Slew	23	9	166	11	18	19	399,378
Loustrous Bid	11	6	101	19	7	9	346,131
Love That Mac	3	2	29	2	4	6	18,162
Lover Boy Leslie	5	1	31	1	1	2	6,974
Lover's Trust	3	2	16	2	2	0	28,825
Low Son	2	1	12	1	1	1	10,575
Loyal Double	1	1	9	1	2	2	26,860
Lt. Stevens	17	8	118	15	16	6	197,426

Broodmare Sire	Perf	Wnrs	Sts	1st	2d	3d	Purses
Lucence	12	6	86	7	11	9	65,194
Luckey Jin Beau	4	3	56	5	7	8	119,864
Lucky Colonel S.	7	5	40	8	3	3	54,386
Lucky Gray	1	1	4	1	0	1	5,430
Lucky Legend	7	2	32	2	3	2	21,941
Lucky Mike	3	1	19	1	0	1	4,928
Lucky North	81	47	627	97	75	74	2,379,626
Lucky Prospect	2	1	6	1	1	0	6,622
Lucky Saros	1	1	4	1	0	1	6,403
Lucky So n' So	8	7	63	12	12	6	182,287
Lucky Sovereign	1	1	8	1	0	2	1,985
Lucy's Axe	12	5	68	10	8	9	119,637
Lugnaquilla (IRE)	3	2	23	2	3	2	16,960
Lumberton	2	1	13	3	2	1	14,135
Lunar Probe (NZ)	1	1	5	1	1	0	2,417
Lunar Ray	3	1	11	2	0	1	18,150
Lustra	5	3	34	3	4	6	30,067
Luthier (FR)	5	3	30	3	2	4	81,922
Lycius	4	1	23	4	4	4	252,515
Lydian (FR)	21	8	136	20	10	15	332,160
Lyllos (FR)	4	3	39	6	4	4	58,615
Lympstone	2	2	17	3	1	2	16,680
Lyphaness	2	1	15	1	1	3	7,162
Lyphard	120	50	763	81	76	92	2,654,074
Lyphard's Ridge	20	10	121	20	17	19	616,322
Lyphard's Wish (FR)	114	44	779	62	88	76	1,024,000
Lypheor (GB)	42	22	286	37	32	31	771,824
Lytrump	4	1	32	2	1	3	9,857
M. Double M.	15	9	99	16	8	14	152,683
Mac Corkle	6	2	40	2	4	6	31,292
Mac Diarmida	18	8	98	15	8	12	261,651
Macarthur Park	5	1	23	1	3	3	9,478
Machiavellian	6	3	47	4	6	8	54,158
Macho Hombre	12	3	77	6	5	3	40,265
Mad Lane	2	1	16	1	2	1	16,531
Mad Scientist	3	1	26	3	5	3	32,329
Maelstrom Lake (IRE)	6	2	27	4	1	2	32,658
Magesterial	96	45	624	87	70	73	1,942,577
Magic Banner	5	5	38	12	6	3	179,890
Magic Hope II	1	1	11	1	1	0	24,543
Magic Moment II (FR)	4	2	39	4	3	6	205,344
Magic Prospect	14	3	81	5	13	11	113,382
Magic Rascal	1	1	11	1	2	0	25,830
Magical Mile	5	2	26	6	4	2	57,199
Magical Wonder	7	3	47	9	8	6	117,157
Magloire	6	1	21	1	1	2	13,876
Maha Baba	9	3	60	4	7	11	80,318
Maheras	16	8	80	12	11	17	104,675
Main Debut	14	9	91	13	15	7	79,938
Majestic Fun	2	1	24	1	3	3	6,042
Majestic Light	218	112	1,535	205	195	169	3,550,633
Majestic Man	4	2	15	3	0	0	7,503
Majestic Marvel	2	1	15	2	0	5	37,819
Majestic Native	1	1	7	1	0	1	9,219
Majestic Prince	23	8	154	18	18	16	174,152
Majestic Red	4	1	29	2	3	3	19,649
Majestic Regent	1	1	13	1	1	1	41,936
Majestic Shore	6	3	57	8	7	9	208,079
Majestic Venture	18	10	140	20	22	18	331,659
Majesty's Prince	49	24	401	37	42	68	520,550
Major Account	2	2	20	3	1	3	20,826
Major Impact	11	5	50	7	5	5	177,252
Major Moran	13	5	104	7	19	14	409,820
Malaga Bay	1	1	10	2	2	0	10,235
Malagra	24	11	152	13	15	21	304,061
Malinowski	16	7	84	8	8	10	107,158
Mamaison	32	15	194	18	32	27	474,876
Mambo	26	11	153	16	15	15	174,697
Man From Eldorado	5	5	43	11	6	2	108,126
Man of Fire	1	1	10	3	3	2	9,044
Man Tan	3	1	16	2	4	3	32,053
Manado (IRE)	2	1	8	3	2	0	49,440
Manastash Ridge	14	7	101	15	7	10	213,808
Manchego	1	1	11	1	2	2	4,061
Mane Minister	22	11	166	20	23	33	426,078
Mangaki	5	2	15	2	0	0	9,612
Manila	79	36	531	66	62	50	2,036,399
Manlove	4	2	39	6	4	8	124,346
Mannerism	4	1	17	1	1	2	11,698
Manos de Piedra	4	3	46	8	3	6	256,646
Mansingh	2	1	14	2	1	1	29,722
Mantecon (ARG)	3	2	25	3	4	2	46,029
Many a Wish	1	1	8	2	0	0	11,175
Manzotti	32	13	228	21	28	26	279,470
Marcellini	13	7	86	12	12	10	169,076
Marenostrum	1	1	14	4	6	0	26,890
Marfa	88	41	659	78	66	96	1,124,350
Mari's Book	83	49	554	96	79	74	3,981,942
Mariache II	3	1	18	3	2	2	28,856
Maribeau	9	1	47	1	7	5	68,617
Marine Brass	26	10	134	17	22	11	240,719
Marine Patrol	11	4	70	4	4	2	51,182
Marju (IRE)	2	1	3	1	0	0	67,000
Mark Around	1	1	3	1	0	1	3,763
Mark Chip	2	1	18	3	3	1	56,330
Mark in the Sky	4	1	14	1	0	0	3,020
Mark of Nobility	12	4	54	6	10	7	173,562
Markesian	1	1	4	1	0	0	2,899
Market Fever	7	3	38	3	1	3	45,004
Marks Blade	1	1	10	1	3	1	19,963
Marks Mill	1	1	9	1	2	2	3,989
Marquetry	32	15	179	24	27	27	409,256
Marsayas	5	2	18	2	2	2	59,249
Marshua's Dancer	103	51	694	94	98	78	1,423,473
Martial Law	13	5	80	11	7	13	196,585
Martian Spell	1	1	5	2	1	1	15,110
Martins Rullah	3	2	16	3	2	3	24,480
Masher	1	1	10	1	0	1	4,508
Masked Dancer	32	13	191	24	22	29	437,177
Masked Marvel (IRE)	2	1	16	1	3	4	33,816
Masked Native	4	1	34	2	4	3	18,705
Maskos	3	2	31	2	11	6	56,478
Master Buck	1	1	2	1	1	0	17,700
Master Builder	1	1	12	2	2	3	10,538
Master Christopher	5	2	30	4	2	6	84,184
Master Derby	88	48	702	88	74	66	867,131
Master Hand	11	9	78	12	12	4	92,724
Master Holmes	1	1	6	1	0	1	10,677
Master Pruner	10	6	77	8	7	10	50,011
Master Robery	3	2	25	6	5	2	37,957
Master Salls	4	1	26	2	3	2	7,124
Master Style	3	2	21	6	4	1	29,043
Master Willie (GB)	14	9	96	13	13	13	239,055
Masterful Advocate	4	4	41	4	2	8	61,627
Mat-Boy (ARG)	9	4	61	11	10	10	221,877
Match the Hatch	18	5	94	7	9	10	104,959
Matchlite	13	8	100	11	7	16	265,012
Mateor	10	2	51	3	2	5	25,581
Matsadoon	30	14	195	25	37	20	463,351
Matsadoon's Honey	1	1	7	1	2	3	20,780
Mattei's Tavern	1	1	6	1	0	0	5,933
Matter of Honor	10	1	49	4	5	3	66,243
Matto Grosso II	5	2	36	5	5	5	64,508
Matzalon Shelter	1	1	5	1	1	2	3,585
Mau Mau (BRZ)	1	1	5	1	0	2	14,445
Maudlin	54	28	393	46	56	49	916,548
Maui Lypheor Jack (JPN)	2	1	13	2	6	1	16,077
Maui No Ka Oi	1	1	4	2	0	0	12,125
Mawsuff (GB)	2	1	14	3	4	4	129,840
Maxistar	4	2	25	4	3	4	25,028
May I Rule	5	4	44	5	5	9	68,600
McCann	9	3	55	4	8	7	64,106
McGinty (NZ)	4	3	35	8	5	5	199,890
McKim	3	3	31	4	5	4	34,060
Me and My Troy	2	1	15	1	3	2	7,660
Meadow Flight	1	1	3	1	2	0	15,365
Meadowlake	164	94	1,047	148	128	144	3,507,431
Medaille d'Or	28	9	149	18	21	21	345,558
Mediatore	1	1	7	2	0	0	53,340
Medieval Man	77	45	562	75	67	56	1,049,605
Medieval Victory	3	2	21	2	3	4	21,858
Megaturn	21	12	146	22	19	19	324,216
Mehmet	73	41	513	72	52	61	1,138,364
Mehmetori	1	1	15	2	2	3	7,660
Meinberg	2	2	26	4	7	4	69,691
Melodisk	3	1	21	3	0	2	16,336

Broodmare Sire	Perf	Wnrs	Sts	1st	2d	3d	Purses
Melyno (IRE)	7	4	67	6	8	8	55,470
Memo (CHI)	2	1	5	2	1	0	16,697
Menderes	1	1	16	1	1	0	7,097
Mendez (FR)	1	1	4	1	0	0	17,600
Meneval	5	3	42	7	4	5	229,618
Menocal	5	3	46	5	5	2	69,586
Mercedes Won	19	12	136	26	13	12	436,441
Merger	1	1	7	3	3	0	13,990
Meritable	33	16	182	23	22	23	123,223
Mertzon	27	10	165	13	12	17	131,546
Meshach	8	3	51	4	2	4	31,350
Messenger of Song	35	14	199	23	20	33	187,048
Metfield	38	15	229	22	35	30	529,622
Metropolis	9	5	75	7	8	10	68,851
Mi Cielo	3	1	13	1	0	1	3,628
Mi Selecto	14	8	93	12	18	15	271,468
Mia's Boy	5	2	33	2	5	3	29,147
Mickey McGuire	17	13	171	22	27	28	275,512
Mickey Mocha	1	1	16	2	0	2	8,973
Midnight Cocktail	1	1	3	1	0	0	1,197
Midway Circle	16	6	94	10	11	9	180,286
Midyan	6	2	23	2	5	1	200,507
Might	1	1	6	1	0	1	1,417
Mighty Adversary	31	19	288	34	37	40	390,345
Mighty Appealing	17	9	133	21	20	24	452,946
Mighty Courageous	6	2	47	3	2	4	11,150
Miglietti	2	1	17	1	4	2	18,569
Mike Fogarty (IRE)	2	1	20	2	1	1	11,262
Milford	3	3	19	4	0	3	85,054
Mill Native	17	5	91	7	7	13	136,201
Mill Reef	9	6	54	9	7	6	247,072
Mille Balles (FR)	1	1	7	2	2	1	36,730
Miner's Mark	11	4	59	4	0	8	124,317
Minera	1	1	7	1	0	2	7,274
Mining	124	64	762	101	123	86	2,632,038
Ministry	1	1	6	2	0	1	7,740
Minneapple	10	3	48	5	3	4	107,585
Minnesota Gus	2	1	23	1	4	1	19,043
Minnesota Mac	10	4	30	4	5	5	62,549
Minshaanshu Amad	19	9	157	12	24	19	244,689
Minstrel Glory	4	3	32	5	7	1	150,810
Mirabeau (GB)	1	1	13	1	2	3	6,166
Miracle Hand	4	1	26	2	2	5	12,306
Miracle Heights	2	1	12	2	0	2	13,170
Misrepresentation	3	1	17	1	1	3	39,910
Missionary Ridge (GB)	9	3	54	4	9	4	72,826
Mississipian	5	3	44	5	3	4	20,022
Mista Vap	1	1	8	1	1	2	20,233
Mister Baileys (GB)	1	1	3	1	1	0	28,140
Mister Jacket	2	1	21	2	5	3	10,896
Mister Lorenzo	2	1	15	1	0	1	8,407
Mister Modesty	1	1	16	2	7	2	65,548
Mister Pitt	1	1	6	1	0	0	5,376
Misty Flight	5	2	37	3	3	4	68,915
Miswaki	237	117	1,443	198	198	187	4,729,285
Miteas Well Laff	14	6	96	12	11	10	151,318
Mitey Prince	1	1	7	1	0	2	11,880
Mo Bay	7	3	27	3	4	3	50,669
Mo Exception	5	3	40	6	4	3	66,857
Mo Power	2	1	12	1	5	1	31,620
Mocito Guapo	9	1	26	1	3	3	261,704
Mocito Serio	1	1	11	1	2	1	90,420
Mock Bird	1	1	6	2	2	0	55,894
Mogambo	42	15	278	31	39	28	643,233
Mohawker	1	1	12	2	1	1	8,988
Mokhieba	10	5	73	7	6	11	112,489
Moleolus	3	1	13	2	2	1	39,785
Mombo Jumbo	7	5	57	10	8	4	59,463
Moment of Crisis	1	1	2	1	0	0	6,600
Moment of Hope	30	19	234	32	22	24	598,451
Moment of Reality	2	1	9	2	1	1	12,882
Momento (CHI)	1	1	15	1	0	2	6,790
Mon Ami Gus	3	1	17	3	1	3	39,314
Mon Classique	1	1	11	1	3	1	7,646
Monetary Crisis	1	1	2	1	0	0	6,570
Monetary Gift	31	19	231	28	23	33	398,531
Money by Orleans	3	1	16	1	0	0	22,474
Moneychanger	5	1	19	1	2	2	7,520
Mongo's Image	1	1	14	1	1	5	12,346
Monsieur Champlain	12	6	89	9	13	9	114,445
Montana Rick	1	1	3	1	0	0	11,358
Montbrook	7	3	32	6	2	5	86,271
Montelimar	1	1	3	1	0	0	9,000
Monteverdi (IRE)	23	9	153	16	21	14	418,262
Montparnasse II	4	2	26	4	1	1	11,730
Moon Prospector	3	3	28	7	5	3	83,040
Moon Up T. C.	12	5	75	9	12	4	43,260
Moonsplash	16	7	96	10	12	10	63,038
Moontrip	2	2	18	2	3	2	40,426
Moorestyle (GB)	2	1	17	2	2	4	34,190
More Horsepower	1	1	10	2	1	1	8,965
More Pleasure	2	1	10	1	0	0	21,161
Morning Bob	54	20	373	30	31	46	566,989
Morning Came	2	2	12	2	2	3	6,115
Morning Charge	2	1	21	3	2	2	8,953
Moro	4	4	42	7	6	7	53,295
Moscow Ballet	105	56	656	89	79	97	1,555,505
Most Welcome (GB)	1	1	3	1	0	1	8,946
Mouktar	1	1	2	2	0	0	67,500
Mount Hagen (FR)	21	9	163	17	13	18	230,400
Mountain Cat	28	10	144	16	14	18	239,928
Mountain Express	6	2	37	2	1	1	9,937
Mountain Lure	7	1	34	1	3	4	29,117
Mountain Native	8	4	41	5	4	7	43,340
Mountdrago (ARG)	4	3	21	6	4	1	236,448
Move Off	2	1	8	1	1	1	15,040
Mr R. T. F.	1	1	13	3	4	2	8,025
Mr. Badger	9	3	38	3	1	8	36,609
Mr. Bold Tea Arr	2	2	23	2	5	6	20,702
Mr. Brilliant	4	2	30	3	2	5	24,621
Mr. Clinch	6	6	64	11	17	5	83,534
Mr. Cockatoo	10	6	77	10	15	13	137,918
Mr. Cool M.	2	1	11	1	0	0	3,914
Mr. Crimson Ruler	3	2	23	3	4	2	39,432
Mr. Exclusive	1	1	4	1	1	1	5,580
Mr. Free Spirit	4	3	32	5	2	3	17,049
Mr. Goldust	6	1	14	1	0	0	9,525
Mr. Howard	6	4	36	5	6	10	52,084
Mr. Inspector	4	1	21	3	2	3	25,953
Mr. Integrity	10	4	49	7	6	7	88,382
Mr. Justice	9	3	61	3	4	10	58,009
Mr. K.	1	1	7	1	0	1	6,870
Mr. Kaskaskia	5	3	46	3	3	10	56,930
Mr. Larkspur	1	1	7	2	0	1	15,514
Mr. Leader	188	97	1,329	179	149	174	3,338,628
Mr. Long	12	5	74	7	5	10	92,494
Mr. Nasty	1	1	7	2	0	1	20,820
Mr. Oct Oil	3	2	21	3	3	3	34,400
Mr. Paul	3	3	36	5	8	8	77,885
Mr. Pleasure	1	1	10	1	1	2	9,830
Mr. Pow Wow	1	1	7	1	0	1	5,191
Mr. Prospector	261	135	1,625	250	207	204	9,847,587
Mr. Ralph	6	4	56	8	9	5	80,020
Mr. Redoy	69	37	550	55	71	66	790,071
Mr. Secretary	1	1	12	1	2	0	5,896
Mr. Sparkles	7	1	36	2	3	6	44,909
Mr. Tattoo	1	1	8	1	1	3	1,955
Mr. Torsion	2	1	7	1	0	1	7,971
Mr. Ward	2	2	23	3	2	3	8,547
Mr. Washington	2	2	16	4	2	1	55,310
Mt. Livermore	193	99	1,275	161	161	162	3,549,320
Mt. Magazine	4	1	17	2	4	3	30,345
Mt. Ruritania	8	3	54	6	8	4	68,791
Mt. Vernon	3	1	18	1	3	5	3,388
Mtoto	4	1	20	2	1	3	30,780
Mud and Water	5	2	14	2	3	1	21,465
Mufti	3	3	24	7	5	2	114,091
Mugassas	6	1	40	1	3	1	16,534
Mugatea	16	10	114	17	7	23	227,406
Mujtahid	2	1	11	1	4	2	48,720
Mullineaux	4	2	39	4	4	6	38,416
Mummy's Pet (GB)	11	8	81	13	10	9	110,670
Murrtheblurr	26	12	163	15	13	12	199,218
Murtaugh	2	2	17	2	5	2	33,332
Muscovite	13	6	77	12	8	8	106,588
Music Master	1	1	3	3	0	0	22,638

Broodmare Sire	Perf	Wnrs	Sts	1st	2d	3d	Purses
Music On Ice	7	5	68	8	8	10	66,039
Music Prince	2	1	10	1	1	1	6,384
Mustard Plaster	2	1	18	3	1	2	14,020
Muttering	20	5	108	6	5	13	59,371
My Boy Adam	5	1	34	4	0	0	129,288
My Dad George	4	3	35	6	2	6	48,830
My Dear Charlie	2	1	4	1	1	0	26,047
My Favorite Moment	6	4	45	10	6	5	172,532
My Gallant	23	12	182	22	25	20	500,451
My Habitony	13	6	85	12	9	5	166,560
My Man Stan	2	1	15	1	2	2	5,018
My Memoirs (GB)	2	2	13	3	0	1	23,503
My Omen	2	1	16	1	2	4	4,693
My Phillipe	3	1	21	1	3	1	26,932
My Ship's In	1	1	1	1	0	0	5,896
Mythical Ruler	16	8	104	17	19	20	499,434
Nabeel Dancer	2	2	12	3	1	2	32,986
Naevus	79	45	483	66	69	48	1,079,906
Nain Bleu (FR)	18	6	106	15	10	11	323,129
Naked Sky	36	16	221	25	27	35	555,879
Nalees Man	54	21	328	28	31	34	374,153
Nalees Rialto	4	1	30	2	2	4	29,717
Nantequos	5	4	37	8	6	5	71,409
Nashaglo	3	1	24	1	2	7	13,083
Nasharco	1	1	14	5	3	2	6,498
Nashua	10	5	96	7	17	15	109,847
Nashwan	16	7	71	9	5	7	343,714
Naskra	126	53	853	112	91	97	4,390,031
Nasty and Bold	110	51	780	93	91	97	1,746,721
Nataraja	11	3	88	7	4	8	53,945
Nathan Detroit	4	1	16	1	1	2	7,850
National Zenith	15	6	106	7	11	12	133,974
Native Aid	3	1	18	1	1	4	14,161
Native Born	6	3	25	5	6	3	40,702
Native Cadet	1	1	11	2	0	1	7,244
Native Charger	44	24	322	37	29	43	419,671
Native Factor	2	1	10	2	1	4	10,895
Native Host	4	1	17	2	4	3	18,737
Native John	2	1	8	2	0	3	17,851
Native of Kentucky	3	2	23	3	2	2	16,068
Native of Seattle	1	1	14	2	3	2	11,132
Native Orbit	3	1	20	1	1	2	4,277
Native Prospector	57	26	343	41	50	40	1,122,943
Native Royalty	67	34	487	53	37	54	823,175
Native Rythm	3	2	22	4	6	3	44,441
Native Secret	5	2	40	3	1	2	17,343
Native Supreme	2	1	19	1	5	7	12,940
Native Tactics	25	10	163	12	25	24	161,126
Native Uproar	26	14	217	25	21	42	438,167
Native Wizard	7	3	46	6	5	7	65,472
Nativo	1	1	7	2	0	1	13,748
Natomas	5	2	18	2	2	2	12,166
Natural (NZ)	1	1	14	1	3	4	11,359
Naturals Grand	3	1	16	1	0	5	14,028
Naughty Jake	3	3	25	4	1	1	18,444
Navajo	36	17	271	30	25	45	369,334
Navajo Trail	3	1	22	1	4	4	23,832
Navy Admiral	3	1	18	2	0	2	12,593
Near the High Sea	1	1	6	1	0	1	18,578
Nearctic Traveller	4	2	26	4	1	4	19,715
Nearly On Time	4	4	37	6	4	6	77,324
Neat Native	2	2	21	3	3	4	32,543
Nebos	4	2	30	3	8	2	213,429
Needles	1	1	8	1	1	3	7,446
Negroni	2	1	23	1	4	3	21,462
Nehoc's Bullet	2	1	13	1	2	0	15,539
Nelson	2	1	5	1	1	0	17,380
Nepal	26	14	164	21	15	17	531,066
Neptuno (ARG)	3	2	8	2	0	1	6,029
Nevada Reality	4	2	40	7	6	6	86,854
Never a Lark	6	4	52	9	3	3	123,123
Never Bend	6	4	57	6	8	6	48,405
Never Dance	2	1	15	1	2	0	7,006
Never Return	1	1	11	1	3	1	5,613
Never Tabled	56	30	314	46	53	47	597,001
New Prospect	13	5	95	15	13	10	535,092
Newsprobe	2	2	20	2	3	0	29,005
Nias	5	4	39	7	1	2	52,719
Niccolo Polo	1	1	6	1	1	0	11,077
Nice Catch	19	6	124	12	16	15	216,594
Nice Dancer	5	3	36	4	3	4	64,182
Nicholas	10	3	42	4	4	5	184,587
Nickel Slot	1	1	9	1	0	0	12,998
Nielbueh	2	1	18	1	0	2	7,318
Night Above	2	1	4	3	0	0	11,748
Night Eagle	3	2	17	2	0	4	13,830
Night Invader	9	2	42	4	6	7	54,428
Night Mover	18	9	107	10	12	22	180,205
Night Musical	7	4	45	4	3	5	11,496
Night Shift	30	15	214	20	22	23	679,378
Night Time	2	2	14	2	1	2	4,939
Nijinsky II	150	75	1,079	142	139	132	3,654,511
Nijinsky Model	5	3	18	3	0	1	43,730
Nijinsky's Secret	16	5	138	5	14	24	112,622
Nijinsky's Table	2	1	20	3	2	3	22,383
Nikoli (IRE)	5	3	44	3	11	4	46,136
Nikos	5	4	32	6	6	4	118,738
Nile Delta	24	7	111	9	9	4	144,672
Nimble Square	1	1	8	1	0	1	5,202
Niniski	5	5	53	7	13	3	84,888
Nishapour	2	2	18	2	1	0	15,200
Nisswa	1	1	9	1	1	3	15,570
Nizon	1	1	2	1	0	0	12,900
No Back Talk	11	8	62	14	8	12	56,071
No Bend	4	3	34	5	2	6	31,872
No Excuses	2	1	10	1	2	0	8,600
No House Call	7	2	62	7	12	9	147,327
No Louder	36	18	265	33	41	31	564,982
No No Billy	3	2	28	6	1	2	40,989
No Points	9	5	64	10	6	8	92,586
No Robbery	25	16	181	26	26	21	343,571
No Sale George	23	9	148	15	16	17	228,176
Noactor	6	1	38	1	8	11	31,601
Noble Assembly	12	6	89	12	15	15	212,388
Noble Commander	1	1	11	1	1	1	3,316
Noble Dancer (GB)	13	5	91	12	9	10	262,163
Noble Decree	1	1	10	1	0	2	7,140
Noble Descent	3	1	10	1	2	1	14,898
Noble Fighter	1	1	5	2	1	1	192,860
Noble Kingdom	2	1	13	1	1	3	6,914
Noble Moment	1	1	10	1	0	0	1,458
Noble Monk (IRE)	3	3	40	3	3	6	41,022
Noble Nashua	29	15	220	28	25	25	393,228
Noble Novice	1	1	4	1	1	0	15,560
Noble Orphan	1	1	9	2	2	2	43,873
Noble Peer	3	1	8	2	2	1	32,930
Noble Saint	4	1	15	2	1	3	72,517
Noble Shamus (IRE)	4	1	16	1	0	1	8,452
Noble Table	6	1	62	2	11	4	58,697
Noble Title	7	4	50	14	4	4	202,569
Noblequest	1	1	7	1	0	2	54,120
Nodouble	92	46	668	70	77	88	1,028,942
Nohesitator	2	2	37	3	6	5	32,307
Noholme II	21	4	125	11	12	8	122,834
Noholme Way	4	2	22	3	4	4	63,666
Nonno (IRE)	3	2	36	4	3	1	25,259
Nonoalco	1	1	9	2	2	0	10,134
Nonparrell	13	4	92	8	7	9	47,601
Noon Time Spender	3	2	24	2	4	3	40,941
Norbot	3	2	41	2	3	6	35,282
Norcliffe	32	14	230	25	37	28	921,817
Nordic Legend	12	5	76	7	11	9	79,909
Nordic Prince	10	5	45	7	2	8	133,081
Nordico	5	3	42	7	6	6	82,258
Normandy Bay	1	1	11	2	1	0	7,380
Norquestor	44	18	249	34	27	34	649,282
North Flight	5	2	49	3	6	0	51,533
North Lad	1	1	22	2	2	4	13,007
North of Eden	3	1	21	1	2	2	9,106
North Pole	19	9	124	16	18	15	228,723
North Prospect	18	8	129	16	17	16	219,965
North Sea	15	5	137	9	18	24	236,838
North Tower	24	13	169	20	22	30	305,720
Northair	1	1	7	1	1	1	47,021
Northern Answer	7	6	41	8	4	3	141,830
Northern Baby	136	62	926	110	135	112	2,868,547

RECORDS OF BROODMARE SIRES

Broodmare Sire	Perf	Wnrs	Sts	1st	2d	3d	Purses
Northern Best	4	2	26	6	2	3	34,811
Northern Birdie	1	1	13	1	0	1	5,516
Northern Classic	4	2	16	3	2	4	43,430
Northern Dancer	50	28	376	50	53	56	1,729,543
Northern Fashion	9	5	68	5	9	6	240,212
Northern Flagship	42	21	225	33	27	29	453,800
Northern Fling	24	9	122	12	13	20	199,904
Northern Horizon	33	13	231	30	27	34	221,459
Northern Invader	1	1	10	1	2	1	2,316
Northern Jove	152	81	1,071	145	145	128	2,413,756
Northern Legend	1	1	11	2	0	1	20,870
Northern Magus	7	6	66	12	3	5	181,565
Northern Majesty	13	7	78	11	2	5	85,163
Northern Monarch	1	1	10	2	2	0	30,453
Northern Mystic	16	5	76	8	11	5	96,580
Northern Native	3	1	28	1	6	5	29,017
Northern No Trump	1	1	10	1	2	0	8,297
Northern Prospect	104	51	632	78	81	69	1,654,519
Northern Raja	11	1	53	1	7	2	35,420
Northern Ringer	9	3	46	4	3	7	80,545
Northern Score	27	13	158	20	19	29	315,384
Northern Smartee	6	5	54	9	8	3	81,968
Northern Spell	3	2	33	5	4	4	44,765
Northern State	1	1	6	1	0	2	30,800
Northern Sun	3	1	15	1	2	2	6,765
Northern Supremo	22	14	165	23	24	18	242,559
Northern Symphony	2	1	12	2	1	0	39,110
Northern Taste	1	1	9	2	0	0	5,544
Northern Treat	2	2	29	5	5	5	111,450
Northern Wolf	14	6	81	7	4	5	98,540
Northfields	14	6	91	7	4	13	571,423
Northiam	11	7	77	13	10	3	167,191
Northjet (IRE)	53	26	410	38	55	50	547,627
Northrop	43	17	275	33	28	47	618,669
Northstar Prospect	1	1	11	2	1	3	11,254
Northwest Passage	5	3	24	3	5	3	47,688
Nose for Money	3	2	12	3	1	0	14,888
Nostalgia	13	4	80	6	7	11	99,052
Nostalgia's Star	19	6	104	7	16	11	102,083
Nostrum	41	23	280	31	33	46	443,336
Notebook	66	42	503	83	61	70	1,721,995
Notna's Prince	4	4	52	7	5	9	72,680
Nova Scotia	6	3	36	3	6	8	38,450
Numa Pompilius	12	7	72	12	10	8	69,883
Numchuek	1	1	15	1	0	1	3,198
Nunneley	2	1	9	2	1	1	27,600
Nureyev	110	55	643	100	86	83	5,296,035
Nureyev Dancer	1	1	6	1	0	0	16,152
O Big Al	3	2	27	4	3	4	21,813
O. K. by You	5	2	24	2	4	6	38,414
O. K. So Far	6	3	39	5	8	3	23,578
Oak Dancer (GB)	5	2	17	3	2	0	92,830
Oats and Corn	1	1	8	2	1	1	6,589
Obligato	16	9	120	11	15	10	183,977
Obraztsovy	9	4	66	7	4	7	69,503
Ocala Slew	2	1	13	1	1	2	38,965
Ocean Bird	1	1	16	1	2	1	6,542
Ocean Trick	6	2	33	3	4	1	73,472
Odd Time	4	1	22	1	4	3	8,831
Ogygian	121	67	784	111	106	99	2,257,468
Oh My Windland	6	3	41	5	9	4	57,242
Oh Oh Canty	1	1	12	2	1	2	4,584
Oh Say	106	55	722	97	92	77	1,670,585
Oka Revolt	2	1	10	1	0	0	7,078
Olantengy (FR)	9	4	59	8	5	5	79,616
Old Broadway	2	2	12	3	0	2	27,467
Old Chronicle	2	1	23	1	7	2	20,400
Old Frankfort Pike	3	1	15	1	1	0	4,190
Old Line	3	1	12	1	0	0	8,400
Old Man (FR)	2	1	15	2	0	4	9,788
Old Pueblo	1	1	10	1	2	2	9,395
Olden Days	1	1	2	1	0	0	3,120
Olden Times	70	30	415	44	46	54	655,092
Ole Bob Bowers	23	9	170	18	21	21	162,701
Ole'	8	3	66	6	9	7	137,004
Olympiad King	10	3	68	4	14	8	65,887
Olympian King	2	2	25	5	3	1	30,093
Olympic Native	10	2	60	5	9	5	140,738
Olympio	23	14	124	24	12	15	670,432
On the Sauce	13	4	75	5	10	13	120,860
On the Sly	11	2	58	2	5	7	60,275
On the Warpath	7	1	29	1	2	4	11,305
On to Glory	83	41	632	72	73	76	1,218,275
Once Wild	29	9	173	10	20	20	195,752
One for All	69	32	476	49	68	69	1,023,603
One in a Mil	8	6	55	9	4	5	31,222
One Little Hustler	1	1	6	4	1	1	106,580
One Magic Moment	2	1	16	1	4	2	103,860
One More Slew	3	2	19	2	3	3	25,949
One Pound Sterling	3	1	16	5	0	1	69,600
Ongoing Mister	1	1	20	2	0	5	12,821
Ono Tarboosh (IRE)	1	1	6	1	3	1	25,155
Onyxly	2	2	23	3	7	3	53,283
Opachisco	2	2	18	2	2	2	30,880
Opening Lead	12	6	104	12	9	11	119,500
Opening Verse	38	18	273	35	29	31	504,268
Opus Dei (FR)	3	2	13	2	3	0	6,012
Oraibi	7	2	17	2	2	1	8,175
Orbit Dancer	48	20	340	29	32	34	303,129
Orbit Ruler	7	4	57	6	9	8	135,773
Orbit's Scene	2	1	12	3	3	0	24,726
Orchestrate	3	1	13	1	1	0	5,772
Order	7	5	44	7	5	3	127,393
Ormonte	4	3	28	5	3	3	111,542
Orono	1	1	10	1	1	2	18,094
Oscar's Gold	1	1	8	1	0	0	2,940
Osorno (ARG)	3	1	31	1	3	0	23,155
Our Blue Chip	8	2	53	3	3	7	47,822
Our Boy Kirk	2	2	17	2	0	0	14,841
Our Captain Willie	4	1	25	1	4	3	23,025
Our City	2	1	19	1	1	1	14,578
Our Escapade	1	1	19	2	1	2	10,518
Our Gary	22	9	170	12	15	12	116,293
Our Hero	17	5	104	7	14	11	97,145
Our Knight	1	1	8	2	0	1	37,210
Our Liberty	6	4	70	8	10	13	97,160
Our Michael	55	19	355	30	47	49	424,482
Our Native	176	79	1,208	146	144	143	2,668,231
Our Recital	2	2	14	2	2	2	14,723
Our Talisman	2	1	27	1	5	6	40,558
Out of Place	16	7	115	8	11	15	164,987
Out of the East	4	3	47	6	5	5	40,784
Outward Bound	3	1	30	2	5	3	33,553
Over Arranged	7	3	83	8	12	11	120,033
Over Mountain	5	2	37	2	6	4	21,484
Over the Rainbow	4	3	41	5	6	6	84,713
Overdressed	2	1	18	2	4	3	28,412
Overskate	43	22	343	38	32	43	690,444
Oxford Flight	3	1	23	1	0	3	16,986
P. R. Man	1	1	17	5	1	2	36,227
P. Vik	2	1	6	1	0	0	6,776
Paavo	8	3	76	7	8	11	51,260
Pac Mania	6	3	47	6	7	4	65,958
Pacclad	1	1	6	1	0	0	3,780
Pachuto	14	5	92	13	5	3	304,355
Pacific Native	19	8	119	16	12	12	117,271
Page	3	1	42	1	6	8	21,258
Page Nijinsky	3	1	12	2	2	0	13,810
Pago Pago	5	3	33	4	6	3	65,670
Pah Check	2	1	32	1	1	7	8,739
Pahaska	2	1	19	1	6	1	8,973
Painted Wagon	8	4	71	5	13	6	54,030
Pair of Deuces	6	4	59	9	5	4	98,441
Palace Music	68	27	479	43	55	57	847,820
Palmetto Prince	1	1	12	3	0	0	10,496
Palton (CHI)	1	1	2	1	0	0	1,098
Pancho Villa	122	71	827	116	113	101	1,725,715
Panorama	1	1	8	1	0	0	4,752
Pappa Max	3	3	29	6	5	4	51,776
Pappa Riccio	22	10	182	19	19	22	263,316
Pappa Steve	5	3	46	5	1	4	53,978
Pappagallo (FR)	17	9	135	16	20	19	120,697

Broodmare Sire	Perf	Wnrs	Sts	1st	2d	3d	Purses
Pappy	5	2	34	4	6	3	42,464
Par Five	2	2	16	2	4	2	24,427
Parade Marshal	4	2	30	3	1	3	47,837
Parade of Stars	6	1	37	2	4	5	57,618
Paradise Bay (GB)	4	1	27	3	2	3	58,536
Paramount Jet	8	4	65	7	11	9	134,398
Parfaitement	29	19	186	33	23	27	861,002
Paris Dust	4	2	31	2	5	2	34,849
Paristo	12	6	99	13	10	9	127,703
Park Regent	7	5	55	10	8	9	99,469
Partez	42	11	240	16	22	26	215,150
Partner's Hope	11	3	52	5	9	1	60,496
Pas de Cheval	2	1	20	3	5	1	24,389
Pas Seul	23	7	145	10	21	13	179,230
Pass and Turn	1	1	4	1	1	0	6,668
Pass Catcher	22	8	124	10	10	11	87,414
Pass the Glass	38	14	241	20	29	32	362,582
Pass the Line	43	17	291	30	30	34	495,858
Pass the Tab	41	19	281	34	37	39	1,326,896
Passing Zone	11	6	60	7	1	2	45,103
Pat's Victory	2	2	21	4	1	5	38,088
Patch of Sun	4	1	16	3	1	1	45,687
Patriot's Dream	2	1	15	2	2	1	18,839
Patriotically	9	3	41	6	3	0	104,445
Patrolman	1	1	3	1	2	0	2,660
Paul's Stark	1	1	13	1	1	2	15,258
Pauper Prince	8	4	48	7	4	6	51,763
Pax Nobiscum	2	1	16	1	0	0	8,498
Pay Tribute	7	3	53	10	5	5	113,744
Peace Arch	5	1	35	1	2	3	5,225
Peace Corps	11	3	65	4	6	4	77,078
Peace for Peace	11	3	65	8	6	11	164,370
Peaked	4	2	27	3	2	2	31,986
Pellinore	2	1	9	1	3	1	8,835
Pellinore's Point	1	1	9	1	1	1	8,651
Pencil Point (IRE)	11	6	79	16	8	9	112,104
Pennine Walk (IRE)	2	1	4	1	0	0	19,630
Pentaquod	5	3	39	7	5	11	84,876
Pentelicus	76	38	432	59	51	50	1,386,533
Pep Up	2	1	14	1	2	3	20,121
Pepenador	9	2	51	4	5	7	74,324
Perceive Arrogance	2	2	27	5	5	5	40,126
Percifal	1	1	5	2	1	0	18,100
Peregrinator (IRE)	3	2	13	4	5	0	33,604
Perfect Parade	3	1	30	6	0	2	113,720
Perfect Player	1	1	17	1	0	0	13,910
Perfect Tan	1	1	15	3	2	2	22,785
Perkin Warbeck	4	3	22	4	3	3	57,810
Perrault (GB)	30	11	198	16	29	25	322,020
Persevered	8	4	52	5	4	4	82,753
Persian Bold (IRE)	19	7	64	8	10	10	267,735
Persian Emperor	5	4	28	5	5	4	34,123
Persian Heights (GB)	2	2	17	2	3	4	63,353
Persifleur	2	2	14	4	0	2	38,251
Personal Flag	102	57	734	102	96	92	2,509,129
Personal Hope	23	14	135	22	18	21	424,120
Personality	9	5	80	10	11	6	137,820
Peter Prompt	1	1	9	3	1	0	44,700
Peterhof	45	21	281	41	48	27	581,960
Petersburg	12	5	55	11	14	4	137,191
Petes Innate	2	1	12	2	3	0	5,122
Peteski	16	10	101	14	8	13	183,492
Petong	5	1	32	1	4	7	132,575
Petorius	1	1	17	2	4	2	27,372
Petrel's Flight	1	1	6	4	0	0	14,015
Petrone	20	9	167	18	21	26	182,054
Pevero (IRE)	1	1	8	1	0	0	6,345
Pharly	15	7	69	7	14	4	183,332
Pheidas (IRE)	1	1	4	1	0	1	5,810
Philosopher	1	1	2	1	0	0	4,500
Phone Order	13	8	82	10	12	11	92,080
Phone Trick	194	94	1,231	159	139	175	3,107,706
Pia Star	11	3	65	3	5	11	50,926
Piaster	5	3	32	7	6	1	67,677
Piccolino	9	6	65	9	5	2	79,786
Picturesque	3	2	26	3	4	3	40,197
Piedmont Pete	3	2	10	2	0	1	25,158
Piker	19	14	154	29	24	22	431,330
Pilgrim	36	17	194	28	20	26	359,851
Pillar of Wisdom	2	2	21	3	0	3	28,485
Pilot Khal	1	1	19	2	0	3	24,926
Pilot Ship	10	4	67	8	11	7	154,388
Pine Bluff	41	20	228	34	25	29	785,022
Pine Circle	5	1	21	3	3	1	36,873
Pipe of Peace	1	1	10	3	0	2	17,745
Pirate's Bounty	188	98	1,316	171	174	189	3,218,600
Pirateer	27	10	180	17	29	21	272,153
Pistols and Roses	1	1	7	1	1	0	12,170
Pitching Wedge	1	1	10	1	1	2	13,208
Pitso Cassello	16	9	89	16	12	13	88,470
Plain Dealing	30	9	168	16	23	27	260,331
Planetarium	3	1	14	1	0	1	4,897
Plastic Surgeon	4	2	31	5	3	6	90,474
Platinum King	2	1	16	1	6	1	46,885
Platoon Leader	5	1	31	3	1	2	21,757
Play Fellow	73	34	556	64	70	73	826,094
Play for Time	1	1	13	3	3	2	252,064
Play It My Way	4	1	45	1	4	2	47,483
Play On	18	7	99	11	11	10	197,070
Play On the Sly	2	1	22	3	3	4	31,809
Play the Ace	2	2	19	2	2	0	24,400
Play the Red	3	1	15	1	3	2	9,554
Pleasant Colony	208	107	1,287	193	186	187	5,278,602
Pleasant Tap	23	10	96	16	10	10	355,141
Pleasure Bent	3	2	21	3	3	3	31,516
Pledge Allegiance	1	1	4	1	0	0	4,950
Pledge Card	3	1	7	1	0	0	1,457
Plenty Old	1	1	3	1	0	0	2,300
Plenum	8	2	40	3	10	9	35,982
Plinth	5	4	40	6	0	4	57,010
Plotting	7	2	44	2	1	4	22,190
Plugged Nickle	77	36	551	50	72	67	1,003,393
Pluie's Sylvester	7	5	67	8	3	11	85,922
Plum Bold	8	3	61	7	4	10	46,048
Pocket Coin	3	3	36	3	4	5	27,210
Pocket Park	9	4	60	6	10	9	57,098
Pocket Zipper	1	1	11	1	1	1	5,383
Pocketful in Vail	5	1	20	3	2	0	55,628
Podium	1	1	12	1	1	1	15,858
Point of Fact	5	2	33	2	4	7	32,421
Poison Ivory	6	3	52	5	9	10	64,999
Poker	13	5	74	5	7	8	89,472
Polar Night	2	1	10	2	1	2	20,690
Polar Palace	3	1	25	2	2	7	17,845
Pole Position	18	10	126	16	15	26	169,908
Poleax	11	5	75	9	3	15	166,830
Poles Apart	9	2	59	7	8	6	48,135
Police Car	26	17	169	27	18	25	232,688
Police Dust	5	2	43	3	4	2	12,928
Police Inspector	9	4	69	6	6	9	62,233
Policeman (FR)	6	2	48	6	4	7	46,667
Polish Navy	93	52	650	89	92	83	1,935,202
Polish Numbers	39	10	185	16	19	18	359,818
Polish Patriot	4	1	14	1	2	0	53,222
Polish Precedent	4	2	21	4	3	0	55,625
Political Ambition	8	3	43	4	4	8	81,492
Polka	1	1	4	1	1	2	17,068
Pollinize	21	5	153	12	16	16	189,399
Poly's Blade	9	3	45	5	7	12	82,370
Polynesian Flyer	6	3	44	4	5	7	45,798
Pondelli	3	1	14	2	0	3	10,512
Pontoise	9	5	69	9	8	5	90,089
Pool Court	2	1	16	1	2	4	5,167
Port Authority	4	2	24	4	2	2	73,190
Port Master	10	4	64	8	11	8	78,298
Posen	3	2	19	3	0	2	15,599
Position Leader	1	1	6	1	0	3	22,320
Positiveness	3	2	16	4	3	1	48,618
Posse	5	3	28	4	3	4	102,461
Potrillazo	5	2	23	2	5	1	126,302
Powder Horn	5	2	31	2	7	3	12,627
Power Break	5	2	21	3	4	3	10,139

RECORDS OF BROODMARE SIRES

Broodmare Sire	Perf	Wnrs	Sts	1st	2d	3d	Purses
Practicante	6	4	59	8	11	4	152,370
Practitioner	13	5	85	9	11	9	104,899
Pranke (ARG)	2	2	22	4	3	3	65,994
Precious Man	3	1	12	1	1	5	6,675
Precisionist	5	3	19	3	1	0	16,751
Preemptive	1	1	9	2	1	3	51,120
Preking	1	1	6	2	2	1	23,550
Premier Ministre	6	2	59	6	9	4	75,644
Premiership	168	86	1,187	141	134	139	2,396,871
Present Value	25	6	176	13	23	28	155,285
President (FR)	3	1	14	1	2	1	11,145
Presidential	1	1	12	1	1	2	10,427
Presidium (GB)	2	1	8	2	3	1	73,740
Press Card	2	1	6	1	0	1	17,036
Presto Lad	14	4	92	6	17	12	67,839
Preston Road	1	1	5	1	1	1	10,090
Prete Khale	1	1	8	1	0	0	13,663
Pretense	22	13	160	16	21	19	192,122
Prima Voce	3	2	20	3	0	4	14,498
Primo Dominie (GB)	4	2	36	4	3	6	27,513
Prince Aly	3	1	20	1	3	1	24,612
Prince Alydar	3	2	17	4	2	2	88,238
Prince Aries	4	1	27	1	0	0	21,505
Prince Astro	10	7	77	11	12	7	132,844
Prince Card	12	2	54	3	6	4	34,711
Prince Dantan	5	2	28	3	2	3	23,756
Prince Forli	11	6	71	7	11	7	74,553
Prince Gala	7	4	24	5	0	1	14,630
Prince Hagley	2	1	10	1	1	0	8,910
Prince Hedstart	2	2	25	3	4	4	25,446
Prince Jaipur	1	1	17	1	3	4	3,746
Prince John	4	1	25	2	1	4	47,518
Prince of Fame	5	3	50	3	4	5	50,869
Prince of Proteus	1	1	10	3	1	1	15,522
Prince of Saron	3	1	22	1	3	5	16,736
Prince Orient	1	1	5	1	1	0	13,397
Prince Regent	1	1	7	1	0	2	3,771
Prince Sabo	3	3	16	8	2	4	719,642
Prince Spellbound	8	4	58	4	3	8	42,941
Prince Street	5	2	40	3	3	7	45,828
Prince Tenderfoot	2	1	11	2	1	0	124,375
Prince Valiant	1	1	10	2	1	3	44,902
Prince Valid	18	6	132	10	9	15	192,244
Princely Native	34	14	200	29	20	26	420,014
Princely Pleasure	22	11	185	18	15	18	315,341
Princely Song	3	2	25	4	2	1	13,773
Private Account	246	119	1,580	195	182	208	4,991,108
Private Express	8	1	28	1	4	4	64,957
Private Terms	85	39	622	71	77	69	1,116,558
Private Thoughts	38	19	291	35	26	37	430,733
Privato	1	1	3	1	1	0	37,150
Prize Ring	2	1	10	1	1	1	9,488
Prized	29	12	179	22	30	21	486,772
Pro Consul	3	2	25	7	4	2	181,600
Probable	4	3	25	3	2	4	21,330
Procida	64	32	436	55	61	51	913,686
Proctor	2	1	16	1	4	2	8,381
Professor Blue	14	5	113	10	8	6	110,200
Proliferate	1	1	12	1	2	4	10,533
Promised City	9	4	52	8	5	5	58,750
Pron Regard	4	1	22	2	1	5	25,193
Proof	16	10	113	17	11	14	225,969
Propelled	2	1	21	1	1	2	14,519
Proper Reality	64	26	394	49	52	48	955,557
Properantes	12	7	78	16	10	10	164,911
Proponent	4	1	24	2	3	3	11,385
Propulsion	1	1	3	1	1	0	2,815
Prospect North	21	8	164	14	22	19	97,944
Prospective Star	28	13	197	24	24	14	278,594
Prospector's Bid	10	5	85	8	6	16	138,899
Prospector's Gold	19	5	142	26	15	16	243,772
Prospector's Halo	21	10	156	17	15	28	472,617
Prospector's Joy	4	3	28	4	3	3	81,400
Prospector's Music	4	1	20	1	4	5	47,800
Prospector's Pick	2	1	11	2	3	1	83,759
Prospectors Gamble	59	35	464	69	66	50	1,279,156
Prosper Fager	7	3	39	6	2	3	52,829
Prosperous	10	6	82	8	7	11	126,266
Proud Appeal	45	22	280	34	39	38	634,821
Proud Arion	2	1	16	1	2	0	12,724
Proud Birdie	89	42	594	65	59	73	1,155,174
Proud Clarion	13	5	92	6	9	11	64,236
Proud Dhabi	3	1	20	3	3	4	51,778
Proud Irish	4	2	25	5	3	3	109,011
Proud Northern	2	2	25	3	6	5	20,208
Proud Pocket	5	3	39	3	5	4	33,500
Proud Romeo	1	1	10	1	1	2	28,500
Proud Truth	65	32	499	49	60	56	886,858
Proudest Doon	2	2	22	5	5	1	35,432
Proudest Duke	3	2	25	5	2	3	40,916
Proudest Roman	40	15	290	25	51	34	441,428
Prove It	4	2	25	3	5	1	27,378
Prove Out	7	2	34	3	3	3	34,444
Proven Reserve	1	1	9	1	0	1	5,750
Proverb	1	1	6	3	0	0	37,200
Providential (IRE)	15	4	78	5	7	5	75,034
Prowess Prince	2	1	9	1	1	2	27,676
Public Finance	2	1	10	1	2	0	9,210
Publicity	3	1	14	2	1	0	13,457
Puchilingui	1	1	14	2	1	3	27,583
Pukka Gent	10	5	61	5	7	11	101,091
Pumpkin Moonshine	14	5	86	11	7	8	117,254
Pumpkin Time	2	1	18	1	4	1	9,858
Punctilio	1	1	4	1	0	0	5,895
Puntivo	7	3	49	5	12	4	55,190
Pure Jest	2	1	11	4	1	1	14,470
Purely Pleasure	6	2	27	3	3	3	73,400
Purple Comet	5	2	32	4	2	4	24,508
Pursuit	10	5	89	12	8	15	183,103
Pursuit of Love	1	1	7	1	2	0	114,270
Pyrite	4	3	38	8	9	6	92,795
Quack	70	34	415	49	42	57	793,315
Quack Attack	1	1	8	1	1	0	6,024
Quadrangle	3	2	33	3	7	5	47,954
Quadratic	52	26	448	47	63	55	913,590
Queen City Lad	13	5	93	9	6	23	89,244
Queen's Splendour	7	5	60	11	6	13	171,309
Quest for Fame (GB)	7	3	26	9	3	2	158,785
Qui Native	22	12	128	16	16	10	162,030
Quick Dance	3	2	18	2	4	0	35,239
Quick Dip	5	3	29	3	4	6	37,991
Quick Style	6	1	35	2	2	2	12,184
Quid Pro Quo	3	1	23	3	2	4	23,430
Quiero Dinero	1	1	10	1	2	1	12,748
Quiet American	39	24	249	39	31	27	718,038
Quiet Fling	8	2	41	3	6	9	52,752
Quiet Jay	3	1	12	1	1	0	9,545
R. B. Chesne	2	1	22	2	3	5	156,931
Racconto	2	2	11	2	2	1	37,190
Racing Room	2	1	15	1	1	2	14,427
Racing Star	11	7	100	11	14	11	154,966
Raconteur	3	2	19	2	2	0	14,244
Radar Ahead	3	2	17	3	4	1	16,498
Raft	10	3	51	4	5	7	53,418
Raggle	1	1	11	2	1	1	8,346
Ragtime Band	7	5	73	11	12	9	152,046
Rahy	147	73	909	132	103	112	3,976,340
Rainbow Quest	24	8	119	11	22	14	1,148,783
Rainy Lake	10	5	85	8	13	8	108,884
Raise a Bid	64	30	431	53	36	46	605,000
Raise a Champion	9	6	66	6	10	9	85,197
Raise a Cup	67	29	385	42	60	51	1,167,489
Raise a Govenor	1	1	3	1	1	1	6,132
Raise a Man	75	34	459	43	54	47	505,280
Raise a Mike	2	2	15	2	1	3	14,016
Raise a Native	126	54	734	92	81	75	1,714,533
Raise a Racer	6	3	31	3	2	2	28,763
Raise a Regal	14	9	118	15	22	10	177,604
Raise an Orphan	4	2	43	3	5	7	50,470
Raise Caine	1	1	7	1	1	1	9,985
Raise Your Glass	6	2	45	2	3	4	15,798
Raised On Stage	6	3	33	3	8	6	65,710

Broodmare Sire	Perf	Wnrs	Sts	1st	2d	3d	Purses
Raised Socially	70	42	508	64	68	61	832,362
Raisor Smart	3	1	20	1	2	4	16,011
Raj Kapoor	2	2	41	5	7	2	34,469
Raja Baba	103	47	740	77	83	84	1,354,884
Raja Native	3	1	10	1	2	1	21,163
Raja's Best Boy	11	9	89	14	6	12	132,521
Raja's Revenge	14	12	130	25	17	21	644,824
Rajab	56	28	430	68	61	42	1,838,373
Raleigh	2	1	5	1	1	1	3,940
Ramadan	2	2	22	2	1	2	12,070
Ramannolie (FR)	1	1	15	2	2	2	3,784
Ramblin Road	1	1	10	1	1	3	5,971
Rambling Rector	5	2	35	4	3	5	128,168
Rambo (IRE)	6	2	62	3	1	4	37,781
Rambo Dancer	2	2	16	3	1	5	65,090
Rambunctious	6	3	30	4	3	4	25,648
Ramirez	17	8	105	14	8	16	132,042
Rampage	8	6	58	11	8	7	218,359
Ramplett	3	1	29	3	4	3	23,700
Ramsinga	11	5	85	10	3	18	117,651
Rare Brick	54	29	346	50	33	41	805,372
Rare Performer	92	49	682	90	78	88	1,451,169
Rarerullah	7	1	31	1	2	2	13,145
Rash Move	7	3	52	5	5	6	74,577
Rattle Dancer	2	1	22	2	3	2	17,194
Ray's Pegasus	4	2	20	2	3	4	24,123
Ray's Pride	1	1	11	1	2	0	5,941
Ray's Word	5	5	66	12	10	7	74,555
Raykour (IRE)	3	1	12	2	1	3	18,594
Reach for More	7	3	46	3	5	4	44,933
Reack Boldly	1	1	8	2	1	3	12,809
Reading Room	7	4	52	5	9	4	35,363
Real Courage	26	15	173	25	16	17	386,550
Real Emperor	3	1	12	1	3	0	43,995
Real Landing	3	3	31	4	3	4	113,822
Real Top Deal	3	1	13	2	1	3	9,033
Real Value	9	4	51	5	5	4	53,877
Real Way	3	1	25	2	3	7	23,700
Reality and Reason	7	4	49	7	7	8	71,722
Really Awesome	3	1	21	2	4	3	29,089
Really Cooking	3	2	28	7	1	6	153,594
Really Secret	4	1	18	3	1	1	203,792
Really Spectacular	2	1	4	1	0	1	2,759
Reasonable Bid	4	1	20	1	2	1	13,503
Reasonably Fair	4	4	47	6	6	6	100,167
Reasoric	3	3	26	4	1	8	28,228
Reb's Policy	10	5	51	6	4	4	89,220
Recaptured	2	1	9	1	0	2	7,596
Recent Issue	1	1	6	1	0	0	3,725
Recitation	6	2	34	2	1	3	34,799
Reckless Blade	5	4	30	6	6	1	121,228
Reckoner	1	1	7	1	2	1	7,552
Record Catch	2	2	16	2	2	3	27,040
Rectory	10	3	73	4	12	11	88,266
Rectus	1	1	13	2	2	2	39,497
Recusant	12	6	101	13	9	10	116,200
Red Anchor	5	1	17	2	1	1	11,014
Red Attack	43	22	291	40	44	33	692,246
Red Clay Country	5	2	43	3	3	2	70,085
Red Crescent	5	3	39	9	4	4	159,246
Red Monk	7	4	43	5	7	6	88,312
Red Ransom	114	55	664	81	85	70	3,009,800
Red Ryder	67	36	587	59	67	57	894,379
Red Sultan	1	1	7	1	0	0	9,279
Red Sunset	2	2	15	4	3	0	131,650
Red Tempo (NZ)	3	1	16	1	1	3	22,210
Red Wing Bold	23	12	139	22	23	13	226,458
Red's Copy	1	1	6	2	1	1	9,190
Redtop III	1	1	15	2	1	1	20,950
Reef Searcher	6	3	35	3	6	4	78,602
Reel On Reel	7	3	36	5	3	5	52,265
Reference Point	9	4	47	7	3	4	97,617
Reflected Glory	17	9	106	13	12	9	112,508
Regal and Royal	66	36	457	71	42	61	1,326,535
Regal Bearing (GB)	8	4	55	6	10	6	73,395
Regal Chief	1	1	22	1	2	1	9,159
Regal Classic	119	61	788	114	86	109	2,629,869
Regal Companion	6	4	44	8	4	7	84,377
Regal Embrace	15	7	107	10	15	18	444,476
Regal Flag	3	3	27	5	3	4	34,892
Regal Humor	4	3	20	4	1	2	68,385
Regal Intention	35	15	232	27	23	35	744,552
Regal Remark	60	37	365	54	40	64	733,484
Regal Search	41	24	239	42	39	26	525,949
Regal Song	2	2	13	2	1	1	18,020
Regalberto	10	8	77	12	11	7	123,106
Regent Cat	1	1	9	1	2	1	24,908
Regent's Dancer	2	1	17	3	3	3	18,654
Rehearing	1	1	5	1	0	0	12,696
Reinvested	8	3	56	5	4	9	76,284
Relaunch	332	191	2,089	347	282	254	8,067,738
Relaunch a Tune	9	4	60	7	5	13	76,791
Religiously	2	1	8	1	0	2	2,080
Relish the Dawn	2	2	19	3	2	3	24,562
Remedial	8	4	46	7	4	5	62,314
Rengold	1	1	17	1	0	0	5,718
Reno City	3	1	20	2	4	1	72,855
Replant	8	4	59	4	5	7	124,903
Repriced	1	1	12	1	2	1	7,785
Reprized	1	1	11	4	2	1	33,050
Requested Honor	1	1	4	1	1	2	2,010
Resound	5	3	38	4	6	2	52,216
Restivo	11	3	64	6	9	9	86,615
Restless Con	2	1	5	2	1	0	38,153
Restless Jet	6	2	35	5	4	3	56,225
Restless Native	18	10	118	19	14	19	265,150
Restless Restless	6	3	37	5	6	0	106,937
Restless Wind	2	2	20	5	4	2	31,885
Retsina Run	7	1	29	1	2	3	19,419
Returnee	8	3	39	3	3	5	32,594
Reverse Mulligan	1	1	11	1	1	1	6,032
Reviewer	9	5	78	9	13	8	142,202
Rewana	5	2	46	4	4	5	48,020
Rewarded	2	2	17	3	2	3	23,729
Rex (CHI)	4	2	23	3	2	2	36,534
Rex Imperator	2	1	17	3	3	1	21,217
Rex Lake	3	1	24	2	4	5	15,530
Rexson	21	11	171	20	15	30	166,882
Rexson's Hope	34	14	247	21	23	26	355,587
Rheffic	1	1	13	2	1	1	17,475
Rhinflo	5	2	37	2	6	2	54,358
Rhodes	6	4	37	6	2	4	37,435
Rhoman Rule	1	1	11	2	2	1	24,425
Rhymeroni	1	1	9	1	2	3	7,665
Riab	2	2	22	3	2	3	9,360
Riad	4	1	30	3	1	3	20,735
Ribet	4	1	32	1	4	2	26,542
Riboronde	1	1	16	2	1	2	9,012
Ribot	1	1	12	2	0	0	7,576
Ribots Verset	2	1	23	1	6	1	36,672
Rich Cream	57	24	314	35	29	41	448,373
Rich Doctor	2	1	16	2	2	1	11,134
Ridan Clarion	1	1	9	3	0	1	157,582
Ridge Fighter	4	2	32	2	2	3	26,160
Right Combination	7	3	41	4	3	5	35,003
Right Con	4	1	33	2	0	0	10,189
Right Honorable	1	1	5	1	2	1	15,312
Right n Ready	2	1	16	1	2	1	12,160
Right of Light (IRE)	1	1	9	1	4	1	10,335
Right Off (ARG)	1	1	8	2	0	2	12,315
Right On Blue	5	4	42	5	8	8	54,466
Riley Ridge	1	1	14	3	2	1	36,246
Ringaro	8	7	77	11	19	13	329,301
Ringside	6	2	29	4	1	1	23,394
Rinoso	18	7	136	12	14	14	131,296
Rio Bravo	2	1	8	1	0	3	3,602
Rio Carmelo (FR)	7	4	52	11	8	10	139,277
Rise Jim	10	4	58	7	7	9	85,800
Risen Star	64	42	452	72	60	71	1,978,146
Rising Market	26	14	168	20	22	19	237,010
Riva Ridge	34	17	226	27	19	25	238,917
Rivelin	1	1	3	1	1	0	3,205

Broodmare Sire	Perf	Wnrs	Sts	1st	2d	3d	Purses
River of Kings (IRE)	3	2	25	3	2	3	18,551
River Special	5	2	27	2	2	3	57,927
Riverman	109	44	662	74	71	62	2,188,318
Riverton (FR)	1	1	13	1	4	1	13,301
Rivotious	1	1	10	1	2	1	62,620
Road At Sea	1	1	11	4	1	2	52,440
Road Checker	2	1	9	2	1	1	6,198
Roanoke	39	21	235	33	29	21	703,101
Roanoke Island	16	11	115	16	16	17	295,619
Robellino	28	16	199	30	21	30	487,344
Roberto	95	43	624	57	72	75	1,317,460
Robin des Pins	7	4	69	9	5	6	128,144
Robin's Song	5	4	56	7	6	6	57,791
Robyn Dancer	18	5	97	8	14	9	167,722
Rock City (IRE)	1	1	16	4	0	2	31,255
Rock Lives	2	2	26	4	7	4	36,973
Rock of Cashel	3	2	25	2	1	3	18,087
Rock Point	5	2	24	2	3	2	74,610
Rock Royalty	6	2	40	6	3	5	63,358
Rock Talk	18	6	105	12	10	17	162,837
Rocket Pocket	2	1	11	2	3	0	38,052
Rockport Crossing	3	1	19	3	1	2	7,643
Rockwall	4	3	35	6	3	2	78,284
Rocky Mountain	1	1	4	1	0	0	5,700
Roderic	6	4	63	7	4	9	71,185
Rogrox	1	1	10	1	3	4	16,360
Roi Danzig	4	2	27	2	0	7	92,199
Rokeby (GB)	2	1	14	1	3	3	19,830
Rolfson	10	4	84	5	8	13	69,881
Rollick 'n Roll	4	3	51	11	4	5	88,408
Rollicking	71	32	463	62	57	65	1,072,001
Rollicking's Image	1	1	6	2	1	1	20,895
Rollin Count	1	1	3	1	1	0	23,637
Rollin On Over	12	4	57	6	4	7	193,846
Rolls Aly	14	7	82	15	9	9	155,407
Roman Diplomat	14	5	101	11	12	11	178,972
Roman Majesty	4	1	12	1	3	0	93,078
Roman Missile	1	1	7	2	0	1	123,000
Roman Reasoning	9	7	78	7	6	9	137,879
Romantic Lead	10	6	58	8	5	5	172,147
Romeo	25	8	138	16	16	16	472,061
Roo Art	12	8	88	13	6	11	116,348
Rouge Sang	1	1	12	1	2	2	11,456
Rougemont	5	1	39	1	3	4	29,880
Rough Iron	1	1	14	3	1	2	20,202
Roulette Wheel	6	4	62	6	9	9	99,532
Round Table	5	1	26	1	3	0	16,579
Round Table Jr.	5	2	50	7	6	2	34,726
Rousillon	10	5	61	9	5	1	92,283
Roxbury Park	8	3	42	5	2	3	58,629
Roy	13	8	78	16	13	7	296,389
Royal Academy	14	6	84	12	14	12	512,100
Royal Air Forbes	1	1	10	1	0	2	17,083
Royal and Regal	28	13	199	24	14	28	238,784
Royal Cap	1	1	9	1	0	4	6,288
Royal Chocolate	11	7	84	23	8	10	442,545
Royal Design	7	1	43	1	7	5	32,347
Royal Express O.	1	1	8	1	2	2	11,340
Royal Hawaiian	1	1	9	1	0	0	1,178
Royal Hierarchy	4	1	23	2	2	4	35,515
Royal Knight	2	1	16	2	0	2	9,026
Royal Mandarin	1	1	7	1	1	0	6,376
Royal Pavilion	4	1	23	1	2	3	13,783
Royal Pennant	6	5	41	6	9	8	51,609
Royal Prayer (GB)	3	1	38	1	3	6	17,531
Royal Reasoning	3	1	22	2	2	1	47,325
Royal Roberto	40	19	321	37	44	41	640,512
Royal Saxon	1	1	13	2	0	1	6,291
Royal Ski	10	6	55	10	9	3	161,576
Royal Surrender	4	3	32	5	4	3	29,090
Royal Value	2	1	12	1	3	1	56,754
Rubiano	45	23	243	38	39	29	1,438,624
Ruff Mark	3	1	24	3	1	3	22,609
Ruffinal	14	8	106	11	15	9	247,392
Ruffled Feathers	3	2	23	4	3	2	27,376
Ruhlmann	30	14	181	23	24	22	248,415
Ruler's Downfall	1	1	12	1	1	2	3,745
Ruling Eagle	2	1	14	2	0	1	7,916
Ruling One	2	1	12	2	2	2	7,667
Rumbo	7	5	45	6	4	3	84,971
Run Dusty Run	15	7	97	16	15	8	379,553
Run Fool Run	2	2	20	3	1	4	17,211
Run Johnny Run	3	1	18	1	4	0	13,823
Run of Luck	32	16	234	21	36	33	352,063
Run the Gantlet	24	13	149	16	7	16	236,495
Runaway Groom	174	71	1,043	107	111	129	2,145,042
Runnett (GB)	3	1	19	2	1	2	241,383
Running Gold	4	4	43	7	10	5	111,591
Rupert's Wing	4	2	37	3	2	4	31,236
Ruritania	3	3	30	6	5	5	144,477
Rustic Ruler	12	7	105	12	12	14	217,073
Ruthie's Native	30	13	196	22	23	28	316,426
Ryeko	2	1	13	1	2	2	15,516
S. S. Hot Sauce	6	2	26	3	2	2	34,862
S. W. Wildcard	1	1	10	2	0	1	12,840
Sabona	10	5	49	7	8	3	101,144
Sadair	4	2	21	2	1	4	22,344
Sadler's Wells	47	20	236	27	34	23	876,059
Safawan	1	1	15	1	1	2	16,300
Sagace (FR)	5	3	38	4	3	5	32,604
Sail Ahoy	6	1	35	1	1	4	11,409
Sain Et Sauf	2	1	11	2	0	2	9,570
Saint Ballado	32	15	183	29	26	24	658,986
Saint Cyrien	4	2	32	6	4	4	77,345
Saint Sever (FR)	4	2	31	2	4	1	58,185
Saint Tropez	3	2	24	2	0	4	30,337
Salem	13	5	105	9	16	10	237,656
Salem Drive	18	8	132	21	13	16	257,401
Salem End Road	2	1	9	1	1	2	12,650
Sallust	5	3	28	3	3	5	135,415
Salmon Leap	2	2	15	2	0	5	65,935
Salse	3	2	27	2	4	5	27,636
Salt Lake	51	33	267	58	32	31	1,416,697
Salt Marsh	4	3	23	5	3	2	176,988
Saltville	1	1	5	1	1	1	2,240
Saltwell	2	2	29	4	3	7	24,413
Salutely	40	17	269	26	29	28	367,864
Sam M.	1	1	14	2	4	4	67,034
Sam Ransom (VEN)	5	1	22	1	3	2	15,308
Sam the Lion	1	1	18	2	6	4	39,405
Samarid	4	2	23	5	4	3	91,525
Samba Boy	1	1	5	3	1	0	3,977
Same Direction	12	8	62	9	6	12	226,493
San Feliou (FR)	8	5	57	6	4	10	71,544
Sanglamore	1	1	3	1	0	0	22,200
Sanhedrin	4	3	38	5	3	8	32,047
Santana Sands	1	1	11	2	0	4	10,565
Santiago Peak	10	7	83	19	13	8	205,820
Saratoga Legend	1	1	12	1	3	1	9,847
Saratoga Six	185	108	1,218	191	165	178	4,148,419
Sarawak	6	2	50	7	6	2	149,931
Sarof Jr.	1	1	7	2	0	0	3,509
Saros (GB)	48	15	232	26	22	21	453,668
Sassafras (FR)	41	23	319	39	38	40	557,868
Satan's Chief	2	1	8	1	0	0	10,557
Satan's Flame	3	3	34	5	3	6	53,254
Satan's Gem	1	1	12	1	1	3	11,065
Satan's Hills	3	3	32	7	2	2	33,506
Satan's Parade	1	1	14	1	0	2	10,164
Satan's Secretary	3	2	26	4	4	2	45,797
Satan's Thunder	4	1	17	3	1	1	54,148
Sauce Boat	135	57	856	94	108	85	1,229,060
Saumarez (GB)	2	1	13	1	2	3	48,466
Sauvage (FR)	4	1	26	3	2	3	25,452
Savings	12	8	121	14	16	16	145,146
Savona Tower	2	1	19	2	1	4	7,664
Sawbones	33	15	215	31	18	33	609,366
Say I'm Smart	2	2	23	5	5	5	41,574
Sayyaf	2	2	23	3	4	1	29,679
Scarlet 'n Gray	4	1	35	3	4	1	33,486
Scarlet Ibis	17	8	126	16	7	14	172,304
Scenic (IRE)	2	1	13	1	0	1	34,450

Broodmare Sire	Perf	Wnrs	Sts	1st	2d	3d	Purses	Broodmare Sire	Perf	Wnrs	Sts	1st	2d	3d	Purses
Schaufuss	3	1	16	1	1	0	5,875	Shantung (FR)	1	1	7	2	0	0	14,326
School Hero	3	2	18	3	3	1	74,780	Shardari (IRE)	1	1	5	1	0	0	23,246
Score Twenty Four	4	2	33	2	5	8	23,245	Shareef Dancer	14	8	89	18	13	13	1,009,992
Scorpio	1	1	8	2	2	1	15,207	Sharif	2	2	26	5	5	3	19,329
Scotchman	2	1	13	1	1	0	20,835	Sharp Hoofer	4	2	23	2	4	9	40,214
Scott's Poppy	1	1	15	3	2	3	12,442	Sharp Kid	3	2	25	4	3	5	26,438
Scottish Reel	1	1	12	1	1	1	8,743	Sharp Reason	2	1	7	1	0	0	3,975
Scout Leader	6	1	24	1	2	3	21,643	Sharp Terdankim	2	1	13	2	0	2	7,169
Scouts Oath	2	2	20	4	1	1	17,360	Sharp Victor	7	3	41	9	2	3	219,782
Screaming Fife	6	2	33	4	6	2	108,779	Sharpen Up (GB)	56	18	312	23	44	36	882,426
Screen King	49	24	373	43	42	43	755,521	Sharper One	28	13	175	21	23	28	484,108
Screen Trend	2	1	8	2	1	0	28,895	Sharpman	1	1	10	1	1	1	10,416
Scroll	4	2	42	2	6	6	28,033	Sharpo	3	1	11	1	0	1	16,105
Scythian	1	1	2	1	0	0	8,586	Sharrood	5	2	24	2	4	5	43,626
Sea Aglo	17	8	151	20	13	22	101,362	Shawklit Won	12	7	75	11	10	10	154,756
Sea Hero	3	2	19	2	3	2	26,391	Shecky Greene	28	16	197	25	13	16	246,207
Sea Songster	9	3	58	3	5	5	52,268	Sheet Anchor	1	1	11	2	3	0	8,534
Seafood	12	8	83	13	9	9	99,993	Sheikh Albadou (GB)	18	7	96	9	11	8	215,689
Search for Gold	33	16	207	22	22	24	265,687	Shelbyville	1	1	9	1	0	0	2,443
Search Tradition	1	1	6	1	0	2	13,275	Shelter Half	54	23	351	43	37	42	647,626
Seat of Power	8	2	56	3	6	11	54,557	Shenadoah River	5	3	44	8	4	7	85,951
Seattle Battle	6	5	27	5	2	2	53,759	Sherry Prince	2	1	8	1	0	1	6,021
Seattle Dancer	94	47	577	85	77	78	2,267,932	Shifty Sheik	2	2	13	5	3	2	45,674
Seattle Knight	10	6	70	8	9	4	74,882	Shimatoree	30	13	237	16	31	28	343,655
Seattle Sleet	5	4	44	7	8	6	163,520	Shining So Bright	1	1	9	1	1	1	67,320
Seattle Slew	224	113	1,422	194	173	174	5,333,587	Ship Leave	9	4	41	7	4	5	47,301
Seattle Song	79	39	473	68	60	61	1,950,381	Shipmate Sam	6	2	32	2	5	5	32,924
Seattle Sun	3	1	15	1	0	0	7,732	Shipping Magnate	7	3	54	11	5	4	145,375
Seclusive	17	6	115	6	13	10	77,933	Shirley Heights (GB)	20	7	95	13	19	6	494,738
Second Pleasure	1	1	14	1	1	0	6,666	Shirley's Champion	6	4	42	6	5	5	40,996
Secret Claim	15	8	111	13	17	12	373,782	Shot Gun Scott	7	4	55	5	5	7	105,874
Secret Counsel	3	1	35	3	5	5	20,235	Shotiche	3	1	23	2	4	4	136,211
Secret Fleet	1	1	7	1	0	2	1,989	Show Dancer	28	12	213	25	16	22	335,944
Secret Hello	19	7	117	15	13	17	305,193	Show'em Slew	4	1	33	4	4	5	124,056
Secret Prince	17	13	128	24	18	24	691,403	Shy Guy	2	1	22	1	2	1	32,570
Secret Slew	14	5	94	10	17	12	266,061	Shy Native	8	1	56	1	3	9	37,739
Secretariat	230	108	1,638	196	217	193	4,589,893	Siberian Express	19	7	123	16	17	12	853,683
Secretary of State	2	1	7	1	2	0	10,690	Sibirri	2	1	12	1	4	0	5,690
Secretary of War	12	4	81	5	8	9	76,469	Sicyos	4	3	38	7	4	6	71,387
Secreto	83	36	573	68	78	68	1,498,714	Sifounas	7	3	50	6	4	3	63,053
Security Council	2	2	9	2	1	0	6,658	Signed Contract	4	1	19	5	2	3	24,451
Seeking the Gold	106	60	624	96	77	96	2,842,451	Silent Cal	14	5	95	10	5	13	141,650
Sefapiano	2	1	15	3	3	2	52,118	Silent Code	2	1	21	2	3	2	5,951
Sejm	10	6	68	9	12	7	147,715	Silent Dignity	15	8	135	12	18	8	148,133
Selkirk	1	1	1	1	0	0	20,400	Silent Fox	18	8	91	9	15	12	108,849
Sellout	2	2	7	2	0	1	26,201	Silent King	10	3	55	4	5	3	89,801
Selous Scout	3	1	15	1	1	6	10,940	Silent Landing	4	3	36	7	4	3	69,648
Semaj	1	1	10	2	3	0	52,420	Silent Review	9	8	74	15	9	7	238,106
Semenenko	7	5	38	10	10	3	485,264	Silent Screen	148	79	976	136	116	109	1,995,460
Semi Northern	3	3	21	5	4	2	26,570	Silent Tempest	1	1	2	1	0	0	8,658
Semipalatinsk	1	1	8	2	0	1	43,400	Silk Or Satin	4	2	31	2	2	1	25,110
Senate Whip	2	1	21	1	1	0	14,580	Silken Reality	1	1	5	1	0	0	6,060
Senator Amo	2	1	28	1	6	2	24,388	Silky Baby	9	3	57	4	7	5	60,194
Senor Pete	4	3	22	5	2	2	91,305	Sillery	3	2	14	3	5	1	301,375
Senor Speedy	7	2	53	11	2	6	115,035	Silly Season	1	1	6	1	2	0	11,420
Sensitive Music	4	4	40	6	5	6	62,742	Silver Badge	6	3	66	11	17	9	190,826
Sensitive Prince	28	13	190	21	24	25	254,665	Silver Buck	140	70	912	108	107	114	1,876,309
Sentimental Slew	10	5	62	8	6	12	92,982	Silver Canyon	1	1	22	2	3	1	15,885
Septieme Ciel	49	23	312	44	46	28	848,613	Silver Deputy	92	56	547	105	77	67	2,494,530
Set Free	10	6	73	7	6	9	73,463	Silver Florin	2	2	15	2	2	1	12,355
Settlement Day	18	9	104	12	6	8	171,094	Silver Ghost	90	42	536	66	72	55	1,409,454
Sevastopol	8	4	45	8	7	6	186,294	Silver Hawk	135	65	809	88	104	110	2,220,296
Sewickley	17	13	122	25	12	17	457,698	Silver Nitrate	3	3	28	3	2	6	38,543
Sexist	4	3	34	12	1	5	199,879	Silver Series	11	4	83	6	7	7	108,104
Sezyou	55	30	430	57	54	47	827,621	Silver Spade	1	1	6	1	0	0	8,189
Shadeed	60	37	405	64	42	66	1,377,319	Silver Supreme	18	10	132	21	20	8	295,030
Shady Character	2	2	16	2	2	1	16,382	Silver Survivor	4	1	16	1	2	2	30,017
Shady Fellow	3	2	30	7	0	3	42,381	Silveyville	20	13	152	21	12	15	247,699
Shahrastani	28	13	188	20	24	20	395,749	Simi Dancer	5	2	27	2	1	2	18,658
Shakapour	2	1	13	1	0	0	9,970	Simply Great	2	1	12	2	1	1	18,062
Shake Rattl'n Fly	3	2	19	2	1	1	11,793	Simply Majestic	39	24	327	43	34	29	540,678
Sham	90	43	570	62	63	74	1,891,049	Sing Sing	9	4	60	5	10	9	76,858
Shamgo	5	3	48	3	4	4	47,433	Singh	8	4	60	8	8	4	143,231
Shamtastic	2	1	7	1	0	1	7,583	Singh America	2	1	22	1	4	4	8,703
Shananie	42	23	307	38	38	34	643,602	Single Lane	2	1	15	3	2	1	45,617
Shanekite	43	21	328	36	48	35	630,607	Sings (ARG)	3	1	15	3	4	3	163,958

Broodmare Sire	Perf	Wnrs	Sts	1st	2d	3d	Purses	Broodmare Sire	Perf	Wnrs	Sts	1st	2d	3d	Purses
Singular	36	14	266	31	21	40	449,637	Smoked Salmon	2	1	9	1	2	0	14,790
Sinister Purpose	6	2	34	3	6	6	93,210	Smoken Tobin	1	1	10	4	0	2	10,542
Sir Ack	7	5	52	8	7	5	128,005	Smokester	7	4	49	10	8	8	250,368
Sir Claudius	1	1	11	1	1	1	4,996	Smokey Oso	2	1	10	1	1	2	10,280
Sir Concorde	2	1	9	1	1	2	9,240	Smoking Gun	7	4	47	8	7	4	81,333
Sir Eric	6	3	48	5	7	5	68,308	Smooth Commander	1	1	5	2	1	1	13,622
Sir Gaylord	6	3	40	6	5	3	49,560	Smooth Dancer	6	2	23	2	0	1	20,011
Sir Godfrey (FR)	2	1	16	1	2	5	20,490	Smooth Dude	4	1	25	1	0	3	10,762
Sir Grundy	1	1	16	1	6	2	13,211	Smugglin George	2	1	11	1	2	1	4,909
Sir Habitat (GB)	5	2	26	2	3	4	6,948	Snake Oil Man	5	2	33	2	4	4	10,406
Sir Halo	3	2	27	6	4	3	24,093	Snohomish County	5	2	22	2	2	2	18,027
Sir Harry Lewis	20	9	135	14	18	12	786,122	Snow Chief	41	18	246	27	26	37	600,048
Sir Ivor	106	45	645	72	70	66	1,532,086	Snow Knight	8	3	47	9	5	2	62,126
Sir Ivor Again	22	9	153	17	30	20	486,727	Snow Satyr (ARG)	3	1	9	1	1	0	9,362
Sir Jinsky	11	8	83	12	12	9	133,703	Snow Sporting	3	2	18	6	1	1	86,060
Sir Leon	5	1	26	2	3	5	30,071	So Blessed	1	1	6	1	3	0	2,790
Sir Macamillion	1	1	5	1	0	0	8,780	So Oh Fast	1	1	6	2	0	1	8,145
Sir Naskra	7	3	29	8	4	2	224,107	Social Diamond	7	3	47	3	10	8	86,093
Sir Optimist	1	1	16	3	5	3	46,860	Society Max	14	6	69	10	14	9	106,479
Sir Paulus	6	4	35	5	4	4	18,197	Society Scion	4	1	20	1	3	3	12,841
Sir Raleigh	14	5	79	6	7	8	85,661	Solar City	32	14	274	22	39	48	358,967
Sir Richard Lewis	8	5	36	7	4	2	107,823	Solar Launch	1	1	3	1	0	0	12,920
Sir Session	10	8	94	13	9	13	80,512	Solar Salute	3	2	21	3	4	3	15,557
Sir Wiggle	1	1	14	2	0	1	11,343	Solarstern (FR)	2	1	3	1	0	0	18,600
Sir Wimborne	32	15	215	29	26	19	430,640	Solazo	2	1	24	1	4	3	51,212
Sir Winzalot	1	1	4	1	0	0	5,175	Soldier Boy	3	1	13	1	1	0	6,066
Sir Woodley	5	1	21	1	1	1	12,938	Solford	17	8	98	12	10	11	169,011
Sirtaki	1	1	10	1	2	3	9,603	Solid Print	2	2	14	3	1	3	26,053
Sisters Prince	2	1	15	1	2	1	2,901	Solinus (IRE)	2	1	23	1	0	3	10,455
Sitzmark	5	1	21	1	6	1	87,971	Solo Bold (ARG)	1	1	4	1	0	2	29,520
Six Speed	4	3	39	6	6	5	87,437	Solo Guy	3	3	22	5	4	5	21,705
Siyah Kalem	44	26	320	44	49	48	934,179	Solo Landing	2	1	16	1	2	1	7,297
Ski Racer	5	1	16	1	0	0	10,663	Solo Road	1	1	9	2	0	2	10,861
Ski Resort	6	6	41	7	6	5	80,056	Some One Frosty	2	2	19	6	1	2	82,212
Skin Head	5	3	56	6	9	7	70,087	Something Lucky	18	7	117	10	14	14	226,164
Skip Trial	74	38	576	75	75	57	1,309,164	Something Wrong	4	1	7	1	0	1	1,020
Sky Classic	44	24	254	33	25	30	744,605	Somethingfabulous	67	37	464	56	58	69	667,735
Sky Filou (NZ)	2	2	9	3	0	1	139,720	Somethingpoetic	3	2	20	4	4	0	84,693
Skylar Alois	1	1	3	1	1	0	4,880	Somethingwonderful	2	1	10	2	1	0	23,693
Skytrick (GB)	1	1	12	2	1	1	24,420	Son Ange	12	7	73	7	5	8	96,717
Skywalker	85	39	452	68	59	62	1,626,225	Son Excellence	8	4	69	8	6	6	98,188
Slady Castle	15	7	106	10	12	15	211,088	Son of Bagdad	2	2	17	3	3	2	50,007
Slew Baby	5	4	52	9	12	7	143,896	Son of Briartic	77	44	568	83	76	88	1,503,196
Slew Bunny	2	1	10	3	3	1	26,046	Sonaskra	2	1	10	1	1	3	4,055
Slew City Slew	59	37	454	71	69	54	1,346,233	Song of Delta	5	1	33	2	2	3	9,904
Slew d'Orsay	2	1	11	1	1	1	10,279	Songhay	1	1	8	2	4	0	7,175
Slew Dancer	1	1	6	1	0	1	14,795	Sonny Fleet	1	1	17	1	4	1	9,425
Slew Express	1	1	1	1	0	0	18,840	Sonny Jay	2	1	9	1	0	0	5,473
Slew Machine	21	8	115	11	15	13	167,574	Sonny's Solo Halo	5	2	13	3	3	0	20,540
Slew o' Gold	136	66	943	122	131	110	2,701,439	Sort	2	1	7	1	0	2	16,953
Slew o' the North	8	3	51	9	7	6	79,031	Sound Off	1	1	12	5	3	0	60,570
Slew of Angels	3	1	10	1	2	2	11,038	Sound Reason	4	3	14	4	2	2	246,081
Slew the Bride	17	7	115	12	21	14	171,658	South Pass	2	2	8	2	4	1	20,355
Slew the Coup	21	9	148	14	16	18	195,220	Southern Halo	19	12	94	15	6	10	398,105
Slew the Knight	6	3	30	4	1	4	77,002	Southern Slugger	2	1	12	2	0	2	14,620
Slew the Slewor	6	3	55	6	7	4	72,707	Southern Sultan	12	9	90	19	7	20	478,953
Slew's Folly	6	1	27	5	3	2	83,679	Sovereign	1	1	9	2	0	3	3,534
Slew's Royalty	39	25	222	41	18	24	384,464	Sovereign Dancer	227	128	1,731	236	194	229	4,141,414
Slewabration	3	1	9	1	0	2	5,342	Sovereign Dignity	3	2	22	5	2	2	27,516
Slewacide	86	40	537	62	59	61	2,710,147	Sovereign Don	16	7	116	13	12	12	125,725
Slewdledo	29	15	205	28	34	30	355,928	Sovereignty	6	1	41	2	3	6	19,067
Slewdonza	6	2	28	2	3	1	24,481	Soviet Lad	3	1	12	1	0	1	8,203
Slewpy	100	48	656	77	84	93	1,749,163	Soviet Star	17	9	106	16	8	10	237,698
Slick	6	3	43	6	6	6	95,484	Soy Numero Uno	31	20	212	26	33	33	389,792
Slip Anchor (GB)	5	4	49	12	2	5	169,847	Space Cup	3	1	27	2	3	1	60,601
Sluggard	3	1	22	1	3	2	16,644	Space Mountain	3	1	18	1	1	1	20,607
Smart Review	3	2	20	4	4	2	99,049	Spanish Drums	16	4	85	5	8	10	170,984
Smart Style	9	3	67	9	3	5	180,324	Spare Card	5	1	16	1	3	1	28,215
Smarten	180	80	1,149	142	141	159	3,165,221	Sparky Rullah	3	1	15	1	1	2	13,080
Smartness	2	1	14	1	0	2	5,220	Speak John	9	2	61	3	4	8	107,373
Smasher	3	1	16	1	1	1	2,058	Spec o' Motion	2	1	17	1	1	1	8,307
Smead	5	2	41	3	8	5	42,500	Special Blend	4	2	41	5	9	5	43,235
Smelly	2	2	20	5	6	3	97,600	Special Lineage	16	7	91	9	15	13	118,272
Smile	82	35	566	56	53	81	1,198,224	Special Secret	14	5	102	7	9	9	71,581
Smiling Forli	1	1	3	1	0	1	7,344	Specialmante	1	1	3	2	0	1	2,037
Smoggy (GB)	9	5	66	8	10	7	197,785	Spectacular Bid	204	92	1,270	152	176	150	4,749,819

Broodmare Sire	Perf	Wnrs	Sts	1st	2d	3d	Purses
Spectacular Turn	4	2	16	3	0	2	10,591
Spectaculardynasty	1	1	9	1	0	2	37,446
Speed Play	1	1	10	1	2	1	5,963
Speeding Moment	1	1	4	2	2	0	109,535
Speedy Idiot	3	1	14	5	4	0	63,505
Speedy Prospect	10	5	105	12	7	9	153,777
Spellcaster	6	3	44	4	6	4	36,209
Spence Bay (IRE)	3	1	20	1	2	1	14,014
Spend a Buck	133	71	865	122	110	100	2,442,034
Spicy Monarch	3	2	23	3	4	4	51,298
Spicy Story	8	4	51	4	12	5	95,236
Spin Off	6	2	40	2	2	6	32,962
Spirit Rock	8	3	39	4	5	2	64,585
Spirit Son	1	1	15	1	1	0	5,623
Spirited Boy	8	6	73	12	7	5	109,711
Splendid Courage	13	6	86	8	11	12	142,707
Splendid Hour	8	2	28	2	0	2	12,109
Splendid Peace	1	1	12	1	0	1	8,506
Splendid Son	1	1	10	2	2	1	29,029
Splinter Group	2	1	8	1	0	0	8,788
Split Infinitive	2	1	8	1	0	0	5,700
Splitting Headache	6	2	48	7	9	8	65,684
Sportful	2	2	17	6	4	1	20,581
Sportin' Life	60	23	426	35	45	46	496,863
Sports View	5	2	24	5	1	2	61,138
Spotter Bay	5	2	28	3	3	4	38,760
Spouting Horn	1	1	11	1	1	1	10,969
Spread the Rumor	27	11	164	24	19	16	248,164
Spring Double	31	10	206	12	29	30	308,652
Springhill (IRE)	9	2	38	4	3	3	55,773
Spruce Bouquet	6	5	49	11	11	3	239,067
Spruce Needles	6	4	58	5	5	8	56,896
Spy Signal	11	6	76	9	7	9	80,731
Squad Car	2	1	6	1	1	1	4,384
Square Your Hat	1	1	12	2	3	3	21,970
Squire	4	1	26	1	4	2	34,925
Sr. Diplomat	7	5	64	6	8	7	121,768
St Puckle (GB)	1	1	4	1	0	0	30,000
St. Forbes	4	1	14	3	0	1	12,370
St. Hilarion	3	1	15	1	2	2	11,025
St. Jovite	23	14	155	17	16	23	394,138
St. Petersburg	6	2	56	2	5	7	40,646
Stacked Pack	22	7	123	8	17	18	217,365
Staff Riot	6	4	38	5	6	4	46,361
Staff Writer	116	63	805	119	97	117	1,302,322
Stage Boss	1	1	7	2	0	0	9,220
Stage Director	2	2	22	4	1	5	39,582
Stage Door Johnny	75	34	492	57	53	60	1,003,331
Stage Fool	1	1	13	2	3	3	36,063
Stage Presence	4	3	34	3	5	3	97,697
Stake Knife	2	1	17	2	4	2	7,931
Stalwars	1	1	4	1	0	0	6,555
Stalwart	171	89	1,060	144	140	127	2,815,352
Stancharry	4	2	18	2	2	4	11,687
Stanford	2	1	4	1	1	1	186,507
Stanstead	12	5	76	11	9	8	207,614
Star Appeal	6	4	41	10	7	2	226,304
Star Choice	24	10	165	19	24	30	285,099
Star de Naskra	174	84	1,144	144	153	118	2,804,964
Star Envoy	14	6	118	11	13	8	87,644
Star Gallant	27	15	190	29	34	13	887,794
Star of Erin (IRE)	5	2	30	3	4	1	20,473
Star of the Crop	6	2	33	4	10	7	91,865
Star Royal	1	1	4	1	1	0	8,844
Star Spangled	15	6	97	9	16	8	209,418
Star Way (GB)	2	1	20	1	2	1	18,407
Starbinia	1	1	13	2	1	0	6,391
State Dinner	84	31	518	46	61	63	887,777
Stately Cielo	3	1	21	2	1	3	67,225
Stately Don	32	18	253	34	40	38	807,360
Stately Native	2	1	11	1	0	2	11,660
Staunch Avenger	46	16	357	24	28	37	285,849
Stay the Course	7	3	49	5	7	8	96,716
Steady Beat	10	3	64	8	7	10	80,440
Steady Growth	35	19	257	28	38	37	752,125
Steel	4	1	26	1	0	2	10,596

Broodmare Sire	Perf	Wnrs	Sts	1st	2d	3d	Purses
Steel Emperor	3	2	24	4	5	3	25,587
Steel Heart	3	1	16	1	0	4	19,226
Steel Robbing	4	3	27	7	1	4	34,002
Steelinctive (GB)	7	2	36	4	11	1	54,389
Steinlen (GB)	13	2	60	2	9	6	95,250
Step Nicely	5	3	26	4	2	1	33,797
Sterling Key	3	1	10	1	0	1	6,446
Steve's Friend	5	4	39	5	10	5	129,166
Steward	5	1	34	2	2	4	19,196
Stifelius (GB)	6	2	38	3	3	3	67,057
Stiff Sentence	10	8	84	17	13	10	224,681
Stomping Ground	1	1	3	1	0	0	6,883
Stone County Kid	1	1	9	1	1	0	3,510
Stone Manor	1	1	27	1	9	5	23,205
Stonewalk	14	5	76	7	7	7	71,111
Stop the Bells	3	1	16	1	2	1	25,634
Stop the Fighting (IRE)	3	1	15	1	2	2	35,946
Stop the Music	191	86	1,267	149	147	141	2,846,320
Stopgap	3	3	26	5	2	4	84,637
Storm a Head	1	1	13	2	2	2	17,148
Storm Bird	225	118	1,440	221	184	205	6,654,708
Storm Boot	5	1	25	1	3	2	33,269
Storm Brewing	6	2	40	2	5	3	34,697
Storm Cat	184	90	1,074	150	156	140	4,739,075
Storm Tracker	1	1	11	1	1	0	10,200
Storm Velocity	1	1	7	1	1	0	3,980
Stradavinsky (IRE)	2	1	19	4	7	0	43,425
Straight Flush	4	2	31	4	4	4	26,522
Strate Stuff	5	1	19	1	1	2	6,541
Strategic Command	6	3	36	3	5	4	84,484
Stratford	5	1	29	1	0	0	7,893
Strawberry Road (AUS)	130	67	819	117	116	119	3,303,751
Strength in Unity	2	1	25	1	0	3	10,464
Strike Gold	96	38	575	56	87	84	1,086,390
Strike the Anvil	25	12	186	17	16	22	439,409
Strike the Gold	24	13	186	19	15	24	365,706
Stripper's Zipper	5	1	45	2	6	4	42,594
Strolling Along	6	3	36	5	2	6	109,847
Strong Bid	3	2	18	3	3	3	33,379
Strong Performance	3	1	15	1	1	1	9,520
Strong Ruler	1	1	1	1	0	0	5,640
Struck Out	4	1	24	2	1	1	9,119
Stuka	7	4	35	5	4	12	74,256
Stupid Pleasure	3	1	28	2	0	3	5,550
Stutz Blackhawk	64	28	527	50	57	50	735,555
Stutz Keys	2	2	17	3	1	4	26,165
Stylish King	4	2	28	4	2	3	106,982
Subpet	4	1	39	2	3	7	33,125
Sucha Pleasure	11	6	78	7	7	8	72,747
Suffice	1	1	8	1	1	3	14,290
Summer Advocate	12	7	64	12	6	8	133,735
Summer Squall	58	32	368	48	51	39	947,775
Summer Time Guy	7	5	43	7	7	6	158,387
Summing	84	44	594	80	66	53	1,164,527
Sun and Shine (GB)	1	1	10	1	3	1	66,120
Sun Master	7	1	35	1	1	5	45,881
Sun Power	15	6	75	9	5	7	70,028
Sun War Dancer	6	2	21	3	5	2	122,911
Sun Worship (IRE)	2	1	7	3	0	0	23,700
Sunbury	2	2	16	2	0	0	26,949
Sunday Guest	2	1	15	2	0	2	8,191
Sunny Clime	82	37	573	61	86	85	1,209,248
Sunny Feet	8	4	72	8	10	13	56,035
Sunny North	23	10	172	15	30	21	264,997
Sunny Songster	1	1	9	1	5	1	6,794
Sunny South	8	3	53	5	4	6	68,006
Sunny Winters	2	1	8	1	3	0	12,685
Sunny's Halo	154	78	1,059	120	112	137	1,703,708
Sunshine Drive	2	1	7	1	1	0	7,700
Sunshine Forever	53	25	332	41	31	36	705,366
Sunshine Today	8	1	39	1	3	5	19,704
Super Concorde	39	10	281	19	27	33	281,632
Super Gun	2	1	13	1	0	1	14,952
Super Moment	20	8	131	20	16	16	255,359
Super Native	3	2	17	5	3	3	99,804
Super Pleasure	2	1	12	2	0	1	5,457

RECORDS OF BROODMARE SIRES

Broodmare Sire	Perf	Wnrs	Sts	1st	2d	3d	Purses
Super Smile	2	2	22	3	1	1	33,373
Superbity	43	13	280	24	32	31	336,670
Superoyale	10	4	42	5	4	4	52,464
Superpower	1	1	4	1	0	0	36,580
Supremity	2	2	18	3	5	1	14,092
Sure Blade	6	2	22	4	2	4	127,971
Surface Raider	1	1	7	1	3	0	23,448
Surgeon Sam	1	1	11	1	1	3	17,112
Surreal	17	6	120	12	15	16	232,674
Surumu (GER)	3	2	18	5	2	1	70,763
Sutter's Prospect	14	10	84	13	7	15	248,328
Swain	1	1	14	2	2	1	11,379
Swap's Fire	2	2	27	7	7	1	48,602
Sweet Candy (VEN)	10	4	65	7	12	6	165,836
Sweet Pete	2	2	20	7	7	2	54,635
Swelegant	7	3	56	3	4	8	67,230
Swift Pursuit	1	1	4	2	0	1	10,060
Swift Swallow	4	2	29	7	4	2	31,565
Swing Music	2	2	24	3	5	3	30,591
Swing Till Dawn	52	24	347	40	43	43	490,419
Swingin Sway	4	1	15	1	4	1	62,404
Switch Partners	12	6	85	9	9	14	168,541
Swoon	11	6	74	11	11	10	84,248
Swoon Swept	2	2	16	4	3	1	35,704
Swoon's Son	1	1	4	1	1	0	6,606
Sword Dance (IRE)	38	15	228	20	31	24	335,858
Sword Devil	3	1	14	1	0	2	6,094
Swordtail	1	1	6	2	0	1	7,758
Synastry	43	19	258	40	22	40	497,382
Syncopate	15	3	92	4	13	12	148,845
Syntariat	5	3	33	4	3	4	31,807
Syrian Silver	2	1	12	2	2	2	39,782
Syrian Star	2	2	17	2	0	1	5,064
Syrian Time	2	1	21	1	3	2	15,629
Szerbusz	2	1	12	1	1	0	2,449
T. Bill Syndrome	3	2	17	3	3	1	14,828
T. Brooke	3	1	24	2	3	2	23,885
T. V. Alliance	5	1	34	2	4	4	52,255
T. V. Charger	4	3	35	3	6	4	26,809
T. V. Commercial	44	18	339	32	52	38	921,342
T. V. Count	2	1	14	1	4	1	10,412
T. V. Gentleman	1	1	9	1	0	2	2,632
T. V. Lark	4	3	38	7	4	3	45,846
Tabasco Cat	3	1	8	1	3	0	112,175
Table Express	5	2	24	2	2	3	9,252
Table Play	3	3	16	4	3	3	45,490
Table Run	55	28	329	47	42	51	520,117
Tabun Bogdo	5	4	43	6	5	6	35,751
Taconeando (ARG)	2	2	26	4	2	9	67,234
Tactical Advantage	3	3	17	3	2	4	117,097
Taga	2	1	25	2	3	3	28,102
Tagish	9	3	47	3	6	3	79,964
Tahitian King (IRE)	2	1	10	1	2	1	11,990
Tai	7	5	62	6	2	8	38,365
Taj Alriyadh	18	9	103	19	7	13	417,280
Take Action	4	3	38	5	3	3	31,839
Take by Storm	6	3	46	6	3	3	22,946
Take Me Out	4	1	26	3	2	6	26,780
Take the Floor	10	5	91	13	13	11	194,032
Take the Rap	5	3	54	7	6	9	62,411
Take Your Partner (AUS)	3	1	21	1	0	3	31,764
Take Your Place	5	1	34	2	1	2	15,182
Talc	116	61	784	99	90	85	2,098,320
Talent Town	5	3	26	4	2	2	68,278
Talented Native	5	1	37	2	1	5	10,478
Talinum	52	28	343	44	39	53	686,646
Tall and Stately	4	1	15	1	0	0	6,620
Tall Ships	2	1	16	4	1	2	47,618
Tally Ho the Fox	13	6	94	17	17	10	250,709
Tammany	3	1	18	2	1	2	25,642
Tampa Trouble	2	1	15	1	2	3	16,797
Tan Pronto	2	1	13	1	2	1	40,435
Taneb	1	1	13	1	1	2	4,343
Tank's Prospect	65	32	364	52	48	55	1,032,388
Tanthem	27	12	193	20	25	17	274,367
Tantoul	22	9	136	14	20	12	199,507
Tap On Wood	3	2	18	4	2	4	43,483
Tap Shoes	12	8	63	13	6	7	120,033
Tapping Wood	3	1	14	2	0	2	22,008
Tarboosh	2	1	9	1	0	0	5,135
Targowice	5	2	30	2	4	5	63,466
Tariffic Prince	1	1	12	2	0	1	26,362
Tarleton Oak	10	5	76	9	11	7	169,082
Tarmoud	5	2	27	3	1	5	43,884
Tarr Road	6	1	29	1	0	2	18,160
Tarsal	18	8	121	18	15	15	163,685
Tartar Chief	3	2	27	4	2	4	17,700
Tasso	62	27	367	42	49	50	796,631
Tasting	13	6	97	7	11	8	57,710
Tasty Victory	1	1	8	1	0	2	7,990
Tate Gallery	2	1	15	2	2	2	68,065
Taufan	7	3	38	4	1	5	87,004
Taunton	6	2	47	2	4	6	33,142
Taxachusetts	4	2	39	3	7	9	40,760
Taylor	1	1	6	2	0	1	10,903
Taylor Road	2	1	11	1	0	0	3,838
Taylor's Falls	70	38	528	69	71	64	1,129,316
Taylor's Special	26	14	172	20	18	22	439,807
Te Vega	1	1	12	2	0	0	12,232
Team Captain	3	1	19	1	0	0	3,702
Technology	4	2	18	4	2	1	67,603
Teddy's Courage	6	1	27	3	2	2	22,992
Tejabo	4	2	13	2	0	2	17,325
Tejano	69	34	429	54	49	46	682,981
Tell	29	8	159	13	17	22	182,225
Tell the Tale	7	4	34	4	2	1	53,323
Tella Fib	3	1	9	2	1	2	22,250
Temerity Prince	17	6	113	9	16	12	86,321
Temperence Hill	166	75	1,165	133	148	140	2,122,033
Tempest Ways	2	1	17	1	6	3	19,366
Temptor	3	2	22	3	5	3	29,966
Ten Gold Pots	27	17	240	30	19	29	870,717
Ten Keys	2	2	12	4	1	3	135,175
Tenacious Jr.	1	1	18	2	0	4	10,410
Tenacious Tom	2	2	13	2	0	3	18,118
Tenagain	2	1	13	2	0	1	7,970
Tender King (IRE)	2	2	12	2	2	1	99,636
Tennessee Rite	1	1	7	3	0	0	29,702
Tentam	24	12	188	17	25	18	720,137
Tentiltwo	3	2	22	4	7	3	37,016
Terete	7	1	31	3	5	5	19,189
Terlago	2	1	19	1	8	3	7,780
Terresto	3	1	19	1	1	3	9,065
Texas City	10	6	60	10	6	5	87,119
Texas Dancer	6	1	28	1	3	3	8,429
Text	22	11	156	20	19	21	328,992
Thalassocrat	1	1	7	1	2	0	6,302
Thaliard (GB)	1	1	7	1	1	0	2,069
Thanks to Tony	8	4	70	5	10	7	64,200
That's a Nice	22	8	137	14	15	13	165,155
Thatching (IRE)	14	8	88	12	18	8	331,617
The Astonisher	17	5	95	10	6	9	88,353
The Axe II	14	6	94	10	18	16	316,518
The Bart	10	2	71	6	3	4	44,561
The Breeze	4	2	28	2	2	8	26,415
The Captain	5	4	31	4	10	4	87,105
The Carpenter	6	5	55	8	8	6	123,996
The Cool Virginian	22	11	154	18	14	14	261,248
The Drizzler	1	1	10	4	1	4	20,547
The Great Carl	1	1	10	1	1	4	6,355
The Hague	8	4	40	6	4	4	49,245
The Home Secretary	1	1	13	5	2	3	84,840
The Irish Lord	62	20	338	29	35	45	417,700
The Minstrel	116	45	716	78	72	99	1,687,394
The Prime Minister	14	6	83	13	12	13	266,096
The Prince's Pants	3	2	31	3	4	4	34,463
The Pruner	14	4	74	7	6	14	95,670
The Real McCoy	2	1	11	1	0	0	5,479
The Reprobate	5	4	47	5	12	3	166,961
The Scotsman	1	1	2	1	0	0	1,625
The Very Best	8	7	66	10	14	7	88,723
The Watcher	3	1	13	3	1	0	173,257

Broodmare Sire	Perf	Wnrs	Sts	1st	2d	3d	Purses
The Wicked North	4	2	23	3	3	2	65,953
The Wonder (FR)	5	3	22	6	4	0	83,730
Theatre Critic (IRE)	3	2	30	5	0	7	42,052
Theatrical (IRE)	112	57	712	93	80	90	2,429,597
Theologist	1	1	8	1	1	2	2,722
Think Snow	4	1	22	1	2	6	7,483
Third and Lex	1	1	12	1	1	1	4,692
Third Martini	2	1	19	2	0	4	19,214
Third World	3	2	24	6	0	4	39,040
Thirty Eight Paces	58	28	396	42	45	42	657,632
Thirty Six Red	51	22	333	34	39	42	648,666
Three Bagger	4	3	37	6	5	10	29,979
Three Martinis	27	17	207	33	29	27	405,893
Three Royal K's	1	1	3	1	0	0	1,515
Thunder Cat	2	2	12	2	2	0	12,787
Thunder O'Shay	2	1	11	1	1	0	15,445
Thunder Puddles	13	5	112	8	10	11	116,066
Thunder Runner	3	1	16	2	3	2	13,622
Thurloe Square	5	2	43	2	4	5	17,215
Tibaut Two	4	4	30	6	3	5	113,731
Tiffany Ice	21	6	83	8	16	5	135,120
Tilt the Odds	6	3	33	4	4	3	69,323
Tilt Top	3	2	22	3	5	5	55,913
Tilt Up	56	20	351	39	41	49	574,801
Tim Plum	1	1	7	1	2	0	5,100
Tim the Tiger	9	4	54	9	12	7	102,799
Timbo	1	1	5	1	0	0	11,170
Time for a Change	156	77	973	120	97	115	2,282,685
Time Tested	4	3	51	6	5	9	43,575
Time to Explode	70	38	496	55	67	62	1,017,120
Time Whisper	2	1	30	3	2	3	10,354
Timeless Moment	112	55	776	89	106	85	1,502,738
Timeless Native	71	29	391	44	34	37	938,293
Timely One	11	4	66	4	10	10	120,387
Tinajero	9	4	60	5	7	5	89,064
Tinsley	1	1	13	1	3	2	13,924
Tirol	3	1	9	1	0	0	66,520
Tisab	6	2	32	2	3	4	11,202
Titanic	15	8	96	11	4	6	173,003
Title Game	1	1	6	1	1	0	8,125
To B. Or Not	6	4	53	9	11	8	71,147
To the Quick	44	15	297	28	29	36	496,269
To-Agori-Mou (IRE)	1	1	12	1	1	0	9,858
Tobin Bronze	13	7	101	10	10	14	103,905
Tobin Town	2	1	17	2	1	2	8,324
Today 'n Tomorrow	1	1	13	1	0	1	7,531
Told	11	6	82	10	9	11	95,408
Tolstoy	4	2	21	4	4	4	42,587
Tom Buck	17	11	110	16	13	21	72,851
Tom Rolfe	85	45	604	72	84	76	1,595,418
Tom Swift	5	2	25	3	0	2	56,029
Tom Tulle	13	4	117	8	10	14	92,701
Tommy Bruce	1	1	9	1	1	0	2,471
Tong Po	8	4	54	5	4	5	50,628
Tonkaton	17	4	91	6	13	10	90,329
Tonzarun	8	1	23	1	1	1	17,096
Toomuchholme	1	1	8	1	0	2	23,640
Toonder	3	1	26	1	1	1	8,814
Toooverprime (IRE)	16	4	75	5	10	12	47,756
Toot'n Tudor	2	1	16	1	0	1	10,521
Top Avenger	32	14	245	20	27	31	401,240
Top Command	25	16	182	26	19	15	345,867
Top Rank	3	1	13	1	1	3	9,231
Top Trojan	1	1	14	2	2	1	32,010
Top Ville	14	4	65	8	9	10	233,468
Topsider	160	96	1,133	179	157	127	3,970,917
Toronto	3	1	17	1	0	1	9,232
Torrontes	1	1	9	1	0	1	6,994
Torsion	57	27	379	47	58	47	570,053
Total Departure	7	4	56	6	6	6	76,850
Totality	1	1	3	1	0	1	7,587
Tough Assignment	12	5	83	7	12	9	137,626
Tough Critic	1	1	9	2	3	0	57,100
Tough Envoy	2	1	8	3	1	1	11,584
Tough Knight	22	15	115	18	13	19	265,944
Toughness	1	1	14	1	0	1	4,697
Tour d'Or	9	3	60	6	9	5	84,330
Touring Dancer	2	1	13	1	0	0	8,341
Tout	7	1	40	1	2	6	14,751
Towson	1	1	11	2	1	1	20,775
Track Barron	86	44	600	73	76	77	1,150,352
Track Dance	4	1	27	2	2	6	17,893
Track Reward	1	1	9	1	1	2	19,108
Trade	1	1	9	2	2	1	17,267
Trader Tom	2	2	20	3	3	2	30,932
Traffic Breaker	7	2	43	4	5	5	21,776
Traffic Cop	6	1	42	1	0	3	12,471
Traffic Mark	8	3	68	5	12	8	52,298
Training Table	4	1	18	3	5	1	20,374
Tralos	17	9	158	24	17	24	503,548
Transworld	40	14	265	26	30	27	539,590
Trapp Mountain	15	6	105	11	12	12	256,530
Travelling Music	12	7	78	14	10	11	255,439
Travelling Victor	31	22	254	36	36	37	696,691
Treasure Kay	3	2	29	4	3	5	70,887
Treasury Secretary	6	4	53	4	3	10	344,370
Treatise	1	1	14	2	3	2	44,865
Tree of Knowledge	10	6	80	9	12	8	56,117
Trempolino	48	26	279	44	28	25	2,025,014
Trench Digger	5	2	30	2	5	5	47,028
Trenchant	3	3	34	11	2	6	197,135
Trepan	3	2	28	4	2	2	24,941
Tri Jet	128	65	897	114	107	101	2,509,570
Tri Swaps	3	1	17	3	1	3	15,068
Trial by Error	2	2	20	3	1	4	12,532
Triangulate	1	1	7	1	1	0	2,985
Tribal Crown	1	1	9	1	0	1	6,109
Tribal Line	2	1	6	1	1	1	2,992
Tribal Ruler	3	3	30	3	5	3	34,417
Tribal Unity	3	3	18	4	2	3	11,833
Trick Me	4	1	13	2	1	1	41,719
Tricky Creek	13	7	73	16	5	5	635,245
Tridessus	12	4	85	8	7	11	77,800
Triocala	10	6	78	9	11	5	110,287
Triomphe	6	2	20	2	0	0	28,990
Triple Bend	17	8	101	13	11	10	174,819
Triple Crown	2	1	12	3	2	2	21,936
Triple Schnap	4	1	40	2	6	1	44,373
Triple Sec	30	16	211	25	29	22	221,701
Tromos (GB)	1	1	2	1	1	0	19,590
Trooper Seven	10	5	55	7	7	8	59,336
Tropic Wave	2	2	19	2	3	3	54,530
Tropular	3	1	7	1	2	0	15,820
Truce Maker	11	8	87	12	7	11	128,017
True Colors	32	14	183	22	17	26	352,335
True Knight	18	5	118	5	11	10	78,669
Trulo	7	2	37	2	2	1	24,704
Truly Vain (AUS)	3	2	17	4	1	4	130,820
Trumpeteer	4	3	22	3	4	2	36,823
Trust a Native	1	1	8	1	0	0	3,698
Trust the Kid	2	1	9	1	1	1	13,656
Truxton King	7	3	45	4	4	2	28,731
Try My Best	7	2	39	4	2	5	98,781
Tsuba	2	1	18	1	2	3	12,006
Tsunami Slew	76	40	536	61	61	72	1,233,975
Tudor Black	5	2	22	2	4	1	21,074
Tudor Gleeman	1	1	15	1	3	2	11,670
Tudor Grey	9	3	64	4	10	6	65,373
Tumble Lane	1	1	6	1	0	1	4,144
Tumble Lark	2	1	16	2	1	3	52,100
Tumble Wind	3	2	29	5	1	2	18,007
Tumbler	8	3	50	5	4	5	51,950
Tumiga	7	3	64	4	5	7	73,494
Tuneful Tip	2	1	30	1	7	3	27,278
Tunerup	69	36	445	54	70	47	1,462,098
Tunic	3	2	10	2	1	2	32,330
Tunnel of Love	3	2	23	3	3	3	41,561
Turf Hero	1	1	18	1	2	4	9,461
Turkey Shoot	26	15	206	30	14	23	419,015
Turkoman	107	52	749	100	96	116	2,130,573
Turn and Count	12	6	91	9	13	6	176,694
Turn of Coin	2	1	22	2	3	5	44,450

RECORDS OF BROODMARE SIRES

Broodmare Sire	Perf	Wnrs	Sts	1st	2d	3d	Purses	Broodmare Sire	Perf	Wnrs	Sts	1st	2d	3d	Purses
Turn Right	2	2	15	3	2	6	17,781	Vencedor	19	12	121	21	22	12	339,620
Turn to Bo	6	3	45	5	6	6	51,924	Vent du Nord	6	1	26	2	3	2	25,111
Turn to Mars	18	5	163	8	22	21	121,310	Verbago	1	1	11	2	1	0	32,042
Turn to Reason	9	6	75	8	8	9	151,384	Verbatim	87	51	684	98	77	79	1,492,848
Turnberry	7	4	29	7	3	2	88,049	Verge	4	3	29	4	2	4	29,242
Turnbuckle	10	4	93	8	3	19	67,704	Verification	7	3	58	5	11	8	222,158
Turnverein	3	2	24	3	0	1	39,840	Vermont	2	1	10	1	1	1	9,635
Turville (FR)	4	3	41	6	6	5	34,904	Vernon Castle	11	8	85	17	6	11	167,148
Twice Bold	5	3	38	7	4	5	102,180	Vertee	2	1	14	4	1	0	63,464
Twice Burned	15	5	100	6	8	10	61,197	Vertex	1	1	3	1	0	0	4,226
Twice Elegant	1	1	8	3	1	1	11,110	Verzy	11	6	75	7	12	5	102,791
Twice Worthy	9	5	54	6	4	11	104,696	Vested Power	4	1	35	1	4	7	13,903
Twilight Agenda	22	9	131	10	3	18	120,336	Vice Regal (NZ)	3	1	9	1	2	1	18,500
Twin Time	4	1	10	1	1	0	8,408	Vice Regent	255	127	1,797	226	246	216	5,514,011
Twist the Axe	4	1	31	1	4	4	18,318	Viceregal	2	1	14	2	0	1	10,940
Two Davids	11	6	83	8	9	13	301,346	Vicksburg	8	6	47	8	3	5	114,511
Two Punch	118	64	778	112	121	96	2,744,776	Victor's Gent	3	1	13	1	4	1	23,104
Two's a Plenty	15	10	114	20	12	12	391,312	Victoria Park	7	1	58	3	5	6	39,881
Twoballsidepocket	5	3	29	3	1	4	11,689	Victorian Double	1	1	6	1	0	1	4,540
Tyrant	28	7	195	9	29	20	159,629	Victorian Line	3	2	39	4	6	8	52,007
Tyrone Terrific	3	1	10	1	3	1	15,780	Victorian Prince	10	7	93	9	15	15	232,248
Tywhapity	2	2	18	2	0	0	24,117	Victoriate	2	2	24	4	4	6	143,116
U Pos Ent	5	3	28	4	3	5	47,594	Victorious	11	7	110	11	19	16	201,282
U. S. Flag	23	14	201	22	34	26	476,568	Victory Stride	26	13	169	21	24	19	252,420
Ulan	6	3	27	3	2	5	15,244	Victory Times	1	1	10	1	2	4	11,190
Ultimate Pleasure	2	1	13	1	1	5	11,431	Vigors	123	49	830	83	95	106	1,378,503
Ultimate Pride	3	1	22	1	5	3	35,518	Vikingson	5	1	26	4	5	1	25,702
Ulysses	6	4	41	4	5	5	44,188	Villa Nova	1	1	4	2	0	1	2,363
Unbridled	62	30	333	41	35	39	1,091,835	Villamor	28	14	222	19	29	29	215,733
Uncle Georger	1	1	3	1	1	0	1,260	Vilzak	22	11	122	15	19	14	404,508
Uncle Jeff	3	1	21	1	2	2	29,285	Vindaloo	3	2	25	3	3	3	55,723
Unconscious	4	3	37	3	2	3	27,190	Virginia Boy	2	1	20	3	2	2	7,927
Under Orders	1	1	6	1	0	1	9,697	Vis-a-Vis	2	2	20	5	2	2	51,871
Under Tack	7	3	53	5	7	8	60,458	Visible	7	3	64	5	4	9	120,732
Under the Table	6	2	42	2	4	2	23,725	Visier	3	1	30	4	6	5	137,642
Unfold	4	2	33	2	4	6	42,857	Vision	4	3	30	9	5	3	323,695
Unfuwain	4	2	10	3	2	1	117,940	Vital Envoy	2	1	10	2	3	2	9,402
Unite	8	3	38	3	5	6	46,752	Vitriolic	12	3	67	5	7	8	68,727
United Holme	10	3	64	6	6	7	100,871	Vittorioso	6	3	56	12	8	8	88,555
Unmistaken	6	5	59	10	7	8	88,971	Viva Deputy	1	1	6	1	0	3	13,740
Uno Roberto	7	1	35	5	4	4	86,687	Vodika Collins	3	2	16	3	4	2	20,561
Unpredictable	37	17	243	34	22	31	448,788	Voom Voom	3	2	32	3	3	5	17,471
Unreal Currency	3	1	12	1	2	3	17,020	Vuela Vuela	2	2	16	2	2	5	25,827
Unreal Zeal	65	37	517	75	85	65	1,745,010	Vying Victor	2	1	17	6	0	1	76,225
Unzipped	12	7	118	17	17	13	285,288	W. D. Jacks	10	3	85	4	9	12	72,357
Upmost	7	7	56	13	12	3	292,139	Waajib (IRE)	1	1	10	6	0	1	42,234
Upper Case	33	11	217	17	26	31	382,170	Wage Raise	5	2	33	2	6	8	55,475
Upper Nile	39	21	265	32	31	36	492,330	Wait Till Monday (IRE)	2	1	19	1	0	1	10,884
Uprising	5	3	26	5	0	3	40,676	Wajima	63	31	439	53	55	56	716,248
Ups	2	1	14	2	1	1	28,329	Waki Bob	1	1	9	1	0	1	6,900
Upset Victory	1	1	3	1	0	0	5,640	Waldmeister	3	1	18	4	2	1	139,201
Upton	3	1	26	1	2	7	16,855	Walesa	6	2	17	3	0	0	39,812
Uzi	2	1	15	2	1	0	14,140	Wall Street Dancer	2	1	14	1	7	1	21,210
Vaal Reef	16	8	119	15	17	18	295,660	Wallenda	3	1	15	1	0	2	5,194
Vacarme	2	1	6	1	0	0	29,040	Wallet Lifter	1	1	21	8	2	1	9,571
Vaguely Noble	61	25	434	44	44	48	726,474	Wander Kind	29	16	212	23	26	35	385,070
Vaigly Great	1	1	6	1	1	0	21,140	Waquoit	75	42	499	78	65	51	1,399,567
Val de l'Orne (FR)	94	40	660	71	67	72	1,520,459	War	15	8	116	12	11	12	217,850
Val du Fier (FR)	1	1	3	1	2	0	12,300	War Hawk II (GB)	2	2	24	4	2	3	41,897
Valdez	29	13	186	16	18	18	276,422	War of Words	4	1	16	1	1	1	10,385
Valedor	1	1	6	1	0	0	21,230	War Trouble	1	1	8	1	1	1	5,580
Valet de Pied (FR)	5	3	44	5	4	7	63,257	Ward McAllister	6	2	40	2	2	5	19,707
Valiant Lark	2	2	12	2	1	3	45,252	Ward Off Trouble	5	1	32	2	5	3	25,231
Valid Appeal	268	167	1,975	302	271	254	7,138,795	Wardlaw	17	5	93	7	12	13	112,317
Valioso	3	1	37	4	2	2	39,139	Warm Front	7	1	35	1	3	5	14,073
Valiyar	3	2	8	2	1	0	52,810	Warning (GB)	5	2	31	4	2	5	104,919
Valley Crossing	4	2	18	3	4	2	36,392	Warrshan	2	1	8	1	1	0	11,390
Van Go	3	1	13	1	1	2	26,955	Washington County	11	2	46	2	3	5	24,756
Van Houten (IRE)	1	1	11	3	5	2	22,505	Wassl	7	3	36	3	3	2	89,038
Vanlandingham	68	36	436	67	52	36	1,086,000	Watch Your Step	1	1	14	1	2	3	5,778
Varick	9	4	48	6	7	5	158,646	Water Bank	35	15	223	25	27	21	328,534
Variety Road	17	6	105	8	15	15	150,283	Water Gate	3	1	17	1	0	2	14,809
Vast Empire	2	2	20	3	1	4	43,135	Wavering Monarch	129	50	762	93	84	92	2,311,601
Vatina	1	1	15	1	1	0	8,301	Wayne's Crane	32	17	201	32	30	32	422,442
Vegas Vic	3	2	28	4	7	2	23,211	Wayward Ace	2	1	17	3	4	2	56,004

Broodmare Sire	Perf	Wnrs	Sts	1st	2d	3d	Purses
Wedding Ring	5	2	18	2	4	0	32,261
Weekend Guest	2	1	9	2	0	0	10,006
Welcome Suitor	3	1	13	3	4	1	16,668
Well Decorated	201	106	1,415	150	196	170	2,548,383
Well Mannered	8	2	39	2	7	7	47,520
Well Selected	2	2	14	2	1	0	34,335
Well Written	2	1	14	2	3	3	6,038
Welsh Idol (GB)	1	1	8	1	1	3	9,535
Welsh Legend	2	1	11	1	3	0	32,268
Welsh Pageant (FR)	4	1	21	1	3	9	43,518
Welsh Saint	2	1	20	5	2	2	24,998
Weshaam	9	2	42	2	3	3	61,999
West by West	11	3	56	4	6	8	65,396
West Coast Scout	6	2	38	4	5	10	106,341
Western Playboy	4	3	36	8	5	6	119,557
Western Series	4	2	29	4	4	3	37,930
Western Symphony	1	1	4	1	0	1	10,850
Western Trick	12	5	68	8	12	11	117,513
Westheimer	18	6	147	10	10	12	135,840
What a Gent	5	5	54	11	6	9	78,978
What a Hoist	5	2	24	5	4	4	39,731
What a Pleasure	44	21	323	36	32	36	497,655
What a Rogue	5	2	29	2	4	1	56,896
What a Romance	3	2	34	7	6	2	124,350
What a Spell	5	1	17	1	1	1	15,182
What a Spy	1	1	3	1	0	0	1,400
What a Threat	5	3	30	4	5	3	21,635
What Luck	68	31	495	64	78	66	1,153,254
What's Dat	7	1	24	1	0	1	11,475
Whatsyourpleasure	2	1	15	3	4	2	21,956
Wheatly Hall	7	2	39	2	2	6	39,003
Whirling Saucer	2	1	23	3	0	2	13,331
Whiskey Road	4	4	31	7	3	5	247,886
Whistling Kettle	1	1	16	2	3	0	15,904
White Fir	12	5	75	8	8	13	141,056
White Mischief	4	2	27	2	1	2	63,930
White Rammer	7	3	45	4	4	5	117,912
Whitesburg	55	16	338	28	41	29	630,186
Whitney Tower	1	1	7	1	1	0	30,514
Who's Fleet	9	5	58	7	10	8	80,636
Who's for Dinner	19	10	161	24	27	18	467,263
Wig Out	6	3	32	3	4	1	30,272
Wild Again	225	103	1,414	187	169	166	4,628,235
Wild and Foolish	1	1	15	1	1	0	4,690
Wild Bill	4	2	21	3	2	0	8,521
Wild Catch	2	2	15	3	1	3	23,005
Wild Jose	3	1	31	1	0	3	14,676
Wild Surf (IRE)	8	2	31	5	2	3	69,058
Will Hays	5	1	11	2	1	1	9,398
Will Win	11	2	54	2	2	5	62,337
Willard Scott	5	2	30	3	6	2	65,051
William Lawrence	4	1	22	1	0	3	13,877
Willie Pleasant	1	1	14	1	1	2	37,036
Willow Hour	24	11	160	18	19	20	208,376
Winaben	1	1	4	1	1	1	1,560
Wind and Wuthering	16	9	114	12	10	9	126,161
Wind Flyer	3	1	14	5	1	3	24,211
Winds of Thought	6	3	66	6	5	5	26,964
Winds of Winter	11	3	68	6	4	5	87,864
Windtex	1	1	15	3	2	1	24,703
Windy Sands	8	6	42	7	8	7	48,167
Windy Sea	1	1	10	2	1	0	11,887
Windy Tide	12	2	79	3	9	7	31,775
Wing Out	18	9	141	13	18	20	130,831
Winged T.	14	6	73	10	12	6	166,386
Winning	2	1	7	4	1	0	599,530
Winning Bull	2	1	13	2	1	3	16,767
Winning Hit	27	15	212	21	31	29	275,391
Winright	8	3	49	5	4	5	96,751
Winter Flower (ARG)	1	1	9	2	0	1	36,810
Winterset	5	1	24	1	1	1	13,289
Wise Exchange	15	9	99	14	9	9	242,492
Wise Times	17	13	165	28	22	20	410,447
Wishful Thinker	1	1	7	1	0	3	4,088
With Approval	95	46	620	69	76	71	2,449,686
With Caution	4	3	35	5	4	7	31,726
Within Hail	4	4	27	5	1	2	75,732
Without Fail	2	2	18	2	0	4	15,435
Witness Tree	8	4	58	6	6	6	65,256
Wolf Power (SAF)	137	65	979	122	123	125	2,748,073
Wolf Touch	2	1	7	1	0	2	10,170
Wolfgang	4	1	38	2	6	6	54,691
Wolfie's Rascal	4	1	19	1	1	2	6,500
Wolver Hollow (GB)	1	1	2	2	0	0	27,000
Wonder Lark	7	2	38	3	5	4	75,900
Woodland Lad	1	1	16	1	0	2	4,813
Woodman	197	99	1,166	170	135	130	5,692,256
World Appeal	82	39	580	76	82	69	1,188,001
World Court	8	3	49	6	5	6	105,924
Worldwatch	5	4	35	5	6	5	448,512
Worthy Piper	1	1	6	1	0	0	4,758
Wrangle	1	1	9	1	0	3	16,003
Write Off	2	2	15	3	1	2	40,214
Wronsky	5	3	23	3	2	6	26,299
Wynslew	4	2	15	2	1	0	30,095
Yacqui	1	1	5	2	1	0	12,060
Yarnallton Native	4	2	43	5	4	5	28,603
Ye	6	2	27	2	3	3	20,465
Yes I'm Blue	4	2	27	5	4	2	45,527
Yesterdays Hero	8	2	55	6	8	10	103,184
Yosi Boy	2	1	10	1	0	1	5,352
You and I	3	2	25	5	5	4	98,561
Youmadeyourpoint	13	6	80	10	9	10	152,760
Young Bob	8	6	82	8	9	6	148,832
Young Commander	4	3	20	3	3	2	48,103
Young Devil	3	2	14	2	3	1	12,858
Young Generation (IRE)	3	1	9	1	0	0	4,480
Young Native	2	1	5	1	0	0	7,768
Young Ralph	2	1	12	1	1	2	48,127
Young Spirit	1	1	8	2	1	1	3,803
Youth	10	4	66	10	7	7	150,112
Yukon	66	29	487	53	75	50	854,952
Yukon Eagle	5	4	34	7	2	3	45,776
Yukon Trail	2	1	7	1	0	0	2,220
Zacky Do	2	2	19	4	3	0	18,285
Zafarrancho (ARG)	11	6	107	15	14	13	343,480
Zaizoom	9	4	54	5	9	5	44,433
Zamboni	14	7	123	12	25	14	235,019
Zanthe	17	4	118	8	7	11	170,059
Zarbyev	12	5	65	6	3	9	133,082
Zein (FR)	3	1	14	2	1	1	108,527
Zen	59	24	348	40	28	41	570,172
Zephyr Bay (AUS)	1	1	6	1	0	1	955
Zevi	2	1	12	1	1	1	6,937
Ziad	20	12	164	18	25	13	273,547
Zie World	6	2	18	3	0	0	31,187
Ziggy's Boy	30	11	224	21	23	18	239,686
Zilzal	20	13	149	22	23	18	1,559,589
Zingalong	6	3	40	4	3	4	43,872
Zinov	11	6	73	11	11	9	263,406
Zodiac	2	2	21	3	4	1	25,061
Zografos	3	2	25	4	0	4	40,887
Zonic	9	2	46	5	4	4	86,398
Zoning	10	2	61	2	7	6	52,506
Zoot Alors	11	7	102	15	15	8	88,602
Zulu Tom	4	2	26	6	3	5	15,884
Zuppardo's Love	2	1	16	2	1	1	40,895
Zuppardo's Prince	54	25	279	36	29	27	500,572